TALMUD BAVLI
תלמוד בבלי

THE SCHOTTENSTEIN EDITION

The ArtScroll Series®

THE DAVIDOWITZ FAMILY
RENOV STAHLER ROSENWALD PERLYSKY EDITION OF SEDER NEZIKIN

מסכת סנהדרין
TRACTATE SANHEDRIN

THE DAVIDOWITZ FAMILY
RENOV STAHLER ROSENWALD PERLYSKY EDITION OF SEDER NEZIKIN

מסכת סנהדרין

TRACTATE SANHEDRIN

VOLUME III

Elucidated by
Rabbi Asher Dicker (chapter 10)
Rabbi Joseph Elias and Rabbi Dovid Katz
(chapter 11)

under the General Editorship of
Rabbi Yisroel Simcha Schorr
in collaboration with a team of Torah Scholars

R' Hersh Goldwurm זצ״ל
General Editor
תש״נ-תשנ״ג / 1990-1993

The Schottenstein Edition

THE GEMARA: THE CLASSIC VILNA EDITION,
WITH AN ANNOTATED, INTERPRETIVE ELUCIDATION,
AS AN AID TO TALMUD STUDY

The Hebrew folios are reproduced from
the newly typeset and enhanced
Oz Vehadar Edition of the Classic Vilna Talmud

Published by
Mesorah Publications, ltd

We gratefully acknowledge the outstanding
Torah scholars who contributed to this volume:

Rabbi Yisroel Simcha Schorr, Rabbi Dovid Cohen
and **Rabbi Chaim Malinowitz**
who reviewed and commented on the manuscript,
Rabbis Hillel Danziger, Yosef Davis, David Fohrman, Henoch Moshe Levin, Eliezer Herzka, Nesanel Kasnett, Zev Meisels, Henoch Morris, Avrohom Yoseif Rosenberg, Moshe Rosenblum, Yitzchok Meir Schorr, Feivel Wahl, and **Yosaif Asher Weiss**
who edited, and assisted in the production of this volume.
Rabbi Yehezkel Danziger, Editorial Director

We are also grateful to our proofreaders: Mrs. Judi Dick, Mrs. Mindy Stern, and Mrs. Faigie Weinbaum, and our typesetters: Mr. Yehuda Gordon, Miss Toby Brander, Mrs. Mindy Breier, Mrs. Estie Dicker, Miss Devory Glatzer, Mrs. Bassie Gutman, Miss Udi Hershkowitz, Mrs. Raitze Leah Levin, Mrs. Miryam Stavsky, Mrs. Leah Bracha Steinharter, Miss Chaya Gitty Zaidman

FIRST EDITION
First Impression . . . March 1995
SECOND EDITION
First Impression . . . July 2002

Published and Distributed by
MESORAH PUBLICATIONS, Ltd.
4401 Second Avenue
Brooklyn, New York 11232

Distributed in Europe by
LEHMANNS
Unit E, Viking Industrial Park
Rolling Mill Road
Jarow, Tyne & Wear NE32 3DP
England

Distributed in Israel by
SIFRIATI / A. GITLER – BOOKS
10 Hashomer Street
Bnei Brak 51361

Distributed in Australia & New Zealand by
GOLDS BOOK & GIFT CO.
36 William Street
Balaclava 3183, Vic., Australia

Distributed in South Africa by
KOLLEL BOOKSHOP
Shop 8A Norwood Hypermarket
Norwood 2196, Johannesburg, South Africa

THE ARTSCROLL SERIES® / SCHOTTENSTEIN EDITION
TALMUD BAVLI / TRACTATE SANHEDRIN VOL. III

ISBN: 0-89906-743-3

Typography by CompuScribe at ArtScroll Studios, Ltd.
Custom bound by **Sefercraft, Inc.,** Brooklyn, N.Y.

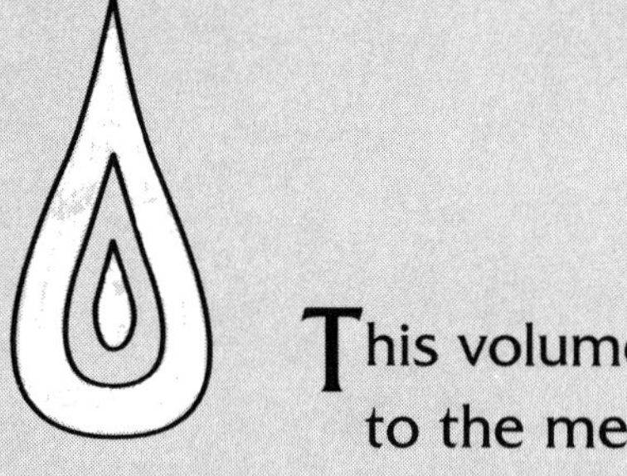

This volume is dedicated to the memory of

Mr. and Mrs. Harry Russak	**צבי הירש ורחל רוסק ע״ה**
Mr. and Mrs. Eliezer Deutsch	**אליעזר ובריינדל דייטש ע״ה**
Mr. and Mrs. Jacob Feiner	**יעקב ורבקה לאה פיינר ע״ה**

אֵלּוּ דְבָרִים שֶׁאָדָם אוֹכֵל פֵּרוֹתֵיהֶן בָּעוֹלָם הַזֶּה וְהַקֶּרֶן קַיֶּמֶת לוֹ לָעוֹלָם הַבָּא: כִּבּוּד אָב וָאֵם . . . (פאה א.א.)

These are the precepts whose fruits a person enjoys in This World but whose principal remains intact for him in the World to Come. They are: the honor due to one's fatherand mother . . . (*Pe'ah* 1:1)

In this volume of Sanhedrin (91b), the Talmud states:

אָמַר לֵיהּ אַנְטוֹנִינוּס לְרַבִּי: מִפְּנֵי מַה חַמָּה יוֹצְאָה בַּמִּזְרָח וְשׁוֹקַעַת בַּמַּעֲרָב? אָמַר לֵיהּ, אִי הֲוָה אִיפְּכָא נַמִּי הָכִי הֲוָה אָמְרַתְּ לִי.

Antoninus asked Rebbi: Why does the sun rise in the east and set in the west? Rebbi said to him: It it were reversed, you would also have asked me the same question.

The one way to learn is to ask. Our parents taught the value of questioning everything. May this volume hold the answers to some of your questions.

Joseph and Adina Russak
Dr. Leonard and Bobbee Feiner
Larry and Rochelle Russak

is reverently dedicated to the memory of
the patron of this Talmud
and of countless other noble causes in Jewish life

יעקב מאיר חיים בן אפרים אליעזר הכהן ע״ה

נפטר ה׳ אדר ב׳ תשנ״ב

Jerome Schottenstein ע״ה

and to the memory of his parents

אפרים אליעזר בן יהושע הכהן ע״ה **חנה בת צבי הירש ע״ה**

נפטר ב׳ אייר תשט״ז נפטרה ט״ו מנחם אב תשט״ו

Ephraim and Anna Schottenstein ע״ה

by

Geraldine Schottenstein

Saul and Sonia Schottenstein

and

Jay and Jeanie Schottenstein

and their children
Joseph Aaron, Jonathan Richard, Jeffrey Adam

Ann and Ari Deshe

and their children
Elie Michael, David Scott, Dara Lauren, Daniel Matthew

Susan and Jon Diamond

and their children
Jillian Leigh, Joshua Louis, Jacob Meyer

and

Lori Schottenstein

PATRONS OF THE SEDARIM

Recognizing the need for the holy legacy of the Talmud
to be available to its heirs in their own language,
these generous and visionary patrons have each dedicated
one of the six Sedarim/Orders of the Talmud.

THE FORMAN EDITION OF SEDER ZERAIM

is lovingly dedicated by

Mr. and Mrs. Sam Forman, Brett and Wendy

in memory of their beloved parents and grandparents

Mr. and Mrs. George Forman ע״ה **Dr. and Mrs. Morey Chapman ע״ה**

THE HORN EDITION OF SEDER MOED

is lovingly dedicated to the memory of

ר׳ משה מניס ב״ר יעקב יצחק ע״ה — Moishe Horn ע״ה

נפטר ב׳ מנחם אב תשנ״ד

by his wife **Malkie**

his parents **Jacob ע״ה and Genia Horn שתחי׳**

and her children

Shimmie and Alissa
Ari Shana Michal Tali

Devorah and Dov Elias
Moishe Ariella Eli Chaviva

Shandi and Sruli Glaser
Ruthi Jack

THE ELLIS A. SAFDEYE EDITION OF SEDER NASHIM

is reverently dedicated to the memory of

המנוח יהודה אצלאן ומרת צלחה ויקטוריא ע״ה

Aslan and Victoria Safdeye ע״ה

and

המנוח יהודה ומרת מרגלית ע״ה

Judah and Margie Sultan ע״ה

by their children

Ellis A. and Altoon Safdeye

and grandchildren

Alan Judah and Rachel Safdeye
Ezra and Victoria Esses
Joseph and Rochelle Safdeye
Michael and Bobbi Safdeye

PATRONS OF THE SEDARIM

THE DAVIDOWITZ FAMILY
RENOV STAHLER ROSENWALD PERLYSKY EDITION OF SEDER NEZIKIN

is lovingly dedicated to

Rozi and Morty Davis-Davidowitz

builders of this dynasty

by their children and grandchildren

Esti and Ushi Stahler

Jamie, Danny, Duvi, Lisi, Avi, Eli, Malka and Loni

Rivki and Lindsay Rosenwald

Doni, Joshy, Demi, Davey and Tamar Rina

Ruki and Kal Renov

Tova, Tani, Eli, Ari, Yoni, Yael, Emi and Benji

Laya and Dov Perlysky

Ayala Malka, Tova Batsheva, Naftali Yonatan, Atara Yael, Eitan Moshe and Shira Avital

and is lovingly dedicated to the memory of our grandparents

Emily and Nathan Selengut ע״ה

נפתלי ב״ר יעקב ע״ה ומלכה בת ר׳ אלתר חיים ע״ה

THE SCHWARTZ EDITION OF SEDER KODASHIM

is lovingly dedicated by

Avrohom Yeshaya and Sally Schwartz

and their children

Ari, Moshe, Dani, and Dovi

in memory of their beloved parents and grandparents

Isaac and Rebecca Jarnicki ז״ל — ר׳ יצחק ב״ר אשר ז״ל וחיה רבקה בת הרב בצלאל הירש ז״ל

נפ׳ יג׳ תמוז תשנ״ז נפ׳ ג׳ אדר תשס״ד

and their beloved grandmother

Mrs. Pearl Septytor ע״ה — פערל בת ר׳ מרדכי ע״ה

and in honor of יבלח״ט their parents and grandparents

Rabbi and Mrs. Gedalia Dov Schwartz שליט״א

and in memory of our grandparents

Rabbi Eliezer and Pesha Chaya Poupko ז״ל   **Abraham Schwartz ז״ל**

Betzalel Hersh and Hendel Berliner ז״ל   **Asher and Gittel Jarnicki ז״ל**

THE WINKLER EDITION OF SEDER TOHOROS

is lovingly dedicated by

Marvin and Sherri Winkler

Jason, Eric, Sam, Nicole

in honor of their parents

Michel and Irene Winkler

in memory of their grandparents who perished in the Holocaust הי״ד

Moshe and Leah Jacobowitz ע״ה   **Joseph and Shaindel Winkler ע״ה**

and in memory of their aunt

Tera Hirsch ע״ה

PATRONS OF THE TALMUD

With generosity, vision, and devotion to the perpetuation of Torah study, the following patrons have dedicated individual volumes of the Talmud

Reference/ Introduction: **George and Vita Kolber**
In loving memory of
Joseph and Frieda Hirschfeld **ע"ה**

BERACHOS I: In memory of
Jerome Schottenstein ע"ה
יעקב מאיר חיים בן אפרים אליעזר הכהן ע"ה

BERACHOS II: **Zvi and Betty Ryzman**
in honor of their children שיחיו
Mickey and Shelly Fenig — Aliza, Yissachar David, and Batsheva
Elie and Adina Ryzman — Leora and Yonatan Zev
Avi Rafi

Malcolm and Joy Lyons
in honour of their parents שיחיו
Eve Lyons
Cecil and Mona Jacobs
and in memory of his father
יהודה בן גרשון ע"ה נפ' כ"ב שבט תשס"ג — Leopold Lyons ע"ה

SHABBOS I: **Nachshon and Bruria Minucha [Nuchi] Draiman and Family**
in memory of
הר"ר יהודה ליב מנדלקורן זצ"ל בן הר"ר צבי הי"ו
Rabbi Yehuda Leib Mandelcorn זצ"ל — נפטר כ' תמוז, תשנ"ג

SHABBOS II: **David and Bonnie Anfang** — **Rachel, Julie and Elliot**
Chaim and Ruthie Anfang — **Ariella Hope** **Michael Brett**
In loving memory of
ר' אריה ליב ב"ר דוד אביגדור ע"ה — Leib Anfang ע"ה
בשה לאה בת ר' אלימלך דוב ע"ה — Barbara Anfang ע"ה

Mimi and Steven Rosenbaum — **Stacey and Danny**
Joseph and Sharon Prawer — **Dena, Dovid, Alana, Naomi**
Alan and Louisa Prawer — **Ruben Pinchas**
In loving memory of
ר' פנחס ב"ר יוסף ברוך הלוי ע"ה גילה בת אשר יונה ע"ה — Pinkus and Genia Prawer ע"ה, and
שרה בת שמעון ליב ע"ה — Sarah Cukierman ע"ה

A Hebrew edition of the Talmud Bavli is now in progress.
The Hebrew edition is dedicated by

Jay and Jeanie Schottenstein

and their children

Joseph Aaron, Jonathan Richard, and Jeffrey Adam

— in honor of their cherished loved ones who have left indelible marks on their own lives and the lives of countless others, as models of inspiration, generosity, integrity, and devotion to the noblest causes in Jewish life:
his parents **JEROME ז"ל AND GERALDINE SCHOTTENSTEIN**,
her parents **LEONARD AND HEDDY RABE**
and **SAUL AND SONIA SCHOTTENSTEIN**

❧ ❧ ❧

JAY AND JEANIE SCHOTTENSTEIN
have a perspective that transcends time and community.
Through their dedication of these editions of the Talmud, they spread Torah study around the globe and across generations.
Multitudes yet unborn will be indebted to them for their vision and generosity.

PATRONS OF THE TALMUD

SHABBOS II: [continued]
Rabbi Eliyahu and Yehudit Fishman
Rivka and Zvi Silberstein and Leah   **Akiva Yitzchak Fishman**
Rabbi Yechiel Meir and Chagit Fishman   **Rabbi Yosef and Aliza Fishman**
Talia Chanah, Ariel Yishai and Daniel
In loving memory of
ר' יוסף ב"ר טוביה ע"ה רודע רבקה בת ר' הירש מאיר ע"ה — Yosef and Rude Rivka Fishman ע"ה
and their children Yechiel Meir, Leah and Chanah הי"ד who perished in the Holocaust

SHABBOS III: **Stanley and Ellen Wasserman**
and their children
Alan Wasserman   **Mark and Anne Wasserman**
Neil and Yael Wasserman   **Stuart and Rivka Berger**
and families
In loving memory of
יוסף בן דוב בער ע"ה   בילא בת יעקב ע"ה — Joseph and Bess Wasserman ע"ה, and
שמריהו בן משה ע"ה   רבקה בת הרב יוסף הכהן ע"ה — Sascha and Regina (Czaczkes) Charles ע"ה

SHABBOS IV: לעילוי נשמות
הורינו היקרים **ר' לוי ב"ר יהודה הלוי ע"ה   וצירל בת ר' מרדכי ע"ה לוינגר**
זקנינו היקרים **ר' יהודה ב"ר אליעזר צבי הלוי ע"ה   וטלצא בת פרומט ע"ה לוינגר**
ר' מרדכי ב"ר שמואל ע"ה   ומלכה בת ר' נתן ע"ה אדלר
אחינו **שמואל הלוי ע"ה   יהודה הלוי ע"ה   יהונתן הלוי הי"ד**
אחותנו **לאה בת ר' לוי סג"ל ע"ה   ובעלה ר' טוביה ע"ה**
גיסינו **ר' מיכאל ב"ר ברוך שמואל ע"ה שוויצר   ר' שמואל ב"ר יעקב ע"ה מיכל**
ולעילוי נשמות דודינו ודודותינו ויוצאי חלוציהם שנפטרו ושנהרגו על קידוש השם הי"ד
Dedicated by **Louis and Morris Lowinger**
Teri Schweitzer   **Kato Michel**   **Margit Baldinger**   **Eva Lowinger**

ERUVIN: [two volumes]
Jerome and Geraldine Schottenstein   **Saul and Sonia Schottenstein**
Jay and Jeanie Schottenstein   **Ann and Ari Deshe**
Susan and Jon Diamond   **Lori Schottenstein**
in memory of
אפרים אליעזר בן יהושע הכהן ע"ה — Ephraim Schottenstein ע"ה
חנה בת צבי הירש ע"ה — Anna Schottenstein ע"ה

PESACHIM I: **Vera and Soli Spira and Family**
in memory of
ברוך בן חיים ע"ה — Baruch Spira ע"ה
בילה בת נתן שלום ע"ה — Bella Spira ע"ה
שמואל בן אברהם ע"ה — Shmuel Lebovits ע"ה
and their respective families הי"ד who perished in the Holocaust
and in honor of
שפרה בת משה — Caroline Lebovits תחי'

The Edmond J. Safra Edition of the Talmud Bavli in French,
adapted from the Schottenstein Edition, is now in progress.

The Edmond J. Safra Edition
is dedicated by
Lily Safra
in memory of her beloved husband
Edmond J. Safra רפאל אדמון עזרא בן אסתר ע"ה

His desire is in the Torah of HASHEM, and in His Torah he meditates day and night.
He shall be like a tree deeply rooted alongside brooks of water;
that yields its fruit in due season, and whose leaf never withers,
and everything that he does will succeed (Psalms 1:2-3).

PATRONS OF THE TALMUD

PESACHIM II: **Vera and Soli Spira and Family**
in memory of an uncle who was like a father
and a cousin who was like a brother
ישראל בן נתן שלום ע״ה — Israel Stern ע״ה
נתן שלום בן ישראל ע״ה — Noussi Stern ע״ה

PESACHIM III: **Lorraine and Mordy Sohn** **Ann and Pinky Sohn**
in memory of
ר׳ צבי ב״ר אלעזר ע״ה — Dr. Harry Sohn ע״ה
מרת הענדיל דבורה ב״ר אברהם שלמה ע״ה — Dora F. Sohn ע״ה
ר׳ יחזקאל ב״ר אליקים חנוך הלוי ע״ה — Harold Levine ע״ה
רבקה הענא בת שמעון הלוי ע״ה — Ruth Levine ע״ה
רייזל ב״ר שמשון ע״ה — Rosalie Sohn ע״ה

SHEKALIM: In loving memory of
Mr. Maurice Lowinger ז״ל
ר׳ מאיר משה ב״ר בן ציון הלוי ז״ל
נפ׳ כ״ז אדר תשס״א

YOMA I: **A. Joseph and Rochelle Stern**
Moshe Dov, Zev, Shani, Esty, and Shaye
in honor of their parents and grandparents
Eli and Frieda Stern שיחיו
Frida Weiss שתחי׳
and in memory of
ר׳ ישעי׳ בן ר׳ ישראל שמואל ווייס ז״ל

YOMA II: **A. Leibish and Edith Elbogen and Family**
לזכר נשמות
מוה״ר אהרן בן מוה״ר יעקב קאפל עלבוגן ז״ל
וזו׳ אלטע חנה חיה מלכה בת מוה״ר חיים יצחק מאיר ע״ה
אחותי פערל עם בעלה ושבע בנים ובנות
ושלשה אחי: חיים יצחק מאיר, משה יוסף, יעקב קאפל הי״ד
בני אהרן עלבוגן שנהרגו עקד״ה
מוה״ר נתן פייטל בן מוה״ר אברהם וואלד ז״ל
וזו׳ ברכה בת מוה״ר דוד יהודה הי״ד שנאספה עקד״ה באוישוויץ

SUCCAH I: **Howard and Roslyn Zuckerman** **Steven and Shellie Zuckerman**
Leo and Rochelle Goldberg
in memory of their parents
ר׳ פסח יהודה ב״ר יצחק אייזיק ע״ה וחוה בת ר׳ יהודה לייב ע״ה — Philip and Evelyn Zuckerman ע״ה

in honor of their children
Yisroel and Shoshana Pesi Zuckerman שיחי׳
Pesach Yehudah and Asher Anshel שיחי׳
Michael (Ezra) and Lauren Zuckerman שיחי׳
Adrianne & Shawn Meller, Elliot, & Joshua Goldberg שיחי׳

in honor of their children
Glenn and Heidi, Jamie Elle, Benjamin,
Brett and Robin, Brandon Noah, Ross and T.J. שיחי׳
and in honor of their parents
Marilyn and Aaron Feinerman שיחי׳

in memory of
ר׳ ישראל צבי ב״ר ברוך ע״ה ושיינדל בת ר׳ ישראל ע״ה — Israel and Shaindel Ray ע״ה
and in memory of Mrs. Rose Ray (Glass) ע״ה

Arthur and Randi Luxenberg
in honor of their parents
Irwin and Joan Luxenberg שיחי׳ Bernard and Evelyn Beeber שיחי׳
their children Elizabeth Jewel and Jacqueline Paige שיחי׳
in memory of his grandparents
ר׳ אברהם בן אהרן מרדכי ז״ל ורחל בת ר׳ משה ע״ה — Abraham and Rose Luxenberg ע״ה
ישעיהו צבי בן הרב טוביה ז״ל ושרה צירל בת ר׳ יעקב ע״ה — Jesse and Celia Aronson ע״ה

PATRONS OF THE TALMUD

SUCCAH II: **Thomas and Lea Schottenstein** **William and Amy Schottenstein**
in memory of
אריה ליב בן אפרים אליעזר הכהן ע״ה — Leon Schottenstein ע״ה
מאיר אבנר בן דוד הלוי ע״ה — Meir Avner Levy ע״ה
and in honor of
Mrs. Jean S. Schottenstein שתחי׳ Bertram and Corinne Natelson שיחי׳
Mrs. Flory Levy שתחי׳

BEITZAH: **Paul and Suzanne Peyser** **Irwin and Bea Peyser**
in memory of
פריידע רייזעל בת יהושע ע״ה דוד בן פינחס ע״ה — David and Rose Peyser ע״ה

ROSH HASHANAH: **Steve and Genie Savitsky** **David and Roslyn Savitsky**
In memory of
יואל בן אברהם ע״ה — Jerry J. Savitsky ע״ה
ישראל בן מנחם מאנעס ע״ה — Irving Tennenbaum ע״ה
שמואל בן יצחק ע״ה — George Hillelsohn ע״ה
רחל בת דוד הלוי ע״ה — Ruth Hillelsohn ע״ה
אהרן בן יהודה אריה ע״ה — Aaron Seif ע״ה

TAANIS: **David and Jean Bernstein, and Scott**
Matthew Bernstein
Albert and Gail Nassi, **Jessica and Garrett**
in memory of
Mr. and Mrs. Harry Bernstein ע״ה Mr. and Mrs. Joseph Furman ע״ה
Mr. Samuel Nassi ע״ה

MEGILLAH: Special Commemorative Edition published in conjunction
with the *Sh'loshim* of the patron of this edition of the Talmud
Jerome Schottenstein ע״ה
יעקב מאיר חיים בן אפרים אליעזר הכהן ע״ה

MOED KATAN: **Solomon T. and Leah Scharf**
and their children
David and Tzipi Diamond **Alexander and Naomi Scharf**
Joseph Scharf **Dovid and Chani Scharf**
לזכרון עולם
ר׳ אליהו בן משה יעקב ע״ה — R' Eliyahu Scharf ע״ה
שרה בת אלכסנדר זיסקינד ע״ה — Sara Scharf ע״ה
ר׳ יוסף בן צבי הירש ע״ה — R' Joseph Felder ע״ה

CHAGIGAH: **The Alvin E. Schottenstein Family**
In memory of
חיים אברהם יונה בן אפרים אליעזר הכהן ע״ה — Alvin E. Schottenstein ע״ה
יצחק אייזיק בן עקיבא הכהן ע״ה — Irving Altman ע״ה

YEVAMOS I: **Phillip and Ruth Wojdyslawski and Family**
In memory of his beloved parents
Abraham Michel and Ora Wojdyslawski ע״ה
ר׳ אברהם מיכאל ב״ר פינחס ע״ה
אורה בת ר׳ צבי הירש ע״ה

YEVAMOS II: **Phillip and Ruth Wojdyslawski and Family**
In memory of her beloved mother
Chaya (Cytryn) Valt ע״ה
חיה צירל בת ר׳ שלמה זלמן ע״ה

PATRONS OF THE TALMUD

YEVAMOS III: **Phillip and Ruth Wojdyslawski and Family**
In honor of
Benjamin C. Fishoff לאוי"ט
To the public he is a leader with vision and dedication.
To us he has always been a role model, a father,
and a constant inspiration.

KESUBOS I: **The Fishoff Families**
in memory of their beloved mother
מינדל בת ר' ישראל ע"ה — Mrs. Marilyn Fishoff ע"ה
נפ' כד תשרי תשמ"ט
and in memory of their dear grandparents
Fishoff — ר' דוב ב"ר מנחם אשר ע"ה מרת מירל בת ר' מנחם מענדל ע"ה
Neider — ר' ישראל ב"ר אברהם ע"ה מרת חיה זיסא בת ר' שרגא פייוועל ע"ה

KESUBOS II **Arthur A. and Carla Rand**
in memory of their parents
ר' ישראל ב"ר צבי Rand ומרת ליבא מלכה ב"ר יהודה Marcus ע"ה
ר' שלמה ב"ר מרדכי יהודה Ratzersdorfer ומרת חוה ב"ר חיים Finkelstein ע"ה
and in honor of their children
ר' אריה יהושע ב"ר אליהו דוב ומרת ליבא מלכה שיחי' — Lydia M. and Lionel S. Zuckier
ר' יואל אשר ב"ר חיים שלמה ומרת גנענדל חנה שיחי' — Gigi A. and Joel A. Baum
ר' ישראל יהודה ומרת צפורה געלא ב"ר יצחק חיים שיחי' — Jay J. and Cyndi G. Finkel-Rand
and grandchildren
דניאל יעקב, נפתלי צבי, חוה, בנימין, צפורה מרים, רחל, בתשבע Baum שיחי'
שלמה יצחק, שירה חיה, צבי, שפרה לאה, בן ציון Zuckier שיחי'
אליהו אריה לייב, יעקב שלמה, צבי, חסיה ליבא, מתתיהו דוד Rand שיחי'

KESUBOS III **ישימך אלהים כשרה רבקה רחל ולאה**
May God make you like Sarah, Rebecca, Rachel and Leah

NEDARIM I: **Mrs. Goldy Golombeck**
Hyman P. and Elaine Golombeck **Blanche B. Lerer**
Moishe Zvi and Sara Leifer **Avrohom Chaim and Renee Fruchthandler**
In memory of
ר' משה יוסף ב"ר חיים פנחס ע"ה — Morris J. Golombeck ע"ה
and by Moishe Zvi and Sara Leifer in memory of
הרב ברוך יוסף ב"ר משה צבי ע"ה — האשה הצנועה מרים יוטא בת ר' לוי יצחק ע"ה
Mr. and Mrs. Baruch Leifer ע"ה

NEDARIM II: **The Rothstein Family**
In loving memory of
וועלוועל ב"ר יוסף ע"ה — Warren Rothstein ע"ה
David and Esther Rothstein ע"ה Max and Gussie Gottlieb ע"ה
and in honor of
Howard and Beatrice Rothstein

NAZIR I: **Albert and Gail Nassi**
Garrett A. Nassi
Jessica Lea Nassi
in memory of
Samuel Nassi ע"ה
Albert and Leona Nassi ע"ה
Benjamin and Adell Eisenberg ע"ה
Arthur and Sarah Dector ע"ה

Daniel and Susan Kane
Jessica, Adam and Stacey
in memory of
Abraham and Rose Kanofsky ע"ה
Benjamin and Sophie Gornstein ע"ה
Elie and Irma Darsa ע"ה
Mack and Naomi Mann ע"ה

NAZIR II: **Alan and Myrna Cohen,** **Alison and Matthew**
in memory of
Harry and Kate Cohen ע"ה Harry and Pauline Katkin ע"ה

PATRONS OF THE TALMUD

SOTAH: **Motty and Malka Klein**
for the merit of their children שיחי׳
Esther and Chaim Baruch Fogel Dovid and Chavie Binyomin Zvi
Elana Leah Moshe Yosef Yaakov Eliyahu
In honor of his mother שתחי׳
Mrs. Suri Klein לאוי״ט
In memory of his father
ר׳ יהודה ב״ר דוד הלוי ז״ל נפ׳ כ״ז אדר ב׳ תשס״ג – Yidel Klein
In memory of her parents
ר׳ אשר אנשיל ב״ר משה יוסף ז״ל נפ׳ ג׳ שבט תשנ״ט – Anchel Gross
שרה בת ר׳ חיים אליהו ע״ה נפ׳ כ״ד סיון תשס״א – Suri Gross
And in memory of their grandparents who perished על קידוש השם in the Holocaust
ר׳ דוד ב״ר יעקב הלוי ע״ה ופערל בת ר׳ צבי ע״ה הי״ד – Klein
ר׳ מרדכי ב״ר דוד הלוי ע״ה ולאה בת ר׳ יעקב הלוי ע״ה הי״ד – Klein
ר׳ משה יוסף ב״ר בנימין צבי ע״ה ומלכה בת ר׳ יחיאל מיכל ע״ה הי״ד – Gross
ר׳ חיים אליהו ב״ר מרדכי ע״ה ויוטא בת ר׳ שלמה אליעזר ע״ה הי״ד – Gartenberg

GITTIN I: **Mrs. Kate Tannenbaum**
Elliot and Debra Tannenbaum Edward and Linda Zizmor and Families
commemorating the first *yahrzeit* of beloved husband, father and grandfather
ר׳ נפתלי ב״ר יהודה אריה ע״ה – Fred Tannenbaum ע״ה
נפטר ח׳ ניסן תשנ״ב

GITTIN II: **Richard and Bonnie Golding**
in honor of Julian and Frances Golding Lawrence Cohen and Helen Lee Cohen
and in memory of Vivian Cohen ע״ה
Irving and Ethel Tromberg Clarence and Jean Permut
in memory of
Benjamin and Sara Tromberg ע״ה Harry and Lena Brown ע״ה
Molly and Julius Permut ע״ה Lizzie and Meyer Moscovitz ע״ה

KIDDUSHIN I: **Ellis A. and Altoon Safdeye**
in memory of their beloved parents
המנוח יהודה אצלאן ומרת צלחה ויקטוריא ע״ה – Aslan and Victoria Safdeye ע״ה
המנוח יהודה ומרת מרגלית ע״ה – Judah and Margie Sultan ע״ה
and in memory of his brother יוסף ע״ה – Joseph Safdeye ע״ה

KIDDUSHIN II: **Mr. and Mrs. Ben Heller**
in memory of his father
יואל נתן ב״ר חיים הלוי ע״ה – Joseph Heller ע״ה
and in honor of his mother
צפורה שתחי׳ לאוי״ט בת ר׳ בנימין ע״ה – Fanya Gottesfeld-Heller שתחי׳

BAVA KAMMA I: **Yitzchok and Shoshana Ganger and Children**
in memory of
ר׳ יצחק ישעיהו ב״ר שלמה זלמן ע״ה–רויזא גיטל בת ר׳ משה ע״ה – Ganger
מיכאל ב״ר אברהם מרדכי ע״ה–מרים יוכבד בת ר׳ בנימין ע״ה – Ferber
ר׳ משה דוד ב״ר יצחק זעליג מקוצק ע״ה–פיגא בת ר׳ אברהם מרדכי ע״ה – Morgenstern
ר׳ מתתיהו ב״ר שמואל דוב ע״ה–אסתר מלכה בת ר׳ אריה ליב ע״ה – Newman

BAVA KAMMA II: **William and Esther Bein, and**
Joseph Hillel, Abraham Chaim Zev, and Bella Leah
In memory of parents and grandparents
מנחם מענדל ב״ר שמואל יצחק הכהן ע״ה – Edward (Mendus) Bein ע״ה
לאה בת חיים זאב הכהן ע״ה – Ilus Hartstein Bein ע״ה
מרדכי בן יוסף ע״ה – Mordochej Szer ע״ה
בילה בת אברהם ע״ה – Baila Silber Szer ע״ה
שמואל יצחק הכהן ושרה ביין ע״ה – חיים זאב הכהן ושרה הרטשטיין ע״ה
יוסף ויענטה שער ע״ה – אברהם ואסתר זילבר ע״ה

PATRONS OF THE TALMUD

BAVA KAMMA III: **Dedicated to Klal Yisrael,**
and particularly to the Six Million.
הקב״ה שוכן בתוך בני ישראל והוא חד עם כנסת ישראל
"The Holy One Blessed is He dwells among the children of Israel;
He and the congregation of Israel are one."
— *Tzidkas Hatzaddik* 179

BAVA METZIA I: **Drs. Robert and Susan Schulman**
Howard and Tzila Schulman **Fred and Cindy Schulman**
and Families
in memory of
מיכאל בן צבי הירש ע״ה ומלכה בת ר׳ יוסף ע״ה — Milton and Molly Schulman ע״ה

BAVA METZIA II: **Donald E. and Eydie R. Garlikov, and Jennifer**
in memory of beloved son and brother
צבי שלמה בן דן ע״ה — Kenneth Scott Garlikov ע״ה
and in memory of parents and grandparents
עזריאל וועלוויל ב״ר אנשיל ע״ה טשארנא בת ר׳ אריה לייב ע״ה
Irve W. and Cecelia (Kiki) Garlikov ע״ה
and in honor of parents and grandparents, brother and uncle
מרדכי ואסתר פריידל ריטטער — Marcus and Elfrieda Ritter
נפתלי חיים ריטטער — Dr. Nathaniel Ritter

BAVA METZIA III: **The David H. Gluck Foundation**
in memory of
The Gluck Family
זאב בן דוד צבי ע״ה ואסתר בת אשר זעליג ע״ה — Zev and Esther Gluck ע״ה
ליבא, אשר זעליג, דוד צבי, שמואל, מנשה, יחזקאל שרגא ע״ה —
Lee, George, David H., Samuel C., Emanuel M., Henry ע״ה, and
יעקב יצחק בן זאב ע״ה ומיימי בת זאב ע״ה — Dr. Jack I. and Mrs. Mae Saks ע״ה
and in memory of
זאב בן חיים דוד וחיה ביילע בת יצחק יעקב ע״ה — Wolf and Chaye Beilah Saks ע״ה
יחיאל בן משה ע״ה — Elie Neustadter ע״ה

BAVA BASRA I: In memory of
מנחם מענדל בן אלימלך יהושע העשל ע״ה
חיה בת יהושע הכהן ע״ה

BAVA BASRA II: **Paul and Beth Guez and Family**
in memory of
Felix (Mazal) Guez ע״ה

BAVA BASRA III: **Irving and Frances Schottenstein**
in honor of their beloved parents
מאיר בן יהושע הכהן ע״ה ליבא בת הרב יצחק משה ע״ה — Meyer and Libbie Schottenstein
טוביה ע״ה ויבדל״ח שיינדל תחי׳ — Tobias ע״ה and Jennie Polster תחי׳
Melvin ע״ה and Lenore תחי׳ Schottenstein
in honor of their beloved parents
אברהם יוסף בן יהושע הכהן ע״ה ויבדל״ח בליה זילפה בת יצחק תחי׳
Abe J. ע״ה and Bessie (Stone) תחי׳ Schottenstein
יצחק ע״ה ויבדל״ח שרה תחי׳ — Isadore J. ע״ה and Sophie תחי׳ Green

PATRONS OF THE TALMUD

SANHEDRIN I: **Mortimer and Barbara Klaus** **Lester and Esther Klaus**
Arthur and Vivian Klaus
in memory of their beloved parents
ר׳ שמשון ב״ר יעקב ע״ה באשא בת ר׳ מרדכי נתן ע״ה
Samuel and Bessie Klaus ע״ה
and in memory of their sister
רייזל בת ר׳ שמשון ע״ה – **Rosalie Klaus Sohn**

SANHEDRIN II: Dedicated by a fellowship of people who revere the Talmud, its sanctity and wisdom, who foster its study, and who join in helping bring its treasures to future generations, the world over.

SANHEDRIN III: **Joseph and Adina Russak**
Dr. Leonard and Bobbee Feiner
Larry and Rochelle Russak
in memory of
צבי הירש ורחל רוסק ע״ה – Mr. and Mrs. Harry Russak ע״ה
אליעזר ובריינדל דייטש ע״ה – Mr. and Mrs. Eliezer Deutsch ע״ה
יעקב ורבקה לאה פיינר ע״ה – Mr. and Mrs. Jacob Feiner ע״ה

MAKKOS: **Mr. and Mrs. Marcos Katz**
in honor of הרב אפרים לייבוש בן הרב מרדכי דוד הכהן כ״ץ שליט״א
Rabbi Ephraim Leibush Katz שליט״א

SHEVUOS: Dedicated by
Michael and Danielle Gross
(London)

AVODAH ZARAH I: **The Kuhl Family**
in memory of
יחיאל ב״ר יצחק אייזיק ע״ה Dr. Julius Kuhl ע״ה
פרומט בת ר׳ שמואל הלוי ע״ה Mrs. Yvonne Kuhl ע״ה
שמואל ב״ר יחיאל ע״ה Sydney Kuhl ע״ה

AVODAH ZARAH II: In memory of
Jerome Schottenstein ע״ה
יעקב מאיר חיים בן אפרים אליעזר הכהן ע״ה

HORAYOS-EDUYOS: **Woli and Chaja Stern** (Sao Paulo, Brazil)
in memory of his parents
ר׳ צבי בן ר׳ חיים הלוי ומרת מרים ז״ל – Stern
מרת דאכא בת ר׳ פרץ ומרת ברכה ע״ה – Tager
and in memory of her parents
ר׳ דוד אריה בן ר׳ יעקב ומרת שיינדל ז״ל – Brenner
מרת איטלה בת ר׳ חיים ומרת מדל ע״ה – Stern
and in memory of their mechutanim
ר׳ ישראל מרדכי ב״ר צבי יוסף סג״ל ז״ל – Landau
ר׳ יששכר טוביה ב״ר יוסף ז״ל – Weitman
ר׳ שמואל עקיבא ב״ר שלמה צבי ז״ל – Kierszenbaum
and in memory of their sister-in-law
מרת זלטה פסל בת ר׳ אברהם יעקב ומרת חנה גיטל ע״ה – Stern
and in honor of their children
Jacques and Ariane Stern Jaime and Ariela Landau Michäel and Annete Kierszenbaum

ZEVACHIM I: **Mr. and Mrs. Samson Bitensky**

ZEVACHIM II: **Victor Posner**

PATRONS OF THE TALMUD

ZEVACHIM III: **Friends of Value City Department Stores**
In memory of
יעקב מאיר חיים בן אפרים אליעזר הכהן ע״ה — Jerome Schottenstein ע״ה

MENACHOS I: **Terumah Foundation**

MENACHOS II: **Terumah Foundation**

MENACHOS III: **Terumah Foundation**

CHULLIN I: **The Kassin Family**
in memory of
הרב יעקב שאול קצין זצ״ל — Rabbi Dr. Jacob Saul Kassin זצ״ל
The late Chief Rabbi of the Syrian-Sephardic Community
and in honor of
הרב שאול יעקב קצין שליט״א — Rabbi Saul Jacob Kassin שליט״א
Chief Rabbi of the Syrian-Sephardic Community

CHULLIN II: **Marty Silverman**
in memory of
Joseph and Fannie Silverman ע״ה and Dorothy Silverman ע״ה

CHULLIN III: **Harold and Ann Platt**
in memory of their beloved parents
אליעזר ושרה פיגא ע״ה — Eliezer and Sarah Feiga (Olshak) Platkowski ע״ה of Malkinia, Poland
ברוך ולאה ע״ה — Baruch and Laura Bienstock ע״ה of Lwow, Poland
and in memory of their entire families who perished in the Holocaust

CHULLIN IV: **Terumah Foundation**

BECHOROS I: **Howard Tzvi and Chaya Friedman**
Gabrielle Aryeh Yerachmiel Alexander and Daniella
in memory of their father and grandfather
הרב ירחמיאל ברוך בן הרה״ח ר׳ אלעזר ז״ל — Yerachmiel Friedman ז״ל

BECHOROS II: **Howard and Chaya Balter**
Perri Naftali Aryeh Akiva
in memory of his mother and their grandmother
רחל בת ר׳ חיים ע״ה, נפ׳ ז׳ שבט תשנ״ט — **Ruth Balter** ע״ה
and in honor of their parents and grandparents שיחי׳
David Balter
Noah and Shirley Schall
and in beloved memory of their grandparents and great grandparents
ר׳ שלמה ב״ר דוד זאב ז״ל אדי בת ר׳ זאב ע״ה — Balter
ר׳ חיים ב״ר לייב ז״ל פערל בת ר׳ בייניש ע״ה — Lelling
ר׳ דוב בער ב״ר אליעזר ז״ל ליבה בת ר׳ ישראל ע״ה — Zabrowsky
ר׳ נפתלי ב״ר יעקב שלמה ז״ל שרה בת ר׳ רפאל ע״ה — Schall

ARACHIN: **Chanoch and Hadassah Weisz and Family**
in memory of his father:
לעי״נ אביו ר׳ צבי ב״ר שמחה הלוי ע״ה, נפ׳ כ״ז מנחם אב תשמ״ה — Weisz
his maternal grandfather:
לעי״נ ר׳ שלמה ב״ר יצחק ע״ה, נפ׳ ה׳ סיון תש״א — Grunwald
his maternal grandmother and their children who perished in the Holocaust:
לעי״נ מרת גנדל בת ר׳ חנוך העניך ע״ה, שנהרגה עקה״ש כ״ז סיון תש״ד הי״ד — Grunwald
ולעי״נ בניהם משה ב״ר שלמה, יעקב ב״ר שלמה, יצחק ב״ר שלמה, בנימין ב״ר שלמה,
שנהרגו עקה״ש כ״ז סיון תש״ד הי״ד
and in memory of her grandparents:
לעי״נ ר׳ חייא בן חכם ר׳ רפאל ע״ה, נפ׳ כ״ד מנחם אב תשל״ה — Aryeh
וזוגתו מרת מלכה בת ר׳ אליהו ע״ה, נפ׳ י״ח טבת תשל״ד

PATRONS OF THE TALMUD

TEMURAH: **Dr. and Mrs. Walter Silver**
Shlomo, Chani, and Avi Cohen
Sheri, Terri, Jennifer and Michelle Kraut
Evan and Alison Silver
in memory of our parents, and great grandparents
צבי יצחק ב"ר שמואל ע"ה – Harry Silver ע"ה
שרה פיגא בת מענדל ע"ה – Sarah Silver ע"ה
אברהם משה בן הרב שלמה זאלי ע"ה – Morris Bienenfeld ע"ה
גוטקה טובה בת אברהם דוד ע"ה – Gertrude Bienenfeld ע"ה

KEREISOS: **Mouki and Charlotte Landau** (Antwerp)
in honor of their children
Natalie and Chemi Friedman   Yanky and Miriam Landau
Steve and Nechama Landau
and in beloved memory of their parents
חיים יעקב ב"ר יהושע ז"ל – Chaim Yaakov Landau ז"ל
אסתר בת ר' יעקב קאפל הכהן ע"ה – Esther Landau ע"ה
בן ציון ב"ר יצחק צבי ז"ל – Benzion Gottlob ז"ל
צילה בת ר' שמואל יהודה לייב ע"ה – Cila Herskovic ע"ה
and in beloved memory of our partner
מורנו הרב ר' יוסף יצחק בן מורנו ורבנו הרה"ג ר' מרדכי רוטנברג זצ"ל אבדק"ק אנטווערפן

ME'ILAH, TAMID, MIDDOS, KINNIM: **Steven and Renée Adelsberg**
Sarita and Rubin Gober   David   Sammy   Avi
in loving memory of
שמואל שמעלקא ב"ר גדליה ז"ל – Samuel Adelsberg ז"ל
and in honor of
Helen Adelsberg Weinberg שתחי'
and
Chaim and Rose Fraiman שיחי'

NIDDAH I: In memory of
Joseph and Eva Hurwitz ע"ה
יוסף ב"ר מרדכי הלוי וחוה פיגא ב"ר אליעזר הלוי ע"ה
and
Lorraine Hurwitz Greenblott – לאה בילא חיה בת ר' יוסף ע"ה
by
Marc and Rachel Hurwitz,
Elisheva Ruchama, Michal, and Nechama Leah;

Martin and Geraldine Schottenstein Hoffman,
Jay and Jeanie Schottenstein, Ann and Ari Deshe,
Susan and Jon Diamond, and Lori Schottenstein;

and Pam and Neil Lazaroff, Frank Millman, and Dawn Petel

NIDDAH II: In memory of
Jerome Schottenstein ע"ה
יעקב מאיר חיים בן אפרים אליעזר הכהן ע"ה

Guardians of the Talmud*

A society of visionary people who recognize the primacy of the Jewish people's commitment to intellect, ethics, integrity, law, and religion — and pursue it by presenting the treasures of the eternal Talmud in the language of today . . . for the generations of tomorrow.

❦ ❦ ❦

David and Jean Bernstein
Matthew Bernstein
Scott and Andrea Bernstein

in memory of
Mr. and Mrs. Harry Bernstein ע״ה
Mr. and Mrs. Joseph Furman ע״ה

❦ ❦ ❦

The publishers pay tribute to the memory of a couple that embodied Torah knowledge and service to our people

הרב יצחק בן ר׳ שמואל ז״ל – Rabbi Yitzchok Filler ז״ל
נפטר ל״ג בעומר תש״ל

הרבנית דבורה בת ר׳ אברהם בצלאל ע״ה – Mrs. Dorothy Filler ע״ה
נפטרה כ״א מרחשון תשס״ג

and the memory of a man of integrity and sensitivity,

ר׳ יוסף בן הרב יהודה אריה ז״ל – George May ז״ל
נפטר כ״ז שבט תש״ס

תנצב״ה

We also honor a matriarch and role model
Mrs. Sylvia May תחי׳

❦ ❦ ❦

Stephen and Terri Geifman
Jacquelyn and Julie

in loving memory of
משה מרדכי בן יחיאל מיכאל ז״ל — Morris M. Geifman
and in honor of
Geraldine G. Geifman

❦ ❦ ❦

Avrohom Chaim and Elisa Taub
Hadassah, Yaakov Yehuda Aryeh, Shifra, Faige, Devorah Raizel, and Golda Leah

in loving memory of his father
ר׳ יעקב ב״ר יהודה אריה ע״ה – Taub
נפ׳ ד׳ מנחם אב תשל״ט

and in memory of the Sanz-Klausenburger Rebbe זצוק״ל
מרן הרהגה״צ ר׳ יקותיאל יהודה בהרהגה״צ ר׳ צבי זצוק״ל כ״ק אדמו״ר אבדק״ק צאנז-קלויזענבורג זי״ע
נלב״ע ש״ק פ׳ חקת, ט׳ תמוז תשנ״ד

*In formation

The Written Word is Forever

Guardians of the Talmud*

A society of visionary people who recognize the primacy of the Jewish people's commitment to intellect, ethics, integrity, law, and religion — and pursue it by presenting the treasures of the eternal Talmud in the language of today . . . for the generations of tomorrow.

❦ ❦ ❦

Milton and Rita Kramer

in honor of their 50th wedding anniversary and Milton's 80th birthday (April 1999),
in honor of the marriage of Ellen to George Gross (September 18, 2000),
and in honor of their children and grandchildren

Daniel and Gina Kramer and Children **Jonathan and Marian Kramer and Children**

Ellen K. and George Gross and their Children

and in everlasting memory of their beloved parents and grandparents
חיים שניאור זלמן הלוי (חזק) ופייגע דינה ע״ה — Hyman S. and Fannie D. Kramer ע״ה
חיים אלטער ושרה חנה ע״ה — Adolph H. and Sadie A. Gross ע״ה
משה אליעזר הלוי ורחל עלקא ע״ה — Morris L. and Rachel E. Kramer ע״ה
דוב בער הכהן ודבורה ע״ה — Barney and Dvorah Cohen ע״ה
משולם צבי ולאה ע״ה — Herman M. and Leah Gross ע״ה
פסח אלכסנדר וחנה ע״ה — Peisach and Hannah Neustadter ע״ה

❦ ❦ ❦

Helene and Moshe Talansky **Ida Bobrowsky** **Irene and Kalman Talansky** **Shoshana Silbert**

in honor of

Rebecca Talansky's 100th birthday עמו״ש

and in memory of
הרב דוד בן הרב אברהם חיים ז״ל — Rabbi David Talansky ז״ל
בלומא בת ר׳ שלמה הלוי ע״ה — Blanche Moshel ע״ה
ר׳ אברהם חיים בן הרב דוד ז״ל — Abraham R. Talansky ז״ל
הרב יעקב בן ר׳ אברהם ז״ל — Rabbi Jacob Bobrowsky ז״ל
תמר בת הרב יעקב ע״ה — Tema Bobrowsky ע״ה
ר׳ משה בן ר׳ לייב ז״ל — בריינה בת ר׳ זלמן ע״ה — Rebecca and Morris Weisinger ז״ל
הרב אברהם בן ר׳ נחמיה ז״ל — Rabbi Avraham Silbert ז״ל
ר׳ מרדכי בן ר׳ שאול ז״ל — שפרה רייזל בת ר׳ צבי ע״ה — Ruth and Marek Stromer ז״ל
ר׳ אהרון בן ר׳ שלמה אריה ז״ל — רחל בת ר׳ יהושע אהרון ע״ה — Rose and Aaron Lerer ז״ל

❦ ❦ ❦

Thomas R. and Janet F. Ketteler

in memory of his mentor

Jerome Schottenstein ע״ה

❦ ❦ ❦

Alan and Myrna Cohen

in honor of

their children

Alison and Matthew

*In formation

The Written Word is Forever

Guardians of the Talmud*

A society of visionary people who recognize the primacy of the Jewish people's commitment to intellect, ethics, integrity, law, and religion — and pursue it by presenting the treasures of the eternal Talmud in the language of today . . . for the generations of tomorrow.

Rona and Edward Jutkowitz

In honor of our family's continuing commitment to Torah learning and Klal Yisrael.
We dedicate this volume to our daughters, **Rebecca and Mollie,**
who are the light of our lives and our blessings, and always fill our hearts with nachas;
and to their zeide, **Mr. Herman Jutkowitz**, who is a constant source of guidance and inspiration;
and in memory of our beloved parents
משה בן מאניס ז״ל ורחל בת אברהם הכהן ע״ה — Martin W. and Ruth Trencher ז״ל
ברכה בת שניאור זלמן ע״ה — Bernice Jutkowitz ע״ה
May our daughters have the honor to teach the value of Torah to their own children,
and may Torah be the guiding light for all of Klal Yisrael.

לעלוי נשמת

הבחור מרדכי גדליהו ז״ל בן משה ואסתר שיחי׳ — Franky Ehrenberg

נפ׳ כ״ג סיון תשס״ג / June 22, 2003

With a life of Torah study and service to Klal Yisrael ahead of him,
our beloved son, brother, and uncle was plucked from this life at only twenty-three.

כי מרדכי . . . דרש טוב לעמו ודבר שלום לכל זרעו

Dr. Martin and Esther Ehrenberg
Scott Leon **Judy and Hillel Olshin**
Yonatan Eliezer **Sara Elisheva**

Richard Bookstaber and Janice Horowitz

In memory of his son

May his memory be a blessing
to all those whose lives he touched.

Michael and Patricia Schiff
Sophia and Juliette
in memory and appreciation of
Jerome Schottenstein ז״ל
and in honor of beloved parents and grandparents
Shirlie and Milton Levitin **Solange and Joseph Fretas** **Judy and Robert Schiff**
and Torah scholars
Rabbi Mordechai Schiff ז״ל and **Rabbi Ephraim Schiff ז״ל**

May we all bring honor to Hashem

*In formation

The Written Word is Forever

The Talmud Associates*

A fellowship of benefactors dedicated to
the dissemination of the Talmud

Dr. Mark and Dr. Barbara Bell,
Bentzion Yosef and Mordechai Yehudah

The Belz Family

Richard Bookstaber and Janice Horowitz
In memory of his son

Michael and Bettina Bradfield
Gabrielle and Matthew
(London)

Nachi and Zippi Brown,
Jessica, Daniella, Shachar and Mindy
in honor of their parents and grandparents

Columbus Jewish Foundation

Milton Cooper and Family

Dr. and Mrs. David Diamond

Nahum and Feige Hinde Dicker and Family

Sophia, Alberto and Rose Djmal

Dr. Richard Dubin

Kenneth and Cochava Dubin

Dr. Martin and Esther Ehrenberg

David and Simone Eshaghian

Louis, Reuben and Larry Feder and Family

Rabbi Judah and Ruth Feinerman

In honor of
Mr. and Mrs. Yehoshua Chaim Fischman
by their children

Mayer and Ruthy Friedman
Ari, Yitzy, Suri, Dovi

Dr. Michael and Susan Friedman
לזכות בניהם, כלתם, ונכדם; בנותיהם, וחתניהם שיחי׳

Yeshaya and Perel Friedman

Julius Frishman

David and Sally Frenkel
לזכות בניהם וכלתם היקרים שיחיו:
דניאל שמואל ומאשה שושנה, אורי גבריאל, רונית פרימיט

Sander and Tracy Gerber
לזכות בניהם היקרים יעקב עקיבא, אסתר פערל, טליה גולדה,
חנה טובה, ורותי רבקה שיחי׳ שיתעלו בתורה ויראת שמים

Leon and Agi Goldenberg
in honor of the marriage of their children
Mendy and Estie Blau

Robert and Rita Gluck
לרפו״ש טויבא רחל בת פריידא שתחי׳

Shari and Jay Gold and Family

Dr. Martin and Shera Goldman and Famil

Esther Henzel

Hirtz, Adler and Zupnick Families

Hashi and Miriam Herzka

Norman and Sandy Nissel Horowitz

Mrs. Farokh Imanuel, Kamram Imanuel
Dr. Mehran and Sepideh Imanuel
Eli and Fariba Maghen

David and Trudy Justin and Family
in honor of their parents
Zoltan and Kitty Justin

Nosson Shmuel and Ann Kahn and Famil
ולזכות בניהם היקרים שיחיו:
חיים דוד, צבי מנחם, אברהם יצחק, ומשפחתם
ולכבוד אמו מרת גיטל שתחי׳ לאויוש״ט

David J. and Dora Kleinbart

In honor of
Mr. and Mrs. Label Kutoff
by their children

The Landowne Family

Ezriel and Miriam Langer

Mr. and Mrs. Chaim Leibel

Yehuda and Rasie Levi

Donald Light

Rudolph and Esther Lowy

Raphael and Blimie Manela
לזכות בניהם היקרים שיחיו:
מתתיהו, ישראל, ישעיהו, חיים משה, ושמעון

Howard and Debra Margolin and Family

Mendy and Phyllis Mendlowitz

*In formation

The Written Word is Forever

The Talmud Associates*

A fellowship of benefactors dedicated to
the dissemination of the Talmud

✣

Robby and Judy Neuman and Family
לזכות בניהם היקרים שיחיו:
אברהם לייב, שרה מאטיל, מרדכי שרגא, שמואל שמעלקא,
רחל ברכה ומנשה ברוך

RoAnna and Moshe Pascher

Naftali Binyomin and Zypora Perlman
In honor of
Mr. and Mrs. Yosef Perlman עמו״ש

Kenneth Ephraim and Julie Pinczower
לרפו״ש ישראל חיים בן פייגלא שיחי׳

Dr. Douglas and Vivian Rabin

Michael G. Reiff

Ingeborg and Ira Leon Rennert

Alan Jay and Hindy Rosenberg

Aviva and Oscar Rosenberg

John and Sue Rossler Family

Mr. and Mrs. David Rubin and Family

Dinah Rubinoff and Family

Ms. Ruth Russ

Mr. and Mrs. Alexander Scharf

Avi and Michou Schnur

Rubin and Marta Schron

Rivie and Leba Schwebel and Family

Shlomo Segev (Smouha)

Bernard and Chaya Shafran
לזכות בניהם היקרים שיחיו:
דבורה, יעקב חיים, דוד זאב, אסתר מנוחה

Steven J. Shaer

Joel and Malka Shafran
לזכות בניהם היקרים שיחיו:
אשר נחמן, טובה חיה, תמר פעסיל, שרה חוה

Robin and Warren Shimoff

Nathan B. and Malka Silberman

The Soclof Family

Dr. Edward L. and Judith Steinberg

Max Taub
and his son Yitzchak

Jay and Sari Tepper

Walter and Adele Wasser

Melvin, Armond and Larry Waxman

William and Noémie Wealcatch

The Wegbreit Family

Robert and Rachel Weinstein and Family

Dr. Zelig and Evelyn (Gutwein) Weinstein
Yaakov, Daniella, Aliza and Zev

Erwin and Myra Weiss

Morry and Judy Weiss

Shlomo and Esther Werdiger

Leslie M. and Shira Westreich

Willie and Blimie Wiesner

The Yad Velvel Foundation

Moshe and Venezia Zakheim

Dr. Harry and Holly Zinn

Mrs. Edith Zukor and Family

*In formation

In Memoriam — לזכרון עולם

Dedicated by the Talmud Associates
to those who forged eternal links

Abraham — שמחה בן ר׳ יהודה לייב הכהן ע״ה
דוד חי ב״ר שלום הכהן ע״ה וחנה בת ר׳ עזרא ע״ה
אהרן בן חיים זאב ע״ה גאלדע בת ר׳ דוד ע״ה
Ashkenazy – ר׳ שלמה ב״ר יצחק זצ״ל ורעיתו עלי׳ מינדעל בת ר׳ יעקב ע״ה
Sarah T. Belz — שרה בת אהרן צבי הלוי ע״ה
Ben-Ari — אליעזר בן מרדכי ע״ה ושרה בת ר׳ אברהם ע״ה
Ben-Ari — מרדכי בן אליעזר ע״ה
Berber — משה ורחל
Bernath – מנשה ב״ר שמואל שמעלקא ע״ה Meizner – מרדכי חיים ב״ר זבולן יצחק חייא ע״ה
Biegeleisen — שמעון דוד ז״ל ב״ר יעקב שלמה שיחי׳ לאוי״ט
Blitz — דוב מאיר ב״ר דוד הכהן ע״ה
Freddy Bradfield — יעקב בן צבי ע״ה
אהרן ב״ר דוד הכהן ז״ל
Cooperberg — שימה רייזל בת ר׳ אהרן שלמה ע״ה
Cooperberg — אברהם אשר בן ר׳ מאיר ע״ה
Cumsky – דוב בער בן אברהם יששכר ע״ה ופעשא מאטלא בת יוסף ע״ה
צבי טעביל בן ישראל ע״ה וליבע בת דוד ע״ה
Diamant — אשר ב״ר יהושע מרדכי הכהן ע״ה
Diamant — שרה בת ר׳ אריה ע״ה
Diamant — ר׳ דוב ב״ר משה ע״ה ורייזל בת ר׳ אברהם ע״ה
Diamond — דר. ר׳ יצחק ב״ר ברוך בענדיט ע״ה
Dicker — מרדכי צבי ב״ר יעקב ע״ה
Dicker — קיילא בת ר׳ משה ע״ה
Djmal — טופיק טוביה בן משה ושושנה ע״ה
Paul and Jeannette Dubin ע״ה
Mollie Dubinsky ע״ה
Abram B. Efroymson ע״ה
Sylvia Spira Efroymson ע״ה
Ehrenberg — אברהם בן עמנואל ע״ה ויוכבד בת ר׳ אלימלך ע״ה
Einhorn — משה בן ברוך ז״ל ורבקה נעכא בת חיים צבי ע״ה
Eshaghian — אברהם בן דוד ע״ה
Esrig — דוד בן שלמה ע״ה וחיה אייגא בת שלום ע״ה
Feder — מלכה בת ירחמיאל הכהן ע״ה
Feiden — ישראל בן אהרן ע״ה
Feinerman — אליעזר בן יוסף ע״ה ולאה בת ישראל יצחק ע״ה
יוסף בן צבי יחזקאל ע״ה ושרה בת ר׳ משה ע״ה
Freier — ישעיה צבי ב״ר חיים אלכסנדר יוסף ע״ה
Freier — שיינדל בת ר׳ משה הלוי ע״ה
Freilich — הרב יצחק דוב ב״ר אברהם יעקב ז״ל
Frenkel – גרשון בן יחיאל דוד ע״ה Rottenstreich – דוד בן עקיבא ע״ה
Friedman — ר׳ אהרן ב״ר יעקב מאיר ע״ה
Friedman — ר׳ אברהם ב״ר אלטר יצחק אייזיק ע״ה

Frishman — מרים בת ר׳ יוסף מרדכי ע״ה
Frishman — יצחק אריה ב״ר יהודה ע״ה ומרים לאה בת ר׳ יצחק ע״ה
Goldman — אמו, שפרה בת ר׳ קלונימוס קלמן ע״ה
Gugenheim — החבר אפרים בן רפאל ע״ה
Gugenheim — בריינדל בת החבר נתן הכהן ע״ה
Hanz — חיים בן מרדכי הי״ד
Henzel — אברהם בן ר׳ מנחם זאב ע״ה
Hirtz — אליעזר בן ישעיה ז״ל ולאה בת יוסף הלוי ע״ה
Horowitz – שלמה יהודה ב״ר זלמן יוסף הלוי ז״ל ומרים בת אברהם הכהן ע״ה
Imanuel — מרדכי בן רחמים ז״ל
Kahn — ר׳ ישראל אריה ב״ר שמואל הכהן ז״ל
Katzef — פרומה באדענה בת אלחנן ע״ה
Kleinbart — משה ב״ר אריה לייב ע״ה
Kleinbart — בתיה בת ר׳ משה אברהם ע״ה
Kriegel — רויזא מינצא בת הרב ישראל יהודה ע״ה
Kulefsky — הילד יהודה לייב ע״ה בן נתן נטע לאי״ט
Langer — משה בן יצחק הי״ד
Landowne — שלמה בן יוסף ע״ה
Lasry — שאול ב״ר אברהם ע״ה וזהרה אסתר בת משה ע״ה
Lazar — אליעזר שאול בן זאב מאיר ע״ה
Lefkovich — ר׳ זאב וועלוול ב״ר יצחק אייזיק ע״ה
Lemberger — יצחק בן אריה ע״ה
Leibel — יחזקאל שרגא ב״ר חיים ע״ה
Leibel — רויזא בת ר׳ אברהם משה ע״ה
Levi — הרב חיים מאיר בן ר׳ מנחם ע״ה
Levi — שושנה טייבא רייזל בת ר׳ יחזקאל גרשון ע״ה
Light — משה גבריאל בן אברהם אליהו ז״ל וחנה בת נתן ע״ה
Lowy – מרדכי אריה ב״ר רפאל הלוי ז״ל ומינדל בת ר׳ שלמה זלמן ע״ה
May — ר׳ יוסף בן הרב יהודה אריה ע״ה
Moskowitz – אליעזר ב״ר אברהם ברוך ז״ל וזהבה בת ר׳ משה ע״ה
Neuman — יצחק אייזיק ב״ר אהרן ע״ה
Nissel — שלמה מאיר בן הרב חיים לייב עזריאל ז״ל
Paneth — אלטע חיה שרה ע״ה בת ר׳ פנחס שיחי׳ לאוי״ט
Parnes – אריה לייבש בן יוסף יצחק ועטיא בת אשר ראובן ע״ה
Parnes — הרב אברהם זאב ב״ר ישכר ע״ה
Parsons — משה זלמן בן אהרן דוב ע״ה
Perlowitz — הרב משה ב״ר אליעזר הלל ע״ה
Pinczower — אפרים ב״ר ישראל חיים ופייגלא בת ר׳ יעקב ע״ה
Rabin — ישראל בן נחום ע״ה
Reiff — לוי יצחק ב״ר עזריאל ז״ל ויהודית בת ר׳ יצחק אייזיק ע״ה
Rennert — שרה בת יצחק יעקב ע״ה
Rennert — יונה מנחם בן אהרן ע״ה

תנצב״ה

In Memoriam — לזכרון עולם

Dedicated by the Talmud Associates
to those who forged eternal links

Rosenberg — חיים נחמן ב״ר דוד ולאה בת יוסף ע״ה
Sam and Leah Rosenbloom ע״ה
Roth — ר׳ צבי יהודה ז״ל ב״ר אברהם יצחק שיחי׳ לאוי״ט
Roth — משה ב״ר יעקב הכהן ע״ה Weisner — יצחק ב״ר זאב ע״ה
Scharf — אליהו ב״ר משה יעקב ושרה בת אלכסנדר זיסקינד ע״ה
Scherman — ר׳ אברהם דוב ב״ר שמואל נטע ע״ה
Scherman — ליבא בת ר׳ זאב וואלף ע״ה
Schnur — אברהם יצחק בן אהרן הי״ד וחנה בת חיים יעקב ע״ה
Schoenbrun — שרגא פייבל ב״ר יעקב הכהן ומאטל אסתר בת מרדכי הלוי ע״ה
Schron — אליעזר דוב בן חיים משה ע״ה
Schron — חוה בת שמעון ע״ה
Schulman — חיים חייקל בן ר׳ שמואל ע״ה
Schulman — חיה בת הרב ישראל יהודה ע״ה
Schwebel — אברהם זכריה מנחם בן יוסף ומחלה בת ישראל מרדכי ע״ה
Scherman — חיים שמואל ב״ר אברהם דוב ע״ה
Scherman — הילד אברהם דוב ע״ה ב״ר זאב יוסף שיחי׳
Rose Schwartz — רייזל בת הרה״ג ר׳ אברהם יצחק ע״ה
Shafran — ר׳ יהושע ב״ר אברהם ע״ה
Shayovich — משה יעקב ב״ר נחום ועטיא פייגא בת מרדכי ע״ה
Shimoff — ר׳ ישראל דוב ב״ר אהרן יעקב ז״ל
Shimoff — חיה רבקה לאה בת ר׳ אליעזר יהודה ע״ה
Shubow — יוסף שלום בן משה ע״ה
Silberman — ר׳ צבי ב״ר זאב הלוי ע״ה
Silberman — דבורה אסתר בת ישראל ע״ה
Silbermintz — יהושע ב״ר יוסף שמריהו ע״ה
Singer — צבי בן ר׳ חיים ע״ה
Singer — הינדי בת ר׳ שלמה ע״ה
Soclof — אברהם אבא ב״ר שמריהו ע״ה
Soclof — חיה ברכה בת צבי הירש הלוי ע״ה
Smouha — הרב אליהו בן מאיר הלוי ע״ה

Steir — משה בן מיכאל ע״ה
Steinberg — יצחק גדליה בן יהודה לייב ע״ה
Steinberg — מלכה בת מאיר לוי ע״ה
Stern — ר׳ חיים מאיר ב״ר שמחה ז״ל ובינה בת ר׳ יוסף מרדכי ע״ה
Tabak — שיינא רחל בת יוסף מרדכי ע״ה
Taub — אליעזר יוסף בן מענדל ע״ה
Taub — מענדל בן אליעזר יוסף חיה בת הירש ע״ה
Wealcatch — חיים דוב ב״ר זאב ואסתר בת ר׳ יוסף אייזיק ע״ה
Weiss — צבי בן יואל ע״ה
Weiss — גיטל בת ישראל ע״ה
Werdiger — ר׳ שלמה אלימלך ב״ר ישראל יצחק ע״ה
Westreich — הרב יהושע בן הרב יוסף יאסקא ז״ל
Leo Werter ע״ה
Wiesner — הרב שמעיה בן הרב זאב ע״ה
Wiesner — שרה לאה בת ר׳ צבי אריה ע״ה
Zakheim-Brecher — בתיה רחל ע״ה בת ר׳ משה יוסף שיחי׳ לאוי״ט
Zalstain — שמעון בן מרדכי יוסף הלוי ע״ה
Zimmer — ר׳ אברהם יעקב בן אהרן אליעזר ע״ה
הרב אהרן ב״ר מאיר יעקב ע״ה
הרבנית פרומא בת ר׳ חיים צבי ע״ה
Zinn — צבי יהודה בן שמעון ע״ה
Zinn — דבורה בת יחיאל מרדכי ע״ה
Leslie Zukor — ר׳ יצחק חיים ב״ר יוסף ע״ה
Zlatow — ר׳ שמואל דוד ב״ר מאיר יעקב ז״ל
הרב אהרן ב״ר מאיר יעקב זצ״ל
הרבנית פרומא בת ר׳ חיים צבי ע״ה
צבי יהודה ז״ל בן אברהם יצחק לאוי״ט
חיים מאיר בן שמחה ז״ל ובינה בת יוסף מרדכי הכהן ע״ה
אליעזר ב״ר אברהם ברוך ז״ל וגולדה זהבה בת משה הלוי ע״ה

תנצב״ה

Pillars of The Talmud

We wish to acknowledge in this volume the friendship of the following:

Murray Zvi Bohnenfield
in memory of his father
Henry Bohnenfield חיים ישראל דוד בן משה צבי ע״ה

Howard D. and Rita Geller
in memory of
יהודה ליב ב״ר יהושע ע״ה
חנה בת יעקב מאיר ע״ה

Dr. Yedidiah and Mrs. Aviva Ghatan

Leighton A. Rosenthal
in memory of
Samuel and Sadie Rosenthal ע״ה

We express our appreciation to the distinguished patrons
who have dedicated volumes in the

HEBREW ELUCIDATION OF THE SCHOTTENSTEIN EDITION OF THE TALMUD

Dedicated by

JAY AND JEANIE SCHOTTENSTEIN

and their children

Joseph Aaron, Jonathan Richard, and Jeffrey Adam

SEDER ZERA'IM:	**Mrs. Margot Guez and Family** **Paul Vivianne Michelle Hubert Monique Gerard Aline Yves**
SEDER NASHIM:	**Ellis A. and Altoon Safdeye and Family**
SEDER NEZIKIN:	**Yisrael and Gittie Ury and Family** (Los Angeles)
BERACHOS I:	**Jay and Jeanie Schottenstein** (Columbus, Ohio)
BERACHOS II:	**Zvi and Betty Ryzman** (Los Angeles)
SHABBOS I:	**Moshe and Hessie Neiman** (New York)
ERUVIN I:	**The Schottenstein Family** (Columbus, Ohio)
ERUVIN II:	**The Schottenstein Family** (Columbus, Ohio)
PESACHIM I:	**Serge and Nina Muller** (Antwerp)
PESACHIM III:	**Morris and Devora Smith** (New York / Jerusalem)
YOMA I:	**Peretz and Frieda Friedberg** (Toronto)
YOMA II:	**Avi Klein and Family** (New York)
SUCCAH I:	**The Pruwer Family** (Jerusalem)
SUCCAH II:	**The Pruwer Family** (Jerusalem)
BEITZAH:	**Chaim and Chava Fink** (Tel Aviv)
ROSH HASHANAH:	**Avi and Meira Schnur** (Savyon)
TAANIS:	**Mendy and Itta Klein** (Cleveland)
MEGILLAH:	**In memory of Jerome Schottenstein ז״ל**
MOED KATTAN:	**Yisroel and Shoshana Lefkowitz** (New York)
CHAGIGAH:	**Steven and Hadassah Weisz** (New York)
YEVAMOS I:	**Phillip and Ruth Wojdyslawski** (Sao Paulo, Brazil)
YEVAMOS II:	**Phillip and Ruth Wojdyslawski** (Sao Paulo, Brazil)
YEVAMOS III:	**Phillip and Ruth Wojdyslawski** (Sao Paulo, Brazil)
KESUBOS I:	**Ben Fishoff and family** (New York)
KESUBOS II:	**Jacob and Esther Gold** (New York)
KESUBOS III:	**David and Roslyn Lowy** (Forest Hills)
NEDARIM I:	**Soli and Vera Spira** (New York / Jerusalem)
NAZIR:	**Shlomo and Esther Ben Arosh** (Jerusalem)
SOTAH:	**Motty and Malka Klein** (New York)
GITTIN I:	**Mrs. Kate Tannenbaum;** **Elliot and Debra Tannenbaum; Edward and Linda Zizmor**

פטרוני התלמוד

KIDDUSHIN I:	**Ellis A. and Altoon Safdeye** (New York)
KIDDUSHIN II:	**Jacqui and Patty Oltuski** (Israel)
BAVA KAMMA I:	**Lloyd and Hadassah Keilson** (New York)
BAVA KAMMA II:	**Faivel and Roiza Weinreich** (New York)
BAVA METZIA I:	**Joseph and Rachel Leah Neumann** (Monsey)
BAVA METZIA II:	**Shlomo and Tirzah Eisenberg** (Bnei Brak)
BAVA METZIA III:	**A. George and Stephanie Saks** (New York)
SANHEDRIN I:	**Martin and Rivka Rapaport** (Jerusalem)
SANHEDRIN III:	In honor of **Joseph and Anita Wolf** (Tel Aviv)
MAKKOS:	**Hirsch and Raquel Wolf** (New York)
SHEVUOS:	**Jacques and Miriam Monderer** (Antwerp)
HORAYOS-EDUYOS:	**Woli and Chaja Stern** (Sao Paulo, Brazil)
ZEVACHIM I:	**Mr. and Mrs. Eli Kaufman**
ZEVACHIM II:	**Mr. and Mrs. Eli Kaufman**
CHULLIN I:	**The Pluczenik Families** (Antwerp)
CHULLIN II:	**Avrohom David and Chaya Baila Klein** (Monsey)
CHULLIN III:	**Avrohom David and Chaya Baila Klein** (Monsey)
CHULLIN IV:	**The Frankel Family**
BECHOROS II:	**Howard and Chaya Balter**
ARACHIN:	**Mr. and Mrs. Eli Kaufman**

PATRONS OF THE TALMUD • DAF YOMI EDITION

We express our appreciation to the distinguished patrons
who have dedicated volumes in the

Dedicated by

JAY AND JEANIE SCHOTTENSTEIN

and their children

Joseph Aaron, Jonathan Richard, and Jeffrey Adam

BERACHOS I: **Jay and Jeanie Schottenstein** (Columbus, Ohio)
BERACHOS II: **Zvi and Betty Ryzman** (Los Angeles)
SHABBOS I: **Dr. Paul and Esther Rosenstock**
SHABBOS II: **Stanley and Ellen Wasserman**
SHABBOS III: **Stanley and Ellen Wasserman**
SHABBOS IV: **Malkie and Nachum Silberman,**
Leonard and Cassia Friedlander, Elkie Friedlander
PESACHIM III: **Lorraine and Mordy Sohn** **Ann and Pinky Sohn**
BEITZAH: **Eric and Joyce Austein**
ROSH HASHANAH: **Steve and Genie Savitsky**
SUCCAH II: **The Lowy and Fasman Families** (Los Angeles)
TAANIS: **David and Jean Bernstein**
MEGILLAH: **Jay and Jeanie Schottenstein** (Columbus, Ohio)
MOED KATAN: **Leon and Olga Klein** **Allen and Sylvia Klein** **Daniel and Esther Ollech**
CHAGIGAH: **Benzi and Esther Dunner**
KESUBOS I: **The Fishoff Families**
KESUBOS II: **Mrs. Moselle Hendeles** **Cecille** **Moise** **Hayim** (Los Angeles)
KESUBOS III: **Brenda and Isaac Gozdzik** (Los Angeles)
NEDARIM I: **Fradie Rapp and Children**
NEDARIM II: **In memory of Laurence A. Tisch**
NAZIR I: **Andrew and Nancy Neff**
NAZIR II: **Andrew and Nancy Neff**
SOTAH I: **Motty and Malka Klein and Family**
SOTAH II: **Motty and Malka Klein and Family**
GITTIN I: **Mrs. Kate Tannenbaum;**
Elliot and Debra Tannenbaum **Edward and Linda Zizmor**
GITTIN II: **Mrs. Kate Tannenbaum;**
Elliot and Debra Tannenbaum **Edward and Linda Zizmor**
KIDDUSHIN I: **Ellis A. and Altoon Safdeye**
KIDDUSHIN II: **Malcolm and Joy Lyons**
BAVA KAMMA I: **Yitzchok and Shoshana Ganger and Family**
BAVA KAMMA II: **The Maggid Families** (Sao Paulo, Brazil)
BAVA KAMMA III: **Robert and Malka Friedlander** (Sao Paulo, Brazil)
BAVA METZIA I: **Fred and Cindy Schulman**
BAVA METZIA II: **Suzy and Yussie Ostreicher**
BAVA METZIA III: **Stephanie and George Saks**

BAVA BASRA I:	**Nachum and Malkie Silberman**
BAVA BASRA II:	**Roger and Caroline Markfield**
BAVA BASRA III:	**Jaime and Marilyn Sohacheski**
SANHEDRIN I:	**Martin and Riva Rapaport**
SANHEDRIN II:	**Martin and Riva Rapaport**
SANHEDRIN III:	**Marvin and Roz Samuels**
SHEVUOS:	**Michael and Danielle Gross** (Herzlia and London)
MAKKOS:	**David and Joan Tepper and Family**
AVODAH ZARAH I:	**The Kuhl Family**
AVODAH ZARAH II:	**In memory of Mr. Jerome Schottenstein ז״ל**
HORAYOS-EDUYOS:	**Woli and Chaja Stern**
ZEVACHIM I:	**Robin and Warren Shimoff**
ZEVACHIM II:	**Abbie Spetner Ari and Chaya Sara and Dovi Nussbaum Chanoch Moshe**
ZEVACHIM III:	**Yaakov and Yona Spinner Dovi Elisheva Yitzy Shiri**
MENACHOS I:	**Terumah Foundation**
MENACHOS II:	**Terumah Foundation**
MENACHOS III:	**Terumah Foundation**
CHULLIN I:	**Rabbi Heshie and Rookie Billet**
CHULLIN II:	**Elly and Brochie Kleinman**
CHULLIN IV:	**Terumah Foundation**
BECHOROS I:	**Jeff and Leslie Gould**
BECHOROS II:	**Hilda and Yitz Applbaum**
ARACHIN:	**The Brown Family**
TEMURAH:	**Dr. Thomas and Anne Kohn Dr. Allan and Susan Seidenfeld**
KEREISOS:	**In memory of Rabbi Meir Shapiro זצ״ל, the Lubliner Rav**
ME'ILAH, TAMID, MIDDOS KINNIM:	**Steven and Renée Adelsberg**
NIDDAH II:	**In memory of Mr. Jerome Schottenstein ז״ל**

The Schottenstein Edition of the Talmud

This pioneering elucidation of the entire Talmud was named THE SCHOTTENSTEIN EDITION in memory of EPHRAIM AND ANNA SCHOTTENSTEIN ז״ל, of Columbus, Ohio. Mr. and Mrs. Schottenstein came to the United States as children, but they never surrendered the principles of Judaism or the love of Torah that they had absorbed in their native Lithuania. Tenacious was their devotion to the Sabbath, kashruth, and halachah; their support of needy Jews in a private, sensitive manner; their generosity to Torah institutions; and their refusal to speak ill of others.

They never surrendered the principles of Judaism or the love of Torah that they had absorbed in Lithuania.

This noble and historic gesture of dedication was made by their sons and daughters-in-law JEROME ז״ל AND GERALDINE SCHOTTENSTEIN and SAUL AND SONIA SCHOTTENSTEIN.

With the untimely passing of JEROME SCHOTTENSTEIN ז״ל, it became our sad privilege to rededicate THE SCHOTTENSTEIN EDITION to his memory, in addition to that of his parents.

Jerome left numerous memorials of accomplishment and generosity, but surely the Schottenstein Edition of the Talmud – spanning centuries – will be the most enduring.

Jerome Schottenstein ז״ל was a dear friend and inspirational patron. He saw the world through the lens of eternity, and devoted his mind, heart and resources to the task of assuring that the Torah would never be forgotten by its people. He left numerous memorials of accomplishment and generosity, but surely the SCHOTTENSTEIN EDITION OF THE TALMUD – spanning centuries – will be the most enduring.

The Schottensteins are worthy heirs to the traditions and principles of Jerome and his parents. Gracious and generous, kind and caring, they have opened their hearts to countless causes and people.

The Schottensteins are worthy heirs to the traditions and principles of Jerome and his parents. Gracious and generous, kind and caring, they have opened their hearts to countless causes and people. Quietly and considerately, they elevate the dignity and self-respect of those they help; they make their beneficiaries feel like benefactors; they imbue institutions with a new sense of mission to be worthy of the trust placed in them.

THE MESORAH HERITAGE FOUNDATION is proud and grateful to be joined with the Schottenstein family as partners in this monumental endeavor.

We pray that this great undertaking will be a source of merit for the continued health and success of the entire Schottenstein family, including the children and grandchildren:

JAY **and** JEANIE SCHOTTENSTEIN and their children, Joseph Aaron, Jonathan Richard, and Jeffrey Adam; ANN **and** ARI DESHE and their children, Elie Michael, David Scott, Dara Lauren, and Daniel Matthew; SUSAN **and** JON DIAMOND and their children, Jillian Leigh, Joshua Louis, and Jacob Meyer; and LORI SCHOTTENSTEIN.

The Schottensteins will be remembered with gratitude for as long as English-speaking Jews are nourished by the eternity of the Talmud's wisdom, for, thanks to them, millions of Jews over the generations will become closer to their heritage.

A Jew can accomplish nothing more meaningful or lasting in his sojourn on earth.

The Davidowitz Family

Renov Stahler Rosenwald Perlysky Edition of Seder Nezikin

An appreciation: By the children of Mr. and Mrs. J. Morton Davis/Davidowitz

The family dynasty created by **ROZI AND MORTY DAVIS/DAVIDOWITZ** is an inspiring, living legend.

ROZI, crowned with goodness, is the exquisite epitome of perfection, with her radiant smile, embracing warmth, brilliance, grace and charm. She was always inspired by her exceptional parents, Emily and Nathan Selengut. Her four daughters seek to emulate this outstanding mother and *aishes chayil.*

Rozi was always inspired by her exceptional parents. Her four daughters seek to emulate this exquisite mother and aishes chayil.

MORTY is renowned as a genius of Wall Street and acclaimed as an eminent author, charismatic lecturer, and innovative financier. With Rozi, he raised himself from humble beginnings through Harvard Business School, until he became President and Chairman of D.H. Blair and Company, Inc.

Morty is renowned as a genius of Wall Street and acclaimed as an eminent author, charismatic lecturer, and innovative financier.

With humility and grateful recognition of Hashem's goodness, Morty and Rozi have become generous supporters of important Jewish causes. Together, Rozi and Morty have created a distinguished and learned family, and imbued their children with Torah values and a heritage of learning, *middos* and *maassim tovim*. Their four daughters and outstanding sons-in-law have created loving, warm, Torah-centered homes. Each couple is uniquely talented and outstanding. Each of their own children is a constant source of joy, nachas, and fun for their grandparents, Rozi and Morty – their "Ema" and "Zidy." These are their greatest dividends and true wealth.

How infinitely blessed we are to have Rozi and Morty as parents, to be part of their dynasty. How infinitely blessed are Rozi and Morty to be enjoying this splendid flow of generations. How blessed are we to be able to express our gratitude for their love and generosity by supporting this eternal Talmud.

How blessed are we to be able to express our gratitude for their love and generosity by supporting this eternal Talmud.

Seder Nezikin is lovingly dedicated in honor of our extraordinary mother and father – Rozi and Morty Davis/Davidowitz: whose achievement brings us honor; whose humor brings us joy; whose teaching brings us direction; whose wisdom brings us understanding; whose values bring us character; whose charity brings us humility; and whose love and totality elevates us to a deeper appreciation of life and G-d.

ESTI AND USHI STAHLER
Jamie, Danny, Duvi, Lisi, Avi, Eli, Malka and Loni

RUKI AND KAL RENOV
Tova, Tani, Eli, Ari, Yoni, Yael, Emi and Benji

RIVKI AND LINDSAY ROSENWALD
Doni, Joshy, Demi and Davey

LAYA AND DOV PERLYSKY
Ayala and Shevi

As this volume goes to press we join in the grief of
Klal Yisrael over the very recent passing of
MARAN HAGAON HARAV SHLOMO ZALMAN AUERBACH זצ״ל
and
HAGAON HARAV SHIMON SCHWAB זצ״ל
They were giants in Torah, in *yiras Shamayim,*
in kindness, in wisdom. They were an inspiration
for the future and bridges to the past.
Their warm support of this edition of the Talmud
was a pillar of strength and a beacon of guidance.

ACKNOWLEDGMENTS

We are grateful to the distinguished *roshei hayeshivah* and rabbinic leaders שליט״א in Israel and the United States whose guidance and encouragement have been indispensable to the success of this Talmud, from its inception. They are named in volume 1 of this tractate.

RABBI ASHER DICKER, a member of the Kollel of Beth Medrash Govoha in Lakewood, who wrote large parts of the first two volumes of this tractate, is the author of chapter 10 of this volume.

Perek Cheilek, the final chapter of Tractate *Sanhedrin,* is one of the seminal aggadic chapters of the Talmud, and it was clear from the start that it must be written by scholars of exceptional competence. We proudly acknowledge their work.

HARAV JOSEPH ELIAS שליט״א is justly regarded as one of this generation's leading educators and expositors of Torah thought. His breadth of knowledge and depth of insight have immeasurably enhanced every page of the commentary of *Perek Cheilek,* especially through his carefully distilled treatments of profound issues. We are grateful that he consented to lend his brilliance to the volume.

RABBI DOVID KATZ, a member of the Kollel of Ner Israel Rabbinical College in Baltimore and a rebbe in the Talmudical Academy of Baltimore, has contributed to previous volumes of this Talmud. As the primary translator and elucidator of *Perek Cheilek,* he painstakingly and efficiently crafted the work until the final editing process. May Rabbi Katz's work bring merit to the soul of his father ר׳ יהודה ליב בן זוסמאן הכהן ע״ה.

Virtually no aspect of our work goes forward without the guidance and counsel of HARAV DAVID FEINSTEIN שליט״א, who makes himself available unstintingly, despite the urgent questions that come to him from throughout the country and the world. This volume, too, has benefited significantly from his inexhaustible knowledge and excellent judgment.

HARAV DAVID COHEN שליט״א has made himself available whenever needed since the inception of the ArtScroll Series, and it has been our privilege to acknowledge his inspirational participation. The stamp of his majesterial knowledge is on every page of this volume.

The taped lectures of HARAV AVIGDOR MILLER שליט״א are justly famous for their incisiveness and illuminating insights. Significant use was made of his shiurim on *Perek Cheilek,* and the editorial staff expresses its gratitude to him.

RABBI ZEV MEISELS read and commented with rare insight and discernment. We are grateful for his help and many valuable suggestions.

A huge investment of time and resources was required to make this edition of the Talmud a reality. Only through the generous support of many people is it possible not only to undertake and sustain such a huge and ambitious undertaking, but to keep the price of the volumes within reach of the average family and student. We are grateful to them all.

The Trustees and Governors of the MESORAH HERITAGE FOUNDATION saw the need to support the scholarship and production of this and other outstanding works of Torah literature. Their names are listed on an earlier page.

In addition, we are grateful to:

ALBERT REICHMANN, whose quiet magnanimity is legend, and LAURENCE A. TISCH and his sons JAMES S. and THOMAS J., who have been more than gracious on numerous occasions;

IRVING I. STONE, whose sponsorship of the STONE EDITION OF THE CHUMASH, SAPIRSTEIN EDITION OF RASHI, and the forthcoming STONE EDITION OF TANACH is bringing a new awareness of the Torah to Jews around the world; MORRY WEISS, who is a shining example of responsible and dynamic lay leadership;

ELLIS A. SAFDEYE, a legendary supporter of worthy causes and a treasured friend; ABRAHAM FRUCHTHANDLER, who has placed support for Torah institutions on a new plateau; LOUIS GLICK, whose sponsorship of the ArtScroll Mishnah Series with the *Yad Avraham* commentary is a jewel in the crown of Torah scholarship and dissemination; JOEL L. FLEISHMAN, whose sage advice and active intervention was a turning point in our work; A. JOSEPH STERN, whose warmth and concern for people and causes are justly legendary; HIRSCH WOLF, a leader in many causes and a valued friend; SHLOMO SEGEV of Bank Leumi, who has been a responsible and effective friend; JUDAH SEPTIMUS and NATHAN SILBERMAN, who make their skills and resources available in too many ways to mention; REUVEN D. DESSLER, a leader in Torah life who brings credit to his distinguished lineage;

and to many other friends who have come forward when their help was needed most: JOSEPH BERLINER, DR. YISRAEL BLUMENFRUCHT, AARON DRILLICK, RABBI YECHEZKEL KAMINSKY, MICHAEL AND GEORGE KARFUNKEL, YEHUDAH LEVI, ABE ROTH, NOCHUM STEIN, DAN AND MOSHE SUKENIK, ZEV WOLLMARK, and MENDY YARMISH.

We conclude with gratitude to *Hashem Yisbarach* for his infinite blessings and for the privilege of being the vehicle to disseminate His word. May this work continue so that all who thirst for His word may find what they seek in the refreshing words of the Torah.

Rabbi Nosson Scherman/ Rabbi Meir Zlotowitz

Adar II, 5755 / March 1995

מסכת סנהדרין
TRACTATE SANHEDRIN

עין משפט
נר מצוה

א א מיי׳ פ״ה מהלכות ממרים הל״ה ופט״ו מהלכות סנהדרין הל״ג סמג לאוין ריט ועשין קו טוש״ע יו״ד סי׳ רמא סעיף א בהג״ה:
ב ב מיי׳ פט״ו מהלכות סנהדרין שם ופרק ט מהלכות גניבה הל״א סמג לאוין קלד:
ג ג מיי׳ פט״ו מהלכות סנהדרין שם ופ״ג מהלכות ממרים הלכה ח סמג לאוין קיג:
ד ד מיי׳ פט״ו מהלכות סנהדרין שם ופ״ט מהלכות יסודי התורה הל״א ופ״ה מהלכות ע״ז הל״א סמג לאוין לה:
ה ה מיי׳ פט״ו מהלכות סנהדרין שם ופרק ה׳ מהלכות ע״ז הלכה ו סמג לאוין לב:
ו ו מיי׳ פט״ו מהלכות סנהדרין שם ופ״א מהלכות איסורי ביאה הל״ו סמג לאוין קג:
ז ז מיי׳ פ״כ מהלכות עדות הל״י:
ח ח מיי׳ פ״ג מהלכות איסורי ביאה הל״ג:
ט ט מיי׳ שם פ״א הלכה ו:
י י מיי׳ פ״ה מהלכות ממרים הלכה ז סמג לאוין רי״ט טור שו״ע יו״ד סימן רמא סעיף ג:
יא כ מיי׳ פכ״ה מהלכו׳ שבת הל״ח סמג לאוין סה טוש״ע או״ח סימן שח סעיף יא:
יב ל מיי׳ פ״א מהלכות שבת הל״ז ופ״ח הל״ז ופ״י הל״י ופי״ב הל״א ופ״ד מהלכות חובל הל״א סמג לאוין סה ועשין ע:

אלו הן הנחנקין: **ה״ג** ואצטריך למכתב מכה איש ומת ואצטריך למכתב ואיש כי יכה כל נפש. ולא כמו שכתוב בספרים כל מכה נפש דבפרק יוצא דופן (נדה מד: ושם) גמרינן בן יום אחד דההורגו חייב ומפיק ליה מדכתיב ואיש כי יכה כל נפש נפש כל דהו ח):

איש דבר מצוה אין. יש ספרים שכתוב בהן אשה לא ואע״ג דהשוה הכתוב אשה לאיש וכו׳ ט) הני מילי בפרשה שנאמרה בלשון זכר אבל היכא דכתיב איש בהדיא ממעטין אשה כדפירש שלהי פרק ד׳ מיתות (לעיל סו.) גבי מקלל אביו ואמו:

הוה אמינא אפילו נפלים. תימה א״כ היכי מיחייב דמי וולדות הא מיחייב מיתה וי״ל דה״א דהכא גזירת הכתוב היא היכא דלא נתכוין לוולדות כדאשכחן לרבי י) ונתתה נפש תחת נפש ממון אי נמי נהי דהוה מיחייב אנפל לאחר שנולד קודם שנולד לא מיחייב: **הכחישה** באבנים כו׳. בהכחשה דלא הדרא איירי דאם לא כן לא שייך נזק דמקרי שבת מידי דהוה אהכהו על ידו ולמחר וסופה לחזור ובבהמה ° לא שייכי ד׳ דברים:

אלא למאן דלית ליה דתנא דבי חזקיה. פירשתי לעיל בפ׳ הנשרפין (דף עט: ד״ה בין):

מאן שמעת ליה דאמר מקלקל בחבורה חייב ר״ש. פלוגתא דר׳ יהודה ור״ש במקלקל בחבורה ומקלקל בהבערה לא מצינו בפירוש לא במשנה ולא בברייתא ובפרק האורג (שבת דף קו. ושם) דחק רש״י לפרש דנפקא מפלוגתא דמלאכה שאינה צריכה לגופה פטור עליה הלכך אין לך חובל ומבעיר שאינו מקלקל ואפילו מבעיר עלים לתבשילו מקלקל הוא אבל העלים ומה שהוא מתקן אבל אחרים לרבי שמעון לא חשיב ליה דהא מלאכה שאינה צריכה לגופה היא אם כן כי חייב הכתוב חובל ומבעיר מדאצטריך למשרי מילה ומדאסר הבערה דבת כהן על כרחיך במקלקל נמי חייב אבל רבי יהודה סבירא ליה מלאכה שאינה צריכה לגופה חייב עליה הלכך חיוב דחובל בצריך לכלבו ומבעיר בצריך לאפרו משכחת לה ואע״פ שמקלקל הוא אבל מלאכה עצמה מתקן הוא אבל אחרים ולרבי יהודה בכי האי גוונא מלאכה היא משום תיקון דאחרים אבל מקלקל ואינו מתקן פטור לשון הקונט׳ כתבתי השתא הא דאמרי׳ התם בפרק האורג (שם) תני רבי אבהו קמיה דר׳ יוחנן כל המקלקלין פטורים חוץ מחובל ומבעיר אמר ליה פוק תני לברא חובל ומבעיר אינה משנה כו׳ משמע מתוך פי׳ הקונטרס דר׳ אבהו כר״ש ורבי יוחנן דבעי צריך לכלבו ולאפרו כר׳ יהודה וזהו תימה א״כ אמאי א״ל פוק תני לברא אטו משום דס״ל כרבי יהודה מאן דתני כר״ש משתיק ליה דכי האי גוונא פריך פרק קמא דחולין (דף טו.) ועוד אי חשיב תיקון גמור צריך לכלבו ולאפרו אמאי נקט חובל ומבעיר ועוד דר״ש אפי׳ בחובל ומבעיר בעי שתהא צריכה לגופה כדמסיק בשמעתין גבי חובל ובשלהי ספק אכל (כריתות דף כ:) גבי הבערה על כן נראה דר׳ אבהו ור׳ יוחנן אליבא דר״ש פליגי דר׳ אבהו כר״ש כדאיתא בפרק האורג (שבת דף קו.) ורבי יוחנן סבר דאפילו ר׳ שמעון בעי תיקון קצת ומיהו לא חשיב תיקון שיתחייב בכך לר׳ יהודה דאין דרך לחבול בחבירו ליתן לכלב ולשרוף גדיש בשביל אפר ופלוגתא דמקלקל בחבורה דרבי יהודה ורבי שמעון קים ליה להש״ס או בקבלה או שמא ברייתא שנויה בשום מקום וכי תימא לרבי אבהו כיון דליכא תיקון א״כ צריכה לגופה היכי משכחת לה הא משכחת לה באיסורי הנאה שסבור שיכול ליהנות וליתן לכלבו וכן מבעיר באיסורי הנאה שסבור שיכול לבשל קדירה ועוד יש לדקדק פלוגתא דמקלקל בחבורה מדתנן בפסחים פר׳ אלו דברים (דף עג: ושם עג. ושם) ושאר כל הזבחים ששחטן לשם פסח אם אין ראוין חייב ואמרי׳ בגמ׳ מאן תנא דשני ליה בין ראוין לשאין ראוין ר״ש הוא ואמרינן התם לעיל מיניה דאיירי בטועה אלמא מחייבינן מתעסק ואמרינן בפ׳ ספק אכל (כריתות ד׳ יט:) הנח לתינוקות הואיל ומקלקל בחבורה חייב מתעסק נמי חייב ומדמחייב רבי שמעון מתעסק בחבורה שמע מינה מקלקל

אלו הן הנחנקין א המכה אביו ואמו ב וגונב נפש מישראל ג וזקן ממרא ע״פ ב״ד ד ונביא השקר ה והמתנבא בשם עבודת כוכבים ו והבא על אשת איש ז וזוממי בת כהן ח ובועלה: **גמ׳** מכה אביו ואמו מנלן דכתיב א) מכה אביו ואמו מות יומת א) ט וכל מיתה האמורה בתורה סתם אינה אלא חנק אימא עד דקטיל ליה מיקטל ס״ד קטל חד בסייף ואביו בחנק ב) הניחא למ״ד חנק קל אלא למאן דאמר חנק חמור מאי איכא למימר אלא מדכתיב ב) מכה איש ומת מות יומת וכתיב ג) או באיבה הכהו בידו וימות שמע מינה כל היכא דאיכא הכאה סתם לאו מיתה הוא ואצטריך למיכתב מכה איש ואיצטריך למכתב ד) כל מכה נפש דאי כתב רחמנא מכה איש ומת הוה אמינא איש דבר מצוה אין קטן לא ג) כתב רחמנא כל מכה נפש ואי כתב רחמנא כל מכה נפש הוה אמינא אפילו נפלים אפילו בן שמונה צריכי ואימא אע״ג דלא עביד ביה חבורה אלמה תנן ד) המכה אביו ואמו אינו חייב עד שיעשה בהן חבורה אמר קרא ה) מכה אדם ומכה בהמה מה מכה בהמה עד דעביד בה חבורה דכתיב בה ו) נפש אף מכה אדם עד דעביד חבורה מתקיף לה רב ירמיה אלא מעתה הכחישה באבנים הכי נמי דלא מיחייב אלא אם אינו ענין לנפש בהמה דהא אי נמי הכחישה באבנים חייב תניהו ענין לנפש אדם אלא הקישא למה לי לכדתניא ה) דבי חזקיה הניחא למאן דאית ליה תנא דבי חזקיה אלא למאן דלית ליה תנא דבי חזקיה היקישא למה לי מה מכה בהמה לרפואה פטור אף מכה אדם לרפואה פטור דאיבעיא להו בן מהו שיקיז דם לאביו רב מתנא אמר ז) ואהבת לרעך כמוך רב דימי בר חיננא אמר מכה אדם ומכה בהמה מה מכה בהמה לרפואה פטור אף מכה אדם לרפואה פטור (א) רב ו לא שביק לבריה למישקל ליה סילוא מר בריה דרבינא לא שביק לבריה למיפתח ליה ו) כוותא דילמא חביל והוה ליה שגגת איסור אי הכי אחר נמי אחר שיגגת לאו בנו שגגת חנק ז) והדתנן כ מחט של יד ליטול בה את הקוץ ליחוש דילמא חביל והויא לה שגגת סקילה התם מקלקל הוא הניחא למאן דאמר ל מקלקל פטור אלא למ״ד חייב מאי איכא למימר מאן שמעת ליה דאמר מקלקל בחבורה חייב ר׳ שמעון היא ורבי

אלו הן הנחנקין: ממרא על פי בית דין. כמו ממרים הייתם עם ה׳ (דברים ט) שמסרב על פי ב״ד הגדול שבלשכת הגזית: וזוממי בת כהן. אע״פ שהם היו מחייבין אותה שריפה אין נדונין אלא במיתה שהיו מחייבין לבועל והיינו חנק כשאר בא על אשת איש כדמפרש קרא היא תשרף ולא בועלה וזוממיה ילפינן מכאשר זמם לעשות לאחיו לאחיו ולא לאחותו: ובועלה. בנשואה בת כהן קמיירי אבל ארוסה בועלה בסקילה: **גמ׳** ס״ד. בתמיה: קטל חד בסייף. כדתנן בפרקין לעיל (דף עו:) אלו הן הנהרגים הרולח ועיר הנדחת: מאי איכא למימר. הכא ליכא למדרש דאביו בחנק: **אלא** מדכתיב מכה איש ומת. היכא דבעי מיתה מפרש מיתה בהדיא: אפילו נפלים. כגון בן תשעה וראשו אטום או שיש לו שני גבין דלא חיי: דכתיב ביה נפש. ונפש משמע דם דהוה חבורה: הכחישה. לבהמה: באבנים. דלא עשה בה חבורה: לנפש אדם. דהיינו אביו דאף על גב דלא בעינן מיתה חבורה מיהא בעינן: **אלא** הקישא למה לי. דאתקש מכה אדם למכה בהמה בחד קרא הואיל וילפת ליה מאם אינו ענין: לכדתניא דבי חזקיה. בב״ק [בהמניח] (דף לה.) לפטור חייבי מיתות שוגגין מן התשלומין מה מכה בהמה לא חלקת בו וכו׳: הניחא וכו׳. פלוגתא דרבי יוחנן ורשב״ל בכתובות באלו נערות (דף לד:): מה מכה בהמה לרפואה. כגון מקיז דם פטור מן התשלומין שהרי לא הזיקה: אף מכה אדם. דהיינו אביו: לרפואה פטור. ממיתה ואע״ג דחבורה היא: ואהבת לרעך כמוך. לא הוזהרו ישראל מלעשות לחבריהם אלא דבר שאינו חפץ לעשות לעצמו: סילוא. קוץ ישב לו בבשרו: למפתח ליה כוותא. כויה להוציא ליחה ממנה: אי הכי אחר נמי. לא ליפתח שהרי כל ישראל הוזהרו על חבלת חבירו דכתיב (דברים כה) לא יוסיף פן יוסיף: שגגת לאו. כשאין מתכוין הוי שגגה באיסור שזדונו לאו בעלמא דקיל: מחט של יד. היא מחט קטנה שתופרין בה בגדים ניטלת בשבת ליטול בה את הקוץ ומשום דקתני לה להלן במסכת שבת בפרק כל הכלים (דף קכב:) גבי ושל שקאין לפתוח בו את הדלת קרי ליה להא קטנה מחט של יד: דילמא חביל. ועביד חבורה בשבת: מקלקל הוא. וכל המקלקלין פטורין בחלול שבת דמלאכת מחשבת כתיב ואין מחייב אמקלקל אלא רבי שמעון ומקלקל בחבורה רבי שמעון נמי לא מחייב אלא במתכוון לכך דהוי צריך לחבלה אבל הנוטל קוץ אין צריך לחבלה וברצונו לא יחבל:

מסורת הש״ס

א) [לעיל נג: לקמן פט.], ב) [לעיל טו: נג:], ג) נדה מד: [ע״ש תוס׳], ד) [לקמן פה:], ה) [לעיל עט: ושם נסמן], ו) [בערוך ערך בע ד׳ איתא בועתא], ז) שבת קז. קכב:, ח) [עי׳ תוס׳ נדה מד: ד״ה איש כי יכה], ט) [כדאיתא פסחים מג.], י) [לעיל עט.].

הגהות הב״ח

(א) גמ׳ רב פפא לא שביק לבריה:

ליקוטי רש״י

מכה אביו ואמו. בחנק. דכתיב ביה (שמות כא) יומת סתמא וקיימא לן (סנהדרין נב:) כל מיתה האמורה בתורה סתם אינו אלא חנק [לעיל נ.]. זקן ממרא. שהמרה על ב״ד של לשכת הגזית ומיתתו בחנק [סוטה כה.]. זוממי בת כהן. לעשות לאחיו מה תלמוד לומר לאחיו למד על זוממי בת כהן נשואה שאינן בשריפה אלא כמיתת הבועל שהוא בחנק שנאמר היא באש תשרף (ויקרא כא, ט) היא ולא בועלה לכך נאמר כאן לאחיו כאשר זמם לעשות לאחיו ולא כאשר זמם לעשות לאחותו אבל בכל שאר מיתות השוה הכתוב אשה לאיש וזוממי אשה נהרגין כזוממי איש כגון שהעידוה שהרגה את הנפש שחללה את השבת נהרגין במיתתה שלא מיעט כאן אחותו אלא במקום שיש לקיים בהן הזמה במיתת הבועל [דברים יט, יט]. שהיא והן נהרגין ולא במיתה אחת דהיא בשריפה והן במיתת הבועל כגון באו עדים והזימו את הראשונים וחייבום מיתת הבועל ולא מיתתה דכתיב (דברים יט) כאשר זמם לעשות לאחיו ולא לאחותו כדאמר באלו הן הנחנקין (סנהדרין נ). בועלה. דהיא בשריפה אבל בועלה נידון כשאר בועל בת ישראל דבועל ארוסה בסקילה ובועל נשואה בחנק דכתיב (ויקרא כא) היא באש תשרף היא ולא בועלה היא ולא זוממיה [לעיל מו.]. מכה אביו ואמו. לפי שלמדנו על החובל בחבירו שהוא בתשלומין ולא במיתה הוצרך לומר על החובל באביו שהוא במיתה ואינו חייב אלא בהכאה שיש בה חבורה [שמות כא, טו]. למאן דאמר חנק חמור. מסייף בפרק ארבע מיתות (סנהדרין נ:) [לעיל טו:]. מכה איש ומת. למה נאמר לפי שנאמר (ויקרא כד, יז) ואיש כי יכה כל נפש אדם מות יומת שומע אני בהכאה בלא מיתה תלמוד לומר מכה איש ומת אינו חייב אלא בהכאה של מיתה ואם נאמר מכה איש ולא נאמר ואיש כי יכה הייתי אומר אינו חייב עד שיכה איש היכה את האשה ואת הקטן מנין תלמוד לומר כי יכה כל נפש אדם אפילו קטן ואפילו אשה ועוד אלו נאמר מכה איש שומע אני אפילו קטן שהכה והרג יהא חייב תלמוד לומר ואיש כי יכה ולא קטן שהכה ועוד כי יכה כל נפש אדם אפילו נפלים במשמע תלמוד לומר מכה איש אינו חייב עד שיכה בן קיימא ראוי להיות איש [שם פסוק יב]. מכה אדם ומכה בהמה. ומכה אדם יומת, אפילו לא הרגו אלא עשה בו חבורה שלא נאמר כאן נפש ובמכה אביו ואמו דבר הכתוב ובא להקישו למכה בהמה מה מכה בהמה מחיים אף מכה אביו ואמו מחיים פרט למכה לאחר מיתה לפי שמצינו שהמקללו לאחר מיתה חייב הוצרך לומר במכה שפטור ומה בבהמה בחבלה שאם אין חבלה אין תשלומין אף מכה אביו ואמו אינו חייב עד שיעשה בהם חבורה [ויקרא כד, כא]. כדתני דבי חזקיה. מכה נפש בהמה ישלמנה מכה אדם יומת מה מכה בהמה לא חלקת בו בין שוגג למזיד לפטרו ממון אף מכה אדם לא תחלק בו בין שוגג למזיד לפטרו ממון [ב״ק כו]. כדאמרי׳ (ב״ק לה.) אדם מועד לעולם אף מכה אדם לפטוריה קרא מתשלומין דכתיב יומת ואפילו בשוגג פטור הואיל ולמזיד מיתה [ב״ק לה.]. מחט של יד. מחט קטן שתופרין בה בגדים [שבת קכב:]. מחט של יד. ניטלת לכתחילה ליטול בה את הקוץ. וביתו דומיא דלחבלה למצער ליה ואינו חושש אם יצא דם מיד [שם קז.]. [המשך בדף פה.]

גליון הש״ס

תוס׳ ד״ה הכחישה וכו׳. לא שייכי ד׳ דברים. עי׳ גיטין דף מב ע״ב תוס׳ ד״ה ושור:

תורה אור השלם

א) וּמַכֵּה אָבִיו וְאִמּוֹ מוֹת יוּמָת: [שמות כא, טו]
ב) מַכֵּה אִישׁ וָמֵת מוֹת יוּמָת: [שמות כא, יב]
ג) אוֹ בְאֵיבָה הִכָּהוּ בְיָדוֹ וַיָּמֹת מוֹת יוּמַת הַמַּכֶּה רֹצֵחַ הוּא גֹּאֵל הַדָּם יָמִית אֶת הָרֹצֵחַ בְּפִגְעוֹ בוֹ: [במדבר לה, כא]
ד) כָּל מַכֵּה נֶפֶשׁ לְפִי עֵדִים יִרְצַח אֶת הָרֹצֵחַ וְעֵד אֶחָד לֹא יַעֲנֶה בְנֶפֶשׁ לָמוּת: [במדבר לה, ל]
[לפי תוס׳] וְאִישׁ כִּי יַכֶּה כָּל נֶפֶשׁ אָדָם מוֹת יוּמָת: [ויקרא כד, יז]
ה) וּמַכֵּה בְהֵמָה יְשַׁלְּמֶנָּה וּמַכֵּה אָדָם יוּמָת: [ויקרא כד, כא]
ו) וּמַכֵּה נֶפֶשׁ בְּהֵמָה יְשַׁלְּמֶנָּה נֶפֶשׁ תַּחַת נָפֶשׁ: [ויקרא כד, יח]
ז) לֹא תִקֹּם וְלֹא תִטֹּר אֶת בְּנֵי עַמֶּךָ וְאָהַבְתָּ לְרֵעֲךָ כָּמוֹךָ אֲנִי יְיָ: [ויקרא יט, יח]

Chapter Ten

Mishnah The previous three chapters list and explain the transgressions for which one incurs the first three methods of execution mentioned on 49b. This chapter discusses the sins for which one incurs the fourth method of execution – strangulation.[1]

אֵלּוּ הֵן הַנֶּחְנָקִין – These are the ones who are strangled:
הַמַּכֶּה אָבִיו וְאִמּוֹ – One who strikes his father or his mother;[2] **וְגוֹנֵב נֶפֶשׁ מִיִּשְׂרָאֵל – one who kidnaps a Jewish person;**[3] **וְזָקֵן מַמְרֵא עַל פִּי בֵית דִּין – a sage who rebels against the word of the** High **Court;**[4] **וּנְבִיא הַשֶּׁקֶר – a false prophet;**[5] **וְהַמִּתְנַבֵּא בְּשֵׁם עֲבוֹדַת כּוֹכָבִים – one who prophesies in the name of a false god;**[6] **וְהַבָּא עַל אֵשֶׁת אִישׁ – one who commits adultery; וְזוֹמְמֵי בַת כֹּהֵן – the** ***zomemin*** witnesses **of the daughter of a Kohen;**[7] **וּבוֹעֲלָהּ – and the man who** illicitly **cohabited with [the daughter]** of a Kohen.[8]

Gemara The Mishnah listed the sins that are punishable with death by strangulation. The Gemara now provides the Scriptural source for the first sin, striking a parent: **מַכֵּה אָבִיו וְאִמּוֹ מְנָלַן – From where do we know** that **one who strikes his father or mother** is punished with strangulation? **דִּכְתִיב ,,וּמַכֵּה אָבִיו וְאִמּוֹ מוֹת יוּמָת" – For it is written:**[9] ***And one who strikes his father or his mother shall surely be put to death.*** The Torah does not specify how he is to be executed, **וְכָל מִיתָה הָאֲמוּרָה בַּתּוֹרָה סְתָם – and** the rule is that **whenever** putting to **death is mentioned by the Torah in an undefined manner,** i.e. without specifying the type of death, **אֵינָהּ אֶלָּא חֶנֶק – it refers to no other** death **than strangulation.**[10] Hence, the verse is stating that one who strikes a parent is killed by strangulation.

The Gemara asks:

אֵימָא עַד דְּקָטִיל לֵיהּ מִיקְטַל – Let us say that he does not receive this punishment **unless he kills [a parent].**[11] How do we know that one is executed for striking a parent even if the parent survived?

The Gemara responds rhetorically:

סָלְקָא דַעְתָּךְ – Can you really **think** this? **קָטַל חַד בְּסַיִיף – Is it** possible that **if [a person] kills someone** other than his parent, he is executed **by beheading,**[12] a relatively severe method of execution, **וְאָבִיו בְּחֶנֶק – but** if he kills **his father,** he is killed **by strangulation,** the most lenient form of execution? Surely not![13] Thus, the Torah must be stating that one is subject to strangulation for striking a parent even if the parent survives.

The Gemara examines this response:

הָנִיחָא לְמַאן דְּאָמַר חֶנֶק קַל – This is understandable according to the one who states that death by **strangulation is more lenient** than beheading.[14] According to him, the Torah could not possibly

NOTES

1. The method by which the court performs strangulation is detailed above (52b).

There is some question about the correct sequence of chapters in this tractate. In the standard edition of the Gemara, this chapter immediately follows the ninth chapter and *Chelek* is the eleventh chapter. The reason for this sequence is that our chapter, like the three preceding ones, discusses the sins punishable by the four methods of execution. *Chelek,* on the other hand, discusses one unrelated topic: which sinners lose their share in the World to Come. Accordingly, it follows our chapter (see *Rashi* to 90a ד״ה כל ישראל). In the standard edition of the Mishnah, however, *Chelek* is the tenth chapter and our chapter is the eleventh. For an explanation of that sequence, see *Chidushei HaRan* at length.

2. And inflicts a wound (see Gemara below).

3. And works with him, and then sells him as a slave (see *Exodus* 21:16 and Gemara 85b).

4. This refers to a sage who refuses to accept a ruling of the Great Sanhedrin, which is located in the Chamber of Hewn Stone on the Temple Mount. [The Gemara (86b-88b) will discuss precisely what the sage must do to be subject to the death penalty.]

Our Mishnah uses מַמְרֵא to mean *rebel* based on the verse in *Deuteronomy* (9:24): *You have been rebels* (*mamrim*) *against Hashem* (*Rashi*).

5. I.e. one who falsely claims to have received a prophecy from God.

6. I.e. one who claims to have received a prophecy not from God but from a false god. The Mishnah and Gemara on 89a will explain the details of these cases.

7. Witnesses become *zomemin* (sing. *zomeim*) when a second set of witnesses states that the first ones could not have seen the incident to which they testified because they were in a different place at the time. This process, known as *hazamah,* discredits the first witnesses and establishes the second set as the ones whose testimony is accepted. The Torah (*Deuteronomy* 19:16-21) prescribes that if false witnesses succeeded in having a person convicted based on their false testimony and they are then found to be *zomemin,* they are to be punished with the very consequences they planned to inflict upon the victim of their plot.

In our Mishnah's case, a pair of witnesses appear in court and testify that a certain woman – a daughter of a Kohen – committed adultery with a certain man. This woman, if convicted, would be executed through burning (see 75a). Then a second set of witnesses discredits the first ones through *hazamah*; that is, they state that the first witnesses could not have seen what they allege because at the time, they were in a different place. The first witnesses then become *zomemim,* but they are not executed through burning, the punishment they tried to impose upon the woman. Rather, they are executed through strangulation, because the Torah exegetically indicates that the woman's partner in adultery is put to death through this form of execution (see above, 51a, and also following note). The source for punishing the *zomemim* witnesses with the type of execution appropriate for the adulterer rather than that appropriate for the adulteress is the verse in *Deuteronomy* 19:19: *You shall do to him* (a *zomeim* witness) *as he conspired to do to* ***his brother.*** This implies that if the witnesses conspired to kill two people – a man and a woman – through different types of execution, they are put to death with the type they tried to impose upon the man (*Rashi*; see *Tosafos* to 51b ד״ה לאחיו).

8. The Torah (*Leviticus* 21:9) specifies that if the daughter of a Kohen commits adultery, she is executed by the method of שְׂרֵיפָה, *burning.* However, only the woman is killed by these means; her male partner is killed in the same way as any man who commits adultery (see previous note). That is, if the Kohen's daughter was a betrothed *naarah,* he is stoned, and if she had already completed marriage through *nisuin,* he is executed through strangulation. Our Mishnah, which imposes strangulation upon the adulterer, discusses a case where the Kohen's daughter had undergone *nisuin* before she committed adultery (see *Rashi*; see also *Aruch LaNer* and *Margaliyos HaYam*).

9. *Exodus* 21:15.

10. This is a הֲלָכָה לְמֹשֶׁה מִסִּינַי, a law taught orally to Moses at Sinai (see *Rambam, Hil. Sanhedrin* 14:1 with *Radbaz*). See above, 52b, 53a.

11. For the word מַכֶּה, which means *to smite* or *to strike,* is often used to denote an act of killing. The Gemara below will cite some examples of such usage. See also *Chidushei HaRan.*

12. As taught in the Mishnah above, 76b.

13. For the Torah would surely not impose a more lenient punishment for murdering a parent than for killing a stranger!

14. The Mishnah on 49b cites a Tannaic dispute about the relative severity of the various types of execution. The Tanna Kamma maintains that strangulation is more lenient than beheading, whereas R' Shimon maintains that it is more severe.

אלו הן הנחנקין [א] המכה אביו ואמו [ב] וגונב נפש מישראל [ג] וזקן ממרא ע"פ ב"ד [ד] ונביא השקר [ה] והמתנבא בשם עבודת כוכבים [ו] והבא על אשת איש [ז] וזוממי בת כהן [ח] ובועלה: **גמ'** מכה אביו ואמו מנלן דכתיב (א) מכה אביו ואמו מות יומת (א) [ט] וכל מיתה האמורה בתורה סתם אינה אלא חנק אימא עד דקטיל ליה מיקטל ס"ד קטל חד בסייף ואביו בחנק (ב) הניחא למ"ד חנק קל אלא למאן דאמר חנק חמור מאי איכא למימר אלא מדכתיב (ב) מכה איש ומת מות יומת וכתיב (ג) או באיבה הכהו בידו וימות שמע מינה כל היכא דאיכא הכאה סתם לאו מיתה הוא ואצטריך למיכתב מכה איש ואיצטריך למכתב (ד) כל מכה נפש דאי כתב רחמנא מכה איש ומת הוה אמינא איש דבר מצוה אין קטן לא (ג) כתב רחמנא כל מכה נפש ואי כתב רחמנא כל מכה נפש הוה אמינא אפילו נפלים אפילו בן שמונה צריכי ואימא אע"ג דלא עביד ביה חבורה אלמה תנן (ד) המכה אביו ואמו אינו חייב עד שיעשה בהן חבורה אמר קרא (ה) מכה אדם ומכה בהמה מה מכה בהמה עד דעביד בה חבורה דכתיב בה (ו) נפש אף מכה אדם עד דעביד חבורה מתקיף לה רב ירמיה אלא מעתה הכחישה באבנים הכי נמי דלא מיחייב אלא אם אינו ענין לנפש בהמה דהא אי נמי הכחישה באבנים חייב תניהו ענין לנפש אדם אלא הקישא למה לי לכדתניא (ה) דבי חזקיה הניחא למאן דאית ליה תנא דבי חזקיה אלא למאן דלית ליה תנא דבי חזקיה היקישא למה לי מה מכה בהמה לרפואה פטור אף מכה אדם לרפואה פטור דאיבעיא להו בן מהו שיקיז דם לאביו רב מתנא אמר (ז) ואהבת לרעך כמוך רב דימי בר חיננא אמר מכה אדם ומכה בהמה מה מכה בהמה לרפואה פטור אף מכה אדם לרפואה פטור (א) רב' לא שביק לבריה למישקל ליה סילוא מר בריה דרבינא לא שביק לבריה למיפתח ליה (ו) כוותא דילמא חביל והוה ליה שגגת איסור אי הכי אחר נמי אחר שיגגת לאו בנו שגגת חנק (ז) והדתנן [כ] מחט של יד ליטול בה את הקוץ ליחוש דילמא חביל והויא לה שגגת סקילה התם מקלקל הוא הניחא למאן דאמר [ל] מקלקל פטור אלא למ"ד חייב מאי איכא למימר מאן שמעת ליה דאמר מקלקל בחבורה חייב ר' שמעון היא ורבי

אלו הן הנחנקין: ממרא על פי בית דין. כמו ממרים הייתם עם ה' (דברים ט) שמסרב על פי ב"ד הגדול שבלשכת הגזית: וזוממי בת כהן. אע"פ שהם היו מחייבין אותה שריפה אין נדונין אלא במיתה שהיו מחייבין לבועל והיינו חנק כשאר בא על אשת איש כדמפרש קרא היא תשרף ולא בועלה וזוממיה ילפינן מכאשר זמם לעשות לאחיו לאחיו ולא לאחותו: ובועלה. בנשואה בת כהן קמיירי אבל ארוסה בועלה בסקילה: **גמ'** ס"ד. בתמיה: קטל חד בסייף. כדתנן בפרקין לעיל (דף עו:) אלו הן הנהרגים הרוצח ועיר הנדחת: **מאי איכא** למימר. הכא ליכא למדרש דאביו בחנק: **אלא** מדכתיב מכה איש ומת. היכא דבעי מיתה מפרש מיתה בהדיא: **אפילו** נפלים. כגון בן תשעה וראשו אטוס או שיש לו שני גבין דלא חיי: **דכתיב** ביה נפש. ונפש משמע דם דהוה חבורה: **הכחישה.** לבהמה: **באבנים.** דלא עשה בה חבורה: **לנפש אדם.** דהיינו אביו דאף על גב דלא בעינן מיתה חבורה מיהא בעינן: **אלא** הקישא למה לי. דאתקש מכה אדם למכה בהמה בחד קרא הואיל וילפת ליה מאם אינו ענין: **לכדתניא דבי** חזקיה. בב"ק [בהמניח] (דף לה.) לפטור חייבי מיתות שוגגין מן התשלומין מה מכה בהמה לא חלקת בו וכו': **הניחא** וכו'. פלוגתא דרבי יוחנן ורשב"ל בכתובות באלו נערות (דף לד:): **מה מכה בהמה לרפואה.** כגון מקיז דם פטור מן התשלומין שהרי לא הזיקה: **אף מכה אדם.** דהיינו אביו: **לרפואה פטור.** ממיתה ואע"ג דחבורה היא: **ואהבת לרעך כמוך.** לא הוזהרו ישראל מלעשות לחבריהם אלא דבר שאינו חפץ לעשות לעצמו: **סילוא.** קוץ ישב לו בבשרו: **למפתח** ליה כוותא. כויה להוציא ליחה ממנה: **אי הכי אחר נמי.** לא ליפתח שהרי כל ישראל הוזהרו על חבלת חבירו דכתיב (דברים כה) לא יוסיף פן יוסיף: **שגגת לאו.** כשאין מתכוין הוי שגגה באיסור שזדונו לאו בעלמא דקיל: **מחט של יד.** היא מחט קטנה שתופרין בה בגדים ניטלת בשבת ליטול בה את הקוץ ומשום דקתני לה להכן במסכת שבת בפרק כל הכלים (דף קכב:) גבי ושל שקאין לפתוח בו את הדלת קרי ליה להא קטנה מחט של יד: **דילמא** חביל. ועביד חבורה בשבת: **מקלקל** הוא. וכל המקלקלין פטורין בחלול שבת דמלאכת מחשבת כתיב ואין מחייב אמקלקל אלא רבי שמעון ומקלקל בחבורה רבי שמעון נמי לא מחייב אלא במתכוון לכך דהוי צריך לחבלה אבל הנוטל קוץ אין צריך לחבלה וברצונו לא יחבל:

אלו הן הנחנקין: **ה"ג** ואצטריך למכתב מכה איש ומת ואצטריך למכתב ואיש כי יכה כל נפש. ולא כמו שכתוב בספרים כל מכה נפש דבפרק יוצא דופן (נדה מד: ושם) גמרינן בן יום אחד דההורגו חייב ומפיק ליה מדכתיב ואיש כי יכה כל נפש נפש כל דהו [ח]:

איש דבר מצוה אין. יש ספרים שכתוב בהן אשה לא ואע"ג דהשוה הכתוב אשה לאיש וכו' [ט] הני מילי בפרשה שנאמרה בלשון זכר אבל היכא דכתיב איש בהדיא ממעטין אשה כדפירש שלהי פרק ד' מיתות (לעיל סו.) גבי מקלל אביו ואמו:

הוה אמינא אפילו נפלים. תימה א"כ היכי מיחייב דמי וולדות הא מיחייב מיתה וי"ל דה"א דהכא גזירת הכתוב היא היכא דלא נתכוין לוולדות כדאשכחן לרבי [י] ונתתה נפש תחת נפש ממון אי נמי נהי דהוה מיחייב אנפל לאחר שנולד קודם שנולד לא מיחייב: **הכחישה** באבנים כו'. בהכחשה דלא הדרא איירי דאם לא כן לא שייך נזק דמקרי שבח מידי דהוה אהכהו על ידו ולמתה וסופה לחזור ובבהמה ° לא שייכי ד' דברים:

אלא למאן דלית ליה דתנא דבי חזקיה. פירשתי לעיל בפ' הנשרפין (דף עט: ד"ה בין):

מאן שמעת ליה דאמר מקלקל בחבורה חייב ר"ש. פלוגתא דר' יהודה ור"ש במקלקל בחבורה ומקלקל בהבערה לא מצינו בפירוש לא במשנה ולא בברייתא ובפרק האורג (שבת דף קו. ושם) דחק רש"י לפרש דנפקא מפלוגתא דמלאכה שאינה צריכה לגופה פטור עליה הלכך אין לך חובל ומבעיר שאינו מקלקל ואפילו מבעיר עצים לתבשילו מקלקל הוא אצל העצים ומה שהוא מתקן אצל אחרים לרבי שמעון לא חשיב ליה דהא מלאכה שאינה צריכה לגופה היא אם כן כי חייב הכתוב חובל ומבעיר מדאצטריך למשרי מילה ומדאסר הבערה דבת כהן על כרחיך במקלקל נמי חייב אבל רבי יהודה סבירא ליה מלאכה שאינה צריכה לגופה חייב עליה הלכך חיוב דחובל בצריך לכלבו ומבעיר בצריך לאפרו משכחת לה ואע"פ שמקלקל הוא אצל מלאכה עצמה מתקן הוא אצל אחרים ולרבי יהודה בכי האי גוונא מלאכה היא משום תיקון דאחרים אבל מקלקל ואינו מתקן פטור לשון הקונט' כתבתי השתא הא דאמרי' התם בפרק האורג (שם) תני רבי אבהו קמיה דר' יוחנן כל המקלקלין פטורים חוץ מחובל ומבעיר אמר ליה פוק תני לברא חובל ומבעיר אינה משנה כו' משמע מתוך פי' הקונטרס דר' אבהו כר"ש ורבי יוחנן דבעי צריך לכלבו ולאפרו כר' יהודה וזהו תימה א"כ אמאי א"ל פוק תני לברא אטו משום דס"ל כרבי יהודה מאן דתני כר"ש משתיק ליה דכי האי גוונא פריך פרק קמא דחולין (דף טו.) ועוד אי חשיב תיקון גמור צריך לכלבו ולאפרו אמאי נקט חובל ומבעיר ועוד דר"ש אפי' בחובל ומבעיר בעי שתהא צריכה לגופה כדמסיק בשמעתין גבי חובל ובשלהי ספק אכל (כריתות דף כ:) גבי הבערה על כן נראה דר' אבהו ור' יוחנן אליבא דר"ש פליגי דר' אבהו כר"ש כדאיתא בפרק האורג (שבת דף קו.) ורבי יוחנן סבר דאפילו ר' שמעון בעי תיקון קצת ומיהו לא חשיב תיקון שיתחייב בכך לר' יהודה דאין דרך לחבול בחבירו ליתן לכלב ולשרוף גדיש בשביל אפר ופלוגתא דמקלקל בחבורה דרבי יהודה ורבי שמעון קים ליה להש"ס או בקבלה או שמא ברייתא שנויה בשום מקום וכי תימא לרבי אבהו כיון דליכא תיקון א"כ צריכה לגופה היכי משכחת לה הא משכחת לה באיסורי הנאה שסבור שיכול ליהנות וליתן לכלבו וכן מבעיר באיסורי הנאה שסבור שיכול לבשל קדירה ועוד יש לדקדק פלוגתא דמקלקל בחבורה מדתנן בפסחים פר' אלו דברים (דף עב: ושם עג. ושם) ושאר כל הזבחים ששחטן לשם פסח אם אינן ראויין חייב ואמרי' בגמ' מאן תנא דשני ליה בין ראוין לשאין ראוין ר"ש הוא ואמרינן התם לעיל מיניה דאיירי בטועה אלמא מחייבינן מתעסק ואמרינן בפ' ספק אכל (כריתות ד' יט:) הנח לתינוקות הואיל ומקלקל בחבורה חייב מתעסק נמי חייב ומדמחייב רבי שמעון מתעסק בחבורה שמע מינה מקלקל

עין משפט נר מצוה

א א מיי' פ"ה מהלכות ממרים הל"ה ופט"ו מהלכות סנהדרין הלי"ג סמג לאוין ריט ועשין קו טוש"ע יו"ד סי' רמא סעיף א בהג"ה:

ב ב מיי' פט"ו מהלכות סנהדרין שם ופרק ט מהלכות גניבה הל"א סמג לאוין קלד:

ג ג מיי' פט"ו מהלכות סנהדרין שם ופ"ג מהלכות ממרים הלכה ח סמג לאוין קיג:

ד ד מיי' פט"ו מהלכות סנהדרין שם ופ"ט מהלכות יסודי התורה הל"א ופ"ה מהלכות ע"ז הל"א סמג לאוין לה:

ה ה מיי' פט"ו מהלכות סנהדרין שם ופרק ה' מהלכות ע"ז הלכה ו סמג לאוין לב:

ו ו מיי' פט"ו מהלכות סנהדרין שם ופ"א מהלכות איסורי ביאה הל"ו סמג לאוין קג:

ז ז מיי' פ"כ מהלכות עדות הל"י:

ח ח מיי' פ"ג מהלכות איסורי ביאה הל"ג:

ט ט מיי' שם פ"א הלכה ו:

י י מיי' פ"ה מהלכות ממרים הלכה ז סמג לאוין רי"ט טור שו"ע יו"ד סימן רמא סעיף ג:

יא כ מיי' פכ"ה מהלכו' שבת הל"ח סמג לאוין סה טוש"ע או"ח סימן שח סעיף יא:

יב ל מיי' פ"א מהלכות שבת הלי"ז ופ"ח הל"ז ופ"י הל"י ופי"ב הל"א ופ"ד מהלכות חובל הל"א סמג לאוין סה ועשין ע:

גליון הש"ס

תוס' ד"ה הכחישה וכו'. לא שייכי ד' דברים. עי' גיטין דף מג ע"ב תוס' ד"ה ושור:

תורה אור השלם

א) וּמַכֵּה אָבִיו וְאִמּוֹ מוֹת יוּמָת: [שמות כא, טו]

ב) מַכֵּה אִישׁ וָמֵת מוֹת יוּמָת: [שמות כא, יב]

ג) אוֹ בְאֵיבָה הִכָּהוּ בְיָדוֹ וַיָּמֹת מוֹת יוּמַת הַמַּכֶּה רֹצֵחַ הוּא גֹּאֵל הַדָּם יָמִית אֶת הָרֹצֵחַ בְּפִגְעוֹ בוֹ: [במדבר לה, כא]

ד) כָּל מַכֵּה נֶפֶשׁ לְפִי עֵדִים יִרְצַח אֶת הָרֹצֵחַ וְעֵד אֶחָד לֹא יַעֲנֶה בְנֶפֶשׁ לָמוּת: [במדבר לה, ל]

[לפי תוס'] וְאִישׁ כִּי יַכֶּה כָּל נֶפֶשׁ אָדָם מוֹת יוּמָת: [ויקרא כד, יז]

ה) וּמַכֵּה בְהֵמָה יְשַׁלְּמֶנָּה וּמַכֵּה אָדָם יוּמָת: [ויקרא כד, כא]

ו) וּמַכֵּה נֶפֶשׁ בְּהֵמָה יְשַׁלְּמֶנָּה נֶפֶשׁ תַּחַת נָפֶשׁ: [ויקרא כד, יח]

ז) לֹא תִקֹּם וְלֹא תִטֹּר אֶת בְּנֵי עַמֶּךָ וְאָהַבְתָּ לְרֵעֲךָ כָּמוֹךָ אֲנִי יְיָ: [ויקרא יט, יח]

מסורת הש"ס

א) [לעיל נב: לקמן פט.], ב) [לעיל טו: נב:], ג) נדה מד: [ע"ש תוס'], ד) [לקמן פה:], ה) [לעיל עט: ושם נסמן], ו) [בערוך ערך בע ד' איתא בועתא], ז) שבת קז. קכב:, ח) [עי' תוס' נדה מד: ד"ה איש כי יכה], ט) [כדאיתא פסחים מג.], י) [לעיל עט.].

הגהות הב"ח

(א) גמ' רב פפא לא שביק לבריה:

ליקוטי רש"י

מכה אביו ואמו. בחנק. דכתיב ביה (שמות כא) יומת סתמא וקיימא לן (סנהדרין נב:) כל מיתה האמורה בתורה סתם אינו אלא חנק [לעיל נ.]. **זקן ממרא.** שהמרה על ב"ד של לשכת הגזית ומיתתו בחנק [סוטה כה.]. **זוממי בת כהן.** לעשות לאחיו מה תלמוד לומר לאחיו למד על זוממי בת כהן נשואה שאינן בשריפה אלא כמיתת הבועל שהוא בחנק שנאמר היא באש תשרף (ויקרא כא, ט) היא ולא בועלה לכך נאמר כאן לאחיו כאשר זמם לעשות לאחיו ולא כאשר זמם לעשות לאחותו אבל בכל שאר מיתות השוה הכתוב אשה לאיש וזוממי אשה נהרגין כזוממי איש כגון שהעידוה שהרגה את הנפש שחללה את השבת נהרגין במיתתה שלא מיעט כאן אחותו אלא במקום שיש לקיים בהן הזמה במיתת הבועל [דברים יט, יט]. שהיא והן נהרגין ולא במיתה אחת דהיא בשריפה והן במיתת הבועל כגון באו עדים והזימו את הראשונים וחייבום מיתת הבועל (דברים יט) כאשר זמם לעשות לאחיו ולא לאחותו דאמר באלו הן הנחנקין (סנהדרין נ:). **בועלה.** דהיא בשריפה אבל הוא נידון כשאר בועל נערה המאורסה דבסקילה ובועל נשואה בחנק דכתיב (ויקרא כא) היא באש תשרף היא ולא בועלה [לעיל נ:]. **מכה אביו ואמו.** לפי שלמדנו על החובל בחבירו שהוא בתשלומין ולא במיתה הוצרך לומר על החובל באביו שהוא במיתה ואינו חייב אלא בהכאה שיש בה חבורה [שמות כא, טו]. **למאן דאמר חנק חמור.** מפרש בפרק ארבע מיתות (סנהדרין נ:) [לעיל נו.]. **מכה איש ומת.** למה נאמר לפי שנאמר (ויקרא כד, יז) ואיש כי יכה כל נפש אדם מות יומת שומע אני בהכאה בלא מיתה תלמוד לומר מכה איש ומת אינו חייב אלא בהכאה של מיתה ואם נאמר מכה איש ולא נאמר ואיש כי יכה הייתי אומר אינו חייב עד שיכה איש היכה את האשה ואת הקטן מנין תלמוד לומר כי יכה כל נפש אדם אפילו קטן ואפילו אשה ועוד אלו נאמר מכה איש שומע אני אפילו קטן שהכה והרג יהא חייב תלמוד לומר ואיש כי יכה ולא קטן שהכה ועוד כי יכה כל נפש אדם אפילו נפלים במשמע תלמוד לומר מכה איש אינו חייב עד שיכה בן קיימא ראוי להיות איש [שם פסוק יב]. **מכה אדם ומכה בהמה.** ומכה אדם יומת, אפילו לא הרגו אלא עשה בו חבורה שלא נאמר כאן נפש ובמכה אביו ואמו דבר הכתוב ובא להקישו למכה בהמה מה מכה בהמה מחיים אף מכה אביו ואמו מחיים פרט למכה לאחר מיתה לפי שמצינו שהמקללו לאחר מיתה חייב הוצרך לומר במכה שפטור ומה בבהמה בחבלה שאם אין חבלה אין תשלומין אף מכה אביו ואמו אינו חייב עד שיעשה בהם חבורה [ויקרא כד, כא]. **כדתני דבי חזקיה.** מכה נפש בהמה ישלמנה ומכה אדם יומת הוקשו יחד דמה מכה בהמה לעולם משלם ואפי' בשוגג כדאמרי' (ב"ק כו) אדם מועד לעולם אף מכה אדם דפטריה קרא מתשלומין דכתיב יומת לעולם פטור ואפילו בשוגג הואיל ובמזיד שייכא מיתה [ב"ק לה.]. **מחט של יד.** מחט קטן שתופר בו בגדים [שבת קכב:]. מחט של יד ניטלת בשבת. **ליטול בה את הקוץ.** והיינו דומיא דלחה דמצער ליה ואינו חושש אם יצא ממנו דם מיד וקאמר ניטלת לכתחילה מחט של יד היא מחט שתופרין בה בגדים ומשום דקתני בהדה ושל שק לפתוח בה את הדלת קרי לה להאי מחט של יד [שם קו.].

[המשך בדף פה.]

be decreeing death by strangulation for one who murders his parent, because ordinary murder is punished more severely, i.e. with beheading. Hence, the Torah must be imposing strangulation for merely striking a parent. אֶלָּא לְמַאן דְּאָמַר חֶנֶק חָמוּר – **But according to the one who states that** death by **strangulation is** more **severe** than beheading, מַאי אִיכָּא לְמֵימַר – **what is there to say?** What is *his* source for stating that someone is subject to death by strangulation for striking a parent even if the parent survives?[15]

In response, the Gemara proves that, according to all, the verse quoted above clearly refers to striking that did not kill the parent: אֶלָּא מִדִּכְתִיב ,,מַכֵּה אִישׁ וָמֵת מוֹת יוּמָת" – **Rather, from** the fact **that it is written** in another verse:[16] ***One who strikes a man so that he dies shall surely be put to death,*** וּכְתִיב ,,אוֹ בְאֵיבָה הִכָּהוּ בְיָדוֹ וַיָּמֹת" – **and it is** also **written:**[17] ***Or in enmity he struck him with his hand and he died.*** שְׁמַע מִינָּהּ – **Learn from these** verses, which specify that the striking killed the victim, כָּל הֵיכָא דְּאִיכָּא הַכָּאָה סְתָם – that **wherever there is** mention in the Torah of **unspecified striking without further qualification,**[18] לָאו מִיתָה הוּא – **it** does **not** refer to a blow that caused **death.**[19] Accordingly, when our verse imposes strangulation for "striking" a parent without mentioning that the parent died, it clearly refers to where the parent survived the blow.

Having quoted a verse that imposes the death penalty for murder, the Gemara digresses to cite a second verse that teaches the same thing, and to explain why both verses are needed:

וְאִיצְטְרִיךְ לְמִכְתַּב ,,מַכֵּה אִישׁ" – **And it was necessary** for the Torah **to write:**[20] ***One who strikes a man*** *so that he dies shall surely be put to death.* וְאִיצְטְרִיךְ לְמִכְתַּב ,,כָּל־מַכֵּה־נֶפֶשׁ" – **And it was necessary** also **to write:**[21] ***Whoever strikes a human soul*** *. . . one shall kill the murderer.* דְּאִי כָּתַב רַחֲמָנָא ,,מַכֵּה אִישׁ וָמֵת" – **For if the Merciful One had written** only: ***one who strikes a man so that he dies,*** הֲוָה אֲמִינָא אִישׁ דְּבַר מִצְוָה אִין – **I would have said** that when someone murders an adult **man, who is subject to** mitzvos, the murderer is **indeed** executed, קָטָן לֹא – **but** if someone murders **a minor,** who is exempt from mitzvos, the murderer is **not** executed.[22] כָּתַב רַחֲמָנָא ,,כָּל־מַכֵּה־נֶפֶשׁ" – Therefore, **the Merciful One wrote** in His Torah: ***whoever strikes a human soul.***[23] This teaches that a murderer is subject to the death penalty whether he killed an adult or a minor. וְאִי כָּתַב רַחֲמָנָא ,,כָּל מַכֵּה נֶפֶשׁ" – **And if the Merciful One had written** only: ***whoever strikes a human soul,*** הֲוָה אֲמִינָא אֲפִילוּ נְפָלִים – **I would have said** that the death penalty is imposed **even** for killing **nonviable babies**[24] אֲפִילוּ בֶּן שְׁמוֹנָה – **and even** for killing a **baby** born **of** an **eight**-month pregnancy.[25] Therefore, the Torah also writes *one who strikes* a *"man,"* thereby indicating that the victim must have a viable life for the murderer to be liable to execution. צְרִיכִי – Thus, **both** verses **are** indeed **needed** to teach when the death penalty is imposed for murder.[26]

Having digressed to discuss the death penalty for murder, the Gemara returns to consider when the death penalty is imposed for striking a parent:

וְאֵימָא אַף עַל גַּב דְּלָא עָבֵיד בֵּיהּ חַבּוּרָה – **Let us say** that one is executed for striking a parent **even if he did not inflict a wound upon him.** אַלְמָה תְּנַן – **Why,** then, **have we learned in a Mishnah:**[27] הַמַּכֶּה אָבִיו וְאִמּוֹ – ONE WHO STRIKES HIS FATHER OR MOTHER אֵינוֹ חַיָּיב עַד שֶׁיַּעֲשֶׂה בָּהֶן חַבּוּרָה – IS NOT LIABLE for this act UNLESS HE INFLICTS A WOUND UPON THEM?

The Gemara answers:

אָמַר קְרָא ,,מַכֵּה אָדָם" וּ,,מַכֵּה בְהֵמָה" – **Scripture mentions *one who strikes a person* and *one who strikes an animal*** in the same verse.[28] Since the Torah juxtaposes these two laws, we employ a *hekeish* to compare them:[29] מַה מַּכֵּה בְהֵמָה עַד דְּעָבֵיד בָּהּ חַבּוּרָה – **Just as one who strikes an animal** is not obligated to pay for the damage **unless he inflicts a wound in [the animal],** דִּכְתִיב בָּהּ ,,נֶפֶשׁ" – **for** the word ***soul*** **is written in connection with** striking **[an animal],**[30] אַף מַכֵּה אָדָם עַד דְּעָבֵיד חַבּוּרָה –

NOTES

15. If strangulation is a more severe punishment than beheading, as this view maintains, then the verse decreeing strangulation for "striking" a parent could well apply only if the parent dies from the blow. In other words, the Torah might be stating that although an ordinary murderer is punished with beheading, one who murders his parent is punished more stringently with strangulation. How is it known, then, that the Torah in fact means to impose strangulation for merely striking?

16. *Exodus* 21:12.

17. *Numbers* 35:21.

18. I.e. where the Torah mentions striking without specifying that it resulted in death.

19. For these two verses explicitly state that someone strikes [a man] and he dies. From the fact that the verses specified the victim's death, it is evident that the term strike ordinarily means to deal a blow that does not kill the victim. (For an explanation as to why the Gemara cited two verses to prove its point, see *Aruch LaNer.*)

20. *Exodus* 21:12.

21. *Numbers* 35:30.

22. For when the Torah imposes the death penalty for murdering an אִישׁ, a *man,* this would be interpreted to mean that the murder victim must have been an adult who performs mitzvos; if he was a minor, who is exempt from mitzvos, the murderer is not executed.

23. And the expression *human soul* includes any human being, i.e. both adults and minors.

Tosafos challenge the accuracy of our text from *Niddah* 44b. The Gemara there cites a verse in *Leviticus* (24:17): וְאִישׁ כִּי יַכֶּה כָּל־נֶפֶשׁ אָדָם, *and a man if he strikes* any *human soul,* as the source that the death penalty is imposed for killing a minor, whereas our Gemara cites the verse in *Numbers* 35:30. Because of this question, *Tosafos* emend our text so that it presents *Leviticus* 24:17 as the second verse. *Rashi* to *Leviticus* loc. cit. apparently had this emendation as well.

24. [נְפָלִים, *nonviable babies,* are fetuses, or newborn infants, who clearly cannot survive for thirty days after birth.] In our Gemara, they refer specifically to full-term babies born with severe deformities, e.g. a grossly misshapen head or two spines (*Rashi*, see *Margaliyos HaYam*). If the Torah had stated only that the death penalty is imposed for killing "any human soul," it could have been thought that one is executed even for killing such babies.

25. A baby born of an eight-month pregnancy is considered nonviable (see *Yevamos* 80a-b).

26. I.e. the verse in *Exodus* – *one who strikes* ***a man*** – teaches that there is no death penalty for killing a nonviable baby. The verse in *Numbers* – *whoever strikes* ***any human soul*** – teaches that there is a death penalty for murdering a minor.

27. Below, 85b.

28. *Leviticus* 24:21. The verse states: וּמַכֵּה בְהֵמָה יְשַׁלְּמֶנָּה וּמַכֵּה אָדָם יוּמָת, *One who strikes an animal shall make restitution, and one who strikes a person shall be put to death.* (The person being discussed is obviously a parent, because there is no death penalty for simply striking anyone else – see above, note 19.)

29. *Hekeish* – Scriptural analogy. When two subjects are juxtaposed in a single verse, and we have a tradition which links the two through a *hekeish,* the laws of one are applied to the other.

30. The verse in *Leviticus* 24:18 states: וּמַכֵּה נֶפֶשׁ־בְּהֵמָה יְשַׁלְּמֶנָּה. Essentially, the verse is teaching that someone who damages an animal must compensate the owner, but the literal translation of this verse is: *A man who strikes* ***the soul*** *(nefesh) of an animal shall make restitution.* Now the Torah elsewhere associates the term נֶפֶשׁ, *soul,* with blood (see *Leviticus* 17:11,14). Hence, our Gemara now expounds our verse to mean that one is not obligated to pay for having damaged an animal unless he made it bleed [either externally or internally] (*Rashi,* see *Margaliyos HaYam*).

אלו הן הנחנקין [א]המכה אביו ואמו [ב]וגונב נפש מישראל [ג]וזקן ממרא ע"פ ב"ד [ד]ונביא השקר [ה]והמתנבא בשם עבודת כוכבים [ו]והבא על אשת איש [ז]וזוממי בת כהן [ח]ובועלה: גמ' מכה אביו ואמו מנלן דכתיב (א) מכה אביו ואמו מות יומת (א) [ט]וכל מיתה האמורה בתורה סתם אינה אלא חנק אימא עד דקטיל ליה מיקטל ס"ד קטל חד בסייף ואביו בחנק (ג) הניחא למ"ד חנק קל אלא למאן דאמר חנק חמור מאי איכא למימר אלא מדכתיב (ב) מכה איש ומת מות יומת וכתיב (ג) או באיבה הכהו בידו וימות שמע מינה כל היכא דאיכא הכאה סתם לאו מיתה הוא ואצטריך למיכתב מכה איש ואיצטריך למכתב (ד) כל מכה נפש דאי כתב רחמנא מכה איש ומת הוה אמינא איש דבר מצוה אין קטן לא (ה) כתב רחמנא כל מכה נפש ואי כתב רחמנא כל מכה נפש הוה אמינא אפילו נפלים אפילו בן שמונה צריכי ואימא אע"ג דלא עביד ביה חבורה אלמה תנן (ז) המכה אביו ואמו אינו חייב עד שיעשה בהן חבורה אמר קרא (ה) מכה אדם ומכה בהמה מה מכה בהמה עד דעביד בה חבורה דכתיב בה (ו) נפש אף מכה אדם עד דעביד חבורה מתקיף לה רב ירמיה אלא מעתה הכחישה באבנים הכי נמי דלא מיחייב אלא אם אינו ענין לנפש בהמה דהא אי נמי הכחישה באבנים חייב תנידהו ענין לנפש אדם אלא הקישא למה לי לכדתניא (ט) דבי חזקיה הניחא למאן דאית ליה תנא דבי חזקיה אלא למאן דלית ליה תנא דבי חזקיה היקישא למה לי מה מכה בהמה לרפואה פטור אף מכה אדם לרפואה פטור דאיבעיא להו בן מהו שיקיז דם לאביו רב מתנא אמר (ז) ואהבת לרעך כמוך רב דימי בר חיננא אמר מכה אדם ומכה בהמה מה מכה בהמה לרפואה פטור אף מכה אדם לרפואה פטור (א) רב לא שביק לבריה למישקל ליה סילוא מר בריה דרבינא לא שביק לבריה למיפתח ליה (י) כוותא דילמא חביל והוה ליה שגגת איסור אי הכי אחר נמי אחר שיגגת לאו בנו שגגת חנק (יא) והדתנן [כ]מחט של יד ליטול בה את הקוץ ליחוש דילמא חביל והויא לה שגגת סקילה התם מקלקל הוא הניחא למאן דאמר [ל]מקלקל פטור אלא למ"ד חייב מאי איכא למימר מאן שמעת ליה דאמר מקלקל בחבורה חייב ר' שמעון היא ורבי

אלו הן הנחנקין: ממרא על פי בית דין. כמו ממרים הייתם עם ה' (דברים ט) שמסרב על פי ב"ד הגדול שבלשכת הגזית: וזוממי בת כהן. אע"פ שהם היו מחייבין אותה שריפה אין נדונין אלא במיתה שהיו מחייבין לבועל והיינו חנק כשאר בא על אשת איש כדמפרש קרא היא תשרף ולא בועלה וזוממיה ילפינן מכאשר זמם לעשות לאחיו לאחיו ולא לאחותו: ובועלה. בנשואה בת כהן קמיירי אבל ארוסה בועלה בסקילה: גמ' ס"ד. בתמיה: קטל חד בסייף. כדתנן בפרקין לעיל (דף עו:) אלו הן הנהרגים הרוצח ועיר הנדחת: מאי איכא למימר. הכא דאיכא למדרש דאביו בחנק: אלא מדכתיב מכה איש ומת. היכא דבעי מיתה מפרש מיתה בהדיא: אפילו נפלים. כגון בן תשעה וראשו אטום או שיש לו שני גבין דלא חיי: דכתיב ביה נפש. ונפש משמע דם דהוה חבורה: הכחישה. לבהמה: באבנים. דלא עשה בה חבורה: לנפש אדם. דהיינו אביו דאף על גב דלא בעינן מיתה חבורה מיהא בעינן: אלא הקישא למה לי. דאתקש מכה אדם למכה בהמה בחד קרא הואיל וילפת ליה מאם אינו ענין: לכדתניא דבי חזקיה. בב"ק [בהמניח] (דף לה.) לפטור חייבי מיתות שוגגין מן התשלומין מה מכה בהמה לא חלקת בו וכו': הניחא וכו'. פלוגתא דרבי יוחנן ורשב"ל בכתובות באלו נערות (דף לד:): מה מכה בהמה לרפואה. כגון מקיז דם פטור מן התשלומין שהרי לא הזיקה: אף מכה אדם. דהיינו אביו: לרפואה פטור. ממיתה ואע"ג דחבורה היא: ואהבת לרעך כמוך. לא הוזהרו ישראל מלעשות לחבריהם אלא דבר שאינו חפץ לעשות לעצמו: סילוא. קוץ ישב לו בבשרו: למפתח ליה כוותא. כויה להוציא ליחה ממנה: אי הכי אחר נמי. לא ליפתח שהרי כל ישראל הוזהרו על חבלת חבירו דכתיב (דברים כה) לא יוסיף פן יוסיף: שגגת לאו. כשאין מתכוין הוי שגגה באיסור שזדונו לאו בעלמא דקיל: מחט של יד. היא מחט קטנה שתופרין בה בגדים ניטלת בשבת ליטול בה את הקוץ ומשום דקתני לה להלן במסכת שבת בפרק כל הכלים (דף קכב:) גבי ושל שקאין לפתוח בו את הדלת קרי ליה להא קטנה מחט של יד: דילמא חביל. ועביד חבורה בשבת: מקלקל הוא. וכל המקלקלין פטורין בחלול שבת דמלאכת מחשבת כתיב ואין מחייב אמקלקל אלא רבי שמעון ומקלקל בחבורה רבי שמעון נמי לא מחייב אלא במתכוון לכך דהוי צריך לחבלה אבל הנוטל קוץ אין צריך לחבלה ורצונו לא יחבל:

אלו הן הנחנקין: **ה"ג** ואצטריך למכתב מכה איש ומת ואצטריך למכתב ואיש כי יכה כל נפש. ולא כמו שכתוב בספרים כל מכה נפש דבפרק יוצא דופן (נדה מד: ושם) גמרינן בן יום אחד דההורגו חייב ומפיק ליה מדכתיב ואיש כי יכה כל נפש נפש כל דהו [ח]:

איש דבר מצוה אין. יש ספרים שכתוב בהן אשה לא ואע"ג דהשוה הכתוב אשה לאיש וכו' [ט] הני מילי בפרשה שנאמרה בלשון זכר אבל היכא דכתיב איש בהדיא ממעטין אשה כדפירש שלהי פרק ד' מיתות (לעיל סו.) גבי מקלל אביו ואמו:

הוה אמינא אפילו נפלים. תימה א"כ היכי מיחייב דמי וולדות הא מיחייב מיתה וי"ל דה"א דהכא גזירת הכתוב היא היכא דלא נתכוין לוולדות כדאשכחן לרבי [י] ונתתה נפש תחת נפש ממון אי נמי נהי דהוה מיחייב אנפל לאחר שנולד קודם שנולד לא מיחייב: **הכחישה** באבנים כו'. בהכחשה דלא הדרא איירי דאם לא כן לא שייך נזק דמקרי שבת מידי דהוה אהכהו על ידו ולמתה וסופה לחזור ובבהמה [ס] לא שייכי ד' דברים:

אלא למאן דלית ליה דתנא דבי חזקיה. פירשתי לעיל בפ' הנשרפין (דף עט: ד"ה בין):

מאן שמעת ליה דאמר מקלקל בחבורה חייב ר"ש. פלוגתא דר' יהודה ור"ש במקלקל בחבורה ומקלקל בהבערה לא מצינו בפירוש לא במשנה ולא בברייתא ובפרק האורג (שבת דף קו. ושם) דחק רש"י לפרש דנפקא מפלוגתא דמלאכה שאינה צריכה לגופה פטור עליה הלכך אין לך חובל ומבעיר שאינו מקלקל ואפילו מבעיר עצים לתבשילו מקלקל הוא אצל העצים ומה שהוא מתקן אצל אחרים לרבי שמעון לא חשיב ליה דהא מלאכה שאינה צריכה לגופה היא אם כן כי חייב הכתוב חובל ומבעיר מדאצטריך למשרי מילה ומדאסר הבערה דבת כהן על כרחיך במקלקל נמי חייב אבל רבי יהודה סבירא ליה מלאכה שאינה צריכה לגופה חייב עליה הלכך חיוב דחובל בצריך לכלבו ומבעיר בצריך לאפרו משכחת לה ואע"פ שמקלקל הוא אצל מלאכה עצמה מתקן הוא אצל אחרים ולרבי יהודה בכי האי גוונא מלאכה היא משום תיקון דאחרים אבל מקלקל ואינו מתקן פטור לשון הקונט' כתבתי השתא הא דאמרי' התם בפרק האורג (שם) תני רבי אבהו קמיה דר' יוחנן כל המקלקלין פטורים חוץ מחובל ומבעיר אמר ליה פוק תני לברא חובל ומבעיר אינה משנה כו' משמע מתוך פי' הקונטרס דר' אבהו כר"ש ורבי יוחנן דבעי צריך לכלבו ולאפרו כר' יהודה וזהו תימה א"כ אמאי א"ל פוק תני לברא אטו משום דס"ל כרבי יהודה מאן דתני כר"ש משתיק ליה דכי האי גוונא פריך פרק קמא דחולין (דף טו.) ועוד אי חשיב תיקון גמור צריך לכלבו ולאפרו אמאי נקט חובל ומבעיר ועוד דר"ש אפי' בחובל ומבעיר בעי שתהא צריכה לגופה כדמסיק בשמעתין גבי חובל ובשלהי ספק אכל (כריתות דף כ:) גבי הבערה על כן נראה דר' אבהו ור' יוחנן אליבא דר"ש פליגי דר' אבהו כר"ש כדאיתא בפרק האורג (שבת דף קו.) ורבי יוחנן סבר דאפילו ר' שמעון בעי תיקון קצת ומיהו לא חשיב תיקון שיתחייב בכך לר' יהודה דאין דרך לחבול בחבירו ליתן לכלב ולשרוף גדיש בשביל אפר ופלוגתא דמקלקל בחבורה דרבי יהודה ורבי שמעון קים ליה להש"ס או בקבלה או שמא ברייתא שנויה בשום מקום וכי תימא לרבי אבהו כיון דליכא תיקון א"כ צריכה לגופה היכי משכחת לה הא משכחת לה באיסורי הנאה שסבור שיכול ליהנות וליתן לכלבו וכן מבעיר באיסורי הנאה שסבור שיכול לבשל קדירה ועוד יש לדקדק פלוגתא דמקלקל בחבורה מדתנן בפסחים פר' אלו דברים (דף עב: ושם עג. ושם) ושאר כל הזבחים ששחטן לשם פסח אם אינן ראויין חייב ואמרי' בגמ' מאן תנא דשני ליה בין ראוין לשאינן ראוין ר"ש הוא ואמרינן התם לעיל מיניה דאיירי בטועה אלמא מחייבינן מתעסק ואמרינן בפ' ספק אכל (כריתות ד' יט:) הנח לתינוקות הואיל ומקלקל בחבורה חייב מתעסק נמי חייב ומדמחייב רבי שמעון מתעסק בחבורה שמע מינה מקלקל

ליקוטי רש"י

מכה אביו ואמו. בחנק. דכתיב ביה (שמות כא) יומת סתמא וקיימא לן (סנהדרין נב:) כל מיתה האמורה בתורה סתם אינו אלא חנק [לעיל נ.]. **זקן ממרא.** שהמרה על ב"ד של לשכת הגזית ומיתתו בחנק [סוטה כה.]. **זוממי בת כהן.** לעשות לאחיו מה תלמוד לומר לאחיו למד על זוממי בת כהן נשואה שאינן בשריפה אלא כמיתת הבועל שהוא בחנק שנאמר היא באש תשרף (ויקרא כא, ט) היא ולא בועלה לכך נאמר כאן לאחיו כאשר זמם לעשות לאחיו ולא כאשר זמם לעשות לאחותו אבל בכל שאר מיתות השוה הכתוב אשה לאיש חוזמי אשה נהרגין כזוממי איש כגון שהעידוה שהרגה את הנפש שחללה את השבת נהרגין במיתתה שלא מיעט כאן אחותו אלא במקום שיש לקיים בהן הזמה במיתת הבועל [דברים יט, יט]. שהיא והן נהרגין ולא במיתה אחת דהיא בשריפה והן במיתת הבועל כגון באו עדים והזימו את הראשונים וחייבום מיתת הבועל ולא מיתתה דכתיב (דברים יט) כאשר זמם לעשות לאחיו ולא לאחותו כדאמר באלו הן הנחנקין (סנהדרין נ). **בועלה.** דהיא בשריפה אבל בועלה נידון כשאר בועל בת ישראל דבועל ארוסה בסקילה ובועל נשואה בחנק דכתיב (ויקרא כא) היא באש תשרף היא ולא בועלה היא ולא זוממיה [לעיל מו.]. **מכה אביו ואמו.** לפי שלמדנו על החובל בחבירו שהוא בתשלומין ולא במיתה הוצרך לומר על החובל באביו שהוא במיתה ואינו חייב אלא בהכאה שיש בה חבורה [שמות כא, טו]. **למאן דאמר חנק חמור.** מסייף בפרק ארבע מיתות (סנהדרין נ:) [לעיל טו:]. **מכה איש ומת.** למה נאמר לפי שנאמר (ויקרא כד, יז) ואיש כי יכה כל נפש אדם מות יומת שומע אני בהכאה בלא מיתה תלמוד לומר מכה איש ומת ואינו חייב אלא בהכאה של מיתה ואם נאמר מכה איש ולא נאמר ואיש כי יכה הייתי אומר אינו חייב עד שיכה איש היכה את האשה ואת הקטן מנין תלמוד לומר כי יכה כל נפש אדם אפילו קטן ואפילו אשה ועוד אלו נאמר מכה איש שומע אני אפילו קטן שהכה והרג יהא חייב תלמוד לומר ואיש כי יכה ולא קטן שהכה ועוד כי יכה כל נפש אדם אפילו נפלים במשמע תלמוד לומר מכה איש אינו חייב עד שיכה בן קיימא ראוי להיות איש [שם פסוק יב]. **מכה אדם ומכה בהמה.** ומכה אדם יומת, אפילו לא הרגו אלא עשה בו חבורה שלא נאמר כאן נפש ובמכה אביו ואמו דבר הכתוב וכא להקישו למכה בהמה מה מכה בהמה מחיים אף מכה אביו ואמו מחיים פרט למכה לאחר מיתה לפי שמצינו שהמקללו לאחר מיתה חייב הוצרך לומר במכה שפטור ומה בבהמה בחבלה שאם אין חבלה אין תשלומין אף באביו ואמו אינו חייב עד שיעשה בהם חבורה [ויקרא כד, כא]. **כדתני דבי חזקיה.** מכה נפש בהמה ישלמנה ומכה אדם יומת הוקשו יחד מה מכה בהמה לעולם משלם ואפי' בשוגג כדאמרי' (ב"ק כו) אדם מועד לעולם אף מכה אדם לפטרים קרא מתשלומין דכתיב יומת לעולם פטור ואפילו בשוגג הואיל ובמזיד שייכא מיתה [ב"ק לה.]. **מחט של יד.** מחט קטן שתופר בו בגדים [שבת קכב:]. מחט של יד ניטלת בשבת. **ליטול בה את הקוץ.** והיינו דומיא דלחה דמצער ליה ואינו חושש אם יפתח מיד וקאמר ניטלת לכתחילה מחט של יד היא מחט שתופרין בה בגדים ומשום דקתני בהדה ושל שק לפתוח בה את הדלת קרי לה להאי מחט של יד [שם קז.]. [המשך בדף פה.]

עין משפט נר מצוה

א א מיי' פ"ג מהלכות ממרים הל"ה ופט"ו מהלכות סנהדרין הל"ג סמג לאוין ריט ועשין קד טוש"ע יו"ד סי' רמא סעיף א בהג"ה:

ב ב מיי' פט"ו מהלכות סנהדרין שם ופרק ט מהלכות גניבה הל"א סמג לאוין קלד:

ג ג מיי' פט"ו מהלכות סנהדרין שם ופ"ג מהלכות ממרים הלכה ח סמג לאוין קיג:

ד ד מיי' פט"ו מהלכות סנהדרין שם ופ"ט מהלכות יסודי התורה הל"ג ופ"ה מהלכות ע"ז הל"ט סמג לאוין לב:

ה ה מיי' פט"ו מהלכות סנהדרין שם ופרק ה' מהלכות ע"ז הלכה ו סמג לאוין לג:

ו ו מיי' פט"ו מהלכות סנהדרין שם ופ"א מהלכות איסורי ביאה הל"ו סמג לאוין קג:

ז ז מיי' פ"כ מהלכות עדות הל"י:

ח ח מיי' פ"ג מהלכות איסורי ביאה הל"ג:

ט ט מיי' שם פ"א הלכה ו:

י י מיי' פ"ה מהלכות ממרים הלכה ו סמג לאוין ריט טור ש"ע יו"ד סימן רמא סעיף ג:

יא כ מיי' פכ"ה מהלכו' שבת הל"ח סמג לאוין סה טוש"ע או"ח סימן שח סעיף יא:

יב ל מיי' פ"י מהלכות שבת הל"ו ופ"ח הל"ו ופי"ב הל"א ופ"ד מהלכות חובל הל"א סמג לאוין קפ ועשין ע:

מסורת הש"ס

א) [לעיל נב: לקמן פט.], ב) [לעיל טו: נב:], ג) נדה מד: [ע"ש תוס'], ד) [לקמן פה:], ה) [לעיל עט: ושם נסמן], ו) [בערוך ערך בע ד' איתא בועתא], ז) שבת קז. קכב:, ח) [עי' תוס' נדה מד: ד"ה איש כי יכה], ט) [כדאיתא פסחים מג.], י) [לעיל עט.].

הגהות הב"ח

(א) גמ' רב פפא לא שביק לבריה:

גליון הש"ס

תוס' ד"ה הכחישה וכו'. לא שייכי ד' דברים. עי' גיטין דף מב ע"ב תוס' ד"ה ושור:

תורה אור השלם

א) וּמַכֵּה אָבִיו וְאִמּוֹ מוֹת יוּמָת: [שמות כא, טו]

ב) מַכֵּה אִישׁ וָמֵת מוֹת יוּמָת: [שמות כא, יב]

ג) אוֹ בְאֵיבָה הִכָּהוּ בְיָדוֹ וַיָּמֹת מוֹת יוּמַת הַמַּכֶּה רֹצֵחַ הוּא גֹּאֵל הַדָּם יָמִית אֶת הָרֹצֵחַ בְּפִגְעוֹ בוֹ: [במדבר לה, כא]

ד) כָּל מַכֵּה נֶפֶשׁ לְפִי עֵדִים יִרְצַח אֶת הָרֹצֵחַ וְעֵד אֶחָד לֹא יַעֲנֶה בְנֶפֶשׁ לָמוּת: [במדבר לה, ל]

[לפי תוס'] וְאִישׁ כִּי יַכֶּה כָּל נֶפֶשׁ אָדָם מוֹת יוּמָת: [ויקרא כד, יז]

ה) וּמַכֵּה בְהֵמָה יְשַׁלְּמֶנָּה וּמַכֵּה אָדָם יוּמָת: [ויקרא כד, כא]

ו) וּמַכֵּה נֶפֶשׁ בְּהֵמָה יְשַׁלְּמֶנָּה נֶפֶשׁ תַּחַת נָפֶשׁ: [ויקרא כד, יח]

ז) לֹא תִקֹּם וְלֹא תִטֹּר אֶת בְּנֵי עַמֶּךָ וְאָהַבְתָּ לְרֵעֲךָ כָּמוֹךָ אֲנִי יְיָ: [ויקרא יט, יח]

similarly one who strikes a person (i.e. a parent) is not executed **unless he makes a wound.** This is the Mishnah's source for the ruling that the death penalty is not imposed for striking a parent unless the parent was wounded.

The Gemara rejects the exposition upon which this answer is based:

מַתְקִיף לָהּ רַב יִרְמְיָה – Rav Yirmiyah challenged [the answer]: אֶלָּא מֵעַתָּה – But now הַכְחִישָׁהּ בַּאֲבָנִים – if one weakens another's **[animal]** by overloading it **with stones** without wounding the animal,[31] **הָכִי נַמִּי דְּלָא מִיחַיַּיב – is it** indeed **so that he is not liable** to pay for damaging it? No, that is untrue! One is surely liable for damaging an animal even if he does not wound it.[32]

The Gemara now gives the actual source for the ruling that one is not executed for striking a parent unless the parent was wounded:

אֶלָּא – Rather, we must apply the exegetic principle that **אִם אֵינוֹ עִנְיָן לְנֶפֶשׁ בְּהֵמָה – since [the word]** *soul* **has no application to an animal's** *soul* (i.e. blood), **דְּהָא אִי נַמִּי הַכְחִישָׁהּ בַּאֲבָנִים חַיָּיב – because even if one weakens** another's **[animal]** by overloading it **with stones** without wounding it, **he is liable** for damages, **תְּנֵיהוּ עִנְיָן לְנֶפֶשׁ אָדָם** – you must therefore remove the phrase from its plain meaning and **assign it an application to the soul of a person,** i.e. a parent.[33] This, then, is the source mandating that one who strikes his parent must wound him to be subject to the death penalty.

The Gemara mentioned that the laws of damaging an animal and striking a parent are linked through *hekeish.* The Gemara now returns to discuss the *hekeish*:

אֶלָּא הֶקֵּישָׁא לָמָּה לִי – But why is the ***hekeish*** **necessary?** What does it teach us? **לְכִדְתַנְיָא דְּבֵי חִזְקִיָּה** – It is needed **to** teach the rule **that was taught in the Baraisa of the academy of Chizkiyah,** i.e. if someone unintentionally commits an act that, if transgressed intentionally, would subject him to a death penalty, he is exempt from a monetary obligation which he incurs at the same time.[34]

The Gemara asks:

הָנִיחָא לְמַאן דְּאִית לֵיהּ תַּנָּא דְּבֵי חִזְקִיָּה – This is understandable according to the one who subscribes to the view of the Baraisa of the academy of Chizkiyah, אֶלָּא לְמַאן דְּלֵית לֵיהּ תַּנָּא דְּבֵי חִזְקִיָּה – but according to the one who does not subscribe to the view of the Baraisa of the academy of Chizkiyah,[35] **הֶיקֵּישָׁא לָמָּה לִי – why is the** ***hekeish*** **necessary?**

The Gemara answers that the *hekeish* teaches as follows:

מָה מַכֵּה בְהֵמָה לִרְפוּאָה פָּטוּר – Just as one who strikes an animal for therapeutic purposes **is exempt** from liability,[36] **אַף מַכֵּה אָדָם לִרְפוּאָה פָּטוּר – so too, one who strikes a person,** i.e. a parent, **for therapeutic purposes is exempt** from the death penalty.[37]

The Gemara cites a similar exchange:

דְּאִיבַּעְיָא לְהוּ – For they inquired: בֵּן מַהוּ שֶׁיַּקִּיז דָּם לְאָבִיו – May a son let the blood of his father for therapeutic purposes? **רַב מַתְנָא אָמַר – Rav Masna said: ,,וְאָהַבְתָּ לְרֵעֲךָ כָּמוֹךָ״** – Scripture states: ***You shall love your fellow as yourself.***[38] Hence, since you would want someone to let your blood, you are permitted to let your parent's blood.

רַב דִּימִי בַּר חִינָּנָא אָמַר – Rav Dimi bar Chinana said: ,,מַכֵּה אָדָם״ וּ,,מַכֵּה בְהֵמָה״ – Scripture juxtaposes the laws about ***one who strikes a person*** and ***one who strikes an animal.*** We may

NOTES

31. [The Gemara discusses a case where someone overloads an animal and, as a result, permanently weakens it. If the animal will eventually recover its strength, however, there is no obligation to compensate the owner for the temporary incapacitation of his animal (see *Tosafos* for a fuller explanation of this idea).]

32. For once the Torah holds a person responsible for damaging a fellow's animal, what difference does it make if he inflicted a wound? Obviously none! Thus, logic dictates that one is liable for damaging an animal whether he wounded it or not (*Aruch LaNer*).

33. One of the rules of Biblical exposition is: אִם אֵינוֹ עִנְיָן לָזֶה תְּנֵהוּ עִנְיָן לָזֶה, *If [a Scriptural passage] has no application to this* (its own context), *assign it an application to that* (some other context). That is, if a certain word in the Torah cannot be understood to be teaching a point regarding its own context (because, for example, the law it seems to be teaching is untenable), then it must be understood to be teaching a point in regard to a different context. [This rule is the twentieth in the list of rules of Biblical exposition of R' Eliezer ben R' Yose HaGlili. See *Sefer HaKrisus, Nesivos Olam* 20 for an elaboration of this rule.]

In the present case, we apply this principle as follows. When the Torah discusses the liability of one who strikes an animal, it uses the expression נֶפֶשׁ בְּהֵמָה, *an animal soul,* which would seem to indicate that one must wound the animal to be held liable (see note 30). This, however, is illogical; a person is clearly responsible for any damage that he causes, whether he inflicts a wound or not (see previous note). Therefore, we apply the word *soul* to the verse discussing the striking of a parent. That is, we understand the verse to be teaching that one is not executed for striking a parent unless the parent is wounded.

34. There is a general rule that someone who simultaneously commits a capital offense and a lesser offense (such as an offense that would ordinarily make him monetarily liable) is liable only to the death penalty and not to any lesser penalty that he otherwise would have incurred (קָם לֵיהּ בִּדְרַבָּה מִינֵּיהּ). The Baraisa of the academy of Chizkiyah added that this rule applies even if the offender was not technically subject to the death penalty. For example, even if he committed the sin unintentionally, still he is exempt from the monetary punishment as well (see above, 79b).

This application of the rule is derived from the *hekeish* that compares he laws of damaging an animal with those of murdering a person. (See *Tosafos* to 79b ד״ה מכה, who discuss whether, in the final analysis, the verse refers to murder or the hitting of a parent.) These laws state that whoever damages an animal, whether intentionally or unintentionally, must pay for the damage; in turn, a murderer is exempt from any monetary obligation (because murder is a capital offense). The *hekeish* between these laws teaches that just as someone who damages an animal, whether intentionally or unintentionally, must compensate the owner, so is a murderer exempt from any monetary obligation incurred at the time of the killing, whether the killing was intentional or unintentional.

35. See the dispute between R' Yochanan and Reish Lakish quoted in *Kesubos* 34b-35a (*Rashi*; cf. *Tosafos* to 79b ד״ה בין).

36. Because the wound he inflicted caused no damage; in fact, he actually healed the animal! (*Rashi*). *Rashi* cites bloodletting as an example of striking [and wounding] for therapeutic purposes. See *Shabbos* 129b and *Rambam* (*Hil. Deos* 4:18) with *Kesef Mishneh,* where the therapeutic value of bloodletting is discussed.

37. For example, if someone let his parent's blood, he is exempt from punishment, because he made the wound to heal his parent and not to cause injury (*Rashi*).

The Gemara here requires a *hekeish* to exempt one from liability for wounding his parent for therapeutic purposes even though the Gemara simply *assumes* that there is no liability for wounding an animal to heal it. Presumably, the distinction is as follows: Only when someone damages an animal must he compensate the owner for these damages. Thus, the fact that bloodletting is a therapeutic procedure is in itself a reason to exempt one from liability, because he has caused no damage. But when someone strikes a parent, he is executed not because of any damage he has caused but because of the nature of the act itself – it is a grave sin to wound a parent. Accordingly, it would have been thought that he is punished for any wound – even if it was inflicted for therapeutic purposes – had the *hekeish* not taught otherwise (see *Aruch LaNer*).

38. *Leviticus* 19:18. Our Gemara understands this verse to be establishing a general rule that governs all Torah prohibitions involving personal relationships: These prohibitions apply only to things that you would not wish to be done to yourself – but whatever you would want done to yourself, you may do to others. Thus, it is permitted to let a parent's blood – in spite of the prohibition against wounding a parent – because you would want others to let your blood (*Rashi*).

אלו הן הנחנקין [א]המכה אביו ואמו [ב]וגונב נפש מישראל [ג]וזקן ממרא ע"פ ב"ד [ד]ונביא השקר [ה]והמתנבא בשם עבודת כוכבים [ו]והבא על אשת איש [ז]וזוממי בת כהן [ח]ובועלה: **גמ'** מכה אביו ואמו מנלן דכתיב א) מכה אביו ואמו מות יומת [א] [ט]וכל מיתה האמורה בתורה סתם אינה אלא חנק אימא עד דקטיל ליה מיקטל ס"ד קטל חד בסייף ואביו בחנק ג) הניחא למ"ד חנק קל אלא למאן דאמר חנק חמור מאי איכא למימר אלא מדכתיב ב) מכה איש ומת מות יומת וכתיב ג) או באיבה הכהו בידו וימות שמע מינה כל היכא דאיכא הכאה סתם לאו מיתה הוא ואצטריך למיכתב מכה איש ואיצטריך למכתב ד) כל מכה נפש דאי כתב רחמנא מכה איש ומת הוה אמינא איש דבר מצוה אין קטן לא ט) כתב רחמנא כל מכה נפש ואי כתב רחמנא כל מכה נפש הוה אמינא אפילו נפלים אפילו בן שמונה צריכי ואימא אע"ג דלא עביד ביה חבורה אלמה תנן ד) המכה אביו ואמו אינו חייב עד שיעשה בהן חבורה אמר קרא ה) מכה אדם ומכה בהמה מה מכה בהמה עד דעביד בה חבורה דכתיב בה ו) נפש אף מכה אדם עד דעביד חבורה מתקיף לה רב ירמיה אלא מעתה הכחישה באבנים הכי נמי דלא מיחייב אלא אם אינו ענין לנפש בהמה דהא אי נמי הכחישה באבנים חייב תניהו ענין לנפש אדם אלא הקישא למה לי לכדתניא ה) דבי חזקיה הניחא למאן דאית ליה תנא דבי חזקיה אלא למאן דלית ליה תנא דבי חזקיה היקישא למה לי מה מכה בהמה לרפואה פטור אף מכה אדם לרפואה פטור דאיבעיא להו בן מהו שיקיז דם לאביו רב מתנא אמר ז) ואהבת לרעך כמוך רב דימי בר חיננא אמר מכה אדם ומכה בהמה מה מכה בהמה לרפואה פטור אף מכה אדם לרפואה פטור (א) רב לא שביק לבריה למישקל ליה סילוא מר בריה דרבינא לא שביק לבריה למיפתח ליה ו) כוותא דילמא חביל והוה ליה שגגת איסור אי הכי אחר נמי אחר שיגגת לאו בנו שגגת חנק ז) והדתנן [כ]מחט של יד ליטול בה את הקוץ ליחוש דילמא חביל והויא לה שגגת סקילה התם מקלקל הוא הניחא למאן דאמר [ל]מקלקל פטור אלא למ"ד חייב מאי איכא למימר מאן שמעת ליה דאמר מקלקל בחבורה חייב ר' שמעון היא ורבי

אלו הן הנחנקין: ממרא על פי בית דין. כמו ממרים הייתם עם ה' (דברים ט) שמסרב על פי ב"ד הגדול שבלשכת הגזית: וזוממי בת כהן. אע"פ שהם היו מחייבין אותה שריפה אין נדונין אלא במיתה שהיו מחייבין לבועל והיינו חנק כשאר בא על אשת איש כדמפרש קרא היא תשרף ולא בועלה וזוממיה ילפינן מכאשר זמם לעשות לאחיו לאחיו ולא לאחותו: ובועלה. בנשואה בת כהן קמיירי אבל ארוסה בועלה בסקילה: **גמ'** ס"ד. בתמיה: קטל חד בסייף. כדתנן בפרקין לעיל (דף עו:) אלו הן הנהרגים הרוצח ועיר הנדחת: מאי איכא למימר. הכא ליכא למדרש דאביו בחנק: אלא מדכתיב מכה איש ומת. היכא דבעי מיתה מפרש מיתה בהדיא: אפילו נפלים. כגון בן תשעה וראשו אטום או שיש לו שני גבין דלא חיי: דכתיב ביה נפש. ונפש משמע דם דהוה חבורה: הכחישה. לבהמה: באבנים. דלא עשה בה חבורה: לנפש אדם. דהיינו אביו דאף על גב דלא בעינן מיתה חבורה מיהא בעינן: אלא הקישא למה לי. דאתקש מכה אדם למכה בהמה בחד קרא הואיל וילפת ליה מאם אינו ענין: לכדתניא דבי חזקיה. בב"ק [בהמניח] (דף לה.) לפטור חייבי מיתות שוגגין מן התשלומין מה מכה בהמה לא חלקת בו וכו': הניחא וכו'. פלוגתא דרבי יוחנן ורשב"ל בכתובות באלו נערות (דף לד:): מה מכה בהמה לרפואה. כגון מקיז דם פטור מן התשלומין שהרי לא הזיקה: אף מכה אדם. דהיינו אביו: לרפואה פטור. ממיתה ואע"ג דחבורה היא: ואהבת לרעך כמוך. לא הוזהרו ישראל מלעשות לחבריהם אלא דבר שאינו חפץ לעשות לעצמו: סילוא. קוץ ישב לו בבשרו: למפתח ליה כוותא. כויה להוציא ליחה ממנה: אי הכי אחר נמי. לא ליפתח שהרי כל ישראל הוזהרו על חבלת חבירו דכתיב (דברים כה) לא יוסיף פן יוסיף: שגגת לאו. כשאין מתכוין הוי שגגה באיסור שזדונו לאו בעלמא דקיל: מחט של יד. היא מחט קטנה שתופרין בה בגדים ניטלת בשבת ליטול בה את הקוץ ומשום דקתני לה להלן במסכת שבת בפרק כל הכלים (דף קכב:) גבי ושל שקאין לפתוח בו את הדלת קרי ליה להא קטנה מחט של יד: דילמא חביל. ועביד חבורה בשבת: מקלקל הוא. וכל המקלקלין פטורין בחלול שבת דמלאכת מחשבת כתיב ואין מחייב אמקלקל אלא רבי שמעון ומקלקל בחבורה רבי שמעון נמי לא מחייב אלא במתכוון לכך דהוי צריך לחבלה אבל הנוטל קוץ אין צריך לחבלה וברצונו לא יחבל:

אלו הן הנחנקין: **ה"ג** ואצטריך למכתב מכה איש ומת ואצטריך למכתב ואיש כי יכה כל נפש. ולא כמו שכתוב בספרים כל מכה נפש דבפרק יוצא דופן (נדה מד: ושם) גמרינן בן יום אחד דההורגו חייב ומפיק ליה מדכתיב ואיש כי יכה כל נפש נפש כל דהו [ח]:

איש דבר מצוה אין. יש ספרים שכתוב בהן אשה לא ואע"ג דהשוה הכתוב אשה לאיש וכו' [ט] הני מילי בפרשה שנאמרה בלשון זכר אבל היכא דכתיב איש בהדיא ממעטין אשה כדפירש שלהי פרק ד' מיתות (לעיל סו.) גבי מקלל אביו ואמו:

הוה אמינא אפילו נפלים. תימה א"כ היכי מיחייב דמי וולדות הא מיחייב מיתה וי"ל דה"א דהכא גזירת הכתוב היא היכא דלא נתכוין לוולדות כדאשכחן לרבי [י] ונתתה נפש תחת נפש ממון אי נמי נהי דהוה מיחייב אנפל לאחר שנולד קודם שנולד לא מיחייב: **הכחישה** באבנים כו'. בהכחשה דלא הדרא איירי דאם לא כן לא שייך נזק דמקרי שבת מידי דהוה אהכהו על ידו ולמתה וסופה לחזור ובבהמה [°]לא שייכי ד' דברים:

אלא למאן דלית ליה דתנא דבי חזקיה. פירשתי לעיל בפ' הנשרפין (דף עט: ד"ה בין):

מאן שמעת ליה דאמר מקלקל בחבורה חייב ר"ש. פלוגתא דר' יהודה ור"ש במקלקל בחבורה ומקלקל בהבערה לא מצינו בפירוש לא במשנה ולא בברייתא ובפרק האורג (שבת דף קו. ושם) דחק רש"י לפרש דנפקא מפלוגתא דמלאכה שאינה צריכה לגופה פטור עליה הלכך אין לך חובל ומבעיר שאינו מקלקל ואפילו מבעיר עלים לתבשילו מקלקל הוא אבל העלים ומה שהוא מתקן אבל אחרים לרבי שמעון לא חשיב ליה דהא מלאכה שאינה צריכה לגופה היא אם כן כי חייב הכתוב חובל ומבעיר מדאצטריך למשרי מילה ומדאסר הבערה דבת כהן על כרחך במקלקל נמי חייב אבל רבי יהודה סבירא ליה מלאכה שאינה צריכה לגופה חייב עליה הלכך חיוב דחובל בצריך לכלבו ומבעיר בצריך לאפרו משכחת לה ואע"פ שמקלקל הוא אבל מלאכה עצמה מתקן הוא אבל אחרים ולרבי יהודה בכי האי גוונא מלאכה היא משום תיקון דאחרים אבל מקלקל ואינו מתקן פטור לשון הקונט' כתבתי השתא הא דאמרי' התם בפרק האורג (שם) תני רבי אבהו קמיה דר' יוחנן כל המקלקלין פטורים חוץ מחובל ומבעיר אמר ליה פוק תני לברא חובל ומבעיר אינה משנה כו' משמע מתוך פי' הקונטרס דר' אבהו כר"ש ורבי יוחנן דבעי צריך לכלבו ולאפרו כר' יהודה וזהו תימה א"כ אמאי א"ל פוק תני לברא אטו משום דס"ל כרבי יהודה מאן דתני כר"ש משתיק ליה דכי האי גוונא פריך פרק קמא דחולין (דף טו.) ועוד אי חשיב תיקון גמור צריך לכלבו ולאפרו אמאי נקט חובל ומבעיר ועוד דר"ש אפי' בחובל ומבעיר בעי שתהא צריכה לגופה כדמסיק בשמעתין גבי חובל ובשלהי ספק אכל (כריתות דף כ:) גבי הבערה על כן נראה דר' אבהו ור' יוחנן אליבא דר"ש פליגי דר' אבהו כר"ש כדאיתא בפרק האורג (שבת דף קו.) ורבי יוחנן סבר דאפילו ר' שמעון בעי תיקון קצת ומיהו לא חשיב תיקון שיתחייב בכך לר' יהודה דאין דרך לחבול בחבירו ליתן לכלב ולשרוף גדיש בשביל אפר ופלוגתא דמקלקל בחבורה דרבי יהודה ורבי שמעון קים ליה להש"ס או בקבלה או שמא ברייתא שנויה בשום מקום וכי תימא לרבי אבהו כיון דליכא תיקון א"כ צריכה לגופה היכי משכחת לה הא משכחת לה באיסורי הנאה שסבור שיכול ליהנות וליתן לכלבו וכן מבעיר באיסורי הנאה שסבור שיכול לבשל קדירה ועוד יש לדקדק פלוגתא דמקלקל בחבורה מדתנן בפסחים פר' אלו דברים (דף עב: ושם עג. ושם) ושאר כל הזבחים ששחטן לשם פסח אם אין ראוין חייב ואמרי' בגמ' מאן תנא דשני ליה בין ראוין לשאין ראוין ר"ש הוא ואמרינן התם לעיל מיניה דאיירי בטועה אלמא מחייבינן מתעסק ואמרינן בפ' ספק אכל (כריתות ד' יט:) הנח לתינוקות הואיל ומקלקל בחבורה חייב מתעסק נמי חייב ומדמחייב רבי שמעון מתעסק בחבורה שמע מינה מקלקל

[המשך בדף פה.]

עין משפט
נר מצוה

א א מיי' פ"ה מהלכות ממרים הל"ה ופט"ו מהלכות סנהדרין הל"ג סמג לאוין ריט ועשין קו טוש"ע יו"ד סי' רמא סעיף א בהג"ה:

ב ב מיי' פט"ו מהלכות סנהדרין שם ופרק ט מהלכות גניבה הל"א סמג לאוין קלד:

ג ג מיי' פט"ו מהלכות סנהדרין שם ופ"ג מהלכות ממרים הלכה ח סמג לאוין קיג:

ד ד מיי' פט"ו מהלכות סנהדרין שם ופ"ט מהלכות יסודי התורה הל"א ופ"ה מהלכות ע"ז הל"א סמג לאוין לה:

ה ה מיי' פט"ו מהלכות סנהדרין שם ופרק ה' מהלכות ע"ז הלכה ו סמג לאוין לג:

ו ו מיי' פט"ו מהלכות סנהדרין שם ופ"א מהלכות איסורי ביאה הל"ו סמג לאוין קג:

ז ז מיי' פ"ב מהלכות עדות הל"י:

ח ח מיי' פ"ג מהלכות איסורי ביאה הל"ג:

ט ט מיי' שם פ"א הלכה ו:

י י מיי' פ"ה מהלכות ממרים הלכה ז סמג לאוין רי"ט טור שו"ע יו"ד סימן רמא סעיף ג:

יא כ מיי' פכ"ה מהלכו' שבת הל"ח סמג לאוין סה טוש"ע או"ח סימן שח סעיף יא:

יב ל מיי' פ"א מהלכות שבת הל"ז ופ"ח הל"ז ופ"י הל"י ופי"ב הל"א ופ"ד מהלכות חובל הל"א סמג לאוין סה ועשין ע:

גליון הש"ס

תוס' ד"ה הכחישה וכו'. לא שייכי ד' דברים. עי' גיטין דף מב ע"ב תוס' ד"ה ושור:

תורה אור השלם

א) וּמַכֵּה אָבִיו וְאִמּוֹ מוֹת יוּמָת: [שמות כא, טו]

ב) מַכֵּה אִישׁ וָמֵת מוֹת יוּמָת: [שמות כא, יב]

ג) אוֹ בְאֵיבָה הִכָּהוּ בְיָדוֹ וַיָּמֹת מוֹת יוּמַת הַמַּכֶּה רֹצֵחַ הוּא גֹּאֵל הַדָּם יָמִית אֶת הָרֹצֵחַ בְּפִגְעוֹ בוֹ: [במדבר לה, כא]

ד) כָּל מַכֵּה נֶפֶשׁ לְפִי עֵדִים יִרְצַח אֶת הָרֹצֵחַ וְעֵד אֶחָד לֹא יַעֲנֶה בְנֶפֶשׁ לָמוּת: [במדבר לה, ל]

[לפי תוס'] וְאִישׁ כִּי יַכֶּה כָּל נֶפֶשׁ אָדָם מוֹת יוּמָת: [ויקרא כד, יז]

ה) וּמַכֵּה בְהֵמָה יְשַׁלְּמֶנָּה וּמַכֵּה אָדָם יוּמָת: [ויקרא כד, כא]

ו) וּמַכֵּה נֶפֶשׁ בְּהֵמָה יְשַׁלְּמֶנָּה נֶפֶשׁ תַּחַת נָפֶשׁ: [ויקרא כד, יח]

ז) לֹא תִקֹּם וְלֹא תִטֹּר אֶת בְּנֵי עַמֶּךָ וְאָהַבְתָּ לְרֵעֲךָ כָּמוֹךָ אֲנִי ה': [ויקרא יט, יח]

מסורת הש"ס

א) [לעיל נג: לקמן פט.], ב) [לעיל טו: נג:], ג) נדה מד: [ע"ש תוס'], ד) [לקמן פה:], ה) [לעיל עט: ושם נסמן], ו) [בערוך ערך בע ד' איתא בועתא], ז) שבת קז. קכב:, ח) [ע' תוס' נדה מד: ד"ה איש כי יכה], ט) [כדאיתא פסחים מג.], י) [לעיל עט.].

הגהות הב"ח

(א) גמ' רב פפא לא שביק לבריה:

ליקוטי רש"י

מכה אביו ואמו. בחנק. דכתיב ביה (שמות כא) יומת סתמא וקיימא לן (סנהדרין נב:) כל מיתה האמורה בתורה סתם אינו אלא חנק [לעיל נ.]. **זקן ממרא.** שממרה על ב"ד של לשכת הגזית ומיתתו בחנק [סוטה כה.]. **זוממי בת כהן.** לעשות לאחיו מה תלמוד לומר לאחיו למד על זוממי בת כהן נשואה שאינן בשריפה אלא כמיתת הבועל שהוא בחנק שנאמר היא באש תשרף (ויקרא כא, ט) היא ולא בועלה לכך נאמר כאן לאחיו כאשר זמם לעשות לאחיו ולא כאשר זמם לעשות לאחותו אבל בכל שאר מיתות השוה הכתוב אשה לאיש וזוממי אשה נהרגין כזוממי איש כגון שהעידוה שהרגה את הנפש שחללה את השבת נהרגין במיתתה שלא מיעט כאן אחותו אלא במקום שיש לקיים בהן הזמה במיתת הבועל [דברים יט, יט]. שהיא והן נהרגין ולא במיתה אחת דהיא בשריפה והן במיתת הבועל כגון באו עדים והזימו את הראשונים וחייבום מיתת הבועל ולא מיתתה דכתיב (דברים יט) כאשר זמם לעשות לאחיו ולא לאחותו כדאמר באלו הן הנחנקין (סנהדרין צ). **בועלה.** דהיא בשריפה אבל בועלה נידון כשאר בועל בת ישראל דבועל ארוסה בסקילה ובועל נשואה בחנק דכתיב (ויקרא כא) היא באש תשרף היא ולא בועלה היא ולא זוממיה [לעיל מו.]. **מכה אביו ואמו.** לפי שלמדנו על החובל בחבירו שהוא בתשלומין ולא במיתה הוצרך לומר על החובל באביו שהוא במיתה ואינו חייב אלא בהכאה שיש בה חבורה [שמות כא, טו]. **למאן דאמר חנק חמור.** מסייף בפרק ארבע מיתות (סנהדרין נ:) [לעיל טו:]. **מכה איש ומת.** למה נאמר לפי שנאמר (ויקרא כד, יז) ואיש כי יכה כל נפש אדם מות יומת שומע אני בהכאה בלא מיתה תלמוד לומר מכה איש ומת אינו חייב אלא בהכאה של מיתה ואם נאמר מכה איש ולא נאמר ואיש כי יכה הייתי אומר אינו חייב עד שיכה איש הכה את האשה ואת הקטן מנין תלמוד לומר כי יכה כל נפש אדם אפילו קטן ואפילו אשה ועוד אלו נאמר מכה איש שומע אני אפילו קטן שהכה והרג יהא חייב תלמוד לומר ואיש כי יכה ולא קטן שהכה ועוד כי יכה כל נפש אדם אפילו נפלים במשמע תלמוד לומר מכה איש אינו חייב עד שיכה בן קיימא ראוי להיות איש [שם פסוק יב]. **מכה אדם ומכה בהמה.** ומכה אדם יומת, אפילו לא הרגו אלא עשה בו חבורה שלא נאמר כאן נפש ובמכה אביו ואמו דבר הכתוב ובא להקישו למכה בהמה מה מכה בהמה מחיים אף מכה אביו ואמו מחיים פרט למכה לאחר מיתה לפי שמצינו שהמקללו לאחר מיתה חייב הוצרך לומר במכה שפטור ומה בבהמה בחבלה שאם אין חבלה אין תשלומין אף מכה אביו ואמו אינו חייב עד שיעשה בהם חבורה [ויקרא כד, כא]. **כדתני דבי חזקיה.** מכה נפש בהמה ישלמנה ומכה אדם יומת הוקשו יחד מה מכה בהמה לעולם משלם ואפי' בשוגג כדאמרי' (ב"ק כו) אדם מועד לעולם אף מכה אדם דפטריה קרא מתשלומין דכתיב יומת לעולם פטור ואפילו בשוגג הואיל ובמזיד שייכא מיתה [ב"ק לה.]. **מחט של יד.** מחט קטן שתופר בו בגדים [שבת קכב:]. מחט של יד ניטלת בשבת. **ליטול בה את הקוץ.** והיינו דומיא דלהא דמצער ליה ואינו חושש אם יפתח מיד וקאמר ניטלת לכתחילה מחט של יד היא מחט שתופרין בה בגדים ומשום דקתני בהדה ושל שק לפתוח בה את הדלת קרי לה להאי מחט של יד [שם קו.].

[המשך בדף פה.]

therefore compare them through the principle of *hekeish*: מַה מַכֵּה בְהֵמָה לִרְפוּאָה פָּטוּר – **Just as one who strikes an animal for therapeutic** purposes **is exempt** from liability, אַף מַכֵּה אָדָם לִרְפוּאָה פָּטוּר – **so, too, one who strikes a person,** i.e. a parent, **for therapeutic** purposes **is exempt** from the death penalty.

The Gemara cites some incidents that relate to these rulings: רַב לֹא שָׁבִיק לִבְרֵיהּ לְמִישְׁקַל לֵיהּ סִילְוָא – **Rav did not allow his son to remove a splinter from his** skin מַר בְּרֵיהּ דְּרָבִינָא לֹא שָׁבִיק לִבְרֵיהּ לְמִיפְתַּח לֵיהּ כַּוְותָא – and **Mar the son of Ravina did not allow his son to lance his boil,** דִּילְמָא חָבִיל וַהֲוָה לֵיהּ שְׁגָגַת אִיסּוּר – for **perhaps [the son]** would inadvertently **inflict a wound, which for him would be an inadvertent** transgression **of a prohibition.**[39]

The Gemara asks:

אִי הָכִי – **If** it is **so** that they were concerned about the son inflicting a wound, אַחֵר נַמִּי – then they should have forbidden **other** people from treating them **as well** since it is prohibited to wound *anyone.*[40] – ? –

The Gemara answers:

אַחֵר שִׁיגְגַת לָאו – If any **other** person inflicted the wound, it would be only **an inadvertent** transgression **of a negative commandment,**[41] a comparatively lenient sin, בְּנוֹ שִׁגְגַת חֶנֶק – but if **one's son** wounds him, it is **an inadvertent** transgression **of** a sin punishable by **strangulation,** a much more serious sin.[42] As such, a son should not remove a splinter from his parent or lance the parent's boil, because there is a risk that he will inflict a wound.

The Gemara challenges the conclusion that one should not perform an act if there is a risk that he will inadvertently transgress a capital sin:

וְהָדְתְנַן – **And** what about **that which we have learned in a Mishnah:**[43] מַחַט שֶׁל יָד לִיטּוֹל בָּהּ אֶת הַקּוֹץ – On the Sabbath one may move A HAND NEEDLE[44] in order TO REMOVE A THORN WITH IT. This Mishnah is clearly stating that one may remove a thorn from his skin on the Sabbath even though this might cause bleeding. But why is that so? לֵיחוּשׁ דִּילְמָא חָבִיל – **Let us be concerned** that **perhaps he will** inadvertently **inflict a wound,** which is a forbidden activity on the Sabbath, וְהָוְיָא לַהּ שְׁגָגַת סְקִילָה – **and this would be an inadvertent** transgression **of a prohibition punishable by stoning.**[45] Evidently, then, the Mishnah permits one to perform an act even if, while doing so, he might inadvertently commit a capital crime. This refutes the Gemara's conclusion to the contrary. – ? –

The Gemara distinguishes between the Mishnah's case and the one discussed above:

הָתָם מְקַלְקֵל הוּא – **There,** in the Mishnah's case, even if the fellow inflicts a wound while removing the thorn, **he is performing a destructive act,** which is not forbidden on the Biblical level.[46] But if someone wounds his parent while removing a splinter, he

NOTES

39. *Beis Yosef* (*Yoreh Deah* 241 ד״ה לפיכך) states that there is some question about whether Rav and Mar the son of Ravina dispute the answers provided above to the Gemara's inquiry. Some maintain that Rav and Mar essentially agree with the position of Rav Masna and Rav Dimi; according to the letter of the law, a son may wound his father for therapeutic purposes. Rav and Mar are adding, however, that it is preferable for the parent not to be treated by his child if other [competent] help is available (see *Rambam, Hil. Mamrim* 5:7 with *Lechem Mishneh; Ramban, Toras HaAdam* [printed in *Kisvei HaRamban,* vol. II, p. 43]; *Rama*, *Yoreh Deah* 241:3). The reason for this, *Ramban* explains, is that a doctor sometimes makes a larger wound than necessary for therapeutic purposes. If the doctor is the patient's child, this is an inadvertent transgression of the prohibition against striking a parent.

Others maintain, however, that there *is* an Amoraic dispute as to whether it is actually forbidden to wound a parent for therapeutic purposes. Rav Masna and Rav Dimi hold that this is permitted, as stated above, but Rav and Mar bar Ravina hold that it is forbidden. Moreover, they maintain that one may not remove a thorn from his parent's skin or lance his parent's boil even though it is merely possible that these procedures will wound the parent (*Rif* and *Rosh* according to *Beis Yosef*; cf. *Bach* ibid. and *Chidushei HaRan*).

40. As the Torah states in *Deuteronomy* (25:3): *Forty shall he strike him, he shall not add; lest he strike him an additional blow beyond these* (*Rashi*). The verse states that an agent of the court may flog someone who was sentenced to lashes but the agent may not continue to strike the offender after the prescribed number of lashes were meted out. This also teaches that nobody is permitted to strike a fellow without a court order (see *Rambam, Hil. Sanhedrin* 16:12).

41. That is, if someone unintentionally wounds anyone except his parent, he performs an act that, if done intentionally, would have been a transgression of a negative commandment (*Rashi*).

42. Our Gemara is stating that there is nothing wrong with inadvertently transgressing a negative commandment, but one must make sure that he does not commit a capital crime unintentionally. *Chidushei HaRan* explains this as follows. When someone inadvertently transgresses a negative commandment, the law does not require him to atone for his act (e.g. by offering a sacrifice). Hence, one is permitted to remove a fellow's thorn because even if this makes a wound, he will, at worst, be inadvertently transgressing a negative commandment. But a capital sin is much more serious. [If someone inadvertently commits most capital sins, he is obligated to atone by bringing a *chatas* offering. (For an explanation of why atonement is needed for an inadvertent sin, see *Ramban* to *Leviticus* 4:2.)] Hence, one should not remove a thorn from his parent's skin, since he might thereby wound the parent, which would be an inadvertent transgression of a capital sin (see *Chidushei HaRan*). [*Chidushei HaRan* adds that if someone inadvertently wounds a fellow (other than his parent) while removing a thorn, he might not even be morally culpable, because he was actually trying to help the person.]

Ramban and *Chidushei HaRan* ask why, given the above, it is permitted to practice medicine at all, since there is always a remote risk that a procedure or medication might kill the patient. Hence, whenever, a doctor treats a patient, it is possible that he will inadvertently transgress the capital crime of murder! They answer that when the Torah permits doctors to practice medicine (see *Bava Kamma* 85a), it implicitly licenses them to treat their patients as well as they can. Hence, they are not liable if they accidentally cause a patient's death.

43. *Shabbos* 122b. This Mishnah discusses some laws of *muktzeh,* objects that may not be handled or moved on the Sabbath. There are several categories of *muktzeh,* one of which is כְּלִי שֶׁמְּלַאכְתּוֹ לְאִסּוּר, *a utensil used primarily for work prohibited on the Sabbath.* Items in this category may not be moved to prevent them from being damaged, but they may be moved if they are needed for a permitted activity (or if they are taking up needed space). The Mishnah lists several examples of such items and situations where it would be permitted to move them. Our Gemara cites one of these examples, a hand (i.e. sewing) needle needed to remove a thorn or splinter embedded in one's skin.

44. I.e. a needle used for sewing clothes. The Mishnah calls this small needle a hand needle in contrast to the other needle listed there – a sackmaker's needle, which is much bigger, and can be used as a lock pick (*Rashi*).

45. For one who intentionally performs a forbidden act on the Sabbath is subject to death by stoning. (For a discussion about the nature of the prohibition against inflicting a wound, see *Magen Avraham, Orach Chaim* 316:15).

46. For the Torah states that on the Sabbath one may not perform מְלֶאכֶת מַחֲשֶׁבֶת, *calculated labor.* Based on this, the Mishnah in *Shabbos* (105b) states that work done in a destructive manner does not constitute "forbidden labor," and one is not punished for doing it on the Sabbath [although it is Rabbinically prohibited] (*Rashi*). Thus, the Mishnah does not refute the rulings of Rav and Mar the son of Ravina (that one may not do anything that could lead to the inadvertent transgression of a capital crime) for in the Mishnah's case, it is not a capital sin to make a wound. [In fact, it is not Biblically forbidden at all!]

עין משפט נר מצוה

א א מיי' פ"ה מהלכות ממרים הל"ה ופט"ו מהלכות סנהדרין הלי"ג סמג לאוין ריט ועשין קו טוש"ע יו"ד סי' רמא סעיף א בהג"ה:
ב ב מיי' פט"ו מהלכות סנהדרין שם ופרק ט מהלכות גניבה הל"א סמג לאוין קלד:
ג ג מיי' פט"ו מהלכות סנהדרין שם ופ"ג מהלכות ממרים הלכה ח סמג לאוין קיג:
ד ד מיי' פט"ו מהלכות סנהדרין שם ופ"ט מהלכות יסודי התורה הל"א ופ"ה מהלכות ע"ז הל"א סמג לאוין לה:
ה ה מיי' פט"ו מהלכות סנהדרין שם ופרק ה' מהלכות ע"ז הלכה ו סמג לאוין לב:
ו ו מיי' פט"ו מהלכות סנהדרין שם ופ"א מהלכות איסורי ביאה הל"ו סמג לאוין קג:
ז ז מיי' פ"ב מהלכות עדות הל"י:
ח ח מיי' פ"ג מהלכות איסורי ביאה הל"ג:
ט ט מיי' שם פ"א הלכה ו:
י י מיי' פ"ה מהלכות ממרים הלכה ז סמג לאוין ריט טור שו"ע יו"ד סימן רמא סעיף ג:
יא כ מיי' פכ"ה מהלכו' שבת הל"א סמג לאוין סה טוש"ע או"ח סימן שח סעיף יא:
יב ל מיי' פ"א מהלכות שבת הלי"ז ופ"ח הל"ז ופ"י הל"י ופי"ב הל"א ופ"ד מהלכות חובל הל"א סמג לאוין סה ועשין ע:

גליון הש"ס

תוס' ד"ה הכחישה וכו'. לא שייכי ד' דברים. עי' גיטין דף מב ע"ב תוס' ד"ה ושור:

תורה אור השלם

א) וּמַכֵּה אָבִיו וְאִמּוֹ מוֹת יוּמָת: [שמות כא, טו]
ב) מַכֵּה אִישׁ וָמֵת מוֹת יוּמָת: [שמות כא, יב]
ג) אוֹ בְאֵיבָה הִכָּהוּ בְיָדוֹ וַיָּמֹת מוֹת יוּמַת הַמַּכֶּה רֹצֵחַ הוּא גֹּאֵל הַדָּם יָמִית אֶת הָרֹצֵחַ בְּפִגְעוֹ בוֹ: [במדבר לה, כא]
ד) כָּל מַכֵּה נֶפֶשׁ לְפִי עֵדִים יִרְצַח אֶת הָרֹצֵחַ וְעֵד אֶחָד לֹא יַעֲנֶה בְנֶפֶשׁ לָמוּת: [במדבר לה, ל]
[לפי תוס'] וְאִישׁ כִּי יַכֶּה כָּל נֶפֶשׁ אָדָם מוֹת יוּמָת: [ויקרא כד, יז]
ה) וּמַכֵּה בְהֵמָה יְשַׁלְּמֶנָּה וּמַכֵּה אָדָם יוּמָת: [ויקרא כד, כא]
ו) וּמַכֵּה נֶפֶשׁ בְּהֵמָה יְשַׁלְּמֶנָּה נֶפֶשׁ תַּחַת נָפֶשׁ: [ויקרא כד, יח]
ז) לֹא תִקֹּם וְלֹא תִטֹּר אֶת בְּנֵי עַמֶּךָ וְאָהַבְתָּ לְרֵעֲךָ כָּמוֹךָ אֲנִי יְיָ: [ויקרא יט, יח]

אלו הן הנחנקין א המכה אביו ואמו ב וגונב נפש מישראל ג וזקן ממרא ע"פ ב"ד ד ונביא השקר ה והמתנבא בשם עבודת כוכבים ו והבא על אשת איש ז וזוממי בת כהן ח ובועלה: **גמ'** מכה אביו ואמו מנלן דכתיב א) מכה אביו ואמו מות יומת א) ט וכל מיתה האמורה בתורה סתם אינה אלא חנק אימא עד דקטיל ליה מיקטל ס"ד קטל חד בסייף ואביו בחנק ב) הניחא למ"ד חנק קל אלא למאן דאמר חנק חמור מאי איכא למימר אלא מדכתיב ב) מכה איש ומת מות יומת וכתיב ג) או באיבה הכהו בידו וימות שמע מינה כל היכא דאיכא הכאה סתם לאו מיתה הוא ואצטריך למיכתב מכה איש ואיצטריך למכתב ד) כל מכה נפש דאי כתב רחמנא מכה איש ומת הוה אמינא איש דבר מצוה אין קטן לא ג) כתב רחמנא כל מכה נפש ואי כתב רחמנא כל מכה נפש הוה אמינא אפילו נפלים אפילו בן שמונה צריכי ואימא אע"ג דלא עביד ביה חבורה אלמה תנן ד) המכה אביו ואמו אינו חייב עד שיעשה בהן חבורה אמר קרא ה) מכה אדם ומכה בהמה מה מכה בהמה עד דעביד בה חבורה דכתיב בה ו) נפש אף מכה אדם עד דעביד חבורה מתקיף לה רב ירמיה אלא מעתה הכחישה באבנים הכי נמי דלא מיחייב אלא אם אינו ענין לנפש בהמה דהא אי נמי הכחישה באבנים חייב תניהו ענין לנפש אדם אלא הקישא למה לי לכדתניא ה) דבי חזקיה הניחא למאן דאית ליה תנא דבי חזקיה אלא למאן דלית ליה תנא דבי חזקיה היקישא למה לי מה מכה בהמה לרפואה פטור אף מכה אדם לרפואה פטור דאיבעיא להו בן מהו שיקיז דם לאביו רב מתנא אמר ז) ואהבת לרעך כמוך רב דימי בר חיננא אמר מכה אדם ומכה בהמה מה מכה בהמה לרפואה פטור אף מכה אדם לרפואה פטור (א) רב לא שביק לבריה למישקל ליה סילוא מר בריה דרבינא לא שביק לבריה למיפתח ליה ו) כוותא דילמא חביל והוה ליה שגגת איסור אי הכי אחר נמי אחר שיגגת לאו בנו שגגת חנק ז) והדתנן כ מחט של יד ליטול בה את הקוץ ליחוש דילמא חביל והויא לה שגגת סקילה התם מקלקל הוא הניחא למאן דאמר ל מקלקל פטור אלא למ"ד חייב מאי איכא למימר מאן שמעת ליה דאמר מקלקל בחבורה חייב ר' שמעון היא ורבי

אלו הן הנחנקין: ממרא על פי בית דין. כמו ממרים הייתם עם ה' (דברים ט) שמסרב על פי ב"ד הגדול שבלשכת הגזית: וזוממי בת כהן. אע"פ שהם היו מחייבין אותה שריפה אין נדונין אלא במיתה שהיו מחייבין לבועל והיינו חנק כשאר בא על אשת איש כדמפרש קרא היא תשרף ולא בועלה וזוממיה ילפינן מכאשר זמם לעשות לאחיו לאחיו ולא לאחותו: ובועלה. בנשואה בת כהן קמיירי אבל ארוסה בועלה בסקילה: **גמ'** ס"ד. בתמיה: קטל חד בסייף. כדתנן בפרקין לעיל (דף עו:) אלו הן הנהרגים הרוצח ועיר הנדחת: מאי איכא למימר. הכא דאיכא למדרש דאביו בחנק: אלא מדכתיב מכה איש ומת. היכא דבעי מיתה מפרש מיתה בהדיא: אפילו נפלים. כגון בן תשעה וראשו אטום או שיש לו שני גבין דלא חיי: דכתיב ביה נפש. ונפש משמע דם דהוה חבורה: הכחישה. לבהמה: באבנים. דלא עשה בה חבורה: לנפש אדם. דהיינו אביו דאף על גב דלא בעינן מיתה חבורה מיהא בעינן: אלא הקישא למה לי. דאתקש מכה אדם למכה בהמה בחד קרא הואיל וילפת ליה מאם אינו ענין: לכדתניא דבי חזקיה. בב"ק [בהמניח] (דף לה.) לפטור חייבי מיתות שוגגין מן התשלומין מה מכה בהמה לא חלקת בו וכו': הניחא וכו'. פלוגתא דרבי יוחנן ורשב"ל בכתובות באלו נערות (דף לד:): מה מכה בהמה לרפואה. כגון מקיז דם פטור מן התשלומין שהרי לא הזיקה: אף מכה אדם. דהיינו אביו: לרפואה פטור. ממיתה ואע"ג דחבורה היא: ואהבת לרעך כמוך. לא הוזהרו ישראל מלעשות לחבריהם אלא דבר שאינו חפץ לעשות לעצמו: סילוא. קוץ ישב לו בבשרו: למפתח ליה כוותא. כויה להוציא ליחה ממנה: אי הכי אחר נמי. לא ליפתח שהרי כל ישראל הוזהרו על חבלת חבירו דכתיב (דברים כה) לא יוסיף פן יוסיף: שגגת לאו. כשאין מתכוין הוי שגגה באיסור שזדונו לאו בעלמא דקיל: מחט של יד. היא מחט קטנה שתופרין בה בגדים ניטלת בשבת ליטול בה את הקוץ ומשום דקתני לה להלן במסכת שבת בפרק כל הכלים (דף קכב:) גבי ושל שקאין לפתוח בו את הדלת קרי ליה להא קטנה מחט של יד: דילמא חביל. ועביד חבורה בשבת: מקלקל הוא. וכל המקלקלין פטורין בחלול שבת דמלאכת מחשבת כתיב ואין מחייב אמקלקל אלא רבי שמעון ומקלקל בחבורה רבי שמעון נמי לא מחייב אלא במתכוין לכך דהוי צריך לחבלה אבל הנוטל קוץ אין צריך לחבלה וברצונו לא יחבל:
ורבי

אלו הן הנחנקין: ה"ג ואצטריך למכתב מכה איש ומת ואצטריך למכתב ואיש כי יכה כל נפש. ולא כמו שכתוב בספרים כל מכה נפש דבפרק יוצא דופן (נדה מד: ושם) גמרינן בן יום אחד דההורגו חייב ומפיק ליה מדכתיב ואיש כי יכה כל נפש נפש כל דהו ח):

איש דבר מצוה אין. יש ספרים שכתוב בהן אשה לא ואע"ג דהשוה הכתוב אשה לאיש וכו' ט) הני מילי בפרשה שנאמרה בלשון זכר אבל היכא דכתיב איש בהדיא ממעטין אשה כדפירש שלהי פרק ד' מיתות (לעיל סו.) גבי מקלל אביו ואמו:

הוה אמינא אפילו נפלים. תימה א"כ היכי מיחייב דמי וולדות הא מיחייב מיתה וי"ל דה"א דהכא גזירת הכתוב היא היכא דלא נתכוין לוולדות כדאשכחן לרבי י) ונתתה נפש תחת נפש ממון אי נמי נהי דהוה מיחייב אנפל לאחר שנולד קודם שנולד לא מיחייב: **הכחישה** באבנים כו'. בהכחשה דלא הדרא איירי דאם לא כן לא שייך נזק דמקרי שבת מידי דהוה אהכהו על ידו ולמתה וסופה לחזור ובבהמה ט לא שייכי ד' דברים:

אלא למאן דלית ליה דתנא דבי חזקיה. פירשתי לעיל בפ' הנשרפין (דף עט: ד"ה בין):

מאן שמעת ליה דאמר מקלקל בחבורה חייב ר"ש. פלוגתא דר' יהודה ור"ש במקלקל בחבורה ומקלקל בהבערה לא מצינו בפירוש לא במשנה ולא בברייתא ובפרק האורג (שבת דף קו. ושם) דחק רש"י לפרש דנפקא מפלוגתא דמלאכה שאינה צריכה לגופה פטור עליה הלכך אין לך חובל ומבעיר שאינו מקלקל ואפילו מבעיר עצים לתבשילו מקלקל הוא אבל העצים ומה שהוא מתקן אבל אחרים לרבי שמעון לא חשיב ליה דהא מלאכה שאינה צריכה לגופה היא אם כן כי חייב הכתוב חובל ומבעיר מדאצטריך למשרי מילה ומדאסר הבערה דבת כהן על כרחיך במקלקל נמי חייב אבל רבי יהודה סבירא ליה מלאכה שאינה צריכה לגופה חייב עליה הלכך חיוב דחובל בצריך לכלבו ומבעיר בצריך לאפרו משכחת לה ואע"פ שמקלקל הוא אבל מלאכה עצמה מתקן הוא אבל אחרים ולרבי יהודה בכי האי גוונא מלאכה היא משום תיקון דאחרים אבל מקלקל ואינו מתקן פטור לשון הקונט' כתבתי השתא הא דאמרי' התם בפרק האורג (שם) תני רבי אבהו קמיה דר' יוחנן כל המקלקלין פטורים חוץ מחובל ומבעיר אמר ליה פוק תני לברא חובל ומבעיר אינה משנה כו' משמע מתוך פי' הקונטרס דר' אבהו כר"ש ורבי יוחנן דבעי צריך לכלבו ולאפרו כר' יהודה וזהו תימה א"כ אמאי א"ל פוק תני לברא אטו משום דס"ל כרבי יהודה מאן דתני כר"ש משתיק ליה דכי האי גוונא פריך פרק קמא דחולין (דף טו.) ועוד אי חשיב תיקון גמור צריך לכלבו ולאפרו אמאי נקט חובל ומבעיר ועוד דר"ש אפי' בחובל ומבעיר בעי שתהא צריכה לגופה כדמסיק בשמעתין גבי חובל ובשלהי ספק אכל (כריתות דף כ:) גבי הבערה על כן נראה דר' אבהו ור' יוחנן אליבא דר"ש פליגי דר' אבהו כר"ש כדאיתא בפרק האורג (שבת דף קו.) ורבי יוחנן סבר דאפילו ר' שמעון בעי תיקון קצת ומיהו לא חשיב תיקון שיתחייב בכך לר' יהודה דאין דרך לחבול בחבירו ליתן לכלב ולשרוף גדיש בשביל אפר ופלוגתא דמקלקל בחבורה דרבי יהודה ורבי שמעון קים ליה להש"ס או בקבלה או שמא ברייתא שנויה בשום מקום וכי תימא לרבי אבהו כיון דליכא תיקון א"כ צריכה לגופה היכי משכחת לה הא משכחת לה באיסורי הנאה שסבור שיכול ליהנות וליתן לכלבו וכן מבעיר באיסורי הנאה שסבור שיכול לבשל קדירה ועוד יש לדקדק פלוגתא דמקלקל בחבורה מדתנן בפסחים פר' אלו דברים (דף עג: ושם עג. ושם) ושאר כל הזבחים ששחטן לשם פסח אם אין ראויין חייב ואמרי' בגמ' מאן תנא דשני ליה בין ראוין לשאין ראוין ר"ש הוא ואמרינן התם לעיל מיניה דאיירי בטועה אלמא מחייבינן מתעסק ואמרינן בפ' ספק אכל (כריתות ד' יט:) הנח לתינוקות הואיל ומקלקל בחבורה חייב מתעסק נמי חייב ומדמחייב רבי שמעון מתעסק בחבורה שמע מינה מקלקל

מסורת הש"ס

א) [לעיל נב: לקמן פט.], ב) [לעיל טו: נב:], ג) נדה מד: [ע"ש תוס'], ד) [לקמן פה:], ה) [לעיל עט: ושם נסמן], ו) [בערוך ערך בע ד' איתא בועתא], ז) שבת קו. קכב., ח) [עי' תוס' נדה מד: ד"ה איש כי יכה], ט) [כדאיתא פסחים מג.], י) [לעיל עט.].

הגהות הב"ח

(א) גמ' רב פפא לא שביק לבריה:

ליקוטי רש"י

מכה אביו ואמו. בחנק. דכתיב ביה (שמות כא) יומת סתמא וקיימא לן (סנהדרין נב:) כל מיתה האמורה בתורה סתם אינו אלא חנק [לעיל נ.]. **זקן ממרא.** שהמרה על ב"ד של לשכת הגזית ומיתתו בחנק [סוטה כה.]. **זוממי בת כהן.** לעשות לאחיו מה תלמוד לומר לאחיו למד על זוממי בת כהן נשואה שאינן בשריפה אלא כמיתת הבועל שהוא בחנק שנאמר היא באש תשרף (ויקרא כא, ט) היא ולא בועלה לכך נאמר כאן לאחיו כאשר זמם לעשות לאחיו ולא כאשר זמם לעשות לאחותו אבל בכל שאר מיתות השוה הכתוב אשה לאיש וזוממי אשה נהרגין כזוממי איש כגון שהעידוה שהרגה את הנפש שחללה את השבת נהרגין במיתתה שלא מיעט כאן אחותו אלא במקום שיש לקיים בהן הזמה במיתת הבועל [דברים יט, יט]. שהיא והן נהרגין ולא במיתה אחת דהיא בשריפה והן במיתת הבועל כגון באו עדים והזימו את הראשונים וחייבום מיתת הבועל ולא מיתתה דכתיב (דברים יט) כאשר זמם לעשות לאחיו ולא לאחותו כדאמר באלו הן הנחנקין (סנהדרין ל). **בועלה.** דהיא בשריפה אבל בועלה נידון כשאר בועל בת ישראל דבועל ארוסה בסקילה ובועל נשואה בחנק דכתיב (ויקרא כא) היא באש תשרף היא ולא בועלה היא ולא זוממיה [לעיל מו.]. **מכה אביו ואמו.** לפי שלמדנו על החובל בחבירו שהוא בתשלומין ולא במיתה הוצרך לומר על החובל באביו שהוא במיתה ואינו חייב אלא בהכאה שיש בה חבורה [שמות כא, טו]. **למאן דאמר חנק חמור.** מסייף בפרק ארבע מיתות (סנהדרין נ:) [לעיל טו:]. **מכה איש ומת.** למה נאמר לפי שנאמר (ויקרא כד, יז) ואיש כי יכה כל נפש אדם מות יומת שומע אני בהכאה בלא מיתה תלמוד לומר מכה איש ומת אינו חייב אלא בהכאה של מיתה ואם נאמר מכה איש ולא נאמר ואיש כי יכה הייתי אומר אינו חייב עד שיכה איש היכה את האשה ואת הקטן מנין תלמוד לומר כי יכה כל נפש אדם אפילו קטן ואפילו אשה ועוד אלו נאמר מכה איש שומע אני אפילו קטן שהכה והרג יהא חייב תלמוד לומר ואיש כי יכה ולא קטן שהכה ועוד כי יכה כל נפש אדם אפילו נפלים במשמע תלמוד לומר מכה איש אינו חייב עד שיכה בן קיימא הראוי להיות איש [שם פסוק יב]. **מכה אדם ומכה בהמה.** ומכה אדם יומת, אפילו לא הרגו אלא עשה בו חבורה שלא נאמר כאן נפש ומכה אביו ואמו דבר הכתוב ובא להקישו למכה בהמה מה מכה בהמה מחיים אף מכה אביו ואמו מחיים פרט למכה לאחר מיתה לפי שמצינו שהמקללו לאחר מיתה חייב הוצרך לומר במכה שפטור ומה בבהמה בחבלה שאם אין חבלה אין תשלומין אף מכה אביו ואמו אינו חייב עד שיעשה בהם חבורה [ויקרא כד, כא]. **כדתני דבי חזקיה.** מכה נפש בהמה ישלמנה ומכה אדם יומת הוקשו יחד דמה מכה בהמה לעולם משלם ואפי' בשוגג כדאמרי' (ב"ק כו) אדם מועד לעולם אף מכה אדם לפטריה קרא מתשלומין דכתיב יומת לעולם פטור ואפילו בשוגג הואיל ובמזיד שייכא מיתה [ב"ק לה.]. **מחט של יד.** מחט קטן שתופר בו בגדים [שבת קכב:]. מחט של יד ניטלת בשבת. **ליטול בה את הקוץ.** והיינו דומיא דלאה דמלעבר ליה ואינו חושש אם יתפס מיד וקאמר ניטלת לכתחילה מחט של יד היא מחט שתופרין בה בגדים ומשום דקתני בהדה ושל שק לפתוח בה את הדלת קרי לה להאי מחט של יד [שם קז.].

[המשך בדף פה.]

transgresses a sin that, if done intentionally, is punishable with death under Biblical law.

The Gemara asks:

הָנִיחָא לְמַאן דְּאָמַר מְקַלְקֵל פָּטוּר – This is understandable according to the one who maintains that **one who** inflicts a wound in a **destructive** way **is not liable. אֶלָּא לְמַאן דְּאָמַר חַיָּיב – But according to the one who maintains that one is liable** for such an act, **מַאי אִיכָּא לְמֵימַר – what is there to say?** Why may one remove a thorn on the Sabbath when it is possible that he will cause bleeding in the process? It should be forbidden on the grounds that drawing blood on the Sabbath, if done intentionally, is punishable with death.[47] **– ? –**

The Gemara answers:

מַאן שָׁמְעַתְּ לֵיהּ דְּאָמַר מְקַלְקֵל בְּחַבּוּרָה חַיָּיב – Who have you heard maintain that **one who performs a destructive act of wounding is liable? רַבִּי שִׁמְעוֹן הִיא – It is R' Shimon,**

NOTES

47. Granted that the person would not actually be subject to the death penalty if he inflicts a wound, because he did not intend to make the person bleed. Still, he will have done something that, if done intentionally, would subject him to stoning, which, according to the previous Gemara, is forbidden to do! (see *Rashi* and *Maharsha*).

וְרַבִּי שִׁמְעוֹן הָאָמַר כָּל מְלָאכָה שֶׁאֵינָהּ צְרִיכָה לְגוּפָהּ פָּטוּר עָלֶיהָ – **and R' Shimon states that** if someone performs **any** forbidden **labor** on the Sabbath **that is not needed for its defined purpose, he is exempt** from being punished **for it.**[1] According to him, then, even someone who *intended* to cause bleeding while removing a thorn would not be punished with death. For this reason, a person is actually *permitted* to remove the thorn, even though he might unintentionally cause bleeding during the procedure.[2]

The Gemara considers whether a son may strike his father in one exceptional case:

בָּעוּ מִינֵּיהּ מֵרַב שֵׁשֶׁת – **They inquired of Rav Sheishess:** בֵּן מַהוּ שֶׁיֵּעָשֶׂה שָׁלִיחַ לְאָבִיו – **May a son be made an agent** of the court **to** punish **his father,** לְהַכּוֹתוֹ וּלְקַלְּלוֹ – that is, **to strike him or to curse him** on behalf of the court?[3]

The Gemara responds rhetorically:

אָמַר לְהוּ – **[Rav Sheishess] answered them:** וְאַחֵר מִי הִתִּירוּ – **And who** do you think **permitted** someone **other** than a son to carry out these acts on the court's behalf?[4] אֶלָּא כְּבוֹד שָׁמַיִם עָדִיף – **Rather,** we must say that maintaining the **honor of Heaven supersedes** the prohibitions against striking or cursing another Jew. הָכָא נַמִּי כְּבוֹד שָׁמַיִם עָדִיף – **Here too,** maintaining the **honor of Heaven supersedes** the prohibition against striking or cursing one's father. Accordingly, a court may appoint a sentenced man's son to curse or strike him.

The Gemara cites a cryptic Baraisa that seems to contradict Rav Sheishess' response:

מֵיתִיבֵי – **The Gemara challenged this from a Baraisa:**[5] וּמַה מִי שֶׁמְּצֻוֶּה לְהַכּוֹתוֹ – NOW, IF ONE WHO IS COMMANDED TO STRIKE [A CERTAIN PERSON] מְצֻוֶּה שֶׁלֹּא לְהַכּוֹתוֹ – IS COMMANDED NOT TO STRIKE [THAT PERSON] מִי שֶׁאֵינוֹ מְצֻוֶּה לְהַכּוֹתוֹ – then ONE WHO IS NOT COMMANDED TO STRIKE [A CERTAIN PERSON] אֵינוֹ דִּין שֶׁמְּצֻוֶּה שֶׁלֹּא לְהַכּוֹתוֹ – IS SURELY COMMANDED NOT TO STRIKE [THAT PERSON].

The Gemara suggests an interpretation of this cryptic Baraisa and, based on this interpretation, challenges Rav Sheishess' statement:

מַאי לָאו אִידִי וְאִידִי בִּמְקוֹם מִצְוָה – **Is** it **not** true that in this Baraisa **both** clauses **refer to a situation where** there is a **mitzvah** to strike, i.e. where the court has appointed an agent to flog a man. הָא בִּבְנוֹ – And **this** second clause deals with a case **where** the agent is the **son of [the sentenced man],** הָא בְּאַחֵר – whereas **this** first clause deals with a case **where** the agent is someone **other** than his son.[6] If so, the Baraisa's second clause clearly assumes that even an agent of the court may not strike his father. This contradicts the ruling of Rav Sheishess. – ? –

The Gemara reinterprets the Baraisa, thereby removing the challenge:

לֹא – **No,** אִידִי וְאִידִי לֹא שְׁנָא בְּנוֹ וְלֹא שְׁנָא אַחֵר – actually in **both** clauses **there is no difference whether** the fellow was struck by **his son or** by **another** person, וְלֹא קַשְׁיָא – **and** the Baraisa thus presents **no difficulty** for Rav Sheishess' position, because we interpret the Baraisa as follows: כָּאן בִּמְקוֹם מִצְוָה – **Here** in the first clause, the Baraisa discusses **a situation where** there is **a mitzvah** to strike the fellow, because the fellow had been sentenced to lashes, כָּאן שֶׁלֹּא בִּמְקוֹם מִצְוָה – while **here** the second clause discusses **a situation in which there is no mitzvah** to strike the fellow, because there was no court order to

NOTES

1. *Rashi* to *Shabbos* 93b ד״ה ור׳ שמעון interprets "the defined purpose" of a labor as the creative purpose inherent in the labor itself. However, a labor performed only in reaction to an undesirable condition – either to prevent it or to rectify it – has no inherently creative purpose, and one is therefore not liable for doing it. For example, one who carries boards from the domain they are in to the domain in which they are needed is performing a labor that contributes toward a creative design, namely, the erection of a building. Hence, a person who does so intentionally is subject to stoning. One who carries a corpse out of his house, however, is not contributing toward a creative design since he does not need the corpse; he is merely ridding his house of it. R' Shimon therefore maintains that he is not subject to punishment for carrying the corpse out (see also *Tosafos* to *Shabbos* 94a ד״ה רבי שמעון). Similarly, when someone intends to cause bleeding while removing a thorn, he has no need for the bleeding per se; he is making the wound only in order to remove the thorn. This, too, is a forbidden labor that is not needed for its defined purpose. Thus, although R' Shimon considers it a punishable offense to wound someone in a destructive way, still there is no punishment for intentionally causing bleeding while removing a thorn, because such a wound is not needed for its defined purpose. (For an example of wounding that *is* done for its defined purpose, see *Shabbos* 106a with *Tosafos* ד״ה בחובל.)

2. Because even if he causes bleeding, he has not done anything that, if done intentionally, would make him subject to the death penalty.

3. The court would appoint an agent to flog someone who was sentenced to lashes and to curse someone who was being excommunicated [for the court would, at times, decide to curse a person who was being excommunicated (see *Tur Yoreh Deah* 334)]. What is the law, the Gemara inquires, if the court wishes to appoint the son of the sentenced man as the agent to strike or curse? Does the general prohibition against striking or cursing a parent extend to a court's agent, in which case the son may not be appointed to carry out these sentences? Or is a court agent excluded from these prohibitions? (see *Rashi* and *Meiri,* cf. *Aruch LaNer*).

4. Rav Sheishess' point is this: Under Torah law, it is forbidden to strike or curse any fellow Jew (see Gemara below, *Shevuos* 36a and *Tosafos* above, 67b ד״ה מאי), and yet Scripture explicitly permits an agent of the court to do so in specific cases; a court officer may flog someone who was sentenced to lashes (*Deuteronomy* 25:2-3), and the Kohen carrying out the ritual of a *sotah* may curse her (*Numbers* 5:21). Evidently, then, the prohibitions against striking an ordinary Jew or cursing him do not apply to an agent of the court (see *Rashi*).

5. See *Mechilta, Mishpatim* ch. 5. The Baraisa uses a *kal vachomer* argument to prove that certain individuals are commanded not to strike others, but it is not at all clear to whom the Baraisa refers. After quoting the Baraisa, the Gemara will suggest an interpretation and, based on this, challenge Rav Sheishess' response above.

6. That is, both rulings of the Baraisa involve a court officer who struck a man who had been sentenced to flogging; the difference between the two cases is the relationship between the officer and the sentenced man. In the first ruling, the officer was not the man's son and he therefore *was* commanded to carry out the court's instructions and strike him. In the second ruling, the officer was the man's son, which means, according to the Baraisa, that he was *not* commanded to strike. According to this interpretation of the Baraisa, the *kal vachomer* would be understood as follows: When the court appoints an officer to flog someone, the officer is commanded to do so (unless he is that person's son), and yet the Torah warns him against meting out more lashes than decreed by the court (*Deuteronomy* 25:3). Is it not logical, then, that since one *is commanded* never *to strike* his father – *even as a court officer* – he is surely warned against striking the father who does not deserve to be struck! (*Rashi*).

Given the above interpretation of the Baraisa, the Baraisa is clearly assuming that the son of a sentenced man may not be appointed as the court's agent to strike his father (see italicized portion of previous sentence). This refutes Rav Sheishess' assertion to the contrary!

Rashi notes that the above *kal vachomer* would be teaching an *azharah, a Scriptural warning,* not to strike one's parents. [The *azharah* is needed even though a different verse explicitly imposes a death penalty for this sin, because every punishable transgression requires two Scriptural sources. One, called *azharah* (אַזְהָרָה) or *Scriptural warning,* states what is forbidden; the second describes the punishment incurred (עוֹנֶשׁ). The function of the *azharah* is to convey the Torah's warning not to commit the sin on pain of incurring the specified punishment (see *Tosafos* and *Chamra VeChayei*; see there also a justification for deriving the *azharah* from a *kal vachomer*).]

ורבי שמעון האמר (א) כל מלאכה שאינה צריכה לגופה פטור עליה בעו מיניה מרב ששת בן מהו שיעשה שליח לאביו להכותו ולקללו א"ל ואחר מי התירו אלא כבוד שמים עדיף הכא נמי כבוד שמים עדיף מיתיבי ומה מי שמצוה להכותו מצוה שלא להכותו מי שאינו מצוה להכותו אינו דין שמצוה שלא להכותו מאי לאו אידי ואידי במקום מצוה הא בבנו הא באחר לא אידי ואידי לא שנא בנו ולא שנא אחר ולא קשיא כאן במקום מצוה כאן שלא במקום מצוה והכי קתני ומה במקום מצוה שמצוה להכותו מצוה שלא להכותו שלא במקום מצוה שאינו מצוה להכותו אינו דין שמצוה שלא להכותו תא שמע [א] היוצא ליהרג ובא בנו והכהו וקיללו חייב בא אחר והכהו וקיללו פטור והוינן בה מאי שנא בנו ומאי שנא אחר ואמר רב חסדא במסרבין בו לצאת ואינו יוצא רב ששת מוקי לה בשאין מסרבין בו לצאת אי הכי אחר נמי אחר גברא קטילא הוא והאמר רב ששת (ב) [ב] ביישו ישן ומת חייב הכא במאי עסקינן בשהכהו הכאה שאין בה שוה פרוטה (ג) והאמר רבי אמי אמר ר' יוחנן [ג] הכהו הכאה שאין בה שוה פרוטה לוקה מאי פטור דקאמר פטור ממנון מכלל דבנו חייב בממון אלא בדינו הכא נמי בדינו אלא אחר היינו טעמא דפטור דאמר קרא (א) ונשיא בעמך לא תאור (ד) בעושה מעשה עמך התינח קללה הכאה מנלן (ה) דמקשינן הכאה לקללה אי הכי בנו נמי (ו) כדאמר רב פינחס בשעשה תשובה הכא נמי [ד] בשעשה תשובה אי הכי אחר נמי אמר רב מרי בעמך במקוים שבעמך אי הכי בנו נמי מידי

רש"י

ור' שמעו'ן אית ליה מלאכה שאינה צריכה לגופה פטור עליה. בפרק המצניע (שבת ד' צג:) גבי המוציא את המת במטה: מהו שיעשה שליח. ב"ד לאביו אם נתחייב אביו נדוי או מלקות: ואחר מי התירו. לקללו ולהכות את חבירו והלא כל ישראל הוזהרו על הכאת חביריהם ועל קללתם כדילפינן בד' מיתות (לעיל ד' נח:) אפ"ה נעשה שליח ב"ד לכך דכתיב (דברים כה) ארבעים יכנו וכתיב (במדבר ה) יתן ה' אותך: ומה מי שמצוה להכותו. ברייתא תניא הכי במכילתא: מאי לאו אידי ואידי. מצוה ואינה מצוה תרוייהו במקום מצוה והא בבנו והא באחר והכי קאמר ויליף אזהרה למכה אביו: ומה אחר שמצוה להכותו במקום מצוה. דכתיב יכנו: מצוה שלא להכותו. יותר מארבעים דכתיב (דברים כה) ולא יוסיף פן יוסיף בנו שאינו מצוה להכותו אפילו במקום מצוה אלמא אינו נעשה שליח לכך אינו דין שמוזהר שלא להכותו שלא במקום מצוה: ומה במקום מצוה שמצוה להכותו מצוה שלא להכותו. יותר מארבעים שלא במקום מצוה לא כל שכן ויליף אזהרה למכה אביו או חבירו מהכא: בא אחר והכהו וקיללו פטור. קס"ד פטור ממלקות: ואינו יוצא. ואשמעי' דבנו אינו נעשה שליח בית דין לכופו לצאת וקשיא לרב ששת: ה"ג והאמר רב ששת ביישו ישן ומת חייב. ביישו ישן ומת תוך שינתו: חייב. דהא מתביישין בניו והאי נמי ל"ש: מכלל. דחייב דקתני גבי בנו ממון קאמר בתמיה והא באין בה שוה פרוטה מוקמת לה: אלא. על כרחך חייב בדינו קאמר מיתה: הכא נמי. דתני גבי אחר פטור בדינו קאמר וממלקות פטר ליה ואכתי מאי שנא: בעושה מעשה עמך. וזה שעובר עבירה שחייב מיתה לאו עושה מעשה עמך הוא: התינח קללה. דכתיב ביה בעמך: מקשינן. כלומר גמרינן במה מצינו ואיכא דאמרי היקשא דכתיב מכה אביו ומקלל אביו גבי הדדי באלה המשפטים אלא שמקרא אחד מפסיק בינתים: אי הכי בנו נמי. דהא לא כתיב אזהרה במקלל אביו אלא במקלל חברו שאביו בכלל עמך בפ' ד' מיתות (לעיל ד' סו.): דרב פנחס. משמיה דרבא במסכת חגיגה בסוף חומר בקודש: במקוים. הראוי להתקיים ולא זה שנגמר דינו: מידי

תוספות

מקלקל נמי מיחייב ור' יהודה יש לדקדק דפטר מדתנן בפ' כל הכלים (שבת ד' קכב:) ומייתי בסמוך דמחט של יד (מותר) ליטול בה את הקוץ דמשמע ליה להש"ס דאתיא ככולי עלמא כי ההיא דשלהי שבת (ד' קמז.) דאמרי' אבל מוקצה מחמת חסרון כיס אפילו ר' שמעון מודה דתנן כל הכלים ניטלין בשבת חוץ ממסר הגדול ויתד של מחרישה ומנא ליה דמודה ר' שמעון בה אלא משמע ליה דבסתמא דהתם מודו כ"ע היכא דלא משכח פלוגתא וכיון דר' יהודה מחייב במלאכה שאינה צריכה לגופה לא אפשר למישרי מחט של יד ליטול בה את הקוץ אי לאו משום דסבירא ליה מקלקל בחבורה פטור ואע"ג דאמרי' בפ' כירה (שם דף מב.) דשמואל במלאכה שאינה צריכה לגופה סבר לה כרבי יהודה ובפ' ספק אכל (כריתות דף יט:) מסיק ר"נ אליבא דשמואל הנח לתינוקות הואיל ומקלקל בחבורה חייב לאו משום דסבירא ליה הכי לשמואל אלא אליבא דמאן דמחייב קאמר ותדע דבשילהי האורג (שבת דף קז.) אמר שמואל כל פטורי דשבת פטור אבל אסור לבר מהני תלת דפטור ומותר המפיס מורסא ומנא לן דפטור ומותר דתנן מחט של יד (מותר) ליטול בה את הקוץ ומדשרי ליטול הקוץ ש"מ דקסבר מקלקל בחבורה פטור דמטעם מלאכה שאינה צריכה לגופה לא שרינא דהא סבירא ליה דחייב:

ורבי שמעון האמר מלאכה שאינה וכו'. הא דקיימא לן הלכה כר' שמעון בגרירה לאו שגגת סקילה היא דאי עביד חריץ הוי כלאחר יד כדאיתא שלהי פ' כירה (שם דף מו: ושם) ועוד דאינה צריכה לגופה ועוד דאפי' לר' יהודה כל אין מתכוין דלא פסיק רישיה פטור מדאורייתא דלא הוי מלאכת מחשבת וכן משמע ביומא (דף לד:) גבי עששיות דאמרי' צירוף דרבנן פי' כי האי משום דאין מתכוין ולא הוי מלאכת מחשבת והתירו משום דאין שבות במקדש וכן מוכח בההיא (ז) דהמכבד והמרבץ דהא רבנן דסבירא להו כרבי יהודה בדבר שאין מתכוין ופטרי אפילו ישוה גומות וכן בפרק ספק אכל (כריתות דף כ.) דמתעסק שאינו מתכוין למלאכה פטור כ"ש היכא דאינו מתכוין אלא לגרירה והא דמחייב רבי יהודה בכריתות נתכוין לכבות את העליונות והובערו התחתונות מאליהן היינו התם משום דהוי פסיק רישיה וחשיב מלאכת מחשבת כיון שיודע שיבעיר ור' שמעון דפוטר משום דאינה צריכה לגופה ולא בעי מלאכת מחשבת דהא ר' שמעון מחייב מקלקל בהבערה ומקלקל דמיפטר בשאר מלאכות היינו משום דלא הוי מלאכת מחשבת כדמוכח שלהי פרק קמא דחגיגה (דף י.) מכלל דבהבערה לא חיישינן והא דשרינן לבעול לכתחלה בשבת אם להנאת עצמו הוא צריך אפילו דם חבורי מחבר ה"ט משום דאינה צריכה לגופה ור' אליעזר דמחייב חטאת (ח) במכבד ומרבץ לאו משום דליהוי פסיק רישיה דהא שרי לר' שמעון לכתחלה אלא חשיב תיקון לכיבוד ולריבוץ כעין בנין ואפילו בלא השוואת גומות דבדבר מועט מיחייב משום בונה כדאשכחן (ט) גודלת ופוקסת ובס"פ כירה (שבת דף מז:) דהוי שרי לטלטל נר הדולק בשבת אי לאו משום דבסיס לדבר האסור היינו משום דאי מכבה בלא מתכוין אינה צריכה לגופה היא ומיהו תימה דהא לשמואל קאמר בפרק כירה (י) דבדבר שאין מתכוין סבר לה כר"ש ובמלאכה שאינה צריכה לגופה סבר לה כר' יהודה וכיון דסבר כר"י במלאכה שאינה צריכה לגופה היכי שרי דבר שאין מתכוין דשרי התם (דף מא:) גבי מיחם שפינהו לתת לתוכו מים להפשיר אפי' שיעור לצרף דהוה ליה שגגת סקילה וי"ל דהא דאסרינן הכא קוץ וסילוא משום דחיישינן כשמתחיל להסיר שמא יתהפך דלא סגי אי לא הוי פסיק רישיה ולא יניח בשביל כך אבל שאר דבר שאין מתכוין דלא פסיק רישיה הוא שרי וליטול קוץ בשבת מודה שמואל אע"ג דמחייב במלאכה שאינה צריכה לגופה דקסבר מקלקל בחבורה פטור:

הא בבנו הא באחר. רוצה ללמד מכאן אזהרה למכה אביו דלא נפיק מפן יוסיף כיון דאינו מצווה להכותו ומשמע בסמוך דאפי' ביוצא ליהרג נפקא לן אזהרה לבנו דחייב דמוקי לה רב חסדא במסרבין בו לצאת ואע"ג דאין מזהירין מן הדין הני מילי להלקותו ומיהו קשה היכי אתא בנו בקל וחומר מאחר כיון דאחר פטור במסרבין בו לצאת ואינו יוצא ושמא גלויי מילתא בעלמא הוא דפן יוסיף איירי אפי' בבנו אע"ג דארבעים יכנו לא איירי בבנו: **והאמר** רב ששת ביישו וכו'. תימה דבפ' החובל (ב"ק דף פו: ושם) בעי רבי אבא בר ממל ביישו ישן ומת מהו ולא איפשיטא והכא פריך בפשיטות ויש ספרים דגרסינן והאמר רב ששת ביישו ישן חייב ולא גרס ומת ולא נהירא דמה ענין ישן ליוצא ליהרג ועוד מאי קמ"ל רב ששת מתניתין היא בפרק החובל (כ) המבייש את הישן חייב ור"ת גרים והאמר רב ששת ביישו חייב ויוצא ליהרג קאי מיהו אין כל כך תימה אם לא הביא דברי רב ששת בפרק החובל למיפשט ההיא בעיא דכי האי גוונא אשכחן בנדרים בפרק אין בין המודר (ד' לה: ושם) דאיבעיא לן הנהו כהני שלוחי דידן או שלוחי דשמיא ולא מייתי התם דברי רב הונא בריה דרב יהושע דאמר בפרק קמא דקדושין (דף כג: ושם) הני כהני שלוחי דרחמנא נינהו דאי שלוחי דידן מי איכא מידי דאנן לא מצינן עבדין ושלוחי דידן עבדי (ל): **הכהו** הכאה שאין בה וכו'. תימה אמאי לקי הא פן יוסיף לאו שניתן לאזהרת מיתת ב"ד הוא דמיניה נפקא לן אזהרה למכה אביו כדאיתא בספרי ובירושלמי:

שיכול

מסורת הש"ס

א) [שבת קה: קו: קמא: כריתות כ:], ב) ב"ק פו:, ג) כתובות לב: מכות ט., ד) [יבמות כב: וש"נ], ה) [שם קא.], ו) [ב"ק לד: ב"מ סב. חגיגה כו. יבמות כב:], ז) [שבת לה.], ח) [שבת לה.], ט) [שם], י) [דף מב.], כ) [דף פו:], ל) [ועי' היטב תוס' יומא יט: ד"ה מי איכא ותוס' ב"מ יז: ד"ה מן].

תורה אור השלם

א) אֱלֹהִים לֹא תְקַלֵּל וְנָשִׂיא בְעַמְּךָ לֹא תָאֹר: [שמות כב, כז]

עין משפט נר מצוה

יג א מיי' פ"ה מהל' ממרים הל' יב ועיין בכ"מ סמג לאוין ריט טוש"ע י"ד סי' רמא סעיף ד:

יד ב מיי' פ"ג מהל' חובל ומזיק הל' ג סמג עשין ע טוש"ע ח"מ סי' תכ סעיף לה:

טו ג מיי' שם פ"ה הלכה ג סמג שם טוש"ע שם סעיף ג:

טז ד מיי' פ"ה מהל' ממרים הלכה יב סמג לאוין ריט טוש"ע י"ד סי' רמא סעיף ד:

ליקוטי רש"י

מקלקל הוא. כל מקלקל דשבת הוי פטור דלאו היינו מלאכת מחשבת וסותר דתנן באבות מלאכות דמיחייב סותר על מנת לבנות הוא ואינו יכול לבנות אלא אם כן סותרו והשתא לאו קלקול הוא ורבי יהודה סבר דאם במקומו חוזר ובונה הוא דמחייב אסתירה ואי לא לא ומכבה דומיא דסותר הוא וכן קורע דומיא דסותר ולהכי תנן הקורע על מנת לתפור וכן מוחק תנן על מנת לכתוב דכולם סותר נינהו [שם לא:]. הניחא למ"ד מקלקל פטור. ר' יהודה דאית ליה מקלקל בחבורה פטור ולא איפרש היכא ולי נראה מתניתין ר' יהודה היא דאמר מלאכה שאינה צריכה לגופה חייב עליה הלכך מיבעא דחובל בצריך לכלבו ומבעיר בצריך לאפרו משכחת לה דלאף על פי דמקלקל הוא אצל מלאכה עצמה מתקן הוא אצל אחרים ולר' יהודה כי האי גוונא מלאכה הוא משום תקון אחרים אבל מקלקל ואינו מתקן פטור. אלא למ"ד חייב. ר' שמעון היא דאמר מלאכה שאינה צריכה לגופה פטור עליה הלכך אין לך חובל ומבעיר שאין מקלקל ואפילו מבעיר עצים לקדרתו מקלקל הוא אצל עצים ומה שהוא מתקן אצל אחרים לר' שמעון לא חשיב דהא מלאכה שאינה צריכה לגופה היא אלא משום דמקלקל בחבלה והבערה חייב כדיליף לקמיה מדאיצטריך קרא וביום השמיני ביום יתירא ואפילו בשבת ומילה חובל הוא מכלל דשאר מקלקלין בחבורה חייב ומדאסר רחמנא הבערה דבת כהן [שבת קו. ועיין תוס' כאן]. מקלקל בחבורה חייב. דהכי אמרינן בבבא קמא בפרק המניח את הכד (דף לד:) כל המקלקלין פטורין חוץ מחובל ומבעיר [כריתות יט:]. כל המקלקלין פטורין לענין שבת חוץ מחובל ומבעיר כדמפרש טעמא במס' שבת בפרק האורג מדאיצטריך קרא למישרי מילה מכלל דשאר חובל חייב ומדאסר רחמנא שריפת בת כהן בשבת דמקלקל הוא מכלל דמקלקל בהבערה חייב כגון השורף כלי דמקלקל הוא [ב"ק לד:].

[עד כאן שייך לדף פד:]

ורבי שמעון האמר מלאכה שאינה צריכה לגופה. כמו מוציא את המת לקוברו אינו צריך לגופה דהוצאה ולא למת אלא לפנות ביתו והוצאה הצריכה לגופה כגון שהוא צריך לחפץ זה במקום אחר [שבת עג:]. מלאכה שאינה צריכה לגופה שברצונו לא תעשה ואינו צריך לעיקר (תחלתה) [תכליתה] [שם יב.]. ר' שמעון פוטר אפילו במת שלם דהוי מלאכה שאינה צריכה לגופה וכל מלאכה שאינה צריכה (לגופה) אלא לסלקה מעליו הוי מלאכה שאינה צריכה לגופה דברצונו לא באה לו ולא היה צריך לה הלכך לאו מלאכת מחשבת היא לר' שמעון [שם צג:]. ר' שמעון דאמר מלאכה שאינה צריכה לגופה פטור עליה הלכך אין לך חובל ומבעיר שאין מקלקל ואפילו מבעיר עצים לקדרתו מקלקל הוא אצל עצים ומה שהוא מתקן אצל אחרים לר' שמעון לא חשיב דהא מלאכה שאינה צריכה לגופה היא אלא משום דמקלקל בחבלה ובהבערה חייב כדיליף לקמיה [שם קו. וצ"ע מסוגיין עי' תוס' כאן]. ביישו ישן. בייש אדם ישן. ומת. מתוך שנתו ולא הכיר בבשתו שעשה לו זה מהו [ב"ק פו:]. בעושה מעשה עמך. וזה לא עשה מעשה עמו ואין חייבין בכבודו [שם צד]. שאין בה שוה פרוטה. שאם יש בה תשלומי פרוטה משלם ואינו לוקה דילפינן בכתובות באלו נערות (דף לב:) בפירוש ריבתה תורה חובל בחבירו לתשלומין וכי אין בה שוה פרוטה לוקה שעבר על לא תוסיף פן יוסיף (דברים כה). מקשינן הכאה לקללה. לומר שכשם שאינו לוקה על קללתו דכתיב בעמך כך לא ילקה על הכאתו [מכות ט.].

do so.[7] וְהָכִי קָתָנֵי – **And this is what the Baraisa teaches:** וּמָה בִּמְקוֹם מִצְוָה שֶׁמִּצְוָה לְהַכּוֹתוֹ – **If in a mitzvah situation, where someone is commanded to strike [a certain fellow],** מִצְוָה שֶׁלֹּא לְהַכּוֹתוֹ – **he is commanded not to strike [the fellow]** an extra time, שֶׁלֹּא בִּמְקוֹם מִצְוָה שֶׁאֵינוֹ מִצְוָה לְהַכּוֹתוֹ – then **when it is not a mitzvah situation, where [a person] is not commanded to strike [the fellow],** אֵינוֹ דִּין שֶׁמִּצְוָה שֶׁלֹּא לְהַכּוֹתוֹ – **is it not logical that [the person] is commanded not to strike [the fellow]** at all!?[8]

Having defended Rav Sheishess against a challenge from one Baraisa, the Gemara presents a challenge from another:

תָּא שְׁמַע – **Come, learn** a refutation to Rav Sheishess from a Baraisa: הַיּוֹצֵא לֵיהָרֵג – If A PERSON IS BEING TAKEN OUT FOR EXECUTION, וּבָא בְנוֹ וְהִכָּהוּ וְקִילְלוֹ – AND HIS SON CAME, STRUCK HIM and wounded him or [THE SON] CURSED HIM, חַיָּיב – [THE SON IS] LIABLE to execution for his act. בָּא אַחֵר וְהִכָּהוּ וְקִילְלוֹ – IF anyone OTHER than the son CAME AND STRUCK [THE MAN] OR CURSED HIM, פָּטוּר – HE IS EXEMPT from punishment for the act.[9]

The Gemara explores the logic of this ruling:

וְהָוֵינַן בָּהּ – **And we asked about [the Baraisa]:** מַאי שְׁנָא בְּנוֹ וּמַאי שְׁנָא אַחֵר – **What is the difference between the son of [the condemned man],** who is punished for striking him, **and another** person, who is not? וְאָמַר רַב חִסְדָּא – **And Rav Chisda said** in response: בִּמְסָרְבִין בּוֹ לָצֵאת וְאֵינוֹ יוֹצֵא – The Baraisa discusses a case **where the** court **[officers] are insisting that [the condemned man] go out** to execution, **and [the man] does not go;** an officer then strikes or curses the man to force him to comply with the court order. Now, the Baraisa states that if the officer was the man's son, he is liable to execution even though he was acting as the court's agent. This refutes Rav Sheishess' view that the court may appoint a son to strike or curse his father.[10] – ? –

The Gemara responds that Rav Sheishess would interpret the Baraisa differently:

רַב שֵׁשֶׁת מוּקֵי לָהּ בְּשֶׁאֵין מְסָרְבִין בּוֹ לָצֵאת – **Rav Sheishess interprets [the Baraisa]** to be discussing a case **in which [the officers] did not** have to **insist that [the condemned man] go out** to his execution, because he was willing to cooperate. Thus, the son is subject to execution because he struck or cursed his father for no reason.[11]

The Gemara asks:

אִי הָכִי – **If** it is **so** that the condemned man was not resisting, אַחֵר נָמֵי – **then even** if a person **other** than the man's son strikes or curses him, that person should be punished![12] – ? –

The Gemara defends Rav Sheishess' interpretation of the Baraisa:

אַחֵר גַּבְרָא קְטִילָא הוּא – Someone **other** than the son is exempt, because **[the condemned man] is** legally considered **a dead man.** Therefore, there is no punishment for striking him.[13]

The Gemara counters:

וְהָאָמַר רַב שֵׁשֶׁת – **But Rav Sheishess said:** בִּיּישׁוֹ יָשֵׁן וָמֵת – **If one disgraces a sleeping person who then dies** in his sleep, חַיָּיב – **he is obligated** to compensate the person's children for having shamed them.[14] Accordingly, someone who strikes a condemned man who then dies should at least be obligated to compensate the children for their shame![15] – ? –

Having rejected the previous defense of Rav Sheishess, the Gemara suggests a second:

הָכָא בְּמַאי עַסְקִינַן – **Here, with what case are we dealing?** בְּשֶׁהִכָּהוּ הַכָּאָה שֶׁאֵין בָּהּ שָׁוֶה פְּרוּטָה – **With** a case **where** the condemned man agreed to be led to execution and **someone struck him with a blow whose** injury **did not amount to a** ***perutah.*** In such a case, there is no monetary obligation.

NOTES

7. The Gemara is retracting its previous assumption that both clauses of the Baraisa discuss a court officer. According to this explanation, when the second clause mentions "one who is not commanded to strike a certain person," it refers not to a court officer striking his father, as previously thought, but rather to an ordinary person striking any fellow for no lawful reason. Thus, the Baraisa does not even discuss Rav Sheishess' case and it surely does not refute his ruling.

8. In other words, the *kal vachomer* is as follows: If the Torah warns a court officer, who is commanded to flog a sentenced man, not to exceed the specified number of lashes, then it is surely warning an ordinary man, who is prohibited to strike anyone, against transgressing this prohibition. Thus, the *kal vachomer* provides the *azharah* against striking anyone – one's father or any other fellow (*Rashi*).

[This interpretation of the Baraisa, unlike the previous one, assumes that the clauses do not differentiate between a father and son; rather, they contrast a court officer who carries out a sentence of flogging and an ordinary person who strikes a fellow for no lawful reason. The first clause (*one who is commanded to strike*) refers to a court officer, and the second clause (*one who is not commanded to strike*) refers to an ordinary person.]

9. At this point, the Gemara assumes that the Baraisa is discussing the punishment of flogging [that is imposed for striking someone] (*Rashi*). The Gemara below will explain why monetary liability is not being discussed.

10. For if he were permitted to strike his father as an agent of the court, he obviously would not be subject to execution for doing so! (see *Yad David*).

11. However, if the man refused to go to execution, his son would be permitted to strike him as an agent of the court, just as Rav Sheishess maintains.

12. Because it is forbidden to strike anyone for no reason! (see notes 4 and 8).

13. That is, once someone is condemned to die, he has no value at all, which means that he is not damaged when he is struck. [This status, however, does not affect the prohibition which applies to the son.] The Gemara now assumes that the striking of the condemned man is legally insignificant and as such, one who strikes him is not punished with flogging. [The Gemara will retract this assumption below; see note 17.]

14. For children are embarrassed when their parent is disgraced (*Rashi*). [When someone damages another, he is obligated to pay not only for any monetary loss, but for any embarrassment that he causes (see *Bava Kama* 83b).]

The Gemara in *Bava Kama* 86b cites the case of a fellow who was disgraced in his sleep and died without awakening; it considers whether the one who disgraced the fellow must pay even though the fellow never realized what happened. Rav Pappa there explains the uncertainty as follows: Perhaps the payment for damages is meant only to compensate the victim himself for his embarrassment. If so, since the sleeping man experienced no embarrassment himself, there would be no obligation to pay damages. Perhaps, however, it is meant to compensate the family for the embarrassment that *they* suffered when their relative was shamed. If so, then damages must be paid to the sleeping man's family. Thus, when Rav Sheishess rules in our Gemara that damages must be paid, he clearly maintains that the damages are paid to compensate the shamed person's *family* for the embarrassment they suffered (see *Rashi* and *Ran*; cf. *Tosafos*).

15. [This refutes the Gemara's previous contention that according to Rav Sheishess, the Baraisa is saying that there is no punishment at all for striking the "dead" man.]

The Gemara's comparison between the sleeping person discussed by Rav Sheishess and the condemned man of the Baraisa seems to be as follows. A sleeping person who is disgraced feels no shame until he awakens; if he dies in his sleep, he never feels the shame. Thus, if someone is liable for disgracing a sleeping man who then dies, the obligation must be to compensate the man's children for *their* shame. If so, it follows that someone who strikes a condemned man should also pay for the children's shame even though the man himself is legally dead! (*Aruch LaNer,* see *Ran*).

מסורת הש"ס

א) [שבת קה: קו: קמא: כריתות כ:], ב) ב"ק פו:, ג) כתובות לב: מכות ט., ד) [יבמות כב: וש"נ], ה) [שם קא.], ו) [ב"ק לד: ב"מ סב. חגיגה כו. יבמות כב:], ז) [שבת לה.], ח) [שבת לה.], ט) [שם], י) [דף מב.], כ) [דף פו:], ל) [ועי' היטב תוס' יומא יט: ד"ה מי איכא ותוס' ב"מ יז: ד"ה מן].

תורה אור השלם

א) אֱלֹהִים לֹא תְקַלֵּל וְנָשִׂיא בְעַמְּךָ לֹא תָאֹר: [שמות כב, כז]

עין משפט נר מצוה

יג א מיי' פ"ה מהל' ממרים הל' יב ועיין בכ"מ סמג לאוין ריט טוש"ע י"ד סי' רמא סעיף ד:

יד ב מיי' פ"ג מהל' חובל ומזיק הל' ג סמג עשין ע טוש"ע ח"מ סי' תכ סעיף לה:

טו ג מיי' שם פ"ה הלכה ג סמג שם טוש"ע שם סעיף ג:

טז ד מיי' פ"ה מהל' ממרים הלכה יב סמג לאוין ריט טוש"ע י"ד סי' רמא סעיף ד:

ורבי שמעון האמר [א] כל מלאכה שאינה צריכה לגופה פטור עליה בעו מיניה מרב ששת בן מהו שיעשה שליח לאביו להכותו ולקללו א"ל ואחר מי התירו אלא כבוד שמים עדיף הכא נמי כבוד שמים עדיף מיתיבי ומה מי שמצוה להכותו מצוה שלא להכותו מי שאינו מצוה להכותו אינו דין שמצוה שלא להכותו מאי לאו אידי ואידי במקום מצוה הא בבנו הא באחר לא אידי ואידי לא שנא בנו ולא שנא אחר ולא קשיא כאן במקום מצוה כאן שלא במקום מצוה והכי קתני ומה במקום מצוה שמצוה להכותו מצוה שלא להכותו שלא במקום מצוה שאינו מצוה להכותו אינו דין שמצוה שלא להכותו תא שמע [א] היוצא ליהרג ובא בנו והכהו וקיללו חייב בא אחר והכהו וקיללו פטור והוינן בה מאי שנא בנו ומאי שנא אחר ואמר רב חסדא במסרבין בו לצאת ואינו יוצא רב ששת מוקי לה בשאין מסרבין בו לצאת אי הכי אחר נמי אחר גברא קטילא הוא והאמר רב ששת [ב] [ב] ביישו ישן ומת חייב הכא במאי עסקינן בשהכהו הכאה שאין בה שוה פרוטה [ג] והאמר רבי אמי אמר ר' יוחנן [ג] הכהו הכאה שאין בה שוה פרוטה לוקה מאי פטור דקאמר פטור ממון מכלל דבנו חייב בממון אלא בדינו הכא נמי בדינו אלא אחר היינו טעמא דפטור דאמר קרא [א] ונשיא בעמך לא תאור [ד] בעושה מעשה עמך התינח קללה הכאה מנלן [ה] דמקשינן הכאה לקללה אי הכי בנו נמי [ו] כדאמר רב פנחס בשעשה תשובה הכא נמי [ד] בשעשה תשובה אי הכי אחר נמי אמר רב מרי בעמך במקוים שבעמך אי הכי בנו נמי מידי

ור' שמעון אית ליה מלאכה שאינה צריכה לגופה פטור עליה. בפרק המצניע (שבת ד' צג:) גבי המוציא את המת במטה: מהו שיעשה שליח. ב"ד לאביו אם נתחייב אביו נדוי או מלקות: ואחר מי התירו. לקללו ולהכות את חבירו והלא כל ישראל הוזהרו על הכאת חביריהם ועל קללתם כדילפינן בד' מיתות (לעיל ד' נח:) אפ"ה נעשה שליח ב"ד לכך דכתיב (דברים כה) ארבעים יכנו וכתיב (במדבר ה) יתן ה' אותך: ומה מי שמצוה להכותו. ברייתא תניא הכי במכילתא: מאי לאו אידי ואידי. מצוה ואינה מצוה תרוייהו במקום מצוה והא בבנו והא באחר והכי קאמר ויליף אזהרה למכה אביו: ומה אחר שמצוה להכותו במקום מצוה. דכתיב יכנו: מצוה שלא להכותו. יותר מארבעים דכתיב (דברים כה) ולא יוסיף פן יוסיף בנו שאינו מצוה להכותו אפילו במקום מצוה אלמא אינו נעשה שליח לכך אינו דין שמוזהר שלא להכותו שלא במקום מצוה: ומה במקום מצוה שמצוה להכותו מצוה שלא להכותו. יותר מארבעים שלא במקום מצוה לא כל שכן ויליף אזהרה למכה אביו או חבירו מהכא: בא אחר והכהו וקיללו פטור. קס"ד פטור ממלקות: ואינו יוצא. ואשמעי' דבנו אינו נעשה שליח בית דין לכופו לצאת וקשיא לרב ששת: ה"ג והאמר רב ששת ביישו ישן ומת חייב. ביישו ישן ומת תוך שינתו: חייב. דהא מתביישין בניו והאי נמי ל"ש: מכלל. דחייב דקתני גבי בנו ממון קאמר בתמיה והא באין בה שוה פרוטה מוקמת לה: אלא. על כרחך חייב בדינו קאמר מיתה: הכא נמי. דתני גבי אחר פטור בדינו קאמר וממלקות פטר ליה ואכתי מאי שנא: בעושה מעשה עמך. וזה שעובר עבירה שחייב מיתה לאו עושה מעשה עמך הוא: התינח קללה. דכתיב ביה בעמך: מקשינן. כלומר גמרינן במה מצינו ואיכא דאמרי היקשא דכתיב מכה אביו ומקלל אביו גבי הדדי באלה המשפטים אלא שמקרא אחד מפסיק בינתים: אי הכי בנו נמי. דהא לא כתיב אזהרה במקלל אביו אלא במקלל חברו שאביו בכלל עמך בפ' ד' מיתות (לעיל ד' סו.): דרב פנחס. משמיה דרבא במסכת חגיגה בסוף חומר בקודש: במקוים. הראוי להתקיים ולא זה שנגמר דינו:

מידי

מקלקל נמי מיחייב ור' יהודה יש לדקדק דפטר מדתנן בפ' כל הכלים (שבת ד' קכב:) ומייתי בסמוך דמחט של יד (מותר) ליטול בה את הקוץ דמשמע ליה להש"ס דאתיא ככולי עלמא כי ההיא דשלהי שבת (ד' קמז.) דאמרי' אבל מוקצה מחמת חסרון כיס אפילו ר' שמעון מודה דתנן כל הכלים ניטלין בשבת חוץ ממסר הגדול ויתד של מחרישה ומנא ליה דמודה ר' שמעון בה אלא משמע ליה דבסתמא דהתם מודו כ"ע היכא דלא משכח פלוגתא וכיון דר' יהודה מחייב במלאכה שאינה צריכה לגופה לא אפשר למישרי מחט של יד ליטול בה את הקוץ אי לאו משום דסבירא ליה מקלקל בחבורה פטור ואע"ג דאמרי' בפ' כירה (שם דף מב.) דשמואל במלאכה שאינה צריכה לגופה סבר לה כרבי יהודה ובפ' ספק אכל (כריתות דף יט:) מסיק ר"נ אליבא דשמואל הנח לתינוקות הואיל ומקלקל בחבורה חייב לאו משום דסבירא ליה הכי לשמואל אלא אליבא דמאן דמחייב קאמר ותדע דבשילהי האורג (שבת דף קז.) אמר שמואל כל פטורי דשבת פטור אבל אסור לבר מהני תלת דפטור ומותר המפיס מורסא ומנא לן דפטור ומותר דתנן מחט של יד (מותר) ליטול בה את הקוץ ומדשרי ליטול הקוץ ש"מ דקסבר מקלקל בחבורה פטור דמטעם מלאכה שאינה צריכה לגופה לא שריא דהא סבירא ליה דחייב:

ורבי שמעון האמר מלאכה שאינה וכו'. הא דקיימא לן הלכה כר' שמעון בגרירה לאו שגגת סקילה היא דאי עביד חריץ הוי כלאחר יד כדאיתא שלהי פ' כירה (שם דף מו: ושם) ועוד דאינה צריכה לגופה ועוד דאפי' לר' יהודה כל אין מתכוין דלא פסיק רישיה פטור מדאורייתא דלא הוי מלאכת מחשבת וכן משמע ביומא (דף לד:) גבי עששיות דאמרי' צירוף דרבנן פי' כי האי משום דאין מתכוין ולא הוי מלאכת מחשבת והתירו משום דאין שבות במקדש וכן מוכח בההיא [ז] דהמכבד והמרבץ דהא רבנן דסבירא להו כרבי יהודה בדבר שאין מתכוין ופטרי אפילו ישוה גומות וכן בפרק ספק אכל (כריתות דף כ.) דמתעסק שאינו מתכוין למלאכה פטור כ"ש היכא דאינו מתכוין אלא לגרירה והא דמחייב רבי יהודה בכריתות נתכוין לכבות את העליונות והובערו התחתונות מאליהן היינו התם משום דהוי פסיק רישיה וחשיב מלאכת מחשבת כיון שיודע שיבעיר ור' שמעון דפוטר משום דאינה צריכה לגופה ולא בעי מלאכת מחשבת דהא ר' שמעון מחייב מקלקל בהבערה ומקלקל דמיפטר בשאר מלאכות היינו משום דלא הוי מלאכת מחשבת כדמוכח שלהי פרק קמא דחגיגה (דף י.) מכלל דבהבערה לא חיישינן והא דשרינן לבעול לכתחלה בשבת אם להנאת עצמו הוא צריך אפילו דם חבורי מחבר ה"ט משום דאינה צריכה לגופה ור' אליעזר דמחייב חטאת [ח] במכבד ומרבץ לאו משום דליהוי פסיק רישיה דהא שרי לר' שמעון לכתחלה אלא חשיב תיקון לכיבוד ולריבוץ כעין בנין ואפילו בלא השוואת גומות דבדבר מועט מיחייב משום בונה כדאשכחן [ט] גודלת ופוקסת ובס"פ כירה (שבת דף מז:) דהוי שרי לטלטל נר הדולק בשבת אי לאו משום דבסיס לדבר האסור היינו משום דאי מכבה בלא מתכוין אינה צריכה לגופה היא ומיהו תימה דהא לשמואל קאמר בפרק כירה [י] דבדבר שאין מתכוין סבר לה כר"ש ובמלאכה שאינה צריכה לגופה סבר לה כר' יהודה וכיון דסבר כר"י במלאכה שאינה צריכה לגופה היכי שרי דבר שאין מתכוין דשרי התם (דף מא:) גבי מיחם שפינהו לתת לתוכו מים להפשיר אפי' שיעור לצרף דהוה ליה שגגת סקילה וי"ל דהא דאסרינן הכא קוץ וסילוא משום דחיישינן כשמתחיל להסיר שמא יתהפך דלא סגי אי לא הוי פסיק רישיה ולא יניח בשביל כך אבל שאר דבר שאין מתכוין דלא פסיק רישיה הוא שרי וליטול קוץ בשבת מודה שמואל אע"ג דמחייב במלאכה שאינה צריכה לגופה דקסבר מקלקל בחבורה פטור:

הא בבנו הא באחר. רוצה ללמד מכאן אזהרה למכה אביו דלא נפיק מפן יוסיף כיון דאינו מצווה להכותו ומשמע בסמוך דאפי' ביוצא ליהרג נפקא לן אזהרה לבנו דחייב דמוקי לה רב חסדא במסרבין בו לצאת ואע"ג דאין מזהירין מן הדין הני מילי להלקותו ומיהו קשה היכי אתא בנו בקל וחומר מאחר כיון דאחר פטור במסרבין בו לצאת ואינו יוצא ושמא גלויי מילתא בעלמא הוא דפן יוסיף מיירי אפי' בבנו אע"ג דארבעים יכנו לא מיירי בבנו: והאמר רב ששת ביישו וכו'. תימה דבפ' החובל (ב"ק דף פו: ושם) בעי רבי אבא בר ממל ביישו ישן ומת מהו ולא איפשיטא והכא פריך בפשיטות ויש ספרים דגרסינן והאמר רב ששת ביישו ישן חייב ולא גרס ומת ולא נהירא דמה ענין ישן ליוצא ליהרג ועוד מאי קמ"ל רב ששת מתניתין היא בפרק החובל [כ] המבייש את הישן חייב ור"ת גריס והאמר רב ששת ביישו חייב ויוצא ליהרג קאי מיהו אין כל כך תימה אם לא הביא דברי רב ששת בפרק החובל למיפשט ההיא בעיא דכי האי גוונא אשכחן בנדרים בפרק אין בין המודר (ד' לה: ושם) דאיבעיא לן הנהו כהני שלוחי דידן או שלוחי דשמיא ולא מייתי התם דברי רב הונא בריה דרב יהושע דאמר בפרק קמא דקדושין (דף כג: ושם) הני כהני שלוחי דרחמנא נינהו דאי שלוחי דידן מי איכא מידי דאנן לא מצינן עבדין ושלוחי דידן עבדי [ל]: הכהו הכאה שאין בה וכו'. תימה אמאי לקי הא פן יוסיף לאו שניתן לאזהרת מיתת ב"ד הוא דמיניה נפקא לן אזהרה למכה אביו כדאיתא בספרי ובירושלמי:

שיכול

ליקוטי רש"י

מקלקל הוא. כל מקלקל דשבת הוי פטור דלאו היינו מלאכת מחשבת וסותר דתנן באבות מלאכות דמיחייב סותר על מנת לבנות הוא ואינו יכול לבנות אלא אם כן סותרו והשתא לאו קלקול הוא ורבי יהודה סבר דאם במקומו חוזר ובונה הוא דמחייב אסתירה ואי לא לא ומכבה דומיא דסותר הוא וכן קורע דומיא דסותר ולהכי תנן הקורע על מנת לתפור וכן מוחק תנן על מנת לכתוב דכולם סותר נינהו [שם לא:]. הניחא למ"ד מקלקל פטור. ר' יהודה דאית ליה מקלקל בחבורה פטור ולא איתפרש היכא ולי נראה מתניתין ר' יהודה היא דאמר מלאכה שאינה צריכה לגופה חייב עליה הלכך חיובא דחובל בצריך לכלבו ומבעיר בצריך לאפרו משכחת לה דאף על פי דמקלקל הוא אצל מלאכה עצמה מתקן הוא אצל אחרים ולר' יהודה כי האי גוונא מלאכה הוא משום תקון אחרים אבל מקלקל ואינו מתקן פטור. אלא למ"ד חייב. ר' שמעון היא דאמר מלאכה שאינה צריכה לגופה פטור עליה הלכך אין לך חובל ומבעיר שאין מקלקל ואפילו מבעיר עלים לקדרתו מקלקל הוא אצל עלים ומה שהוא מתקן אצל אחרים לר' שמעון לא חשיב דהא מלאכה שאינה צריכה לגופה היא אלא משום דמקלקל בחבלה ובהבערה חייב כדיליף לקמיה מדאיצטריך קרא וביום השמיני ביום יתירא ואפילו בשבת ומילה חובל הוא מכלל דשאר מקלקלין בחבורה חייב ומדאסר רחמנא הבערה דבת כהן [שבת קו. ועיין תוס' כאן]. מקלקל בחבורה חייב. דהכי אמרינן בבבא קמא בפרק המניח את הכד (דף לד:) כל המקלקלין פטורין חוץ מחובל ומבעיר [כריתות יט:]. כל המקלקלין פטורין לענין שבת חוץ מחובל ומבעיר כדמפרש טעמא במס' שבת בפרק האורג מדאיצטריך קרא למישרי מילה מכלל דשאר חובל חייב ומדאסר רחמנא שריפת בת כהן בשבת דמקלקל הוא מכלל דמקלקל בהבערה חייב כגון השורף כלי דמקלקל הוא [ב"ק לד:]. [עד כאן שייך לדף פד:] ורבי שמעון האמר מלאכה שאינה צריכה לגופה. כמו מוציא את המת לקוברו אינו צריך לגופה דהוצאה ולא למת אלא לפנות ביתו והוצאה הצריכה לגופה כגון שהוא צריך לחפץ זה במקום אחר [שבת עג:]. מלאכה שאינה צריכה לגופה שברצונו לא תעשה ואינו צריך לעיקר (תכליתה) [תכליתה] [שם יב.]. ר' שמעון פוטר אפילו במת שלם דהוי מלאכה שאינה צריכה לגופה וכל מלאכה שאינה צריכה (לגופה) אלא לסלקה מעליו הוי מלאכה שאינה צריכה לגופה דברצונו לא באה לו ולא היה צריך לה הלכך לאו מלאכת מחשבת היא לר' שמעון [שם צג:]. ר' שמעון דאמר מלאכה שאינה צריכה לגופה פטור עליה הלכך אין לך חובל ומבעיר שאין מקלקל ואפילו מבעיר עלים לקדרתו מקלקל הוא אצל עלים ומה שהוא מתקן אצל אחרים לר' שמעון לא חשיב דהא מלאכה שאינה צריכה לגופה היא אלא משום דמקלקל בחבלה ובהבערה חייב כדיליף לקמיה [שם קו. וצ"ע מסוגיין עי' תוס' כאן]. ביישו ישן. בייש אדם ישן. ומת. מתוך שנתו ולא הכיר בבשתו שעשה לו זה מהו [ב"ק פו:]. בעושה מעשה עמך. וזה לא עשה מעשה עמו ואין חייבין בכבודו [שם צד]. שאין בה שוה פרוטה. שאם יש בה תשלומי פרוטה משלם ואינו לוקה דילפינן בכתובות באלו נערות (דף לב:) בפירוש ריבתה תורה חובל בחבירו לתשלומין וכי אין בה שוה פרוטה לוקה שעבר על לא תוסיף פן יוסיף (דברים כה). מקשינן הכאה לקללה. לומר שכשם שאינו לוקה על קללתו דכתיב בעמך כך לא ילקה על הכאתו [מכות ט.].

The Gemara objects:

וְהָאָמַר רַבִּי אַמִּי אָמַר רַבִּי יוֹחָנָן – **But R' Ami said in the name of R' Yochanan:** הִכָּהוּ הַכָּאָה שֶׁאֵין בָּהּ שָׁוֶה פְּרוּטָה לוֹקֶה – **Someone who struck [a fellow] with a blow whose** injury **does not amount to a *perutah* is flogged.**[16] How can Rav Sheishess say, then, that the Baraisa exempts a person from punishment when he deals such a blow to the condemned man?[17]

The Gemara answers:

מַאי פָּטוּר דְּקָאָמַר – **What is** the meaning of the term EXEMPT, **which [the Baraisa] mentions?** פָּטוּר מִמָּמוֹן – It means only that **he is exempt from monetary** liability, because the injury did not amount to a *perutah.* He does receive lashes, however, as R' Yochanan stated.

The Gemara questions this interpretation of the Baraisa:

מִכְּלָל דִּבְנוֹ חַיָּיב בְּמָמוֹן – If so, then **we may infer that [the condemned man's] son would be monetarily liable** for striking him.[18] But why should he be monetarily liable if he caused damage amounting to less than a *perutah*. – ? –

The Gemara continues:

אֶלָּא בְּדִינוֹ – **Rather,** when the Baraisa implies that the son is liable, **it** must **refer to the** death **sentence to** which **he** is subject. הָכָא נַמִּי בְּדִינוֹ – **Here too** in the latter clause, when the Baraisa mentions exemption, this **refers to the sentence** of lashes **to** which **he** could be subject. Accordingly, the Gemara's objection to Rav Sheishess' second defense reasserts itself: If the Baraisa deals with a blow whose injury did not amount to a *perutah,* as Rav Sheishess maintains, then why does the latter clause exempt the striker from lashes?

Having rejected two defenses of Rav Sheishess, the Gemara advances a third way for Rav Sheishess to interpret our Baraisa:

אֶלָּא אַחֵר – **Rather,** when someone **other** than the son of the condemned man strikes him, הַיְינוּ טַעְמָא דְּפָטוּר – **this is the reason that he is exempt** from lashes: דְּאָמַר קְרָא ,,וְנָשִׂיא בְעַמְּךָ לֹא תָאֹר" – It is **because Scripture has stated:**[19] *And* a *prince among your people you shall not curse.* בְּעוֹשֶׂה מַעֲשֵׂה עַמְּךָ – The phrase *among your people* **refers to** cursing **one who acts in** accord with **the deeds of your people;** that is, he acts in a manner that is proper for your people.[20] Now, a man who is condemned to die for having committed a capital crime obviously did not act in such a manner. Therefore, one who curses him is exempt from lashes.[21]

The Gemara notes that this explanation does not suffice:

הָתֵינַח קְלָלָה – **This** explanation **is fine** in regard to **cursing** a condemned man, who has performed a sinful act, הַכָּאָה מְנָלַן – **but from where do we know** that one who deals a **blow** to a condemned man is exempt?

The Gemara responds:

דְּמַקְּשִׁינַן הַכָּאָה לִקְלָלָה – **For we compare** the laws of **striking to** the laws of **cursing.**[22] Just as there is no prohibition against cursing a sinner, so is there no prohibition against striking him.

The Gemara challenges its interpretation of the Baraisa:

אִי הָכִי – But **if so,** בְּנוֹ נַמִּי – then **even** if **the [condemned man's] son** curses him, the son should be exempt from punishment.[23] Why does the Baraisa state, then, that he is liable?

The Gemara answers:

כִּדְאָמַר רַב פִּינְחָס – It is **as Rav Pinchas said** elsewhere[24] to answer a similar question: בְּשֶׁעָשָׂה תְּשׁוּבָה – It refers to a case **where he repented.** הָכָא נַמִּי בְּשֶׁעָשָׂה תְּשׁוּבָה – **Here too,** we can answer that our Baraisa refers to a case **in which [the condemned man] repented** before being led to execution.[25] Therefore his son is punished for striking or cursing him.

The Gemara rejects this answer:

אִי הָכִי – **If** it is **so** that the Baraisa discusses a condemned man who repented, אַחֵר נַמִּי – then **even** someone **other** than the son should be held liable for striking or cursing the man. – ? –

NOTES

16. For striking another Jew is forbidden by a negative commandment and as a general rule, whoever violates a negative commandment is flogged. [R' Yochanan of course agrees that if the injury amounted to more than a *perutah,* there is a monetary obligation. In such a case, the guilty party is not flogged, because we never impose a double penalty of lashes and monetary obligation (see *Kesubos* 32b-33a). As long as the damage amounts to less than a *perutah,* though, there is no monetary obligation and we therefore impose the punishment of flogging.]

17. At this point, the Gemara changes its previous assumption. The Gemara thus far assumed that when someone strikes a condemned man, who has no value, the blow is so insignificant that the striker is not punished at all. The Gemara now notes that whenever someone inflicts a blow whose damage amounts to less than a *perutah,* he is flogged; it thus stands to reason that one who strikes a condemned man should be flogged as well. Why then, asks the Gemara, does the Baraisa state that he is exempt from punishment?

18. For the Baraisa contains two clauses about someone who strikes a condemned man: a) If the striker is his son, he is "liable"; b) if the striker is anyone else, he is "exempt." Thus, if the latter clause speaks of exemption from monetary obligation, it follows that the former clause also discusses monetary liability.

19. *Exodus* 22:27. The Gemara above (66a) derives that this prohibition applies not only to cursing a prince, but also to cursing an ordinary Jew; see there.

20. I.e. he is not a flagrant sinner (רָשָׁע), whose personal conduct sets him apart from the masses of his people.

21. Whereas the prohibition against cursing a father does not specify that the father must act "in [accord with the] deeds of your people." Hence, if someone cursed his father who had committed a capital crime, he is subject to the death penalty, as the first clause of the Baraisa rules. [The Gemara below will challenge the above assumption that the Torah's warning against cursing applies even to a father who acts in a sinful manner.]

22. Through the principle called מָה מָצִינוּ. This principle dictates that whenever a commonality of law is found in two separate areas of Torah law, analogies may be drawn from one to another, and the limitations of one apply to the other as well. In this case, for example, we derive that just as there is no prohibition against cursing a sinner, so is there no prohibition against striking him.

Alternatively, we may compare striking to cursing by means of a *hekeish.* The Torah states in *Exodus* 21:15: *One who strikes his father or mother shall surely be put to death*; two verses later, it states: *One who curses his father or mother shall surely be put to death.* Since the Torah juxtaposes two subjects, cursing and striking, we may apply the laws of one to the other. According to this second interpretation, the Tanna of our Baraisa maintains that a *hekeish* is established even if the two verses in which the subjects appear are separated by an intervening verse (*Rashi*; see *Toras Chaim*; *Aruch LaNer* to 85b indicates that *Rashi* there seems to prefer the second interpretation).

23. For the *azharah* against cursing a parent is also derived from the verse cited above: *And a prince among your people you shall not curse.* Since that verse does not apply to cursing a sinner, we do not punish someone for cursing a sinful parent (see *Rashi,* see also *Yad David*).

24. See *Chagigah* 26a, where Rav Pinchas quotes this answer in the name of Rava (*Rashi*).

25. A person's sins are atoned for through repentance. Consequently, a sinner who repents is henceforth considered "one who acts in accord with the deeds of your people," and his son is therefore punished for striking or cursing him.

ורבי שמעון האמר א) כל מלאכה שאינה צריכה לגופה פטור עליה בעו מיניה מרב ששת בן מהו שיעשה שליח לאביו להכותו ולקללו א"ל ואחר מי התירו אלא כבוד שמים עדיף הכא נמי כבוד שמים עדיף מיתיבי ומה מי שמצוה להכותו מצוה שלא להכותו מי שאינו מצוה להכותו אינו דין שמצוה שלא להכותו מאי לאו אידי ואידי במקום מצוה הא בבנו הא באחר לא אידי ואידי לא שנא בנו ולא שנא אחר ולא קשיא כאן במקום מצוה כאן שלא במקום מצוה והכי קתני ומה במקום מצוה שמצוה להכותו מצוה שלא להכותו שלא במקום מצוה שאינו מצוה להכותו אינו דין שמצוה שלא להכותו תא שמע א היוצא ליהרג ובא בנו והכהו וקיללו חייב בא אחר והכהו וקיללו פטור והוינן בה מאי שנא בנו ומאי שנא אחר ואמר רב חסדא במסרבין בו לצאת ואינו יוצא רב ששת מוקי לה בשאין מסרבין בו לצאת אי הכי אחר נמי אחר גברא קטילא הוא והאמר רב ששת ב) ב ביישו ישן ומת חייב הכא במאי עסקינן בשהכהו הכאה שאין בה שוה פרוטה ג) והאמר רבי אמי אמר ר' יוחנן ג הכהו הכאה שאין בה שוה פרוטה לוקה מאי פטור דקאמר פטור ממממון מכלל דבנו חייב בממון אלא בדינו הכא נמי בדינו אלא אחר היינו טעמא דפטור דאמר קרא א) ונשיא בעמך לא תאור ד) בעושה מעשה עמך התינח קללה הכאה מנלן ה) דמקשינן הכאה לקללה אי הכי בנו נמי ו) כדאמר רב פינחס בשעשה תשובה הכא נמי ד בשעשה תשובה אי הכי אחר נמי אמר רב מרי בעמך במקוים שבעמך אי הכי בנו נמי מידי

רש"י

ור' שמעון אית ליה מלאכה שאינה צריכה לגופה פטור עליה. בפרק המצניע (שבת ד' לג:) גבי המוציא את המת במטה: מהו שיעשה שליח. ב"ד לאביו אם נתחייב אביו נדוי או מלקות: ואחר מי התירו. לקללו ולהכות את חבירו והלא כל ישראל הוזהרו על הכאת חביריהם ועל קללתם כדילפינן בד' מיתות (לעיל ד' נח:) אפ"ה נעשה שליח ב"ד לכך דכתיב (דברים כה) ארבעים יכנו וכתיב (במדבר ה) יתן ה' אותך: ומה מי שמצוה להכותו. ברייתא תניא הכי במכילתא: מאי לאו אידי ואידי. מצוה ואינה מצוה תרוייהו במקום מצוה והא בבנו והא באחר והכי קאמר ויליף אזהרה למכה אביו: ומה אחר שמצוה להכותו במקום מצוה. דכתיב יכנו: מצוה שלא להכותו. יותר מארבעים דכתיב (דברים כה) ולא יוסיף פן יוסיף בנו שאינו מצוה להכותו אפילו במקום מצוה אלמא אינו נעשה שליח לכך אינו דין שמוזהר שלא להכותו שלא במקום מצוה: ומה במקום מצוה שמצוה להכותו מצוה שלא להכותו. יותר מארבעים שלא במקום מצוה לא כל שכן ויליף אזהרה למכה אביו או חבירו מהכא: בא אחר והכהו וקיללו פטור. קס"ד פטור ממלקות: ואינו יוצא. ואשמעי' דבנו אינו נעשה שליח בית דין לכופו לצאת וקשיא לרב ששת: ה"ג והאמר רב ששת ביישו ישן ומת חייב. ביישו ישן ומת תוך שינתו: חייב. דהא מתביישין בניו והאי נמי ל"ש: מכלל. דחייב דקתני גבי בנו ממון קאמר בתמיה והא באין בה שוה פרוטה מוקמת לה: אלא. על כרחך חייב בדינו קאמר מיתה: הכא נמי. דתני גבי אחר פטור בדינו קאמר וממלקות פטר ליה ואכתי מאי שנא: בעושה מעשה עמך. וזה שעובר עבירה שחייב מיתה לאו עושה מעשה עמך הוא: התינח קללה. דכתיב ביה בעמך: מקשינן. כלומר גמרינן במה מצינו ואיכא דאמרי היקשא דכתיב מכה אביו ומקלל אביו גבי הדדי באלה המשפטים אלא שמקרא אחד מפסיק בינתים: אי הכי בנו נמי. דהא לא כתיב אזהרה במקלל אביו אלא במקלל חברו שאביו בכלל עמך בפ' ד' מיתות (לעיל ד' סו.): דרב פנחס. משמיה דרבא במסכת חגיגה בסוף חומר בקודש: במקוים. הראוי להתקיים ולא זה שנגמר דינו: מידי

תוספות

מקלקל נמי מיחייב ור' יהודה יש לדקדק דפטר מדתנן בפ' כל הכלים (שבת ד' קכג:) ומייתי בסמוך דמחט של יד (מותר) ליטול בה את הקוץ דמשמע ליה להש"ס דאתיא ככולי עלמא כי ההיא דשלהי שבת (ד' קמ.) דאמרי' אבל מוקצה מחמת חסרון כיס אפילו ר' שמעון מודה דתנן כל הכלים ניטלין בשבת חוץ ממסר הגדול ויתד של מחרישה ומנא ליה דמודה ר' שמעון בה אלא משמע ליה דבסתמא דהתם מודו כ"ע היכא דלא משכח פלוגתא וכיון דר' יהודה מחייב במלאכה שאינה צריכה לגופה לא אפשר למישרי מחט של יד ליטול בה את הקוץ אי לאו משום דסבירא ליה מקלקל בחבורה פטור ואע"ג דאמרי' בפ' כירה (שם דף מב.) דשמואל במלאכה שאינה צריכה לגופה סבר לה כרבי יהודה ובפ' ספק אכל (כריתות דף יט:) מסיק ר"נ אליבא דשמואל הנח לתינוקות הואיל ומקלקל בחבורה חייב לאו משום דסבירא ליה הכי לשמואל אלא אליבא דמאן דמחייב קאמר ותדע דבשילהי האורג (שבת דף קז.) אמר שמואל כל פטורי דשבת פטור אבל אסור לבר מהני תלת דפטור ומותר המפיס מורסא ומנא לן דפטור ומותר דתנן מחט של יד (מותר) ליטול בה את הקוץ ומדשרי ליטול הקוץ ש"מ דקסבר מקלקל בחבורה פטור דמטעם מלאכה שאינה צריכה לגופה לא שרינא דהא סבירא ליה דחייב:

ורבי שמעון האמר מלאכה שאינה וכו'. הא דקיימא לן הלכה כר' שמעון בגרירה לאו שגגת סקילה היא דאי עביד חריץ הוי כלאחר יד כדאיתא שלהי פ' כירה (שם דף מו: ושם) ועוד דאינה צריכה לגופה ועוד דאפי' לר' יהודה כל אין מתכוין דלא פסיק רישיה פטור מדאורייתא דלא הוי מלאכת מחשבת וכן משמע ביומא (דף לד:) גבי עששיות דאמרי' צירוף דרבנן פי' כי האי משום דאין מתכוין ולא הוי מלאכת מחשבת והתירו משום דאין שבות במקדש וכן מוכח בההיא ז) דהמכבד והמרבץ דהא רבנן דסבירא להו כרבי יהודה בדבר שאין מתכוין ופטרי אפילו ישוה גומות וכן בפרק ספק אכל (כריתות דף כ.) דמתעסק שאינו מתכוין למלאכה פטור כ"ש היכא דאינו מתכוין אלא לגרירה והא דמחייב רבי יהודה בכריתות נתכוין לכבות את העליונות והובערו התחתונות מאליהן היינו התם משום דהוי פסיק רישיה וחשיב מלאכת מחשבת כיון שיודע שיבעיר ור' שמעון דפוטר משום דאינה צריכה לגופה ולא בעי מלאכת מחשבת דהא ר' שמעון מחייב מקלקל בהבערה ומקלקל דמיפטר בשאר מלאכות היינו משום דלא הוי מלאכת מחשבת כדמוכח שלהי פרק קמא דחגיגה (דף י.) מכלל דבהבערה לא חיישינן והא דשרינן לבעול לכתחלה בשבת אם להנאת עצמו הוא צריך אפילו דם חבורי מחבר ה"ט משום דאינה צריכה לגופה ור' אליעזר דמחייב חטאת ח) במכבד ומרבץ לאו משום דליהוי פסיק רישיה דהא שרי לר' שמעון לכתחלה אלא חשיב תיקון לכיבוד ולריבוץ כעין בנין ואפילו בלא השוואת גומות דבדבר מועט מיחייב משום בונה כדאשכחן ט) גודלת ופוקסת ובס"פ כירה (שבת דף מז:) דהוי שרי לטלטל נר הדולק בשבת אי לאו משום דבסים לדבר האסור היינו משום דאי מכבה בלא מתכוין אינה צריכה לגופה היא ומיהו תימה דהא לשמואל קאמר בפרק כירה י) דבדבר שאין מתכוין סבר לה כר"ש ובמלאכה שאינה צריכה לגופה סבר לה כר' יהודה וכיון דסבר כר"י במלאכה שאינה צריכה לגופה היכי שרי דבר שאין מתכוין דשרי התם (דף מא:) גבי מיחם שפינהו לתת לתוכו מים להפשיר אפי' שיעור לצרף דהוה ליה שגגת סקילה וי"ל דהא דאסרינן הכא קוץ וסילוא משום דחיישינן כשמתחיל להסיר שמא יתהפך דלא סגי אי לא הוי פסיק רישיה ולא יניח בשביל כך אבל שאר דבר שאין מתכוין דלא פסיק רישיה הוא שרי וליטול קוץ בשבת מודה שמואל אע"ג דמחייב במלאכה שאינה צריכה לגופה דקסבר מקלקל בחבורה פטור:

הא בבנו הא באחר. רוצה ללמד מכאן אזהרה למכה אביו דלא נפיק מפן יוסיף כיון דאינו מצווה להכותו ומשמע בסמוך דאפי' ביוצא ליהרג נפקא לן אזהרה לבנו דחייב דמוקי לה רב חסדא במסרבין בו לצאת ואע"ג דאין מזהירין מן הדין הני מילי להלקותו ומיהו קשה היכי אתא בנו בקל וחומר מאחר כיון דאחר פטור במסרבין בו לצאת ואינו יוצא ושמא גלויי מילתא בעלמא הוא דפן יוסיף מיירי אפי' בבנו אע"ג דארבעים יכנו לא מיירי בבנו: **והאמר** רב ששת ביישו וכו'. תימה דבפ' החובל (ב"ק דף פו: ושם) בעי רבי אבא בר ממל ביישו ישן ומת מהו ולא איפשיטא והכא פריך בפשיטות ויש ספרים דגרסינן והאמר רב ששת ביישו ישן חייב ולא גרס ומת ולא נהירא דמה ענין ישן ליוצא ליהרג ועוד מאי קמ"ל רב ששת מתניתין היא בפרק החובל כ) המבייש את הישן חייב ור"ת גרים והאמר רב ששת ביישו חייב ויוצא ליהרג קאי מיהו אין כל כך תימה אם לא הביא דברי רב ששת בפרק החובל למיפשט ההיא בעיא דכי האי גוונא אשכחן בנדרים בפרק אין בין המודר (ד' לה: ושם) דאיבעיא לן הנהו כהני שלוחי דידן או שלוחי דשמיא ולא מייתי התם דברי רב הונא בריה דרב יהושע דאמר בפרק קמא דקדושין (דף כג: ושם) הני כהני שלוחי דרחמנא נינהו דאי שלוחי דידן מי איכא מידי דאנן לא מצינן עבדין ושלוחי דידן עבדי ל): **הכהו** הכאה שאין בה וכו'. תימה אמאי לקי הא פן יוסיף לאו שניתן לאזהרת מיתת ב"ד הוא דמיניה נפקא לן אזהרה למכה אביו כדאיתא בספרי ובירושלמי:

סיכול

מסורת הש"ס

א) [שבת קה: קו. קמא: כריתות כ:], ב) ב"ק פו:, ג) כתובות לב: מכות ט., ד) [יבמות כב: וש"נ], ה) [שם קא.], ו) [ב"ק לד: ב"מ סב. חגיגה כו. יבמות כב.], ז) [שבת לה.], ח) [שבת לה.], ט) [שם], י) [דף מב.], כ) [דף פו.], ל) [ועי' היטב תוס' יומא יט: ד"ה מי איכא ותוס' ב"מ י: ד"ה מן].

תורה אור השלם

א) אֱלֹהִים לֹא תְקַלֵּל וְנָשִׂיא בְעַמְּךָ לֹא תָאֹר: [שמות כב, כז]

עין משפט נר מצוה

יג א מיי' פ"ה מהל' ממרים הל' יב ועיין בכ"מ סמג לאוין ריט טוש"ע י"ד סי' רמא סעיף ד:

יד ב מיי' פ"ג מהל' חובל ומזיק הל' ג סמג עשין ע טוש"ע ח"מ סי' תכ סעיף לה:

טו ג מיי' שם פ"ה הלכה ג סמג שם טוש"ע שם סעיף ג:

טז ד מיי' פ"ה מהל' ממרים הלכה יב סמג לאוין ריט טוש"ע י"ד סי' רמא סעיף ד:

ליקוטי רש"י

מקלקל הוא. כל מקלקל דשבת הוי פטור דלאו היינו מלאכת מחשבת וסותר דתנן באבות מלאכות דמיחייב סותר על מנת לבנות הוא ואינו יכול לבנות אלא אם כן סותרו והשתא לאו קלקול הוא ורבי יהודה סבר דאם במקומו חוזר ובונה הוא דמחייב אסתירה ואי לא לא ומכבה דומיא דסותר הוא וכן קורע דומיא דסותר ולהכי תנן הקורע על מנת לתפור וכן מוחק תנן על מנת לכתוב דכולם סותר נינהו [שם לא:]. הניחא למ"ד מקלקל פטור. ר' יהודה דאית ליה מקלקל בחבורה פטור ולא איתפרש היכא ולי נראה מתניתין ר' יהודה היא דאמר מלאכה שאינה צריכה לגופה חייב עליה הלכך חיובא דחובל בצריך לכלבו ומבעיר בצריך לאפרו משכחת לה דאף על פי דמקלקל הוא אצל מלאכה עצמה מתקן הוא אצל אחרים ולר' יהודה כי האי גוונא מלאכה הוא משום תקון אחרים אבל מקלקל ואינו מתקן פטור. אלא למ"ד חייב. ר' שמעון היא דאמר מלאכה שאינה צריכה לגופה פטור עליה הלכך אין לך חובל ומבעיר שאין מקלקל ואפילו מבעיר עצים לקדרתו מקלקל הוא אצל עצים ומה שהוא מתקן אצל אחרים לר' שמעון לא חשיב דהא מלאכה שאינה צריכה לגופה היא אלא משום דמקלקל בחבלה ובהבערה חייב כדיליף לקמיה מדאיצטריך קרא וביום השמיני ימול ואפילו בשבת ומילה הוא מכלל דשאר מקלקלין בחבורה חייב ומדאסר רחמנא הבערה דבת כהן [שבת קו. ועיין תוס' כאן]. מקלקל בחבורה חייב. דהכי אמרינן בבבא קמא בפרק המניח (דף לד:) כל המקלקלין פטורין חוץ מחובל ומבעיר [כריתות יט:]. כל המקלקלין פטורין לענין שבת חוץ מחובל ומבעיר דמחמת טעמא דמצ' שבת בפרק האורג מדאצטריך קרא למישרי מילה מכלל דמקלקל חובל חייב ומדאסר רחמנא שריפת בת כהן בשבת דמקלקל הוא מכלל דמקלקל בהבערה חייב כגון השורף כלי דמקלקל הוא [ב"ק לד:]. [עד כאן שייך לדף פד:]

ורבי שמעון האמר מלאכה שאינה צריכה לגופה. כמו מוציא את המת לקוברו אינו צריך לגופה ולא למת עצמו ולא לצאת ממנו והוצאה הצריכה לגופה כגון שהוא צריך לחפץ זה במקום אחר [שבת צג.]. פטור עליה. מלאכה שאינה צריכה לגופה שברצונו לא תעשה ואינו צריך לעיקר (תחלתה) [תכליתה] [שם יב.]. ר' שמעון פוטר אפילו במת שלם דהוי מלאכה שאינה צריכה לגופה וכל מלאכה שאינה צריכה (לגופה) אלא לסלקה מעליו הוי מלאכה דברצונו לא באה לו ולא היה צריך לה הלכך לאו מלאכת מחשבת היא לר' שמעון [שם צג:]. ר' שמעון דאמר מלאכה שאינה צריכה לגופה פטור עליה הלכך אין לך חובל ומבעיר שאין מקלקל ואפילו מבעיר עצים אצל עצים ומה שהוא מתקן אצל אחרים לר' שמעון לא חשיב דהא מלאכה שאינה צריכה לגופה היא אלא משום דמקלקל בחבלה ובהבערה חייב כדיליף לקמיה [שם קו. וצ"ע מסוגיין עי' תוס' כאן]. ביישו ישן. ביש אדם ישן. ומת. מתוך שנתו ולא הכיר בבשתו שעשה לו זה מהו [ב"ק פו:]. בעושה מעשה עמך. וזה לא עשה מעשה עמו ואין חייבין בכבודו [שם צד.]. שאין בה שוה פרוטה. שאם יש בה תשלומי פרוטה משלם ואינו לוקה דילפינן בכתובות בפלוגתא נערות (דף לב:) בפירוש ריבתא חובל בחבירו לתשלומין ולא לחוקה ואין יש בה שוה פרוטה לוקה שנאמר על לא תוסיף פן יוסיף (דברים כה). מקשינן הכאה לקללה. לומר שכשם שאינו לוקה על קללתו דכתיב בעמך כך לא ילקה על הכאתו [מכות ט.].

After rejecting the third defense of Rav Sheishess, the Gemara presents its final explanation of how Rav Sheishess interprets the Baraisa:

אָמַר רַב מָרִי – **Rav Mari said:** ,,בְּעַמְּךָ" – **Scripture states:** ***among your people.*** בְּמְקוּיָם שֶׁבְּעַמְּךָ – This **refers to someone who will survive among your people.** This excludes a condemned man, who is about to die. For this reason, the Baraisa's second clause imposes no punishment for cursing (or striking) a condemned man.[26]

The Gemara asks:

אִי הָכִי – **If so,** בְּנוֹ נַמִּי – then **even a son** who strikes or curses his condemned father should be exempt for the same reason.[27] Why, then, does the Baraisa's first clause state that he is liable?

NOTES

26. For the verse teaches that there is no punishment for cursing a condemned man, and the prohibition against striking is exegetically compared to the one against cursing (see note 22).

27. For the *azharah* that warns a son against cursing his father is derived from this very verse (see note 23). Why, then, does the Baraisa state that the son is punished?

ורבי שמעון האמר [א] כל מלאכה שאינה צריכה לגופה פטור עליה בעו מיניה מרב ששת בן מהו שיעשה שליח לאביו להכותו ולקללו א"ל ואחר מי התירו אלא כבוד שמים עדיף הכא נמי כבוד שמים עדיף מיתיבי ומה מי שמצוה להכותו מצוה שלא להכותו מי שאינו מצוה להכותו אינו דין שמצוה שלא להכותו מאי לאו אידי ואידי במקום מצוה הא בבנו הא באחר לא אידי ואידי לא שנא בנו ולא שנא אחר ולא קשיא כאן במקום מצוה כאן שלא במקום מצוה והכי קתני ומה במקום מצוה שמצוה להכותו מצוה שלא להכותו שלא במקום מצוה שאינו מצוה להכותו אינו דין שמצוה שלא להכותו תא שמע [א] היוצא ליהרג ובא בנו והכהו וקיללו חייב בא אחר והכהו וקיללו פטור והוינן בה מאי שנא בנו ומאי שנא אחר ואמר רב חסדא במסרבין בו לצאת ואינו יוצא רב ששת מוקי לה בשאין מסרבין בו לצאת אי הכי אחר נמי אחר גברא קטילא הוא והאמר רב ששת [ב] [ב] ביישו ישן ומת חייב הכא במאי עסקינן בשהכהו הכאה שאין בה שוה פרוטה [ג] והאמר רבי אמי אמר ר' יוחנן [ג] הכהו הכאה שאין בה שוה פרוטה לוקה מאי פטור דקאמר פטור ממון מכלל דבנו חייב בממון אלא בדינו הכא נמי בדינו אלא אחר היינו טעמא דפטור דאמר קרא [א] ונשיא בעמך לא תאור [ד] בעושה מעשה עמך התינח קללה הכאה מנלן [ה] דמקשינן הכאה לקללה אי הכי בנו נמי [ו] כדאמר רב פינחס בשעשה תשובה הכא נמי [ד] בשעשה תשובה אי הכי אחר נמי אמר רב מרי בעמך במקיימים שבעמך אי הכי בנו נמי מידי

רש"י

ור' שמעון אית ליה מלאכה שאינה צריכה לגופה פטור עליה. בפרק המצניע (שבת ד' צג:) גבי המוציא את המת במטה: מהו שיעשה שליח. ב"ד לאביו אם נתחייב אביו נדוי או מלקות: ואחר מי התירו. לקללו ולהכות את חבירו והלא כל ישראל הוזהרו על הכאת חביריהם ועל קללתם כדילפינן בד' מיתות (לעיל ד' נח:) אפ"ה נעשה שליח ב"ד לכך דכתיב (דברים כה) ארבעים יכנו וכתיב (במדבר ה) יתן ה' אותך: ומה מי שמצוה להכותו. ברייתא תניא הכי במכילתא: מאי לאו אידי ואידי. מצוה ואינה מצוה תרוייהו במקום מצוה והא בבנו והא באחר והכי קאמר ויליף אזהרה למכה אביו: ומה אחר שמצוה להכותו במקום מצוה. דכתיב יכנו: מצוה שלא להכותו. יותר מארבעים דכתיב (דברים כה) ולא יוסיף פן יוסיף בנו שאינו מצוה להכותו אפילו במקום מצוה אלמא אינו נעשה שליח לכך אינו דין שמוזהר שלא להכותו שלא במקום מצוה: ומה במקום מצוה שמצוה להכותו מצוה שלא להכותו. יותר מארבעים שלא במקום מצוה לא כל שכן ויליף אזהרה למכה אביו או חבירו מהכא: בא אחר והכהו וקיללו פטור. קס"ד פטור ממלקות: ואינו יוצא. ואשמעי' דבנו אינו נעשה שליח בית דין לכופו לצאת וקשיא לרב ששת: ה"ג והאמר רב ששת ביישו ישן ומת חייב. ביישו ישן ומת תוך שינתו: חייב. דהא מתביישין בניו והאי נמי ל"ש: מכלל. דחייב דקתני גבי בנו ממון קאמר בתמיה והא באין בה שוה פרוטה מוקמת לה: אלא. על כרחך חייב בדינו קאמר מיתה: הכא נמי. דתני גבי אחר פטור בדינו קאמר וממלקות פטר ליה ואכתי מאי שנא: בעושה מעשה עמך. וזה שעובר עבירה שחייב מיתה לאו עושה מעשה עמך הוא: התינח קללה. דכתיב ביה בעמך: מקשינן. כלומר גמרינן במה מצינו ואיכא דאמרי היקשא דכתיב מכה אביו ומקלל אביו גבי הדדי באלה המשפטים אלא שמקרא אחד מפסיק בינתים: אי הכי בנו נמי. דהא לא כתיב אזהרה במקלל אביו אלא במקלל חברו שאביו בכלל עמך בפ' ד' מיתות (לעיל ד' סו.): דרב פנחס. משמיה דרבא במסכת חגיגה בסוף חומר בקודש: במקיימים. הראוי להתקיים ולא זה שנגמר דינו:

תוספות

מקלקל נמי מיחייב ור' יהודה יש לדקדק דפטור מדתנן בפ' כל הכלים (שבת ד' קכג:) ומייתי בסמוך דמחט של יד (מותר) ליטול בה את הקוץ דמשמע ליה להש"ס דאתיא ככולי עלמא כי ההיא דשלהי שבת (ד' קמז.) דאמרי' אבל מוקצה מחמת חסרון כיס אפילו ר' שמעון מודה דתנן כל הכלים ניטלין בשבת חוץ ממסר הגדול ויתד של מחרישה ומנא ליה דמודה ר' שמעון בה אלא משמע ליה דבסתמא דהתם מודו כ"ע היכא דלא משכח פלוגתא וכיון דר' יהודה מחייב במלאכה שאינה צריכה לגופה לא אפשר למישרי מחט של יד ליטול בה את הקוץ אי לאו משום דסבירא ליה מקלקל בחבורה פטור ואע"ג דאמרי' בפ' כירה (שם דף מב.) דשמואל במלאכה שאינה צריכה לגופה סבר לה כרבי יהודה ובפ' ספק אכל (כריתות דף יט:) מסיק ר"נ אליבא דשמואל הנח לתינוקות הואיל ומקלקל בחבורה חייב לאו משום דסבירא ליה הכי לשמואל אלא אליבא דמאן דמחייב קאמר ותדע דבשילהי האורג (שבת דף קו.) אמר שמואל כל פטורי דשבת פטור אבל אסור לבר מהני תלת דפטור ומותר המפיס מורסא ומנא לן דפטור ומותר דתנן מחט של יד (מותר) ליטול בה את הקוץ ומדשרי ליטול הקוץ ש"מ דקסבר מקלקל בחבורה פטור דמטעם מלאכה שאינה צריכה לגופה לא שרינא דהא סבירא ליה דחייב:

ורבי שמעון האמר מלאכה שאינה וכו'. הא דקיימא לן הלכה כר' שמעון בגרירה לאו שגגת סקילה היא דאי עביד חריץ הוי כלאחר יד כדאיתא שלהי פ' כירה (שם דף מו: ושם) ועוד דאינה צריכה לגופה ועוד דאפי' לר' יהודה כל אין מתכוין דלא פסיק רישיה פטור מדאורייתא דלא הוי מלאכת מחשבת וכן משמע ביומא (דף לד:) גבי עששיות דאמרי' לירוף דרבנן פי' כי האי משום דאין מתכוין ולא הוי מלאכת מחשבת והתירו משום דאין שבות במקדש וכן מוכח בההיא [ז] דהמכבד והמרבץ דהא רבנן דסבירא להו כרבי יהודה בדבר שאין מתכוין ופטרי אפילו ישוה גומות וכן בפרק ספק אכל (כריתות דף כ.) דמתעסק שאינו מתכוין למלאכה פטור כ"ש היכא דאינו מתכוין אלא לגרירה והא דמחייב רבי יהודה בכריתות נתכוין לכבות את העליונות והובערו התחתונות מאליהן היינו התם משום דהוי פסיק רישיה וחשיב מלאכת מחשבת כיון שיודע שיבעיר ור' שמעון דפוטר משום דאינה צריכה לגופה ולא בעי מלאכת מחשבת דהא ר' שמעון מחייב מקלקל בהבערה ומקלקל דמיפטר בשאר מלאכות היינו משום דלא הוי מלאכת מחשבת כדמוכח שלהי פרק קמא דחגיגה (דף י.) מכלל דבהבערה לא חיישינן והא דשרינן לבעול לכתחלה בשבת אם להנאת עצמו הוא צריך אפילו דם חבורי מחבר ה"ט משום דאינה צריכה לגופה ור' אליעזר דמחייב חטאת [ח] במכבד ומרבץ לאו משום דליהוי פסיק רישיה דהא שרי לר' שמעון לכתחלה אלא חשיב תיקון לכיבוד ולריבוץ כעין בנין ואפילו בלא השוואת גומות דבדבר מועט מיחייב משום בונה כדאשכחן [ט] גודלת ופוקסת ובס"פ כירה (שבת דף מז:) דהוי שרי לטלטל נר הדולק בשבת אי לאו משום דבסיס לדבר האסור היינו משום דאי מכבה בלא מתכוין אינה צריכה לגופה היא ומיהו תימה דהא לשמואל קאמר בפרק כירה [י] דבדבר שאין מתכוין סבר לה כר"ש ובמלאכה שאינה צריכה לגופה סבר לה כר' יהודה וכיון דסבר כר"י במלאכה שאינה צריכה לגופה היכי שרי דבר שאין מתכוין דשרי התם (דף מא:) גבי מיחם שפינהו לתת לתוכו מים להפשיר אפי' שיעור לצרף דהוה ליה שגגת סקילה וי"ל דהא דאסרינן הכא קוץ וסילוא משום דחיישינן כשמתחיל להסיר שמא יתהפך דלא סגי אי לא הוי פסיק רישיה ולא יניח בשביל כך אבל שאר דבר שאין מתכוין דלא פסיק רישיה הוא שרי וליטול קוץ בשבת מודה שמואל אע"ג דמחייב במלאכה שאינה צריכה לגופה דקסבר מקלקל בחבורה פטור:

הא בבנו הא באחר. רוצה ללמד מכאן אזהרה למכה אביו דלא נפיק מפן יוסיף כיון דאינו מצווה להכותו ומשמע בסמוך דאפי' ביוצא ליהרג נפקא לן אזהרה לבנו דחייב דמוקי לה רב חסדא במסרבין בו לצאת ואע"ג דאין מזהירין מן הדין הני מילי להלקותו ומיהו קשה היכי אתא בנו בקל וחומר מאחר כיון דאחר פטור במסרבין בו לצאת ואינו יוצא ושמא גלויי מילתא בעלמא הוא דפן יוסיף מיירי אפי' בבנו אע"ג דארבעים יכנו לא מיירי בבנו: והאמר רב ששת ביישו וכו'. תימה דבפ' החובל (ב"ק דף פו: ושם) בעי רבי אבא בר ממל ביישו ישן ומת מהו ולא איפשיטא והכא פריך בפשיטות ויש ספרים דגרסינן והאמר רב ששת ביישו ישן חייב ולא גרס ומת ולא נהירא דמה ענין ישן ליוצא ליהרג ועוד מאי קמ"ל רב ששת מתניתין היא בפרק החובל [כ] המבייש את הישן חייב ור"ת גריס והאמר רב ששת ביישו חייב ויוצא ליהרג קאי ומיהו אין כל כך תימה אם לא הביא דברי רב ששת בפרק החובל למיפשט ההיא בעיא דכי האי גוונא אשכחן בנדרים בפרק אין בין המודר (ד' לה: ושם) דאיבעיא לן הנהו כהני שלוחי דידן או שלוחי דשמיא ולא מייתי התם דברי רב הונא בריה דרב יהושע דאמר בפרק קמא דקדושין (דף כג: ושם) הני כהני שלוחי דרחמנא נינהו דאי שלוחי דידן מי איכא מידי דאנן לא מצינן עבדין ושלוחי דידן עבדי [ל]: הכהו הכאה שאין בה וכו'. תימה אמאי לקי הא פן יוסיף לאו שניתן לאזהרת מיתת ב"ד הוא דמיניה נפקא לן אזהרה למכה אביו כדאיתא בספרי ובירושלמי:

סיכול

[עד כאן שייך לדף פד:]

עין משפט נר מצוה

יג א מיי' פ"ה מהל' ממרים הל' יב ועיין בכ"מ סמג לאוין ריט טוש"ע י"ד סי' רמא סעיף ז:

יד ב מיי' פ"ג מהל' חובל ומזיק הל' ג סמג עשין ע טוש"ע ח"מ סי' תכ סעיף לה:

טו ג מיי' שם פ"ה הלכה ג סמג שם טוש"ע שם סעיף ג:

טז ד מיי' פ"ה מהל' ממרים הלכה יב סמג לאוין ריט טוש"ע י"ד סי' רמא סעיף ז:

ליקוטי רש"י

מקלקל הוא. כל מקלקל דשבת הוי פטור דלאו היינו מלאכת מחשבת וסותר דתנן באבות מלאכות דמיחייב סותר על מנת לבנות הוא ואינו יכול לבנות אלא אם כן סותרו והשתא לאו קלקול הוא ורבי יהודה סבר דאם במקומו חוזר ובונה הוא דמחייב אסתירה ואי לא לא ומכבה דומיא דסותר הוא וכן קורע דומיא דסותר ולהכי תנן הקורע על מנת לתפור וכן מוחק תנן על מנת לכתוב דכולם סותר נינהו [שם לא:]. הניחא למ"ד מקלקל פטור. ר' יהודה דאית ליה מקלקל בחבורה פטור ולא איתפרש היכא ולי נראה מתניתין ר' יהודה היא דאמר מלאכה שאינה צריכה לגופה חייב עליה הלכך חובל דחובל בצריך לכלבו ומבעיר בצריך לאפרו משכחת לה דאף על פי דמקלקל הוא אבל מלאכה עצמה מתקן הוא אבל אחרים ולר' יהודה כי האי גוונא מלאכה הוא משום תקון אחרים אבל מקלקל ואינו מתקן פטור. אלא למ"ד חייב. ר' שמעון היא דאמר מלאכה שאינה צריכה לגופה פטור עליה הלכך אין לך חובל ומבעיר שאין מקלקל ואפילו מבעיר עלים לקדרתו מקלקל הוא אבל עלים ומה שהוא מתקן אבל אחרים לר' שמעון לא חשיב דהא מלאכה שאינה צריכה לגופה היא אלא משום דמקלקל בחבלה ובהבערה חייב כדיליף לקמיה מדאיצטריך קרא וביום השמיני ביום יתירא ואפילו בשבת ומילה חובל הוא מכלל דשאר מקלקלין בחבורה חייב ומדאסר רחמנא הבערה דבת כהן [שבת קו. ועיין תוס' כאן]. מקלקל בחבורה חייב. דהכי אמרינן בבבא קמא בפרק המניח את הכד (דף לד:) כל המקלקלין פטורין חוץ מחובל ומבעיר [כריתות יט:]. כל המקלקלין פטורין לענין שבת חוץ מחובל ומבעיר כדמפרש טעמא במס' שבת בפרק האורג מדאצטריך קרא למישרי מילה מכלל דשאר חובל חייב ומדאסר רחמנא שריפת בת כהן בשבת דמקלקל הוא מכלל דמקלקל בהבערה חייב כגון השורף כלי דמקלקל הוא [ב"ק לד:].

ורבי שמעון האמר מלאכה שאינה צריכה לגופה. כמו מוציא את המת לקוברו אינו צריך לגופה דהוצאה ולא למת אלא לפנות ביתו והוצאה הצריכה לגופה כגון שהוא צריך לחפץ זה במקום אחר [שבת עג:]. מלאכה שאינה צריכה לגופה שברצונו לא תעשה ואינו צריך לעיקר (תחלתה) [תכליתה] [שם יב.]. ר' שמעון פוטר אפילו במת שלם דהוי מלאכה שאינה צריכה לגופה וכל מלאכה שאינה צריכה (לגופה) אלא לסלקה מעליו הוי מלאכה שאינה צריכה לגופה דברצונו לא באה לו ולא היה צריך לה הלכך לאו מלאכת מחשבת היא לר' שמעון [שם צג:]. ר' שמעון דאמר מלאכה שאינה צריכה לגופה פטור עליה הלכך אין לך חובל ומבעיר שאין מקלקל ואפילו מבעיר עלים לקדרתו מקלקל הוא אבל עלים ומה שהוא מתקן אבל אחרים לר' שמעון לא חשיב דהא מלאכה שאינה צריכה לגופה היא אלא משום דמקלקל בחבלה ובהבערה חייב כדיליף לקמיה [שם קו. וצ"ע מסוגיין עי' תוס' כאן]. ביישו ישן. ביישו אדם ישן. ומת. מתוך שנתו ולא הכיר בבשתו שעשה לו זה מהו [ב"ק פו:]. בעושה מעשה עמך. וזה לא עשה מעשה עמו ואין חייבין בכבודו [שם צד]. שאין בה שוה פרוטה. שאם יש בה תשלומי פרוטה משלם ואינו לוקה דילפינן בכתובות באלו נערות (דף לב:) בפירוש ריבתה תורה חובל בחבירו לתשלומין וכי אין בה שוה פרוטה לוקה שעבר על לא תוסיף פן יוסיף (דברים כה). מקשינן הכאה לקללה. לומר שכשם שאינו לוקה על קללתו דכתיב בעמך כך לא ילקה על הכאתו [מכות ט.].

מסורת הש"ס

א) [שבת קה: קו: קמא: כריתות כ:], ב) ב"ק פו:, ג) כתובות לב: מכות ט., ד) [יבמות כב: וש"נ], ה) [שם קא.], ו) [ב"ק לד: ב"מ סב. חגיגה כו. יבמות כב:], ז) [שבת לה.], ח) [שבת לה.], ט) [שם], י) [דף מב.], כ) [דף פו:], ל) [ועי' היטב תוס' יומא יט: ד"ה מי איכא ותוס' ב"מ י: ד"ה מן].

תורה אור השלם

א) אֱלֹהִים לֹא תְקַלֵּל וְנָשִׂיא בְעַמְּךָ לֹא תָאֹר: [שמות כב, כז]

מידי דהוה לאחר מיתה מאי הוה עלה (א) אמר רבה בר רב הונא וכן תנא דבי רבי ישמעאל א לכל אין הבן נעשה שליח לאביו להכותו ולקללו ב חוץ ממסית שהרי אמרה תורה א) לא תחמול ולא תכסה עליו: **מתני'** ב) ג המכה אביו ואמו אינו חייב עד שיעשה בהן חבורה זה חומר במקלל מבמכה ד שהמקלל לאחר מיתה חייב ג) ה והמכה לאחר מיתה פטור: **גמ'** ת"ר ב) אביו ואמו קלל לאחר מיתה שיכול הואיל וחייב במכה וחייב במקלל מה מכה אינו חייב אלא מחיים אף המקלל אינו חייב אלא מחיים ועוד ק"ו ומה מכה שעשה בו שלא בעמך כבעמך לא חייב בו לאחר מיתה מקלל שלא עשה בו שלא בעמך כבעמך אינו דין שלא חייב בו לאחר מיתה ת"ל אביו ואמו קלל לאחר מיתה הניחא לר' יונתן דמייתר ליה קרא אביו ואמו (א) אלא לר' יאשיה מאי איכא למימר ד) דתניא ב) איש איש מה ת"ל איש איש ו לרבות בת טומטום ואנדרוגינוס ב) אשר יקלל את אביו ואת אמו ה) אין לי אלא אביו ואמו אביו שלא אמו אמו שלא אביו מניין ת"ל אביו ואמו קלל אביו קלל אמו קלל דברי ר' יאשיה ר' יונתן אומר משמע שניהן כאחד ומשמע אחד ואחד בפני עצמו ו) עד שיפרט לך הכתוב יחדיו מנא ליה נפקא ליה ג) ומקלל אביו ואמו מות יומת ואידך ההוא מיבעי ליה לרבות בת טומטום ואנדרוגינוס ותיפוק ליה מאיש איש ז) דברה תורה כלשון בני אדם וליתני חומר במכה מבמקלל שהמכה עשה בו שלא בעמך כבעמך משא"כ במקלל קסבר ח) מקשינן הכאה לקללה לימא הני תנאי כהני תנאי דתני חדא כותי אתה מצווה על הכאתו ואי אתה מצווה על קללתו ותניא אידך אי אתה מצווה לא על קללתו ולא על הכאתו סברוה דכולי עלמא כותים גירי אמת הן מאי לאו בהא קמיפלגי דמר סבר מקשינן הכאה לקללה ומר סבר ט) לא מקשינן הכאה לקללה לא דכ"ע לא מקשינן הכאה לקללה והכא בהא קמיפלגי מר סבר כותים גירי אמת הן ומר סבר י) כותים גירי אריות הן אי הכי היינו דקתני עלה ושורו כישראל אלא שמע מינה בהיקישא פליגי ש"מ: **מתני'** ז הגונב נפש מישראל אינו חייב עד שיכניסנו לרשותו רבי יהודה אומר עד שיכניסנו לרשותו וישתמש בו שנאמר ד) והתעמר בו ומכרו הגונב את בנו רבי ישמעאל בנו של ר' יוחנן בן ברוקה מחייב וחכמים ח פוטרין גנב מי שחציו עבד וחציו בן חורין ר' יהודה מחייב וחכמים פוטרין: **גמ'** ותנא קמא לא בעי עימור א"ר אחא בריה דרבא ט עימור פחות משוה פרוטה איכא בינייהו י בעי ר' ירמיה גנבו ומכרו ישן מהו כ מכר אשה לעוברה מהו יש דרך עימור בכך או אין דרך עימור בכך ותיפוק ליה דליכא עימור כלל לא צריכא ישן דזגא עליה אשה דאוקמא באפי זיקא דרך עימור בכך או ל אין דרך עימור בכך מאי תיקו ת"ר ד) כי ימצא איש גונב נפש מאחיו אין לי אלא איש שגנב אשה מניין ת"ל ה) וגונב איש אין לי אלא איש שגנב בין אשה ובין איש ואשה שגנבה איש אשה שגנבה אשה מניין ת"ל ד) ומת הגנב ההוא מ מכל מקום תניא אידך כ) כי ימצא איש גונב נפש מאחיו אחד הגונב את האיש ואחד הגונב את האשה נ ואחד גר ואחד עבד משוחרר וקטן חייב ס גנבו ולא מכרו מכרו ועדיין ישנו ברשותו פטור מכרו לאביו או לאחיו או לאחד מן הקרובים חייב ע הגונב את העבדים פטור

תני

רש"י

מידי דהוה לאחר מיתה. דילפינן לקמן מקלל לאחר מיתה חייב וא"ת והתנן מכה לאחר מיתה פטור והכא מיחייב ליה אהכאה דקתני הכהו וקללו היינו טעמא דפטור מכה לאחר מיתה משום דבעינן חבורה ולאחר מיתה ליכא חבורה דליכא נפש דנפקא ליה לעיל מנפש ויוצא ליהרג איכא חבורה דחי הוא אלא דסופו למות: **מתני'** שהמקלל לאחר מיתה חייב. כדיליף בגמרא: והמכה לאחר מיתה פטור. דחבורה ליכא: **גמ'** אביו ואמו קלל. קרא יתירא הוא דהא כתיב רישיה דקרא אשר יקלל את אביו ואת אמו: מכה שעשה שלא בעמך כבעמך. דגבי הכאה לא כתיב בעמך למעוטי שאינו עושה מעשה עמך והאי תנא סבר לא מקשינן הכאה לקללה מפני המקרא המפסיק בינתים: לא חייב בו לאחר מיתה. דהא חבורה כתיב: לרבות בת. טומטום ואנדרוגינוס: אין לי אלא אביו ואמו. שניהם יחד: אביו קילל ואמו קילל. בראש המקרא סמך קללה לאביו ובסוף סמך לאמו: עד שיפרט לך הכתוב יחדו. וכמו שפרט בחורש בשור ובחמור מדפרט לך ש"מ דאי לא הוי יחדו הוה משמע שור לבדו וחמור לבדו והא אביו ואמו דרישא דרשינן נמי או אביו או אמו וסיפא לאתויי לאחר מיתה: ומקלל אביו. דואלה המשפטים: ואידך. דמפיק לאחר מיתה מאביו ואמו קילל: וליתני נמי וכו'. אמתניתין קאי דקתני זה חומר במקלל מבמכה: לימא הני תנאי. תנא דמתניתין דלא תנא חומר במכה שעשה בו שלא בעמך כבעמך ותנא דברייתא דלעיל דתנא ומה מכה שעשה בו: גירי אמת הן. מתחילתן גרים גמורים היו ועכשיו הרשיעו וישראל שאינו עושה מעשה עמך הוא וכי היכי דעל קללתו פטור על הכאתו נמי פטור: גירי אריות הן. והרי הם כעובדי כוכבים גמורים: אי הכי. דטעמא דפטור משום דגירי אריות הן: היינו דתנא עלה. בתמיה בהך מתני' דקתני אינו מצווה לא על הכאתו ולא על קללתו קתני ושורו כישראל שור שלנו שנגח את שורו ושורו שנגח שלנו תם משלם חצי נזק ומועד משלם נזק שלם ואילו דעובד כוכבים תנן שור של ישראל שנגח שור של עובד כוכבים פטור ושל עובד כוכבים שנגח שור של ישראל בין תם בין מועד משלם נזק שלם: **מתני'** שיכניסנו לרשותו. דכתיב (שמות כב) ונמצא בידו ותניא במכילתא ונמצא אין מציאה בכל מקום אלא בעדים בידו אין בידו אלא ברשותו וכן הוא אומר (במדבר כא) ויקח את כל ארצו מידו: **גמ'** עמור. שמוש: גנבו ומכרו כשהוא ישן מהו. לקמן מפרש לה הבעיא: מכר אשה לעוברה. גנב אשה מעוברת ומכרה לעוברה שלא מכר הגוף שלה אלא שיהא עובר מכור: דליכא עימור. לא בישן ולא בעובר: דזוגא עליה. דסמך עליו: דאוקמא באפי זיקא. וכל כמה שהיא עבה מועיל יותר להגין בפני הרוח: אין לי אלא איש. כשהגנב איש: וגונב איש. שהנגנב איש ולא אשה וקרא קמא דלא קפיד אנגנב למהוי איש דכתיב נפש הלכך אין לי אלא איש שגנב בין איש בין אשה דהיכא דגנב הוי איש כתוב גונב נפש ואשה שגנבה איש דכתיב וגונב איש וגונב אפילו אשה גונבת משמע: הגנב. מ"מ וההוא דרשינן ליה בספרי למעוטי גונב עבד: ועדיין ישנו ברשותו. ברשות הנגנב עצמו שעדיין לא הכניסו גנב ברשותו: פטור. שהרי לא גנבו: לאביו. אביו של נגנב:

תני

תוספות

שיכול הואיל וחייב במכה כו'. הוי מצי למימר הואיל וכתיב בעמך כדאמר לעיל במקיים שבעמך: **ומה** מכה אביו כו'. ואם תאמר מה למכה שכן בחנק תאמר במקלל דבסקילה וי"ל דהיא גופה ילפינן השתא דמכה אביו בסקילה מקל וחומר ממקלל ומיהו קשה לבסוף דיליף דמקלל לאחר מיתה חייב נילף ליה שלא נעשה בו שלא בעמך כבעמך ממקלל דחייב ביה לאחר מיתה ומכה פטור דבעינן נפש כדדרשינן לעיל (דף פד:) עד דעביד חבורה: **איש** איש מה תלמוד לומר איש איש. פירשתי שלהי פ' ד' מיתות (לעיל דף סו. ד"ה לרבות): **ושורו** כישראל. לאו לגמרי כישראל דשור של ישראל שנגח לשור של כותי פטור משום דקנסינן להו כדאמר בריש פ' ד' וה' (ב"ק דף לח:) ומיהו לגבי הכי הוי כישראל דשור של כותי שנגח לשור של ישראל תם משלם חצי נזק ומועד נזק שלם ושור של עובד כוכבים שנגח לשור של ישראל בין תם בין מועד משלם נזק שלם: **עד** שיכניסנו לרשותו. משום דכתיב ונמצא בידו ואע"ג דבפ"ק דבבא מציעא (דף י:) גבי גט וגניבה מצרכינן תרי קראי לרבויי ידו לאו דווקא דהוא הדין גגו חצירו קרפיפו דלמא כאן נמי יש שום ריבוי ואפשר דאם הגביהו אפילו ברשות בעלים חייב כדאשכחן גבי גניבה בפרק מרובה (ב"ק דף עט: ושם) דתנן היה מושכו ויוצא כו' אי נמי הכא דפטר ר' שמעון מכרו לקרובים דבעינן שיוציאנו מרשות אחיו כ"ש דברשות בעלים לא מהני כלל:

מונמצא

עין משפט נר מצוה

יז א מיי' פ"ה מהל' ממרים הל' יד סמג לאוין ריט טוש"ע י"ד סי' רמא סעיף ה:

יח ב מיי' שם הלכה יד [וברב אלפס עוד ביבמות פרק ב דף ה: והכי גרס חוץ ממסית ומדיח שהרי אמרה תורה וכו' וכן איתא בשאלתות בלק ס"ס קלד חוץ ממסית ומדיח שהרי וכו']:

יט ג מיי' שם הלכה ה סמג שם טוש"ע שם סעיף א בהג"ה:

כ ד מיי' שם הלכה א טוש"ע שם סעיף א:

כא ה מיי' שם הלכה ה טוש"ע שם בהג"ה:

כב ו מיי' שם הלכה א (טוש"ע שם סעי' א):

כג ז מיי' פ"ט מהלכות גניבה הלכה ב סמג לאוין קכד:

כד ח מיי' שם הלכה ה סמג שם:

כה ט מיי' שם הל' ג:

כו י מיי' שם הלכה ג:

כז כ ל מיי' שם הל' ד:

כח מ נ מיי' שם הל' ו:

כט ס מיי' שם הל' ג:

ל ע מיי' שם הלכה ו:

תורה אור השלם

א) לא תֹאבֶה לוֹ וְלֹא תִשְׁמַע אֵלָיו וְלֹא תָחוֹס עֵינְךָ עָלָיו וְלֹא תַחְמֹל וְלֹא תְכַסֶּה עָלָיו: [דברים יג, ט]

ב) כִּי אִישׁ אִישׁ אֲשֶׁר יְקַלֵּל אֶת אָבִיו וְאֶת אִמּוֹ מוֹת יוּמָת אָבִיו וְאִמּוֹ קִלֵּל דָּמָיו בּוֹ: [ויקרא כ, ט]

ג) וּמְקַלֵּל אָבִיו וְאִמּוֹ מוֹת יוּמָת: [שמות כא, יז]

ד) כִּי יִמָּצֵא אִישׁ גֹּנֵב נֶפֶשׁ מֵאֶחָיו מִבְּנֵי יִשְׂרָאֵל וְהִתְעַמֶּר בּוֹ וּמְכָרוֹ וּמֵת הַגַּנָּב הַהוּא וּבִעַרְתָּ הָרָע מִקִּרְבֶּךָ: [דברים כד, ז]

ה) וְגֹנֵב אִישׁ וּמְכָרוֹ וְנִמְצָא בְיָדוֹ מוֹת יוּמָת: [שמות כא, טז]

מסורת הש"ס

א) מכות יב., ב) [לעיל פד:], ג) [בס"ח סי' תקע"ו אסבריה טעם דחמור מקלל יותר ממכה מפני שבקללה יש היזק לאב לנשמתו], ד) לעיל סו., ה) [שם] ב"מ לד: לה: שבועות כז. חולין עח., ו) [יומא נז: מנחות ל: לא.], ז) [ברכות לא: קדושין יז: וש"נ], ח) [יבמות דף קא.], ט) [מכות ט.], י) יבמות כד: ב"ק לח: נדה נו: חולין ג: קידושין עה., כ) [תוספ' דב"ק פ"ח].

הגהות הב"ח

(א) גמ' אביו ואמו קלל אלא לר' יאשיה:

ליקוטי רש"י

לכל אין הבן נעשה וכו'. לכל עבירות שבתורה אין הבן נעשה שליח ב"ד על אביו לא להלקותו ולא לנדותו חוץ ממסית [מכות יב.]. טומטום. שאין ניכר בו לא זכרות ולא נקבות [ב"ב קכו:]. וכל זמן שלא נקרע מספקינן ליה בזכר ובנקבה. אנדרוגינוס. שיש לו זכרות ונקבות [שם קכז.]. אביו ואמו קלל. לרבות לאחר מיתה [ויקרא כ, ט]. הניחא לר' יונתן. דאמר אע"ג דלא כתיב או כמאן דכתיב או דמי וכל היכא דכתיב פלוני ופלוני או האי או האי משמע. דתניא איש. אשר יקלל את אביו ואת אמו אין לי אלא קלל שניהם אחד מהם מנין. ת"ל. בסיפיה אביו ואמו קלל. אביו קלל ואמו קלל. כלומר בתחלת המקרא סמך קללה לאביו ובסוף המקרא סמך קללה לאמו למימרא דאו האי או האי. ר' יונתן אומר. אביו ואמו משמע נמי או האי או האי וסיפיה דקרא לדרשא אחרינא להביא את המקלל לאחר מיתה שחייב [חולין עח.]. איש איש כי יקלל וגו' לרבות בת. שקללה, או טומטום שקלל. אין לי אלא אביו ואמו. כאחד. אביו שלא אמו ואמו שלא אביו מניין תלמוד לומר אביו ואמו קלל. כלומר סמך קללה בראש המקרא לאביו ובסופו סמך לאמו. ר' יונתן אומר. מתחלת המקרא משמע את אביו ואת אמו דאף על גב דוי"ו מוסיף על ענין ראשון משמע נמי אחד מהם עד שיפרט לך הכתוב יחדיו כדרך שהוצרך לפרוט בכלאים שכתוב בו (דברים כב) לא תחרוש בשור ובחמור ופרט בו יחדיו שלא תאמר אסור לחרוש בשור לבדו ובחמור לבדו ואביו ואמו קלל דסיפא דריש ליה ר' יונתן לקמן באלו הן הנחנקין לרבות את המקלל לאחר מיתה [לעיל סו:]. אביו קלל אמו קלל. בתחילתו סמך קללה לאביו בסופו סמך קללה לאמו. עד שיפרוט לך הכתוב יחד׳ כמו שפרט לך הכתוב (דברים כב) בחורש שור וחמור דמדאיצטריך למיכתב יחדי שמעינן דאי לא כתביה הוה משמע שלא יחרוש לא בשור ולא בחמור ואביו ואמו קלל דריש לה בסנהדרין (פה.) להביא את המקלל לאחר מיתה [ב"מ צד:]. דברה תורה כלשון בני אדם וכו'. ואף על גב דאיכא למדרש לא דרשינן כדמוכח בפ"ב דב"מ (דף לא:) [נדרים ג.]. מקשינן הכאה לקללה. לומר שכשם שאינו לוקה על קללתו דכתיב בעמך כך לא ילקה על הכאתו ופלוגתא היא בסנהדרין דאיכא דמקיש ואיכא דלא מקיש [מכות ט.]. והפסיק הענין וכתב וגונב איש, בין מכה אביו ואמו למקלל אביו ואמו, ונראה לי היינו פלוגתא, דמר סבר מקשינן הכאה לקללה, ומר סבר לא מקשינן [שמות כא, טז]. כותים גירי אריות. כותים אותם שהושיב סנחריב בערי שומרון כדכתיב (מלכים ב יז) ויבא מלך אשור (אנשים מספרויים) מבבל ומכותה וגו' ועל שם שהביאם מכותה נקראו כותים ונתגיירו מאימת האריות כדכתיב (מלכים ב' יז) וישלח (בם את) ה' בהם האריות וגו' וכולה עניניה במלכים [קידושין עד.]. גירי אריות כגון כותים דכתיב בספר מלכים (ב' יז) וישלח ה' בהם את האריות ונתגיירו כדכתיב התם בגלות שומרון [יבמות כד:]. בספר מלכים (ב יז) מפורש וישלח ה' בהם את האריות וכותים כתיבי התם ויבא מלך אשור (אנשים) מכותה וקא חשיב שאר מקומות [ב"ק לח:]. והתעמר בו. אינו חייב עד שישתמש בו [דברים כד, ז]. וגנב איש ומכרו. למה נאמר לפי שנאמר (דברים כד, ז) כי ימצא איש גונב נפש מאחיו אין לי אלא איש שגנב נפש אשה או טומטום או אנדרוגינוס שגנבו מנין תלמוד לומר וגונב איש ומכרו ולפי שנאמר כאן וגונב איש אין לי אלא גונב איש גונב אשה מנין תלמוד לומר (שם) גונב נפש לכך הוצרכו שניהם מה שחסר זה גלה זה [שמות כא, טז].

The Gemara answers:

מִידֵי דַהֲוָה לְאַחַר מִיתָה – It is **just as if** he had pronounced the curse **after** his father's **death,** in which case he is subject to execution.[1] Since a son is punished for cursing his father who has actually died, he is surely punished if his father was merely condemned to die![2]

The Gemara concludes:

מַאי הֲוָה עֲלָה – **How was the question resolved?** May someone be appointed by the court to flog his parent or not? אָמַר רַבָּה בַּר רַב הוּנָא – **Rabbah bar Rav Huna said,** וְכֵן תָּנָא דְּבֵי רַבִּי יִשְׁמָעֵאל – **and so it was taught in a Baraisa of the academy of R' Yishmael:** לַכֹּל – If a man was sentenced **for any** sin, אֵין הַבֵּן נַעֲשֶׂה שָׁלִיחַ לְאָבִיו לְהַכּוֹתוֹ וּלְקַלְלוֹ – the law is that **the** man's **son may not be appointed** to be **an agent** of the court **to** punish **his father,** that is, **to strike him or to curse [him]** חוּץ מִמֵּסִית – **except for one who instigates others** to engage in idolatry. The son of such a person *may* be appointed by the court to carry out the execution שֶׁהֲרֵי אָמְרָה תּוֹרָה ,,וְלֹא־תַחְמֹל וְלֹא־תְכַסֶּה עָלָיו" – **for the Torah has stated** regarding an instigator:[3] ***You shall not be compassionate nor conceal him.***[4]

Mishnah

The previous Mishnah listed transgressions for which one is punished with strangulation. The coming Mishnahs explain the transgressions in more detail:

הַמַּכֶּה אָבִיו וְאִמּוֹ – **One who strikes his father or mother** אֵינוֹ חַיָּיב עַד שֶׁיַּעֲשֶׂה בָּהֶן חַבּוּרָה – **is not liable** to execution **unless he wounds them.**[5]

זֶה חוֹמֶר בִּמְקַלֵּל מִבְּמַכֶּה – **This,** then, is a **stringency of one who curses** his parent **over one who strikes** him; שֶׁהַמְקַלֵּל לְאַחַר מִיתָה חַיָּיב – **that** is, **one who curses** his parent **after** the parent's **death is liable** to execution,[6] וְהַמַּכֶּה לְאַחַר מִיתָה פָּטוּר – **but one who strikes** his parent **after** the parent's **death is exempt.**[7]

Gemara

The Mishnah stated that one is punished for cursing a parent who has died. The Gemara cites the source of this ruling:

תָּנוּ רַבָּנָן – **The Rabbis taught in a Baraisa:** ,,אָבִיו וְאִמּוֹ קִלֵּל" – Scripture writes a redundant clause:[8] ***HIS FATHER OR HIS MOTHER HE HAS CURSED.*** לְאַחַר מִיתָה – This teaches that the prohibition against cursing a parent applies even **AFTER** the parent's **DEATH.**

NOTES

1. The Gemara below derives this exegetically.

2. But since one is not punished for cursing a dead person who is not his parent, he is likewise not punished for cursing a condemned man. This explains why the Baraisa states that the condemned man's son is liable for cursing him but anyone else is not liable.

Rashi notes that it is indeed understandable why a son is liable for *cursing* his condemned father, since one is punished for cursing his father even after the father's death. However, one is punished only for striking a father while the father is alive. Why then, *Rashi* asks, is a son liable for *striking* his condemned father? *Rashi* answers that a son who strikes his dead father is exempt only due to a technicality: A son is never punished for striking his father unless the father is wounded, and it is impossible to wound a dead man. Accordingly, since a father who is merely condemned to die *can* be wounded, the son is indeed punished if he does so (see also below, note 7).

This concludes the Gemara's discussion of the second Baraisa cited on 85a. That discussion can be summarized as follows:

The Baraisa's case: Someone who was sentenced to death is being led to execution.

First ruling: If the condemned man's child strikes or curses him, the son is liable.

Second ruling: If anyone but a son strikes or curses him, he is exempt.

Rav Chisda's interpretation: The condemned man was struck by a court officer forcing him to go to execution. If the officer was not the man's child, he is merely acting as an agent of the court and is therefore exempt from punishment. If he is the man's child, however, he is forbidden to strike or curse his father even as an agent of the court, and he is therefore punished if he does so.

Rav Sheishess: Rejects Rav Chisda's interpretation, asserting that one is in fact permitted to strike or curse his father as an agent of the court. Instead, he interprets the Baraisa to be discussing a man who went to execution willingly. This makes the second ruling difficult to understand; why should the striker be exempt if he hit the condemned man for no reason? The Gemara then suggests four ways in which Rav Sheishess might interpret the Baraisa, but rejects the first three:

1) A condemned man is considered legally dead. Since one incurs no monetary liability for striking such a person, this indicates that the striking is legally insignificant and for this reason, he is also exempt from lashes. Only a son, who is liable for acts even against a dead parent, is punished.

This interpretation is rejected, based on Rav Sheishess' ruling that if someone disgraces a sleeping man who then dies, he *is* obligated to pay.

2) Baraisa exempts a person who struck someone and caused damage amounting to less than a *perutah* unless the damaged party was his father.

This explanation, too, is rejected, for R' Yochanan states that one *is* flogged for striking someone when the damage caused amounts to less than a *perutah*.

3) The Baraisa exempts one for striking or cursing a condemned man who does not keep all the mitzvos.

This explanation is rejected as well, for a son would also be exempt for striking or cursing such a man.

4) The verse exegetically indicates that there is no punishment for striking or cursing an ordinary person who is condemned to die. But one *is* punished for doing these things to his parent since he would be liable for doing such acts even after the parent actually died.

3. *Deuteronomy* 13:9.

4. I.e. have no mercy upon an instigator; just kill him. The section of the Torah dealing with instigation to idolatry opens with a verse discussing someone who instigates any of several relatives, including a father who instigates his son (see *Sifri* and *Rashi* to *Deuteronomy* 13:7 ד״ה אשר כנפשך). Two verses later, the Torah forbids showing compassion to the instigator, and commands the one who was instigated to participate in the execution. This teaches that even the son of an instigator may carry out the execution as an agent of the court (*Toras Chaim*). [For an explanation as to why a son may not strike or curse his father to carry out the court's sentence for any other crime, see *Rosh* to *Yevamos* ch. 2 §3, *Tur Yoreh Deah* 241 and *Bach* there, *Shulchan Aruch* 241:4 with *Beur HaGra*; cf. *Chidushei HaRan* here.]

5. I.e. unless he causes internal or external bleeding (see *Bava Kamma* 86a). If he strikes a parent without wounding him, he does not commit the capital crime of striking a parent, but he does transgress the general prohibition against striking any Jew (*Rambam, Hil. Mamrim* 5:5, *Meiri* to *Bava Kama* 87a).

6. The Gemara will cite the Mishnah's source (*Rashi*).

7. [This stringency is based on the first law of the Mishnah: One is punished for striking a parent only if he inflicts a wound (*Toras Chaim*).] Since a person cannot be wounded after death, one is not liable for striking his dead parent (*Rashi*; cf. *Meiri*). Thus, even if he punctures the parent's cadaver and thereby causes the blood to emerge, he is still not liable.

8. *Leviticus* 20:9. The verse in full states: כִּי־אִישׁ אִישׁ אֲשֶׁר יְקַלֵּל אֶת־אָבִיו וְאֶת־אִמּוֹ מוֹת יוּמָת אָבִיו וְאִמּוֹ קִלֵּל דָּמָיו בּוֹ, *For any man* (literally: a man, a man) *who will curse his father or his mother shall be put to death; his father or his mother he has cursed, his blood is upon himself.* Once the verse states *for any man who will curse his father or his mother,* the final clause *his father or his mother he has cursed* is redundant (*Rashi*). [The Gemara below will expound the redundancy of *a man, a man* that appears in the first clause.]

מידי דהוה לאחר מיתה מאי הוה עלה
א) אמר רבה בר רב הונא וכן תנא דבי רבי
ישמעאל א לכל אין הבן נעשה שליח לאביו
להכותו ולקללו ב חוץ ממסית שהרי אמרה
תורה א) לא תחמול ולא תכסה עליו:
מתני' ג המכה אביו ואמו אינו חייב עד
שיעשה בהן חבורה זה חומר במקלל מבמכה
ד שהמקלל לאחר מיתה חייב ה והמכה לאחר
מיתה פטור: גמ' ת"ר ב) אביו ואמו קלל
לאחר מיתה שיכול הואיל וחייב במכה
וחייב במקלל מה מכה אינו חייב אלא מחיים
אף המקלל אינו חייב אלא מחיים ועוד ק"ו
ומה מכה שעשה בו שלא בעמך כבעמך
לא חייב בו לאחר מיתה מקלל שלא עשה
בו שלא בעמך כבעמך אינו דין שלא חייב
בו לאחר מיתה ת"ל אביו ואמו קלל לאחר
מיתה הניחא לר' יונתן דמייתר ליה קרא
אביו ואמו (א) אלא לר' יאשיה מאי איכא למימר
ד) דתניא ב) איש איש מה ת"ל איש איש
ו לרבות בת טומטום ואנדרוגינוס ב) אשר יקלל
את אביו ואת אמו ה) אין לי אלא אביו ואמו
אביו שלא אמו אמו שלא אביו מניין ת"ל
אביו ואמו קלל אביו קלל אמו קלל דברי ר'
יאשיה ר' יונתן אומר משמע שניהן כאחד
ומשמע אחד ואחד בפני עצמו ו) עד שיפרט
לך הכתוב יחדיו מנא ליה נפקא ליה ג) מומקלל
אביו ואמו מות יומת ואידך ההוא מיבעי
ליה לרבות בת טומטום ואנדרוגינוס ותיפוק
ליה מאיש איש ז) דברה תורה כלשון בני אדם וליתני חומר במכה מבמקלל
שהמכה עשה בו שלא בעמך כבעמך משא"כ במקלל קסבר ח) מקשינן הכאה
לקללה לימא הני תנאי כהני תנאי דתני חדא כותי אתה מצווה על הכאתו
ואי אתה מצווה על קללתו ותניא אידך אי אתה מצווה לא על קללתו ולא
על הכאתו סברוה דכולי עלמא כותים גירי אמת הן מאי לאו בהא קמיפלגי
דמר סבר מקשינן הכאה לקללה ומר סבר ט) לא מקשינן הכאה לקללה לא
דכ"ע לא מקשינן הכאה לקללה והכא בהא קמיפלגי מר סבר כותים גירי אמת
הן ומר סבר י) כותים גירי אריות הן אי הכי היינו דקתני עלה ושורו כישראל
אלא שמע מינה בהיקישא פליגי ש"מ: מתני' ז הגונב נפש מישראל אינו
חייב עד שיכניסנו לרשותו רבי יהודה אומר עד שיכניסנו לרשותו וישתמש
בו שנאמר ד) והתעמר בו ומכרו הגונב את בנו רבי ישמעאל בנו של ר'
יוחנן בן ברוקה מחייב וחכמים פוטרין ח פוטרין גנב מי שחציו עבד וחציו בן חורין ר'
יהודה מחייב וחכמים פוטרין: גמ' ותנא קמא לא בעי עימור א"ר אחא בריה
דרבא ט עימור פחות משוה פרוטה איכא בינייהו י בעי ר' ירמיה גנבו ומכרו ישן
מהו כ מכר אשה לעוברה מהו יש דרך עימור בכך או אין דרך עימור בכך
ותיפוק ליה דליכא עימור כלל לא צריכא ישן דזגא עליה אשה דאוקמא באפי
זיקא דרך עימור בכך או ל אין דרך עימור בכך מאי תיקו ת"ר ד) כי ימצא איש
גונב נפש מאחיו אין לי אלא איש מניין ת"ל ה) וגונב איש אין לי
אלא איש שגנב בין אשה ובין איש ואשה שגנבה איש אשה שגנבה אשה
מניין ת"ל ד) ומת הגנב ההוא מ מכל מקום תניא אידך כ) כי ימצא איש גונב נפש
מאחיו אחד הגונב את האיש ואחד הגונב את האשה נ ואחד גר ואחד עבד
משוחרר וקטן חייב ס גנבו ולא מכרו מכרו ועדיין ישנו ברשותו פטור מכרו
לאביו או לאחיו או לאחד מן הקרובים חייב ע הגונב את העבדים פטור
תני

מידי דהוה לאחר מיתה. דילפינן לקמן מקלל לאחר מיתה חייב וא"ת והתנן מכה לאחר מיתה פטור והכא מיחייב ליה אהכאה דקתני הכהו וקללו היינו טעמא דפטור מכה לאחר מיתה משום דבעינן חבורה ולאחר מיתה ליכא חבורה דליכא נפש דנפקא ליה לעיל מנפש ויוצא ליהרג איכא חבורה דחי הוא אלא דסופו למות: מתני' שהמקלל לאחר מיתה חייב. כדיליף בגמרא: והמכה לאחר מיתה פטור. דחבורה ליכא: גמ' אביו ואמו קלל. קרא יתירא הוא דהא כתיב רישיה דקרא אשר יקלל את אביו ואת אמו: מכה שעשה שלא בעמך כבעמך. דגבי הכאה לא כתיב בעמך למעוטי שאינו עושה מעשה עמך והאי תנא סבר לא מקשינן הכאה לקללה מפני המקרא המפסיק בינתים: לא חייב בו לאחר מיתה. דהא חבורה כתיב: לרבות בת. טומטום ואנדרוגינוס: אין לי אלא אביו ואמו. שניהם יחד: אביו קילל ואמו קילל. בראש המקרא סמך קללה לאביו ובסוף סמך לאמו: עד שיפרט לך הכתוב יחדו. וכמו שפרט בחורש בשור ובחמור מדפרט לך ש"מ דאי לא הוי יחדו הוה משמע שור לבדו וחמור לבדו והא אביו ואמו דרישא דרשינן נמי או אביו או אמו וסיפא לאתויי לאחר מיתה: מומקלל אביו. דואלה המשפטים: ואידך. דמפיק לאחר מיתה מאביו ואמו קילל: וליתני נמי וכו'. אמתניתין קאי דקתני זה חומר במקלל מבמכה: לימא הני תנאי. תנא דמתניתין דלא תנא חומר במכה שעשה בו שלא בעמך כבעמך ותנא דברייתא דלעיל דתנא ומה מכה שעשה בו: גירי אמת הן. מתחילתן גרים גמורים היו ועכשיו הרשיעו וישראל שאינו עושה מעשה עמך הוא וכי היכי דעל קללתו פטור על הכאתו נמי פטור: גירי אריות הן. והרי הם כעובדי כוכבים גמורים: אי הכי. דטעמא דפטור משום דגירי אריות הן: היינו דתנא עלה. בתמיה בהך מתני' דקתני אינו מצווה לא על הכאתו ולא על קללתו קתני ושורו כישראל שור שלנו שנגח את שורו ושורו שנגח שלנו תם משלם חצי נזק ומועד משלם נזק שלם ואילו דעובד כוכבים תנן שור של ישראל שנגח שור של עובד כוכבים פטור ושל עובד כוכבים שנגח שור של ישראל בין תם בין מועד משלם נזק שלם: מתני' שיכניסנו לרשותו. דכתיב (שמות כב) ונמצא בידו ותניא במכילתא ונמצא אין מציאה בכל מקום אלא בעדים בידו אין בידו אלא ברשותו וכן הוא אומר (במדבר כא) ויקח את כל ארצו מידו: גמ' עמור. שמוש: גנבו ומכרו כשהוא ישן מהו. לקמן מפרש לה הבעיא: מכר אשה לעוברה. גנב אשה מעוברת ומכרה לעוברה שלא מכר הגוף שלה אלא שיהא עובר מכור: דליכא עימור. לא בישן ולא בעובר: דזגא עליה. דסמך עליו: דאוקמא באפי זיקא. וכל כמה שהיא עבה מועיל יותר להגין בפני הרוח: אין לי אלא איש. כשהגנב איש: וגונב איש. שהנגנב איש ולא אשה וקרא קמא דלא קפיד אגונב למהוי איש דכתיב נפש הלכך אין לי אלא איש שגנב בין איש בין אשה דהיכא דגנב הוי איש כתוב גונב נפש ואשה שגנבה איש דכתיב וגונב איש וגונב אפילו אשה גונבת משמע: הגנב. מ"מ והוא דרשינן ליה בספרי למעוטי גונב עבד: ועדיין ישנו ברשותו. ברשות הנגנב עצמו שעדיין לא הכניסו גנב לרשותו: פטור. שהרי לא גנבו: לאביו. אביו של נגנב:
תני

שיכול הואיל וחייב במכה כו'. הוי מצי למימר הואיל וכתיב בעמך כדאמר לעיל במקיים שבעמך: ומה מכה אביו כו'. ואם תאמר מה למכה שכן בחנק תאמר במקלל דבסקילה וי"ל דהיא גופה ילפינן השתא דמכה אביו בסקילה מקל וחומר ממקלל ומיהו קשה לבסוף דיליף דמקלל לאחר מיתה חייב נילף ליה שלא נעשה בו שלא בעמך כבעמך ממקלל דחייב ביה לאחר מיתה ומכה פטור דבעינן נפש כדדרשינן לעיל (דף פד:) עד דעביד חבורה: איש איש מה תלמוד לומר איש איש. פירשתי שלהי פ' ד' מיתות (לעיל דף סו. ד"ה לרבות): ושורו כישראל. לאו לגמרי כישראל דשור של ישראל שנגח לשור של כותי פטור משום דקנסינן להו כדאמר בריש פ' ד' וה' (ב"ק דף לז:) ומיהו לגבי הכי הוי כישראל דשור של כותי שנגח לשור של ישראל תם משלם חצי נזק ומועד נזק שלם ושור של עובד כוכבים שנגח לשור של ישראל בין תם בין מועד משלם נזק שלם: עד שיכניסנו לרשותו. משום דכתיב ונמצא בידו ואע"ג דבפ"ק דבבא מציעא (דף י:) גבי גט וגניבה מצרכינן תרי קראי לרבויי ידו לאו דווקא דהוא הדין גגו חצירו קרפיפו דלמא כאן נמי יש שום ריבוי ואפשר דאם הגביהו אפילו ברשות בעלים חייב כדאשכחן גבי גניבה בפרק מרובה (ב"ק דף עט: ושם) דתנן היה מושכו ויוצא כו' אי נמי הכא דפטר ר' שמעון מכרו לקרובים דבעינן שיוציאנו מרשות אחיו כ"ש דברשות בעלים לא מהני כלל:
מונמצא

עין משפט
נר מצוה

יז א מיי' פ"ה מהל' ממרים הל' יד סמג לאוין ריט טוש"ע י"ד סי' רמא סעיף ה:
יח ב מיי' שם הלכה יד [וברב אלפס עוד ביבמות פרק ב דף ה: והכי גרס חוץ ממסית ומדיח שהרי אמרה תורה וכו' וכן איתא בשאילתות בלק ס"ס קלד חוץ ממסית ומדיח שהרי וכו']:
יט ג מיי' שם הלכה ה סמג שם טוש"ע שם סעיף א בהג"ה:
כ ד מיי' שם הלכה א טוש"ע שם סעיף א:
כא ה מיי' שם הלכה ה טוש"ע שם בהג"ה:
כב ו מיי' שם הלכה א (טוש"ע שם סעי' א):
כג ז מיי' פ"ט מהלכות גניבה הלכה ב סמג לאוין קכד:
כד ח מיי' שם הלכה ה סמג שם:
כה ט מיי' שם הל' ב:
כו י מיי' שם הלכה ג:
כז כ ל מיי' שם הל' ד:
כח מ נ מיי' שם הל' ו:
כט ס מיי' שם הל' ג:
ל ע מיי' שם הלכה ו:

תורה אור השלם

א) לֹא תֹאבֶה לוֹ וְלֹא תִשְׁמַע אֵלָיו וְלֹא תָחוֹס עֵינְךָ עָלָיו וְלֹא תַחְמֹל וְלֹא תְכַסֶּה עָלָיו: [דברים יג, ט]

ב) כִּי אִישׁ אִישׁ אֲשֶׁר יְקַלֵּל אֶת אָבִיו וְאֶת אִמּוֹ מוֹת יוּמָת אָבִיו וְאִמּוֹ קִלֵּל דָּמָיו בּוֹ: [ויקרא כ, ט]

ג) וּמְקַלֵּל אָבִיו וְאִמּוֹ מוֹת יוּמָת: [שמות כא, יז]

ד) כִּי יִמָּצֵא אִישׁ גֹּנֵב נֶפֶשׁ מֵאֶחָיו מִבְּנֵי יִשְׂרָאֵל וְהִתְעַמֶּר בּוֹ וּמְכָרוֹ וּמֵת הַגַּנָּב הַהוּא וּבִעַרְתָּ הָרָע מִקִּרְבֶּךָ: [דברים כד, ז]

ה) וְגֹנֵב אִישׁ וּמְכָרוֹ וְנִמְצָא בְיָדוֹ מוֹת יוּמָת: [שמות כא, טז]

מסורת הש"ס

א) מכות יב., ב) [לעיל פד:], ג) [בס"ח סי' תקע"ו אסבריה טעם דחמור מקלל יותר ממכה מפני שבקללה יש היזק לאב לנשמתו], ד) לעיל סו., ה) [שם] ב"מ לד: לה: שבועות כז. חולין עח., ו) [יומא נז: מנחות ל: לא.], ז) [ברכות לא: קדושין יז: וש"נ], ח) [יבמות דף קא.], ט) [מכות ט.], י) יבמות כד: ב"ק לח: נדה נו: חולין ג: קידושין עה:, כ) [תוספ' דב"ק פ"ח].

הגהות הב"ח

(א) גמ' אביו ואמו קלל אלא לר' יאשיה:

ליקוטי רש"י

לכל אין הבן נעשה וכו'. לכל עבירות שבתורה אין הבן נעשה שליח ב"ד על אביו לא להלקותו ולא לנדותו חוץ ממסית [מכות יב.]. טומטום. שאין ניכר בו לא זכרות ולא נקבות [ב"ב קכו:]. וכל זמן שלא נקרע מספקינן ליה בזכר ובנקבה. אנדרוגינוס. שיש לו זכרות ונקבות [שם קכז.]. אביו ואמו קלל. לרבות לאחר מיתה [ויקרא כ, ט]. הניחא לר' יונתן. דאמר אע"ג דלא כתיב או כמאן דכתיב או דמי וכל היכא דכתיב פלוני ופלוני או האי או האי משמע. דתניא איש. אשר יקלל את אביו ואת אמו אין לי אלא קלל שניהם אחד מהם מנין. ת"ל. בסיפיה אביו ואמו קלל. אביו קלל ואמו קלל. כלומר בתחלת המקרא סמך קללה לאביו ובסוף המקרא סמך קללה לאמו למימרא דאו האי או האי. ר' יונתן אומר. אביו ואמו משמע נמי או האי או האי וסיפיה דקרא לדרשא אחרינא להביא את המקלל לאחר מיתה שחייב [חולין עח.]. איש איש כי יקלל וגו' לרבות בת. שקללה, או טומטום שקלל. אין לי אלא אביו ואמו. כאחד. אביו שלא אמו ואמו שלא אביו מניין תלמוד לומר אביו ואמו קלל. כלומר סמך קללה בראש המקרא לאביו ובסופו סמך לאמו. ר' יונתן אומר. מתחלת המקרא משמע את אביו ואת אמו דאף על גב דוי"ו מוסיף על ענין ראשון משמע נמי אחד מהם עד שיפרט לך הכתוב יחדיו כדרך שהוצרך לפרוט בכלאים שכתוב בו (דברים כב) לא תחרוש בשור ובחמור ופרט בו יחדיו שלא תאמר אסור לחרוש בשור לבדו ובחמור לבדו ואביו ואמו קלל דסיפא דריש ליה ר' יונתן לקמן באלו הן הנחנקין לרבות את המקלל לאחר מיתה [לעיל סו:]. אביו קלל אמו קלל. בתחילתו סמך קללה לאביו בסופו סמך קללה לאמו. עד שיפרוט לך הכתוב יחד׳ כמו שפרט לך הכתוב (דברים כב) בחורש שור וחמור דמדאיצטריך למיכתב יחדיו שמעינן דאי לא כתביה הוה משמע שלא יחרוש לא בשור ולא

בחמור ואביו ואמו קלל דריש לה בסנהדרין (פה:) להביא את המקלל לאחר מיתה [ב"מ צד:]. דברה תורה כלשון בני אדם וכו'. ואף על גב דאיכא למדרש לא דרשינן כדמוכח בפ"ב דב"מ (דף לא:) [נדרים ג.]. מקשינן הכאה לקללה. לומר שכשם שאינו לוקה על קללתו דכתיב בעמך כך לא ילקה על הכאתו ופלוגתא היא בסנהדרין דאיכא דמקיש ואיכא דלא מקיש [מכות ט.]. והפסיק הענין וכתב וגונב איש, בין מכה אביו ואמו למקלל אביו ואמו, ונראה לי היינו פלוגתא, דמר סבר מקשינן הכאה לקללה, ומר סבר לא מקשינן [שמות כא, טז]. כותים גירי אריות. כותים אותם שהושיב סנחריב בערי שומרון כדכתיב (מלכים ב יז) ויבא מלך אשור (אנשים מספרוים) מבבל ומכותה וגו' ועל שם שהביאם מכותה נקראו כותים ונתגיירו מאימת האריות כדכתיב (מלכים ב' יז) וישלח (בם את) ה' בהם האריות וגו' וכולה ענייה במלכים [קידושין עד.]. גירי אריות כגון כותים דכתיב בספר מלכים (ב' יז) וישלח ה' בהם את האריות ונתגיירו כדכתיב התם בגלות שומרון [יבמות כד:]. בספר מלכים (ב יז) מפורש וישלח ה' בהם את האריות וכותים כתיבי התם ויבא מלך אשור (אנשים) מכותה וקא חשיב שאר מקומות [ב"ק לח:]. והתעמר בו. אינו חייב עד שישתמש בו [דברים כד, ז]. וגנב איש ומכרו. למה נאמר לפי שנאמר (דברים כד, ז) כי ימצא איש גונב נפש מאחיו אין לי אלא איש שגנב נפש אשה או טומטום או אנדרוגינוס שגנבו מנין תלמוד לומר וגונב איש ומכרו ולפי שנאמר כאן וגונב איש גונב אשה מנין תלמוד לומר (שם) גונב נפש לכך הוצרכו שניהם מה שחסר זה גלה זה [שמות כא, טז].

The Baraisa cites two reasons why this derivation is necessary:[9] שֶׁיָּכוֹל – FOR I COULD HAVE thought הוֹאִיל וְחַיָּיב בְּמַכֶּה וְחַיָּיב בִּמְקַלֵּל – that SINCE ONE IS LIABLE FOR STRIKING a parent AND ONE IS LIABLE FOR CURSING a parent, we can draw the following analogy: מַה מַּכֶּה אֵינוֹ חַיָּיב אֶלָּא מֵחַיִּים – JUST AS ONE WHO STRIKES a parent IS NOT LIABLE UNLESS the parent was struck DURING his LIFETIME, אַף הַמְקַלֵּל אֵינוֹ חַיָּיב אֶלָּא מֵחַיִּים – SO TOO, ONE WHO CURSES a parent SHOULD NOT BE LIABLE UNLESS the parent was cursed DURING his LIFETIME. וְעוֹד – AND FURTHERMORE, קַל וָחוֹמֶר – I could have advanced the following *KAL VACHOMER*:[10] וּמַה מַּכֶּה – IF concerning the prohibition against STRIKING a parent, שֶׁעָשָׂה בּוֹ שֶׁלֹּא בְעַמְּךָ כִּבְעַמְּךָ – WHERE [THE TORAH] stringently EQUATED a parent WHO IS NOT included IN the term *YOUR NATION* (i.e. a sinner) WITH ONE WHO IS included IN *YOUR NATION*,[11] לֹא חִיֵּיב בּוֹ לְאַחַר מִיתָה – [THE TORAH] DID NOT MAKE [A SON] LIABLE for striking a parent AFTER the parent's DEATH; מְקַלֵּל – then concerning the prohibition against CURSING a parent, שֶׁלֹּא עָשָׂה בּוֹ שֶׁלֹּא בְעַמְּךָ כִּבְעַמְּךָ – WHERE [THE TORAH] was lenient in that it DID NOT EQUATE a parent WHO IS NOT included IN the term *YOUR NATION* WITH ONE WHO IS included IN *YOUR NATION*,[12] אֵינוֹ דִּין שֶׁלֹּא חִיֵּיב בּוֹ לְאַחַר מִיתָה – IS IT NOT CERTAIN THAT [THE TORAH] DOES NOT HOLD [A SON] LIABLE for cursing his parent AFTER the parent's DEATH![13] תַּלְמוּד לוֹמַר ,,אָבִיו וְאִמּוֹ קִלֵּל'' – SCRIPTURE therefore TAUGHT a redundant clause: *HIS FATHER OR HIS MOTHER HE HAS CURSED*. לְאַחַר מִיתָה – This teaches that one who curses AFTER his parent's DEATH is liable to execution.[14]

The Gemara analyzes this exposition:

הָנִיחָא לְרַבִּי יוֹנָתָן – This is understandable according to R' Yonasan, דְּמִיַּיתַּר לֵיהּ קְרָא ,,אָבִיו וְאִמּוֹ'' **– for** according to **him the verse *his father or his mother* he has cursed is extra.** אֶלָּא לְרַבִּי יֹאשִׁיָּה **– But according to R' Yoshiyah,** who states that the verse is not extra, מַאי אִיכָּא לְמֵימַר **– what is there to say?** How do we know that one is punished for cursing a dead parent?

The Gemara first cites the Baraisa that records R' Yoshiyah's view, and then returns to complete its question:

דְּתַנְיָא **– For it has been taught in a Baraisa:** ,,אִישׁ אִישׁ'' – Scripture states:[15] *A MAN, A MAN*. מַה תַּלְמוּד לוֹמַר ,,אִישׁ אִישׁ'' – WHY DID THE TORAH STATE repetitively *A MAN, A MAN*? לְרַבּוֹת בַּת טוּמְטוּם וְאַנְדְּרוֹגִינוֹס – The Torah uses the repetitive expression TO INCLUDE A DAUGHTER, A *TUMTUM* AND AN ANDROGYNE among those who are liable to be put to death if they curse their parents.[16] ,,אֲשֶׁר יְקַלֵּל אֶת־אָבִיו וְאֶת־אִמּוֹ'' – The verse then states: *WHO WILL CURSE HIS FATHER AND HIS MOTHER shall be put to death.* אֵין לִי אֶלָּא אָבִיו וְאִמּוֹ – I HAVE ESTABLISHED ONLY that one is liable to capital punishment if he curses HIS FATHER AND HIS MOTHER together. אָבִיו שֶׁלֹּא אִמּוֹ אִמּוֹ שֶׁלֹּא אָבִיו מִנַּיִין – But FROM WHERE can I derive that one is similarly liable if he curses HIS FATHER WITHOUT cursing HIS MOTHER, or he curses HIS MOTHER WITHOUT cursing HIS FATHER? תַּלְמוּד לוֹמַר ,,אָבִיו וְאִמּוֹ קִלֵּל'' – SCRIPTURE therefore STATES further in that same verse: *HIS FATHER AND HIS MOTHER HE HAS CURSED.* אָבִיו קִלֵּל אִמּוֹ קִילֵּל – The carefully phrased repetitions teach that one is liable if HE CURSED HIS FATHER separately or if HE CURSED HIS MOTHER separately.[17] דִּבְרֵי רַבִּי יֹאשִׁיָּה – THESE ARE THE WORDS OF R' YOSHIYAH. רַבִּי יוֹנָתָן אוֹמֵר – R' YONASAN SAYS: מַשְׁמַע שְׁנֵיהֶן כְּאֶחָד – When a verse states a law regarding two subjects and connects the subjects with the conjunction *vav*, IT IMPLIES that the law is applicable to BOTH of them TOGETHER וּמַשְׁמַע אֶחָד וְאֶחָד בִּפְנֵי עַצְמוֹ – AND IT also IMPLIES that the law is applicable to either ONE of them BY ITSELF, עַד שֶׁיְּפָרֵט לְךָ הַכָּתוּב ,,יַחְדָּיו'' – UNLESS SCRIPTURE SPECIFIES FOR YOU that it applies to both of them *TOGETHER*.[18]

NOTES

9. That is, it would seem that once the Torah enacted a prohibition against cursing a parent, we would simply *assume* that this prohibition remains in effect after the parent's death. However, the Baraisa gives two reasons as to why we would have limited the prohibition to the parent's lifetime if the derivation had not indicated otherwise.

10. A *kal vachomer* is an a fortiori argument, one of the thirteen methods of Biblical exegesis. In this Baraisa, it involves the following reasoning: If a particular leniency applies in a usually stringent case, it must surely apply in a less stringent case as well.

11. That is, the prohibition against striking a parent is stringent in that one is punished for striking *any* parent; the Torah makes no distinction between a sinful parent — who is not considered *in your nation* (see 85a note 23) — and a law-abiding one (*Exodus* 21:15). But although the prohibition is stringent in this sense, one is not punished for striking a parent who is dead (*Rashi*).

Rashi notes that on 85a the Gemara did distinguish between striking sinful parents and law-abiding ones based on a *hekeish* to the law of cursing. Evidently, *Rashi* asserts, the Tanna of this Baraisa rejects the *hekeish* between striking and cursing because the verses discussing these subjects are separated by another verse (see 85a note 22). Without the *hekeish*, we must assume that there is no difference whether the struck parent was law-abiding or not, since the verse does not explicitly differentiate between the two.

12. That is, the Torah imposed a punishment only for cursing a law-abiding parent but not for cursing a sinful one.

13. In short, the Gemara's argument is as follows: The prohibition against striking a parent applies even if the parent is sinful, whereas the prohibition against cursing does not. Having thus established that the prohibition against striking is more stringent, we may advance the following *kal vachomer*: The prohibition against striking is relatively stringent, and yet one is not punished for striking a dead parent. Is it not logical, then, that since cursing is relatively lenient, one is surely not punished for cursing a dead parent!? [*Chidushei HaRan* notes that there is a practical reason for not punishing one who strikes a dead parent that does not apply to cursing: A dead parent cannot be wounded and there is no punishment for striking a parent without wounding him. Nevertheless, the Baraisa argues that the prohibition against striking, which is more stringent, in fact applies only during the parent's lifetime. Thus, if the more lenient prohibition against cursing applied even after the parent's death, the Torah should have explicitly said so.]

14. In other words, the superfluous verse teaches us that in spite of the *kal vachomer*, one is punished for cursing a parent after the parent's death.

15. *Leviticus* 20:9.

16. A *tumtum* is a person whose reproductive organs are enclosed within the body. Such a person is of unknown gender. An androgyne is a person with both male and female genitals.

Ordinarily, we would expound the word *man* to *exclude* someone who is not a man, i.e. a daughter, a person of indeterminate gender, and an androgynous person. However, the rule is אֵין מִיעוּט אַחַר מִיעוּט אֶלָּא לְרַבּוֹת: Two exclusionary terms, placed one after the other, have the effect of a double negative; they *include* that which they seem to exclude. Thus, the double exclusion *a man, a man* teaches that even a daughter, a person of indeterminate gender or an androgyne is punished for cursing his parent (see *Tosafos* and *Yad Ramah* to 66a).

17. The first part of the verse juxtaposes יְקַלֵּל (*will curse*) and אָבִיו (*his father*); the second part juxtaposes קִלֵּל (*has cursed*) and אִמּוֹ (*his mother*). This unusual construction intimates that a child is liable for cursing either parent separately. [Had the Torah stated only one of the phrases and joined *his father* and *his mother* with the conjunction ו, we would have translated the ו as *and*, and would have interpreted the verse to mean that the child must curse his father *and* mother together in order to be liable] (see *Rashi*).

18. R' Yonasan is referring to the language of the prohibition stated in *Deuteronomy* (22:10): לֹא־תַחֲרֹשׁ בְּשׁוֹר־וּבַחֲמֹר יַחְדָּו, *You shall not plow with an ox and a donkey together.* Since according to him וּבַחֲמֹר can mean *or with a donkey*, R' Yonasan holds that had the Torah not stated *together,* we would think that plowing with either beast individually is also forbidden (see *Ritva* to *Bava Metzia* 94b). It is only because the Torah specified *an ox and a donkey together* that the prohibition is limited to where beasts of different species pull the plow together. Similarly, in the

מידי דהוה לאחר מיתה מאי הוה עלה א) אמר רבה בר רב הונא וכן תנא דבי רבי ישמעאל א לכל אין הבן נעשה שליח לאביו להכותו ולקללו ב חוץ ממסית שהרי אמרה תורה א) לא תחמול ולא תכסה עליו: **מתני'** ב) ג המכה אביו ואמו אינו חייב עד שיעשה בהן חבורה זה חומר במקלל מבמכה ד שהמקלל לאחר מיתה חייב ג) ה והמכה לאחר מיתה פטור: **גמ'** ת"ר ב) אביו ואמו קלל לאחר מיתה שיכול הואיל וחייב במכה וחייב במקלל מה מכה אינו חייב אלא מחיים אף המקלל אינו חייב אלא מחיים ועוד ק"ו ומה מכה שעשה בו שלא בעמך כבעמך לא חייב בו לאחר מיתה מקלל שלא עשה בו שלא בעמך כבעמך אינו דין שלא חייב בו לאחר מיתה ת"ל אביו ואמו קלל לאחר מיתה הניחא לר' יונתן דמייתר ליה קרא אביו ואמו (א) אלא לר' יאשיה מאי איכא למימר ד) דתניא ב) איש איש מה ת"ל איש איש ו לרבות בת טומטום ואנדרוגינוס ב) אשר יקלל את אביו ואת אמו ה) אין לי אלא אביו ואמו אביו שלא אמו אמו שלא אביו מניין ת"ל אביו ואמו קלל אביו קלל אמו קלל דברי ר' יאשיה ר' יונתן אומר משמע שניהן כאחד ומשמע אחד ואחד בפני עצמו ו) עד שיפרט לך הכתוב יחדו מנא ליה נפקא ליה ג) מומקלל אביו ואמו מות יומת ואידך ההוא מיבעי ליה לרבות בת טומטום ואנדרוגינוס ותיפוק ליה מאיש איש ז) דברה תורה כלשון בני אדם וליתני חומר במכה מבמקלל שהמכה עשה בו שלא בעמך כבעמך משא"כ במקלל קסבר ח) מקשינן הכאה לקללה לימא הני תנאי כהני תנאי דתני חדא כותי אתה מצווה על הכאתו ואי אתה מצווה על קללתו ותניא אידך אי אתה מצווה לא על קללתו ולא על הכאתו סברוה דכולי עלמא כותים גירי אמת הן מאי לאו בהא קמיפלגי דמר סבר מקשינן הכאה לקללה ומר סבר ט) לא מקשינן הכאה לקללה לא דכ"ע לא מקשינן הכאה לקללה והכא בהא קמיפלגי מר סבר כותים גירי אמת הן ומר סבר י) כותים גירי אריות הן אי הכי היינו דקתני עלה ושורו כישראל אלא שמע מינה בהיקישא פליגי ש"מ: **מתני'** ז הגונב נפש מישראל אינו חייב עד שיכניסנו לרשותו רבי יהודה אומר עד שיכניסנו לרשותו וישתמש בו שנאמר ד) והתעמר בו ומכרו הגונב את בנו רבי ישמעאל בנו של ר' יוחנן בן ברוקה מחייב וחכמים ח פוטרין גנב מי שחציו עבד וחציו בן חורין ר' יהודה מחייב וחכמים פוטרין: **גמ'** ותנא קמא לא בעי עימור א"ר אחא בריה דרבא ט עימור פחות משוה פרוטה איכא בינייהו י בעי ר' ירמיה גנבו ומכרו ישן מהו כ מכר אשה לעוברה מהו יש דרך עימור בכך או אין דרך עימור בכך ותיפוק ליה דליכא עימור כלל לא צריכא ישן דזגא עליה אשה דאוקמא באפי זיקא דרך עימור בכך או ל אין דרך עימור בכך מאי תיקו ת"ר ד) כי ימצא איש גונב נפש מאחיו אין לי אלא איש שגנב אשה מניין ת"ל ה) וגונב איש אין לי אלא איש שגנב בין אשה ובין איש ואשה שגנבה איש אשה שגנבה אשה מניין ת"ל ד) ומת הגנב ההוא מ מכל מקום תניא אידך ד) כי ימצא איש גונב נפש מאחיו אחד הגונב את האיש ואחד הגונב את האשה נ ואחד גר ואחד עבד משוחרר וקטן חייב ס גנבו ולא מכרו מכרו ועדיין ישנו ברשותו פטור מכרו לאביו או לאחיו או לאחד מן הקרובים חייב ע הגונב את העבדים פטור

תני

תוספות

שיכול הואיל וחייב במכה כו'. הוי מצי למימר הואיל וכתיב בעמך כדאמר לעיל במקיים שבעמך: **ומה** מכה אביו כו'. ואם תאמר מה למכה שכן בחנק תאמר במקלל דבסקילה וי"ל דהיא גופה ילפינן השתא דמכה אביו בסקילה מקל וחומר ממקלל ומיהו קשה לבסוף דיליף דמקלל לאחר מיתה חייב נילף ליה שלא נעשה בו שלא בעמך כבעמך ממקלל דחייב ביה לאחר מיתה ומכה פטור דבעינן נפש כדדרשינן לעיל (דף פד:) עד דעביד חבורה: **איש** איש מה תלמוד לומר איש איש. פירשתי שלהי פ' ד' מיתות (לעיל דף סו. ד"ה לרבות):

ושורו כישראל. לאו לגמרי כישראל דשור של ישראל שנגח לשור של כותי פטור משום דקנסינן להו כדאמר בריש פ' ד' וה' (ב"ק דף לח:) ומיהו לגבי הכי הוי כישראל דשור של כותי שנגח לשור של ישראל תם משלם חצי נזק ומועד נזק שלם ושור של עובד כוכבים שנגח לשור של ישראל בין תם בין מועד משלם נזק שלם: **עד** שיכניסנו לרשותו. משום דכתיב ונמצא בידו ואע"ג דבפ"ק דבבא מציעא (דף י:) גבי גט וגניבה מצרכינן תרי קראי לרבויי ידו לאו דווקא דהוא הדין גגו חצירו קרפיפו דלמא כאן נמי יש שום ריבוי ואפשר דאם הגביהו אפילו ברשות בעלים חייב כדאשכחן גבי גניבה בפרק מרובה (ב"ק דף עט: ושם) דתנן היה מושכו ויוצא כו' אי נמי הכא דפטר ר' שמעון מכרו לקרובים דבעינן שיוציאנו מרשות אחיו כ"ש דברשות בעלים לא מהני כלל:

מוגמגא

רש"י

מידי דהוה לאחר מיתה. דילפינן לקמן מקלל לאחר מיתה חייב וא"ת והתנן מכה לאחר מיתה פטור והכא מיחייב ליה אהכאה דקתני הכהו וקללו היינו טעמא דפטור מכה לאחר מיתה משום דבעינן חבורה ולאחר מיתה ליכא חבורה דליכא נפש דנפקא ליה לעיל מנפש ויוצא ליהרג. איכא חבורה דחי הוא אלא דסופו למות: **מתני'** שהמקלל לאחר מיתה חייב. כדיליף בגמרא: והמכה לאחר מיתה פטור. דחבורה ליכא: **גמ'** אביו ואמו קלל. קרא יתירא הוא דהא כתיב רישיה דקרא אשר יקלל את אביו ואת אמו: מכה שעשה שלא בעמך כבעמך. דגבי הכאה לא כתיב בעמך למעוטי שאינו עושה מעשה עמך והאי תנא סבר לא מקשינן הכאה לקללה מפני המקרא המפסיק בינתים: לא חייב בו לאחר מיתה. דהא חבורה כתיב: לרבות בת. טומטום ואנדרוגינוס: אין לי אלא אביו ואמו. שניהם יחד: אביו קילל ואמו קילל. בראש המקרא סמך קללה לאביו ובסוף סמך לאמו: עד שיפרט לך הכתוב יחדו. וכמו שפרט בחורש בשור ובחמור מדפרט לך ש"מ דאי לא הוי יחדו הוה משמע שור לבדו וחמור לבדו והא אביו ואמו דרישא דרשינן נמי או אביו או אמו וסיפא לאתויי לאחר מיתה: מומקלל אביו. דואלה המשפטים: ואידך. דמפיק לאחר מיתה מאביו ואמו קילל: וליתני נמי וכו'. אמתניתין קאי דקתני זה חומר במקלל מבמכה: לימא הני תנאי. תנא דמתניתין דלא תנא חומר במכה שעשה בו שלא בעמך כבעמך ותנא דברייתא דלעיל דתנא ומה מכה שעשה בו: גירי אמת הן. מתחילתן גרים גמורים היו ועכשיו הרשיעו וישראל שאינו עושה מעשה עמך הוא וכי היכי דעל קללתו פטור על הכאתו נמי פטור: גירי אריות הן. והרי הם כעובדי כוכבים גמורים: אי הכי. דטעמא דפטור משום דגירי אריות הן: היינו דתנא עלה. בתמיה בהך מתני' דקתני אינו מצווה לא על הכאתו ולא על קללתו קתני ושורו כישראל שור שלנו שנגח את שורו ושורו שנגח שלנו תם משלם חצי נזק ומועד משלם נזק שלם ואילו דעובד כוכבים תנן שור של ישראל שנגח שור של עובד כוכבים פטור ושל עובד כוכבים שנגח שור של ישראל בין תם בין מועד משלם נזק שלם: **מתני'** שיכניסנו לרשותו. דכתיב (שמות כב) ונמצא בידו ותניא במכילתא ונמצא אין מציאה בכל מקום אלא בעדים בידו אין בידו אלא ברשותו וכן הוא אומר (במדבר כא) ויקח את כל ארצו מידו: **גמ'** עמור. שמוש: גנבו ומכרו כשהוא ישן מהו. לקמן מפרש לה הבעיא: מכר אשה לעוברה. גנב אשה מעוברת ומכרה לעוברה שלא מכר הגוף שלה אלא שיהא עובר מכור: דליכא עימור. לא בישן ולא בעובר: דזגא עליה. דסמך עליו: **דאוקמא באפי זיקא.** וכל כמה שהיא עבה מועיל יותר להגין בפני הרוח: **אין לי אלא איש.** כשהגנב איש: **וגונב איש.** שהגנב איש ולא אשה וקרא קמא דלא קפיד אגנב למהוי איש דכתיב נפש הלכך אין לי אלא איש שגנב בין איש בין אשה דהיכא דגנב הוי איש כתוב גונב נפש ואשה שגנבה איש דכתיב וגונב איש וגונב אפילו אשה גונבת משמע: **הגנב.** מ"מ וההוא דרשינן ליה בספרי למעוטי גונב עבד: **ועדיין ישנו ברשותו.** ברשות הנגנב עצמו שעדיין לא הכניסו גנב ברשותו: **פטור.** שהרי לא גנבו: **לאביו.** אביו של נגנב:

תני

עין משפט נר מצוה

יז א מיי' פ"ה מהל' ממרים הל' יד סמג לאוין ריט טוש"ע י"ד סי' רמא סעיף ה:

יח ב מיי' שם הלכה יד [וברב אלפס עוד ביבמות פרק ב דף ה: וכתוב גרם חוץ ממסית ומדיח שהרי אמרה תורה וכו' וכן איתא בשאלתות בלק ס"ס קלד חוץ ממסית ומדיח שהרי וכו']:

יט ג מיי' שם הלכה ה סמג שם טוש"ע שם סעיף א בהג"ה:

כ ד מיי' שם הלכה א טוש"ע שם סעיף א:

כא ה מיי' שם הלכה ה טוש"ע שם בהג"ה:

כב ו מיי' שם הלכה א (טוש"ע שם סעי' א):

כג ז מיי' פ"ט מהלכות גניבה הלכה ב סמג לאוין קכד:

כד ח מיי' שם הלכה ה סמג שם:

כה ט מיי' שם הל' ג:

כו י מיי' שם הלכה ג:

כז כ מיי' שם הל' ד:

כח ל מ נ מיי' שם הל' ו:

כט ס מיי' שם הל' ג:

ל ע מיי' שם הלכה ו:

מסורת הש"ס

א) מכות יב., ב) [לעיל סד:], ג) [בס"ח סי' תקע"ג מסביר טעם דהמכה מקלל יותר ממכה מפני שבקללה יש היזק לנשמתו], ד) לעיל סו., ה) [שם], ו) ב"מ לד: לה: שבועות כו. חולין עח., ז) [יומא נז: מנחות לג.], ח) [ברכות לא: קדושין יז: וש"נ], ט) [יבמות דף קא.], י) [מכות ט.], י) יבמות כד: ב"ק לח. נדה נו: חולין ג. קידושין עה:, כ) [תוספ' דב"ק פ"ח].

הגהות הב"ח

(א) גמ' אביו ואמו קלל אלא לר' יאשיה:

ליקוטי רש"י

לכל אין הבן נעשה וכו'. לכל עבירות שבתורה אין הבן נעשה שליח ב"ד על אביו לא להלקותו ולא לנדותו חוץ ממסית [מכות יב.]. טומטום. שאין ניכר בו לא זכרות ולא נקבות [ב"ב קכו:]. וכל זמן שלא נקרע מספקינן ליה בזכר ובנקבה. אנדרוגינוס. שיש לו זכרות ונקבות [שם קכז.]. אביו ואמו קלל. לרבות לאחר מיתה [ויקרא כ, ט]. הניחא לר' יונתן. דאמר אע"ג דלא כתיב או לא כמאן דכתיב או דמי וכל היכא דכתיב פלוני ופלוני או האי או האי משמע. דתניא איש. אשר יקלל את אביו ואת אמו אין לי אלא שניהם אחד מהם מנין. ת"ל. בסיפיה אביו ואמו קלל. אביו קלל ואמו קלל. כלומר בתחלת המקרא סמך קללה לאביו ובסוף המקרא סמך קללה לאמו למימרא דלא בעי האי בהאי. ר' יונתן אומר. אביו או אמו משמע נמי או האי או האי וסיפיה דקרא לדרשא אחריתא להביא את המקלל לאחר מיתה חייב [חולין עח.]. איש איש כי יקלל וגו'. לרבות בת. טומטום שקלל. אין לי אלא אביו ואמו. כאחד. אביו שלא אמו ואמו שלא אביו מניין תלמוד לומר אביו ואמו קלל. כלומר בתחילתו סמך קללה לאביו בסופו סמך קללה לאמו. עד שיפרוט לך הכתוב יחדו כמו שפרט הכתוב (דברים כב) בחורש שור וחמור דמדאיצטריך למיכתב יחדי שמעינן דאי לא כתביה הוה משמע שלא יחרוש לא בשור ולא בחמור ואביו ואמו קלל דריש לה בסנהדרין (פה:) להביא את המקלל לאחר מיתה [ב"מ צד:]. דברה תורה כלשון בני אדם וכו'. ואף על גב דאיכא למדרש לא דרשינן כדמוכח בפ"ב דב"מ (דף לא:) [נדרים ג.]. מקשינן הכאה לקללה. לומר שכשם שאינו לוקה על קללתו דכתיב בעמך כך לא ילקה על הכאתו ופלוגתא היא בסנהדרין דאיכא דמקיש ואיכא דלא מקיש [מכות ט.]. והפסיק הענין וכתב וגונב איש, בין מכה אביו ואמו למקלל אביו ואמו, ונראה לי היינו פלוגתא, דמר סבר מקשינן הכאה לקללה, ומר סבר לא מקשינן [שמות כא, טז]. כותים גירי אריות. כותים אותם שהושיב סנחריב בערי שומרון כדכתיב (מלכים ב יז) ויבא מלך אשור (אנשים מספרויים) מבבל ומכותה וגו' ועל שם שהביאם מכותה נקראו כותים ונתגיירו מאימת האריות כדכתיב (מלכים ב' יז) וישלח (בם את) ה' בהם האריות וגו' וכולה ענייניה במלכים [קידושין עד.]. גירי אריות. כגון כותים דכתיב בספר מלכים (ב' יז) וישלח ה' בהם את האריות ונתגיירו כדכתיב התם בגלות שומרון [יבמות כד:]. בספר מלכים (ב יז) מפורש וישלח ה' בהם את האריות וכותים כתיבי התם ויבא מלך אשור (אנשים) מכותה וקא חשיב שאר מקומות [ב"ק לח:]. והתעמר בו. אינו חייב עד שישתמש בו [דברים כד, ז]. וגנב איש ומכרו. למה נאמר לפי שנאמר (דברים כד, ז) כי ימצא איש גונב נפש מאחיו אין לי אלא איש שגנב נפש אשה או טומטום או אנדרוגינוס שגנבו מנין תלמוד לומר וגונב איש ומכרו ולפי שנאמר כאן וגונב איש אין לי אלא גונב איש גונב אשה מנין תלמוד לומר (שם) גונב נפש לכך הוצרכו שניהם מה שחסר זה גלה זה [שמות כא, טז].

תורה אור השלם

א) לא תֹאבֶה לוֹ וְלֹא תִשְׁמַע אֵלָיו וְלֹא תָחוֹס עֵינְךָ עָלָיו וְלֹא תַחְמֹל וְלֹא תְכַסֶּה עָלָיו: [דברים יג, ט]

ב) כִּי אִישׁ אִישׁ אֲשֶׁר יְקַלֵּל אֶת אָבִיו וְאֶת אִמּוֹ מוֹת יוּמָת אָבִיו וְאִמּוֹ קִלֵּל דָּמָיו בּוֹ: [ויקרא כ, ט]

ג) וּמְקַלֵּל אָבִיו וְאִמּוֹ מוֹת יוּמָת: [שמות כא, יז]

ד) כִּי יִמָּצֵא אִישׁ גֹּנֵב נֶפֶשׁ מֵאֶחָיו מִבְּנֵי יִשְׂרָאֵל וְהִתְעַמֶּר בּוֹ וּמְכָרוֹ וּמֵת הַגַּנָּב הַהוּא וּבִעַרְתָּ הָרָע מִקִּרְבֶּךָ: [דברים כד, ז]

ה) וְגֹנֵב אִישׁ וּמְכָרוֹ וְנִמְצָא בְיָדוֹ מוֹת יוּמָת: [שמות כא, טז]

Thus, the clause *his father or his mother he has cursed* is extra according to R' Yonasan but not according to R' Yoshiyah.

Having cited R' Yoshiyah's position, the Gemara returns to its question:

מְנָא לֵיהּ – **From where does [R' Yoshiyah] know** that one is punished for cursing his dead parent? R' Yonasan learns this from the superfluous clause *his father or his mother he has cursed,* but according to R' Yoshiyah, that clause is not superfluous! – ? –

The Gemara answers:

נַפְקָא לֵיהּ מִ,,וּמְקַלֵּל אָבִיו וְאִמּוֹ מוֹת יוּמָת" – **He derives** that **[one is punished]** for cursing a dead parent **from** the verse:[19] ***One who curses his father or his mother shall surely be put to death.***

The Gemara now considers how R' Yonasan [who derives the punishment for cursing a dead parent from a different source – viz. *his father and his mother he has cursed*] expounds the above verse:

וְאִידָךְ – **And the other** disputant, i.e. R' Yonasan, what does he derive from: *One who curses his father or his mother shall surely be put to death?*

הַהוּא מִיבָּעֵי לֵיהּ לְרַבּוֹת בַּת טוּמְטוּם וְאַנְדְּרוֹגִינוּס – According to R' Yonasan, **that** verse **is needed to include a daughter, a** ***tumtum*** **and an androgyne** among those who are liable for cursing their parents.[20]

The Gemara objects:

וְתִיפּוֹק לֵיהּ מִ,,אִישׁ אִישׁ" – **But let [R' Yonasan] derive this from** the repetitive phrase ***a man, a man*** as the previous Baraisa does.[21] – ? –

The Gemara answers:

דִּבְּרָה תוֹרָה כִּלְשׁוֹן בְּנֵי אָדָם – R' Yonasan maintains that there is no special significance in this repetition, for **the Torah** simply **spoke in the** common **language** used by **men.** Thus, the repetitive phraseology is merely a manner of speech, and we therefore derive no new laws from it.

The Mishnah explained how the prohibition against cursing one's parent was more stringent than the prohibition against striking him. The Gemara therefore asks:

וְלִיתְנֵי חוֹמֶר בְּמַכֶּה מִבִּמְקַלֵּל – **Let the Mishnah** also **teach the stringency of striking** one's parent **over cursing** him, שֶׁהַמַּכֶּה – **for concerning** the liability to punishment for **striking** a parent, עָשָׂה בּוֹ שֶׁלֹּא בְעַמְּךָ כִּבְעַמְּךָ – **[the Torah] equated** a parent **who is not** included **in** the expression ***your nation*** **with one who is** included **in** ***your nation,*** holding a person liable for striking both these types of parents, מַה שֶּׁאֵין כֵּן בִּמְקַלֵּל – **while this is not the case concerning** the prohibition against **cursing,** where one is not liable for cursing a sinful parent.[22] – ? –

The Gemara answers:

קָסָבַר מַקְשִׁינַן הַכָּאָה לִקְלָלָה – **[The Tanna]** of our Mishnah **held that we compare** the laws of **striking to** the laws of **cursing.**[23] Accordingly, just as one is not punished for cursing a sinful parent, so is he not punished for striking one.

We have established that the Tanna of our Mishnah compares striking and cursing, which means that he disputes the Tanna of the Baraisa cited above. The Gemara considers whether this dispute parallels another Tannaic debate:[24]

לֵימָא הָנֵי תַּנָּאֵי כְּהָנֵי תַּנָּאֵי – **Shall we say** that the dispute between **these Tannaim** involves **the same** matter **as** that between **these Tannaim** recorded in the following Baraisos? דְּתָנֵי חֲדָא – **For it was taught in one Baraisa:** כּוּתִי – In the case of A CUTHEAN,[25] אַתָּה מְצוּוֶּה עַל הַכָּאָתוֹ – YOU ARE COMMANDED WITH REGARD TO STRIKING HIM, i.e. you may not strike him, וְאִי אַתָּה מְצוּוֶּה עַל קִלְלָתוֹ – BUT YOU ARE NOT COMMANDED WITH REGARD TO CURSING HIM, i.e. there is no prohibition against cursing him.

וְתַנְיָא אִידָךְ – **And in another Baraisa it was taught:** אִי אַתָּה מְצוּוֶּה לֹא עַל קִלְלָתוֹ וְלֹא עַל הַכָּאָתוֹ – YOU ARE COMMANDED NEITHER WITH REGARD TO CURSING HIM NOR WITH REGARD TO STRIKING HIM. That is, there is no prohibition against either cursing a Cuthean or striking him.

The Gemara attempts to clarify their point of dispute:

סָבְרוּהָ – **They**[26] **assumed** דְּכוּלֵּי עָלְמָא כּוּתִים גֵּירֵי אֱמֶת הֵן – **that** according to **everyone** (i.e. both these Baraisos), **Cutheans are true converts** who later reverted to idol worship.[27] As such, they are considered Jewish sinners.

The Gemara now states its understanding of the dispute between the Baraisos:

מַאי לָאו בְּהָא קָמִיפְלְגֵי – **Is it not that [the Baraisos] disagree over this** point? דְּמַר סָבַר מַקְשִׁינַן הַכָּאָה לִקְלָלָה – **One master** [the Tanna of the second Baraisa] **maintains that we compare** the laws of **striking to** the laws of **cursing:** Just as there is no prohibition against cursing a Jewish sinner (e.g. a Cuthean), so is there no prohibition against striking him.[28] וּמַר סָבַר לֹא מַקְשִׁינַן

NOTES

Baraisa's case, R' Yonasan maintains that since the Torah did not state, "for any man who will curse his father and his mother *together*," אֶת־אָבִיו וְאֶת־אִמּוֹ is rendered "his father and/or his mother," thus teaching that liability accrues even when the child curses either parent.

Given the fact that according to R' Yonasan, the liability for cursing one parent is derived from the first part of the verse, the second part (*his father or his mother he has cursed*) is superfluous. R' Yonasan therefore derives from the second part of the verse that one is liable to execution for cursing his parent even if the parent has died. But according to R' Yoshiyah, the second part of the verse is needed, as explained in the previous note. The Gemara will therefore question how R' Yoshiyah knows that one is liable for cursing a dead parent.

19. *Exodus* 21:17.

20. For rather than writing *a man who curses,* the verse uses the general expression *one* who curses; this includes all genders (*Imrei Binah*).

21 See above, note 16.

22. See 85a note 23.

23. See 85a note 22.

24. The forthcoming Gemara will discuss two Tannaic disputes. The first dispute centers on whether we compare the laws of striking to those of cursing; the Tanna of our Mishnah holds that we do, but the Baraisa (quoted immediately after our Mishnah) holds that we do not (see note 11 above). The Gemara will now cite a second Tannaic dispute and consider whether it parallels the first one.

25. The Cutheans were a pagan group transplanted by the Assyrian emperor from their native Cutha to Eretz Yisrael to replace the exiled Ten Tribes of Israel. Motivated by an outbreak of lion attacks, which they attributed to their failure to serve the God of the Land, they converted to Judaism (see *II Kings* ch. 17). Even after their conversion, however, the Cutheans continued to serve their pagan deities (see ibid. v. 33). This raised the question as to whether their conversion was valid, for a *sincere* acceptance of Torah law is a prerequisite for conversion. As will be seen below, there is a Tannaic disagreement about the validity of their conversions.

26. I.e. those who are suggesting that this Tannaic dispute parallels the previous one (see note 24).

27. According to this view, the Cutheans originally converted wholeheartedly but *later* reverted to their pagan worship (*Rashi*; cf. *Tosafos* to *Chullin* 3b ד״ה קסבר). This gave them the status of sinful Jews "who do not act in accord with the deeds of your nation" (see 85a). Hence, both Baraisos agree that there is no prohibition against cursing them (*Rashi*, see 85a). The Gemara is about to explain why the Baraisos disagree as to whether there is a prohibition against striking them.

28. As explained on 85a, the Torah prohibits cursing a Jew who acts "in accord with the deeds of your people" (i.e. one who observes the laws of the Torah), but there is no prohibition against cursing one who worships idols, as the Cutheans do. As such, if we compare striking to cursing, then there is no prohibition against striking a Cuthean either, as the second Baraisa states (*Rashi*).

מידי דהוה לאחר מיתה מאי הוה עלה (א) אמר רבה בר רב הונא וכן תנא דבי רבי ישמעאל א לכל אין הבן נעשה שליח לאביו להכותו ולקללו ב חוץ ממסית שהרי אמרה תורה (א) לא תחמול ולא תכסה עליו: **מתני'** (ב) ג המכה אביו ואמו אינו חייב עד שיעשה בהן חבורה זה חומר במקלל מבמכה ד שהמקלל לאחר מיתה חייב (ג) ה והמכה לאחר מיתה פטור: **גמ'** ת"ר (ב) אביו ואמו קלל לאחר מיתה שיכול הואיל וחייב במכה וחייב במקלל מה מכה אינו חייב אלא מחיים אף המקלל אינו חייב אלא מחיים ועוד ק"ו ומה מכה שעשה בו שלא בעמך כבעמך לא חייב בו לאחר מיתה מקלל שלא עשה בו שלא בעמך כבעמך אינו דין שלא חייב בו לאחר מיתה ת"ל אביו ואמו קלל לאחר מיתה הניחא לר' יונתן דמייתר ליה קרא אביו ואמו (א) אלא לר' יאשיה מאי איכא למימר (ד) דתניא (ב) איש איש מה ת"ל איש איש ו לרבות בת טומטום ואנדרוגינוס (ב) אשר יקלל את אביו ואת אמו (ה) אין לי אלא אביו ואמו אביו שלא אמו אמו שלא אביו מניין ת"ל אביו ואמו קלל אביו קלל אמו קלל דברי ר' יאשיה ר' יונתן אומר משמע שניהן כאחד ומשמע אחד ואחד בפני עצמו (ו) עד שיפרט לך הכתוב יחדיו מנא ליה נפקא ליה (ג) ומקלל אביו ואמו מות יומת ואידך ההוא מיבעי ליה לרבות בת טומטום ואנדרוגינוס ותיפוק ליה מאיש איש (ז) דברה תורה כלשון בני אדם וליתני חומר במכה מבמקלל שהמכה עשה בו שלא בעמך כבעמך משא"כ במקלל קסבר (ח) מקשינן הכאה לקללה לימא הני תנאי כהני תנאי דתני חדא כותי אתה מצווה על הכאתו ואי אתה מצווה על קללתו ותניא אידך אי אתה מצווה לא על קללתו ולא על הכאתו סברוה דכולי עלמא כותים גירי אמת הן מאי לאו בהא קמיפלגי דמר סבר מקשינן הכאה לקללה ומר סבר (ט) לא מקשינן הכאה לקללה לא דכ"ע לא מקשינן הכאה לקללה והכא בהא קמיפלגי מר סבר כותים גירי אמת הן ומר סבר (י) כותים גירי אריות הן אי הכי היינו דקתני עלה ושורו כישראל אלא שמע מינה בהיקישא פליגי ש"מ: **מתני'** ז הגונב נפש מישראל אינו חייב עד שיכניסנו לרשותו רבי יהודה אומר עד שיכניסנו לרשותו וישתמש בו שנאמר (ד) והתעמר בו ומכרו הגונב את בנו רבי ישמעאל בנו של ר' יוחנן בן ברוקה מחייב וחכמים ח פוטרין גנב מי שחציו עבד וחציו בן חורין ר' יהודה מחייב וחכמים פוטרין: **גמ'** ותנא קמא לא בעי עימור א"ר אחא בריה דרבא ט עימור פחות משוה פרוטה איכא בינייהו י בעי ר' ירמיה גנבו ומכרו ישן מהו כ מכר אשה לעוברה מהו יש דרך עימור בכך או אין דרך עימור בכך ותיפוק ליה דליכא עימור כלל לא צריכא ישן דזגא עליה אשה דאוקמא באפי זיקא דרך עימור בכך או ל אין דרך עימור בכך מאי תיקו ת"ר (ד) כי ימצא איש גונב נפש מאחיו אין לי אלא איש שגנב אשה מניין ת"ל (ה) וגונב איש אין לי אלא איש שגנב בין אשה ובין איש ואשה שגנבה איש אשה שגנבה אשה מניין ת"ל (ד) ומת הגנב ההוא מ מכל מקום תניא אידך (כ) כי ימצא איש גונב נפש מאחיו אחד הגונב את האיש ואחד הגונב את האשה נ ואחד גר ואחד עבד משוחרר וקטן חייב ס גנבו ולא מכרו מכרו ועדיין ישנו ברשותו פטור מכרו לאביו או לאחיו או לאחד מן הקרובים חייב ע הגונב את העבדים פטור

תני

שיכול הואיל וחייב במכה כו'. הוי מצי למימר הואיל וכתיב בעמך כדאמר לעיל במקוים שבעמך: **ומה** מכה אביו כו'. ואם תאמר מה למכה שכן בחנק תאמר במקלל דבסקילה וי"ל דהיא גופה ילפינן השתא דמכה אביו בסקילה מקל וחומר ממקלל ומיהו קשה לבסוף דיליף דמקלל לאחר מיתה חייב נילף ליה שלא נעשה בו שלא בעמך כבעמך ממקלל דחייב ביה לאחר מיתה ומכה פטור דבעינן נפש כדדרשינן לעיל (דף פד:) עד דעביד חבורה: **איש** איש מה תלמוד לומר איש איש. פירשתי שלהי פ' ד' מיתות (לעיל דף סו. ד"ה לרבות): **ושורו** כישראל. לאו לגמרי כישראל דשור של ישראל שנגח לשור של כותי פטור משום דקנסינן להו כדאמר בריש פ' ד' וה' (ב"ק דף לח:) ומיהו לגבי הכי הוי כישראל דשור של כותי שנגח לשור של ישראל תם משלם חצי נזק ומועד נזק שלם ושור של עובד כוכבים שנגח לשור של ישראל בין תם בין מועד משלם נזק שלם: **עד** שיכניסנו לרשותו. משום דכתיב ונמצא בידו ואע"ג דבפ"ק דבבא מציעא (דף י:) גבי גט וגניבה מצרכינן תרי קראי לרבויי ידו לאו דווקא דהוא הדין גגו חצירו קרפיפו דלמא כאן נמי יש שום ריבוי ואפשר דאם הגביהו אפילו ברשות בעלים חייב כדאשכחן גבי גניבה בפרק מרובה (ב"ק דף עט: ושם) דתנן היה מושכו ויוצא כו' אי נמי הכא דפטר ר' שמעון מכרו לקרובים דבעינן שיוציאנו מרשות אחיו כ"ש דברשות בעלים לא מהני כלל: מונמלא

מידי דהוה לאחר מיתה. דילפינן לקמן מקלל לאחר מיתה חייב וא"ת והתנן מכה לאחר מיתה פטור והכא מיחייב ליה אהכאה דקתני הכהו וקללו היינו טעמא דפטור מכה לאחר מיתה משום דבעינן חבורה ולאחר מיתה ליכא חבורה דליכא נפש דנפקא ליה לעיל מנפש ויוצא ליהרג איכא חבורה דחי הוא אלא דסופו למות: **מתני'** שהמקלל לאחר מיתה חייב. כדיליף בגמרא: והמכה לאחר מיתה פטור. דחבורה ליכא: **גמ'** אביו ואמו קלל. קרא יתירא הוא דהא כתיב רישיה דקרא אשר יקלל את אביו ואת אמו: מכה שעשה שלא בעמך כבעמך. דגבי הכאה לא כתיב בעמך למעוטי שאינו עושה מעשה עמך והאי תנא סבר לא מקשינן הכאה לקללה מפני המקרא המפסיק בינתים: **לא חייב בו לאחר** מיתה. דהא חבורה כתיב: **לרבות** בת. טומטום ואנדרוגינוס: **אין** לי אלא אביו ואמו. שניהם יחד: **אביו** קילל ואמו קילל. בראש המקרא סמך קללה לאביו ובסוף סמך לאמו: **עד** שיפרט לך הכתוב יחדו. וכמו שפרט בחורש בשור ובחמור מדפרט לך ש"מ דאי לא הוי יחדו הוה משמע שור לבדו וחמור לבדו והא אביו ואמו דרישא דרשינן נמי או אביו או אמו וסיפא לאתויי לאחר מיתה: מומקלל **אביו**. דואלה המשפטים: **ואידך**. דמפיק לאחר מיתה מאביו ואמו קילל: **ולתני נמי וכו'**. אמתניתין קאי דקתני זה חומר במקלל מבמכה: **לימא הני תנאי**. תנא דמתניתין דלא תנא חומר במכה שעשה בו שלא בעמך כבעמך ותנא דברייתא דלעיל דתנא ומה מכה שעשה בו: גירי **אמת** הן. מתחילתן גרים גמורים היו ועכשיו הרשיעו וישראל שאינו עושה מעשה עמך הוא וכי היכי דעל קללתו פטור על הכאתו נמי פטור: גירי **אריות** הן. והרי הם כעובדי כוכבים גמורים: **אי הכי**. דטעמא דפטור משום דגירי אריות הן: היינו דתנא **עלה**. בתמיה בהך מתני' דקתני אינו מצווה לא על הכאתו ולא על קללתו קתני ושורו כישראל שור שלנו שנגח את שורו ושורו שנגח שלנו תם משלם חצי נזק ומועד משלם נזק שלם ואילו דעובד כוכבים תנן שור של ישראל שנגח שור של עובד כוכבים פטור ושל עובד כוכבים שנגח שור של ישראל בין תם בין מועד משלם נזק שלם: **מתני'** שיכניסנו לרשותו. דכתיב (שמות כב) ונמצא בידו ותניא במכילתא ונמצא אין מציאה בכל מקום אלא בעדים בידו אין בידו אלא ברשותו וכן הוא אומר (במדבר כא) ויקח את כל ארצו מידו: **גמ'** עמור. שמוש: גנבו ומכרו כשהוא **ישן** מהו. לקמן מפרש לה הבעיא: **מכר אשה לעוברה**. גנב אשה מעוברת ומכרה לעוברה שלא מכר הגוף שלה אלא שיהא עובר מכור: **דליכא** עימור. לא בישן ולא בעובר: **דזגא** עליה. דסמך עליו: דאוקמא **באפי** זיקא. וכל כמה שהיא עבה מועיל יותר להגין בפני הרוח: **אין לי אלא איש**. כשהגנב איש: **וגונב איש**. שהנגנב איש ולא אשה וקרא קמא דלא קפיד אנגנב למהוי איש דכתיב נפש הלכך אין לי אלא איש שגנב בין איש בין אשה דהיכא דגנב הוי איש כתוב גונב נפש ואשה שגנבה איש דכתיב וגונב איש וגונב אפילו אשה גונבת משמע: **הגנב**. מ"מ והההוא דרשינן ליה בספרי למעוטי גונב עבד: **ועדיין ישנו ברשותו**. ברשות הנגנב עצמו שעדיין לא הכניסו גנב ברשותו: **פטור**. שהרי לא גנבו: **לאביו**. אביו של נגנב:

תני

בחמור ואביו ואמו קלל דריש לה בסנהדרין (פה:) להביא את המקלל לאחר מיתה [ב"מ צד:]. **דברה תורה כלשון בני אדם וכו'**. ואף על גב דאיכא למדרש לא דרשינן כדמוכח בפ"ב דב"מ (דף לא:) [נדרים ג.]. מקשינן **הכאה לקללה**. לומר שכשם שאינו לוקה על קללתו דכתיב בעמך כך לא ילקה על הכאתו ופלוגתא היא בסנהדרין דאיכא דמקיש ואיכא דלא מקיש [מכות ט.]. והפסיק הענין וכתב וגונב איש, בין מכה אביו ואמו למקלל אביו ואמו, ונראה לי היינו פלוגתא, דמר סבר מקשינן הכאה לקללה, ומר סבר לא מקשינן [שמות כא, טז]. **כותים גירי אריות**. כותים אותם שהושיב סנחריב בערי שומרון כדכתיב (מלכים ב יז) ויבא מלך אשור (אנשים מספרויים) מבבל ומכותה וגו' ועל שם שהביאם מכותה נקראו כותים ונתגיירו מאימת האריות כדכתיב (מלכים ב' יז) וישלח (בם את) ה' בהם האריות וגו' וכולה ענייניה במלכים [קידושין עה:]. גירי אריות כגון כותים דכתיב בספר מלכים (ב' יז) וישלח ה' בהם את האריות ונתגיירו כדכתיב התם בגלות שומרון [יבמות כד:]. בספר מלכים (ב יז) מפורש וישלח ה' בהם את האריות וכותים כתיבי התם ויבא מלך אשור (אנשים) מכותה וקא חשיב שאר מקומות [ב"ק לח:]. **והתעמר בו**. אינו חייב עד שישתמש בו [דברים כד, ז]. **וגנב איש ומכרו**. למה נאמר לפי שנאמר (דברים כד, ז) כי ימצא איש גונב נפש מאחיו אין לי אלא איש שגנב או טומטום או אנדרוגינוס שגנבו מנין תלמוד לומר וגונב איש ומכרו ולפי שנאמר כאן וגונב איש אין לי אלא גונב איש גונב אשה מנין תלמוד לומר (שם) גונב נפש לכך הוצרכו שניהם מה שחסר זה גלה זה [שמות כא, טז].

עין משפט
נר מצוה

יז א מיי' פ"ה מהל' ממרים הל' יד סמג לאוין ריט טוש"ע י"ד סי' רמא סעיף ה:
יח ב מיי' שם הלכה יד [וברב אלפס עוד ביבמות פרק ב דף ה: והכי גרס חוץ ממסית ומדיח שהרי אמרה תורה וכו' וכן איתא בשאילתות בלק ס"ס קלד חוץ ממסית ומדיח שהרי וכו']:
יט ג מיי' שם הלכה ה סמג שם טוש"ע שם סעיף א בהג"ה:
כ ד מיי' שם הלכה א טוש"ע שם סעיף א:
כא ה מיי' שם הלכה ה טוש"ע שם בהג"ה:
כב ו מיי' שם הלכה א (טוש"ע שם סעי' א):
כג ז מיי' פ"ט מהלכות גניבה הלכה ב סמג לאוין קכד:
כד ח מיי' שם הלכה ה סמג שם:
כה ט מיי' שם הל' ב:
כו י מיי' שם הלכה ג:
כז כ ל מיי' שם הל' ד:
כח מ נ מיי' שם הל' ו:
כט ס מיי' שם הל' ג:
ל ע מיי' שם הלכה ו:

תורה אור השלם

א) לֹא תֹאבֶה לוֹ וְלֹא תִשְׁמַע אֵלָיו וְלֹא תָחוֹס עֵינְךָ עָלָיו וְלֹא תַחְמֹל וְלֹא תְכַסֶּה עָלָיו: [דברים יג, ט]

ב) כִּי אִישׁ אִישׁ אֲשֶׁר יְקַלֵּל אֶת אָבִיו וְאֶת אִמּוֹ מוֹת יוּמָת אָבִיו וְאִמּוֹ קִלֵּל דָּמָיו בּוֹ: [ויקרא כ, ט]

ג) וּמְקַלֵּל אָבִיו וְאִמּוֹ מוֹת יוּמָת: [שמות כא, יז]

ד) כִּי יִמָּצֵא אִישׁ גֹּנֵב נֶפֶשׁ מֵאֶחָיו מִבְּנֵי יִשְׂרָאֵל וְהִתְעַמֶּר בּוֹ וּמְכָרוֹ וּמֵת הַגַּנָּב הַהוּא וּבִעַרְתָּ הָרָע מִקִּרְבֶּךָ: [דברים כד, ז]

ה) וְגֹנֵב אִישׁ וּמְכָרוֹ וְנִמְצָא בְיָדוֹ מוֹת יוּמָת: [שמות כא, טז]

מסורת הש"ס

א) מכות יב., ב) [לעיל פד:], ג) [בס"ח סי' תקע"ו אסבריה טעם דחמור מקלל יותר ממכה מפני שבקללה יש היזק לאב לנשמתו], ד) לעיל סו., ה) [שם] ב"מ לד: לה: שבועות כז. חולין עח:, ו) [יומא נז: מנחות ל: לא.], ז) [ברכות לא: קידושין יז: וש"נ], ח) [יבמות דף קא.], ט) [מכות ט.], י) יבמות כד: ב"ק לח: נדה נו: חולין ג: קידושין עה:, כ) [תוספ' דב"ק פ"ח].

הגהות הב"ח

(א) גמ' אביו ואמו קלל אלא לר' יאשיה:

ליקוטי רש"י

לכל אין הבן נעשה וכו'. לכל עבירות שבתורה אין הבן נעשה שליח ב"ד על אביו לא להלקותו ולא לנדותו חוץ ממסית [מכות יב.]. **טומטום**. שאין ניכר בו לא זכרות ולא נקבות [ב"ב קכו:]. וכל זמן שלא נקרע מספקינן ליה בזכר ובנקבה. **אנדרוגינוס**. שיש לו זכרות ונקבות [שם קכז.]. **אביו ואמו קלל**. לרבות לאחר מיתה [ויקרא כ, ט]. **הניחא לר' יונתן**. דאמר אע"ג דלא כתיב או כמאן דכתיב או דמי וכל היכא דכתיב פלוני ופלוני או האי או האי משמע. **דתניא איש**. אשר יקלל את אביו ואת אמו אין לי אלא קלל שניהם אחד מהם מנין. ת"ל. בסיפיה אביו ואמו קלל. **אביו קלל ואמו קלל**. כלומר בתחלת המקרא סמך קללה לאביו ובסוף המקרא סמך קללה לאמו למימרא דאו האי או האי. ר' **יונתן אומר**. אביו ואמו משמע נמי או האי או האי וסיפיה דקרא לדרשא אחרינא להביא את המקלל לאחר מיתה שחייב [חולין עח.]. **איש איש** כי יקלל וגו' **לרבות בת**. שקללה, או טומטום שקלל. **אין לי אלא אביו ואמו**. כאחד. **אביו שלא אמו ואמו שלא אביו מניין** תלמוד **לומר אביו ואמו קלל**. כלומר סמך קללה בראש המקרא לאביו ובסופו סמך לאמו. ר' **יונתן אומר**. מתחלת המקרא משמע את אביו ואת אמו דאף על גב דוי"ו מוסיף על ענין ראשון משמע נמי אחד מהם עד שיפרט לך הכתוב יחדיו כדרך שהוצרך לפרוט בכלאים שכתוב בו (דברים כב) לא תחרוש בשור ובחמור ופרט בו יחדיו שלא תאמר אסור לחרוש בשור לבדו ובחמור לבדו ואביו ואמו קלל דסיפא דריש ליה ר' יונתן לקמן באלו הן הנחנקין לרבות את המקלל לאחר מיתה [לעיל סו:]. **אביו קלל אמו קלל**. בתחילתו סמך קללה לאביו בסופו סמך קללה לאמו. **עד שיפרוט לך הכתוב יחדיו**. כמו שפרט לך הכתוב (דברים כב) בחורש שור וחמור דמאיצטריך למיכתב יחדיו שמעינן דאי לא כתביה הוה משמע שלא יחרוש לא בשור ולא

הַכָּאָה לִקְלָלָה – But the other master [the Tanna of the first Baraisa] maintains that we do not compare the laws of striking to the laws of cursing and for this reason, it is prohibited to strike a Jewish sinner, such as a Cuthean.[29] Thus, the dispute between these two Baraisos parallels the one between our Mishnah and the Baraisa quoted above!

The Gemara suggests that the dispute between these two Baraisos can be interpreted differently:

לֹא – No! The disputes are not necessarily parallel. דְּכוּלֵּי עָלְמָא לֹא מַקְשִׁינַן הַכָּאָה לִקְלָלָה – For it might well be that according to everyone (i.e. these two Baraisos), we do not compare the laws of striking to the laws of cursing, and thus both Baraisos maintain that it is forbidden to strike any Jew, even a Jewish sinner.

וְהָכָא בְּהָא קָמִיפַּלְגֵי – And here, it is about this following matter that they disagree: מַר סָבַר כּוּתִים גֵּירֵי אֱמֶת הֵן – One master [the Tanna of the first Baraisa] maintains that Cutheans are true converts, and as such, full-fledged Jews. Hence, it is forbidden to strike them. וּמַר סָבַר כּוּתִים גֵּירֵי אֲרָיוֹת הֵן – But the other master [the Tanna of the second Baraisa] maintains that Cutheans are lion-inspired converts, whose conversions were invalid.[30] Thus, they still have the status of idolaters, and for this reason, there is also no prohibition against striking them.

The Gemara rejects this interpretation of the dispute:

אִי הָכִי – If it were so that according to the second Baraisa, the Cutheans have the status of idolaters,[31] הַיְינוּ דְּקָתָנֵי עֲלָהּ – then what about that law which this very same Baraisa teaches about [a Cuthean]: וְשׁוֹרוֹ כְּיִשְׂרָאֵל – AND HIS OX IS treated LIKE an ox belonging to A JEW rather than like an idolater's ox? If a Cuthean has the status of an idolater, then his ox should be judged like an idolater's ox![32] אֶלָּא שְׁמַע מִינָּהּ בְּהֶיקֵּישָׁא פְּלִיגֵי – Rather, learn from this that [the Baraisos] disagree over whether to draw a comparison between striking and cursing, as first suggested. שְׁמַע מִינָּהּ – Indeed, you may learn from this. Thus, the dispute between these Baraisos indeed parallels the debate between our Mishnah and the Baraisa quoted above.

Mishnah The Mishnah now discusses the details of the second crime listed in the Mishnah on 84b: הַגּוֹנֵב נֶפֶשׁ מִיִּשְׂרָאֵל – **One who kidnaps a Jew** אֵינוֹ חַיָּיב עַד שֶׁיַּכְנִיסֶנּוּ לִרְשׁוּתוֹ – **is not liable** to strangulation **unless he takes him into his possession.**[33] רַבִּי יְהוּדָה אוֹמֵר – **R' Yehudah says:** עַד שֶׁיַּכְנִיסֶנּוּ לִרְשׁוּתוֹ וְיִשְׁתַּמֵּשׁ בּוֹ – He is not liable **unless [the kidnaper] takes [his victim] into his possession and makes use of him,** שֶׁנֶּאֱמַר ,,וְהִתְעַמֶּר־בּוֹ וּמְכָרוֹ" – **as it is stated:** ***And he made use of him and sold him.***[34]

The Mishnah discusses two specific types of kidnaping:

הַגּוֹנֵב אֶת בְּנוֹ – If **one kidnaps his** own **son,** רַבִּי יִשְׁמָעֵאל בְּנוֹ שֶׁל רַבִּי יוֹחָנָן בֶּן בְּרוֹקָה מְחַיֵּיב – **R' Yishmael the son of R' Yochanan ben Berokah renders him liable,** וַחֲכָמִים פּוֹטְרִין – **but the Sages exempt him.**[35] גָּנַב מִי שֶׁחֶצְיוֹ עֶבֶד וְחֶצְיוֹ בֶּן חוֹרִין – If **he kidnaped someone who was half slave and half freeman,**[36] רַבִּי יְהוּדָה מְחַיֵּיב – **R' Yehudah renders him liable,** וַחֲכָמִים פּוֹטְרִין – **but the Sages exempt him.**

Gemara R' Yehudah stated that a kidnaper is not liable unless he makes use of his victim, but the Tanna Kamma mentioned no such requirement. The Gemara therefore asks:

וְתַנָּא קַמָּא לֹא בָּעֵי עִימּוּר – And as for the Tanna Kamma, does he not require that the kidnaper make use of his victim? But the verse cited by R' Yehudah clearly states this requirement! – ? –

The Gemara answers:

אָמַר רַבִּי אַחָא בְּרֵיהּ דְּרָבָא – R' Acha the son of Rava said: עִימּוּר פָּחוֹת מִשָּׁוֶה פְּרוּטָה אִיכָּא בֵּינַיְיהוּ – The point of dispute between them [the Tanna Kamma and R' Yehudah] emerges where the kidnaper used his victim for work that was worth less than the

NOTES

29. Even though there is no prohibition against cursing him. Thus, the first Baraisa rules that there is a prohibition against striking a Cuthean but not against cursing him.

30. That is, they decided to convert only out of fear of the lions and not out of a genuine desire for conversion. This can be seen from the fact that they continued to worship pagan deities after their conversions (*Tosafos* to *Chullin* 3b ד״ה קסבר). Hence, their conversions were insincere, which made them meaningless.

31. And this is why there is no prohibition against striking or cursing them (*Rashi*).

32. The Torah (*Exodus* 21:35-36) states a Jew's liability if his ox damaged the ox of another Jew. The first three times that the animal inflicts damage in a violent manner, such as goring, the owner is liable to pay for only half the damage. [At this stage, the animal is known as a תָּם, *tam* (literally: ordinary).] If the owner fails to restrain his animal after the third attack, he is liable to pay full damages for the fourth and subsequent attacks. [At that stage, the animal is known as a מוּעָד, *muad* (literally: warned).]

The ox of an idolater, however, is not subject to the above laws. If the ox of an idolater gores a Jew's ox, the idolater is obligated to pay full damages whether his ox was a *tam* or *muad*. If the ox of a Jew gored the ox of an idolater, the Jew has no monetary liability at all. (For a discussion of why a Jew and idolater are treated differently, see ArtScroll Mishnah Series, *Bava Kamma* p. 82.)

This Baraisa teaches that the ox of a Cuthean is treated like the ox of a Jew. This refutes the suggested interpretation of the Baraisa, which maintains that the Baraisa considers Cutheans to be idolaters! (*Rashi*, cf. *Tosafos*; and *Chidushei HaRan*; see also *Aruch LaNer* and *Binyan Shlomo*).

33. That is, a man is not liable for kidnaping unless he takes the victim into his possession; he is not liable for merely imprisoning the victim in his own house. [He must also work the victim, and sell the victim as a slave; see Mishnah and Gemara below.]

Our Mishnah's ruling is based on the verse in *Exodus* 21:16: וְגֹנֵב אִישׁ וּמְכָרוֹ וְנִמְצָא בְיָדוֹ מוֹת יוּמָת, *One who kidnaps a man and sells him, and he was found to have been in his hand, shall surely be put to death.* The expression בְיָדוֹ, *in his hand,* generally connotes *in his legal possession*; see for example, *Numbers* 21:26 [see also *Tosafos* ד״ה עד for a discussion of the form of acquisition (קִנְיָן) that legally brings the victim into the kidnaper's possession]. The expression וְנִמְצָא, *and he was found,* generally implies that witnesses have come forward and testified to what has occurred. In this case, it indicates that witnesses must have found the victim in the kidnaper's possession and then testify to that effect (*Rashi* from *Mechilta* §63, 64; cf. Gemara below, 86a; see also *Tosafos, Aruch LaNer* and *Binyan Shlomo*).

34. *Deuteronomy* 24:7. This verse also discusses the punishment for kidnaping. It adds that after taking the victim into his possession, the kidnaper must put him to work and then sell him; otherwise, the kidnaper is not liable to execution.

35. The Gemara will explain this dispute.

36. I.e. a slave was owned by two partners and one of them emancipated his share, leaving the slave part free and part slave. Although the death penalty does not apply to one who kidnaps a full-fledged slave (see Gemara below), our Mishnah quotes a Tannaic dispute as to whether it applies if the kidnaping victim is part slave, part free. (The Gemara below will explain the dispute.)

מידי דהוה לאחר מיתה מאי הוה עלה [א] אמר רבה בר רב הונא וכן תנא דבי רבי ישמעאל [א]לכל אין הבן נעשה שליח לאביו להכותו ולקללו [ב]חוץ ממסית שהרי אמרה תורה א) לא תחמול ולא תכסה עליו: **מתני'** [ב] [ג]המכה אביו ואמו אינו חייב עד שיעשה בהן חבורה זה חומר במקלל מבמכה [ד]שהמקלל לאחר מיתה חייב [ג] [ה]והמכה לאחר מיתה פטור: **גמ'** ת"ר ב) אביו ואמו קלל לאחר מיתה שיכול הואיל וחייב במכה וחייב במקלל מה מכה אינו חייב אלא מחיים אף המקלל אינו חייב אלא מחיים ועוד ק"ו ומה מכה שעשה בו שלא בעמך כבעמך לא חייב בו לאחר מיתה מקלל שלא עשה בו שלא בעמך כבעמך אינו דין שלא חייב בו לאחר מיתה ת"ל אביו ואמו קלל לאחר מיתה הניחא לר' יונתן דמייתר ליה קרא אביו ואמו (א) אלא לר' יאשיה מאי איכא למימר [ד]דתניא ב) איש איש מה ת"ל איש איש [ו]לרבות בת טומטום ואנדרוגינוס ב) אשר יקלל את אביו ואת אמו [ה]אין לי אלא אביו ואמו אביו שלא אמו אמו שלא אביו מניין ת"ל אביו ואמו קלל אביו קלל אמו קלל דברי ר' יאשיה ר' יונתן אומר משמע שניהן כאחד ומשמע אחד ואחד בפני עצמו [ו]עד שיפרט לך הכתוב יחדיו מנא ליה נפקא ליה ג) ומקלל אביו ואמו מות יומת ואידך ההוא מיבעי ליה לרבות בת טומטום ואנדרוגינוס ותיפוק ליה מאיש איש [ז]דברה תורה כלשון בני אדם וליתני חומר במכה מבמקלל שהמכה עשה בו שלא בעמך כבעמך משא"כ במקלל קסבר [ח]מקשינן הכאה לקללה לימא הני תנאי כהני תנאי דתני חדא כותי אתה מצווה על הכאתו ואי אתה מצווה על קללתו ותניא אידך אי אתה מצווה לא על קללתו ולא על הכאתו סברוה דכולי עלמא כותים גירי אמת הן מאי לאו בהא קמיפלגי דמר סבר מקשינן הכאה לקללה ומר סבר [ט]לא מקשינן הכאה לקללה לא דכ"ע לא מקשינן הכאה לקללה והכא בהא קמיפלגי מר סבר כותים גירי אמת הן ומר סבר [י]כותים גירי אריות הן אי הכי היינו דקתני עלה ושורו כישראל אלא שמע מינה בהיקישא פליגי ש"מ: **מתני'** [י]הגונב נפש מישראל אינו חייב עד שיכניסנו לרשותו רבי יהודה אומר עד שיכניסנו לרשותו וישתמש בו שנאמר ד) והתעמר בו ומכרו הגונב את בנו רבי ישמעאל בנו של ר' יוחנן בן ברוקה מחייב וחכמים [ח]פוטרין גנב מי שחציו עבד וחציו בן חורין ר' יהודה מחייב וחכמים פוטרין: **גמ'** ותנא קמא לא בעי עימור א"ר אחא בריה דרבא [ט]עימור פחות משוה פרוטה איכא בינייהו [י]בעי ר' ירמיה גנבו ומכרו ישן מהו [כ]מכר אשה לעוברה מהו יש דרך עימור בכך או אין דרך עימור בכך ותיפוק ליה דליכא עימור כלל לא צריכא ישן דזגא עליה אשה דאוקמא באפי זיקא דרך עימור בכך או [ל]אין דרך עימור בכך מאי תיקו ת"ר ד) כי ימצא איש גונב נפש מאחיו אין לי אלא איש שגנב אשה מניין ת"ל ה) וגונב איש אין לי אלא איש שגנב בין אשה ובין איש ואשה שגנבה אשה מניין ת"ל ד) ומת הגנב ההוא [מ]מכל מקום תניא אידך [ס]כי ימצא איש גונב נפש מאחיו אחד הגונב את האיש ואחד הגונב את האשה [נ]ואחד גר ואחד עבד משוחרר וקטן חייב [ס]גנבו ולא מכרו מכרו ועדיין ישנו ברשותו פטור מכרו לאביו או לאחיו או לאחד מן הקרובים חייב [ע]הגונב את העבדים פטור

תני

רש"י

מידי דהוה לאחר מיתה. דילפינן לקמן מקלל לאחר מיתה חייב וא"ת והתנן מכה לאחר מיתה פטור והכא מיחייב ליה אהכאה דקתני הכהו וקללו היינו טעמא דפטור מכה לאחר מיתה משום דבעינן חבורה ולאחר מיתה ליכא חבורה דליכא נפש דנפקא ליה לעיל מנפש ויוצא ליהרג איכא חבורה דחי הוא אלא דסופו למות: **מתני'** שהמקלל לאחר מיתה חייב. כדיליף בגמרא: והמכה לאחר מיתה פטור. דחבורה ליכא: **גמ'** אביו ואמו קלל. קרא יתירא הוא דהא כתיב רישיה דקרא אשר יקלל את אביו ואת אמו: מכה שעשה שלא בעמך כבעמך. דגבי הכאה לא כתיב בעמך למעוטי שאינו עושה מעשה עמך והאי תנא סבר לא מקשינן הכאה לקללה מפני המקרא המפסיק בינתים: לא חייב בו לאחר מיתה. דהא חבורה כתיב: לרבות בת. טומטום ואנדרוגינוס: אין לי אלא אביו ואמו. שניהם יחד: אביו קילל ואמו קילל. בראש המקרא סמך קללה לאביו ובסוף סמך לאמו: עד שיפרט לך הכתוב יחדו. וכמו שפרט בחורש בשור ובחמור מדפרט לך ש"מ דאי לא הוי יחדו הוה משמע שור לבדו וחמור לבדו והא אביו ואמו דרישא דרשינן נמי או אביו או אמו וסיפא לאתויי לאחר מיתה: מומקלל אביו. דואלה המשפטים: ואידך. דמפיק לאחר מיתה מאביו ואמו קילל: ולתני נמי וכו'. אמתניתין קאי דקתני זה חומר במקלל מבמכה: לימא הני תנאי. תנא דמתניתין דלא תנא חומר במכה שעשה בו שלא בעמך כבעמך ותנא דברייתא דלעיל דתנא ומה מכה שעשה בו: גירי אמת הן. מתחילתן גרים גמורים היו ועכשיו הרשיעו וישראל שאינו עושה מעשה עמך הוא וכי היכי דעל קללתו פטור על הכאתו נמי פטור: גירי אריות הן. והרי הם כעובדי כוכבים גמורים: אי הכי. דטעמא דפטור משום דגירי אריות הן: היינו דתנא עלה. בתמיה בהך מתני' דקתני אינו מצווה לא על הכאתו ולא על קללתו קתני ושורו כישראל שור שלנו שנגח את שורו ושורו שנגח שלנו תם משלם חצי נזק ומועד משלם נזק שלם ואילו דעובד כוכבים תנן שור של ישראל שנגח שור של עובד כוכבים פטור ושל עובד כוכבים שנגח שור של ישראל בין תם בין מועד משלם נזק שלם: **מתני'** שיכניסנו לרשותו. דכתיב (שמות כב) ונמצא בידו ותניא במכילתא ונמצא אין מציאה בכל מקום אלא בעדים בידו אין בידו אלא ברשותו וכן הוא אומר (במדבר כא) ויקח את כל ארצו מידו: **גמ'** עמור. שמוש: גנבו ומכרו כשהוא ישן מהו. לקמן מפרש לה הבעיא: מכר אשה לעוברה. גנב אשה מעוברת ומכרה לעוברה שלא מכר הגוף שלה אלא שיהא עובר מכור: דליכא עימור. לא בישן ולא בעובר: דזגא עליה. דסמך עליו: דאוקמא באפי זיקא. וכל כמה שהיא עבה מועיל יותר להגין בפני הרוח: אין לי אלא איש. כשהגנב איש: וגונב איש. שהגנב איש ולא אשה וקרא קמא דלא קפיד אנגנב למהוי איש דכתיב נפש הלכך אין לי אלא איש שגנב בין איש בין אשה דהיכא דגנב הוי איש כתוב גונב נפש ואשה שגנבה איש דכתיב וגונב איש וגונב אפילו אשה גונבת משמע: הגנב. מ"מ וההוא דרשינן ליה בספרי למעוטי גונב עבד: ועדיין ישנו ברשותו. ברשות הנגנב עצמו שעדיין לא הכניסו גנב ברשותו: פטור. שהרי לא גנבו: לאביו. אביו של נגנב:

תני

תוספות

שיכול הואיל וחייב במכה כו'. הוי מצי למימר הואיל וכתיב בעמך כדאמר לעיל במקוים שבעמך: ומה מכה אביו כו'. ואם תאמר מה למכה שכן בחנק תאמר במקלל דבסקילה וי"ל דהיא גופה ילפינן השתא דמכה אביו בסקילה מקל וחומר ממקלל ומיהו קשה לבסוף דיליף דמקלל לאחר מיתה חייב נילף ליה שלא נעשה בו שלא בעמך כבעמך ממקלל דחייב ביה לאחר מיתה ומכה פטור דבעינן נפש כדדרשינן לעיל (דף פד:) עד דעביד חבורה: איש איש מה תלמוד לומר איש איש. פירשתי שלהי פ' ד' מיתות (לעיל דף סו. ד"ה לרבות): ושורו כישראל. לאו לגמרי כישראל דשור של ישראל שנגח לשור של כותי פטור משום דקנסינן להו כדאמר בריש פ' ד' וה' (ב"ק דף לח:) ומיהו לגבי הכי הוי כישראל דשור של כותי שנגח לשור של ישראל תם משלם חצי נזק ומועד נזק שלם ושור של עובד כוכבים שנגח לשור של ישראל בין תם בין מועד משלם נזק שלם: עד שיכניסנו לרשותו. משום דכתיב ונמצא בידו ואע"ג דבפ"ק דבבא מציעא (דף י:) גבי גט וגניבה מצרכינן תרי קראי לרבויי ידו לאו דווקא דהוא הדין גגו חצירו קרפיפו דלמא כאן נמי יש שום ריבוי ואפשר דאם הגביהו אפילו ברשות בעלים חייב כדאשכחן גבי גניבה בפרק מרובה (ב"ק דף עט: ושם) דתנן היה מושכו ויוצא כו' אי נמי הכא דפטר ר' שמעון מכרו לקרובים דבעינן שיוציאנו מרשות אחיו כ"ש דברשות בעלים לא מהני כלל:

מונמלא

עין משפט נר מצוה

יז א מיי' פ"ה מהל' ממרים הל' יד סמג לאוין ריט טוש"ע י"ד סי' רמא סעיף ה:
יח ב מיי' שם הלכה יד [וברב אלפס עוד ביבמות פרק ב דף ה: והכי גרס חוץ ממסית ומדיח שהרי אמרה תורה וכו' וכן איתא בשאילתות בלק ס"ס קלד חוץ ממסית ומדיח שהרי וכו']:
יט ג מיי' שם הלכה ה סמג שם טוש"ע שם סעיף א בהג"ה:
כ ד מיי' שם הלכה א טוש"ע שם סעיף א:
כא ה מיי' שם הלכה ה טוש"ע שם בהג"ה:
כב ו מיי' שם הלכה א (טוש"ע שם סעי' א):
כג ז מיי' פ"ט מהלכות גניבה הלכה ב סמג לאוין קכד:
כד ח מיי' שם הלכה ה סמג שם:
כה ט מיי' שם הל' ב:
כו י מיי' שם הלכה ג:
כז כ ל מיי' שם הל' ד:
כח מ נ מיי' שם הל' ו:
כט ס מיי' שם הל' ג:
ל ע מיי' שם הלכה ו:

תורה אור השלם

א) לֹא תֹאבֶה לוֹ וְלֹא תִשְׁמַע אֵלָיו וְלֹא תָחוֹס עֵינְךָ עָלָיו וְלֹא תַחְמֹל וְלֹא תְכַסֶּה עָלָיו: [דברים יג, ט]

ב) כִּי אִישׁ אִישׁ אֲשֶׁר יְקַלֵּל אֶת אָבִיו וְאֶת אִמּוֹ מוֹת יוּמָת אָבִיו וְאִמּוֹ קִלֵּל דָּמָיו בּוֹ: [ויקרא כ, ט]

ג) וּמְקַלֵּל אָבִיו וְאִמּוֹ מוֹת יוּמָת: [שמות כא, יז]

ד) כִּי יִמָּצֵא אִישׁ גֹּנֵב נֶפֶשׁ מֵאֶחָיו מִבְּנֵי יִשְׂרָאֵל וְהִתְעַמֶּר בּוֹ וּמְכָרוֹ וּמֵת הַגַּנָּב הַהוּא וּבִעַרְתָּ הָרָע מִקִּרְבֶּךָ: [דברים כד, ז]

ה) וְגֹנֵב אִישׁ וּמְכָרוֹ וְנִמְצָא בְיָדוֹ מוֹת יוּמָת: [שמות כא, טז]

מסורת הש"ס

א) מכות יב., ב) [לעיל פד:], ג) [בס"ח סי' תקע"ו אסבריה טעם דחמור מקלל יותר ממכה מפני שבקללה יש היזק לאב לנשמתו], ד) לעיל סו., ה) [שם] ב"מ לד: לה: שבועות כז. חולין עח., ו) [יומא נז: מנחות ל: לא.], ז) [ברכות לא: קדושין יז: וש"נ], ח) [יבמות דף קא.], ט) [מכות ט.], י) יבמות כד: ב"ק לח: נדה נו: חולין ג: קידושין עה., כ) [תוספ' דב"ק פ"ח].

הגהות הב"ח

(א) גמ' אביו ואמו קלל אלא לר' יאשיה:

ליקוטי רש"י

לכל אין הבן נעשה וכו'. לכל עבירות שבתורה אין הבן נעשה שליח ב"ד על אביו לא להלקותו ולא לנדותו חוץ ממסית [מכות יב.]. טומטום. שאין ניכר בו לא זכרות ולא נקבות [ב"ב קכו:]. וכל זמן שלא נקרע מספקינן ליה בזכר ובנקבה. אנדרוגינוס. שיש לו זכרות ונקבות [שם קכז.]. אביו ואמו קלל. לרבות לאחר מיתה [ויקרא כ, ט]. הניחא לר' יונתן. דאמר אע"ג דלא כתיב או כמאן דכתיב או דמי וכל היכא דכתיב פלוני ופלוני או האי או האי משמע. דתניא איש. אשר יקלל את אביו ואת אמו אין לי אלא קלל שניהם אחד מהם מנין. ת"ל. בסיפיה אביו ואמו קלל. אביו קלל ואמו קלל. כלומר בתחלת המקרא סמך קללה לאביו ובסוף המקרא סמך קללה לאמו למימרא דאו האי או האי. ר' יונתן אומר. אביו ואמו נשמע נמי או האי או האי וסיפיה דקרא לדרשא אחרינא להביא את המקלל לאחר מיתה שחייב [חולין עח.]. איש איש כי יקלל וגו' לרבות בת. שקללה, או טומטום שקלל. אין לי אלא אביו ואמו. כאחד. אביו שלא אמו ואמו שלא אביו מניין תלמוד לומר אביו ואמו קלל. כלומר סמך קללה בראש המקרא לאביו ובסופו סמך קללה לאמו. ר' יונתן אומר. מתחלת המקרא משמע אביו ואמו או זה או זה דו"ו מוסיף על ענין ראשון משמע נמי אחד מהם עד שיפרט לך הכתוב יחדיו כדרך שהולכך לפרוט בכלאים שכתוב בו (דברים כב) לא תחרוש בשור ובחמור ופרט בו יחדיו שלא תאמר אסור לחרוש בשור לבדו ובחמור לבדו ואביו ואמו קלל דסיפא דריש ליה ר' יונתן לקמן באלו הן הנחנקין לרבות את המקלל לאחר מיתה (לעיל סו:). אביו קלל אמו קלל. בתחילתו סמך קללה לאביו ובסופו סמך קללה לאמו. עד שיפרוט לך הכתוב יחדו כמו שפרט הכתוב (דברים כב) בשור וחמור דמדאיצטריך למיכתב יחדיו שמעינן דאי לא כתביה הוה משמע שלא יחרוש לא בשור

בחמור ואביו ואמו קלל דריש לה בסנהדרין (פס:) לרבות את המקלל לאחר מיתה [ב"מ צד:]. דברה תורה כלשון בני אדם וכו'. ואף על גב דאיכא למדרש לא דרשינן כדמוכח בפ"ב דב"מ (דף לא:) [נדרים ג.]. מקשינן הכאה לקללה. לומר שכשם שאינו לוקה על קללתו דכתיב בעמך כך לא ילקה על הכאתו ופלוגתא היא בסנהדרין דאיכא דמקיש ואיכא דלא מקיש [מכות ט.]. והפסיק הענין וכתב וגונב איש, בין מכה אביו ואמו למקלל אביו ואמו, ונראה לי היינו פלוגתא, דמר סבר מקשינן הכאה לקללה, ומר סבר לא מקשינן [שמות כא, טו]. כותים גירי אריות. כותים אותם שהושיב סנחריב בערי שומרון כדכתיב (מלכים ב יז) ויבא מלך אשור (אנשים מספרויים) מבבל ומכותה וגו' ועל שם שהביאם מכותה נקראו כותים ונתגיירו מאימת האריות כדכתיב (מלכים ב' יז) וישלח (בם את) ה' בהם האריות וגו' וכולה ענייה במלכים [קידושין עה.]. גירי אריות כגון כותים דכתיב בספר מלכים (ב' יז) וישלח ה' בהם את האריות ונתגיירו מחמת פחד האריות והם בגלות שומרון [יבמות כד:]. בספר מלכים (ב יז) מפורש וישלח ה' בהם את האריות וכותים כתיבי התם ויבא מלך אשור (אנשים) מכותה וקא חשיב שאר מקומות [ב"ק לח:]. והתעמר בו. אינו חייב עד שישתמש בו [דברים כד, ז]. וגנב איש ומכרו. למה נאמר לפי שנאמר (דברים כד, ז) כי ימצא איש גונב נפש מאחיו אין לי אלא איש שגנב נפש או טומטום או אנדרוגינוס שגנבו מנין תלמוד לומר וגונב איש ומכרו ולפי שנאמר כאן וגונב איש אין לי אלא גונב איש גונב אשה מנין תלמוד לומר (שם) גונב נפש לכך הוצרכו שניהם מה שחסר זה גלה זה [שמות כא, טז].

value of a ***perutah.*** According to the Tanna Kamma, the kidnaper is liable to execution, whereas according to R' Yehudah, he is not.[37]

The Gemara discusses two specific cases of kidnapings:

בָּעֵי רַבִּי יִרְמְיָה – **R' Yirmiyah inquired:** גְּנָבוֹ וּמְכָרוֹ יָשֵׁן מַהוּ – **If someone kidnaped and sold [a victim]** who was **asleep, what** is the law? מָכַר אִשָּׁה לְעוּבָּרָהּ מַהוּ – **If [a kidnaper] sold a** pregnant **woman for her baby, what** is the law?[38]

The Gemara explains the inquiries:

יֵשׁ דֶּרֶךְ עִימּוּר בְּכָךְ – **Is there a normal manner of usage** in these cases אוֹ אֵין דֶּרֶךְ עִימּוּר בְּכָךְ – **or is there no normal manner of usage?**

The Gemara argues that the law in these cases should be obvious:

וְתֵיפוֹק לֵיהּ – **But derive** that **[the law]** exempts the kidnaper in these cases דְּלֵיכָּא עִימּוּר כְּלָל – **because there was no usage at all!**[39] – ? –

The Gemara answers that the victims were indeed used:

לֹא צְרִיכָא – **[The inquiries] require** consideration **only** if the victims were in fact used, יָשֵׁן דְּזָגָא עֲלֵיהּ – such as if the victim was **asleep** and **[the kidnaper] leaned upon him;** אִשָּׁה דְאוֹקְמָא בְּאַפֵּי זִיקָא – or if the victim was a pregnant **woman** and **[the kidnaper] stood her in front of the wind** to protect himself from its blasts.[40]

Having explained where the inquiry is relevant, the Gemara restates the inquiry:

דֶּרֶךְ עִימּוּר בְּכָךְ אוֹ אֵין דֶּרֶךְ עִימּוּר בְּכָךְ – If the kidnaper uses his victim in one of these ways, **is this a normal manner of usage or is this not a normal manner of usage?**[41] מַאי – **What** is the law?

The Gemara does not resolve these questions, and concludes:

תֵּיקוּ – **Let [these questions] stand.**

The Gemara cites a related Baraisa:[42]

תָּנוּ רַבָּנַן – **The Rabbis taught in a Baraisa:** ,,כִּי־יִמָּצֵא אִישׁ גֹּנֵב נֶפֶשׁ מֵאֶחָיו'' – One verse states:[43] ***IF A MAN IS FOUND KIDNAPING A PERSON OF HIS BRETHREN.*** ,,אִישׁ'' שֶׁגָּנַב – אֵין לִי אֶלָּא – I KNOW FROM HERE ONLY that A *MAN* WHO KIDNAPS someone is liable to execution.[44] אִשָּׁה מִנַּיִין – FROM WHERE DO I KNOW that A WOMAN who kidnaps is liable? תַּלְמוּד לוֹמַר ,,וְגֹנֵב אִישׁ'' – SCRIPTURE therefore TEACHES in another verse: ***ONE WHO KIDNAPS A MAN.***[45] אֵין לִי אֶלָּא אִישׁ שֶׁגָּנַב בֵּין אִשָּׁה וּבֵין אִישׁ – From these two phrases I KNOW ONLY that the death penalty is imposed upon A MAN WHO KIDNAPS EITHER A MAN OR A WOMAN, וְאִשָּׁה שֶׁגָּנְבָה אִישׁ – AND upon A WOMAN WHO KIDNAPS A MAN.[46] אִשָּׁה שֶׁגָּנְבָה אִשָּׁה מִנַּיִין – FROM WHERE DO I KNOW that A WOMAN WHO KIDNAPS A WOMAN is liable? תַּלְמוּד לוֹמַר ,,וּמֵת הַגַּנָּב הַהוּא'' – SCRIPTURE therefore TEACHES[47]: ***THAT KIDNAPER SHALL DIE***, מִכָּל מָקוֹם – indicating that one is liable for kidnaping IN ANY MANNER.[48]

A second Baraisa:

תַּנְיָא אִידָךְ – **It was taught in another Baraisa:** ,,כִּי־יִמָּצֵא אִישׁ גֹּנֵב נֶפֶשׁ מֵאֶחָיו'' – Scripture states: ***IF A MAN IS FOUND KIDNAPING A PERSON OF HIS BRETHREN.*** אֶחָד הַגּוֹנֵב אֶת הָאִישׁ וְאֶחָד הַגּוֹנֵב אֶת הָאִשָּׁה – This teaches that WHETHER ONE KIDNAPS A MAN OR HE KIDNAPS A WOMAN, וְאֶחָד גֵּר וְאֶחָד עֶבֶד מְשׁוּחְרָר וְקָטָן – WHETHER he kidnaps A CONVERT, FREED SLAVE OR A MINOR, חַיָּיב – HE IS LIABLE for his act.[49]

The Baraisa now teaches under what conditions someone is liable for kidnaping:

גְּנָבוֹ וְלֹא מְכָרוֹ – IF HE KIDNAPED ONE of the above people BUT DID NOT SELL HIM, מְכָרוֹ וַעֲדַיִין יֶשְׁנוֹ בִּרְשׁוּתוֹ – or HE SOLD HIM, BUT [THE VICTIM] IS STILL IN HIS own DOMAIN,[50] פָּטוּר – [THE

NOTES

37. That is, the Tanna Kamma certainly admits that the kidnaper is not liable to execution unless he put his victim to work before selling him. Nevertheless, he made no mention of this in order to indicate that even the most insignificant usage makes the kidnaper liable (*Imrei Binah*; cf. *Sanhedrei Ketanah*).

38. That is, what if someone kidnaps a pregnant woman and then sells the rights to the unborn child, without selling the woman herself? (*Rashi*). Is the kidnaper liable to execution for kidnaping the unborn child or not? (*Margaliyos HaYam*).

39. For presumably, the sleeping victim and the unborn child were never used, just sold (*Rashi*).

40. So that her additional girth (resulting from her pregnancy) sheltered the kidnaper from the wind (*Rashi*). R' Yirmiyah inquires as to whether this makes the kidnaper liable to execution for having kidnaped the baby, used it and sold it (cf. *Ein Mishpat* §8 in *Likutei Halachos*).

[The case must be one in which the woman's additional girth afforded extra protection from a draft, because the kidnaper sold only the fetus and not the woman herself. Hence, the kidnaper would not be liable for merely using the woman; he must use the baby, e.g. by taking advantage of the protection afforded as a result of the pregnancy (see *Imrei Binah* and *Margaliyos HaYam;* see also *Rashash*).]

41. In other words, are these usages (of a sleeping person and a fetus) considered a normal way of using a person or not?

Our elucidation reflects *Rashi*'s understanding of the Gemara. However, *Rambam* (*Hil. Geneivah* 9:3,4) apparently understood the Gemara very differently, possibly based on a different text (see *Aruch LaNer, Toras Chaim* and *Even HaEzel* to *Rambam* loc. cit.).

42. This Baraisa expounds two verses that discuss the laws of kidnaping: 1) *Exodus* 21:16: וְגֹנֵב אִישׁ וּמְכָרוֹ וְנִמְצָא בְיָדוֹ מוֹת יוּמָת, *One who kidnaps a man and sells him, and he was found to have been in his hand, shall surely be put to death.*
2) *Deuteronomy* 24:7: כִּי־יִמָּצֵא אִישׁ גֹּנֵב נֶפֶשׁ מֵאֶחָיו מִבְּנֵי יִשְׂרָאֵל וְהִתְעַמֶּר־בּוֹ וּמְכָרוֹ וּמֵת הַגַּנָּב הַהוּא. . ., *If a man is found kidnaping a person from his brethren among the Children of Israel, and he uses him and sells him, that kidnaper shall die...*

43. *Deuteronomy* 24:7.

44. For this verse specifically mentions a *man* who kidnaps (*Rashi*).

45. *Exodus* 21:16. In this verse, the Torah makes no reference to the kidnaper's gender, which indicates that a woman, too, is liable for kidnaping.

46. For the verse in *Deuteronomy* states that a *man* who kidnaps a *person* is executed. Since the Torah does not specify the victim's gender, this indicates that a male is liable for kidnaping anyone — either male or female. The verse in *Exodus* states that *one* who kidnaps a *man* is executed. Since the kidnaper's gender is not specified, this indicates that anyone — man or woman — is liable for kidnaping a man. But there seems to be no explicit source that a woman is liable for kidnaping another woman! (*Rashi*).

47. *Deuteronomy* 24:7.

48. That is, a kidnaper of any gender is liable for kidnaping anyone — male or female.

Rashi explains that the Gemara's derivation is based upon the superfluity of this clause. The verse in *Deuteronomy* (24:7) could simply have stated that if a man is found kidnaping a person . . . and he uses him and sells him, "he shall die" (וּמֵת), but the verse adds the expression הַגַּנָּב הַהוּא, *that kidnaper*. Our Gemara therefore expounds the extra word *kidnaper* to be teaching that a woman who kidnaps a woman is also subject to execution. *Sifri* expounds the extra word *that* to be teaching that the death penalty is not imposed for kidnaping a slave (*Rashi*).

49. The word נֶפֶשׁ, *person,* includes men, women and minors. The word מֵאֶחָיו, *from his brethren,* includes converts and freed slaves, since they too are commanded in some mitzvos (see *Rambam, Hil. Geneivah* 9:6).

50. That is, if the victim was imprisoned and sold to another person while still on his own property, the kidnaper is not liable to execution. If the kidnaper removed the victim to his (the kidnaper's) property, however, the death penalty is imposed even if the purchaser did not actually take possession of the victim (see *Rashi* and *Rambam, Hil. Geneivah* 9:3 with *Maggid Mishneh*).

Ramban to *Exodus* (21:16) understands this clause of the Baraisa

מידי דהוה לאחר מיתה מאי הוה עלה [א] אמר רבה בר רב הונא וכן תנא דבי רבי ישמעאל לכל אין הבן נעשה שליח לאביו להכותו ולקללו חוץ ממסית שהרי אמרה תורה (א) לא תחמול ולא תכסה עליו: **מתני'** (ב) המכה אביו ואמו אינו חייב עד שיעשה בהן חבורה זה חומר במקלל מבמכה שהמקלל לאחר מיתה חייב (ג) והמכה לאחר מיתה פטור: **גמ'** ת"ר (ב) אביו ואמו קלל לאחר מיתה שיכול הואיל וחייב במכה וחייב במקלל מה מכה אינו חייב אלא מחיים אף המקלל אינו חייב אלא מחיים ועוד ק"ו ומה מכה שעשה בו שלא בעמך כבעמך לא חייב בו לאחר מיתה מקלל שלא עשה בו שלא בעמך כבעמך אינו דין שלא חייב בו לאחר מיתה ת"ל אביו ואמו קלל לאחר מיתה הניחא לר' יונתן דמייתר ליה קרא אביו ואמו (א) אלא לר' יאשיה מאי איכא למימר (ד) דתניא (ב) איש איש מה ת"ל איש איש לרבות בת טומטום ואנדרוגינוס (ב) אשר יקלל את אביו ואת אמו (ה) אין לי אלא אביו ואמו אביו שלא אמו אמו שלא אביו מניין ת"ל אביו ואמו קלל אביו קלל אמו קלל דברי ר' יאשיה ר' יונתן אומר משמע שניהן כאחד ומשמע אחד ואחד בפני עצמו (ו) עד שיפרט לך הכתוב יחדיו מנא ליה נפקא ליה (ג) מומקלל אביו ואמו מות יומת ואידך ההוא מיבעי ליה לרבות בת טומטום ואנדרוגינוס ותיפוק ליה מאיש איש (ז) דברה תורה כלשון בני אדם וליתני חומר במכה מבמקלל שהמכה עשה בו שלא בעמך כבעמך משא"כ במקלל קסבר (ח) מקשינן הכאה לקללה לימא הני תנאי כהני תנאי דתני חדא כותי אתה מצווה על הכאתו ואי אתה מצווה על קללתו ותניא אידך אי אתה מצווה לא על קללתו ולא על הכאתו סברוה דכולי עלמא כותים גירי אמת הן מאי לאו בהא קמיפלגי דמר סבר מקשינן הכאה לקללה ומר סבר (ט) לא מקשינן הכאה לקללה לא דכ"ע לא מקשינן הכאה לקללה והכא בהא קמיפלגי מר סבר כותים גירי אמת הן ומר סבר (י) כותים גירי אריות הן אי הכי היינו דקתני עלה ושורו כישראל אלא שמע מינה בהיקישא פליגי ש"מ: **מתני'** הגונב נפש מישראל אינו חייב עד שיכניסנו לרשותו רבי יהודה אומר עד שיכניסנו לרשותו וישתמש בו שנאמר (ד) והתעמר בו ומכרו הגונב את בנו רבי ישמעאל בנו של ר' יוחנן בן ברוקה מחייב וחכמים פוטרין גנב מי שחציו עבד וחציו בן חורין ר' יהודה מחייב וחכמים פוטרין: **גמ'** ותנא קמא לא בעי עימור א"ר אחא בריה דרבא עימור פחות משוה פרוטה איכא בינייהו בעי ר' ירמיה גנבו ומכרו ישן מהו מכר אשה לעוברה מהו יש דרך עימור בכך או אין דרך עימור בכך ותיפוק ליה דליכא עימור כלל לא צריכא ישן דזגא עליה אשה דאוקמא באפי זיקא דרך עימור בכך או אין דרך עימור בכך מאי תיקו ת"ר (ד) כי ימצא איש גונב נפש מאחיו אין לי אלא איש שגנב אשה מניין ת"ל (ה) וגונב איש אין לי אלא איש שגנב בין אשה ובין איש ואשה שגנבה איש אשה שגנבה אשה מניין ת"ל (ד) ומת הגנב ההוא מכל מקום תניא אידך (ד) כי ימצא איש גונב נפש מאחיו אחד הגונב את האיש ואחד הגונב את האשה ואחד גר ואחד עבד משוחרר וקטן חייב גנבו ולא מכרו מכרו ועדיין ישנו ברשותו פטור מכרו לאביו או לאחיו או לאחד מן הקרובים חייב הגונב את העבדים פטור

תני

רש"י

מידי דהוה לאחר מיתה. דילפינן לקמן מקלל לאחר מיתה חייב וא"ת והתנן מכה לאחר מיתה פטור והכא מיחייב ליה אהכאה דקתני הכהו וקללו היינו טעמא דפטור מכה לאחר מיתה משום דבעינן חבורה ולאחר מיתה ליכא חבורה דליכא נפש דנפקא ליה לעיל מנפש ויוצא ליהרג איכא חבורה דחי הוא אלא דסופו למות: **מתני'** שהמקלל לאחר מיתה חייב. כדיליף בגמרא: והמכה לאחר מיתה פטור. דחבורה ליכא: **גמ'** אביו ואמו קלל. קרא יתירא הוא דהא כתיב רישיה דקרא אשר יקלל את אביו ואת אמו: מכה שעשה שלא בעמך כבעמך. דגבי הכאה לא כתיב בעמך למעוטי שאינו עושה מעשה עמך והאי תנא סבר לא מקשינן הכאה לקללה מפני המקרא המפסיק בינתים: לא חייב בו לאחר מיתה. דהא חבורה כתיב: לרבות בת. טומטום ואנדרוגינוס: אין לי אלא אביו ואמו. שניהם יחד: אביו קילל ואמו קילל. ברחש המקרא סמך קללה לאביו ובסוף סמך לאמו: עד שיפרט לך הכתוב יחדו. וכמו שפרט בחורש בשור ובחמור מדפרט לך ש"מ דאי לא הוי יחדו הוה משמע שור לבדו וחמור לבדו והא אביו ואמו דרישא דרשינן נמי או אביו או אמו וסיפא לאתויי לאחר מיתה: מומקלל אביו. דואלה המשפטים: ואידך. דמפיק לאחר מיתה מאביו ואמו קילל: וליתני נמי וכו'. אמתניתין קאי דקתני זה חומר במקלל מבמכה: לימא הני תנאי. תנא דמתניתין דלא תנא חומר במכה שעשה בו שלא בעמך כבעמך ותנא דברייתא דלעיל דתנא ומה מכה שעשה בו: גירי אמת הן. מתחילתן גרים גמורים היו ועכשיו הרשיעו וישראל שאינו עושה מעשה עמך הוא וכי היכי דעל קללתו פטור על הכאתו נמי פטור: גירי אריות הן. והרי הם כעובדי כוכבים גמורים: אי הכי. דטעמא דפטור משום דגירי אריות הן: היינו דתנא עלה. בתמיה בהך מתני' דקתני אינו מצווה לא על הכאתו ולא על קללתו קתני ושורו כישראל שור שלנו שנגח את שורו ושורו שנגח שלנו תם משלם חצי נזק ומועד משלם נזק שלם ואילו דעובד כוכבים תנן שור של ישראל שנגח שור של עובד כוכבים פטור ושל עובד כוכבים שנגח שור של ישראל בין תם בין מועד משלם נזק שלם: **מתני'** שיכניסנו לרשותו. דכתיב (שמות כב) ונמצא בידו ותניא במכילתא ונמצא אין מציאה בכל מקום אלא בעדים בידו אין בידו אלא ברשותו וכן הוא אומר (במדבר כא) ויקח את כל ארצו מידו: **גמ'** עמור. שמוש: גנבו ומכרו כשהוא ישן מהו. לקמן מפרש לה הבעיא: מכר אשה לעוברה. גנב אשה מעוברת ומכרה לעוברה שלא מכר הגוף שלה אלא שיהא עובר מכור: דליכא עימור. לא בישן ולא בעובר: דזגא עליה. דסמך עליו: דאוקמא באפי זיקא. וכל כמה שהיא עבה מועיל יותר להגין בפני הרוח: אין לי אלא איש. כשהגנב איש: וגונב איש. שהנגנב איש ולא אשה וקרא קמא דלא קפיד אנגנב למהוי איש דכתיב נפש הלכך אין לי אלא איש שגנב בין איש בין אשה דהיכא דגנב הוי איש כתוב גונב נפש ואשה שגנבה איש דכתיב וגונב איש וגונב אפילו אשה גונבת משמע: הגנב. מ"מ וההוא דרשינן ליה בספרי למעוטי גונב עבד: ועדיין ישנו ברשותו. ברשות הנגנב עצמו שעדיין לא הכניסו גנב ברשותו: פטור. שהרי לא גנבו: לאביו. אביו של נגנב:

תני

תוספות

שיכול הואיל וחייב במכה כו'. הוי מצי למימר הואיל וכתיב בעמך כדאמר לעיל במקוים שבעמך: **ומה** מכה אביו כו'. ואם תאמר מה למכה שכן בחנק תאמר במקלל דבסקילה וי"ל דהיא גופה ילפינן השתא דמכה אביו בסקילה מקל וחומר ממקלל ומיהו קשה לבסוף דיליף דמקלל לאחר מיתה חייב נילף ליה שלא נעשה בו שלא בעמך כבעמך ממקלל דחייב ביה לאחר מיתה ומכה פטור דבעינן נפש כדדרשינן לעיל (דף פד:) עד דעביד חבורה: **איש** איש מה תלמוד לומר איש איש. פירשתי שלהי פ' ד' מיתות (לעיל דף סו. ד"ה לרבות):

ושורו כישראל. לאו לגמרי כישראל דשור של ישראל שנגח לשור של כותי פטור משום דקנסינן להו כדאמר בריש פ' ד' וה' (ב"ק דף לח:) ומיהו לגבי הכי הוי כישראל דשור של כותי שנגח לשור של ישראל תם משלם חצי נזק ומועד נזק שלם ושור של עובד כוכבים שנגח לשור של ישראל בין תם בין מועד משלם נזק שלם: **עד** שיכניסנו לרשותו. משום דכתיב ונמצא בידו ואע"ג דבפ"ק דבבא מציעא (דף י:) גבי גט וגניבה מצרכינן תרי קראי לרבויי דידו לאו דווקא דהוא הדין גגו חצירו קרפיפו דלמא כאן נמי יש שום ריבוי ואפשר דאם הגביהו אפילו ברשות בעלים חייב כדאשכחן גבי גניבה בפרק מרובה (ב"ק דף עט: ושם) דתנן היה מושכו ויוצא כו' אי נמי הכא דפטר ר' שמעון מכרו לקרובים דבעינן שיוציאנו מרשות אחיו כ"ש דברשות בעלים לא מהני כלל:

מונמלא

תורה אור השלם

א) לא תאבה לו ולא תשמע אליו ולא תחוס עינך עליו ולא תחמל ולא תכסה עליו: [דברים יג, ט]

ב) כי איש איש אשר יקלל את אביו ואת אמו מות יומת אביו ואמו קלל דמיו בו: [ויקרא כ, ט]

ג) ומקלל אביו ואמו מות יומת: [שמות כא, יז]

ד) כי ימצא איש גנב נפש מאחיו מבני ישראל והתעמר בו ומכרו ומת הגנב ההוא ובערת הרע מקרבך: [דברים כד, ז]

ה) וגנב איש ומכרו ונמצא בידו מות יומת: [שמות כא, טז]

KIDNAPER] IS EXEMPT from punishment.[51] מְכָרוֹ לְאָבִיו אוֹ לְאָחִיו – **IF [THE KIDNAPER] SOLD [HIS VICTIM] TO [THE VICTIM'S] FATHER OR BROTHER,** אוֹ לְאֶחָד מִן הַקְּרוֹבִים – **OR TO ANY ONE OF [THE VICTIM'S] RELATIVES,** חַיָּיב – **[THE KIDNAPER] IS LIABLE** for his act.[52] הַגּוֹנֵב אֶת הָעֲבָדִים פָּטוּר – **ONE WHO KIDNAPS SLAVES IS EXEMPT** from punishment.[53]

NOTES

somewhat differently. According to *Ramban,* when the Baraisa states that the victim is still in *his* domain, it refers to the domain of the kidnaper. In other words, the kidnaper is not liable to execution for selling his victim unless the purchaser actually took possession of him.

51. Kidnaping means removing someone from his own domain; as long as he is on his own domain, he has not been kidnaped and thus the "kidnaper" who sold him is not liable to execution. [According to *Ramban* (cited in previous note), the victim must also have left the legal possession of the kidnaper and entered that of the purchaser. Until he does, his sale is not complete, and a kidnaper is not liable unless he sells his victim.]

52. The Gemara will explain the novelty of this ruling.

53. See note 48.

תָּנֵי תַּנָּא קַמֵּיהּ דְּרַב שֵׁשֶׁת – **A Tanna**[1] **taught the** above **Baraisa in the presence of Rav Sheishess.**[2] אָמַר לֵיהּ – **[Rav Sheishess] said to him:** אֲנִי שׁוֹנֶה – **I have learned** the following Baraisa: רַבִּי שִׁמְעוֹן אוֹמֵר – R' SHIMON SAYS: ,,מֵאֶחָיו'' עַד שֶׁיּוֹצִיאֶנּוּ מֵרְשׁוּת אֶחָיו – The verse states that the kidnaper stole the victim *FROM HIS BRETHREN,*[3] which teaches that he is not liable UNTIL HE REMOVES [THE VICTIM] FROM THE DOMAIN OF HIS BRETHREN. וְאַתְּ אָמְרַתְּ חַיָּיב – **And you say** that **[a kidnaper] is liable** if he sells the victim to his father or brothers.[4] That is clearly impossible!

תְּנֵי פָּטוּר – Rather, revise the text of your Baraisa and TEACH it as follows: [THE KIDNAPER] IS EXEMPT if he sells the victim to his (the victim's) relative.

The Gemara asks:

מַאי קוּשְׁיָא – **What was** Rav Sheishess' **difficulty** reconciling his Baraisa with the one quoted to him? דִּילְמָא הָא רַבִּי שִׁמְעוֹן הָא רַבָּנָן – **Perhaps this** Baraisa taught by Rav Sheishess reflects the opinion of **R' Shimon,** whereas **this** Baraisa that the Tanna quoted to Rav Sheishess reflects the view of **the Rabbis.** – ? –

The Gemara answers:

לֹא סָלְקָא דַּעְתָּךְ – **Do not let that** answer **enter your mind,** דְּאָמַר רַבִּי יוֹחָנָן – **for R' Yochanan said:** סְתָם מַתְנִיתִין רַבִּי מֵאִיר – **An anonymous Mishnah** generally reflects the view of **R' Meir,**[5] סְתָם תּוֹסֶפְתָּא רַבִּי נְחֶמְיָה – **an anonymous** ***Tosefta*** generally reflects the view of **R' Nechemiah,**[6] סְתָם סִפְרָא רַבִּי יְהוּדָה – **an anonymous** ***Sifra*** generally reflects the view of **R' Yehudah,**[7] סְתָם סִפְרֵי רַבִּי שִׁמְעוֹן – **an anonymous** ***Sifrei*** generally reflects the view of **R' Shimon**[8] וְכוּלְּהוּ אַלִּיבָּא דְּרַבִּי עֲקִיבָא – **and all these** Tannaim stated their opinions **based on** the opinion **of R' Akiva.**[9] Thus, the Baraisa quoted to Rav Sheishess, which is codified in *Sifrei* anonymously, clearly reflects the view of R' Shimon and not that of the Sages, and thus should be emended.

The Gemara quotes a section of our Mishnah:

הַגּוֹנֵב בְּנוֹ – If ONE KIDNAPS HIS SON, R' Yishmael the son of R' Yochanan ben Berokah renders him liable, but the Sages exempt him.

The Gemara analyzes the Mishnah's ruling:

מַאי טַעְמָא דְּרַבָּנָן – **What is the reasoning of the Rabbis?** אָמַר אַבַּיֵי – **Abaye said:** דְּאָמַר קְרָא ,,כִּי־יִמָּצֵא'' – **For the verse states:**[10] ***If*** *a man* ***is found*** *kidnaping a person,* פְּרָט לְמָצוּי – which **excludes** a case where **[the victim] was** readily **accessible** to the kidnaper, e.g. the kidnaper's own son.[11]

The Gemara asks:

אָמַר לֵיהּ רַב פָּפָּא לְאַבַּיֵי – **Rav Pappa said to Abaye:** אֶלָּא מֵעַתָּה – **But now,** ,,כִּי־יִמָּצֵא אִישׁ שֹׁכֵב עִם־אִשָּׁה בְעֻלַת־בַּעַל'' – when discussing adultery, Scripture states:[12] ***If a man is found lying with a woman who is married to a husband***; הָכִי נַמִּי ,,כִּי־יִמָּצֵא'' פְּרָט לְמָצוּי – is it **indeed so** that there too, the expression *if a man* ***will be found*** **excludes** a case **where [the woman] was** readily **accessible** to the adulterer? כְּגוֹן שֶׁל בֵּית פְּלוֹנִי – **For example,** take the married women **of the house of So-and-so,** דִּשְׁכִיחָן גַּבַּיְיהוּ – **who are readily accessible to [men]** other than their husbands;[13] הָכִי נַמִּי דִּפְטִירֵי – is it **indeed so that [the men]** would be **exempt** if they committed adultery with these women? Surely not! Evidently, then, the expression *if a man is found* cannot be expounded as was previously suggested.[14] – ? –

NOTES

1. In this context, "Tanna" means a scholar who had memorized the texts of numerous Tannaic teachings.

2. Specifically, the clause stating that a kidnaper is liable for selling the victim to his (the victim's) father [or brothers] (*Rashi*).

3. *Deuteronomy* 24:7.

4. R' Shimon expounds the *mem* prefix of מֵאֶחָיו, ***from*** *his brethren,* to mean that the kidnaper is not liable unless he separates the victim from his family. Hence, he is surely not liable if he sells the victim to his own family.

5. R' Yehudah HaNasi, redactor of the Mishnah, organized the Tannaic teachings and included many of them in that work. Those teachings that he recorded anonymously generally reflect the view of R' Meir.

There are several compilations of Tannaic teachings not included in R' Yehudah HaNasi's Mishnah; see next three notes.

6. *Tosefta* is a collection of Tannaic teachings that explain and elaborate on the Mishnah (*Mevo HaTalmud*). When *Tosefta* anonymously cites a ruling, it generally reflects the opinion of R' Nechemiah. [The *Tosefta* referred to by the Gemara is *not* the same *Tosefta* printed in the back of the Gemara (see *Kitzur Klalei HaTalmud,* citing *Sefer HaKerisus*).]

7. *Sifra* (also called *Toras Kohanim*) is a collection of Baraisos that expound the Book of *Leviticus.* [It is also known as *Sifra D'vei Rav* – The Book of the *Yeshiva* – because the students in Talmudical academies were well versed in this work (*Rashi* to *Chullin* 66a ד״ה תנא דבי רב).] When a *Sifra* anonymously cites a ruling, it generally reflects the opinion of R' Yehudah.

8. *Sifrei* is a collection of Baraisos that expound the Books of *Numbers* and *Deuteronomy.* [It is called *Sifrei* (plural) because it expounds both *Numbers* and *Deuteronomy* in contrast to *Sifra* (singular), which expounds only *Leviticus* (*Aruch* ע׳ ספר; *Rabbeinu Chananel* to *Yoma* 40b).] When *Sifrei* anonymously cites a ruling, it generally reflects the opinion of R' Shimon. [There is some discussion as to whether R' Yehudah and R' Shimon actually recorded anonymous rulings in the *Sifra* and *Sifrei* respectively, or if the anonymous Baraisos were recorded by others but reflect the view of these Tannaim. See *Sdei Chemed, Kelalei HaPoskim* ch. 2:4.]

The anonymous Baraisa on 85b, which a Tanna quoted to Rav Sheishess, expounds a verse in *Deuteronomy* and is found in *Sifrei.* Since it is anonymous, it presumably reflects the opinion of R' Shimon rather than, as previously suggested, the Rabbis who dispute his view (*Rashi*).

9. That is, all quoted teachings that they heard from R' Akiva (*Rashi*).

10. *Deuteronomy* 24:7.

11. [Generally the term יִמָּצֵא, *is found,* connotes that a person or thing was found by chance, not that it was readily accessible. Since we would not expect the Torah to use this expression in connection with a kidnaper, we apply it to the victim. In other words, if someone chanced upon a victim, kidnaped, used and sold him, he is liable to execution. If the victim was readily accessible, however, such as when one kidnaped his son, the kidnaper is not liable to execution. See *Ran* ד״ה אנא.]

12. *Deuteronomy* 22:22.

13. There was a certain house where several married couples lived. The men, of course, never secluded themselves with other people's wives, but those wives were nonetheless accessible to them.

The Gemara refers to these people simply as the residents of the house of So-and-so rather than identifying them, because they were reputable people who were lax in one area; they all lived in the same house, which made the men and women accessible to each other. Thus, the Talmudic Sages looked askance at these living arrangements, but they saw no reason to publicize the identities of the people involved (*Rashi*).

14. The Gemara's point is as follows: The Torah uses the expression כִּי־יִמָּצֵא אִישׁ, *if a man will be found,* in two verses, one dealing with a kidnaper and the other with an adulterer; presumably, the expression means the same thing in both contexts. Thus, if we derive that the kidnaper must chance upon his victim in order to be liable, then the same must be true of an adulterer; an adulterer, too, must not be liable unless he chanced upon the adulteress. But this second derivation is absolutely illogical; a man is surely liable to execution if he commits adultery with any married woman, whether she was readily accessible or not. We must therefore conclude that כִּי־יִמָּצֵא אִישׁ, *if a man will be found,* does not mean to stipulate that the kidnaper or adulterer must chance upon the victim, as previously suggested.

תני תנא קמיה דרב ששת א"ל אני שונה רבי שמעון אומר א) מאחיו עד שיוציאנו מרשות אחיו ואת אמרת חייב [א]תני פטור מאי קושיא דילמא הא ר"ש הא רבנן לא ס"ד דאמר ר' יוחנן ב) סתם מתני' ר' מאיר סתם תוספתא ר' נחמיה ג) סתם ספרא רבי יהודה סתם ספרי ר"ש וכולהו אליבא דר"ע: הגונב בנו: מאי טעמא דרבנן אמר אביי דאמר קרא א) כי ימצא פרט למצוי א"ל רב פפא לאביי אלא מעתה ב) כי ימצא איש שוכב עם אשה בעולת בעל הכי נמי כי ימצא פרט למצוי כגון של בית פלוני דשכיחן גביידהו הכי נמי דפטירי א"ל אנא ג) מונמצא בידו קאמינא אמר רבא [ב]הלכך הני מיקרי דרדקי ומתנו רבנן כמצויין בידן דמו ופטירי: גנב מי שחציו וכו': ג) תנן התם רבי יהודה אומר אין לעבדים בושת ד) מאי טעמא דר' יהודה אמר קרא ד) כי ינצו אנשים יחדיו איש ואחיו מי שיש לו אחוה יצא עבד שאין לו אחוה ורבנן אחיו הוא במצות והכא היכי דריש ר' יהודה סבר א) מאחיו לאפוקי עבדים בני ישראל למעוטי מי שחציו עבד וחציו בן חורין מבני ישראל למעוטי מי שחציו עבד וחציו בן חורין הוי מיעוט אחר מיעוט ה) ואין מיעוט אחר מיעוט אלא לרבות ורבנן מאחיו לאפוקי עבדים לא משמע להו דהא אחיו הוא במצות בני ישראל מבני ישראל חד למעוטי עבד וחד למעוטי מי שחציו עבד וחציו בן חורין אזהרה לגונב נפש מנין רבי יאשיה אמר ה) מלא תגנב רבי יוחנן אמר ו) מלא ימכרו ממכרת עבד ולא פליגי מר קא חשיב לאו דגניבה ומר קא חשיב לאו דמכירה ת"ר ה) לא תגנוב [ג]בגונב נפשות הכתוב מדבר אתה אומר בגונב נפשות או אינו אלא בגונב ממון אמרת צא ולמד משלש עשרה מדות שהתורה נדרשת בהן דבר הלמד מעניינו במה הכתוב מדבר בנפשות אף כאן בנפשות תניא אידך ז) לא תגנובו בגונב ממון הכתוב מדבר אתה אומר בגונב ממון או אינו אלא בגונב נפשות אמרת צא ולמד משלש עשרה מדות שהתורה נדרשת בהן י) דבר הלמד מעניינו במה הכתוב מדבר בממון אף כאן בממון איתמר עידי גניבה ועידי מכירה בנפש שהוזמו חזקיה אמר אין נהרגין רבי יוחנן אמר נהרגין חזקיה דאמר כר"ע י) דאמר ח) דבר ולא חצי דבר ורבי יוחנן אמר כרבנן דאמרי דבר ואפי' חצי דבר ומודה חזקיה בעדים האחרונים של בן סורר ומורה שהוזמו שנהרגין מתוך שיכולים לומר הראשונים להלקותו

רש"י

תני תנא. להך מתני' דקתני מכר לאביו חייב: **סתם ספרא.** תורת כהנים: **סתם ספרי.** ספר וידבר ומשנה תורה והאי סתמא דכי ימצא איש במשנה תורה הוא: **אליבא דרבי עקיבא.** ממה שלמדו מר' עקיבא אמרום: **של בית פלוני.** לא רצה להזכיר שמם שחשובין היו וזה לא היו נוהגין כדת שהיו הרבה דרין בבית אחד אנשים ונשים והיו מצויין תמיד עם נשי חביריהן ולא שמתייחדין: **ונמצא.** קרא יתירא הוא דאי ללמד שימצא בעדים מכי ימצא נפקא: **כמצויין בידן דמו.** התלמידים מצויין תמיד בבית הרב ואם גנב הרב אחד מתלמידיו ומכרו אינו נהרג: **אין לעבדים בושת.** המבייש את העבד לא חייבתו תורה לתת דמי בשתו: **וכי ינצו אנשים יחדיו והכה איש וגו'.** מהתם נפקא לן חיוב בשת דכתיב וקצותה את כפה ממון אתה אומר ממון או אינו אלא ממש נאמר כאן לא תחוס עינך ונאמר להלן בעדים זוממין (דברים יט) לא תחוס עינך מה להלן ממון אף כאן ממון: **עבד שאין לו אחוה.** ואפי' עם אחיו בני אביו דכתיב (בראשית כב) עם החמור עם הדומה לחמור אינו אלא כבהמה: **אחיו הוא במצות.** בכל מצות שהאשה חייבת בהן עבד חייב בהן דגמר לה לה מאשה: **והכא.** במתני' בגונב נפש דכתיב מאחיו: **היכי דריש.** רבי יהודה לחייב על מי שחציו עבד: **מאחיו למעוטי עבדים.** דהא לרבי יהודה אין לו אחוה: **מבני.** יתירא דריש ליה דהוה ליה למכתב מאחיו בני ישראל: **מלא תגנוב.** האמור בעשרת הדברות דבגונב נפשות מתוקם לקמן בשמעתין: **דבר הלמד מעניינו.** אם אי אתה יודע במה הכתוב מדבר צא ולמד מפרשה שכתוב בה ולפי הפרשה הוא נכתב אצלה וכאן במה כל הענין מדבר בנפשות לא תרצח ולא תנאף כל אלה חייבי מיתות ב"ד אף לא תגנוב בגניבה שיש בה מיתת ב"ד: **לא תגנובו.** בפרשת קדושים תהיו: **משלש עשרה מדות.** זו היא אחת מהן שיהא הדבר מעניינו למד: **במה הכתוב מדבר.** הענין של מטה ושל מעלה מזו: **בממון.** לא תעשוק את רעך (ויקרא יט): **עידי גניבה ועידי מכירה.** שני כיתי עדים אחת העידה שגנב את הנפש ואחת העידה שמכר אין נהרגין כדמפרש טעמא ואזיל וכיון דאינהו לא מקטלי איהו נמי אם לא הוזמו לא מקטיל דהוי' לה עדות שאי אתה יכול להזימה ולא משכחת לה דמקטיל אלא בכת אחת שמעידין על הגניבה ועל המכירה: **פלוגתא דר"ע ורבנן.** בבבא בתרא בחזקת הבתים על פי שנים עדים יקום דבר ולא חצי דבר והאי חצי דבר הוא אבל כל כת וכת דאי לאו עידי גניבה אינו נהרג משום עידי מכירה שיכול לומר עבדי מכרתי ואי לאו מכירה נמי לא מיחייב אגניבה: **בעדים האחרונים של בן סורר ומורה.** דתנן לעיל (דף עא.) מתרין בו בפני ג' ומלקין אותו חזר וקלקל נדון בעשרים ושלשה מתרין בו אביו ואמו בפני הדיינין וכשבאין עדים ראשונים ומעידין עליו שאכל תרטימר בשר ושתה חצי לוג יין מגניבה מלקין אותו כדכתיב ויסרו אותו דהיינו מלקות חזר וקלקל נדון בכ"ג למיתה ומודה חזקיה בהנך אחרונים שהעידו שחזר וקלקל שהוזמו שנהרגין ולא אמרינן שחצי דבר הוא דאי לאו סהדותא דקמאי לא מקטיל בסהדותא דהני אלא אמרינן הואיל ויש עונש על פי ראשונים שזה לקה על ידה תו לא שייכא ההוא סהדותא קמייתא בהני בתרייתא והני בתראי כוליה דבר קא עבדי:

תוספות

מונמצא בידו קא אמינא. ° תימה דבסוטה פ' עגלה ערופה (דף מה:) דרשינן כי ימצא חלל פרט למצוי ופטרינן עיר שרובה עובדי כוכבים וי"ל דהתם כתיב באדמה והוי כמו בידו דהכא ואכתי קשה דדרשינן בפ' בתרא דערכין (דף ל:) גבי בתי ערי חומה ומצא פרט למצוי שלא ימכור ברחוק ויגאל בקרוב (א) וי"ל (ח) כדפי' בקונטרס דהכא מריבויא דקרא:

יצא עבד שאין לו אחוה. פירש בקונטרס עבד אין לו אחוה ואפילו עם אחיו בני אביו דכתיב עם החמור עם הדומה לחמור וקשה דאם כן גר ומשוחרר נמי ונראה לפרש שאין לו אחוה שאין יוצאי חלציו קרויין אחוה משא"כ בגר:

בני ישראל למעוטי מי שחציו וכו'. אבל כולו משוחרר וגר לא ממעט מבני ישראל וכן בפרק בנות כותים (נדה דף לד. ושם) בני ישראל מיטמאין בזיבה וכו' אבל גרים ומשוחררים לא ממעט וכן שלהי (ט) פ"י דמנחות גבי סמיכה בני ישראל סומכין ואין העובדי כוכבים סומכין ומשוחרר וגר לא ממעטינן וכן בפ"ק דערכין (דף ה:) בני ישראל מעריכין ואין העובדי כוכבים מעריכין ולא ממעטין גרים ולא עבדים משוחררין ותימה דבפרק כל המנחות באות מצה (מנחות דף סא: ושם) גבי תנופה אמרינן בני ישראל מניפין ואין העובדי כוכבים מניפין ואין לי אלא בני ישראל גרים ועבדים משוחררים מניין תלמוד לומר המקריב וכן בפ' הערל (יבמות דף עד: ושם) ובשלהי פ"ק דכריתות (דף ז:) אשה כי תזריע אין לי אלא בני ישראל גיורת ושפחה משוחררת מניין ת"ל אשה ושמא בכל הני יש שום רבוי דמרבינן מיניה גרים ומשוחררין (י):

דבר ואפי' חצי דבר. וא"ת הא אמרינן לקמן (דף צ.) קיים מקצת וביטל מקצת דשאר מצות דברי הכל פטור ופי' בקונטרס משום דכתיב אך הנביא אשר יזיד לדבר דבר ולא חצי דבר וי"ל דרבנן נמי מודו דדרשינן ולא חצי דבר והא דפליגי אדרבי עקיבא היינו משום דחשבי ליה דבר שלם כדמוכח במרובה (ב"ק דף ע:) ובחזקת הבתים (ב"ב דף נו: ושם) וצריך לחלק בדברים דיש מקומות כה"ג בפ' ד' וה' (ב"ק דף מ. ושם) כופר שלם אמר רחמנא ולא חצי כופר ובפרק יש בכור (בכורות דף מח:) חומש ולא חצי חומש ובמרובה (ב"ק דף עא:) חמשה בקר אמר רחמנא ואפי' חמשה חצאי בקר ובפרק אותו ואת בנו (חולין דף עט: ושם) פליגי ר' אליעזר ורבנן בשה ואפילו מקצת שה ולענין כיסוי בצבי ואפילו מקצת צבי ובפרק הבא על יבמתו (יבמות דף נט: ושם) בבתולה מקצת בתולים ובכתובות פרק אלמנה (דף לז: ושם) במקצת כסף ככל כסף ושלהי כסוי הדם (חולין דף פח. ושם) דם ואפילו מקצת דם ובריש בכורות (דף ג. ושם) בכור ואפילו מקצת בכור:

מתוך שיכולים עדים הראשונים כו'. אין הטעם תלוי באמירתם אלא במאי דעידי גניבה ראשונה לא צריכי לעידי גניבה שניה כדאמרינן במרובה (ב"ק דף ע: ושם) דמודה רבי עקיבא בשנים אומרים קידש ושנים אומרים בעל אע"ג דעידי ביאה צריכי לעידי קדושין [הואיל] והן לא צריכי לעידי ביאה כוליה דבר הוא:

עין משפט נר מצוה

לא א מיי' פ"ט מהל' גניבה הלכה ג סמג שם:
לב ב מיי' שם הל' ה:
לג ג מיי' שם הל' א:

ליקוטי רש"י

סתם ספרא רבי יהודה. ספרא דבי רב היינו תורת כהנים ברייתא של ספר ויקרא שאר ספרי דבי רב קרי למדרש של ספר במדבר מוישלחו מן המחנה עד סוף הספר אלה הדברי' כו' ומכילתא דהיינו מדרש אלה שמות מהחדש הזה לכם עד סוף הספר כולהו אקרי שאר ספרי דבי רב והיינו דאמרינן בעלמא (סנהדרין דף פו) סתם מתני' רבי מאיר סתם ספרא רבי יהודה סתם ספרי רבי שמעון סתם סדר עולם ר' יוסי סתם תוספתא רבי נחמיה וכולן אליבא דר' עקיבא [ב"ב קכד:]. **וכולהו אליבא דר' עקיבא.** [יש מפרשים רבי עקיבא סתימתאה דאמרינן בסנהדרין באלו הן הנחנקין (דף פו) סתם משנה רבי מאיר סתם ברייתא רבי נתן וכולהו אליבא דרבי עקיבא ולאו מילתא היא דהא בכמה דוכתין אמרינן רבי מנחם סתימתאה רבי שמעון סתימתאה אלא רוב משניות איכא בהש"ס סתומות אליבא דר' עקיבא [בכורות ל.]. **יצא עבד שאין לו אחוה.** עם ישראל שאין בא בקהל. **במצות.** כל מצוה שאשה חייבת בה עבד חייב בה דגמר לה לה מאשה [ב"ק פח.]. **לא תגנב.** בגונב נפשות הכתוב מדבר. לא תגנובו (ויקרא יט, יא) בגונב ממון או אינו אלא זה בגונב ממון ולהלן בגונב נפשות אמרת דבר הלמד מעניינו מה לא תרצח לא תנאף מדבר בדבר שחייבין עליהם מיתת בית דין אף לא תגנוב דבר שחייב עליו מיתת בית דין [שמות כ, יב]. **דבר הלמד מעניינו.** דבר סתום שאין מפורש בו במה מדבר הוי לומדו מן הענין פרשה שנכתב בה במה הענין מיירי [חולין קטו:]. זה אחד מי"ג מדות מקרא שכתוב סתם ואין אנו יודעין במה מדבר הוי לומדו מעניינו [שם מ:]. **דבר ולא חצי דבר.** האי דבר למעוטי חצי דבר דכי האי גוונא כגון שנים אומרים אחת בגבה ראינו ולא בזקנו יותר ושנים אומרים אנו בזקנו מלפניה וראינו אחת בכריסה ואי לאו מיעוטא דקרא דבר ולא חצי דבר לא היה לנו לפסול עדות זה דעדות זה כשר הוא מאחר שיש ב' עדים על כל שיער שהרי אין מכחישין כלל זה את זה אלא כת זו בדקו מגבה וכת שניה בדקו מלפניה ובשעה אחת ראו ב' שערות אלו מכאן ואלו מכאן דליכא למימר שומא ניגהו השתא דכתיב דבר עדותן בטלה דב' שערות דבר אחד הוא ואין מועילין אלא כשהן ביחד בבת אחת שאם נראה אחד היום מכאן ולמחר גדל שני במקום אחר וכבר נשר הראשון אמרינן שומא ניגהו ואין כלום אלא אם כן ישנן ביחד וכל כת וכת יכול לראות ב' השערות דהא ביחד היו נמצא שכל כת עדות של חצי דבר מעידין וכל אחד אינו מעיד שהיא גדולה אלא חצי סימני גדלות ראינו [ב"ב נו:].

מסורת הש"ס

א) [ערובין לו: גיטין ד.], ב) [עירובין שם שבת קלז. יומא מא. קידושין נג. שבועות יג. בכורות סא. כריתות כב.], ג) ב"ק פז., ד) [שם פח.], ה) [יומא מג. וש"נ], ו) [חולין קטו: קמ.], ז) לעיל ל: ב"ק עו: ב"ב נו:, ח) ע' רש"ל, ט) [צ"ל פרק שתי מדות דף עג.], י) [וע"ע תוספות סוכה כח: ד"ה לרבות ותוספות מנחות סא: ד"ה אין לי].

הגהות הב"ח

(א) תוס' ד"ה מונמצא וכו' בפ' בתרא דערכין גבי שדה אחוזה ומצא פרט וכו' ויגאל בקרוב נ"ב ול"ע דהרי בערכין איתא להדיא משום דהכא מעניינא דקרא ולכך דרשינן אע"פ דלא כתיב בידו:

גליון הש"ס

תוס' ד"ה מונמצא וכו' תימה דבסוטה. עי' בריטב"א מכות דף ח' ע"א ד"ה התם מעניינא דקרא:

תורה אור השלם

א) כִּי יִמָּצֵא אִישׁ גֹּנֵב נֶפֶשׁ מֵאֶחָיו מִבְּנֵי יִשְׂרָאֵל וְהִתְעַמֶּר בּוֹ וּמְכָרוֹ וּמֵת הַגַּנָּב הַהוּא וּבִעַרְתָּ הָרָע מִקִּרְבֶּךָ: [דברים כד, ז]

ב) כִּי יִמָּצֵא אִישׁ שֹׁכֵב עִם אִשָּׁה בְעֻלַת בַּעַל וּמֵתוּ גַּם שְׁנֵיהֶם הָאִישׁ הַשֹּׁכֵב עִם הָאִשָּׁה וְהָאִשָּׁה וּבִעַרְתָּ הָרָע מִיִּשְׂרָאֵל: [דברים כב, כב]

ג) וְגֹנֵב אִישׁ וּמְכָרוֹ וְנִמְצָא בְיָדוֹ מוֹת יוּמָת: [שמות כא, טז]

ד) כִּי יִנָּצוּ אֲנָשִׁים יַחְדָּו אִישׁ וְאָחִיו וְקָרְבָה אֵשֶׁת הָאֶחָד לְהַצִּיל אֶת אִישָׁהּ מִיַּד מַכֵּהוּ וְשָׁלְחָה יָדָהּ וְהֶחֱזִיקָה בִּמְבֻשָׁיו: [דברים כה, יא]

ה) לֹא תִרְצָח לֹא תִנְאָף לֹא תִגְנֹב לֹא תַעֲנֶה בְרֵעֲךָ עֵד שָׁקֶר: [שמות כ, יג]

ו) כִּי עֲבָדַי הֵם אֲשֶׁר הוֹצֵאתִי אֹתָם מֵאֶרֶץ מִצְרָיִם לֹא יִמָּכְרוּ מִמְכֶּרֶת עָבֶד: [ויקרא כה, מב]

ז) לֹא תִּגְנֹבוּ וְלֹא תְכַחֲשׁוּ וְלֹא תְשַׁקְּרוּ אִישׁ בַּעֲמִיתוֹ: [ויקרא יט, יא]

ח) לֹא יָקוּם עֵד אֶחָד בְּאִישׁ לְכָל עָוֹן וּלְכָל חַטָּאת בְּכָל חֵטְא אֲשֶׁר יֶחֱטָא עַל פִּי שְׁנֵי עֵדִים אוֹ עַל פִּי שְׁלֹשָׁה עֵדִים יָקוּם דָּבָר: [דברים יט, טו]

Abaye clarifies what he meant:

אָמַר לֵיהּ – **[Abaye] said to [Rav Pappa]:** אֲנָא מ,,וְנִמְצָא בְיָדוֹ'' קָאָמִינָא – **I meant** that the Rabbis derive their law **from** the phrase[15] ***and he was found to have been in his hand.*** This superfluous phrase teaches that one who kidnaps his son is not liable to execution.

The Gemara suggests a logical extension of Abaye's explanation:

אָמַר רָבָא – **Rava said:** הִלְכָּךְ – **Therefore,** הָנֵי מִיקְרֵי דַּרְדְּקֵי וּמַתְנוּ רַבָּנָן – we can say about **those who teach** Scripture to **children and** Talmud **to Rabbis,** כִּמְצוּיִין בְּיָדָן דָּמוּ – that **[their students] are considered readily accessible to [the teachers],**[16] וּפְטִירֵי – **and [the teachers] are** thus **exempt** from execution if they kidnap a student.

The Mishnah taught:

גָּנַב מִי שֶׁחֶצְיוֹ וכו׳ – IF ONE KIDNAPED SOMEONE WHO WAS HALF, etc. [slave and half freeman, R' Yehudah considers him liable (to the death penalty), but the Sages exempt him.].

The Gemara proceeds to explain the basis for the dispute between R' Yehudah and the Sages. It begins by examining what will be shown to be a related dispute between these same two Tannaim:

תְּנַן הָתָם – **We learned in a Mishnah there:**[17] רַבִּי יְהוּדָה אוֹמֵר – R' YEHUDAH SAYS: אֵין לַעֲבָדִים בּוֹשֶׁת – THERE IS NO liability for DISGRACE IN the case OF SLAVES.[18] The Sages, however, state that there is a claim of damages for disgrace to a slave.

R' Yehudah's opinion is explained:

מַאי טַעְמָא דְּרַבִּי יְהוּדָה – **What is R' Yehudah's reasoning?** It is as follows: אָמַר קְרָא ,,כִּי־יִנָּצוּ אֲנָשִׁים יַחְדָּו אִישׁ וְאָחִיו'' – **The verse** that introduces the obligation to pay for disgrace **states:**[19] ***If men should fight with one another, a man and his brother...*** מִי שֶׁיֵּשׁ לוֹ אַחֲוָה – The mention of the word "brother" implies: Only **someone who has** the possibility of **brotherhood** is entitled to damages for disgrace; יָצָא עֶבֶד שֶׁאֵין לוֹ אַחֲוָה – **this excludes a slave, who does not have** the possibility of **brotherhood.**[20]

The Gemara explains the view of the Sages:

וְרַבָּנָן – **And the Sages** maintain: אָחִיו הוּא בְּמִצְוֹת – **A slave is [his assailant's] brother with** respect to certain **mitzvos.**[21] Hence, payment for disgrace is applicable to him as well.

The Gemara proceeds to show that the reasoning of each of the Tannaim in their dispute about payment for disgrace can illuminate their dispute about kidnaping, too.

וְהָכָא – **And here,** concerning kidnaping, Scripture also employs the term "brother" when it refers to the victim as *of his* [the abductor's] *brethren.*[22] הֵיכִי דָּרִישׁ רַבִּי יְהוּדָה – **How,** then, **does R' Yehudah expound** that verse? סָבַר ,,מֵאֶחָיו'' לְאַפּוּקֵי עֲבָדִים – **He maintains:** This phrase, ***from his brethren,*** **excludes slaves;**[23] it conveys that one is not liable to the death penalty for kidnaping a slave. ,,בְּנֵי יִשְׂרָאֵל'' – The verse then continues, identifying the person who was kidnaped as being a member of ***the Children of Israel.*** לְמַעוּטֵי מִי שֶׁחֶצְיוֹ עֶבֶד וְחֶצְיוֹ בֶּן חוֹרִין – **This excludes someone who is a half slave and half freeman** [i.e. it teaches that if the victim was such a person, the kidnaper is likewise exempt from the death penalty].[24] ,,מִבְּנֵי יִשְׂרָאֵל'' – Finally, the verse adds the prefix מִ, *among,* to the phrase ***the Children of Israel.***[25] לְמַעוּטֵי מִי שֶׁחֶצְיוֹ עֶבֶד וְחֶצְיוֹ בֶּן חוֹרִין – **This** once again **excludes someone who is a half slave and half freeman.** הָוֵי מִיעוּט אַחַר מִיעוּט – **Thus, it is** a case of **one exclusion following another exclusion;** that is, the verse twice excludes one who is a half slave-half freeman from the general law of kidnaping, וְאֵין מִיעוּט אַחַר מִיעוּט אֶלָּא לְרַבּוֹת – **and** the hermeneutic rule is that **an exclusion after an exclusion is** meant **only as an inclusion.**[26] Thus, the two exclusions result in this person's *inclusion* in the law of kidnaping.

Having explained R' Yehudah's reasoning, the Gemara turns to consider the view of the Sages:

וְרַבָּנָן – **And as for the Sages,** how would they expound the verse concerning kidnaping? ,,מֵאֶחָיו'' לְאַפּוּקֵי עֲבָדִים לָא מַשְׁמַע לְהוּ – **They do not interpret** the phrase ***from his brethren*** **as excluding slaves** at all, דְּהָא אָחִיו הוּא בְּמִצְוֹת – **since** they argue that **a slave *is* the brother of [his kidnaper] with** respect to certain **mitzvos.**[27] They are thus left with only two exclusionary indications: ,,בְּנֵי יִשְׂרָאֵל'' – The phrase ***Children of Israel,*** ,,מִבְּנֵי יִשְׂרָאֵל'' – and the prefix מִ, which, when added to that phrase, causes it to read ***among the Children of Israel.*** חַד לְמַעוּטֵי עֶבֶד

NOTES

15. *Exodus* 21:16. In other words, Abaye concedes that the term כִּי־יִמָּצֵא does not exclude a victim who was accessible. [Rather, it teaches that witnesses must come forward and testify that the kidnaping victim was found in the kidnaper's possession. Since the expression כִּי־יִמָּצֵא, which appears in *Deuteronomy,* teaches the witness requirement, it emerges that a similar expression appearing in *Exodus,* וְנִמְצָא בְיָדוֹ, *and it is found to have been in his hand,* is superfluous. Accordingly,] the Rabbis expound the superfluous expression to mean that one is not liable to execution for kidnaping a readily accessible victim (*Rashi;* cf. *Tosafos* and *Maharshal;* see also *Imrei Binah* and *Aruch LaNer* to 85b רש״י ד״ה שיכניסנו).

16. Because the students are regularly at their teachers' homes (*Rashi*).

17. *Bava Kamma* 87a.

18. When someone assails another person, one of the things the victim may claim from his assailant is compensation for the disgrace or humiliation he suffered from the attack (see *Bava Kamma* 84b). R' Yehudah states, however, that the claim for disgrace is not applicable when the injured party is a slave. The Gemara proceeds to explain the reason for this.

[As it is used here, the term "slaves" refers to Canaanite slaves owned by a Jew. Canaanite slaves, who undergo a modified form of conversion upon entering the service of a Jew, have a quasi-Jewish status, and are required to observe all commandments binding upon Jewish women.]

19. *Deuteronomy* 25:11.

20. In a legal sense, a Canaanite slave is not considered the kin of any of his blood relatives (the Scriptural basis for this is *Genesis* 22:5; see *Yevamos* 62a). Thus, a slave is not considered a "brother" even to another son of his own father (*Rashi;* cf. *Tosafos* and *Rashi, Bava Kamma* 88a ד״ה יצא).

21. As mentioned above (note 18), a Canaanite slave is obligated to perform all mitzvos incumbent upon a Jewish woman. (The exegetical derivation of this is given in *Chagigah* 4a.) Thus, in the Sages' view, a slave can be viewed as the "brother" of his assailant, for he shares in common with him an obligation to perform certain mitzvos (*Rashi*).

22. *Deuteronomy* 24:7. The full verse states: *If a man is found kidnaping a person of his brethren* [מֵאֶחָיו] *among the Children of Israel, and he uses him and sells him, that kidnaper shall die, and you shall remove the evil from your midst.* [The Gemara here understands the word מֵאֶחָיו to mean *of his brethren,* rather than *from his brethren,* as in the Gemara above.]

23. This follows the same logic R' Yehudah employed above: The term "brother" excludes a slave, since a slave lacks the potential to be someone's brother (*Rashi;* see above, note 20).

24. The words *Children of Israel* are understood as broadening the previous exclusion. It teaches that *everyone* who is not yet a complete member of the Children of Israel is excluded by the verse. The Gemara takes this to mean that the exclusion applies not just to full slaves, but even to half slaves.

25. In the plain meaning of the verse, this prefix is superfluous. Scripture could simply have stated: מֵאֶחָיו בְּנֵי יִשְׂרָאֵל, . . .*[kidnaping a person] from his brethren, the Children of Israel* (*Rashi*). The words ***among the Children of Israel*** thus reiterate the previous exclusion, for they imply that the verse is dealing with only some, but not all, members of Israel.

26. I.e. two exclusionary phrases, placed one after the other, have the effect of a double negative; they *include* that which they both seem to exclude. This rule is applied widely throughout the Talmud.

27. See above, note 21.

תני תנא קמיה דרב ששת א"ל אני שונה רבי שמעון אומר א) מאחיו עד שיוציאנו מרשות אחיו ואת אמרת חייב [א]תני פטור מאי קושיא דילמא הא ר"ש הא רבנן לא ס"ד דאמר ר' יוחנן ה) סתם מתני' ר' מאיר סתם תוספתא ר' נחמיה ט) סתם ספרא רבי יהודה סתם ספרי ר"ש וכולהו אליבא דר"ע: הגונב בנו: מאי טעמא דרבנן אמר אביי דאמר קרא א) כי ימצא פרט למצוי א"ל רב פפא לאביי אלא מעתה ב) כי ימצא איש שוכב עם אשה בעולת בעל הכי נמי כי ימצא פרט למצוי כגון של בית פלוני דשכיחן גבייהו הכי נמי דפטירי א"ל אנא ג) מונמצא בידו קאמינא אמר רבא [ב]הלכך הני מיקרי דרדקי ומתנו רבנן כמצויין בידן דמו ופטירי: גנב מי שחציו וכו': [ג]תנן התם רבי יהודה אומר אין לעבדים בושת ד) מאי טעמא דר' יהודה אמר קרא ד) כי ינצו אנשים יחדיו איש ואחיו מי שיש לו אחוה יצא עבד שאין לו אחוה ורבנן אחיו הוא במצות והכא היכי דריש ר' יהודה סבר א) מאחיו לאפוקי עבדים בני ישראל למעוטי מי שחציו עבד וחציו בן חורין מבני ישראל למעוטי מי שחציו עבד וחציו בן חורין הוי מיעוט אחר מיעוט ט) ואין מיעוט אחר מיעוט אלא לרבות ורבנן מאחיו לאפוקי עבדים לא משמע להו דהא אחיו הוא במצות בני ישראל מבני ישראל חד למעוטי עבד וחד למעוטי מי שחציו עבד וחציו בן חורין אזהרה לגונב נפש מנין רבי יאשיה אמר ה) מלא תגנב רבי יוחנן אמר ו) מלא ימכרו ממכרת עבד ולא פליגי מר קא חשיב לאו דגניבה ומר קא חשיב לאו דמכירה ת"ר ה) לא תגנוב [ג]בגונב נפשות הכתוב מדבר אתה אומר בגונב נפשות או אינו אלא בגונב ממון אמרת צא ולמד משלש עשרה מדות שהתורה נדרשת בהן דבר הלמד מעניינו במה הכתוב מדבר בנפשות אף כאן בנפשות תניא אידך ז) לא תגנובו בגונב ממון הכתוב מדבר אתה אומר בגונב ממון או אינו אלא בגונב נפשות אמרת צא ולמד משלש עשרה מדות שהתורה נדרשת בהן י) דבר הלמד מעניינו במה הכתוב מדבר בממון אף כאן בממון איתמר עידי גניבה ועידי מכירה בנפש שהוזמו חזקיה אמר אין נהרגין רבי יוחנן אמר נהרגין חזקיה דאמר כר"ע ז) דאמר ח) דבר ולא חצי דבר ורבי יוחנן אמר כרבנן דאמרי דבר ואפי' חצי דבר ומודה חזקיה בעדים האחרונים של בן סורר ומורה שהוזמו שנהרגין מתוך שיכולים לומר הראשונים

להלקותו

רש"י

תני תנא. להך מתני' דקתני מכר לאביו חייב: סתם ספרא. תורת כהנים: סתם ספרי. ספר וידבר ומשנה תורה והאי סתמא דכי ימצא איש במשנה תורה הוא: אליבא דרבי עקיבא. ממה שלמדו מר' עקיבא אמרום: של בית פלוני. לא רצה להזכיר שמם שחשובין היו וזה לא היו נוהגין כדת שהיו הרבה דרין בבית אחד אנשים ונשים והיו מלויין תמיד עם נשי חביריהן ולא שמתייחדין: ונמצא. קרא יתירא הוא דאי ללמד שימצא בעדים מכי ימצא נפקא: כמצויין בידן דמו. התלמידים מלויין תמיד בבית הרב ואם גנב הרב אחד מתלמידיו ומכרו אינו נהרג: אין לעבדים בושת. המבייש את העבד לא חייבתו תורה לתת דמי בשתו: וכי ינצו אנשים יחדיו והכה איש וגו'. מהתם נפקא לן חיוב בשת דכתיב וקצותה את כפה ממון אתה אומר ממון או אינו אלא ממש נאמר כאן לא תחוס עינך ונאמר להלן בעדים זוממין (דברים יט) לא תחוס עינך מה להלן ממון אף כאן ממון: עבד שאין לו אחוה. ואפי' עם אחיו בני אביו דכתיב (בראשית כב) עם החמור עם הדומה לחמור אינו אלא כבהמה: אחיו הוא במצות. בכל מצות שהאשה חייבת בהן עבד חייב בהן דגמר לה לה מאשה: והכא. במתני' בגונב נפש דכתיב מאחיו: היכי דריש. רבי יהודה לחייב על מי שחציו עבד: מאחיו למעוטי עבדים. דהא לרבי יהודה אין לו אחוה: מבני. יתירא דריש ליה דהוה ליה למכתב מאחיו בני ישראל: מלא תגנוב. האמור בעשרת הדברות דבגונב נפשות מתוקם לקמן בשמעתין: דבר הלמד מעניינו. אם אי אתה יודע במה הכתוב מדבר לא ולמד מפרשה שכתוב בה ולפי הפרשה הוא נכתב אצלה וכאן במה כל הענין מדבר בנפשות לא תרצח ולא תנאף כל אלה חייבי מיתות ב"ד אף לא תגנוב בגניבה שיש בה מיתת ב"ד: לא תגנובו. בפרשת קדושים תהיו: משלש עשרה מדות. זו היא אחת מהן שיהא הדבר מעניינו למד: במה הכתוב מדבר. הענין של מטה ושל מעלה מזו: בממון. לא תעשוק את רעך (ויקרא יט): עידי גניבה ועידי מכירה. שני כיתי עדים אחת העידה שגנב את הנפש ואחת העידה שמכר אין נהרגין כדמפרש טעמא ואזיל וכיון דאינהו לא מקטלי איהו נמי אם לא הוזמו לא מקטיל דהוי' לה עדות שאי אתה יכול להזימה ולא משכחת לה דמקטיל אלא בכת אחת שמעידין על הגניבה ועל המכירה: פלוגתא דר"ע ורבנן. בבבא בתרא בחזקת הבתים על פי שנים עדים יקום דבר ולא חצי דבר והאי חצי דבר הוא אלא כל כת וכת דאי לאו עידי גניבה אינו נהרג משום עידי מכירה שיכול לומר עבדי מכרתי ואי לאו מכירה נמי לא מיחייב אגניבה: בעדים האחרונים של בן סורר ומורה. דתנן לעיל (דף עא.) מתרין בו בפני ג' ומלקין אותו חזר וקלקל נדון בעשרים ושלשה מתרין בו אביו ואמו בפני הדיינין וכשבאין עדים ראשונים ומעידין עליו שאכל תרטימר בשר ושתה חצי לוג יין מגניבה מלקין אותו כדכתיב ויסרו אותו דהיינו מלקות חזר וקלקל נדון בכ"ג למיתה ומודה חזקיה בהנך אחרונים שהעידו שחזר וקלקל שהוזמו שנהרגין ולא אמרינן שחצי דבר הוא דאי לאו סהדותא דקמאי לא מקטיל בסהדותא דהני אלא אמרינן הואיל ויש עונש על פי ראשונים שזה לקה על ידה תו לא שייכא ההוא סהדותא קמייתא בהני בתרייתא והני בתראי כוליה דבר קא עבדי:

להלקותו

תוספות

מונמצא בידו קא אמינא. ° תימה דבסוטה פ' עגלה ערופה (דף מה:) דרשינן כי ימצא חלל פרט למצוי ופטרינן עיר שרובה עובדי כוכבים וי"ל דהתם כתיב באדמה והוי כמו בידו דהכא ואכתי קשה דדרשינן בפ' בתרא דערכין (דף ל:) גבי בתי ערי חומה ומצא פרט למצוי שלא ימכור ברחוק ויגאל בקרוב (א) וי"ל ח) כדפי' בקונטרס דהכא מריבויא דקרא:

יצא עבד שאין לו אחוה. פירש בקונטרס עבד אין לו אחוה ואפילו עם אחיו בני אביו דכתיב עם החמור עם הדומה לחמור וקשה דאם כן גר ומשוחרר נמי ונראה לפרש שאין לו אחוה שאין יוצאי חלציו קרויין אחוה משא"כ בגר:

בני ישראל למעוטי מי שחציו וכו'. אבל כולו משוחרר וגר לא ממעט מבני ישראל וכן בפרק בנות כותים (נדה דף לד. ושם) בני ישראל מיטמאין בזיבה וכו' אבל גרים ומשוחררים לא ממעט וכן שלהי ט) פ"ק דמנחות גבי סמיכה בני ישראל סומכין ואין העובדי כוכבים סומכין ומשוחרר וגר לא ממעטינן וכן בפ"ק דערכין (דף ה:) בני ישראל מעריכין ואין העובדי כוכבים מעריכין ולא ממעטין גרים ולא עבדים משוחררין ותימה דבפרק כל המנחות באות מצה (מנחות דף סא: ושם) גבי תנופה אמרינן בני ישראל מניפין ואין העובדי כוכבים מניפין ואין לי אלא בני ישראל גרים ועבדים משוחררים מניין תלמוד לומר המקריב וכן בפ' הערל (יבמות דף עד: ושם) ובשלהי פ"ק דכריתות (דף ז:) אשה כי תזריע אין לי אלא בני ישראל גיורת ושפחה משוחררת מניין ת"ל אשה ושמא בכל הני יש שום רבוי דמרבינן מיניה גרים ומשוחררין י):

דבר ואפי' חצי דבר. וא"ת הא אמרינן לקמן (דף ל.) קיים מקצת וביטל מקצת דשאר מצות דברי הכל פטור ופי' בקונטרס משום דכתיב אך הנביא אשר יזיד לדבר דבר ולא חצי דבר וי"ל דרבנן נמי מודו דדרשינן ולא חצי דבר והא דפליגי אדרבי עקיבא היינו משום דחשבי ליה דבר שלם כדמוכח במרובה (ב"ק דף ע:) ובחזקת הבתים (ב"ב דף נו: ושם) וצריך לחלק בדברים דיש מקומות כה"ג בפ' ד' וה' (ב"ק דף מ. ושם) כופר שלם אמר רחמנא ולא חצי כופר ובפרק יש בכור (בכורות דף מח:) חומש ולא חצי חומש ובמרובה (ב"ק דף עא:) חמשה בקר אמר רחמנא ואפי' חמשה חצאי בקר ובפרק אותו ואת בנו (חולין דף עט: ושם) פליגי ר' אליעזר ורבנן בשה ואפילו מקצת שה ולענין כיסוי בצבי ואפילו מקצת צבי ובפרק הבא על יבמתו (יבמות דף נט: ושם) בבתולה מקצת בתולים ובכתובות פרק אלמנה (דף לו: ושם) במקצת כסף ככל כסף ושלהי כסוי הדם (חולין דף פח. ושם) דם ואפילו מקצת דם ובריש בכורות (דף ג. ושם) בכור ואפילו מקצת בכור:

מתוך שיכולים עדים הראשונים כו'. אין הטעם תלוי באמירתם אלא במאי דעידי גניבה ראשונה לא צריכי לעידי גניבה שניה כדאמרינן במרובה (ב"ק דף ע: ושם) דמודה רבי עקיבא בשנים אומרים קידש ושנים אומרים בעל אע"ג דעידי ביאה צריכי לעידי קדושין [הואיל] והן לא צריכי לעידי ביאה כוליה דבר הוא:

גניבה

מסורת הש"ס

א) [עירובין לו: גיטין ד.], ב) [עירובין שם שבת קלז. יומא מא. קידושין נג. שבועות יג. בכורות סא. כריתות כב.], ג) ב"ק פז., ד) [שם פח.], ה) [יומא מג. וש"נ], ו) [חולין קטו: קמ.], ז) לעיל ל: ב"ק ע: ב"ב נו:, ח) עי' רש"ל, ט) [צ"ל פרק שתי מדות דף לג.], י) [וע"ע תוספות סוכה כח: ד"ה לרבות ותוספות מנחות סא: ד"ה אין לי].

הגהות הב"ח

(א) תוס' ד"ה מונמצא וכו' בפ' בתרא דערכין גבי שדה אחוזה ומצא פרט וכו' ויגאל בקרוב נ"ב ול"ע דהרי בערכין איתא להדיא משום דהכא מעניינא דקרא ולכך דרשינן אע"פ דלא כתיב בידו:

גליון הש"ס

תוס' ד"ה מונמצא וכו' תימה דבסוטה. עי' בריטב"א מכות דף ח' ע"א ד"ה התם מענינא דקרא:

תורה אור השלם

א) כִּי יִמָּצֵא אִישׁ גֹּנֵב נֶפֶשׁ מֵאֶחָיו מִבְּנֵי יִשְׂרָאֵל וְהִתְעַמֶּר בּוֹ וּמְכָרוֹ וּמֵת הַגַּנָּב הַהוּא וּבִעַרְתָּ הָרָע מִקִּרְבֶּךָ: [דברים כד, ז]

ב) כִּי יִמָּצֵא אִישׁ שֹׁכֵב עִם אִשָּׁה בְעֻלַת בַּעַל וּמֵתוּ גַּם שְׁנֵיהֶם הָאִישׁ הַשֹּׁכֵב עִם הָאִשָּׁה וְהָאִשָּׁה וּבִעַרְתָּ הָרָע מִיִּשְׂרָאֵל: [דברים כב, כב]

ג) וְגֹנֵב אִישׁ וּמְכָרוֹ וְנִמְצָא בְיָדוֹ מוֹת יוּמָת: [שמות כא, טז]

ד) כִּי יִנָּצוּ אֲנָשִׁים יַחְדָּו אִישׁ וְאָחִיו וְקָרְבָה אֵשֶׁת הָאֶחָד לְהַצִּיל אֶת אִישָׁהּ מִיַּד מַכֵּהוּ וְשָׁלְחָה יָדָהּ וְהֶחֱזִיקָה בִּמְבֻשָׁיו: [דברים כה, יא]

ה) לֹא תִרְצָח לֹא תִנְאָף לֹא תִגְנֹב לֹא תַעֲנֶה בְרֵעֲךָ עֵד שָׁקֶר: [שמות כ, יג]

ו) כִּי עֲבָדַי הֵם אֲשֶׁר הוֹצֵאתִי אֹתָם מֵאֶרֶץ מִצְרָיִם לֹא יִמָּכְרוּ מִמְכֶּרֶת עָבֶד: [ויקרא כה, מב]

ז) לֹא תִּגְנֹבוּ וְלֹא תְכַחֲשׁוּ וְלֹא תְשַׁקְּרוּ אִישׁ בַּעֲמִיתוֹ: [ויקרא יט, יא]

ח) לֹא יָקוּם עֵד אֶחָד בְּאִישׁ לְכָל עָוֹן וּלְכָל חַטָּאת בְּכָל חֵטְא אֲשֶׁר יֶחֱטָא עַל פִּי שְׁנֵי עֵדִים אוֹ עַל פִּי שְׁלֹשָׁה עֵדִים יָקוּם דָּבָר: [דברים יט, טו]

עין משפט נר מצוה

לא א מיי' פ"ט מהל' גניבה הלכה ג סמג שם:
לב ב מיי' שם הל' ה:
לג ג מיי' שם הל' א:

ליקוטי רש"י

סתם ספרא רבי יהודה. ספרא דבי רב היינו תורת כהנים ברייתא של ספר ויקרא שאר ספרי דבי רב קרי למדרש של ספר במדבר מוישלחו מן המחנה עד סוף הספר אלה הדברי' כו' ומכילתא דהיינו מדרש אלה שמות מהחדש הזה לכם עד סוף הספר כולהו אקרי שאר ספרי דבי רב והיינו דאמרינן בעלמא (סנהדרין דף פו) סתם מתני' רבי מאיר סתם ספרא רבי יהודה סתם ספרי רבי שמעון סתם סדר עולם ר' יוסי סתם תוספתא רבי נחמיה וכולן אליבא דר' עקיבא [ב"ב קכד:]. וכולהו אליבא דר' עקיבא. [יש מפרשים רבי עקיבא שמימתאה דאמרינן בסנהדרין באלו הן הנחנקין (דף פו) סתם משנה רבי מאיר סתם ברייתא רבי נתן וכולהו אליבא דרבי עקיבא ולאו מילתא היא דהא בכמה דוכתין אמרינן רבי מנחם שמימתאה רבי שמעון שמימתאה אלא רוב משניות איכא בהש"ס סתומות אליבא דר' עקיבא [בכורות ל.]. יצא עבד שאין לו אחוה. עם ישראל שאין בא בקהל. במצות. כל מצוה שאשה חייבת בה עבד חייב בה דגמר לה לה מאשה [ב"ק פח.]. לא תגנב. בגונב נפשות הכתוב מדבר. לא תגנובו (ויקרא יט, יא) בגונב ממון או אינו אלא זה בגונב ממון ולהלן בגונב נפשות אמרת דבר הלמד מעניינו מה לא תרצח לא תנאף מדבר בדבר שחייבין עליהם מיתת בית דין אף לא תגנוב דבר שחייב עליו מיתת בית דין [שמות כ, יב]. דבר הלמד מענינו. דבר סתום שאין מפורש בו במה מדבר הוי לומדו מן הענין פרשה שנכתב בה במה הענין מיירי [חולין קטו:]. זה אחד מי"ג מדות מקרא שכתוב סתם ואין אנו יודעין במה מדבר הוי לומדו מענינו [שם מ:]. דבר ולא חצי דבר. האי דבר למעוטי חצי דבר דכי האי גוונא כגון שנים אומרים אחת בגבה ראינו ולא בדקנו יותר ושנים אומרים אנו בדקנו מלפניה וראינו אחת בכריסה ואי לאו מיעוטא דקרא דבר ולא חצי דבר לא היה לנו לפסול עדות זה דעדות זה כשר הוא מאחר שיש ב' עדים על כל שיעור שערי אינן מכחישין כלל זה את זה אלא כת זו בדקו מגבה וכת שניה בדקו מלפניה ובשעה אחת ראו ב' שערות אלו מכאן ואלו מכאן דליכא למימר שומא ניהו השתא דכתיב דבר עדותן בטלה דב' שערות דבר אחד הוא ואין מועילין אלא כשהן ביחד בבת אחת שאם נראה אחד היום מכאן ולמחר גדל שני במקום אחר וכבר נשר הראשון אמרינן שומא ניהו ואין כלום אלא אם כן ישנן ביחד וכל כת וכת יכול לראות ב' השערות דהא ביחד היו ונמצא של כת עדות על אחד ואינו מעיד על חבירו וכל אחד אינו מעיד שהיא גדולה אלא חצי סימני גדלות ראוי [ב"ב נו:].

– They thus hold that **one excludes a** full **slave** from the law of kidnaping, וְחַד לְמַעוּטֵי מִי שֶׁחֶצְיוֹ עֶבֶד וְחֶצְיוֹ בֶּן חוֹרִין – **and the other excludes someone who is a half slave and half freeman.** The Sages therefore conclude that the one is not liable to the death sentence for kidnaping a half slave.

Until this point, the Gemara has dealt with the circumstances under which the death penalty applies for kidnaping. The Gemara now searches for the verse in Scripture that gives the prohibition for kidnaping:[28]

אַזְהָרָה לְגוֹנֵב נֶפֶשׁ מִנַּיִן – **From where do we know the Scriptural warning against kidnaping?** רַבִּי יֹאשִׁיָּה אָמַר – **R' Yoshiyah said:** מ,,לֹא תִּגְנֹב" – **From** the verse:[29] ***You shall not steal.*** רַבִּי יוֹחָנָן אָמַר – **R' Yochanan said:** מ,,לֹא יִמָּכְרוּ מִמְכֶּרֶת עָבֶד" – **From** the verse:[30] ***They shall not be sold in the manner of a slave.***

The Gemara comments:

וְלֹא פְּלִיגֵי – **And [these Amoraim] do not dispute** one another. מַר קָא חָשֵׁיב לָאו דִּגְנֵיבָה – For one **master** [R' Yoshiyah] **is delineating the prohibition against kidnaping** itself, וּמַר קָא חָשֵׁיב לָאו דִּמְכִירָה – **while** the other **master** [R' Yochanan] **is delineating the prohibition against** subsequently **selling** the kidnap victim as a slave.

The Gemara has stated that the prohibition against kidnaping is stated in the verse *you shall not steal.* A Baraisa now shows how it was known that this verse refers to kidnaping as opposed to monetary theft:

תָּנוּ רַבָּנָן – **The Rabbis taught in a Baraisa:** ,,לֹא תִּגְנֹב" בְּגוֹנֵב נְפָשׁוֹת הַכָּתוּב מְדַבֵּר – In the verse ***YOU SHALL NOT STEAL,***[29] **SCRIPTURE SPEAKS OF ONE WHO KIDNAPS.** אַתָּה אוֹמֵר בְּגוֹנֵב נְפָשׁוֹת – Now, **YOU SAY** that the verse deals **WITH ONE WHO KIDNAPS;** אוֹ אֵינוֹ אֶלָּא בְּגוֹנֵב מָמוֹן – **BUT** perhaps it speaks **ONLY OF ONE WHO STEALS MONEY?** אָמַרְתָּ – To this **YOU CAN RESPOND:** צֵא וּלְמַד מִשְּׁלֹשׁ עֶשְׂרֵה מִדּוֹת שֶׁהַתּוֹרָה נִדְרֶשֶׁת בָּהֶן – **GO AND LEARN** the meaning of the verse **FROM** one of **THE THIRTEEN METHODS OF EXEGESIS THROUGH WHICH THE TORAH IS EXPOUNDED;** דָּבָר הַלָּמֵד מֵעִנְיָנוֹ – specifically, the method of **"A MATTER THAT IS LEARNED FROM ITS CONTEXT."**[31] בַּמֶּה הַכָּתוּב מְדַבֵּר – Let us examine the context in which this phrase *you shall not steal* appears: **WHAT** general topic **IS SCRIPTURE DISCUSSING** in the adjacent verses? בִּנְפָשׁוֹת – It is dealing **WITH CAPITAL CRIMES,** such as murder and adultery.[32] אַף כָּאן בִּנְפָשׁוֹת – **HERE TOO,** then, the prohibition expressed in the words *you shall not steal* is one that involves **A CAPITAL CRIME.** Thus, the verse can only be referring to kidnaping.[33]

A corresponding Baraisa elucidates the meaning of a similar phrase:

תַּנְיָא אִידָךְ – **It was taught in another Baraisa:** ,,לֹא תִּגְנֹבוּ" בְּגוֹנֵב מָמוֹן הַכָּתוּב מְדַבֵּר – In the verse ***YOU*** [plural form] ***SHALL NOT STEAL,***[34] **SCRIPTURE SPEAKS OF ONE WHO STEALS MONEY.** אַתָּה אוֹמֵר בְּגוֹנֵב מָמוֹן – Now, **YOU SAY** that the verse deals with **ONE WHO STEALS MONEY;** אוֹ אֵינוֹ אֶלָּא בְּגוֹנֵב נְפָשׁוֹת – **BUT** perhaps it speaks **ONLY OF ONE WHO KIDNAPS?** אָמַרְתָּ – To this, **YOU CAN RESPOND:** צֵא וּלְמַד מִשְּׁלֹשׁ עֶשְׂרֵה מִדּוֹת שֶׁהַתּוֹרָה נִדְרֶשֶׁת בָּהֶן – **GO AND LEARN** the true meaning of the verse **FROM** one of **THE THIRTEEN METHODS OF EXEGESIS THROUGH WHICH THE TORAH IS EXPOUNDED,** דָּבָר הַלָּמֵד מֵעִנְיָנוֹ – specifically, the method of **"A MATTER THAT IS LEARNED FROM ITS CONTEXT."** בַּמֶּה הַכָּתוּב מְדַבֵּר – Let us examine the context in which this phrase *you shall not steal* appears: **WHAT** general topic **IS SCRIPTURE DISCUSSING** in the surrounding verses? בְּמָמוֹן – It is dealing **WITH** transgressions **INVOLVING MONEY.**[35] אַף כָּאן בְּמָמוֹן – **HERE TOO,** then, the prohibition expressed in the words *you shall not steal* is one that **INVOLVES MONEY;** i.e. it refers to monetary theft, not to kidnaping.

We have learned that one is not liable to execution for kidnaping unless he subsequently sold the victim into slavery. The Gemara discusses a case in which two sets of witnesses separately testified to these two aspects of the crime:

אִיתְּמַר – **It was stated:** עֵידֵי גְנֵיבָה וְעֵידֵי מְכִירָה בְּנֶפֶשׁ שֶׁהוּזְמוּ – If one set of **witnesses** testifies **to a kidnaping and** another set of **witnesses** testifies **to the** victim's **sale** into slavery, and **they** [both sets of witnesses] **are discredited through *hazamah,***[36] חִזְקִיָּה אָמַר – **Chizkiyah says** that אֵין נֶהֱרָגִין – **they are not executed,**[37] רַבִּי יוֹחָנָן אָמַר – while **R' Yochanan says** that

NOTES

28. In the Torah's system, in order for a sin to be subject to a corporal punishment, the Torah must not only clearly state the punishment for that activity but it must also clearly and separately state the prohibition of that activity. See above, 85a note 6.

29. *Exodus* 20:13. The Gemara below will explain how it is known that this verse refers to kidnaping rather than to monetary theft (*Rashi*).

30. *Leviticus* 25:42. The plain meaning of the verse is that a Jewish servant shall not be sold on the auction block, in the manner that a Canaanite slave is sold (see *Toras Kohanim* ibid.). The verse is expounded, however, to refer to kidnaping, as the Gemara proceeds to explain.

31. This rule is the twelfth of R' Yishmael's thirteen rules of Biblical interpretation. It teaches that a verse whose meaning is not clear must be interpreted in light of the context in which it appears (see *Rashi*).

32. The command *you shall not steal* appears immediately after the two commands, *you shall not kill* and *you shall not commit adultery* (see *Exodus* 20:13).

33. The only type of "stealing" punishable by death is kidnaping (see *Exodus* 21:16; *Deuteronomy* 24:7). Thus, it must be this type of theft to which the verse refers (*Rashi*; cf. *Aruch LaNer*).

34. This verse appears in *Leviticus* 19:11. It differs from the above-cited phrase in *Exodus* 20:13 in that the verb *steal* is stated in the plural form (see *Margaliyos HaYam* and *Toras Chaim*).

35. *Leviticus* 19:13 states: *You shall not cheat your fellow,* and *you shall not rob,* two sins connected with the misappropriation of money. We can surmise, then, that the verse stated earlier (v. 11), *you shall not steal,* also refers to a sin involving money (*Rashi*).

36. For the definition of *hazamah,* see 84b note 7.

37. The Gemara assumes that Chizkiyah refers to both sets of witnesses.

If the testimony of both sets of witnesses would have been accepted, the kidnaper would have been put to death. Hence, now that the witnesses have been discredited through *hazamah,* the law of reciprocal punishment for *zomemin* should dictate that they are executed. Chizkiyah, however, maintains that they are not executed. The Gemara below discusses the reason for Chizkiyah's ruling.

[Chizkiyah's ruling applies not only to the witnesses but also to the defendant himself. That is, even if the witnesses are not discredited through *hazamah,* the defendant is not liable to execution. It was not necessary for Chizkiyah to mention the law of the defendant, because it is evident from his ruling about the witnesses. As we learned above (78a), wherever witnesses cannot receive the reciprocal punishment if they are found to be *zomemin,* their testimony is inadmissible in the first place. (Such testimony is termed עֵדוּת שֶׁאִי אַתָּה יָכוֹל לַהֲזִימָהּ, *testimony that cannot be refuted through hazamah.*) Hence, once Chizkiyah has ruled that the witnesses are not executed (if they are discredited), it automatically follows that the defendant cannot be convicted on the basis of their testimony (even if they are not discredited). According to Chizkiyah, the only case in which a kidnaper (or the witnesses who testify against him) can be executed is where the same set of witnesses testified to both the kidnaping and the selling (*Rashi,* as explained by *Binyan Shlomo;* see *Ran* and *Maharsha*).]

תני תנא קמיה דרב ששת א"ל אני שונה רבי שמעון אומר א) מאחיו עד שיוציאנו מרשות אחיו ואת אמרת חייב *תני פטור מאי קושיא דילמא הא ר"ש הא רבנן לא ס"ד דאמר ר' יוחנן א) סתם מתני' ר' מאיר סתם תוספתא ר' נחמיה ב) סתם ספרא רבי יהודה סתם ספרי ר"ש וכולהו אליבא דר"ע: הגונב בנו: מאי טעמא דרבנן אמר אביי דאמר קרא א) כי ימצא פרט למצוי א"ל רב פפא לאביי אלא מעתה ב) כי ימצא איש שוכב עם אשה בעולת בעל הכי נמי כי ימצא פרט למצוי כגון של בית פלוני דשכיחן גבייהו הכי נמי דפטירי א"ל אנא ג) מונמצא בידו קאמינא אמר רבא ב הלכך הני מיקרי דרדקי ומתנו רבנן כמצויין בידן דמו ופטירי: גנב מי שחציו וכו': ג) תנן התם רבי יהודה אומר אין לעבדים בושת ד) מאי טעמא דר' יהודה אמר קרא ד) כי ינצו אנשים יחדיו איש ואחיו מי שיש לו אחוה יצא עבד שאין לו אחוה ורבנן אחיו הוא במצות והכא היכי דריש ר' יהודה סבר א) מאחיו לאפוקי עבדים בני ישראל למעוטי מי שחציו עבד וחציו בן חורין מבני ישראל למעוטי מי שחציו עבד וחציו בן חורין הוי מיעוט אחר מיעוט ה) ואין מיעוט אחר מיעוט אלא לרבות ורבנן מאחיו לאפוקי עבדים לא משמע להו דהא אחיו הוא במצות בני ישראל מבני ישראל חד למעוטי עבד וחד למעוטי מי שחציו עבד וחציו בן חורין אזהרה לגונב נפש מנין רבי יאשיה אמר ה) מלא תגנב רבי יוחנן אמר ו) מלא ימכרו ממכרת עבד ולא פליגי מר קא חשיב לאו דגניבה ומר קא חשיב לאו דמכירה ת"ר ה) לא תגנוב ג בגונב נפשות הכתוב מדבר אתה אומר בגונב נפשות או אינו אלא בגונב ממון אמרת צא ולמד משלש עשרה מדות שהתורה נדרשת בהן דבר הלמד מעניינו במה הכתוב מדבר בנפשות אף כאן בנפשות תניא אידך ז) לא תגנובו בגונב ממון הכתוב מדבר אתה אומר בגונב ממון או אינו אלא בגונב נפשות אמרת צא ולמד משלש עשרה מדות שהתורה נדרשת בהן ו) דבר הלמד מעניינו במה הכתוב מדבר בממון אף כאן בממון איתמר עידי גניבה ועידי מכירה בנפש שהוזמו חזקיה אמר אין נהרגין רבי יוחנן אמר נהרגין חזקיה דאמר כר"ע ז) דאמר ח) דבר ולא חצי דבר ורבי יוחנן אמר כרבנן דאמרי דבר ואפי' חצי דבר ומודה חזקיה בעדים האחרונים של בן סורר ומורה שהוזמו שנהרגין מתוך שיכולים לומר הראשונים להלקותו

רש"י

תני תנא. להך מתני' דקתני מכר לאביו חייב: סתם ספרא. תורת כהנים: סתם ספרי. ספר וידבר ומשנה תורה והאי סתמא דכי ימצא איש במשנה תורה הוא: אליבא דרבי עקיבא. ממה שלמדו מר' עקיבא אמרום: של בית פלוני. לא רצה להזכיר שמם שחשובין היו ובזה לא היו נוהגין כדת שהיו הרבה דרין בבית אחד אנשים ונשים והיו מצויין תמיד עם נשי חביריהן ולא שמתייחדין: ונמצא. קרא יתירא הוא דאי ללמד שימצא בעדים מכי ימצא נפקא: כמצויין בידן דמו. התלמידים מצויין תמיד בבית הרב ואם גנב הרב אחד מתלמידיו ומכרו אינו נהרג: אין לעבדים בושת. המבייש את העבד לא חייבתו תורה לתת דמי בשתו: וכי ינצו אנשים יחדיו והכה איש וגו'. מהתם נפקא לן חיוב בשת דכתיב וקצותה את כפה ממון אתה אומר ממון או אינו אלא ממש נאמר כאן לא תחוס עינך ונאמר להלן בעדים זוממין (דברים יט) לא תחוס עינך מה להלן ממון אף כאן ממון: עבד שאין לו אחוה. ואפי' עם אחיו בני אביו דכתיב (בראשית כב) עם החמור עם הדומה לחמור אינו אלא כבהמה: אחיו הוא במצות. בכל מצות שהאשה חייבת בהן עבד חייב בהן דגמר לה לה מאשה: והכא. במתני' בגונב נפש דכתיב מאחיו: היכי דריש. רבי יהודה לחייב על מי שחציו עבד: מאחיו למעוטי עבדים. דהא לרבי יהודה אין לו אחוה: מבני. יתירא דריש ליה דהוה ליה למכתב מאחיו בני ישראל: מלא תגנוב. האמור בעשרת הדברות דבגונב נפשות מתוקם לקמן בשמעתין: דבר הלמד מעניינו. אם אי אתה יודע במה הכתוב מדבר לא ולמד מפרשה שכתוב בה ולפי הפרשה הוא נכתב אצלה וכאן במה כל הענין מדבר בנפשות לא תרצח ולא תנאף כל אלה חייבי מיתות ב"ד אף לא תגנוב בגניבה שיש בה מיתת ב"ד: לא תגנובו. בפרשת קדושים תהיו: משלש עשרה מדות. זו היא אחת מהן שיהא הדבר מעניינו למד: במה הכתוב מדבר. הענין של מטה ושל מעלה מזו: בממון. לא תעשוק את רעך (ויקרא יט): עידי גניבה ועידי מכירה. שני כיתי עדים אחת העידה שגנב את הנפש ואחת העידה שמכר אין נהרגין כדמפרש טעמא ואזיל וכיון דאינהו לא מקטלי איהו נמי אם לא הוזמו לא מקטיל דהוי' לה עדות שאי אתה יכול להזימה ולא משכחת לה דמקטיל אלא בכת אחת שמעידין על הגניבה ועל המכירה: פלוגתא דר"ע ורבנן. בבבא בתרא בחזקת הבתים על פי שנים עדים יקום דבר ולא חצי דבר והאי חצי דבר הוא אבל כל כת וכת דאי לאו עידי גניבה אינו נהרג משום עידי מכירה שיכול לומר עבדי מכרתי ואי לאו מכירה נמי לא מיחייב אגניבה: בעדים האחרונים של בן סורר ומורה. דתנן לעיל (דף עא.) מתרין בו בפני ג' ומלקין אותו חזר וקלקל נדון בעשרים ושלשה מתרין בו אביו ואמו בפני הדיינין וכשבאין עדים ראשונים ומעידין עליו שאכל תרטימר בשר ושתה חצי לוג יין מגניבה מלקין אותו כדכתיב ויסרו אותו דהיינו מלקות חזר וקלקל נדון בכ"ג למיתה ומודה חזקיה בהנך אחרונים שהעידו שחזר וקלקל שהוזמו שנהרגין ולא אמרינן שחצי דבר הוא דאי לאו סהדותא דקמאי לא מקטיל בסהדותא דהני אלא אמרינן הואיל ויש עונש על פי ראשונים שזה לקה על ידה תו לא שייכא ההוא סהדותא קמייתא בהני בתרייתא והני בתראי כוליה דבר קא עבדי:

להלקותו

תוספות

מונמצא בידו קא אמינא. ° תימה דבסוטה פ' עגלה ערופה (דף מה:) דרשינן כי ימצא חלל פרט למצוי ופטרינן עיר שרובה עובדי כוכבים וי"ל דהתם כתיב באדמה והוי כמו בידו דהכא ואכתי קשה דדרשינן בפ' בתרא דערכין (דף לב:) גבי בתי ערי חומה ומצא פרט למצוי שלא ימכור ברחוק ויגאל בקרוב (א) וי"ל ח) כדפי' בקונטרס דהכא מריבויא דקרא:

יצא עבד שאין לו אחוה. פירש בקונטרס עבד אין לו אחוה ואפילו עם אחיו בני אביו דכתיב עם החמור עם הדומה לחמור וקשה דאם כן גר ומשוחרר נמי ונראה לפרש שאין לו אחוה שאין יוצאי חלציו קרויין אחוה משא"כ בגר:

בני ישראל למעוטי מי שחציו וכו'. אבל כולו משוחרר וגר לא ממעט מבני ישראל וכן בפרק בנות כותים (נדה דף לד. ושם) בני ישראל מיטמאין בזיבה וכו' אבל גרים ומשוחררים לא ממעט וכן שלהי ט) פ"ו דמנחות גבי סמיכה בני ישראל סומכין ואין העובדי כוכבים סומכין ומשוחרר וגר לא ממעטינן וכן בפ"ק דערכין (דף ה:) בני ישראל מעריכין ואין העובדי כוכבים מעריכין ולא ממעטין גרים ולא עבדים משוחררין ותימה דבפרק כל המנחות באות מצה (מנחות דף סא: ושם) גבי תנופה אמרינן בני ישראל מניפין ואין העובדי כוכבים מניפין ואין לי אלא בני ישראל גרים ועבדים משוחררים מניין תלמוד לומר המקריב וכן בפ' הערל (יבמות דף עד: ושם) ובשלהי פ"ק דכריתות (דף ז:) אשה כי תזריע אין לי אלא בני ישראל גיורת ושפחה משוחררת מניין ת"ל אשה ושמא בכל הני יש שום רבוי דמרבינן מיניה גרים ומשוחררין י):

דבר ואפי' חצי דבר. וא"ת הא אמרינן לקמן (דף ל.) קיים מקצת וביטל מקצת דשאר מצות דברי הכל פטור ופי' בקונטרס משום דכתיב אך הנביא אשר יזיד לדבר דבר דבר ולא חצי דבר וי"ל דרבנן נמי מודו דדרשינן ולא חצי דבר והא דפליגי אדרבי עקיבא היינו משום דחשבי ליה דבר שלם כדמוכח במרובה (ב"ק דף ע:) ובחזקת הבתים (ב"ב דף נו: ושם) וצריך לחלק בדברים דיש מקומות כה"ג בפ' ד' וה' (ב"ק דף מ. ושם) כופר שלם אמר רחמנא ולא חצי כופר ובפרק יש בכור (בכורות דף מח:) חומש ולא חצי חומש ובמרובה (ב"ק דף עח:) חמשה בקר אמר רחמנא ואפי' חמשה חצאי בקר ובפרק אותו ואת בנו (חולין דף עט: ושם) פליגי ר' אליעזר ורבנן בשה ואפילו מקצת שה ולענין כיסוי בצבי ואפילו מקצת צבי ובפרק הבא על יבמתו (יבמות דף נט: ושם) בבתולה מקצת בתולים ובכתובות פרק אלמנה (דף לז: ושם) במקצת כסף ככל כסף ושלהי כסוי הדם (חולין דף פח. ושם) דם ואפילו מקצת דם וכריש בכורות (דף ג. ושם) בכור ואפילו מקצת בכור:

מתוך שיכולים עדים הראשונים כו'. אין הטעם תלוי באמירתם אלא במאי דעידי גניבה ראשונה לא צריכי לעידי גניבה שניה כדאמרינן במרובה (ב"ק דף ע: ושם) דמודה רבי עקיבא בשנים אומרים קידש ושנים אומרים בעל אע"ג דעידי ביאה צריכי לעידי קדושין [הואיל] והן לא צריכי לעידי ביאה כוליה דבר הוא:

גניבה

מסורת הש"ס

א) [עירובין לו: גיטין ד.], ב) [עירובין שם שבת קלז. יומא מא. קידושין נג. שבועות יג. בכורות סא. כריתות כב.], ג) ב"ק פז., ד) [שם פח.], ה) [יומא מג. וש"נ], ו) [חולין קטו: קמ.], ז) לעיל ל: ב"ק ע: ב"ב נו:, ח) עי' רש"ל, ט) [נ"ל פרק שתי מדות דף צג.], י) [וע"ע תוספות סוכה כח: ד"ה לרבות ותוספות מנחות סא: ד"ה אין לי].

הגהות הב"ח

(א) תוס' ד"ה מונמצא וכו' בפ' בתרא דערכין גבי שדה אחוזה ומצא פרט וכו' ויגאל בקרוב נ"ב וע"ע דהרי בערכין איתא להדיא משום דהכא מעניינא דקרא ולכך דרשינן אע"פ דלא כתיב בידו:

גליון הש"ס

תוס' ד"ה מונמצא וכו' תימה דבסוטה. עי' בריטב"א מכות דף ח' ע"א ד"ה התם מעניינא דקרא:

תורה אור השלם

א) כִּי יִמָּצֵא אִישׁ גֹּנֵב נֶפֶשׁ מֵאֶחָיו מִבְּנֵי יִשְׂרָאֵל וְהִתְעַמֶּר בּוֹ וּמְכָרוֹ וּמֵת הַגַּנָּב הַהוּא וּבִעַרְתָּ הָרָע מִקִּרְבֶּךָ: [דברים כד, ז]

ב) כִּי יִמָּצֵא אִישׁ שֹׁכֵב עִם אִשָּׁה בְעֻלַת בַּעַל וּמֵתוּ גַּם שְׁנֵיהֶם הָאִישׁ הַשֹּׁכֵב עִם הָאִשָּׁה וְהָאִשָּׁה וּבִעַרְתָּ הָרָע מִיִּשְׂרָאֵל: [דברים כב, כב]

ג) וְגֹנֵב אִישׁ וּמְכָרוֹ וְנִמְצָא בְיָדוֹ מוֹת יוּמָת: [שמות כא, טז]

ד) כִּי יִנָּצוּ אֲנָשִׁים יַחְדָּו אִישׁ וְאָחִיו וְקָרְבָה אֵשֶׁת הָאֶחָד לְהַצִּיל אֶת אִישָׁהּ מִיַּד מַכֵּהוּ וְשָׁלְחָה יָדָהּ וְהֶחֱזִיקָה בִּמְבֻשָׁיו: [דברים כה, יא]

ה) לֹא תִרְצָח לֹא תִנְאָף לֹא תִגְנֹב לֹא תַעֲנֶה בְרֵעֲךָ עֵד שָׁקֶר: [שמות כ, יג]

ו) כִּי עֲבָדַי הֵם אֲשֶׁר הוֹצֵאתִי אֹתָם מֵאֶרֶץ מִצְרָיִם לֹא יִמָּכְרוּ מִמְכֶּרֶת עָבֶד: [ויקרא כה, מב]

ז) לֹא תִּגְנֹבוּ וְלֹא תְכַחֲשׁוּ וְלֹא תְשַׁקְּרוּ אִישׁ בַּעֲמִיתוֹ: [ויקרא יט, יא]

ח) לֹא יָקוּם עֵד אֶחָד בְּאִישׁ לְכָל עָוֹן וּלְכָל חַטָּאת בְּכָל חֵטְא אֲשֶׁר יֶחֱטָא עַל פִּי שְׁנֵי עֵדִים אוֹ עַל פִּי שְׁלֹשָׁה עֵדִים יָקוּם דָּבָר: [דברים יט, טו]

עין משפט נר מצוה

לא א מיי' פ"ט מהל' גניבה הלכה ג סמג שם:
לב ב מיי' שם הל' ה:
לג ג מיי' שם הל' א:

ליקוטי רש"י

סתם ספרא רבי יהודה. ספרא דבי רב היינו תורת כהנים ברייתא של ספר ויקרא שאר ספרי דבי רב קרי למדרש של ספר במדבר מוישלחו מן המחנה עד סוף הספר אלה הדברי' כו' ומכילתא דהיינו מדרש אלה שמות מהחדש הזה לכם עד סוף הספר כולהו אקרי שאר ספרי דבי רב והיינו דאמרינן בעלמא (סנהדרין דף פו) סתם מתני' רבי מאיר סתם ספרא רבי יהודה סתם ספרי רבי שמעון סתם סדר עולם ר' יוסי סתם תוספתא רבי נחמיה וכולן אליבא דר' עקיבא [ב"ב קכד:]. וכולהו אליבא דר' עקיבא. [יש מפרשים רבי עקיבא סתימתאה דאמרינן בסנהדרין באלו הן הנחנקין (דף פו) סתם משנה רבי מאיר סתם ברייתא רבי נתן וכולהו אליבא דרבי עקיבא ולאו מילתא היא דהא בכמה דוכתין אמרינן רבי מנחם סתימתאה רבי שמעון סתימתאה אלא רוב משניות איכא בהש"ס סתומות אליבא דר' עקיבא [בכורות ל.]. יצא עבד שאין לו אחוה. עם ישראל שאין בא בקהל. במצות. כל מצוה שאשה חייבת בה עבד חייב בה דגמר לה לה מאשה [ב"ק פח.]. לא תגנב. בגונב נפשות הכתוב מדבר. לא תגנובו (ויקרא יט, יא) בגונב ממון או אינו אלא זה בגונב ממון ולהלן בגונב נפשות אמרת דבר הלמד מעניינו מה לא תרצח לא תנאף מדבר בדבר שחייבין עליהם מיתת בית דין אף לא תגנוב דבר שחייב עליו מיתת בית דין [שמות כ, יב]. דבר הלמד מעניינו. דבר סתום שאין מפורש בו במה מדבר הוי לומדו מן הענין פרשה שנכתב בה במה הענין מיירי [חולין קטו:]. זה אחד מי"ג מדות מקרא שכתוב סתם ואין אנו יודעין במה מדבר הוי לומדו מעניינו [שם מ:]. דבר ולא חצי דבר. האי דבר למעוטי חצי דבר דכי האי גוונא כגון שנים אומרים אחת בגבה ראינו ולא בדקנו יותר ושנים אומרים אנו בדקנו מלפניה וראינו אחת בכריסה ואי לאו מיעוטא דקרא דבר ולא חצי דבר לא היה לנו לפסול עדות זה דעדות זה כשר הוא מאחר שיש ב' עדים על כל שיער שהרי אין מכחישין כלל זה את זה אלא כת זו בדקו מגבה וכת שניה בדקו מלפניה ובשעה אחת ראו ב' שערות אלו מכאן ואלו מכאן דליכא למימר שומא נינהו השתא דכתיב דבר עדותן בטלה דב' שערות דבר אחד הוא ואין מועילין אלא כשהן ביחד בבת אחת שאם נראה אחד היום מכאן ולמחר גדל שני במקום אחר וכבר נשר הראשון אמרינן שומא נינהו ואין כלום אלא אם כן ישנן ביחד וכל כת וכת יכול לראות ב' השערות דהא ביחד היו נמצא שכל כת עדות של חצי דבר מעידין וכל אחד אינו מעיד שהיא גדולה אלא חצי סימני גדלות ראינו [ב"ב נו:].

נֶהֱרָגִין – **they are executed.**

The Gemara explains the two sides of the dispute:

חִזְקִיָּה דְּאָמַר כְּרַבִּי עֲקִיבָא – **Chizkiyah agrees with R' Akiva,** דְּאָמַר ,,דָּבָר" וְלֹא חֲצִי דָבָר – **who maintains** that when the Torah says, [witnesses shall establish] *a matter,*[38] it means ***a*** complete ***matter*** **and not half a matter.** That is, testimony is unacceptable unless it establishes a complete matter.[39] In our case, therefore, where each set of witnesses testified to only part of the kidnaper's capital offense, their testimony is unacceptable.[40]

וְרַבִּי יוֹחָנָן אָמַר כְּרַבָּנָן – **But R' Yochanan agrees with the Sages,** דְּאָמְרֵי ,,דָּבָר" וַאֲפִילוּ חֲצִי דָבָר – **who maintain** that when the Torah says *a matter,* it means ***a*** complete ***matter*** **and even half a matter.** That is, testimony is acceptable even if it establishes just part of a matter. Hence, in this case, although each set of witnesses testified to only part of the capital offense, their testimony is acceptable.[41]

The Gemara adds:

וּמוֹדֶה חִזְקִיָּה – **And Chizkiyah would agree** בְּעֵדִים הָאַחֲרוֹנִים שֶׁל בֵּן סוֹרֵר וּמוֹרֶה שֶׁהוּזְמוּ – that **if the second witnesses** involved in the prosecution **of a *ben sorer umoreh* are discredited through *hazamah*,**[42] שֶׁנֶּהֱרָגִין – **they are executed.** Although their testimony on its own does not suffice to have the *ben sorer umoreh* put to death, it is nevertheless acceptable, for the following reason: מִתּוֹךְ שֶׁיְּכוֹלִים לוֹמַר הָרִאשׁוֹנִים – **Since the first [witnesses] can say,**

NOTES

38. *Deuteronomy* 19:15. עַל־פִּי שְׁנֵי עֵדִים ... יָקוּם דָּבָר, *According to two witnesses... shall a matter be established.*

39. R' Akiva maintains that testimony which is relevant only in conjunction with the testimony of other witnesses is not valid at all. (This concept is elaborated on below.)

40. When taken separately, the testimony of each set of witnesses does not suffice to render the defendant liable to execution. The first set's testimony (viz. one person kidnaped another) will not, by itself, result in a death penalty, for only a kidnaping followed by the victim's sale is punishable by death. And the second set's testimony (viz. one person sold another) will not, by itself, result in the death penalty, since the defendant can claim that he was selling his own slave. Thus, each testimony is relevant only in conjunction with that of other witnesses (*Rashi*).

Chizkiyah, following R' Akiva's opinion, maintains that such testimonies are unacceptable, and thus could not have rendered the defendant liable to execution even when taken together. Accordingly, if the witnesses are found to be *zomemin,* they are not executed.

[According to this reasoning, viz. that partial testimony is inadmissible, the defendant himself cannot be executed on account of it. Why, then, did *Rashi* (above, note 37) give a different explanation as to why the defendant cannot be executed, viz. that the testimony against him is עֵדוּת שֶׁאִי אַתָּה יָכוֹל לַהֲזִימָהּ, *testimony that cannot be refuted through hazamah*? The answer is that *Rashi* cited that point only to demonstrate that since the law of the defendant automatically follows from the law of the witnesses (irrespective of the reason for the law of the witnesses), it was not necessary for Chizkiyah to mention the law of the defendant (*Binyan Shlomo;* cf. *Maharsha, Aruch LaNer*).]

41. The Sages [R' Akiva's disputants] maintain that even testimony which is relevant only in conjunction with that of other witnesses is valid. R' Yochanan, following the Sages' opinion, maintains therefore that the combination of the testimonies from the two sets of witnesses *were* capable of resulting in a death penalty. Hence, when the witnesses are found to be *zomemin,* they are liable to execution.

42. As taught above (Mishnah 71a), a *ben sorer umoreh* is one who stole money in certain specific circumstances, and ate specific quantities of meat and wine that he had bought with the stolen money. The first time he performs this offense, he is brought to court and flogged. If he subsequently repeats the offense, he is liable to execution.

The Gemara discusses a case where one set of witnesses testified to the first offense, another set testified to the second offense, and then the second set was discredited through *hazamah.*

תני תנא קמיה דרב ששת א"ל אני שונה רבי שמעון אומר א) מאחיו עד שיוציאנו מרשות אחיו ואת אמרת חייב א תני פטור מאי קושיא דילמא הא ר"ש הא רבנן לא ס"ד דאמר ר' יוחנן ב) סתם מתני' ר' מאיר סתם תוספתא ר' נחמיה ג) סתם ספרא רבי יהודה סתם ספרי ר"ש וכולהו אליבא דר"ע: הגונב בנו: מאי טעמא דרבנן אמר אביי דאמר קרא א) כי ימצא פרט למצוי א"ל רב פפא לאביי אלא מעתה ב) כי ימצא איש שוכב עם אשה בעולת בעל הכי נמי כי ימצא פרט למצוי כגון של בית פלוני דשכיחן גביידהו הכי נמי דפטירי א"ל אנא ג) מונמצא בידו קאמינא אמר רבא ב הלכך הני מיקרי דרדקי ומתנו רבנן כמצויין בידן דמו ופטירי: גנב מי שחציו וכו': ג) תנן התם רבי יהודה אומר אין לעבדים בושת ד) מאי טעמא דר' יהודה אמר קרא ד) כי ינצו אנשים יחדיו איש ואחיו מי שיש לו אחוה יצא עבד שאין לו אחוה ורבנן אחיו הוא במצות והכא היכי דריש ר' יהודה סבר א) מאחיו לאפוקי עבדים בני ישראל למעוטי מי שחציו עבד וחציו בן חורין מבני ישראל למעוטי מי שחציו עבד וחציו בן חורין הוי מיעוט אחר מיעוט ה) ואין מיעוט אחר מיעוט אלא לרבות ורבנן מאחיו לאפוקי עבדים לא משמע להו דהא אחיו הוא במצות בני ישראל מבני ישראל חד למעוטי עבד וחד למעוטי מי שחציו עבד וחציו בן חורין אזהרה לגונב נפש מנין רבי יאשיה אמר ה) מלא תגנב רבי יוחנן אמר ו) מלא ימכרו ממכרת עבד ולא פליגי מר קא חשיב לאו דגניבה ומר קא חשיב לאו דמכירה ת"ר ה) לא תגנוב ג בגונב נפשות הכתוב מדבר אתה אומר בגונב נפשות או אינו אלא בגונב ממון אמרת צא ולמד משלש עשרה מדות שהתורה נדרשת בהן דבר הלמד מעניינו במה הכתוב מדבר בנפשות אף כאן בנפשות תניא אידך ז) לא תגנובו בגונב ממון הכתוב מדבר אתה אומר בגונב ממון או אינו אלא בגונב נפשות אמרת צא ולמד משלש עשרה מדות שהתורה נדרשת בהן י) דבר הלמד מעניינו במה הכתוב מדבר בממון אף כאן בממון איתמר עידי גניבה ועידי מכירה בנפש שהוזמו חזקיה אמר אין נהרגין רבי יוחנן אמר נהרגין חזקיה דאמר כר"ע ז) דאמר ח) דבר ולא חצי דבר ורבי יוחנן אמר כרבנן דאמרי דבר ואפי' חצי דבר ומודה חזקיה בעדים האחרונים של בן סורר ומורה שהוזמו שנהרגין מתוך שיכולים לומר הראשונים להלקותו

תני תנא. להך מתני' דקתני מכר לאביו חייב: סתם ספרא. תורת כהנים: סתם ספרי. ספר וידבר ומשנה תורה והאי סתמא דכי ימצא איש במשנה תורה הוא: אליבא דרבי עקיבא. ממה שלמדו מר' עקיבא אמרום: של בית פלוני. לא רצה להזכיר שמם שחשובין היו וזה לא היו נוהגין כדת שהיו הרבה דרין בבית אחד אנשים ונשים והיו מלוין תמיד עם נשי חביריהן ולא שמתייחדין: ונמצא. קרא יתירא הוא דאי ללמד שימצא בעדים מכי ימצא נפקא: כמצויין בידן דמו. התלמידים מלוין תמיד בבית הרב ואם גנב הרב אחד מתלמידיו ומכרו אינו נהרג: אין לעבדים בושת. המבייש את העבד לא חייבתו תורה לתת דמי בשתו: וכי ינצו אנשים יחדיו והכה איש וגו'. מהתם נפקא לן חיוב בשת דכתיב וקצותה את כפה ממון אתה אומר ממון או אינו אלא ממש נאמר כאן לא תחוס עינך ונאמר להלן בעדים זוממין (דברים יט) לא תחוס עינך מה להלן ממון אף כאן ממון: עבד שאין לו אחוה. ואפי' עם אחיו בני אביו דכתיב (בראשית כב) עם החמור עם הדומה לחמור אינו אלא כבהמה: אחיו הוא במצות. בכל מצות שהאשה חייבת בהן עבד חייב בהן דגמר לה לה מאשה: והכא. במתני' בגונב נפש דכתיב מאחיו: היכי דריש. רבי יהודה לחייב על מי שחציו עבד: מאחיו למעוטי עבדים. דהא לרבי יהודה אין לו אחוה: מבני. יתירא דריש ליה דהוה ליה למכתב מאחיו בני ישראל: מלא תגנוב. האמור בעשרת הדברות דבגונב נפשות מתוקם לקמן בשמעתין: דבר הלמד מעניינו. אם אי אתה יודע במה הכתוב מדבר לא ולמד מפרשה שכתוב בה ולפי הפרשה הוא נכתב אצלה וכאן במה כל הענין מדבר בנפשות לא תרצח ולא תנאף כל אלה חייבי מיתות ב"ד אף לא תגנוב בגניבה שיש בה מיתת ב"ד: לא תגנובו. בפרשת קדושים תהיו: משלש עשרה מדות. זו היא אחת מהן שיהא הדבר מעניינו למד: במה הכתוב מדבר. הענין של מטה ושל מעלה מזו: בממון. לא תעשוק את רעך (ויקרא יט): עידי גניבה ועידי מכירה. שני כיתי עדים אחת העידה שגנב את הנפש ואחת העידה שמכר אין נהרגין כדמפרש טעמא ואזיל וכיון דאינהו לא מקטלי איהו נמי אם לא הוזמו לא מקטיל דהוי' לה עדות שאי אתה יכול להזימה ולא משכחת לה דמקטיל אלא בכת אחת שמעידין על הגניבה ועל המכירה: פלוגתא דר"ע ורבנן. בבבא בתרא בחזקת הבתים על פי שנים עדים יקום דבר ולא חצי דבר והאי חצי דבר הוא אלא כל כת וכת דאי לאו עידי גניבה אינו נהרג משום עידי מכירה שיכול לומר עבדי מכרתי ואי לאו מכירה נמי לא מיחייב אגניבה: בעדים האחרונים של בן סורר ומורה. דתנן לעיל (דף עא.) מתרין בו בפני ג' ומלקין אותו חזר וקלקל נדון בעשרים ושלשה מתרין בו אביו ואמו בפני הדיינין וכשבאין עדים ראשונים ומעידין עליו שאכל תרטימר בשר ושתה חצי לוג יין מגניבה מלקין אותו כדכתיב ויסרו אותו דהיינו מלקות חזר וקלקל נדון בכ"ג למיתה ומודה חזקיה בהנך אחרונים שהעידו שחזר וקלקל שהוזמו שנהרגין ולא אמרינן שחצי דבר הוא דאי לאו סהדותא דקמאי לא מקטיל בסהדותא דהני אלא אמרינן הואיל ויש עונש על פי ראשונים שזה לקה על ידה תו לא שייכא ההוא סהדותא קמייתא בהני בתרייתא והני בתראי כוליה דבר קא עבדי: להלקותו

מונמצא בידו קא אמינא. *תימה דבסוטה פ' עגלה ערופה (דף מה:) דרשינן כי ימצא חלל פרט למצוי ופטרינן עיר שרובה עובדי כוכבים וי"ל דהתם כתיב באדמה והוי כמו בידו דהכא ואכתי קשה דדרשינן בפ' בתרא דערכין (דף ל:) גבי בתי ערי חומה ומצא פרט למצוי שלא ימכור ברחוק ויגאל בקרוב (א) וי"ל ח) כדפי' בקונטרס דהכא מריבויא דקרא:

יצא עבד שאין לו אחוה. פירש בקונטרס עבד אין לו אחוה ואפילו עם אחיו בני אביו דכתיב עם החמור עם הדומה לחמור וקשה דאם כן גר ומשוחרר נמי ונראה לפרש שאין לו אחוה שאין יוצאי חלציו קרויין אחוה משא"כ בגר:

בני ישראל למעוטי מי שחציו וכו'. אבל כולו משוחרר וגר לא ממעט מבני ישראל וכן בפרק בנות כותים (נדה דף לד. ושם) בני ישראל מיטמאין בזיבה וכו' אבל גרים ומשוחררים לא ממעט וכן שלהי ט) פ"ב דמנחות גבי סמיכה בני ישראל סומכין ואין העובדי כוכבים סומכין ומשוחרר וגר לא ממעטין וכן בפ"ק דערכין (דף ה:) בני ישראל מעריכין ואין העובדי כוכבים מעריכין ולא ממעטין גרים ולא עבדים משוחררין ותימה דבפרק כל המנחות באות מצה (מנחות דף סא: ושם) גבי תנופה אמרינן בני ישראל מניפין ואין העובדי כוכבים מניפין ואין לי אלא בני ישראל גרים ועבדים משוחררים מניין תלמוד לומר המקריב וכן בפ' הערל (יבמות דף עד: ושם) ובשלהי פ"ק דכריתות (דף ז:) אשה כי תזריע אין לי אלא בני ישראל גיורת ושפחה משוחררת מניין ת"ל אשה ושמא בכל הני יש שום רבוי דמרבינן מיניה גרים ומשוחררין י):

דבר ואפי' חצי דבר. וא"ת הא אמרינן לקמן (דף ל.) קיים מקצת וביטל מקצת דשאר מצות דברי הכל פטור ופי' בקונטרס משום דכתיב אך הנביא אשר יזיד לדבר דבר דבר ולא חצי דבר וי"ל דרבנן נמי מודו דדרשינן ולא חצי דבר והא דפליגי אדרבי עקיבא היינו משום דחשבי ליה דבר שלם כדמוכח במרובה (ב"ק דף ע:) ובחזקת הבתים (ב"ב דף נו: ושם) וצריך לחלק בדברים דיש מקומות כה"ג בפ' ד' וה' (ב"ק דף מ. ושם) כופר שלם אמר רחמנא ולא חצי כופר ובפרק יש בכור (בכורות דף מח:) חומש ולא חצי חומש ובמרובה (ב"ק דף עא:) חמשה בקר אמר רחמנא ואפי' חמשה חצאי בקר ובפרק אותו ואת בנו (חולין דף עט: ושם) פליגי ר' אליעזר ורבנן בשה ואפילו מקצת שה ולענין כיסוי בצבי ואפילו מקצת צבי ובפרק הבא על יבמתו (יבמות דף נט: ושם) בבתולה מקצת בתולים ובכתובות פרק אלמנה (דף לז: ושם) במקצת כסף ככל כסף ושלהי כסוי הדם (חולין דף פח. ושם) דם ואפילו מקצת דם וכריש בכורות (דף ג. ושם) בכור ואפילו מקצת בכור:

מתוך שיכולים עדים הראשונים כו'. אין הטעם תלוי באמירתם אלא במאי דעידי גניבה ראשונה לא צריכי לעידי גניבה שניה כדאמרינן במרובה (ב"ק דף ע: ושם) דמודה רבי עקיבא בשנים אומרים קידש ושנים אומרים בעל אע"ג דעידי ביאה צריכי לעידי קדושין [הואיל] והן לא צריכי לעידי ביאה כוליה דבר הוא: גניבה

מסורת הש"ס

א) [עירובין לו: גיטין ד.], ב) [עירובין שם שבת קלז. יומא מא. קידושין נג. שבועות יג. בכורות סא. כריתות כב.], ג) ב"ק פז., ד) [שם פח.], ה) [יומא מג. וש"נ], ו) [חולין קטו: קמ.], ז) לעיל ל: ב"ק ע: ב"ב נו:, ח) עי' רש"ל, ט) [צ"ל פרק שתי מדות דף סג.], י) [וע"ע תוספות סוכה כח: ד"ה לרבות ותוספות מנחות סא: ד"ה אין לי].

הגהות הב"ח

(א) תוס' ד"ה מונמצא וכו' בפ' בתרא דערכין גבי שדה אחוזה ומצא פרט וכו' ויגאל בקרוב נ"ב ול"ע דהרי בערכין איתא להדיא משום דהכא מעניינא דקרא ולכך דרשינן אע"פ דלא כתיב בידו:

גליון הש"ס

תוס' ד"ה מונמצא וכו' תימה דבסוטה. עי' בריטב"א מכות דף ח' ע"א ד"ה התם מענינא דקרא:

תורה אור השלם

א) כִּי יִמָּצֵא אִישׁ גֹּנֵב נֶפֶשׁ מֵאֶחָיו מִבְּנֵי יִשְׂרָאֵל וְהִתְעַמֶּר בּוֹ וּמְכָרוֹ וּמֵת הַגַּנָּב הַהוּא וּבִעַרְתָּ הָרָע מִקִּרְבֶּךָ: [דברים כד, ז]

ב) כִּי יִמָּצֵא אִישׁ שֹׁכֵב עִם אִשָּׁה בְעֻלַת בַּעַל וּמֵתוּ גַּם שְׁנֵיהֶם הָאִישׁ הַשֹּׁכֵב עִם הָאִשָּׁה וְהָאִשָּׁה וּבִעַרְתָּ הָרָע מִיִּשְׂרָאֵל: [דברים כב, כב]

ג) וְגֹנֵב אִישׁ וּמְכָרוֹ וְנִמְצָא בְיָדוֹ מוֹת יוּמָת: [שמות כא, טז]

ד) כִּי יִנָּצוּ אֲנָשִׁים יַחְדָּו אִישׁ וְאָחִיו וְקָרְבָה אֵשֶׁת הָאֶחָד לְהַצִּיל אֶת אִישָׁהּ מִיַּד מַכֵּהוּ וְשָׁלְחָה יָדָהּ וְהֶחֱזִיקָה בִּמְבֻשָׁיו: [דברים כה, יא]

ה) לֹא תִרְצָח לֹא תִנְאָף לֹא תִגְנֹב לֹא תַעֲנֶה בְרֵעֲךָ עֵד שָׁקֶר: [שמות כ, יג]

ו) כִּי עֲבָדַי הֵם אֲשֶׁר הוֹצֵאתִי אֹתָם מֵאֶרֶץ מִצְרָיִם לֹא יִמָּכְרוּ מִמְכֶּרֶת עָבֶד: [ויקרא כה, מב]

ז) לֹא תִּגְנֹבוּ וְלֹא תְכַחֲשׁוּ וְלֹא תְשַׁקְּרוּ אִישׁ בַּעֲמִיתוֹ: [ויקרא יט, יא]

ח) לֹא יָקוּם עֵד אֶחָד בְּאִישׁ לְכָל עָוֹן וּלְכָל חַטָּאת בְּכָל חֵטְא אֲשֶׁר יֶחֱטָא עַל פִּי שְׁנֵי עֵדִים אוֹ עַל פִּי שְׁלֹשָׁה עֵדִים יָקוּם דָּבָר: [דברים יט, טו]

עין משפט נר מצוה

לא א מיי' פ"ט מהל' גניבה הלכה ג סמג שם:
לב ב מיי' שם הל' ה:
לג ג מיי' שם הל' א:

ליקוטי רש"י

סתם ספרא רבי יהודה. ספרא דבי רב היינו תורת כהנים ברייתא של ספר ויקרא שאר ספרי דבי רב קרי למדרש של ספר במדבר מושלחו מן המחנה עד סוף הספר אלה הדברי' כו' ומכילתא דהיינו מדרש אלה שמות מהחדש הזה לכם עד סוף הספר כולהו אקרי שאר ספרי דבי רב והיינו דאמרינן בעלמא (סנהדרין דף פו) סתם מתני' רבי מאיר סתם ספרא רבי יהודה סתם ספרי רבי שמעון סתם סדר עולם ר' יוסי סתם תוספתא רבי נחמיה וכולן אליבא דר' עקיבא [ב"ב קכד:]. וכולהו אליבא דר' עקיבא. [יש מפרשים רבי עקיבא שמתמהא דאמרינן בסנהדרין באלו הן הנחנקין (דף פו) סתם משנה רבי מאיר סתם ברייתא רבי נתן וכולהו אליבא דרבי עקיבא ולאו מילתא היא דהא בכמה דוכתין אמרינן רבי מנחם שמתמהא רבי שמעון שמתמהא אלא רוב משניות איכא בהש"ס סתומות אליבא דר' עקיבא [בכורות ל.]. יצא עבד שאין לו אחוה. עם ישראל שאין בא בקהל. במצות. כל מצוה שאשה חייבת בה עבד חייב בה דגמר לה לה מאשה [ב"ק פח.]. לא תגנב. בגונב נפשות הכתוב מדבר. לא תגנובו (ויקרא יט, יא) בגונב ממון או אינו אלא זה בגונב ממון ולהלן בגונב נפשות אמרת דבר הלמד מעניינו מה לא תרצח לא תנאף מדבר בדבר שחייבין עליהם מיתת בית דין אף לא תגנוב דבר שחייב עליו מיתת בית דין [שמות כ, יב]. דבר הלמד מעניינו. דבר סתום שאין מפורש בו במה מדבר הוי לומדו מן הענין פרשה שנכתב בה במה הענין מיירי [חולין קטו:]. זה אחד מי"ג מדות מקרא שכתוב סתם ואין אנו יודעין במה מדבר הוי לומדו מענינו [שם מ:]. דבר ולא חצי דבר. האי דבר למעוטי חצי דבר דכי האי גוונא כגון שנים אומרים אחת בגבה ראינו ולא בדקנו יותר ושנים אומרים אנו בדקנו מלפניה וראינו אחת בכריסה ואי לאו מיעוטא דקרא דבר ולא חצי דבר לא היה לנו לפסול עדות זו דעדות זה כשר הוא מאחר שיש ב' עדים על כל שיער שהרי אין מכחישין כלל זה את זה אלא כת זו בדקו מגבה וכת שניה בדקו מלפניה ובשעה אחת ראו ב' שערות אלו מכאן ואלו מכאן דליכא למימר שומא נינהו השתא דכתיב דבר עדותן בטלה דב' שערות דבר אחד הוא ואין מועילין אלא כשהן ביחד בבת אחת שאם נראה אחד היום מכאן ולמחר גדל שני במקום אחר וכבר נשר הראשון אמרינן שומא נינהו ואין כלום אלא אם כן ישנן ביחד וכל כת וכת יכול לראות ב' השערות דהא ביחד היו נמצא שכל כת עדות של חצי דבר מעידין וכל אחד אינו מעיד שהיא גדולה אלא חצי סימני גדלות ראינו [ב"ב נו:].

להלקותו באנו והני אחריני כולי דבר קא עבדי ליה מתקיף לה רב פפא אי הכי עידי מכירה נמי (א) ליקטליה מתוך שיכולין עידי גניבה לומר להלקותו באנו וכי תימא דקסבר חזקיה דלא לקי והא איתמר עידי גניבה בנפש שהוזמו חזקיה ורבי יוחנן חד אמר לוקין וחד אמר אין לוקין ואמרינן תסתיים דחזקיה דאמר לוקין מדאמר חזקיה אין נהרגין דאי ר' יוחנן כיון דאמר נהרגין הוה ליה לאו שניתן לאזהרת מיתת ב"ד וכל [א]לאו שניתן לאזהרת מיתת ב"ד אין לוקין עליו איהו לא לקי אינהו היכי לקו אלא אמר רב פפא [א]בעידי מכירה דכולי עלמא לא פליגי דנהרגין כי פליגי בעידי גניבה חזקיה אמר אין נהרגין גניבה לחודה קיימא ומכירה לחודה קיימא ר' יוחנן אמר [ב]נהרגין גניבה אתחלתא דמכירה היא [ג]ומודה רבי יוחנן בעדים הראשונים של בן סורר ומורה שהוזמו שאין נהרגין מתוך שיכולין לומר להלקותו באנו אמר אביי הכל מודים בבן סורר ומורה והכל מודים בבן סורר ומורה ומחלוקת בבן סורר ומורה הכל מודים בבן סורר ומורה בעדים הראשונים שאין נהרגין מתוך שיכולין לומר להלקותו באנו והכל מודים בבן סורר ומורה בעדים אחרונים [ד]שנהרגים מתוך שעדים הראשונים יכולין לומר להלקותו באנו והני כוליה דבר קא עבדי ליה ומחלוקת בבן סורר ומורה [ה]שנים אומרים בפנינו גנב ושנים אומרים בפנינו אכל אמר רב אסי עידי מכירה בנפש שהוזמו [ו]אין נהרגין מתוך שיכול לומר עבדי מכרתי אמר רב יוסף כמאן אזלא הא שמעתא דרב אסי כר"ע דאמר דבר ולא חצי דבר א"ל אביי דאי כרבנן נהרגין הא מתוך קאמר אלא אפילו תימא רבנן [ז]ובדלא אתו עידי גניבה אי הכי מאי למימרא לא צריכא דאע"ג [ח]דאתו לבסוף ואכתי מאי למימרא לא צריכא [ט]דקא מרמזי רמוזי מהו דתימא רמיזא מילתא היא קמ"ל [ט]רמיזא לאו כלום הוא: **מתני'** זקן ממרא על פי ב"ד שנאמר (א) כי יפלא ממך דבר למשפט [י]שלשה בתי דינין היו שם אחד יושב על פתח הר הבית ואחד יושב על פתח העזרה ואחד יושב בלשכת הגזית [כ]באין לזה שעל פתח הר הבית ואומר כך דרשתי וכך דרשו חבירי כך לימדתי וכך לימדו חבירי אם שמעו (ג) אמר להם ואם לאו באין להן לאותן שעל פתח עזרה ואומר כך דרשתי וכך דרשו חבירי כך לימדתי וכך לימדו חבירי אם שמעו אמר להם ואם לאו אלו ואלו באין לב"ד הגדול שבלשכת הגזית שממנו יוצא תורה לכל ישראל שנאמר (ב) מן המקום ההוא אשר יבחר ה' (ד) חזר לעירו שנה ולמד בדרך שהיה למד פטור ואם הורה לעשות חייב שנאמר (ג) והאיש אשר יעשה בזדון אינו חייב עד שיורה לעשות [ל]תלמיד שהורה לעשות פטור נמצא חומרו קולו: **גמ'** תנו רבנן (א) כי יפלא ממך דבר במופלא

רש"י

להלקותו באנו. ולא הועדנו להמיתו שלא ידענו שסופו לחזור ולקלקל: להלקותו באנו. על הגניבה ולא ידענו שימכרנו: דלא לקי. אגניבה לחודה משום דהוה ליה לאו שניתן לאזהרת מיתת ב"ד שאם ימכרנו יהרג: עידי גניבה בנפש. שהעידוהו שגנב נפש: מדאמר חזקיה אין נהרגין. אם הוזמו לאחר שבאו עידי מכירה משום הכי לוקין שהרי אין סופן למות על עדות זו ולא הוי לגבייהו לאו שניתן לאזהרת מיתת ב"ד: דאי ר' יוחנן כיון דאמר נהרגין. אם באו עידי מכירה אחרי כן קודם הזמה ונגמר דינו ע"פ שתי הכתות והוזמו היכי לקו אם הוזמו קודם שבאו עידי מכירה הא הוה ליה לאו דלא תענה לגבייהו בשעה שהעידו לאו שניתן לאזהרה שלא להעיד כן שאם יעידו ולא יוזמו עד שיבאו עידי מכירה ויגמר דינו ויוזמו ימותו: וכל לאו שניתן לאזהרת ב"ד אין לוקין עליו. ואפילו יפטרו מן המיתה שהרי לא לאזהרת מלקות ניתן: אינהו היכי לקו. הא לאו כאשר זמם הוא ואי משום לא תענה (שמות כ) לאו שאין בו מעשה הוא: בעידי מכירה כולי עלמא לא פליגי דנהרגין. אם נגמר דינו על פי שתי הכתות: לחודה קיימא. ועידי גניבה אינן באין להורגו אלא להלקותו אבל עידי מכירה שבאין עמהן ואומרין שהתרו בו למיתה מונעין אותו ממלקות ומחייבין אותו מיתה והויא לה מכירה דבר שלם: אתחלתא דמכירה. דקסבר ר' יוחנן לא לקי עלה דלאו שניתן לאזהרת מיתת ב"ד ואינן באין אלא להורגו ואף על גב דשתיהן צריכות זו לזו והוה ליה כל חדא וחדא חצי דבר מיקטל כרבנן: ומודה ר' יוחנן בעדים הראשונים של בן סורר ומורה שהוזמו דאין נהרגין. דאינהו ודאי למלקות אתו כדכתיב ויסרו אותו (דברים כא): הכל מודים כו'. כלומר יש עדים בבן סורר ומורה שהכל מודים באחת כתותיו לפטור ויש כת שהכל מודים בו לחיוב ויש כת בבן סורר ומורה שנחלקו חזקיה ורבי יוחנן לפי מה ששמענו במחלוקתן: שנים אומרים בפנינו גנב. משל אביו מעות לקנות בשר ויין בפעם שניה אחר שלקה: ושנים אומרים בפנינו אכל. הבשר ברשות אחרים דאינו חייב עד שיגנוב משל אביו ויאכל ברשות אחרים הנך שתי כתות צריכות זו לזו ואין הראשונים יכולין לומר להלקותו באנו והוה ליה חצי דבר לחזקיה דסבר לה כר"ע דאמר אין נהרגין ולר' יוחנן דאמר נהרגין כרבנן: עידי מכירה בנפש. ולא באו עידי גניבה על כך לפנינו: הא מתוך קאמר. אפי' חצי דבר אין כאן שהרי היה לו להציל נפשו מב"ד בטענה זו: ובדלא אתו עידי גניבה. קאמר רב אסי וכדפרישית שהיה יכול לומר עבדי מכרתי: לבסוף. אחר שהעידו עידי מכירה באו עידי גניבה ונגמר הדין ע"פ שניהם: ואכתי מאי למימרא. כשהעידו הראשונים לא היה הדין ראוי ליגמר על פיהם ויכולין לומר לא היינו יודעין שיבואו עידי גניבה עלינו: דקא מרמזי רמוזי. הני להני: **מתני'** ג' בתי דינין היו שם. בירושלים דמשתעי בה קרא וקמת ועלית: אחד יושב על פתח הר הבית. הוא שער המזרחי שלפנים מן החיל לפני עזרת נשים: ואחד יושב למעלה הימנו. כשעברו עזרת נשים ובאין לפני עזרת ישראל: ואחד בלשכת הגזית. שהיא בנויה בתוך העזרה חציה בקודש וחציה בחול כדאמרינן בסדר יומא (דף כה.): באין לזה שעל פתח הר הבית. זקן זה שהורה בעירו ונחלק ב"ד שבעירו עליו והזקיקו הכתוב לעלות לירושלים ולשאול ובאין הוא ובית דין שבעירו לב"ד זה שעל פתח הר הבית שהרי בו פוגעין תחילה: תלמיד שהורה לעשות. תלמיד שלא הגיע להוראה ונחלק על ב"ד שבעירו ובאו לב"ד הגדול ושאלו וחזר לעירו והורה כבתחילה פטור שאין לסמוך על הוראתו והתורה לא חייבה אלא מופלא ומומחה לב"ד כדאמרי' בגמ': נמצא חומרו קולו. חומר שהחמירו עליו שאינו ראוי להוראה (ה) עד שיהא בן ארבעים שנה נעשה לו קל לפוטרו מן המיתה:

גמרא

תוספות

גניבה אתחלתא דמכירה היא. וא"ת אמאי מקטלי הא מצו למימר לפוסלו לעדות באנו וכ"ת דבעו התראה וכיון דאמרי שהתרו בו למיתה אלמא למיקטליה קא אתו אם כן לחזקיה נמי לקטלו אע"ג דאתו נמי להלקותו כדאשכחן בפ"ב דב"ק (דף כד. ושם) דעידי נגיחה ראשונה ושניה אע"ג דאתו לחיובי' חצי נזק כיון דאתו נמי לייעודי משלמי חצי נזק של העדאה עם הכת השלישית כשהוזמו השלש כתות וי"ל דקסבר חזקיה דגניבה לחודה קיימא כמו עידי קדושין ועידי ביאה ואע"ג דמיירי באתרו ביה מדמקטלי לרבי יוחנן מ"מ לא שייך בהו חיוב מיתה ואפשר דלחזקיה לא בעי התראה ולר' יוחנן בעי אי נמי הש"ס לא חש בטעמא דלפוסלו לעדות באנו מדאיצטריך לעיל למימר להלקותו ושמא איצטריך היכא דמפסיל מעיקרא וקאי:

עבדי מכרתי. וא"ת אי לאו למקטליה קא אתו אם יבאו עדים שאינו עבדו אם כן למאי קא אתו וי"ל דאתו לקיים המקח וא"ת אי דלא אתרו ביה למה לן טעמא דעבדי מכרתי אלא ודאי אתרו ביה אם כן למקטליה קאתי וי"ל דאתרו ביה אחריני ואינהו לא ידעי וכי האי גוונא הוה מצי לשנויי בריש פרק היו בודקין (לעיל דף מא.) גבי נערה המאורסה:

אמר רב יוסף כו'. סלקא דעתך דרב יוסף בדאתו עידי גניבה וה"פ מתוך שהוא יכול לומר עבדי מכרתי אם לא היו באים עידי גניבה אם כן אין בעדותם ממש וחצי דבר הוא ואביי פריך ליה הא מתוך קאמר דמשמע הלשון דאפילו השתא נמי בתר דאתו עידי גניבה מצי למימר הכי: **קמ"ל** רמיזה לאו כלום הוא. בפ"ב דב"ק (דף כד: ושם) גבי לייעודי תורא ולייעודי גברא דמסקינן התם אלא דקא מרמזי רמוזי לא דמי לרמיזה דהכא דהתם מיירי ברמיזה חשובה שבכל השלשה ימים באו אלו עם אלו וקא מרמזי אבל הכא ברמיזה גרועה איירי דלאו מילתא היא אי נמי דיני נפשות שאני:

עין משפט נר מצוה

ד א ב ג ד ה ו ז ח ט מיי' פכ"א מהל' עדות הלכה ט:

ה י מיי' פ"א מהל' סנהדרין הלכה ג:

ו כ מיי' פ"ג מהלכות ממרים הלכה ח:

ז ל מיי' שם הל' ה:

ליקוטי רש"י

אזהרת מיתת בית דין. ניתן דלא ענש מיתה אלא אם כן הזהיר הלכך עיקר אזהרתו למקום שיש מיתה אתאי ולא למלקות [שבת קנד.]. וכל לאו שניתן לאזהרת שלא יעשה כן שמתחייב עליו מיתת בית דין אין לוקין עליו אפילו לא התרו בו מיתה והתרו בו למלקות דהשתא לא מיקטיל אפילו הכי לא לקי דלאזהרת מיתה ניתן ולא למלקות [עירובין יז:]. לאו שניתן לאזהרת [כו'] שלא יעשה שלא ימיתוהו בית דין אין לוקין עליו דמיתת ב"ד הוא עונשו של לאו [ב"ק עד:]. לאזהרת דבר שמחייבין עליו מיתת ב"ד אין לוקין עליו כשהתרו בו למלקות בלא מיתה לפי שלא ניתן לאו זה לאזהרת עונש מלקות כשאר לאוין שהרי הוצרך להזהירו שאם לא כן לא היה יכול לחייבו מיתה [מכות יג:]. כגון דקא מרמזי רמוזי. כת עידי ראשונה לעידי כת [שניה] שיעידו הלכך ודאי אחרונים נמי לכך נתכוונו שהיו יודעים בראשונים וכך משמעתי [ב"ק כד:]. זקן ממרא. שהמרה על ב"ד שבלשכת הגזית ומיתתו בחנק [סוטה כה.]. על פי ב"ד. זקן אינו נהרג אלא אם כן המרה על פי בית דין הגדול דכתיב (שם דברים י"ז) וקמת ועלית [לעיל טז.]. באין לב"ד הגדול שבלשכת הגזית. בשבעים ואחד דכתיב (דברים יז) מן המקום ההוא מקום המיוחד דהיינו לשכת הגזית ואפילו מצאן אבי פגי שהמרה עליהן ילפינן מיניה דאין המראתו המראה (סנהדרין יד) [סוטה ז:]. חזר. זקן ממרא לעירו וכו' הורה לעשות דמשמע דקאמר ואתרין אתם לעשות גמרה הוראתו חייב [הוריות ב.].

מסורת הש"ס

א) [שבת קנד. עירובין יז: בבא קמא עד: מכות יג: שבועות ד.], ב) [ב"ק כד:], ג) [נ"ל אומרים כך הגי' במשנה שבמשניות ועי' תוי"ט], ד) הוריות ב., ה) [סוטה כב.].

הגהות הב"ח

(א) גמ' עדי מכירה נמי ליקטלו:

תורה אור השלם

א) כִּי יִפָּלֵא מִמְּךָ דָבָר לַמִּשְׁפָּט בֵּין דָּם לְדָם בֵּין דִּין לְדִין וּבֵין נֶגַע לָנֶגַע דִּבְרֵי רִיבֹת בִּשְׁעָרֶיךָ וְקַמְתָּ וְעָלִיתָ אֶל הַמָּקוֹם אֲשֶׁר יִבְחַר יְיָ אֱלֹהֶיךָ בּוֹ: [דברים יז, ח]

ב) וְעָשִׂיתָ עַל פִּי הַדָּבָר אֲשֶׁר יַגִּידוּ לְךָ מִן הַמָּקוֹם הַהוּא אֲשֶׁר יִבְחַר יְיָ וְשָׁמַרְתָּ לַעֲשׂוֹת כְּכֹל אֲשֶׁר יוֹרוּךָ: [דברים יז, י]

ג) וְהָאִישׁ אֲשֶׁר יַעֲשֶׂה בְזָדוֹן לְבִלְתִּי שְׁמֹעַ אֶל הַכֹּהֵן הָעֹמֵד לְשָׁרֶת שָׁם אֶת יְיָ אֱלֹהֶיךָ אוֹ אֶל הַשֹּׁפֵט וּמֵת הָאִישׁ הַהוּא וּבִעַרְתָּ הָרָע מִיִּשְׂרָאֵל: [דברים יז, יב]

וַהֲנֵי אַחֲרִינֵי לְהַלְקוֹתוֹ בָּאנוּ – "We came only **to give him lashes,**" – **and these second [witnesses]** כּוּלֵּי דָּבָר קָא עָבְדֵי לֵיהּ – **are perpetrating a "whole matter" on him,** i.e. they alone are seen as trying to have the defendant executed.[1]

The Gemara challenges this distinction between a kidnaper and a *ben sorer umoreh*:

מַתְקִיף לָהּ רַב פָּפָּא – **Rav Pappa objected:** אִי הָכִי – **If so,** that the second witnesses against a *ben sorer umoreh* can be executed since they perpetrated a "whole matter," עֵידֵי מְכִירָה נַמִּי לִיקְטְלֵיהּ – then **the witnesses to the sale** of a kidnaped person can **also be executed,** מִתּוֹךְ שֶׁיְּכוֹלִין עֵדֵי גְנֵיבָה לוֹמַר – **because the witnesses to the kidnaping** itself **could say:** לְהַלְקוֹתוֹ בָּאנוּ – **"We came** only **to give him lashes,"**[2] and thus the witnesses to the sale perpetrated a "whole matter."[3] – ? –

The Gemara suggests a resolution and then rejects it:

וְכִי תֵּימָא דְּקָסָבַר חִזְקִיָּה דְּלֹא לָקֵי – **And if you say that Chizkiyah maintains that [a kidnaper] does not incur lashes** for kidnaping alone,[4] this cannot be so, וְהָא אִיתְּמַר – **for it was stated:** עֵידֵי גְנֵיבָה בְּנֶפֶשׁ שֶׁהוּזְמוּ – If **witnesses to a kidnaping were discredited through** ***hazamah,*** חִזְקִיָּה וְרַבִּי יוֹחָנָן – their fate is the subject of another dispute between **Chizkiyah and R' Yochanan.** חַד אָמַר לוֹקִין – **One says** that **they incur lashes;** וְחַד אָמַר אֵין לוֹקִין – **and one says** that **they do not incur lashes.**[5]

From this dispute about discredited witnesses to a kidnaping, Rav Pappa proves that according to Chizkiyah the very act of kidnaping is punishable by lashes. As the first stage of the proof, Rav Pappa shows that Chizkiyah (not R' Yochanan) was the one who said that discredited witnesses to a kidnaping incur lashes:

וְאַמְרִינַן – **And we said:** תִּסְתַּיֵּים דְּחִזְקִיָּה דְּאָמַר לוֹקִין – **Conclude that Chizkiyah was the one who said** that **they incur lashes,** מִדְּאָמַר חִזְקִיָּה אֵין נֶהֱרָגִין – **for Chizkiyah said** above that where one set of witnesses testified to a kidnaping and another set to the victim's sale and both sets were discredited through *hazamah,* **they are not executed.**[6] דְּאִי רַבִּי יוֹחָנָן – **For if R' Yochanan** was the one who said that they incur lashes, the following difficulty arises: כֵּיוָן דְּאָמַר נֶהֱרָגִין – **Since [R' Yochanan] said** above **that** where one set of witnesses testified to a kidnaping and another set to the victim's sale, and both sets were discredited through *hazamah,* **they are executed,** הָוֶה לֵיהּ לָאו שֶׁנִּיתַּן לְאַזְהָרַת מִיתַת בֵּית דִּין – it transpires that this **prohibition** against their testifying falsely **serves as their warning** not to testify on pain of liability **to court-imposed execution,**[7] וְכָל לָאו שֶׁנִּיתַּן לְאַזְהָרַת מִיתַת בֵּית דִּין אֵין לוֹקִין עָלָיו – **and any prohibition that serves as a warning for a court-imposed execution does not carry the penalty of lashes.**[8] Therefore, R' Yochanan could not have been the one who said that those who testify falsely to a kidnaping incur lashes. Since it was not R' Yochanan, it must have been Chizkiyah, his disputant, who said it.

Having shown that, in Chizkiyah's view, those who falsely testify to a kidnaping incur lashes, Rav Pappa now proves that the same must apply to the kidnaper himself:

אִיהוּ לֹא לָקֵי – Now, if **he** [the kidnaper] **does not incur lashes,**

NOTES

1. We have learned that if a legal proceeding is dependent on the occurrence of two events and these events are attested to by different sets of witnesses, then each of their testimonies is viewed as effecting a "half matter." The Gemara now introduces an exception to this definition: If the first event effects some independent consequence and the witnesses to that event did not know that the second event will occur, it is assumed that they intended to establish only that independent consequence and not to lay the groundwork for the later proceeding. The second witnesses, therefore, are viewed as establishing the later proceeding on their own. Thus, each set of witnesses establishes a "whole matter" – the first set establishes the "whole matter" of the consequence effected by their testimony alone, and the second set establishes the "whole matter" of the later proceeding.

[For example: In order to convict a married woman of adultery, the fact that she is married must have been established by witnesses. It would thus seem that the witnesses to the cohabitation are establishing only a "half matter," for without the testimony to the woman's marriage their testimony amounts to nothing. However, since the witnesses to the woman's marriage effected an independent consequence (viz. that she is forbidden to all men other than her husband), they are not considered to be testifying regarding the matter of her illicit relations. Accordingly, if other witnesses testify that she committed adultery, they *alone* are establishing this matter. Thus, the second pair, too, is considered to be establishing a "whole matter" (see *Bava Kamma* 70b).]

In the case of a *ben sorer umoreh*, upon the first witnesses' testimony the defendant is liable to lashes, and upon the second witnesses' testimony he is liable to execution. Since the testimony of the first witnesses effects a distinct punishment (viz. lashes), and they testified without knowing that the defendant would repeat the offense (and thereby become liable to execution), their testimony is considered independent, and not the basis for the penalty of execution. Accordingly, it is only the second witnesses who are seen as responsible for rendering the defendant liable to execution (they establish a "whole matter"). Hence, even according to Chizkiyah, the second witnesses' testimony is valid and, if discredited, they can be executed on account of it.

2. Rav Pappa assumes that (according to Chizkiyah) one who kidnaps a person and does not sell him is liable to lashes for violating the negative commandment of לֹא תִגְנֹב, *you shall not steal* [a person] (see 86a).

3. The case of a kidnaper is apparently the same as that of a *ben sorer umoreh.* In both cases one set of witnesses renders the defendant liable to lashes and then a second set renders him liable to execution. Accordingly, there are no grounds for the Gemara's preceding distinction: viz. that the second testimony against a kidnaper effects only a "half matter," but the second testimony against a *ben sorer umoreh* effects a "whole matter."

4. [If this would be so, those who testified to the kidnaping would be seen as attempting to execute the defendant, in which case, their testimony and that of the witnesses to the sale would each effect only a "half matter."]

The reason why one might have thought that kidnaping alone does not bear lashes is that there is a rule which states: לָאו שֶׁנִּיתַּן לְאַזְהָרַת מִיתַת בֵּית דִּין אֵין לוֹקִין עָלָיו, *A prohibition that serves as a warning for a court-imposed execution does not carry the penalty of lashes.* That is, although the standard punishment for violating a prohibition is lashes, if one violates a prohibition which carries the death penalty, he does not incur liability to lashes, even if in fact he does not become liable to the death penalty. Now, kidnaping someone (and then selling him) carries the penalty of execution. Hence, it could be argued on the basis of the aforementioned rule that one should not incur lashes for kidnaping even if he does not sell the victim (see *Rashi*; see also *Maharsha, Binyan Shlomo, Aruch LaNer*).

5. This dispute concerns a case in which witnesses testified to the kidnaping but no witnesses testified to the victim's sale. In the dispute between Chizkiyah and R' Yochanan recorded above (86a) there were witnesses to kidnaping and to the sale.

6. Chizkiyah ruled above (86a) that even where there are witnesses to both the kidnaping and the selling, and the witnesses are found to be *zomemin,* they are not executed. Thus, according to Chizkiyah, witnesses who falsely testify to a kidnaping cannot become liable to execution. Since they cannot be executed for this transgression of false testimony, the rule stated in note 4 does not apply, and thus it is possible that they do incur lashes (*Rashi*).

7. I.e. through committing this transgression, the witnesses can become liable to the death penalty. For if the witnesses to the kidnaping are not found to be *zomemin* until after other witnesses have testified to the sale and the accused is sentenced to death, they are executed (*Rashi*).

8. See note 4; see also *Tosafos* to *Shabbos* 154b ד"ה בלאו, who discuss different applications of this concept. Since, according to R' Yochanan, witnesses who testify falsely to a kidnaping *can* be executed for doing so (see previous note), they do not incur lashes even if they do not actually become liable to execution (e.g. they are discredited *before* the other witnesses testify).

להלקותו באנו והני אחריני כולי דבר קא עבדי ליה מתקיף לה רב פפא אי הכי עידי מכירה נמי (א) ליקטליה מתוך שיכולין עידי גניבה לומר להלקותו באנו וכי תימא דקסבר חזקיה דלא לקי והא איתמר עידי גניבה בנפש שהוזמו חזקיה ורבי יוחנן חד אמר לוקין וחד אמר אין לוקין ואמרינן תסתיים דחזקיה דאמר לוקין מדאמר חזקיה אין נהרגין דאי ר' יוחנן כיון דאמר נהרגין הוה ליה לאו שניתן לאזהרת מיתת ב"ד וכל [א] לאו שניתן לאזהרת מיתת ב"ד אין לוקין עליו איהו לא לקי אינהו היכי לקו אלא אמר רב פפא [א] בעידי מכירה דכולי עלמא לא פליגי דנהרגין כי פליגי בעידי גניבה חזקיה אמר אין נהרגין גניבה לחודה קיימא ומכירה לחודה קיימא ר' יוחנן אמר [ב] נהרגין גניבה אתחלתא דמכירה היא [ג] ומודה רבי יוחנן בעדים הראשונים של בן סורר ומורה שהוזמו שאין נהרגין מתוך שיכולין לומר להלקותו באנו אמר אביי הכל מודים בבן סורר ומורה והכל מודים בבן סורר ומורה ומחלוקת בבן סורר ומורה הכל מודים בבן סורר ומורה בעדים הראשונים שאין נהרגין מתוך שיכולין לומר להלקותו באנו והכל מודים בבן סורר ומורה בעדים אחרונים [ד] שנהרגים מתוך שעדים הראשונים יכולין לומר להלקותו באנו והני כוליה דבר קא עבדי ליה ומחלוקת בבן סורר ומורה [ה] שנים אומרים בפנינו גנב ושנים אומרים בפנינו אכל אמר רב אסי עידי מכירה בנפש שהוזמו [ו] אין נהרגין מתוך שיכול לומר עבדי מכרתי אמר רב יוסף כמאן אזלא הא שמעתא דרב אסי כר"ע דאמר דבר ולא חצי דבר א"ל אביי דאי כרבנן נהרגין הא מתוך קאמר אלא אפילו תימא רבנן [ז] ובדלא אתו עידי גניבה אי הכי מאי למימרא לא צריכא דאע"ג [ח] דאתו לבסוף ואכתי מאי למימרא לא צריכא [ג] דקא מרמזי רמוזי מהו דתימא [ט] רמיזא מילתא היא קמ"ל [ט] רמיזא לאו כלום הוא: **מתני'** זקן ממרא על פי ב"ד שנאמר [א] כי יפלא ממך דבר למשפט [י] שלשה בתי דינין היו שם אחד יושב על פתח הר הבית ואחד יושב על פתח העזרה ואחד יושב בלשכת הגזית [כ] באין לזה שעל פתח הר הבית ואומר כך דרשתי וכך דרשו חבירי כך לימדתי וכך לימדו חבירי אם שמעו [ג] אמר להם ואם לאו באין להן לאותן שעל פתח עזרה ואומר כך דרשתי וכך דרשו חבירי כך לימדתי וכך לימדו חבירי אם שמעו אמר להם ואם לאו אלו ואלו באין לב"ד הגדול שבלשכת הגזית שממנו יוצא תורה לכל ישראל שנאמר [ב] מן המקום ההוא אשר יבחר ה' [ד] חזר לעירו שנה ולמד בדרך שהיה למד פטור ואם הורה לעשות חייב שנאמר [ג] והאיש אשר יעשה בזדון אינו חייב עד שיורה לעשות [ל] תלמיד שהורה לעשות פטור נמצא חומרו קולו: **גמ'** תנו רבנן [א] כי יפלא ממך דבר

במופלא

רש"י

להלקותו באנו. ולא הועדנו להמיתו שלא ידענו שסופו לחזור ולקלקל: להלקותו באנו. על הגניבה ולא ידענו שימכרנו: דלא לקי. אגניבה לחודה משום דהוה ליה לאו שניתן לאזהרת מיתת ב"ד שאם ימכרנו יהרג: עידי גניבה בנפש. שהעידוהו שגנב נפש: מדאמר חזקיה אין נהרגין. אם הוזמו לאחר שבאו עידי מכירה משום הכי לוקין שהרי אין סופן למות על עדות זו ולא הוי לגבייהו לאו שניתן לאזהרת מיתת ב"ד: דאי ר' יוחנן כיון דאמר נהרגין. אם באו עידי מכירה אחרי כן קודם הזמה ונגמר דינו ע"פ שתי הכתות והוזמו היכי לקו אם הוזמו קודם שבאו עידי מכירה הא הוה ליה לאו דלא תענה לגבייהו בשעה שהעידו לאו שניתן לאזהרה שלא להעיד כן שאם יעידו ולא יוזמו עד שיבאו עידי מכירה ויגמר דינו ויוזמו ימותו: וכל לאו שניתן לאזהרת ב"ד אין לוקין עליו. ואפילו יפטרו מן המיתה שהרי לא לאזהרת מלקות ניתן: אינהו היכי לקו. הא לאו כאשר זמם הוא ואי משום לא תענה (שמות כ) לאו שאין בו מעשה הוא: בעידי מכירה כולי עלמא לא פליגי דנהרגין. אם נגמר דינו על פי שתי הכתות: לחודה קיימא. ועידי גניבה אינן באין להורגו אלא להלקותו אבל עידי מכירה שבאין עמהן ואומרין שהתרו בו למיתה מונעין אותו ממלקות ומחייבין אותו מיתה והויא לה מכירה דבר שלם: אתחלתא דמכירה. דקסבר ר' יוחנן לא לקי עלה דלאו שניתן לאזהרת מיתת ב"ד ואינן באין אלא להורגו ואף על גב דשתיהן צריכות זו לזו והוה ליה כל חדא וחדא חצי דבר מיקטל כרבנן: ומודה ר' יוחנן בעדים הראשונים של בן סורר ומורה שהוזמו דאין נהרגין. דאינהו ודאי למלקות אתו כדכתיב ויסרו אותו (דברים כא): הכל מודים כו'. כלומר יש עדים בבן סורר ומורה שהכל מודים באחת כתותיו לפטור ויש כת שהכל מודים בו לחיוב ויש כת בבן סורר ומורה שנחלקו חזקיה ורבי יוחנן לפי מה שמשמעו במחלוקתן: שנים אומרים בפנינו גנב. משל אביו מעות לקנות בשר ויין בפעם שניה אחר שלקה: ושנים אומרים בפנינו אכל. הבשר ברשות אחרים דאינו חייב עד שיגנוב משל אביו ויאכל ברשות אחרים הנך שתי כתות צריכות זו לזו ואין הראשונים יכולין לומר להלקותו באנו והוה ליה חצי דבר לחזקיה דסבר לה כר"ע דאמר אין נהרגין ולר' יוחנן דאמר נהרגין כרבנן: עידי מכירה בנפש. ולא באו עידי גניבה על כך לפנינו: הא מתוך קאמר. אפי' חצי דבר אין כאן שהרי היה לו להציל נפשו מב"ד בטענה זו: ובדלא אתו עידי גניבה. קאמר רב אשי וכדפרישית שהיה יכול לומר עבדי מכרתי: לבסוף. אחר שהעידו עידי מכירה באו עידי גניבה ונגמר הדין ע"פ שניהם: ואכתי מאי למימרא. כשהעידו הראשונים לא היה הדין ראוי ליגמר על פיהם ויכולין לומר לא היינו יודעין שיבואו עידי גניבה עלינו: דקא מרמזי רמוזי. הני להני: מתני' ג' בתי דינין היו שם. בירושלים דמשתעי בה קרא וקמת ועלית: אחד יושב על פתח הר הבית. הוא שער המזרחי שלפנים מן החיל לפני עזרת נשים: ואחד יושב למעלה הימנו. כשעברו עזרת נשים ובאין לפני עזרת ישראל: ואחד בלשכת הגזית. שהיא בנויה בתוך העזרה חציה בקודש וחציה בחול כדאמרינן בסדר יומא (דף כה.): באין לזה שעל פתח הר הבית. זקן זה שהורה בעירו ונחלק ב"ד שבעירו עליו והזקיקו הכתוב לעלות לירושלים ולשאול ובאין הוא ובית דין שבעירו לב"ד זה שעל פתח הר הבית שהרי בו פוגעין תחילה: תלמיד שהורה לעשות. תלמיד שלא הגיע להוראה ונחלק על ב"ד שבעירו ובאו לב"ד הגדול ושאלו וחזר לעירו והורה כבתחילה פטור שאין לסמוך על הוראתו והתורה לא חייבה אלא מופלא ומומחה לב"ד כדאמרי' בגמ': נמצא חומרו קולו. חומר שהחמירו עליו שאינו ראוי להוראה [ה] עד שיהא בן ארבעים שנה נעשה לו קל לפוטרו מן המיתה:

גמרא

תוספות

גניבה אתחלתא דמכירה היא. וא"ת אמאי מקטלי הא מצו למימר לפוסלו לעדות באנו וכ"ת דבעו התראה וכיון דאמרי שהתרו בו למיתה אלמא למיקטליה קא אתו אם כן לחזקיה נמי לקטלו אע"ג דאתו נמי להלקותו כדאשכחן בפ"ב דב"ק (דף כד. ושם) דעידי נגיחה ראשונה ושניה אע"ג דאתו לחיובי' חצי נזק כיון דאתו נמי לייעודי משלמי חצי נזק של העדאה עם הכת השלישית כשהוזמו השלש כתות וי"ל דקסבר חזקיה דגניבה לחודה קיימא כמו עידי קדושין ועידי ביאה ואע"ג דמיירי באתרו ביה מדמקטלי לרבי יוחנן מ"מ לא שייך בהו חיוב מיתה ואפשר דלחזקיה לא בעי התראה ולר' יוחנן בעי אי נמי הש"ס לא חש בטעמא דלפוסלו לעדות באנו מדאיצטריך לעיל למימר להלקותו ושמא איצטריך היכא דמפסיל מעיקרא וקאי:

עבדי מכרתי. וא"ת אי לאו למקטליה קא אתו אם יבאו עדים שאינו עבדו אם כן למאי קא אתו וי"ל דאתו לקיים המקח וא"ת אי דלא אתרו ביה למה לן טעמא דעבדי מכרתי אלא ודאי אתרו ביה אם כן למקטליה קאתי וי"ל דאתרו ביה אחריני ואינהו לא ידעי וכי האי גוונא הוה מצי לשנויי בריש פרק היו בודקין (לעיל דף מא.) גבי נערה המאורסה:

אמר רב יוסף כו'. סלקא דעתך דרב יוסף בדאתו עידי גניבה וה"פ מתוך שהוא יכול לומר עבדי מכרתי אם לא היו באים עידי גניבה אם כן אין בעדותם ממש וחצי דבר הוא ואביי פריך ליה הא מתוך קאמר דמשמע הלשון דאפילו השתא נמי בתר דאתו עידי גניבה מצי למימר הכי: קמ"ל רמיזה לאו כלום הוא. בפ"ב דב"ק (דף כד: ושם) גבי לייעודי תורא ולייעודי גברא דמסקינן התם אלא דקא מרמזי רמוזי לא דמי לרמיזה דהכא דהתם מיירי ברמיזה חשובה שבכל השלשה ימים באו אלו עם אלו וקא מרמזי אבל הכא ברמיזה גרועה איירי דלאו מילתא היא אי נמי דיני נפשות שאני:

במופלא

עין משפט נר מצוה

ד א ב ג ד ה ו ז ח ט מיי' פכ"א מהל' עדות הלכה ט:
ה י מיי' פ"א מהל' סנהדרין הלכה ג:
ו כ מיי' פ"ג מהלכות ממרים הלכה ח:
ז ל מיי' שם הל' ה:

ליקוטי רש"י

אזהרת מיתת בית ין. ניתן דלא ענש מיתה :א אם כן הזהיר הלכך יקר אזהרתו למקום שיש מיתה אתאי ולא זלקות [שבת קנד.]. וכל זו שניתן לאזהרה שלא :שה כן שמתחייב עליו יתת בית דין אין לוקין ליו אפילו לא התרו בו זיתה והתרו בו למלקות :שמא לא מיקטיל אפילו כי לא לקי דלאזהרת יתה ניתן ולא למלקות ירובין יז:]. לאו שניתן זזהרת [כו'] שלא יעשה שלא ימיתוהו בית דין זין לוקין עליו דמיתת "ד הוא עונשו של לאו :"ק עד:]. לאזהרת דבר חייבין עליו מיתת ב"ד ץ לוקין עליו כשהתרו בו לקות בלא מיתה לפי לא ניתן לאו זה לאזהרת וגם מלקות כשאר לאוין הרי הוצרך להזהירו שאם ן כן לא היה יכול לחייבו יתה [מכות יג:]. כגון קא מרמזי רמוזי. כת ידי ראשונה לעידי כת ג' שיעידו הלכך ודאי חרונים נמי לכך נתכוונו זיו יודעים בראשונים וכך מעתי [ב"ק כד:]. זקן מרא. שהמרה על ב"ד ל לשכת הגזית ומיתתו זנק [סוטה כה.]. על פי "ד. זקן אינו נהרג אלא ס כן המרה על פי בית ין הגדול דכתיב (שם ברים י"ז) וקמת ועלית עיל טז.]. באין לב"ד גדול שבלשכת גזית. בשבעים ואחד :תיב (דברים יז) מן מקום ההוא מקום יוחד דהיינו לשכת הגזית אפילו מצאן אבי פגי זמרה עליהן ילפינן יניה דאין המראתו מראה (סנהדרין יד) וטה ז:]. חזר. זקן מרא לעירו וכו' הורה נשות דמשמע דקאמר ותרין אתם לעשות :גמרה הוראתו חייב [הוריות ב.].

מסורת הש"ס

א) [שבת קנד. עירובין יז: בבא קמא עד: מכות יג: שבועות ד.], ב) [ב"ק כד:], ג) [נ"ל אומרים כך הגי' במשנה שבמשניות ועי' תוי"ט], ד) הוריות ב., ה) [סוטה כג.].

הגהות הב"ח

(א) גמ' עדי מכירה נמי ליקטלו:

תורה אור השלם

א) כִּי יִפָּלֵא מִמְּךָ דָבָר לַמִּשְׁפָּט בֵּין דָּם לְדָם בֵּין דִּין לְדִין וּבֵין נֶגַע לָנֶגַע דִּבְרֵי רִיבֹת בִּשְׁעָרֶיךָ וְקַמְתָּ וְעָלִיתָ אֶל הַמָּקוֹם אֲשֶׁר יִבְחַר יְיָ אֱלֹהֶיךָ בּוֹ: [דברים יז, ח]

ב) וְעָשִׂיתָ עַל פִּי הַדָּבָר אֲשֶׁר יַגִּידוּ לְךָ מִן הַמָּקוֹם הַהוּא אֲשֶׁר יִבְחַר יְיָ וְשָׁמַרְתָּ לַעֲשׂוֹת כְּכֹל אֲשֶׁר יוֹרוּךָ: [דברים יז, י]

ג) וְהָאִישׁ אֲשֶׁר יַעֲשֶׂה בְזָדוֹן לְבִלְתִּי שְׁמֹעַ אֶל הַכֹּהֵן הָעֹמֵד לְשָׁרֶת שָׁם אֶת יְיָ אֱלֹהֶיךָ אוֹ אֶל הַשֹּׁפֵט וּמֵת הָאִישׁ הַהוּא וּבִעַרְתָּ הָרָע מִיִּשְׂרָאֵל: [דברים יז, יב]

אִינְהוּ הֵיכִי לָקוּ – **how can they** [those who falsely testified to a kidnaping] **incur lashes?**[9] Certainly, then, Chizkiyah maintains that the kidnaper himself incurs lashes.

This concludes Rav Pappa's proof that according to Chizkiyah, kidnaping only carries the penalty of lashes, and thus the original difficulty still remains: Since those who testify to a kidnaping can claim that they intended only to render the defendant liable to lashes, the witnesses to the sale are establishing the entire matter of the defendant's execution. Why, then, did Chizkiyah rule that the witnesses to the sale are not executed?

In view of this difficulty, Rav Pappa qualifies the first dispute between Chizkiyah and R' Yochanan:

אֶלָּא אָמַר רַב פָּפָּא – **Rather, Rav Pappa said,** בְּעֵידֵי מְכִירָה דְּכוּלֵּי עָלְמָא לֹא פְּלִיגֵי דְּנֶהֱרָגִין – **all agree that** false **witnesses** who testified **to the sale** of a kidnaped person **are executed.**[10] כִּי פְּלִיגֵי – **Where do they disagree?** בְּעֵידֵי גְנֵיבָה – They disagree **regarding** false **witnesses** who testified **to the kidnaping** itself. חִזְקִיָּה אָמַר – **Chizkiyah says** that אֵין נֶהֱרָגִין – **they are not executed,** גְּנֵיבָה לְחוּדָהּ קַיְימָא וּמְכִירָה לְחוּדָהּ קַיְימָא – because **the** testimony to the **kidnaping stands by itself and** the testimony to the **selling stands by itself.**[11] רַבִּי יוֹחָנָן אָמַר – But **R' Yochanan says** that נֶהֱרָגִין – **they are executed,** גְּנֵיבָה אַתְחַלְתָּא דִּמְכִירָה הִיא – because testimony to **a kidnaping is** viewed as **the beginning of the** testimony to the victim's **sale.**[12]

The Gemara adds:

וּמוֹדֶה רַבִּי יוֹחָנָן – **And R' Yochanan would agree** that בְּעֵדִים הָרִאשׁוֹנִים שֶׁל בֵּן סוֹרֵר וּמוֹרֶה שֶׁהוּזְמוּ – **if the first witnesses** involved in the prosecution **of a *ben sorer umoreh* are discredited through *hazamah*,**[13] שֶׁאֵין נֶהֱרָגִין – **they are not executed,** מִתּוֹךְ שֶׁיְּכוֹלִין לוֹמַר לְהַלְקוֹתוֹ בָּאנוּ – **because they can say: "We came** only **to give him lashes."**[14]

The Gemara discusses three cases involving false witnesses who accuse someone of being a *ben sorer umoreh,* and it teaches how Chizkiyah and R' Yochanan would rule in each case:

אָמַר אַבָּיֵי – **Abaye said:** הַכֹּל מוֹדִים בְּבֵן סוֹרֵר וּמוֹרֶה – There is a group of witnesses involved **in** the prosecution of **a *ben sorer umoreh*** that **everyone agrees** is not liable to execution; וְהַכֹּל מוֹדִים בְּבֵן סוֹרֵר וּמוֹרֶה – there is another group of witnesses involved **in** the prosecution of **a *ben sorer umoreh*** that **everyone agrees** *is* liable to execution; וּמַחֲלוֹקֶת בְּבֵן סוֹרֵר וּמוֹרֶה – **and** there is a third group of witnesses involved **in** the prosecution of **a *ben sorer umoreh*** regarding which there is **a dispute.**

Abaye explains the first case:

הַכֹּל מוֹדִים בְּבֵן סוֹרֵר וּמוֹרֶה – **Everyone** agrees **regarding a *ben sorer umoreh*** בְּעֵדִים הָרִאשׁוֹנִים שֶׁאֵין נֶהֱרָגִין – that **if the first witnesses** are discredited through *hazamah*, **they are not executed,** מִתּוֹךְ שֶׁיְּכוֹלִין לוֹמַר לְהַלְקוֹתוֹ בָּאנוּ – **for they can say: "We came** only **to give him lashes."**[15]

Abaye explains the second case:

וְהַכֹּל מוֹדִים בְּבֵן סוֹרֵר וּמוֹרֶה – **And everyone agrees regarding a *ben sorer umoreh*** בְּעֵדִים אַחֲרוֹנִים שֶׁנֶּהֱרָגִים – that **if the second witnesses** are discredited through *hazamah,* **they are executed.** מִתּוֹךְ שֶׁעֵדִים הָרִאשׁוֹנִים יְכוֹלִין לוֹמַר לְהַלְקוֹתוֹ בָּאנוּ – **Since the first witnesses can say: "We came** only **to give him lashes,"** וְהָנֵי – **and these** second witnesses כּוּלֵּיהּ דָּבָר קָא עָבְדֵי לֵיהּ – **are perpetrating a "whole matter" on him,** i.e. they alone are seen as trying to have the defendant executed.[16]

Abaye explains the third case:

וּמַחֲלוֹקֶת בְּבֵן סוֹרֵר וּמוֹרֶה – **And there is a dispute regarding a *ben sorer umoreh*** where the testimony to his second offense is divided in the following manner: שְׁנַיִם אוֹמְרִים בְּפָנֵינוּ גָּנַב – **Two** witnesses **say: "He stole** money **before us,"** וּשְׁנַיִם אוֹמְרִים בְּפָנֵינוּ אָכַל – **and two** other witnesses **say: "He consumed** the prescribed quantities of meat and wine **before**

NOTES

9. *Zomemin* witnesses are punished with the consequences they had sought to inflict on the subject of their false testimony. Hence, if Chizkiyah maintains that a kidnaper does not incur lashes, how could he rule that *zomemin* witnesses who testified to a kidnaping *do* incur lashes? (*Rashi*).

It cannot be answered that they incur lashes on account of the prohibition (*Exodus* 20:13): לֹא־תַעֲנֶה בְרֵעֲךָ עֵד שָׁקֶר, *You shall not bear false witness against your fellow*. This is because one does not incur lashes for violating a prohibition unless one performed an action, and giving testimony (i.e. speech) is not deemed an action (*Rashi;* see *Makkos* 2b; see *Ran*, *Aruch LaNer;* see also *Kehilos Yaakov* to *Makkos* 1:5).

10. That is, if one set of witnesses testifies to a kidnaping and one set to the victim's sale, and the defendant is sentenced to death (*Rashi*), and then the witnesses are found to be *zomemin*, both Chizkiyah and R' Yochanan agree that the witnesses to the selling are executed. However, their reasons are different:

According to Chizkiyah, since the witnesses to the kidnaping render the accused liable to lashes, the witnesses to the sale effect the "whole matter" of his execution (see note 1). Hence, regardless of whether Chizkiyah accepts partial testimony or not, he will accept the testimony to the sale. Consequently, if those who testified to the sale are found to be *zomemin*, they are executed (see *Rashi* ד״ה לחודה; see *Maharsha;* see also *Ran* and *Aruch LaNer*).

According to R' Yochanan, however, kidnaping (without selling) does not carry the penalty of lashes (see notes 4 and 8). Those who testify to a kidnaping, therefore, since they do not render the defendant liable to lashes, are viewed as setting him up for execution. Consequently, the testimony to the *sale* effects only "half" the matter of the defendant's execution. Nevertheless, if those who testified to the sale are found to be *zomemin*, they are executed, because R' Yochanan rules that even partial testimony is valid (*Rashi* below ד״ה אתחלתא).

11. In Chizkiyah's opinion, kidnaping (without selling) carries the penalty of lashes (see Gemara above). Hence, those who testify to a kidnaping are viewed only as attempting to subject the defendant to lashes, not as trying to set the stage for a capital prosecution (*Rashi;* see note 1). Accordingly, even if a kidnaper is sentenced to death due to their testimony (as well as testimony to the victim's sale) and then they are found to be *zomemin,* they are not executed for attempting to kill the defendant.

12. R' Yochanan maintains that kidnaping is *not* punishable by lashes. Hence, those who testify to a kidnaping are seen as attempting to have the defendant executed (*Rashi*). Thus, if discredited, they are liable to execution (see end of note 10).

[According to Rav Pappa's approach, the point of contention between Chizkiyah and R' Yochanan is whether a kidnaper is liable to lashes. This is in contrast to the Gemara's initial understanding, according to which the dispute centered on the issue of whether partial testimony is acceptable (see note 19).]

13. See 86a note 42.

14. In contrast to the crime of kidnaping (without selling), for which the Torah does not specify a punishment, the first offense of a *ben sorer umoreh* is designated the penalty of lashes. This is derived from the verse (*Deuteronomy* 21:18): וְיִסְּרוּ אֹתוֹ, *and they discipline him,* which is interpreted as referring to lashes (*Rashi*). Hence, even R' Yochanan would agree that witnesses who testify to a *ben sorer umoreh's* first offense intend to render him liable to lashes, and not to lay the groundwork for a death penalty. Consequently, if such witnesses are found to be *zomemin*, they are liable to lashes and not execution.

15. Even R' Yochanan agrees to this, as the Gemara stated above (see previous note).

16. Even Chizkiyah agrees to this, as stated at the end of 86a (see also note 1 above).

להלקותו באנו והני אחריני כולי דבר קא עבדי ליה מתקיף לה רב פפא אי הכי עידי מכירה נמי (א) ליקטליה מתוך שיכולין עידי גניבה לומר להלקותו באנו וכי תימא דקסבר חזקיה דלא לקי והא איתמר עידי גניבה בנפש שהוזמו חזקיה ורבי יוחנן חד אמר לוקין וחד אמר אין לוקין ואמרינן תסתיים דחזקיה דאמר לוקין מדאמר חזקיה אין נהרגין דאי ר' יוחנן כיון דאמר נהרגין הוה ליה לאו שניתן לאזהרת מיתת ב"ד וכל [א] לאו שניתן לאזהרת מיתת ב"ד אין לוקין עליו איהו לא לקי אינהו היכי לקו אלא אמר רב פפא [א] בעידי מכירה דכולי עלמא לא פליגי דנהרגין כי פליגי בעידי גניבה חזקיה אמר אין נהרגין גניבה לחודה קיימא ומכירה לחודה קיימא ר' יוחנן אמר [ב] נהרגין גניבה אתחלתא דמכירה היא [ג] ומודה רבי יוחנן בעדים הראשונים של בן סורר ומורה שהוזמו שאין נהרגין מתוך שיכולין לומר להלקותו באנו אמר אביי הכל מודים בבן סורר ומורה והכל מודים בבן סורר ומורה ומחלוקת בבן סורר ומורה הכל מודים בבן סורר ומורה בעדים הראשונים שאין נהרגין מתוך שיכולין לומר להלקותו באנו והכל מודים בבן סורר ומורה בעדים אחרונים [ד] שנהרגים מתוך שעדים הראשונים יכולין לומר להלקותו באנו והני כוליה דבר קא עבדי ליה ומחלוקת בבן סורר ומורה [ה] שנים אומרים בפנינו גנב ושנים אומרים בפנינו אכל אמר רב אסי עידי מכירה בנפש שהוזמו [ו] אין נהרגין מתוך שיכול לומר עבדי מכרתי אמר רב יוסף כמאן אזלא הא שמעתא דרב אסי כר"ע דאמר דבר ולא חצי דבר א"ל אביי דאי כרבנן נהרגין הא מתוך קאמר אלא אפילו תימא רבנן [ז] ובדלא אתו עידי גניבה אי הכי מאי למימרא לא צריכא דאע"ג [ח] דאתו לבסוף ואכתי מאי למימרא לא צריכא (ג) דקא מרמזי רמוזי מהו דתימא רמיזא מילתא היא קמ"ל [ט] רמיזא לאו כלום הוא: **מתני'** זקן ממרא על פי ב"ד שנאמר א) כי יפלא ממך דבר למשפט [י] שלשה בתי דינין היו שם אחד יושב על פתח הר הבית ואחד יושב על פתח העזרה ואחד יושב בלשכת הגזית [כ] באין לזה שעל פתח הר הבית ואומר כך דרשתי וכך דרשו חבירי כך לימדתי וכך לימדו חבירי אם שמעו (ג) אמר להם ואם לאו באין להן לאותן שעל פתח עזרה ואומר כך דרשתי וכך דרשו חבירי כך לימדתי וכך לימדו חבירי אם שמעו אמר להם ואם לאו אלו ואלו באין לב"ד הגדול שבלשכת הגזית שממנו יוצא תורה לכל ישראל שנאמר ב) מן המקום ההוא אשר יבחר ה' (ד) חזר לעירו שנה ולמד בדרך שהיה למד פטור ואם הורה לעשות חייב שנאמר ג) והאיש אשר יעשה בזדון אינו חייב עד שיורה לעשות [ל] תלמיד שהורה לעשות פטור נמצא חומרו קולו: **גמ'** תנו רבנן א) כי יפלא ממך דבר

במופלא

להלקותו באנו. ולא הועדנו להמיתו שלא ידענו שסופו לחזור ולקלקל: להלקותו באנו. על הגניבה ולא ידענו שימכרנו: דלא לקי. אגניבה לחודה משום דהוה ליה לאו שניתן לאזהרת מיתת ב"ד שאם ימכרנו יהרג: עידי גניבה בנפש. שהעידוהו שגנב נפש: מדאמר חזקיה אין נהרגין. אם הוזמו לאחר שבאו עידי מכירה משום הכי לוקין שהרי אין סופן למות על עדות זו ולא הוי לגבייהו לאו שניתן לאזהרת מיתת ב"ד: דאי ר' יוחנן כיון דאמר נהרגין. אם באו עידי מכירה אחרי כן קודם הזמה ונגמר דינו ע"פ שתי הכתות והוזמו היכי לקו אם הוזמו קודם שבאו עידי מכירה הא הוה ליה לאו דלא תענה לגבייהו בשעה שהעידו לאו שניתן לאזהרה שלא להעיד כן שאם יעידו ולא יוזמו עד שיבאו עידי מכירה ויגמר דינו ויוזמו ימותו: וכל לאו שניתן לאזהרת ב"ד אין לוקין עליו. ואפילו יפטרו מן המיתה שהרי לא לאזהרת מלקות ניתן: אינהו היכי לקו. הא לאו כאשר זמם הוא ואי משום לא תענה (שמות כ) לאו שאין בו מעשה הוא: בעידי מכירה כולי עלמא לא פליגי דנהרגין. אם נגמר דינו על פי שתי הכתות: לחודה קיימא. ועידי גניבה אינן באין להורגו אלא להלקותו אבל עידי מכירה שבאין עמהן ואומרין שהתרו בו למיתה מונעין אותו ממלקות ומחייבין אותו מיתה והויא לה מכירה דבר שלם: אתחלתא דמכירה. דקסבר ר' יוחנן לא לקי עלה דלאו שניתן לאזהרת מיתת ב"ד ואינן באין אלא להורגו ואף על גב דשתיהן צריכות זו לזו והוה ליה כל חדא וחדא חצי דבר מיקטל כרבנן: ומודה ר' יוחנן בעדים הראשונים של בן סורר ומורה שהוזמו דאין נהרגין. דאינהו ודאי למלקות אתו כדכתיב ויסרו אותו (דברים כא): הכל מודים כו'. כלומר יש עדים בבן סורר ומורה שהכל מודים באחת כתותיו לפטור ויש כת שהכל מודים בו לחיוב ויש כת בבן סורר ומורה שנחלקו חזקיה ורבי יוחנן לפי מה ששמענו במחלוקתן: שנים אומרים בפנינו גנב. משל אביו מעות לקנות בשר ויין בפעם שניה אחר שלקה: ושנים אומרים בפנינו אכל. הבשר ברשות אחרים דאינו חייב עד שיגנוב משל אביו ויאכל ברשות אחרים הנך שתי כתות צריכות זו לזו ואין הראשונים יכולין לומר להלקותו באנו והוה ליה חצי דבר לחזקיה דסבר לה כר"ע דאמר אין נהרגין ולר' יוחנן דאמר נהרגין כרבנן: עידי מכירה בנפש. ולא באו עידי גניבה על כך לפנינו: הא מתוך קאמר. אפי' חצי דבר אין כאן שהרי היה לו להציל נפשו מב"ד בטענה זו: ובדלא אתו עידי גניבה. קאמר רב אשי וכדפרישית שהיה יכול לומר עבדי מכרתי: לבסוף. אחר שהעידו עידי מכירה באו עידי גניבה ונגמר הדין ע"פ שניהם: ואכתי מאי למימרא. כשהעידו הראשונים לא היה הדין ראוי ליגמר על פיהם ויכולין לומר לא היינו יודעין שיבואו עידי גניבה עליו: דקא מרמזי רמוזי. הני להני: **מתני'** ג' בתי דינין היו שם. בירושלים דמשתעי בה קרא וקמת ועלית: אחד יושב על פתח הר הבית. הוא שער המזרחי שלפנים מן החיל לפני עזרת נשים: ואחד יושב למעלה הימנו. כשעברו עזרת נשים ובאין לפני עזרת ישראל: ואחד בלשכת הגזית. שהיא בנויה בתוך העזרה חציה בקודש וחציה בחול כדאמרינן בסדר יומא (דף כה.): באין לזה שעל פתח הר הבית. זקן זה שהורה בעירו ונחלק ב"ד שבעירו עליו והזקיקו הכתוב לעלות לירושלים ולשאול ובאין הוא ובית דין שבעירו לב"ד זה שעל פתח הר הבית שהרי בו פוגעין תחילה: תלמיד שהורה לעשות. תלמיד שלא הגיע להוראה ונחלק על ב"ד שבעירו ובאו לב"ד הגדול ושאלו וחזר לעירו והורה כבתחילה פטור שאין לסמוך על הוראתו והתורה לא חייבה אלא מופלא ומומחה לב"ד כדאמרי' בגמ': נמצא חומרו קולו. חומר שהחמירו עליו שאינו ראוי להוראה (ה) עד שיהא בן ארבעים שנה נעשה לו קל לפוטרו מן המיתה:

גמרא

גניבה אתחלתא דמכירה היא. וא"ת אמאי מקטלי הא מצו למימר לפוסלו לעדות באנו וכ"ת דבעו התראה וכיון דאמרי שהתרו בו למיתה אלמא למיקטליה קא אתו אם כן לחזקיה נמי לקטלו אע"ג דאתו נמי להלקותו כדאשכחן בפ"ב דב"ק (דף כד. ושם) דעידי נגיחה ראשונה ושניה אע"ג דאתו לחיובי' חצי נזק כיון דאתו נמי לייעודי משלמי חצי נזק של העדאה עם הכת השלישית כשהוזמו השלש כתות וי"ל דקסבר חזקיה דגניבה לחודה קיימא כמו עידי קדושין ועידי ביאה ואע"ג דמיירי באתרו ביה מדמקטלי לרבי יוחנן מ"מ לא שייך בהו חיוב מיתה ואפשר דלחזקיה לא בעי התראה ולר' יוחנן בעי אי נמי הש"ס לא חש בטעמא דלפוסלו לעדות באנו מדאיצטריך לעיל למימר להלקותו ושמא איצטריך היכא דמפסיל מעיקרא וקאי:

עבדי מכרתי. וא"ת אי לאו למקטליה קא אתו אם יבאו עדים שאינו עבדו אם כן למאי קא אתו וי"ל דאתו לקיים המקח וא"ת אי דלא אתרו ביה למה לן טעמא דעבדי מכרתי אלא ודאי אתרו ביה אם כן למקטליה קאתי וי"ל דאתרו ביה אחריני ואינהו לא ידעי וכי האי גוונא הוה מצי לשנויי בריש פרק היו בודקין (לעיל דף מא.) גבי נערה המאורסה:

אמר רב יוסף כו'. סלקא דעתך דרב יוסף בדאתו עידי גניבה וה"פ מתוך שהוא יכול לומר עבדי מכרתי אם לא היו באים עידי גניבה אם כן אין בעדותם ממש וחצי דבר הוא ואביי פריך ליה הא מתוך קאמר דמשמע הלשון דאפילו השתא נמי בתר דאתו עידי גניבה מצי למימר הכי: **קמ"ל** רמיזה לאו כלום הוא. בפ"ב דב"ק (דף כד: ושם) גבי לייעודי תורא ולייעודי גברא דמסקינן התם אלא דקא מרמזי רמוזי לא דמי לרמיזה דהכא דהתם מיירי ברמיזה חשובה שבכל השלשה ימים באו אלו עם אלו וקא מרמזי אבל הכא ברמיזה גרועה איירי דלאו מילתא היא אי נמי דיני נפשות שאני:

במופלא

עין משפט נר מצוה

ד א ב ג ד ה ו ז ח ט מיי' פכ"א מהל' עדות הלכה ט:
ה י מיי' פ"א מהל' סנהדרין הלכה ג:
ו כ מיי' פ"ג מהלכות ממרים הלכה ח:
ז ל מיי' שם הל' ה:

ליקוטי רש"י

אזהרת מיתת בית ...ין. ניתן דלא ענש מיתה ...לא אם כן הזהיר הלכך ...יקר אזהרתו למקום שיש ... מיתה אתאי ולא ...מלקות [שבת קנד.]. וכל ...או שניתן לאזהרת שלא ...שה כן שמתחייב עליו ...יתת בית דין אין לוקין ...ליו אפילו לא התרו בו ...יתה והתרו בו למלקות ...השתא לא מיקטיל אפילו ...כי לא לקי דלאזהרת ...יתה ניתן ולא למלקות [...ירובין יז:]. לאו שניתן ...אזהרת [כו'] שלא יעשה ... שלא ימיתוהו בית דין ...אין לוקין עליו דמיתת ...ב"ד הוא עונשו של לאו [...ב"ק עד:]. לאזהרת דבר ...מחייבין עליו מיתת ב"ד ...אין לוקין עליו כשהתרו בו ...מלקות בלא מיתה לפי ...לא ניתן לאו זה לאזהרת ...וגם מלקות כשאר לאוין ...הרי הוצרך להזהירו שאם ...אז כן לא היה יכול לחייבו ...מיתה [מכות יג:]. כגון ...דקא מרמזי רמוזי. כת ...עידי ראשונה לעידי כת ...ב' שיעידו הלכך ודאי ...אחרונים נמי לכך נתכוונו ...היו יודעים בראשונים וכך ...מעתי [ב"ק כד:]. זקן ...ממרא. שהמרה על ב"ד ...של לשכת הגזית ומיתתו ...בחנק [סוטה כה.]. על פי ...ב"ד. זקן אינו נהרג אלא ...אם כן המרה על פי בית ...דין הגדול דכתיב (שם ...דברים י"ז) וקמת ועלית ...[לעיל טז.]. באין לב"ד ...הגדול שבלשכת ...הגזית. בשבעים ואחד ...כתיב (דברים יז) מן ...המקום ההוא מקום ...המיוחד דהיינו לשכת הגזית ...אפילו מצאן אבי פגי ...וזמרה עליהן ילפינן ...מיניה דאין המראתו ...המראה (סנהדרין יד) [...סוטה ז:]. חזר. זקן ...ממרא לעירו וכו' הורה ...בנשות דמשמע דקאמר ...ותרין אתם לעשות ...בגמרה הוראתו חייב [הוריות ב.].

מסורת הש"ס

א) [שבת קנד. עירובין יז: בבא קמא עד: מכות יג: שבועות ד.], ב) [ב"ק כד:], ג) [נ"ל אומרים כך הגי' במשנה שבמשניות ועי' תוי"ט], ד) הוריות ב., ה) [סוטה כה.].

הגהות הב"ח

(א) גמ' עדי מכירה נמי ליקטלו:

תורה אור השלם

א) כִּי יִפָּלֵא מִמְּךָ דָבָר לַמִּשְׁפָּט בֵּין דָּם לְדָם בֵּין דִּין לְדִין וּבֵין נֶגַע לָנֶגַע דִּבְרֵי רִיבֹת בִּשְׁעָרֶיךָ וְקַמְתָּ וְעָלִיתָ אֶל הַמָּקוֹם אֲשֶׁר יִבְחַר יְיָ אֱלֹהֶיךָ בּוֹ: [דברים יז, ח]

ב) וְעָשִׂיתָ עַל פִּי הַדָּבָר אֲשֶׁר יַגִּידוּ לְךָ מִן הַמָּקוֹם הַהוּא אֲשֶׁר יִבְחַר יְיָ וְשָׁמַרְתָּ לַעֲשׂוֹת כְּכֹל אֲשֶׁר יוֹרוּךָ: [דברים יז, י]

ג) וְהָאִישׁ אֲשֶׁר יַעֲשֶׂה בְזָדוֹן לְבִלְתִּי שְׁמֹעַ אֶל הַכֹּהֵן הָעֹמֵד לְשָׁרֶת שָׁם אֶת יְיָ אֱלֹהֶיךָ אוֹ אֶל הַשֹּׁפֵט וּמֵת הָאִישׁ הַהוּא וּבִעַרְתָּ הָרָע מִיִּשְׂרָאֵל: [דברים יז, יב]

us."[17] Both sets of witnesses were then discredited through *hazamah.* In this case, each set of witnesses established only "half" the matter of the defendant's execution.[18] Hence, Chizkiyah, who maintains that partial testimony is invalid, will rule that the discredited witnesses are not executed, while R' Yochanan, who accepts even partial testimony, will rule that they are executed.[19]

The Gemara now discusses a case in which witnesses testified to the sale of a kidnap victim, but no witnesses testified to the kidnaping itself:

אָמַר רַב אַסִּי – **Rav Assi said:** עֵדֵי מְכִירָה בְּנֶפֶשׁ שֶׁהוּזַמּוּ – **If witnesses to the sale of a kidnap victim are discredited through** ***hazamah,*** אֵין נֶהֱרָגִין – **they are not executed.** The reason is that their testimony could not have resulted in the defendant's execution anyway, מִתּוֹךְ שֶׁיָּכוֹל לוֹמַר עַבְדִּי מָכַרְתִּי – **because he could plead: "I was selling my slave."**[20]

The Gemara cites a different explanation of Rav Assi's ruling:

אָמַר רַב יוֹסֵף – **Rav Yosef said:** כְּמַאן אָזְלָא הָא שְׁמַעְתָּא דְּרַב אַסִּי – **Whose opinion does Rav Assi's teaching follow?** כְּרַבִּי עֲקִיבָא – **It follows** the opinion of **R' Akiva,** דְּאָמַר ,,דָּבָר" וְלֹא חֲצִי דָּבָר – **who maintains** that when the Torah says, [witnesses shall establish] *a matter,* it means ***a*** complete ***matter*** **and not a half matter.** Therefore, since the testimony to the sale can establish only "half" the matter of the defendant's execution, it was not acceptable in the first place, and thus the false witnesses cannot be executed on account of it.

Abaye rejects Rav Yosef's explanation:

אָמַר לֵיהּ אַבַּיֵי – **Abaye said to [Rav Yosef]:** דְּאִי כְּרַבָּנָן נֶהֱרָגִין – You imply **that if** Rav Assi would maintain, **as the Rabbis** do, that partial testimony is valid, he would rule that **[these witnesses] are executed.** הָא מִתּוֹךְ קָאָמַר – **But** that cannot be, for **[Rav Assi]** himself **stated** that they are not executed **because** the defendant could plead: "I was selling my own slave." This reason applies regardless of whether partial testimony is valid.[21] – ? –

Abaye concludes:

אֶלָּא אֲפִילּוּ תֵּימָא רַבָּנָן – **Rather, you can say** that Rav Assi's ruling holds true **even** according to **the Rabbis,** וּבִדְלָא אָתוּ עֵידֵי גְנֵיבָה – **and** it applies **where no witnesses to the kidnaping came** forward to testify.[22]

The Gemara asks:

אִי הָכִי – **If so,** that Rav Assi speaks of a case in which there was no testimony to the kidnaping itself, מַאי לְמֵימְרָא – **what** was the need for Rav Assi **to state** this ruling?[23]

The Gemara answers:

לֹא צְרִיכָא – Rav Assi's ruling is **not required except** to teach דְּאַף עַל גַּב דְּאָתוּ לְבַסּוֹף – **that even though [witnesses to the kidnaping] came** forward **later,** after the witnesses to the sale had testified, the witnesses to the sale are not liable to execution.[24]

The Gemara asks:

וְאַכַּתִּי מַאי לְמֵימְרָא – **Still, what** was the need **to state** this ruling?[25]

The Gemara answers:

לֹא צְרִיכָא – Rav Assi's ruling is **not required except** דְּקָא מְרַמְּזֵי רַמּוּזֵי – in a case **where [the witnesses to the kidnaping] signaled** to the witnesses to the sale that they were about to testify to the kidnaping. מַהוּ דְּתֵימָא רְמִיזָא מִילְּתָא הִיא – **You might have thought that signaling carries** legal **significance** and thus the witnesses to the sale should be considered as though testifying with prior knowledge of the kidnaping.[26] קָא מַשְׁמַע לָן רְמִיזָא לָאו כְּלוּם הוּא – **[Rav Assi]** therefore **teaches us that signaling carries no** legal **significance.**[27]

Mishnah The Mishnah now discusses the details of the third sinner executed by strangulation – the *zakein mamrei,* the sage who rebels against the ruling of the High Court:

זָקֵן מַמְרֵא עַל פִּי בֵית דִּין – Also executed by strangulation is **a sage who rebels against the word of the** High **Court,**

NOTES

17. As taught above (71a), a *ben sorer umoreh* stole money from his parents, used it to purchase meat and wine, and then consumed the meat and wine on someone else's property. For the first offense, he incurs lashes. If he does it again, he is liable to execution.

The case of dispute is where two separate sets of witnesses testify to the *ben sorer umoreh's* second offense: One set testifies to the stealing and another set testifies to his consuming of the meat and wine (*Rashi*).

18. The first witnesses (i.e. the witnesses to the theft) cannot claim that their intent was to render the defendant liable to lashes (*Rashi*), for this act does not carry the penalty of lashes.

19. *Rashi.* [Actually, according to Rav Pappa's understanding of Chizkiyah's ruling, his ruling (in the case of kidnaping) holds true regardless of whether partial testimony is acceptable (see notes 10 and 12). Why, then, does Abaye assume that Chizkiyah disqualifies such testimony? It may be answered that Abaye (who lived before Rav Pappa) does not take Rav Pappa's approach. He follows the Gemara's initial understanding of Chizkiyah's ruling according to which Chizkiyah does indeed disqualify partial testimony, as explained above, 86a (*Maharsha,* in explanation of *Rashi;* see *Ran* and *Aruch LaNer*).]

20. Unless it had been previously established that the sold person had been kidnaped, the accused may claim that he was selling his legally owned slave. Since the accused could not have been sentenced to death on the basis of these witnesses' testimony, they are not executed if they are found to be *zomemin* (*Rambam, Hil. Eidus* 21:9).

21. For according to this reason (viz. the defendant can claim that he was selling his slave), the testimony to the sale does not accomplish anything at all, not even a "half matter" (*Rashi*).

22. Since the Rabbis accept partial testimony, Rav Assi's ruling (viz. those who testified to the selling are not executed) applies only where the testimony to the selling is invalid for some other reason. Such a situation arises where there were no witnesses to the kidnaping and thus the defendant can claim that he was selling his slave.

This is in contrast to R' Akiva's view, according to which Rav Assi's ruling applies even in a case where there were witnesses to the kidnaping. Since R' Akiva disqualifies partial testimony, the testimony to the selling is invalid even where the defendant cannot claim that he was selling his slave.

23. One who sells a person into slavery is not liable to the death penalty unless he had kidnaped that person. Hence, if the court receives testimony only to the selling and not to the kidnaping, it cannot execute the defendant. In such a case, therefore, if the witnesses to the selling are found to be *zomemin,* it goes without saying that they are not liable to execution.

24. Even though the defendant was ultimately sentenced to death on the basis of the two sets of testimony, the discredited witnesses to the sale are not executed (*Rashi*). [This is because their testimony had no legal import at the time they testified, since the defendant could have claimed at that point that he was selling his slave.]

25. When the witnesses to the sale gave their testimony, the defendant could not have been convicted of a capital offense. Furthermore, these witnesses can claim that they did not know that the court would ever receive testimony to the kidnaping (*Rashi*). Hence, they cannot be accused of participating in a plot to kill the defendant.

26. If this were so, it would be assumed that they plotted to kill the defendant, since they knew that their testimony would result in the defendant's execution.

27. And thus the witnesses to the sale can still claim that they were not aware that the court will receive testimony to the kidnaping (see note 25).

להלקותו באנו והני אחריני כולי דבר קא עבדי ליה מתקיף לה רב פפא אי הכי עידי מכירה נמי (א) ליקטליה מתוך שיכולין עידי גניבה לומר להלקותו באנו וכי תימא דקסבר חזקיה דלא לקי והא איתמר עידי גניבה בנפש שהוזמו חזקיה ורבי יוחנן חד אמר לוקין וחד אמר אין לוקין ואמרינן תסתיים דחזקיה דאמר לוקין מדאמר חזקיה אין נהרגין דאי ר' יוחנן כיון דאמר נהרגין הוה ליה לאו שניתן לאזהרת מיתת ב"ד וכל [א]לאו שניתן לאזהרת מיתת ב"ד אין לוקין עליו איהו לא לקי אינהו היכי לקו אלא אמר רב פפא [א]בעידי מכירה דכולי עלמא לא פליגי דנהרגין כי פליגי בעידי גניבה חזקיה אמר אין נהרגין גניבה לחודה קיימא ומכירה לחודה קיימא ר' יוחנן אמר [ב]נהרגין גניבה אתחלתא דמכירה היא [ג]ומודה רבי יוחנן בעדים הראשונים של בן סורר ומורה שהוזמו שאין נהרגין מתוך שיכולין לומר להלקותו באנו אמר אביי הכל מודים בבן סורר ומורה והכל מודים בבן סורר ומורה ומחלוקת בבן סורר ומורה הכל מודים בבן סורר ומורה בעדים הראשונים שאין נהרגין מתוך שיכולין לומר להלקותו באנו והכל מודים בבן סורר ומורה בעדים אחרונים [ד]שנהרגים מתוך שעדים הראשונים יכולין לומר להלקותו באנו והני כוליה דבר קא עבדי ליה ומחלוקת בבן סורר ומורה [ה]שנים אומרים בפנינו גנב ושנים אומרים בפנינו אכל אמר רב אסי עידי מכירה בנפש שהוזמו [ו]אין נהרגין מתוך שיכול לומר עבדי מכרתי אמר רב יוסף כמאן אזלא הא שמעתא דרב אסי כר"ע דאמר דבר ולא חצי דבר א"ל אביי דאי כרבנן נהרגין הא מתוך קאמר אלא אפילו תימא רבנן [ז]ובדלא אתו עידי גניבה אי הכי מאי למימרא לא צריכא דאע"ג [ח]דאתו לבסוף ואכתי מאי למימרא לא צריכא (ג) דקא מרמזי רמוזי מהו דתימא רמיזא מילתא היא קמ"ל [ט]רמיזא לאו כלום הוא:

מתני' זקן ממרא על פי ב"ד שנאמר (א) כי יפלא ממך דבר למשפט [י]שלשה בתי דינין היו שם אחד יושב על פתח הר הבית ואחד יושב על פתח העזרה ואחד יושב בלשכת הגזית [כ]באין לזה שעל פתח הר הבית ואומר כך דרשתי וכך דרשו חבירי כך לימדתי וכך לימדו חבירי אם שמעו (ג) אמר להם ואם לאו באין להן לאותן שעל פתח עזרה ואומר כך דרשתי וכך דרשו חבירי כך לימדתי וכך לימדו חבירי אם שמעו אמר להם ואם לאו אלו ואלו באין לב"ד הגדול שבלשכת הגזית שממנו יוצא תורה לכל ישראל שנאמר (ב) מן המקום ההוא אשר יבחר ה' (ד) חזר לעירו שנה ולמד בדרך שהיה למד פטור ואם הורה לעשות חייב שנאמר (ג) והאיש אשר יעשה בזדון אינו חייב עד שיורה לעשות [ל]תלמיד שהורה לעשות פטור נמצא חומרו קולו: **גמ'** תנו רבנן (א) כי יפלא ממך דבר

במופלא

רש"י

להלקותו באנו. ולא הועדנו להמיתו שלא ידענו שסופו לחזור ולקלקל: להלקותו באנו. על הגניבה ולא ידענו שימכרנו: דלא לקי. אגניבה לחודה משום דהוה ליה לאו שניתן לאזהרת מיתת ב"ד שאם ימכרנו יהרג: עידי גניבה בנפש. שהעידוהו שגנב נפש: מדאמר חזקיה אין נהרגין. אם הוזמו לאחר שבאו עידי מכירה משום הכי לוקין שהרי אין סופן למות על עדות זו ולא הוי לגבייהו לאו שניתן לאזהרת מיתת ב"ד: דאי ר' יוחנן כיון דאמר נהרגין. אם באו עידי מכירה אחרי כן קודם הזמה ונגמר דינו ע"פ שתי הכתות והוזמו היכי לקו אם הוזמו קודם שבאו עידי מכירה הא הוה ליה לאו דלא תענה לגבייהו בשעה שהעידו לאו שניתן לאזהרה שלא להעיד כן שאם יעידו ולא יוזמו עד שיבאו עידי מכירה ויגמר דינו ויוזמו ימותו: וכל לאו שניתן לאזהרת ב"ד אין לוקין עליו. ואפילו יפטרו מן המיתה שהרי לא לאזהרת מלקות ניתן: אינהו היכי לקו. הא לאו כאשר זמם הוא ואי משום לא תענה (שמות כ) לאו שאין בו מעשה הוא: בעידי מכירה כולי עלמא לא פליגי דנהרגין. אם נגמר דינו על פי שתי הכתות: לחודה קיימא. ועידי גניבה אינן באין להורגו אלא להלקותו אבל עידי מכירה שבאין עמהן ואומרין שהתרו בו למיתה מונעין אותו ממלקות ומחייבין אותו מיתה והויא לה מכירה דבר שלם: אתחלתא דמכירה. דקסבר ר' יוחנן לא לקי עלה דלאו שניתן לאזהרת מיתת ב"ד ואינן באין אלא להורגו ואף על גב דשתיהן צריכות זו לזו והוה ליה כל חדא וחדא חצי דבר מיקטל כרבנן: ומודה ר' יוחנן בעדים הראשונים של בן סורר ומורה שהוזמו דאין נהרגין. דאינהו ודאי למלקות אתו כדכתיב ויסרו אותו (דברים כא): הכל מודים כו'. כלומר יש עדים בבן סורר ומורה שהכל מודים באחת כתותיו לפטור ויש כת שהכל מודים בו לחיוב ויש כת בבן סורר ומורה שנחלקו חזקיה ורבי יוחנן לפי מה ששמענו במחלוקתן: שנים אומרים בפנינו גנב. משל אביו מעות לקנות בשר ויין בפעם שניה אחר שלקה: ושנים אומרים בפנינו אכל. הבשר ברשות אחרים דאינו חייב עד שיגנוב משל אביו ויאכל ברשות אחרים הנך שתי כתות צריכות זו לזו ואין הראשונים יכולין לומר להלקותו באנו והוה ליה חצי דבר לחזקיה דסבר לה כר"ע דאמר אין נהרגין ולר' יוחנן דאמר נהרגין כרבנן: עידי מכירה בנפש. ולא באו עידי גניבה על כך לפנינו: הא מתוך קאמר. אפי' חצי דבר אין כאן שהרי היה לו להציל נפשו מב"ד בטענה זו: ובדלא אתו עידי גניבה. קאמר רב אסי וכדפרישית שהיה יכול לומר עבדי מכרתי: לבסוף. אחר שהעידו עידי מכירה באו עידי גניבה ונגמר הדין ע"פ שניהם: ואכתי מאי למימרא. כשהעידו הראשונים לא היה הדין ראוי ליגמר על פיהם ויכולין לומר לא היינו יודעין שיבואו עידי גניבה עלינו: דקא מרמזי רמוזי. הני להני: **מתני'** ג' בתי דינין היו שם. בירושלים דמשתעי בה קרא וקמת ועלית: אחד יושב על פתח הר הבית. הוא שער המזרחי שלפנים מן החיל לפני עזרת נשים: ואחד יושב למעלה הימנו. כשעברו עזרת נשים ובאין לפני עזרת ישראל: ואחד בלשכת הגזית. שהיא בנויה בתוך העזרה חציה בקודש וחציה בחול כדאמרינן בסדר יומא (דף כה.): באין לזה שעל פתח הר הבית. זקן זה שהורה בעירו ונחלק ב"ד שבעירו עליו והזקיקו הכתוב לעלות לירושלים ולשאול ובאין הוא ובית דין שבעירו לב"ד זה שעל פתח הר הבית שהרי בו פוגעין תחילה: תלמיד שהורה לעשות. תלמיד שלא הגיע להוראה ונחלק על ב"ד שבעירו ובאו לב"ד הגדול ושאלו וחזר לעירו והורה כבתחילה פטור שאין לסמוך על הוראתו והתורה לא חייבה אלא מופלא ומומחה לב"ד כדאמרי' בגמ': נמצא חומרו קולו. חומר שהחמירו עליו שאינו ראוי להוראה (ה) עד שיהא בן ארבעים שנה נעשה לו קל לפוטרו מן המיתה:

גמרא

תוספות

גניבה אתחלתא דמכירה היא. וא"ת אמאי מקטלי הא מצו למימר לפוסלו לעדות באנו וכ"ת דבעו התראה וכיון דאמרי שהתרו בו למיתה אלמא למיקטליה קא אתו אם כן לחזקיה נמי לקטלו אע"ג דאתו נמי להלקותו כדאשכחן בפ"ב דב"ק (דף כד. ושם) דעידי נגיחה ראשונה ושניה אע"ג דאתו לחיובי' חצי נזק כיון דאתו נמי לייעודי משלמי חצי נזק של העדאה עם הכת השלישית כשהוזמו השלש כתות וי"ל דקסבר חזקיה דגניבה לחודה קיימא כמו עידי קדושין ועידי ביאה ואע"ג דמיירי באתרו ביה מדמקטלי לרבי יוחנן מ"מ לא שייך בהו חיוב מיתה ואפשר דלחזקיה לא בעי התראה ולר' יוחנן בעי אי נמי הש"ס לא חש בטעמא דלפוסלו לעדות באנו מדאיצטריך לעיל למימר להלקותו ושמא איצטריך היכא דמפסיל מעיקרא וקאי:

עבדי מכרתי. וא"ת אי לאו למקטליה קא אתו אם יבאו עדים שאינו עבדו אם כן למאי קא אתו וי"ל דאתו לקיים המקח וא"ת אי דלא אתרו ביה למה לן טעמא דעבדי מכרתי אלא ודאי אתרו ביה אם כן למקטליה קאתי וי"ל דאתרו ביה אחריני ואינהו לא ידעי וכי האי גוונא הוה מצי לשנויי בריש פרק היו בודקין (לעיל דף מא.) גבי נערה המאורסה:

אמר רב יוסף כו'. סלקא דעתך דרב יוסף בדאתו עידי גניבה וה"פ מתוך שהוא יכול לומר עבדי מכרתי אם לא היו באים עידי גניבה אם כן אין בעדותם ממש וחצי דבר הוא ואביי פריך ליה הא מתוך קאמר דמשמע הלשון דאפילו השתא נמי בתר דאתו עידי גניבה מצי למימר הכי: **קמ"ל** רמיזה לאו כלום הוא. בפ"ב דב"ק (דף כד: ושם) גבי לייעודי תורא ולייעודי גברא דמסקינן התם אלא דקא מרמזי רמוזי לא דמי לרמיזה דהכא דהתם מיירי ברמיזה חשובה שבכל השלשה ימים באו אלו עם אלו וקא מרמזי אבל הכא ברמיזה גרועה איירי דלאו מילתא היא אי נמי דיני נפשות שאני:

במופלא

עין משפט נר מצוה

ד א ב ג ד ה ו ז ח ט מיי' פכ"א מהל' עדות הלכה ט:
ה י מיי' פ"א מהל' סנהדרין הלכה ג:
ו כ מיי' פ"ג מהלכות ממרים הלכה ח:
ז ל מיי' שם הל' ה:

ליקוטי רש"י

אזהרת מיתת בית [ד]ין. ניתן דלא ענש מיתה [א]לא אם כן הזהיר הלכך [ע]יקר אזהרתו למקום שיש [ב]ו מיתה אתאי ולא [למ]לקות [שבת קנד.]. וכל [לא]ו שניתן לאזהרת שלא [יע]שה כן שמתחייב עליו [מ]יתת בית דין אין לוקין [על]יו אפילו לא התרו בו [למ]יתה והתרו בו למלקות [ד]השתא לא מיקטיל אפילו [ה]כי לא לקי דלאזהרת [מ]יתה ניתן ולא למלקות [ע]ירובין יז:]. לאו שניתן [לא]זהרת [כו'] שלא יעשה [כן]ו שלא ימיתוהו בית דין [א]ין לוקין עליו דמיתת [ב]"ד הוא עונשו של לאו [ב]"ק עד:]. לאזהרת דבר [שמ]חייבין עליו מיתת ב"ד [אי]ן לוקין עליו כשהתרו בו [למ]לקות בלא מיתה לפי [של]א ניתן לאו זה לאזהרת [ו]גם מלקות כשאר לאוין [ש]הרי הוצרך להזהירו שאם [כ]ן לא היה יכול לחייבו [מ]יתה [מכות יג:]. כגון [ד]קא מרמזי רמוזי. כת [עי]די ראשונה לעידי כת [ב]' שיעידו הלכך ודאי [א]חרונים נמי לכך נתכוונו [ש]יו יודעים בראשונים וכך [ש]מעתי [ב"ק כד:]. זקן [מ]מרא. שהמרה על ב"ד [ש]ל לשכת הגזית ומיתתו [ב]חנק [סוטה כה.]. על פי [ב]"ד. זקן אינו נהרג אלא [א]ם כן המרה על פי בית [די]ן הגדול דכתיב (שם [ד]ברים י"ז) וקמת ועלית [ל]עיל טז.]. באין לב"ד גדול שבלשכת גזית. בשבעים ואחד [כ]תיב (דברים יז) מן מקום ההוא מקום יוחד דהיינו לשכת הגזית אפילו מצאן אבי פגי [ה]מרה עליהן ילפינן [מ]יניה דאין המראתו מראה (סנהדרין יד) [ס]וטה ז:]. חזר. זקן [מ]מרא לעירו וכו' הורה [ב]נשות דמשמע דקאמר [ו]תרין אתם לעשות [ב]גמרה הוראתו חייב [הוריות ב.].

מסורת הש"ס

א) [שבת קנד. עירובין יז: בבא קמא עד: מכות יג: שבועות ד.], ב) [ב"ק כד:], ג) [נ"ל אומרים כך הגי' במשנה שבמשניות ועי' תוי"ט], ד) הוריות ב., ה) [סוטה כב.].

הגהות הב"ח

(א) גמ' עדי מכירה נמי ליקטלו:

תורה אור השלם

א) כִּי יִפָּלֵא מִמְּךָ דָבָר לַמִּשְׁפָּט בֵּין דָּם לְדָם בֵּין דִּין לְדִין וּבֵין נֶגַע לָנֶגַע דִּבְרֵי רִיבֹת בִּשְׁעָרֶיךָ וְקַמְתָּ וְעָלִיתָ אֶל הַמָּקוֹם אֲשֶׁר יִבְחַר יְיָ אֱלֹהֶיךָ בּוֹ: [דברים יז, ח]

ב) וְעָשִׂיתָ עַל פִּי הַדָּבָר אֲשֶׁר יַגִּידוּ לְךָ מִן הַמָּקוֹם הַהוּא אֲשֶׁר יִבְחַר יְיָ וְשָׁמַרְתָּ לַעֲשׂוֹת כְּכֹל אֲשֶׁר יוֹרוּךָ: [דברים יז, י]

ג) וְהָאִישׁ אֲשֶׁר יַעֲשֶׂה בְזָדוֹן לְבִלְתִּי שְׁמֹעַ אֶל הַכֹּהֵן הָעֹמֵד לְשָׁרֶת שָׁם אֶת יְיָ אֱלֹהֶיךָ אוֹ אֶל הַשֹּׁפֵט וּמֵת הָאִישׁ הַהוּא וּבִעַרְתָּ הָרָע מִיִּשְׂרָאֵל: [דברים יז, יב]

שֶׁנֶּאֱמַר ,,כִּי יִפָּלֵא מִמְּךָ דָבָר לַמִּשְׁפָּט'' – as it is stated: ***If there be hidden from you a matter of judgment . . .***[28]

The Mishnah now proceeds to elaborate on the process described in the passage detailing the law of the rebellious sage:

שְׁלֹשָׁה בָּתֵּי דִינִין הָיוּ שָׁם – There were three courts there in Jerusalem:[29] **אֶחָד יוֹשֵׁב עַל פֶּתַח הַר הַבַּיִת – One sitting at the entrance to the Temple Mount,**[30] **וְאֶחָד יוֹשֵׁב עַל פֶּתַח הָעֲזָרָה – one** higher up on the Temple mount **sitting at the entrance to the Temple Courtyard,**[31] **וְאֶחָד יוֹשֵׁב בְּלִשְׁכַּת הַגָּזִית – and one** even higher up the Mount **sitting in the Chamber of Hewn Stone.**[32] **בָּאִין לָזֶה שֶׁעַל פֶּתַח הַר הַבַּיִת וְאוֹמֵר – They** [the dissenting sage and his disputants on the local court][33] **come to the court at the entrance to the Temple Mount,**[34] **and [the dissenting sage] says** before the court at the entrance to the Temple Mount: **כַּךְ דָּרַשְׁתִּי וְכַךְ דָּרְשׁוּ חֲבֵירַי – Thus have I expounded and thus have my colleagues expounded; כַּךְ לִימַּדְתִּי וְכַךְ לִימְּדוּ חֲבֵירַי – thus have I taught and thus have my colleagues taught.**[35] **אִם שָׁמְעוּ – If they** [the court at the entrance of the Temple Mount] **have heard** from their teachers a tradition in this matter, **אָמַר לָהֶם – they tell them**[36] the law. **וְאִם לָאו – But if they have not heard** a tradition in this matter,[37] **בָּאִין לָהֶן לְאוֹתָן שֶׁעַל פֶּתַח עֲזָרָה וְאוֹמֵר – they come**[38] **before those** judges **sitting at the entrance of the Courtyard, and [the dissenting sage]** says before this higher court: **כַּךְ דָּרַשְׁתִּי וְכַךְ דָּרְשׁוּ חֲבֵירַי – Thus have I expounded and thus have my colleagues expounded; כַּךְ לִימַּדְתִּי וְכַךְ לִימְּדוּ חֲבֵירַי – thus have I taught and thus have my colleagues taught. אִם שָׁמְעוּ אָמַר לָהֶם – If they** [the court sitting at the entrance to the Courtyard] **have heard** a tradition in this matter, **they tell them** the law. **וְאִם לָאו – But if** they have **not** heard a tradition in this matter, **אֵלּוּ וָאֵלּוּ בָּאִין לְבֵית דִּין הַגָּדוֹל שֶׁבְּלִשְׁכַּת הַגָּזִית – these and those**[39] **come before the High Court** that sits **in the Chamber of Hewn Stone, שֶׁמִּמֶּנּוּ יוֹצֵא תּוֹרָה לְכָל יִשְׂרָאֵל – from which Torah goes forth to all of Israel,**[40] **שֶׁנֶּאֱמַר ,,מִן־הַמָּקוֹם הַהוּא אֲשֶׁר יִבְחַר ה׳ '' – as it is stated: *from that place which Hashem shall choose.***[41]

חָזַר לְעִירוֹ – If **[the sage]** then **returned to his town שָׁנָה וְלִמֵּד בְּדֶרֶךְ שֶׁהָיָה לָמֵד –** and **he taught and interpreted in the manner he was used to** before being instructed otherwise by the High Court, **פָּטוּר – he is not liable** as a *zakein mamrei*; **וְאִם הוֹרָה לַעֲשׂוֹת – but if he instructed** people **to act** in accordance with his overruled opinion, **חַיָּיב – he is liable** to the death penalty as a *zakein mamrei.* **שֶׁנֶּאֱמַר ,,וְהָאִישׁ אֲשֶׁר יַעֲשֶׂה בְזָדוֹן'' – For it is stated: *but the man who will "act" with willfulness,***[42] which indicates that **אֵינוֹ חַיָּיב עַד שֶׁיּוֹרֶה לַעֲשׂוֹת – he is not liable**

NOTES

28. *Deuteronomy* 17:8. The Mishnah cites but the beginning of the passage, which reads in its entirety (vs. 8-13): כִּי יִפָּלֵא מִמְּךָ דָבָר לַמִּשְׁפָּט בֵּין־דָּם לְדָם בֵּין־דִּין לְדִין וּבֵין נֶגַע לָנֶגַע דִּבְרֵי רִיבֹת בִּשְׁעָרֶיךָ וְקַמְתָּ וְעָלִיתָ אֶל־הַמָּקוֹם אֲשֶׁר יִבְחַר ה׳ אֱלֹהֶיךָ בּוֹ. וּבָאתָ אֶל־הַכֹּהֲנִים הַלְוִיִּם וְאֶל־הַשֹּׁפֵט אֲשֶׁר יִהְיֶה בַּיָּמִים הָהֵם וְדָרַשְׁתָּ וְהִגִּידוּ לְךָ אֵת דְּבַר הַמִּשְׁפָּט. וְעָשִׂיתָ עַל־פִּי הַדָּבָר אֲשֶׁר יַגִּידוּ לְךָ מִן־הַמָּקוֹם הַהוּא אֲשֶׁר יִבְחַר ה׳ וְשָׁמַרְתָּ לַעֲשׂוֹת כְּכֹל אֲשֶׁר יוֹרוּךָ. עַל־פִּי הַתּוֹרָה אֲשֶׁר יוֹרוּךָ וְעַל־הַמִּשְׁפָּט אֲשֶׁר־יֹאמְרוּ לְךָ תַּעֲשֶׂה לֹא תָסוּר מִן־הַדָּבָר אֲשֶׁר־יַגִּידוּ לְךָ יָמִין וּשְׂמֹאל. וְהָאִישׁ אֲשֶׁר־יַעֲשֶׂה בְזָדוֹן לְבִלְתִּי שְׁמֹעַ אֶל־הַכֹּהֵן הָעֹמֵד לְשָׁרֶת שָׁם אֶת־ה׳ אֱלֹהֶיךָ אוֹ אֶל־הַשֹּׁפֵט וּמֵת הָאִישׁ הַהוּא וּבִעַרְתָּ הָרָע מִיִּשְׂרָאֵל. וְכָל־הָעָם יִשְׁמְעוּ וְיִרָאוּ וְלֹא יְזִידוּן עוֹד., *If there be hidden from you a matter of judgment, between blood and blood, between verdict and verdict, between affliction and affliction, matters of disputes in your gates — then you shall rise up and you shall ascend to the place that Hashem, your God, shall choose. And you shall come to the Levite Kohanim, and to the judge who will be in those days; and you shall inquire and they will tell you the word of judgment. And you shall do according to the word that they will tell you, from that place which Hashem will choose, and you shall be careful to do according to everything that they will teach you. According to the law that they will teach you and according to the judgment that they will say to you shall you do; you shall not deviate from the word that they will tell you, right or left. And the man that will act with willfulness, not listening to the Kohen who stands to serve there Hashem, your God, or to the judge, that man shall die, and you shall remove the evil from Israel. And the entire nation shall hear and fear, and they shall not act willfully any more.*

29. Jerusalem is the place alluded to in the verse: *Then you shall rise up and ascend to "the place that Hashem, your God, shall choose"* (*Rashi*; see below, 87a).

30. This does not refer to the entrance at the foot of the Temple Mount but to the eastern gate of the Women's Courtyard (*Rashi*), the gate by which one entered and exited the actual Temple complex. It is called here the entrance to the Temple Mount because it is through this gate that one entered the Temple Mount area upon *exiting* the Temple complex (*Tosefos Yom Tov*; see *Aruch LaNer*; cf. *Rambam, Hil. Mamrim* 1:4, 3:8 and *Hil. Sanhedrin* 1:3).

31. I.e. by the gate between the Women's Courtyard and the main Temple Courtyard (*Rashi*). These first two courts consisted of twenty-three judges (*Meiri,* from Baraisa on 88b).

32. This chamber was built in [the wall of] the Temple Courtyard itself; half the chamber was within the sanctified area and half outside of it (*Rashi, from Yoma* 25a). [The Gemara (ibid.) describes this chamber as "a great basilica." See *Margaliyos HaYam*.] Here sat the Great Sanhedrin of seventy-one judges (*Meiri,* from Baraisa on 88b).

33. As stated in the Torah, if a sage in a town ruled on a point of Torah law and his ruling was disputed by the members of the court of that town, the sage is required to ascend to Jerusalem to inquire about the matter before the Jerusalem court [see v. 8]. The Mishnah teaches that the local court accompanies the sage to the Jerusalem court (*Rashi*).

34. For this is the first court that they come upon (*Rashi*).

35. He relates the dispute between himself and his colleagues, and the reasons for their respective positions, whether these had first been propounded in public lectures [כַּךְ דָּרַשְׁתִּי וְכַךְ דָּרְשׁוּ חֲבֵירַי] or in private study with disciples [כַּךְ לִימַּדְתִּי וְכַךְ לִימְּדוּ חֲבֵירַי] (*Tos. Yom Tov*).

36. [The reading: אוֹמְרִים לָהֶם, *they say to them,* found in other texts, seems more correct (*Mesoras HaShas*).]

37. If this court has a tradition regarding the law in this matter, they repeat it to the disputants. If, however, they have no tradition on the matter, but bring the matter to a vote, their own decision is not binding on the sages who come to ask, who then bring the matter before the next highest court (*Rambam, Commentary to Mishnah*; see *Tosefos Yom Tov* and *Kesef Mishneh* to *Hil. Mamrim* 3:8).

38. See end of note 41.

39. I.e. the original disputants as well as the subsequent courts that were uncertain about the matter.

40. This court is the final authority on the law. If they have no tradition in a matter, they decide it according to the rules of Biblical interpretation, and their decision is binding (*Rambam, Commentary to Mishnah*).

41. *Deuteronomy* 17:10 (cited above). The verse states that the court empowered to render final decisions on matters of Torah law is the one that meets in the Temple itself (see *Tosefos Yom Tov* ד״ה אם שמעו, citing *Tosafos*; see also *Tosafos* above, 14b ד״ה מלמד).

The Mishnah's omission of the expression "these and those" in the earlier stages (viz. when the question moves up from the first Temple Mount court to the second) would seem to indicate that the members of that first court do not accompany the original disputants to the second court. (For the second court, too, is but a court of twenty-three, and their decision is not binding on the members of the first court.) From *Rambam* (*Hil. Mamrim* 1:4 and 3:8), however, it appears that even in the first case, the first court accompanies the disputants to the proceedings before the next highest court (*Tosefos Yom Tov*).

42. *Deuteronomy* 17:12 (cited above in note 28).

ד א ב ג ד ה ו ז ח ט מיי' פכ"א מהל' עדות הלכה ט:
ה י מיי' פ"א מהל' סנהדרין הלכה ג:
י כ מיי' פ"ג מהלכות ממרים הלכה ח:
ו ל מיי' שם הל' ה:

ליקוטי רש"י

אזהרת מיתת בית [ד]ין. ניתן דלא ענש מיתה [ל]א אם כן הזהיר הלכך [ע]יקר אזהרתו למקום שיש [בו] מיתה אתאי ולא [למ]לקות [שבת קנד.]. וכל [לא]ו שניתן לאזהרת שלא [יע]שה כן שמתחייב עליו [מ]יתת בית דין אין לוקין [על]יו אפילו לא התרו בו [למ]יתה והתרו בו למלקות [ד]השתא לא מיקטיל אפילו [ה]כי לא לקי דלאזהרת [מ]יתה ניתן ולא למלקות [ע]ירובין יז:]. לאו שניתן [לא]זהרת [כו'] שלא יעשה [כ]י שלא ימיתוהו בית דין [א]ין לוקין עליו דמיתת [ב]"ד הוא עונשו של לאו [ב]"ק עד:]. לאזהרת דבר [שח]ייבין עליו מיתת ב"ד [אי]ן לוקין עליו כשהתרו בו [מ]לקות בלא מיתה לפי [ש]לא ניתן לאו זה לאזהרת [עו]נש מלקות כשאר לאוין [ש]הרי הוצרך להזהירו שאם [לא] כן לא היה יכול לחייבו [מ]יתה [מכות יג:]. כגון [ד]קא מרמזי רמוזי. כת [ע]ידי ראשונה לעידי כת [ב]' שיעידו הלכך ודאי [א]חרונים נמי לכך נתכוונו [וה]יו יודעים בראשונים וכך [ש]מעתי [ב"ק כד:]. זקן [מ]מרא. שהמרה על ב"ד [ש]ל לשכת הגזית ומיתתו [ב]חנק [סוטה כה.]. על פי [ב]"ד. זקן אינו נהרג אלא [א]ם כן המרה על פי בית [די]ן הגדול דכתיב (שם [דב]רים י"ז) וקמת ועלית [ל]עיל טז.]. באין לב"ד גדול שבלשכת [ה]גזית. בשבעים ואחד [כ]תיב (דברים יז) מן [ה]מקום ההוא מקום [המ]יוחד דהיינו לשכת הגזית [וא]פילו מלאן אבי פגי [המ]מרה עליהן ילפינן [בב]יניה דאין המראתו מראה (סנהדרין יד) [ס]וטה ז:]. חזר. זקן [מ]מרא לעירו וכו' הורה [כ]נשות דמשמע דקאמר [ה]ותרין אתם לעשות [ו]גמרה הוראתו חייב [הוריות ב.].

להלקותו באנו והני אחריני כולי דבר קא עבדי ליה מתקיף לה רב פפא אי הכי עידי מכירה נמי (א) ליקטליה מתוך שיכולין עידי גניבה לומר להלקותו באנו וכי תימא דקסבר חזקיה דלא לקי והא איתמר עידי גניבה בנפש שהוזמו חזקיה ורבי יוחנן חד אמר לוקין וחד אמר אין לוקין ואמרינן תפתיים דחזקיה דאמר לוקין מדאמר חזקיה אין נהרגין דאי ר' יוחנן כיון דאמר נהרגין הוה ליה לאו שניתן לאזהרת מיתת ב"ד וכל [א]לאו שניתן לאזהרת מיתת ב"ד אין לוקין עליו איהו לא לקי אינהו היכי לקו אלא אמר רב פפא [א]בעידי מכירה דכולי עלמא לא פליגי דנהרגין כי פליגי בעידי גניבה חזקיה אמר אין נהרגין גניבה לחודה קיימא ומכירה לחודה קיימא ר' יוחנן אמר [ב]נהרגין גניבה אתחלתא דמכירה היא [ג]ומודה רבי יוחנן בעדים הראשונים של בן סורר ומורה שהוזמו שאין נהרגין מתוך שיכולין לומר להלקותו באנו אמר אביי הכל מודים בבן סורר ומורה והכל מודים בבן סורר ומורה ומחלוקת בבן סורר ומורה הכל מודים בבן סורר ומורה בעדים הראשונים שאין נהרגין מתוך שיכולין לומר להלקותו באנו והכל מודים בבן סורר ומורה בעדים אחרונים [ד]שנהרגים מתוך שעדים הראשונים יכולין לומר להלקותו באנו והני כוליה דבר קא עבדי ליה ומחלוקת בבן סורר ומורה [ה]שנים אומרים בפנינו גנב ושנים אומרים בפנינו אכל אמר רב אסי עידי מכירה בנפש שהוזמו [ו]אין נהרגין מתוך שיכול לומר עבדי מכרתי אמר רב יוסף כמאן אזלא הא שמעתא דרב אסי כר"ע דאמר דבר ולא חצי דבר א"ל אביי דאי כרבנן נהרגין הא מתוך קאמר אלא אפילו תימא רבנן [ז]ובדלא אתו עידי גניבה אי הכי מאי למימרא לא צריכא דאע"ג [ח]דאתו לבסוף ואכתי מאי למימרא לא צריכא [ט]דקא מרמזי רמוזי מהו דתימא רמיזא מילתא היא קמ"ל [ט]רמיזא לאו כלום הוא:

מתני' זקן ממרא על פי ב"ד שנאמר [א] כי יפלא ממך דבר למשפט [י]שלשה בתי דינין היו שם אחד יושב על פתח הר הבית ואחד יושב על פתח העזרה ואחד יושב בלשכת הגזית [כ]באין לזה שעל פתח הר הבית ואומר כך דרשתי וכך דרשו חבירי כך לימדתי וכך לימדו חבירי אם שמעו [ג] אמר להם ואם לאו באין להן לאותן שעל פתח עזרה ואומר כך דרשתי וכך דרשו חבירי כך לימדתי וכך לימדו חבירי אם שמעו אמר להם ואם לאו אלו ואלו באין לב"ד הגדול שבלשכת הגזית שממנו יוצא תורה לכל ישראל שנאמר [ב] מן המקום ההוא אשר יבחר ה' [ד] חזר לעירו שנה ולמד בדרך שהיה למד פטור ואם הורה לעשות חייב שנאמר [ג] והאיש אשר יעשה בזדון אינו חייב עד שיורה לעשות [ל]תלמיד שהורה לעשות פטור נמצא חומרו קולו: **גמ'** תנו רבנן [א] כי יפלא ממך דבר במופלא

תוספות

גניבה אתחלתא דמכירה היא. וא"ת אמאי מקטלי הא מצו למימר לפוסלו לעדות באנו וכ"ת דבעו התראה וכיון דאמרי שהתרו בו למיתה אלמא למיקטליה קא אתו אם כן לחזקיה נמי לקטלו אע"ג דאתו נמי להלקותו כדאשכחן בפ"ב דב"ק (דף כד. ושם) דעידי נגיחה ראשונה ושניה אע"ג דאתו לחיובי' חצי נזק כיון דאתו נמי לייעודי משלמי חצי נזק של העדאה עם הכת השלישית כשהוזמו השלש כתות וי"ל דקסבר חזקיה דגניבה לחודה קיימא כמו עידי קדושין ועידי ביאה ואע"ג דמיירי באתרו ביה מדמקטלי לרבי יוחנן מ"מ לא שייך בהו חיוב מיתה ואפשר דלחזקיה לא בעי התראה ולר' יוחנן בעי אי נמי הש"ס לא חש בטעמא דלפוסלו לעדות באנו מדאיצטריך לעיל למימר להלקותו ושמא איצטריך היכא דמפסיל מעיקרא וקאי:

עבדי מכרתי. וא"ת אי לאו למקטליה קא אתו אם יבאו עדים שאינו עבדו אם כן למאי קא אתו וי"ל דאתו לקיים המקח וא"ת אי דלא אתרו ביה למה לן טעמא דעבדי מכרתי אלא ודאי אתרו ביה אם כן למקטליה קאתי וי"ל דאתרו ביה אחריני ואינהו לא ידעי וכי האי גוונא הוה מצי לשנויי בריש פרק היו בודקין (לעיל דף מא.) גבי נערה המאורסה:

אמר רב יוסף כו'. סלקא דעתך דרב יוסף בדאתו עידי גניבה וה"פ מתוך שהוא יכול לומר עבדי מכרתי אם לא היו באים עידי גניבה אם כן אין בעדותם ממש וחצי דבר הוא ואביי פריך ליה הא מתוך קאמר דמשמע הלשון דאפילו השתא נמי בתר דאתו עידי גניבה מצי למימר הכי: **קמ"ל** רמיזה לאו כלום הוא. בפ"ב דב"ק (דף כד: ושם) גבי לייעודי תורא ולייעודי גברא דמסקינן התם אלא דקא מרמזי רמוזי לא דמי לרמיזה דהכא דהתם מיירי ברמיזה חשובה שבכל השלשה ימים באו אלו עם אלו וקא מרמזי אבל הכא ברמיזה גרועה איירי דלאו מילתא היא אי נמי דיני נפשות שאני:

רש"י

להלקותו באנו. ולא הועדנו להמיתו שלא ידענו שסופו לחזור ולקלקל: להלקותו באנו. על הגניבה ולא ידענו שימכרנו: דלא לקי. אגניבה לחודה משום דהוה ליה לאו שניתן לאזהרת מיתת ב"ד שאם ימכרנו יהרג: עידי גניבה בנפש. שהעידוהו שגנב נפש: מדאמר חזקיה אין נהרגין. אם הוזמו לאחר שבאו עידי מכירה משום הכי לוקין שהרי אין סופן למות על עדות זו ולא הוי לגבייהו לאו שניתן לאזהרת מיתת ב"ד: דאי ר' יוחנן כיון דאמר נהרגין. אם באו עידי מכירה אחרי כן קודם הזמה ונגמר דינו ע"פ שתי הכתות והוזמו היכי לקו אם הוזמו קודם שבאו עידי מכירה הא הוה ליה לאו דלא תענה לגבייהו בשעה שהעידו לאו שניתן לאזהרה שלא להעיד כן שאם יעידו ולא יוזמו עד שיבאו עידי מכירה ויגמר דינו ויוזמו ימותו: וכל לאו שניתן לאזהרת ב"ד אין לוקין עליו. ואפילו יפטרו מן המיתה שהרי לא לאזהרת מלקות ניתן: אינהו היכי לקו. הא לאו כאשר זמם הוא ואי משום לא תענה (שמות כ) לאו שאין בו מעשה הוא: בעידי מכירה כולי עלמא לא פליגי דנהרגין. אם נגמר דינו על פי שתי הכתות: לחודה קיימא. ועידי גניבה אינן באין להורגו אלא להלקותו אבל עידי מכירה שבאין עמהן ואומרין שהתרו בו למיתה מונעין אותו ממלקות ומחייבין אותו מיתה והויא לה מכירה דבר שלם: אתחלתא דמכירה. דקסבר ר' יוחנן לא לקי עלה דלאו שניתן לאזהרת מיתת ב"ד ואינן באין אלא להורגו ואף על גב דשתיהן צריכות זו לזו והוה ליה כל חדא וחדא חצי דבר מיקטל כרבנן: ומודה ר' יוחנן בעדים הראשונים של בן סורר ומורה שהוזמו דאין נהרגין. דאינהו ודאי למלקות אתו כדכתיב ויסרו אותו (דברים כא): הכל מודים כו'. כלומר יש עדים בבן סורר ומורה שהכל מודים באחת כתותיו לפטור ויש כת שהכל מודים בו לחיוב ויש כת בבן סורר ומורה שנחלקו חזקיה ורבי יוחנן לפי מה ששמענו במחלוקתן: שנים אומרים בפנינו גנב. משל אביו מעות לקנות בשר ויין בפעם שניה אחר שלקה: ושנים אומרים בפנינו אכל. הבשר ברשות אחרים דאינו חייב עד שיגנוב משל אביו ויאכל ברשות אחרים הנך שתי כתות צריכות זו לזו ואין הראשונים יכולין לומר להלקותו באנו והוה ליה חצי דבר לחזקיה דסבר לה כר"ע דאמר אין נהרגין ולר' יוחנן דאמר נהרגין כרבנן: עידי מכירה בנפש. ולא באו עידי גניבה על כך לפנינו: הא מתוך קאמר. אפי' חצי דבר אין כאן שהרי היה לו להציל נפשו מב"ד בטענה זו: ובדלא אתו עידי גניבה. קאמר רב אסי וכדפרישית שהיה יכול לומר עבדי מכרתי: לבסוף. אחר שהעידו עידי מכירה באו עידי גניבה ונגמר הדין ע"פ שניהם: ואכתי מאי למימרא. כשהעידו הראשונים לא היה הדין ראוי ליגמר על פיהם ויכולין לומר לא היינו יודעין שיבואו עידי גניבה עלינו: דקא מרמזי רמוזי. הני להני: **מתני'** ג' בתי דינין היו שם. בירושלים דמשתעי בה קרא וקמת ועלית: אחד יושב על פתח הר הבית. הוא שער המזרחי שלפנים מן החיל לפני עזרת נשים: ואחד יושב למעלה הימנו. כשעברו עזרת נשים ובאין לפני עזרת ישראל: ואחד בלשכת הגזית. שהיא בנויה בתוך העזרה חציה בקודש וחציה בחול כדאמרינן בסדר יומא (דף כה.): באין לזה שעל פתח הר הבית. זקן זה שהורה בעירו ונחלק ב"ד שבעירו עליו והזקיקו הכתוב לעלות לירושלים ולשאול ובאין הוא ובית דין שבעירו לב"ד זה שעל פתח הר הבית שהרי בו פוגעין תחילה: תלמיד שהורה לעשות. תלמיד שלא הגיע להוראה ונחלק על ב"ד שבעירו ובאו לב"ד הגדול ושאלו וחזר לעירו והורה כבתחילה פטור שאין לסמוך על הוראתו והתורה לא חייבה אלא מופלא ומומחה לב"ד כדאמרי' בגמ': נמצא חומרו קולו. חומר שהחמירו עליו שאינו ראוי להוראה [ה] עד שיהא בן ארבעים שנה נעשה לו קל לפוטרו מן המיתה:

גמרא

מסורת הש"ס

א) [שבת קנד. עירובין יז: בבא קמא עד: מכות יג: שבועות ז.], ב) [ב"ק כד:], ג) [נ"ל אומרים כך הגי' במשנה שבמשניות ועי' תוי"ט], ד) הוריות ב., ה) [סוטה כב.].

הגהות הב"ח

(א) גמ' עדי מכירה נמי ליקטלו:

תורה אור השלם

א) כִּי יִפָּלֵא מִמְּךָ דָבָר לַמִּשְׁפָּט בֵּין דָּם לְדָם בֵּין דִּין לְדִין וּבֵין נֶגַע לָנֶגַע דִּבְרֵי רִיבֹת בִּשְׁעָרֶיךָ וְקַמְתָּ וְעָלִיתָ אֶל הַמָּקוֹם אֲשֶׁר יִבְחַר יְיָ אֱלֹהֶיךָ בּוֹ: [דברים יז, ח]

ב) וְעָשִׂיתָ עַל פִּי הַדָּבָר אֲשֶׁר יַגִּידוּ לְךָ מִן הַמָּקוֹם הַהוּא אֲשֶׁר יִבְחַר יְיָ וְשָׁמַרְתָּ לַעֲשׂוֹת כְּכֹל אֲשֶׁר יוֹרוּךָ: [דברים יז, י]

ג) וְהָאִישׁ אֲשֶׁר יַעֲשֶׂה בְזָדוֹן לְבִלְתִּי שְׁמֹעַ אֶל הַכֹּהֵן הָעֹמֵד לְשָׁרֶת שָׁם אֶת יְיָ אֱלֹהֶיךָ אוֹ אֶל הַשֹּׁפֵט וּמֵת הָאִישׁ הַהוּא וּבִעַרְתָּ הָרָע מִיִּשְׂרָאֵל: [דברים יז, יב]

until he instructs people **to *act*** in accordance with his opinion.[43]

תַּלְמִיד שֶׁהוֹרָה לַעֲשׂוֹת פָּטוּר – **A disciple who instructed** people **to act** in accordance with an opinion of his that was overruled by the High Court **is not liable** to punishment as a *zakein mamrei.*[44] **נִמְצָא חוּמְרוֹ קוּלּוֹ** – **It emerges that his stringency is his leniency.**[45]

Gemara The Gemara cites a Baraisa that expounds the first verse of the *zakein mamrei* passage:[46]

תָּנוּ רַבָּנַן – **The Rabbis taught in a Baraisa:** **,,כִּי יִפָּלֵא מִמְּךָ דָבָר''** – The verse states: ***IF THERE BE HIDDEN FROM YOU A MATTER . . .***

NOTES

43. Since the verse states that the penalty is for one who will act with *willfulness,* it clearly refers to the judge who willfully ignores the ruling he received from the High Court, not to the person who acts on the rebel judge's ruling – since the latter is not acting willfully, but faithfully following the judge whose opinion he sought. Accordingly, the verse's reference to *acting* with willfulness (rather than to *ruling* with willfulness) is understood to teach that the ruling must be in regard to a course of action, not merely an abstract teaching (*Sifre,* as explained by *Malbim*).

44. A scholar is generally not granted the authority to issue rulings [i.e. *semichah,* the original form of ordination] until he is at least forty years old (*Rashi,* from *Sotah* 22a). Before he has the authority to rule, he is called a *talmid* [disciple]. If a disciple disputes the ruling of the court of his town and the matter is brought before the High Court, who rule against him, he is not deemed a *zakein mamrei* even if he returns home and instructs people to follow his own opinion. For a disciple's ruling is not to be relied upon altogether, and the law of *zakein mamrei* applies only to a duly ordained sage, as the Gemara will explain (*Rashi*).

45. I.e. the stringency that the youthful scholar not be ordained (since he is not yet forty) is what causes him to be treated leniently and not be executed as a *zakein mamrei.* For had he been ordained, he would have been executed as a *zakein mamrei* (*Rashi*; see *Rashash*).

46. *Deuteronomy* 17:8, cited in full in note 28.

בְּמוּפְלָא שֶׁבְּבֵית דִּין הַכָּתוּב מְדַבֵּר – SCRIPTURE IS SPEAKING OF A RECOGNIZED MEMBER OF THE COURT.[1] The verse states next: "מִמְּךָ" – ***FROM YOU***; **זֶה יוֹעֵץ – THIS** alludes to **ONE WHO GIVES COUNSEL** in the matter of intercalation,[2] **וְכֵן הוּא אוֹמֵר "מִמֵּךְ יָצָא חֹשֵׁב עַל־ה׳ רָעָה יֹעֵץ בְּלִיָּעַל" – AND SO IT STATES: *"FROM YOU" CAME OUT ONE WHO PLOTS EVIL AGAINST HASHEM, ONE WHO GIVES WICKED COUNSEL.***[3]

The verse in *Deuteronomy* states next:

"דָּבָר" – ***A MATTER***; **זוֹ הֲלָכָה – THIS** alludes to **A *HALACHAH*** *LeMoshe MiSinai.*[4]

"לַמִּשְׁפָּט" – ***OF JUDGMENT***; **זֶה הַדִּין – THIS** alludes to **THE RULE** of *gezeirah shavah.*[5]

"בֵּין דָּם לְדָם" – ***BETWEEN BLOOD AND BLOOD***; **בֵּין דַּם נִדָּה דַּם לֵידָה דַּם זִיבָה** – this alludes to a dispute **BETWEEN** sages regarding **THE BLOOD OF *NIDDAH*, THE BLOOD AFTER CHILDBIRTH** or **THE BLOOD OF *ZIVAH*.**[6]

"בֵּין־דִּין לְדִין" – ***BETWEEN VERDICT AND VERDICT***; **בֵּין דִּינֵי נְפָשׁוֹת דִּינֵי מָמוֹנוֹת דִּינֵי מַכּוֹת** – this alludes to a dispute **BETWEEN** sages regarding **CAPITAL CASES, MONETARY CASES** or **CASES CONCERNING LASHES.**

"בֵּין נֶגַע לָנֶגַע" – ***BETWEEN AFFLICTION AND AFFLICTION***; **בֵּין נִגְעֵי אָדָם נִגְעֵי בָתִּים נִגְעֵי בְגָדִים** – this alludes to a dispute **BETWEEN** sages regarding ***TZARAAS* OF PEOPLE, *TZARAAS* OF HOUSES** or ***TZARAAS* OF CLOTHING.**[7]

"דִּבְרֵי" – ***MATTERS OF***; **אֵלּוּ הַחֲרָמִים וְהָעֲרָכִין וְהַהֶקְדֵּשׁוֹת – THESE** are disputes regarding ***CHEREM* VOWS,**[8] ***ERECH*-VOWS**[9] **OR CONSECRATION VOWS.**[10]

"רִיבֹת" – ***DISPUTES***; **זוֹ הַשְׁקָאַת סוֹטָה וַעֲרִיפַת עֶגְלָה וְטָהֳרַת מְצוֹרָע – THIS** alludes to disputes regarding **MAKING A *SOTAH* DRINK** the bitter waters,[11] **DECAPITATION OF THE CALF**[12] **AND THE PURIFICATION OF A *METZORA*.**[13]

"בִּשְׁעָרֶיךָ" – ***IN YOUR GATES***; **זוֹ לֶקֶט שִׁכְחָה וּפֵאָה – THIS** alludes to disputes regarding ***LEKET*, *SHICH'CHAH* AND *PE'AH*.**[14]

The Baraisa continues its exposition of the verse:

NOTES

1. I.e. an ordained sage, and not a disciple (see *Rashi*). [The use of the term מוּפְלָא as referring simply to an ordained sage is unlike the use of this term elsewhere, where it refers to the Chief of the High Court (*Av Beis Din*), the highest ranking member of the court after the *Nasi* (see *Tosafos* here and to 16b ד״ה אחד ממונה).]

This exposition would seem to be based on the similarity of the words יִפָּלֵא and מוּפְלָא. *Rambam* (*Commentary to the Mishnah* and *Hil. Mamrim* 3:5), however, explains that the requirement is implicit in the simple meaning of the verse. The Torah speaks of a sage who is unclear about the law only in an abstruse case, which excludes a non-ordained disciple, who is not yet expert and to whom the law even in simpler matters is unclear.

2. I.e. he is wise in the esoteric calculations needed to determine whether a month should be made into a "full" month by intercalating a thirtieth day, or whether a leap year should be established by intercalating a thirteenth month. One possessed of this esoteric wisdom is called "one who gives counsel" (see *Rashi*, and Gemara below). [Intercalation may be implemented only by the High Court itself or by a panel of judges authorized by them (*Rambam, Hil. Kiddush HaChodesh* 5:1). See also *Rambam* and *Ramban, Sefer HaMitzvos, Aseh* §153.]

This exposition of the Baraisa teaches that if a sage disputed the High Court's ruling regarding whether an extra month should be added to the year, and he issued a ruling in accordance with his own view, he is liable as a *zakein mamrei*. [Similarly, the next several expositions of the Baraisa deal with other questions of law that can be the issue of dispute for which a *zakein mamrei* is executed.]

3. *Nahum* 1:11. The Baraisa's exposition is supported by this verse, which juxtaposes "from you" and "one who gives counsel" (*Rashi*).

4. A *Halachah LeMoshe MiSinai* is a law or detail of a law taught to Moshe at Sinai, but for which there is no Scriptural allusion.

The reference to *Halachah LeMoshe MiSinai* is apparently based on translating דָּבָר as *word*; a *Halachah LeMoshe MiSinai* is based only on word of mouth – an oral tradition going back to Moses at Sinai (*Rashash*).

Thus, the Baraisa teaches that a sage can become a *zakein mamrei* even by disputing the High Court concerning a Biblical law that has no basis in Scripture.

5. Since the verse later makes explicit reference to *legal* judgment by its mention of דִּין, *verdict*, the Baraisa construes the expression מִשְׁפָּט, *judgment*, as alluding to the rule of *gezeirah shavah* (*Rashi*).

Thus, a sage can become a *zakein mamrei* by disputing the High Court in a law derived from a *gezeirah shavah*.

6. When a woman discharges uterine blood, her *tumah* status will depend on whether the blood was discharged during her *niddah* period, her *zivah* period, or one of several periods following childbirth. In general, on the Biblical level, the onset of normal menstrual flow begins a seven-day *niddah* period, followed by an eleven-day *zivah* period, during which any discharge of blood will be deemed *zivah* [abnormal flow] blood. After childbirth, a woman is *tamei* for a week (in the case of a baby boy) or two weeks (in the case of a baby girl); from day 8 to day 40 (in the case of a boy) or from day 15 to day 80 (in the case of a girl), any blood she discharges is deemed to be *tohar* blood, meaning that it does not render her *tamei*. After day forty or eighty (respectively), her next discharge of blood begins her *niddah* cycle anew. [Further details of these laws will be discussed below; see note 36.]

A sage can become a *zakein mamrei* disputing by the High Court in one of these matters.

7. *Tzaraas* is a discoloration of a person's skin, clothing, or house, which renders the affected object *tamei* and requires a special purification procedure (see *Leviticus* chs. 13 ff). The Torah (loc. cit.) consistently refers to the discoloration as a נֶגַע, *affliction*.

A sage can become a *zakein mamrei* by disputing the High Court in the matter of *tzaraas*.

8. A *cherem* is a vow in which one uses the expression "*cherem*" to consecrate property, placing it under the jurisdiction of *hekdesh* (the Temple Estate). (For a description of various types of *charamim*, see *Rambam, Hil. Arachin VeCharamim* 6:1-4.)

9. An *erech* vow is one in which one pledges the "set value" of a person to the Holy Estate. The Torah (*Leviticus* 27:1-8) sets these values for each of eight different categories, classified by age and gender.

10. This refers to various vows in which one consecrates property to *hekdesh*.

The Torah could have written דְּבַר רִיב, *a matter of dispute*, instead of the plural דִּבְרֵי רִיבֹת, *matters of disputes*. The unnecessary plural דִּבְרֵי, which can also be rendered *words*, is taken as an allusion to these various types of vows, whereby legal conditions are effected through the mere pronouncement of words (*Rashi*; see *Aruch LaNer*).

11. This refers to the suspected adulteress, who is taken to Jerusalem and is made to drink the specially prepared waters that will demonstrate her innocence or guilt. If she is guilty, the waters miraculously cause her to die a horrible death; if she is innocent, she remains completely unharmed and is permitted to return to her husband (see *Numbers* 5:11-31).

12. If the body of a murder victim is found outside a town in Eretz Yisrael and it is not known who killed him, the Torah requires the elders of the town nearest the body to take a calf and decapitate it according to a prescribed procedure (see *Deuteronomy* 21:1-9).

13. A *metzora* is a person who has contracted *tzaraas* (see note 7). When cured of the *tzaraas*, he must undergo the purification procedure described in *Leviticus* ch. 14.

The unnecessary plural expression רִיבֹת, *disputes* (see note 10), alludes to these laws, which involve dispute and strife. *Sotah* is the product of marital discord, the murder victim has been killed in a dispute, and we are taught that the *metzora* contracts his condition as punishment for לְשׁוֹן הָרָע – disparaging talk concerning his fellow man – which creates much strife (see *Rashi*).

14. לֶקֶט, *leket* (gleanings), refers to the ears of grain that fall from the reaper and which must be left for the poor (see *Leviticus* 19:9, 23:22). שִׁכְחָה, *shich'chah* (forgotten produce), refers to sheaves forgotten in the field during the removal of sheaves to the threshing floor (as well as to standing produce that the harvester overlooked), which must be left for the poor (see *Deuteronomy* 24:19). פֵּאָה, *pe'ah* (the edge), refers to the portion of standing crop that the farmer may not harvest but must leave for the poor (see *Leviticus* 19:9, 23:22).

These three categories are alluded to by the expression בִּשְׁעָרֶיךָ, *in your*

א במופלא שבב"ד הכתוב מדבר ממך זה יועץ וכן הוא אומר א) ממך יצא חושב על ה' רעה יועץ בליעל דבר זו הלכה למשפט זה הדין בין דם לדם בין דם נדה דם לידה דם זיבה בין דין לדין בין דיני נפשות דיני ממונות דיני מכות בין נגע לנגע בין נגעי אדם נגעי בתים נגעי בגדים דברי אלו החרמים והערכין וההקדשות ריבות זו השקאת סוטה ועריפת עגלה וטהרת מצורע בשעריך זו לקט שכחה ופאה וקמת מב"ד ועלית א) מלמד שבית המקדש גבוה מא"י וא"י גבוה מכל הארצות אל המקום ב) ב מלמד שהמקום גורם בשלמא בית המקדש גבוה מא"י דכתיב ועלית אלא א"י גבוה מכל הארצות מנא ליה דכתיב ב) לכן הנה ימים באים נאם ה' (ג) לא יאמר) חי ה' אשר העלה את בני ישראל מארץ מצרים כי אם חי ה' אשר העלה ואשר הביא את זרע בית ישראל מארץ צפונה ומכל הארצות אשר הדחתים שם וישבו על אדמתם תנו רבנן ג זקן ממרא אינו חייב אלא על דבר שזדונו כרת ושגגתו חטאת דברי ר"מ רבי יהודה אומר על דבר שעיקרו מדברי תורה ופירושו מדברי סופרים ר"ש אומר אפילו דקדוק אחד מדקדוקי סופרים מאי טעמא דר"מ ד) גמר דבר דבר כתיב הכא ג) כי יפלא ממך דבר למשפט וכתיב התם ד) ונעלם דבר מעיני הקהל מה להלן דבר שחייב על זדונו כרת ועל שגגתו חטאת אף כאן דבר שחייב על זדונו כרת ועל שגגתו חטאת ור' יהודה ה) על פי התורה אשר יורוך עד דאיכא תורה ויורוך ור"ש ו) אשר יגידו לך מן המקום ההוא אפילו כל דהו א"ל רב הונא בר חיננא לרבא תרגמא לי להא מתניתא אליבא דר"מ א"ל רבא לרב פפא פוק תרגמא ליה ג) כי יפלא במופלא שבב"ד הכתוב מדבר ממך זה יועץ ה) שיודע לעבר שנים ולקבוע חדשים ו) כדתנן ד הן העידו שמעברים את השנה כל אדר שהיו אומרים עד הפורים דאי להאי גיסא קא שרי חמץ בפסח ואי להאי גיסא קא שרי חמץ בפסח דבר זה הלכה זו הלכות אחד עשר דאיתמר ז) עשירי ר' יוחנן אמר עשירי כתשיעי ור"ש בן לקיש אמר עשירי כאחד עשר רבי יוחנן אמר עשירי כתשיעי מה תשיעי בעי שימור ה אף עשירי בעי שימור ר"ל אמר עשירי כאחד עשר מה אחד עשר לא בעי שימור אף עשירי לא בעי שימור משפט זה הדין [א]

דין

רש"י

גמ' במופלא שבב"ד. במומחה לב"ד למעוטי תלמיד: ממך זה יועץ. שנחלק בעיבור השנה הקרוי סוד ועצה כדמפרש לקמן: וכן הוא אומר. דגבי יועץ כתוב ממך: זו הלכה למשה מסיני. שאף עליה הוא נהרג: למשפט זה הדין. אם נחלק בדבר הלמד בדין ג"ש גם הוא נהרג דאילו דין ממש כתיב להדיא בין דין לדין: בין דם נדה דם לידה כו'. שנחלקו בדם נדה או בדם לידה או בדם זיבה: ובין נגע לנגע. שנחלקו בנגעי אדם או בנגעי בגדים: דברי ריבות. ה"ל למכתב דבר ריב וכתיב דברי ריבות לרבות חרמין וערכין והקדשות שהן באין וחלים ע"י דיבור הפה: זו השקאת סוטה. שהיא על ידי ריב שבינה ובין בעלה: ועריפת העגלה. שהחלל נהרג ע"י מריבה: וטהרת מצורע. שאף נגעים ע"י ריב של לשון הרע הם באים: זה לקט שכחה ופאה. שהן לעניים שכתוב בהן ואכלו בשעריך: וקמת מבית דין. מדכתיב וקמת מכלל דיושבין עסקינן והיינו ב"ד שיושבין במקום הקבוע להם עד עת האוכל ושם באין כל הצריכין לדין ולהוראה בכל עיר ועיר ואזהר רחמנא לב"ד של אותה העיר שהמחלוקת ביניהם לילך ולישאל: מלמד שבית המקדש גבוה מא"י. וקמת ועלית אל המקום ש"מ אין לך עיר בא"י שאין ירושלים גבוה ממנה: וא"י גבוה מכל הארצות. תנא דברייתא קא מסיק למלתיה ולאו מהאי קרא יליף ולקמן מפרש מנלן: אשר העלה וגו' מכל הארצות אשר הדחתים שם וישבו על אדמתם. ש"מ דאדמתם גבוה מכל הארצות דכתיב העלה: מה להלן דבר שחייבים כו'. כדילפינן בהוריות: תרגמא לי. להאי מתניתא דלעיל דקתני דמיקטיל אכל הני דחשיב בה הלכה וגזירה שוה וערכים והקדשות וכולהו הנך דתנא בה דתיובתא כר"מ דאמר אין חייב אלא על דבר שזדונו כרת וכו': כדתנן הם העידו. כלומר אי אפלוגתא דהנך תנאי פליגי זקן ממרא ורבנן: הם העידו. ר' יהושע ור' פפיים במס' עדיות: שמעברין את השנה כל אדר. ואע"פ שלא נמלכו לעבר קודם הפורים וקראו את המגילה באדר הראשון ואחר כך ראו שהשנה צריכה להתעבר ועברוה: שהיו אומרים כו'. לפיכך הוצרכו להעיד כן שהיו שאר חכמים אומרים עד הפורים מעברין ושוב אין מעברין וטעמא מפרש במס' ר"ה דמן הפורים התחילו לדרוש בהלכות הפסח דתניא שואלים בהלכות הפסח קודם לפסח ל' יום וכי מרחק להו לא לייתי לשלוחי ב"ד שכבר שמעו מן הדרשנים לעשות הפסח בסוף ל' ואתי לזלזולי בחמץ: דאי להאי גיסא. אם אמרו ב"ד שבלשכת הגזית שמעברים אחר הפורים מעוברת כר' יהושע ור' פפיים והוא אמר אינה מעוברת קא שרי חמץ בפסח: ואי איפכא. נמי שרי חמץ בפסח דזדונו כרת: הלכות אחד עשר. יום אחרון של י"א שבין נדה לנדה קיימא לן י"א יום שבין נדה לנדה הלכה למשה מסיני משעברו ז' ימי הנדה אינה חוזרת להיות נדה עד שיעברו י"א יום דכל דמים שרואה בהם דם זיבה הם ואם ראתה בהם יום או יומים רצופים שומרת יום ג' ואם פסקה ולא ראתה בו טובלת בו ביום וטהורה ואם ראתה ג' ימים רצופים הויא זיבה לקרבן ולטבילת מים חיים ואפליגו רבי יוחנן ורשב"ל בהלכות יום האחרון: רבי יוחנן אמר הלכה אחת נאמרה בו ר"ל אמר שתי הלכות נאמרו בו ליחלק משלפניו והך פלוגתא בשילהי מסכת נדה ואתמר בתרתי לישני וחד מינייהו נקט הכא: עשירי רבי יוחנן אמר הרי הוא כתשיעי. מה הרואה בתשיעי צריכה להיות שומרת עשירי שהרי ראויה בצירוף ג' לזיבה ושמא תראה בעשירי הרי שנים ותחזור ותראה באחד עשר הרי ג' אף הרואה בעשירי צריכה להיות שומרת אחד עשר ואע"פ שעשירי אינו ראוי לצירוף ג' שאין שנים עשר מצטרף עמהם לזיבה דהיכא דלא ראתה ג' רצופין להיות זבה בהנך י"א יום הוי יום שנים עשר תחלת נדה והיינו דקאמר רבי יוחנן התם הלכתא י"א הלכה אחת נאמרה בו ליחלק משלפניו ומאי איהו דלא בעי שימור להיות שומרת שנים עשר נגדו דהא לאו מימי זיבה הוא אבל שוה לשלפניו להיות שימור לראיית עשירי כשם שהעשירי שימור לראיית תשיעי: ור"ל אמר עשירי כאחד עשר. מה אחד עשר לא בעי שימור שנים עשר שהרי אין השנים עשר מימי הזיבה אף עשירי לא בעי שימור להיות שומרת י"א דלא נאמרה שומרת יום נגד יום אלא בראויה לצירוף ג' הלכך לר"ל שתי הלכות נאמרו ביום אחד עשר ליחלק משאר ימים שלפניו אחת שאינו צריך שימור ואחת שאין נעשה שימור לראיית עשירי ואי איפלוג זקן ממרא ורבנן בהלכות אחד עשר כדאיפליגו ר"ל ורבי יוחנן הוי דבר שזדונו כרת על שומרת יום כנגד יום חייב כרת כדכתיב (ויקרא טו) כל ימי זוב טומאתה וגו' ודרשינן ימי וכל ימי:

דרב

תוספות

במופלא שבב"ד. מומחה למעוטי תלמיד ואין זה כשאר מופלא דבכל דוכתין כדפרישית שלהי פרק קמא (דף טז:): שבית המקדש גבוה. לאו מכל א"י דאיכא עין עיטם דמידלי מיניה כדאמר באיזהו מקומן (זבחים דף נד:) סבור למבנייה בעין עיטם דמידלי אי נמי כותלי בהמ"ק גבוה מעין עיטם שגובהן ק' אמה: מלמד שהמקום גורם. לאפוקי מצאן בבית פאגי והמרה עליהם כדאמרינן לעיל בפרק קמא (שם יד:): דאי להאי גיסא קא שרי חמץ בפסח. תימה הא מ"ד עד הפורים מודה דאם עברוה אחר הפורים מעוברת דדוקא בניסן הוא דאמר בפרק קמא (דף יב: ושם) זה ניסן ואין אחר ניסן אבל מאן דאמר עד הפורים מדרבנן בעלמא הוא דאסור כדמפרש בפרק קמא דר"ה (דף ז. ושם) מ"ט דמ"ד עד הפורים כיון דאמר מר שואלין בהלכות הפסח קודם הפסח ל' יום אתי לזלזולי בחמץ וכיון דאם עברוה כ"ע מודו דמעוברת לא קא שרי חמץ בפסח: ורשב"ל אומר עשירי כאחד עשר. וא"ת ולרשב"ל אי אמר זקן ממרא כרבי יוחנן אמאי מיחייב הרי מחמיר הוא ואין כאן דבר שזדונו כרת וי"ל דמשכחת לה אי נגעה בככר של תרומה וקידש בו את האשה דאי טמא הוא אין בו שוה פרוטה דלא חזי אלא להסקה ואינה מקודשת ואי טהור הוא יש בו שוה פרוטה דחזי לאכילה ומקודשת:

דין

עין משפט נר מצוה

לח א מיי' פ"ג מהלכות ממרים הלכה ה:

לט ב מיי' שם הלכה ז:

מ ג מיי' שם הלכה ה ופ"ד הלכה א והלכה ב ועיי' שם הכל:

מא ד מיי' פ"ד מהל' קידוש החדש הלכה יג יד:

מב ה מיי' פ"ה מהל' מטמאי משכב ומושב הלכה ח טור י"ד סי' קפג:

הגהות הגר"א

[א] גמ' זה הדין דין. נמחק דין שני:

תורה אור השלם

א) מִמֵּךְ יָצָא חֹשֵׁב עַל יְיָ רָעָה יֹעֵץ בְּלִיָּעַל: [נחום א, יא]

ב) לָכֵן הִנֵּה יָמִים בָּאִים נְאֻם יְיָ וְלֹא יֹאמְרוּ עוֹד חַי יְיָ אֲשֶׁר הֶעֱלָה אֶת בְּנֵי יִשְׂרָאֵל מֵאֶרֶץ מִצְרָיִם: כִּי אִם חַי יְיָ אֲשֶׁר הֶעֱלָה וַאֲשֶׁר הֵבִיא אֶת זֶרַע בֵּית יִשְׂרָאֵל מֵאֶרֶץ צָפוֹנָה וּמִכֹּל הָאֲרָצוֹת אֲשֶׁר הִדַּחְתִּים שָׁם וְיָשְׁבוּ עַל אַדְמָתָם: [ירמיה כג, ז-ח]

ג) כִּי יִפָּלֵא מִמְּךָ דָבָר לַמִּשְׁפָּט בֵּין דָּם לְדָם בֵּין דִּין לְדִין וּבֵין נֶגַע לָנֶגַע דִּבְרֵי רִיבֹת בִּשְׁעָרֶיךָ וְקַמְתָּ וְעָלִיתָ אֶל הַמָּקוֹם אֲשֶׁר יִבְחַר יְיָ אֱלֹהֶיךָ בּוֹ: [דברים יז, ח]

ד) וְאִם כָּל עֲדַת יִשְׂרָאֵל יִשְׁגּוּ וְנֶעְלַם דָּבָר מֵעֵינֵי הַקָּהָל וְעָשׂוּ אַחַת מִכָּל מִצְוֹת יְיָ אֲשֶׁר לֹא תֵעָשֶׂינָה וְאָשֵׁמוּ: [ויקרא ד, יג]

ה) עַל פִּי הַתּוֹרָה אֲשֶׁר יוֹרוּךָ וְעַל הַמִּשְׁפָּט אֲשֶׁר יֹאמְרוּ לְךָ תַּעֲשֶׂה לֹא תָסוּר מִן הַדָּבָר אֲשֶׁר יַגִּידוּ לְךָ יָמִין וּשְׂמֹאל: [דברים יז, יא]

ו) וְעָשִׂיתָ עַל פִּי הַדָּבָר אֲשֶׁר יַגִּידוּ לְךָ מִן הַמָּקוֹם הַהוּא אֲשֶׁר יִבְחַר יְיָ וְשָׁמַרְתָּ לַעֲשׂוֹת כְּכֹל אֲשֶׁר יוֹרוּךָ: [דברים יז, י]

מסורת הש"ס

א) [קידושין סט.] זבחים נד:, ב) [לעיל יד: ע"ז ח:], ג) [ל"ל ולא יאמרו עוד], ד) הוריות ד., ה) [חגיגה יד.], ו) ר"ה ז. עדיות פ"ז מ"ז, ז) נדה עב ע"ב.

ליקוטי רש"י

יועץ. יודע לעבר שנים ולקבוע חדשים [ישעיהו ג, ג]. בין דם לדם. בין דם טמא לדם טהור. בין דין לדין. בין דין זכאי לדין חייב. בין נגע לנגע. בין נגע טמא לנגע טהור. דברי ריבות. שיהו חכמי העיר חולקים בדבר זה מטמא וזה מטהר זה מחייב וזה מזכה. וקמת ועלית. מלמד שבית המקדש גבוה מכל המקומות [דברים יז, ח]. בית המקדש גבוה. דברי ריבות בשעריך וקמת ועלית וגו', מכאן שהמקדש גבוה מכל ארץ ישראל דכל לגדיה סתם וכתב ועלית [קידושין סט:]. ועלית, בכל שעריך קרי עלייה ומשם לבית המקדש מלמד שבית המקדש היה גבוה מכל ארץ ישראל [זבחים נד:]. ארץ ישראל גבוה. לא מיבעיא לן הכא ולאו מהכא נפקא לן אלא מקרא אחרינא דכתיב (ירמיהו טז וכג) לא יאמר עוד חי וגו' כי אם חי ה' אשר העלה ואשר הביא את בני ישראל מארץ צפון ומכל המקומות אשר הדחתים שם וגו' [זבחים נד:]. ועלו אל אבי. ארץ ישראל גבוה מכל הארצות [בראשית מה, ט]. הנה שמעונה באפרתה, וכו' ד"א שמעונה באפרתה בספר יהושע (ט"ו) שבא מאפרים בכל התחומין הוא אומר (יהושע ט"ו) ועלה הגבול ותאר הגבול וכאן הוא אומר ועלה הגבול אל כתף היבוסי ירושלים נמצאת ירושלים גבוה מכל הארצות והוא ראוי לבית המקדש שנאמר (דברים יז) וקמת ועלית אל המקום וגו' מלמד שבית המקדש גבוה מכל ארץ ישראל כך נדרש בשחיטת קדשים [תהלים קלב, ו]. לכן הנה ימים באים נאם ה' לא יאמר עוד חי ה' אשר העלה את בני ישראל מארץ מצרים, כי אם חי ה' אשר העלה ואשר הביא את בני ישראל מארץ צפון דהיינו בבל ומכל הארצות אשר הדחתים שם וכתיב אשר העלה [קידושין סט:]. שהמקום. המיוחד למשפט והוא לשכת הגזית [סוטה מה.]. המקום גורם לחייב הנדון ואם אינם שם לא ידונו והאי קרא בדיני נפשות קאי כי יפלא ממך דבר בפרשת שופטים ושוטרים בזקן ממרא [ע"ז ח:]. דקדוקי סופרים. שהוסיפו לדקדק אחר מעשה הבריות ולהחמיר ולעשות סייג ואזנים לתורה וגזרו גזרות להרחיק את האדם מן העבירה ודכוותה בבכורות (ל:) גר הבא לקבל תורה עליו חוץ מדבר אחד אין מקבלין אותו ר' יוסי אומר אפילו דקדוק אחד מדקדוקי סופרים [סוכה כח.]. שדקדקו האחרונים מלשון משנת הראשונים [מגילה יט:]. כגון גזירות שגזרו חכמים שלא יבא לידי איסור תורה [ב"ב קלד.]. חומרא דרבנן [בכורות ל:]. ונעלם דבר. טעו להורות באחת מכל כריתות שבתורה שהוא מותר [ויקרא ד, יג]. הם העידו. רבי יהושע ורבי פפיים שמעברין את השנה כל אדר, אם ראו בית דין לאחר הפורים שהשנה צריכה להתעבר מעברין אותה. שהיו אומרים עד הפורים. לפי שהיו חכמים אומרים שאין מעברין אלא אם כן נתישבו בדבר לפני הפורים, לכך הוזקקו לעדות זו. קא שרי חמץ בפסח. אתי לזלזולי בחמץ שכבר מן הפורים ואילך התחילו הדרשנים לדרוש ברבים בהלכות הפסח הוזקקו השומעים לעשות פסח לסוף שלושים יום ואם יעברו בית דין את השנה לא יתקבלו דברי שלוחי בית דין לשומעין לדחות את הפסח שכבר שמעו מן הדרשנים [ר"ה ז.]. הלכות אחד עשר. שזה דין נדה לאורייתא ראתה היום מונה ששה והוא ראתה שנים מונה חמשה והן ואפילו ראתה כל שבעה ופסקה לערב טובלת ומשמשת ומיום שביעי ואילך הוויין ימי זיבה אחד עשר יום שאם ראתה בהן יום אחד או שנים שומרת יום כנגד יום וטובלת ואם ראתה בהן ג' רצופין הויא זבה גמורה וטעונה ספירה ז' נקיים וקרבן ואם משכו ימי זובה חדש או שנה אינה חוזרת לתחילת נדות עד שתשב שבעה נקיים ישבה ז' נקיים וראתה הויא תחילת נדה ומונה ששה והוא חוזרת לענינה ככל המפורש ואם לא ראתה באותן י"א יום ג' רצופין אינה זבה וכשתראה אחרי כן בין ראתה סמוך בין שהרחיקה ראייתה הויא תחילת נדה ואפילו תראה שלשה רצופין אינה מונה אלא ארבעה והן שאין ימי זוב אלא באותן י"א יום שבין סוף נדה זו לתחלת נדה הבאה וכן מפורש בהלכה אחרונה של מסכת נדה (דף עב) [ערכין ח.]. אחד עשר. לאחר שכלה שבעה ימי נדה נכנסין אחד עשר יום הקרויין ימי זיבה שאם תראה בהן שלשה ימים רצופין הרי היא זבה וטעונה ספירת שבעה וקרבן ואם תראה יום אחד שומרת יום למחרת וטובלת ומקראי יליף לה בתורת כהנים [מגילה כ.]. אחד עשר יום יש בין סוף נדה לתחלת נדה שכל שלשה רצופין שתראה באחד עשר יום הללו תהא זבה [ויקרא טו, כה]. עשירי. אין לו צרוף לזיבה שאין מצטרף עמו אלא י"א דהוי להו תרי. כתשיעי. דפשיטא לן ביה דבעי שימור אם ראתה בו דהא ראוי להביאה לידי זבה גמורה. בעי שימור. אם התחילה לראות בו. אף עשירי. י"א כנגדו אע"ג דאינה ראויה לבא לידי זבה גמורה. כי"א. לב"ה דאמרי לא בעי שימור [נדה עב:].

"וְקַמְתָּ" – *THEN YOU SHALL RISE UP;* מִבֵּית דִּין – this means that you shall rise up FROM THE COURT in your city.[15] "וְעָלִיתָ" – *AND YOU SHALL ASCEND;* מְלַמֵּד שֶׁבֵּית הַמִּקְדָּשׁ גָּבוֹהַּ מֵאֶרֶץ יִשְׂרָאֵל – THIS TEACHES THAT THE HOLY TEMPLE IS HIGHER THAN other points in ERETZ YISRAEL.[16] וְאֶרֶץ יִשְׂרָאֵל גְּבוֹהָה מִכָּל הָאֲרָצוֹת – AND furthermore, ERETZ YISRAEL IS HIGHER THAN ALL OTHER LANDS.[17]

The verse continues: "אֶל־הַמָּקוֹם" – *TO THE PLACE;* מְלַמֵּד שֶׁהַמָּקוֹם גּוֹרֵם – THIS TEACHES THAT THE LOCATION of the High Court CAUSES the law of *zakein mamrei* to take effect.[18]

The Gemara questions the second-to-last statement of the Baraisa:

בִּשְׁלָמָא בֵּית הַמִּקְדָּשׁ גָּבוֹהַּ מֵאֶרֶץ יִשְׂרָאֵל – It is understandable how the Tanna of the Baraisa derives from the verse that **the Holy Temple is higher than** other points in **Eretz Yisrael, דִּכְתִיב "וְעָלִיתָ" – for it is written:** ***and you shall ascend.*** **אֶלָּא אֶרֶץ יִשְׂרָאֵל גְּבוֹהָה מִכָּל הָאֲרָצוֹת מְנָא לֵיהּ – But from where does he know** that **Eretz Yisrael is higher than all other lands?** The verse cited in the Baraisa provides no proof of this! – ? –

The Gemara answers that he knows it from a different verse, not cited in the Baraisa:

דִּכְתִיב "לָכֵן הִנֵּה־יָמִים בָּאִים נְאֻם־ה' וְלֹא־יֹאמְרוּ עוֹד חַי־ה' אֲשֶׁר הֶעֱלָה אֶת־בְּנֵי יִשְׂרָאֵל מֵאֶרֶץ מִצְרַיִם – For it is written:[19] ***Therefore, behold days are coming, says Hashem, and they will no longer say*** [when taking an oath]: ***As Hashem lives, Who took up the Children of Israel from the land of Egypt;*** כִּי אִם־ – ***but rather:*** חַי־ה' אֲשֶׁר הֶעֱלָה וַאֲשֶׁר הֵבִיא אֶת־זֶרַע בֵּית יִשְׂרָאֵל מֵאֶרֶץ צָפוֹנָה וּמִכֹּל הָאֲרָצוֹת אֲשֶׁר הִדַּחְתִּים שָׁם וְיָשְׁבוּ עַל־אַדְמָתָם" – ***As Hashem lives, Who took up and Who brought the seed of the house of Israel from the northern country*** [Babylonia] ***and from all the countries to which I had driven them; and they shall dwell in their land.***[20]

The Gemara cites another Baraisa regarding the types of disputes for which a sage can be executed as a *zakein mamrei*:

תָּנוּ רַבָּנָן – The Rabbis taught in a Baraisa: זָקֵן מַמְרֵא אֵינוֹ חַיָּיב אֶלָּא עַל דָּבָר שֶׁזְּדוֹנוֹ כָּרֵת וְשִׁגְגָתוֹ חַטָּאת – A REBELLIOUS SAGE IS LIABLE ONLY FOR disputing the High Court's ruling in A MATTER WHOSE INTENTIONAL TRANSGRESSION IS punishable by *KARES* AND WHOSE INADVERTENT TRANSGRESSION makes the transgressor liable to A SIN OFFERING; דִּבְרֵי רַבִּי מֵאִיר – these are THE WORDS OF R' MEIR.[21] רַבִּי יְהוּדָה אוֹמֵר עַל דָּבָר שֶׁעִיקָּרוֹ מִדִּבְרֵי תוֹרָה וּפֵירוּשׁוֹ מִדִּבְרֵי סוֹפְרִים – R' YEHUDAH SAYS: He is liable FOR disputing the High Court's ruling in A MATTER WHOSE ESSENCE IS STATED IN THE written TORAH AND WHOSE ELABORATION IS STATED BY THE *SOFERIM*.[22] רַבִּי שִׁמְעוֹן אוֹמֵר אֲפִילּוּ דִּקְדּוּק אֶחָד מִדִּקְדּוּקֵי סוֹפְרִים – R' SHIMON SAYS: He is liable EVEN if he disputes the High Court in regard to ONE INFERENCE INFERRED BY THE *SOFERIM* from the Torah.[23]

NOTES

gates, since the Torah (*Deuteronomy* 26:12) states concerning the gifts left for the poor: *And [the poor] shall eat "in your gates" and be satisfied* (*Rashi*; see *Aruch LaNer*).

15. "You shall rise up" indicates that the disputants were sitting. This, then, is a reference to the local court, which sits in session in its regular place, and hears matters of litigation or halachic query that are brought before it. The verse, then, alludes to the law that it is incumbent on the local court (which had been "sitting") that cannot resolve a point of law to travel [to Jerusalem] to inquire of the courts there (*Rashi*).

16. Since the Torah [refers to matters of doubt that arise "in your gates," i.e. in any of your cities, and] commands the local court to "ascend" to Jerusalem, we can deduce that Jerusalem is higher than all other cities in Eretz Yisrael (*Rashi*; see *Tosafos*).

17. The Tanna adds this part in order to conclude the teaching about the relative height of Jerusalem, but he does not derive it from the verse cited; rather, it is derived from a different verse, as the Gemara will explain below (*Rashi*).

Concerning the statement that Eretz Yisrael is higher than all other lands, *Maharsha* (to *Kiddushin* 69a) suggests that since the earth is a sphere and Eretz Yisrael is the center (i.e. focus) of the sphere, it is viewed as the top of the sphere. Thus, traveling from anywhere to Eretz Yisrael is viewed as an ascent (see also *Sefer HaMiknah* there).

Maharal (there) contends that since the world is a sphere, the designation of any one area as the highest – i.e. the center of the sphere's surface – is totally arbitrary. Therefore, argues *Maharal,* the designation of Eretz Yisrael as the most elevated place must not be meant in a topographical sense, but in a spiritual sense. [See *Chasam Sofer* (there), who suggests that since in the tradition of the Sages the creation of the earth began from the place of the Temple (see *Yoma* 54b), it is not arbitrary to view that part of the globe as the center of the sphere.]

Still others suggest that the Gemara's statement is meant in a topographical sense but only relative to the surrounding lands. Eretz Yisrael is higher than these lands, so that when approaching Eretz Yisrael from any direction, one ascends (*Meromei Sadeh* there). [Although some of the mountains of Lebanon have a higher altitude than the mountains of present-day Israel, most of Lebanon is part of Biblical Israel.] See also *Einayim LaMishpat* here.

18. That is, the dissenting sage is deemed a *zakein mamrei* only if he ignores a ruling of the High Court issued while in session *in the Temple.* But if the High Court issued its decision while convened elsewhere – even in the environs of Jerusalem – the sage is not deemed a *zakein mamrei* (*Tosafos,* from Gemara 14b).

19. *Jeremiah* 23:7,8.

20. The verse refers to all lands of the dispersion, and states that the exiled Jews will be "brought" up to their land, i.e. Eretz Yisrael. This demonstrates that Eretz Yisrael is higher than all other lands (*Rashi*; see *Rashash*).

21. *Chidushei HaRan* (end of ד״ה ר׳ יהודה) explains R' Meir to mean specifically that the rebellious sage instructs a person to perform an act that renders him liable to *kares* in the opinion of the High Court. But if the High Court holds the *lenient* position and the sage instructs the person to act *stringently,* the sage is not a *zakein mamrei* in R' Meir's view. (This is also the view of *Rashi* and *Tosafos* – see *Toras Chaim* 87b ד״ה ריש לקיש.) *Rambam* (*Hil. Mamrim* 4:1-2), however, explains that the sage is a *zakein mamrei* for disputing the High Court in a matter of *kares* regardless of whether he instructs the person to adopt the stringent position or the lenient one (see also *Toras Chaim* loc. cit.; cf. *Ran's* comments on *Rambam's* view).

22. I.e. the early Sages (see *Keilim* 13:7, *Rosh Hashanah* 34a and *Kiddushin* 30a; see *Doros HaRishonim* vol. 5, בבל וארץ ישראל, ch. 4, p. 174).

As explained by *Chidushei HaRan,* R' Yehudah widens the scope of matters for which the sage can be liable as a *zakein mamrei.* For while R' Meir restricts the law of *zakein mamrei* to matters of *kares,* R' Yehudah extends it to *any* matter whose essence is in the Written Torah and whose elaboration comes to us through the Rabbis. Cf. *Tosafos* to 88b ד״ה ואין לנו.

[Furthermore, *Ran* contends, R' Meir is *less* restrictive than R' Yehudah in one point: Whereas R' Yehudah requires that the essence of the law in dispute must be contained in the Written Torah, R' Meir (like R' Shimon below) allows the law to be one based entirely on Rabbinic tradition or exegesis. No one, however, holds that the law in dispute must be contained entirely in the Written Torah. For, on the contrary, the Mishnah below (88b) states that if the *zakein mamrei* rules contrary to an explicit verse, he is not liable as a *zakein mamrei,* since his obvious error cannot be deemed a ruling altogether (see *Rashi* there).]

23. R' Shimon agrees that the law in dispute must be Biblical, but he maintains – unlike R' Yehudah – that even its essence need not be contained in the Written Torah. Rather, the law may be based entirely on Rabbinic tradition or exegesis (*Chidushei HaRan*; cf. *Rambam* in *Sefer HaMitzvos, Shoresh* 1 and *Ramban* there, but see *Megillas Esther* to *Sefer HaMitzvos* ad loc. and *Radvaz* to *Hil. Mamrim* 4:1).

To summarize the three Tannaic views, as explained by *Ran*:

1) **R' Meir:** The law in dispute must be one that is punishable by *kares* and requires a *chatas* if transgressed inadvertently. Its essence,

[א]במופלא שבב"ד הכתוב מדבר ממך זה יועץ וכן הוא אומר א) ממך יצא חושב על ה' רעה יועץ בליעל דבר זו הלכה למשפט זה הדין בין דם לדם בין דם נדה דם לידה דם זיבה בין דין לדין בין דיני נפשות דיני ממונות דיני מכות בין נגע לנגע בין נגעי אדם נגעי בתים נגעי בגדים דברי אלו החרמים והערכין וההקדשות ריבות זו השקאת סוטה ועריפת עגלה וטהרת מצורע בשעריך זו לקט שכחה ופאה וקמת מב"ד ועלית א) מלמד שבית המקדש גבוה מא"י וא"י גבוה מכל הארצות אל המקום ג) [ב]מלמד שהמקום גורם בשלמא בית המקדש גבוה מא"י דכתיב ועלית אלא א"י גבוה מכל הארצות מנא ליה דכתיב ב) לכן הנה ימים באים נאם ה' (ג) לא יאמר) חי ה' אשר העלה את בני ישראל מארץ מצרים כי אם חי ה' אשר העלה ואשר הביא את זרע בית ישראל מארץ צפונה ומכל הארצות אשר הדחתים שם וישבו על אדמתם תנו רבנן [ג]זקן ממרא אינו חייב אלא על דבר שזדונו כרת ושגגתו חטאת דברי ר"מ רבי יהודה אומר על דבר שעיקרו מדברי תורה ופירושו מדברי סופרים ר"ש אומר אפילו דקדוק אחד מדקדוקי סופרים מאי טעמא דר"מ ד) גמר דבר דבר כתיב הכא ג) כי יפלא ממך דבר למשפט וכתיב התם ד) ונעלם דבר מעיני הקהל מה להלן דבר שחייב על זדונו כרת ועל שגגתו חטאת אף כאן דבר שחייב על זדונו כרת ועל שגגתו חטאת ור' יהודה ה) על פי התורה אשר יורוך עד דאיכא תורה ויורוך ור"ש ו) אשר יגידו לך מן המקום ההוא אפילו כל דהו א"ל רב הונא בר חיננא לרבא תרגמא לי להא מתניתא אליבא דר"מ א"ל רבא לרב פפא פוק תרגמא ליה ג) כי יפלא במופלא שבב"ד הכתוב מדבר ממך זה יועץ ה) שיודע לעבר שנים ולקבוע חדשים ו) כדתנן [ד]הן העידו שמעברים את השנה כל אדר שהיו אומרים עד הפורים דאי להאי גיסא קא שרי חמץ בפסח ואי להאי גיסא קא שרי חמץ בפסח דבר זה הלכה זו הלכות אחד עשר דאיתמר ז) עשירי ר' יוחנן אמר עשירי כתשיעי ור"ש בן לקיש אמר עשירי כאחד עשר רבי יוחנן אמר עשירי כתשיעי מה תשיעי בעי שימור [ה]אף עשירי בעי שימור ר"ל אמר עשירי כאחד עשר מה אחד עשר לא בעי שימור אף עשירי לא בעי שימור משפט זה הדין [א] דין

גמ' במופלא שבב"ד. במומחה לב"ד למעוטי תלמיד: ממך זה יועץ. שנחלק בעיבור השנה הקרוי סוד ועצה כדמפרש לקמן: וכן הוא אומר. דגבי יועץ כתוב ממך: זו הלכה למשה מסיני. שאף עליה הוא נהרג: למשפט זה הדין. אם נחלק בדבר הלמד בדין ג"ש גם הוא נהרג דאילו דין ממש כתיב להדיא בין דין לדין: בין דם נדה דם לידה כו'. שנחלקו בדם נדה או בדם לידה או בדם זיבה: ובין נגע לנגע. שנחלקו בנגעי אדם או בנגעי בגדים: דברי ריבות. ה"ל למכתב דבר ריב וכתיב דברי ריבות לרבות חרמין וערכין והקדשות שהן באין וחלים ע"י דיבור הפה: זו השקאת סוטה. שהיא על ידי ריב שבינה ובין בעלה: ועריפת העגלה. שהחלל נהרג ע"י מריבה: וטהרת מצורע. שאף נגעים ע"י ריב של לשון הרע הם באים: זה לקט שכחה ופאה. שהן לעניים שכתוב בהן ואכלו בשעריך: וקמת מבית דין. מדכתיב וקמת מכלל דיושבין עסקינן והיינו ב"ד שיושבין במקום הקבוע להם עד עת האוכל ושם באין כל הצריכין לדין ולהוראה בכל עיר ועיר ואזהר רחמנא לב"ד של אותה העיר שהמחלוקת ביניהם לילך ולישאל: מלמד שבית המקדש גבוה מא"י. וקמת ועלית אל המקום ש"מ אין לך עיר בא"י שאין ירושלים גבוה ממנה: וא"י גבוה מכל הארצות. תנא דברייתא קא מסיק למלתיה ולאו מהאי קרא יליף ולקמן מפרש מנלן: אשר העלה וגו' מכל הארצות אשר הדחתים שם וישבו על אדמתם. ש"מ דאדמתם גבוה מכל הארצות דכתיב העלה: מה להלן דבר שחייבים כו'. כדילפינן בהוריות: תרגמא לי. להאי מתניתא דלעיל דקתני דמיקטיל אכל הני דחשיב בה הלכה וגזירה שוה וערכים והקדשות וכולהו הנך דתנא בה דתיתוקם כר"מ דאמר אין חייב אלא על דבר שזדונו כרת וכו': כדתנן הם העידו. כלומר אי אפלוגתא דהנך תנאי פליגי זקן ממרא ורבנן: הם העידו. ר' יהושע ור' פפיים במס' עדיות: שמעברין את השנה כל אדר. ואע"פ שלא נמלכו לעבר קודם הפורים וקראו את המגילה באדר הראשון ואחר כך ראו שהשנה צריכה להתעבר ועברוה: שהיו אומרים כו'. לפיכך הוצרכו להעיד כן שהיו שאר חכמים אומרים עד הפורים מעברין ושוב אין מעברין וטעמא מפרש במס' ר"ה דמן הפורים התחילו לדרוש בהלכות הפסח דתניא שואלים בהלכות הפסח קודם לפסח ל' יום וכי מרחק להו לא צייתי לשלוחי ב"ד שכבר שמעו מן הדרשנים לעשות הפסח בסוף ל' ואתי לזלזולי בחמץ: דאי להאי גיסא. אם אמרו ב"ד שבלשכת הגזית שמעברים אחר הפורים מעוברת כר' יהושע ור' פפיים והוא אמר אינה מעוברת קא שרי חמץ בפסח: ואי איפכא. נמי שרי חמץ בפסח דזדונו כרת: הלכות אחד עשר. יום אחרון של י"א שבין נדה לנדה קיימא לן י"א יום שבין נדה לנדה הלכה למשה מסיני משעברו ז' ימי הנדה אינה חוזרת להיות נדה עד שיעברו י"א יום דכל דמים שרואה בהם דם זיבה הם ואם ראתה בהם יום או יומים רצופים שומרת יום ג' ואם פסקה ולא ראתה בו טובלת בו ביום וטהורה ואם ראתה ג' ימים רצופים הויא זיבה לקרבן ולטבילת מים חיים ואפליגו רבי יוחנן ורשב"ל בהלכות יום האחרון: רבי יוחנן אמר הלכה אחת נאמרה בו ר"ל אמר שתי הלכות נאמרו בו ליחלק משלפניו והך פלוגתא בשילהי מסכת נדה ואתמר בתרתי לישני וחד מינייהו נקט הכא: עשירי רבי יוחנן אמר הרי הוא כתשיעי. מה הרואה בתשיעי צריכה להיות שומרת עשירי שהרי ראויה בצירוף ג' לזיבה ושמא תראה בעשירי הרי שנים ותחזור ותראה באחד עשר הרי ג' אף הרואה בעשירי צריכה להיות שומרת אחד עשר ואע"פ שעשירי אינו ראוי לצירוף ג' שאין שנים עשר מצטרף עמהם לזיבה דהיכא דלא ראתה ג' רצופין להיות זבה בהנך י"א יום הוי יום שנים עשר תחלת נדה והיינו דקאמר רבי יוחנן התם הלכתא י"א הלכה אחת נאמרה בו ליחלק משלפניו ומאי איהו דלא בעי שימור להיות שומרת שנים עשר נגדו דהא לאו מימי זיבה הוא אבל שוה לשלפניו להיות שימור לראיית עשירי כשם שהעשירי שימור לראיית תשיעי: ור"ל אמר עשירי כאחד עשר. מה אחד עשר לא בעי שימור שנים עשר שהרי אין השנים עשר מימי הזיבה אף עשירי לא בעי שימור להיות שומרת י"א דלא נאמרה שומרת יום נגד יום אלא בראויה לצירוף ג' הלכך לר"ל שתי הלכות נאמרו ביום אחד עשר ליחלק משאר ימים שלפניו אחת שאינו צריך שימור ואחת שאין נעשה שימור לראיית עשירי ואי איפלוג זקן ממרא ורבנן בהלכות אחד עשר כדאיפליגו ר"ל ורבי יוחנן הוי דבר שזדונו כרת על שומרת יום כנגד יום חייב כרת כדכתיב (ויקרא טו) כל ימי זוב טומאתה וגו' ודרשינן ימי וכל ימי: דרכ

במופלא שבב"ד. מומחה למעוטי תלמיד ואין זה כשאר מופלא דבכל דוכתין כדפרישית שלהי פרק קמא (דף טו:): שבית המקדש גבוה. לאו מכל א"י דאיכא עין עיטם דמידלי מיניה כדאמר באיזהו מקומן (זבחים דף נד:) סבור למבנייה בעין עיטם דמידלי אי נמי כותלי בהמ"ק גבוה מעין עיטם שגובהן ק' אמה: מלמד שהמקום גורם. לאפוקי מלאן בבית פאגי והמרה עליהם כדאמרינן לעיל בפרק קמא (שם יד:): דאי להאי גיסא קא שרי חמץ בפסח. תימה הא מ"ד עד הפורים מודה דאם עברוה אחר הפורים מעוברת דדוקא בניסן הוא דאמר בפרק קמא (דף יב: ושם) זה ניסן ואין אחר ניסן אבל מאן דאמר עד הפורים מדרבנן בעלמא הוא דאסור כדמפרש בפרק קמא דר"ה (דף ז. ושם) מ"ט דמ"ד עד הפורים כיון דאמר מר שואלין בהלכות הפסח קודם הפסח ל' יום אתי לזלזולי בחמץ וכיון דאם עברוה כ"ע מודו דמעוברת לא קא שרי חמץ בפסח: ורשב"ל אומר עשירי כאחד עשר. וא"ת ולרשב"ל אי אמר זקן ממרא כרבי יוחנן אמאי מיחייב הרי מחמיר הוא ואין כאן דבר שזדונו כרת וי"ל דמשכחת לה אי נגעה בככר של תרומה וקידש בו את האשה דאי טמא הוא אין בו שוה פרוטה דלא חזי אלא להסקה ואינה מקודשת ואי טהור הוא יש בו שוה פרוטה דחזי לאכילה ומקודשת: דין

מסורת הש"ס

א) [קידושין סט.] זבחים נד:, ב) [לעיל יד: ע"ז ח:], ג) [נ"ל ולא יאמרו עוד], ד) הוריות ד., ה) [חגיגה יז.], ו) ר"ה ז. עדיות פ"ז מ"ז, ז) נדה עב ע"ב.

עין משפט נר מצוה

לח א מיי' פ"ג מהלכות ממרים הלכה ה:

לט ב מיי' שם הלכה ז:

מ ג מיי' שם הלכה ה ופ"ד הלכה א והלכה ב ועיי' שם הכל:

מא ד מיי' פ"ד מהל' קידוש החדש הלכה יג יד:

מב ה מיי' פ"ה מהל' מטמאי משכב ומושב הלכה ח טור י"ד סי' קפג:

הגהות הגר"א

[א] גמ' זה הדין דין. נמחק דין שני:

תורה אור השלם

א) מִמֵּךְ יָצָא חֹשֵׁב עַל יְיָ רָעָה יֹעֵץ בְּלִיָּעַל: [נחום א, יא]

ב) לָכֵן הִנֵּה יָמִים בָּאִים נְאֻם יְיָ וְלֹא יֹאמְרוּ עוֹד חַי יְיָ אֲשֶׁר הֶעֱלָה אֶת בְּנֵי יִשְׂרָאֵל מֵאֶרֶץ מִצְרָיִם: כִּי אִם חַי יְיָ אֲשֶׁר הֶעֱלָה וַאֲשֶׁר הֵבִיא אֶת זֶרַע בֵּית יִשְׂרָאֵל מֵאֶרֶץ צָפוֹנָה וּמִכֹּל הָאֲרָצוֹת אֲשֶׁר הִדַּחְתִּים שָׁם וְיָשְׁבוּ עַל אַדְמָתָם: [ירמיה כג, ז-ח]

ג) כִּי יִפָּלֵא מִמְּךָ דָבָר לַמִּשְׁפָּט בֵּין דָּם לְדָם בֵּין דִּין לְדִין וּבֵין נֶגַע לָנֶגַע דִּבְרֵי רִיבֹת בִּשְׁעָרֶיךָ וְקַמְתָּ וְעָלִיתָ אֶל הַמָּקוֹם אֲשֶׁר יִבְחַר יְיָ אֱלֹהֶיךָ בּוֹ: [דברים יז, ח]

ד) וְאִם כָּל עֲדַת יִשְׂרָאֵל יִשְׁגּוּ וְנֶעְלַם דָּבָר מֵעֵינֵי הַקָּהָל וְעָשׂוּ אַחַת מִכָּל מִצְוֹת יְיָ אֲשֶׁר לֹא תֵעָשֶׂינָה וְאָשֵׁמוּ: [ויקרא ד, יג]

ה) עַל פִּי הַתּוֹרָה אֲשֶׁר יוֹרוּךָ וְעַל הַמִּשְׁפָּט אֲשֶׁר יֹאמְרוּ לְךָ תַּעֲשֶׂה לֹא תָסוּר מִן הַדָּבָר אֲשֶׁר יַגִּידוּ לְךָ יָמִין וּשְׂמֹאל: [דברים יז, יא]

ו) וְעָשִׂיתָ עַל פִּי הַדָּבָר אֲשֶׁר יַגִּידוּ לְךָ מִן הַמָּקוֹם הַהוּא אֲשֶׁר יִבְחַר יְיָ וְשָׁמַרְתָּ לַעֲשׂוֹת כְּכֹל אֲשֶׁר יוֹרוּךָ: [דברים יז, י]

ליקוטי רש"י

יועץ. יודע לעבר שנים ולקבוע חדשים [ישעיהו ג, ג]. בין דם לדם. בין דם טמא לדם טהור. בין דין לדין. בין דין זכאי לדין חייב. בין נגע לנגע. בין נגע טמא לנגע טהור. דברי ריבות. שיהו חכמי העיר חולקים בדבר זה מטמא וזה מטהר זה מחייב וזה מזכה. וקמת ועלית. מלמד שבית המקדש גבוה מכל המקומות [דברים יז, ח]. בית המקדש גבוה. דברי ריבות בשעריך וקמת ועלית וגו', מכאן שהמקדש גבוה מכל ארץ ישראל דכל לגביה סתם וכתב ועלית [קידושין סט:]. ועלית, בכל שעריך קרי עלייה ומשם לבית המקדש מלמד שבית המקדש היה גבוה מכל ארץ ישראל [זבחים נד:]. ארץ ישראל גבוה. לא מיבעיא לן הכא ולאו מהכא נפקא לן אלא מקרא אחרינא דכתיב (ירמיהו טז וכג) לא יאמר עוד חי וגו' כי אם חי ה' אשר העלה ואשר הביא את בני ישראל מארץ צפון ומכל המקומות אשר הדחתים שם וגו' [זבחים נד:]. ועלו אל אבי. ארץ ישראל גבוה מכל הארצות [בראשית מה, ט]. הנה שמענוה באפרתה, וכו' ד"א שמענוה באפרתה בספר יהושע (ט"ו) שבא מאפרים בכל התחומין הוא אומר (יהושע ט"ו) ועלה הגבול ותאר הגבול וכאן הוא אומר ועלה הגבול אל כתף היבוסי ירושלים נמצאת ירושלים גבוה מכל הארצות והוא ראוי לבית המקדש שנאמר (דברים יז) וקמת ועלית אל המקום וגו' מלמד שבית המקדש גבוה מכל ארץ ישראל כך נדרש בשחיטת קדשים [תהלים קלב, ו]. לכן הנה ימים באים נאם ה' לא יאמר עוד חי ה' אשר העלה את בני ישראל מארץ מצרים, כי אם חי ה' אשר העלה ואשר הביא את בני ישראל מארץ צפון דהיינו בבל ומכל הארצות אשר הדחתים שם וכתיב אשר העלה [קידושין סט:]. שהמקום. המיוחד למשפט והוא לשכת הגזית [סוטה מה.]. המקום גורם לחייב הנדון ואם אינם שם לא ידונו והאי קרא בדיני נפשות קאי כי יפלא ממך דבר בפרשת שופטים ושוטרים בזקן ממרא [ע"ז ח:]. דקדוקי סופרים. שהוסיפו לדקדק אחר מעשה הבריות ולהחמיר ולעשות סייג ואזנים לתורה וגזרו גזרות להרחיק את האדם מן העבירה ודכוותה בבכורות (ל:) גר הבא לקבל תורה עליו חוץ מדבר אחד אין מקבלין אותו ר' יוסי אומר אפילו דקדוק אחד מדקדוקי סופרים [סוכה כח.]. שדקדקו האחרונים מלשון משנת הראשונים [מגילה יט:]. כגון גזירות שגזרו חכמים שלא יבא לידי איסור תורה [ב"ב קלד.]. חומרא דרבנן [בכורות ל:]. ונעלם דבר. טעו להורות באחת מכל כריתות שבתורה שהוא מותר [ויקרא ד, יג]. הם העידו. רבי יהושע ורבי פפייס שמעברין את השנה כל אדר, אם ראו בית דין לאחר הפורים שהשנה צריכה להתעבר מעברין אותה. שהיו אומרים עד הפורים. לפי שהיו חכמים אומרים שאין מעברין אלא אם כן נתישבו בדבר לפני הפורים, לכך הוזקקו לעדות זו. קא שרי חמץ בפסח. אתי לזלזולי בחמץ שכבר מן הפורים ואילך התחילו הדרשנים לדרוש ברבים בהלכות הפסח הוזקקו השומעים לעשות פסח לסוף שלשים יום ואם יעברו בית דין את השנה לא יתקבלו דברי שלוחי בית דין לשומעין לדחות את הפסח שכבר שמעו מן הדרשנים [ר"ה ז.]. הלכות אחד עשר. שזה דין נדה לאורייתא ראתה היום מונה שבעה והוא ראתה שנים מונה חמשה וכן ואפילו ראתה כל שבעה ופסקה לערב טובלת ומשמשת ומיום שמיני ואילך הויין ימי זיבה אחד עשר יום שאם ראתה בהן יום אחד או שנים שומרת יום כנגד יום וטובלת ואם ראתה בהן ג' רצופין הויא זבה גמורה וטעונה ספירה ז' נקיים וקרבן ואם משכו ימי זובה חדש או שנה אינה חוזרת לתחלת נדות עד שתשב שבעה נקיים ישבה ז' נקיים וראתה הויא תחלת נדה ומונה ששה והוא חוזרת לעניינה ככל המפורש ואם לא ראתה באותן י"א יום ג' רצופין אינה זבה וכשתראה אחרי כן בין ראתה סמוך בין שהרחיקה ראייתה הויא תחילת נדה ואפילו תראה שלשה רצופין אינה מונה אלא ארבעה והן שאין ימי זוב אלא באותן י"א יום שבין סוף נדה זו לתחלת נדה הבאה וכן מפורש בהלכה אחרונה של מסכת נדה (דף עב) [ערכין ח.]. אחד עשר. לאחר שכלה שבעה ימי נדה נכנסין אחד עשר יום הקרויין ימי זיבה שאם תראה בהן שלשה ימים רצופין הרי היא זבה וטעונה ספירת שבעה וקרבן ואם תראה יום אחד שומרת יום למחרת וטובלת ומקראי יליף לה בתורת כהנים [מגילה כ.]. אחד עשר יום יש בין סוף נדה לתחלת נדה שכל שלשה רצופין שתראה באחד עשר יום הללו תהא זבה [ויקרא טו, כה]. עשירי. אין לו צרוך לזיבה שאין מצטרף עמו אלא י"א דהוי להו תרי. כתשיעי. דפשיטא לן ביה דבעי שימור אם ראתה בו דהא ראוי להביאה לידי זבה גמורה. בעי שימור. י"א כנגדו אע"ג דאינה ראויה לבא לידי זבה גמורה. כי"א. לב"ה דאמרי לא בעי שימור [נדה עב:].

The Gemara cites the respective sources for the opinions of these Tannaim:

מַאי טַעֲמָא דְּרַבִּי מֵאִיר – **What is R' Meir's reason** for ruling as he does? גָּמַר ,,דָּבָר'' ,,דָּבָר'' – **He derives** it through a *gezeirah shavah* established by the words ***matter, matter.*** כְּתִיב הָכָא ,,כִּי יִפָּלֵא מִמְּךָ דָבָר לַמִּשְׁפָּט'' – **It is written here** in the passage of *zakein mamrei*: ***if there be hidden from you "a matter" of judgment,*** וּכְתִיב הָתָם ,,וְנֶעְלַם דָּבָר מֵעֵינֵי הַקָּהָל'' – **and it is written there** in the passage concerning a sin offering brought for a transgression caused by an incorrect ruling of the High Court: ***And "the matter" became hidden from the eyes of the congregation.***[24] מַה לְהַלָּן דָּבָר שֶׁחַיָּיב עַל זְדוֹנוֹ כָּרֵת וְעַל שִׁגְגָתוֹ חַטָּאת – **Just as there,** in the case of the congregation's sin offering, the reference is to **a matter for which one is liable to *kares* for its intentional transgression and to a sin offering for its inadvertent transgression,**[25] אַף כָּאן דָּבָר שֶׁחַיָּיב עַל זְדוֹנוֹ כָּרֵת וְעַל שִׁגְגָתוֹ חַטָּאת – **so too, here** in the case of *zakein mamrei,* the reference is to **a matter for which one is liable to *kares* for its intentional transgression and to a sin offering for its inadvertent transgression.**

R' Yehudah's reason:

וְרַבִּי יְהוּדָה – **And R' Yehudah** derives his opinion from that which the Torah states: ,,עַל־פִּי הַתּוֹרָה אֲשֶׁר יוֹרוּךָ'' – ***According to the "law" that "they will teach you,"***[26] עַד דְּאִיכָּא תּוֹרָה וְיוֹרוּךָ – which indicates that a *zakein mamrei* is not liable **until there is** in the matter that he disputes both **"law" and "they will teach you."**[27]

R' Shimon's reason:

וְרַבִּי שִׁמְעוֹן – **And R' Shimon** derives his opinion from that which the Torah states: ,,אֲשֶׁר יַגִּידוּ לְךָ מִן־הַמָּקוֹם הַהוּא'' – *And you shall do in accordance with the word* ***that they will tell you, from that place,***[28] אֲפִילוּ כָּל דְּהוּ – which includes **even the slightest** instruction that they give you.[29]

The Gemara relates a discussion concerning the Baraisa (cited above) that saw various types of law alluded to in the *zakein mamrei* passage:

אָמַר לֵיהּ רַב הוּנָא בַּר חִינָנָא לְרָבָא – **Rav Huna bar Chinana said to Rava:** תַּרְגְּמָא לִי לְהָא מַתְנִיתָא אַלִּיבָּא דְּרַבִּי מֵאִיר – **Interpret this Baraisa for me according to the view of R' Meir,** who holds that a *zakein mamrei* is liable only if the issue in dispute involves a matter of *kares.* At first glance, none of the laws listed in the Baraisa involves *kares.* אָמַר לֵיהּ רָבָא לְרַב פָּפָּא – **Rava said to Rav Pappa:** פּוּק תַּרְגְּמָא לֵיהּ – **Go interpret it for [Rav Huna bar Chinana].**

Rav Pappa recites the Baraisa, interspersing his citation with interpretive comments:

,,כִּי יִפָּלֵא'' בְּמוּפְלָא – The verse states: *IF THERE BE HIDDEN* . . . שֶׁבְּבֵית דִּין הַכָּתוּב מְדַבֵּר – SCRIPTURE IS SPEAKING OF A RECOGNIZED MEMBER OF THE COURT. ,,מִמְּךָ'' זֶה יוֹעֵץ – *FROM YOU*; THIS alludes to ONE WHO GIVES COUNSEL; שֶׁיּוֹדֵעַ לְעַבֵּר שָׁנִים וְלִקְבּוֹעַ חֳדָשִׁים – that is, one **who knows** how **to intercalate** months into **years and to fix months.**[30] כִּדְתְנַן – And the point that the *zakein mamrei* disputes is **like** the one about which **we learned in a Mishnah:**[31] הֵן הֵעִידוּ שֶׁמְּעַבְּרִים אֶת הַשָּׁנָה כָּל אֲדָר – THEY TESTIFIED THAT WE MAY INTERCALATE a month into THE YEAR during THE ENTIRE MONTH OF ADAR.[32] שֶׁהָיוּ אוֹמְרִים עַד הַפּוּרִים – This testimony was necessary BECAUSE THERE WERE THOSE WHO SAID THAT the leap year can be declared only UNTIL PURIM, i.e. the fourteenth/fifteenth of Adar.[33] The Baraisa, then, could refer to where the sage and the Sanhedrin disagreed as to whether or not the leap year could be declared after Purim, and this dispute leads to a matter of *kares*: דְּאִי לְהַאי גִּיסָא קָא שָׁרֵי חָמֵץ בְּפֶסַח – **For if** the sage takes **this side** of the question, **he is permitting *chametz* on Pesach,**[34] וְאִי לְהַאי גִּיסָא קָא שָׁרֵי חָמֵץ בְּפֶסַח – **and if** he takes **the other side** of the question, **he is also permitting *chametz* on Pesach.**[35]

Rav Pappa continues his interpretive citation of the Baraisa:

,,דָּבָר'' זֶה הֲלָכָה – *A MATTER*; THIS alludes to A HALACHAH *LeMoshe MiSinai*. Rav Pappa explains: זוּ הִלְכוֹת אַחַד עָשָׂר – **This** refers to the ***Halachos** LeMoshe MiSinai* **concerning the**

NOTES

however, need not be contained in the Written Torah.

2) **R' Yehudah:** The law in dispute need not involve a matter of *kares,* but its essence must be contained in the Written Torah.

3) **R' Shimon:** The law in dispute need not involve a matter of *kares,* nor must its essence be contained in the Written Torah.

24. *Leviticus* 4:13. The verse discusses a case in which the High Court issued a mistaken ruling, which resulted in the majority of the nation violating a prohibition. The congregation must bring a sin offering to atone.

25. As derived in Tractate *Horayos* [8a] (*Rashi*).

26. *Deuteronomy* 17:11 (cited in full on 86b in note 28).

27. ["Law" refers to something explicit in the Written Torah. "That they will teach you" indicates something that we know only because the Rabbis taught it to us.]

28. Ibid. v. 10 (cited in full on 86b in note 28).

29. ["In accordance with the word that they will tell you" implies "regardless of what they tell you" (as long as they assert that it is a Biblical law). Alternatively, R' Shimon might be expounding the superfluous word הַהוּא to mean *whatever it is.*]

30. See above, note 2.

31. *Eduyos* 7:7. [The Mishnahs there record the testimonies (*eduyos*) of many Tannaim as to their received traditions concerning various laws about which disputes had arisen.] This Mishnah records the testimony of R' Yehoshua and R' Pappayis, who were the "witnesses" offering the forthcoming testimony (*Rashi*).

32. When the court proclaims a leap year, it adds a second Adar as the intercalary month. R' Yehoshua and R' Pappayis testified that the Court may decide to proclaim a leap year at the very end of Adar, even if they did not consider doing so before Purim (the fourteenth/fifteenth) and the Megillah was thus read on Purim [from which point people began to discuss the laws of the upcoming Pesach festival – see next note] (*Rashi*). [In a leap year, the celebration of Purim is postponed until the fourteenth/fifteenth of the Second Adar.]

33. The Gemara (*Rosh Hashanah* 7a) explains their reasoning: The law is that one should start inquiring into the laws of Pesach thirty days prior to Pesach [i.e. on Purim], in order to familiarize himself with its laws. Now, once people have celebrated Purim and have thus begun discussing the laws of Pesach, they have it in their minds that Pesach will occur in thirty days. The court cannot then proclaim a leap year (pushing up Pesach by a month), for the distant communities, which have no direct knowledge of the court's actions but must rely on messengers of the court to apprise them of the court's decisions, will not believe the messengers. Rather, they will observe Pesach a month early and eat *chametz* on the real festival of Pesach a month later (*Rashi*).

34. I.e. if a leap year is proclaimed after Purim, and the High Court rules in accordance with the testimony of R' Yehoshua and R' Pappayis that it is valid even at this late date, whereas the rebellious sage disputes them and rules that the year is *not* a leap year, he is permitting the consumption of *chametz* on the real Pesach one month after his own. And the consumption of *chametz* on Pesach is a sin for which one is liable to *kares* or a *chatas* (*Rashi*).

35. I.e. if the High Court decides that the late proclamation is *not* valid (unlike the testimony of R' Yehoshua and R' Pappayis), whereas the rebellious sage rules that it is valid and thus pushes Pesach off for a month, he is permitting the consumption of *chametz* on the true Pesach [which is the earlier one, as set by the High Court] (see *Rashi*; cf. *Tosafos*; see *Binyan Shlomo, Toras Chaim* and *Aruch LaNer*).

גמ' **במופלא** שבב"ד. במומחה לב"ד למעוטי תלמיד: **ממך** זה יועץ. שנחלק בעיבור השנה הקרוי סוד ועלה כדמפרש לקמן: **וכן הוא אומר.** דגבי יועץ כתוב ממך: **זו הלכה** למשה מסיני. שאף עליה הוא נהרג: **למשפט** זה הדין. אם נחלק בדבר הלמד בדין ג"ש גם הוא נהרג דאילו דין ממש כתיב להדיא בין דין לדין: **בין דם** נדה דם לידה כו'. שנחלקו בדם נדה או בדם לידה או בדם זיבה: **ובין** נגע לנגע. שנחלקו בנגעי אדם או בנגעי בגדים: **דברי ריבות.** ה"ל למכתב דבר ריב וכתיב דברי ריבות לרבות חרמין וערכין והקדשות שהן באין וחלים ע"י דיבור הפה: **זו השקאת סוטה.** שהיא על ידי ריב שבינה ובין בעלה: **ועריפת העגלה.** שהחלל נהרג ע"י מריבה: **וטהרת מצורע.** שאף נגעים ע"י ריב של לשון הרע הם באים: **זה לקט שכחה ופאה.** שהן לעניים שכתוב בהן ואכלו בשעריך: **וקמת מבית דין.** מדכתיב וקמת מכלל דיושבין עסקינן והיינו ב"ד שיושבין במקום הקבוע להם עד עת האוכל ושם באין כל הצריכין לדין ולהוראה בכל עיר ועיר ואזהר רחמנא לב"ד של אותה העיר שהמחלוקת ביניהם לילך ולישאל: **מלמד שבית המקדש גבוה** מא"י. וקמת ועלית אל המקום ש"מ אין לך עיר בא"י שאין ירושלים גבוה ממנה: **וא"י גבוה מכל הארצות.** הנא דברייתא קא מסיק למלתיה ולאו מהאי קרא יליף ולקמן מפרש מנלן: **אשר העלה וגו' מכל הארצות אשר הדחתים שם וישבו על אדמתם.** ש"מ דאדמתם גבוה מכל הארצות דכתיב העלה: **מה להלן דבר שחייבים כו'.** כדילפינן בהוריות: **תרגמא לי.** להאי מתניתא דלעיל דקתני דמיקטיל אכל הני דחשיב בה הלכה וגזירה שוה וערכים והקדשות וכולהו הנך דתנא בה דתיתוקם כר"מ דאמר אין חייב אלא על דבר שזדונו כרת וכו': **כדתנן הם העידו.** כלומר אי אפלוגתא דהנך תנאי פליגי זקן ממרא ורבנן: **הם העידו.** ר' יהושע ור' פפיים במס' עדיות: **שמעברין את השנה כל אדר.** ואע"פ שלא נמלכו לעבר קודם הפורים וקראו את המגילה באדר הראשון ואחר כך ראו שהשנה צריכה להתעבר ועברוה: **שהיו אומרים כו'.** לפיכך הוצרכו להעיד כן שהיו שאר חכמים אומרים עד הפורים מעברין ושוב אין מעברין וטעמא מפרש במס' ר"ה דמן הפורים התחילו לדרוש בהלכות הפסח דתניא שואלים בהלכות הפסח קודם לפסח ל' יום וכי מרחק להו לא לייתי לשלוחי ב"ד שכבר שמעו מן הדרשנים לעשות הפסח בסוף ל' ואתי לזלזולי בחמץ: **דאי להאי גיסא.** אם אמרו ב"ד שבלשכת הגזית שמעברים אחר הפורים מעוברת כר' יהושע ור' פפיים והוא אמר אינה מעוברת קא שרי חמץ בפסח: **ואי איפכא.** נמי שרי חמץ בפסח דזדונו כרת: **הלכות אחד עשר.** יום אחרון של י"א שבין נדה לנדה קיימא לן י"א יום שבין נדה לנדה הלכה למשה מסיני משעברו ז' ימי הנדה אינה חוזרת להיות נדה עד שיעברו י"א יום דכל דמים שרואה בהם דם זיבה הם ואם ראתה בהם יום או יומים רצופים שומרת יום ג' ואם פסקה ולא ראתה בו טובלת בו ביום וטהורה ואם ראתה ג' ימים רצופים הויא זיבה לקרבן ולטבילת מים חיים ואפליגו רבי יוחנן ורשב"ל בהלכות יום האחרון: רבי יוחנן אמר הלכה אחת נאמרה בו ר"ל אמר שתי הלכות נאמרו בו ליחלק משלפניו והך פלוגתא בשילהי מסכת נדה ואתמר בתרתי לישני וחד מינייהו נקט הכא: **עשירי רבי יוחנן אמר** הרי הוא כתשיעי. מה הרואה בתשיעי צריכה להיות שומרת עשירי שהרי ראויה בצירוף ג' לזיבה ושמא תראה בעשירי הרי שנים ותחזור ותראה באחד עשר הרי ג' אף הרואה בעשירי צריכה להיות שומרת אחד עשר ואע"פ שעשירי אינו ראוי לצירוף ג' שאין שנים עשר מצטרף עמהם לזיבה דהיכא דלא ראתה ג' רצופין להיות זבה בהנך י"א יום הוי יום שנים עשר תחלת נדה והיינו דקאמר רבי יוחנן התם הלכתא י"א הלכה אחת נאמרה בו ליחלק משלפניו ומאי איהו דלא בעי שימור להיות שומרת שנים עשר נגדו דהא לאו מימי זיבה הוא אבל שוה לשלפניו להיות שימור לראיית עשירי כשם שהעשירי שימור לראיית תשיעי: **ור"ל אמר עשירי כאחד עשר.** מה אחד עשר לא בעי שימור שנים עשר שהרי אין השנים עשר מימי הזיבה אף עשירי לא בעי שימור להיות שומרת י"א דלא נאמרה שומרת יום נגד יום אלא בראויה לצירוף ג' הלכך לר"ל שתי הלכות נאמרו ביום אחד עשר ליחלק משאר ימים שלפניו אחת שאינו צריך שימור ואחת שאין נעשה שימור לראיית עשירי ואי איפלוג זקן ממרא ורבנן בהלכות אחד עשר כדאיפליגו ר"ל ורבי יוחנן הוי דבר שזדונו כרת על שומרת יום כנגד יום חייב כרת כדכתיב (ויקרא טו) כל ימי זוב טומאתה וגו' ודרשינן ימי וכל ימי:

במופלא שבב"ד. מומחה למעוטי תלמיד ואין זה כשאר מופלא דבכל דוכתין כדפרישית שלהי פרק קמא (דף טז:):

שבית המקדש גבוה. לאו מכל א"י דאיכא עין עיטם דמידלי מיניה כדאמר באיזהו מקומן (זבחים דף נד:) סבור למבנייה בעין עיטם דמידלי אי נמי כותלי בהמ"ק גבוה מעין עיטם שגובהן ק' אמה: **מלמד** שהמקום גורם. לאפוקי מלאן בבית פאגי והמרה עליהם כדאמרינן לעיל בפרק קמא (שם יד:): **דאי** להאי גיסא קא שרי חמץ בפסח. תימה הא מ"ד עד הפורים מודה דאם עברוה אחר הפורים מעוברת דדוקא בניסן הוא דאמר בפרק קמא (דף יב: ושם) זה ניסן ואין אחר ניסן אבל מאן דאמר עד הפורים מדרבנן בעלמא הוא דאסור כדמפרש בפרק קמא דר"ה (דף ז. ושם) מ"ט דמ"ד עד הפורים כיון דאמר מר שואלין בהלכות הפסח קודם הפסח ל' יום אתי לזלזולי בחמץ וכיון דאם עברוה כ"ע מודו דמעוברת לא קא שרי חמץ בפסח:

ורשב"ל אומר עשירי כאחד עשר. וא"ת ולרשב"ל אי אמר זקן ממרא כרבי יוחנן אמאי מיחייב הרי מחמיר הוא ואין כאן דבר שזדונו כרת וי"ל דמשכחת לה אי נגעה בככר של תרומה וקידש בו את האשה דאי טמא הוא אין בו שוה פרוטה דלא חזי אלא להסקה ואינה מקודשת ואי טהור הוא יש בו שוה פרוטה דחזי לאכילה ומקודשת:

גמ' [א] במופלא שבב"ד הכתוב מדבר ממך זה יועץ וכן הוא אומר (א) ממך יצא חושב על ה' רעה יועץ בליעל דבר זו הלכה למשפט זה הדין בין דם לדם בין דם נדה דם לידה דם זיבה בין דין לדין בין דיני נפשות דיני ממונות דיני מכות בין נגע לנגע בין נגעי אדם נגעי בתים נגעי בגדים דברי אלו החרמים והערכין וההקדשות ריבות זו השקאת סוטה ועריפת עגלה וטהרת מצורע בשעריך זו לקט שכחה ופאה וקמת מב"ד ועלית (א) מלמד שבית המקדש גבוה מא"י וא"י גבוה מכל הארצות אל המקום (ב) ב מלמד שהמקום גורם בשלמא בית המקדש גבוה מא"י דכתיב ועלית אלא א"י גבוה מכל הארצות מנא ליה דכתיב (ב) לכן הנה ימים באים נאם ה' (ג) לא יאמר) חי ה' אשר העלה את בני ישראל מארץ מצרים כי אם חי ה' אשר העלה ואשר הביא את זרע בית ישראל מארץ צפונה ומכל הארצות אשר הדחתים שם וישבו על אדמתם תנו רבנן ג זקן ממרא אינו חייב אלא על דבר שזדונו כרת ושגגתו חטאת דברי ר"מ רבי יהודה אומר על דבר שעיקרו מדברי תורה ופירושו מדברי סופרים ר"ש אומר אפילו דקדוק אחד מדקדוקי סופרים מאי טעמא דר"מ (ד) גמר דבר דבר כתיב הכא (ג) כי יפלא ממך דבר למשפט וכתיב התם (ד) ונעלם דבר מעיני הקהל מה להלן דבר שחייב על זדונו כרת ועל שגגתו חטאת אף כאן דבר שחייב על זדונו כרת ועל שגגתו חטאת ור' יהודה (ה) על פי התורה אשר יורוך עד דאיכא תורה ויורוך ור"ש (ו) אשר יגידו לך מן המקום ההוא אפילו כל דהו א"ל רב הונא בר חיננא לרבא תרגמא לי להא מתניתא אליבא דר"מ א"ל רבא לרב פפא פוק תרגמא ליה (ג) כי יפלא במופלא שבב"ד הכתוב מדבר ממך זה יועץ (ה) שיודע לעבר שנים ולקבוע חדשים (ו) כדתנן ד הן העידו שמעברים את השנה כל אדר שהיו אומרים עד הפורים דאי להאי גיסא קא שרי חמץ בפסח ואי להאי גיסא קא שרי חמץ בפסח דבר זה הלכה זו הלכות אחד עשר דאיתמר (ז) עשירי ר' יוחנן אמר עשירי כתשיעי ור"ש בן לקיש אמר עשירי כאחד עשר רבי יוחנן אמר עשירי כתשיעי מה תשיעי בעי שימור ה אף עשירי בעי שימור ר"ל אמר עשירי כאחד עשר מה אחד עשר לא בעי שימור אף עשירי לא בעי שימור משפט זה הדין [א] דין

דרב

ורשב"ל (continued) — דין

מסורת הש"ס

א) [קידושין סו.] זבחים נד:, ב) [לעיל יד: ע"ש], ג) [נ"ל ולא יאמרו עוד], ד) הוריות ד., ה) [חגיגה יז.], ו) ר"ה ז. עדיות פ"ז מ"ז, ז) נדה עב ע"ב.

עין משפט נר מצוה

לח א מיי' פ"ג מהלכות ממרים הלכה ה:
לט ב מיי' שם הלכה ה:
מ ג מיי' שם הלכה ה ופ"ד הלכה א והלכה ב ועיי' שם הלכה:
מא ד מיי' פ"ד מהל' קידוש החדש הלכה יג:
מב ה מיי' פ"ה מהל' מטמאי משכב ומושב הלכה ח טור י"ד סי' קפג:

הגהות הגר"א

[א] גמ' זה הדין דין. נמחק דין שני:

תורה אור השלם

א) מִמֵּךְ יָצָא חֹשֵׁב עַל יְיָ רָעָה יֹעֵץ בְּלִיָּעַל: [נחום א, יא]

ב) לָכֵן הִנֵּה יָמִים בָּאִים נְאֻם יְיָ וְלֹא יֹאמְרוּ עוֹד חַי יְיָ אֲשֶׁר הֶעֱלָה אֶת בְּנֵי יִשְׂרָאֵל מֵאֶרֶץ מִצְרָיִם: כִּי אִם חַי יְיָ אֲשֶׁר הֶעֱלָה וַאֲשֶׁר הֵבִיא אֶת זֶרַע בֵּית יִשְׂרָאֵל מֵאֶרֶץ צָפוֹנָה וּמִכֹּל הָאֲרָצוֹת אֲשֶׁר הִדַּחְתִּים שָׁם וְיָשְׁבוּ עַל אַדְמָתָם: [ירמיה כג, ז-ח]

ג) כִּי יִפָּלֵא מִמְּךָ דָבָר לַמִּשְׁפָּט בֵּין דָּם לְדָם בֵּין דִּין לְדִין וּבֵין נֶגַע לָנֶגַע דִּבְרֵי רִיבֹת בִּשְׁעָרֶיךָ וְקַמְתָּ וְעָלִיתָ אֶל הַמָּקוֹם אֲשֶׁר יִבְחַר יְיָ אֱלֹהֶיךָ בּוֹ: [דברים יז, ח]

ד) וְאִם כָּל עֲדַת יִשְׂרָאֵל יִשְׁגּוּ וְנֶעְלַם דָּבָר מֵעֵינֵי הַקָּהָל וְעָשׂוּ אַחַת מִכָּל מִצְוֹת יְיָ אֲשֶׁר לֹא תֵעָשֶׂינָה וְאָשֵׁמוּ: [ויקרא ד, יג]

ה) עַל פִּי הַתּוֹרָה אֲשֶׁר יוֹרוּךָ וְעַל הַמִּשְׁפָּט אֲשֶׁר יֹאמְרוּ לְךָ תַּעֲשֶׂה לֹא תָסוּר מִן הַדָּבָר אֲשֶׁר יַגִּידוּ לְךָ יָמִין וּשְׂמֹאל: [דברים יז, יא]

ו) וְעָשִׂיתָ עַל פִּי הַדָּבָר אֲשֶׁר יַגִּידוּ לְךָ מִן הַמָּקוֹם הַהוּא אֲשֶׁר יִבְחַר יְיָ וְשָׁמַרְתָּ לַעֲשׂוֹת כְּכֹל אֲשֶׁר יוֹרוּךָ: [דברים יז, י]

ליקוטי רש"י

יועץ. יודע לעבר שנים ולקבוע חדשים [ישעיהו ג, ג]. בין דם לדם. בין דם טמא לדם טהור. בין דין לדין. בין דין זכאי לדין חייב. בין נגע לנגע. בין נגע טמא לנגע טהור. דברי ריבות. שיהו חכמי העיר חולקים בדבר זה מטמא וזה מטהר זה מחייב וזה מזכה. וקמת ועלית. מלמד שבית המקדש גבוה מכל המקומות [דברים יז, ח]. בית המקדש גבוה. דברי ריבות בשעריך וקמת ועלית וגו', מכאן שהמקדש גבוה מכל ארץ ישראל דכל לעלייה סתם וכתב ועלית [קידושין סו:]. ועלית. שבשעריך קרי עליה ומשם לבית המקדש מלמד שבית המקדש היה גבוה מכל ארץ ישראל [זבחים נד:]. ארץ ישראל גבוה. לא מינעילה גן הכא ולאו מהכא נפקא לן אלא מקרא אחרינא דכתיב (ירמיהו כג וכו) לא יאמר עוד חי ה' כי אם חי ה' אשר העלה ואשר הביא את בני ישראל מארץ צפון ומכל הארצות אשר הדחתים שם וגו' [זבחים נד:]. ועלו אל אחי. ארץ ישראל גבוה מכל הארצות [בראשית מה, ט]. הנה שמעוני באפרתה, וכו' ד"א שמענו באפרתה בספר יהושע (ע"ו) שבא מאפרים בכל התחומין הוא אומר (יהושע ע"ו) ועלה הגבול ואתר הגבול וכלכן הוא אומר ועלה הגבול אל כתף היבוסי ירושלים נמצאת ירושלים גבוה מכל הארצות והוא ראוי לבית המקדש שנאמר (דברים יז) וקמת ועלית אל המקום וגו' מלמד שבית המקדש גבוה מכל ארץ ישראל כך נדרש בשמועות קדשים [תהלים קלב, ו]. לכן הנה ימים באים וגו' לא יאמר עוד חי ה' אשר העלה את בני ישראל מארץ מצרים, כי אם חי ה' אשר העלה ואשר הביא את זרע בית ישראל מארץ לפון ומכל הארצות אשר הדחתים שם וכתיב בהם אשר העלה [קידושין סו.]. שהמקום. שהמיוחד למשפט והוא לשכת הגזית [סוטה מה.]. המקום גורם שאם חייב המקום אם הוא מוצא מורידין אותו לשם ולא ימרה [עיין ספרי]. שנקראו מופלא ממך דבר דמעכב נפשות דאי כי יפלא ממך דבר במשפטים ושוטרים שבזקן ממרא [עיין ח.]. דקדוקי סופרים. שסופרים להקדק אחר מעשה הברייתא ולהחמיר ולעשות סייג ואזנים לתורה וגזרו גזרות להרחיק את האדם מן העבירה ודכותה בבכורות (ל:) גר הבא לקבל תורה עליו חוץ מדבר אחד אין מקבלין אותו ר' יוסי אומר אפילו דקדוק אחד מדקדוקי סופרים [סוכה כח.]. שדקדקו האחרונים מלשון משנת הראשונים [מגילה יט:]. כגון גזירות שגזרו חכמים שלא יבא לידי איסור תורה [ב"ב קלד.]. ונעלם דבר. טעו להורות באחת מכל כריתות שבתורה שהוא מותר [ויקרא ד, יג]. הם העידו. ... כל אדר, אם ראו בית דין לאחר הפורים שהשנה צריכה להתעבר מעברין אותה. שהיו אומרים עד הפורים. לפי שהיו חכמים אומרים שאין מעברין אלא אם כן נתישבו בדבר לפני הפורים, לכך הוזקקו לעדות ... בחמץ שכבר מן הפורים ואילך התחילו הדרשנים לדרוש ברבים בהלכות הפסח הוזקקו השומעים לעשות פסח לסוף שלשים יום ואם יעברו בית דין את השנה לא יתקבלו דברי שלוחי בית דין לשומעין לדחות את ה... הלכות אחד עשר. שזה דין נדה דאורייתא ראתה היום מונה ששה והוא ראתה שנים מונה חמשה והן ואפילו ראתה כל שבעה ופסקה לערב טובלת ומשמשת ומיום שביעי ואילך הוין ימי זיבה אחד עשר יום שאם ... כנגד יום וטובלת ואם ראתה בהן ג' רצופין הויא זבה גמורה וטעונה ספירה ז' נקיים וקרבן ואם משכו ימי זובה חדש או שנה אינה חוזרת לתחילת נדות עד שתשב שבעה נקיים ישבה ז' נקיים וראתה הויא תח... בכלל המפורש ואם לא ראתה באותן י"א יום ג' רצופין אינה זבה וכשתראה אחרי כן בין שהרחיקה ראייתה הויא תחילת נדה ואפילו תראה שלשה רצופין אינה מונה אלא ארבעה והן שאין ימי זו... תחלת נדה הבאה וכן מפורש בהלכה אחרונה של מסכת נדה (דף עב) [ערכין ח.]. אחד עשר. לאחר שכלה שבעה ימי נדה נכנסין אחד עשר יום הקרויין ימי זיבה שאם תראה בהן שלשה ימים רצופין הרי היא זבה וטעונה ... שומרת יום למחרת וטובלת ומקראי יליף לה בתורת כהנים [מגילה כ.]. אחד עשר יום יש בין סוף נדה לתחלת נדה שכל שלשה רצופין שתראה באחד עשר יום הללו תהא זבה [ויקרא טו, כה]. עשירי. אין לו צרוף לזיבה ... כתשיעי. דפשיטא לן ביה דבעי שימור אם ראתה בו דהא ראוי להביאה לידי זבה גמורה. בעי שימור. י"א כנגדו אע"ג דאינה ראויה לבא לידי זבה גמורה. כר"א. לב"ה דאמרי לא בעי...

eleventh day of the *zivah* cycle.[36] דְּאִיתְּמַר – **For** a dispute of Amoraim **was stated:** עֲשִׂירִי – Concerning **the tenth** day of the *zivah* cycle,[37] רַבִּי יוֹחָנָן אָמַר עֲשִׂירִי כִּתְשִׁיעִי – **R' Yochanan says: The tenth** day **is like the ninth** day. וְרַבִּי שִׁמְעוֹן בֶּן לָקִישׁ אָמַר עֲשִׂירִי כְּאַחַד עָשָׂר – **Whereas R' Shimon ben Lakish says: The tenth** day **is like the eleventh** day.

These opinions are now explained:

רַבִּי יוֹחָנָן אָמַר עֲשִׂירִי כִּתְשִׁיעִי – **R' Yochanan says** that **the tenth** day **is like the ninth** day, meaning that מָה תְּשִׁיעִי בָּעֵי שִׁימּוּר – **just as the ninth** day **requires** the tenth day as a day of **observation,**[38] אַף עֲשִׂירִי בָּעֵי שִׁימּוּר – **so too, the tenth** day **requires** the eleventh day as a day of **observation.**[39]

רֵישׁ לָקִישׁ אָמַר עֲשִׂירִי כְּאַחַד עָשָׂר – **Reish Lakish,** however, **says** that **the tenth** day **is like the eleventh** day, meaning that מָה אַחַד עָשָׂר לֹא בָּעֵי שִׁימּוּר – **just as the eleventh** day **does not require** the twelfth day as a day of **observation,**[40] אַף עֲשִׂירִי לֹא בָּעֵי שִׁימּוּר – **so too, the tenth** day **does not require** the eleventh day as a day of **observation.**[41] This, then, is the *Halachah LeMoshe MiSinai* referred to by the Baraisa, for this question involves a matter of *kares* and *chatas.*[42]

Rav Pappa continues:

,,מִשְׁפָּט'' זֶה הַדִּין – *OF JUDGMENT*; **THIS** alludes to **THE INFERENCE** of *gezeirah shavah.* To which *gezeirah shavah* does this refer?

NOTES

36. As mentioned in note 6, following the seven-day *niddah* period, a woman enters her time of זִיבָה, *zivah,* the period of unusual flow. For the next eleven days (for now, though, we will limit the discussion to the first nine days; the law for the last two days will be discussed below), should she experience a flow of blood at any time, she becomes *tamei* (and forbidden to her husband) according to the following rules: If she experiences a discharge on only one day – or even on two consecutive days – she is *tamei* for the entire day of the discharge, and she must observe the next day as a "clean day" (i.e. one day entirely free of blood). She may immerse herself any time after daybreak of that clean day, and if she experiences no further discharges that day, she is *tahor* that evening. A woman in these circumstances is known as a זָבָה קְטַנָּה, *minor zavah,* and also as a שׁוֹמֶרֶת יוֹם כְּנֶגֶד יוֹם, *a woman who observes a day* [free of discharge] *against the day* [or two days on which she experienced a discharge of blood]. If, however, she experiences a flow of blood on three consecutive days during the eleven days of *zivah,* she becomes a זָבָה גְּדוֹלָה, *a major zavah,* and she must count seven clean days before she may immerse herself. She is then permitted to her husband on the night after the seventh clean day, but she must bring a bird offering on the next day (the eighth day) to complete her *taharah* in regard to sanctified things (see *Leviticus* 15:29). [*Rashi* here mentions that the *major zavah* must immerse herself specifically in spring water (a requirement that the Torah states in regard to a male *zav*). However, this view, though mentioned in the Geonim, is one that *Rashi* himself emphatically rejects in *Shabbos* 65b (see *Rashash* and various sources cited in *Margaliyos HaYam*). Rather, unlike her male counterpart, the *major zavah* can fulfill her immersion requirement in an ordinary *mikveh.*]

If the woman has not become a *major zavah* during these eleven days, her next discharge of blood will start her *niddah*-cycle anew. If she does become a *major zavah,* her *niddah*-cycle resumes the first time she experiences a flow after her seven clean days (see *Rashi*).

[The above details the Biblical law in these matters. However, already in Talmudic times, it became the practice to treat every *niddah* as a *major zavah,* so that no *niddah* can become *tahor* until she counts seven clean days. This is the practice that is followed today. The Gemara here, however, refers to the Biblical law.]

Now, all agree that there is a *Halachah LeMoshe MiSinai* which teaches that a discharge of blood on the eleventh day does not require observing the next day as a clean day, since that next day is after the conclusion of the eleven-day *zivah*-period. Rather, if the woman discharges blood on the eleventh day (or even on the tenth *and* eleventh) and the blood stops before the end of the eleventh day, she may immerse in a *mikveh* after nightfall and is permitted to her husband (see, however, *Tur Yoreh Deah* §183, and *Beis Yosef* ד״ה ואם and ד״ה וביום, with commentaries there). Any subsequent discharge of blood will begin her *niddah*-period anew. [Of course, if she discharged blood on the ninth, tenth and eleventh, then she is a *major zavah* and must count seven clean days.] The Gemara, however, now cites a dispute whether the *Halachah LeMoshe MiSinai* concerning the eleventh day distinguishes this day from the others in yet another respect (see *Rashi*).

37. [Though the Gemara cites the dispute in terms of the tenth day, it is the question about the *Halachah LeMoshe MiSinai* stated regarding the eleventh day that is at the root of the dispute, as will be explained below.]

38. I.e. if a woman experiences a discharge of blood on the ninth day, she certainly must observe the next day as a "clean day," just as if she had experienced the discharge on any of the previous days of the *zivah*-period. For the discharge she experiences on the ninth day can combine with a second discharge on day ten and a third on day eleven to render her a *major zavah*; thus, the discharge of day nine has the same potential as a discharge of any previous day of the cycle (*Rashi*).

39. I.e. although an initial discharge of blood on day ten cannot lead to the woman becoming a *major zavah* (which requires three consecutive days of discharge, and day twelve is already after the *zivah*-period), it nevertheless requires the observation of the next day (day eleven) as a clean day; that is, she is not permitted to her husband until the night after day eleven.

40. I.e. if the woman experiences her first or second discharge on day eleven, she need not observe the next day as a clean day, but is permitted to her husband that night (see end of note 36).

41. Rather, a woman who experiences her initial discharge of blood on day ten need wait only until that night (if the flow has stopped) to immerse herself and be permitted to her husband.

According to Reish Lakish, this special feature of day ten derives from a second *Halachah LeMoshe MiSinai* said in regard to day eleven: That is, not only does the *Halachah LeMoshe MiSinai* teach that day eleven is unique in that a discharge on that day does not require the observation of a clean day, but it also teaches that day eleven is unique in that it does not *serve* as a clean day for a discharge experienced on day ten. [This second *Halachah LeMoshe MiSinai* is another way of saying that a discharge on day ten does not require the observation of day eleven as a clean day.]

Thus, according to Reish Lakish, there were two *Halachos LeMoshe MiSinai* said concerning day eleven. According to R' Yochanan, however, there was only one *Halachah LeMoshe MiSinai* said concerning it: that a discharge on that day does not require the observation of day twelve as a clean day. But, in R' Yochanan's view, there is no second *Halachah LeMoshe MiSinai* preventing day eleven from serving as a clean day for day ten (*Rashi*).

42. For example, the dissenting sage ruled that a discharge on day ten does not require the observance of day eleven as a clean day (as Reish Lakish rules) and the High Court ruled that it does (as R' Yochanan rules). If the rebellious sage instructs the woman to immerse on the night after day ten and be permitted to her husband, he instructs her to do what is punishable by *kares* according to the High Court, since one who cohabits with a *minor zavah* that immerses before observing a clean day is liable to *kares* (see *Rashi* and *Aruch LaNer*; see also *Tosafos*).

א במופלא שבב"ד הכתוב מדבר ממך זה יועץ וכן הוא אומר (א) ממך יצא חושב על ה' רעה יועץ בליעל דבר זו הלכה למשפט זה הדין בין דם לדם בין דם נדה דם לידה דם זיבה בין דין לדין בין דיני נפשות דיני ממונות דיני מכות בין נגע לנגע בין נגעי אדם נגעי בתים נגעי בגדים דברי אלו החרמים והערכין וההקדשות ריבות זו השקאת סוטה ועריפת עגלה וטהרת מצורע בשעריך זו לקט שכחה ופאה וקמת מב"ד ועלית (א) מלמד שבית המקדש גבוה מא"י וא"י גבוה מכל הארצות אל המקום (ג) ב מלמד שהמקום גורם בשלמא בית המקדש גבוה מא"י דכתיב ועלית אלא א"י גבוה מכל הארצות מנא ליה דכתיב (ב) לכן הנה ימים באים נאם ה' (ג) לא יאמר) חי ה' אשר העלה את בני ישראל מארץ מצרים כי אם חי ה' אשר העלה ואשר הביא את זרע בית ישראל מארץ צפונה ומכל הארצות אשר הדחתים שם וישבו על אדמתם תנו רבנן ג זקן ממרא אינו חייב אלא על דבר שזדונו כרת ושגגתו חטאת דברי ר"מ רבי יהודה אומר על דבר שעיקרו מדברי תורה ופירושו מדברי סופרים ר"ש אומר אפילו דקדוק אחד מדקדוקי סופרים מאי טעמא דר"מ (ד) גמר דבר דבר כתיב הכא (ג) כי יפלא ממך דבר למשפט וכתיב התם (ד) ונעלם דבר מעיני הקהל מה להלן דבר שחייב על זדונו כרת ועל שגגתו חטאת אף כאן דבר שחייב על זדונו כרת ועל שגגתו חטאת ור' יהודה (ה) על פי התורה אשר יורוך עד דאיכא תורה ויורוך ור"ש (ו) אשר יגידו לך מן המקום ההוא אפילו כל דהו א"ל רב הונא בר חיננא לרבא תרגמא לי להא מתניתא אליבא דר"מ א"ל רבא לרב פפא פוק תרגמא ליה (ג) כי יפלא במופלא שבב"ד הכתוב מדבר ממך זה יועץ (ה) שיודע לעבר שנים ולקבוע חדשים (ו) כדתנן ד הן העידו שמעברים את השנה כל אדר שהיו אומרים עד הפורים דאי להאי גיסא קא שרי חמץ בפסח ואי להאי גיסא קא שרי חמץ בפסח דבר זה הלכה זו הלכות אחד עשר דאיתמר (ז) עשירי ר' יוחנן אמר עשירי כתשיעי ור"ש בן לקיש אמר עשירי כאחד עשר רבי יוחנן אמר עשירי כתשיעי מה תשיעי בעי שימור ה אף עשירי בעי שימור ר"ל אמר עשירי כאחד עשר מה אחד עשר לא בעי שימור אף עשירי לא בעי שימור משפט זה הדין [א]

דין

גמ' במופלא שבב"ד. במומחה לב"ד למעוטי תלמיד: **ממך זה יועץ.** שנחלק בעיבור השנה הקרוי סוד ועלה כדמפרש לקמן: **וכן הוא אומר.** דגבי יועץ כתוב ממך: **זו הלכה** למשה מסיני. שאף עליה הוא נהרג: **למשפט זה הדין.** אם נחלק בדבר הלמד בדין ג"ש גם הוא נהרג דאילו דין ממש כתיב להדיא בין דין לדין: **בין דם נדה דם לידה כו'.** שנחלקו בדם נדה או בדם לידה או בדם זיבה: **ובין נגע לנגע.** שנחלקו בנגעי אדם או בנגעי בגדים: **דברי ריבות.** ה"ל למכתב דבר ריב וכתיב דברי ריבות לרבות חרמין וערכין והקדשות שהן באין וחלים ע"י דיבור הפה: **זו השקאת סוטה.** שהיא על ידי ריב שבינה ובין בעלה: **ועריפת העגלה.** שהחלל נהרג ע"י מריבה: **וטהרת מצורע.** שאף נגעים ע"י ריב של לשון הרע הם באים: **זה לקט שכחה ופאה.** שהן לעניים שכתוב בהן ואכלו בשעריך: **וקמת מבית דין.** מדכתיב וקמת מכלל דיושבין עסקינן והיינו ב"ד שיושבין במקום הקבוע להם עד עת האוכל ושם באין כל הצריכין לדין ולהוראה בכל עיר ועיר ואזהר רחמנא לב"ד של אותה העיר שהמחלוקת ביניהם לילך ולישאל: **מלמד שבית המקדש גבוה מא"י.** וקמת ועלית אל המקום ש"מ אין לך עיר בא"י שאין ירושלים גבוה ממנה: **וא"י גבוה מכל הארצות.** תנא דברייתא קא מסיק למלתיה ולאו מהאי קרא יליף ולקמן מפרש מנלן: **אשר העלה וגו' מכל הארצות אשר הדחתים שם וישבו על אדמתם.** ש"מ דאדמתם גבוה מכל הארצות דכתיב העלה: **מה להלן דבר שחייבים כו'.** כדילפינן בהוריות: **תרגמא לי.** להאי מתניתא דלעיל דקתני דמיקטיל אכל הני דחשיב בה הלכה וגזירה שוה וערכים והקדשות וכולהו הנך דתנא בה דתיתוקם כר"מ דאמר אין חייב אלא על דבר שזדונו כרת וכו': **כדתנן הם העידו.** כלומר אי אפלוגתא דהנך תנאי פליגי זקן ממרא ורבנן: **הם העידו.** ר' יהושע ור' פפייס במס' עדיות: **שמעברין את השנה כל אדר.** ואע"פ שלא נמלכו לעבר קודם הפורים וקראו את המגילה באדר הראשון ואחר כך ראו שהשנה צריכה להתעבר ועברוה: **שהיו אומרים כו'.** לפיכך הוצרכו להעיד כן שהיו שאר חכמים אומרים עד הפורים מעברין ושוב אין מעברין וטעמא מפרש במס' ר"ה דמן הפורים התחילו לדרוש בהלכות הפסח דתניא שואלים בהלכות הפסח קודם לפסח ל' יום וכי מרחק להו לא לייתי לשלוחי ב"ד שכבר שמעו מן הדרשנים לעשות הפסח בסוף ל' ואתי לזלזולי בחמץ: **דאי להאי גיסא.** אם אמרו ב"ד שבלשכת הגזית שמעברים אחר הפורים מעוברת כר' יהושע ור' פפייס והוא אמר אינה מעוברת קא שרי חמץ בפסח: **ואי איפכא.** נמי שרי חמץ בפסח דזדונו כרת: **הלכות אחד עשר.** יום אחרון של י"א יום שבין נדה לנדה הלכה למשה מסיני משעברו ז' ימי הנדה אינה חוזרת להיות נדה עד שיעברו י"א יום דכל דמים שרואה בהם דם זיבה הם ואם ראתה בהם יום או יומים רצופים שומרת יום ג' ואם פסקה ולא ראתה בו טובלת בו ביום וטהורה ואם ראתה ג' ימים רצופים הויא זיבה לקרבן ולטבילת מים חיים ואפליגו רבי יוחנן ורשב"ל בהלכות יום האחרון: רבי יוחנן אמר הלכה אחת נאמרה בו ר"ל אמר שתי הלכות נאמרו בו ליחלק משלפניו והך פלוגתא בשילהי מסכת נדה ואתמר בתרתי לישני וחד מינייהו נקט הכא: **עשירי רבי יוחנן אמר הרי הוא כתשיעי.** מה הרואה בתשיעי צריכה להיות שומרת עשירי שהרי ראויה בצירוף ג' לזיבה ושמא תראה בעשירי הרי שנים ותחזור ותראה באחד עשר הרי ג' אף הרואה בעשירי צריכה להיות שומרת אחד עשר ואע"פ שעשירי אינו ראוי לצירוף ג' שאין שנים עשר מצטרף עמהם לזיבה דהיכא דלא ראתה ג' רצופין להיות זבה בהנך י"א יום הוי יום שנים עשר תחלת נדה והיינו דקאמר רבי יוחנן התם הלכתא י"א הלכה אחת נאמרה בו ליחלק משלפניו ומאי איהו דלא בעי שימור להיות שומרת שנים עשר נגדו דהא לאו מימי זיבה הוא אבל שוה לשלפניו להיות שימור לראיית עשירי כשם שהעשירי שימור לראיית תשיעי: **ור"ל אמר עשירי כאחד עשר.** מה אחד עשר לא בעי שימור שהרי אין השנים עשר מימי הזיבה אף עשירי לא בעי שימור להיות שומרת י"א דלא נאמרה שומרת יום נגד יום אלא בראויה לצירוף ג' הלכך לר"ל שתי הלכות נאמרו ביום אחד עשר ליחלק משאר ימים שלפניו אחת שאינו צריך שימור ואחת שאין נעשה שימור לראיית עשירי ואי איפלוג זקן ממרא ורבנן בהלכות אחד עשר כדאיפליגו ר"ל ורבי יוחנן הוי דבר שזדונו כרת על שומרת יום כנגד יום חייב כרת כדכתיב (ויקרא טו) כל ימי זוב טומאתה וגו' ודרשינן ימי וכל ימי:

דרב

במופלא שבב"ד. מומחה למעוטי תלמיד ואין זה כשאר מופלא דבכל דוכתין כדפרישית שלהי פרק קמא (דף טז:): **שבית** המקדש גבוה. לאו מכל א"י דאיכא עין עיטם דמידלי מיניה כדאמר באיזהו מקומן (זבחים דף נד:) סבור למבנייה בעין עיטם דמידלי אי נמי כותלי בהמ"ק גבוה מעין עיטם שגובהן ק' אמה: **מלמד** שהמקום גורם. לאפוקי מלאן בבית פאגי והמרה עליהם כדאמרינן לעיל בפרק קמא (שם יד:): **דאי** להאי גיסא קא שרי חמץ בפסח. תימה הא מ"ד עד הפורים מודה דאם עברוה אחר הפורים מעוברת דדוקא בניסן הוא דאמר בפרק קמא (דף יב: ושם) זה ניסן ואין אחר ניסן אבל מאן דאמר עד הפורים מדרבנן בעלמא הוא דאסור כדמפרש בפרק קמא דר"ה (דף ז. ושם) מ"ט דמ"ד עד הפורים כיון דאמר מר שואלין בהלכות הפסח קודם הפסח ל' יום אתי לזלזולי בחמץ וכיון דאם עברוה כ"ע מודו דמעוברת לא קא שרי חמץ בפסח: **ורשב"ל** אומר עשירי כאחד עשר. וא"ת ולרשב"ל אי אמר זקן ממרא כרבי יוחנן אמאי מיחייב הרי מחמיר הוא ואין כאן דבר שזדונו כרת וי"ל דמשכחת לה אי נגעה בככר של תרומה וקידש בו את האשה דאי טמא הוא אין בו שוה פרוטה דלא חזי אלא להסקה ואינה מקודשת ואי טהור הוא יש בו שוה פרוטה דחזי לאכילה ומקודשת:

דין

מסורת הש"ס

א) [קידושין סט.] זבחים נד:, ב) [לעיל יד: ע"ז ח:], ג) [צ"ל ולא יאמרו עוד], ד) הוריות ד., ה) [חגיגה יד.], ו) ר"ה ז. עדיות פ"ז מ"ז, ז) נדה עב ע"ב.

ליקוטי רש"י

יועץ. יודע לעבר שנים ולקבוע חדשים [ישעיהו ג, ג]. **בין דם לדם.** בין דם טמא לדם טהור. **בין דין לדין.** בין דין זכאי לדין חייב. **בין נגע לנגע.** בין נגע טמא לנגע טהור. **דברי ריבות.** שיהו חכמי העיר חולקים בדבר זה מטמא וזה מטהר זה מחייב וזה מזכה. **וקמת ועלית.** מלמד שבית המקדש גבוה מכל המקומות [דברים יז, ח]. **בית המקדש גבוה.** דברי ריבות בשעריך וקמת ועלית וגו', מכאן שהמקדש גבוה מכל ארץ ישראל דכל צדדיה סתם וכתב ועלית [קידושין סט:]. **ועלית,** בכל שעריך קרי עלייה ומשם לבית המקדש מלמד שבית המקדש היה גבוה מכל ארץ ישראל [זבחים נד:]. **ארץ ישראל גבוה.** לא מיבעיא לן הכא ולאו מהכא נפקא לן אלא מקרא אחרינא דכתיב (ירמיהו טז וכג) לא יאמר עוד חי וגו' כי אם חי ה' אשר העלה ואשר הביא את בני ישראל מארץ צפון ומכל המקומות אשר הדחתים שם וגו' [זבחים נד:]. **ועלו אל אבי.** ארץ ישראל גבוה מכל הארצות [בראשית מה, ט]. **הנה** שמעגוה באפרתה, וכו' ד"א שמעגוה באפרתה בספר יהושע (ט"ו) שבא מאפרים בכל התחומין הוא אומר (יהושע ט"ו) ועלה הגבול ותאר הגבול וכאן הוא אומר ועלה הגבול אל כתף היבוסי ירושלים נמצאת ירושלים גבוה מכל הארצות והוא ראוי לבית המקדש שנאמר (דברים יז) וקמת ועלית אל המקום וגו' מלמד שבית המקדש גבוה מכל ארץ ישראל כך נדרש בשחיטת קדשים [תהלים קלב, ו]. **לכן הנה ימים** באים נאם ה' לא יאמר עוד חי ה' אשר העלה את בני ישראל מארץ מצרים, כי אם חי ה' אשר העלה ואשר הביא את בני ישראל מארץ צפון דהיינו בבל ומכל הארצות אשר הדחתים שם וכתיב אשר העלה [קידושין סט:]. **שהמקום.** המיוחד למשפט והוא לשכת הגזית [סוטה מה.]. **המקום גורם** לחייב הנדון ואם אינם שם לא ידונו והאי קרא בדיני נפשות קאי כי יפלא ממך דבר בפרשת שופטים ושוטרים בזקן ממרא [ע"ז ח:]. **דקדוקי סופרים.** שהוסיפו לדקדק אחר מעשה הבריות ולהחמיר ולעשות סייג ואזנים לתורה וגזרו גזרות להרחיק את האדם מן העבירה ודכוותה בבכורות (ל:) גר הבא לקבל תורה עליו חוץ מדבר אחד אין מקבלין אותו ר' יוסי אומר אפילו דקדוק אחד מדקדוקי סופרים [סוכה כח.]. שדקדקו האחרונים מלשון משנת הראשונים [מגילה יט:]. כגון גזירות שגזרו חכמים שלא יבא לידי איסור תורה [ב"ב קלד.]. חומרא דרבנן [בכורות ל:]. **ונעלם דבר.** טעו להורות באחת מכל כריתות שבתורה שהוא מותר [ויקרא ד, יג]. **הם העידו.** רבי יהושע ורבי פפייס שמעברין את השנה כל אדר, אם ראו בית דין לאחר הפורים שהשנה צריכה להתעבר מעברין אותה. **שהיו אומרים עד הפורים.** לפי שהיו חכמים אומרים שאין מעברין אלא אם כן נתישבו בדבר לפני הפורים, לכך הוזקקו לעדות זו. **קא שרי חמץ בפסח.** אתי לזלזולי בחמץ שכבר מן הפורים ואילך התחילו הדרשנים לדרוש ברבים בהלכות הפסח הוזקקו השומעים לעשות פסח לסוף שלושים יום ואם יעברו בית דין את השנה לא יתקבלו דברי שלוחי בית דין לשומעין לדחות את הפסח שכבר שמעו מן הדרשנים [ר"ה ז.]. **הלכות אחד עשר.** שזה דין נדה דאורייתא ראתה היום מונה ששה והוא ראתה שנים מונה חמשה והן ואפילו ראתה כל שבעה ופסקה לערב טובלת ומשמשת ומיום שביעי ואילך הויין ימי זיבה אחד עשר יום שאם ראתה בהן יום אחד או שנים שומרת יום כנגד יום וטובלת ואם ראתה בהן ג' רצופין הויא זבה גמורה וטעונה ספירה ז' נקיים וקרבן ואם משכו ימי זובה חדש או שנה אינה חוזרת לתחילת נדות עד שתשב שבעה נקיים ישבה ז' נקיים וראתה הויא תחילת נדה ומונה ששה והוא חוזרת לעניינה ככל המפורש ואם לא ראתה באותן י"א יום ג' רצופין אינה זבה וכשתראה אחרי כן בין ראתה סמוך בין שהרחיקה ראייתה הויא תחילת נדה ואפילו תראה שלשה רצופין אינה מונה אלא ארבעה והן שאין ימי זוב אלא באותן י"א יום שבין סוף נדה זה לתחלת נדה הבאה וכן מפורש בהלכה אחרונה של מסכת נדה (דף עב) [ערכין ח.]. **אחד עשר.** לאחר שכלה שבעה ימי נדה נכנסין אחד עשר יום הקרויין ימי זיבה שאם תראה בהן שלשה ימים רצופין הרי היא זבה וטעונה ספירת שבעה וקרבן ואם תראה יום אחד שומרת יום למחרת וטובלת ומקראי יליף לה בתורת כהנים [מגילה כ.]. אחד עשר יום יש בין סוף נדה לתחלת נדה שכל שלשה רצופין שתראה באחד עשר יום הללו תהא זבה [ויקרא טו, כה]. **עשירי.** אין לו צרוף לזיבה שאין מצטרף עמו אלא י"א דהוי להו תרי. **כתשיעי.** דפשיטא לן ביה דבעי שימור אם ראתה בו דהא ראוי להביאה לידי זבה גמורה. **אף עשירי.** אם התחילה לראות בו. **בעי שימור.** י"א כנגדו אע"ג דאינה ראויה לבא לידי זבה גמורה. **כי"א.** לב"ה דאמרי לא בעי שימור [נדה עב:].

עין משפט נר מצוה

לח א מיי' פ"ג מהלכות ממרים הלכה ה:

לט ב מיי' שם הלכה ז:

מ ג מיי' שם הלכה ה ופ"ד הלכה א והלכה ב ועיי' שם הכל:

מא ד מיי' פ"ד מהל' קידוש החדש הלכה יג יד:

מב ה מיי' פ"ה מהל' מטמאי משכב ומושב הלכה ח טור י"ד סי' קפג:

הגהות הגר"א

[א] גמ' זה הדין דין. נמחק דין שני:

תורה אור השלם

א) מִמֵּךְ יָצָא חֹשֵׁב עַל יְיָ רָעָה יֹעֵץ בְּלִיָּעַל: [נחום א, יא]

ב) לָכֵן הִנֵּה יָמִים בָּאִים נְאֻם יְיָ וְלֹא יֹאמְרוּ עוֹד חַי יְיָ אֲשֶׁר הֶעֱלָה אֶת בְּנֵי יִשְׂרָאֵל מֵאֶרֶץ מִצְרָיִם: כִּי אִם חַי יְיָ אֲשֶׁר הֶעֱלָה וַאֲשֶׁר הֵבִיא אֶת זֶרַע בֵּית יִשְׂרָאֵל מֵאֶרֶץ צָפוֹנָה וּמִכֹּל הָאֲרָצוֹת אֲשֶׁר הִדַּחְתִּים שָׁם וְיָשְׁבוּ עַל אַדְמָתָם: [ירמיה כג, ז-ח]

ג) כִּי יִפָּלֵא מִמְּךָ דָבָר לַמִּשְׁפָּט בֵּין דָּם לְדָם בֵּין דִּין לְדִין וּבֵין נֶגַע לָנֶגַע דִּבְרֵי רִיבֹת בִּשְׁעָרֶיךָ וְקַמְתָּ וְעָלִיתָ אֶל הַמָּקוֹם אֲשֶׁר יִבְחַר יְיָ אֱלֹהֶיךָ בּוֹ: [דברים יז, ח]

ד) וְאִם כָּל עֲדַת יִשְׂרָאֵל יִשְׁגּוּ וְנֶעְלַם דָּבָר מֵעֵינֵי הַקָּהָל וְעָשׂוּ אַחַת מִכָּל מִצְוֹת יְיָ אֲשֶׁר לֹא תֵעָשֶׂינָה וְאָשֵׁמוּ: [ויקרא ד, יג]

ה) עַל פִּי הַתּוֹרָה אֲשֶׁר יוֹרוּךָ וְעַל הַמִּשְׁפָּט אֲשֶׁר יֹאמְרוּ לְךָ תַּעֲשֶׂה לֹא תָסוּר מִן הַדָּבָר אֲשֶׁר יַגִּידוּ לְךָ יָמִין וּשְׂמֹאל: [דברים יז, יא]

ו) וְעָשִׂיתָ עַל פִּי הַדָּבָר אֲשֶׁר יַגִּידוּ לְךָ מִן הַמָּקוֹם הַהוּא אֲשֶׁר יִבְחַר יְיָ וְשָׁמַרְתָּ לַעֲשׂוֹת כְּכֹל אֲשֶׁר יוֹרוּךָ: [דברים יז, י]

דין בתו מאנוסתו [א] דאמר רבא א"ל רב יצחק בר אבודימי אתיא [א] הנה [ב] הנה אתיא זימה [ג] זימה בין דם לדם בין דם נדה דם לידה דם זיבה דם נדה בפלוגתא עקביא בן מהללאל ורבנן דתנן [ג] דם הירוק עקביא בן מהללאל מטמא וחכמים [א] מטהרין דם לידה בפלוגתא דרב ולוי דאתמר [ג] רב אמר [ב] מעין אחד הוא התורה טימאתו והתורה טיהרתו ולוי אמר שני מעיינות הן נסתם הטמא נפתח הטהור נסתם הטהור נפתח הטמא: דם זיבה בפלוגתא דר"א ורבי יהושע דתנן [ד] קישתה שלשה ימים בתוך אחד עשר יום אם שפתה מעת לעת וילדה [ג] הרי זו יולדת בזוב דברי ר"א ור' יהושע אומר לילה ויום כלילי שבת ויומו ששפתה מן הצער ולא מן הדם בין דין לדין בין דיני ממונות דיני נפשות דיני מכות דיני ממונות בפלוגתא דשמואל ורבי אבהו [ה] דאמר שמואל שנים שדנו דיניהם דין אלא שנקראין בית דין חצוף ורבי אבהו אמר [ו] לדברי הכל אין דיניהן דין דיני נפשות בפלוגתא דרבי ורבנן דתניא [ז] רבי אומר [ד] ונתת נפש תחת נפש ממון אתה אומר ממון או אינו אלא נפש ממש נאמר [ה] נתינה למעלה ונאמר נתינה למטה מה להלן ממון אף כאן ממון דיני מכות בפלוגתא דרבי ישמעאל ורבנן דתנן [ח] מכות בג' משום רבי ישמעאל אמרו בכ"ג בין נגע לנגע בין נגעי אדם נגעי בתים נגעי בגדים נגעי אדם בפלוגתא דרבי יהושע ורבנן [ט] דתנן [ד] אם בהרת קדם לשער הלבן טמא אם שער לבן קדם לבהרת טהור ספק [ה] טמא רבי יהושע אומר כהה מאי כהה אמר [י] רבא כהה טהור נגעי בתים בפלוגתא דרבי אלעזר ברבי שמעון ורבנן [כ] דתנן רבי אליעזר ברבי שמעון אומר לעולם אין הבית טמא עד שיראה כשני גריסין על שתי אבנים בשתי כתלים בקרן זוית ארכו כשני גריסין ורחבו כגרים מאי טעמא דר' אלעזר בר"ש כתיב [ו] קיר וכתיב [ו] קירות איזהו קיר שהוא כקירות הוי אומר זה קרן זוית נגעי בגדים בפלוגתא דר' ([ל] יונתן) בן אבטולמוס ורבנן [מ] דתניא ר' ([ל] יונתן) בן אבטולמוס אומר מנין לפריחה

רש"י

דרב יצחק בר אבודימי. באלו הן הנשרפין פרישית לה גבי בתו מאנוסתו דמהאי דינא ילפינן והוא דבר שזדונו כרת: הירוק עקביא בן מהללאל מטמא. דם הירוק הוי דם הנדה ואם אמר זקן ממרא כעקביא בן מהללאל מייתי לה לחיוב כרת שפעמים שרואה דם הירוק בתחלת נדותה ולבסוף ב' ימים רואה דם אדום ופוסקת והיא מתחלת למנות שבעה ימים מראיית דם ירוק וטובלת ומשמשת עם בעלה ב' ימים בנדותה לפי שדם הירוק טהור הוא והיה לה להתחיל למנות מראיית דם אדום: מעין אחד הוא. דם הבא בשבועיים של נקיבה שהוא טמא ודם הבא לאחר שבועיים שהוא טהור ממעין אחד הוא: התורה טימאתו. כל שבועיים: והתורה טיהרתו. לאחר שבועיים וחזרה וטימאתו לאחר שכלין ימי טוהר: ולוי אמר ב' מעיינות הן. נסתם הטמא לאחר שבועיים ונפתח הטהור וכשנסתם הטהור בסוף ימי טוהר נפתח הטמא ואמרי' במס' נדה מאי בינייהו בשופעת מתוך שבועיים לאחר שבועיים או מתוך שמונים לאחר שמונים לרב אע"פ שלא פסק מעיינה בתוך שבועיים ויצא דם לאחר שבועיים ממנה טהור וללוי טמא עד שתפסוק שעה דנימא נסתם הטמא והשופעת מתוך שמונים לאחר שמונים לרב טמאה ואע"פ שזהו מעין עצמו של ימי טוהר וללוי טהורה עד שיפסוק מעין הטהור ויפתח מעין הטמא ואי איפלוג זקן ממרא ורבנן בהא קאתי לידי כרת אי רבנן כרב והוא כלוי איכא כרת לאחר ימי טוהר ואי רבנן כלוי והוא כרב איכא כרת בתחלת ימי טוהר דרב לקולא ולוי לחומרא: קישתה ג' ימים בתוך אחד עשר יום כו'. כתיב בפרשת זבה באחד עשר יום שבין נדה לנדה שהם הימים המביאין לידי זיבה ואשה כי יזוב זוב דמה ימים רבים ותניא בפרק בנות כותים (נדה לו:) דמה מחמת עצמה ולא מחמת ולד מגיד שדם הקישוי שילא קודם הולד מחמת צער הקישוי אינו מביאה לידי זיבה וכ"ש דם שלאחר הולד אבל אם ראתה ג' ימים רצופין בהן מתוך קושי ושפתה קודם יציאת הולד יום אחד מעת לעת ששקטה ונחה מצערה ואח"כ ילדה בין מתוך קושי בין מתוך שופי הרי זו יולדת בזוב לפי שכיון שלאחר ג' שפתה איגלאי מילתא דלאו מחמת ולד אתא ונעשית בהן זבה למנות ז' נקיים כדין זבה וכל זמן שלא תספור ז' נקיים לא יהא דם שלה דם טוהר ואפילו לאחר שבועיים ואחר מלאת שמונים שלה צריכה שני קרבנות אחד ללידתה ואחד לזיבתה: לילה ויום. אבל מעת לעת לא חשיב שופי אם שפתה משש שעות של שלישי עד שש שעות של ד' הואיל וה"ל מקצת קושי ביום השופי לא הויא יולדת בזוב ור"א לחומרא ורבי יהושע לקולא והיינו דבר שזדונו כרת: ששפתה מן הצער. ואין אנו חוששין אם לא שפתה מן הדם: בפלוגתא דשמואל ור' אבהו. וכיון דאפיקי הני בי תרי ממונא מהאי ויהבו להאי בדינא דידהו והלך זה וקידש אשה באותו ממון לשמואל מקודשת לרבי אבהו אינה מקודשת דה"ל קידשה בגזל וקי"ל בפ"ב דקידושין (דף נב.) גבי מעשה דה' נשים שנתקדשו בכלכלה קידשה בגזל אינה מקודשת דהשתא אתי לידי כרת אי רבנן כשמואל וזקן ממרא כרבי אבהו וא"נ רבנן כרבי אבהו וזקן ממרא כשמואל אתי לידי כרת דקא משוי להו קידושין ואי אתי איניש אחרינא לבתר הכי וקדשה מפיק לה מבתרא בלא גט וה"ל דבר שזדונו כרת בלא עדים ובלא התראה דאי איכא עדים והתראה הוי מיתת ב"ד ואי ליכא לא זה ולא זה הוי כרת: ונתתה נפש תחת נפש. במתכוין להרוג את זה והרג את זה ומיחייב ליה רבי ממון ורבנן פטרי וכפלוגתא באלו הן הנשרפין [ס] ואי תפסו יורשין דהרוג ממונא דהורג ופטר ליה זקן ממרא וקידשו בו את האשה לרבי מקודשת לרבנן אינה מקודשת ואי אתי איניש אחרינא וקידשה מקודשת לשני הרי חיוב כרת בדבר: נתינה למעלה. גבי נוגף אשה הרה ונתן בפלילים (שמות כא) דמי ולדות: בכ"ג. ואם הלקוהו ג' לר' ישמעאל חייבין לו ממון כשאר חובל בחבירו ומקדש בו את האשה ולרבנן בדין הלקוהו ואם תפס ממונו וקידש בו אינה מקודשת: ספק. אם זה קדם אם זה קדם: כהה. כאילו כהה הנגע דהוי מסימני טהרה כשמשתנה הלובן לאחר הסגר ולרבנן אם נכנס למקדש חייב כרת ולר' יהושע פטור: עד שיראה כשני גריסין. שיעור הנגע כגרים על גרים וכתיב את האבנים אשר בהן הנגע שיהא הנגע על שתי אבנים על כל אחד ואחד שיעור נגע על ב' כתלים ובקרן זוית כגון מקלוע דרומית מזרחית אורכו כשני גריסין ורחבו כגרים שיהא בקיר הדרומי גרים וכן בקיר המזרחי והנגע כולו מחובר כאחד: מאי טעמא דר' אליעזר. דבעי קרן זוית: כתיב. ומראיהן שפל מן הקיר (ויקרא יד) וכתיב והנה הנגע בקירות הבית: זה קרן זוית. ורבנן לא בעו קרן זוית והיכא דליתיה בקרן זוית ונכנס בה אדם ואח"כ נכנס למקדש לרבנן חייב כרת לר' אלעזר בר"ש פטור:

תוספות

דין בתו מאנוסתו. בכולהו משכח פלוגתא בר מהאי ורוצה לומר דאין זקן ממרא מודה בגזירה שוה זו: עקביא בן מהללאל מטמא. ואף על גב דעקביא מחמיר זמנין דהויא קולא כגון שרואה דם אדום ומשלימתו לדם ירוק: כלילי שבת ויומו. לאפוקי יום תחלה ואח"כ לילה אלא אע"כ שפתה לילה שלם ואחר כך יום שלם כלילי שבת ויום שהיום הולך אחר הלילה: בפלוגתא דרבי יהושע ורבנן. פי' בקונטרס לרבנן אם נכנס למקדש חייב ולרבי יהושע פטור ולא יתכן דלכי האי גוונא לא מחייב זקן ממרא כיון שהוא בעולה ויורד דהא ילפינן לעיל דבר דבר מונעלם דבר דתנן בפ' [הורי'] כהן משוח (הוריות דף ט.) מביאין עולה ויורד על טומאת מקדש וקדשיו ויש לפרש כדפרישית לעיל [ע] בככר של תרומה: רבי יהושע אומר כיהה. פירש בקונטרס כאילו כיהה הנגע דהוא מסימני טהרה כשמשתנה בו לובן שלו לאחר הסגר וקשה היכי פריך בשילהי נזיר (דף סה:) ודילמא כיהה וטמא הא לפירושו כל כיהה טהור ועוד אי כיהה וטמא היינו ת"ק ונראה כגירסת ר"ח קהה בקו"ף ול"ג אומר כלומר ר' יהושע הקשה ודקדק בדבר כמו [פ] הקהה את שיניו וכן מקהו אקהייתא בשוקא (יבמות דף קי:) מאספים אסופות של בני אדם כלומר עמדו למניין ולא ידע הש"ס אם להביא ראיה לת"ק או לסתור ולהכי בעי מאי קיהה וקאמר קיהה וטיהר ומיהו בירושלמי דריש שבועות משמע דיש כיהה טמא דאמר התם והתורה אמרה והנה כהה הנגע הכהה טמא וכהה מן הכהה טהור:

מרחו

מג א מיי' פ"ה מהל' איסורי ביאה הלכה ו סמג לאוין קיא ועשין רמג טוש"ע י"ד סי' קפח סעיף א:
מד ב מיי' שם פ"ו הלכה א סמג שם:
מה ג מיי' שם פ"ו הלכה א סמג שם:
מו ד מיי' פ"ב מהלכות טומאת צרעת הלכה ו סמג עשין רלד:
מז ה מיי' שם הלכה ט:

ליקוטי רש"י

דין בתו מאנוסתו. דהיינו בתו ובת בנו ובת בתו מאנוסתו דלאו בכלל אשה ובתה דקרא נינהו דהתם באשתו על ידי קידושין קאמר דדרשינן לה ביבמות [צז.] מקראי דרבה רמי כתיב ערות בת בנך או בת בתך וגו' הא בת בנה ובת בתה שלא ילדה ממך גלה וכתיב ערות אשה ובתה לא תגלה משמע בין שילדתו לך בין שילדתו לאיש אחר לא קשיא כאן באנוסין כאן בנישואין אם אנוסתך או מפותה לך היא אי אתה מוזהר על בתה אלא אם כן ממך היא ואם אשתך היא אתה מוזהר אף על בת שילדה לאיש אחר. אתיא הנה הנה אתיא זמה זמה. מעיקרא מייתינן לה בהנה הנה והדר בזמה זמה כתיב הכא (ויקרא יח) כי ערותך הנה וכתיב בשאר אשתו (שם ויקרא יח) שארה הנה מה להלן זמה עמו אף כאן זמה עמו ובתר דאייתינן זמה לשאר דידיה ילפינן בה שריפה בזמה זמה נאמר כאן (שם ויקרא י"ח) זמה ונאמר להלן (שם כ) בשריפה זמה מה להלן שריפה אף כאן שריפה [לעיל עה:]. מעין אחד הוא. דם הבא בתוך ז' של לידה ודם הבא לאחר שבעה ממעין אחד הוא. התורה טמאתו. תוך שבעה לזכר וי"ד לנקבה. שני מעיינות הן. נפתח הטמא כל ימי הלידה ונסתם הטהור ולסוף שבעה לזכר וי"ד לנקבה נסתם הטמא ונפתח הטהור [נדה יא.]. מעין אחד הוא. דם הבא בימי לידה ודם הבא בימי טוהר ממעין אחד הן באין. התורה טמאתו. כל שבעה לזכר וי"ד לנקבה. והתורה טהרתו. אחר מכן. נסתם הטמא. לאחר שבועים ונפתח הטהור. נסתם הטהור. לאחר שמנים ונפתח הטמא [שם לה:]. קשתה ג' ימים. דקיי"ל (נדה דף לו:) בנדה דאורייתא המקשה בתוך י"א שבין נדה לנדה ורואה דם ג' ימים רצופים מחמת צער וולדה אינה באה לידי זיבה להיות צריכה ספירת ז' נקיים כיולדת בזוב אלא ימי טומאת לידה כיולדת גרידתא דתניא (שם) כי יזוב זוב דמה דמה מחמת עצמה ולא מחמת ולד [יבמות פג.]. קשתה. מחמת ולד. ג' ימים. בתוך אחד עשר יום שבין נדה לנדה וראתה כל שלשתן הימים רצופין. ושפתה. מצערה. מעת לעת. ברביעי. וילדה. איגלאי מילתא דדמים שראתה לא באו מחמת ולד הלכך הרי זו יולדת בזוב אבל אם לא שפתה סמוך ללידתה כל דמים שראתה מחמת ולד הוא ורחמנא טהרינהו מזיבה דכתיב זוב דמה דמה מחמת עצמה ולא דמה מחמת ולד. לילה ויום. דאם שפתה בתאי יום שלישי וילדה יום רביעי דשפתה מעת לעת אין זו שופי אלא אם כן שפתה לילה ויום שלאחר הלילה כלילי שבת ויומו. ששפתה מן הצער ולא מן הדם. לאע"ג דחזיא דם הוי שופי [שם לו:]. בית דין חצוף. שעברו על תקנת חכמים. דברי הכל. לקמן סנהדרין (ו.) קאי דפליגי בפשרה אשמעינן ר' אבהו דבדין כולהו מודו דבעינן שלשה [לעיל ב:]. דכתיב נפש תחת נפש. אם אסון יהיה שמתה האשה יתן ממון דמי האשה ליורשיה שאין עליה חיוב מיתה שלא נתכוון לה אלא לחברו נתכוון דכתיב וכי ינצו אנשים יחדיו קסבר רבי נתכוון להרוג את זה והרג את זה פטור ממיתה ומשלם ממון. נתינה למעלה. לענין דמי וולדות כתיב ונתן בפלילים (שמות כא). נתינה למטה. ונתתה נפש תחת נפש ממון ומאי נפש דמי הנפש [חגיגה יא.]. גבי לא יהיה אסון ונתן בפלילים (שמות כא) דמי ולדות [לעיל עט:]. ואם אסון יהיה. באשה. ונתתה נפש תחת נפש. רבותינו חולקין בדבר. יש אומרים נפש ממש ויש אומרים ממון אבל לא נפש ממש שהמתכוין להרוג את זה והרג את זה פטור ממיתה ומשלם ליורשיו דמיו כמו שהיה נמכר בשוק [שמות כא, כג]. מכות. מלקות ארבעים טעמא דר' ישמעאל ורבנן מפרש בגמרא סנהדרין (י.) מקראי [לעיל ב.]. אם בהרת קדמה לשער לבן טמא. דשער לבן ספרת בו הוא סימן לטומאה, כדכתיב (ויקרא יג) והנה נהפך שער לבן בבהרת. טהור. לפי מה שכתוב בתורה [ב"מ פו.]. טמא. דהכי כתיב קרא (ויקרא יג) שער לבן בבהרת. רבי יהושע אומר כהה. כלמפרש רבה. כהה טהור. הרי הוא ככהה הנגע ממראהו שהוא טהור ואמם ר' משה הדרשן שמעתי ורבי יהושע קיהה מאי קיהה אמר רבה קיהה וטיהר כלומר קיהה בדבר ונחלק עליהם וטיהר [כאדם שנקהו שיניו על אדם שאין משגיח לדבריו] וכן מצאתי בת"כ ור' יהושע קיהה טיהר אלמא העמד הגוף על חזקתו ולא תטמאהו מספק [כתובות עה:]. אם בהרת קודמת לשער לבן טמא. דשער לבן מסימני טומאה וכגון שקדמתו בהרת דכתיב (ויקרא יג) והנה נהפך שער לבן בבהרת. הרי הוא כנגע שכהה מראיתו בשבוע של הסגר שהוא סימן טהרה דכתיב (שם) והנה כהה הנגע וגו' ובשם רבי משה הדרשן שמעתי קיהה כלומר קיהה בדבר ונחלק עליו וכן מצאתי בת"כ ר' יהושע קיהה וטיהר. שיעור נגע כגרים. לאורך ולרוחב. כשני גריסין על שני אבנים שבקרן זוית. אחד בכותל זה ואחד בכותל זה. ארכו כשני גריסין ורחבו כגרים. דכשהוא מוטל ארכו על ב' אבנים נמצא בכל אבן גרים על גרים כשיעור נגע ושתי אבנים בעינן דכתיב (ויקרא יד) וחלצו את האבנים. כתיב קיר. ומראיהן שפל מן הקיר (שם) [נדה יט.]. גרים. זה שיעור נגעים ושתי גריסין על שתי אבנים דכתיב (ויקרא יד) וחלצו את האבנים תרתי משמע ובכל אחת שיעור נגע. בקרן זוית. ואומן שתי אבנים יהיו בקרן זוית אחד בכותל זה ואחד בכותל זה והנגע משוך בשתיהן ארכו שני גריסין ורחבו כגרים שיהא בכל אבן כגרים על גרים. מאי טעמא דר' אלעזר. דבעי קרן זוית. כתיב קיר. ומראיהן שפל מן הקיר [לעיל עא.].

א) לעיל נא. עה: עו. חגיגה יא: יבמות ג. כריתות ה., ב) נדה יט., ג) [נדה לה:], ד) נדה לו:, ה) לעיל ג. ה: ו. כתובות כב., ו) [לעיל ג: ו.], ז) חגיגה יא. [לעיל עט.], ח) לעיל ב. [ט.], ט) ב"מ פו. נדה יט. נזיר סה: ע"ש כתובות עה: נגעים פ"ד מי"א, י) [לפי גיר' תוס' בכתובות ובנדה רבה ובנזיר איתא רב יהודה], כ) לעיל עא. נדה יט. נגעים פי"ב מ"ג, ל) [צ"ל נתן], מ) [נדה יט. זבחים מט:], נ) [עמוד א ד"ה ורשב"ל], ס) [בהגדה של פסח].

גליון הש"ס

רש"י ד"ה בפלוגתא וכו' ואי תפסו יורשין. עי' טורי אבן חגיגה באבני שהם דף י ע"א ד"ה נפש:

תורה אור השלם

א) עֶרְוַת בַּת בִּנְךָ אוֹ בַת בִּתְּךָ לֹא תְגַלֶּה עֶרְוָתָן כִּי עֶרְוָתְךָ הֵנָּה: [ויקרא יח, י]

ב) עֶרְוַת אִשָּׁה וּבִתָּהּ לֹא תְגַלֵּה אֶת בַּת בְּנָהּ וְאֶת בַּת בִּתָּהּ לֹא תִקַּח לְגַלּוֹת עֶרְוָתָהּ שַׁאֲרָה הֵנָּה זִמָּה הִוא: [ויקרא יח, יז]

ג) וְאִישׁ אֲשֶׁר יִקַּח אֶת אִשָּׁה וְאֶת אִמָּהּ זִמָּה הִוא בָּאֵשׁ יִשְׂרְפוּ אֹתוֹ וְאֶתְהֶן וְלֹא תִהְיֶה זִמָּה בְּתוֹכְכֶם: [ויקרא כ, יד]

ד) וְאִם אָסוֹן יִהְיֶה וְנָתַתָּה נֶפֶשׁ תַּחַת נָפֶשׁ: [שמות כא, כג]

ה) וְכִי יִנָּצוּ אֲנָשִׁים וְנָגְפוּ אִשָּׁה הָרָה וְיָצְאוּ יְלָדֶיהָ וְלֹא יִהְיֶה אָסוֹן עָנוֹשׁ יֵעָנֵשׁ כַּאֲשֶׁר יָשִׁית עָלָיו בַּעַל הָאִשָּׁה וְנָתַן בִּפְלִלִים: [שמות כא, כב]

ו) וְרָאָה אֶת הַנֶּגַע וְהִנֵּה הַנֶּגַע בְּקִירֹת הַבַּיִת שְׁקַעֲרוּרֹת יְרַקְרַקֹּת אוֹ אֲדַמְדַּמֹּת וּמַרְאֵיהֶן שָׁפָל מִן הַקִּיר: [ויקרא יד, לז]

דִּין בִּתּוֹ מֵאֲנוּסָתוֹ – This refers to **the** *gezeirah shavah* **inference** that teaches the prohibition **of one's daughter** born **of his rape victim.**[1] דְּאָמַר רָבָא – **For Rava said:** אָמַר לִי רַב יִצְחָק בַּר אֲבוּדִימִי – **Rav Yitzchak bar Avudimi told me:** אַתְיָא ,,הֵנָּה" ,,הֵנָּה" אַתְיָא ,,זִמָּה" ,,זִמָּה" – **It** [the law regarding one's illegitimate daughter] **is derived** through the *gezeirah shavah* ***"heinnah, heinnah"*** and **it is derived** through the *gezeirah shavah* ***"zimmah, zimmah."***[2]

Rav Pappa continues his interpretive citation of the Baraisa: ,,בֵּין דָּם לְדָם" – *BETWEEN BLOOD AND BLOOD*; בֵּין דַּם נִדָּה דַּם לֵידָה דַּם זִיבָה – this alludes to a dispute BETWEEN the sages regarding THE BLOOD OF *NIDDAH,* THE BLOOD AFTER CHILDBIRTH or THE BLOOD OF *ZIVAH.*

Rav Pappa explains each case separately:

דַּם נִדָּה – To what dispute regarding **the blood of** ***niddah*** does the Baraisa refer? בִּפְלוּגְתָּא עֲקַבְיָא בֶּן מַהֲלַלְאֵל וְרַבָּנָן – **It refers to** where the sage and the High Court had **the** same **dispute** as the one **between Akavya ben Mahalalel and the Sages.** דִּתְנַן – **For we learned in a Mishnah:**[3] דַּם הַיָּרוֹק – Regarding YELLOWISH BLOOD,[4] עֲקַבְיָא בֶּן מַהֲלַלְאֵל מְטַמֵּא – AKAVYA BEN MAHALALEL DECLARES it *TAMEI,* וַחֲכָמִים מְטַהֲרִין – AND THE SAGES DECLARE it *TAHOR.*[5]

Rav Pappa explains the next case of "blood":

דַּם לֵידָה – To what dispute regarding **the blood after childbirth** does the Baraisa refer? בִּפְלוּגְתָּא דְּרַב וְלֵוִי – **It refers to** where the sage and the High Court had **the** same **dispute** as the one **between Rav and Levi.** דְּאִתְּמַר – **For** the following dispute **was stated** concerning the blood that a woman discharges in the days following childbirth:[6] רַב אָמַר מַעְיָן אֶחָד הוּא – **Rav says: There is but one source** that emits both the *tamei* and *tahor* bloods; הַתּוֹרָה טִמְּאַתּוּ וְהַתּוֹרָה טִיהֲרַתּוּ – **the Torah has declared [this source]** ***tamei*** **and the Torah has declared [this source]** ***tahor.***[7] וְלֵוִי אָמַר שְׁנֵי מַעְיָינוֹת – **Whereas Levi says: There are two sources** of blood – one which produces the *tamei* blood and one which produces the *tahor* blood: נִסְתַּם הַטָּמֵא נִפְתַּח הַטָּהוֹר – **The** ***tamei*** source **is sealed** at the end of the fourteenth day, whereupon **the** ***tahor*** source **opens;** נִסְתַּם הַטָּהוֹר נִפְתַּח

NOTES

1. I.e. his out-of-wedlock daughter. [The usual case of a child born out of wedlock is the case of a child born to a rape victim.]

2. The *gezeirah shavah* of *heinnah, heinnah* teaches that she is prohibited to him, and the *gezeirah shavah* of *zimmah, zimmah* teaches that the penalty for violating the prohibition is burning.

As explained on 51a (see note 18 there; see also 75b), there are two verses in the Torah which teach that it is forbidden to commit incest with one's daughter. *Leviticus* 18:10 states: עֶרְוַת בַּת־בִּנְךָ אוֹ בַת־בִּתְּךָ לֹא תְגַלֶּה עֶרְוָתָן כִּי עֶרְוָתְךָ הֵנָּה, *The nakedness of your son's daughter or your daughter's daughter – you shall not uncover their nakedness; for they are (heinnah) your own nakedness. Leviticus* 18:17 states: עֶרְוַת אִשָּׁה וּבִתָּהּ לֹא תְגַלֵּה אֶת־בַּת־בְּנָהּ וְאֶת־בַּת־בִּתָּהּ לֹא תִקַּח לְגַלּוֹת עֶרְוָתָהּ שַׁאֲרָה הֵנָּה זִמָּה הִוא, *The nakedness of a woman and her daughter you shall not uncover; you shall not take her son's daughter or her daughter's daughter to uncover her nakedness – they are (heinnah) close relatives, it is a sinful counsel (zimmah)*. The first verse, which (as explained in *Yevamos* 97a) refers to the daughter of one's *illegitimate* son or daughter, does not explicitly prohibit the illegitimate daughter herself. The second verse, which does prohibit the daughter herself, speaks only of one's *wife's* daughter – whether or not he is the father. Since the two verses are linked to each other through the common expression *heinnah* that both contain, we derive that just as in the second verse the daughter herself is prohibited, so too is she prohibited in the first verse (which refers to one's illegitimate daughter). The penalty for the forbidden unions mentioned in both these linked verses is derived through another *gezeirah shavah,* which links the word *zimmah* stated in the second verse to the word *zimmah* stated in *Leviticus* 20:14: וְאִישׁ אֲשֶׁר יִקַּח אֶת־אִשָּׁה וְאֶת־אִמָּהּ זִמָּה הִוא בָּאֵשׁ יִשְׂרְפוּ אֹתוֹ וְאֶתְהֶן, *And a man who will take a woman and her mother, it is a sinful counsel (zimmah); with fire shall they burn him and them.* Just as the penalty in the case of the latter verse is burning, so too in the cases of *Leviticus* 18:17 and 10.

Now, the derived prohibition of one's illegitimate daughter also bears the penalty of *kares* (*Rashi*) [just as the source prohibitions from which it is derived do]. Accordingly, if the rebellious sage rejects the *gezeirah shavah* and permits a man to cohabit with his illegitimate daughter, he will have disputed the High Court in a matter whose intentional transgression bears the penalty of *kares* and whose inadvertent transgression creates a *chatas* obligation.

3. *Niddah* 19a. The Mishnah there discusses which shades of red a discharge of blood must be to render the woman *tamei.*

4. [In classical Hebrew, there is no separate word for the color yellow. Rather, the term יָרוֹק is used for both green and yellow, and differentiation between the two colors is made by the addition of a modifier, i.e. "*yarok* like leek" (green) or "*yarok* like the yolk of an egg" (yellow). See *Einayim LaMishpat* here.] The question here concerns a discharge of blood that has a golden or "yellowish" color.

5. According to Akavya ben Mahalalel, a woman who discharges the yellowish blood is *tamei,* whereas according to the Sages she remains *tahor.*

Thus, if the rebellious sage disputes the High Court in this matter, he is a *zakein mamrei,* since it is a matter of *kares* and *chatas.*

Obviously, if the High Court adopts the ruling of Akavya and the rebellious sage that of the Sages, and the rebellious sage proceeds to permit a woman who experiences a discharge of yellowish blood to have relations with her husband, he thereby instructs her to do something that is punishable by *kares* in the eyes of the High Court. But even if the positions are reversed, it may come about that the rebellious sage permits an offense punishable by *kares.* For Akavya's position in this matter is not always the stringent one, as the following case demonstrates: The law is that a woman who discharges blood (not during the *zivah*-period) is a *niddah* and is automatically *tamei* for seven days, regardless of whether her flow stops abruptly or continues for the duration of the seven days. Now, let us consider a case in which a woman, say, had a discharge of yellowish blood on day one, and then had a discharge of red blood on day three. According to Akavya, the yellowish discharge on day one began her *niddah*-period and she may (on the Biblical level) immerse herself after day seven and become *tahor.* According to the Sages (who disregard the yellowish discharge), however, her seven-day *niddah*-period does not start until day *three* when she experiences her first discharge of *red* blood. The Sages, then, would not allow her to immerse in the *mikveh* until after day *nine* (which is the seventh day from day three), and she would remain *tamei* in their view if she immersed any earlier. Thus, if the rebellious sage adopted Akavya's "stringent" view and allowed the woman to immerse on the night following day seven, whereas the High Court adopted the Sages' view, the rebellious sage has permitted the woman to be with her husband in a manner that renders them liable to *kares* or *chatas* in the eyes of the High Court (*Rashi* and *Tosafos*).

6. As explained on 87a in note 6, a woman who gives birth thereupon goes through several periods of *tumah* and *taharah,* the durations of which depend on whether she has given birth to a boy or a girl. For the sake of convenience, we will follow *Rashi's* lead and use (both in the text and the notes) the example of a woman who has given birth to a girl. The woman is thereupon *tamei* for two weeks and any blood she discharges during this time is *tamei* (i.e. it renders *tamei* any people, utensils or food that come into contact with it). For the next sixty-six days (i.e. from day 15 until day 80), any blood that she discharges is *tohar*-blood, which is not *tamei* nor does its discharge render her *tamei.* Therefore, she may immerse in a *mikveh* after day fourteen and be permitted to her husband even if she will still experience a discharge of blood. [This is the law as it applied in Talmudic times. See, however, *Yoreh Deah* 194 concerning the law as it applies today.] If she experiences a discharge of blood after day eighty, she thereby becomes an ordinary *niddah.*

7. According to Rav, the *tamei* blood (discharged between days 1 and 14, or after day 80) and the *tahor* blood (discharged between days 15 and 80) are identical in every respect except for the time period in which they are discharged. The Torah has declared them *tamei* or *tahor* solely on the basis of the time in which they are discharged.

מג א מיי' פ"ט מהל' איסורי ביאה הלכה ו סמג לאוין קיא ועשין רמג טוש"ע י"ד סי' קפח סעיף א:
מד ב מיי' שם פ"ו הלכה א סמג שם:
מה ג מיי' שם פ"ז הלכה א סמג שם:
מו ד מיי' פ"ב מהלכות טומאת צרעת הלכה ו סמג עשין רלד:
מז ה מיי' שם הלכה ט:

דין בתו מאנוסתו ^(א) דאמר רבא א"ל רב יצחק בר אבודימי אתיא ^(א) הנה ^(ב) הנה אתיא זימה ^(ג) זימה בין דם לדם בין דם נדה דם לידה דם זיבה דם נדה בפלוגתא עקביא בן מהללאל ורבנן דתנן ^(ג) דם הירוק עקביא בן מהללאל מטמא וחכמים ^(א) מטהרין דם לידה בפלוגתא דרב ולוי דאתמר ^(ג) רב אמר ^(ב) מעין אחד הוא התורה טימאתו והתורה טיהרתו ולוי אמר שני מעיינות הן נסתם הטמא נפתח הטהור נסתם הטהור נפתח הטמא: דם זיבה בפלוגתא דר"א ורבי יהושע דתנן ^(ד) קישתה שלשה ימים בתוך אחד עשר יום אם שפתה מעת לעת וילדה ^(ג) הרי זו יולדת בזוב דברי ר"א ור' יהושע אומר לילה ויום כלילי שבת ויומו ששפתה מן הצער ולא מן הדם בין דין לדין בין דיני ממונות דיני נפשות דיני מכות דיני ממונות בפלוגתא דשמואל ורבי אבהו ^(ה) דאמר שמואל שנים שדנו דיניהם דין אלא שנקראין בית דין חצוף ורבי אבהו אמר ^(ו) לדברי הכל אין דיניהן דין דיני נפשות בפלוגתא דרבי ורבנן דתניא ^(ז) רבי אומר ^(ד) ונתת נפש תחת נפש ממון אתה אומר ממון או אינו אלא נפש ממש נאמר ^(ה) נתינה למעלה ונאמר נתינה למטה מה להלן ממון אף כאן ממון דיני מכות בפלוגתא דרבי ישמעאל ורבנן דתנן ^(ח) מכות בג' משום רבי ישמעאל אמרו בכ"ג בין נגע לנגע בין נגעי אדם נגעי בתים נגעי בגדים נגעי אדם בפלוגתא דרבי יהושע ורבנן ^(ט) דתנן ^(ד) אם בהרת קדם לשער הלבן טמא אם שער לבן קדם לבהרת טהור ספק ^(ה) טמא רבי יהושע אומר כהה מאי כהה אמר ^(י) רבא כהה טהור נגעי בתים בפלוגתא דרבי אלעזר ברבי שמעון ורבנן ^(כ) דתנן רבי אליעזר ברבי שמעון אומר לעולם אין הבית טמא עד שיראה כשני גריסין על שתי אבנים בשתי כתלים בקרן זוית ארכו כשני גריסין ורחבו כגריס מאי טעמא דר' אלעזר בר"ש כתיב ^(ו) קיר וכתיב ^(ז) קירות איזהו קיר שהוא כקירות הוי אומר זה קרן זוית נגעי בגדים בפלוגתא דר' (^(ל) יונתן) בן אבטולמוס ורבנן ^(מ) דתניא ר' (^(ל) יונתן) בן אבטולמוס אומר מנין לפריחה

רש"י

דין בתו מאנוסתו. דאלו הן הנשרפין פרישית לה גבי בתו מאנוסתו דמהאי דינא ילפינן והוא דבר שזדונו כרת: הירוק עקביא בן מהללאל מטמא. דם הירוק הוי דם הנדה ואם אמר זקן ממרא כעקביא בן מהללאל מייתי לה לחיוב כרת שפעמים שרואה דם הירוק בתחלת נדותה ולבסוף ז' ימים רואה דם אדום ופוסקת והיא מתחלת למנות שבעה ימים מראיית דם ירוק וטובלת ומשמשת עם בעלה ב' ימים בנדותה לפי שדם הירוק טהור הוא והיה לה להתחיל למנות מראיית דם אדום: מעין אחד הוא. דם הבא בשבועיים של נקיבה שהוא טמא ודם הבא לאחר שבועיים שהוא טהור ממעין אחד הוא: התורה טימאתו. כל שבועיים: והתורה טיהרתו. לאחר שבועיים וחזרה וטימאתו לאחר שכלין ימי טוהר: ולוי אמר ב' מעיינות הן. נסתם הטמא לאחר שבועיים ונפתח הטהור וכשנסתם הטהור בסוף ימי טוהר נפתח הטמא ואמרי' במס' נדה מאי בינייהו בשופעת מתוך שבועיים לאחר שבועיים או מתוך שמונים לאחר שמונים לרב אע"פ שלא פסק מעיינה בתוך שבועיים ויולא דם לאחר שבועיים ממנה טהור וללוי טמא עד שתפסוק שעה דנימא נסתם הטמא והשופעת מתוך שמונים לאחר שמונים לרב טמאה ואע"פ שזהו מעין עלמו של ימי טוהר וללוי טהורה עד שיפסוק מעין הטהור ויפתח מעין הטמא ואי איפלוג זקן ממרא ורבנן בהא קאתי לידי כרת אי רבנן כרב והוא כלוי איכא כרת לאחר ימי טוהר ואי רבנן כלוי והוא כרב איכא כרת בתחלת ימי טוהר דרב לקולא ולוי לחומרא: קישתה ג' ימים בתוך אחד עשר יום כו'. כתיב בפרשת זבה באחד עשר יום שבין נדה לנדה שהם הימים המביאין לידי זיבה ואשה כי יזוב זוב דמה ימים רבים ותניא בפרק בנות כותים (נדה לו:) דמה מחמת עלמה ולא מחמת ולד מגיד שדם הקישוי שילא קודם הולד מחמת לער הקישוי אינו מביאה לידי זיבה וכ"ש דם שלאחר הולד אבל אם ראתה ג' ימים רלופין בהן מתוך קושי ושפתה קודם יליאת הולד יום אחד מעת לעת ששקטה ונחה מלערה ואח"כ ילדה בין מתוך קושי בין מתוך שופי הרי זו יולדת בזוב לפי שכיון שלאחר ג' שפתה איגלאי מילתא דלאו מחמת ולד אתא ונעשית בהן זבה למנות ז' נקיים כדין זבה וכל זמן שלא תספור ז' נקיים לא יהא דם שלה דם טוהר ואפילו לאחר שבועיים ואחר מלאת שמונים שלה לריכה שני קרבנות אחד ללידתה ואחד לזיבתה: לילה ויום. אבל מעת לעת לא חשיב שופי אם שפתה משש שעות של שלישי עד שש שעות של ד' הואיל וה"ל מקלת קושי ביום השופי לא הויא יולדת בזוב ור"א לחומרא ורבי יהושע לקולא והיינו דבר שזדונו כרת: ששפתה מן הצער. ואין אנו חוששין אם לא שפתה מן הדם: בפלוגתא דשמואל ור' אבהו. וכיון דאפיקי הני בי תרי ממונא מהאי ויהבו להאי בדינא דידהו והלך זה וקידש אשה באותו ממון לשמואל מקודשת לרבי אבהו אינה מקודשת דה"ל קידשה בגזל וקי"ל בפ"ב דקידושין (דף נב.) גבי מעשה דה' נשים שנתקדשו בכלכלה קידשה בגזל אינה מקודשת דהשתא אתי לידי כרת אי רבנן כשמואל וזקן ממרא כרבי אבהו וא"נ רבנן כרבי אבהו וזקן ממרא כשמואל אתי לידי כרת דקא משוי להו קידושין ואי אתי איניש אחרינא לבתר הכי וקדשה מפיק לה מבתרא בלא גט וה"ל דבר שזדונו כרת בלא עדים ובלא התראה דאי איכא עדים והתראה הוי מיתת ב"ד ואי ליכא לא זה ולא זה הוי כרת: ונתתה נפש תחת נפש. במתכוין להרוג את זה והרג את זה ומיחייב ליה רבי ממון ורבנן פטרי וכפלוגתא באלו הן הנשרפין ^(ס) ואי תפסו יורשין דהרוג ממונא דהורג ופטר ליה זקן ממרא וקידשו בו את האשה לרבי מקודשת לרבנן אינה מקודשת ואי אתי איניש אחרינא וקידשה מקודשת לשני הרי חיוב כרת בדבר: נתינה למעלה. גבי נוגף אשה הרה ונתן בפלילים (שמות כא) דמי ולדות: בכ"ג. ואם הלקוהו ג' לר' ישמעאל חייבין לו ממון כשאר חובל בחבירו ומקדש בו את האשה ולרבנן בדין הלקוהו ואם תפס ממונו וקידש בו אינה מקודשת: ספק. אם זה קדם אם זה קדם: כהה. כאילו כהה הנגע דהוי מסימני טהרה כשמשתנה הלובן לאחר הסגר ולרבנן אם נכנס למקדש חייב כרת ולר' יהושע פטור: עד שיראה כשני גריסין. שיעור הנגע כגריס על גריס וכתיב את האבנים אשר בהן הנגע שיהא הנגע על שתי אבנים על כל אחד ואחד שיעור נגע על ב' כתלים ובקרן זוית כגון מקלוע דרומית מזרחית אורכו כשני גריסין ורחבו כגריס שיהא בקיר הדרומי גריס וכן בקיר המזרחי והנגע כולו מחובר כאחד: מאי טעמא דר' אליעזר. דבעי קרן זוית: כתיב. ומראיהן שפל מן הקיר (ויקרא יד) וכתיב והנה הנגע בקירות הבית: זה קרן זוית. ורבנן לא בעו קרן זוית והיכא דליתיה בקרן זוית ונכנס בה אדם ואח"כ נכנס למקדש לרבנן חייב כרת לר' אלעזר בר"ש פטור: לפריחה

תוספות

דין בתו מאנוסתו. בכולהו משכח פלוגתא בר מהאי ורוצה לומר דאין זקן ממרא מודה בגזירה שוה זו:

עקביא בן מהללאל מטמא. ואף על גב דעקביא מחמיר זמנין דהויא קולא כגון שרואה דם אדום ומשלימתו לדם ירוק:

כלילי שבת ויומו. לאפוקי יום תחלה ואח"כ לילה אלא א"כ שפתה לילה שלם ואחר כך יום שלם כלילי שבת ויום שהיום הולך אחר הלילה:

בפלוגתא דרבי יהושע ורבנן. פי' בקונטרס לרבנן אם נכנס למקדש חייב ולרבי יהושע פטור ולא יתכן דהכי האי גוונא לא מחייב זקן ממרא כיון שהוא בעולה ויורד דהא ילפינן לעיל דבר דבר מונעלם דבר דתנן בפ' [הור'] כהן משוח (הוריות דף ט.) מביאין עולה ויורד על טומאת מקדש וקדשיו ויש לפרש כדפרישית לעיל ^(י) בככר של תרומה:

רבי יהושע אומר כיהה. פירש בקונטרס כאילו כיהה הנגע דהוא מסימני טהרה כשמשתנה בו לובן שלו לאחר הסגר וקשה היכי פריך בשילהי נזיר (דף סה:) ודילמא כיהה וטמא הא לפירושו כל כיהה טהור ועוד אי כיהה וטמא היינו ת"ק ונראה כגירסת ר"ח קהה בקו"ף ול"ג אומר כלומר ר' יהושע הקשה ודקדק בדבר כמו ^(פ) הקהה את שיניו וכן מקהו אקהייתא בשוקא (יבמות דף קי:) מאספים אסופות של בני אדם כלומר עמדו למניין ולא ידע הש"ס אם להביא ראיה לת"ק או לסתור ולהכי בעי מאי קיהה וקאמר קיהה וטיהר ומיהו בירושלמי דריש שבועות משמע דיש כיהה טמא דאמר התם והתורה אמרה והנה כהה הנגע הכהה טמא וכהה מן הכהה טהור:

מרחו

ליקוטי רש"י

דין בתו מאנוסתו. דהיינו בתו ובת בנו ובת בתו מאנוסתו דלאו בכלל אשה ובתה קא נינהו דהתם באשתו על ידי קידושין קאמר דדרשינן לה ביבמות [צז.] מקראי דרבה למי ערות בת בנך או בת בתך וגו' הא בת שילדה ממך גלה וכתיב ערות אשה ובתה לא תגלה משמע בין שילדתו לך בין שילדתו לאיש אחר לא קשיא כאן באנוסין כאן בנשואין או באשתו שם אנוסתו אי מפותה לך היא אי אתה מוזהר על בתה אלא אם היא בתך אבל אשתו אתה מוזהר אף על בת שילדה לאיש אחר. אתיא הנה הנה אתיא זמה זמה. מעיקרא מייתינן לה בהנה הנה והדר בזמה זמה כתיב הכא (ויקרא יח) כי ערותך הנה וכתיב באשה ובתה (שם) שארה הנה זמה מה להלן זמה עמו אף כאן זמה עמו ובתר דילפינן זימה לשאר דודיה ילפינן בה שריפה בזמה זמה נאמר כאן זמה ונאמר להלן (שם כ) בשריפה זמה מה להלן שריפה אף כאן שריפה [לעיל עה.]. מעין אחד הוא. דם הבא בתוך ז' של לידה ודם הבא בימי טוהר ממעין אחד הוא. התורה טמאתו. כל שבעה לזכר וי"ד לנקבה. והתורה טהרתו. אחר מכן. נסתם הטמא. לאחר שבועיים ונפתח הטהור ולסוף שבעה לזכר וי"ד לנקבה נסתם הטמא ונפתח הטהור [נדה יא.]. מעין אחד הוא. דם הבא בימי לידה ודם הבא בימי טוהר ממעין אחד הוא. התורה טמאתו. כל שבעה לזכר וי"ד לנקבה. והתורה טהרתו. אחר מכן. נסתם הטמא. לאחר שבועיים ונפתח הטהור. נסתם הטהור. לאחר מלאת שמונים ונפתח הטמא [בכ לה:]. קשתה ג' ימים. דקי"ל (נדה דף לו.) כנדה דאורייתא המקשה בתוך י"א שבין נדה לנדה ורואה דם ג' ימים רצופים מחמת צער וולדה אינה באה לידי זיבה להיות צריכה ספירת ז' נקיים כיולדת בזוב אלא ימי לידה כיולדת גרידתא דתניא (שם) כי יזוב זוב דמה דמה מחמת עצמה ולא מחמת ולד [יבמות פג.]. קשתה. מחמת ולד. ג' ימים. בתוך אחד עשר יום שבין נדה לנדה וראתה כל שלשתן הימים רצופין. ושפתה. מצערה. מעת לעת. ברביעי. וילדה. איגלאי מילתא דדמים שראתה לא באו מחמת ולד הלכך הרי זו יולדת בזוב אבל אם לא שפתה סמוך ללידתה כל דמים שראתה מחמת ולד הוא ורחמנא טהרינהו מזיבה דכתיב זוב דמה דמה מחמת עצמה ולא דמה מחמת ולד. לילה ויום. דאם שפתה בתלי יום שלישי וילדה יום רביעי דשפתה מעת לעת אין זו שופי אלא אם כן שפתה לילה ויום שלאחר הלילה כלילי שבת ויומו. ששפתה מן הצער ולא מן הדם. דאע"ג דחזיא דם הוי שופי [שם לו:]. בית דין חצוף. שעברו על תקנת חכמים. דברי הכל. לקמן סנהדרין (ו.) קאי דפליגי בפשרה אשמעינן ר' אבהו דבדין כולהו מודו דבעינן שלשה [לעיל ב:]. דכתיב נפש תחת נפש. אם אסון יהיה שמתה האשה יתן ממון דמי האשה ליורשיה שאין עליה חיוב מיתה שלא נתכוון לה אלא לחברו נתכוון דכתיב וכי ינצו אנשים יחדיו קסבר רבי נתכוון להרוג את זה והרג את זה פטור ממיתה ומשלם ממון. נתינה למעלה. לענין דמי וולדות כתיב ונתן בפלילים (שמות כא). נתינה למטה. ונתתה נפש תחת נפש ממון ומאי נפש דמי הנפש [חגיגה יא.]. נתינה למעלה. גבי לא יהיה אסון ונתן בפלילים (שמות כא) דמי ולדות [לעיל עט:]. ואם אסון יהיה. באשה. ונתתה נפש תחת נפש. רבותינו חולקין בדבר. יש אומרים נפש ממש ויש אומרים ממון אבל לא נפש ממש שהמתכוין להרוג את זה והרג את זה פטור ממיתה ומשלם ליורשיו דמיו כמו שהיה נמכר בשוק [שמות כא, כג]. מכות. מלקות ארבעים טעמא דר' ישמעאל ורבנן מפרש בגמרא סנהדרין (י.) מקראי [לעיל ב.]. אם בהרת קדמה לשער לבן טמא. דשער לבן שפרח בו הוא סימן לטומאה, כדכתיב (ויקרא יג) והנה נהפך שער לבן בבהרת. טהור. לפי מה שכתוב בתורה [ב"מ פו.]. טמא. דהכי כתיב קרא (ויקרא יג) שער לבן בבהרת. רבי יהושע אומר כהה. כדמפרש רבה. כהה טהור. הרי הוא ככהה הנגע ממראהו שהוא טהור ומשם ר' משה הדרשן שמעתי ורבי יהושע קיהה מאי קיהה אמר רבה קיהה וטיהר כלומר קיהה בדבר ונחלק עליהם וטיהר [כאדם שנקהו שיניו על אדם שאין משגיח לדבריו] וכן מצאתי בת"כ ור' יהושע קיהה טיהר אלמא העמד הגוף על חזקתו ולא תטמאנו מספק [כתובות עה:]. אם בהרת קודמת לשער לבן טמא. דשער לבן מסימני טומאה וכגון שקדמתו בהרת דכתיב (ויקרא יג) והנה נהפך שער לבן בבהרת. כהה טהור. הרי הוא כנגע שכהה מראיתו בשבוע של הסגר שהוא סימן טהרה דכתיב (שם) והנה כהה הנגע וגו' ובשם רבי משה הדרשן שמעתי קיהה כלומר קיהה בדבר ונחלק עליו וכן מצאתי בת"כ ר' יהושע קיהה וטיהר. שיעור נגע כגרים. לאורך ולרוחב. כשני גריסין על שני אבנים שבקרן זוית. אחד בכותל זה ואחד בכותל זה. ארכו כשני גריסין ורחבו כגרים. דכשהוא מוטל ארכו על ב' אבנים נמלא בכל אבן גרים על גרים כשיעור נגע ושתי אבנים בעינן דכתיב (ויקרא יד) וחלצו את האבנים. כתיב קיר. ומראיהן שפל מן הקיר (שם) [נדה יט.]. גרים. זה שיעור נגעים ושתי גריסין על שתי אבנים דכתיב (ויקרא יד) וחלצו את האבנים תרתי משמע ובכל אחת שיעור נגע. בקרן זוית. ואותן שתי אבנים יהיו בקרן זוית אחד בכותל זה ואחד בכותל זה והנגע משוך בשתיהן ארכו שני גריסין ורחבו כגרים שיהא בכל אבן כגרים על גרים. מאי טעמא דר' אלעזר. דבעי קרן זוית. כתיב קיר. ומראיהן שפל מן הקיר [לעיל עא.]

מסורת הש"ס

א) לעיל נא. עה: עו. חגיגה יא: יבמות ג. כריתות ה., ב) נדה יט, ג) נדה לה:, ד) נדה לו:, ה) לעיל ב. ג: כתובות כב., ו) [לעיל ב: ו.], ז) חגיגה יא: [לעיל עט.], ח) לעיל ב. [ע.], ט) ב"מ פו. נדה יט. נזיר סה: ע"ש כתובות עה: נגעים פ"ד מי"א, י) [לפי גיר' תוס' בכתובות ובנדה רבה ובנזיר איתא רב יהודה], כ) לעיל עא. נדה יט. נגעים פי"ב מ"ג, ל) [צ"ל נתן], מ) [נדה יט. זבחים מט.], נ) [עמוד ג' ד"ה ורשב"ם], ס) [בהגדה של פסח].

גליון הש"ס

רש"י ד"ה בפלוגתא וכו' ואי תפסו יורשין. עי' טורי אבן חגיגה באבני שהם דף ע"א ד"ה נפש.

תורה אור השלם

א) עֶרְוַת בַּת בִּנְךָ אוֹ בַת בִּתְּךָ לֹא תְגַלֶּה עֶרְוָתָן כִּי עֶרְוָתְךָ הֵנָּה: [ויקרא יח, י]

ב) עֶרְוַת אִשָּׁה וּבִתָּהּ לֹא תְגַלֵּה אֶת בַּת בְּנָהּ וְאֶת בַּת בִּתָּהּ לֹא תִקַּח לְגַלּוֹת עֶרְוָתָהּ שַׁאֲרָה הֵנָּה זִמָּה הִוא: [ויקרא יח, יז]

ג) וְאִישׁ אֲשֶׁר יִקַּח אֶת אִשָּׁה וְאֶת אִמָּהּ זִמָּה הִוא בָּאֵשׁ יִשְׂרְפוּ אֹתוֹ וְאֶתְהֶן וְלֹא תִהְיֶה זִמָּה בְּתוֹכְכֶם: [ויקרא כ, יד]

ד) וְאִם אָסוֹן יִהְיֶה וְנָתַתָּה נֶפֶשׁ תַּחַת נָפֶשׁ: [שמות כא, כג]

ה) וְכִי יִנָּצוּ אֲנָשִׁים וְנָגְפוּ אִשָּׁה הָרָה וְיָצְאוּ יְלָדֶיהָ וְלֹא יִהְיֶה אָסוֹן עָנוֹשׁ יֵעָנֵשׁ כַּאֲשֶׁר יָשִׁית עָלָיו בַּעַל הָאִשָּׁה וְנָתַן בִּפְלִלִים: [שמות כא, כב]

ו) וְרָאָה אֶת הַנֶּגַע וְהִנֵּה הַנֶּגַע בְּקִירֹת הַבַּיִת שְׁקַעֲרוּרֹת יְרַקְרַקֹּת אוֹ אֲדַמְדַּמֹּת וּמַרְאֵיהֶן שָׁפָל מִן הַקִּיר: [ויקרא יד, לז]

הַטָּמֵא – and **the *tahor*** source **is sealed** at the end of the eightieth day and **the *tamei*** source **opens.**[8]

Rav Pappa explains the third case of "blood":

דַּם זִיבָה – To what dispute regarding **the blood of *zivah*** does the Baraisa refer? בִּפְלוּגְתָּא דְּרַבִּי אֱלִיעֶזֶר וְרַבִּי יְהוֹשֻׁעַ – **It refers to** where the sage and the High Court had **the** same **dispute** as the one **between R' Eliezer and R' Yehoshua.** דִּתְנַן – **For we learned in a Mishnah:**[9] קִישְׁתָה שְׁלֹשָׁה יָמִים בְּתוֹךְ אַחַד עָשָׂר יוֹם – This is the law for A WOMAN who bleeds IN LABOR FOR THREE DAYS WITHIN the ELEVEN DAYS of her *zivah*-period:[10] אִם שֶׁפָּתָה מֵעֵת לְעֵת וְיָלְדָה – IF SHE HAD RELIEF FOR TWENTY-FOUR HOURS[11] AND THEN SHE GAVE BIRTH, הֲרֵי זוֹ יוֹלֶדֶת בְּזוֹב – SHE IS deemed to be ONE WHO HAS GIVEN BIRTH IN a state of *ZIVAH*;[12] דִּבְרֵי רַבִּי אֱלִיעֶזֶר – these are THE WORDS OF R' ELIEZER. וְרַבִּי יְהוֹשֻׁעַ אוֹמֵר – BUT R' YEHOSHUA SAYS: לַיְלָה וְיוֹם כְּלֵילֵי שַׁבָּת וְיוֹמוֹ – The labor pains must have subsided for A NIGHT AND A DAY LIKE THE NIGHT OF THE SABBATH AND ITS DAY.[13] The Mishnah adds a word of explanation concerning what it means by "relief": שֶׁשָּׁפְתָה מִן הַצַּעַר וְלֹא מִן הַדָּם – It means that SHE HAD RELIEF FROM THE PAIN, BUT NOT necessarily FROM THE flow of BLOOD.[14]

Rav Pappa continues:

בֵּין דִּינֵי "בֵּין דִּין לְדִין" – *BETWEEN VERDICT AND VERDICT*; מָמוֹנוֹת דִּינֵי נְפָשׁוֹת דִּינֵי מַכּוֹת – this alludes to a dispute BETWEEN the sages regarding MONETARY CASES, CAPITAL CASES, OR CASES CONCERNING LASHES.

Rav Pappa explains each case separately:

דִּינֵי מָמוֹנוֹת – To what dispute concerning **monetary cases** does the Baraisa refer? בִּפְלוּגְתָּא דִּשְׁמוּאֵל וְרַבִּי אַבָּהוּ – **It refers to** where the sage and the High Court had **the** same **dispute** as the one **between Shmuel and R' Abahu.** דְּאָמַר שְׁמוּאֵל – **For Shmuel said:** שְׁנַיִם שֶׁדָּנוּ דִּינֵיהֶם דִּין – If **two** judges **adjudicated** a loan dispute, **their verdict is a** valid **verdict,** אֶלָּא שֶׁנִּקְרָאִין בֵּית דִּין חָצוּף – **but they are called an insolent court.**[15] וְרַבִּי אַבָּהוּ אָמַר – **And R' Abahu says:** If two judges adjudicate a case, לְדִבְרֵי הַכֹּל אֵין דִּינֵיהֶן דִּין – **according to all opinions, their verdict is not a** valid **verdict.**[16]

NOTES

8. According to Levi, the Torah did not declare the blood *tamei* or *tahor* solely on the basis of the period during which it is emitted. Rather, the Torah informs us that the *tamei* source of blood closes at the end of day fourteen, whereupon the *tahor* source opens, and the process is reversed at the end of day eighty. The true basis for the *tumah* or *taharah* of the blood, then, is the source from which it emanates.

The Gemara in *Niddah* (35b) explains that the legal difference between Rav and Levi emerges in a case where the cut-off time (i.e. the expiration of day fourteen or of day eighty) occurred during a continuous flow of blood. According to Rav (who holds that both bloods derive from the same source and the sole determinant of their *tumah* and *taharah* is the time at which they are discharged), the fact that the cut-off time occurs during a continuous flow does not change the law at all: Whatever blood is discharged between days 15 and 80 is *tahor*; whatever blood is discharged before or after this time is *tamei*. According to Levi, however, the law *is* different in this case. For once a source begins discharging blood, you cannot say that it has closed until the discharge stops. Thus, if a woman had a continuous flow from day 10 through day 20, Levi would declare all the blood *tamei* (and declare the woman forbidden to her husband) until the blood stops on day 20, for the continuous flow indicates that the *tamei* source is still open. Similarly, if the woman had a continuous flow from day 75 to day 85, Levi would declare the woman *tahor* even though she is discharging blood after the eightieth day, since the continuous flow of blood indicates that it is the *tahor* source that is still open.

Thus, if the rebellious sage disputed the High Court in this matter, it could emerge that he permits a matter of *kares* and *chatas*. If he adopts Rav's view and the High Court adopts Levi's, the rebellious sage will be permitting a *kares* infraction where the woman has a continuous flow running into the fifteenth day and he declares her *tahor*. If the positions are reversed (with the sage following Levi and the High Court Rav), then the rebellious sage will be permitting a *kares* infraction where the woman has a continuous flow running into the eighty-first day and he declares her *tahor* (*Rashi*).

9. *Niddah* 36b.

10. For example, she became a *niddah* one week before she went into labor; thus, her labor begins on the first day of her eleven-day *zivah*-period (see 87a notes 6 and 36). Now, ordinarily if a woman bleeds (i.e. she experiences a discharge of uterine blood) for three consecutive days of the *zivah*-period, she is a *major zavah* and must count seven clean days. However, a Baraisa in *Niddah* (loc. cit.) teaches that this applies only when the woman bleeds naturally, but not if she bleeds as a result of labor. [Regarding what the woman's status is as a result of blood discharged in the course of labor, see Mishnah and Gemara there.] This special law of "bleeding as a result of labor" applies, though, only if the labor is true labor, resulting from the actual impending birth of the child. If, however, the labor subsides for a time and only afterwards does she give birth, then it shows that the labor she had experienced previously was not true labor and the bleeding that she experienced then did indeed render her a *major zavah* (*Rashi*). The Mishnah now considers how long the labor pains must subside in order for the relief to be taken as an indication that the labor was not true labor.

11. As the end of the Mishnah explains, this means that her labor pains eased.

12. A *major zavah* who gives birth cannot begin her days of *tohar*-blood [see above, note 6] until she first counts seven clean days. Furthermore, she will have to bring the bird offerings of a *major zavah* in addition to those of a new mother at the conclusion of eighty days (*Rashi*).

13. I.e. the labor pains must subside for a full night followed by a full day. [This must be like the day of Sabbath is reckoned, with the day following the night, not the other way around (*Tosafos*).] But if they subside merely for a twenty-four-hour period (e.g. from noon Tuesday until noon Wednesday), the relief does not indicate that the labor was false, and she is *not* deemed to be one who has given birth in a state of *zivah* (*Rashi*). [R' Yehoshua holds that the subsiding of labor for a complete night and day is more indicative of false labor than a cessation for a mere twenty-four hours (*Tosafos* to *Niddah* 36b).]

Thus (in the above example), if a woman bled for three days in labor during her *zivah*-period and the labor pains then subsided from noon Tuesday until noon Wednesday, after which she gave birth (whether or not the labor pains resumed), she is considered by R' Eliezer to be one who has given birth in a state of *zivah*. According to R' Yehoshua, however, she is not considered to be one who has given birth in a state of *zivah,* since the labor pains resumed (or she gave birth) before Wednesday night. Accordingly, R' Eliezer adopts the stringent position (ruling that she is a *major zavah* and that she cannot begin her days of *tohar*-blood until after she counts seven clean days), whereas R' Yehoshua adopts the lenient position (ruling that she is not a *major zavah* and that her days of *tohar*-blood start on day fifteen after birth even if she has not counted seven clean days). This dispute, then, involves a matter of *kares* (*Rashi*). Thus, if the rebellious sage rules in accordance with R' Yehoshua's lenient position and the High Court holds the stringent position of R' Eliezer, the sage will be a *zakein mamrei.*

14. I.e. even if her bleeding continues unabated after the labor pains subside, it is considered to be relief from labor, and the day-long cessation of labor indicates that the labor preceding it was false (see *Rashi*).

15. Shmuel maintains that by Torah law, a court that adjudicates certain monetary disputes (e.g. loans) may consist of a single judge (see above, 2b-3a); a three-judge panel is required only by Rabbinic decree. Shmuel thus maintains that a verdict of two judges is valid after the fact, although the court is considered insolent for violating the Rabbinic decree.

16. The Gemara (5b-6a) cites a Tannaic dispute regarding the use of fewer than three judges for cases in which the litigants agree to submit their case for arbitrated compromise. R' Abahu observes that the Tannaic dispute is only in regard to compromise; concerning judgment according to the strict dictates of Torah law, however, all agree that three judges are required.

Now, if a loan dispute were to be adjudicated by only two judges, and money was extracted from one litigant and given to the other based on

דין בתו מאנוסתו [א] דאמר רבא א"ל רב יצחק בר אבודימי אתיא א) הנה ב) הנה אתיא זימה ג) זימה בין דם לדם בין דם נדה דם לידה דם זיבה דם נדה בפלוגתא עקביא בן מהללאל ורבנן דתנן [ג] דם הירוק עקביא בן מהללאל מטמא וחכמים [א] מטהרין דם לידה בפלוגתא דרב ולוי דאתמר [ג] רב אמר [ב] מעין אחד הוא התורה טימאתו והתורה טיהרתו ולוי אמר שני מעיינות הן נסתם הטמא נפתח הטהור נסתם הטהור נפתח הטמא: דם זיבה בפלוגתא דר"א ורבי יהושע דתנן [ד] קישתה שלשה ימים בתוך אחד עשר יום אם שפתה מעת לעת וילדה [ג] הרי זו יולדת בזוב דברי ר"א ור' יהושע אומר לילה ויום כלילי שבת ויומו ששפתה מן הצער ולא מן הדם בין דין לדין בין דיני ממונות דיני נפשות דיני מכות דיני ממונות בפלוגתא דשמואל ורבי אבהו [ה] דאמר שמואל שנים שדנו דיניהם דין אלא שנקראין בית דין חצוף ורבי אבהו אמר [ו] לדברי הכל אין דיניהן דין דיני נפשות בפלוגתא דרבי ורבנן דתניא [ז] רבי אומר ד) ונתת נפש תחת נפש ממון אתה אומר ממון או אינו אלא נפש ממש נאמר ה) נתינה למעלה ונאמר נתינה למטה מה להלן ממון אף כאן ממון דיני מכות בפלוגתא דרבי ישמעאל ורבנן דתנן [ח] מכות בג' משום רבי ישמעאל אמרו בכ"ג בין נגע לנגע בין נגעי אדם נגעי בתים נגעי בגדים נגעי אדם בפלוגתא דרבי יהושע ורבנן [ט] דתנן [ד] אם בהרת קדם לשער הלבן טמא אם שער לבן קדם לבהרת טהור ספק [ה] טמא רבי יהושע אומר כהה מאי כהה אמר [י] רבא כהה טהור נגעי בתים בפלוגתא דרבי אלעזר ברבי שמעון ורבנן [כ] דתנן רבי אליעזר ברבי שמעון אומר לעולם אין הבית טמא עד שיראה כשני גריסין על שתי אבנים בשתי כתלים בקרן זוית ארכו כשני גריסין ורחבו כגריס מאי טעמא דר' אלעזר בר"ש כתיב ו) קיר וכתיב ו) קירות איזהו קיר שהוא כקירות הוי אומר זה קרן זוית נגעי בגדים בפלוגתא דר' ([ל] יונתן) בן אבטולמוס ורבנן [מ] דתניא ר' ([ל] יונתן) בן אבטולמוס אומר מנין לפריחה

רש"י

דרב יצחק בר אבודימי. באלו הן הנשרפין פרישית לה גבי בתו מאנוסתו דמהאי דינא ילפינן והוא דבר שזדונו כרת: הירוק עקביא בן מהללאל מטמא. דם הירוק הוי דם הנדה ואם אמר זקן ממרא כעקביא בן מהללאל מייתי לה לחיוב כרת שפעמים שרואה דם הירוק בתחלת נדותה ולבסוף ב' ימים רואה דם אדום ופוסקת והיא מתחלת למנות שבעה ימים מראיית דם ירוק וטובלת ומשמשת עם בעלה ב' ימים בנדותה לפי שדם הירוק טהור הוא והיה לה להתחיל למנות מראיית דם אדום: מעין אחד הוא. דם הבא בשבועיים של נקיבה שהוא טמא ודם הבא לאחר שבועיים שהוא טהור ממעין אחד הוא: התורה טימאתו. כל שבועיים: והתורה טיהרתו. לאחר שבועיים וחזרה וטימאתו לאחר שכלין ימי טוהר: ולוי אמר ב' מעיינות הן. נסתם הטמא לאחר שבועיים ונפתח הטהור וכשנסתם הטהור בסוף ימי טוהר נפתח הטמא ואמרי' במס' נדה מאי בינייהו בשופעת מתוך שבועיים לאחר שבועיים או מתוך שמונים לאחר שמונים לרב אע"פ שלא פסק מעיינה בתוך שבועיים ויוצא דם לאחר שבועיים ממנה טהור וללוי טמא עד שתפסוק שעה דנימא נסתם הטמא והשופעת מתוך שמונים לאחר שמונים לרב טמאה ואע"פ שזהו מעין עצמו של ימי טוהר וללוי טהורה עד שיפסוק מעין הטהור ויפתח מעין הטמא ואי איפלוג זקן ממרא ורבנן בהא קאתי לידי כרת אי רבנן כרב והוא כלוי איכא כרת לאחר ימי טוהר ואי רבנן כלוי והוא כרב איכא כרת בתחלת ימי טוהר דרב לקולא ולוי לחומרא: קישתה ג' ימים בתוך אחד עשר יום כו'. כתיב בפרשת זבה באחד עשר יום שבין נדה לנדה שהם הימים המביאין לידי זיבה ואשה כי יזוב זוב דמה ימים רבים ותניא בפרק בנות כותים (נדה לו:) דמה מחמת עצמה ולא מחמת ולד מגיד שדם הקישוי שילא קודם הולד מחמת צער הקישוי אינו מביאה לידי זיבה וכ"ש דם שלאחר הולד אבל אם ראתה ג' ימים רצופין בהן מתוך קושי ושפתה קודם יציאת הולד יום אחד מעת לעת ששקטה ונחה מצערה ואח"כ ילדה בין מתוך קושי בין מתוך שופי הרי זו יולדת בזוב לפי שכיון שלאחר ג' שפתה איגלאי מילתא דלאו מחמת ולד אתא ונעשית בהן זבה למנות ז' נקיים כדין זבה וכל זמן שלא תספור ז' נקיים לא יהא דם שלה דם טוהר ואפילו לאחר שבועיים ואחר מלאת שמונים שלה צריכה שני קרבנות אחד ללידתה ואחד לזיבתה: לילה ויום. אבל מעת לעת לא חשיב שופי אם שפתה משש שעות של שלישי עד שש שעות של ד' הואיל וה"ל מקצת קושי ביום השופי לא הויא יולדת בזוב ור"א לחומרא ורבי יהושע לקולא והיינו דבר שזדונו כרת: ששפתה מן הצער. ואין אנו חוששין אם לא שפתה מן הדם: בפלוגתא דשמואל ור' אבהו. וכיון דאפיקי הני בי תרי ממונא מהאי ויהבו להאי בדינא דידהו והלך זה וקידש אשה באותו ממון לשמואל מקודשת לרבי אבהו אינה מקודשת דה"ל קידשה בגזל וקי"ל בפ"ב דקידושין (דף נב.) גבי מעשה דה' נשים שנתקדשו בכלכלה קידשה בגזל אינה מקודשת דהשתא אתי לידי כרת אי רבנן כשמואל וזקן ממרא כרבי אבהו וא"נ רבנן כרבי אבהו וזקן ממרא כשמואל אתי לידי כרת דקא משוי להו קידושין ואי אתי איניש אחרינא לבתר הכי וקדשה מפיק לה מבתרא בלא גט וה"ל דבר שזדונו כרת בלא עדים ובלא התראה דאי איכא עדים והתראה הוי מיתת ב"ד ואי ליכא לא זה ולא זה הוי כרת: ונתתה נפש תחת נפש. במתכוין להרוג את זה והרג את זה ומיחייב ליה רבי ממון ורבנן פטרי וכפלוגתא באלו הן הנשרפין [ס] ואי תפסו יורשין דהרוג ממונא דהורג ופטר ליה זקן ממרא וקידשו בו את האשה לרבי מקודשת לרבנן אינה מקודשת ואי אתי איניש אחרינא וקידשה מקודשת לשני הרי חיוב כרת בדבר: נתינה למעלה. גבי נוגף אשה הרה ונתן בפלילים (שמות כא) דמי ולדות: בכ"ג. ואם הלקוהו ג' לר' ישמעאל חייבין לו ממון כשאר חובל בחבירו ומקדש בו את האשה ולרבנן בדין הלקוהו ואם תפס ממונו וקידש בו אינה מקודשת: ספק. אם זה קדם אם זה קדם: כהה. כאילו כהה הנגע דהוי מסימני טהרה כשמשתנה הלובן לאחר הסגר ולרבנן אם נכנס למקדש חייב כרת ולר' יהושע פטור: עד שיראה כשני גריסין. שיעור הנגע כגריס על גריס וכתיב את האבנים אשר בהן הנגע שיהא הנגע על שתי אבנים על כל אחד ואחד שיעור נגע על ב' כתלים ובקרן זוית כגון מקצוע דרומית מזרחית אורכו כשני גריסין ורחבו כגריס שיהא בקיר הדרומי גריס וכן בקיר המזרחי והנגע כולו מחובר כאחד: מאי טעמא דר' אליעזר. דבעי קרן זוית: כתיב. ומראיהן שפל מן הקיר (ויקרא יד) וכתיב והנה הנגע בקירות הבית: זה קרן זוית. ורבנן לא בעו קרן זוית והיכא דליתיה בקרן זוית ונכנס בה אדם ואח"כ נכנס למקדש לרבנן חייב כרת לר' אלעזר בר"ש פטור:

תוספות

דין בתו מאנוסתו. בכולהו משכח פלוגתא בר מהאי ורוצה לומר דאין זקן ממרא מודה בגזירה שוה זו:

עקביא בן מהללאל מטמא. ואף על גב דעקביא מחמיר זמנין דהויא קולא כגון שרואה דם אדום ומשלימתו לדם ירוק:

כלילי שבת ויומו. לאפוקי יום תחלה ואח"כ לילה אלא א"כ שפתה לילה שלם ואחר כך יום שלם כלילי שבת ויום שהיום הולך אחר הלילה: בפלוגתא דרבי יהושע ורבנן. פי' בקונטרס לרבנן אם נכנס למקדש חייב ולרבי יהושע פטור ולא יתכן דאכי האי גוונא לא מחייב זקן ממרא כיון שהוא בעולה ויורד דהא ילפינן לעיל דבר דבר מונעלם דבר דתנן בפ' [הור'] כהן משוח (הוריות דף ט.) מביאין עולה ויורד על טומאת מקדש וקדשיו ויש לפרש כדפרישית לעיל [י] בככר של תרומה:

רבי יהושע אומר כיהה. פירש בקונטרס כאילו כיהה הנגע דהוא מסימני טהרה כשמשתנה בו לובן שלו לאחר הסגר וקשה היכי פריך בשילהי נזיר (דף סה:) ודילמא כיהה וטמא הא לפירושו כל כיהה טהור ועוד אי כיהה וטמא היינו ת"ק ונראה כגירסת ר"ח קהה בקו"ף ול"ג אומר כלומר ר' יהושע הקשה ודקדק בדבר כמו [ס] הקהה את שיניו וכן מקהו אקהייתא בשוקא (יבמות דף קי:) מאספים אסופות של בני אדם כלומר עמדו למניין ולא ידע הש"ס אם להביא ראיה לת"ק או לסתור ולהכי בעי מאי קיהה וקאמר קיהה וטיהר ומיהו בירושלמי דריש שבועות משמע דיש כיהה טמא דאמר התם והתורה אמרה והנה כהה הנגע הכהה טמא וכהה מן הכהה טהור:

מרחו

ליקוטי רש"י

דין בתו מאנוסתו. דהיינו בתו ובת בנו ובת בתו מאנוסתו דלאו בכלל אשה ובתה דקרא נינהו דהתם באשתו על ידי קידושין קאמר דדרשינן לה ביבמות [צז.] מקראי דרבה רמי כתיב ערות בת בנך או בת בתך וגו' הא בת בנה ובת בתה שלא ילדה ממך גלה וכתיב ערות אשה ובתה לא תגלה משמע בין שילדתו לך בין שילדתו לאיש אחר לא קשיא כאן באנוסין כאן בנישואין אם אנוסתך או מפותה לך היא אי אתה מוזהר על בתה אלא אם כן ממך היא ואם אשתך היא אתה מוזהר אף על בת שילדה לאיש אחר. אתיא הנה הנה אתיא זמה זמה. מעיקרא מייתינן לה בהנה הנה והדר בזמה וזמה כתיב הכא (ויקרא יח) כי ערותך הנה וכתיב בשאר אשתו (שם ויקרא יח) שארה הנה מה להלן זמה עמו אף כאן זמה עמו ובתר דאייתינן זמה לשאר דידיה ילפינן בה שריפה בזמה וזמה נאמר כאן (שם ויקרא י"ח) זמה ונאמר להלן (שם כ) בשריפה זמה מה להלן שריפה אף כאן שריפה [לעיל עה:]. מעין אחד הוא. דם הבא בתוך ז' של לידה ודם הבא לאחר שבעה ממעין אחד הוא. התורה טמאתו. תוך שבעה לזכר וי"ד לנקבה. שני מעיינות הן. נפתח הטמא כל ימי הלידה ונסתם הטהור ולסוף שבעה לזכר וי"ד לנקבה נסתם הטמא ונפתח הטהור [נדה יא.]. מעין אחד הוא. דם הבא בימי לידה ודם הבא בימי טוהר ממעין אחד הן באין. התורה טמאתו. כל שבעה לזכר וי"ד לנקבה. והתורה טהרתו. אחר מכן. נסתם הטמא. לאחר שבועים ונפתח הטהור. נסתם הטהור. לאחר שמנים ונפתח הטמא [שם לה:]. קשתה ג' ימים. דקיי"ל (נדה דף לו:) בנדה דאורייתא המקשה בתוך י"א שבין נדה לנדה ורואה דם ג' ימים רצופים מחמת צער וולדה אינה באה לידי זיבה להיות צריכה ספירת ז' נקיים כיולדת בזוב אלא ימי טומאת לידה כיולדת גרידתא דתניא (שם) כי יזוב זוב דמה דמה מחמת עצמה ולא מחמת ולד [יבמות פג.]. קשתה. מחמת ולד. ג' ימים. בתוך אחד עשר יום שבין נדה לנדה וראתה כל שלשתן הימים רצופין. ושפתה. מצערה. מעת לעת. כרביעי. וילדה. איגלאי מילתא דדמים שראתה לא באו מחמת ולד הלכך הרי זו יולדת בזוב אבל אם לא שפתה סמוך ללידתה כל דמים שראתה מחמת ולד הוא ורחמנא טהרינהו מזיבה דכתיב זוב דמה דמה מחמת עצמה ולא דמה מחמת ולד. לילה ויום. דאם שפתה בחצי יום שלישי וילדה יום רביעי דשפתה מעת לעת אין זו שופי אלא אם כן שפתה לילה ויום שלאחר הלילה כלילי שבת ויומו. ששפתה מן הצער ולא מן הדם. דלא"ג דחזיא דם הוי שופי [שם לו:]. בית דין חצוף. שעברו על תקנת חכמים. דברי הכל. לקמן סנהדרין (ו.) קאי דפליגי בפשרה אשמעינן ר' אבהו דבדין כולהו מודו דבעינן שלשה [לעיל ב:]. דכתיב נפש תחת נפש. אם אסון יהיה שמתה האשה יתן ממון דמי האשה ליורשיה שאין עליה חיוב מיתה שלא נתכוון לה אלא לחברו נתכוון דכתיב וכי ינצו אנשים יחדיו קסבר רבי נתכוון להרוג את זה והרג את זה פטור ממיתה ומשלם ממון. נתינה למעלה. לענין דמי וולדות כתיב ונתן בפלילים (שמות כא). נתינה למטה. ונתתה נפש תחת נפש ממון ומאי נפש דמי הנפש [חגיגה יא.]. נתינה למעלה. גבי לא יהיה אסון ונתן בפלילים (שמות כא) דמי ולדות [לעיל עט:]. ואם אסון יהיה. באשה. ונתתה נפש תחת נפש. רבותינו חולקין בדבר. יש אומרים נפש ממש ויש אומרים ממון אבל לא נפש ממש שהמתכוין להרוג את זה והרג את זה פטור ממיתה ומשלם ליורשיו דמיו כמו שהיה נמכר בשוק [שמות כא, כג]. מכות. מלקות ארבעים טעמא דר' ישמעאל ורבנן מפרש בגמרא סנהדרין (י.) מקראי [לעיל ב.]. אם בהרת קדמה לשער לבן טמא. דשער לבן שפרח בו הוא סימן לטומאה, כדכתיב (ויקרא יג) והנה נהפך שער לבן בבהרת. טהור. לפי מה שכתוב בתורה [ב"מ פו.]. טמא. דהכי כתיב קרא (ויקרא יג) שער לבן בבהרת. רבי יהושע אומר כהה. כדמפרש רבה. כהה טהור. הרי הוא ככהה הנגע ממראהו שהוא טהור ומשם ר' משה הדרשן שמעתי ורבי יהושע קיהה מאי קיהה אמר רבה קיהה וטיהר כלומר קיהה בדבר ונחלק עליהם וטיהר [כאדם שנקהו שיניו על אדם שאין משגיח לדבריו] וכן מצאתי בת"כ ור' יהושע קיהה טיהר אלמא העמד הגוף על חזקתו ולא תטמאנו מספק [כתובות עה:]. אם בהרת קודמת לשער לבן טמא. דשער לבן מסימני טומאה וכגון שקדמתו בהרת דכתיב (ויקרא יג) והנה נהפך שער לבן בבהרת. כהה טהור. הרי הוא כנגע שכהה מראיתו בשבוע של הסגר שהוא סימן טהרה דכתיב (שם) והנה כהה הנגע וגו' ובשם רבי משה הדרשן שמעתי קיהה כלומר קיהה בדבר ונחלק עליו וכן מצאתי בת"כ ר' יהושע קיהה וטיהר. שיעור נגע כגריס. לאורך ולרוחב. כשני גריסין על שני אבנים שבקרן זוית. אחד בכותל זה ואחד בכותל זה. ארכו כשני גריסין ורחבו כגריס. דכשהוא מוטל ארכו על ב' אבנים נמצא בכל אבן גריס על גריס כשיעור נגע ושתי אבנים בעינן דכתיב (ויקרא יד) וחלצו את האבנים תרתי משמע ובכל אחת שיעור נגע. בקרן זוית. ואותן שתי אבנים יהיו בקרן זוית אחד בכותל זה ואחד בכותל זה והנגע משוך בשתיהן ארכו שני גריסין ורחבו כגריס שיהא בכל אבן כגריס על גריס. מאי טעמא דר' אלעזר. דבעי קרן זוית. כתיב קיר. ומראיהן שפל מן הקיר [לעיל עא.].

עין משפט נר מצוה

מג א מיי' פ"א מהל' איסורי ביאה הלכה ו סמג לאוין קיא ועשין רמג טוש"ע י"ד סי' קפח סעיף א:
מד ב מיי' שם פ"ו הלכה א סמג שם:
מה ג מיי' שם פ"ו הלכה א סמג שם:
מו ד מיי' פ"ב מהלכות טומאת צרעת הלכה ו סמג עשין רלד:
מז ה מיי' שם הלכה ט:

מסורת הש"ס

א) לעיל נא. עה: עו. חגיגה יא: יבמות ג. כריתות ה., ב) נדה יט., ג) [נדה לה:], ד) נדה לו:, ה) לעיל ג. ה: ל. כתובות כב., ו) [לעיל ג: ו.], ז) חגיגה יא. [לעיל עט.], ח) לעיל ב. [ט.], ט) ב"מ פו. נדה יט. נזיר סה: ע"ש כתובות עה: נגעים פ"ד מי"א, י) [לפי גיר' תוס' בכתובות ובנדה רבה ובנזיר איתא רב יהודה], כ) לעיל עא. נדה יט. נגעים פי"ב מ"ג, ל) [נ"ל נתן], מ) [נדה יט. זבחים מט:], נ) [עמוד א ד"ה ורשב"ל], ס) [בהגדה של פסח].

גליון הש"ס

רש"י ד"ה בפלוגתא וכו' ואי תפסו יורשין. עי' טורי אבן חגיגה באבני שהם דף י ע"א ד"ה נפש:

תורה אור השלם

א) עֶרְוַת בַּת בִּנְךָ אוֹ בַת בִּתְּךָ לֹא תְגַלֶּה עֶרְוָתָן כִּי עֶרְוָתְךָ הֵנָּה: [ויקרא יח, י]

ב) עֶרְוַת אִשָּׁה וּבִתָּהּ לֹא תְגַלֵּה אֶת בַּת בְּנָהּ וְאֶת בַּת בִּתָּהּ לֹא תִקַּח לְגַלּוֹת עֶרְוָתָהּ שַׁאֲרָה הֵנָּה זִמָּה הִוא: [ויקרא יח, יז]

ג) וְאִישׁ אֲשֶׁר יִקַּח אֶת אִשָּׁה וְאֶת אִמָּהּ זִמָּה הִוא בָּאֵשׁ יִשְׂרְפוּ אֹתוֹ וְאֶתְהֶן וְלֹא תִהְיֶה זִמָּה בְּתוֹכְכֶם: [ויקרא כ, יד]

ד) וְאִם אָסוֹן יִהְיֶה וְנָתַתָּה נֶפֶשׁ תַּחַת נָפֶשׁ: [שמות כא, כג]

ה) וְכִי יִנָּצוּ אֲנָשִׁים וְנָגְפוּ אִשָּׁה הָרָה וְיָצְאוּ יְלָדֶיהָ וְלֹא יִהְיֶה אָסוֹן עָנוֹשׁ יֵעָנֵשׁ כַּאֲשֶׁר יָשִׁית עָלָיו בַּעַל הָאִשָּׁה וְנָתַן בִּפְלִלִים: [שמות כא, כב]

ו) וְרָאָה אֶת הַנֶּגַע וְהִנֵּה הַנֶּגַע בְּקִירֹת הַבַּיִת שְׁקַעֲרוּרֹת יְרַקְרַקֹּת אוֹ אֲדַמְדַּמֹּת וּמַרְאֵיהֶן שָׁפָל מִן הַקִּיר: [ויקרא יד, לז]

Rav Pappa explains the next case of a "verdict":

דִּינֵי נְפָשׁוֹת – To what dispute concerning **capital cases** does the Baraisa refer? בִּפְלוּגְתָּא דְּרַבִּי וְרַבָּנָן – **It refers to** where the sage and the High Court had **the** same **dispute** as the one **between Rebbi and the Rabbis.** דְּתַנְיָא – **For it was taught in a Baraisa:**[17] רַבִּי אוֹמֵר – REBBI SAYS: "וְנָתַתָּה נֶפֶשׁ תַּחַת נָפֶשׁ" – When the verse states: *AND YOU SHALL AWARD A LIFE FOR A LIFE,* מָמוֹן – it refers to MONETARY COMPENSATION.[18] אַתָּה אוֹמֵר מָמוֹן – Now, YOU SAY it refers to MONETARY COMPENSATION, אוֹ אֵינוֹ אֶלָּא נֶפֶשׁ מַמָּשׁ – BUT PERHAPS that is NOT so; rather, it means LITERALLY A "LIFE," i.e. the murderer is executed. To this we may answer: נֶאֱמַר נְתִינָה לְמַעְלָה – IT IS STATED "GIVING" ABOVE, in the preceding verse,[19] וְנֶאֱמַר נְתִינָה לְמַטָּה – AND IT IS STATED "GIVING" BELOW, in our verse. The common use of the expression "giving" establishes a link between these verses, from which we derive: מָה לְהַלָּן מָמוֹן – JUST AS THERE the reference is to MONETARY COMPENSATION, אַף כָּאן מָמוֹן – SO HERE TOO the reference is to MONETARY COMPENSATION.[20]

Rav Pappa explains the final case of "verdict":

דִּינֵי מַכּוֹת – To what dispute regarding **cases concerning lashes** does the Baraisa refer? בִּפְלוּגְתָּא דְּרַבִּי יִשְׁמָעֵאל וְרַבָּנָן – **It refers to** where the sage and the High Court had **the** same **dispute** as the one **between R' Yishmael and the Rabbis.** דִּתְנַן – **For we learned in a Mishnah:**[21] מַכּוֹת בִּשְׁלֹשָׁה – Cases where the defendant is accused of being liable for LASHES are judged BY a court of THREE. מִשּׁוּם רַבִּי יִשְׁמָעֵאל אָמְרוּ – IN THE NAME OF R' YISHMAEL THEY SAID: בְּעֶשְׂרִים וּשְׁלֹשָׁה – Cases of lashes are judged BY a court of TWENTY-THREE.[22]

Rav Pappa continues his interpretive citation of the Baraisa: "בֵּין נֶגַע לָנֶגַע" – *BETWEEN AFFLICTION AND AFFLICTION;* בֵּין נִגְעֵי אָדָם נִגְעֵי בָתִּים נִגְעֵי בְגָדִים – this alludes to a dispute BETWEEN the sages regarding *TZARAAS* OF PEOPLE, *TZARAAS* OF HOUSES, OR *TZARAAS* OF CLOTHING.

Rav Pappa explains each case separately:

נִגְעֵי אָדָם – To what dispute concerning ***tzaraas*** **of people** does the Baraisa refer? בִּפְלוּגְתָּא דְּרַבִּי יְהוֹשֻׁעַ וְרַבָּנָן – **It refers to** where the sage and the High Court had **the** same **dispute** as the one **between R' Yehoshua and the Rabbis.** דִּתְנַן – **For we learned in a Mishnah:**[23] אִם בַּהֶרֶת קָדַם לְשֵׂעָר הַלָּבָן – IF THE *BAHERES*[24] PRECEDED THE WHITE HAIR, טָמֵא – [THE *BAHERES*] IS *TAMEI.* אִם שֵׂעָר לָבָן קָדַם לַבַּהֶרֶת – BUT IF THE WHITE HAIR PRECEDED THE *BAHERES,* טָהוֹר – IT IS *TAHOR.*[25] סָפֵק טָמֵא – If there is DOUBT about which came first, it is ruled *TAMEI.* רַבִּי יְהוֹשֻׁעַ אוֹמֵר – BUT R' YEHOSHUA SAYS: כֵּהָה – IT IS FAINT.

The Gemara explains R' Yehoshua's statement:

מַאי כֵּהָה – **What is** meant by "**it is faint**"? אָמַר רָבָא – **Rava**

NOTES

their ruling, the following dispute would result. Shmuel would maintain that the money was rightfully extracted and it legally belongs to the victorious litigant, while R' Abahu would maintain that it is stolen money in the hands of the "victorious" litigant. Now, the law is that if a man betroths a woman with stolen money, the betrothal, or *kiddushin,* is not valid (see *Kiddushin* 52a). Thus, if a dissenting sage were to rule as R' Abahu while the High Court ruled as Shmuel, and the victor were to use the money extracted by the two-member court for money of *kiddushin,* the sage would rule the marriage invalid while the High Court would rule it valid. The sage would thus be permitting other men to this married woman, a sin punishable by *kares.* [Indeed, when there are witnesses to the sin or the sinner is properly warned, he is *executed* for this transgression. In absence of either witnesses or a warning, however, the intentional sinner incurs *kares*; if the transgression is inadvertent, he is liable to a *chatas.*]

Furthermore, even if the dissenting sage were to rule as Shmuel, his ruling could result in a matter of *kares.* For the sage, following Shmuel, would have ruled in the above case that the woman was married, while the High Court, ruling as R' Abahu, would have ruled her to be unmarried. Now, if *another* man were then to present this woman with legitimate *kiddushin* money, the High Court would recognize this second marriage and require her to obtain a *get* from the second man before allowing her to remain with her first husband (or marry anyone else). The sage, on the other hand, would not require her to obtain a *get* from the second "husband" and would allow her to remain with the first husband even though according to the High Court she is legally married to the second man (*Rashi*).

[In truth, the Gemara could have avoided mentioning Shmuel and R' Abahu and simply stated that the sage and the High Court disputed a particular monetary law – e.g. the sage ruled that Reuven owed Shimon one hundred *zuz,* while the High Court ruled that he did not. Shimon then seized the "owed" money, and betrothed a woman with it. This could result in a sin of *kares* as explained above. Indeed, *Rambam* (*Hil. Mamrim* 4:2) includes such a case (see *Toras Chaim* and *Aruch LaNer*).]

17. The Baraisa discusses *Exodus* 21:23, which deals with a case in which two men were fighting with intent to kill each other, and a woman bystander was inadvertently struck and killed by a blow that one of the combatants had intended for his opponent. The Rabbis maintain that the intent that the combatant had to kill the other is sufficient to consider the killing of the woman "intentional," and the killer is himself executed. The Baraisa now records Rebbi's opinion.

18. Rebbi maintains that the woman's killing cannot be legally considered "intentional," and the Torah cannot have meant that the killer be put to death. Rather, the phrase must refer to monetary damages; i.e. he must give to the woman's heirs the "value" of her life, determined by how much she would fetch if sold on the auction block as a maidservant.

19. Ibid. v. 22. The Torah there speaks of a case in which the woman is not killed due to the combatant's blow but suffers a miscarriage as a result of it. The Torah rules: *and he shall give by order of judges,* i.e. he shall pay monetary compensation for causing the woman to miscarry.

20. The Rabbis and Rebbi dispute whether the woman's heirs are entitled to monetary damages. If the heirs would on their own seize money belonging to the murderer to satisfy the monetary damages, the Rabbis would consider the money as stolen in their hands. Rebbi, however, would consider it rightfully theirs. Thus, if this money was used to betroth a woman it could result in a sin punishable by *kares;* see note 16 (*Rashi*).

21. Above, 2a.

22. According to R' Yishmael, lashes meted out by a three-member court are illegal, being unauthorized by a proper Jewish court. Those judges authorizing the lashes are liable to pay compensatory damages to the defendant, just as though he were struck by a person on the street (see Aruch LaNer who explains why the judges are held liable when it was not they, but an officer of the court, who inflicted the lashes). According to the Rabbis, however, since the three-member court was authorized to mete out the lashes, no damages are owed. If money was extracted from the judges to pay damages to the defendant, the Rabbis would consider it stolen money, while R' Yishmael would consider it the rightful property of the defendant. Thus, if that money was used by the defendant to betroth a woman, it could result in a sin punishable by *kares,* as explained in note 16 (*Rashi*).

[As above, the Gemara could have omitted the dispute of R' Yishmael and the Rabbis and simply stated that the sage and the High Court disputed a particular law involving lashes. This could result in a *kares* penalty, as explained above. Again, *Rambam* (ad loc.) includes such a case.]

23. *Negaim* 4:11.

24. A snow-white spot, one of the skin discolorations symptomatic of *tzaraas* (*Negaim* 1:1). If the spot contains two white hairs, it is confirmed as *tzaraas* immediately. However, as this Mishnah explains, not all white hairs result in such confirmation.

25. In order to be declared *tamei,* the discoloration must appear first and the white hairs later. If the order is reversed, the affliction is *tahor* (i.e. it is not confirmed as *tamei,* and it is treated as if the hairs were not present).

עין משפט
נר מצוה

מג א מיי' פ"ה מהל' איסורי ביאה הלכה ו סמג לאוין קיא ועשין רמג טוש"ע י"ד סי' קפח סעיף א:
מד ב מיי' שם פ"ו הלכה א סמג שם:
מה ג מיי' שם פ"ז הלכה א סמג שם:
מו ד מיי' פ"ב מהלכות טומאת צרעת הלכה ו סמג עשין רלד:
מז ה מיי' שם הלכה ט:

דין בתו מאנוסתו [א] דאמר רבא א"ל רב יצחק בר אבודימי אתיא [א] הנה [ב] הנה אתיא זימה [ג] זימה בין דם לדם בין דם נדה דם לידה דם זיבה דם נדה בפלוגתא עקביא בן מהללאל ורבנן דתנן [ד] דם הירוק עקביא בן מהללאל מטמא וחכמים [א] מטהרין דם לידה בפלוגתא דרב ולוי דאתמר [ה] רב אמר [ב] מעין אחד הוא התורה טימאתו והתורה טיהרתו ולוי אמר שני מעיינות הן נסתם הטמא נפתח הטהור נסתם הטהור נפתח הטמא: דם זיבה בפלוגתא דר"א ורבי יהושע דתנן [ו] קישתה שלשה ימים בתוך אחד עשר יום אם שפתה מעת לעת וילדה [ג] הרי זו יולדת בזוב דברי ר"א ור' יהושע אומר לילה ויום כלילי שבת ויומו ששפתה מן הצער ולא מן הדם בין דין לדין בין דיני ממונות דיני נפשות דיני מכות דיני ממונות בפלוגתא דשמואל ורבי אבהו [ז] דאמר שמואל שנים שדנו דיניהם דין אלא שנקראין בית דין חצוף ורבי אבהו אמר [ח] לדברי הכל אין דיניהן דין דיני נפשות בפלוגתא דרבי ורבנן דתניא [י] רבי אומר [ד] ונתת נפש תחת נפש ממון אתה אומר ממון או אינו אלא נפש ממש נאמר [ה] נתינה למעלה ונאמר נתינה למטה מה להלן ממון אף כאן ממון דיני מכות בפלוגתא דרבי ישמעאל ורבנן דתנן [ט] מכות בג' משום רבי ישמעאל אמרו בכ"ג בין נגע לנגע בין נגעי אדם נגעי בתים נגעי בגדים נגעי אדם בפלוגתא דרבי יהושע ורבנן [ט] דתנן [ד] אם בהרת קדם לשער הלבן טמא אם שער לבן קדם לבהרת טהור ספק [ה] טמא רבי יהושע אומר כהה מאי כהה אמר [י] רבא כהה טהור נגעי בתים בפלוגתא דרבי אלעזר ברבי שמעון ורבנן [כ] דתנן רבי אליעזר ברבי שמעון אומר לעולם אין הבית טמא עד שיראה כשני גריסין על שתי אבנים בשתי כתלים בקרן זוית ארכו כשני גריסין ורחבו כגריס מאי טעמא דר' אלעזר בר"ש כתיב [ו] קיר וכתיב [ו] קירות איזהו קיר שהוא כקירות הוי אומר זה קרן זוית נגעי בגדים בפלוגתא דר' ([ל] יונתן) בן אבטולמוס ורבנן [מ] דתניא ר' ([ל] יונתן) בן אבטולמוס אומר מנין

לפריחה

רש"י

דין בתו מאנוסתו. בכולהו משכח פלוגתא בר מהאי ורוצה לומר דאין זקן ממרא מודה בגזירה שוה זו: עקביא בן מהללאל מטמא. ואף על גב דעקביא מחמיר זמנין דהויא קולא כגון שרואה דם אדום ומשלימתו לדם ירוק: דרב יצחק בר אבודימי. באלו הן הנשרפין פרישית לה גבי בתו מאנוסתו דמהאי דינא ילפינן והוא דבר שזדונו כרת: הירוק עקביא בן מהללאל מטמא. דם הירוק הוי דם הנדה ואם אמר זקן ממרא כעקביא בן מהללאל מייתי לה לחיוב כרת שפעמים שרואה דם הירוק בתחלת נדותה ולבסוף ב' ימים רואה דם אדום ופוסקת והיא מתחלת למנות שבעה ימים מראיית דם ירוק וטובלת ומשמשת עם בעלה ב' ימים בנדותה לפי שדם הירוק טהור הוא והיה לה להתחיל למנות מראיית דם אדום: מעין אחד הוא. דם הבא בשבועיים של נקיבה שהוא טמא ודם הבא לאחר שבועיים שהוא טהור ממעין אחד הוא: התורה טימאתו. כל שבועיים: והתורה טיהרתו. לאחר שבועיים וחזרה וטימאתו לאחר שכלין ימי טוהר: ולוי אמר ב' מעיינות הן. נסתם הטמא לאחר שבועיים ונפתח הטהור וכשנסתם הטהור בסוף ימי טוהר נפתח הטמא ואמרי' במס' נדה מאי בינייהו בשופעת מתוך שבועיים לאחר שבועיים או מתוך שמונים לאחר שמונים לרב אע"פ שלא פסק מעיינה בתוך שבועיים ויוצא דם לאחר שבועיים ממנה טהור וללוי טמא עד שתפסוק שעה דנימא נסתם הטמא והשופעת מתוך שמונים לאחר שמונים לרב טמאה ואע"פ שזהו מעין עצמו של ימי טוהר וללוי טהורה עד שיפסוק מעין הטהור ויפתח מעין הטמא ואי איפלוג זקן ממרא ורבנן בהא קאתי לידי כרת אי רבנן כרב והוא כלוי איכא כרת לאחר ימי טוהר ואי רבנן כלוי והוא כרב איכא כרת בתחלת ימי טוהר דרב לקולא ולוי לחומרא: קישתה ג' ימים בתוך אחד עשר יום כו'. כתיב בפרשת זבה באחד עשר יום שבין נדה לנדה שהם הימים המביאין לידי זיבה ואשה כי יזוב זוב דמה ימים רבים ותניא בפרק בנות כותים (נדה לו:) דמה מחמת עצמה ולא מחמת ולד מגיד שדם הקישוי שילא קודם הולד מחמת צער הקישוי אינו מביאה לידי זיבה וכ"ש דם שלאחר הולד אבל אם ראתה ג' ימים רצופין בהן מתוך קושי ושפתה קודם יציאת הולד יום אחד מעת לעת ששקטה ונחה מצערה ואח"כ ילדה בין מתוך קושי בין מתוך שופי הרי זו יולדת בזוב לפי שכיון שלאחר ג' שפתה איגלאי מילתא דלאו מחמת ולד אתא ונעשית בהן זבה למנות ז' נקיים כדין זבה וכל זמן שלא תספור ז' נקיים לא יהא דם שלה דם טוהר ואפילו לאחר שבועיים ואחר שלשת שמונים שלה צריכה שני קרבנות אחד ללידתה ואחד לזיבתה: לילה ויום. אבל מעת לעת לא חשיב שופי אם שפתה משש שעות של שלישי עד שש שעות של ד' הואיל וה"ל מקצת קושי ביום השופי לא הויא יולדת בזוב ור"א לחומרא ורבי יהושע לקולא והיינו דבר שזדונו כרת: ששפתה מן הצער. ואין אנו חוששין אם לא שפתה מן הדם: בפלוגתא דשמואל ור' אבהו. וכיון דאפיקי הני בי תרי ממונא מהאי ויהבו להאי בדינא דידהו והלך זה וקידש אשה באותו ממון לשמואל מקודשת לרבי אבהו אינה מקודשת דה"ל קידשה בגזל וקי"ל בפ"ב דקידושין (דף נב.) גבי מעשה דה' נשים שנתקדשו בכלכלה קידשה בגזל אינה מקודשת דהשתא אתי לידי כרת אי רבנן כשמואל וזקן ממרא כרבי אבהו וא"כ רבנן כרבי אבהו וזקן ממרא כשמואל אתי לידי כרת דקא משוי להו קידושין ואי אתי איניש אחרינא לבתר הכי וקדשה מפיק לה מבתרא בלא גט וה"ל דבר שזדונו כרת בלא עדים ובלא התראה דאי איכא עדים והתראה הוי מיתת ב"ד ואי ליכא לא זה ולא זה הוי כרת: ונתתה נפש תחת נפש. במתכוין להרוג את זה והרג את זה ומיחייב ליה רבי ממון ורבנן פטרי וכפלוגתא באלו הן הנשרפין [°] ואי תפסו יורשין דהרוג ממונא דהורג ופטר ליה זקן ממרא וקידשו בו את האשה לרבי מקודשת לרבנן אינה מקודשת ואי אתי איניש אחרינא וקידשה מקודשת לשני הרי חיוב כרת בדבר: נתינה למעלה. גבי נוגף אשה הרה ונתן בפלילים (שמות כא) דמי ולדות: בכ"ג. ואם הלקוהו ג' לר' ישמעאל חייבין לו ממון כשאר חובל בחבירו ומקדש בו את האשה ולרבנן בדין הלקוהו ואם תפס ממונו וקידש בו אינה מקודשת: ספק. אם זה קדם אם זה קדם: כהה. כאילו כהה הנגע דהוי מסימני טהרה כשמשתנה הלובן לאחר הסגר ולרבנן אם נכנס למקדש חייב כרת ולר' יהושע פטור: עד שיראה כשני גריסין. שיעור הנגע כגרים על גרים וכתיב את האבנים אשר בהן הנגע שיהא הנגע על שתי אבנים על כל אחד ואחד שיעור נגע על ב' כתלים ובקרן זוית כגון מקלוע דרומית מזרחית אורכו כשני גריסין ורחבו כגרים שיהא בקיר הדרומי גרים וכן בקיר המזרחי והנגע כולו מחובר כאחד: מאי טעמא דר' אליעזר. דבעי קרן זוית: כתיב. ומראיהן שפל מן הקיר (ויקרא יד) וכתיב והנה הנגע בקירות הבית: זה קרן זוית. ורבנן לא בעו קרן זוית והיכא דליתיה בקרן זוית ונכנס בה אדם ואח"כ נכנס למקדש לרבנן חייב כרת לר' אלעזר בר"ש פטור:

לפריחה

תוספות

כלילי שבת ויומו. לאפוקי יום תחלה ואח"כ לילה אלא א"כ שפתה לילה שלם ואחר כך יום שלם כלילי שבת ויום שהיום הולך אחר הלילה: בפלוגתא דרבי יהושע ורבנן. פי' בקונטרס לרבנן אם נכנס למקדש חייב ולרבי יהושע פטור ולא יתכן דאכי האי גוונא לא מחייב זקן ממרא כיון שהוא בעולה ויורד דהא ילפינן לעיל דבר דבר מונעלם דבר דתנן בפ' [הור'] כהן משוח (הוריות דף ט.) מביאין עולה ויורד על טומאת מקדש וקדשיו ויש לפרש כדפרישית לעיל[ט] בככר של תרומה: רבי יהושע אומר כיהה. פירש בקונטרס כאילו כיהה הנגע דהוא מסימני טהרה כשמשתנה בו לובן שלו לאחר הסגר וקשה היכי פריך בשילהי נזיר (דף סה:) ודילמא כיהה וטמא הא לפירושו כל כיהה טהור ועוד אי כיהה וטמא היינו ת"ק ונראה כגירסת ר"ח קהה בקו"ף ול"ג אומר כלומר ר' יהושע הקשה ודקדק בדבר כמו [פ] הקהה את שיניו וכן מקהו אקהייתא בשוקא (יבמות דף קי:) מאספים אסופות של בני אדם כלומר עמדו למניין ולא ידע הש"ס אם להביא ראיה לת"ק או לסתור ולהכי בעי מאי קיהה וקאמר קיהה וטיהר ומיהו בירושלמי דריש שבועות משמע דיש כיהה טמא דאמר התם והתורה אמרה והנה כהה הנגע הכהה טמא וכהה מן הכהה טהור:

מרחו

מסורת הש"ס

א) לעיל נא. עה: עו. חגיגה יא: יבמות ג. כריתות ה., ב) נדה יט., ג) [נדה לה:], ד) נדה לו:, ה) לעיל ג. ה: ל. כתובות כב., ו) [לעיל ג: ו.], ז) חגיגה יא. [לעיל עט.], ח) לעיל ג. [ט.], ט) ב"מ פו. נדה יט. נזיר סה: ע"ש כתובות עה: נגעים פ"ד מי"א, י) [לפי גיר' תוס' בכתובות ובנדה רבה ובנזיר איתא רב יהודה], כ) לעיל עא. נדה יט. נגעים פי"ב מ"ג, ל) [נ"ל נתן], מ) [נדה יט. זבחים מט:], נ) [עמוד א ד"ה ורשב"א], ס) [בהגדה של פסח].

גליון הש"ס

רש"י ד"ה בפלוגתא וכו' ואי תפסו יורשין. עי' טורי אבן חגיגה באבני שהם דף י ע"א ד"ה נפש:

תורה אור השלם

א) עֶרְוַת בַּת בִּנְךָ אוֹ בַת בִּתְּךָ לֹא תְגַלֶּה עֶרְוָתָן כִּי עֶרְוָתְךָ הֵנָּה: [ויקרא יח, י]

ב) עֶרְוַת אִשָּׁה וּבִתָּהּ לֹא תְגַלֵּה אֶת בַּת בְּנָהּ וְאֶת בַּת בִּתָּהּ לֹא תִקַּח לְגַלּוֹת עֶרְוָתָהּ שַׁאֲרָה הֵנָּה זִמָּה הִוא: [ויקרא יח, יז]

ג) וְאִישׁ אֲשֶׁר יִקַּח אֶת אִשָּׁה וְאֶת אִמָּהּ זִמָּה הִוא בָּאֵשׁ יִשְׂרְפוּ אֹתוֹ וְאֶתְהֶן וְלֹא תִהְיֶה זִמָּה בְּתוֹכְכֶם: [ויקרא כ, יד]

ד) וְאִם אָסוֹן יִהְיֶה וְנָתַתָּה נֶפֶשׁ תַּחַת נָפֶשׁ: [שמות כא, כג]

ה) וְכִי יִנָּצוּ אֲנָשִׁים וְנָגְפוּ אִשָּׁה הָרָה וְיָצְאוּ יְלָדֶיהָ וְלֹא יִהְיֶה אָסוֹן עָנוֹשׁ יֵעָנֵשׁ כַּאֲשֶׁר יָשִׁית עָלָיו בַּעַל הָאִשָּׁה וְנָתַן בִּפְלִלִים: [שמות כא, כב]

ו) וְרָאָה אֶת הַנֶּגַע וְהִנֵּה הַנֶּגַע בְּקִירֹת הַבַּיִת שְׁקַעֲרוּרֹת יְרַקְרַקֹּת אוֹ אֲדַמְדַּמֹּת וּמַרְאֵיהֶן שָׁפָל מִן הַקִּיר: [ויקרא יד, לז]

ליקוטי רש"י

דין בתו מאנוסתו. דהיינו בתו ובת בנו ובת בתו מאנוסתו דלאו בכלל אשה ובתה דקרא נינהו דהתם באשתו על ידי קידושין קאמר דדרשינן לה ביבמות [צז.] מקראי דרבה רמי כתיב ערות בת בנך או בת בתך וגו' הא בת בנה ובת בתה שלא ילדה ממך גלה וכתיב ערות אשה ובתה לא תגלה משמע בין שילדתו לך בין שילדתו לאיש אחר לא קשיא כאן באנוסין כאן בנישואין אם אנוסתך או מפותה לך היא אי אתה מוזהר על בתה אלא אם כן ממך היא ואם אשתך היא אתה מוזהר אף על בת שילדה לאיש אחר. אתיא הנה הנה אתיא זמה זמה. מעיקרא מייתינן לה בהנה הנה והדר בזמה זמה כתיב הכא (ויקרא יח) כי ערותך הנה וכתיב בשאר אשתו (שם ויקרא יח) שארה הנה מה להלן זמה עמו אף כאן זמה עמו ובתר דאייתינן זמה לשאר דידיה ילפינן בה שריפה בזמה זמה נאמר כאן (שם ויקרא י"ח) זמה ונאמר להלן (שם כ) בשריפה זמה מה להלן שריפה אף כאן שריפה [לעיל עה:]. מעין אחד הוא. דם הבא בתוך ז' של לידה ודם הבא לאחר שבעה ממעין אחד הוא. התורה טמאתו. תוך שבעה לזכר וי"ד לנקבה. שני מעיינות הן. נפתח הטמא כל ימי הלידה ונסתם הטהור ולסוף שבעה לזכר וי"ד לנקבה נסתם הטמא ונפתח הטהור [נדה יא.]. מעין אחד הוא. דם הבא בימי לידה ודם הבא בימי טוהר ממעין אחד הן באין. התורה טמאתו. כל שבעה לזכר וי"ד לנקבה. והתורה טהרתו. אחר מכן. נסתם הטמא. לאחר שבועים ונפתח הטהור. נסתם הטהור. לאחר שמנים ונפתח הטמא [שם לה:]. קשתה ג' ימים. דקיי"ל (נדה דף לו:) בנדה דאורייתא המקשה בתוך י"א שבין נדה לנדה ורואה דם ג' ימים רצופים מחמת צער וולדה אינה באה לידי זיבה להיות צריכה ספירת ז' נקיים כיולדת בזוב אלא ימי טומאת לידה כיולדת גרידתא דתניא (שם) כי יזוב זוב דמה דמה מחמת עצמה ולא מחמת ולד [יבמות פג.]. קשתה. מחמת ולד. ג' ימים. בתוך אחד עשר יום שבין נדה לנדה וראתה כל שלשתן הימים רצופין. ושפתה. מצערה. מעת לעת. ברביעי. וילדה. איגלאי מילתא דדמים שראתה לא באו מחמת ולד הלכך הרי זו יולדת בזוב אבל אם לא שפתה סמוך ללידתה כל דמים שראתה מחמת ולד הוא ורחמנא טהרינהו מזיבה דכתיב זוב דמה דמה מחמת עצמה ולא דמה מחמת ולד. לילה ויום. דאם שפתה בחצי יום שלישי וילדה יום רביעי דשפתה מעת לעת [illegible] שופי אלא אם כן שפתה לילה ויום שלאחר הלילה כלילי שבת ויומו. ששפתה מן הצער ולא מן הדם. דאע"ג דחזיא דם הוי שופי [שם לו:]. בית דין חצוף. שעברו על תקנת חכמים. דברי הכל. לקמן סנהדרין (ו.) קאי דפליגי בפשרה אשמעינן ר' [illegible] דבדין כולהו מודו דבעינן שלשה [לעיל ב:]. דכתיב נפש תחת נפש. אם אסון יהיה שמתה האשה יתן ממון דמי האשה ליורשיה שאין עליה חיוב מיתה שלא נתכוון לה אלא לחברו נתכוון דכתיב וכי ינצו אנשים יחדיו קסבר רבי נתכוון להרוג את זה והרג את [illegible] פטור ממיתה ומשלם ממון. נתינה למעלה. לענין דמי וולדות כתיב ונתן בפלילים (שמות כא). נתינה למטה. ונתתה נפש תחת נפש ממון ומאי נפש דמי הנפש [חגיגה יא.]. נתינה למעלה. גבי לא יהיה אסון ונתן בפלילים (שמות כא) דמי ולדות [illegible] עט:]. ואם אסון יהיה. באשה. ונתתה נפש תחת נפש. רבותינו חולקין בדבר. יש אומרים נפש ממש ויש אומרים ממון אבל לא נפש ממש שהמתכוין להרוג את זה והרג את זה פטור ממיתה ומשלם ליורשיו דמיו כמו שהיה נמכר בשוק [שמות כא, [illegible] מכות. מלקות ארבעים טעמא דר' ישמעאל ורבנן מפרש בגמרא סנהדרין (י.) מקראי [לעיל ב.]. אם בהרת קדמה לשער לבן טמא. דשער לבן שפרח בו הוא סימן לטומאה, כדכתיב (ויקרא יג) והנה נהפך שער לבן בבהרת. טהור. לפי מה שכתוב בה [illegible] [ב"מ פו.]. טמא. דהכי כתיב קרא (ויקרא יג) שער לבן בבהרת. רבי יהושע אומר כהה. כדמפרש רבה. כהה טהור. הרי הוא ככהה הנגע ממראהו שהוא טהור ומשם ר' משה הדרשן שמעתי ורבי יהושע קיהה מאי קיהה אמר רבה קיהה וטיהר כל [illegible] קיהה בדבר ונחלק עליהם וטיהר [כאדם שנקהו שיניו על אדם שאין משגיח לדבריו] וכן מצאתי בת"כ ור' יהושע קיהה טיהר אלמא העמד הגוף על חזקתו ולא תטמאנו מספק [כתובות עה:]. אם בהרת קודמת לשער לבן טמא. דשער לבן מסימני טו[illegible] [illegible] כתיב קיר. ומראיהן שפל מן הקיר [לעיל עא.].

said: כֵּהָה טָהוֹר – **It is** as if it is **faint,** and it is ***tahor.***[26]

Rav Pappa explains the next case of "affliction":

נִגְעֵי בָתִּים – To what dispute concerning ***tzaraas* of houses** does the Baraisa refer? בִּפְלוּגְתָּא דְּרַבִּי אֶלְעָזָר בְּרַבִּי שִׁמְעוֹן וְרַבָּנָן – **It refers to** where the sage and the High Court had **the** same **dispute** as the one **between R' Elazar the son of R' Shimon and the Rabbis.** דִּתְנַן – **For we learned in a Mishnah:**[27] רַבִּי אֶלְעָזָר בְּרַבִּי שִׁמְעוֹן אוֹמֵר – R' ELAZAR THE SON OF R' SHIMON SAYS: לְעוֹלָם אֵין הַבַּיִת טָמֵא – A HOUSE NEVER BECOMES *TAMEI* as a result of *tzaraas* עַד שֶׁיֵּרָאֶה כִּשְׁנֵי גְרִיסִין עַל שְׁתֵּי אֲבָנִים – UNTIL a *tzaraas* marking THE SIZE OF TWO *GRIS* IS SEEN ON TWO STONES[28] בִּשְׁתֵּי כְתָלִים בְּקֶרֶן זָוִית – located ON TWO WALLS that form A CORNER. אָרְכּוֹ כִּשְׁנֵי גְרִיסִין וְרָחְבּוֹ כִּגְרִיס – Thus, THE LENGTH OF [THE *TZARAAS* MARKING] must be at least TWO *GRIS* AND ITS WIDTH must be at least ONE *GRIS*.

The Gemara asks:

מַאי טַעֲמָא דְּרַבִּי אֶלְעָזָר בְּרַבִּי שִׁמְעוֹן – **What is the reason of R' Elazar the son of R' Shimon?** Why does he require that the *tzaraas* affliction appear in a corner?

The Gemara cites a Biblical source:

כְּתִיב ,,קִיר" וּכְתִיב ,,קִירֹת" – In the second section of the verse, **it is written *wall*, but** in the first section **it is written: *walls.***[29] This suggests that the verse is discussing one continuous wall that in a sense is like two walls. אֵיזֶהוּ קִיר שֶׁהוּא כִּקִירוֹת – **Which wall** do you find **that is like** two **walls?** הֱוֵי אוֹמֵר זֶה קֶרֶן זָוִית – **I would say that this is a corner,** where two walls meet to become like one.[30]

Rav Pappa explains the final case of "affliction":

נִגְעֵי בְגָדִים – To what dispute concerning ***tzaraas* of clothing** does the Baraisa refer? בִּפְלוּגְתָּא דְּרַבִּי יוֹנָתָן בֶּן אַבְטוֹלְמוֹס וְרַבָּנָן – **It refers to** where the sage and the High Court had **the** same **dispute** as the one **between R' Yonasan ben Avtolmos and the Rabbis.** דְּתַנְיָא – **For it was taught in a Baraisa:** רַבִּי יוֹנָתָן בֶּן אַבְטוֹלְמוֹס אוֹמֵר – R' YONASAN BEN AVTOLMOS SAYS: מִנַּיִן – FROM WHERE DO WE KNOW

NOTES

26. The ruling of *tahor* here has nothing to do with appearing faint. It is merely an expression borrowed from *Leviticus* 13:6 to denote a *tahor* affliction (*Rashi*; cf. *Tosafos* and *Binyan Shlomo*).

The law is that a person who enters the confines of the Temple with a *tzaraas* affliction is subject to *kares*. Thus, if the High Court were to rule as the Rabbis, they would prohibit someone with a *baheres* concerning which there is doubt [whether it appeared before the white hairs or after them] from entering the Temple on penalty of *kares*. If a sage were to dispute the High Court's ruling and maintain as R' Yehoshua, he would allow such an afflicted person to enter the Temple, and cause him to incur *kares* (*Rashi;* see *Yad David* and *Margaliyos HaYam*).

27. *Negaim* 12:3.

28. [A *gris* is a bean large enough for 36 hairs to grow on it (*Negaim* 6:1).] This is the minimum size needed to render a person or garment *tamei*. In regard to houses, however, R' Elazar the son of R' Shimon maintains that the minimum size is double, for the Torah states: *the stones* (plural) *that contain the affliction;* i.e. one *gris* per stone (*Rashi*).

29. Concerning the original examination of the *tzaraas* (*Leviticus* 14:37), Scripture states: וְהִנֵּה הַנֶּגַע בְּקִירֹת הַבַּיִת . . . וּמַרְאֵיהֶן שָׁפָל מִן־הַקִּיר, *And behold, if the affliction be in the* ***walls*** *of the house . . . and their appearance is deeper than the* ***wall*** (*Rashi*).

30. Based on this verse, R' Elazer requires that a two *gris* by one *gris* marking appear in the corner, with a square of one *gris* by one *gris* on each wall. Other Tannaim in the Mishnah, referred to here as "the Rabbis," maintain that the marking need not appear in a corner (see Mishnah ibid.).

The law is that a person who enters an afflicted house and then enters the Temple is subject to *kares*. Thus, if the High Court were to rule as the Rabbis, they would prohibit someone who had entered a house with an affliction that did not appear in a corner from entering the Temple on pain of *kares*. If a sage were to dispute the High Court's ruling and maintain as R' Elazer, he would allow such a person to enter the Temple and cause him to incur *kares* (*Rashi*).

לִפְרִיחָה בִּבְגָדִים שֶׁהִיא טְהוֹרָה – that REGARDING GARMENTS, A *tzaraas* ERUPTION that spread over the entire garment IS *TAHOR*?[1] It is derived by way of a *gezeirah shavah*, as follows: נֶאֶמְרָה קָרַחַת וְגַבַּחַת בָּאָדָם – The expressions *KARACHAS* AND *GABACHAS* WERE STATED IN REGARD TO *tzaraas* of A PERSON,[2] וְנֶאֶמְרָה קָרַחַת וְגַבַּחַת בִּבְגָדִים – AND the expressions *KARACHAS* AND *GABACHAS* WERE also STATED IN REGARD TO *tzaraas* of GARMENTS.[3] מַה לְהַלָּן – JUST AS THERE, in regard to a person, פָּרַח בְּכוּלוֹ טָהוֹר – if [THE AFFLICTION] ERUPTED OVER THE ENTIRE [PERSON], HE IS *TAHOR,* אַף כָּאן – SO TOO HERE, in regard to garments, פָּרַח בְּכוּלוֹ טָהוֹר – if [THE AFFLICTION] ERUPTED OVER THE ENTIRE garment, [THE GARMENT] IS *TAHOR.*[4]

Rav Pappa continues his interpretive citing of the Baraisa: ,,דִּבְרֵי'' – *MATTERS OF;* אֵלּוּ הָעֲרָכִין וְהַחֲרָמִים וְהֶקְדֵּישׁוֹת – THESE are disputes regarding *ERECH* VOWS, *CHEREM* VOWS AND CONSECRATION VOWS.

Rav Pappa explains each case separately:

הָעֲרָכִין – To what dispute concerning ***erech* vows** does the Baraisa refer? בִּפְלוּגְתָּא דְּרַבִּי מֵאִיר וְרַבָּנָן – **It refers to the dispute between R' Meir and the Rabbis,** (דתנן) [דְּתַנְיָא] – **as it was taught in a Baraisa:**[5] הַמַּעֲרִיךְ פָּחוֹת מִבֶּן חֹדֶשׁ – ONE WHO VOWS to give THE *ERECH* OF a child LESS THAN A MONTH OLD,[6] רַבִּי מֵאִיר אוֹמֵר – R' MEIR SAYS: נוֹתֵן דָּמָיו – HE MUST GIVE [THE CHILD'S] actual VALUE.[7] וַחֲכָמִים אוֹמְרִים – AND THE SAGES SAY: לֹא אָמַר כְּלוּם – HE HAS SAID NOTHING, i.e. the vow is meaningless.[8]

Rav Pappa explains the next case derived from "matters of": הַחֲרָמִים – To what dispute concerning ***cherem* vows** does the Baraisa refer? בִּפְלוּגְתָּא דְּרַבִּי יְהוּדָה בֶּן בְּתֵירָה וְרַבָּנָן – **It refers to the dispute between R' Yehudah ben Beseirah and the Rabbis,** דִּתְנַן – **as we learned in a Mishnah:**[9] רַבִּי יְהוּדָה בֶּן בְּתֵירָה אוֹמֵר – R' YEHUDAH BEN BESEIRAH SAYS: סְתָם חֲרָמִים לְבֶדֶק הַבַּיִת – UNSPECIFIED *CHEREM* VOWS, i.e. *cherem* vows formulated simply as "This is *cherem*" without any further clarification, ARE FOR THE UPKEEP OF THE TEMPLE, שֶׁנֶּאֱמַר ,,כָּל חֵרֶם קֹדֶשׁ־קָדָשִׁים הוּא לַה' '' – AS IT IS STATED: *ANY CHEREM IS MOST HOLY TO HASHEM.*[10] וַחֲכָמִים אוֹמְרִים – AND THE SAGES SAY: סְתָם חֲרָמִים לַכֹּהֵן – UNSPECIFIED *CHEREM* VOWS ARE FOR THE KOHEN, שֶׁנֶּאֱמַר ,,כִּשְׂדֵה הַחֵרֶם לַכֹּהֵן תִּהְיֶה אֲחֻזָּתוֹ'' – AS IT SAYS: *LIKE THE CHEREM FIELD, HIS ANCESTRAL HOLDING SHALL GO TO THE KOHEN.*[11] אִם כֵּן – IF SO, מַה תַּלְמוּד לוֹמַר ,,קֹדֶשׁ־קָדָשִׁים הוּא לַה' '' – WHY DOES SCRIPTURE SAY: *[ANY CHEREM] IS MOST HOLY TO HASHEM?*

NOTES

1. The Torah decrees (*Leviticus* 13:12,13) that if a *tzaraas* affliction that originally rendered a person *tamei* subsequently spread over the person's entire body, he is rendered *tahor*. R' Yonasan extends this law to *tzaraas* afflictions of garments.

2. Ibid v. 40-43.

3. Ibid. v. 55 (see *Rashi* there vs. 41 and 55 for definitions of the terms *karachas* and *gabachas*).

4. This is the opinion of R' Yonasan. The Rabbis, however, maintain that this law applies only to *tzaraas* afflicting a person. Concerning garments, even if the *tzaraas* affliction covers the entire garment, the garment remains *tamei.*

Now, the law is that a person who touches an afflicted garment and then enters the Temple, or one who brings such a garment into the Temple, is subject to *kares* (cf. *Rashi* to *Leviticus* 17:16 ד״ה ובשרו; see also *Rashi* to *Eruvin* 104b ד״ה חייב with *Hagahos HaGra, Mishneh LaMelech Hil. Bias HaMikdash* 3:18 [near end], *Aruch LaNer* here). Thus, if the High Court were to rule as the Rabbis, they would prohibit such a person from entering the Temple on penalty of *kares.* If a sage were to dispute this ruling and maintain as R' Yonasan, he would allow such a person to enter the Temple and cause him to incur *kares* (*Rashi*).

5. Emendation follows *Mesoras HaShas.*

6. [The *erech* of a person is the amount of money fixed by the Torah (*Leviticus* 27:1-8) for each of eight different groupings, classified by age and gender. If a person vows and says, "I take upon myself to give my *erech,*" or "I take upon myself to give the *erech* of So-and-so," the subject of the vow is assessed by the Torah's *erech* valuation for that grouping, and the person who made the vow must give that amount to the Temple, regardless of the individual's true market value.] The Torah does not specify, however, an *erech* for anyone less than thirty days old (*Rashi*).

7. R' Meir maintains that אֵין אָדָם מוֹצִיא דְּבָרָיו לְבַטָּלָה, *A person does not utter his words* (i.e. a legal declaration) *in vain.* Hence, we reinterpret the words of an ineffective vow to make it halachically meaningful. Accordingly, in our case, R' Meir maintains that since the vower realizes that the Torah did not fix a value for a newborn child less than thirty days old, he must have intended to pledge the market value of the child [as determined on the slave market] (*Rashi*).

8. The Rabbis maintain that a person might utter a vow in vain. Thus, a vow to give to the Temple the *erech* of a newborn less than thirty days old is meaningless, for the vow is not reinterpreted.

Now, if a Temple treasurer would extract the value of the child from the above vower, R' Meir would maintain that the money becomes *hekdesh* (Temple property), since the person did in fact owe that sum to the Temple. The Rabbis, on the other hand, who maintain that he never owed this money to the Temple, would maintain that it remains his personal property.

If the vower were then to inadvertently use the extracted money in betrothing a woman, the Rabbis would hold the betrothal valid, since the money was entirely his. R' Meir, however, would maintain that the betrothal is invalid, for *kiddushin* inadvertently performed with *hekdesh* funds is ineffective (*Mishnah Kiddushin* 52b, according to R' Meir's view). Thus, if the High Court were to rule as the Rabbis and the dissenting sage as R' Meir, the sage would rule the marriage invalid while the High Court would consider it valid. The sage would thus be permitting other men to this married woman, a sin punishable by *kares.*

We would find the opposite result if another person, other than the vower, knowingly used the funds extracted by the treasurer to betroth a woman. If the High Court were to rule as R' Meir (who maintains that the funds are considered *hekdesh* property), the woman would be betrothed, following the rule stated by R' Meir in the Mishnah in *Kiddushin* 52b that *kiddushin* knowingly performed with *hekdesh* funds is valid (see ibid. 53b, 54b as to why this is so). If the dissenting sage would then rule as the Rabbis (who maintain that the extracted funds are considered the vower's personal property), a betrothal performed by another person with those funds is certainly invalid, since they are considered stolen from the vower (*Rashi* with *Maharsha*).

Another example of how following the dissenting sage's ruling in this matter will result in *kares:* According to R' Meir, since the money is *hekdesh* property, if someone were to mistakenly commit *me'ilah* with it (i.e. use it for his own purposes), he would be required to bring an *asham*-offering, while according to the Rabbis, since the money is not *hekdesh,* no offering would be necessary.

Now, if the High Court were to rule as R' Meir, they would prohibit someone who is *tamei* from eating the *asham* on penalty of *kares.* A sage who would dissent and rule as the Rabbis, however, would rule that the *"asham"* has no legal standing of an offering, and, based on that, would allow a *tamei* person to eat of it. The sage's ruling could thus lead to a sin punishable by *kares* (*Rashi*).

9. *Arachin* 28b. A *cherem* is a declaration used to dedicate something as property of the Kohanim or as property of the Temple itself, depending on what the declarer specifies in his dedication. If, however, a person states only, "This calf is *cherem,*" without specifying whether for the Temple or the Kohanim, the status of the animal is a subject of dispute in this Mishnah.

10. *Leviticus* 27:28. R' Yehudah ben Beseirah maintains that if one declares his property *cherem* without specifying the type of *cherem, it* is considered a Temple *cherem.* The money pledged is used for the Temple upkeep.

11. Ibid. v. 21. This verse refers to a consecrated ancestral field. The verse states that if the original owner did not redeem it before *yovel* (the Jubilee year), *then the field, when it goes out in yovel, shall be holy to Hashem like the cherem field, his ancestral holding shall go to the Kohen.* This teaches that the unspecified *cherem* is given to Kohanim.

לפריחה בבגדים שהיא טהורה נאמרה קרחת וגבחת באדם ונאמרה קרחת וגבחת בבגדים מה להלן פרח בכולו טהור אף כאן פרח בכולו טהור א) דברי אלו הערכין והחרמים והקדישות הערכין בפלוגתא דר"מ ורבנן א) דתנן ב) המעריך פחות מבן חדש ר"מ אומר נותן דמיו וחכמים אומרים א לא אמר כלום החרמים בפלוגתא דרבי יהודה בן בתירה ורבנן דתנן ג) ר' יהודה בן בתירה אומר סתם חרמים לבדק הבית שנאמר ב) כל חרם קדש קדשים הוא לה' וחכמים אומרים ב סתם חרמים לכהן שנאמר ג) כשדה החרם לכהן תהיה אחוזתו אם כן מה תלמוד לומר קדש קדשים הוא לה' ג שחל על קדשי קדשים ועל קדשים קלים הקדשות בפלוגתא דרבי אליעזר בן יעקב ורבנן דתניא ד) ר' אליעזר בן יעקב אומר אפילו צינורא של הקדש ה) צריכה עשרה בני אדם לפדותה א) ריבות זה השקאת סוטה ועריפת העגלה וטהרת מצורע השקאת סוטה בפלוגתא דרבי אליעזר ור' יהושע דתנן ו) המקנא לאשתו ר"א אומר מקנא על פי שנים ומשקה על פי עד אחד או על פי עצמו ר' יהושע אומר ד מקנא על פי שנים ומשקה על פי שנים עריפת עגלה בפלוגתא דרבי אליעזר ורבי עקיבא דתנן ז) מאין היו מודדין רבי אליעזר אומר מטיבורו ר' עקיבא אומר ה מחוטמו ר' אליעזר בן יעקב אומר ממקום שנעשה חלל מצוארו טהרת מצורע בפלוגתא דר' שמעון ורבנן דתנן ח) אין לו בהן יד בהן רגל אוזן ימנית אין לו טהרה עולמית ר' אליעזר אומר נותן לו על מקומו ויוצא רבי שמעון אומר ט) נותן על של שמאל ויוצא א) בשעריך זה לקט שכחה פיאה לקט דתנן י) ו שני שבלין לקט שלשה אינן לקט שכחה שני עומרין שכחה שלשה אינן שכחה ועל כולן ב"ש אומרים שלש לעני וארבע לבעל הבית פיאה בפלוגתא דר' ישמעאל ורבנן כ) דתנן ל) מצות פיאה להפריש מן הקמה לא הפריש מן הקמה יפריש מן העומרין לא הפריש מן העומרין יפריש מן הכרי עד שלא מירחו מירחו מעשר ונותן לו משום רבי ישמעאל אמרו ז אף מפריש מן העיסה: ג' בתי דינין וכו': אמר רב כהנא הוא אומר מפי השמועה והן אומרין מפי השמועה אינו נהרג הוא אומר כך הוא בעיני והן אומרין כך הוא בעינינו אינו נהרג וכל שכן הוא אומר מפי השמועה והן אומרין כך הוא בעינינו אינו נהרג עד שיאמר כך הוא בעיני והן אומרים מפי השמועה תדע שהרי לא הרגו את עקביא בן מהללאל ור' אלעזר אומר ח אפילו הוא אומר מפי השמועה והן אומרין כך הוא בעינינו נהרג כדי שלא ירבו מחלוקות בישראל ואם תאמר מפני מה לא הרגו את עקביא בן מהללאל מפני שלא הורה הלכה למעשה תנן כך דרשתי וכך דרשו חבירי כך למדתי וכך למדו חבירי מאי לאו דהוא אמר מפי השמועה והם אומרין כך הוא בעינינו לא הוא אומר כך הוא בעיני והם אומרים מפי השמועה ת"ש מ) דאמר רבי יאשיה שלשה דברים סח לי זעירא מאנשי ירושלים ט בעל שמחל על קינויו קינויו מחול

בן

לפריחה בבגדים. אם פרוח תפרח הצרעת ונתמלא כל הבגד: אדם שפרחה בכולו טהור. דכתיב (ויקרא יג) אם פרוח תפרח הצרעת וגו' ופליגי רבנן עליה והיכא דפרחה בבגד כולו והכניסו למקדש או הנוגע בו נכנס למקדש לרבנן חייב ולר' יונתן פטור: המעריך פחות מבן חדש. אמר על פחות מבן חדש ערכו עלי והתורה לא נתנה לו ערך דגבי ערכין כתיב (ויקרא כז) ואם מבן חדש וגו': ר"מ אומר נותן דמיו. כמה שהוא נמכר בשוק דקסבר אין אדם מוציא דבריו לבטלה ויודע שאין ערך לפחות מבן חדש וגמר ואמר לשם דמים ולרבנן פטור ואם בא גיזבר ומשכנו לר"מ הוי הקדש ואין אשה מתקדשת בו אלא אם כן יודע בו כדתנן (קידושין דף נג:) וההקדש במזיד קידש בשוגג לא קידש ולרבנן לא הוי הקדש והרי הוא של בעלים לקדש בו האשה והאחר שקדש בו אינה מקודשת א"נ לר"מ הוי הקדש והנהנה ממנו מביא אשם מעילות והרי אותו אשם קדש קדשים והאוכלו בטומאת גופו חייב כרת ולרבנן לא הוי הקדש והרי של בעלים הוא והנהנה ממנו לא מעל ואם הביא אשם מעילות חולין לעזרה הוא ואין חייבין עליו משום טומאה: לבדק הבית. ומועלין בהן: לכהנים. ואין מועלין בהם: שחל על קדשי קדשים. כדתנן (ערכין דף כח:) מחרים אדם את קדשיו אם נדר נותן דמיהם ואם נדבה נותן את טובתם כפי חלק שיש לו בה כדמפרש במסכת ערכין בפ' המקדיש: צינורא. מזלג קטן שטווין בו זהב: י' כהנים. כדמפרש בפרק קמא י' כהנים כתובין בפרשה אם נפדית בפחות מעשרה בני אדם עדיין הקדש היא ומועלין בה ולרבנן אין מועלין בה: המקנא לאשתו. המתרה באשתו אל תסתרי עם איש פלוני: ומשקה על פי עד אחד. שבא ואמר אני ראיתיה שנסתרה ואם לא השקה נאסרת עליו ותנן (סוטה דף כד.) אלו לא שותות ולא נוטלות כתובתן האומרת איני שותה והיכא דליכא עידי סתירה ואמרה איני שותה לרבי אליעזר אין לה כתובה לרבי יהושע יש לה כתובה שאינה נאסרת עליו ואם מכרה לאחר כתובתה קנה ואם תופס ממונו של זה כדי כתובה הרי הוא שלו לקדש בו את האשה ולרבי אליעזר הוי גזל ולא קידש: מאין היו מודדין. לידע אי זו עיר קרובה אל החלל: מטבורו. ואותה שקרובה לטבורו תביא את העגלה ולא הקרובה לחוטמו: ר' עקיבא אומר מחוטמו. ובמסכת סוטה מפרש טעמא מר סבר עיקר חיותיה באפיה ומר סבר עיקר חיותיה בטבוריה: ממקום שנעשה חלל. דהיינו מצואריה דשם חלל מן הצואר כדמפרש התם לתת אותך על צוארי חללי רשעים ותנן (קידושין דף נז:) המקדש בעגלה ערופה אינה מקודשת ואם מדד זקן ממרא מטיבורו וב"ד מחוטמו והביאו אלו עגלה ואלו עגלה למר זו עגלה אסורה ואין מקדשין בה וזו אינה עגלה ומקדשין בה ולמר הוי איפכא: אין לו טהרה עולמית. דבעינן קרא כדכתיב כדאמרן בנגמר הדין: נותן על מקומו. על מקום הבוהן נותן דם האשם וטהור ליכנס למקדש ולאכול קודש דהיינו זדונו כרת: שלש אינן לקט. שאין דרך להפקירן: שלשה אינן שכחה. בסיפרא יליף לה מקראי בפרשת שכחה ואם נחלק זקן ממרא ואמר אף שלשה שכחה ובא עני ונטלן ובא בעל הבית ונטלן הימנו לזקן ממרא הוי גזל ואין מקדשין בו אשה ולרבנן מקודשת: מצות פיאה מפריש מן הקמה. דכתיב לא תכלה אלא הנח לפניהם והם יקצרוהו: מרחו. י) בכרי נתחייב במעשר דנגמרה מלאכתו הלכך מעשר תחילה את הכרי מכל מעשרותיו ונותן לו את הפאה שאילו הפרישה לא היו עניים צריכין לעשרה דלקט שכחה פאה פטורין מן המעשר: אף מפריש מן העיסה. אם טחנה ולשה ולת"ק טחנה פטור דקנייה בשינוי ואם בא עני ונטל כדי פאה משטחנה לר' ישמעאל לא הוי גזל לרבנן הוי גזל: עקביא בן מהללאל. נחלק על חכמים בלשכת הגזית בד' דברים במסכת עדיות (פ"ה משנה ו) שהיה אומר לבנו בשעת מיתתו חזור בך בד' דברים שהייתי אומר אמר לו אבא ואתה מפני מה לא חזרת בהם אמר לו אני שמעתי מפי המרובים והם שמעו מפי המרובים הם עמדו בשמועתן ואני עמדתי בשמועתי אבל אתה שמעת מפי היחיד וכו': על קינויו. שקינא לאשתו אל תסתרי עם פלוני: קינויו מחול. ואם נסתרה אינה נאסרת עליו:

בן

מרחו מעשר ונותן לו. ואפילו למאן דאית ליה ברירה כל זמן שלא הפריש פיאה ולא ביררה היה הכל שלו ונתחייב הכל במעשר ושוב לא יפטר וא"ת תרומה נמי לתני שתורם ונותן לו וכ"ת דתרומה בלאו הכי יפריש העני דכל פיאה חייבת בתרומה חדא דאם כן הרי הוא מקדים מעשר לתרומה גדולה ועוד דתנן במסכת תרומות פ"ק [מ"ה] אין תורמין מן הלקט מן השכחה ומן הפיאה וי"מ דלהכי לא תני תורם דאפילו הפקיר לאחר מירוח פטור מן התרומה ס) (דתנן במסכת מעשרות פ' שלשה מינין) פירות ממורחין בשדה מכונסין אסורים משום גזל מפוזרים מותרין בין כך בין כך חייבין במעשר ופטורים מן התרומה וליתא דבירושל' מפרש דלהכי פטורין מן התרומה לפי שאי אפשר לגורן שתעקר אלא אם כן נתרמה ממנו תרומה גדולה לפיכך אין צריך לתרום כשמצא פירות דמסתמא הופרשה מהם תרומה גדולה ונראה לפרש דמשום דתרומה דבר מועט לא חש להזכיר ע):

קינויו מחול. היינו דוקא קודם שנמחקה המגילה אבל לאחר מיכן אין יכול למחול:

מסית

מסורת הש"ס

א) [נ"ל דתניא], ב) ערכין ה., ג) ערכין כח:, ד) לעיל יד:, ה) [עי' תוספות תמורה כז: ד"ה לא אמרו], ו) סוטה ב., ז) סוטה מה:, ח) לעיל מה: נזיר מו: ע"ש יומא סא: נגעים פי"ד מ"ט, ט) [בנגעים איתא אם נתן על של שמאל יצא], י) פאה פ"ו מ"ה ע"ש, כ) [נ"ל דתניא], ל) תמורה ו. מכות טז: ב"ק לז., מ) סוטה כה., נ) רש"ל גורס כבר, ס) [מהרש"א גרים כדתניא בירושלמי במס' מעשרות פרק ג], ע) [ועי' תוס' ב"ק ד. ד"ה מירחו].

תורה אור השלם

א) כִּי יִפָּלֵא מִמְּךָ דָבָר לַמִּשְׁפָּט בֵּין דָּם לְדָם בֵּין דִּין לְדִין וּבֵין נֶגַע לָנֶגַע דִּבְרֵי רִיבֹת בִּשְׁעָרֶיךָ וְקַמְתָּ וְעָלִיתָ אֶל הַמָּקוֹם אֲשֶׁר יִבְחַר יְיָ אֱלֹהֶיךָ בּוֹ: [דברים יז, ח]

ב) אַךְ כָּל חֵרֶם אֲשֶׁר יַחֲרִם אִישׁ לַייָ מִכָּל אֲשֶׁר לוֹ מֵאָדָם וּבְהֵמָה וּמִשְּׂדֵה אֲחֻזָּתוֹ לֹא יִמָּכֵר וְלֹא יִגָּאֵל כָּל חֵרֶם קֹדֶשׁ קָדָשִׁים הוּא לַייָ: [ויקרא כז, כח]

ג) וְהָיָה הַשָּׂדֶה בְּצֵאתוֹ בַיֹּבֵל קֹדֶשׁ לַייָ כִּשְׂדֵה הַחֵרֶם לַכֹּהֵן תִּהְיֶה אֲחֻזָּתוֹ: [ויקרא כז, כא]

עין משפט נר מצוה

מח א מיי' פ"א מהל' ערכין הל' ג סמג עשין קכח:

מט ב מיי' שם פ"ו הל' א סמג עשין קלב:

נ ג מיי' שם הלכה יא:

נא ד מיי' פ"א מהל' סוטה הל' א ב סמג עשין מח נו [וטוש"ע אה"ע סי' קעח סעי' ב ד]:

נב ה מיי' פ"ט מהל' רוצח הל' ט סמג עשין עה:

נג ו מיי' פ"ד מהל' מתנות עניים הל' א:

נד ז מיי' פ"א שם הלכה ב:

נה ח מיי' פ"ד מהל' ממרים הל' א סמג עשין קיא ולאוין רטז:

נו ט מיי' פ"א מהל' סוטה הל' ז סמג עשין נו טוש"ע אה"ע סי' קעח סעיף יב:

ליקוטי רש"י

לפריחה. אם פרחה הצרעת בכל הבגד. מה להלן פרח בכולה טהור. דכתיב אם פרוח תפרח וגו' (ויקרא יג) [זבחים מט:]. המעריך פחות מבן חודש. רבי מאיר במסכת ערכין (דף ה) דאמר אין אדם מוציא דבריו לבטלה דתנן המעריך פחות מבן חדש ר"מ אומר נותן דמיו דאדם יודע שאין ערך לפחות מבן חדש וגמר ואמר לשם דמים [כתובות נח:]. נותן דמיו. כמה שהוא נמכר בשוק [ערכין ה.]. החרמים בפלוגתא דר' יהודה בן בתירא ורבנן. אך כל חרם וגו', נחלקו רבותינו בדבר יש אומרים סתם חרמים להקדש ומה אני מקיים (במדבר יח יד) כל חרם בישראל לך יהיה בחרמי כהנים שפירש ואמר הרי זה חרם לכהן ויש שאמרו סתם חרמים לכהנים. כל חרם קדש קדשים הוא. האומר סתם חרמים לבדק הבית מביא ראיה מכאן והאומר סתם חרמים לכהנים מפרש כל חרם קדש קדשים הוא לה' ללמד שחרמי כהנים חלים על קדשי קדשים ועל קדשים קלים ונותן לכהן כמו ששנינו במסכת ערכין (כח:) אם נדר נותן דמיהם ואם נדבה נותן את טובתה [ויקרא כז, כח]. שחל על קדשי קדשים. כדמפרש מחרים אדם את קדשיו וכו' והיאך מוחרמים והלא אינו שלו אלא אם נדר הן דאמר הרי עלי עולה והפריש בהמה לנדרו ואחר כך החרימה הואיל והוא חייב באחריותה אם מתה או נגנבה נמצאת שלו היא והוא נותן כל דמיה לכהן ואת הבהמה יקריב לנדרו דהא ודאי אית ליה פדיון דלאו גופה איחרם דלאו דידיה הוא [ערכין כח:]. צריכה עשרה בני אדם. עשרה כהנים כתובין בפדיון הקדישות שלשה בפרשת ערכין שהיא ראשונה ושלשה בפדיון בהמה וארבעה בקרקעות [לעיל יד:]. המקנא לאשתו. לישנא דקרא נקט וקנא את אשתו (במדבר ה) ולקמן בגמ' מפרש מאי לשון קינוי ובמתניתין מפרש כילד מקנא לה אומר לה אל תסתרי עם איש פלוני.

מקנא לה ע"פ שנים. אם בא להשקותה צריך להביא שני עדים שאמר לה בפניהם אל תסתרי עמו ואם לא קינא לה בפני שנים אינה נאסרת עליו בסתירתה ואינו משקה. ומשקה ע"פ עד א' או ע"פ עצמו. ואפי' אין עדים שנסתרה אלא עד אחד או הוא עצמו אומר ראיתיה שנסתרה אחר שקינאתי לה נאסרת בסתירה עד שתשתה ולקמן ילפינן מקראי שסתירתה אוסרתה עליו מספק. ר' יהושע אומר. צריך ב' עדים אף לסתירתה [סוטה ב.]. אין לו בהן יד בהן רגל אין לו טהרה עולמית. לפי שאין יכול לקיים בו מתן דם ושמן על בהן ידו [נזיר מו:]. אין לו טהרה עולמית. דבעינן קרא כדכתיב [יומא סא:]. ר' אליעזר. לא בעי קרא כדכתיב וכן ר' שמעון [לעיל מה:]. שני עומרים שכחה שלשה אינן שכחה. בספרי מפיק ליה מהאי קרא ושכחת עומר בשדה (דברים כד) ולא גדיש וגם עומר שיש בו סאתים מפיק ליה התם מדכתיב לקחתו למעוטי האי דלאו ניקח בפעם אחת יפה [ב"ב עב:]. מצות פאה להפריש מן הקמה. דכתיב לא תכלה פאת שדך לקצור (ויקרא יט). מרחו. מחליק את הכרי ברחת ומירוח הוי גמר מלאכה למעשר הלכך מעשר כל מעשרותיו תחלה ואחר כך נותן לו פאה כדי שלא יפסיד עני שאילו היה נותנו קודם מירוח אע"פ שעני מגרף לקט שכחה ופאה הרבה ועושה מהן כרי פטור מן המעשר שהרי הפקר הוא אבל עכשיו שנתמרח ביד בעל הבית נתחייב במעשר דהכי אמרינן במסכת ברכות (דף מ:) לקט שכחה ופאה שעשאן בגורן הוקבעו. אף מפריש מן העיסה. פאה אם לא נתנה כבר ואילו לת"ק מן העיסה לא דקנייה בשינוי והוי ממון שאין לו תובעים דעד השתא דישה לאו שינוי הוא דאוכל הוא כמו שהיה [ב"ק צד.]. מירחו. ונתחייב במעשר מעשר תחלה את הכרי ואחר כך נותן לו הפאה שלא להפסיד את העני שהלקט והשכחה והפאה פטורין מן המעשר וזה הביאן לידי חיוב [מכות טז:]. סח לי זעירא. שהיה מאנשי ירושלים.

שֶׁחָל עַל קָדְשֵׁי קָדָשִׁים וְעַל קָדָשִׁים קַלִּים – To teach THAT IT TAKES EFFECT UPON *KODSHEI KODASHIM* AND UPON *KODASHIM KALIM*.[12]

Rav Pappa explains the final case derived from the phrase "matters of":

הֶקְדֵּשׁוֹת – To what dispute concerning **consecration vows** does the Baraisa refer? בִּפְלוּגְתָּא דְּרַבִּי אֱלִיעֶזֶר בֶּן יַעֲקֹב וְרַבָּנָן – **It refers to the dispute between R' Eliezer ben Yaakov and the Rabbis,** דְּתַנְיָא – **as it was taught in a Baraisa:** רַבִּי אֱלִיעֶזֶר בֶּן יַעֲקֹב אוֹמֵר – R' ELIEZER BEN YAAKOV SAYS: אֲפִילּוּ צִינּוֹרָא שֶׁל הֶקְדֵּשׁ צְרִיכָה עֲשָׂרָה בְּנֵי אָדָם לִפְדוֹתָהּ – EVEN A SPINNING FORK[13] THAT BELONGS TO THE TEMPLE TREASURY REQUIRES that TEN PEOPLE appraise it if one wishes TO REDEEM IT.[14]

Rav Pappa continues his interpretive explanation of the Baraisa:

"רִיבֹת" – *DISPUTES;* זוֹ הַשְׁקָאַת סוֹטָה וַעֲרִיפַת הָעֶגְלָה וְטָהֳרַת מְצוֹרָע – THIS alludes to disputes regarding MAKING A *SOTAH* DRINK the bitter waters, DECAPITATION OF THE CALF, AND PURIFICATION OF THE *METZORA.*

Rav Pappa explains each case separately:

הַשְׁקָאַת סוֹטָה – To what dispute concerning **making a *sotah* drink** does the Baraisa refer? בִּפְלוּגְתָּא דְּרַבִּי אֱלִיעֶזֶר וְרַבִּי יְהוֹשֻׁעַ – **It refers to the dispute between R' Eliezer and R' Yehoshua,** דִּתְנַן – **as we learned in a Mishnah:**[15] הַמְקַנֵּא לְאִשְׁתּוֹ – ONE WHO WARNS HIS WIFE not to seclude herself with another man – רַבִּי אֱלִיעֶזֶר אוֹמֵר – R' ELIEZER SAYS: מְקַנֵּא עַל פִּי שְׁנַיִם – HE MUST WARN her IN THE PRESENCE OF TWO witnesses, וּמַשְׁקָה עַל פִּי עֵד אֶחָד אוֹ עַל פִּי עַצְמוֹ – BUT HE CAN MAKE her DRINK the bitter waters ON THE TESTIMONY OF ONE witness OR even HIS OWN TESTIMONY.[16] רַבִּי יְהוֹשֻׁעַ אוֹמֵר – R' YEHOSHUA SAYS: מְקַנֵּא עַל פִּי שְׁנַיִם – HE MUST WARN her IN THE PRESENCE OF TWO witnesses, וּמַשְׁקָה עַל פִּי שְׁנַיִם – AND HE CAN MAKE her DRINK only ON THE TESTIMONY OF TWO witnesses.[17]

Rav Pappa explains the next case derived from "disputes":

עֲרִיפַת עֶגְלָה – To what dispute concerning **decapitation of the calf** does the Baraisa refer? בִּפְלוּגְתָּא דְּרַבִּי אֱלִיעֶזֶר וְרַבִּי עֲקִיבָא – **It refers to the dispute between R' Eliezer and R' Akiva,** דִּתְנַן – **as we learned in a Mishnah:**[18] מֵאַיִן הָיוּ מוֹדְדִין – FROM WHICH PART of the corpse WOULD THEY MEASURE the distance to the nearest city? רַבִּי אֱלִיעֶזֶר אוֹמֵר – R' ELIEZER SAYS: מִטִּיבּוּרוֹ – FROM HIS NAVEL. רַבִּי עֲקִיבָא אוֹמֵר – R' AKIVA SAYS:

NOTES

12. All sacrificial offerings fall into one of two categories, *kodshei kodashim* (literally: most-holy offerings) and *kodashim kalim* (literally: offerings of lesser holiness), the former having stricter laws than the latter.

Although an animal designated as an offering is no longer the property of its owner, and it is therefore not his to give away, we learn from this verse that he can nonetheless declare a Kohanic *cherem* in regard to it. In this case the animal itself does not go to the Kohen, since it is an offering, but the declarer must instead give the Kohanim an amount equal to his financial interest in the offering, as explained in the continuation of the Mishnah in *Arachin* (*Rashi*).

Now, if an article was dedicated as an unspecified *cherem,* R' Yehudah ben Beseirah would maintain that it is Temple property and is subject to the prohibition of *me'ilah*. The Sages, however, would maintain that it is the personal property of the Kohanim and not subject to *me'ilah.* Thus, if the dissenting sage were to rule as the Sages and the High Court as R' Yehudah ben Beseirah, following the sage's ruling could result in *kares,* as explained in the last paragraph of note 8.

13. A small forked [needle] used for spinning gold thread (*Rashi*).

14. However, as the Gemara above (14b) notes, the Tanna of the Mishnah (above, 2a) disagrees and maintains that *hekdesh* may be redeemed based on an appraisal by a court of three.

Thus, if someone were to redeem an item belonging to the Temple treasury based on an appraisal by a three-member court, R' Eliezer ben Yaakov would maintain that it is still *hekdesh* and is subject to the prohibition of *me'ilah,* while the Rabbis (i.e. the Tanna of the Mishnah on 2a) would maintain that it is redeemed and not subject to *me'ilah*. Consequently, if a dissenting sage were to rule as the Rabbis and the High Court as R' Eliezer ben Yaakov, following the sage's ruling could result in *kares,* as explained in note 8 (see *Rashi*).

15. *Sotah* 2a. A woman who is legally under suspicion of committing adultery is known as a *sotah.* That is, if the husband warns his wife before witnesses not to seclude herself with a certain man, and then witnesses testify that she did seclude herself, she is legally suspected of committing adultery. If the woman persists in her claim of innocence, a procedure (outlined in *Numbers* 5:11-31) is prescribed to ascertain the truth. She is given certain water (the "bitter waters") to drink. If she is guilty, she dies; if she is innocent, she lives.

Now, all opinions in the Mishnah agree that the husband's warning must have been witnessed by two people. There is a dispute, however, as to how many witnesses to the seclusion are required.

16. In contrast to the evidence required to establish the warning, R' Eliezer does not require that the seclusion be attested to by two witnesses, but considers the testimony of even one witness, and even the testimony of the husband himself, sufficient to establish that the seclusion took place.

17. R' Yehoshua requires that two witnesses establish that seclusion has taken place just as two witnesses are needed to attest to the warning.

The Mishnah (*Sotah* 24a) further teaches that there are women who become prohibited to their husbands as a result of warning and seclusion but who nevertheless cannot be tested by the bitter waters. As a result, they must be divorced, and they forfeit whatever payments are due them under their *kesubah* (marriage contract). One of these women is one who declares, "I will not drink," i.e. a woman who, without confessing her guilt, refuses to drink the bitter waters. Now, consider a case in which there was only one witness to the seclusion, and the *sotah* says, "I will not drink." R' Eliezer, who considers the testimony of one witness sufficient to establish that the seclusion has taken place and to require the woman to drink, would rule that the woman forfeits her *kesubah* payment. R' Yehoshua, who considers one witness' testimony insufficient to require a woman to drink, would rule that the woman does not forfeit her payment.

Now, let us say that someone bought the woman's rights to the *kesubah* payments from her on the speculation that the husband would eventually pay out (i.e. he would divorce or predecease her). The above scenario then occurred, where seclusion was attested to by a single witness, the woman refused to drink, the husband divorced her, and the purchaser of the *kesubah* rights then seized assets from the husband to cover the *kesubah* payment. According to R' Eliezer, the seized assets are considered stolen property in the hand of the purchaser, since the woman had already forfeited her rights to the payment. R' Yehoshua, on the other hand, would maintain that the woman did not forfeit her *kesubah,* and in case of divorce, for example, the man who purchased the rights to the *kesubah* may rightfully keep the seized assets to cover the payment.

If the dissenting sage were to rule as R' Eliezer and the High Court were to rule as R' Yehoshua, then if the purchaser of the *kesubah* rights were to use the seized assets to betroth a woman, the sage would rule the marriage invalid, while the High Court would rule it valid. The sage would thus be permitting other men to this married woman, a sin punishable by *kares* (*Rashi*; see above, 87b note 16 for an explanation of how, even if the sage and the High Court had taken the reverse positions, following the sage could result in *kares*).

18. *Sotah* 45b. If the body of a murder victim is discovered outside a town in Eretz Yisrael and it is not known who killed him, the Torah requires the elders of the town nearest the body to take a calf that was never worked and bring it to a valley of unworked ground, where it is decapitated.

This Mishnah discusses a case in which the body is nearly equidistant to two cities, so that the part of the body from which they would measure would determine the city to which the body is closest.

לפריחה בבגדים שהיא טהורה נאמרה קרחת וגבחת באדם ונאמרה קרחת וגבחת בבגדים מה להלן פרח בכולו טהור אף כאן פרח בכולו טהור א) דברי אלו הערכין והחרמים והקדישות הערכין בפלוגתא דר"מ ורבנן א) דתנן ב) המעריך פחות מבן חדש ר"מ אומר נותן דמיו וחכמים אומרים א לא אמר כלום החרמים בפלוגתא דרבי יהודה בן בתירה ורבנן דתנן ג) ר' יהודה בן בתירה אומר סתם חרמים לבדק הבית שנאמר ב) כל חרם קדש קדשים הוא לה' וחכמים אומרים ב סתם חרמים לכהן שנאמר ג) כשדה החרם לכהן תהיה אחוזתו אם כן מה תלמוד לומר קדש קדשים הוא לה' ג שחל על קדשי קדשים ועל קדשים קלים הקדשות בפלוגתא דרבי אליעזר בן יעקב ורבנן דתניא ד) ר' אליעזר בן יעקב אומר אפילו צינורא של הקדש ה) צריכה עשרה בני אדם לפדותה א) ריבות זה השקאת סוטה ועריפת העגלה וטהרת מצורע השקאת סוטה בפלוגתא דרבי אליעזר ור' יהושע דתנן ו) המקנא לאשתו ר"א אומר מקנא על פי שנים ומשקה על פי עד אחד או על פי עצמו ר' יהושע אומר ד מקנא על פי שנים ומשקה על פי שנים עריפת עגלה בפלוגתא דרבי אליעזר ורבי עקיבא דתנן ז) מאין היו מודדין רבי אליעזר אומר מטיבורו ר' עקיבא אומר ה מחוטמו ר' אליעזר בן יעקב אומר ממקום שנעשה חלל מצוארו טהרת מצורע בפלוגתא דר' שמעון ורבנן דתנן ח) אין לו בהן יד בהן רגל אוזן ימנית אין לו טהרה עולמית ר' אליעזר אומר נותן לו על מקומו ויוצא רבי שמעון אומר ט) נותן על של שמאל ויוצא א) בשעריך זה לקט שכחה פיאה לקט דתנן י) ו שני שבלין לקט שלשה אינן לקט שכחה שני עומרין שכחה שלשה אינן שכחה ועל כולן ב"ש אומרים שלש לעני וארבע לבעל הבית פיאה בפלוגתא דר' ישמעאל ורבנן כ) דתנן ל) מצות פיאה להפריש מן הקמה לא הפריש מן הקמה יפריש מן העומרין לא הפריש מן העומרין יפריש מן הכרי עד שלא מירחו מירחו מעשר ונותן לו משום רבי ישמעאל אמרו ז אף מפריש מן העיסה: ג' בתי דינין וכו': אמר רב כהנא הוא אומר מפי השמועה והן אומרין מפי השמועה אינו נהרג הוא אומר כך הוא בעיני והן אומרין כך הוא בעינינו אינו נהרג וכל שכן הוא אומר מפי השמועה והן אומרין כך הוא בעינינו אינו נהרג עד שיאמר כך הוא בעיני והן אומרים מפי השמועה תדע שהרי לא הרגו את עקביא בן מהללאל ור' אלעזר אומר ח אפילו הוא אומר מפי השמועה והן אומרין כך הוא בעינינו נהרג כדי שלא ירבו מחלוקות בישראל ואם תאמר מפני מה לא הרגו את עקביא בן מהללאל מפני שלא הורה הלכה למעשה תנן כך דרשתי וכך דרשו חבירי כך למדתי וכך למדו חבירי מאי לאו דהוא אמר מפי השמועה והם אומרין כך הוא בעינינו לא הוא אומר כך הוא בעיני והם אומרים מפי השמועה ת"ש מ) דאמר רבי יאשיה שלשה דברים סח לי זעירא מאנשי ירושלים ט בעל שמחל על קינויו קינויו מחול

בן

רש"י

לפריחה בבגדים. אם פרוח תפרח הצרעת ונתמלא כל הבגד: אדם שפרחה בכולו טהור. דכתיב (ויקרא יג) אם פרוח תפרח הצרעת וגו' ופליגי רבנן עליה והיכא דפרחה בבגד כולו והכניסו למקדש או הנוגע בו נכנס למקדש לרבנן חייב ולר' יונתן פטור: המעריך פחות מבן חדש. אמר על פחות מבן חדש ערכו עלי והתורה לא נתנה לו ערך דגבי ערכין כתיב (ויקרא כז) ואם מבן חדש וגו': ר"מ אומר נותן דמיו. כמה שהוא נמכר בשוק דקסבר אין אדם מוציא דבריו לבטלה ויודע שאין ערך לפחות מבן חדש וגמר ואמר לשם דמים ולרבנן פטור ואם בא גיזבר ומשכנו לר"מ הוי הקדש ואין אשה מתקדשת בו אלא אם כן יודע בו כדתנן (קידושין דף נב:) ובהקדש במזיד קידש בשוגג לא קידש ולרבנן לא הוי הקדש והרי הוא של בעלים לקדש בו האשה והאחר שקדש בו אינה מקודשת א"נ לר"מ הוי הקדש והנהנה ממנו מביא אשם מעילות והרי אותו אשם קדש קדשים והאוכלו בטומאת גופו חייב כרת ולרבנן לא הוי הקדש והרי של בעלים הוא והנהנה ממנו לא מעל ואם הביא אשם מעילות חולין לעזרה הוא ואין חייבין עליו משום טומאה: לבדק הבית. ומועלין בהן: לכהנים. ואין מועלין בהם: שחל על קדשי קדשים. כדתנן (ערכין דף כח:) מחרים אדם את קדשיו אם נדר נותן דמיהם ואם נדבה נותן את טובתם כפי חלק שיש לו בה כדמפרש במסכת ערכין בפ' המקדיש: צינורא. מזלג קטן שטווין בו זהב: י' כהנים. כדמפרש בפרק קמא י' כהנים כתובין בפרשה אם נפדית בפחות מעשרה בני אדם עדיין הקדש היא ומועלין בה ולרבנן אין מועלין בה: המקנא לאשתו. המתרה באשתו אל תסתרי עם איש פלוני: ומשקה על פי עד אחד. שבא ואמר אני ראיתיה שנסתרה ואם לא השקה נאסרת עליו ותנן (סוטה דף כד.) אלו לא שותות ולא נוטלות כתובתן האומרת איני שותה והיכא דליכא עידי סתירה ואמרה איני שותה לרבי אליעזר אין לה כתובה לרבי יהושע יש לה כתובה שאינה נאסרת עליו ואם מכרה לאחר כתובתה קנה ואם תופס ממונו של זה כדי כתובה הרי הוא שלו לקדש בו את האשה ולרבי אליעזר הוי גזל ולא קידש: מאין היו מודדין. לידע אי זו עיר קרובה אל החלל: מטבורו. ואותה שקרובה לטבורו תביא את העגלה ולא הקרובה לחוטמו: ר' עקיבא אומר מחוטמו. ובמסכת סוטה מפרש טעמא מר סבר עיקר חיותיה באפיה ומר סבר עיקר חיותיה בטבוריה: ממקום שנעשה חלל. דהיינו מצואריה דסתם חלל מן הצואר כדמפרש התם לתת אותך על צוארי חלל רשעים ותנן (קידושין דף טו:) המקדש בעגלה ערופה אינה מקודשת ואם מלד זקן ממרא מטיבורו וב"ד מחוטמו והביאו אלו עגלה ואלו עגלה למר זו עגלה אסורה ואין מקדשין בה וזו אינה עגלה ומקדשין בה ולמר הוי איפכא: אין לו טהרה עולמית. דבעינן קרא כדכתב כדאמרן בנגמר הדין: נותן על מקומו. על מקום הבוהן נותן דם האשם וטהור ליכנס למקדש ולאכול קודש דהיינו זדונו כרת: שלש אינן לקט. שאין דרך להפקירן: שלשה אינן שכחה. בסיפרא יליף לה מקראי בפרשת שכחה ואם נחלק זקן ממרא ואמר אף שלשה שכחה ובא עני ונטלן ובא בעל הבית ונטלן הימנו לזקן ממרא הוי גזל ואין מקדשין בו אשה ולרבנן מקודשת: מצות פיאה מפריש מן הקמה. דכתיב לא תכלה אלא הנח לפניהם והם יקצרוהו: מרחו. ס) בכרי נתחייב במעשר דנגמרה מלאכתו הלכך מעשר תחילה את הכרי מכל מעשרותיו ונותן לו את הפאה שאילו הפרישה לא היו עניים צריכין לעשרה דלקט שכחה פאה פטורין מן המעשר: אף מפריש מן העיסה. אם טחנה ולשה ולת"ק טחנה פטור דקנייה בשינוי ואם בא עני ונטל כדי פאה משטחנה לר' ישמעאל לא הוי גזל לרבנן הוי גזל: עקביא בן מהללאל. נחלק על חכמים בלשכת הגזית בד' דברים במסכת עדיות (פ"ה משנה ו) שהיה אומר לבנו בשעת מיתתו חזור בך בד' דברים שהייתי אומר אמר לו אבא ואתה מפני מה לא חזרתה בהם אמר לו אני שמעתי מפי המרובים והם שמעו מפי המרובים הם עמדו בשמועתן ואני עמדתי בשמועתי אבל אתה שמעת מפי היחיד וכו': על קינויו. שקינא לאשתו אל תסתרי עם פלוני: קינויו מחול. ואם נסתרה אינה נאסרת עליו:

תוספות

מרחו מעשר ונותן לו. ואפילו למאן דאית ליה ברירה כל זמן שלא הפריש פיאה ולא בירה היה הכל שלו ונתחייב הכל במעשר ושוב לא יפטר וא"ת תרומה נמי לתני שתורם ונותן לו וכ"ת דתרומה בלאו הכי יפריש העני דכל פיאה חייבת בתרומה חדא דאם כן הרי הוא מקדים מעשר לתרומה גדולה ועוד דתנן במסכת תרומות פ"ק [מ"ה] אין תורמין מן הלקט מן השכחה ומן הפיאה וי"מ דלהכי לא תני תורם דאפילו הפקיר לאחר מירוח פטור מן התרומה ס) (דתנן במסכת מעשרות פ' שלשה מינין) פירות ממורחין בשדה מכונסין אסורים משום גזל מפוזרים מותרין בין כך בין כך חייבין במעשר ופטורים מן התרומה וליתא דבירושל' מפרש דלהכי פטורין מן התרומה לפי שאי אפשר לגורן שתעקר אלא אם כן נתרמה ממנו תרומה גדולה לפיכך אין צריך לתרום כשמצא פירות דמסתמא הופרשה מהם תרומה גדולה ונראה לפרש דמשום דתרומה דבר מועט לא חש להזכיר ע):

קינויו מחול. הייני דוקא קודם שנמחקה המגילה אבל לאחר מיכן אין יכול למחול:

מסית

עין משפט נר מצוה

מח א מיי' פ"א מהל' ערכין הל' ג סמג עשין קכח:

מט ב מיי' שם פ"ו הל' א סמג עשין קלב:

נ ג מיי' שם הלכה יא:

נא ד מיי' פ"א מהל' סוטה הל' א ב סמג עשין מח נו [וטוש"ע אה"ע סי' קעח סעי' ב ד]:

נב ה מיי' פ"ט מהל' רוצח הל' ט סמג עשין עה:

נג ו מיי' פ"ד מהל' מתנות עניים הל' א:

נד ז מיי' פ"א שם הלכה ב:

נה ח מיי' פ"ד מהל' ממרים הל' א סמג עשין קיא ולאוין רטו:

נו ט מיי' פ"א מהל' סוטה הל' ז סמג עשין נו טוש"ע אה"ע סי' קעח סעיף יג:

ליקוטי רש"י

לפריחה. אם פרחה הצרעת בכל הבגד. מה להלן פרח בכולה טהור. כדכתיב אם פרוח תפרח וגו' (ויקרא יג) [זבחים מט:]. המעריך פחות מבן חודש. רבי מאיר במסכת ערכין (דף ה) דאמר אין אדם מוציא דבריו לבטלה דתנן המעריך פחות מבן חדש ר"מ אומר נותן דמיו דאדם יודע שאין ערך לפחות מבן חדש וגמר ואמר לשם דמים [כתובות נח:]. נותן דמיו. כמה שהוא נמכר בשוק [ערכין ה.]. החרמים בפלוגתא דר' יהודה בן בתירא ורבנן. אך כל חרם וגו', נחלקו רבותינו בדבר יש אומרים סתם חרמים להקדש ומה אני מקיים (במדבר יח יד) כל חרם בישראל לך יהיה בחרמי כהנים שפירש ואמר הרי זה חרם לכהן ויש שאמרו סתם חרמים לכהנים. כל חרם קדש קדשים הוא. האומר סתם חרמים לבדק הבית מביא ראיה מכאן והאומר סתם חרמים לכהנים מפרש כל חרם קדש קדשים הוא לה' ללמד שחרמי כהנים חלים על קדשי קדשים ועל קדשים קלים ונותן לכהן כמו ששנינו במסכת ערכין (כח:) אם נדר נותן דמיהם ואם נדבה נותן את טובתם [ויקרא כז, כח]. שחל על קדשי קדשים. כדמפרש מחרים אדם את קדשיו וכו' והיאך מוחרמים והלא אינו שלו אלא אם נדר הן דאמר הרי עלי עולה והפריש בהמה לנדרו ואחר כך החרימה הואיל והוא חייב באחריותה אם מתה או נגנבה נמצאת שלו היא והוא נותן כל דמיה לכהן ואת הבהמה יקריב לנדרו דהא ודאי אית ליה פדיון דלאו גופה איחרם דלאו דידיה הוא [ערכין כח:]. צריכה עשרה בני אדם. עשרה כהנים כתובין בפדיון הקדישות שלשה בפרשת ערכין שהיא ראשונה ושלשה בפדיון בהמה וארבעה בקרקעות [לעיל יד:]. המקנא לאשתו. לישנא דקרא נקט וקנא את אשתו (במדבר ה) ולקמן בגמ' מפרש מאי לשון קינוי ובמתניתין מפרש כיצד מקנא לה אומר לה אל תסתרי עם איש פלוני. מקנא לה ע"פ שנים. אם בא להשקותה צריך להביא שני עדים שאמר לה בפניהם אל תסתרי עמו ואם לא קינא לה בפני שנים אינה נאסרת עליו בסתירתה ואינו משקה. ומשקה ע"פ עד א' או ע"פ עצמו. ואפי' אין עדים שנסתרה אלא עד אחד או הוא עצמו אומר ראיתיה שנסתרה אחר שקינאתי לה נאסרת בסתירה עד שתשתה ולקמן ילפינן מקראי שסתירתה אוסרתה עליו מספק. ר' יהושע אומר. צריך ב' עדים אף לסתירתה [סוטה ב.]. אין לו בהן יד בהן רגל אין לו טהרה עולמית. לפי שאין יכול לקיים בו מתן דם ושמן על בהן ידו [נזיר מו:]. אין לו טהרה עולמית. דבעינן קרא כדכתיב [יומא סא:]. ר' אליעזר. לא בעי קרא כדכתיב וכן ר' שמעון [לעיל מה:]. שני עומרים שכחה שלשה אינן שכחה. בספרי מפיק ליה מהאי קרא ושכחת עומר בשדה (דברים כד) ולא גדיש וגם עומר שיש בו סאתים מפיק ליה התם מדכתיב לקחתו למעוטי האי דאינו ניקח בפעם אחת יפה [ב"ב עב:]. מצות פאה להפריש מן הקמה. דכתיב לא תכלה פאת שדך לקצור (ויקרא יט). מרחו. מחליק את הכרי ברחת ומירוח הוי גמר מלאכה למעשר הלכך מעשר כל מעשרותיו תחלה ואחר כך נותן לו פאה כדי שלא יפסיד עני שאילו היה נותנו קודם מירוח אע"פ שעני מצרף לקט שכחה ופאה הרבה ועושה מהן כרי פטור מן המעשר שהרי הפקר הוא אבל עכשיו שנתמרח ביד בעל הבית נתחייב במעשר דהכי אמרינן במסכת ברכות (דף מ:) לקט שכחה ופאה שעשאן בגורן הוקבעו. אף מפריש מן העיסה. פאה אם לא נתנה ככר ואילו לת"ק מן העיסה לא דקנייה בשינוי והוי ממון שאין לו תובעים דעד השתא דישה לאו שינוי הוא דאוכל הוא כמו שהיה [ב"ק צד.]. מירחו. ונתחייב במעשר מעשר תחלה את הכרי ואחר כך נותן לו הפאה שלא להפסיד את העני שהלקט והשכחה והפאה פטורין מן המעשר וזה הביאן לידי חיוב [מכות טז:]. סח לי זעירא. שהיה מאנשי ירושלים.

מסורת הש"ס

א) [צ"ל דתניא], ב) ערכין ה., ג) ערכין כח:, ד) לעיל יד:, ה) [עי' תוספות תמורה כו: ד"ה לא אמרן], ו) סוטה ב., ז) סוטה מה:, ח) לעיל מה: נזיר מו: ע"ש יומא סא: נגעים פי"ד מ"ט, ט) [בנגעים איתא אם נתן על של שמאל יצא], י) פאה פ"ו מ"ה ע"ש, כ) [צ"ל דתניא], ל) תמורה ו. מכות טז: ב"ק לד., מ) סוטה כה., נ) רש"ל גורס ככר, ס) [מהרש"א גריס כדתניא בירושלמי במס' מעשרות פרק ג], ע) [ועי' תוס' ב"ק ד. ד"ה מירחו].

תורה אור השלם

א) כִּי יִפָּלֵא מִמְּךָ דָבָר לַמִּשְׁפָּט בֵּין דָּם לְדָם בֵּין דִּין לְדִין וּבֵין נֶגַע לָנֶגַע דִּבְרֵי רִיבֹת בִּשְׁעָרֶיךָ וְקַמְתָּ וְעָלִיתָ אֶל הַמָּקוֹם אֲשֶׁר יִבְחַר יְיָ אֱלֹהֶיךָ בּוֹ: [דברים יז, ח]

ב) אַךְ כָּל חֵרֶם אֲשֶׁר יַחֲרִם אִישׁ לַייָ מִכָּל אֲשֶׁר לוֹ מֵאָדָם וּבְהֵמָה וּמִשְּׂדֵה אֲחֻזָּתוֹ לֹא יִמָּכֵר וְלֹא יִגָּאֵל כָּל חֵרֶם קֹדֶשׁ קָדָשִׁים הוּא לַייָ: [ויקרא כז, כח]

ג) וְהָיָה הַשָּׂדֶה בְּצֵאתוֹ בַיֹּבֵל קֹדֶשׁ לַייָ כִּשְׂדֵה הַחֵרֶם לַכֹּהֵן תִּהְיֶה אֲחֻזָּתוֹ: [ויקרא כז, כא]

מֵחוֹטְמוֹ – FROM HIS NOSE.[19] רַבִּי אֱלִיעֶזֶר בֶּן יַעֲקֹב אוֹמֵר – R' ELIEZER BEN YAAKOV SAYS: מִמָּקוֹם שֶׁנַּעֲשָׂה חָלָל – FROM THE PLACE THAT HE BECAME A CORPSE, מִצַּוָּארוֹ – i.e. FROM HIS NECK.[20]

Rav Pappa explains the final case derived from "disputes": טָהֳרַת מְצוֹרָע – To what dispute concerning **purification of the *metzora*** does the Baraisa refer? בִּפְלוּגְתָּא דְּרַבִּי שִׁמְעוֹן וְרַבָּנָן – **It refers to the dispute between R' Shimon and the Rabbis,** דִּתְנַן – **as we learned in a Mishnah** concerning the purification ritual of a *metzora:*[21] אֵין לוֹ בֹּהֶן יָד בֹּהֶן רֶגֶל אוֹזֶן יְמָנִית – If [A *METZORA*] DOES NOT HAVE A THUMB on his right hand, A BIG TOE on his right foot, or if he lacks A RIGHT EAR, אֵין לוֹ טָהֳרָה עוֹלָמִית – HE CAN NEVER ACHIEVE PURIFICATION.[22] רַבִּי אֱלִיעֶזֶר אוֹמֵר – R' ELIEZER SAYS: נוֹתֵן לוֹ עַל מְקוֹמוֹ וְיוֹצֵא – [THE KOHEN] SHOULD PLACE the blood of the offering ON THE LOCATION [OF THE MISSING MEMBER], AND [THE *METZORA*] WILL thereby DISCHARGE his obligation. רַבִּי שִׁמְעוֹן אוֹמֵר – R' SHIMON SAYS: נוֹתֵן עַל שֶׁל שְׂמֹאל וְיוֹצֵא – [THE KOHEN] SHOULD PLACE the blood ON the thumb or the big toe of THE LEFT hand or foot, or on the left ear, AND [THE *METZORA*] WILL thereby DISCHARGE his obligation.[23]

Rav Pappa continues his interpretive citing of the Baraisa: "בִּשְׁעָרֶיךָ" – *IN YOUR GATES;* זוֹ לֶקֶט שִׁכְחָה וּפֵאָה – THIS alludes to a dispute regarding *LEKET, SHICH'CHAH,* AND *PE'AH.*

Rav Pappa explains the first two cases derived from "in your gates": לֶקֶט – To what dispute concerning ***leket*** does the Baraisa refer? דִּתְנַן – **As we learned in a Mishnah:**[24] שְׁנֵי שִׁבֳּלִין לֶקֶט – TWO EARS that fall together ARE *LEKET;* שְׁלֹשָׁה אֵינָן לֶקֶט – THREE ARE NOT *LEKET.*[25]

שִׁכְחָה – To what dispute concerning ***shich'chah*** does the Baraisa refer? As we learned in the previously cited Mishnah: שְׁנֵי עוֹמָרִין שִׁכְחָה – TWO SHEAVES that are forgotten ARE *SHICH'CHAH;* שְׁלֹשָׁה אֵינָן שִׁכְחָה – THREE ARE NOT *SHICH'CHAH.*[26] וְעַל כּוּלָּן – AND CONCERNING ALL OF THEM, i.e. both *leket* and *shich'chah,* בֵּית שַׁמַּאי אוֹמְרִים – BEIS SHAMMAI SAY: שָׁלֹשׁ לֶעָנִי – THREE ears or sheaves BELONG TO THE POOR וְאַרְבַּע לְבַעַל הַבַּיִת – AND FOUR BELONG TO THE OWNER.[27]

Rav Pappa explains the final case derived from "in your gates": פֵּאָה – To what dispute concerning ***pe'ah***[28] does the Baraisa refer? בִּפְלוּגְתָּא דְּרַבִּי יִשְׁמָעֵאל וְרַבָּנָן – **It refers to the dispute between R' Yishmael and the Rabbis,** דִּתְנַן – **as it was taught in a Baraisa:**[29] מִצְוַת פֵּאָה לְהַפְרִישׁ מִן הַקָּמָה – THE MITZVAH OF *PE'AH* IS performed BY SEPARATING IT FROM THE STANDING CROP. לֹא הִפְרִישׁ מִן הַקָּמָה – If [THE FARMER] DID NOT SEPARATE it FROM THE STANDING CROP,[30] יַפְרִישׁ מִן הָעוֹמָרִין – HE MUST SEPARATE it FROM THE SHEAVED PRODUCE. לֹא הִפְרִישׁ מִן הָעוֹמָרִין – If HE DID NOT SEPARATE it FROM THE SHEAVED PRODUCE, יַפְרִישׁ מִן הַכְּרִי עַד שֶׁלֹּא מֵירְחוֹ – HE MUST SEPARATE it

NOTES

19. The city closest to the corpse's navel according to R' Eliezer [or to its nose according to R' Akiva] must bring the *eglah arufah* (*Rashi*).

As the Gemara there explains, they argue which body part is [most representative of] the body's vitality (*Rashi*); the nose, through which one breaths, or the navel, which is opposite the organs that process the body's food (*Rambam* in *Commentary to Mishnah* there).

20. When Scripture uses the term "corpse" (*chalal*) in an unspecified manner, it refers to one killed from the neck, as it states: (*Ezekiel* 21:34): *to place [your necks] with the necks of the corpses of the wicked* (*Rashi* from *Sotah* 45b).

Now, the Mishnah (*Kiddushin* 56b) teaches that if one betroths a woman with an *eglah arufah*, the woman is not betrothed, for since it is forbidden to derive benefit from this animal, it is valueless. Thus, consider the following case: A body was found between two towns. The High Court ruled as R' Akiva and instructed the city closest to the corpse's nose to bring an *eglah arufah,* while a dissenting sage ruled as R' Eliezer and instructed another city, closest to the corpse's navel, to do so. If someone were to betroth a woman with the *eglah arufah* of the second city, the High Court would validate the marriage (since that city was never supposed to bring an *eglah arufah*), while the sage would invalidate it, thereby permitting a married woman to other men (see *Rashi*).

21. *Negaim* 14:9. As part of the purification ritual of a *metzora* the Torah commands (*Leviticus* 14:14): וְלָקַח הַכֹּהֵן מִדַּם הָאָשָׁם וְנָתַן הַכֹּהֵן עַל־תְּנוּךְ אֹזֶן הַמִּטַּהֵר הַיְמָנִית וְעַל־בֹּהֶן יָדוֹ הַיְמָנִית וְעַל־בֹּהֶן רַגְלוֹ הַיְמָנִית, *The Kohen shall take from the blood of the asham offering, and the Kohen shall place it on the middle part of the right ear of the person being purified and on the thumb of his right hand and the big toe of his right foot.*

22. In the Tanna Kamma's opinion, a *metzora* who is missing, for example, his right thumb or right big toe can never be purified, because the purification is not effected unless the procedure is carried out exactly as it is spelled out in the verse (*Rashi*, from Gemara above, 45b).

23. Both R' Eliezer and R' Shimon maintain that the procedure can effect purification even if it is not carried out exactly as stated in the verse (*Rashi*). However, R' Eliezer holds that in the absence of a right thumb or right big toe it is preferable to put the blood on the location of the thumb or toe, for one thereby fulfills the stipulation of placing it on the right side. R' Shimon, on the other hand, deems it preferable to place the blood on the left thumb or left big toe so as to fulfill the stipulation that the blood be placed on a thumb and big toe (*Chazon Ish, Negaim* 12:22).

Now since a *metzora* incurs *kares* upon entering the Temple without purification, if the High Court were to rule as the Rabbis (the Tanna Kamma), they would prohibit such a *metzora* from entering the Temple. If the dissenting sage rules as either of the other views and "purifies" the *metzora,* he may cause the *metzora* to incur *kares.*

24. *Pe'ah* 6:5. This Mishnah discusses both *leket* and *shich'chah. Leket* (gleanings) are those ears of grains that fall from within the sickle or from within the reaper's hand when he gathers the ears and harvests; see *Leviticus* 19:9, 23:22. *Shich'chah* (forgotten produce) are those sheaves forgotten in the field during the removal to the threshing floor, as well as the standing produce which the harvester overlooked; see *Deuteronomy* 24:19.

25. If one or two ears fall together from within the harvester's sickle or hand, they are *leket* and belong to the poor. If three ears fall, they are not *leket* and belong to the owner, for it is not usual for an owner to relinquish as many as three ears at a time (*Rashi*, see *Rashash* and *Aruch LaNer*).

26. If the farmer forgot two sheaves, they are both rendered *shich'chah* and belong to the poor. If, however, he forgot three or more consecutive sheaves, they do not become *shich'chah*, and remain the property of the owner. This is derived in *Sifrei* to *Deuteronomy* 24:19 (*Rashi*).

27. Beis Shammai maintain that for *leket* and *shich'chah* a set of three is still awarded by the Torah to the poor, but a set of four or more is retained by the owner.

Now, consider a case in which a poor person took three ears of *leket* or three sheaves of *shich'chah,* and the owner of the field repossessed them from him. The owner then betrothed a woman with it. According to Beis Shammai, the ears and sheaves are stolen property in the owner's hands, for they rightfully belong to the poor person. According to Beis Hillel, they are considered the property of the owner, the poor person having had no right to them in the first place. Thus, if the High Court were to rule as Beis Hillel, they would validate the owner's betrothal. If the dissenting sage were to rule as Beis Shammai, he would invalidate the owner's betrothal, and thereby permit a married woman to other men (*Rashi*; see *Maharsha*).

28. *Pe'ah* (the edge) is a portion of the crop that the farmer must leave standing for the benefit of the poor, in keeping with the Torah's prohibition against harvesting one's field entirely. The Torah (see *Leviticus* 19:9, 23:22) states: *And when you reap the harvest of your land, you shall not finish off the edge of your field.*

29. Translation follows emendation of *Mesores HaShas*.

30. Rather, he violated the prohibition and reaped his entire crop.

לפריחה בבגדים שהיא טהורה נאמרה קרחת וגבחת באדם ונאמרה קרחת וגבחת בבגדים מה להלן פרח בכולו טהור אף כאן פרח בכולו טהור (א) דברי אלו הערכין והחרמים והקדישות הערכין בפלוגתא דר"מ ורבנן (א) דתנן (ב) המעריך פחות מבן חדש ר"מ אומר נותן דמיו וחכמים אומרים [א] לא אמר כלום החרמים בפלוגתא דרבי יהודה בן בתירה ורבנן דתנן (ג) ר' יהודה בן בתירה אומר סתם חרמים לבדק הבית שנאמר (ב) כל חרם קדש קדשים הוא לה' וחכמים אומרים [ב] סתם חרמים לכהן שנאמר (ג) כשדה החרם לכהן תהיה אחוזתו אם כן מה תלמוד לומר קדש קדשים הוא לה' [ג] שחל על קדשי קדשים ועל קדשים קלים הקדשות בפלוגתא דרבי אליעזר בן יעקב ורבנן דתניא (ד) ר' אליעזר בן יעקב אומר אפילו צינורא של הקדש (ה) צריכה עשרה בני אדם לפדותה (א) ריבות זה השקאת סוטה ועריפת העגלה וטהרת מצורע השקאת סוטה בפלוגתא דרבי אליעזר ור' יהושע דתנן (ו) המקנא לאשתו ר"א אומר מקנא על פי שנים ומשקה על פי עד אחד או על פי עצמו ר' יהושע אומר [ד] מקנא על פי שנים ומשקה על פי שנים עריפת עגלה בפלוגתא דרבי אליעזר ורבי עקיבא דתנן (ז) מאין היו מודדין רבי אליעזר אומר מטיבורו ר' עקיבא אומר [ה] מחוטמו ר' אליעזר בן יעקב אומר ממקום שנעשה חלל מצוארו טהרת מצורע בפלוגתא דר' שמעון ורבנן דתנן (ח) אין לו בהן יד בהן רגל אוזן ימנית אין לו טהרה עולמית ר' אליעזר אומר נותן לו על מקומו ויוצא רבי שמעון אומר (ט) נותן על של שמאל ויוצא (א) בשעריך זה לקט שכחה פיאה לקט דתנן (י) [ו] שני שבלין לקט שלשה אינן לקט שכחה שני עומרין שכחה שלשה אינן שכחה ועל כולן ב"ש אומרים שלש לעני וארבע לבעל הבית פיאה בפלוגתא דר' ישמעאל ורבנן (כ) דתנן (ל) מצות פיאה להפריש מן הקמה לא הפריש מן הקמה יפריש מן העומרין לא הפריש מן העומרין יפריש מן הכרי עד שלא מירחו מירחו מעשר ונותן לו משום רבי ישמעאל אמרו [ז] אף מפריש מן העיסה: ג' בתי דינין וכו': אמר רב כהנא הוא אומר מפי השמועה והן אומרין מפי השמועה אינו נהרג הוא אומר כך הוא בעיני והן אומרין כך הוא בעינינו אינו נהרג וכל שכן הוא אומר מפי השמועה והן אומרין כך הוא בעינינו אינו נהרג עד שיאמר כך הוא בעיני והן אומרים מפי השמועה תדע שהרי לא הרגו את עקביא בן מהללאל ור' אלעזר אומר [ח] אפילו הוא אומר מפי השמועה והן אומרין כך הוא בעינינו נהרג כדי שלא ירבו מחלוקות בישראל ואם תאמר מפני מה לא הרגו את עקביא בן מהללאל מפני שלא הורה הלכה למעשה תנן כך דרשתי וכך דרשו חבירי כך למדתי וכך למדו חבירי מאי לאו דהוא אמר מפי השמועה והם אומרין כך הוא בעינינו לא הוא אומר כך הוא בעיני והם אומרים מפי השמועה ת"ש (מ) דאמר רבי יאשיה שלשה דברים סח לי זעירא מאנשי ירושלים [ט] בעל שמחל על קינויו קינויו מחול

בן

לפריחה בבגדים. אם פרות תפרח הצרעת ונתמלא כל הבגד: אדם שפרחה בכולו טהור. דכתיב (ויקרא יג) אם פרוח תפרח הצרעת וגו' ופליגי רבנן עליה והיכא דפרחה בבגד כולו והכניסו למקדש או הנוגע בו נכנס למקדש לרבנן חייב ולר' יונתן פטור: המעריך פחות מבן חדש. אמר על פחות מבן חדש ערכו עלי והתורה לא נתנה לו ערך דגבי ערכין כתיב (ויקרא כז) ואם מבן חדש וגו': ר"מ אומר נותן דמיו. כמה שהוא נמכר בשוק דקסבר אין אדם מוציא דבריו לבטלה ויודע שאין ערך לפחות מבן חדש וגמר ואמר לשם דמים ולרבנן פטור ואם בא גיזבר ומשכנו לר"מ הוי הקדש ואין אשה מתקדשת בו אלא אם כן יודע בו כדתנן (קידושין דף נג:) והמקדש במזיד קידש בשוגג לא קידש ולרבנן לא הוי הקדש והרי הוא של בעלים לקדש בו האשה והאחר שקדש בו אינה מקודשת א"נ לר"מ הוי הקדש והנהנה ממנו מביא אשם מעילות והרי אותו אשם קדש קדשים והאוכלו בטומאת גופו חייב כרת ולרבנן לא הוי הקדש והרי של בעלים הוא והנהנה ממנו לא מעל ואם הביא אשם מעילות חולין לעזרה הוא ואין חייבין עליו משום טומאה: לבדק הבית. ומועלין בהן: לכהנים. ואין מועלין בהם: שחל על קדשי קדשים. כדתנן (ערכין דף כח:) מחרים אדם את קדשיו אם נדר נותן דמיהם ואם נדבה נותן את טובתם כפי חלק שיש לו בה כדמפרש במסכת ערכין בפ' המקדיש: צינורא. מזלג קטן שטווין בו זהב: י' כהנים. כדמפרש בפרק קמא י' כהנים כתובין בפרשה אם נפדית בפחות מעשרה בני אדם עדיין הקדש היא ומועלין בה ולרבנן אין מועלין בה: המקנא לאשתו. המתרה באשתו אל תסתרי עם איש פלוני: ומשקה על פי עד אחד. שבא ואמר אני ראיתיה שנסתרה ואם לא השקה נאסרת עליו ותנן (סוטה דף כד.) אלו לא שותות ולא נוטלות כתובתן האומרת איני שותה והיכא דליכא עידי סתירה ואמרה איני שותה לרבי אליעזר אין לה כתובה לרבי יהושע יש לה כתובה שאינה נאסרת עליו ואם מכרה לאחר כתובתה קנה ואם תופס ממונו של זה כדי כתובה הרי הוא שלו לקדש בו את האשה ולרבי אליעזר הוי גזל ולא קידש: מאין היו מודדין. לידע אי זו עיר קרובה אל החלל: מטבורו. ואותה שקרובה לטבורו תביא את העגלה ולא הקרובה לחוטמו: ר' עקיבא אומר מחוטמו. ובמסכת סוטה מפרש טעמא מר סבר עיקר חיותיה באפיה ומר סבר עיקר חיותיה בטבוריה: ממקום שנעשה חלל. דהיינו מצואריה דסתם חלל מן הצואר כדמפרש התם לתת אותך על צוארי חלל רשעים ותנן (קידושין דף נו:) המקדש בעגלה ערופה אינה מקודשת ואם מדד זקן ממרא מטיבורו וב"ד מחוטמו והביאו אלו עגלה ואלו עגלה למר זו עגלה אסורה ואין מקדשין בה וזו אינה עגלה ומקדשין בה ולמר הוי איפכא: אין לו טהרה עולמית. דבעינן קרא כדכתב כדאמרן בנגמר הדין: נותן על מקומו. על מקום הבוהן נותן דם האשם וטהור ליכנס למקדש ולאכול קודש דהיינו זדונו כרת: שלש אינן לקט. שאין דרך להפקירן: שלשה אינן שכחה. בסיפרא יליף לה מקראי בפרשת שכחה ואם נחלק זקן ממרא ואמר אף שלשה שכחה ובא עני ונטלן ובא בעל הבית ונטלן הימנו לזקן ממרא הוי גזל ואין מקדשין בו אשה ולרבנן מקודשת: מצות פיאה מפריש מן הקמה. דכתיב לא תכלה אלא הנח לפניהם והם יקצרוהו: מרחו. (י) בכרי נתחייב במעשר דנגמרה מלאכתו הלכך מעשר תחילה את הכרי מכל מעשרותיו ונותן לו את הפאה שאילו הפרישה לא היו עניים צריכין לעשרה דלקט שכחה פאה פטורין מן המעשר: אף מפריש מן העיסה. אם טחנה ולשה ולת"ק טחנה פטור דקנייה בשינוי ואם בא עני ונטל כדי פאה משטחנה לר' ישמעאל לא הוי גזל לרבנן הוי גזל: עקביא בן מהללאל. נחלק על חכמים בלשכת הגזית בד' דברים במסכת עדיות (פ"ה משנה ו) שהיה אומר לבנו בשעת מיתתו חזור בך בד' דברים שהייתי אומר אמר לו אבא ואתה מפני מה לא חזרת בהם אמר לו אני שמעתי מפי המרובים והם שמעו מפי המרובים הם עמדו בשמועתן ואני עמדתי בשמועתי אבל אתה שמעת מפי היחיד וכו': על קינויו. שקינא לאשתו אל תסתרי עם פלוני: קינויו מחול. ואם נסתרה אינה נאסרת עליו:

בן

מרחו מעשר ונותן לו. ואפילו למאן דאית ליה ברירה כל זמן שלא הפריש פיאה ולא ביררה היה הכל שלו ונתחייב הכל במעשר ושוב לא יפטר וא"ת תרומה נמי לתני שתורם ונותן לו וכ"ת דתרומה בלאו הכי יפריש העני דכל פיאה חייבת בתרומה חדא דאם כן הרי הוא מקדים מעשר לתרומה גדולה ועוד דתנן במסכת תרומות פ"ק [מ"ה] אין תורמין מן הלקט מן השכחה ומן הפיאה וי"מ דלהכי לא תני תורם דאפילו הפקיר לאחר מירוח פטור מן התרומה (ס) (דתנן במסכת מעשרות פ' שלשה מינין) פירות ממורחין בשדה מכונסין אסורים משום גזל מפוזרים מותרין בין כך בין כך חייבין במעשר ופטורים מן התרומה וליתא דבירושל' מפרש דלהכי פטורין מן התרומה לפי שאי אפשר לגורן שתעקר אלא אם כן נתרמה ממנו תרומה גדולה לפיכך אין צריך לתרום כשמצא פירות דמסתמא הופרשה מהם תרומה גדולה ונראה לפרש דמשום דתרומה דבר מועט לא חש להזכיר (ע):

קינויו מחול. היינו דוקא קודם שנמחקה המגילה אבל לאחר מיכן אין יכול למחול:

מסית

עין משפט נר מצוה

מח א מיי' פ"א מהל' ערכין הל' ג סמג עשין קכח:

מט ב מיי' שם פ"ו הל' א סמג עשין קלב:

נ ג מיי' שם הלכה יא:

נא ד מיי' פ"א מהל' סוטה הל' א ב סמג עשין מח נו [וטוש"ע אה"ע סי' קעח סעי' ב ד]:

נב ה מיי' פ"ט מהל' רוצח הל' ט סמג עשין עה:

נג ו מיי' פ"ד מהל' מתנות עניים הל' א:

נד ז מיי' פ"א שם הלכה ב:

נה ח מיי' פ"ד מהל' ממרים הל' א סמג עשין קיא ולאוין רטז:

נו ט מיי' פ"א מהל' סוטה הל' ז סמג עשין נו טוש"ע אה"ע סי' קעח סעיף יב:

ליקוטי רש"י

לפריחה. אם פרחה הצרעת בכל הבגד. מה להלן פרח בכולה טהור. כדכתיב אם פרוח תפרח וגו' (ויקרא יג) [זבחים מט:]. המעריך פחות מבן חודש. רבי מאיר במסכת ערכין (דף ה) דאמר אין אדם מוציא דבריו לבטלה דתנן המעריך פחות מבן חדש ר"מ אומר נותן דמיו דאדם יודע שאין ערך לפחות מבן חדש וגמר ואמר לשם דמים [כתובות נח:]. נותן דמיו. כמה שהוא נמכר בשוק [ערכין ה.]. החרמים בפלוגתא דר' יהודה בן בתירא ורבנן. אך כל חרם וגו', נחלקו רבותינו בדבר יש אומרים סתם חרמים להקדש ומה אני מקיים (במדבר יח יד) כל חרם בישראל לך יהיה בחרמי כהנים שפירש ואמר הרי זה חרם לכהן ויש שאמרו סתם חרמים לכהנים. כל חרם קדש קדשים הוא. האומר סתם חרמים לבדק הבית מביא ראיה מכאן והאומר סתם חרמים לכהנים מפרש כל חרם קדש קדשים הוא לה' ללמד שחרמי כהנים חלים על קדשי קדשים ועל קדשים קלים ונותן לכהן כמו ששנינו במסכת ערכין (כח:) אם נדר נותן דמיהם ואם נדבה נותן את טובתה [ויקרא כז, כח]. שחל על קדשי קדשים. כדמפרש מחרים אדם את קדשיו וכו' והיאך מוחרמים והלא אינו שלו אלא אם נדר הן דאמר הרי עלי עולה והפריש בהמה לנדרו ואחר כך החרימה הואיל והוא חייב באחריותה אם מתה או נגנבה נמצאת שלו היא והוא נותן כל דמיה לכהן ואת הבהמה יקריב לנדרו דהא ודאי אית ליה פדיון דלאו גופה איחרם דלאו דידיה הוא [ערכין כח:]. צריכה עשרה בני אדם. עשרה כהנים כתובין בפדיון הקדישות שלשה בפרשת ערכין שהיא ראשונה ושלשה בפדיון בהמה וארבעה בקרקעות [לעיל יד:]. המקנא לאשתו. לישנא דקרא נקט וקנא את אשתו (במדבר ה) ולקמן בגמ' מפרש מאי לשון קינוי ובמתניתין מפרש כילד מקנא לה אומר לה אל תסתרי עם איש פלוני. מקנא לה ע"פ שנים. אם בא להשקותה צריך להביא שני עדים שאמר לה בפניהם אל תסתרי עמו ואם לא קינא לה בפני שנים אינה נאסרת עליו בסתירתה ואינו משקה. ומשקה ע"פ עד א' או ע"פ עצמו. ואפי' אין עדים שנסתרה אלא עד אחד או הוא עצמו אומר ראיתיה שנסתרה אחר שקינאתי לה נאסרת בסתירה עד שתשתה ולקמן ילפינן מקראי שסתירתה אוסרתה עליו מספק. ר' יהושע אומר. צריך ב' עדים אף לסתירתה [סוטה ב.]. אין לו בהן יד בהן רגל אין לו טהרה עולמית. לפי שאין יכול לקיים בו מתן דם ושמן על בהן ידו [נזיר מו:]. אין לו טהרה עולמית. דבעינן קרא כדכתיב [יומא סא:]. ר' אליעזר. לא בעי קרא כדכתיב וכן ר' שמעון [לעיל מה:]. שני עומרים שכחה שלשה אינן שכחה. בספרי מפיק ליה מהאי קרא ושכחת עומר בשדה (דברים כד) ולא גדיש וגם עומר שיש בו סאתים מפיק ליה התם מדכתיב לקחתו למעוטי האי דאינו ניקח בפעם אחת יפה [ב"ב עב:]. מצות פאה להפריש מן הקמה. דכתיב לא תכלה פאת שדך לקצור (ויקרא יט). מרחו. מחליק את הכרי ברחת ומירוח הוי גמר מלאכה למעשר הלכך מעשר כל מעשרותיו תחלה ואחר כך נותן לו פאה כדי שלא יפסיד עני שאילו היה נותנו קודם מירוח אע"פ שעני מצרף לקט שכחה ופאה הרבה ועושה מהן כרי פטור מן המעשר שהרי הפקר הוא אבל עכשיו שנתמרח ביד בעל הבית נתחייב במעשר דהכי אמרינן במסכת ברכות (דף מ:) לקט שכחה ופאה שעשאן בגורן הוקבעו. אף מפריש מן העיסה. פאה אם לא נתנה כבר ואילו לת"ק מן העיסה לא דקנייה בשינוי והוי ממון שאין לו תובעים דעד השתא דישה לאו שינוי הוא דאוכל הוא כמו שהיה [ב"ק צד.]. מירחו. ונתחייב במעשר מעשר תחלה את הכרי ואחר כך נותן לו הפאה שלא להפסיד את העני שהלקט והשכחה והפאה פטורין מן המעשר וזה הביאן לידי חיוב [מכות טז:]. סח לי זעירא. שהיה מאנשי ירושלים.

מסורת הש"ס

א) [נ"ל דתניא], ב) ערכין ה., ג) ערכין כח:, ד) לעיל יד:, ה) [עי' תוספות תמורה כז: ד"ה לא אמרו], ו) סוטה ב., ז) סוטה מה:, ח) לעיל מה: נזיר מו: ע"ש יומא סא:, נגעים פי"ד מ"ט, ט) [בנגעים איתא אם נתן על של שמאל יצא], י) פאה פ"ו מ"ה ע"ש, כ) [נ"ל דתניא], ל) תמורה ו. מכות טז: ב"ק לד., מ) סוטה כה., נ) רש"ל גורס כבר, ס) [מהרש"א גרים כדתניא בירושלמי במס' מעשרות פרק ג], ע) [ועי' תוס' ב"ק ז. ד"ה מירחו].

תורה אור השלם

א) כִּי יִפָּלֵא מִמְּךָ דָבָר לַמִּשְׁפָּט בֵּין דָּם לְדָם בֵּין דִּין לְדִין וּבֵין נֶגַע לָנֶגַע דִּבְרֵי רִיבֹת בִּשְׁעָרֶיךָ וְקַמְתָּ וְעָלִיתָ אֶל הַמָּקוֹם אֲשֶׁר יִבְחַר יְיָ אֱלֹהֶיךָ בּוֹ: [דברים יז, ח]

ב) אַךְ כָּל חֵרֶם אֲשֶׁר יַחֲרִם אִישׁ לַייָ מִכָּל אֲשֶׁר לוֹ מֵאָדָם וּבְהֵמָה וּמִשְּׂדֵה אֲחֻזָּתוֹ לֹא יִמָּכֵר וְלֹא יִגָּאֵל כָּל חֵרֶם קֹדֶשׁ קָדָשִׁים הוּא לַייָ: [ויקרא כז, כח]

ג) וְהָיָה הַשָּׂדֶה בְּצֵאתוֹ בַיֹּבֵל קֹדֶשׁ לַייָ כִּשְׂדֵה הַחֵרֶם לַכֹּהֵן תִּהְיֶה אֲחֻזָּתוֹ: [ויקרא כז, כא]

FROM THE PILE of kernels AS LONG AS HE HAD NOT SMOOTHED IT.[31] מֵירְחוֹ – BUT ONCE HE HAS SMOOTHED IT, מְעַשֵּׂר וְנוֹתֵן לוֹ – HE MUST first TITHE the produce AND then GIVE it TO [THE POOR PERSON].[32] מִשּׁוּם רַבִּי יִשְׁמָעֵאל אָמְרוּ – IN THE NAME OF R' YISHMAEL THEY SAID: אַף מַפְרִישׁ מִן הָעִיסָּה – HE MAY EVEN SEPARATE *pe'ah* FROM THE DOUGH.[33]

The Gemara discusses the next part of the Mishnah, which stated:

שְׁלֹשָׁה בָּתֵּי דִינִין וכו׳ – There were THREE COURTS there **etc.** The Mishnah then quoted the basis for the sage's and the High Court's arguments. The Gemara now expands upon that:

אָמַר רַב כַּהֲנָא – **Rav Kahana said:** הוּא אוֹמֵר מִפִּי הַשְּׁמוּעָה – If **[the sage] states** his ruling based on **what he heard** as a tradition from his teachers, וְהֵן אוֹמְרִין מִפִּי הַשְּׁמוּעָה – **and [the High Court] states** their ruling based on **what they heard** as a tradition from their teachers, אֵינוֹ נֶהֱרָג – **[the sage]** is not deemed a *zakein mamrei,* and **is not killed.**

הוּא אוֹמֵר כָּךְ הוּא בְּעֵינַי – **If [the sage] states, "It appears thus in my eyes,"** i.e. he bases his ruling on his own reasoning, not on his received tradition, וְהֵן אוֹמְרִין כָּךְ הוּא בְּעֵינֵינוּ – **and [the High Court] states, "It appears thus in our eyes,"** i.e. they, too, base their ruling on their own reasoning, not on their received tradition, אֵינוֹ נֶהֱרָג – **[the sage]** is not deemed a *zakein mamrei*, and **is not killed.** וְכָל שֶׁכֵּן הוּא אוֹמֵר מִפִּי הַשְּׁמוּעָה – **And certainly if [the sage] states** his ruling based on **what he heard** as a tradition from his teachers, וְהֵן אוֹמְרִין כָּךְ הוּא בְּעֵינֵינוּ אֵינוֹ נֶהֱרָג – **and [the High Court] states, "It appears thus in our eyes," he is not killed** as a *zakein mamrei.*[34] עַד שֶׁיֹּאמַר כָּךְ הוּא בְּעֵינַי – For a sage is not killed as a *zakein mamrei* **unless he states, "It appears thus in my eyes,"** וְהֵן אוֹמְרִים מִפִּי הַשְּׁמוּעָה – **and [the High Court] state** their ruling based on **what they heard** as a tradition from their teachers. תֵּדַע – **And you should know** that this is so, שֶׁהֲרֵי לֹא הָרְגוּ אֶת עֲקַבְיָא בֶּן מַהֲלַלְאֵל – **for they did not execute Akavya ben Mahalalel.**[35]

The Gemara cites a different opinion:

וְרַבִּי אֶלְעָזָר אוֹמֵר – **But R' Elazar says:** אֲפִילּוּ הוּא אוֹמֵר מִפִּי הַשְּׁמוּעָה – **Even if [the sage] states** his ruling based on **what he heard** as a tradition from his teachers, וְהֵן אוֹמְרִין כָּךְ הוּא בְּעֵינֵינוּ – **and [the High Court] states, "It appears thus in our eyes,"** נֶהֱרָג – **[the sage]** is deemed a *zakein mamrei* and **is killed.**

R'Elazar explains why the sage is killed even if the source for his ruling is a tradition he received, and that of the High Court is their own reasoning:

כְּדֵי שֶׁלֹּא יִרְבּוּ מַחֲלוֹקוֹת בְּיִשְׂרָאֵל – The sage is killed **so that disputes will not proliferate in** the nation of **Israel.**

R' Elazar now refutes Rav Kahana's proof:

וְאִם תֹּאמַר – **And if you should say:** מִפְּנֵי מָה לֹא הָרְגוּ אֶת עֲקַבְיָא בֶּן מַהֲלַלְאֵל – **Why,** then, **did they not execute Akavya ben Mahalalel?** The answer is: מִפְּנֵי שֶׁלֹּא הוֹרָה הֲלָכָה לְמַעֲשֶׂה – **Because he did not instruct** anyone to adopt his ruling as **a course of action.**[36]

The Gemara adduces support for R' Elazar from our Mishnah:

תְּנַן – **We learned in our Mishnah** that the sage and his disputants come to the court at the entrance to the Temple Mount, where the sage says: כָּךְ דָּרַשְׁתִּי וְכָךְ דָּרְשׁוּ חֲבֵירַי – THUS I HAVE EXPOUNDED AND THUS MY COLLEAGUES HAVE EXPOUNDED; כָּךְ לִמַּדְתִּי וְכָךְ לִמְּדוּ חֲבֵירַי – THUS I HAVE TAUGHT AND THUS MY COLLEAGUES HAVE TAUGHT.

The Gemara analyzes the Mishnah:

מַאי לָאו דְּהוּא אָמַר מִפִּי הַשְּׁמוּעָה – **What** is the case here? Is the Mishnah **not** speaking of **where [the sage] states** his ruling based on **what he heard** as a tradition from his teachers, וְהֵם אוֹמְרִין כָּךְ הוּא בְּעֵינֵינוּ – **and [the High Court] states, "It appears**

NOTES

31. Before the pile has been smoothed, *pe'ah* can still be separated from the untithed produce.

The sheaved produce is moved to the threshing floor, where it is threshed and winnowed to separate the kernels from the straw and ears. The kernels are then concentrated into a pile, whose sides are then smoothed. This smoothing of the pile, called מירוח, *meiruach,* represents the completion of the processing of the raw produce and it activates the tithing obligation for that produce.

Once the tithing obligation has been activated, a person may not eat this produce without first separating the appropriate *maasros* from what he wishes to eat. Prior to the *meiruach,* however, one is permitted to eat a casual snack from the produce without tithing it (although the Sages forbade a regular meal).

32. The gift of *pe'ah* is ordinarily exempt from all *maasros*. However, if the farmer delays separating the *pe'ah* until after the *meiruach*, he has already activated the tithing obligation, and the *pe'ah* that he separates at that point will be subject to *maasros.* Accordingly, the poor person's share of *pe'ah* will be reduced by the amount of *maasros* that he must separate from it. Therefore, the Rabbis required the farmer to tithe the produce and then separate the *pe'ah,* in order not to reduce the poor person's share (*Rashi*).

33. R' Yishmael rules that the mitzvah to separate *pe'ah* must be fulfilled even if the grain has already been made into flour or dough [or even baked into bread]. The Tanna Kamma, however, maintains that by effecting a change in the grain by grinding it into flour, the field owner legally acquires the *pe'ah* produce, and the poor no longer have a claim on it.

Thus, if the field owner did not separate *pe'ah* and processed the grain into flour, and then a poor person came and took some of the flour as *pe'ah,* according to the Tanna Kamma, the flour is stolen property in his hands; while according to R' Yishmael, it is rightfully his. If the poor person were to betroth a woman with the flour, the validity of the betrothal would hinge on this dispute; thus, a dissenting sage who differed with the High Court regarding this dispute would be disputing a matter that could lead to *kares* [see note 27] (see *Rashi*).

The Gemara has thus shown how all the cases cited by the Baraisa on 87a can be explained even according to R' Meir's opinion that the dissenting sage's ruling must involve a sin punishable by *kares.*

34. [According to Rav Kahana, a sage is executed as a *zakein mamrei* only if, based upon his own reasoning, he disputes a ruling grounded in tradition. If, however, his ruling, too, is based on tradition, he is not executed.]

35. The Mishnah in *Eduyos* (5:6) states that Akavya ben Mahalalel testified about four specific rulings (before the High Court in the *Lishkas HaGazis,*) and stood by these rulings despite their rejection by the High Court. The next Mishnah there states that at the time of his death Akavya instructed his son to follow the Sages' opinion in these matters and not his own. Akavya's son then asked his father why he himself had not renounced those rulings, inasmuch as he was now instructing his son to do so. Akavya responded that he had been taught those rulings by his teachers, just as the Sages had been taught their rulings by their teachers. Akavya's son, on the other hand, had to choose between the positions of the Sages and of his father. Akavya thus advised him to follow the view of many Sages, and not adopt the lone dissenting opinion of his father [see *Rav* there] (*Rashi*).

Now, Akavya was not executed as a *zakein mamrei* for standing by his rulings in the face of the High Court's opposition. Rav Kahana thus proves from here that a sage does not become a *zakein mamrei* unless he follows his own reasoning over the tradition-based ruling of the High Court. Akavya's source, however, was equal to that of the High Court, and thus he did not become a *zakein mamrei*.

36. As stated in the Mishnah, a sage does not become a *zakein mamrei* unless he instructs that his ruling be followed in practice. Akavya, however, taught his ruling hypothetically; he agreed that in practice the High Court's ruling must be followed.

לפריחה בבגדים שהיא טהורה נאמרה קרחת וגבחת באדם ונאמרה קרחת וגבחת בבגדים מה להלן פרח בכולו טהור אף כאן פרח בכולו טהור א) דברי אלו הערכין והחרמים והקדישות הערכין בפלוגתא דר"מ ורבנן א) דתנן ב) המעריך פחות מבן חדש ר"מ אומר נותן דמיו וחכמים אומרים *לא אמר כלום החרמים בפלוגתא דרבי יהודה בן בתירה ורבנן דתנן ג) ר' יהודה בן בתירה אומר סתם חרמים לבדק הבית שנאמר ב) כל חרם קדש קדשים הוא לה' וחכמים אומרים ב סתם חרמים לכהן שנאמר ג) כשדה החרם לכהן תהיה אחוזתו אם כן מה תלמוד לומר קדש קדשים הוא לה' ג שחל על קדשי קדשים ועל קדשים קלים הקדשות בפלוגתא דרבי אליעזר בן יעקב ורבנן דתניא ד) ר' אליעזר בן יעקב אומר אפילו צינורא של הקדש ה) צריכה עשרה בני אדם לפדותה א) ריבות זה השקאת סוטה ועריפת העגלה וטהרת מצורע השקאת סוטה בפלוגתא דרבי אליעזר ור' יהושע דתנן ו) המקנא לאשתו ר"א אומר מקנא על פי שנים ומשקה על פי עד אחד או על פי עצמו ר' יהושע אומר ד מקנא על פי שנים ומשקה על פי שנים עריפת עגלה בפלוגתא דרבי אליעזר ורבי עקיבא דתנן ז) מאין היו מודדין רבי אליעזר אומר מטיבורו ר' עקיבא אומר ה מחוטמו ר' אליעזר בן יעקב אומר ממקום שנעשה חלל מצוארו טהרת מצורע בפלוגתא דר' שמעון ורבנן דתנן ח) אין לו בהן יד בהן רגל אוזן ימנית אין לו טהרה עולמית ר' אליעזר אומר נותן לו על מקומו ויוצא רבי שמעון אומר ט) נותן על של שמאל ויוצא א) בשעריך זה לקט שכחה פיאה לקט דתנן י) ו שני שבלין לקט שלשה אינן לקט שכחה שני עומרין שכחה שלשה אינן שכחה ועל כולן ב"ש אומרים שלש לעני וארבע לבעל הבית פיאה בפלוגתא דר' ישמעאל ורבנן כ) דתנן ז מצות פיאה להפריש מן הקמה לא הפריש מן הקמה יפריש מן העומרין לא הפריש מן העומרין יפריש מן הכרי עד שלא מירחו מירחו מעשר ונותן לו משום רבי ישמעאל אמרו ז אף מפריש מן העיסה: ג' בתי דינין וכו': אמר רב כהנא הוא אומר מפי השמועה והן אומרין מפי השמועה אינו נהרג הוא אומר כך הוא בעיני והן אומרין כך הוא בעינינו אינו נהרג וכל שכן הוא אומר מפי השמועה והן אומרין כך הוא בעינינו אינו נהרג עד שיאמר כך הוא בעיני והן אומרים מפי השמועה תדע שהרי לא הרגו את עקביא בן מהללאל ור' אלעזר אומר ח אפילו הוא אומר מפי השמועה והן אומרין כך הוא בעינינו נהרג כדי שלא ירבו מחלוקות בישראל ואם תאמר מפני מה לא הרגו את עקביא בן מהללאל מפני שלא הורה הלכה למעשה תנן כך דרשתי וכך דרשו חבירי כך למדתי וכך למדו חבירי מאי לאו דהוא אמר מפי השמועה והם אומרין כך הוא בעינינו לא הוא אומר כך הוא בעיני והם אומרים מפי השמועה ת"ש מ) דאמר רבי יאשיה שלשה דברים סח לי זעירא מאנשי ירושלים ט בעל שמחל על קינויו קינויו מחול

בן

רש"י

לפריחה בבגדים. אם פרחה תפרת הצרעת ונתמלא כל הבגד: אדם שפרחה בכולו טהור. דכתיב (ויקרא יג) אם פרוח תפרח הצרעת וגו' ופליגי רבנן עליה והיכא דפרחה בבגד כולו והכניסו למקדש או הנוגע בו נכנס למקדש לרבנן חייב ולר' יונתן פטור: המעריך פחות מבן חדש. אמר על פחות מבן חדש ערכו עלי והתורה לא נתנה לו ערך דגבי ערכין כתיב (ויקרא כז) ואם מבן חדש וגו': ר"מ אומר נותן דמיו. כמה שהוא נמכר בשוק דקסבר אין אדם מוציא דבריו לבטלה ויודע שאין ערך לפחות מבן חדש וגמר ואמר לשם דמים ולרבנן פטור ואם בא גיזבר ומשכנו לר"מ הוי הקדש ואין אשה מתקדשת בו אלא אם כן יודע בו כדתנן (קידושין דף נג:) וההקדש במזיד קידש בשוגג לא קידש ולרבנן לא הוי הקדש והרי הוא של בעלים לקדש בו האשה והאחר שקדש בו אינה מקודשת א"נ לר"מ הוי הקדש והנהנה ממנו מביא אשם מעילות והרי אותו אשם קדש קדשים והאוכלו בטומאת גופו חייב כרת ולרבנן לא הוי הקדש והרי של בעלים הוא והנהנה ממנו לא מעל ואם הביא אשם מעילות חולין לעזרה הוא ואין חייבין עליו משום טומאה: לבדק הבית. ומועלין בהן: לכהנים. ואין מועלין בהם: שחל על קדשי קדשים. כדתנן (ערכין דף כח:) מחרים אדם את קדשיו אם נדר נותן דמיהם ואם נדבה נותן את טובתם כפי חלק שיש לו בה כדמפרש במסכת ערכין בפ' המקדיש: צינורא. מזלג קטן שטווין בו זהב: י' כהנים. כדמפרש בפרק קמא י' כהנים כתובין בפרשה אם נפדית בפחות מעשרה בני אדם עדיין הקדש היא ומועלין בה ולרבנן אין מועלין בה: המקנא לאשתו. המתרה באשתו אל תסתרי עם איש פלוני: ומשקה על פי עד אחד. שבא ואמר אני ראיתיה שנסתרה ואם לא השקה נאסרת עליו ותנן (סוטה דף כד.) אלו לא שותות ולא נוטלות כתובתן האומרת איני שותה והיכא דליכא עידי סתירה ואמרה איני שותה לרבי אליעזר אין לה כתובה לרבי יהושע יש לה כתובה שאינה נאסרת עליו ואם מכרה לאחר כתובתה קנה ואם תופס ממונו של זה כדי כתובה הרי הוא שלו לקדש בו את האשה ולרבי אליעזר הוי גזל ולא קידש: מאין היו מודדין. לידע אי זו עיר קרובה אל החלל: מטבורו. ואותה שקרובה לטבורו תביא את העגלה ולא הקרובה לחוטמו: ר' עקיבא אומר מחוטמו. ובמסכת סוטה מפרש טעמא מר סבר עיקר חיותיה באפיה ומר סבר עיקר חיותיה בטבוריה: ממקום שנעשה חלל. דהיינו מצואריה דשם חלל מן הצואר כדמפרש התם לתת אותך על צוארי חלל רשעים ותנן (קידושין דף נז:) המקדש בעגלה ערופה אינה מקודשת ואם מדד זקן ממרא מטיבורו וב"ד מחוטמו והביאו אלו עגלה ואלו עגלה למר זו עגלה אסורה ואין מקדשין בה וזו אינה עגלה ומקדשין בה ולמר הוי איפכא: אין לו טהרה עולמית. דבעינן קרא כדכתב כדאמרן בנגמר הדין: נותן על מקומו. על מקום הבוהן נותן דם האשם וטהור ליכנס למקדש ולאכול קודש דהיינו זדונו כרת: שלש אינן לקט. שאין דרך להפקירן: שלשה אינן שכחה. בסיפרא יליף לה מקראי בפרשת שכחה ואם נחלק זקן ממרא ואמר אף שלשה שכחה ובא עני ונטלן ובא בעל הבית ונטלן הימנו לזקן ממרא הוי גזל ואין מקדשין בו אשה ולרבנן מקודשת: מצות פיאה מפריש מן הקמה. דכתיב לא תכלה אלא הנח לפניהם והם יקצרוהו: מרחו. י) בכרי נתחייב במעשר דנגמרה מלאכתו הלכך מעשר תחילה את הכרי מכל מעשרותיו ונותן לו את הפאה שאילו הפרישה לא היו עניים צריכין לעשרה דלקט שכחה פאה פטורין מן המעשר: אף מפריש מן העיסה. אם טחנה ולשה ולת"ק טחנה פטור דקנייה בשינוי ואם בא עני ונטל כדי פאה משטחנה לר' ישמעאל לא הוי גזל לרבנן הוי גזל: עקביא בן מהללאל. נחלק על חכמים בלשכת הגזית בד' דברים במסכת עדיות (פ"ה משנה ו) שהיה אומר לבנו בשעת מיתתו חזור בך בד' דברים שהייתי אומר אמר לו אבא ואתה מפני מה לא חזרתה בהם אמר לו אני שמעתי מפי המרובים והם שמעו מפי המרובים הם עמדו בשמועתן ואני עמדתי בשמועתי אבל אתה שמעת מפי היחיד וכו': על קינויו. שקינא לאשתו אל תסתרי עם פלוני: קינויו מחול. ואם נסתרה אינה נאסרת עליו:

בן

תוספות

מרחו מעשר ונותן לו. ואפילו למאן דאית ליה ברירה כל זמן שלא הפריש פיאה ולא בירדה היה הכל שלו ונתחייב הכל במעשר ושוב לא יפטר וא"ת תרומה נמי לתני שתורם ונותן לו וכ"ת דתרומה בלאו הכי יפריש העני דכל פיאה חייבת בתרומה חדא דאם כן הרי הוא מקדים מעשר לתרומה גדולה ועוד דתנן במסכת תרומות פ"ק [מ"ה] אין תורמין מן הלקט מן השכחה ומן הפיאה וי"מ דלהכי לא תני תורם דאפילו הפקיר לאחר מירוח פטור מן התרומה ס) (דתנן במסכת מעשרות פ' שלשה מינין) פירות ממורחין בשדה מכונסין אסורים משום גזל מפוזרים מותרין בין כך בין כך חייבין במעשר ופטורים מן התרומה וליתא דבירושל' מפרש דלהכי פטורין מן התרומה לפי שאי אפשר לגורן שתעקר אלא אם כן נתרמה ממנו תרומה גדולה לפיכך אין צריך לתרום כשמלא פירות דמסתמא הופרשה מהם תרומה גדולה ונראה לפרש דמשום דתרומה דבר מועט לא חש להזכיר ע):

קינוין מחול. היינו דוקא קודם שנמחקה המגילה אבל לאחר מיכן אין יכול למחול:

מסית

מסורת הש"ס

א) [צ"ל דתניא], ב) ערכין ה., ג) ערכין כח., ד) לעיל יד:, ה) [עי' תוספות תמורה כז: ד"ה לא אמרו], ו) סוטה ב., ז) סוטה מה:, ח) לעיל מה: נזיר מו: ע"ש יומא סא: נגעים פי"ד מ"ט, ט) [בנגעים איתא אם נתן על של שמאל יצא], י) פאה פ"ו מ"ה ע"ש, כ) [צ"ל דתניא], ל) תמורה ו. מכות טז: ב"ק לד., מ) סוטה כה., נ) רש"ל גורס כבר, ס) [מהרש"א גרים כדתניא בירושלמי במס' מעשרות פרק ג], ע) [ועי' תוס' ב"ק ז. ד"ה מירחו].

תורה אור השלם

א) כִּי יִפָּלֵא מִמְּךָ דָבָר לַמִּשְׁפָּט בֵּין דָּם לְדָם בֵּין דִּין לְדִין וּבֵין נֶגַע לָנֶגַע דִּבְרֵי רִיבֹת בִּשְׁעָרֶיךָ וְקַמְתָּ וְעָלִיתָ אֶל הַמָּקוֹם אֲשֶׁר יִבְחַר יְיָ אֱלֹהֶיךָ בּוֹ: [דברים יז, ח]

ב) אַךְ כָּל חֵרֶם אֲשֶׁר יַחֲרִם אִישׁ לַייָ מִכָּל אֲשֶׁר לוֹ מֵאָדָם וּבְהֵמָה וּמִשְּׂדֵה אֲחֻזָּתוֹ לֹא יִמָּכֵר וְלֹא יִגָּאֵל כָּל חֵרֶם קֹדֶשׁ קָדָשִׁים הוּא לַייָ: [ויקרא כז, כח]

ג) וְהָיָה הַשָּׂדֶה בְּצֵאתוֹ בַיֹּבֵל קֹדֶשׁ לַייָ כִּשְׂדֵה הַחֵרֶם לַכֹּהֵן תִּהְיֶה אֲחֻזָּתוֹ: [ויקרא כז, כא]

עין משפט נר מצוה

מח א מיי' פ"א מהל' ערכין הל' ג סמג עשין קכח:

מט ב מיי' שם פ"ו הל' א סמג עשין קלב:

נ ג מיי' שם הלכה יא:

נא ד מיי' פ"א מהל' סוטה הל' א ב סמג עשין מח נו [וטוש"ע אה"ע סי' קעח סעי' ב ד]:

נב ה מיי' פ"ט מהל' רוצח הל' ט סמג עשין עה:

נג ו מיי' פ"ד מהל' מתנות עניים הל' א:

נד ז מיי' פ"א שם הלכה ב:

נה ח מיי' פ"ד מהל' ממרים הל' א סמג עשין קיא ולאוין רטז:

נו ט מיי' פ"א מהל' סוטה הל' ז סמג עשין נו טוש"ע אה"ע סי' קעח סעיף יג:

ליקוטי רש"י

לפריחה. אם פרחה הצרעת בכל הבגד. מה להלן פרח בכולה טהור. כדכתיב אם פרוח תפרח וגו' (ויקרא יג) [זבחים מט:]. המעריך פחות מבן חודש. רבי מאיר במסכת ערכין (דף ה) דאמר אין אדם מוציא דבריו לבטלה דתנן המעריך פחות מבן חדש ר"מ אומר נותן דמיו דאדם יודע שאין ערך לפחות מבן חדש וגמר ואמר לשם דמים [כתובות נח:]. נותן דמיו. כמה שהוא נמכר בשוק [ערכין ה.]. החרמים בפלוגתא דר' יהודה בן בתירא ורבנן. אך כל חרם וגו', נחלקו רבותינו בדבר יש אומרים סתם חרמים להקדש ומה אני מקיים (במדבר יח יד) כל חרם בישראל לך יהיה בחרמי כהנים שפירש ואמר הרי זה חרם לכהן ויש שאמרו סתם חרמים לכהנים. כל חרם קדש קדשים הוא. האומר סתם חרמים לבדק הבית מביא ראיה מכאן והאומר סתם חרמים לכהנים מפרש כל חרם קדש קדשים הוא לה' ללמד שחרמי כהנים חלים על קדשי קדשים ועל קדשים קלים ונותן לכהן כמו ששנינו במסכת ערכין (כח:) אם נדר נותן דמיהם ואם נדבה נותן את טובתה [ויקרא כז, כח]. שחל על קדשי קדשים. כדמפרש מחרים אדם את קדשיו וכו' והיאך מוחרמים והלא אינו שלו אלא אם נדר הן דאמר הרי עלי עולה והפריש בהמה לנדרו ואחר כך החרימה הואיל והוא חייב באחריותה אם מתה או נגנבה נמצאת שלו היא והוא נותן כל דמיה לכהן ואת הבהמה יקריב לנדרו דהא ודאי אית ליה פדיון דלאו גופה איחרם דלאו דידיה הוא [ערכין כח:]. צריכה עשרה בני אדם. עשרה כהנים כתובין בפדיון הקדישות שלשה בפרשת ערכין שהיא ראשונה ושלשה בפדיון בהמה וארבעה בקרקעות [לעיל יד:]. המקנא לאשתו. לישנא דקרא נקט וקנא את אשתו (במדבר ה) ולקמן בגמ' מפרש מאי לשון קינוי ובמתניתין מפרש כיצד מקנא לה אומר לה אל תסתרי עם איש פלוני. מקנא לה ע"פ שנים. אם בא להשקותה צריך להביא שני עדים שאמר לה בפניהם אל תסתרי עמו ואם לא קינא לה בפני שנים אינה נאסרת עליו בסתירתה ואינו משקה. ומשקה ע"פ עד א' או ע"פ עצמו. ואפי' אין עדים שנסתרה אלא עד אחד או הוא עצמו אומר ראיתיה שנסתרה אחר שקינאתי לה נאסרת בסתירה עד שתשתה ולקמן ילפינן מקראי שסתירתה אוסרתה עליו מספק. ר' יהושע אומר. צריך ב' עדים אף לסתירתה [סוטה ב.]. אין לו בהן יד בהן רגל אין לו טהרה עולמית. לפי שאין יכול לקיים בו מתן דם ושמן על בהן ידו [נזיר מו:]. אין לו טהרה עולמית. דבעינן קרא כדכתיב [יומא סא:]. ר' אליעזר. לא בעי קרא כדכתיב וכן ר' שמעון [לעיל מה:]. שני עומרים שכחה שלשה אינן שכחה. בספרי מפיק ליה מהאי קרא ושכחת עומר בשדה (דברים כד) ולא גדיש וגם עומר שיש בו סאתים מפיק ליה התם מדכתיב לקחתו למעוטי האי דאינו ניקח בפעם אחת יפה [ב"ב עב:]. מצות פאה להפריש מן הקמה. דכתיב לא תכלה פאת שדך לקצור (ויקרא יט). מרחו. מחליק את הכרי ברחת ומירוח הוי גמר מלאכה למעשר הלכך מעשר כל מעשרותיו תחלה ואחר כך נותן לו פאה כדי שלא יפסיד עני שאילו היה נותנו קודם מירוח אע"פ שעני מצרף לקט שכחה ופאה הרבה ועושה מהן כרי פטור מן המעשר שהרי הפקר הוא אבל עכשיו שנתמרח ביד בעל הבית נתחייב במעשר דהכי אמרינן במסכת ברכות (דף מ:) לקט שכחה ופאה שעשאן בגורן הוקבעו. אף מפריש מן העיסה. פאה אם לא נתנה כבר ואילו לת"ק מן העיסה לא דקנייה בשינוי והוי ממון שאין לו תובעים דעד השתא דישה לאו שינוי הוא דאוכל הוא כמו שהיה [ב"ק צד.]. מירחו. ונתחייב במעשר מעשר תחלה את הכרי ואחר כך נותן לו הפאה שלא להפסיד את העני שהלקט והשכחה והפאה פטורין מן המעשר וזה הביאן לידי חיוב [מכות טז:]. סח לי זעירא. שהיה מאנשי ירושלים.

thus in our eyes"?[37] Apparently, then, even when the source of his ruling is superior, a sage may become a *zakein mamrei*, which refutes Rav Kahana's view. – ? –

The Gemara rejects this interpretation:

לא – No, our Mishnah discusses a case where **הוּא אוֹמֵר כָּךְ הוּא בְּעֵינַי – [the sage] states, "It appears thus in my eyes,"** **וְהֵם אוֹמְרִים מִפִּי הַשְּׁמוּעָה – and [the High Court] states** its ruling based on **what they heard** as a tradition from their teachers, and only in such a case[38] will a sage become a *zakein mamrei*.[39]

The Gemara corroborates R' Elazar's opinion from a different source:

תָּא שְׁמַע – Come learn a proof to R' Elazar from the following Baraisa: **דְּאָמַר רַבִּי יֹאשִׁיָּה – FOR R' YOSHIYAH SAYS:** **שְׁלֹשָׁה דְבָרִים סָח לִי זְעִירָא מֵאַנְשֵׁי יְרוּשָׁלַיִם – ZE'IRA,** one **OF THE MEN OF JERUSALEM, TOLD ME THREE LAWS,** as follows: **בַּעַל שֶׁמָּחַל עַל קִינּוּיוֹ –** In the case of **A HUSBAND WHO CANCELS HIS WARNING,**[40] **קִינּוּיוֹ מָחוּל – HIS WARNING IS CANCELED.**[41]

NOTES

37. The Gemara assumes that this was the scenario, because when the sage repeated the opinions to the Jerusalem courts, he cited his own opinion before that of the disputing court. The Gemara inferred that the sage presented the opinions in this order because his own opinion was based on a source [his teachers] that preceded the source of his disputants [their own reasoning] (*Aruch LaNer, Toras Chaim*).

38. I.e. where the sage uses his own reasoning to refute a tradition.

39. And the *zakein mamrei* cited his own ruling first because the local court issued its ruling *only after* the sage taught his ruling (*Aruch LaNer*).

40. A husband had warned his wife not to seclude herself with a certain man. Were she subsequently to do so, she would have to drink "bitter waters" to prove that she had not cohabited with him (see above, note 15). Ze'ira spoke of where the husband wishes to rescind his warning before his wife secludes herself with the other man.

41. Hence, if his wife should subsequently seclude herself with the other man, she does not drink the bitter waters, and she is not forbidden to her husband (*Rashi*).

Rashi implies that if the woman had secluded herself *before* the husband rescinded his warning, the rescission would not take effect and the woman would have to drink the bitter waters. This is, in fact, the conclusion of the Gemara (*Sotah* 25a). See, however, *Tosafos*, *Toras Chaim* and *Aruch LaNer*.

לפריחה בבגדים שהיא טהורה נאמרה קרחת וגבחת באדם ונאמרה קרחת וגבחת בבגדים מה להלן פרח בכולו טהור אף כאן פרח בכולו טהור א) דברי אלו הערכין והחרמים והקדישות הערכין בפלוגתא דר"מ ורבנן א) דתנן ב) המעריך פחות מבן חדש ר"מ אומר נותן דמיו וחכמים אומרים א לא אמר כלום החרמים בפלוגתא דרבי יהודה בן בתירה ורבנן דתנן ג) ר' יהודה בן בתירה אומר סתם חרמים לבדק הבית שנאמר ב) כל חרם קדש קדשים הוא לה' וחכמים אומרים ב סתם חרמים לכהן שנאמר ג) כשדה החרם לכהן תהיה אחוזתו אם כן מה תלמוד לומר קדש קדשים הוא לה' ג שחל על קדשי קדשים ועל קדשים קלים הקדשות בפלוגתא דרבי אליעזר בן יעקב ורבנן דתניא ד) ר' אליעזר בן יעקב אומר אפילו צינורא של הקדש ה) צריכה עשרה בני אדם לפדותה א) ריבות זה השקאת סוטה ועריפת העגלה וטהרת מצורע השקאת סוטה בפלוגתא דרבי אליעזר ור' יהושע דתנן ו) המקנא לאשתו ר"א אומר מקנא על פי שנים ומשקה על פי עד אחד או על פי עצמו ר' יהושע אומר ד מקנא על פי שנים ומשקה על פי שנים עריפת עגלה בפלוגתא דרבי אליעזר ורבי עקיבא דתנן ז) מאין היו מודדין רבי אליעזר אומר מטיבורו ר' עקיבא אומר ה מחוטמו ר' אליעזר בן יעקב אומר ממקום שנעשה חלל מצוארו טהרת מצורע בפלוגתא דר' שמעון ורבנן דתנן ח) אין לו בהן יד בהן רגל אוזן ימנית אין לו טהרה עולמית ר' אליעזר אומר נותן לו על מקומו ויוצא רבי שמעון אומר ט) נותן על של שמאל ויוצא א) בשעריך זה לקט שכחה פיאה לקט דתנן י) ו שני שבלין לקט שלשה אינן לקט שכחה שני עומרין שכחה שלשה אינן שכחה ועל כולן ב"ש אומרים שלש לעני וארבע לבעל הבית פיאה בפלוגתא דר' ישמעאל ורבנן כ) דתנן ל) מצות פיאה להפריש מן הקמה לא הפריש מן הקמה יפריש מן העומרין לא הפריש מן העומרין יפריש מן הכרי עד שלא מירחו מירחו מעשר ונותן לו משום רבי ישמעאל אמרו ז אף מפריש מן העיסה: ג' בתי דינין וכו': אמר רב כהנא הוא אומר מפי השמועה והן אומרין מפי השמועה אינו נהרג הוא אומר כך הוא בעיני והן אומרין כך הוא בעינינו אינו נהרג וכל שכן הוא אומר מפי השמועה והן אומרין כך הוא בעינינו אינו נהרג עד שיאמר כך הוא בעיני והן אומרים מפי השמועה תדע שהרי לא הרגו את עקביא בן מהללאל ור' אלעזר אומר ח אפילו הוא אומר מפי השמועה והן אומרין כך הוא בעינינו נהרג כדי שלא ירבו מחלוקות בישראל ואם תאמר מפני מה לא הרגו את עקביא בן מהללאל מפני שלא הורה הלכה למעשה תנן כך דרשתי וכך דרשו חבירי כך למדתי וכך למדו חבירי מאי לאו דהוא אמר מפי השמועה והם אומרין כך הוא בעינינו לא הוא אומר כך הוא בעיני והם אומרים מפי השמועה ת"ש מ) דאמר רבי יאשיה שלשה דברים סח לי זעירא מאנשי ירושלים ט בעל שמחל על קינויו קינויו מחול

בן

רש"י

לפריחה בבגדים. אם פרוח תפרח הצרעת ונתמלא כל הבגד: אדם שפרחה בכולו טהור. דכתיב (ויקרא יג) אם פרוח תפרח הצרעת וגו' ופליגי רבנן עליה והיכא דפרחה בבגד כולו והכניסו למקדש או הנוגע בו נכנס למקדש לרבנן חייב ולר' יונתן פטור: המעריך פחות מבן חדש. אמר על פחות מבן חדש ערכו עלי והתורה לא נתנה לו ערך דגבי ערכין כתיב (ויקרא כז) ואם מבן חדש וגו': ר"מ אומר נותן דמיו. כמה שהוא נמכר בשוק דקסבר אין אדם מוציא דבריו לבטלה ויודע שאין ערך לפחות מבן חדש וגמר ואמר לשם דמים ולרבנן פטור ואם בא גיזבר ומשכנו לר"מ הוי הקדש ואין אשה מתקדשת בו אלא אם כן יודע בו כדתנן (קידושין דף נג:) ובהקדש במזיד קידש בשוגג לא קידש ולרבנן לא הוי הקדש והרי הוא של בעלים לקדש בו האשה והאחר שקדש בו אינה מקודשת א"נ לר"מ הוי הקדש והנהנה ממנו מביא אשם מעילות והרי אותו אשם קדש קדשים והאוכלו בטומאת גופו חייב כרת ולרבנן לא הוי הקדש והרי של בעלים הוא והנהנה ממנו לא מעל ואם הביא אשם מעילות חולין לעזרה הוא ואין חייבין עליו משום טומאה: לבדק הבית. ומועלין בהן: לכהנים. ואין מועלין בהם: שחל על קדשי קדשים. כדתנן (ערכין דף כח:) מחרים אדם את קדשיו אם נדר נותן דמיהם ואם נדבה נותן את טובתם כפי חלק שיש לו בה כדמפרש במסכת ערכין בפ' המקדיש: צינורא. מזלג קטן שטווין בו זהב: י' כהנים. כדמפרש בפרק קמא י' כהנים כתובין בפרשה אם נפדית בפחות מעשרה בני אדם עדיין הקדש היא ומועלין בה ולרבנן אין מועלין בה: המקנא לאשתו. המתרה באשתו אל תסתרי עם איש פלוני: ומשקה על פי עד אחד. שבא ואמר אני ראיתיה שנסתרה ואם לא השקה נאסרת עליו ותנן (סוטה דף כד.) אלו לא שותות ולא נוטלות כתובתן האומרת איני שותה והיכא דליכא עידי סתירה ואמרה איני שותה לרבי אליעזר אין לה כתובה לרבי יהושע יש לה כתובה שאינה נאסרת עליו ואם מכרה לאחר כתובתה קנה ואם תופס ממונו של זה כדי כתובה הרי הוא שלו לקדש בו את האשה ולרבי אליעזר הוי גזל ולא קידש: מאין היו מודדין. לידע אי זו עיר קרובה אל החלל: מטבורו. ואותה שקרובה לטבורו תביא את העגלה ולא הקרובה לחוטמו: ר' עקיבא אומר מחוטמו. ובמסכת סוטה מפרש טעמא מר סבר עיקר חיותיה באפיה ומר סבר עיקר חיותיה בטבוריה: ממקום שנעשה חלל. דהיינו מצואריה דשם חלל מן הצואר כדמפרש התם לתת אותך על צוארי חלל רשעים ותנן (קידושין דף נז:) המקדש בעגלה ערופה אינה מקודשת ואם מדד זקן ממרא מטיבורו וב"ד מחוטמו והביאו אלו עגלה ואלו עגלה למר זו עגלה אסורה ואין מקדשין בה וזו אינה עגלה ומקדשין בה ולמר הוי איפכא: אין לו טהרה עולמית. דבעינן קרא כדכתב כדאמרן בנגמר הדין: נותן על מקומו. על מקום הבוהן נותן דם האשם וטהור ליכנס למקדש ולאכול קודש דהיינו זדונו כרת: שלש אינן לקט. שאין דרך להפקירן: שלשה אינן שכחה. בסיפרא יליף לה מקראי בפרשת שכחה ואם נחלק זקן ממרא ואמר אף שלשה שכחה ובא עני ונטלן ובא בעל הבית ונטלן הימנו לזקן ממרא הוי גזל ואין מקדשין בו אשה ולרבנן מקודשת: מצות פיאה מפריש מן הקמה. דכתיב לא תכלה אלא הנח לפניהם והם יקצרוהו: מרחו. י) בכרי נתחייב במעשר דנגמרה מלאכתו הלכך מעשר תחילה את הכרי מכל מעשרותיו ונותן לו את הפאה שאילו הפרישה לא היו עניים צריכין לעשרה דלקט שכחה פאה פטורין מן המעשר: אף מפריש מן העיסה. אם טחנה ולשה ולת"ק טחנה פטור דקנייה בשינוי ואם בא עני ונטל כדי פאה משטחנה לר' ישמעאל לא הוי גזל לרבנן הוי גזל: עקביא בן מהללאל. נחלק על חכמים בלשכת הגזית בד' דברים במסכת עדיות (פ"ה משנה ו) שהיה אומר לבנו בשעת מיתתו חזור בך בד' דברים שהייתי אומר אמר לו אבא ואתה מפני מה לא חזרת בהם אמר לו אני שמעתי מפי המרובים והם שמעו מפי המרובים הם עמדו בשמועתן ואני עמדתי בשמועתי אבל אתה שמעת מפי היחיד וכו': על קינויו. שקינא לאשתו אל תסתרי עם פלוני: קינויו מחול. ואם נסתרה אינה נאסרת עליו:

בן

תוספות

מרחו מעשר ונותן לו. ואפילו למאן דאית ליה ברירה כל זמן שלא הפריש פיאה ולא ביררה היה הכל שלו ונתחייב הכל במעשר ושוב לא יפטר וא"ת תרומה נמי לתני שתורם ונותן לו וכ"ת דתרומה בלאו הכי יפריש העני דכל פיאה חייבת בתרומה חדא דאם כן הרי הוא מקדים מעשר לתרומה גדולה ועוד דתנן במסכת תרומות פ"ק [מ"ה] אין תורמין מן הלקט מן השכחה ומן הפיאה וי"מ דלהכי לא תני תורם דאפילו הפקיר לאחר מירוח פטור מן התרומה ס) (דתנן במסכת מעשרות פ' שלשה מינין) פירות ממורחין בשדה מכונסין אסורים משום גזל מפוזרים מותרין בין כך בין כך חייבין במעשר ופטורים מן התרומה וליתא דבירושל' מפרש דלהכי פטורין מן התרומה לפי שאי אפשר לגורן שתעקר אלא אם כן נתרמה ממנו תרומה גדולה לפיכך אין צריך לתרום כשמצא פירות דמסתמא הופרשה מהם תרומה גדולה ונראה לפרש דמשום דתרומה דבר מועט לא חש להזכיר ע):

קינויו מחול. היינו דוקא קודם שנמחקה המגילה אבל לאחר מיכן אין יכול למחול:

מסית

עין משפט נר מצוה

מח א מיי' פ"א מהל' ערכין הל' ג סמג עשין קכח:
מט ב מיי' שם פ"ו הל' א סמג עשין קלב:
נ ג מיי' שם הלכה יא:
נא ד מיי' פ"א מהל' סוטה הל' א ב סמג עשין מח נו [וטוש"ע אה"ע סי' קעח סעי' ב ד]:
נב ה מיי' פ"ט מהל' רוצח הל' ט סמג עשין עה:
נג ו מיי' פ"ד מהל' מתנות עניים הל' א:
נד ז מיי' פ"א שם הלכה ב:
נה ח מיי' פ"ד מהל' ממרים הל' א סמג עשין קיא ולאוין רטז:
נו ט מיי' פ"א מהל' סוטה הל' ז סמג עשין נו טוש"ע אה"ע סי' קעח סעיף יג:

מסורת הש"ס

א) [צ"ל דתניא], ב) ערכין ה., ג) ערכין כח., ד) לעיל יד:, ה) [עי' תוספות תמורה כז: ד"ה לא אמרו], ו) סוטה ב., ז) סוטה מה:, ח) לעיל מה: נזיר מו: ע"ש יומא סא: נגעים פי"ד מ"ט, ט) [בנגעים איתא אם נתן על של שמאל יצא], י) פאה פ"ו מ"ה ע"ש, כ) [צ"ל דתניא], ל) תמורה ו. מכות טז: ב"ק לד., מ) סוטה כה., נ) רש"ל גורס ככר, ס) [מהרש"א גרים כדתניא בירושלמי במס' מעשרות פרק ג], ע) [ועי' תוס' ב"ק ד. ד"ה מירחו].

תורה אור השלם

א) כִּי יִפָּלֵא מִמְּךָ דָבָר לַמִּשְׁפָּט בֵּין דָּם לְדָם בֵּין דִּין לְדִין וּבֵין נֶגַע לָנֶגַע דִּבְרֵי רִיבֹת בִּשְׁעָרֶיךָ וְקַמְתָּ וְעָלִיתָ אֶל הַמָּקוֹם אֲשֶׁר יִבְחַר יְיָ אֱלֹהֶיךָ בּוֹ: [דברים יז, ח]

ב) אַךְ כָּל חֵרֶם אֲשֶׁר יַחֲרִם אִישׁ לַייָ מִכָּל אֲשֶׁר לוֹ מֵאָדָם וּבְהֵמָה וּמִשְּׂדֵה אֲחֻזָּתוֹ לֹא יִמָּכֵר וְלֹא יִגָּאֵל כָּל חֵרֶם קֹדֶשׁ קָדָשִׁים הוּא לַייָ: [ויקרא כז, כח]

ג) וְהָיָה הַשָּׂדֶה בְּצֵאתוֹ בַיֹּבֵל קֹדֶשׁ לַייָ כִּשְׂדֵה הַחֵרֶם לַכֹּהֵן תִּהְיֶה אֲחֻזָּתוֹ: [ויקרא כז, כא]

ליקוטי רש"י

לפריחה. אם פרחה הצרעת בכל הבגד. מה להלן פרח בכולה טהור. דכתיב אם פרוח תפרח וגו' (ויקרא יג) [זבחים מט:]. המעריך פחות מבן חודש. רבי מאיר במסכת ערכין (דף ה) דאמר אין אדם מוציא דבריו לבטלה דתנן המעריך פחות מבן חדש ר"מ אומר נותן דמיו דאדם יודע שאין ערך לפחות מבן חדש וגמר ואמר לשם דמים [כתובות נח:]. נותן דמיו. כמה שהוא נמכר בשוק [ערכין ה.]. החרמים בפלוגתא דר' יהודה בן בתירא ורבנן. אך כל חרם וגו', נחלקו רבותינו בדבר יש אומרים סתם חרמים להקדש ומה אני מקיים (במדבר יח יד) כל חרם בישראל לך יהיה בחרמי כהנים שפירש ואמר הרי זה חרם לכהן ויש שאמרו סתם חרמים לכהנים. כל חרם קדש קדשים הוא. האומר סתם חרמים לבדק הבית מביא ראיה מכאן והאומר סתם חרמים לכהנים מפרש כל חרם קדש קדשים הוא לה' ללמד שחרמי כהנים חלים על קדשי קדשים ועל קדשים קלים ונותן לכהן כמו ששנינו במסכת ערכין (כח:) אם נדר נותן דמיהם ואם נדבה נותן את טובתה [ויקרא כז, כח]. שחל על קדשי קדשים. כדמפרש מחרים אדם את קדשיו וכו' והיאך מוחרמים והלא אינו שלו אלא אם נדר הן דאמר הרי עלי עולה והפריש בהמה לנדרו ואחר כך החרימה הואיל והוא חייב באחריותה אם מתה או נגנבה נמצאת שלו היא והוא נותן כל דמיה לכהן ואת הבהמה יקריב לנדרו דהא ודאי אית ליה פדיון דלאו גופה איחרם דלאו דידיה הוא [ערכין כח:]. צריכה עשרה בני אדם. עשרה כהנים כתובין בפדיון הקדישות שלשה בפרשת ערכין שהיא ראשונה ושלשה בפדיון בהמה וארבעה בקרקעות [לעיל יד:]. המקנא לאשתו. לישנא דקרא נקט וקנא את אשתו (במדבר ה) ולקמן בגמ' מפרש מאי לשון קינוי ובמתניתין מפרש כילד מקנא לה אומר לה אל תסתרי עם איש פלוני.

מקנא לה ע"פ שנים. אם בא להשקותה צריך להביא שני עדים שאמר לה בפניהם אל תסתרי עמו ואם לא קינא לה בפני שנים אינה נאסרת עליו בסתירתה ואינו משקה. ומשקה ע"פ עד א' או ע"פ עצמו. ואפי' אין עדים שנסתרה אלא עד אחד או הוא עצמו אומר ראיתיה שנסתרה אחר שקינאתי לה נאסרת בסתירה עד שתשתה ולקמן ילפינן מקראי שסתירתה אוסרתה עליו מספק. ר' יהושע אומר. צריך ב' עדים אף לסתירתה [סוטה ב.]. אין לו בהן יד בהן רגל אין לו טהרה עולמית. לפי שאין יכול לקיים בו מתן דם ושמן על בהן ידו [נזיר מו:]. אין לו טהרה עולמית. דבעינן קרא כדכתיב [יומא סא:]. ר' אליעזר. לא בעי קרא כדכתיב וכן ר' שמעון [לעיל מה:]. שני עומרים שכחה שלשה אינן שכחה. בספרי מפיק ליה מהאי קרא ושכחת עומר בשדה (דברים כד) ולא גדיש וגם עומר שיש בו סאתים מפיק ליה התם מדכתיב לקחתו למעוטי האי דלאו ניקח בפעם אחת יפה [ב"ב עב:]. מצות פאה להפריש מן הקמה. דכתיב לא תכלה פאת שדך לקצור (ויקרא יט). מרחו. מחליק את הכרי ברחת ומירוח הוי גמר מלאכה למעשר הלכך מעשר כל מעשרותיו תחלה ואחר כך נותן לו פאה כדי שלא יפסיד עני שאילו היה נותנו קודם מירוח אע"פ שעני מצרף לקט שכחה ופאה הרבה ועושה מהן כרי פטור מן המעשר שהרי הפקר הוא אבל עכשיו שנתמרח ביד בעל הבית נתחייב במעשר דהכי אמרינן במסכת ברכות (דף מ:) לקט שכחה ופאה שעשאן בגורן הוקבעו. אף מפריש מן העיסה. פאה אם לא נתנה כבר ואילו לת"ק מן העיסה לא דקנייה בשינוי והוי ממון שאין לו תובעים דעד השתא דישה לאו שינוי הוא דלגבל הוא כמו שהיה [ב"ק צד.]. מירחו. ונתחייב במעשר מעשר תחלה את הכרי ואחר כך נותן לו הפאה שלא להפסיד את העני שהלקט והשכחה והפאה פטורין מן המעשר וזה הביאן לידי חיוב [מכות טז:]. סח לי זעירא. שהיה מאנשי ירושלים.

עין משפט
נר מצוה

נז א מיי׳ פ״ג מהלכות ממרים הלכה ח:
נח ב מיי׳ שם הל׳ ד סמג עשין קיא ולאוין רין:
נט ג מיי׳ פ״א הל׳ ד סמג שם:
ס ד ה מיי׳ פ״ג מהל׳ סנהדרין הלכה א:
סא ו מיי׳ פ״א מהל׳ ממרים הל׳ ד סמג עשין קיא ולאוין רין:
סב ז מיי׳ פ״ב מהל׳ סנהדרין הלכה ח:
סג ח מיי׳ שם פ״א ממרים הל׳ ה ופ״ד הלכה ה סמג עשין קיא ולאוין רין:
סד ט י מיי׳ שם פ״ג הלכה ח:
סה כ מיי׳ פ״ד שם הלכה ג סמג עשין קיא ולאוין רין:
סו מ מיי׳ פ״ז מהל׳ לולב הלכה ו סמג עשין מד טוש״ע א״ח סי׳ תרנא סעיף א:

גליון הש״ס

תוס׳ ד״ה ואין וכו׳ לא חייש. עיין בטורי אבן באבני שהם לר״ה דף כ״ז ע״א ד״ה מלות.

מסית דלא בעי התראה מאי איכא למימר. לאו אליבא דר׳ מאיר פריך דאמסית לא מיחייב דאין בו כרת:
ואין לנו אלא תפילין ואליבא דר׳ יהודה. כל הנך דרשות דדרשינן לעיל מקרא דכי יפלא ° לא חייש: **אי** סבירא לן דלולב אין צריך אגד וכו׳. משמע אבל אי סבירא לן דצריך אגד לא אמרינן האי לחודיה קאי והאי לחודיה קאי והכי נמי אמרי׳ בריש לולב הגזול (סוכה דף לא.) דקאמר רבי יהודה אין אוגדין את הלולב אלא במינו מאי טעמא דכיון דאמר ר׳ יהודה לולב צריך אגד אי עבדי ליה ממין אחר הוה ליה ה׳ מינין ותימה דאמר התם (שם:) ד׳ מינין שבלולב כשם שאין פוחתין מהן כך אין מוסיפין עליהם ופריך פשיטא ומשני מהו דתימא הואיל ואמר רבי יהודה לולב צריך אגד אי אייתי מינא אחרינא האי לחודיה קאי והאי לחודיה קאי קמ״ל מאי קא תלי טעמא דהאי לחודיה קאי משום דלולב צריך אגד אדרבה מטעם זה יש לנו לומר יותר דאסור ומיהו י״ל דהתם בדמנח ליה חוץ לאגד אבל קשה דמשמע דמסיק לר׳ יהודה דלא אמר האי לחודיה וכ״ש לרבנן והכא משמע דלרבנן אמר האי לחודיה קאי וי״ל דהתם מדרבנן אסור ור״ת ל״ג התם הואיל ואמר ר׳ יהודה וזהו לשונו מהו דתימא הואיל ואמרו חכמים בין אגוד בין שאינו אגוד כשר הלכך אין צריך אגד והאי יתירה דמוסיף על הד׳ לחודיה קאי ולא מיפסל ביה קמ״ל ומיהו תימה אמאי לא משכח לולב לרבי יהודה בכי האי גוונא שאגד ג׳ מינין בפני עצמן דנעשה בכשרות ואחר כך אגד עמהן מין אחר דהוה ליה מוסיף גורע ויש לומר כיון דקודם נטילתו נפסל הוה ליה גרוע ועומד אבל תפילין אם הניחן בראשו בכשרות והניח גבייהו בית חמישי הרי זה מוסיף גורע שפוסלן ומבטל מצות שעל ראשו ולא דמי ללולב דאם נטלו ובעודו בידו הוסיף מין חמישי אין זה מבטל מצותו דמדאגביה נפק ביה:

קשר

בן סורר ומורה. אף לאחר שהתרו בו וקלקל והלקוהו וחזר וקלקל אם רצו למחול ולא הביאוהו לבית דין מוחלין לו שהכתוב תלה בהם ותפסו בו: **תיובתא.** מדתלי טעמא בשלא ירבו מחלוקת ש״מ אפי׳ הוא אומר מפי השמועה והן אומרין כך הוא בעינינו: **יושבין בחיל.** מפני שהעם רב ומקום צר להם בלשכה אי נמי שלא יהו נראים כיושבין בדין שבלשכת הגזית היו דנים וזה עיקר: **משם מעלין אותו.** להיות דיין בהר הבית כשמת אחד מהם ויושב שם עד שמת אחד משל עזרה ומעלין את זה שם וכולן יש בהם מעלה זה מזה: **שייף.** שוחה נכנס ושוחה יוצא והכי אמרי׳ בב״ב (דף ז.) גבי תקרת הבית שנחבטה שוף עול שוף פוק: **מעיקרא.** קודם שבא לבית דין שבלשכת הגזית לישאל לא הוה מיחייב קטלא כל כמה דלא עביד איהו גופיה: **מעיקרא נמי בר קטלא הוא.** אם עושה עבירה שיש בה מיתת בית דין הוה מיקטיל: **מסית דלא בעי התראה.** אם היה מסית ומורה טעם היתר ולומר אין בלשון הזה הסתה מעיקרא נמי מקטיל בלא התראה: **אי אמר טעמא לזכותא.** לאצוליה אבל השתא אי אמר טעמא לא מקבלינן שהרי שמע מפי ב״ד שלא לעשות והמרה: **מתני׳ האומר אין תפילין פטור.** דאין זו הוראה דזיל קרי בי רב הוא: **חמש טוטפות יש.** שאע״פ שאין דבר זה אלא להוסיף על דברי סופרים חייב דמדרש דסופרים הוא לטטפת לטטפת לטוטפות הרי כאן ד׳: **גמ׳ ויש בו להוסיף.** על מה שפירשו חכמים: **ואם הוסיף גורע.** ופוסל הראשון בתוספתו: **ואין לנו אלא תפילין.** שעיקרן בתורה ופירושן מדברי סופרים שהם ד׳ בתים ויש להוסיף חמשה או יותר ואם הוסיף גורע דקא עבר בבל תוסיף ולא עבד מצוה: **ואליבא דרבי יהודה.** אמר ר׳ אושעיא למילתיה דאמר לעיל עד דאיכא תורה ויורוך ואית דאמרי אין לנו אלא תפילין ואליבא דרבי יהודה דאמר צריך להדביק במנחות בהקומץ רבה (דף לד:) ולא נהירא לי דההיא בתפילין של יד קאי ומתני׳ טוטפות תאני והיינו דראש ועוד מדקא מקשי בסיפא אי דעבד ארבעה בתים כו׳ שמע מינה בשל ראש קיימין דאי בשל יד בית אחד הוא דקא הוי: **האי לחודיה קאי.** ואין זה גורע: **גרוע ועומד.** דמתחילתו לא עשה כהוגן שאגד שם תוספת מצוה ואנן בעינן גורע דהשתא שהיה מתחילתו כשר ופוסלו בתוספתו: **ופירושו מדברי סופרים.** ד׳ חוטין דילפינן גדיל ב׳ גדילים ד׳: **קשר עליון.** שעושין סמוך לכנף כשנתלו החוטין ועל ידיהן נעשין חיבור לטלית לאו דאורייתא (ס) אלא) הלכה למשה מסיני דפלוגתא היא במנחות ט) (דף לט.): **האי לחודיה קאי.** דכיון דלא נקשר אינו חיבור עם השאר והראוי למצוה היא המצוה והעודף כמי שאינו:

שאינו

א בן סורר ומורה שרצו אביו ואמו למחול לו מוחלין לו זקן ממרא שרצו בית דינו למחול לו מוחלין לו וכשבאתי אצל חבירי שבדרום על שנים הודו לי על זקן ממרא ב לא הודו לי כדי שלא ירבו מחלוקת בישראל תיובתא תניא א) אמר רבי יוסי ג מתחילה לא היו מרבין מחלוקת בישראל אלא בית דין של שבעים ואחד יושבין בלשכת הגזית ושני בתי דינין של עשרים ושלשה אחד יושב על פתח הר הבית ואחד יושב על פתח העזרה ושאר בתי דינין של עשרים ושלשה יושבין בכל עיירות ישראל הוצרך הדבר לשאול שואלין מבית דין שבעירן אם שמעו אמרו להן ואם לאו באין לזה שסמוך לעירן אם שמעו אמרו להם ואם לאו באין לזה שעל פתח הר הבית אם שמעו אמרו להם ואם לאו באין לזה שעל פתח העזרה ואומר כך דרשתי וכך דרשו חבירי כך למדתי וכך למדו חבירי אם שמעו אמרו להם ואם לאו אלו ואלו באין ללשכת הגזית ד ששם יושבין מתמיד של שחר עד תמיד של בין הערבים ה ובשבתות ובימים טובים יושבין בחיל ו נשאלה שאלה בפניהם אם שמעו אמרו להם ואם לאו עומדין למנין רבו המטמאים טמאו רבו המטהרין טהרו ב) משרבו תלמידי שמאי והלל שלא שמשו כל צרכן רבו מחלוקת בישראל ונעשית תורה כשתי תורות ז משם כותבין ושולחין בכל מקומות כל מי שהוא חכם ושפל ברך ודעת הבריות נוחה הימנו יהא דיין בעירו ג) משם מעלין אותו להר הבית משם לעזרה משם ללשכת הגזית ד) שלחו מתם איזהו בן העולם הבא ענוותן ה) ושפל ברך שייף עייל שייף ונפיק וגריס באורייתא תדירא ולא מחזיק טיבותא לנפשיה יהבו ביה רבנן עינייהון ברב עולא בר אבא: חזר לעירו ושנה: ת״ר ח אינו חייב עד שיעשה כהוראתו או שיורה לאחרים ויעשו כהוראתו בשלמא יורה לאחרים ויעשו כהוראתו מעיקרא לאו בר קטלא הוא והשתא בר קטלא הוא אלא שיעשה כהוראתו מעיקרא נמי בר קטלא הוא התינח היכא דאורי בחלב ודם דמעיקרא לאו בר קטלא הוא והשתא בר קטלא הוא אלא היכא דאורי בחייבי מיתות ב״ד מעיקרא נמי בר קטלא הוא מעיקרא בעי התראה השתא ט לא בעי התראה מסית דלא בעי התראה מאי איכא למימר מעיקרא אי אמר טעמא מקבלינן מיניה השתא אי אמר טעמא י לא מקבלינן מיניה: **מתני׳** חומר בדברי סופרים מבדברי תורה האומר אין תפילין כדי לעבור על ד״ת פטור כ חמש טוטפות להוסיף על דברי סופרים חייב: **גמ׳** אמר ר׳ אלעזר אמר ר׳ אושעיא אינו חייב אלא על דבר שעיקרו מדברי תורה ופירושו מדברי סופרים ויש בו להוסיף ואם הוסיף גורע ואין לנו ו) אלא תפילין אליבא דרבי יהודה והאיכא לולב דעיקרו מדברי תורה ופירושו מדברי סופרים ויש בו להוסיף ואם הוסיף גורע בלולב מאי סבירא לן אי סבירא לן ז) דלולב מ אין צריך אגד האי לחודיה קאי והאי לחודיה קאי ואי סבירא לן ח) דצריך אגד גרוע ועומד הוא והאיכא ציצית דעיקרו מדברי תורה ופירושו מדברי סופרים ויש בו להוסיף ואם הוסיף גורע בציצית מאי סבירא לן אי סבירא לן דקשר העליון לאו דאורייתא האי לחודיה קאי והאי לחודיה קאי ואי סבירא לן

דקשר

מיעט כאן אחותו אלא במקום שיש לקיים בהן הזמה במיתת הבועל [דברים יט, יט]. שהיא והן נהרגין ולא במיתה אחת דהיא בשריפה והן במיתת הבועל כגון באו עדים והזימו את הראשונים וחייבום מיתת הבועל ולא מיתתה דכתיב (דברים יט) כאשר זמם לעשות לאחיו ולא לאחותו כדאמר באלו הן הנחנקין (סנהדרין ל). **בועלה.** דהיא בשריפה אבל בועלה נידון כשאר בועל בת ישראל דבועל ארוסה בסקילה ובועל נשואה בחנק דכתיב (ויקרא כא) היא באש תשרף היא ולא בועלה היא ולא זוממיה [לעיל מו.]. **וזוממי בת כהן.** אף על פי שהם היו מחייבין אותה שריפה אין נדונין אלא במיתה שהיו מחייבין לבועל והיינו חנק כשאר בא על אשת איש כדמפרש קרא היא תשרף ולא בועלה וזוממיה ילפינן מכאשר זמם לעשות לאחיו ולא לאחותו. **ובועלה.** בנשואה בת כהן קמיירי אבל ארוסה בועלה בסקילה [לעיל פד:]. **אשר לא צויתיו לדבר.** אבל צויתיו לחבירו. **ואשר ידבר בשם אלהים אחרים.** אפילו כיון את ההלכה לאסור את האסור ולהתיר את המותר. **ומת.** בחנק שלשה מיתתן בידי אדם המתנבא מה שלא שמע ומה שלא נאמר לו ונאמר לחבירו והמתנבא בשם עבודה זרה אבל הכובש את נבואתו והעובר על דברי נביא והעובר על דברי עצמו מיתתו בידי שמים שנאמר (פסוק יט) אנכי אדרוש מעמו [דברים יח, כ]. **ויצא הרוח.** פתרון ויצא המלאך שהרי אומר לעיל וכל צבא השמים וגו׳ ועתה יצא אחד מן המלאכים ויאמר אני אפתנו כדאמר (תהלים קד) עושה מלאכיו רוחות ולפיכך קדם ואמר לעיל וכל צבא השמים עומדים שלא תתמה כשתאמר ויצא הרוח מי הוא ומהיכן יצא וכשאמר וכל צבא השמים עומדים כדי להודיע מהיכן יצא משאר הרוחות העומדים עליו, ורבותינו פירשו זהו רוחו של נבות. **בפי כל נביאיו.** שישים דבר בפיהם לאמר עלה והצלח ויעלה ויפול מכלל שהיו נביאי אמת שלא היו מתנבאים כי אם מה שישים השם בפיהם [דה״ב יח]. **זה בכה.** אני אפתנו בכה [שבת קמט:]. **תפתה וגם תוכל.** לפי שיש מפתה הבא לפתות חבירו פעמים שהמפותה מבין שזה רוצה לפתותו והוא נזהר ואינו שומע להתפתות אבל באחאב תפתה וגם תוכל [דה״ב שם]. **צא ממחיצתי.** הפורע נוקם חמתו וקנאתו מחריב ביתיה, כרות של נבות שנקם כעסו מאחאב ויצא ממחיצתו של הקדוש ברוך הוא. **רוחו של נבות.** שלפי שהוא הרג נבות היה רוחו מחזר לפתותו ולהפילו [לקמן קב:]. **תפלצתך.** ל׳ בהלה שהיית ממהר ונבהל לעורר שטימתך לאחיך ויש לועזין לשון פלצות ויש לועזין לשון מפלצת [ירמיהו מט, טז]. **האין פה נביא לה׳ עוד.** מקובלני אין ב׳ נביאים מתנבאים בל׳ א׳ ואלה כולם לשון א׳ אומרים [מ״א כב, ז]. **את קשת עילם.** את תקות עילם [ירמיהו מט, לה]. **שברתי את עול מלך בבל.** אמרו רבותינו מי הטעה את חנניה שמע שהיה ירמיה מתנב׳ בשוק העליון הנני שובר את קשת עילם (ירמיה מט) ונבואה זו בסוף הספר נאמרה בראשית ממלכת צדקיהו כמו שמפורש שם ולפי שעילם סמוכה לבבל עמד הוא בשוק התחתון ודרש ודן קל וחומר ומה עילם שלא באה אלא לעזור את הכשדים וכו׳ כמה שהיא בסנהדרין [שם כח, א].

מסורת הש״ס

א) [תוספ׳ פ״ז תוספ׳ חגיגה פרק ב], ב) [סוטה מז:], ג) [תוספ׳ שקלים ספ״ג], ד) [לעיל יז: וש״נ], ה) [בתענית טז. פירש״י שפל ברך עניו וצ״ל דכמה עניי ענוה יש ועי׳ רש״א ח״א], ו) [סוכה לג:], ז) [סוכה לא.], ח) [צ״ל כלומר], ט) [עי׳ תוס׳ פט. לקמן בסמוך ד״ה קשר].

ליקוטי רש״י

זקן ממרא. שהמרה על ב״ד של לשכת הגזית ומיתתו בחנק [סוטה כה:]. **האומר אין תפילין.** זקן ממרא מן הדבר ולא כל דבר דהא כתי׳ מן הדבר ותנן באלו הן הנחנקין (סנהדרין דף פח:) האומר אין תפלין לעבור על דברי תורה פטור חמש טוטפות להוסיף על דברי סופרים חייב דהיינו מן הדבר ולא כל דבר [הוריות ד.]. **לולב צריך אגד.** הלכך כל הנאגד עמו הוי מן המצוה ונמצא עובר בבל תוסיף אם יאגד מין חמישי [סוכה לא.].

[מכאן שייך לדף פט.].

קשר עליון. היינו נמי ההוא קשר למטה הלכה למשה מסיני כלומר קשר אחד בגלילת מיהא דאורייתא והכי נקט עליון משום דאי לא עביד אלא חד קשר בסופו עביד ליה שמקיים את הגדיל כולו. **דאורייתא.** ואפי׳ יכול לכרוך יפה ולהתקיים בלא קשר יום או יומים פסולה [מנחות לט.]. **וכל העם ישמעו.** מכאן שממתינין לו עד הרגל וממיתין אותו ברגל [דברים יז, יג]. **לרשות הבעל.** כגון מסרה האב לשלוחי הבעל ועדיין היא בדרך ולא קרינן בה בית אביה. **לאותה מיתה.** שהיו מחייבין את הנידון. **ובועלה.** כלומר וכל הבועלים נידונין כמיתת הנבעלת חוץ מבועל בת כהן [לקמן צ.]. **מקדימים לאותה מיתה.** כלומר אין להם לצפות מיתה אחרת אלא משכימין לאותה מיתה שנגמר בה דינו של נדון. **חוץ מזוממי בת כהן.** נשואה שאע״פ שנגמר דינה לשריפה על פיהם הם בחנק כדילפינן התם סנהדרין (דף נ) היא בשריפה ואין בועלה בשריפה אלא בחנק כשאר אשת איש והזוממין משכימין למיתה שחייבו את הבועל דכתיב כאשר זמם לעשות לאחיו ולא לאחותו [מכות ב.]. **זוממי בת כהן.** לעשות לאחיו מה תלמוד לומר לאחיו למד על זוממי בת כהן נשואה שאין בשריפה אלא כמיתת הבועל שהוא בחנק שנאמר היא באש תשרף (ויקרא כא, ט) היא ולא בועלה לכך נאמר כאן לאחיו כאשר זמם לעשות לאחיו ולא כאשר זמם לעשות לאחותו אבל בכל שאר מיתות השוה הכתוב אשה לאיש וזוממי אשה נהרגין כזוממי איש כגון שהעידוה שהרגה את הנפש שחללה את השבת נהרגין במיתתה שלא

בֵּן סוֹרֵר וּמוֹרֶה שֶׁרָצוּ אָבִיו וְאִמּוֹ לִמְחוֹל לוֹ – In the case of A WAYWARD AND REBELLIOUS SON WHOSE PARENTS WISH TO PARDON HIM to spare him from execution for his gluttonous behavior, מוֹחֲלִין לוֹ – THEY MAY PARDON HIM.[1] זָקֵן מַמְרֵא שֶׁרָצוּ בֵּית דִּינוֹ לִמְחוֹל לוֹ – In the case of A REBELLIOUS SAGE WHOM THE HIGH COURT, whose ruling he disputed, WISHES TO PARDON, מוֹחֲלִין לוֹ – THEY MAY PARDON HIM.

R' Yoshiyah relates that the Sages did not agree with the last of the three rulings:

וּכְשֶׁבָּאתִי אֵצֶל חֲבֵירַי שֶׁבַּדָּרוֹם – However, WHEN I CAME TO MY COLLEAGUES IN THE SOUTH, עַל שְׁנַיִם הוֹדוּ לִי – THEY AGREED WITH ME CONCERNING the first TWO rulings, עַל זָקֵן מַמְרֵא לֹא הוֹדוּ לִי – BUT THEY DID NOT AGREE WITH ME CONCERNING the ruling about THE REBELLIOUS SAGE. Rather, they maintained that a *zakein mamrei* may not be pardoned, כְּדֵי שֶׁלֹּא יִרְבּוּ מַחֲלוֹקֶת בְּיִשְׂרָאֵל – SO THAT DISPUTES WILL NOT PROLIFERATE IN the nation of ISRAEL. Now, this very argument is the stated rationale of R' Elazar's opinion; hence, the Baraisa refutes Rav Kahana's opinion.[2] – ? –

תְּיוּבְתָּא – This is indeed **a refutation.**

The Gemara cites a Baraisa that details how cases were adjudicated before disputes proliferated in the nation:

תַּנְיָא – **It was taught in a Baraisa:** אָמַר רַבִּי יוֹסֵי – R' YOSE SAID: מִתְּחִילָּה לֹא הָיוּ מַרְבִּין מַחֲלוֹקֶת בְּיִשְׂרָאֵל – INITIALLY, DISPUTE WAS NOT EXCESSIVE IN the nation of ISRAEL. אֶלָּא בֵּית דִּין שֶׁל שִׁבְעִים וְאֶחָד יוֹשְׁבִין בְּלִשְׁכַּת הַגָּזִית – RATHER, THE COURT OF SEVENTY-ONE judges WOULD SIT IN THE CHAMBER OF HEWN STONE, וּשְׁנֵי בָתֵּי דִינִין שֶׁל עֶשְׂרִים וּשְׁלֹשָׁה – AND there would be TWO COURTS OF TWENTY-THREE judges, אֶחָד יוֹשֵׁב עַל פֶּתַח הַר הַבַּיִת – ONE SITTING AT THE ENTRANCE OF THE TEMPLE MOUNT וְאֶחָד יוֹשֵׁב עַל פֶּתַח הָעֲזָרָה – AND ONE SITTING AT THE ENTRANCE OF THE COURTYARD. וּשְׁאָר בָּתֵּי דִינִין שֶׁל עֶשְׂרִים וּשְׁלֹשָׁה – AND THE REMAINING COURTS OF TWENTY-THREE judges יוֹשְׁבִין בְּכָל עֲיָירוֹת יִשְׂרָאֵל – WERE SITTING IN ALL ISRAELITE CITIES.

הוּצְרַךְ הַדָּבָר לִשְׁאוֹל – IF IT WAS NECESSARY TO INQUIRE in court about A particular MATTER, שׁוֹאֲלִין מִבֵּית דִּין שֶׁבְּעִירָן – [THE LITIGANTS] WOULD INQUIRE OF THE COURT IN THEIR CITY. אִם שָׁמְעוּ – IF [THE LOCAL JUDGES] HAD HEARD the correct ruling in that matter, אָמְרוּ לָהֶן – THEY WOULD TELL it TO [THE LITIGANTS], וְאִם לָאו – BUT IF they had NOT heard the correct ruling,[3] בָּאִין לְזֶה שֶׁסָּמוּךְ לְעִירָן – [THE LITIGANTS] WOULD COME TO THE court in the city ADJACENT TO THEIR OWN CITY, and present the case to the judges there.[4] אִם שָׁמְעוּ – IF [THOSE JUDGES] HAD HEARD the correct ruling, אָמְרוּ לָהֶם – THEY WOULD TELL it TO [THE LITIGANTS], וְאִם לָאו – BUT IF they had NOT heard it, בָּאִין לְזֶה שֶׁעַל פֶּתַח הַר הַבַּיִת – [THE LITIGANTS] WOULD COME TO [THIS COURT] AT THE ENTRANCE OF THE TEMPLE MOUNT.

אִם שָׁמְעוּ – IF [THOSE JUDGES] HAD HEARD the correct ruling in the matter, אָמְרוּ לָהֶם – THEY WOULD TELL it TO [THE LITIGANTS], וְאִם לָאו – BUT IF they had NOT heard it, בָּאִין לְזֶה שֶׁעַל פֶּתַח הָעֲזָרָה – [THE LITIGANTS] WOULD COME TO [THIS COURT] AT THE ENTRANCE OF THE COURTYARD, וְאוֹמֵר – AND [THE SAGE] WOULD SAY: כָּךְ דָּרַשְׁתִּי וְכָךְ דָּרְשׁוּ חֲבֵירַי – "THUS I HAVE EXPOUNDED AND THUS MY COLLEAGUES HAVE EXPOUNDED; כָּךְ לִמַּדְתִּי וְכָךְ לִמְּדוּ חֲבֵירַי – THUS I HAVE TAUGHT AND THUS MY COLLEAGUES HAVE TAUGHT." אִם שָׁמְעוּ – IF THOSE JUDGES HAD HEARD the correct ruling, אָמְרוּ לָהֶם – THEY WOULD TELL it TO [THE LITIGANTS], וְאִם לָאו – BUT IF they had NOT heard it, אֵלּוּ וָאֵלּוּ בָּאִין לְלִשְׁכַּת הַגָּזִית – both THESE AND THOSE disputants[5] COME TO THE CHAMBER OF HEWN STONE, שֶׁשָּׁם יוֹשְׁבִין מִתָּמִיד שֶׁל שַׁחַר – FOR THERE [THE SANHEDRIN] SITS FROM the time THE MORNING *TAMID* sacrifice is offered עַד תָּמִיד שֶׁל בֵּין הָעַרְבַּיִם – UNTIL the time THE AFTERNOON *TAMID* sacrifice is offered,[6] וּבְשַׁבָּתוֹת וּבְיָמִים טוֹבִים יוֹשְׁבִין בַּחֵיל – AND ON THE SABBATH AND FESTIVALS THE SANHEDRIN SITS IN THE *CHEIL*.[7] נִשְׁאֲלָה שְׁאֵלָה בִּפְנֵיהֶם – THE QUESTION under advisement WAS ASKED BEFORE THEM. אִם שָׁמְעוּ – IF [THE MEMBERS OF THE SANHEDRIN] HAD HEARD the correct ruling, אָמְרוּ לָהֶם – THEY WOULD TELL it TO [THE LITIGANTS]. וְאִם לָאו – BUT IF they had NOT heard it, עוֹמְדִין לַמִּנְיָן – THEY WOULD TAKE A VOTE. רַבּוּ הַמְטַמְּאִים – If THOSE judges WHO RULED the object *TAMEI* WERE MORE NUMEROUS than those who did not, טִמְּאוּ – THEY RULED IT *TAMEI*. רַבּוּ הַמְטַהֲרִין – And if THOSE judges WHO RULED the object *TAHOR* WERE MORE NUMEROUS, טִהֲרוּ – THEY RULED IT *TAHOR*.[8]

The Baraisa relates that this ideal situation did not last:

מִשֶּׁרַבּוּ תַּלְמִידֵי שַׁמַּאי וְהִלֵּל שֶׁלֹּא שִׁמְּשׁוּ כָּל צָרְכָּן – But ONCE THERE INCREASED the number of STUDENTS OF SHAMMAI AND HILLEL WHO HAD NOT STUDIED SUFFICIENTLY,[9] רַבּוּ מַחֲלוֹקֶת בְּיִשְׂרָאֵל –

NOTES

1. A young adult becomes a "wayward and rebellious son" if he initially commits the sins of theft and gluttony with certain amounts of meat and wine (see above, 70a), and is warned by his parents before witnesses to stop this behavior. If he does not stop, he is brought to court and is flogged there. If he persists in this decadent behavior pattern, his parents return him to court, where he is killed.

R' Yoshiyah teaches that even if a son continued to indulge in gluttony after being flogged by the court, his parents may decline to return him to court to receive the death penalty, for the Torah states (*Deuteronomy* 21:19): *His father and his mother shall seize him.* That is, the Torah allows the parents discretion in the matter of bringing the child to court for execution (*Rashi*; cf. *Meiri*).

2. Since preventing dissension is of paramount importance, it follows that a sage becomes a *zakein mamrei* even when the source of his ruling is a tradition (*Rashi*; see *Aruch LaNer*).

3. See above, 86b note 37.

4. *Rambam* (*Hil. Mamrim* 1:4) does not record this step in the process. Either he felt it was obvious that all local courts were consulted before the litigants brought their case to Jerusalem, or he did not have this section in his text of the Gemara (*Kesef Mishneh* ad loc.; see there). Alternatively, he maintained that our Mishnah, which does not mention this step, disputes the Baraisa's ruling (*Aruch LaNer*).

5. See above, 86b notes 39 and 41.

6. There were two *tamid* (literally: constant) sacrifices offered in the Temple each day — the morning *tamid*, brought early in the morning, and the afternoon *tamid*, brought in mid-afternoon (see *Rambam, Hil. Temidin U'Mussafin* 1:2,3).

7. Within the walls of the Temple Mount and just ten cubits from the walls of the Temple Courtyard was a low wall called a *soreg*. The space between the *soreg* and the Courtyard wall was called the *Cheil* (see Mishnah *Keilim* 1:8 and *Midos* 2:3).

Rashi offers two reasons why the Sanhedrin met in this area on the Sabbath and Festivals: 1) The crowd that gathered on these days was too large for the Chamber of Hewn Stone to hold. 2) Adjudication on the Sabbath and Festival days is prohibited. On those days the Sanhedrin did not congregate in the Chamber of Hewn Stone, its usual venue, so as not to give the false impression that they were then sitting in judgment. *Rashi* prefers the second reason.

8. [That is, the law on each issue was authoritatively decided.] Furthermore, even after the Sanhedrin was disbanded following the destruction of the Temple, an established judicial system functioned to determine the halachah (*Meiri*). It was for this reason that neither legal disputes nor disparate practices existed in the nation up until that time.

9. The Gemara is stating that essential to the development of one who wishes to render halachic decisions is שִׁימּוּשׁ תַּלְמִידֵי חֲכָמִים, *apprenticeship to Torah scholars.* That is because the aspiring decisor must be well versed in the logic and reasoning behind the many Tannaic opinions found throughout the Mishnah. This expertise is crucial, for Tannaim may appear to have similar views regarding one matter, but when their rationales are revealed it is clear that they would disagree in

א בן סורר ומורה שרצו אביו ואמו למחול לו מוחלין לו זקן ממרא שרצו בית דינו למחול לו מוחלין לו וכשבאתי אצל חבירי שבדרום על שנים הודו לי על זקן ממרא ב לא הודו לי כדי שלא ירבו מחלוקת בישראל תיובתא תניא א) אמר רבי יוסי ג מתחילה לא היו מרבין מחלוקת בישראל אלא בית דין של שבעים ואחד יושבין בלשכת הגזית ושני בתי דינין של עשרים ושלשה אחד יושב על פתח הר הבית ואחד יושב על פתח העזרה ושאר בתי דינין של עשרים ושלשה יושבין בכל עיירות ישראל הוצרך הדבר לשאול שואלין מבית דין שבעירן אם שמעו אמרו להן ואם לאו באין לזה שסמוך לעירן אם שמעו אמרו להם ואם לאו באין לזה שעל פתח הר הבית אם שמעו אמרו להם ואם לאו באין לזה שעל פתח העזרה ואומר כך דרשתי וכך דרשו חבירי כך למדתי וכך למדו חבירי אם שמעו אמרו להם ואם לאו אלו ואלו באין ללשכת הגזית ד ששם יושבין מתמיד של שחר עד תמיד של בין הערבים ה ובשבתות ובימים טובים יושבין בחיל ו נשאלה שאלה בפניהם אם שמעו אמרו להם ואם לאו עומדין למנין רבו המטמאים טמאו רבו המטהרין טהרו ב) משרבו תלמידי שמאי והלל שלא שמשו כל צרכן רבו מחלוקת בישראל ונעשית תורה כשתי תורות ז משם כותבין ושולחין בכל מקומות כל מי שהוא חכם ושפל ברך ודעת הבריות נוחה הימנו יהא דיין בעירו ג) משם מעלין אותו להר הבית משם לעזרה משם ללשכת הגזית ד) שלחו מתם איזהו בן העולם הבא ענוותן ה) ושפל ברך שייף עייל שייף ונפיק וגריס באורייתא תדירא ולא מחזיק טיבותא לנפשיה יהבו ביה רבנן עינייהון ברב עולא בר אבא: חזר לעירו ושנה: ת"ר ח אינו חייב עד שיעשה כהוראתו או שיורה לאחרים ויעשו כהוראתו בשלמא יורה לאחרים ויעשו כהוראתו מעיקרא לאו בר קטלא הוא והשתא בר קטלא הוא אלא שיעשה כהוראתו מעיקרא נמי בר קטלא הוא התינח היכא דאורי בחלב ודם דמעיקרא לאו בר קטלא הוא והשתא בר קטלא הוא אלא היכא דאורי בחייבי מיתות ב"ד מעיקרא נמי בר קטלא הוא מעיקרא בעי התראה השתא ט לא בעי התראה מסית דלא בעי התראה מאי איכא למימר מעיקרא אי אמר טעמא מקבלינן מיניה השתא אי אמר טעמא י לא מקבלינן מיניה: **מתני'** חומר בדברי סופרים מבדברי תורה האומר אין תפילין כדי לעבור על ד"ת פטור כ חמש טוטפות להוסיף על דברי סופרים חייב: **גמ'** אמר ר' אלעזר אמר ר' אושעיא אינו חייב אלא על דבר שעיקרו מדברי תורה ופירושו מדברי סופרים ויש בו להוסיף ואם הוסיף גורע ואין לנו ל אלא תפילין אליבא דרבי יהודה והאיכא לולב דעיקרו מדברי תורה ופירושו מדברי סופרים ויש בו להוסיף ואם הוסיף גורע בלולב מאי סבירא לן אי סבירא לן ו) דלולב מ אין צריך אגד האי לחודיה קאי והאי לחודיה קאי ואי סבירא לן ז) דצריך אגד גרוע ועומד הוא והאיכא ציצית דעיקרו מדברי תורה ופירושו מדברי סופרים ויש בו להוסיף ואם הוסיף גורע בציצית מאי סבירא לן אי סבירא לן דקשר העליון לאו דאורייתא האי לחודיה קאי והאי לחודיה קאי ואי סבירא לן

דקשר

בן סורר ומורה. אף לאחר שהתרו בו וקלקל והלקוהו וחזר וקלקל אם רצו למחול ולא הביאוהו לבית דין מוחלין לו שהכתוב תלה בהם ותפסו בו: **תיובתא.** מדתלי טעמא בשלא ירבו מחלוקת ש"מ אפי' הוא אומר מפי השמועה והן אומרין כך הוא בעינינו: **יושבין בחיל.** מפני שהעם רב ומקום צר להם בלשכה אי נמי שלא יהו נראים כיושבין בדין שבלשכת הגזית היו דנים וזה עיקר: **משם מעלין אותו.** להיות דיין בהר הבית כשמת אחד מהם ויושב שם עד שמת אחד משל עזרה ומעלין את זה שם וכולן יש בהם מעלה זה מזה: **שייף.** שוחה נכנס ושוחה יוצא והכי אמרי' בב"ב (דף ז.) גבי תקרת הבית שנחבטה שוף עול שוף פוק: **מעיקרא.** קודם שבא לבית דין שבלשכת הגזית לישאל לא הוה מיחייב קטלא כל כמה דלא עביד איהו גופיה: **מעיקרא נמי בר קטלא הוא.** אם עושה עבירה שיש בה מיתת בית דין הוה מיקטיל: **מסית דלא בעי התראה.** אם היה מסית ומורה טעם היתר ולומר אין בלשון הזה הסתה מעיקרא נמי מקטיל בלא התראה: **אי אמר טעמא לזכותא.** לאצוליה אבל השתא אי אמר טעמא לא מקבלינן שהרי שמע מפי ב"ד שלא לעשות והמרה: **מתני' האומר אין תפילין פטור.** דאין זו הוראה דזיל קרי בי רב הוא: **חמש טוטפות יש.** שאע"פ שאין דבר זה אלא להוסיף על דברי סופרים חייב דמדרש דסופרים הוא לטטפת לטטפת לטוטפות הרי כאן ד': **גמ' ויש בו להוסיף.** על מה שפירשו חכמים: **ואם הוסיף גורע.** ופוסל הראשון בתוספתו: **ואין לנו אלא תפילין.** שעיקרן בתורה ופירושן מדברי סופרים שהם ד' בתים ויש להוסיף חמשה או יותר ואם הוסיף גורע דקא עבר בבל תוסיף ולא עבד מצוה: **ואליבא דרבי יהודה.** אמר ר' אושעיא למילתיה דאמר לעיל עד דאיכא תורה ויורוך ואית דאמרי אין לנו אלא תפילין ואליבא דרבי יהודה דאמר צריך להדביק במנחות בהקומץ רבה (דף לד:) ולא נהירא לי דהיא בתפילין של יד קאי ומתני' טוטפות תאני והיינו דראש ועוד מדקא מקשי בסיפא אי דעבד ארבעה בתים כו' שמע מינה בשל ראש קיימין דאי בשל יד בית אחד הוא דקא הוי: **האי לחודיה קאי.** ואין זה גורע: **גרוע ועומד.** דמתחילתו לא עשה כהוגן שאגד שם תוספת מצוה ואנן בעינן גורע דהשתא שהיה מתחילתו כשר ופוסלו בתוספתו: **ופירושו מדברי סופרים.** ד' חוטין דילפינן גדיל ב' גדילים ד': **קשר עליון.** שעושין סמוך לכנף כשנתלו החוטין ועל ידיהן נעשין חיבור לטלית לאו דאורייתא (ח) אלא) הלכה למשה מסיני דפלוגתא היא במנחות ט) (דף לט.): **האי לחודיה קאי.** דכיון דלא נקשר אינו חיבור עם השאר והראוי למצוה היא המצוה והעודף כמי שאינו:

שאינו

מסית דלא בעי התראה מאי איכא למימר. לאו אליבא דר' מאיר פריך דלאמסית לא מיחייב דאין בו כרת: **ואין** לנו אלא תפילין ואליבא דר' יהודה. כל הנך דרשות דדרשינן לעיל מקרא דכי יפלא ° לא חייש: **אי** סבירא לן דלולב אין צריך אגד וכו'. משמע אבל אי סבירא לן דצריך אגד לא אמרינן האי לחודיה קאי והאי לחודיה קאי והכי נמי אמרי' בריש לולב הגזול (סוכה דף לא.) דקאמר רבי יהודה אין אוגדין את הלולב אלא במינו מאי טעמא דכיון דאמר ר' יהודה לולב צריך אגד אי עבדי ליה ממין אחר הוה ליה ה' מינין ותימה דאמר התם (שם:) ד' מינין שבלולב כשם שאין פוחתין מהן כך אין מוסיפין עליהם ופריך פשיטא ומשני מהו דתימא הואיל ואמר רבי יהודה לולב צריך אגד אי אייתי מינא אחרינא האי לחודיה קאי והאי לחודיה קאי קמ"ל מאי קא תלי טעמא דהאי לחודיה קאי משום דלולב צריך אגד אדרבה מטעם זה יש לנו לומר יותר דאסור ומיהו י"ל דהתם בדמנח ליה חוץ לאגד אבל קשה דמשמע דמסיק לר' יהודה דלא אמר האי לחודיה וכ"ש לרבנן והכא משמע דלרבנן אמר האי לחודיה קאי וי"ל דהתם מדרבנן אסור ור"ח ל"ג התם הואיל ואמר ר' יהודה וזהו לשונו מהו דתימא הואיל ואמרו חכמים בין אגוד בין שאינו אגוד כשר הלכך אין צריך אגד והאי יתירה דמוסיף על הד' לחודיה קאי ולא מיפסל ביה קמ"ל ומיהו תימה אמאי לא משכח לולב לרבי יהודה בכי האי גוונא שאגד ג' מינין בפני עצמן דנעשה בכשרות ואחר כך אגד עמהן מין אחר דהוה ליה מוסיף גורע ויש לומר כיון דקודם נטילתו נפסל הוה ליה גרוע ועומד אבל תפילין אם הניחן בראשו בכשרות והניח גבייהו בית חמישי הרי זה מוסיף גורע שפוסלן ומבטל מצות שעל ראשו ולא דמי ללולב דאם נטלו ובעודו בידו הוסיף מין חמישי אין זה מבטל מצותו דמדאגביה נפק ביה:

קשר

עין משפט נר מצוה

נז א מיי' פ"ז מהלכות ממרים הלכה ח:
נח ב מיי' פ"ג שם הל' ד סמג עשין קיא ולאוין ריז:
נט ג מיי' שם פ"א הל' ד סמג שם:
ס ד ה מיי' פ"ג מהל' סנהדרין הלכה א:
סא ו מיי' פ"א מהל' ממרים הל' ד סמג עשין קיא ולאוין ריז:
סב ז מיי' פ"ב מהל' סנהדרין הלכה ח:
סג ח מיי' פ"ג מהל' ממרים הל' ה ופ"ד הלכה א סמג עשין קיא ולאוין ריז:
סד ט י מיי' שם פ"ג הלכה ח:
סה כ ל מיי' פ"ד שם הלכה ג סמג עשין קיא ולאוין ריז:
סו מ מיי' פ"ז מהל' לולב הלכה ו סמג עשין מד טוש"ע א"ח סי' תרנא סעיף א:

גליון הש"ס

תוס' ד"ה ואין וכו' לא חייש. עיין בטורי אבן בחגיגה שם לר"ה דף כ"ז ע"א ד"ה מצות:

מסורת הש"ס

א) [תוספ' פ"ז תוספ' חגיגה פרק ב], ב) [סוטה מז:], ג) [תוספ' שקלים ספ"ג], ד) [לעיל יז: וש"נ], ה) [בתענית טז. פירש"י שפל ברך עניו וצ"ל דכמה עניני ענוה יש ועי' רש"א ח"א], ו) [סוכה לו:], ז) [סוכה לא.], ח) [צ"ל כלומר], ט) [עי' תוס' פט. לקמן בסמוך ד"ה קשר].

ליקוטי רש"י

זקן ממרא. שהמרה על ב"ד של לשכת הגזית ומיתתו בחנק [סוטה כה:]. **האומר אין תפילין.** זקן ממרא מן הדבר ולא כל דבר דהא כתי' מן הדבר ותנן באלו הן הנחנקין (סנהדרין דף פח:) האומר אין תפלין לעבור על דברי תורה פטור חמש טוטפות להוסיף על דברי סופרים חייב דהיינו מן הדבר ולא כל דבר [הוריות ד.]. **לולב צריך אגד.** הלכך כל הנאגד עמו הוי מן המצוה ונמצא עובר בבל תוסיף אם יאגד מין חמישי [סוכה לא.].

[מכאן שייך לדף פט.]

קשר עליון. היינו נמי ההוא קשר למטה הלכה למשה מסיני כלומר קשר אחד בלילית מיהא דאורייתא והכי נקט עליון משום דאי לא עביד אלא חד קשר בסופו עביד ליה שמקיים את הגדיל כולו. **דאורייתא.** ואפי' יכול לכרוך יפה ולהתקיים בלא קשר יום או יומים פסולה [מנחות לט.]. **וכל העם ישמעו.** מכאן שממתינין לו עד הרגל וממיתין אותו ברגל [דברים יז, יג]. **לרשות הבעל.** כגון מסרה האב לשלוחי הבעל ועדיין היא בדרך ולא קרינן בה בית אביה. **לאותה מיתה.** שהיו מחייבין את הנידון. **ובועלה.** כלומר וכל הבועלים נידונין כמיתת הנבעלת חוץ מבועל בת כהן [לקמן צ.]. **מקדימים לאותה מיתה.** כלומר אין להם לצפות מיתה אחרת אלא מסכימין לאותה מיתה שנגמר בה דינו של נדון. **חוץ מזוממי בת כהן.** נשואה שאע"פ שנגמר דינה לשריפה על פיהם הם בחנק כדילפינן התם סנהדרין (דף נ) היא בשריפה ואין בועלה בשריפה אלא בחנק כשאר אשת איש והזוממין מסכימין למיתה שחייבו את הבועל דכתיב כאשר זמם לעשות לאחיו ולא לאחותו [מכות ב.]. **זוממי בת כהן.** לעשות לאחיו מה תלמוד לומר לאחיו למד על זוממי בת כהן נשואה שאינן בשריפה אלא כמיתת הבועל שהוא בחנק שנאמר היא באש תשרף (ויקרא כא, ט) היא ולא בועלה לכך נאמר כאן לאחיו כאשר זמם לעשות לאחיו ולא כאשר זמם לעשות לאחותו אבל בכל שאר מיתות השוה הכתוב אשה לאיש וזוממי אשה נהרגין כזוממי איש כגון שהעידוה שהרגה את הנפש שחללה את השבת נהרגין במיתתה שלא מיעט כאן אחותו אלא במקום שיש לקיים בהן הזמה במיתת הבועל [דברים יט, יט]. **שהיא והן נהרגין** ולא במיתה אחת דהיא בשריפה והן במיתת הבועל כגון באו עדים והזימו את הראשונים וחייבום מיתת הבועל ולא מיתתה דכתיב (דברים יט) כאשר זמם לעשות לאחיו ולא לאחותו כדאמר באלו הן הנחנקין (סנהדרין ל). **בועלה.** דהיא בשריפה אבל בועלה נידון כשאר בועל בת ישראל דבועל ארוסה בסקילה ובועל נשואה בחנק דכתיב (ויקרא כא) היא באש תשרף היא ולא בועלה היא ולא זוממיה [לעיל מו.]. **וזוממי בת כהן.** אף על פי שהם היו מחייבין אותה שריפה אין נדונין אלא במיתה שהיו מחייבין לבועל והיינו חנק כשאר בא על אשת איש כדמפרש קרא היא תשרף ולא בועלה וזוממיה ילפינן מכאשר זמם לעשות לאחיו ולא לאחותו. **ובועלה.** בנשואה בת כהן קמיירי אבל ארוסה בועלה בסקילה [לעיל פד:]. **אשר לא צויתיו לדבר.** אבל צויתיו לחבירו. **ואשר ידבר בשם אלהים אחרים.** אפילו כיון את ההלכה לאסור את האסור ולהתיר את המותר. **ומת.** בחנק שלשה מיתתן בידי אדם המתנבא מה שלא שמע ומה שלא נאמר לו ונאמר לחבירו והמתנבא בשם עבודה זרה אבל הכובש את נבואתו והעובר על דברי נביא והעובר על דברי עצמו מיתתן בידי שמים שנאמר (פסוק יט) אנכי אדרוש מעמו [דברים יח, כ]. **ויצא הרוח.** פתרון ויצא המלאך שהרי אומר לעיל וכל צבא השמים וגו' ועתה יצא אחד מן המלאכים ויאמר אני אפתנו כדאמר (תהלים קד) עושה מלאכיו רוחות ולפיכך קדם ואמר לעיל וכל צבא השמים עומדים שאל תתמה כשתאמר ויצא הרוח מי הוא ומהיכן יצא וכשאמר וכל צבא השמים עומדים כדי להודיע מהיכן יצא מאשר הרוחות העומדים עליו, ורבותינו פירשו זהו רוחו של נבות. **בפי כל נביאיו.** שישים דבר בפיהם לאמר עלה והצלח ויעלה ויפול מכלל שהיו נביאי אמת שלא היו מתנבאים כי אם מה שישים השם בפיהם [דה"ב יח]. **זה בכה.** אני אפתנו בכה [שבת קמט:]. **תפתה וגם תוכל.** לפי שיש מפתה הבא לפתות חבירו פעמים שהמפותה מבין שזה רוצה לפתותו והוא נזהר ואינו שומע להתפתות אבל באחאב תפתה וגם תוכל [דה"ב שם]. **צא ממחיצתי.** הפורע נוקם חמתו וקנאתו מחריב ביתיה, כרוח של נבות שנקם כעסו מאחאב ויצא ממחיצתו של הקדוש ברוך הוא. **רוחו של נבות.** שלפי שהוא הרג נבות היה רוחו מחזר לפתותו ולהפילו [לקמן קב:]. **תפלצתך.** ל' בהלה שהיית ממהר ונבהל לעורר שטימתך לאחיך ויש לועזין לשון פלצות ויש לועזין לשון מפלצת [ירמיהו מט, טז]. **האין פה נביא לה' עוד.** מקובלני אין ב' נביאים מתנבאים בל' א' ואלה כולם לשון א' אומרים [מ"א כב, ז]. **את קשת עילם.** את תקות עילם [ירמיהו מט, לה]. **שברתי את עול מלך בבל.** אמרו רבותינו מי הטעה את חנניה שמע שהיה ירמיה מתנב' בשוק העליון הנני שובר את קשת עילם (ירמיה מט) ונבואה זו בסוף הספר נאמרה בראשית ממלכת צדקיהו כמו שמפורש שם ולפי שעילם סמוכה לבבל עמד הוא בשוק התחתון ודרש ודן קל וחומר ומה עילם שלא באה אלא לעזור את הכשדים וכו' כמה שהיא בסנהדרין [שם כח, א].

DISPUTE IN the nation of ISRAEL PROLIFERATED, וְנַעֲשֵׂית תּוֹרָה כִּשְׁתֵּי תוֹרוֹת – AND THE TORAH BECAME AS TWO TORAHS because of the many conflicting rulings.

The Baraisa now discusses the qualifications that a candidate for appointment to the lower courts must possess:

מִשָּׁם כּוֹתְבִין וְשׁוֹלְחִין בְּכָל מְקוֹמוֹת – FROM THERE, the seat of the Great Sanhedrin, [THE JUDGES] WRITE AND SEND the following directive to the lower courts IN ALL PLACES: כָּל מִי שֶׁהוּא חָכָם וּשְׁפַל בֶּרֶךְ – ANYONE WHO IS WISE AND HUMBLE וְדַעַת הַבְּרִיּוֹת נוֹחָה הֵימֶנּוּ – AND WHOM THE PEOPLE FIND AGREEABLE יְהֵא דַיָּין בְּעִירוֹ – SHALL BE A JUDGE IN HIS CITY.[10]

The professional advancement of a judge is described:

מִשָּׁם מַעֲלִין אוֹתוֹ לְהַר הַבַּיִת – FROM THERE, i.e. from the municipal courts, THEY ELEVATE [A DESERVING JUDGE] TO the court that sits at the entrance OF THE TEMPLE MOUNT.[11] מִשָּׁם לָעֲזָרָה – FROM THERE, i.e. from the court at the Temple Mount, they elevate him TO the court that sits at the entrance of THE COURTYARD. מִשָּׁם לְלִשְׁכַּת הַגָּזִית – FROM THERE, i.e. from the court at the Courtyard, they elevate him TO the Sanhedrin, which sits in THE CHAMBER OF HEWN STONE.

The Gemara cites another teaching, which mentions some of the aforecited attributes:

שָׁלְחוּ מִתָּם – **They sent from there**[12] the following teaching: אֵיזֶהוּ בֶּן הָעוֹלָם הַבָּא – **Which is the one destined for** a share in **the World to Come?**[13] עַנְוְותָן וּשְׁפַל בֶּרֶךְ – One who is **modest and humble,** שָׁיֵיף עָיֵיל שָׁיֵיף וְנָפֵיק – and who **enters bowing and leaves bowing**[14] וְגָרִיס בְּאוֹרַיְיתָא תְּדִירָא וְלָא מַחֲזִיק טֵיבוּתָא לְנַפְשֵׁיהּ – **and** who **learns Torah constantly but does not take credit for himself** for it.[15] יָהֲבוּ בֵּיהּ רַבָּנָן עֵינַיְיהוּ בְּרַב עוּלָּא בַּר אַבָּא – Upon hearing this description **the Rabbis placed their eyes upon Rav Ulla bar Abba,** who possessed all of these qualities.

The Mishnah continued:

חָזַר לְעִירוֹ וְשָׁנָה – IF [THE SAGE] RETURNED TO HIS TOWN, AND HE TAUGHT and interpreted in the manner he was used to, he is not liable. But if he instructed people to act in accordance with his overruled opinion, he is liable.

The Gemara cites a related Baraisa:

תָּנוּ רַבָּנָן – **The Rabbis taught in a Baraisa:** אֵינוֹ חַיָּיב עַד שֶׁיַּעֲשֶׂה כְּהוֹרָאָתוֹ – A [REBELLIOUS SAGE] IS NOT LIABLE to the death penalty UNLESS HE himself ACTS IN ACCORDANCE WITH HIS OWN RULING אוֹ שֶׁיּוֹרֶה לַאֲחֵרִים וְיַעֲשׂוּ כְּהוֹרָאָתוֹ – OR HE INSTRUCTS OTHERS THAT THEY SHOULD ACT IN ACCORDANCE WITH HIS RULING.[16]

We can infer from the Baraisa that if the sage would follow his own ruling *before* the Sanhedrin overruled his opinion, he would not be liable to the death penalty.[17] The Gemara explores this:

בִּשְׁלָמָא יוֹרֶה לַאֲחֵרִים וְיַעֲשׂוּ כְּהוֹרָאָתוֹ – The second clause of the Baraisa – that if [THE SAGE] INSTRUCTS OTHERS TO ACT IN ACCORDANCE WITH HIS RULING he is liable to the death penalty as a rebellious sage – **is understandable,** מֵעִיקָּרָא לָאו בַּר קְטָלָא הוּא – for if he had done this **before** the Sanhedrin overruled his opinion, **he would not have been liable to the death penalty,** וְהַשְׁתָּא בַּר קְטָלָא הוּא – **whereas now** that the Sanhedrin overruled him, **he is liable to the death penalty** for rebelling against them.[18] אֶלָּא שֶׁיַּעֲשֶׂה כְּהוֹרָאָתוֹ – **But** the first clause of the Baraisa – that if [THE SAGE] himself ACTS IN ACCORDANCE WITH HIS OWN RULING he is liable to the death penalty as a rebellious sage – is difficult, מֵעִיקָּרָא נַמִּי בַּר קְטָלָא הוּא – for **even before** the Sanhedrin overruled him, **he** could have been **liable to the death penalty** for following his own erroneous opinion.[19] – ? –

The Gemara qualifies the question:

הָתֵינַח הֵיכָא דְּאוֹרֵי בְּחֵלֶב וְדָם – **This** statement of the Baraisa **fits well** in regard to a case **where [the sage] ruled** and acted **in** a matter such as the prohibition against eating ***cheilev* or** drinking **blood.**[20] דְּמֵעִיקָּרָא לָאו בַּר קְטָלָא הוּא – **For** in such a case, **before** the Sanhedrin overruled him, **he would not** have been **liable to the death penalty** for acting in accordance with his own ruling,[21] וְהַשְׁתָּא בַּר קְטָלָא הוּא – **whereas now** that the Sanhedrin overruled him, **he is liable to the death penalty**

NOTES

other, related matters (see *Sotah* 22a, and *Rashi* there ד״ה ולא שימש). Thus, only when their underlying logic is known is it possible to apply their teachings.

However, those students not well-versed in Tannaic logic will marshal incorrect proofs to support their legal decisions, for their proofs will be based on their faulty understanding of the Tannaic sources. Thus, legal disputes will ensue, and ultimately, since each student will follow his own opinion in practice, it will appear to others that there are "two Torahs" (see *Maharsha*). This is the situation described by the Baraisa.

10. A prospective judge must possess all three qualifications, for a wise man will not merit to determine the correct ruling unless he is humble as well. Furthermore, unless people are pleased with him on a personal level, they may not willingly accept his rulings as truth, or comply with them (*Ben Yehoyada*; cf. *Iyun Yaakov*; see also *Rambam, Hil. Sanhedrin* 2:7).

11. If a member of the court sitting at the entrance of the Temple Mount dies, he is replaced by a qualified judge from one of the municipal courts. Further promotion is possible for this judge when a member of the next higher court dies (*Rashi*).

12. I.e. from Eretz Yisrael.

13. While all Jews are guaranteed a share in the World to Come, sin may cause one person's share to be given to another. The Gemara thus wonders which type of person surely will not lose his share to another, so that it may *now* be said that he is "destined for a share in the World to Come" (*Ben Yehoyada*; cf. *Toras Chaim*).

14. The Gemara recognizes that there are three strengths that can cause a person to be haughty: his mental prowess, his physical prowess and his monetary wealth. A person destined for a share in the World to Come must be free of haughtiness in all three areas. He must be an עָנָיו, *modest,* with regard to his intellectual capabilities, and שְׁפַל בֶּרֶךְ, *humble* (literally: low of knee), with regard to his physical capabilities, just as a *knee* (בֶּרֶךְ) is physically low on a person's body. Furthermore, he must be modest with his wealth, possessing a home so unpretentious that people have to bend over when entering or exiting through the doorway (*Maharsha*; cf. *Ben Yehoyada*).

15. Although he exceeds the minimum time requirements for Torah study, he does not become proud (*Maharsha*; cf. *Ben Yehoyada*).

16. If a sage merely preaches his view as an alternative to the view of the Sanhedrin, he is not liable. But if he commits his opinion to practice by instructing others to follow his opinion, or even by himself acting in accordance with his opinion, he is liable. [If he instructs others to follow his ruling he is liable regardless of whether they actually follow it] (*Rambam, Hil. Mamrim* 3:5 with *Radvaz*).

17. [For the Baraisa holds him liable for rebelling against the Sanhedrin, not for the transgression that he commits by following his own erroneous opinion.]

18. [Only a sage who rebels against the Sanhedrin is liable to the death penalty, not one who issues an incorrect ruling on a matter that he did not present to the Sanhedrin.]

19. If his ruling pertained to a capital offense and he acted in accordance with his own misguided opinion, which is in conflict with the accepted halachah, he would have been liable to the death penalty for the act even if it had not placed him in the category of *zakein mamrei* (*Rashi*).

20. I.e. the sage ruled that some form of blood or *cheilev* (the forbidden fat of a slaughtered animal) is permitted, while in fact it is prohibited.

21. The penalty for transgressing the prohibitions of consuming *cheilev* or blood is *kares,* not capital punishment.

[א]בן סורר ומורה שרצו אביו ואמו למחול לו מוחלין לו זקן ממרא שרצו בית דינו למחול לו מוחלין לו וכשבאתי אצל חבירי שבדרום על שנים הודו לי על זקן ממרא [ב]לא הודו לי כדי שלא ירבו מחלוקת בישראל תיובתא תניא [א]אמר רבי יוסי [ג]מתחילה לא היו מרבין מחלוקת בישראל אלא בית דין של שבעים ואחד יושבין בלשכת הגזית ושני בתי דינין של עשרים ושלשה אחד יושב על פתח הר הבית ואחד יושב על פתח העזרה ושאר בתי דינין של עשרים ושלשה יושבין בכל עיירות ישראל הוצרך הדבר לשאול שואלין מבית דין שבעירן אם שמעו אמרו להן ואם לאו באין לזה שסמוך לעירן אם שמעו אמרו להם ואם לאו באין לזה שעל פתח הר הבית אם שמעו אמרו להם ואם לאו באין לזה שעל פתח העזרה ואומר כך דרשתי וכך דרשו חבירי כך למדתי וכך למדו חבירי אם שמעו אמרו להם ואם לאו אלו ואלו באין ללשכת הגזית [ד]ששם יושבין מתמיד של שחר עד תמיד של בין הערבים [ה]ובשבתות ובימים טובים יושבין בחיל [ו]נשאלה שאלה בפניהם אם שמעו אמרו להם ואם לאו עומדין למנין רבו המטמאים טמאו רבו המטהרין טהרו [ב]משרבו תלמידי שמאי והלל שלא שמשו כל צרכן רבו מחלוקת בישראל ונעשית תורה כשתי תורות [ז]משם כותבין ושולחין בכל מקומות כל מי שהוא חכם ושפל ברך ודעת הבריות נוחה הימנו יהא דיין בעירו [ג]משם מעלין אותו להר הבית משם לעזרה משם ללשכת הגזית [ד]שלחו מתם איזהו בן העולם הבא ענוותן [ה]ושפל ברך שייף עייל שייף ונפיק וגריס באורייתא תדירא ולא מחזיק טיבותא לנפשיה יהבו ביה רבנן עינייהון ברב עולא בר אבא: חזר לעירו ושנה: ת"ר [ח]אינו חייב עד שיעשה כהוראתו או שיורה לאחרים ויעשו כהוראתו בשלמא יורה לאחרים ויעשו כהוראתו מעיקרא לאו בר קטלא הוא והשתא בר קטלא הוא אלא שיעשה כהוראתו מעיקרא נמי בר קטלא הוא התינח היכא דאורי בחלב ודם דמעיקרא לאו בר קטלא הוא והשתא בר קטלא הוא אלא היכא דאורי בחייבי מיתות ב"ד מעיקרא נמי בר קטלא הוא מעיקרא בעי התראה השתא [ט]לא בעי התראה מסית דלא בעי התראה מאי איכא למימר מעיקרא אי אמר טעמא מקבלינן מיניה השתא אי אמר טעמא [י]לא מקבלינן מיניה: **מתני'** חומר בדברי סופרים מבדברי תורה האומר אין תפילין כדי לעבור על ד"ת פטור [כ]חמש טוטפות להוסיף על דברי סופרים חייב: **גמ'** אמר ר' אלעזר אמר ר' אושעיא אינו חייב אלא על דבר שעיקרו מדברי תורה ופירושו מדברי סופרים ויש בו להוסיף ואם הוסיף גורע ואין לנו [ל]אלא תפילין אליבא דרבי יהודה והאיכא לולב דעיקרו מדברי תורה ופירושו מדברי סופרים ויש בו להוסיף ואם הוסיף גורע בלולב מאי סבירא לן אי סבירא לן [ו]דלולב [מ]אין צריך אגד האי לחודיה קאי והאי לחודיה קאי ואי סבירא לן [ז]דצריך אגד גרוע ועומד הוא והאיכא ציצית דעיקרו מדברי תורה ופירושו מדברי סופרים ויש בו להוסיף ואם הוסיף גורע בציצית מאי סבירא לן אי סבירא לן דקשר העליון לאו דאורייתא האי לחודיה קאי והאי לחודיה קאי ואי סבירא לן

דקשר

בן סורר ומורה. אף לאחר שהתרו בו וקלקל והלקוהו וחזר וקלקל אם רצו למחול ולא הביאוהו לבית דין מוחלין לו שהכתוב תלה בהם ותפשו בו: **תיובתא.** מדתלי טעמא בשלא ירבו מחלוקת ש"מ אפי' הוא אומר מפי השמועה והן אומרין כך הוא בעינינו: **יושבין בחיל.** מפני שהעם רב ומקום צר להם בלשכה אי נמי שלא יהו נראים כיושבין בדין שבלשכת הגזית היו דנים וזה עיקר: **משם מעלין אותו.** להיות דיין בהר הבית כשמת אחד מהם ויושב שם עד שמת אחד משל עזרה ומעלין את זה שם וכולן יש בהם מעלה זה מזה: **שייף.** שוחה נכנס ושוחה יוצא והכי אמרי' בב"ב (דף ז.) גבי תקרת הבית שנחבטה שוף עול שוף פוק: **מעיקרא.** קודם שבא לבית דין שבלשכת הגזית לישאל לא הוה מחייב קטלא כל כמה דלא עביד איהו גופיה: **מעיקרא נמי בר קטלא הוא.** אם עושה עבירה שיש בה מיתת בית דין הוה מיקטיל: **מסית דלא בעי התראה.** אם היה מסית ומורה טעם היתר ולומר אין בלשון הזה הסתה מעיקרא נמי מקטיל בלא התראה: **אי אמר טעמא לזכותא.** לאלוליה אבל השתא אי אמר טעמא לא מקבלינן שהרי שמע מפי ב"ד שלא לעשות והמרה: **מתני' האומר אין תפילין פטור.** דאין זו הוראה דזיל קרי בי רב הוא: **חמש טוטפות יש.** שאע"פ שאין דבר זה אלא להוסיף על דברי סופרים חייב דמדרש דסופרים הוא לטטפת לטטפת לטוטפות הרי כאן ד': **גמ' ויש בו להוסיף.** על מה שפירשו חכמים: **ואם הוסיף גורע.** ופוסל הראשון בתוספתו: **ואין לנו אלא תפילין.** שעיקרן בתורה ופירושן מדברי סופרים שהם ד' בתים ויש להוסיף חמשה או יותר ואם הוסיף גורע דקא עבר בבל תוסיף ולא עבד מצוה: **ואליבא דרבי יהודה.** אמר ר' אושעיא למילתיה דאמר לעיל עד דאיכא תורה ויורוך ואית דאמרי אין לנו אלא תפילין ואליבא דרבי יהודה דאמר צריך להדביק במנחות בהקומץ רבה (דף לד:) ולא נהירא לי דההיא בתפילין של יד קאי ומתני' טוטפות תאני והיינו דראש ועוד מדקא מקשי בסיפא אי דעבד ארבעה בתים כו' שמע מינה בשל ראש קיימין דאי בשל יד בית אחד הוא דקא הוי: **האי לחודיה קאי.** ואין זה גורע: **גרוע ועומד.** דמתחילתו לא עשה כהוגן שאגד שם תוספת מצוה ואנן בעינן גורע דהשתא שהיה מתחילתו כשר ופוסלו בתוספתו: **ופירושו מדברי סופרים.** ד' חוטין דילפינן גדיל ב' גדילים ד': **קשר עליון.** שעושין סמוך לכנף כשנתלו החוטין ועל ידיהן נעשין חיבור לטלית לאו דאורייתא ([ח] אלא) הלכה למשה מסיני דפלוגתא היא במנחות [ט] (דף לט.): **האי לחודיה קאי.** דכיון דלא נקשר אינו חיבור עם השאר והראוי למצוה היא המצוה והעודף כמי שאינו:

שאינו

מסית דלא בעי התראה מאי איכא למימר. לאו אליבא דר' מאיר פריך דאמסית לא מחייב דאין בו כרת: **ואין** לנו אלא תפילין ואליבא דר' יהודה. כל הנך דרשות דדרשינן לעיל מקרא דכי יפלא ° לא חייש: **אי** סבירא לן דלולב אין צריך אגד וכו'. משמע אבל אי סבירא לן דצריך אגד לא אמרינן האי לחודיה קאי והאי לחודיה קאי והכי נמי אמרי' בריש לולב הגזול (סוכה דף לא.) דקאמר רבי יהודה אין אוגדין את הלולב אלא במינו מאי טעמא דכיון דאמר ר' יהודה לולב צריך אגד אי עבדי ליה ממין אחר הוה ליה ה' מינין ותימה דאמר התם (שם:) ד' מינין שבלולב כשם שאין פוחתין מהן כך אין מוסיפין עליהם ופריך פשיטא ומשני מהו דתימא הואיל ואמר רבי יהודה לולב צריך אגד אי אייתי מינא אחרינא האי לחודיה קאי והאי לחודיה קאי קמ"ל מאי קא תלי טעמא דהאי לחודיה קאי משום דלולב צריך אגד אדרבה מטעם זה יש לנו לומר יותר דאסור ומיהו י"ל דהתם בדמנח ליה חוץ לאגד אבל קשה דמשמע דמסיק לר' יהודה דלא אמר האי לחודיה וכ"ש לרבנן והכא משמע דלרבנן אמר האי לחודיה קאי וי"ל דהתם מדרבנן אסור ור"ח ל"ג התם הואיל ואמר ר' יהודה וזהו לשונו מהו דתימא הואיל ואמרו חכמים בין אגוד בין שאינו אגוד כשר הלכך אין צריך אגד והאי יתירה דמוסיף על הד' לחודיה קאי ולא מיפסל ביה קמ"ל ומיהו תימה אמאי לא משכח לולב לרבי יהודה בכי האי גוונא שאגד ג' מינין בפני עצמן דנעשה בכשרות ואחר כך אגד עמהן מין אחר דהוה ליה מוסיף גורע ויש לומר כיון דקודם נטילתו נפסל הוה ליה גרוע ועומד אבל תפילין אם הניחן בראשו בכשרות והניח גבייהו בית חמישי הרי זה מוסיף גורע שפוסלן ומבטל מצות שעל ראשו ולא דמי ללולב דאם נטלו ובעודו בידו הוסיף מין חמישי אין זה מבטל מצותו דמלאגביה נפק ביה:

קשר

עין משפט נר מצוה

נז א מיי' פ"ז מהלכות ממרים הלכה ח:

נח ב מיי' פ"ג שם הל' ד סמג עשין קיא ולאוין ריז:

נט ג מיי' שם פ"א הל' ד סמג שם:

ס ד ה מיי' פ"ג מהל' סנהדרין הלכה א:

סא ו מיי' פ"א מהל' ממרים הל' ד סמג עשין קיא ולאוין ריז:

סב ז מיי' פ"ב מהל' סנהדרין הלכה ח:

סג ח מיי' פ"ג מהל' ממרים הל' ה ופ"ד הלכה א סמג עשין קיא ולאוין ריז:

סד ט י מיי' שם פ"ג הלכה ח:

סה כ ל מיי' פ"ד שם הלכה ג סמג עשין קיא ולאוין ריז:

סו מ מיי' פ"ז מהל' לולב הלכה ו סמג עשין מד טוש"ע א"ח סי' תרנא סעיף א:

מסורת הש"ס

א) [תוספ' פ"ז תוספ' חגיגה פרק ב], ב) [סוטה מז:], ג) [תוספ' שקלים ספ"ג], ד) [לעיל יז: וש"נ], ה) [בתענית טז. פירש"י שפל ברך עניו וצ"ל דכמה עניני ענוה יש ועי' רש"א ח"א], ו) [סוכה ל:], ז) [סוכה לא.], ח) [צ"ל כלומר], ט) [עי' תוס' פט. לקמן בסמוך ד"ה קשר].

גליון הש"ס

תוס' ד"ה ואין וכו' לא חייש. עיין בטורי אבן באבני שהם לר"ה דף כ"ז ע"א ד"ה מצות:

ליקוטי רש"י

זקן ממרא. שהמרה על ב"ד של לשכת הגזית ומיתתו בחנק [סוטה כה:]. **האומר אין תפילין.** זקן ממרא מן הדבר ולא כל דבר דהא כתי' מן הדבר ותנן באלו הן הנחנקין (סנהדרין דף פח:) האומר אין תפלין לעבור על דברי תורה פטור חמש טוטפות להוסיף על דברי סופרים חייב דהיינו מן הדבר ולא כל דבר [הוריות ד.]. **לולב צריך אגד.** הלכך כל הנאגד עמו הוי מן המצוה ונמצא עובר בבל תוסיף אם יאגד מין חמישי [סוכה לא.].

[מכאן שייך לדף פט.].

קשר עליון. היינו נמי ההוא קשר למטה הלכה למשה מסיני כלומר קשר אחד בלילית מיהא דאורייתא ולהכי נקט עליון משום דאי לא עביד אלא חד קשר בסופו עביד ליה שמקיים את הגדיל כולו. **דאורייתא.** ואפי' יכול לכרוך יפה ולהתקיים בלא קשר יום או יומים פסולה [מנחות לט.]. **וכל העם ישמעו.** מכאן שממתינין לו עד הרגל וממיתין אותו ברגל [דברים יז, יג]. **לרשות הבעל.** כגון מסרה האב לשלוחי הבעל ועדיין היא בדרך ולא קרינן בה בית אביה. **לאותה מיתה.** שהיו מחייבין את הנידון. **ובועלה.** כלומר וכל הבועלים נידונין כמיתת הנבעלת חוץ מבועל בת כהן [לקמן צ.]. **מקדימים לאותה מיתה.** כלומר אין להם לצפות מיתה אחרת אלא מסכימין לאותה מיתה שנגמר בה דינו של נדון. **חוץ מזוממי בת כהן.** נשואה שאע"פ שנגמר דינה לשריפה על פיהם הם בחנק כדילפינן התם סנהדרין (דף נ) היא בשריפה ואין בועלה בשריפה אלא בחנק כשאר אשת איש והזוממין מסכימין למיתה שחייבו את הבועל דכתיב כאשר זמם לעשות לאחיו ולא לאחותו [מכות ב.]. **זוממי בת כהן.** לעשות לאחיו מה תלמוד לומר לאחיו למד על זוממי בת כהן נשואה שאינן בשריפה אלא כמיתת הבועל שהוא בחנק שנאמר היא באש תשרף (ויקרא כא, ט) היא ולא בועלה לכך נאמר כאן לאחיו כאשר זמם לעשות לאחיו ולא כאשר זמם לעשות לאחותו אבל בכל שאר מיתות השוה הכתוב אשה לאיש וזוממי אשה נהרגין כזוממי איש כגון שהעידוה שהרגה את הנפש שחללה את השבת נהרגין במיתתה שלא מיעט כאן אחותו אלא במקום שיש לקיים בהן הזמה במיתת הבועל [דברים יט, יט]. **שהיא והן נהרגין** ולא במיתה אחת דהיא בשריפה והן במיתת הבועל כגון באו עדים והזימו את הראשונים וחייבום מיתת הבועל ולא מיתתה דכתיב (דברים יט) כאשר זמם לעשות לאחיו ולא לאחותו כדאמר באלו הן הנחנקין (סנהדרין נ). **בועלה.** דהיא בשריפה אבל בועלה נידון כשאר בועל בת ישראל דבועל ארוסה בסקילה ובועל נשואה בחנק דכתיב (ויקרא כא) היא באש תשרף היא ולא בועלה היא ולא זוממיה [לעיל מו.]. **וזוממי בת כהן.** אף על פי שהם היו מחייבין אותה שריפה אין נדונין אלא במיתה שהיו מחייבין לבועל והיינו חנק כשאר בא על אשת איש כדמפרש קרא היא תשרף ולא בועלה וזוממיה ילפינן מכאשר זמם לעשות לאחיו ולא לאחותו. **ובועלה.** בנשואה בת כהן קמיירי אבל ארוסה בועלה בסקילה [לעיל פד:]. **אשר לא צויתיו לדבר.** אבל צויתיו לחבירו. **ואשר ידבר בשם אלהים אחרים.** אפילו כיון את ההלכה לאסור את האסור ולהתיר את המותר. **ומת.** בחנק שלשה מיתתן בידי אדם המתנבא מה שלא שמע ומה שלא נאמר לו ונאמר לחבירו והמתנבא בשם עבודה זרה אבל הכובש את נבואתו והעובר על דברי נביא והעובר על דברי עצמו מיתתן בידי שמים שנאמר (פסוק יט) אנכי אדרוש מעמו [דברים יח, כ]. **ויצא הרוח.** פתרון ויצא המלאך שהרי אומר לעיל וכל צבא השמים וגו' ועתה יצא אחד מן המלאכים ויאמר אני אפתנו כדאמר (תהלים קד) עושה מלאכיו רוחות ולפיכך קדם ואמר לעיל וכל צבא השמים עומדים שאל תתמה כשתאמר ויצא הרוח מי הוא ומהיכן יצא וכשאמר וכל צבא השמים עומדים כדי להודיע מהיכן יצא משאר הרוחות העומדים עליו, ורבותינו פירשו זהו רוחו של נבות. **בפי כל נביאיו.** שישים דבר בפיהם לאמר עלה והצלח ויעלה ויפול מכלל שהיו נביאי אמת שלא היו מתנבאים כי אם מה שישים השם בפיהם [דה"ב יח]. **זה בכה.** אני אפתנו בכה [שבת קמט:]. **תפתה וגם תוכל.** לפי שיש מפתה הבא לפתות חבירו פעמים שהמפותה מבין שזה רוצה לפתותו והוא נזהר ואינו שומע להתפתות אבל באחאב תפתה וגם תוכל [דה"ב שם]. **צא ממחיצתי.** הפורע נוקם חמתו וקנאתו מחריב ביתיה, כרוח של נבות שנקם כעסו מאחאב ויצא ממחיצתו של הקדוש ברוך הוא. **רוחו של נבות.** שלפי שהוא הרג נבות היה רוחו מחזר לפתותו ולהפילו [לקמן קב:]. **תפלצתך.** ל' בהלה שהיית ממהר ונבהל לעורר שטימתך לאחיך ויש לועזין לשון פלצות ויש לועזין לשון מפלצת [ירמיהו מט, טז]. **האין פה נביא לה' עוד.** מקובלני אין ב' נביאים מתנבאים בל' א' ואלה כולם לשון א' אומרים [מ"א כב, ז]. **את קשת עילם.** את תקות עילם [ירמיהו מט, לה]. **שברתי את עול מלך בבל.** אמרו רבותינו מי הטעה את חנניה שמע שהיה ירמיה מתנב' בשוק העליון הנני שובר את קשת עילם (ירמיה מט) ונבואה זו בסוף הספר נאמרה בראשית ממלכת צדקיהו כמו שמפורש שם ולפי שעילם סמוכה לבבל עמד הוא בשוק התחתון ודרש ודן קל וחומר ומה עילם שלא באה אלא לעזור את הכשדים וכו' כמה שהיא בסנהדרין [שם כח, א].

for rebelling against them.

אֶלָּא הֵיכָא דְאוֹרֵי בְּחַיָּיבֵי מִיתוֹת בֵּית דִּין – **But** in regard to a case **where [the sage] ruled in** a matter that is **subject to capital punishment,** the Baraisa's statement is difficult, מֵעִיקָּרָא נַמִּי בַּר קְטָלָא הוּא – for **even before** the Sanhedrin overruled him, **[the sage]** would have been **liable to the death penalty** if he acted in accordance with his own erroneous opinion. Of what import is the Baraisa's statement – that if he follows his own ruling he is considered a rebellious sage – in regard to such a case?

The Gemara answers:

מֵעִיקָּרָא בָּעֵי הַתְרָאָה – **Before** the Sanhedrin overruled him, **[the sage]** would have **required warning** to incur the death penalty for his sin.[22] הַשְׁתָּא לֹא בָּעֵי הַתְרָאָה – But **now** that the Sanhedrin overruled the opinion of the sage, **he does not require warning** to incur the death penalty.[23]

The Gemara counters:

מֵסִית דְּלֹא בָּעֵי הַתְרָאָה מַאי אִיכָּא לְמֵימַר – If a sage rebels by being **an instigator** to idolatry, **who does not** normally **require warning** to incur the death penalty, **what is there to say?**[24] Of what import is the Baraisa's ruling in regard to that case?

The Gemara answers:

מֵעִיקָּרָא אִי אָמַר טַעְמָא – **Before** the Sanhedrin overruled him, **if [the sage] would say a reason** to acquit himself of liability for his instigation,[25] מְקַבְּלִינַן מִינֵּיה – **we would accept it from him.**[26] הַשְׁתָּא אִי אָמַר טַעְמָא – But **now** that the Sanhedrin overruled him and he defied the Sanhedrin, **if he says a reason** to acquit himself, לֹא מְקַבְּלִינַן מִינֵּיה – **we do not accept it from him.**[27]

Mishnah חוֹמֶר בְּדִבְרֵי סוֹפְרִים מִבְּדִבְרֵי תוֹרָה – There is **a greater stringency** attached **to the words of the *Soferim* than to the words of the Torah**, with respect to the law of a rebellious sage.[28]

For example:

הָאוֹמֵר אֵין תְּפִילִּין – **If [a sage] states, "There is no** commandment of **tefillin"** – כְּדֵי לַעֲבוֹר עַל דִּבְרֵי תוֹרָה – **in order to transgress the words of the Torah** – פָּטוּר – **he is exempt.**[29] חָמֵשׁ טוֹטָפוֹת – But if he states, "There are **five compartments** to tefillin," rather than four – לְהוֹסִיף עַל דִּבְרֵי סוֹפְרִים – in order **to add to the words of the *Soferim*** – חַיָּיב – **he is liable.**[30][31]

Gemara The Gemara cites a related ruling:

אָמַר רַבִּי אֶלְעָזָר אָמַר רַבִּי אוֹשַׁעְיָא – **R' Elazar said in the name of R' Oshaya:** אֵינוֹ חַיָּיב אֶלָּא עַל דָּבָר שֶׁעִיקָּרוֹ מִדִּבְרֵי תוֹרָה – **[The rebellious sage] is liable only for** contradicting the Sanhedrin in **a matter whose essence is stated in the Torah,** וּפֵירוּשׁוֹ מִדִּבְרֵי סוֹפְרִים – **and whose elaboration is stated by the *Soferim*,** וְיֵשׁ בּוֹ לְהוֹסִיף – **and which has** an element **to** which one can **add,**[32] וְאִם הוֹסִיף גּוֹרֵעַ – **and if one adds** to that

NOTES

22. As a rule, the death penalty is not imposed on a capital offender unless he was warned before committing the transgression that it is a capital offense.

23. The *zakein mamrei* is put to death for acting in defiance of the Sanhedrin, not for the actual offense that he commits. Thus, he need not be forewarned that it is a capital offense. He must, however, be forewarned that rebelling against the Sanhedrin is a capital offense (*Tos. HaRosh*; see also *Rambam, Commentary to the Mishnah,* 89a).

24. One who instigates a fellow Jew to idolatry is liable to death even if he was not forewarned (see 67a). If a sage ruled erroneously that a certain statement is not considered instigation and he acted in accord with his own ruling, he would incur the death penalty without warning even if he was not acting in defiance of the Sanhedrin (*Rashi*).

25. I.e. he would argue that his statement was not considered instigation.

26. I.e. although according to the accepted halachah his statement was regarded as instigation, if he offered a valid reason that it should not be regarded as such, the Sanhedrin would weigh his arguments in consideration of overturning the accepted halachah (cf. *Riaz, Kuntres HaRaayos*).

27. Since he heard the ruling of the Sanhedrin and he defied them, he is liable to the death penalty as a rebellious sage regardless of the validity of his argument (*Rashi*).

28. I.e. the laws of the Torah that are understood only through the elucidation of the *Soferim* have a greater stringency attached to them than the laws of the Torah that are stated explicitly. The *Soferim* were the early Sages.

29. He is exempt from punishment as a rebellious sage because this is such an obvious distortion that it cannot be viewed as a ruling of Torah law (*Rashi*).

30. The number of compartments in the tefillin box that is worn upon the head is not stated explicitly in the Torah. Rather, the *Soferim* found an allusion in the Torah that it is to be made of four compartments (see above, 4b). [Each compartment contains a scroll inscribed with a certain Scriptural passage. In contrast, the tefillin box that is worn on the arm consists of only one compartment. It contains one scroll inscribed with all four Scriptural passages.] Since the law that the tefillin box worn on the head contains four compartments is known to us only through the exposition of the *Soferim,* a ruling by a sage that there should be five compartments instead of four is considered a legal (albeit incorrect) ruling. It is in this respect that contradicting the words of the *Soferim* invokes a greater stringency than contradicting a law stated explicitly in the Torah (see *Rashi*).

[*Maharal* (*Be'er HaGolah* §2) adds the following explanation: The reason the Torah imposed the death penalty on a rebellious sage is to preclude the proliferation of halachic disputes in matters decided by the Sanhedrin, thus ensuring the continuity of Torah law. It is necessary to deter people only from disputing the Sages' clarifications of the Torah's commandments. If a scholar contradicts an explicit Scriptural statement nobody will follow his ruling since its folly will be patently evident.]

31. The Gemara above (87a) cited a Tannaic dispute concerning the type of ruling for which a rebellious sage is liable. R' Meir maintains that one is not liable to the special punishment for a rebellious sage unless his ruling involved a matter that is subject to *kares* when transgressed intentionally and to a *chatas* offering when transgressed unintentionally. R' Yehudah maintains that the rebellious sage must rule on a matter whose essence is in the written Torah but was elucidated by the *Soferim.* R' Shimon maintains that the matter need not be mentioned in the Torah; rather, one is considered a rebellious sage even if his ruling involves a matter whose essence is not found in the written Torah.

All three Tannaim agree with the first statement of this Mishnah: If a sage denies an explicit commandment of the Torah he is exempt from the punishment imposed on a rebellious sage, because his decision cannot be viewed as a ruling of Torah law.

The second statement of the Mishnah, however, cannot follow the opinion of R' Meir, for one who transgresses the commandment of tefillin is not liable to *kares* if he sins intentionally nor to a *chatas* offering if he sins unintentionally. Rather, the Mishnah follows the opinion of R' Yehudah [or that of R' Shimon] (*Ran* to 87a ד״ה ר׳ יהודה; see below, note 35).

32. I.e. it must be a commandment which, according to the explanation handed down by the *Soferim,* is performed with an element [e.g. the tefillin box] that contains a specific number of units [e.g. four compartments] to which a rebellious sage can add by ruling that it is to contain a greater number of units [e.g. five compartments] (*Rashi*).

[א]בן סורר ומורה שרצו אביו ואמו למחול לו מוחלין לו זקן ממרא שרצו בית דינו למחול לו מוחלין לו וכשבאתי אצל חבירי שבדרום על שנים הודו לי על זקן ממרא [ב]לא הודו לי כדי שלא ירבו מחלוקת בישראל תיובתא תניא (א) אמר רבי יוסי [ג]מתחילה לא היו מרבין מחלוקת בישראל אלא בית דין של שבעים ואחד יושבין בלשכת הגזית ושני בתי דינין של עשרים ושלשה אחד יושב על פתח הר הבית ואחד יושב על פתח העזרה ושאר בתי דינין של עשרים ושלשה יושבין בכל עיירות ישראל הוצרך הדבר לשאול שואלין מבית דין שבעירן אם שמעו אמרו להן ואם לאו באין לזה שסמוך לעירן אם שמעו אמרו להם ואם לאו באין לזה שעל פתח הר הבית אם שמעו אמרו להם ואם לאו באין לזה שעל פתח העזרה ואומר כך דרשתי וכך דרשו חבירי כך למדתי וכך למדו חבירי אם שמעו אמרו להם ואם לאו אלו ואלו באין ללשכת הגזית [ד]ששם יושבין מתמיד של שחר עד תמיד של בין הערבים [ה]ובשבתות ובימים טובים יושבין בחיל [ו]נשאלה שאלה בפניהם אם שמעו אמרו להם ואם לאו עומדין למנין רבו המטמאים טמאו רבו המטהרין טהרו (ב) משרבו תלמידי שמאי והלל שלא שמשו כל צרכן רבו מחלוקת בישראל ונעשית תורה כשתי תורות [ז]משם כותבין ושולחין בכל מקומות כל מי שהוא חכם ושפל ברך ודעת הבריות נוחה הימנו יהא דיין בעירו (ג) משם מעלין אותו להר הבית משם לעזרה משם ללשכת הגזית (ד) שלחו מתם איזהו בן העולם הבא ענוותן (ה) ושפל ברך שייף עייל שייף ונפיק וגרים באורייתא תדירא ולא מחזיק טיבותא לנפשיה יהבו ביה רבנן עינייהון ברב עולא בר אבא: חזר לעירו ושנה: ת"ר [ח]אינו חייב עד שיעשה כהוראתו או שיורה לאחרים ויעשו כהוראתו בשלמא יורה לאחרים ויעשו כהוראתו מעיקרא לאו בר קטלא הוא והשתא בר קטלא הוא אלא שיעשה כהוראתו מעיקרא נמי בר קטלא הוא התינח היכא דאורי בחלב ודם דמעיקרא לאו בר קטלא הוא והשתא בר קטלא הוא אלא היכא דאורי בחייבי מיתות ב"ד מעיקרא נמי בר קטלא הוא מעיקרא בעי התראה השתא [ט]לא בעי התראה מסית דלא בעי התראה מאי איכא למימר מעיקרא אי אמר טעמא מקבלינן מיניה השתא אי אמר טעמא [י]לא מקבלינן מיניה: **מתני'** חומר בדברי סופרים מבדברי תורה האומר אין תפילין כדי לעבור על ד"ת פטור [כ]חמש טוטפות להוסיף על דברי סופרים חייב: **גמ'** אמר ר' אלעזר אמר ר' אושעיא אינו חייב אלא על דבר שעיקרו מדברי תורה ופירושו מדברי סופרים ויש בו להוסיף ואם הוסיף גורע ואין לנו [ל]אלא תפילין אליבא דרבי יהודה והאיכא לולב דעיקרו מדברי תורה ופירושו מדברי סופרים ויש בו להוסיף ואם הוסיף גורע בלולב מאי סבירא לן אי סבירא לן (ו) דלולב [מ]אין צריך אגד האי לחודיה קאי והאי לחודיה קאי ואי סבירא לן (ז) דצריך אגד גרוע ועומד הוא והאיכא ציצית דעיקרו מדברי תורה ופירושו מדברי סופרים ויש בו להוסיף ואם הוסיף גורע בציצית מאי סבירא לן אי סבירא לן דקשר העליון לאו דאורייתא האי לחודיה קאי והאי לחודיה קאי ואי סבירא לן

דקשר

בן סורר ומורה. אף לאחר שהתרו בו וקלקל והלקוהו וחזר וקלקל אם רצו למחול ולא הביאוהו לבית דין מוחלין לו שהכתוב תלה בהם ותפשו בו: **תיובתא.** מדתלי טעמא בשלא ירבו מחלוקת ש"מ אפי' הוא אומר מפי השמועה והן אומרין כך הוא בעינינו: **יושבין בחיל.** מפני שהעם רב ומקום צר להם בלשכה אי נמי שלא יהו נראים כיושבין בדין שבלשכת הגזית היו דנים וזה עיקר: **משם מעלין אותו.** להיות דיין בהר הבית כשמת אחד מהם ויושב שם עד שמת אחד משל עזרה ומעלין את זה שם וכולן יש בהם מעלה זה מזה: **שייף.** שוחה נכנס ושוחה יוצא והכי אמרי' בב"ב (דף ז.) גבי תקרת הבית שנחבטה שוף עול שוף פוק: **מעיקרא.** קודם שבא לבית דין שבלשכת הגזית לישאל לא הוה מיחייב קטלא כל כמה דלא עביד איהו גופיה: **מעיקרא נמי בר קטלא הוא.** אם עושה עבירה שיש בה מיתת בית דין הוה מיקטיל: **מסית דלא בעי התראה.** אם היה מסית ומורה טעם היתר ולומר אין בלשון הזה הסתה מעיקרא נמי מקטיל בלא התראה: **אי אמר טעמא לזכותא.** לאצוליה אבל השתא אי אמר טעמא לא מקבלינן שהרי שמע מפי ב"ד שלא לעשות והמרה: **מתני' האומר אין תפילין פטור.** דאין זו הוראה דזיל קרי בי רב הוא: **חמש טוטפות יש.** שאע"פ שאין דבר זה אלא להוסיף על דברי סופרים חייב דמדרש דסופרים הוא לטטפת לטטפת לטוטפות הרי כאן ד': **גמ' ויש בו להוסיף.** על מה שפירשו חכמים: **ואם הוסיף גורע.** ופוסל הראשון בתוספתו: **ואין לנו אלא תפילין.** שעיקרן בתורה ופירושן מדברי סופרים שהם ד' בתים ויש להוסיף חמשה או יותר ואם הוסיף גורע דקא עבר בבל תוסיף ולא עבד מצוה: **ואליבא דרבי יהודה.** אמר ר' אושעיא למילתיה דאמר לעיל עד דאיכא תורה ויורוך ואית דאמרי אין לנו אלא תפילין ואליבא דרבי יהודה דאמר צריך להדביק במנחות בהקומץ רבה (דף לד:) ולא נהירא לי דההיא בתפילין של יד קאי ומתני' טוטפות תאני והיינו דראש ועוד מדקא מקשי בסיפא אי דעבד ארבעה בתים כו' שמע מינה בשל ראש קיימין דאי בשל יד בית אחד הוא דקא הוי: **האי לחודיה קאי.** ואין זה גורע: **גרוע ועומד.** דמתחילתו לא עשה כהוגן שאגד שם תוספת מצוה ואנן בעינן גורע דהשתא שהיה מתחילתו כשר ופוסלו בתוספתו: **ופירושו מדברי סופרים.** ד' חוטין דילפינן גדיל ב' גדילים ד': **קשר עליון.** שעושין סמוך לכנף כשנתלו החוטין ועל ידיהן נעשין חיבור לטלית לאו דאורייתא ((ח) אלא) הלכה למשה מסיני דפלוגתא היא במנחות (ט) (דף לט.): **האי לחודיה קאי.** דכיון דלא נקשר אינו חיבור עם השאר והראוי למצוה היא המצוה והעודף כמי שאינו:

שאינו

מסית דלא בעי התראה מאי איכא למימר. לאו אליבא דר' מאיר פריך דאמסית לא מיחייב דאין בו כרת:

ואין לנו אלא תפילין ואליבא דר' יהודה. כל הנך דרשות דדרשינן לעיל מקרא דכי יפלא ° לא חייש:

אי סבירא לן דלולב אין צריך אגד וכו'. משמע אבל אי סבירא לן דצריך אגד לא אמרינן האי לחודיה קאי והאי לחודיה קאי והכי נמי אמרי' בריש לולב הגזול (סוכה דף לא.) דקאמר רבי יהודה אין אוגדין את הלולב אלא במינו מאי טעמא דכיון דאמר ר' יהודה לולב צריך אגד אי עבדי ליה ממין אחר הוה ליה ה' מינין ותימה דאמר התם (שם:) ד' מינין שבלולב כשם שאין פוחתין מהן כך אין מוסיפין עליהם ופריך פשיטא ומשני מהו דתימא הואיל ואמר רבי יהודה לולב צריך אגד אי אייתי מינא אחרינא האי לחודיה קאי והאי לחודיה קאי קמ"ל מאי קא תלי טעמא דהאי לחודיה קאי משום דלולב צריך אגד אדרבה מטעם זה יש לנו לומר יותר דאסור ומיהו י"ל דהתם בדמנח ליה חוץ לאגד אבל קשה דמשמע דמסיק לר' יהודה דלא אמר האי לחודיה וכ"ש לרבנן והכא משמע דלרבנן אמר האי לחודיה קאי וי"ל דהתם מדרבנן אסור ור"ח ל"ג התם הואיל ואמר ר' יהודה וזהו לשונו מהו דתימא הואיל ואמרו חכמים בין אגוד בין שאינו אגוד כשר הלכך אין צריך אגד והאי יתירה דמוסיף על הד' לחודיה קאי ולא מיפסל ביה קמ"ל ומיהו תימה אמאי לא משכח לולב לרבי יהודה בכי האי גוונא שאגד ג' מינין בפני עצמן דנעשה בכשרות ואחר כך אגד עמהן מין אחר דהוה ליה מוסיף גורע ויש לומר כיון דקודם נטילתו נפסל הוה ליה גרוע ועומד אבל תפילין אם הניחן בראשו בכשרות והניח גבייהו בית חמישי הרי זה מוסיף גורע שפוסלן ומבטל מצות שעל ראשו ולא דמי ללולב דאם נטלו ובעודו בידו הוסיף מין חמישי אין זה מבטל מצותו דמדאגביה נפק ביה:

קשר

עין משפט נר מצוה

נז א מיי' פ"ז מהלכות ממרים הלכה ח:
נח ב מיי' פ"ג שם הל' ד סמג עשין קיא ולאוין ריז:
נט ג מיי' שם פ"א הל' ד סמג שם:
ס ד ה מיי' פ"ג מהל' סנהדרין הלכה א:
סא ו מיי' פ"א מהל' ממרים הל' ד סמג עשין קיא ולאוין ריז:
סב ז מיי' פ"ב מהל' סנהדרין הלכה ח:
סג ח מיי' פ"ג מהל' ממרים הל' ה ופ"ד הלכה א סמג עשין קיא ולאוין ריז:
סד ט י מיי' שם פ"ג הלכה ח:
סה כ ל מיי' פ"ד שם הלכה ג סמג עשין קיא ולאוין ריז:
סו מ מיי' פ"ז מהל' לולב הלכה ו סמג עשין מד טוש"ע א"ח סי' תרנא סעיף א:

גליון הש"ס

תוס' ד"ה ואין וכו' לא חייש. עיין בטורי אבן באבני שהם לר"ה דף כ"ז ע"א ד"ה מצות:

מסורת הש"ס

א) [תוספ' פ"ז תוספ' חגיגה פרק ב], ב) [סוטה מז:], ג) [תוספ' שקלים ספ"ג], ד) [לעיל יז: וש"נ], ה) [בתענית טז. פירש"י שפל ברך עניו וצ"ל דכמה עניני ענוה יש ועי' רש"א ח"א], ו) [סוכה ל:], ז) [סוכה לא.], ח) [צ"ל כלומר], ט) [עי' תוס' פט. לקמן בסמוך ד"ה קשר].

ליקוטי רש"י

זקן ממרא. שהמרה על ב"ד של לשכת הגזית ומיתתו בחנק [סוטה כה:]. **האומר אין תפילין.** זקן ממרא מן הדבר ולא כל דבר דהא כתי' מן הדבר ותנן באלו הן הנחנקין (סנהדרין דף פח:) האומר אין תפלין לעבור על דברי תורה פטור חמש טוטפות להוסיף על דברי סופרים חייב דהיינו מן הדבר ולא כל דבר [הוריות ד.]. **לולב צריך אגד.** הלכך כל הנאגד עמו הוי מן המצוה ונמצא עובר בבל תוסיף אם יאגד מין חמישי [סוכה לא.].

[מכאן שייך לדף פט.].

קשר עליון. היינו נמי ההוא קשר למטה הלכה למשה מסיני כלומר קשר אחד בציצית מיהא דאורייתא והכי נקט עליון משום דאי לא עביד אלא חד קשר בסופו עביד ליה שמקיים את הגדיל כולו. **דאורייתא.** ואפי' יכול לכרוך יפה ולהתקיים בלא קשר יום או יומים פסולה [מנחות לט.]. **וכל העם ישמעו.** מכאן שממתינין לו עד הרגל וממיתין אותו ברגל [דברים יז, יג]. **לרשות הבעל.** כגון מסרה האב לשלוחי הבעל ועדיין היא בדרך ולא קרינן בה בית אביה. **לאותה מיתה.** שהיו מחייבין את הנידון. **ובועלה.** כלומר וכל הבועלים נידונין כמיתת הנבעלת חוץ מבועל בת כהן [לקמן צ.]. **מקדימים לאותה מיתה.** כלומר אין להם לצפות מיתה אחרת אלא מסכימין לאותה מיתה שנגמר בה דינו של נדון. **חוץ מזוממי בת כהן.** נשואה שאע"פ שנגמר דינה לשריפה על פיהם הם בחנק כדילפינן התם סנהדרין (דף נ) היא בשריפה ואין בועלה בשריפה אלא בחנק כשאר אשת איש והזוממין מסכימין למיתה שחייבו את הבועל דכתיב כאשר זמם לעשות לאחיו ולא לאחותו [מכות ב.]. **זוממי בת כהן.** לעשות לאחיו מה תלמוד לומר לאחיו למד על זוממי בת כהן נשואה שאינן בשריפה אלא כמיתת הבועל שהוא בחנק שנאמר היא באש תשרף (ויקרא כא, ט) היא ולא בועלה לכך נאמר כאן לאחיו כאשר זמם לעשות לאחיו ולא כאשר זמם לעשות לאחותו אבל בכל שאר מיתות השוה הכתוב אשה לאיש וזוממי אשה נהרגין כזוממי איש כגון שהעידוה שהרגה את הנפש שחללה את השבת נהרגין במיתתה שלא מיעט כאן אחותו אלא במקום שיש לקיים בהן הזמה במיתת הבועל [דברים יט, יט]. שהיא והן נהרגין ולא במיתה אחת דהיא בשריפה והן במיתת הבועל כגון באו עדים והזימו את הראשונים וחייבום מיתת הבועל ולא מיתתה דכתיב (דברים יט) כאשר זמם לעשות לאחיו ולא לאחותו כדאמר באלו הן הנחנקין (סנהדרין נ). **בועלה.** דהיא בשריפה אבל בועלה נידון כשאר בועל בת ישראל דבועל ארוסה בסקילה ובועל נשואה בחנק דכתיב (ויקרא כא) היא באש תשרף היא ולא בועלה היא ולא זוממיה [לעיל מה.]. **וזוממי בת כהן.** אף על פי שהם היו מחייבין אותה שריפה אין נדונין אלא במיתה שהיו מחייבין לבועל והיינו חנק כשאר בא על אשת איש כדמפרש קרא היא תשרף ולא בועלה וזוממיה ילפינן מכאשר זמם לעשות לאחיו ולא לאחותו. **ובועלה.** בנשואה בת כהן קמיירי אבל ארוסה בועלה בסקילה [לעיל פד:]. **אשר לא צויתיו לדבר.** אבל צויתיו לחבירו. **ואשר ידבר בשם אלהים אחרים.** אפילו כיון את ההלכה לאסור את האסור ולהתיר את המותר. **ומת.** בחנק שלשה מיתתן בידי אדם המתנבא מה שלא שמע ומה שלא נאמר לו ונאמר לחבירו והמתנבא בשם עבודה זרה אבל הכובש את נבואתו והעובר על דברי נביא והעובר על דברי עצמו מיתתו בידי שמים שנאמר (פסוק יט) אנכי אדרוש מעמו [דברים יח, כ]. **ויצא הרוח.** פתרון ויצא המלאך שהרי אומר לעיל וכל צבא השמים וגו' ועתה יצא אחד מן המלאכים ויאמר אני אפתנו כדאמר (תהלים קד) עושה מלאכיו רוחות ולפיכך קדם ואמר לעיל וכל צבא השמים עומדים שלא תתמה כשתאמר ויצא הרוח מי הוא ומהיכן יצא וכשאמר וכל צבא השמים עומדים כדי להודיע מהיכן יצא משאר הרוחות העומדים עליו, ורבותינו פירשו זהו רוחו של נבות. **בפי כל נביאיו.** שישים דבר בפיהם לאמר עלה והצלח ויעלה ויפול מכלל שהיו נביאי אמת שלא היו מתנבאים כי אם מה שישים השם בפיהם [דה"ב יח]. **זה בכה.** אני אפתנו ככה [שבת קמט:]. **תפתה וגם תוכל.** לפי שיש מפתה הבא לפתות חבירו פעמים שהמפותה מבין שזה רוצה לפתותו והוא נזהר ואינו שומע להתפתות אבל באחאב תפתה וגם תוכל [דה"ב שם]. **צא ממחיצתי.** הפורע נוקם חמתו וקנאתו מחריב ביתיה, כרוח של נבות שנקם כעסו מאחאב ויצא ממחיצתו של הקדוש ברוך הוא. **רוחו של נבות.** שלפי שהוא הרג נבות היה רוחו מחזר לפתותו ולהפילו [לקמן קב:]. **תפלצתך.** ל' בהלה שהיית ממהר ונבהל לעורר שטימתך לאחיך ויש לועזין לשון פלצות ויש לועזין לשון מפלצת [ירמיהו מט, טז]. **האין פה נביא לה' עוד.** מקובלני אין ב' נביאים מתנבאים בל' א' ואלו כולם לשון א' אומרים [מ"א כב, ז]. **את קשת עילם.** את תקות עילם [ירמיהו מט, לה]. **שברתי את עול מלך בבל.** אמרו רבותינו מי הטעה את חנניה שמע שהיה ירמיה מתנב' בשוק העליון הנני שובר את קשת עילם (ירמיה מט) ונבואה זו בסוף הספר נאמרה בראשית ממלכת צדקיהו כמו שמפורש שם ולפי שעילם סמוכה לבבל עמד הוא בשוק התחתון ודרש ודן קל וחומר ומה עילם שלא באה אלא לעזור את הכשדים וכו' כמה שהיא בסנהדרין [שם כח, א].

element **he detracts.**[33]

R' Elazar concludes:

וְאֵין לָנוּ אֶלָּא תְּפִילִּין אַלִיבָּא דְּרַבִּי יְהוּדָה – And the only commandment **we have** that fulfills these criteria **is** the commandment of **tefillin,**[34] and R' Oshaya's ruling is **in accordance with** the opinion of **R' Yehudah.**[35]

The Gemara objects to the statement that the only commandment that meets these criteria is that of tefillin:

וְהָאִיכָּא לוּלָב – But there is also the commandment of ***lulav*,**[36] **דְּעִיקָּרוֹ מִדִּבְרֵי תוֹרָה וּפֵירוּשׁוֹ מִדִּבְרֵי סוֹפְרִים** – which is a matter **whose essence is stated in the Torah and whose elaboration is stated by the *Soferim*, וְיֵשׁ בּוֹ לְהוֹסִיף וְאִם הוֹסִיף גּוֹרֵעַ – and it has** an element **to** which one can **add, and if one adds** to it **he detracts.**[37] **– ? –**

The Gemara responds:

בְּלוּלָב מַאי סְבִירָא לָן – What opinion **do we hold in regard to *lulav***, i.e. in regard to whether the species that are taken with the *lulav* must be bound together?[38] **אִי סְבִירָא לָן דְּלוּלָב אֵין צָרִיךְ אֶגֶד – If we hold** the opinion **that the** species taken with the ***lulav* need not be bound** together, **הַאי לְחוּדֵיהּ קָאֵי וְהַאי לְחוּדֵיהּ קָאֵי** – then even if one adds to the commandment by taking an extra species, **this one** (the required species) **stands by itself and that one** (the extra species) **stands by itself.** I.e. the extra species does not detract from the validity of the others.[39] **וְאִי סְבִירָא לָן דְּצָרִיךְ אֶגֶד – And if we hold** the opinion **that** the species taken with **[the *lulav*] need be bound** together, **גָּרוּעַ וְעוֹמֵד הוּא** – then if one adds to the commandment by binding an extra species with the *lulav,* **[the bound species] lack** validity **from the outset.**[40] And according to the criteria set forth by R' Elazar, the law of the rebellious sage, applies only to a case where the element used in the performance of a commandment was initially valid and one detracted by adding to it.[41] Thus, the commandment of *lulav* does not meet those criteria.

NOTES

33. I.e. and by adding to the element, he disqualifies it from use in the performance of the mitzvah (*Rashi*).

34. The mitzvah of tefillin is stated explicitly in the Torah (*Deuteronomy* 6:8); the number of compartments in the tefillin box that is placed upon the head was clarified by the *Soferim;* it is possible to add to the tefillin box by making five or more compartments; and if one adds any compartments to the tefillin he detracts. If one dons tefillin that contain an extra compartment he transgresses the prohibition (*Deuteronomy* 13:1): לֹא־תֹסֵף עָלָיו, *You shall not add to it* (any commandment of the Torah), and he does not fulfill the commandment of wearing tefillin (*Rashi*; see *Binyan Shlomo*).

35. For it is R' Yehudah who maintains (above, 87a) that the the law of *zakein mamrei* applies only with respect to commandments that are written in the Torah and were clarified by the *Soferim* (*Rashi*; see also *Aruch LaNer*).

Ran (87a) raises the following questions: It seems implausible that according to R' Yehudah the law of *zakein mamrei* applies only if a sage issues one specific ruling concerning the commandment of tefillin. Furthermore, the Gemara stated above that the Sanhedrin may not pardon a *zakein mamrei* lest halachic disputes proliferate. Need we fear the proliferation of disputes concerning the number of compartments in the tefillin box? And furthermore, the Gemara above (87a-88a) expounded the Scriptural passage of *zakein mamrei* as alluding to disputes concerning many different commandments, not only tefillin. How can all this be reconciled with our Gemara?

Ran therefore explains that the Gemara means to single out tefillin as the only *positive commandment* to which the law of *zakein mamrei* applies. But with respect to negative commandments, R' Yehudah maintains that the law of *zakein mamrei* applies to any number of Biblical prohibitions that were stated in the Torah and clarified by the Sages. This includes, but is not limited to, the laws of *niddah, tzaraas* and all the other cases listed above (87a-88a). The reason for this distinction is the following: A *zakein mamrei* is liable only if he rules that one is to *act* contrary to a ruling of the Sanhedrin. Thus, if a sage permits doing something that the Sanhedrin defined as the subject of a negative commandment, he is liable. However, if he rules that one is to refrain from doing something that the Sanhedrin defined as the subject of a positive commandment, he is not liable. The only case in which a sage can possibly issue a ruling whereby one would actively transgress a positive commandment is that of tefillin, for only in the case of tefillin can one actively ruin his performance of the mitzvah — by adding a fifth compartment to the box.

According to this explanation, the Tannaic dispute between R' Meir, R' Yehudah and R' Shimon runs as follows: R' Meir maintains that the law of *zakein mamrei* applies in regard to any commandment that is subject to *kares* when transgressed intentionally and requires a *chatas* offering when transgressed unintentionally. R' Yehudah maintains that *kares* and *chatas* are not critical factors. Rather, the law of *zakein mamrei* applies in regard to any commandment whose essence is in the written Torah but required the clarification of the *Soferim.* This includes the positive commandment of tefillin, as well as many negative commandments that are not subject to *kares*. However, it excludes commandments — even *kares*-type commandments — that did not require the clarification of the *Soferim* as well as commandments that are not mentioned at all in the written Torah. R' Shimon maintains that the law of *zakein mamrei* applies even in regard to laws whose essence is not in the written Torah. All agree, however, that the *zakein mamrei* is liable only if his ruling leads to an *active* transgression (*Chidushei HaRan* ibid.; see also 87a note 23, cf. *Tosafos* ד״ה ואין לנו and *Rambam, Hil. Mamrim* ch. 4; see also *Turei Aven* [*Avnei Shoham*] to *Rosh Hashanah* 27a ד״ה מצות).

36. I.e. the mitzvah to take in one's hand four species of plants on the festival of Sukkos. The four species are the *lulav* (palm branch), *esrog* (citron), *hadasim* (myrtle branches) and *aravos* (willow branches).

37. The commandment to take four species is stated explicitly in the Torah (*Leviticus* 23:40); however, the Torah does not explicitly name these species. Rather, the *Soferim* explained that the species to which the Torah alludes are the *lulav, esrog, hadasim* and *aravos* (see *Sukkah* 32a,b; 33b; 35a). It is possible to add to this commandment by ruling that a fifth species is to be taken. And if one follows such a ruling and takes five species instead of four, he spoils his performance of the mitzvah and he transgresses the prohibition (*Deuteronomy* ibid.): *You shall not add to it* (*Chidushei HaRan*, second explanation; see *Sukkah* 31a; see also *Tosafos* ד״ה אי and *Rashi* to *Deuteronomy* 4:2 and 13:1).

38. It is customary to bind together the *lulav, hadasim* and *aravos.* The Gemara (*Sukkah* 31a) cites a dispute whether it is obligatory to bind them together or it is merely a way of beautifying the mitzvah [הִדּוּר מִצְוָה].

39. If one holds an extra species in his hand while he takes the four required species, he does not spoil his performance of the mitzvah, since the fifth species is unconnected with the others. [This holds true even if one binds the extra species with the others, since the binding is legally insignificant (*Aruch LaNer;* see also *Margaliyos HaYam*).] Although by holding a fifth species one transgresses the prohibition (ibid.), *you shall not add* (cf. *Chidushei HaRan*), he nevertheless fulfills the mitzvah of *lulav* with the first four species. Hence, a *zakein mamrei* does not incur the death penalty for ruling that one is to take five species (*Tosafos, Sukkah* 31b ד״ה הואיל; see also *Raavad, Hil. Mamrim* 4:3 and *Rashi* to *Deuteronomy* ibid., and *Binyan Shlomo*).

40. I.e. they were bound together faultily in the first place, since an extra species was combined with the others (*Rashi*).

41. *Rashi.* As explained above (note 35), the *zakein mamrei* must issue a ruling whereby one would actively violate a mitzvah. And if one began his performance of a mitzvah with a faulty article (e.g. five species bound together) he merely failed to perform the mitzvah rather than actively violating it (*Binyan Shlomo*). Rather, we must be discussing a case where the mitzvah was being performed, and he then "violated" it by adding something to it.

Even if one would initially bind together only the proper number of species and then add another one he would also not detract from a valid performance of the mitzvah. For if he did not take the species in his hand until the extra one was bound with the others, he began his performance with a faulty article. And if he took the proper species in his hand and he then bound in the extra one, he had successfully performed the mitzvah before binding in the extra one. The mitzvah of *lulav* requires

[א]בן סורר ומורה שרצו אביו ואמו למחול לו מוחלין לו זקן ממרא שרצו בית דינו למחול לו מוחלין לו וכשבאתי אצל חבירי שבדרום על שנים הודו לי על זקן ממרא [ב]לא הודו לי כדי שלא ירבו מחלוקת בישראל תיובתא תניא [א]אמר רבי יוסי [ג]מתחילה לא היו מרבין מחלוקת בישראל אלא בית דין של שבעים ואחד יושבין בלשכת הגזית ושני בתי דינין של עשרים ושלשה אחד יושב על פתח הר הבית ואחד יושב על פתח העזרה ושאר בתי דינין של עשרים ושלשה יושבין בכל עיירות ישראל הוצרך הדבר לשאול שואלין מבית דין שבעירן אם שמעו אמרו להן ואם לאו באין לזה שסמוך לעירן אם שמעו אמרו להם ואם לאו באין לזה שעל פתח הר הבית אם שמעו אמרו להם ואם לאו באין לזה שעל פתח העזרה ואומר כך דרשתי וכך דרשו חבירי כך למדתי וכך למדו חבירי אם שמעו אמרו להם ואם לאו אלו ואלו באין ללשכת הגזית [ד]ששם יושבין מתמיד של שחר עד תמיד של בין הערבים [ה]ובשבתות ובימים טובים יושבין בחיל [ו]נשאלה שאלה בפניהם אם שמעו אמרו להם ואם לאו עומדין למנין רבו המטמאים טמאו רבו המטהרין טהרו [ב]משרבו תלמידי שמאי והלל שלא שמשו כל צרכן רבו מחלוקת בישראל ונעשית תורה כשתי תורות [ז]משם כותבין ושולחין בכל מקומות כל מי שהוא חכם ושפל ברך ודעת הבריות נוחה הימנו יהא דיין בעירו [ג]משם מעלין אותו להר הבית משם לעזרה משם ללשכת הגזית [ד]שלחו מתם איזהו בן העולם הבא ענוותן [ה]ושפל ברך שייף עייל שייף ונפיק וגרים באורייתא תדירא ולא מחזיק טיבותא לנפשיה יהבו ביה רבנן עינייהון ברב עולא בר אבא: חזר לעירו ושנה: ת"ר [ח]אינו חייב עד שיעשה כהוראתו או שיורה לאחרים ויעשו כהוראתו בשלמא יורה לאחרים ויעשו כהוראתו מעיקרא לאו בר קטלא הוא והשתא בר קטלא הוא אלא שיעשה כהוראתו מעיקרא נמי בר קטלא הוא התינח היכא דאורי בחלב ודם דמעיקרא לאו בר קטלא הוא והשתא בר קטלא הוא אלא היכא דאורי בחייבי מיתות ב"ד מעיקרא נמי בר קטלא הוא מעיקרא בעי התראה השתא [ט]לא בעי התראה מסית דלא בעי התראה מאי איכא למימר מעיקרא אי אמר טעמא מקבלינן מיניה השתא אי אמר טעמא [י]לא מקבלינן מיניה: **מתני'** חומר בדברי סופרים מבדברי תורה האומר אין תפילין כדי לעבור על ד"ת פטור [כ]חמש טוטפות להוסיף על דברי סופרים חייב: **גמ'** אמר ר' אלעזר אמר ר' אושעיא אינו חייב אלא על דבר שעיקרו מדברי תורה ופירושו מדברי סופרים ויש בו להוסיף ואם הוסיף גורע ואין לנו [ל]אלא תפילין אליבא דרבי יהודה והאיכא לולב דעיקרו מדברי תורה ופירושו מדברי סופרים ויש בו להוסיף ואם הוסיף גורע בלולב מאי סבירא לן אי סבירא לן [ו]דלולב [מ]אין צריך אגד האי לחודיה קאי והאי לחודיה קאי ואי סבירא לן [ז]דצריך אגד גרוע ועומד הוא והאיכא ציצית דעיקרו מדברי תורה ופירושו מדברי סופרים ויש בו להוסיף ואם הוסיף גורע בציצית מאי סבירא לן אי סבירא לן דקשר העליון לאו דאורייתא האי לחודיה קאי והאי לחודיה קאי ואי סבירא לן

דקשר

רש"י

בן סורר ומורה. אף לאחר שהתרו בו וקלקל והלקוהו וחזר וקלקל אם רצו למחול ולא הביאוהו לבית דין מוחלין לו שהכתוב תלה בהם ותפשו בו: תיובתא. מדתלי טעמא בשלא ירבו מחלוקת ש"מ אפי' הוא אומר מפי השמועה והן אומרין כך הוא בעינינו: יושבין בחיל. מפני שהעם רב ומקום צר להם בלשכה אי נמי שלא יהו נראים כיושבין בדין שבלשכת הגזית היו דנים וזה עיקר: משם מעלין אותו. להיות דיין בהר הבית כשמת אחד מהם ויושב שם עד שמת אחד משל עזרה ומעלין את זה שם וכולן יש בהם מעלה זה מזה: שייף. שוחה נכנס ושוחה יוצא והכי אמרי' בב"ב (דף ז.) גבי תקרת הבית שנחבטה שוף עול שוף פוק: מעיקרא. קודם שבא לבית דין שבלשכת הגזית לישאל לא הוה מיחייב קטלא כל כמה דלא עביד איהו גופיה: מעיקרא נמי בר קטלא הוא. אם עושה עבירה שיש בה מיתת בית דין הוה מיקטיל: מסית דלא בעי התראה. אם היה מסית ומורה טעם היתר ולומר אין בלשון הזה הסתה מעיקרא נמי מקטיל בלא התראה: אי אמר טעמא לזכותא. לאלוליה אבל השתא אי אמר טעמא לא מקבלינן שהרי שמע מפי ב"ד שלא לעשות והמרה: **מתני'** האומר אין תפילין פטור. דאין זו הוראה דזיל קרי בי רב הוא: חמש טוטפות יש. שאע"פ שאין דבר זה אלא להוסיף על דברי סופרים חייב דמדרש דסופרים הוא לטטפת לטטפת לטוטפות הרי כאן ד': **גמ'** ויש בו להוסיף. על מה שפירשו חכמים: ואם הוסיף גורע. ופוסל הראשון בתוספתו: ואין לנו אלא תפילין. שעיקרן בתורה ופירושן מדברי סופרים שהם ד' בתים ויש להוסיף חמשה או יותר ואם הוסיף גורע דקא עבר בבל תוסיף ולא עבד מצוה: ואליבא דרבי יהודה. אמר ר' אושעיא למילתיה דאמר לעיל עד דאיכא תורה ויורוך ואית דאמרי אין לנו אלא תפילין ואליבא דרבי יהודה דאמר צריך להדביק במנחות בהקומץ רבה (דף לד:) ולא נהירא לי דההיא בתפילין של יד קאי ומתני' טוטפות תאני והיינו דראש ועוד מדקא מקשי בסיפא אי דעבד ארבעה בתים כו' שמע מינה בשל ראש קיימין דאי בשל יד בית אחד הוא דקא הוי: האי לחודיה קאי. ואין זה גורע: גרוע ועומד. דמתחילתו לא עשה כהוגן שאגד שם תוספת מצוה ואין בעינן גורע דהשתא שהיה מתחילתו כשר ופוסלו בתוספתו: ופירושו מדברי סופרים. ד' חוטין דילפינן גדיל ב' גדילים ד': קשר עליון. שעושין סמוך לכנף כשנתלו החוטין ועל ידיהן נעשין חיבור לטלית לאו דאורייתא ([ח]אלא) הלכה למשה מסיני דפלוגתא היא במנחות [ט](דף לט.): האי לחודיה קאי. דכיון דלא נקשר אינו חיבור עם השאר והראוי למצוה היא המצוה והעודף כמי שאינו:

שאינו

תוספות

מסית דלא בעי התראה מאי איכא למימר. לאו אליבא דר' מאיר פריך דאמסית לא מיחייב דאין בו כרת:

ואין לנו אלא תפילין ואליבא דר' יהודה. כל הנך דרשות דדרשינן לעיל מקרא דכי יפלא [°]לא חייש:

אי סבירא לן דלולב אין צריך אגד וכו'. משמע אבל אי סבירא לן דצריך אגד לא אמרינן האי לחודיה קאי והאי לחודיה קאי והכי נמי אמרי' בריש לולב הגזול (סוכה דף לא.) דקאמר רבי יהודה אין אוגדין את הלולב אלא במינו מאי טעמא דכיון דאמר ר' יהודה לולב צריך אגד אי עבדי ליה ממין אחר הוה ליה ה' מינין ותימה דאמר התם (שם:) ד' מינין שבלולב כשם שאין פוחתין מהן כך אין מוסיפין עליהם ופריך פשיטא ומשני מהו דתימא הואיל ואמר רבי יהודה לולב צריך אגד אי אייתי מינא אחרינא האי לחודיה קאי והאי לחודיה קאי קמ"ל מאי קא תלי טעמא דהאי לחודיה קאי משום דלולב צריך אגד אדרבה מטעם זה יש לנו לומר יותר דאסור ומיהו י"ל דהתם בדמנח ליה חוץ לאגד אבל קשה דמשמע דמסיק לר' יהודה דלא אמר האי לחודיה וכ"ש לרבנן והכא משמע דלרבנן אמר האי לחודיה קאי וי"ל דהתם מדרבנן אסור ור"ת ל"ג התם הואיל ואמר ר' יהודה וזהו לשונו מהו דתימא הואיל ואמרו חכמים בין אגוד בין שאינו אגוד כשר הלכך אין צריך אגד והאי יתירה דמוסיף על הד' לחודיה קאי ולא מיפסל ביה קמ"ל ומיהו תימה אמאי לא משכח לולב לרבי יהודה בכי האי גוונא שאגד ג' מינין בפני עצמן דנעשה בכשרות ואחר כך אגד עמהן מין אחר דהוה ליה מוסיף גורע ויש לומר כיון דקודם נטילתו נפסל הוה ליה גרוע ועומד אבל תפילין אם הניחן בראשו בכשרות והניח גבייהו בית חמישי הרי זה מוסיף גורע שפוסלן ומבטל מצות שעל ראשו ולא דמי ללולב דאם נטלו ובעודו בידו הוסיף מין חמישי אין זה מבטל מצותו דמדאגביה נפק ביה:

קשר

עין משפט נר מצוה

נז א מיי' פ"ז מהלכות ממרים הלכה ח:
נח ב מיי' פ"ג שם הל' ד סמג עשין קיא ולאוין ריז:
נט ג מיי' שם פ"א הל' ד סמג שם:
ס ד ה מיי' פ"ג מהל' סנהדרין הלכה א:
סא ו מיי' פ"א מהל' ממרים הל' ד סמג עשין קיא ולאוין ריז:
סב ז מיי' פ"ב מהל' סנהדרין הלכה ח:
סג ח מיי' פ"ג מהל' ממרים הל' ה ופ"ד הלכה א סמג עשין קיא ולאוין ריז:
סד ט י מיי' שם פ"ג הלכה ח:
סה כ ל מיי' פ"ד שם הלכה ג סמג עשין קיא ולאוין ריז:
סו מ מיי' פ"ז מהל' לולב הלכה ו סמג עשין מד טוש"ע א"ח סי' תרנא סעיף א:

מסורת הש"ס

א) [תוספ' פ"ז תוספ' חגיגה פרק ב], ב) [סוטה מז:], ג) [תוספ' שקלים ספ"ג], ד) [לעיל יז: וש"נ], ה) [בתענית טז. פירש"י שפל ברך ענוו ול"ל דכמה עניני ענוה יש ועי' רש"א ח"א], ו) [סוכה ל:], ז) [סוכה לא.], ח) [נ"ל כלומר], ט) [עי' תוס' פט. לקמן בסמוך ד"ה קשר].

גליון הש"ס

תוס' ד"ה ואין וכו' לא חייש. עיין בטורי אבן באבני שהם לר"ה דף כ"ז ע"א ד"ה מצות:

ליקוטי רש"י

זקן ממרא. שהמרה על ב"ד של לשכת הגזית ומיתתו בחנק [סוטה כה:]. האומר אין תפילין. זקן ממרא מן הדבר ולא כל דבר דהא כתי' מן הדבר ותנן באלו הן הנחנקין (סנהדרין דף פח:) האומר אין תפלין לעבור על דברי תורה פטור חמש טוטפות להוסיף על דברי סופרים חייב דהיינו מן הדבר ולא כל דבר [הוריות ד.]. לולב צריך אגד. הלכך כל הנאגד עמו הוי מן המצוה ונמצא עובר בבל תוסיף אם יאגד מין חמישי [סוכה לא.].

[מכאן שייך לדף פט.].

קשר עליון. היינו נמי ההוא קשר למטה הלכה למשה מסיני כלומר קשר אחד בגלילת מיהא דאורייתא והכי נקט עליון משום דאי לא עביד אלא חד קשר בסופו עביד ליה שמקיים את הגדיל כולו. דאורייתא. ואפי' יכול לכרוך יפה ולהתקיים בלא קשר יום או יומים פסולה [מנחות לט.]. וכל העם ישמעו. מכאן שממתינין לו עד הרגל וממיתין אותו ברגל [דברים יז, יג]. לרשות הבעל. כגון מסרה האב לשלוחי הבעל ועדיין היא בדרך ולא קרינן בה בית אביה. לאותה מיתה. שהיו מחייבין את הנידון. ובועלה. כלומר וכל הבועלים נידונין כמיתת הנבעלת חוץ מבועל בת כהן [לקמן צ.]. מקדימים לאותה מיתה. כלומר אין להם לצפות מיתה אחרת אלא מסכימין לאותה מיתה שנגמר בה דינו של נדון. חוץ מזוממי בת כהן. נשואה שאע"פ שנגמר דינה לשריפה על פיהם הם בחנק כדילפינן התם סנהדרין (דף נ) היא בשריפה ואין בועלה בשריפה אלא בחנק כשאר אשת איש והזוממין מסכימין למיתה שחייבו את הבועל דכתיב כאשר זמם לעשות לאחיו ולא לאחותו [מכות ב.]. זוממי בת כהן. לעשות לאחיו מה תלמוד לומר לאחיו למד על זוממי בת כהן נשואה שאינן בשריפה אלא כמיתת הבועל שהוא בחנק שנאמר היא באש תשרף (ויקרא כא, ט) היא ולא בועלה לכך נאמר כאן לאחיו כאשר זמם לעשות לאחיו ולא כאשר זמם לעשות לאחותו אבל בכל שאר מיתות השוה הכתוב אשה לאיש וזוממי אשה נהרגין כזוממי איש כגון שהעידוה שהרגה את הנפש שחללה את השבת נהרגין במיתתה שלא מיעט כאן אחותו אלא במקום שיש לקיים בהן הזמה במיתת הבועל [דברים יט, יט]. שהיא והן נהרגין ולא במיתה אחת דהיא בשריפה והן במיתת הבועל כגון באו עדים והזימו את הראשונים וחייבום מיתת הבועל ולא מיתתה דכתיב (דברים יט) כאשר זמם לעשות לאחיו ולא לאחותו כדאמר באלו הן הנחנקין (סנהדרין נ). בועלה. דהיא בשריפה אבל בועלה נידון כשאר בועל בת ישראל דבועל ארוסה בסקילה ובועל נשואה בחנק דכתיב (ויקרא כא) היא באש תשרף היא ולא בועלה היא ולא זוממיה [לעיל מו.]. וזוממי בת כהן. אף על פי שהם היו מחייבין אותה שריפה אין נדונין אלא במיתה שהיו מחייבין לבועל והיינו חנק כשאר בא על אשת איש כדמפרש קרא היא תשרף ולא בועלה וזוממיה ילפינן מכאשר זמם לעשות לאחיו ולא לאחותו. ובועלה. בנשואה בת כהן קמיירי אבל ארוסה בועלה בסקילה [לעיל פד:]. אשר לא צויתיו לדבר. אבל צויתיו לחבירו. ואשר ידבר בשם אלהים אחרים. אפילו כיון את ההלכה לאסור את האסור ולהתיר את המותר. ומת. בחנק שלשה מיתתן בידי אדם המתנבא מה שלא שמע ומה שלא נאמר לו ונאמר לחבירו והמתנבא בשם עבודה זרה אבל הכובש את נבואתו והעובר על דברי נביא והעובר על עצמו מיתתן בידי שמים שנאמר (פסוק יט) אנכי אדרוש מעמו [דברים יח, כ]. ויצא הרוח. פתרון ויצא המלאך שהרי אומר לעיל וכל צבא השמים וגו' ועתה יצא אחד מן המלאכים ויאמר אני אפתנו כדאמר (תהלים קד) עושה מלאכיו רוחות ולפיכך קדם ואמר לעיל וכל צבא השמים עומדים שאל תתמה כשתאמר ויצא הרוח מי הוא ומהיכן יצא וכשאמר וכל צבא השמים עומדים כדי להודיע מהיכן יצא משאר הרוחות העומדים עליו, ורבותינו פירשו זהו רוחו של נבות. בפי כל נביאיו. שישים דבר בפיהם לאמר עלה והצלח ויעלה ויפול מכלל שהיו נביאי אמת שלא היו מתנבאים כי אם מה שישים השם בפיהם [דה"ב יח]. זה בכה. אני אפתנו בכה [שבת קמט:]. תפתה וגם תוכל. לפי שיש מפתה הבא לפתות חבירו פעמים שהמפותה מבין שזה רוצה לפתותו והוא נזהר ואינו שומע להתפתות אבל באחאב תפתה וגם תוכל [דה"ב שם]. צא ממחיצתי. הפורע נוקם חמתו וקנאתו מחריב ביתיה, כרוח של נבות שנקם כעסו מאחאב ויצא ממחילתו של הקדוש ברוך הוא. רוחו של נבות. שלפי שהוא הרג נבות היה רוחו מחזר לפתותו ולהפילו [לקמן קב:]. תפלצתך. ל' בהלה שהיית ממהר ונבהל לעורר שטימתך לאחיך ויש לועזין לשון פלצות ויש לועזין לשון מפלצת [ירמיהו מט, טז]. האין פה נביא לה' עוד. מקובלני אין ב' נביאים מתנבאים בל' א' ואלה כולם לשון א' אומרים [מ"א כב, ז]. את קשת עילם. את תקות עילם [ירמיהו מט, לה]. שברתי את עול מלך בבל. אמרו רבותינו מי הטעה את חנניה שמע שהיה ירמיה מתנב' בשוק העליון הנני שובר את קשת עילם (ירמיה מט) ונבואה זו בסוף הספר נאמרה ברשית ממלכת צדקיהו כמו שמפורש שם ולפי שעילם סמוכה לבבל עמד הוא בשוק התחתון ודרש ודן קל וחומר ומה עילם שלא באה אלא לעזור את הכשדים וכו' כמה שהיא בסנהדרין [שם כח, א].

The Gemara identifies another commandment that seems to meet the aforementioned criteria:

וְהָאִיכָּא צִיצִית – **But there is** also the commandment of ***tzitzis,*** **דְּעִיקָּרוֹ מִדִּבְרֵי תוֹרָה וּפֵירוּשׁוֹ מִדִּבְרֵי סוֹפְרִים** – which is a matter **whose essence is** stated **in the Torah and whose elaboration is stated by the *Soferim*,** **וְיֵשׁ בּוֹ לְהוֹסִיף וְאִם הוֹסִיף גּוֹרֵעַ** – **and it has** an element **to** which one can **add, and if one adds** to it **he detracts.**[42] – ? –

The Gemara responds:

בְּצִיצִית מַאי סְבִירָא לָן – **What** opinion **do we hold in regard to *tzitzis***, i.e. in regard to the requirement of knotting the *tzitzis* to the garment?[43] **אִי סְבִירָא לָן דְּקֶשֶׁר הָעֶלְיוֹן לָאו דְּאוֹרָיְיתָא** – **If we hold** the opinion **that the upper knot** of the *tzitzis* **is not** required under **Biblical** law,[44] **הַאי לְחוּדֵיהּ קָאֵי וְהַאי לְחוּדֵיהּ קָאֵי** – then even if one adds an extra string to the *tzitzis,* **this one** (the required strings) **stands by itself and that one** (the extra string) **stands by itself.** I.e. the extra string does not detract from the validity of the others.[45]

וְאִי סְבִירָא לָן – **And if we hold** the opinion

NOTES

only that the species be held for a moment, and thus, adding a fifth species after the others were taken does not detract at all. In contrast, tefillin are supposed to be worn all day. Thus, if one begins with valid tefillin and then adds an extra compartment he actively spoils his subsequent performance of the mitzvah (*Tosafos* ד״ה אי, *Chidushei HaRan*).

42. The Torah states explicitly (*Deuteronomy* 22:12) that *tzitzis* should be placed on the corners of garments, but does not specify the details of this mitzvah. The *Soferim* expounded (*Yevamos* 5b) that four threads are to be inserted in the corners of a four-cornered garment. [The threads are doubled over so that "eight" strings hang from the corners of the garment] (see *Rashi*). It is possible to add to this commandment by hanging a fifth string from the corner of the garment, and if one does so he invalidates the *tzitzis* (*Chidushei HaRan*).

43. There is a dispute (*Menachos* 39a) whether under Biblical law the *tzitzis* must be knotted to the garment or it is sufficient to form a fringe by hanging the threads from the corner of the garment and winding one thread around the others (*Rashi*; see *Chidushei HaRan; cf. Tosafos* 89a ד״ה קשר).

44. The "upper" knot refers to the knot closest to the garment. (It is the "upper" knot in relation to the knots further away from the garment.) The question at hand does not pertain to any particular knot, but rather to whether any knot at all is required under Biblical law. The Gemara refers specifically to the upper knot because the Biblical requirement, if it exists, is fulfilled by tying one double knot, and the upper knot is the first one that is tied (see *Rashi* and *Chidushei HaRan*; cf. *Rashi* and *Tosafos* to *Menachos* 39a).

45. For since the threads are not knotted, the extra one is not attached to the others. Accordingly, the mitzvah is fulfilled with the required number of threads and the extra one may be ignored (*Rashi*). [Even if one would knot the threads he would not detract from the validity of the *tzitzis*, since the knot is inconsequential under Biblical law.]

דְּקֶשֶׁר הָעֶלְיוֹן דְּאוֹרַיְיתָא – **that the upper knot is** required under **Biblical** law, גָּרוּעַ וְעוֹמֵד – then if one adds to the commandment by knotting an extra thread with his *tzitzis,* [**the** *tzitzis*] **lack** validity **from the outset.**[1] Thus, the commandment of *tzitzis* does not meet the criteria set forth by R' Elazar.

The Gemara asks:

אִי הָכִי – **If so,** תְּפִילִּין נַמִּי – the commandment of **tefillin also** does not fit the criteria outlined above. אִי עָבֵיד אַרְבָּעָה בָּתֵּי – For **if one** originally **made** a tefillin box with **four compartments** וְאַיְיתֵי אַחֲרִינָא וְאַנַּח גַּבַּיְיהוּ – **and he** then **brought another** compartment **and placed it alongside them,** הַאי לְחוּדֵיהּ קָאֵי וְהַאי לְחוּדֵיהּ קָאֵי – **then this one** (the original set of boxes) **stands by itself and that one** (the new compartment) **stands by itself.**[2] וְאִי עָבֵיד חַמְשָׁה בָּתֵּי – **And if he** originally **made** a tefillin box with **five compartments,** גָּרוּעַ וְעוֹמֵד הוּא – **[the tefillin] lack** validity **from the outset. – ? –**

The Gemara answers:

הָאָמַר רַבִּי זֵירָא – **R' Zeira said:** בַּיִת חִיצוֹן שֶׁאֵינוֹ רוֹאֶה אֶת הָאֲוִיר פָּסוּל – **If the outer compartment** of the tefillin box **is not exposed to the air,** the tefillin are **invalid.**[3] Thus, if one originally made four compartments and he then added a fifth one, the addition detracts by rendering the tefillin invalid.

Mishnah

The Mishnah discusses the place and time at which the execution of a *zakein mamrei* is carried out:

אֵין מְמִיתִין אוֹתוֹ לֹא בְּבֵית דִּין שֶׁבְּעִירוֹ – **They do not execute him in the court of his town**[4] וְלֹא בְּבֵית דִּין שֶׁבְּיַבְנֶה – **nor** do they execute him **in the court in Yavneh.**[5] אֶלָּא מַעֲלִין אוֹתוֹ לְבֵית דִּין הַגָּדוֹל שֶׁבִּירוּשָׁלַיִם – **Rather, they bring him up to the High Court in Jerusalem,** וּמְשַׁמְּרִין אוֹתוֹ עַד הָרֶגֶל – **and they guard him until the** next **Festival,** וּמְמִיתִין אוֹתוֹ בָּרֶגֶל – **and they execute him** there **during** that **Festival;**[6] שֶׁנֶּאֱמַר ,,וְכָל־הָעָם יִשְׁמְעוּ וְיִרָאוּ וְלֹא יְזִידוּן עוֹד" – **for it is stated:** ***And the entire nation shall hear and fear, and they shall not act willfully any more.***[7] דִּבְרֵי רַבִּי עֲקִיבָא – These are **the words of R' Akiva.**

רַבִּי יְהוּדָה אוֹמֵר – However, **R' Yehudah says:** אֵין מְעַנִּין אֶת דִּינוֹ שֶׁל זֶה – **We do not delay** carrying out **this one's judgment** by postponing his execution.[8] אֶלָּא מְמִיתִין אוֹתוֹ מִיָּד – **Rather, they execute him immediately,** וְכוֹתְבִין וְשׁוֹלְחִין שְׁלוּחִין בְּכָל הַמְּקוֹמוֹת – **and** then **they write** out proclamations **and send messengers to all places,** saying: אִישׁ פְּלוֹנִי מִתְחַיֵּיב מִיתָה בְּבֵית דִּין – **"So-and-so was sentenced to death by the court."**

Gemara

A Baraisa puts forth an expanded version of the dispute recorded in our Mishnah:

תָּנוּ רַבָּנָן – **The Rabbis taught in a Baraisa:** אֵין מְמִיתִין אוֹתוֹ לֹא בְּבֵית דִּין שֶׁבְּעִירוֹ – THEY DO NOT EXECUTE HIM IN THE COURT OF HIS TOWN וְלֹא בְּבֵית דִּין שֶׁבְּיַבְנֶה – NOR do they execute him IN THE COURT IN YAVNEH. אֶלָּא מַעֲלִין אוֹתוֹ לְבֵית דִּין הַגָּדוֹל שֶׁבִּירוּשָׁלַיִם – RATHER, THEY BRING HIM UP TO THE HIGH COURT IN JERUSALEM, וּמְשַׁמְּרִין אוֹתוֹ עַד הָרֶגֶל – AND THEY GUARD HIM UNTIL THE next FESTIVAL, וּמְמִיתִין אוֹתוֹ בָּרֶגֶל – AND THEY EXECUTE HIM there DURING that FESTIVAL; שֶׁנֶּאֱמַר ,,וְכָל־הָעָם יִשְׁמְעוּ וְיִרָאוּ" – FOR IT IS STATED: *AND THE ENTIRE NATION SHALL HEAR AND FEAR, AND THEY SHALL NOT ACT WILLFULLY ANY MORE.* דִּבְרֵי רַבִּי עֲקִיבָא – These are THE WORDS OF R' AKIVA.

R' Akiva asserts that this verse conveys that the nation must actually witness the execution of the *zakein mamrei.* R' Yehudah challenges this notion: אָמַר לוֹ רַבִּי יְהוּדָה – R' YEHUDAH SAID TO [R' AKIVA]: וְכִי נֶאֱמַר יִרְאוּ וְיִירָאוּ – DOES [THE TORAH] SAY: *"And the entire nation* SHALL *SEE* AND *FEAR"?* וַהֲלֹא לֹא נֶאֱמַר אֶלָּא ,,יִשְׁמְעוּ וְיִרָאוּ" – WHY, IT SAYS ONLY: *And the entire nation SHALL HEAR AND FEAR,* which conveys only that the

NOTES

1. And the law of *zakein mamrei* applies only to a case where one begins with a valid element and subsequently detracts by adding to the element (see 88b note 41).

[If one would initially knot four *tzitzis* threads to his garment and then undo the knot and add a fifth thread, he would not be detracting from valid *tzitzis* with the additional thread. For the original *tzitzis* are invalidated when the knot is undone, and when a new knot is made with five threads the new *tzitzis* are invalid from the outset (*Kessef Mishneh, Hil. Mamrim* 4:3).]

2. The extra compartment does not detract from the validity of the original tefillin box since it is not crafted of the same piece of leather (see *Rashash* and *Margaliyos HaYam*; see also *Menachos* 34b).

3. [Each of the outer compartments contains a scroll inscribed with a specific Scriptural passage.] The outer compartments must be exposed. If a fifth compartment, or any other object, is attached to the tefillin box, the tefillin are invalidated (*Rashi*).

4. A sage who continues to rule in accordance with his view even after the High Court has ruled otherwise is tried and sentenced in the court of his own town. However, that court is not permitted to carry out the death sentence itself (*Meiri*), for, as R' Akiva will soon explain, his execution must be well publicized. He is thus executed by the High Court in Jerusalem, where masses of people will witness his death and be dissuaded from following in his ways (see *Rashi*).

5. The Mishnah refers to a case where a sage received the ruling of the High Court while it was still in Jerusalem (as is required in order for him to be liable for execution; see 87a note 18, and *Hil. Mamrim* 3:7), but he did not defy its ruling until after the court was exiled to Yavneh, just prior to the destruction of the Second Temple. In such a case, the *zakein mamrei* is not to be executed at Yavneh, for even though the Sanhedrin has gathered there, masses of people were not present. Instead, the execution is to take place during a Festival at the Temple in Jerusalem (see *Rashash*), for in this way we can fulfill the requirement (stated below) that "all Israel" must witness the sage's punishment (see *Rashi;* cf. *Tosafos*).

6. The *zakein mamrei* was not executed immediately upon his conviction as were all other convicts, but he was incarcerated and held until the next Festival (i.e. Pesach, Shavuos or Succos), at which time he was executed. [The execution was not carried out on the Festival *itself,* for no executions are performed on Festivals (see *Tiferes Yisrael* §26).]

7. *Deuteronomy* 17:13. Since the Torah specifies that the entire populace must hear about the execution in order to instill in them a fear of repeating this transgression, it is necessary to carry out the execution at a time when it will be publicized so that it will serve as a deterrent (see *Rashi*). Consequently, they postponed the execution until the people gathered in Jerusalem for one of the Festivals.

[*Aruch LaNer* points out that the case of *zakein mamrei* is not the only one in which the Torah states that *the entire nation shall hear....* Indeed, a similar language is stated with reference to the punishments of a מֵסִית (an instigator), a *ben sorer umoreh,* and *zomemim* witnesses (see below, notes 13 and 14). He thus questions why R' Akiva does not require that these persons, too, be executed during a Festival at the Temple. For a resolution to this difficulty, see *Aruch LaNer.* (It should also be noted that although *Aruch LaNer* takes it for granted that the execution of those others is not delayed until the Festival, and his assumption is shared by *Kesef Mishneh* to *Hil. Mamrim* 3:8, there are indications to the contrary; see *Sefer HaMitzvos* of *R' Saadiah Gaon* vol. III pp. 125-126 for a lengthy discussion of this topic.)]

8. In general, once someone is convicted of a capital crime, his sentence must be carried out that very day, so as not to keep him waiting in agony for his punishment (see *Rambam, Hil. Sanhedrin* 12:4). R' Yehudah holds that a *zakein mamrei* is accorded the same treatment.

The Gemara below explains the basis for R' Yehudah's view.

דקשר העליון דאורייתא גרוע ועומד אי הכי תפילין נמי אי עביד ארבעה בתי ואייתי אחרינא ואנח גבייהו האי לחודיה קאי והאי לחודיה קאי ואי עביד חמשה בתי גרוע ועומד הוא האמר ר' זירא (א) א בית חיצון שאינו רואה את האויר פסול: **מתני'** ב אין ממיתין אותו לא בבית דין שבעירו ולא בבית דין שביבנה אלא מעלין אותו לבית דין הגדול שבירושלים ומשמרין אותו עד הרגל וממיתין אותו ברגל שנאמר א) וכל העם ישמעו ויראו ולא יזידון עוד דברי ר' עקיבא ר' יהודה אומר אין מענין את דינו של זה אלא ממיתין אותו מיד וכותבין ושולחין שלוחין בכל המקומות איש פלוני ג) מתחייב מיתה בבית דין: **גמ'** תנו רבנן ג) אין ממיתין אותו לא בבית דין שבעירו ולא בבית דין שביבנה אלא מעלין אותו לב"ד הגדול שבירושלים ומשמרין אותו עד הרגל וממיתין אותו ברגל שנאמר וכל העם ישמעו ויראו דברי רבי עקיבא אמר לו ר' יהודה וכי נאמר יראו וייראו והלא לא נאמר אלא ישמעו וייראו למה מענין דינו של זה אלא ממיתין אותו מיד וכותבין ושולחין בכל מקום איש פלוני נתחייב מיתה בבית דין ת"ר ארבעה צריכין הכרזה ג המסית ד ובן סורר ומורה ה וזקן ממרא ו ועדים זוממין בכולהו כתיב בהו א) וכל העם ב) ג) וכל ישראל בעדים זוממין כתיב ד) והנשארי' דלא כולי עלמא חזו לסהדותא: **מתני'** נביא השקר ז המתנבא מה שלא שמע ומה שלא נאמר לו מיתתו בידי אדם ח אבל הכובש את נבואתו ט והמוותר על דברי נביא י ונביא שעבר על דברי עצמו מיתתו בידי שמים שנאמר ה) אנכי אדרש מעמו כ המתנבא בשם עבודת כוכבים ואומר כך אמרה עבודת כוכבים אפי' כוון את ההלכה לטמא את הטמא ולטהר את הטהור ל הבא על אשת איש כיון שנכנסה ד) לרשות הבעל לנשואין אע"פ שלא נבעלה הבא עליה הרי זה בחנק וזוממי בת כהן ובועלה מ שכל המוזמין ה) מקדימין לאותה מיתה נ חוץ מזוממי בת כהן ובועלה: **גמ'** תנו רבנן שלשה מיתתן בידי אדם ושלשה מיתתן בידי שמים המתנבא מה שלא שמע ומה שלא נאמר לו והמתנבא בשם עבודת כוכבים מיתתן בידי אדם הכובש את נבואתו והמוותר על דברי נביא ונביא שעבר על דברי עצמו מיתתן בידי שמים מנהני מילי אמר רב יהודה אמר רב דאמר קרא ו) אך הנביא אשר יזיד לדבר דבר בשמי זה המתנבא מה שלא שמע ו) ואשר לא צויתיו הא לחבירו צויתיו זה המתנבא מה שלא נאמר לו ו) ואשר ידבר בשם אלהים אחרים זה המתנבא בשם עבודת כוכבים וכתיב ו) ומת הנביא ההוא ו) וכל מיתה האמורה בתורה סתם אינה אלא חנק הכובש את נבואתו והמוותר על דברי נביא ונביא שעבר על דברי עצמו מיתתן בידי שמים [א] דכתיב ה) והאיש אשר לא ישמע (א) קרי ביה לא ישמיע וקרי ביה לא ישמע אל דברי וכתיב אנכי אדרש מעמו בידי שמים: המתנבא מה שלא שמע: כגון צדקיה בן כנענה דכתיב ז) ויעש לו צדקיה בן כנענה קרני ברזל מאי הוה ליה למיעבד רוח נבות אטעיתיה דכתיב ח) ויאמר ה' מי יפתה את אחאב ויעל ויפול ברמות גלעד ט) ויצא הרוח ויעמד לפני ה' ויאמר אני אפתנו ויאמר י) תפתה וגם תוכל צא ועשה כן אמר רב יהודה מאי צא צא ממחיצתי י) מאי רוח אמר רבי יוחנן רוחו של נבות היזרעאלי הוה ליה למידק כדרבי יצחק דאמר רבי יצחק סיגנון אחד עולה לכמה נביאים ואין שני נביאים מתנבאין בסיגנון אחד עובדיה אמר כ) זדון לבך השיאך ירמיה אמר ל) תפלצתך השיא אותך זדון לבך והני מדקאמרי כולהו כהדדי שמע מינה לא כלום קאמרי דילמא לא הוה ידע ליה להא דרבי יצחק יהושפט הוה התם וקאמר להו דכתיב מ) ויאמר יהושפט האין פה נביא מ) (עוד לה') אמר ליה הא איכא כל הני אמר ליה כך מקובלני מבית אבי אבא סיגנון אחד עולה לכמה נביאים ואין שני נביאים מתנבאים בסיגנון אחד. המתנבא מה שלא נאמר לו כגון חנניה בן עזור דקאי ירמיה בשוק העליון וקאמר נ) כה אמר ה' [צבאות] הנני שובר את קשת עילם נשא חנניה ק"ו בעצמו מה עילם שלא בא אלא לעזור את בבל אמר הקב"ה הנני שובר את קשת עילם כשדים עצמן על אחת כמה וכמה אתא איהו בשוק התחתון אמר ס) כה אמר ה' וגו' שברתי את עול מלך בבל א"ל רב פפא לאביי האי לחבירו נמי לא נאמר א"ל כיון דאיתיהיב ק"ו למידרש כמאן דאיתמר ליה דמי הוא ניהו דלא נאמר לו המתנבא בשם עבודת כוכבים כגון נביאי הבעל הכובש את נבואתו כגון יונה בן אמיתי והמוותר על דברי נביא כגון חבריה

רש"י

שאינו רואה את האויר. כגון שהוסיף בית חמישי עליהם בצדו או דבר אחר: **מתני'** כל ישראל ישמעו. צריך להשמיע מיתתו לרבים שלא יעשה אדם עוד כן: לא בבית דין שביבנה. אם נשאלו לבית דין שבלשכת הגזית ואמרו להם וחזר לעירו ושהה ימים עד שגלתה סנהדרי גדולה ליבנה ועדיין הבית קיים ואחרי כן הורה כבתחלה אין ממיתין אותו ביבנה ואע"פ ששם סנהדרי גדולה שסוף סוף אין נקבצים שם: **גמ'** וכי נאמר וכל העם יראו וייראו. דבעינן שיהו רואין במיתתו: הכרזה. פלוני מת בב"ד על שעבר עבירה זו כדי לרדות את האחרים: וכל ישראל. ישמעו וייראו: ובעדים זוממים כתיב והנשארים. ישמעו וייראו משום דלא שייך למיכתב וכל העם דלאו כולי עלמא חזו לסהדותא שיש גזלנין ומלוי ברבית ומועלים בשביעית שהן פסולים לעדות: **מתני'** ומה שלא נאמר לו. אע"פ שנאמר לחבירו ובגמרא יליף לה: הכובש נבואתו. שלא אמרה כגון יונה בן אמיתי: והמוותר על דברי נביא. המפקירם שלא חשש למה שאמר לו הנביא: **גמ'** והאיש אשר לא ישמע. היינו מוותר: קרי ביה איש אשר לא ישמיע. היינו כובש וקרי ביה לא ישמע שהוא עצמו אינו נשמע היינו עובר על דברי עצמו: ויצא הרוח ויאמר אני אפתנו. אצא והייתי רוח שקר בפי כל נביאיו: סיגנון. דבר מליצות של רוח הקודש: עולה לכמה נביאים. נכנס בלבם לזה בלשון זה ולזה בלשון זה והכל אחד: ואין שני נביאים מתנבאין בסיגנון אחד. בלשון אחד ואלו כולן לשון אחד היו אומרים דכתיב הנה נא כל הנביאים אומרים פה אחד טוב: חבריה

תוספות

קשר העליון דאורייתא. פי' בקונט' דפלוגתא היא בפ' התכלת (מנחות דף לט. ושם) וליתיה אלא דמסקינן התם ט) שמע מינה קשר העליון דאורייתא: **ולא** בבית דין שביבנה. פירש בקונטרס אם נשאלו בבית דין שבלשכת הגזית ואמרו להם וחזר לעירו ושהה ימים עד שגלתה סנהדרי גדולה ותימה דסוף סוף כשממתינין עד הרגל היאך ממיתין הא כיון דגלתה סנהדרין אין דנין דיני נפשות כדאמר בפרק היו בודקין (לעיל דף מא.) וכי תימא דברגל חוזרים ב"ד הגדול ויושבין בלשכת הגזית אף לאחר שגלו ואז דנין אותו חדא דאם כן משכחת ליה לרבן יוחנן בן זכאי דהוה בסנהדרין ובפרק היו בודקין (שם) לא משמע הכי ועוד מאי עינוי הדין יש הא אין שייך עינוי הדין אלא כשמשהין אותו אחר גמר דינו כדמוכח בפרק אחד דיני ממונות (לעיל דף לה.) דפריך לגמרוהו לדיניה בשבתא וליקטלוהו וכו' ומשני אתה מענה את דינו והדר פריך לדיינוהו במעלי שבתא וכו' ועוד מאי אריא זקן ממרא בשאר עבירות נמי ועוד אמאי נקט יבנה לימא לא בב"ד שבחנות ודוחק לומר דלעבירה דקודם שגלתה סנהדרין דנין אף לאחר שגלתה ולא אמרינן מקום גורם כיון דבשעת עבירה סנהדרי גדולה במקומן ור"ת אומר דמיירי כשנגמר דינו קודם שגלתה סנהדרי: י) **הכובש** נבואתו לוקה. לית ביה לאו ועוד דאין בו מעשה אלא מכין אותו עד שתצא נפשו כמו עשה סוכה ואינו עושה כ): אליהו

מסורת הש"ס

א) [בערוך ערך פלש א' גריס בית המפולש לחבירו פסול פי' אי מתחלה עבדינהו ה' בתי ופליש חד בית לחבריה דהיינו ד' בתי וכו' ע"ש], ב) [במשנה שבמשניות ובברייתא הסמוכה איתא נתחייב], ג) [תוספתא פי"א], ד) [פירש"י על בבא זו עי' ברש"י לקמן צ. וע"ע בפירש"י דמכות ג. ד"ה התם קאי וכו' ובמ"ש תוס' שם ד"ה כל כו' ובד"ה זוממי], ה) מכות ב. [ע"ש], ו) [לעיל נב: פד:], ז) שבת קמט: [לקמן קג:], ח) [נ"ל לה' עוד], ט) [דף לט.], י) זה שייך לע"ב, כ) [כתובות פו.].

הגהות הב"ח

(א) גמ' דכתיב והאיש אשר לא ישמע וקרי ביה לא ישמיע וקרי ביה לא יִשָּׁמַע:

הגהות הגר"א

[א] גמ' והאיש אשר לא ישמע וגו'. נ"ב גי' הגאונים והיה וכו' אשר וגו' וכתיב אנכי וגו'. והיא הנכונה:

ליקוטי רש"י

[נדפס בדרך פח:]

תורה אור השלם

א) וְכָל הָעָם יִשְׁמְעוּ וְיִרָאוּ וְלֹא יְזִידוּן עוֹד: [דברים יז, יג]

ב) וְכָל יִשְׂרָאֵל יִשְׁמְעוּ וְיִרָאוּן וְלֹא יוֹסִפוּ לַעֲשׂוֹת כַּדָּבָר הָרָע הַזֶּה בְּקִרְבֶּךָ: [דברים יג, יב]

ג) וּרְגָמֻהוּ כָּל אַנְשֵׁי עִירוֹ בָאֲבָנִים וָמֵת וּבִעַרְתָּ הָרָע מִקִּרְבֶּךָ וְכָל יִשְׂרָאֵל יִשְׁמְעוּ וְיִרָאוּ: [דברים כא, כא]

ד) וְהַנִּשְׁאָרִים יִשְׁמְעוּ וְיִרָאוּ וְלֹא יֹסִפוּ לַעֲשׂוֹת עוֹד כַּדָּבָר הָרָע הַזֶּה בְּקִרְבֶּךָ: [דברים יט, כ]

ה) וְהָיָה הָאִישׁ אֲשֶׁר לֹא יִשְׁמַע אֶל דְּבָרַי אֲשֶׁר יְדַבֵּר בִּשְׁמִי אָנֹכִי אֶדְרֹשׁ מֵעִמּוֹ: [דברים יח, יט]

ו) אַךְ הַנָּבִיא אֲשֶׁר יָזִיד לְדַבֵּר דָּבָר בִּשְׁמִי אֵת אֲשֶׁר לֹא צִוִּיתִיו לְדַבֵּר וַאֲשֶׁר יְדַבֵּר בְּשֵׁם אֱלֹהִים אֲחֵרִים וּמֵת הַנָּבִיא הַהוּא: [דברים יח, כ]

ז) וַיַּעַשׂ לוֹ צִדְקִיָּהוּ בֶן כְּנַעֲנָה קַרְנֵי בַרְזֶל וַיֹּאמֶר כֹּה אָמַר יְיָ בְּאֵלֶּה תְּנַגַּח אֶת אֲרָם עַד כַּלּוֹתָם: [דברי הימים ב' יח, י]

ח) וַיֹּאמֶר יְיָ מִי יְפַתֶּה אֶת אַחְאָב וְיַעַל וְיִפֹּל בְּרָמֹת גִּלְעָד וַיֹּאמֶר זֶה בְּכֹה וְזֶה אֹמֵר בְּכֹה: [מלכים א' כב, כ]

ט) וַיֵּצֵא הָרוּחַ וַיַּעֲמֹד לִפְנֵי יְיָ וַיֹּאמֶר אֲנִי אֲפַתֶּנּוּ וַיֹּאמֶר יְיָ אֵלָיו בַּמָּה: [מלכים א' כב, כא] י) וַיֹּאמֶר אֵצֵא וְהָיִיתִי רוּחַ שֶׁקֶר בְּפִי כָּל נְבִיאָיו וַיֹּאמֶר תְּפַתֶּה וְגַם תּוּכָל צֵא וַעֲשֵׂה כֵן: [מלכים א' כב, כב] כ) זְדוֹן לִבְּךָ הִשִּׁיאֶךָ שֹׁכְנִי בְחַגְוֵי סֶלַע מְרוֹם שִׁבְתּוֹ אֹמֵר בְּלִבּוֹ מִי יוֹרִדֵנִי אָרֶץ: [עובדיה א, ג] ל) תִּפְלַצְתְּךָ הִשִּׁיא אֹתָךְ זְדוֹן לִבֶּךָ שֹׁכְנִי בְּחַגְוֵי הַסֶּלַע תֹּפְשִׂי מְרוֹם גִּבְעָה כִּי תַגְבִּיהַּ כַּנֶּשֶׁר קִנֶּךָ מִשָּׁם אוֹרִידְךָ נְאֻם יְיָ: [ירמיה מט, טז] מ) וַיֹּאמֶר יְהוֹשָׁפָט הַאֵין פֹּה נָבִיא לַייָ עוֹד וְנִדְרְשָׁה מֵאֹתוֹ: [מלכים א' כב, ז] נ) כֹּה אָמַר יְיָ צְבָאוֹת הִנְנִי שֹׁבֵר אֶת קֶשֶׁת עֵילָם רֵאשִׁית גְּבוּרָתָם: [ירמיה מט, לה] ס) כֹּה אָמַר יְיָ צְבָאוֹת אֱלֹהֵי יִשְׂרָאֵל לֵאמֹר שָׁבַרְתִּי אֶת עֹל מֶלֶךְ בָּבֶל: [ירמיה כח, ב]

עין משפט נר מצוה

סז א מיי' פ"ד מהל' ממרים הלכה ג:
סח ב ג מיי' פ"ג שם הלכה ח:
סט ד מיי' שם ופי"ח שם הלכה יג:
ע ה מיי' שם פ"ג הלכה ח:
עא ו מיי' שם ופי"ח מהל' עדות הל' ז:
עב ז מיי' פ"ה מהל' ע"ז הלכה ח סמג לאוין לב:
עג ח מיי' פ"ט מהלכות יסודי התורה הל' ג סמג לאוין לג:
עד ט מיי' שם הל' ב סמג עשין ו:
עה י מיי' שם הלכה ג סמג לאוין לב:
עו כ מיי' פ"ה מהל' ע"ז הל' ו סמג שם:
עז ל מיי' פ"ג מהל' איסורי ביאה הל' ד:
עח מ מיי' פ"ח מהל' עדות הלכה א סמג עשין קי:
עט נ מיי' שם פ"כ הל' י:

רבינו חננאל

אמרי היכי דמי אי נימא דעבד ד' בתי בטבלא ואייתי בית אחרינא אנח גבייהו ולא חבריה בהדייהו אמאי חייב האי לחודיה קאי והני לחודייהו קיימי ואי מתחלה עבדינהו ה' בתי ופילש בית חד לחבריה דהיינו ד' כיון דעבדינהו שלא כהלכתן לאו תפלין דכתיבי באורייתא נינהו כלל והאי לא איגרע לפי שהוסיף עליו אלא גרוע ועומד הוה מעיקרא דהא פסול הוא כר' זירא דאמר בית המפולש לחבירו פסול ופרישנ' לא צריכא כגון דעבד טוטפת בת ד' בתי דהויא כהלכתא תפילין מעילאי ואייתי בית אחרינא וחבריה בהדייהו דהיינו כל המוסיף גורע העיקר וכדרבא דאמר בית החיצון שאינו רואה את האויר פסול והאי כיון דאייתי בית מאבראי ואוקמיה קמי החיצון נעשה החיצון פנימי ואינו רואה אויר לפיכך הוא פסול ואתינן להשוויי לולב וציצית לתפילין ונדחו דלא דמו: ת"ר אין ממיתין אותו אלא בב"ד הגדול שבירושלים ואין ממיתין אותו אלא ברגל דברי ר' עקיבא. ר' יהודה אומר ממיתין אותו מיד לפי שאין מענין דינו כו': ת"ר ד' צריכין הכרזה מסית ובן סורר ומורה וזקן ממרא ועדים זוממין כולהו משום [דכתיב בהו] וכל ישראל וכל העם. בעדים זוממין כתיב והנשארים דלאו כולי עלמא חזו לסהדותא: ת"ר ג' מיתתן בידי אדם המתנבא מה שלא שמע ומה שלא נאמר לו והמתנבא בשם ע"ז. מנא הני מילי אמר רב יהודה אמר רב דאמר קרא אך הנביא אשר יזיד לדבר דבר בשמי זה המתנבא מה שלא שמע את אשר לא צויתיו הא לנביא אחר צויתיו זה המתנבא מה שלא נאמר לו. ואשר ידבר בשם אלהים אחרים זה המתנבא בשם ע"ז וכתיב ומת הנביא ההוא (שכל) [וכל] מיתה האמורה בתורה סתם חנק הוא. אבל נביא הכובש נבואתו והמוותר על דברי הנביא ונביא שעבר על דברי עצמו מיתתן בידי שמים. ואסיקנא המתנבא מה שלא שמע כגון צדקיה בן כנענה. ואע"ג דאמרינן מדכתיב ויאמר אצא והייתי רוח שקר בפי כל נביאיו שמעינן מינה רוח נבות אטעיתיה מדהוה ליה למבדק בהא דאין סיגנון אחד עולה לשני נביאים. כלומר אין ב' נביאים מתנבאים בסיגנון אחד. והני כולהו עלה להן סיגנון אחד כלומר דבר אחד (וכולן מתנבאין בסיגנון אחד). כדכתיב עלה ויתן ה' ביד המלך ש"מ אין נבואה זו כהוגן דא"ר יצחק סיגנון אחד עולה לכמה נביאים ואין ב' נביאים מתנבאים בסיגנון אחד. סיגנון אחד עולה לכמה נביאים זה עובדיה וירמיה עובדיה הוציא בלשון זדון לבך השיאך. וירמיה אמר תפלצתך השיא אותך זדון לבך ודחינן ודלמא צדקיה בן כנענה לא הוה ידע הא שמעתא דר' יצחק ופרקינן יהושפט הוה התם ואמר להו כך מקובל אני מבית אבי אבא שאין שני נביאים מתנבאין בסיגנון אחד. והיינו דכתיב ויאמר יהושפט האין פה נביא לה' עוד ונדרשה מאתו. כלומר אלו כולן אינן נביאי ה': **המתנבא** מה שלא נאמר לו כגון חנניה בן עזור דשמע לירמיה דאמר כה אמר ה' צבאות הנני שובר את קשת עילם וגו' נשא ק"ו כה אמר ה' צבאות אלהי ישראל לאמר שברתי את עול מלך בבל וזה הק"ו יש לו לירמיה לשאת אותו אבל לזולתו לא. המתנבא בשם ע"ז כגון נביאי [הבעל] אלו כולן מיתתן בידי אדם. אבל הכובש את נבואתו כגון יונה בן אמיתי דינו בידי שמים

people must hear of – not actually witness – the *zakein mamrei's* demise. לָמָּה מְעַנִּין דִּינוֹ שֶׁל זֶה – Thus, **WHY SHOULD WE DELAY THIS ONE'S JUDGMENT** by postponing his execution until the Festival? אֶלָּא מְמִיתִין אוֹתוֹ מִיָּד – **INSTEAD, THEY MUST EXECUTE HIM IMMEDIATELY,** וְכוֹתְבִין וְשׁוֹלְחִין בְּכָל מָקוֹם – **AND** to make certain that the nation "hears" of the execution, **THEY MUST WRITE** proclamations **AND SEND** messengers **TO ALL PLACES,** saying: אִישׁ פְּלוֹנִי נִתְחַיֵּיב מִיתָה בְּבֵית דִּין – **"SO-AND-SO WAS SENTENCED TO DEATH BY THE COURT."**

The Mishnah stated R' Yehudah's view that the execution of the *zakein mamrei* is proclaimed publicly. The Gemara cites a Baraisa that lists other people whose executions are also publicly proclaimed:

תָּנוּ רַבָּנַן – **The Rabbis taught in a Baraisa:** אַרְבָּעָה צְרִיכִין הַכְרָזָה – **THERE ARE FOUR** categories of people **WHO REQUIRE PROCLAMATION** after their sentences are carried out.[9] These are: הַמֵּסִית – **THE INSTIGATOR,**[10] וּבֵן סוֹרֵר וּמוֹרֶה – **A *BEN SORER UMOREH,***[11] וְזָקֵן מַמְרֵא – **A REBELLIOUS SAGE,** וְעֵדִים זוֹמְמִין – **AND *ZOMEMIM* WITNESSES.**[12]

In respect to each of these four offenders, the Torah declares that others shall "hear" of their punishments, and shall "fear" committing similar crimes. The Gemara notes, however, that the language in one of the four passages differs from the other three: בְּכוּלְּהוּ כְּתִיב בְּהוּ ,,וְכָל־הָעָם'' ,,וְכָל יִשְׂרָאֵל'' – **With respect to each** of the first three offenders mentioned in the Baraisa, **it is written: *The entire nation*** *shall hear and fear. . .,* or ***all of Israel*** *shall hear and fear. . .,*[13] בְּעֵדִים זוֹמְמִין כְּתִיב ,,וְהַנִּשְׁאָרִים'' – whereas **in respect to *zomemin* witnesses it is written:**[14] ***And those who remain*** *shall hear and fear.* דְּלֹא כּוּלֵּי עָלְמָא חָזוּ לְסָהֲדוּתָא – The reason for this change in expression is **BECAUSE NOT EVERYONE** in the nation **IS QUALIFIED TO** give **TESTIMONY.**[15]

Mishnah The opening Mishnah of this chapter (84b) enumerated the offenses punishable by strangulation. The following Mishnah delineates the laws of the last four of these offenses:

נְבִיא הַשֶּׁקֶר – **The false prophet,** הַמִּתְנַבֵּא מַה שֶּׁלֹּא שָׁמַע – i.e. **one who prophesies that which he did not hear**[16] וּמַה שֶּׁלֹּא נֶאֱמַר לוֹ – **or that which was not said to him,** even though it was said to another prophet,[17] מִיתָתוֹ בִּידֵי אָדָם – is subject to death and **his death is at the hands of man**; i.e. he is executed by the courts.[18] אֲבָל הַכּוֹבֵשׁ אֶת נְבוּאָתוֹ – **However, one who suppresses his prophecy,**[19] וְהַמְוַותֵּר עַל דִּבְרֵי נָבִיא – **and one who disregards the**

NOTES

9. The proclamation, whose purpose it was to deter others from committing the same crimes, would state: "So-and-so has died at the hands of the court for having perpetrated such and such a deed" (*Rashi*). The requirement for such a proclamation is derived from the fact that in each of the Biblical passages that speaks of these four criminals, the verse states that all Israel shall "hear" of their punishment, and shall be fearful of committing similar acts themselves.

10. I.e. one who instigates a fellow Jew to commit idolatry; see Mishnah above, 67a.

11. See 86a note 42.

12. See 84b note 7.

[*Rambam* (*Hil. Eidus* 18:7) states that *all* punishments decreed upon *zomemim* witnesses – whether capital, corporal or monetary – are publicly proclaimed.]

13. Regarding the instigator and the *ben sorer umoreh,* the Torah writes *And all of Israel shall hear and fear* (*Deuteronomy* 13:12 and 21:21), and in the passage describing the fate of the *zakein mamrei* the Torah states *The entire nation shall hear and fear* (ibid. 17:13).

14. Ibid. 19:20.

15. There are a number of persons who are disqualified from testifying in court – e.g. a gambler, one who lends money at interest, and one who sells produce of the *sheviis* year. Thus, in the case of *zomemim* – where the proclamation is intended to discourage people from giving false testimony – it is not necessary for "the entire nation" to take heed of the *zomemim's* punishment. Rather, only "those who remain" among the ranks of qualified witnesses need take heed (*Rashi*).

[*Ran* takes issue with this explanation. He notes that just as a gambler is disqualified from testifying, he is also disqualified from acting as a judge. Thus, why does the verse regarding a *zakein mamrei* state that *all of Israel* must hear if this verse cannot be addressing itself to a gambler? Similarly, he argues, the law is that one can be designated as a *ben sorer umoreh* only in the first three months of his adulthood (see 69a). If so, why does the Torah state that *the entire nation* must take heed of the *ben sorer umoreh's* demise? Only persons in the relevant age category need be addressed!

Ran thus suggests that there is a deeper meaning in the warnings set forth by the Torah in the cases of *zakein mamrei* and *ben sorer umoreh.* The passage that appears in connection with *zakein mamrei,* for example, is not simply a warning addressed to judges that they not defy the High Court. Rather, it is a more encompassing public warning to all Jews that they subordinate themselves to the halachah as interpreted by the present judiciary. Similarly, in the case of *ben sorer umoreh,* the warning is not simply meant to caution youths not to become a *ben sorer umoreh.* Rather, it is counsel to all Jewish parents to train their children to act properly. Thus, it was indeed appropriate for the Torah to address *all* Israel in these matters. In the case of *zomemim witnesses,* the warning was indeed meant in a more narrow sense, so the Torah addressed only those Jews who could indeed have the opportunity to testify falsely (cf. *Ramban,* commentary to *Deuteronomy* 21:18, *Rashash* and *Toras Chaim*).]

16. I.e. he proclaims as a prophecy from God something that he did not hear from God (*Rambam, Hil. Avodas Kochavim* 5:8).

[Accordingly, one should be careful not to say – even in jest – "God told me . . ." (*Hagahos Maimonios*, citing *R' Eliezer of Metz*). Nevertheless, if one did say so but it is clear to all that he is not a prophet (and that the statement was not truly meant as a declaration of prophecy), the person is not subject to the death penalty, though he has transgressed a prohibition (*Minchas Chinuch* 517:4).]

17. A prophet who hears a prophecy from another prophet may not then proclaim that prophecy as his own. Doing so is also a form of false prophecy and is subject to the death penalty. The Gemara will explain the source for this.

18. He is executed by strangulation (Mishnah 84b).

In order to execute him, the court must know that he did not receive such a prophecy. But how can the court determine that the prophet did not hear what he claims to have heard? One way is in a case where a prophet foretells the future and his prediction does not come to pass (*Deuteronomy* 18:21-22; see *Rambam, Hil. Yesodei HaTorah* 10:1). [This rule does not, however, apply to predictions of tragedy, since the repentance of people may bring about a retraction of the evil decree (see *Jeremiah* 28:7 and *Rashi* there).]

Another instance is where a prophet declares in the Name of God that a law of the Torah has been revoked. Since God has stated that the Torah's laws are everlasting, any statement to the contrary is clearly false (*Rambam, Hil. Yesodei HaTorah* 9:1,3; see Gemara below, 90a). [Here too there is an exception in the case of an established prophet who states in the Name of God that a law of the Torah should be violated on a *temporary* basis, to meet a special need. In such a case, the prophet is believed and the Torah law is *temporarily* suspended. This is learned from the well-known incident in which the prophet Elijah sacrificed an offering on Mount Carmel during his confrontation with the prophets of *Baal* (*I Kings* ch. 18), even though sacrifices at that time were forbidden outside the Temple in Jerusalem (see Gemara below, 90a, and *Yevamos* 90b).]

Yet a third instance is where a prophet commands the people to worship an idol, even temporarily. The prohibition of idolatry cannot be suspended even temporarily (see Gemara 90a).

19. I.e. he refrains from delivering the prophecy he was commanded by God to deliver.

דקשר העליון דאורייתא גרוע ועומד אי הכי תפילין נמי אי עביד ארבעה בתי ואייתי אחרינא ואנח גבייהו האי לחודיה קאי והאי לחודיה קאי ואי עביד חמשה בתי גרוע ועומד הוא האמר ר' זירא (א) א בית חיצון שאינו רואה את האויר פסול: **מתני'** ב אין ממיתין אותו לא בבית דין שבעירו ולא בבית דין שביבנה אלא מעלין אותו לבית דין הגדול שבירושלים ומשמרין אותו עד הרגל וממיתין אותו ברגל שנאמר א) וכל העם ישמעו ויראו ולא יזידון עוד דברי ר' עקיבא ר' יהודה אומר אין מענין את דינו של זה אלא ממיתין אותו מיד וכותבין ושולחין בכל המקומות איש פלוני ג) מתחייב מיתה בבית דין: **גמ'** תנו רבנן ג) אין ממיתין אותו לא בבית דין שבעירו ולא בבית דין שביבנה אלא מעלין אותו לב"ד הגדול שבירושלים ומשמרין אותו עד הרגל וממיתין אותו ברגל שנאמר וכל העם ישמעו ויראו דברי רבי עקיבא אמר לו ר' יהודה וכי נאמר יראו וייראו והלא לא נאמר אלא ישמעו וייראו למה מענין דינו של זה אלא ממיתין אותו מיד וכותבין ושולחין בכל מקום איש פלוני נתחייב מיתה בבית דין ת"ר ארבעה צריכין הכרזה ג המסית ד ובן סורר ומורה ה וזקן ממרא ו ועדים זוממין בכולהו כתיב בהו א) וכל העם ב) ג) וכל ישראל בעדים זוממין כתיב ד) והנשארי' דלא כולי עלמא חזו לסהדותא: **מתני'** נביא השקר ז המתנבא מה שלא שמע ומה שלא נאמר לו מיתתו בידי אדם ח אבל הכובש את נבואתו ט והמוותר על דברי נביא י ונביא שעבר על דברי עצמו מיתתו בידי שמים שנאמר ה) אנכי אדרש מעמו כ המתנבא בשם עבודת כוכבים ואומר כך אמרה עבודת כוכבים אפי' כוון את ההלכה לטמא את הטמא ולטהר את הטהור ל הבא על אשת איש כיון שנכנסה ד) לרשות הבעל לנשואין אע"פ שלא נבעלה הבא עליה הרי זה בחנק וזוממי בת כהן ובועלה מ שכל המוזמין ה) מקדימין לאותה מיתה נ חוץ מזוממי בת כהן ובועלה: **גמ'** תנו רבנן שלשה מיתתן בידי אדם ושלשה מיתתן בידי שמים המתנבא מה שלא שמע ומה שלא נאמר לו והמתנבא בשם עבודת כוכבים מיתתן בידי אדם הכובש את נבואתו והמוותר על דברי נביא ונביא שעבר על דברי עצמו מיתתן בידי שמים מנהני מילי אמר רב יהודה אמר רב דאמר קרא ו) אך הנביא אשר יזיד לדבר דבר בשמי זה המתנבא מה שלא שמע ו) ואשר לא צויתיו הא לחבירו צויתיו זה המתנבא מה שלא נאמר לו ו) ואשר ידבר בשם אלהים אחרים זה המתנבא בשם עבודת כוכבים וכתיב ו) ומת הנביא ההוא ו) וכל מיתה האמורה בתורה סתם אינה אלא חנק הכובש את נבואתו והמוותר על דברי נביא ונביא שעבר על דברי עצמו מיתתן בידי שמים [א] דכתיב ה) והאיש אשר לא ישמע (א) קרי ביה לא ישמיע וקרי ביה לא ישמע אל דברי וכתיב אנכי אדרש מעמו בידי שמים: המתנבא מה שלא שמע: כגון צדקיה בן כנענה דכתיב ז) ויעש לו צדקיה בן כנענה קרני ברזל מאי הוה ליה למיעבד רוח נבות אטעיתיה דכתיב ח) ויאמר ה' מי יפתה את אחאב ויעל ויפול ברמות גלעד ט) ויצא הרוח ויעמד לפני ה' ויאמר אני אפתנו ויאמר י) תפתה וגם תוכל צא ועשה כן אמר רב יהודה מאי צא צא ממחיצתי י) מאי רוח אמר רבי יוחנן רוחו של נבות היזרעאלי הוה ליה למידק כדרבי יצחק דאמר רבי יצחק סיגנון אחד עולה לכמה נביאים ואין שני נביאים מתנבאין בסיגנון אחד עובדיה אמר כ) זדון לבך השיאך ירמיה אמר ל) תפלצתך השיא אותך זדון לבך והני מדקאמרי כולהו כהדדי שמע מינה לא כלום קאמרי דילמא לא הוה ידע ליה להא דרבי יצחק יהושפט הוה התם וקאמר להו דכתיב מ) ויאמר יהושפט האין פה נביא ס) (עוד לה') אמר ליה הא איכא כל הני אמר ליה כך מקובלני מבית אבי אבא סיגנון אחד עולה לכמה נביאים ואין שני נביאים מתנבאים בסיגנון אחד. המתנבא מה שלא נאמר לו כגון חנניה בן עזור דקאי ירמיה בשוק העליון וקאמר נ) כה אמר ה' [צבאות] הנני שובר את קשת עילם נשא חנניה ק"ו בעצמו מה עילם שלא בא אלא לעזור את בבל אמר הקב"ה הנני שובר את קשת עילם כשדים עצמן על אחת כמה וכמה אתא איהו בשוק התחתון אמר ס) כה אמר ה' וגו' שברתי את עול מלך בבל א"ל רב פפא לאביי האי לחבירו נמי לא נאמר א"ל כיון דאיתיהיב ק"ו למידרש כמאן דאיתמר ליה דמי הוא ניהו דלא נאמר לו המתנבא בשם עבודת כוכבים כגון נביאי הבעל הכובש את נבואתו כגון יונה בן אמיתי והמוותר על דברי נביא כגון

חבריה

רש"י

שאינו רואה את האויר. כגון שהוסיף בית חמישי עליהם בלדו או דבר אחר: **מתני'** כל ישראל ישמעו. לריך להשמיע מיתתו לרבים שלא יעשה אדם עוד כן: לא בבית דין שביבנה. אם נשאלו לבית דין שבלשכת הגזית ואמרו להם וחזר לעירו ושהה ימים עד שגלתה סנהדרי גדולה ליבנה ועדיין הבית קיים ואחרי כן הורה כבתחילה אין ממיתין אותו ביבנה ואע"פ ששם סנהדרי גדולה שסוף סוף אין נקבלים שם: **גמ'** וכי נאמר וכל העם יראו וייראו. דבעינן שיהו רואין במיתתו: הכרזה. פלוני מת בב"ד על שעבר עבירה זו כדי לרדות את האחרים: וכל ישראל. ישמעו וייראו: ובעדים זוממים כתיב והנשארים. ישמעו וייראו משום דלא שייך למיכתב וכל העם דלאו כולי עלמא חזו לסהדותא שיש גזלנין ומלוי ברבית ומועלים בשביעית שהן פסולים לעדות: **מתני'** ומה שלא נאמר לו. אע"פ שנאמר לחבירו ובגמרא יליף לה: הכובש נבואתו. שלא אמרה כגון יונה בן אמיתי: והמוותר על דברי נביא. המפקירם שלא חשש למה שאמר לו הנביא: **גמ'** והאיש אשר לא ישמע. היינו מוותר: קרי ביה איש אשר לא ישמיע. היינו כובש וקרי ביה לא ישמע שהוא עלמו אינו נשמע היינו עובר על דברי עלמו: ויצא הרוח ויאמר אני אפתנו. אלא והייתי רוח שקר בפי כל נביאיו: סיגנון. דבר מליצות של רוח הקודש: עולה לכמה נביאים. נכנס בלבם לזה בלשון זה ולזה בלשון זה והכל אחד: ואין שני נביאים מתנבאין בסיגנון אחד. בלשון אחד ואלו כולן לשון אחד היו אומרים דכתיב הנה נא כל הנביאים אומרים פה אחד טוב:

חבריה

תוספות

קשר העליון דאורייתא. פי' בקונט' דפלוגתא היא בפ' התכלת (מנחות דף לט. ושם) וליתיה אלא דמסקינן התם ט) שמע מינה קשר העליון דאורייתא: **ולא** בבית דין שביבנה. פירש בקונטרס אם נשאלו בבית דין שבלשכת הגזית ואמרו להם וחזר לעירו ושהה ימים עד שגלתה סנהדרי גדולה ותימה דסוף סוף כשממתינין עד הרגל היאך ממיתין הא כיון דגלתה סנהדרין אין דנין דיני נפשות כדאמר בפרק היו בודקין (לעיל דף מא.) וכי תימא דברגל חוזרים ב"ד הגדול ויושבין בלשכת הגזית אף לאחר שגלו ואז דנין אותו חדא דאם כן משכחת ליה לרבן יוחנן בן זכאי דהוה בסנהדרין ובפרק היו בודקין (שם) לא משמע הכי ועוד מאי עינוי הדין יש הא אין שייך עינוי הדין אלא כשמשהין אותו אחר גמר דינו כדמוכח בפרק אחד דיני ממונות (לעיל דף לה.) דפריך לגמרוהו לדיניה בשבתא וליקטלוהו וכו' ומשני אתה מענה את דינו והדר פריך לדיינוהו במעלי שבתא וכו' ועוד מאי אריא זקן ממרא בשאר עבירות נמי ועוד אמאי נקט יבנה לימא לא בב"ד שבחנות ודוחק לומר דאעבירה דקודם שגלתה סנהדרין דנין אף לאחר שגלתה ולא אמרינן מקום גורם כיון דבשעת עבירה סנהדרי גדולה במקומן ור"ת אומר דמיירי כשנגמר דינו קודם שגלתה סנהדרי: **הכובש** י) נבואתו לוקה. לית ביה לאו ועוד דאין בו מעשה אלא מכין אותו עד שתצא נפשו כמו עשה סוכה ואינו עושה כ):

אליהו

מסורת הש"ס

א) [בערוך ערך פלש א' גריס בית המפולש לחבירו פסול פי' אי מתחלה עבדינהו ה' בתי ופליש חד בית לחבריה דהיינו ד' בתי וכו' ע"ש], ב) [במשנה שבמשניות ובברייתא הסמוכה איתא נתחייב], ג) [תוספתא פי"א], ד) [פירש"י על בבא זו עי' ברש"י לקמן צ. וע"ע בפירש"י דמכות ב. ד"ה התם קאי וכו' ובמ"ש תוס' שם ד"ה כל כו' ובד"ה זוממי], ה) מכות ב. [ע"ש], ו) [לעיל נב: פד:], ז) שבת קמט: [לקמן קג:], ח) [צ"ל לה' עוד], ט) [דף לט.], י) זה שייך לע"ב, כ) [כתובות פו.].

הגהות הב"ח

(א) גמ' דכתיב והאיש אשר לא ישמע וקרי ביה לא ישמיע וקרי ביה לא יִשָּׁמַע:

הגהות הגר"א

[א] גמ' והאיש אשר לא ישמע וגו'. נ"ב גי' הגאונים והיה וגו' אשר וגו' וכתיב אנכי וגו'. והיא הנכונה:

ליקוטי רש"י

[נדפס בדף פח:]

תורה אור השלם

א) וְכָל הָעָם יִשְׁמְעוּ וְיִרָאוּ וְלֹא יְזִידוּן עוֹד: [דברים יז, יג]

ב) וְכָל יִשְׂרָאֵל יִשְׁמְעוּ וְיִרָאוּן וְלֹא יוֹסִפוּ לַעֲשׂוֹת כַּדָּבָר הָרָע הַזֶּה בְּקִרְבֶּךָ: [דברים יג, יב]

ג) וּרְגָמֻהוּ כָּל אַנְשֵׁי עִירוֹ בָאֲבָנִים וָמֵת וּבִעַרְתָּ הָרָע מִקִּרְבֶּךָ וְכָל יִשְׂרָאֵל יִשְׁמְעוּ וְיִרָאוּ: [דברים כא, כא]

ד) וְהַנִּשְׁאָרִים יִשְׁמְעוּ וְיִרָאוּ וְלֹא יֹסִפוּ לַעֲשׂוֹת עוֹד כַּדָּבָר הָרָע הַזֶּה בְּקִרְבֶּךָ: [דברים יט, כ]

ה) וְהָיָה הָאִישׁ אֲשֶׁר לֹא יִשְׁמַע אֶל דְּבָרַי אֲשֶׁר יְדַבֵּר בִּשְׁמִי אָנֹכִי אֶדְרֹשׁ מֵעִמּוֹ: [דברים יח, יט]

ו) אַךְ הַנָּבִיא אֲשֶׁר יָזִיד לְדַבֵּר דָּבָר בִּשְׁמִי אֵת אֲשֶׁר לֹא צִוִּיתִיו לְדַבֵּר וַאֲשֶׁר יְדַבֵּר בְּשֵׁם אֱלֹהִים אֲחֵרִים וּמֵת הַנָּבִיא הַהוּא: [דברים יח, כ]

ז) וַיַּעַשׂ לוֹ צִדְקִיָּהוּ בֶן כְּנַעֲנָה קַרְנֵי בַרְזֶל וַיֹּאמֶר כֹּה אָמַר יְיָ בְּאֵלֶּה תְּנַגַּח אֶת אֲרָם עַד כַּלּוֹתָם: [דברי הימים ב' יח, י]

ח) וַיֹּאמֶר יְיָ מִי יְפַתֶּה אֶת אַחְאָב וְיַעַל וְיִפֹּל בְּרָמֹת גִּלְעָד וַיֹּאמֶר זֶה בְּכֹה וְזֶה אֹמֵר בְּכֹה: [מלכים א' כב, כ]

ט) וַיֵּצֵא הָרוּחַ וַיַּעֲמֹד לִפְנֵי יְיָ וַיֹּאמֶר אֲנִי אֲפַתֶּנּוּ וַיֹּאמֶר יְיָ אֵלָיו בַּמָּה: [מלכים א' כב, כא] י) וַיֹּאמֶר אֵצֵא וְהָיִיתִי רוּחַ שֶׁקֶר בְּפִי כָּל נְבִיאָיו וַיֹּאמֶר תְּפַתֶּה וְגַם תּוּכָל צֵא וַעֲשֵׂה כֵן: [מלכים א' כב, כב] כ) זְדוֹן לִבְּךָ הִשִּׁיאֶךָ שֹׁכְנִי בְחַגְוֵי סֶלַע מְרוֹם שִׁבְתּוֹ אֹמֵר בְּלִבּוֹ מִי יוֹרִדֵנִי אָרֶץ: [עובדיה א, ג] ל) תִּפְלַצְתְּךָ הִשִּׁיא אֹתָךְ זְדוֹן לִבֶּךָ שֹׁכְנִי בְּחַגְוֵי הַסֶּלַע תֹּפְשִׂי מְרוֹם גִּבְעָה כִּי תַגְבִּיהַּ כַּנֶּשֶׁר קִנֶּךָ מִשָּׁם אוֹרִידְךָ נְאֻם יְיָ: [ירמיה מט, טז] מ) וַיֹּאמֶר יְהוֹשָׁפָט הַאֵין פֹּה נָבִיא לַייָ עוֹד וְנִדְרְשָׁה מֵאֹתוֹ: [מלכים א' כב, ז] נ) כֹּה אָמַר יְיָ צְבָאוֹת הִנְנִי שֹׁבֵר אֶת קֶשֶׁת עֵילָם רֵאשִׁית גְּבוּרָתָם: [ירמיה מט, לה] ס) כֹּה אָמַר יְיָ צְבָאוֹת אֱלֹהֵי יִשְׂרָאֵל לֵאמֹר שָׁבַרְתִּי אֶת עֹל מֶלֶךְ בָּבֶל: [ירמיה כח, ב]

עין משפט נר מצוה

סז א מיי' פ"ד מהל' ממרים הלכה ג:
סח ב ג מיי' פ"ג שם הלכה ח:
סט ד מיי' שם ופ"ז שם הלכה יג:
ע ה מיי' שם פ"ג הלכה ח:
עא ו מיי' שם ופי"ח מהל' עדות הל' ז:
עב ז מיי' פ"ה מהל' ע"ז הלכה ח סמג לאוין לה:
עג ח מיי' פ"ט מהלכות יסודי התורה הל' ג סמג לאוין לג:
עד ט מיי' שם הל' ב סמג עשין ו:
עה י מיי' שם הלכה ג סמג לאוין שם:
עו כ מיי' פ"ה מהל' ע"ז הל' ו סמג שם:
עז ל מיי' פ"ג מהל' איסורי ביאה הל' ד:
עח מ מיי' פי"ח מהל' עדות הלכה א סמג עשין קי:
עט נ מיי' שם פ"כ הל' י:

רבינו חננאל

אמרי היכי דמי אי נימא דעבד ד' בתי בטבלא ואייתי בית אחרינא אנח גבייהו ולא חבריה בהדייהו אמאי חייב האי לחודיה קאי והני לחודייהו קיימי ואי מתחלה עבדינהו ה' בתי ופילש בית חד לחבריה דהיינו ד' כיון דעבדינהו שלא כהלכתן לאו תפלין דכתיבי באורייתא נינהו כלל והאי לא איגרע לפי שהוסיף עליו אלא גרוע ועומד הוה מעיקרא דהא פסול הוא כר' זירא דאמר בית המפולש לחבירו פסול ופרישנ' לא צריכא כגון דעבד טוטפת בת ד' בתי דהויא כהלכתא תפילין מעילאי ואייתי בית אחרינא וחבריה בהדייהו דהיינו כל המוסיף גורע העיקר וכדרבא דאמר בית החיצון שאינו רואה את האויר פסול והאי כיון דאייתי בית מאבראי ואוקמיה קמי החיצון נעשה החיצון פנימי ואינו רואה אויר לפיכך הוא פסול ואתינן להשוויי לולב וציצית לתפילין ונדחו דלא דמו: **ת"ר** אין ממיתין אותו אלא בב"ד הגדול שבירושלים ואין ממיתין אותו אלא ברגל דברי ר' עקיבא. ר' יהודה אומר ממיתין אותו מיד לפי שאין מענין דינו כו': **ת"ר** ד' צריכין הכרזה מסית ובן סורר ומורה וזקן ממרא ועדים זוממין כולהו משום [דכתיב בהו] וכל ישראל וכל העם. בעדים זוממין כתיב והנשארים דלאו כולי עלמא חזו לסהדותא: **ת"ר** ג' מיתתן בידי אדם המתנבא מה שלא שמע ומה שלא נאמר לו והמתנבא בשם ע"ז. מנא הני מילי אמר רב יהודה אמר רב דאמר קרא אך הנביא אשר יזיד לדבר דבר בשמי זה המתנבא מה שלא שמע את אשר לא צויתיו הא לנביא אחר צויתיו זה המתנבא מה שלא נאמר לו. ואשר ידבר בשם אלהים אחרים זה המתנבא בשם ע"ז וכתיב ומת הנביא ההוא (שכל) [וכל] מיתה האמורה בתורה סתם חנק הוא. אבל נביא הכובש נבואתו והמוותר על דברי הנביא ונביא שעבר על דברי עצמו מיתתן בידי שמים. ואסיקנא המתנבא מה שלא שמע כגון צדקיה בן כנענה. ואע"ג דאמרינן מדכתיב ויאמר אצא והייתי רוח שקר בפי כל נביאיו שמעינן מינה רוח נבות אטעיתיה מדהוה ליה למבדק בהא דאין סיגנון אחד עולה לשני נביאים. כלומר אין ב' נביאים מתנבאים בסיגנון אחד. והני כולהו עלה להן סיגנון אחד כלומר דבר אחד (וכולן מתנבאין בסיגנון אחד). כדכתיב עלה ויתן ה' ביד המלך ש"מ אין נבואה זו כהוגן דא"ר יצחק סיגנון אחד עולה לכמה נביאים ואין ב' נביאים מתנבאים בסיגנון אחד. סיגנון אחד עולה לכמה נביאים זה עובדיה וירמיה עובדיה הוציא בלשון זדון לבך השיאך. וירמיה אמר תפלצתך השיא אותך זדון לבך ודחינן ודלמא צדקיה בן כנענה לא הוה ידע הא שמעתא דר' יצחק ופרקינן יהושפט הוה התם ואמר להו כך מקובל אני מבית אבי אבא שאין שני נביאים מתנבאין בסיגנון אחד. והיינו דכתיב ויאמר יהושפט האין פה נביא לה' עוד ונדרשה מאתו. כלומר אלו כולן אינן נביאי ה': **המתנבא** מה שלא נאמר לו כגון חנניה בן עזור דשמע לירמיה דאמר כה אמר ה' צבאות הנני שובר את קשת עילם וגו' נשא ק"ו כה אמר ה' צבאות אלהי ישראל לאמר שברתי את עול מלך בבל וזה הק"ו יש לו לירמיה לשאת אותו אבל לזולתו לא. המתנבא בשם ע"ז כגון נביאי [הבעל] אלו כולן מיתתן בידי אדם. אבל הכובש את נבואתו כגון יונה בן אמיתי דינו בידי שמים

words of a prophet, וְנָבִיא שֶׁעָבַר עַל דִּבְרֵי עַצְמוֹ – **or a prophet who transgresses his own** prophetic **words,** מִיתָתוֹ בִּידֵי שָׁמַיִם – is subject to death, but **his death is at the hands of Heaven;** שֶׁנֶּאֱמַר – **as it says:** ,,אָנֹכִי אֶדְרֹשׁ מֵעִמּוֹ" – ***I*** [God] ***will demand it from him.***[20]

הַמִּתְנַבֵּא בְּשֵׁם עֲבוֹדַת כּוֹכָבִים – **One who prophesies in the name of an idol** וְאוֹמֵר כָּךְ אָמְרָה עֲבוֹדַת כּוֹכָבִים – **and says, "So said this idol,"** אֲפִילּוּ כִּוֵּון אֶת הַהֲלָכָה לְטַמֵּא אֶת הַטָּמֵא וּלְטַהֵר אֶת הַטָּהוֹר – **even if he accorded with the law**[21] – **to render *tamei* that which is *tamei,* and to render *tahor* that which is *tahor*** – he is subject to death by strangulation as a prophet of idolatry.[22]

הַבָּא עַל אֵשֶׁת אִישׁ – **One who cohabits with a married woman** כֵּיוָן שֶׁנִּכְנְסָה לִרְשׁוּת הַבַּעַל לְנִשּׂוּאִין – **once she has entered the domain of the husband for marriage,** אַף עַל פִּי שֶׁלֹּא נִבְעֲלָה – **even though she has not yet cohabited** with him – הַבָּא עָלֶיהָ הֲרֵי זֶה בְּחֶנֶק – **one who cohabits with her** adulterously **is subject to** death by **strangulation.**[23]

וְזוֹמְמֵי בַּת כֹּהֵן – **The *zomemim* witnesses of the daughter of a Kohen,**[24] וּבוֹעֲלָהּ – **as well as the one who cohabits with her** adulterously, are all subject to strangulation;[25] שֶׁכָּל הַמּוּזָמִין מַקְדִּימִין לְאוֹתָהּ מִיתָה – **for** the rule is that **all those who are proven to be *zomemim* advance to that** very **death** that they sought to impose upon their victim, חוּץ מִזּוֹמְמֵי בַּת כֹּהֵן – **with the exception** of the ***zomemim*** **witnesses of the daughter of a Kohen;** וּבוֹעֲלָהּ – **and the one who cohabits with her** as well.[26]

Gemara The Gemara cites a Baraisa that summarizes the death-penalty laws related to prophecy:

תָּנוּ רַבָּנָן – **The Rabbis taught in a Baraisa:** שְׁלֹשָׁה מִיתָתָן בִּידֵי אָדָם – There are THREE WHOSE DEATHS for prophecy-related offenses ARE AT THE HANDS OF MAN, i.e. the courts, where they are executed by strangulation, וּשְׁלֹשָׁה מִיתָתָן בִּידֵי שָׁמַיִם – AND THREE WHOSE DEATHS ARE AT THE HANDS OF HEAVEN. הַמִּתְנַבֵּא מַה שֶּׁלֹּא שָׁמַע – ONE WHO PROPHESIES THAT WHICH HE DID NOT HEAR וּמַה שֶּׁלֹּא נֶאֱמַר לוֹ – and one who prophesies THAT WHICH WAS NOT SAID TO HIM, even though it was said to another prophet, וְהַמִּתְנַבֵּא בְּשֵׁם עֲבוֹדַת כּוֹכָבִים – AND ONE WHO PROPHESIES IN THE NAME OF AN IDOL – מִיתָתָן בִּידֵי אָדָם – THEIR DEATHS ARE AT THE HANDS OF MAN. הַכּוֹבֵשׁ אֶת נְבוּאָתוֹ – ONE WHO SUPPRESSES HIS PROPHECY, וְהַמְוַותֵּר עַל דִּבְרֵי נָבִיא – AND ONE WHO DISREGARDS THE WORDS OF A PROPHET, וְנָבִיא שֶׁעָבַר עַל דִּבְרֵי עַצְמוֹ – AND A PROPHET WHO TRANSGRESSES HIS OWN WORDS – מִיתָתָן בִּידֵי שָׁמַיִם – THEIR DEATHS ARE AT THE HANDS OF HEAVEN.

The Gemara explains the Scriptural source for these laws:

מְנָהָנֵי מִילֵּי – **From where** in Scripture **are these matters** derived? אָמַר רַב יְהוּדָה אָמַר רַב – **Rav Yehudah said in the name of Rav:** דְּאָמַר קְרָא – **For the verse says:**[27] ,,אַךְ הַנָּבִיא אֲשֶׁר יָזִיד לְדַבֵּר דָּבָר בִּשְׁמִי" – ***But the prophet who will willfully speak a word in My Name*** – זֶה הַמִּתְנַבֵּא מַה שֶּׁלֹּא שָׁמַע – **this refers to one who prophesies that which he did not hear.** ,,וַאֲשֶׁר לֹא־צִוִּיתִיו" – **And** the phrase: ***that which I have not commanded him to speak*** – הָא לַחֲבֵירוֹ צִוִּיתִיו – **which implies that I did command his fellow** prophet to speak these words – זֶה הַמִּתְנַבֵּא מַה שֶּׁלֹּא נֶאֱמַר לוֹ – **this** phrase **refers to one who prophesies that which was not said to *him*** even though it was said to another prophet.[28] ,,וַאֲשֶׁר יְדַבֵּר בְּשֵׁם אֱלֹהִים אֲחֵרִים" – And the next phrase: ***or who will speak in the***

NOTES

20. *Deuteronomy* 18:19. This verse refers to one who does not follow the dictates of a prophet. The full verse reads: וְהָיָה הָאִישׁ אֲשֶׁר לֹא־יִשְׁמַע אֶל־דְּבָרַי אֲשֶׁר יְדַבֵּר בִּשְׁמִי אָנֹכִי אֶדְרֹשׁ מֵעִמּוֹ, *And it shall be that the man who does not hearken to My words that he will speak in My name, I will demand it from him*; i.e. his punishment will be at the hands of God, not the courts. [This is in contrast to the statement made in connection with the false prophet in the very next verse – *he shall die* – which implies that he is to be *put to death.*]

21. I.e. even if his declaration coincided with the Torah's law in this matter.

22. Since he speaks in the name of an alien god.

23. Marriage under Torah law is effected in two stages – *erusin* (betrothal) and *nisuin* (full marriage). Adulterous relations with a betrothed *naarah* are subject to death by stoning (Mishnah 66b); adultery with a fully married woman is punishable by strangulation. The state of *nisuin* takes effect when a betrothed woman enters her husband's premises for the purpose of completing the marriage (or the ceremony known as *chuppah).* The Mishnah teaches here that as far as punishment for adultery is concerned, the changeover in her status does not depend on this formality of *chuppah* but on her entrance into the "domain" of her husband. This can take place (independently of *chuppah*) when her father entrusts her to the emissaries of her husband to bring her to him for the completion of the marriage (*Rashi* 90a ד״ה לרשות הבעל based on *Kesubos* 48b; see also conclusion of *sugya* there, 49a).

[The reason for this distinction is that the Torah decrees stoning for a betrothed *naarah* for adultery committed *in her father's house* (*Deuteronomy* 22:21). Once her father has entrusted her to the husband's emissaries to go to the place of *chuppah,* she has departed "her father's house." Thus, although she is still only betrothed, her adultery is treated like that of a fully married woman and is subject to strangulation, not stoning (*Rashi* ibid.).]

24. That is, those who testified falsely that she committed adultery and were proven to have lied by means of *hazamah* (see above, 84b note 7).

25. The daughter of a Kohen is subject to death by burning if she commits adultery (*Leviticus* 21:9, Mishnah 75a), and the man with whom she sinned is subject to death by strangulation. Similarly, witnesses who testified falsely that a Kohen's daughter committed adultery are subject to death by strangulation (not burning), despite the general rule that *zomemim* witnesses are subject to whatever punishment they attempted to impose upon their victim. The Gemara (90a) will explain the reason for this.

26. I.e. just as adultery with a Kohen's daughter involves an exception to the reciprocal-punishment law of *zomemim* witnesses, it involves also an exception to the death-penalty law for sexual offenders. The general rule for such offenses is that both the man and woman are subject to the same punishment. The exception to this rule, the Mishnah states, is the case of adultery with a Kohen's daughter, where the man is executed by strangulation [in common with other adulterers], whereas the woman is executed by burning [Mishnah above, 75a] (*Rashi* 90a). The Gemara will explain the source for this distinction.

27. *Deuteronomy* 18:20. The full text of the verse is: אַךְ הַנָּבִיא אֲשֶׁר יָזִיד לְדַבֵּר דָּבָר בִּשְׁמִי אֵת אֲשֶׁר לֹא־צִוִּיתִיו לְדַבֵּר וַאֲשֶׁר יְדַבֵּר בְּשֵׁם אֱלֹהִים אֲחֵרִים וּמֵת הַנָּבִיא הַהוּא, *But the prophet who will willfully speak a word in My Name, that which I have not commanded him to speak, or who will speak in the name of the gods of others – that prophet shall die.* The Gemara will expound the verse phrase by phrase.

28. The previous phrase – *who will willfully speak a word in My Name* – already implies that the prophet is proclaiming something that he was not commanded to proclaim; there is no need for the verse to elaborate by adding: *that which I have not commanded him to speak*. The Gemara therefore understands this next phrase to refer to another transgression, as if the verse had said "and [he who speaks] that which I have not commanded him to speak." In this context, the emphasis is on the word *him*. Though God may indeed have commanded this prophecy, He did not command it to *him* – the prophet who now proclaims it (see *Sefer HaMitzvos of R' Saadiah Gaon,* vol. III p. 176).

גמרא

דקשר העליון דאורייתא גרוע ועומד אי הכי תפילין נמי אי עביד ארבעה בתי ואייתי אחרינא ואנח גבייהו האי לחודיה קאי והאי לחודיה קאי ואי עביד חמשה בתי גרוע ועומד הוא האמר ר' זירא (א) [א] בית חיצון שאינו רואה את האויר פסול: מתני' [ב] אין ממיתין אותו לא בבית דין שבעירו ולא בבית דין שביבנה אלא מעלין אותו לבית דין הגדול שבירושלים ומשמרין אותו עד הרגל וממיתין אותו ברגל שנאמר א) וכל העם ישמעו ויראו ולא יזידון עוד דברי ר' עקיבא ר' יהודה אומר אין מענין את דינו של זה אלא ממיתין אותו מיד וכותבין ושולחין בכל המקומות איש פלוני ב) מתחייב מיתה בבית דין: גמ' תנו רבנן ג) אין ממיתין אותו לא בבית דין שבעירו ולא בבית דין שביבנה אלא מעלין אותו לב"ד הגדול שבירושלים ומשמרין אותו עד הרגל וממיתין אותו ברגל שנאמר וכל העם ישמעו ויראו דברי רבי עקיבא אמר לו ר' יהודה וכי נאמר יראו וייראו והלא לא נאמר אלא ישמעו וייראו למה מענין דינו של זה אלא ממיתין אותו מיד וכותבין ושולחין בכל מקום איש פלוני נתחייב מיתה בבית דין ת"ר ארבעה צריכין הכרזה [ג] המסית [ד] ובן סורר ומורה [ה] וזקן ממרא [ו] ועדים זוממין בכולהו כתיב בהו א) וכל העם ב) ג) וכל ישראל בעדים זוממין כתיב ד) והנשארי' דלא כולי עלמא חזו לסהדותא: מתני' נביא השקר [ז] המתנבא מה שלא שמע ומה שלא נאמר לו מיתתו בידי אדם [ח] אבל הכובש את נבואתו [ט] והמוותר על דברי נביא [י] ונביא שעבר על דברי עצמו מיתתו בידי שמים שנאמר ה) אנכי אדרש מעמו [כ] המתנבא בשם עבודת כוכבים ואומר כך אמרה עבודת כוכבים אפי' כוון את ההלכה לטמא את הטמא ולטהר את הטהור [ל] הבא על אשת איש כיון שנכנסה ד) לרשות הבעל לנשואין אע"פ שלא נבעלה הבא עליה הרי זה בחנק וזוממי בת כהן ובועלה [מ] שכל המוזמין ה) מקדימין לאותה מיתה [נ] חוץ מזוממי בת כהן ובועלה: גמ' תנו רבנן שלשה מיתתן בידי אדם ושלשה מיתתן בידי שמים המתנבא מה שלא שמע ומה שלא נאמר לו והמתנבא בשם עבודת כוכבים מיתתן בידי אדם הכובש את נבואתו והמוותר על דברי נביא ונביא שעבר על דברי עצמו מיתתן בידי שמים מנהני מילי אמר רב יהודה אמר רב דאמר קרא ו) אך הנביא אשר יזיד לדבר דבר בשמי זה המתנבא מה שלא שמע ו) ואשר לא צויתיו הא לחבירו צויתיו זה המתנבא מה שלא נאמר לו ו) ואשר ידבר בשם אלהים אחרים זה המתנבא בשם עבודת כוכבים וכתיב ו) ומת הנביא ההוא ו) וכל מיתה האמורה בתורה סתם אינה אלא חנק הכובש את נבואתו והמוותר על דברי נביא ונביא שעבר על דברי עצמו מיתתן בידי שמים [א] דכתיב ה) והאיש אשר לא ישמע (א) קרי ביה לא ישמיע וקרי ביה לא ישמע אל דברי וכתיב אנכי אדרש מעמו בידי שמים: המתנבא מה שלא שמע: כגון צדקיה בן כנענה דכתיב ז) ויעש לו צדקיה בן כנענה קרני ברזל מאי הוה ליה למיעבד רוח נבות אטעיתיה דכתיב ח) ויאמר ה' מי יפתה את אחאב ויעל ויפול ברמות גלעד ט) ויצא הרוח ויעמד לפני ה' ויאמר אני אפתנו ויאמר י) תפתה וגם תוכל צא ועשה כן אמר רב יהודה מאי צא צא ממחיצתי י) מאי רוח אמר רבי יוחנן רוחו של נבות היזרעאלי הוה ליה למידק כדרבי יצחק דאמר רבי יצחק סיגנון אחד עולה לכמה נביאים ואין שני נביאים מתנבאין בסיגנון אחד עובדיה אמר כ) זדון לבך השיאך ירמיה אמר ל) תפלצתך השיא אותך זדון לבך והני מדקאמרי כולהו כהדדי שמע מינה לא כלום קאמרי דילמא לא הוה ידע ליה להא דרבי יצחק יהושפט הוה התם וקאמר להו דכתיב מ) ויאמר יהושפט האין פה נביא ח) (עוד לה') אמר ליה הא איכא כל הני אמר ליה כך מקובלני מבית אבי אבא סיגנון אחד עולה לכמה נביאים ואין שני נביאים מתנבאים בסיגנון אחד. המתנבא מה שלא נאמר לו כגון חנניה בן עזור דקאי ירמיה בשוק העליון וקאמר נ) כה אמר ה' [צבאות] הנני שובר את קשת עילם נשא חנניה ק"ו בעצמו מה עילם שלא בא אלא לעזור את בבל אמר הקב"ה הנני שובר את קשת עילם כשדים עצמן על אחת כמה וכמה אתא איהו בשוק התחתון אמר ס) כה אמר ה' וגו' שברתי את עול מלך בבל א"ל רב פפא לאביי האי לחבירו נמי לא נאמר א"ל כיון דאיתיהיב ק"ו למידרש כמאן דאיתמר ליה דמי הוא ניהו דלא נאמר לו המתנבא בשם עבודת כוכבים כגון נביאי הבעל הכובש את נבואתו כגון יונה בן אמיתי והמוותר על דברי נביא כגון

חבריה

רש"י

שאינו רואה את האויר. כגון שהוסיף בית חמישי עליהם בגלדו או דבר אחר: מתני' כל ישראל ישמעו. צריך להשמיע מיתתו לרבים שלא יעשה אדם עוד כן: לא בבית דין שביבנה. אם נשאלו לבית דין שבלשכת הגזית ואמרו להם וחזר לעירו ושהה ימים עד שגלתה סנהדרי גדולה ליבנה ועדיין הבית קיים ואחרי כן הורה כבתחילה אין ממיתין אותו ביבנה ואע"פ שהם סנהדרי גדולה שסוף סוף אין נקבלים שם: גמ' וכי נאמר וכל העם יראו וייראו. דבעינן שיהו רואין במיתתו: הכרזה. פלוני מת בב"ד על שעבר עבירה זו כדי לרדות את האחרים: וכל ישראל. ישמעו וייראו: ובעדים זוממים כתיב והנשארים. ישמעו וייראו משום דלא שייך למיכתב וכל העם דלאו כולי עלמא חזו לסהדותא שיש גזלנין ומלוי ברבית ומועלים בשביעית שהן פסולים לעדות: מתני' ומה שלא נאמר לו. אע"פ שנאמר לחבירו ובגמרא יליף לה: הכובש נבואתו. שלא אמרה כגון יונה בן אמיתי: והמוותר על דברי נביא. המפקירם שלא חשש למה שאמר לו הנביא: גמ' והאיש אשר לא ישמע. היינו מוותר: קרי ביה איש אשר לא ישמיע. היינו כובש וקרי ביה לא ישמע שהוא עצמו אינו נשמע היינו עובר על דברי עצמו: ויצא הרוח ויאמר אני אפתנו. אצא והייתי רוח שקר בפי כל נביאיו: סיגנון. דבר מליצות של רוח הקודש: עולה לכמה נביאים. נכנס בלבם לזה בלשון זה ולזה בלשון זה והכל אחד: ואין שני נביאים מתנבאין בסיגנון אחד. בלשון אחד ואלו כולן לשון אחד היו אומרים דכתיב הנה נא כל הנביאים אומרים פה אחד טוב:

חבריה

תוספות

קשר העליון דאורייתא. פי' בקונט' דפלוגתא היא בפ' התכלת (מנחות דף לה. ושם) וליתיה אלא דמסקינן התם ט) שמע מינה קשר העליון דאורייתא: ולא בבית דין שביבנה. פירש בקונטרס אם נשאלו בבית דין שבלשכת הגזית ואמרו להם וחזר לעירו ושהה ימים עד שגלתה סנהדרי גדולה ותימה דסוף סוף כשממתינין עד הרגל היאך ממיתין הא כיון דגלתה סנהדרין אין דנין דיני נפשות כדאמר בפרק היו בודקין (לעיל דף מא.) וכי תימא דברגל חוזרים ב"ד הגדול ויושבין בלשכת הגזית אף לאחר שגלו ואז דנין אותו חדא דאם כן משכחת ליה לרבן יוחנן בן זכאי דהוה בסנהדרין ובפרק היו בודקין (שם) לא משמע הכי ועוד מאי עינוי הדין יש הא אין שייך עינוי הדין אלא כשמשהין אותו אחר גמר דינו כדמוכח בפרק אחד דיני ממונות (לעיל דף לה.) דפריך לגמרוהו לדיניה בשבתא וליקטלוהו וכו' ומשני אתה מענה את דינו והדר פריך לדיינוהו במעלי שבתא וכו' ועוד מאי אריא זקן ממרא בשאר עבירות נמי ועוד אמאי נקט יבנה לימא לא בב"ד שבחנות ודוחק לומר דאעבירה דקודם שגלתה סנהדרין דנין אף לאחר שגלתה ולא אמרינן מקום גורם כיון דבשעת עבירה סנהדרי גדולה במקומן ור"ת אומר דמיירי כשנגמר דינו קודם שגלתה סנהדרי: י) הכובש נבואתו לוקה. לית ביה לאו ועוד דאין בו מעשה אלא מכין אותו עד שתצא נפשו כמו עשה סוכה ואינו עושה כ):

אליהו

עין משפט נר מצוה

סז א מיי' פ"ד מהל' ממרים הלכה ג:
סח ב ג מיי' פ"ג שם הלכה ח:
סט ד מיי' שם ופ"ז שם הלכה יג:
ע ה מיי' שם פ"ג הלכה ח:
עא ו מיי' שם ופי"ח מהל' עדות הל' ז:
עב ז מיי' פ"ה מהל' ע"ז הלכה ח סמג לאוין לה:
עג ח מיי' פ"ט מהלכות יסודי התורה הל' ג סמג לאוין לג:
עד ט מיי' שם הל' ב סמג עשין ו:
עה י מיי' שם הלכה ג סמג לאוין שם:
עו כ מיי' פ"ה מהל' ע"ז הל' ו סמג שם:
עז ל מיי' פ"ג מהל' איסורי ביאה הל' ד:
עח מ מיי' פי"ח מהל' עדות הלכה א סמג עשין קי:
עט נ מיי' שם פ"כ הל' י:

רבינו חננאל

אמרי היכי דמי אי נימא דעבד ד' בתי בטבלא ואייתי בית אחרינא אנח גבייהו ולא חבריה בהדייהו אמאי חייב האי לחודיה קאי והני לחודייהו קיימי ואי מתחלה עבדינהו ה' בתי ופילש בית חד לחבריה דהיינו ד' כיון דעבדינהו שלא כהלכתן לאו תפלין דכתיבי באורייתא נינהו כלל והאי לא איגרע לפי שהוסיף עליו אלא גרוע ועומד הוה מעיקרא דהא פסול הוא כר' זירא דאמר בית המפולש לחבירו פסול ופרישנ' לא צריכא כגון דעבד טוטפת בת ד' בתי דהויא כהלכתא תפילין מעילאי ואייתי בית אחרינא וחבריה בהדייהו דהיינו כל המוסיף גורע העיקר וכדרבא דאמר בית החיצון שאינו רואה את האויר פסול והאי כיון דאייתי בית מאבראי ואוקמיה קמי החיצון נעשה החיצון פנימי ואינו רואה אויר לפיכך הוא פסול ואתינן להשוויי לולב וציצית לתפילין ונדחו דלא דמו: ת"ר אין ממיתין אותו אלא בב"ד הגדול שבירושלים ואין ממיתין אותו אלא ברגל דברי ר' עקיבא. ר' יהודה אומר ממיתין אותו מיד לפי שאין מענין דינו כו': ת"ר ד' צריכין הכרזה מסית ובן סורר ומורה וזקן ממרא ועדים זוממין כולהו משום [דכתיב בהו] וכל ישראל וכל העם. בעדים זוממין כתיב והנשארים דלאו כולי עלמא חזו לסהדותא: ת"ר ג' מיתתן בידי אדם המתנבא מה שלא שמע ומה שלא נאמר לו והמתנבא בשם ע"ז. מנא הני מילי אמר רב יהודה אמר רב דאמר קרא אך הנביא אשר יזיד לדבר דבר בשמי זה המתנבא מה שלא שמע את אשר לא צויתיו הא לנביא אחר צויתיו זה המתנבא מה שלא נאמר לו. ואשר ידבר בשם אלהים אחרים זה המתנבא בשם ע"ז וכתיב ומת הנביא ההוא (שכל) [וכל] מיתה האמורה בתורה סתם חנק הוא. אבל נביא הכובש נבואתו והמוותר על דברי הנביא ונביא שעבר על דברי עצמו מיתתן בידי שמים. ואסיקנא המתנבא מה שלא שמע כגון צדקיה בן כנענה. ואע"ג דאמרינן מדכתיב ויאמר אצא והייתי רוח שקר בפי כל נביאיו שמעינן מינה רוח נבות אטעיתיה מדהוה ליה למבדק בהא דאין סיגנון אחד עולה לשני נביאים. כלומר אין ב' נביאים מתנבאים בסיגנון אחד. והני כולהו עלה להן סיגנון אחד כלומר דבר אחד (וכולן מתנבאין בסיגנון אחד). כדכתיב עלה ויתן ה' ביד המלך ש"מ אין נבואה זו כהוגן דא"ר יצחק סיגנון אחד עולה לכמה נביאים ואין ב' נביאים מתנבאים בסיגנון אחד. סיגנון אחד עולה לכמה נביאים זה עובדיה וירמיה עובדיה הוציא בלשון זדון לבך השיאך. וירמיה אמר תפלצתך השיא אותך זדון לבך ודחינן ודלמא צדקיה בן כנענה לא הוה ידע הא שמעתא דר' יצחק ופרקינן יהושפט הוה התם ואמר להו כך מקובל אני מבית אבי אבא שאין שני נביאים מתנבאין בסיגנון אחד. והיינו דכתיב ויאמר יהושפט האין פה נביא לה' עוד ונדרשה מאתו. כלומר אלו כולן אינן נביאי ה': המתנבא מה שלא נאמר לו כגון חנניה בן עזור דשמע לירמיה דאמר כה אמר ה' צבאות הנני שובר את קשת עילם וגו' נשא ק"ו כה אמר ה' צבאות אלהי ישראל לאמר שברתי את עול מלך בבל וזה הק"ו יש לו לירמיה לשאת אותו אבל לזולתו לא. המתנבא בשם ע"ז כגון נביאי [הבעל] אלו כולן מיתתן בידי אדם. אבל הכובש את נבואתו כגון יונה בן אמיתי דינו בידי

שמים

מסורת הש"ס

א) [בערוך ערך פלש א' גרים בית המפולש לחבירו פסול פי' אי מתחלה עבדינהו ה' בתי ופליש חד בית לחבריה דהיינו ד' בתי וכו' ע"ש], ב) [במשנה שבמשניות ובברייתא הסמוכה איתא נתחייב], ג) [תוספתא פי"א], ד) [פירש"י על בבא זו עי' ברש"י לקמן ל. וע"ע בפירש"י דמכות ב. ד"ה התם קאי וכו' ובמ"ש תוס' שם ד"ה כל כו' ובד"ה זוממין], ה) מכות ב. [ע"ש], ו) [לעיל נב: פד:], ז) שבת קמט: [לקמן קב:], ח) [צ"ל לה' עוד], ט) [דף לט.], י) זה שייך לע"ב, כ) [כתובות פו.].

הגהות הב"ח

(א) גמ' דכתיב והאיש אשר לא ישמע וקרי ביה לא ישמיע וקרי ביה לא יִשָּׁמַע:

הגהות הגר"א

[א] גמ' והאיש אשר לא ישמע וגו'. נ"ב גי' הגאונים והיה וגו' אשר וגו' וכתיב אנכי וגו'. והיא הנכונה:

ליקוטי רש"י

[נדפס בדף פח:]

תורה אור השלם

א) וְכָל הָעָם יִשְׁמְעוּ וְיִרָאוּ וְלֹא יְזִידוּן עוֹד: [דברים יז, יג]

ב) וְכָל יִשְׂרָאֵל יִשְׁמְעוּ וְיִרָאוּן וְלֹא יוֹסִפוּ לַעֲשׂוֹת כַּדָּבָר הָרָע הַזֶּה בְּקִרְבֶּךָ: [דברים יג, יב]

ג) וּרְגָמֻהוּ כָּל אַנְשֵׁי עִירוֹ בָאֲבָנִים וָמֵת וּבִעַרְתָּ הָרָע מִקִּרְבֶּךָ וְכָל יִשְׂרָאֵל יִשְׁמְעוּ וְיִרָאוּ: [דברים כא, כא]

ד) וְהַנִּשְׁאָרִים יִשְׁמְעוּ וְיִרָאוּ וְלֹא יֹסִפוּ לַעֲשׂוֹת עוֹד כַּדָּבָר הָרָע הַזֶּה בְּקִרְבֶּךָ: [דברים יט, כ]

ה) וְהָיָה הָאִישׁ אֲשֶׁר לֹא יִשְׁמַע אֶל דְּבָרַי אֲשֶׁר יְדַבֵּר בִּשְׁמִי אָנֹכִי אֶדְרֹשׁ מֵעִמּוֹ: [דברים יח, יט]

ו) אַךְ הַנָּבִיא אֲשֶׁר יָזִיד לְדַבֵּר דָּבָר בִּשְׁמִי אֵת אֲשֶׁר לֹא צִוִּיתִיו לְדַבֵּר וַאֲשֶׁר יְדַבֵּר בְּשֵׁם אֱלֹהִים אֲחֵרִים וּמֵת הַנָּבִיא הַהוּא: [דברים יח, כ]

ז) וַיַּעַשׂ לוֹ צִדְקִיָּהוּ בֶן כְּנַעֲנָה קַרְנֵי בַרְזֶל וַיֹּאמֶר כֹּה אָמַר יְיָ בְּאֵלֶּה תְּנַגַּח אֶת אֲרָם עַד כַּלּוֹתָם: [דברי הימים ב' יח, י]

ח) וַיֹּאמֶר יְיָ מִי יְפַתֶּה אֶת אַחְאָב וְיַעַל וְיִפֹּל בְּרָמֹת גִּלְעָד וַיֹּאמֶר זֶה בְּכֹה וְזֶה אֹמֵר בְּכֹה: [מלכים א' כב, כ]

ט) וַיֵּצֵא הָרוּחַ וַיַּעֲמֹד לִפְנֵי יְיָ וַיֹּאמֶר אֲנִי אֲפַתֶּנּוּ וַיֹּאמֶר יְיָ אֵלָיו בַּמָּה: [מלכים א' כב, כא]

י) וַיֹּאמֶר אֵצֵא וְהָיִיתִי רוּחַ שֶׁקֶר בְּפִי כָּל נְבִיאָיו וַיֹּאמֶר תְּפַתֶּה וְגַם תּוּכָל צֵא וַעֲשֵׂה כֵן: [מלכים א' כב, כב]

כ) זְדוֹן לִבְּךָ הִשִּׁיאֶךָ שֹׁכְנִי בְחַגְוֵי סֶלַע מְרוֹם שִׁבְתּוֹ אֹמֵר בְּלִבּוֹ מִי יוֹרִדֵנִי אָרֶץ: [עובדיה א, ג]

ל) תִּפְלַצְתְּךָ הִשִּׁיא אֹתָךְ זְדוֹן לִבֶּךָ שֹׁכְנִי בְּחַגְוֵי הַסֶּלַע תֹּפְשִׂי מְרוֹם גִּבְעָה כִּי תַגְבִּיהַּ כַּנֶּשֶׁר קִנֶּךָ מִשָּׁם אוֹרִידְךָ נְאֻם יְיָ: [ירמיה מט, טז]

מ) וַיֹּאמֶר יְהוֹשָׁפָט הַאֵין פֹּה נָבִיא לַייָ עוֹד וְנִדְרְשָׁה מֵאוֹתוֹ: [מלכים א' כב, ז]

נ) כֹּה אָמַר יְיָ צְבָאוֹת הִנְנִי שֹׁבֵר אֶת קֶשֶׁת עֵילָם רֵאשִׁית גְּבוּרָתָם: [ירמיה מט, לה]

ס) כֹּה אָמַר יְיָ צְבָאוֹת אֱלֹהֵי יִשְׂרָאֵל לֵאמֹר שָׁבַרְתִּי אֶת עֹל מֶלֶךְ בָּבֶל: [ירמיה כח, ב]

name of the gods of others – זֶה הַמִּתְנַבֵּא בְּשֵׁם עֲבוֹדַת כּוֹכָבִים – **this refers to one who prophesies in the name of an idol.** וּכְתִיב – **Now** at the end of this verse **it is written:** "וּמֵת הַנָּבִיא הַהוּא" – *that prophet shall die,* וְכָל מִיתָה הָאֲמוּרָה בַּתּוֹרָה סְתָם אֵינָהּ אֶלָּא חֶנֶק – **and** we have a rule that **whenever** putting to **death is mentioned by the Torah in an undefined manner,** i.e. without specifying the type of death, **it refers to no other** death **than strangulation.**[29]

The Gemara now gives the source for the three prophecy-related death penalties that are at the hands of Heaven:

הַכּוֹבֵשׁ אֶת נְבוּאָתוֹ – ONE WHO SUPPRESSES HIS PROPHECY, וְהַמְוַותֵּר עַל דִּבְרֵי נָבִיא – AND ONE WHO DISREGARDS THE WORDS OF A PROPHET וְנָבִיא שֶׁעָבַר עַל דִּבְרֵי עַצְמוֹ – AND A PROPHET WHO TRANSGRESSES HIS OWN WORDS – מִיתָתָן בִּידֵי שָׁמַיִם – THEIR DEATHS ARE AT THE HANDS OF HEAVEN. What is the source for this? דִּכְתִיב "וְהָאִישׁ אֲשֶׁר לֹא יִשְׁמַע" – **For it is written:** ***And it shall be that the man who does not hearken*** *to My words that he* [the prophet] *will speak in My Name . . .*[30] According to its simple meaning, the verse refers here to one who disregards the words of a prophet. Exegetically, however, קְרִי בֵּיהּ לֹא יַשְׁמִיעַ – you may **read this as,** ***he*** *who* ***will not proclaim,*** thereby making reference to the prophet who suppresses his prophecy,[31] וּקְרִי בֵּיהּ לֹא יִשָּׁמַע אֶל דְּבָרַי – **and** you may also **read this as,** ***he*** *who* ***will not obey My words,*** referring to one who transgresses his own prophecy.[32] וּכְתִיב – **Now** at the end of this verse **it is written** in regard to the three offenders alluded to in it: "אָנֹכִי אֶדְרֹשׁ מֵעִמּוֹ" – ***I*** [God] ***will demand it from him*** – his punishment is **in the hands of Heaven.**[33]

The Gemara now cites Scriptural examples of the prophecy-related transgressions enumerated above:

הַמִּתְנַבֵּא מַה שֶּׁלֹּא שָׁמַע – ONE WHO PROPHESIES THAT WHICH HE DID NOT HEAR – כְּגוֹן צִדְקִיָּה בֶּן כְּנַעֲנָה – **for example, Tzidkiah ben Kenaanah,** דִּכְתִיב – **as it is written:** "וַיַּעַשׂ לוֹ צִדְקִיָּה בֶן־כְּנַעֲנָה קַרְנֵי בַרְזֶל" – ***And Tzidkiah ben Kenaanah made for himself horns of iron,*** *and said, "Thus has Hashem said: With these shall you gore the Arameans until they are eradicated."*[34]

The Gemara questions this example:

מַאי הֲוָה לֵיהּ לְמֶעֱבַד – **What could he** (Tzidkiah) **have done?** רוּחַ נָבוֹת אַטְעִיתֵיהּ – **The spirit of Navos misled him!**[35] דִּכְתִיב – **As it is written:**[36] "וַיֹּאמֶר ה׳ מִי יְפַתֶּה אֶת־אַחְאָב וְיַעַל וְיִפֹּל בְּרָמֹת גִּלְעָד. . ." – ***And Hashem said, "Who will entice Ahab so that he shall go up and fall at Ramos Gilead?"*** "וַיֵּצֵא הָרוּחַ וַיַּעֲמֹד לִפְנֵי ה׳ וַיֹּאמֶר אֲנִי אֲפַתֶּנּוּ. . ." – ***. . . And the spirit came forth and stood before Hashem and said, "I will entice him."***[37] "וַיֹּאמֶר תְּפַתֶּה וְגַם־תּוּכָל צֵא וַעֲשֵׂה־כֵן" – ***. . . And [Hashem] said, "You will entice and also prevail. Go out and do so."*** The spirit of Navos then induced a spirit of false prophecy that deceived

NOTES

29. This was derived by the Gemara above, at the end of 52b.

30. See above, note 20.

31. [A Torah scroll is written without any vowel markings above or below its letters. The rules of Biblical exegesis therefore permit a word to be expounded not only according to the vowels assigned by tradition, but also according to other plausible combinations of vowels. This in no way detracts from the correctness of the received vowelization; it merely serves as an exegetical basis for additional laws alluded to by the verse.]

The word ישמע found in this verse, which tradition tells should be read as יִשְׁמַע (*yishma*), may also be vowelized יַשְׁמִעַ (*yashmia*), meaning *cause to be heard,* i.e. proclaim. Read this way, the verse refers to a prophet who refuses to proclaim the prophecy given to him (*Rashi*).

The textual indication for this alternative reading is the unexpected wording of our verse. The previous verse concludes with the statement: *and he* [the prophet] *shall speak to them all that I will command him.* It would therefore seem logical that the Torah's injunction in our verse should also refer to the prophet's words, and say: "And . . . the man who will not hearken to *the prophet's* words that he will speak in My Name. . ." Why does our verse say instead, "who will not hearken to *My* [God's] words"? This shift indicates that there is also an alternative reading being alluded to by the verse, according to which the object of the verse must be God's words and not the prophet's. The reading thus indicated is יַשְׁמִעַ, *proclaim,* according to which the verse states: "And the man [i.e. prophet] who will not *proclaim* My words. . ." (*Gur Aryeh* to *Deuteronomy* 18:19, cited by *Tosefos Yom Tov*).

32. The word ישמע can also be vowelized as יִשָּׁמַע (*yishama*). Read this way it refers to *one who does not hearken himself,* i.e. one who does not heed his own prophecy (*Rashi*).

[This alternative reading may also be suggested by a seeming redundancy in the verse. The verse previous to this one concludes with the words: *and he* [the prophet] *shall speak to them all that I will command him.* Accordingly, our verse could simply have continued: וַאֲשֶׁר לֹא יִשְׁמַע אֶל דְּבָרַי, *And he who will not hearken to My words*. . . Why does our verse preface itself by adding: וְהָיָה הָאִישׁ, *And it shall be that the man* [who will not hearken to My words]? This indicates that the verse is speaking of more than one person who refuses to hearken. To accommodate this extra person into the verse's injunction, the key phrase לֹא יִשְׁמַע should also be read as לֹא יִשָּׁמַע, *will not obey*. (See *Tos. Yom Tov* who suggests a somewhat different explanation along these lines.)] See next note.

33. [It is curious that the Gemara should find it necessary to establish a separate Scriptural source for a prophet who transgresses his own prophecy. Why is this not the same as "disregarding the words of a prophet," for which the Gemara cited another source? (Indeed, *Mizrachi* and *Gur Aryeh* in their commentaries to the verse do not seem to make a separate derivation for a prophet transgressing his own prophecy. However, as *Rashi* explains the Gemara here, there is a separate derivation for it.)

It could be argued that the prohibition to disregard the words of a prophet applies only to a prophecy that has been spoken, and the Torah must therefore warn a prophet not to transgress his prophecy even if he has never told it to anyone. However, the Scriptural example the Gemara (89b) will give of this transgression deals with a case in which the prophet (Iddo) did articulate his prophecy before transgressing it. Possibly, the answer is that an ordinary person would be allowed to disregard the words of a prophet if he were later commanded to do so by another prophet (since changing circumstances might result in a new Divine directive). A prophet, however, may never transgress his own prophecy on the basis of another prophet's words (since God would not alter His previous directive to him without telling it to him personally). This is indeed the example given by the Gemara (89b) of a prophet who transgressed his own prophecy. (See *Teshuvos HaRashba* 1:11; see also *Meiri.*)]

34. *I Kings* 22:11. Yehoshafat, the righteous king of Judah, entered into an alliance with Ahab, the wicked king of Israel. Ahab convinced Yehoshafat to join him in attacking Aram, but Yehoshafat asked that a prophet of Hashem first be consulted. Ahab gathered four hundred prophets, all of whom advised him to embark on the campaign. To give substance to their predictions of success, Tzidkiah ben Kenaanah, one of these prophets, forged horns of iron and told Ahab and Yehoshafat in the name of Hashem that with these horns they would succeed in "goring" Aram into extinction. Yehoshafat then asked for yet one more prophet to be consulted. Much against his will, Ahab produced Michayehu ben Yimla, who foretold Ahab's death in battle. The verse states (with the prophet Michayehu speaking to Ahab): *And now behold! Hashem has put a lying spirit in the mouth of all these prophets of yours, and Hashem has spoken evil against you* (ibid. v. 23). Michayehu's prophecy indeed came true.

35. A spirit of prophecy had indeed possessed Tzidkiah ben Kenaanah, but it had been sent from Heaven bearing a false message designed to lure Ahab to his death (ibid. vs. 19-23).

Navos was the name of a man who had owned a vineyard adjacent to the royal estate and Ahab coveted it. When Navos refused to sell the vineyard, Ahab had Navos falsely convicted and executed for blasphemy, and then confiscated his property (*I Kings* ch. 21).

36. *I Kings* 22:20-22.

37. The verse continues: *And Hashem said to him, "With what?" And he said, "I will go forth and I will be a lying spirit in the mouth of all his prophets. . ."*

דקשר העליון דאורייתא גרוע ועומד אי הכי תפילין נמי אי עביד ארבעה בתי ואייתי אחרינא ואנח גבייהו האי לחודיה קאי והאי לחודיה קאי ואי עביד חמשה בתי גרוע ועומד הוא האמר ר' זירא (א) [א] בית חיצון שאינו רואה את האויר פסול: **מתני'** [ב] אין ממיתין אותו לא בבית דין שבעירו ולא בבית דין שביבנה אלא מעלין אותו לבית דין הגדול שבירושלים ומשמרין אותו עד הרגל וממיתין אותו ברגל שנאמר א) וכל העם ישמעו ויראו ולא יזידון עוד דברי ר' עקיבא ר' יהודה אומר אין מענין את דינו של זה אלא ממיתין אותו מיד וכותבין ושולחין בכל המקומות איש פלוני (ב) מתחייב מיתה בבית דין: **גמ'** תנו רבנן (ג) אין ממיתין אותו לא בבית דין שבעירו ולא בבית דין שביבנה אלא מעלין אותו לב"ד הגדול שבירושלים ומשמרין אותו עד הרגל וממיתין אותו ברגל שנאמר וכל העם ישמעו ויראו דברי רבי עקיבא אמר לו ר' יהודה וכי נאמר יראו וייראו והלא לא נאמר אלא ישמעו וייראו למה מענין דינו של זה אלא ממיתין אותו מיד וכותבין ושולחין בכל מקום איש פלוני נתחייב מיתה בבית דין ת"ר ארבעה צריכין הכרזה [ג] המסית [ד] ובן סורר ומורה [ה] וזקן ממרא [ו] ועדים זוממין בכולהו כתיב בהו א) וכל העם ב) (ג) וכל ישראל בעדים זוממין כתיב ד) והנשארי' דלא כולי עלמא חזו לסהדותא: **מתני'** נביא השקר [ז] המתנבא מה שלא שמע ומה שלא נאמר לו מיתתו בידי אדם [ח] אבל הכובש את נבואתו [ט] והמוותר על דברי נביא [י] ונביא שעבר על דברי עצמו מיתתו בידי שמים שנאמר ה) אנכי אדרש מעמו [כ] המתנבא בשם עבודת כוכבים ואומר כך אמרה עבודת כוכבים אפי' כוון את ההלכה לטמא את הטמא ולטהר את הטהור [ל] הבא על אשת איש כיון שנכנסה (ד) לרשות הבעל לנשואין אע"פ שלא נבעלה הבא עליה הרי זה בחנק וזוממי בת כהן ובועלה [מ] שכל המוזמין (ה) מקדימין לאותה מיתה [נ] חוץ מזוממי בת כהן ובועלה: **גמ'** תנו רבנן שלשה מיתתן בידי אדם ושלשה מיתתן בידי שמים המתנבא מה שלא שמע ומה שלא נאמר לו והמתנבא בשם עבודת כוכבים מיתתן בידי אדם הכובש את נבואתו והמוותר על דברי נביא ונביא שעבר על דברי עצמו מיתתן בידי שמים מנהני מילי אמר רב יהודה אמר רב דאמר קרא ו) אך הנביא אשר יזיד לדבר דבר בשמי זה המתנבא מה שלא שמע ו) ואשר לא צויתיו הא לחבירו צויתיו זה המתנבא מה שלא נאמר לו ו) ואשר ידבר בשם אלהים אחרים זה המתנבא בשם עבודת כוכבים וכתיב ו) ומת הנביא ההוא (ו) וכל מיתה האמורה בתורה סתם אינה אלא חנק הכובש את נבואתו והמוותר על דברי נביא ונביא שעבר על דברי עצמו מיתתן בידי שמים [א] דכתיב ה) והאיש אשר לא ישמע (א) קרי ביה לא ישמיע וקרי ביה לא ישמע אל דברי וכתיב אנכי אדרש מעמו בידי שמים: המתנבא מה שלא שמע: כגון צדקיה בן כנענה דכתיב ז) ויעש לו צדקיה בן כנענה קרני ברזל מאי הוה ליה למיעבד רוח נבות אטעיתיה דכתיב ח) ויאמר ה' מי יפתה את אחאב ויעל ויפול ברמות גלעד ט) ויצא הרוח ויעמד לפני ה' ויאמר אני אפתנו ויאמר י) תפתה וגם תוכל צא ועשה כן אמר רב יהודה מאי צא צא ממחיצתי (ז) מאי רוח אמר רבי יוחנן רוחו של נבות היזרעאלי הוה ליה למידק כדרבי יצחק דאמר רבי יצחק סיגנון אחד עולה לכמה נביאים ואין שני נביאים מתנבאין בסיגנון אחד עובדיה אמר כ) זדון לבך השיאך ירמיה אמר ל) תפלצתך השיא אותך זדון לבך והני מדקאמרי כולהו כהדדי שמע מינה לא כלום קאמרי דילמא לא הוה ידע ליה להא דרבי יצחק יהושפט הוה התם וקאמר להו דכתיב מ) ויאמר יהושפט האין פה נביא (ח) (עוד לה') אמר ליה הא איכא כל הני אמר ליה כך מקובלני מבית אבי אבא סיגנון אחד עולה לכמה נביאים ואין שני נביאים מתנבאים בסיגנון אחד. המתנבא מה שלא נאמר לו כגון חנניה בן עזור דקאי ירמיה בשוק העליון וקאמר נ) כה אמר ה' [צבאות] הנני שובר את קשת עילם נשא חנניה ק"ו בעצמו מה עילם שלא בא אלא לעזור את בבל אמר הקב"ה הנני שובר את קשת עילם כשדים עצמן על אחת כמה וכמה אתא איהו בשוק התחתון אמר ס) כה אמר ה' וגו' שברתי את עול מלך בבל א"ל רב פפא לאביי האי לחבירו נמי לא נאמר א"ל כיון דאיתיהיב ק"ו למידרש כמאן דאיתמר ליה דמי הוא ניהו דלא נאמר לו המתנבא בשם עבודת כוכבים כגון נביאי הבעל הכובש את נבואתו כגון יונה בן אמיתי והמוותר על דברי נביא כגון

חבריה

רש"י

שאינו רואה את האויר. כגון שהוסיף בית חמישי עליהם בלדו או דבר אחר: **מתני'** כל ישראל ישמעו. צריך להשמיע מיתתו לרבים שלא יעשה אדם עוד כן: לא בבית דין שביבנה. אם נשאלו לבית דין שבלשכת הגזית ואמרו להם וחזר לעירו ושנה ימים עד שגלתה סנהדרי גדולה ליבנה ועדיין הבית קיים ואחרי כן הורה כבתחילה אין ממיתין אותו ביבנה ואע"פ ששם סנהדרי גדולה שסוף סוף אין נקבצים שם: **גמ'** וכי נאמר וכל העם יראו וייראו. דבעינן שיהו רואין במיתתו: הכרזה. פלוני מת בב"ד על שעבר עבירה זו כדי לרדות את האחרים: וכל ישראל. ישמעו ויראו: ובעדים זוממים כתיב והנשארים. ישמעו ויראו משום דלא שייך למיכתב וכל העם דלאו כולי עלמא חזו לסהדותא שיש גזלנין ומלוי ברבית ומועלים בשביעית שהן פסולים לעדות: **מתני'** ומה שלא נאמר לו. אע"פ שנאמר לחבירו ובגמרא יליף לה: הכובש נבואתו. שלא אמרה כגון יונה בן אמיתי: והמוותר על דברי נביא. המפקירם שלא חשש למה שאמר לו הנביא: **גמ'** והאיש אשר לא ישמע. היינו מוותר: קרי ביה איש אשר לא ישמיע. היינו כובש וקרי ביה לא ישמע שהוא עצמו אינו נשמע היינו עובר על דברי עצמו: ויצא הרוח ויאמר אני אפתנו. אלא והייתי רוח שקר בפי כל נביאיו: סיגנון. דבר מליצות של רוח הקודש: עולה לכמה נביאים. נכנס בלבם לזה בלשון זה ולזה בלשון זה והכל אחד: ואין שני נביאים מתנבאין בסיגנון אחד. בלשון אחד ואלו כולן לשון אחד היו אומרים דכתיב הנה נא כל הנביאים אומרים פה אחד טוב:

חבריה

תוספות

קשר העליון דאורייתא. פי' בקונט' דפלוגתא היא בפ' התכלת (מנחות דף לט. ושם) וליתיה אלא דמסקינן התם (ט) שמע מינה קשר העליון דאורייתא: **ולא** בבית דין שביבנה. פירש בקונטרס אם נשאלו בבית דין שבלשכת הגזית ואמרו להם וחזר לעירו ושנה ימים עד שגלתה סנהדרי גדולה ותימה דסוף סוף כשממתינין עד הרגל היאך ממיתין הא כיון דגלתה סנהדרין אין דנין דיני נפשות כדאמר בפרק היו בודקין (לעיל דף מא.) וכי תימא דברגל חוזרים ב"ד הגדול ויושבין בלשכת הגזית אף לאחר שגלו ואז דנין אותו חדא דאם כן משכחת ליה לרבן יוחנן בן זכאי דהוה בסנהדרין ובפרק היו בודקין (שם) לא משמע הכי ועוד מאי עינוי הדין יש הא אין שייך עינוי הדין אלא כששהין אותו אחר גמר דינו כדמוכח בפרק אחד דיני ממונות (לעיל דף לה.) דפריך לגמרוהו לדיניה בשבתא וליקטלוהו וכו' ומשני אתה מענה את דינו והדר פריך לדיינוהו במעלי שבתא וכו' ועוד מאי אריא זקן ממרא בשאר עבירות נמי ועוד אמאי נקט יבנה לימא לא בב"ד שבחנות ודוחק לומר דאעבירה דקודם שגלתה סנהדרין דנין אף לאחר שגלתה ולא אמרינן מקום גורם כיון דבשעת עבירה סנהדרי גדולה במקומן ור"ת אומר דמיירי כשנגמר דינו קודם שגלתה סנהדרי: (י) **הכובש** נבואתו לוקה. לית ביה לאו ועוד דאין בו מעשה אלא מכין אותו עד שתצא נפשו כמו עשה סוכה ואינו עושה (כ):

אליהו

מסורת הש"ס

א) [בערוך ערך פלש א' גרים בית המפולש לחבירו פסול פי' אי מתחלה עבדינהו ה' בתי ופליש חד בית לחבריה דהיינו ד' בתי וכו' ע"ש], ב) [במשנה שבמשניות ובברייתא הסמוכה איתא נתחייב], ג) [תוספתא פי"א], ד) [פירש"י על בבא זו עי' ברש"י לקמן צ. וע"ע בפירש"י דמכות ב. ד"ה התם קאי וכו' ובמ"ש תוס' שם ד"ה כל כו' ובד"ה זוממי], ה) מכות ב. [ע"ש], ו) [לעיל נב: פד:], ז) שבת קמט: [לקמן קב:], ח) [צ"ל לה' עוד], ט) [דף לט.], י) זה שייך לע"ב, כ) [כתובות פו.].

הגהות הב"ח

(א) גמ' דכתיב והאיש אשר לא ישמע וקרי ביה לא ישמיע וקרי ביה לא ישמע:

הגהות הגר"א

[א] גמ' והאיש אשר לא ישמע וגו'. נ"ב ג"' הגאונים והיה וגו' אשר וגו' וכתיב אנכי וגו'. והיא הנכונה:

ליקוטי רש"י

[נדפס בדף פח:]

תורה אור השלם

א) וְכָל הָעָם יִשְׁמְעוּ וְיִרָאוּ וְלֹא יְזִידוּן עוֹד: [דברים יז, יג]

ב) וְכָל יִשְׂרָאֵל יִשְׁמְעוּ וְיִרָאוּן וְלֹא יוֹסִפוּ לַעֲשׂוֹת כַּדָּבָר הָרָע הַזֶּה בְּקִרְבֶּךָ: [דברים יג, יב]

ג) וּרְגָמֻהוּ כָּל אַנְשֵׁי עִירוֹ בָאֲבָנִים וָמֵת וּבִעַרְתָּ הָרָע מִקִּרְבֶּךָ וְכָל יִשְׂרָאֵל יִשְׁמְעוּ וְיִרָאוּ: [דברים כא, כא]

ד) וְהַנִּשְׁאָרִים יִשְׁמְעוּ וְיִרָאוּ וְלֹא יֹסִפוּ לַעֲשׂוֹת עוֹד כַּדָּבָר הָרָע הַזֶּה בְּקִרְבֶּךָ: [דברים יט, כ]

ה) וְהָיָה הָאִישׁ אֲשֶׁר לֹא יִשְׁמַע אֶל דְּבָרַי אֲשֶׁר יְדַבֵּר בִּשְׁמִי אָנֹכִי אֶדְרֹשׁ מֵעִמּוֹ: [דברים יח, יט]

ו) אַךְ הַנָּבִיא אֲשֶׁר יָזִיד לְדַבֵּר דָּבָר בִּשְׁמִי אֵת אֲשֶׁר לֹא צִוִּיתִיו לְדַבֵּר וַאֲשֶׁר יְדַבֵּר בְּשֵׁם אֱלֹהִים אֲחֵרִים וּמֵת הַנָּבִיא הַהוּא: [דברים יח, כ]

ז) וַיַּעַשׂ לוֹ צִדְקִיָּהוּ בֶן כְּנַעֲנָה קַרְנֵי בַרְזֶל וַיֹּאמֶר כֹּה אָמַר יְיָ בְּאֵלֶּה תְּנַגַּח אֶת אֲרָם עַד כַּלּוֹתָם: [דברי הימים ב' יח, י]

ח) וַיֹּאמֶר יְיָ מִי יְפַתֶּה אֶת אַחְאָב וְיַעַל וְיִפֹּל בְּרָמֹת גִּלְעָד וַיֹּאמֶר זֶה בְּכֹה וְזֶה אֹמֵר בְּכֹה: [מלכים א' כב, כ]

ט) וַיֵּצֵא הָרוּחַ וַיַּעֲמֹד לִפְנֵי יְיָ וַיֹּאמֶר אֲנִי אֲפַתֶּנּוּ וַיֹּאמֶר יְיָ אֵלָיו בַּמָּה: [מלכים א' כב, כא]

י) וַיֹּאמֶר אֵצֵא וְהָיִיתִי רוּחַ שֶׁקֶר בְּפִי כָּל נְבִיאָיו וַיֹּאמֶר תְּפַתֶּה וְגַם תּוּכָל צֵא וַעֲשֵׂה כֵן: [מלכים א' כב, כב]

כ) זְדוֹן לִבְּךָ הִשִּׁיאֶךָ שֹׁכְנִי בְחַגְוֵי סֶלַע מְרוֹם שִׁבְתּוֹ אֹמֵר בְּלִבּוֹ מִי יוֹרִדֵנִי אָרֶץ: [עובדיה א, ג]

ל) תִּפְלַצְתְּךָ הִשִּׁיא אֹתָךְ זְדוֹן לִבֶּךָ שֹׁכְנִי בְּחַגְוֵי הַסֶּלַע תֹּפְשִׂי מְרוֹם גִּבְעָה כִּי תַגְבִּיהַּ כַּנֶּשֶׁר קִנֶּךָ מִשָּׁם אוֹרִידְךָ נְאֻם יְיָ: [ירמיה מט, טז]

מ) וַיֹּאמֶר יְהוֹשָׁפָט הַאֵין פֹּה נָבִיא לַיְיָ עוֹד וְנִדְרְשָׁה מֵאֹתוֹ: [מלכים א' כב, ז]

נ) כֹּה אָמַר יְיָ צְבָאוֹת הִנְנִי שֹׁבֵר אֶת קֶשֶׁת עֵילָם רֵאשִׁית גְּבוּרָתָם: [ירמיה מט, לה]

ס) כֹּה אָמַר יְיָ צְבָאוֹת אֱלֹהֵי יִשְׂרָאֵל לֵאמֹר שָׁבַרְתִּי אֶת עֹל מֶלֶךְ בָּבֶל: [ירמיה כח, ב]

עין משפט נר מצוה

סז א מיי' פ"ד מהל' ממרים הלכה ג:

סח ב ג מיי' פ"ג שם הלכה ח:

סט ד מיי' שם ופ"ז שם הלכה יג:

ע ה מיי' שם פ"ג הלכה ח:

עא ו מיי' שם ופי"ח מהל' עדות הל' ז:

עב ז מיי' פ"ה מהל' ע"ז הלכה ח סמג לאוין לה:

עג ח מיי' פ"ט מהלכות יסודי התורה הל' ג סמג לאוין לג:

עד ט מיי' שם הל' ב סמג עשין ו:

עה י מיי' שם הלכה ג סמג לאוין שם:

עו כ מיי' פ"ה מהל' ע"ז הל' ו סמג שם:

עז ל מיי' פ"ג מהל' איסורי ביאה הל' ד:

עח מ מיי' פי"ח מהל' עדות הלכה א סמג עשין קי:

עט נ מיי' שם פ"כ הל' י:

רבינו חננאל

אמרי היכי דמי אי נימא דעבד ד' בתי בטבלא ואייתי בית אחרינא אנח גבייהו ולא חבריה בהדייהו אמאי חייב האי לחודיה קאי והני לחודייהו קיימי ואי מתחלה עבדינהו ה' בתי ופילש בית חד לחבריה דהיינו ד' כיון דעבדינהו שלא כהלכתן לאו תפלין דכתיבי באורייתא נינהו כלל והאי לא איגרע לפי שהוסיף עליו אלא גרוע ועומד הוה מעיקרא דהא פסול הוא כר' זירא דאמר בית המפולש לחבירו פסול ופרישנ' לא צריכא כגון דעבד טוטפת בת ד' בתי דהויא כהלכתא תפילין מעילאי ואייתי בית אחרינא וחבריה בהדייהו דהיינו כל המוסיף גורע העיקר וכדרבא דאמר בית החיצון שאינו רואה את האויר פסול והאי כיון דאייתי בית מאבראי ואוקמיה קמי החיצון נעשה החיצון פנימי ואינו רואה אויר לפיכך הוא פסול ואתינן להשוויי לולב וציצית לתפילין ונדחו דלא דמו: **ת"ר** אין ממיתין אותו אלא בב"ד הגדול שבירושלים ואין ממיתין אותו אלא ברגל דברי ר' עקיבא. ר' יהודה אומר ממיתין אותו מיד לפי שאין מענין דינו כו': **ת"ר** ד' צריכין הכרזה מסית ובן סורר ומורה וזקן ממרא ועדים זוממין כולהו משום [דכתיב בהו] וכל ישראל וכל העם. בעדים זוממין כתיב והנשארים דלאו כולי עלמא חזו לסהדותא: **ת"ר** ג' מיתתן בידי אדם המתנבא מה שלא שמע ומה שלא נאמר לו והמתנבא בשם ע"ז. מנא הני מילי אמר רב יהודה אמר רב דאמר קרא אך הנביא אשר יזיד לדבר דבר בשמי זה המתנבא מה שלא שמע את אשר לא צויתיו הא לנביא אחר צויתיו זה המתנבא מה שלא נאמר לו. ואשר ידבר בשם אלהים אחרים זה המתנבא בשם ע"ז וכתיב ומת הנביא ההוא (שכל) [וכל] מיתה האמורה בתורה סתם חנק הוא. אבל נביא הכובש נבואתו והמותר על דברי הנביא ונביא שעבר על דברי עצמו מיתתן בידי שמים. ואסיקנא המתנבא מה שלא שמע כגון צדקיה בן כנענה. ואע"ג דאמרינן מדכתיב ויאמר אצא והייתי רוח שקר בפי כל נביאיו שמעינן מינה רוח נבות אטעיתיה מדהוה ליה למבדק בהא דאין סיגנון אחד עולה לשני נביאים. כלומר אין ב' נביאים מתנבאים בסיגנון אחד. והני כולהו עלה להן סיגנון אחד כלומר דבר אחד (וכולן מתנבאין בסיגנון אחד). כדכתיב עלה ויתן ה' ביד המלך ש"מ אין נבואה זו כהוגן דא"ר יצחק סיגנון אחד עולה לכמה נביאים ואין ב' נביאים מתנבאים בסיגנון אחד. סיגנון אחד עולה לכמה נביאים זה עובדיה וירמיה עובדיה הוציא בלשון זדון לבך השיאך. וירמיה אמר תפלצתך השיא אותך זדון לבך ודחינן ודלמא צדקיה בן כנענה לא הוה ידע הא שמעתא דר' יצחק ופרקינן יהושפט הוה התם ואמר להו כך מקובל אני מבית אבי אבא שאין שני נביאים מתנבאין בסיגנון אחד. והיינו דכתיב ויאמר יהושפט האין פה נביא לה' עוד ונדרשה מאתו. כלומר אלו כולן אינן נביאי ה': **המתנבא** מה שלא נאמר לו כגון חנניה בן עזור דשמע לירמיה דאמר כה אמר ה' צבאות הנני שובר את קשת עילם וגו' נשא ק"ו כה אמר ה' צבאות אלהי ישראל לאמר שברתי את עול מלך בבל וזה הק"ו יש לו לירמיה לשאת אותו אבל לזולתו לא. המתנבא בשם ע"ז כגון נביאי [הבעל] אלו כולן מיתתן בידי אדם. אבל הכובש את נבואתו כגון יונה בן אמיתי דינו בידי

שמים

Tzidkiah ben Kenaanah into prophesying the success of Ahab's campaign.[38] Accordingly, why should Tzidkiah ben Kenaanah be held responsible for prophesying this false message?

Before answering the question, the Gemara digresses to explain certain points in the verse just cited:[39]

אָמַר רַב יְהוּדָה – **Rav Yehudah said:** מַאי ,,צֵא'' – **What is** the meaning of ***Go out***? צֵא מִמְּחִיצָּתִי – God said to the spirit, **"Leave My environs."**[40] מַאי ,,רוּחַ'' – **What is the *spirit*** of which the verse speaks? אָמַר רַבִּי יוֹחָנָן רוּחוֹ שֶׁל נָבוֹת הַיִּזְרְעֵאלִי – **Said R' Yochanan:** It refers to **the spirit of Navos the Yizraelite.**[41]

The Gemara now answers its earlier question of how Tzidkiah could be held accountable for false prophecy after being deceived by the lying spirit of Navos:

הֲוָה לֵיהּ לְמֵידַק כִּדְרַבִּי יִצְחָק – **He should have discerned** the falsity of his prophecy, **as R' Yitzchak** explained: דְּאָמַר רַבִּי יִצְחָק – **For R' Yitzchak has said:** סִיגְנוֹן אֶחָד עוֹלֶה לְכַמָּה נְבִיאִים – **One** prophetic **signal** may **come to several prophets,** וְאֵין שְׁנֵי נְבִיאִים מִתְנַבְּאִין בְּסִיגְנוֹן אֶחָד – **but two prophets never communicate a prophecy in** exactly **the same** verbal **signals** (i.e. words). Rather, the message is invariably expressed somewhat differently by each prophet.[42]

The Gemara cites an example of this rule:

עוֹבַדְיָה אָמַר – The prophet **Ovadiah said:** ,,זְדוֹן לִבְּךָ הִשִּׁיאֶךָ'' – ***The malice of your heart has beguiled you.***[43] יִרְמְיָה אָמַר – **Jeremiah said:** ,,תִּפְלַצְתְּךָ הִשִּׁיא אֹתָךְ זְדוֹן לִבֶּךָ'' – ***Your tyranny has beguiled you, even the malice of your heart.***[44] Thus we see the same thought expressed by two different prophets in slightly different fashion.

The Gemara resumes its explanation of Tzidkiah's sin:

וְהָנֵי מִדְקָאָמְרֵי כּוּלְּהוּ כַּהֲדָדֵי – **Now these** four hundred prophets of Ahab who foretold his success in battle, **since they all said** exactly **the same as one another,** שְׁמַע מִינָּהּ לֹא כְּלוּם קָאָמְרֵי – **one could deduce from that** fact alone **that they said nothing at all** that was true. Seeing this, Tzidkiah ben Kenaanah should have refrained from continuing his prophecy.

The Gemara questions how Tzidkiah could have been held accountable on this basis:

דִּילְמָא לֹא הֲוָה יָדַע לֵיהּ לְהָא דְּרַבִּי יִצְחָק – **Perhaps he was unaware of this** rule **of R' Yitzchak.** How does that make him accountable as a false prophet?

The Gemara answers:

יְהוֹשָׁפָט הֲוָה הָתָם וְקָאָמַר לְהוּ – **Yehoshafat was there and he told them** that their prophecy could not be genuine for this reason; דִּכְתִיב – **as it is written:** ,,וַיֹּאמֶר יְהוֹשָׁפָט הַאֵין פֹּה נָבִיא לַה' עוֹד'' – ***And Yehoshafat said, "Is there no other prophet to Hashem here?"***[45] אָמַר לֵיהּ הָא אִיכָּא כָּל הָנֵי – **[Ahab] said to him** [Yehoshafat]: **But there are all these** four hundred whose prophecy you just heard. Why do you ask for yet another prophet? אָמַר לֵיהּ – **[Yehoshafat] replied to him:** כָּךְ מְקוּבְּלַנִי מִבֵּית אֲבִי אַבָּא – **Such** is the tradition that **I have received from the house of my grandfather:**[46] סִיגְנוֹן אֶחָד עוֹלֶה לְכַמָּה נְבִיאִים וְאֵין שְׁנֵי נְבִיאִים מִתְנַבְּאִים בְּסִיגְנוֹן אֶחָד – **One** prophetic **signal** may **come to several prophets, but two prophets never communicate a prophecy in** exactly **the same** verbal **signals** (i.e. words).[47]

The Gemara now gives an example from Scripture of the next type of false prophecy that renders its speaker subject to execution:

הַמִּתְנַבֵּא מַה שֶּׁלֹּא נֶאֱמַר לוֹ – ONE WHO PROPHESIES THAT WHICH WAS NOT SAID TO HIM but rather to another prophet – כְּגוֹן חֲנַנְיָה בֶּן עַזּוּר – **for example, Chananiah ben Azur,** who lived in the days of Jeremiah and prophesied that the Babylonian exile foretold by Jeremiah would not come to pass.[48] What led Chananiah to say this?[49] דְּקָאֵי יִרְמְיָה בְּשׁוּק הָעֶלְיוֹן וְקָאָמַר – **For Jeremiah was standing in the upper marketplace** of Jerusalem **and proclaiming:** ,,כֹּה אָמַר ה' [צְבָאוֹת] הִנְנִי שֹׁבֵר אֶת־קֶשֶׁת עֵילָם'' – ***So said Hashem [Lord of Hosts]: Behold I am about to***

NOTES

38. [It was fitting that Ahab be lured to his destruction by falsity, inasmuch as he killed Navos in this manner, by hiring witnesses to testify falsely that Navos had committed blasphemy (cf. *Maharsha*).]

39. [Although this next point does not seem relevant to the discussion of our Gemara, it is part of an exposition of this verse stated below, on 102b. The Gemara here quotes the entire exposition.]

40. Literally: go out from My partition. God banished the spirit of Navos from His presence. Although it was fulfilling God's purpose by luring Ahab to his death, the instrument of falsehood that it chose to accomplish this task has no place in the presence of God, the source of Truth (*Shabbos* 149b).

Alternatively, whoever is the cause of another's punishment is excluded from the presence of God. It is unbecoming to the righteous that even the wicked should suffer punishment through them, as stated in *Proverbs* (17:26): עֲנוֹשׁ לַצַּדִּיק לֹא־טוֹב, *To punish is for the righteous not good* (*Shabbos* ibid.).

41. Prophecy is often associated with the term "spirit." [See, for example, *Numbers* 11:29: *Would that the entire people of Hashem could be prophets, if Hashem would but place His spirit upon them.*] However, the use of the definite article to identify this spirit ("and *the* spirit came forth... and said, 'I will entice him' ") indicates that the spirit mentioned here is not the one ordinarily associated with prophecy but one associated specifically with Ahab. Thus, the Sages see this as a reference to Navos, whose life was cut short – and whose soul was thereby prematurely returned to the spirit state – through the machinations of Ahab and Jezebel (see *Maharsha* here and 102b).

42. Prophecy did not generally consist of formal statements but rather of images whose meaning was apparent to the prophet (*Rambam, Hil. Yesodei HaTorah* 7:3, based on *Numbers* 12:8). Moreover, the precise form in which the image was comprehended depended on the unique set of qualities and characteristics of each prophet's soul. Its articulation thus varied slightly from prophet to prophet (see *Sefer HaIkkarim* 3:9, cited by *Margaliyos HaYam*).

The word נָבִיא (prophet) primarily means *one who proclaims* or *communicates* (see *Exodus* 7:1) and is related to the expression (*Isaiah* 57:19) נִיב שְׂפָתַיִם, *fruit of the lips* (*Rashi* to *Exodus* 7:1).

43. *Ovadiah* 1:3. This is part of a prophecy foretelling the destruction of Edom.

44. *Jeremiah* 49:16. This prophecy, too, foretells the destruction of Edom.

45. *I Kings* 22:7. After hearing the prophecy of the four hundred prophets and Tzidkiah ben Kenaanah, Yehoshafat inquired if there was yet another prophet of Hashem to ask. Ahab then produced Michayehu ben Yimla, who foretold Ahab's death.

46. I.e. King David; see *Rashi, Berachos* 10a ד״ה מקובלני מבית אבי אבא.

47. Thus, Tzidkiah ben Kenaanah had been properly warned by Yehoshafat that his "prophetic" inspiration could not be true. Since he subsequently fashioned iron horns and prophesied in the name of Hashem that Ahab would destroy Aram with those horns, he was held guilty of false prophecy.

48. Chananiah prophesied in the Name of Hashem that the Babylonian hegemony over Israel would be broken and that within two years' time, the Temple vessels and the people exiled to Babylonia together with King Yechoniah would be returned to the Land of Israel. This contradicted Jeremiah's earlier prophecy that if the king did not submit to Babylonian rule, Jerusalem and the Temple would be destroyed and the rest of the nation would be forced into exile. Following Chananiah's prophecy, Jeremiah was told to confront him and declare his prophecy false. See *Jeremiah* ch. 28.

49. Chananiah had at one time been a true prophet of Hashem (below, 90a). He would not deliberately say something he knew to be false.

דקשר העליון דאורייתא גרוע ועומד אי הכי תפילין נמי אי עביד ארבעה בתי ואייתי אחרינא ואנח גבייהו האי לחודיה קאי והאי לחודיה קאי ואי עביד חמשה בתי גרוע ועומד הוא האמר ר' זירא (א) [א]בית חיצון שאינו רואה את האויר פסול: **מתני'** [ב]אין ממיתין אותו לא בבית דין שבעירו ולא בבית דין שביבנה אלא מעלין אותו לבית דין הגדול שבירושלים ומשמרין אותו עד הרגל וממיתין אותו ברגל שנאמר א) וכל העם ישמעו ויראו ולא יזידון עוד דברי ר' עקיבא ר' יהודה אומר אין מענין את דינו של זה אלא ממיתין אותו מיד וכותבין ושולחין בכל המקומות איש פלוני ב) מתחייב מיתה בבית דין: **גמ'** תנו רבנן ג) אין ממיתין אותו לא בבית דין שבעירו ולא בבית דין שביבנה אלא מעלין אותו לב"ד הגדול שבירושלים ומשמרין אותו עד הרגל וממיתין אותו ברגל שנאמר וכל העם ישמעו ויראו דברי רבי עקיבא אמר לו ר' יהודה וכי נאמר יראו וייראו והלא לא נאמר אלא ישמעו וייראו למה מענין דינו של זה אלא ממיתין אותו מיד וכותבין ושולחין בכל מקום איש פלוני נתחייב מיתה בבית דין ת"ר ארבעה צריכין הכרזה [ג]המסית [ד]ובן סורר ומורה [ה]וזקן ממרא [ו]ועדים זוממין בכולהו כתיב בהו א) וכל העם ב) ג) וכל ישראל בעדים זוממין כתיב ד) והנשארי' דלא כולי עלמא חזו לסהדותא: **מתני'** נביא השקר [ז]המתנבא מה שלא שמע ומה שלא נאמר לו מיתתו בידי אדם [ח]אבל הכובש את נבואתו [ט]והמוותר על דברי נביא [י]ונביא שעבר על דברי עצמו מיתתו בידי שמים שנאמר ה) אנכי אדרש מעמו [כ]המתנבא בשם עבודת כוכבים ואומר כך אמרה עבודת כוכבים אפי' כוון את ההלכה לטמא את הטמא ולטהר את הטהור [ל]הבא על אשת איש כיון שנכנסה ד) לרשות הבעל לנשואין אע"פ שלא נבעלה הבא עליה הרי זה בחנק וזוממי בת כהן ובועלה [מ]שכל המוזמין ה) מקדימין לאותה מיתה [נ]חוץ מזוממי בת כהן ובועלה: **גמ'** תנו רבנן שלשה מיתתן בידי אדם ושלשה מיתתן בידי שמים המתנבא מה שלא שמע ומה שלא נאמר לו והמתנבא בשם עבודת כוכבים מיתתן בידי אדם הכובש את נבואתו והמוותר על דברי נביא ונביא שעבר על דברי עצמו מיתתן בידי שמים מנהני מילי אמר רב יהודה אמר רב דאמר קרא ו) אך הנביא אשר יזיד לדבר דבר בשמי זה המתנבא מה שלא שמע ו) ואשר לא צויתיו הא לחבירו צויתיו זה המתנבא מה שלא נאמר לו ו) ואשר ידבר בשם אלהים אחרים זה המתנבא בשם עבודת כוכבים וכתיב ו) ומת הנביא ההוא ו) וכל מיתה האמורה בתורה סתם אינה אלא חנק הכובש את נבואתו והמוותר על דברי נביא ונביא שעבר על דברי עצמו מיתתן בידי שמים [א] דכתיב ה) והאיש אשר לא ישמע (א) קרי ביה לא ישמיע וקרי ביה לא ישמע אל דברי וכתיב אנכי אדרש מעמו בידי שמים: המתנבא מה שלא שמע: כגון צדקיה בן כנענה דכתיב ז) ויעש לו צדקיה בן כנענה קרני ברזל מאי הוה ליה למיעבד רוח נבות אטעיתיה דכתיב ח) ויאמר ה' מי יפתה את אחאב ויעל ויפול ברמות גלעד ט) ויצא הרוח ויעמד לפני ה' ויאמר אני אפתנו ויאמר י) תפתה וגם תוכל צא ועשה כן אמר רב יהודה מאי צא צא ממחיצתי י) מאי רוח אמר רבי יוחנן רוחו של נבות היזרעאלי הוה ליה למידק כדרבי יצחק דאמר רבי יצחק סיגנון אחד עולה לכמה נביאים ואין שני נביאים מתנבאין בסיגנון אחד עובדיה אמר כ) זדון לבך השיאך ירמיה אמר ל) תפלצתך השיא אותך זדון לבך והני מדקאמרי כולהו כהדדי שמע מינה לא כלום קאמרי דילמא לא הוה ידע ליה להא דרבי יצחק יהושפט הוה התם וקאמר להו דכתיב מ) ויאמר יהושפט האין פה נביא י) (עוד לה') אמר ליה הא איכא כל הני אמר ליה כך מקובלני מבית אבי אבא סיגנון אחד עולה לכמה נביאים ואין שני נביאים מתנבאים בסיגנון אחד. המתנבא מה שלא נאמר לו כגון חנניה בן עזור דקאי ירמיה בשוק העליון וקאמר נ) כה אמר ה' [צבאות] הנני שובר את קשת עילם נשא חנניה ק"ו בעצמו מה עילם שלא בא אלא לעזור את בבל אמר הקב"ה הנני שובר את קשת עילם כשדים עצמן על אחת כמה וכמה אתא איהו בשוק התחתון אמר ס) כה אמר ה' וגו' שברתי את עול מלך בבל א"ל רב פפא לאביי האי לחבירו נמי לא נאמר א"ל כיון דאיתיהיב ק"ו למידרש כמאן דאיתמר ליה דמי הוא ניהו דלא נאמר לו המתנבא בשם עבודת כוכבים כגון נביאי הבעל הכובש את נבואתו כגון יונה בן אמיתי והמוותר על דברי נביא כגון חבריה

רש"י

שאינו רואה את האויר. כגון שהוסיף בית חמישי עליהם בלדו או דבר אחר: **מתני'** כל ישראל ישמעו. לריך להשמיע מיתתו לרבים שלא יעשה אדם עוד כן: לא בבית דין שביבנה. אם נשאלו לבית דין שבלשכת הגזית ואמרו להם וחזר לעירו ושהה ימים עד שגלתה סנהדרי גדולה ליבנה ועדיין הבית קיים ואחרי כן הורה כבתחילה אין ממיתין אותו ביבנה ואע"פ ששם סנהדרי גדולה שסוף סוף אין נקבלים שם: **גמ'** וכי נאמר וכל העם יראו וייראו. דבעינן שיהו רואין במיתתו: הכרזה. פלוני מת בב"ד על שעבר עבירה זו כדי לרדות את האחרים: וכל ישראל. ישמעו וייראו: ובעדים זוממים כתיב והנשארים. ישמעו וייראו משום דלא שייך למיכתב וכל העם דלאו כולי עלמא חזו לסהדותא שיש גזלנין ומלוי בריבית ומועלים בשביעית שהן פסולים לעדות: **מתני'** ומה שלא נאמר לו. אע"פ שנאמר לחבירו ובגמרא יליף לה: הכובש נבואתו. שלא אמרה כגון יונה בן אמיתי: והמוותר על דברי נביא. המפקירם שלא חשש למה שאמר לו הנביא: **גמ'** והאיש אשר לא ישמע. היינו מוותר: קרי ביה איש אשר לא ישמיע. היינו כובש וקרי ביה לא ישמע שהוא עלמו אינו נשמע היינו עובר על דברי עלמו: ויצא הרוח ויאמר אני אפתנו. אלא והייתי רוח שקר בפי כל נביאיו: סיגנון. דבר מליצות של רוח הקודש: עולה לכמה נביאים. נכנס לזה בלשון זה ולזה בלשון זה והכל אחד: ואין שני נביאים מתנבאין בסיגנון אחד. בלשון אחד ואלו כולן לשון אחד היו אומרים דכתיב הנה נא כל הנביאים אומרים פה אחד טוב: חבריה

תוספות

קשר העליון דאורייתא. פי' בקונט' דפלוגתא היא בפ' התכלת (מנחות דף לט. ושם) וליתיה אלא דמסקינן התם ט) שמע מינה קשר העליון דאורייתא: **ולא** בבית דין שביבנה. פירש בקונטרס אם נשאלו בבית דין שבלשכת הגזית ואמרו להם וחזר לעירו ושהה ימים עד שגלתה סנהדרי גדולה ותימה דסוף סוף כשממתינין עד הרגל היאך ממיתין הא כיון דגלתה סנהדרין אין דנין דיני נפשות כדאמר בפרק היו בודקין (לעיל דף מא.) וכי תימא דברגל חוזרים ב"ד הגדול ויושבין בלשכת הגזית אף לאחר שגלו ואז דנין אותו חדא דאם כן משכחת ליה לרבן יוחנן בן זכאי דהוה בסנהדרין ובפרק היו בודקין (שם) לא משמע הכי ועוד מאי עינוי הדין יש הא אין שייך עינוי הדין אלא כששהין אותו אחר גמר דינו כדמוכח בפרק אחד דיני ממונות (לעיל דף לה.) דפריך לגמרוהו לדיניה בשבתא וליקטלוהו וכו' ומשני אתה מענה את דינו והדר פריך לדיינוהו במעלי שבתא וכו' ועוד מאי אריא זקן ממרא בשאר עבירות נמי ועוד אמאי נקט יבנה לימא לא בב"ד שבחנות ודוחק לומר דלעבירה דקודם שגלתה סנהדרין דנין אף לאחר שגלתה ולא אמרינן מקום גורם כיון דבשעת עבירה סנהדרי גדולה במקומן ור"ת אומר דמיירי כשנגמר דינו קודם שגלתה סנהדרי: **הכובש** י) נבואתו לוקה. לית ביה לאו ועוד דאין בו מעשה אלא מכין אותו עד שתלא נפשו כמו עשה סוכה ואינו עושה כ): אליהו

עין משפט נר מצוה

סז א מיי' פ"ד מהל' ממרים הלכה ג:
סח ב ג מיי' פ"ג שם הלכה ח:
סט ד מיי' שם ופ"ז שם הלכה יג:
ע ה מיי' שם פ"ג הלכה ח:
עא ו מיי' שם ופי"ח מהל' עדות הל' ז:
עב ז מיי' פ"ה מהל' ע"ז הלכה ט סמג לאוין לה:
עג ח מיי' פ"ט מהלכות יסודי התורה הל' ג סמג לאוין לג:
עד ט מיי' שם הל' ב סמג עשין ו:
עה י מיי' שם הלכה ג סמג לאוין שם:
עו כ מיי' פ"ה מהל' ע"ז הל' ו סמג שם:
עז ל מיי' פ"ג מהל' איסורי ביאה הל' ד:
עח מ מיי' פי"ח מהל' עדות הלכה א סמג עשין קי:
עט נ מיי' שם פ"כ הל' י:

רבינו חננאל

אמרי היכי דמי אי נימא דעבד ד' בתי בטבלא ואייתי בית אחרינא אנח גבייהו ולא חבריה בהדייהו אמאי חייב האי לחודיה קאי והני לחודייהו קיימי ואי מתחלה עבדינהו ה' בתי ופילש בית חד לחבריה דהיינו ד' כיון דעבדינהו שלא כהלכתן לאו תפלין דכתיבי באורייתא נינהו כלל והאי לא איגרע לפי שהוסיף עליו אלא גרוע ועומד הוה מעיקרא דהא פסול הוא כר' זירא דאמר בית המפולש לחבירו פסול ופרישנ' לא צריכא כגון דעבד טוטפת בת ד' בתי דהויא כהלכתא תפילין מעילאי ואייתי בית אחרינא וחבריה בהדייהו דהיינו כל המוסיף גורע העיקר וכדרבא דאמר בית החיצון שאינו רואה את האויר פסול והאי כיון דאייתי בית מאבראי ואוקמיה קמי החיצון נעשה החיצון פנימי ואינו רואה אויר לפיכך הוא פסול ואתינן להשוויי לולב וציצית לתפילין ונדחו דלא דמו: **ת"ר** אין ממיתין אותו אלא בב"ד הגדול שבירושלים ואין ממיתין אותו אלא ברגל דברי ר' עקיבא. ר' יהודה אומר ממיתין אותו מיד לפי שאין מענין דינו כו': **ת"ר** ד' צריכין הכרזה מסית ובן סורר ומורה וזקן ממרא ועדים זוממין כולהו משום [דכתיב בהו] וכל ישראל וכל העם. בעדים זוממין כתיב והנשארים דלאו כולי עלמא חזו לסהדותא: **ת"ר** ג' מיתתן בידי אדם המתנבא מה שלא שמע ומה שלא נאמר לו והמתנבא בשם ע"ז. מנא הני מילי אמר רב יהודה אמר רב דאמר קרא אך הנביא אשר יזיד לדבר דבר בשמי זה המתנבא מה שלא שמע את אשר לא צויתיו הא לנביא אחר צויתיו זה המתנבא מה שלא נאמר לו. ואשר ידבר בשם אלהים אחרים זה המתנבא בשם ע"ז וכתיב ומת הנביא ההוא (שכל) [וכל] מיתה האמורה בתורה סתם חנק הוא. אבל נביא הכובש נבואתו והמותר על דברי הנביא ונביא שעבר על דברי עצמו מיתתן בידי שמים. ואסיקנא המתנבא מה שלא שמע כגון צדקיה בן כנענה. ואע"ג דאמרינן מדכתיב ויאמר אצא והייתי רוח שקר בפי כל נביאיו שמעינן מינה רוח נבות אטעיתיה מדהוה ליה למבדק בהא דאין סיגנון אחד עולה לשני נביאים. כלומר אין ב' נביאים מתנבאים בסיגנון אחד. והני כולהו עלה להן סיגנון אחד כלומר דבר אחד (וכולן מתנבאין בסיגנון אחד). כדכתיב עלה ויתן ה' ביד המלך ש"מ אין נבואה זו כהוגן דא"ר יצחק סיגנון אחד עולה לכמה נביאים ואין ב' נביאים מתנבאים בסיגנון אחד. סיגנון אחד עולה לכמה נביאים זה עובדיה וירמיה עובדיה הוציא בלשון זדון לבך השיאך. וירמיה אמר תפלצתך השיא אותך זדון לבך ודחינן ודלמא צדקיה בן כנענה לא הוה ידע הא שמעתא דר' יצחק ופרקינן יהושפט הוה התם ואמר להו כך מקובל אני מבית אבי אבא שאין שני נביאים מתנבאין בסיגנון אחד. והיינו דכתיב ויאמר יהושפט האין פה נביא לה' עוד ונדרשה מאתו. כלומר אלו כולן אינן נביאי ה': **המתנבא** מה שלא נאמר לו כגון חנניה בן עזור דשמע לירמיה דאמר כה אמר ה' צבאות הנני שובר את קשת עילם וגו' נשא ק"ו כה אמר ה' צבאות אלהי ישראל לאמר שברתי את עול מלך בבל וזה הק"ו יש לו לירמיה לשאת אותו אבל לזולתו לא. המתנבא בשם ע"ז כגון נביאי [הבעל] אלו כולן מיתתן בידי אדם. אבל הכובש את נבואתו כגון יונה בן אמיתי דינו בידי שמים

מסורת הש"ס

א) [בערך ערך פלש א' גרים בית המפולש לחבירו פסול פי' אי מתחלה עבדינהו ד' בתי ופלש חד בית לחבריה דהיינו ד' בתי וכו' ע"ש], ב) [במתניתא שבמשניות ובבריתא הסמוכה איתא נתחייב], ג) [תוספתא פי"א], ד) [פירש"י על גבא זו ע' רש"י לקמן ל. וע"ע בפירש"י למכות ג. ד"ה הכא קאי וכו' ובתוס' שם ד"ה כל כו' ובד"ה זוממין], ה) מכות ב. [ע"ש], ו) [לעיל נב: פד:], ז) שבת קמו: [לקמן קב:], ח) [נ"ל לה' עוד], ט) [דף לט.], י) יש שייך לע"ב, כ) [כתובות סו.].

הגהות הב"ח

(א) גמ' דכתיב והאיש אשר לא ישמע וקרי ביה לא ישמיע וקרי ביה לא ישמע:

הגהות הגר"א

[א] גמ' והאיש אשר לא ישמע וגו'. נ"ב ג' הגאונים והיה וגו' ואשר וגו' וכתיב אנכי וגו'. והיא הנכונה.

ליקוטי רש"י

[נדפס בדף פח:]

תורה אור השלם

א) וְכָל הָעָם יִשְׁמְעוּ וְיִרָאוּ וְלֹא יְזִידוּן עוֹד: [דברים יז, יג]
ב) וְכָל יִשְׂרָאֵל יִשְׁמְעוּ וְיִרָאוּן וְלֹא יוֹסִפוּ לַעֲשׂוֹת כַּדָּבָר הָרָע הַזֶּה בְּקִרְבֶּךָ: [דברים יג, יב]
ג) וּרְגָמֻהוּ כָּל אַנְשֵׁי עִירוֹ בָאֲבָנִים וָמֵת וּבִעַרְתָּ הָרָע מִקִּרְבֶּךָ וְכָל יִשְׂרָאֵל יִשְׁמְעוּ וְיִרָאוּ: [דברים כא, כא]
ד) וְהַנִּשְׁאָרִים יִשְׁמְעוּ וְיִרָאוּ וְלֹא יֹסִפוּ לַעֲשׂוֹת עוֹד כַּדָּבָר הָרָע הַזֶּה בְּקִרְבֶּךָ: [דברים יט, כ]
ה) וְהָיָה הָאִישׁ אֲשֶׁר לֹא יִשְׁמַע אֶל דְּבָרַי אֲשֶׁר יְדַבֵּר בִּשְׁמִי אָנֹכִי אֶדְרֹשׁ מֵעִמּוֹ: [דברים יח, יט]
ו) אַךְ הַנָּבִיא אֲשֶׁר יָזִיד לְדַבֵּר דָּבָר בִּשְׁמִי אֵת אֲשֶׁר לֹא צִוִּיתִיו לְדַבֵּר וַאֲשֶׁר יְדַבֵּר בְּשֵׁם אֱלֹהִים אֲחֵרִים וּמֵת הַנָּבִיא הַהוּא: [דברים יח, כ]
ז) וַיַּעַשׂ לוֹ צִדְקִיָּהוּ בֶן כְּנַעֲנָה קַרְנֵי בַרְזֶל וַיֹּאמֶר כֹּה אָמַר יְיָ בְּאֵלֶּה תְּנַגַּח אֶת אֲרָם עַד כַּלּוֹתָם: [דברי הימים ב' יח, י]
ח) וַיֹּאמֶר יְיָ מִי יְפַתֶּה אֶת אַחְאָב וְיַעַל וְיִפֹּל בְּרָמֹת גִּלְעָד וַיֹּאמֶר זֶה בְּכֹה וְזֶה אֹמֵר בְּכֹה: [מלכים א' כב, כ]
ט) וַיֵּצֵא הָרוּחַ וַיַּעֲמֹד לִפְנֵי יְיָ וַיֹּאמֶר אֲנִי אֲפַתֶּנּוּ וַיֹּאמֶר יְיָ אֵלָיו בַּמָּה: [מלכים א' כב, כא]
י) וַיֹּאמֶר אֵצֵא וְהָיִיתִי רוּחַ שֶׁקֶר בְּפִי כָּל נְבִיאָיו וַיֹּאמֶר תְּפַתֶּה וְגַם תּוּכָל צֵא וַעֲשֵׂה כֵן: [מלכים א' כב, כב]
כ) זְדוֹן לִבְּךָ הִשִּׁיאֶךָ שֹׁכְנִי בְחַגְוֵי סֶלַע מְרוֹם שִׁבְתּוֹ אֹמֵר בְּלִבּוֹ מִי יוֹרִדֵנִי אָרֶץ: [עובדיה א, ג]
ל) תִּפְלַצְתְּךָ הִשִּׁיא אֹתָךְ זְדוֹן לִבֶּךָ שֹׁכְנִי בְּחַגְוֵי הַסֶּלַע תֹּפְשִׂי מְרוֹם גִּבְעָה כִּי תַגְבִּיהַּ כַּנֶּשֶׁר קִנֶּךָ מִשָּׁם אוֹרִידְךָ נְאֻם יְיָ: [ירמיה מט, טז]
מ) וַיֹּאמֶר יְהוֹשָׁפָט הַאֵין פֹּה נָבִיא לַייָ עוֹד וְנִדְרְשָׁה מֵאֹתוֹ: [מלכים א' כב, ז]
נ) כֹּה אָמַר יְיָ צְבָאוֹת הִנְנִי שֹׁבֵר אֶת קֶשֶׁת עֵילָם רֵאשִׁית גְּבוּרָתָם: [ירמיה מט, לה]
ס) כֹּה אָמַר יְיָ צְבָאוֹת אֱלֹהֵי יִשְׂרָאֵל לֵאמֹר שָׁבַרְתִּי אֶת עֹל מֶלֶךְ בָּבֶל: [ירמיה כח, ב]

break the strength of Eilam.[50] נָשָׂא חֲנַנְיָה קַל וָחוֹמֶר בְּעַצְמוֹ – **Chananiah,** overhearing this prophecy, **drew** from it **a** ***kal vachomer*** **of his own:** מָה עֵילָם שֶׁלֹּא בָא אֶלָּא לַעֲזוֹר אֶת בָּבֶל – **Now if Eilam, which came** and fought against Israel **only to assist Babylonia,**[51] אָמַר הַקָּדוֹשׁ בָּרוּךְ הוּא ,,הִנְנִי שֹׁבֵר אֶת־קֶשֶׁת עֵילָם'' – nevertheless, **the Holy One, Blessed is He,** now **says** about it: ***Behold, I am about to break the strength of Eilam;*** כַּשְׂדִּים עַצְמָן עַל אַחַת כַּמָּה וְכַמָּה – then **how much more so** must it be God's intention to break **the Chaldeans** (i.e. Babylonians) **themselves!** אָתָא אִיהוּ בְּשׁוּק הַתַּחְתּוֹן אָמַר – **He** then **came into the lower marketplace** of Jerusalem **and proclaimed:** ,,כֹּה־אָמַר ה' וגו' שָׁבַרְתִּי אֶת־עֹל מֶלֶךְ בָּבֶל'' – ***So said Hashem*** *Lord of Hosts, the God of Israel, saying:* ***I have broken the yoke of the king of Babylon.***[52]

This example is challenged:

אָמַר לֵיהּ רַב פָּפָּא לְאַבַּיֵי – **Rav Pappa said to Abaye:** הַאי לַחֲבֵירוֹ נַמִּי לֹא נֶאֱמַר – **This prophecy was not said to his fellow prophet either.** How then can you cite the case of Chananiah ben Azur as an example of one who prophesies that which was not said to him, but rather to another prophet?

Abaye responds:

אָמַר לֵיהּ – **He said to [Rav Pappa]:** כֵּיוָן דְּאִיתְיְהִיב קַל וָחוֹמֶר לְמִידְרַשׁ – **Since the principle of** ***kal vachomer*** **was given** by God as a device with which **to expound** the Torah,[53] כְּמַאן דְּאִיתְמַר לֵיהּ דָּמֵי – what is derived from **it may be considered as if it had been said to [Jeremiah].** הוּא נִיהוּ דְּלֹא נֶאֱמַר לוֹ – Therefore, **it is only to him** (Chananiah) **that it was not said,** but it can be seen as having been said to his fellow prophet.[54]

The Gemara provides a Scriptural example of prophets of idolatry:

הַמִּתְנַבֵּא בְּשֵׁם עֲבוֹדַת כּוֹכָבִים – ONE WHO PROPHESIES IN THE NAME OF AN IDOL – כְּגוֹן נְבִיאֵי הַבַּעַל – **for example, the prophets of** ***Baal.***[55]

An example of suppressed prophecy:

הַכּוֹבֵשׁ אֶת נְבוּאָתוֹ – ONE WHO SUPPRESSES HIS PROPHECY – כְּגוֹן יוֹנָה בֶּן אֲמִיתַּי – **for example, Jonah ben Amitai,** who initially refused to go to Nineveh and proclaim the prophecy of destruction ordained by God.[56]

An example of a disregarded prophecy:

וְהַמְוַותֵּר עַל דִּבְרֵי נָבִיא – OR ONE WHO DISREGARDS THE WORDS OF A PROPHET – כְּגוֹן – **for example,**

NOTES

50. *Jeremiah* 49:35. [Literally: the bow of Eilam.] In this chapter Jeremiah prophesies the destruction of a number of nations. Eilam was a kingdom in southwestern Persia (Iran), east of Babylonia. See *Daniel* 8:2.

51. [Units from Eilam would seem to have served in the Babylonian army. Eilam, however, never initiated any conflict with Israel.]

52. *Jeremiah* 28:2. [Thus, God's prophecy to Jeremiah regarding Eilam (in the midst of all the turmoil with Babylonia) was understood by Chananiah to contain a message regarding Babylonia as well. Chananiah reformulated this message and proclaimed it as an explicit statement about Babylonia.]

53. And words of prophecy are considered a part of Torah.

54. This seems puzzling. Since the message proclaimed by Chananiah was in fact untrue – as God Himself declared to Jeremiah (ibid. 28:14) – how can it be considered to have been said to Jeremiah, the *kal vachomer* notwithstanding?

Maharsha suggests that part of Chananiah's "prophecy" was indeed true. God would indeed destroy the yoke of Babylon. But Chananiah added on his own that this would occur in two years time. This part of his statement was not based on the *kal vachomer* and was in fact untrue. Babylon was not destroyed until many years later. Nevertheless, even in declaring that Babylon would be destroyed, Chananiah was guilty of the capital offense of "prophesying that which was not said to him, but to someone else." Thus, the Gemara cites him as an example of this transgression *(Maharsha;* cf. *Chazon Ish, Sanhedrin* 21:3).

55. A pagan deity mentioned many times in Scripture, most notably in connection with Elijah's confrontation with it on Mt. Carmel (*I Kings* ch. 18).

56. See *Jonah* 1:1-3.

דקשר העליון דאורייתא גרוע ועומד אי הכי תפילין נמי אי עביד ארבעה בתי ואייתי אחרינא ואנח גבייהו האי לחודיה קאי והאי לחודיה קאי ואי עביד חמשה בתי גרוע ועומד הוא האמר ר' זירא [א] בית חיצון שאינו רואה את האויר פסול: **מתני'** [ב] אין ממיתין אותו לא בבית דין שבעירו ולא בבית דין שביבנה אלא מעלין אותו לבית דין הגדול שבירושלים ומשמרין אותו עד הרגל וממיתין אותו ברגל שנאמר (א) וכל העם ישמעו ויראו ולא יזידון עוד דברי ר' עקיבא ר' יהודה אומר אין מענין את דינו של זה אלא ממיתין אותו מיד וכותבין ושולחין בכל המקומות איש פלוני [ג] מתחייב מיתה בבית דין: **גמ'** תנו רבנן [ד] אין ממיתין אותו לא בבית דין שבעירו ולא בבית דין שביבנה אלא מעלין אותו לב"ד הגדול שבירושלים ומשמרין אותו עד הרגל וממיתין אותו ברגל שנאמר וכל העם ישמעו ויראו דברי רבי עקיבא אמר לו ר' יהודה וכי נאמר יראו וייראו והלא לא נאמר אלא ישמעו וייראו למה מענין דינו של זה אלא ממיתין אותו מיד וכותבין ושולחין בכל מקום איש פלוני נתחייב מיתה בבית דין ת"ר ארבעה צריכין הכרזה [ג] המסית [ד] ובן סורר ומורה [ה] וזקן ממרא [ו] ועדים זוממין בכולהו כתיב בהו (א) וכל העם (ב) [ג] וכל ישראל בעדים זוממין כתיב (ד) והנשארי' דלא כולי עלמא חזו לסהדותא: **מתני'** נביא השקר [ז] המתנבא מה שלא שמע ומה שלא נאמר לו מיתתו בידי אדם [ח] אבל הכובש את נבואתו [ט] והמוותר על דברי נביא [י] ונביא שעבר על דברי עצמו מיתתו בידי שמים שנאמר (ה) אנכי אדרש מעמו [כ] המתנבא בשם עבודת כוכבים ואומר כך אמרה עבודת כוכבים אפי' כוון את ההלכה לטמא את הטמא ולטהר את הטהור [ל] הבא על אשת איש כיון שנכנסה [ד] לרשות הבעל לנשואין אע"פ שלא נבעלה הבא עליה הרי זה בחנק וזוממי בת כהן ובועלה [מ] שכל המוזמין [ה] מקדימין לאותה מיתה [נ] חוץ מזוממי בת כהן ובועלה: **גמ'** תנו רבנן שלשה מיתתן בידי אדם ושלשה מיתתן בידי שמים המתנבא מה שלא שמע ומה שלא נאמר לו והמתנבא בשם עבודת כוכבים מיתתן בידי אדם הכובש את נבואתו והמוותר על דברי נביא ונביא שעבר על דברי עצמו מיתתן בידי שמים מנהני מילי אמר רב יהודה אמר רב דאמר קרא (ו) אך הנביא אשר יזיד לדבר דבר בשמי זה המתנבא מה שלא שמע (ו) ואשר לא צויתיו הא לחבירו צויתיו זה המתנבא מה שלא נאמר לו (ו) ואשר ידבר בשם אלהים אחרים זה המתנבא בשם עבודת כוכבים וכתיב (ו) ומת הנביא ההוא (ו) וכל מיתה האמורה בתורה סתם אינה אלא חנק הכובש את נבואתו והמוותר על דברי נביא ונביא שעבר על דברי עצמו מיתתן בידי שמים [א] דכתיב (ה) והאיש אשר לא ישמע (א) קרי ביה לא ישמיע וקרי ביה לא ישמע אל דברי וכתיב אנכי אדרש מעמו בידי שמים: המתנבא מה שלא שמע: כגון צדקיה בן כנענה דכתיב (ז) ויעש לו צדקיה בן כנענה קרני ברזל מאי הוה ליה למיעבד רוח נבות אטעיתיה דכתיב (ח) ויאמר ה' מי יפתה את אחאב ויעל ויפול ברמות גלעד (ט) ויצא הרוח ויעמד לפני ה' ויאמר אני אפתנו ויאמר (י) תפתה וגם תוכל צא ועשה כן אמר רב יהודה מאי צא צא ממחיצתי (י) מאי רוח אמר רבי יוחנן רוחו של נבות היזרעאלי הוה ליה למידק כדרבי יצחק דאמר רבי יצחק סיגנון אחד עולה לכמה נביאים ואין שני נביאים מתנבאין בסיגנון אחד עובדיה אמר (כ) זדון לבך השיאך ירמיה אמר (ל) תפלצתך השיא אותך זדון לבך והני מדקאמרי כולהו כהדדי שמע מינה לא כלום קאמרי דילמא לא הוה ידע ליה להא דרבי יצחק יהושפט הוה התם וקאמר להו דכתיב (מ) ויאמר יהושפט האין פה נביא (מ) (עוד לה') אמר ליה הא איכא כל הני אמר ליה כך מקובלני מבית אבי אבא סיגנון אחד עולה לכמה נביאים ואין שני נביאים מתנבאים בסיגנון אחד. המתנבא מה שלא נאמר לו כגון חנניה בן עזור דקאי ירמיה בשוק העליון וקאמר (נ) כה אמר ה' [צבאות] הנני שובר את קשת עילם נשא חנניה ק"ו בעצמו מה עילם שלא בא אלא לעזור את בבל אמר הקב"ה הנני שובר את קשת עילם כשדים עצמן על אחת כמה וכמה אתא איהו בשוק התחתון אמר (ס) כה אמר ה' וגו' שברתי את עול מלך בבל א"ל רב פפא לאביי האי לחבירו נמי לא נאמר א"ל כיון דאיתיהיב ק"ו למידרש כמאן דאיתמר ליה דמי הוא ניהו דלא נאמר לו המתנבא בשם עבודת כוכבים כגון נביאי הבעל הכובש את נבואתו כגון יונה בן אמיתי והמוותר על דברי נביא כגון חבריה

שאינו רואה את האויר. כגון שהוסיף בית חמישי עליהם בצדו או דבר אחר: **מתני'** כל ישראל ישמעו. צריך להשמיע מיתתו לרבים שלא יעשה אדם עוד כן: לא בבית דין שביבנה. אם נשאלו לבית דין שבלשכת הגזית ואמרו להם וחזר לעירו ושהה ימים עד שגלתה סנהדרי גדולה ליבנה ועדיין הבית קיים ואחרי כן הורה כבתחילה אין ממיתין אותו ביבנה ואע"פ ששם סנהדרי גדולה שסוף סוף אין נקבצים שם: **גמ'** וכי נאמר וכל העם יראו וייראו. דבעינן שיהו רואין במיתתו: הכרזה. פלוני מת בב"ד על שעבר עבירה זו כדי לרדות את האחרים: וכל ישראל. ישמעו וייראו: ובעדים זוממים כתיב והנשארים. ישמעו וייראו משום דלא שייך למיכתב וכל העם דלאו כולי עלמא חזו לסהדותא שיש גזלנין ומלוי ברבית ומועלים בשביעית שהן פסולים לעדות: **מתני'** ומה שלא נאמר לו. אע"פ שנאמר לחבירו ובגמרא יליף לה: הכובש נבואתו. שלא אמרה כגון יונה בן אמיתי: והמוותר על דברי נביא. המפקירם שלא חשש למה שאמר לו הנביא: **גמ'** והאיש אשר לא ישמע. היינו מוותר: קרי ביה איש אשר לא ישמיע. היינו כובש וקרי ביה לא ישמע שהוא עצמו אינו נשמע היינו עובר על דברי עצמו: ויצא הרוח ויאמר אני אפתנו. אלא והייתי רוח שקר בפי כל נביאיו: סיגנון. דבר מליצות של רוח הקודש: עולה לכמה נביאים. נכנס בלבם לזה בלשון זה ולזה בלשון זה והכל אחד: ואין שני נביאים מתנבאין בסיגנון אחד. בלשון אחד ואלו כולן לשון אחד היו אומרים דכתיב הנה נא כל הנביאים אומרים פה אחד טוב: חבריה

קשר העליון דאורייתא. פי' בקונט' דפלוגתא היא בפ' התכלת (מנחות דף לט. ושם) וליתיה אלא דמסקינן התם [ט] שמע מינה קשר העליון דאורייתא: **ולא** בבית דין שביבנה. פירש בקונטרס אם נשאלו בבית דין שבלשכת הגזית ואמרו להם וחזר לעירו ושהה ימים עד שגלתה סנהדרי גדולה ותימה דסוף סוף כשממתינין עד הרגל היאך ממיתין הא כיון דגלתה סנהדרין אין דנין דיני נפשות כדאמר בפרק היו בודקין (לעיל דף מא.) וכי תימא דברגל חוזרים ב"ד הגדול ויושבין בלשכת הגזית אף לאחר שגלו ואז דנין אותו חדא דאם כן משכחת ליה לרבן יוחנן בן זכאי דהוה בסנהדרין ובפרק היו בודקין (שם) לא משמע הכי ועוד מאי עינוי הדין יש הא אין שייך עינוי הדין אלא כשמשהין אותו אחר גמר דינו כדמוכח בפרק אחד דיני ממונות (לעיל דף לה.) דפריך לגמרוהו לדיניה בשבתא וליקטלוהו וכו' ומשני אתה מענה את דינו והדר פריך לדיינוהו במעלי שבתא וכו' ועוד מאי אריא זקן ממרא בשאר עבירות נמי ועוד אמאי נקט יבנה לימא לא בב"ד שבחנות ודוחק לומר דאעבירה דקודם שגלתה סנהדרין דנין אף לאחר שגלתה ולא אמרינן מקום גורם כיון דבשעת עבירה סנהדרי גדולה במקומן ור"ת אומר דמיירי כשנגמר דינו קודם שגלתה סנהדרי: [י] **הכובש** נבואתו לוקה. לית ביה לאו ועוד דאין בו מעשה אלא מכין אותו עד שתצא נפשו כמו עשה סוכה ואינו עושה [כ]: אליהו

א) [בערוך ערך פלש א' גרים בית המפולש לחבירו פסול פי' אי מתחלה עבדינהו ה' בתי ופליש חד בית לחבריה דהיינו ד' בתי וכו' ע"ש], ב) [במשנה שבמשניות ובברייתא הסמוכה איתא נתחייב], ג) [תוספתא פי"א], ד) [פירש"י על בבא זו עי' ברש"י לקמן צ. וע"ע בפירש"י דמכות ב. ד"ה התם קאי וכו' ובמ"ש תוס' שם ד"ה כל כו' ובד"ה זוממי], ה) מכות ב. [ע"ש], ו) [לעיל נג: פד:], ז) שבת קמט: [לקמן קב:], ח) [צ"ל לה' עוד], ט) [דף לט.], י) זה שייך לע"ב, כ) [כתובות פו.].

הגהות הב"ח

(א) גמ' דכתיב והאיש אשר לא ישמע וקרי ביה לא ישמיע וקרי ביה לא יִשָּׁמַע:

הגהות הגר"א

[א] גמ' והאיש אשר לא ישמע וגו'. נ"ב גי' הגאונים והיה וגו' אשר וגו' וכתיב אנכי וגו'. והיא הנכונה:

ליקוטי רש"י

[נדפס בדף פח:]

תורה אור השלם

א) וְכָל הָעָם יִשְׁמְעוּ וְיִרָאוּ וְלֹא יְזִידוּן עוֹד: [דברים יז, יג]

ב) וְכָל יִשְׂרָאֵל יִשְׁמְעוּ וְיִרָאוּן וְלֹא יוֹסִפוּ לַעֲשׂוֹת כַּדָּבָר הָרָע הַזֶּה בְּקִרְבֶּךָ: [דברים יג, יב]

ג) וּרְגָמֻהוּ כָּל אַנְשֵׁי עִירוֹ בָאֲבָנִים וָמֵת וּבִעַרְתָּ הָרָע מִקִּרְבֶּךָ וְכָל יִשְׂרָאֵל יִשְׁמְעוּ וְיִרָאוּ: [דברים כא, כא]

ד) וְהַנִּשְׁאָרִים יִשְׁמְעוּ וְיִרָאוּ וְלֹא יֹסִפוּ לַעֲשׂוֹת עוֹד כַּדָּבָר הָרָע הַזֶּה בְּקִרְבֶּךָ: [דברים יט, כ]

ה) וְהָיָה הָאִישׁ אֲשֶׁר לֹא יִשְׁמַע אֶל דְּבָרַי אֲשֶׁר יְדַבֵּר בִּשְׁמִי אָנֹכִי אֶדְרֹשׁ מֵעִמּוֹ: [דברים יח, יט]

ו) אַךְ הַנָּבִיא אֲשֶׁר יָזִיד לְדַבֵּר דָּבָר בִּשְׁמִי אֵת אֲשֶׁר לֹא צִוִּיתִיו לְדַבֵּר וַאֲשֶׁר יְדַבֵּר בְּשֵׁם אֱלֹהִים אֲחֵרִים וּמֵת הַנָּבִיא הַהוּא: [דברים יח, כ]

ז) וַיַּעַשׂ לוֹ צִדְקִיָּהוּ בֶן כְּנַעֲנָה קַרְנֵי בַרְזֶל וַיֹּאמֶר כֹּה אָמַר יְיָ בְּאֵלֶּה תְּנַגַּח אֶת אֲרָם עַד כַּלּוֹתָם: [דברי הימים ב' יח, י]

ח) וַיֹּאמֶר יְיָ מִי יְפַתֶּה אֶת אַחְאָב וְיַעַל וְיִפֹּל בְּרָמֹת גִּלְעָד וַיֹּאמֶר זֶה בְּכֹה וְזֶה אֹמֵר בְּכֹה: [מלכים א' כב, כ]

ט) וַיֵּצֵא הָרוּחַ וַיַּעֲמֹד לִפְנֵי יְיָ וַיֹּאמֶר אֲנִי אֲפַתֶּנּוּ וַיֹּאמֶר יְיָ אֵלָיו בַּמָּה: [מלכים א' כב, כא]

י) וַיֹּאמֶר אֵצֵא וְהָיִיתִי רוּחַ שֶׁקֶר בְּפִי כָּל נְבִיאָיו וַיֹּאמֶר תְּפַתֶּה וְגַם תּוּכָל צֵא וַעֲשֵׂה כֵן: [מלכים א' כב, כב]

כ) זְדוֹן לִבְּךָ הִשִּׁיאֶךָ שֹׁכְנִי בְחַגְוֵי סֶלַע מְרוֹם שִׁבְתּוֹ אֹמֵר בְּלִבּוֹ מִי יוֹרִדֵנִי אָרֶץ: [עובדיה א, ג]

ל) תִּפְלַצְתְּךָ הִשִּׁיא אֹתָךְ זְדוֹן לִבֶּךָ שֹׁכְנִי בְּחַגְוֵי הַסֶּלַע תֹּפְשִׂי מְרוֹם גִּבְעָה כִּי תַגְבִּיהַּ כַּנֶּשֶׁר קִנֶּךָ מִשָּׁם אוֹרִידְךָ נְאֻם יְיָ: [ירמיה מט, טז]

מ) וַיֹּאמֶר יְהוֹשָׁפָט הַאֵין פֹּה נָבִיא לַייָ עוֹד וְנִדְרְשָׁה מֵאוֹתוֹ: [מלכים א' כב, ז]

נ) כֹּה אָמַר יְיָ צְבָאוֹת הִנְנִי שֹׁבֵר אֶת קֶשֶׁת עֵילָם רֵאשִׁית גְּבוּרָתָם: [ירמיה מט, לה]

ס) כֹּה אָמַר יְיָ צְבָאוֹת אֱלֹהֵי יִשְׂרָאֵל לֵאמֹר שָׁבַרְתִּי אֶת עֹל מֶלֶךְ בָּבֶל: [ירמיה כח, ב]

עין משפט נר מצוה

סז א מיי' פ"ד מהל' ממרים הלכה ג:
סח ב ג מיי' פ"ג שם הלכה ח:
סט ד מיי' שם ופ"ז שם הלכה יג:
ע ה מיי' שם פ"ג הלכה ח:
עא ו מיי' שם ופי"ח מהל' עדות הל' ז:
עב ז מיי' פ"ה מהל' ע"ז הלכה ח סמג לאוין לה:
עג ח מיי' פ"ט מהלכות יסודי התורה הל' ג סמג לאוין לג:
עד ט מיי' שם הל' ג סמג עשין ו:
עה י מיי' שם הלכה ג סמג לאוין שם:
עו כ מיי' פ"ה מהל' ע"ז הל' ו סמג שם:
עז ל מיי' פ"ג מהל' איסורי ביאה הל' ד:
עח מ מיי' פי"ח מהל' עדות הלכה א סמג עשין קי:
עט נ מיי' שם פ"כ הל' י:

רבינו חננאל

אמרי היכי דמי אי נימא דעבד ד' בתי בטבלא ואייתי בית אחרינא אנח גבייהו ולא חבריה בהדייהו אמאי חייב האי לחודיה קאי והני לחודייהו קיימי ואי מתחלה עבדינהו ה' בתי ופילש בית חד לחבריה דהיינו ד' כיון דעבדינהו שלא כהלכתן לאו תפלין דכתיבי באורייתא נינהו כלל והאי לא איגרע לפי שהוסיף עליו אלא גרוע ועומד הוה מעיקרא דהא פסול הוא כר' זירא דאמר בית המפולש לחבירו פסול ופרישנ' לא צריכא כגון דעבד טוטפת בת ד' בתי דהויא כהלכתא תפילין מעילאי ואייתי בית אחרינא וחבריה בהדייהו דהיינו כל המוסיף גורע העיקר וכדרבא דאמר בית החיצון שאינו רואה את האויר פסול והאי כיון דאייתי בית מאבראי ואוקמיה קמי החיצון נעשה החיצון פנימי ואינו רואה אויר לפיכך הוא פסול ואתינן להשוויי לולב וציצית לתפילין ונדחו דלא דמו: **ת"ר** אין ממיתין אותו אלא בב"ד הגדול שבירושלים ואין ממיתין אותו אלא ברגל דברי ר' עקיבא. ר' יהודה אומר ממיתין אותו מיד לפי שאין מענין דינו כו': **ת"ר** ד' צריכין הכרזה מסית ובן סורר ומורה וזקן ממרא ועדים זוממין כולהו משום [דכתיב בהו] וכל ישראל וכל העם. בעדים זוממין כתיב והנשארים דלאו כולי עלמא חזו לסהדותא: **ת"ר** ג' מיתתן בידי אדם המתנבא מה שלא שמע ומה שלא נאמר לו והמתנבא בשם ע"ז. מנא הני מילי אמר רב יהודה אמר רב דאמר קרא אך הנביא אשר יזיד לדבר דבר בשמי זה המתנבא מה שלא שמע את אשר לא צויתיו הא לנביא אחר צויתיו זה המתנבא מה שלא נאמר לו. ואשר ידבר בשם אלהים אחרים זה המתנבא בשם ע"ז וכתיב ומת הנביא ההוא (שכל) [וכל] מיתה האמורה בתורה סתם חנק הוא. אבל נביא הכובש נבואתו והמוותר על דברי הנביא ונביא שעבר על דברי עצמו מיתתן בידי שמים. ואסיקנא המתנבא מה שלא שמע כגון צדקיה בן כנענה. ואע"ג דאמרינן מדכתיב ויאמר אצא והייתי רוח שקר בפי כל נביאיו שמעינן מינה רוח נבות אטעיתיה מדהוה ליה למבדק בהא דאין סיגנון אחד עולה לשני נביאים. כלומר אין ב' נביאים מתנבאים בסיגנון אחד. והני כולהו עלה להן סיגנון אחד כלומר דבר אחד (וכולן מתנבאין בסיגנון אחד). כדכתיב עלה ויתן ה' ביד המלך ש"מ אין נבואה זו כהוגן דא"ר יצחק סיגנון אחד עולה לכמה נביאים ואין ב' נביאים מתנבאים בסיגנון אחד. סיגנון אחד עולה לכמה נביאים זה עובדיה וירמיה עובדיה הוציא בלשון זדון לבך השיאך. וירמיה אמר תפלצתך השיא אותך זדון לבך ודחינן ודלמא צדקיה בן כנענה לא הוה ידע הא שמעתא דר' יצחק ופרקינן יהושפט הוה התם ואמר להו כך מקובל אני מבית אבי אבא שאין שני נביאים מתנבאין בסיגנון אחד. והיינו דכתיב ויאמר יהושפט האין פה נביא לה' עוד ונדרשה מאתו. כלומר אלו כולן אינן נביאי ה': **המתנבא** מה שלא נאמר לו כגון חנניה בן עזור דשמע לירמיה דאמר כה אמר ה' צבאות הנני שובר את קשת עילם וגו' נשא ק"ו כה אמר ה' צבאות אלהי ישראל לאמר שברתי את עול מלך בבל וזה הק"ו יש לו לירמיה לשאת אותו אבל לזולתו לא. המתנבא בשם ע"ז כגון נביאי [הבעל] אלו כולן מיתתן בידי אדם. אבל הכובש את נבואתו כגון יונה בן אמיתי דינו בידי שמים

פ א מיי' פ"ט מהלכות יסודי התורה הל' ג:

רבינו חננאל

שמים: **תני** תנא קמיה דרב חסדא לוקה א"ל ומי התרה בו דלקי כלומר מי יודע ששלחו אלהים להינבא והסתיר נבואתו ואמר אביי חבריו הנביאים שגילה כדכתיב כי לא יעשה ה' אלהים דבר כי אם גלה סודו אל עבדיו הנביאים ודלמא הדרו ביה כו': **המוותר** על דברי נביא ואינו עושה כל מה שיאמר לו אלא ממאן לשמוע דבריו כגון חבריה דמיכיהו דכתיב ואיש אחד מבני הנביאים אמר לרעהו בדבר ה' הכני נא וימאן האיש להכותו וכתיב ויאמר לו יען אשר לא שמעת בקול ה' הנך הולך מאתי והכך האריה וילך מאצלו וימצאהו האריה ויכהו דינו בידי שמים. ואקשינן מנא ידע דהוא נביא ואיענש ושנינן מוחזק בנביאות הוה אבל מאן דלא מוחזק לא מיחייב לקבולי מיניה עד דיהיב ליה אות ומופת ומאן דמוחזק מקבלינן מיניה מאליהו בהר הכרמל אילולי שהיה מוחזק בנביאות היכי הוו מקבלי מיניה ועבדי שחוטי חוץ אלא ש"מ היכא דמוחזק שאני. ונביא שעבר על דברי עצמו כגון עדו הנביא שנאמר כי כן צוה אותי בדבר ה' לאמר לא תאכל לחם ולא תשתה מים ולא תשוב בדרך אשר הלכת ויאמר לו גם אני נביא כמוך ומלאך דבר אלי בדבר ה' לאמר השיבהו אתך אל ביתך ויאכל לחם וישתה מים כחש לו דינו בידי שמים שנאמר וימצאהו האריה בדרך וימיתהו. **ירושלמי** א"ר שמואל בר רב יצחק ונביא אחד זקן ישב בבית אל זה אמציהו כהן בית אל: **ויהי** אחר הדברים האלה והאלהים נסה את אברהם אחר מי א"ר יוחנן אחר דברי השטן שאמר לפני הקב"ה רבון כל העולמים זקן זה חננתו למאה פרי [בטן] ומכל סעודות שעש' לא היה לו להקריב לפניך תור או בן יונה אחד. א"ל כלום עשה אלא למען בנו אם אני אומר לו זבח אותו לפני עושה. מיד והאלהים נסה את אברהם כו' ר' לוי אמר אחר דברי ישמעאל שאמר ליצחק אני גדול ממך במצות שאתה נמלתה בן ח' ימים ואני בן י"ג שנה א"ל ובאבר אחד אתה מי יראיני אם אומר לו הקב"ה זבח עצמך מיד אני זובח את עצמי. מיד והאלהים נסה את אברהם: **ת"ר** נביא שהדיח בסקילה מאי טעמא גמרי הדחה הדחה ממסית מה מסית בסקילה אף נביא שהדיח בסקילה רבי שמעון אומר מיתה כתיבא ביה וכל מיתה האמורה בתורה סתם בחנק. מדיחי עיר הנדחת בסקילה גמרי הדחה הדחה אי ממסית אי מנביא שהדיח ר' שמעון אומר בחנק גמר הדחה הדחה מנביא שהדיח.

תוספות

אליהו בהר הכרמל וכו'. משמע דבשם הקב"ה היה מתנבא לעבור וכיון דמוחזק מהימנינן ביה אע"ג דלא יהיב אות ובהאשה רבה (יבמות דף צ: ושם) נפקא לן דכתיב אליו תשמעון אפי' אמר לך עבור על אחת מכל מצות האמורות בתורה כגון אליהו בהר הכרמל ותימה מאי קא פריך התם וליגמר מיניה כיון דע"פ הדיבור היה מתנבא מה שייך למילף מיניה לעבור משום תקנה דרבנן שלא על פי הדיבור ועוד למה לן הכא טעמא משום דאיתחזק בנביאות הא אפילו בלא נביא שרי לב"ד לעבור משום מיגדר מילתא ויש לומר דמדקדק התם מלישנא דברייתא דקתני הכל לפי שעה דמשמע הכל מפני צורך השעה ואי על פי הדיבור למה לי צורך השעה בין לצורך בין שלא לצורך צריך לקיים צוויו של מקום אלא ודאי בנביא שעשה מדעתו קא אמרה ברייתא דמיירי קרא והא דבעי הכא איתחזק היינו משום דכי איתחזק בנביאות סומכין עליו במה שהיה מבטיח לירידת אש ושוחטין על הבטחתו קדשים בחוץ שבזכותו ובתפלתו תרד אש מהשמים ויהיה מגדר מילתא בדבר שיתקדש שמו של הקב"ה ברבים ויחזרו ישראל למוטב ומיהו בקראי משמע שעל פי הדיבור עשה דכתיב באליהו ובדברך עשיתי וגו' ופרש"י מאור הגולה בפירושו לנביאים ובדברך עשיתי שהקרבתי בשעת איסור הבמות ונראה לומר דכיון דעל פי הדיבור שרי משום צורך שעה הוא הדין שלא על פי הדיבור שהרי אין נביא רשאי לחדש דבר כדאיתא בפ"ק דמגילה (דף ג:) ועוד י"ל דהא דקאמר אליהו ובדברך עשיתי לא שאמר לו הקב"ה אלא מקרא היה דורש דכתיב גוי וקהל גוים יהיה ממך ואמרינן [מ] עתידין בניך לעשות כמעשה נכרים פירוש לשחוט בחוץ ואני מסכים על ידו ולפי שהיה נביא מוחזק סמכו עליו שעליו נאמר מקרא זה:

גמרא

חבריה דמיכה דכתיב [א] ואיש אחד מבני הנביאים אמר אל רעהו בדבר ה' הכני נא וימאן האיש להכותו וכתיב [ב] ויאמר לו יען אשר לא שמעת [וגו'] ונביא שעבר על דברי עצמו כגון עדו הנביא דכתיב [ג] כי כן צוה אותי וכתיב [ד] ויאמר לו גם אני נביא כמוך וכתיב [ה] וישב אתו וכתיב [ו] וילך וימצאהו אריה תני תנא קמיה דרב חסדא הכובש את נבואתו לוקה [א] אמר ליה מאן דאכיל תמרי בארבלא לקי מאן מתרי ביה אמר אביי חבריה נביאי מנא ידעי אמר אביי דכתיב [ז] כי לא יעשה ה' [אלהים] דבר כי אם גלה סודו ודילמא הדרי ביה אם איתא דהדרי ביה אודועי הוו מודעי לכלהו נביאי והא יונה דהדרי ביה ולא אודעוהו יונה מעיקרא נינוה נהפכת אמרי ליה איהו לא ידע אי לטובה אי לרעה המוותר על דברי נביא מנא ידע דאיענש דיהב ליה אות והא מיכה דלא יהיב ליה אות ואיענש היכא דמוחזק שאני דאי לא תימא הכי אברהם בהר המוריה היכי שמע ליה יצחק אליהו בהר הכרמל היכי סמכי עליה ועבדי שחוטי חוץ אלא [א]היכא דמוחזק שאני [ח] ויהי אחר הדברים האלה והאלהים נסה את אברהם [ב] (אחר מאי) א"ר יוחנן משום רבי יוסי בן זימרא אחר דבריו של שטן דכתיב [ט] ויגדל הילד ויגמל וגו' אמר שטן לפני הקב"ה רבונו של עולם זקן זה חננתו למאה שנה פרי בטן מכל סעודה שעשה לא היה לו תור אחד או גוזל אחד להקריב לפניך אמר לו כלום עשה אלא בשביל בנו אם אני אומר לו זבח את בנך לפני מיד זובחו מיד והאלהים נסה את אברהם [י] ויאמר קח נא את בנך אמר רבי שמעון בר אבא [ג] אין נא אלא לשון בקשה משל למלך בשר ודם שעמדו עליו מלחמות הרבה והיה לו גבור אחד ונצחן לימים עמדה עליו מלחמה חזקה אמר לו בבקשה ממך עמוד לי במלחמה זו שלא יאמרו ראשונות אין בהם ממש אף הקב"ה אמר לאברהם ניסיתיך בכמה נסיונות ועמדת בכלן עכשיו עמוד לי בנסיון זה שלא יאמרו אין ממש בראשונים את בנך ב' בנים יש לי [י] את יחידך זה יחיד לאמו וזה יחיד לאמו [י] אשר אהבת תרוייהו רחימנא להו [י] את יצחק וכל כך למה כדי שלא תטרף דעתו עליו קדמו שטן לדרך אמר לו [כ] הנסה דבר אליך תלאה הנה יסרת רבים וידים רפות תחזק כושל יקימון מליך כי עתה תבא אליך ותלא אמר לו [ל] אני בתומי אלך אמר לו [ד] [מ] הלא יראתך כסלתך אמר לו [נ] זכר נא מי הוא נקי אבד כיון דחזא דלא קא שמיע ליה אמר ליה [ס] ואלי דבר יגונב כך שמעתי מאחורי הפרגוד [ע] השה לעולה ואין יצחק לעולה אמר לו [ה] כך עונשו של בדאי שאפילו אמר אמת אין שומעין לו ר' לוי אמר אחר דבריו של ישמעאל ליצחק אמר לו ישמעאל ליצחק אני גדול ממך במצות שאתה מלת בן שמנת ימים ואני בן שלש עשרה שנה אמר לו ובאבר אחד אתה מגרה בי אם אומר לי הקב"ה זבח עצמך לפני אני זובח מיד והאלהים נסה את אברהם [ו] תנו רבנן נביא שהדיח בסקילה רבי שמעון אומר בחנק [ז] מדיחי עיר הנדחת בסקילה רבי שמעון אומר בחנק נביא שהדיח בסקילה מ"ט דרבנן אתיא [פ] הדחה [צ] הדחה ממסית מה להלן בסקילה אף כאן בסקילה ור"ש מיתה כתיבא ביה [ח] וכל מיתה האמורה בתורה סתם אינה אלא חנק מדיחי עיר הנדחת בסקילה מ"ט דרבנן גמרי [ק] הדחה הדחה או ממסית או מנביא שהדיח ור"ש גמר [ק] הדחה [פ] הדחה מנביא וליגמר ממסית דנין מסית רבים ממסית רבים ואין דנין מסית רבים ממסית יחיד אדרבה [ט] דנין הדיוט מהדיוט ואין דנין הדיוט מנביא ור"ש [י] כיון שהדיח אין לך הדיוט גדול מזה אמר רב חסדא

מחלוקת

רש"י

חבריה דמיכה. דכתיב ואיש אחד מבני הנביאים אמר אל רעהו בדבר ה' הכני נא זה היה מיכיהו בן ימלא שנתנבא אותו היום על אחאב ליפול ביד ארם מפני שנפל בן הדד בידו ושלחו לשלום והיינו דקאמר אחאב ליהושפט לא ידבר עלי טוב כי אם רע מפני שנתנבא כבר את זו עליו ולא קיבל חבירו את דבריו דכתיב וימאן האיש להכותו: **עדו הנביא.** שנתנבא על מזבח [א] ה' בבית אל שהיה ירבעם מקטר עליו [כ] ובדברי הימים גבי יאשיהו כתיב והוא היה עדו: **כי כן צוה אותי.** בדבר ה' לאמר לא תאכל לחם ולא תשתה מים [ל] (במקום הזה) ועבר על דברי עצמו ושמע לדברי הנביא השקר ואכל ושתה: **תמרי בארבילא.** תמרים הנתונים בכברה: **דילמא הדרו ביה.** פמליא של מעלה וניחם על הרעה והם אינם יודעים והיאך מתרינן בו התראת ספק: **והא יונה דהדרו ביה.** מהפוך את נינוה: **מעיקרא נינוה נהפכת אמרו ליה.** ברוח הקדש ומשמע נמי לטובה שיהפכו מעשיהם מרעה לטובה וכיון ששבו נתקיימה הנבואה ולא מיהדר הוא: **ואיהו דלא ידע.** הוא היה טועה וסבור שהוא לרעה: **מנא ידע.** האי גברא שזה נביא אמת שהקב"ה עונשו והלא שמא סבור שזהו נביא שקר לפיכך מוותר על דבריו: **היכא דהוחזק.** שהוא צדיק ונביא אמת: **שאני.** ולא בעי אות: **היכי שמע ליה יצחק.** שהוא דבר אמת מה שלא נאמר לשום אדם להקריב את בנו: **שחוטי חוץ.** שהרי בית המקדש היה בירושלים: **הנסה דבר אליך תלאה.** וכי היה לאוהבך לנסותך בדבר שהיא תלאה אותך ומכרית את זרעך: **הנה יסרת רבים.** רגילות והיית' לו כל באי העולם בדברים ועתה הנה בא להלאותך ולבהלך: **נביא שהדיח.** שמתנבא בשם הקב"ה לעבוד עבודת כוכבים: **הדחה.** כתיב הכא כי דבר סרה להדיחך וכתיב במסית כי ביקש להדיחך וגו': **מיתה כתב ביה.** והך גזירה שוה לא גמר מרביה דאין אדם דן גזירה שוה מעצמו: **ורבי שמעון גמר הדחה הדחה מנביא.** דבעיר הנדחת אגמריה רביה גזירה שוה מסיני לדון הדחה הדחה ומסתברא דמנביא אגמריה הלכה למשה גזירה שוה זו כדיהיב טעמא למלתיה:

מחלוקת

הדרן עלך אלו הן הנחנקין

מסורת הש"ס

א) מכות כ:, ב) [נ"ל מאי אחר כ"א בע"י], ג) [לעיל מג: ברכות ט. סוטה יד:], ד) [פירושו דמלתא תמלא בתוס' ב"מ נח: סוף ד"ה הלא], ה) [אדר"נ פ"ל], ו) לעיל סז. פד., ז) [לעיל ג.], ח) [לעיל נב: ופד:], ט) [לעיל פד.], י) [שם], כ) לא נמצא שם מפורש ורד"ק כתב רמז לזה, ל) ס"א ל"ג, מ) [ב"ר פ' וישלח].

הגהות מהר"ב רנשבורג

א] רש"י ד"ה עדו הנביא שנתנבא על מזבח בבית אל כו'. כצ"ל:

תורה אור השלם

א) וְאִישׁ אֶחָד מִבְּנֵי הַנְּבִיאִים אָמַר אֶל רֵעֵהוּ בִּדְבַר יְיָ הַכֵּינִי נָא וַיְמָאֵן הָאִישׁ לְהַכֹּתוֹ: [מלכים א' כ, לה]

ב) וַיֹּאמֶר לוֹ יַעַן אֲשֶׁר לֹא שָׁמַעְתָּ בְּקוֹל יְיָ הִנְּךָ הוֹלֵךְ מֵאִתִּי וְהִכְּךָ הָאַרְיֵה וַיֵּלֶךְ מֵאֶצְלוֹ וַיִּמְצָאֵהוּ הָאַרְיֵה וַיַּכֵּהוּ: [מלכים א' כ, לו]

ג) כִּי כֵן צִוָּה אֹתִי בִּדְבַר יְיָ לֵאמֹר לֹא תֹאכַל לֶחֶם וְלֹא תִשְׁתֶּה מָּיִם וְלֹא תָשׁוּב בַּדֶּרֶךְ אֲשֶׁר הָלָכְתָּ: [מלכים א' יג, ט]

ד) וַיֹּאמֶר לוֹ גַּם אֲנִי נָבִיא כָּמוֹךָ וּמַלְאָךְ דִּבֶּר אֵלַי בִּדְבַר יְיָ לֵאמֹר הֲשִׁבֵהוּ אִתְּךָ אֶל בֵּיתֶךָ וְיֹאכַל לֶחֶם וְיֵשְׁתְּ מָיִם כִּחֵשׁ לוֹ: [מלכים א' יג, יח]

ה) וַיָּשָׁב אִתּוֹ וַיֹּאכַל לֶחֶם בְּבֵיתוֹ וַיֵּשְׁתְּ מָיִם: [מלכים א' יג, יט]

ו) וַיֵּלֶךְ וַיִּמְצָאֵהוּ אַרְיֵה בַּדֶּרֶךְ וַיְמִיתֵהוּ וַתְּהִי נִבְלָתוֹ מֻשְׁלֶכֶת בַּדֶּרֶךְ וְהַחֲמוֹר עֹמֵד אֶצְלָהּ וְהָאַרְיֵה עֹמֵד אֵצֶל הַנְּבֵלָה: [מלכים א' יג, כד]

ז) כִּי לֹא יַעֲשֶׂה אֲדֹנָי אֱלֹהִים דָּבָר כִּי אִם גָּלָה סוֹדוֹ אֶל עֲבָדָיו הַנְּבִיאִים: [עמוס ג, ז]

ח) וַיְהִי אַחַר הַדְּבָרִים הָאֵלֶּה וְהָאֱלֹהִים נִסָּה אֶת אַבְרָהָם וַיֹּאמֶר אֵלָיו אַבְרָהָם וַיֹּאמֶר הִנֵּנִי: [בראשית כב, א]

ט) וַיִּגְדַּל הַיֶּלֶד וַיִּגָּמַל וַיַּעַשׂ אַבְרָהָם מִשְׁתֶּה גָדוֹל בְּיוֹם הִגָּמֵל אֶת יִצְחָק: [בראשית כא, ח]

י) וַיֹּאמֶר קַח נָא אֶת בִּנְךָ אֶת יְחִידְךָ אֲשֶׁר אָהַבְתָּ אֶת יִצְחָק וְלֶךְ לְךָ אֶל אֶרֶץ הַמֹּרִיָּה וְהַעֲלֵהוּ שָׁם לְעֹלָה עַל אַחַד הֶהָרִים אֲשֶׁר אֹמַר אֵלֶיךָ: [בראשית כב, ב]

כ) הֲנִסָּה דָבָר אֵלֶיךָ תִּלְאֶה וַעְצֹר בְּמִלִּין מִי יוּכָל: הִנֵּה יִסַּרְתָּ רַבִּים וְיָדַיִם רָפוֹת תְּחַזֵּק: כּוֹשֵׁל יְקִימוּן מִלֶּיךָ וּבִרְכַּיִם כֹּרְעוֹת תְּאַמֵּץ: כִּי עַתָּה תָּבוֹא אֵלֶיךָ וַתֵּלֶא תִּגַּע עָדֶיךָ וַתִּבָּהֵל: [איוב ד, ב-ה]

ל) וַאֲנִי בְּתֻמִּי אֵלֵךְ פְּדֵנִי וְחָנֵּנִי: [תהלים כו, יא] מ) הֲלֹא יִרְאָתְךָ כִּסְלָתֶךָ תִּקְוָתְךָ וְתֹם דְּרָכֶיךָ: [איוב ד, ו] נ) זְכָר נָא מִי הוּא נָקִי אָבָד וְאֵיפֹה יְשָׁרִים נִכְחָדוּ: [איוב ד, ז] ס) וְאֵלַי דָּבָר יְגֻנָּב וַתִּקַּח אָזְנִי שֵׁמֶץ מֶנְהוּ: [איוב ד, יב] ע) וַיֹּאמֶר אַבְרָהָם אֱלֹהִים יִרְאֶה לּוֹ הַשֶּׂה לְעֹלָה בְּנִי וַיֵּלְכוּ שְׁנֵיהֶם יַחְדָּו: [בראשית כב, ח] פ) וְהַנָּבִיא הַהוּא אוֹ חֹלֵם הַחֲלוֹם הַהוּא יוּמָת כִּי דִבֶּר סָרָה עַל יְיָ אֱלֹהֵיכֶם הַמּוֹצִיא אֶתְכֶם מֵאֶרֶץ מִצְרַיִם וְהַפֹּדְךָ מִבֵּית עֲבָדִים לְהַדִּיחֲךָ מִן הַדֶּרֶךְ אֲשֶׁר צִוְּךָ יְיָ אֱלֹהֶיךָ לָלֶכֶת בָּהּ וּבִעַרְתָּ הָרָע מִקִּרְבֶּךָ: [דברים יג, ו] צ) וּסְקַלְתּוֹ בָאֲבָנִים וָמֵת כִּי בִקֵּשׁ לְהַדִּיחֲךָ מֵעַל יְיָ אֱלֹהֶיךָ הַמּוֹצִיאֲךָ מֵאֶרֶץ מִצְרַיִם מִבֵּית עֲבָדִים: [דברים יג, יא] ק) יָצְאוּ אֲנָשִׁים בְּנֵי בְלִיַּעַל מִקִּרְבֶּךָ וַיַּדִּיחוּ אֶת יֹשְׁבֵי עִירָם לֵאמֹר נֵלְכָה וְנַעַבְדָה אֱלֹהִים אֲחֵרִים אֲשֶׁר לֹא יְדַעְתֶּם: [דברים יג, יד]

ליקוטי רש"י

הכני נא. סימן זה רע על אחאב שאמר לו הנביא על פי הגבורה להכות את בן הדד ולא הכהו ואף זה שאמר לו הנביא בדבר ה' הכיני ולא הכהו כשם שנפרע מזה יפרע מאחאב. **בדבר ה'.** הקב"ה אמר שתכה אותי [מ"א כ, לה]. **דאכיל תמרי בארבילא.** האוכל תמרים בכברה יהא לוקה בתמיה [מכות כ:]. **כי לא יעשה אדני אלהים דבר אלא א"כ גלה סודו.** אותו סוד אל עבדיו הנביאים [עמוס ג, ז]. **היכי דמוחזק שאני.** אשר ידבר הנביא, ויאמר דבר זה עתיד לבוא עליכם ותראו שלא יבא הוא הדבר אשר לא דברו ה' והרוג אותו ואם תאמר זו במתנבא על העתידות הרי שבא ואמר עשו כך וכך ומפי הקב"ה אני אומר כבר נצטוו שאם בא להדיחך מאחת מכל המצות לא תשמע לו אלא אם כן מומחה הוא לך שהוא צדיק גמור כגון אליהו בהר הכרמל שהקריב בבמה בשעת איסור הבמות כדי לגדור את ישראל הכל לפי צורך השעה וסייג הפרצה לכך נאמר אליו תשמעון [דברים יח, כב]. כגון אליהו בהר הכרמל שהקריב בבמה ושעת איסור הבמות היתה ואיכא כרת דשחוטי חוץ וכרת דהעלאה [יבמות צ:].

[ההמשך בדף צ.]

חַבְרֵיהּ דְּמִיכָה דִּכְתִיב – **the colleague of Michah,**[1] **as it is written:**[2] "וְאִישׁ אֶחָד מִבְּנֵי הַנְּבִיאִים אָמַר אֶל־רֵעֵהוּ בִּדְבַר ה׳ – ***And a certain man*** [Michah] ***of the disciples of the prophets said to his fellow as the word of Hashem,***[3] הַכֵּינִי נָא וַיְמָאֵן הָאִישׁ לְהַכֹּתוֹ" – ***"Strike me now." But the man refused to strike him.***[4] וּכְתִיב, "וַיֹּאמֶר לוֹ יַעַן אֲשֶׁר לֹא־שָׁמַעְתָּ [וגו׳]" – **And it is written** immediately afterwards: ***Then he*** [Michah] ***said to him, "Because you have not obeyed*** *the voice of Hashem, behold! As soon as you will depart from me, a lion will slay you." And as soon as he departed from him, a lion found him and slew him.*[5]

An example of a prophet who transgresses his own prophecy: וְנָבִיא שֶׁעָבַר עַל דִּבְרֵי עַצְמוֹ – AND A PROPHET WHO TRANSGRESSES HIS OWN WORDS – כְּגוֹן עִדּוֹ הַנָּבִיא דִּכְתִיב – **for example, Iddo the prophet, as it is written** that Iddo said: "כִּי־כֵן צִוָּה אֹתִי" – ***For so he commanded me*** *by the word of Hashem saying, "Eat no bread, nor drink water, nor return by the same way that you came."*[6] Iddo left and began his journey home. On his way, he passed by the home of an old prophet, who invited him to a meal. וּכְתִיב, "וַיֹּאמֶר לוֹ גַּם־אֲנִי נָבִיא כָּמוֹךָ" – **And it is written:** ***He*** [the aged prophet of Bethel] ***said to him*** [Iddo], ***"I am also a prophet just as you are****; and an angel spoke to me by the word of Hashem saying, 'Bring him back with you into your house, so that he may eat bread and drink water.'" [But] he lied to him.*[7] וּכְתִיב, "וַיָּשָׁב אִתּוֹ" – **And it is written:** ***So he*** [Iddo] ***went back with him,*** *and ate bread in his house and drank water.*[8] Thus, Iddo transgressed his own prophetic command and instead followed the words of this false prophet. וּכְתִיב, "וַיֵּלֶךְ וַיִּמְצָאֵהוּ אַרְיֵה" – **And it is written** afterwards: ***And [when] he*** [Iddo] ***went, and a lion found him*** *by the way and slew him.*[9]

The Gemara cites a Baraisa:

תָּנֵי תַּנָּא קַמֵּיהּ דְּרַב חִסְדָּא – **A teacher of Baraisos taught a Baraisa in the presence of Rav Chisda:** הַכּוֹבֵשׁ אֶת נְבוּאָתוֹ לוֹקֶה – ONE WHO SUPPRESSES HIS PROPHECY RECEIVES LASHES.[10]

Rav Chisda questions this ruling:

אָמַר לֵיהּ – **[Rav Chisda] said to him:** מַאן דְּאָכִיל תַּמְרֵי בְּאַרְבְּלָא לָקֵי – **Does one who eats dates out of a sieve receive lashes?**[11] We must see a person doing something wrong before we flog him! Therefore, how can we give lashes to a prophet who suppresses his prophecy? מַאן מַתְרֵי בֵּיהּ – **Who** could possibly **warn him** not to suppress his prophecy?[12]

The Gemara answers:

אָמַר אַבָּיֵי – **Abaye said:** חַבְרֵיהּ נְבִיאֵי – **His fellow prophets** can warn him.

The Gemara asks:

מְנָא יָדְעֵי – **How do they know** that he has received a prophecy which he is suppressing?

The Gemara answers:

אָמַר אַבָּיֵי – **Abaye said:** דִּכְתִיב – **For it is written:**[13] "כִּי לֹא יַעֲשֶׂה ה׳ [אֱלֹהִים] דָּבָר כִּי אִם־גָּלָה סוֹדוֹ" – ***For Hashem God will not do something unless he reveals His secret*** *to His servants, the prophets.* Thus, if a prophet received a prophecy, other prophets received it as well, and they can warn him not to suppress it.[14]

NOTES

1. Michah is a shortened form of Michayehu ben Yimla (*Rashi*; see *II Chronicles* 18:7, 14).

2. *I Kings* 20:35.

3. I.e. he told this to the man as being the word of Hashem (*Rashi* ibid.).

4. This was intended as an object lesson to Ahab for his refusal to kill Ben Hadad (king of Syria) when God had given him into Ahab's hand, as described earlier in the chapter. Pity upon the wicked is misplaced and can only lead to tragedy. Failure to heed the word of God, whether to strike an enemy or a prophet, brings a Heavenly death sentence (see *Rashi* and *Radak* to verse).

5. [Although the Gemara identifies the prophet mentioned in these verses as Michah, this is not explicit in the verses themselves. *Rashi* explains that a later verse (*I Kings* 22:8) implies that he is the prophet of our chapter. The later verse reads: *And the king of Israel [Ahab] said to Yehoshafat, "There is one other man, Michayehu ben Yimla, from whom we may inquire of Hashem; but I hate him, for he does not prophesy good concerning me, but evil."* Ahab's complaint that Michah *does not prophesy good concerning me, but evil* is a reference to the prophecy of doom spoken by the anonymous prophet of our verses.]

6. *I Kings* 13:9. [I.e. for so the angel who spoke the prophecy to me commanded me in the name of *Hashem* (*Metzudos*).]

Yarovam, the wicked king of Israel, had established golden calves and altars in his kingdom. One day, Yarovam himself was offering sacrifices on the altar in Bethel, when Iddo came and prophesied the destruction of both the altar and of Yarovam himself. Upon hearing this, Yarovam pointed to the prophet to order his arrest, but his arm withered instantly. The king begged the prophet to pray for the restoration of his arm and the prophet did so. When he was healed, Yarovam asked Iddo to join him for a meal, but Iddo responded that he was forbidden to do so. [Iddo is not mentioned by name in these verses either. *Rashi* (104a ד״ה ומשרה שכינה) quotes *Seder Olam* 20 which identifies this prophet as Iddo. *Rashi* to *Proverbs* 10:20 cites *Midrash Tanchuma, Ki Sissa* 6 to the same effect. *Radak* to *I Kings* 13:1 finds a clue to this identification in *II Chronicles* 9:29. There is an עִדּוֹ הַחוֹזֶה, *Iddo the Seer,* mentioned in *II Chronicles* 12:15 and 13:22, who may be the Iddo of our discussion. See *Rashi* here and *Chazon Ish, Sanhedrin* 21:3.

7. *I Kings* 13:18. The aged prophet mentioned in this verse was originally a true prophet known to Iddo (*Teshuvos HaRashba* 1:11) who became a false prophet (below, 104a).

8. *I Kings* 13:19. Iddo was confronted with the gravity of his actions immediately: *And it came to pass, as they sat at the table, that the word of Hashem came unto the prophet that brought him back: And he* [the aged prophet] *cried unto the man of God that came from Judah saying, "Thus says Hashem, 'Forasmuch as you have disobeyed the mouth of Hashem, and have not kept the commandment which Hashem your God commanded you, but you came back and have eaten bread and drunk water in the place of which He did say to you, "Eat no bread, and drink no water," your carcass shall not come unto the sepulcher of your fathers'"* (ibid. 13:20-22).

9. *I Kings* 13:24. [We thus see that a prophet who transgresses his own words of prophecy is subject to death at the hands of Heaven.]

10. *Tosafos* (89a ד״ה הכובש) state that these lashes cannot be punishment for having violated a prohibition. There are two reasons for this: a) Although a prophet is certainly obligated to transmit his prophecy, there is no specific negative commandment forbidding him to suppress it (see also *Rambam, Hil. Sanhedrin* 19:3). b) The suppression of a prophecy does not require any action on the prophet's part, and no lashes are incurred for a violation that does not involve action [לַאו שֶׁאֵין בּוֹ מַעֲשֶׂה] (see *Makkos* 4b, 13b and 16a).

Rather, *Tosafos* state, these lashes are given to the prophet to force him to do his duty and communicate his prophecy. They are given again and again until he does so. This is an example of the rule governing failed observance of any positive commandment: The offender may be flogged until he complies (cf. *Chamra VeChayei* in the name of *Talmidei Rabbeinu Peretz*).

11. This is merely an expression used by Rav Chisda to convey the notion that there are no grounds for *malkus* (see also *Makkos* 20b). The court cannot give someone lashes just for eating dates! (see *Ritva* to *Makkos* 20b ד״ה א״ל רב חסדא; *Chasam Sofer* to *Shabbos* 93a; *Rashash*; cf. *Meiri* and *Aruch* ד״ה תמר).

12. [Since the lashes are given to force him to discharge his duty (see note 10), he is obviously not flogged until he has been warned to do his duty and he refuses! (see *Yad David*).]

13. *Amos* 3:7.

14. Abaye deduces from the language of the verse that a single prophetic message ["His secret"] reaches several prophets ["His servants, the prophets"]. The reason for this may be to counter the possibility of a prophet suppressing his prophecy and thereby depriving the intended recipients of the benefit of the prophetic warning (see *HaBoneh* in *Ein Yaakov*).

פ א מיי' פ"ט מהלכות יסודי התורה הל' ג:

רבינו חננאל

שמים: **תני** תנא קמיה דרב חסדא לוקה א"ל ומי התרה בו דלקי כלומר מי יודע ששלחו אלהים להינבא והסתיר נבואתו ואמר אביי חבריו הנביאים שגילה כדכתיב כי לא יעשה ה' אלהים דבר כי אם גלה סודו אל עבדיו הנביאים ודלמא הדרו ביה כו': **המוותר** על דברי נביא ואינו עושה כל מה שיאמר לו אלא ממאן לשמוע דבריו כגון חבריה דמיכיהו כדכתיב ואיש אחד מבני הנביאים אמר לרעהו בדבר ה' הכני נא וימאן האיש להכותו וכתיב ויאמר לו יען אשר לא שמעת בקול ה' הנך הולך מאתי והכך האריה וילך מאצלו וימצאהו האריה ויכהו דינו בידי שמים. ואקשינן מנא ידע דהוא נביא ואיענש ושנינן מוחזק בנביאות הוה אבל מאן דלא מוחזק לא מיחייב לקבולי מיניה עד דיהיב ליה אות ומופת ומאן דמוחזק מקבלינן מיניה מאליהו בהר הכרמל אילולי שהיה מוחזק בנביאות היכי הוו מקבלי מיניה ועבדי שחוטי חוץ אלא ש"מ היכא דמוחזק שאני. ונביא שעבר על דברי עצמו כגון עדו הנביא שנאמר כי כן צוה אותי בדבר ה' לאמר לא תאכל לחם ולא תשתה מים ולא תשוב בדרך אשר הלכת ויאמר לו גם אני נביא כמוך ומלאך דבר אלי בדבר ה' לאמר השיבהו אתך אל ביתך ויאכל לחם וישתה מים כחש לו דינו בידי שמים שנאמר וימצאהו האריה בדרך וימיתהו. **ירושלמי** א"ר שמואל בר רב יצחק ונביא אחד זקן ישב בבית אל זה אמציהו כהן בית אל: **ויהי** אחר הדברים האלה והאלהים נסה את אברהם אחר מי א"ר יוחנן אחר דברי השטן שאמר לפני הקב"ה רבון כל העולמים זקן זה חננתו למאה פרי [בטן] ומכל סעודות שעש' לא היה לו להקריב לפניך תור או בן יונה אחד. א"ל כלום עשה אלא למען בנו אם אני אומר לו זבח אותו לפני עושה. מיד והאלהים נסה את אברהם כו' ר' לוי אמר אחר דברי ישמעאל שאמר ליצחק אני גדול ממך במצות שאתה נמלתה בן ח' ימים ואני בן י"ג שנה א"ל ובאבר אחד אתה מי יראיני אם אומר לו הקב"ה זבח עצמך מיד אני זובח את עצמי. מיד והאלהים נסה את אברהם: **ת"ר** נביא שהדיח בסקילה מאי טעמא גמרי הדחה הדחה ממסית מה מסית בסקילה אף נביא שהדיח בסקילה רבי שמעון אומר מיתה כתיבא ביה וכל מיתה האמורה בתורה סתם בחנק. מדיחי עיר הנדחת בסקילה גמרי הדחה הדחה אי ממסית אי מנביא שהדיח ר' שמעון אומר בחנק גמר הדחה הדחה מנביא שהדיח.

אליהו בהר הכרמל וכו'. משמע דבשם הקב"ה היה מתנבא לעבור וכיון דמוחזק מהימנינן ביה אע"ג דלא יהיב אות ובהאשה רבה (יבמות דף צ: ושם) נפקא לן דכתיב אליו תשמעון אפי' אמר לך עבור על אחת מכל מצות האמורות בתורה כגון אליהו בהר הכרמל ותימה מאי קא פריך התם וליגמר מיניה כיון דע"פ הדיבור היה מתנבא מה שייך למילף מיניה לעבור משום תקנה דרבנן שלא על פי הדיבור ועוד למה לן הכא טעמא משום דאיתחזק בנביאות הא אפילו בלא נביא שרי לב"ד לעבור משום מיגדר מילתא ויש לומר דמדקדק התם מלישנא דברייתא דקתני הכל לפי שעה דמשמע הכל מפני צורך השעה ואי על פי הדיבור למה לי צורך השעה בין לצורך בין שלא לצורך צריך לקיים צוויו של מקום אלא ודאי בנביא שעשה מדעתו קא אמרה ברייתא דמיירי קרא והא דבעי הכא איתחזק היינו משום דכי איתחזק בנביאות סומכין עליו במה שהיה מבטיח לירידת אש ושוחטין על הבטחתו קדשים בחוץ שבזכותו ובתפלתו תרד אש מהשמים ויהיה מגדר מילתא בדבר שיתקדש שמו של הקב"ה ברבים ויחזרו ישראל למוטב ומיהו בקראי משמע שעל פי הדיבור עשה דכתיב באליהו ובדברך עשיתי וגו' ופרש"י מאור הגולה בפירושו לנביאים ובדברך עשיתי שהקרבתי בשעת איסור הבמות ונראה לומר דכיון דעל פי הדיבור שרי משום צורך שעה הוא הדין שלא על פי הדיבור שהרי אין נביא רשאי לחדש דבר כדאיתא בפ"ק דמגילה (דף ג:) ועוד י"ל דהא דקאמר אליהו ובדברך עשיתי לא שאמר לו הקב"ה אלא מקרא היה דורש דכתיב גוי וקהל גוים יהיה ממך ואמרינן [מ] עתידין בניך לעשות כמעשה נכרים פירוש לשחוט בחוץ ואני מסכים על ידו ולפי שהיה נביא מוחזק סמכו עליו שעליו נאמר מקרא זה:

הדרן עלך אלו הן הנחנקין

חבריה דמיכה דכתיב [א] ואיש אחד מבני הנביאים אמר אל רעהו בדבר ה' הכני נא וימאן האיש להכותו וכתיב [ב] ויאמר לו יען אשר לא שמעת [וגו'] ונביא שעבר על דברי עצמו כגון עדו הנביא דכתיב [ג] כי כן צוה אותי וכתיב [ד] ויאמר לו גם אני נביא כמוך וכתיב [ה] וישב אתו וכתיב [ו] וילך וימצאהו אריה תני תנא קמיה דרב חסדא הכובש את נבואתו לוקה [א] אמר ליה מאן דאכיל תמרי בארבלא לקי מאן מתרי ביה אמר אביי חבריה נביאי מנא ידעי אמר אביי דכתיב [ז] כי לא יעשה ה' [אלהים] דבר כי אם גלה סודו ודילמא הדרי ביה אם איתא דהדרי ביה אודועי הוו מודעי לכלהו נביאי והא יונה דהדרי ביה ולא אודעוהו יונה מעיקרא נינוה נהפכת אמרי ליה איהו לא ידע אי לטובה אי לרעה המוותר על דברי נביא מנא ידע דאיענש דיהב ליה אות והא מיכה דלא יהיב ליה אות ואיענש היכא דמוחזק שאני דאי לא תימא הכי אברהם בהר המוריה היכי שמע ליה יצחק אליהו בהר הכרמל היכי סמכי עליה ועבדי שחוטי חוץ אלא [א]היכא דמוחזק שאני [ח] ויהי אחר הדברים האלה והאלהים נסה את אברהם [ב] (אחר מאי) א"ר יוחנן משום רבי יוסי בן זימרא אחר דבריו של שטן דכתיב [ט] ויגדל הילד ויגמל וגו' אמר שטן לפני הקב"ה רבונו של עולם זקן זה חננתו למאה שנה פרי בטן מכל סעודה שעשה לא היה לו תור אחד או גוזל אחד להקריב לפניך אמר לו כלום עשה אלא בשביל בנו אם אני אומר לו זבח את בנך לפני מיד זובחו מיד והאלהים נסה את אברהם [י] ויאמר קח נא את בנך אמר רבי שמעון בר אבא [ג] אין נא אלא לשון בקשה משל למלך בשר ודם שעמדו עליו מלחמות הרבה והיה לו גבור אחד ונצחן לימים עמדה עליו מלחמה חזקה אמר לו בבקשה ממך עמוד לי במלחמה זו שלא יאמרו ראשונות אין בהם ממש אף הקב"ה אמר לאברהם ניסיתיך בכמה נסיונות ועמדת בכלן עכשיו עמוד לי בנסיון זה שלא יאמרו אין ממש בראשונים את בנך ב' בנים יש לי [י] את יחידך זה יחיד לאמו וזה יחיד לאמו [י] אשר אהבת תרוייהו רחימנא להו [י] את יצחק וכל כך למה כדי שלא תטרף דעתו עליו קדמו שטן לדרך אמר לו [כ] הנסה דבר אליך תלאה הנה יסרת רבים וידים רפות תחזק כושל יקימון מליך כי עתה תבא אליך ותלא אמר לו [ל] אני בתומי אלך אמר לו [ד] [מ] הלא יראתך כסלתך אמר לו [נ] זכר נא מי הוא נקי אבד כיון דחזא דלא קא שמיע ליה אמר ליה [ס] ואלי דבר יגונב כך שמעתי מאחורי הפרגוד [ע] השה לעולה ואין יצחק לעולה אמר לו [ה] כך עונשו של בדאי שאפילו אמר אמת אין שומעין לו ר' לוי אמר אחר דבריו של ישמעאל ליצחק אמר לו ישמעאל ליצחק אני גדול ממך במצות שאתה מלת בן שמנת ימים ואני בן שלש עשרה שנה אמר לו ובאבר אחד אתה מגרה בי אם אומר לי הקב"ה זבח עצמך לפני אני זובח מיד והאלהים נסה את אברהם [ו] תנו רבנן נביא שהדיח בסקילה רבי שמעון אומר בחנק [ז] מדיחי עיר הנדחת בסקילה מ"ט דרבנן אתיא [פ] הדחה [צ] הדחה ממסית מה להלן בסקילה אף כאן בסקילה ור"ש מיתה כתיבא ביה [ח] וכל מיתה האמורה בתורה סתם אינה אלא חנק מדיחי עיר הנדחת בסקילה מ"ט דרבנן גמרי [ק] הדחה הדחה או ממסית או מנביא שהדיח ור"ש גמר [ק] הדחה [פ] הדחה מנביא וליגמר ממסית דנין מסית רבים ממסית רבים ואין דנין מסית רבים ממסית יחיד אדרבה [ט] דנין הדיוט מהדיוט ואין דנין הדיוט מנביא ור"ש [י] כיון שהדיח אין לך הדיוט גדול מזה אמר רב חסדא

מחלוקת

חבריה דמיכה. דכתיב ואיש אחד מבני הנביאים אמר אל רעהו בדבר ה' הכני נא זה היה מיכיהו בן ימלא שנתנבא אותו היום על אחאב ליפול ביד ארם מפני שנפל בן הדד בידו ושלחו לשלום והיינו דקאמר אחאב ליהושפט לא ידבר עלי טוב כי אם רע מפני שנתנבא כבר את זו עליו ולא קיבל חבירו את דבריו דכתיב וימאן האיש להכותו: עדו הנביא. שנתנבא על מזבח [א] ה' בבית אל שהיה ירבעם מקטר עליו [כ] ובדברי הימים גבי יאשיהו כתיב והוא היה עדו: כי כן צוה אותי. בדבר ה' לאמר לא תאכל לחם ולא תשתה מים [ל] (במקום הזה) ועבר על דברי עצמו ושמע לדברי הנביא השקר ואכל ושתה: תמרי בארבילא. תמרים הנתונים בכברה: דילמא הדרו ביה. פמליא של מעלה וניחם על הרעה והם אינם יודעים והיאך מתרינן בו התראת ספק: והא יונה דהדרו ביה. מהפוך את נינוה: מעיקרא נינוה נהפכת אמרו ליה. ברוח הקדש ומשמע נמי לטובה שיהפכו מעשיהם מרעה לטובה וכיון ששבו נתקיימה הנבואה ולא מיהדר הוא: ואיהו דלא ידע. הוא היה טועה וסבור שהוא לרעה: מנא ידע. האי גברא שזה נביא אמת שהקב"ה עונשו והלא שמא סבור שזהו נביא שקר לפיכך מוותר על דבריו: היכא דהוחזק. שהוא צדיק ונביא אמת: שאני. ולא בעי אות: היכי שמע ליה יצחק. שהוא דבר אמת מה שלא נאמר לשום אדם להקריב את בנו: שחוטי חוץ. שהרי בית המקדש היה בירושלים: הנסה דבר אליך תלאה. וכי היה לאוהבך לנסותך בדבר שהיא תלאה אותך ומכרית את זרעך: הנה יסרת רבים. רלית והחיית' לו כל באי העולם בדברים ועתה הנה בא להלאותך ולבהלך: נביא שהדיח. שמתנבא בשם הקב"ה לעבוד עבודת כוכבים: הדחה. כתיב הכא כי דבר סרה להדיחך וכתיב במסית כי ביקש להדיחך וגו': מיתה כתב ביה. והך גזירה שוה לא גמר מרביה דאין אדם דן גזירה שוה מעצמו: ורבי שמעון גמר הדחה הדחה מנביא. דבעיר הנדחת אגמריה רביה גזירה שוה מסיני לדון הדחה הדחה ומסתברא דמנביא אגמריה הלכה למשה גזירה שוה זו כדיהיב טעמא למלתיה:

מחלוקת

מסורת הש"ס

א) מכות כ:, ב) [נ"ל מאי אחר כ"א בע"י], ג) [לעיל מג: ברכות ט. סוטה יוד:], ד) [פירושו דמלתא תמלא בתוס' ב"מ נח: סוף ד"ה הלא], ה) [אדר"נ פ"ל], ו) לעיל סז. פד., ז) [לעיל נ.], ח) [לעיל נג: ופד:], ט) [לעיל פד.], י) [שם], כ) לא נמלא שם מפורש וברד"ק כתב רמז לזה, ל) ס"א ל"ג, מ) [ב"ר פ' וישלח].

הגהות מהר"ב רנשבורג

א] רש"י ד"ה עדו הנביא שנתנבא על מזבח בבית אל כו'. כצ"ל:

תורה אור השלם

א) וְאִישׁ אֶחָד מִבְּנֵי הַנְּבִיאִים אָמַר אֶל רֵעֵהוּ בִּדְבַר יְיָ הַכֵּינִי נָא וַיְמָאֵן הָאִישׁ לְהַכֹּתוֹ: [מלכים א' כ, לה]

ב) וַיֹּאמֶר לוֹ יַעַן אֲשֶׁר לֹא שָׁמַעְתָּ בְּקוֹל יְיָ הִנְּךָ הוֹלֵךְ מֵאִתִּי וְהִכְּךָ הָאַרְיֵה וַיֵּלֶךְ מֵאֶצְלוֹ וַיִּמְצָאֵהוּ הָאַרְיֵה וַיַּכֵּהוּ: [מלכים א' כ, לו]

ג) כִּי כֵן צִוָּה אֹתִי בִּדְבַר יְיָ לֵאמֹר לֹא תֹאכַל לֶחֶם וְלֹא תִשְׁתֶּה מָיִם וְלֹא תָשׁוּב בַּדֶּרֶךְ אֲשֶׁר הָלָכְתָּ: [מלכים א' יג, ט]

ד) וַיֹּאמֶר לוֹ גַּם אֲנִי נָבִיא כָּמוֹךָ וּמַלְאָךְ דִּבֶּר אֵלַי בִּדְבַר יְיָ לֵאמֹר הֲשִׁבֵהוּ אִתְּךָ אֶל בֵּיתֶךָ וְיֹאכַל לֶחֶם וְיֵשְׁתְּ מָיִם כִּחֵשׁ לוֹ: [מלכים א' יג, יח]

ה) וַיָּשָׁב אִתּוֹ וַיֹּאכַל לֶחֶם בְּבֵיתוֹ וַיֵּשְׁתְּ מָיִם: [מלכים א' יג, יט]

ו) וַיֵּלֶךְ וַיִּמְצָאֵהוּ אַרְיֵה בַּדֶּרֶךְ וַיְמִיתֵהוּ וַתְּהִי נִבְלָתוֹ מֻשְׁלֶכֶת בַּדֶּרֶךְ וְהַחֲמוֹר עֹמֵד אֶצְלָהּ וְהָאַרְיֵה עֹמֵד אֵצֶל הַנְּבֵלָה: [מלכים א' יג, כד]

ז) כִּי לֹא יַעֲשֶׂה אֲדֹנָי אֱלֹהִים דָּבָר כִּי אִם גָּלָה סוֹדוֹ אֶל עֲבָדָיו הַנְּבִיאִים: [עמוס ג, ז]

ח) וַיְהִי אַחַר הַדְּבָרִים הָאֵלֶּה וְהָאֱלֹהִים נִסָּה אֶת אַבְרָהָם וַיֹּאמֶר אֵלָיו אַבְרָהָם וַיֹּאמֶר הִנֵּנִי: [בראשית כב, א]

ט) וַיִּגְדַּל הַיֶּלֶד וַיִּגָּמַל וַיַּעַשׂ אַבְרָהָם מִשְׁתֶּה גָדוֹל בְּיוֹם הִגָּמֵל אֶת יִצְחָק: [בראשית כא, ח]

י) וַיֹּאמֶר קַח נָא אֶת בִּנְךָ אֶת יְחִידְךָ אֲשֶׁר אָהַבְתָּ אֶת יִצְחָק וְלֶךְ לְךָ אֶל אֶרֶץ הַמֹּרִיָּה וְהַעֲלֵהוּ שָׁם לְעֹלָה עַל אַחַד הֶהָרִים אֲשֶׁר אֹמַר אֵלֶיךָ: [בראשית כב, ב]

כ) הֲנִסָּה דָבָר אֵלֶיךָ תִּלְאֶה וַעְצֹר בְּמִלִּין מִי יוּכָל: הִנֵּה יִסַּרְתָּ רַבִּים וְיָדַיִם רָפוֹת תְּחַזֵּק: כּוֹשֵׁל יְקִימוּן מִלֶּיךָ וּבִרְכַּיִם כֹּרְעוֹת תְּאַמֵּץ: כִּי עַתָּה תָּבוֹא אֵלֶיךָ וַתֵּלֶא תִּגַּע עָדֶיךָ וַתִּבָּהֵל: [איוב ד, ב-ה] ל) וַאֲנִי בְּתֻמִּי אֵלֵךְ פְּדֵנִי וְחָנֵּנִי: [תהלים כו, יא] מ) הֲלֹא יִרְאָתְךָ כִּסְלָתֶךָ תִּקְוָתְךָ וְתֹם דְּרָכֶיךָ: [איוב ד, ו] נ) זְכָר נָא מִי הוּא נָקִי אָבָד וְאֵיפֹה יְשָׁרִים נִכְחָדוּ: [איוב ד, ז] ס) וְאֵלַי דָּבָר יְגֻנָּב וַתִּקַּח אָזְנִי שֵׁמֶץ מֶנְהוּ: [איוב ד, יב] ע) וַיֹּאמֶר אַבְרָהָם אֱלֹהִים יִרְאֶה לּוֹ הַשֶּׂה לְעֹלָה בְּנִי וַיֵּלְכוּ שְׁנֵיהֶם יַחְדָּו: [בראשית כב, ח] פ) וְהַנָּבִיא הַהוּא אוֹ חֹלֵם הַחֲלוֹם הַהוּא יוּמָת כִּי דִבֶּר סָרָה עַל יְיָ אֱלֹהֵיכֶם הַמּוֹצִיא אֶתְכֶם מֵאֶרֶץ מִצְרַיִם וְהַפֹּדְךָ מִבֵּית עֲבָדִים לְהַדִּיחֲךָ מִן הַדֶּרֶךְ אֲשֶׁר צִוְּךָ יְיָ אֱלֹהֶיךָ לָלֶכֶת בָּהּ וּבִעַרְתָּ הָרָע מִקִּרְבֶּךָ: [דברים יג, ו] צ) וּסְקַלְתּוֹ בָאֲבָנִים וָמֵת כִּי בִקֵּשׁ לְהַדִּיחֲךָ מֵעַל יְיָ אֱלֹהֶיךָ הַמּוֹצִיאֲךָ מֵאֶרֶץ מִצְרַיִם מִבֵּית עֲבָדִים: [דברים יג, יא] ק) יָצְאוּ אֲנָשִׁים בְּנֵי בְלִיַּעַל מִקִּרְבֶּךָ וַיַּדִּיחוּ אֶת יֹשְׁבֵי עִירָם לֵאמֹר נֵלְכָה וְנַעַבְדָה אֱלֹהִים אֲחֵרִים אֲשֶׁר לֹא יְדַעְתֶּם: [דברים יג, יד]

ליקוטי רש"י **הכני נא.** סימן זה רע על אחאב [illegible] זה שאמר לו ה[illegible] אמר שתכה אותי [מ"א כ, לה]. **דא**[illegible] **יעשה אדני אלהים דבר אלא** [illegible] אשר ידבר הנביא, ויאמר דבר זה [illegible] זו במתנבא על העתידות הרי שבא [illegible] המצות לא תשמע לו אלא אם כן [illegible] הבמות כדי לגדור את ישראל הכל לפי צורך השעה וסייג הפרצה לכך נאמר אליו תשמעון [דברים יח, כב]. כגון אליהו בהר הכרמל שהקריב בבמה ושעת איסור הבמות היתה ואיכא כרת דשחוטי חוץ וכרת דהעלאה [יבמות צ:].

[ההמשך בדף צ.]

The Gemara objects:

וְדִילְמָא הָדְרֵי בֵּיהּ – But perhaps [the Heavenly Court][15] **will rescind** the prophecy – and they will be unaware of this?[16]

The Gemara answers:

אִם אִיתָא דְּהָדְרֵי בֵּיהּ – If it happened that [the Heavenly Court] rescinded the decree, **אוֹדוּעֵי הֲווּ מוֹדְעֵי לְכֻלְּהוּ נְבִיאֵי – they would certainly have informed all the prophets** who had previously been told of the original decree.[17]

This explanation is challenged:

וְהָא יוֹנָה דְּהָדְרֵי בֵּיהּ – But the case of **Jonah was** one in **which a [prophecy]** of doom **was rescinded, וְלָא אוֹדְעוּהוּ – and** yet **[Jonah] was not informed** of this![18] – ? –

The Gemara answers:

יוֹנָה מֵעִיקָּרָא ,,נִינְוֵה נֶהְפָּכֶת" אָמְרֵי לֵיהּ – Jonah was originally told merely that ***Nineveh shall be overturned.***[19] **אִיהוּ לֹא יָדַע – He** assumed this meant that the city would be destroyed; **he did not know** that this was meant originally **אִי לְטוֹבָה אִי לְרָעָה – either for good or for bad.**[20]

The Gemara turns to the prohibition of disregarding a prophet:

הַמְוַותֵּר עַל דִּבְרֵי נָבִיא – ONE WHO DISREGARDS THE WORDS OF A PROPHET: מְנָא יָדַע דְּאִיעַנַּשׁ – How is one to know that a person claiming to be a prophet is indeed a true prophet, so **that he should be punished** for disregarding him?[21]

The Gemara answers:

דְּיָהַב לֵיהּ אוֹת – Because [the prophet] has given him a sign.[22]

The Gemara challenges this:

וְהָא מִיכָה דְּלָא יָהֵיב לֵיהּ אוֹת – But the case of **Michah** cited above **was** one **where he did not give [his fellow] a sign** when he told the man to strike him, **וְאִיעַנַּשׁ – and** yet **[that man] was punished** for disregarding Michah's words.

The Gemara answers:

הֵיכָא דְּמוּחְזָק שָׁאנֵי – Where he is already **established** as a true prophet, **it is different;** his word must be accepted even without a sign. A prophet need not present a sign every time he communicates a prophecy.[23]

The Gemara cites proof:

דְּאִי לָא תֵּימָא הָכִי – This must be the case, for if you do not say so, אַבְרָהָם בְּהַר הַמּוֹרִיָּה – then when **Abraham** attempted to sacrifice Isaac **on Mt. Moriah, הֵיכִי שָׁמַע לֵיהּ יִצְחָק – how could Isaac have listened to him?**[24] **אֵלִיָּהוּ בְּהַר הַכַּרְמֶל –** Similarly, when **Elijah** ordered people to bring an offering **on Mt. Carmel** in the era of the First Temple, **הֵיכִי סָמְכֵי עֲלֵיהּ – how could they have relied upon him וְעָבְדֵי שְׁחוּטֵי חוּץ – and made an** offering **slaughtered outside** the Temple?[25] **אֶלָּא הֵיכָא דְּמוּחְזָק שָׁאנֵי – Rather,** you must say that **where** a prophet **is** already **established,** the law **is different** and the prophecy must be heeded even if no sign is given.[26]

Having made reference to Abraham's attempted sacrifice of Isaac, the Gemara digresses here to discuss that incident:

,,וַיְהִי אַחַר הַדְּבָרִים הָאֵלֶּה – The opening verse of that chapter

NOTES

15. See *Rashi.*

16. Even though a prophet has already foretold the destruction of a person or persons, God will sometimes withhold the promised devastation (*Rashi*). He may do so either temporarily or permanently, perhaps because the persons have improved their ways or perhaps for some other reason (*Rambam, Introduction to the Mishnah*). [Thus, the prophet would no longer be required to proclaim his testimony.] Therefore, even if it is not known that the prophecy has been rescinded, how can his fellow prophets warn him to declare his prophecy [and threaten him with lashes if he does not; see note 10 above] when they cannot be certain that he is still obligated to declare it (see *Rashi* and *Aruch LaNer*).

17. [Thus, as long as they have not heard of any revocation of the decree, they may assume that the decree, and the prophet's obligation to declare it, are still in force, and he may be flogged for suppressing it.]

18. Jonah was sent to Nineveh to prophesy that the city would be overturned in forty days' time. In response, the people of Nineveh fasted, donned sackcloth, and repented the sins that had initiated this evil decree. God saw their deeds and their penitence and spared the city from the threatened catastrophe (*Jonah* ch. 3). After the forty days had passed, Jonah saw that Nineveh still stood and he stationed himself to the east of the city to see if his prophecy would yet be fulfilled (*Jonah* 4:5 and *Mahari Kara* ad loc. 4:3,5). He was unsure whether God had merely given the Ninevites extra time or had completely pardoned them. Jonah did not know that his prophecy had been rescinded until God told him that He had decided to spare the city, as is recorded in the last verse of the book (*Aruch LaNer*; cf. *Maharsha*).

19. *Jonah* 3:4.

20. I.e. it could also denote a spiritual upheaval, a transformation of their behavior from wicked to worthy. As soon as the people of Nineveh repented, this sense of the prophecy was fulfilled, and it was not necessary to rescind the prophecy in order to avert destruction. It was merely Jonah himself who was unaware of this alternative meaning of his prophecy (*Rashi*: see also *Derech Hashem* III 4:7). [The original prophecy to Jonah as recorded in Scripture does not make mention of the words "Nineveh will be overturned" (see *Jonah* 1:2). These words appear only as part of Jonah's proclamation when he finally came to Nineveh. Nevertheless, these were not Jonah's own words, but the words conveyed to him through the prophetic spirit [רוּחַ הַקֹּדֶשׁ] at the time he received his prophecy (*Rashi,* as explained by *HaBoneh* in *Ein Yaakov*).]

21. Perhaps the person disregarding the prophet's words does so because he deems the prophet to be a false one (*Rashi*). Since one is dutybound to ignore a false prophet (*Deuteronomy* 18:22), why should this person be punished?

22. I.e. he foretells the future; this is one of the prerequisites for establishing the "credentials" of a prophet (see *Ramban* to *Deuteronomy* 13:2).

Prophecy is granted only to a person perfect in his characteristics, scrupulous in his observance of the Torah, known for his saintliness and accustomed to the ways of holiness and self-restraint; in short, a flawless individual in every way. One who does not meet this description is not deemed a prophet even if he presents numerous signs. If he has all these qualifications, then we must believe his claim to be a prophet if he performs a miracle or if he foretells the future and every detail of his predictions comes true (*Rambam, Hil. Yesodei HaTorah* 7:7,10:1 and in his *Introduction to the Mishnah*; *Derashos HaRan* §12 (ד״ה ולפי שבהעלותו).

23. Once a prophet's credentials have been established, his later claims of prophecy are believed without any further proof; it is indeed prohibited to test him further (*Rambam, Yesodei HaTorah* 7:7, 10:5).

24. I.e. how could Isaac have believed that God really asked this of Abraham? After all, God had never asked anyone else to sacrifice his son to Him! (*Rashi*). [Nor is there any indication from Scripture that Abraham performed any wonder at this time to demonstrate the truth of his prophecy.]

25. See *I Kings* 18:17-39. Once the Temple had been built in Jerusalem, it became forever forbidden to offer sacrifices anywhere else (Mishnah, *Zevachim* 112b). Since there is no indication that Elijah performed any wonder at the time he told the people to prepare his offering, how could they have heeded Elijah and violated a Torah commandment, unless it was because Elijah had already been established as a prophet? [From the Gemara it seems that Elijah did not slaughter the offering himself but had others do it for him. Thus, they had to rely on his stature as a prophet to be permitted to do so (see also *Tosafos*). Had Elijah slaughtered the offering himself, however, there would have been no need for anyone to ascertain that he was a prophet other than Elijah himself!]

26. [The Gemara assumes a principle here that is detailed on 90a. If a confirmed prophet directs someone in the name of God to breach the halachah temporarily, the person is dutybound to do so (cf. *Tosafos*; see also *Aruch LaNer* in the name of *Yerushalmi Taanis*).

עין משפט
נר מצוה

פ א מיי' פ"ט מהלכות יסודי התורה הל' ג:

חבריה דמיכה דכתיב א) ואיש אחד מבני הנביאים אמר אל רעהו בדבר ה' הכני נא וימאן האיש להכותו וכתיב ב) ויאמר לו יען אשר לא שמעת [וגו'] ונביא שעבר על דברי עצמו כגון עדו הנביא דכתיב ג) כי כן צוה אותי וכתיב ד) ויאמר לו גם אני נביא כמוך וכתיב ה) וישב אתו וכתיב ו) וילך וימצאהו אריה תני תנא קמיה דרב חסדא הכובש את נבואתו לוקה א) אמר ליה מאן דאכיל תמרי בארבלא לקי מאן מתרי ביה אמר אביי חבריה נביאי מנא ידעי אמר אביי דכתיב ז) כי לא יעשה ה' [אלהים] דבר כי אם גלה סודו ודילמא הדרי ביה אם איתא דהדרי ביה אודועי הוו מודעי לכלהו נביאי והא יונה דהדרי ביה ולא אודעוהו יונה מעיקרא נינוה נהפכת אמרי ליה איהו לא ידע אי לטובה אי לרעה המוותר על דברי נביא מנא ידע דאיענש דיהב ליה אות והא מיכה דלא יהיב ליה אות ואיענש היכא דמוחזק שאני דאי לא תימא הכי אברהם בהר המוריה היכי שמע ליה יצחק אליהו בהר הכרמל היכי סמכי עליה ועבדי שחוטי חוץ אלא *היכא דמוחזק שאני ח) ויהי אחר הדברים האלה והאלהים נסה את אברהם ב) (אחר מאי) א"ר יוחנן משום רבי יוסי בן זימרא אחר דבריו של שטן דכתיב ט) ויגדל הילד ויגמל וגו' אמר שטן לפני הקב"ה רבונו של עולם זקן זה חננתו למאה שנה פרי בטן מכל סעודה שעשה לא היה לו תור אחד או גוזל אחד להקריב לפניך אמר לו כלום עשה אלא בשביל בנו אם אני אומר לו זבח את בנך לפני מיד זובחו מיד והאלהים נסה את אברהם י) ויאמר קח נא את בנך אמר רבי שמעון בר אבא ג) אין נא אלא לשון בקשה משל למלך בשר ודם שעמדו עליו מלחמות הרבה והיה לו גבור אחד ונצחן לימים עמדה עליו מלחמה חזקה אמר לו בבקשה ממך עמוד לי במלחמה זו שלא יאמרו ראשונות אין בהם ממש אף הקב"ה אמר לאברהם ניסיתיך בכמה נסיונות ועמדת בכלן עכשיו עמוד לי בנסיון זה שלא יאמרו אין ממש בראשונים את בנך ב' בנים יש לי ד) את יחידך זה יחיד לאמו וזה יחיד לאמו ה) אשר אהבת תרוייהו רחימנא להו ו) את יצחק וכל כך למה כדי שלא תטרף דעתו עליו קדמו שטן לדרך אמר לו כ) הנסה דבר אליך תלאה הנה יסרת רבים וידים רפות תחזק כושל יקימון מליך כי עתה תבא אליך ותלא אמר לו ל) אני בתומי אלך אמר לו ז) מ) הלא יראתך כסלתך אמר לו נ) זכר נא מי הוא נקי אבד כיון דחזא דלא קא שמיע ליה אמר ליה ס) ואלי דבר יגונב כך שמעתי מאחורי הפרגוד ע) השה לעולה ואין יצחק לעולה אמר לו ח) כך עונשו של בדאי שאפילו אמר אמת אין שומעין לו ר' לוי אמר אחר דבריו של ישמעאל ליצחק אמר לו ישמעאל ליצחק אני גדול ממך במצות שאתה מלת בן שמנת ימים ואני בן שלש עשרה שנה אמר לו ובאבר אחד אתה מגרה בי אם אומר לי הקב"ה זבח עצמך לפני אני זובח מיד והאלהים נסה את אברהם ט) תנו רבנן נביא שהדיח בסקילה רבי שמעון אומר בחנק י) מדיחי עיר הנדחת בסקילה רבי שמעון אומר בחנק נביא שהדיח בסקילה מ"ט דרבנן אתיא פ) הדחה צ) הדחה ממסית מה להלן בסקילה אף כאן בסקילה ור"ש מיתה כתיבא ביה כ) וכל מיתה האמורה בתורה סתם אינה אלא חנק מדיחי עיר הנדחת בסקילה מ"ט דרבנן גמרי ק) הדחה הדחה או ממסית או מנביא שהדיח ור"ש גמר ק) הדחה פ) הדחה מנביא וליגמר ממסית דנין מסית רבים ממסית רבים ואין דנין מסית רבים ממסית יחיד אדרבה ט) דנין הדיוט מהדיוט ואין דנין הדיוט מנביא ור"ש י) כיון שהדיח אין לך הדיוט גדול מזה אמר רב חסדא

מחלוקת

הדרן עלך אלו הן הנחנקין

רש"י

חבריה דמיכה. דכתיב ואיש אחד מבני הנביאים אמר אל רעהו בדבר ה' הכני נא זה היה מיכיהו בן ימלא שנתנבא אותו היום על אחאב ליפול ביד ארם מפני שנפל בן הדד בידו ושלחו לשלום והיינו דקאמר אחאב ליהושפט לא ידבר עלי טוב כי אם רע מפני שנתנבא כבר את זו עליו ולא קיבל חבירו את דבריו דכתיב וימאן האיש להכותו: עדו הנביא. שנתנבא על מזבח א] ה' בבית אל שהיה ירבעם מקטר עליו כ) ובדברי הימים גבי יאשיהו כתיב והוא היה עדו: כי כן צוה אותי. בדבר ה' לאמר לא תאכל לחם ולא תשתה מים ל) (במקום הזה) ועבר על דברי עצמו ושמע לדברי הנביא השקר ואכל ושתה: תמרי בארבילא. תמרים הנתונים בכברה: דילמא הדרו ביה. פמליא של מעלה וניחם על הרעה והם אינם יודעים והיאך מתרינן בו התראת ספק: והא יונה דהדרו ביה. מהפוך את נינוה: מעיקרא נינוה נהפכת אמרו ליה. ברוח הקדש ומשמע נמי לטובה שיהפכו מעשיהם מרעה לטובה וכיון ששבו נתקיימה הנבואה ולא מיהדר הוא: ואיהו דלא ידע. הוא היה טועה וסבור שהוא לרעה: מנא ידע. האי גברא שזה נביא אמת שהקב"ה עונשו והלא שמא סבור שזהו נביא שקר לפיכך מוותר על דבריו: היכא דהוחזק. שהוא צדיק ונביא אמת: שאני. ולא בעי אות: היכי שמע ליה יצחק. שהוא דבר אמת מה שלא נאמר לשום אדם להקריב את בנו: שחוטי חוץ. שהרי בית המקדש היה בירושלים: הנסה דבר אליך תלאה. וכי היה לאוהבך לנסותך בדבר שהיא תלאה אותך ומכרית את זרעך: הנה יסרת רבים. רגית והחיית' לו כל באי העולם בדברים ועתה הנה בא להלאותך ולבהלך: נביא שהדיח. שמתנבא בשם הקב"ה לעבוד עבודת כוכבים: הדחה. כתיב הכא כי דבר סרה להדיחך וכתיב במסית כי בקש להדיחך וגו': מיתה כתב ביה. והך גזירה שוה לא גמר מרביה דאין אדם דן גזירה שוה מעצמו: ורבי שמעון גמר הדחה הדחה מנביא. דבעיר הנדחת אגמריה רביה גזירה שוה מסיני לדון הדחה הדחה ומסתברא דמנביא אגמריה הלכה למשה גזירה שוה זו כדיהיב טעמא למלתיה:

תוספות

אליהו בהר הכרמל וכו'. משמע דבשם הקב"ה היה מתנבא לעבור וכיון דמוחזק מהימנינן ביה אע"ג דלא יהיב אות ובהאשה רבה (יבמות דף צ: ושם) נפקא לן דכתיב אליו תשמעון אפי' אמר לך עבור על אחת מכל מצות האמורות בתורה כגון אליהו בהר הכרמל ותימה מאי קא פריך התם וליגמר מיניה כיון דע"פ הדיבור היה מתנבא מה שייך למילף מיניה לעבור משום תקנה דרבנן שלא על פי הדיבור ועוד למה לן הכא טעמא משום דאיתחזק בנביאות הא אפילו בלא נביא שרי לב"ד לעבור משום מיגדר מילתא ויש לומר דמדקדק התם מלישנא דברייתא דקתני הכל לפי שעה דמשמע הכל מפני צורך השעה ואי על פי הדיבור למה לי צורך השעה בין לצורך בין שלא לצורך צריך לקיים צוויו של מקום אלא ודאי בנביא שעשה מדעתו קא אמרה ברייתא דמיירי קרא והא דבעי הכא איתחזק היינו משום דכי איתחזק בנביאות סומכין עליו במה שהיה מבטיח לירידת אש ושוחטין על הבטחתו קדשים בחוץ שבזכותו ובתפלתו תרד אש מהשמים ויהיה מגדר מילתא בדבר שיתקדש שמו של הקב"ה ברבים ויחזרו ישראל למוטב ומיהו בקראי משמע שעל פי הדיבור עשה דכתיב באליהו ובדברך עשיתי וגו' ופרש"י מאור הגולה בפירושו לנביאים ובדברך עשיתי שהקרבתי בשעת איסור הבמות ונראה לומר דכיון דעל פי הדיבור שרי משום צורך שעה הוא הדין שלא על פי הדיבור שהרי אין נביא רשאי לחדש דבר כדאיתא בפ"ק דמגילה (דף ג:) ועוד י"ל דהא דקאמר אליהו ובדברך עשיתי לא שאמר לו הקב"ה אלא מקרא היה דורש דכתיב גוי וקהל גוים יהיה ממך ואמרינן מ) עתידין בניך לעשות כמעשה גוים פירוש לשחוט בחוץ ואני מסכים על ידו ולפי שהיה נביא מוחזק סמכו עליו שעליו נאמר מקרא זה:

רבינו חננאל

שמים: **תני** תנא קמיה דרב חסדא לוקה א"ל ומי התרה בו דלקי כלומר מי יודע ששלחו אלהים להינבא והסתיר נבואתו ואמר אביי חבריו הנביאים שגילה כדכתיב כי לא יעשה ה' אלהים דבר כי אם גלה סודו אל עבדיו הנביאים ודלמא הדרו ביה כו': **המוותר** על דברי נביא ואינו עושה כל מה שיאמר לו אלא ממאן לשמוע דבריו כגון חבריה דמיכיהו כדכתיב ואיש אחד מבני הנביאים אמר לרעהו בדבר ה' הכני נא וימאן האיש להכותו וכתיב ויאמר לו יען אשר לא שמעת בקול ה' הנך הולך מאתי והכך האריה וילך מאצלו וימצאהו האריה ויכהו דינו בידי שמים. ואקשינן מנא ידע דהוא נביא ואיענש ושנינן מוחזק בנביאות הוה אבל מאן דלא מוחזק לא מיחייב לקבולי מיניה עד דיהיב ליה אות ומופת ומאן דמוחזק מקבלינן מיניה מאליהו בהר הכרמל אילולי שהיה מוחזק בנביאות היכי הוו מקבלי מיניה ועבדי שחוטי חוץ אלא ש"מ היכא דמוחזק שאני. ונביא שעבר על דברי עצמו כגון עדו הנביא שנאמר כי כן צוה אותי בדבר ה' לאמר לא תאכל לחם ולא תשתה מים ולא תשוב בדרך אשר הלכת ויאמר לו גם אני נביא כמוך ומלאך דבר אלי בדבר ה' לאמר השיבהו אתך אל ביתך ויאכל לחם וישתה מים כחש לו דינו בידי שמים שנאמר וימצאהו האריה בדרך וימיתהו. **ירושלמי** א"ר שמואל בר רב יצחק ונביא אחד זקן ישב בבית אל זה אמציהו כהן בית אל: **ויהי** אחר הדברים האלה והאלהים נסה את אברהם אחר מי א"ר יוחנן אחר דברי השטן שאמר לפני הקב"ה רבון כל העולמים זקן זה חננתו למאה פרי [בטן] ומכל סעודות שעש' לא היה לו להקריב לפניך תור או בן יונה אחד. א"ל כלום עשה אלא למען בנו אם אני אומר לו זבח אותו לפני עושה. מיד והאלהים נסה את אברהם כו' ר' לוי אמר אחר דברי ישמעאל שאמר ליצחק אני גדול ממך במצות שאתה נמלתה בן ח' ימים ואני בן י"ג שנה א"ל ובאבר אחד אתה מי יראיני אם אומר לו הקב"ה זבח עצמך מיד אני זובח את עצמי. מיד והאלהים נסה את אברהם: **ת"ר** נביא שהדיח בסקילה מאי טעמא גמרי הדחה הדחה ממסית מה מסית בסקילה אף נביא שהדיח בסקילה רבי שמעון אומר מיתה כתיבא ביה וכל מיתה האמורה בתורה סתם בחנק. מדיחי עיר הנדחת בסקילה גמרי הדחה הדחה אי ממסית אי מנביא שהדיח ר' שמעון אומר בחנק גמר הדחה הדחה מנביא שהדיח.

מסורת הש"ס

א) מכות כ:, ב) [צ"ל מאי אחר כ"א בע"י], ג) [לעיל מג: ברכות ט. סוטה יז:], ד) [פירושו דמלתא תמצא בתוס' ב"מ נח: סוף ד"ה הלא], ה) [אדר"נ פ"ל], ו) לעיל סז. פד., ז) [לעיל נ.], ח) [לעיל נב: ופד:], ט) [לעיל פד.], י) [שם], כ) לא נמצא שם מפורש וברד"ק כתב רמז לזה, ל) ס"א ל"ג, מ) [ב"ר פ' וישלח].

הגהות מהר"ב רנשבורג

א] רש"י ד"ה עדו הנביא שנתנבא על מזבח בבית אל כו'. כצ"ל:

תורה אור השלם

א) וְאִישׁ אֶחָד מִבְּנֵי הַנְּבִיאִים אָמַר אֶל רֵעֵהוּ בִּדְבַר יְיָ הַכֵּינִי נָא וַיְמָאֵן הָאִישׁ לְהַכֹּתוֹ: [מלכים א' כ, לה]

ב) וַיֹּאמֶר לוֹ יַעַן אֲשֶׁר לֹא שָׁמַעְתָּ בְּקוֹל יְיָ הִנְּךָ הוֹלֵךְ מֵאִתִּי וְהִכְּךָ הָאַרְיֵה וַיֵּלֶךְ מֵאֶצְלוֹ וַיִּמְצָאֵהוּ הָאַרְיֵה וַיַּכֵּהוּ: [מלכים א' כ, לו]

ג) כִּי כֵן צִוָּה אֹתִי בִּדְבַר יְיָ לֵאמֹר לֹא תֹאכַל לֶחֶם וְלֹא תִשְׁתֶּה מָּיִם וְלֹא תָשׁוּב בַּדֶּרֶךְ אֲשֶׁר הָלָכְתָּ: [מלכים א' יג, ט]

ד) וַיֹּאמֶר לוֹ גַּם אֲנִי נָבִיא כָּמוֹךָ וּמַלְאָךְ דִּבֶּר אֵלַי בִּדְבַר יְיָ לֵאמֹר הֲשִׁבֵהוּ אִתְּךָ אֶל בֵּיתֶךָ וְיֹאכַל לֶחֶם וְיֵשְׁתְּ מָיִם כִּחֵשׁ לוֹ: [מלכים א' יג, יח]

ה) וַיָּשָׁב אִתּוֹ וַיֹּאכַל לֶחֶם בְּבֵיתוֹ וַיֵּשְׁתְּ מָיִם: [מלכים א' יג, יט]

ו) וַיֵּלֶךְ וַיִּמְצָאֵהוּ אַרְיֵה בַּדֶּרֶךְ וַיְמִיתֵהוּ וַתְּהִי נִבְלָתוֹ מֻשְׁלֶכֶת בַּדֶּרֶךְ וְהַחֲמוֹר עֹמֵד אֶצְלָהּ וְהָאַרְיֵה עֹמֵד אֵצֶל הַנְּבֵלָה: [מלכים א' יג, כד]

ז) כִּי לֹא יַעֲשֶׂה אֲדֹנָי אֱלֹהִים דָּבָר כִּי אִם גָּלָה סוֹדוֹ אֶל עֲבָדָיו הַנְּבִיאִים: [עמוס ג, ז]

ח) וַיְהִי אַחַר הַדְּבָרִים הָאֵלֶּה וְהָאֱלֹהִים נִסָּה אֶת אַבְרָהָם וַיֹּאמֶר אֵלָיו אַבְרָהָם וַיֹּאמֶר הִנֵּנִי: [בראשית כב, א]

ט) וַיִּגְדַּל הַיֶּלֶד וַיִּגָּמַל וַיַּעַשׂ אַבְרָהָם מִשְׁתֶּה גָדוֹל בְּיוֹם הִגָּמֵל אֶת יִצְחָק: [בראשית כא, ח]

י) וַיֹּאמֶר קַח נָא אֶת בִּנְךָ אֶת יְחִידְךָ אֲשֶׁר אָהַבְתָּ אֶת יִצְחָק וְלֶךְ לְךָ אֶל אֶרֶץ הַמֹּרִיָּה וְהַעֲלֵהוּ שָׁם לְעֹלָה עַל אַחַד הֶהָרִים אֲשֶׁר אֹמַר אֵלֶיךָ: [בראשית כב, ב]

כ) הֲנִסָּה דָבָר אֵלֶיךָ תִּלְאֶה וַעְצֹר בְּמִלִּין מִי יוּכָל: הִנֵּה יִסַּרְתָּ רַבִּים וְיָדַיִם רָפוֹת תְּחַזֵּק: כּוֹשֵׁל יְקִימוּן מִלֶּיךָ וּבִרְכַּיִם כֹּרְעוֹת תְּאַמֵּץ: כִּי עַתָּה תָּבוֹא אֵלֶיךָ וַתֵּלֶא תִּגַּע עָדֶיךָ וַתִּבָּהֵל: [איוב ד, ב-ה] ל) וַאֲנִי בְּתֻמִּי אֵלֵךְ פְּדֵנִי וְחָנֵּנִי: [תהלים כו, יא] מ) הֲלֹא יִרְאָתְךָ כִּסְלָתֶךָ תִּקְוָתְךָ וְתֹם דְּרָכֶיךָ: [איוב ד, ו] נ) זְכָר נָא מִי הוּא נָקִי אָבָד וְאֵיפֹה יְשָׁרִים נִכְחָדוּ: [איוב ד, ז] ס) וְאֵלַי דָּבָר יְגֻנָּב וַתִּקַּח אָזְנִי שֵׁמֶץ מֶנְהוּ: [איוב ד, יב] ע) וַיֹּאמֶר אַבְרָהָם אֱלֹהִים יִרְאֶה לּוֹ הַשֶּׂה לְעֹלָה בְּנִי וַיֵּלְכוּ שְׁנֵיהֶם יַחְדָּו: [בראשית כב, ח] פ) וְהַנָּבִיא הַהוּא אוֹ חֹלֵם הַחֲלוֹם הַהוּא יוּמָת כִּי דִבֶּר סָרָה עַל יְיָ אֱלֹהֵיכֶם הַמּוֹצִיא אֶתְכֶם מֵאֶרֶץ מִצְרַיִם וְהַפֹּדְךָ מִבֵּית עֲבָדִים לְהַדִּיחֲךָ מִן הַדֶּרֶךְ אֲשֶׁר צִוְּךָ יְיָ אֱלֹהֶיךָ לָלֶכֶת בָּהּ וּבִעַרְתָּ הָרָע מִקִּרְבֶּךָ: [דברים יג, ו] צ) וּסְקַלְתּוֹ בָאֲבָנִים וָמֵת כִּי בִקֵּשׁ לְהַדִּיחֲךָ מֵעַל יְיָ אֱלֹהֶיךָ הַמּוֹצִיאֲךָ מֵאֶרֶץ מִצְרַיִם מִבֵּית עֲבָדִים: [דברים יג, יא] ק) יָצְאוּ אֲנָשִׁים בְּנֵי בְלִיַּעַל מִקִּרְבֶּךָ וַיַּדִּיחוּ אֶת יֹשְׁבֵי עִירָם לֵאמֹר נֵלְכָה וְנַעַבְדָה אֱלֹהִים אֲחֵרִים אֲשֶׁר לֹא יְדַעְתֶּם: [דברים יג, יד]

ליקוטי רש"י

הכני נא. סימן זה רע על אחאב שאמר לו הנביא על פי הגבורה להכות את בן הדד ולא הכהו ואף זה שאמר לו הנביא בדבר ה' הכיני ולא הכהו כשם שנפרע מזה יפרע מאחאב. בדבר ה'. הקב"ה אמר שתכה אותי [מ"א כ, לה]. דאכיל תמרי בארבילא. האוכל תמרים בכברה יהא לוקה בתמיה [מכות כ:]. כי לא יעשה אדני אלהים דבר אלא א"כ גלה סודו. אותו סוד אל עבדיו הנביאים [עמוס ג, ז]. היכי דמוחזק שאני. אשר ידבר הנביא, ויאמר דבר זה עתיד לבוא עליכם ותראו שלא יבא הוא הדבר אשר לא דברו ה' והרוג אותו ואם תאמר זו במתנבא על העתידות הרי שבא ואמר עשו כך וכך ומפי הקב"ה אני אומר כבר נלטוו שאם בא להדיחך מאחת מכל המצות לא תשמע לו אלא אם כן מומחה הוא לך שהוא צדיק גמור כגון אליהו בהר הכרמל שהקריב בבמה בשעת איסור הבמות כדי לגדור את ישראל הכל לפי צורך השעה וסייג הפרצה לכך נאמר אליו תשמעון [דברים יח, כב]. כגון אליהו בהר הכרמל שהקריב בבמה ושעת איסור הבמות היתה ואיכא כרת דשחוטי חוץ וכרת דהעלאה [יבמות צ:]. [ההמשך בדף צ.]

states: ***And it came to pass after these things*** וְהָאֱלֹהִים נִסָּה אֶת־אַבְרָהָם״ – ***that God tested Abraham.***[27] (אַחַר מַאי – **After which** things?) אָמַר רַבִּי יוֹחָנָן מִשּׁוּם רַבִּי יוֹסֵי בֶּן זִמְרָא – **R' Yochanan said in the name of R' Yose ben Zimra:** אַחַר דְּבָרָיו שֶׁל שָׂטָן – **After the words of Satan,** who seized an opportunity to criticize Abraham before God. דִּכְתִיב – **For it is written:** ,,וַיִּגְדַּל הַיֶּלֶד וַיִּגָּמַל וגו׳ ״ – ***And the child*** [Isaac] ***grew and was weaned, etc.*** *And Abraham made a great feast on the day that Isaac was weaned.*[28] אָמַר שָׂטָן לִפְנֵי הַקָּדוֹשׁ בָּרוּךְ הוּא – **Satan said before the Holy One, Blessed is He,** רִבּוֹנוֹ שֶׁל עוֹלָם – **"Master of the Universe!** זָקֵן זֶה חֲנַנְתּוֹ לְמֵאָה שָׁנָה פְּרִי בֶטֶן – **This old man you have graced with the fruit of the womb at** the age of **a hundred years.** מִכָּל סְעוּדָה שֶׁעָשָׂה – **From the entire feast that he made** to celebrate, לֹא הָיָה לוֹ תּוֹר אֶחָד אוֹ גּוֹזָל אֶחָד לְהַקְרִיב לְפָנֶיךָ – **did he not have one turtledove or one young dove to offer before You?"**[29] אָמַר לוֹ – **[The Holy One, Blessed is He,] said to him:** כְּלוּם עָשָׂה אֶלָּא בִּשְׁבִיל בְּנוֹ – **"Did he make** the feast **for any** reason **other than for his son?** אִם אֲנִי אוֹמֵר לוֹ זְבַח אֶת בִּנְךָ לְפָנַי – **Yet, if I would tell him, 'Sacrifice your son before Me,'** מִיָּד זוֹבְחוֹ – **he would sacrifice him immediately."** מִיָּד ,,וְהָאֱלֹהִים נִסָּה אֶת־אַבְרָהָם״ – **Thereupon,** the verse states: ***And God tested Abraham.***

The Gemara now expounds the next verse of this passage:

,,וַיֹּאמֶר קַח־נָא אֶת־בִּנְךָ״ – Scripture states:[30] ***And he said, "Take*** **now** [*na*] ***your son ..."*** אָמַר רַבִּי שִׁמְעוֹן בַּר אַבָּא – **R' Shimon bar Abba said:** אֵין ,,נָא״ אֶלָּא לְשׁוֹן בַּקָּשָׁה – The word ***na*** here[31] **is none other than a term of appeal.** Thus, God entreated Abraham, as it were, to do His bidding. מָשָׁל לְמֶלֶךְ בָּשָׂר וָדָם – **This is analogous to a king of flesh and blood** שֶׁעָמְדוּ עָלָיו מִלְחָמוֹת הַרְבֵּה – **who had been confronted with many wars,** וְהָיָה לוֹ גִּבּוֹר אֶחָד וְנִצְּחָן – **and he had one mighty warrior who won** all **[the battles].** לְיָמִים – **One day,** עָמְדָה עָלָיו מִלְחָמָה חֲזָקָה – **a** particularly **fierce war confronted [the king].** אָמַר לוֹ – **He** turned to his warrior and **said to him,** בְּבַקָּשָׁה מִמְּךָ – **"I beg of you,** עֲמוֹד לִי בְּמִלְחָמָה זוֹ – **stand** fast **for me in this war,** שֶׁלֹּא יֹאמְרוּ רִאשׁוֹנוֹת אֵין בָּהֶם מַמָּשׁ – **so that [people] should not say that the earlier [wars] were of no substance,** and your victories in them were of no consequence."[32] אַף הַקָּדוֹשׁ בָּרוּךְ הוּא אָמַר לְאַבְרָהָם – **Similarly, the Holy One, Blessed is He, told Abraham:** נִיסִּיתִיךָ בְּכַמָּה נִסְיוֹנוֹת וְעָמַדְתָּ בְּכֻלָּן – **"I have tested you with many trials and you have withstood them all.**[33] עַכְשָׁיו עֲמוֹד לִי בְּנִסָּיוֹן זֶה – **Now, stand** fast **for me in this trial,** שֶׁלֹּא יֹאמְרוּ אֵין מַמָּשׁ בָּרִאשׁוֹנִים – **so that [people] should not say that there was no substance to the earlier [trials]."**[34]

The Gemara expounds the remainder of the statement cited above:

,,אֶת־בִּנְךָ״ – God told Abraham, *"Take now* ***your son."*** שְׁנֵי בָנִים יֵשׁ לִי – Abraham responded, **"I have two sons** – Isaac and Ishmael! Which should I take?" ,,אֶת־יְחִידְךָ״ – God added, ***"Your only one!"*** זֶה יָחִיד לְאִמּוֹ וְזֶה יָחִיד לְאִמּוֹ – Abraham responded, "But **this one is the only son of his mother and that one is the only son of his mother."** ,,אֲשֶׁר־אָהַבְתָּ״ – God added, ***"Whom you love!"*** תַּרְוַיְיהוּ רְחִימְנָא לְהוּ – Abraham responded, "But **I love them both."** ,,אֶת־יִצְחָק״ – Finally, God said, ***"Isaac."***

The Gemara explains the lengthiness of the request:

וְכָל כָּךְ לָמָּה – **And why** was **all of this** necessary? Why did God not immediately say, "Take your son Isaac"? כְּדֵי שֶׁלֹּא תִּטָּרֵף דַּעְתּוֹ עָלָיו – **So that Abraham's mind should not be unbalanced** by a sudden command to sacrifice his beloved son.

The Gemara relates:

קְדָמוֹ שָׂטָן לַדֶּרֶךְ – **Satan came before him on the road.** אָמַר לוֹ – **[Satan] said to him,**[35] . . . ,,הֲנִסָּה דָבָר אֵלֶיךָ תִּלְאֶה – ***"Should He test you with something that will leave you debilitated . . .?*** הִנֵּה יִסַּרְתָּ רַבִּים וְיָדַיִם רָפוֹת תְּחַזֵּק כּוֹשֵׁל יְקִימוּן מִלֶּיךָ . . . – ***Behold, you have chided many, steadying hands that were weak. Your words would raise him who had stumbled,*** *you would brace buckling knees.* כִּי עַתָּה תָּבוֹא אֵלֶיךָ וַתֵּלֶא״ – ***Yet now it comes upon you and you become weary,*** *it touches you, and you become disrupted."*[36] אָמַר לוֹ – **[Abraham] replied to him,** ,,וַאֲנִי בְּתֻמִּי אֵלֵךְ״ – ***"As for me, I will walk in my perfect***

NOTES

27. *Genesis* 22:1.

28. Ibid. 21:8.

29. I.e. could he not present you with even a modest offering, such as a dove, which is a poor man's offering? (*Maharsha;* see *Leviticus* 5:7).

Why indeed did Abraham not make such an offering? We find that he brought sacrifices upon the mere tidings of a son. Certainly he should have offered sacrifices in gratitude for the son himself!

Perhaps Abraham was so overwhelmed by the munificence of what had been given him that he deemed any sacrifices he could offer to be an embarrassingly puny thanks. Thus, he saw no possibility of properly expressing his gratitude and he made no offerings (*Sanhedrei Ketanah*).

30. *Genesis* 22:2.

31. *Maharsha* quoting *Ran*. [The word נָא, *na,* in this context generally means "now," as we translated it. However, the word also carries the connotation of "please," and this is how R' Shimon bar Abba explains it in our verse.]

32. [I.e. so that people should not say that the earlier wars were won over weak opponents, and did not demonstrate true greatness.]

33. Abraham was tested ten times by God (*Avos* 5:3; see *Rashi* and *Rambam* there for an enumeration of them). This trial was the tenth and most severe.

34. The purpose of these tests was not to ascertain whether Abraham had achieved a particular spiritual level; since God is Omniscient, He certainly knew where Abraham stood without testing him. Rather, the purpose of a trial is to set an example of Godliness for bystanders, to demonstrate, in Abraham's case, how far the love and the awe of God can extend. This is done in the hope that others will follow in the footsteps of the righteous people who withstood such trials (*Rambam, Moreh Nevuchim* 3:24; cf. *Ramban* to *Genesis* 22:1). [Had Abraham failed the final trial, people would have unfairly dismissed the other nine trials as less challenging, and their spiritual impact would be considerably lessened.]

35. Much of the ensuing conversation between Satan and Abraham is expressed in verses taken from the fourth chapter of *Job* (one of Eliphaz's speeches to Job). The straightforward meaning of the verses there has little to do with their meaning in the context of our Gemara. Nevertheless, the sages of the Gemara chose to articulate their points in the language of a section of Scripture, as is their wont in many Midrashim (*Maharsha, Iyun Yaakov*).

36. *Job* 4:2-5. Satan argued that someone who loved Abraham would surely not subject him to a test that would enfeeble him and destroy his progeny (*Rashi*). Satan developed this argument further: Abraham's sole ambition and occupation in this world was to teach others that there was a Creator, one God, and to bring them closer to Him. Abraham had been very successful in these endeavors until this point. Now, Satan argued, if Abraham went ahead and sacrificed his son as God had commanded him, all his achievements would be undone (*Rashi,* as explained by *Aruch LaNer*). Disillusionment would be rampant among his followers. They would say that the man who preached against idolatry in the end offered his own son to Molech (*R' Chaim Shmulevitz, Sichos Mussar,* 5731, §11), or that the man who preached kindness represents a god of cruelty (*Emes L'Yaakov*).

Thus, Satan argued, it behooved Abraham to refrain from fulfilling the command regarding Isaac, instead of actively desecrating God's Name among all his followers. At the very least, Satan argued, Abraham could reinterpret his prophetic command, so it would not require him to cause such a desecration (*R' Chaim Shmulevitz* ibid.).

חבריה דמיכה דכתיב א) ואיש אחד מבני הנביאים אמר אל רעהו בדבר ה' הכני נא וימאן האיש להכותו וכתיב ב) ויאמר לו יען אשר לא שמעת [וגו'] ונביא שעבר על דברי עצמו כגון עדו הנביא דכתיב ג) כי כן צוה אותי וכתיב ד) ויאמר לו גם אני נביא כמוך וכתיב ה) וישב אתו וכתיב ו) וילך וימצאהו אריה תני תנא קמיה דרב חסדא הכובש את נבואתו לוקה א) אמר ליה מאן דאכיל תמרי בארבלא לקי מאן מתרי ביה אמר אביי חבריה נביאי מנא ידעי אמר אביי דכתיב ז) כי לא יעשה ה' [אלהים] דבר כי אם גלה סודו ודילמא הדרי ביה אם איתא דהדרי ביה אודועי הוו מודעי לכלהו נביאי והא יונה דהדרי ביה ולא אודעוהו יונה מעיקרא נינוה נהפכת אמרי ליה איהו לא ידע אי לטובה אי לרעה המוותר על דברי נביא מנא ידע דאיענש דיהב ליה אות והא מיכה דלא יהיב ליה אות ואיענש היכא דמוחזק שאני דאי לא תימא הכי אברהם בהר המוריה היכי שמע ליה יצחק אליהו בהר הכרמל היכי סמכי עליה ועבדי שחוטי חוץ אלא [א]היכא דמוחזק שאני ח) ויהי אחר הדברים האלה והאלהים נסה את אברהם ג) (אחר מאי) א"ר יוחנן משום רבי יוסי בן זימרא אחר דבריו של שטן דכתיב ט) ויגדל הילד ויגמל וגו' אמר שטן לפני הקב"ה רבונו של עולם זקן זה חננתו למאה שנה פרי בטן מכל סעודה שעשה לא היה לו תור אחד או גוזל אחד להקריב לפניך אמר לו כלום עשה אלא בשביל בנו אם אני אומר לו זבח את בנך לפני מיד זובחו מיד והאלהים נסה את אברהם י) ויאמר קח נא את בנך אמר רבי שמעון בר אבא ג) אין נא אלא לשון בקשה משל למלך בשר ודם שעמדו עליו מלחמות הרבה והיה לו גבור אחד ונצחן לימים עמדה עליו מלחמה חזקה אמר לו בבקשה ממך עמוד לי במלחמה זו שלא יאמרו ראשונות אין בהם ממש אף הקב"ה אמר לאברהם ניסיתיך בכמה נסיונות ועמדת בכלן עכשיו עמוד לי בנסיון זה שלא יאמרו אין ממש בראשונים את בנך ב' בנים יש לי י) את יחידך זה יחיד לאמו וזה יחיד לאמו י) אשר אהבת תרווייהו רחימנא להו י) את יצחק וכל כך למה כדי שלא תטרף דעתו עליו קדמו שטן לדרך אמר לו כ) הנסה דבר אליך תלאה הנה יסרת רבים וידים רפות תחזק כושל יקימון מליך כי עתה תבא אליך ותלא אמר לו ל) אני בתומי אלך אמר לו מ) הלא יראתך כסלתך אמר לו נ) זכר נא מי הוא נקי אבד כיון דחזא דלא קא שמיע ליה אמר ליה ס) ואלי דבר יגונב כך שמעתי מאחורי הפרגוד ע) השה לעולה ואין יצחק לעולה אמר לו ה) כך עונשו של בדאי שאפילו אמר אמת אין שומעין לו ר' לוי אמר אחר דבריו של ישמעאל ליצחק אמר לו ישמעאל ליצחק אני גדול ממך במצות שאתה מלת בן שמנת ימים ואני בן שלש עשרה שנה אמר לו ובאבר אחד אתה מגרה בי אם אומר לי הקב"ה זבח עצמך לפני אני זובח מיד והאלהים נסה את אברהם י) תנו רבנן נביא שהדיח בסקילה רבי שמעון אומר בחנק ז) מדיחי עיר הנדחת בסקילה רבי שמעון אומר בחנק נביא שהדיח בסקילה מ"ט דרבנן אתיא פ) הדחה צ) הדחה ממסית מה להלן בסקילה אף כאן בסקילה ור"ש מיתה כתיבא ביה ס) וכל מיתה האמורה בתורה סתם אינה אלא חנק מדיחי עיר הנדחת בסקילה מ"ט דרבנן גמרי ק) הדחה הדחה או ממסית או מנביא שהדיח ור"ש גמר ק) הדחה פ) הדחה מנביא וליגמר ממסית דנין מסית רבים ממסית רבים ואין דנין מסית רבים ממסית יחיד אדרבה ט) דנין הדיוט מהדיוט ואין דנין הדיוט מנביא ור"ש י) כיון שהדיח אין לך הדיוט גדול מזה אמר רב חסדא
מחלוקת

רש"י

חבריה דמיכה. דכתיב ואיש אחד מבני הנביאים אמר אל רעהו בדבר ה' הכני נא זה היה מיכיהו בן ימלא שנתנבא אותו היום על אחאב ליפול ביד ארם מפני שנפל בן הדד בידו ושלחו לשלום והיינו דקאמר אחאב ליהושפט לא ידבר עלי טוב כי אם רע מפני שנתנבא כבר את זו עליו ולא קיבל חבירו את דבריו דכתיב וימאן האיש להכותו: עדו הנביא. שנתנבא על מזבח [א] ה' בבית אל שהיה ירבעם מקטר עליו ס) ובדברי הימים גבי יאשיהו כתיב והוא היה עדו: כי כן צוה אותי. בדבר ה' לאמר לא תאכל לחם ולא תשתה מים ל) (במקום הזה) ועבר על דברי עצמו ושמע לדברי הנביא השקר ואכל ושתה: תמרי בארבילא. תמרים הנתונים בכברה: דילמא הדרו ביה. פמליא של מעלה וניחם על הרעה והם אינם יודעים והיאך מתרינן בו התראת ספק: והא יונה דהדרו ביה. מהפוך את נינוה: מעיקרא נינוה נהפכת אמרו ליה. ברוח הקדש ומשמע נמי לטובה שיהפכו מעשיהם מרעה לטובה וכיון ששבו נתקיימה הנבואה ולא מיהדר הוא: ואיהו דלא ידע. הוא היה טועה וסבור שהוא לרעה: מנא ידע. האי גברא שזה נביא אמת שהקב"ה עונשו והלא שמא סבור שזהו נביא שקר לפיכך מוותר על דבריו: היכא דהוחזק. שהוא צדיק ונביא אמת: שאני. ולא בעי אות: היכי שמע ליה יצחק. שהוא דבר אמת מה שלא נאמר לשום אדם להקריב את בנו: שחוטי חוץ. שהרי בית המקדש היה בירושלים: הנסה דבר אליך תלאה. וכי היה לאוהבך לנסותך בדבר שהיא תלאה אותך ומכרית את זרעך: הנה יסרת רבים. רצית והחיית' לו כל באי העולם בדברים ועתה הנה בא להלאותך ולבהלך: נביא שהדיח. שמתנבא בשם הקב"ה לעבוד עבודת כוכבים: הדחה. כתיב הכא כי דבר סרה להדיחך וכתיב במסית כי ביקש להדיחך וגו': מיתה כתב ביה. והך גזירה שוה לא גמר מרביה דאין אדם דן גזירה שוה מעצמו: ורבי שמעון גמר הדחה הדחה מנביא. דבעיר הנדחת אגמריה רביה גזירה שוה מסיני לדון הדחה ומסתברא דמנביא אגמריה הלכה למשה גזירה שוה זו כדיהיב טעמא למלתיה:
מחלוקת

תוספות

אליהו בהר הכרמל וכו'. משמע דבשם הקב"ה היה מתנבא לעבור וכיון דמוחזק מהימנינן ביה אע"ג דלא יהיב אות ובהאשה רבה (יבמות דף צ: ושם) נפקא לן דכתיב אליו תשמעון אפי' אמר לך עבור על אחת מכל מצות האמורות בתורה כגון אליהו בהר הכרמל ותימה מאי קא פריך התם וליגמר מיניה כיון דע"פ הדיבור היה מתנבא מה שייך למילף מיניה לעבור משום תקנה דרבנן שלא על פי הדיבור ועוד למה לן הכא טעמא משום דאיתחזק בנביאות הא אפילו בלא נביא שרי לב"ד לעבור משום מיגדר מילתא ויש לומר דמדקדק התם מלישנא דברייתא דקתני הכל לפי שעה דמשמע הכל מפני צורך השעה ואי על פי הדיבור למה לי צורך השעה בין לצורך בין שלא לצורך צריך לקיים צוויו של מקום אלא ודאי בנביא שעשה מדעתו קא אמרה ברייתא דמיירי קרא והא דבעי הכא איתחזק היינו משום דכי איתחזק בנביאות סומכין עליו במה שהיה מבטיח לירידת אש ושוחטין על הבטחתו קדשים בחוץ שבזכותו ובתפלתו תרד אש מהשמים ויהיה מגדר מילתא בדבר שיתקדש שמו של הקב"ה ברבים ויחזרו ישראל למוטב ומיהו בקראי משמע שעל פי הדיבור עשה דכתיב באליהו ובדברך עשיתי וגו' ופרש"י אמור הגולה בפירושו לנביאים ובדברך עשיתי שהקרבתי בשעת איסור הבמות ונראה לומר דכיון דעל פי הדיבור שרי משום צורך שעה הוא הדין שלא על פי הדיבור שהרי אין נביא רשאי לחדש דבר כדאיתא בפ"ק דמגילה (דף ב:) ועוד י"ל דהא דקאמר אליהו ובדברך עשיתי לא שאמר לו הקב"ה אלא מקרא היה דורש דכתיב גוי וקהל גוים יהיה ממך ואמרינן מ) עתידין בניך לעשות כמעשה נכרים פירוש לשחוט בחוץ ואני מסכים על ידו ולפי שהיה נביא מוחזק סמכו עליו שעליו נאמר מקרא זה:

הדרן עלך אלו הן הנחנקין

עין משפט נר מצוה

פ א מיי' פ"ט מהלכות יסודי התורה הל' ג:

רבינו חננאל

שמים: תני תנא קמיה דרב חסדא לוקה א"ל ומי התרה בו דלקי כלומר מי יודע ששלחו אלהים להינבא והסתיר נבואתו ואמר אביי חבריו הנביאים שגילה כדכתיב כי לא יעשה ה' אלהים דבר כי אם גלה סודו אל עבדיו הנביאים ודלמא הדרו ביה כו': המוותר על דברי נביא ואינו עושה כל מה שיאמר לו אלא ממאן לשמוע דבריו כגון חבריה דמיכיהו כדכתיב ואיש אחד מבני הנביאים אמר לרעהו בדבר ה' הכני נא וימאן האיש להכותו וכתיב ויאמר לו יען אשר לא שמעת בקול ה' הנך הולך מאתי והכך האריה וילך מאצלו וימצאהו האריה ויכהו דינו בידי שמים. ואקשינן מנא ידע דהוא נביא ואיענש ושנינן מוחזק בנביאות הוה אבל מאן דלא מוחזק לא מיחייב לקבולי מיניה עד דיהיב ליה אות ומופת ומאן דמוחזק מקבלינן מיניה מאליהו בהר הכרמל אילולי שהיה מוחזק בנביאות היכי הוו מקבלי מיניה ועבדי שחוטי חוץ אלא ש"מ היכא דמוחזק שאני. ונביא שעבר על דברי עצמו כגון עדו הנביא שנאמר כי כן צוה אותי בדבר ה' לאמר לא תאכל לחם ולא תשתה מים ולא תשוב בדרך אשר הלכת ויאמר לו גם אני נביא כמוך ומלאך דבר אלי בדבר ה' לאמר השיבהו אתך אל ביתך ויאכל לחם וישתה מים כחש לו דינו בידי שמים שנאמר וימצאהו האריה בדרך וימיתהו. ירושלמי א"ר שמואל בר רב יצחק ונביא אחד זקן ישב בבית אל זה אמציהו כהן בית אל: ויהי אחר הדברים האלה והאלהים נסה את אברהם אחר מי א"ר יוחנן אחר דברי השטן שאמר לפני הקב"ה רבון כל העולמים זקן זה חננתו למאה פרי [בטן] ומכל סעודות שעש' לא היה לו להקריב לפניך תור או בן יונה אחד. א"ל כלום עשה אלא למען בנו אם אני אומר לו זבח אותו לפני עושה. מיד והאלהים נסה את אברהם כו' ר' לוי אמר אחר דברי ישמעאל שאמר ליצחק אני גדול ממך במצות שאתה נמלתה בן ח' ימים ואני בן י"ג שנה א"ל ובאבר אחד אתה מי יראיני אם אומר לו הקב"ה זבח עצמך מיד אני זובח את עצמי. מיד והאלהים נסה את אברהם: ת"ר נביא שהדיח בסקילה מאי טעמא גמרי הדחה הדחה ממסית מה מסית בסקילה אף נביא שהדיח בסקילה רבי שמעון אומר מיתה כתיבא ביה וכל מיתה האמורה בתורה סתם בחנק. מדיחי עיר הנדחת בסקילה גמרי הדחה הדחה אי ממסית אי מנביא שהדיח ר' שמעון אומר בחנק גמר הדחה הדחה מנביא שהדיח.

מסורת הש"ס

א) מכות כ:, ב) [נ"ל מאי אחר כ"א בע"י], ג) [לעיל מג: ברכות ע. סוטה יד:], ד) [פירושו דמלתא תמלא בתוס' ב"מ נח: סוף ד"ה הלא], ה) [אדר"נ פ"ל], ו) לעיל סז. פד., ז) [לעיל נ.], ח) [לעיל נג: ופד:], ט) [לעיל פד.], י) [שם], כ) לא נמלא שם מפורש וברד"ק כתב רמז לזה, ל) ס"א ל"ג, מ) [ב"ר פ' וישלח].

הגהות מהר"ב רנשבורג

א] רש"י ד"ה עדו הנביא שנתנבא על מזבח בבית אל כו'. כנ"ל:

תורה אור השלם

א) וְאִישׁ אֶחָד מִבְּנֵי הַנְּבִיאִים אָמַר אֶל רֵעֵהוּ בִּדְבַר יְיָ הַכֵּינִי נָא וַיְמָאֵן הָאִישׁ לְהַכֹּתוֹ: [מלכים א' כ, לה]

ב) וַיֹּאמֶר לוֹ יַעַן אֲשֶׁר לֹא שָׁמַעְתָּ בְּקוֹל יְיָ הִנְּךָ הוֹלֵךְ מֵאִתִּי וְהִכְּךָ הָאַרְיֵה וַיֵּלֶךְ מֵאֶצְלוֹ וַיִּמְצָאֵהוּ הָאַרְיֵה וַיַּכֵּהוּ: [מלכים א' כ, לו]

ג) כִּי כֵן צִוָּה אֹתִי בִּדְבַר יְיָ לֵאמֹר לֹא תֹאכַל לֶחֶם וְלֹא תִשְׁתֶּה מָיִם וְלֹא תָשׁוּב בַּדֶּרֶךְ אֲשֶׁר הָלָכְתָּ: [מלכים א' יג, ט]

ד) וַיֹּאמֶר לוֹ גַּם אֲנִי נָבִיא כָּמוֹךָ וּמַלְאָךְ דִּבֶּר אֵלַי בִּדְבַר יְיָ לֵאמֹר הֲשִׁבֵהוּ אִתְּךָ אֶל בֵּיתֶךָ וְיֹאכַל לֶחֶם וְיֵשְׁתְּ מָיִם כִּחֵשׁ לוֹ: [מלכים א' יג, יח]

ה) וַיָּשָׁב אִתּוֹ וַיֹּאכַל לֶחֶם בְּבֵיתוֹ וַיֵּשְׁתְּ מָיִם: [מלכים א' יג, יט]

ו) וַיֵּלֶךְ וַיִּמְצָאֵהוּ אַרְיֵה בַּדֶּרֶךְ וַיְמִיתֵהוּ וַתְּהִי נִבְלָתוֹ מֻשְׁלֶכֶת בַּדֶּרֶךְ וְהַחֲמוֹר עֹמֵד אֶצְלָהּ וְהָאַרְיֵה עֹמֵד אֵצֶל הַנְּבֵלָה: [מלכים א' יג, כד]

ז) כִּי לֹא יַעֲשֶׂה אֲדֹנָי אֱלֹהִים דָּבָר כִּי אִם גָּלָה סוֹדוֹ אֶל עֲבָדָיו הַנְּבִיאִים: [עמוס ג, ז]

ח) וַיְהִי אַחַר הַדְּבָרִים הָאֵלֶּה וְהָאֱלֹהִים נִסָּה אֶת אַבְרָהָם וַיֹּאמֶר אֵלָיו אַבְרָהָם וַיֹּאמֶר הִנֵּנִי: [בראשית כב, א]

ט) וַיִּגְדַּל הַיֶּלֶד וַיִּגָּמַל וַיַּעַשׂ אַבְרָהָם מִשְׁתֶּה גָדוֹל בְּיוֹם הִגָּמֵל אֶת יִצְחָק: [בראשית כא, ח]

י) וַיֹּאמֶר קַח נָא אֶת בִּנְךָ אֶת יְחִידְךָ אֲשֶׁר אָהַבְתָּ אֶת יִצְחָק וְלֶךְ לְךָ אֶל אֶרֶץ הַמֹּרִיָּה וְהַעֲלֵהוּ שָׁם לְעֹלָה עַל אַחַד הֶהָרִים אֲשֶׁר אֹמַר אֵלֶיךָ: [בראשית כב, ב]

כ) הֲנִסָּה דָבָר אֵלֶיךָ תִּלְאֶה וַעְצֹר בְּמִלִּין מִי יוּכָל: הִנֵּה יִסַּרְתָּ רַבִּים וְיָדַיִם רָפוֹת תְּחַזֵּק: כּוֹשֵׁל יְקִימוּן מִלֶּיךָ וּבִרְכַּיִם כֹּרְעוֹת תְּאַמֵּץ: כִּי עַתָּה תָּבוֹא אֵלֶיךָ וַתֵּלֶא תִּגַּע עָדֶיךָ וַתִּבָּהֵל: [איוב ד, ב-ה]

ל) וַאֲנִי בְּתֻמִּי אֵלֵךְ פְּדֵנִי וְחָנֵּנִי: [תהלים כו, יא] מ) הֲלֹא יִרְאָתְךָ כִּסְלָתֶךָ תִּקְוָתְךָ וְתֹם דְּרָכֶיךָ: [איוב ד, ו] נ) זְכָר נָא מִי הוּא נָקִי אָבָד וְאֵיפֹה יְשָׁרִים נִכְחָדוּ: [איוב ד, ז] ס) וְאֵלַי דָּבָר יְגֻנָּב וַתִּקַּח אָזְנִי שֵׁמֶץ מֶנְהוּ: [איוב ד, יב] ע) וַיֹּאמֶר אַבְרָהָם אֱלֹהִים יִרְאֶה לּוֹ הַשֶּׂה לְעֹלָה בְּנִי וַיֵּלְכוּ שְׁנֵיהֶם יַחְדָּו: [בראשית כב, ח] פ) וְהַנָּבִיא הַהוּא אוֹ חֹלֵם הַחֲלוֹם הַהוּא יוּמָת כִּי דִבֶּר סָרָה עַל יְיָ אֱלֹהֵיכֶם הַמּוֹצִיא אֶתְכֶם מֵאֶרֶץ מִצְרַיִם וְהַפֹּדְךָ מִבֵּית עֲבָדִים לְהַדִּיחֲךָ מִן הַדֶּרֶךְ אֲשֶׁר צִוְּךָ יְיָ אֱלֹהֶיךָ לָלֶכֶת בָּהּ וּבִעַרְתָּ הָרָע מִקִּרְבֶּךָ: [דברים יג, ו] צ) וּסְקַלְתּוֹ בָאֲבָנִים וָמֵת כִּי בִקֵּשׁ לְהַדִּיחֲךָ מֵעַל יְיָ אֱלֹהֶיךָ הַמּוֹצִיאֲךָ מֵאֶרֶץ מִצְרַיִם מִבֵּית עֲבָדִים: [דברים יג, יא] ק) יָצְאוּ אֲנָשִׁים בְּנֵי בְלִיַּעַל מִקִּרְבֶּךָ וַיַּדִּיחוּ אֶת יֹשְׁבֵי עִירָם לֵאמֹר נֵלְכָה וְנַעַבְדָה אֱלֹהִים אֲחֵרִים אֲשֶׁר לֹא יְדַעְתֶּם: [דברים יג, יד]

ליקוטי רש"י

הכני נא. סימן זה רע על אחאב שאמר לו הנביא על פי הגבורה להכות את בן הדד ולא הכהו ואף זה שאמר לו הנביא בדבר ה' הכיני ולא הכהו כשם שנפרע מזה יפרע מאחאב. בדבר ה'. הקב"ה אמר שתכה אותי [מ"א כ, לה]. דאכיל תמרי בארבילא. האוכל תמרים בכברה יהא לוקה בתמיה [מכות כ:]. כי לא יעשה אדני אלהים דבר אלא א"כ גלה סודו. אותו סוד אל עבדיו הנביאים [עמוס ג, ז]. היכי דמוחזק שאני. אשר ידבר הנביא, ויאמר דבר זה עתיד לבוא עליכם ותראו שלא יבא הוא הדבר אשר לא דברו ה' והרוג אותו ואם תאמר זו במתנבא על העתידות הרי שבא ואמר עשו כך וכך ומפי הקב"ה אני אומר כבר נלטוו שאם בא להדיחך מאחת מכל המצות לא תשמע לו אלא אם כן מומחה הוא לך שהוא צדיק גמור כגון אליהו בהר הכרמל שהקריב בבמה בשעת איסור הבמות כדי לגדור את ישראל הכל לפי צורך השעה וסייג הפרצה לכך נאמר אליו תשמעון [דברים יח, כב]. כגון אליהו בהר הכרמל שהקריב בבמה ושעת איסור הבמות היתה ואיכא כרת דשחוטי חוץ וכרת דהעלאה [יבמות צ:]. [ההמשך בדף צ.]

innocence. . .''[37] אָמַר לוֹ – **[Satan] said to him,** ,,הֲלֹא יִרְאָתְךָ כִּסְלָתֶךָ'' – ***"Is not your reverence then your folly?"***[38] אָמַר לוֹ – **[Abraham] said to him,** ,,זְכָר־נָא מִי הוּא נָקִי אָבָד'' – ***"Do recall I beg you: Who is the innocent who was ever lost?"***[39] כֵּיוָן דְּחָזָא דְּלֹא קָא שְׁמִיעַ לֵיהּ – **When [Satan] saw that [Abraham] was not listening to him,** he tried a new tack. אָמַר לֵיהּ – **[Satan] said to him,**[40] ,,וְאֵלַי דָּבָר יְגֻנָּב'' – ***"As for me, a message stole up upon me,*** *my ear picked up just a mite of it.* כַּךְ שָׁמַעְתִּי מֵאֲחוֹרֵי הַפַּרְגּוֹד – **This is what I have heard from behind the curtain,**[41] הַשֶּׂה לְעוֹלָה וְאֵין יִצְחָק לְעוֹלָה – **'The lamb shall be for a burnt offering but Isaac shall not be for a burnt offering.' "**[42] אָמַר לוֹ – **[Abraham] said to him,** כַּךְ עוֹנְשׁוֹ שֶׁל בַּדַּאי – **"This is the punishment of a liar,** שֶׁאֲפִילוּ אָמַר אֱמֶת אֵין שׁוֹמְעִין לוֹ – **that even when he speaks the truth, one does not listen to him."**[43]

The Gemara above cited R' Yochanan's exposition of the word *after* in the opening verse of Abraham's test in regard to the Satan. (*And it came to pass after these things that God tested Abraham.*) The Gemara now cites another exposition of it:

רַבִּי לֵוִי אָמַר – **R' Levi said:** אַחַר דְּבָרָיו שֶׁל יִשְׁמָעֵאל לְיִצְחָק – This incident took place **after Ishmael's words to Isaac.** אָמַר לוֹ יִשְׁמָעֵאל לְיִצְחָק – **Ishmael said to Isaac,** אֲנִי גָּדוֹל מִמְּךָ בְּמִצְוֹת – **"I am greater than you in** the observance of **commandments,** שֶׁאַתָּה מַלְתָּ בֶּן שְׁמֹנַת יָמִים – **for you were circumcised** when you were merely **eight days old,** וַאֲנִי בֶּן שְׁלֹשׁ עֶשְׂרֵה שָׁנָה – **whereas I was circumcised when I was thirteen years old."**[44] אָמַר לוֹ – **[Isaac] replied to him,** וּבְאֵבֶר אֶחָד אַתָּה מְגָרֶה בִּי – **"Do you challenge me then from** merely **one limb?** אִם אוֹמֵר לִי הַקָּדוֹשׁ בָּרוּךְ הוּא – **If the Holy One, Blessed is He, would tell me,** זְבַח עַצְמְךָ לְפָנַי – **'Sacrifice yourself before Me,'** אֲנִי זוֹבֵחַ – **I would sacrifice** myself willingly." מִיָּד ,,וְהָאֱלֹהִים נִסָּה אֶת־אַבְרָהָם'' – **Thereupon,** the verse states: ***And God tested Abraham.***[45]

The Gemara now returns to the subject of false prophets, citing a Baraisa:

תָּנוּ רַבָּנָן – **The Rabbis taught in a Baraisa:** נָבִיא שֶׁהִדִּיחַ בִּסְקִילָה – A PROPHET WHO SUBVERTS others to idolatry[46] is executed BY STONING. רַבִּי שִׁמְעוֹן אוֹמֵר – R' SHIMON SAYS: בְּחֶנֶק – BY STRANGULATION. מַדִּיחֵי עִיר הַנִּדַּחַת בִּסְקִילָה – THE SUBVERTERS OF A CITY are executed BY STONING.[47] רַבִּי שִׁמְעוֹן אוֹמֵר – R' SHIMON SAYS: בְּחֶנֶק – BY STRANGULATION.

The Gemara examines the first dispute recorded in the Baraisa:

נָבִיא שֶׁהִדִּיחַ בִּסְקִילָה – A PROPHET WHO SUBVERTS others to idolatry is executed BY STONING. מַאי טַעְמָא דְּרַבָּנָן – **What is the reason of the Rabbis** for prescribing stoning?

The Gemara explains:

אַתְיָא ,,הַדָּחָה'' ,,הַדָּחָה'' מִמֵּסִית – **This is derived** from a *gezeirah shavah* based on the words **"subverting"** and **"subverting"** used here and **in regard to an instigator.**[48] מַה לְהַלָּן בִּסְקִילָה – **Just as there** the Torah states that the instigator is executed **by stoning,** אַף כַּאן בִּסְקִילָה – **so too here** we learn that the subversive prophet is executed **by stoning.**

The Gemara now explains R' Shimon's view:

וְרַבִּי שִׁמְעוֹן – **R' Shimon, however,** learns the punishment for a subversive prophet from the fact that ,,מִיתָה'' כְּתִיבָא בֵּיהּ – ***"death"* is written** in the Torah **regarding [the subversive prophet],**[49] וְכָל מִיתָה הָאֲמוּרָה בַּתּוֹרָה סְתָם – **and** the rule is

NOTES

37. *Psalms* 26:11. Abraham replied: I know what the clear and simple meaning of God's command is and I shall follow that (*R' Chaim Shmulevitz* ibid.). You may be right about my followers, but it is not my job to make such calculations regarding His orders (*Emes L'Yaakov*).

38. *Job* 4:6. Are you not stumbling over your own religiosity? Your zealousness in this matter will prevent new people from embracing the belief in God and it will force out those already converted! (*Aruch LaNer; cf. Tosafos, Bava Metzia* 58b ד״ה הלא).

39. *Job* 4:7. Ultimately, no one ever lost out by listening to God. If I do my part, with the proper intentions, God will find a way to set everything right (*Aruch LaNer*).

40. *Job* 4:12.

41. I.e. the "partition" that separates, as it were, the Divine Presence from all creation (*Rashi* to *Berachos* 18b ד״ה הפרגוד). [One could nevertheless discern hidden truths from behind this "partition"; see *Berachos* ibid. and *Chagigah* 15a.]

42. This indeed turned out to be true, as the Torah states (*Genesis* 22:9-13).

43. [When a person lies too many times, he is no longer taken seriously. Since Satan had plied Abraham with clearly false arguments until this point, Abraham would no longer give him credence.] Abraham implied that Satan might very well be speaking the truth – even though this was only later confirmed on Mt. Moriah – because this explanation had the ring of truth to it (*Chida* in *Pesach Einayim*).

Alternatively, בַּדַּאי refers to one who embellishes the facts, mixing false details into his stories and statements. His reports are always considered unreliable because he has effectively trained himself never to let an untainted utterance leave his mouth (*Mesillas Yesharim*, ch. 11 ד״ה והנה דבר השקר).

44. Being an infant, you could not have protested your circumcision, whereas I was old enough to have done so (see *Genesis* 17:25) and yet did not (*Eitz Yosef*).

45. The conversation between Isaac and Ishmael took place the night before, when Ishmael had come from the Paran Desert to visit Abraham (*Eitz Yosef* quoting *Pirkei D'Rabbi Eliezer*).

Sanhedrei Ketanah asks: If the purpose of this trial was to verify Isaac's claim that he would be willing to sacrifice himself, why does the verse state *and God tested Abraham*? It should read instead *and God tested Isaac*!

Sanhedrei Ketanah answers that the trial here was Abraham's. Indeed, the ten trials of Abraham were destined from the Six Days of Creation and his passing them justified the world's existence (see *Avos* 5:1,3; *Bereishis Rabbah* 12:9). Now, God was able to administer the first nine tests without any hindrance. When He came to the tenth test, the command to sacrifice Isaac, He did not want to ask this of Abraham as it would obviously pain Isaac. Once Isaac expressed his willingness to be sacrificed, however, God "had a free hand," so to speak, to administer the final test to Abraham.

46. [The Gemara below (90a) will discuss whether the law of a נָבִיא שֶׁהִדִּיחַ, *a prophet who subverts,* refers only to one who prophesies to have people practice idolatry, or whether it refers to a prophet who attempts to subvert people in regard to other Torah laws as well.]

47. [This category refers specifically to those who succeed in subverting the majority of a city's population to idolatry. See above, 67a.]

48. In our instance, an expression of "subverting" appears in *Deuteronomy* 13:6 in connection with a subversive prophet. There Scripture states: וְהַנָּבִיא הַהוּא אוֹ חֹלֵם הַחֲלוֹם הַהוּא יוּמָת כִּי דִבֶּר־סָרָה . . . לְהַדִּיחֲךָ מִן־הַדֶּרֶךְ, *And that prophet or that dreamer of a dream shall be put to death, for he had spoken perversion. . .* ***to subvert you*** *from the path.* It also appears in connection with a מֵסִית, *instigator* (an ordinary person who attempts to persuade individuals to engage in idolatry; see Mishnah 67a), where Scripture states (ibid. v. 11): וּסְקַלְתּוֹ בָאֲבָנִים וָמֵת כִּי בִקֵּשׁ לְהַדִּיחֲךָ מֵעַל ה׳ אֱלֹהֶיךָ, *You shall stone him with stones and he shall die, for he sought* ***to subvert you*** *from near Hashem, your God* (*Rashi*).

49. *Deuteronomy* 13:6: The verse reads: *And that prophet or that dreamer of a dream shall be put to death.*

R' Shimon did not receive the *gezeirah shavah* cited by the Rabbis from his teachers, and one may not expound a *gezeirah shavah* on his own (*Rashi*). [A *gezeirah shavah* is valid only if it has come down to us as part of the body of Oral Law transmitted from generation to generation in an unbroken chain extending back to Moses, who received it from God at Sinai.]

חבריה דמיכה דכתיב א) ואיש אחד מבני הנביאים אמר אל רעהו בדבר ה' הכני נא וימאן האיש להכותו וכתיב ב) ויאמר לו יען אשר לא שמעת [וגו'] ונביא שעבר על דברי עצמו כגון עדו הנביא דכתיב ג) כי כן צוה אותי וכתיב ד) ויאמר לו גם אני נביא כמוך וכתיב ה) וישב אתו וכתיב ו) וילך וימצאהו אריה תני תנא קמיה דרב חסדא הכובש את נבואתו לוקה א) אמר ליה מאן דאכיל תמרי בארבלא לקי מאן מתרי ביה אמר אביי חבריה נביאי מנא ידעי אמר אביי דכתיב ז) כי לא יעשה ה' [אלהים] דבר כי אם גלה סודו ודילמא הדרי ביה אם איתא דהדרי ביה אודועי הוו מודעי לכלהו נביאי והא יונה דהדרי ביה ולא אודעוהו יונה מעיקרא נינוה נהפכת אמרי ליה איהו לא ידע אי לטובה אי לרעה המוותר על דברי נביא מנא ידע דאיענש דיהיב ליה אות והא מיכה דלא יהיב ליה אות ואיענש היכא דמוחזק שאני דאי לא תימא הכי אברהם בהר המוריה היכי שמע ליה יצחק אליהו בהר הכרמל היכי סמכי עליה ועבדי שחוטי חוץ אלא א) היכא דמוחזק שאני ח) ויהי אחר הדברים האלה והאלהים נסה את אברהם ב) (אחר מאי) א"ר יוחנן משום רבי יוסי בן זימרא אחר דבריו של שטן דכתיב ט) ויגדל הילד ויגמל וגו' אמר שטן לפני הקב"ה רבונו של עולם זקן זה חננתו למאה שנה פרי בטן מכל סעודה שעשה לא היה לו תור אחד או גוזל אחד להקריב לפניך אמר לו כלום עשה אלא בשביל בנו אם אני אומר לו זבח את בנך לפני מיד זובחו מיד והאלהים נסה את אברהם י) ויאמר קח נא את בנך אמר רבי שמעון בר אבא ג) אין נא אלא לשון בקשה משל למלך בשר ודם שעמדו עליו מלחמות הרבה והיה לו גבור אחד ונצחן לימים עמדה עליו מלחמה חזקה אמר לו בבקשה ממך עמוד לי במלחמה זו שלא יאמרו ראשונות אין בהם ממש אף הקב"ה אמר לאברהם ניסיתיך בכמה נסיונות ועמדת בכלן עכשיו עמוד לי בנסיון זה שלא יאמרו אין ממש בראשונים את בנך ב' בנים יש לי ד) את יחידך זה יחיד לאמו וזה יחיד לאמו אשר אהבת תרוויהו רחימנא להו ה) את יצחק וכל כך למה כדי שלא תטרף דעתו עליו קדמו שטן לדרך אמר לו ו) כ) הנסה דבר אליך תלאה הנה יסרת רבים וידים רפות תחזק כושל יקימון מליך כי עתה תבא אליך ותלא אמר לו ל) אני בתומי אלך אמר לו ז) מ) הלא יראתך כסלתך אמר לו נ) זכר נא מי הוא נקי אבד כיון דחזא דלא קא שמיע ליה אמר ליה ס) ואלי דבר יגונב כך שמעתי מאחורי הפרגוד ע) השה לעולה ואין יצחק לעולה אמר לו ח) כך עונשו של בדאי שאפילו אמר אמת אין שומעין לו ר' לוי אמר אחר דבריו של ישמעאל ליצחק אמר לו ישמעאל ליצחק אני גדול ממך במצות שאתה מלת בן שמונת ימים ואני בן שלש עשרה שנה אמר לו ובאבר אחד אתה מגרה בי אם אומר לי הקב"ה זבח עצמך לפני אני זובח מיד והאלהים נסה את אברהם ט) תנו רבנן נביא שהדיח בסקילה רבי שמעון אומר בחנק י) מדיחי עיר הנדחת בסקילה רבי שמעון אומר בחנק נביא שהדיח בסקילה מ"ט דרבנן אתיא פ) הדחה צ) הדחה ממסית מה להלן בסקילה אף כאן בסקילה ור"ש מיתה כתיבא ביה פ) וכל מיתה האמורה בתורה סתם אינה אלא חנק מדיחי עיר הנדחת בסקילה מ"ט דרבנן גמרי ק) הדחה הדחה או ממסית או מנביא שהדיח ור"ש גמר ק) הדחה פ) הדחה מנביא וליגמר ממסית דנין מסית רבים ממסית רבים ואין דנין מסית רבים ממסית יחיד אדרבה ל) דנין הדיוט מהדיוט ואין דנין הדיוט מנביא ור"ש כיון שהדיח אין לך הדיוט גדול מזה אמר רב חסדא

מחלוקת

רש"י

חבריה דמיכה. דכתיב ואיש אחד מבני הנביאים אמר אל רעהו בדבר ה' הכני נא זה היה מיכיהו בן ימלא שנתנבא אותו היום על אחאב ליפול ביד ארם מפני שנפל בן הדד בידו ושלחו לשלום והיינו דקאמר אחאב ליהושפט לא ידבר עלי טוב כי אם רע מפני שנתנבא כבר את זו עליו ולא קיבל חבירו את דבריו דכתיב וימאן האיש להכותו: עדו הנביא. שנתנבא על מזבח א] ה' בבית אל שהיה ירבעם מקטר עליו כ) ובדברי הימים גבי יאשיהו כתיב והוא היה עדו: כי כן צוה אותי. בדבר ה' לאמר לא תאכל לחם ולא תשתה מים ל) (במקום הזה) ועבר על דברי עצמו ושמע לדברי הנביא השקר ואכל ושתה: תמרי בארבילא. תמרים הנתונים בכברה: דילמא הדרו ביה. פמליא של מעלה וניחם על הרעה והם אינם יודעים והיאך מתרינן בו התראת ספק: והא יונה דהדרו ביה. מהפוך את נינוה: מעיקרא נינוה נהפכת אמרו ליה. ברוח הקדש ומשמע נמי לטובה שיהפכו מעשיהם מרעה לטובה וכיון שטבו נתקיימה הנבואה ולא מיהדר הוא: ואיהו דלא ידע. הוא היה טועה וסבור שהוא לרעה: מנא ידע. האי גברא שזה נביא אמת שהקב"ה עונשו והלא שמא סבור שזהו נביא שקר לפיכך מוותר על דבריו: היכא דהוחזק. שהוא צדיק ונביא אמת: שאני. ולא בעי אות: היכי שמע ליה יצחק. שהוא דבר אמת מה שלא נאמר לשום אדם להקריב את בנו: שחוטי חוץ. שהרי בית המקדש היה בירושלים: הנסה דבר אליך תלאה. וכי היה לאוהבך לנסותך בדבר שהיא תלאה אותך ומכרית את זרעך: הנה יסרת רבים. ראית והשיית' לו כל באי העולם בדברים ועתה הנה בא להלאותך ולבהלך: נביא שהדיח. שמתנבא בשם הקב"ה לעבוד עבודת כוכבים: הדחה. כתיב הכא כי דבר סרה להדיחך וכתיב במסית כי ביקש להדיחך וגו': מיתה כתב ביה. והך גזירה שוה לא גמר מרביה דאין אדם דן גזירה שוה מעצמו: ורבי שמעון גמר הדחה הדחה מנביא. דבעיר הנדחת לגמריה רביה גזירה שוה מסיני לדון הדחה הדחה ומסתברא דמנביא לגמריה הלכה למשה גזירה שוה זו כדיהיב טעמא למלתיה:

מחלוקת

תוספות

אליהו בהר הכרמל וכו'. משמע דבשם הקב"ה היה מתנבא לעבור וכיון דמוחזק מהימנינן ביה אע"ג דלא יהיב אות ובהאשה רבה (יבמות דף צ: ושם) נפקא לן דכתיב אליו תשמעון אפי' אמר לך עבור על אחת מכל מצות האמורות בתורה כגון אליהו בהר הכרמל ותימה מאי קא פריך התם וליגמר מיניה כיון דע"פ הדיבור היה מתנבא מה שייך למילף מיניה לעבור משום תקנה דרבנן שלא על פי הדיבור ועוד למה לן הכא טעמא משום דאיתחזק בנביאות הא אפילו בלא נביא שרי לב"ד לעבור משום מיגדר מילתא ויש לומר דמדקדק התם מלישנא דברייתא דקתני הכל לפי שעה דמשמע הכל מפני צורך השעה ואי על פי הדיבור למה לי צורך השעה בין לצורך בין שלא לצורך צריך לקיים צוויו של מקום אלא ודאי בנביא שעשה מדעתו קא אמרה ברייתא דמיירי קרא והא דבעי הכא איתחזק היינו משום דכי איתחזק בנביאות סומכין עליו במה שהיה מבטיח לירידת אש ושוחטין על הבטחתו קדשים בחוץ שבזכותו ובתפלתו תרד אש מהשמים ויהיה מגדר מילתא בדבר שיתקדש שמו של הקב"ה ברבים ויחזרו ישראל למוטב ומיהו בקראי משמע שעל פי הדיבור עשה דכתיב באליהו ובדברך עשיתי וגו' ופרש"י מאור הגולה בפירושו לנביאים ובדברך עשיתי שהקרבתי בשעת איסור הבמות ונראה לומר דכיון דעל פי הדיבור שרי משום צורך שעה הוא הדין שלא על פי הדיבור שהרי אין נביא רשאי לחדש דבר כדאיתא בפ"ק דמגילה (דף ב:) ועוד י"ל דהא דקאמר אליהו ובדברך עשיתי לא שאמר לו הקב"ה אלא מקרא היה דורש דכתיב גוי וקהל גוים יהיה ממך ואמרינן מ) עתידין בניך לעשות כמעשה נכרים פירוש לשחוט בחוץ ואני מסכים על ידו ולפי שהיה נביא מוחזק סמכו עליו שעליו נאמר מקרא זה:

הדרן עלך אלו הן הנחנקין

עין משפט נר מצוה

פ א מיי' פ"ט מהלכות יסודי התורה הל' ג:

רבינו חננאל

שמים: **תני** תנא קמיה דרב חסדא לוקה א"ל ומי התרה בו דלקי כלומר מי יודע ששלחו אלהים להינבא והסתיר נבואתו ואמר אביי חבריו הנביאים שגילה כדכתיב כי לא יעשה ה' אלהים דבר כי אם גלה סודו אל עבדיו הנביאים ודלמא הדרו ביה כו': **המוותר** על דברי נביא ואינו עושה כל מה שיאמר לו אלא ממאן לשמוע דבריו כגון חבריה דמיכיהו כדכתיב ואיש אחד מבני הנביאים אמר לרעהו בדבר ה' הכני נא וימאן האיש להכותו וכתיב ויאמר לו יען אשר לא שמעת בקול ה' הנך הולך מאתי והכך האריה וילך מאצלו וימצאהו האריה ויכהו דינו בידי שמים. ואקשינן מנא ידע דהוא נביא ואיענש ושנינן מוחזק בנביאות הוה אבל מאן דלא מוחזק לא מיחייב לקבולי מיניה עד דיהיב ליה אות ומופת ומאן דמוחזק מקבלינן מיניה מאליהו בהר הכרמל אילולי שהיה מוחזק בנביאות היכי הוו מקבלי מיניה ועבדי שחוטי חוץ אלא ש"מ היכא דמוחזק שאני. ונביא שעבר על דברי עצמו כגון עדו הנביא שנאמר כי כן צוה אותי בדבר ה' לאמר לא תאכל לחם ולא תשתה מים ולא תשוב בדרך אשר הלכת ויאמר לו גם אני נביא כמוך ומלאך דבר אלי בדבר ה' לאמר השיבהו אתך אל ביתך ויאכל לחם וישתה מים כחש לו דינו בידי שמים שנאמר וימצאהו האריה בדרך וימיתהו. **ירושלמי** א"ר שמואל בר רב יצחק ונביא אחד זקן ישב בבית אל זה אמציהו כהן בית אל: **ויהי אחר** הדברים האלה והאלהים נסה את אברהם אחר מי א"ר יוחנן אחר דברי השטן שאמר לפני הקב"ה רבון כל העולמים זקן זה חננתו למאה פרי [בטן] ומכל סעודות שעש' לא היה לו להקריב לפניך תור או בן יונה אחד. א"ל כלום עשה אלא למען בנו אם אני אומר לו זבח אותו לפני עושה. מיד והאלהים נסה את אברהם כו' ר' לוי אמר אחר דברי ישמעאל שאמר ליצחק אני גדול ממך במצות שאתה נמלתה בן ח' ימים ואני בן י"ג שנה א"ל ובאבר אחד אתה מי יראיני אם אומר לו הקב"ה זבח עצמך מיד אני זובח את עצמי. מיד והאלהים נסה את אברהם: ת"ר נביא שהדיח בסקילה מאי טעמא גמרי הדחה הדחה ממסית מה מסית בסקילה אף נביא שהדיח בסקילה רבי שמעון אומר מיתה כתיבה ביה וכל מיתה האמורה בתורה סתם בחנק. מדיחי עיר הנדחת בסקילה גמרי הדחה הדחה מנביא שהדיח ר' שמעון אומר בחנק גמר הדחה הדחה מנביא שהדיח.

מסורת הש"ס

א) מכות כ:, ב) [נ"ל מאי אחר כ"א בע"י], ג) [לעיל מג: ברכות ט. סוטה יוד:], ד) [פירושו דמלתא תמצא בתוס' ב"מ נח: סוף ד"ה הלא], ה) [אדר"נ פ"ל], ו) לעיל סז. פד., ז) [לעיל נ.], ח) [לעיל נג: ופד:], ט) [לעיל פד.], י) [שם], כ) לא נמצא שם מפורש וברד"ק כתב רמז לזה, ל) ס"א ל"ג, מ) [ב"ר פ' וישלח].

הגהות מהר"ב רנשבורג

א] רש"י ד"ה עדו הנביא שנתנבא על מזבח בבית אל כו'. כצ"ל:

תורה אור השלם

א) וְאִישׁ אֶחָד מִבְּנֵי הַנְּבִיאִים אָמַר אֶל רֵעֵהוּ בִּדְבַר יְיָ הַכֵּינִי נָא וַיְמָאֵן הָאִישׁ לְהַכֹּתוֹ: [מלכים א' כ, לה]

ב) וַיֹּאמֶר לוֹ יַעַן אֲשֶׁר לֹא שָׁמַעְתָּ בְּקוֹל יְיָ הִנְּךָ הוֹלֵךְ מֵאִתִּי וְהִכְּךָ הָאַרְיֵה וַיֵּלֶךְ מֵאֶצְלוֹ וַיִּמְצָאֵהוּ הָאַרְיֵה וַיַּכֵּהוּ: [מלכים א' כ, לו]

ג) כִּי כֵן צִוָּה אֹתִי בִּדְבַר יְיָ לֵאמֹר לֹא תֹאכַל לֶחֶם וְלֹא תִשְׁתֶּה מָיִם וְלֹא תָשׁוּב בַּדֶּרֶךְ אֲשֶׁר הָלָכְתָּ: [מלכים א' יג, ט]

ד) וַיֹּאמֶר לוֹ גַּם אֲנִי נָבִיא כָּמוֹךָ וּמַלְאָךְ דִּבֶּר אֵלַי בִּדְבַר יְיָ לֵאמֹר הֲשִׁבֵהוּ אִתְּךָ אֶל בֵּיתֶךָ וְיֹאכַל לֶחֶם וְיֵשְׁתְּ מָיִם כִּחֵשׁ לוֹ: [מלכים א' יג, יח]

ה) וַיָּשָׁב אִתּוֹ וַיֹּאכַל לֶחֶם בְּבֵיתוֹ וַיֵּשְׁתְּ מָיִם: [מלכים א' יג, יט]

ו) וַיֵּלֶךְ וַיִּמְצָאֵהוּ אַרְיֵה בַּדֶּרֶךְ וַיְמִיתֵהוּ וַתְּהִי נִבְלָתוֹ מֻשְׁלֶכֶת בַּדֶּרֶךְ וְהַחֲמוֹר עֹמֵד אֶצְלָהּ וְהָאַרְיֵה עֹמֵד אֵצֶל הַנְּבֵלָה: [מלכים א' יג, כד]

ז) כִּי לֹא יַעֲשֶׂה אֲדֹנָי אֱלֹהִים דָּבָר כִּי אִם גָּלָה סוֹדוֹ אֶל עֲבָדָיו הַנְּבִיאִים: [עמוס ג, ז]

ח) וַיְהִי אַחַר הַדְּבָרִים הָאֵלֶּה וְהָאֱלֹהִים נִסָּה אֶת אַבְרָהָם וַיֹּאמֶר אֵלָיו אַבְרָהָם וַיֹּאמֶר הִנֵּנִי: [בראשית כב, א]

ט) וַיִּגְדַּל הַיֶּלֶד וַיִּגָּמַל וַיַּעַשׂ אַבְרָהָם מִשְׁתֶּה גָדוֹל בְּיוֹם הִגָּמֵל אֶת יִצְחָק: [בראשית כא, ח]

י) וַיֹּאמֶר קַח נָא אֶת בִּנְךָ אֶת יְחִידְךָ אֲשֶׁר אָהַבְתָּ אֶת יִצְחָק וְלֶךְ לְךָ אֶל אֶרֶץ הַמֹּרִיָּה וְהַעֲלֵהוּ שָׁם לְעֹלָה עַל אַחַד הֶהָרִים אֲשֶׁר אֹמַר אֵלֶיךָ: [בראשית כב, ב]

כ) הֲנִסָּה דָבָר אֵלֶיךָ תִּלְאֶה וַעְצֹר בְּמִלִּין מִי יוּכָל: הִנֵּה יִסַּרְתָּ רַבִּים וְיָדַיִם רָפוֹת תְּחַזֵּק: כּוֹשֵׁל יְקִימוּן מִלֶּיךָ וּבִרְכַּיִם כֹּרְעוֹת תְּאַמֵּץ: כִּי עַתָּה תָּבוֹא אֵלֶיךָ וַתֵּלֶא תִּגַּע עָדֶיךָ וַתִּבָּהֵל: [איוב ד, ב-ה]

ל) וַאֲנִי בְּתֻמִּי אֵלֵךְ פְּדֵנִי וְחָנֵּנִי: [תהלים כו, יא] מ) הֲלֹא יִרְאָתְךָ כִּסְלָתֶךָ תִּקְוָתְךָ וְתֹם דְּרָכֶיךָ: [איוב ד, ו] נ) זְכָר נָא מִי הוּא נָקִי אָבָד וְאֵיפֹה יְשָׁרִים נִכְחָדוּ: [איוב ד, ז] ס) וְאֵלַי דָּבָר יְגֻנָּב וַתִּקַּח אָזְנִי שֵׁמֶץ מֶנְהוּ: [איוב ד, יב]

ע) וַיֹּאמֶר אַבְרָהָם אֱלֹהִים יִרְאֶה לּוֹ הַשֶּׂה לְעֹלָה בְּנִי וַיֵּלְכוּ שְׁנֵיהֶם יַחְדָּו: [בראשית כב, ח] פ) וְהַנָּבִיא הַהוּא אוֹ חֹלֵם הַחֲלוֹם הַהוּא יוּמָת כִּי דִבֶּר סָרָה עַל יְיָ אֱלֹהֵיכֶם הַמּוֹצִיא אֶתְכֶם מֵאֶרֶץ מִצְרַיִם וְהַפֹּדְךָ מִבֵּית עֲבָדִים לְהַדִּיחֲךָ מִן הַדֶּרֶךְ אֲשֶׁר צִוְּךָ יְיָ אֱלֹהֶיךָ לָלֶכֶת בָּהּ וּבִעַרְתָּ הָרָע מִקִּרְבֶּךָ: [דברים יג, ו] צ) וּסְקַלְתּוֹ בָאֲבָנִים וָמֵת כִּי בִקֵּשׁ לְהַדִּיחֲךָ מֵעַל יְיָ אֱלֹהֶיךָ הַמּוֹצִיאֲךָ מֵאֶרֶץ מִצְרַיִם מִבֵּית עֲבָדִים: [דברים יג, יא] ק) יָצְאוּ אֲנָשִׁים בְּנֵי בְלִיַּעַל מִקִּרְבֶּךָ וַיַּדִּיחוּ אֶת יֹשְׁבֵי עִירָם לֵאמֹר נֵלְכָה וְנַעַבְדָה אֱלֹהִים אֲחֵרִים אֲשֶׁר לֹא יְדַעְתֶּם: [דברים יג, יד]

ליקוטי רש"י

הכני נא. סימן זה רע על אחאב שאמר לו הנביא על פי הגבורה להכות את בן הדד ולא הכהו ואף זה שאמר לו הנביא בדבר ה' הכיני ולא הכהו כשם שנפרע מזה יפרע מאחאב. **בדבר ה'.** הקב"ה אמר שתכה אותי [מ"א כ, לה]. **דאכיל תמרי בארבילא.** האוכל תמרים בכברה יהא לוקה בתמיה [מכות כ:]. **כי לא יעשה אדני אלהים דבר אלא א"כ גלה סודו.** אותו סוד אל עבדיו הנביאים [עמוס ג, ז]. **היכי דמוחזק שאני.** אשר ידבר הנביא, ויאמר דבר זה עתיד לבוא עליכם ותראו שלא יבא הוא הדבר אשר לא דברו ה' והרוג אותו ואם תאמר זו במתנבא על העתידות הרי שבא ואמר עשו כך וכך ומפי הקב"ה אני אומר כבר נצטוו שאם בא להדיחך מאחת מכל המצות לא תשמע לו אלא אם כן מומחה הוא לך שהוא צדיק גמור כגון אליהו בהר הכרמל שהקריב בבמה בשעת איסור הבמות כדי לגדור את ישראל הכל לפי צורך השעה וסייג הפרצה לכך נאמר אליו תשמעון [דברים יח, כב]. כגון אליהו בהר הכרמל שהקריב בבמה ושעת איסור הבמות היתה ואיכא כרת דשחוטי חוץ וכרת דהעלאה [יבמות צ:].

[ההמשך בדף צ.]

that **whenever** putting to **death is mentioned by the Torah in an undefined manner,** i.e. without specifying the type of death, אֵינָהּ אֶלָּא חֶנֶק – **it refers to no other** death **than strangulation.**

The second dispute is examined:

מַדִּיחֵי עִיר הַנִּדַּחַת בִּסְקִילָה – THE SUBVERTERS OF A CITY are executed BY STONING. מַאי טַעְמָא דְּרַבָּנַן – **What is the reason of the Rabbis** in prescribing stoning? גָּמְרֵי ,,הַדָּחָה'' ,,הַדָּחָה'' אוֹ מִמֵּסִית אוֹ מִנָּבִיא שֶׁהִדִּיחַ – **[The Rabbis] learned** this from a *gezeirah shavah* based on the word ***subverting*** stated here (in connection with the subverters of a city) and the word ***subverting*** stated **either in regard to the instigator or in regard to the prophet who subverts** others.[50]

The Gemara explains R' Shimon's view:

וְרַבִּי שִׁמְעוֹן – **R' Shimon, however,** גָּמַר ,,הַדָּחָה'' ,,הַדָּחָה'' מִנָּבִיא – **learns** the punishment of strangulation from a *gezeirah shavah* based on the word ***subverting*** stated here and the word ***subverting*** stated **in regard to the** subversive **prophet.** Since R' Shimon stated above that a subversive prophet is executed by strangulation, he learns from the *gezeirah shavah* that the subverters of a city are also executed by strangulation.

The Gemara asks:

וְלִיגְמַר מִמֵּסִית – **But let [R' Shimon] derive** the *gezeirah shavah* **from the instigator** instead.[51] This would teach that the subverters of a city are stoned. – ? –

The Gemara answers:

דָּנִין מֵסִית רַבִּים מִמֵּסִית רַבִּים – R' Shimon maintains that **we expound** the *gezeirah shavah* **between** one **instigator of the masses and** another **instigator of the masses,** i.e. between the subverters of a city and a prophet who subverts others,[52] וְאֵין דָּנִין מֵסִית רַבִּים מִמֵּסִית יָחִיד – **and we do not expound** the *gezeirah shavah* **between an instigator of the masses and the instigator of an individual,** i.e. between the subverters of a city and the instigator of an individual.

This answer is challenged:

אַדְּרַבָּה – **To the contrary!** דָּנִין הֶדְיוֹט מֵהֶדְיוֹט – It is more reasonable that **we** should **expound** a *gezeirah shavah* **between a commoner and a commoner,** i.e. the subverters of a city and an instigator (neither of whom is a prophet), וְאֵין דָּנִין הֶדְיוֹט מִנָּבִיא – **rather than** that **we** should **expound** it **between a commoner** (the subverters of a city) **and a prophet!** – ? –

The Gemara answers:

וְרַבִּי שִׁמְעוֹן – **R' Shimon, however,** is of the opinion that כֵּיוָן שֶׁהִדִּיחַ – **since he has subverted** others to idolatry, אֵין לְךָ הֶדְיוֹט גָּדוֹל מִזֶּה – **there is** certainly **no** one that deserves to be regarded as a **commoner more than this** one.

Previously, the Gemara stated that R' Shimon and the Rabbis dispute the type of execution mandated for a subversive prophet. The Gemara now defines the kind of subversive prophecy under discussion:

אָמַר רַב חִסְדָּא – **Rav Chisda said:**

NOTES

50. A form of the word "subvert" appears three times in *Deuteronomy* chapter 13: Concerning a subversive prophet (v. 6), an instigator (v. 11) and the subverters of a city (v. 14). [A מֵסִית, *instigator,* is one who attempts to persuade individuals to practice idolatry; a מַדִּיחַ, *subverter,* is one who persuades the majority of a city to practice idolatry (see above, 67a). A prophet who commands in the Name of God to practice idolatry is referred to as נָבִיא הַמַּדִּיחַ; see note 46.] The Gemara stated previously that the Rabbis had the tradition of a *gezeirah shavah* which linked the passages of the subversive prophet and the instigator [מֵסִית]. R' Shimon did not have this tradition. The Gemara now states that there is also a second *gezeirah shavah* using these words, a tradition shared by both the Rabbis and R' Shimon. This *gezeirah shavah* links the passage of the subverters of a city [מַדִּיחַ] with one of the two other passages – which one was not specified by the tradition. As far as the Rabbis are concerned, the point is moot: Whether we derive this from the subversive prophet or from the instigator, the method will be the same according to the Rabbis – stoning. [The question is critical, however, according to R' Shimon, since he does not accept the first *gezeirah shavah* and thus rules that the subversive prophet is executed by strangulation. The Gemara will now elaborate on this.]

51. R' Shimon received from his teacher the tradition that the word הַדָּחָה, *subverting,* stated in connection with the subverters of a city was linked in a *gezeirah shavah* to another such word. He had not, however, received a tradition regarding which other verse it was linked to. [The tradition did not always specify which verses are linked through the *gezeirah shavah*.] R' Shimon concluded on his own that the appropriate link was to the subversive prophet. The Gemara now questions his conclusion (*Rashi*).

52. A prophet who subverts a single individual has exactly the same legal status as a prophet who subverts the public. The Gemara treats him as an "instigator of the public" because the verses discuss him in terms of instigating the public, and it is the *gezeirah shavah* linked to these verses that is at issue here (*Binyan Shlomo*).

[However, *Chazon Ish* (*Sanhedrin* 24:8) infers from our Gemara that a prophet who speaks to an individual (or even several individuals) to worship an idol is classified as a מֵסִית, *an instigator,* the same as an ordinary person who attempts to persuade someone to worship an idol. (Thus, he would be liable to stoning even according to R' Shimon.) Only if he proclaims his "prophecy" for idolatry publicly is he classified as a נָבִיא הַמַּדִּיחַ, *a subversive prophet,* who according to R' Shimon is executed by strangulation rather than stoning. This accords with the simple reading of *Rambam* in *Hil. Avodas Kochavim* 5:1, as noted by *Chazon Ish*. However, *Kesef Mishneh's* explanation of *Rambam's* ruling would seem to assume otherwise.]

מַחֲלוֹקֶת בְּעוֹקֵר הַגּוּף דַּעֲבוֹדַת כּוֹכָבִים – **The dispute** between R' Shimon and the Rabbis regarding a subversive prophet **pertains** both **to one who abolishes** by his prophecy **the whole** of the prohibition of **idolatry,**[1] וְקִיּוּם מִקְצָת וּבִיטּוּל מִקְצָת דַּעֲבוֹדַת כּוֹכָבִים – **and** to one whose prophecy dictates **the preservation of part and the nullification of part** of the prohibition **of idolatry.**[2] דְּרַחֲמָנָא אָמַר ,,מִן־הַדֶּרֶךְ'' – We know this last point **for the Merciful One has stated** in connection with a subversive prophet:[3] *And that prophet . . .shall be put to death, for he has spoken perversion against Hashem, your God . . . to subvert you* ***from the path*** *which Hashem, your God, has commanded you . . .* אֲפִילּוּ מִקְצָת הַדֶּרֶךְ – This implies that **even** if he spoke to subvert you from **just part of the path**, he is considered a subversive prophet.[4] And since this verse appears in the context of a prophet who attempts to subvert others to idol-worship, we may derive that if he attempts to partially subvert them towards idolatry, he is also deemed a subversive prophet.[5] אֲבָל עוֹקֵר הַגּוּף דִּשְׁאָר מִצְוֹת – **But** where a prophet **abolishes** by his prophecy **the whole** of any **of the other mitzvos,** דִּבְרֵי הַכֹּל בְּחֶנֶק – **all agree** that he is put to death **by strangulation**, since he is then classified a false prophet, not a subversive prophet.[6] וְקִיּוּם מִקְצָת וּבִיטּוּל מִקְצָת דִּשְׁאָר מִצְוֹת – **And** if he prophesies **the preservation of part and the nullification of part of any of the other mitzvos,** דִּבְרֵי הַכֹּל פָּטוּר – **all agree that he is exempt** from punishment.[7]

The Gemara questions Rav Chisda's interpretation of the dispute:

מָתִיב רַב הַמְנוּנָא – **Rav Hamnuna challenged** this on the basis of a Baraisa: ,,לָלֶכֶת'' זוּ מִצְוַת עֲשֵׂה – The Torah states: *For he has spoken perversion against Hashem, your God . . . to subvert you from the path which Hashem, your God, has commanded you to go on it.* *TO GO* – THIS REFERS TO A POSITIVE COMMANDMENT, i.e. to a subversive prophet who tells people not to fulfill a positive commandment. ,,בָּהּ'' זוּ מִצְוַת לֹא תַעֲשֶׂה – *ON IT*, THIS REFERS TO A NEGATIVE COMMANDMENT, i.e. to a prophet who tells people to transgress a negative commandment.[8] וְאִי סָלְקָא דַּעְתָּךְ בַּעֲבוֹדַת כּוֹכָבִים – **Now, if you think** that the passage of the subversive prophet deals only with **idolatry** and not with other mitzvos, עֲשֵׂה בַּעֲבוֹדַת כּוֹכָבִים הֵיכִי מַשְׁכַּחַת לָהּ – **where do you find a**

NOTES

1. Literally: who uproots the body of idol worship. That is, he says that he has been prophetically commanded by the Almighty to totally abrogate the Torah's prohibition against idolatry.

2. That is, he says that he was prophetically commanded to partially abrogate the commandment regarding idolatry.

Rav Chisda maintains that the verse, *And that prophet . . . shall be put to death, for he has spoken perversion against Hashem, your God . . . to subvert you . . .* (*Deuteronomy* 13:6), refers specifically to subversion regarding idolatry [and not to subversion regarding other Torah commandments]. Rav Chisda concludes this from the opening verses of this section (vs. 2 and 3), which state: *If there should stand up in your midst a prophet or a dreamer of a dream . . . saying, "Let us follow the gods of others that you did not know and we shall worship them!"* These introductory verses make it clear that this section is dealing specifically with idolatry. Now, the Rabbis rule that a subversive prophet is stoned, having derived this from a *gezeirah shavah* based on the words, *to subvert you,* that appear in verse 6 of the section. Accordingly, Rav Chisda holds, their ruling applies only to one who prophesies the abrogation of the idolatry prohibitions (see *Rashi*). One who prophesies the abrogation of other commandments, however, is not included in the law of the subversive prophet, and he is therefore not subject to stoning.

3. *Deuteronomy* 13:6.

4. [This word מִן, *from,* is generally taken to mean "part of," i.e. *from* – but not all.]

5. [What is meant by "partial subverting" will be explained below in note 7.]

6. One who declares in the Name of God the abolition of any other of the laws of the Torah is certainly a false prophet, since the Torah states a number of times that its commandments are everlasting (e.g. *Deuteronomy* 29:28), and that we may neither add nor subtract from its laws (*Deuteronomy* 13:1), even by the word of a prophet [see *Megillah* 2b, *Yoma* 80a] (from *Rambam, Hil. Yesodei HaTorah* 9:1). Thus, a prophet who declares that he has been commanded to abrogate a Torah law is the subject of the verse regarding the false prophet (*Deuteronomy* 18:20): אַךְ הַנָּבִיא אֲשֶׁר יָזִיד לְדַבֵּר דָּבָר בִּשְׁמִי אֵת אֲשֶׁר לֹא־צִוִּיתִיו לְדַבֵּר . . . וּמֵת הַנָּבִיא הַהוּא, *But the prophet who will willfully speak a matter in My name that which I have not commanded him to speak . . . that prophet shall die.* Now, this verse does not contain any expression of "subversion"; it simply states that a prophet who prophesies that which he did not hear from God is subject to the death penalty. This, as we learned above (89a), means that he is subject to strangulation, as both R' Shimon and the Rabbis agree (*Rashi*).

7. The Torah prescribes the death penalty only for a prophet who abolishes a mitzvah entirely, not for one who partially abolishes a mitzvah. For example, if the prophet proclaims that God has rescinded the mitzvah of the Sabbath, he is put to death; if, however, he proclaims that God has suspended the Sabbath for the duration of the Sabbatical year, the prophet is exempt from punishment, as this represents only the partial abrogation of the mitzvah (see *Horayos* 4b; see below).

This distinction is derived from the words of the verse itself: אַךְ הַנָּבִיא אֲשֶׁר יָזִיד לְדַבֵּר דָּבָר בִּשְׁמִי, *But the prophet who will willfully speak a matter in My Name.* The word דָּבָר, *a matter*, is seemingly redundant, and is therefore expounded to teach that the death penalty mentioned in this verse is only for one who abrogates a whole matter (law), and not just a fraction of a matter (*Rashi*; see *Tosafos* 86a ד״ה דבר).

From the Gemara below it seems that the case of a prophet commanding to preserve part of a mitzvah and to nullify part of it is one in which the prophet declares that the mitzvah should be abrogated for a certain period of time, but not permanently (see *Rashi* below ד״ה היום עובדה; *Rambam, Hil. Yesodei HaTorah* 9:3,5; *Chidushei HaRan;* cf. *Binyan Shlomo*).

Moreover, *Ran* deduces from *Rashi's* citation of a Scriptural decree to exempt partial nullification of a mitzvah from the death penalty, that a prophet who abrogates a mitzvah for a limited time period is not subject to the death penalty even if his prophecy is proven false. [*Ran* challenges this on the grounds that false prophecy about the temporary abrogation of a mitzvah should be treated no more leniently than false prophecy regarding any other matter. Since a false prophet is executed for saying anything in the Name of God that he was not commanded to say – even regarding a completely mundane matter – he should be executed for falsely prophesying the temporary suspension of a mitzvah as well (cf. *Binyan Shlomo*).]

However, from *Rambam* (ibid.) it seems that the exemption in our Gemara refers only to a prophecy that can be assumed to be true. Thus, if an established prophet declares in the Name of God that a certain mitzvah should be suspended temporarily, we accept his prophecy to be true. If, however, he declares it to be permanently abrogated, we execute him as a false prophet. Since God has told us in His Torah that the mitzvos are everlasting, a prophet who states otherwise has demonstrated himself to be a false prophet. By the same token, *Ran* argues, even a prophet who prophesies the temporary suspension of a mitzvah is executed if it can be proven that he lied (*Chidushei HaRan*). [Possibly, *Rashi* means this as well. The verse cited and expounded by *Rashi* may be saying that in the case of a complete (i.e. permanent) nullification of a mitzvah, the prophet is *automatically* proven false. The verse excludes from this categorical rule a case of a partial nullification because it is *possible* in such a case that the prophet is telling the truth. Thus, the verse alludes to the law that we are to follow an established prophet who commands the temporary suspension of a Torah law.]

8. This Baraisa appears in *Sifrei* in connection with the passage of the subversive prophet (*Parashas Re'eh*, §62). The phrase לָלֶכֶת בָּהּ, *to go on it,* seems superfluous in this verse. The Baraisa therefore expounds it. The word לָלֶכֶת, *to go*, connotes a positive act (as opposed to a passive one), and indicates a positive commandment. The word בָּהּ, *on it,* indicates a negative commandment, based on an exposition linking our verse with *Leviticus* 4:23 (see *Rashi*; see also alternative explanation cited by *Maharshal*).

מחלוקת בעוקר הגוף דעבודת כוכבים וקיום מקצת וביטול מקצת דעבודת כוכבים דרחמנא אמר א) מן הדרך אפילו מקצת הדרך אבל עוקר הגוף דשאר מצות דברי הכל בחנק וקיום מקצת וביטול מקצת דבשאר מצות דברי הכל פטור מתיב רב המנונא א) ללכת זו מצות עשה בה זו מצות לא תעשה ואי סלקא דעתך בעבודת כוכבים עשה בעבודת כוכבים היכי משכחת לה תרגמה רב חסדא ב) ונתצתם רב המנונא אמר מחלוקת בעוקר הגוף בין בעבודת כוכבים בין בשאר מצות וקיום מקצת וביטול מקצת דעבודת כוכבים דרחמנא אמר מן הדרך אפילו מקצת הדרך אבל קיום מקצת וביטול מקצת דבשאר מצות דברי הכל פטור ת"ר ה) המתנבא לעקור דבר מן התורה חייב לקיים מקצת ולבטל מקצת ר"ש פוטר ובעבודת כוכבים אפילו אומר היום עיבדוה ולמחר בטלוה דברי הכל חייב אביי סבר לה כרב חסדא ומתרץ לה כרב חסדא רבא סבר לה כרב המנונא ומתרץ לה כרב המנונא אביי סבר לה כרב חסדא ומתרץ לה כרב חסדא המתנבא לעקור דבר מן התורה דברי הכל בחנק לקיים מקצת ולבטל מקצת ר"ש פוטר והוא הדין לרבנן ובעבודת כוכבים אפילו אמר היום עיבדוה ולמחר בטלוה חייב מר כדאית ליה ומר כדאית ליה רבא סבר לה כרב המנונא ומתרץ לה כרב המנונא המתנבא לעקור דבר מן התורה בין בעבודת כוכבים בין בשאר מצות חייב מר כדאית ליה ומר כדאית ליה ו) לקיים מקצת ולבטל מקצת בשאר מצות ר"ש פוטר והוא הדין לרבנן ובעבודת כוכבים אפילו אומר היום עיבדוה ולמחר בטלוה חייב מר כדאית ליה ומר כדאית ליה א"ר אבהו א"ר יוחנן א בכל אם יאמר לך נביא עבור על דברי תורה שמע לו חוץ מעבודת כוכבים שאפילו מעמיד לך חמה באמצע הרקיע אל תשמע לו תניא רבי יוסי הגלילי אומר הגיעה תורה לסוף דעתה של עבודת כוכבים לפיכך נתנה תורה ממשלה בה שאפילו מעמיד לך חמה באמצע הרקיע אל תשמע לו תניא א"ר עקיבא חס ושלום שהקדוש ב"ה מעמיד חמה לעוברי רצונו אלא כגון חנניה בן עזור שמתחלתו נביא אמת ולבסוף נביא שקר: וזוממי בת כהן: מנהני מילי אמר רב אחא בריה דרב איקא דתניא ר' יוסי אומר מה ת"ל ג) ג) ועשיתם לו כאשר זמם לעשות לאחיו לפי שכל ד) המזוממין שבתורה זוממיהן ובועליהן כיוצא בהן בת כהן ה) היא בשריפה ואין בועלה בשריפה זוממין איני יודע אם לו הוקשו אם לה הוקשו כשהוא אומר לעשות לאחיו ו) לאחיו ולא לאחותו:

הדרן עלך אלו הן הנחנקין

כל ישראל ב יש להם חלק לעולם הבא שנאמר ד) ועמך כולם צדיקים לעולם יירשו ארץ נצר מטעי מעשה ידי להתפאר ז) ג ואלו שאין להם חלק לעולם הבא האומר אין תחיית המתים מן התורה ואין תורה מן השמים ואפיקורוס ר"ע אומר אף הקורא בספרים החיצונים ח) והלוחש על המכה ואומר ה) כל המחלה אשר שמתי במצרים לא אשים עליך כי אני ה' רופאך אבא שאול אומר אף ט) ההוגה את השם באותיותיו י) שלשה מלכים וארבעה הדיוטות אין להן חלק לעולם הבא שלשה מלכים ירבעם אחאב ומנשה ר' יהודה אומר מנשה יש לו חלק לעולם הבא שנאמר ו) ויתפלל אליו כ) וישמע תחנתו וישיבהו ירושלים למלכותו אמרו לו למלכותו השיבו ולא לחיי העולם הבא השיבו ארבעה הדיוטות בלעם ודואג ואחיתופל וגחזי: **גמ'** וכל כך למה תנא הוא כפר בתחיית המתים לפיכך לא יהיה לו חלק בתחיית המתים שכל מדותיו של הקב"ה מדה כנגד מדה דאמר ר' שמואל בר נחמני אמר ר' יונתן מניין שכל מדותיו של הקב"ה מדה כנגד מדה שנאמר ז) ויאמר אלישע שמעו דבר ה' [וגו'] כעת מחר סאה סלת בשקל וסאתים שעורים בשקל בשער שומרון וכתיב ח) ויען השליש אשר (ל) המלך) נשען על ידו את איש האלהים ויאמר הנה ה' עושה ארובות בשמים היהיה הדבר הזה ויאמר מ) הנך רואה בעיניך ומשם לא תאכל וכתיב

מחלוקת. דרבנן ורבי שמעון בנביא בעוקר כל הגוף בעבודת כוכבים ואומר נלטויתי ברוח הקודש מפי הגבורה להתנבאות לעקור כל מלות עבודת כוכבים מן התורה או לקיים מקלת ולבטל מקלת בהאי הוא דקאמרי רבנן סקילה משום דבהאי עניינא דכתיבא הדחה בנביא דגמרי סקילה מיניה בע"ז הוא משתעי דכתיב ובא האות והמופת וגו' נלכה ונעבדה היינו עקירת הגוף ובטול מקלת התם נמי כתיב בסיפא יומת כי דבר סרה וגו' להדיחך מן הדרך ואפי' במקלת במשמע ומיהו לא מישתעי קרא אלא בע"ז דדבר למד מעניינו: **אבל עוקר הגוף דשאר מצות דברי הכל בחנק.** דנפקא לן מקרא אחרינא האמור בפרשה אחרינא דלא כתיב בה הדחה אך הנביא אשר יזיד לדבר דבר בשמי (דברים יח) והיינו מה שלא שמע וכתיב ומת הנביא ההוא וכל מיתה האמורה סתם חנק הוא: **פטור.** דהתם דבר כתיב דבר שלם ולא חלי דבר: **ללכת זו מצות עשה.** ברייתא היא בספרי גבי פרשת נביא המדיח דכתב בה הדחה (שם יג) להדיחך מן הדרך אשר לוך ה' אלהיך ללכת בה וגו' ודריש קרא יתירא ללכת זו מלות עשה דמשמע לעשות ולא משמע אזהרה: **בה לא תעשה.** דגמרינן מאשר חטא בה דבלא תעשה מיירי אלמא דשאר מלות נמי הכא גבי הדחה כתיבי דאי לא משתעי קרא אלא בע"ז מאי עשה איכא: **ובין בשאר מצות.** דהאי ללכת בה לא משמע ליה לרב המנונא אונתלתם דרחמנא אמר מן הדרך ואע"ז קאי דאכתי לא איתרבו שאר מלות בהאי עניינא דללכת בה כולה משמע: **ד"ה פטור.** ואפילו מחנק דהתם דבר שלם כתיב ולאו אעוקר דברי תורה האי כי יזיד לדבר דבר קאי דהתם סקילה הוא אלא אדברים בעלמא כגון לדקיה בן כנענה: **היום עובדה.** כלומר היינו קיום מקלת וביטול מקלת: **כרב חסדא.** דאמר בע"ז הוא דפליגי אבל בשאר מלות עוקר הגוף הוא בחנק וביטול מקלת פטור: **ר"ש פוטר והוא הדין לרבנן.** דגבי חנק דבר שלם כתיב ולרב חסדא הא דנקט ר"ש הא קמ"ל דרישא דקתני סתמא חייב ואפילו לרבנן בחנק דרבי שמעון הוא דקא מחייב חנק ולא סקילה דשאר מלות בעניינא הדחה דסקילה לא כתיבי: **מר כדאית ליה כו'.** לרבנן בסקילה לרבי שמעון בחנק י) והוא הדין לרבנן ולרב המנונא האי דנקט ר' שמעון רבותא הוא כלומר ואפילו מחנק דרבי שמעון פטור וכ"ש מסקילה דמחייבי ליה רבנן בעוקר את הכל: **אם יאמר לך נביא.** המוחזק עבור על דברי תורה הכל לפי תקנת השעה כגון אליהו בהר הכרמל בשחוטי חוץ: **נתנה התורה ממשלה בה.** כלומר אפילו תראה אותו נביא מושל ועושה כרלונו דכתיב (דברים יג) ונתן אליך אות או מופת: **שתחילתו נביא אמת.** כגון חנניה הנביא והאי ונתן אליך אות בעודו נביא אמת יתן לך אות בנבואה אחרת ולבסוף כשיחזור להרשיע יאמר לעבוד עבודת כוכבים וסמוך עלי שהרי מוחזק אני על ידי אות ומופת שנתתי לך כבר: ס) (**לרשות הבעל.** כגון מסרה האב לשלוחי הבעל ועדיין היא בדרך ולא קרינן בה בית אביה: **לאותה מיתה.** שהיו מחייבין את הנידון: **ובועלה.** כלומר וכל הבועלים נידונין כמיתת הנבעלת חוץ מבועל בת כהן:) **מה ת"ל לאחיו.** לכתוב כאשר זמם לעשות ולישתוק: **אם לו הוקשו.** לבועל שהיו מחייבין אותו חנק: **אם לה.** שמחייבין אותה שריפה: **לאחיו ולא לאחותו.** כל היכא דבעדותן מחייבין איש ואשה ודינן חלוק כי הכא לו הוקשו:

הדרן עלך אלו הן הנחנקין

כל ישראל יש להם חלק לעולם הבא. מעיקרא איירי בארבע מיתות ומפרש ואזיל להו לכולהו והדר מפרש הני דאין להם חלק לעולם הבא: ה"ג **האומר אין תחיית המתים מן התורה.** ע) שכופר במדרשים דדרשינן בגמרא לקמן מניין לתחיית המתים מן התורה ואפי' יהא מודה ומאמין שיחיו המתים אלא דלא רמיזא באורייתא כופר הוא הואיל ועוקר שיש תחיית המתים מן התורה מה לנו ולאמונתו וכי מהיכן הוא יודע שכן הוא הלכך כופר גמור הוא: **אפיקורוס.** מפרש בגמרא: **ספרים החיצונים.** מפרש בגמרא: **גמ'** ויהי

מסורת הש"ס

א) [הוריות ד:], ב) [שם ד:], ג) [הנהו תמש תיבות ועשיתם לו כאשר זמם לעשות נראה דאינם מן הגירסא אלא עיקר הגי' כדאיתא בפירש"י מה ת"ל לאחיו], ד) [י"ג המזומנין], ה) [לעיל נא. ע"ש], ו) [שם:], ז) [ע"ז יח.], ח) שבועות טו:, ט) ע"ז יח., י) חגיגה טו:, כ) [ויעתר לו], ל) [נ"ל למלך], מ) [נ"ל הנכה], נ) הוא דבור בפ"ע רש"ל, ס) מן ד"ה לרשות עד ד"ה מה ת"ל שייך למתני' לעיל פט., ע) כ' ב"ש שאין זה מדברי רש"י.

גליון הש"ס

מתני' כל ישראל יש להן חלק. עי' כתובות דף קג ע"ב תוס' ד"ה מזומן: שם האומר אין תחיית המתים. עי' סוטה ד"ה ע"א תוד"ה כל: שם ההוגה את השם. עי' סוכה דף ה' ע"א תוד"ה יו"ד ה"א. שבועות דף לד ע"א תוס' ד"ה באלף: גמ' מדה כנגד מדה. עי' סוטה דף ח' ע"ב:

תורה אור השלם

א) וְהַנָּבִיא הַהוּא אוֹ חֹלֵם הַחֲלוֹם הַהוּא יוּמָת כִּי דִבֶּר סָרָה עַל יְיָ אֱלֹהֵיכֶם הַמּוֹצִיא אֶתְכֶם מֵאֶרֶץ מִצְרַיִם וְהַפֹּדְךָ מִבֵּית עֲבָדִים לְהַדִּיחֲךָ מִן הַדֶּרֶךְ אֲשֶׁר צִוְּךָ יְיָ אֱלֹהֶיךָ לָלֶכֶת בָּהּ וּבִעַרְתָּ הָרָע מִקִּרְבֶּךָ: [דברים יג, ו]

ב) וְנִתַּצְתֶּם אֶת מִזְבְּחֹתָם וְשִׁבַּרְתֶּם אֶת מַצֵּבֹתָם וַאֲשֵׁרֵיהֶם תִּשְׂרְפוּן בָּאֵשׁ וּפְסִילֵי אֱלֹהֵיהֶם תְּגַדֵּעוּן וְאִבַּדְתֶּם אֶת שְׁמָם מִן הַמָּקוֹם הַהוּא: [דברים יב, ג]

ג) וַעֲשִׂיתֶם לוֹ כַּאֲשֶׁר זָמַם לַעֲשׂוֹת לְאָחִיו וּבִעַרְתָּ הָרָע מִקִּרְבֶּךָ: [דברים יט, יט]

ד) וְעַמֵּךְ כֻּלָּם צַדִּיקִים לְעוֹלָם יִירְשׁוּ אָרֶץ נֵצֶר מַטָּעַי מַעֲשֵׂה יָדַי לְהִתְפָּאֵר: [ישעיה ס, כא]

ה) וַיֹּאמֶר אִם שָׁמוֹעַ תִּשְׁמַע לְקוֹל יְיָ אֱלֹהֶיךָ וְהַיָּשָׁר בְּעֵינָיו תַּעֲשֶׂה וְהַאֲזַנְתָּ לְמִצְוֹתָיו וְשָׁמַרְתָּ כָּל חֻקָּיו כָּל הַמַּחֲלָה אֲשֶׁר שַׂמְתִּי בְמִצְרַיִם לֹא אָשִׂים עָלֶיךָ כִּי אֲנִי יְיָ רֹפְאֶךָ: [שמות טו, כו]

ו) וַיִּתְפַּלֵּל אֵלָיו וַיֵּעָתֶר לוֹ וַיִּשְׁמַע תְּחִנָּתוֹ וַיְשִׁיבֵהוּ יְרוּשָׁלַיִם לְמַלְכוּתוֹ וַיֵּדַע מְנַשֶּׁה כִּי יְיָ הוּא הָאֱלֹהִים: [דברי הימים ב' לג, יג]

ז) וַיֹּאמֶר אֱלִישָׁע שִׁמְעוּ דְּבַר יְיָ כֹּה אָמַר יְיָ כָּעֵת מָחָר סְאָה סֹלֶת בְּשֶׁקֶל וְסָאתַיִם שְׂעֹרִים בְּשֶׁקֶל בְּשַׁעַר שֹׁמְרוֹן: [מלכים ב' ז, א]

ח) וַיַּעַן הַשָּׁלִישׁ אֲשֶׁר לַמֶּלֶךְ נִשְׁעָן עַל יָדוֹ אֶת אִישׁ הָאֱלֹהִים וַיֹּאמַר הִנֵּה יְיָ עֹשֶׂה אֲרֻבּוֹת בַּשָּׁמַיִם הֲיִהְיֶה הַדָּבָר הַזֶּה וַיֹּאמֶר הִנְּכָה רֹאֶה בְּעֵינֶיךָ וּמִשָּׁם לֹא תֹאכֵל: [מלכים ב' ז, ב]

עין משפט נר מצוה

פא א מיי' פ"ט מהלכות יסודי התורה הל"ג והל"ה והיינו לפי שעה וע"ש:

א ב מיי' פ"ג מהלכות תשובה הלכה ה:

ב ג מיי' שם הלכה ו:

ליקוטי רש"י

אחר הדברים האלה. יש מרבותינו אומרים אחר דבריו של שטן שהיה מקטרג ואומר מכל סעודה שעשה אברהם לא הקריב לפניך פר אחד או איל אחד אמר לו כלום עשה אלא בשביל בנו אילו הייתי אומר לו זבח אותו לפני לא היה מעכב ויש אומרים אחר דבריו של ישמעאל שהיה מתפאר על יצחק שמל בן שלש עשרה שנה ולא מיחה אמר לו יצחק באבר אחד אתה מיראני אילו אמר לי הקב"ה זבח עצמך לפני לא הייתי מעכב [בראשית כב, א]. **קח נא.** אין נא אלא לשון בקשה אמר לו בבקשה ממך עמוד לי בזה הנסיון שלא יאמרו הראשונות לא היה בהן ממש. **את בנך.** אמר לו שני בנים יש לי אמר לו את יחידך אמר לו זה יחיד לאמו וזה יחיד לאמו אמר לו אשר אהבת אמר לו שניהם אני אוהב אמר לו את יצחק ולמה לא גילה לו מתחלה שלא לערבבו פתאום ותזוח דעתו עליו ותטרף וכדי לחבב עליו את המצוה וליתן לו שכר על כל דבור ודבור [שם פוק ב']. **הנסה.** לשון תימה הבעבור שניסה דבר אליך תלאה בנסיון אחד שניסך בוראך ובא אליך אתה נלאה ומעתה עצור במילין מי יוכל מלהשיבך. **הנה יסרתם רבים.** שהרגו דברים הוכחתם ויסרתם. **וידים רפות.** ויגורות מפורענות הבא עליה' אתה היית רגיל לחזקם ולומר אל תירא שכך הוא מדת הדין. **יקימון.** רגילות הם מליך להקים את הכושל. **הלא יראתך כסלתך.** עתה סופך מוכיח על תחלתך שיראתך שהיית ירא שמים כסלתך היא מחמת כסילות היא ולא מדעת שלימה וכן תקותך ותום דרכיך הכל כסילות [איוב ד].

[עד כאן שייך לדף פט:]

המתנבא לעקור דבר מן התורה. כגון שתחלתו נביא של אמת ולבסוף נביא השקר שהתנבא לעקור דבר מדברי תורה חייב ודברי הכל בחנק. **לקיום מקצת ולבטל מקצת.** דשאר מלות ר"ש פוטר וה"ה לרבנן. **ובעבודת כוכבים אפי' אמר לך היום עובדה ולמחר בטלה.** דהיינו קיום מקלת ובטול מקלת דעבודת כוכבים חייב דרחמנא אמר להדיחך מן הדרך אפי' מקלת דרך ובעבודת כוכבי' הוא דכתיב וכי קתני חייב כגון לרבנן בסקילה ולר"ש בחנק וככי מתרץ ליה רב חסדא בפ' אלו הן הנחנקין (סנהדרין דף ל) והיום עובדה ולמחר בטלה כאין שבת בשביעית דמי וקרי להו ביטול מקלת וקיום מקלת ש"מ [הוריות ד:]. **זוממי בת כהן.** עיין בזה ליקוטי רש"י לעיל פט.

positive commandment that bears upon idolatry? The Torah's commandments regarding idolatry are all in the form of prohibitions, not positive commandments![9] – ? –

The Gemara answers:

תַּרְגְּמָה רַב חִסְדָּא – **Rav Chisda interpreted [the Baraisa]** to refer to the following positive commandment: "וְנִתַּצְתֶּם" – ***You shall break apart*** *their altars.*[10]

Rav Hamnuna does not accept Rav Chisda's answer. Rav Hamnuna therefore concludes that the passage of the subversive prophet discusses both idolatry and other mitzvos:

רַב הַמְנוּנָא אָמַר – **Rav Hamnuna said:** מַחֲלוֹקֶת בְּעוֹקֵר הַגּוּף – The **dispute** between R' Shimon and the Rabbis[11] **pertains to** a subversive prophet who **abolishes** by his prophecy **the whole** of any commandment, בֵּין בַּעֲבוֹדַת כּוֹכָבִים בֵּין בִּשְׁאָר מִצְוֹת – **whether in** regard to **idolatry or** any **of the other mitzvos;** וְקִיּוּם מִקְצָת וּבִיטּוּל מִקְצָת דַּעֲבוֹדַת כּוֹכָבִים – it refers **as well** to one whose prophecy dictates **the preservation of part and the nullification of part** of the prohibition **of idolatry.** דְּרַחֲמָנָא אָמַר "מִן־הַדֶּרֶךְ" – **For the Merciful One has stated** in his Torah: *for he has spoken perversion against Hashem, your God . . . to subvert you* ***from the path,*** אֲפִילּוּ מִקְצָת הַדֶּרֶךְ – which implies from **even just part of the path.**[12]

אֲבָל קִיּוּם מִקְצָת וּבִיטּוּל מִקְצָת דִּבִשְׁאָר מִצְוֹת – **However,** if he prophesies **the preservation of part and the nullification of part of any of the other mitzvos,** דִּבְרֵי הַכֹּל פָּטוּר – **all agree that he is exempt** from punishment.[13]

The Gemara cites another Baraisa that addresses the views of R' Shimon and the Rabbis:

תָּנוּ רַבָּנָן – **The Rabbis taught in a Baraisa:** הַמִּתְנַבֵּא לַעֲקוֹר דָּבָר מִן הַתּוֹרָה – ONE WHO PROPHESIES TO ABOLISH SOMETHING FROM THE TORAH, i.e. any mitzvah, חַיָּיב – IS LIABLE to the death penalty. לְקַיֵּים מִקְצָת וּלְבַטֵּל מִקְצָת – If he prophesies TO PRESERVE PART of a mitzvah AND TO NULLIFY PART of it: רַבִּי שִׁמְעוֹן פּוֹטֵר – R' SHIMON EXEMPTS him from the death penalty – where his prophecy concerned mitzvos other than idolatry. וּבַעֲבוֹדַת כּוֹכָבִים – HOWEVER, if he prophesied CONCERNING the laws of IDOLATRY, אֲפִילּוּ אוֹמֵר הַיּוֹם עִיבְדוּהָ וּלְמָחָר בַּטְּלוּהָ – then EVEN IF HE SAYS, "WORSHIP [THIS IDOL] TODAY AND NULLIFY IT TOMORROW!"[14] דִּבְרֵי הַכֹּל חַיָּיב – ALL AGREE that HE IS LIABLE to the death penalty.[15]

This Baraisa seems to contradict both views cited above, for it seems to say that where a prophet attempts to abolish a Torah commandment entirely, there is no dispute between R' Shimon and the Rabbis[16] – implying that they agree even about what the penalty should be. This is certainly not true according to Rav Hamnuna.[17] Secondly, the Baraisa states that for the partial nullification of mitzvos other than idolatry, "R' Shimon exempts," implying that *only* R' Shimon exempts but the Rabbis consider him liable. This is not true according to either opinion.[18] Thirdly, the Baraisa states that in the case of idolatry, all agree that he is liable for partial nullification. However, both according to Rav Chisda and Rav Hamnuna, partial nullification of the idolatry prohibition is included in the law of the subversive

NOTES

9. Thus, the Baraisa must be referring to the positive and negative commandments of mitzvos not related to idolatry. If so, the Baraisa states that the passage of the subversive prophet is not limited to the subject of idolatry, but rather deals with all mitzvos. This would refute Rav Chisda's contention that this passage – and by extension, the dispute between R' Shimon and the Rabbis – pertains only to idolatry.

10. *Deuteronomy* 12:3. The verse states that when the Jewish nation enters Eretz Yisrael, they must utterly destroy any vestiges of idolatry left by the former inhabitants. This is a positive, idolatry-related commandment. The Baraisa thus teaches that if a prophet proclaims in the Name of God that idolatrous altars should not be broken apart, he is deemed a subversive prophet (*Rabbeinu Chananel*).

11. Regarding the manner in which a subversive prophet is executed – stoning (according to the Rabbis) or strangulation (according to R' Shimon).

12. Rav Hamnuna concedes that the part of the verse that refers to *partial* nullification pertains only to idolatry. The reason is as follows: The verses read: *If there should stand up in your midst a prophet . . . saying, "Let us follow the gods of others that you did not know and we shall worship them" . . . that prophet . . . shall be put to death, for he has spoken perversion against Hashem, your God . . . to subvert you from the path which Hashem, your God, has commanded you to go on.* Now, Rav Hamnuna contends, the first portion of this passage certainly deals with idolatry (*Let us follow the gods of others*). It is only the very end of the last verse quoted here (*to go on*) that contains a reference to other mitzvos, as explained in the Baraisa quoted above. However, the phrase *from the path,* from which the penalty for partial nullification is derived, occurs earlier in the passage, at which point the verse has not yet mentioned other mitzvos and is still addressing idolatry alone. As a result, the exposition that a partial nullification is the same as a complete abolition is true only for idolatry, not other mitzvos. [The words *to go on* themselves do not indicate a partial nullification, but refer to a complete abolition] (*Rashi* according to *Maharsha*).

13. He is exempt because there is no verse that discusses the partial nullification of other mitzvos. The passage of the subversive prophet alludes to a partial nullification, but only in connection with idolatry, not other mitzvos (see previous note). The passage of the false prophet also does not mandate execution for the partial nullification of other mitzvos, as explained in note 7 ("*a matter*, and not part of a matter"). Indeed, according to Rav Hamnuna, the passage of the false prophet does not deal with any attempted modification of Torah law; rather, it deals with prophets who make false predictions, such as Tzidkiyah ben Kenaanah (see 89a). Thus, there are no grounds for executing a prophet for declaring the partial nullification of any mitzvah other than idolatry (*Rashi*). [See note 7 for a discussion of whether this refers only to a prophecy that may be accepted as true or even to one that has been proven false.] See chart.

		IDOLATRY		OTHER MITZVOS	
		Complete Nullification	Partial Nullification	Complete Nullification	Partial Nullification
RAV CHISDA	RABBIS	stoning	stoning	strangulation	exempt
	R' SHIMON	strangulation	strangulation	strangulation	exempt
RAV HAMNUNA	RABBIS	stoning	stoning	stoning	exempt
	R' SHIMON	strangulation	strangulation	strangulation	exempt

14. [There is a legal procedure known as בִּיטּוּל עֲבוֹדָה זָרָה, *nullifying an idol.* When certain specific acts are performed to an idol (see *Avodah Zarah* 52a, 53a), its status as a forbidden object can be nullified (see there for further elaboration). Thus, the Baraisa teaches that even if the "prophet" stated that the idol should be nullified the very next day, he is deemed a subversive prophet.]

15. Declaring that an idol should be worshiped temporarily and then abandoned is the case of "preservation of part of the mitzvah and the nullification of part" (*Rashi*). All agree that in the case of idolatry, a prophet is liable to the death penalty for such a prophecy as a subversive prophet [נְבִיא הַמַּדִּיחַ].

16. The Baraisa mentions R' Shimon's view specifically only in regard to *partial* nullification, implying that there is no dispute in regard to complete abolition.

17. According to Rav Hamnuna, the dispute between R' Shimon and the Rabbis regarding the punishment of a subversive prophet extends even to a prophet who commands the complete abolition of *any* mitzvah. [This part of the Baraisa is less problematic according to Rav Chisda, because it may be referring to mitzvos other than idolatry. According to Rav Chisda, abolition of other mitzvos is not included in the law of נְבִיא הַמַּדִּיחַ, *a subversive prophet,* but rather in the law of נְבִיא שֶׁקֶר, *a false prophet*, where all agree that the punishment is strangulation (see below).]

18. Both Rav Chisda and Rav Hamnuna agree that there is no death penalty for the partial nullification of mitzvos other than idolatry even according to the Rabbis (see chart above).

מחלוקת בעוקר הגוף דעבודת כוכבים וקיום מקצת וביטול מקצת דעבודת כוכבים דרחמנא אמר א) מן הדרך אפילו מקצת הדרך אבל עוקר הגוף דשאר מצות דברי הכל בחנק וקיום מקצת וביטול מקצת דבשאר מצות דברי הכל פטור מתיב רב המנונא א) ללכת זו מצות עשה בה זו מצות לא תעשה ואי סלקא דעתך בעבודת כוכבים עשה בעבודת כוכבים היכי משכחת לה תרגמה רב חסדא ב) ונתצתם רב המנונא אמר מחלוקת בעוקר הגוף בין בעבודת כוכבים בין בשאר מצות וקיום מקצת וביטול מקצת דעבודת כוכבים דרחמנא אמר מן הדרך אפילו מקצת הדרך אבל קיום מקצת וביטול מקצת דבשאר מצות דברי הכל פטור ת"ר א) המתנבא לעקור דבר מן התורה חייב לקיים מקצת ולבטל מקצת ר"ש פוטר ובעבודת כוכבים אפילו אומר היום עיבדוה ולמחר בטלוה דברי הכל חייב אביי סבר לה כרב חסדא ומתרץ לה כרב חסדא רבא סבר לה כרב המנונא ומתרץ לה כרב המנונא אביי סבר לה כרב חסדא ומתרץ לה כרב חסדא המתנבא לעקור דבר מן התורה דברי הכל בחנק לקיים מקצת ולבטל מקצת ר"ש פוטר והוא הדין לרבנן ובעבודת כוכבים אפילו אומר היום עיבדוה ולמחר בטלוה חייב מר כדאית ליה ומר כדאית ליה רבא סבר לה כרב המנונא ומתרץ לה כרב המנונא המתנבא לעקור דבר מן התורה בין בעבודת כוכבים בין בשאר מצות חייב מר כדאית ליה ומר כדאית ליה ג) לקיים מקצת ולבטל מקצת בשאר מצות ר"ש פוטר והוא הדין לרבנן ובעבודת כוכבים אפילו אומר היום עיבדוה ולמחר בטלוה חייב מר כדאית ליה ומר כדאית ליה א"ר אבהו א"ר יוחנן א בכל אם יאמר לך נביא עבור על דברי תורה שמע לו חוץ מעבודת כוכבים שאפילו מעמיד לך חמה באמצע הרקיע אל תשמע לו תניא רבי יוסי הגלילי אומר הגיעה תורה לסוף דעתה של עבודת כוכבים לפיכך נתנה תורה ממשלה בה שאפילו מעמיד לך חמה באמצע הרקיע אל תשמע לו תניא א"ר עקיבא חס ושלום שהקדוש ב"ה מעמיד חמה לעוברי רצונו אלא כגון חנניה בן עזור שמתחלתו נביא אמת ולבסוף נביא שקר: וזוממי בת כהן: מנהני מילי אמר רב אחא בריה דרב איקא דתניא ר' יוסי אומר מה ת"ל ג) ג) ועשיתם לו כאשר זמם לעשות לאחיו לפי שכל ד) המזוממין שבתורה זוממיהן ובועליהן כיוצא בהן בת כהן ה) היא בשריפה ואין בועלה בשריפה זוממין איני יודע אם לו הוקשו אם לה הוקשו כשהוא אומר לעשות לאחיו ו) לאחיו ולא לאחותו:

הדרן עלך אלו הן הנחנקין

כל ישראל ב יש להם חלק לעולם הבא שנאמר ד) ועמך כולם צדיקים לעולם יירשו ארץ נצר מטעי מעשה ידי להתפאר ז) ג ואלו שאין להם חלק לעולם הבא האומר אין תחיית המתים מן התורה ואין תורה מן השמים ואפיקורוס ר"ע אומר אף הקורא בספרים החיצונים ח) והלוחש על המכה ואומר ה) כל המחלה אשר שמתי במצרים לא אשים עליך כי אני ה' רופאך אבא שאול אומר אף ט) ההוגה את השם באותיותיו י) שלשה מלכים וארבעה הדיוטות אין להן חלק לעולם הבא שלשה מלכים ירבעם אחאב ומנשה ר' יהודה אומר מנשה יש לו חלק לעולם הבא שנאמר ו) ויתפלל אליו כ) וישמע תחנתו וישיבהו ירושלים למלכותו אמרו לו למלכותו השיבו ולא לחיי העולם הבא השיבו ארבעה הדיוטות בלעם ודואג ואחיתופל וגחזי: **גמ'** וכל כך למה תנא הוא כפר בתחיית המתים לפיכך לא יהיה לו חלק בתחיית המתים שכל מדותיו של הקב"ה מדה כנגד מדה דאמר ר' שמואל בר נחמני אמר ר' יונתן מניין שכל מדותיו של הקב"ה מדה כנגד מדה שנאמר ז) ויאמר אלישע שמעו דבר ה' [וגו'] כעת מחר סאה סלת בשקל וסאתים שעורים בשקל בשער שומרון וכתיב ח) ויען השליש אשר (ל) המלך) נשען על ידו את איש האלהים ויאמר הנה ה' עושה ארובות בשמים היהיה הדבר הזה ויאמר מ) הנך רואה בעיניך ומשם לא תאכל וכתיב

רש"י

מחלוקת. דרבנן ורבי שמעון בנביא בעוקר כל הגוף בעבודת כוכבים ואומר נצטויתי ברוח הקודש מפי הגבורה להתנבאות לעקור כל מצות עבודת כוכבים מן התורה או לקיים מקצת ולבטל מקצת בהאי הוא דקאמרי רבנן סקילה משום דבהאי עניינא דכתיבא הדחה בנביא דגמרי סקילה מיניה בע"ז הוא משתעי דכתיב ובא האות והמופת וגו' נלכה ונעבדה היינו עקירת הגוף ובטול מקצת התם נמי כתיב בסיפא יומת כי דבר סרה וגו' להדיחך מן הדרך ואפי' במקצת במשמע ומיהו לא מישתעי קרא אלא בע"ז דדבר למד מענייני: **אבל עוקר הגוף דשאר מצות דברי הכל בחנק.** דנפקא לן מקרא אחרינא האמור בפרשה אחרינא דלא כתיב בה הדחה אך הנביא אשר יזיד לדבר דבר בשמי (דברים יח) והיינו מה שלא שמע וכתיב ומת הנביא ההוא וכל מיתה האמורה סתם חנק הוא: **פטור.** דהתם דבר כתיב דבר שלם ולא חצי דבר: **ללכת זו מצות עשה.** ברייתא היא בספרי גבי פרשת נביא המדיח דכתב בה הדחה (שם יג) להדיחך מן הדרך אשר צוך ה' אלהיך ללכת בה וגו' ודריש קרא יתירא ללכת זו מצות עשה דמשמע לעשות ולא משמע אזהרה: **בה לא תעשה.** דגמרינן מאשר חטא בה דבלא תעשה מיירי אלמא דשאר מצות נמי הכא גבי הדחה כתיבי דאי לא משתעי קרא אלא בע"ז מאי עשה איכא: **ובין בשאר מצות.** דהאי ללכת בה לא משמע ליה לרב המנונא אונתאס דרחמנא אמר מן הדרך ואע"ז קאי דאכתי לא איתרבו שאר מצות בהאי עניינא דללכת בה כולה משמע: ד"ה **פטור.** ואפילו מחנק דהתם דבר שלם כתיב ולאו אעוקר דברי תורה האי כי יזיד לדבר דבר קאי דהתם סקילה הוא אלא אדברים בעלמא כגון לדקיה בן כנענה: **היום עובדה.** כלומר היינו קיום מקצת וביטול מקצת: **כרב חסדא.** דאמר בע"ז הוא דפליגי אבל בשאר מצות עוקר הגוף הוא בחנק וביטול מקצת פטור: **ר"ש פוטר והוא הדין לרבנן.** דגבי חנק דבר שלם כתיב ולרב חסדא הא דנקט ר"ש הא קמ"ל דרישא דקתני סתמא חייב ואפילו לרבנן בחנק דרבי שמעון הוא דקא מחייב חנק ולא סקילה דשאר מצות בעניינא הדחה דסקילה לא כתיבי: **מר כדאית ליה כו'.** לרבנן בסקילה לרבי שמעון בחנק ק) והוא הדין לרבנן ולרב המנונא האי דנקט ר' שמעון רבותא הוא כלומר ואפילו מחנק דרבי שמעון פטור וכ"ש מסקילה דמחייבי ליה רבנן בעוקר את הכל: **אם יאמר לך נביא.** המוחזק עבור על דברי תורה הכל לפי תקנת השעה כגון אליהו בהר הכרמל בשחוטי חוץ: **נתנה התורה ממשלה בה.** כלומר אפילו תראה אותו נביא מושל ועושה כרצונו דכתיב (דברים יג) ונתן אליך אות או מופת: **שתחילתו נביא אמת.** כגון חנניה הנביא והאי ונתן אליך אות בעודו נביא אמת יתן לך אות בנבואה אחרת ולבסוף כשיחזור להרשיע יאמר לעבוד עבודת כוכבים וסמוך עלי שהרי מוחזק אני על ידי אות ומופת שנתתי לך כבר: פ) (**לרשות הבעל.** כגון מסרה האב לשלוחי הבעל ועדיין היא בדרך ולא קרינן בה בית אביה: **לאותה מיתה.** שהיו מחייבין את הנידון: **ובועלה.** כלומר וכל הבועלים נידונין כמיתת הנבעלת חוץ מבועל בת כהן:) **מה ת"ל לאחיו.** לכתוב כאשר זמם לעשות ולישתוק: **אם לו הוקשו.** לבועל שהיו מחייבין אותו חנק: **אם לה.** שמחייבין אותה שריפה: **לאחיו ולא לאחותו.** כל היכא דבעדותן מחייבין איש ואשה ודינן חלוק כי הכא לו הוקשו:

הדרן עלך אלו הן הנחנקין

כל ישראל יש להם חלק לעולם הבא. מעיקרא איירי בארבע מיתות ומפרש ואזיל להו לכולהו והדר מפרש הני דאין להם חלק לעולם הבא: ה"ג **האומר אין תחיית המתים מן התורה.** ע) שכופר במדרשים דדרשינן בגמרא לקמן מניין לתחיית המתים מן התורה ואפי' יהא מודה ומאמין שיחיו המתים אלא דלא רמיזא באורייתא כופר הוא הואיל ועוקר שיש תחיית המתים מן התורה מה לנו ולאמונתו וכי מהיכן הוא יודע שכן הוא הלכך כופר גמור הוא: **אפיקורוס.** מפרש בגמרא: **ספרים החיצונים.** מפרש בגמרא: **גמ'** ויהי

פא א מיי' פ"ח מהלכות יסודי התורה הל"ג והל"ה והיינו לפי שעה וע"ש:
א ב מיי' פ"ג מהלכות תשובה הלכה ה:
ב ג מיי' שם הלכה ו:

ליקוטי רש"י

אחר הדברים האלה. יש מרבותינו אומרים אחר דבריו של שטן שהיה מקטרג ואומר מכל סעודה שעשה אברהם לא הקריב לפניך פר אחד או איל אחד אמר לו כלום עשה אלא בשביל בנו אילו הייתי אומר לו זבח אותו לפני לא היה מעכב ויש אומרים אחר דבריו של ישמעאל שהיה מתפאר על יצחק שמל בן שלש עשרה שנה ולא מיחה אמר לו יצחק באבר אחד אתה מיראני אילו אמר לי הקב"ה זבח עצמך לפני לא הייתי מעכב [בראשית כב, א]. **קח נא.** אין נא אלא לשון בקשה אמר לו בבקשה ממך עמוד לי בזה הנסיון שלא יאמרו הראשונות לא היה בהן ממש. **את בנך.** אמר לו שני בנים יש לי אמר לו את יחידך אמר לו זה יחיד לאמו וזה יחיד לאמו אמר לו אשר אהבת אמר לו שניהם אני אוהב אמר לו את יצחק ולמה לא גילה לו מתחלה שלא לערבבו פתאום ותזוח דעתו עליו ותטרף וכדי לחבב עליו את המצוה וליתן לו שכר על כל דבור ודבור [שם פוק ב']. **הנסה.** לשון תימה הבעבור שניסה דבר אליך תלאה בנסיון אחד שניסך בוראך ובא אליך אתה נלאה ומעתה עצור במילין מי יוכל מלהשיבך. **הנה יסרתם רבים.** שהרגו דברים הוכחתם ויסרתם. **וידים רפות.** ויגורות מפורענות הבא עליה' אתה היית רגיל לחזקם ולומר אל תירא שכך הוא מדת הדין. **יקימון.** רגילות הם מליך להקים את הכושל. **הלא יראתך כסלתך.** עתה סופך מוכיח על תחלתך שיראתך שהיית ירא שמים כסלתך היא מחמת כסילות היא ולא מדעת שלימה וכן תקותך ותום דרכיך הכל כסילות [איוב ד].

[עד כאן שייך לדף פט:]

המתנבא לעקור דבר מן התורה. כגון שתחלתו נביא של אמת ולבסוף נביא השקר שהתנבא לעקור דבר מדברי תורה חייב ודברי הכל בחנק. **לקיום מקצת ולבטל מקצת.** דשאר מצות ר"ש פוטר וה"ה לרבנן. **ובעבודת כוכבים אפי' אמר לך היום עובדה ולמחר בטלה.** דהיינו קיום מקצת ובטול מקצת דעבודת כוכבים חייב דרחמנא אמר להדיחך מן הדרך אפי' מקצת דרך ובעבודת כוכבי' הוא דכתיב וכי קתני חייב כגון לרבנן בסקילה ולר"ש בחנק והכי מתרץ ליה רב חסדא בפ' אלו הן הנחנקין (סנהדרין דף נ) והיום עובדה ולמחר בטלה כאין שבת בשביעית דמי וקרי להו ביטול מקצת וקיום מקצת ש"מ [הוריות ד:]. **זוממי בת כהן.** עיין בזה ליקוטי רש"י לעיל פט.

מסורת הש"ס

א) [הוריות ד:], ב) [שם ד:], ג) [הנהו חמש תיבות ועשיתם לו כאשר זמם לעשות נראה דאינם מן הגירסא אלא עיקר הגי' כדאיתא בפירש"י מה ת"ל לאחיו], ד) [י"ג המומתין], ה) [לעיל נא. ע"ש], ו) [שם:], ז) [ע"ז יח.], ח) שבועות טו:, ט) ע"ז יח., י) חגיגה טו:, כ) [ויעתר לו], ל) [צ"ל למלך], מ) [צ"ל הנבה], נ) הוא דבור בפ"ע רש"ל, ס) מן ד"ה לרשות עד ד"ה מה ת"ל שייך למתני' לעיל פט., ע) כ' ב"ש שאין זה מדברי רש"י.

גליון הש"ס

מתני' **כל ישראל יש להן חלק.** עי' כתובות דף קג ע"ב תוס' ד"ה מזומן: **שם האומר אין תחיית המתים.** עי' סוטה ד"ה ע"א תוד"ה כל: **שם ההוגה את השם.** עי' סוכה דף ה' ע"א תוד"ה יו"ד ה"א. שבועות דף לד ע"א תוס' ד"ה באלף: **גמ' מדה כנגד מדה.** עי' סוטה דף ח' ע"ב:

תורה אור השלם

א) וְהַנָּבִיא הַהוּא אוֹ חֹלֵם הַחֲלוֹם הַהוּא יוּמָת כִּי דִבֶּר סָרָה עַל יְיָ אֱלֹהֵיכֶם הַמּוֹצִיא אֶתְכֶם מֵאֶרֶץ מִצְרַיִם וְהַפֹּדְךָ מִבֵּית עֲבָדִים לְהַדִּיחֲךָ מִן הַדֶּרֶךְ אֲשֶׁר צִוְּךָ יְיָ אֱלֹהֶיךָ לָלֶכֶת בָּהּ וּבִעַרְתָּ הָרָע מִקִּרְבֶּךָ: [דברים יג, ו]

ב) וְנִתַּצְתֶּם אֶת מִזְבְּחֹתָם וְשִׁבַּרְתֶּם אֶת מַצֵּבֹתָם וַאֲשֵׁרֵיהֶם תִּשְׂרְפוּן בָּאֵשׁ וּפְסִילֵי אֱלֹהֵיהֶם תְּגַדֵּעוּן וְאִבַּדְתֶּם אֶת שְׁמָם מִן הַמָּקוֹם הַהוּא: [דברים יב, ג]

ג) וַעֲשִׂיתֶם לוֹ כַּאֲשֶׁר זָמַם לַעֲשׂוֹת לְאָחִיו וּבִעַרְתָּ הָרָע מִקִּרְבֶּךָ: [דברים יט, יט]

ד) וְעַמֵּךְ כֻּלָּם צַדִּיקִים לְעוֹלָם יִירְשׁוּ אָרֶץ נֵצֶר מַטָּעַי מַעֲשֵׂה יָדַי לְהִתְפָּאֵר: [ישעיה ס, כא]

ה) וַיֹּאמֶר אִם שָׁמוֹעַ תִּשְׁמַע לְקוֹל יְיָ אֱלֹהֶיךָ וְהַיָּשָׁר בְּעֵינָיו תַּעֲשֶׂה וְהַאֲזַנְתָּ לְמִצְוֹתָיו וְשָׁמַרְתָּ כָּל חֻקָּיו כָּל הַמַּחֲלָה אֲשֶׁר שַׂמְתִּי בְמִצְרַיִם לֹא אָשִׂים עָלֶיךָ כִּי אֲנִי יְיָ רֹפְאֶךָ: [שמות טו, כו]

ו) וַיִּתְפַּלֵּל אֵלָיו וַיֵּעָתֶר לוֹ וַיִּשְׁמַע תְּחִנָּתוֹ וַיְשִׁיבֵהוּ יְרוּשָׁלַיִם לְמַלְכוּתוֹ וַיֵּדַע מְנַשֶּׁה כִּי יְיָ הוּא הָאֱלֹהִים: [דברי הימים ב' לג, יג]

ז) וַיֹּאמֶר אֱלִישָׁע שִׁמְעוּ דְּבַר יְיָ כֹּה אָמַר יְיָ כָּעֵת מָחָר סְאָה סֹלֶת בְּשֶׁקֶל וְסָאתַיִם שְׂעֹרִים בְּשֶׁקֶל בְּשַׁעַר שֹׁמְרוֹן: [מלכים ב' ז, א]

ח) וַיַּעַן הַשָּׁלִישׁ אֲשֶׁר לַמֶּלֶךְ נִשְׁעָן עַל יָדוֹ אֶת אִישׁ הָאֱלֹהִים וַיֹּאמַר הִנֵּה יְיָ עֹשֶׂה אֲרֻבּוֹת בַּשָּׁמַיִם הֲיִהְיֶה הַדָּבָר הַזֶּה וַיֹּאמֶר הִנְּכָה רֹאֶה בְּעֵינֶיךָ וּמִשָּׁם לֹא תֹאכֵל: [מלכים ב' ז, ב]

prophet and is therefore subject to the dispute between R' Shimon and the Rabbis regarding the form of punishment imposed – stoning or strangulation. How then can the Baraisa state that they are in agreement in this case?

These questions are answered by the proponents of Rav Chisda and Rav Hamnuna, each according to his respective view: אַבַּיֵי סָבַר לָהּ כְּרַב חִסְדָּא – **Abaye holds like Rav Chisda** וּמְתָרֵץ לָהּ כְּרַב חִסְדָּא – **and he explains [the Baraisa] according to Rav Chisda.** רָבָא סָבַר לָהּ כְּרַב הַמְנוּנָא – **Rava holds like Rav Hamnuna** וּמְתָרֵץ לָהּ כְּרַב הַמְנוּנָא – **and he explains [the Baraisa] according to Rav Hamnuna.**

Abaye's approach:

אַבַּיֵי סָבַר לָהּ כְּרַב חִסְדָּא וּמְתָרֵץ לָהּ כְּרַב חִסְדָּא – **Abaye holds like Rav Chisda and he** therefore **explains [the Baraisa] according to Rav Chisda** in the following way: הַמִּתְנַבֵּא לַעֲקוֹר דָּבָר מִן הַתּוֹרָה – ONE WHO PROPHESIES TO ABOLISH SOMETHING FROM THE TORAH other than idolatry, דִּבְרֵי הַכֹּל בְּחֶנֶק – **all agree** that he is put to death **by strangulation.**[19] לְקַיֵּים מִקְצָת וּלְבַטֵּל מִקְצָת – If he prophesies TO PRESERVE PART of a mitzvah AND TO NULLIFY PART of it: רַבִּי שִׁמְעוֹן פּוֹטֵר – R' SHIMON EXEMPTS him from the death penalty וְהוּא הַדִּין לְרַבָּנָן – **and the same** holds true **for the Rabbis.**[20] וּבַעֲבוֹדַת כּוֹכָבִים – HOWEVER, if he prophesies CONCERNING the laws of IDOLATRY, אֲפִילוּ אָמַר הַיּוֹם עִיבְדוּהָ וּלְמָחָר בַּטְּלוּהָ – then EVEN IF HE SAID, "WORSHIP [THIS IDOL] TODAY AND NULLIFY IT TOMORROW!" חַיָּיב – all agree that HE IS LIABLE to the death penalty, although they differ as to the method of execution: מַר כִּדְאִית לֵיהּ – This **master** (the Rabbis) would execute him **as he maintains,** by stoning, וּמַר כִּדְאִית לֵיהּ – **and** this **master** (R' Shimon) would execute him **as he maintains,** by strangulation.[21]

Rava's approach:

רָבָא סָבַר לָהּ כְּרַב הַמְנוּנָא וּמְתָרֵץ לָהּ כְּרַב הַמְנוּנָא – **Rava holds like Rav Hamnuna and he** therefore **explains [the Baraisa] according to Rav Hamnuna,** as follows: הַמִּתְנַבֵּא לַעֲקוֹר דָּבָר מִן הַתּוֹרָה – ONE WHO PROPHESIES TO ABOLISH SOMETHING FROM THE TORAH, בֵּין בַּעֲבוֹדַת כּוֹכָבִים בֵּין בִּשְׁאָר מִצְוֹת – regardless of **whether** it is **in** regard to **idolatry or in** regard to any **of the other mitzvos,** חַיָּיב – all agree that HE IS LIABLE to the death penalty, although they differ as to the method of execution:[22] מַר כִּדְאִית לֵיהּ – This **master** (the Rabbis) would execute him **as he maintains,** by stoning, וּמַר כִּדְאִית לֵיהּ – **and** this **master** (R' Shimon) would execute him **as he maintains,** by strangulation. לְקַיֵּים מִקְצָת וּלְבַטֵּל מִקְצָת בִּשְׁאָר מִצְוֹת – If he prophesies TO PRESERVE PART AND TO NULLIFY PART of one of the **mitzvos other** than idolatry, רַבִּי שִׁמְעוֹן פּוֹטֵר – R' SHIMON EXEMPTS him from death, וְהוּא הַדִּין לְרַבָּנָן – **and the same** holds true **for the Rabbis.**[23] וּבַעֲבוֹדַת כּוֹכָבִים – HOWEVER, if he prophesies CONCERNING the laws of IDOLATRY, אֲפִילוּ אוֹמֵר הַיּוֹם עִיבְדוּהָ וּלְמָחָר בַּטְּלוּהָ – then EVEN IF HE SAYS, "WORSHIP [THIS IDOL] TODAY AND NULLIFY IT TOMORROW!" חַיָּיב – all agree that HE IS LIABLE to the death penalty, although they differ as to the method of execution: מַר כִּדְאִית לֵיהּ – This **master** (the Rabbis) would execute him **as he maintains,** by stoning, וּמַר כִּדְאִית לֵיהּ – **and** this **master** (R' Shimon) would execute him **as he maintains,** by strangulation.

The Gemara cites a related ruling:

אָמַר רַבִּי אַבָּהוּ אָמַר רַבִּי יוֹחָנָן – **R' Abahu said in the name of R' Yochanan:** בַּכֹּל – **In every case,** אִם יֹאמַר לְךָ נָבִיא עֲבוֹר עַל דִּבְרֵי תוֹרָה – **if a prophet should tell you, "Transgress** this **Torah law** temporarily," שְׁמַע לוֹ – **obey him,**[24] חוּץ מֵעֲבוֹדַת כּוֹכָבִים – **with the exception of idolatry;** שֶׁאֲפִילוּ מַעֲמִיד לְךָ חַמָּה בְּאֶמְצַע הָרָקִיעַ – **for** in the case of idolatry, **even if he makes the sun stand still in the middle of the sky** as a sign that his prophecy is true, אַל תִּשְׁמַע לוֹ – **do not obey him.**[25]

The Gemara cites a supporting Baraisa:

תַּנְיָא – **It was taught in a Baraisa:** רַבִּי יוֹסֵי הַגְּלִילִי אוֹמֵר – R' YOSE HAGLILI SAYS: הִגִּיעַ תּוֹרָה לְסוֹף דַּעְתָּהּ שֶׁל עֲבוֹדַת כּוֹכָבִים – THE TORAH UNDERSTOOD WELL THE MINDSET of the prophets OF IDOLATRY, and realized that they would find ways to delude people into accepting idolatry by performing "wonders" through sorcery. לְפִיכָךְ נָתְנָה תּוֹרָה מֶמְשָׁלָה בָּהּ – THEREFORE, THE TORAH GRANTED DOMINION IN THIS, i.e. the Torah spoke of the prophets of idolatry as being able to perform great wonders in support of their cause. This is meant to warn us שֶׁאֲפִילוּ מַעֲמִיד לְךָ חַמָּה בְּאֶמְצַע הָרָקִיעַ – THAT EVEN IF [THE IDOLATROUS PROPHET] MAKES THE SUN STAND STILL IN THE MIDDLE OF THE SKY, אַל תִּשְׁמַע לוֹ – DO NOT OBEY HIM, for his is not the word of God.[26]

NOTES

19. According to Rav Chisda, abolition of any Torah commandment other than idolatry makes one a false prophet [נְבִיא שֶׁקֶר], not a subversive prophet [נְבִיא הַמַּדִּיחַ]. Thus, both R' Shimon and the Rabbis agree that the punishment is strangulation. See note 6.

20. For, as mentioned above (note 7), the Torah states that the prophet should die if he speaks *"a matter,"* not merely "part of a matter."

Now since *all* agree that the prophet is exempt, why did the Baraisa specify that R' Shimon exempts him? The answer is that this indirectly teaches us the opinion of the Rabbis in the first part of the Baraisa.

The Baraisa starts with the unattributed – and therefore unanimous – ruling that someone who prophesies the abolition of an entire mitzvah is subject to the death penalty. The Baraisa continues: If he prophesies merely a partial suspension of the mitzvah, he is exempt. Which death penalty is meant here? Since R' Shimon is mentioned, it must be strangulation [based on the Baraisa above, 89b]. Since the first part of the Baraisa is unanimous, we may conclude that the Rabbis also prescribe strangulation where the prophet entirely abolished a mitzvah other than idolatry (*Rashi* according to *Maharsha*).

21. Thus, the Baraisa's statement that "all agree that he is liable" means only that they all agree that this is a capital offense, but they do not agree as to the method of execution.

22. According to Rav Hamnuna, complete abolition of *any* mitzvah renders one a subversive prophet [נְבִיא הַמַּדִּיחַ]. Thus, while all agree that he is liable to execution, the type of execution is subject to the dispute between R' Shimon and the Rabbis.

23. We may address the question mentioned in note 20 to Rav Hamnuna's approach as well: Since *everyone* agrees that the prophet is exempt, why did the Baraisa specify that R' Shimon says this? The answer here is that the Gemara wished to show us the novelty in this ruling. For not only is the prophet exempt from the harsher penalty of stoning, as the Rabbis might have ruled, he is exempt even from strangulation, as R' Shimon might have ruled (*Rashi*).

24. [God will sometimes command a prophet to suspend a Torah law temporarily, to deal with a momentary crisis or need.] Therefore, if a prophet declares a *temporary* suspension of a law, we must obey him. The prophet, must, however, be an established prophet (*Rashi;* see also *Rambam, Hil. Yesodei HaTorah* 9:3; see also *Yevamos* 90b).

The classic example of this is the story of Elijah on Mt. Carmel (see 89b note 21). The people of his time listened to him when he prophesied the temporary suspension of the prohibition against offering sacrifices outside the Temple (*Rashi*).

25. For God will never decree even the temporary suspension of the laws of idolatry, as we learned above (see also *Rambam, Hil. Yesodei HaTorah* 9:5).

26. The Torah states (*Deuteronomy* 13:2-4): *If there should stand up in your midst a prophet or a dreamer of a dream, and he will produce to you a sign or a wonder, and the sign or the wonder comes about, of which he spoke to you, saying, "Let us follow the gods of others that you did not know and we shall worship them!" – do not hearken to the words of that prophet or to that dreamer of a dream, for Hashem, your God, is testing you to know whether you love Hashem, your God, with all your heart and with all your soul.* Thus, if you see an idolatrous prophet who exhibits

מחלוקת בעוקר הגוף דעבודת כוכבים וקיום מקצת וביטול מקצת דעבודת כוכבים דרחמנא אמר א) מן הדרך אפילו מקצת הדרך אבל עוקר הגוף דשאר מצות דברי הכל בחנק וקיום מקצת וביטול מקצת דבשאר מצות דברי הכל פטור מתיב רב המנונא א) ללכת זו מצות עשה בה זו מצות לא תעשה ואי סלקא דעתך בעבודת כוכבים עשה בעבודת כוכבים היכי משכחת לה תרגמה רב חסדא ב) ונתצתם רב המנונא אמר מחלוקת בעוקר הגוף בין בעבודת כוכבים בין בשאר מצות וקיום מקצת וביטול מקצת דעבודת כוכבים דרחמנא אמר מן הדרך אפילו מקצת הדרך אבל קיום מקצת וביטול מקצת דבשאר מצות דברי הכל פטור ת"ר ל) המתנבא לעקור דבר מן התורה חייב לקיים מקצת ולבטל מקצת ר"ש פוטר ובעבודת כוכבים אפילו אומר היום עיבדוה ולמחר בטלוה דברי הכל חייב אביי סבר לה כרב חסדא ומתרץ לה כרב חסדא רבא סבר לה כרב המנונא ומתרץ לה כרב המנונא אביי סבר לה כרב חסדא ומתרץ לה כרב חסדא המתנבא לעקור דבר מן התורה דברי הכל בחנק לקיים מקצת ולבטל מקצת ר"ש פוטר והוא הדין לרבנן ובעבודת כוכבים אפילו אומר היום עיבדוה ולמחר בטלוה חייב מר כדאית ליה ומר כדאית ליה רבא סבר לה כרב המנונא ומתרץ לה כרב המנונא המתנבא לעקור דבר מן התורה בין בעבודת כוכבים בין בשאר מצות חייב מר כדאית ליה ומר כדאית ליה נ) לקיים מקצת ולבטל מקצת בשאר מצות ר"ש פוטר והוא הדין לרבנן ובעבודת כוכבים אפילו אומר היום עיבדוה ולמחר בטלוה חייב מר כדאית ליה ומר כדאית ליה א"ר אבהו א"ר יוחנן א בכל אם יאמר לך נביא עבור על דברי תורה שמע לו חוץ מעבודת כוכבים שאפילו מעמיד לך חמה באמצע הרקיע אל תשמע לו תניא רבי יוסי הגלילי אומר הגיעה תורה לסוף דעתה של עבודת כוכבים לפיכך נתנה תורה ממשלה בה שאפילו מעמיד לך חמה באמצע הרקיע אל תשמע לו תניא א"ר עקיבא חס ושלום שהקדוש ב"ה מעמיד חמה לעוברי רצונו אלא כגון חנניה בן עזור שמתחלתו נביא אמת ולבסוף נביא שקר: וזוממי בת כהן: מנהני מילי אמר רב אחא בריה דרב איקא דתניא ר' יוסי אומר מה ת"ל ג) ג) ועשיתם לו כאשר זמם לעשות לאחיו לפי שכל ל) המזוממין שבתורה זוממיהן ובועליהן כיוצא בהן בת כהן ס) היא בשריפה ואין בועלה בשריפה זוממין איני יודע אם לו הוקשו אם לה הוקשו כשהוא אומר לעשות לאחיו ע) לאחיו ולא לאחותו:

הדרן עלך אלו הן הנחנקין

כל ישראל ב יש להם חלק לעולם הבא שנאמר ד) ועמך כולם צדיקים לעולם יירשו ארץ נצר מטעי מעשה ידי להתפאר ו) ג ואלו שאין להם חלק לעולם הבא האומר אין תחיית המתים מן התורה ואין תורה מן השמים ואפיקורוס ר"ע אומר אף הקורא בספרים החיצונים פ) והלוחש על המכה ואומר ה) כל המחלה אשר שמתי במצרים לא אשים עליך כי אני ה' רופאך אבא שאול אומר אף ט) ההוגה את השם באותיותיו י) שלשה מלכים וארבעה הדיוטות אין להן חלק לעולם הבא שלשה מלכים ירבעם אחאב ומנשה ר' יהודה אומר מנשה יש לו חלק לעולם הבא שנאמר ו) ויתפלל אליו פ) וישמע תחנתו וישיבהו ירושלים למלכותו אמרו לו למלכותו השיבו ולא לחיי העולם הבא השיבו ארבעה הדיוטות בלעם ודואג ואחיתופל וגחזי: **גמ'** וכל כך למה תנא הוא כפר בתחיית המתים לפיכך לא יהיה לו חלק בתחיית המתים שכל מדותיו של הקב"ה מדה כנגד מדה דאמר ר' שמואל בר נחמני אמר ר' יונתן מניין שכל מדותיו של הקב"ה מדה כנגד מדה שנאמר ז) ויאמר אלישע שמעו דבר ה' [וגו'] כעת מחר סאה סלת בשקל וסאתים שעורים בשקל בשער שומרון וכתיב ח) ויען השליש אשר (ל) המלך) נשען על ידו את איש האלהים ויאמר הנה ה' עושה ארובות בשמים היהיה הדבר הזה ויאמר מ) הנך רואה בעיניך ומשם לא תאכל וכתיב

מחלוקת. דרבנן ורבי שמעון בנביא בעוקר כל הגוף בעבודת כוכבים ואומר נצטויתי ברוח הקודש מפי הגבורה להתנבאות לעקור כל מצות עבודת כוכבים מן התורה או לקיים מקצת ולבטל מקצת בהאי הוא דקאמרי רבנן סקילה משום דבהאי עניינא דכתיבא הדחה בנביא דגמרי סקילה מינייה בע"ז הוא משתעי דכתיב ובא האות והמופת וגו' נלכה ונעבדה היינו עקירת הגוף ובטול מקצת התם נמי כתיב בסיפא יומת כי דבר סרה וגו' להדיחך מן הדרך ואפי' במקצת במשמע ומיהו לא מישתעי קרא אלא בע"ז דדבר למד מעניינו: **אבל עוקר הגוף דשאר מצות דברי הכל בחנק.** דנפקא לן מקרא אחרינא האמור בפרשה אחרינא דלא כתיב בה הדחה אך הנביא אשר יזיד לדבר דבר בשמי (דברים יח) והיינו מה שלא שמע וכתיב ומת הנביא ההוא וכל מיתה האמורה סתם חנק הוא: **פטור.** דהתם דבר כתיב דבר שלם ולא חצי דבר: **ללכת זו מצות עשה.** ברייתא היא בספרי גבי פרשת נביא המדיח דכתב בה הדחה (שם יג) להדיחך מן הדרך אשר צוך ה' אלהיך ללכת בה וגו' ודריש קרא יתירא ללכת זו מצות עשה דמשמע לעשות ולא משמע אזהרה: **בה לא תעשה.** דגמרינן מאשר תטא בה דבלא תעשה מיירי אלמא דשאר מצות נמי הכא גבי הדחה כתיבי דאי לא משתעי קרא אלא בע"ז מאי עשה איכא: **ובין בשאר מצות.** דהאי ללכת בה לא משמע ליה לרב המנונא אונקלוס דרחמנא אמר מן הדרך ואע"ז קאי דאכתי לא איתרבו שאר מצות בהאי עניינא דללכת בה כולה משמע: **ד"ה פטור.** ואפילו מחנק דהתם דבר שלם כתיב ולאו אעוקר דברי תורה האי כי יזיד לדבר דבר קאי דהתם סקילה הוא אלא אדברים בעלמא כגון צדקיה בן כנענה: **היום עובדה.** כלומר היינו קיום מקצת וביטול מקצת: **כרב חסדא.** דאמר בע"ז הוא דפליגי אבל בשאר מצות עוקר הגוף הוא בחנק וביטול מקצת פטור: **ר"ש פוטר והוא הדין לרבנן.** דגבי חנק דבר שלם כתיב ולרב חסדא הא דנקט ר"ש הא קמ"ל דרישא דקתני סתמא חייב ואפילו לרבנן בחנק דרבי שמעון הוא דקא מחייב חנק ולא סקילה דשאר מצות בעניינא הדחה דסקילה לא כתיבי: **מר כדאית ליה כו'.** לרבנן בסקילה לרבי שמעון בחנק ל) והוא הדין לרבנן ולרב המנונא האי דנקט ר' שמעון רבותא הוא כלומר ואפילו מחנק דרבי שמעון פטור וכ"ש מסקילה דמחייבי ליה רבנן בעוקר את הכל: **אם יאמר לך נביא.** המוחזק עבור על דברי תורה הכל לפי תקנת השעה כגון אליהו בהר הכרמל בשחוטי חוץ: **נתנה התורה ממשלה בה.** כלומר אפילו תראה אותו נביא מושל ועושה כרצונו דכתיב (דברים יג) ונתן אליך אות או מופת: **שתחילתו נביא אמת.** כגון חנניה הנביא והאי ונתן אליך אות בעודו נביא אמת יתן לך אות בנבואה אחרת ולבסוף כשיחזור להרשיע יאמר לעבוד עבודת כוכבים וסמוך עלי שהרי מוחזק אני על ידי אות ומופת שנתתי לך כבר: ס) (לרשות הבעל. כגון מסרה האב לשלוחי הבעל ועדיין היא בדרך ולא קרינן בה בית אביה: **לאותה מיתה.** שהיו מחייבין את הנידון: **ובועלה.** כלומר וכל הבועלים נידונין כמיתת הנבעלת חוץ מבועל בת כהן:) **מה ת"ל לאחיו.** לכתוב כאשר זמם לעשות ולישתוק: **אם לו הוקשו.** לבועל שהיו מחייבין אותו חנק: **אם לה.** שמחייבין אותה שריפה: **לאחיו ולא לאחותו.** כל היכא דבעדותן מחייבין איש ואשה ודינן חלוק כי הכא לו הוקשו:

הדרן עלך אלו הן הנחנקין

כל ישראל יש להם חלק לעולם הבא. מעיקרא איירי בארבע מיתות ומפרש ואזיל להו לכולהו והדר מפרש הני דאין להם חלק לעולם הבא: ה"ג **האומר אין תחיית המתים מן התורה.** ע) שכופר במדרשים דדרשינן בגמרא לקמן מניין לתחיית המתים מן התורה ואפי' יהא מודה ומאמין שיחיו המתים אלא דלא רמיזא באורייתא כופר הוא הואיל ועוקר שיש תחיית המתים מן התורה מה לנו ולאמונתו וכי מהיכן הוא יודע שכן הוא הלכך כופר גמור הוא: **אפיקורוס.** מפרש בגמרא: **ספרים החיצונים.** מפרש בגמרא: **גמ'** ויהי

עין משפט נר מצוה

פא א מיי' פ"ט מהלכות יסודי התורה הל"ג והל"ה והיינו לפי שעה וע"ש:

א ב מיי' פ"ג מהלכות תשובה הלכה ה:

ב ג מיי' שם הלכה ו:

ליקוטי רש"י

אחר הדברים האלה. יש מרבותינו אומרים אחר דבריו של שטן שהיה מקטרג ואומר מכל סעודה שעשה אברהם לא הקריב לפניך פר אחד או איל אחד אמר לו כלום עשה אלא בשביל בנו אילו הייתי אומר לו זבח אותו לפני לא היה מעכב ויש אומרים אחר דבריו של ישמעאל שהיה מתפאר על יצחק שמל בן שלש עשרה שנה ולא מיחה אמר לו יצחק באבר אחד אתה מיראני אילו אמר לי הקב"ה זבח עצמך לפני לא הייתי מעכב [בראשית כב, א]. **קח נא.** אין נא אלא לשון בקשה אמר לו בבקשה ממך עמוד לי בזה הנסיון שלא יאמרו הראשונות לא היה בהן ממש. **את בנך.** אמר לו שני בנים יש לי אמר לו את יחידך אמר לו זה יחיד לאמו וזה יחיד לאמו אמר לו אשר אהבת אמר לו שניהם אני אוהב אמר לו את יצחק ולמה לא גילה לו מתחלה שלא לערבבו פתאום ותזוח דעתו עליו ותטרף וכדי לחבב עליו את המצוה וליתן לו שכר על כל דבור ודבור [שם פוק ב']. **הנסה.** לשון תימה הבעבור שניסה דבר אליך תלאה בנסיון אחד שניסך בורא ובא אליך אתה נלאה ומעתה עצור במילין מי יוכל מלהשיבך. **הנה יסרתם רבים.** שהרבו דברים הוכחתם ויסרתם. **וידים רפות.** ויגורות מפורענות הבא עליה' אתה היית רגיל לחזקם ולומר אל תירא שכך הוא מדת הדין. **יקימון.** רגילות הם מליך להקים את הכושל. **הלא יראתך כסלתך.** עתה סופך מוכיח על תחלתך שיראתך שהיית ירא שמים כסלתך היא מחמת כסילות היא ולא מדעת שלימה וכן תקותך ותום דרכיך הכל כסילות [איוב ד].

[עד כאן שייך לדף פט:]

המתנבא לעקור דבר מן התורה. כגון שתחלתו נביא של אמת ולבסוף נביא השקר שהתנבא לעקור דבר מדברי תורה חייב ודברי הכל בחנק. **לקיים מקצת ולבטל מקצת.** דשאר מצות ר"ש פוטר וה"ה לרבנן. **ובעבודת כוכבים אפי' אמר לך היום עובדה ולמחר בטלה.** דהיינו קיום מקצת ובטול מקצת דעבודת כוכבים חייב דרחמנא אמר להדיחך מן הדרך אפי' מקצת דרך ובעבודת כוכבי' הוא דכתיב וכי קתני חייב כגון לרבנן בסקילה ולר"ש בחנק והכי מתרץ ליה רב חסדא בפ' אלו הן הנחנקין (סנהדרין דף צ) והיום עובדה ולמחר בטלה כאין שבת בשביעית דמי וקרי להו ביטול מקצת וקיום מקצת ש"מ [הוריות ד:]. **זוממי בת כהן.** עיין בזה ליקוטי רש"י לעיל פט.

מסורת הש"ס

א) [הוריות ד:], ב) [שם ד:], ג) [הנהו חמש תיבות ועשיתם לו כאשר זמם לעשות נראה דאינם מן הגירסא אלא עיקר הסגי' כדאיתא בפירש"י מה ת"ל לאחיו], ד) [י"ג המזומתין], ה) [לעיל נא. ע"ש], ו) [שם:], ז) [ע"ז יח.], ח) שבועות טו., ט) ע"ז יח., י) חגיגה טו:, כ) [ויעתר לו], ל) [נ"ל למלך], מ) [נ"ל הנבה], נ) הוא דבור בפ"ע רש"ל, ס) מן ד"ה לרשות עד ד"ה מה ת"ל שייך למתני' לעיל פט., ע) כ' ב"ש שאין זה מדברי רש"י.

גליון הש"ס

מתני' כל ישראל יש להן חלק. עי' כתובות דף קג ע"ב תוס' ד"ה מזומן: שם האומר אין תחיית המתים. עי' סוטה ד"ה ע"א תוד"ה כל: שם ההוגה את השם. עי' סוכה דף ה' ע"א תוד"ה יו"ד ה"א. שבועות דף לד ע"א תוס' ד"ה באלף: גמ' מדה כנגד מדה. עי' סוטה דף ח' ע"ב:

תורה אור השלם

א) וְהַנָּבִיא הַהוּא אוֹ חֹלֵם הַחֲלוֹם הַהוּא יוּמָת כִּי דִבֶּר סָרָה עַל יְיָ אֱלֹהֵיכֶם הַמּוֹצִיא אֶתְכֶם מֵאֶרֶץ מִצְרַיִם וְהַפֹּדְךָ מִבֵּית עֲבָדִים לְהַדִּיחֲךָ מִן הַדֶּרֶךְ אֲשֶׁר צִוְּךָ יְיָ אֱלֹהֶיךָ לָלֶכֶת בָּהּ וּבִעַרְתָּ הָרָע מִקִּרְבֶּךָ: [דברים יג, ו]

ב) וְנִתַּצְתֶּם אֶת מִזְבְּחֹתָם וְשִׁבַּרְתֶּם אֶת מַצֵּבֹתָם וַאֲשֵׁרֵיהֶם תִּשְׂרְפוּן בָּאֵשׁ וּפְסִילֵי אֱלֹהֵיהֶם תְּגַדֵּעוּן וְאִבַּדְתֶּם אֶת שְׁמָם מִן הַמָּקוֹם הַהוּא: [דברים יב, ג]

ג) וַעֲשִׂיתֶם לוֹ כַּאֲשֶׁר זָמַם לַעֲשׂוֹת לְאָחִיו וּבִעַרְתָּ הָרָע מִקִּרְבֶּךָ: [דברים יט, יט]

ד) וְעַמֵּךְ כֻּלָּם צַדִּיקִים לְעוֹלָם יִירְשׁוּ אָרֶץ נֵצֶר מַטָּעַי מַעֲשֵׂה יָדַי לְהִתְפָּאֵר: [ישעיה ס, כא]

ה) וַיֹּאמֶר אִם שָׁמוֹעַ תִּשְׁמַע לְקוֹל יְיָ אֱלֹהֶיךָ וְהַיָּשָׁר בְּעֵינָיו תַּעֲשֶׂה וְהַאֲזַנְתָּ לְמִצְוֹתָיו וְשָׁמַרְתָּ כָּל חֻקָּיו כָּל הַמַּחֲלָה אֲשֶׁר שַׂמְתִּי בְמִצְרַיִם לֹא אָשִׂים עָלֶיךָ כִּי אֲנִי יְיָ רֹפְאֶךָ: [שמות טו, כו]

ו) וַיִּתְפַּלֵּל אֵלָיו וַיֵּעָתֶר לוֹ וַיִּשְׁמַע תְּחִנָּתוֹ וַיְשִׁיבֵהוּ יְרוּשָׁלַיִם לְמַלְכוּתוֹ וַיֵּדַע מְנַשֶּׁה כִּי יְיָ הוּא הָאֱלֹהִים: [דברי הימים ב' לג, יג]

ז) וַיֹּאמֶר אֱלִישָׁע שִׁמְעוּ דְּבַר יְיָ כֹּה אָמַר יְיָ כָּעֵת מָחָר סְאָה סֹלֶת בְּשֶׁקֶל וְסָאתַיִם שְׂעֹרִים בְּשֶׁקֶל בְּשַׁעַר שֹׁמְרוֹן: [מלכים ב' ז, א]

ח) וַיַּעַן הַשָּׁלִישׁ אֲשֶׁר לַמֶּלֶךְ נִשְׁעָן עַל יָדוֹ אֶת אִישׁ הָאֱלֹהִים וַיֹּאמַר הִנֵּה יְיָ עֹשֶׂה אֲרֻבּוֹת בַּשָּׁמַיִם הֲיִהְיֶה הַדָּבָר הַזֶּה וַיֹּאמֶר הִנְּכָה רֹאֶה בְּעֵינֶיךָ וּמִשָּׁם לֹא תֹאכֵל: [מלכים ב' ז, ב]

The Gemara cites a dissenting view:

תַּנְיָא – **It was taught in a Baraisa:** אָמַר רַבִּי עֲקִיבָא – **R' AKIVA SAID:** חַס וְשָׁלוֹם שֶׁהַקָּדוֹשׁ בָּרוּךְ הוּא מַעֲמִיד חַמָּה לְעוֹבְרֵי רְצוֹנוֹ – **HEAVEN FORBID THAT THE HOLY ONE, BLESSED IS HE, WOULD MAKE THE SUN STAND STILL FOR THOSE WHO WOULD TRANSGRESS HIS WILL!** אֶלָּא כְּגוֹן חֲנַנְיָה בֶּן עַזּוּר – **RATHER,** when the Torah speaks of a subversive prophet who has performed a miraculous sign, the reference is to someone **SUCH AS CHANANIAH BEN AZUR,** שֶׁמִּתְּחִלָּתוֹ נְבִיא אֱמֶת – **WHO WAS ORIGINALLY A TRUE PROPHET,** and who performed a sign at the time of his verification as a prophet, וּלְבַסּוֹף נְבִיא שֶׁקֶר – **BUT** who **IN THE END** became **A FALSE PROPHET** and now prophesies for idolatry.[27]

The Gemara now cites the final section of our Mishnah:

וְזוֹמְמֵי בַת כֹּהֵן – **THE *ZOMEMIM* WITNESSES OF THE DAUGHTER OF A KOHEN,** as well as the one who cohabits with her adulterously, are subject to strangulation.

The Gemara gives the sources for these rulings:

מְנָהֲנֵי מִילֵּי – **From where do we know these laws?** אָמַר רַב אַחָא בְּרֵיהּ דְּרַב אִיקָא – **Rav Acha the son of Rav Ika said:** דְּתַנְיָא – **For a Baraisa has taught:** רַבִּי יוֹסֵי אוֹמֵר – **R' YOSE SAYS:** מַה תַּלְמוּד לוֹמַר ,,וַעֲשִׂיתֶם לוֹ כַּאֲשֶׁר זָמַם לַעֲשׂוֹת לְאָחִיו" – **WHAT DOES SCRIPTURE TEACH** when it states: ***YOU SHALL DO TO HIM AS HE PLANNED TO DO TO HIS BROTHER?***[28] Why was it necessary to mention the word "brother"?[29] לְפִי שֶׁכָּל (המזוממין) [הַמּוּמָתִין] שֶׁבַּתּוֹרָה – **BECAUSE** in the case of **ALL** women **WHO ARE CONDEMNED TO DEATH**[30] **BY THE TORAH** for sexual offenses, זוֹמְמֵיהֶן וּבוֹעֲלֵיהֶן כַּיּוֹצֵא בָּהֶן – we find that **THEIR *ZOMEMIM* WITNESSES AND THOSE WHO COHABIT WITH THEM,** i.e. the men who were their partners in the transgression, **ARE** treated **THE SAME AS THEM,** i.e. they are executed by the same method as the offender herself. בַּת כֹּהֵן – In the case of **THE DAUGHTER OF A KOHEN,** however, הִיא בִּשְׂרֵיפָה וְאֵין בּוֹעֲלָהּ בִּשְׂרֵיפָה – **SHE IS** put to death **BY BURNING, WHEREAS THE MAN WHO COHABITED WITH HER IS NOT** put to death **BY BURNING,** but rather by strangulation.[31]

Having established that the Kohen's daughter and her partner are executed by different methods, the Baraisa continues:

זוֹמְמִין – Now, as regards ***ZOMEMIM* WITNESSES** who testify falsely that a Kohen's daughter committed adultery, אֵינִי יוֹדֵעַ אִם לוֹ הוּקְשׁוּ – **I WOULD NOT KNOW WHETHER THEY ARE** to be **COMPARED TO HIM** (the man who allegedly cohabited with her), in which case the witnesses would be executed by strangulation, אִם לָהּ הוּקְשׁוּ – **OR WHETHER THEY ARE** to be **COMPARED TO HER** (the daughter of the Kohen), in which case they would be executed by burning.[32] כְּשֶׁהוּא אוֹמֵר ,,לַעֲשׂוֹת לְאָחִיו" – **HOWEVER, WHEN [SCRIPTURE] STATES:** . . . *As he planned* ***TO DO TO HIS BROTHER,*** the question is resolved; ,,לְאָחִיו" וְלֹא לַאֲחוֹתוֹ – the implication is that he is punished with the same consequences he attempted **TO** inflict on ***HIS BROTHER*** (i.e. the man in the case), **AND NOT** those he intended **TO** inflict on **HIS SISTER** (the Kohen's daughter). We thus execute the *zomemim* with the method of execution that would have applied to their *male* victim.[33]

הדרן עלך אלו הן הנחנקין

WE SHALL RETURN TO YOU, EILU HEIN HANECHNAKIN

NOTES

a mastery over nature, rest assured that his idols are not real even though his miracles may appear to be (*Rashi*; see *Aruch LaNer*, *Malbim* to *Deuteronomy* 13:2).

[The previous explanation follows the reading found in the standard editions of *Rashi*. However, *Dikdukei Soferim* notes that in all the old manuscripts of *Rashi's* commentary, *Rashi* had the reading: לְפִיכָךְ נָתְנָה לְךָ הַתּוֹרָה מֶמְשָׁלָה בָּהּ, *therefore the Torah granted* ***you*** *dominion over it.* That is, the Torah granted us dominion over the idolatrous prophets by warning us that despite their "wonders," they speak falsely and not on behalf of God (see also *Ben Yehoyada*).

27. See above, 89a note 48. R' Akiva rejects R' Yose HaGlili's proof from the Torah that a false prophet might attain seemingly miraculous powers. Rather, R' Akiva contends, the verse speaks of a man who was originally a true prophet and who later became a subversive prophet. When he *first* spoke in the name of God, God enabled him to perform a sign to prove that he was a true prophet — which he indeed was at the time. Afterwards, the prophet turned wicked and called on people to serve idols, saying, "You may rely on my prophecy (to perform idolatry) since I am long established as a prophet through the sign I once gave you" (*Rashi*; see *Rabbeinu Chananel*).

28. *Deuteronomy* 19:19. This is the verse that teaches that witnesses proven to be false through the process of *hazamah* are punished with the same consequences they intended to impose upon their victim.

29. The Torah could merely have stated: "You shall do to him as he planned to do" (*Rashi*).

30. The translation follows the reading of the Baraisa given in the margin by *Mesoras HaShas,* which indeed is the version that appears in *Sifrei* and *Yalkut.* This version replaces the word הַמְזוּמָּמִין found in the Vilna text with the word הַמּוּמָתִין, *those condemned to death.*

31. The source for this is the verse (*Leviticus* 21:9) that states: *And the daughter of a Kohen who profanes herself through adultery,* ***she*** *profanes her father; she shall be burned in fire.* The Gemara (above, 51a) derives from here that only *she* is put to death by burning, while her partner in adultery is put to death by the same method as any other adulterer — strangulation.

32. By testifying that the Kohen's daughter committed adultery, these false witnesses are conspiring to kill both the woman and the man who allegedly cohabited with her. The woman and man, however, would have been executed by different methods — she by burning and he by strangulation. The question thus arises as to which of these methods should be chosen as the punishment for the *zomemim* witnesses.

33. I.e. by using the masculine term "brother," the verse teaches that whenever the testimony of *zomemim* witnesses would result in different penalties for a man and a woman, they are to be punished as the man would have been punished (*Rashi*).

[The simplest application of the Baraisa's law is to a case where the testimony of the *zomemim* would actually have inflicted a punishment on both the man and the woman. *Tosafos* (above, 51b ד״ה לאחיו; *Makkos* 2a ד״ה זוממי בת כהן), however, state that the law also applies even when the man would have suffered no punishment at all [for example, where the witnesses testified that they observed the Kohen's daughter commit adultery, but they could not identify the man]. In such a case, *Tosafos* contend, the *zomemim* are punished with strangulation — the punishment that would have been suffered by the man — even though they did not actually conspire to inflict this fate upon him.

[Whether or not *Rashi* subscribes to *Tosafos'* interpretation is the subject of some discussion. *Ritva* to *Makkos* 2a states that *Rashi* disputes *Tosafos.* See, however, *Tos. Yom Tov* and *Margaliyos HaYam;* see also *Rambam, Hil. Eidus* 20:10; *Rashash*; *Margaliyos HaYam* to 84b §4, and *Aruch LaNer.*]

מחלוקת בעוקר הגוף דעבודת כוכבים וקיום מקצת וביטול מקצת דעבודת כוכבים דרחמנא אמר [א] מן הדרך אפילו מקצת הדרך אבל עוקר הגוף דשאר מצות דברי הכל בחנק וקיום מקצת וביטול מקצת דבשאר מצות דברי הכל פטור מתיב רב המנונא [א] ללכת זו מצות עשה בה זו מצות לא תעשה ואי סלקא דעתך בעבודת כוכבים עשה בעבודת כוכבים היכי משכחת לה תרגמה רב חסדא [ב] ונתצתם רב המנונא אמר מחלוקת בעוקר הגוף בין בעבודת כוכבים בין בשאר מצות וקיום מקצת וביטול מקצת דעבודת כוכבים דרחמנא אמר מן הדרך אפילו מקצת הדרך אבל קיום מקצת וביטול מקצת דבשאר מצות דברי הכל פטור ת"ר [א] המתנבא לעקור דבר מן התורה חייב לקיים מקצת ולבטל מקצת ר"ש פוטר ובעבודת כוכבים אפילו אומר היום עיבדוה ולמחר בטלוה דברי הכל חייב אביי סבר לה כרב חסדא ומתרץ לה כרב חסדא רבא סבר לה כרב המנונא ומתרץ לה כרב המנונא אביי סבר לה כרב חסדא ומתרץ לה כרב חסדא המתנבא לעקור דבר מן התורה דברי הכל בחנק לקיים מקצת ולבטל מקצת ר"ש פוטר והוא הדין לרבנן ובעבודת כוכבים אפילו אמר היום עיבדוה ולמחר בטלוה חייב מר כדאית ליה ומר כדאית ליה רבא סבר לה כרב המנונא ומתרץ לה כרב המנונא המתנבא לעקור דבר מן התורה בין בעבודת כוכבים בין בשאר מצות חייב מר כדאית ליה ומר כדאית ליה [ג] לקיים מקצת ולבטל מקצת בשאר מצות ר"ש פוטר והוא הדין לרבנן ובעבודת כוכבים אפילו אומר היום עיבדוה ולמחר בטלוה חייב מר כדאית ליה ומר כדאית ליה א"ר אבהו א"ר יוחנן [ב] בכל אם יאמר לך נביא עבור על דברי תורה שמע לו חוץ מעבודת כוכבים שאפילו מעמיד לך חמה באמצע הרקיע אל תשמע לו תניא רבי יוסי הגלילי אומר הגיעה תורה לסוף דעתה של עבודת כוכבים לפיכך נתנה תורה ממשלה בה שאפילו מעמיד לך חמה באמצע הרקיע אל תשמע לו תניא א"ר עקיבא חס ושלום שהקדוש ב"ה מעמיד חמה לעוברי רצונו אלא כגון חנניה בן עזור שמתחלתו נביא אמת ולבסוף נביא שקר: וזוממי בת כהן: מנהני מילי אמר רב אחא בריה דרב איקא דתניא ר' יוסי אומר מה ת"ל [ג] ועשיתם לו כאשר זמם לעשות לאחיו לפי שכל [ד] המזוממין שבתורה זוממיהן ובועליהן כיוצא בהן בת כהן [ה] היא בשריפה ואין בועלה בשריפה זוממין איני יודע אם לו הוקשו אם לה הוקשו כשהוא אומר לעשות לאחיו [ו] לאחיו ולא לאחותו:

הדרן עלך אלו הן הנחנקין

כל ישראל [ב] יש להם חלק לעולם הבא שנאמר [ד] ועמך כולם צדיקים לעולם יירשו ארץ נצר מטעי מעשה ידי להתפאר [ו] ואלו שאין להם חלק לעולם הבא האומר אין תחיית המתים מן התורה ואין תורה מן השמים ואפיקורוס ר"ע אומר אף הקורא בספרים החיצונים [ח] והלוחש על המכה ואומר [ה] כל המחלה אשר שמתי במצרים לא אשים עליך כי אני ה' רופאך אבא שאול אומר אף [ט] ההוגה את השם באותיותיו [י] שלשה מלכים וארבעה הדיוטות אין להן חלק לעולם הבא שלשה מלכים ירבעם אחאב ומנשה ר' יהודה אומר מנשה יש לו חלק לעולם הבא שנאמר [ו] ויתפלל אליו [כ] וישמע תחנתו וישיבהו ירושלים למלכותו אמרו לו למלכותו השיבו ולא לחיי העולם הבא השיבו ארבעה הדיוטות בלעם ודואג ואחיתופל וגחזי: **גמ'** וכל כך למה תנא הוא כפר בתחיית המתים לפיכך לא יהיה לו חלק בתחיית המתים שכל מדותיו של הקב"ה מדה כנגד מדה דאמר ר' שמואל בר נחמני אמר ר' יונתן מניין שכל מדותיו של הקב"ה מדה כנגד מדה שנאמר [ז] ויאמר אלישע שמעו דבר ה' [וגו'] כעת מחר סאה סלת בשקל וסאתים שעורים בשקל בשער שומרון וכתיב [ח] ויען השליש אשר ([ל] המלך) נשען על ידו את איש האלהים ויאמר הנה ה' עושה ארובות בשמים היהיה הדבר הזה ויאמר [מ] הנך רואה בעיניך ומשם לא תאכל וכתיב

רש"י

מחלוקת. דרבנן ורבי שמעון בנביא בעוקר כל הגוף בעבודת כוכבים ואומר נלטויתי ברוח הקודש מפי הגבורה להתנבאות לעקור כל מלות עבודת כוכבים מן התורה או לקיים מקלת ולבטל מקלת בהאי הוא דקאמרי רבנן סקילה משום דבהאי עניינא דכתיבא הדחה בנביא דגמרי סקילה מיניה בע"ז הוא משתעי דכתיב ובא האות והמופת וגו' נלכה ונעבדה היינו עקירת הגוף ובטול מקלת התם נמי כתיב בסיפא יומת כי דבר סרה וגו' להדיחך מן הדרך ואפי' במקלת במשמע ומיהו לא מישתעי קרא אלא בע"ז דדבר למד מעניינו: **אבל עוקר הגוף דשאר מצות דברי הכל בחנק.** דנפקא לן מקרא אחרינא האמור בפרשה אחרינא דלא כתיב בה הדחה אך הנביא אשר יזיד לדבר דבר בשמי (דברים יח) והיינו מה שלא שמע וכתיב ומת הנביא ההוא וכל מיתה האמורה סתם חנק הוא: **פטור.** דהתם דבר כתיב דבר שלם ולא חצי דבר: **ללכת זו מצות עשה.** ברייתא היא בספרי גבי פרשת נביא המדיח דכתב בה הדחה (שם יג) להדיחך מן הדרך אשר צוך ה' אלהיך ללכת בה וגו' ודריש קרא יתירא ללכת זו מלות עשה דמשמע לעשות ולא משמע אזהרה: **בה לא תעשה.** דגמרינן מאשר חטא בה דבלא תעשה מיירי אלמא דשאר מלות נמי הכא גבי הדחה כתיבי דאי לא משתעי קרא אלא בע"ז מאי עשה איכא: **ובין בשאר מצות.** דהאי ללכת בה לא משמע ליה לרב המנונא אונקלתס דרחמנא אמר מן הדרך ואע"ז קאי דאכתי לא איתרבו שאר מלות בהאי עניינא דללכת בה כולה משמע: **ד"ה פטור.** ואפילו מחנק דהתם דבר שלם כתיב ולאו אעוקר דברי תורה האי כי יזיד לדבר דבר קאי דהתם סקילה הוא אלא אדברים בעלמא כגון לדקיה בן כנענה: **היום עובדה.** כלומר היינו קיום מקלת וביטול מקלת: **כרב חסדא.** דאמר בע"ז הוא דפליגי אבל בשאר מלות עוקר הגוף הוא בחנק וביטול מקלת פטור: **ר"ש פוטר והוא הדין לרבנן.** דגבי חנק דבר שלם כתיב ולרב חסדא הא דנקט ר"ש הא קמ"ל דרישא דקתני סתמא חייב ואפילו לרבנן בחנק דרבי שמעון הוא דקא מחייב חנק ולא סקילה דשאר מלות בעניינא הדחה דסקילה לא כתיבי: **מר כדאית ליה כו'.** לרבנן בסקילה לרבי שמעון בחנק [י] והוא הדין לרבנן ולרב המנונא האי דנקט ר' שמעון רבותא הוא כלומר ואפילו מחנק דרבי שמעון פטור וכ"ש מסקילה דמחייבי ליה רבנן בעוקר את הכל: **אם יאמר לך נביא.** המוחזק עבור על דברי תורה הכל לפי תקנת השעה כגון אליהו בהר הכרמל בשחוטי חוץ: **נתנה התורה ממשלה בה.** כלומר אפילו תראה אותו נביא מושל ועושה כרלונו דכתיב (דברים יג) ונתן אליך אות או מופת: **שתחילתו נביא אמת.** כגון חנניה הנביא והאי ונתן אליך אות בעודו נביא אמת יתן לך אות בנבואה אחרת ולבסוף כשיחזור להרשיע יאמר לעבוד עבודת כוכבים וסמוך עלי שהרי מוחזק אני על ידי אות ומופת שנתתי לך כבר: [ס] (**לרשות הבעל.** כגון מסרה האב לשלוחי הבעל ועדיין היא בדרך ולא קרינן בה בית אביה: **לאותה מיתה.** שהיו מחייבין את הנידון: **ובועלה.** כלומר וכל הבועלים נידונין כמיתת הנבעלת חוץ מבועל בת כהן:) **מה ת"ל לאחיו.** לכתוב כאשר זמם לעשות ולישתוק: **אם לו הוקשו.** לבועל שהיו מחייבין אותו חנק: **אם לה.** שמחייבין אותה שריפה: **לאחיו ולא לאחותו.** כל היכא דבעדותן מחייבין איש ואשה ודינן חלוק כי הכא לו הוקשו:

כל ישראל יש להם חלק לעולם הבא. מעיקרא איירי בארבע מיתות ומפרש ואזיל להו לכולהו והדר מפרש הני דאין להם חלק לעולם הבא: ה"ג **האומר אין תחיית המתים מן התורה.** [ע] שכופר במדרשים דדרשינן בגמרא לקמן מניין לתחיית המתים מן התורה ואפי' יהא מודה ומאמין שיחיו המתים אלא דלא רמיזא באורייתא כופר הוא הואיל ועוקר שיש תחיית המתים מן התורה מה לנו ולאמונתו וכי מהיכן הוא יודע שכן הוא הלכך כופר גמור הוא: **אפיקורוס.** מפרש בגמרא: **ספרים החיצונים.** מפרש בגמרא: **גמ'** ויהי

עין משפט נר מצוה

פא א מיי' פ"ח מהלכות יסודי התורה הל"ג והל"ה והיינו לפי שעה וע"ש:

א ב מיי' פ"ג מהלכות תשובה הלכה ה:

ב ג מיי' שם הלכה ו:

ליקוטי רש"י

אחר הדברים האלה. יש מרבותינו אומרים אחר דבריו של שטן שהיה מקטרג ואומר מכל סעודה שעשה אברהם לא הקריב לפניך פר אחד או איל אחד אמר לו כלום עשה אלא בשביל בנו אילו הייתי אומר לו זבח אותו לפני לא היה מעכב ויש אומרים אחר דבריו של ישמעאל שהיה מתפאר על יצחק שמל בן שלש עשרה שנה ולא מיחה אמר לו יצחק באבר אחד אתה מיראני אילו אמר לי הקב"ה זבח עצמך לפני לא הייתי מעכב [בראשית כב, א]. **קח נא.** אין נא אלא לשון בקשה אמר לו בבקשה ממך עמוד לי בזה הנסיון שלא יאמרו הראשונות לא היה בהן ממש. **את בנך.** אמר לו שני בנים יש לי אמר לו את יחידך אמר לו זה יחיד לאמו וזה יחיד לאמו אמר לו אשר אהבת אמר לו שניהם אני אוהב אמר לו את יצחק ולמה לא גילה לו מתחלה שלא לערבבו פתאום ותזוח דעתו עליו ותטרף וכדי לחבב עליו את המצוה וליתן לו שכר על כל דבור ודבור [שם פוק ב']. **הנסה.** לשון תימה הבעבור שניסה דבר אליך תלאה בנסיון אחד שניסך בוראך ובא אליך אתה נלאה ומעתה עצור במילין מי יוכל מלהשיבך. **הנה יסרתם רבים.** שהרבו דברים הוכחתם ויסרתם. **וידים רפות.** ויגורות מפורענות הבא עליה' אתה היית רגיל לחזקם ולומר אל תירא שכך הוא מדת הדין. **יקימון.** רגילות הם מליך להקים את הכושל. **הלא יראתך כסלתך.** עתה סופך מוכיח על תחלתך שיראתך שהיית ירא שמים כסלתך היא מחמת כסילות היא ולא מדעת שלימה וכן תקותך ותום דרכיך הכל כסילות [איוב ד].

[עד כאן שייך לדף פט:]

המתנבא לעקור דבר מן התורה. כגון שתחלתו נביא של אמת ולבסוף נביא השקר שהתנבא לעקור דבר מדברי תורה חייב ודברי הכל בחנק. **לקיום מקצת ולבטל מקצת.** דשאר מלות ר"ש פוטר וה"ה לרבנן. **ובעבודת כוכבים אפי' אמר לך היום עובדה ולמחר בטלה.** דהיינו קיום מקלת ובטול מקלת דעבודת כוכבים חייב דרחמנא אמר להדיחך מן הדרך אפי' מקלת דרך ובעבודת כוכבי' הוא דכתיב וכי קתני חייב כגון לרבנן בסקילה ולר"ש בחנק והכי מתרץ ליה רב חסדא בפ' אלו הן הנחנקין (סנהדרין דף נ) והיום עובדה ולמחר בטלה כאין שבת בשביעית דמי וקרי להו ביטול מקלת וקיום מקלת ש"מ [הוריות ד:]. **זוממי בת כהן.** עיין בזה ליקוטי רש"י לעיל פט.

מסורת הש"ס

א) [הוריות ד:], ב) [שם ד:], ג) [הנהו תיבות ועשיתם לו כאשר זמם לעשות נראה דאינם מן הגירסא אלא עיקר הגי' כדאיתא בפירש"י מה ת"ל לאחיו], ד) [י"ג המוזמתין], ה) [לעיל נה. ע"ש], ו) [שם:], ז) [ע"ז יח.], ח) שבועות טו:, ט) ע"ז יח., י) חגיגה טו:, כ) [ויעתר לו], ל) [נ"ל למלך], מ) [נ"ל הנכה], נ) הוא דבור בפ"ע רש"ל, ס) מן ד"ה לרשות עד ד"ה מה ת"ל שייך למתני' לעיל פט., ע) כ' ב"ש שאין זה מדברי רש"י.

גליון הש"ס

מתני' כל ישראל יש להן חלק. עי' כתובות דף קג ע"ב תוס' ד"ה מזומן: שם האומר אין תחיית המתים. עי' סוטה ד"ה ע"א תוד"ה כל: שם ההוגה את השם. עי' סוכה דף ה' ע"א תוד"ה יו"ד ה"א. שבועות דף לד ע"א תוס' ד"ה באלף: גמ' מדה כנגד מדה. עי' סוטה דף ח' ע"ב:

תורה אור השלם

א) וְהַנָּבִיא הַהוּא אוֹ חֹלֵם הַחֲלוֹם הַהוּא יוּמָת כִּי דִבֶּר סָרָה עַל יְיָ אֱלֹהֵיכֶם הַמּוֹצִיא אֶתְכֶם מֵאֶרֶץ מִצְרַיִם וְהַפֹּדְךָ מִבֵּית עֲבָדִים לְהַדִּיחֲךָ מִן הַדֶּרֶךְ אֲשֶׁר צִוְּךָ יְיָ אֱלֹהֶיךָ לָלֶכֶת בָּהּ וּבִעַרְתָּ הָרָע מִקִּרְבֶּךָ: [דברים יג, ו]

ב) וְנִתַּצְתֶּם אֶת מִזְבְּחֹתָם וְשִׁבַּרְתֶּם אֶת מַצֵּבֹתָם וַאֲשֵׁרֵיהֶם תִּשְׂרְפוּן בָּאֵשׁ וּפְסִילֵי אֱלֹהֵיהֶם תְּגַדֵּעוּן וְאִבַּדְתֶּם אֶת שְׁמָם מִן הַמָּקוֹם הַהוּא: [דברים יב, ג]

ג) וַעֲשִׂיתֶם לוֹ כַּאֲשֶׁר זָמַם לַעֲשׂוֹת לְאָחִיו וּבִעַרְתָּ הָרָע מִקִּרְבֶּךָ: [דברים יט, יט]

ד) וְעַמֵּךְ כֻּלָּם צַדִּיקִים לְעוֹלָם יִירְשׁוּ אָרֶץ נֵצֶר מַטָּעַי מַעֲשֵׂה יָדַי לְהִתְפָּאֵר: [ישעיה ס, כא]

ה) וַיֹּאמֶר אִם שָׁמוֹעַ תִּשְׁמַע לְקוֹל יְיָ אֱלֹהֶיךָ וְהַיָּשָׁר בְּעֵינָיו תַּעֲשֶׂה וְהַאֲזַנְתָּ לְמִצְוֹתָיו וְשָׁמַרְתָּ כָּל חֻקָּיו כָּל הַמַּחֲלָה אֲשֶׁר שַׂמְתִּי בְמִצְרַיִם לֹא אָשִׂים עָלֶיךָ כִּי אֲנִי יְיָ רֹפְאֶךָ: [שמות טו, כו]

ו) וַיִּתְפַּלֵּל אֵלָיו וַיֵּעָתֶר לוֹ וַיִּשְׁמַע תְּחִנָּתוֹ וַיְשִׁיבֵהוּ יְרוּשָׁלַיִם לְמַלְכוּתוֹ וַיֵּדַע מְנַשֶּׁה כִּי יְיָ הוּא הָאֱלֹהִים: [דברי הימים ב' לג, יג]

ז) וַיֹּאמֶר אֱלִישָׁע שִׁמְעוּ דְּבַר יְיָ כֹּה אָמַר יְיָ כָּעֵת מָחָר סְאָה סֹלֶת בְּשֶׁקֶל וְסָאתַיִם שְׂעֹרִים בְּשֶׁקֶל בְּשַׁעַר שֹׁמְרוֹן: [מלכים ב' ז, א]

ח) וַיַּעַן הַשָּׁלִישׁ אֲשֶׁר לַמֶּלֶךְ נִשְׁעָן עַל יָדוֹ אֶת אִישׁ הָאֱלֹהִים וַיֹּאמַר הִנֵּה יְיָ עֹשֶׂה אֲרֻבּוֹת בַּשָּׁמַיִם הֲיִהְיֶה הַדָּבָר הַזֶּה וַיֹּאמֶר הִנְּכָה רֹאֶה בְּעֵינֶיךָ וּמִשָּׁם לֹא תֹאכֵל: [מלכים ב' ז, ב]

Chapter Eleven

Introduction

In our editions of Talmud Bavli, this chapter is the eleventh and final chapter of this tractate. However, in Talmud Yerushalmi and in most editions of Mishnayos, it is the tenth and next to last chapter.[1]

Since the preceding chapters of this tractate discuss capital offenses, the current chapter follows to indicate that even those who commit such grievous sins have a share in the World to Come after repenting and receiving their deserved punishment [see Gemara above, 47a-b]. For all of Israel has a share in the World to Come, except those who have forfeited their shares, as enumerated in the Mishnahs of this chapter (*Rambam,* commentary to Mishnah 3 of this chapter; *Maharsha*).[2]

This chapter focuses almost exclusively on Aggadic material and deals extensively with the Future Era. Many different terms are found in the Talmud pertaining to the Future Era or parts thereof. We find reference to: **יְמוֹת הַמָּשִׁיחַ**, *the Days of the Messiah,* or *the Messianic Era*; **לֶעָתִיד לָבֹא**, *in the Future to come*; **עוֹלָם הַבָּא**, *The World to Come*; **תְּחִיַּית הַמֵּתִים**, *The Resurrection of the Dead*; **גַּן עֵדֶן**, *the Garden of Eden,* or *Paradise,* and its counterpart **גֵּיהִנֹּם**, *Gehinnom,* or *Hell.* Sometimes, these terms are used in a general or loose sense; sometimes they refer to very specific epochs in the Future Era; at times, they overlap or even refer to identical things. Moreover, there are different views concerning some of the definitions, as well as the sequence in which these periods will occur and the length of their duration. This introduction will briefly outline some broad definitions and main opinions in these matters, which are treated more fully in the appendix at the end of this volume.

⊲§ The Messianic Era: There is universal agreement regarding the meaning of the Messiah and the Messianic Era. A scion of the Davidic dynasty will gather the Jewish exiles from the lands of their dispersal and return them to Eretz Yisrael, where he will rebuild the Holy Temple and rule over the Jews as their king. The world will thenceforth forever be at peace, show obeisance to the Jewish king and seek his counsel, and be filled with the knowledge of God like the waters that cover the sea (see at great length *Rambam* in *Hil. Melachim* chs. 11-12, based on *Deuteronomy* 30:3-10, *Isaiah* 11:9, *Zephaniah* 3:9 and many other verses; *Hil. Teshuvah* 9:2; and in *Commentary to the Mishnah,* Introduction to this chapter). There is a dispute in the Gemara whether the Messianic Era will usher in a time of supernatural existence or whether the current natural order will prevail, albeit in an especially blessed and idyllic fashion (see Gemara 91b).

NOTES

1. This latter ordering is the one followed by *Rambam* (see *Tos. Yom Tov*) and *Rashi* to *Makkos* 2a (ד״ה התם קאי). *Yad Ramah* (beginning of this chapter) insists that this latter ordering is indeed the one found in older, accurate and authoritative editions of Talmud Bavli as well. *Yad Ramah* supports this ordering by pointing to the appearance of the laws of *ir hanidachas* [the subverted city] in this chapter (111b-113a). This is accounted for if this chapter immediately follows the ninth, which mentioned "the inhabitants of the *ir hanidachas* [subverted city]" among those sinners put to death by the sword (Mishnah 76b). But if the chapter concerning those executed by strangulation (*HaNechnakin*) comes first, then it would be difficult to explain why the Tanna neglected to conclude his discussion of those executed by the sword before going on to a discussion of those executed by strangulation. Rather, we must say that chapter *Cheilek* immediately follows chapter nine. And the chapter opens with a list of those who have no share in the World to Come, because the Mishnah wishes to conclude its discussion of sinners who are punished by Heaven rather than by man (begun at the end of the Mishnah on 81b). [See also *Tos. Yom Tov.*]

Meiri (who has this chapter as the eleventh and final chapter) answers *Yad Ramah's* difficulty by explaining that the Mishnah wished to conclude its discussion of all who are executed as *individuals,* and leave the details of sinful *communities* for the end of the tractate.

Rashi's first comments to this chapter would suggest that he has *Cheilek* as the *final* chapter of the tractate (see version of *Rashi* cited by *Maharshal*), but *Tos. Yom Tov* considers the evidence inconclusive (see there).

[As regards the commentary printed as *Rashi* to this chapter, *Dikdukei Soferim* (to 92b §50) finds that its wording in many places suggests an authorship by one of *Rashi's* disciples rather than by *Rashi* himself. But he yields to the evidence of *Rashi's* own authorship provided by *Yad Ramah,* who throughout this chapter cites in the name of *Rashi* large portions that are indeed found in our commentary.]

2. See preceding note for another explanation of the sequence. From *Rashi* (90a ד״ה כל ישראל) it would seem that the Tanna wishes to follow his treatment of capital crimes with a discussion of those sins for which the punishment is a loss of one's share in the World to Come.

◈ The Resurrection of the Dead:

There is also universal agreement that the deserving soul is eternal and that a person's deeds in this world are rewarded or punished primarily in the afterlife that follows death. When a person dies, his eternal soul enters the World of Souls – *Gan Eden* for reward, and *Gehinnom* for punishment and purification. There is also universal agreement that at some point afterward, God will literally resurrect the dead, reuniting here on this earth the body and soul that were separated through death.

The duration of bodily life after resurrection, however, is the subject of dispute among the Rishonim. *Ramah, Ramban* and many other Rishonim insist that the resurrected state is eternal. Once resurrected, the righteous will live on eternally with body and soul united and delight forever in the splendor of the Divine Presence.[3]

According to *Rambam* and those who follow his view, however, the eternal world is not the world of resurrection but the World of Souls. For, according to *Rambam,* the state of resurrection is *not* permanent. Rather, the resurrected will live the unusually long, happy lives of the idyllic Messianic Era that culminates life on this earth – eating, drinking, and procreating just like the people born initially in that epoch.[4] Eventually, however, body and soul will again be separated, with the souls returning to the eternal World of Souls to delight in the Divine Presence forever.

◈ Terms Used in This Chapter:

יְמוֹת הַמָּשִׁיחַ – *The Days of the Messiah* [also: *the Messianic Era*]. This is the culmination of human history and civilization, when a scion of David will rule in Jerusalem, the entire Jewish nation will be restored to the Land of Israel and all the world will seek the word of God from the Jewish people and their Messianic king.

גַּן עֵדֶן – *Gan Eden* [also: *Paradise*]. This is the reward of the disembodied soul in the World of Souls after one's earthly death. [The term **עוֹלָם הַנְּשָׁמוֹת**, *World of Souls,* is not used in the Talmud, but is used extensively by the Rishonim.]

גֵּיהִנֹּם – *Gehinnom.* This is the counterpart of *Gan Eden,* and refers to the punishment and atonement that the disembodied soul of the sinner undergoes in the World of Souls.

עוֹלָם הַבָּא – *The World to Come.* According to *Ramban* (and those who follow his view), this term is reserved almost exclusively for the eternal world of resurrected life after the Resurrection of the Dead. According to *Rambam,* however, it is a much broader term that can refer to the entire period of the Afterlife or any portion thereof.[5]

לֶעָתִיד לָבֹא – *In the Future to come.* This term is used primarily to refer to the Messianic Era, but can be applied to any point beyond that as well.[6]

Many of these matters, as well as others, such as the time of the resurrection, the people it will encompass, its purpose and the nature of life afterward, are discussed more fully in the appendix at the end of this volume.

NOTES

3. According to this view, the famous dictum of Rav, "In the World to Come there is no eating or drinking . . . rather, the righteous sit with their crowns on their heads and delight in the radiance of the Divine Presence" (*Berachos* 17a), refers to this reunited state of body and soul. Accordingly, the resurrected will not have their present physical needs or functions; rather, their bodies will be sustained through a spiritual nourishment similar to the way Moses was sustained on Mount Sinai for forty days and nights without food or drink (see *Exodus* 24:18; *Deuteronomy* 9:9,18). According to the way this view is presented by *Sefer HaIkkarim* (4:35), the resurrected will *initially* have normal physical function, and only after their natural life span will their bodies be transformed and elevated to an ethereal state, whereupon they will not require any physical sustenance.

4. For according to *Rambam,* when Rav says that "In the World to Come there is no eating and drinking . . . rather, the righteous sit with their crowns on their heads and delight in the radiance of the Divine Presence," he speaks only of the World of Souls, not the world of resurrection.

5. *Rambam* must allow for a broader definition of this term, since there are clearly places where it refers to the eternal world and places where it refers to the world of the resurrected, which – in *Rambam's* view – are not the same (see Appendix).

6. *Meiri* to *Avos* 2:20.

Chapter Eleven

Mishnah כָּל יִשְׂרָאֵל יֵשׁ לָהֶם חֵלֶק לָעוֹלָם הַבָּא – ALL ISRAEL HAS A SHARE IN THE WORLD TO COME,[1] שֶׁנֶּאֱמַר ,,וְעַמֵּךְ כֻּלָּם צַדִּיקִים – **as it is stated:**[2] ***And your people [Israel] are all righteous,*** לְעוֹלָם יִירְשׁוּ אָרֶץ – ***forever shall they inherit the land;*** נֵצֶר מַטָּעַי – ***the branch of My plantings,*** מַעֲשֵׂה יָדַי לְהִתְפָּאֵר" – ***My handiwork, in which to take pride.***[3] וְאֵלוּ שֶׁאֵין לָהֶם חֵלֶק לָעוֹלָם הַבָּא – **However, the following** are the ones **who do not have a share in the World to Come:**[4] הָאוֹמֵר אֵין תְּחִיַּית הַמֵּתִים מִן הַתּוֹרָה – **One who says that there is no** reference to the **Resurrection of the Dead in the Torah,**[5] וְאֵין תּוֹרָה מִן הַשָּׁמַיִם – **or that the Torah is not from Heaven,**[6] וְאַפִּיקוֹרוֹס – **or an** ***apikoros.***[7] רַבִּי עֲקִיבָא אוֹמֵר – **R' Akiva says:** אַף הַקּוֹרֵא

NOTES

1. The term "World to Come" has been explained in the Introduction to this chapter.

"All Israel" does not mean to exclude righteous gentiles (see note 17 below). Rather, the Mishnah means to tell us that *all* Israel – even sinners (including those executed by the courts, as enumerated in the earlier chapters) – have a share in the World to Come, unless they forfeit that share in one of the ways listed further in the Mishnah.

The term "Israel" includes all Jews – even those accounted "wicked" because of their numerous sins – unless they forfeit the title "Israel" by rejecting any of the basic tenets of Judaism (*Rambam,* commentary to this Mishnah, who expounds on what these basic tenets are; see end of note 7 below).

Rashi (here) seems to take the Tanna's main thrust to be the enumeration below of those who do *not* have a share in the World to Come. The Mishnah's opening statement, then, is meant to open the discussion on a positive note (see *Maharshal*).

While all Israel has a share in the World to Come, the shares are not equal, but dependent on the level achieved by each person through his deeds in this life (*Meiri*; *Sefer HaIkkarim* 4:31; *Maharsha*; *Be'er Sheva*).

The Mishnah's terminology חֵלֶק לָעוֹלָם הַבָּא literally means *a share "towards" the World to Come.* This indicates that we gain *olam haba* through working *toward* it by performing good deeds [notably, Torah study – see *Kesubos* 111b] (*Ruach Chaim* to *Avos*).

2. *Isaiah* 60:21.

3. The Mishnah applies this verse to the World to Come, since in this world not all Jews are righteous, nor is there eternal life. Rather, it refers to the World to Come, where all Jews are deemed righteous after having been cleansed of their sins through the punishment they receive upon dying (*Tiferes Yisrael* §3).

The "land" that they shall forever inherit is "the land of the living" (*Psalms* 142:6), which is an allegory for the spiritual reward of the World to Come (*Rambam*). Or it may refer to the bodily existence in the World of Resurrection (*Tiferes Yisrael* ibid.). This "land" is described as being *inherited* forever, because it is the birthright of every Jew, just as every Jew has a portion in the Land of Israel (*Margaliyos HaYam*; see *Ramban* to *Bereishis* 33:18, and *Ikkarim* 4:31).

"The branch of My plantings" may refer to the soul, planted in this world to be nurtured and developed. It has also been explained, variously, as a reference to the Jew planted in the World to Come (*Alshich*), to the World to Come itself (*Tiferes Yisrael*), or to the Jewish people, who are God's children (in *Shabbos* 32b, we find "the work of one's hand" used to describe one's children). Note also *R' Yerucham Levovitz* (*Chever Maamarim*): The Jew is planted in this world in order to grow to fulfillment in the World to Come. Everything in this world gives birth to great consequences in the World to Come, and in that sense the latter is prepared even while we are in this world. See also *Maharsha.*

4. Rather, they are punished eternally for their evil (*Meiri,* based on *Rambam, Hil. Teshuvah* 3:6), if they die without repenting. But one who repents has a share in the World to Come, for there is nothing that stands in the face of repentance (*Rambam, Hil. Teshuvah* 3:14; see *Yerushalmi* to this Mishnah).

[However, the Kabbalists teach that even those Jews cited as having no share in the World to Come will ultimately be included in the eternal bond between the Almighty and the Jewish people. However, they will have no share of their own but will stand among the masses (of such evildoers) and receive these benefits as part of the multitude (*Recanti* to *Exodus* 33:19; *Rabbeinu Bachya* to *Leviticus* 18:29) who are granted this benefit in the merit of the truly righteous through that which God has linked the entire Jewish people together into one general "soul" (see *Derech Hashem* II:3:8).]

5. Even if he personally believes that there will be a resurrection of the dead, but he does not accept that it is alluded to in the Torah, as shown in the Gemara, he is called "a denier of the resurrection." For what significance do his personal feelings have in the matter if he does not accept that the doctrine of Resurrection of the Dead is part of the authentic and original Torah tradition? (see *Rashi* and *Meiri*; see also *Teshuvos HaRashba* 1:9, cited on 90b end of note 22; cf. *Be'er Sheva*).

6. I.e. he denies that the Torah was transmitted by God to Moses. This applies not only to the Written Torah, but to the Oral Explanation that accompanied it, such as the precise description of a *succah* or of tefillin (*Rambam,* commentary to this Mishnah, the Eighth Principle; *Hil. Teshuvah* 3:8; see *Kesef Mishneh* there; see *Emes LeYaakov* here).

The denial of the Divine origin of the Torah is certainly a transgression that deserves the severest punishment, but it also has a direct connection to the exclusion of the denier from the World to Come. For the World to Come can be gained only through Torah, and is obviously closed to anyone who denies the Torah's Divine origin (see *Kesubos* 111b and *Maharal, Tiferes Yisrael,* ch. 15).

7. This is one who disparages a Torah scholar (Gemara 99b).

Apikoros is derived from an Aramaic word meaning *disparagement* [אַפְקִירוּתָא] of the Torah or its teachers, and is used to describe a person who denies any fundamental principle of the Torah or who disparages the sages of the Torah or even a single sage (*Rambam,* commentary to this Mishnah). [*Sefer HaIkkarim* 1:10, however, explains the term to denote followers of the Greek philosopher Epicurus, who declared the world to be a product of chance rather than the creation of God.] The Gemara below defines *apikoros* simply as "one who disparages a Torah scholar" because there are many who cannot know the existence of God on their own, but must learn about it through the traditions conveyed and the proofs advanced by the Torah sages. Thus, one who disparages a Torah scholar in effect cuts himself off from the source of knowledge about God (*Sefer HaIkkarim* loc. cit.). Though the term *apikoros* is commonly used to include anyone who denies the existence of God or His unity, or who worships idols even as intermediaries between man and God, or who denies prophecy or God's awareness, there was no need for the Mishnah to state that such people have no share in the World to Come, since they are not included in the term "Israel" altogether. Therefore, by the term *apikoros,* the Mishnah meant only to include the person who disparages the Torah scholar, for such disparagement leads ultimately to a disparagement of the scholar's Torah and to a denial of all proper beliefs (see *Meiri*; see also *Rashi* to *Chagigah* 5b ד"ה אפיקורסים).

Sefer HaIkkarim (1:4) reduces *Rambam's* thirteen basic tenets of Judaism (see note 1) to three main categories [of which the other tenets are subdivisions]. These three categories are: (1) the existence of God; (2) His providence and reward and punishment; and (3) the Divine origin of the Torah. [*Rambam* provides a similar grouping in *Hil. Teshuvah* 3:7-8.] Furthermore, *Sefer HaIkkarim* (1:10) asserts that these three broad principles are contained in our very Mishnah when it states that the ones who lose their share in the World to Come are: one who denies the Resurrection of the Dead [which encompasses the principle of reward and punishment in general], one who denies that the Torah is divine, or the *apikoros* [which encompasses all who hold improper notions about God and His existence].

[It emerges, then, that those whom our Mishnah lists as forfeiting their share in the World to Come are not accounted part of Israel (see *Rambam,* cited in note 1). *Emes LeYaakov,* however, suggests that the sinners mentioned in our Mishnah, while they forfeit their *olam haba,* retain the title Israel, unlike the sinners enumerated by the Baraisa in *Rosh Hashanah* 17a, who forfeit that title. This would explain the discrepancy between the lists of our Mishnah and that Baraisa.]

מחלוקת בעוקר הגוף דעבודת כוכבים וקיום מקצת וביטול מקצת דעבודת כוכבים דרחמנא אמר (א) מן הדרך אפילו מקצת הדרך אבל עוקר הגוף דשאר מצות דברי הכל בחנק וקיום מקצת וביטול מקצת דבשאר מצות דברי הכל פטור מתיב רב המנונא (א) ללכת זו מצות עשה בה זו מצות לא תעשה ואי סלקא דעתך בעבודת כוכבים עשה בעבודת כוכבים היכי משכחת לה תרגמה רב חסדא (ב) ונתצתם רב המנונא אמר מחלוקת בעוקר הגוף בין בעבודת כוכבים בין בשאר מצות וקיום מקצת וביטול מקצת דעבודת כוכבים דרחמנא אמר מן הדרך אפילו מקצת הדרך אבל קיום מקצת וביטול מקצת דבשאר מצות דברי הכל פטור ת"ר (א) המתנבא לעקור דבר מן התורה חייב לקיים מקצת ולבטל מקצת ר"ש פוטר ובעבודת כוכבים אפילו אומר היום עיבדוה ולמחר בטלוה דברי הכל חייב אביי סבר לה כרב חסדא ומתרץ לה כרב חסדא רבא סבר לה כרב המנונא ומתרץ לה כרב המנונא אביי סבר לה כרב חסדא ומתרץ לה כרב חסדא המתנבא לעקור דבר מן התורה דברי הכל בחנק לקיים מקצת ולבטל מקצת ר"ש פוטר והוא הדין לרבנן ובעבודת כוכבים אפילו אומר היום עיבדוה ולמחר בטלוה חייב מר כדאית ליה ומר כדאית ליה רבא סבר לה כרב המנונא ומתרץ לה כרב המנונא המתנבא לעקור דבר מן התורה בין בעבודת כוכבים בין בשאר מצות חייב מר כדאית ליה ומר כדאית ליה (ב) לקיים מקצת ולבטל מקצת בשאר מצות ר"ש פוטר והוא הדין לרבנן ובעבודת כוכבים אפילו אומר היום עיבדוה ולמחר בטלוה חייב מר כדאית ליה ומר כדאית ליה א"ר אבהו א"ר יוחנן (א) בכל אם יאמר לך נביא עבור על דברי תורה שמע לו חוץ מעבודת כוכבים שאפילו מעמיד לך חמה באמצע הרקיע אל תשמע לו תניא רבי יוסי הגלילי אומר הגיעה תורה לסוף דעתה של עבודת כוכבים לפיכך נתנה תורה ממשלה בה שאפילו מעמיד לך חמה באמצע הרקיע אל תשמע לו תניא א"ר עקיבא חס ושלום שהקדוש ב"ה מעמיד חמה לעוברי רצונו אלא כגון חנניה בן עזור שמתחלתו נביא אמת ולבסוף נביא שקר: וזוממי בת כהן: מנהני מילי אמר רב אחא בריה דרב איקא דתניא ר' יוסי אומר מה ת"ל (ג) (ג) ועשיתם לו כאשר זמם לעשות לאחיו לפי שכל (ד) המזוממין שבתורה זוממיהן ובועליהן כיוצא בהן בת כהן (ה) היא בשריפה ואין בועלה בשריפה זוממין איני יודע אם לו הוקשו אם לה הוקשו כשהוא אומר לעשות לאחיו (ו) לאחיו ולא לאחותו:

הדרן עלך אלו הן הנחנקין

כל ישראל (ב) יש להם חלק לעולם הבא שנאמר (ד) ועמך כולם צדיקים לעולם יירשו ארץ נצר מטעי מעשה ידי להתפאר (ז) (ג) ואלו שאין להם חלק לעולם הבא האומר אין תחיית המתים מן התורה ואין תורה מן השמים ואפיקורוס ר"ע אומר אף הקורא בספרים החיצונים (ח) והלוחש על המכה ואומר (ה) כל המחלה אשר שמתי במצרים לא אשים עליך כי אני ה' רופאך אבא שאול אומר אף (ט) ההוגה את השם באותיותיו (י) שלשה מלכים וארבעה הדיוטות אין להן חלק לעולם הבא שלשה מלכים ירבעם אחאב ומנשה ר' יהודה אומר מנשה יש לו חלק לעולם הבא שנאמר (ו) ויתפלל אליו (כ) וישמע תחנתו וישיבהו ירושלים למלכותו אמרו לו למלכותו השיבו ולא לחיי העולם הבא השיבו ארבעה הדיוטות בלעם ודואג ואחיתופל וגחזי: **גמ'** וכל כך למה תנא הוא כפר בתחיית המתים לפיכך לא יהיה לו חלק בתחיית המתים שכל מדותיו של הקב"ה מדה כנגד מדה דאמר ר' שמואל בר נחמני אמר ר' יונתן מניין שכל מדותיו של הקב"ה מדה כנגד מדה שנאמר (ז) ויאמר אלישע שמעו דבר ה' [וגו'] כעת מחר סאה סלת בשקל וסאתים שעורים בשקל בשער שומרון וכתיב (ח) ויען השליש אשר (ל) (המלך) נשען על ידו את איש האלהים ויאמר הנה ה' עושה ארובות בשמים היהיה הדבר הזה ויאמר (מ) הנך רואה בעיניך ומשם לא תאכל וכתיב

רש"י

מחלוקת. דרבנן ורבי שמעון בנביא בעוקר כל הגוף בעבודת כוכבים ואומר נצטויתי ברוח הקודש מפי הגבורה להתנבאות לעקור כל מצות עבודת כוכבים מן התורה או לקיים מקצת ולבטל מקצת בהאי הוא דקאמרי רבנן סקילה משום דבהאי עניינא דכתיבא הדחה בנביא דגמרי סקילה מיניה בע"ז הוא משתעי דכתיב ובא האות והמופת וגו' נלכה ונעבדה היינו עקירת הגוף ובטול מקצת התם נמי כתיב בסיפא יומת כי דבר סרה וגו' להדיחך מן הדרך ואפי' במקצת במשמע ומיהו לא מישתעי קרא אלא בע"ז דדבר למד מעניינו: אבל עוקר הגוף דשאר מצות דברי הכל בחנק. דנפקא לן מקרא אחרינא האמור בפרשה אחרינא דלא כתיב בה הדחה אך הנביא אשר יזיד לדבר דבר בשמי (דברים יח) והיינו מה שלא שמע וכתיב ומת הנביא ההוא וכל מיתה האמורה סתם חנק הוא: פטור. דהתם דבר כתיב דבר שלם ולא חצי דבר: ללכת זו מצות עשה. ברייתא היא בספרי גבי פרשת נביא המדיח דכתב בה הדחה (שם יג) להדיחך מן הדרך אשר צוך ה' אלהיך ללכת בה וגו' ודריש קרא יתירא ללכת זו מצות עשה דמשמע לעשות ולא משמע אזהרה: בה לא תעשה. דגמרינן מאשר חטא בה דבלא תעשה מיירי אלמא דשאר מצות נמי הכא גבי הדחה כתיבי דאי לא משתעי קרא אלא בע"ז מאי עשה איכא: ובין בשאר מצות. דהאי ללכת בה לא משמע ליה לרב המנונא אונכלתם דרחמנא אמר מן הדרך ואע"ז קאי דהכתי לא איתרבו שאר מצות בהאי עניינא דללכת בה כולה משמע: ד"ה פטור. ואפילו מחנק דהתם דבר שלם כתיב ולאו אעוקר דברי תורה האי כי יזיד לדבר דבר קאי דהתם סקילה הוא אלא אדברים בעלמא כגון צדקיה בן כנענה: היום עובדה. כלומר היינו קיום מקצת וביטול מקצת: כרב חסדא. דאמר בע"ז הוא דפליגי אבל בשאר מצות עוקר הגוף הוא בחנק וביטול מקצת פטור: ר"ש פוטר והוא הדין לרבנן. דגבי חנק דבר שלם כתיב ולרב חסדא הא דנקט ר"ש הא קמ"ל דרישא דקתני סתמא חייב ואפילו לרבנן בחנק דרבי שמעון הוא דקא מחייב חנק ולא סקילה דשאר מצות בעניינא הדחה דסקילה לא כתיבי: מר כדאית ליה כו'. לרבנן בסקילה לרבי שמעון בחנק (י) והוא הדין לרבנן ולרב המנונא האי דנקט ר' שמעון רבותא הוא כלומר ואפילו מחנק דרבי שמעון פטור וכ"ש מסקילה דמחייבי ליה רבנן בעוקר את הכל: אם יאמר לך נביא. המוחזק עבור על דברי תורה הכל לפי תקנת השעה כגון אליהו בהר הכרמל בשחוטי חוץ: נתנה התורה ממשלה בה. כלומר אפילו תראה אותו נביא מושל ועושה כרצונו דכתיב (דברים יג) ונתן אליך אות או מופת: שתחילתו נביא אמת. כגון חנניה הנביא והאי ונתן אליך אות בעודו נביא אמת יתן לך אות בנבואה אחרת ולבסוף כשיחזור להרשיע יאמר לעבוד עבודת כוכבים וסמוך עלי שהרי מוחזק אני על ידי אות ומופת שנתתי לך כבר: (ס) (לרשות הבעל. כגון מסרה האב לשלוחי הבעל ועדיין היא בדרך ולא קרינן בה בית אביה: לאותה מיתה. שהיו מחייבין את הנידון: ובועלה. כלומר וכל הבועלים נידונין כמיתת הנבעלת חוץ מבועל בת כהן:) מה ת"ל לאחיו. לכתוב כאשר זמם לעשות ולישתוק: אם לו הוקשו. לבועל שהיו מחייבין אותו חנק: אם לה. שמחייבין אותה שריפה: לאחיו ולא לאחותו. כל היכא דבעדותן מחייבין איש ואשה ודינן חלוק כי הכא לו הוקשו:

הדרן עלך אלו הן הנחנקין

כל ישראל יש להם חלק לעולם הבא. מעיקרא איירי בארבע מיתות ומפרש ואזיל להו לכולהו והדר מפרש הני דאין להם חלק לעולם הבא: ה"ג האומר אין תחיית המתים מן התורה. (ע) שכופר במדרשים דדרשינן בגמרא לקמן מניין לתחיית המתים מן התורה ואפי' יהא מודה ומאמין שיחיו המתים אלא דלא רמיזא באורייתא כופר הוא הואיל ועוקר שיש תחיית המתים מן התורה מה לנו ולאמונתו וכי מהיכן הוא יודע שכן הוא הלכך כופר גמור הוא: אפיקורוס. מפרש בגמרא: ספרים החיצונים. מפרש בגמרא: **גמ'** ויהי

עין משפט נר מצוה

פא א מיי' פ"ח מהלכות יסודי התורה הל"ג והל"ה והיינו לפי שעה וע"ש:

א ב מיי' פ"ג מהלכות תשובה הלכה ה:

ב ג מיי' שם הלכה ו:

ליקוטי רש"י

אחר הדברים האלה. יש מרבותינו אומרים אחר דבריו של שטן שהיה מקטרג ואומר מכל סעודה שעשה אברהם לא הקריב לפניך פר אחד או איל אחד אמר לו כלום עשה אלא בשביל בנו אילו הייתי אומר לו זבח אותו לפני לא היה מעכב ויש אומרים אחר דבריו של ישמעאל שהיה מתפאר על יצחק שמל בן שלש עשרה שנה ולא מיחה אמר לו יצחק באבר אחד אתה מיראני אילו אמר לי הקב"ה זבח עצמך לפני לא הייתי מעכב [בראשית כב, א]. קח נא. אין נא אלא לשון בקשה אמר לו בבקשה ממך עמוד לי בזה הנסיון שלא יאמרו הראשונות לא היה בהן ממש. את בנך. אמר לו שני בנים יש לי אמר לו את יחידך אמר לו זה יחיד לאמו וזה יחיד לאמו אמר לו אשר אהבת אמר לו שניהם אני אוהב אמר לו את יצחק ולמה לא גילה לו מתחלה שלא לערבבו פתאום ותזוח דעתו עליו ותטרף וכדי לחבב עליו את המצוה וליתן לו שכר על כל דבור ודבור [שם פוק ב']. הנסה. לשון תימה הבעבור שניסה דבר אליך תלאה בנסיון אחד שניסך בוראך ובא אליך אתה נלאה ומעתה עצור במילין מי יוכל מלהשיבך. הנה יסרתם רבים. שהרבו דברים הוכחתם ויסרתם. וידים רפות. ויגורות מפורענות הבא עליה' אתה היית רגיל לחזקם ולומר אל תירא שכך הוא מדת הדין. יקימון. רגילות הם מליך להקים את הכושל. הלא יראתך כסלתך. עתה סופך מוכיח על תחלתך שיראתך שהיית ירא שמים כסלתך היא מחמת כסילות היא ולא מדעת שלימה וכן תקותך ותום דרכיך הכל כסילות [איוב ד].

[עד כאן שייך לדף פט:]

המתנבא לעקור דבר מן התורה. כגון שתחלתו נביא של אמת ולבסוף נביא השקר שהתנבא לעקור דבר מדברי תורה חייב ודברי הכל בחנק. לקיום מקצת ולבטל מקצת. דשאר מצות ר"ש פוטר וה"ה לרבנן. ובעבודת כוכבים אפי' אמר לך היום עובדה ולמחר בטלה. דהיינו קיום מקצת ובטול מקצת דעבודת כוכבים חייב דרחמנא אמר להדיחך מן הדרך אפי' מקצת דרך ובעבודת כוכבי' הוא דכתיב וכי קתני חייב כגון לרבנן בסקילה ולר"ש בחנק והכי מתרץ ליה רב חסדא בפ' אלו הן הנחנקין (סנהדרין דף צ) והיום עובדה ולמחר בטלה כאין שבת בשביעית דמי וקרי להו ביטול מקצת וקיום מקצת ש"מ [הוריות ד:]. זוממי בת כהן. עיין בזה ליקוטי רש"י לעיל פט.

מסורת הש"ס

א) [הוריות ד:], ב) [שם ד:], ג) [הנהו תמה תיבות ועשיתם לו כאשר זמם לעשות נראה דאינם מן הגירסא אלא עיקר הגי' כדאיתא בפירש"י מה ת"ל לאחיו], ד) [י"ג המזומנין], ה) [לעיל נה. ע"ש], ו) [שם:], ז) [ע"ז יח.], ח) שבועות טו:, ט) ע"ז יח., י) חגיגה טו:, כ) [ויעתר לו], ל) [נ"ל למלך], מ) [נ"ל הנכה], נ) הוא דבור בפ"ע רש"ל, ס) מן ד"ה לרשות עד ד"ה מה ת"ל שייך למתני' לעיל פט., ע) כ' ב"ש שאין זה מדברי רש"י.

גליון הש"ס

מתני' כל ישראל יש להן חלק. עי' כתובות דף קג ע"ב תוס' ד"ה מזומן: שם האומר אין תחיית המתים. עי' סוטה ד"ה ע"א תוד"ה כל: שם ההוגה את השם. עי' סוכה דף ה' ע"א תוד"ה יו"ד ה"א. שבועות דף לג ע"א תוס' ד"ה באלף: גמ' מדה כנגד מדה. עי' סוטה דף ח' ע"ב:

תורה אור השלם

א) וְהַנָּבִיא הַהוּא אוֹ חֹלֵם הַחֲלוֹם הַהוּא יוּמָת כִּי דִבֶּר סָרָה עַל יְיָ אֱלֹהֵיכֶם הַמּוֹצִיא אֶתְכֶם מֵאֶרֶץ מִצְרַיִם וְהַפֹּדְךָ מִבֵּית עֲבָדִים לְהַדִּיחֲךָ מִן הַדֶּרֶךְ אֲשֶׁר צִוְּךָ יְיָ אֱלֹהֶיךָ לָלֶכֶת בָּהּ וּבִעַרְתָּ הָרָע מִקִּרְבֶּךָ: [דברים יג, ו]

ב) וְנִתַּצְתֶּם אֶת מִזְבְּחֹתָם וְשִׁבַּרְתֶּם אֶת מַצֵּבֹתָם וַאֲשֵׁרֵיהֶם תִּשְׂרְפוּן בָּאֵשׁ וּפְסִילֵי אֱלֹהֵיהֶם תְּגַדֵּעוּן וְאִבַּדְתֶּם אֶת שְׁמָם מִן הַמָּקוֹם הַהוּא: [דברים יב, ג]

ג) וַעֲשִׂיתֶם לוֹ כַּאֲשֶׁר זָמַם לַעֲשׂוֹת לְאָחִיו וּבִעַרְתָּ הָרָע מִקִּרְבֶּךָ: [דברים יט, יט]

ד) וְעַמֵּךְ כֻּלָּם צַדִּיקִים לְעוֹלָם יִירְשׁוּ אָרֶץ נֵצֶר מַטָּעַי מַעֲשֵׂה יָדַי לְהִתְפָּאֵר: [ישעיה ס, כא]

ה) וַיֹּאמֶר אִם שָׁמוֹעַ תִּשְׁמַע לְקוֹל יְיָ אֱלֹהֶיךָ וְהַיָּשָׁר בְּעֵינָיו תַּעֲשֶׂה וְהַאֲזַנְתָּ לְמִצְוֹתָיו וְשָׁמַרְתָּ כָּל חֻקָּיו כָּל הַמַּחֲלָה אֲשֶׁר שַׂמְתִּי בְמִצְרַיִם לֹא אָשִׂים עָלֶיךָ כִּי אֲנִי יְיָ רֹפְאֶךָ: [שמות טו, כו]

ו) וַיִּתְפַּלֵּל אֵלָיו וַיֵּעָתֶר לוֹ וַיִּשְׁמַע תְּחִנָּתוֹ וַיְשִׁיבֵהוּ יְרוּשָׁלַיִם לְמַלְכוּתוֹ וַיֵּדַע מְנַשֶּׁה כִּי יְיָ הוּא הָאֱלֹהִים: [דברי הימים ב' לג, יג]

ז) וַיֹּאמֶר אֱלִישָׁע שִׁמְעוּ דְּבַר יְיָ כֹּה אָמַר יְיָ כָּעֵת מָחָר סְאָה סֹלֶת בְּשֶׁקֶל וְסָאתַיִם שְׂעֹרִים בְּשֶׁקֶל בְּשַׁעַר שֹׁמְרוֹן: [מלכים ב' ז, א]

ח) וַיַּעַן הַשָּׁלִישׁ אֲשֶׁר לַמֶּלֶךְ נִשְׁעָן עַל יָדוֹ אֶת אִישׁ הָאֱלֹהִים וַיֹּאמַר הִנֵּה יְיָ עֹשֶׂה אֲרֻבּוֹת בַּשָּׁמַיִם הֲיִהְיֶה הַדָּבָר הַזֶּה וַיֹּאמֶר הִנְּכָה רֹאֶה בְּעֵינֶיךָ וּמִשָּׁם לֹא תֹאכֵל: [מלכים ב' ז, ב]

בַּסְּפָרִים הַחִיצוֹנִים – Also one who reads external books,[8] **וְהַלּוֹחֵשׁ עַל הַמַּכָּה וְאוֹמֵר ,,כָּל־הַמַּחֲלָה אֲשֶׁר־שַׂמְתִּי בְמִצְרַיִם לֹא־אָשִׂים עָלֶיךָ כִּי אֲנִי ה׳ רֹפְאֶךָ״ – or one who incants over a wound**[9] **and says** the verse: ***All the diseases that I have placed upon Egypt I shall not place upon you because I am HASHEM your healer.***[10] **אַבָּא שָׁאוּל אוֹמֵר – Abba Shaul says: אַף הַהוֹגֶה אֶת הַשֵּׁם בְּאוֹתִיּוֹתָיו – Also one who pronounces the Name** of God **according to its letters.**[11]

The Mishnah now lists specific historical individuals who forfeited their share in the World to Come:

שְׁלֹשָׁה מְלָכִים וְאַרְבָּעָה הֶדְיוֹטוֹת אֵין לָהֶן חֵלֶק לָעוֹלָם הַבָּא – Three kings and four commoners have no share in the World to Come.[12] **שְׁלֹשָׁה מְלָכִים יָרָבְעָם אַחְאָב וּמְנַשֶּׁה** – The **three kings** are: **Yarovam,**[13] **Ahab,**[14] **and Menasheh.**[15] **רַבִּי יְהוּדָה אוֹמֵר – R' Yehudah says: מְנַשֶּׁה יֵשׁ לוֹ חֵלֶק לָעוֹלָם הַבָּא – Menasheh has a portion in the World to Come, שֶׁנֶּאֱמַר ,,וַיִּתְפַּלֵּל אֵלָיו . . . וַיִּשְׁמַע תְּחִנָּתוֹ וַיְשִׁיבֵהוּ יְרוּשָׁלַםִ לְמַלְכוּתוֹ״ – as it is stated:** ***And he prayed to Him . . ., and He*** allowed Himself to be entreated and ***heard his plea, and He returned him to Jerusalem to his kingdom.***[16] **אָמְרוּ לוֹ – [The Sages] said to [R' Yehudah]: לְמַלְכוּתוֹ הֱשִׁיבוֹ** – From this very verse we infer that only **to his *kingdom* did [God] return him, וְלֹא לְחַיֵּי הָעוֹלָם הַבָּא הֱשִׁיבוֹ – but He did not return him to the life of the World to Come.**

אַרְבָּעָה הֶדְיוֹטוֹת בִּלְעָם וְדוֹאֵג וַאֲחִיתוֹפֶל וְגֵחֲזִי – The **four commoners** are: **Bilam,**[17] **Doeg,**[18] **Achithophel,**[19] **and Geichazi.**[20]

Gemara

The Gemara addresses the Mishnah's statement that one who denies that the Resurrection of the Dead is a Scriptural doctrine forfeits his share in the World to Come:

וְכָל כַּךְ לָמָּה – Why so much?[21] **תָּנָא הוּא כָּפַר בִּתְחִיַּית הַמֵּתִים – An explanatory Baraisa taught: HE DENIED THE RESURRECTION OF THE DEAD; לְפִיכָךְ לֹא יִהְיֶה לוֹ חֵלֶק בִּתְחִיַּית הַמֵּתִים – THEREFORE HE SHALL HAVE NO SHARE IN THE RESURRECTION OF THE DEAD.** The Gemara elaborates: **שֶׁכָּל מִדּוֹתָיו שֶׁל הַקָּדוֹשׁ בָּרוּךְ הוּא מִדָּה כְּנֶגֶד מִדָּה – For all of the measures of the Holy One, Blessed is He, are**

NOTES

8. See the Gemara below, 100b, which explains which books are meant here.

9. I.e. he utters an incantation over a wound to heal it.

10. *Exodus* 15:26. The Gemara (101a) will explain what is meant here and why the sin is considered so grave.

11. This will be explained in the Gemara (101b) and notes there.

The Mishnah's list of sins that cause a person to lose his share in the World to Come does not include many others enumerated in other Talmudic passages (e.g. *Rosh Hashanah* 17a, *Sotah* 5a, *Kesubos* 110b, *Avos* 3:11 and *Avos DeRabbi Nassan* §36). *Rambam* (*Hil. Teshuvah* 3:6-14) enumerates twenty-four categories, and then adds other sins, which – if habitually transgressed – cause the sinner to forfeit his share in the World to Come. Why does the Mishnah here omit mention of those other sins? (see *Tosafos* to *Sotah* 5a ד״ה כל אדם).

Possibly, many of those other categories could fall under the general heading *apikoros* mentioned in our Mishnah (*Meiri*; see above, note 7). *R' Elchanan Wasserman* (*Kovetz Maamarim,* part 2, "An explanation of the Mishnah in *Cheilek*") answers that our Mishnah here appears in the chain of Mishnahs listing the penalties for various sins, and thus lists only those who lose their share in the World to Come as a *punishment* for their sin. Thus, the Mishnah here lists only those sins for which a single transgression warrants loss of the World to Come [which indicates that the loss is a punishment for the sin], but does not list those sins that must be habitual [which indicates that the loss is not a punishment for the sin, but rather the result of the person's basic unworthiness]. Nor does the Mishnah mention those who do not have a share in the World to Come because they lack the basic attainments needed to qualify for the World to Come [such as Torah study or a connection to it (see *Michtav MeEliyahu* vol I, p. 215)]. See *Maharal* (*Tiferes Yisrael* ch. 15); see also *Emes LeYaakov* (cited at the end of note 7 above).

12. Actually, there have been many other wicked people who have forfeited their share in the World to Come. Our Mishnah singles out these, however, for one might have thought that they have a share in the World to Come because of their great wisdom and in the merit of the Torah, which they knew profoundly. Therefore, the Mishnah teaches us that they do not have a share in the World to Come, because their notions regarding some of the fundamental tenets of Judaism were corrupt (*Rambam,* commentary to this Mishnah; see also *Rabbeinu Yehonasan,* cited in *Chamra VeChayei*, and *Meiri*). The Gemara will explain their failings.

13. Yarovam (Jeroboam) revolted against the sovereignty of Rechavam, the son of King Solomon, and led the Ten Tribes in a break from the kingdom of the House of David. Fearing that if his subjects would go to the Temple in Jerusalem to offer sacrifices to God on the Three Festivals they would gradually resume their loyalty to the House of David, he established two golden calves within his kingdom for his people to serve, and thus led them to idolatry (see *I Kings* 12:25-33). For this, he lost his share in the World to Come – see Gemara 101b.

14. Ahab was king of the Ten Tribes who, together with his wicked wife Jezebel, introduced Baal idolatry to Israel (see *Radak* to *I Kings* 21:25). See Gemara 102b.

15. Menasheh (Manasseh), the son of the righteous King Chizkiah, king of Judah, was an idolatrous king who is compared by Scripture to Ahab (*II Kings* 21:2-3). See Gemara 102b.

16. *II Chronicles* 33:13. After twenty-two years on the throne, during which Menasheh spread idolatry throughout the land, God delivered Menasheh into the hands of the Assyrians, who brought him in chains to Babylon. There, in his pain, Menasheh called out to God *and became greatly humbled before the God of his fathers* (ibid. v. 12). As the verse quoted here states, God accepted his prayer and returned him to his throne in Jerusalem, where for the next thirty-three years he attempted to repair the spiritual damage he had wrought during the first part of his reign. R' Yehudah maintains that God's acceptance of Menasheh's prayer indicates that his penitence was accepted and he regained his share in the World to Come.

17. Bilam (Balaam) was the gentile soothsayer hired by Balak, king of Moab, to curse the Israelites in the Wilderness (*Numbers* chs. 22-24). See Gemara 105a.

From the Mishnah's listing of the wicked Bilam, who was a non-Jew, it is evident that *righteous* non-Jews *do* have a share in the World to Come (see Gemara 105a; *Rambam, Hil. Teshuvah* 3:5). Though the Mishnah's primary subject here is the Jewish nation (as evidenced by its opening statement), it excludes Bilam so that one should not be misled into thinking that his great powers of foretelling the future indicate that he was one of the righteous men of the nations (*Meiri*).

18. Doeg was the advisor of King Saul who slandered David to him and thereby brought about the destruction of Nob, the city of Kohanim (see *I Samuel* 22:9-22). See Gemara 106b.

19. Achithophel was the highly regarded sage and advisor to King David who deserted the king in favor of David's renegade son, Absalom (see *II Samuel* 17). See Gemara 106b.

20. Geichazi was the servant of the prophet Elisha, but he disparaged Torah scholars and led others to sin (see Gemara 107b).

21. Apparently, the Gemara means to ask why the denier of the resurrection should be punished so severely. *Maharsha,* however, notes that denying the resurrection is certainly a grave denial [of one of the fundamental tenets of Judaism, as enumerated by *Rambam,* and warrants the denier's loss of his share in the World to Come]. Rather, he explains, the Gemara means to ask why the denial of the resurrection heads the Mishnah's list, preceding even one who denies the Divine origin of the Torah and the *apikoros.* [See also *Yad Ramah,* and note 23 below.]

מחלוקת בעוקר הגוף דעבודת כוכבים וקיום מקצת וביטול מקצת דעבודת כוכבים דרחמנא אמר [א] מן הדרך אפילו מקצת הדרך אבל עוקר הגוף דשאר מצות דברי הכל בחנק וקיום מקצת וביטול מקצת דבשאר מצות דברי הכל פטור מתיב רב המנונא [א] ללכת זו מצות עשה בה זו מצות לא תעשה ואי סלקא דעתך בעבודת כוכבים עשה בעבודת כוכבים היכי משכחת לה תרגמה רב חסדא [ב] ונתצתם רב המנונא אמר מחלוקת בעוקר הגוף בין בעבודת כוכבים בין בשאר מצות וקיום מקצת וביטול מקצת דעבודת כוכבים דרחמנא אמר מן הדרך אפילו מקצת הדרך אבל קיום מקצת וביטול מקצת דבשאר מצות דברי הכל פטור ת"ר [ה] המתנבא לעקור דבר מן התורה חייב לקיים מקצת ולבטל מקצת ר"ש פוטר ובעבודת כוכבים אפילו אומר היום עיבדוה ולמחר בטלוה דברי הכל חייב אביי סבר לה כרב חסדא ומתרץ לה כרב חסדא רבא סבר לה כרב המנונא ומתרץ לה כרב המנונא אביי סבר לה כרב חסדא ומתרץ לה כרב חסדא המתנבא לעקור דבר מן התורה דברי הכל בחנק לקיים מקצת ולבטל מקצת ר"ש פוטר והוא הדין לרבנן ובעבודת כוכבים אפילו אומר היום עיבדוה ולמחר בטלוה חייב מר כדאית ליה ומר כדאית ליה רבא סבר לה כרב המנונא ומתרץ לה כרב המנונא המתנבא לעקור דבר מן התורה בין בעבודת כוכבים בין בשאר מצות חייב מר כדאית ליה ומר כדאית ליה [ג] לקיים מקצת ולבטל מקצת בשאר מצות ר"ש פוטר והוא הדין לרבנן ובעבודת כוכבים אפילו אומר היום עיבדוה ולמחר בטלוה חייב מר כדאית ליה ומר כדאית ליה א"ר אבהו א"ר יוחנן [א] בכל אם יאמר לך נביא עבור על דברי תורה שמע לו חוץ מעבודת כוכבים שאפילו מעמיד לך חמה באמצע הרקיע אל תשמע לו תניא רבי יוסי הגלילי אומר הגיעה תורה לסוף דעתה של עבודת כוכבים לפיכך נתנה תורה ממשלה בה שאפילו מעמיד לך חמה באמצע הרקיע אל תשמע לו תניא א"ר עקיבא חס ושלום שהקדוש ב"ה מעמיד חמה לעוברי רצונו אלא כגון חנניה בן עזור שמתחלתו נביא אמת ולבסוף נביא שקר: וזוממי בת כהן: מנהני מילי אמר רב אחא בריה דרב איקא דתניא ר' יוסי אומר מה ת"ל [ג] [ג] ועשיתם לו כאשר זמם לעשות לאחיו לפי שכל [ד] המזוממין שבתורה זוממיהן ובועליהן כיוצא בהן בת כהן [ה] היא בשריפה ואין בועלה בשריפה זוממין איני יודע אם לו הוקשו אם לה הוקשו כשהוא אומר לעשות לאחיו [ו] לאחיו ולא לאחותו:

הדרן עלך אלו הן הנחנקין

כל ישראל [ב] יש להם חלק לעולם הבא שנאמר [ד] ועמך כולם צדיקים לעולם יירשו ארץ נצר מטעי מעשה ידי להתפאר [ז] ואלו שאין להם חלק לעולם הבא האומר אין תחיית המתים מן התורה ואין תורה מן השמים ואפיקורוס ר"ע אומר אף הקורא בספרים החיצונים [ס] והלוחש על המכה ואומר [ה] כל המחלה אשר שמתי במצרים לא אשים עליך כי אני ה' רופאך אבא שאול אומר אף [ט] ההוגה את השם באותיותיו [י] שלשה מלכים וארבעה הדיוטות אין להן חלק לעולם הבא שלשה מלכים ירבעם אחאב ומנשה ר' יהודה אומר מנשה יש לו חלק לעולם הבא שנאמר [ו] ויתפלל אליו [כ] וישמע תחנתו וישיבהו ירושלים למלכותו אמרו לו למלכותו השיבו ולא לחיי העולם הבא השיבו ארבעה הדיוטות בלעם ודואג ואחיתופל וגחזי: **גמ'** וכל כך למה תנא הוא כפר בתחיית המתים לפיכך לא יהיה לו חלק בתחיית המתים שכל מדותיו של הקב"ה מדה כנגד מדה דאמר ר' שמואל בר נחמני אמר ר' יונתן מניין שכל מדותיו של הקב"ה מדה כנגד מדה שנאמר [ז] ויאמר אלישע שמעו דבר ה' [וגו'] כעת מחר סאה סלת בשקל וסאתים שעורים בשקל בשער שומרון וכתיב [ח] ויען השליש אשר ([ל] המלך) נשען על ידו את איש האלהים ויאמר הנה ה' עושה ארובות בשמים היהיה הדבר הזה ויאמר [מ] הנך רואה בעיניך ומשם לא תאכל וכתיב

רש"י

מחלוקת. דרבנן ורבי שמעון בנביא בעוקר כל הגוף בעבודת כוכבים ואומר נצטויתי ברוח הקודש מפי הגבורה להתנבאות לעקור כל מצות עבודת כוכבים מן התורה או לקיים מקצת ולבטל מקצת בהאי הוא דקאמרי רבנן סקילה משום דבהאי עניינא דכתיבא הדחה בנביא דגמרי סקילה מיניה בע"ז הוא משתעי דכתיב ובא האות והמופת וגו' נלכה ונעבדה היינו עקירת הגוף ובטול מקצת התם נמי כתיב בסיפא יומת כי דבר סרה וגו' להדיחך מן הדרך ואפי' במקצת במשמע ומיהו לא מישתעי קרא אלא בע"ז דדבר למד מעניינו: **אבל עוקר הגוף דשאר מצות דברי הכל בחנק.** דנפקא לן מקרא אחרינא האמור בפרשה אחרינא דלא כתיב בה הדחה אך הנביא אשר יזיד לדבר דבר בשמי (דברים יח) והיינו מה שלא שמע וכתיב ומת הנביא ההוא וכל מיתה האמורה סתם חנק הוא: **פטור.** דהתם דבר כתיב דבר שלם ולא חצי דבר: **ללכת זו מצות עשה.** ברייתא היא בספרי גבי פרשת נביא המדיח דכתב בה הדחה (שם יג) להדיחך מן הדרך אשר צוך ה' אלהיך ללכת בה וגו' ודריש קרא יתירא ללכת זו מצות עשה דמשמע לעשות ולא משמע אזהרה: **בה לא תעשה.** דגמרינן מאשר חטא בה דבלא תעשה מיירי אלמא דשאר מצות נמי הכא גבי הדחה כתיבי דאי לא משתעי קרא אלא בע"ז מאי עשה איכא: **ובין בשאר מצות.** דהאי ללכת בה לא משמע ליה לרב המנונא אונקלוס דרחמנא אמר מן הדרך ואע"ז קאי דאכתי לא איתרבו שאר מצות בהאי עניינא דללכת בה כולה משמע: **ד"ה פטור.** ואפילו מחנק דהתם דבר שלם כתיב ולאו אעוקר דברי תורה האי כי יזיד לדבר דבר קאי דהתם סקילה הוא אלא אדברים בעלמא כגון לדקיה בן כנענה: **היום עובדה.** כלומר היינו קיום מקצת וביטול מקצת: **כרב חסדא.** דאמר בע"ז הוא דפליגי אבל בשאר מצות עוקר הגוף הוא בחנק וביטול מקצת פטור: **ר"ש פוטר והוא הדין לרבנן.** דגבי חנק דבר שלם כתיב ולרב חסדא הא דנקט ר"ש הא קמ"ל דרישא דקתני סתמא חייב ואפילו לרבנן בחנק דרבי שמעון הוא דקא מחייב חנק ולא סקילה דשאר מצות בעניינא הדחה דסקילה לא כתיבי: **מר כדאית ליה כו'.** לרבנן בסקילה לרבי שמעון בחנק [י] והוא הדין לרבנן ולרב המנונא האי דנקט ר' שמעון רבותא הוא כלומר ואפילו מחנק דרבי שמעון פטור וכ"ש מסקילה דמחייבי ליה רבנן בעוקר את הכל: **אם יאמר לך נביא.** המוחזק עבור על דברי תורה הכל לפי תקנת השעה כגון אליהו בהר הכרמל בשחוטי חוץ: **נתנה התורה ממשלה בה.** כלומר אפילו תראה אותו נביא מושל ועושה כרצונו דכתיב (דברים יג) ונתן אליך אות או מופת: **שתחילתו נביא אמת.** כגון חנניה הנביא והאי ונתן אליך אות בעודו נביא אמת יתן לך אות בנבואה אחרת ולבסוף כשיחזור להרשיע יאמר לעבוד עבודת כוכבים וסמוך עלי שהרי מוחזק אני על ידי אות ומופת שנתתי לך כבר: [ס] (**לרשות הבעל.** כגון מסרה האב לשלוחי הבעל ועדיין היא בדרך ולא קרינן בה בית אביה: **לאותה מיתה.** שהיו מחייבין את הנידון: **ובועלה.** כלומר וכל הבועלים נידונין כמיתת הנבעלת חוץ מבועל בת כהן:) **מה ת"ל לאחיו.** לכתוב כאשר זמם לעשות ולישתוק: **אם לו הוקשו.** לבועל שהיו מחייבין אותו חנק: **אם לה.** שמחייבין אותה שריפה: **לאחיו ולא לאחותו.** כל היכא דבעדותן מחייבין איש ואשה ודינן חלוק כי הכא לו הוקשו:

הדרן עלך אלו הן הנחנקין

כל ישראל יש להם חלק **לעולם הבא.** מעיקרא איירי בארבע מיתות ומפרש ואזיל להו לכולהו והדר מפרש הני דאין להם חלק לעולם הבא: ה"ג **האומר אין תחיית המתים מן התורה.** [ע] שכופר במדרשים דדרשינן בגמרא לקמן מניין לתחיית המתים מן התורה ואפי' יהא מודה ומאמין שיחיו המתים אלא דלא רמיזא באורייתא כופר הוא הואיל ועוקר שיש תחיית המתים מן התורה מה לנו ולאמונתו וכי מהיכן הוא יודע שכן הוא הלכך כופר גמור הוא: **אפיקורוס.** מפרש בגמרא: **ספרים החיצונים.** מפרש בגמרא: **גמ'** ויהי

מסורת הש"ס

א) [הוריות ד:], ב) [שם ד:], ג) [הנהו תמש תיבות ועשיתם לו כאשר זמם לעשות נראה דאינם מן הגירסא אלא עיקר הגי' כדאיתא בפירש"י מה ת"ל לאחיו], ד) [י"ג המומתין], ה) [לעיל נא. ע"ש], ו) [שם:], ז) [ע"ז יח.], ח) שבועות טו:, ט) ע"ז יח., י) חגיגה טו:, כ) [ויעתר לו], ל) [נ"ל למלך], מ) [נ"ל הנבהו], נ) הוא דבור בפ"ע רש"ל, ס) מן ד"ה לרשות עד ד"ה מה ת"ל שייך למתני' לעיל פט., ע) כ' ב"ש שאין זה מדברי רש"י.

גליון הש"ס

מתני' כל ישראל יש להן חלק. עי' כתובות דף קג ע"ב תוס' ד"ה מזומן: שם האומר אין תחיית המתים. עי' סוטה ד"ה ע"א תוד"ה כל: שם ההוגה את השם. עי' סוכה דף ה' ע"א תוד"ה יו"ד ה"א. שבועות דף לד ע"א תוס' ד"ה באלף: גמ' מדה כנגד מדה. עי' סוטה דף ח' ע"ב:

תורה אור השלם

א) וְהַנָּבִיא הַהוּא אוֹ חֹלֵם הַחֲלוֹם הַהוּא יוּמָת כִּי דִבֶּר סָרָה עַל יְיָ אֱלֹהֵיכֶם הַמּוֹצִיא אֶתְכֶם מֵאֶרֶץ מִצְרַיִם וְהַפֹּדְךָ מִבֵּית עֲבָדִים לְהַדִּיחֲךָ מִן הַדֶּרֶךְ אֲשֶׁר צִוְּךָ יְיָ אֱלֹהֶיךָ לָלֶכֶת בָּהּ וּבִעַרְתָּ הָרָע מִקִּרְבֶּךָ: [דברים יג, ו]

ב) וְנִתַּצְתֶּם אֶת מִזְבְּחֹתָם וְשִׁבַּרְתֶּם אֶת מַצֵּבֹתָם וַאֲשֵׁרֵיהֶם תִּשְׂרְפוּן בָּאֵשׁ וּפְסִילֵי אֱלֹהֵיהֶם תְּגַדֵּעוּן וְאִבַּדְתֶּם אֶת שְׁמָם מִן הַמָּקוֹם הַהוּא: [דברים יב, ג]

ג) וַעֲשִׂיתֶם לוֹ כַּאֲשֶׁר זָמַם לַעֲשׂוֹת לְאָחִיו וּבִעַרְתָּ הָרָע מִקִּרְבֶּךָ: [דברים יט, יט]

ד) וְעַמֵּךְ כֻּלָּם צַדִּיקִים לְעוֹלָם יִירְשׁוּ אָרֶץ נֵצֶר מַטָּעַי מַעֲשֵׂה יָדַי לְהִתְפָּאֵר: [ישעיה ס, כא]

ה) וַיֹּאמֶר אִם שָׁמוֹעַ תִּשְׁמַע לְקוֹל יְיָ אֱלֹהֶיךָ וְהַיָּשָׁר בְּעֵינָיו תַּעֲשֶׂה וְהַאֲזַנְתָּ לְמִצְוֹתָיו וְשָׁמַרְתָּ כָּל חֻקָּיו כָּל הַמַּחֲלָה אֲשֶׁר שַׂמְתִּי בְמִצְרַיִם לֹא אָשִׂים עָלֶיךָ כִּי אֲנִי יְיָ רֹפְאֶךָ: [שמות טו, כו]

ו) וַיִּתְפַּלֵּל אֵלָיו וַיֵּעָתֶר לוֹ וַיִּשְׁמַע תְּחִנָּתוֹ וַיְשִׁיבֵהוּ יְרוּשָׁלַיִם לְמַלְכוּתוֹ וַיֵּדַע מְנַשֶּׁה כִּי יְיָ הוּא הָאֱלֹהִים: [דברי הימים ב' לג, יג]

ז) וַיֹּאמֶר אֱלִישָׁע שִׁמְעוּ דְּבַר יְיָ כֹּה אָמַר יְיָ כָּעֵת מָחָר סְאָה סֹלֶת בְּשֶׁקֶל וְסָאתַיִם שְׂעֹרִים בְּשֶׁקֶל בְּשַׁעַר שֹׁמְרוֹן: [מלכים ב' ז, א]

ח) וַיַּעַן הַשָּׁלִישׁ אֲשֶׁר לַמֶּלֶךְ נִשְׁעָן עַל יָדוֹ אֶת אִישׁ הָאֱלֹהִים וַיֹּאמַר הִנֵּה יְיָ עֹשֶׂה אֲרֻבּוֹת בַּשָּׁמַיִם הֲיִהְיֶה הַדָּבָר הַזֶּה וַיֹּאמֶר הִנְּכָה רֹאֶה בְּעֵינֶיךָ וּמִשָּׁם לֹא תֹאכֵל: [מלכים ב' ז, ב]

עין משפט נר מצוה

פא א מיי' פ"ט מהלכות יסודי התורה הל"ג והל"ה והיינו לפי שעה וע"ש:

א ב מיי' פ"ג מהלכות תשובה הלכה ה:

ב ג מיי' שם הלכה ו:

ליקוטי רש"י

אחר הדברים האלה. יש מרבותינו אומרים אחר דבריו של שטן שהיה מקטרג ואומר מכל סעודה שעשה אברהם לא הקריב לפניך פר אחד או איל אחד אמר לו כלום עשה אלא בשביל בנו אילו הייתי אומר לו זבח אותו לפני לא היה מעכב ויש אומרים אחר דבריו של ישמעאל שהיה מתפאר על יצחק שמל בן שלש עשרה שנה ולא מיחה אמר לו יצחק באבר אחד אתה מיראני אילו אמר לי הקב"ה זבח עצמך לפני לא הייתי מעכב [בראשית כב, א]. **קח נא.** אין נא אלא לשון בקשה אמר לו בבקשה ממך עמוד לי בזה הנסיון שלא יאמרו הראשונות לא היה בהן ממש. **את בנך.** אמר לו שני בנים יש לי אמר לו את יחידך אמר לו זה יחיד לאמו וזה יחיד לאמו אמר לו אשר אהבת אמר לו שניהם אני אוהב אמר לו את יצחק ולמה לא גילה לו מתחלה שלא לערבבו פתאום ותזוח דעתו עליו ותטרף וכדי לחבב עליו את המצוה וליתן לו שכר על כל דבור ודבור [שם פוק ב']. **הנסה.** לשון תימה הבעבור שניסה דבר אליך תלאה בנסיון אחד שניסך בוראך ובא אליך אתה נלאה ומעתה עצור במילין מי יוכל מלהשיבך. **הנה יסרתם רבים.** שהרבו דברים הוכחתם ויסרתם. **וידים רפות.** ויגורות מפורענות הבא עליה' אתה היית רגיל לחזקם ולומר אל תירא שכך הוא מדת הדין. **יקימון.** רגילות הם מליך להקים את הכושל. **הלא יראתך כסלתך.** עתה סופך מוכיח על תחלתך שיראתך שהיית ירא שמים כסלתך היא מחמת כסילות היא ולא מדעת שלימה וכן תקותך ותום דרכיך הכל כסילות [איוב ד].

[עד כאן שייך לדף פט:]

המתנבא לעקור דבר מן התורה. כגון שתחלתו נביא של אמת ולבסוף נביא השקר שהתנבא לעקור דבר מדברי תורה חייב ודברי הכל בחנק. **לקיום מקצת ולבטל מקצת.** דשאר מצות ר"ש פוטר וה"ה לרבנן. **ובעבודת כוכבים אפי' אמר לך היום עובדה ולמחר בטלה.** דהיינו קיום מקצת ובטול מקצת דעבודת כוכבים חייב דרחמנא אמר להדיחך מן הדרך אפי' מקצת דרך ובעבודת כוכבי' הוא דכתיב וכי קתני חייב כגון לרבנן בסקילה ולר"ש בחנק והכי מתרץ ליה רב חסדא בפ' אלו הן הנחנקין (סנהדרין דף ל) והיום עובדה ולמחר בטלה כאין שבת בשביעית דמי וקרי להו ביטול מקצת וקיום מקצת ש"מ [הוריות ד:]. **זוממי בת כהן.** עיין בזה לליקוטי רש"י לעיל פט.

measure for measure.[22] דְּאָמַר רַבִּי שְׁמוּאֵל בַּר נַחְמָנִי אָמַר רַבִּי יוֹנָתָן – **For R' Shmuel bar Nachmani said in the name of R' Yonasan:** מִנַּיִין שֶׁכָּל מִדּוֹתָיו שֶׁל הַקָּדוֹשׁ בָּרוּךְ הוּא מִדָּה כְּנֶגֶד מִדָּה – **From where** do we know **that all the measures of the Holy One, Blessed is He, are measure for measure?** שֶׁנֶּאֱמַר ,,וַיֹּאמֶר אֱלִישָׁע שִׁמְעוּ דְּבַר־ה׳ [וגו׳] – **For it is stated:**[23] ***And Elisha said, "Hear the word of God [etc.].*** כָּעֵת מָחָר סְאָה־סֹלֶת בְּשֶׁקֶל וְסָאתַיִם שְׂעֹרִים בְּשֶׁקֶל בְּשַׁעַר שֹׁמְרוֹן״ – ***At this time tomorrow, a se'ah of fine flour shall go for a shekel, and two se'ahs of barley for a shekel, in the gate of Shomron!"*** וּכְתִיב ,,וַיַּעַן הַשָּׁלִישׁ אֲשֶׁר לַמֶּלֶךְ נִשְׁעָן עַל־יָדוֹ אֶת־אִישׁ הָאֱלֹהִים וַיֹּאמַר – **And it is written** further:[24] ***Then the captain on whose hand the king leaned answered the man of God, and said:*** הִנֵּה ה׳ עֹשֶׂה אֲרֻבּוֹת בַּשָּׁמַיִם הֲיִהְיֶה הַדָּבָר הַזֶּה – ***"Behold, if God should make windows in heaven, might this thing be?"*** וַיֹּאמֶר הִנְּכָה רֹאֶה בְּעֵינֶיךָ וּמִשָּׁם לֹא תֹאכֵל״ – ***And [Elisha] said: "Behold, you shall see it with your eyes, but you will not eat therefrom."***

NOTES

22. I.e. all punishments meted out by God ("measures") correspond exactly to the nature of the sin [and the same holds true for rewards] (see below, 100a, and 100b note 2).

Since the principle of "measure for measure" is most directly evident in the punishment for one who denies the resurrection, the Mishnah opens its list of exclusions with such a person (*Maharsha*; see preceding note).

The person denied the Resurrection of the Dead, yet he loses his share in the World to Come. What is the connection? This Baraisa would seem to support the view of *Ramban* (see Introduction) that the World to Come refers to the eternal life that follows the Resurrection of the Dead. Accordingly, the one who will not be resurrected (because he denied that doctrine) has no share in the World to Come that follows. See *Tiferes Yisrael* here, who reconciles this Baraisa with *Rambam's* view, that *olam haba* refers primarily to the world of disembodied souls. See also *Chidushei HaRan* here.

This Gemara presents us with a subtle difficulty: *Rambam* counts the tenet of resurrection among the fundamental principles, whose denial places the person outside the pale of Judaism, causing him to forfeit his innate Jewish right to the World to Come. This seems to be at odds with our Gemara, which asks, "Why so much?" suggesting that the actual denial of this principle would *not* seem to place the person outside the pale. Moreover, the Gemara's answer of "measure for measure" accounts only for the person's loss of his share in the World to Come; it does *not* explain his being accounted beyond the pale. *R' Yitzchak Hutner* (*Pachad Yitzchak, Shaar Chodesh HaAviv* §9 [5730]) provides an incisive solution: Unlike the denial of other fundamental principles, denial of the resurrection places the person outside the pale precisely *because* he loses his share in the World to Come as a result of "measure for measure"; for one who has no share in the ultimate redemption and fulfillment of the Jewish people cannot be reckoned as being among them. [*Maharsha's* explanation of this Gemara (cited above) would also seem to provide a solution to this difficulty.]

23. *II Kings* 7:1. Shomron, the capital of the northern kingdom of Israel, was besieged by an Aramean army, and its populace was slowly starving. The prophet Elisha then prophesied that on the morrow there would be such an abundance of food in the gates of Shomron that large quantities could be bought for a *shekel.* The king's captain did not believe the prophecy, and mocked it.

24. Ibid. v. 2.

מחלוקת בעוקר הגוף דעבודת כוכבים וקיום מקצת וביטול מקצת דעבודת כוכבים דרחמנא אמר [א] מן הדרך אפילו מקצת הדרך אבל עוקר הגוף דשאר מצות דברי הכל בחנק וקיום מקצת וביטול מקצת דבשאר מצות דברי הכל פטור מתיב רב המנונא [א] ללכת זו מצות עשה בה זו מצות לא תעשה ואי סלקא דעתך בעבודת כוכבים עשה בעבודת כוכבים היכי משכחת לה תרגמה רב חסדא [ב] ונתצתם רב המנונא אמר מחלוקת בעוקר הגוף בין בעבודת כוכבים בין בשאר מצות וקיום מקצת וביטול מקצת דעבודת כוכבים דרחמנא אמר מן הדרך אפילו מקצת הדרך אבל קיום מקצת וביטול מקצת דבשאר מצות דברי הכל פטור ת"ר [א] המתנבא לעקור דבר מן התורה חייב לקיים מקצת ולבטל מקצת ר"ש פוטר ובעבודת כוכבים אפילו אומר היום עיבדוה ולמחר בטלוה דברי הכל חייב אביי סבר לה כרב חסדא ומתרץ לה כרב חסדא רבא סבר לה כרב המנונא ומתרץ לה כרב המנונא אביי סבר לה כרב חסדא ומתרץ לה כרב חסדא המתנבא לעקור דבר מן התורה דברי הכל בחנק לקיים מקצת ולבטל מקצת ר"ש פוטר והוא הדין לרבנן ובעבודת כוכבים אפילו אומר היום עיבדוה ולמחר בטלוה חייב מר כדאית ליה ומר כדאית ליה רבא סבר לה כרב המנונא ומתרץ לה כרב המנונא המתנבא לעקור דבר מן התורה בין בעבודת כוכבים בין בשאר מצות חייב מר כדאית ליה ומר כדאית ליה [ג] לקיים מקצת ולבטל מקצת בשאר מצות ר"ש פוטר והוא הדין לרבנן ובעבודת כוכבים אפילו אומר היום עיבדוה ולמחר בטלוה חייב מר כדאית ליה ומר כדאית ליה א"ר אבהו א"ר יוחנן [א] בכל אם יאמר לך נביא עבור על דברי תורה שמע לו חוץ מעבודת כוכבים שאפילו מעמיד לך חמה באמצע הרקיע אל תשמע לו תניא רבי יוסי הגלילי אומר הגיעה תורה לסוף דעתה של עבודת כוכבים לפיכך נתנה תורה ממשלה בה שאפילו מעמיד לך חמה באמצע הרקיע אל תשמע לו תניא א"ר עקיבא חס ושלום שהקדוש ב"ה מעמיד חמה לעוברי רצונו אלא כגון חנניה בן עזור שמתחלתו נביא אמת ולבסוף נביא שקר: וזוממי בת כהן: מנהני מילי אמר רב אחא בריה דרב איקא דתניא ר' יוסי אומר מה ת"ל [ג] [ג] ועשיתם לו כאשר זמם לעשות לאחיו לפי שכל [ד] המזוממין שבתורה זוממיהן ובועליהן כיוצא בהן בת כהן [ה] היא בשריפה ואין בועלה בשריפה זוממין איני יודע אם לו הוקשו אם לה הוקשו כשהוא אומר לעשות לאחיו [ו] לאחיו ולא לאחותו:

הדרן עלך אלו הן הנחנקין

כל ישראל [ב] יש להם חלק לעולם הבא שנאמר [ד] ועמך כולם צדיקים לעולם יירשו ארץ נצר מטעי מעשה ידי להתפאר [ז] [ג] ואלו שאין להם חלק לעולם הבא האומר אין תחיית המתים מן התורה ואין תורה מן השמים ואפיקורוס ר"ע אומר אף הקורא בספרים החיצונים [ח] והלוחש על המכה ואומר [ה] כל המחלה אשר שמתי במצרים לא אשים עליך כי אני ה' רופאך אבא שאול אומר אף [ט] ההוגה את השם באותיותיו [י] שלשה מלכים וארבעה הדיוטות אין להן חלק לעולם הבא שלשה מלכים ירבעם אחאב ומנשה ר' יהודה אומר מנשה יש לו חלק לעולם הבא שנאמר [ו] ויתפלל אליו [כ] וישמע תחנתו וישיבהו ירושלים למלכותו אמרו לו למלכותו השיבו ולא לחיי העולם הבא השיבו ארבעה הדיוטות בלעם ודואג ואחיתופל וגחזי: **גמ'** וכל כך למה תנא הוא כפר בתחיית המתים לפיכך לא יהיה לו חלק בתחיית המתים שכל מדותיו של הקב"ה מדה כנגד מדה דאמר ר' שמואל בר נחמני אמר ר' יונתן מניין שכל מדותיו של הקב"ה מדה כנגד מדה שנאמר [ז] ויאמר אלישע שמעו דבר ה' [וגו'] כעת מחר סאה סלת בשקל וסאתים שעורים בשקל בשער שומרון וכתיב [ח] ויען השליש אשר ([ל] המלך) נשען על ידו את איש האלהים ויאמר הנה ה' עושה ארובות בשמים היהיה הדבר הזה ויאמר [מ] הנך רואה בעיניך ומשם לא תאכל וכתיב

מחלוקת. דרבנן ורבי שמעון בנביא בעוקר כל הגוף בעבודת כוכבים ואומר נצטויתי ברוח הקודש מפי הגבורה להתנבאות לעקור כל מצות עבודת כוכבים מן התורה או לקיים מקצת ולבטל מקצת בהאי הוא דקאמרי רבנן סקילה משום דבהאי עניינא דכתיבא הדחה בנביא דגמרי סקילה מיניה בע"ז הוא משתעי דכתיב ובא האות והמופת וגו' נלכה ונעבדה היינו עקירת הגוף וביטול מקצת התם נמי כתיב בסיפא יומת כי דבר סרה וגו' להדיחך מן הדרך ואפי' במקצת במשמע ומיהו לא מישתעי קרא אלא בע"ז דדבר למד מעניינו: **אבל עוקר הגוף דשאר מצות דברי הכל בחנק.** דנפקא לן מקרא אחרינא האמור בפרשה אחרינא דלא כתיב בה הדחה אך הנביא אשר יזיד לדבר דבר בשמי (דברים יח) והיינו מה שלא שמע וכתיב ומת הנביא ההוא וכל מיתה האמורה סתם חנק הוא: **פטור.** דהתם דבר כתיב דבר שלם ולא חצי דבר: **ללכת זו מצות עשה.** ברייתא היא בספרי גבי פרשת נביא המדיח דכתב בה הדחה (שם יג) להדיחך מן הדרך אשר צוך ה' אלהיך ללכת בה וגו' ודריש קרא יתירא ללכת זו מצות עשה דמשמע לעשות ולא משמע אזהרה: **בה לא תעשה.** דגמרינן מאשר חטא בה דבלא תעשה מיירי אלמא דשאר מצות נמי הכא גבי הדחה כתיבי דאי לא משתעי קרא אלא בע"ז מאי עשה איכא: **ובין בשאר מצות.** דהאי ללכת בה לא משמע ליה לרב המנונא אונכתם דרחמנא אמר מן הדרך ואע"ז קאי דאכתי לא איתרבו שאר מצות בהאי עניינא דללכת בה כולה משמע: **ד"ה פטור.** ואפילו מחנק דהתם דבר שלם כתיב ולאו אעוקר דברי תורה האי כי יזיד לדבר דבר קאי דהתם סקילה הוא אלא אדברים בעלמא כגון צדקיה בן כנענה: **היום עובדה.** כלומר היינו קיום מקצת וביטול מקצת: **כרב חסדא.** דאמר בע"ז הוא דפליגי אבל בשאר מצות עוקר הגוף הוא בחנק וביטול מקצת פטור: **ר"ש פוטר והוא הדין לרבנן.** דגבי חנק דבר שלם כתיב ולרב חסדא הא דנקט ר"ש הא קמ"ל דרישא דקתני סתמא חייב ואפילו לרבנן בחנק דרבי שמעון הוא דקא מחייב חנק ולא סקילה דשאר מצות בעניינא הדחה דסקילה לא כתיבי: **מר כדאית ליה כו'.** לרבנן בסקילה לרבי שמעון בחנק [י] והוא הדין לרבנן ולרב המנונא האי דנקט ר' שמעון רבותא הוא כלומר ואפילו מחנק דרבי שמעון פטור וכ"ש מסקילה דמחייבי ליה רבנן בעוקר את הכל: **אם יאמר לך נביא.** המוחזק עבור על דברי תורה הכל לפי תקנת השעה כגון אליהו בהר הכרמל בשחוטי חוץ: **נתנה התורה ממשלה בה.** כלומר אפילו תראה אותו נביא מושל ועושה כרצונו דכתיב (דברים יג) ונתן אליך אות או מופת: **שתחילתו נביא אמת.** כגון חנניה הנביא והאי ונתן אליך אות בעודו נביא אמת יתן לך אות בנבואה אחרת ולבסוף כשיחזור להרשיע יאמר לעבוד עבודת כוכבים וסמוך עלי שהרי מוחזק אני על ידי אות ומופת שנתתי לך כבר: [ס] (לרשות הבעל. כגון מסרה האב לשלוחי הבעל ועדיין היא בדרך ולא קרינן בה בית אביה: **לאותה מיתה.** שהיו מחייבין את הנידון: **ובועלה.** כלומר וכל הבועלים נידונין כמיתת הנבעלת חוץ מבועל בת כהן:) **מה ת"ל לאחיו.** לכתוב כאשר זמם לעשות ולישתוק: **אם לו הוקשו.** לבועל שהיו מחייבין אותו חנק: **אם לה.** שמחייבין אותה שריפה: **לאחיו ולא לאחותו.** כל היכא דבעדותן מחייבין איש ואשה ודינן חלוק כי הכא לו הוקשו:

הדרן עלך אלו הן הנחנקין

כל ישראל יש להם חלק לעולם הבא. מעיקרא איירי בארבע מיתות ומפרש ואזיל להו לכולהו והדר מפרש הני דאין להם חלק לעולם הבא: **ה"ג האומר אין תחיית המתים מן התורה.** [ע] שכופר במדרשים דדרשינן בגמרא לקמן מניין לתחיית המתים מן התורה ואפי' יהא מודה ומאמין שיחיו המתים אלא דלא רמיזא באורייתא כופר הוא הואיל ועוקר שיש תחיית המתים מן התורה מה לנו ולאמונתו וכי מהיכן הוא יודע שכן הוא הלכך כופר גמור הוא: **אפיקורוס.** מפרש בגמרא: **ספרים החיצונים.** מפרש בגמרא: **גמ'** ויהי

מסורת הש"ס

א) [הוריות ד:], ב) [שם ד:], ג) [הנהו תמש תיבות ועשיתם לו כאשר זמם לעשות נראה דאינם מן הגירסא אלא עיקר הגי' כדאיתא בפירש"י מה ת"ל לאחיו], ד) [י"ג המזומתין], ה) [לעיל נא. ע"ש], ו) [שם:], ז) [ע"ז יח.], ח) שבועות טו:, ט) ע"ז יח., י) חגיגה טו:, כ) [ויעתר לו], ל) [נ"ל למלך], מ) [נ"ל הנכה], נ) הוא דבור בפ"ע רש"ל, ס) מן ד"ה לרשות עד ד"ה מה ת"ל שייך למתני' לעיל פט., ע) כ' ב"ש שאין זה מדברי רש"י.

גליון הש"ס

מתני' כל ישראל יש להן חלק. עי' כתובות דף קג ע"ב תוס' ד"ה מזומן: **שם האומר אין תחיית המתים.** עי' סוטה ד"ה ע"א תוד"ה כל: **שם ההוגה את השם.** עי' סוכה דף ה' ע"א תוד"ה יו"ד ה"א. שבועות דף לד ע"א תוס' ד"ה באלף: **גמ' מדה כנגד מדה.** עי' סוטה דף ח' ע"ב:

תורה אור השלם

א) וְהַנָּבִיא הַהוּא אוֹ חֹלֵם הַחֲלוֹם הַהוּא יוּמָת כִּי דִבֶּר סָרָה עַל יְיָ אֱלֹהֵיכֶם הַמּוֹצִיא אֶתְכֶם מֵאֶרֶץ מִצְרַיִם וְהַפֹּדְךָ מִבֵּית עֲבָדִים לְהַדִּיחֲךָ מִן הַדֶּרֶךְ אֲשֶׁר צִוְּךָ יְיָ אֱלֹהֶיךָ לָלֶכֶת בָּהּ וּבִעַרְתָּ הָרָע מִקִּרְבֶּךָ: [דברים יג, ו]

ב) וְנִתַּצְתֶּם אֶת מִזְבְּחֹתָם וְשִׁבַּרְתֶּם אֶת מַצֵּבֹתָם וַאֲשֵׁרֵיהֶם תִּשְׂרְפוּן בָּאֵשׁ וּפְסִילֵי אֱלֹהֵיהֶם תְּגַדֵּעוּן וְאִבַּדְתֶּם אֶת שְׁמָם מִן הַמָּקוֹם הַהוּא: [דברים יב, ג]

ג) וַעֲשִׂיתֶם לוֹ כַּאֲשֶׁר זָמַם לַעֲשׂוֹת לְאָחִיו וּבִעַרְתָּ הָרָע מִקִּרְבֶּךָ: [דברים יט, יט]

ד) וְעַמֵּךְ כֻּלָּם צַדִּיקִים לְעוֹלָם יִירְשׁוּ אָרֶץ נֵצֶר מַטָּעַי מַעֲשֵׂה יָדַי לְהִתְפָּאֵר: [ישעיה ס, כא]

ה) וַיֹּאמֶר אִם שָׁמוֹעַ תִּשְׁמַע לְקוֹל יְיָ אֱלֹהֶיךָ וְהַיָּשָׁר בְּעֵינָיו תַּעֲשֶׂה וְהַאֲזַנְתָּ לְמִצְוֹתָיו וְשָׁמַרְתָּ כָּל חֻקָּיו כָּל הַמַּחֲלָה אֲשֶׁר שַׂמְתִּי בְמִצְרַיִם לֹא אָשִׂים עָלֶיךָ כִּי אֲנִי יְיָ רֹפְאֶךָ: [שמות טו, כו]

ו) וַיִּתְפַּלֵּל אֵלָיו וַיֵּעָתֶר לוֹ וַיִּשְׁמַע תְּחִנָּתוֹ וַיְשִׁיבֵהוּ יְרוּשָׁלַיִם לְמַלְכוּתוֹ וַיֵּדַע מְנַשֶּׁה כִּי יְיָ הוּא הָאֱלֹהִים: [דברי הימים ב' לג, יג]

ז) וַיֹּאמֶר אֱלִישָׁע שִׁמְעוּ דְּבַר יְיָ כֹּה אָמַר יְיָ כָּעֵת מָחָר סְאָה סֹלֶת בְּשֶׁקֶל וְסָאתַיִם שְׂעֹרִים בְּשֶׁקֶל בְּשַׁעַר שֹׁמְרוֹן: [מלכים ב' ז, א]

ח) וַיַּעַן הַשָּׁלִישׁ אֲשֶׁר לַמֶּלֶךְ נִשְׁעָן עַל יָדוֹ אֶת אִישׁ הָאֱלֹהִים וַיֹּאמַר הִנֵּה יְיָ עֹשֶׂה אֲרֻבּוֹת בַּשָּׁמַיִם הֲיִהְיֶה הַדָּבָר הַזֶּה וַיֹּאמֶר הִנְּכָה רֹאֶה בְּעֵינֶיךָ וּמִשָּׁם לֹא תֹאכֵל: [מלכים ב' ז, ב]

עין משפט נר מצוה

פא א מיי' פ"ט מהלכות יסודי התורה הל"ג והל"ה והיינו לפי שעה וע"ש:

א ב מיי' פ"ג מהלכות תשובה הלכה ה:

ב ג מיי' שם הלכה ו:

ליקוטי רש"י

אחר הדברים האלה. יש מרבותינו אומרים אחר דבריו של שטן שהיה מקטרג ואומר מכל סעודה שעשה אברהם לא הקריב לפניך פר אחד או איל אחד אמר לו כלום עשה אלא בשביל בנו אילו הייתי אומר לו זבח אותו לפני לא היה מעכב ויש אומרים אחר דבריו של ישמעאל שהיה מתפאר על יצחק שמל בן שלש עשרה שנה ולא מיחה אמר לו יצחק באבר אחד אתה מיראני אילו אמר לי הקב"ה זבח עצמך לפני לא הייתי מעכב [בראשית כב, א]. **קח נא.** אין נא אלא לשון בקשה אמר לו בבקשה ממך עמוד לי בזה הנסיון שלא יאמרו הראשונות לא היה בהן ממש. **את בנך.** אמר לו שני בנים יש לי אמר לו את יחידך אמר לו זה יחיד לאמו וזה יחיד לאמו אמר לו אשר אהבת אמר לו שניהם אני אוהב אמר לו את יצחק ולמה לא גילה לו מתחלה שלא לערבבו פתאום ותזוח דעתו עליו ותטרף וכדי לחבב עליו את המצוה וליתן לו שכר על כל דבור ודבור [שם פוק ב']. **הנסה.** לשון תימה הבעבור שניסה דבר אליך תלאה בנסיון אחד שניסך בוראך ובא אליך אתה נלאה ומעתה עצור במילין מי יוכל להשיבך. **הנה יסרתם רבים.** שהרבו דברים הוכחתם ויסרתם. **וידים רפות.** ויגורות מפורענות הבא עליה' אתה היית רגיל לחזקם ולומר אל תירא שכך הוא מדת הדין. **יקימון.** רגילות הם מליך להקים את הכושל. **הלא יראתך כסלתך.** עתה סופך מוכיח על תחלתך שיראתך שהיית ירא שמים כסלתך היא מחמת כסילות היא ולא מדעת שלימה וכן תקותך ותום דרכיך הכל כסילות [איוב ד].

[עד כאן שייך לדף פט:]

המתנבא לעקור דבר מן התורה. כגון שתחלתו נביא של אמת ולבסוף נביא השקר שהתנבא לעקור דבר מדברי תורה חייב ודברי הכל בחנק. **לקיום מקצת ולבטל מקצת.** דשאר מצות ר"ש פוטר וה"ה לרבנן. **ובעבודת כוכבים אפי' אמר לך היום עובדה ולמחר בטלה.** דהיינו קיום מקצת ובטול מקצת דעבודת כוכבים חייב דרחמנא אמר להדיחך מן הדרך אפי' מקצת דרך ובעבודת כוכבי' הוא דכתיב וכי קתני חייב כגון לרבנן בסקילה ולר"ש בחנק והכי מתרץ ליה רב חסדא בפ' אלו הן הנחנקין (סנהדרין דף צ) והיום עובדה ולמחר בטלה כאין שבת בשביעית דמי וקרי להו ביטול מקצת וקיום מקצת ש"מ [הוריות ד:]. **זוממי בת כהן.** עיין בזה ליקוטי רש"י לעיל פט.

וכתיב ^{א)} ויהי לו כן וירמסו אותו העם בשער וימות ודילמא קללת אלישע גרמה ליה [א] דאמר רב יהודה אמר רב קללת חכם אפי' על חנם היא באה אם כן לכתוב קרא וירמסוהו וימות מאי בשער על עסקי שער (ב) אמר ר' יוחנן) מניין לתחיית המתים מן התורה שנאמר ב) ונתתם ממנו [את] תרומת ה' לאהרן הכהן וכי אהרן לעולם קיים והלא לא נכנס לארץ ישראל שנותנין לו תרומה אלא מלמד שעתיד לחיות וישראל נותנין לו תרומה מכאן לתחיית המתים מן התורה דבי רבי ישמעאל תנא לאהרן כאהרן מה אהרן חבר אף בניו חברים [ג] [ד] א"ר שמואל בר נחמני אמר רבי יונתן מניין שאין נותנין תרומה לכהן עם הארץ שנאמר ג) ויאמר לעם ליושבי ירושלים לתת מנת (ה) לכהנים ולוים) למען יחזקו בתורת ה' כל המחזיק בתורת ה' יש לו מנת ושאינו מחזיק בתורת ה' אין לו מנת אמר רב אחא בר אדא אמר רב יהודה כל הנותן תרומה לכהן עם הארץ כאילו נותנה לפני ארי [ו] מה ארי ספק דורס ואוכל ספק אינו דורס ואוכל אף כהן עם הארץ ספק אוכלה בטהרה ספק אוכלה בטומאה ר' יוחנן אמר אף גורם לו מיתה שנאמר ד) ומתו בו כי יחללוהו דבי ר"א בן יעקב תנא אף משיאו עון אשמה שנאמר ה) והשיאו אותם עון אשמה באכלם את קדשיהם תניא ר' סימאי אומר מניין לתחיית המתים מן התורה שנאמר ו) וגם הקימותי את בריתי אתם לתת להם את ארץ כנען לכם לא נאמר אלא להם מכאן לתחיית המתים מן התורה: [א] (צד"ק ג"ם גש"ם ק"ם סימן): שאלו מינין את רבן גמליאל מניין שהקדוש ברוך הוא מחיה מתים אמר להם מן התורה ומן הנביאים ומן הכתובים ולא קיבלו ממנו מן התורה דכתיב ז) ויאמר ה' אל משה הנך שוכב עם אבותיך וקם אמרו לו ודילמא וקם העם הזה וזנה מן הנביאים דכתיב ח) יחיו מתיך נבלתי יקומון הקיצו ורננו שוכני עפר כי טל אורות טלך וארץ רפאים תפיל ודילמא מתים שהחיה יחזקאל מן הכתובים דכתיב ט) וחכך כיין הטוב הולך לדודי למישרים דובב שפתי ישנים ודילמא רחושי מרחשן שפוותיה בעלמא כר' יוחנן [ז] דאמר ר' יוחנן משום ר"ש בן יהוצדק כל מי שנאמרה הלכה בשמו בעולם הזה שפתותיו דובבות בקבר שנאמר דובב שפתי ישנים עד שאמר להם מקרא זה י) אשר נשבע ה' לאבותיכם לתת להם לכם לא נאמר אלא להם מיכן לתחיית המתים מן התורה וי"א מן המקרא הזה אמר להם כ) ואתם הדבקים בה' אלהיכם חיים כלכם היום (ח) פשיטא דחיים כולכם היום אלא אפילו ביום שכל העולם כולם מתים אתם חיים) מה היום כולכם קיימין אף לעוה"ב כולכם קיימין שאלו רומיים את רבי יהושע בן חנניה מניין שהקב"ה מחיה מתים ויודע מה שעתיד להיות אמר להו תרווייהו מן המקרא הזה שנאמר ז) ויאמר ה' אל משה הנך שוכב עם אבותיך וקם העם הזה וזנה ודילמא וקם העם הזה וזנה אמר להו [ט] נקוטו מיהא פלגא בידייכו דיודע מה שעתיד להיות איתמר נמי א"ר יוחנן משום רבי שמעון בן יוחאי מניין שהקדוש ברוך הוא מחיה מתים ויודע מה שעתיד להיות שנאמר הנך שוכב עם אבותיך וקם וגו' תניא א"ר אליעזר בר' יוסי בדבר זה זייפתי ספרי מינים שהיו אומרים אין תחיית המתים מן התורה אמרתי להן זייפתם תורתכם ולא העליתם בידכם כלום שאתם אומרים אין תחיית המתים מן התורה הרי הוא אומר ל) הכרת תכרת הנפש ההיא עונה בה הכרת בעולם הזה עונה בה לאימת לאו לעולם הבא א"ל רב פפא לאביי ולימא להו תרוייהו מהכרת תכרת אינהו הוו אמרי ליה [י] דברה תורה כלשון בני אדם כתנאי [כ] הכרת תכרת [א]הכרת בעולם הזה תכרת לעולם הבא דברי ר"ע אמר לו ר' ישמעאל והלא כבר נאמר מ) את ה' הוא מגדף ונכרתה וכי שלשה עולמים יש אלא ונכרתה בעולם הזה הכרת לעולם הבא הכרת תכרת דברה תורה כלשון בני אדם בין ר' ישמעאל ובין ר"ע עונה בה מאי עבדי ביה לכדתניא [ל] יכול אפילו עשה תשובה ת"ל עונה בה לא אמרתי אלא בזמן שעונה בה שאלה קליאופטרא מלכתא את ר"מ אמרה ידענא דחיי שכבי דכתיב נ) ויציצו מעיר כעשב הארץ אלא כשהן עומדין עומדין ערומין או בלבושיהן עומדין אמר לה [מ] ק"ו מחיטה [ב] ומה חיטה שנקברה ערומה יוצאה בכמה לבושין צדיקים שנקברים בלבושיהן על אחת כמה וכמה א"ל קיסר לרבן גמליאל אמריתו דשכבי חיי הא הוו עפרא ועפרא מי קא חיי

אמרה

רש"י

ויהי לו כן וירמסו אותו. דבדבר שכפר בו נדון שלא אכל מסס ונרמס ברגלי הבאים לקנות: [י] (וכי אהרן קיים לעולם. כלומר וכי אהרן חיה כל כך שתנתן לו תרומה והלא לא נכנס לארץ ישראל ומאי האי דקאמר ונתתם ממנו תרומת ה' לאהרן הכהן): לעולם קיים. לאו דווקא אלא כלומר הלא לא נגזר עליו שיחיה כל כך: שעתיד לחיות. לעולם הבא: דבי רבי ישמעאל תנא. הא דכתיב לאהרן לאו להכי הוא דאתא אלא לומר לך כאהרן וכו': מה ארי ספק דורס ואוכל. ואין אנו יודעין כשנוטל בהמה מן העדר אם דעתו לדורסה ולאוכלה מיד קודם שתסריח או לא אלא לטרוף ולמלא (חורו) [תאותו] ולאחר זמן יאכלנה כשתסריח וה"נ כהן עם הארץ כשאנו נותנין לו תרומה בידו אין אנו יודעין אם יאכלנה בטהרה או בטומאה [אי נמי] ספק דורס שארי דרכו לדרוס ולרמוס בהמה ברגליו ואוכלה כשהיא דרוסה מנוולת ופעמים שנותנה בחורו ואינה מנוולת: עון אשמה. עונות הרבה מטעין עליו: באכלם את קדשיהם. ומתרגמינן במיכלהון בסואבא ית קודשיהון: אלא להם. דמשמע שהבטיח הקב"ה לאבותינו אברהם יצחק ויעקב שיתן להם ארץ ישראל וכי להם ניתנה והלא לבניהם ניתנה אלא מלמד שעתידין לחיות ועתיד הקב"ה ליתן להם את ארץ ישראל: הנך שוכב עם אבותיך וקם. הנה אתה מת שוכב והנה אתה קם שתחיה לעתיד לבא והאי וקם אהנך קאי: דילמא וקם העם וזנה. דלקמי' קאי ולאו אדלעיל והיינו אחד [ס] (מג') מקראות שאין להם הכרע [ע]: יחיו מתיך. דמתים שבארץ ישראל יחיו: נבלתי יקומון. אפי' נפלים יחיו במסכת כתובות [פ]: ודילמא מתים שהחיה יחזקאל. דהסיא קרא יחיו מתיך ישעיה אמרו והוא קדם ליחזקאל שנתנבא בימי חזקיה והיה מתנבא פסוק זה על שהיה עתיד יחזקאל להחיות מתים אבל לעולם הבא לא: דובב. פרונמיי"ש בלע"ז כלומר נעות ומתנודדות שפתי ישיני עפר מכלל שיחיו: מרחשן שפוותיהו בעלמא. שפתותיהן נעות מעט בתוך הקבר אבל אין חיין ויוצאין לאויר העולם וכרבי יוחנן וכו': ולא קבלו ממנו. עד שאמר להם וכו': חיים כלכם היום. דהאי [צ] יום מיותר הוא דמצי למכתב חיים כלכם מה תלמוד לומר היום כהיום מה היום וכו' כך שמעתי: הנך שוכב עם אבותיך וקם. הרי תחיית המתים העם הזה וזנה הרי מה שעתיד להיות: פלגא בידך. דמהאי קרא נפקא דיודע מה שעתיד: זייפתם ולא העליתם. כזב אתם אומרים ואין ממש בדבריכם: לאו לעולם הבא. אלמא יש תחיית המתים: מהכרת תכרת. הכרת בעולם הזה תכרת לעולם הבא: אינהו הוו אמרי ליה דברה תורה כלשון בני אדם. ולהכי אמר להו הכי כי היכי דלא להוי להו פתחון פה: הכרת תכרת. בעבודת כוכבים כתיב: והלא כבר נאמר. בעבודת כוכבים את ה' הוא מגדף ונכרתה דס"ל מגדף [ק] היינו עובד עבודת כוכבים: וכי שלשה עולמים יש וכו'. ור"ע סבירא ליה דמגדף היינו מברך השם: והשתא בין לרבי ישמעאל בין לר"ע עונה בה מאי עבדי ליה מבעי ליה וכו': שעונה בה. שלא שב קודם מיתה הוי בכרת אבל שב לא: דחיי שכבי. שהמתים חיים: ויציצו מעיר. שעתידין ישראל לציץ ולפרוח מעיר ירושלים וכדאמרינן (כתובות דף קיא.) הקב"ה עושה להם מחילות לצדיקים והולכין ועולין לירושלים:

עין משפט נר מצוה

ג א מיי' פ"ח מהלכות תשובה הל"א:

ד ב מיי' שם הלכה ג בהשגו' ובהפירוש שהביא בעל מ"ע בשם הרמב"ן:

תורה אור השלם

א) וַיְהִי לוֹ כֵּן וַיִּרְמְסוּ אֹתוֹ הָעָם בַּשַּׁעַר וַיָּמֹת: [מלכים ב' ז, כ]

ב) כֵּן תָּרִימוּ גַם אַתֶּם תְּרוּמַת יְיָ מִכֹּל מַעְשְׂרֹתֵיכֶם אֲשֶׁר תִּקְחוּ מֵאֵת בְּנֵי יִשְׂרָאֵל וּנְתַתֶּם מִמֶּנּוּ אֶת תְּרוּמַת יְיָ לְאַהֲרֹן הַכֹּהֵן: [במדבר יח, כח]

ג) וַיֹּאמֶר לָעָם לְיוֹשְׁבֵי יְרוּשָׁלַיִם לָתֵת מְנָת הַכֹּהֲנִים וְהַלְוִיִּם לְמַעַן יֶחֶזְקוּ בְּתוֹרַת יְיָ: [דברי הימים ב' לא, ד]

ד) וְשָׁמְרוּ אֶת מִשְׁמַרְתִּי וְלֹא יִשְׂאוּ עָלָיו חֵטְא וּמֵתוּ בוֹ כִּי יְחַלְּלֻהוּ אֲנִי יְיָ מְקַדְּשָׁם: [ויקרא כב, ט]

ה) וְהִשִּׂיאוּ אוֹתָם עֲוֹן אַשְׁמָה בְּאׇכְלָם אֶת קׇדְשֵׁיהֶם כִּי אֲנִי יְיָ מְקַדְּשָׁם: [ויקרא כב, טז]

ו) וְגַם הֲקִמֹתִי אֶת בְּרִיתִי אִתָּם לָתֵת לָהֶם אֶת אֶרֶץ כְּנָעַן אֵת אֶרֶץ מְגֻרֵיהֶם אֲשֶׁר גָּרוּ בָהּ: [שמות ו, ד]

ז) וַיֹּאמֶר יְיָ אֶל מֹשֶׁה הִנְּךָ שֹׁכֵב עִם אֲבֹתֶיךָ וְקָם הָעָם הַזֶּה וְזָנָה אַחֲרֵי אֱלֹהֵי נֵכַר הָאָרֶץ אֲשֶׁר הוּא בָא שָׁמָּה בְּקִרְבּוֹ וַעֲזָבַנִי וְהֵפֵר אֶת בְּרִיתִי אֲשֶׁר כָּרַתִּי אִתּוֹ: [דברים לא, טז]

ח) יִחְיוּ מֵתֶיךָ נְבֵלָתִי יְקוּמוּן הָקִיצוּ וְרַנְּנוּ שֹׁכְנֵי עָפָר כִּי טַל אוֹרֹת טַלֶּךָ וָאָרֶץ רְפָאִים תַּפִּיל: [ישעיה כו, יט]

ט) וְחִכֵּךְ כְּיֵין הַטּוֹב הוֹלֵךְ לְדוֹדִי לְמֵישָׁרִים דּוֹבֵב שִׂפְתֵי יְשֵׁנִים: [שיר השירים ז, י]

י) לְמַעַן יִרְבּוּ יְמֵיכֶם וִימֵי בְנֵיכֶם עַל הָאֲדָמָה אֲשֶׁר נִשְׁבַּע יְיָ לַאֲבֹתֵיכֶם לָתֵת לָהֶם כִּימֵי הַשָּׁמַיִם עַל הָאָרֶץ: [דברים יא, כא]

כ) וְאַתֶּם הַדְּבֵקִים בַּייָ אֱלֹהֵיכֶם חַיִּים כֻּלְּכֶם הַיּוֹם: [דברים ד, ד]

ל) כִּי דְבַר יְיָ בָּזָה וְאֶת מִצְוָתוֹ הֵפַר הִכָּרֵת תִּכָּרֵת הַנֶּפֶשׁ הַהִוא עֲוֹנָה בָהּ: [במדבר טו, לא]

מ) וְהַנֶּפֶשׁ אֲשֶׁר תַּעֲשֶׂה בְּיָד רָמָה מִן הָאֶזְרָח וּמִן הַגֵּר אֶת יְיָ הוּא מְגַדֵּף וְנִכְרְתָה הַנֶּפֶשׁ הַהִוא מִקֶּרֶב עַמָּהּ: [במדבר טו, ל]

נ) יְהִי פִסַּת בַּר בָּאָרֶץ בְּרֹאשׁ הָרִים יִרְעַשׁ כַּלְּבָנוֹן פִּרְיוֹ וְיָצִיצוּ מֵעִיר כְּעֵשֶׂב הָאָרֶץ: [תהלים עב, טז]

מסורת הש"ס

א) מכות יא. ברכות נו., ב) [ליתא בע"י], ג) ס"א מכאן אמרו שאין נותנין מתנה לכהן ע"ה, ד) חולין קל:, ה) [נ"ל הכהנים והלוים], ו) [פסחים מט: ע"ש], ז) יבמות צז: ע"ש בכורות לא: ע"ש, ח) רש"ל מ"ז, ט) [מו"ק כח.], י) [קידושין יז. וש"נ], כ) לעיל סד: [שבועות יג.], ל) [שבועות דף יג.], מ) [כתובות קיא: ועי' תוספות חולין קיז: ד"ה חטה], נ) רש"ל מ"ז, ס) [נ"ל מחמשה], ע) [יומא נב.], פ) [דף קיא.], צ) [נ"ל היום], ק) [לעיל סד: כריתות ז:].

הגהות הגר"א

[א] גמ' סימן צדיק גם גשם קם. נ"ב לדיק ק"ם גש"ם ג"ם סי' כצ"ל:

ליקוטי רש"י

ויאמר לעם. ביהושפט כתיב בדברי הימים סיפיה דקרא למען יחזקו בתורת ה'. מנת. חלק כהונה [חולין קל:]. למען יחזקו בתורת ה'. יוחר ברצון ועוד בעוד שיהא להם פרנסה מזומנת יכלו לעשות ולעסוק בתורת ה' לפי שלא נתנה התורה אלא לאוכלי המן ושניים להם אוכלי תרומה [דה"ב לא, ד]. ומתו בו. למדנו שהיא מיתה בידי שמים [ויקרא כב, ט]. יחיו מתיך. כאן התפלל שיחיו הצדיקים בבקשה ממך יחיו אותן שמומתין עליך יצא דבר מלכות מלפניך לומר נבלתי יקומון נבלות עמי שנבלו עצמן עלי להם תהי תקומה זו חילוף למה שכתוב למעלה רפאים בל יקומו אבל אלו יקומון. הקיצו ורננו. כל זה יאמר להם הקב"ה הקיצו ורננו ל' צווי הוא זה. כי טל אורות טלך. כי נאה לך לעשות כן שיהא טל תורתך ומצותיך להם טל של אור. וארץ רפאים תפיל. ולארץ ולעפר תפיל את ארץ רפאים שריפו ידיהם מתורתך [ישעיה כו, יט]. ודילמא רחושי מרחשן שפוותיה בעלמא. כיין הטוב שהוא דובב שפתי ישני' אף אבותי בקבר ישמחו בי ויודו על חלקם דובב מרחיש פרומ"יר בלע"ז ויסודו לשון דיבור [שה"ש ז, י]. דובבות. נעות לשון דבר [ס"א, דבב] שמרחיש ומבצבץ [יבמות צז.]. נעות והנאה הוא לו שדומה כחי [בכורות לא:]. והלא כבר נאמר את ה' הוא מגדף ונכרתה. באותה פרשה עצמה גבי מגדף ור' עקיבא סבירא ליה מגדף היינו מברך את השם כדאמר בכריתות ועולם הבא לא נפקא ליה בעבודה זרה אלא מהכרת תכרת ור' ישמעאל לאו לר' עקיבא פריך והלא כבר נאמר ונכרתה דהא ר' עקיבא במברך את השם מוקים לה אלא טעמא דנפשיה קאמר והלא כבר נאמרה ונכרתה ואנא סבירא ליה דבעבודה זרה כתיבא. וכי שלשה עולמים יש וכו'. ודומה לו בשחיטת חולין והלא במוקדשין האומר רגלה של זו עולה כולה עולה דהא פרקא לאו לכשנגדו פריך דאיהו סבירא ליה אפילו במוקדשין דאין כולה עולה אלא טעמא דנפשיה אמר בפרק [בהמה המקשה] (חולין סט.) [לעיל סד:]. דברה תורה כלשון בני אדם וכו'. הכי משתעו בני אדם ודברה תורה כלשון בני אדם וליכא למידרש מינה כלום [נדרים ג.]. ואף על גב דאיכא למדרש לא דרשינן כדמוכח בפ"ב דב"מ (לא:) [ר"ן שם]. לא אמרתי אלא בזמן שעונה בה. שאם עשה תשובה ואין עונה בה מיתה ממרקת ולא תכרת לעולם הבא [שבועות יג.]. ויציצו. ישראל. מעיר. מתוך ירושלים כעשב הארץ [תהלים עב, טז].

וּכְתִיב – **And it is written:** ,,וַיְהִי־לוֹ כֵּן וַיִּרְמְסוּ אֹתוֹ הָעָם בַּשַּׁעַר וַיָּמֹת" – ***And so it happened to him, that the people trampled him in the gate, and he died.***[1]

The Gemara asks:

וְדִילְמָא קִלְלַת אֱלִישָׁע גָּרְמָה לֵיהּ – **But perhaps Elisha's curse caused him** [the captain] to die, rather than Divine "measure for measure" punishment. דְּאָמַר רַב יְהוּדָה אָמַר רַב – **For Rav Yehudah said in the name of Rav:** קִלְלַת חָכָם אֲפִילוּ עַל חִנָּם הִיא בָאָה – **The curse of a sage – even when it is gratuitous – comes** to pass.[2] – ? –

The Gemara answers:

אִם כֵּן – **If so,** that Elisha's curse was the cause, לִכְתּוֹב קְרָא ,,וַיִּרְמְסוּהוּ וַיָּמֹת" – then **the verse should write** simply: ***And they trampled him and he died.*** מַאי ,,בַּשַּׁעַר" – **What** is the significance of the verse stating that they trampled him ***in the gate***? עַל עִסְקֵי שַׁעַר – It is to indicate that he died **on account of matters pertaining to the gate.**[3]

R' Yochanan demonstrates how a Pentateuchal passage alludes to the Resurrection of the Dead:

(אָמַר רַבִּי יוֹחָנָן – **R' Yochanan said:**) מִנַּיִין לִתְחִיַּית הַמֵּתִים מִן הַתּוֹרָה – **Where** do we find an allusion **to the Resurrection of the Dead in the** Written **Torah?**[4] שֶׁנֶּאֱמַר ,,וּנְתַתֶּם מִמֶּנּוּ [אֶת־] תְּרוּמַת ה' לְאַהֲרֹן הַכֹּהֵן" – **For it states:** ***And you shall give from it HASHEM's terumah to Aaron the Kohen.***[5] וְכִי אַהֲרֹן לְעוֹלָם קַיָּים – **Now, is Aaron alive forever?** וַהֲלֹא לֹא נִכְנַס לְאֶרֶץ יִשְׂרָאֵל – **Why, he never** even **entered Eretz Yisrael** שֶׁנּוֹתְנִין לוֹ תְּרוּמָה – **that they should give him *terumah*!**[6] אֶלָּא מְלַמֵּד שֶׁעָתִיד לִחְיוֹת – **Rather, this teaches that [Aaron] is destined to live** again in bodily form, וְיִשְׂרָאֵל נוֹתְנִין לוֹ תְּרוּמָה – **and** the people of **Israel will** then **give him *terumah.***[7] מִכָּאן לִתְחִיַּית הַמֵּתִים מִן הַתּוֹרָה – **Here** we have an allusion **to the Resurrection of the Dead in the** Written **Torah.**

A Baraisa, however, interprets the mention of Aaron in this passage differently:

דְּבֵי רַבִּי יִשְׁמָעֵאל תָּנָא – **In R' Yishmael's academy, a Tanna taught** that Aaron is mentioned in this passage for a different reason: ,,לְאַהֲרֹן" כְּאַהֲרֹן – By stating that the *terumah* is to be given *TO AARON,* Scripture indicates that *terumah* is to be given specifically to a Kohen LIKE AARON. מָה אַהֲרֹן חָבֵר – JUST AS AARON was A *CHAVER,*[8] אַף בָּנָיו חֲבֵרִים – SO TOO, HIS CHILDREN must be *CHAVERIM* in order to receive *terumah.*[9] According to this exposition, we cannot find an allusion to Resurrection of the Dead in this passage.

Another source for the rule that *terumah* may be given to a Kohen only if he is a *chaver*:

אָמַר רַבִּי שְׁמוּאֵל בַּר נַחְמָנִי אָמַר רַבִּי יוֹנָתָן – **R' Shmuel bar Nachmani said in the name of R' Yonasan:** מִנַּיִין שֶׁאֵין נוֹתְנִין תְּרוּמָה

NOTES

1. *II Kings* 7:20. Elisha's prediction came true. The besieging army fled during the night, leaving all their food behind in their camp. In the morning, people went out and despoiled the abandoned camp of the enemy, bringing an abundance of food to the city. The captain, who was stationed at the gate, was trampled to death by the stampede of people.

His death was an example of a Divine punishment that corresponded exactly to the nature of the sin. He had sinned by denying God's ability to provide an abundance of food on the morrow. He was punished by witnessing that abundance yet being denied the opportunity to partake of it, and by being trampled in the very stampede caused by the abundance he had declared impossible (see *Rashi*).

2. See *Makkos* 11a. [*Ritva* (there) asserts that the curse must nonetheless be somewhat deserved. But regarding a curse that is *entirely* undeserved, the verse (*Proverbs* 26:2, cited earlier by the Gemara there) states: כַּצִּפּוֹר לָנוּד כַּדְּרוֹר לָעוּף כֵּן קִלְלַת חִנָּם לֹא תָבֹא, *Like a wandering bird, like a flying swallow, so will a gratuitous curse not come to pass.* Cf. *Maharal, Nesivos Olam, Nesiv HaTorah* §12, cited by *Einayim LaMishpat* here.]

If the curse of a sage comes to pass even if gratuitous, then certainly it comes to pass if pronounced for good reason, as in the case of the captain cursed by Elisha. Perhaps, then, it was Elisha's curse that caused the captain to die in this way (*Be'er Sheva*; cf. *Sanhedrei Katanah*).

3. Since the word בַּשַּׁעַר is superfluous, it is expounded not as "*in* the gate" (designating the place of the captain's death) but rather as "*on account of* the gate," i.e. for having scoffed at what the prophet foretold would happen in the gate of Shomron. [*Maharsha* explains that the Gemara means to expound the word שַׁעַר, *shaar,* in the sense of "market price," a usage common in the Talmud. Thus, the captain was punished for having scoffed at the drastic fall in the price of food foretold by the prophet.]

[Had the captain's end come about as a result of Elisha's curse, however, the verse would not describe it as resulting from the captain's remarks concerning the *shaar,* though those remarks prompted Elisha's curse.]

4. Though the verse that will be cited is from the Pentateuch itself, the expression מִן הַתּוֹרָה can refer to all of Scripture, as evident from the end of 91b, where this same expression is used regarding proofs brought from prophets (*Neviim*) and the Holy Writings (*Kesuvim*).

5. *Numbers* 18:28. This commandment is addressed to the Leviim, who are bidden to tithe the tithe *they* receive from the produce growers and give that tithe of the tithe (*terumas maaser*) to the Kohanim.

6. [Translation follows the printed text. The words וַהֲלֹא לֹא נִכְנַס לְאֶרֶץ יִשְׂרָאֵל, however, seem to interrupt the flow of the statement and are indeed absent in *Yalkut Shimoni* §759; see also *Ein Yaakov* and *Dikdukei Soferim.*]

Aaron died in the Wilderness in the fortieth year after the Exodus, and never entered Eretz Yisrael (see *Numbers* 20:28, 33:38). The obligation to separate *terumos* and *maasros,* however, did not commence until the Jews entered Eretz Yisrael (see *Kiddushin* 36b ff.). Thus, the Torah's command that *terumah* be given to Aaron was never fulfilled! [Though the mention here of "Aaron the Kohen" could be understood as reference to Kohanim in general, who are all his descendants, elsewhere the Torah refers to Kohanim in general as "the *sons* of Aaron" (see, for example, *Leviticus* 6:2). The specific mention of Aaron himself, then, indicates that it is Aaron himself who is meant.]

7. The Gemara here, which states that Aaron will be given *terumah* upon his resurrection, seems to indicate that the resurrected will engage in eating and drinking (and all bodily functions). This presents a difficulty according to the view of *Ramban* et al. (which maintains that the time of the Resurrection is what is meant by "the World to Come") in light of Rav's teaching (*Berachos* 17a) that "in the World to Come there is no eating or drinking . . ." (see Introduction to this chapter). *Aruch LaNer* suggests (on the basis of *Yoma* 5b; see also *Ritva* to *Niddah* ad loc. at great length) that Moses and Aaron [and other great *tzaddikim*] will be resurrected at the *beginning* of the Messianic reign, at which time the natural order of the world – including all bodily functions – will remain in force. The other statements cited above concerning the era of the Resurrection, apply to the era of the *general* resurrection, which will take place at the end of the Messianic reign. (See also *Sefer HaIkkarim,* cited above in note 4 to the chapter introduction.)

[Another issue that has bearing here is the applicability of *mitzvos* (such as *terumah*) upon resurrection – see *Niddah* 61b, with *Ritva* at length; see also *Kovetz Shiurim II* 29.]

8. A *chaver* is one who has accepted upon himself the meticulous observance of the *tumah* laws with all their attendant customs (see *Tosefta Demai* 2:2). This is in contrast to an *am haaretz,* who – although basically an observant Jew – is one whose observance of certain laws, especially those with numerous and complex details, cannot be relied upon due to his ignorance. A Kohen *chaver* is careful never to eat *terumah* that is *tamei* or to eat any *terumah* while he is *tamei.*

9. Some texts (see margin of Vilna edition; see also *Sifri* ad loc.) have here a concluding statement of the Baraisa: *Based on this, [the sages] said that we do not give a priestly gift to a Kohen who is an am haaretz.* Thus, the rule taught here concerns not only *terumah* (which is but one of the twenty-four priestly gifts) but all the priestly gifts as well. There is, however, a distinction between *terumah* and non-*terumah* gifts. In the case of other gifts, one does give them to a Kohen *am haaretz* if no Kohen *chaver* is available [as stated in *Tosafos* to *Chullin* 130b ד"ה מנין]. Under no circumstances, though, should *terumah* be given to a Kohen *am haaretz* (*Be'er Sheva*; see Mishnah *Challah* 4:9 with commentaries).

עין משפט
נר מצוה

ג א מיי' פ"ח מהלכות תשובה הל"א:
ד ב מיי' שם הלכה ב בהשגו' ובהפירוש שהביא בעל מ"ע בשם הרמב"ן:

וכתיב א) ויהי לו כן וירמסו אותו העם בשער וימות ודילמא קללת אלישע גרמה ליה א) דאמר רב יהודה אמר רב קללת חכם אפי' על חנם היא באה אם כן לכתוב קרא וירמסוהו וימות מאי בשער על עסקי שער (ב) אמר ר' יוחנן) מניין לתחיית המתים מן התורה שנאמר ב) ונתתם ממנו [את] תרומת ה' לאהרן הכהן וכי אהרן לעולם קיים והלא לא נכנס לארץ ישראל שנותנין לו תרומה אלא מלמד שעתיד לחיות וישראל נותנין לו תרומה מכאן לתחיית המתים מן התורה דבי רבי ישמעאל תנא לאהרן כאהרן מה אהרן חבר אף בניו חברים ג) ד) א"ר שמואל בר נחמני אמר רבי יונתן מניין שאין נותנין תרומה לכהן עם הארץ שנאמר ג) ויאמר לעם ליושבי ירושלים לתת מנת (ה) לכהנים ולוים) למען יחזקו בתורת ה' כל המחזיק בתורת ה' יש לו מנת ושאינו מחזיק בתורת ה' אין לו מנת אמר רב אחא בר אדא אמר רב יהודה כל הנותן תרומה לכהן עם הארץ כאילו נותנה לפני ארי ו) מה ארי ספק דורס ואוכל ספק אינו דורס ואוכל אף כהן עם הארץ ספק אוכלה בטהרה ספק אוכלה בטומאה ר' יוחנן אמר אף גורם לו מיתה שנאמר ד) ומתו בו כי יחללוהו דבי ר"א בן יעקב תנא אף משיאו עון אשמה שנאמר ה) והשיאו אותם עון אשמה באכלם את קדשיהם תניא ר' סימאי אומר מניין לתחיית המתים מן התורה שנאמר ו) וגם הקימותי את בריתי אתם לתת להם את ארץ כנען לכם לא נאמר אלא להם מכאן לתחיית המתים מן התורה: [א] (צד"ק ג"ם גש"ם ק"ם סימן): שאלו מינין את רבן גמליאל מניין שהקדוש ברוך הוא מחיה מתים אמר להם מן התורה ומן הנביאים ומן הכתובים ולא קיבלו ממנו מן התורה דכתיב ז) ויאמר ה' אל משה הנך שוכב עם אבותיך וקם אמרו לו ודילמא וקם העם הזה וזנה מן הנביאים דכתיב ח) יחיו מתיך נבלתי יקומון הקיצו ורננו שוכני עפר כי טל אורות טלך וארץ רפאים תפיל ודילמא מתים שהחיה יחזקאל מן הכתובים דכתיב ט) וחכך כיין הטוב הולך לדודי למישרים דובב שפתי ישנים ודילמא רחושי מרחשן שפוותיה בעלמא כר' יוחנן י) דאמר ר' יוחנן משום ר"ש בן יהוצדק כל מי שנאמרה הלכה בשמו בעולם הזה שפתותיו דובבות בקבר שנאמר דובב שפתי ישנים עד שאמר להם מקרא זה י) אשר נשבע ה' לאבותיכם לתת להם לכם לא נאמר אלא להם מיכן לתחיית המתים מן התורה וי"א מן המקרא הזה אמר להם כ) ואתם הדבקים בה' אלהיכם חיים כלכם היום (נ) פשיטא דחיים כולכם היום אלא אפילו ביום שכל העולם כולם מתים אתם חיים) מה היום כולכם קיימין אף לעוה"ב כולכם קיימין שאלו רומיים את רבי יהושע בן חנניה מניין שהקב"ה מחיה מתים ויודע מה שעתיד להיות אמר להו תרווייהו מן המקרא הזה שנאמר ז) ויאמר ה' אל משה הנך שוכב עם אבותיך וקם העם הזה וזנה ודילמא וקם העם הזה וזנה אמר להו ט) נקוטו מיהא פלגא בידייכו דיודע מה שעתיד להיות איתמר נמי א"ר יוחנן משום רבי שמעון בן יוחאי מניין שהקדוש ברוך הוא מחיה מתים ויודע מה שעתיד להיות שנאמר הנך שוכב עם אבותיך וקם וגו' תניא א"ר אליעזר בר' יוסי בדבר זה זייפתי ספרי מינים שהיו אומרים אין תחיית המתים מן התורה אמרתי להן זייפתם תורתכם ולא העליתם בידכם כלום שאתם אומרים אין תחיית המתים מן התורה הרי הוא אומר ל) הכרת תכרת הנפש ההיא עונה בה הכרת תכרת בעולם הזה עונה בה לאימת לאו לעולם הבא א"ל רב פפא לאביי ולימא להו תרווייהו מהכרת תכרת אינהו הוו אמרי ליה י) דברה תורה כלשון בני אדם כתנאי נ) הכרת תכרת א הכרת בעולם הזה תכרת לעולם הבא דברי ר"ע אמר לו ר' ישמעאל והלא כבר נאמר מ) את ה' הוא מגדף ונכרתה וכי שלשה עולמים יש אלא ונכרתה בעולם הזה הכרת לעולם הבא הכרת תכרת דברה תורה כלשון בני אדם בין ר' ישמעאל ובין ר"ע עונה בה מאי עבדי ביה לכדתניא ל) יכול אפילו עשה תשובה ת"ל עונה בה לא אמרתי אלא בזמן שעונה בה שאלה קליאופטרא מלכתא את ר"מ אמרה ידענא דחיי שכבי דכתיב נ) ויציצו מעיר כעשב הארץ אלא כשהן עומדין עומדין ערומין או בלבושיהן עומדין אמר לה מ) ק"ו מחיטה ב ומה חיטה שנקברה ערומה יוצאה בכמה לבושין צדיקים שנקברים בלבושיהן על אחת כמה וכמה א"ל קיסר לרבן גמליאל אמריתו דשכבי חיי הא הוו עפרא ועפרא מי קא חיי

אמרה

ויהי לו כן וירמסו אותו. דבדבר שכפר בו נדון שלא אכל משם ונרמס ברגלי הבאים לקנות: ס) (וכי אהרן קיים לעולם. כלומר וכי אהרן חיה כל כך שתנתן לו תרומה והלא לא נכנס לארץ ישראל ומאי האי דקאמר ונתתם ממנו תרומת ה' לאהרן הכהן): לעולם קיים. לאו דווקא אלא כלומר הלא לא נגזר עליו שיחיה כל כך: שעתיד לחיות. לעולם הבא: דבי רבי ישמעאל תנא. הא דכתיב לאהרן לאו להכי הוא דאתא אלא לומר לך כאהרן וכו': מה ארי ספק דורס ואוכל. ואין אנו יודעין כשנוטל בהמה מן העדר אם דעתו לדורסה ולאוכלה מיד קודם שתסריח או לא אלא לטרוף ולמלא (חורו) [תאותו] ולאחר זמן יאכלנה כשתסריח וה"נ כהן עם הארץ כשאנו נותנין לו תרומה בידו אין אנו יודעין אם יאכלנה בטהרה או בטומאה [אי נמי] ספק דורס שארי דרכו לדרוס ולרמוס בהמה ברגליו ואוכלה כשהיא דרוסה מנוולת ופעמים שנותנה בחורו ואינה מנוולת: עון אשמה. עונות הרבה מטעין עליו: באכלם את קדשיהם. ומתרגמינן במיכלהון בסואבא ית קודשיהון: אלא להם. דמשמע שהבטיח הקב"ה לאבותינו אברהם יצחק ויעקב שיתן להם ארץ ישראל וכי להם ניתנה והלא לבניהם ניתנה אלא מלמד שעתידין לחיות ועתיד הקב"ה ליתן להם את ארץ ישראל: הנך שוכב עם אבותיך וקם. הנה אתה מת שוכב והנה אתה קם שתחיה לעתיד לבא והאי וקם אהנך קאי: דילמא וקם העם וזנה. דלקמי' קאי ולאו אדלעיל והיינו אחד פ) (מג') מקראות שאין להם הכרע צ): יחיו מתיך. דמתים שבארץ ישראל יחיו: נבלתי יקומון. אפי' נפלים יחיו במסכת כתובות ק): ודילמא מתים שהחיה יחזקאל. דההיא קרא יחיו מתיך ישעיה אמרו והוא קדם ליחזקאל שנתנבא בימי חזקיה והיה מתנבא פסוק זה על שהיה עתיד יחזקאל להחיות מתים אבל לעולם הבא לא: דובב. פרונמיי"ש בלע"ז כלומר נעות ומתנודדות שפתי ישיני עפר מכלל שיחיו: מרחשן שפוותיהו בעלמא. שפתותיהן נעות מעט בתוך הקבר אבל אין חיין ויוצאין לאויר העולם וכרבי יוחנן וכו': ולא קבלו ממנו. עד שאמר להם וכו': חיים כלכם היום. דהאי ר) יום מיותר הוא דמצי למכתב חיים כלכם מה תלמוד לומר היום כהיום מה היום וכו' כך שמעתי: הנך שוכב עם אבותיך וקם. הרי תחיית המתים העם הזה וזנה הרי מה שעתיד להיות: פלגא בידך. דמהאי קרא נפקא דיודע מה שעתיד: זייפתם ולא העליתם. כזב אתם אומרים ואין ממש בדבריכם: לאו לעולם הבא. אלמא יש תחיית המתים: מהכרת תכרת. הכרת בעולם הזה תכרת לעולם הבא: אינהו הוו אמרי ליה דברה תורה כלשון בני אדם. ולהכי אמר להו הכי כי היכי דלא להוי להו פתחון פה: הכרת תכרת. בעבודת כוכבים כתיב: והלא כבר נאמר. בעבודת כוכבים את ה' הוא מגדף ונכרתה דס"ל מגדף ק) היינו עובד עבודת כוכבים: וכי שלשה עולמים יש וכו'. ור"ע סבירא ליה דמגדף היינו מברך השם: והשתא בין לרבי ישמעאל בין לר"ע עונה בה מאי עבדי ליה מבעי ליה וכו': שעונה בה. שלא שב קודם מיתה הוי בכרת אבל שב לא: דחיי שכבי. שהמתים חיים: ויציצו מעיר. שעתידין ישראל לציץ ולפרוח מעיר ירושלים וכדאמרינן (כתובות דף קיא.) הקב"ה עושה להם מחילות לצדיקים והולכין ועולין לירושלים:

רגלה של זו עולה כולה עולה דהא פרכא לאו לכשנגדו פריך דאיהו סבירא ליה אפילו במוקדשין דאין כולה עולה אלא טעמא דנפשיה אמר בפרק [בהמה המקשה] (חולין סט.) [לעיל סד:]. דברה תורה כלשון בני אדם וכו'. הכי משתעו בני אדם ודברה תורה כלשון בני אדם וליכא למידרש מינה כלום [נדרים ג.]. ואף על גב דאיכא למדרש לא דרשינן כדמוכח בפ"ב דב"מ (לא:) [ר"ן שם]. לא אמרתי אלא בזמן שעונה בה. שאם עשה תשובה ואין עונה בה מיתה ממרקת ולא תכרת לעולם הבא [שבועות יג.]. ויציצו. ישראל. מעיר. מתוך ירושלים כעשב הארץ [תהלים עב, טז].

תורה אור השלם

א) וַיְהִי לוֹ כֵּן וַיִּרְמְסוּ אֹתוֹ הָעָם בַּשַּׁעַר וַיָּמֹת: [מלכים ב' ז, כ]

ב) כֵּן תָּרִימוּ גַם אַתֶּם תְּרוּמַת יְיָ מִכֹּל מַעְשְׂרֹתֵיכֶם אֲשֶׁר תִּקְחוּ מֵאֵת בְּנֵי יִשְׂרָאֵל וּנְתַתֶּם מִמֶּנּוּ אֶת תְּרוּמַת יְיָ לְאַהֲרֹן הַכֹּהֵן: [במדבר יח, כח]

ג) וַיֹּאמֶר לָעָם לְיוֹשְׁבֵי יְרוּשָׁלִַם לָתֵת מְנָת הַכֹּהֲנִים וְהַלְוִיִּם לְמַעַן יֶחֶזְקוּ בְּתוֹרַת יְיָ: [דברי הימים ב' לא, ד]

ד) וְשָׁמְרוּ אֶת מִשְׁמַרְתִּי וְלֹא יִשְׂאוּ עָלָיו חֵטְא וּמֵתוּ בוֹ כִּי יְחַלְּלֻהוּ אֲנִי יְיָ מְקַדְּשָׁם: [ויקרא כב, ט]

ה) וְהִשִּׂיאוּ אוֹתָם עֲוֹן אַשְׁמָה בְּאָכְלָם אֶת קָדְשֵׁיהֶם כִּי אֲנִי יְיָ מְקַדְּשָׁם: [ויקרא כב, טז]

ו) וְגַם הֲקִמֹתִי אֶת בְּרִיתִי אִתָּם לָתֵת לָהֶם אֶת אֶרֶץ כְּנָעַן אֵת אֶרֶץ מְגֻרֵיהֶם אֲשֶׁר גָּרוּ בָהּ: [שמות ו, ד]

ז) וַיֹּאמֶר יְיָ אֶל מֹשֶׁה הִנְּךָ שֹׁכֵב עִם אֲבֹתֶיךָ וְקָם הָעָם הַזֶּה וְזָנָה אַחֲרֵי אֱלֹהֵי נֵכַר הָאָרֶץ אֲשֶׁר הוּא בָא שָׁמָּה בְּקִרְבּוֹ וַעֲזָבַנִי וְהֵפֵר אֶת בְּרִיתִי אֲשֶׁר כָּרַתִּי אִתּוֹ: [דברים לא, טז]

ח) יִחְיוּ מֵתֶיךָ נְבֵלָתִי יְקוּמוּן הָקִיצוּ וְרַנְּנוּ שֹׁכְנֵי עָפָר כִּי טַל אוֹרֹת טַלֶּךָ וָאָרֶץ רְפָאִים תַּפִּיל: [ישעיה כו, יט]

ט) וְחִכֵּךְ כְּיֵין הַטּוֹב הוֹלֵךְ לְדוֹדִי לְמֵישָׁרִים דּוֹבֵב שִׂפְתֵי יְשֵׁנִים: [שיר השירים ז, י]

י) לְמַעַן יִרְבּוּ יְמֵיכֶם וִימֵי בְנֵיכֶם עַל הָאֲדָמָה אֲשֶׁר נִשְׁבַּע יְיָ לַאֲבֹתֵיכֶם לָתֵת לָהֶם כִּימֵי הַשָּׁמַיִם עַל הָאָרֶץ: [דברים יא, כא]

כ) וְאַתֶּם הַדְּבֵקִים בַּייָ אֱלֹהֵיכֶם חַיִּים כֻּלְּכֶם הַיּוֹם: [דברים ד, ד]

ל) כִּי דְבַר יְיָ בָּזָה וְאֶת מִצְוָתוֹ הֵפַר הִכָּרֵת תִּכָּרֵת הַנֶּפֶשׁ הַהִוא עֲוֹנָה בָהּ: [במדבר טו, לא]

מ) וְהַנֶּפֶשׁ אֲשֶׁר תַּעֲשֶׂה בְּיָד רָמָה מִן הָאֶזְרָח וּמִן הַגֵּר אֶת יְיָ הוּא מְגַדֵּף וְנִכְרְתָה הַנֶּפֶשׁ הַהִוא מִקֶּרֶב עַמָּהּ: [במדבר טו, ל]

נ) יְהִי פִסַּת בַּר בָּאָרֶץ בְּרֹאשׁ הָרִים יִרְעַשׁ כַּלְּבָנוֹן פִּרְיוֹ וְיָצִיצוּ מֵעִיר כְּעֵשֶׂב הָאָרֶץ: [תהלים עב, טז]

מסורת הש"ס

א) מכות יא. ברכות נו., ב) [ליתא בע"י], ג) ס"א מכאן אמרו שאין נותנין מתנה לכהן ע"ה, ד) חולין קל:, ה) [צ"ל הכהנים והלוים], ו) [פסחים מט: ע"ש], ז) יבמות לו: ע"ש בכורות לא: ע"ש, ח) רש"ל מ"ז, ט) [מו"ק כח.], י) [קידושין יז. וש"נ], כ) לעיל סד: [שבועות יג.], ל) [שבועות דף יג.], מ) [כתובות קיא: ועי' תוספות חולין קיז: ד"ה חטה], נ) רש"ל מ"ז, ס) [צ"ל מחמשה], ע) [יומא נב.], פ) [דף קיא.], צ) [צ"ל היום], ק) [לעיל סד: כריתות ז:].

הגהות הגר"א

[א] גמ' סימן צדיק גם גשם קם. נ"ב לדיק ק"ס גש"ס ג"ס סי' כצ"ל:

ליקוטי רש"י

ויאמר לעם. ביהושפט כתיב בדברי הימים סיפיה דקרא למען יחזקו בתורת ה'. מנת. חלק כהונה [חולין קל:]. למען יחזקו בתורת ה'. יותר ברצון ועוד בעוד שיהא להם פרנסה' מזומנת יכלו לעשות ולעסוק בתורת ה' לפי שלא נתנה התורה אלא לאוכלי המן ושניים להם אוכלי תרומה [דה"ב לא, ד]. ומתו בו. למדנו שהיא מיתה בידי שמים [ויקרא כב, ט]. יחיו מתיך. כאן התפלל שיחיו הצדיקים בבקשה ממך יחיו אותן שמומתין עליך יצא דבר מלכות מלפניך לומר נבלתי יקומון נבלות עמי שנבלו עצמן עלי להם תהי תקומה זו חילוף למה שכתוב למעלה רפאים בל יקומו אבל אלו יקומון. הקיצו ורננו. כל זה יאמר להם הקב"ה הקיצו ורננו ל' צווי הוא זה. כי טל אורות טלך. כי נאה לך לעשות כן שיהא טל תורתך ומצותיך להם טל של אור. וארץ רפאים תפיל. ולארץ ולעפר תפיל את ארץ רפאים שריפו ידיהם מתורתך [ישעיה כו, יט]. ודילמא רחושי מרחשן שפוותיה בעלמא. כיין הטוב שהוא דובב שפתי ישני' אף אבותי בקבר ישמחו בי ויודו על חלקם דובב מרחיש פרומ"יר בלע"ז ויסודו לשון דיבור [שה"ש ז, י]. דובבות. נעות לשון דבר [ס"א, דבב] שמרחיש ומגלגל [יבמות צז.]. נעות והנאה הוא לו שדומה כחי [בכורות לא:]. והלא כבר נאמר את ה' הוא מגדף ונכרתה. באותה פרשה עצמה גבי מגדף ור' עקיבא סבירא ליה מגדף היינו מברך את השם כדאמר בכריתות ועולם הבא לא נפקא ליה בעבודה זרה אלא מהכרת תכרת ור' ישמעאל לאו לר' עקיבא פריך והלא כבר נאמר ונכרתה דהא ר' עקיבא במברך את השם מוקים לה אלא טעמא דנפשיה קאמר והלא כבר נאמרה ונכרתה ואנא סבירא ליה דבעבודה זרה כתיבא. וכי שלשה עולמים יש וכו'. ודומה לו בשחיטת חולין והלא במוקדשין האומר

לְכֹהֵן עַם הָאָרֶץ – **From where** in Scripture do we know **that we do not give** ***terumah*** **to a Kohen** who is an ***am haaretz?*** שֶׁנֶּאֱמַר ,,וַיֹּאמֶר לָעָם לְיוֹשְׁבֵי יְרוּשָׁלַם לָתֵת מְנָת הַכֹּהֲנִים וְהַלְוִיִּם לְמַעַן יֶחֶזְקוּ בְּתוֹרַת ה׳" – **For it is stated:** ***And [Chizkiah] instructed the people, the inhabitants of Jerusalem, to give the portion of the Kohanim and the Leviim so that [the Kohanim and Leviim] might be strong in*** **H*ASHEM*'s** ***Torah.***[10] From Scripture's description of *terumah* as being intended to support the Kohanim in their adherence to the Torah, we can derive that כָּל הַמַּחֲזִיק בְּתוֹרַת ה׳ יֵשׁ לוֹ מְנָת – **any** Kohen **who holds strongly to Hashem's Torah is entitled to a** *terumah* **portion,** וְשֶׁאֵינוֹ מַחֲזִיק בְּתוֹרַת ה׳ אֵין לוֹ מְנָת – **whereas one who does not hold strongly to Hashem's Torah is not entitled to a** *terumah* **portion.**

The Gemara elaborates on the impropriety of giving *terumah* to a Kohen *am haaretz,* by citing several teachings in this matter:

אָמַר רַב אַחָא בַּר אַדָּא אָמַר רַב יְהוּדָה – **Rav Acha bar Ada said in the name of Rav Yehudah:** כָּל הַנּוֹתֵן תְּרוּמָה לְכֹהֵן עַם הָאָרֶץ – **Whoever gives** ***terumah*** **to a Kohen** ***am haaretz*** כְּאִילּוּ נוֹתְנָהּ לִפְנֵי אֲרִי – **is as if he places it in front of a lion:** מָה אֲרִי סָפֵק דּוֹרֵס וְאוֹכֵל – **Just as** when **a lion** attacks its prey, **it is uncertain** to us **whether [the lion] will maul** its prey **and devour** it immediately, סָפֵק אֵינוֹ דּוֹרֵס וְאוֹכֵל – **or whether it will not maul and devour** its prey immediately,[11] אַף כֹּהֵן עַם הָאָרֶץ – **similarly,** when one gives *terumah* to **a Kohen** ***am haaretz,*** סָפֵק אוֹכְלָהּ בְּטָהֳרָה סָפֵק אוֹכְלָהּ בְּטוּמְאָה – **it is uncertain whether he will eat it in** a state of ***taharah*** **or whether he will eat it in** a state of ***tumah.***[12]

רַבִּי יוֹחָנָן אָמַר – **R' Yochanan says:** אַף גּוֹרֵם לוֹ מִיתָה – By giving *terumah* to a Kohen *am haaretz,* **one even causes death to [the Kohen],** שֶׁנֶּאֱמַר ,,וּמֵתוּ בוֹ כִּי יְחַלְּלֻהוּ" – **as it is stated:** ***And die through it, for they will have desecrated it.***[13]

דְּבֵי רַבִּי אֱלִיעֶזֶר בֶּן יַעֲקֹב תָּנָא – **In the academy of R' Eliezer ben Yaakov, a Tanna taught:** אַף מַשִּׂיאוֹ עֲוֹן אַשְׁמָה – By giving *terumah* to a Kohen *am haaretz,* ONE EVEN BURDENS HIM WITH SIN AND GUILT,[14] שֶׁנֶּאֱמַר ,,וְהִשִּׂיאוּ אוֹתָם עֲוֹן אַשְׁמָה בְּאָכְלָם אֶת־קָדְשֵׁיהֶם" – **as it states:** ***And they will burden them with sin and guilt when they eat their holy foods.***[15]

The Gemara returns to its discussion concerning allusions in the Torah to the doctrine of the Resurrection of the Dead:

תַּנְיָא – **It was taught in a Baraisa:** רַבִּי סִימַאי אוֹמֵר – R' SIMAI SAYS: מִנַּיִין לִתְחִיַּית הַמֵּתִים מִן הַתּוֹרָה – WHERE do we find an allusion TO THE RESURRECTION OF THE DEAD IN THE Written TORAH? שֶׁנֶּאֱמַר ,,וְגַם הֲקִמֹתִי אֶת־בְּרִיתִי אִתָּם לָתֵת לָהֶם אֶת־אֶרֶץ כְּנָעַן" – FOR IT IS STATED: *AND I HAVE ALSO ESTABLISHED MY COVENANT WITH THEM TO GIVE TO THEM THE LAND OF CANAAN.*[16] ,,לָכֶם" לֹא נֶאֱמַר – Note that *TO "YOU"* IS NOT STATED, אֶלָּא ,,לָהֶם" – BUT RATHER *TO "THEM."* מִכָּאן לִתְחִיַּית הַמֵּתִים מִן הַתּוֹרָה – HERE we have an allusion TO THE RESURRECTION OF THE DEAD IN THE Written TORAH.[17]

(צר״ק ק״ם גש״ם ג״ם סִימָן[18] – **Tzr"k k"m, gsh"m g"m – a mnemonic** for five non-believers and the Jewish sages they questioned concerning the Resurrection of the Dead.)[19]

שָׁאֲלוּ מִינִין אֶת רַבָּן גַּמְלִיאֵל – **The sectarians**[20] **asked Rabban Gamliel:** מִנַּיִין שֶׁהַקָּדוֹשׁ בָּרוּךְ הוּא מְחַיֶּה מֵתִים – **From where** in Scripture can it be seen **that the Holy One, Blessed is He, resurrects the dead?** אָמַר לָהֶם מִן הַתּוֹרָה וּמִן הַנְּבִיאִים וּמִן הַכְּתוּבִים – **He cited to them** sources **from the Pentateuch and from the Prophets and from the** Holy **Writings,** וְלֹא קִיבְּלוּ מִמֶּנּוּ

NOTES

10. *II Chronicles* 31:4. The righteous king Chizkiah, as part of his campaign to reverse the spiritual decline wrought during the reign of his father, the wicked king Achaz, ordered the people of his kingdom to be rigorous in giving the mandatory *terumos* and *maasros* to the Kohanim and Leviim, so that these servants of Hashem be free to devote themselves entirely to their holy tasks.

11. When a lion attacks its prey, we cannot ascertain whether it intends to maul and devour its prey immediately [while the meat is still fresh], or whether it intends to maul its prey and carry it off to its lair, where it will devour the meat after it has become rancid (*Rashi*). Alternatively, the meaning is that we cannot ascertain whether the lion intends to maul its prey so thoroughly that the carcass is repulsive [to onlookers] or whether it means only to kill the prey and carry it to its lair, in which case the carcass is not repulsive (ibid.).

12. The state of *tumah* is analogous to the rancid or repulsive carcass, and the state of *taharah* is analogous to the fresh or intact one (see *Rashi*; cf. *Maharsha*). When one gives *terumah* to a Kohen *am haaretz,* one has no way of knowing whether the Kohen will guard the sanctity of that *terumah* and eat it only in a state of *taharah* (see *Aruch LaNer*).

13. *Leviticus* 22:9. The verse cautions the Kohanim not to eat *terumah* while they are *tamei,* and states: וְשָׁמְרוּ אֶת־מִשְׁמַרְתִּי וְלֹא־יִשְׂאוּ עָלָיו חֵטְא וּמֵתוּ בוֹ כִּי יְחַלְּלֻהוּ אֲנִי ה׳ מְקַדְּשָׁם, *And they [the Kohanim] shall protect My charge* [i.e. they shall guard against eating *terumah* while they are *tamei*] *and not bear a sin on account of it and die through it, for they will have desecrated it.*

14. I.e. with many sins (*Rashi*; see next note).

15. *Leviticus* 22:16. [We have rendered עֲוֹן אַשְׁמָה as *Rashi* apparently renders it. This is also the rendering of *Targum Onkelos,* who translates: עֲוָיָן וְחוֹבִין.] The verse refers to Kohanim who eat *terumah* while they are *tamei,* as stated by *Targum Onkelos* ad loc. (*Rashi*; cf. *Rashi* ad loc.).

[The previous verse states: וְלֹא יְחַלְּלוּ אֶת־קָדְשֵׁי בְּנֵי יִשְׂרָאֵל אֵת אֲשֶׁר־יָרִימוּ לַה׳, *And they shall not desecrate the holy foods of the Children of Israel – that which they separate for* H*ASHEM*. This Baraisa apparently interprets that verse to mean that the Children of Israel shall not desecrate what they separate as *terumah* by giving it to a Kohen lax in observance. For, as the next verse continues, the Children of Israel would thereby burden the Kohen with many sins upon his eating of that *terumah* while he is *tamei* (see *Maharsha*). See a different interpretation of the verse cited by *Rashi* ad loc.]

16. *Exodus* 6:4. In this verse, God speaks to Moses, describing to him the covenant He made with the Patriarchs Abraham, Isaac and Jacob to give them the Land of Canaan.

17. If the Torah referred to God's promise to the Patriarchs that their *descendants* – the generation of Moses – would inherit the Land of Canaan, the verse should have stated: *to give to "you" the Land of Canaan,* which would have indicated that the Divine promise was to be fulfilled in the time of Moses' generation. By stating instead: *to give to "them" the Land of Canaan,* the verse implies that the Patriarchs themselves were to inherit the Land of Canaan. And since the Patriarchs had already died, the promise can only be fulfilled in the future when the Patriarchs will be resurrected.

18. [We have emended the mnemonic in accordance with *Maharsha* and *Hagahos HaGra.*]

19. This mnemonic, which facilitates recall of the next five discussions in the Gemara, consists of two parts. צר״ק ק״ם is an acronym for the five who questioned the sages. They are צְדוּקִים (Sadducees, but sometimes it applies to the "sectarians" or *minim*); רוֹמִיִּים (Romans); קְלֵיאוֹפַּטְרָא (Cleopatra); קֵיסָר (Caesar, the Roman emperor); and מִין (sectarian).

גש״ם ג״ם is an acronym for the five sages who were questioned and responded: Rabban **G**amliel, R' Yeho**sh**ua, R' **M**eir; Rabban **G**amliel, R' A**m**i.

20. *Minim* [sectarians] ordinarily refers to sectarian Jews, who often challenged Rabban Gamliel to defend the traditional interpretation of Scripture. Indeed, it was in response to their attacks on traditional Judaism that Rabban Gamliel directed Shmuel HaKatan to compose the nineteenth benediction of the *Shemoneh Esrei,* which begins: "May there be no hope for the *minim*" (see *Berachos* 28b). In light of the Gemara's mnemonic, it would seem that the reference is specifically to the sectarian צְדוּקִים, *Sadducees,* who denied the doctrine of Resurrection and also frequently disagreed with the Rabbinic interpretation of Scripture. [See *Rambam, Commentary to the Mishnah* above, end of chapter 4.]

וכתיב (א) ויהי לו כן וירמסו אותו העם בשער וימות ודילמא קללת אלישע גרמה ליה (א) דאמר רב יהודה אמר רב קללת חכם אפי' על חנם היא באה אם כן לכתוב קרא וירמסוהו וימות מאי בשער על עסקי שער (ב) אמר ר' יוחנן) מניין לתחיית המתים מן התורה שנאמר (ב) ונתתם ממנו [את] תרומת ה' לאהרן הכהן וכי אהרן לעולם קיים והלא לא נכנס לארץ ישראל שנותנין לו תרומה אלא מלמד שעתיד לחיות וישראל נותנין לו תרומה מכאן לתחיית המתים מן התורה דבי רבי ישמעאל תנא לאהרן כאהרן מה אהרן חבר אף בניו חברים (ג) (ד) א"ר שמואל בר נחמני אמר רבי יונתן מניין שאין נותנין תרומה לכהן עם הארץ שנאמר (ג) ויאמר לעם ליושבי ירושלים לתת מנת (ה) לכהנים ולוים) למען יחזקו בתורת ה' כל המחזיק בתורת ה' יש לו מנת ושאינו מחזיק בתורת ה' אין לו מנת אמר רב אחא בר אדא אמר רב יהודה כל הנותן תרומה לכהן עם הארץ כאילו נותנה לפני ארי (ו) מה ארי ספק דורס ואוכל ספק אינו דורס ואוכל אף כהן עם הארץ ספק אוכלה בטהרה ספק אוכלה בטומאה ר' יוחנן אמר אף גורם לו מיתה שנאמר (ד) ומתו בו כי יחללוהו דבי ר"א בן יעקב תנא אף משיאו עון אשמה שנאמר (ה) והשיאו אותם עון אשמה באכלם את קדשיהם תניא ר' סימאי אומר מניין לתחיית המתים מן התורה שנאמר (ו) וגם הקימותי את בריתי אתם לתת להם את ארץ כנען לכם לא נאמר אלא להם מכאן לתחיית המתים מן התורה: [א] (צד"ק ג"ם גש"ם ק"ם סימן): שאלו מינין את רבן גמליאל מניין שהקדוש ברוך הוא מחיה מתים אמר להם מן התורה ומן הנביאים ומן הכתובים ולא קיבלו ממנו מן התורה דכתיב (ז) ויאמר ה' אל משה הנך שוכב עם אבותיך וקם אמרו לו ודילמא וקם העם הזה וזנה מן הנביאים דכתיב (ח) יחיו מתיך נבלתי יקומון הקיצו ורננו שוכני עפר כי טל אורות טלך וארץ רפאים תפיל ודילמא מתים שהחיה יחזקאל מן הכתובים דכתיב (ט) וחכך כיין הטוב הולך לדודי למישרים דובב שפתי ישנים ודילמא רחושי מרחשן שפוותיה בעלמא כר' יוחנן (ז) דאמר ר' יוחנן משום ר"ש בן יהוצדק כל מי שנאמרה הלכה בשמו בעולם הזה שפתותיו דובבות בקבר שנאמר דובב שפתי ישנים עד שאמר להם מקרא זה (י) אשר נשבע ה' לאבותיכם לתת להם לכם לא נאמר אלא להם מיכן לתחיית המתים מן התורה וי"א מן המקרא הזה אמר להם (כ) ואתם הדבקים בה' אלהיכם חיים כלכם היום (ח) פשיטא דחיים כולכם היום אלא אפילו ביום שכל העולם כולם מתים אתם חיים) מה היום כולכם קיימין אף לעוה"ב כולכם קיימין שאלו רומיים את רבי יהושע בן חנניה מניין שהקב"ה מחיה מתים ויודע מה שעתיד להיות אמר להו תרווייהו מן המקרא הזה שנאמר (ז) ויאמר ה' אל משה הנך שוכב עם אבותיך וקם העם הזה וזנה ודילמא וקם העם הזה וזנה אמר להו (ט) נקוטו מיהא פלגא בידייכו דיודע מה שעתיד להיות איתמר נמי א"ר יוחנן משום רבי שמעון בן יוחאי מניין שהקדוש ברוך הוא מחיה מתים ויודע מה שעתיד להיות שנאמר הנך שוכב עם אבותיך וקם וגו' תניא א"ר אליעזר בר' יוסי בדבר זה זייפתי ספרי מינים שהיו אומרים אין תחיית המתים מן התורה אמרתי להן זייפתם תורתכם ולא העליתם בידכם כלום שאתם אומרים אין תחיית המתים מן התורה הרי הוא אומר (ל) הכרת תכרת הנפש ההיא עונה בה הכרת תכרת בעולם הזה עונה בה לאימת לאו לעולם הבא א"ל רב פפא לאביי ולימא להו תרווייהו מהכרת תכרת אינהו הוו אמרי ליה (י) דברה תורה כלשון בני אדם כתנאי (כ) הכרת תכרת * הכרת בעולם הזה תכרת לעולם הבא דברי ר"ע אמר לו ר' ישמעאל והלא כבר נאמר (מ) את ה' הוא מגדף ונכרתה וכי שלשה עולמים יש אלא ונכרתה בעולם הזה הכרת לעולם הבא הכרת תכרת דברה תורה כלשון בני אדם בין ר' ישמעאל ובין ר"ע עונה בה מאי עבדי ביה לכדתניא (ל) יכול אפילו עשה תשובה ת"ל עונה בה לא אמרתי אלא בזמן שעונה בה שאלה קליאופטרא מלכתא את ר"מ אמרה ידענא דחיי שכבי דכתיב (נ) ויציצו מעיר כעשב הארץ אלא כשהן עומדין עומדין ערומין או בלבושיהן עומדין אמר לה (מ) ק"ו מחיטה (נ) ומה חיטה שנקברה ערומה יוצאה בכמה לבושין צדיקים שנקברים בלבושיהן על אחת כמה וכמה א"ל קיסר לרבן גמליאל אמריתו דשכבי חיי הא הוו עפרא ועפרא מי קא חיי

אמרה

רש"י

ויהי לו כן וירמסו אותו. דבדבר שכפר בו נדון שלא אכל משם ונרמס ברגלי הבאים לקנות: (ע) (וכי אהרן קיים לעולם. כלומר וכי אהרן חיה כל כך שתנתן לו תרומה והלא לא נכנס לארץ ישראל ומאי האי דקאמר ונתתם ממנו תרומת ה' לאהרן הכהן): לעולם קיים. לאו דווקא אלא כלומר הלא לא נגזר עליו שיחיה כל כך: שעתיד לחיות. לעולם הבא: דבי רבי ישמעאל תנא. הא דכתיב לאהרן לאו להכי הוא דאתא אלא לומר לך כאהרן וכו': מה ארי ספק דורס ואוכל. ואין אנו יודעין כשנוטל בהמה מן העדר אם דעתו לדורסה ולאוכלה מיד קודם שתסריח או לא אלא לטרוף ולמלא (חורו) [תאותו] ולאחר זמן יאכלנה כשתסריח וה"נ כהן עם הארץ כשאנו נותנין לו תרומה בידו אין אנו יודעין אם יאכלנה בטהרה או בטומאה [אי נמי] ספק דורס שאחרי דרכו לדרוס ולרמוס בהמה ברגליו ואוכלה כשהיא דרוסה מנוולת ופעמים שנותנה בחורו ואינה מנוולת: עון אשמה. עונות הרבה מטעין עליו: באכלם את קדשיהם. ומתרגמינן במיכלהון בסואבא ית קודשיהון: אלא להם. דמשמע שהבטיח הקב"ה לאבותינו אברהם יצחק ויעקב שיתן להם ארץ ישראל וכי להם ניתנה והלא לבניהם ניתנה אלא מלמד שעתידין לחיות ועתיד הקב"ה ליתן להם את ארץ ישראל: הנך שוכב עם אבותיך וקם. הנה אתה מת שוכב והנה אתה קם שתחיה לעתיד לבא והאי וקם אהנך קאי: דילמא וקם העם וזנה. דלקמי' קאי ולאו אדלעיל והיינו אחד (ס) (מג') מקראות שאין להם הכרע (ע): יחיו מתיך. דמתים שבארץ ישראל יחיו: נבלתי יקומון. אפי' נפלים יחיו במסכת כתובות (פ): ודילמא מתים שהחיה יחזקאל. דהסיק קרא יחיו מתיך ישעיה אמרו והוא קדם ליחזקאל שנתנבא בימי חזקיה והיה מתנבא פסוק זה על שהיה עתיד יחזקאל להחיות מתים אבל לעולם הבא לא: דובב. פרונמיי"ש בלע"ז כלומר נעות ומתנודדות שפתי ישיני עפר מכלל שיחיו: מרחשן שפוותיהו בעלמא. שפתותיהן נעות מעט בתוך הקבר אבל אין חיין ויוצאין לאויר העולם וכרבי יוחנן וכו': ולא קבלו ממנו. עד שאמר להם וכו': חיים כלכם היום. דהאי (צ) יום מיותר הוא דמצי למכתב חיים כלכם מה תלמוד לומר היום כהיום מה היום וכו' כך שמעתי: הנך שוכב עם אבותיך וקם. הרי תחיית המתים העם הזה וזנה הרי מה שעתיד להיות: פלגא בידך. דמהאי קרא נפקא דיודע מה שעתיד: זייפתם ולא העליתם. כזב אתם אומרים ואין ממש בדבריכם: לאו לעולם הבא. אלמא יש תחיית המתים: מהכרת תכרת. הכרת בעולם הזה תכרת לעולם הבא: אינהו הוו אמרי ליה דברה תורה כלשון בני אדם. ולהכי אמר להו הכי כי היכי דלא להוי להו פתחון פה: הכרת תכרת. בעבודת כוכבים כתיב: והלא כבר נאמר. בעבודת כוכבים את ה' הוא מגדף ונכרתה דס"ל מגדף (ק) היינו עובד עבודת כוכבים: וכי שלשה עולמים יש וכו'. ור"ע סבירא ליה דמגדף היינו מברך השם: והשתא בין לרבי ישמעאל בין לר"ע עונה בה מאי עבדי ליה מבעי ליה וכו': שעונה בה. שלא שב קודם מיתה הוי בכרת אבל שב לא: דחיי שכבי. שהמתים חיים: ויציצו מעיר. שעתידין ישראל לציץ ולפרוח מעיר ירושלים וכדאמרינן (כתובות דף קיא.) הקב"ה עושה להם מחילות לצדיקים והולכין ועולין לירושלים:

אמרה

עין משפט נר מצוה

ג א מיי' פ"ח מהלכות תשובה הל"א:

ד ב מיי' שם הלכה ב בהשגו' ובהפירוש שהביא בעל מ"ע בשם הרמב"ן:

תורה אור השלם

א) וַיְהִי לוֹ כֵּן וַיִּרְמְסוּ אֹתוֹ הָעָם בַּשַּׁעַר וַיָּמֹת: [מלכים ב' ז, כ]

ב) כֵּן תָּרִימוּ גַם אַתֶּם תְּרוּמַת יְיָ מִכֹּל מַעְשְׂרֹתֵיכֶם אֲשֶׁר תִּקְחוּ מֵאֵת בְּנֵי יִשְׂרָאֵל וּנְתַתֶּם מִמֶּנּוּ אֶת תְּרוּמַת יְיָ לְאַהֲרֹן הַכֹּהֵן: [במדבר יח, כח]

ג) וַיֹּאמֶר לָעָם לְיוֹשְׁבֵי יְרוּשָׁלַיִם לָתֵת מְנָת הַכֹּהֲנִים וְהַלְוִיִּם לְמַעַן יֶחֶזְקוּ בְּתוֹרַת יְיָ: [דברי הימים ב' לא, ד]

ד) וְשָׁמְרוּ אֶת מִשְׁמַרְתִּי וְלֹא יִשְׂאוּ עָלָיו חֵטְא וּמֵתוּ בוֹ כִּי יְחַלְּלֻהוּ אֲנִי יְיָ מְקַדְּשָׁם: [ויקרא כב, ט]

ה) וְהִשִּׂיאוּ אוֹתָם עֲוֹן אַשְׁמָה בְּאָכְלָם אֶת קָדְשֵׁיהֶם כִּי אֲנִי יְיָ מְקַדְּשָׁם: [ויקרא כב, טז]

ו) וְגַם הֲקִמֹתִי אֶת בְּרִיתִי אִתָּם לָתֵת לָהֶם אֶת אֶרֶץ כְּנָעַן אֵת אֶרֶץ מְגֻרֵיהֶם אֲשֶׁר גָּרוּ בָהּ: [שמות ו, ד]

ז) וַיֹּאמֶר יְיָ אֶל מֹשֶׁה הִנְּךָ שֹׁכֵב עִם אֲבֹתֶיךָ וְקָם הָעָם הַזֶּה וְזָנָה אַחֲרֵי אֱלֹהֵי נֵכַר הָאָרֶץ אֲשֶׁר הוּא בָא שָׁמָּה בְּקִרְבּוֹ וַעֲזָבַנִי וְהֵפֵר אֶת בְּרִיתִי אֲשֶׁר כָּרַתִּי אִתּוֹ: [דברים לא, טז]

ח) יִחְיוּ מֵתֶיךָ נְבֵלָתִי יְקוּמוּן הָקִיצוּ וְרַנְּנוּ שֹׁכְנֵי עָפָר כִּי טַל אוֹרֹת טַלֶּךָ וָאָרֶץ רְפָאִים תַּפִּיל: [ישעיה כו, יט]

ט) וְחִכֵּךְ כְּיֵין הַטּוֹב הוֹלֵךְ לְדוֹדִי לְמֵישָׁרִים דּוֹבֵב שִׂפְתֵי יְשֵׁנִים: [שיר השירים ז, י]

י) לְמַעַן יִרְבּוּ יְמֵיכֶם וִימֵי בְנֵיכֶם עַל הָאֲדָמָה אֲשֶׁר נִשְׁבַּע יְיָ לַאֲבֹתֵיכֶם לָתֵת לָהֶם כִּימֵי הַשָּׁמַיִם עַל הָאָרֶץ: [דברים יא, כא]

כ) וְאַתֶּם הַדְּבֵקִים בַּייָ אֱלֹהֵיכֶם חַיִּים כֻּלְּכֶם הַיּוֹם: [דברים ד, ד]

ל) כִּי דְבַר יְיָ בָּזָה וְאֶת מִצְוָתוֹ הֵפַר הִכָּרֵת תִּכָּרֵת הַנֶּפֶשׁ הַהִוא עֲוֹנָה בָהּ: [במדבר טו, לא]

מ) וְהַנֶּפֶשׁ אֲשֶׁר תַּעֲשֶׂה בְּיָד רָמָה מִן הָאֶזְרָח וּמִן הַגֵּר אֶת יְיָ הוּא מְגַדֵּף וְנִכְרְתָה הַנֶּפֶשׁ הַהִוא מִקֶּרֶב עַמָּהּ: [במדבר טו, ל]

נ) יְהִי פִסַּת בַּר בָּאָרֶץ בְּרֹאשׁ הָרִים יִרְעַשׁ כַּלְּבָנוֹן פִּרְיוֹ וְיָצִיצוּ מֵעִיר כְּעֵשֶׂב הָאָרֶץ: [תהלים עב, טז]

מסורת הש"ס

א) מכות יא. ברכות כו., ב) [ליתא בע"י], ג) ס"א מכאן אמרו שאין נותנין מתנה לכהן ע"ה, ד) חולין קל:, ה) [צ"ל הכהנים והלוים], ו) [פסחים מט: ע"ש], ז) יבמות לו: ע"ש בכורות לא: ע"ש, ח) רש"ל מ"ז, ט) [מו"ק כח.], י) [קידושין יז. וש"נ], כ) לעיל סד: [שבועות יג.], ל) [שבועות דף יג.], מ) [כתובות קיא: ועי' תוספות חולין קיז: ד"ה סטה], נ) רש"ל מ"ז, ס) [צ"ל מחמשה], ע) [יומא נב.], פ) [דף קיא.], צ) [צ"ל היום], ק) [לעיל סד: כריתות ז:].

הגהות הגר"א

[א] גמ' סימן צדיק גם גשם קם. נ"ב צדיק ק"ם גש"ם ג"ם סי' כצ"ל:

ליקוטי רש"י

ויאמר לעם. ביהושפט כתיב בדברי הימים סיפיה דקרא למען יחזקו בתורת ה'. מנת. חלק כהונה [חולין קל:]. למען יחזקו בתורת ה'. יותר ברצון ועוד בעוד שיהא להם פרנסה' מזומנת יכלו לעשות ולעסוק בתורת ה' לפי שלא נתנה התורה אלא לאוכלי המן ושניים להם אוכלי תרומה [דה"ב לא, ד]. ומתו בו. למדנו שהיא מיתה בידי שמים [ויקרא כב, ט]. יחיו מתיך. כאן התפלל שיחיו הצדיקים בבקשה ממך יחיו אותן שמומתין עליך יצא דבר מלכות מלפניך לומר נבלתי יקומון נבלות עמי שנבלו עצמן עלי להם תהי תקומה זו חילוף למה שכתוב למעלה רפאים בל יקומו אבל אלו יקומון. הקיצו ורננו. כל זה יאמר להם הקב"ה הקיצו ורננו ל' לווי הוא זה. כי טל אורות טלך. כי נאה לך לעשות כן שיהא טל תורתך ומצותיך להם טל של אור. וארץ רפאים תפיל. ולארץ ולעפר תפיל את ארץ רפאים שריפו ידיהם מתורתך [ישעיה כו, יט]. ודילמא רחושי מרחשן שפוותיה בעלמא. כיין הטוב שהוא דובב שפתי ישני' אף אבותי בקבר ישמחו בי ויודו על חלקם דובב מרחיש פרומ"יר בלע"ז ויקודו לשון דיבור [שה"ש ז, י]. דובבות. נעות לשון דבר [ס"א, דבב] שמרחיש ומבלבל [יבמות צז.]. נעות והנאה הוא לו שדומה כחי [בכורות לא:]. והלא כבר נאמר את ה' הוא מגדף ונכרתה. באותה פרשה עצמה גבי מגדף ור' עקיבא סבירא ליה מגדף היינו מברך את השם כדאמר בכריתות ועולם הבא לא נפקא ליה בעבודה זרה אלא מהכרת תכרת ור' ישמעאל לאו לר' עקיבא פריך והלא כבר נאמר ונכרתה דהא ר' עקיבא במברך את השם מוקים לה אלא טעמא דנפשיה קאמר והלא כבר נאמרה ונכרתה ואנא סבירא ליה דבעבודה זרה כתיבא. וכי שלשה עולמים יש וכו'. ודומה לו בשחיטת חולין והלא במוקדשין האומר רגלה של זו עולה כולה עולה דהא פרכא לאו לכשנגדו פריך דאיהו סבירא ליה אפילו במוקדשין דאין כולה עולה אלא טעמא דנפשיה אמר בפרק [בהמה המקשה] (חולין סט.) [לעיל סד:]. דברה תורה כלשון בני אדם וכו'. הכי משתעו בני אדם ודברה תורה כלשון בני אדם וליכא למידרש מינה כלום [נדרים ג.]. ואף על גב דאיכא למדרש לא דרשינן כדמוכח בפ"ב דב"מ (לא:) [ר"ן שם]. לא אמרתי אלא בזמן שעונה בה. שאם עשה תשובה ואין עונה בה מיתה ממרקת ולא תכרת לעולם הבא [שבועות יג.]. ויציצו. ישראל. מעיר. מתוך ירושלים כעשב הארץ [תהלים עב, טז].

– **but they did not accept** the proofs **from him** as convincing . . .[21]

The Gemara elaborates:

מִן הַתּוֹרָה – The source Rabban Gamliel cited **from the Pentateuch** **דִּכְתִיב** – was from **that** which **is written:** ,,וַיֹּאמֶר ה׳ אֶל־מֹשֶׁה הִנְּךָ שֹׁכֵב עִם־אֲבֹתֶיךָ וְקָם״ – *And HASHEM said to Moses: "Behold, you will lie with your forefathers and rise."*[22] **אָמְרוּ לוֹ** – **[The sectarians] replied to [Rabban Gamliel]:** **וְדִילְמָא** ,,וְקָם הָעָם הַזֶּה וְזָנָה״ – **But perhaps** the verse means instead: *And rise will this nation and go astray . . .*[23]

מִן הַנְּבִיאִים – The source Rabban Gamliel cited **from the Prophets** **דִּכְתִיב** – was from **that** which **is written:**[24] ,,יִחְיוּ מֵתֶיךָ נְבֵלָתִי יְקוּמוּן הָקִיצוּ וְרַנְּנוּ שֹׁכְנֵי עָפָר כִּי טַל אוֹרֹת טַלֶּךָ וָאָרֶץ רְפָאִים תַּפִּיל״ – *May Your dead live. [O, command:] "My [people's] corpses shall rise! Awake and sing, you who dwell in the earth!" For a dew of lights is Your dew. And [to] the ground You shall cast the refaim.*[25] This verse clearly predicts a future resurrection. **וְדִילְמָא מֵתִים שֶׁהֶחֱיָה יְחֶזְקֵאל** – The sectarians retorted: **But perhaps** Isaiah refers to **the dead whom** the prophet **Ezekiel resurrected,**[26] not to a universal resurrection that is yet to occur.

מִן הַכְּתוּבִים – The source Rabban Gamliel cited **from the** Holy **Writings** **דִּכְתִיב** – was from **that** which **is written:** ,,וְחִכֵּךְ כְּיֵין הַטּוֹב הוֹלֵךְ לְדוֹדִי לְמֵישָׁרִים דּוֹבֵב שִׂפְתֵי יְשֵׁנִים״ – *And [the words of] your palate shall be like the choicest wine; going to my Beloved with sincerity, stirring the lips of those who sleep [in the grave].*[27] **וְדִילְמָא רַחוּשֵׁי מְרַחְשָׁן שִׂפְוָתֵיהּ בְּעָלְמָא** – The sectarians retorted: **But perhaps** the verse means only that **their lips will merely move** slightly in the grave, not that they will be fully resurrected. And the interpretation of the verse could then be **כְּרַבִּי יוֹחָנָן** – **as R' Yochanan** taught. **דְּאָמַר רַבִּי יוֹחָנָן מִשּׁוּם רַבִּי שִׁמְעוֹן בֶּן יְהוֹצָדָק** – **For R' Yochanan said in the name of R' Shimon ben Yehotzadak:** **כָּל מִי שֶׁנֶּאֶמְרָה הֲלָכָה בִּשְׁמוֹ בָּעוֹלָם הַזֶּה** – **Whenever a halachah is recited in the name of someone in this world,** i.e. when a deceased scholar is cited as the source of a certain halachah, **שִׂפְתוֹתָיו דּוֹבְבוֹת בַּקֶּבֶר** – **his lips move in the grave,** **שֶׁנֶּאֱמַר** ,,דּוֹבֵב שִׂפְתֵי יְשֵׁנִים״ – **as it is stated:** *stirring the lips of those who sleep [in the grave].*

עַד שֶׁאָמַר לָהֶם מִקְרָא זֶה – And Rabban Gamliel was not able to give them a convincing proof **until he cited to them this** following **verse:** ,,אֲשֶׁר נִשְׁבַּע ה׳ לַאֲבֹתֵיכֶם לָתֵת לָהֶם״ – *On the land that HASHEM swore to your forefathers to give to them.*[28] ,,לָכֶם״ לֹא נֶאֱמַר אֶלָּא ,,לָהֶם״ – Note that *to "you"* **is not stated, but rather** *to "them."* **מִיכָּן לִתְחִיַּית הַמֵּתִים מִן הַתּוֹרָה** – **Here** we have an allusion **to the Resurrection of the Dead in the** Written **Torah.**[29] **וְיֵשׁ אוֹמְרִים מִן הַמִּקְרָא הַזֶּה אָמַר לָהֶם** – **And some say** that it was **from this** following **verse that he adduced to them** the convincing proof: ,,וְאַתֶּם הַדְּבֵקִים בַּה׳ אֱלֹהֵיכֶם חַיִּים כֻּלְּכֶם הַיּוֹם״ – *And you who cleave to HASHEM your God are alive all of you today.*[30] **פְּשִׁיטָא (דְּחַיִּים כּוּלְּכֶם הַיּוֹם)** – **Obviously, all of you are alive** *today.* Why, then, did Moses add the word "today"?[31] **אֶלָּא אֲפִילּוּ בְּיוֹם שֶׁכָּל הָעוֹלָם כּוּלָּם מֵתִים** – **Rather,** it indicates that **even on the day when all** others in **the world are dead,**[32] **אַתֶּם חַיִּים** – **you** who cleave to God **are alive,** because God will

NOTES

21. [The Gemara stops here in mid-sentence to detail the proofs that the sectarians did *not* find convincing. The sentence is completed below, when the Gemara continues: "until he cited them [a proof] from this verse . . ."]

22. *Deuteronomy* 31:16. The verse in its entirety reads: וַיֹּאמֶר ה׳ אֶל־מֹשֶׁה הִנְּךָ שֹׁכֵב עִם־אֲבֹתֶיךָ וְקָם הָעָם הַזֶּה וְזָנָה אַחֲרֵי אֱלֹהֵי נֵכַר־הָאָרֶץ אֲשֶׁר הוּא בָא־שָׁמָּה בְּקִרְבּוֹ וַעֲזָבַנִי וְהֵפֵר אֶת־בְּרִיתִי אֲשֶׁר כָּרַתִּי אִתּוֹ, *And Hashem said to Moses: Behold, you will lie with your forefathers and rise will this nation and stray after the gods of peoples of the land in whose midst it is coming and it will forsake Me and annul My covenant that I have sealed with it.* According to the superficial meaning of the verse, the word וְקָם, *and rise,* begins a new clause (*and rise will this nation* . . .), and in no way alludes to a future resurrection. However, the Gemara in *Yoma* (52a-b) lists this word among the five in the Pentateuch שֶׁאֵין לָהֶם הֶכְרֵעַ, *regarding which the balance cannot be tilted,* i.e. it is indeterminate whether the word is connected to what precedes or to what follows. If the word וְקָם, *and rise,* is connected to the preceding, then it indeed indicates that Moses will be resurrected (see *Rashi* below).

[*Maharal* here explains that the word וְקָם, *and rise,* is certainly connected to what follows as well, which is otherwise incomplete. What the Gemara in *Yoma* means, asserts *Maharal,* is that the Torah *also* meant the word to relate to the preceding, since it purposely constructed the verse so that the naturally connected concepts of "lying" and "rising" be in juxtaposition. See further in *Maharal*; see also *Maharsha* and *Anaf Yosef*; cf. *Tosefos Yeshanim* to *Yoma* ad loc.]

Certainly, no sage of Israel would derive the doctrine of the Resurrection of the Dead based on his own exposition of the verse in this way. Rather, in light of the authentic tradition [concerning the Resurrection of the Dead], it is known to us that this doctrine is alluded to in this verse (*Teshuvos HaRashba* 1:9).

23. Perhaps, the word וְקָם, *and rise,* is connected *only* with what follows and thus in no way indicates a resurrection of the dead (see *Maharsha*). Thus, they did not accept Rabban Gamliel's proof from the Pentateuch.

24. *Isaiah* 26:19. The entire chapter until this verse describes the song of deliverance that will be sung in the Land of Judea at the time of the Final Redemption (*Radak* ad loc.). Now, Isaiah speaks of the Resurrection of the Dead.

25. [Our rendering and explanation of the verse follows *Rashi* ad loc.] Isaiah prays, *"May Your dead* [i.e. the *tzaddikim,* who gave their lives for You] *live."* O God, command, *"My [people's] corpses shall rise! Awake and sing you who dwell in the earth!" For a dew of lights is Your dew.* [I.e. it is fitting for You to resurrect the righteous so that the refreshing dew of Your Torah and mitzvos be a dew of lights unto them.] *And [to] the ground You shall cast the refaim.* [I.e. in contrast to the righteous whom You shall resurrect, cast down the *refaim* – those who have relinquished (from the root רפה, *to relax one's grip*) Your Torah.]

[*Rashi* to our Gemara, however, interprets *your dead* as a reference to those who are buried in Eretz Yisrael, and *corpses* as a reference to those who were stillborn in this world (see *Kesubos* 111a). See also *Maharsha.*]

26. The prophet Ezekiel resurrected the dead of the Valley of the Dry Bones (see *Ezekiel* 37:1-14). It is possible, then, that the prophet Isaiah, who lived a century before Ezekiel, referred in the verse cited by Rabban Gamliel to the resurrection wrought by Ezekiel and not to some future general resurrection of the dead in or after the Messianic era (see *Rashi*).

27. *Song of Songs* 7:10. Israel's pledge of loyalty to God will stir the lips of their departed forebears, who will give praise for their joyous lot of having such descendants (see *Rashi* ad loc.). If the lips of the dead will be stirred to utter praise, does that not presume that the dead will be resurrected?! [See also *Maharsha.*]

28. The Gemara's reference seems to be to *Deuteronomy* 11:21 (see *Sifri* and *Rashi* ad loc.). Cf. end of next note.

29. The verse implies that the Patriarchs themselves were to inherit the Land of Canaan. And since the Patriarchs had already died, the promise can only be fulfilled in the future when the Patriarchs will be resurrected. See above, note 17.

[Actually, there are many other verses that speak explicitly of the land being given "to the Patriarchs *and* to their descendants," indicating that the Patriarchs themselves are meant, and not only their seed (e.g. *Genesis* 13:15, 17:8, 26:3; *Deuteronomy* 1:8, 11:9). Why, then, did the Gemara not cite them? See *Be'er Sheva,* and *Margaliyos HaYam* §7.]

30. *Deuteronomy* 4:4.

31. He need have said only "you are all alive" (this is how *Rashi* explains the thrust of the proof, though he may not have had this actual reading in the Gemara – see note 33).

32. [The word הַיּוֹם should not be rendered "today," but rather "on *the* day," i.e. the day of the Resurrection of the Dead.]

עין משפט
נר מצוה

ג א מיי' פ"ח מהלכות תשובה הל"א:
ד ב מיי' שם הלכה ב בהשגו' ובהפירוש שהביא בעל מ"ע בשם הרמב"ן:

תורה אור השלם

א) וַיְהִי לוֹ כֵּן וַיִּרְמְסוּ אֹתוֹ הָעָם בַּשַּׁעַר וַיָּמֹת: [מלכים ב' ז, כ]

ב) כֵּן תָּרִימוּ גַם אַתֶּם תְּרוּמַת יְיָ מִכֹּל מַעְשְׂרֹתֵיכֶם אֲשֶׁר תִּקְחוּ מֵאֵת בְּנֵי יִשְׂרָאֵל וּנְתַתֶּם מִמֶּנּוּ אֶת תְּרוּמַת יְיָ לְאַהֲרֹן הַכֹּהֵן: [במדבר יח, כח]

ג) וַיֹּאמֶר לָעָם לְיוֹשְׁבֵי יְרוּשָׁלַיִם לָתֵת מְנָת הַכֹּהֲנִים וְהַלְוִיִּם לְמַעַן יֶחֶזְקוּ בְּתוֹרַת יְיָ: [דברי הימים ב' לא, ד]

ד) וְשָׁמְרוּ אֶת מִשְׁמַרְתִּי וְלֹא יִשְׂאוּ עָלָיו חֵטְא וּמֵתוּ בוֹ כִּי יְחַלְּלֻהוּ אֲנִי יְיָ מְקַדְּשָׁם: [ויקרא כב, ט]

ה) וְהִשִּׂיאוּ אוֹתָם עֲוֹן אַשְׁמָה בְּאָכְלָם אֶת קָדְשֵׁיהֶם כִּי אֲנִי יְיָ מְקַדְּשָׁם: [ויקרא כב, טז]

ו) וְגַם הֲקִמֹתִי אֶת בְּרִיתִי אִתָּם לָתֵת לָהֶם אֶת אֶרֶץ כְּנָעַן אֵת אֶרֶץ מְגֻרֵיהֶם אֲשֶׁר גָּרוּ בָהּ: [שמות ו, ד]

ז) וַיֹּאמֶר יְיָ אֶל מֹשֶׁה הִנְּךָ שֹׁכֵב עִם אֲבֹתֶיךָ וְקָם הָעָם הַזֶּה וְזָנָה אַחֲרֵי אֱלֹהֵי נֵכַר הָאָרֶץ אֲשֶׁר הוּא בָא שָׁמָּה בְּקִרְבּוֹ וַעֲזָבַנִי וְהֵפֵר אֶת בְּרִיתִי אֲשֶׁר כָּרַתִּי אִתּוֹ: [דברים לא, טז]

ח) יִחְיוּ מֵתֶיךָ נְבֵלָתִי יְקוּמוּן הָקִיצוּ וְרַנְּנוּ שֹׁכְנֵי עָפָר כִּי טַל אוֹרֹת טַלֶּךָ וָאָרֶץ רְפָאִים תַּפִּיל: [ישעיה כו, יט]

ט) וְחִכֵּךְ כְּיֵין הַטּוֹב הוֹלֵךְ לְדוֹדִי לְמֵישָׁרִים דּוֹבֵב שִׂפְתֵי יְשֵׁנִים: [שיר השירים ז, י]

י) לְמַעַן יִרְבּוּ יְמֵיכֶם וִימֵי בְנֵיכֶם עַל הָאֲדָמָה אֲשֶׁר נִשְׁבַּע יְיָ לַאֲבֹתֵיכֶם לָתֵת לָהֶם כִּימֵי הַשָּׁמַיִם עַל הָאָרֶץ: [דברים יא, כא]

כ) וְאַתֶּם הַדְּבֵקִים בַּייָ אֱלֹהֵיכֶם חַיִּים כֻּלְּכֶם הַיּוֹם: [דברים ד, ד]

ל) כִּי דְבַר יְיָ בָּזָה וְאֶת מִצְוָתוֹ הֵפַר הִכָּרֵת תִּכָּרֵת הַנֶּפֶשׁ הַהִוא עֲוֹנָה בָהּ: [במדבר טו, לא]

מ) וְהַנֶּפֶשׁ אֲשֶׁר תַּעֲשֶׂה בְּיָד רָמָה מִן הָאֶזְרָח וּמִן הַגֵּר אֶת יְיָ הוּא מְגַדֵּף וְנִכְרְתָה הַנֶּפֶשׁ הַהִוא מִקֶּרֶב עַמָּהּ: [במדבר טו, ל]

נ) יְהִי פִסַּת בַּר בָּאָרֶץ בְּרֹאשׁ הָרִים יִרְעַשׁ כַּלְּבָנוֹן פִּרְיוֹ וְיָצִיצוּ מֵעִיר כְּעֵשֶׂב הָאָרֶץ: [תהלים עב, טז]

וכתיב א) ויהי לו כן וירמסו אותו העם בשער וימות ודילמא קללת אלישע גרמה ליה א) דאמר רב יהודה אמר רב קללת חכם אפי' על חנם היא באה אם כן לכתוב קרא וירמסוהו וימות מאי בשער על עסקי שער (ג) אמר ר' יוחנן) מניין לתחיית המתים מן התורה שנאמר ב) ונתתם ממנו [את] תרומת ה' לאהרן הכהן וכי אהרן לעולם קיים והלא לא נכנס לארץ ישראל שנותנין לו תרומה אלא מלמד שעתיד לחיות וישראל נותנין לו תרומה מכאן לתחיית המתים מן התורה דבי רבי ישמעאל תנא לאהרן כאהרן מה אהרן חבר אף בניו חברים ג) ד) א"ר שמואל בר נחמני אמר רבי יונתן מניין שאין נותנין תרומה לכהן עם הארץ שנאמר ג) ויאמר לעם ליושבי ירושלים לתת מנת (ה) לכהנים ולוים) למען יחזקו בתורת ה' כל המחזיק בתורת ה' יש לו מנת ושאינו מחזיק בתורת ה' אין לו מנת אמר רב אחא בר אדא אמר רב יהודה כל הנותן תרומה לכהן עם הארץ כאילו נותנה לפני ארי ו) מה ארי ספק דורס ואוכל ספק אינו דורס ואוכל אף כהן עם הארץ ספק אוכלה בטהרה ספק אוכלה בטומאה ר' יוחנן אמר אף גורם לו מיתה שנאמר ד) ומתו בו כי יחללוהו דבי ר"א בן יעקב תנא אף משיאו עון אשמה שנאמר ה) והשיאו אותם עון אשמה באכלם את קדשיהם תניא ר' סימאי אומר מניין לתחיית המתים מן התורה שנאמר ו) וגם הקימותי את בריתי אתם לתת להם את ארץ כנען לכם לא נאמר אלא להם מכאן לתחיית המתים מן התורה: [א] (צד"ק ג"ם גש"ם ק"ם סימן): שאלו מינין את רבן גמליאל מניין שהקדוש ברוך הוא מחיה מתים אמר להם מן התורה ומן הנביאים ומן הכתובים ולא קיבלו ממנו מן התורה דכתיב ז) ויאמר ה' אל משה הנך שוכב עם אבותיך וקם אמרו לו ודילמא וקם העם הזה וזנה מן הנביאים דכתיב ח) יחיו מתיך נבלתי יקומון הקיצו ורננו שוכני עפר כי טל אורות טלך וארץ רפאים תפיל ודילמא מתים שהחיה יחזקאל מן הכתובים דכתיב ט) וחכך כיין הטוב הולך לדודי למישרים דובב שפתי ישנים ודילמא רחושי מרחשן שפוותיה בעלמא כר' יוחנן י) דאמר ר' יוחנן משום ר"ש בן יהוצדק כל מי שנאמרה הלכה בשמו בעולם הזה שפתותיו דובבות בקבר שנאמר דובב שפתי ישנים עד שאמר להם מקרא זה י) אשר נשבע ה' לאבותיכם לתת להם לכם לא נאמר אלא להם מיכן לתחיית המתים מן התורה וי"א מן המקרא הזה אמר להם כ) ואתם הדבקים בה' אלהיכם חיים כולכם היום (ל) פשיטא דחיים כולכם היום אלא אפילו ביום שכל העולם כולם מתים אתם חיים) מה היום כולכם קיימין אף לעוה"ב כולכם קיימין שאלו רומיים את רבי יהושע בן חנניה מניין שהקב"ה מחיה מתים ויודע מה שעתיד להיות אמר להו תרוייהו מן המקרא הזה שנאמר ז) ויאמר ה' אל משה הנך שוכב עם אבותיך וקם העם הזה וזנה ודילמא וקם העם הזה וזנה אמר להו נ) נקוטו מיהא פלגא בידייכו דיודע מה שעתיד להיות איתמר נמי א"ר יוחנן משום רבי שמעון בן יוחאי מניין שהקדוש ברוך הוא מחיה מתים ויודע מה שעתיד להיות שנאמר הנך שוכב עם אבותיך וקם וגו' תניא א"ר אליעזר בר' יוסי בדבר זה זייפתי ספרי מינים שהיו אומרים אין תחיית המתים מן התורה אמרתי להן זייפתם תורתכם ולא העליתם בידכם כלום שאתם אומרים אין תחיית המתים מן התורה הרי הוא אומר ל) הכרת תכרת הנפש ההיא עונה בה הכרת תכרת בעולם הזה עונה בה לאימת לאו לעולם הבא א"ל רב פפא לאביי ולימא להו תרוייהו מהכרת תכרת אינהו הוו אמרי ליה ס) דברה תורה כלשון בני אדם כתנאי א) הכרת תכרת הכרת בעולם הזה תכרת לעולם הבא דברי ר"ע אמר לו ר' ישמעאל והלא כבר נאמר מ) את ה' הוא מגדף ונכרתה וכי שלשה עולמים יש אלא ונכרתה בעולם הזה הכרת לעולם הבא הכרת תכרת דברה תורה כלשון בני אדם בין ר' ישמעאל ובין ר"ע עונה בה מאי עבדי ביה לכדתניא ע) יכול אפילו עשה תשובה ת"ל עונה בה לא אמרתי אלא בזמן שעונה בה שאלה קליאופטרא מלכתא את ר"מ אמרה ידענא דחיי שכבי דכתיב נ) ויציצו מעיר כעשב הארץ אלא כשהן עומדין עומדין ערומין או בלבושיהן עומדין אמר לה פ) ק"ו מחיטה ב) ומה חיטה שנקברה ערומה יוצאה בכמה לבושין צדיקים שנקברים בלבושיהן על אחת כמה וכמה א"ל קיסר לרבן גמליאל אמריתו דשכבי חיי הא הוו עפרא ועפרא מי קא חיי

אמרה

ויהי לו כן וירמסו אותו. דבדבר שכפר בו נדון שלא אכל משם ונרמס ברגלי הבאים לקנות: ס) (וכי אהרן קיים לעולם. כלומר וכי אהרן חיה כל כך שתנתן לו תרומה והלא לא נכנס לארץ ישראל ומאי האי דקאמר ונתתם ממנו תרומת ה' לאהרן הכהן): לעולם קיים. לאו דווקא אלא כלומר הלא לא נגזר עליו שיחיה כל כך: שעתיד לחיות. לעולם הבא: דבי רבי ישמעאל תנא. הא דכתיב לאהרן לאו להכי הוא דאתא אלא לומר לך כאהרן וכו': מה ארי ספק דורס ואוכל. ואין אנו יודעין כשנוטל בהמה מן העדר אם דעתו לדורסה ולאוכלה מיד קודם שתסריח או לא אלא לטרוף ולמלא (חורו) [תאותו] ולאחר זמן יאכלנה כשתסריח וה"נ כהן עם הארץ כשאנו נותנין לו תרומה בידו אין אנו יודעין אם יאכלנה בטהרה או בטומאה [אי נמי] ספק דורס שאחרי דרכו לדרוס ולרמוס בהמה ברגליו ואוכלה כשהיא דרוסה מנוולת ופעמים שנותנה בחורו ואינה מנוולת: עון אשמה. עונות הרבה מטעין עליו: באכלם את קדשיהם. ומתרגמינן במיכלהון בסואבא ית קודשיהון: אלא להם. דמשמע שהבטיח הקב"ה לאבותינו אברהם יצחק ויעקב שיתן להם ארץ ישראל וכי להם ניתנה והלא לבניהם ניתנה אלא מלמד שעתידין לחיות ועתיד הקב"ה ליתן להם את ארץ ישראל: הנך שוכב עם אבותיך וקם. הנה אתה מת שוכב והנה אתה קם שתחיה לעתיד לבא והאי וקם אהנך קאי: דילמא וקם העם וזנה. דלקמי' קאי ולאו אדלעיל והיינו אחד ס) (מג') מקראות שאין להם הכרע ע): יחיו מתיך. דמתים שבארץ ישראל יחיו: נבלתי יקומון. אפי' נפלים יחיו במסכת כתובות פ): ודילמא מתים שהחיה יחזקאל. דהסיא קרא יחיו מתיך ישעיה אמרו והוא קדם ליחזקאל שנתנבא בימי חזקיה והיה מתנבא פסוק זה על שהיה עתיד יחזקאל להחיות מתים אבל לעולם הבא לא: דובב. פרונמיי"ש בלע"ז כלומר נעות ומתנודדות שפתי ישיני עפר מכלל שיחיו: מרחשן שפוותיהו בעלמא. שפתותיהן נעות מעט בתוך הקבר אבל אין חיין ויוצאין לאויר העולם וכרבי יוחנן וכו': ולא קבלו ממנו. עד שאמר להם וכו': חיים כלכם היום. דהאי צ) יום מיותר הוא דמצי למכתב חיים כלכם מה תלמוד לומר היום כהיום מה היום וכו' כך שמעתי: הנך שוכב עם אבותיך וקם. הרי תחיית המתים העם הזה וזנה הרי מה שעתיד להיות: פלגא בידך. דמהאי קרא נפקא דיודע מה שעתיד: זייפתם ולא העליתם. כזב אתם אומרים ואין ממש בדבריכם: לאו לעולם הבא. אלמא יש תחיית המתים: מהכרת תכרת. הכרת בעולם הזה תכרת לעולם הבא: אינהו הוו אמרי ליה דברה תורה כלשון בני אדם. ולהכי אמר להו הכי כי היכי דלא להוי להו פתחון פה: הכרת תכרת. בעבודת כוכבים כתיב: והלא כבר נאמר. בעבודת כוכבים את ה' הוא מגדף ונכרתה דס"ל מגדף ק) היינו עובד עבודת כוכבים: וכי שלשה עולמים יש וכו'. ור"ע סבירא ליה דמגדף היינו מברך השם: והשתא בין לרבי ישמעאל בין לר"ע עונה בה מאי עבדי ליה מבעי ליה וכו': שעונה בה. שלא שב קודם מיתה הוי בכרת אבל שב לא: דחיי שכבי. שהמתים חיים: ויציצו מעיר. שעתידין ישראל לצוץ ולפרוח מעיר ירושלים וכדאמרינן (כתובות דף קיא.) הקב"ה עושה להם מחילות לצדיקים והולכין ועולין לירושלים:

מסורת הש"ס

א) מכות יא. ברכות נו., ב) [ליתא בע"י], ג) ס"א מכאן אמרו שאין נותנין מתנה לכהן ע"ה, ד) חולין קל:, ה) [נ"ל הכהנים והלוים], ו) [פסחים מט: ע"ש], ז) יבמות לו: ע"ש בכורות לא: ע"ש, ח) רש"ל מ"ז, ט) [מו"ק כח.], י) [קידושין יז. וש"נ], כ) לעיל סד: [שבועות יג.], ל) [שבועות דף יג.], מ) [כתובות קיא: ועי' תוספות חולין קיז: ד"ה חטה], נ) רש"ל מ"ז, ס) [נ"ל מחמשה], ע) [יומא נב.], פ) [דף קיא.], צ) [נ"ל היום], ק) [לעיל סד: כריתות ז:].

הגהות הגר"א

[א] גמ' סימן צדיק גם גשם קם. נ"ב לדיק ק"ם גש"ם ג"ם סי' כל"ל:

ליקוטי רש"י

ויאמר לעם. ביהושפט כתיב בדברי הימים סיפיה דקרא למען יחזקו בתורת ה'. מנת. חלק כהונה [חולין קל:]. למען יחזקו בתורת ה'. יותר ברצון ועוד בעוד שיהא להם פרנסת' מזומנת יכלו לעשות ולעסוק בתורת ה' לפי שלא נתנה התורה אלא לאוכלי המן ושניים להם אוכלי תרומה [דה"ב לא, ד]. ומתו בו. למדנו שהיא מיתה בידי שמים [ויקרא כב, ט]. יחיו מתיך. כאן התפלל שיחיו הצדיקים בבקשה ממך יחיו אותן שמומתין עליך יצא דבר מלכות מלפניך לומר נבלתי יקומון נבלות עמי שנבלו עצמן עלי להם תהי תקומה זו חילוף למה שכתוב למעלה רפאים בל יקומו אבל אלו יקומון. הקיצו ורננו. כל זה יאמר להם הקב"ה הקיצו ורננו ל' צווי הוא זה. כי טל אורות טלך. כי נאה לך לעשות כן שיהא טל תורתך ומצותיך להם טל של אור. וארץ רפאים תפיל. ולארץ ולעפר תפיל את ארץ רפאים שריפו ידיהם מתורתך [ישעיה כו, יט]. ודילמא רחושי מרחשן שפוותיה בעלמא. כיין הטוב שהוא דובב שפתי ישני' אף אבותי בקבר ישמחו בי ויודו על חלקם דובב מרחיש פרומ"יר בלע"ז ויסודו לשון דיבור [שה"ש ז, י]. דובבות. נעות לשון דבר [ס"א, דבב] שמרחיש ומבלבך [יבמות צז.]. נעות והנאה הוא לו שדומה כחי [בכורות לא:]. והלא כבר נאמר את ה' הוא מגדף ונכרתה. באותה פרשה עצמה גבי מגדף ור' עקיבא סבירא ליה מגדף היינו מברך את השם כדאמר בכריתות ועולם הבא לא נפקא ליה בעבודה זרה אלא מהכרת תכרת ור' ישמעאל לאו לר' עקיבא פריך והלא כבר נאמר ונכרתה דהא ר' עקיבא במברך את השם מוקים לה אלא טעמא דנפשיה קאמר והלא כבר נאמרה ונכרתה ואנא סבירא ליה דבעבודה זרה כתיבא. וכי שלשה עולמים יש וכו'. ודומה לו בשחיטת חולין והלא במוקדשין האומר רגלה של זו עולה כולה עולה דהא פרכא לאו לכשנגדו פריך דאיהו סבירא ליה אפילו במוקדשין דאין כולה עולה אלא טעמא דנפשיה אמר בפרק [בהמה המקשה] (חולין סט.) [לעיל סד:]. דברה תורה כלשון בני אדם וכו'. הכי משתעו בני אדם ודברה תורה כלשון בני אדם וליכא למידרש מינה כלום [נדרים ג.]. ואף על גב דאיכא למדרש לא דרשינן כדמוכח בפ"ב דב"מ (לא:) [ר"ן שם]. לא אמרתי אלא בזמן שעונה בה. שאם עשה תשובה ואין עונה בה מיתה ממרקת ולא תכרת לעולם הבא [שבועות יג.]. ויציצו. ישראל. מעיר. מתוך ירושלים כעשב הארץ [תהלים עב, טז].

resurrect you.) מָה הַיּוֹם כּוּלְּכֶם קַיָּימִין – The superfluous word "today" indicates:[33] **Just as today you are all alive,** אַף לָעוֹלָם הַבָּא כּוּלְּכֶם קַיָּימִין – **so too, in the World to Come you will all be alive.**[34]

The second exchange:

שָׁאֲלוּ רוֹמִיִּים אֶת רַבִּי יְהוֹשֻׁעַ בֶּן חֲנַנְיָה – **The Romans asked R' Yehoshua ben Chananiah** the following two questions: מִנַּיִין שֶׁהַקָּדוֹשׁ בָּרוּךְ הוּא מְחַיֶּה מֵתִים – **From where** in Scripture is it known **that the Holy One, Blessed is He, resurrects the dead,** וְיוֹדֵעַ מַה שֶּׁעָתִיד לִהְיוֹת – **and that He knows what will be in the future?**[35] אָמַר לְהוּ – **He said to them:** תַּרְוַיְיהוּ מִן הַמִּקְרָא הַזֶּה – **Both** principles are evident **from this** following **verse:** שֶׁנֶּאֱמַר ,,וַיֹּאמֶר ה׳ אֶל־מֹשֶׁה הִנְּךָ שֹׁכֵב עִם־אֲבֹתֶיךָ וְקָם הָעָם הַזֶּה וְזָנָה" – **For it is stated:** ***And Hashem said to Moses, "Behold, you will lie with your forefathers and rise will this nation and stray*** *after the gods of the peoples of the land . . .*[36] וְדִילְמָא ,,וְקָם הָעָם הַזֶּה וְזָנָה" – The Romans retorted: **But perhaps** the verse means only ***and rise will this nation and go astray . . .,***[37] and thus in no way indicates a future resurrection. אָמַר לְהוּ – **[R' Yehoshua] said to them:** נְקוּטוּ מִיהָא פַּלְגָא בִּידַיְיכוּ – **Take, at any rate, half** the proof **in your hands** – דְּיוֹדֵעַ מַה שֶּׁעָתִיד לִהְיוֹת – namely, **that [God] knows what will be in the future;** for even you concede that the second part of the verse indicates God's knowledge of the future.[38]

The Gemara cites another Tanna who employed the same proof:

אִיתְּמַר נַמִּי – **Similarly, it was stated:** אָמַר רַבִּי יוֹחָנָן מִשּׁוּם רַבִּי שִׁמְעוֹן בֶּן יוֹחַאי – **R' Yochanan said in the name of R' Shimon ben Yochai:** מִנַּיִין שֶׁהַקָּדוֹשׁ בָּרוּךְ הוּא מְחַיֶּה מֵתִים וְיוֹדֵעַ מַה שֶּׁעָתִיד לִהְיוֹת – **From where** in Scripture is it known **that the Holy One, Blessed is He, resurrects the dead and knows what will be in the future?** שֶׁנֶּאֱמַר ,,הִנְּךָ שֹׁכֵב עִם־אֲבֹתֶיךָ וְקָם וגו׳" – **For it is stated:** ***Behold, you will lie with your forefathers and rise etc.***

The Gemara cites a related Baraisa:

תַּנְיָא – **It was taught in a Baraisa:** אָמַר רַבִּי אֱלִיעֶזֶר בְּרַבִּי יוֹסֵי – **R' ELIEZER THE SON OF R' YOSE SAID:** בְּדָבָר זֶה זִייַּפְתִּי סִפְרֵי מִינִים – **IN THIS MATTER, I SHOWED THE BOOKS OF THE SECTARIANS TO BE FALSE.**[39] שֶׁהָיוּ אוֹמְרִים אֵין תְּחִיַּית הַמֵּתִים מִן הַתּוֹרָה – **FOR THEY WOULD SAY THAT THERE IS NO** indication of the **RESURRECTION OF THE DEAD IN THE** Written **TORAH.** אָמַרְתִּי לָהֶן – **I SAID TO THEM:** זִייַּפְתֶּם תּוֹרַתְכֶם – **YOU HAVE FALSIFIED YOUR SCRIPTURES,** וְלֹא הֶעֱלִיתֶם בְּיֶדְכֶם כְּלוּם – **BUT YOU HAVE ACCOMPLISHED NOTHING** thereby. שֶׁאַתֶּם אוֹמְרִים אֵין תְּחִיַּית הַמֵּתִים מִן הַתּוֹרָה – **FOR YOU SAY THAT THERE IS NO** indication of the **RESURRECTION OF THE DEAD IN THE** Written **TORAH.** הֲרֵי הוּא אוֹמֵר ,,הִכָּרֵת תִּכָּרֵת הַנֶּפֶשׁ הַהִוא עֲוֹנָה בָהּ" – **BUT SURELY IT STATES:**[40] ***THAT SOUL SHALL BE UTTERLY CUT OFF, ITS SIN IS UPON IT.*** ,,הִכָּרֵת תִּכָּרֵת" בָּעוֹלָם הַזֶּה – Now, the phrase ***IT SHALL BE UTTERLY CUT OFF*** can mean **IN THIS WORLD;** that is, the sinner will die. ,,עֲוֹנָה בָהּ" לְאֵימַת – But if the sinner is already dead, then **WHEN** does ***ITS SIN IS UPON IT*** apply? לָאו לָעוֹלָם הַבָּא – **MUST IT NOT BE** that this refers **TO THE WORLD TO COME?**[41] Thus I proved to them that the Pentateuch clearly alludes to the Resurrection of the Dead.[42]

The Gemara explains why R' Eliezer the son of R' Yose did not adduce his proof differently:

אָמַר לֵיהּ רַב פָּפָּא לְאַבַּיֵי – **Rav Pappa said to Abaye:** וְלֵימָא לְהוּ תַּרְוַיְיהוּ מִ,,הִכָּרֵת תִּכָּרֵת" – **But let [R' Eliezer the son of R' Yose] cite to them** the proof for punishment in **both** worlds **from the** words ***it shall be utterly cut off.***[43] The answer is: אִינְהוּ הֲווּ אָמְרֵי לֵיהּ – Had he done so, **they would have replied to him** that no proof can be brought from the double expression, since דִּבְּרָה תּוֹרָה כִּלְשׁוֹן בְּנֵי אָדָם – **the Torah speaks the language of men.**[44]

NOTES

33. [What follows is not a continuation of the preceding phrase (which has been placed in parentheses) but rather an alternative formulation of the meaning of the superfluous word הַיּוֹם (see *Maharshal* and *Ein Yaakov,* who omit the portion in parentheses altogether; *Rashi's* comments also indicate that those words were absent from his text).]

34. [The superfluous word "today" indicates that there will come a time when you will all be alive as you are today. Cf. *Ben Yehoyada.*]

35. Certainly, God's knowledge of the future is evident from all the prophecies mentioned in Scripture. What the Romans asked, rather, concerned God's knowledge of those future events that will be determined by man's free will. How do we know that God's knowledge of the future extends even to such matters? (*Emes LeYaakov*).

36. *Deuteronomy* 31:16; see above, note 22. The first part of the verse (*you will lie with your forefathers and rise*) indicates that Moses will be resurrected. The second part of the verse (that the nation will stray after the gods of Canaan) indicates that God knows what man will choose to do of his own free will [since God does not coerce man to sin] (see *Rashi*).

37. See above, note 23.

38. See *Rashi*; cf. *Maharsha* and *Ben Yehoyada.*

39. *Rashi* seems to explain this to mean simply that he disproved the sectarian doctrine that denies the Resurrection of the Dead. See, however, *Maharsha* (cited in note 42).

40. *Numbers* 15:31, concerning one who worships idols.

41. And the verse means that after the sinner's death, his soul will endure eternal punishment for his sin (*Ramban* ad loc., citing *Pirkei DeRabbi Eliezer*). [This apparently proves only the existence of the soul in the Afterlife, not that the soul will be restored to its resurrected body. However, the two doctrines are interrelated and both were denied by the sectarians. Thus, R' Eliezer the son of R' Yose did indeed disprove the sectarian doctrine.]

42. *Maharsha* explains that the sectarians had deliberately altered their copies of the Holy Scriptures to eliminate all allusions to the Resurrection of the Dead. Thus, for example, they altered the expression *to them* (in the verses cited by the Gemara above) to read *to you.* [Some versions of this Gemara read: סִפְרֵי כּוּתִים, *the books of the Samaritans* (Cutheans), rather than סִפְרֵי מִינִים, *the books of the sectarians* (see *Ein Yaakov*; see also *Sotah* 33b). Indeed, *R' David Zvi Hoffman* (*Melamed LeHo'il* 3:79) notes that to this very day the Samaritan scrolls contain altered versions of various Scriptural proof texts for the Resurrection of the Dead (specifically, in *Deuteronomy* 1:8 and 11:9, which speak about the land that God swore to our forefathers *to give to them and to their children,* the Samaritans delete: "to them and").] R' Eliezer the son of R' Yose pointed out to the sectarians that their efforts to suppress the Scriptural message in this matter were of no avail, for they had neglected to alter another crucial passage that alludes to resurrection. [Thus, R' Eliezer the son of R' Yose means: "I have shown that you are falsifiers, since your assertion that *you* possess the authentic Scriptural text, as your version contains no mention of the Resurrection of the Dead, is belied by the appearance of a proof text even in your versions." Thus, "you have falsified your versions of the Holy Scriptures but have not achieved your objective." Alternatively, *Rif* in *Ein Yaakov* explains: You maintain that all Scriptural allusions to the Resurrection of the Dead are later additions. You thereby indict your own versions of Scripture as altered, since even *your* versions contain allusions that you neglected to expunge!]

43. Why the double expression הִכָּרֵת תִּכָּרֵת [literally: *cutting it shall be cut off*]? Is it not evident, then, that the first mention of כָּרֵת refers to This World and the second refers to the World to Come? (*Rashi*).

44. The Torah might express itself in terms used by human beings, who occasionally are redundant in their speech. Thus, a person might say, "Cut off shall he be, utterly cut off!" by way of angry emphasis, even though he does not mean that the other person will be punished more than once.

Anticipating this possible objection to the proof from the double expression, R' Eliezer the son of R' Yose used a different proof [though, in truth, the double expression *does* allude to the World to Come] (*Rashi*).

וכתיב א) ויהי לו כן וירמסו אותו העם בשער וימות ודילמא קללת אלישע גרמה ליה א) דאמר רב יהודה אמר רב קללת חכם אפי' על חנם היא באה אם כן לכתוב קרא וירמסוהו וימות מאי בשער על עסקי שער (ב) אמר ר' יוחנן) מניין לתחיית המתים מן התורה שנאמר ב) ונתתם ממנו [את] תרומת ה' לאהרן הכהן וכי אהרן לעולם קיים והלא לא נכנס לארץ ישראל שנותנין לו תרומה אלא מלמד שעתיד לחיות וישראל נותנין לו תרומה מכאן לתחיית המתים מן התורה דבי רבי ישמעאל תנא לאהרן כאהרן מה אהרן חבר אף בניו חברים ג) ד) א"ר שמואל בר נחמני אמר רבי יונתן מניין שאין נותנין תרומה לכהן עם הארץ שנאמר ג) ויאמר לעם ליושבי ירושלים לתת מנת (ה) לכהנים ולוים) למען יחזקו בתורת ה' כל המחזיק בתורת ה' יש לו מנת ושאינו מחזיק בתורת ה' אין לו מנת אמר רב אחא בר אדא אמר רב יהודה כל הנותן תרומה לכהן עם הארץ כאילו נותנה לפני ארי ו) מה ארי ספק דורס ואוכל ספק אינו דורס ואוכל אף כהן עם הארץ ספק אוכלה בטהרה ספק אוכלה בטומאה ר' יוחנן אמר אף גורם לו מיתה שנאמר ד) ומתו בו כי יחללוהו דבי ר"א בן יעקב תנא אף משיאו עון אשמה שנאמר ה) והשיאו אותם עון אשמה באכלם את קדשיהם תניא ר' סימאי אומר מניין לתחיית המתים מן התורה שנאמר ו) וגם הקימותי את בריתי אתם לתת להם את ארץ כנען לכם לא נאמר אלא להם מכאן לתחיית המתים מן התורה: [א] (צד"ק ג"ם גש"ם ק"ם סימן): שאלו מינין את רבן גמליאל מניין שהקדוש ברוך הוא מחיה מתים אמר להם מן התורה ומן הנביאים ומן הכתובים ולא קיבלו ממנו מן התורה דכתיב ז) ויאמר ה' אל משה הנך שוכב עם אבותיך וקם אמרו לו ודילמא וקם העם הזה וזנה מן הנביאים דכתיב ח) יחיו מתיך נבלתי יקומון הקיצו ורננו שוכני עפר כי טל אורות טלך וארץ רפאים תפיל ודילמא מתים שהחיה יחזקאל מן הכתובים דכתיב ט) וחכך כיין הטוב הולך לדודי למישרים דובב שפתי ישנים ודילמא רחושי מרחשן שפוותיה בעלמא כר' יוחנן י) דאמר ר' יוחנן משום ר"ש בן יהוצדק כל מי שנאמרה הלכה בשמו בעולם הזה שפתותיו דובבות בקבר שנאמר דובב שפתי ישנים עד שאמר להם מקרא זה י) אשר נשבע ה' לאבותיכם לתת להם לכם לא נאמר אלא להם מיכן לתחיית המתים מן התורה וי"א מן המקרא הזה אמר להם כ) ואתם הדבקים בה' אלהיכם חיים כלכם היום (ס) פשיטא דחיים כולכם היום אלא אפילו ביום שכל העולם כולם מתים אתם חיים) מה היום כולכם קיימין אף לעוה"ב כולכם קיימין שאלו רומיים את רבי יהושע בן חנניה מניין שהקב"ה מחיה מתים ויודע מה שעתיד להיות אמר להו תרווייהו מן המקרא הזה שנאמר ז) ויאמר ה' אל משה הנך שוכב עם אבותיך וקם העם הזה וזנה ודילמא וקם העם הזה וזנה אמר להו ט) נקוטו מיהא פלגא בידייכו דיודע מה שעתיד להיות איתמר נמי א"ר יוחנן משום רבי שמעון בן יוחאי מניין שהקדוש ברוך הוא מחיה מתים ויודע מה שעתיד להיות שנאמר הנך שוכב עם אבותיך וקם וגו' תניא א"ר אליעזר בר' יוסי בדבר זה זייפתי ספרי מינים שהיו אומרים אין תחיית המתים מן התורה אמרתי להן זייפתם תורתכם ולא העליתם בידכם כלום שאתם אומרים אין תחיית המתים מן התורה הרי הוא אומר ל) הכרת תכרת הנפש ההיא עונה בה הכרת תכרת בעולם הזה עונה בה לאימת לאו לעולם הבא א"ל רב פפא לאביי ולימא להו תרווייהו מהכרת תכרת אינהו הוו אמרי ליה י) דברה תורה כלשון בני אדם כתנאי כ) הכרת תכרת א) הכרת בעולם הזה תכרת לעולם הבא דברי ר"ע אמר לו ר' ישמעאל והלא כבר נאמר מ) את ה' הוא מגדף ונכרתה וכי שלשה עולמים יש אלא ונכרתה בעולם הזה הכרת לעולם הבא הכרת תכרת דברה תורה כלשון בני אדם בין ר' ישמעאל ובין ר"ע עונה בה מאי עבדי ביה לכדתניא ל) יכול אפילו עשה תשובה ת"ל עונה בה לא אמרתי אלא בזמן שעונה בה שאלה קליאופטרא מלכתא את ר"מ אמרה ידענא דחיי שכבי דכתיב נ) ויציצו מעיר כעשב הארץ אלא כשהן עומדין עומדין ערומין או בלבושיהן עומדין אמר לה מ) ק"ו מחיטה ב ומה חיטה שנקברה ערומה יוצאה בכמה לבושין צדיקים שנקברים בלבושיהן על אחת כמה וכמה א"ל קיסר לרבן גמליאל אמריתו דשכבי חיי הא הוו עפרא ועפרא מי קא חיי אמרה

רש"י

ויהי לו כן וירמסו אותו. דדבר שכפר בו נדון שלא אכל משם ונרמס ברגלי הבאים לקנות: ו) (וכי אהרן קיים לעולם. כלומר וכי אהרן חיה כל כך שתנתן לו תרומה והלא לא נכנס לארץ ישראל ומאי האי דקאמר ונתתם ממנו תרומת ה' לאהרן הכהן): לעולם קיים. לאו דווקא אלא כלומר הלא לא נגזר עליו שיחיה כל כך: שעתיד לחיות. לעולם הבא: דבי רבי ישמעאל תנא. הא דכתיב לאהרן לאו להכי הוא דאתא אלא לומר לך כאהרן וכו': מה ארי ספק דורס ואוכל. ואין אנו יודעין כשנוטל בהמה מן העדר אם דעתו לדורסה ולאוכלה מיד קודם שתסריח או לא אלא לטרוף ולמלא (חורו) [תאותו] ולאחר זמן יאכלנה כשתסריח וה"נ כהן עם הארץ כשאנו נותנין לו תרומה בידו אין אנו יודעין אם יאכלנה בטהרה או בטומאה [אי נמי] ספק דורס שארי דרכו לדרוס ולרמוס בהמה ברגליו ואוכלה כשהיא דרוסה מנוולת ופעמים שנותנה בחורו ואינה מנוולת: עון אשמה. עונות הרבה מטעין עליו: באכלם את קדשיהם. ומתרגמינן במיכלהון בסואבא ית קודשיהון: אלא להם. דמשמע שהבטיח הקב"ה לאבותינו אברהם יצחק ויעקב שיתן להם ארץ ישראל וכי להם ניתנה והלא לבניהם ניתנה אלא מלמד שעתידין לחיות ועתיד הקב"ה ליתן להם את ארץ ישראל: הנך שוכב עם אבותיך וקם. הנה אתה מת שוכב והנה אתה קם שתחיה לעתיד לבא והאי וקם אהנך קאי: דילמא וקם העם וזנה. דלקמי' קאי ולאו אדלעיל והיינו אחד ס) (מג') מקראות שאין להם הכרע ע): יחיו מתיך. דמתים שבארץ ישראל יחיו: נבלתי יקומון. אפי' נפלים יחיו במסכת כתובות פ): ודילמא מתים שהחיה יחזקאל. דההיא קרא יחיו מתיך ישעיה אמרו והוא קדם ליחזקאל שנתנבא בימי חזקיה והיה מתנבא פסוק זה על שהיה עתיד יחזקאל להחיות מתים אבל לעולם הבא לא: דובב. פרונמיי"ש בלע"ז כלומר נעות ומתנודדות שפתי ישיני עפר מכלל שיחיו: מרחשן שפוותיהו בעלמא. שפתותיהן נעות מעט בתוך הקבר אבל אין חיין ויוצאין לאויר העולם וכרבי יוחנן וכו': ולא קבלו ממנו. עד שאמר להם וכו': חיים כלכם היום. דהאי צ) יום מיותר הוא דמצי למכתב חיים כלכם מה תלמוד לומר היום כהיום מה היום וכו' כך שמעתי: הנך שוכב עם אבותיך וקם. הרי תחיית המתים העם הזה וזנה הרי מה שעתיד להיות: פלגא בידך. דמהאי קרא נפקא דיודע מה שעתיד: זייפתם ולא העליתם. כזב אתם אומרים ואין ממש בדבריכם: לאו לעולם הבא. אלמא יש תחיית המתים: מהכרת תכרת. הכרת בעולם הזה תכרת לעולם הבא: אינהו הוו אמרי ליה דברה תורה כלשון בני אדם. ולהכי אמר להו הכי כי היכי דלא להוי להו פתחון פה: הכרת תכרת. בעבודת כוכבים כתיב: והלא כבר נאמר. בעבודת כוכבים את ה' הוא מגדף ונכרתה דס"ל מגדף ק) היינו עובד עבודת כוכבים: וכי שלשה עולמים יש וכו'. ור"ע סבירא ליה דמגדף היינו מברך השם: והשתא בין לרבי ישמעאל בין לר"ע עונה בה מאי עבדי ליה מבעי ליה וכו': שעונה בה. שלא שב קודם מיתה הוי בכרת אבל שב לא: דחיי שכבי. שהמתים חיים: ויציצו מעיר. שעתידין ישראל לציץ ולפרוח מעיר ירושלים וכדאמרינן (כתובות דף קיא.) הקב"ה עושה להם מחילות לצדיקים והולכין ועולין לירושלים:

עין משפט נר מצוה

ג א מיי' פ"ח מהלכות תשובה הל"א:

ד ב מיי' שם הלכה ב בהשגו' ובהפירוש שהביא בעל מ"ע בשם הרמב"ן:

תורה אור השלם

א) וַיְהִי לוֹ כֵּן וַיִּרְמְסוּ אֹתוֹ הָעָם בַּשַּׁעַר וַיָּמֹת: [מלכים ב' ז, כ]

ב) כֵּן תָּרִימוּ גַם אַתֶּם תְּרוּמַת יְיָ מִכֹּל מַעְשְׂרֹתֵיכֶם אֲשֶׁר תִּקְחוּ מֵאֵת בְּנֵי יִשְׂרָאֵל וּנְתַתֶּם מִמֶּנּוּ אֶת תְּרוּמַת יְיָ לְאַהֲרֹן הַכֹּהֵן: [במדבר יח, כח]

ג) וַיֹּאמֶר לָעָם לְיוֹשְׁבֵי יְרוּשָׁלַיִם לָתֵת מְנָת הַכֹּהֲנִים וְהַלְוִיִּם לְמַעַן יֶחֶזְקוּ בְּתוֹרַת יְיָ: [דברי הימים ב' לא, ד]

ד) וְשָׁמְרוּ אֶת מִשְׁמַרְתִּי וְלֹא יִשְׂאוּ עָלָיו חֵטְא וּמֵתוּ בוֹ כִּי יְחַלְּלֻהוּ אֲנִי יְיָ מְקַדְּשָׁם: [ויקרא כב, ט]

ה) וְהִשִּׂיאוּ אוֹתָם עֲוֹן אַשְׁמָה בְּאָכְלָם אֶת קָדְשֵׁיהֶם כִּי אֲנִי יְיָ מְקַדְּשָׁם: [ויקרא כב, טז]

ו) וְגַם הֲקִמֹתִי אֶת בְּרִיתִי אִתָּם לָתֵת לָהֶם אֶת אֶרֶץ כְּנָעַן אֵת אֶרֶץ מְגֻרֵיהֶם אֲשֶׁר גָּרוּ בָהּ: [שמות ו, ד]

ז) וַיֹּאמֶר יְיָ אֶל מֹשֶׁה הִנְּךָ שֹׁכֵב עִם אֲבֹתֶיךָ וְקָם הָעָם הַזֶּה וְזָנָה אַחֲרֵי אֱלֹהֵי נֵכַר הָאָרֶץ אֲשֶׁר הוּא בָא שָׁמָּה בְּקִרְבּוֹ וַעֲזָבַנִי וְהֵפֵר אֶת בְּרִיתִי אֲשֶׁר כָּרַתִּי אִתּוֹ: [דברים לא, טז]

ח) יִחְיוּ מֵתֶיךָ נְבֵלָתִי יְקוּמוּן הָקִיצוּ וְרַנְּנוּ שֹׁכְנֵי עָפָר כִּי טַל אוֹרֹת טַלֶּךָ וָאָרֶץ רְפָאִים תַּפִּיל: [ישעיה כו, יט]

ט) וְחִכֵּךְ כְּיֵין הַטּוֹב הוֹלֵךְ לְדוֹדִי לְמֵישָׁרִים דּוֹבֵב שִׂפְתֵי יְשֵׁנִים: [שיר השירים ז, י]

י) לְמַעַן יִרְבּוּ יְמֵיכֶם וִימֵי בְנֵיכֶם עַל הָאֲדָמָה אֲשֶׁר נִשְׁבַּע יְיָ לַאֲבֹתֵיכֶם לָתֵת לָהֶם כִּימֵי הַשָּׁמַיִם עַל הָאָרֶץ: [דברים יא, כא]

כ) וְאַתֶּם הַדְּבֵקִים בַּיְיָ אֱלֹהֵיכֶם חַיִּים כֻּלְּכֶם הַיּוֹם: [דברים ד, ד]

ל) כִּי דְבַר יְיָ בָּזָה וְאֶת מִצְוָתוֹ הֵפַר הִכָּרֵת תִּכָּרֵת הַנֶּפֶשׁ הַהִוא עֲוֹנָה בָהּ: [במדבר טו, לא]

מ) וְהַנֶּפֶשׁ אֲשֶׁר תַּעֲשֶׂה בְּיָד רָמָה מִן הָאֶזְרָח וּמִן הַגֵּר אֶת יְיָ הוּא מְגַדֵּף וְנִכְרְתָה הַנֶּפֶשׁ הַהִוא מִקֶּרֶב עַמָּהּ: [במדבר טו, ל]

נ) יְהִי פִסַּת בַּר בָּאָרֶץ בְּרֹאשׁ הָרִים יִרְעַשׁ כַּלְּבָנוֹן פִּרְיוֹ וְיָצִיצוּ מֵעִיר כְּעֵשֶׂב הָאָרֶץ: [תהלים עב, טז]

מסורת הש"ס

א) מכות יא. ברכות נו., ב) [ליתא בע"י], ג) ס"א מכאן אמרו שאין נותנין מתנה לכהן ע"ה, ד) חולין קל:, ה) [נ"ל הכהנים והלוים], ו) [פסחים מט: ע"ש], ז) יבמות נו: ע"ש בכורות לא: ע"ש, ח) רש"ל מ"ז, ט) [מו"ק כח.], י) [קידושין יז. וש"נ], כ) לעיל סד: [שבועות יג.], ל) [שבועות דף יג.], מ) [כתובות קיא: ועי' תוספות חולין קיז: ד"ה חטה], נ) רש"ל מ"ז, ס) [נ"ל מחמשה], ע) [יומא נב.], פ) [דף קיא.], צ) [נ"ל היום], ק) [לעיל סד: כריתות ז:].

הגהות הגר"א

[א] גמ' סימן צדיק גם גשם קם. נ"ב צדיק ק"ם גש"ם ג"ם סי' כצ"ל:

ליקוטי רש"י

ויאמר לעם. ביהושפט כתיב בדברי הימים סיפיה דקרא למען יחזקו בתורת ה'. מנת. חלק כהונה [חולין קל:]. למען יחזקו בתורת ה'. יותר ברצון ועוד בעוד שיהא להם פרנסת' מזומנת יכלו לעשות ולעסוק בתורת ה' לפי שלא נתנה התורה אלא לאוכלי המן ושניים להם אוכלי תרומה [דה"ב לא, ד]. ומתו בו. למדנו שהיא מיתה בידי שמים [ויקרא כב, ט]. יחיו מתיך. כאן התפלל שיחיו הצדיקים בבקשה ממך יחיו אותן שמומתין עליך יצא דבר מלכות מלפניך לומר נבלתי יקומון נבלות עמי שנבלו עצמן עלי להם תהי תקומה זו חילוף למה שכתוב למעלה רפאים בל יקומו אבל אלו יקומון. הקיצו ורננו. כל זה יאמר להם הקב"ה הקיצו ורננו ל' צווי הוא זה. כי טל אורות טלך. כי נאה לך לעשות כן שיהא טל תורתך ומצותיך להם טל של אור. וארץ רפאים תפיל. ולארץ ולעפר תפיל את ארץ רפאים שריפו ידיהם מתורתך [ישעיה כו, יט]. ודילמא רחושי מרחשן שפוותיה בעלמא. כיין הטוב שהוא דובב שפתי ישני' אף אבותי בקבר ישמחו בי ויודו על חלקם דובב מרחיש פרומ"יר בלע"ז ויסודו לשון דיבור [שה"ש ז, י]. דובבות. נעות לשון דבר [ס"א, דבב] שמרחים ומבלבן [יבמות צז.]. נעות והנאה הוא לו שדומה כחי [בכורות לא:]. והלא כבר נאמר את ה' הוא מגדף ונכרתה. באותה פרשה עצמה גבי מגדף ור' עקיבא סבירא ליה מגדף היינו מברך את השם כדאמר בכריתות ועולם הבא לא נפקא ליה בעבודה זרה אלא מהכרת תכרת ור' ישמעאל לאו לר' עקיבא פריך והלא כבר נאמר ונכרתה דהא ר' עקיבא במברך את השם מוקים לה אלא טעמא דנפשיה קאמר והלא כבר נאמרה ונכרתה ואנא סבירא ליה דבעבודה זרה כתיבא. וכי שלשה עולמים יש וכו'. ודומה לו בשחיטת חולין והלא במוקדשין האומר רגלה של זו עולה כולה עולה דהא פרכא לאו לכשנגדו פריך דאיהו סבירא ליה אפילו במוקדשין דאין כולה עולה אלא טעמא דנפשיה אמר בפרק [בהמה המקשה] (חולין סט.) [לעיל סד:]. דברה תורה כלשון בני אדם וכו'. הכי משמעו בני אדם ודברה תורה כלשון בני אדם וליכא למידרש מינה כלום [נדרים ג.]. ואף על גב דאיכא למדרש לא דרשינן כדמוכח בפ"ב דב"מ (לא:) [ר"ן שם]. לא אמרתי אלא בזמן שעונה בה. שאם עשה תשובה ואין עונה בה מיתה ממרקת ולא תכרת לעולם הבא [שבועות יג.]. ויציצו. ישראל. מעיר. מתוך ירושלים כעשב הארץ [תהלים עב, טז].

The Gemara notes:

כְּתַנָּאֵי – This is **like** the following dispute between **Tannaim.** I.e. both the question and answer are rooted in different Tannaic approaches to this verse. For a Baraisa[45] teaches: ,,הִכָּרֵת תִּכָּרֵת'' – When Scripture states: ***CUTTING OFF IT SHALL BE CUT OFF,*** it means: ,,הִכָּרֵת'' בָּעוֹלָם הַזֶּה ,,תִּכָּרֵת'' לָעוֹלָם הַבָּא דִּבְרֵי רַבִּי עֲקִיבָא – ***CUTTING OFF*** from life **IN THIS WORLD,** and ***IT SHALL BE CUT OFF*** from life **IN THE WORLD TO COME.** These are **THE WORDS OF R' AKIVA.** אָמַר לוֹ רַבִּי יִשְׁמָעֵאל – **R' YISHMAEL SAID TO HIM:** וַהֲלֹא כְּבָר נֶאֱמַר ,,אֶת־ה' הוּא מְגַדֵּף וְנִכְרְתָה'' – **BUT IT IS ALREADY STATED** in the previous verse: ***IT IS HASHEM WHOM HE IS BLASPHEMING, CUT OFF SHALL BE*** *that soul.*[46] וְכִי שְׁלֹשָׁה עוֹלָמִים יֵשׁ – **ARE THERE THEN *THREE* WORLDS** that *kares* might apply to?[47] אֶלָּא ,,וְנִכְרְתָה'' בָּעוֹלָם הַזֶּה – **RATHER,** the verses should be interpreted as follows: ***CUT OFF SHALL BE*** that soul from life **IN THIS WORLD.** ,,הִכָּרֵת'' לָעוֹלָם הַבָּא – ***CUTTING OFF*** refers to life **IN THE WORLD TO COME.** ,,הִכָּרֵת תִּכָּרֵת'' דִּבְּרָה תּוֹרָה כִּלְשׁוֹן בְּנֵי אָדָם – And as for the double expression ***CUTTING OFF IT SHALL BE CUT OFF,*** there is no special significance in this repetition, for **THE TORAH SPEAKS THE LANGUAGE OF MEN.**

The Gemara asks:

בֵּין רַבִּי יִשְׁמָעֵאל וּבֵין רַבִּי עֲקִיבָא ,,עֲוֹנָה בָהּ'' מַאי עָבְדֵי בֵּיהּ – **Both** according to **R' Yishmael and R' Akiva,** we could ask: **What do they do with** the last part of the second verse, which states: ***its sin is upon it?***[48]

The Gemara answers:

לִכְדְתַנְיָא – They will explain that this expression is needed **for what has been taught in the** following **Baraisa:** יָכוֹל אֲפִילוּ עָשָׂה תְשׁוּבָה – **IT WOULD BE POSSIBLE** to say that the sinner is cut off **EVEN IF HE REPENTS.** תַּלְמוּד לוֹמַר ,,עֲוֹנָה בָהּ'' – Therefore **THE TORAH SAYS:** ***ITS SIN IS UPON IT,*** which indicates that לֹא אָמַרְתִּי אֶלָּא בִּזְמַן שֶׁעֲוֹנָהּ בָּהּ – **I DO NOT SAY** that the sinner's soul is cut off **EXCEPT WHEN ITS SIN IS** still **UPON IT,** i.e. if he dies unrepentant.[49]

The third exchange:

שָׁאֲלָה קְלֵיאוֹפַּטְרָא מַלְכְּתָא אֶת רַבִּי מֵאִיר – **Queen Cleopatra**[50] **asked R' Meir.** אָמְרָה יָדַעְנָא דְּחַיֵּי שָׁכְבֵי – **She said: I know that the dead** will **live** again, דִּכְתִיב ,,וְיָצִיצוּ מֵעִיר כְּעֵשֶׂב הָאָרֶץ'' – **as it is written:** ***And they shall blossom forth from the city like the grass of the earth.***[51] אֶלָּא כְּשֶׁהֵן עוֹמְדִין – **But** what I want to know is whether **when they rise** from the dead, עוֹמְדִין עֲרוּמִין – **do they rise naked** אוֹ בִּלְבוּשֵׁיהֶן עוֹמְדִין – **or do they rise in their clothes?** אָמַר לָהּ – **He said to her:** קַל וָחוֹמֶר מֵחִיטָּה – The answer can be inferred through **an *a fortiori* analysis of a wheat kernel:** וּמַה חִיטָּה שֶׁנִּקְבְּרָה עֲרוּמָּה – **If a wheat grain, which was buried** in the ground **naked,** יוֹצְאָה בְּכַמָּה לְבוּשִׁין – **emerges** from the ground fully grown and **wearing several garments,** צַדִּיקִים שֶׁנִּקְבָּרִים בִּלְבוּשֵׁיהֶן עַל אַחַת כַּמָּה וְכַמָּה – **then how much more so will the righteous, who are buried in their clothes,** emerge fully clothed at the resurrection![52]

The fourth exchange:

אָמַר לֵיהּ קֵיסָר לְרַבָּן גַּמְלִיאֵל – **Caesar said to Rabban Gamliel:** אָמְרִיתוּ דְּשָׁכְבֵי חַיֵּי – **You** Jews **say that the dead will live** again. How can this be? הָא הָווּ עַפְרָא – **Why, they become dust,** וְעַפְרָא מִי קָא חַיֵּי – **and can dust come alive?!**

NOTES

45. Above, 64b.

46. *Numbers* 15:30. R' Yishmael holds that the "blasphemy" mentioned here is nothing other than the act of idolatry (*Rashi*; see above, 64b). If so, then according to R' Akiva's interpretation that the double expression *cutting off it shall be cut off* alludes to two *kares* penalties, we have *three* such penalties stated for idolatry – one in v. 30 and two in v. 31.

47. Certainly, there are only two. Thus, we cannot interpret the double expression *cutting off it shall be cut off* as alluding to two *kares* penalties. [As explained in the preceding note, R' Yishmael's objection is predicated on his own view that the blasphemer of v. 30 is none other than the idolater of v. 31. This objection, then, does not pose any difficulty for R' Akiva, who holds that v. 30 refers to an actual blasphemer, not to an idolater (*Rashi* to 64b).]

[*Toras Chaim* considers why R' Yishmael could not answer that there are indeed three worlds to which *kares* might apply: this world, the world of the soul in the Afterlife, and the world in which the dead are resurrected. He answers that the latter two are interrelated – only those who merit the Afterlife will be resurrected. But he then points to *Tosafos, Rosh Hashanah* 16b ד״ה ליום הדין, who explain the Gemara there to mean that there are some who merit the Afterlife but not the resurrection. Might the three mentions of *kares,* then, not refer to being cut off from: this life, the resurrection, and the Afterlife?]

48. This expression apparently indicates an additional punishment of the soul (see Gemara above and note 41 there). But what punishment could this be if punishment in both worlds is already indicated earlier – whether according to R' Akiva's interpretation or R' Yishmael's?

49. According to this interpretation, the words *its sin is upon it* does not indicate another punishment, but rather means that the aforementioned punishment applies only if the sinner has not repented.

50. Cleopatra was the name used by a long line of Egyptian queens. The one mentioned here is *not* the one most commonly known, who lived a century before the time of R' Meir.

51. *Psalms* 72:16. "The city" is Jerusalem, and the meaning is that at the time of the resurrection, the bodies of the righteous will be transported from their place of burial to Jerusalem through underground tunnels (*Rashi,* from *Kesubos* 111b).

52. There is a question whether this refers to the very clothing in which they were buried or to different clothing (see *Tosafos* to *Kesubos* 111b and *Gilyon HaShas* there; R' Yannai's statement in *Shabbos* 114a and *Maharal* here; see also references cited in *Margaliyos HaYam* and *Michtav MeEliyahu* IV:154).

אָמְרָה לֵיהּ בְּרַתֵּיהּ – **[Caesar's] daughter said to [Rabban Gamliel]:** שִׁבְקֵיהּ – Rabbi, **leave him be** וַאֲנָא מַהְדַרְנָא לֵיהּ – **and I will answer him** for you. She then turned to her father and said: שְׁנֵי יוֹצְרִים יֵשׁ בְּעִירֵנוּ – Suppose **there were two potters in our city,** אֶחָד יוֹצֵר מִן הַמַּיִם – **one** who **fashions** pottery **out of water** וְאֶחָד יוֹצֵר מִן הַטִּיט – **and one** who **fashions** pottery **out of clay.** אֵיזֶה מֵהֶן מְשׁוּבָּח – **Which one of them** would you say **is superior?** אָמַר לָהּ – **[Caesar] replied to her:** זֶה שֶׁיּוֹצֵר מִן הַמַּיִם – **The one who fashions** pottery **out of water.**[1] אָמְרָה לוֹ – **She** then **said to him:** מִן הַמַּיִם צָר – By the same token, **if [God] fashions** human beings **out of water,**[2] מִן הַטִּיט לֹא כָּל שֶׁכֵּן – **is it not certain** that He can fashion them **out of clay** or dust?!

Another version:

דְּבֵי רַבִּי יִשְׁמָעֵאל תָּנָא – **In R' Yishmael's academy, a Tanna taught** a different version of what Caesar's daughter replied to her father: קַל וָחוֹמֶר מִכְּלֵי זְכוּכִית – The plausibility of resurrection can be inferred through AN *A FORTIORI* ANALYSIS OF GLASSWARE: מַה כְּלֵי זְכוּכִית שֶׁעֲמָלָן בְּרוּחַ בָּשָׂר וָדָם – IF GLASSWARE, WHOSE WORKING into shape IS done BY THE BREATH OF FLESH AND BLOOD,[3] נִשְׁבְּרוּ יֵשׁ לָהֶן תַּקָּנָה – CAN BE FIXED IF THEY ARE BROKEN,[4] בָּשָׂר וָדָם שֶׁבְּרוּחוֹ שֶׁל הַקָּדוֹשׁ בָּרוּךְ הוּא – then a person of FLESH AND BLOOD, WHO is fashioned BY THE BREATH OF THE HOLY ONE, BLESSED IS HE,[5] עַל אַחַת כַּמָּה וְכַמָּה – HOW MUCH MORE SO is it understandable that he can be resurrected after he has disintegrated into dust!

The fifth exchange:

אָמַר לֵיהּ הַהוּא מִינָא לְרַבִּי אַמִּי – **A certain sectarian said to R' Ami:** אָמְרִיתוּ דִּשְׁכְבֵי חַיֵּי – **You** Jews **say that the dead will live** again. How can this be? וְהָא הָווּ עַפְרָא – **Why, they become dust,** וְעַפְרָא מִי קָא חַיֵּי – **and can dust come alive?** אָמַר לֵיהּ – **[R' Ami] replied to him:** אֶמְשׁוֹל לְךָ מָשָׁל – **I will give you a parable:** לְמָה הַדָּבָר דּוֹמֶה – **To what can the matter** of your objection **be compared?** לְמֶלֶךְ בָּשָׂר וָדָם שֶׁאָמַר לַעֲבָדָיו – **To a king of flesh and blood who said to his servants:** לְכוּ וּבְנוּ לִי פַּלְטְרִין גְּדוֹלִים – **"Go and build me a great palace** בְּמָקוֹם שֶׁאֵין מַיִם וְעָפָר – **in a place where there is no water or earth** with which to make bricks." הָלְכוּ וּבָנוּ אוֹתוֹ – **They went and built it** using other materials. לְיָמִים נָפְלוּ – **Some days** later, **[the palace] collapsed.** אָמַר לָהֶם – **[The king] said to them:** חִזְרוּ וּבְנוּ אוֹתוֹ בְּמָקוֹם שֶׁיֵּשׁ עָפָר וּמַיִם – **"Rebuild it in a place where there is earth and water."** אָמְרוּ לוֹ אֵין אָנוּ יְכוֹלִין – **They said to him: "We are unable** to do so." כָּעַס עֲלֵיהֶם וְאָמַר לָהֶן – **[The king] became angry with them and said to them:** בְּמָקוֹם שֶׁאֵין מַיִם וְעָפָר בְּנִיתֶם – **"If you built** the palace **in a place where there is no water or earth** with which to make bricks, עַכְשָׁיו שֶׁיֵּשׁ מַיִם וְעָפָר עַל אַחַת כַּמָּה וְכַמָּה – **now that there is water and earth, how much more so** should you be able to build it!"[6] אִם אִי אַתָּה מַאֲמִין – **And if you do not** find yourselves able to **believe** that living beings can be formed from dust, צֵא לַבִּקְעָה – **go out to the field** וּרְאֵה עַכְבָּר שֶׁהַיּוֹם חֶצְיוֹ בָּשָׂר וְחֶצְיוֹ אֲדָמָה – **and see the squirrel**[7] **that one day is half flesh and half earth** לְמָחָר הִשְׁרִיץ וְנַעֲשָׂה כֻּלּוֹ בָּשָׂר – **and by the morrow it has metamorphosed into a creeping thing and become entirely flesh!**[8] Thus, such a thing is not only possible, but takes place before our very eyes! שֶׁמָּא תֹּאמַר לִזְמַן מְרוּבֶּה – **Perhaps you will say** that **it takes a long time** for this creature to develop from the earth.[9] עֲלֵה לָהָר – Then **go up to the mountain** וּרְאֵה שֶׁהַיּוֹם אֵין בּוֹ אֶלָּא חִלָּזוֹן אֶחָד – **and see that one day there is but a single *chilazon***[10] there, לְמָחָר יָרְדוּ גְשָׁמִים – **and on the morrow rain falls** וְנִתְמַלֵּא כּוּלּוֹ חִלְזוֹנוֹת – **and the whole [mountain] is full of *chilzonos*!**[11]

The Gemara records additional debates with enemies of the Jews and Jewish belief:

אָמַר לֵיהּ הַהוּא מִינָא לְגְבִיהָא בֶּן פְּסִיסָא – **A certain sectarian said to Geviha ben Pesisa:** וַוי לְכוֹן חַיָּיבַיָּא – **Woe to you, O sinners,** דְּאָמְרִיתוּן מֵיתֵי חַיִּין – **for you say that the dead will live.** דְּחַיִּין מֵיתִי דְּמֵיתֵי חַיִּין – Now, if even **the living** eventually **die,** is it credible that **the dead will live?** אָמַר לֵיהּ – **[Geviha] said to him:** וַוי לְכוֹן חַיָּיבַיָּא – **Woe to *you*, O sinners,**[12] דְּאָמְרִיתוּן מֵיתֵי לָא חַיִּין – **for you say that the dead will *not* live.** דְּלָא הָווּ חַיֵּי – Now, if even **the non-existent come to life,**[13] דַּהֲווּ חַיֵּי לֹא כָּל שֶׁכֵּן – **is it not all the more** possible that **those who once lived** will live again? אָמַר לֵיהּ – **[The sectarian] retorted** angrily:

NOTES

1. For any potter can fashion pottery out of clay, but it is quite a feat to fashion a piece of solid pottery out of water!

2. I.e. from a fluid — a fetid drop [of semen] (*Rashi*).

3. The glassmaker shapes his wares by blowing into the molten glass through a tube (*Rashi*).

4. By melting the shards and reshaping them.

5. As stated in *Genesis* 2:7: *And He blew into his nostrils the breath of life.*

6. Similarly, your objection to the notion of resurrection on grounds that earth cannot be infused with life is specious. For even you admit that God fashions human beings from a mere drop of semen. Will you now claim it inconceivable that He should do so from earth, which is more substantive? (*Rashi*). Alternatively, if you admit that He created the world out of nothing, will you now claim it inconceivable that He should fashion man out of dust? (ibid.).

The water in this parable represents the "Dew of Resurrection" [see *Shabbos* 88b and *Chagigah* 12b] (see *Rif* in *Ein Yaakov*).

7. *Rashi.*

8. Ancient explorers and naturalists (notably Pliny in his *Natural History*) report the existence of such a creature, which does not appear to reproduce sexually, but rather to be generated spontaneously from the earth. It is discussed by the Mishnah and Gemara in *Chullin* 126b-127a. *Rambam* (*Commentary to the Mishnah* there) writes: "The existence of such a creature is widely known, and uncounted people have told me that they have seen one, though the existence of such a creature is baffling." *Tiferes Yisrael* there cites a German scholar by the name of Link, who describes in his book (*Urwelt*, I:327) this type of creature, called *springmaus* in German, found in Egypt in the area of Thebes. He writes that the front quarters of the body, viz. the head, the chest and the forelegs are well formed, while the rear quarters still appear to be unformed earth. A few days later, the entire mouse turns to flesh. [This description, however, does not appear to exactly match the one stated in the *Gemara* in *Chullin.*] (See also note to ArtScroll Mishnah *Chullin* 9:6.)

9. That is, a week or two. Thus, you cannot accept that as a precedent for an immediate resurrection (see *Rashi*).

10. See next note.

11. *Rashi* identifies the *chilazon* discussed here as the Mediterranean sea creature whose blood is used to manufacture the *techeiles* dye. This creature emerges from the sea once every seventy years and climbs onto the land. At first only one *chilazon* appears, but after rain falls, its eggs hatch very quickly and the whole mountain is covered with them. [Others object to this identification (for a variety of reasons) and explain that *chilazon* here refers to a different creature (see *Yad Ramah, Aruch* ע׳ חלזון and *Be'er Sheva*).]

The rapid development of *chilazon,* then, should illustrate to you God's ability to resurrect the dead very quickly.

12. *Maharsha* explains why each said to the other, "Woe to you, O sinner." As it would seem from the Gemara further in this chapter, there are sinners who forfeit all share in the World to Come and others who will be resurrected to be punished on the Great Day of Judgment. Thus, the sectarian called Geviha "sinner" — i.e. you, who believe in a resurrection, will have to suffer for your sins at that time. We, however, who do not believe in a resurrection, are free of this worry. To which Geviha replied that the sectarian was in fact the unfortunate sinner, since one who denies the resurrection has no share in it and thus loses the opportunity to be purified through punishment upon resurrection and thereby gain an eternal share in the World to Come.

13. For every day babies are born who have never previously been alive.

אמרה ליה ברתיה שבקיה ואנא מהדרנא ליה שני יוצרים יש בעירנו אחד יוצר מן המים ואחד יוצר מן הטיט איזה מהן משובח א"ל זה שיוצר מן המים א"ל מן המים צר מן הטיט לא כל שכן דבי ר' ישמעאל תנא ק"ו מכלי זכוכית מה כלי זכוכית שעמלן ברוח בשר ודם נשברו יש להן תקנה בשר ודם שברוחו של הקב"ה על אחת כמה וכמה א"ל ההוא מינא לר' אמי אמריתו דשכבי חיי והא הוו עפרא ועפרא מי קא חיי א"ל אמשול לך משל למה הדבר דומה למלך בשר ודם שאמר לעבדיו לכו ובנו לי פלטרין גדולים במקום שאין מים ועפר הלכו ובנו אותו לימים נפלו אמר להם חזרו ובנו אותו במקום שיש עפר ומים אמרו לו אין אנו יכולין כעס עליהם ואמר להן במקום שאין מים ועפר בניתם [א] עכשיו שיש מים ועפר על אחת כמה וכמה ואם אי אתה מאמין צא לבקעה וראה עכבר שהיום חציו בשר וחציו אדמה למחר השריץ ונעשה כלו בשר שמא תאמר לזמן מרובה עלה להר וראה שהיום [ב] אין בו אלא חלזון אחד למחר ירדו גשמים ונתמלא כולו חלזונות א"ל ההוא מינא לגביהא בן פסיסא ווי לכון חייביא דאמריתון מיתי חיין דחיין מיתי דמיתי חיין א"ל ווי לכון חייביא דאמריתון מיתי לא חיין דלא הוו חיי דהוי חיי לא כ"ש א"ל חייביא קרית לי אי קאימנא בעיטנא בך ופשיטנא לעקמותך מינך א"ל אם אתה עושה כן רופא אומן תקרא ושכר הרבה תטול ת"ר [ג] בעשרים וארבעה בניסן איתנטילו דימוסנאי מיהודה ומירושלים כשבאו בני אפריקיא לדון עם ישראל לפני אלכסנדרוס מוקדון אמרו לו ארץ כנען שלנו היא דכתיב [א] ארץ כנען לגבולותיה וכנען אבוהון דהנהו אינשי הוה אמר להו גביהא בן פסיסא לחכמים תנו לי רשות ואלך ואדון עמהן לפני אלכסנדרוס מוקדון אם ינצחוני אמרו הדיוט שבנו נצחתם ואם אני אנצח אותם אמרו להם תורת משה נצחתכם נתנו לו רשות והלך ודן עמהם אמר להם מהיכן אתם מביאים ראיה אמרו לו מן התורה אמר להן אף אני לא אביא לכם ראיה אלא מן התורה שנאמר [ב] ויאמר ארור כנען עבד עבדים יהיה לאחיו [ד] עבד שקנה נכסים עבד למי ונכסים למי ולא עוד אלא שהרי כמה שנים שלא עבדתונו אמר להם אלכסנדרוס מלכא החזירו לו תשובה אמרו לו תנו לנו זמן שלשה ימים נתן להם זמן בדקו ולא מצאו תשובה מיד ברחו והניחו שדותיהן כשהן זרועות וכרמיהן כשהן נטועות ואותה שנה שביעית היתה שוב [א] פעם אחת באו בני מצרים לדון עם ישראל לפני אלכסנדרוס מוקדון אמרו לו הרי הוא אומר [ג] וה' נתן את חן העם בעיני מצרים וישאילום תנו לנו כסף וזהב שנטלתם ממנו אמר גביהא בן פסיסא לחכמים תנו לי רשות ואלך ואדון עמהן לפני אלכסנדרוס אם ינצחוני אמרו להם הדיוט שבנו נצחתם ואם אני אנצח אותם אמרו להם תורת משה רבינו נצחתכם נתנו לו רשות והלך ודן עמהן אמר להן מהיכן אתם מביאין ראיה אמרו לו מן התורה אמר להן אף אני לא אביא לכם ראיה אלא מן התורה שנאמר [ד] ומושב בני ישראל אשר ישבו במצרים שלשים שנה וארבע מאות שנה תנו לנו שכר עבודה של ששים ריבוא ששיעבדתם במצרים שלשים שנה וארבע מאות שנה אמר להן אלכסנדרוס מוקדון החזירו לו תשובה אמרו לו תנו לנו זמן שלשה ימים נתן להם זמן בדקו ולא מצאו תשובה מיד הניחו שדותיהן כשהן זרועות וכרמיהן כשהן נטועות וברחו ואותה שנה שביעית היתה ושוב פעם אחת באו בני ישמעאל ובני קטורה לדון עם ישראל לפני אלכסנדרוס מוקדון אמרו לו ארץ כנען שלנו ושלכם דכתיב [ה] ואלה תולדות ישמעאל בן אברהם וכתיב [ו] אלה תולדות יצחק בן אברהם אמר להן גביהא בן פסיסא לחכמים תנו לי רשות ואלך ואדון עמהם לפני אלכסנדרוס מוקדון אם ינצחוני אמרו הדיוט שבנו נצחתם ואם אני אנצח אותם אמרו להם תורת משה רבינו נצחתכם נתנו לו רשות הלך ודן עמהן אמר להם מהיכן אתם מביאין ראיה אמרו לו מן התורה אמר להן אף אני לא אביא ראיה אלא מן התורה שנאמר [ז] ויתן אברהם את כל אשר לו ליצחק ולבני הפילגשים אשר לאברהם נתן אברהם מתנות [ה] אב שנתן אגטין לבניו בחייו ושיגר זה מעל זה כלום יש לזה על זה כלום מאי מתנות אמר ר' ירמיה בר אבא מלמד שמסר להם שם טומאה אמר ליה אנטונינוס לרבי גוף ונשמה יכולין לפטור עצמן מן הדין כיצד גוף אומר נשמה חטאת שמיום שפירשה ממני הריני מוטל כאבן דומם בקבר ונשמה אומרת גוף חטא שמיום שפירשתי ממנו הריני פורחת באויר כצפור אמר ליה אמשול לך משל למה הדבר דומה למלך בשר ודם שהיה לו פרדס נאה והיה בו

בכורות

אמרה ליה ברתיה. דקיסר לרבן גמליאל שבקיה: שני יוצרים וכו'. משל הוא אלו היו שני יוצרים בעירנו אחד יוצר כלים מן המים וכו': אמרה לו. א"כ הקב"ה אם מן המים הוא מצייר דמטפה סרוחה שהיא כמים הוא מוליד: מן העפר לא כל שכן. שבידו: דבי רבי ישמעאל תנא קל וחומר מכלי זכוכית. וזו היא תשובה שהשיבה לאביה: מה כלי זכוכית שעמלן ברוח של אדם. שכשהוא עושה אותו יש לו שפופרת ונופח לתוכה וכן נשמע מפי האומנין: יש להם תקנה. להתיכן ולחזור ולעשות מהן כלי והא דאמרינן בחגיגה (דף טו.) ונוחין לאבדם ככלי זכוכית לא שאין להם תקנה אלא שנפסדין לשעתן ואין מתקיימין: עכשיו שיש מים. והכי נמי הקב"ה יוצר את האדם מטפה קטנה שאין בה ממש וכ"ש שיכול לבראתו מן העפר אי נמי כל העולם כולו יצר מתוהו: ואם אי אתה מאמין. שהקב"ה יוצר מן העפר: עכבר. שקורין אשקרו"ל ויש במינן שאין נבראין על ידי תולדה: היום. מתחיל לברא ולצאת מן העפר ולמחר מהלך כשהוא נברא כדאמרי' בשחיטת חולין בהעור והרוטב (דף קכו.): ושמא תאמר לזמן מרובה. שאותו שרץ אינו נברא לאלתר אלא לזמן מרובה שבוע או שבועיים ותהא סבור שאין הקב"ה מחיה המתים לפי שעה: לך עלה להר וכו': חלזון. תולעת ° שיוצא מן הים אחד לשבעים שנה [ו] וצובעין בדמו תכלת ולכתחלה אינו נראה בכל ההר אלא חלזון אחד: ולמחר. שהגשמים יורדין מתמלא כולו חלזונות ונראה למורי שבילי חלזון ([ז] ראשון) משרילין כולן אלמא יש בידו לחיות לפי שעה: גביהא בן פסיסא. כך שמו והיתה לו עקמומיות בגבו כדמוכח לקמן: ווי לכון חיביא. אוי לכם לרשעים: דחיי מתים. אותן שהן חיין רואין אנו שמתין והיאך יעלה על דעתנו שהמתים חוזרין וחיים: דלא הוו. אותן שלא היו מעולם נולדין ונולדין וחיין אותן שהיו כבר לא כ"ש שחוזרין וחיין: א"ל. מינא: חייבא קרית לי וכו'. בא לקנתרו: דימוסנאי. עוררין בעלי חמס שהיו רוצין ליטול חלק ביהודה ובירושלים: שבאו בני אפריקא לדון וכו'. ובמגלת תענית חשיב להו כל אותן ימים שנעשה בהן נסים לישראל וקבעום יו"ט ולהכי קאמר הכא בעשרים וארבעה בניסן לומר דיום טוב הוא ואסור בהספד משום נס זה: ארץ כנען לגבולותיה. דלהך ארעא קרי ארץ כנען ואתם ירשתם שלא כדין דשלנו הוא דכנען אבינו היה: אגטין. כתבים שלא יטול אחד בחלק חבירו כמו שעשה אברהם לישמעאל שלא ליטול במה שנתן ליצחק כלום יש לזה על זה כלום: שם טומאה. כשוף ומעשה שדים:

בכורות

מסורת הש"ס

א) [התשבי בשורש עכשיו כתב יש כותבין ביו"ד ואינו לריך], ב) גי' הערוך ערך חלזון ג' אין שם חלזון אפי' אחד, ג) [עי' מגילת תענית פ"ג], ד) [לקמן קה. מגילה טז.], ה) [גי' הערוך ערך גט אב שכתב לגטין וכו' פי' שטר לוואה ודע עוד דבילקוט איתא אב שכתב לקיטין], ו) [מנחות דף מד.], ז) [ברש"י שבע"י ליתא].

ליקוטי רש"י

חלזון. כמין דג קטן ועולה אחת לשבעים שנה [שבת עד:]. חלזון עולה מן הים להרים וצובעין בדמו תכלת ונמכר בדמים יקרים [מגילה ו.]. שהחלזון מן הים הוא עולה אחת לשבעים שנה (מנחות מד.) ומראית דמו דומה לים [חולין פט.]. עולה מן הארץ [מנחות מד. ועיי"ש ובגה"ש]. וישאילום. אף מה שלא היו שואלים מהם היו נותנים להם אתה אומר אחד טול שנים ולך [שמות יב, לו]. אשר ישבו במצרים. אחר שאר הישיבות שישבו גרים בארץ לא להם. שלשים שנה וארבע מאות שנה. בין הכל משנולד יצחק עד עכשיו היו ארבע מאות שנה. משהיה לו זרע לאברהם נתקיים (בראשית טו יג) כי גר יהיה זרעך, ושלשים שנה היו משנגזרה גזירת בין הבתרים עד שנולד יצחק וכו' וכשתמנה ארבע מאות שנה משנולד יצחק, תמצא מביאתן למצרים עד יציאתן מאתים ועשר שנה, וזה אחד מן הדברים ששינו לתלמי המלך [שם, מ ועי' במהרש"א בח"א]. הפילגשים. חסר כתיב שלא היתה אלא פלגש אחת היא הגר היא קטורה נשים בכתובה פילגשים בלא כתובה כדאמרינן בסנהדרין (כא.) בנשים ופילגשים לדוד [בראשית כה, ו].

הגהות הגר"א

[א] גמ' פעם אחת. נמחק:

גליון הש"ס

רש"י ד"ה חלזון וכו' שיצא מן הים. עיין בלשון רש"י מנחות דף מד ע"א ד"ה ועולה:

תורה אור השלם

א) צַו אֶת בְּנֵי יִשְׂרָאֵל וְאָמַרְתָּ אֲלֵהֶם כִּי אַתֶּם בָּאִים אֶל הָאָרֶץ כְּנָעַן זֹאת הָאָרֶץ אֲשֶׁר תִּפֹּל לָכֶם בְּנַחֲלָה אֶרֶץ כְּנַעַן לִגְבֻלֹתֶיהָ: [במדבר לד, ב]

ב) וַיֹּאמֶר אָרוּר כְּנָעַן עֶבֶד עֲבָדִים יִהְיֶה לְאֶחָיו: [בראשית ט, כה]

ג) וַיְיָ נָתַן אֶת חֵן הָעָם בְּעֵינֵי מִצְרַיִם וַיַּשְׁאִלוּם וַיְנַצְּלוּ אֶת מִצְרָיִם: [שמות יב, לו]

ד) וּמוֹשַׁב בְּנֵי יִשְׂרָאֵל אֲשֶׁר יָשְׁבוּ בְּמִצְרָיִם שְׁלֹשִׁים שָׁנָה וְאַרְבַּע מֵאוֹת שָׁנָה: [שמות יב, מ]

ה) וְאֵלֶּה תֹּלְדֹת יִשְׁמָעֵאל בֶּן אַבְרָהָם אֲשֶׁר יָלְדָה הָגָר הַמִּצְרִית שִׁפְחַת שָׂרָה לְאַבְרָהָם: [בראשית כה, יב]

ו) וְאֵלֶּה תּוֹלְדֹת יִצְחָק בֶּן אַבְרָהָם אַבְרָהָם הוֹלִיד אֶת יִצְחָק: [בראשית כה, יט]

ז) וַיִּתֵּן אַבְרָהָם אֶת כָּל אֲשֶׁר לוֹ לְיִצְחָק: וְלִבְנֵי הַפִּילַגְשִׁים אֲשֶׁר לְאַבְרָהָם נָתַן אַבְרָהָם מַתָּנֹת וַיְשַׁלְּחֵם מֵעַל יִצְחָק בְּנוֹ בְּעוֹדֶנּוּ חַי קֵדְמָה אֶל אֶרֶץ קֶדֶם: [בראשית כה, ה-ו]

חַיָּבַיָּא קָרֵית לִי – You dare call *me* "sinners"? אִי קָאֵימְנָא בְּעִיטְנָא בָּךְ – Why, if I arise, I will kick you so hard וּפָשִׁיטְנָא לַעֲקָמוּתָךְ מִינָּךְ – that I will straighten out your hump![14] אֲמַר לֵיהּ – [Geviha] said to him: אִם אַתָּה עוֹשֶׂה כֵּן – If you do that, רוֹפֵא אוּמָּן תִּקָּרֵא – you will be called a skilled doctor וְשָׂכָר הַרְבֵּה תִּטּוֹל – and command a large fee for your medical services!

The Gemara relates how Geviha ben Pesisa defended the Jewish claim to Eretz Yisrael against the descendants of Canaan:

תָּנוּ רַבָּנָן – The Rabbis taught in a Baraisa:[15] בְּעֶשְׂרִים וְאַרְבָּעָה בְּנִיסָן – ON THE TWENTY-FOURTH OF NISSAN,[16] אִיתְנְטִילוּ דִּימוֹסְנָאֵי מִיהוּדָה וּמִירוּשָׁלַיִם – THE CHALLENGERS[17] WERE REMOVED FROM JUDEA AND FROM JERUSALEM: כְּשֶׁבָּאוּ בְּנֵי אַפְרִיקְיָא לָדוּן עִם יִשְׂרָאֵל לִפְנֵי אֲלֶכְּסַנְדְּרוֹס מוֹקְדוֹן – For WHEN THE AFRICANS CAME TO CONTEND WITH THE JEWS BEFORE ALEXANDER THE MACEDONIAN,[18] אָמְרוּ לוֹ אֶרֶץ כְּנַעַן שֶׁלָּנוּ הִיא – [THE AFRICANS] SAID TO HIM: THE LAND OF CANAAN IS rightfully OURS. דִּכְתִיב ,,אֶרֶץ כְּנַעַן לִגְבֻלֹתֶיהָ'' – FOR IT IS WRITTEN in the Torah of the Jews that they were to take as their inheritance *THE LAND OF CANAAN ACCORDING TO ITS BORDERS.*[19] וּכְנַעַן אֲבוּהוֹן דְּהָנְהוּ אִינְשֵׁי הֲוָה – AND CANAAN WAS THE ANCESTOR OF THESE very PEOPLE standing before you (i.e. we Africans). אָמַר לְהוּ גְּבִיהָא בֶּן פְּסִיסָא לַחֲכָמִים – Whereupon GEVIHA BEN PESISA SAID TO THE SAGES who had to respond to the Africans' claim: תְּנוּ לִי רְשׁוּת – GIVE ME PERMISSION וְאֵלֵךְ וְאָדוּן עִמָּהֶן לִפְנֵי אֲלֶכְּסַנְדְּרוֹס מוֹקְדוֹן – AND I WILL GO AND DEBATE THEM BEFORE ALEXANDER THE MACEDONIAN. אִם יְנַצְּחוּנִי – IF THEY DEFEAT ME in the debate, אִמְרוּ הֶדְיוֹט שֶׁבָּנוּ נִצַּחְתֶּם – SAY TO THEM, "It is but AN ORDINARY ONE AMONG US that YOU HAVE DEFEATED, so your victory proves nothing." וְאִם אֲנִי אֲנַצֵּחַ אוֹתָם – AND IF I DEFEAT THEM, אִמְרוּ לָהֶם תּוֹרַת מֹשֶׁה נִצַּחְתְּכֶם – SAY TO THEM, "THE TORAH OF MOSES HAS DEFEATED YOU!" נָתְנוּ לוֹ רְשׁוּת – [THE SAGES] GAVE HIM PERMISSION וְהָלַךְ וְדָן עִמָּהֶם – AND HE WENT AND DEBATED [THE AFRICANS]. אָמַר לָהֶם מֵהֵיכָן אַתֶּם מְבִיאִים רְאָיָה – HE SAID TO THEM: FROM WHERE DO YOU BRING PROOF to your claim that the former Land of Canaan belongs to you? אָמְרוּ לוֹ מִן הַתּוֹרָה – THEY SAID TO HIM: FROM THE TORAH.[20] אָמַר לָהֶן אַף אֲנִי לֹא אָבִיא לָכֶם רְאָיָה אֶלָּא מִן הַתּוֹרָה – HE SAID TO THEM: I, TOO, WILL BRING YOU PROOF ONLY FROM THE TORAH! שֶׁנֶּאֱמַר ,,וַיֹּאמֶר אָרוּר כְּנָעַן עֶבֶד עֲבָדִים יִהְיֶה לְאֶחָיו'' – FOR IT IS STATED in the Torah: *AND [NOAH] SAID, "ACCURSED IS CANAAN; A SLAVE OF SLAVES SHALL HE BE TO HIS BROTHERS."*[21] עֶבֶד שֶׁקָּנָה נְכָסִים עֶבֶד לְמִי וּנְכָסִים לְמִי – Now, IF A SLAVE ACQUIRES PROPERTY, TO WHOM belongs THE SLAVE AND TO WHOM THE PROPERTY? Certainly to the master! Since your ancestor Canaan was the slave of Shem and Japheth, the Land of Canaan belongs to us, the descendants of Shem![22] וְלֹא עוֹד אֶלָּא שֶׁהֲרֵי כַּמָּה שָׁנִים שֶׁלֹּא עֲבַדְתּוּנוּ – AND NOT ONLY THAT, BUT IT IS now MANY YEARS THAT YOU HAVE NOT SERVED US![23] אָמַר לָהֶם אֲלֶכְּסַנְדְּרוֹס מַלְכָּא – ALEXANDER THE KING SAID TO THEM: הַחֲזִירוּ לוֹ תְּשׁוּבָה – "RESPOND TO HIM!" אָמְרוּ לוֹ – THEY SAID TO [ALEXANDER]: תְּנוּ לָנוּ זְמַן שְׁלֹשָׁה יָמִים – "GIVE US THREE DAYS' TIME to prepare a reply." נָתַן לָהֶם זְמַן – HE GAVE THEM the TIME, during which בָּדְקוּ וְלֹא מָצְאוּ תְּשׁוּבָה – THEY SEARCHED BUT DID NOT FIND AN adequate ANSWER. מִיָּד בָּרְחוּ – Realizing their untenable position in the eyes of Alexander, THEY FLED IMMEDIATELY, וְהִנִּיחוּ שְׂדוֹתֵיהֶן כְּשֶׁהֵן זְרוּעוֹת – ABANDONING THEIR FIELDS, SOWN AS THEY WERE, וְכַרְמֵיהֶן כְּשֶׁהֵן נְטוּעוֹת – AND THEIR VINEYARDS, PLANTED AS THEY WERE. וְאוֹתָהּ שָׁנָה שְׁבִיעִית הָיְתָה – AND THAT YEAR WAS *SHEVIIS.*[24]

The Baraisa continues:

שׁוּב פַּעַם אַחַת – ANOTHER TIME,[25] בָּאוּ בְּנֵי מִצְרַיִם לָדוּן עִם יִשְׂרָאֵל לִפְנֵי אֲלֶכְּסַנְדְּרוֹס מוֹקְדוֹן – THE EGYPTIANS CAME TO CONTEND WITH THE JEWS BEFORE ALEXANDER THE MACEDONIAN. אָמְרוּ לוֹ – [THE EGYPTIANS] SAID TO HIM: הֲרֵי הוּא אוֹמֵר ,,וַה' נָתַן אֶת־חֵן הָעָם בְּעֵינֵי מִצְרַיִם וַיַּשְׁאִלוּם'' – BEHOLD IT SAYS in the Torah of the Jews:[26] *AND HASHEM GAVE THE [JEWISH] PEOPLE FAVOR IN THE EYES OF THE EGYPTIANS AND THEY LENT THEM* gold and silver and other valuables, which the Jews never returned. Thus, we claim from the Jews: תְּנוּ לָנוּ כֶּסֶף וְזָהָב שֶׁנְּטַלְתֶּם מִמֶּנּוּ – "GIVE US THE SILVER AND GOLD THAT YOU TOOK FROM US!" אָמַר גְּבִיהָא בֶּן פְּסִיסָא לַחֲכָמִים – Whereupon GEVIHA BEN PESISA SAID TO THE SAGES: תְּנוּ לִי רְשׁוּת – GIVE ME PERMISSION וְאֵלֵךְ וְאָדוּן עִמָּהֶן לִפְנֵי אֲלֶכְּסַנְדְּרוֹס – AND I WILL GO AND DEBATE THEM BEFORE

NOTES

14. Geviha was a hunchback.

The sectarian denied the resurrection, but declared that if he was wrong and he and Geviha *would* be resurrected, he would straighten out Geviha's hump for him (see *Hagahos Yavetz*).

15. This Baraisa appears, with some variations (see next note), in the third chapter of *Megillas Taanis* [the Scroll of Fasts], a compendium recorded by Chananyah ben Chizkiah and his colleagues during the period of the Second Temple (see *Shabbos* 13b). In it are recorded all the days on which great miracles and victories occurred for the Jewish people during the Second Commonwealth – days which were thereafter celebrated every year as minor holidays. On some of these days, fasting was forbidden but eulogies were permitted; while on others, even eulogies were forbidden. Thus, the Baraisa mentions that this incident occurred on the twenty-fourth of Nissan to inform us that the date is a minor festival on which eulogies are forbidden (see *Rashi*). [After the destruction of the Holy Temple, all of these days lost their special status except Chanukah and Purim (see *Rosh Hashanah* 18b, 19b).]

16. In *Megillas Taanis,* the date of this incident is given as the twenty-fifth of Sivan (more than two months after the date given here), and there are other differences of detail as well. *Megillas Taanis* also has the three incidents recorded in this Baraisa occurring on the same day (as does *Bereishis Rabbah* §61).

17. Translation follows *Rashi*. [*Aruch,* however, provides the alternative rendering of *foreign governors,* who had ruled in Jerusalem until that day. (This is closer to the meaning of the word in Greek, which is *tax officers* – see *R' Yaakov Emden* to *Megillas Taanis* ad loc.)]

18. Who had conquered Eretz Yisrael.

[These Africans were the Girgashites, who heeded Joshua's call to leave the Land of Canaan in advance of the Israelite conquest, whereupon God gave them a comparable land in Africa [see *Yerushalmi, Sheviis* 6:1] (*Rabbeinu David Bonfils*; *Maharsha*). [Indeed, the Greek historian Procopius speaks of the city of "Girgish" in North Africa (*Aruch HaShalem*).]

19. *Numbers* 34:2. Thus, the land the Jews are currently in possession of is the Land of Canaan, which they usurped from us! (*Rashi*).

20. Though the Torah itself states that the Jews were to dispossess the Canaanites, it also states that the land would vomit out the Jews if they would disobey God (*Leviticus* 20:22 et al.). As the Jews had already been exiled by Nebuchadnezzar for their sins, the Canaanite descendants claimed that the Jews' title to the land had lapsed, and they laid claim to the land as its original inhabitants (*Maharsha*).

21. *Genesis* 9:25. Thus, Canaan's own grandfather, Noah, designated him as a slave to his brothers – the children of Shem and of Japheth.

22. The Jews are "Semites" – descended from Shem. [See *Ben Yehoyada* and *Margaliyos HaYam* §9, regarding why Geviha was not concerned that Alexander, too, would lay claim to the land as a descendant of Japheth, co-master of Canaan.]

23. [Thus, in addition to your land, we lay claim to compensation for the centuries of servitude that you owe us!]

24. The Jews are forbidden to cultivate the land during *sheviis* (see *Leviticus* 25:1-7). Thus, food was scarce that year, and the cultivated fields abandoned by the Africans that year in Eretz Yisrael left an unexpected windfall of needed food for the Jews.

25. *Hagahos HaGra* deletes these words. [It should be noted that *Megillas Taanis* records all these debates as occurring on the same occasion, when the Ishmaelites joined with the Africans and Egyptians in petitioning Alexander against the Jews (see note 16).]

26. *Exodus* 12:36.

אמרה ליה ברתיה שבקיה ואנא מהדרנא ליה שני יוצרים יש בעירנו אחד יוצר מן המים ואחד יוצר מן הטיט איזה מהן משובח א"ל זה שיוצר מן המים א"ל מן המים צר מן הטיט לא כל שכן דבי ר' ישמעאל תנא ק"ו מכלי זכוכית מה כלי זכוכית שעמלן ברוח בשר ודם נשברו יש להן תקנה בשר ודם שברוחו של הקב"ה על אחת כמה וכמה א"ל ההוא מינא לר' אמי אמריתו דשכבי חיי והא הוו עפרא ועפרא מי קא חיי א"ל אמשול לך משל למה הדבר דומה למלך בשר ודם שאמר לעבדיו לכו ובנו לי פלטרין גדולים במקום שאין מים ועפר הלכו ובנו אותו לימים נפלו אמר להם חזרו ובנו אותו במקום שיש עפר ומים אמרו לו אין אנו יכולין כעס עליהם ואמר להן במקום שאין מים ועפר בניתם [ו] עכשיו שיש מים ועפר על אחת כמה וכמה ואם אי אתה מאמין צא לבקעה וראה עכבר שהיום חציו בשר וחציו אדמה למחר השריץ ונעשה כלו בשר שמא תאמר לזמן מרובה עלה להר וראה שהיום [ג] אין בו אלא חלזון אחד למחר ירדו גשמים ונתמלא כולו חלזונות א"ל ההוא מינא לגביהא בן פסיסא ווי לכון חייביא דאמריתון מיתי חיין דחיין מיתי מיתי דמיתי חיין א"ל ווי לכון חייביא דאמריתון מיתי לא חיין דלא הוו חיי דהוו חיי לא כ"ש א"ל חייביא קרית לי אי קאימנא בעיטנא בך ופשיטנא לעקמותך מינך א"ל אם אתה עושה כן רופא אומן תקרא ושכר הרבה תטול ת"ר [ד] בעשרים וארבעה בניסן איתנטילו דימוסנאי מיהודה ומירושלים כשבאו בני אפריקיא לדון עם ישראל לפני אלכסנדרוס מוקדון אמרו לו ארץ כנען שלנו היא דכתיב [א] ארץ כנען לגבולותיה וכנען אבוהון דהנהו אינשי הוה אמר להו גביהא בן פסיסא לחכמים תנו לי רשות ואלך ואדון עמהן לפני אלכסנדרוס מוקדון אם ינצחוני אמרו הדיוט שבנו נצחתם ואם אני אנצח אותם אמרו להם תורת משה נצחתכם נתנו לו רשות והלך ודן עמהם אמר להם מהיכן אתם מביאים ראייה אמרו לו מן התורה אמר להן אף אני לא אביא לכם ראייה אלא מן התורה שנאמר [ב] ויאמר ארור כנען עבד עבדים יהיה לאחיו [ז] עבד שקנה נכסים עבד למי ונכסים למי ולא עוד אלא שהרי כמה שנים שלא עבדתונו אמר להם אלכסנדרוס מלכא החזירו לו תשובה אמרו לו תנו לנו זמן שלשה ימים נתן להם זמן בדקו ולא מצאו תשובה מיד ברחו והניחו שדותיהן כשהן זרועות וכרמיהן כשהן נטועות ואותה שנה שביעית היתה שוב **[א]** פעם אחת באו בני מצרים לדון עם ישראל לפני אלכסנדרוס מוקדון אמרו לו הרי הוא אומר [ג] וה' נתן את חן העם בעיני מצרים וישאילום תנו לנו כסף וזהב שנטלתם ממנו אמר גביהא בן פסיסא לחכמים תנו לי רשות ואלך ואדון עמהן לפני אלכסנדרוס אם ינצחוני אמרו להם הדיוט שבנו נצחתם ואם אני אנצח אותם אמרו להם תורת משה רבינו נצחתכם נתנו לו רשות והלך ודן עמהן אמר להן מהיכן אתם מביאין ראייה אמרו לו מן התורה אמר להן אף אני לא אביא לכם ראייה אלא מן התורה שנאמר [ד] ומושב בני ישראל אשר ישבו במצרים שלשים שנה וארבע מאות שנה תנו לנו שכר עבודה של ששים ריבוא ששיעבדתם במצרים שלשים שנה וארבע מאות שנה אמר להן אלכסנדרוס מוקדון החזירו לו תשובה אמרו לו תנו לנו זמן שלשה ימים נתן להם זמן בדקו ולא מצאו תשובה מיד הניחו שדותיהן כשהן זרועות וכרמיהן כשהן נטועות ואותה שנה שביעית היתה ושוב פעם אחת באו בני ישמעאל ובני קטורה לדון עם ישראל לפני אלכסנדרוס מוקדון אמרו לו ארץ כנען שלנו ושלכם דכתיב [ה] ואלה תולדות ישמעאל בן אברהם וכתיב [ו] אלה תולדות יצחק בן אברהם אמר להן גביהא בן פסיסא לחכמים תנו לי רשות ואלך ואדון עמהם לפני אלכסנדרוס מוקדון אם ינצחוני אמרו הדיוט שבנו נצחתם ואם אני אנצח אותם אמרו להם תורת משה רבינו נצחתכם נתנו לו רשות הלך ודן עמהן אמר להם מהיכן אתם מביאין ראייה אמרו לו מן התורה אמר להן אף אני לא אביא אלא מן התורה שנאמר [ז] ויתן אברהם את כל אשר לו ליצחק ולבני הפילגשים אשר לאברהם נתן אברהם מתנות [ה] אב שנתן אגטין לבניו בחייו ושיגר זה מעל זה כלום יש לזה על זה כלום מאי מתנות אמר ר' ירמיה בר אבא מלמד שמסר להם שם טומאה אמר ליה אנטונינוס לרבי גוף ונשמה יכולין לפטור עצמן מן הדין כיצד גוף אומר נשמה חטאת שמיום שפירשה ממני הריני מוטל כאבן דומם בקבר ונשמה אומרת גוף חטא שמיום שפירשתי ממנו הריני פורחת באויר כצפור אמר ליה אמשול לך משל למה הדבר דומה למלך בשר ודם שהיה לו פרדס נאה והיה בו

בכורות

רש"י

אמרה ליה ברתיה. דקיסר לרבן גמליאל שבקיה: **שני יוצרים וכו'.** משל הוא אלו היו שני יוצרים בעירנו אחד יוצר כלים מן המים וכו': **אמרה לו.** א"כ הקב"ה אם מן המים הוא מצייר דמטפה סרוחה שהיא כמים הוא מוליד: **מן העפר לא כל שכן.** שבידו: **דבי רבי ישמעאל תנא קל וחומר מכלי זכוכית.** וזו היא תשובה שהשיבה לאביה: **מה כלי זכוכית שעמלן ברוח של אדם.** שכשהוא עושה אותו יש לו שפופרת ונופח לתוכה וכן נשמע מפי האומנין: **יש להם תקנה.** להתיכן ולחזור ולעשות מהן כלי והא דאמרינן בחגיגה (דף טו.) ונוחין לאבדם ככלי זכוכית לא שאין להם תקנה אלא שנפסדין לשעתן ואין מתקיימין: **עכשיו שיש מים.** והכי נמי הקב"ה יוצר את האדם מטפה קטנה שאין בה ממש וכ"ש שיכול לבראתו מן העפר אי נמי כל העולם כולו יצר מתוהו: **ואם אי אתה מאמין.** שהקב"ה יוצר מן העפר: **עכבר.** שקורין אשקרו"ל ויש במינן שאין נבראין על ידי תולדה: **היום.** מתחיל לברא ולצאת מן העפר ולמחר מהלך כשהוא נברא כדאמרי' בשחיטת חולין בהעור והרוטב (דף קכו.): **ושמא תאמר לזמן מרובה.** שאותו שרץ אינו נברא לאלתר אלא לזמן מרובה שבוע או שבועיים ותהא סבור שאין הקב"ה מחיה המתים לפי שעה: **לך עלה להר וכו':** **חלזון.** תולעת [ב] שיוצא מן הים אחד לשבעים שנה [ו] וצובעין בדמו תכלת ולכתחלה אינו נראה בכל ההר אלא חלזון אחד: **ולמחר.** שהגשמים יורדין מתמלא כולו חלזונות ונראה למורי שבילי חלזון ([ז] ראשון) משרצין כולן אלמא יש בידו לחיות לפי שעה: **גביהא בן פסיסא.** כך שמו והיתה לו עקמומיות בגבו כדמוכח לקמן: **ווי לכון חייביא.** אוי לכם לרשעים: **דחיי מתים.** אותן שהן חיין רואין אנו שמתין והיאך יעלה על דעתנו שהמתים חוזרין וחיים: **דלא הוו.** אותן שלא היו מעולם נוצרין ונולדין וחיין אותן שהיו כבר לא כ"ש שחוזרין וחיין: **א"ל.** מינא: **חייבא קרית לי וכו'.** בא לקנתרו: **דימוסנאי.** עוררין בעלי חמס שהיו רוצין ליטול חלק ביהודה ובירושלים: **שבאו בני אפריקא לדון וכו'.** ובמגלת תענית חשיב להו כל אותן ימים שנעשה בהן נסים לישראל וקבעום יו"ט ולהכי קאמר הכא בעשרים וארבעה בניסן לומר דיום טוב הוא ואסור בהספד משום נס זה: **ארץ כנען לגבולותיה.** דלהך ארעא קרי ארץ כנען ואתם ירשתם שלא כדין דשלנו הוא דכנען אבינו היה: **אגטין.** כתבים שלא יטול אחד בחלק חבירו כמו שעשה אברהם לישמעאל שלא ליטול במה שנתן ליצחק כלום יש לזה על זה כלום: **שם טומאה.** כשוף ומעשה שדים:

בכורות

מסורת הש"ס

א) [התשבי בשורש עכשיו כתב יש כותבין ביו"ד ואינו צריך], ב) גי' הערוך ערך חלזון ג' **אין שם חלזון אפי' אחד**, ג) [עי' מגילת תענית פ"ג], ד) [לקמן קה. מגילה טז.], ה) [גי' הערוך ערך גט **אב שכתב** לגטין וכו' פי' שטר צוואה ודע עוד דבילקוט איתא **אב שכתב** לקיטין], ו) [מנחות דף מד.], ז) [ברש"י שבע"י ליתא].

ליקוטי רש"י

חלזון. כמין דג קטן ועולה אחת לשבעים שנה [שבת עד:]. חלזון עולה מן הים להרים וצובעין בדמו תכלת ונמכר בדמים יקרים [מגילה ו.]. שהחלזון מן הים הוא עולה אחת לשבעים שנה (מנחות מד.) ומראית דמו דומה לים [חולין פט.]. עולה מן הארץ [מנחות מד. ועיי"ש ובגה"ש]. **וישאילום.** אף מה שלא היו שואלים מהם היו נותנים להם אתה אומר אחד טול שנים ולך [שמות יב, לו]. **אשר ישבו במצרים.** אחר שאר הישיבות שישבו גרים בארץ לא להם. **שלשים שנה וארבע מאות שנה.** בין הכל משנולד יצחק עד עכשיו היו ארבע מאות שנה. משהיה לו זרע לאברהם נתקיים (בראשית טו יג) כי גר יהיה זרעך, ושלשים שנה היו משנגזרה גזירת בין הבתרים עד שנולד יצחק וכו' וכשתמנה ארבע מאות שנה משנולד יצחק, תמצא מביאתן למצרים עד יציאתן מאתים ועשר שנה, וזה אחד מן הדברים ששינו לתלמי המלך [שם, מ ועי' במהרש"א בח"א]. **הפילגשים.** חסר כתיב שלא היתה אלא פלגש אחת היא הגר היא קטורה נשים בכתובה פילגשים בלא כתובה כדאמרינן בסנהדרין (כא.) בנשים ופילגשים דדוד [בראשית כה, ו].

הגהות הגר"א

[א] גמ' פעם אחת. נמחק:

גליון הש"ס

רש"י ד"ה חלזון וכו' **שיצא מן הים.** עיין בלשון רש"י מנחות דף מד ע"א ד"ה ועולה:

תורה אור השלם

א) צַו אֶת בְּנֵי יִשְׂרָאֵל וְאָמַרְתָּ אֲלֵהֶם כִּי אַתֶּם בָּאִים אֶל הָאָרֶץ כְּנָעַן זֹאת הָאָרֶץ אֲשֶׁר תִּפֹּל לָכֶם בְּנַחֲלָה אֶרֶץ כְּנַעַן לִגְבֻלֹתֶיהָ: [במדבר לד, ב]

ב) וַיֹּאמֶר אָרוּר כְּנָעַן עֶבֶד עֲבָדִים יִהְיֶה לְאֶחָיו: [בראשית ט, כה]

ג) וַייָ נָתַן אֶת חֵן הָעָם בְּעֵינֵי מִצְרַיִם וַיַּשְׁאִלוּם וַיְנַצְּלוּ אֶת מִצְרָיִם: [שמות יב, לו]

ד) וּמוֹשַׁב בְּנֵי יִשְׂרָאֵל אֲשֶׁר יָשְׁבוּ בְּמִצְרָיִם שְׁלֹשִׁים שָׁנָה וְאַרְבַּע מֵאוֹת שָׁנָה: [שמות יב, מ]

ה) וְאֵלֶּה תֹּלְדֹת יִשְׁמָעֵאל בֶּן אַבְרָהָם אֲשֶׁר יָלְדָה הָגָר הַמִּצְרִית שִׁפְחַת שָׂרָה לְאַבְרָהָם: [בראשית כה, יב]

ו) וְאֵלֶּה תּוֹלְדֹת יִצְחָק בֶּן אַבְרָהָם אַבְרָהָם הוֹלִיד אֶת יִצְחָק: [בראשית כה, יט]

ז) וַיִּתֵּן אַבְרָהָם אֶת כָּל אֲשֶׁר לוֹ לְיִצְחָק: וְלִבְנֵי הַפִּילַגְשִׁים אֲשֶׁר לְאַבְרָהָם נָתַן אַבְרָהָם מַתָּנֹת וַיְשַׁלְּחֵם מֵעַל יִצְחָק בְּנוֹ בְּעוֹדֶנּוּ חַי קֵדְמָה אֶל אֶרֶץ קֶדֶם: [בראשית כה, ה-ו]

ALEXANDER. אִם יְנַצְּחוּנִי – IF THEY DEFEAT ME in the debate, אִמְרוּ לָהֶם הֶדְיוֹט שֶׁבָּנוּ נִצַּחְתֶּם – SAY TO THEM, "It is but AN ORDINARY ONE AMONG US that YOU HAVE DEFEATED." וְאִם אֲנִי אֲנַצַּח אוֹתָם – AND IF I DEFEAT THEM, אִמְרוּ לָהֶם תּוֹרַת מֹשֶׁה רַבֵּינוּ נִצַּחְתֶּכֶם – SAY TO THEM, "THE TORAH OF MOSES OUR TEACHER HAS DEFEATED YOU!" נָתְנוּ לוֹ רְשׁוּת וְהָלַךְ וְדָן עִמָּהֶן – [THE SAGES] GAVE HIM PERMISSION AND HE WENT AND DEBATED [THE EGYPTIANS]. אָמַר לָהֶן מֵהֵיכָן אַתֶּם מְבִיאִין רְאָיָיה – HE SAID TO THEM: FROM WHERE DO YOU BRING PROOF that we took gold and silver from you in Egypt? אָמְרוּ לוֹ מִן הַתּוֹרָה – THEY SAID TO HIM: FROM THE TORAH. אָמַר לָהֶן אַף אֲנִי לֹא אָבִיא לָכֶם רְאָיָיה אֶלָּא מִן הַתּוֹרָה – HE SAID TO THEM: I, TOO, WILL BRING YOU PROOF ONLY FROM THE TORAH! שֶׁנֶּאֱמַר ,,וּמוֹשַׁב בְּנֵי יִשְׂרָאֵל אֲשֶׁר יָשְׁבוּ בְּמִצְרָיִם שְׁלשִׁים שָׁנָה וְאַרְבַּע מֵאוֹת שָׁנָה" – FOR IT IS STATED in the Torah:[27] *AND THE STAY OF THE CHILDREN OF ISRAEL THAT THEY STAYED IN EGYPT WAS FOUR HUNDRED AND THIRTY YEARS.* תְּנוּ לָנוּ שְׂכַר עֲבוֹדָה שֶׁל שִׁשִּׁים רִיבּוֹא – GIVE US, then, THE WAGES FOR THE LABOR OF the SIX HUNDRED THOUSAND men שֶׁשִּׁיעְבַּדְתֶּם בְּמִצְרַיִם שְׁלֹשִׁים שָׁנָה וְאַרְבַּע מֵאוֹת שָׁנָה – THAT YOU ENSLAVED IN EGYPT FOR FOUR HUNDRED AND THIRTY YEARS![28] This sum surely far exceeds anything we might owe you. אָמַר לָהֶן אֲלֶכְסַנְדְּרוֹס מוֹקְדוֹן הַחֲזִירוּ לוֹ תְּשׁוּבָה – ALEXANDER THE MACEDONIAN SAID TO THEM: "RESPOND TO HIM!" אָמְרוּ לוֹ תְּנוּ לָנוּ זְמַן שְׁלֹשָׁה יָמִים – THEY SAID TO [ALEXANDER]: "GIVE US THREE DAYS' TIME to prepare a reply." נָתַן לָהֶם זְמַן – HE GAVE THEM the TIME, during which בָּדְקוּ וְלֹא מָצְאוּ תְּשׁוּבָה – THEY SEARCHED BUT DID NOT FIND AN adequate ANSWER. מִיַּד הִנִּיחוּ שְׂדוֹתֵיהֶן כְּשֶׁהֶן זְרוּעוֹת – IMMEDIATELY, THEY ABANDONED THEIR FIELDS, SOWN AS THEY WERE, וְכַרְמֵיהֶן כְּשֶׁהֶן נְטוּעוֹת – AND THEIR VINEYARDS, PLANTED AS THEY WERE, וּבָרְחוּ – AND THEY FLED. וְאוֹתָהּ שָׁנָה שְׁבִיעִית הָיְתָה – AND THAT YEAR WAS *SHEVIIS.*

The Baraisa continues:

וְשׁוּב פַּעַם אַחַת – AND YET ANOTHER TIME, בָּאוּ בְּנֵי יִשְׁמָעֵאל וּבְנֵי קְטוּרָה לָדוּן עִם יִשְׂרָאֵל לִפְנֵי אֲלֶכְסַנְדְּרוֹס מוֹקְדוֹן – THE DESCENDANTS OF ISHMAEL AND THE DESCENDANTS OF KETURAH[29] CAME TO CONTEND WITH THE JEWS BEFORE ALEXANDER THE MACEDONIAN. אָמְרוּ לוֹ אֶרֶץ כְּנַעַן שֶׁלָּנוּ וְשֶׁלָּכֶם – THEY [these enemies of the Jews] SAID TO HIM: THE LAND OF CANAAN BELONGS TO US *AND* TO YOU [i.e. to the Jews]. דִּכְתִיב ,,וְאֵלֶּה תֹּלְדֹת יִשְׁמָעֵאל בֶּן־אַבְרָהָם" – FOR IT IS WRITTEN in your Torah: *AND THESE ARE THE DESCENDANTS OF ISHMAEL THE SON OF ABRAHAM.*[30] וּכְתִיב ,,וְאֵלֶּה תּוֹלְדֹת יִצְחָק בֶּן־אַבְרָהָם" – AND IT IS also WRITTEN: *AND THESE ARE THE DESCENDANTS OF ISAAC THE SON OF ABRAHAM.*[31] אָמַר לָהֶן גְּבִיהָא בֶּן פְּסִיסָא לַחֲכָמִים – Whereupon GEVIHA BEN PESISA SAID TO THE SAGES: תְּנוּ לִי רְשׁוּת – GIVE ME PERMISSION וְאֵלֵךְ וְאָדוּן עִמָּהֶם לִפְנֵי אֲלֶכְסַנְדְּרוֹס מוֹקְדוֹן – AND I WILL GO AND DEBATE THEM BEFORE ALEXANDER THE MACEDONIAN. אִם יְנַצְּחוּנִי – IF THEY DEFEAT ME, אִמְרוּ הֶדְיוֹט שֶׁבָּנוּ נִצַּחְתֶּם – SAY TO THEM, "It is but AN ORDINARY ONE AMONG US that YOU HAVE DEFEATED." וְאִם אֲנִי אֲנַצַּח אוֹתָם – AND IF I DEFEAT THEM, אִמְרוּ לָהֶם תּוֹרַת מֹשֶׁה רַבֵּינוּ נִצַּחְתֶּכֶם – SAY TO THEM, "THE TORAH OF MOSES OUR TEACHER HAS DEFEATED YOU!" נָתְנוּ לוֹ רְשׁוּת – [THE SAGES] GAVE HIM PERMISSION, הָלַךְ וְדָן עִמָּהֶן – Whereupon HE WENT AND DEBATED WITH [THE DESCENDANTS OF ISHMAEL AND OF KETURAH]. אָמַר לָהֶן מֵהֵיכָן אַתֶּם מְבִיאִין רְאָיָיה – HE SAID TO THEM: FROM WHERE DO YOU BRING PROOF to your claim to part of the land? אָמְרוּ לוֹ מִן הַתּוֹרָה – THEY SAID TO HIM: FROM THE TORAH. אָמַר לָהֶן אַף אֲנִי לֹא אָבִיא רְאָיָיה אֶלָּא מִן הַתּוֹרָה – HE SAID TO THEM: I, TOO, WILL BRING PROOF ONLY FROM THE TORAH! שֶׁנֶּאֱמַר ,,וַיִּתֵּן אַבְרָהָם אֶת־כָּל־אֲשֶׁר־לוֹ לְיִצְחָק – FOR IT IS STATED:[32] *AND ABRAHAM GAVE ALL THAT WAS HIS TO ISAAC.* וְלִבְנֵי הַפִּילַגְשִׁים אֲשֶׁר לְאַבְרָהָם נָתַן אַבְרָהָם מַתָּנֹת" – *AND TO THE CONCUBINE-CHILDREN*[33] *WHOM ABRAHAM HAD, ABRAHAM GAVE PRESENTS and he sent them away from Isaac, his son, while he was still alive – eastward to the east country.* אָב שֶׁנָּתַן אֲגָטִין לְבָנָיו בְּחַיָּיו – Now, if A FATHER GAVE LEGACIES TO HIS SONS IN HIS LIFETIME[34] וְשִׁיגֵּר זֶה מֵעַל זֶה – AND then SENT ONE son AWAY FROM THE OTHER to prevent rivalry after his death, כְּלוּם יֵשׁ לָזֶה עַל זֶה כְּלוּם – DOES ONE son HAVE ANY CLAIM WHATEVER ON THE OTHER? Certainly not! Therefore you have no claim on Eretz Yisrael, for Abraham gave your ancestors part of his possessions and then sent them out of Eretz Yisrael to a different land, thereby indicating that they were to have no part in Eretz Yisrael.

The Gemara elaborates on the verse cited here concerning the gifts Abraham gave to his other sons:

מַאי ,,מַתָּנוֹת" – What is meant by *gifts?*[35] אָמַר רַבִּי יִרְמְיָה בַּר אַבָּא – **R' Yirmiyah bar Abba said:** מְלַמֵּד שֶׁמָּסַר לָהֶם שֵׁם טוּמְאָה – **This teaches** us **that he gave over to them the** knowledge of **unholy utterance.**[36]

NOTES

27. *Exodus* 12:40.

28. Geviha spoke of 430 years, since that is the number mentioned in the verse cited. In truth, however, the verse does not mean that the Jews were even in Egypt that long, as they were only there for 210 years, and the period of enslavement was even shorter [see commentaries ad loc.] (*Maharsha*).

Chida (*Rosh David*) explains that Geviha arrived at the figure 430 as follows: The period of actual enslavement was only 86 years (*Seder Olam* §3; *Shir HaShirim Rabbah* to 2:11; cited by *Rashi* to *Shir HaShirim Rabbah* 2:13) but, as our Sages teach, four-fifths of the Jews died before the Exodus during the plague of darkness. Thus, the 600,000 men who left Egypt represented only one-fifth the work force that had toiled in Egypt. The Egyptians therefore owed *five times* the 86 workyears of 600,000 men, which is the equivalent of 430 workyears of 600,000 [5x86=430], and this is what Geviha meant by "the enslavement of 430 years."

29. Ishmael was Abraham's oldest son, and Keturah was the wife Abraham took after Sarah's death (see *Genesis* 16:15 and 25:1).

30. *Genesis* 25:12.

31. Ibid. v. 19. [As the Torah in these verses explicitly identifies both Ishmael and Isaac as Abraham's sons, it follows that both sons – and their progeny – have equal claim to the land that God gave to Abraham.] And though the Torah specifically assigns Eretz Yisrael to the Jews, that applies only as long as they do not sin [as explained in note 20] (see *Maharsha*).

32. *Genesis* 25:5-6.

33. [Both Ishmael and the sons of Keturah were concubine-children.]

34. That is, he distributes his property in writing among his sons so that there should be no dispute as to how to divide his estate after his death (see *Rashi*; see also *Maharsha* and *Yad David*).

35. For the verse does not seem to refer to *tangible* gifts, as the preceding verse states that "Abraham gave *all* that was his to Isaac" (*Rashbatz, Milchemess Mitzvah* §11; see also *Yad David*).

36. I.e. he imparted to them the secrets of the unclean arts of sorcery and demonology (*Rashi*).

According to *Rashi's* explanation, R' Yirmiyah bar Abba must follow the view that non-Jews are permitted to practice sorcery (see above, 56b). For according to the view that they are forbidden to do so (ibid.), how could Abraham abet his children in sinful practices? (*Maharsha*). Others explain, however, that Abraham did not teach his sons these arts so that they would practice them. Rather, since he was sending these sons away to the eastern lands of idolatry, he wanted them to know the means through which the idolaters were able to perform their seemingly miraculous feats and prognostications, so that his sons not be misled to ascribe powers to the idols (cited by *Be'er Sheva*). The Torah does not forbid the *study* of these arts, but only their practice. Indeed, the great Sages of the Sanhedrin were obligated to have detailed knowledge of these arts [so that they could judge the cases of sorcery brought before them (see above, 68a)] (*Rashbatz* loc. cit.). *Gur Aryeh* (to *Genesis* 25:6) explains the Gemara to mean that Abraham taught his sons how to *defend themselves* against the practitioners of these arts.

Alternatively, the meaning is that Abraham taught them how to

אמרה ליה ברתיה שבקיה ואנא מהדרנא ליה שני יוצרים יש בעירנו אחד יוצר מן המים ואחד יוצר מן הטיט איזה מהן משובח א"ל זה שיוצר מן המים א"ל מן המים צר מן הטיט לא כל שכן דבי ר' ישמעאל תנא ק"ו מכלי זכוכית מה כלי זכוכית שעמלן ברוח בשר ודם נשברו יש להן תקנה בשר ודם שברוחו של הקב"ה על אחת כמה וכמה א"ל ההוא מינא לר' אמי אמריתו דשכבי חיי והא הוו עפרא ועפרא מי קא חיי א"ל אמשול לך משל למה הדבר דומה למלך בשר ודם שאמר לעבדיו לכו ובנו לי פלטרין גדולים במקום שאין מים ועפר הלכו ובנו אותו לימים נפלו אמר להם חזרו ובנו אותו במקום שיש עפר ומים אמרו לו אין אנו יכולין כעס עליהם ואמר להן במקום שאין מים ועפר בניתם [א]עכשיו שיש מים ועפר על אחת כמה וכמה ואם אי אתה מאמין צא לבקעה וראה עכבר שהיום חציו בשר וחציו אדמה למחר השריץ ונעשה כלו בשר שמא תאמר לזמן מרובה עלה להר וראה שהיום [ב]אין בו אלא חלזון אחד למחר ירדו גשמים ונתמלא כולו חלזונות א"ל ההוא מינא לגביהא בן פסיסא ווי לכון חייביא דאמריתון מיתי חיין דחיין מיתי דמיתי חיין א"ל ווי לכון חייביא דאמריתון מיתי לא חיין דלא הוו חיי דהוי חיי לא כ"ש א"ל חייביא קרית לי אי קאימנא בעיטנא בך ופשיטנא לעקמותך מינך א"ל אם אתה עושה כן רופא אומן תקרא ושכר הרבה תטול ת"ר [ג]בעשרים וארבעה בניסן איתנטילו דימוסנאי מיהודה ומירושלים כשבאו בני אפריקיא לדון עם ישראל לפני אלכסנדרוס מוקדון אמרו לו ארץ כנען שלנו היא דכתיב [א]ארץ כנען לגבולותיה וכנען אבוהון דהנהו אינשי הוה אמר להו גביהא בן פסיסא לחכמים תנו לי רשות ואלך ואדון עמהן לפני אלכסנדרוס מוקדון אם ינצחוני אמרו הדיוט שבנו נצחתם ואם אני אנצח אותם אמרו להם תורת משה נצחתכם נתנו לו רשות והלך ודן עמהם אמר להם מהיכן אתם מביאים ראייה אמרו לו מן התורה אמר להן אף אני לא אביא לכם ראייה אלא מן התורה שנאמר [ב]ויאמר ארור כנען עבד עבדים יהיה לאחיו [ד]עבד שקנה נכסים עבד למי ונכסים למי ולא עוד אלא שהרי כמה שנים שלא עבדתונו אמר להם אלכסנדרוס מלכא החזירו לו תשובה אמרו לו תנו לנו זמן שלשה ימים נתן להם זמן בדקו ולא מצאו תשובה מיד ברחו והניחו שדותיהן כשהן זרועות וכרמיהן כשהן נטועות ואותה שנה שביעית היתה שוב [א] פעם אחת באו בני מצרים לדון עם ישראל לפני אלכסנדרוס מוקדון אמרו לו הרי הוא אומר [ג]וה' נתן את חן העם בעיני מצרים וישאילום תנו לנו כסף וזהב שנטלתם ממנו אמר גביהא בן פסיסא לחכמים תנו לי רשות ואלך ואדון עמהן לפני אלכסנדרוס אם ינצחוני אמרו להם הדיוט שבנו נצחתם ואם אני אנצח אותם אמרו להם תורת משה רבינו נצחתכם נתנו לו רשות והלך ודן עמהן אמר להן מהיכן אתם מביאין ראייה אמרו לו מן התורה אמר להן אף אני לא אביא לכם ראייה אלא מן התורה שנאמר [ד]ומושב בני ישראל אשר ישבו במצרים שלשים שנה וארבע מאות שנה תנו לנו שכר עבודה של ששים ריבוא ששיעבדתם במצרים שלשים שנה וארבע מאות שנה אמר להן אלכסנדרוס מוקדון החזירו לו תשובה אמרו לו תנו לנו זמן שלשה ימים נתן להם זמן בדקו ולא מצאו תשובה מיד הניחו שדותיהן כשהן זרועות וכרמיהן כשהן נטועות וברחו ואותה שנה שביעית היתה ושוב פעם אחת באו בני ישמעאל ובני קטורה לדון עם ישראל לפני אלכסנדרוס מוקדון אמרו לו ארץ כנען שלנו ושלכם דכתיב [ה]ואלה תולדות ישמעאל בן אברהם וכתיב [ו]אלה תולדות יצחק בן אברהם אמר להן גביהא בן פסיסא לחכמים תנו לי רשות ואלך ואדון עמהם לפני אלכסנדרוס מוקדון אם ינצחוני אמרו הדיוט שבנו נצחתם ואם אני אנצח אותם אמרו להם תורת משה רבינו נצחתכם נתנו לו רשות הלך ודן עמהן אמר להם מהיכן אתם מביאין ראייה אמרו לו מן התורה אמר להן אף אני לא אביא ראייה אלא מן התורה שנאמר [ז]ויתן אברהם את כל אשר לו ליצחק ולבני הפילגשים אשר לאברהם נתן אברהם מתנות [ה]אב שנתן אגטין לבניו בחייו ושיגר זה מעל זה כלום יש לזה על זה כלום מאי מתנות אמר ר' ירמיה בר אבא מלמד שמסר להם שם טומאה אמר ליה אנטונינוס לרבי גוף ונשמה יכולין לפטור עצמן מן הדין כיצד גוף אומר נשמה חטאת שמיום שפירשה ממני הריני מוטל כאבן דומם בקבר ונשמה אומרת גוף חטא שמיום שפירשתי ממנו הריני פורחת באויר כצפור אמר ליה אמשול לך משל למה הדבר דומה למלך בשר ודם שהיה לו פרדס נאה והיה בו

בכורות

רש"י

אמרה ליה ברתיה. דקיסר לרבן גמליאל שבקיה: שני יוצרים וכו'. משל הוא אלו היו שני יוצרים בעירנו אחד יוצר כלים מן המים וכו': אמרה לו. א"כ הקב"ה אם מן המים הוא מצייר דמטפה סרוחה שהיא כמים הוא מוליד: מן העפר לא כל שכן. שבידו: דבי רבי ישמעאל תנא קל וחומר מכלי זכוכית. וזו היא תשובה שהשיבה לאביה: מה כלי זכוכית שעמלן ברוח של אדם. שכשהוא עושה אותו יש לו שפופרת ונופח לתוכה וכן נשמע מפי האומנין: יש להם תקנה. להתיכן ולחזור ולעשות מהן כלי והא דאמרינן בחגיגה (דף טו.) ונוחין לאבדם ככלי זכוכית לא שאין להם תקנה אלא שנפסדין לשעתן ואין מתקיימין: עכשיו שיש מים. והכי נמי הקב"ה יוצר את האדם מטפה קטנה שאין בה ממש וכ"ש שיכול לבראתו מן העפר אי נמי כל העולם כולו יצר מתוהו: ואם אי אתה מאמין. שהקב"ה יוצר מן העפר: עכבר. שקורין אשקרו"ל ויש במינן שאין נבראין על ידי תולדה: היום. מתחיל לברא ולצאת מן העפר ולמחר מהלך כשהוא נברא כדאמרי' בשחיטת חולין בהעור והרוטב (דף קכו.): ושמא תאמר לזמן מרובה. שאותו שרץ אינו נברא לאלתר אלא לזמן מרובה שבוע או שבועיים ותהא סבור שאין הקב"ה מחיה המתים לפי שעה: לך עלה להר וכו': חלזון. תולעת [ו]שעולה מן הים אחד לשבעים שנה [ז]וצובעין בדמו תכלת ולכתחלה אינו נראה בכל ההר אלא חלזון אחד: ולמחר. שהגשמים יורדין מתמלא כולו חלזונות ונראה למורי שבילי חלזון ([ז] ראשון) משריצין כולן אלמא יש בידו לחיות לפי שעה: גביהא בן פסיסא. כך שמו והיתה לו עקמומיות בגבו כדמוכח לקמן: ווי לכון חיביא. אוי לכם לרשעים: דחיי מתים. אותן שהן חיין רואין אנו שמתין והיאך יעלה על דעתנו שהמתים חוזרין וחיים: דלא הוו. אותן שלא היו מעולם נוצרין ונולדין וחיין אותן שהיו כבר לא כ"ש שחוזרין וחיין: א"ל. מינא: חייבא קרית לי וכו'. בא לקנתרו: דימוסנאי. עוררין בעלי חמס שהיו רוצין ליטול חלק ביהודה ובירושלים: שבאו בני אפריקא לדון וכו'. ובמגלת תענית חשיב להו כל אותן ימים שנעשה בהן נסים לישראל וקבעום יו"ט ולהכי קאמר הכא בעשרים וארבעה בניסן לומר דיום טוב הוא ואסור בהספד משום נס זה: ארץ כנען לגבולותיה. דלהך ארעא קרי ארץ כנען ואתם ירשתם שלא כדין דשלנו הוא דכנען אבינו היה: אגטין. כתבים שלא יטול אחד בחלק חבירו כמו שעשה אברהם לישמעאל שלא ליטול במה שנתן ליצחק כלום יש לזה על זה כלום: שם טומאה. כשוף ומעשה שדים:

בכורות

מסורת הש"ס

א) [התשבי בשורש עכשיו כתב יש כותבין ביו"ד ואינו צריך], ב) גי' הערוך ערך חלזן ג' אין שם חלזון אפי' אחד, ג) [עי' מגילת תענית פ"ג], ד) [לקמן קה. מגילה טז.], ה) [גי' הערוך ערך גט אב שכתב לגטין וכו' פי' שטר צוואה ודע עוד דבילקוט איתא אב שכתב לקיטין], ו) [מנחות דף מד.], ז) [ברש"י שבע"י ליתא].

ליקוטי רש"י

חלזון. כמין דג קטן ועולה אחת לשבעים שנה [שבת עד:]. חלזון עולה מן הים להרים וצובעין בדמו תכלת ונמכר בדמים יקרים [מגילה ו.]. שהחלזון מן הים הוא עולה אחת לשבעים שנה (מנחות מד.) ומראית דמו דומה לים [חולין פט.]. עולה מן הארץ [מנחות מד. ועיי"ש ובגה"ש]. וישאילום. אף מה שלא היו שואלים מהם היו נותנים להם אתה אומר אחד טול שנים ולך [שמות יב, לו]. אשר ישבו במצרים. אחר שאר הישיבות שישבו גרים בארץ לא להם. שלשים שנה וארבע מאות שנה. בין הכל משנולד יצחק עד עכשיו היו ארבע מאות שנה. משהיה לו זרע לאברהם נתקיים (בראשית טו יג) כי גר יהיה זרעך, ושלשים שנה היו משנגזרה גזירת בין הבתרים עד שנולד יצחק וכו' וכשתמנה ארבע מאות שנה משנולד יצחק, תמצא מביאתן למצרים עד יציאתן מאתים ועשר שנה, וזה אחד מן הדברים ששינו לתלמי המלך [שם, מ ועי' במהרש"א בח"א]. הפילגשים. חסר כתיב שלא היתה אלא פלגש אחת היא הגר היא קטורה נשים בכתובה פילגשים בלא כתובה כדאמרינן בסנהדרין (כא.) בנשים ופילגשים דדוד [בראשית כה, ו].

הגהות הגר"א

[א] גמ' פעם אחת. נמחק:

גליון הש"ס

רש"י ד"ה חלזון וכו' שיצא מן הים. עיין בלשון רש"י מנחות דף מד ע"א ד"ה ועולה:

תורה אור השלם

א) צַו אֶת בְּנֵי יִשְׂרָאֵל וְאָמַרְתָּ אֲלֵהֶם כִּי אַתֶּם בָּאִים אֶל הָאָרֶץ כְּנָעַן זֹאת הָאָרֶץ אֲשֶׁר תִּפֹּל לָכֶם בְּנַחֲלָה אֶרֶץ כְּנַעַן לִגְבֻלֹתֶיהָ: [במדבר לד, ב]

ב) וַיֹּאמֶר אָרוּר כְּנָעַן עֶבֶד עֲבָדִים יִהְיֶה לְאֶחָיו: [בראשית ט, כה]

ג) וַיְיָ נָתַן אֶת חֵן הָעָם בְּעֵינֵי מִצְרַיִם וַיַּשְׁאִלוּם וַיְנַצְּלוּ אֶת מִצְרָיִם: [שמות יב, לו]

ד) וּמוֹשַׁב בְּנֵי יִשְׂרָאֵל אֲשֶׁר יָשְׁבוּ בְּמִצְרָיִם שְׁלֹשִׁים שָׁנָה וְאַרְבַּע מֵאוֹת שָׁנָה: [שמות יב, מ]

ה) וְאֵלֶּה תֹּלְדֹת יִשְׁמָעֵאל בֶּן אַבְרָהָם אֲשֶׁר יָלְדָה הָגָר הַמִּצְרִית שִׁפְחַת שָׂרָה לְאַבְרָהָם: [בראשית כה, יב]

ו) וְאֵלֶּה תּוֹלְדֹת יִצְחָק בֶּן אַבְרָהָם אַבְרָהָם הוֹלִיד אֶת יִצְחָק: [בראשית כה, יט]

ז) וַיִּתֵּן אַבְרָהָם אֶת כָּל אֲשֶׁר לוֹ לְיִצְחָק: וְלִבְנֵי הַפִּילַגְשִׁים אֲשֶׁר לְאַבְרָהָם נָתַן אַבְרָהָם מַתָּנֹת וַיְשַׁלְּחֵם מֵעַל יִצְחָק בְּנוֹ בְּעוֹדֶנּוּ חַי קֵדְמָה אֶל אֶרֶץ קֶדֶם: [בראשית כה, ה-ו]

The Gemara records a discussion between Antoninus and his friend and mentor, Rebbi, which leads to the mention of reuniting body and soul:

אָמַר לֵיהּ אַנְטוֹנִינוּס לְרַבִּי – Antoninus[37] **said to Rebbi:** גּוּף וּנְשָׁמָה יְכוֹלִין לִפְטוֹר עַצְמָן מִן הַדִּין – Seemingly, a person's **body and soul are** each **able to excuse themselves from judgment,** i.e. from being punished for their sins after death. כֵּיצַד – **How so?** גּוּף אוֹמֵר נְשָׁמָה חָטָאת – The **body says:** It is **the soul** that **has sinned,** שֶׁמִּיּוֹם שֶׁפֵּירְשָׁה מִמֶּנִּי הֲרֵינִי מוּטָל כְּאֶבֶן דּוּמָם בַּקֶּבֶר – for **from the day that it has departed from me, I have been lying** – unable to sin – **like a silent rock in the grave.** וּנְשָׁמָה אוֹמֶרֶת גּוּף חָטָא – **And the soul says:** It is **the body** that **has sinned,** שֶׁמִּיּוֹם שֶׁפֵּירַשְׁתִּי מִמֶּנּוּ הֲרֵינִי פּוֹרַחַת בָּאֲוִיר כְּצִפּוֹר – **for from the day that I have departed from it, I have been flying in the air like a bird,**[38] unable to sin.

Rebbi answered:

אָמַר לֵיהּ – **[Rebbi] said to him:** אֶמְשׁוֹל לְךָ מָשָׁל – **I will give you a parable.** לְמָה הַדָּבָר דּוֹמֶה – **To what can this matter be compared?** לְמֶלֶךְ בָּשָׂר וָדָם שֶׁהָיָה לוֹ פַּרְדֵּס נָאֶה – **To a king of flesh and blood who had a beautiful orchard,** וְהָיָה בּוֹ – **which contained**

NOTES

address God while one is in a state of impurity since he knew they would live impure lives and would not be permitted to utter God's holy Names (*Sifsei Chachamim* to *Genesis* 25:6).

[*R' Avigdor Miller* (taped lectures to this chapter) suggests that R' Yirmiyah bar Abba refers to profound knowledge of natural sciences. Abraham's sons kept secret this knowledge they had learned from him, and used it to perform seemingly magical feats before the uninformed masses and thereby delude them into ascribing to them occult powers. Thus, they misused the perfectly legitimate scientific knowledge they received from Abraham and represented it to the masses as "knowledge of unholy utterance."]

37. *Doros HaRishonim* identifies him as the Roman emperor Marcus Aurelius Antoninus, who ruled from 161-180 C.E. In the course of his travels through the empire, he visited Judea. There he met Rebbi, with whom he formed a lifelong friendship, which was of great benefit to the Jewish people. Antoninus engaged Rebbi in many discussions of religious and philosophical matters [see *Avodah Zarah* 10a ff.].

38. *Maharsha* explains that this simile applies only to the soul of a sinner, which knows no peace in the World to Come. But the souls of the righteous find tranquility in the bond of eternal life.

אמרה ליה ברתיה שבקיה ואנא מהדרנא ליה שני יוצרים יש בעירנו אחד יוצר מן המים ואחד יוצר מן הטיט איזה מהן משובח א"ל זה שיוצר מן המים א"ל מן המים צר מן הטיט לא כל שכן דבי ר' ישמעאל תנא ק"ו מכלי זכוכית מה כלי זכוכית שעמלן ברוח בשר ודם נשברו יש להן תקנה בשר ודם שברוחו של הקב"ה על אחת כמה וכמה א"ל ההוא מינא לר' אמי אמריתו דשכבי חיי והא הוו עפרא ועפרא מי קא חיי א"ל אמשול לך משל למה הדבר דומה למלך בשר ודם שאמר לעבדיו לכו ובנו לי פלטרין גדולים במקום שאין מים ועפר הלכו ובנו אותו לימים נפלו אמר להם חזרו ובנו אותו במקום שיש עפר ומים אמרו לו אין אנו יכולין כעס עליהם ואמר להן במקום שאין מים ועפר בניתם [א] עכשיו שיש מים ועפר על אחת כמה וכמה ואם אי אתה מאמין צא לבקעה וראה עכבר שהיום חציו בשר וחציו אדמה למחר השריץ ונעשה כלו בשר שמא תאמר לזמן מרובה עלה להר וראה שהיום [ב] אין בו אלא חלזון אחד למחר ירדו גשמים ונתמלא כולו חלזונות א"ל ההוא מינא לגביהא בן פסיסא ווי לכון חייביא דאמריתון מיתי חיין דחיין מיתי דמיתי חיין א"ל ווי לכון חייביא דאמריתון מיתי לא חיין דלא הוו חיי דהוי חיי לא כ"ש א"ל חייביא קרית לי אי קאימנא בעיטנא בך ופשיטנא לעקמותך מינך א"ל אם אתה עושה כן רופא אומן תקרא ושכר הרבה תטול ת"ר [ג] בעשרים וארבעה בניסן איתנטילו דימוסנאי מיהודה ומירושלים כשבאו בני אפריקיא לדון עם ישראל לפני אלכסנדרוס מוקדון אמרו לו ארץ כנען שלנו היא דכתיב [א] ארץ כנען לגבולותיה וכנען אבוהון דהנהו אינשי הוה אמר להו גביהא בן פסיסא לחכמים תנו לי רשות ואלך ואדון עמהן לפני אלכסנדרוס מוקדון אם ינצחוני אמרו הדיוט שבנו נצחתם ואם אני אנצח אותם אמרו להם תורת משה נצחתכם נתנו לו רשות והלך ודן עמהם אמר להם מהיכן אתם מביאים ראייה אמרו לו מן התורה אמר להן אף אני לא אביא לכם ראייה אלא מן התורה שנאמר [ב] ויאמר ארור כנען עבד עבדים יהיה לאחיו [ד] עבד שקנה נכסים עבד למי ונכסים למי ולא עוד אלא שהרי כמה שנים שלא עבדתונו אמר להם אלכסנדרוס מלכא החזירו לו תשובה אמרו לו תנו לנו זמן שלשה ימים נתן להם זמן בדקו ולא מצאו תשובה מיד ברחו והניחו שדותיהן כשהן זרועות וכרמיהן כשהן נטועות ואותה שנה שביעית היתה שוב [א] פעם אחת באו בני מצרים לדון עם ישראל לפני אלכסנדרוס מוקדון אמרו לו הרי הוא אומר [ג] וה' נתן את חן העם בעיני מצרים וישאילום תנו לנו כסף וזהב שנטלתם ממנו אמר גביהא בן פסיסא לחכמים תנו לי רשות ואלך ואדון עמהן לפני אלכסנדרוס אם ינצחוני אמרו להם הדיוט שבנו נצחתם ואם אני אנצח אותם אמרו להם תורת משה רבינו נצחתכם נתנו לו רשות והלך ודן עמהן אמר להן מהיכן אתם מביאין ראייה אמרו לו מן התורה אמר להן אף אני לא אביא לכם ראייה אלא מן התורה שנאמר [ד] ומושב בני ישראל אשר ישבו במצרים שלשים שנה וארבע מאות שנה תנו לנו שכר עבודה של ששים ריבוא ששיעבדתם במצרים שלשים שנה וארבע מאות שנה אמר להן אלכסנדרוס מוקדון החזירו לו תשובה אמרו לו תנו לנו זמן שלשה ימים נתן להם זמן בדקו ולא מצאו תשובה מיד הניחו שדותיהן כשהן זרועות וכרמיהן כשהן נטועות וברחו ואותה שנה שביעית היתה ושוב פעם אחת באו בני ישמעאל ובני קטורה לדון עם ישראל לפני אלכסנדרוס מוקדון אמרו לו ארץ כנען שלנו ושלכם דכתיב [ה] ואלה תולדות ישמעאל בן אברהם וכתיב [ו] אלה תולדות יצחק בן אברהם אמר להן גביהא בן פסיסא לחכמים תנו לי רשות ואלך ואדון עמהם לפני אלכסנדרוס מוקדון אם ינצחוני אמרו הדיוט שבנו נצחתם ואם אני אנצח אותם אמרו להם תורת משה רבינו נצחתכם נתנו לו רשות הלך ודן עמהן אמר להם מהיכן אתם מביאין ראייה אמרו לו מן התורה אמר להן אף אני לא אביא ראייה אלא מן התורה שנאמר [ז] ויתן אברהם את כל אשר לו ליצחק ולבני הפילגשים אשר לאברהם נתן אברהם מתנות [ה] אב שנתן אגטין לבניו בחייו ושיגר זה מעל זה כלום יש לזה על זה כלום מאי מתנות אמר ר' ירמיה בר אבא מלמד שמסר להם שם טומאה אמר ליה אנטונינוס לרבי גוף ונשמה יכולין לפטור עצמן מן הדין כיצד גוף אומר נשמה חטאת שמיום שפירשה ממני הריני מוטל כאבן דומם בקבר ונשמה אומרת גוף חטא שמיום שפירשתי ממנו הריני פורחת באויר כצפור אמר ליה אמשול לך משל למה הדבר דומה למלך בשר ודם שהיה לו פרדס נאה והיה בו

בכורות

אמרה ליה. ברתיה. דקיסר לרבן גמליאל שבקיה: שני יוצרים וכו'. משל הוא אלו היו שני יוצרים בעירנו אחד יוצר כלים מן המים וכו': אמרה לו. א"כ הקב"ה אם מן המים הוא מצייר דמטפה סרוחה שהיא כמים הוא מוליד: מן העפר לא כל שכן. שבידו: דבי רבי ישמעאל תנא קל וחומר מכלי זכוכית. וזו היא תשובה שהשיבה לאביה: מה כלי זכוכית שעמלן ברוח של אדם. שכשהוא עושה אותו יש לו שפופרת ונופח לתוכה וכן נשמע מפי האומנין: יש להם תקנה. להתיכן ולחזור ולעשות מהן כלי והא דאמרינן בחגיגה (דף טו.) ונוחין לאבדם ככלי זכוכית לא שאין להם תקנה אלא שנפסדין לשעתן ואין מתקיימין: עכשיו שיש מים. והכי נמי הקב"ה יוצר את האדם מטפה קטנה שאין בה ממש וכ"ש שיכול לבראתו מן העפר אי נמי כל העולם כולו יצר מתוהו: ואם אי אתה מאמין. שהקב"ה יוצר מן העפר: עכבר. שקורין אשקרו"ל ויש במינן שאין נבראין על ידי תולדה: היום. מתחיל לברא ולצאת מן העפר ולמחר מהלך כשהוא נברא כדאמרי' בשחיטת חולין בהעור והרוטב (דף קכז.): ושמא תאמר לזמן מרובה. שאותו שרץ אינו נברא לאלתר אלא לזמן מרובה שבוע או שבועיים ותהא סבור שאין הקב"ה מחיה המתים לפי שעה: לך עלה להר וכו': חלזון. תולעת [ו] שיוצא מן הים אחד לשבעים שנה [ז] וצובעין בדמו תכלת ולכתחלה אינו נראה בכל ההר אלא חלזון אחד: ולמחר. שהגשמים יורדין מתמלא כולו חלזונות ונראה למורי שבילי חלזון ([ז] ראשון משרצין כולן אלמא יש בידו לחיות לפי שעה: גביהא בן פסיסא. כך שמו והיתה לו עקמומיות בגבו כדמוכח לקמן: ווי לכון חייביא. אוי לכם לרשעים: דחיי מתים. אותן שהן חיין רואין אנו שמתין והיאך יעלה על דעתנו שהמתים חוזרין וחיים: דלא הוו. אותן שלא היו מעולם נוצרין ונולדין וחיין אותן שהיו כבר לא כ"ש שחוזרין וחיין: א"ל. מינא: חייבא קרית לי וכו'. בא לקנתרו: דימוסנאי. עוררין בעלי חמס שהיו רוצין ליטול חלק ביהודה ובירושלים: שבאו בני אפריקא לדון וכו'. ובמגלת תענית חשיב להו כל אותן ימים שנעשה בהן נסים לישראל וקבעום יו"ט ולהכי קאמר הכא בעשרים וארבעה בניסן לומר דיום טוב הוא ואסור בהספד משום נס זה: ארץ כנען לגבולותיה. דלהך ארעא קרי ארץ כנען ואתם ירשתם שלא כדין דשלנו הוא דכנען אבינו היה: אגטין. כתבים שלא יטול אחד בחלק חבירו כמו שעשה אברהם לישמעאל שלא ליטול במה שנתן ליצחק כלום יש לזה על זה כלום: שם טומאה. כשוף ומעשה שדים:

בכורות

מסורת הש"ס

א) [התשבי בשורש עכשיו כתב יש כותבין ביו"ד ואינו צריך], ב) גי' הערוך ערך חלזון ג' אין שם חלזון אפי' אחד, ג) [עי' מגילת תענית פ"ג], ד) [לקמן קה. מגילה טז.], ה) [גי' הערוך ערך גט אב שכתב לגטין וכו' פי' שטר צוואה ודע עוד דבילקוט איתא אב שכתב לקיטין], ו) [מנחות דף מד.], ז) [ברש"י שבע"י ליתא].

ליקוטי רש"י

חלזון. כמין דג קטן ועולה אחת לשבעים שנה [שבת עד:]. חלזון עולה מן הים להרים וצובעין בדמו תכלת ונמכר בדמים יקרים [מגילה ו.]. שהחלזון מן הים הוא עולה אחת לשבעים שנה (מנחות מד.) ומראית דמו דומה לים [חולין פט.]. עולה מן הארץ [מנחות מד. ועיי"ש ובגה"ש]. וישאילום. אף מה שלא היו שואלים מהם היו נותנים להם אתה אומר אחד טול שנים ולך [שמות יב, לו]. אשר ישבו במצרים. אחר שאר הישיבות שישבו גרים בארץ לא להם. שלשים שנה וארבע מאות שנה. בין הכל משנולד יצחק עד עכשיו היו ארבע מאות שנה. משהיה לו זרע לאברהם נתקיים (בראשית טו יג) כי גר יהיה זרעך, ושלשים שנה היו משנגזרה גזירת בין הבתרים עד שנולד יצחק וכו' וכשתמנה ארבע מאות שנה משנולד יצחק, תמצא מביאתן למצרים עד יציאתן מאתים ועשר שנה, וזה אחד מן הדברים ששינו לתלמי המלך [שם, מ ועי' במהרש"א בח"א]. הפילגשים. חסר כתיב שלא היתה אלא פלגש אחת היא הגר היא קטורה נשים בכתובה פילגשים בלא כתובה כדאמרינן בסנהדרין (כא.) בנשים ופילגשים דדוד [בראשית כה, ו].

הגהות הגר"א

[א] גמ' פעם אחת. נמחק:

גליון הש"ס

רש"י ד"ה חלזון וכו' שיצא מן הים. עיין בלשון רש"י מנחות דף מד ע"א ד"ה ועולה:

תורה אור השלם

א) צַו אֶת בְּנֵי יִשְׂרָאֵל וְאָמַרְתָּ אֲלֵהֶם כִּי אַתֶּם בָּאִים אֶל הָאָרֶץ כְּנָעַן זֹאת הָאָרֶץ אֲשֶׁר תִּפֹּל לָכֶם בְּנַחֲלָה אֶרֶץ כְּנַעַן לִגְבֻלֹתֶיהָ: [במדבר לד, ב]

ב) וַיֹּאמֶר אָרוּר כְּנָעַן עֶבֶד עֲבָדִים יִהְיֶה לְאֶחָיו: [בראשית ט, כה]

ג) וַיְיָ נָתַן אֶת חֵן הָעָם בְּעֵינֵי מִצְרַיִם וַיַּשְׁאִלוּם וַיְנַצְּלוּ אֶת מִצְרָיִם: [שמות יב, לו]

ד) וּמוֹשַׁב בְּנֵי יִשְׂרָאֵל אֲשֶׁר יָשְׁבוּ בְּמִצְרָיִם שְׁלֹשִׁים שָׁנָה וְאַרְבַּע מֵאוֹת שָׁנָה: [שמות יב, מ]

ה) וְאֵלֶּה תֹּלְדֹת יִשְׁמָעֵאל בֶּן אַבְרָהָם אֲשֶׁר יָלְדָה הָגָר הַמִּצְרִית שִׁפְחַת שָׂרָה לְאַבְרָהָם: [בראשית כה, יב]

ו) וְאֵלֶּה תּוֹלְדֹת יִצְחָק בֶּן אַבְרָהָם אַבְרָהָם הוֹלִיד אֶת יִצְחָק: [בראשית כה, יט]

ז) וַיִּתֵּן אַבְרָהָם אֶת כָּל אֲשֶׁר לוֹ לְיִצְחָק: וְלִבְנֵי הַפִּילַגְשִׁים אֲשֶׁר לְאַבְרָהָם נָתַן אַבְרָהָם מַתָּנֹת וַיְשַׁלְּחֵם מֵעַל יִצְחָק בְּנוֹ בְּעוֹדֶנּוּ חַי קֵדְמָה אֶל אֶרֶץ קֶדֶם: [בראשית כה, ה-ו]

בכורות נאות והושיב בו שני שומרים אחד חיגר ואחד סומא אמר לו חיגר לסומא בכורות נאות אני רואה בפרדס בא והרכיבני ונביאם לאכלם רכב חיגר על גבי סומא והביאום ואכלום לימים בא בעל פרדס אמר להן בכורות נאות היכן הן אמר לו חיגר כלום יש לי רגלים להלך בהן אמר לו סומא כלום יש לי עינים לראות מה עשה הרכיב חיגר על גבי סומא ודן אותם כאחד אף הקב"ה מביא נשמה וזורקה בגוף ודן אותם כאחד שנאמר [א] יקרא אל השמים מעל ואל הארץ לדין עמו יקרא אל השמים מעל זו נשמה ואל הארץ לדין עמו זה הגוף: א"ל אנטונינוס לרבי מפני מה חמה יוצאה במזרח ושוקעת במערב א"ל אי הוה איפכא נמי הכי הוה אמרת לי א"ל הכי קאמינא לך מפני מה שוקעת במערב א"ל כדי ליתן שלום לקונה שנאמר [ב] וצבא השמים לך משתחוים א"ל ותיתי עד פלגא דרקיע ותתן שלמא ותיעול משום פועלים ומשום עוברי דרכים וא"ל אנטונינוס לרבי נשמה מאימתי ניתנה באדם משעת פקידה או משעת יצירה א"ל משעת יצירה א"ל אפשר חתיכה של בשר עומדת שלשה ימים בלא מלח ואינה מסרחת אלא משעת פקידה אמר רבי דבר זה למדני אנטונינוס ומקרא מסייעו שנאמר [ג] ופקודתך שמרה רוחי ואמר ליה אנטונינוס לרבי מאימתי יצה"ר שולט באדם משעת יצירה או משעת יציאה א"ל משעת יצירה א"ל א"כ בועט במעי אמו ויוצא אלא משעת יציאה אמר רבי דבר זה למדני אנטונינוס ומקרא מסייעו שנאמר [ד] לפתח חטאת רובץ ר"ל רמי כתיב [ה] בם עור ופסח הרה ויולדת יחדו וכתיב [ו] אז ידלג כאיל פסח ותרון לשון אלם כי נבקעו במדבר מים ונחלים בערבה הא כיצד עומדין במומן ומתרפאין [א] עולא רמי כתיב [ז] בלע המות לנצח ומחה ה' דמעה מעל כל פנים וכתיב [ב] [ח] כי הנער בן מאה שנה ימות לא יהיה משם עוד עול ימים לא קשיא כאן בישראל כאן בעובדי כוכבים ועובדי כוכבים מאי בעו התם הנך דכתיב בהו [ט] ועמדו זרים ורעו צאנכם ובני נכר אכריכם וכורמיכם רב חסדא רמי כתיב [י] וחפרה הלבנה ובושה החמה כי מלך ה' צבאות וכתיב [כ] והיה אור הלבנה כאור החמה ואור החמה יהיה שבעתים כאור שבעת הימים לא קשיא כאן לימות המשיח כאן לעוה"ב ולשמואל [ג] דאמר [א] אין בין העוה"ז לימות המשיח אלא שיעבוד גליות בלבד לא קשיא כאן במחנה צדיקים כאן במחנה שכינה [ד] רבא רמי כתיב [ל] אני אמית ואחיה וכתיב [ל] מחצתי ואני ארפא אמר הקב"ה מה שאני ממית אני מחיה והדר מה שמחצתי ואני ארפא ת"ר אני אמית ואחיה יכול שתהא מיתה באחד וחיים באחד כדרך שהעולם נוהג ת"ל מחצתי ואני ארפא מה מחיצה ורפואה באחד אף מיתה וחיים באחד מיכן תשובה לאומרין אין תחיית המתים מן התורה תניא אמר רבי מאיר מניין לתחיית המתים מן התורה שנאמר [מ] אז ישיר משה ובני ישראל את השירה הזאת לה' שר לא נאמר אלא ישיר מכאן לתחיית המתים מן התורה כיוצא בדבר אתה אומר [נ] אז יבנה יהושע מזבח לה' בנה לא נאמר אלא יבנה מכאן לתחיית המתים מן התורה אלא מעתה [ס] אז יבנה שלמה במה לכמוש שקוץ מואב הכי נמי דיבנה [ה] אלא מעלה עליו הכתוב כאילו בנה א"ר יהושע בן לוי מניין לתחיית המתים מן התורה שנאמר [ע] אשרי יושבי ביתך עוד יהללוך סלה היללוך לא נאמר אלא יהללוך מכאן לתחיית המתים מן התורה וא"ר יהושע בן לוי כל האומר שירה בעוה"ז זוכה ואומרה לעולם הבא שנאמר אשרי יושבי ביתך עוד יהללוך סלה א"ר חייא בר אבא א"ר יוחנן מניין לתחיית המתים מן התורה שנאמר [פ] קול צופיך נשאו קול יחדו ירננו וגו' רינו לא נאמר אלא ירננו מכאן לתחיית המתים מן התורה וא"ר חייא בר אבא א"ר יוחנן עתידין כל הנביאים כולן אומרים שירה בקול אחד שנאמר קול צופיך נשאו קול יחדו ירננו אמר רב יהודה אמר רב כל המונע הלכה מפי תלמיד כאילו גוזלו מנחלת אבותיו שנאמר [צ] תורה צוה לנו משה מורשה קהילת יעקב מורשה היא לכל ישראל מששת ימי בראשית אמר רב חנא בר ביזנא אמר רבי שמעון חסידא כל המונע הלכה מפי תלמיד אפילו עוברין שבמעי אמו מקללין אותו שנאמר [ק] מונע בר

יקבוהו

רש"י

בכורות. תאני הבכורות: **יקרא אל השמים מעל.** כלומר יקרא הקב"ה לנשמה הבאה לו לתוך גופו של אדם [א] מאל השמים מעל ויקרא אף אל הגוף שבא מן הארץ: **מפני מה שוקעת במערב.** תסובב את כל העולם עד שתחזור למקום זריחתה למזרח ותשקע דאי הוה הכי לא הוה אמינא לך מפני מה שוקעת במזרח דנוהג העולם כך הוא ממקום שיצא שם נכנס: **כדי ליתן שלום לקונה.** להקב"ה שהשכינה במערב וכיון שמגעת עד מערב הולכת ומשתחוה לפני הקב"ה שבראה ולכך שוקעת ונכנסת כפופה לפני הקב"ה: **ותיתי עד פלגא דרקיעא.** דאם לכך מתכוונת למה הולכת בתוך המערב תבא עד אמצעו של רקיע ותשקע לשם ומשם תשתחוה כלפי מערב שכן דרך ב"א שמשתחוה ברחוק לפני המלך ואינו מתקרב כל כך: **משום פועלים.** דאילו כן היה מחשיך פתאום שכשחמה באמצע הרקיע מאירה ביותר וסבורים שעדיין יש שהות ביום והיו פועלין שוהין במלאכתן עד שחשיכה ועוברי דרכים נמי לא היו יודעין מתי יחשוך לבקש להם בית לינה ולכך שוקעת במערב שכשהולכת ומשתפלת והולכת וכלה אורה יודעין שמגיע שעת חשיכה: **משעת יצירה.** שנקרם כולו בבשר וגידין ועצמות: **פקידה.** משעה שהמלאך פוקד הטיפה ומביאה לפני המקום מה תהא עליה כדאמרינן בפרק כל היד במסכת נדה (דף טז:) מיד נזרקה בו נשמה וחיות: **אמר ליה.** רבי משעת יצירה: **ואמר לו.** אנטונינוס וכי אפשר לחתיכה שתתקיים אפילו ג' ימים בלא מלח שאינה מסרחת וה"נ אילו לא היתה נשמה נתונה עד שעת יצירה היאך תתקיים הטיפה שלא תסריח במעיה וכיון שטיפה מסרחת שוב אינה מולדת: **למדני אנטונינוס.** מדבריו למדתי: **ופקודתך שמרה רוחי.** משעת פקידה נשמר רוחי: **משעת יציאה.** כשיוצא ממעי אמו או משעת יצירה: **א"ל.** רבי משעת יצירה: **אמר לו אנטונינוס א"כ בועט במעי אמו ויוצא.** אלא משעת יציאתה: **בם עור ופסח.** שחיין עם מומן: **וכתיב אז ידלג כאיל פסח.** דמשמע שמתרפאין: **עומדין במומן.** ואח"כ מתרפאין: **בלע המות לנצח.** דלעתיד לבא מאחר שחיין שוב אין מתין: **כי הנער.** כלומר כשימות אדם לעתיד ומת בן מאה שנה יאמרו נער הוא מת כי הנער בן מאה שנה ימות אלמא מתין: **וחפרה הלבנה ובושה החמה.** משמע שיהא אורם כהה וכתיב והיתה אור הלבנה כאור החמה: **כאן לימות המשיח.** כשיכלה השיעבוד והיתה אור הלבנה כאור החמה ולעתיד לבא וחפרה הלבנה ובושה החמה מרוב נגהם של צדיקים: **ולשמואל דאמר.** בדוכתא אחריתי אין בין העולם הזה וכו'. אידי ואידי לעוה"ב: **אלא כאן במחנה שכינה.** וחפרה מזיו השכינה: **כאן במחנה צדיקים.** כאן במחנה רשעים לא גרסינן: **כתיב אני אמית ואחיה.** דמשמע כשם שאני אמית את האדם כך אני מחייהו כשמת בעל מום עומד וחי בעל מום: **וכתיב מחצתי ואני ארפא.** שכשהוא מחיה מרפא את המחץ ועומד שלם: **והדר מה שמחצתי.** שלאחר כן מתרפא וכדלעיל עומדין במומן ומתרפאין: **מיתה באחד וחיים באחד.** וה"ק אני ממית אדם זה ומחיה אדם אחר: **כדרך שהעולם נוהג.** שזה מת וזה נולד: **מה מחץ ורפוי באחד.** ואין רפואה אלא במקום מחץ: **ישיר.** משמע לעתיד: **נשאו קול יחדיו.** היינו קול אחד: **המונע הלכה.** מללמדו: **מששת ימי בראשית.** דכתיב בראשית ברא בשביל התורה שהיא ראשית וישראל נקראו [ו] ראשית תבואתה שעתידין להנחיל' ברא אלהים את השמים וגו': **בר.** תורה:

יקבוהו

עין משפט נר מצוה

ה א מיי' פי"ב מהל' מלכים הל' ב' ופ"ט מהל' תשובה הלכה ב:

ליקוטי רש"י

בכורות. תאני הבכורות, שבישלו כל צרכן בתחלת בכורי תאנים שהם חביבות על אוכליהם בראשיתם [ירמיה כד, ב]. **בכורות.** תאנים חשובות הממהרות להתבשל [עירובין כא:]. **שמרה רוחי.** בבטן אמי [איוב י, יב]. **לפתח חטאת רובץ.** משעה שנולד הולד הוא נתון בו [קהלת ד, יג]. **בלע המות.** יכסנו ויעלימנו עולמי' מישראל [ישעיה כה, ח]. יבולע מלאך המות שלא ישלוט. **עול ימים.** נער כמו עולל (איכה ב) עול ימים קטן בשנים [שם סה, כ]. **בישראל.** כתיב ובלע המות וגו'. **אכריכם.** מנהיגי המחרישה [שם סא, ה]. **ובושה החמה** שלא תאיר [פסחים סח.]. **יהיה שבעתים כאור שבעת הימים.** שבעתים שבע שבעיות כאור של שבעת הימים הרי ארבעים ותשע שבעיות העולים לשלש מאות וארבעים ושלשה [ישעיה ל, כו]. שבעתים הן ארבעים ותשע וכתיב כאור שבעת הימים ארבעים ותשע כאור שבעת ימים של עכשיו נמצא עודף על אור של עכשיו שלש מאות וארבעים ושלשה. **לימות המשיח.** יהיה אור הלבנה כאור החמה. **לעולם הבא.** וחפרה הלבנה ובושה החמה שלא יהא בעולם אלא זיו זוהר ומראה שכינה. **ולשמואל.** דאמר ימות המשיח אין משתנין משל עכשיו מה הוא מקיים והיה אור הלבנה כאור החמה. **מה שאני ממית אני מחיה והדר מה שמחצתי ואני ארפא.** שכדרך שהן מתים חגרים סומים אלמים כך הן חיין במומן ואחר כך מתרפאים כדכתיב אז ידלג כאיל פסח (ישעיה לה). **מיתה באחד וחיים באחד.** אני ממית את המתים ואני מחיה וזן את החיים. **ת"ל מחצתי ואני ארפא.** הא אתא לאשמועינן דלא תימא אמית ואחיה לאו דמתים חיים קאמר אלא אני אמית את המתים ואני מחיה וזן את החיים ובורא את הנולדים להכי כתיב בתריה מחצתי ואני ארפא כשם שמחצתי אני ארפא דאין רפואה אלא במוכה כך אותו עצמו שאני ממית אני מחיה [פסחים שם]. **אז ישיר משה.** אז כשראה הנס עלה בלבו שישיר שירה וכן (יהושע י, יב) אז ידבר יהושע וכן (מ"א ז, ח) ובית יעשה לבת פרעה חשב בלבו שיעשה לה אף כאן ישיר אמר לו לבו שישיר וכן עשה ויאמרו לאמר אשירה לה' וכן ביהושע כשראה הנס אמר לו לבו שידבר וכן עשה (יהושע י, יב) ויאמר לעיני ישראל וכן שירת הבאר שפתח בה (במדבר כא, יז) אז ישיר ישראל פירש אחריו עלי באר ענו לה (מ"א יא, ז) אז יבנה שלמה במה פירשו בו חכמי ישראל שבקש לבנות ולא בנה למדנו שהיו"ד על שם המחשבה נאמרה זהו ליישב פשוטו אבל מדרשו אמרו רבותינו זכרונם לברכה מכאן רמז לתחיית המתים מן התורה וכן בכולן חוץ משל שלמה שפירשוהו בקש לבנות ולא בנה ואין לומר וליישב הלשון הזה כשאר דברים הנכתבים בלשון עתיד והן מיד כגון (איוב א, ה) ככה יעשה איוב (במדבר ט, כג) על פי ה' יחנו (שם כ) ויש אשר יהיה הענן לפי שהן דבר ההוה תמיד ונופל בו בין לשון עתיד בין לשון עבר אבל זה שלא היה אלא לשעה אינו יכול ליישבו בלשון הזה [שמות טו, א ועי' במהרש"א בח"א]. **אז יבנה שלמה במה.** רבותינו אמרו מתוך שלא מיחה בנשיו נקראת על שמו [מ"א יא, ז]. **צופיך.** נביאי הדורות [מגילה ב: ע"ש בתוס']. **תורה.** אשר צוה לנו משה מורשה היא לקהלת יעקב אחזוה ולא נעזבנה [דברים לג, ד]. **מונע בר.** מלמד תורה [משלי יא, כו].

מסורת הש"ס

א) פסחים סח., ב) [בפסוק כתיב מהופך ועי' ס"א שמישבו], ג) שבת סג. ודף קנא. ברכות לד: [פסחים סח: לקמן לט.], ד) [פסחים סח. ע"ש], ה) [שבת נו: ועי' תוס' שם ד"ה אלא מעתה], ו) [ירמיה ב].

הגהות הב"ח

(א) רש"י ד"ה יקרא וכו' גופו של אדם מעל השמים ממעל ויקרא:

תורה אור השלם

א) יִקְרָא אֶל הַשָּׁמַיִם מֵעָל וְאֶל הָאָרֶץ לָדִין עַמּוֹ: [תהלים נ, ד]

ב) אַתָּה הוּא יְיָ לְבַדֶּךָ אַתָּה עָשִׂיתָ אֶת הַשָּׁמַיִם שְׁמֵי הַשָּׁמַיִם וְכָל צְבָאָם הָאָרֶץ וְכָל אֲשֶׁר עָלֶיהָ הַיַּמִּים וְכָל אֲשֶׁר בָּהֶם וְאַתָּה מְחַיֶּה אֶת כֻּלָּם וּצְבָא הַשָּׁמַיִם לְךָ מִשְׁתַּחֲוִים: [נחמיה ט, ו]

ג) חַיִּים וָחֶסֶד עָשִׂיתָ עִמָּדִי וּפְקֻדָּתְךָ שָׁמְרָה רוּחִי: [איוב י, יב]

ד) הֲלוֹא אִם תֵּיטִיב שְׂאֵת וְאִם לֹא תֵיטִיב לַפֶּתַח חַטָּאת רֹבֵץ וְאֵלֶיךָ תְּשׁוּקָתוֹ וְאַתָּה תִּמְשָׁל בּוֹ: [בראשית ד, ז]

ה) הִנְנִי מֵבִיא אוֹתָם מֵאֶרֶץ צָפוֹן וְקִבַּצְתִּים מִיַּרְכְּתֵי אָרֶץ בָּם עִוֵּר וּפִסֵּחַ הָרָה וְיֹלֶדֶת יַחְדָּו קָהָל גָּדוֹל יָשׁוּבוּ הֵנָּה: [ירמיה לא, ז]

ו) אָז יְדַלֵּג כָּאַיָּל פִּסֵּחַ וְתָרֹן לְשׁוֹן אִלֵּם כִּי נִבְקְעוּ בַמִּדְבָּר מַיִם וּנְחָלִים בָּעֲרָבָה: [ישעיה לה, ו]

ז) בִּלַּע הַמָּוֶת לָנֶצַח וּמָחָה אֲדֹנָי אֱלֹהִים דִּמְעָה מֵעַל כָּל פָּנִים וְחֶרְפַּת עַמּוֹ יָסִיר מֵעַל כָּל הָאָרֶץ כִּי יְיָ דִּבֵּר: [ישעיה כה, ח]

ח) לֹא יִהְיֶה מִשָּׁם עוֹד עוּל יָמִים וְזָקֵן אֲשֶׁר לֹא יְמַלֵּא אֶת יָמָיו כִּי הַנַּעַר בֶּן מֵאָה שָׁנָה יָמוּת וְהַחוֹטֶא בֶּן מֵאָה שָׁנָה יְקֻלָּל: [ישעיה סה, כ]

ט) וְעָמְדוּ זָרִים וְרָעוּ צֹאנְכֶם וּבְנֵי נֵכָר אִכָּרֵיכֶם וְכֹרְמֵיכֶם: [ישעיה סא, ה]

י) וְחָפְרָה הַלְּבָנָה וּבוֹשָׁה הַחַמָּה כִּי מָלַךְ יְיָ צְבָאוֹת בְּהַר צִיּוֹן וּבִירוּשָׁלַיִם וְנֶגֶד זְקֵנָיו כָּבוֹד: [ישעיה כד, כג]

כ) וְהָיָה אוֹר הַלְּבָנָה כְּאוֹר הַחַמָּה וְאוֹר הַחַמָּה יִהְיֶה שִׁבְעָתַיִם כְּאוֹר שִׁבְעַת הַיָּמִים בְּיוֹם חֲבֹשׁ יְיָ אֶת שֶׁבֶר עַמּוֹ וּמַחַץ מַכָּתוֹ יִרְפָּא: [ישעיה ל, כו]

ל) רְאוּ עַתָּה כִּי אֲנִי אֲנִי הוּא וְאֵין אֱלֹהִים עִמָּדִי אֲנִי אָמִית וַאֲחַיֶּה מָחַצְתִּי וַאֲנִי אֶרְפָּא וְאֵין מִיָּדִי מַצִּיל: [דברים לב, לט]

מ) אָז יָשִׁיר מֹשֶׁה וּבְנֵי יִשְׂרָאֵל אֶת הַשִּׁירָה הַזֹּאת לַייָ וַיֹּאמְרוּ לֵאמֹר אָשִׁירָה לַייָ כִּי גָאֹה גָּאָה סוּס וְרֹכְבוֹ רָמָה בַיָּם: [שמות טו, א] נ) אָז יִבְנֶה יְהוֹשֻׁעַ מִזְבֵּחַ לַייָ אֱלֹהֵי יִשְׂרָאֵל בְּהַר עֵיבָל: [יהושע ח, ל] ס) אָז יִבְנֶה שְׁלֹמֹה בָּמָה לִכְמוֹשׁ שִׁקֻּץ מוֹאָב בָּהָר אֲשֶׁר עַל פְּנֵי יְרוּשָׁלָיִם וּלְמֹלֶךְ שִׁקֻּץ בְּנֵי עַמּוֹן: [מלכים א' יא, ז] ע) אַשְׁרֵי יוֹשְׁבֵי בֵיתֶךָ עוֹד יְהַלְלוּךָ סֶּלָה: [תהלים פד, ה] פ) קוֹל צֹפַיִךְ נָשְׂאוּ קוֹל יַחְדָּו יְרַנֵּנוּ כִּי עַיִן בְּעַיִן יִרְאוּ בְּשׁוּב יְיָ צִיּוֹן: [ישעיה נב, ח] צ) תּוֹרָה צִוָּה לָנוּ מֹשֶׁה מוֹרָשָׁה קְהִלַּת יַעֲקֹב: [דברים לג, ד] ק) מֹנֵעַ בָּר יִקְּבֻהוּ לְאוֹם וּבְרָכָה לְרֹאשׁ מַשְׁבִּיר: [משלי יא, כו]

בְּכוּרוֹת נָאוֹת – **beautiful early figs.**[1] וְהוֹשִׁיב בּוֹ שְׁנֵי שׁוֹמְרִים – **and he stationed in [the orchard] two guards,** אֶחָד חִיגֵּר וְאֶחָד סוּמָא – **one lame and the other blind.** אָמַר לוֹ חִיגֵּר לְסוּמָא – **The lame one said to the blind one:** בְּכוּרוֹת נָאוֹת אֲנִי רוֹאֶה בְּפַרְדֵּס – **"I see beautiful early figs in the orchard.** בֹּא וְהַרְכִּיבֵנִי – **Come, mount me** on your shoulders וּנְבִיאֵם לְאָכְלָם – **and** together **we will bring [the figs]** here **to eat them."** רָכַב חִיגֵּר עַל גַּבֵּי סוּמָא – **The lame one mounted the back of the blind person** וֶהֱבִיאוּם וַאֲכָלוּם – **and they brought [the figs] and they ate them.** לְיָמִים בָּא בַּעַל פַּרְדֵּס – **Some days later, the** royal **owner of the orchard came,** and found his prized figs missing. אָמַר לָהֶם – **He said to [the guards]** accusingly: בְּכוּרוֹת נָאוֹת הֵיכָן הֵן – **"The beautiful early figs – where are they?"** אָמַר לוֹ חִיגֵּר כְּלוּם יֵשׁ לִי רַגְלַיִם לְהַלֵּךְ בָּהֶן – **The lame one said to him, "Do I have any feet with which to travel** to the figs? I certainly could not have taken them." אָמַר לוֹ סוּמָא כְּלוּם יֵשׁ לִי עֵינַיִם לִרְאוֹת – And **the blind one said to him, "Do I have any eyes** with which **to see** where the figs are? I certainly could not have taken them." מֶה עָשָׂה – **What did [the king] do?** הִרְכִּיב חִיגֵּר עַל גַּבֵּי סוּמָא – **He mounted the lame one on the back of the blind one,** וְדָן אוֹתָם כְּאֶחָד – **and he judged them as a unit.**[2] אַף הַקָּדוֹשׁ בָּרוּךְ הוּא מֵבִיא נְשָׁמָה וְזוֹרְקָהּ בַּגּוּף – **So too,** on the Day of Judgment, **the Holy One, Blessed is He, brings the soul and injects it into the body,** וְדָן אוֹתָם כְּאֶחָד – **and judges them as a unit** for the sins they committed together in this life. שֶׁנֶּאֱמַר ,,יִקְרָא אֶל־הַשָּׁמַיִם מֵעָל וְאֶל־הָאָרֶץ לָדִין עַמּוֹ" – **As it is stated:**[3] ***He [God] will call to the heavens above, and to the earth to judge His people.*** Rebbi explains the verse: ,,יִקְרָא אֶל־הַשָּׁמַיִם מֵעָל" – ***He will call to the heavens above*** – זוֹ נְשָׁמָה – **this** refers to **the soul;** ,,וְאֶל־הָאָרֶץ לָדִין עַמּוֹ" – ***and to the earth to judge His people*** – זֶה הַגּוּף – **this** refers to **the body.**[4]

Antoninus questions Rebbi regarding the movement of the sun: אָמַר לֵיהּ אַנְטוֹנִינוּס לְרַבִּי – **Antoninus asked Rebbi:** מִפְּנֵי מָה חַמָּה יוֹצְאָה בַּמִּזְרָח וְשׁוֹקַעַת בַּמַּעֲרָב – **Why does the sun rise in the east and set in the west?** אָמַר לֵיהּ – **[Rebbi] said to him:** אִי הֲוָה אִיפְּכָא נַמִּי הָכִי הֲוָה אָמְרַתְּ לִי – **If it were reversed, you would also have asked me this** question![5] אָמַר לֵיהּ – **[Antoninus] said to him:** הָכִי קָאָמִינָא לָךְ – **This is what I** mean to **ask you:** מִפְּנֵי מָה שׁוֹקַעַת בַּמַּעֲרָב – Given that the sun rises in the east, **why does it set in the west,** rather than in the same place from which it rose?[6] אָמַר לֵיהּ – **[Rebbi] said to him:** כְּדֵי לִיתֵּן שָׁלוֹם לְקוֹנָהּ – **In order to offer greetings to its Creator,**[7] שֶׁנֶּאֱמַר ,,וּצְבָא הַשָּׁמַיִם לְךָ מִשְׁתַּחֲוִים" – **as it is stated:** ***And the hosts of the heavens bow to You.***[8] אָמַר לֵיהּ – **[Antoninus]** then **said to [Rebbi]:** וְתֵיתֵי עַד פַּלְגָא דִּרְקִיעַ – If that is why the sun does so, **then it should travel to the middle of the sky,** i.e. to its noontime position, halfway between east and west, וְתִתֵּן שְׁלָמָא וְתֵיעוּל – **offer greetings and set** there.[9] מִשּׁוּם פּוֹעֲלִים וּמִשּׁוּם עוֹבְרֵי דְרָכִים – Rebbi answered him: The sun proceeds to the end of the west **on account of workers and on account of wayfarers.**[10]

NOTES

1. The early ripening figs are greatly prized (*Rashi* to *Jeremiah* 24:2).

2. Finding them guilty of the crime of which they were jointly capable.

3. *Psalms* 50:4.

4. God will summon the soul [which comes into a man from Heaven] and the body [which comes from the earth] (*Rashi*) and reunite them in order to judge them as a unit. [*Toras Chaim* sees this alluded to in the verse (*Psalms* 19:10): מִשְׁפְּטֵי־ה׳ אֱמֶת צָדְקוּ יַחְדָּו, *The judgments of* H*ASHEM* *are true, they are righteous together.* When the body and soul are judged *together,* then Hashem's judgments *are righteous.*]

Rebbi's parable apparently indicates that even the wicked will be resurrected in order to stand in judgment for their misdeeds (see *Yad Ramah* p. 159 column 1). [This view, however, is not universally held (see Appendix). *Sefer HaIkkarim* (end of 3:33) explains that Rebbi's parable refers not to a reuniting of the body and soul, but rather allegorically to the punishment of the sinful soul in the "body" of Gehinnom. *Ben Yehoyada* suggests that the reference is to suffering in the grave (חִבּוּט הַקֶּבֶר). *R' Avigdor Miller* (taped lectures on this chapter) suggests that the "body" mentioned by this Gemara does not refer to the physical body, but rather to the human personality with which one "clothes" his pure soul through his free-willed activities in this world. That personality becomes attached to the soul, which is in itself pure and incapable of sin.]

5. I.e. why does the sun rise in the west and set in the east? [The sun had to rise from some direction and set in another. Thus, the question of why God made it rise here and set there rather than the other way around is inappropriate (cf. *Moreh Nevuchim* end of 3:26).]

6. Why does the sun not travel every day in a complete circle above the horizon, returning to its starting point in the east? This would have seemed more reasonable, given the fact that things ordinarily go back the same way in which they came (*Rashi*; cf. *Yad Ramah*).

7. Whose Presence is manifest in the west [as the Divine Presence rests on the Holy Ark in the Holy of Holies, which is at the western end of the Beis HaMikdash] (*Rashi,* from *Bava Basra* 25a). Thus, the sun sets in the west, disappearing from view in bowed submissiveness before its Creator (ibid.).

Bowing is the mark of submission to a greater authority. The setting of the sun is, metaphorically, the ultimate sign of its submission. Thus, the direction in which it sets is the direction of its "bow" (*Maharal, Chidushei Aggados* to *Bava Basra* 25a). Though the apparent "bowing" of the sun is actually its disappearance from view in the course of its regular orbit [i.e. in the course of the earth's rotation], the discussion focuses on the way things appear to the human observer [and the conceptions the natural phenomena were meant to impress upon him] (ibid.).

8. *Nehemiah* 9:6.

9. After all, when one gives obeisance to a king, one does so from a respectful distance. Similarly, the sun should not descend all the way into the west, but should "bow" from its zenith [by descending slightly to the west] and set immediately at that point (*Rashi*). [Antoninus's question apparently reflects the notion that the sun sets by leaving the "dome" of the sky. Accordingly, the sun could exit the dome at any point in its path and disappear from view behind the dome (see *Bava Basra* 25a-b). Rebbi answers Antoninus even according to the premise assumed by the question.]

Alternatively, *Maharal* suggests that Antoninus did not mean that the sun should actually disappear from the middle of the sky, which is impossible [as the world is presently constructed]. Rather, he meant that Rebbi's explanation of its movement towards the west would have been acceptable if the sun would then disappear from view. But given the fact that it must proceed to the horizon, it does not then appear to us that the sun's movement to the west is a mark of obeisance.

10. If the sun were to set from the middle of the sky, there would be an abrupt shift from bright sunshine to darkness. This would adversely affect [field] workers and wayfarers, who would have no advance warning that night is about to fall so that they could return home or seek lodging before dark. The gradual darkening caused by the progressive setting of the sun to the western extremity, on the other hand, alerts them to the advent of night and enables them to plan accordingly (*Rashi*).

According to *Maharal,* this discussion between Rebbi and Antoninus is not about whether the sun, under the present astronomical conditions, could move differently. Rather, Antoninus asked why the world was not created in such a way that the sun would never disappear from our eyesight. This would have given us the picture of a world created in perfect symmetry. Rebbi replied that, if so, the sun would give the impression to the human observer that it was eternal and divine; its setting in the west, in contrast, is a sign of subservience to God, Who alone is forever. Antoninus argued that this point would have been made had the sun set in the middle of the sky, to which Rebbi replied that this was not desirable for practical reasons.

This interpretation makes it clear that the discussion was not about how the laws of nature function but about what impression they are meant to have on the human observer. (Cf. *Chever Ma'amorim,* who notes that the moon itself does not change, but it *seems* to wax and wane, and thereby gives the impression of constant renewal on which our Blessing of the Moon is based.) God could have created the world quite

בכורות נאות והושיב בו שני שומרים אחד חיגר ואחד סומא אמר לו חיגר לסומא בכורות נאות אני רואה בפרדס בא והרכיבני ונביאם לאכלם רכב חיגר על גבי סומא והביאום ואכלום לימים בא בעל פרדס אמר להן בכורות נאות היכן הן אמר לו חיגר כלום יש לי רגלים להלך בהן אמר לו סומא כלום יש לי עינים לראות מה עשה הרכיב חיגר על גבי סומא ודן אותם כאחד אף הקב"ה מביא נשמה וזורקה בגוף ודן אותם כאחד שנאמר א) יקרא אל השמים מעל ואל הארץ לדין עמו יקרא אל השמים מעל זו נשמה ואל הארץ לדין עמו זה הגוף: א"ל אנטונינוס לרבי מפני מה חמה יוצאה במזרח ושוקעת במערב א"ל אי הוה איפכא נמי הכי הוה אמרת לי א"ל הכי קאמינא לך מפני מה שוקעת במערב א"ל כדי ליתן שלום לקונה שנאמר ב) וצבא השמים לך משתחוים א"ל ותיתי עד פלגא דרקיע ותתן שלמא ותיעול משום פועלים ומשום עוברי דרכים וא"ל אנטונינוס לרבי נשמה מאימתי ניתנה באדם משעת פקידה או משעת יצירה א"ל משעת יצירה א"ל אפשר חתיכה של בשר עומדת שלשה ימים בלא מלח ואינה מסרחת אלא משעת פקידה אמר רבי דבר זה למדני אנטונינוס ומקרא מסייעו שנאמר ג) ופקודתך שמרה רוחי ואמר ליה אנטונינוס לרבי מאימתי יצה"ר שולט באדם משעת יצירה או משעת יציאה א"ל משעת יצירה א"ל א"כ בועט במעי אמו ויוצא אלא משעת יציאה אמר רבי דבר זה למדני אנטונינוס ומקרא מסייעו שנאמר ד) לפתח חטאת רובץ ר"ל רמי כתיב ה) בם עור ופסח הרה ויולדת יחדו וכתיב ו) אז ידלג כאיל פסח ותרון לשון אלם כי נבקעו במדבר מים ונחלים בערבה הא כיצד עומדין במומן ומתרפאין [א] עולא רמי כתיב ז) בלע המות לנצח ומחה ה' דמעה מעל כל פנים וכתיב [ב] ח) כי הנער בן מאה שנה ימות לא יהיה משם עוד עול ימים לא קשיא כאן בישראל כאן בעובדי כוכבים ועובדי כוכבים מאי בעו התם הנך דכתיב בהו ט) ועמדו זרים ורעו צאנכם ובני נכר אכריכם וכורמיכם רב חסדא רמי כתיב י) וחפרה הלבנה ובושה החמה כי מלך ה' צבאות וכתיב כ) והיה אור הלבנה כאור החמה ואור החמה יהיה שבעתים כאור שבעת הימים לא קשיא כאן לימות המשיח כאן לעוה"ב ולשמואל [ג] דאמר [א] אין בין העוה"ז לימות המשיח אלא שיעבוד גליות בלבד לא קשיא כאן במחנה צדיקים כאן במחנה שכינה [ד] רבא רמי כתיב ל) אני אמית ואחיה וכתיב ל) מחצתי ואני ארפא אמר הקב"ה מה שאני ממית אני מחיה והדר מה שמחצתי ואני ארפא ת"ר אני אמית ואחיה יכול שתהא מיתה באחד וחיים באחד כדרך שהעולם נוהג ת"ל מחצתי ואני ארפא מה מחיצה ורפואה באחד אף מיתה וחיים באחד מיכן תשובה לאומרין אין תחיית המתים מן התורה תניא אמר רבי מאיר מניין לתחיית המתים מן התורה שנאמר מ) אז ישיר משה ובני ישראל את השירה הזאת לה' שר לא נאמר אלא ישיר מכאן לתחיית המתים מן התורה כיוצא בדבר אתה אומר נ) אז יבנה יהושע מזבח לה' בנה לא נאמר אלא יבנה מכאן לתחיית המתים מן התורה אלא מעתה ס) אז יבנה שלמה במה לכמוש שקוץ מואב הכי נמי דיבנה ס) אלא מעלה עליו הכתוב כאילו בנה א"ר יהושע בן לוי מניין לתחיית המתים מן התורה שנאמר ע) אשרי יושבי ביתך עוד יהללוך סלה הללוך לא נאמר אלא יהללוך מכאן לתחיית המתים מן התורה וא"ר יהושע בן לוי כל האומר שירה בעוה"ז זוכה ואומרה לעולם הבא שנאמר אשרי יושבי ביתך עוד יהללוך סלה א"ר חייא בר אבא א"ר יוחנן מניין לתחיית המתים מן התורה שנאמר פ) קול צופיך נשאו קול יחדו ירננו וגו' רננו לא נאמר אלא ירננו מכאן לתחיית המתים מן התורה וא"ר חייא בר אבא א"ר יוחנן עתידין כל הנביאים כולן אומרים שירה בקול אחד שנאמר קול צופיך נשאו קול יחדו ירננו אמר רב יהודה אמר רב כל המונע הלכה מפי תלמיד כאילו גוזלו מנחלת אבותיו שנאמר צ) תורה צוה לנו משה מורשה קהילת יעקב מורשה היא לכל ישראל מששת ימי בראשית אמר רב חנא בר ביזנא אמר רבי שמעון חסידא כל המונע הלכה מפי תלמיד אפילו עוברין שבמעי אמו מקללין אותו שנאמר ק) מונע בר יקבוהו

בכורות. תאני הבכורות: יקרא אל השמים מעל. כלומר יקרא הקב"ה לנשמה הבאה לו לתוך גופו של אדם (א) מאל השמים מעל ויקרא אף אל הגוף שבא מן הארץ: מפני מה שוקעת במערב. תסובב את כל העולם עד שתחזור למקום זריחתה למזרח ותשקע דאי הוה הכי לא הוה אמינא לך מפני מה שוקעת במזרח דנוהג העולם כך הוא ממקום שיצא שם נכנס: כדי ליתן שלום לקונה. להקב"ה שהשכינה במערב וכיון שמגעת עד מערב הולכת ומשתחוה לפני הקב"ה שבראה ולכך שוקעת ונכנסת כפופה לפני הקב"ה: ותיתי עד פלגא דרקיעא. דאם לכך מתכוונת למה הולכת בתוך המערב תבא עד אמצעו של רקיע ותשקע לשם ומשם תשתחוה כלפי מערב שכן דרך ב"א שמשתחוה ברחוק לפני המלך ואינו מתקרב כל כך: משום פועלים. דאילו כן היה מחשיך פתאום שכשחמה באמצע הרקיע מאירה ביותר וסבורים שעדיין יש שהות ביום והיו פועלין שוהין במלאכתן עד שחשיכה ועוברי דרכים נמי לא היו יודעין מתי יחשוך לבקש להם בית לינה ולכך שוקעת במערב שכשהולכת ומשתפלת והולכת וכלה אורה יודעין שמגיע שעת חשיכה: משעת יצירה. שנקרם כולו בבשר וגידין ועצמות: פקידה. משעה שהמלאך פוקד הטיפה ומביאה לפני המקום מה תהא עליה כדאמרינן בפרק כל היד במסכת נדה (דף טז:) מיד נזרקה בו נשמה וחיות: אמר ליה. רבי משעת יצירה: ואמר לו. אנטונינוס וכי אפשר לחתיכה שתתקיים אפילו ג' ימים בלא מלח שאינה מסרחת וה"נ אילו לא היתה נשמה נתונה עד שעת יצירה היאך תתקיים הטיפה שלא תסריח במעיה וכיון שטיפה מסרחת שוב אינה מולדת: למדני אנטונינוס. מדבריו למדתי: ופקודתך שמרה רוחי. משעת פקידה נשמר רוחי: משעת יציאה. כשיוצא ממעי אמו או משעת יצירה: א"ל. רבי משעת יצירה: אמר לו אנטונינוס א"כ בועט במעי אמו ויוצא. אלא משעת יציאתה: בם עור ופסח. שחיין עם מומן: וכתיב אז ידלג כאיל פסח. דמשמע שמתרפאין: עומדין במומן. ואח"כ מתרפאין: בלע המות לנצח. דלעתיד לבא מאחר שחיין שוב אינן מתין: כי הנער. כלומר כשימות אדם לעתיד ומת בן מאה שנה יאמרו נער הוא מת כי הנער בן מאה שנה ימות אלמא מתין: וחפרה הלבנה ובושה החמה. משמע שיהא אורם כהה וכתיב והיתה אור הלבנה כאור החמה: כאן לימות המשיח. כשיכלה השיעבוד והיתה אור הלבנה כאור החמה ולעתיד לבא וחפרה הלבנה ובושה החמה מרוב נגהם של צדיקים: ולשמואל דאמר. בדוכתא אחריתי אין בין העולם הזה וכו'. אידי ואידי לעוה"ב: אלא כאן במחנה שכינה. וחפרה מזיו השכינה: כאן במחנה צדיקים. כאן במחנה רשעים לא גרסינן: כתיב אני אמית ואחיה. דמשמע כשם שאני אמית את האדם כך אני מחייהו כשמת בעל מום עומד וחי בעל מום: וכתיב מחצתי ואני ארפא. שכשהוא מחיה מרפא את המחץ ועומד שלם: והדר מה שמחצתי. שלאחר כן מתרפא וכדלעיל עומדין במומן ומתרפאין: מיתה באחד וחיים באחד. וה"ק אני ממית אדם זה ומחיה אדם אחר: כדרך שהעולם נוהג. שזה מת וזה נולד: מה מחץ ורפוי באחד. ואין רפואה אלא במקום מחץ: ישיר. משמע לעתיד: נשאו קול יחדיו. היינו קול אחד: המונע הלכה. מללמדו: מששת ימי בראשית. דכתיב בראשית ברא בשביל התורה שהיא ראשית וישראל נקראו ו) ראשית תבואתה שעתידין להנחיל' ברא אלהים את השמים וגו': בר. תורה:

יקבוהו

עין משפט
נר מצוה

ה א מיי' פי"ב מהל' מלכים הל' ב' ופ"ט מהל' תשובה הלכה ב:

ליקוטי רש"י

בכורות. תאני הבכרות, שבישלו כל צרכן בתחלת בכורי תאינים שהם חביבות על מוצאיהם בראשיתם [ירמיה כד, ב]. בכורות. תאנים חשובות הממהרות להתבשל [עירובין כא:]. שמרה רוחי. בבטן אמי [איוב י, יב]. לפתח חטאת רובץ. משעה שנולד הולד הוא נתון בו [קהלת ד, יג]. בלע המות. יכסנו ויעלימנו עולמי' מישראל [ישעיה כה, ח]. יבולע מלאך המות שלא ישלוט. עול ימים. נער כמו עולל (איכה ב) עול ימים קטן בשנים [שם סה, כ]. בישראל. כתיב ובלע המות וגו'. אכריכם. מנהיגי המחרישה [שם סא, ה]. ובושה החמה שלא תאיר [פסחים סח.]. יהיה שבעתים כאור שבעת הימים. שבעתים שבע שבעיות כאור של שבעת הימים הרי ארבעים ותשע שבעיות העולים לשלש מאות וארבעים ושלשה [ישעיה ל, כו]. שבעתים הן ארבעים ותשע וכתיב כאור שבעת הימים ארבעים ותשע כאור שבעת ימים של עכשיו נמצא עודף על אור של עכשיו שלש מאות וארבעים ושלשה. לימות המשיח. יהיה אור הלבנה כאור החמה. לעולם הבא. וחפרה הלבנה ובושה החמה שלא יהא בעולם אלא זיו זוהר ומראה שכינה. ולשמואל. דאמר ימות המשיח אין משתנין משל עכשיו מה הוא מקיים והיה אור הלבנה כאור החמה. מה שאני ממית אני מחיה והדר מה שמחצתי ואני ארפא. שכדרך שהן מתים חגרים סומים אלמים כך הן חיין במומן ואחר כך מתרפאים כדכתיב אז ידלג כאיל פסח (ישעיה לה). מיתה באחד וחיים באחד. אני ממית את המתים ואני מחיה וזן את החיים. ת"ל מחצתי ואני ארפא. הא אתא לאשמועינן דלא תימא אמית ואחיה לאו דמתים חיים קאמר אלא אני אמית את המתים ואני מחיה וזן את החיים ובורא את הנולדים להכי כתיב בתריה מחצתי ואני ארפא כשם שמחצתי אני ארפא דאין רפואה אלא במוכה כך אותו עצמו שאני ממית אני מחיה [פסחים שם]. אז ישיר משה. אז כשראה הנס עלה בלבו שישיר שירה וכן (יהושע י, יב) אז ידבר יהושע וכן (מ"א ז, ח) ובית יעשה לבת פרעה חשב בלבו שיעשה לה אף כאן ישיר אמר לו לבו שישיר וכן עשה ויאמרו לאמר אשירה לה' וכן ביהושע כשראה הנס אמר לו לבו שידבר וכן עשה (יהושע י, יב) ויאמר לעיני ישראל וכן שירת הבאר שפתח בה (במדבר כא, יז) אז ישיר ישראל פירש אחריו עלי באר ענו לה (מ"א יא, ז) אז יבנה שלמה במה פירשו בו חכמי ישראל שבקש לבנות ולא בנה על שם המחשבה נאמרה זהו ליישב פשוטו אבל מדרשו אמרו רבותינו זכרונם לברכה מכאן רמז לתחיית המתים מן התורה וכן בכולן חוץ מזה משל שלמה שפירשוהו בקש לבנות ולא בנה ואין לומר וליישב הלשון הזה כשאר דברים הנכתבים בלשון הזה כגון (איוב א, ה) ככה יעשה איוב (במדבר ט, כג) על פי ה' יחנו (שם כ) ויש אשר יהיה הענן לפני שכן לשון דבר ההווה ונופל בו בין לשון עתיד בין לשון עבר אבל זה שלא היה אלא לשעה אינו יכול ליישבו בלשון הזה [שמות טו, א ועי' במהרש"א בח"א]. אז יבנה שלמה במה. רבותינו אמרו מתוך שלא מיחה בנשיו נקראת על שמו [מ"א יא, ז]. צופיך. נביאי הדורות [מגילה ב: ע"ש בתוס']. תורה. אשר צוה לנו משה מורשה היא לקהלת יעקב אחזנוה ולא נעזבנה [דברים לג, ד]. מונע בר. מלמד תורה [משלי יא, כו].

מסורת הש"ס

א) פסחים סח., ב) [בפסוק כתיב מהופך ועי' מ"א שמישבו], ג) שבת סג. ודף קנא. ברכות לד: [פסחים סח: לקמן צט.], ד) [פסחים סח. ע"ש], ה) [שבת נו: ועי' תוס' שם ד"ה אלא מעתה], ו) [ירמיה ב].

הגהות הב"ח

(א) רש"י ד"ה יקרא וכו' גופו של אדם מעל השמים ממעל ויקרא:

תורה אור השלם

א) יִקְרָא אֶל הַשָּׁמַיִם מֵעָל וְאֶל הָאָרֶץ לָדִין עַמּוֹ: [תהלים נ, ד]

ב) אַתָּה הוּא יי לְבַדֶּךָ אַתָּה עָשִׂיתָ אֶת הַשָּׁמַיִם שְׁמֵי הַשָּׁמַיִם וְכָל צְבָאָם הָאָרֶץ וְכָל אֲשֶׁר עָלֶיהָ הַיַּמִּים וְכָל אֲשֶׁר בָּהֶם וְאַתָּה מְחַיֶּה אֶת כֻּלָּם וּצְבָא הַשָּׁמַיִם לְךָ מִשְׁתַּחֲוִים: [נחמיה ט, ו]

ג) חַיִּים וָחֶסֶד עָשִׂיתָ עִמָּדִי וּפְקֻדָּתְךָ שָׁמְרָה רוּחִי: [איוב י, יב]

ד) הֲלוֹא אִם תֵּיטִיב שְׂאֵת וְאִם לֹא תֵיטִיב לַפֶּתַח חַטָּאת רֹבֵץ וְאֵלֶיךָ תְּשׁוּקָתוֹ וְאַתָּה תִּמְשָׁל בּוֹ: [בראשית ד, ז]

ה) הִנְנִי מֵבִיא אוֹתָם מֵאֶרֶץ צָפוֹן וְקִבַּצְתִּים מִיַּרְכְּתֵי אָרֶץ בָּם עִוֵּר וּפִסֵּחַ הָרָה וְיֹלֶדֶת יַחְדָּו קָהָל גָּדוֹל יָשׁוּבוּ הֵנָּה: [ירמיה לא, ז]

ו) אָז יְדַלֵּג כָּאַיָּל פִּסֵּחַ וְתָרֹן לְשׁוֹן אִלֵּם כִּי נִבְקְעוּ בַמִּדְבָּר מַיִם וּנְחָלִים בָּעֲרָבָה: [ישעיה לה, ו]

ז) בִּלַּע הַמָּוֶת לָנֶצַח וּמָחָה אֲדֹנָי אֱלֹהִים דִּמְעָה מֵעַל כָּל פָּנִים וְחֶרְפַּת עַמּוֹ יָסִיר מֵעַל כָּל הָאָרֶץ כִּי יי דִּבֵּר: [ישעיה כה, ח]

ח) לֹא יִהְיֶה מִשָּׁם עוֹד עוּל יָמִים וְזָקֵן אֲשֶׁר לֹא יְמַלֵּא אֶת יָמָיו כִּי הַנַּעַר בֶּן מֵאָה שָׁנָה יָמוּת וְהַחוֹטֶא בֶּן מֵאָה שָׁנָה יְקֻלָּל: [ישעיה סה, כ]

ט) וְעָמְדוּ זָרִים וְרָעוּ צֹאנְכֶם וּבְנֵי נֵכָר אִכָּרֵיכֶם וְכֹרְמֵיכֶם: [ישעיה סא, ה]

י) וְחָפְרָה הַלְּבָנָה וּבוֹשָׁה הַחַמָּה כִּי מָלַךְ יי צְבָאוֹת בְּהַר צִיּוֹן וּבִירוּשָׁלַיִם וְנֶגֶד זְקֵנָיו כָּבוֹד: [ישעיה כד, כג]

כ) וְהָיָה אוֹר הַלְּבָנָה כְּאוֹר הַחַמָּה וְאוֹר הַחַמָּה יִהְיֶה שִׁבְעָתַיִם כְּאוֹר שִׁבְעַת הַיָּמִים בְּיוֹם חֲבֹשׁ יי אֶת שֶׁבֶר עַמּוֹ וּמַחַץ מַכָּתוֹ יִרְפָּא: [ישעיה ל, כו]

ל) רְאוּ עַתָּה כִּי אֲנִי אֲנִי הוּא וְאֵין אֱלֹהִים עִמָּדִי אֲנִי אָמִית וַאֲחַיֶּה מָחַצְתִּי וַאֲנִי אֶרְפָּא וְאֵין מִיָּדִי מַצִּיל: [דברים לב, לט]

מ) אָז יָשִׁיר מֹשֶׁה וּבְנֵי יִשְׂרָאֵל אֶת הַשִּׁירָה הַזֹּאת לַיי וַיֹּאמְרוּ לֵאמֹר אָשִׁירָה לַיי כִּי גָאֹה גָּאָה סוּס וְרֹכְבוֹ רָמָה בַיָּם: [שמות טו, א]

נ) אָז יִבְנֶה יְהוֹשֻׁעַ מִזְבֵּחַ לַיי אֱלֹהֵי יִשְׂרָאֵל בְּהַר עֵיבָל: [יהושע ח, ל]

ס) אָז יִבְנֶה שְׁלֹמֹה בָּמָה לִכְמוֹשׁ שִׁקֻּץ מוֹאָב בָּהָר אֲשֶׁר עַל פְּנֵי יְרוּשָׁלָיִם וּלְמֹלֶךְ שִׁקֻּץ בְּנֵי עַמּוֹן: [מלכים א' יא, ז]

ע) אַשְׁרֵי יוֹשְׁבֵי בֵיתֶךָ עוֹד יְהַלְלוּךָ סֶּלָה: [תהלים פד, ה]

פ) קוֹל צֹפַיִךְ נָשְׂאוּ קוֹל יַחְדָּו יְרַנֵּנוּ כִּי עַיִן בְּעַיִן יִרְאוּ בְּשׁוּב יי צִיּוֹן: [ישעיה נב, ח]

צ) תּוֹרָה צִוָּה לָנוּ מֹשֶׁה מוֹרָשָׁה קְהִלַּת יַעֲקֹב: [דברים לג, ד]

ק) מֹנֵעַ בָּר יִקְּבֻהוּ לְאוֹם וּבְרָכָה לְרֹאשׁ מַשְׁבִּיר: [משלי יא, כו]

Antoninus and Rebbi discuss the precise moment the soul enters the person:

וְאָמַר לוֹ אַנְטוֹנִינוּס לְרַבִּי – **And Antoninus** also **asked Rebbi:** נְשָׁמָה מֵאֵימָתַי נִיתְּנָה בָּאָדָם – **When is the soul placed into man?** מִשְּׁעַת פְּקִידָה – Is it **from the moment of "attention"**[11] אוֹ מִשְּׁעַת יְצִירָה – **or from the moment of** the embryo's **formation?**[12] אָמַר לוֹ – **[Rebbi] said to him:** מִשְּׁעַת יְצִירָה – It is **from the moment of** the embryo's **formation** that it receives a soul. אָמַר לוֹ – **[Antoninus] said to him:** אֶפְשָׁר חֲתִיכָה שֶׁל בָּשָׂר עוֹמֶדֶת שְׁלֹשָׁה יָמִים בְּלֹא מֶלַח – **Can a piece of meat remain for** even **three days without salt** וְאֵינָהּ מַסְרַחַת – **and not become putrid?**[13] אֶלָּא מִשְּׁעַת פְּקִידָה – Must it not be, **rather,** that the soul enters the person **from the moment of "attention"?**[14] אָמַר רַבִּי – **Rebbi remarked:** דָּבָר זֶה לִמְּדַנִי אַנְטוֹנִינוּס – **This matter did Antoninus teach me,**[15] וּמִקְרָא מְסַיְּיעוֹ – **and Scripture supports him,** שֶׁנֶּאֱמַר ,,וּפְקֻדָּתְךָ שָׁמְרָה רוּחִי'' – **for it is stated:** ***And "Your attention" has guarded my spirit.***[16]

Antoninus and Rebbi discuss the precise moment the Evil Inclination begins to assert itself in a person:

וְאָמַר לוֹ אַנְטוֹנִינוּס לְרַבִּי – **And Antoninus** also **asked Rebbi:** מֵאֵימָתַי יֵצֶר הָרַע שׁוֹלֵט בָּאָדָם – **From when does the Evil Inclination have influence over a person?** מִשְּׁעַת יְצִירָה – Is it **from the moment of** the embryo's **formation** אוֹ מִשְּׁעַת יְצִיאָה – **or from the moment of birth?**[17] אָמַר לוֹ מִשְּׁעַת יְצִירָה – **[Rebbi] said to him: From the moment of** the embryo's **formation.** אָמַר לוֹ אִם כֵּן בּוֹעֵט בִּמְעֵי אִמּוֹ וְיוֹצֵא – **[Antoninus] said to him: If so, [the fetus] would kick against its mother's womb and leave** the womb prematurely![18] אֶלָּא מִשְּׁעַת יְצִיאָה – Must it not be, **rather,** that the Evil Inclination begins to have influence over a person **from the moment of birth?** אָמַר רַבִּי – **Rebbi remarked:** דָּבָר זֶה לִמְּדַנִי אַנְטוֹנִינוּס – **This matter did Antoninus teach me** [that the Evil Inclination does not begin to have influence over a person until birth], וּמִקְרָא מְסַיְּיעוֹ – **and Scripture supports him,** שֶׁנֶּאֱמַר ,,לַפֶּתַח חַטָּאת רֹבֵץ'' – **for it is stated:** ***Sin crouches at the door.***[19]

The Gemara presents a series of teachings about the Future World expounded by contrasting various verses in Scripture:

רֵישׁ לָקִישׁ רָמֵי – **Reish Lakish contrasted** two verses: כְּתִיב ,,בָּם עִוֵּר וּפִסֵּחַ הָרָה וְיֹלֶדֶת יַחְדָּו'' – On the one hand **it is written:** *Behold I will bring them from the north country and gather them from the ends of the earth,* ***among them the blind and the lame, the pregnant woman and the woman who has given birth, all together;*** *a great assembly shall return hither.*[20] וּכְתִיב ,,אָז יְדַלֵּג כָּאַיָּל פִּסֵּחַ וְתָרֹן לְשׁוֹן אִלֵּם כִּי־נִבְקְעוּ בַמִּדְבָּר מַיִם וּנְחָלִים בָּעֲרָבָה'' – **Yet** on the other hand **it is written:** ***Then the lame will leap like a hart and the tongue of the mute will sing; for water will break out in the desert, and streams in the barren land.***[21] הָא כֵּיצַד – **How is this** contradiction to be reconciled? עוֹמְדִין בְּמוּמָן וּמִתְרַפְּאִין – **They will rise** at the resurrection **with their defects** [as indicated by the first verse] **and** then **they will be healed** of their deformities [as indicated by the second verse].[22]

עוּלָּא רָמֵי – **Ulla contrasted** two verses: כְּתִיב ,,בִּלַּע הַמָּוֶת לָנֶצַח וּמָחָה ה' [אֱלֹהִים] דִּמְעָה מֵעַל כָּל־פָּנִים'' – On the one hand **it is**

NOTES

differently; the way it was created was designed to convey certain impressions and lessons to us, even though these might be the product of erroneous interpretations of the natural phenomena. The Sages were concerned with these impressions, not with teaching us about the actual laws of nature.

Maharal distinguishes between the immediate causes of natural events, which correspond to the laws of nature, and the ultimate and real causes, which express God's will and work through the laws of nature set by the Creator. When the Sages discuss natural phenomena, they are not talking about the natural causes which are the subject of the scientist, but about God's purposes (see *Be'er HaGolah*).

R' Moshe Chaim Luzzatto makes this point most forcefully when he stresses that we all know the course of the sun and "all that you find in the statements of our Sages about the sun and stars that do not correspond to what we observe speak about their innermost hidden aspects which are concealed in their physical nature" (cited here in *Margalios HaYam* §4).

11. I.e. from the moment the angel appointed to oversee conception turns his attention to the human germ and brings it before God, Who decrees what its physical and intellectual qualities will be (*Rashi,* based on *Niddah* 16b). [*Yad Ramah,* however, dismisses this explanation of פְּקִידָה, and explains מִשְּׁעַת פְּקִידָה to mean simply *from the moment of conception.*]

12. I.e. when the embryo is fully formed with flesh, sinews and bones (*Rashi*). [The term גידין, used by *Rashi,* which we have translated as *sinews,* refers in Talmudic usage to tendons, ligaments, nerves and even blood vessels – in short, any part of the anatomy that is long and string-like.] The Mishnah in *Niddah* (30a) teaches that the human embryo is fully formed by the forty-first day after conception. [See also *Menachos* 99b, where R' Yochanan and R' Elazar both state that "the soul is formed in forty days" (*Margaliyos HaYam*).]

13. Just as meat will spoil in three days if not preserved, so too would the human seed spoil without the animating force of the soul, and never develop into an embryo (*Rashi*).

14. And Rebbi conceded that it must indeed be so (see *Ein Yaakov* and *Rashi* thereon). [Initially, however, Rebbi had assumed that the mother's soul preserves the developing embryo until the fortieth day (*Rif* in *Ein Yaakov*).]

15. I.e. from his analogy to unsalted meat, I learned that the soul indeed enters the person at the moment of "attention" (see *Rashi*).

16. *Job* 10:12. I.e. from the moment of "attention" my spirit (or "soul") has been guarded in my body (see *Rashi*). [Alternatively, Rebbi means to render: "And from the moment of Your "attention" has my spirit (soul) guarded [my body]" (*Maharsha*).]

17. Literally: from the moment of departure [from the womb] (*Rashi*). Regarding the definition of "formation," see note 12. [Does the human characteristic of self-assertion (which is at the root of all sin) begin in the womb, or only upon birth?]

18. [Perhaps, the expression בּוֹעֵט בִּמְעֵי אִמּוֹ is used in the sense of *rebelling against* (see end of *Sotah* 22a) the mother's womb, in favor of independence.]

19. *Genesis* 4:7. That is, the capacity for sin waits at the door of the womb to enter the person upon his birth.

[*Maharsha* and other commentators point out that this conclusion apparently conflicts with the well-known Midrash that Esau was drawn to houses of idol worship while still in his mother's womb. See *Be'er Sheva, Yad David* and sources cited in *Margaliyos HaYam* for resolutions.]

[Though the Evil Inclination has influence over a person, it does not mean that the person is powerless to resist. On the contrary, the very verse quoted here, which states that *sin crouches at the door,* concludes: ,,וְאֵלֶיךָ תְּשׁוּקָתוֹ וְאַתָּה תִּמְשָׁל־בּוֹ, *its desire is to [make] you [sin], yet you can have mastery over it* (see *Rashi* ad loc.). Man's capacity for mature choice gives him this mastery.] *Piskei HaTosafos* (to *Nedarim* §62) write: "The Good Inclination is given to a person in his mother's womb, where he knows the entire Torah. And at the time of birth the Evil Inclination enters and then banishes the Good Inclination until the person becomes intellectually mature and the Good Inclination enters [once again]."

20. *Jeremiah* 31:7. [According to its simple meaning, the verse describes the ingathering of the exiles in the Messianic era. Reish Lakish interprets the verse as referring to the resurrection as well.] The verse indicates that those who died while crippled or deformed will be resurrected with their deformities (*Rashi*).

21. *Isaiah* 35:6. This verse indicates that the deformed will be cured of their deformities.

22. The dead will be resurrected initially with their deformities so that the wicked living at that time will not be able to deny that God has resurrected the very people who were dead (*Tanchuma* to *Vayigash,* cited by *Eitz Yosef*; *Bereishis Rabbah* §95; see also *Maharal*).

עין משפט
נר מצוה

ה א מיי' פי"ב מהל' מלכים הל' ב' ופ"ט מהל' תשובה הלכה ב:

בכורות נאות והושיב בו שני שומרים אחד חיגר ואחד סומא אמר לו חיגר לסומא בכורות נאות אני רואה בפרדס בא והרכיבני ונביאם לאכלם רכב חיגר על גבי סומא והביאום ואכלום לימים בא בעל פרדס אמר להן בכורות נאות היכן הן אמר לו חיגר כלום יש לי רגלים להלך בהן אמר לו סומא כלום יש לי עינים לראות מה עשה הרכיב חיגר על גבי סומא ודן אותם כאחד אף הקב"ה מביא נשמה וזורקה בגוף ודן אותם כאחד שנאמר א) יקרא אל השמים מעל ואל הארץ לדין עמו יקרא אל השמים מעל זו נשמה ואל הארץ לדין עמו זה הגוף: א"ל אנטונינוס לרבי מפני מה חמה יוצאה במזרח ושוקעת במערב א"ל אי הוה איפכא נמי הכי הוה אמרת לי א"ל הכי קאמינא לך מפני מה שוקעת במערב א"ל כדי ליתן שלום לקונה שנאמר ב) וצבא השמים לך משתחוים א"ל ותיתי עד פלגא דרקיע ותתן שלמא ותיעול משום פועלים ומשום עוברי דרכים וא"ל אנטונינוס לרבי נשמה מאימתי ניתנה באדם משעת פקידה או משעת יצירה א"ל משעת יצירה א"ל אפשר חתיכה של בשר עומדת שלשה ימים בלא מלח ואינה מסרחת אלא משעת פקידה אמר רבי דבר זה למדני אנטונינוס ומקרא מסייעו שנאמר ג) ופקודתך שמרה רוחי ואמר ליה אנטונינוס לרבי מאימתי יצה"ר שולט באדם משעת יצירה או משעת יציאה א"ל משעת יצירה א"ל א"כ בועט במעי אמו ויוצא אלא משעת יציאה אמר רבי דבר זה למדני אנטונינוס ומקרא מסייעו שנאמר ד) לפתח חטאת רובץ ר"ל רמי כתיב ה) בם עור ופסח הרה ויולדת יחדו וכתיב ו) אז ידלג כאיל פסח ותרון לשון אלם כי נבקעו במדבר מים ונחלים בערבה הא כיצד עומדין במומן ומתרפאין [א] עולא רמי כתיב ז) בלע המות לנצח ומחה ה' דמעה מעל כל פנים וכתיב ח) כי הנער בן מאה שנה ימות לא יהיה משם עוד עול ימים לא קשיא כאן בישראל כאן בעובדי כוכבים ועובדי כוכבים מאי בעו התם הנך דכתיב בהו ט) ועמדו זרים ורעו צאנכם ובני נכר אכריכם וכורמיכם רב חסדא רמי כתיב י) וחפרה הלבנה ובושה החמה כי מלך ה' צבאות וכתיב כ) והיה אור הלבנה כאור החמה ואור החמה יהיה שבעתים כאור שבעת הימים לא קשיא כאן לימות המשיח כאן לעוה"ב ולשמואל ג) דאמר [א] אין בין העוה"ז לימות המשיח אלא שיעבוד גליות בלבד לא קשיא כאן במחנה צדיקים כאן במחנה שכינה ד) רבא רמי כתיב ל) אני אמית ואחיה וכתיב ל) מחצתי ואני ארפא אמר הקב"ה מה שאני ממית אני מחיה והדר מה שמחצתי ואני ארפא ת"ר אני אמית ואחיה יכול שתהא מיתה באחד וחיים באחד כדרך שהעולם נוהג ת"ל מחצתי ואני ארפא מה מחיצה ורפואה באחד אף מיתה וחיים באחד מיכן תשובה לאומרין אין תחיית המתים מן התורה תניא אמר רבי מאיר מניין לתחיית המתים מן התורה שנאמר מ) אז ישיר משה ובני ישראל את השירה הזאת לה' שר לא נאמר אלא ישיר מכאן לתחיית המתים מן התורה כיוצא בדבר אתה אומר נ) אז יבנה יהושע מזבח לה' בנה לא נאמר אלא יבנה מכאן לתחיית המתים מן התורה אלא מעתה ס) אז יבנה שלמה במה לכמוש שקוץ מואב הכי נמי דיבנה אלא מעלה עליו הכתוב כאילו בנה א"ר יהושע בן לוי מניין לתחיית המתים מן התורה שנאמר ע) אשרי יושבי ביתך עוד יהללוך סלה הללוך לא נאמר אלא יהללוך מכאן לתחיית המתים מן התורה וא"ר יהושע בן לוי כל האומר שירה בעוה"ז זוכה ואומרה לעולם הבא שנאמר אשרי יושבי ביתך עוד יהללוך סלה א"ר חייא בר אבא א"ר יוחנן מניין לתחיית המתים מן התורה שנאמר פ) קול צופיך נשאו קול יחדו ירננו וגו' רננו לא נאמר אלא ירננו מכאן לתחיית המתים מן התורה וא"ר חייא בר אבא א"ר יוחנן עתידין כל הנביאים כולן אומרים שירה בקול אחד שנאמר קול צופיך נשאו קול יחדו ירננו אמר רב יהודה אמר רב כל המונע הלכה מפי תלמיד כאילו גוזלו מנחלת אבותיו שנאמר צ) תורה צוה לנו משה מורשה קהלת יעקב מורשה היא לכל ישראל מששת ימי בראשית אמר רב חנא בר ביזנא אמר רבי שמעון חסידא כל המונע הלכה מפי תלמיד אפילו עוברין שבמעי אמו מקללין אותו שנאמר ק) מונע בר יקבוהו

בכורות. תאני הבכורות: יקרא אל השמים מעל. כלומר יקרא הקב"ה לנשמה הבאה לו לתוך גופו של אדם (א) מאל השמים מעל ויקרא אף אל הגוף שבא מן הארץ: מפני מה שוקעת במערב. תסובב את כל העולם עד שתחזור למקום זריחתה למזרח ותשקע דאי הוה הכי לא הוה אמינא לך מפני מה שוקעת במזרח דנוהג העולם כך הוא ממקום שיצא שם נכנס: כדי ליתן שלום לקונה. להקב"ה שהשכינה במערב וכיון שמגעת עד מערב הולכת ומשתחוה לפני הקב"ה שבראה ולכך שוקעת ונכנסת כפופה לפני הקב"ה: ותיתי עד פלגא דרקיעא. דאם לכך מתכוונת למה הולכת בתוך המערב תבא עד אמצעו של רקיע ותשקע לשם ומשם תשתחוה כלפי מערב שכן דרך ב"א שמשתחוה ברחוק לפני המלך ואינו מתקרב כל כך: משום פועלים. דאילו כן היה מחשיך פתאום שכשחמה באמצע הרקיע מאירה ביותר וסבורים שעדיין יש שהות ביום והיו פועלין שוהין במלאכתן עד שחשיכה ועוברי דרכים נמי לא היו יודעין מתי יחשוך לבקש להם בית לינה ולכך שוקעת במערב שכשהולכת ומשתפלת והולכת וכלה אורה יודעין שמגיע שעת חשיכה: משעת יצירה. שנקרם כולו בבשר וגידין ועצמות: פקידה. משעה שהמלאך פוקד הטיפה ומביאה לפני המקום מה תהא עליה כדאמרינן בפרק כל היד במסכת נדה (דף טז:) מיד נזרקה בו נשמה וחיות: אמר ליה. רבי משעת יצירה: ואמר לו. אנטונינוס וכי אפשר לחתיכה שתתקיים אפילו ג' ימים בלא מלח שאינה מסרחת וה"נ אילו לא היתה נשמה נתונה עד שעת יצירה היאך תתקיים הטיפה שלא תסריח במעיה וכיון שטיפה מסרחת שוב אינה מולדת: למדני אנטונינוס. מדבריו למדתי: ופקודתך שמרה רוחי. משעת פקידה נשמר רוחי: משעת יציאה. כשיוצא ממעי אמו או משעת יצירה: א"ל. רבי משעת יצירה: אמר לו אנטונינוס א"כ בועט במעי אמו ויוצא. אלא משעת יציאתה: בם עור ופסח. שחיין עם מומן: וכתיב אז ידלג כאיל פסח. דמשמע שמתרפאין: עומדין במומן. ואח"כ מתרפאין: בלע המות לנצח. דלעתיד לבא מאחר שחיין שוב אין מתין: כי הנער. כלומר כשימות אדם לעתיד ומת בן מאה שנה יאמרו נער הוא מת כי הנער בן מאה שנה ימות אלמא מתין: וחפרה הלבנה ובושה החמה. משמע שיהא אורם כהה וכתיב והיתה אור הלבנה כאור החמה: כאן לימות המשיח. כשיכלה השיעבוד והיתה אור הלבנה כאור החמה ולעתיד לבא וחפרה הלבנה ובושה החמה ירוב נגהם של לדיקים: ולשמואל דאמר. בדוכתא אחריתי אין בין העולם הזה וכו'. אידי ואידי לעוה"ב: אלא כאן במחנה שכינה. וחפרה מזיו השכינה: כאן במחנה צדיקים. כאן במחנה רשעים לא גרסינן: כתיב אני אמית ואחיה. דמשמע כשם שאני אמית את האדם כך אני מחייהו כשמת בעל מום עומד וחי בעל מום: וכתיב מחצתי ואני ארפא. שכשהוא מחיה מרפא את המחץ ועומד שלם: והדר מה שמחצתי. שלאחר כן מתרפא וכדלעיל עומדין במומן ומתרפאין: מיתה באחד וחיים באחד. וה"ק אני ממית אדם זה ומחיה אדם אחר: כדרך שהעולם נוהג. שזה מת וזה נולד: מה מחץ ורפוי באחד. ואין רפואה אלא במקום מחץ: ישיר. משמע לעתיד: נשאו קול יחדיו. היינו קול אחד: המונע הלכה. מללמדו: מששת ימי בראשית. דכתיב בראשית ברא בשביל התורה שהיא ראשית וישראל נקראו [ו] ראשית תבואתה שעתידין להנחיל' ברא אלהים את השמים וגו': בר. תורה:

ליקוטי רש"י

בכורות. תאני הבכרות, שבישלו כל צרכן בתחלת בכורי תאנים שהם חביבות על מוצאיהם בראשיתם [ירמיה כד, ב]. בכורות. תאנים חשובות הממהרות להתבשל [עירובין כא:]. שמרה רוחי. בבטן אמי [איוב י, יב]. לפתח חטאת רובץ. משעה שנולד הולד הוא נתון בו [קהלת ד, יג]. בלע המות. יכסנו ויעלימנו עולמי' מישראל [ישעיה כה, ח]. יבולע מלאך המות שלא ישלוט. עול ימים. נער כמו עולל (איכה ב) עול ימים קטן בשנים [שם סה, כ]. בישראל. כתיב ובלע המות וגו'. אכריכם. מנהיגי המחרישה [שם סא, ה]. ובושה החמה שלא תאיר [פסחים סח.]. יהיה שבעתים כאור שבעת הימים. שבעתים שבע שבעיות כאור של שבעת הימים הרי ארבעים ותשע שבעיות העולים לשלש מאות וארבעים ושלשה [ישעיה ל, כו]. שבעתים הן ארבעים ותשע וכתיב כאור שבעת הימים ארבעים ותשע כאור שבעת ימים של עכשיו נמצא עודף על אור של עכשיו שלש מאות וארבעים ושלשה. לימות המשיח. יהיה אור הלבנה כאור החמה. לעולם הבא. וחפרה הלבנה ובושה החמה שלא יהא בעולם אלא זיו זוהר ומראה שכינה. ולשמואל. דאמר ימות המשיח אין משתנין משל עכשיו מה הוא מקיים והיה אור הלבנה כאור החמה. מה שאני ממית אני מחיה והדר מה שמחצתי ואני ארפא. שכדרך שהן מתים חגרים סומים אלמים כך הן חיין במומן ואחר כך מתרפאים כדכתיב אז ידלג כאיל פסח (ישעיה לה). מיתה באחד וחיים באחד. אני ממית את המתים ואני מחיה וזן את החיים. ת"ל מחצתי ואני ארפא. הא אתא לאשמועינן דלא תימא אמית ואחיה לאו דמתים חיים קאמר אלא אני אמית את המתים ואני מחיה וזן את החיים ובורא את הנולדים להכי כתיב בתריה מחצתי ואני ארפא כשם שמחצתי אני ארפא דאין רפואה אלא במוכה כך אותו עצמו שאני ממית אני מחיה [פסחים שם]. אז ישיר משה. אז כשראה הנס עלה בלבו שישיר שירה וכן (יהושע י, יב) אז ידבר יהושע וכן (מ"א ז, ח) ובית יעשה לבת פרעה חשב בלבו שיעשה לה אף כאן ישיר אמר לו לבו שישיר וכן עשה ויאמרו לאמר אשירה לה' וכן ביהושע כשראה הנס אמר לו לבו שידבר וכן עשה (יהושע י, יב) ויאמר לעיני ישראל וכן שירת הבאר שפתח בה (במדבר כא, יז) אז ישיר ישראל פירש אחריו עלי באר ענו לה (מ"א יא, ז) אז יבנה שלמה במה פירשו בו חכמי ישראל שבקש לבנות ולא בנה למדנו שהיו"ד על שם המחשבה נאמרה זהו ליישב פשוטו אבל מדרשו אמרו רבותינו זכרונם לברכה מכאן רמז לתחיית המתים מן התורה וכן בכולן חוץ משל שלמה שפירשוהו בקש לבנות ולא בנה ואין לומר וליישב הלשון הזה כשאר דברים הנכתבים בלשון עתיד והן מיד כגון (איוב א, ה) ככה יעשה איוב (במדבר ט, כג) על פי ה' יחנו (שם כ) ויש אשר יהיה הענן לפי שהן דבר ההוה תמיד ונופל בו בין לשון עתיד בין לשון עבר אבל זה שלא היה אלא לשעה אינו יכול ליישבו בלשון הזה [שמות טו, א ועי' במהרש"א בח"א]. אז יבנה שלמה במה. רבותינו אמרו מתוך שלא מיחה בנשיו נקראת על שמו [מ"א יא, ז]. צופיך. נביאי הדורות [מגילה ב: ע"ש בתוס']. תורה. אשר צוה לנו משה מורשה היא לקהלת יעקב אחזנוה ולא נעזבנה [דברים לג, ד]. מונע בר. מלמד תורה [משלי יא, כו].

מסורת הש"ס

א) פסחים סח., ב) [בפסוק כתיב מהופך ועי' ח"א שמישבו], ג) שבת סג. ודף קנא. ברכות לד: [פסחים סח: לקמן לט.], ד) [פסחים סח. ע"ש], ה) [שבת נו: ועי' תוס' שם ד"ה אלא מעתה], ו) [ירמיה ב].

הגהות הב"ח

(א) רש"י ד"ה יקרא וכו' גופו של אדם מעל השמים ממעל ויקרא:

תורה אור השלם

א) יִקְרָא אֶל הַשָּׁמַיִם מֵעָל וְאֶל הָאָרֶץ לָדִין עַמּוֹ: [תהלים נ, ד]

ב) אַתָּה הוּא יְיָ לְבַדֶּךָ אַתָּה עָשִׂיתָ אֶת הַשָּׁמַיִם שְׁמֵי הַשָּׁמַיִם וְכָל צְבָאָם הָאָרֶץ וְכָל אֲשֶׁר עָלֶיהָ הַיַּמִּים וְכָל אֲשֶׁר בָּהֶם וְאַתָּה מְחַיֶּה אֶת כֻּלָּם וּצְבָא הַשָּׁמַיִם לְךָ מִשְׁתַּחֲוִים: [נחמיה ט, ו]

ג) חַיִּים וָחֶסֶד עָשִׂיתָ עִמָּדִי וּפְקֻדָּתְךָ שָׁמְרָה רוּחִי: [איוב י, יב]

ד) הֲלוֹא אִם תֵּיטִיב שְׂאֵת וְאִם לֹא תֵיטִיב לַפֶּתַח חַטָּאת רֹבֵץ וְאֵלֶיךָ תְּשׁוּקָתוֹ וְאַתָּה תִּמְשָׁל בּוֹ: [בראשית ד, ז]

ה) הִנְנִי מֵבִיא אוֹתָם מֵאֶרֶץ צָפוֹן וְקִבַּצְתִּים מִיַּרְכְּתֵי אָרֶץ בָּם עִוֵּר וּפִסֵּחַ הָרָה וְיֹלֶדֶת יַחְדָּו קָהָל גָּדוֹל יָשׁוּבוּ הֵנָּה: [ירמיה לא, ז]

ו) אָז יְדַלֵּג כָּאַיָּל פִּסֵּחַ וְתָרֹן לְשׁוֹן אִלֵּם כִּי נִבְקְעוּ בַמִּדְבָּר מַיִם וּנְחָלִים בָּעֲרָבָה: [ישעיה לה, ו]

ז) בִּלַּע הַמָּוֶת לָנֶצַח וּמָחָה אֲדֹנָי אֱלֹהִים דִּמְעָה מֵעַל כָּל פָּנִים וְחֶרְפַּת עַמּוֹ יָסִיר מֵעַל כָּל הָאָרֶץ כִּי יְיָ דִּבֵּר: [ישעיה כה, ח]

ח) לֹא יִהְיֶה מִשָּׁם עוֹד עוּל יָמִים וְזָקֵן אֲשֶׁר לֹא יְמַלֵּא אֶת יָמָיו כִּי הַנַּעַר בֶּן מֵאָה שָׁנָה יָמוּת וְהַחוֹטֶא בֶּן מֵאָה שָׁנָה יְקֻלָּל: [ישעיה סה, כ]

ט) וְעָמְדוּ זָרִים וְרָעוּ צֹאנְכֶם וּבְנֵי נֵכָר אִכָּרֵיכֶם וְכֹרְמֵיכֶם: [ישעיה סא, ה]

י) וְחָפְרָה הַלְּבָנָה וּבוֹשָׁה הַחַמָּה כִּי מָלַךְ יְיָ צְבָאוֹת בְּהַר צִיּוֹן וּבִירוּשָׁלַיִם וְנֶגֶד זְקֵנָיו כָּבוֹד: [ישעיה כד, כג]

כ) וְהָיָה אוֹר הַלְּבָנָה כְּאוֹר הַחַמָּה וְאוֹר הַחַמָּה יִהְיֶה שִׁבְעָתַיִם כְּאוֹר שִׁבְעַת הַיָּמִים בְּיוֹם חֲבֹשׁ יְיָ אֶת שֶׁבֶר עַמּוֹ וּמַחַץ מַכָּתוֹ יִרְפָּא: [ישעיה ל, כו]

ל) רְאוּ עַתָּה כִּי אֲנִי אֲנִי הוּא וְאֵין אֱלֹהִים עִמָּדִי אֲנִי אָמִית וַאֲחַיֶּה מָחַצְתִּי וַאֲנִי אֶרְפָּא וְאֵין מִיָּדִי מַצִּיל: [דברים לב, לט]

מ) אָז יָשִׁיר מֹשֶׁה וּבְנֵי יִשְׂרָאֵל אֶת הַשִּׁירָה הַזֹּאת לַייָ וַיֹּאמְרוּ לֵאמֹר אָשִׁירָה לַייָ כִּי גָאֹה גָּאָה סוּס וְרֹכְבוֹ רָמָה בַיָּם: [שמות טו, א]

נ) אָז יִבְנֶה יְהוֹשֻׁעַ מִזְבֵּחַ לַייָ אֱלֹהֵי יִשְׂרָאֵל בְּהַר עֵיבָל: [יהושע ח, ל]

ס) אָז יִבְנֶה שְׁלֹמֹה בָּמָה לִכְמוֹשׁ שִׁקֻּץ מוֹאָב בָּהָר אֲשֶׁר עַל פְּנֵי יְרוּשָׁלָםִ וּלְמֹלֶךְ שִׁקֻּץ בְּנֵי עַמּוֹן: [מלכים א' יא, ז]

ע) אַשְׁרֵי יוֹשְׁבֵי בֵיתֶךָ עוֹד יְהַלְלוּךָ סֶּלָה: [תהלים פד, ה]

פ) קוֹל צֹפַיִךְ נָשְׂאוּ קוֹל יַחְדָּו יְרַנֵּנוּ כִּי עַיִן בְּעַיִן יִרְאוּ בְּשׁוּב יְיָ צִיּוֹן: [ישעיה נב, ח]

צ) תּוֹרָה צִוָּה לָנוּ מֹשֶׁה מוֹרָשָׁה קְהִלַּת יַעֲקֹב: [דברים לג, ד]

ק) מֹנֵעַ בָּר יִקְּבֻהוּ לְאוֹם וּבְרָכָה לְרֹאשׁ מַשְׁבִּיר: [משלי יא, כו]

written: ***He will conceal death forever, and Adonai Elohim will wipe tears off every face.***[23] וּכְתִיב ,,כִּי הַנַּעַר בֶּן־מֵאָה שָׁנָה יָמוּת" ,,לֹא־יִהְיֶה מִשָּׁם עוֹד עוּל יָמִים" – **Yet** on the other hand **it is written:** ***For the youth will die one hundred years old,*** and ***There shall be no more thenceforth one young in years*** *nor one old who shall not fill his days,*[24] which implies that people *will* die in the Future World. How is this contradiction to be resolved? Ulla answers: לֹא קַשְׁיָא – **It is not a difficulty.** כָּאן בְּיִשְׂרָאֵל – **Here,** in the first verse, which states that death will cease altogether, **it refers to the Jews,** כָּאן בְּעוֹבְדֵי כוֹכָבִים – whereas **here,** in the second verse, which speaks of eventual death after exceptionally long life, **it refers to idolaters.**

The Gemara asks:

וְעוֹבְדֵי כוֹכָבִים מַאי בָּעוּ הָתָם – **But what are idolaters doing there** in the Future World altogether?

The Gemara answers:

הָנָךְ דִּכְתִיב בְּהוּ ,,וְעָמְדוּ זָרִים וְרָעוּ צֹאנְכֶם וּבְנֵי נֵכָר אִכָּרֵיכֶם וְכֹרְמֵיכֶם" – It refers to **those** idolaters **regarding whom it is written:** ***And strangers will stand and tend your flocks, and foreigners will be your plowmen and your vinedressers.***[25]

רַב חִסְדָּא רָמֵי – **Rav Chisda contrasted** two verses: כְּתִיב ,,וְחָפְרָה הַלְּבָנָה וּבוֹשָׁה הַחַמָּה כִּי־מָלַךְ ה׳ צְבָאוֹת" – On the one hand **it is written:** ***Then the moon shall be abashed and the sun ashamed, for Hashem Lord of Hosts shall reign*** *in Mount Zion and in Jerusalem.*[26] וּכְתִיב ,,וְהָיָה אוֹר־הַלְּבָנָה כְּאוֹר הַחַמָּה וְאוֹר הַחַמָּה יִהְיֶה שִׁבְעָתַיִם כְּאוֹר שִׁבְעַת הַיָּמִים" – **Yet** on the other hand **it is written:** ***And the light of the moon shall be like the light of the sun, and the light of the sun shall be sevenfold as the light of a septenary of days.***[27] How is this contradiction to be resolved? Rav Chisda answers: לֹא קַשְׁיָא – **It is not a difficulty.** כָּאן לִימוֹת הַמָּשִׁיחַ – **Here,** in the second verse, which speaks of the luminaries becoming more intense, **it refers to the Messianic era,**[28] כָּאן לָעוֹלָם הַבָּא – whereas **here,** in the first verse, which speaks of the luminaries ceasing to shine altogether, **it refers to the World to Come.**

The Gemara asks:

וְלִשְׁמוּאֵל דְּאָמַר אֵין בֵּין הָעוֹלָם הַזֶּה לִימוֹת הַמָּשִׁיחַ אֶלָּא שִׁיעְבּוּד גָּלֻיּוֹת בִּלְבַד – **And according to Shmuel, who says, "There is no** difference **between this world and the Messianic era except** for **the subjugation of** the Jews **in the** various **exiles,"**[29] how is the contradiction between the verses to be reconciled? The verse that speaks of an intensification of the luminaries cannot refer to the Messianic era, for Shmuel rejects the notion that the Messianic era will contain any changes in the laws of nature. – ? –

The Gemara answers:

לֹא קַשְׁיָא – **This is not a difficulty,** i.e. Shmuel will reconcile the verses differently: Both refer to the World to Come.[30] כָּאן בְּמַחֲנֵה צַדִּיקִים – **Here,** in the verse which speaks of the luminaries intensifying, **it refers to the camp of the righteous,** כָּאן בְּמַחֲנֵה שְׁכִינָה – whereas **here,** in the verse which speaks of the luminaries paling, **it refers to the camp of the Divine Presence,** where the radiance of that Presence will blot out the light of the luminaries.[31]

רָבָא רָמֵי – **Rava contrasted** two verses: כְּתִיב ,,אֲנִי אָמִית וַאֲחַיֶּה"

NOTES

23. *Isaiah* 25:8. This verse states that in the Future World, there will be no death, as God will not give the Angel of Death any dominion (see *Rashi* to *Pesachim* 68a).

[*Radak* (ad loc.), however, understands the verse according to its simple meaning as referring to the time when the nations who will gather around Jerusalem to attack Israel during the war of Gog and Magog will be defeated. God will put a final end to the nations' persecution of the Jewish people, whose tears and sorrow will cease forevermore.]

24. *Isaiah* 65:20. [The Gemara here cites two halves of the same verse, but in inverted order; see *Maharsha.*] The entire verse reads: לֹא־יִהְיֶה מִשָּׁם עוֹד עוּל יָמִים וְזָקֵן אֲשֶׁר לֹא־יְמַלֵּא אֶת־יָמָיו כִּי הַנַּעַר בֶּן־מֵאָה שָׁנָה יָמוּת וְהַחוֹטֶא בֶּן־מֵאָה שָׁנָה יְקֻלָּל, *There shall be no more thenceforth one young in years nor one old who shall not fill his days; for the youth will die one hundred years old, and the sinner one hundred years old shall be accursed.* All will live long lives. One who dies at the age of one hundred will be accounted as having died a youth, as the result of his sins, due to the extreme longevity which will be normal then (see *Rashi* here and *Radak* ad loc.).

25. *Isaiah* 61:5. These non-Jews will survive into the era of the Future World and attend to the physical needs of Israel so that the latter be free to devote themselves exclusively to the Torah, service, and knowledge of God (see v. 6 there and *Radak*).

After living a long life, however, these non-Jews will die. The souls of those who are deserving will return to the World of Souls, normally the place for those who die, unlike the Jews who will live forever in the World to Come.

Yad Ramah explains that Ulla's entire discussion relates to the Messianic Era, when there will still be physical needs to be attended to; it does not relate to the World to Come (after the resurrection), in which (according to *Yad Ramah*) there are no physical needs and hence no need for "plowmen and vinedressers." And Shmuel, who cannot hold that death will cease in the days of Messiah (see Gemara below), but only in the World to Come, will resolve Ulla's contradiction differently.

Ulla's distinction here between Jews and idolaters is actually the subject of a dispute in *Bereishis Rabbah* (26:2). There, R' Chanina reconciles the two verses as Ulla does. R' Yehoshua ben Levi, however, explains that *He will conceal death forever and . . . wipe tears off "every" face* applies to non-Jews as well. And how does he explain the verse *for the youth will die one hundred years old*? It means that at that time one hundred (rather than twenty) will be the minimum age at which one can be liable to death by the hands of Heaven for his sins. [Thus, although *natural* death will cease at that time, one might still become liable to death by the hands of Heaven for his sins (*Tiferes Zion* ad loc.; cf. *Maharzav* ad loc.).]

26. *Isaiah* 24:23. The light of the sun and moon will pale before the intense luminosity of the righteous at that time (*Rashi* below ד״ה כאן לימות המשיח). Alternatively, the sun and the moon will cease to shine, and the only light in the world will be the visible splendor of the Divine Presence (*Rashi* to *Pesachim* 68a.).

27. *Isaiah* 30:26. This passage describes the extraordinary intensity of the light of the sun and the moon in the Future World. The moon will shine as brightly as the sun does today, and the sun will shine "sevenfold as the light of a septenary of days." The term שִׁבְעָתַיִם (which we have rendered *sevenfold*) is interpreted by *Targum Yonasan,* followed by *Rashi* ad loc. and to *Pesachim* 68a, as meaning: "seven seven." Thus, the sun will have 49 times the light of seven days, i.e. 343 times its present brightness (7x7x7=343). ["A septenary of days" means seven present-days of sunlight (*Rashi* to *Pesachim* 68a). Alternatively, the verse means: "the light of the seven days" – the special light that was concealed after the Seven Days of Creation (see *Toras Chaim*).]

28. When the Jews will be redeemed from the subjugation of the nations (*Rashi*). The Messianic era precedes the World to Come (see Chapter Introduction).

29. Shmuel (*Berachos* 34b, *Shabbos* 63a, 151b) maintains that the Messianic era does not usher in any change in the natural order. What *will* change is that all Jews will return to Eretz Yisrael from the lands of their exile and dwell there in complete security and independence (see also *Rambam, Hil. Melachim* chs. 11-12 at length).

30. In which the laws of nature will no longer prevail, even in Shmuel's view.

31. The splendor of the camp of the Divine Presence is just as intense today. The meaning here is that in the World to Come that splendor will be revealed to all (*Yad Ramah*).

This distinction between "the camp of the Divine Presence" and "the camp of the righteous" is indicated in this very verse (*Isaiah* 24:23), which reads in its entirety: וְחָפְרָה הַלְּבָנָה וּבוֹשָׁה הַחַמָּה כִּי־מָלַךְ ה׳ צְבָאוֹת בְּהַר צִיּוֹן וּבִירוּשָׁלַםִ וְנֶגֶד זְקֵנָיו כָּבוֹד, *Then the moon shall be abashed and the sun ashamed; for Hashem Lord of Hosts shall reign in Mount Zion and in Jerusalem, and before His elders shall be glory. For Hashem . . . shall reign . . .* refers to the camp of the Divine Presence; *and before His elders . . .* refers to the camp of the righteous (*Rif* in *Ein Yaakov*).

עין משפט נר מצוה

ה א מיי' פי"ב מהל' מלכים הל' ב' ופ"ט מהל' תשובה הלכה ב:

בכורות נאות והושיב בו שני שומרים אחד חיגר ואחד סומא אמר לו חיגר לסומא בכורות נאות אני רואה בפרדס בא והרכיבני ונביאם לאכלם רכב חיגר על גבי סומא והביאום ואכלום לימים בא בעל פרדס אמר להן בכורות נאות היכן הן אמר לו חיגר כלום יש לי רגלים להלך בהן אמר לו סומא כלום יש לי עינים לראות מה עשה הרכיב חיגר על גבי סומא ודן אותם כאחד אף הקב"ה מביא נשמה וזורקה בגוף ודן אותם כאחד שנאמר א) יקרא אל השמים מעל ואל הארץ לדין עמו יקרא אל השמים מעל זו נשמה ואל הארץ לדין עמו זה הגוף: א"ל אנטונינוס לרבי מפני מה חמה יוצאה במזרח ושוקעת במערב א"ל אי הוה איפכא נמי הכי הוה אמרת לי א"ל הכי קאמינא לך מפני מה שוקעת במערב א"ל כדי ליתן שלום לקונה שנאמר ב) וצבא השמים לך משתחוים א"ל ותיתי עד פלגא דרקיע ותתן שלמא ותיעול משום פועלים ומשום עוברי דרכים וא"ל אנטונינוס לרבי נשמה מאימתי ניתנה באדם משעת פקידה או משעת יצירה א"ל משעת יצירה א"ל אפשר חתיכה של בשר עומדת שלשה ימים בלא מלח ואינה מסרחת אלא משעת פקידה אמר רבי דבר זה למדני אנטונינוס ומקרא מסייעו שנאמר ג) ופקודתך שמרה רוחי ואמר ליה אנטונינוס לרבי מאימתי יצה"ר שולט באדם משעת יצירה או משעת יציאה א"ל משעת יצירה א"ל א"כ בועט במעי אמו ויוצא אלא משעת יציאה אמר רבי דבר זה למדני אנטונינוס ומקרא מסייעו שנאמר ד) לפתח חטאת רובץ ר"ל רמי כתיב ה) בם עור ופסח הרה ויולדת יחדו וכתיב ו) אז ידלג כאיל פסח ותרון לשון אלם כי נבקעו במדבר מים ונחלים בערבה הא כיצד עומדין במומן ומתרפאין [א] עולא רמי כתיב ז) בלע המות לנצח ומחה ה' דמעה מעל כל פנים וכתיב[ב] ח) כי הנער בן מאה שנה ימות לא יהיה משם עוד עול ימים לא קשיא כאן בישראל כאן בעובדי כוכבים ועובדי כוכבים מאי בעו התם הנך דכתיב בהו ט) ועמדו זרים ורעו צאנכם ובני נכר אכריכם וכורמיכם רב חסדא רמי כתיב י) וחפרה הלבנה ובושה החמה כי מלך ה' צבאות וכתיב כ) והיה אור הלבנה כאור החמה ואור החמה יהיה שבעתים כאור שבעת הימים לא קשיא כאן לימות המשיח כאן לעוה"ב ולשמואל [ג] דאמר [א] אין בין העוה"ז לימות המשיח אלא שיעבוד גליות בלבד לא קשיא כאן במחנה צדיקים כאן במחנה שכינה [ד] רבא רמי כתיב ל) אני אמית ואחיה וכתיב ל) מחצתי ואני ארפא אמר הקב"ה מה שאני ממית אני מחיה והדר מה שמחצתי ואני ארפא ת"ר אני אמית ואחיה יכול שתהא מיתה באחד וחיים באחד כדרך שהעולם נוהג ת"ל מחצתי ואני ארפא מה מחיצה ורפואה באחד אף מיתה וחיים באחד מיכן תשובה לאומרין אין תחיית המתים מן התורה תניא אמר רבי מאיר מניין לתחיית המתים מן התורה שנאמר מ) אז ישיר משה ובני ישראל את השירה הזאת לה' שר לא נאמר אלא ישיר מכאן לתחיית המתים מן התורה כיוצא בדבר אתה אומר נ) אז יבנה יהושע מזבח לה' בנה לא נאמר אלא יבנה מכאן לתחיית המתים מן התורה אלא מעתה ס) אז יבנה שלמה במה לכמוש שקוץ מואב הכי נמי דיבנה [ה] אלא מעלה עליו הכתוב כאילו בנה א"ר יהושע בן לוי מניין לתחיית המתים מן התורה שנאמר ע) אשרי יושבי ביתך עוד יהללוך סלה הילל לא נאמר אלא יהללוך מכאן לתחיית המתים מן התורה וא"ר יהושע בן לוי כל האומר שירה בעוה"ז זוכה ואומרה לעולם הבא שנאמר אשרי יושבי ביתך עוד יהללוך סלה א"ר חייא בר אבא א"ר יוחנן מניין לתחיית המתים מן התורה שנאמר פ) קול צופיך נשאו קול יחדו ירננו וגו' רינני לא נאמר אלא ירננו מכאן לתחיית המתים מן התורה וא"ר חייא בר אבא א"ר יוחנן עתידין כל הנביאים כולן אומרים שירה בקול אחד שנאמר קול צופיך נשאו קול יחדו ירננו אמר רב יהודה אמר רב כל המונע הלכה מפי תלמיד כאילו גוזלו מנחלת אבותיו שנאמר צ) תורה צוה לנו משה מורשה קהילת יעקב מורשה היא לכל ישראל מששת ימי בראשית אמר רב חנא בר ביזנא אמר רבי שמעון חסידא כל המונע הלכה מפי תלמיד אפילו עוברין שבמעי אמו מקללין אותו שנאמר ק) מונע בר יקבוהו

רש"י

בכורות. תאני הבכורות: יקרא אל השמים מעל. כלומר יקרא הקב"ה לנשמה הבאה לו לתוך גופו של אדם (א) מאל השמים מעל ויקרא אף אל הגוף שבא מן הארץ: מפני מה שוקעת במערב. תסובב את כל העולם עד שתחזור למקום זריחתה למזרח ותשקע דאי הוה הכי לא הוה אמינא לך מפני מה שוקעת במזרח דנוהג העולם כך הוא ממקום שיצא שם נכנס: כדי ליתן שלום לקונה. להקב"ה שהשכינה במערב וכיון שמגעת עד מערב הולכת ומשתחוה לפני הקב"ה שבראה ולכך שוקעת ונכנסת כפופה לפני הקב"ה: ותיתי עד פלגא דרקיעא. דאם לכך מתכוונת למה הולכת בתוך המערב תבא עד אמצעו של רקיע ותשקע לשם ומשם תשתחוה כלפי מערב שכן דרך ב"א שמשתחוה ברחוק לפני המלך ואינו מתקרב כל כך: משום פועלים. דאילו כן היה מחשיך פתאום שכשחמה באמצע הרקיע מאירה ביותר וסבורים שעדיין יש שהות ביום והיו פועלין שוהין במלאכתן עד שתחשיכה ועוברי דרכים נמי לא היו יודעין מתי יחשוך לבקש להם בית לינה ולכך שוקעת במערב שכשהולכת ומשתפלת והולכת וכלה אורה יודעין שמגיע שעת חשיכה: משעת יצירה. שנקרם כולו בבשר וגידין ועצמות: פקידה. משעה שהמלאך פוקד הטיפה ומביאה לפני המקום מה תהא עליה כדאמרינן בפרק כל היד במסכת נדה (דף טז:) מיד נזרקה בו נשמה וחיות: אמר ליה. רבי משעת יצירה: ואמר לו. אנטונינוס וכי אפשר לחתיכה שתתקיים אפילו ג' ימים בלא מלח שאינה מסרחת וה"נ אילו לא היתה נשמה נתונה עד שעת יצירה היאך תתקיים הטיפה שלא תסריח במעיה וכיון שטיפה מסרחת שוב אינה מולדת: למדני אנטונינוס. מדבריו למדתי: ופקודתך שמרה רוחי. משעת פקידה נשמר רוחי: משעת יציאה. כשיוצא ממעי אמו או משעת יצירה: א"ל. רבי משעת יצירה: אמר לו אנטונינוס א"כ בועט במעי אמו ויוצא. אלא משעת יציאתה: בם עור ופסח. שחיין עם מומן: וכתיב אז ידלג כאיל פסח. דמשמע שמתרפאין: עומדין במומן. ואח"כ מתרפאין: בלע המות לנצח. דלעתיד לבא מאחר שחיין שוב אין מתין: כי הנער. כלומר כשימות אדם לעתיד ומת בן מאה שנה יאמרו נער הוא מת כי הנער בן מאה שנה ימות אלמא מתין: וחפרה הלבנה ובושה החמה. משמע שיהא אורם כהה וכתיב והיתה אור הלבנה כאור החמה: כאן לימות המשיח. כשיכלה השיעבוד והיתה אור הלבנה כאור החמה ולעתיד לבא וחפרה הלבנה ובושה החמה מרוב נגהם של צדיקים: ולשמואל דאמר. בדוכתא אחריתי אין בין העולם הזה וכו'. אידי ואידי לעוה"ב: אלא כאן במחנה שכינה. וחפרה מזיו השכינה: כאן במחנה צדיקים. כאן במחנה רשעים לא גרסינן: כתיב אני אמית ואחיה. דמשמע כשם שאני אמית את האדם כך אני מחייהו כשמת בעל מום עומד וחי בעל מום: וכתיב מחצתי ואני ארפא. שכשהוא מחיה מרפא את המחץ ועומד שלם: והדר מה שמחצתי. שלאחר כן מתרפא וכדלעיל עומדין במומן ומתרפאין: מיתה באחד וחיים באחד. וה"ק אני ממית אדם זה ומחיה אדם אחר: כדרך שהעולם נוהג. שזה מת וזה נולד: מה מחץ ורפוי באחד. ואין רפואה אלא במקום מחץ: ישיר. משמע לעתיד: נשאו קול יחדיו. היינו קול אחד: המונע הלכה. מללמדו: מששת ימי בראשית. דכתיב בראשית ברא בשביל התורה שהיא ראשית וישראל נקראו [ו] ראשית תבואתה שעתידין להנחיל' ברא אלהים את השמים וגו': בר. תורה: יקבוהו

ליקוטי רש"י

בכורות. תאני הבכרות, שבישלו כל צרכן בתחלת בכורי תאנים שהם חביבות על מוצאיהם בראשיתם [ירמיה כד, ב]. בכורות. תאנים חשובות הממהרות להתבשל [עירובין כא:]. שמרה רוחי. בבטן אמי [איוב י, יב]. לפתח חטאת רובץ. משעה שנולד הולד הוא נתון בו [קהלת ד, יג]. בלע המות. יכסנו ויעלימנו עולמי' מישראל [ישעיה כה, ח]. יבולע מלאך המות שלא ישלוט. עול ימים. נער כמו עולל (איכה ב) עול ימים קטן בשנים [שם סה, כ]. בישראל. כתיב ובלע המות וגו'. אכריכם. מנהיגי המחרישה [שם סא, ה]. ובושה החמה שלא תאיר [פסחים סח.]. יהיה שבעתים כאור שבעת הימים. שבעתים שבע שבעיות כאור של שבעת הימים הרי ארבעים ותשע שבעיות העולים לשלש מאות וארבעים ושלשה [ישעיה ל, כו]. שבעתים הן ארבעים ותשע וכתיב כאור שבעת הימים ארבעים ותשע כאור שבעת ימים של עכשיו נמצא עודף על אור של עכשיו שלש מאות וארבעים ושלשה. לימות המשיח. יהיה אור הלבנה כאור החמה. לעולם הבא. וחפרה הלבנה ובושה החמה שלא יהא בעולם אלא זיו זוהר ומראה שכינה. ולשמואל. דאמר ימות המשיח אין משתנין משל עכשיו מה הוא מקיים והיה אור הלבנה כאור החמה. מה שאני ממית אני מחיה והדר מה שמחצתי ואני ארפא. שכדרך שהן מתים חגרים סומים אלמים כך הן חיין במומן ואחר כך מתרפאים כדכתיב אז ידלג כאיל פסח (ישעיה לה). מיתה באחד וחיים באחד. אני ממית את המתים ואני מחיה וזן את החיים. ת"ל מחצתי ואני ארפא. הא אתא לאשמועינן דלא תימא אמית ואחיה לאו דמתים חיים קאמר אלא אני אמית את המתים ואני מחיה וזן את החיים ובורא את הנולדים להכי כתיב בתריה מחצתי ואני ארפא כשם שמחצתי אני ארפא דאין רפואה אלא במוכה כך אותו עצמו שאני ממית אני מחיה [פסחים שם]. אז ישיר משה. אז כשראה הנס עלה בלבו שישיר שירה וכן (יהושע י, יב) אז ידבר יהושע וכן (מ"א ז, ח) ובית יעשה לבת פרעה חשב בלבו שיעשה לה אף כאן ישיר אמר לו לבו שישיר וכן עשה ויאמרו לאמר אשירה לה' וכן ביהושע כשראה הנס אמר לו לבו שידבר וכן עשה (יהושע י, יב) ויאמר לעיני ישראל וכן שירת הבאר שפתח בה (במדבר כא, יז) אז ישיר ישראל פירש אחריו עלי באר ענו לה (מ"א יא, ז) אז יבנה שלמה במה פירשו בו חכמי ישראל שבקש לבנות ולא בנה למדנו שהיו"ד על שם המחשבה נאמרה זהו ליישב פשוטו אבל מדרשו אמרו רבותינו זכרונם לברכה מכאן רמז לתחיית המתים מן התורה וכן בכולן חוץ משל שלמה שפירשוהו בקש לבנות ולא בנה ואין לומר ולישב הלשון הזה כשאר דברים הנכתבים בלשון עתיד והן מיד כגון (איוב א, ה) ככה יעשה איוב (במדבר ט, כג) על פי ה' יחנו (שם כ) ויש אשר יהיה הענן לפי שהן דבר ההוה תמיד ונופל בו בין לשון עתיד בין לשון עבר אבל זה שלא היה אלא לשעה אינו יכול ליישבו בלשון הזה [שמות טו, א ועי' במהרש"א בח"א]. אז יבנה שלמה במה. רבותינו אמרו מתוך שלא מיחה בנשיו נקראת על שמו [מ"א יא, ז]. צופיך. נביאי הדורות [מגילה ב: ע"ש בתוס']. תורה. אשר צוה לנו משה מורשה היא לקהלת יעקב אחזוה ולא נעזבנה [דברים לג, ד]. מונע בר. מלמד תורה [משלי יא, כו].

מסורת הש"ס

א) פסחים סח., ב) [בפסוק כתיב מהופך ועי' מ"א שמישבו], ג) שבת סג. ודף קנא. ברכות לד: [פסחים סח: לקמן לט.], ד) [פסחים סח. ע"ש], ה) [שבת נו: ועי' תוס' שם ד"ה אלא מעתה], ו) [ירמיה ב].

הגהות הב"ח

(א) רש"י ד"ה יקרא וכו' גופו של אדם מעל השמים ממעל ויקרא:

תורה אור השלם

א) יִקְרָא אֶל הַשָּׁמַיִם מֵעָל וְאֶל הָאָרֶץ לָדִין עַמּוֹ: [תהלים נ, ד]

ב) אַתָּה הוּא יְיָ לְבַדֶּךָ אַתָּה עָשִׂיתָ אֶת הַשָּׁמַיִם שְׁמֵי הַשָּׁמַיִם וְכָל צְבָאָם הָאָרֶץ וְכָל אֲשֶׁר עָלֶיהָ הַיַּמִּים וְכָל אֲשֶׁר בָּהֶם וְאַתָּה מְחַיֶּה אֶת כֻּלָּם וּצְבָא הַשָּׁמַיִם לְךָ מִשְׁתַּחֲוִים: [נחמיה ט, ו]

ג) חַיִּים וָחֶסֶד עָשִׂיתָ עִמָּדִי וּפְקֻדָּתְךָ שָׁמְרָה רוּחִי: [איוב י, יב]

ד) הֲלוֹא אִם תֵּיטִיב שְׂאֵת וְאִם לֹא תֵיטִיב לַפֶּתַח חַטָּאת רֹבֵץ וְאֵלֶיךָ תְּשׁוּקָתוֹ וְאַתָּה תִּמְשָׁל בּוֹ: [בראשית ד, ז]

ה) הִנְנִי מֵבִיא אוֹתָם מֵאֶרֶץ צָפוֹן וְקִבַּצְתִּים מִיַּרְכְּתֵי אָרֶץ בָּם עִוֵּר וּפִסֵּחַ הָרָה וְיֹלֶדֶת יַחְדָּו קָהָל גָּדוֹל יָשׁוּבוּ הֵנָּה: [ירמיה לא, ז]

ו) אָז יְדַלֵּג כָּאַיָּל פִּסֵּחַ וְתָרֹן לְשׁוֹן אִלֵּם כִּי נִבְקְעוּ בַמִּדְבָּר מַיִם וּנְחָלִים בָּעֲרָבָה: [ישעיה לה, ו]

ז) בִּלַּע הַמָּוֶת לָנֶצַח וּמָחָה אֲדֹנָי אֱלֹהִים דִּמְעָה מֵעַל כָּל פָּנִים וְחֶרְפַּת עַמּוֹ יָסִיר מֵעַל כָּל הָאָרֶץ כִּי יְיָ דִּבֵּר: [ישעיה כה, ח]

ח) לֹא יִהְיֶה מִשָּׁם עוֹד עוּל יָמִים וְזָקֵן אֲשֶׁר לֹא יְמַלֵּא אֶת יָמָיו כִּי הַנַּעַר בֶּן מֵאָה שָׁנָה יָמוּת וְהַחוֹטֶא בֶּן מֵאָה שָׁנָה יְקֻלָּל: [ישעיה סה, כ]

ט) וְעָמְדוּ זָרִים וְרָעוּ צֹאנְכֶם וּבְנֵי נֵכָר אִכָּרֵיכֶם וְכֹרְמֵיכֶם: [ישעיה סא, ה]

י) וְחָפְרָה הַלְּבָנָה וּבוֹשָׁה הַחַמָּה כִּי מָלַךְ יְיָ צְבָאוֹת בְּהַר צִיּוֹן וּבִירוּשָׁלַיִם וְנֶגֶד זְקֵנָיו כָּבוֹד: [ישעיה כד, כג]

כ) וְהָיָה אוֹר הַלְּבָנָה כְּאוֹר הַחַמָּה וְאוֹר הַחַמָּה יִהְיֶה שִׁבְעָתַיִם כְּאוֹר שִׁבְעַת הַיָּמִים בְּיוֹם חֲבֹשׁ יְיָ אֶת שֶׁבֶר עַמּוֹ וּמַחַץ מַכָּתוֹ יִרְפָּא: [ישעיה ל, כו]

ל) רְאוּ עַתָּה כִּי אֲנִי אֲנִי הוּא וְאֵין אֱלֹהִים עִמָּדִי אֲנִי אָמִית וַאֲחַיֶּה מָחַצְתִּי וַאֲנִי אֶרְפָּא וְאֵין מִיָּדִי מַצִּיל: [דברים לב, לט]

מ) אָז יָשִׁיר מֹשֶׁה וּבְנֵי יִשְׂרָאֵל אֶת הַשִּׁירָה הַזֹּאת לַייָ וַיֹּאמְרוּ לֵאמֹר אָשִׁירָה לַייָ כִּי גָאֹה גָּאָה סוּס וְרֹכְבוֹ רָמָה בַיָּם: [שמות טו, א] נ) אָז יִבְנֶה יְהוֹשֻׁעַ מִזְבֵּחַ לַייָ אֱלֹהֵי יִשְׂרָאֵל בְּהַר עֵיבָל: [יהושע ח, ל] ס) אָז יִבְנֶה שְׁלֹמֹה בָּמָה לִכְמוֹשׁ שִׁקֻּץ מוֹאָב בָּהָר אֲשֶׁר עַל פְּנֵי יְרוּשָׁלָיִם וּלְמֹלֶךְ שִׁקֻּץ בְּנֵי עַמּוֹן: [מלכים א' יא, ז] ע) אַשְׁרֵי יוֹשְׁבֵי בֵיתֶךָ עוֹד יְהַלְלוּךָ סֶּלָה: [תהלים פד, ה] פ) קוֹל צֹפַיִךְ נָשְׂאוּ קוֹל יַחְדָּו יְרַנֵּנוּ כִּי עַיִן בְּעַיִן יִרְאוּ בְּשׁוּב יְיָ צִיּוֹן: [ישעיה נב, ח] צ) תּוֹרָה צִוָּה לָנוּ מֹשֶׁה מוֹרָשָׁה קְהִלַּת יַעֲקֹב: [דברים לג, ד] ק) מֹנֵעַ בָּר יִקְּבֻהוּ לְאוֹם וּבְרָכָה לְרֹאשׁ מַשְׁבִּיר: [משלי יא, כו]

– On the one hand **it is written:** ***I [God] put to death and I make live,***[32] implying that God resurrects the dead exactly the way they were in their first life.[33] וּכְתִיב ,,מָחַצְתִּי וַאֲנִי אֶרְפָּא'' – **Yet** on the other hand **it is written** in the very same verse: ***I have wounded and I will heal,*** implying that the deformities of the resurrected *will* be healed. How are these two parts of the verse to be reconciled? Rava answers: אָמַר הַקָּדוֹשׁ בָּרוּךְ הוּא – In this verse, **the Holy One, Blessed is He, said:** מַה שֶּׁאֲנִי מֵמִית אֲנִי מְחַיֶּה – **What I put to death I bring to life,** וַהֲדַר מַה שֶּׁמָּחַצְתִּי וַאֲנִי אֶרְפָּא – **and then what I have wounded I will heal.**[34]

A Baraisa discusses the meaning of the verse just cited: תָּנוּ רַבָּנָן – **The Rabbis taught in a Baraisa:** ,,אֲנִי אָמִית וַאֲחַיֶּה'' – The verse states: *I PUT TO DEATH AND I MAKE LIVE.* יָכוֹל שֶׁתְּהֵא מִיתָה בְּאֶחָד וְחַיִּים בְּאֶחָד – IT WOULD BE POSSIBLE to interpret this to mean THAT DEATH IS inflicted UPON ONE person AND LIFE is bestowed UPON another ONE, כְּדֶרֶךְ שֶׁהָעוֹלָם נוֹהֵג – IN THE MANNER THAT THE WORLD presently FUNCTIONS.[35] תַּלְמוּד לוֹמַר ,,מָחַצְתִּי וַאֲנִי אֶרְפָּא'' – Therefore THE TORAH STATES: *I HAVE WOUNDED AND I WILL HEAL;* the juxtaposition teaches that מַה מְּחִיצָה וּרְפוּאָה בְּאֶחָד – JUST AS the WOUNDING AND HEALING mentioned here ARE IN reference to ONE and the same person (for only one who was wounded can be healed), אַף מִיתָה וְחַיִּים בְּאֶחָד – SO TOO DEATH AND LIFE mentioned here ARE IN reference to ONE and the same person, meaning that the dead will be resurrected. מִיכָּן תְּשׁוּבָה לָאוֹמְרִין אֵין תְּחִיַּית הַמֵּתִים מִן הַתּוֹרָה – FROM HERE we have A REFUTATION TO THOSE WHO SAY that THERE IS NO allusion to the RESURRECTION OF THE DEAD IN THE Written TORAH.

The Gemara presents a series of Scriptural allusions to the Resurrection of the Dead:

תַּנְיָא – **It was taught in a Baraisa:** אָמַר רַבִּי מֵאִיר – R' MEIR SAID: מִנַּיִין לִתְחִיַּית הַמֵּתִים מִן הַתּוֹרָה – WHERE do we find an allusion TO THE RESURRECTION OF THE DEAD IN THE Written TORAH? שֶׁנֶּאֱמַר ,,אָז יָשִׁיר־מֹשֶׁה וּבְנֵי יִשְׂרָאֵל אֶת־הַשִּׁירָה הַזֹּאת לַה' '' – FOR IT IS STATED: *THEN WILL MOSES AND THE CHILDREN OF ISRAEL SING THIS SONG TO HASHEM.*[36] ,,שָׁר'' לֹא נֶאֱמַר אֶלָּא ,,יָשִׁיר'' – *HE SANG* IS NOT STATED, BUT RATHER: *HE WILL SING.*[37] מִכָּאן לִתְחִיַּית הַמֵּתִים מִן הַתּוֹרָה – HERE we have an allusion TO THE RESURRECTION OF THE DEAD IN THE Written TORAH. כַּיּוֹצֵא בַּדָּבָר אַתָּה אוֹמֵר – SIMILARLY YOU MAY SAY regarding the verse: ,,אָז יִבְנֶה יְהוֹשֻׁעַ מִזְבֵּחַ לַה' '' – *THEN WILL JOSHUA BUILD AN ALTAR UNTO HASHEM,*[38] that ,,בָּנָה'' לֹא נֶאֱמַר אֶלָּא ,,יִבְנֶה'' – *HE BUILT* IS NOT STATED, BUT RATHER: *HE WILL BUILD.* מִכָּאן לִתְחִיַּית הַמֵּתִים מִן הַתּוֹרָה – HERE we have an allusion TO THE RESURRECTION OF THE DEAD IN THE Written TORAH.[39]

The Gemara objects:

אֶלָּא מֵעַתָּה – **But accordingly,** if Scripture's use of the future in such cases alludes to the time of the resurrection, then regarding the verse: ,,אָז יִבְנֶה שְׁלֹמֹה בָּמָה לִכְמוֹשׁ שִׁקֻּץ מוֹאָב'' – ***Then will Solomon build a high place for Kemosh, the abomination of Moab,***[40] הָכִי נַמִּי דִּיבְנֶה – would you say **also** that it means **that** the righteous **[Solomon] will build** a pagan altar when he is resurrected in the future? Such a notion is patently absurd! – ? –

The Gemara answers that the future tense is used in that verse for a different reason:

אֶלָּא מַעֲלֶה עָלָיו הַכָּתוּב כְּאִילּוּ בָּנָה – **Rather,** there the use of the future tense indicates that **Scripture regards him** ***as though*** **he built** it.[41]

Another Scriptural allusion to resurrection:

אָמַר רַבִּי יְהוֹשֻׁעַ בֶּן לֵוִי – **R' Yehoshua the son of Levi said:** מִנַּיִין לִתְחִיַּית הַמֵּתִים מִן הַתּוֹרָה – **Where** do we find an allusion **to the Resurrection of the Dead in the** Written **Torah?** שֶׁנֶּאֱמַר ,,אַשְׁרֵי יוֹשְׁבֵי בֵיתֶךָ עוֹד יְהַלְלוּךָ סֶּלָה'' – **For it is stated:**[42] ***Happy are those who dwell in Your house; yet again shall they praise You, selah.*** ,,הִילְלוּךָ'' לֹא נֶאֱמַר אֶלָּא ,,יְהַלְלוּךָ'' – **It does not say** ***they have praised You,*** **but rather** ***they will praise You*** in the future, i.e. after resurrection. מִכָּאן לִתְחִיַּית הַמֵּתִים מִן הַתּוֹרָה – **Here** we have an allusion **to the Resurrection of the Dead in the** Written **Torah.**

R' Yehoshua ben Levi further expounds this verse:

וְאָמַר רַבִּי יְהוֹשֻׁעַ בֶּן לֵוִי – **And R' Yehoshua ben Levi** also **said** in exposition of this verse: כָּל הָאוֹמֵר שִׁירָה בָּעוֹלָם הַזֶּה – **Whoever sings praise** to God **in this world** זוֹכֶה וְאוֹמְרָהּ לָעוֹלָם הַבָּא – **merits to sing it in the World to Come,** שֶׁנֶּאֱמַר ,,אַשְׁרֵי יוֹשְׁבֵי בֵיתֶךָ עוֹד יְהַלְלוּךָ סֶּלָה'' – **for it is stated:** ***Happy are those who dwell in Your house; yet again shall they praise You, selah,*** i.e. in the World to Come.[43]

Another Scriptural allusion to resurrection:

אָמַר רַבִּי חִיָּיא בַּר אַבָּא אָמַר רַבִּי יוֹחָנָן – **R' Chiya bar Abba said in the name of R' Yochanan:** מִנַּיִין לִתְחִיַּית הַמֵּתִים מִן הַתּוֹרָה – **Where** do we find an allusion **to the Resurrection of the Dead in the** Written **Torah?** שֶׁנֶּאֱמַר ,,קוֹל צֹפַיִךְ נָשְׂאוּ קוֹל יַחְדָּו יְרַנֵּנוּ וגו' '' –

NOTES

32. *Deuteronomy* 32:39.

33. That is, if they were injured or deformed in this life, that is the state to which they are restored upon resurrection (*Rashi*).

34. In other words, the deformed will be resurrected with their deformities and only afterwards will God heal them, as was taught above by Reish Lakish (*Rashi*).

35. In the present order of things, one person dies and another person is born (*Rashi*). The one who has died is not the same one that is brought to life. Accordingly, this verse would not refer to the Resurrection of the Dead.

36. *Exodus* 15:1, introducing the Song by the Sea. See next note.

37. Now, according to the simple meaning of the verse, the future יָשִׁיר, *he will sing,* is used because it refers to the *intent* to sing. That is, Moses and the Children of Israel decided to sing to God *in the very near future*; and indeed that decision was carried out, as stated further in that verse: וַיֹּאמְרוּ לֵאמֹר, *and they said the following* . . . The sages, however, see a deeper meaning in the use of the future tense here; namely, an allusion to the song that Moses and the Children of Israel will sing upon their resurrection (*Rashi* ad loc.).

38. *Joshua* 8:30. [The simple meaning is that Joshua *decided* to build the altar in the very near future, which he did (see preceding note, and *Rashi* cited there; cf. *Iyun Yaakov*).]

39. This verse is not in the Pentateuch but in the Prophets, yet the Baraisa refers to the proof as an allusion from "the Torah." This shows that the Gemara uses the term "Torah" as a reference to the entire Written Torah, i.e. all of Scripture (*Emes L'Yaakov*).

40. *I Kings* 11:7. This passage states how *at the time of Solomon's old age, his wives turned away his heart after other gods . . . Then did Solomon build a high place . . .* (see next note). Here, too, Scripture uses the future expression אָז יִבְנֶה שְׁלֹמֹה [literally: then will Solomon build].

41. Solomon did not worship other gods at all. But he did not do everything in his power to prevent his backsliding convert wives from doing so. Thus, when these wives built the altar to the pagan deity Kemosh, Scripture accounts it as if Solomon built it himself. The future tense *he will build* is used to indicate that he did not actually build it, but it is accounted as *if* he did (see *Rashi* to *I Kings* 11:7 and *Shabbos* 56b; cf. *Maharsha* here).

42. *Psalms* 84:5.

43. Though the verse does not state explicitly that those who dwelt in the House of God in this world sang praise, it is indicated in the end of the verse: *"yet again" shall they praise You*; that is, just as they praised you in this world, so will they praise You in the next (*Maharsha*).

בכורות נאות והושיב בו שני שומרים אחד חיגר ואחד סומא אמר לו חיגר לסומא בכורות נאות אני רואה בפרדס בא והרכיבני ונביאם לאכלם רכב חיגר על גבי סומא והביאום ואכלום לימים בא בעל פרדס אמר להן בכורות נאות היכן הן אמר לו חיגר כלום יש לי רגלים להלך בהן אמר לו סומא כלום יש לי עינים לראות מה עשה הרכיב חיגר על גבי סומא ודן אותם כאחד אף הקב"ה מביא נשמה וזורקה בגוף ודן אותם כאחד שנאמר (א) יקרא אל השמים מעל ואל הארץ לדין עמו יקרא אל השמים מעל זו נשמה ואל הארץ לדין עמו זה הגוף: א"ל אנטונינוס לרבי מפני מה חמה יוצאה במזרח ושוקעת במערב א"ל אי הוה איפכא נמי הכי הוה אמרת לי א"ל הכי קאמינא לך מפני מה שוקעת במערב א"ל כדי ליתן שלום לקונה שנאמר (ב) וצבא השמים לך משתחוים א"ל ותיתי עד פלגא דרקיע ותתן שלמא ותיעול משום פועלים ומשום עוברי דרכים וא"ל אנטונינוס לרבי נשמה מאימתי ניתנה באדם משעת פקידה או משעת יצירה א"ל משעת יצירה א"ל אפשר חתיכה של בשר עומדת שלשה ימים בלא מלח ואינה מסרחת אלא משעת פקידה אמר רבי דבר זה למדני אנטונינוס ומקרא מסייעו שנאמר (ג) ופקודתך שמרה רוחי ואמר ליה אנטונינוס לרבי מאימתי יצה"ר שולט באדם משעת יצירה או משעת יציאה א"ל משעת יצירה א"ל א"כ בועט במעי אמו ויוצא אלא משעת יציאה אמר רבי דבר זה למדני אנטונינוס ומקרא מסייעו שנאמר (ד) לפתח חטאת רובץ ר"ל רמי כתיב (ה) בם עור ופסח הרה ויולדת יחדו וכתיב (ו) אז ידלג כאיל פסח ותרון לשון אלם כי נבקעו במדבר מים ונחלים בערבה הא כיצד עומדין במומן ומתרפאין א עולא רמי כתיב (ז) בלע המות לנצח ומחה ה' דמעה מעל כל פנים וכתיב ב (ח) כי הנער בן מאה שנה ימות לא יהיה משם עוד עול ימים לא קשיא כאן בישראל כאן בעובדי כוכבים ועובדי כוכבים מאי בעו התם הנך דכתיב בהו (ט) ועמדו זרים ורעו צאנכם ובני נכר אכריכם וכורמיכם רב חסדא רמי כתיב (י) וחפרה הלבנה ובושה החמה כי מלך ה' צבאות וכתיב (כ) והיה אור הלבנה כאור החמה ואור החמה יהיה שבעתים כאור שבעת הימים לא קשיא כאן לימות המשיח כאן לעוה"ב ולשמואל ג דאמר א אין בין העוה"ז לימות המשיח אלא שיעבוד גליות בלבד לא קשיא כאן במחנה צדיקים כאן במחנה שכינה ד רבא רמי כתיב (ל) אני אמית ואחיה וכתיב (ל) מחצתי ואני ארפא אמר הקב"ה מה שאני ממית אני מחיה והדר מה שמחצתי ואני ארפא ת"ר אני אמית ואחיה יכול שתהא מיתה באחד וחיים באחד כדרך שהעולם נוהג ת"ל מחצתי ואני ארפא מה מחיצה ורפואה באחד אף מיתה וחיים באחד מיכן תשובה לאומרין אין תחיית המתים מן התורה תניא אמר רבי מאיר מניין לתחיית המתים מן התורה שנאמר (מ) אז ישיר משה ובני ישראל את השירה הזאת לה' שר לא נאמר אלא ישיר מכאן לתחיית המתים מן התורה כיוצא בדבר אתה אומר (נ) אז יבנה יהושע מזבח לה' בנה לא נאמר אלא יבנה מכאן לתחיית המתים מן התורה אלא מעתה (ס) אז יבנה שלמה במה לכמוש שקוץ מואב הכי נמי דיבנה ה אלא מעלה עליו הכתוב כאילו בנה א"ר יהושע בן לוי מניין לתחיית המתים מן התורה שנאמר (ע) אשרי יושבי ביתך עוד יהללוך סלה הללוך לא נאמר אלא יהללוך מכאן לתחיית המתים מן התורה וא"ר יהושע בן לוי כל האומר שירה בעוה"ז זוכה ואומרה לעולם הבא שנאמר אשרי יושבי ביתך עוד יהללוך סלה א"ר חייא בר אבא א"ר יוחנן מניין לתחיית המתים מן התורה שנאמר (פ) קול צופיך נשאו קול יחדו ירננו וגו' רננו לא נאמר אלא ירננו מכאן לתחיית המתים מן התורה וא"ר חייא בר אבא א"ר יוחנן עתידין כל הנביאים כולן אומרים שירה בקול אחד שנאמר קול צופיך נשאו קול יחדו ירננו אמר רב יהודה אמר רב כל המונע הלכה מפי תלמיד כאילו גוזלו מנחלת אבותיו שנאמר (צ) תורה צוה לנו משה מורשה קהילת יעקב מורשה היא לכל ישראל משעת ששת ימי בראשית אמר רב חנא בר ביזנא אמר רבי שמעון חסידא כל המונע הלכה מפי תלמיד אפילו עוברין שבמעי אמו מקללין אותו שנאמר (ק) מונע בר יקבוהו

רש"י

בכורות. תאני הבכורות: יקרא אל השמים מעל. כלומר יקרא הקב"ה לנשמה הבאה לו לתוך גופו של אדם (א) מאל השמים מעל ויקרא אף אל הגוף שבא מן הארץ: מפני מה שוקעת במערב. תסובב את כל העולם עד שתחזור למקום זריחתה למזרח ותשקע דאי הוה הכי לא הוה אמינא לך מפני מה שוקעת במזרח דנוהג העולם כך הוא ממקום שיצא שם נכנס: כדי ליתן שלום לקונה. להקב"ה שהשכינה במערב וכיון שמגעת עד מערב הולכת ומשתחוה לפני הקב"ה שבראה ולכך שוקעת ונכנסת כפופה לפני הקב"ה: ותיתי עד פלגא דרקיעא. דאם לכך מתכוונת למה הולכת בתוך המערב תבא עד אמצעו של רקיע ותשקע לשם ומשם תשתחוה כלפי מערב שכן דרך ב"א שמשתחוה ברחוק לפני המלך ואינו מתקרב כל כך: משום פועלים. דאילו כן היה מחשיך פתאום שכשחמה באמצע הרקיע מאירה ביותר וסבורים שעדיין יש שהות ביום והיו פועלין שוהין במלאכתן עד שתחשיכה ועוברי דרכים נמי לא היו יודעין מתי יחשוך לבקש להם בית לינה ולכך שוקעת במערב שכשהולכת ומשפלת והולכת וכלה אורה יודעין שמגיע שעת חשיכה: משעת יצירה. שנקרם כולו בבשר וגידין ועצמות: פקידה. משעה שהמלאך פוקד הטיפה ומביאה לפני המקום מה תהא עליה כדאמרינן בפרק כל היד במסכת נדה (דף טז:) מיד נזרקה בו נשמה וחיות: אמר ליה. רבי משעת יצירה: ואמר לו. אנטונינוס וכי אפשר לחתיכה שתתקיים אפילו ג' ימים בלא מלח שאינה מסרחת וה"נ אילו לא היתה נשמה נתונה עד שעת יצירה היאך תתקיים הטיפה שלא תסריח במעיה וכיון שטיפה מסרחת שוב אינה מולדת: למדני אנטונינוס. מדבריו למדתי: ופקודתך שמרה רוחי. משעת פקידה נשמר רוחי: משעת יציאה.

כשיוצא ממעי אמו או משעת יצירה: א"ל. רבי משעת יצירה: אמר לו אנטונינוס א"כ בועט במעי אמו ויוצא. אלא משעת יציאתה: בם עור ופסח. שחיין עם מומן: וכתיב אז ידלג כאיל פסח. דמשמע שמתרפאין: עומדין במומן. ואח"כ מתרפאין: בלע המות לנצח. דלעתיד לבא מאחר שחיין שוב אינן מתין: כי הנער. כלומר כשימות אדם לעתיד ומת בן מאה שנה יאמרו נער הוא מת כי הנער בן מאה שנה ימות אלמא מתין: וחפרה הלבנה ובושה החמה. משמע שיהא אורם כהה וכתיב והיתה אור הלבנה כאור החמה: כאן לימות המשיח. כשיכלה השיעבוד והיתה אור הלבנה כאור החמה ולעתיד לבא וחפרה הלבנה ובושה החמה מרוב נגהם של צדיקים: ולשמואל דאמר. בדוכתא אחריתי אין בין העולם הזה וכו'. אידי ואידי לעוה"ב: אלא כאן במחנה שכינה. וחפרה מזיו השכינה: כאן במחנה צדיקים. כאן במחנה רשעים לא גרסינן: כתיב אני אמית ואחיה. דמשמע כשם שאני אמית את האדם כך אני מחייהו כשמת בעל מום עומד וחי בעל מום: וכתיב מחצתי ואני ארפא. שכשהוא מחיה מרפא את המחץ ועומד שלם: והדר מה שמחצתי. שלאחר כן מתרפא וכדלעיל עומדין במומן ומתרפאין: מיתה באחד וחיים באחד. וה"ק אני ממית אדם זה ומחיה אדם אחר: כדרך שהעולם נוהג. שזה מת וזה נולד: מה מחץ ורפוי באחד. ואין רפואה אלא במקום מחץ: ישיר. משמע לעתיד: נשאו קול יחדיו. היינו קול אחד: המונע הלכה. מללמדו: משעת ששת ימי בראשית. דכתיב בראשית ברא בשביל התורה שהיא ראשית וישראל נקראו (ו) ראשית תבואתה שעתידין להנחיל' ברא אלהים את השמים וגו': בר. תורה: יקבוהו

ה א מיי' פי"ב מהל' מלכים הל' ב' ופ"ט מהל' תשובה הלכה ב:

ליקוטי רש"י

בכורות. תאני הבכרות, שבישלו כל צרכן בתחלת בכורי תאנים שהם חביבות על מוצאיהם בראשיתם [ירמיה כד, ב]. בכורות. תאנים חשובות הממהרות להתבשל [עירובין כא:]. שמרה רוחי. בבטן אמי [איוב י, יב]. לפתח חטאת רובץ. משעה שנולד הולד הוא נתון בו [קהלת ד, יג]. בלע המות. יכסנו ויעלימנו עולמי' מישראל [ישעיה כה, ח]. יבולע מלאך המות שלא ישלוט. עול ימים. נער כמו עולל (איכה ב) עול ימים קטן בשנים [שם סה, כ]. בישראל. כתיב ובלע המות וגו'. אכריכם. מנהיגי המחרישה [שם סא, ה]. ובושה החמה שלא תאיר [פסחים סח.]. יהיה שבעתים כאור שבעת הימים. שבעתים שבע שבעיות כאור של שבעת הימים הרי ארבעים ותשע שבעיות העולים לשלש מאות וארבעים ושלשה [ישעיה ל, כו]. שבעתים הן ארבעים ותשע וכתיב כאור שבעת הימים ארבעים ותשע כאור שבעת ימים של עכשיו נמצא עודף על אור של עכשיו שלש מאות וארבעים ושלשה. לימות המשיח. יהיה אור הלבנה כאור החמה. לעולם הבא. וחפרה הלבנה ובושה החמה שלא יהא בעולם אלא זיו זוהר ומראה שכינה. ולשמואל. דאמר ימות המשיח אין משתנין משל עכשיו מה הוא מקיים והיה אור הלבנה כאור החמה. מה שאני ממית אני מחיה והדר מה שמחצתי ואני ארפא. שכדרך שהן מתים חגרים סומים אלמים כך הן חיין במומן ואחר כך מתרפאים כדכתיב אז ידלג כאיל פסח (ישעיה לה). מיתה באחד וחיים באחד. אני ממית את המתים ואני מחיה וזן את החיים. ת"ל מחצתי ואני ארפא. הא אתא לאשמועינן דלא תימא אמית ואחיה לאו דמתים חיים קאמר אלא אני אמית את המתים ואני מחיה וזן את החיים ובורא את הנולדים להכי כתיב בתריה מחצתי ואני ארפא כשם שמה שמחצתי אני ארפא דאין רפואה אלא במוכה כך אותו עצמו שאני ממית אני מחיה [פסחים שם]. אז ישיר משה. אז כשראה הנס עלה בלבו שישיר שירה וכן (יהושע י, יב) אז ידבר יהושע וכן (מ"א ז, ח) ובית יעשה לבת פרעה חשב בלבו שיעשה לה אף כאן ישיר אמר לו לבו שישיר וכן עשה ויאמרו לאמר אשירה לה' וכן ביהושע כשראה הנס אמר לו לבו שידבר וכן עשה (יהושע י, יב) ויאמר לעיני ישראל וכן שירת הבאר שפתח בה (במדבר כא, יז) אז ישיר ישראל פירש אחריו עלי באר ענו לה (מ"א יא, ז) אז יבנה שלמה במה פירשו בו חכמי ישראל שבקש לבנות ולא בנה למדנו שהיו"ד על שם המחשבה נאמרה זהו ליישב פשוטו אבל מדרשו אמרו רבותינו זכרונם לברכה מכאן רמז לתחיית המתים מן התורה וכן בכולן חוץ משל שלמה שפירשוהו בקש לבנות ולא בנה ואין לומר וליישב הלשון הזה כשאר דברים הנכתבים בלשון עתיד והן מיד כגון (איוב א, ה) ככה יעשה איוב (במדבר ט, כג) על פי ה' יחנו (שם כ) ויש אשר יהיה הענן לפי שהן דבר ההוה תמיד ונופל בו בין לשון עתיד בין לשון עבר אבל זה שלא היה אלא לשעה אינו יכול ליישבו בלשון הזה [שמות טו, א ועי' במהרש"א בח"א]. אז יבנה שלמה במה. רבותינו אמרו מתוך שלא מיחה בנשיו נקראת על שמו [מ"א יא, ז]. צופיך. נביאי הדורות [מגילה ב: ע"ש בתוס']. תורה. אשר צוה לנו משה מורשה היא לקהלת יעקב אחזנוה ולא נעזבנה [דברים לג, ד]. מונע בר. מלמד תורה [משלי יא, כו].

מסורת הש"ס

א) פסחים סח., ב) [בפסוק כתיב מהופך ועי' מ"א שמישבון], ג) שבת סג. ודף קנא. ברכות לד: [פסחים סח: לקמן צט.], ד) [פסחים סח. ע"ש], ה) [שבת נו: ועי' תוס' שם ד"ה אלא מעתה], ו) [ירמיה ב].

הגהות הב"ח

(א) רש"י ד"ה יקרא וכו' גופו של אדם מעל השמים ממעל ויקרא:

תורה אור השלם

א) יִקְרָא אֶל הַשָּׁמַיִם מֵעָל וְאֶל הָאָרֶץ לָדִין עַמּוֹ: [תהלים נ, ד]

ב) אַתָּה הוּא יְיָ לְבַדֶּךָ אַתָּה עָשִׂיתָ אֶת הַשָּׁמַיִם שְׁמֵי הַשָּׁמַיִם וְכָל צְבָאָם הָאָרֶץ וְכָל אֲשֶׁר עָלֶיהָ הַיַּמִּים וְכָל אֲשֶׁר בָּהֶם וְאַתָּה מְחַיֶּה אֶת כֻּלָּם וּצְבָא הַשָּׁמַיִם לְךָ מִשְׁתַּחֲוִים: [נחמיה ט, ו]

ג) חַיִּים וָחֶסֶד עָשִׂיתָ עִמָּדִי וּפְקֻדָּתְךָ שָׁמְרָה רוּחִי: [איוב י, יב]

ד) הֲלוֹא אִם תֵּיטִיב שְׂאֵת וְאִם לֹא תֵיטִיב לַפֶּתַח חַטָּאת רֹבֵץ וְאֵלֶיךָ תְּשׁוּקָתוֹ וְאַתָּה תִּמְשָׁל בּוֹ: [בראשית ד, ז]

ה) הִנְנִי מֵבִיא אוֹתָם מֵאֶרֶץ צָפוֹן וְקִבַּצְתִּים מִיַּרְכְּתֵי אָרֶץ בָּם עִוֵּר וּפִסֵּחַ הָרָה וְיֹלֶדֶת יַחְדָּו קָהָל גָּדוֹל יָשׁוּבוּ הֵנָּה: [ירמיה לא, ז]

ו) אָז יְדַלֵּג כָּאַיָּל פִּסֵּחַ וְתָרֹן לְשׁוֹן אִלֵּם כִּי נִבְקְעוּ בַמִּדְבָּר מַיִם וּנְחָלִים בָּעֲרָבָה: [ישעיה לה, ו]

ז) בִּלַּע הַמָּוֶת לָנֶצַח וּמָחָה אֲדֹנָי אֱלֹהִים דִּמְעָה מֵעַל כָּל פָּנִים וְחֶרְפַּת עַמּוֹ יָסִיר מֵעַל כָּל הָאָרֶץ כִּי יְיָ דִּבֵּר: [ישעיה כה, ח]

ח) לֹא יִהְיֶה מִשָּׁם עוֹד עוּל יָמִים וְזָקֵן אֲשֶׁר לֹא יְמַלֵּא אֶת יָמָיו כִּי הַנַּעַר בֶּן מֵאָה שָׁנָה יָמוּת וְהַחוֹטֶא בֶּן מֵאָה שָׁנָה יְקֻלָּל: [ישעיה סה, כ]

ט) וְעָמְדוּ זָרִים וְרָעוּ צֹאנְכֶם וּבְנֵי נֵכָר אִכָּרֵיכֶם וְכֹרְמֵיכֶם: [ישעיה סא, ה]

י) וְחָפְרָה הַלְּבָנָה וּבוֹשָׁה הַחַמָּה כִּי מָלַךְ יְיָ צְבָאוֹת בְּהַר צִיּוֹן וּבִירוּשָׁלַיִם וְנֶגֶד זְקֵנָיו כָּבוֹד: [ישעיה כד, כג]

כ) וְהָיָה אוֹר הַלְּבָנָה כְּאוֹר הַחַמָּה וְאוֹר הַחַמָּה יִהְיֶה שִׁבְעָתַיִם כְּאוֹר שִׁבְעַת הַיָּמִים בְּיוֹם חֲבֹשׁ יְיָ אֶת שֶׁבֶר עַמּוֹ וּמַחַץ מַכָּתוֹ יִרְפָּא: [ישעיה ל, כו]

ל) רְאוּ עַתָּה כִּי אֲנִי אֲנִי הוּא וְאֵין אֱלֹהִים עִמָּדִי אֲנִי אָמִית וַאֲחַיֶּה מָחַצְתִּי וַאֲנִי אֶרְפָּא וְאֵין מִיָּדִי מַצִּיל: [דברים לב, לט]

מ) אָז יָשִׁיר מֹשֶׁה וּבְנֵי יִשְׂרָאֵל אֶת הַשִּׁירָה הַזֹּאת לַייָ וַיֹּאמְרוּ לֵאמֹר אָשִׁירָה לַייָ כִּי גָאֹה גָּאָה סוּס וְרֹכְבוֹ רָמָה בַיָּם: [שמות טו, א]

נ) אָז יִבְנֶה יְהוֹשֻׁעַ מִזְבֵּחַ לַייָ אֱלֹהֵי יִשְׂרָאֵל בְּהַר עֵיבָל: [יהושע ח, ל]

ס) אָז יִבְנֶה שְׁלֹמֹה בָּמָה לִכְמוֹשׁ שִׁקֻּץ מוֹאָב בָּהָר אֲשֶׁר עַל פְּנֵי יְרוּשָׁלָיִם וּלְמֹלֶךְ שִׁקֻּץ בְּנֵי עַמּוֹן: [מלכים א' יא, ז]

ע) אַשְׁרֵי יוֹשְׁבֵי בֵיתֶךָ עוֹד יְהַלְלוּךָ סֶּלָה: [תהלים פד, ה]

פ) קוֹל צֹפַיִךְ נָשְׂאוּ קוֹל יַחְדָּו יְרַנֵּנוּ כִּי עַיִן בְּעַיִן יִרְאוּ בְּשׁוּב יְיָ צִיּוֹן: [ישעיה נב, ח]

צ) תּוֹרָה צִוָּה לָנוּ מֹשֶׁה מוֹרָשָׁה קְהִלַּת יַעֲקֹב: [דברים לג, ד]

ק) מֹנֵעַ בָּר יִקְּבֻהוּ לְאוֹם וּבְרָכָה לְרֹאשׁ מַשְׁבִּיר: [משלי יא, כו]

For it is stated: ***The voice of your seers – they have shouted! In unison shall they sing!*** *For eye to eye shall they see the return of* H*ASHEM* *to Zion.*[44] ,,יְרַנֵּנוּ" לֹא נֶאֱמַר אֶלָּא ,,רִינְּנוּ" – **It is not stated** ***they sang,*** **but rather** ***they shall sing*** – in the future. מִכָּאן לִתְחִיַּית הַמֵּתִים מִן הַתּוֹרָה – **Here** we have an allusion **to the Resurrection of the Dead in the** Written **Torah.**[45]

R' Chiya bar Abba further expounds this verse:

וְאָמַר רַבִּי חִיָּיא בַּר אַבָּא אָמַר רַבִּי יוֹחָנָן – **And R' Chiya bar Abba** also **said in the name of R' Yochanan:** עֲתִידִין כָּל הַנְּבִיאִים כּוּלָּן אוֹמְרִים שִׁירָה בְּקוֹל אֶחָד – **All the prophets – every one of them – are destined to sing praise in one voice,** שֶׁנֶּאֱמַר ,,קוֹל צֹפַיִךְ נָשְׂאוּ קוֹל יַחְדָּו יְרַנֵּנוּ" – **as it is stated:** ***The voice of your seers – they have shouted! In unison shall they sing.***

The Gemara digresses momentarily to a different topic:[46]

אָמַר רַב יְהוּדָה אָמַר רַב – **Rav Yehudah said in the name of Rav:** כָּל הַמּוֹנֵעַ הֲלָכָה מִפִּי תַלְמִיד – **Whoever withholds** the teaching of **the law from the mouth of a student,** i.e. whoever neglects to teach Torah to a student, כְּאִילּוּ גּוֹזְלוֹ מִנַּחֲלַת אֲבוֹתָיו – **is as if he robs [the student] of his ancestral heritage.** שֶׁנֶּאֱמַר ,,תּוֹרָה צִוָּה־לָנוּ מֹשֶׁה מוֹרָשָׁה קְהִלַּת יַעֲקֹב" – **For it is stated:**[47] ***The Torah that Moses commanded us is the heritage of the congregation of Jacob.*** This means: מוֹרָשָׁה הִיא לְכָל יִשְׂרָאֵל – **It is a heritage to all of Israel** מִשֵּׁשֶׁת יְמֵי בְרֵאשִׁית – **since the six days of Creation.**[48]

A related teaching:

אָמַר רַב חָנָא בַּר בִּיזְנָא אָמַר רַבִּי שִׁמְעוֹן חֲסִידָא – **Rav Chana bar Bizna said in the name of R' Shimon Chasida:** כָּל הַמּוֹנֵעַ הֲלָכָה מִפִּי תַלְמִיד – **Whoever withholds** the teaching of **the law from a student** is so reprehensible that אֲפִילּוּ עוּבָּרִין שֶׁבִּמְעֵי אִמּוֹ מְקַלְּלִין אוֹתוֹ – **even fetuses in the mother's womb curse him!**[49] שֶׁנֶּאֱמַר ,,מֹנֵעַ בָּר – **For it is stated:** ***He who withholds grain*** (*"bar"*)

NOTES

44. *Isaiah* 52:8. [*Rashi* (ad loc.) renders צֹפַיִךְ as *your lookouts* – those stationed atop the city walls to alert the inhabitants about those who approach. They will be the first to espy the approaching liberation and they will shout the joyful news to the people below. The Gemara below, however, takes צֹפַיִךְ in the sense of *your seers* or *prophets,* and this is also the way it is rendered by *Radak* ad loc.]

45. The prophets who *have shouted* (i.e. who prophesied about the ultimate redemption, but who did not live to see the fulfilment of their prophecies) will *sing in unison when they* are resurrected and *see with their very own eyes the return of* H*ASHEM* *to Zion* (see *Maharsha*).

46. This topic will include the statement below (92a) that "whoever teaches Torah in this world merits to teach it in the World to Come," which parallels the analogous teaching cited above regarding one who sings praise in this world (see *Rashash*; see also *Teshuvos Noda BiYehudah, Yoreh Deah* II:190).

47. *Deuteronomy* 33:4.

48. Torah introduces Creation with the expression בְּרֵאשִׁית [literally: in the beginning], which the sages expound to mean: Because of the Torah, which is called "*the beginning* of His way" (*Proverbs* 8:22); and because of Israel, who is called "*the beginning* of His produce" (*Jeremiah* 2:3). That is, for the sake of Israel, which is destined to inherit the Torah, God created heaven and earth (*Rashi*).

Maharsha explains as follows: One must not withhold the study of Torah from *the mouth of* a student. That is, just as R' Pareida taught his slow student the same lesson *four hundred times* until the student had mastered it (*Eruvin* 54b), so too must a teacher teach every student until each is *fluent* in it. The teacher who claims that the student is unfit and unteachable robs that student of his ancestral heritage! For the Torah is the heritage of every Jew from the time of Creation – that is, each Jew by his very nature is suited to the study of Torah!

49. I.e. he is cursed even by fetuses, who are presently not affected by his withholding of Torah, as they are taught the entire Torah by the angels [see *Niddah* 30b] (*Toras Chaim*; *Yavetz*).

„יִקְּבֻהוּ לְאוֹם" – ***the nation*** *("le'om")* ***will curse him.***[1] וְאֵין לְאוֹם אֶלָּא עוּבָּרִין – **And** the word ***le'om*** here **means nothing other than "fetuses,"** שֶׁנֶּאֱמַר „וּלְאֹם מִלְאֹם יֶאֱמָץ" – **as it is stated** in another verse: ***And one nation*** *("le'om")* ***will be stronger than the other nation*** *("le'om").*[2] וְאֵין קָבָה אֶלָּא קְלָלָה – **And** ***kavo,*** which is the root of *yikevuhu,* **means nothing other than "curse,"** שֶׁנֶּאֱמַר „מָה אֶקֹּב לֹא קַבֹּה אֵל" – **as it is stated** in another verse: ***How can I curse*** *("ekov")*? ***God has not cursed,*** etc.[3] וְאֵין בַּר אֶלָּא תּוֹרָה – **And** the word ***bar*** here **means nothing other than Torah,** שֶׁנֶּאֱמַר „נַשְּׁקוּ־בַר פֶּן־יֶאֱנַף" – **as it is stated** in another verse: ***Arm yourselves with purity [of heart]*** *("bar")* ***lest He grow wrathful.***[4] עוּלָּא בַּר יִשְׁמָעֵאל אוֹמֵר – **Ulla bar Yishmael** expounds the verse further and **says:** מְנַקְּבִין אוֹתוֹ כִּכְבָרָה – If one withholds teaching of Torah from a student, **he is pierced** full of holes **like a sieve.**[5] כְּתִיב הָכָא „יִקְּבֻהוּ לְאוֹם" – For **it is written here,** in the verse cited above, that if one withholds Torah from a student, ***the nation "yikevuhu,"*** וּכְתִיב הָתָם „וַיִּקֹּב חֹר בְּדַלְתּוֹ" – **and it is written there:**[6] ***And he pierced*** *("vayikov")* ***a hole in its door.*** Just as the word *vayikov* refers to "piercing," so too does the similar word *yikevuhu* refer to "piercing." וְאָמַר אַבַּיֵי – **And Abaye said:** כִּי אוּכְלָא דְקַצְרֵי – He is pierced **like a launderer's sprinkler.**[7]

The Gemara continues:

וְאִם לִמְּדוֹ מַה שְּׂכָרוֹ – **But if [the teacher]** ***does*** **teach [his student]** Torah, **what is [the teacher's] reward?** אָמַר רָבָא אָמַר רַב שֵׁשֶׁת – **Rava said in the name of Rav Sheishess:** זוֹכֶה לִבְרָכוֹת כְּיוֹסֵף – **He merits blessings like Joseph.** שֶׁנֶּאֱמַר „וּבְרָכָה לְרֹאשׁ מַשְׁבִּיר" – **For it is stated** at the end of the verse: ***But a blessing upon the head of the provider.***[8] וְאֵין מַשְׁבִּיר אֶלָּא יוֹסֵף – **And "the provider" is none other than Joseph,** שֶׁנֶּאֱמַר „וְיוֹסֵף הוּא [הַשַּׁלִּיט עַל־הָאָרֶץ הוּא] הַמַּשְׁבִּיר לְכָל־עַם הָאָרֶץ" – **as it is stated:**[9] ***And Joseph was the viceroy over the land, he was "the provider" to all the populace.***

The Gemara continues this theme:

אָמַר רַב שֵׁשֶׁת – **Rav Sheishess said:** כָּל הַמְלַמֵּד תּוֹרָה בָּעוֹלָם הַזֶּה – **Whoever teaches Torah in this world** זוֹכֶה וּמְלַמְּדָהּ לָעוֹלָם הַבָּא – **merits to teach it in the World to Come,** שֶׁנֶּאֱמַר „וּמַרְוֶה גַּם־הוּא יוֹרֶא" – **as it is stated:** ***And he who sates [others] – he too shall be sated.***[10]

The Gemara resumes its original discussion concerning Scriptural allusions to the Resurrection of the Dead:

אָמַר רָבָא – **Rava said:** מִנַּיִן לִתְחִיַּית הַמֵּתִים מִן הַתּוֹרָה – **Where** do we find an allusion **to the Resurrection of the Dead in the** Written **Torah?** שֶׁנֶּאֱמַר „יְחִי רְאוּבֵן וְאַל־יָמֹת" – **For it is stated:** ***May Reuben live and not die.***[11] This means: „יְחִי רְאוּבֵן" בָּעוֹלָם הַזֶּה – ***May Reuben live*** **in this world,** „וְאַל־יָמֹת" לָעוֹלָם הַבָּא – ***and not die*** **in the World to Come.**[12] Thus, this verse alludes to the Resurrection of the Dead.

Ravina provides another source:

רָבִינָא אָמַר מֵהָכָא – **Ravina says** that we know the tenet of Resurrection of the Dead **from the following** verse: „וְרַבִּים מִיְּשֵׁנֵי אַדְמַת־עָפָר יָקִיצוּ אֵלֶּה לְחַיֵּי עוֹלָם וְאֵלֶּה לַחֲרָפוֹת לְדִרְאוֹן עוֹלָם" – ***And many of those who sleep in the dusty earth shall awaken; these for everlasting life, and these for shame – for everlasting abhorrence.***[13]

Rav Ashi provides another source:

רַב אַשִׁי אָמַר מֵהָכָא – **Rav Ashi says** that we know the tenet of Resurrection of the Dead **from the following** verse: „וְאַתָּה לֵךְ לַקֵּץ וְתָנוּחַ וְתַעֲמֹד לְגֹרָלְךָ לְקֵץ הַיָּמִין" – ***And as for you [Daniel], go to the end; and you will repose, and you will arise to your lot at the end of days.***[14]

The Gemara now quotes a series of R' Elazar's teachings:[15]

אָמַר רַבִּי אֶלְעָזָר – **R' Elazar said:** כָּל פַּרְנָס שֶׁמַּנְהִיג אֶת הַצִּבּוּר בְּנַחַת – **Any community leader who leads the community with gentleness**[16] זוֹכֶה וּמַנְהִיגָם לָעוֹלָם הַבָּא – **merits to lead them in**

NOTES

1. *Proverbs* 11:26. The Gemara will now show how "fetuses," "cursing," and "Torah" are contained in this verse.

2. *Genesis* 25:23. Rebecca was expecting twins, who struggled within her. She inquired of God, Who informed her that she was carrying two nations that would contend with each other for supremacy. At this point, each *le'om* [nation] was but a fetus; hence the connection of the word *le'om* to "fetus."

3. *Numbers* 23:8. This was stated by the gentile soothsayer Bilam, who had been hired by Balak, king of Moab, to curse the Israelites in the Wilderness. His designs thwarted by God, Bilam proclaimed that he could not curse the Israelites, whom God had not cursed. See also below, 105b.

4. *Psalms* 2:12. "Purity of heart" is adherence to the Torah.

5. Since he withholds his Torah from others, he will forget the Torah knowledge he has amassed, like the grain that runs out of a sieve leaving only the chaff (*Maharsha* and *Toras Chaim*).

6. *II Kings* 12:10.

7. A perforated metal vessel used by launderers to sprinkle water on garments (*Rashi*; cf. *Aruch*). Abaye employs the simile of a sprinkler rather than a sieve, because Torah is likened to water (*Maharsha*; cf. *Maharal*).

8. *Proverbs* 11:26. The verse contrasts the "withholder of grain," who is cursed, with "the provider," who is blessed (see *Maharsha*).

9. *Genesis* 42:6.

10. *Proverbs* 11:25, which precedes the verse cited above. [Rav Sheishess expounds the word יוֹרֶא, *he shall be sated,* to mean יוֹרֶה, *he shall teach.*] Thus, *he who sates* others with Torah in this world will teach it in the World to Come (*Rashi*). Alternatively, the word מַרְוֶה, too, is expounded as deriving from the root ירה and meaning *he who teaches* (ibid.).

11. *Deuteronomy* 33:6. Before his death, Moses blessed each tribe individually. The verse cited here was part of his blessing to the tribe of Reuben, and was stated to indicate that Reuben would not be punished further for the incident of Bilhah [see *Genesis* 35:22] (*Rashi* to *Deuteronomy* 33:6).

12. [The verse seems redundant – "*May Reuben live*" and "*not die.*" Therefore,] the Gemara expounds: *May Reuben live* in this world – i.e. [each member of his tribe] will live out his natural life, or [at any rate] will not die in battle [or, as *Ramban* to *Deuteronomy* loc. cit. explains the simple sense of the verse: Reuben's tribe will forever be one of the twelve tribes]. *And not die* in the World to Come – i.e. Reuben [himself] will be resurrected and live in the World to Come, despite his actions in the incident of Bilhah (see *Be'er Sheva*) for God has forgiven that sin (*Maharsha*).

13. *Daniel* 12:2. *Rambam* (cited by *Abarbanel* in *Mayenei HaYeshuah* 11:9) considers this verse to be the most explicit of any in Scripture about the tenet of Resurrection of the Dead (see *Maamar Techiyas HaMeisim* §8), and one that does not admit a figurative explanation (*Maamar Techiyas HaMeisim* §4).

14. Ibid. v. 13. *Go to the end* means: You will pass from this world to your eternal reward in the Afterlife (see *Rashi* to *Daniel* ad loc.). The angel indicates to Daniel that he will die before the culmination of the events foretold, but that he will be resurrected at the end of days (*Rashi*).

Rashi to *Daniel* (loc. cit.) insists on rendering לְקֵץ הַיָּמִין as *to the end of days,* pointing to the Masoretic note listing the word הַיָּמִין here as one of the words that should end with a *mem* but end instead with a *nun. Rashi* to our Gemara, however, presents the interpretation (see *Midrash Shocher Tov* 137:7) of הַיָּמִין as *the right hand.* For from the time the Second Temple was destroyed, God *withdrew His right hand behind Him in the presence of the enemy* (*Lamentations* 2:3), i.e. He did not fight on behalf of His children, the people of Israel, against their enemies (*Rashi* ad loc.). *At the end of the right hand* – at the time God has designated to return His right hand to His front (i.e. to redeem Israel and destroy her enemies) – Daniel will be resurrected and arise to his lot.

15. [Apparently, they are recorded here because the first of them parallels the teaching of Rav Sheishess that was quoted tangentially above.]

16. For [as stated in *Ecclesiastes* 9:17] *the words of the wise [spoken] gently are accepted* (*Iyun Yaakov*).

יקבוהו לאום ואין [א] לאום אלא עוברין שנאמר
א) ולאום מלאום יאמץ ואין קבה אלא קללה
שנאמר ב) מה אקב לא קבה אל ואין בר אלא
תורה שנאמר ג) נשקו בר פן יאנף עולא בר
ישמעאל אומר מנקבין אותו ככברה כתיב
הכא ד) יקבוהו לאום וכתיב התם ה) ויקב חור
בדלתו ואמר אביי כי [ב] אוכלא דקצרי ואם
למדו מה שכרו אמר רבא אמר רב ששת
זוכה לברכות כיוסף שנאמר ד) וברכה לראש
משביר ואין משביר אלא יוסף שנאמר ו) ויוסף
הוא [השליט על הארץ הוא] המשביר לכל
עם הארץ אמר רב ששת כל המלמד תורה
בעוה"ז זוכה ומלמדה לעולם הבא שנאמר
ז) ומרוה גם הוא [ג] יורה אמר רבא מניין לתחיית
המתים מן התורה שנאמר ח) יחי ראובן ואל
ימות יחי ראובן בעולם הזה ואל ימות לעולם
הבא רבינא אמר מהכא ט) ורבים מישני
אדמת עפר יקיצו אלה לחיי עולם ואלה
לחרפות לדראון עולם רב אשי אמר מהכא
י) ואתה לך [לקץ] ותנוח ותעמוד לגורלך לקץ
הימין אמר רבי אלעזר כל פרנס שמנהיג את
הצבור בנחת זוכה ומנהיגם לעוה"ב שנאמר
יא) כי מרחמם ינהגם ועל מבועי מים ינהלם
[ד] וא"ר אלעזר גדולה דעה שניתנה בין שתי
אותיות שנאמר יב) כי אל דעות ה' וא"ר
אלעזר גדול מקדש שניתן בין שתי אותיות
שנאמר יג) פעלת ה' מקדש ה' כוננו ידיך
מתקיף לה רב אדא [ה] קרחינאה אלא מעתה
גדולה נקמה שניתנה בין שתי אותיות
דכתיב יד) אל נקמות ה' אל נקמות הופיע
אמר ליה למילתיה הכי נמי כדעולא דאמר
עולא שתי הופעיות הללו למה אחת
למדת טובה ואחת למדת פורענות ואמר ר' אלעזר כל אדם שיש בו
דעה כאילו נבנה בית המקדש בימיו שזה ניתן בין שתי אותיות וזה ניתן
בין שתי אותיות ואמר ר' אלעזר כל אדם שיש בו דעה לסוף מתעשר שנאמר טו) ובדעת חדרים ימלאו
כל הון יקר ונעים ואמר ר' אלעזר כל אדם שאין בו דעה אסור לרחם עליו שנאמר טז) כי לא עם בינות
הוא על כן לא ירחמנו עושהו ויוצרו לא יחוננו וא"ר אלעזר כל הנותן פיתו למי שאין בו דעה יסורין
באין עליו שנאמר יז) לחמך ישימו מזור תחתיך אין תבונה בו ואין מזור אלא יסורין שנאמר יח) וירא אפרים
את חליו ויהודה את מזורו ואמר ר' אלעזר כל אדם שאין בו דעה לסוף גולה שנאמר יט) לכן גלה עמי מבלי
דעת ואמר ר"א [ו] [א] כל בית שאין דברי תורה נשמעים בו בלילה אש אוכלתו שנאמר כ) כל חשך טמון לצפוניו
תאכלהו אש לא נופח ירע שריד באהלו [ז] אין שריד אלא ת"ח שנאמר כא) ובשרידים אשר ה' קורא ואמר
ר' אלעזר כל שאינו מהנה תלמידי חכמים מנכסיו אינו רואה סימן ברכה לעולם שנאמר כב) אין שריד
לאכלו על כן לא יחיל טובו אין שריד אלא תלמידי חכמים שנאמר ובשרידים אשר ה' קורא ואמר
רבי אלעזר [ב] כל שאינו משייר פת על שלחנו אינו רואה סימן ברכה לעולם שנאמר אין שריד לאכלו
על כן לא יחיל טובו והאמר רבי אלעזר כל המשייר פתיתים על שלחנו כאילו עובד ע"ז שנאמר
כג) העורכים לגד שלחן והממלאים למני ממסך לא קשיא [ג] הא דאיכא שלימה בהדיה הא דליכא שלימה
בהדיה ואמר רבי אלעזר [ז] כל המחליף בדבורו כאילו עובד ע"ז כתיב הכא כד) והייתי בעיניו כמתעתע
וכתיב התם כה) הבל המה מעשה תעתועים ואמר רבי אלעזר כל המסתכל בערוה קשתו ננערת שנאמר
כו) עריה תעור קשתך [ח] ואמר רבי אלעזר לעולם הוי קבל וקיים אמר רבי זירא אף אנן נמי תנינא
ט) [ד] בית אפל אין פותחין לו חלונות לראות נגעו ש"מ [י] אמר ר' טבי אמר ר' יאשיה מאי דכתיב כז) שאול
ועוצר רחם ארץ לא שבעה מים וכי מה ענין שאול אצל רחם אלא לומר לך מה רחם מכנים ומוציא אף
שאול מכנים ומוציא והלא דברים קל וחומר ומה רחם שמכניסין בו בחשאי מוציאין ממנו בקולי קולות שאול
שמכניסין [כ] בו בקולות אינו דין שמוציאין ממנו בקולי קולות מיכן תשובה לאומרין אין תחיית המתים מן
התורה תנא דבי אליהו צדיקים שעתיד הקדוש ברוך הוא להחיותן [ה] אינן חוזרין לעפרן שנאמר כח) והיה הנשאר
בציון והנותר בירושלים קדוש יאמר לו כל הכתוב לחיים בירושלים מה קדוש לעולם קיים אף הם לעולם קיימין

ואם

רש"י

יקבוהו. מנקבים אותו לשון (מלכים ב יב) ויקוב חור בדלתו: אוכלא דקצרי. כלי של כובסין שהוא מנוקב ומזלפין בו מים על הבגדים: ומרוה גם הוא יורה. מי שמרווה את תלמידו בדבר הלכה גם הוא יורה לעולם הבא ל"א ומרוה לשון מורה: ואתה לך לקץ ותנוח ותעמוד וגו'. רמז לו שימות ויעמוד לאחר מכן לקץ הימין לקץ שעתיד הקב"ה להחזיר ימינו לפניו שהרי השיב אחור ימינו: מרחמם בעוה"ז. ינהגם לעוה"ב: שתי אותיות. של שם. כך שמעתי. ל"א כל שמות על שם דאמרי' בעלמא (חגיגה דף טז.) לצבאות אות הוא בצבא שלו קרי להו אותיות לשון מופלא: גדול מקדש. חשוב הוא: למילתיה הכי נמי. דגדולה היא וכדעולא: שתי הופעיות. דכתיב אל נקמות ה' אל נקמות הופיע ואיכא תרי נקמות וחדא הופעה בתרוייהו ודמי כמאן דאיכא אכל נקמה ונקמה חדא הופעה: חדא לטובה. של ישראל שסילק שכינתו מאומות העולם ובא על ישראל וקרי ליה נקמות משום דתגמול טוב הוא שזכו לשכינה על שאמרו נעשה ונשמע ונקמה היינו תגמול ואחת לפורענות לעובדי כוכבים שנפרע מהן ליום הדין כדאמרינן בפרק קמא דמסכת ע"ז (דף ד.) נוקם ה' ובעל חמה לעכו"ם שהוא בעצמו ובכבודו נפרע מהן והיינו הופעה: ובדעת. מפני הדעת מלאו כל החדרים הון: בשביל לחמך. שנתת למי שאין בו דעה ישימו מזור תחתיך: כל חשך טמון לצפוניו. כל לילה לפון ונחבא ממלפוני התורה שאין דברי תורה נשמעין באותו בית: תאכלהו אש לא נופח. זה אשו של גיהנם שאין צריך נפוח: ירע שריד באהלו. מי שרע בעיניו שיש שריד באהלו: כל שאינו משייר פתיתין. דצריך לשייר כדכתיב אכול והותר (מלכים ב ד): והא אמר רבי אלעזר כל המשייר פתיתין על שולחנו כאילו עובד ע"ז שנאמר העורכים לגד שולחן. שכן עושין שמניחין שלחן ערוך במאכל ומשתה לשם אותה ע"ז שקורין גד וממלאים כוסות של מרקחים נסוכים לע"ז ששמה מני: הא. דקאמר אסור: דאיכא שלימה בהדיה. שמניח שלימה לאחר שאכל ונותן על השלחן עם הפתיתין ששייר דמחזי דלשם ע"ז עביד הכי: והא. דליכא שלימה בהדייהו דמזומנין לעני: הא גדא לביתיה לא גרסי': המחליף בדבורו. משנה בדבורו שלא יהא ניכר: קשתו ננערת. כח קושי אבר שלו ננער שאינו מוליד שנאמר עריה תעור קשתך עריה שאתה מסתכל בה ממש בערותה היא תעיר קשתך ד"א המסתכל המחשב בעריות דאשת איש קשתו גבורת ידו ננערת מתהלכת ומתמעטת כמו (ב"מ דף כט:) מלא כסות מנערה אחת לשלשים יום א"נ כמו (שמות יד) וינער ה': הוי קבל. הוי עניו ותחיה. קבל לשון אפל עשה עצמך אפל ושפל: בית אפל אין פותחין בו חלונות לראות את נגעו. כנגע נראה לי בבית כתיב דמשמע נראה ממילא ועוד דכתיב לי [נ] ולא לאורי נמצא שאפלתו הצלתו דכל זמן שאין כהן רואהו אין מטמא בנגעים: שאול ועוצר רחם ארץ לא שבעה מים. קבר לא שבע ממתים ועוצר רחם בית הרחם שהוא קצור ועצור לא ישבע מבעילות וכן ארץ לא שבעה מים: וכי מה ענין שאול וכו'. למה נסמכו הני אהדדי: מכנים. הזרע ומוציא הולד אף שאול מכנים ומוציא לתחיית המתים: שמכניסין בה בקולי קולות. בבכי גדול קוברין את המת: אינו דין שמוציאין אותו בקולי קולות. שנאמר יתקע בשופר גדול: שעתיד הקב"ה להחיות. לימות המשיח: לאחר שיחיו שוב אין חוזרין לעפרם. בין [מ] (לימות המשיח בין לעולם הבא) אלא הבשר מתקיים עליהם עד שישובו ויחיו לעתיד לבא:

ואותן

מסורת הש"ס

א) סוטה מא:, ב) [גי' הערוך ערך אבל אובלא בבי"ת וע"ש שני פירושים], ג) בקרא כתיב יורא באל"ף, ד) ברכות לג. ע"ש, ה) [שם. ע"ש], ו) חולין קלג., ז) [מס' כלה], ח) לעיל יד., ט) [נגעים פ"ב מ"ג] חולין י:, י) ברכות טו:, כ) בד"י אותו, ל) [מועד קטן ח.], מ) ימות המשיח ולעולם הבא. רש"ל.

גליון הש"ס

גמ' כל בית שאין ד"ת נשמעין. עיין עירובין דף יח ע"ב:

תורה אור השלם

א) וַיֹּאמֶר יְיָ לָהּ שְׁנֵי גוֹיִם בְּבִטְנֵךְ וּשְׁנֵי לְאֻמִּים מִמֵּעַיִךְ יִפָּרֵדוּ וּלְאֹם מִלְאֹם יֶאֱמָץ וְרַב יַעֲבֹד צָעִיר: [בראשית כה, כג]

ב) מָה אֶקֹּב לֹא קַבֹּה אֵל וּמָה אֶזְעֹם לֹא זָעַם יְיָ: [במדבר כג, ח]

ג) נַשְּׁקוּ בַר פֶּן יֶאֱנַף וְתֹאבְדוּ דֶרֶךְ כִּי יִבְעַר כִּמְעַט אַפּוֹ אַשְׁרֵי כָּל חוֹסֵי בוֹ: [תהלים ב, יב]

ד) מֹנֵעַ בָּר יִקְּבֻהוּ לְאוֹם וּבְרָכָה לְרֹאשׁ מַשְׁבִּיר: [משלי יא, כו]

ה) וַיִּקַּח יְהוֹיָדָע הַכֹּהֵן אֲרוֹן אֶחָד וַיִּקֹּב חֹר בְּדַלְתּוֹ וַיִּתֵּן אֹתוֹ אֵצֶל הַמִּזְבֵּחַ מִיָּמִין בְּבוֹא אִישׁ בֵּית יְיָ וְנָתְנוּ שָׁמָּה הַכֹּהֲנִים שֹׁמְרֵי הַסַּף אֶת כָּל הַכֶּסֶף הַמּוּבָא בֵית יְיָ: [מלכים ב' יב, י]

ו) וְיוֹסֵף הוּא הַשַּׁלִּיט עַל הָאָרֶץ הוּא הַמַּשְׁבִּיר לְכָל עַם הָאָרֶץ וַיָּבֹאוּ אֲחֵי יוֹסֵף וַיִּשְׁתַּחֲווּ לוֹ אַפַּיִם אָרְצָה: [בראשית מב, ו]

ז) נֶפֶשׁ בְּרָכָה תְדֻשָּׁן וּמַרְוֶה גַּם הוּא יוֹרֶא: [משלי יא, כה]

ח) יְחִי רְאוּבֵן וְאַל יָמֹת וִיהִי מְתָיו מִסְפָּר: [דברים לג, ו]

ט) וְרַבִּים מִיְּשֵׁנֵי אַדְמַת עָפָר יָקִיצוּ אֵלֶּה לְחַיֵּי עוֹלָם וְאֵלֶּה לַחֲרָפוֹת לְדִרְאוֹן עוֹלָם: [דניאל יב, ב]

י) וְאַתָּה לֵךְ לַקֵּץ וְתָנוּחַ וְתַעֲמֹד לְגֹרָלְךָ לְקֵץ הַיָּמִין: [דניאל יב, יג]

יא) לֹא יִרְעָבוּ וְלֹא יִצְמָאוּ וְלֹא יַכֵּם שָׁרָב וָשָׁמֶשׁ כִּי מְרַחֲמָם יְנַהֲגֵם וְעַל מַבּוּעֵי מַיִם יְנַהֲלֵם: [ישעיה מט, י]

יב) אַל תַּרְבּוּ תְדַבְּרוּ גְּבֹהָה גְבֹהָה יֵצֵא עָתָק מִפִּיכֶם כִּי אֵל דֵּעוֹת יְיָ וְלוֹ נִתְכְּנוּ עֲלִלוֹת: [שמואל א' ב, ג]

יג) תְּבִאֵמוֹ וְתִטָּעֵמוֹ בְּהַר נַחֲלָתְךָ מָכוֹן לְשִׁבְתְּךָ פָּעַלְתָּ יְיָ מִקְּדָשׁ אֲדֹנָי כּוֹנְנוּ יָדֶיךָ: [שמות טו, יז]

יד) אֵל נְקָמוֹת יְיָ אֵל נְקָמוֹת הוֹפִיעַ: [תהלים צד, א] טו) וּבְדַעַת חֲדָרִים יִמָּלְאוּ כָּל הוֹן יָקָר וְנָעִים: [משלי כד, ד] טז) בִּיבֹשׁ קְצִירָהּ תִּשָּׁבַרְנָה נָשִׁים בָּאוֹת מְאִירוֹת אוֹתָהּ כִּי לֹא עַם בִּינוֹת הוּא עַל כֵּן לֹא יְרַחֲמֶנּוּ עֹשֵׂהוּ וְיֹצְרוֹ לֹא יְחֻנֶּנּוּ: [ישעיה כז, יא] יז) עַד הַגְּבוּל שִׁלְּחוּךָ כֹּל אַנְשֵׁי בְרִיתֶךָ הִשִּׁיאוּךָ יָכְלוּ לְךָ אַנְשֵׁי שְׁלֹמֶךָ לַחְמְךָ יָשִׂימוּ מָזוֹר תַּחְתֶּיךָ אֵין תְּבוּנָה בּוֹ: [עובדיה א, ז] יח) וַיַּרְא אֶפְרַיִם אֶת חָלְיוֹ וִיהוּדָה אֶת מְזֹרוֹ וַיֵּלֶךְ אֶפְרַיִם אֶל אַשּׁוּר וַיִּשְׁלַח אֶל מֶלֶךְ יָרֵב וְהוּא לֹא יוּכַל לִרְפֹּא לָכֶם וְלֹא יִגְהֶה מִכֶּם מָזוֹר: [הושע ה, יג] יט) לָכֵן גָּלָה עַמִּי מִבְּלִי דָעַת וּכְבוֹדוֹ מְתֵי רָעָב וַהֲמוֹנוֹ צִחֵה צָמָא: [ישעיה ה, יג] כ) כָּל חֹשֶׁךְ טָמוּן לִצְפוּנָיו תְּאָכְלֵהוּ אֵשׁ לֹא נֻפָּח יֵרַע שָׂרִיד בְּאָהֳלוֹ: [איוב כ, כו] כא) וְהָיָה כֹּל אֲשֶׁר יִקְרָא בְּשֵׁם יְיָ יִמָּלֵט כִּי בְּהַר צִיּוֹן וּבִירוּשָׁלַיִם תִּהְיֶה פְלֵיטָה כַּאֲשֶׁר אָמַר יְיָ וּבַשְּׂרִידִים אֲשֶׁר יְיָ קֹרֵא: [יואל ג, ה] כב) אֵין שָׂרִיד לְאָכְלוֹ עַל כֵּן לֹא יָחִיל טוּבוֹ: [איוב כ, כא] כג) וְאַתֶּם עֹזְבֵי יְיָ הַשְּׁכֵחִים אֶת הַר קָדְשִׁי הַעֹרְכִים לַגַּד שֻׁלְחָן וְהַמְמַלְאִים לַמְנִי מִמְסָךְ: [ישעיה סה, יא] כד) אוּלַי יְמֻשֵּׁנִי אָבִי וְהָיִיתִי בְעֵינָיו כִּמְתַעְתֵּעַ וְהֵבֵאתִי עָלַי קְלָלָה וְלֹא בְרָכָה: [בראשית כז, יב] כה) הֶבֶל הֵמָּה מַעֲשֵׂה תַּעְתֻּעִים בְּעֵת פְּקֻדָּתָם יֹאבֵדוּ: [ירמיה י, טו] כו) עֶרְיָה תֵעוֹר קַשְׁתֶּךָ שְׁבֻעוֹת מַטּוֹת אֹמֶר סֶלָה נְהָרוֹת תְּבַקַּע אָרֶץ: [חבקוק ג, ט] כז) שְׁאוֹל וְעֹצֶר רָחַם אֶרֶץ לֹא שָׂבְעָה מַּיִם וְאֵשׁ לֹא אָמְרָה הוֹן: [משלי ל, טז] כח) וְהָיָה הַנִּשְׁאָר בְּצִיּוֹן וְהַנּוֹתָר בִּירוּשָׁלַיִם קָדוֹשׁ יֵאָמֶר לוֹ כָּל הַכָּתוּב לַחַיִּים בִּירוּשָׁלָיִם: [ישעיה ד, ג]

עין משפט נר מצוה

ו א מיי' פ"ג מהל' ת"ת הל' יג סמג עשין יב טוש"ע יו"ד סי' רמו סעיף כד:
ז ב ג טוש"ע או"ח סי' קפ סעיף ב:
ח ד מיי' פי"ד מהל' טומאת צרעת הל' ה:
ט ה מיי' פ"ח מהל' תשובה הל' א:

ליקוטי רש"י

אוכלא דקצרי. כלי נחושת העשוי כנפה נקבים נקבים והוא של כובסים ונותנו על הבגדים ומזלף בו המים עליהן ויש מפרשים שמגמרין מוגמר מתחתיו והבגדים מונחין עליו ומתגמרין דרך הנקבים [שבת קכג:]. כלי שמשימין בו הכובסין בגדיהן [נדרים כג.]. קצרי. הכובס נקרא קצרי בלשון ארמי [ב"ק קיט:]. כך שמם בלשון ישמעאל והם כובסין שמעתי אומרים על שם שמקצרין בגדי למר כשדורסין אותן ברגליהן במים שקורין פורלוי"ר והיינו דמתרגמינן עין רוגל (ש"ב יז) עינא דקצרא [תענית כט:]. ואל ימות לעולם הבא. שלא יזכר לו מעשה בלהה [דברים לג, ו]. ורבים מישני אדמת עפר יקיצו. יחיו המתים [דניאל יב, ב]. לך לקץ. תפטר לבית עולמך. לגורלך. לקבל חלקך עם הצדיקים. לקץ הימין. כמו באחרית הימים ואין לפרש הימין לשון יד הימנית שהרי הוא מנוי במסורת הגדולה בשיטת תיבות המיוחדין בנו"ן זקופה בסוף תיבה המשמשת במקום מ"ם ולית דכותיהון כגון ועליה יכרעון אחרין (איוב לא) יקום ולא יאמין בחיין (שם כד) קח לך חטין (יחזקאל ד) יחרדון איין (שם כו) למחות מלכין (משלי לא) לקץ הימין (כאן) [שם, יג]. שיחזיר ימינו לפניו שהשיב אחור ימינו מפני אויב [פסחים נו:]. בין שתי אותיות. בין שתי הזכרות. למילתיה הכי נמי. במקום שצריכה נקמה דבר גדול הוא [ברכות לג.]. הופיע. הראה וגלה לנו את נקמתך [תהלים צד, א]. מזורו. לשון חולי [הושע ה, יג]. מבלי דעת. לפי שהיה לבם בלי דעת [ישעיה ה, יג]. ובשרידים. בשארית אשר יותיר. אשר ה' קורא. לשון קרואים לסעודה או לעבודת המלך לשון הזמנה [יואל ג, ה]. אין שריד לאכלו. לא השרה תלמידי חכמים על שלחנו כמו ובשרידים אשר ה' קורא. על כן לא יחיל טובו. לא יצליח כמו (תהלים י) יחילו דרכיו. כל שאינו משייר וכו' שנאמר אין שריד לאכלו. לא שייר ממאכלו לחלק לעניים [איוב כ, כא]. העורכים לגד. שם עכו"ם העשוים על שם המזל ובלשון משנה יש גד גדי וסינוק לא. למני. למניין חשבון הכומרים היו ממלאים אגנות מזג יין. ממסך. יין מזוג במים כמשפטו כמו לחקור ממסך (משלי כג) מסכה יינה (משלי ט) [ישעיה סה, יא]. הוי קבל. אפל.

וקיים. ותחיה כלומר הרחק מן הרבנות שמקברת את בעליה אפילו מתרגם קבלה (שמות י) [לעיל יד.]. בית אפל. שצריך לפתוח לו חלונות לראות הנגע פוטרין אותו לגמרי דכתיב (ויקרא יד) כנגע נראה לי בבית ולא לאורי שאם עמד במקום אפל וצריך שם להדליק את הנר אינו נגע [חולין י:]. שאול ועוצר רחם. פסוק הוא בספר משלי שלש הנה לא תשבענה. שאול. קבר. שמכניסין בו בקולות. של בכי ומספד [ברכות טו:]. והיה הנשאר. בהם בציון יתיישבו. והנותר. בכל מקום ישכנו בירושלים. קדוש יאמר לו. כולם יהיו צדיקים וא"ת צדיקים המתים לפני אותו היום אבד כבודם ת"ל כל הכתוב לחיי העוה"ב יחיו בירושלים (כת"י) [ישעיה ד, ג].

the World to Come, שֶׁנֶּאֱמַר ,,כִּי־מְרַחֲמָם יְנַהֲגֵם וְעַל־מַבּוּעֵי מַיִם יְנַהֲלֵם" – **as it is stated:** ***For he who has mercy on them shall lead them, and to springs of water he shall guide them.***[17]

Some other teachings of R' Elazar:

וְאָמַר רַבִּי אֶלְעָזָר – **And R' Elazar** also **said:** גְּדוֹלָה דֵּעָה שֶׁנִּתְּנָה בֵּין שְׁתֵּי אוֹתִיּוֹת – **Great is understanding, for it was placed** in Scripture **between two letters** of the Divine Name,[18] שֶׁנֶּאֱמַר ,,כִּי אֵל דֵּעוֹת ה' " – **as it is stated:** ***For the God of de'os is Hashem.***[19]

וְאָמַר רַבִּי אֶלְעָזָר – **And R' Elazar** also **said:** גָּדוֹל מִקְדָּשׁ שֶׁנִּיתַּן בֵּין שְׁתֵּי אוֹתִיּוֹת – **Great is the Sanctuary,**[20] **for it was placed** in Scripture **between two letters** of the Divine Name, שֶׁנֶּאֱמַר ,,פָּעַלְתָּ ה' מִקְּדָשׁ אֲדֹנָי כּוֹנְנוּ יָדֶיךָ" – **as it is stated:** *The foundation of Your dwelling place* ***that You have made, O Hashem, the Sanctuary, my Lord, that Your hands have established.***[21]

Rav Adda Karchinaah challenges these last two expositions of R' Elazar:

מַתְקִיף לָהּ רַב אַדָּא קַרְחִינָאָה – **Rav Adda Karchinaah objected:** אֶלָּא מֵעַתָּה גְּדוֹלָה נְקָמָה שֶׁנִּיתְּנָה בֵּין שְׁתֵּי אוֹתִיּוֹת – **But accordingly,** you would also have to say: **Great is vengeance, for it was placed** in Scripture **between two letters** of the Divine Name. דִּכְתִיב ,,אֵל־נְקָמוֹת ה' אֵל נְקָמוֹת הוֹפִיעַ" – **For it is written:** ***O God of vengeance, Hashem! O God of vengeance, appear!***[22] Would you indeed submit that vengeance is a great thing?!

אָמַר לֵיהּ – **[R' Elazar] said to him:** לְמִילְּתֵיהּ הָכִי נַמִּי – When used **for its** proper **purpose,** vengeance is **indeed** a great thing. The Gemara elaborates: כִּדְעוּלָּא – **And this** sentiment that vengeance is at times a great thing is **as Ulla** taught. דְּאָמַר עוּלָּא – **For Ulla said:** שְׁתֵּי הוֹפָעוֹת הַלָּלוּ לָמָּה – **Why these two "appearances"** in this verse?[23] אַחַת לְמִדַּת טוֹבָה – **One is for the meting out of benefit** [i.e. reward] וְאַחַת לְמִדַּת פּוּרְעָנוּת – **and one is for the meting out of punishment.**[24]

The Gemara presents an additional five teachings of R' Elazar concerning "understanding":

וְאָמַר רַבִּי אֶלְעָזָר – **And R' Elazar** also **said:** כָּל אָדָם שֶׁיֵּשׁ בּוֹ דֵּעָה – **If a person has understanding,** כְּאִילּוּ נִבְנָה בֵּית הַמִּקְדָּשׁ בְּיָמָיו – it is **as if the Sanctuary were built in his days.** שֶׁזֶּה נִיתַּן בֵּין שְׁתֵּי אוֹתִיּוֹת – **For this** [i.e. understanding] **was placed** in Scripture **between two letters** of the Divine Name (as demonstrated above) וְזֶה נִיתַּן בֵּין שְׁתֵּי אוֹתִיּוֹת – **and this** [i.e. the Sanctuary] **was** likewise **placed between two letters** of the Divine Name (as demonstrated above).[25]

NOTES

17. *Isaiah* 49:10. I.e. *he who has mercy on them* in this world *shall lead them* in the World to Come (*Rashi*). *And to the springs of water he shall guide them* – i.e. the foregoing holds true provided the gentle manner of leadership guides the people to the wellsprings of Torah observance; otherwise, sternness is in order, if that is the only way to insure Torah observance (*Maharsha*).

18. *Rashi*. Alternatively, אוֹתִיּוֹת here is not used in the sense of *letters,* but rather in the sense of *sublime things* and thus refers to the Divine Names themselves (ibid.). [See *HaKoseiv* in *Ein Yaakov* to *Berachos* 33a for an exposition of the difference between *Rashi's* two explanations.]

19. *I Samuel* 2:3. In the context of that passage, the meaning is that Hashem is the God Who knows all thoughts [דֵּעוֹת] of man (see *Rashi* ad loc.). R' Elazar's exposition notes the placement of the word דֵּעוֹת (plural of דֵּעָה, *understanding*) between two Divine Names אֵל and ה'.

The Name אֵל represents God's attribute of stern justice; the Name ה' [the Tetragrammaton] represents His attribute of mercy. The world could not exist purely according to the dictates of one without the other. [According to the dictates of stern justice, all would perish, as no person is entirely free of sin. According to the dictates of mercy, the wicked would never be punished, and there would be no way to differentiate between the righteous and the wicked (*Rashba,* in his response to a Dominican priest, printed at the end of *Rashba, Chidushei Aggados,* edition Mossad HaRav Kook).] God therefore relates to the world with a mixture of these two attributes. Accordingly, "understanding" was placed *in the midst* of these two Divine Names, for someone who is in the midst of something perceives its true nature. Thus, one who has understanding can attain the ultimate knowledge possible to a human being of God and His providence in the world, which is the goal of human understanding (*Rashba, Chidushei Aggados* to *Berachos* 33a; cf. *Maharsha* here).

Iyun Yaakov explains the progression from אֵל to דֵּעוֹת to ה'. One who experiences Divine justice and still remains firm in his righteousness with clear understanding will eventually experience God's mercy as well. [See also *Darash Moshe,* cited by *Chidushei Geonim* in *Ein Yaakov.*]

20. I.e. it is important (*Rashi*).

21. *Exodus* 15:17. In this verse, the word מִקְדָּשׁ, *Sanctuary* [or: *Temple*] appears between the Divine Names ה' and אֲדֹנָי.

Rashba (*Chidushei Aggados* to *Berachos* loc. cit.) explains this statement of R' Elazar to mean that the knowledge of God and His providence represented by the two Divine Names (as explained in note 19) can be gained through "the Temple, which is called [in this very verse] *the foundation of God's dwelling place,* and is built with glory and splendor, and whose components and operation signify conceptual matters, as the verse states: *And see and make [the vessels] according to their form that you are shown at the mountain* (*Exodus* 25:40). And [stationed] in that place are the authorities of the Torah and expositors of wisdom, and from there is *ruach hakodesh* drawn" [see *Yerushalmi, Succah* 5:1; *Bereishis Rabbah* 70:8].

22. *Psalms* 94:1. In this verse, the word *vengeance* appears between the Divine Names אֵל and ה'.

23. Though the word "appear" is mentioned only once in the verse, it is preceded by a double call to the *God of vengeance.* Thus, it is as if God is called upon to appear twice – once for each vengeance (*Rashi* and *Yad Ramah*). [In *Berachos* 33a, however, the text indeed reads: "two vengeances" instead of "two appearances."]

24. The first refers to God's withdrawal of His Presence from the nations of the world [when they rejected the Torah – see *Deuteronomy* 33:2 with *Rashi*] and His resting of that Presence [His "appearance"] exclusively upon Israel in reward for their unanimous declaration at Sinai, *"We will fulfill and we will obey!"* This, too, is called נְקָמוֹת, *vengeance,* which fundamentally refers to *retribution* – whether for good or for bad. The second is a call for God [upon the final Redemption] to "appear," i.e. to "personally," so to speak, take vengeance upon the nations of the world for their wickedness [as stated by the Gemara in *Avodah Zarah* 4a] (*Rashi*; cf. *Rashi* to *Berachos* loc. cit.). [See also *Yad Ramah.*]

In keeping with the explanation of *Rashba* cited in note 19, the following explanation emerges: The word *vengeance* is flanked by two Divine Names – אֵל and ה', one representing stern justice and the other mercy. When God appears and takes vengeance against the nations of the world, it is a manifestation of "stern justice" vis-a-vis the nations and a manifestation of "mercy" vis-a-vis Israel (see *Maharsha* here and to *Berachos* loc. cit.).

[*R' Avigdor Miller* (taped lectures to *Cheilek*) explains that God's "appearance" – i.e. the evidence of His handiwork in this world – is made known to us both through the myriad *beneficial measures* that He metes out to His creatures, and through the *retributive measures* He metes out to those who violate His will.]

25. *Rashba* (cited in note 21) explains that one who has understanding can, through the use of his intellect, reach the level of understanding that was formerly attainable through the Temple, its components, and the Torah authorities that were stationed there. Thus, if one utilizes his understanding to this degree, it is "as if the Temple were built in his days." According to *Rama* (Introduction to *Toras HaOlah,* cited in *Anaf Yosef* to *Berachos* 33a), that level of understanding is still available through the study and contemplation of the Temple and its service, even though they are not physically present today. Thus, "if one has understanding, it is as if the Temple were built in his days," for he has realized their intended purpose [see also *Menachos* 110a].

Others explain that one who is filled with a knowledge and understanding of God causes the Divine Presence to rest upon him. Such a person resembles the Temple, which was built to serve as a dwelling place for the Divine Presence among men [*Exodus* 25:8] (see *Toras Chaim* here and *Ben Yehoyada* to *Berachos* loc. cit.).

יקבוהו לאום ואין [א] לאום אלא עוברין שנאמר [א] ולאום מלאום יאמץ ואין קבה אלא קללה שנאמר [ב] מה אקב לא קבה אל ואין בר אלא תורה שנאמר [ג] נשקו בר פן יאנף עולא בר ישמעאל אומר מנקבין אותו ככברה כתיב הכא [ד] יקבוהו לאום וכתיב התם [ה] ויקב חור בדלתו ואמר אביי כי [ב] אוכלא דקצרי ואם למדו מה שכרו אמר רבא אמר רב ששת זוכה לברכות כיוסף שנאמר [ד] וברכה לראש משביר ואין משביר אלא יוסף שנאמר [ו] ויוסף הוא [השליט על הארץ הוא] המשביר לכל עם הארץ אמר רב ששת כל המלמד תורה בעוה"ז זוכה ומלמדה לעולם הבא שנאמר [ז] ומרוה גם הוא [ג] יורה אמר רבא מניין לתחיית המתים מן התורה שנאמר [ח] יחי ראובן ואל ימות יחי ראובן בעולם הזה ואל ימות לעולם הבא רבינא אמר מהכא [ט] ורבים מישני אדמת עפר יקיצו אלה לחיי עולם ואלה לחרפות לדראון עולם רב אשי אמר מהכא [י] ואתה לך [לקץ] ותנוח ותעמוד לגורלך לקץ הימין אמר רבי אלעזר כל פרנס שמנהיג את הצבור בנחת זוכה ומנהיגם לעוה"ב שנאמר [יא] כי מרחמם ינהגם ועל מבועי מים ינהלם [ד] וא"ר אלעזר גדולה דעה שניתנה בין שתי אותיות שנאמר [יב] כי אל דעות ה' וא"ר אלעזר גדול מקדש שניתן בין שתי אותיות שנאמר [יג] פעלת ה' מקדש ה' כוננו ידיך מתקיף לה רב אדא [ה] קרחינאה אלא מעתה גדולה נקמה שניתנה בין שתי אותיות דכתיב [יד] אל נקמות ה' אל נקמות הופיע אמר ליה למילתיה הכי נמי כדעולא דאמר עולא שתי הופעיות הללו למה אחת למדת טובה ואחת למדת פורענות ואמר ר' אלעזר כל אדם שיש בו דעה כאילו נבנה בית המקדש בימיו שזה ניתן בין שתי אותיות וזה ניתן בין שתי אותיות ואמר ר' אלעזר כל אדם שיש בו דעה לסוף מתעשר שנאמר [טו] ובדעת חדרים ימלאו כל הון יקר ונעים ואמר ר' אלעזר כל אדם שאין בו דעה אסור לרחם עליו שנאמר [טז] כי לא עם בינות הוא על כן לא ירחמנו עושהו ויוצרו לא יחוננו וא"ר אלעזר כל הנותן פיתו למי שאין בו דעה יסורין באין עליו שנאמר [יז] לחמך ישימו מזור תחתיך אין תבונה בו ואין מזור אלא יסורין שנאמר [יח] וירא אפרים את חליו ויהודה את מזורו ואמר ר' אלעזר כל אדם שאין בו דעה לסוף גולה שנאמר [יט] לכן גלה עמי מבלי דעת ואמר ר"א [ו] [א] כל בית שאין דברי תורה נשמעים בו בלילה אש אוכלתו שנאמר [כ] כל חשך טמון לצפוניו תאכלהו אש לא נופח ירע שריד באהלו [י] אין שריד אלא ת"ח שנאמר [כא] ובשרידים אשר ה' קורא ואמר ר' אלעזר כל שאינו מהנה תלמידי חכמים מנכסיו אינו רואה סימן ברכה לעולם שנאמר [כב] אין שריד לאכלו על כן לא יחיל טובו אין שריד אלא תלמידי חכמים שנאמר ובשרידים אשר ה' קורא ואמר רבי אלעזר [ב] כל שאינו משייר פת על שלחנו אינו רואה סימן ברכה לעולם שנאמר אין שריד לאכלו על כן לא יחיל טובו והאמר רבי אלעזר כל המשייר פתיתים על שלחנו כאילו עובד ע"ז שנאמר [כג] העורכים לגד שלחן והממלאים למני ממסך לא קשיא [ג] הא דאיכא שלימה בהדיה הא דליכא שלימה בהדיה ואמר רבי אלעזר [ז] כל המחליף בדבורו כאילו עובד ע"ז כתיב הכא [כד] והייתי בעיניו כמתעתע וכתיב התם [כה] הבל המה מעשה תעתועים ואמר רבי אלעזר כל המסתכל בערוה קשתו ננערת שנאמר [כו] עריה תעור קשתך [ח] ואמר רבי אלעזר לעולם הוי קבל וקיים אמר רבי זירא אף אנן נמי תנינא [ט] [ד] בית אפל אין פותחין לו חלונות לראות נגעו ש"מ [י] אמר ר' טבי אמר ר' יאשיה מאי דכתיב [כז] שאול ועוצר רחם ארץ לא שבעה מים וכי מה ענין שאול אצל רחם אלא לומר לך מה רחם מכנים ומוציא אף שאול מכנים ומוציא והלא דברים קל וחומר ומה רחם שמכניסין בו בחשאי מוציאין ממנו בקולי קולות שאול שמכניסין [כ] בו בקולות אינו דין שמוציאין ממנו בקולי קולות מיכן תשובה לאומרין אין תחיית המתים מן התורה תנא דבי אליהו צדיקים שעתיד הקדוש ברוך הוא להחיותן [ה] אינן חוזרין לעפרן שנאמר [כח] והיה הנשאר בציון והנותר בירושלים קדוש יאמר לו כל הכתוב לחיים בירושלים מה קדוש לעולם קיים אף הם לעולם קיימין

ואם

רש"י

יקבוהו. מנקבים אותו לשון (מלכים ב יב) ויקוב חור בדלתו: אוכלא דקצרי. כלי של כובסין שהוא מנוקב ומזלפין בו מים על הבגדים: ומרוה גם הוא יורה. מי שמרווה את תלמידו בדבר הלכה גם הוא יורה לעולם הבא ל"א ומרוה לשון מורה: ואתה לך לקץ ותנוח ותעמוד וגו'. רמז לו שימות ויעמוד לאחר מכן לקץ הימין לקץ שעתיד הקב"ה להחזיר ימינו לפניו שהרי השיב אחור ימינו: מרחמם בעוה"ז. ינהגם לעוה"ב: שתי אותיות. של שם. כך שמעתי. ל"א כל שמות על שם דאמרי' בעלמא (חגיגה דף טז.) צבאות אות הוא בצבא שלו קרי להו אותיות לשון מופלא: גדול מקדש. חשוב הוא: למילתיה הכי נמי. דגדולה היא ודעולא: שתי הופעיות. דכתיב אל נקמות ה' אל נקמות הופיע ואיכא תרי נקמות וחדא הופעה בתרוייהו ודמי כמאן דאיכא אכל נקמה ונקמה חדא הופעה: חדא לטובה. של ישראל שסילק שכינתו מאומות העולם ובא על ישראל וקרי ליה נקמות משום דתגמול טוב הוא שזכו לשכינה על שאמרו נעשה ונשמע ונקמה היינו תגמול ואחת לפורענות לעובדי כוכבים שנפרע מהן ליום הדין כדאמרינן בפרק קמא דמסכת ע"ז (דף ד.) נוקם ה' ובעל חמה לעכו"ם שהוא בעצמו ובכבודו נפרע מהן והיינו הופעה: ובדעת. מפני הדעת מלאו כל החדרים הון: בשביל לחמך. שנתת למי שאין בו דעה ישימו מזור תחתיך: כל חשך טמון לצפוניו. כל לילה צפון ונחבא ממצפוני התורה שאין דברי תורה נשמעין באותו בית: תאכלהו אש לא נופח. זה אשו של גיהנם שאין צריך נפוח: ירע שריד באהלו. מי שרע בעיניו שיש שריד באהלו: כל שאינו משייר פתיתין. דצריך לשייר כדכתיב אכול והותר (מלכים ב ד): והא אמר רבי אלעזר כל המשייר פתיתין על שולחנו כאילו עובד ע"ז שנאמר העורכים לגד שולחן. שכן עושין שמניחין שלחן ערוך במאכל ומשתה לשם אותה ע"ז שקורין גד וממלאים כוסות של מרקחים נסוכים לע"ז ששמה מני: הא. דקאמר אסור: דאיכא שלימה בהדיה. שמביא שלימה לאחר שאכל ונותן על השלחן עם הפתיתין ששייר דמחזי דלשם ע"ז עביד הכי: והא. דליכא שלימה בהדייהו דמזומנין לעני: הא גדא לביתיה לא גרסי': המחליף בדבורו. משנה בדבורו שלא יהא ניכר: קשתו ננערת. כח קושי אבר שלו ננער שאינו מוליד שנאמר עריה תעור קשתך עריה שאתה מסתכל בה ממש בערותה היא תעיר קשתך ד"א המסתכל המחשב בעריות דאשת איש קשתו גבורת ידו ננערת מתהלכת ומתמעטת כמו (ב"מ דף כט:) מלא כסות מנערה אחת לשלשים יום א"נ כמו (שמות יד) וינער ה': הוי קבל. הוי עניו ותחיה. קבל לשון אפל עשה עצמך אפל ושפל: בית אפל אין פותחין בו חלונות לראות את נגעו. כנגע נראה לי בבית כתיב דמשמע נראה ממילא ועוד דכתיב לי [נ] ולא לאורי נמצא שאפלתו הצלתו דכל זמן שאין כהן רואהו אין מטמא בנגעים: שאול ועוצר רחם ארץ לא שבעה מים. קבר לא שבע ממתים ועוצר רחם בית הרחם שהוא קצור ועצור לא ישבע מבעילות וכן ארץ לא שבעה מים: וכי מה ענין שאול וכו'. למה נסמכו הני אהדדי: מכנים. הזרע ומוציא הולד אף שאול מכניס ומוציא לתחיית המתים: שמכניסין בה בקולי קולות. בבכי גדול קוברין את המת: אינו דין שמוציאין אותו בקולי קולות. שנאמר יתקע בשופר גדול: שעתיד הקב"ה להחיות. לימות המשיח: לאחר שיחיו שוב אין חוזרין לעפרם. בין [מ] (לימות המשיח בין לעולם הבא) אלא הבשר מתקיים עליהם עד שישובו ויחיו לעתיד לבא:

ואותן

מסורת הש"ס

א) סוטה מא:, ב) [גי' הערוך ערך אכל אוכלא בכי"מ וע"ש שני פירושים], ג) בקרא כתיב יורא באל"ף, ד) ברכות לג. ע"ש, ה) [שם. ע"ש], ו) חולין קלג., ז) [מס' כלה], ח) לעיל יד., ט) [נגעים פ"ב מ"ג] חולין י:, י) ברכות טו:, כ) בד"י אותו, ל) [מועד קטן ח.], מ) ימות המשיח ולעולם הבא. רש"ל.

גליון הש"ס

גמ' כל בית שאין ד"ת נשמעין. עיין עירובין דף יח ע"ב:

תורה אור השלם

א) ויאמר יי לה שני גוים בבטנך ושני לאמים ממעיך יפרדו ולאם מלאם יאמץ ורב יעבד צעיר: [בראשית כה, כג]

ב) מה אקב לא קבה אל ומה אזעם לא זעם יי: [במדבר כג, ח]

ג) נשקו בר פן יאנף ותאבדו דרך כי יבער כמעט אפו אשרי כל חוסי בו: [תהלים ב, יב]

ד) מנע בר יקבהו לאום וברכה לראש משביר: [משלי יא, כו]

ה) ויקח יהוידע הכהן ארון אחד ויקב חר בדלתו ויתן אתו אצל המזבח מימין בבוא איש בית יי ונתנו שמה הכהנים שמרי הסף את כל הכסף המובא בית יי: [מלכים ב' יב, י]

ו) ויוסף הוא השליט על הארץ הוא המשביר לכל עם הארץ ויבאו אחי יוסף וישתחוו לו אפים ארצה: [בראשית מב, ו]

ז) נפש ברכה תדשן ומרוה גם הוא יורא: [משלי יא, כה]

ח) יחי ראובן ואל ימת ויהי מתיו מספר: [דברים לג, ו]

ט) ורבים מישני אדמת עפר יקיצו אלה לחיי עולם ואלה לחרפות לדראון עולם: [דניאל יב, ב]

י) ואתה לך לקץ ותנוח ותעמד לגרלך לקץ הימין: [דניאל יב, יג]

יא) לא ירעבו ולא יצמאו ולא יכם שרב ושמש כי מרחמם ינהגם ועל מבועי מים ינהלם: [ישעיה מט, י]

יב) אל תרבו תדברו גבהה גבהה יצא עתק מפיכם כי אל דעות יי ולו נתכנו עללות: [שמואל א' ב, ג]

יג) תבאמו ותטעמו בהר נחלתך מכון לשבתך פעלת יי מקדש אדני כוננו ידיך: [שמות טו, יז]

יד) אל נקמות יי אל נקמות הופיע: [תהלים צד, א] טו) ובדעת חדרים ימלאו כל הון יקר ונעים: [משלי כד, ד] טז) כי לא עם בינות הוא על כן לא ירחמנו עשהו ויצרו לא יחננו: [ישעיה כז, יא] יז) עד הגבול שלחוך כל אנשי בריתך השיאוך יכלו לך אנשי שלמך לחמך ישימו מזור תחתיך אין תבונה בו: [עובדיה א, ז] יח) וירא אפרים את חליו ויהודה את מזורו וילך אפרים אל אשור וישלח אל מלך ירב והוא לא יוכל לרפא לכם ולא יגהה מכם מזור: [הושע ה, יג] יט) לכן גלה עמי מבלי דעת וכבודו מתי רעב והמונו צחה צמא: [ישעיה ה, יג] כ) כל חשך טמון לצפוניו תאכלהו אש לא נפח ירע שריד באהלו: [איוב כ, כו] כא) והיה כל אשר יקרא בשם יי ימלט כי בהר ציון ובירושלים תהיה פליטה כאשר אמר יי ובשרידים אשר יי קרא: [יואל ג, ה] כב) אין שריד לאכלו על כן לא יחיל טובו: [איוב כ, כא] כג) ואתם עזבי יי השכחים את הר קדשי הערכים לגד שלחן והממלאים למני ממסך: [ישעיה סה, יא] כד) אולי ימשני אבי והייתי בעיניו כמתעתע והבאתי עלי קללה ולא ברכה: [בראשית כז, יב] כה) הבל המה מעשה תעתעים בעת פקדתם יאבדו: [ירמיה י, טו] כו) עריה תעור קשתך שבעות מטות אמר סלה נהרות תבקע ארץ: [חבקוק ג, ט] כז) שאול ועצר רחם ארץ לא שבעה מים ואש לא אמרה הון: [משלי ל, טז] כח) והיה הנשאר בציון והנותר בירושלים קדוש יאמר לו כל הכתוב לחיים בירושלים: [ישעיה ד, ג]

עין משפט נר מצוה

ו א מיי' פ"ג מהל' ת"ת הל' יג סמג עשין יב טוש"ע יו"ד סי' רמו סעיף כד:

ז ב ג טוש"ע או"ח סי' קפ סעיף ב:

ח ד מיי' פי"ד מהל' טומאת צרעת הל' ה:

ט ה מיי' פ"ח מהל' תשובה הל' א:

ליקוטי רש"י

אוכלא דקצרי. כלי נחושת העשוי כנפה נקבים נקבים והוא של כובסים ונותנו על הבגדים ומזלף בו המים עליהן ויש מפרשים שמגמרין מוגמר מתחתיו והבגדים מונחין עליו ומתגמרין דרך הנקבים [שבת קכג:]. כלי שמשימין בו הכובסין בגדיהן [נדרים כג.]. קצרי. הכובס נקרא קצרא בלשון ארמי [ב"ק קיט:]. כך שמם בלשון ישמעאל והם כובסין שמעתי אומרים על שם שמקצרין בגדי צמר כשדורסין אותן ברגליהן במים שקורין פורלוי"ר והיינו דמתרגמינן עין רוגל (ש"ב יז) עינא דקצרא [תענית כט:]. ואל ימות לעולם הבא. שלא יזכר לו מעשה בלהה [דברים לג, ו]. ורבים מישני אדמת עפר יקיצו. יחיו המתים [דניאל יב, ב]. לך לקץ. תפטר לבית עולמך. לגורלך. לקבל חלקך עם הצדיקים. לקץ הימין. כמו באחרית הימים ואין לפרש הימין לשון יד הימנית שהרי הוא מנוי במסורת הגדולה בשיטת תיבות המיוחדין בנו"ן זקופה בסוף תיבה המשמשת במקום מ"ם ולית דכותיהון כגון ועליה יכרעון אחרין (איוב לא) יקום ולא יאמין בחיין (שם כד) קח לך חטין (יחזקאל ד) יתרדון אין (שם כו) למחות מלכין (משלי לא) לקץ הימין (כאן) [שם, יג]. שיחזיר ימינו לפניו שהשיב אחור ימינו מפני אויב [פסחים נו:]. בין שתי אותיות. בין שתי הזכרות. למילתיה הכי נמי. במקום שצריכה נקמה דבר גדול הוא [ברכות לג.]. הופיע. הראה וגלה לנו את נקמתך [תהלים צד, א]. מזורו. לשון חולי [הושע ה, יג]. מבלי דעת. לפי שהיה להם בלי דעת [ישעיה ה, יג]. ובשרידים. בשארית אשר יותיר. אשר ה' קורא. לשון קרואים לסעודה או לעבודת המלך לשון הזמנה [יואל ג, ה]. אין שריד לאכלו. לא השרה תלמידי חכמים על שלחנו כמו ובשרידים אשר ה' קורא. על כן לא יחיל טובו. לא יצליח כמו (תהלים י) יחילו דרכיו. כל שאינו משייר וכו' שנאמר אין שריד לאכלו. לא שייר ממאכלו לחלק לעניים [איוב כ, כא]. העורכים לגד. שם עכו"ם העשוים על שם המזל ובלשון משנה יש גד גדי וסינוק לא. למני. למניין חשבון הכומרים היו ממלאים אגנות מזג יין. ממסך. יין מזוג במים כמשפטו כמו לחקור ממסך (משלי כג) מסכה יינה (משלי ט) [ישעיה סה, יא]. הוי קבל. אפל וקיים. ותחיה כלומר הרחק מן הרבנות שמקברת את בעליה אפילה מתרגם קבלה (שמות י) [לעיל יד.]. בית אפל. שצריך לפתוח לו חלונות לראות הנגע פוטרין אותו לגמרי דכתיב (ויקרא יד) כנגע נראה לי בבית לי ולא לאורי שאם עמד במקום אפל וצריך שם להדליק את הנר אינו נגע [חולין י:]. שאול ועוצר רחם. פסוק הוא בספר משלי שלש הנה לא תשבענה. שאול. קבר. שמכניסין בו בקולות. של בכי ומספד [ברכות טו:]. והיה הנשאר. בהם בציון יתיישבו. והנותר. בכל מקום ישכנו בירושלים. קדוש יאמר לו. כולם יהיו צדיקים וא"ת צדיקים המתים לפני אותו היום אבד כבודם ת"ל כל הכתוב לחיי העוה"ב יהיו בירושלים (כת"י) [ישעיה ד, ג].

כָּל אָדָם שֶׁאֵין בּוֹ דֵעָה – וְאָמַר רַבִּי אֶלְעָזָר – And R' Elazar also said: **Any person who does not have understanding** לְסוֹף גּוֹלֶה – **eventually goes into exile.** שֶׁנֶּאֱמַר ,,לָכֵן גָּלָה עַמִּי מִבְּלִי־דָעַת'' – **For it is stated:** ***Therefore, My people has gone into exile from lack of understanding.***[31]

כָּל בַּיִת שֶׁאֵין דִּבְרֵי – וְאָמַר רַבִּי אֶלְעָזָר – **And R' Elazar** also **said:** תּוֹרָה נִשְׁמָעִים בּוֹ בַּלַּיְלָה – **Any house in which words of Torah are not heard at night** אֵשׁ אוֹכַלְתּוֹ – **is** eventually **consumed by fire.**[32] שֶׁנֶּאֱמַר ,,כָּל־חֹשֶׁךְ טָמוּן לִצְפוּנָיו תְּאָכְלֵהוּ אֵשׁ לֹא־נֻפָּח יֵרַע שָׂרִיד בְּאָהֳלוֹ'' – **For it is stated:** ***Every darkness is hidden away for his treasures; a fire not blown shall consume him; it will be bad for the remnant in his tent.***[33] אֵין שָׂרִיד אֶלָּא תַּלְמִיד חָכָם – **And "remnant"** here **is nothing other than a Torah scholar,** שֶׁנֶּאֱמַר ,,וּבַשְּׂרִידִים אֲשֶׁר ה' קֹרֵא'' – **as it is stated** elsewhere: ***And among the remnants whom Hashem calls.***[34]

כָּל שֶׁאֵינוֹ מְהַנֶּה – וְאָמַר רַבִּי אֶלְעָזָר – **And R' Elazar** also **said:** תַּלְמִידֵי חֲכָמִים מִנְּכָסָיו – **Whoever does not benefit Torah scholars from his property** אֵינוֹ רוֹאֶה סִימַן בְּרָכָה לְעוֹלָם – **will never see a sign of blessing.**[35] שֶׁנֶּאֱמַר ,,אֵין־שָׂרִיד לְאָכְלוֹ עַל־כֵּן לֹא־יָחִיל טוּבוֹ'' – **For it is stated:** ***There is no remnant to his food; therefore his goods shall not prosper.***[36] אֵין שָׂרִיד אֶלָּא תַּלְמִידֵי חֲכָמִים – And **"remnant"** here **is nothing other than**

כָּל אָדָם שֶׁיֵּשׁ בּוֹ דֵעָה – וְאָמַר רַבִּי אֶלְעָזָר – **And R' Elazar** also **said:** לְסוֹף מִתְעַשֵּׁר – **Any person who has understanding eventually becomes wealthy.** שֶׁנֶּאֱמַר ,,וּבְדַעַת חֲדָרִים יִמָּלְאוּ כָּל־הוֹן יָקָר וְנָעִים'' – **For it is stated:** ***Through understanding the rooms are filled, [with] all riches precious and pleasant.***[26]

כָּל אָדָם שֶׁאֵין בּוֹ דֵעָה – וְאָמַר רַבִּי אֶלְעָזָר – **And R' Elazar** also **said:** אָסוּר לְרַחֵם עָלָיו – **If a person does not have understanding,**[27] **it is forbidden to have mercy on him.** שֶׁנֶּאֱמַר ,,כִּי לֹא עַם־בִּינוֹת הוּא עַל־כֵּן לֹא־יְרַחֲמֶנּוּ עֹשֵׂהוּ וְיֹצְרוֹ לֹא יְחֻנֶּנּוּ'' – **For it is stated:** ***For it is not a people of understanding; therefore, its Maker shall not have compassion on it, and He who formed it shall not grant it favor.***[28]

כָּל הַנּוֹתֵן פִּיתּוֹ לְמִי – וְאָמַר רַבִּי אֶלְעָזָר – **And R' Elazar** also **said:** שֶׁאֵין בּוֹ דֵעָה – **If one gives his bread to someone who does not have understanding,** יִסּוּרִין בָּאִין עָלָיו – **suffering comes upon him** [the misguided donor]. שֶׁנֶּאֱמַר ,,לַחְמְךָ יָשִׂימוּ מָזוֹר תַּחְתֶּיךָ אֵין תְּבוּנָה בּוֹ'' – **For it is stated:** ***[Because of] your bread, they will lay "mazor" under you; there is no discernment in him.***[29] וְאֵין מָזוֹר אֶלָּא יִסּוּרִין – **And** the word ***mazor*** here **means nothing other than "suffering,"** שֶׁנֶּאֱמַר ,,וַיַּרְא אֶפְרַיִם אֶת־חָלְיוֹ וִיהוּדָה אֶת־מְזֹרוֹ'' – **as it is stated:** ***And Ephraim saw his sickness, and Yehudah his suffering*** ("*mezoro*").[30]

NOTES

26. *Proverbs* 24:4. Beginning with the preceding verse, the passage reads: בְּחָכְמָה יִבָּנֶה בָּיִת וּבִתְבוּנָה יִתְכּוֹנָן, *Through knowledge a house is built, and through insight it is established.* וּבְדַעַת חֲדָרִים יִמָּלְאוּ כָּל־הוֹן יָקָר וְנָעִים, *And through understanding the rooms are filled, [with] all riches precious and pleasant.* These are the three levels of intellectual faculties in ascending order: חָכְמָה [the amassing of *knowledge* from other sources]; תְּבוּנָה [the *insight* to deduce new things based on one's existing corpus of knowledge]; and דַּעַת [*understanding*] (see *Rashi* to *Exodus* 31:3; see also *Iyun Yaakov* to *Berachos* loc. cit. ד״ה גדולה דעה).

Maharsha explains R' Elazar's statement in light of the Gemara in *Niddah* (70b), which records that the people of Alexandria asked R' Yehoshua ben Chananiah what a person should do in order to become wealthy. He answered: One should work long hours [cf. *Hagahos HaGra* ad loc.] and deal honestly. They replied: But many have done so and not become wealthy! He answered: Rather, one should beseech the One to Whom all wealth belongs. Accordingly, explains *Maharsha,* one who has understanding and comes to the realization that it is not his own commercial efforts that grant wealth will eventually beseech God for success and thereby become wealthy.

[Moreover, it is possible that the wealth achieved as a result of "understanding" is not to be understood as material wealth, but in the light of the dictum: "Who is truly rich? He who is happy with his lot" (*Avos* 4:1). The person who possesses true understanding will find true wealth in the inner contentment that the so-called "rich" man who is bereft of such knowledge vainly seeks in an abundance of material possessions. *R' Nachum of Chernobyl* explains in a similar manner the statement of the Sages that he who tithes will become rich: He becomes wealthy through inner contentment, not necessarily through material abundance (see *Margaliyos HaYam*).]

27. I.e. he does not bother to utilize his mind to think and understand (*Be'er Sheva*).

28. *Isaiah* 27:11. Israel fails to realize that its suffering is due to its sins. Therefore, God will not have compassion and alleviate that suffering, in the hope that the nation's continued suffering will lead them to repentance (*Radak* ad loc.). [Similarly, R' Elazar teaches that it is forbidden to have compassion and alleviate the suffering of a person who fails to realize that the suffering is meant to stir him to repentance.]

Margaliyos HaYam (citing incidents recorded in *Sefer Chasidim* and *Leket Yosher*) explains R' Elazar's intent to be that one must not submit to the entreaties of a fool who does not realize that what he seeks is in fact detrimental to him.

29. *Obadiah* v. 7. Because of your bread, which you gave to one who has no discernment, they will lay suffering under you [i.e. in the end, you will be hurt] (*Rashi*; see *Sanhedrei Ketanah*).

30. *Hosea* 5:13.

31. *Isaiah* 5:13. [In keeping with his explanation of the earlier Gemara, *Maharsha* (see note 26) explains that one who lacks understanding will fail to beseech God for success, and will thus — despite all his efforts — be reduced to such penury that he will have to sell everything and be exiled from his place.]

32. R' Elazar warns of the punishment in store for a man in whose house Torah is not studied at night; this is the counterpart of R' Yirmiyah ben Elazar's statement (*Eruvin* 18b) that any house in which words of Torah are heard at night will never be destroyed. Why the stress on Torah study at night? *Maharsha* explains that the reference is to a man who must work all day for a living. If he does not at least study Torah at night when he is free, his house will be consumed by the fire of Gehinnom. Alternatively, the emphasis is on the sound of Torah being *heard* in one's house at night, because the lack of such sounds by day does not prove that Torah is not being studied — it may simply be drowned out by the hubbub of daytime sounds.

Rambam (*Hil. Talmud Torah* 3:13) stresses the special significance of nocturnal study of Torah: "Even though it is a mitzvah to study by day and by night, a person learns most of his wisdom only at night. Therefore, whoever aspires to attain the "crown of Torah" should be careful with all of his nights and not waste even one of them with sleeping, eating, drinking, chatting, and the like; rather, [he should occupy himself] in the study of Torah and wisdom." Various Talmudic statements emphasize this point (see *Chagigah* 12b, *Avodah Zarah* 3b, *Menachos* 110a, *Tamid* 32b, and other sources cited here by *Margaliyos HaYam*).

33. *Job* 20:26. The passage describes the punishment of the wicked man. He will lose his ill-gotten gain and in its place, all manner of misfortune [*every darkness*] will be his lot; he will be consumed by *a fire [that does] not [need to be] blown* by any bellows, i.e. the fires of Gehinnom (see *Rashi* ad loc.).

Homiletically, R' Elazar expounds the beginning of the verse to mean: *Every darkness* [i.e. every night] *is hidden from its treasures* [i.e. the treasured words of Torah are absent from his house]; *therefore, a fire not blown shall consume him — the one who begrudges that there be a "remnant"* [i.e. one who studies Torah] *in his tent* (*Rashi*; see also *Margaliyos HaYam*).

34. *Joel* 3:5. The "remnants whom Hashem calls" are those who study Torah.

35. [I.e. his labors will never be blessed with success.]

36. *Job* 20:21. R' Elazar again expounds "remnant" as a reference to Torah scholars, as the Gemara will state shortly.

R' Elazar speaks of a person who is himself not a Torah scholar. Such a person can earn a portion in the World to Come as a reward for Torah learning — even if he personally does not study Torah — by supporting

יקבוהו לאום ואין [א] לאום אלא עוברין שנאמר א) ולאום מלאום יאמץ ואין קבה אלא קללה שנאמר ב) מה אקב לא קבה אל ואין בר אלא תורה שנאמר ג) נשקו בר פן יאנף עולא בר ישמעאל אומר מנקבין אותו ככברה כתיב הכא ד) יקבוהו לאום וכתיב התם ה) ויקב חור בדלתו ואמר אביי כי [ב] אוכלא דקצרי ואם למדו מה שכרו אמר רבא אמר רב ששת זוכה לברכות כיוסף שנאמר ד) וברכה לראש משביר ואין משביר אלא יוסף שנאמר ו) ויוסף הוא [השליט על הארץ הוא] המשביר לכל עם הארץ אמר רב ששת כל המלמד תורה בעוה"ז זוכה ומלמדה לעולם הבא שנאמר ז) ומרוה גם הוא [ג] יורה אמר רבא מניין לתחיית המתים מן התורה שנאמר ח) יחי ראובן ואל ימות יחי ראובן בעולם הזה ואל ימות לעולם הבא רבינא אמר מהכא ט) ורבים מישני אדמת עפר יקיצו אלה לחיי עולם ואלה לחרפות לדראון עולם רב אשי אמר מהכא י) ואתה לך [לקץ] ותנוח ותעמוד לגורלך לקץ הימין אמר רבי אלעזר כל פרנס שמנהיג את הצבור בנחת זוכה ומנהיגם לעוה"ב שנאמר יא) כי מרחמם ינהגם ועל מבועי מים ינהלם [ד] וא"ר אלעזר גדולה דעה שניתנה בין שתי אותיות שנאמר יב) כי אל דעות ה' וא"ר אלעזר גדול מקדש שניתן בין שתי אותיות שנאמר יג) פעלת ה' מקדש ה' כוננו ידיך מתקיף לה רב אדא [ה] קרחינאה אלא מעתה גדולה נקמה שניתנה בין שתי אותיות דכתיב יד) אל נקמות ה' אל נקמות הופיע אמר ליה למילתיה הכי נמי כדעולא דאמר עולא שתי הופעיות הללו למה אחת למדת טובה ואחת למדת פורענות ואמר ר' אלעזר כל אדם שיש בו דעה כאילו נבנה בית המקדש בימיו שזה ניתן בין שתי אותיות וזה ניתן בין שתי אותיות ואמר ר' אלעזר כל אדם שיש בו דעה לסוף מתעשר שנאמר טו) ובדעת חדרים ימלאו כל הון יקר ונעים ואמר ר' אלעזר כל אדם שאין בו דעה אסור לרחם עליו שנאמר טז) כי לא עם בינות הוא על כן לא ירחמנו עושהו ויוצרו לא יחוננו וא"ר אלעזר כל הנותן פיתו למי שאין בו דעה יסורין באין עליו שנאמר יז) לחמך ישימו מזור תחתיך אין תבונה בו ואין מזור אלא יסורין שנאמר יח) וירא אפרים את חליו ויהודה את מזורו ואמר ר' אלעזר כל אדם שאין בו דעה לסוף גולה שנאמר יט) לכן גלה עמי מבלי דעת ואמר ר"א [ו] א כל בית שאין דברי תורה נשמעים בו בלילה אש אוכלתו שנאמר כ) כל חשך טמון לצפוניו תאכלהו אש לא נופח ירע שריד באהלו [ז] אין שריד אלא ת"ח שנאמר כא) ובשרידים אשר ה' קורא ואמר ר' אלעזר כל שאינו מהנה תלמידי חכמים מנכסיו אינו רואה סימן ברכה לעולם שנאמר כב) אין שריד לאכלו על כן לא יחיל טובו אין שריד אלא תלמידי חכמים שנאמר ובשרידים אשר ה' קורא ואמר רבי אלעזר ב כל שאינו משייר פת על שלחנו אינו רואה סימן ברכה לעולם שנאמר אין שריד לאכלו על כן לא יחיל טובו והאמר רבי אלעזר כל המשייר פתיתים על שלחנו כאילו עובד ע"ז שנאמר כג) העורכים לגד שלחן והממלאים למני ממסך לא קשיא ג הא דאיכא שלימה בהדיה הא דליכא שלימה בהדיה ואמר רבי אלעזר [ח] כל המחליף בדבורו כאילו עובד ע"ז כתיב הכא כד) והייתי בעיניו כמתעתע וכתיב התם כה) הבל המה מעשה תעתועים ואמר רבי אלעזר כל המסתכל בערוה קשתו ננערת שנאמר כו) עריה תעור קשתך [ט] ואמר רבי אלעזר לעולם הוי קבל וקיים אמר רבי זירא אף אנן נמי תנינא [י] ד בית אפל אין פותחין לו חלונות לראות נגעו ש"מ [כ] אמר ר' טבי אמר ר' יאשיה מאי דכתיב כז) שאול ועוצר רחם ארץ לא שבעה מים וכי מה ענין שאול אצל רחם אלא לומר לך מה רחם מכנים ומוציא אף שאול מכנים ומוציא והלא דברים קל וחומר ומה רחם שמכניסין בו בחשאי מוציאין ממנו בקולי קולות שאול שמכניסין [ל] בו בקולות אינו דין שמוציאין ממנו בקולי קולות מיכן תשובה לאומרין אין תחיית המתים מן התורה תנא דבי אליהו צדיקים שעתיד הקדוש ברוך הוא להחיותן ה אינן חוזרין לעפרן שנאמר כח) והיה הנשאר בציון והנותר בירושלים קדוש יאמר לו כל הכתוב לחיים בירושלים מה קדוש לעולם קיים אף הם לעולם קיימין

ואם

רש"י

יקבוהו. מנקבים אותו לשון (מלכים ב יב) ויקוב חור בדלתו: אוכלא דקצרי. כלי של כובסין שהוא מנוקב ומזלפין בו מים על הבגדים: ומרוה גם הוא יורה. מי שמרווה את תלמידו בדבר הלכה גם הוא יורה לעולם הבא ל"א ומרוה לשון מורה: ואתה לך לקץ ותנוח ותעמוד וגו'. רמז לו שימות ויעמוד לאחר מכן לקץ הימין לקץ שעתיד הקב"ה להחזיר ימינו לפניו שהרי השיב אחור ימינו: מרחמם בעוה"ז. ינהגם לעוה"ב: שתי אותיות. של שם. כך שמעתי. ל"א כל שמות על שם דאמרי' בעלמא (חגיגה דף טז.) לבאות אות הוא בצבא שלו קרי להו אותיות לשון מופלא: גדול מקדש. חשוב הוא: למילתיה הכי נמי. דגדולה היא וכדעולא: שתי הופעיות. דכתיב אל נקמות ה' אל נקמות הופיע ואיכא תרי נקמות וחדא הופעה בתרוייהו ודמי כמאן דאיכא אכל נקמה ונקמה חדא הופעה: חדא לטובה. של ישראל שסילק שכינתו מאומות העולם ובא על ישראל וקרי ליה נקמות משום דתגמול טוב הוא שזכו לשכינה על שאמרו נעשה ונשמע ונקמה היינו תגמול ואחת לפורענות לעובדי כוכבים שנפרע מהן ליום הדין כדאמרינן בפרק קמא דמסכת ע"ז (דף ד.) נוקם ה' ובעל חמה לעכו"ם שהוא בעצמו ובכבודו נפרע מהן והיינו הופעה: ובדעת. מפני הדעת מלאו כל החדרים הון: בשביל לחמך. שנתת למי שאין בו דעה ישימו מזור תחתיך: כל חשך טמון לצפוניו. כל לילה לפון ונחבא ממלפוני התורה שאין דברי תורה נשמעין באותו בית: תאכלהו אש לא נופח. זה אשו של גיהנם שאין צריך נפוח: ירע שריד באהלו. מי שרע בעיניו שיש שריד באהלו: כל שאינו משייר פתיתין. דצריך לשייר כדכתיב אכול והותר (מלכים ב ד): והא אמר רבי אלעזר כל המשייר פתיתין על שולחנו כאילו עובד ע"ז שנאמר העורכים לגד שולחן. שכן עושין שמניחין שלחן ערוך במאכל ומשתה לשם אותה ע"ז שקורין גד וממלאים כוסות של מרקחים נסוכים לע"ז ששמה מני: הא. דקאמר אסור: דאיכא שלימה בהדיה. שמביא שלימה לאחר שאכל ונותן על השלחן עם הפתיתין ששייר דמחזי דלשם ע"ז עביד הכי: והא. דליכא שלימה בהדייהו דמזומנין לעני: הא גדא לביתיה לא גרסי': המחליף בדבורו. משנה בדבורו שלא יהא ניכר: קשתו ננערת. כח קושי אבר שלו ננער שאינו מוליד שנאמר עריה תעור קשתך עריה שאתה מסתכל בה ממש בערותה היא תעיר קשתך ד"א המסתכל המחשב בעריות דאשת איש קשתו גבורת ידו ננערת מתהלכת ומתמעטת כמו (ב"מ דף כט:) מלא כסות מנערה אחת לשלשים יום א"נ כמו (שמות יד) וינער ה': הוי קבל. הוי עניו ותחיה. קבל לשון אפל עשה עצמך אפל ושפל: בית אפל אין פותחין בו חלונות לראות את נגעו. כנגע נראה לי בבית כתיב דמשמע נראה ממילא ועוד דכתיב לי [ל] ולא לאורי נמצא שאפלתו הצלתו דכל זמן שאין כהן רואהו אין מטמא בנגעים: שאול ועוצר רחם ארץ לא שבעה מים. קבר לא שבע ממתים ועוצר רחם בית הרחם שהוא קצור ועצור לא ישבע מבעילות וכן ארץ לא שבעה מים: וכי מה ענין שאול וכו'. למה נסמכו הני אהדדי: מכנים. הזרע ומוציא הולד אף שאול מכנים ומוציא לתחיית המתים: שמכניסין בה בקולי קולות. בבכי גדול קוברין את המת: אינו דין שמוציאין אותו בקולי קולות. שנאמר יתקע בשופר גדול: שעתיד הקב"ה להחיות. לימות המשיח: לאחר שיחיו שוב אין חוזרין לעפרם. בין [מ] (לימות המשיח בין לעולם הבא) אלא הבשר מתקיים עליהם עד שיסובו ויחיו לעתיד לבא: ואותן

מסורת הש"ס

א) סוטה מח:, ב) [גי' הערוך ערך אבל אובלא בבי"ת וע"ש שני פירושים], ג) בקרא כתיב יורא באל"ף, ד) ברכות לג. ע"ש, ה) [שם. ע"ש], ו) חולין קלג., ז) [מס' כלה], ח) לעיל יד., ט) [נגעים פ"ב מ"ג] חולין י:, י) ברכות טו:, כ) בד"י אותו, ל) [מועד קטן ח.], מ) ימות המשיח ולעולם הבא. רש"ל.

גליון הש"ס

גמ' כל בית שאין ד"ת נשמעין. עיין עירובין דף יח ע"ב:

עין משפט נר מצוה

ו א מיי' פ"ג מהל' ת"ת הל' יג סמג עשין יב טוש"ע יו"ד סי' רמו סעיף כד:
ז ב ג טוש"ע או"ח סי' קפ סעיף ג:
ח ד מיי' פי"ד מהל' טומאת צרעת הל' ה:
ט ה מיי' פ"ח מהל' תשובה הל' א:

ליקוטי רש"י

אוכלא דקצרי. כלי נחושת העשוי כנפה נקבים נקבים והוא של כובסים ונותנו על הבגדים ומזלף בו המים עליהן ויש מפרשים שמגמרין מוגמר מתחתיו והבגדים מונחין עליו ומתגמרין דרך הנקבים [שבת קכג:]. כלי שמשימין בו הכובסין בגדיהן [נדרים כג.]. קצרי. הכובס נקרא קצרי בלשון ארמי [ב"ק קיט:]. כך שמם בלשון ישמעאל והם כובסין שמעתי אומרים על שם שמקצרין בגדי צמר כשדורסין אותן ברגליהן במים שקורין פורלוי"ר והיינו דמתרגמינן עין רוגל (ש"ב יז) עינא דקצרא [תענית כט:]. ואל ימות לעולם הבא. שלא יזכר לו מעשה בלהה [דברים לג, ו]. ורבים מישני אדמת עפר יקיצו. יחיו המתים [דניאל יב, ב]. לך לקץ. תפטר לבית עולמך. לגורלך. לקבל חלקך עם הצדיקים. לקץ הימין. כמו באחרית הימים ואין לפרש הימין לשון יד הימנית שהרי הוא מנוי במסורת הגדולה בשיטת תיבות המיוחדין בנו"ן זקופה בסוף תיבה המשמשת במקום מ"ם ולית דכוותיהון כגון ועליה יכרעון אחרין (איוב לא) יקום ולאמון כחיין (יחזקאל כד) קם לך קמין (יחזקאל ד) יחרדון אימין (שם כו) למחות מלכין (משלי לא) לקץ הימין (כאן) [שם, יג]. שיחזיר ימינו לפניו שהשיב אחור ימינו מפני אויב [פסחים נו.]. בין שתי אותיות. בין שתי הזכרות. למילתיה הכי נמי. נקמה במקום שצריכה נקמה דבר גדול הוא [ברכות לג.]. הופיע. הראה וגלה לנו את נקמתך [תהלים צד, א]. מזורו. לשון חולי [הושע ה, יג]. מבלי דעת. לפי שהיה להם בלי דעת [ישעיה ה, יג]. ובשרידים. ובשארית אשר יותר. אשר ה' קורא. לשון קרואים לסעודה או לעבודת המלך לשון הזמנה [יואל ג, ה]. אין שריד לאכלו. לא השאיר ולא הניח לתלמידי חכמים על שלחנו כמו ובשרידים אשר ה' קורא. על כן לא יחיל טובו. לא יצליח כמו (תהלים י) יחילו דרכיו. כל שאינו משייר וכו' שנאמר אין שריד לאכלו. לא שייר ממאכלו לחלק לעניים [איוב כ, כא]. העורכים לגד. שם עכו"ם העשוים על שם המזל ולשון מזל יש גד גדי ויסוק לא. למני. למניין משמש הכומרים היו ממלאים אגנות מזג יין. ממסך. יין מזוג במים כמשפטו כמו לחקור ממסך (משלי כג) מסכה יינה (משלי ט) [ישעיה סה, יא]. הוי קבל. אפל. וקיים. ותחיה כלומר הרחק מן הרבנות שמקברת את בעליה אפילו מתרגם קבלה (שמות י) [לעיל יד.]. בית אפל. שצריך לפתוח לו חלונות לראות הנגע פוטרין אותו לגמרי כדכתיב (ויקרא יד) כנגע נראה לי בבית ולא לאורי עמד במקום אפל וצריך שם להדליק את הנר אינו נגע [חולין י:]. שאול ועוצר רחם. קבר. שמכניסין בו בקולות. של בכי ומספד [ברכות טו:]. והיה הנשאר. כל מקום ישבו בירושלים. קדוש יאמר לו. כלם יהיו צדיקים. והנותר. היום אשר נשאר כלם יהיו הכתוב לחיי העוה"ב שיהיו בירושלים [ישעיה ד, ג].

תורה אור השלם

א) וַיֹּאמֶר יְיָ לָהּ שְׁנֵי גוֹיִם בְּבִטְנֵךְ וּשְׁנֵי לְאֻמִּים מִמֵּעַיִךְ יִפָּרֵדוּ וּלְאֹם מִלְאֹם יֶאֱמָץ וְרַב יַעֲבֹד צָעִיר: [בראשית כה, כג]
ב) מָה אֶקֹּב לֹא קַבֹּה אֵל וּמָה אֶזְעֹם לֹא זָעַם יְיָ: [במדבר כג, ח]
ג) נַשְּׁקוּ בַר פֶּן יֶאֱנַף וְתֹאבְדוּ דֶרֶךְ כִּי יִבְעַר כִּמְעַט אַפּוֹ אַשְׁרֵי כָּל חוֹסֵי בוֹ: [תהלים ב, יב]
ד) מֹנֵעַ בָּר יִקְּבֻהוּ לְאוֹם וּבְרָכָה לְרֹאשׁ מַשְׁבִּיר: [משלי יא, כו]
ה) וַיִּקַּח יְהוֹיָדָע הַכֹּהֵן אֲרוֹן אֶחָד וַיִּקֹּב חֹר בְּדַלְתּוֹ וַיִּתֵּן אֹתוֹ אֵצֶל הַמִּזְבֵּחַ מִיָּמִין בְּבוֹא אִישׁ בֵּית יְיָ וְנָתְנוּ שָׁמָּה הַכֹּהֲנִים שֹׁמְרֵי הַסַּף אֶת כָּל הַכֶּסֶף הַמּוּבָא בֵית יְיָ: [מלכים ב' יב, י]
ו) וְיוֹסֵף הוּא הַשַּׁלִּיט עַל הָאָרֶץ הוּא הַמַּשְׁבִּיר לְכָל עַם הָאָרֶץ וַיָּבֹאוּ אֲחֵי יוֹסֵף וַיִּשְׁתַּחֲווּ לוֹ אַפַּיִם אָרְצָה: [בראשית מב, ו]
ז) נֶפֶשׁ בְּרָכָה תְדֻשָּׁן וּמַרְוֶה גַּם הוּא יוֹרֶא: [משלי יא, כה]
ח) יְחִי רְאוּבֵן וְאַל יָמֹת וִיהִי מְתָיו מִסְפָּר: [דברים לג, ו]
ט) וְרַבִּים מִיְּשֵׁנֵי אַדְמַת עָפָר יָקִיצוּ אֵלֶּה לְחַיֵּי עוֹלָם וְאֵלֶּה לַחֲרָפוֹת לְדִרְאוֹן עוֹלָם: [דניאל יב, ב]
י) וְאַתָּה לֵךְ לַקֵּץ וְתָנוּחַ וְתַעֲמֹד לְגֹרָלְךָ לְקֵץ הַיָּמִין: [דניאל יב, יג]
יא) לֹא יִרְעָבוּ וְלֹא יִצְמָאוּ וְלֹא יַכֵּם שָׁרָב וָשָׁמֶשׁ כִּי מְרַחֲמָם יְנַהֲגֵם וְעַל מַבּוּעֵי מַיִם יְנַהֲלֵם: [ישעיה מט, י]
יב) אַל תַּרְבּוּ תְדַבְּרוּ גְּבֹהָה גְבֹהָה יֵצֵא עָתָק מִפִּיכֶם כִּי אֵל דֵּעוֹת יְיָ וְלוֹ נִתְכְּנוּ עֲלִלוֹת: [שמואל א ב, ג]
יג) תְּבִאֵמוֹ וְתִטָּעֵמוֹ בְּהַר נַחֲלָתְךָ מָכוֹן לְשִׁבְתְּךָ פָּעַלְתָּ יְיָ מִקְּדָשׁ אֲדֹנָי כּוֹנְנוּ יָדֶיךָ: [שמות טו, יז]
יד) אֵל נְקָמוֹת יְיָ אֵל נְקָמוֹת הוֹפִיעַ: [תהלים צד, א]
טו) וּבְדַעַת חֲדָרִים יִמָּלְאוּ כָּל הוֹן יָקָר וְנָעִים: [משלי כד, ד]
טז) בִּיבֹשׁ קְצִירָהּ תִּשָּׁבַרְנָה נָשִׁים בָּאוֹת מְאִירוֹת אוֹתָהּ כִּי לֹא עַם בִּינוֹת הוּא עַל כֵּן לֹא יְרַחֲמֶנּוּ עֹשֵׂהוּ וְיֹצְרוֹ לֹא יְחֻנֶּנּוּ: [ישעיה כז, יא]
יז) עַד הַגְּבוּל שִׁלְּחוּךָ כֹּל אַנְשֵׁי בְרִיתֶךָ הִשִּׁיאוּךָ יָכְלוּ לְךָ אַנְשֵׁי שְׁלֹמֶךָ לַחְמְךָ יָשִׂימוּ מָזוֹר תַּחְתֶּיךָ אֵין תְּבוּנָה בּוֹ: [עובדיה א, ז]
יח) וַיַּרְא אֶפְרַיִם אֶת חָלְיוֹ וִיהוּדָה אֶת מְזֹרוֹ וַיֵּלֶךְ אֶפְרַיִם אֶל אַשּׁוּר וַיִּשְׁלַח אֶל מֶלֶךְ יָרֵב וְהוּא לֹא יוּכַל לִרְפֹּא לָכֶם וְלֹא יִגְהֶה מִכֶּם מָזוֹר: [הושע ה, יג]
יט) לָכֵן גָּלָה עַמִּי מִבְּלִי דָעַת וּכְבוֹדוֹ מְתֵי רָעָב וַהֲמוֹנוֹ צִחֵה צָמָא: [ישעיה ה, יג]
כ) כָּל חֹשֶׁךְ טָמוּן לִצְפוּנָיו תְּאָכְלֵהוּ אֵשׁ לֹא נֻפָּח יֵרַע שָׂרִיד בְּאָהֳלוֹ: [איוב כ, כו]
כא) וְהָיָה כֹּל אֲשֶׁר יִקְרָא בְּשֵׁם יְיָ יִמָּלֵט כִּי בְּהַר צִיּוֹן וּבִירוּשָׁלַיִם תִּהְיֶה פְלֵיטָה כַּאֲשֶׁר אָמַר יְיָ וּבַשְּׂרִידִים אֲשֶׁר יְיָ קֹרֵא: [יואל ג, ה]
כב) אֵין שָׂרִיד לְאָכְלוֹ עַל כֵּן לֹא יָחִיל טוּבוֹ: [איוב כ, כא]
כג) וְאַתֶּם עֹזְבֵי יְיָ הַשְּׁכֵחִים אֶת הַר קָדְשִׁי הָעֹרְכִים לַגַּד שֻׁלְחָן וְהַמְמַלְאִים לַמְנִי מִמְסָךְ: [ישעיה סה, יא]
כד) אוּלַי יְמֻשֵּׁנִי אָבִי וְהָיִיתִי בְעֵינָיו כִּמְתַעְתֵּעַ וְהֵבֵאתִי עָלַי קְלָלָה וְלֹא בְרָכָה: [בראשית כז, יב]
כה) הֶבֶל הֵמָּה מַעֲשֵׂה תַּעְתֻּעִים בְּעֵת פְּקֻדָּתָם יֹאבֵדוּ: [ירמיה י, טו]
כו) עֶרְיָה תֵעוֹר קַשְׁתֶּךָ שְׁבֻעוֹת מַטּוֹת אֹמֶר סֶלָה נְהָרוֹת תְּבַקַּע אָרֶץ: [חבקוק ג, ט]
כז) שְׁאוֹל וְעֹצֶר רָחַם אֶרֶץ לֹא שָׂבְעָה מַּיִם וְאֵשׁ לֹא אָמְרָה הוֹן: [משלי ל, טז]
כח) וְהָיָה הַנִּשְׁאָר בְּצִיּוֹן וְהַנּוֹתָר בִּירוּשָׁלַיִם קָדוֹשׁ יֵאָמֶר לוֹ כָּל הַכָּתוּב לַחַיִּים בִּירוּשָׁלָיִם: [ישעיה ד, ג]

Torah scholars, שֶׁנֶּאֱמַר ,,וּבַשְּׂרִידִים אֲשֶׁר ה׳ קֹרֵא״ – **as it is stated** elsewhere: ***And among the remnants whom HASHEM calls.***[37]

וְאָמַר רַבִּי אֶלְעָזָר – **And R' Elazar** also **said** in exposition of the verse cited above: כָּל שֶׁאֵינוֹ מְשַׁיֵּיר פַּת עַל שֻׁלְחָנוֹ – **Whoever does not leave over bread on his table** after his meal אֵינוֹ רוֹאֶה סִימַן בְּרָכָה לְעוֹלָם – **will never see a sign of blessing.**[38] שֶׁנֶּאֱמַר ,,אֵין שָׂרִיד לְאָכְלוֹ עַל כֵּן לֹא יָחִיל טוּבוֹ״ – **For it is stated: *There is no remnant to his food; therefore his goods shall not prosper.***[39]

The Gemara asks:

וְהָאָמַר רַבִּי אֶלְעָזָר – **But R' Elazar said** elsewhere: כָּל הַמְשַׁיֵּיר פְּתִיתִים עַל שֻׁלְחָנוֹ – **If one leaves over pieces of bread on his table,** כְּאִילּוּ עוֹבֵד עֲבוֹדָה זָרָה – **it is as if he worships idols!** שֶׁנֶּאֱמַר ,,הָעֹרְכִים לַגַּד שֻׁלְחָן וְהַמְמַלְאִים לַמְנִי מִמְסָךְ״ – **For it is stated: *Those who set a table for Gad and fill [cups of] spiced wine for Meni.***[40] How, then, does R' Elazar in his first statement advocate leaving bread over on one's table?

The Gemara answers:

לָא קַשְׁיָא – **It is not a difficulty,** i.e. there is no contradiction. הָא דְּאִיכָּא שְׁלֵימָה בַּהֲדֵיהּ – In **this** second statement, where he prohibits leaving over pieces of bread, R' Elazar refers to **where there is a whole loaf together with [the pieces].**[41] הָא דְּלֵיכָּא שְׁלֵימָה בַּהֲדֵיהּ – In **this** first statement, where he condemns one who does *not* leave over bread on his table, R' Elazar refers to **where there is not a whole loaf together with [the pieces].**[42]

וְאָמַר רַבִּי אֶלְעָזָר – **And R' Elazar** also **said:** כָּל הַמַּחֲלִיף בְּדִיבּוּרוֹ – **Whoever disguises his speech** so that he should not be recognized[43] כְּאִילּוּ עוֹבֵד עֲבוֹדָה זָרָה – **is considered as if he worships idols.** כְּתִיב הָכָא ,,וְהָיִיתִי בְעֵינָיו כִּמְתַעְתֵּעַ״ – For **it is written here,** in one verse, concerning Jacob's impersonation of Esau: ***And I shall appear in his eyes as a deceiver.***[44] וּכְתִיב הָתָם ,,הֶבֶל הֵמָּה מַעֲשֵׂה תַּעְתֻּעִים״ – **And it is written there,** in reference to idol worship: ***They are vanity, the work of deception.***[45]

וְאָמַר רַבִּי אֶלְעָזָר – **And R' Elazar** also **said:** כָּל הַמִּסְתַּכֵּל בָּעֶרְוָה – **If one gazes upon the nakedness** of a woman,[46] קַשְׁתּוֹ נִנְעֶרֶת – **his bow is emptied.**[47] שֶׁנֶּאֱמַר ,,עֶרְיָה תֵעוֹר קַשְׁתֶּךָ״ – **For it is stated: *Nakedness shall empty your bow.***[48]

וְאָמַר רַבִּי אֶלְעָזָר – **And R' Elazar** also **said:** לְעוֹלָם הֱוֵי קָבֵל וְקַיָּים – **Always be humble and** thereby **live.**[49] אָמַר רַבִּי זֵירָא – **R' Zeira said:** אַף אֲנַן נַמִּי תְּנֵינָא – **We, too, have learned** this **in a Mishnah,** which states: בַּיִת אָפֵל אֵין פּוֹתְחִין לוֹ חַלּוֹנוֹת לִרְאוֹת נִגְעוֹ – In **A DARK HOUSE, WE DO NOT MAKE WINDOWS TO EXAMINE ITS *TZARAAS* SPOT.**[50] שְׁמַע מִינָּהּ – **Learn from this** that humility causes long life.[51]

The Gemara returns to its earlier discussion of the Scriptural sources for resurrection:

אָמַר רַבִּי טָבִי אָמַר רַבִּי יֹאשִׁיָּה – **R' Tavi said in the name of R'**

NOTES

those who do study (see *Sotah* 21a). However, if a person neither studies Torah himself nor supports others who study, then he is unworthy of enjoying his wealth, for the Torah and its study are the root of all blessing (see *Maharsha*).

37. See note 34 above.

38. See note 35 above.

39. One should leave over some of his meal on his table, as it is written *eat and leave over* [*II Kings* 4:43] (*Rashi*), so that a poor, unexpected guest might find something ready to eat (*Rashi* below ד״ה והוא; *Rabbeinu Yehonasan,* cited in *Chamra VeChayei*; see also *Rashi* to *Job* ad loc.). Alternatively, some food should be left over so that the person who has eaten can thank God for His gift which is so bounteous that one has eaten to satiety and still has food left over (*Levush,* cited by *Mishnah Berurah* 180:1-2).

40. *Isaiah* 65:11. Gad and Meni were pagan deities. Gad was worshiped by leaving a table set with food and drink; Meni was worshiped by filling cups of specially mixed drinks (*Rashi*). Since leaving food over on one's table is a mode of idol worship, R' Elazar forbids one to leave pieces of bread over on his table lest it appear that he is engaging in this pagan rite (see *Rashi* below).

41. I.e. where after the meal, the person brings a whole loaf of bread and places it on the table together with the pieces. This has the semblance of the pagan rite (*Rashi*) since it does not [then] seem likely that he placed an entire loaf on the table just for some poor person who might happen by (*Derishah, Orach Chaim* 180:1). [*Beur HaGra* (cited by *Mishnah Berurah* 180:4) deduces from *Rashi* here that if there are no pieces left on the table, then one *may* place a whole loaf there.]

42. In this case, it is praiseworthy so they will be readily available for a poor man who might happen by [and all realize that it is not being done as a pagan rite] (see *Rashi* printed in *Ein Yaakov*).

Yad Ramah cites a different version of the Gemara's answer, which states that R' Elazar forbids leaving bread on the table: וְהוּא דְּאָמַר הָנֵי לְגַדָּא דְבֵיתָא וְהוּא דְלֵיכָּא שְׁלֵמָה בֵּינֵיהֶן, *provided that he says, "These are for the guardian spirit of the house," provided that there is* ***no*** *whole loaf among [the pieces].* According to this reading, it is specifically *pieces* of bread that present a problem, not a *whole* loaf. See, however, *Orach Chaim* 180:1-2.

43. *Rashi. Meiri* explains that this refers to one who does not keep his word.

44. *Genesis* 27:12.

45. *Jeremiah* 10:15. Thus, Scripture employs the root תעתע for both a deceiver and for idol worship, thereby equating the two. See *Maharal.*

46. I.e. her private parts (*Rashi,* first explanation; see also note 48).

47. I.e. he becomes impotent (*Rashi,* first explanation). ["Bow" is a reference to the male organ, which shoots forth the seed like a bow (*R' Yehudah Almadari*).] See also *Ben Yehoyada.*

48. *Habakkuk* 3:9. [The simple meaning of the verse is: *Starkly revealed is Your bow,* i.e. God's power is manifestly displayed (see *Rashi* and *Radak* ad loc.). R' Elazar expounds the verse homiletically.]

Alternatively, R' Elazar refers to one who *contemplates* another man's wife, allowing his thoughts to dwell upon her. This causes his might to be sapped. Accordingly, the verse would be rendered: *Nakedness shall sap your strength* (*Rashi,* second explanation; see *Maharsha,* who explains why *Rashi* singles out the married woman from among the many types of forbidden women).

49. קָבֵל means literally *remain in the dark*; i.e. stay out of the limelight (see *Rashi*). This leads to long life.

50. *Negaim* 2:3. The appearance of a *tzaraas* spot on the inside walls of the house can result in the entire house being razed to the ground (see *Leviticus* 14:33 ff.). This Mishnah teaches, however, that a *tzaraas* spot appearing in a darkened house [where the spot cannot be properly seen by the sunlight that filters in] is disregarded. For the verse states that the *tzaraas* process of a house is initiated when the homeowner comes to the Kohen and declares: *Something like a tzaraas spot has appeared to me in the house* (*Leviticus* 14:35). The expression *has appeared* suggests that it has appeared under natural lighting conditions [i.e. the light that filters in through windows and doors], without the need for artificial light. Furthermore, the superfluous expression *to me* indicates an exclusion — to *me* but not to *my lamp.* And we learn from here that the Kohen's examination of the spot (which is essential for his declaring it *tamei*) may also be conducted only under similar conditions [see *Moed Katan* 8a]. Though we could break open a new window in the wall opposite the spot, thereby illuminating the spot with natural light, the Mishnah teaches that this need not be done. Since the spot is in the dark as the house is currently constructed, the spot is disregarded entirely. Thus, it emerges that the house's lack of light is what saves it from destruction (see *Rashi*).

51. Like the dark house, one who is humble lives long. For the one who is not humble and flaunts his talent or wealth arouses jealousy and thereby brings "the evil eye" upon himself (see 93a note 14), which could be the cause of his downfall (see *Maharsha*).

This sentiment is echoed by the Talmudic statement that leadership shortens the life of a person, as evidenced by Joseph, who died before his brothers [*Berachos* 55a] (*Rabbeinu Yehonasan,* cited in *Chamra VeChayei*).

יקבוהו לאום ואין א) לאום אלא עוברין שנאמר א) ולאום מלאום יאמץ ואין קבה אלא קללה שנאמר ב) מה אקב לא קבה אל ואין בר אלא תורה שנאמר ג) נשקו בר פן יאנף עולא בר ישמעאל אומר מנקבין אותו ככברה כתיב הכא ד) יקבוהו לאום וכתיב התם ה) ויקב חור בדלתו ואמר אביי כי ב) אוכלא דקצרי ואם למדו מה שכרו אמר רבא אמר רב ששת זוכה לברכות כיוסף שנאמר ד) וברכה לראש משביר ואין משביר אלא יוסף שנאמר ו) ויוסף הוא [השליט על הארץ הוא] המשביר לכל עם הארץ אמר רב ששת כל המלמד תורה בעוה"ז זוכה ומלמדה לעולם הבא שנאמר ז) ומרוה גם הוא ג) יורה אמר רבא מניין לתחיית המתים מן התורה שנאמר ח) יחי ראובן ואל ימות יחי ראובן בעולם הזה ואל ימות לעולם הבא רבינא אמר מהכא ט) ורבים מישני אדמת עפר יקיצו אלה לחיי עולם ואלה לחרפות לדראון עולם רב אשי אמר מהכא י) ואתה לך [לקץ] ותנוח ותעמוד לגורלך לקץ הימין אמר רבי אלעזר כל פרנס שמנהיג את הצבור בנחת זוכה ומנהיגם לעוה"ב שנאמר יא) כי מרחמם ינהגם ועל מבועי מים ינהלם ד) וא"ר אלעזר גדולה דעה שניתנה בין שתי אותיות שנאמר יב) כי אל דעות ה' וא"ר אלעזר גדול מקדש שניתן בין שתי אותיות שנאמר יג) פעלת ה' מקדש ה' כוננו ידיך מתקיף לה רב אדא ה) קרחינאה אלא מעתה גדולה נקמה שניתנה בין שתי אותיות דכתיב יד) אל נקמות ה' אל נקמות הופיע אמר ליה למילתיה הכי נמי כדעולא דאמר עולא שתי הופעיות הללו למה אחת למדת טובה ואחת למדת פורענות ואמר ר' אלעזר כל אדם שיש בו דעה כאילו נבנה בית המקדש בימיו שזה ניתן בין שתי אותיות וזה ניתן בין שתי אותיות ואמר ר' אלעזר כל אדם שיש בו דעה לסוף מתעשר שנאמר טו) ובדעת חדרים ימלאו כל הון יקר ונעים ואמר ר' אלעזר כל אדם שאין בו דעה אסור לרחם עליו שנאמר טז) כי לא עם בינות הוא על כן לא ירחמנו עושהו ויוצרו לא יחוננו וא"ר אלעזר כל הנותן פיתו למי שאין בו דעה יסורין באין עליו שנאמר יז) לחמך ישימו מזור תחתיך אין תבונה בו ואין מזור אלא יסורין שנאמר יח) וירא אפרים את חליו ויהודה את מזורו ואמר ר' אלעזר כל אדם שאין בו דעה לסוף גולה שנאמר יט) לכן גלה עמי מבלי דעת ואמר ר"א א כל בית שאין דברי תורה נשמעים בו בלילה אש אוכלתו שנאמר כ) כל חשך טמון לצפוניו תאכלהו אש לא נופח ירע שריד באהלו ו) אין שריד אלא ת"ח שנאמר כא) ובשרידים אשר ה' קורא ואמר ר' אלעזר כל שאינו מהנה תלמידי חכמים מנכסיו אינו רואה סימן ברכה לעולם שנאמר כב) אין שריד לאכלו על כן לא יחיל טובו אין שריד אלא תלמידי חכמים שנאמר ובשרידים אשר ה' קורא ואמר רבי אלעזר ב כל שאינו משייר פת על שלחנו אינו רואה סימן ברכה לעולם שנאמר אין שריד לאכלו על כן לא יחיל טובו והאמר רבי אלעזר כל המשייר פתיתים על שלחנו כאילו עובד ע"ז שנאמר כג) העורכים לגד שלחן והממלאים למני ממסך לא קשיא ג הא דאיכא שלימה בהדיה הא דליכא שלימה בהדיה ואמר רבי אלעזר ז) כל המחליף בדבורו כאילו עובד ע"ז כתיב הכא כד) והייתי בעיניו כמתעתע וכתיב התם כה) הבל המה מעשה תעתועים ואמר רבי אלעזר כל המסתכל בערוה קשתו נגערת שנאמר כו) עריה תעור קשתך ח) ואמר רבי אלעזר לעולם הוי קבל וקיים אמר רבי זירא אף אנן נמי תנינא ד בית אפל אין פותחין לו חלונות לראות נגעו ש"מ ט) אמר ר' טבי אמר ר' יאשיה מאי דכתיב כז) שאול ועוצר רחם ארץ לא שבעה מים וכי מה ענין שאול אצל רחם אלא לומר לך מה רחם מכנים ומוציא אף שאול מכנים ומוציא והלא דברים קל וחומר ומה רחם שמכניסין בו בחשאי מוציאין ממנו בקולי קולות שאול שמכניסין י) בו בקולות אינו דין שמוציאין ממנו בקולי קולות מיכן תשובה לאומרין אין תחיית המתים מן התורה תנא דבי אליהו צדיקים שעתיד הקדוש ברוך הוא להחיותן ה אינן חוזרין לעפרן שנאמר כח) והיה הנשאר בציון והנותר בירושלים קדוש יאמר לו כל הכתוב לחיים בירושלים מה קדוש לעולם קיים אף הם לעולם קיימין ואם

רש"י

יקבוהו. מנקבים אותו לשון (מלכים ב יב) ויקוב חור בדלתו: אוכלא דקצרי. כלי של כובסין שהוא מנוקב ומזלפין בו מים על הבגדים: ומרוה גם הוא יורה. מי שמרווה את תלמידו בדבר הלכה גם הוא יורה לעולם הבא ל"א ומרוה לשון מורה: ואתה לך לקץ ותנוח ותעמוד וגו'. רמז לו שימות ויעמוד לאחר מכן לקץ הימין לקץ שעתיד הקב"ה להחזיר ימינו לפניו שהרי השיב אחור ימינו: מרחמם בעוה"ז. ינהגם לעוה"ב: שתי אותיות. של שם. כך שמעתי. ל"א כל שמות על שם דאמרי' בעלמא (חגיגה דף טז.) צבאות אות הוא בצבא שלו קרי להו אותיות לשון מופלא: גדול מקדש. חשוב הוא: למילתיה הכי נמי. דגדולה היא וכדעולא: שתי הופעיות. דכתיב אל נקמות ה' אל נקמות הופיע ואיכא תרי נקמות וחדא הופעה בתרוייהו ודמי כמאן דאיכא אכל נקמה ונקמה חדא הופעה: חדא לטובה. של ישראל שסילק שכינתו מאומות העולם ובא על ישראל וקרי ליה נקמות משום דתגמול טוב הוא שזכו לשכינה על שאמרו נעשה ונשמע ונקמה היינו תגמול ואחת לפורענות לעובדי כוכבים שנפרע מהן ליום הדין כדאמרינן בפרק קמא דמסכת ע"ז (דף ד.) נוקם ה' ובעל חמה לעכו"ם שהוא בעצמו ובכבודו נפרע מהן והיינו הופעה: ובדעת. מפני הדעת מלאו כל החדרים הון: בשביל לחמך. שנתת למי שאין בו דעה ישימו מזור תחתיך: כל חשך טמון לצפוניו. כל לילה לפון ונחבא ממלפוני התורה שאין דברי תורה נשמעין באותו בית: תאכלהו אש לא נופח. זה אשו של גיהנם שאין צריך נפוח: ירע שריד באהלו. מי שרע בעיניו שיש שריד באהלו: כל שאינו משייר פתיתין. דצריך לשייר כדכתיב אכול והותר (מלכים ב ד): והא אמר רבי אלעזר כל המשייר פתיתין על שולחנו כאילו עובד ע"ז שנאמר העורכים לגד שולחן. שכן עושין שמניחין שלחן ערוך במאכל ומשתה לשם אותה ע"ז שקורין גד וממלאים כוסות של מרקחים נסוכים לע"ז ששמה מני: הא. דקאמר אסור: דאיכא שלימה בהדיה. שמביא שלימה לאחר שאכל ונותן על השלחן עם הפתיתין ששייר דמחזי דלשם ע"ז עביד הכי: והא. דליכא שלימה בהדייהו דמזומנין לעני: הא גדא לביתיה לא גרסי': המחליף בדבורו. משנה בדבורו שלא יהא ניכר: קשתו ננערת. כח קושי אבר שלו ננער שאינו מוליד שנאמר עריה תעור קשתך עריה שאתה מסתכל בה ממש בערותה היא תעיר קשתך ד"א המסתכל המחשב בעריות דאשת איש קשתו גבורת ידו ננערת מתהלכת ומתמעטת כמו (ב"מ דף כט:) מלא כסות מנערה אחת לשלשים יום א"נ כמו (שמות יד) וינער ה': הוי קבל. הוי עניו ותחיה. קבל לשון אפל עשה עצמך אפל ושפל: בית אפל אין פותחין בו חלונות לראות את נגעו. כנגע נראה לי בבית כתיב דמשמע נראה ממילא ועוד דכתיב לי ל) ולא לאורי נמצא שאפלתו הצלתו דכל זמן שאין כהן רואהו אין מטמא בנגעים: שאול ועוצר רחם ארץ לא שבעה מים. קבר לא שבע ממתים ועוצר רחם בית הרחם שהוא קצור ועצור לא ישבע מבעילות וכן ארץ לא שבעה מים: וכי מה ענין שאול וכו'. למה נסמכו הני אהדדי: מכנים. הזרע ומוציא הולד אף שאול מכנים ומוציא לתחיית המתים: שמכניסין בה בקולי קולות. בבכי גדול קוברין את המת: אינו דין שמוציאין אותו בקולי קולות. שנאמר יתקע בשופר גדול: שעתיד הקב"ה להחיות. לימות המשיח: לאחר שיחיו שוב אין חוזרין לעפרם. בין מ) (לימות המשיח בין לעולם הבא) אלא הבשר מתקיים עליהם עד שישובו ויחיו לעתיד לבא: ואותן

מסורת הש"ס

א) סוטה מא:, ב) [גי' הערוך ערך אכל אוכלא דקצרי ב"ח וע"ש שני פירושים], ג) בקרא כתיב יורא בגלי', ד) ברכות נג. ע"ש, ה) [שם. ע"ש], ו) חולין קלג., ז) [מ' כלה], ח) לעיל יד., ט) [נגעים פ"ב מ"ג] חולין י., י) ברכות טו: כד"י אותו, ל) [מועד קטן ח.], מ) ימות המשיח ולעולם הבא. רש"ל.

גליון הש"ס

גמ' כל בית שאין ד"ת נשמעין. עיין עירובין דף יח ע"ב:

תורה אור השלם

א) ויאמר יי לה שני גוים בבטנך ושני לאמים ממעיך יפרדו ולאם מלאם יאמץ ורב יעבד צעיר: [בראשית כה, כג]

ב) מה אקב לא קבה אל ומה אזעם לא זעם יי: [במדבר כג, ח]

ג) נשקו בר פן יאנף ותאבדו דרך כי יבער כמעט אפו אשרי כל חוסי בו: [תהלים ב, יב]

ד) מנע בר יקבהו לאום וברכה לראש משביר: [משלי יא, כו]

ה) ויקח יהוידע הכהן ארון אחד ויקב חר בדלתו ויתן אתו אצל המזבח מימין בבוא איש בית יי ונתנו שמה הכהנים שמרי הסף את כל הכסף המובא בית יי: [מלכים ב' יב, י]

ו) ויוסף הוא השליט על הארץ הוא המשביר לכל עם הארץ ויבאו אחי יוסף וישתחוו לו אפים ארצה: [בראשית מב, ו]

ז) נפש ברכה תדשן ומרוה גם הוא יורא: [משלי יא, כה]

ח) יחי ראובן ואל ימת ויהי מתיו מספר: [דברים לג, ו]

ט) ורבים מישני אדמת עפר יקיצו אלה לחיי עולם ואלה לחרפות לדראון עולם: [דניאל יב, ב]

י) ואתה לך לקץ ותנוח ותעמד לגרלך לקץ הימין: [דניאל יב, יג]

יא) לא ירעבו ולא יצמאו ולא יכם שרב ושמש כי מרחמם ינהגם ועל מבועי מים ינהלם: [ישעיה מט, י]

יב) אל תרבו תדברו גבהה גבהה יצא עתק מפיכם כי אל דעות יי ולו נתכנו עללות: [שמואל א' ב, ג]

יג) תבאמו ותטעמו בהר נחלתך מכון לשבתך פעלת יי מקדש אדני כוננו ידיך: [שמות טו, יז]

יד) אל נקמות יי אל נקמות הופיע: [תהלים צד, א]

טו) ובדעת חדרים ימלאו כל הון יקר ונעים: [משלי כד, ד] טז) ביבש קצירה תשברנה נשים באות מאירות אותה כי לא עם בינות הוא על כן לא ירחמנו עשהו ויצרו לא יחננו: [ישעיה כז, יא] יז) עד הגבול שלחוך כל אנשי בריתך השיאוך יכלו לך אנשי שלמך לחמך ישימו מזור תחתיך אין תבונה בו: [עובדיה א, ז] יח) וירא אפרים את חליו ויהודה את מזרו וילך אפרים אל אשור וישלח אל מלך ירב והוא לא יוכל לרפא לכם ולא יגהה מכם מזור: [הושע ה, יג] יט) לכן גלה עמי מבלי דעת וכבודו מתי רעב והמונו צחה צמא: [ישעיה ה, יג] כ) כל חשך טמון לצפוניו תאכלהו אש לא נפח ירע שריד באהלו: [איוב כ, כו] כא) והיה כל אשר יקרא בשם יי ימלט כי בהר ציון ובירושלים תהיה פליטה כאשר אמר יי ובשרידים אשר יי קרא: [יואל ג, ה] כב) אין שריד לאכלו על כן לא יחיל טובו: [איוב כ, כא] כג) ואתם עזבי יי השכחים את הר קדשי הערכים לגד שלחן והממלאים למני ממסך: [ישעיה סה, יא] כד) אולי ימשני אבי והייתי בעיניו כמתעתע והבאתי עלי קללה ולא ברכה: [בראשית כז, יב] כה) הבל המה מעשה תעתעים בעת פקדתם יאבדו: [ירמיה י, טו] כו) עריה תעור קשתך שבעות מטות אמר סלה נהרות תבקע ארץ: [חבקוק ג, ט] כז) שאול ועצר רחם ארץ לא שבעה מים ואש לא אמרה הון: [משלי ל, טז] כח) והיה הנשאר בציון והנותר בירושלים קדוש יאמר לו כל הכתוב לחיים בירושלים: [ישעיה ד, ג]

עין משפט נר מצוה

ו א מיי' פ"ג מהל' ת"ת הל' יג סמג עשין יג טוש"ע יו"ד סי' רמו סעיף כד:

ז ב ג טוש"ע או"ח סי' קפ סעיף ג:

ח ד מיי' פ"ד מהל' טומאת צרעת הל' ה:

ט ה מיי' פ"ח מהל' תשובה הל' ד:

ליקוטי רש"י

אוכלא דקצרי. כלי נחושת העשוי כנפה נקבים נקבים והוא של כובסים ונותנו על הבגדים ומזלף בו המים עליהן ויש מפרשים שמגמרין מוגמר מתחתיו והבגדים מונחין עליו ומתגמרין דרך הנקבים [שבת קכג:]. כלי שמשימין בו הכובסין בגדיהן [נדרים כג.]. קצרי. הכובס נקרא קצרי בלשון ארמי [ב"ק קיט:]. כך שם בלשון ישמעאל והם כובסין שמעתי אומרים על שם שמקצרין בגדי לבנות כשדורסין אותן ברגליהן במים שקורין פורלו"ר והיינו דמתרגמינן עין רוגל (ש"ב יז) עינא דקצרא [תענית כט.]. ואל ימות לעולם הבא. שלא יזכר לו מעשה בלהה [דברים לג, ו]. ורבים מישני אדמת עפר יקיצו. יחיו המתים [דניאל יב, ב]. לך לקץ. תפטר לבית עולמך. לגורלך. לקבל חלקך עם הצדיקים. לקץ הימין. כמו באחרית הימים ואין לפרש הימין לשון יד ימינית שהרי הוא מנוי במסורת הגדולה בשיטת תיבות המיוחדין בנו"ן וקופה בסוף תיבה המשמשת במקום מ"ם ולית דכוותיהון כגון ועליה יכרעון אחרין (איוב לא) יקום ולא יאמין בחיין (שם כד) קח חטין (יחזקאל ד) ימרדון אורין (שם כד) למחות מלכין לקץ הימין [שם יג]. לקץ הימין שיחזיר ימינו לפני שהשיב אחור ימינו מפני אויב [פסחים נג:]. בין שתי אותיות. בין שתי הזכרות. למילתיה הכי נמי. נקמה דבר גדול הוא [ברכות לג.]. הופיע. הראה נקמתך [תהלים צד, א]. מזורו. לשון חולי [הושע ה, יג]. מבלי דעת. שהיה לבם בלי דעת [ישעיה ה, יג]. ובשרידים. בשארית אשר יואיל. אשר ה' קורא. לשון קרואים לסעודה או לעבודת המלך לשון הזמנה [יואל ג, ה]. אין שריד לאכלו. לא השרה תלמידי חכמים על שלחנו כמו ובשרידים אשר ה' קורא. על כן לא יחיל טובו. לא יצליח כמו (תהלים י) יחילו דרכיו. כל שאינו משייר וכו' שנאמר אין שריד לאכלו. לא שייר ממאכלו לחלק לעניים [איוב כ, כא]. העורכים לגד. שם עכו"ם העשוים על שם המזל ובלשון משנה יש גד גדי וסיעוק לא. למני. למניין חשבון הכומרים היו ממלאים אגנות מזג יין. ממסך. יין מזוג במים כמשפטו כמו לחקור ממסך (משלי כג) מסכה יינה (משלי ט) [ישעיה סה, יא]. הוי קבל. אפל. וקיים. ותחיה כלומר הרחק מן הרבנות שמקברת את בעליה אפילה מתרגם קבלה (שמות י) [לעיל יד.]. בית אפל. שצריך לפתוח לו חלונות לראות הנגע פוטרין אותו לגמרי כדכתיב (ויקרא יד) כנגע נראה לי בבית לי ולא לאורי שאם עמד במקום אפל וצריך שם להדליק את הנר אינו נגע [חולין י:]. שאול ועוצר רחם. פסוק הוא בספר משלי שלש הנה לא תשבענה. שאול. קבר. שמכניסין בו בקולות. של בכי ומספד [ברכות טו:]. והיה הנשאר. בהם בציון יתיישבו. והנותר. בכל מקום ישכנו בירושלים. קדוש יאמר לו. כולם יהיו צדיקים וא"ת צדיקים המתים לפני אותו היום אבל כבודם ת"ל כל הכתוב לחיי העוה"ב יהיו בירושלים (כת"י) [ישעיה ד, ג].

Yoshiyah: מַאי דִּכְתִיב ,,שְׁאוֹל וְעֹצֶר רָחַם אֶרֶץ לֹא־שָׂבְעָה מַּיִם'' – **What is the meaning of that which is written:** *There are three things that are never satisfied . . .* ***The grave, the narrow part of the womb,***[52] ***and the earth that is not sated with water?***[53] וְכִי מָה עִנְיַן שְׁאוֹל אֵצֶל רֶחֶם – **Now, what connection is there between the grave and the womb** that would account for their juxtaposition in this verse? אֶלָּא לוֹמַר לָךְ – **Rather, it is to tell you** מָה רֶחֶם מַכְנִיס וּמוֹצִיא – that **just as the womb takes in and sends forth,**[54] אַף שְׁאוֹל מַכְנִיס וּמוֹצִיא – **so too does the grave take in** the corpse **and send forth** that very person, alive, at the time of resurrection. וַהֲלֹא דְּבָרִים קַל וָחוֹמֶר – **Now, is the matter not a *kal vachomer*?** וּמָה רֶחֶם שֶׁמַּכְנִיסִין בּוֹ בַּחֲשַׁאי מוֹצִיאִין מִמֶּנּוּ בְּקוֹלֵי קוֹלוֹת – **If the womb, which takes in** the sperm **in silence** subsequently **sends forth** the baby **amidst great noise,** שְׁאוֹל שֶׁמַּכְנִיסִין בּוֹ בְּקוֹלוֹת אֵינוֹ דִּין שֶׁמּוֹצִיאִין מִמֶּנּוּ בְּקוֹלֵי קוֹלוֹת – then **is it not evident that the grave, which takes in** the corpse **amidst great noise,**[55] **will** eventually **bring** it **forth amidst great noise?!**[56] מִיכָּן תְּשׁוּבָה לָאוֹמְרִין אֵין תְּחִיַּית הַמֵּתִים מִן הַתּוֹרָה – **From here is a refutation to those who say** that **there is no** allusion to **the Resurrection of the Dead in the** Written **Torah.**

A Baraisa concerning the fate of the righteous after resurrection:

תָּנָא דְּבֵי אֵלִיָּהוּ – **A Baraisa was taught in the academy of Eliyahu:**[57] צַדִּיקִים שֶׁעָתִיד הַקָּדוֹשׁ בָּרוּךְ הוּא לְהַחֲיוֹתָן – THE RIGHTEOUS THAT THE HOLY ONE, BLESSED IS HE, IS DESTINED TO RESURRECT אֵינָן חוֹזְרִין לַעֲפָרָן – WILL NOT RETURN TO THEIR DUST,[58] שֶׁנֶּאֱמַר ,,וְהָיָה הַנִּשְׁאָר בְּצִיּוֹן וְהַנּוֹתָר בִּירוּשָׁלַם קָדוֹשׁ יֵאָמֶר לוֹ כָּל־הַכָּתוּב לַחַיִּים בִּירוּשָׁלָם'' – AS IT IS STATED: *AND IT SHALL COME TO PASS THAT THE REMNANT WILL BE IN ZION AND THE LEFT OVER WILL BE IN JERUSALEM – "HOLY" SHALL BE SAID OF HIM; EVERYONE INSCRIBED FOR LIFE SHALL BE IN JERUSALEM.*[59] מָה קָדוֹשׁ לְעוֹלָם קַיָּים – From the fact that the resurrected are called "holy," we derive that JUST AS THE HOLY ONE [God] ENDURES FOREVER, אַף הֵם לְעוֹלָם קַיָּימִין – SO TOO THEY [the righteous resurrected at that time] ENDURE FOREVER.

NOTES

52. I.e. the corridor leading to the womb (*Rashi*).

53. *Proverbs* 30:16. The grave is never sated with corpses, nor the corridor to the womb with intercourse, nor the earth with water (*Rashi*).

54. The womb takes in the male's sperm and sends forth the child that has thereby been conceived (*Rashi*).

55. The wailing and weeping of the mourners (*Rashi*).

56. As it is written (*Isaiah* 27:13): *And it will be on that day a great shofar will be blown* (*Rashi*).

57. *Be'er Sheva* here insists that this does not refer to Elijah the Prophet, but rather to a Tanna by the name of Eliyahu, whom *Rambam* (*Introduction to the Mishnah*) lists together with Choni HaMe'agel. *Chida* (*Shem HaGedolim, Maareches Sefarim* ד״ה סדר, based on *Kesubos* 106a), however, presents a refutation of *Be'er Sheva's* explanation, and insists that the reference is to a collection of Baraisos that the prophet Elijah taught – after his ascent to heaven – to the Amora, Rav Anan.

58. That is, the righteous who will be resurrected in the Messianic Era will not revert to dust between the end of the Messianic Era and the World to Come. Rather, their bodies will remain intact until they come to life again in the World to Come (*Rashi*, as emended by *Maharshal*; cf. *Aruch LaNer*). See 92b note 2, where the meaning of this statement will be elaborated upon.

59. *Isaiah* 4:3. This passage describes the period following the cataclysmic wars at the advent of the Messianic Era. Anyone who survives those terrible times will return to Jerusalem and be regarded as a holy person. Similarly, "all inscribed for life" – the righteous who have died but who merit resurrection – will be resurrected and returned to Jerusalem (see *Rashi* ad loc.).

יקבוהו לאום ואין [א] לאום אלא עוברין שנאמר א) ולאום מלאום יאמץ ואין קבה אלא קללה שנאמר ב) מה אקב לא קבה אל ואין בר אלא תורה שנאמר ג) נשקו בר פן יאנף עולא בר ישמעאל אומר מנקבין אותו ככברה כתיב הכא ד) יקבוהו לאום וכתיב התם ה) ויקב חור בדלתו ואמר אביי כי [ב] אוכלא דקצרי ואם למדו מה שכרו אמר רבא אמר רב ששת זוכה לברכות כיוסף שנאמר ד) וברכה לראש משביר ואין משביר אלא יוסף שנאמר ו) ויוסף הוא [השליט על הארץ הוא] המשביר לכל עם הארץ אמר רב ששת כל המלמד תורה בעוה"ז זוכה ומלמדה לעולם הבא שנאמר ז) ומרוה גם הוא [ג] יורה אמר רבא מניין לתחיית המתים מן התורה שנאמר ח) יחי ראובן ואל ימות יחי ראובן בעולם הזה ואל ימות לעולם הבא רבינא אמר מהכא ט) ורבים מישני אדמת עפר יקיצו אלה לחיי עולם ואלה לחרפות לדראון עולם רב אשי אמר מהכא י) ואתה לך [לקץ] ותנוח ותעמוד לגורלך לקץ הימין אמר רבי אלעזר כל פרנס שמנהיג את הצבור בנחת זוכה ומנהיגם לעוה"ב שנאמר יא) כי מרחמם ינהגם ועל מבועי מים ינהלם [ד] וא"ר אלעזר גדולה דעה שניתנה בין שתי אותיות שנאמר יב) כי אל דעות ה' וא"ר אלעזר גדול מקדש שניתן בין שתי אותיות שנאמר יג) פעלת ה' מקדש ה' כוננו ידיך מתקיף לה רב אדא [ה] קרחינאה אלא מעתה גדולה נקמה שניתנה בין שתי אותיות דכתיב יד) אל נקמות ה' אל נקמות הופיע אמר ליה למילתיה הכי נמי כדעולא דאמר עולא שתי הופעיות הללו למה אחת למדת טובה ואחת למדת פורענות ואמר ר' אלעזר כל אדם שיש בו דעה כאילו נבנה בית המקדש בימיו שזה ניתן בין שתי אותיות וזה ניתן בין שתי אותיות ואמר ר' אלעזר כל אדם שיש בו דעה לסוף מתעשר שנאמר טו) ובדעת חדרים ימלאו כל הון יקר ונעים ואמר ר' אלעזר כל אדם שאין בו דעה אסור לרחם עליו שנאמר טז) כי לא עם בינות הוא על כן לא ירחמנו עושהו ויוצרו לא יחוננו וא"ר אלעזר כל הנותן פיתו למי שאין בו דעה יסורין באין עליו שנאמר יז) לחמך ישימו מזור תחתיך אין תבונה בו ואין מזור אלא יסורין שנאמר יח) וירא אפרים את חליו ויהודה את מזורו ואמר ר' אלעזר כל אדם שאין בו דעה לסוף גולה שנאמר יט) לכן גלה עמי מבלי דעת ואמר ר"א [א] כל בית שאין דברי תורה נשמעים בו בלילה אש אוכלתו שנאמר כ) כל חשך טמון לצפוניו תאכלהו אש לא נופח ירע שריד באהלו [ו] אין שריד אלא ת"ח שנאמר כא) ובשרידים אשר ה' קורא ואמר ר' אלעזר כל שאינו מהנה תלמידי חכמים מנכסיו אינו רואה סימן ברכה לעולם שנאמר כב) אין שריד לאכלו על כן לא יחיל טובו אין שריד אלא תלמידי חכמים שנאמר ובשרידים אשר ה' קורא ואמר רבי אלעזר [ב] כל שאינו משייר פת על שלחנו אינו רואה סימן ברכה לעולם שנאמר אין שריד לאכלו על כן לא יחיל טובו והאמר רבי אלעזר כל המשייר פתיתים על שלחנו כאילו עובד ע"ז שנאמר כג) העורכים לגד שלחן והממלאים למני ממסך לא קשיא [ג] הא דאיכא שלימה בהדיה הא דליכא שלימה בהדיה ואמר רבי אלעזר [ז] כל המחליף בדבורו כאילו עובד ע"ז כתיב הכא כד) והייתי בעיניו כמתעתע וכתיב התם כה) הבל המה מעשה תעתועים ואמר רבי אלעזר כל המסתכל בערוה קשתו נוערת שנאמר כו) עריה תעור קשתך [ח] ואמר רבי אלעזר לעולם הוי קבל וקיים אמר רבי זירא אף אנן נמי תנינא [ט] בית אפל אין פותחין לו חלונות לראות נגעו ש"מ [י] אמר ר' טבי אמר ר' יאשיה מאי דכתיב כז) שאול ועוצר רחם ארץ לא שבעה מים וכי מה ענין שאול אצל רחם אלא לומר לך מה רחם מכנים ומוציא אף שאול מכנים ומוציא והלא דברים קל וחומר ומה רחם שמכניסין בו בחשאי מוציאין ממנו בקולי קולות שאול שמכניסין [כ] בו בקולות אינו דין שמוציאין ממנו בקולי קולות מיכן תשובה לאומרין אין תחיית המתים מן התורה תנא דבי אליהו צדיקים שעתיד הקדוש ברוך הוא להחיותן [ה] אינן חוזרין לעפרן שנאמר כח) והיה הנשאר בציון והנותר בירושלים קדוש יאמר לו כל הכתוב לחיים בירושלים מה קדוש לעולם קיים אף הם לעולם קיימין

ואם

רש"י

יקבוהו. מנקבים אותו לשון (מלכים ב יב) ויקוב חור בדלתו: אוכלא דקצרי. כלי של כובסין שהוא מנוקב ומזלפין בו מים על הבגדים: ומרוה גם הוא יורה. מי שמרווה את תלמידו בדבר הלכה גם הוא יורה לעולם הבא ל"א ומרוה לשון מורה: ואתה לך לקץ ותנוח ותעמוד וגו'. רמז לו שימות ויעמוד לאחר מכן לקץ הימין לקץ שעתיד הקב"ה להחזיר ימינו לפניו שהרי השיב אחור ימינו: מרחמם בעוה"ז. ינהגם לעוה"ב: שתי אותיות. של שם. כך שמעתי. ל"א כל שמות על שם דאמרי' בעלמא (חגיגה דף טז.) צבאות אות הוא בצבא שלו קרי להו אותיות לשון מופלא: גדול מקדש. חשוב הוא: למילתיה הכי נמי. דגדולה היא וכדעולא: שתי הופעיות. דכתיב אל נקמות ה' אל נקמות הופיע ואיכא תרי נקמות וחדא הופעה בתרוייהו ודמי כמאן דאיכא אכל נקמה ונקמה חדא הופעה: חדא לטובה. של ישראל שסילק שכינתו מאומות העולם ובא על ישראל וקרי ליה נקמות משום דתגמול טוב הוא שזכו לשכינה על שאמרו נעשה ונשמע ונקמה היינו תגמול ואחת לפורענות לעובדי כוכבים שנפרע מהן ליום הדין כדאמרינן בפרק קמא דמסכת ע"ז (דף ד.) נוקם ה' ובעל חמה לעכו"ם שהוא בעצמו ובכבודו נפרע מהן והיינו הופעה: ובדעת. מפני הדעת מלאו כל החדרים הון: בשביל לחמך. שנתת למי שאין בו דעה ישימו מזור תחתיך: כל חשך טמון לצפוניו. כל לילה צפון ונחבא ממצפוני התורה שאין דברי תורה נשמעין באותו בית: תאכלהו אש לא נופח. זה אשו של גיהנם שאין צריך נפוח: ירע שריד באהלו. מי שרע בעיניו שיש שריד באהלו: כל שאינו משייר פתיתין. דצריך לשייר כדכתיב אכול והותר (מלכים ב ד): והא אמר רבי אלעזר כל המשייר פתיתין על שולחנו כאילו עובד ע"ז שנאמר העורכים לגד שולחן. שכן עושין שמניחין שלחן ערוך במאכל ומשתה לשם אותה ע"ז שקורין גד וממלאים כוסות של מרקחים נסוכים לע"ז ששמה מני: הא. דקאמר אסור: דאיכא שלימה בהדיה. שמביא שלימה לאחר שאכל ונותן על השלחן עם הפתיתין ששייר דמחזי דלשם ע"ז עביד הכי: והא. דליכא שלימה בהדייהו דמזומנין לעני: הא גדא לביתיה לא גרסי': המחליף בדבורו. משנה בדבורו שלא יהא ניכר: קשתו ננערת. כח קושי אבר שלו ננער שאינו מוליד שנאמר עריה תעור קשתך עריה שאתה מסתכל בה ממש בערותה היא תעיר קשתך ד"א המסתכל המחשב בעריות דאשת איש קשתו גבורת ידו ננערת מתהלכת ומתמעטת כמו (ב"מ דף כט:) מלא כסות מנערה אחת לשלשים יום א"נ כמו (שמות יד) וינער ה': הוי קבל. הוי עניו ותחיה. קבל לשון אפל עשה עצמך אפל ושפל: בית אפל אין פותחין בו חלונות לראות את נגעו. כנגע נראה לי בבית כתיב דמשמע נראה ממילא ועוד דכתיב לי [ל] ולא לאורי נמצא שאפלתו הצלתו דכל זמן שאין כהן רואהו אין מטמא בנגעים: שאול ועוצר רחם ארץ לא שבעה מים. קבר לא שבע ממתים ועוצר רחם בית הרחם שהוא קצור ועצור לא ישבע מבעילות וכן ארץ לא שבעה מים: וכי מה ענין שאול וכו'. למה נסמכו הני אהדדי: מכנים. הזרע ומוציא הולד אף שאול מכנים ומוציא לתחיית המתים: שמכניסין בה בקולי קולות. בבכי גדול קוברין את המת: אינו דין שמוציאין אותו בקולי קולות. שנאמר יתקע בשופר גדול: שעתיד הקב"ה להחיות. לימות המשיח: לאחר שיחיו שוב אין חוזרין לעפרם. בין [מ] (לימות המשיח בין לעולם הבא) אלא הבשר מתקיים עליהם עד שישובו ויחיו לעתיד לבא: ואותן

עין משפט נר מצוה

ו א מיי' פ"ג מהל' ת"ת הל' יג סמג עשין יב טוש"ע יו"ד סי' רמו סעיף כד:

ז ב ג טוש"ע או"ח סי' קפ סעיף ב:

ח ד מיי' פי"ד מהל' טומאת צרעת הל' ה:

ט ה מיי' פ"ח מהל' תשובה הל' א:

ליקוטי רש"י

אוכלא דקצרי. כלי נחושת העשוי כנפה נקבים נקבים והוא של כובסים ונותנו על הבגדים ומזלף בו המים עליהן ויש מפרשים שמגמרין מוגמר מתחתיו והבגדים מונחין עליו ומתגמרין דרך הנקבים [שבת קכג:]. כלי שמשימין בו הכובסין בגדיהן [נדרים כג.]. קצרי. הכובס נקרא קצרי בלשון ארמי [ב"ק קיט:]. כך שמם בלשון ישמעאל והם כובסין שמעתי אומרים על שם שמקצרין בגדי צמר כשדורסין אותן ברגליהן במים שקורין פורלוי"ר והיינו דמתרגמינן עין רוגל (ש"ב יז) עינא דקצרא [תענית כט:]. ואל ימות לעולם הבא. שלא יזכר לו מעשה בלהה [דברים לג, ו]. ורבים מישני אדמת עפר יקיצו. יחיו המתים [דניאל יב, ב]. לך לקץ. תפטר לבית עולמך. לגורלך. לקבל חלקך עם הצדיקים. לקץ הימין. כמו באחרית הימים ואין לפרש הימין לשון יד הימנית שהרי הוא מנוי במסורת הגדולה בשיטת תיבות המיוחדין בנו"ן זקופה בסוף תיבה המשמשת במקום מ"ם ולית דכותיהון כגון ועליה יכרעון אחרין (איוב לא) יקום ולא יאמין בחיין (שם כד) קח לך חטין (יחזקאל ד) יחרדון איין (שם כו) למחות מלכין (משלי לא) לקץ הימין (כאן) [שם, יג]. שיחזיר ימינו לפניו שהשיב אחור ימינו מפני אויב [פסחים נו:]. בין שתי אותיות. בין שתי הזכרות. למילתיה הכי נמי. במקום שצריכה נקמה דבר גדול הוא [ברכות לג.]. הופיע. הראה וגלה לנו את נקמתך [תהלים צד, א]. מזורו. לשון חולי [הושע ה, יג]. מבלי דעת. לפי שהיה לבם בלי דעת [ישעיה ה, יג]. ובשרידים. בשארית אשר יותיר. אשר ה' קורא. לשון קרואים לסעודה או לעבודת המלך לשון הזמנה [יואל ג, ה]. אין שריד לאכלו. לא השרה תלמידי חכמים על שלחנו כמו ובשרידים אשר ה' קורא. על כן לא יחיל טובו. לא יצליח כמו (תהלים י) יחילו דרכיו. כל שאינו משייר וכו' שנאמר אין שריד לאכלו. לא שייר ממאכלו לחלק לעניים [איוב כ, כא]. העורכים לגד. שם עכו"ם העשוים על שם המזל ובלשון משנה יש גד גדי וסינוק לא. למני. למניין חשבון הכומרים היו ממלאים אגנות מזג יין. ממסך. יין מזוג במים כמשפטו כמו לחקור ממסך (משלי כג) מסכה יינה (משלי ט) [ישעיה סה, יא]. הוי קבל. אפל. וקיים. ותחיה כלומר הרחק מן הרבנות שמקברת את בעליה אפילה מתרגם קבלה (שמות י) [לעיל יד.]. בית אפל. שצריך לפתוח לו חלונות לראות הנגע פוטרין אותו לגמרי כדכתיב (ויקרא יד) כנגע נראה לי בבית לי ולא לאורי שאם עמד במקום אפל וצריך שם להדליק את הנר אינו נגע [חולין י:]. שאול ועוצר רחם. פסוק הוא בספר משלי שלש הנה לא תשבענה. שאול. קבר. שמכניסין בו בקולות. של בכי ומספד [ברכות טו:]. והיה הנשאר. בהם בציון יתיישבו. והנותר. בכל מקום ישכנו בירושלים. קדוש יאמר לו. כולם יהיו צדיקים וא"ת צדיקים המתים לפני אותו היום אבד כבודם ת"ל כל הכתוב לחיי העוה"ב יהיו בירושלים (כת"י) [ישעיה ד, ג].

מסורת הש"ס

א) סוטה מא:, ב) [ג"ז הערוך ערך אכל אוכלא בבי"ת וע"ש שני פירושים], ג) בקהלת כתיב יורא באל"ף, ד) ברכות לג. ע"ש, ה) [שם. ע"ש], ו) חולין קלג., ז) [מס' כלה], ח) [לעיל יד.], ט) [נגעים פ"ב מ"ג] חולין י:, י) ברכות טו:, כ) כד"י אותה, ל) [מועד קטן ח.], מ) ימות המשיח ולעולם הבא. רש"ל.

גליון הש"ס

גמ' כל בית שאין ד"ת נשמעין. עיין עירובין דף יח ע"ב:

תורה אור השלם

א) וַיֹּאמֶר יְיָ לָהּ שְׁנֵי גוֹיִם בְּבִטְנֵךְ וּשְׁנֵי לְאֻמִּים מִמֵּעַיִךְ יִפָּרֵדוּ וּלְאֹם מִלְאֹם יֶאֱמָץ וְרַב יַעֲבֹד צָעִיר: [בראשית כה, כג]

ב) מָה אֶקֹּב לֹא קַבֹּה אֵל וּמָה אֶזְעֹם לֹא זָעַם יְיָ: [במדבר כג, ח]

ג) נַשְּׁקוּ בַר פֶּן יֶאֱנַף וְתֹאבְדוּ דֶרֶךְ כִּי יִבְעַר כִּמְעַט אַפּוֹ אַשְׁרֵי כָּל חוֹסֵי בוֹ: [תהלים ב, יב]

ד) מֹנֵעַ בָּר יִקְּבֻהוּ לְאוֹם וּבְרָכָה לְרֹאשׁ מַשְׁבִּיר: [משלי יא, כו]

ה) וַיִּקַּח יְהוֹיָדָע הַכֹּהֵן אֲרוֹן אֶחָד וַיִּקֹּב חֹר בְּדַלְתּוֹ וַיִּתֵּן אֹתוֹ אֵצֶל הַמִּזְבֵּחַ מִיָּמִין בְּבוֹא אִישׁ בֵּית יְיָ וְנָתְנוּ שָׁמָּה הַכֹּהֲנִים שֹׁמְרֵי הַסַּף אֶת כָּל הַכֶּסֶף הַמּוּבָא בֵית יְיָ: [מלכים ב' יב, י]

ו) וְיוֹסֵף הוּא הַשַּׁלִּיט עַל הָאָרֶץ הוּא הַמַּשְׁבִּיר לְכָל עַם הָאָרֶץ וַיָּבֹאוּ אֲחֵי יוֹסֵף וַיִּשְׁתַּחֲווּ לוֹ אַפַּיִם אָרְצָה: [בראשית מב, ו]

ז) נֶפֶשׁ בְּרָכָה תְדֻשָּׁן וּמַרְוֶה גַּם הוּא יוֹרֶא: [משלי יא, כה]

ח) יְחִי רְאוּבֵן וְאַל יָמֹת וִיהִי מְתָיו מִסְפָּר: [דברים לג, ו]

ט) וְרַבִּים מִיְּשֵׁנֵי אַדְמַת עָפָר יָקִיצוּ אֵלֶּה לְחַיֵּי עוֹלָם וְאֵלֶּה לַחֲרָפוֹת לְדִרְאוֹן עוֹלָם: [דניאל יב, ב]

י) וְאַתָּה לֵךְ לַקֵּץ וְתָנוּחַ וְתַעֲמֹד לְגֹרָלְךָ לְקֵץ הַיָּמִין: [דניאל יב, יג]

יא) לֹא יִרְעָבוּ וְלֹא יִצְמָאוּ וְלֹא יַכֵּם שָׁרָב וָשָׁמֶשׁ כִּי מְרַחֲמָם יְנַהֲגֵם וְעַל מַבּוּעֵי מַיִם יְנַהֲלֵם: [ישעיה מט, י]

יב) אַל תַּרְבּוּ תְדַבְּרוּ גְּבֹהָה גְבֹהָה יֵצֵא עָתָק מִפִּיכֶם כִּי אֵל דֵּעוֹת יְיָ וְלוֹ נִתְכְּנוּ עֲלִלוֹת: [שמואל א' ב, ג]

יג) תְּבִאֵמוֹ וְתִטָּעֵמוֹ בְּהַר נַחֲלָתְךָ מָכוֹן לְשִׁבְתְּךָ פָּעַלְתָּ יְיָ מִקְּדָשׁ אֲדֹנָי כּוֹנְנוּ יָדֶיךָ: [שמות טו, יז]

יד) אֵל נְקָמוֹת יְיָ אֵל נְקָמוֹת הוֹפִיעַ: [תהלים צד, א] טו) וּבְדַעַת חֲדָרִים יִמָּלְאוּ כָּל הוֹן יָקָר וְנָעִים: [משלי כד, ד] טז) בִּיבֹשׁ קְצִירָהּ תִּשָּׁבַרְנָה נָשִׁים בָּאוֹת מְאִירוֹת אוֹתָהּ כִּי לֹא עַם בִּינוֹת הוּא עַל כֵּן לֹא יְרַחֲמֶנּוּ עֹשֵׂהוּ וְיֹצְרוֹ לֹא יְחֻנֶּנּוּ: [ישעיה כז, יא] יז) עַד הַגְּבוּל שִׁלְּחוּךָ כֹּל אַנְשֵׁי בְרִיתֶךָ הִשִּׁיאוּךָ יָכְלוּ לְךָ אַנְשֵׁי שְׁלֹמֶךָ לַחְמְךָ יָשִׂימוּ מָזוֹר תַּחְתֶּיךָ אֵין תְּבוּנָה בּוֹ: [עובדיה א, ז] יח) וַיַּרְא אֶפְרַיִם אֶת חָלְיוֹ וִיהוּדָה אֶת מְזֹרוֹ וַיֵּלֶךְ אֶפְרַיִם אֶל אַשּׁוּר וַיִּשְׁלַח אֶל מֶלֶךְ יָרֵב וְהוּא לֹא יוּכַל לִרְפֹּא לָכֶם וְלֹא יִגְהֶה מִכֶּם מָזוֹר: [הושע ה, יג] יט) לָכֵן גָּלָה עַמִּי מִבְּלִי דָעַת וּכְבוֹדוֹ מְתֵי רָעָב וַהֲמוֹנוֹ צִחֵה צָמָא: [ישעיה ה, יג] כ) כָּל חֹשֶׁךְ טָמוּן לִצְפּוּנָיו תְּאָכְלֵהוּ אֵשׁ לֹא נֻפָּח יֵרַע שָׂרִיד בְּאָהֳלוֹ: [איוב כ, כו] כא) וְהָיָה כֹּל אֲשֶׁר יִקְרָא בְּשֵׁם יְיָ יִמָּלֵט כִּי בְּהַר צִיּוֹן וּבִירוּשָׁלַיִם תִּהְיֶה פְלֵיטָה כַּאֲשֶׁר אָמַר יְיָ וּבַשְּׂרִידִים אֲשֶׁר יְיָ קֹרֵא: [יואל ג, ה] כב) אֵין שָׂרִיד לְאָכְלוֹ עַל כֵּן לֹא יָחִיל טוּבוֹ: [איוב כ, כא] כג) וְאַתֶּם עֹזְבֵי יְיָ הַשְּׁכֵחִים אֶת הַר קָדְשִׁי הַעֹרְכִים לַגַּד שֻׁלְחָן וְהַמְמַלְאִים לַמְנִי מִמְסָךְ: [ישעיה סה, יא] כד) אוּלַי יְמֻשֵּׁנִי אָבִי וְהָיִיתִי בְעֵינָיו כִּמְתַעְתֵּעַ וְהֵבֵאתִי עָלַי קְלָלָה וְלֹא בְרָכָה: [בראשית כז, יב] כה) הֶבֶל הֵמָּה מַעֲשֵׂה תַּעְתֻּעִים בְּעֵת פְּקֻדָּתָם יֹאבֵדוּ: [ירמיה י, טו] כו) עֶרְיָה תֵעוֹר קַשְׁתֶּךָ שְׁבֻעוֹת מַטּוֹת אֹמֶר סֶלָה נְהָרוֹת תְּבַקַּע אָרֶץ: [חבקוק ג, ט] כז) שְׁאוֹל וְעֹצֶר רָחַם אֶרֶץ לֹא שָׂבְעָה מַּיִם וְאֵשׁ לֹא אָמְרָה הוֹן: [משלי ל, טז] כח) וְהָיָה הַנִּשְׁאָר בְּצִיּוֹן וְהַנּוֹתָר בִּירוּשָׁלַיִם קָדוֹשׁ יֵאָמֶר לוֹ כָּל הַכָּתוּב לַחַיִּים בִּירוּשָׁלָיִם: [ישעיה ד, ג]

ואם תאמר אותן שנים שעתיד הקב"ה לחדש בהן את עולמו שנאמר א) ונשגב ה' לבדו ביום ההוא צדיקים מה הן עושין הקב"ה עושה להם כנפים כנשרים ושטין על פני המים שנאמר ב) על כן לא נירא בהמיר ארץ במוט הרים בלב ימים ושמא תאמר יש להם צער ת"ל ג) וקווי ה' יחליפו כח יעלו אבר כנשרים ירוצו ולא ייגעו ילכו ולא ייעפו ונילף ממתים שהחיה יחזקאל סבר לה כמאן דאמר באמת משל היה דתניא ר"א אומר מתים שהחיה יחזקאל עמדו על רגליהם ואמרו שירה ומתו מה שירה אמרו ה' ממית בצדק ומחיה ברחמים ר' יהושע אומר שירה זו אמרו ד) ה' ממית ומחיה מוריד שאול ויעל ר' יהודה אומר אמת משל היה אמר לו רבי נחמיה אם אמת למה משל ואם משל למה אמת אלא באמת משל היה ר"א בנו של ר' יוסי הגלילי אומר מתים שהחיה יחזקאל עלו לארץ ישראל ונשאו נשים והולידו בנים ובנות עמד ר"י בן בתירא על רגליו ואמר אני מבני בניהם והללו תפילין שהניח לי אבי אבא מהם ומאן נינהו מתים שהחיה יחזקאל אמר רב אלו בני אפרים שמנו לקץ וטעו שנאמר ה) ובני אפרים שותלח וברד בנו ותחת בנו ואלעדה בנו ותחת בנו וזבד בנו ושותלח בנו ועזר (ואלעזר) [ואלעד] והרגום אנשי גת הנולדים בארץ וגו' וכתיב ו) ויתאבל אפרים אביהם ימים רבים ויבאו אחיו לנחמו ושמואל אמר אלו בני אדם שכפרו בתחיית המתים שנאמר ז) ויאמר אלי בן אדם העצמות האלה כל בית ישראל המה הנה אומרים יבשו עצמותינו ואבדה תקותנו נגזרנו לנו ר' ירמיה בר אבא אמר אלו בני אדם שאין בהן לחלוחית של מצוה שנאמר ח) העצמות היבשות שמעו דבר ה' ר' יצחק נפחא אמר אלו בני אדם שחיפו את ההיכל כולו שקצים ורמשים שנאמר ט) ואבוא ואראה והנה כל תבנית רמש ובהמה שקץ וכל גלולי בית ישראל מחוקה על הקיר סביב וגו' וכתיב התם י) והעבירני עליהם סביב סביב ר' יוחנן אמר אלו מתים שבבקעת דורא וא"ר יוחנן מנהר אשל עד רבת בקעת דורא שבשעה שהגלה נבוכדנצר הרשע את ישראל היו בהן בחורים שהיו מגנין את החמה ביופיין והיו כשדיות רואות אותן ושופעות זבות אמרו לבעליהן ובעליהן למלך צוה המלך והרגום ועדיין היו שופעות זבות צוה המלך ורמסום תנו רבנן בשעה שהפיל נבוכדנצר הרשע את חנניה מישאל ועזריה לכבשן האש אמר לו הקב"ה ליחזקאל לך והחיה מתים בבקעת דורא כיון שהחיה אותן באו עצמות וטפחו לו [א] לאותו רשע על פניו אמר מה טיבן של אלו אמרו לו חבריהן של אלו מחיה מתים בבקעת דורא פתח ואמר כ) אתוהי כמה רברבין ותמהוהי כמה תקיפין מלכותיה מלכות עלם ושלטניה עם דר ודר וגו' א"ר יצחק יוצק זהב רותח לתוך פיו [ב] של אותו רשע שאילמלא (א) לא) בא מלאך וסטרו על פיו ביקש לגנות כל שירות ותושבחות שאמר דוד בספר תהלים ת"ר ששה נסים נעשו באותו היום ואלו הן צף הכבשן ונפרץ הכבשן והומק סודו ונהפך צלם על פניו ונשרפו ארבע מלכיות והחיה יחזקאל את המתים בבקעת דורא וכולהו גמרא וארבע מלכיות קרא דכתיב ל) ונבוכדנצר מלכא שלח למכנש לאחשדרפניא סגניא ופחוותא אדרגזריא גדבריא דתבריא תפתיא וכל שלטוני מדינתא וגו' וכתיב מ) איתי גוברין יהודאין וגו' וכתיב נ) ומתכנשין אחשדרפניא סגניא ופחוותא והדברי מלכא חזיין לגבריא אלך וגו' תני דבי רבי אליעזר בן יעקב אפילו בשעת הסכנה לא ישנה אדם את עצמו מן הרבנות שלו שנאמר ס) באדין גבריא אלך כפתו בסרבליהון פטשיהון וכרבלתהון וגו' אמר רבי יוחנן

גדולים

ואותן שנים שעתיד הקב"ה לחדש את עולמו. ויהיה עולם זה חרב אלף שנים אותן לדיקים היכן הם הואיל ואינן נקברין בארץ: לא נירא בהמיר ארץ. כשמחליף הקב"ה את הארץ לא נירא לפי שאנו בלב ימים: וקווי ה' יחליפו כח. שיהא להם כח לשוט ולעופף בלי לער: ונילף ממתים שהחיה יחזקאל. שחזרו ומתו כך לדיקים שעתיד להחיות יחזרו לעפרם כך שמעתי יחזקאל הגלהו נבוכדנלר עם יכניה מלך יהודה והיה יחזקאל מתנבא בבבל וירמיה בארץ ישראל באותן אחת עשרה שנה שמלך לדקיה: באמת. בברור: משל היה. שהיה מרמז להם על הגלות כאדם מת שחוזר וחי כך ישראל ישובו מן הגלות: מהם. שאותן תפילין היו שלהם: שמנו לקץ. של יציאת מלרים: וטעו. שלא היה להם למנות גזירת ועבדום וענו אותם אלא משנולד ילחק דהא כתיב (בראשית טו) כי גר יהיה זרעך זה ילחק דכתיב (שם כא) כי בילחק יקרא לך זרע והם מנו משעת הדיבור לאברהם ותניא בסדר עולם אברהם אבינו בשעה שנדבר עמו בין הבתרים בן שבעים שנה היה ומבין הבתרים עד שנולד ילחק היה ל' שנה כדכתיב (בראשית כא) ואברהם בן מאת שנה בהולד לו את ילחק בנו נמלאת אומר משדבר עמו בין הבתרים עד שילאו ממלרים היו ארבע מאות ואותן ל' שמן הדבור עד לידת ילחק טעו בני אפרים. ומניין שבני אפרים הן שילאו קודם זמנן ונהרגו שנאמר ובני אפרים שותלח וגו' והרגום אנשי גת: ושמואל אמר. מתים שהחיה יחזקאל אלו בני אדם שכפרו בתחיית המתים שנאמר (יחזקאל לז) אבדה תקותנו: העצמות האלה כל בית ישראל המה. עלמות הללו סימן לכל ישראל הן שעתידה להם תחיית המתים כמו לאלו שהרי אלו אמרו אבדה תקותנו ועכשו ידעו שאני מחיה את המתים וסימן זה לכל ישראל שגם הם עתידין להחיות ולא מן הדין חיו דהא אמרן ג) הכופר בתחיית המתים אין לו חלק לעוה"ב אלא משום סימן חיו: שחיפו להיכל. שהיו מליירין ללמים על קירות ההיכל דכתיב ואבא ואראה מחוקה על הקיר סביב: וכתיב והעבירני עליהם סביב סביב. כלומר על אותן אנשים שכתוב עליהם סביב עבר עליהם יחזקאל להחיותם: אלו מתים שבבקעת דורא. שהמית נבוכדנלר מלך בבל על שהיו יפים כדלקמן: מנהר אשל עד רבת. מקומות הן היו בבקעת דורא: שופעות. מחמת תאוה: וצוה המלך והרגן ועדיין היו שופעות. שהיתה נראית זיו תארם ולוה המלך ורמסום: ובאו עצמות מן הבקעה וטפחו לו לאותו רשע על פניו. והלכו להם ואית דאמרי שמאותן עלמות היה לו כלים וכשהגיעה שעה שחיו טפחו לו על פיו כשהיה רולה לשתות בהם: חבריהם של אלו מחיה מתים. על יחזקאל היו אומרין שהיה חבירן של חנניה מישאל ועזריה ונבוכדנלר היה יודע שהיה הקב"ה מחיה אותם: פתח ואמר. להקב"ה אתוהי כמה רברבין פסוק הוא (דניאל ג): יוצק זהב רותח. משום דקא מיירי בשבחו דנבוכדנלר נקיט נמי לישנא מעליא ולשון קללה: סטרו. הכהו מאחורי ידו: לגנות. שהיה מסדר שבחות נאות יותר מדוד ואילו אמרן הקב"ה היה נוטה אחריהן יותר מאחרי השירות שעשה דוד: באותו יום. שהשליכן לכבשן: צף הכבשן. שהכבשן היה משוקע בארץ כעין כבשן של סיד ולף ועומד על גבי קרקע כדי שיראוהו כל העולם: נפרץ הכבשן. נפלו קלת כותליו כדי שיוכלו כולם לראות בתוכו: הומק סורו. נשפל גאותו כמו סורו רע (קדושין דף פב.) ל"א הומק סודו כמו יסודו נשתלשל וכן לימדני רבי יעקב בן יקר אבל מורי גרס והומק סידו סיד הכבשן נמסה מרוב חמימות כך שמעתי והיתה מושכת למרחוק ומהבל של אותו הסיד נשרפו אותן שהשליכו חנניה מישאל ועזריה לתוך כבשן האש: ונהפך. צלם של זהב על פניו: ארבע מלכיות. מלכים ואנשיהם שסייעו לנבוכדנלר להשליך חנניה מישאל ועזריה לתוך האור: מקראי נפקי. דכתיב (דניאל ג) נבוכדנלר שלח למכנש לאחשדרפניא סגניא ולבסוף לאחר שבאו מן הכבשן כתיב ומתכנשין אחשדרפניא סגניא ופחותא והנך דלא כתיבי נשרפו: אל ישנה מן הרבנות שלו. שהרי חנניה מישאל ועזריה היו לבושין בגדי תפארתן כשהושלכו לכבשן אל ישנה שלא יראה מבוהל ומפוחד ומתביישין שונאיו מפניו: פטשיהון וכרבלתהון. עניני מלבושין:

גדולים

הגהות הגר"א

[א] גמ' נ"ל לאותו רשע שחיק טמי': [ב] שם נ"ל של אותו רשע שחיק טמי':

תורה אור השלם

א) וְשַׁח גַּבְהוּת הָאָדָם וְשָׁפֵל רוּם אֲנָשִׁים וְנִשְׂגַּב יְיָ לְבַדּוֹ בַּיּוֹם הַהוּא: [ישעיה ב, יז]

ב) עַל כֵּן לֹא נִירָא בְּהָמִיר אָרֶץ וּבְמוֹט הָרִים בְּלֵב יַמִּים: [תהלים מו, ג]

ג) וְקוֹיֵ יְיָ יַחֲלִיפוּ כֹחַ יַעֲלוּ אֵבֶר כַּנְּשָׁרִים יָרוּצוּ וְלֹא יִיגָעוּ יֵלְכוּ וְלֹא יִיעָפוּ: [ישעיה מ, לא]

ד) יְיָ מֵמִית וּמְחַיֶּה מוֹרִיד שְׁאוֹל וַיָּעַל: [שמואל א' ב, ו]

ה) וּבְנֵי אֶפְרַיִם שׁוּתָלַח וּבֶרֶד בְּנוֹ וְתַחַת בְּנוֹ וְאֶלְעָדָה בְנוֹ וְתַחַת בְּנוֹ: וְזָבָד בְּנוֹ וְשׁוּתֶלַח בְּנוֹ וְעֵזֶר וְאֶלְעָד וַהֲרָגוּם אַנְשֵׁי גַת הַנּוֹלָדִים בָּאָרֶץ כִּי יָרְדוּ לָקַחַת אֶת מִקְנֵיהֶם: [דברי הימים א' ז, כ-כא]

ו) וַיִּתְאַבֵּל אֶפְרַיִם אֲבִיהֶם יָמִים רַבִּים וַיָּבֹאוּ אֶחָיו לְנַחֲמוֹ: [דברי הימים א' ז, כב]

ז) וַיֹּאמֶר אֵלַי בֶּן אָדָם הָעֲצָמוֹת הָאֵלֶּה כָּל בֵּית יִשְׂרָאֵל הֵמָּה הִנֵּה אֹמְרִים יָבְשׁוּ עַצְמוֹתֵינוּ וְאָבְדָה תִקְוָתֵנוּ נִגְזַרְנוּ לָנוּ: [יחזקאל לז, יא]

ח) וַיֹּאמֶר אֵלַי הִנָּבֵא עַל הָעֲצָמוֹת הָאֵלֶּה וְאָמַרְתָּ אֲלֵיהֶם הָעֲצָמוֹת הַיְבֵשׁוֹת שִׁמְעוּ דְּבַר יְיָ: [יחזקאל לז, ד]

ט) וָאָבוֹא וָאֶרְאֶה וְהִנֵּה כָל תַּבְנִית רֶמֶשׂ וּבְהֵמָה שֶׁקֶץ וְכָל גִּלּוּלֵי בֵּית יִשְׂרָאֵל מְחֻקֶּה עַל הַקִּיר סָבִיב סָבִיב: [יחזקאל ח, י]

י) וְהֶעֱבִירַנִי עֲלֵיהֶם סָבִיב סָבִיב וְהִנֵּה רַבּוֹת מְאֹד עַל פְּנֵי הַבִּקְעָה וְהִנֵּה יְבֵשׁוֹת מְאֹד: [יחזקאל לז, ב]

כ) אָתוֹהִי כְּמָה רַבְרְבִין וְתִמְהוֹהִי כְּמָה תַקִּיפִין מַלְכוּתֵהּ מַלְכוּת עָלַם וְשָׁלְטָנֵהּ עִם דָּר וְדָר: [דניאל ג, לג]

ל) וּנְבוּכַדְנֶצַּר מַלְכָּא שְׁלַח לְמִכְנַשׁ לַאֲחַשְׁדַּרְפְּנַיָּא סִגְנַיָּא וּפַחֲוָתָא אֲדַרְגָּזְרַיָּא גְדָבְרַיָּא דְּתָבְרַיָּא תִּפְתָּיֵא וְכֹל שִׁלְטֹנֵי מְדִינָתָא לְמֵתֵא לַחֲנֻכַּת צַלְמָא דִּי הֲקֵים נְבוּכַדְנֶצַּר מַלְכָּא: [דניאל ג, ב]

מ) אִיתַי גֻּבְרִין יְהוּדָאִין דִּי מַנִּיתָ יָתְהוֹן עַל עֲבִידַת מְדִינַת בָּבֶל שַׁדְרַךְ מֵישַׁךְ וַעֲבֵד נְגוֹ גֻּבְרַיָּא אִלֵּךְ לָא שָׂמוּ עֲלָךְ מַלְכָּא טְעֵם לֵאלָהָךְ לָא פָלְחִין וּלְצֶלֶם דַּהֲבָא דִּי הֲקֵימְתָּ לָא סָגְדִין: [דניאל ג, יב]

נ) וּמִתְכַּנְּשִׁין אֲחַשְׁדַּרְפְּנַיָּא סִגְנַיָּא וּפַחֲוָתָא וְהַדָּבְרֵי מַלְכָּא חָזַיִן לְגֻבְרַיָּא אִלֵּךְ דִּי לָא שְׁלֵט נוּרָא בְּגֶשְׁמְהוֹן וּשְׂעַר רֵאשְׁהוֹן לָא הִתְחָרַךְ וְסָרְבָּלֵיהוֹן לָא שְׁנוֹ וְרֵיחַ נוּר לָא עֲדָת בְּהוֹן: [דניאל ג, כז]

ס) בֵּאדַיִן גֻּבְרַיָּא אִלֵּךְ כְּפִתוּ בְּסַרְבָּלֵיהוֹן פַּטְּשֵׁיהוֹן וְכַרְבְּלָתְהוֹן וּלְבֻשֵׁיהוֹן וּרְמִיו לְגוֹא אַתּוּן נוּרָא יָקִדְתָּא: [דניאל ג, כא]

מסורת הש"ס

א) [עי' תוס' מגילה כא.], ב) [לעיל נ.].

ליקוטי רש"י

אותן שנים. דהיינו אלף שביעי. ונשגב ה' לבדו ביום ההוא. יומו של הקב"ה אלף שנה שנאמר כי אלף שנים בעיניך כיום אתמול כי יעבור [לקמן צז.]. בהמיר ארץ. לעתיד לבא ביום שנאמר והארץ כבגד תבלה (ישעיה נא) ראו בני קרח נס שנעש' להם שנבלעו כל סביבותיה' והם עמדו באויר ואמרו לישראל ברוח הקדש שדוגמת הנס הזה יהיה עשוי להם לעתיד [תהלים מו, ג]. אבר. כנף [ישעיה מ, לא]. שקץ. עשוין לשקוץ עכו"ם. מחוקה. חקוקין על הקיר [יחזקאל ח, י]. בקעת דורא. שם מקום [דניאל ג, א]. לאחשדרפניא. דוכסין. ופחוותא. שלטונין. אדרגזריא גדבריא וגומר. כולם שם עכו"ם הם [שם, ב]. איתי. יש. יהודאין. משבט יהודה [שם, יב]. ומתכנשין אחשדרפניא. ד' אומות נמנו למעלה באסיפה הראשונה שלא נמנו כאן אדרגזריא דתבריא גדבריא תפתיא הם גבורי החיל אשר הרגם שביב האש בהשליכם את חנניה וחבריו לאור. חזיין לגבריא אלך. רואין את האנשים האלה חנניה וחבריו [שם, כז]. גבריא אלך. אנשים אלו. כפתו בסרבליהון. נתקשרו בבגדי מעטפותן. פטשיהון וכרבלתהון. מיני מלבוש מלכות שהיה להם ואע"פ שהיו יוצאין לידון לפני נ"נ דיני מיתה לא שנו בגדיהם להשפיל את גדולתם מכאן למדו חכמים שאפי' בשעת הסכנה לא ישנה אדם מן השררה שהוחזק בה. וכרבלתהון. יש לו דוגמא (בד"ה א' טו) ודוד מכורבל [שם, כא].

וְאִם תֹּאמַר אוֹתָן שָׁנִים שֶׁעָתִיד הַקָּדוֹשׁ בָּרוּךְ הוּא לְחַדֵּשׁ בָּהֶן אֶת עוֹלָמוֹ – AND PERHAPS YOU WILL ASK: In THOSE YEARS DURING WHICH THE HOLY ONE, BLESSED IS HE, IS DESTINED TO RENEW HIS WORLD – שֶׁנֶּאֱמַר ,,וְנִשְׂגַּב ה׳ לְבַדּוֹ בַּיּוֹם הַהוּא" – AS IT IS STATED: *AND HASHEM ALONE WILL BE EXALTED ON THAT DAY*[1] – צַדִּיקִים מָה הֵן עוֹשִׂין – WHAT WILL THE RIGHTEOUS BE DOING?[2] הַקָּדוֹשׁ בָּרוּךְ הוּא עוֹשֶׂה לָהֶם כְּנָפַיִם כַּנְּשָׁרִים – The answer is: THE HOLY ONE, BLESSED IS HE, WILL MAKE THEM WINGS LIKE THE EAGLES וְשָׁטִין עַל פְּנֵי הַמַּיִם – AND THEY WILL GLIDE OVER THE WATER in safety, שֶׁנֶּאֱמַר ,,עַל־כֵּן לֹא־נִירָא בְּהָמִיר אָרֶץ וּבְמוֹט הָרִים בְּלֵב יַמִּים" – AS IT IS STATED: *THEREFORE WE SHALL NOT FEAR WHEN THE EARTH IS TRANSFORMED AND WHEN THE MOUNTAINS COLLAPSE IN THE HEART OF THE SEAS.*[3] וְשֶׁמָּא תֹּאמַר יֵשׁ לָהֶם צַעַר – AND PERHAPS YOU WILL SAY that THEY WILL SUFFER PAIN from the constant exertion needed to stay aloft. תַּלְמוּד לוֹמַר ,,וְקוֵֹי ה׳ יַחֲלִיפוּ כֹחַ יַעֲלוּ אֵבֶר כַּנְּשָׁרִים יָרוּצוּ וְלֹא יִיגָעוּ יֵלְכוּ וְלֹא יִיעָפוּ" – Therefore SCRIPTURE STATES: *AND THOSE WHO HOPE IN HASHEM SHALL HAVE RENEWED STRENGTH, THEY SHALL SPROUT WINGS LIKE EAGLES; THEY SHALL RUN AND NOT BE WEARY, THEY SHALL WALK AND NOT BE FAINT.*[4]

The Gemara asks:

וְנֵילַף מִמֵּתִים שֶׁהֶחֱיָה יְחֶזְקֵאל – How can this Tanna say that the resurrected righteous will not return to dust? **Let us learn** otherwise **from** the precedent of **the dead whom Ezekiel resurrected!**[5] – ? –

The Gemara answers:

סָבַר לָהּ כְּמַאן דְּאָמַר בֶּאֱמֶת מָשָׁל הָיָה – **[This Tanna] holds as** does **the one who says that in truth it** [the account of resurrection in the Book of *Ezekiel*] **was a parable.**[6] The Gemara records the dispute in this matter: דְּתַנְיָא – **For it was taught in a Baraisa:** רַבִּי אֱלִיעֶזֶר אוֹמֵר – R' ELIEZER SAYS: מֵתִים שֶׁהֶחֱיָה יְחֶזְקֵאל עָמְדוּ עַל רַגְלֵיהֶם וְאָמְרוּ שִׁירָה וָמֵתוּ – THE DEAD THAT EZEKIEL RESURRECTED STOOD ON THEIR FEET, UTTERED SONG, AND then DIED.[7] מָה שִׁירָה אָמְרוּ – WHAT SONG DID THEY UTTER? ה׳ מֵמִית בְּצֶדֶק וּמְחַיֶּה בְּרַחֲמִים – "HASHEM PUTS TO DEATH WITH JUSTICE AND BRINGS TO LIFE WITH MERCY." רַבִּי יְהוֹשֻׁעַ אוֹמֵר שִׁירָה זוֹ אָמְרוּ – R' YEHOSHUA SAYS that THEY UTTERED THE FOLLOWING SONG: ,,ה׳ מֵמִית וּמְחַיֶּה מוֹרִיד שְׁאוֹל וַיָּעַל" – *HASHEM PUTS TO DEATH AND BRINGS TO LIFE, HE BRINGS DOWN TO THE GRAVE AND RAISES UP.*[8] רַבִּי יְהוּדָה אוֹמֵר אֱמֶת מָשָׁל הָיָה – R' YEHUDAH SAYS: IT IS TRUE; IT WAS A PARABLE.[9] אָמַר לוֹ רַבִּי נְחֶמְיָה – R' NECHEMIAH SAID TO [R' YEHUDAH]: אִם אֱמֶת לָמָּה מָשָׁל – What you say is unclear: IF "IT IS TRUE," then WHY do you say "A PARABLE"? וְאִם מָשָׁל לָמָּה אֱמֶת – AND IF it was "A PARABLE," then WHY do you say "IT IS TRUE"? אֶלָּא בֶּאֱמֶת מָשָׁל הָיָה – Say RATHER: IN TRUTH IT WAS A PARABLE.[10] רַבִּי אֱלִיעֶזֶר בְּנוֹ שֶׁל רַבִּי יוֹסֵי הַגְּלִילִי אוֹמֵר – R' ELIEZER THE SON OF R' YOSE HAGLILI SAYS: מֵתִים שֶׁהֶחֱיָה יְחֶזְקֵאל עָלוּ לְאֶרֶץ יִשְׂרָאֵל – THE DEAD THAT EZEKIEL RESURRECTED WENT UP TO ERETZ YISRAEL, וְנָשְׂאוּ נָשִׁים וְהוֹלִידוּ בָּנִים וּבָנוֹת – MARRIED AND FATHERED SONS AND DAUGHTERS. עָמַד רַבִּי יְהוּדָה בֶּן בְּתֵירָא עַל רַגְלָיו וְאָמַר – R' YEHUDAH BEN BESEIRA ROSE TO HIS FEET AND DECLARED: אֲנִי מִבְּנֵי בְנֵיהֶם – I AM ONE OF THEIR DESCENDANTS, וְהַלָּלוּ תְּפִילִּין שֶׁהִנִּיחַ לִי אֲבִי אַבָּא מֵהֶם – AND THESE ARE THE TEFILLIN THAT MY FATHER'S FATHER LEFT ME FROM THEM.[11]

NOTES

1. *Isaiah* 2:11. The Gemara below (end of 97a) states on the basis of this verse that the world will last for six thousand years and will lie wasted for one thousand years, during which "God alone will be exalted" [after which He will renew His world and usher in the World to Come] (*Rashi*; see Gemara there).

2. I.e if the righteous who were resurrected in the Messianic Era are not buried at the end of the world, then where will their bodies be during the thousand years that the world will lie in waste? (*Rashi*). The apparent meaning of *Rashi's* remarks here and to the beginning of the Baraisa is that the righteous who are resurrected during the Messianic Era will indeed die prior to the World to Come, but their bodies will neither disintegrate nor be buried. This way of interpreting *Rashi's* remarks, however, is – for various reasons – rejected by *Radbaz* (2:839), who seeks to demonstrate that *Rashi* in fact means that the righteous will not die at all. See below, note 4, where this is elaborated upon.

3. *Psalms* 46:3. The verse is expounded to mean that we, the righteous, *shall not fear when the earth is transformed and when the mountains collapse [because we will be] in the heart of the seas* – i.e. gliding over the waters of the sea (see *Rashi*).

4. *Isaiah* 40:31. Thus, the righteous will be granted the necessary strength to stay aloft without suffering pain or fatigue (*Rashi*). *Radbaz* (loc. cit.) explains that "wings" and "effortless flight" are metaphors for the supreme purification and elevation of their bodies to the point that they delight in the splendor of the Divine Presence without requiring any physical sustenance.

Radbaz (loc. cit.) takes *Rashi* here as agreeing with many other commentators, who interpret this Baraisa to mean that the righteous who are resurrected will not die with the advent of the seventh millennium, but rather will enter a higher and purified state of existence (symbolized by "wings" and "effortless flight").

Radbaz also reports a tradition from many earlier authorities that there will be two resurrections. One resurrection will occur at the early part of the Messianic era, when the truly righteous will be resurrected to share in the glory of that sublime epoch. The second, general resurrection will occur at the end of the sixth millennium, when all will arise for the Great Day of Judgment. Accordingly, the Baraisa means that the righteous who will be resurrected at the beginning of the Messianic Era, as well as those resurrected for judgment at the end of the sixth millennium and found worthy of *olam haba,* will not die with the advent of the seventh millennium, but will enter a more sublime state. (Those alive when the Messiah comes as well as those born afterwards will live long, idyllic lives and then taste death [after which they will eventually be resurrected].)

This is fundamentally also the interpretation of *Ramchal* (see *Daas Tevunos* §72 ff and *Maamar HaIkkarim* §8 [*Geulah*] and *Michtav MeEliyahu* (vol. IV p. 150 ff.). See also *Rif* in *Ein Yaakov, Yad Yosef* and *Ben Yehoyada*; see below, 97a note 59.

5. In *Ezekiel* ch. 37 (vs. 1-10), it is related that the prophet Ezekiel was transported to a valley filled with dry bones, where he resurrected them at God's behest. These resurrected people eventually died and were buried like anyone else. Accordingly, we should use this established precedent of resurrection as an indication that those who come alive at the Resurrection of the Dead might also eventually die and be buried, unlike the teaching of the *Tanna Devei Eliyahu* (see *Rashi*; cf. *R' David Bonfils* and *Maharsha,* cited below in note 11).

6. [The dry bones represent the soon-to-be-exiled House of Israel, which would despair of redemption and of return to their land. Indeed, they will be resurrected from the "grave" of their exile and restored to the Land of Israel (*Ezekiel* 37:11-14; see *Rashi* here, and end of ד״ה ונילף).] If the account of resurrection is but a parable, it cannot serve as a precedent for the actual resurrection that is yet to occur.

7. The fact that they stood on their feet to utter song is perhaps a source for ruling that one should stand when reciting songs of praise to God (*Iyun Yaakov*; see *Mishnah Berurah* 422:28).

8. This is the song that Hannah uttered in *I Samuel* 2:6 upon the birth of her son Samuel after many years of being childless. [See *Maharsha* and *Maharal* for discussions of the dispute between R' Eliezer and R' Yehoshua.]

9. I.e. the vision shown to Ezekiel symbolized the restoration of the exiled Jewish people, which is akin to the deceased rising from the dead (see *Rashi*).

10. The expression "in truth" is used to indicate that what follows is considered definitive (see *Bava Metzia* 60a). Thus, the intent is that the view which considers the account of resurrection in *Ezekiel* to be a parable is the definitive one (*Sefer HaIkkarim* 4:35; *Toras Chaim*; see next note).

11. R' Yehudah ben Beseira states that his grandfather left him the tefillin that had been handed down to him in turn from *his* ancestor, who had been resurrected by Ezekiel (see *Rashi*).

[Since the expression "in truth" (when used in regard to halachic matters) indicates the definitive view, the Gemara's conclusion would

ואותן שנים שעתיד הקב"ה לחדש את עולמו. ויהיה עולם זה חרב אלף שנים אותן צדיקים היכן הם הואיל ואינן נקברין בארץ: לא נירא בהמיר ארץ. כשמחליף הקב"ה את הארץ לא ניראה לפי שאנו בלב ימים: וקווי ה' יחליפו כח. שיהא להם כח לשוט ולעופף בלי צער: ונילף ממתים שהחיה יחזקאל. שחזרו ומתו כך צדיקים שעתיד להחיות יחזרו לעפרם כך שמעתי יחזקאל הגלהו נבוכדנצר עם יכניה מלך יהודה והיה יחזקאל מתנבא בבבל וירמיה בארץ ישראל באותן אחת עשרה שנה שמלך צדקיה: באמת. בברור: משל היה. שהיה מרמז להם על הגלות כאדם מת שחוזר וחי כך ישראל ישובו מן הגלות: מהם. שאותן תפילין היו שלהם: שמנו לקץ. של יציאת מצרים: וטעו. שלא היה להם למנות גזירת ועבדום ועינו אותם אלא משנולד יצחק דהא כתיב (בראשית טו) כי גר יהיה זרעך זה יצחק דכתיב (שם כא) כי ביצחק יקרא לך זרע והם מנו משעת הדיבור לאברהם ותניא בסדר עולם אברהם אבינו בשעה שנדבר עמו בין הבתרים בן שבעים שנה היה ומבין הבתרים עד שנולד יצחק היה ל' שנה כדכתיב (בראשית כא) ואברהם בן מאת שנה בהולד לו את יצחק בנו נמצאת אומר משדבר עמו בין הבתרים עד שיצאו ממצרים היו ארבע מאות ואותן ל' שמן הדבור עד לידת יצחק טעו בני אפרים. ומניין שבני אפרים הן שיצאו קודם זמנן ונהרגו שנאמר ובני אפרים שותלח וגו' והרגום אנשי גת: ושמואל אמר. מתים שהחיה יחזקאל אלו בני אדם שכפרו בתחיית המתים שנאמר (יחזקאל לז) אבדה תקותנו: העצמות האלה כל בית ישראל המה. עצמות הללו סימן לכל ישראל הן שעתידה להם תחיית המתים כמו לאלו שהרי אלו אמרו אבדה תקותנו ועכשיו ידעו שאני מחיה את המתים וסימן זה לכל ישראל שגם הם עתידין להחיות ולא מן הדין חיו דהא אמרן ב) הכופר בתחיית המתים אין לו חלק לעוה"ב אלא משום סימן חיו: שחיפו להיכל. שהיו מציירין צלמים על קירות ההיכל דכתיב ואבא ואראה מחוקה על הקיר סביב: וכתיב והעבירני עליהם סביב סביב. כלומר על אותן אנשים שכתוב עליהם סביב עבר עליהם יחזקאל להחיותם: אלו מתים שבבקעת דורא. שהמית נבוכדנצר מלך בבל על שהיו יפים כדלקמן: מנהר אשל עד רבת. מקומות הן היו בבקעת דורא: שופעות. מחמת תאוה: וצוה המלך והרגן ועדיין היו שופעות. שהיתה נראית זיו תארם ונוה המלך ורמסום: ובאו עצמות מן הבקעה וטפחו לו לאותו רשע על פניו. והלכו להם ואית דאמרי שמאותן עצמות היה לו כלים וכשהגיעה שעה שחיו טפחו לו על פיו כשהיה רוצה לשתות בהם: חבריהם של אלו מחיה מתים. על יחזקאל היו אומרין שהיה חבירן של חנניה מישאל ועזריה ונבוכדנצר היה יודע שהיה הקב"ה מחיה אותם: פתח ואמר. להקב"ה אתוהי כמה רברבין פסוק הוא (דניאל ג): יוצק זהב רותח. משום דקא מיירי בשבחו דנבוכדנצר נקיט נמי לישנא מעליא ולשון קללה: סטרו. הכהו מאחורי ידו: לגנות. שהיה מסדר שבחות נאות יותר מדוד ואילו אמרן הקב"ה היה נוטה אחריהן יותר מאחרי השירות שעשה דוד: באותו יום. שהשליכן לכבשן: צף הכבשן. שהכבשן היה משוקע בארץ כעין כבשן של סיד וצף ועומד על גבי קרקע כדי שיראוהו כל העולם: נפרץ הכבשן. נפלו קצת כותליו כדי שיוכלו כולם לראות בתוכו: הומק סורו. נשפל גאותו כמו סורו רע (קדושין דף פב.) ל"א הומק סודו כמו יסודו נשתלשל וכן לימדני רבי יעקב בן יקר אבל מורי גרס והומק סידו סיד הכבשן נמסה מרוב חמימות כך שמעתי והיתה מושכת למרחוק ומהבל של אותו הסיד נשרפו אותן שהשליכו חנניה מישאל ועזריה לתוך כבשן האש: ונהפך. צלם של זהב על פניו: ארבע מלכיות. מלכים ואנשיהם שסייעו לנבוכדנצר להשליך חנניה מישאל ועזריה לתוך האור: מקראי נפקי. דכתיב (דניאל ג) נבוכדנצר שלח למכנש לאחשדרפניא סגניא ולבסוף לאחר שבאו מן הכבשן כתיב ומתכנשין אחשדרפניא סגניא ופחותא והנך דלא כתיבי נשרפו: אל ישנה מן הרבנות שלו. שהרי חנניה מישאל ועזריה היו לבושין בגדי תפארתן כשהושלכו לכבשן אל ישנה שלא יראה מבוהל ומפוחד ומתביישין שונאיו מפניו: פטשיהון וכרבלתהון. עניני מלבושין: גדולים

ואם תאמר אותן שנים שעתיד הקב"ה לחדש בהן את עולמו שנאמר א) ונשגב ה' לבדו ביום ההוא צדיקים מה הן עושין הקב"ה עושה להם כנפים כנשרים ושטין על פני המים שנאמר ב) על כן לא נירא בהמיר ארץ במוט הרים בלב ימים ושמא תאמר יש להם צער ת"ל ג) וקווי ה' יחליפו כח יעלו אבר כנשרים ירוצו ולא ייגעו ילכו ולא ייעפו ונילף ממתים שהחיה יחזקאל סבר לה כמאן דאמר באמת משל היה דתניא ר"א אומר מתים שהחיה יחזקאל עמדו על רגליהם ואמרו שירה ומתו מה שירה אמרו ה' ממית בצדק ומחיה ברחמים ר' יהושע אומר שירה זו אמרו ד) ה' ממית ומחיה מוריד שאול ויעל ר' יהודה אומר אמת משל היה אמר לו רבי נחמיה אם אמת למה משל ואם משל למה אמת אלא באמת משל היה ר"א בנו של ר' יוסי הגלילי אומר מתים שהחיה יחזקאל עלו לארץ ישראל ונשאו נשים והולידו בנים ובנות עמד ר"י בן בתירא על רגליו ואמר אני מבני בניהם והללו תפילין שהניח לי אבי אבא מהם ומאן נינהו מתים שהחיה יחזקאל אמר רב אלו בני אפרים שמנו לקץ וטעו שנאמר ה) ובני אפרים שותלח וברד בנו ותחת בנו ואלעדה בנו ותחת בנו וזבד בנו ושותלח בנו ועזר (ואלעזר) [ואלעד] והרגום אנשי גת הנולדים בארץ וגו' וכתיב ו) ויתאבל אפרים אביהם ימים רבים ויבאו אחיו לנחמו ושמואל אמר אלו בני אדם שכפרו בתחיית המתים שנאמר ז) ויאמר אלי בן אדם העצמות האלה כל בית ישראל המה הנה אומרים יבשו עצמותינו ואבדה תקותנו נגזרנו לנו ר' ירמיה בר אבא אמר אלו בני אדם שאין בהן לחלוחית של מצוה שנאמר ח) העצמות היבשות שמעו דבר ה' ר' יצחק נפחא אמר אלו בני אדם שחיפו את ההיכל כולו שקצים ורמשים שנאמר ט) ואבוא ואראה והנה כל תבנית רמש ובהמה שקץ וכל גלולי בית ישראל מחוקה על הקיר סביב וגו' וכתיב התם י) והעבירני עליהם סביב סביב ר' יוחנן אמר אלו מתים שבבקעת דורא וא"ר יוחנן מנהר אשל עד רבת בקעת דורא שבשעה שהגלה נבוכדנצר הרשע את ישראל היו בהן בחורים שהיו מגנין את החמה ביופיין והיו כשדיות רואות אותן ושופעות זבות אמרו לבעליהן ובעליהן למלך צוה המלך והרגום ועדיין היו שופעות זבות צוה המלך ורמסום תנו רבנן בשעה שהפיל נבוכדנצר הרשע את חנניה מישאל ועזריה לכבשן האש אמר לו הקב"ה ליחזקאל לך והחייה מתים בבקעת דורא כיון שהחייה אותן באו עצמות וטפחו לו [א] לאותו רשע על פניו אמר מה טיבן של אלו אמרו לו חבריהן של אלו מחיה מתים בבקעת דורא פתח ואמר כ) אתוהי כמה רברבין ותמהוהי כמה תקיפין מלכותיה מלכות עלם ושלטניה עם דר ודר וגו' א"ר יצחק יוצק זהב רותח לתוך פיו [ב] של אותו רשע שאילמלא (א) לא) בא מלאך וסטרו על פיו ביקש לגנות כל שירות ותושבחות שאמר דוד בספר תהלים ת"ר ששה נסים נעשו באותו היום ואלו הן צף הכבשן ונפרץ הכבשן והומק סודו ונהפך צלם על פניו ונשרפו ארבע מלכיות והחייה יחזקאל את המתים בבקעת דורא וכולהו גמרא וארבע מלכיות קרא דכתיב ל) ונבוכדנצר מלכא שלח למכנש לאחשדרפניא סגניא ופחוותא אדרגזריא גדבריא דתבריא תפתיא וכל שלטוני מדינתא וגו' וכתיב מ) איתי גוברין יהודאין וכתיב נ) ומתכנשין אחשדרפניא סגניא ופחוותא והדברי מלכא חזיין לגבריא אלך וגו' תני דבי רבי אליעזר בן יעקב אפילו בשעת הסכנה לא ישנה אדם את עצמו מן הרבנות שלו שנאמר ס) באדין גבריא אלך כפתו בסרבליהון פטשיהון וכרבלתהון וגו' אמר רבי יוחנן גדולים

הגהות הגר"א

[א] גמ' נ"ל לאותו רשע שחיק טמי': [ב] שם נ"ל של אותו רשע שחיק טמי':

תורה אור השלם

א) וְשַׁח גַּבְהוּת הָאָדָם וְשָׁפֵל רוּם אֲנָשִׁים וְנִשְׂגַּב יְיָ לְבַדּוֹ בַּיּוֹם הַהוּא: [ישעיה ב, יז]

ב) עַל כֵּן לֹא נִירָא בְּהָמִיר אָרֶץ וּבְמוֹט הָרִים בְּלֵב יַמִּים: [תהלים מו, ג]

ג) וְקוֵֹי יְיָ יַחֲלִיפוּ כֹחַ יַעֲלוּ אֵבֶר כַּנְּשָׁרִים יָרוּצוּ וְלֹא יִיגָעוּ יֵלְכוּ וְלֹא יִיעָפוּ: [ישעיה מ, לא]

ד) יְיָ מֵמִית וּמְחַיֶּה מוֹרִיד שְׁאוֹל וַיָּעַל: [שמואל א' ב, ו]

ה) וּבְנֵי אֶפְרַיִם שׁוּתָלַח וּבֶרֶד בְּנוֹ וְתַחַת בְּנוֹ וְאֶלְעָדָה בְנוֹ וְתַחַת בְּנוֹ: וְזָבָד בְּנוֹ וְשׁוּתֶלַח בְּנוֹ וְעֵזֶר וְאֶלְעָד וַהֲרָגוּם אַנְשֵׁי גַת הַנּוֹלָדִים בָּאָרֶץ כִּי יָרְדוּ לָקַחַת אֶת מִקְנֵיהֶם: [דברי הימים א' ז, כ-כא]

ו) וַיִּתְאַבֵּל אֶפְרַיִם אֲבִיהֶם יָמִים רַבִּים וַיָּבֹאוּ אֶחָיו לְנַחֲמוֹ: [דברי הימים א' ז, כב]

ז) וַיֹּאמֶר אֵלַי בֶּן אָדָם הָעֲצָמוֹת הָאֵלֶּה כָּל בֵּית יִשְׂרָאֵל הֵמָּה הִנֵּה אֹמְרִים יָבְשׁוּ עַצְמוֹתֵינוּ וְאָבְדָה תִקְוָתֵנוּ נִגְזַרְנוּ לָנוּ: [יחזקאל לז, יא]

ח) וַיֹּאמֶר אֵלַי הִנָּבֵא עַל הָעֲצָמוֹת הָאֵלֶּה וְאָמַרְתָּ אֲלֵיהֶם הָעֲצָמוֹת הַיְבֵשׁוֹת שִׁמְעוּ דְּבַר יְיָ: [יחזקאל לז, ד]

ט) וָאָבוֹא וָאֶרְאֶה וְהִנֵּה כָל תַּבְנִית רֶמֶשׂ וּבְהֵמָה שֶׁקֶץ וְכָל גִּלּוּלֵי בֵּית יִשְׂרָאֵל מְחֻקֶּה עַל הַקִּיר סָבִיב סָבִיב: [יחזקאל ח, י]

י) וְהֶעֱבִירַנִי עֲלֵיהֶם סָבִיב סָבִיב וְהִנֵּה רַבּוֹת מְאֹד עַל פְּנֵי הַבִּקְעָה וְהִנֵּה יְבֵשׁוֹת מְאֹד: [יחזקאל לז, ב]

כ) אָתוֹהִי כְּמָה רַבְרְבִין וְתִמְהוֹהִי כְּמָה תַקִּיפִין מַלְכוּתֵהּ מַלְכוּת עָלַם וְשָׁלְטָנֵהּ עִם דָּר וְדָר: [דניאל ג, לג]

ל) וּנְבוּכַדְנֶצַּר מַלְכָּא שְׁלַח לְמִכְנַשׁ לַאֲחַשְׁדַּרְפְּנַיָּא סִגְנַיָּא וּפַחֲוָתָא אֲדַרְגָּזְרַיָּא גְדָבְרַיָּא דְּתָבְרַיָּא תִּפְתָּיֵא וְכֹל שִׁלְטֹנֵי מְדִינָתָא לְמֵתֵא לַחֲנֻכַּת צַלְמָא דִּי הֲקֵים נְבוּכַדְנֶצַּר מַלְכָּא: [דניאל ג, ב]

מ) אִיתַי גֻּבְרִין יְהוּדָאיִן דִּי מַנִּיתָ יָתְהוֹן עַל עֲבִידַת מְדִינַת בָּבֶל שַׁדְרַךְ מֵישַׁךְ וַעֲבֵד נְגוֹ גֻּבְרַיָּא אִלֵּךְ לָא שָׂמוּ עֲלָךְ מַלְכָּא טְעֵם לֵאלָהָךְ לָא פָלְחִין וּלְצֶלֶם דַּהֲבָא דִּי הֲקֵימְתָּ לָא סָגְדִין: [דניאל ג, יב]

נ) וּמִתְכַּנְּשִׁין אֲחַשְׁדַּרְפְּנַיָּא סִגְנַיָּא וּפַחֲוָתָא וְהַדָּבְרֵי מַלְכָּא חָזַיִן לְגֻבְרַיָּא אִלֵּךְ דִּי לָא שְׁלֵט נוּרָא בְּגֶשְׁמְהוֹן וּשְׂעַר רֵאשְׁהוֹן לָא הִתְחָרַךְ וְסָרְבָּלֵיהוֹן לָא שְׁנוֹ וְרֵיחַ נוּר לָא עֲדָת בְּהוֹן: [דניאל ג, כז]

ס) בֵּאדַיִן גֻּבְרַיָּא אִלֵּךְ כְּפִתוּ בְּסַרְבָּלֵיהוֹן פַּטְּשֵׁיהוֹן וְכַרְבְּלָתְהוֹן וּלְבֻשֵׁיהוֹן וּרְמִיו לְגוֹא אַתּוּן נוּרָא יָקִדְתָּא: [דניאל ג, כא]

מסורת הש"ס

א) [עי' תוס' מגילה כא.], ב) [לעיל צ.].

ליקוטי רש"י

אותן שנים. דהיינו אלף שביעי. ונשגב ה' לבדו ביום ההוא. יומו של הקב"ה אלף שנה שנאמר כי אלף שנים בעיניך כיום אתמול כי יעבור [לקמן צז.]. בהמיר ארץ. לעתיד לבא ביום שנאמר והארץ כבגד תבלה (ישעיה נא) ראו בני קרח נס שנעש' להם שנבלעו כל סביבותיה' והם עמדו באויר ואמרו לישראל ברוח הקדש שדוגמת הנס הזה יהיה עשוי להם לעתיד [תהלים מו, ג]. אבר. כנף [ישעיה מ, לא]. שקץ. עשוין לשקוץ עכו"ם. מחוקה. חקוקין על הקיר [יחזקאל ח, י]. בקעת דורא. שם מקום [דניאל ג, א]. לאחשדרפניא. דוכסין. ופחוותא. שלטונין. אדרגזריא גדבריא וגומר. כולם שם עכו"ם הם [שם, ב]. איתי. יש. יהודאין. משבט יהודה [שם, יב]. ומתכנשין אחשדרפניא. ד' אומות נמנו למעלה באסיפה הראשונה שלא נמנו כאן אדרגזריא דתבריא גדבריא תפתיא הם גבורי החיל אשר הרגם שביב האש בהשליכם את חנניה וחבריו לאור. חזיין לגבריא אלך. רואין את האנשים האלה חנניה וחבריו [שם, כז]. גבריא אלך. אנשים אלו. כפתו בסרבליהון. נתקשרו בבגדי מעטפותן. פטשיהון וכרבלתהון. מיני מלבוש מלכות שהיה להם ואע"פ שהיו יוצאין לידון לפני ב"ד דיני מיתה לא שנו בגדיהם להשפיל את גדולתם מכאן למדו חכמים שאפי' בשעת הסכנה לא ישנה אדם מן השררה שהוחזק בה. וכרבלתהון. יש לו דוגמא (בד"ה א' טו) ודוד מכורבל [שם, כא].

In line with the view that the account in *Ezekiel* refers to an actual resurrection, the Gemara presents five opinions as to the identity of the dead who were resurrected:

וּמַאן נִינְהוּ מֵתִים שֶׁהֶחֱיָה יְחֶזְקֵאל – **And who were the dead that Ezekiel resurrected?**

אָמַר רַב – **Rav said:** אֵלּוּ בְּנֵי אֶפְרַיִם שֶׁמָּנוּ לַקֵּץ וְטָעוּ – **These were the sons of** the tribe of **Ephraim, who calculated the end** of the slavery in Egypt **and erred** in their count, and were killed after escaping Egypt,[12] שֶׁנֶּאֱמַר "וּבְנֵי אֶפְרַיִם שׁוּתָלַח וּבֶרֶד בְּנוֹ וְתַחַת בְּנוֹ וְאֶלְעָדָה בְנוֹ וְתַחַת בְּנוֹ. וְזָבָד בְּנוֹ וְשׁוּתֶלַח בְּנוֹ וְעֵזֶר וְאֶלְעָד וַהֲרָגוּם אַנְשֵׁי־גַת הַנּוֹלָדִים בָּאָרֶץ וגו׳" – *as it is stated: And the sons of Ephraim: Shuthelach; and his son Bered, and his son Tachath, and his son El'adah, and his son Tachath. And his son Zavad, and his son Shuthelach, and Ezer and El'ad. But the men of Gath, who were born in the land, killed them* etc.[13] וּכְתִיב "וַיִּתְאַבֵּל אֶפְרַיִם אֲבִיהֶם יָמִים רַבִּים וַיָּבֹאוּ אֶחָיו לְנַחֲמוֹ" – **And it is written** in the next verse: *And Ephraim, their father, mourned many days, and his brothers came to console him.*[14]

וּשְׁמוּאֵל אָמַר – **And Shmuel says:** אֵלּוּ בְּנֵי אָדָם שֶׁכָּפְרוּ בִּתְחִיַּית הַמֵּתִים – **These** dead whom Ezekiel resurrected **were people who denied** that there would be **the Resurrection of the Dead,** שֶׁנֶּאֱמַר "וַיֹּאמֶר אֵלַי בֶּן־אָדָם הָעֲצָמוֹת הָאֵלֶּה כָּל־בֵּית יִשְׂרָאֵל הֵמָּה הִנֵּה אֹמְרִים יָבְשׁוּ עַצְמוֹתֵינוּ וְאָבְדָה תִקְוָתֵנוּ נִגְזַרְנוּ לָנוּ" – **as it is stated** in that passage: *Then He said to me: Son of man, these bones – they are all of the House of Israel; behold they say, "Our bones have dried up, our hope is lost, we are doomed."*[15]

רַבִּי יִרְמְיָה בַּר אַבָּא אָמַר – **R' Yirmiyah bar Abba says:** אֵלּוּ בְּנֵי אָדָם שֶׁאֵין בָּהֶן לַחְלוּחִית שֶׁל מִצְוָה – **These** dead whom Ezekiel resurrected **were people who lack** even **the "moisture" of a mitzvah** (that is, they were totally bereft of even the slightest merit), שֶׁנֶּאֱמַר "הָעֲצָמוֹת הַיְבֵשׁוֹת שִׁמְעוּ דְּבַר־ה׳" – **as it is stated** in that passage: *O dry bones, hear the word of* HASHEM.[16]

רַבִּי יִצְחָק נַפְחָא אָמַר – **R' Yitzchak Nafcha says:** אֵלּוּ בְּנֵי אָדָם שֶׁחִיפּוּ אֶת הַהֵיכָל כּוּלּוֹ שְׁקָצִים וּרְמָשִׂים – **These** dead whom Ezekiel resurrected **were the people who covered the entire** Temple **Sanctuary** with pictures of pagan **abominations and creeping things.** שֶׁנֶּאֱמַר "וָאָבוֹא וָאֶרְאֶה וְהִנֵּה כָל־תַּבְנִית רֶמֶשׂ וּבְהֵמָה שֶׁקֶץ וְכָל־גִּלּוּלֵי בֵּית יִשְׂרָאֵל מְחֻקֶּה עַל־הַקִּיר סָבִיב וגו׳" – **For it is stated:** *So I entered and I looked, and behold there was every form of creeping thing and animal – abominable idols – and every manner of idol of the House of Israel; carved into the wall "round* **etc.** *and round."*[17] וּכְתִיב הָתָם "וְהֶעֱבִירַנִי עֲלֵיהֶם סָבִיב סָבִיב" – **And it is written there,** in the passage of the resurrection wrought by Ezekiel: *And He led me over them "round and round."*[18]

רַבִּי יוֹחָנָן אָמַר – **R' Yochanan says:** אֵלּוּ מֵתִים שֶׁבְּבִקְעַת דּוּרָא – **These** dead whom Ezekiel resurrected **were the dead of the Plain of Dura.**[19] וְאָמַר רַבִּי יוֹחָנָן – **And R' Yochanan** also **said:** מִנְּהַר אֶשֶׁל עַד רַבַּת בִּקְעַת דּוּרָא – **From the Eshel River until Rabbas is the Plain of Dura.** And what was the incident

NOTES

appear to be that the episode of resurrection recorded in *Ezekiel* was indeed a parable (see preceding note). Accordingly, we would have to assume that R' Yehudah ben Beseira issued his claim of descent from those resurrected by Ezekiel and his possession of their tefillin as no more than an exaggerated statement (*Sefer HaIkkarim* 4:35).] It should be noted, however, that *Rambam* declares (in regard to a different dispute) that the fixing of a definitive view is not applicable to *aggadic* matters that have no practical ramifications (see *Peirush HaMishnah* to 110b).

According to *Rashi's* explanation of the Gemara's question and answer, it emerges that those who take the resurrection recorded in *Ezekiel* to be factual might dispute the teaching of the *Tanna Devei Eliyahu* that the righteous to be resurrected in the future will not return to dust. [Indeed, this might be the source for *Rambam's* view that the bodies of the resurrected will indeed return to dust – see Introduction.] *R' David Bonfils* (see also *Maharsha*), however, rejects the notion that all these Tannaim and Amoraim would dispute the teaching of the *Tanna Devei Eliyahu*. Furthermore, he argues, there would be no reasonable basis for the Gemara to derive the fate of the truly righteous that God will resurrect in the future from that of the people resurrected by Ezekiel (who were sinners, according to many opinions – see Gemara below). Therefore, he differs with *Rashi* and explains the Gemara's statement, *"Let us learn from the dead whom Ezekiel resurrected,"* to be: As recorded above, the Sages have gone to great length to refute those who reject the notion of resurrection. Why do we not simply prove the notion of resurrection from the actual resurrection wrought by Ezekiel? To this the Gemara answers that such proof would be insufficient, since some Tannaim maintain that the resurrection recorded in *Ezekiel* was but a parable. [See further in *R' David Bonfils* for a defense of his explanation against anticipated objections. Cf. *Iyun Yaakov*. See also *Teshuvos Radbaz* 2:839.]

12. At the Covenant between the Parts, God told Abraham that *your seed will be strangers in a land that is not theirs, and they will enslave them and oppress them – four hundred years* (*Genesis* 15:13). Now, in truth these four hundred years began with the birth of Isaac (as stated: *your seed*) thirty years later. The Ephraimites, however, counted four hundred years from the time of the covenant and thus miscalculated by thirty years the end of the Egyptian bondage. Based on their erroneous calculation, they escaped from Egypt prematurely and were killed by the people of Gath, as recounted in the verse the Gemara will now cite (*Rashi*). [For a more extensive discussion of this subject, see ArtScroll *Divrei Hayamim I* pp. 411-414.]

13. *I Chronicles* 7:20-21. [*Radak* (ad loc.) explains that Shuthelach, Bered and Tachath were Ephraim's actual sons, and the rest were descendants; alternatively, even Bered and Tachath were grandchildren.]

14. Ibid. v. 22. [This second verse places the event in Ephraim's own lifetime and thus during the Egyptian bondage, since it is assumed that Ephraim died before the Exodus. Cf. *Toras Chaim.*]

[*Toras Chaim* suggests that Rav's identification of Ezekiel's resurrected as the killed Ephraimites is based on the verse in the passage describing that resurrection: וּפְחִי בַּהֲרוּגִים הָאֵלֶּה וְיִחְיוּ, *and blow into these "killed ones" and they shall live* (*Ezekiel* 37:9). "Killed ones" is a reference to the Ephraimites, about whom it is written (as cited in the Gemara from *I Chronicles* 7:21): וַהֲרָגוּם אַנְשֵׁי־גַת, *and the men of Gath "killed them."*]

15. *Ezekiel* 37:11. The statement *our hope is lost* indicates a denial of the Resurrection of the Dead. Accordingly, the verse means: *Then He said to me: Son of man, these bones – they are* a sign to *all of the House of Israel,* who will eventually be resurrected. For *behold they say* [i.e. those whom you have resurrected used to deny the resurrection and say]: *Our bones have dried up, our hope is lost, we are doomed,* yet they were indeed resurrected. Though by rights they should have forfeited the privilege of resurrection, as stated in our Mishnah, they were especially resurrected as a sign to all of Israel (*Rashi*).

16. Ibid. v. 4. The bones which were completely dry (see v. 2) are a metaphor for persons who are completely "dry" of merit.

These people did not deny the resurrection; they merely considered themselves unworthy of it because of their total lack of merit. They were resurrected to indicate that even such sinners will merit the resurrection after undergoing the requisite atonement of Gehinnom (see *Maharsha*).

17. *Ezekiel* 8:10. This passage relates how an angel led Ezekiel into the Temple and showed him the rampant idol worship that was taking place there during the last years before its destruction. [For a fuller treatment of this matter, see ArtScroll *Ezekiel* pp. 159-168.]

18. Ibid. 37:2. Thus, it is as if the verse states that *He led me over them – [those about whom it is written elsewhere] "round and round"* (*Rashi*). See *Maharsha,* who discusses why precisely these people were resurrected.

19. The Babylonian Plain of Dura was the place where Nebuchadnezzar erected his golden colossus, before which he ordered all to bow on pain of being cast into the fiery furnace. Chananyah, Mishael and Azaryah refused to bow, were cast into the furnace and emerged unscathed (see *Daniel* 3:1 ff). See *Toras Chaim,* who discusses R' Yochanan's source.

ואם תאמר אותן שנים שעתיד הקב"ה לחדש בהן את עולמו שנאמר א) ונשגב ה' לבדו ביום ההוא צדיקים מה הן עושין הקב"ה עושה להם כנפים כנשרים ושטין על פני המים שנאמר ב) על כן לא נירא בהמיר ארץ במוט הרים בלב ימים ושמא תאמר יש להם צער ת"ל ג) וקווי ה' יחליפו כח יעלו אבר כנשרים ירוצו ולא ייגעו ילכו ולא ייעפו ונילף ממתים שהחיה יחזקאל סבר לה כמאן דאמר באמת משל היה דתניא ר"א אומר מתים שהחיה יחזקאל עמדו על רגליהם ואמרו שירה ומתו מה שירה אמרו ה' ממית בצדק ומחיה ברחמים ר' יהושע אומר שירה זו אמרו ד) ה' ממית ומחיה מוריד שאול ויעל ר' יהודה אומר אמת משל היה אמר לו רבי נחמיה אם אמת למה משל ואם משל למה אמת אלא באמת משל היה ר"א בנו של ר' יוסי הגלילי אומר מתים שהחיה יחזקאל עלו לארץ ישראל ונשאו נשים והולידו בנים ובנות עמד ר"י בן בתירא על רגליו ואמר אני מבני בניהם והללו תפילין שהניח לי אבי אבא מהם ומאן נינהו מתים שהחיה יחזקאל אמר רב אלו בני אפרים שמנו לקץ וטעו שנאמר ה) ובני אפרים שותלח וברד בנו ותחת בנו ואלעדה בנו ותחת בנו וזבד בנו ושותלח בנו ועזר (ואלעזר) [ואלעד] והרגום אנשי גת הנולדים בארץ וגו' וכתיב ו) ויתאבל אפרים אביהם ימים רבים ויבאו אחיו לנחמו ושמואל אמר אלו בני אדם שכפרו בתחיית המתים שנאמר ז) ויאמר אלי בן אדם העצמות האלה כל בית ישראל המה הנה אומרים יבשו עצמותינו ואבדה תקותנו נגזרנו לנו ר' ירמיה בר אבא אמר אלו בני אדם שאין בהן לחלוחית של מצוה שנאמר ח) העצמות היבשות שמעו דבר ה' ר' יצחק נפחא אמר אלו בני אדם שחיפו את ההיכל כולו שקצים ורמשים שנאמר ט) ואבוא ואראה והנה כל תבנית רמש ובהמה שקץ וכל גלולי בית ישראל מחוקה על הקיר סביב וגו' וכתיב התם י) והעבירני עליהם סביב סביב ר' יוחנן אמר אלו מתים שבבקעת דורא וא"ר יוחנן מנהר אשל עד רבת בקעת דורא שבשעה שהגלה נבוכדנצר הרשע את ישראל היו בהן בחורים שהיו מגנין את החמה ביופיין והיו כשדיות רואות אותן ושופעות זבות אמרו לבעליהן ובעליהן למלך צוה המלך והרגום ועדיין היו שופעות זבות צוה המלך ורמסום תנו רבנן בשעה שהפיל נבוכדנצר הרשע את חנניה מישאל ועזריה לכבשן האש אמר לו הקב"ה ליחזקאל לך והחייה מתים בבקעת דורא כיון שהחייה אותן באו עצמות וטפחו לו [א] לאותו רשע על פניו אמר מה טיבן של אלו אמרו לו חבריהן של אלו מחיה מתים בבקעת דורא פתח ואמר כ) אתוהי כמה רברבין ותמהוהי כמה תקיפין מלכותיה מלכות עלם ושלטניה עם דר ודר וגו' א"ר יצחק יוצק זהב רותח לתוך פיו [ב] של אותו רשע שאילמלא (א) לא) בא מלאך וסטרו על פיו ביקש לגנות כל שירות ותושבחות שאמר דוד בספר תהלים ת"ר ששה נסים נעשו באותו היום ואלו הן צף הכבשן ונפרץ הכבשן והומק סודו ונהפך צלם על פניו ונשרפו ארבע מלכיות והחייה יחזקאל את המתים בבקעת דורא וכולהו גמרא וארבע מלכיות קרא דכתיב ל) ונבוכדנצר מלכא שלח למכנש לאחשדרפניא סגניא ופחוותא אדרגזריא גדבריא דתבריא תפתיא וכל שלטוני מדינתא וגו' וכתיב מ) איתי גוברין יהודאין וכתיב נ) ומתכנשין אחשדרפניא סגניא ופחוותא והדברי מלכא חזיין לגבריא אלך וגו' תני דבי רבי אליעזר בן יעקב אפילו בשעת הסכנה לא ישנה אדם את עצמו מן הרבנות שלו שנאמר ס) באדין גבריא אלך כפתו בסרבליהון פטשיהון וכרבלתהון וגו' אמר רבי יוחנן

גדולים

ואותן שנים שעתיד הקב"ה לחדש את עולמו. ויהיה עולם זה חרב אלף שנים אותן לדיקים היכן הם הואיל ואינן נקברין בארץ: לא נירא בהמיר ארץ. כשמחליף הקב"ה את הארץ לא נירא לפי שאנו בלב ימים: וקווי ה' יחליפו כח. שיהא להם כח לשוט ולעופף בלי לער: ונילף ממתים שהחיה יחזקאל. שחזרו ומתו כך לדיקים שעתיד להחיות יחזרו לעפרם כך שמעתי יחזקאל הגלהו נבוכדנלר עם יכניה מלך יהודה והיה יחזקאל מתנבא בבבל וירמיה בארץ ישראל באותן אחת עשרה שנה שמלך לדקיה: באמת. בברור: משל היה. שהיה מרמז להם על הגלות כאדם מת שחוזר וחי כך ישראל ישובו מן הגלות: מהם. שאותן תפילין היו שלהם: שמנו לקץ. של יליאת מלרים: וטעו. שלא היה להם למנות גזירת ועבדום וענו אותם אלא משנולד ילחק דהא כתיב (בראשית טו) כי גר יהיה זרעך זה ילחק דכתיב (שם כא) כי בילחק יקרא לך זרע והם מנו משעת הדיבור לאברהם ותניא בסדר עולם אברהם אבינו בשעה שנדבר עמו בין הבתרים בן שבעים שנה היה ומבין הבתרים עד שנולד ילחק היה ל' שנה כדכתיב (בראשית כא) ואברהם בן מאת שנה בהולד לו את ילחק בנו נמלאת אומר משדבר עמו בין הבתרים עד שילאו ממלרים היו ארבע מאות ואותן ל' שמן הדבור עד לידת ילחק טעו בני אפרים. ומניין שבני אפרים הן שילאו קודם זמנן ונהרגו שנאמר ובני אפרים שותלח וגו' והרגום אנשי גת: ושמואל אמר. מתים שהחיה יחזקאל אלו בני אדם שכפרו בתחיית המתים שנאמר (יחזקאל לז) אבדה תקותנו: העצמות האלה כל בית ישראל המה. עלמות הללו סימן לכל ישראל הן שעתידה להם תחיית המתים כמו לאלו שהרי אלו אמרו אבדה תקותנו ועכשיו ידעו שאני מחיה את המתים וסימן זה לכל ישראל שגם הם עתידין להחיות ולא מן הדין חיו דהא אמרן ג) הכופר בתחיית המתים אין לו חלק לעוה"ב אלא משום סימן חיו: שחיפו להיכל. שהיו מליירין ללמים על קירות ההיכל דכתיב ואבא ואראה מחוקה על הקיר סביב: וכתיב והעבירני עליהם סביב סביב. כלומר על אותן אנשים שכתוב עליהם סביב עבר עליהם יחזקאל להחיותם: אלו מתים שבבקעת דורא. שהמית נבוכדנלר מלך בבל על שהיו יפים כדלקמן: מנהר אשל עד רבת. מקומות הן היו בבקעת דורא: שופעות. מחמת תאוה: וצוה המלך והרגן ועדיין היו שופעות. שהיתה נראית זיו תארם ולוה המלך ורמסום: ובאו עצמות מן הבקעה וטפחו לו לאותו רשע על פניו. והלכו להם ואית דאמרי שמאותן עלמות היה לו כליס וכשהגיעה שעה שחיו טפחו לו על פיו כשהיה רולה לשתות בהם: חבריהם של אלו מחיה מתים. על יחזקאל היו אומרין שהיה חבירן של חנניה מישאל ועזריה ונבוכדנלר היה יודע שהיה הקב"ה מחיה אותם: פתח ואמר. להקב"ה אתוהי כמה רברבין פסוק הוא (דניאל ג): יוצק זהב רותח. משום דקא מיירי בשבחו דנבוכדנלר נקיט נמי לישנא מעליא ולשון קללה: סטרו. הכהו מאחורי ידו: לגנות. שהיה מסדר שבחות נאות יותר מדוד ואילו אמרן הקב"ה היה נוטה אחריהן יותר מאחרי השירות שעשה דוד: באותו יום. שהשליכן לכבשן: צף הכבשן. שהכבשן היה משוקע בארץ כעין כבשן של סיד וצף ועומד על גבי קרקע כדי שיראוהו כל העולם: נפרץ הכבשן. נפלו קצת כותליו כדי שיוכלו כולם לראות בתוכו: הומק סודו. נשפל גאותו כמו סורו רע (קדושין דף פב.) ל"א הומק סודו כמו יסודו נשתלשל וכן לימדני רבי יעקב בן יקר אבל מורי גרס והומק סידו סיד הכבשן נמסה מרוב חמימות כך שמעתי והיתה מושכת למרחוק ומהבל של אותו הסיד נשרפו אותן שהשליכו חנניה מישאל ועזריה לתוך כבשן האש: ונהפך. צלם של זהב על פניו: ארבע מלכיות. מלכים ואנשיהם שסייעו לנבוכדנלר להשליך חנניה מישאל ועזריה לתוך האור: מקראי נפקי. דכתיב (דניאל ג) נבוכדנלר שלח למכנש לאחשדרפניא סגניא ולבסוף לאחר שבאו מן הכבשן כתיב ומתכנשין אחשדרפניא סגניא ופחותא והנך דלא כתיבי נשרפו: אל ישנה מן הרבנות שלו. שהרי חנניה מישאל ועזריה היו לבושין בגדי תפארתן כשהושלכו לכבשן אל ישנה שלא יראה מבוהל ומפוחד ומתביישין שונאיו מפניו: פטשיהון וכרבלתהון. עניני מלבושין גדולים

[א] גמ' נ"ל לאותו רשע שחיק טמי': [ב] שם נ"ל של אותו רשע שחיק טמי':

תורה אור השלם

א) וְשַׁח גַּבְהוּת הָאָדָם וְשָׁפֵל רוּם אֲנָשִׁים וְנִשְׂגַּב יְיָ לְבַדּוֹ בַּיּוֹם הַהוּא: [ישעיה ב, יז]

ב) עַל כֵּן לֹא נִירָא בְּהָמִיר אָרֶץ וּבְמוֹט הָרִים בְּלֵב יַמִּים: [תהלים מו, ג]

ג) וְקוֵֹי יְיָ יַחֲלִיפוּ כֹחַ יַעֲלוּ אֵבֶר כַּנְּשָׁרִים יָרוּצוּ וְלֹא יִיגָעוּ יֵלְכוּ וְלֹא יִיעָפוּ: [ישעיה מ, לא]

ד) יְיָ מֵמִית וּמְחַיֶּה מוֹרִיד שְׁאוֹל וַיָּעַל: [שמואל א' ב, ו]

ה) וּבְנֵי אֶפְרַיִם שׁוּתָלַח וּבֶרֶד בְּנוֹ וְתַחַת בְּנוֹ וְאֶלְעָדָה בְנוֹ וְתַחַת בְּנוֹ: וְזָבָד בְּנוֹ וְשׁוּתֶלַח בְּנוֹ וְעֵזֶר וְאֶלְעָד וַהֲרָגוּם אַנְשֵׁי גַת הַנּוֹלָדִים בָּאָרֶץ כִּי יָרְדוּ לָקַחַת אֶת מִקְנֵיהֶם: [דברי הימים א' ז, כ-כא]

ו) וַיִּתְאַבֵּל אֶפְרַיִם אֲבִיהֶם יָמִים רַבִּים וַיָּבֹאוּ אֶחָיו לְנַחֲמוֹ: [דברי הימים א' ז, כב]

ז) וַיֹּאמֶר אֵלַי בֶּן אָדָם הָעֲצָמוֹת הָאֵלֶּה כָּל בֵּית יִשְׂרָאֵל הֵמָּה הִנֵּה אֹמְרִים יָבְשׁוּ עַצְמוֹתֵינוּ וְאָבְדָה תִקְוָתֵנוּ נִגְזַרְנוּ לָנוּ: [יחזקאל לז, יא]

ח) וַיֹּאמֶר אֵלַי הִנָּבֵא עַל הָעֲצָמוֹת הָאֵלֶּה וְאָמַרְתָּ אֲלֵיהֶם הָעֲצָמוֹת הַיְבֵשׁוֹת שִׁמְעוּ דְּבַר יְיָ: [יחזקאל לז, ד]

ט) וָאָבוֹא וָאֶרְאֶה וְהִנֵּה כָל תַּבְנִית רֶמֶשׂ וּבְהֵמָה שֶׁקֶץ וְכָל גִּלּוּלֵי בֵּית יִשְׂרָאֵל מְחֻקֶּה עַל הַקִּיר סָבִיב סָבִיב: [יחזקאל ח, י]

י) וְהֶעֱבִירַנִי עֲלֵיהֶם סָבִיב סָבִיב וְהִנֵּה רַבּוֹת מְאֹד עַל פְּנֵי הַבִּקְעָה וְהִנֵּה יְבֵשׁוֹת מְאֹד: [יחזקאל לז, ב]

כ) אָתוֹהִי כְּמָה רַבְרְבִין וְתִמְהוֹהִי כְּמָה תַקִּיפִין מַלְכוּתֵהּ מַלְכוּת עָלַם וְשָׁלְטָנֵהּ עִם דָּר וְדָר: [דניאל ג, לג]

ל) וּנְבוּכַדְנֶצַּר מַלְכָּא שְׁלַח לְמִכְנַשׁ לַאֲחַשְׁדַּרְפְּנַיָּא סִגְנַיָּא וּפַחֲוָתָא אֲדַרְגָּזְרַיָּא גְדָבְרַיָּא דְּתָבְרַיָּא תִּפְתָּיֵא וְכֹל שִׁלְטֹנֵי מְדִינָתָא לְמֵתֵא לַחֲנֻכַּת צַלְמָא דִּי הֲקֵים נְבוּכַדְנֶצַּר מַלְכָּא: [דניאל ג, ב]

מ) אִיתַי גֻּבְרִין יְהוּדָאִין דִּי מַנִּיתָ יָתְהוֹן עַל עֲבִידַת מְדִינַת בָּבֶל שַׁדְרַךְ מֵישַׁךְ וַעֲבֵד נְגוֹ גֻּבְרַיָּא אִלֵּךְ לָא שָׂמוּ עֲלָךְ מַלְכָּא טְעֵם לֵאלָהָךְ לָא פָלְחִין וּלְצֶלֶם דַּהֲבָא דִּי הֲקֵימְתָּ לָא סָגְדִין: [דניאל ג, יב]

נ) וּמִתְכַּנְּשִׁין אֲחַשְׁדַּרְפְּנַיָּא סִגְנַיָּא וּפַחֲוָתָא וְהַדָּבְרֵי מַלְכָּא חָזַיִן לְגֻבְרַיָּא אִלֵּךְ דִּי לָא שְׁלֵט נוּרָא בְּגֶשְׁמְהוֹן וּשְׂעַר רֵאשְׁהוֹן לָא הִתְחָרַךְ וְסָרְבָּלֵיהוֹן לָא שְׁנוֹ וְרֵיחַ נוּר לָא עֲדָת בְּהוֹן: [דניאל ג, כז]

ס) בֵּאדַיִן גֻּבְרַיָּא אִלֵּךְ כְּפִתוּ בְּסַרְבָּלֵיהוֹן פַּטְּשֵׁיהוֹן וְכַרְבְּלָתְהוֹן וּלְבֻשֵׁיהוֹן וּרְמִיו לְגוֹא אַתּוּן נוּרָא יָקִדְתָּא: [דניאל ג, כא]

א) [עי' תוס' מגילה כא.], ב) [לעיל נ.].

ליקוטי רש"י

אותן שנים. דהיינו אלף שביעי. ונשגב ה' לבדו ביום ההוא. יומו של הקב"ה אלף שנה שנאמר כי אלף שנים בעיניך כיום אתמול כי יעבור [לקמן צז.]. בהמיר ארץ. לעתיד לבא ביום שנאמר והארץ כבגד תבלה (ישעיה נא) ראו בני קרח נס שנעשה להם שנבלעו כל סביבותיה' והם עמדו באויר ואמרו לישראל ברוח הקדש שדוגמת הנס הזה יהיה עשוי להם לעתיד [תהלים מו, ג]. אבר. כנף [ישעיה מ, לא]. שקץ. עשוין לשקוץ עכו"ם. מחוקה. מקוקין על הקיר [יחזקאל ח, י]. בקעת דורא. שם מקום [דניאל ג, א]. לאחשדרפניא. דוכסין. ופחוותא. שלטונין. אדרגזריא גדבריא וגומר. כולם שם עכו"ם הם [שם, ב]. איתי. יש. יהודאין. משבט יהודה [שם, יב]. ומתכנשין אחשדרפניא. ד' אומות נמנו למעלה באסיפה הראשונה שלא נמנו כאן אדרגזריא דתבריא גדבריא תפתיא הם גבורי החיל אשר הרגם שביב האש בהשליכם את חנניה וחבריו לאור. חזיין לגבריא אלך. רואין את האנשים האלה חנניה וחבריו [שם, כז]. גבריא אלך. אנשים אלו. כפתו בסרבליהון. נתקשרו בבגדי מעטפותן. פטשיהון וכרבלתהון. מיני מלבוש מלכות שהיה להם ואע"פ שהיו יוצאין לידון לפני נ"נ דיני מיתה לא שנו בגדיהם להשפיל את גדולתם מכאן למדו חכמים שאפי' בשעת הסכנה לא ישנה אדם מן השררה שהוחזק בה. וכרבלתהון. יש לו דוגמא (בד"ה א' טו) ודוד מכורבל [שם, כא].

surrounding "the dead of the Plain of Dura"? שֶׁבְּשָׁעָה שֶׁהֶגְלָה נְבוּכַדְנֶצַּר הָרָשָׁע אֶת יִשְׂרָאֵל – **For at the time that the wicked Nebuchadnezzar exiled Israel,** הָיוּ בָּהֶן בַּחוּרִים שֶׁהָיוּ מְגַנִּין אֶת הַחַמָּה בְּיוֹפְיָין – **there were among [the exiles] youths who put the sun to shame with their beauty.** וְהָיוּ כַּשְׂדִּיּוֹת רוֹאוֹת אוֹתָן וְשׁוֹפְעוֹת זָבוֹת – **And the Chaldean women would see them and experience untimely flow** from their great arousal at the sight of these beautiful captives. אָמְרוּ לְבַעֲלֵיהֶן – **They told** this to **their husbands,** וּבַעֲלֵיהֶן לַמֶּלֶךְ – **and their husbands** told **the king.** צִוָּה הַמֶּלֶךְ וַהֲרָגוּם – **The king** then **gave the order and had [the captive youths] killed.** וַעֲדַיִין הָיוּ שׁוֹפְעוֹת זָבוֹת – **And still [the Chaldean women] experienced untimely flow** from the sight of the lustrous corpses, צִוָּה הַמֶּלֶךְ וּרְמָסוּם – whereupon **the king gave the order and had [the corpses] trampled** to destroy their beauty. This occurred in the Plain of Dura.

The Gemara cites a Baraisa:

תָּנוּ רַבָּנַן – **The Rabbis taught in a Baraisa:** בְּשָׁעָה שֶׁהִפִּיל נְבוּכַדְנֶצַּר הָרָשָׁע אֶת חֲנַנְיָה מִישָׁאֵל וַעֲזַרְיָה לְכִבְשַׁן הָאֵשׁ – WHEN THE WICKED NEBUCHADNEZZAR CAST CHANANYAH, MISHAEL AND AZARYAH INTO THE FIERY FURNACE, אָמַר לוֹ הַקָּדוֹשׁ בָּרוּךְ הוּא לִיחֶזְקֵאל – THE HOLY ONE, BLESSED IS HE, SAID TO EZEKIEL: לֵךְ וְהַחֲיֵה מֵתִים בְּבִקְעַת דּוּרָא – GO RESURRECT THE DEAD IN THE PLAIN OF DURA.[20] כֵּיוָן שֶׁהֶחֱיָה אוֹתָן – AS SOON AS HE HAD RESURRECTED THEM, בָּאוּ עֲצָמוֹת וְטָפְחוּ לוֹ לְאוֹתוֹ רָשָׁע עַל פָּנָיו – THE BONES CAME AND SLAPPED THAT EVIL ONE [Nebuchadnezzar] ON HIS FACE.[21] אָמַר מַה טִּיבָן שֶׁל אֵלּוּ – [NEBUCHADNEZZAR] ASKED his courtiers: WHAT IS THE NATURE OF THESE strange bones?! אָמְרוּ לוֹ חַבְרֵיהֶן שֶׁל אֵלּוּ מְחַיֶּה מֵתִים בְּבִקְעַת דּוּרָא – THEY SAID TO HIM: THE FRIEND OF THESE three men that you have cast into the furnace IS RESURRECTING THE DEAD IN THE PLAIN OF DURA! פָּתַח וְאָמַר – Immediately,[22] [NEBUCHADNEZZAR] BEGAN RECITING his paean of praise to God: "אָתוֹהִי כְּמָה רַבְרְבִין, וְתִמְהוֹהִי כְּמָה תַקִּיפִין – *HOW GREAT ARE HIS SIGNS, AND HOW MIGHTY HIS WONDERS!* מַלְכוּתֵהּ מַלְכוּת עָלַם וְשָׁלְטָנֵהּ עִם־דָּר וְדָר וגו' " – *HIS KINGDOM IS AN EVERLASTING KINGDOM, AND HIS DOMINION IS WITH EVERY GENERATION!*[23] אָמַר רַבִּי יִצְחָק – R' YITZCHAK SAID: יוּצַק זָהָב רוֹתֵחַ לְתוֹךְ פִּיו שֶׁל אוֹתוֹ רָשָׁע – MOLTEN GOLD BE POURED INTO THE MOUTH OF THAT EVIL ONE![24] שֶׁאִילְמָלֵא (לא) בָּא מַלְאָךְ וּסְטָרוֹ עַל פִּיו – FOR HAD AN ANGEL NOT COME AND STRUCK HIM ON HIS MOUTH, interrupting his paean of praise, בִּיקֵּשׁ לְגַנּוֹת כָּל שִׁירוֹת וְתוּשְׁבָּחוֹת שֶׁאָמַר דָּוִד בְּסֵפֶר תְּהִלִּים – HE WOULD HAVE THREATENED TO PUT TO SHAME ALL THE SONGS AND PRAISES THAT DAVID SAID IN THE BOOK OF *PSALMS*![25]

A Baraisa describes the various miracles which took place when Chananyah, Mishael, and Azaryah were cast into Nebuchadnezzar's fiery furnace:

תָּנוּ רַבָּנַן – **The Rabbis taught in a Baraisa:** שִׁשָּׁה נִסִּים נַעֲשׂוּ בְּאוֹתוֹ הַיּוֹם – SIX MIRACLES OCCURRED ON THAT DAY.[26] וְאֵלּוּ הֵן – THEY ARE: צָף הַכִּבְשָׁן – THE FURNACE ROSE to ground level; וְנִפְרַץ הַכִּבְשָׁן – AND the wall of the THE FURNACE WAS BREACHED;[27] וְהוּמַק סוּדוֹ – AND ITS FOUNDATION CAVED IN;[28] וְנֶהְפַּךְ צֶלֶם עַל פָּנָיו – AND THE golden IMAGE that Nebuchadnezzar had erected and ordered worshiped WAS OVERTURNED ONTO ITS FACE; וְנִשְׂרְפוּ אַרְבַּע מַלְכִיּוֹת – AND FOUR ROYAL PARTIES WERE BURNED;[29] וְהֶחֱיָה יְחֶזְקֵאל אֶת הַמֵּתִים בְּבִקְעַת דּוּרָא – AND EZEKIEL RESURRECTED THE DEAD IN THE PLAIN OF DURA.[30] The Gemara adds: וְכוּלְּהוּ גְּמָרָא – **And all of these** miracles are known solely

NOTES

20. [This Baraisa supports R' Yochanan's identification of the dead resurrected by Ezekiel with the dead of the Plain of Dura.]

The intent was to teach Nebuchadnezzar that it is God Who decrees life and death – not the king of Babylon. Though Nebuchadnezzar murdered the innocent captives on the Plain of Dura and had them trampled into the dirt, God restored them to life, thwarting the king's designs against them! (*Maharsha*).

21. These were the very bones that Ezekiel had brought to life [but before they became clothed with flesh]. Alternatively, the bones of some of the martyrs of the Plain of Dura had been fashioned into vessels, from which Nebuchadnezzar would drink. At the moment Ezekiel began resurrecting the bones in the Plain of Dura, Nebuchadnezzar was attempting to drink from one of these bone utensils, whereupon the utensil struck him on the mouth (*Rashi*).

22. Realizing that it was actually God Who was resurrecting them (*Rashi*).

23. *Daniel* 3:33.

24. "Molten gold be poured" is really a euphemistic curse [in place of "molten dung" (cited in *Eitz Yosef*)]. The euphemism is used to parallel the praise of Nebuchadnezzar that follows (*Rashi*).

25. [After the one verse of praise (cited here by the Baraisa), Nebuchadnezzar abruptly shifts to a narrative of what happened to him, rather than continuing his praise of God (see *Daniel* 4:1 ff). R' Yitzchak explains that Nebuchadnezzar's paean was cut short by an angel who struck him on the mouth.] For had he been allowed to continue, Nebuchadnezzar would have arranged praises more beautiful and more pleasing to God than the psalms of David (*Rashi*; see also *Rif* in *Ein Yaakov*).

Rashash and *Ben Yehoyada,* however, find it unthinkable that compositions of the vile Nebuchadnezzar could possibly approach the divinely inspired psalms of the holy David, far less eclipse them! Rather, they suggest, the Baraisa means that Nebuchadnezzar would have composed lengthier psalms and trumpeted them as superior to David's. Moreover, Nebuchadnezzar's elaborate compositions might indeed have seemed in the eyes of the undiscriminating masses to outshine the truly masterful psalms of David.

The *Kotzker Rebbe* interprets the angel's slap in a different way. It was not meant to silence Nebuchadnezzar but to test him. King David praised God even when he was suffering. Nebuchadnezzar recited his words of praise while he was at the height of his rule. The angel slapped him to determine whether, like David, he would pay homage to God even if unfavorable things happened to him; hence the slap – and, indeed, a silencing of Nebuchadnezzar's praise (see *Lahavos Kodesh* pg. 109).

26. The incident of Chananyah, Mishael and Azaryah being cast into the furnace is related in *Daniel* ch. 3. In brief, Nebuchadnezzar erected a colossal golden image in the Plain of Dura and ordered all to prostrate themselves before it on pain of being cast into a fiery furnace. Chananyah, Mishael and Azaryah refused and were cast into the furnace, which Nebuchadnezzar had ordered specially overheated for the occasion. So hot was the fire that those who had cast Chananyah, Mishael and Azaryah into it were themselves killed by the heat of the flames, but – to Nebuchadnezzar's utter consternation – Chananyah, Mishael and Azaryah could be seen walking around in the furnace amid the roaring flames, completely unharmed. Thereupon, Nebuchadnezzar praised the God of Chananyah, Mishael and Azaryah, Who had rescued His servants that refused to worship any other god.

27. The furnace was a kiln dug into the ground and lined with masonry walls. The depth of the furnace as well as the walls surrounding it would have prevented anyone from seeing what was happening inside. However, two miracles occurred: The furnace rose to ground level and the walls were breached so that all could see Chananyah, Mishael and Azaryah walking around unharmed in the flames (*Rashi*).

28. [I.e. the floor of the furnace disintegrated from the intense heat.] Rendered according to *Rashi* in the name of *R' Yaakov ben Yakar.* Another reading cited by *Rashi* is: והומק סידו, *[the furnaces's] plaster dissolved* from the intense heat. A stream of molten plaster flowed away from the furnace and it was the heat of this stream that killed those who cast Chananyah, Mishael and Azaryah into the furnace [see *Daniel* 3:22] (see also *Ben Yehoyada*). Another reading is: והומק סורו, *its arrogance was deflated* (*Rashi*; *Yad Ramah*); i.e. the intensity of the flame was diminished (see *Yad Ramah*; see also *Pesachim* 118a,b).

29. The elite of Nebuchadnezzar's guard that were consumed by the flames as they cast Chananyah, Mishael and Azaryah into the furnace (*Daniel* 3:20-22) were actually four subject kings and their courtiers (see *Rashi* here and to *Daniel* 3:27).

30. [See the Baraisa cited earlier in the Gemara.] The wind that toppled

ואם תאמר אותן שנים שעתיד הקב"ה לחדש בהן את עולמו שנאמר א) ונשגב ה' לבדו ביום ההוא צדיקים מה הן עושין הקב"ה עושה להם כנפים כנשרים ושטין על פני המים שנאמר ב) על כן לא נירא בהמיר ארץ במוט הרים בלב ימים ושמא תאמר יש להם צער ת"ל ג) וקווי ה' יחליפו כח יעלו אבר כנשרים ירוצו ולא ייגעו ילכו ולא ייעפו ונילף ממתים שהחיה יחזקאל סבר לה כמאן דאמר באמת משל היה דתניא ר"א אומר מתים שהחיה יחזקאל עמדו על רגליהם ואמרו שירה ומתו מה שירה אמרו ה' ממית בצדק ומחיה ברחמים ר' יהושע אומר שירה זו אמרו ד) ה' ממית ומחיה מוריד שאול ויעל ר' יהודה אומר אמת משל היה אמר לו רבי נחמיה אם אמת למה משל ואם משל למה אמת אלא באמת משל היה ר"א בנו של ר' יוסי הגלילי אומר מתים שהחיה יחזקאל עלו לארץ ישראל ונשאו נשים והולידו בנים ובנות עמד ר"י בן בתירא על רגליו ואמר אני מבני בניהם והללו תפילין שהניח לי אבי אבא מהם ומאן נינהו מתים שהחיה יחזקאל אמר רב אלו בני אפרים שמנו לקץ וטעו שנאמר ה) ובני אפרים שותלח וברד בנו ותחת בנו ואלעדה בנו ותחת בנו וזבד בנו ושותלח בנו ועזר (ואלעזר) [ואלעד] והרגום אנשי גת הנולדים בארץ וגו' וכתיב ו) ויתאבל אפרים אביהם ימים רבים ויבאו אחיו לנחמו ושמואל אמר אלו בני אדם שכפרו בתחיית המתים שנאמר ז) ויאמר אלי בן אדם העצמות האלה כל בית ישראל המה הנה אומרים יבשו עצמותינו ואבדה תקותנו נגזרנו לנו ר' ירמיה בר אבא אמר אלו בני אדם שאין בהן לחלוחית של מצוה שנאמר ח) העצמות היבשות שמעו דבר ה' ר' יצחק נפחא אמר אלו בני אדם שחיפו את ההיכל כולו שקצים ורמשים שנאמר ט) ואבוא ואראה והנה כל תבנית רמש ובהמה שקץ וכל גלולי בית ישראל מחוקה על הקיר סביב וגו' וכתיב התם י) והעבירני עליהם סביב סביב ר' יוחנן אמר אלו מתים שבבקעת דורא וא"ר יוחנן מנהר אשל עד רבת בקעת דורא שבשעה שהגלה נבוכדנצר הרשע את ישראל היו בהן בחורים שהיו מגנין את החמה ביופיין והיו כשדיות רואות אותן ושופעות זבות אמרו לבעליהן ובעליהן למלך צוה המלך והרגום ועדיין היו שופעות זבות צוה המלך ורמסום תנו רבנן בשעה שהפיל נבוכדנצר הרשע את חנניה מישאל ועזריה לכבשן האש אמר לו הקב"ה ליחזקאל לך והחייה מתים בבקעת דורא כיון שהחייה אותן באו עצמות וטפחו לו [א] לאותו רשע על פניו אמר מה טיבן של אלו אמרו לו חבריהן של אלו מחיה מתים בבקעת דורא פתח ואמר כ) אתוהי כמה רברבין ותמהוהי כמה תקיפין מלכותיה מלכות עלם ושלטניה עם דר ודר וגו' א"ר יצחק יוצק זהב רותח לתוך פיו [ב] של אותו רשע שאילמלא (א) לא) בא מלאך וסטרו על פיו ביקש לגנות כל שירות ותושבחות שאמר דוד בספר תהלים ת"ר ששה נסים נעשו באותו היום ואלו הן צף הכבשן ונפרץ הכבשן והומק סודו ונהפך צלם על פניו ונשרפו ארבע מלכיות והחייה יחזקאל את המתים בבקעת דורא וכולהו גמרא וארבע מלכיות קרא דכתיב ל) ונבוכדנצר מלכא שלח למכנש לאחשדרפניא סגניא ופחוותא אדרגזריא גדבריא דתבריא תפתיא וכל שלטוני מדינתא וגו' וכתיב מ) איתי גוברין יהודאין וכתיב נ) ומתכנשין אחשדרפניא סגניא ופחוותא והדברי מלכא חזיין לגבריא אלך וגו' תני דבי רבי אליעזר בן יעקב אפילו בשעת הסכנה לא ישנה אדם את עצמו מן הרבנות שלו שנאמר ס) באדין גבריא אלך כפתו בסרבליהון פטשיהון וכרבלתהון וגו' אמר רבי יוחנן
גדולים

ואותן שנים שעתיד הקב"ה לחדש את עולמו. ויהיה עולם זה חרב אלף שנים אותן צדיקים היכן הם הואיל ואינן נקברין בארץ: לא נירא בהמיר ארץ. כשמחליף הקב"ה את הארץ לא נירא לפי שאנו בלב ימים: וקווי ה' יחליפו כח. שיהא להם כח לשוט ולעופף בלי צער: ונילף ממתים שהחיה יחזקאל. שחזרו ומתו כך צדיקים שעתיד להחיות יחזרו לעפרם כך שמעתי יחזקאל הגלהו נבוכדנצר עם יכניה מלך יהודה והיה יחזקאל מתנבא בבבל וירמיה בארץ ישראל באותן אחת עשרה שנה שמלך צדקיה: באמת. בברור: משל היה. שהיה מרמז להם על הגלות כאדם מת שחוזר וחי כך ישראל ישובו מן הגלות: מהם. שאותן תפילין היו שלהם: שמנו לקץ. של יציאת מצרים: וטעו. שלא היה להם למנות גזירת ועבדום וענו אותם אלא משנולד יצחק דהא כתיב (בראשית טו) כי גר יהיה זרעך זה יצחק דכתיב (שם כא) כי ביצחק יקרא לך זרע והם מנו משעת הדיבור לאברהם ותניא בסדר עולם אברהם אבינו בשעה שנדבר עמו בין הבתרים בן שבעים שנה היה ומבין הבתרים עד שנולד יצחק היה ל' שנה כדכתיב (בראשית כא) ואברהם בן מאת שנה בהולד לו את יצחק בנו נמצאת אומר משדבר עמו בין הבתרים עד שיצאו ממצרים היו ארבע מאות ואותן ל' שמן הדבור עד לידת יצחק טעו בני אפרים. ומניין שבני אפרים הן שיצאו קודם זמנן ונהרגו שנאמר ובני אפרים שותלח וגו' והרגום אנשי גת: ושמואל אמר. מתים שהחיה יחזקאל אלו בני אדם שכפרו בתחיית המתים שנאמר (יחזקאל לז) אבדה תקותנו: העצמות האלה כל בית ישראל המה. עצמות הללו סימן לכל ישראל הן שעתידה להם תחיית המתים כמו לאלו שהרי אלו אמרו אבדה תקותנו ועכשו ידעו שאני מחיה את המתים וסימן זה לכל ישראל שגם הם עתידין להחיות ולא מן הדין חיו דהא אמרן [ג] הכופר בתחיית המתים אין לו חלק לעוה"ב אלא משום סימן חיו: שחיפו להיכל. שהיו מציירין צלמים על קירות ההיכל דכתיב ואבא ואראה מחוקה על הקיר סביב: וכתיב והעבירני עליהם סביב סביב. כלומר על אותן אנשים שכתוב עליהם סביב עבר עליהם יחזקאל להחיותם: אלו מתים שבבקעת דורא. שהמית נבוכדנצר מלך בבל על שהיו יפים כדלקמן: מנהר אשל עד רבת. מקומות הן היו בבקעת דורא: שופעות. מחמת תאוה: וצוה המלך והרגן ועדיין היו שופעות. שהיתה נראית זיו תארם וצוה המלך ורמסום: ובאו עצמות מן הבקעה וטפחו לו לאותו רשע על פניו. והלכו להם ואית דאמרי שמאותן עצמות היה לו כלים וכשהגיעה שעה שחיו טפחו לו על פיו כשהיה רוצה לשתות בהם: חבריהם של אלו מחיה מתים. על יחזקאל היו אומרין שהיה חבירן של חנניה מישאל ועזריה ונבוכדנצר היה יודע שהיה הקב"ה מחיה אותם: פתח ואמר. להקב"ה אתוהי כמה רברבין פסוק הוא (דניאל ג): יוצק זהב רותח. משום דקא מיירי בשבחו דנבוכדנצר נקיט נמי לישנא מעליא ולשון קללה: סטרו. הכהו מאחורי ידו: לגנות. שהיה מסדר שבחות נאות יותר מדוד ואילו אמרן הקב"ה היה נוטה אחריהן יותר מאחרי השירות שעשה דוד: באותו יום. שהשליכן לכבשן: צף הכבשן. שהכבשן היה משוקע בארץ כעין כבשן של סיד וצף ועומד על גבי קרקע כדי שיראוהו כל העולם: נפרץ הכבשן. נפלו קצת כותליו כדי שיוכלו כולם לראות בתוכו: הומק סורו. נשפל גאותו כמו סורו רע (קדושין דף פב.) ל"א הומק סודו כמו יסודו נשתלשל וכן לימדני רבי יעקב בן יקר אבל מורי גרס והומק סידו סיד הכבשן נמסה מרוב חמימות כך שמעתי והיתה מושכת למרחוק ומהבל של אותו הסיד נשרפו אותן שהשליכו חנניה מישאל ועזריה לתוך כבשן האש: ונהפך. צלם של זהב על פניו: ארבע מלכיות. מלכים ואנשיהם שסייעו לנבוכדנצר להשליך חנניה מישאל ועזריה לתוך האור: מקראי נפקי. דכתיב (דניאל ג) נבוכדנצר שלח למכנש לאחשדרפניא סגניא ולבסוף לאחר שבאו מן הכבשן כתיב ומתכנשין אחשדרפניא סגניא ופחותא והנך דלא כתיבי נשרפו: אל ישנה מן הרבנות שלו. שהרי חנניה מישאל ועזריה היו לבושין בגדי תפארתן כשהושלכו לכבשן אל ישנה שלא יראה מבוהל ומפוחד ומתביישין שונאיו מפניו: פטשיהון וכרבלתהון. עניני מלבושין:
גדולים

הגהות הגר"א

[א] גמ' נ"ל לאותו רשע שחיק טמי': [ב] שם נ"ל של אותו רשע שחיק טמי':

תורה אור השלם

א) וְשַׁח גַּבְהוּת הָאָדָם וְשָׁפֵל רוּם אֲנָשִׁים וְנִשְׂגַּב יְיָ לְבַדּוֹ בַּיּוֹם הַהוּא: [ישעיה ב, יז]

ב) עַל כֵּן לֹא נִירָא בְּהָמִיר אָרֶץ וּבְמוֹט הָרִים בְּלֵב יַמִּים: [תהלים מו, ג]

ג) וְקוֵֹי יְיָ יַחֲלִיפוּ כֹחַ יַעֲלוּ אֵבֶר כַּנְּשָׁרִים יָרוּצוּ וְלֹא יִיגָעוּ יֵלְכוּ וְלֹא יִיעָפוּ: [ישעיה מ, לא]

ד) יְיָ מֵמִית וּמְחַיֶּה מוֹרִיד שְׁאוֹל וַיָּעַל: [שמואל א' ב, ו]

ה) וּבְנֵי אֶפְרַיִם שׁוּתָלַח וּבֶרֶד בְּנוֹ וְתַחַת בְּנוֹ וְאֶלְעָדָה בְנוֹ וְתַחַת בְּנוֹ: וְזָבָד בְּנוֹ וְשׁוּתֶלַח בְּנוֹ וְעֵזֶר וְאֶלְעָד וַהֲרָגוּם אַנְשֵׁי גַת הַנּוֹלָדִים בָּאָרֶץ כִּי יָרְדוּ לָקַחַת אֶת מִקְנֵיהֶם: [דברי הימים א' ז, כ-כא]

ו) וַיִּתְאַבֵּל אֶפְרַיִם אֲבִיהֶם יָמִים רַבִּים וַיָּבֹאוּ אֶחָיו לְנַחֲמוֹ: [דברי הימים א' ז, כב]

ז) וַיֹּאמֶר אֵלַי בֶּן אָדָם הָעֲצָמוֹת הָאֵלֶּה כָּל בֵּית יִשְׂרָאֵל הֵמָּה הִנֵּה אֹמְרִים יָבְשׁוּ עַצְמוֹתֵינוּ וְאָבְדָה תִקְוָתֵנוּ נִגְזַרְנוּ לָנוּ: [יחזקאל לז, יא]

ח) וַיֹּאמֶר אֵלַי הִנָּבֵא עַל הָעֲצָמוֹת הָאֵלֶּה וְאָמַרְתָּ אֲלֵיהֶם הָעֲצָמוֹת הַיְבֵשׁוֹת שִׁמְעוּ דְּבַר יְיָ: [יחזקאל לז, ד]

ט) וָאָבוֹא וָאֶרְאֶה וְהִנֵּה כָל תַּבְנִית רֶמֶשׂ וּבְהֵמָה שֶׁקֶץ וְכָל גִּלּוּלֵי בֵּית יִשְׂרָאֵל מְחֻקֶּה עַל הַקִּיר סָבִיב סָבִיב: [יחזקאל ח, י]

י) וְהֶעֱבִירַנִי עֲלֵיהֶם סָבִיב סָבִיב וְהִנֵּה רַבּוֹת מְאֹד עַל פְּנֵי הַבִּקְעָה וְהִנֵּה יְבֵשׁוֹת מְאֹד: [יחזקאל לז, ב]

כ) אָתוֹהִי כְּמָה רַבְרְבִין וְתִמְהוֹהִי כְּמָה תַקִּיפִין מַלְכוּתֵהּ מַלְכוּת עָלַם וְשָׁלְטָנֵהּ עִם דָּר וְדָר: [דניאל ג, לג]

ל) וּנְבוּכַדְנֶצַּר מַלְכָּא שְׁלַח לְמִכְנַשׁ לַאֲחַשְׁדַּרְפְּנַיָּא סִגְנַיָּא וּפַחֲוָתָא אֲדַרְגָּזְרַיָּא גְדָבְרַיָּא דְתָבְרַיָּא תִּפְתָּיֵא וְכֹל שִׁלְטֹנֵי מְדִינָתָא לְמֵתֵא לַחֲנֻכַּת צַלְמָא דִּי הֲקֵים נְבוּכַדְנֶצַּר מַלְכָּא: [דניאל ג, ב]

מ) אִיתַי גֻּבְרִין יְהוּדָאיִן דִּי מַנִּיתָ יָתְהוֹן עַל עֲבִידַת מְדִינַת בָּבֶל שַׁדְרַךְ מֵישַׁךְ וַעֲבֵד נְגוֹ גֻּבְרַיָּא אִלֵּךְ לָא שָׂמוּ עֲלָךְ מַלְכָּא טְעֵם לֵאלָהָךְ לָא פָלְחִין וּלְצֶלֶם דַּהֲבָא דִּי הֲקֵימְתָּ לָא סָגְדִין: [דניאל ג, יב]

נ) וּמִתְכַּנְּשִׁין אֲחַשְׁדַּרְפְּנַיָּא סִגְנַיָּא וּפַחֲוָתָא וְהַדָּבְרֵי מַלְכָּא חָזַיִן לְגֻבְרַיָּא אִלֵּךְ דִּי לָא שְׁלֵט נוּרָא בְּגֶשְׁמְהוֹן וּשְׂעַר רֵאשְׁהוֹן לָא הִתְחָרַךְ וְסָרְבָּלֵיהוֹן לָא שְׁנוֹ וְרֵיחַ נוּר לָא עֲדָת בְּהוֹן: [דניאל ג, כז] ס) בֵּאדַיִן גֻּבְרַיָּא אִלֵּךְ כְּפִתוּ בְּסַרְבָּלֵיהוֹן פַּטְּשֵׁיהוֹן וְכַרְבְּלָתְהוֹן וּלְבֻשֵׁיהוֹן וּרְמִיו לְגוֹא אַתּוּן נוּרָא יָקִדְתָּא: [דניאל ג, כא]

מסורת הש"ס

א) [עי' תוס' מגילה כא.], ב) [לעיל ל.].

ליקוטי רש"י

אותן שנים. דהיינו אלף שביעי. ונשגב ה' לבדו ביום ההוא. יומו של הקב"ה אלף שנה שנאמר כי אלף שנים בעיניך כיום אתמול כי יעבור [לקמן צז.]. בהמיר ארץ. לעתיד לבא ביום שנאמר והארץ כבגד תבלה (ישעיה נא) ראו בני קרח נס שנעש' להם שנבלעו כל סביבותיה' והם עמדו באויר ואמרו לישראל ברוח הקדש שדוגמת הנס הזה יהיה עשוי להם לעתיד [תהלים מו, ג]. אבר. כנף [ישעיה מ, לא]. שקץ. עשוין לשקוץ עכו"ם. מחוקה. חקוקין על הקיר [יחזקאל ח, י]. בקעת דורא. שם מקום [דניאל ג, א]. לאחשדרפניא. דוכסין. ופחוותא. שלטונין. אדרגזריא גדבריא וגומר. כולם שם עכו"ם הם [שם, ב]. איתי. יש. יהודאין. משבט יהודה [שם, יב]. ומתכנשין אחשדרפניא. ד' אומות נמנו למעלה באסיפה הראשונה שלא נמנו כאן אדרגזריא דתבריא גדבריא תפתיא הם גבורי החיל אשר הרגם שביב האש בהשליכם את חנניה וחבריו לאור. חזיין לגבריא אלך. רואין את האנשים האלה חנניה וחבריו [שם, כז]. גבריא אלך. אנשים אלו. כפתו בסרבליהון. נתקשרו בבגדי מעטפותן. פטשיהון וכרבלתהון. מיני מלבוש מלכות שהיה להם ואע"פ שהיו יוצאין לידון לפני נ"נ דיני מיתה לא שנו בגדיהם להשפיל את גדולתם מכאן למדו חכמים שאפי' בשעת הסכנה לא ישנה אדם מן השררה שהוחזק בה. וכרבלתהון. יש לו דוגמא (דה"א טו) ודוד מכורבל [שם, כא].

from oral **tradition,** וְאַרְבַּע מַלְכִיּוֹת קְרָא – **except** for the miracle of the burning of **the four kingdoms, which is** even evident in **Scripture.** דִּכְתִיב ,,וּנְבוּכַדְנֶצַּר מַלְכָּא שְׁלַח לְמִכְנַשׁ לַאֲחַשְׁדַּרְפְּנַיָּא סִגְנַיָּא וּפַחֲוָתָא אֲדַרְגָּזְרַיָּא גְדָבְרַיָּא דְּתָבְרַיָּא תִּפְתָּיֵא וְכֹל שִׁלְטֹנֵי מְדִינָתָא וגו׳ ״ – **For it is written** in one verse: ***Then King Nebuchadnezzar sent to assemble the satraps, the nobles, and the governors; the Adargazraya, the Gedavraya, the Desavraya, the Tiftayei, and all the provincial officials, etc.***[31] All these officials were commanded to attend the dedication ceremonies of Nebuchadnezzar's golden image. At the ceremonies, all were commanded to prostrate themselves before the image, but Chananyah, Mishael and Azaryah refused. וּכְתִיב ,,אִיתַי גֻּבְרִין יְהוּדָאִין״ – **And it is written** afterwards that certain Chaldean men stepped forward and informed Nebuchadnezzar:[32] ***There are Jewish men*** *. . . who have not accepted upon themselves, O king, your decree; your gods they do not worship, nor before the golden image which you set up do they prostrate themselves.* וּכְתִיב ,,וּמִתְכַּנְּשִׁין אֲחַשְׁדַּרְפְּנַיָּא סִגְנַיָּא וּפַחֲוָתָא וְהַדָּבְרֵי מַלְכָּא חָזַיִן לְגֻבְרַיָּא אִלֵּךְ וגו׳ ״ – **And it is written** afterwards that Chananyah, Mishael and Azaryah emerged unscathed from the flames: ***And the satraps, the nobles, the governors, and the ministers of the king assembled, saw these men*** **etc.** *over whose bodies the fire had had no effect . . .*[33]

A Baraisa derives a general lesson from the conduct of Chananyah, Mishael and Azaryah:

תָּנֵי דְּבֵי רַבִּי אֱלִיעֶזֶר בֶּן יַעֲקֹב – **A Baraisa was taught in the academy of R' Eliezer ben Yaakov:** אֲפִילּוּ בִּשְׁעַת הַסַּכָּנָה – EVEN AT A TIME OF MORTAL DANGER, לֹא יְשַׁנֶּה אָדָם אֶת עַצְמוֹ מִן הָרַבָּנוּת שֶׁלּוֹ – A PERSON SHOULD NOT ABANDON HIS DIGNIFIED BEARING, שֶׁנֶּאֱמַר ,,בֵּאדַיִן גֻּבְרַיָּא אִלֵּךְ כְּפִתוּ בְּסַרְבָּלֵיהוֹן פַּטְּשֵׁיהוֹן וְכַרְבְּלָתְהוֹן וגו׳ ״ – AS IT IS STATED: *THEN THESE MEN WERE BOUND IN THEIR CLOAKS, THEIR PANTS, THEIR ROBES . . .*[34]

אָמַר רַבִּי יוֹחָנָן – **R' Yochanan said:**

NOTES

the golden image was the very same wind that resurrected the dead in the Plain of Dura (*Shir HaShirim Rabbah* 7:9).

31. *Daniel* 3:2.

32. Ibid. v. 12.

33. *Daniel* 3:27. Of the seven categories enumerated in v. 2, only the first three are mentioned here. But the *Adargazraya, Gedavraya, Desavraya* and *Tiftayei* are omitted here, because they were the ones killed when casting Chananyah, Mishael and Azaryah into the flames (*Rashi*).

Thus, the miracle of the death of these "four royalties" is indicated in Scripture.

34. Ibid. v. 21. Chananyah, Mishael and Azaryah knew they were about to be cast into the flames, but they maintained their dignified bearing and did not remove the vestments of their high office. This is a lesson for others to maintain their dignity even in the face of death, and not appear bewildered or frightened. When one retains such bearing in the face of his enemies, they are shamed in his presence (*Rashi*) and one demonstrates that he accepts the Divine judgment with love and happiness (*Maharsha*).

גְּדוֹלִים צַדִּיקִים יוֹתֵר מִמַּלְאֲכֵי הַשָּׁרֵת – **The righteous are greater than the ministering angels.** שֶׁנֶּאֱמַר ,,עָנֵה וְאָמַר – **For it is written** that upon seeing Chananyah, Mishael and Azaryah walking around unscathed in the furnace: ***[Nebuchadnezzar] exclaimed and said:*** הָא־אֲנָה חָזֵה גֻּבְרִין אַרְבְּעָה שְׁרַיִן מַהְלְכִין בְּגוֹא־נוּרָא – ***Behold I see four unbound men walking in the midst of the fire*** וַחֲבָל לָא־אִיתַי בְּהוֹן – ***and there is no wound upon them,*** וְרֵוֵהּ דִּי רְבִיעָאָה דָּמֵה לְבַר־אֱלָהִין״ – ***and the appearance of the fourth is like an angel.***[1]

The Gemara continues to discuss the episode of the miraculous delivery of Chananyah, Mishael, and Azaryah from the fiery furnace:

אָמַר רַבִּי תַּנְחוּם בַּר חֲנִילַאי – **R' Tanchum bar Chanilai said:** בְּשָׁעָה שֶׁיָּצְאוּ חֲנַנְיָה מִישָׁאֵל וַעֲזַרְיָה מִכִּבְשַׁן הָאֵשׁ – **When Chananyah, Mishael, and Azaryah came out of the fiery furnace** unharmed, בָּאוּ כָּל אוּמּוֹת הָעוֹלָם – **all the nations of the world came** וְטָפְחוּ לְשׂוֹנְאֵיהֶן שֶׁל יִשְׂרָאֵל עַל פְּנֵיהֶם – **and struck the enemies of Israel**[2] **on their faces,** אָמְרוּ לָהֶם – and **said to them** incredulously: יֵשׁ לָכֶם אֱלוֹהַּ כָּזֶה וְאַתֶּם מִשְׁתַּחֲוִים לְצֶלֶם – **You have such a** powerful **God and yet you** submit to Nebuchadnezzar's threat and **bow to the idol?!** מִיַּד פָּתְחוּ וְאָמְרוּ ,,לְךָ ה׳ הַצְּדָקָה וְלָנוּ בֹּשֶׁת הַפָּנִים כַּיּוֹם הַזֶּה״ – Ashamed of the conduct of their fellow Jews, **[Chananyah, Mishael and Azaryah] immediately began to declare: *Yours, O Lord, is the righteousness; and ours is the shamefacedness as of this day.***[3]

A verse in *Song of Songs* is expounded as a reference to these events:

אָמַר רַבִּי שְׁמוּאֵל בַּר נַחְמָנִי אָמַר רַבִּי יוֹנָתָן – **R' Shmuel bar Nachmani said in the name of R' Yonasan:** מַאי דִּכְתִיב ,,אָמַרְתִּי אֶעֱלֶה בְתָמָר אֹחֲזָה בְּסַנְסִנָּיו״ – **What is** the meaning of **that which is written: *I said I would be exalted through the palm tree, [but] I take hold [only] of the branches?***[4] ,,אָמַרְתִּי אֶעֱלֶה בְתָמָר״ אֵלּוּ יִשְׂרָאֵל – God says: ***I said I would be exalted through the palm tree*** – **this is Israel.** וְעַכְשָׁיו לֹא עָלָה בְּיָדִי אֶלָּא סַנְסָן אֶחָד שֶׁל חֲנַנְיָה מִישָׁאֵל וַעֲזַרְיָה – **But now, all that has come up in My hand is the single branch of Chananyah, Mishael, and Azaryah.**[5]

R' Yochanan expounds a Scriptural verse in a similar vein: אָמַר רַבִּי יוֹחָנָן – **R' Yochanan said:** מַאי דִּכְתִיב ,,רָאִיתִי הַלַּיְלָה וְהִנֵּה־אִישׁ רֹכֵב עַל־סוּס אָדֹם וְהוּא עֹמֵד בֵּין הַהֲדַסִּים אֲשֶׁר בַּמְּצֻלָה [וגו׳]״ – **What is** the meaning of **that which is written** in the prophecy of Zechariah: ***I saw in the night and behold a man was riding on a red horse, and he was standing among the myrtles that were in the pool etc.?***[6] R' Yochanan proceeds to expound the verse phrase by phrase: מַאי ,,רָאִיתִי הַלַּיְלָה״ – **What is** the meaning of ***I saw in the night?*** בִּיקֵּשׁ הַקָּדוֹשׁ בָּרוּךְ הוּא לַהֲפוֹךְ אֶת כָּל הָעוֹלָם כּוּלּוֹ לְלַיְלָה – **The Holy One, Blessed is He, was ready to turn the entire world into "night,"** i.e. to destroy it, because the Jews were submitting to Nebuchadnezzar's command to bow to the idol.[7] ,,וְהִנֵּה־אִישׁ רֹכֵב״ אֵין אִישׁ אֶלָּא הַקָּדוֹשׁ בָּרוּךְ הוּא – ***And behold a man was riding*** – **"a man"** here alludes to **none other than the Holy One, Blessed is He,** שֶׁנֶּאֱמַר ,,ה׳ אִישׁ מִלְחָמָה ה׳ שְׁמוֹ״ – **as it is stated** elsewhere: ***HASHEM is "a man" of war, HASHEM is His name.***[8] ,,עַל־סוּס אָדֹם״ בִּיקֵּשׁ הַקָּדוֹשׁ בָּרוּךְ הוּא לַהֲפוֹךְ אֶת הָעוֹלָם כּוּלּוֹ לְדָם – And He was riding ***on a red horse,*** which indicates that **the Holy One, Blessed is He, was ready to turn the entire world into blood,** i.e. to destroy it. כֵּיוָן שֶׁנִּסְתַּכֵּל בַּחֲנַנְיָה מִישָׁאֵל וַעֲזַרְיָה נִתְקָרְרָה דַּעְתּוֹ – **But once He looked upon Chananyah, Mishael, and Azaryah,** who were willing to die rather than worship the idol, **He was appeased** and refrained from destroying the world, שֶׁנֶּאֱמַר ,,וְהוּא עֹמֵד בֵּין הַהֲדַסִּים אֲשֶׁר בַּמְּצֻלָה״ – **as it is stated** further in the verse: ***and He was standing among the myrtles*** *(hadassim)* ***that were in the pool*** *(metzulah).* וְאֵין הֲדַסִּים אֶלָּא צַדִּיקִים – **Now** the word ***hadassim*** in this verse **refers to nothing other than the righteous,** שֶׁנֶּאֱמַר ,,וַיְהִי אֹמֵן אֶת־הֲדַסָּה״ – **as it is stated** elsewhere: ***And [Mordechai] raised Hadassah.***[9] וְאֵין מְצוּלָה אֶלָּא בָּבֶל – **And** the word ***metzulah*** in this verse **means nothing other than Babylon,** שֶׁנֶּאֱמַר ,,הָאֹמֵר לַצּוּלָה חֳרָבִי וְנַהֲרֹתַיִךְ אוֹבִישׁ״ – **as it is stated** elsewhere: ***[I am God] Who says to the deep*** *(tzulah)*: ***"Be dry! And I will dry up your rivers."***[10] מִיַּד מְלֵאִים רוֹגֶז נַעֲשִׂים שְׂרוּקִים וַאֲדוּמִים – **Immediately those full of anger, which had become colored and red,** נַעֲשׂוּ לְבָנִים – **became white.**[11] אָמַר רַב פַּפָּא – **Rav Pappa said:**

NOTES

1. *Daniel* 3:25. Nebuchadnezzar referred to the angel as "the fourth one," indicating that the three righteous men, Chananyah, Mishael, and Azaryah, were more important (*Rashi*; see *Maharsha*; see also *Toras Chaim*).

2. A euphemism for the Jews themselves.

3. Ibid. 9:7. The end of the verse "as of this day" refers to the day of Chananyah, Mishael and Azaryah's deliverance from the fiery furnace, when the gentiles shamed the Jews (*Maharsha*). [We have explained that this confession was proclaimed by Chananyah, Mishael and Azaryah, in accordance with *Midrash Tanchuma,* cited by *Margaliyos HaYam* §7.]

4. *Song of Songs* 7:9. [Literally: *I said I would ascend the palm tree, I would take hold of its branches.*]

5. The people of Israel are compared to a palm tree, which has but one "heart" – i.e. unlike other trees, such as nut trees and grapevines, which have pith in the branches as well as in the trunk, the date palm has pith only in the trunk. Just as the palm has but one heart, so too does Israel have but one heart, bound to its Father in Heaven (*Succah* 45b with *Rashi*).

God had intended that His Name be exalted through the entire palm tree – i.e. that all Israel would have courageously withstood Nebuchadnezzar's threats and would have refused to bow to the idol (see *Rashi*).

See *Toras Chaim,* who explains why the Gemara refers to Chananyah, Mishael, and Azaryah as a single branch. See also note 9.

Midrash Shir HaShirim Rabbah states that Ezekiel told Chananya, Mishael and Azaryah not to sacrifice themselves, and that God had told him that He would not save them; yet the three persisted because they wanted to sanctify God's name. One sanctifies God's name not because *God* needs it but so that *people* should learn from it. If God had not saved them, their action would have amounted to but a minor protest against idol worship; yet, they were ready all the same to sacrifice themselves, and as a result, when they were saved, the nations despised their idols (*Michtav MeEliyahu* III, pp. 318-319). Why did God say He would not save them? For had they let themselves be thrown into the furnace counting on a miracle to save them, their action would not have been a true sacrifice and they would not have merited a miracle (cf. *Targum Yonasan, Bereishis* 11:28).

6. *Zechariah* 1:8. The verse concludes: וְאַחֲרָיו סוּסִים אֲדֻמִּים שְׂרֻקִּים וּלְבָנִים, *and after him were horses that were red, colored, and white.* [*Rashi* here renders שְׂרֻקִּים simply as *colored.* In his commentary to *Zechariah, Rashi* states that he does not know what color is referred to.]

7. Idol worship is one of the three cardinal sins that a Jew must resist even under threat of death (see *Iyun Yaakov*).

8. *Exodus* 15:3.

9. *Esther* 2:7. I.e. the righteous Esther. Thus, we see that the righteous are called *hadassim* (see *Megillah* 13a). Moreover, myrtle leaves grow in groups of threes, and Chananyah, Mishael and Azaryah were three (*Toras Chaim*).

10. *Isaiah* 44:27. Here, God declares the destruction of Babylon, which is referred to as "the deep" because it is abundantly watered by the mighty Tigris and Euphrates Rivers between which it is situated (see *Rashi* ad loc.). Thus, we see that Babylon is referred to as צוּלָה, which is a short form of מְצוּלָה.

Hence, *and He was standing among the myrtles* is expounded to mean that God *stood Himself,* i.e. He stayed Himself from carrying forward with the destruction of the world, *because of the myrtles* – in the merit of the righteous Chananyah, Mishael and Azaryah (*Rashi*).

11. This is based on the conclusion of the verse, which (as cited above in note 6) states: *and after him were horses that were red, colored, and*

מסורת הש"ס

א) [עי' בילקוט זכרי' ושם איתא מאמר זה קצת בנוסחא אחרינא], ב) [לקמן לו: סוטה מב: מח.], ג) [מגילה יג. ע"ש ועי' תוס' ברכות כו: ד"ה ואין שיחה כו'], ד) [עיין ברכות נו:], ה) [צ"ל והתנן], ו) לעיל לג. בכורות כח:, ז) בקרא כתיב וכאחב.

גמרא

גדולים צדיקים יותר ממלאכי השרת שנאמר א) ענה ואמר הא אנא חזי גוברין ארבעה שריין מהלכין בגו נורא וחבל לא איתי בהון ורויה די רביעאה דמה לבר אלהין אמר ר' תנחום בר חנילאי בשעה שיצאו חנניה מישאל ועזריה מכבשן האש באו כל אומות העולם וטפחו לשונאיהן של ישראל על פניהם אמרו להם יש לכם אלוה כזה ואתם משתחוים לצלם מיד פתחו ואמרו ב) לך ה' הצדקה ולנו בושת הפנים כיום הזה אמר ר' שמואל בר נחמני אמר ר' יונתן מאי דכתיב ג) אמרתי אעלה בתמר אוחזה בסנסניו אמרתי אעלה בתמר אלו ישראל ועכשיו לא עלה בידי אלא סנסן אחד של חנניה מישאל ועזריה א) אמר רבי יוחנן מאי דכתיב ד) ראיתי הלילה והנה איש רוכב על סוס אדום והוא עומד בין ההדסים אשר במצולה [וגו'] מאי ראיתי הלילה ביקש הקב"ה להפוך את כל העולם כולו ללילה והנה איש רוכב ג) אין איש אלא הקב"ה שנאמר ה) ה' איש מלחמה ה' שמו על סוס אדום ביקש הקב"ה להפוך את העולם כולו לדם כיון שנסתכל בחנניה מישאל ועזריה נתקררה דעתו שנאמר ד) והוא עומד בין ההדסים אשר במצולה ואין הדסים אלא צדיקים ג) שנאמר ו) ויהי אומן את הדסה ואין מצולה אלא בבל שנאמר ז) האומר לצולה חרבי ונהרותיך אוביש מיד מלאים רוגז נעשים שרוקים ואדומים נעשו לבנים אמר רב פפא שמע מינה ד) סוסיא חיורא מעלי לחלמא: ורבנן להיכא (אזול) [אזלו] אמר רב בעין [הרע] מתו ושמואל אמר ברוק טבעו ור' יוחנן אמר עלו לארץ ישראל ונשאו נשים והולידו בנים ובנות כתנאי ר' אליעזר אומר בעין [הרע] מתו ר' יהושע אומר ברוק טבעו וחכ"א עלו לא"י ונשאו נשים והולידו בנים ובנות שנאמר ח) שמע נא יהושע הכהן הגדול אתה ורעיך היושבים לפניך כי אנשי מופת המה איזו הם אנשים שנעשה להן מופת הוי אומר זה חנניה מישאל ועזריה ודניאל להיכן אזל אמר רב למיכרא נהרא רבא בטבריא ושמואל אמר לאתויי ביזרא דאספסתא ור' יוחנן אמר לאתויי חזירי דאלכסנדריא של מצרים איני ה) והתניא ו) תודוס הרופא אמר אין פרה וחזירה יוצאה מאלכסנדריא של מצרים שאין חותכין האם שלה בשביל שלא תלד זוטרי אייתי בלא דעתייהו ת"ר שלשה היו באותה עצה הקב"ה ודניאל ונבוכדנצר הקב"ה אמר ניזיל דניאל מהכא דלא לימרו בזכותיה איתנצל ודניאל אמר איזיל מהכא דלא ליקיים בי ט) פסילי אלהיהם תשרפון באש ונבוכדנצר אמר יזיל דניאל מהכא דלא לימרו קלייה לאלהיה בנורא ומניין דסגיד ליה דכתיב י) באדין מלכא נבוכדנצר נפל על אנפוהי ולדניאל סגיד וגו': כ) כה אמר ה' צבאות אלהי ישראל אל אחאב בן קוליה ואל צדקיה בן מעשיה הנבאים לכם בשמי לשקר וגו' וכתיב ל) ולוקח מהם קללה לכל גלות יהודה אשר בבבל לאמר ישימך ה' כצדקיהו ז) וכאחאב אשר קלם מלך בבל באש אשר שרפם לא נאמר אלא אשר קלם אמר רבי יוחנן משום ר' שמעון בן יוחי מלמד שעשאן כקליות מ) יען אשר עשו נבלה בישראל וינאפו את נשי רעיהם מאי עבוד אזול לגבי ברתיה דנבוכדנצר אחאב אמר לה כה אמר ה' השמיעי אל צדקיה וצדקיה אמר כה אמר ה' השמיעי אל אחאב אזלה ואמרה ליה לאבוה אמר לה אלהיהם של אלו שונא זימה הוא כי אתו לגבך שדרינהו לגבאי כי אתו לגבה שדרתנהו לגבי אבוה אמר להו מאן אמר לכון אמרו הקדוש ברוך הוא והא חנניה מישאל ועזריה שאלתינהו ואמרו לי אסור אמרו ליה אנן נמי נביאי כוותייהו לדידהו לא אמר להו לדידן אמר לן אמר להו אנא בעינא דאיבדקינכו כי היכי דבדקתינהו לחנניה מישאל ועזריה אמרו ליה אינון (א) תלתא הוו ואנן תרין אמר להו בחרו לכון מאן דבעיתו בהדייכו אמרו יהושע כהן גדול סברי ליתי יהושע דנפיש זכותיה ומגנא עלן אחתיוהו שדינהו אינהו איקלו יהושע כהן גדול איחרוכי מאניה שנאמר נ) ויראני את יהושע הכהן הגדול עומד לפני מלאך ה' וגו' וכתיב ס) ויאמר ה' אל השטן יגער ה' בך וגו' א"ל ידענא דצדיקא את אלא מאי טעמא אהניא בך פורתא נורא חנניה מישאל ועזריה לא אהניא בהו כלל א"ל אינהו תלתא הוו ואנא חד א"ל והא אברהם יחיד הוה התם לא הוו רשעים בהדיה ולא אתיהיב רשותא לנורא הכא הוו רשעים בהדי ואתיהיב רשותא לנורא היינו דאמרי אינשי תרי אודי יבישי וחד רטיבא אוקדן יבישי לרטיבא מאי טעמא איענש אמר רב פפא שהיו בניו נושאין נשים שאינן הגונות לכהונה ולא מיחה בהן שנאמר ע) ויהושע היה לבוש בגדים צואים וכי דרכו של יהושע ללבוש בגדים צואים אלא מלמד שהיו בניו נושאים נשים שאינן הגונות לכהונה ולא מיחה בהן אמר רבי תנחום דרש בר קפרא בציפורי מאי דכתיב פ) שש השעורים האלה נתן לי מאי שש השעורים אילימא שש שעורים ממש וכי דרכו של בועז ליתן מתנה שש שעורים

אלא

רש"י

גדולים צדיקים יותר ממלאכי השרת. דרביעא חשיב לתלתא צדיקי ומלאך לבסוף דכתיב ורויה די רביעאה דמי לבר אלהין: וטפחו לישראל על פניהם. שהשתחוו לצלם: אני אמרתי שכל התמר שלי הוא. שיהיו בהם צדיקים הרבה ולא עלתה בידי וכו' ישראל נמשלו לתמר כדאמרי' (סוכה דף מה:) מה תמר זה אין לו אלא לב אחד וכו': והנה איש רוכב על סוס אדום. בזכריה כתיב: כל העולם כולו ללילה. מפני שהשתחוו לצלם: והוא עומד. העמיד הקב"ה עצמו בזכות ההדסים שבמצולה: האומר לצולה חרבי. לבבל שיושבת במצולה: חרבי. לשון חרבו המים (בראשית ח): שרוקים. צבועים ואח"כ נעשו לבנים כשנסתכל בצדיקים נח מכעסו: סוסיא חיורא מעלי לחלמא. מדקאמר שאדום הוי רמז לקללה: ורבנן. חנניה מישאל ועזריה: להיכן אזלו. כשיצאו מן הכבשן דתו לא מדכר להו בכולהו כתובי: בעין הרע מתו. שהיו מסתכלים בהן על שהיו תמהין בהן: ברוק טבעו. באותו רוק שרקקו אומות העולם בישראל שאומרין אלוה כזה יש לכם והשתחויתם לצלם: הוי אומר זה חנניה מישאל ועזריה. אלמא חזרו לארץ אצל יהושע כהן גדול: ודניאל להיכן אזל. כשהושלכו חביריו לתוך כבשן האש שלא הושלך עמהם: למכרא נהרא רבא בטבריא. לחפור ולהוציא נהר בטבריא ל"א למכרא נהרא בטורא בהר: לאתויי בירי דאספסתא. להביא זרע של עשב שהוא מאכל בהמה שלחו נבוכדנצר הכי הוה קים להו: לאתויי חזירי ממצרים. שלחו כדי לגדלם לולדות שחזירי מצרים גדולים הם: והתניא אמר תודוס הרופא לחכמים שהיו אומרים ניטלה האם טרפה והא אין פרה וחזירה יוצאה ממצרים וכו' כדי שלא יהיו מצויין במקומות אחרים ואעפ"כ חיו: זוטרי אייתינהו. ולא העלו על לבם דלפריה ורביה בעי והניחו להוציאן בלא חתוך האם: באותה עצה. שהלך משם דניאל: דלא לקיים בי פסילי אלהיהם תשרפון באש. דנבוכדנצר עשאו אלוה כדכתיב ולדניאל הוה סגיד והוה ליה כפסילי אלהיהם שהמקרא הזה היה צוח עליהם לשורפן לכך היה מתירא: קליות. שבלים המהובהבין באש: השמיעי. השמשי: תלתא. ונפישי זכותייהו: הלא זה אוד. מה אוד נחרך אף הוא נחרך: אהני. הועיל: אקדו. שרפו: מאי טעמא איענוש. יהושע דאהני נורא למאניה דהאי דאהדר איהו לנבוכדנצר דחייה בעצמא דחייה: שש שעורים. שש גרעינים שעורים ממש: וכי דרכו של בועז ליתן שש שבלים. והא תנן (פאה פ"ח מ"ה) אין פוחתין לעני בגורן פחות מחצי קב שעורים:

אלא

תורה אור השלם

א) ענה ואמר הא אנה חזה גברין ארבעה שרין מהלכין בגוא נורא וחבל לא איתי בהון ורוה די רביעאה דמה לבר אלהין: [דניאל ג, כה]

ב) לך אדני הצדקה ולנו בשת הפנים כיום הזה לאיש יהודה וליושבי ירושלים ולכל ישראל הקרבים והרחקים בכל הארצות אשר הדחתם שם במעלם אשר מעלו בך: [דניאל ט, ז]

ג) אמרתי אעלה בתמר אחזה בסנסניו ויהיו נא שדיך כאשכלות הגפן וריח אפך כתפוחים: [שיר השירים ז, ט]

ד) ראיתי הלילה והנה איש רכב על סוס אדם והוא עמד בין ההדסים אשר במצלה ואחריו סוסים אדמים שרקים ולבנים: [זכריה א, ח]

ה) יי איש מלחמה יי שמו: [שמות טו, ג]

ו) ויהי אמן את הדסה היא אסתר בת דדו כי אין לה אב ואם והנערה יפת תאר וטובת מראה ובמות אביה ואמה לקחה מרדכי לו לבת: [אסתר ב, ז]

ז) האמר לצולה חרבי ונהרתיך אוביש: [ישעיה מד, כז]

ח) שמע נא יהושע הכהן הגדול אתה ורעיך הישבים לפניך כי אנשי מופת המה כי הנני מביא את עבדי צמח: [זכריה ג, ח]

ט) פסילי אלהיהם תשרפון באש לא תחמד כסף וזהב עליהם ולקחת לך פן תוקש בו כי תועבת יי אלהיך הוא: [דברים ז, כה]

י) באדין מלכא נבוכדנצר נפל על אנפוהי ולדניאל סגד ומנחה וניחחין אמר לנסכה לה: [דניאל ב, מו]

כ) כה אמר יי צבאות אלהי ישראל אל אחאב בן קוליה ואל צדקיהו בן מעשיה הנבאים לכם בשמי שקר הנני נתן אתם ביד נבוכדראצר מלך בבל והכם לעיניכם: [ירמיה כט, כא]

ל) ולקח מהם קללה לכל גלות יהודה אשר בבבל לאמר ישמך יי כצדקיהו וכאחב אשר קלם מלך בבל באש: [ירמיה כט, כב]

מ) יען אשר עשו נבלה בישראל וינאפו את נשי רעיהם וידברו דבר בשמי שקר אשר לוא צויתם ואנכי הוידע ועד נאם יי: [ירמיה כט, כג]

נ) ויראני את יהושע הכהן הגדול עמד לפני מלאך יי והשטן עמד על ימינו לשטנו: [זכריה ג, א]

ס) ויאמר יי אל השטן יגער יי בך השטן ויגער יי בך הבחר בירושלים הלוא זה אוד מצל מאש: [זכריה ג, ב]

ע) ויהושע היה לבש בגדים צואים ועמד לפני המלאך: [זכריה ג, ג]

פ) ותאמר שש השערים האלה נתן לי כי אמר אלי אל תבואי ריקם אל חמותך: [רות ג, יז]

הגהות הב"ח

(א) גמ' תלתא הוו ואנן תרין. נ"ב וקשה מיד הכא הוה ליה לאקשויי והא אברהם יחיד הוה כמו שהקשה בתר הכי ליהושע כ"ג:

ליקוטי רש"י

שריין מהלכין בגו נורא. מותרין מאסוריהן והולכים בתוך האש. וחבל לא איתי בהון. וחבלה לא יש בהם. ורויה די רביעאה. ותוארו של רביעי. דמה לבר אלהין. דומה למלאך שראיתי בהיותי עם סנחרב כשנשרפו אוכלוסיו שנאמר (ישעיה לז) ויך במחנה אשור ונבוכדנצר היה שם ונמלט בתוך עשרה שנמלטו מהם [דניאל ג, כה]. לך ה' הצדקה. כלומר משפטיך ופורענות שהבאת עלינו הדין והצדק עמך. ולנו בושת הפנים. כדי לנו להתבייש על המאורע לנו כי אנחנו גרמנו לעצמנו. כיום הזה. כאשר אנחנו רואים היום [שם ט, ז]. בסנסניו. סנסנים, ענפים [שה"ש ז, ט]. ה' איש מלחמה. בעל מלחמות כמו (רות א, ג) איש נעמי וכל איש ואיש מתורגמין בעל וכן (מ"א ב, ב) וחזקת והיית לאיש לגבור. ה' שמו. מלחמותיו לא בכלי זיין אלא בשמו הוא נלחם כמו שאמר דוד (ש"א יז, מה) ואנכי בא אליך בשם ה' צבאות. דבר אחר ה' שמו אף בשעה שהוא נלחם ונוקם מאויביו אוחז הוא במדתו לרחם על ברואיו ולזון את כל באי עולם ולא כמדת מלכי אדמה כשהוא עוסק במלחמה פונה עצמו מכל עסקים ואין בו כח לעשות זו וזו [שמות טו, ג]. בין ההדסים אשר במצולה. בין אילני ההדסים [זכריה א, ח]. בין הצדיקים שגלו ונשמעו... קרא [מגילה יג.]. האומר לצולה חרבי. האומר לבבל... ונהרותיך אוביש. לפי שהיא יושבת על נהרות מדמה הריגת אוכלוסיה ליובש נהרות [ישעיה מד, כז]. שרוקים. לא ידעתי מה צבע הוא ויונתן תרגם קוחין [זכריה שם]. אתה ורעיך. חנניה מישאל ועזריה הם. אנשי מופת. גברין כשרין למיעבד להון ניסין אף להם נעשה נס [זכריה ג, ח]. אין פרה וחזירה כו'. לפי שטובות הן ואין רוצין שיהיו מצויות במקומות אחרות [לעיל לג.]. מפני פרות וחזירות שלכן מעולין מאד ומוכרין אותן ביוקר ורוצין שלא ילדו במלכות אחרת כדי שיהו צריכין להם וחותכין האם שלה... אשר קלם. לשון קלוי באש (ויקרא ב) [ירמיה כט, כב]. יגער ה' בך השטן. ...בך הוא הבוחר בירושלים שלא תכנס לפניו לקטרג על הצדיק ...שלא הוא וזכה לכך שהוצל מאש השריפה [זכריה ג, ב]. נשים שאינן הגונות לכהונה. שהיו בניו נשואות נשים נכריות כמו שכ' בספר עזרא וימצא מבני הכהנים אשר הושיבו נשים נכריות מבני יהושע בן יוזדק [שם, א]. לבוש בגדים צואים. כתרגומו הוו ליה בנין דנסבין להון נשין דלא כשרין לכהונתא והיה נענש הוא על שלא מיחה בידם [שם, ג].

שְׁמַע מִינָּהּ סוּסְיָא חִיוָּרָא מַעֲלֵי לְחֶלְמָא – **Learn from this that a white horse is** a **favorable** omen **in a dream.**[12]

The Gemara inquires:

וְרַבָּנָן לְהֵיכָא אֲזוּל – **And where did these dignitaries** [i.e. Chananyah, Mishael, and Azaryah] **go** after this incident?[13]

The Gemara presents three opinions:

אָמַר רַב בְּעַיִן [הָרַע] מֵתוּ – **Rav said: They died through the "evil eye."**[14] וּשְׁמוּאֵל אָמַר בָּרוֹק טָבְעוּ – **And Shmuel says: They drowned in spittle.**[15] וְרַבִּי יוֹחָנָן אָמַר עָלוּ לְאֶרֶץ יִשְׂרָאֵל – **And R' Yochanan says: They went up to the Land of Israel,**[16] וְנָשְׂאוּ נָשִׁים וְהוֹלִידוּ בָּנִים וּבָנוֹת – **married, and fathered sons and daughters.**

The Gemara notes:

כְּתַנָּאֵי – The above is the same **as** the dispute among the following **Tannaim:** רַבִּי אֱלִיעֶזֶר אוֹמֵר בְּעַיִן [הָרַע] מֵתוּ – R' ELIEZER SAYS: THEY DIED THROUGH THE "EVIL EYE." רַבִּי יְהוֹשֻׁעַ אוֹמֵר בָּרוֹק טָבְעוּ – R' YEHOSHUA SAYS: THEY DROWNED IN SPITTLE. וַחֲכָמִים אוֹמְרִים עָלוּ לְאֶרֶץ יִשְׂרָאֵל וְנָשְׂאוּ נָשִׁים וְהוֹלִידוּ בָּנִים וּבָנוֹת – AND THE SAGES SAY: THEY WENT UP TO THE LAND OF ISRAEL, MARRIED, AND FATHERED SONS AND DAUGHTERS, שֶׁנֶּאֱמַר ,,שְׁמַע־נָא יְהוֹשֻׁעַ הַכֹּהֵן הַגָּדוֹל אַתָּה וְרֵעֶיךָ הַיֹּשְׁבִים לְפָנֶיךָ כִּי־אַנְשֵׁי מוֹפֵת הֵמָּה" – AS IT IS STATED: *HEAR NOW, O JOSHUA THE HIGH PRIEST – YOU AND YOUR COMPANIONS WHO SIT BEFORE YOU, FOR THEY ARE MEN OF MIRACLE.*[17] אֵיזוּ הֵם אֲנָשִׁים שֶׁנַּעֲשָׂה לָהֶן מוֹפֵת – WHO ARE THE MEN TO WHOM A MIRACLE WAS PERFORMED? הֱוֵי אוֹמֵר זֶה חֲנַנְיָה מִישָׁאֵל וַעֲזַרְיָה – SAY, THEN, THAT THIS IS a reference to CHANANYAH, MISHAEL, AND AZARYAH. Thus, we find them in Eretz Yisrael in the presence of Joshua the High Priest long after the death of Nebuchadnezzar.

Daniel, the friend of Chananyah, Mishael, and Azaryah, is not mentioned in the account of the miracle of the furnace, indicating that he was absent.[18] The Gemara presents three opinions as to where Daniel was at the time:

וְדָנִיאֵל לְהֵיכָן אָזַל – **And where did Daniel go** that he was absent when this incident occurred? אָמַר רַב לְמִיכְרָא נַהֲרָא רַבָּא בִּטְבֶרְיָא – **Rav said:** He was sent by Nebuchadnezzar **to dig a great river in Tiberias.**[19] וּשְׁמוּאֵל אָמַר לְאַתוּיֵי בִּיזְרָא דְּאַסְפַּסְתָּא – **And Shmuel says:** He was sent **to import *aspasta* seed** to Babylon.[20] וְרַבִּי יוֹחָנָן אָמַר לְאַתוּיֵי חֲזִירֵי דַּאֲלֶכְּסַנְדְּרִיָּא שֶׁל מִצְרַיִם – **And R' Yochanan says:** He was sent **to import Alexandrian hogs** to Babylon to be bred there.[21]

The Gemara asks:

אִינִי – **Is that so?** וְהָתַנְיָא תּוֹדוֹס הָרוֹפֵא אָמַר – **But it was taught in a Mishnah:**[22] TODOS THE PHYSICIAN SAID: אֵין פָּרָה וַחֲזִירָה יוֹצֵא מֵאֲלֶכְּסַנְדְּרִיָּא שֶׁל מִצְרַיִם שֶׁאֵין חוֹתְכִין הָאֵם שֶׁלָּהּ בִּשְׁבִיל שֶׁלֹּא תֵּלֵד – NO COW OR SOW LEAVES EGYPTIAN ALEXANDRIA WITHOUT THEIR CUTTING OUT HER WOMB SO THAT SHE

NOTES

white. [The whitening of the dark horses] symbolizes the appeasement of God's anger (*Rashi*).

[We have rendered this phrase so that it conforms in intent to the reading cited by *Maharsha* from *Yalkut*: מִיַּד מְלָאִים רוֹגֶז שְׂרוּקִים וַאֲדוּמִים וְאַחַר כָּךְ נַעֲשׂוּ לְבָנִים. I.e. after the red horses came on the scene, symbolizing God's wrath toward the world, God's notice of the righteous "myrtles" caused His anger to abate, and the horses turned white (*Maharsha*). *Maharsha* also cites the reading cited by *Radak* (ad loc.): מִיַּד שְׁחוֹרִים נַעֲשׂוּ שְׂרוּקִים וַאֲדוּמִים לְבָנִים, *Immediately, the black became colored, and the red [became] white. Dikdukei Soferim,* too, cites a version that omits the words מִיַּד מְלָאִים רוֹגֶז entirely, and reads simply: מִיַּד שְׂרוּקִים וַאֲדוּמִים נַעֲשׂוּ וכו׳, *Immediately, the colored and red became (white).*]

12. For the white horses in Zechariah's vision symbolized the appeasement of Divine wrath (see *Rashi* and *Rashash*). [Since dreams are one-sixtieth of prophecy (*Berachos* 57b), a good omen in a prophetic vision is accounted a good omen in a dream as well (*Maharsha*).]

13. For there is no further reference to them in Scripture (*Rashi*). One would have expected that Nebuchadnezzar would have promoted such highly regarded dignitaries to even higher rank after such a miraculous display of their Divine favor [and the fact that such promotion is not mentioned in Scripture indicates that they departed the scene abruptly] (*Maharsha*). [Chananyah, Mishael and Azaryah are referred to here as רַבָּנָן, *leaders* or *dignitaries,* in keeping with the lesson derived from them in the Gemara above (end of 92b) that one should never abandon רַבְּנוּת שֶׁלּוֹ, *his dignified bearing* (*Maharsha*).]

14. *Chazon Ish* (*Choshen Mishpat, Likkutim* ch. 21 ד״ה יהבו ביה רבנן עינייהו, p. 255) states that the human mind has the ability to trigger a variety of natural phenomena that can cascade and eventually lead to the destruction of even large physical bodies. [For a lengthy treatment of this subject, see *Maharal* (*Chidushei Agaddos* to *Bava Metzia* 84a, and *Nesivos Olam, Nesiv Ayin Tov,* ch. 1).]

Others suggest that the mechanism through which the "evil eye" operates is an ethical one. The blessings bestowed by God upon an individual should not serve as a source of anguish to others. If one allows his blessings (e.g. wealth, children, etc.) to cause pain to others less fortunate – and certainly if one flaunts his blessings – one arouses a Divine judgment against himself and a re-evaluation of his fitness for those blessings. This can lead to their eventual retraction (*Michtav MeEliyahu* III, p. 313; IV, pp. 5-6; *R' Avigdor Miller*).

In the present instance, the extraordinary miracle performed for Chananyah, Mishael, and Azaryah made them the object of everyone's attention. In attributing the deaths of Chananyah, Mishael and Azaryah to the evil eye, Rav is consistent with his teaching in *Bava Metzia* (107b) that "ninety-nine [out of a hundred] die through the evil eye and only one through natural causes" (*Yad Ramah*; see also R' Eliezer's statement in *Avos* 2:9).

15. I.e. in the pool of spittle generated by the spitting of the gentiles who (as stated above) scorned the Jews who had succumbed to Nebuchadnezzar's threats. The enormous amount of spittle they heaped upon the disloyal Jews drowned Chananyah, Mishael and Azaryah (*Rashi*). *Yad Ramah* explains "drowning in spittle" as a metaphor for death through humiliation. The terrible humiliation of their fellow Jews from the reproach of these gentiles so mortified Chananyah, Mishael, and Azaryah that they died. See also *Maharsha* and *Ben Yehoyada.*

16. Rather than serve as ministers to Nebuchadnezzar; that is why no further mention of them is found in Scripture (*Maharsha*).

17. *Zechariah* 3:8. In this prophetic vision, which took place subsequent to the reign of Nebuchadnezzar, in the second year of the reign of Darius, King of Persia (ibid. 1:1), an angel brought Zechariah to the Temple in Jerusalem and showed him the High Priest, Joshua, in the company of other persons, who are identified as "men of miracle."

18. Had he been present, he, too, would certainly have refused to bow to the image, and would have been cast into the furnace along with Chananyah, Mishael and Azaryah (see *Rashi*).

19. Some have the reading: נַהֲרָא רַבָּא בְּטוּרָא, *a great river at the mountain* (see *Rashi, Yad Ramah*), i.e. to dig canals so that the various springs in the mountain would converge and form a great river (*Yad Ramah*). [In our editions of *Rashi,* the reading בִּטְבֶרְיָא, *in Tiberias,* appears as the first version, and the reading בְּטוּרָא, *at the mountain,* as an alternative. *Dikdukei Sofrim* reports, however, that in certain early editions of *Rashi,* the reading בִּטְבֶרְיָא, *in Tiberias,* does not appear altogether.]

This time-consuming task was specially designed so that Daniel would be absent from the capital until matters returned to normal (*Yad Ramah*). [In explaining the views of the next two Amoraim, *Rashi* writes explicitly that Daniel was sent on his mission by Nebuchadnezzar himself. The same would apply to the present view – that of Rav (see *Maharal* ד״ה וקאמר רב). For, as explained in the Baraisa below, Nebuchadnezzar was involved in the plan to absent Daniel from the dedication of the image.]

20. *Aspasta* is a grain used for animal fodder (*Rashi*). These Amoraim report Daniel's whereabouts based on traditions they had received (*Rashi, Yad Ramah*). See also *Maharal.*

21. For the Alexandrian hogs were larger (*Rashi*) and superior (*Yad Ramah*).

22. This Mishnah appears in the fourth chapter of *Bechoros* (28b). *Mesoras HaShas* emends the text here to read וְהָתְנַן, *but we learned in a Mishnah,* rather than וְהָתַנְיָא, which is used to refer to a Baraisa.

גדולים צדיקים יותר ממלאכי השרת שנאמר [א] ענה ואמר הא אנא חזי גוברין ארבעה שריין מהלכין בגו נורא וחבל לא איתי בהון ורויה די רביעאה דמה לבר אלהין אמר ר' תנחום בר חנילאי בשעה שיצאו חנניה מישאל ועזריה מכבשן האש באו כל אומות העולם וטפחו לשונאיהן של ישראל על פניהם אמרו להם יש לכם אלוה כזה ואתם משתחוים לצלם מיד פתחו ואמרו [ב] לך ה' הצדקה ולנו בושת הפנים כיום הזה אמר ר' שמואל בר נחמני אמר ר' יונתן מאי דכתיב [ג] אמרתי אעלה בתמר אוחזה בסנסניו אמרתי אעלה בתמר אלו ישראל ועכשיו לא עלה בידי אלא סנסן אחד של חנניה מישאל ועזריה [א] אמר רבי יוחנן מאי דכתיב [ד] ראיתי הלילה והנה איש רוכב על סוס אדום והוא עומד בין ההדסים אשר במצולה [וגו'] מאי ראיתי הלילה ביקש הקב"ה להפוך את כל העולם כולו ללילה והנה איש רוכב [ב] אין איש אלא הקב"ה שנאמר [ה] ה' איש מלחמה ה' שמו על סוס אדום ביקש הקב"ה להפוך את העולם כולו לדם כיון שנסתכל בחנניה מישאל ועזריה נתקררה דעתו שנאמר [ד] והוא עומד בין ההדסים אשר במצולה ואין הדסים אלא צדיקים [ג] שנאמר [ו] ויהי אומן את הדסה ואין מצולה אלא בבל שנאמר [ז] האומר לצולה חרבי ונהרותיך אוביש מיד מלאים רוגז נעשים שרוקים ואדומים נעשו לבנים אמר רב פפא שמע מינה [ד] סוסיא חיורא מעלי לחלמא: ורבנן להיכא (אזול) [אזלו] אמר רב בעין [הרע] מתו ושמואל אמר ברוק טבעו ור' יוחנן אמר עלו לארץ ישראל ונשאו נשים והולידו בנים ובנות כתנאי ר' אליעזר אומר בעין [הרע] מתו ר' יהושע אומר ברוק טבעו וחכ"א עלו לא"י ונשאו נשים והולידו בנים ובנות שנאמר [ח] שמע נא יהושע הכהן הגדול אתה ורעיך היושבים לפניך כי אנשי מופת המה איזו הם אנשים שנעשה להן מופת הוי אומר זה חנניה מישאל ועזריה ודניאל להיכן אזל אמר רב למיכרא נהרא רבא בטבריא ושמואל אמר לאתויי ביזרא דאספסתא ור' יוחנן אמר לאתויי חזירי דאלכסנדריא של מצרים איני [ה] והתניא [ו] תודוס הרופא אמר אין פרה וחזירה יוצאה מאלכסנדריא של מצרים שאין חותכין האם שלה בשביל שלא תלד זוטרי אייתי בלא דעתייהו ת"ר שלשה היו באותה עצה הקב"ה ודניאל ונבוכדנצר הקב"ה אמר ניזיל דניאל מהכא דלא לימרו בזכותיה איתנצל ודניאל אמר איזיל מהכא דלא ליקיים בי [ט] פסילי אלהיהם תשרפון באש ונבוכדנצר אמר יזיל דניאל מהכא דלא לימרו קלייה לאלהיה בנורא ומניין דסגיד ליה דכתיב [י] באדין מלכא נבוכדנצר נפל על אנפוהי ולדניאל סגיד וגו': [כ] כה אמר ה' צבאות אלהי ישראל אל אחאב בן קוליה ואל צדקיה בן מעשיה הנבאים לכם בשמי לשקר וגו' וכתיב [ל] ולוקח מהם קללה לכל גלות יהודה אשר בבבל לאמר ישימך ה' כצדקיהו [ז] וכאחאב אשר קלם מלך בבל באש אשר שרפם לא נאמר אלא אשר קלם אמר רבי יוחנן משום ר' שמעון בן יוחי מלמד שעשאן כקליות [מ] יען אשר עשו נבלה בישראל וינאפו את נשי רעיהם מאי עבוד אזול לגבי ברתיה דנבוכדנצר אחאב אמר לה כה אמר ה' השמיעי אל צדקיה וצדקיה אמר כה אמר ה' השמיעי אל אחאב אזלה ואמרה ליה לאבוה אמר לה אלהיהם של אלו שונא זימה הוא כי אתו לגבך שדרינהו לגבאי כי אתו לגבה שדרתנהו לגבי אבוה אמר להו מאן אמר לכון אמרו הקדוש ברוך הוא והא חנניה מישאל ועזריה שאלתינהו ואמרו לי אסור אמרו ליה אנן נמי נביאי כוותייהו לדידהו לא אמר להו לדידן אמר לן אמר להו אנא בעינא דאיבדקינכו כי היכי דבדקתינהו לחנניה מישאל ועזריה אמרו ליה אינון (א) תלתא הוו ואנן תרין אמר להו בחרו לכון מאן דבעיתו בהדייכו אמרו יהושע כהן גדול סברי ליתי יהושע דנפיש זכותיה ומגנא עלן אחתיוהו שדינהו אינהו איקלו יהושע כהן גדול איחרוכי מאניה שנאמר [נ] ויראני את יהושע הכהן הגדול עומד לפני מלאך ה' וגו' וכתיב [ס] ויאמר ה' אל השטן יגער ה' בך וגו' א"ל ידענא דצדיקא את אלא מאי טעמא אהניא בך פורתא נורא חנניה מישאל ועזריה לא אהניא בהו כלל א"ל אינהו תלתא הוו ואנא חד א"ל והא אברהם יחיד הוה התם לא הוו רשעים בהדיה ולא אתיהיב רשותא לנורא הכא הוו רשעים בהדי ואתיהיב רשותא לנורא היינו דאמרי אינשי תרי אודי יבישי וחד רטיבא אוקדן יבישי לרטיבא מאי טעמא איענש אמר רב פפא שהיו בניו נושאין נשים שאינן הגונות לכהונה ולא מיחה בהן שנאמר [ע] ויהושע היה לבוש בגדים צואים וכי דרכו של יהושע ללבוש בגדים צואים אלא מלמד שהיו בניו נושאים נשים שאינן הגונות לכהונה ולא מיחה בהן אמר רבי תנחום דרש בר קפרא בציפורי מאי דכתיב [פ] שש השעורים האלה נתן לי מאי שש השעורים אילימא שש שעורים ממש וכי דרכו של בועז ליתן מתנה שש שעורים

אלא

רש"י

גדולים צדיקים יותר ממלאכי השרת. דברישא חשיב לתלתא צדיקי ומלאך לבסוף דכתיב ורויה די רביעאה דמי לבר אלהין: וטפחו לישראל על פניהם. שהשתחוו לצלם: אני אמרתי שכל התמר שלי הוא. שיהיו בהם צדיקים הרבה ולא עלתה בידי וכו' ישראל נמשלו לתמר כדאמרי' (סוכה דף מה:) מה תמר זה אין לו אלא לב אחד וכו': והנה איש רוכב על סוס אדום. בזכריה כתיב: כל העולם כולו ללילה. מפני שהשתחוו לצלם: והוא עומד. העמיד הקב"ה עצמו בזכות ההדסים שבמצולה: האומר לצולה חרבי. לבבל שיושבת במצולה: חרבי. לשון חרבו המים (בראשית ח): שרוקים. צבועים ואח"כ נעשו לבנים כשנסתכל בצדיקים נח מכעסו: סוסיא חיורא מעלי לחלמא. מדקאמר שאדום הוי רמז לקללה: ורבנן. חנניה מישאל ועזריה: להיכן אזלו. כשיצאו מן הכבשן דתו לא מדכר להו בכולהו כתובי: בעין הרע מתו. שהיו מסתכלים בהן על שהיו תמהין בהן: ברוק טבעו. באותו רוק שרקקו אומות העולם בישראל שאומרין אלוה כזה יש לכם והשתחויתם לצלם: הוי אומר זה חנניה מישאל ועזריה. אלמא חזרו לארץ אצל יהושע כהן גדול: ודניאל להיכן אזל. כשהושלכו חביריו לתוך כבשן האש שלא הושלך עמהם: למכרא נהרא רבא בטבריא. לחפור ולהוציא נהר בטבריא ל"א למכרא נהרא בטורא בהר: לאתויי בירי דאספסתא. להביא זרע של עשב שהוא מאכל בהמה שלחו נבוכדנצר הכי הוה קים להו: לאתויי חזירי ממצרים. שלחו כדי לגדלם לולדות שחזירי מצרים גדולים הם: והתניא אמר תודוס הרופא לחכמים שהיו אומרים ניטלה האם טרפה והא אין פרה וחזירה יוצאה ממצרים וכו' כדי שלא יהיו מצויין במקומות אחרים ואעפ"כ חיו: זוטרי אייתינהו. ולא העלו על לבם דלפריה ורביה בעי והניחו להוציאן בלא חתוך האם: באותה עצה. שהלך משם דניאל: דלא לקיים בי פסילי אלהיהם תשרפון באש. דנבוכדנצר עשאו אלוה כדכתיב ולדניאל הוה סגיד והוה ליה כפסילי אלהיהם שהמקרא הזה היה צוות עליהם לשורפן לכך היה מתירא: קליות. שבלים המהובהבין באש: השמיעי. השתמשי: תלתא. ונפישי זכותייהו: הלא זה אוד. מה אוד נחרך אף הוא נחרך: אהני. הועיל: אקדו. שרפו: מאי טעמא איענוש. יהושע דאהני נורא למאניה דהאי דאהדר איהו לנבוכדנצר דחייה בעלמא דחייה: שש שעורים. שש גרעינים שעורים ממש: וכי דרכו של בועז ליתן שש שבלים. והא תנן (פאה פ"ח מ"ה) אין פוחתין לעני בגורן פחות מחצי קב שעורים:

אלא

מסורת הש"ס

א) [עי' בילקוט זכרי' ושם איתא מאמר זה קצת בנוסחא אחרינא], ב) [לקמן צו: סוטה מג: מח.], ג) [מגילה יג. ע"ש ועי' תוס' ברכות כו: ד"ה ואין שיחה כו'], ד) [עיין ברכות נו:], ה) [נ"ל והתנן], ו) לעיל לג. בכורות כח:, ז) בקרא כתיב וכאחב.

הגהות הב"ח

(א) גמ' תלתא הוו ואנן תרין. נ"ב וקשה מיד הכא הוה ליה לאקשויי והא אברהם יחיד הוה כמו שהקשה בתר הכי ליהושע כ"ג:

ליקוטי רש"י

שריין מהלכין בגו נורא. מותרין מאסוריהן והולכים בתוך האש. וחבל לא איתי בהון. וחבלה אין יש בהם. ורויה די רביעאה. ותוארו של רביעי. דמה לבר אלהין. דומה למלאך שראיתי בהיותי עם סנחריב כשנשרפו אוכלוסיו שנאמר (ישעיה לז) ויך במחנה אשור ונבוכדנצר היה שם ונמלט בתוך עשרה שנמלטו מהם [דניאל ג, כה]. לך ה' הצדקה. כלומר משפטיך ופורענות שהבאת עלינו הדין והצדק עמך. ולנו בושת הפנים. כדי אנו להתבייש על המאורע לנו כי אנחנו גרמנו לעצמנו. כיום הזה. כאשר אנחנו רואים היום [שם ט, ז]. בסנסניו. סנסנים, ענפים [שה"ש ז, ט]. ה' איש מלחמה. בעל מלחמות כמו (רות א, ג) איש נעמי וכל איש ואישך מתורגמין בעל וכן (מ"א ב, ב) וחזקת והיית לאיש לגבור. ה' שמו. מלחמותיו לא בכלי זיין אלא בשמו הוא נלחם כמו שאמר דוד (ש"א יז, מה) ואנכי בא אליך בשם ה' צבאות. דבר אחר ה' שמו אף בשעה שהוא נלחם ונוקם מאויביו אוחז הוא במדתו לרחם על ברואיו ולזון את כל באי עולם ולא כמדת מלכי אדמה כשהוא עוסק במלחמה פונה עצמו מכל עסקים ואין בו כח לעשות זו וזו [שמות טו, ג]. בין ההדסים אשר במצולה. בין אילני הדסים דבבל [זכריה א, ח]. בין הצדיקים שגלו לבבל ושכינה משמעי קרא [מגילה יג.]. האומר לצולה חרבי. האומר לבבל התיבשי. ונהרותיך אוביש. לפי שהיא יושבת על נהרות מדמה הריגת אוכלוסיה ליובש נהרות [ישעיה מד, כז]. שרוקים. לא ידעתי מה צבע הוא ויונתן תרגם קוחין [זכריה שם]. אתה ורעיך. חנניה מישאל ועזריה היו. אנשי מופת. גברין כשרין למיעבד להון ניסין שאף להם נעשה נס [זכריה ג, ח]. ביזרא. הזרע [ב"מ עד:]. אין פרה וחזירה כו'. לפי שטובות הן ואין רוצין שיהיו מצויות במקומות אחרות וקא חזינן דמתקיימות [לעיל לג.]. מפני ספרות וחזירות שלהן מעולין מאד ומוכרין אותן ביוקר ורוצין שלא ילדו במלכות אחרת כדי שיהו צריכין להם וחותכין האם שלה ואינה מתה. האם שלה. רחם שלה [בכורות כח:]. אשר קלם. לשון קלוי באש (ויקרא ב) [ירמיה כט, כב]. יגער ה' בך השטן. יגער הקב"ה בך אתה השטן וחוזר ואומר ויגער ה' בך הוא הבוחר בירושלים שלא תכנס לפניו לקטרג על הצדיק הזה הלא ראוי הוא וזכה לכך שהוצל מאש השריפה [זכריה ג, ב]. נשים שאינן הגונות לכהונה. שהיו בניו נשואות נשים נכריות כמו שכ' בספר עזרא וימצא מבני הכהנים אשר הושיבו נשים נכריות מבני יהושע בן יהוצדק [שם, א]. לבוש בגדים צואים. כתרגומו הוו ליה בנין דנסבין להון נשין דלא כשרין לכהונתא והיה נענש הוא על שלא מיחה בידם [שם, ג].

תורה אור השלם

א) עָנֵה וְאָמַר הָא אֲנָה חָזֵה גֻּבְרִין אַרְבְּעָה שְׁרַיִן מַהְלְכִין בְּגוֹא נוּרָא וַחֲבָל לָא אִיתַי בְּהוֹן וְרֵוֵהּ דִּי רְבִיעָאָה דָּמֵה לְבַר אֱלָהִין: [דניאל ג, כה]

ב) לְךָ אֲדֹנָי הַצְּדָקָה וְלָנוּ בֹּשֶׁת הַפָּנִים כַּיּוֹם הַזֶּה לְאִישׁ יְהוּדָה וּלְיוֹשְׁבֵי יְרוּשָׁלַיִם וּלְכָל יִשְׂרָאֵל הַקְּרֹבִים וְהָרְחֹקִים בְּכָל הָאֲרָצוֹת אֲשֶׁר הִדַּחְתָּם שָׁם בְּמַעֲלָם אֲשֶׁר מָעֲלוּ בָךְ: [דניאל ט, ז]

ג) אָמַרְתִּי אֶעֱלֶה בְתָמָר אֹחֲזָה בְּסַנְסִנָּיו וְיִהְיוּ נָא שָׁדַיִךְ כְּאֶשְׁכְּלוֹת הַגֶּפֶן וְרֵיחַ אַפֵּךְ כַּתַּפּוּחִים: [שיר השירים ז, ט]

ד) רָאִיתִי הַלַּיְלָה וְהִנֵּה אִישׁ רֹכֵב עַל סוּס אָדֹם וְהוּא עֹמֵד בֵּין הַהֲדַסִּים אֲשֶׁר בַּמְּצֻלָה וְאַחֲרָיו סוּסִים אֲדֻמִּים שְׂרֻקִּים וּלְבָנִים: [זכריה א, ח]

ה) יְיָ אִישׁ מִלְחָמָה יְיָ שְׁמוֹ: [שמות טו, ג]

ו) וַיְהִי אֹמֵן אֶת הֲדַסָּה הִיא אֶסְתֵּר בַּת דֹּדוֹ כִּי אֵין לָהּ אָב וָאֵם וְהַנַּעֲרָה יְפַת תֹּאַר וְטוֹבַת מַרְאֶה וּבְמוֹת אָבִיהָ וְאִמָּהּ לְקָחָהּ מָרְדֳּכַי לוֹ לְבַת: [אסתר ב, ז]

ז) הָאֹמֵר לַצּוּלָה חֳרָבִי וְנַהֲרֹתַיִךְ אוֹבִישׁ: [ישעיה מד, כז]

ח) שְׁמַע נָא יְהוֹשֻׁעַ הַכֹּהֵן הַגָּדוֹל אַתָּה וְרֵעֶיךָ הַיֹּשְׁבִים לְפָנֶיךָ כִּי אַנְשֵׁי מוֹפֵת הֵמָּה כִּי הִנְנִי מֵבִיא אֶת עַבְדִּי צֶמַח: [זכריה ג, ח]

ט) פְּסִילֵי אֱלֹהֵיהֶם תִּשְׂרְפוּן בָּאֵשׁ לֹא תַחְמֹד כֶּסֶף וְזָהָב עֲלֵיהֶם וְלָקַחְתָּ לָךְ פֶּן תִּוָּקֵשׁ בּוֹ כִּי תוֹעֲבַת יְיָ אֱלֹהֶיךָ הוּא: [דברים ז, כה]

י) בֵּאדַיִן מַלְכָּא נְבוּכַדְנֶצַּר נְפַל עַל אַנְפּוֹהִי וּלְדָנִיֵּאל סְגִד וּמִנְחָה וְנִיחֹחִין אֲמַר לְנַסָּכָה לֵהּ: [דניאל ב, מו]

כ) כֹּה אָמַר יְיָ צְבָאוֹת אֱלֹהֵי יִשְׂרָאֵל אֶל אַחְאָב בֶּן קוֹלָיָה וְאֶל צִדְקִיָּהוּ בֶן מַעֲשֵׂיָה הַנִּבְּאִים לָכֶם בִּשְׁמִי שָׁקֶר הִנְנִי נֹתֵן אֹתָם בְּיַד נְבוּכַדְרֶאצַּר מֶלֶךְ בָּבֶל וְהִכָּם לְעֵינֵיכֶם: [ירמיה כט, כא]

ל) וְלֻקַּח מֵהֶם קְלָלָה לְכֹל גָּלוּת יְהוּדָה אֲשֶׁר בְּבָבֶל לֵאמֹר יְשִׂמְךָ יְיָ כְּצִדְקִיָּהוּ וּכְאֶחָב אֲשֶׁר קָלָם מֶלֶךְ בָּבֶל בָּאֵשׁ: [ירמיה כט, כב]

מ) יַעַן אֲשֶׁר עָשׂוּ נְבָלָה בְּיִשְׂרָאֵל וַיְנַאֲפוּ אֶת נְשֵׁי רֵעֵיהֶם וַיְדַבְּרוּ דָבָר בִּשְׁמִי שֶׁקֶר אֲשֶׁר לוֹא צִוִּיתִם וְאָנֹכִי הַיּוֹדֵעַ וָעֵד נְאֻם יְיָ: [ירמיה כט, כג]

נ) וַיַּרְאֵנִי אֶת יְהוֹשֻׁעַ הַכֹּהֵן הַגָּדוֹל עֹמֵד לִפְנֵי מַלְאַךְ יְיָ וְהַשָּׂטָן עֹמֵד עַל יְמִינוֹ לְשִׂטְנוֹ: [זכריה ג, א]

ס) וַיֹּאמֶר יְיָ אֶל הַשָּׂטָן יִגְעַר יְיָ בְּךָ הַשָּׂטָן וְיִגְעַר יְיָ בְּךָ הַבֹּחֵר בִּירוּשָׁלָיִם הֲלוֹא זֶה אוּד מֻצָּל מֵאֵשׁ: [זכריה ג, ב]

ע) וִיהוֹשֻׁעַ הָיָה לָבֻשׁ בְּגָדִים צוֹאִים וְעֹמֵד לִפְנֵי הַמַּלְאָךְ: [זכריה ג, ג]

פ) וַתֹּאמֶר שֵׁשׁ הַשְּׂעֹרִים הָאֵלֶּה נָתַן לִי כִּי אָמַר אֵלַי אַל תָּבוֹאִי רֵיקָם אֶל חֲמוֹתֵךְ: [רות ג, יז]

NOT BEAR YOUNG.[23]

The Gemara answers:

זוּטְרֵי אַיְיתֵי בְּלֹא דַּעְתַּיְיהוּ – [Daniel] **brought young ones** out of Egypt **without their knowledge** of his intended purpose.[24]

A Baraisa concerning Daniel's absence from dedication ceremonies for Nebuchadnezzar's idol:

תָּנוּ רַבָּנָן – **The Rabbis taught in a Baraisa:** שְׁלֹשָׁה הָיוּ בְּאוֹתָהּ עֵצָה – THREE WERE involved IN THAT STRATAGEM of absenting Daniel from Babylon at the time the idol was dedicated: הַקָּדוֹשׁ בָּרוּךְ הוּא וְדָנִיֵּאל וּנְבוּכַדְנֶצַּר – THE HOLY ONE, BLESSED IS HE, DANIEL, AND NEBUCHADNEZZAR. The Gemara explains that each had a different reason: הַקָּדוֹשׁ בָּרוּךְ הוּא אָמַר – **The Holy One, Blessed is He, said:** נֵיזִיל דָּנִיֵּאל מֵהָכָא – **Let Daniel go away from here** [Babylon] דְּלֹא לֵימְרוּ בִּזְכוּתֵיהּ אִיתְנַצַּל – **so that people not say, "In his merit were [Chananyah, Mishael, and Azaryah] saved!"**[25] וְדָנִיֵּאל אָמַר – **And Daniel said:** אֵיזִיל מֵהָכָא – **I will go away from here** דְּלֹא לִיקַּיֵּים בִּי ,,פְּסִילֵי אֱלֹהֵיהֶם תִּשְׂרְפוּן בָּאֵשׁ" – **so that it not be fulfilled in me** the Scriptural declaration: ***Their idolatrous statues shall you burn in fire.***[26] וּנְבוּכַדְנֶצַּר אָמַר – **And Nebuchadnezzar said:** יֵיזִיל דָּנִיֵּאל מֵהָכָא – **Let Daniel go away from here** דְּלֹא לֵימְרוּ קַלְיֵיהּ לֶאֱלָהֵיהּ בְּנוּרָא – **so that people should not say** about me, **"He burned his** own **god in fire!"**[27] וּמִנַּיִין דִּסְגִיד לֵיהּ – **And from where** do we know **that [Nebuchadnezzar] prostrated himself before [Daniel]?** דִּכְתִיב ,,בֵּאדַיִן מַלְכָּא נְבוּכַדְנֶצַּר נְפַל עַל־אַנְפּוֹהִי וּלְדָנִיֵּאל סְגִד וגו׳" – **For it is written:** ***Then King Nebuchadnezzar fell upon his face and prostrated himself before Daniel etc.***[28]

The Gemara relates how the false prophets Achav ben Kolayah and Tzidkiahu ben Maaseyah sought to equate themselves with Chananyah, Mishael and Azaryah, and the subsequent fate of these false prophets:

,,כֹּה־אָמַר ה׳ צְבָאוֹת אֱלֹהֵי יִשְׂרָאֵל אֶל־אַחְאָב בֶּן־קוֹלָיָה וְאֶל־צִדְקִיָּהוּ בֶן־מַעֲשֵׂיָה הַנִּבְּאִים לָכֶם בִּשְׁמִי שָׁקֶר וגו׳" – The prophet Jeremiah was told: ***Thus said Hashem Lord of Hosts, the God of Israel, concerning Achav the son of Kolayah and concerning Tzidkiahu the son of Maaseyah, who prophesy to you in My Name falsely, etc.***[29] וּכְתִיב ,,וְלֻקַּח מֵהֶם קְלָלָה לְכֹל גָּלוּת יְהוּדָה אֲשֶׁר בְּבָבֶל לֵאמֹר יְשִׂמְךָ ה׳ כְּצִדְקִיָּהוּ וּכְאֶחָב אֲשֶׁר־קָלָם מֶלֶךְ־בָּבֶל בָּאֵשׁ" – **And it is written** further: ***And a curse shall be taken from them by the entire exile of Judah which is in Babylon, saying: May Hashem make you like Tzidkiahu and like Echav, whom the king of Babylon scorched in the fire.***[30] ,,אֲשֶׁר שְׂרָפָם" לֹא נֶאֱמַר אֶלָּא ,,אֲשֶׁר־קָלָם" – Now, **Scripture does not state** *whom [the king of Babylon] "burned,"* **but rather** *whom [the king of Babylon] "scorched."* אָמַר רַבִּי יוֹחָנָן מִשּׁוּם רַבִּי שִׁמְעוֹן בֶּן יוֹחַי – To explain this, **R' Yochanan reported in the name of R' Shimon ben Yochai:** מְלַמֵּד שֶׁעֲשָׂאָן כִּקְלָיוֹת – **This teaches that [Nebuchadnezzar] made them like toasted grain.**[31] Scripture continues that Achav and Tzidkiahu were punished so: ,,יַעַן אֲשֶׁר עָשׂוּ נְבָלָה בְּיִשְׂרָאֵל וַיְנַאֲפוּ אֶת־נְשֵׁי רֵעֵיהֶם" – ***Because they committed a disgrace in Israel and consorted with the wives of their fellows...***[32] מַאי עֲבוּד – **What** exactly **had they done?** אֲזוּל לְגַבֵּי בְּרַתֵּיהּ דִּנְבוּכַדְנֶצַּר – **They had gone to Nebuchadnezzar's daughter.** אַחְאָב אָמַר לָהּ כֹּה אָמַר ה׳ הִשָּׁמְעִי אֶל צִדְקִיָּה – **Achav said to her, "Thus said Hashem: Consent to Tzidkiah** when he approaches to lie with you," וְצִדְקִיָּה אָמַר כֹּה אָמַר ה׳ הִשָּׁמְעִי אֶל אַחְאָב – **while Tzidkiah said** to her, **"Thus said Hashem: Consent to Achav** when *he* approaches you." אֲזַלָה וְאָמְרָה לֵיהּ לַאֲבוּהָ – **She went and told her father about it.** אָמַר לָהּ – **[Nebuchadnezzar] said to her:** אֱלֹהֵיהֶם שֶׁל אֵלּוּ שׂוֹנֵא זִימָּה הוּא – I know that **the God of these** Jews **hates immorality.** How could it be that He has given them such instructions?! כִּי אָתוּ לְגַבָּךְ שַׁדְּרִינְהוּ לְגַבַּאי – **When they come to you** again, **send them to me.** כִּי אָתוּ לְגַבָּהּ שַׁדְּרִינְהוּ לְגַבֵּי אֲבוּהָ – **When they came to her, she sent them to her father.** אָמַר לְהוּ – **He said to them:** מַאן אָמַר לְכוּן – **Who told you** to instruct my daughter so? אָמְרוּ הַקָּדוֹשׁ בָּרוּךְ הוּא – **They replied: The Holy One, Blessed is He,** instructed us so. וְהָא חֲנַנְיָה מִישָׁאֵל וַעֲזַרְיָה שְׁאֶלְתִּינְהוּ וְאָמְרוּ לִי אָסוּר – Nebuchadnezzar said to them: **But I asked Chananyah, Mishael, and Azaryah** about it **and they told me** that **it is** absolutely **forbidden** and God would never say such a thing! אָמְרוּ לֵיהּ –

NOTES

23. The Egyptians sought thereby to preserve their monopoly on these high-quality breeds (*Rashi*).

24. Daniel's export of these young hogs was done with the knowledge of the Egyptians, but they did not suspect that he was exporting them in order to establish herds elsewhere. Thus, they neglected to remove the wombs (*Rashi*). *Yad Ramah,* however, explains that the hogs were so small that Daniel was able to smuggle them out of Egypt.

[Though Egypt was then a vassal state of Nebuchadnezzar, who could have ordered the open export of Alexandrian hogs to Babylon, he desired Daniel's mission to remain secret, so that people not realize that he had deliberately engineered Daniel's absence at the time of the dedication of the image. Daniel, therefore, could not reveal his official standing in the Babylonian government, and had to obtain the hogs through ordinary means (*Ben Yehoyada*).]

25. [Had Daniel been present, he too would have refused to bow to the idol, would have been cast into the furnace and saved. People would have then said that Chananyah, Mishael and Azaryah were saved not because of their own willingness to sacrifice their lives for God and His commandments, but because they were incidental beneficiaries of the miracle God wished to perform on behalf of Daniel.]

26. *Deuteronomy* 7:25. As the Gemara will cite shortly, Nebuchadnezzar worshiped Daniel as a deity. Therefore, Daniel was afraid [that when he would be cast into the fiery furnace upon refusing to bow before the idol, he would be consumed in the fiery furnace in keeping with the Scriptural declaration consigning pagan deities to the flames] (*Rashi*). Though Daniel would gladly have given his life to sanctify God's Name, the magnitude of the miracle would have been diminished in the eyes of the people if only Chananyah, Mishael and Azaryah had emerged unscathed and Daniel had been burned (see *Maharal*).

27. [Nebuchadnezzar knew that Daniel would refuse to bow before the idol, and that he would have no choice but to have Daniel cast into the furnace. And since he had worshiped Daniel as a deity, his pagan subjects would consider his casting of Daniel into the flames an act of the most fearful impiety — one does not destroy one's own god! To avoid this dilemma, he sent Daniel abroad.]

28. *Daniel* 2:46. The verse concludes: וּמִנְחָה וְנִיחֹחִין אֲמַר לְנַסָּכָה לֵהּ, *and with sacrifice and incense he wished to exalt him.* This indicates that Nebuchadnezzar worshiped Daniel as a god (see *Rashi* and *Ibn Ezra* ad loc.; cf. commentary of *R' Saadiah* ad loc.).

29. *Jeremiah* 29:21. After declaring that the prophets who foretell an imminent return of the Jews from Babylon prophesy falsely (ibid. v. 8 ff), God declares to the exiles through His prophet Jeremiah that the false prophets Achav ben Kolayah and Tzidkiahu ben Maaseyah will be delivered into the hands of Nebuchadnezzar, who will burn them in fire. This will be their punishment for committing adultery as well as for being false prophets (ibid. v. 23). The Gemara here elaborates on these incidents.

30. Ibid. v. 22. The execution of these two false prophets will be so striking that they will become a byword for misfortune; people will use their example when they utter a curse: "May God do unto you what He did unto Echav and Tzidkiahu!" [In this verse, the demeaning diminutive אֶחָב is used in place of his real name אַחְאָב (*Radak* ad loc.).]

31. *Maharal* suggests that Nebuchadnezzar never intended to burn them in fire, but simply to test whether they would be impervious to fire as Chananyah, Mishael, and Azaryah had been. The two false prophets died quickly in the flames, however, and Nebuchadnezzar immediately withdrew their bodies. Thus, their bodies were simply scorched like toasted grain, not thoroughly burned. See also *Toras Chaim* and *Ben Yehoyada.*

32. Ibid. v. 23.

גדולים צדיקים יותר ממלאכי השרת שנאמר א) ענה ואמר הא אנא חזי גוברין ארבעה שריין מהלכין בגו נורא וחבל לא איתי בהון ורויה די רביעאה דמה לבר אלהין אמר ר' תנחום בר חנילאי בשעה שיצאו חנניה מישאל ועזריה מכבשן האש באו כל אומות העולם וטפחו לשונאיהן של ישראל על פניהם אמרו להם יש לכם אלוה כזה ואתם משתחוים לצלם מיד פתחו ואמרו ב) לך ה' הצדקה ולנו בושת הפנים כיום הזה אמר ר' שמואל בר נחמני אמר ר' יונתן מאי דכתיב ג) אמרתי אעלה בתמר אוחזה בסנסניו אמרתי אעלה בתמר אלו ישראל ועכשיו לא עלה בידי אלא סנסן אחד של חנניה מישאל ועזריה (א) אמר רבי יוחנן מאי דכתיב ד) ראיתי הלילה והנה איש רוכב על סוס אדום והוא עומד בין ההדסים אשר במצולה [וגו'] מאי ראיתי הלילה ביקש הקב"ה להפוך את כל העולם כולו ללילה והנה איש רוכב (ב) אין איש אלא הקב"ה שנאמר ה) ה' איש מלחמה ה' שמו על סוס אדום ביקש הקב"ה להפוך את העולם כולו לדם כיון שנסתכל בחנניה מישאל ועזריה נתקררה דעתו שנאמר ד) והוא עומד בין ההדסים אשר במצולה ואין הדסים אלא צדיקים (ג) שנאמר ו) ויהי אומן את הדסה ואין מצולה אלא בבל שנאמר ז) האומר לצולה חרבי ונהרותיך אוביש מיד מלאים רוגז נעשים שרוקים ואדומים נעשו לבנים אמר רב פפא שמע מינה (ד) סוסיא חיורא מעלי לחלמא: ורבנן להיכא (אזול) [אזלו] אמר רב בעין [הרע] מתו ושמואל אמר ברוק טבעו ור' יוחנן אמר עלו לארץ ישראל ונשאו נשים והולידו בנים ובנות כתנאי ר' אליעזר אומר בעין [הרע] מתו ר' יהושע אומר ברוק טבעו וחכ"א עלו לא"י ונשאו נשים והולידו בנים ובנות שנאמר ח) שמע נא יהושע הכהן הגדול אתה ורעיך היושבים לפניך כי אנשי מופת המה איזו הם אנשים שנעשה להן מופת הוי אומר זה חנניה מישאל ועזריה ודניאל להיכן אזל אמר רב למיכרא נהרא רבא בטבריא ושמואל אמר לאתויי ביזרא דאספסתא ור' יוחנן אמר לאתויי חזירי דאלכסנדריא של מצרים איני (ה) והתניא ו) תודוס הרופא אמר אין פרה וחזירה יוצאה מאלכסנדריא של מצרים שאין חותכין האם שלה בשביל שלא תלד זוטרי אייתי בלא דעתייהו ת"ר שלשה היו באותה עצה הקב"ה ודניאל ונבוכדנצר הקב"ה אמר ניזיל דניאל מהכא דלא לימרו בזכותיה איתנצל ודניאל אמר איזיל מהכא דלא ליקיים בי ט) פסילי אלהיהם תשרפון באש ונבוכדנצר אמר יזיל דניאל מהכא דלא לימרו קלייה לאלהיה בנורא ומניין דסגיד ליה דכתיב י) באדין מלכא נבוכדנצר נפל על אנפוהי ולדניאל סגיד וגו': כ) כה אמר ה' צבאות אלהי ישראל אל אחאב בן קוליה ואל צדקיה בן מעשיה הנבאים לכם בשמי לשקר וגו' וכתיב ל) ולוקח מהם קללה לכל גלות יהודה אשר בבבל לאמר ישימך ה' כצדקיהו ז) וכאחאב אשר קלם מלך בבל באש אשר שרפם לא נאמר אלא אשר קלם אמר רבי יוחנן משום ר' שמעון בן יוחי מלמד שעשאן כקליות מ) יען אשר עשו נבלה בישראל וינאפו את נשי רעיהם מאי עבוד אזול לגבי ברתיה דנבוכדנצר אחאב אמר לה כה אמר ה' השמיעי אל צדקיה וצדקיה אמר כה אמר ה' השמיעי אל אחאב אזלה ואמרה ליה לאבוה אמר לה אלהיהם של אלו שונא זימה הוא כי אתו לגבך שדרינהו לגבאי כי אתו לגבה שדרתנהו לגבי אבוה אמר להו מאן אמר לכון אמרו הקדוש ברוך הוא והא חנניה מישאל ועזריה שאלתינהו ואמרו לי אסור אמרו ליה אנן נמי נביאי כוותייהו לדידהו לא אמר להו לדידן אמר לן אמר להו אנא בעינא דאיבדקינכו כי היכי דבדקתינהו לחנניה מישאל ועזריה אמרו ליה אינון (א) תלתא הוו ואנן תרין אמר להו בחרו לכון מאן דבעיתו בהדייכו אמרו יהושע כהן גדול סברי ליתי יהושע דנפיש זכותיה ומגנא עלן אחתיוהו שדינהו אינהו איקלו יהושע כהן גדול איחרוכי מאניה שנאמר נ) ויראני את יהושע הכהן הגדול עומד לפני מלאך ה' וגו' וכתיב ס) ויאמר ה' אל השטן יגער ה' בך וגו' א"ל ידענא דצדיקא את אלא מאי טעמא אהניא בך פורתא נורא חנניה מישאל ועזריה לא אהניא בהו כלל א"ל אינהו תלתא הוו ואנא חד א"ל והא אברהם יחיד הוה התם לא הוו רשעים בהדיה ולא אתיהיב רשותא לנורא הכא הוו רשעים בהדי ואתיהיב רשותא לנורא היינו דאמרי אינשי תרי אודי יבישי וחד רטיבא אוקדן יבישי לרטיבא מאי טעמא איענש אמר רב פפא שהיו בניו נושאין נשים שאינן הגונות לכהונה ולא מיחה בהן שנאמר ע) ויהושע היה לבוש בגדים צואים וכי דרכו של יהושע ללבוש בגדים צואים אלא מלמד שהיו בניו נושאים נשים שאינן הגונות לכהונה ולא מיחה בהן אמר רבי תנחום דרש בר קפרא בציפורי מאי דכתיב פ) שש השעורים האלה נתן לי מאי שש השעורים אילימא שש שעורים ממש וכי דרכו של בועז ליתן מתנה שש שעורים

אלא

רש"י

גדולים צדיקים יותר ממלאכי השרת. דברישא חשיב לתלתא צדיקי ומלאך לבסוף דכתיב ורויה די רביעאה דמי לבר אלהין: וטפחו לישראל על פניהם. שהשתחוו לצלם: אני אמרתי שכל התמר שלי הוא. שיהיו בהם צדיקים הרבה ולא עלתה בידי וכו' ישראל נמשלו לתמר כדאמרי' (סוכה דף מה:) מה תמר זה אין לו אלא לב אחד וכו': והנה איש רוכב על סוס אדום. בזכריה כתיב: כל העולם כולו ללילה. מפני שהשתחוו לצלם: והוא עומד. העמיד הקב"ה עצמו בזכות ההדסים שבמצולה: האומר לצולה חרבי. לבבל שיושבת במצולה: חרבי. לשון חרבו המים (בראשית ח): שרוקים. צבועים ואח"כ נעשו לבנים כשנסתכל בצדיקים נח מכעסו: סוסיא חיורא מעלי לחלמא. מדקאמר שאדום הוי רמז לקללה: ורבנן. חנניה מישאל ועזריה: להיכן אזלו. כשיצאו מן הכבשן דתו לא מדכר להו בכולהו כתובי: בעין הרע מתו. שהיו מסתכלים בהן על שהיו תמהין בהן: ברוק טבעו. באותו רוק שרקקו אומות העולם בישראל שאומרין אלוה כזה יש לכם והשתחויתם לצלם: הוי אומר זה חנניה מישאל ועזריה. אלמא חזרו לארץ אצל יהושע כהן גדול: ודניאל להיכן אזל. כשהושלכו חביריו לתוך כבשן האש שלא הושלך עמהם: למכרא נהרא רבא בטבריא. לחפור ולהוציא נהר בטבריא ל"א למכרא נהרא בטורא בהר: לאתויי בירי דאספסתא. להביא זרע של עשב שהוא מאכל בהמה שלחו נבוכדנצר הכי הוה קים להו: לאתויי חזירי ממצרים. שלחו כדי לגדלם לולדות שחזירי מצרים גדולים הם: והתניא אמר תודוס הרופא לחכמים שהיו אומרים ניטלה האם טרפה והא אין פרה וחזירה יוצאה ממצרים וכו' כדי שלא יהיו מצויין במקומות אחרים ואעפ"כ חיו: זוטרי אייתינהו. ולא העלו על לבם לפריה ורביה בעי והניחו להוציאן בלא חתוך האם: באותה עצה. שהלך משם דניאל: דלא ליקיים בי פסילי אלהיהם תשרפון באש. דנבוכדנצר עשאו אלוה כדכתיב ולדניאל הוה סגיד והוה ליה כפסילי אלהיהם שהמקרא הזה היה צוח עליהם לשורפן לכך היה מתירא: קליות. שבלים המהובהבין באש: השמיעי. השתמשי: תלתא. ונפישי זכותייהו: הלא זה אוד. מה אוד נחרך אף הוא נחרך: אהני. הועיל: אקדו. שרפו: מאי טעמא איענש. יהושע דאהני נורא למאניה דהאי דאהדר איהו לנבוכדנצר דקייה בעלמא דקייה: שש שעורים. שש גרעינים שעורים ממש: וכי דרכו של בועז ליתן שש שבלים. והא תנן (פאה פ"ח מ"ה) אין פוחתין לעני בגורן פחות מחצי קב שעורים:

אלא

מסורת הש"ס

א) [עי' בילקוט זכרי' ושם איתא מאמר זה קצת בנוסחא אחרינא], ב) [לקמן צו: סוטה מב: מח.], ג) [מגילה יג. ע"ש ועי' תוס' ברכות כו: ד"ה ואין שיחה כו'], ד) [עיין ברכות נו:], ה) [צ"ל והתנן], ו) לעיל לג. בכורות כח., ז) בקרא כתיב וכאחב.

הגהות הב"ח

(א) גמ' תלתא הוו ואנן תרין. נ"ב וקשה מיד הכא הוה ליה לאקשויי והא אברהם יחיד הוה כמו שהקשה בתר הכי ליהושע כ"ג:

ליקוטי רש"י

שריין מהלכין בגו נורא. מותרין מאסוריהן והולכים בתוך האש. וחבל לא איתי בהון. וחבלה לא יש בהם. ורויה די רביעאה. ותוארו של רביעי. דמה לבר אלהין. דומה למלאך שראיתי בהיותי עם סנחריב כשנשרפו אוכלוסיו שנאמר (ישעיה לז) ויך במחנה אשור ונבוכדנצר היה שם ונמלטו בתוך עשרה שנמלטו משם [דניאל ג, כה]. לך ה' הצדקה. כלומר משפטיך ופורענות שהבאת עלינו הדין והצדק עמך. ולנו בושת הפנים. כדי אנו להתבייש על המאורע לנו כי אנחנו גרמנו לעצמנו. כיום הזה. כאשר אנחנו רואים היום [שם ט, ז]. בסנסניו. סנסנים, ענפים [שה"ש ז, ט]. ה' איש מלחמה. בעל מלחמות כמו (רות א, ג) איש נעמי וכל איש ואישך מתורגמין בעל וכן (מ"א ב, ב) וחזקת והיית לאיש לגבור. ה' שמו. מלחמותיו לא בכלי זיין אלא בשמו הוא נלחם כמו שאמר דוד (ש"א יז, מה) ואנכי בא אליך בשם ה' צבאות. דבר אחר ה' שמו אף בשעה שהוא נלחם ונוקם מאויביו אוחז הוא במדתו לרחם על ברואיו ולזון את כל באי עולם ולא כמדת מלכי אדמה כשהוא עוסק במלחמה פונה עצמו מכל עסקים ואין בו כח לעשות זו וזו [שמות טו, ג]. בין ההדסים אשר במצולה. בין אילני הדסים דבבל [זכריה א, ח]. בין הצדיקים שגלו לבבל ושכינה משתעי קרא [מגילה יג.]. האומר לצולה חרבי. האומר לבבל התייבשי. ונהרותיך אוביש. לפי שהיא יושבת על נהרות מדמה הריגת אוכלוסיה ליובש נהרות [ישעיה מד, כז]. שרוקים. לא ידעתי מה צבע הוא ויונתן תרגם קוחין [זכריה שם]. אתה ורעיך. חנניה מישאל ועזריה היו. אנשי מופת. גברין כשרין למיעבד להון ניסין שאף להם נעשה נס [זכריה ג, ח]. ביזרא. הזרע [ב"מ עד:]. אין פרה וחזירה כו'. לפי שטובות הן ואין רוצין שיהיו מצויות במקומות אחרות וקא חזינן דמתקיימות [לעיל לג.]. מפני שפרות וחזירות שלהן מעולין מאד ומוכרין אותן ביוקר ורוצין שלא ילדו במלכות אחרת כדי שיהו צריכין להם וחותכין האם שלה ואינה מתה. האם שלה. רחם שלה [בכורות כח:]. אשר קלם. לשון קלוי באש (ויקרא ב) [ירמיה כט, כב]. יגער ה' בך השטן. יגער הקב"ה בך אתה השטן וחוזר ואומר ויגער ה' בך הוא הבוחר בירושלים שלא תכנס לפניו לקטרג על הצדיק הזה הלא ראוי הוא וזכה לכך שהוצל מאש השריפה [זכריה ג, ב]. נשים שאינן הגונות לכהונה. שהיו בניו נשואות נשים נכריות כמו שכ' בספר עזרא וימצא מבני הכהנים אשר הושיבו נשים נכריות מבני יהושע בן יהוצדק [שם, א]. לבוש בגדים צואים. כתרגומו הוו ליה בנין דנסבין להון נשין דלא כשרין לכהונתא והיה נענש הוא על שלא מיחה בידם [שם, ג].

תורה אור השלם

א) ענה ואמר הא אנה חזה גברין ארבעה שרין מהלכין בגוא נורא וחבל לא איתי בהון ורוה די רביעאה דמה לבר אלהין: [דניאל ג, כה]

ב) לך אדני הצדקה ולנו בשת הפנים כיום הזה לאיש יהודה וליושבי ירושלים ולכל ישראל הקרבים והרחקים בכל הארצות אשר הדחתם שם במעלם אשר מעלו בך: [דניאל ט, ז]

ג) אמרתי אעלה בתמר אחזה בסנסניו ויהיו נא שדיך כאשכלות הגפן וריח אפך כתפוחים: [שיר השירים ז, ט]

ד) ראיתי הלילה והנה איש רכב על סוס אדם והוא עמד בין ההדסים אשר במצלה ואחריו סוסים אדמים שרקים ולבנים: [זכריה א, ח]

ה) יי איש מלחמה יי שמו: [שמות טו, ג]

ו) ויהי אמן את הדסה היא אסתר בת דדו כי אין לה אב ואם והנערה יפת תאר וטובת מראה ובמות אביה ואמה לקחה מרדכי לו לבת: [אסתר ב, ז]

ז) האמר לצולה חרבי ונהרתיך אוביש: [ישעיה מד, כז]

ח) שמע נא יהושע הכהן הגדול אתה ורעיך הישבים לפניך כי אנשי מופת המה כי הנני מביא את עבדי צמח: [זכריה ג, ח]

ט) פסילי אלהיהם תשרפון באש לא תחמד כסף וזהב עליהם ולקחת לך פן תוקש בו כי תועבת יי אלהיך הוא: [דברים ז, כה]

י) באדין מלכא נבוכדנצר נפל על אנפוהי ולדניאל סגד ומנחה וניחחין אמר לנסכה לה: [דניאל ב, מו]

כ) כה אמר יי צבאות אלהי ישראל אל אחאב בן קוליה ואל צדקיהו בן מעשיה הנבאים לכם בשמי שקר הנני נתן אתם ביד נבוכדראצר מלך בבל והכם לעיניכם: [ירמיה כט, כא]

ל) ולקח מהם קללה לכל גלות יהודה אשר בבבל לאמר ישמך יי כצדקיהו וכאחב אשר קלם מלך בבל באש: [ירמיה כט, כב]

מ) יען אשר עשו נבלה בישראל וינאפו את נשי רעיהם וידברו דבר בשמי שקר אשר לוא צויתם ואנכי הוידע ועד נאם יי: [ירמיה כט, כג]

נ) ויראני את יהושע הכהן הגדול עמד לפני מלאך יי והשטן עמד על ימינו לשטנו: [זכריה ג, א]

ס) ויאמר יי אל השטן יגער יי בך השטן ויגער יי בך הבחר בירושלים הלוא זה אוד מצל מאש: [זכריה ג, ב]

ע) ויהושע היה לבש בגדים צואים ועמד לפני המלאך: [זכריה ג, ג]

פ) ותאמר שש השערים האלה נתן לי כי אמר אלי אל תבואי ריקם אל חמותך: [רות ג, יז]

[Achav and Tzidkiah] replied to him: אֲנַן נַמִּי נְבִיאֵי כְּוָותַיְיהוּ – **We, too, are prophets just like them;** לְדִידְהוּ לֹא אָמַר לְהוּ לְדִידָן אָמַר לָן – **to them [God] did not tell** it, but **to us He did tell** it. אָמַר לְהוּ – **[Nebuchadnezzar] said to them:** אֲנָא בָּעֵינָא דְּאִיבְדְּקִינְכוּ – **I wish to test you** to see if you are true prophets, כִּי הֵיכִי דִּבְדַקְתִּינְהוּ לַחֲנַנְיָה מִישָׁאֵל וַעֲזַרְיָה – **just as I tested Chananyah, Mishael, and Azaryah** by casting them into the fiery furnace. אָמְרוּ לֵיהּ – **[Achav and Tzidkiah] said to him:** אִינוּן תְּלָתָא הֲווּ וַאֲנַן תְּרֵין – The test you propose would not prove anything, because **they were three, while we are two,** and to be saved from the furnace requires the collective merit of three righteous people. אָמַר לְהוּ – **[Nebuchadnezzar] said to them:** בַּחֲרוּ לְכוֹן מַאן דְּבָעֵיתוּ בַּהֲדַיְיכוּ – Very well. **Choose for yourselves anyone you wish** to be cast in the furnace together **with you.** You will then have the collective merit of three! אָמְרוּ יְהוֹשֻׁעַ כֹּהֵן גָּדוֹל – **They said,** "We choose **Joshua the High Priest,**" סָבְרֵי לֵיתֵי יְהוֹשֻׁעַ דְּנַפִּישׁ זְכוּתֵיהּ וּמַגְנָא עֲלָן – **thinking: Let Joshua come** and join us, **for his merit is great and it will shield us** from the heat of the furnace. אַחְתִּיוּהוּ – **They brought [Joshua the High Priest] down**[33] שְׁדִינְהוּ – and **cast** all three of **them** into the furnace. אִינְהוּ אִיקְלוּ – **[Achav and Tzidkiah] were scorched** by the flames and died; יְהוֹשֻׁעַ כֹּהֵן גָּדוֹל אִיחֲרוּכֵי מָאנֵיהּ – and as for **Joshua the High Priest, his clothes were singed,** שֶׁנֶּאֱמַר ,,וַיַּרְאֵנִי אֶת־יְהוֹשֻׁעַ הַכֹּהֵן הַגָּדוֹל עֹמֵד לִפְנֵי מַלְאַךְ ה׳ וגו׳ ״ – **as it is stated:** ***And [the angel] showed me Joshua the High Priest standing before the angel of God,* etc.** *and the Accuser was standing by his right to accuse him.*[34] וּכְתִיב ,,וַיֹּאמֶר ה׳ אֶל־הַשָּׂטָן יִגְעַר ה׳ בְּךָ וגו׳ ״ הֲלוֹא זֶה אוּד מֻצָּל מֵאֵשׁ״ – **And it is written** in the next verse: ***And God said to the Accuser: May God rebuke you, O Accuser . . . is this one not a brand saved from the fire?***[35] אָמַר לֵיהּ – **[Nebuchadnezzar] said to [Joshua]:** יָדַעְנָא דְּצַדִּיקָא אַתְּ – **I know that you are a righteous person,** as you personally were not harmed by the flames. אֶלָּא מַאי טַעְמָא אַהֲנְיָא בָּךְ פּוּרְתָּא נוּרָא – **So why did the fire have a slight effect on you,** singeing your clothes, חֲנַנְיָה מִישָׁאֵל וַעֲזַרְיָה לֹא אַהֲנְיָא בְּהוּ כְּלָל – whereas in the case of **Chananyah, Mishael, and Azaryah, it had no effect on them whatsoever?** אָמַר לֵיהּ – **He replied to [Nebuchadnezzar]:** אִינְהוּ תְּלָתָא הֲווּ וַאֲנָא חַד – **They were three, whereas I was** only **one.** Their collective merit succeeded in making them totally impervious to the flames. אָמַר לֵיהּ – **[Nebuchadnezzar] said to him:** וְהָא אַבְרָהָם יָחִיד הֲוָה – **But Abraham was a lone** individual when Nimrod cast him into the furnace, yet he emerged with even his clothes unscathed by the fire.[36] הָתָם לֹא הֲווּ רְשָׁעִים בַּהֲדֵיהּ – Joshua answered: **There,** in the case of Abraham, **there were no wicked people with him** in the furnace, וְלֹא אִתְיְהִיב רְשׁוּתָא לְנוּרָא – **thus no permission was granted to the fire** by Heaven to have any effect whatsoever. הָכָא הֲווּ רְשָׁעִים בַּהֲדַי – **Here** in my case, however, **there were wicked people with me** in the furnace, וְאִתְיְהִיב רְשׁוּתָא לְנוּרָא – **thus permission was granted to the fire** by Heaven to have an effect and burn them. Once the flames were granted the power to consume, they were also able to singe my clothes. הַיְינוּ דְּאָמְרֵי אִינָשֵׁי – And **thus do people say:** תְּרֵי אוּדֵי יְבִישֵׁי וְחַד רְטִיבָא – If you have **two dry brands and one that is wet,** אוֹקְדָן יְבִישֵׁי לִרְטִיבָא – **the two dry ones will ignite the wet one.**

The Gemara inquires:

מַאי טַעְמָא אִיעֲנַשׁ – **Why was [Joshua] punished** in that his clothes were singed?[37]

The Gemara answers:

אָמַר רַב פָּפָּא – **Rav Pappa said:** שֶׁהָיוּ בָּנָיו נוֹשְׂאִין נָשִׁים שֶׁאֵינָן הֲגוּנוֹת לִכְהוּנָּה וְלֹא מִיחָה בָּהֶן – **Because his sons married women who were unfit for the Kehunah**[38] **and he did not protest against them,** שֶׁנֶּאֱמַר ,,וִיהוֹשֻׁעַ הָיָה לָבֻשׁ בְּגָדִים צוֹאִים״ – **as it is stated:** ***And Joshua was wearing soiled clothes.***[39] וְכִי דַּרְכּוֹ שֶׁל יְהוֹשֻׁעַ לִלְבּוֹשׁ בְּגָדִים צוֹאִים – **Now, was it the practice of Joshua,** who was the High Priest, **to wear soiled clothes?** Certainly not! אֶלָּא מְלַמֵּד שֶׁהָיוּ בָּנָיו נוֹשְׂאִים נָשִׁים שֶׁאֵינָן הֲגוּנוֹת לִכְהוּנָּה וְלֹא מִיחָה בָּהֶן – **Rather, this teaches that his sons married women who were unfit for the Kehunah, and he did not protest against them.**[40]

The Gemara presents a Scriptural exposition of Bar Kappara that relates, among other things, to Chananyah, Mishael, and Azaryah:

אָמַר רַבִּי תַּנְחוּם דָּרַשׁ בַּר קַפָּרָא בְּצִיפּוֹרִי – **R' Tanchum said: Bar Kappara expounded in Tzipori:** מַאי דִּכְתִיב ,,שֵׁשׁ־הַשְּׂעֹרִים הָאֵלֶּה נָתַן לִי״ – **What is** the meaning of **that which is written:** ***[Ruth] said: These six barleys did he give me?***[41] מַאי ,,שֵׁשׁ־הַשְּׂעֹרִים״ – Now, **what is** meant by ***six barleys?*** אִילֵימָא שֵׁשׁ שְׂעוֹרִים מַמָּשׁ – **If you say** it means **literally "six barleys,"** i.e. six kernels of barley – וְכִי דַּרְכּוֹ שֶׁל בּוֹעַז לִיתֵּן מַתָּנָה שֵׁשׁ שְׂעוֹרִים – **but was it the practice of** the wealthy **Boaz to give a present** as trifling as **six barleycorns?** Certainly not!

NOTES

33. [I.e. from Eretz Yisrael to Babylon.] The reading in *Ein Yaakov* is אַחְתִּיוּהּ, *they brought him down.*

34. *Zechariah* 3:1. In this prophetic vision, Zechariah was shown Joshua the High Priest about to be accused by Satan [because Joshua's sons had married unlawful wives – see *Rashi* ad loc., and note 40 below].

35. Ibid. v. 2. How dare you threaten to accuse the righteous Joshua, who is a "brand saved from the fire"!

Just as the outside of a firebrand is charred by the fire, so too were Joshua's clothes charred by the flames (*Rashi*).

36. Abraham was thrown into a fiery furnace by King Nimrod because he refused to worship idols. He emerged completely unscathed (see *Eruvin* 53a and *Bereishis Rabbah* 38:13).

37. Apparently, the Gemara knows that the reason Joshua gave Nebuchadnezzar was meant only to deflect the question, and not the true reason (*Rashi*). Alternatively, the reason Joshua gave Nebuchadnezzar was indeed the true one. And the Gemara here is not asking why Joshua's clothes were singed, but seeks rather to discover what accusation the Accuser sought to bring against him [see note 34] (*Iyun Yaakov*). See also *Maharsha.*

38. A Kohen may not marry a *zonah, chalalah,* or a divorcee (*Leviticus* 21:7; see *Shulchan Aruch, Even HaEzer* §6).

39. *Zechariah* 3:3. [This is the verse that follows God's rebuke of the Accuser (see above, note 35).]

40. Since the Kohanim are set apart from the rest of the nation by their special priestly vestments, a profaning of their priestly status is symbolized in the prophetic vision by "soiled" clothes (*Maharsha*). [And failure to protest against a sin is tantamount in a way to having personally committed it, as stated in Tractate *Shabbos* (56b) regarding King Solomon.] See also *Hagahos Yavetz.*

Indeed, it is recorded in *Ezra* 10:18 that the children of the Kohen "Yeshua ben Yotzadak" married "foreign women." This "Yeshua ben Yotzadak" is none other than Joshua the High Priest (see *Rashi* to *Zechariah* 3:1 [cf. *Haggai* 1:1]). [As explained in the Gemara here, "foreign women" refers to Jewish women who were "foreign" to the Kehunah. Or perhaps, it refers to foreign women who subsequently converted to Judaism, who – although full-fledged Jewesses – are not permitted to Kohanim.]

41. *Ruth* 3:17. At the threshing floor, where Ruth had gone to Boaz at her mother-in-law Naomi's behest, Boaz gave Ruth this present so that she not return emptyhanded to her mother-in-law.

גדולים צדיקים יותר ממלאכי השרת שנאמר א) ענה ואמר הא אנא חזי גוברין ארבעה שריין מהלכין בגו נורא וחבל לא איתי בהון ורויה די רביעאה דמה לבר אלהין אמר ר' תנחום בר חנילאי בשעה שיצאו חנניה מישאל ועזריה מכבשן האש באו כל אומות העולם וטפחו לשונאיהן של ישראל על פניהם אמרו להם יש לכם אלוה כזה ואתם משתחוים לצלם מיד פתחו ואמרו ב) לך ה' הצדקה ולנו בושת הפנים כיום הזה אמר ר' שמואל בר נחמני אמר ר' יונתן מאי דכתיב ג) אמרתי אעלה בתמר אוחזה בסנסניו אמרתי אעלה בתמר אלו ישראל ועכשיו לא עלה בידי אלא סנסן אחד של חנניה מישאל ועזריה (א) אמר רבי יוחנן מאי דכתיב ד) ראיתי הלילה והנה איש רוכב על סוס אדום והוא עומד בין ההדסים אשר במצולה [וגו'] מאי ראיתי הלילה ביקש הקב"ה להפוך את כל העולם כולו ללילה והנה איש רוכב ב) אין איש אלא הקב"ה שנאמר ה) ה' איש מלחמה ה' שמו על סוס אדום ביקש הקב"ה להפוך את העולם כולו לדם כיון שנסתכל בחנניה מישאל ועזריה נתקררה דעתו שנאמר ד) והוא עומד בין ההדסים אשר במצולה ואין הדסים אלא צדיקים ג) שנאמר ו) ויהי אומן את הדסה ואין מצולה אלא בבל שנאמר ז) האומר לצולה חרבי ונהרותיך אוביש מיד מלאים רוגז נעשים שרוקים ואדומים נעשו לבנים אמר רב פפא שמע מינה ד) סוסיא חיורא מעלי לחלמא: ורבנן להיכא (אזול) [אזלו] אמר רב בעין [הרע] מתו ושמואל אמר ברוק טבעו ור' יוחנן אמר עלו לארץ ישראל ונשאו נשים והולידו בנים ובנות כתנאי ר' אליעזר אומר בעין [הרע] מתו ר' יהושע אומר ברוק טבעו וחכ"א עלו לא"י ונשאו נשים והולידו בנים ובנות שנאמר ח) שמע נא יהושע הכהן הגדול אתה ורעיך היושבים לפניך כי אנשי מופת המה איזו הם אנשים שנעשה להן מופת הוי אומר זה חנניה מישאל ועזריה ודניאל להיכן אזל אמר רב למיכרא נהרא רבא בטבריא ושמואל אמר לאתויי ביזרא דאספסתא ור' יוחנן אמר לאתויי חזירי דאלכסנדריא של מצרים איני ה) והתניא ו) תודוס הרופא אמר אין פרה וחזירה יוצאה מאלכסנדריא של מצרים שאין חותכין האם שלה בשביל שלא תלד זוטרי אייתי בלא דעתייהו ת"ר שלשה היו באותה עצה הקב"ה ודניאל ונבוכדנצר הקב"ה אמר ניזיל דניאל מהכא דלא לימרו בזכותיה איתנצל ודניאל אמר איזיל מהכא דלא ליקיים בי ט) פסילי אלהיהם תשרפון באש ונבוכדנצר אמר יזיל דניאל מהכא דלא לימרו קלייה לאלהיה בנורא ומניין דסגיד ליה דכתיב י) באדין מלכא נבוכדנצר נפל על אנפוהי ולדניאל סגיד וגו': כ) כה אמר ה' צבאות אלהי ישראל אל אחאב בן קוליה ואל צדקיה בן מעשיה הנבאים לכם בשמי לשקר וגו' וכתיב ל) ולוקח מהם קללה לכל גלות יהודה אשר בבבל לאמר ישימך ה' כצדקיהו ז) וכאחאב אשר קלם מלך בבל באש אשר שרפם לא נאמר אלא אשר קלם אמר רבי יוחנן משום ר' שמעון בן יוחי מלמד שעשאן כקליות מ) יען אשר עשו נבלה בישראל וינאפו את נשי רעיהם מאי עבוד אזול לגבי ברתיה דנבוכדנצר אחאב אמר לה כה אמר ה' השמיעי אל צדקיה וצדקיה אמר כה אמר ה' השמיעי אל אחאב אזלה ואמרה ליה לאבוה אמר לה אלהיהם של אלו שונא זימה הוא כי אתו לגבך שדרינהו לגבאי כי אתו לגבה שדרתנהו לגבי אבוה אמר להו מאן אמר לכון אמרו הקדוש ברוך הוא והא חנניה מישאל ועזריה שאלתינהו ואמרו לי אסור אמרו ליה אנן נמי נביאי כוותייהו לדידהו לא אמר להו לדידן אמר לן אמר להו אנא בעינא דאיבדקינכו כי היכי דבדקתינהו לחנניה מישאל ועזריה אמרו ליה אינון (א) תלתא הוו ואנן תרין אמר להו בחרו לכון מאן דבעיתו בהדייכו אמרו יהושע כהן גדול סברי ליתי יהושע דנפיש זכותיה ומגנא עלן אחתיוהו שדינהו אינהו איקלו יהושע כהן גדול איחרוכי מאניה שנאמר נ) ויראני את יהושע הכהן הגדול עומד לפני מלאך ה' וגו' וכתיב ס) ויאמר ה' אל השטן יגער ה' בך וגו' א"ל ידענא דצדיקא את אלא מאי טעמא אהניא בך פורתא נורא חנניה מישאל ועזריה לא אהניא בהו כלל א"ל אינהו תלתא הוו ואנא חד א"ל והא אברהם יחיד הוה התם לא הוו רשעים בהדיה ולא אתיהיב רשותא לנורא הכא הוו רשעים בהדי ואתיהיב רשותא לנורא היינו דאמרי אינשי תרי אודי יבישי וחד רטיבא אוקדן יבישי לרטיבא מאי טעמא איענש אמר רב פפא שהיו בניו נושאין נשים שאינן הגונות לכהונה ולא מיחה בהן שנאמר ע) ויהושע היה לבוש בגדים צואים וכי דרכו של יהושע ללבוש בגדים צואים אלא מלמד שהיו בניו נושאים נשים שאינן הגונות לכהונה ולא מיחה בהן אמר רבי תנחום דרש בר קפרא בציפורי מאי דכתיב פ) שש השעורים האלה נתן לי מאי שש השעורים אילימא שש שעורים ממש וכי דרכו של בועז ליתן מתנה שש שעורים

אלא

רש"י

גדולים צדיקים יותר ממלאכי השרת. דברישא חשיב לתלתא צדיקי ומלאך לבסוף דכתיב ורויה די רביעאה דמי לבר אלהין: וטפחו לישראל על פניהם. שהשתחוו לצלם: אני אמרתי שכל התמר שלי הוא. שיהיו בהם צדיקים הרבה ולא עלתה בידי וכו' ישראל נמשלו לתמר כדאמרי' (סוכה דף מה:) מה תמר זה אין לו אלא לב אחד וכו': והנה איש רוכב על סוס אדום. בזכריה כתיב: כל העולם כולו ללילה. מפני שהשתחוו לצלם: והוא עומד. העמיד הקב"ה עצמו בזכות ההדסים שבמצולה: האומר לצולה חרבי. לבבל שיושבת במצולה: חרבי. לשון חרבו המים (בראשית ח): שרוקים. צבועים ואח"כ נעשו לבנים כשנסתכל בצדיקים נח מכעסו: סוסיא חיורא מעלי לחלמא. מדקאמר שאדום הוי רמז לקללה: ורבנן. חנניה מישאל ועזריה: להיכן אזלו. כשיצאו מן הכבשן דתו לא מדכר להו בכולהו כתובי: בעין הרע מתו. שהיו מסתכלים בהן על שהיו תמהין בהן: ברוק טבעו. באותו רוק שרקקו אומות העולם בישראל שאומרין אלוה כזה יש לכם והשתחויתם לצלם: הוי אומר זה חנניה מישאל ועזריה. אלמא חזרו לארץ אצל יהושע כהן גדול: ודניאל להיכן אזל. כשהושלכו חביריו לתוך כבשן האש שלא הושלך עמהם: למכרא נהרא רבא בטבריא. לחפור ולהוציא נהר בטבריא נ"א למכרא נהרא בטורא בהר: לאתויי ביזרי דאספסתא. להביא זרע של עשב שהוא מאכל בהמה שלחו נבוכדנצר הכי הוה קים להו: לאתויי חזירי ממצרים. שלחו כדי לגדלם לולדות שחזירי מצרים גדולים הם: והתניא אמר תודוס הרופא לחכמים שהיו אומרים ניטלה האם טרפה והא אין פרה וחזירה יוצאה ממצרים וכו' כדי שלא יהיו מצויין במקומות אחרים ואעפ"כ חיו: זוטרי אייתינהו. ולא העלו על לבם לפריה ורביה בעי והניחו להוציאן בלא חתוך האם: באותה עצה. שהלך משם דניאל: דלא לקיים בי פסילי אלהיהם תשרפון באש. דנבוכדנצר עשאו אלוה כדכתיב ולדניאל הוה סגיד והוה ליה כפסילי אלהיהם שהמקרא הזה היה צוות עליהם לשורפן לכך היה מתירא: קליות. שבלים המהובהבין באש: השמיעי. השתמשי: תלתא. ונפישי זכותייהו: הלא זה אוד. מה אוד נחרך אף הוא נחרך: אהני. הועיל: אקדו. שרפו: מאי טעמא איענוש. יהושע דאהני נורא למאניה דהאי דאהדר איהו לנבוכדנצר דחייה בעלמא דחייה: שש שעורים. שש גרעינים שעורים ממש: וכי דרכו של בועז ליתן שש שבלים. והא תנן (פאה פ"ח מ"ה) אין פוחתין לעני בגורן פחות מחצי קב שעורים:

אלא

מפני ספרות וחזירות שלהן מעולין מאד ומוכרין אותן ביוקר ורוצין שלא ילדו במלכות אחרת כדי שיהו צריכין להם ותותכין האם שלה ואינה מתה. האם שלה. רחם שלה [בכורות כח:]. אשר קלם. לשון קלוי באש (ויקרא ב) [ירמיה כט, כב]. יגער ה' בך השטן. יגער הקב"ה בך אתה השטן וחוזר ואומר ויגער ה' בך הוא הבוחר בירושלים שלא תכנס לפניו לקטרג על הצדיק הזה הלא ראוי הוא וזכה לכך שהוצל מאש השריפה [זכריה ג, ב]. נשים שאינן הגונות לכהונה. שהיו בניו נשואות נשים נכריות כמו שכ' בספר עזרא וימלא מבני הכהנים אשר הושיבו נשים נכריות מבני יהושע בן יהוצדק [שם, א]. לבוש בגדים צואים. כתרגומו הוו ליה בנין דנסבין להון נשין דלא כשרין לכהונתא והיה נענש הוא על שלא מיחה בידם [שם, ג].

מסורת הש"ס

א) [עי' בילקוט זכרי' ושם איתא מאמר זה קצת בנוסחא אחרינא], ב) [לקמן צו: סוטה מב: מח.], ג) [מגילה יג. ע"ש ועי' תוס' ברכות כו: ד"ה ואין שיחה כו'], ד) [עיין ברכות נו:], ה) [נ"ל והתנן], ו) לעיל לג. בכורות כח., ז) בקרא כתיב וכאחב.

הגהות הב"ח

(א) גמ' תלתא הוו ואנן תרין. נ"ב וקשה מיד הכא הוה ליה לאקשויי והא אברהם יחיד הוה כמו שהקשה בתר הכי ליהושע כ"ג:

ליקוטי רש"י

שריין מהלכין בגו נורא. מותרין מאסוריהן והולכים בתוך האש. וחבל לא איתי בהון. וחבלה לא יש בהם. ורויה די רביעאה. ותוארו של רביעי. דמה לבר אלהין. דומה למלאך שראיתי בהיותי עם סנחרב כשנשרפו אוכלוסיו שנאמר (ישעיה לז) ויך במחנה אשור ונבוכדנצר היה שם ונמלט בתוך עשרה שנמלטו מהם [דניאל ג, כה]. לך ה' הצדקה. כלומר משפטיך ופורענות שהבאת עלינו הדין והצדק עמך. ולנו בושת הפנים. כדי אנו להתבייש על המאורע לנו כי אנחנו גרמנו לעצמנו. כיום הזה. כאשר אנחנו רואים היום [שם ט, ז]. בסנסניו. סנסנים, ענפים [שה"ש ז, ט]. ה' איש מלחמה. בעל מלחמות כמו (רות א, ג) איש נעמי וכל איש ואישך מתורגמין בעל וכן (מ"א ב, ב) וחזקת והיית לאיש לגבור. ה' שמו. מלחמותיו לא בכלי זיין אלא בשמו הוא נלחם כמו שאמר דוד (ש"א יז, מה) ואנכי בא אליך בשם ה' צבאות. דבר אחר ה' שמו אף בשעה שהוא נלחם ונוקם מאויביו אוחז הוא במדתו לרחם על ברואיו ולזון את כל באי עולם ולא כמדת מלכי אדמה כשהוא עוסק במלחמה פונה עצמו מכל עסקים ואין בו כח לעשות זו וזו [שמות טו, ג]. בין ההדסים אשר במצולה. בין אילני הדסים דבבל [זכריה א, ח]. בין הצדיקים שגלו לבבל ושכינה משתעי קרא [מגילה יג.]. האומר לצולה חרבי. האומר לבבל התיבשי. ונהרותיך אוביש. לפי שהיא יושבת על נהרות מדמה הריגת אוכלוסיה ליובש נהרות [ישעיה מד, כז]. שרוקים. לא ידעתי מה צבע הוא ויונתן תרגם קוחין [זכריה שם]. אתה ורעיך. חנניה מישאל ועזריה היו. אנשי מופת. גברין כשרין למיעבד להון ניסין שאף להם נעשה נס [זכריה ג, ח]. ביזרא. הזרע [ב"מ עד:]. אין פרה וחזירה כו'. לפי שטובות הן ואין רוצין שיהיו מצויות במקומות אחרות וקא חזינן דמתקיימות [לעיל לג.]. נכריות כמו שכ' בספר עזרא

תורה אור השלם

א) עָנֵה וְאָמַר הָא אֲנָה חָזֵה גֻּבְרִין אַרְבְּעָה שְׁרַיִן מַהְלְכִין בְּגוֹא נוּרָא וַחֲבָל לָא אִיתַי בְּהוֹן וְרֵוֵהּ דִּי רְבִיעָאָה דָּמֵה לְבַר אֱלָהִין: [דניאל ג, כה]

ב) לְךָ אֲדֹנָי הַצְּדָקָה וְלָנוּ בֹּשֶׁת הַפָּנִים כַּיּוֹם הַזֶּה לְאִישׁ יְהוּדָה וּלְיוֹשְׁבֵי יְרוּשָׁלַיִם וּלְכָל יִשְׂרָאֵל הַקְּרֹבִים וְהָרְחֹקִים בְּכָל הָאֲרָצוֹת אֲשֶׁר הִדַּחְתָּם שָׁם בְּמַעֲלָם אֲשֶׁר מָעֲלוּ בָךְ: [דניאל ט, ז]

ג) אָמַרְתִּי אֶעֱלֶה בְתָמָר אֹחֲזָה בְּסַנְסִנָּיו וְיִהְיוּ נָא שָׁדַיִךְ כְּאֶשְׁכְּלוֹת הַגֶּפֶן וְרֵיחַ אַפֵּךְ כַּתַּפּוּחִים: [שיר השירים ז, ט]

ד) רָאִיתִי הַלַּיְלָה וְהִנֵּה אִישׁ רֹכֵב עַל סוּס אָדֹם וְהוּא עֹמֵד בֵּין הַהֲדַסִּים אֲשֶׁר בַּמְּצֻלָה וְאַחֲרָיו סוּסִים אֲדֻמִּים שְׂרֻקִּים וּלְבָנִים: [זכריה א, ח]

ה) יְיָ אִישׁ מִלְחָמָה יְיָ שְׁמוֹ: [שמות טו, ג]

ו) וַיְהִי אֹמֵן אֶת הֲדַסָּה הִיא אֶסְתֵּר בַּת דֹּדוֹ כִּי אֵין לָהּ אָב וָאֵם וְהַנַּעֲרָה יְפַת תֹּאַר וְטוֹבַת מַרְאֶה וּבְמוֹת אָבִיהָ וְאִמָּהּ לְקָחָהּ מָרְדֳּכַי לוֹ לְבַת: [אסתר ב, ז]

ז) הָאֹמֵר לַצּוּלָה חֳרָבִי וְנַהֲרֹתַיִךְ אוֹבִישׁ: [ישעיה מד, כז]

ח) שְׁמַע נָא יְהוֹשֻׁעַ הַכֹּהֵן הַגָּדוֹל אַתָּה וְרֵעֶיךָ הַיֹּשְׁבִים לְפָנֶיךָ כִּי אַנְשֵׁי מוֹפֵת הֵמָּה כִּי הִנְנִי מֵבִיא אֶת עַבְדִּי צֶמַח: [זכריה ג, ח]

ט) פְּסִילֵי אֱלֹהֵיהֶם תִּשְׂרְפוּן בָּאֵשׁ לֹא תַחְמֹד כֶּסֶף וְזָהָב עֲלֵיהֶם וְלָקַחְתָּ לָךְ פֶּן תִּוָּקֵשׁ בּוֹ כִּי תוֹעֲבַת יְיָ אֱלֹהֶיךָ הוּא: [דברים ז, כה]

י) בֵּאדַיִן מַלְכָּא נְבוּכַדְנֶצַּר נְפַל עַל אַנְפּוֹהִי וּלְדָנִיֵּאל סְגִד וּמִנְחָה וְנִיחֹחִין אֲמַר לְנַסָּכָה לֵהּ: [דניאל ב, מו]

כ) כֹּה אָמַר יְיָ צְבָאוֹת אֱלֹהֵי יִשְׂרָאֵל אֶל אַחְאָב בֶּן קוֹלָיָה וְאֶל צִדְקִיָּהוּ בֶן מַעֲשֵׂיָה הַנִּבְּאִים לָכֶם בִּשְׁמִי שָׁקֶר הִנְנִי נֹתֵן אֹתָם בְּיַד נְבוּכַדְרֶאצַּר מֶלֶךְ בָּבֶל וְהִכָּם לְעֵינֵיכֶם: [ירמיה כט, כא]

ל) וְלֻקַּח מֵהֶם קְלָלָה לְכֹל גָּלוּת יְהוּדָה אֲשֶׁר בְּבָבֶל לֵאמֹר יְשִׂמְךָ יְיָ כְּצִדְקִיָּהוּ וּכְאֶחָב אֲשֶׁר קָלָם מֶלֶךְ בָּבֶל בָּאֵשׁ: [ירמיה כט, כב]

מ) יַעַן אֲשֶׁר עָשׂוּ נְבָלָה בְּיִשְׂרָאֵל וַיְנַאֲפוּ אֶת נְשֵׁי רֵעֵיהֶם וַיְדַבְּרוּ דָבָר בִּשְׁמִי שֶׁקֶר אֲשֶׁר לוֹא צִוִּיתִם וְאָנֹכִי הַיּוֹדֵעַ וָעֵד נְאֻם יְיָ: [ירמיה כט, כג]

נ) וַיַּרְאֵנִי אֶת יְהוֹשֻׁעַ הַכֹּהֵן הַגָּדוֹל עֹמֵד לִפְנֵי מַלְאַךְ יְיָ וְהַשָּׂטָן עֹמֵד עַל יְמִינוֹ לְשִׂטְנוֹ: [זכריה ג, א]

ס) וַיֹּאמֶר יְיָ אֶל הַשָּׂטָן יִגְעַר יְיָ בְּךָ הַשָּׂטָן וְיִגְעַר יְיָ בְּךָ הַבֹּחֵר בִּירוּשָׁלָיִם הֲלוֹא זֶה אוּד מֻצָּל מֵאֵשׁ: [זכריה ג, ב]

ע) וִיהוֹשֻׁעַ הָיָה לָבֻשׁ בְּגָדִים צוֹאִים וְעֹמֵד לִפְנֵי הַמַּלְאָךְ: [זכריה ג, ג]

פ) וַתֹּאמֶר שֵׁשׁ הַשְּׂעֹרִים הָאֵלֶּה נָתַן לִי כִּי אָמַר אֵלַי אַל תָּבוֹאִי רֵיקָם אֶל חֲמוֹתֵךְ: [רות ג, יז]

אלא שש סאין וכי דרכה של אשה ליטול שש סאין אלא רמז [רמז] לה שעתידין ששה בנים לצאת ממנה שמתברכין בשש [שש] ברכות ואלו הן דוד ומשיח דניאל חנניה מישאל ועזריה דוד דכתיב א) ויען אחד מהנערים ויאמר הנה ראיתי בן לישי בית הלחמי יודע נגן וגבור חיל ואיש מלחמה ונבון דבר ואיש תואר וה' עמו [א] וגו' ואמר רב יהודה אמר רב כל הפסוק הזה לא אמרו דואג אלא בלשון הרע יודע נגן שיודע לישאל גבור שיודע להשיב איש מלחמה שיודע לישא וליתן במלחמתה של תורה א) (איש תואר שמראה פנים בהלכה ונבון דבר שמבין דבר מתוך דבר) וה' עמו שהלכה כמותו בכל מקום בכולהו אמר להו יהונתן בני כמוהו כיון דאמר ליה [וה' עמו] מילתא דבדידיה נמי לא הוה ביה חלש דעתיה ואיקניא ביה דבשאול כתיב ב) ובכל אשר יפנה ירשיע ובדוד כתיב ג) ובכל אשר יפנה יצליח מנלן דדואג הוה כתיב הכא א) ויען אחד מהנערים מיוחד שבנערים וכתיב התם ג) ושם איש מעבדי שאול ביום ההוא נעצר לפני ה' ושמו דואג האדומי אביר הרועים אשר לשאול משיח דכתיב ד) ונחה עליו רוח ה' רוח חכמה ובינה רוח עצה וגבורה רוח דעת ויראת ה' וגו' [ב] וכתיב ה) והריחו ביראת ה' אמר רבי אלכסנדרי מלמד שהטעינו מצות ויסורין כריחיים רבא אמר דמורח ודאין דכתיב ה) ולא למראה עיניו ישפוט ו) ושפט בצדק דלים והוכיח במישור לענוי ארץ בר כוזיבא מלך תרתין שנין ופלגא אמר להו לרבנן אנא משיח אמרו ליה במשיח כתיב דמורח ודאין נחזי אנן אי מורח ודאין כיון דחזיוהו דלא מורח ודאין קטלוהו דניאל חנניה מישאל ועזריה דכתיב בהו ז) אשר אין בהם כל מאום וטובי מראה ומשכילים בכל חכמה ויודעי דעת ומביני מדע ואשר כח בהם לעמוד בהיכל המלך וללמדם ספר ולשון כשדים מאי אשר אין בהם כל מום אמר רבי חמא (ג) בר חנניא) אפילו כריבדא דכוסילתא לא הוה בהו מאי ואשר כח בהם לעמוד בהיכל המלך אמר רבי חמא ברבי חנינא מלמד שהיו אונסין את עצמן מן השחוק ומן השיחה ומן השינה ומעמידין על עצמן בשעה שנצרכין לנקביהם מפני אימת מלכות ח) ויהיו בהם מבני יהודה דניאל חנניה מישאל ועזריה אמר רבי (ד) אליעזר) כולן מבני יהודה הם ורבי שמואל בר נחמני אמר דניאל מבני יהודה חנניה מישאל ועזריה משאר שבטים ט) ומבניך אשר יצאו ממך אשר תוליד יקחו והיו סריסים בהיכל מלך בבל מאי סריסים רב אמר סריסים ממש ורבי חנינא אמר שנסתרסה ע"ז בימיהם בשלמא למאן דאמר שנסתרסה ע"ז בימיהם היינו דכתיב י) וחבל לא איתי בהון אלא למאן דאמר סריסים ממש מאי וחבל לא איתי בהון חבלא דנורא והכתיב כ) וריח נור לא עדת בהן לא חבלא ולא ריחא בשלמא למאן דאמר שנסתרסה ע"ז בימיהם היינו דכתיב ל) כה אמר ה' לסריסים אשר ישמרו את שבתותי וגו' אלא למאן דאמר סריסים ממש משתעי קרא בגנותא דצדיקי הא והא הוה בהו בשלמא למאן דאמר סריסים ממש היינו דכתיב מ) בביתי ובחומותי יד ושם טוב מבנים ומבנות אלא למאן דאמר שנסתרסה ע"ז בימיהם מאי טוב מבנים ומבנות אמר רב נחמן בר יצחק מבנים שהיו להם כבר ומתו מאי מ) שם עולם אתן לו אשר לא יכרת אמר ר' תנחום דרש בר קפרא בצפורי זה ספר דניאל שנקרא על שמו מכדי כל מילי דעזרא נחמיה בן חכליה אמרינהו ונחמיה בן חכליה מ"ט לא איקרי סיפרא על שמיה אמר רבי ירמיה בר אבא מפני שהחזיק טובה לעצמו שנאמר נ) זכרה לי אלהי לטובה דוד נמי מימר אמר ס) זכרני ה' ברצון עמך פקדני בישועתך דוד רחמי הוא דקבעי רב יוסף אמר מפני שסיפר בגנותן של ראשונים שנאמר ע) והפחות הראשונים אשר לפני הכבידו על העם ויקחו מהם בלחם ויין אחר כסף שקלים ארבעים וגו' ואף על דניאל שגדול ממנו סיפר ומנלן דגדול ממנו דכתיב פ) וראיתי אני דניאל לבדי את המראה והאנשים אשר היו עמי לא ראו את המראה אבל חרדה גדולה נפלה עלידם ויברחו בהחבא [ג] והאנשים אשר היו עמי לא ראו את המראה ומאן נינהו אנשים אמר רבי ירמיה ואיתימא ר' חייא בר אבא זה חגי זכריה ומלאכי

אינהו

רש"י

אלא שש סאין. דשש קבין או שש לוגין ליכא למימר דלא מייתי בגורן מדה פחותה מסאה: ליטול שש סאין. ולישא משוי כזה: רמז לה. דשש גרעינין נתן לה לסימן ורמז שעתידין לצאת שש בנים ממנה: יודע נגן גבור חיל ואיש מלחמה ונבון דבר ואיש תאר וה' עמו. היינו שש ברכות: לא אמרן דואג. לקמן מפרש האחד מן הנערים היינו דואג: אלא בלשון הרע. שהיה מספר בשבחו של דוד כדי שיקנא בו שאול ויהרגהו: לישא וליתן במלחמתה של תורה. להתוכח בתלמוד: פנים בהלכה. שמביא ראיה לדבריו: דבדידיה נמי לא הוה. דשאול נמי לא הוה הלכה כמותו כדאמרינן בעירובין (דף נג.) דוד דגלי מסכתא כתיב ביה יראיך יראוני וישמחו שאול דלא גלי מסכתא כתיב ביה בכל אשר יפנה ירשיע: נעצר לפני ה'. ללמוד תורה הרבה: אביר הרועים אשר לשאול. אלמא ההוא מיוחד שבנערים דהיינו דואג דחזינן הכא דקרי אביר הרועים: ונחה עליו רוח ה'. איזה רוח רוח חכמה ובינה רוח עצה וגבורה רוח דעת ויראת ה' הרי ששה: ה"ג והריחו ביראת ה' א"ר אלכסנדריא שהטעינו במצות ויסורין כריחים והיינו והריחו לשון רחים ולא גרסינן וכתיב והריחו: רבא אמר. מאי והריחו דמורח ודאין שמריח באדם ושופט ויודע מי החייב שנאמר לא למראה עיניו ישפוט ולא למשמע אזניו יוכיח ואפילו הכי ושפט בצדק דלים כגון על ידי הרחה: בר כוזיבא. (עס) י) ממלכי הורדוס היה: אשר אין בהם כל מום וטובי מראה משכילים בכל חכמה יודעי דעת ומביני מדע ואשר כח בהם הרי ו': אפי' ריבדא דכוסילתא לא היתה בגופם. שלא היו צריכין להקזה. ריבדא פוניור"א בלעז כוסילתא שם כלי המקיז פלנמא"ל: מן השיחה. שלא היו מספרין בדברים בטלים כדי שלא יתגנו בפני המלך: כלם מבני יהודה. כדחשיב לעיל ששה בנים העתידים לצאת מרות וחשיב בהדייהו חנניה מישאל ועזריה: דניאל. לחוד קאי אבני יהודה אבל חנניה מישאל ועזריה לא ולית ליה הך דרשה דלעיל דשש שעורים: מבניך אשר יצאו ממעיך. בחזקיהו מלך יהודה כתיב: סריסים ממש. שסירסו לחנניה מישאל ועזריה שכן דרכן של מלכים לסרס את האדם כדי שלא ישא אשה ויהא פנוי לעבודת המלך ולית ליה הא דחכמים דאמרי לעיל שעלו לארץ ישראל ונשאו נשים והולידו בנים ובנות: ר' חנניה אומר. לא סרסם אלא להכי קרו ליה סריסים שנסתרסה ע"ז בימיהם שבימיהם נודע לכל שאין ממש בע"ז ופורענות שהיה נביא מתנבא לחזקיהו שיהיו גולים מארצם ויוליכם בהיכל מלך בבל ור' שמואל בר נחמני דאמר חנניה מישאל ועזריה משאר שבטים היו מוקים האי קרא בדניאל לחוד: מאי חבל לא איתי בהון. והלא חבלה היא זו שנסתרסו ומהאי קרא דלעיל ילדים אשר אין בהם כל מום לא מצי פריך דאיכא למימר בשעה שבאו לנבוכדנצר תמימים הוו וסרסן: חבל די נורא. לא איתי בהון אבל חבלת הגוף מיהא איכא ופריך לחבלא דנורא לא איצטריך דהא כתיב קרא וריח נור לא עדת בהון: ולא ריחא. עשן האש: הא והא היו. סריסים ממש ושנסתרסה ע"ז בימיהם: טוב מבנים ומבנות. מכלל דבנים לא הוו להו דסריסים היו: מאי טוב מבנים ומבנות. הכא לא מצי לתרוצי הא והא הוו דא"כ במאי פליגי: בנים שהיו להן כבר ומתו. דלא חיו בניהם ומיהו לא היו סריסים: אתן לו. להם לא נאמר אלא לו לאחד מהם והיינו ספר דניאל שנקרא על שמו והשתא קא פריך פירכא באפי נפשה אגב דאתי בידו ספר דניאל: מכדי וכו'. רוב דברים שבספר עזרא ונחמיה אמרם: דוד נמי מימר אמר. הכי כלומר מאי מחזיק טובה איכא: רב יוסף אמר. לאו אהכי איענש דהא דוד נמי אמר כי האי גוונא אלא לכך נענש שספר בגנותן של ראשונים: מאי נינהו. שהיו עמו חגי זכריה מלאכי וכיון שהם לא ראו והוא ראה אלמא גדול מהם הוה ומדאשכחן דדניאל הוה חשיב טפי מחגי זכריה ומלאכי דהוו נביאי שמע מינה דגדול הוה מנחמיה בן חכליה דלא הוה נביא ואפי' הכי ספר עליו דלא אפקיה מכלל גנות הראשונים. דניאל היה מבאי הגולה עם החרש והמסגר ונחמיה הוה מעולי הגולה זמן מרובה לאחר מיכן:

אינהו

תורה אור השלם

א) וַיַּעַן אֶחָד מֵהַנְּעָרִים וַיֹּאמֶר הִנֵּה רָאִיתִי בֵּן לְיִשַׁי בֵּית הַלַּחְמִי יֹדֵעַ נַגֵּן וְגִבּוֹר חַיִל וְאִישׁ מִלְחָמָה וּנְבוֹן דָּבָר וְאִישׁ תֹּאַר וַיְיָ עִמּוֹ: [שמואל א' טז, יח]

ב) וְשָׁאוּל לָכַד הַמְּלוּכָה עַל יִשְׂרָאֵל וַיִּלָּחֶם סָבִיב בְּכָל אֹיְבָיו בְּמוֹאָב וּבִבְנֵי עַמּוֹן וּבֶאֱדוֹם וּבְמַלְכֵי צוֹבָה וּבַפְּלִשְׁתִּים וּבְכֹל אֲשֶׁר יִפְנֶה יַרְשִׁיעַ: [שמואל א' יד, מז]

ג) וְשָׁם אִישׁ מֵעַבְדֵי שָׁאוּל בַּיּוֹם הַהוּא נֶעְצָר לִפְנֵי יְיָ וּשְׁמוֹ דֹּאֵג הָאֲדֹמִי אַבִּיר הָרֹעִים אֲשֶׁר לְשָׁאוּל: [שמואל א' כא, ח]

ד) וְנָחָה עָלָיו רוּחַ יְיָ רוּחַ חָכְמָה וּבִינָה רוּחַ עֵצָה וּגְבוּרָה רוּחַ דַּעַת וְיִרְאַת יְיָ: [ישעיה יא, ב]

ה) וַהֲרִיחוֹ בְּיִרְאַת יְיָ וְלֹא לְמַרְאֵה עֵינָיו יִשְׁפּוֹט וְלֹא לְמִשְׁמַע אָזְנָיו יוֹכִיחַ: [ישעיה יא, ג]

ו) וְשָׁפַט בְּצֶדֶק דַּלִּים וְהוֹכִיחַ בְּמִישׁוֹר לְעַנְוֵי אָרֶץ וְהִכָּה אֶרֶץ בְּשֵׁבֶט פִּיו וּבְרוּחַ שְׂפָתָיו יָמִית רָשָׁע: [ישעיה יא, ד]

ז) יְלָדִים אֲשֶׁר אֵין בָּהֶם כָּל מוּם וְטוֹבֵי מַרְאֶה וּמַשְׂכִּילִים בְּכָל חָכְמָה וְיֹדְעֵי דַעַת וּמְבִינֵי מַדָּע וַאֲשֶׁר כֹּחַ בָּהֶם לַעֲמֹד בְּהֵיכַל הַמֶּלֶךְ וּלְלַמְּדָם סֵפֶר וּלְשׁוֹן כַּשְׂדִּים: [דניאל א, ד]

ח) וַיְהִי בָהֶם מִבְּנֵי יְהוּדָה דָּנִיֵּאל חֲנַנְיָה מִישָׁאֵל וַעֲזַרְיָה: [דניאל א, ו]

ט) וּמִבָּנֶיךָ אֲשֶׁר יֵצְאוּ מִמְּךָ אֲשֶׁר תּוֹלִיד יִקָּחוּ וְהָיוּ סָרִיסִים בְּהֵיכַל מֶלֶךְ בָּבֶל: [ישעיה לט, ז]

י) עָנֵה וְאָמַר הָא אֲנָה חָזֵה גֻּבְרִין אַרְבְּעָה שְׁרַיִן מַהְלְכִין בְּגוֹא נוּרָא וַחֲבָל לָא אִיתַי בְּהוֹן וְרֵוֵהּ דִּי רְבִיעָאָה דָּמֵה לְבַר אֱלָהִין: [דניאל ג, כה]

כ) וּמִתְכַּנְּשִׁין אֲחַשְׁדַּרְפְּנַיָּא סִגְנַיָּא וּפַחֲוָתָא וְהַדָּבְרֵי מַלְכָּא חָזַיִן לְגֻבְרַיָּא אִלֵּךְ דִּי לָא שְׁלֵט נוּרָא בְּגֶשְׁמְהוֹן וּשְׂעַר רֵאשְׁהוֹן לָא הִתְחָרַךְ וְסָרְבָּלֵיהוֹן לָא שְׁנוֹ וְרֵיחַ נוּר לָא עֲדָת בְּהוֹן: [דניאל ג, כז]

ל) כִּי כֹה אָמַר יְיָ לַסָּרִיסִים אֲשֶׁר יִשְׁמְרוּ אֶת שַׁבְּתוֹתַי וּבָחֲרוּ בַּאֲשֶׁר חָפָצְתִּי וּמַחֲזִיקִים בִּבְרִיתִי: [ישעיה נו, ד]

מ) וְנָתַתִּי לָהֶם בְּבֵיתִי וּבְחוֹמֹתַי יָד וָשֵׁם טוֹב מִבָּנִים וּמִבָּנוֹת שֵׁם עוֹלָם אֶתֶּן לוֹ אֲשֶׁר לֹא יִכָּרֵת: [ישעיה נו, ה]

נ) זָכְרָה לִּי אֱלֹהַי לְטוֹבָה כֹּל אֲשֶׁר עָשִׂיתִי עַל הָעָם הַזֶּה: [נחמיה ה, יט]

ס) זָכְרֵנִי יְיָ בִּרְצוֹן עַמֶּךָ פָּקְדֵנִי בִּישׁוּעָתֶךָ: [תהלים קו, ד]

ע) וְהַפַּחוֹת הָרִאשֹׁנִים אֲשֶׁר לְפָנַי הִכְבִּידוּ עַל הָעָם וַיִּקְחוּ מֵהֶם בְּלֶחֶם וָיַיִן אַחַר כֶּסֶף שְׁקָלִים אַרְבָּעִים גַּם נַעֲרֵיהֶם שָׁלְטוּ עַל הָעָם וַאֲנִי לֹא עָשִׂיתִי כֵן מִפְּנֵי יִרְאַת אֱלֹהִים: [נחמיה ה, טו]

פ) וְרָאִיתִי אֲנִי דָנִיֵּאל לְבַדִּי אֶת הַמַּרְאָה וְהָאֲנָשִׁים אֲשֶׁר הָיוּ עִמִּי לֹא רָאוּ אֶת הַמַּרְאָה אֲבָל חֲרָדָה גְדֹלָה נָפְלָה עֲלֵיהֶם וַיִּבְרְחוּ בְּהֵחָבֵא: [דניאל י, ז]

מסורת הש"ס

א) [צ"ל ונבון דבר שמבין דבר מתוך דבר איש תואר שמראה פנים בהלכה כ"א בילקוט], ב) לא נמצא במקרא לשון זה ועי' רש"א בח"א [ואולי שצ"ל דבכל דרכיו משכיל פרש"י בשמואל א יח מצליח ודע דבילקוט ליתא להך דבשאול כתיב כו' ובדוד כתיב], ג) צ"ל בר' חנינא, ד) [צ"ל אלעזר], ה) מגילה ג., ו) צ"ל אחר מלכי הורדוס.

הגהות הגר"א

[א] גמ' עמו וגו'. נמחק תיבת וגו': [ב] שם וכתיב והריחו. נמחק תיבת וגו' וכתיב: [ג] שם והאנשים אשר היו עמי לא ראו את המראה. נמחק:

ליקוטי רש"י

וכי דרכה של אשה ליטול שש סאין. אי אפשר לומר שש סאין שאין דרכה של אשה לשאת כמשאוי זה אלא שש שעורים ממש [רות ג, טו]. אחד מהנערים. מיוחד שבהם דואג האדומי. לא אמרו דואג אלא בלשון הרע. כל עצמו נתכוון להכניס עין רעה של שאול בדוד שיתקנא בו [ש"א טז, יח]. דואג אביר הרועים וגדול שבתלמידים היה ונתקנא בדוד שראהו נבון דבר ואיש תואר ומראה פנים בהלכה כדכתיב (ש"א טז) הנה ראיתי בן לישי בית הלחמי וגו' ואמר באגדה דחלק סנהדרין (צג:) דכל הפסוק הזה דואג אמרו בלשון הרע [סוטה ט:]. דבדידיה נמי לא הוי. שאול גדול בתורה היה אלא שלא לימד לאחרים כדאמר' בעירובין (נג.) שאול לא גלי מסכתא להכי כתיב ביה בכל אשר יפנה ירשיע [גיטין נט.]. ירשיע. לא היה זוכה להורות כהלכה [עירובין נג:]. נעצר לפני ה'. עוצר עצמו לפני אהל מועד לעסוק בתורה. אביר הרועים. אב בית דין [ש"א כא, ח]. במישור. לשון נוח ורך [ישעיה יא, ד]. בר כוזיבא מלך. בכרך ביתר ומלך על ישראל שתי שנים ומחצה [יבמות עב.]. וללמדם ספר. מוסב על אשר כח בהם [דניאל א, ד]. ריבדא דכוסילתא. נקבי כלי האומן שבבשרו, פלימ"א [שבת קכט.]. כלי אומן המקיז בכתפים רידבא מכת הכלי ובלעז פיינדר"א [ע"ז כז.]. פולטוייר"א דפלמוא"ה בלע"ז. רידבא. ניקור. כוסילתא. כלי אומן מקיז [כתובות לט:]. רידבא. מכה. כוסילתא. כלי שמכה בו בלע"ז פליימא [מכות כא.]. ומבניך. הם חנניה מישאל ועזריה [ישעיה לט, ז]. וחבל לא איתי בהון. וחבלה לא יש בהם [דניאל ג, כה]. לא עדת בהן לא סרה לתוכ' [שם, כז]. ברצון עמך. בהרצותך לעמך [תהלים קו, ד]. הכבידו על העם. הכבידו מס על העם. ויקחו. והיו לוקחים מהם בשביל המס לחם ויין אחר נתינת ארבעים שקלים של כסף וכך היו רגילים בכל שנה [נחמיה ה, טו].

אֶלָּא שֵׁשׁ סְאִין – And if you say, **rather,** that it means he gave her **six** *se'ahs* of barley,[1] which is a sizable gift – וְכִי דַּרְכָּהּ שֶׁל אִשָּׁה לִיטּוֹל שֵׁשׁ סְאִין – **but is it the practice of a woman to carry** a burden as heavy as **six *se'ahs*** of grain? How did Boaz expect Ruth to carry that much barley back to her home?[2] אֶלָּא רֶמֶז [רָמַז] לָהּ – **Rather,** it indeed means that he gave her six barleycorns – not as an ordinary gift but for a symbolic purpose.[3] For **he was indicating to her** שֶׁעֲתִידִין שִׁשָּׁה בָנִים לָצֵאת מִמֶּנָּה שֶׁמִּתְבָּרְכִין בְּשֵׁשׁ [שֵׁשׁ] בְּרָכוֹת – **that six sons** [i.e. descendants] **were destined to descend from her who would each be blessed with six blessings.**[4] וְאֵלּוּ הֵן דָּוִד וּמָשִׁיחַ דָּנִיֵּאל חֲנַנְיָה מִישָׁאֵל וַעֲזַרְיָה – **And these** six descendants **were: David, and the Messiah, Daniel, Chananyah, Mishael, and Azaryah.**[5]

The Gemara shows how the six blessings of these six descendants are indicated in Scripture:

דָּוִד דִּכְתִיב ,,וַיַּעַן אֶחָד מֵהַנְּעָרִים וַיֹּאמֶר הִנֵּה רָאִיתִי בֵּן לְיִשַׁי בֵּית הַלַּחְמִי יֹדֵעַ נַגֵּן וְגִבּוֹר חַיִל וְאִישׁ מִלְחָמָה וּנְבוֹן דָּבָר וְאִישׁ תֹּאַר וה׳ עִמּוֹ (וגו׳)" – The six blessings of **David** are indicated in that **which is written:** ***And one of the retainers spoke up and said: "Behold I have seen a son of Jesse, the Bethlehemite, one who knows how to play [the harp], and one mighty in courage, and a warrior, and understanding in [all] matters, and a man of appealing looks; and Hashem is with him*** **(etc).**[6] Thus, David is described here as being blessed with six qualities. וְאָמַר רַב יְהוּדָה אָמַר רַב – **And Rav Yehudah said in the name of Rav:** כָּל הַפָּסוּק הַזֶּה לֹא אֲמָרוֹ דּוֹאֵג אֶלָּא בְּלָשׁוֹן הָרַע – **All** the praises of David mentioned in **this verse were said by Doeg only with an evil tongue.**[7] Rav explains what Doeg meant to intimate with each of his praises: ,,יֹדֵעַ נַגֵּן" שֶׁיּוֹדֵעַ לִישָּׁאֵל – David is ***one who knows how to play*** – he is one **who knows how to ask** incisive Torah inquiries.[8] ,,גִּבּוֹר" שֶׁיּוֹדֵעַ לְהָשִׁיב – ***Mighty*** – he is one **who knows how to answer** difficult Torah questions.[9] ,,אִישׁ מִלְחָמָה" שֶׁיּוֹדֵעַ לִישָּׂא וְלִיתֵּן בְּמִלְחַמְתָּהּ שֶׁל תּוֹרָה – ***A warrior*** – he is one **who knows how to** engage in the **give and take of Torah debate.** ,,אִישׁ תֹּאַר" שֶׁמַּרְאֶה פָּנִים בַּהֲלָכָה – ***A man of appealing looks*** – he is one **who displays** the appealing **face** of his opinions **in halachah,** i.e. his arguments are convincing. ,,וּנְבוֹן דָּבָר" שֶׁמֵּבִין דָּבָר מִתּוֹךְ דָּבָר – ***And understanding in [all] matters*** – he is one **who understands one matter from** his knowledge of **another,** i.e. he possesses keen deductive abilities.[10] ,,וַה׳ עִמּוֹ" שֶׁהֲלָכָה כְּמוֹתוֹ בְּכָל מָקוֹם – ***And Hashem is with him*** – this means **that the halachah accords with his opinion in every instance.**[11] בְּכוּלְּהוּ אָמַר לְהוּ יְהוֹנָתָן בְּנִי כָּמוֹהוּ – **In** response to **each** successive praise of David, Saul **said to them: My son Jonathan is** also **like him** in that regard. כֵּיוָן דְּאָמַר לֵיהּ [,,וַה׳ עִמּוֹ"] מִילְּתָא דִּבְדִידֵיהּ נַמִּי לָא הֲוָה בֵּיהּ – **Once,** however, **[Doeg] said to him *and Hashem is with him,*** i.e. the halachah always accords with his opinion – **a quality that he** [Saul], **too, did not have**[12] – חָלַשׁ דַּעְתֵּיהּ וְאִיקַּנְיָא בֵּיהּ – **[Saul] became disheartened and jealous of [David].** And how do we know that Saul did not possess this quality but David did? דִּבְשָׁאוּל כְּתִיב ,,וּבְכֹל אֲשֶׁר־יִפְנֶה יַרְשִׁיעַ" – **For concerning Saul it is written: *Wherever he would turn, he would condemn,***[13] וּבְדָוִד כְּתִיב ,,וּבְכֹל אֲשֶׁר יִפְנֶה יַצְלִיחַ" – **whereas concerning David it is written: *Wherever he would turn, he would succeed.***[14]

NOTES

1. [A *se'ah* is the volume of 144 eggs.] If the verse does not mean that he gave her six barleycorns, it must be that he gave her six *measures* of barley. This would refer, then, to six *se'ahs,* since the *se'ah* is the smallest measure used on the threshing floor (*Rashi*; cf. *Maharsha*).

2. If the load borne at one time by the average *man* is but five *se'ahs* [see *Rashi* to *Bava Metzia* 80b ד״ה קב לכתף], how could Ruth have carried six? (*Margaliyos HaYam*).

3. He indeed gave her six measures of barley as well (to be transported in several trips) as stated (*Ruth* 3:15): וַיָּמָד שֵׁשׁ־שְׂעֹרִים וַיָּשֶׁת עָלֶיהָ, *and he measured six barleys and placed [it] upon her.* The expression: *he measured* certainly cannot refer to *barleycorns,* which are simply counted, not measured [nor would the verse state that *he placed it upon her*]. The Gemara here means that in addition to the six *measures* of barley mentioned in the earlier verse, Boaz also gave her six barleycorns – all of which she had in hand upon returning to Naomi, as it states: *"these" six barleys did he give me.* [The second verse cannot refer to the same "six barleys" mentioned in the first verse, as she could not have had all six measures with her when she returned to Naomi] (see *Toras Chaim* and *Eitz Yosef*; see also *Maharsha*). [See, however, *Rashi* to *Ruth* 3:15, who in fact cites our Gemara's exposition of six *kernels* on that *first* mention of "six barleys."]

4. [The double portent of six (*six* sons and *six* blessings) is indicated by the two sixes given to her – six measures and six barleycorns; see preceding note (*Toras Chaim* and *Eitz Yosef*; cf. *Maharal*).]

5. David was a direct descendant of Ruth (*Ruth* 4:13-17) and the Messiah is a direct descendant of David (*Isaiah* 11:1; *Jeremiah* 23:5 ff). Regarding the descent from Ruth of Daniel, Chananyah, Mishael and Azaryah, see end of note 24 below.

6. *I Samuel* 16:18. God had withdrawn His Divine spirit from King Saul and replaced it with a spirit of depression. Saul therefore ordered his servants to seek a skilled harpist to stand in attendance, so that he might dispel the king's dark moods with music. One of Saul's retainers announced that he knew of a suitable candidate – David, son of Jesse – who, in addition to being a skilled musician, was blessed with the five other qualities enumerated in the verse.

7. [The Gemara below identifies "one of the retainers" in this verse as Doeg (*Rashi*).] Rav asserts that Doeg's lavish praise of David – though accurate – was not sincere, but was calculated to arouse Saul's jealousy, so that Saul would seek to destroy David. [Rav's following exposition shows how each of the six praises alludes to some special Torah quality. Thus, the six praises are truly six "blessings."]

8. Rav's exposition is prompted by the fact that Saul had accepted his servants' suggestion that *one who knows how to play on the harp* be sought (*I Samuel* 16:16), whereas Doeg responded that he knew of someone who simply "knows how to *play,*" curiously omitting the word "harp." Moreover, Doeg added accolades clearly having nothing to do with the musical talents sought by Saul (*one mighty in courage, and a warrior,* etc.). Accordingly, Rav understands that Doeg meant to allude to David's great prowess in Torah and thereby arouse Saul's jealousy (*Maharsha*).

9. These two abilities – to ask proper questions and to give proper answers – are essential for accomplishment in Torah (see *Avos* 6:6).

10. [In *Yalkut* (cited by *Mesoras HaShas*) the order of these last two expositions is inverted, thereby corresponding to the sequence of the verse.]

11. [He is the recipient of special Divine assistance, as evident from the fact that his views invariably become established as the accepted halachah.]

12. As taught in *Eruvin* (53a): "David illuminated treatises of law, [whereas] Saul did not illuminate treatises of law. In reference to David . . . it is written (*Psalms* 119:74): *Those who revere You shall see me and rejoice* [i.e. in the accuracy of my halachic rulings]. In reference to Saul it is written (*I Samuel* 14:47): *And wherever he would turn he would condemn* [i.e. his halachic rulings would be inaccurate – see Gemara below] (*Rashi*).

13. *I Samuel* 14:47. This verse describes Saul's successful military campaigns against Israel's enemies. Accordingly, the plain meaning is that he would condemn – i.e. defeat – his enemies. As expounded here, however, the verse alludes to Saul's failure to arrive at the correct halachah in his rulings. See *Radak* loc. cit.

14. *Maharsha* (see also *Rashash*) points out that there is no such verse in Scripture. *Mesoras HaShas* and *Eitz Yosef* suggest that the Gemara should read: וּבְדָוִד כְּתִיב ,,וַיְהִי דָוִד לְכָל־דְּרָכָו מַשְׂכִּיל וַה׳ עִמּוֹ", *whereas concerning David it is written: And David was successful in all his ways, and Hashem was with him* (*I Samuel* 18:14). [*Mesoras HaShas* points out that *Yalkut's* version of this Gemara entirely omits any citation of these last two verses (*Yalkut Shimoni* is a medieval compilation of various *aggados*). *Dikdukei Sofrim,* too, observes that these verses are not cited in the earliest prints of the Talmud and *Ein Yaakov,* and first appear in

אלא שש סאין וכי דרכה של אשה ליטול שש סאין אלא רמז [רמז] לה שעתידין ששה בנים לצאת ממנה שמתברכין בשש [שש] ברכות ואלו הן דוד ומשיח דניאל חנניה מישאל ועזריה דוד דכתיב א) ויען אחד מהנערים ויאמר הנה ראיתי בן לישי בית הלחמי יודע נגן וגבור חיל ואיש מלחמה ונבון דבר ואיש תואר וה' עמו [א] וגו' ואמר רב יהודה אמר רב כל הפסוק הזה לא אמרו דואג אלא בלשון הרע יודע נגן שיודע לישאל גבור שיודע להשיב איש מלחמה שיודע לישא וליתן במלחמתה של תורה א) (איש תואר שמראה פנים בהלכה ונבון דבר שמבין דבר מתוך דבר) וה' עמו שהלכה כמותו בכל מקום בכולהו אמר להו יהונתן בני כמוהו כיון דאמר ליה [וה' עמו] מילתא דבדידיה נמי לא הוה ביה חלש דעתיה ואיקניא ביה דבשאול כתיב ב) ובכל אשר יפנה ירשיע ובדוד כתיב ב) ובכל אשר יפנה יצליח מנלן דדואג הוה כתיב הכא א) ויען אחד מהנערים מיוחד שבנערים וכתיב התם ג) ושם איש מעבדי שאול ביום ההוא נעצר לפני ה' ושמו דואג האדומי אביר הרועים אשר לשאול משיח דכתיב ד) ונחה עליו רוח ה' רוח חכמה ובינה רוח עצה וגבורה רוח דעת ויראת ה' וגו' [ב] וכתיב ה) והריחו ביראת ה' אמר רבי אלכסנדרי מלמד שהטעינו מצות ויסורין כריחיים רבא אמר דמורח ודאין דכתיב ה) ולא למראה עיניו ישפוט ו) ושפט בצדק דלים והוכיח במישור לענוי ארץ בר כוזיבא מלך תרתין שנין ופלגא אמר להו לרבנן אנא משיח אמרו ליה במשיח כתיב דמורח ודאין נחזי אנן אי מורח ודאין כיון דחזיוהו דלא מורח ודאין קטלוהו דניאל חנניה מישאל ועזריה דכתיב בהו ז) אשר אין בהם כל מאום וטובי מראה ומשכילים בכל חכמה ויודעי דעת ומביני מדע ואשר כח בהם לעמוד בהיכל המלך וללמדם ספר ולשון כשדים מאי אשר אין בהם כל מום אמר רבי חמא (ג) בר חנניא) אפילו כריבדא דכוסילתא לא הוה בהו מאי ואשר כח בהם לעמוד בהיכל המלך אמר רבי חמא ברבי חנינא מלמד שהיו אונסין את עצמן מן השחוק ומן השינה ומן השיחה ומעמידין על עצמן בשעה שנצרכין לנקביהם מפני אימת מלכות ח) ויהיו בהם מבני יהודה דניאל חנניה מישאל ועזריה אמר רבי (ד) אליעזר) כולן מבני יהודה הם ורבי שמואל בר נחמני אמר דניאל מבני יהודה חנניה מישאל ועזריה משאר שבטים ט) ומבניך אשר יצאו ממך אשר תוליד יקחו והיו סריסים בהיכל מלך בבל מאי סריסים רב אמר סריסים ממש ורבי חנינא אמר שנסתרסה ע"ז בימיהם בשלמא למאן דאמר שנסתרסה ע"ז בימיהם היינו דכתיב י) וחבל לא איתי בהון אלא למאן דאמר סריסים ממש מאי וחבל לא איתי בהון חבלא דנורא והכתיב כ) וריח נור לא עדת בהן לא חבלא ולא ריחא בשלמא למאן דאמר שנסתרסה ע"ז בימיהם היינו דכתיב ל) כה אמר ה' לסריסים אשר ישמרו את שבתותי וגו' אלא למאן דאמר סריסים ממש משתעי קרא בגנותא דצדיקי הא והא הוה בהו בשלמא למאן דאמר סריסים ממש היינו דכתיב מ) בביתי ובחומותי יד ושם טוב מבנים ומבנות אלא למאן דאמר שנסתרסה ע"ז בימיהם מאי טוב מבנים ומבנות אמר רב נחמן בר יצחק מבנים שהיו להם כבר ומתו מאי מ) שם עולם אתן לו אשר לא יכרת אמר ר' תנחום דרש בר קפרא בצפורי זה ספר דניאל שנקרא על שמו מכדי כל מילי דעזרא נחמיה בן חכליה אמרינהו ונחמיה בן חכליה מ"ט לא איקרי סיפרא על שמיה אמר רבי ירמיה בר אבא מפני שהחזיק טובה לעצמו שנאמר נ) זכרה לי אלהי לטובה דוד נמי מימר אמר ס) זכרני ה' ברצון עמך פקדני בישועתך דוד רחמי הוא דקבעי רב יוסף אמר מפני שסיפר בגנותן של ראשונים שנאמר ע) והפחות הראשונים אשר לפני הכבידו על העם ויקחו מהם בלחם ויין אחר כסף שקלים ארבעים וגו' ואף על דניאל שגדול ממנו סיפר ומנלן דגדול ממנו דכתיב פ) וראיתי אני דניאל לבדי את המראה והאנשים אשר היו עמי לא ראו את המראה אבל חרדה גדולה נפלה עליהם ויברחו בהחבא [ג] והאנשים אשר היו עמי לא ראו את המראה ה) ומאן נינהו אנשים אמר רבי ירמיה ואיתימא ר' חייא בר אבא זה חגי זכריה ומלאכי

אינהו

רש"י

אלא שש סאין. דשש קבין או שש לוגין ליכא למימר דלא מייתי בגורן מדה פחותה מסאה: ליטול שש סאין. וליטא משוי כזה: רמז לה. דשש גרעינין נתן לה לסימן ורמז שעתידין לצאת שש בנים ממנה: יודע נגן גבור חיל ואיש מלחמה ונבון דבר ואיש תאר וה' עמו. היינו שש ברכות: לא אמרן דואג. לקמן מפרש האחד מן הנערים היינו דואג: אלא בלשון הרע. שהיה מספר בשבחו של דוד כדי שיקנא בו שאול ויהרגהו: לישא וליתן במלחמתה של תורה. להתווכח בתלמוד: פנים בהלכה. שמביא ראיה לדבריו: דבדידיה נמי לא הוה. דשאול נמי לא הוה הלכה כמותו כדאמרינן בעירובין (דף נג.) דוד דגלי מסכתא כתיב ביה יראיך יראוני וישמחו שאול דלא גלי מסכתא כתיב ביה בכל אשר יפנה ירשיע: נעצר לפני ה'. ללמוד תורה הרבה: אביר הרועים אשר לשאול. אלמא ההוא מיוחד שבנערים דהיינו דואג דחזינן הכא דקרי אביר הרועים: ונחה עליו רוח ה'. איזה רוח רוח חכמה ובינה רוח עצה וגבורה רוח דעת ויראת ה' הרי ששה: ה"ג והריחו ביראת ה' א"ר אלכסנדריא שהטעינו במצות ויסורין כריחים והיינו והריחו לשון רחים ולא גרסינן וכתיב והריחו: רבא אמר. מאי והריחו דמורח ודאין שמריח באדם ושופט ויודע מי החייב שנאמר לא למראה עיניו ישפוט ולא למשמע אזניו יוכיח ואפילו הכי ושפט בצדק דלים כגון על ידי הרחה: בר כוזיבא. (עם) ו) ממלכי הורדוס היה: אשר אין בהם כל מום וטובי מראה משכילים בכל חכמה יודעי דעת ומביני מדע ואשר כח בהם הרי ו': אפי' ריבדא דכוסילתא לא היתה בגופם. שלא היו צריכין להקזה. ריבדא פוניור"א בלעז כוסילתא שם כלי המקיז פלנמא"ל: מן השיחה. שלא היו מספרין בדברים בטלים כדי שלא יתגנו בפני המלך: כלם מבני יהודה. כדחשיב לעיל ששה בנים העתידים לצאת מרות וחשיב בהדייהו חנניה מישאל ועזריה: דניאל. לחוד קאי אבני יהודה אבל חנניה מישאל ועזריה לא ולית ליה הך דרשה דלעיל שש שעורים: מבניך אשר יצאו ממעיך. בחזקיהו מלך יהודה כתיב: סריסים ממש. שסירסו לחנניה מישאל ועזריה שכן דרכן של מלכים לסרס את האדם כדי שלא ישא אשה ויהא פנוי לעבודת המלך ולית ליה הא דחכמים דאמרי לעיל שעלו לארץ ישראל ונשאו נשים והולידו בנים ובנות: ר' חנניה אומר. לא סרסם אלא להכי קרו ליה סריסים שנסתרסה ע"ז בימיהם שבימיהם נודע לכל שאין ממש בע"ז ופורענות שהיה נביא מתנבא לחזקיהו שיהיו גולים מארצם ויוליכם בהיכל מלך בבל ור' שמואל בר נחמני דאמר חנניה מישאל ועזריה משאר שבטים היו מוקים האי קרא בדניאל לחוד: מאי חבל לא איתי בהון. והלא חבלה היא זו שנסתרסו ומהאי קרא דלעיל ילדים אשר אין בהם כל מום לא מצי פריך דאיכא למימר בשעה שבאו לנבוכדנצר תמימים הוו וסרסן: חבל די נורא. לא איתי בהון אבל חבלת הגוף מיהא איכא ופריך לחבלא דנורא לא איצטריך דהא כתיב קרא וריח נור לא עדת בהון: ולא ריחא. עשן האש: הא והא היו. סריסים ממש ושנסתרסה ע"ז בימיהם: טוב מבנים ומבנות. מכלל דבנים לא הוו להו דסריסים היו: מאי טוב מבנים ומבנות. הכא לא מצי לתרוצי הא והא הוו דא"כ במאי פליגי: בנים שהיו להן כבר ומתו. דלא חיו בניהם ומיהו לא היו סריסים: אתן לו. להם לא נאמר אלא לו לאחד מהם והיינו ספר דניאל שנקרא על שמו והשתא קא פריך פירכא באפי נפשה אגב דאתי בידו ספר דניאל: מכדי וכו'. רוב דברים שבספר עזרא ונחמיה אמרם: דוד נמי מימר אמר. הכי כלומר מאי מחזיק טובה איכא: רב יוסף אמר. לאו אהכי איענש דהא דוד נמי אמר כי האי גוונא אלא לכך נענש שספר בגנותן של ראשונים: מאי נינהו. שהיו עמו חגי זכריה מלאכי וכיון שהם לא ראו והוא ראה אלמא גדול מהם הוה ומדאשכחן דדניאל הוה חשיב טפי מחגי זכריה ומלאכי דהוו נביאי שמע מינה דגדול הוה מנחמיה בן חכליה דלא הוה נביא ואפי' הכי ספר עליו דלא אפקיה מכלל גנות הראשונים. דניאל היה מבאי הגולה עם החרש והמסגר ונחמיה הוה מעולי הגולה זמן מרובה לאחר מיכן:

אינהו

תורה אור השלם

א) ויען אחד מהנערים ויאמר הנה ראיתי בן לישי בית הלחמי ידע נגן וגבור חיל ואיש מלחמה ונבון דבר ואיש תאר וי' עמו: [שמואל א' טז, יח]

ב) ושאול לכד המלוכה על ישראל וילחם סביב בכל איביו במואב ובבני עמון ובאדום ובמלכי צובה ובפלשתים ובכל אשר יפנה ירשיע: [שמואל א' יד, מז]

ג) ושם איש מעבדי שאול ביום ההוא נעצר לפני י' ושמו דאג האדמי אביר הרעים אשר לשאול: [שמואל א' כא, ח]

ד) ונחה עליו רוח י' רוח חכמה ובינה רוח עצה וגבורה רוח דעת ויראת י': [ישעיה יא, ב]

ה) והריחו ביראת י' ולא למראה עיניו ישפוט ולא למשמע אזניו יוכיח: [ישעיה יא, ג]

ו) ושפט בצדק דלים והוכיח במישור לענוי ארץ והכה ארץ בשבט פיו וברוח שפתיו ימית רשע: [ישעיה יא, ד]

ז) ילדים אשר אין בהם כל מאום וטובי מראה ומשכילים בכל חכמה וידעי דעת ומביני מדע ואשר כח בהם לעמד בהיכל המלך וללמדם ספר ולשון כשדים: [דניאל א, ד]

ח) ויהי בהם מבני יהודה דניאל חנניה מישאל ועזריה: [דניאל א, ו]

ט) ומבניך אשר יצאו ממך אשר תוליד יקחו והיו סריסים בהיכל מלך בבל: [ישעיה לט, ז]

י) ענה ואמר הא אנה חזה גברין ארבעה שרין מהלכין בגוא נורא וחבל לא איתי בהון ורוה די רביעאה דמה לבר אלהין: [דניאל ג, כה]

כ) ומתכנשין אחשדרפניא סגניא ופחותא והדברי מלכא חזין לגבריא אלך די לא שלט נורא בגשמהון ושער ראשהון לא התחרך וסרבליהון לא שנו וריח נור לא עדת בהון: [דניאל ג, כז]

ל) כי כה אמר י' לסריסים אשר ישמרו את שבתותי ובחרו באשר חפצתי ומחזיקים בבריתי: [ישעיה נו, ד]

מ) ונתתי להם בביתי ובחומתי יד ושם טוב מבנים ומבנות שם עולם אתן לו אשר לא יכרת: [ישעיה נו, ה]

נ) זכרה לי אלהי לטובה כל אשר עשיתי על העם הזה: [נחמיה ה, יט]

ס) זכרני י' ברצון עמך פקדני בישועתך: [תהלים קו, ד]

ע) והפחות הראשנים אשר לפני הכבידו על העם ויקחו מהם בלחם ויין אחר כסף שקלים ארבעים גם נעריהם שלטו על העם ואני לא עשיתי כן מפני יראת אלהים: [נחמיה ה, טו]

פ) וראיתי אני דניאל לבדי את המראה והאנשים אשר היו עמי לא ראו את המראה אבל חרדה גדלה נפלה עליהם ויברחו בהחבא: [דניאל י, ז]

מסורת הש"ס

א) [צ"ל ונבון דבר שמבין דבר מתוך דבר איש תואר שמראה פנים בהלכה כ"א בילקוט], ב) לא נמצא במקרא לשון זה ועי' רש"א בח"א [ואולי שצ"ל לכל דרכיו משכיל פרש"י בשמואל א יח מלכים ודע דבילקוט ליתא להך דבשאול כתיב כו' ובדוד כתיב], ג) צ"ל בר' חנינא, ד) [צ"ל אלעזר], ה) מגילה ג., ו) צ"ל אחד מלכי הורדוס.

הגהות הגר"א

[א] גמ' עמו וגו'. נמחק תיבת וגו': [ב] שם וכתיב והריחו. נמחק תיבת וגו' וכתיב: [ג] שם והאנשים אשר היו עמי לא ראו את המראה. נמחק:

ליקוטי רש"י

וכי דרכה של אשה ליטול שש סאין. אי אפשר לומר שש סאין שאין דרכה של אשה לשאת כמשאוי זה אלא שש שעורים ממש [רות ג, טו]. אחד מהנערים. מיוחד שבהם דואג האדומי. לא אמרו דואג אלא בלשון הרע. כל עצמו נתכוון להכניס עין רעה של שאול בדוד שיתקנא בו [ש"א טז, יח]. דואג אביר הרועים וגדול שבתלמידים היה ונתקנא בדוד שראהו נבון דבר ואיש תואר ומראה פנים בהלכה כדכתיב (ש"א טז) הנה ראיתי בן לישי בית הלחמי וגו' ואמר באגדה דחלק סנהדרין (צג:) דכל הפסוק הזה דואג אמרו בלשון הרע [סוטה ט:]. דבדידיה נמי לא הוי. שאול גדול בתורה היה אלא שלא לימד לאחרים כדאמרי' בעירובין (נג.) שאול לא גלי מסכתא להכי כתיב ביה בכל אשר יפנה ירשיע [גיטין נט.]. ירשיע. לא היה זוכה להורות כהלכה [עירובין נג:]. נעצר לפני ה'. עוצר עצמו לפני אהל מועד לעסוק בתורה. אביר הרועים. אב בית דין [ש"א כא, ח]. במישור. לשון נוח ורך [ישעיה יא, ד]. בר כוזיבא מלך. בכרך ביתר ומלך על ישראל שתי שנים ומחצה [יבמות עב.]. וללמדם ספר. מוסב על אשר כח בהם [דניאל א, ד]. ריבדא דכוסילתא. נקבי כלי האומן שבבשרו, פלימ"א [שבת קכט.]. כלי אומן המקיז בכתפים ריבדא מכת הכלי ובלעז פיינדר"א [ע"ז כז.]. פולטוייר"א דפלמוא"ה בלע"ז. ריבדא. ניקור. כוסילתא. כלי אומן מקיז [כתובות לט:]. ריבדא. מכה. כוסילתא. כלי שמכה בו בלע"ז פליימא [מכות כא.]. ומבניך. הם חנניה מישאל ועזריה [ישעיה לט, ז]. וחבל לא איתי בהון. וחבלה לא יש בהם [דניאל ג, כה]. לא עדת בהן לא סרה לתוך' [שם, כז]. ברצון עמך. בהרצותך לעמך [תהלים קו, ד]. הכבידו על העם. הכבידו מס על העם. ויקחו. והיו לוקחים מהם בשביל המס לחם ויין אחר נתינת ארבעים שקלים של כסף וכך היו רגילים בכל שנה [נחמיה ה, טו].

The Gemara proves its earlier assertion that "one of the retainers" was Doeg:

מְנָלָן דְּדוֹאֵג הֲוָה – From where is it known **to us that it was Doeg** who praised David to Saul? **כְּתִיב הָכָא ,,וַיַּעַן אֶחָד מֵהַנְּעָרִים" – It is written here** in the verse cited above: ***And "one" of the retainers spoke up,*** **מְיוּחָד שֶׁבַּנְּעָרִים** – indicating **"the outstanding one" among the retainers, וּכְתִיב הָתָם ,,וְשָׁם אִישׁ מֵעַבְדֵי שָׁאוּל בַּיּוֹם הַהוּא נֶעְצָר לִפְנֵי ה׳ וּשְׁמוֹ דֹּאֵג הָאֲדֹמִי אַבִּיר הָרֹעִים אֲשֶׁר לְשָׁאוּל" – and it is written there** in another verse: ***And there [in Nov] was a man – one of Saul's servants – on that day, detained before HASHEM, and his name was Doeg the Edomite; the chief of Saul's shepherds.***[15]

The Gemara now shows how the six blessings of the second descendant of Ruth are indicated in Scripture:

מָשִׁיחַ דִּכְתִיב ,,וְנָחָה עָלָיו רוּחַ ה׳ רוּחַ חָכְמָה וּבִינָה רוּחַ עֵצָה וּגְבוּרָה רוּחַ דַּעַת וְיִרְאַת ה׳ (וגו׳)" – The six blessings of **the Messiah** are indicated in that **which is written: *And the spirit of HASHEM shall rest upon him – a spirit of wisdom and insight, a spirit of counsel and strength, a spirit of understanding and fear of HASHEM.***[16]

The Gemara digresses to expound on a verse in the passage just cited:[17]

(וכתיב) ,,וַהֲרִיחוֹ בְּיִרְאַת ה׳ " – The next verse reads: ***He shall be inspired*** (*vaharicho*) ***with the fear of HASHEM,***[18] **אָמַר רַבִּי אֲלֶכְּסַנְדְּרִי מְלַמֵּד שֶׁהִטְעִינוֹ מִצְוֹת וְיִסּוּרִין כָּרֵיחַיִם** – on which **R' Alexandri remarked: This teaches that [God] loaded [the Messiah] with commandments and suffering like a millstone** (*rechayim*).[19] **רָבָא אָמַר דְּמוֹרַח וְדָאִין – Rava says:** This means **that he "sniffs and judges,"** i.e. he can sense unerringly which of the litigants is the guilty party without having to actually weigh the evidence,[20] **דִּכְתִיב ,,וְלֹא־לְמַרְאֵה עֵינָיו יִשְׁפּוֹט . . . וְשָׁפַט בְּצֶדֶק דַּלִּים וְהוֹכִיחַ בְּמִישׁוֹר לְעַנְוֵי־אָרֶץ" – for it is written** in the very next words: ***and not by the sight of his eyes shall he judge*** *nor by the hearing of his ears shall he decide.* ***Yet he will judge the poor justly and decide with fairness for the humble of the land.***[21]

The Gemara relates how a false messiah was exposed because he did not possess this prophetic power:

בַּר כּוֹזִיבָא מָלַךְ תַּרְתֵּין שְׁנִין וּפַלְגָּא – Bar Koziva[22] **ruled two-and-a-half years. אָמַר לְהוּ לְרַבָּנָן אֲנָא מָשִׁיחַ – He declared to the Rabbis: I am the** awaited **Messiah! אָמְרוּ לֵיהּ – They said to him: בְּמָשִׁיחַ כְּתִיב דְּמוֹרַח וְדָאִין – Regarding the Messiah it is written that "he sniffs and judges." נֶחֱזֵי אֲנַן אִי מוֹרַח וְדָאִין – Let us see for ourselves whether he** [i.e. you] **can "sniff and judge"! כֵּיוָן דַּחֲזְיוּהוּ דְּלֹא מוֹרַח וְדָאִין קַטְלוּהוּ – Once they saw that he could not "sniff and judge,"** proving that his messianic claim was false, **they killed him.**[23]

The Gemara now shows how the six blessings of the other four descendants of Ruth are indicated in Scripture:

דָּנִיֵּאל חֲנַנְיָה מִישָׁאֵל וַעֲזַרְיָה דִּכְתִיב בְּהוּ ,,אֲשֶׁר אֵין־בָּהֶם כָּל־מאוּם וְטוֹבֵי מַרְאֶה – The six blessings of **Daniel, Chananyah, Mishael and Azaryah** are indicated in that **which is written** that Nebuchadnezzar ordered *Ashpenaz, the chief of his courtiers, to bring from the Children of Israel and from the royal seed and from the nobles: Youths* ***in whom there is no blemish, good-looking,*** **וּמַשְׂכִּלִים בְּכָל־חָכְמָה וְיֹדְעֵי דַעַת וּמְבִינֵי מַדָּע** – ***skillful in all wisdom, discriminating in knowledge, perceptive in learning,*** **וַאֲשֶׁר כֹּחַ בָּהֶם לַעֲמֹד בְּהֵיכַל הַמֶּלֶךְ וּלְלַמְּדָם סֵפֶר וּלְשׁוֹן כַּשְׂדִּים"** – ***and who have the stamina to stand in the king's palace; and to teach them the script and language of the Chaldeans.***[24]

NOTES

later editions. *Rashi's* citation of the Gemara in *Eruvin* (see note 12) to support our Gemara's contention would also indicate that his version of our Gemara did not contain any Scriptural support of its own.]

15. *I Samuel* 21:8. [The verse states that at that time (i.e. when David arrived in Nov, the site of the Sanctuary), Doeg was present – *detained before HASHEM,* i.e. he had detained himself there to occupy himself in Torah study (*Rashi* ad loc.).] We see from this verse, in which Doeg is described as "the chief of Saul's shepherds," that he was chief among Saul's men (*Rashi*). Thus, he is also "the outstanding one among the retainers" referred to in the earlier verse.

16. *Isaiah* 11:2, concerning the Messianic scion of David. The spirit of Hashem that will be conferred upon him is described here in six terms: the spirit of wisdom, insight, counsel, strength, understanding and fear of Hashem. Thus, the Messiah will be blessed with these six qualities (*Rashi*).

17. This follows *Rashi,* who deletes the word וּכְתִיב, *and it is written,* indicating that what follows is an independent exposition and not an integral component of the Gemara's preceding statement.

18. Ibid. v. 3.

19. An exposition based on the homophony of וַהֲרִיחוֹ, *vaharicho,* and רֵיחַיִם, *rechayim.* [The millstone is sometimes used as the metaphor for the heavy burden a person is forced to bear (see *Kiddushin* 29b).]

Maharsha explains the symbolism as follows: The Messiah will be loaded with mitzvos (in whose merit he will be chosen as Israel's redeemer), and with suffering (through which he will bear Israel's sins – see Gemara below, 98b and note 59 there). Just as the great exertion expended in turning the millstone produces the great benefit of flour, so too will the Messiah's great exertions produce for Israel the great benefit of the redemption.

Maharal (*Netzach Yisrael* ch. 32) explains that the Messiah's ability to unerringly sense the truth (see the exposition of Rava that follows) derives from the purification from material impediments he has achieved through mitzvos and suffering.

20. *Rashi.* Alternatively, we are to vowelize: שֶׁמְּרִיחַ וַדָּאִין, *that he sniffs certainties*; the general intent, however, is the same (*Yad Ramah*).

21. Ibid. vs. 3-4.

22. This was Shimon Bar Kochba, the Jewish king who revolted against Rome under Emperor Hadrian after the destruction of the Second Temple, and whom R' Akiva and other Sages supposed to be the Messiah (see *Yerushalmi, Taanis* 4:5 and *Rambam, Hilchos Melachim* 11:3; see also below, 97b note 24; see *Rashi* as emended by *Mesoras HaShas*; cf. *Yad Ramah*). [From *Yerushalmi Taanis* (loc. cit.) it appears that his real name was Bar Koziva, but he was called Bar Kochba because R' Akiva had applied to him the verse (*Numbers* 24:17, referring to the Messiah): *a star ("kochav") has issued from Jacob* (see *Seder HaDoros,* Year 3880).]

According to *Doros HaRishonim* (vol. 4 §621), the two-and-a-half years referred to here are the years Bar Kochba ruled in the city of Jerusalem he had liberated from Roman rule.

23. Why did Bar Koziva's false messianic claim make him liable to death? *Yad Ramah* suggests that since the messianic claim includes the ability to "sniff and judge," which is a form of prophetic power, one who lays false claim to such powers is a false prophet, who is liable to the death penalty [see *Deuteronomy* 18:20, and Gemara above, 89a].

From our Gemara, it would seem that the Jews put Bar Koziva to death. *Yerushalmi* (*Taanis* 4:5) and *Midrash Eichah* (2:4), however, indicate that the Romans killed him (see also *Rambam, Hil. Taaniyos* 5:3). *Radvaz* (to *Hil. Melachim* 11:3) explains that our Gemara might not mean that the Jews literally killed him. Rather, upon determining that he was not the real Messiah, the Jews deserted Bar Koziva, making him vulnerable to the Romans, who killed him. Alternatively, these *aggados* disagree regarding how Bar Koziva met his end. [*Yerushalmi* and *Midrash Eichah* (loc. cit.) attribute Bar Koziva's death to a Divine punishment for his striking of his uncle, R' Elazar HaModa'i, who died from the powerful blow.]

24. See *Daniel* 1:3-4. Ashpenaz was ordered to recruit Jewish youths endowed with six qualities (unblemished, good looking, wise, discriminating, perceptive, possessing stamina) and to teach them the Chaldean script and language (*Metzudos* ad loc.; *Rashi* there, however, explains that *to teach them the script and language of the Chaldeans* is a continuation of *and who have the stamina* – i.e. they have the ability to learn this new script and language). Verse 6 goes on to say that among these youths were Daniel, Chananyah, Mishael and Azaryah. Thus, we see

אלא שש סאין וכי דרכה של אשה ליטול שש סאין אלא רמז [רמז] לה שעתידין ששה בנים לצאת ממנה שמתברכין בשש [שש] ברכות ואלו הן דוד ומשיח דניאל חנניה מישאל ועזריה דוד דכתיב א) ויען אחד מהנערים ויאמר הנה ראיתי בן לישי בית הלחמי יודע נגן וגבור חיל ואיש מלחמה ונבון דבר ואיש תואר וה' עמו [א] וגו' ואמר רב יהודה אמר רב כל הפסוק הזה לא אמרו דואג אלא בלשון הרע יודע נגן שיודע לישאל גבור שיודע להשיב איש מלחמה שיודע לישא וליתן במלחמתה של תורה א) (איש תואר שמראה פנים בהלכה ונבון דבר שמבין דבר מתוך דבר) וה' עמו שהלכה כמותו בכל מקום בכולהו אמר להו יהונתן בני כמוהו כיון דאמר ליה [וה' עמו] מילתא דבדידיה נמי לא הוה ביה חלש דעתיה ואיקניא ביה דבשאול כתיב ב) ובכל אשר יפנה ירשיע ובדוד כתיב ב) ובכל אשר יפנה יצליח מנלן דדואג הוה כתיב הכא א) ויען אחד מהנערים מיוחד שבנערים וכתיב התם ג) ושם איש מעבדי שאול ביום ההוא נעצר לפני ה' ושמו דואג האדומי אביר הרועים אשר לשאול משיח דכתיב ד) ונחה עליו רוח ה' רוח חכמה ובינה רוח עצה וגבורה רוח דעת ויראת ה' וגו' [ב] וכתיב ה) והריחו ביראת ה' אמר רבי אלכסנדרי מלמד שהטעינו מצות ויסורין כריחיים רבא אמר דמורח ודאין דכתיב ה) ולא למראה עיניו ישפוט ו) ושפט בצדק דלים והוכיח במישור לענוי ארץ בר כוזיבא מלך תרתין שנין ופלגא אמר להו לרבנן אנא משיח אמרו ליה במשיח כתיב דמורח ודאין נחזי אנן אי מורח ודאין כיון דחזיוהו דלא מורח ודאין קטלוהו דניאל חנניה מישאל ועזריה דכתיב בהו ז) אשר אין בהם כל מאום וטובי מראה ומשכילים בכל חכמה ויודעי דעת ומביני מדע ואשר כח בהם לעמוד בהיכל המלך וללמדם ספר ולשון כשדים מאי אשר אין בהם כל מום אמר רבי חמא (ג) בר חנניא) אפילו כריבדא דכוסילתא לא הוה בהו מאי ואשר כח בהם לעמוד בהיכל המלך אמר רבי חמא ברבי חנינא מלמד שהיו אונסין את עצמן מן השחוק ומן השינה ומן השיחה ומעמידין על עצמן בשעה שנצרכין לנקביהם מפני אימת מלכות ח) ויהיו בהם מבני יהודה דניאל חנניה מישאל ועזריה אמר רבי (ד) אליעזר) כולן מבני יהודה הם ורבי שמואל בר נחמני אמר דניאל מבני יהודה חנניה מישאל ועזריה משאר שבטים ט) ומבניך אשר יצאו ממך אשר תוליד יקחו והיו סריסים בהיכל מלך בבל מאי סריסים רב אמר סריסים ממש ורבי חנינא אמר שנסתרסה ע"ז בימיהם בשלמא למאן דאמר שנסתרסה ע"ז בימיהם היינו דכתיב י) וחבל לא איתי בהון אלא למאן דאמר סריסים ממש מאי וחבל לא איתי בהון חבלא דנורא והכתיב כ) וריח נור לא עדת בהן לא חבלא ולא ריחא בשלמא למאן דאמר שנסתרסה ע"ז בימיהם היינו דכתיב ל) כה אמר ה' לסריסים אשר ישמרו את שבתותי וגו' אלא למאן דאמר סריסים ממש משתעי קרא בגנותא דצדיקי הא והא הוה בהו בשלמא למאן דאמר סריסים ממש היינו דכתיב מ) בביתי ובחומותי יד ושם טוב מבנים ומבנות אלא למאן דאמר שנסתרסה ע"ז בימיהם מאי טוב מבנים ומבנות אמר רב נחמן בר יצחק מבנים שהיו להם כבר ומתו מאי מ) שם עולם אתן לו אשר לא יכרת אמר ר' תנחום דרש בר קפרא בצפורי זה ספר דניאל שנקרא על שמו מכדי כל מילי דעזרא נחמיה בן חכליה אמרינהו ונחמיה בן חכליה מ"ט לא איקרי סיפרא על שמיה אמר רבי ירמיה בר אבא מפני שהחזיק טובה לעצמו שנאמר נ) זכרה לי אלהי לטובה דוד נמי מימר אמר ס) זכרני ה' ברצון עמך פקדני בישועתך דוד רחמי הוא דקבעי רב יוסף אמר מפני שסיפר בגנותן של ראשונים שנאמר ע) והפחות הראשונים אשר לפני הכבידו על העם ויקחו מהם בלחם ויין אחד כסף שקלים ארבעים וגו' ואף על דניאל שגדול ממנו סיפר ומנלן דגדול ממנו דכתיב פ) וראיתי אני דניאל לבדי את המראה והאנשים אשר היו עמי לא ראו את המראה אבל חרדה גדולה נפלה עליהם ויברחו בהחבא [ג] והאנשים אשר היו עמי לא ראו את המראה ו) ומאן נינהו אנשים אמר רבי ירמיה ואיתימא ר' חייא בר אבא זה חגי זכריה ומלאכי

אינהו

אלא שש סאין. דשש קבין או שש לוגין ליכא למימר דלא מייתי בגורן מדה פחותה מסאה: ליטול שש סאין. ולישא משוי כזה: רמז לה. דשש גרעינין נתן לה לסימן ורמז שעתידין לצאת שש בנים ממנה: יודע נגן גבור חיל ואיש מלחמה ונבון דבר ואיש תאר וה' עמו. היינו שש ברכות: לא אמרן דואג. לקמן מפרש האחד מן הנערים היינו דואג: אלא בלשון הרע. שהיה מספר בשבחו של דוד כדי שיקנא בו שאול ויהרגהו: לישא וליתן במלחמתה של תורה. להתוכח בתלמוד: פנים בהלכה. שמביא ראיה לדבריו: דבדידיה נמי לא הוה. דשאול נמי לא הוה הלכה כמותו כדאמרינן בעירובין (דף נג.) דוד דגלי מסכתא כתיב ביה יראיך יראוני וישמחו שאול דלא גלי מסכתא כתיב ביה בכל אשר יפנה ירשיע: נעצר לפני ה'. ללמוד תורה הרבה: אביר הרועים אשר לשאול. אלמא ההוא מיוחד שבנערים דהיינו דואג דחזינן הכא דקרי אביר הרועים: ונחה עליו רוח ה'. איזה רוח רוח חכמה ובינה רוח עצה וגבורה רוח דעת ויראת ה' הרי ששה: ה"ג והריחו ביראת ה' א"ר אלכסנדריא שהטעינו במצות ויסורין כריחים והיינו והריחו לשון רחים ולא גרסינן וכתיב והריחו: רבא אמר. מאי והריחו דמורח ודאין שמריח באדם ושופט ויודע מי החייב שנאמר לא למראה עיניו ישפוט ולא למשמע אזניו יוכיח ואפילו הכי ושפט בצדק דלים כגון על ידי הרחה: בר כוזיבא. (עס) ו) ממלכי הורדוס היה: אשר אין בהם כל מום וטובי מראה משכילים בכל חכמה יודעי דעת ומביני מדע ואשר כח בהם הרי ו': אפי' ריבדא דכוסילתא לא היתה בגופם. שלא היו צריכין להקיזה. ריבדא פוניור"א בלעז כוסילתא שם כלי המקיז פלנמא"ל: מן השיחה. שלא היו מספרין בדברים בטלים כדי שלא יתגנו בפני המלך: כלם מבני יהודה. כדחשיב לעיל ששה בנים העתידים לצאת מרות וחשיב בהדייהו חנניה מישאל ועזריה: דניאל. לחוד קאי אבני יהודה אבל חנניה מישאל ועזריה לא ולית ליה הך דרשה דלעיל גבי שש שעורים: מבניך אשר יצאו ממעיך. בחזקיהו מלך יהודה כתיב:

סריסים ממש. שסירסו לחנניה מישאל ועזריה שכן דרכן של מלכים לסרס את האדם כדי שלא ישא אשה ויהא פנוי לעבודת המלך ולית ליה הא דחכמים דאמרי לעיל שעלו לארץ ישראל ונשאו נשים והולידו בנים ובנות: ר' חנניה אומר. לא סרסם אלא להכי קרו ליה סריסים שנסתרסה ע"ז בימיהם שבימיהם נודע לכל שאין ממש בע"ז ופורענות שהיה נביא מתנבא לחזקיהו שיהיו גולים מארצם ויוליכם בהיכל מלך בבל ור' שמואל בר נחמני דאמר חנניה מישאל ועזריה משאר שבטים היו מוקים האי קרא בדניאל לחוד: מאי חבל לא איתי בהון. והלא חבלה היא זו שנסתרסו ומהאי קרא דלעיל ילדים אשר אין בהם כל מום לא מצי פריך דאיכא למימר בשעה שבאו לנבוכדנצר תמימים הוו וסרסן: חבל די נורא. לא איתי בהון אבל חבלת הגוף מיהא איכא ופריך לחבלא דנורא לא איצטריך דהא כתיב קרא וריח נור לא עדת בהון: ולא ריחא. עשן האש: הא והא היו. סריסים ממש ושנסתרסה ע"ז בימיהם: טוב מבנים ומבנות. מכלל דבנים לא הוו להו דסריסים היו: מאי טוב מבנים ומבנות. הכא לא מצי לתרוצי הא והא הוו דא"כ במאי פליגי: בנים שהיו להן כבר ומתו. דלא חיו בניהם ומיהו לא היו סריסים: אתן לו. להם לא נאמר אלא לו לאחד מהם והיינו ספר דניאל שנקרא על שמו והשתא קא פריך פירכא באפי נפשה אגב דאתי בידו ספר דניאל: מכדי וכו'. רוב דברים שבספר עזרא ונחמיה אמרם: דוד נמי מימר אמר. הכי כלומר מאי מחזיק טובה איכא: רב יוסף אמר. לאו אהכי איענש דהא דוד נמי אמר כי האי גוונא אלא לכך נענש שספר בגנותן של ראשונים: מאי נינהו. שהיו עמו חגי זכריה מלאכי וכיון שהם לא ראו והוא ראה אלמא גדול מהם הוה ומדאשכחן דדניאל הוה חשיב טפי מחגי זכריה ומלאכי דהוו נביאי שמע מינה דגדול הוה מנחמיה בן חכליה דלא הוה נביא ואפי' הכי ספר עליו דלא אפקיה מכלל גנות הראשונים. דניאל היה מבאי הגולה עם החרש והמסגר ונחמיה הוה מעולי הגולה זמן מרובה לאחר מיכן:

אינהו

תורה אור השלם

א) וַיַּעַן אֶחָד מֵהַנְּעָרִים וַיֹּאמֶר הִנֵּה רָאִיתִי בֵּן לְיִשַׁי בֵּית הַלַּחְמִי יֹדֵעַ נַגֵּן וְגִבּוֹר חַיִל וְאִישׁ מִלְחָמָה וּנְבוֹן דָּבָר וְאִישׁ תֹּאַר וַיְיָ עִמּוֹ: [שמואל א' טז, יח]

ב) וְשָׁאוּל לָכַד הַמְּלוּכָה עַל יִשְׂרָאֵל וַיִּלָּחֶם סָבִיב בְּכָל אֹיְבָיו בְּמוֹאָב וּבִבְנֵי עַמּוֹן וּבֶאֱדוֹם וּבְמַלְכֵי צוֹבָה וּבַפְּלִשְׁתִּים וּבְכֹל אֲשֶׁר יִפְנֶה יַרְשִׁיעַ: [שמואל א' יד, מז]

ג) וְשָׁם אִישׁ מֵעַבְדֵי שָׁאוּל בַּיּוֹם הַהוּא נֶעְצָר לִפְנֵי יְיָ וּשְׁמוֹ דֹּאֵג הָאֲדֹמִי אַבִּיר הָרֹעִים אֲשֶׁר לְשָׁאוּל: [שמואל א' כא, ח]

ד) וְנָחָה עָלָיו רוּחַ יְיָ רוּחַ חָכְמָה וּבִינָה רוּחַ עֵצָה וּגְבוּרָה רוּחַ דַּעַת וְיִרְאַת יְיָ: [ישעיה יא, ב]

ה) וַהֲרִיחוֹ בְּיִרְאַת יְיָ וְלֹא לְמַרְאֵה עֵינָיו יִשְׁפּוֹט וְלֹא לְמִשְׁמַע אָזְנָיו יוֹכִיחַ: [ישעיה יא, ג]

ו) וְשָׁפַט בְּצֶדֶק דַּלִּים וְהוֹכִיחַ בְּמִישׁוֹר לְעַנְוֵי אָרֶץ וְהִכָּה אֶרֶץ בְּשֵׁבֶט פִּיו וּבְרוּחַ שְׂפָתָיו יָמִית רָשָׁע: [ישעיה יא, ד]

ז) יְלָדִים אֲשֶׁר אֵין בָּהֶם כָּל מוּם וְטוֹבֵי מַרְאֶה וּמַשְׂכִּילִים בְּכָל חָכְמָה וְיֹדְעֵי דַעַת וּמְבִינֵי מַדָּע וַאֲשֶׁר כֹּחַ בָּהֶם לַעֲמֹד בְּהֵיכַל הַמֶּלֶךְ וּלְלַמְּדָם סֵפֶר וּלְשׁוֹן כַּשְׂדִּים: [דניאל א, ד]

ח) וַיְהִי בָהֶם מִבְּנֵי יְהוּדָה דָּנִיֵּאל חֲנַנְיָה מִישָׁאֵל וַעֲזַרְיָה: [דניאל א, ו]

ט) וּמִבָּנֶיךָ אֲשֶׁר יֵצְאוּ מִמְּךָ אֲשֶׁר תּוֹלִיד יִקָּחוּ וְהָיוּ סָרִיסִים בְּהֵיכַל מֶלֶךְ בָּבֶל: [ישעיה לט, ז]

י) עָנֵה וְאָמַר הָא אֲנָה חָזֵה גֻּבְרִין אַרְבְּעָה שְׁרַיִן מַהְלְכִין בְּגוֹא נוּרָא וַחֲבָל לָא אִיתַי בְּהוֹן וְרֵוֵהּ דִּי רְבִיעָאָה דָּמֵה לְבַר אֱלָהִין: [דניאל ג, כה]

כ) וּמִתְכַּנְּשִׁין אֲחַשְׁדַּרְפְּנַיָּא סִגְנַיָּא וּפַחֲוָתָא וְהַדָּבְרֵי מַלְכָּא חָזַיִן לְגֻבְרַיָּא אִלֵּךְ דִּי לָא שְׁלֵט נוּרָא בְּגֶשְׁמְהוֹן וּשְׂעַר רֵאשְׁהוֹן לָא הִתְחָרַךְ וְסָרְבָּלֵיהוֹן לָא שְׁנוֹ וְרֵיחַ נוּר לָא עֲדָת בְּהוֹן: [דניאל ג, כז]

ל) כִּי כֹה אָמַר יְיָ לַסָּרִיסִים אֲשֶׁר יִשְׁמְרוּ אֶת שַׁבְּתוֹתַי וּבָחֲרוּ בַּאֲשֶׁר חָפָצְתִּי וּמַחֲזִיקִים בִּבְרִיתִי: [ישעיה נו, ד]

מ) וְנָתַתִּי לָהֶם בְּבֵיתִי וּבְחוֹמֹתַי יָד וָשֵׁם טוֹב מִבָּנִים וּמִבָּנוֹת שֵׁם עוֹלָם אֶתֶּן לוֹ אֲשֶׁר לֹא יִכָּרֵת: [ישעיה נו, ה]

נ) זָכְרָה לִּי אֱלֹהַי לְטוֹבָה כֹּל אֲשֶׁר עָשִׂיתִי עַל הָעָם הַזֶּה: [נחמיה ה, יט]

ס) זָכְרֵנִי יְיָ בִּרְצוֹן עַמֶּךָ פָּקְדֵנִי בִּישׁוּעָתֶךָ: [תהלים קו, ד]

ע) וְהַפַּחוֹת הָרִאשֹׁנִים אֲשֶׁר לְפָנַי הִכְבִּידוּ עַל הָעָם וַיִּקְחוּ מֵהֶם בְּלֶחֶם וָיַיִן אַחַר כֶּסֶף שְׁקָלִים אַרְבָּעִים גַּם נַעֲרֵיהֶם שָׁלְטוּ עַל הָעָם וַאֲנִי לֹא עָשִׂיתִי כֵן מִפְּנֵי יִרְאַת אֱלֹהִים: [נחמיה ה, טו]

פ) וְרָאִיתִי אֲנִי דָנִיֵּאל לְבַדִּי אֶת הַמַּרְאָה וְהָאֲנָשִׁים אֲשֶׁר הָיוּ עִמִּי לֹא רָאוּ אֶת הַמַּרְאָה אֲבָל חֲרָדָה גְדֹלָה נָפְלָה עֲלֵיהֶם וַיִּבְרְחוּ בְּהֵחָבֵא: [דניאל י, ז]

מסורת הש"ס

א) [צ"ל ונבון דבר שמבין דבר מתוך דבר איש תואר שמראה פנים בהלכה כ"א בילקוט], ב) לא נמצא במקרא לשון זה ועי' רש"א בח"א [ואולי שצ"ל לכל דרכיו משכיל פרש"י בשמואל א יח מצליח ודע דבילקוט ליתא להך דבשאול כתיב כו' ובדוד כתיב], ג) צ"ל בר' חנינא, ד) [צ"ל אלעזר], ה) מגילה ג., ו) צ"ל אחר מלכי הורדוס.

הגהות הגר"א

[א] גמ' עמו וגו'. נמחק תיבת וגו': [ב] שם וכתיב והריחו. נמחק תיבת וגו' וכתיב: [ג] שם והאנשים אשר היו עמי לא ראו את המראה. נמחק:

ליקוטי רש"י

וכי דרכה של אשה ליטול שש סאין. אי אפשר לומר שש סאין שאין דרכה של אשה לשאת כמשאוי זה אלא שש שעורים ממש [רות ג, טו]. אחד מהנערים. מיוחד שבהם דואג האדומי. לא אמרו דואג אלא בלשון הרע. כל עצמו נתכוון להכניס עין רעה של שאול בדוד שיתקנא בו [ש"א טז, יח]. דואג אביר הרועים וגדול שבתלמידים היה ונתקנא בדוד שראהו נבון דבר ואיש תואר ומראה פנים בהלכה כדכתיב (ש"א טז) הנה ראיתי בן לישי בית הלחמי וגו' ואמר באגדה דחלק סנהדרין (צג:) דכל הפסוק הזה דואג אמרו בלשון הרע [סוטה ט:]. דבדידיה נמי לא הוי. שאול גדול בתורה היה אלא שלא לימד לאחרים כדאמרי' בעירובין (נג.) שאול לא גלי מסכתא להכי כתיב ביה בכל אשר יפנה ירשיע [גיטין נט.]. ירשיע. לא היה זוכה להורות כהלכה [עירובין נג:]. נעצר לפני ה'. עוצר עצמו לפני אהל מועד לעסוק בתורה. אביר הרועים. אב בית דין [ש"א כא, ח]. במישור. לשון נוח ורך [ישעיה יא, ד]. בר כוזיבא מלך. בכרך ביתר ומלך על ישראל שתי שנים ומחצה [יבמות עב.]. וללמדם ספר. מוסב על אשר כח בהם [דניאל א, ד]. ריבדא דכוסילתא. נקבי כלי האומן שבבשרו, פלימ"א [שבת קכט.]. כלי אומן המקיז בכתפים ריבדא מכת הכלי ובלעז פיינדר"א [ע"ז כז.]. פולטויי"ר דפלמו"ה בלע"ז. ריבדא. ניקור. כוסילתא. כלי אומן מקיז [כתובות לט:]. ריבדא. מכה. כוסילתא. כלי שמכה בו בלע"ז פליימא [מכות כא.]. ומבניך. הם חנניה מישאל ועזריה [ישעיה לט, ז]. וחבל לא איתי בהון. וחבלה לא יש בהם [דניאל ג, כה]. לא עדת בהן לא סרה לתוכ' [שם, כז]. ברצון עמך. בהרצותך לעמך [תהלים קו, ד]. הכבידו על העם. הכבידו מס על העם. ויקחו. והיו לוקחים מהם בשביל המס לחם ויין אחר נתינת ארבעים שקלים של כסף וכך היו רגילים בכל שנה [נחמיה ה, טו].

The Gemara digresses to expound the verse just cited:

מַאי ,,אֲשֶׁר אֵין־בָּהֶם כָּל־מאום״ – **What is** the meaning of ***in whom there is no blemish?*** אָמַר רַבִּי חָמָא (בר חנניא) [בְּרַבִּי חֲנִינָא] – **R' Chama the son of R' Chanina said:** אֲפִילוּ כְּרִיבְדָּא דְכוּסִילְתָּא לֹא הֲוָה בְּהוּ – **There was not in them even so much as a lancet puncture.**[25] מַאי ,,וַאֲשֶׁר כֹּחַ בָּהֶם לַעֲמֹד בְּהֵיכַל הַמֶּלֶךְ״ – **What is** the meaning of ***and who have the stamina to stand in the king's palace?*** אָמַר רַבִּי חָמָא בְּרַבִּי חֲנִינָא – **R' Chama the son of R' Chanina said:** מְלַמֵּד שֶׁהָיוּ אוֹנְסִין אֶת עַצְמָן מִן הַשְּׂחוֹק וּמִן הַשִּׂיחָה וּמִן הַשֵּׁינָה – **This teaches that** while in the royal presence, **they would deprive themselves of laughter, conversation, and sleep,** וּמַעֲמִידִין עַל עַצְמָן בְּשָׁעָה שֶׁנִּצְרָכִין לְנִקְבֵיהֶם – **and they would stay themselves when feeling the need to relieve themselves** – מִפְּנֵי אֵימַת מַלְכוּת – all this **out of** reverential **fear of the royal majesty.**

The Gemara records a dispute concerning the ancestry of Chananyah, Mishael and Azaryah:

,,וַיְהִי בָהֶם מִבְּנֵי יְהוּדָה דָּנִיֵּאל חֲנַנְיָה מִישָׁאֵל וַעֲזַרְיָה״ – Scripture states: ***And among them, from the children of Judah, were Daniel, Chananyah, Mishael, and Azaryah.***[26] אָמַר רַבִּי (אליעזר) [אֶלְעָזָר] כּוּלָּן מִבְּנֵי יְהוּדָה הֵם – **R' Elazar said: All of them were from the tribe of Judah.**[27] וְרַבִּי שְׁמוּאֵל בַּר נַחְמָנִי אָמַר – **But R' Shmuel bar Nachmani says:** דָּנִיֵּאל מִבְּנֵי יְהוּדָה – **Daniel was from the tribe of Judah;** חֲנַנְיָה מִישָׁאֵל וַעֲזַרְיָה מִשְּׁאָר שְׁבָטִים – **Chananyah, Mishael, and Azaryah,** however, **were from other tribes.**[28]

The Gemara analyzes another verse said in reference to Daniel, Chananyah, Mishael and Azaryah:

,,וּמִבָּנֶיךָ אֲשֶׁר יֵצְאוּ מִמְּךָ אֲשֶׁר תּוֹלִיד יִקָּחוּ וְהָיוּ סָרִיסִים בְּהֵיכַל מֶלֶךְ בָּבֶל״ – Scripture states: ***And from your sons that will issue from you, that you will bear, they will take to be eunuchs in the palace of the king of Babylon.***[29] מַאי ,,סָרִיסִים״ – **What is** the meaning of the word ***eunuchs*** in this verse? רַב אָמַר סָרִיסִים מַמָּשׁ – **Rav says:** It means that they were **actual eunuchs.**[30] וְרַבִּי חֲנִינָא אָמַר שֶׁנִּסְתָּרְסָה עֲבוֹדָה זָרָה בִּימֵיהֶם – **And R' Chanina says:** It means only **that idolatry was emasculated in their days.**[31]

The Gemara asks:

בִּשְׁלָמָא לְמַאן דְּאָמַר שֶׁנִּסְתָּרְסָה עֲבוֹדָה זָרָה בִּימֵיהֶם הַיְינוּ דִּכְתִיב ,,וַחֲבָל לָא־אִיתַי בְּהוֹן״ – **It is well according to the one who says "that idolatry was emasculated in their days" that which is written** in regard to Chananyah, Mishael and Azaryah: ***and there is no wound upon them,***[32] for – according to this view – they were never physically mutilated. אֶלָּא לְמַאן דְּאָמַר סָרִיסִים מַמָּשׁ – **But according to the one who says that** they were made into **actual eunuchs,** מַאי ,,וַחֲבָל לָא־אִיתַי בְּהוֹן״ – **what is** the meaning of ***there is no wound upon them?*** How could Nebuchadnezzar say this if they had previously been castrated?

The Gemara answers:

חַבְלָא דְנוּרָא – Nebuchadnezzar meant only that there was no **wound caused by fire** upon them.[33]

The Gemara asks:

וְהָכְתִיב ,,וְרֵיחַ נוּר לָא עֲדָת בְּהוֹן״ – **But it is written** elsewhere in the passage: ***and [even] the smoke of the fire had not seeped into them,***[34] which already tells us that they were untouched by the flames. Does not the verse *there is no wound upon them,* then, refer to the absence of any physical defect?

The Gemara answers:

לֹא חַבְלָא וְלֹא רֵיחָא – No, the purpose of both verses may be to teach that there was **neither wound nor smell** of smoke upon them.[35]

NOTES

that they were endowed with six blessings.

[Ashpenaz was ordered to recruit youths *from the Children of Israel and from the royal seed and from the nobles.* If we take this to mean that the youths had to have all three characteristics – i.e. they must be noble Israelite youths from the Royal House of David – then it follows that Daniel, Chananyah, Mishael and Azaryah were all descended from David and were thus descendants of Ruth. See, however, Gemara below and note 28 there.]

25. I.e. a puncture made by a bloodletter's lancet; a venesection scar. [Bloodletting was, until recent times, a medical procedure performed at regular intervals to promote general health, as well as to treat certain illnesses.] Daniel and his three companions enjoyed such perfect health that they never required bloodletting [a rare phenomenon in those days] (see *Rashi*).

Rif in *Ein Yaakov* and *Malbim* loc. cit. remark on the unusual spelling מאום instead of the usual מום. The word מאום is related to מְאוּמָה, *a thing.* Thus, we expound that these were youths *in whom there was not a thing [wrong],* not even the slightest physical imperfection.

26. *Daniel* 1:6.

27. R' Elazar follows Bar Kappara (above), who considers all four to be descended from Ruth (*Rashi*; see also note 24 above).

28. [Accordingly, the verse would be interpreted: *And among them: from the children of Judah, Daniel; Chananyah, Mishael, and Azaryah* (see *Rashi*). Possibly, R' Shmuel bar Nachmani interprets the phrase in v. 3: *from the children of Israel and from the royal seed and from the nobles* as referring to three distinct categories, meaning that Nebuchadnezzar sought youths from the children of Israel *as well as* from the royal seed *as well as* from the nobles. Thus, not all the recruits were from the royal seed (see ArtScroll Commentary to *Daniel* ad loc.).]

R' Shmuel bar Nachmani does not subscribe to Bar Kappara's exposition (above), which takes all four to be descended from Ruth (*Rashi*).

29. *II Kings* 20:18 and *Isaiah* 39:7. This prophecy, told by Isaiah to King Chizkiah, states Chizkiah's punishment for exhibiting Israel's most precious treasures before the Babylonian emissaries sent to him. This prophecy was fulfilled in the descendants of Chizkiah who were taken to serve in the palace of Nebuchadnezzar, king of Babylon – Chananyah, Mishael and Azaryah (*Rashi* to *Isaiah* loc. cit.) and Daniel (*Radak* to *II Kings* loc. cit.). According to R' Shmuel bar Nachmani, however, who holds that Chananyah, Mishael and Azaryah were *not* from the tribe of Judah, Isaiah's prophecy referred to Daniel alone (*Rashi* below ד״ה ר׳ חנניא אומר).

30. It was the custom of kings to castrate male royal attendants so that they should not marry, but be devoted exclusively to the service of the king (*Rashi*). Rav maintains that this was the humiliating fate that befell Chizkiah's descendants. And Rav does not accept the view of the Sages in the Baraisa (93a) that Chananyah, Mishael and Azaryah eventually married and raised families (*Rashi*).

31. I.e. [as a result of their miraculous deliverance from the fiery furnace (*Daniel* ch. 3) and from the lions' den (*Daniel* ch. 6) for refusing to abandon their devotion to God] everyone realized the futility of idolatry (*Aruch* ע׳ סרס; *Yad Ramah*). *Ben Yehoyada* explains that had they not been saved, idolatry would have proliferated, or – in figurative terms – the original idols would have "begotten children." By halting the proliferation of idolatry, they in effect "emasculated" the original idols.

According to R' Chanina, the humiliating fate foretold by Isaiah to Chizkiah was that his descendants would be exiled from their land and carried off to serve in the palace of a foreign king (*Rashi*).

Maharsha and *Be'er Sheva* consider why the Gemara did not explain simply that the term סָרִיס, *eunuch,* here is a borrowed term referring to a high royal officer, even if not castrated, as rendered many times by *Targum* (see, for example, *Targum Onkelos* to *Genesis* 37:36). [See solutions proposed by *Maharsha* and *Iyun Yaakov.*]

32. *Daniel* 3:25, cited above at the beginning of 93a.

33. Nebuchadnezzar was expressing incredulity that they were inside the flaming furnace without being burned in the least.

34. Ibid. v. 27.

35. [The two verses can be seen as forming a progression of increasingly incredulous observations: Not only was there no wound upon their persons (v. 25) but they had not even been tainted by the smell of smoke (v. 27)!]

The Gemara could not challenge Rav's view that they were actual eunuchs from the other verse cited above: *youths in whom there is no blemish* (*Daniel* 1:4), as that verse speaks of their state upon being *recruited* to serve Nebuchadnezzar, who might *subsequently* have castrated them (*Rashi*).

אלא שש סאין וכי דרכה של אשה ליטול שש סאין אלא רמז [רמז] לה שעתידין ששה בנים לצאת ממנה שמתברכין בשש [שש] ברכות ואלו הן דוד ומשיח דניאל חנניה מישאל ועזריה דוד דכתיב א) ויען אחד מהנערים ויאמר הנה ראיתי בן לישי בית הלחמי יודע נגן וגבור חיל ואיש מלחמה ונבון דבר ואיש תואר וה' עמו [א] וגו' ואמר רב יהודה אמר רב כל הפסוק הזה לא אמרו דואג אלא בלשון הרע יודע נגן שיודע לישאל גבור שיודע להשיב איש מלחמה שיודע לישא וליתן במלחמתה של תורה א) (איש תואר שמראה פנים בהלכה ונבון דבר שמבין דבר מתוך דבר) וה' עמו שהלכה כמותו בכל מקום בכולהו אמר להו יהונתן בני כמוהו כיון דאמר ליה [וה' עמו] מילתא דבדידיה נמי לא הוה ביה חלש דעתיה ואיקניא ביה דבשאול כתיב ב) ובכל אשר יפנה ירשיע ובדוד כתיב ב) ובכל אשר יפנה יצליח מנלן דדואג הוה כתיב הכא א) ויען אחד מהנערים מיוחד שבנערים וכתיב התם ג) ושם איש מעבדי שאול ביום ההוא נעצר לפני ה' ושמו דואג האדומי אביר הרועים אשר לשאול משיח דכתיב ד) ונחה עליו רוח ה' רוח חכמה ובינה רוח עצה וגבורה רוח דעת ויראת ה' וגו' [ב] וכתיב ה) והריחו ביראת ה' אמר רבי אלכסנדרי מלמד שהטעינו מצות ויסורין כריחיים רבא אמר דמורח ודאין דכתיב ה) ולא למראה עיניו ישפוט ו) ושפט בצדק דלים והוכיח במישור לענוי ארץ בר כוזיבא מלך תרתין שנין ופלגא אמר להו לרבנן אנא משיח אמרו ליה במשיח כתיב דמורח ודאין נחזי אנן אי מורח ודאין כיון דחזיוהו דלא מורח ודאין קטלוהו דניאל חנניה מישאל ועזריה דכתיב בהו ז) אשר אין בהם כל מאום וטובי מראה ומשכילים בכל חכמה ויודעי דעת ומביני מדע ואשר כח בהם לעמוד בהיכל המלך וללמדם ספר ולשון כשדים מאי אשר אין בהם כל מום אמר רבי חמא (ג) בר חנניא) אפילו כריבדא דכוסילתא לא הוה בהו מאי ואשר כח בהם לעמוד בהיכל המלך אמר רבי חמא ברבי חנינא מלמד שהיו אונסין את עצמן מן השחוק ומן השינה ומן השיחה ומעמידין על עצמן בשעה שנצרכין לנקביהם מפני אימת מלכות ח) ויהיו בהם מבני יהודה דניאל חנניה מישאל ועזריה אמר רבי (ד) אליעזר) כולן מבני יהודה הם ורבי שמואל בר נחמני אמר דניאל מבני יהודה חנניה מישאל ועזריה משאר שבטים ט) ומבניך אשר יצאו ממך אשר תוליד יקחו והיו סריסים בהיכל מלך בבל מאי סריסים רב אמר סריסים ממש ורבי חנינא אמר שנסתרסה ע"ז בימיהם בשלמא למאן דאמר שנסתרסה ע"ז בימיהם היינו דכתיב י) וחבל לא איתי בהון אלא למאן דאמר סריסים ממש מאי וחבל לא איתי בהון חבלא דנורא והכתיב כ) וריח נור לא עדת בהן לא חבלא ולא ריחא בשלמא למאן דאמר שנסתרסה ע"ז בימיהם היינו דכתיב ל) כה אמר ה' לסריסים אשר ישמרו את שבתותי וגו' אלא למאן דאמר סריסים ממש משתעי קרא בגנותא דצדיקי הא והא הוה בהו בשלמא למאן דאמר סריסים ממש היינו דכתיב מ) בביתי ובחומותי יד ושם טוב מבנים ומבנות אלא למאן דאמר שנסתרסה ע"ז בימיהם מאי טוב מבנים ומבנות אמר רב נחמן בר יצחק מבנים שהיו להם כבר ומתו מאי מ) שם עולם אתן לו אשר לא יכרת אמר ר' תנחום דרש בר קפרא בצפורי זה ספר דניאל שנקרא על שמו מכדי כל מילי דעזרא נחמיה בן חכליה אמרינהו ונחמיה בן חכליה מ"ט לא איקרי סיפרא על שמיה אמר רבי ירמיה בר אבא מפני שהחזיק טובה לעצמו שנאמר נ) זכרה לי אלהי לטובה דוד נמי מימר אמר ס) זכרני ה' ברצון עמך פקדני בישועתך דוד רחמי הוא דקבעי רב יוסף אמר מפני שסיפר בגנותן של ראשונים שנאמר ע) והפחות הראשונים אשר לפני הכבידו על העם ויקחו מהם בלחם ויין אחר כסף שקלים ארבעים וגו' ואף על דניאל שגדול ממנו סיפר ומנלן דגדול ממנו דכתיב פ) וראיתי אני דניאל לבדי את המראה והאנשים אשר היו עמי לא ראו את המראה אבל חרדה גדולה נפלה עליהם ויברחו בהחבא [ג] והאנשים אשר היו עמי לא ראו את המראה צ) ומאן נינהו אנשים אמר רבי ירמיה ואיתימא ר' חייא בר אבא זה חגי זכריה ומלאכי

אינהו

רש"י

אלא שש סאין. דשש קבין או שש לוגין ליכא למימר דלא מייתי בגורן מדה פחותה מסאה: ליטול שש סאין. ולישא משוי כזה: רמז לה. דשש גרעינין נתן לה לסימן ורמז שעתידין לצאת שש בנים ממנה: יודע נגן גבור חיל ואיש מלחמה ונבון דבר ואיש תאר וה' עמו. הוינו שש ברכות: לא אמרן דואג. לקמן מפרש האחד מן הנערים היינו דואג: אלא בלשון הרע. שהיה מספר בשבחו של דוד כדי שיקנא בו שאול ויהרגהו: לישא וליתן במלחמתה של תורה. להתוכח בתלמוד: פנים בהלכה. שמביא ראיה לדבריו: דבדידיה נמי לא הוה. דשאול נמי לא הוה הלכה כמותו כדאמרינן בעירובין (דף נג.) דוד דגלי מסכתא כתיב ביה יראיך יראוני וישמחו שאול דלא גלי מסכתא כתיב ביה בכל אשר יפנה ירשיע: נעצר לפני ה'. ללמוד תורה הרבה: אביר הרועים אשר לשאול. אלמא ההוא מיוחד שבנערים דהיינו דואג דחזינן הכא דקרי אביר הרועים: ונחה עליו רוח ה'. איזה רוח רוח חכמה ובינה רוח עצה וגבורה רוח דעת ויראת ה' הרי ששה: ה"ג והריחו ביראת ה' א"ר אלכסנדריא שהטעינו במצות ויסורין כריחים והיינו והריחו לשון רחים ולא גרסינן וכתיב והריחו: רבא אמר. מאי והריחו דמורח ודאין שמריח באדם ושופט ויודע מי החייב שנאמר לא למראה עיניו ישפוט ולא למשמע אזניו יוכיח ואפילו הכי ושפט בצדק דלים כגון על ידי הרחה: בר כוזיבא. (עס) ו) ממלכי הורדוס היה: אשר אין בהם כל מום וטובי מראה משכילים בכל חכמה יודעי דעת ומביני מדע ואשר כח בהם הרי ו': אפי' ריבדא דכוסילתא לא היתה בגופם. שלא היו צריכין להקזה. ריבדא פוניור"א בלעז כוסילתא שם כלי המקיז פלנמא"ל: מן השיחה. שלא היו מספרין בדברים בטלים כדי שלא יתגנו בפני המלך: כלם מבני יהודה. כדחשיב לעיל ששה בנים העתידים לצאת מרות וחשיב בהדייהו חנניה מישאל ועזריה: דניאל. לחוד קאי אבני יהודה אבל חנניה מישאל ועזריה לא ולית ליה הך דרשה דלעיל שם שעורים: מבניך אשר יצאו ממעיך. בחזקיהו מלך יהודה כתיב: סריסים ממש. שסירסו לחנניה מישאל ועזריה שכן דרכן של מלכים לסרס את האדם כדי שלא ישא אשה ויהא פנוי לעבודת המלך ולית ליה הא דחכמים דאמרי לעיל שעלו לארץ ישראל ונשאו נשים והולידו בנים ובנות: ר' חנניה אומר. לא סרסם אלא להכי קרו ליה סריסים שנסתרסה ע"ז בימיהם שבימיהם נודע לכל שאין ממש בע"ז ופורענות שהיה נביא מתנבא לחזקיהו שיהיו גולים מארצם ויוליכם בהיכל מלך בבל ור' שמואל בר נחמני דאמר חנניה מישאל ועזריה משאר שבטים היו מוקים האי קרא בדניאל לחוד: מאי חבל לא איתי בהון. והלא חבלה היא זו שנסתרסו ומהאי קרא דלעיל ילדים אשר אין בהם כל מום לא מצי פריך דאיכא למימר בשעה שבאו לנבוכדנצר תמימים הוו וסרסן: חבל די נורא. לא איתי בהון אבל חבלת הגוף מיהא איכא ופריך לחבלא דנורא לא איצטריך דהא כתיב קרא וריח נור לא עדת בהון: ולא ריחא. עשן האש: הא והא היו. סריסים ממש ושנסתרסה ע"ז בימיהם: טוב מבנים ומבנות. מכלל דבנים לא הוו להו דסריסים היו: מאי טוב מבנים ומבנות. הכא לא מצי לתרולי הא והא הוו דא"כ במאי פליגי: בנים שהיו להן כבר ומתו. דלא היו בניהם ומיהו לא היו סריסים: אתן לו. להם לא נאמר אלא לו לאחד מהם והיינו ספר דניאל שנקרא על שמו והשתא קא פריך פירכא באפי נפשה אגב דאתי בידו ספר דניאל: מכדי וכו'. רוב דברים שבספר עזרא ונחמיה אמרם: דוד נמי מימר אמר. הכי כלומר מאי מחזיק טובה איכא: רב יוסף אמר. לאו אהכי איענש דהא דוד נמי אמר כי האי גוונא אלא לכך נענש שספר בגנותן של ראשונים: מאי נינהו. שהיו עמו חגי זכריה מלאכי וכיון שהם לא ראו והוא ראה אלמא גדול מהם הוה ומדאשכחן דדניאל הוה חשיב טפי מחגי זכריה ומלאכי דהוו נביאי שמע מינה דגדול הוה מנחמיה בן חכליה דלא הוה נביא ואפי' הכי ספר עליו דלא אפקיה מכלל גנות הראשונים. דניאל היה מבאי הגולה עם החרש והמסגר ונחמיה הוה מעולי הגולה זמן מרובה לאחר מיכן:

אינהו

תורה אור השלם

א) וַיַּעַן אֶחָד מֵהַנְּעָרִים וַיֹּאמֶר הִנֵּה רָאִיתִי בֵּן לְיִשַׁי בֵּית הַלַּחְמִי יֹדֵעַ נַגֵּן וְגִבּוֹר חַיִל וְאִישׁ מִלְחָמָה וּנְבוֹן דָּבָר וְאִישׁ תֹּאַר וַיְיָ עִמּוֹ: [שמואל א' טז, יח]

ב) וְשָׁאוּל לָכַד הַמְּלוּכָה עַל יִשְׂרָאֵל וַיִּלָּחֶם סָבִיב בְּכָל אֹיְבָיו בְּמוֹאָב וּבִבְנֵי עַמּוֹן וּבֶאֱדוֹם וּבְמַלְכֵי צוֹבָה וּבַפְּלִשְׁתִּים וּבְכֹל אֲשֶׁר יִפְנֶה יַרְשִׁיעַ: [שמואל א' יד, מז]

ג) וְשָׁם אִישׁ מֵעַבְדֵי שָׁאוּל בַּיּוֹם הַהוּא נֶעְצָר לִפְנֵי יְיָ וּשְׁמוֹ דֹּאֵג הָאֲדֹמִי אַבִּיר הָרֹעִים אֲשֶׁר לְשָׁאוּל: [שמואל א' כא, ח]

ד) וְנָחָה עָלָיו רוּחַ יְיָ רוּחַ חָכְמָה וּבִינָה רוּחַ עֵצָה וּגְבוּרָה רוּחַ דַּעַת וְיִרְאַת יְיָ: [ישעיה יא, ב]

ה) וַהֲרִיחוֹ בְּיִרְאַת יְיָ וְלֹא לְמַרְאֵה עֵינָיו יִשְׁפּוֹט וְלֹא לְמִשְׁמַע אָזְנָיו יוֹכִיחַ: [ישעיה יא, ג]

ו) וְשָׁפַט בְּצֶדֶק דַּלִּים וְהוֹכִיחַ בְּמִישׁוֹר לְעַנְוֵי אָרֶץ וְהִכָּה אֶרֶץ בְּשֵׁבֶט פִּיו וּבְרוּחַ שְׂפָתָיו יָמִית רָשָׁע: [ישעיה יא, ד]

ז) יְלָדִים אֲשֶׁר אֵין בָּהֶם כָּל מוּם וְטוֹבֵי מַרְאֶה וּמַשְׂכִּילִים בְּכָל חָכְמָה וְיֹדְעֵי דַעַת וּמְבִינֵי מַדָּע וַאֲשֶׁר כֹּחַ בָּהֶם לַעֲמֹד בְּהֵיכַל הַמֶּלֶךְ וּלְלַמְּדָם סֵפֶר וּלְשׁוֹן כַּשְׂדִּים: [דניאל א, ד]

ח) וַיְהִי בָהֶם מִבְּנֵי יְהוּדָה דָּנִיֵּאל חֲנַנְיָה מִישָׁאֵל וַעֲזַרְיָה: [דניאל א, ו]

ט) וּמִבָּנֶיךָ אֲשֶׁר יֵצְאוּ מִמְּךָ אֲשֶׁר תּוֹלִיד יִקָּחוּ וְהָיוּ סָרִיסִים בְּהֵיכַל מֶלֶךְ בָּבֶל: [ישעיה לט, ז]

י) עָנֵה וְאָמַר הָא אֲנָה חָזֵה גֻּבְרִין אַרְבְּעָה שְׁרַיִן מַהְלְכִין בְּגוֹא נוּרָא וַחֲבָל לָא אִיתַי בְּהוֹן וְרֵוֵהּ דִּי רְבִיעָאָה דָּמֵה לְבַר אֱלָהִין: [דניאל ג, כה]

כ) וּמִתְכַּנְּשִׁין אֲחַשְׁדַּרְפְּנַיָּא סִגְנַיָּא וּפַחֲוָתָא וְהַדָּבְרֵי מַלְכָּא חָזַיִן לְגֻבְרַיָּא אִלֵּךְ דִּי לָא שְׁלֵט נוּרָא בְּגֶשְׁמְהוֹן וּשְׂעַר רֵאשְׁהוֹן לָא הִתְחָרַךְ וְסַרְבָּלֵיהוֹן לָא שְׁנוֹ וְרֵיחַ נוּר לָא עֲדָת בְּהוֹן: [דניאל ג, כז]

ל) כִּי כֹה אָמַר יְיָ לַסָּרִיסִים אֲשֶׁר יִשְׁמְרוּ אֶת שַׁבְּתוֹתַי וּבָחֲרוּ בַּאֲשֶׁר חָפָצְתִּי וּמַחֲזִיקִים בִּבְרִיתִי: [ישעיה נו, ד]

מ) וְנָתַתִּי לָהֶם בְּבֵיתִי וּבְחוֹמֹתַי יָד וָשֵׁם טוֹב מִבָּנִים וּמִבָּנוֹת שֵׁם עוֹלָם אֶתֶּן לוֹ אֲשֶׁר לֹא יִכָּרֵת: [ישעיה נו, ה]

נ) זָכְרָה לִּי אֱלֹהַי לְטוֹבָה כֹּל אֲשֶׁר עָשִׂיתִי עַל הָעָם הַזֶּה: [נחמיה ה, יט]

ס) זָכְרֵנִי יְיָ בִּרְצוֹן עַמֶּךָ פָּקְדֵנִי בִּישׁוּעָתֶךָ: [תהלים קו, ד]

ע) וְהַפַּחוֹת הָרִאשֹׁנִים אֲשֶׁר לְפָנַי הִכְבִּידוּ עַל הָעָם וַיִּקְחוּ מֵהֶם בְּלֶחֶם וָיַיִן אַחַר כֶּסֶף שְׁקָלִים אַרְבָּעִים גַּם נַעֲרֵיהֶם שָׁלְטוּ עַל הָעָם וַאֲנִי לֹא עָשִׂיתִי כֵן מִפְּנֵי יִרְאַת אֱלֹהִים: [נחמיה ה, טו]

פ) וְרָאִיתִי אֲנִי דָנִיֵּאל לְבַדִּי אֶת הַמַּרְאָה וְהָאֲנָשִׁים אֲשֶׁר הָיוּ עִמִּי לֹא רָאוּ אֶת הַמַּרְאָה אֲבָל חֲרָדָה גְדֹלָה נָפְלָה עֲלֵיהֶם וַיִּבְרְחוּ בְּהֵחָבֵא: [דניאל י, ז]

מסורת הש"ס

א) [נ"ל ונבון דבר שמבין דבר מתוך דבר איש תואר שמראה פנים בהלכה כ"א בילקוט], ב) לא נמצא במקרא לשון זה ועי' רש"א בח"א [ואולי שצ"ל לכל דרכיו משכיל פרש"י בשמואל א יח מגליה ודע דבילקוט ליתא להך דבשאול כתיב כו' ובדוד כתיב], ג) נ"ל בר' חנינא, ד) [נ"ל אלעזר], ה) מגילה ג., ו) נ"ל אחר מלכי הורדוס.

הגהות הגר"א

[א] גמ' עמו וגו'. נמחק תיבת וגו': [ב] שם וכתיב והריחו. נמחק תיבת וגו' וכתיב: [ג] שם והאנשים אשר היו עמי לא ראו את המראה. נמחק:

ליקוטי רש"י

וכי דרכה של אשה ליטול שש סאין. אי אפשר לומר שש סאין שאין דרכה של אשה לשאת כמשאוי זה אלא שש שעורים ממש [רות ג, טו]. אחד מהנערים. מיוחד שבהם דואג האדומי. לא אמרו דואג אלא בלשון הרע. כל עצמו נתכוון להכניס עין רעה של שאול בדוד שיתקנא בו [ש"א טז, יח]. דואג אביר הרועים וגדול שבתלמידים היה ונתקנא בדוד שראהו נבון דבר ואיש תואר ומראה פנים בהלכה כדכתיב (ש"א טז) הנה ראיתי בן לישי בית הלחמי וגו' ואמר באגדה דחלק סנהדרין (צג:) דכל הפסוק הזה דואג אמרו בלשון הרע [סוטה ט:]. דבדידיה נמי לא הוי. שאול גדול בתורה היה אלא שלא לימד לאחרים כדאמרי' בעירובין (נג.) שאול לא גלי מסכתא להכי כתיב ביה בכל אשר יפנה ירשיע [גיטין נט.]. ירשיע. לא היה זוכה להורות כהלכה [עירובין נג:]. נעצר לפני ה'. עוצר עצמו לפני אהל מועד לעסוק בתורה. אביר הרועים. אב בית דין [ש"א כא, ח]. במישור. לשון נוח ורך [ישעיה יא, ד]. בר כוזיבא מלך. בכרך ביתר ומלך על ישראל שתי שנים ומחצה [יבמות עב.]. וללמדם ספר. מוסב על אשר כח בהם [דניאל א, ד]. ריבדא דכוסילתא. נקבי כלי האומן שבבשרו, פלימ"א [שבת קכט.]. כלי אומן המקיז בכתפים רידא מכת הכלי ובלעז פיינדר"א [ע"ז כז.]. פולטוייר"א דפלמו"ה בלע"ז. רידא. ניקור. כוסילתא. כלי אומן מקיז [כתובות לט:]. רידא. מכה. כוסילתא. כלי שמכה בו בלע"ז פליימא [מכות כא.]. ומבניך. הם חנניה מישאל ועזריה [ישעיה לט, ז]. וחבל לא איתי בהון. ומכה לא יש בהם [דניאל ג, כה]. לא עדת בהן לא סרה לתוכ' [שם, כז]. ברצון עמך. בהרצותך לעמך [תהלים קו, ד]. הכבידו על העם. הכבידו מס על העם. ויקחו. והיו לוקחים מהם בשביל המס לחם ויין אחר נתינת ארבעים שקלים של כסף וכך היו רגילים כל שנה [נחמיה ה, טו].

The Gemara asks:

בִּשְׁלָמָא לְמַאן דְּאָמַר שֶׁנִּסְתָּרְסָה עֲבוֹדָה זָרָה בִּימֵיהֶם הַיְינוּ דִּכְתִיב ,,כֹּה אָמַר ה׳ לַסָּרִיסִים אֲשֶׁר יִשְׁמְרוּ אֶת־שַׁבְּתוֹתַי וגו׳״ – It is well according to the one who says "that idolatry was emasculated in their days" that which is written: ***Thus says HASHEM to the eunuchs who will keep My Sabbaths*** **etc.**[36] **אֶלָּא לְמַאן דְּאָמַר סָרִיסִים מַמָּשׁ – However, according to the one who says that** the term as applied to Daniel, Chananyah, Mishael and Azaryah means that they were **actual eunuchs, מִשְׁתָּעֵי קְרָא בִּגְנוּתָא דְּצַדִּיקֵי – would the verse speak disparagingly of the righteous?!**[37]

The Gemara answers:

הָא וְהָא הֲוָה בְּהוּ – Rav will hold that **both were true of them,** i.e. they were called "eunuchs" because of their literal mutilation as well as because idolatry was emasculated in their days.[38]

R' Chanina's opinion is challenged:

בִּשְׁלָמָא לְמַאן דְּאָמַר סָרִיסִים מַמָּשׁ הַיְינוּ דִּכְתִיב ,,בְּבֵיתִי וּבְחוֹמֹתַי יָד וָשֵׁם טוֹב מִבָּנִים וּמִבָּנוֹת״ – It is well according to the one who says "they were **actual eunuchs" that which is written:** *And I will give them* ***within My house and walls a monument and memorial better than sons and daughters.***[39] Such assurance is appropriate to actual eunuchs, who cannot achieve earthly continuity through children. **אֶלָּא לְמַאן דְּאָמַר שֶׁנִּסְתָּרְסָה עֲבוֹדָה זָרָה בִּימֵיהֶם – But according to the one who says "that idolatry was emasculated in their days,"** but they were not actual eunuchs, **מַאי ,,טוֹב מִבָּנִים וּמִבָּנוֹת״ – what is** the assurance ***better than sons and daughters*** doing in this verse?[40]

The Gemara answers:

אָמַר רַב נַחְמָן בַּר יִצְחָק – Rav Nachman bar Yitzchak said: מִבָּנִים שֶׁהָיוּ לָהֶם כְּבָר וָמֵתוּ – The verse means: greater **than the children they had previously, who had died.**[41]

The Gemara further expounds the verse just cited:

מַאי ,,שֵׁם עוֹלָם אֶתֶּן־לוֹ אֲשֶׁר לֹא יִכָּרֵת״ – What is the meaning of the conclusion of the verse just cited: ***an everlasting name I will give him, which will not be cut off?*** **אָמַר רַבִּי תַּנְחוּם דָּרַשׁ בַּר קַפָּרָא בְּצִפּוֹרִי – R' Tanchum said: Bar Kappara expounded in Tzipori: זֶה סֵפֶר דָּנִיֵּאל שֶׁנִּקְרָא עַל שְׁמוֹ – This refers to the Book of** ***Daniel,*** **which was named after him** and thus gave him an everlasting name.[42]

Having given a reason why the Book of *Daniel* is named for him, the Gemara digresses to discuss why a different book was *not* named for its author:[43]

מִכְּדִי כָּל מִילֵּי דְּעֶזְרָא נְחֶמְיָה בֶּן חֲכַלְיָה אַמְרִינְהוּ – Now, let us see. **All the matters of** the Book of ***Ezra*** **were said** [i.e. authored] **by Nehemiah the son of Chachaliah.**[44] **וּנְחֶמְיָה בֶּן חֲכַלְיָה מַאי טַעְמָא לֹא אִיקְרֵי סִיפְרָא עַל שְׁמֵיהּ – So why,** then, **is the book not named after Nehemiah the son of Chachaliah,** its author? **אָמַר רַבִּי יִרְמְיָה בַּר אַבָּא – R' Yirmiyah bar Abba said: מִפְּנֵי שֶׁהֶחֱזִיק טוֹבָה לְעַצְמוֹ** – It was not named for Nehemiah **because he took personal credit** for his achievements,[45] **שֶׁנֶּאֱמַר ,,זָכְרָה־לִּי אֱלֹהַי לְטוֹבָה״ – as it is stated:** ***Remember me, my God, for good.***[46]

The Gemara asks:

דָּוִד נַמִּי מֵימַר אָמַר ,,זָכְרֵנִי ה׳ בִּרְצוֹן עַמֶּךָ פָּקְדֵנִי בִּישׁוּעָתֶךָ״ – But **surely David, too, said:** ***Remember me, O HASHEM, when You favor Your People; think of me at Your salvation.***[47] **– ? –**

NOTES

36. *Isaiah* 56:4. The Gemara assumes that the סָרִיסִים, *eunuchs,* mentioned here are none other than Daniel, Chananyah, Mishael and Azaryah referred to earlier in *Isaiah* (39:7) by this term. For the context in which the "eunuchs" are not specifically identified can be clarified on the basis of the context in which they are identified in the very same book (*Maharal*). According to R' Chanina, there is nothing derogatory about referring to these righteous men a second time as "eunuchs," since the term as applied to them alludes to the fact that they emasculated idolatry. [The context of the verse seems to indicate that the reference is to actual eunuchs, since the next verse assures them that *I will give them within My house and My walls a monument and memorial better than sons and daughters.* The Gemara below will raise this question.]

37. [In the earlier verse (39:7) they were spoken of in these terms in order to indicate the humiliating punishment that would befall Chizkiah. But here, it seems to be a gratuitous humiliation to allude to them in these terms.]

38. [And the reference to them as "eunuchs" in the second verse (56:4) is not considered humiliating, since it also alludes to the fact that idolatry was emasculated in their days.]

39. *Isaiah* 56:5. [יָד וָשֵׁם means literally: *a hand and a name.* When one has children, he enjoys *a supporting hand* in his old age, and a *continued name* after death. God promises the righteous who are childless greater support and greater continuity than that provided by children (*Toras Chaim*).]

40. If they were not actual eunuchs, then they very well might have had sons and daughters of their own! Why, then, would they need to be reassured that their continuity would be greater than that provided by offspring?

[The Gemara could not answer (as it did according to Rav) that R' Chanina means that *both* were fulfilled in them – they were actual eunuchs *and* idolatry was emasculated in their days. For if that were what R' Chanina meant, then his view would be identical with Rav's, which cannot be, as their views are presented above in the form of a dispute (*Rashi*).]

41. True, they were not eunuchs and had once had children, but these children had since died (*Rashi*). Thus, it was appropriate to reassure them that their continuity would exceed that generally assured by offspring, which were no longer living.

42. [The Book of *Daniel* was written by the Men of the Great Assembly (*Bava Basra* 15a). Nonetheless, the Gemara is stating that it is called "*Daniel*" in order to provide him with an everlasting name. See *Ben Yehoyada.*] *Chida* (cited by *Margaliyos HaYam,* end of §19) notes that the Hebrew words סֵפֶר [book] and שֵׁם [name] have the same numerical value [340].

Bar Kappara's exposition of this verse as a reference specifically to Daniel [rather than to Chananyah, Mishael and Azaryah] is based on [the shift from the plural used at the beginning of the verse – וְנָתַתִּי לָהֶם, *And I will give to "them"* – to] the singular used at the end – אֶתֶּן־לוֹ, *I will give to "him"* (*Rashi*).

43. See *Rashi.*

44. [Though printed editions of Scripture have a Book of *Ezra* followed by a Book of *Nehemiah,* both actually form but one large book known in the Talmud as the Book of *Ezra.*] The Gemara here says that "all the matters of the Book of *Ezra* were said by Nehemiah," but *Rashi* explains it to mean simply that *most* of it was said by Nehemiah [as the greater part of the book (from *Nehemiah* 1:1 onward) is prefaced with the introduction: *The words of Nehemiah son of Chachaliah* (ibid.; see *Rashi* ad loc.)].

[In any event, this Gemara seems to be at odds with the Baraisa quoted in *Bava Basra* 15a, which states that the Book of *Ezra* was authored by Ezra himself. See ArtScroll Commentary to *Ezra* (p. 59) for a proposed resolution. See also *Maharshal* to *Bava Basra* 15a.]

45. *Avos* 2:9 states: "If you have studied much Torah, do not take credit for yourself, for that is what you were created for."

46. *Nehemiah* 5:19, 13:31. Nehemiah was appointed by the Persian king as governor of the newly returned Jewish colony in Jerusalem, which was in desperate straits. As governor, Nehemiah undertook a series of needed reforms, including building a wall around the city, and fighting against intermarriage, Sabbath desecration, and social injustice. After listing some of his accomplishments, especially his own refusal to take a salary from his heavily burdened fellow Jews, he calls upon God to remember his good deeds and count them to his credit.

Maharal explains that Nehemiah was punished "measure for measure": He aggrandized himself; therefore, God removed his name from the title of his Scriptural book.

47. *Psalms* 106:4. [And we do not find that this was accounted presumptuous of him.] Obviously, then, such a statement does not constitute improper "taking credit for oneself" (*Rashi*).

אלא שש סאין וכי דרכה של אשה ליטול שש סאין אלא רמז [רמז] לה שעתידין ששה בנים לצאת ממנה שמתברכין בשש [שש] ברכות ואלו הן דוד ומשיח דניאל חנניה מישאל ועזריה דוד דכתיב א) ויען אחד מהנערים ויאמר הנה ראיתי בן לישי בית הלחמי יודע נגן וגבור חיל ואיש מלחמה ונבון דבר ואיש תואר וה' עמו [א] וגו' ואמר רב יהודה אמר רב כל הפסוק הזה לא אמרו דואג אלא בלשון הרע יודע נגן שיודע לישאל גבור שיודע להשיב איש מלחמה שיודע לישא וליתן במלחמתה של תורה א) (איש תואר שמראה פנים בהלכה ונבון דבר שמבין דבר מתוך דבר) וה' עמו שהלכה כמותו בכל מקום בכולהו אמר להו יהונתן בני כמוהו כיון דאמר ליה [וה' עמו] מילתא דבדידיה נמי לא הוה ביה חלש דעתיה ואיקניא ביה דבשאול כתיב ב) ובכל אשר יפנה ירשיע ובדוד כתיב ב) ובכל אשר יפנה יצליח מנלן דדואג הוה כתיב הכא א) ויען אחד מהנערים מיוחד שבנערים וכתיב התם ג) ושם איש מעבדי שאול ביום ההוא נעצר לפני ה' ושמו דואג האדומי אביר הרועים אשר לשאול משיח דכתיב ד) ונחה עליו רוח ה' רוח חכמה ובינה רוח עצה וגבורה רוח דעת ויראת ה' וגו' [ב] וכתיב ה) והריחו ביראת ה' אמר רבי אלכסנדרי מלמד שהטעינו מצות ויסורין כריחיים רבא אמר דמורח ודאין דכתיב ה) ולא למראה עיניו ישפוט ו) ושפט בצדק דלים והוכיח במישור לענוי ארץ בר כוזיבא מלך תרתין שנין ופלגא אמר להו לרבנן אנא משיח אמרו ליה במשיח כתיב דמורח ודאין נחזי אנן אי מורח ודאין כיון דחזיוהו דלא מורח ודאין קטלוהו דניאל חנניה מישאל ועזריה דכתיב בהו ז) אשר אין בהם כל מאום וטובי מראה ומשכילים בכל חכמה ויודעי דעת ומביני מדע ואשר כח בהם לעמוד בהיכל המלך וללמדם ספר ולשון כשדים מאי אשר אין בהם כל מום אמר רבי חמא (ג) בר חנניא) אפילו כריבדא דכוסילתא לא הוה בהו מאי ואשר כח בהם לעמוד בהיכל המלך אמר רבי חמא ברבי חנינא מלמד שהיו אונסין את עצמן מן השחוק ומן השיחה ומן השינה ומעמידין על עצמן בשעה שנצרכין לנקביהם מפני אימת מלכות ח) ויהיו בהם מבני יהודה דניאל חנניה מישאל ועזריה אמר רבי (ד) אליעזר) כולן מבני יהודה הם ורבי שמואל בר נחמני אמר דניאל מבני יהודה חנניה מישאל ועזריה משאר שבטים ט) ומבניך אשר יצאו ממך אשר תוליד יקחו והיו סריסים בהיכל מלך בבל מאי סריסים רב אמר סריסים ממש ורבי חנינא אמר שנסתרסה ע"ז בימיהם בשלמא למאן דאמר שנסתרסה ע"ז בימיהם היינו דכתיב י) וחבל לא איתי בהון אלא למאן דאמר סריסים ממש מאי וחבל לא איתי בהון חבלא דנורא והכתיב כ) וריח נור לא עדת בהן לא חבלא ולא ריחא בשלמא למאן דאמר שנסתרסה ע"ז בימיהם היינו דכתיב ל) כה אמר ה' לסריסים אשר ישמרו את שבתותי וגו' אלא למאן דאמר סריסים ממש משתעי קרא בגנותא דצדיקי הא והא הוה בהו בשלמא למאן דאמר סריסים ממש היינו דכתיב מ) בביתי ובחומותי יד ושם טוב מבנים ומבנות אלא למאן דאמר שנסתרסה ע"ז בימיהם מאי טוב מבנים ומבנות אמר רב נחמן בר יצחק מבנים שהיו להם כבר ומתו מאי מ) שם עולם אתן לו אשר לא יכרת אמר ר' תנחום דרש בר קפרא בצפורי זה ספר דניאל שנקרא על שמו מכדי כל מילי דעזרא נחמיה בן חכליה אמרינהו ונחמיה בן חכליה מ"ט לא איקרי סיפרא על שמיה אמר רבי ירמיה בר אבא מפני שהחזיק טובה לעצמו שנאמר נ) זכרה לי אלהי לטובה דוד נמי מימר אמר ס) זכרני ה' ברצון עמך פקדני בישועתך דוד רחמי הוא דקבעי רב יוסף אמר מפני שסיפר בגנותן של ראשונים שנאמר ע) והפחות הראשונים אשר לפני הכבידו על העם ויקחו מהם בלחם ויין אחד כסף שקלים ארבעים וגו' ואף על דניאל שגדול ממנו סיפר ומנלן דגדול ממנו דכתיב פ) וראיתי אני דניאל לבדי את המראה והאנשים אשר היו עמי לא ראו את המראה אבל חרדה גדולה נפלה עליהם ויברחו בהחבא [ג] והאנשים אשר היו עמי לא ראו את המראה צ) ומאן נינהו אנשים אמר רבי ירמיה ואיתימא ר' חייא בר אבא זה חגי זכריה ומלאכי

אינהו

רש"י

אלא שש סאין. דשש קבין או שש לוגין ליכא למימר דלא מייתי בגורן מדה פחותה מסאה: ליטול שש סאין. ולישא משוי כזה: רמז לה. דשש גרעינין נתן לה לסימן ורמז שעתידין לצאת שש בנים ממנה: יודע נגן גבור חיל ואיש מלחמה ונבון דבר ואיש תאר וה' עמו. היינו שש ברכות: לא אמרן דואג. לקמן מפרש האחד מן הנערים היינו דואג: אלא בלשון הרע. שהיה מספר בשבחו של דוד כדי שיקנא בו שאול ויהרגהו: לישא וליתן במלחמתה של תורה. להתוכח בתלמוד: פנים בהלכה. שמביא ראיה לדבריו: דבדידיה נמי לא הוה. דשאול נמי לא הוה הלכה כמותו כדאמרינן בעירובין (דף נג.) דוד דגלי מסכתא כתיב ביה יראיך יראוני וישמחו שאול דלא גלי מסכתא כתיב ביה בכל אשר יפנה ירשיע: נעצר לפני ה'. ללמוד תורה הרבה: אביר הרועים אשר לשאול. אלמא ההוא מיוחד שבנערים דהיינו דואג דחזינן הכא דקרי אביר הרועים: ונחה עליו רוח ה'. איזה רוח רוח חכמה ובינה רוח עצה וגבורה רוח דעת ויראת ה' הרי ששה: ה"ג והריחו ביראת ה' א"ר אלכסנדריא שהטעינו במצות ויסורין כריחים והיינו והריחו לשון רחים ולא גרסינן וכתיב והריחו: רבא אמר. מאי והריחו דמורח ודאין שמריח באדם ושופט ויודע מי החייב שנאמר לא למראה עיניו ישפוט ולא למשמע אזניו יוכיח ואפילו הכי ושפט בצדק דלים כגון על ידי הרחה: בר כוזיבא. (עם) ו) ממלכי הורדוס היה: אשר אין בהם כל מום וטובי מראה משכילים בכל חכמה יודעי דעת ומביני מדע ואשר כח בהם הרי ו': אפי' ריבדא דכוסילתא לא היתה בגופם. שלא היו צריכין להקזה. רידא פוניור"א בלעז כוסילתא שם כלי המקיז פלנמא"ל: מן השיחה. שלא היו מספרין בדברים בטלים כדי שלא יתגנו בפני המלך: כלם מבני יהודה. כדחשיב לעיל ששה בנים העתידים לצאת מרות וחשיב בהדייהו חנניה מישאל ועזריה: דניאל. לחוד קאי אבני יהודה אבל חנניה מישאל ועזריה לא ולית ליה הך דרשה דלעיל שש שעורים: מבניך אשר יצאו ממעיך. בחזקיהו מלך יהודה כתיב:

סריסים ממש. שסירסו לחנניה מישאל ועזריה שכן דרכן של מלכים לסרס את האדם כדי שלא ישא אשה ויהא פנוי לעבודת המלך ולית ליה הא דחכמים דאמרי לעיל שעלו לארץ ישראל ונשאו נשים והולידו בנים ובנות: ר' חנניה אומר. לא סרסם אלא להכי קרו ליה סריסים שנסתרסה ע"ז בימיהם שבימיהם נודע לכל שאין ממש בע"ז ופורענות שהיה נביא מתנבא לחזקיהו שיהיו גולים מארצם ויוליכם בהיכל מלך בבל ור' שמואל בר נחמני דאמר חנניה מישאל ועזריה משאר שבטים היו מוקים האי קרא בדניאל לחוד: מאי חבל לא איתי בהון. והלא חבלה היא זו שנסתרסו ומהאי קרא דלעיל ילדים אשר אין בהם כל מום לא מצי פריך דאיכא למימר בשעה שבאו לנבוכדנצר תמימים הוו וסרסן: חבל די נורא. לא איתי בהון אבל חבלת הגוף מיהא איכא ופריך לחבלא דנורא לא איצטריך דהא כתיב קרא וריח נור לא עדת בהון: ולא ריחא. עשן האש: הא והא היו. סריסים ממש ושנסתרסה ע"ז בימיהם: טוב מבנים ומבנות. מכלל דבנים לא הוו להו דסריסים היו: מאי טוב מבנים ומבנות. הכא לא מצי לתרוצי הא והא הוו דא"כ במאי פליגי: בנים שהיו להן כבר ומתו. דלא חיו בניהם ומיהו לא היו סריסים: אתן לו. להם לא נאמר אלא לו לאחד מהם והיינו ספר דניאל שנקרא על שמו והשתא קא פריך פירכא באפי נפשה אגב דאתי בידו ספר דניאל: מכדי וכו'. רוב דברים שבספר עזרא ונחמיה אמרם: דוד נמי מימר אמר. הכי כלומר מאי מחזיק טובה איכא: רב יוסף אמר. לאו אהכי איענש דהא דוד נמי אמר כי האי גוונא אלא לכך נענש שספר בגנותן של ראשונים: מאי נינהו. שהיו עמו חגי זכריה מלאכי וכיון שהם לא ראו והוא ראה אלמא גדול מהם הוה ומדאשכחן דדניאל הוה חשיב טפי מחגי זכריה ומלאכי דהוו נביאי שמע מינה דגדול הוה מנחמיה בן חכליה דלא הוה נביא ואפי' הכי ספר עליו דלא אפקיה מכלל גנות הראשונים. דניאל היה מבאי הגולה עם החרש והמסגר ונחמיה הוה מעולי הגולה זמן מרובה לאחר מיכן:

אינהו

תורה אור השלם

א) וַיַּעַן אֶחָד מֵהַנְּעָרִים וַיֹּאמֶר הִנֵּה רָאִיתִי בֵּן לְיִשַׁי בֵּית הַלַּחְמִי יֹדֵעַ נַגֵּן וְגִבּוֹר חַיִל וְאִישׁ מִלְחָמָה וּנְבוֹן דָּבָר וְאִישׁ תֹּאַר וַיְיָ עִמּוֹ: [שמואל א' טז, יח]

ב) וְשָׁאוּל לָכַד הַמְּלוּכָה עַל יִשְׂרָאֵל וַיִּלָּחֶם סָבִיב בְּכָל אֹיְבָיו בְּמוֹאָב וּבִבְנֵי עַמּוֹן וּבֶאֱדוֹם וּבְמַלְכֵי צוֹבָה וּבַפְּלִשְׁתִּים וּבְכֹל אֲשֶׁר יִפְנֶה יַרְשִׁיעַ: [שמואל א' יד, מז]

ג) וְשָׁם אִישׁ מֵעַבְדֵי שָׁאוּל בַּיּוֹם הַהוּא נֶעְצָר לִפְנֵי יְיָ וּשְׁמוֹ דֹּאֵג הָאֲדֹמִי אַבִּיר הָרֹעִים אֲשֶׁר לְשָׁאוּל: [שמואל א' כא, ח]

ד) וְנָחָה עָלָיו רוּחַ יְיָ רוּחַ חָכְמָה וּבִינָה רוּחַ עֵצָה וּגְבוּרָה רוּחַ דַּעַת וְיִרְאַת יְיָ: [ישעיה יא, ב]

ה) וַהֲרִיחוֹ בְּיִרְאַת יְיָ וְלֹא לְמַרְאֵה עֵינָיו יִשְׁפּוֹט וְלֹא לְמִשְׁמַע אָזְנָיו יוֹכִיחַ: [ישעיה יא, ג]

ו) וְשָׁפַט בְּצֶדֶק דַּלִּים וְהוֹכִיחַ בְּמִישׁוֹר לְעַנְוֵי אָרֶץ וְהִכָּה אֶרֶץ בְּשֵׁבֶט פִּיו וּבְרוּחַ שְׂפָתָיו יָמִית רָשָׁע: [ישעיה יא, ד]

ז) יְלָדִים אֲשֶׁר אֵין בָּהֶם כָּל מוּם וְטוֹבֵי מַרְאֶה וּמַשְׂכִּילִים בְּכָל חָכְמָה וְיֹדְעֵי דַעַת וּמְבִינֵי מַדָּע וַאֲשֶׁר כֹּחַ בָּהֶם לַעֲמֹד בְּהֵיכַל הַמֶּלֶךְ וּלְלַמְּדָם סֵפֶר וּלְשׁוֹן כַּשְׂדִּים: [דניאל א, ד]

ח) וַיְהִי בָהֶם מִבְּנֵי יְהוּדָה דָּנִיֵּאל חֲנַנְיָה מִישָׁאֵל וַעֲזַרְיָה: [דניאל א, ו]

ט) וּמִבָּנֶיךָ אֲשֶׁר יֵצְאוּ מִמְּךָ אֲשֶׁר תּוֹלִיד יִקָּחוּ וְהָיוּ סָרִיסִים בְּהֵיכַל מֶלֶךְ בָּבֶל: [ישעיה לט, ז]

י) עָנֵה וְאָמַר הָא אֲנָה חָזֵה גֻּבְרִין אַרְבְּעָה שְׁרַיִן מַהְלְכִין בְּגוֹא נוּרָא וַחֲבָל לָא אִיתַי בְּהוֹן וְרֵוֵהּ דִּי רְבִיעָאָה דָּמֵה לְבַר אֱלָהִין: [דניאל ג, כה]

כ) וּמִתְכַּנְּשִׁין אֲחַשְׁדַּרְפְּנַיָּא סִגְנַיָּא וּפַחֲוָתָא וְהַדָּבְרֵי מַלְכָּא חָזַיִן לְגֻבְרַיָּא אִלֵּךְ דִּי לָא שְׁלֵט נוּרָא בְּגֶשְׁמְהוֹן וּשְׂעַר רֵאשְׁהוֹן לָא הִתְחָרַךְ וְסָרְבָּלֵיהוֹן לָא שְׁנוֹ וְרֵיחַ נוּר לָא עֲדָת בְּהוֹן: [דניאל ג, כז]

ל) כִּי כֹה אָמַר יְיָ לַסָּרִיסִים אֲשֶׁר יִשְׁמְרוּ אֶת שַׁבְּתוֹתַי וּבָחֲרוּ בַּאֲשֶׁר חָפָצְתִּי וּמַחֲזִיקִים בִּבְרִיתִי: [ישעיה נו, ד]

מ) וְנָתַתִּי לָהֶם בְּבֵיתִי וּבְחוֹמֹתַי יָד וָשֵׁם טוֹב מִבָּנִים וּמִבָּנוֹת שֵׁם עוֹלָם אֶתֶּן לוֹ אֲשֶׁר לֹא יִכָּרֵת: [ישעיה נו, ה]

נ) זָכְרָה לִּי אֱלֹהַי לְטוֹבָה כֹּל אֲשֶׁר עָשִׂיתִי עַל הָעָם הַזֶּה: [נחמיה ה, יט]

ס) זָכְרֵנִי יְיָ בִּרְצוֹן עַמֶּךָ פָּקְדֵנִי בִּישׁוּעָתֶךָ: [תהלים קו, ד]

ע) וְהַפַּחוֹת הָרִאשֹׁנִים אֲשֶׁר לְפָנַי הִכְבִּידוּ עַל הָעָם וַיִּקְחוּ מֵהֶם בְּלֶחֶם וָיַיִן אַחַר כֶּסֶף שְׁקָלִים אַרְבָּעִים גַּם נַעֲרֵיהֶם שָׁלְטוּ עַל הָעָם וַאֲנִי לֹא עָשִׂיתִי כֵן מִפְּנֵי יִרְאַת אֱלֹהִים: [נחמיה ה, טו]

פ) וְרָאִיתִי אֲנִי דָנִיֵּאל לְבַדִּי אֶת הַמַּרְאָה וְהָאֲנָשִׁים אֲשֶׁר הָיוּ עִמִּי לֹא רָאוּ אֶת הַמַּרְאָה אֲבָל חֲרָדָה גְדֹלָה נָפְלָה עֲלֵיהֶם וַיִּבְרְחוּ בְּהֵחָבֵא: [דניאל י, ז]

מסורת הש"ס

א) [צ"ל ונבון דבר שמבין דבר מתוך דבר איש תואר שמראה פנים בהלכה כ"א בילקוט], ב) לא נמצא במקרא לשון זה ועי' רש"א בח"א [ואולי שצ"ל לכל דרכיו משכיל פרש"י בשמואל א יח מצליח ודע דבילקוט ליתא להך דבשאול כתיב כו' ובדוד כתיב], ג) צ"ל בר' חנינא, ד) [צ"ל אלעזר], ה) מגילה ג., ו) צ"ל אחד מלכי הורדוס.

הגהות הגר"א

[א] גמ' עמו וגו'. נמחק תיבת וגו': [ב] שם וכתיב והריחו. נמחק תיבת וגו' וכתיב: [ג] שם והאנשים אשר היו עמי לא ראו את המראה. נמחק:

ליקוטי רש"י

וכי דרכה של אשה ליטול שש סאין. אי אפשר לומר שש סאין שאין דרכה של אשה לשאת כמשאוי זה אלא שש שעורים ממש [רות ג, טו]. אחד מהנערים. מיוחד שבהם דואג האדומי. לא אמרו דואג אלא בלשון הרע. כל עצמו נתכוון להכניס עין רעה של שאול בדוד שיתקנא בו [ש"א טז, יח]. דואג אביר הרועים וגדול שבתלמידים היה ונתקנא בדוד שראהו נבון דבר ואיש תואר ומראה פנים בהלכה כדכתיב (ש"א טז) הנה ראיתי בן לישי בית הלחמי וגו' ואמר באגדה דחלק סנהדרין (צג:) דכל הפסוק הזה דואג אמרו בלשון הרע [סוטה ט:]. דבדידיה נמי לא הוי. שאול גדול בתורה היה אלא שלא לימד לאחרים כדאמרי' בעירובין (נג.) שאול לא גלי מסכתא להכי כתיב ביה בכל אשר יפנה ירשיע [גיטין נט.]. ירשיע. לא היה זוכה להורות כהלכה [עירובין נג:]. נעצר לפני ה'. עוצר עצמו לפני אהל מועד לעסוק בתורה. אביר הרועים. אב בית דין [ש"א כא, ח]. במישור. לשון נוח ורך [ישעיה יא, ד]. בר כוזיבא מלך. בכרך ביתר ומלך על ישראל שתי שנים ומחצה [יבמות עב.]. וללמדם ספר. מוסב על אשר כח בהם [דניאל א, ד]. ריבדא דכוסילתא. נקבי כלי האומן שבבשרו, פלימ"א [שבת קכט.]. כלי אומן המקיז בכתפים רידא מכת הכלי ובלעז פיינדר"א [ע"ז כז.]. פולטוייר"א דפלמות"ה בלע"ז. רידא. ניקור. כוסילתא. כלי אומן מקיז [כתובות לט:]. רידא. מכה. כוסילתא. כלי שמכה בו בלע"ז פליימא [מכות כא.]. ומבניך. הם חנניה מישאל ועזריה [ישעיה לט, ז]. וחבל לא איתי בהון. וחבלה לא יש בהם [דניאל ג, כה]. לא עדת בהן לא סרה לתוכ' [שם, כז]. ברצון עמך. בהרצותך לעמך [תהלים קו, ד]. הכבידו על העם. הכבידו מס על העם. ויקחו. והיו לוקחים מהם בשביל המס לחם ויין אחר נתינת ארבעים שקלים של כסף וכך היו רגילים בכל שנה [נחמיה ה, טו].

The Gemara answers:

דָּוִד רַחֲמֵי הוּא דְּקָבָעֵי – **David was simply appealing for Divine mercy.**[48]

Rav Yosef advances a different reason for Nehemiah's punishment:[49]

רַב יוֹסֵף אָמַר – **Rav Yosef says:** מִפְּנֵי שֶׁסִּיפֵּר בִּגְנוּתָן שֶׁל רִאשׁוֹנִים – Nehemiah's book was not called by his name **because he spoke disparagingly of the earlier ones,** i.e. the governors that preceded him. שֶׁנֶּאֱמַר ,,וְהַפַּחוֹת הָרִאשֹׁנִים אֲשֶׁר־לְפָנַי הִכְבִּידוּ עַל־הָעָם – **For it is stated:** ***And the earlier governors who preceded me burdened the people*** וַיִּקְחוּ מֵהֶם בְּלֶחֶם וָיַיִן אַחַר כֶּסֶף־שְׁקָלִים אַרְבָּעִים וגו׳ ״ – ***and took from them [taxes] in [the form of] bread and wine, after [taking] forty silver shekels,* etc.** *but I did not do so, for fear of God.*[50] וְאַף עַל דָּנִיֵּאל שֶׁגָּדוֹל מִמֶּנּוּ סִיפֵּר – **And even against Daniel, who was** clearly **greater than he, did he speak.**[51] וּמְנָלָן דְּגָדוֹל מִמֶּנּוּ – **And from where** in Scripture do we know **that [Daniel] was greater than he?** דִּכְתִיב ,,וְרָאִיתִי אֲנִי דָנִיֵּאל לְבַדִּי אֶת־הַמַּרְאָה – **For it is written:** ***And I, Daniel, alone saw the vision,*** וְהָאֲנָשִׁים אֲשֶׁר־הָיוּ עִמִּי לֹא רָאוּ אֶת־הַמַּרְאָה – ***whereas the men who were with me did not see the vision;*** אֲבָל חֲרָדָה גְדֹלָה נָפְלָה עֲלֵיהֶם וַיִּבְרְחוּ בְּהֵחָבֵא״ – ***yet a great fear fell upon them, and they fled into hiding.***[52] ,,וְהָאֲנָשִׁים אֲשֶׁר הָיוּ עִמִּי לֹא רָאוּ אֶת־הַמַּרְאָה״ – The verse stated: ***And the men who were with me did not see the vision.*** וּמַאן נִינְהוּ אֲנָשִׁים – **Now, who were** these **men?** אָמַר רַבִּי יִרְמְיָה וְאִיתֵימָא רַבִּי חִיָּיא בַּר אַבָּא – **R' Yirmiyah said, and some say** it was **R' Chiya bar Abba** who said: זֶה חַגַּי זְכַרְיָה וּמַלְאָכִי – **This** refers to the prophets **Haggai, Zechariah and Malachi.**[53]

NOTES

48. David's statement was an appeal for Divine mercy, not a call for deserved reward. But Nehemiah's statements [as evident from their context] were a call for deserved reward (see *Maharsha*). Thus, he was punished for "taking credit for himself."

Anaf Yosef explains that no person – however righteous – has any claim on God, nor could the person even have done any righteous deed without Divine assistance. Any appeal to God for favor must be based solely on a plea for Divine mercy. David appealed to God using the Name ה׳, *Hashem,* which represents the Attribute of Mercy. Nehemiah, however, invoked the Name אֱלֹהַי, *My God,* which represents the Attribute of Justice.

49. Rav Yosef considers Nehemiah's statement to be substantively identical to David's. Thus, it cannot be that Nehemiah was punished for making it (*Rashi*).

50. *Nehemiah* 5:15. Though these criticisms were accurate, it is a grave sin to glorify oneself through belittling others [see *Yerushalmi Chagigah* 2:1; *Rambam, Hil. De'os* 6:3 and *Hil. Teshuvah* 3:14] (*Iyun Yaakov*).

51. Daniel was among those exiled to Babylon with the *charash* and the *masger* (the "craftsmen" and the "locksmiths" – see 103a note 9) eleven years before the destruction of the First Temple [see *II Kings* 24:16 and *Gittin* 88a]. Nehemiah was among those who returned to Eretz Yisrael many years (nearly a century) later (*Rashi*). [Thus, with respect to Nehemiah, Daniel is accounted "an earlier one."]

[Although Scripture makes no explicit mention of Daniel's having been Nehemiah's predecessor as governor of Judea, Midrashic sources identify Daniel with Sheshbazzar, who was sent by Cyrus to return the sacred vessels to the Temple, and who led the laborers in the laying of the Temple foundation [*Ezra* 5:13 ff] (*Pesikta Rabbasi* §6 [23b]; *Yalkut Shimoni* to *Ezra* ch. 5; *Rashi* to *Ezra* 1:8; see also ArtScroll Commentary to *Ezra,* p. 72). Accordingly, Daniel was in fact one of the predecessors of Nehemiah as governor of Judea. Cf. *Rif* in *Ein Yaakov.*] And since Nehemiah derogated the preceding governors collectively, without especially excepting Daniel, he in effect derogated Daniel as well (*Rashi*).

Sefer Chasidim (282) derives from here the lesson that one should not criticize a group of people as sinners if even one of that group is blameless, for he thereby denigrates the blameless individual as well.

52. *Daniel* 10:7.

53. The verse must refer to people of prophetic stature who are generally capable of beholding a vision; otherwise, it would not have mentioned that they did not see the vision in this case. R' Yirmiyah bar Abba therefore concludes that they were the prophets Haggai, Zechariah, and Malachi (*Geon Yaakov* in *Ein Yaakov* to *Megillah* 3a). Since Daniel was greater than these prophets, he certainly was greater than Nehemiah, who was not a prophet (*Rashi*; see also *Rashi* to *Megillah* 3b).

The Gemara adds incidentally:[1] אִינְהוּ עֲדִיפֵי מִינֵּיהּ – In one way they [Haggai, Zechariah and Malachi were superior to him [Daniel], וְאִיהוּ עָדִיף מִנַּיְיהוּ – and in another way he was superior to them. אִינְהוּ עֲדִיפֵי מִינֵּיהּ – They were superior to him דְּאִינְהוּ נְבִיאֵי וְאִיהוּ לַאו נָבִיא – in that they were prophets whereas he was not a prophet.[2] וְאִיהוּ עָדִיף מִנַּיְיהוּ – And he was superior to them דְּאִיהוּ חֲזָא וְאִינְהוּ לֹא חֲזוּ – in that he saw the vision and they did not see the vision.

The Gemara returns to the verse cited above in order to explain a point. The Gemara asks:

וְכִי מֵאַחַר דְּלֹא חֲזוּ מַאי טַעְמָא אִיבְּעוּת – Now since they [Haggai, Zechariah, and Malachi] did not see the vision, why were they frightened?[3]

The Gemara answers:

אַף עַל גַּב דְּאִינְהוּ לֹא חֲזוּ מִידֵּי – Even though they did not see anything, מַזָּלַיְיהוּ חֲזֵי – their *mazal*[4] did see the vision. אָמַר רָבִינָא – Ravina commented: שְׁמַע מִינָּהּ הַאי מַאן דְּמִבְּעִית – Learn from this that when one becomes frightened for no apparent reason, אַף עַל גַּב דְּאִיהוּ לֹא חָזֵי מַזָּלֵיהּ חָזֵי – even though he has not seen the cause of his fear, his *mazal* has seen it.

The Gemara continues:

מַאי תַּקַּנְתֵּיהּ – What is his remedy? How can he defend himself against this threat which he senses but cannot see? לִינְשׁוֹף מִדּוּכְתֵּיהּ אַרְבָּעָה גַּרְמִידֵי – He should jump four *amos* from his place.[5] אִי נַמִּי לִיקְרֵי קְרִיַּת שְׁמַע – Alternatively, he should recite *Krias Shema.*[6] וְאִי קָאֵי בִּמְקוֹם הַטִּנּוֹפֶת – And if he is standing in a place of filth, where it is prohibited to recite *Krias Shema,*[7] לֵימָא הָכִי – he should say the following incantation: עִיזָּא דְּבֵי טַבָּחָא שְׁמִינָא מִינַּאי – "The goat at the slaughterhouse is fatter than I."[8]

The Gemara introduces another of Bar Kappara's expositions, this one concerning King Chizkiah of the Kingdom of Judah.[9] After this exposition, the Gemara begins an extended discussion of Chizkiah and his rule:

״לְםַרְבֵּה הַמִּשְׂרָה וּלְשָׁלוֹם אֵין־קֵץ וגו׳״ – Scripture states: ***To him who increases [God's] authority; and for [him there shall be] peace without end, etc.***[10] אָמַר רַבִּי תַּנְחוּם – R' Tanchum said: דָּרַשׁ בַּר קַפָּרָא בְּצִיפּוֹרִי – In Tzippori, Bar Kappara expounded this verse as follows: מִפְּנֵי מַה כָּל מ״ם שֶׁבְּאֶמְצַע תֵּיבָה פָּתוּחַ – Why is it that every letter *mem* that appears in the middle of a word is always open, וְזֶה סָתוּם – but this letter *mem* that appears in the word *lemarbeh* is closed?[11] בִּיקֵּשׁ הַקָּדוֹשׁ בָּרוּךְ הוּא לַעֲשׂוֹת חִזְקִיָּהוּ מָשִׁיחַ – This *mem* is closed to indicate that the Holy One, Blessed is He, sought to make King Chizkiah the Messiah, וְסַנְחֵרִיב גּוֹג וּמָגוֹג – and he sought to make Sancheiriv, Chizkiah's enemy, Gog and Magog.[12] אָמְרָה מִדַּת הַדִּין לִפְנֵי הַקָּדוֹשׁ בָּרוּךְ הוּא – However, the Divine Attribute of Justice exclaimed before the Holy One, Blessed is He:[13] רִבּוֹנוֹ שֶׁל

NOTES

1. *Rashi,* who notes that most Gemara texts do not have this following passage at all.

2. In fact, Daniel was also a prophet, but unlike Haggai, Zechariah and Malachi, he was never sent with a prophetic message to the people (*Rashi* to *Megillah* 3a; *Tos. HaRosh* ad loc.).

3. As stated in the end of the verse: *yet a great fear fell upon them* (*Rashi*). The word אֲבָל, *yet,* implies that their fear was caused by the vision mentioned in the verse, even though they did not see it, and was not the result of some other factor (*Yad David,* cited by *Menachem Meishiv Nefesh* to *Megillah* 3a, in explanation of *Rashi*; cf. *Dikdukei Soferim* to 93b §2).

4. "*Mazal*" here refers to the angel designated in heaven to represent each person (*Rashi* to *Megillah* 3a; see *Michtav MeEliyahu* II:287). *R' Avraham Min Hahar* (to *Megillah* loc. cit.) explains that *mazal* here refers to one's imaginative faculties, which can sense what his physical senses do not.

5. As evidenced by the fact that Haggai, Zechariah and Malachi fled from their place (*Toras Chaim*). [The "place" that a person occupies is defined as the four *amos* that surround him. By jumping four *amos,* the person leaves his original place, where the source of his fear was located.] See, however, note 8 below.

6. These are the verses beginning with "*Shema Yisrael . . .*" (*Deuteronomy* 6:4) recited as part of the morning and evening prayers. The recitation of *Krias Shema* has the power to ward off destructive forces (see *Berachos* 5a).

7. See *Orach Chaim* §76 and §79 for the details of this law.

8. As if to say to the unseen menace: *Go to the goats and leave me alone* (*Rashi*).

In *Megillah* 3a, the remedy of "jumping four *amos* from one's place" immediately precedes the remedy of reciting this incantation. According to that ordering, it is possible that the intent is that one should move four *amos* away from the source of the filth, so that he should then be able to recite *Krias Shema* [see *Orach Chaim* 79:1] (see *R' Avraham Min Hahar* to *Megillah* loc. cit.).

9. King Chizkiah [Hezekiah] was the son of Achaz and the father of Menasheh. Both Achaz and Menasheh are characterized by Scripture as wicked kings, but Chizkiah himself was exceedingly righteous. He brought a spiritual revival to the Jewish people, eradicating the *bamos* [see Glossary] that had been used for sacrifice outside of the Temple, and smashing the copper serpent that Moses had made (see *Numbers* 21:9) because it had become worshiped as an independent deity.

In Chizkiah's time, Assyria invaded Eretz Yisrael, conquering and exiling the Ten Tribes that comprised the Northern Israelite Kingdom. Assyria then turned to threaten the Kingdom of Judah, and it laid siege to Jerusalem. Chizkiah, however, beseeched God to turn back the Assyrian onslaught, and God indeed did so. A plague miraculously descended upon the Assyrian army, killing a hundred and eighty-five thousand men in one night, and causing Sancheiriv — the king of Assyria — to retreat to Nineveh.

The Gemara now addresses the spiritual implications of these historic events.

10. *Isaiah* 9:6. In the previous verse, the prophet Isaiah relates that God has named King Chizkiah the "Prince of Peace." The present verse relates that Chizkiah merited this distinction because he has "increased God's authority [over himself]," i.e. he has feared God (*Rashi* to *Isaiah* ad loc.).

The Gemara here focuses on the fact that the letter *mem* that appears in the word לְםַרְבֵּה is written as a final *mem* (ם). This is unusual, for this *mem* appears in the *middle* of the word, and it thus should have been written as an ordinary *mem* (מ). The Gemara interprets this deviation as indicative of a larger truth, as it now proceeds to explain.

11. I.e. it is a closed, or final, *mem* (ם) rather than an ordinary open one (מ). See previous note.

12. Scripture indicates that the coming of the Messiah will be connected with the invasion of the Land of Israel by the armies of Magog, led by their king, Gog (see *Ezekiel* chs. 38-39, and *Zechariah* ch. 14). These invading armies represent the final effort of the nations to block the attainment of God's goal, the universal establishment of His Kingship on earth. Scripture foretells that God will destroy the invading armies, and the Messianic Era shall then begin.

The invasion of Judah by Sancheiriv and his army, the miraculous destruction of the invaders, and the presence of a righteous leader such as Chizkiah on the throne, all seemed to fit the description of the Gog and Magog episode. Thus, the Gemara states that Chizkiah's struggle with Sancheiriv could potentially have been the final war, the precursor of the Messianic era. Nevertheless, the Messianic potential inherent in these events was not realized, as the Gemara goes on to explain (cf. *Ben Yehoyada*).

13. [In concession to Man's fragility, God generally deals with Man in a way that balances strict Justice with deep and abiding Mercy. When Man is particularly undeserving, however, God sometimes restrains His attribute of Mercy, and allows the harsh demands of Justice to be met uncompromisingly. Such was the case in this particular instance.]

מסורת הש"ס

א) [מגילה ג.], ב) [שם ע"ש היטב], ג) [כתובות קיב: פירוש באים שודדים על ארץ ישראל ובאים שודדים אחרים ושודדים המשודדים וישראל עמהן. ערוך בערך בז ד'], ד) ילקוט איתא רב פפא, ה) [שבת קיג:], ו) שבת קיג. ב"ק לא:, ז) [ועי' היטב (תוס') בשבת קיג: תראה שם בגמרא ובפרש"י דהתם שינויים גדולים בלשון ובגרס' אחרת וצריך ישוב למאד], ח) [לעיל נב. וש"נ].

א) אינהו עדיפי מיניה ואיהו עדיף מנייהו אינהו עדיפי מיניה דאינהו נביאי ואיהו לאו נביא ואיהו עדיף מנייהו דאיהו חזא ואינהו לא חזו וכי מאחר דלא חזו מאי טעמא איבעות אע"ג דאינהו לא חזו מידי מזלייהו חזי אמר רבינא ש"מ האי מאן דמבעית אף על גב דאיהו לא חזי מזליה חזי מאי תקנתיה ב) לינשוף מדוכתיה ארבעה גרמידי אי נמי ליקרי קרית שמע ואי קאי במקום הטנופת לימא הכי עיזא דבי טבחא שמינא מינאי א) למרבה המשרה ולשלום אין קץ וגו' א"ר תנחום דרש בר קפרא בציפורי מפני מה כל מ"ם שבאמצע תיבה פתוח וזה סתום ביקש הקב"ה לעשות חזקיהו משיח וסנחריב גוג ומגוג אמרה מדת הדין לפני הקב"ה רבש"ע ומה דוד מלך ישראל שאמר כמה שירות ותשבחות לפניך לא עשיתו משיח חזקיה שעשית לו כל הנסים הללו ולא אמר שירה לפניך תעשהו משיח לכך נסתתם מיד פתחה הארץ ואמרה לפניו רבש"ע אני אומרת לפניך שירה תחת צדיק זה ועשהו משיח פתחה ואמרה שירה לפניו שנאמר ב) מכנף הארץ זמירות שמענו צבי לצדיק וגו' אמר שר העולם לפניו רבש"ע צביונו עשה לצדיק זה יצאה בת קול ואמרה רזי לי רזי לי אמר נביא אוי לי אוי לי עד מתי יצאה בת קול ואמרה ב) בוגדים בגדו ובגד בוגדים בגדו ואמר רבא ואיתימא ר' יצחק ג) עד דאתו בוזזי ובזוזי דבזוזי ג) משא דומה אלי קורא משעיר שומר מה מלילה שומר מה מליל וגו' א"ר יוחנן אותו מלאך הממונה על הרוחות דומה שמו נתקבצו כל הרוחות אצל דומה אמרו לו שומר מה מלילה שומר מה מליל [א] ד) אמר שומר אתא בקר וגם לילה אם תבעיון בעיו שובו אתיו תנא משום רבי פפיים גנאי הוא לחזקיה וסייעתו שלא אמרו שירה עד שפתחה הארץ ואמרה שירה שנא' ב) מכנף הארץ זמירות שמענו צבי לצדיק וגו' כיוצא בדבר אתה אומר ה) ויאמר יתרו ברוך ה' אשר הציל אתכם תנא משום רבי פפיים גנאי הוא למשה וששים ריבוא שלא אמרו ברוך עד שבא יתרו ואמר ברוך ה' ו) ויחד יתרו רב ושמואל רב אמר שהעביר חרב חדה על בשרו ושמואל אמר שנעשה חדודים חדודים כל בשרו אמר רב ד) [ב] היינו דאמרי אינשי גיורא עד עשרה דרי לא תבזה ארמאי קמיה ז) לכן ישלח האדון ה' צבאות במשמניו רזון מאי במשמניו רזון אמר הקב"ה יבא חזקיהו שיש לו שמונה שמות ויפרע מסנחריב שיש לו שמונה שמות חזקיה דכתיב ח) כי ילד יולד לנו בן ניתן לנו ותהי המשרה על שכמו ויקרא שמו פלא יועץ אל גבור אבי עד שר שלום והאיכא חזקיה שחזקו יה דבר אחר חזקיה שחיזק את ישראל לאביהם שבשמים סנחריב דכתיב ביה [ג] ט) תגלת פלאסר י) פלנאסר כ) שלמנאסר ל) פול מ) סרגון (סרגין) נ) אסנפר רבא ויקירא והאיכא סנחריב שסיחתו ריב דבר אחר שסח וניחר דברים כלפי מעלה א"ר יוחנן מפני מה זכה אותו רשע לקרותו אסנפר רבא ויקירא מפני שלא סיפר בגנותה של ארץ ישראל שנאמר ס) עד בואי ולקחתי אתכם אל ארץ כארצכם רב ושמואל חד אמר מלך פקח היה וחד אמר מלך טיפש היה למאן דאמר מלך פקח היה אי אמינא להו עדיפא מארעייכו אמרו קא משקרת ומאן דאמר מלך טיפש היה אם כן מאי רבותיה להיכא אגלי להו מר זוטרא אמר לאפריקי ורבי חנינא אמר להרי סלוג אבל ישראל ספרו בגנותה של ארץ ישראל כי מטו שוש אמרי שויא כי ארעין כי מטו עלמין אמרו כעלמין כי מטו שוש תרי אמרי על חד תרין ז) ע) ותחת כבודו [יקד] יקוד כיקוד אש א"ר יוחנן תחת כבודו ולא כבודו ממש ו) כי הא דרבי יוחנן קרי ליה למאני מכבדותי ו) רבי אלעזר אמר תחת כבודו ממש כשריפת בני אהרן מה להלן פ) שריפת נשמה וגוף קיים אף כאן שריפת נשמה וגוף קיים תנא משמיה דרבי יהושע בן קרחה פרעה שחירף בעצמו נפרע ממנו הקב"ה בעצמו סנחריב שחירף

ע"י

אינהו עדיפי מיניה וכו'. איידי דגררא בעלמא קתני הכא ומילתא באפי נפשה היא וברוב ספרים אינה כתובה: מ"ט איבעות. דכתיב אבל חרדה גדולה נפלה עליהם: לנשוף. לדלוג: במקום הטנופת. דלא מצי קרי: לימא הכי. לאם כלומר לך אצל העזים והניחני: מ"ס שבתיבת למרבה המשרה סתום לכך נסתם לומר נסתמו הדברים שעלו במחשבה ולא נעשה ל"א שביקש הקב"ה לסתום צרותיהן של ישראל שבקש לעשותו משיח ומורי רבי פירש לפי שנסתם פיו של חזקיה ולא אמר שירה: כל הנסים הללו. שניצל מסנחריב ונתרפא מחליו: שר העולם. מלאך שכל העולם מסור בידו: שמענו צבי לצדיק. שר העולם שאמר עשה צביונו של צדיק: רזי לי רזי לי. נסתרות שלי הן ואני יודע על מה מעכב: אמר נביא אוי לי עד מתי. יבא משיח: עד דאתי בוזזי ובזוזי דבזוזי. עד שנתבזזו שונאי ישראל כמה פעמים: שר הרוחות. שהנשמות נפקדות אצלו והיינו משא דומה כך אמר דומה אלי קורין הרוחות על עסקי שעיר עשו ואומר לי שומר מה מלילה הקב"ה שהוא שומר מה אומר מן הגלות שהוא כלילה: שומר מה מליל. מה דבר מתי קץ הגאולה מליל זה: אתא בקר. בתמיה ואית ספרים דלא כתיב בהו ונכון אמר להם השר כך אמר שומר הקב"ה אתא בקר גאולה תבא וגם לילה אבל מתחלה תהיה גלות הרבה ל"א שיגאלו ויבנה מקדש שני ויחזרו ויגלו גלות זה ל"א וגם לילה לרשעים וכן תרגומו מוכיח אית אגר לצדיקיא ואית פורענות לרשיעיא: אם תבעיון. אם תבקשו להגאל: בעיו. בקשו רחמים: שובו. בתשובה ואתיו לגאולה: גנאי הוא. דבר מגונה עשו: חרב חדה. שמל את עצמו ונתגייר: חדודין חדודין. קמטין קמטין שהיה מיצר מאד על מפלת מצרים: גיורא עד עשרה דרי. הכי הוא משל בני אדם ומיהו יתרו °לאו עשירי הוה: פלא יועץ אל גבור אבי עד שר שלום: שחיזק ישראל. העוסקין בתורה כדלקמן: תגלת פלאסר. שם אחד הוא דכתיב בימי פקח בן רמליה בא תגלת פלאסר מלך אשור: אסנפר חד רבא חד ויקירא חד: כלפי מעלה. כדלקמן שחירף ע"י מלאך: אל ארץ כארצכם. ולא אמר מוטבת מארצכם: קא משקרת. שהרי אין ארץ מעולה הימנה ולכן לא אמר מוטבת מארצכם: להיכא אגלינהו. סנחריב לעשרת השבטים דכתיב (מלכים ב יח) וינחם בחלח ובחבור נהר גוזן וערי מדי הי נינהו אותן מקומות: אבל ישראל. כי אגלינהו סנחריב ספרו בגנותה של א"י דכי מטו לאותו מקום ששמו שוש אמרו שויא לארעין זאת הארץ שויא לארצנו וכשבאו למקום ששמו עלמין אמרו כי עלמין זה המקום שוה לירושלים שנקראת בית עולמים: כשבאו למקום ששמו שוש תרי אמרו על חד תרין. כלומר זה יפה פי שנים כמקומנו ועל שם כך נקראו כל אותן מקומות כך: ה"ג תחת כבודו ולא כבודו ממש. דכבודו ממש משמע בשרו וגופו תחת כבודו משמע תחת הגוף והבשר כלומר נשמה שבתוך הגוף והשתא אמר תחת כבודו ולא כבודו ממש נשמה שבתוך הגוף אלא האי כבודו היינו בגדיו דתחת בגדיהם נשרפו וכי הא דרבי יוחנן וכו' דכל הגוף נשרף תחת הבגדים ולא גרסי' תחת כבודו ולא תחת כבודו ממש דמשמע דמקרא נפקא לזה דהאי תחת כבודו לא תחת כבודו ממש ומהיכא תיפוק ליה האי אבל השתא דדרשא בעלמא דריש ליה: תחת כבודו ממש. תחת גופו ממש שהגוף קיים ונשמה נשרפת: בעצמו. הוא עצמו ולא ע"י שליח לא היה בזיון כל כך ולכך הקב"ה כמו כן נפרע ממנו בעצמו ולא נתבייש כל כך דאינו דומה מתבייש מן הגדול למתבייש מן הקטן:

על

הגהות הגר"א

[א] גמ' שומר מה מליל. נ"ב לא אתא בוקר. כן גי' רש"י: [ב] שם אמר רב. נ"ב פפא: [ג] שם תגלת פלאסר. נ"ב פלסר פלנסר וזה סדרן פול תגלת פלאסר (מ"ב טו) תגלת פלסר (שם טז) תלגת פלנאסר תלגת פלנסר (דה"א ה) שלמנאסר סרגון אסנפר (ובזה א"ש למה שדחק רש"י בד"ה אסנפר):

תורה אור השלם

א) לְםַרְבֵּה הַמִּשְׂרָה וּלְשָׁלוֹם אֵין קֵץ עַל כִּסֵּא דָוִד וְעַל מַמְלַכְתּוֹ לְהָכִין אֹתָהּ וּלְסַעֲדָהּ בְּמִשְׁפָּט וּבִצְדָקָה מֵעַתָּה וְעַד עוֹלָם קִנְאַת יְיָ צְבָאוֹת תַּעֲשֶׂה זֹּאת: [ישעיה ט, ו]

ב) מִכְּנַף הָאָרֶץ זְמִרֹת שָׁמַעְנוּ צְבִי לַצַּדִּיק וָאֹמַר רָזִי לִי רָזִי לִי אוֹי לִי בֹּגְדִים בָּגָדוּ וּבֶגֶד בּוֹגְדִים בָּגָדוּ: [ישעיה כד, טז]

ג) מַשָּׂא דּוּמָה אֵלַי קֹרֵא מִשֵּׂעִיר שֹׁמֵר מַה מִּלַּיְלָה שֹׁמֵר מַה מִּלֵּיל: [ישעיה כא, יא]

ד) אָמַר שֹׁמֵר אָתָה בֹקֶר וְגַם לָיְלָה אִם תִּבְעָיוּן בְּעָיוּ שֻׁבוּ אֵתָיוּ: [ישעיה כא, יב]

ה) וַיֹּאמֶר יִתְרוֹ בָּרוּךְ יְיָ אֲשֶׁר הִצִּיל אֶתְכֶם מִיַּד מִצְרַיִם וּמִיַּד פַּרְעֹה אֲשֶׁר הִצִּיל אֶת הָעָם מִתַּחַת יַד מִצְרָיִם: [שמות יח, י]

ו) וַיִּחַדְּ יִתְרוֹ עַל כָּל הַטּוֹבָה אֲשֶׁר עָשָׂה יְהוָה לְיִשְׂרָאֵל אֲשֶׁר הִצִּילוֹ מִיַּד מִצְרָיִם: [שמות יח, ט]

ז) לָכֵן יְשַׁלַּח הָאָדוֹן יְיָ צְבָאוֹת בְּמִשְׁמַנָּיו רָזוֹן וְתַחַת כְּבֹדוֹ יֵקַד יְקֹד כִּיקוֹד אֵשׁ: [ישעיה י, טז]

ח) כִּי יֶלֶד יֻלַּד לָנוּ בֵּן נִתַּן לָנוּ וַתְּהִי הַמִּשְׂרָה עַל שִׁכְמוֹ וַיִּקְרָא שְׁמוֹ פֶּלֶא יוֹעֵץ אֵל גִּבּוֹר אֲבִי עַד שַׂר שָׁלוֹם: [ישעיה ט, ה]

ט) בִּימֵי פֶּקַח מֶלֶךְ יִשְׂרָאֵל בָּא תִּגְלַת פִּלְאֶסֶר מֶלֶךְ אַשּׁוּר וַיִּקַּח אֶת עִיּוֹן וְאֶת אָבֵל בֵּית מַעֲכָה וְאֶת יָנוֹחַ וְאֶת קֶדֶשׁ וְאֶת חָצוֹר וְאֶת הַגִּלְעָד וְאֶת הַגָּלִילָה כֹּל אֶרֶץ נַפְתָּלִי וַיַּגְלֵם אַשּׁוּרָה: [מלכים ב' טו, כט]

י) וַיָּבֹא עָלָיו תִּלְגַת פִּלְנְאֶסֶר מֶלֶךְ אַשּׁוּר וַיָּצַר לוֹ וְלֹא חֲזָקוֹ: [דברי הימים ב' כח, כ]

כ) עָלָיו עָלָה שַׁלְמַנְאֶסֶר מֶלֶךְ אַשּׁוּר וַיְהִי לוֹ הוֹשֵׁעַ עֶבֶד וַיָּשֶׁב לוֹ מִנְחָה: [מלכים ב' יז, ג]

ל) בָּא פוּל מֶלֶךְ אַשּׁוּר עַל הָאָרֶץ וַיִּתֵּן מְנַחֵם לְפוּל אֶלֶף כִּכַּר כָּסֶף לִהְיוֹת יָדָיו אִתּוֹ לְהַחֲזִיק הַמַּמְלָכָה בְּיָדוֹ: [מלכים ב' טו, יט]

מ) בִּשְׁנַת בֹּא תַרְתָּן אַשְׁדּוֹדָה בִּשְׁלֹחַ אֹתוֹ סַרְגוֹן מֶלֶךְ אַשּׁוּר וַיִּלָּחֶם בְּאַשְׁדּוֹד וַיִּלְכְּדָהּ: [ישעיה כ, א]

נ) וּשְׁאָר אֻמַיָּא דִּי הַגְלִי אָסְנַפַּר רַבָּא וְיַקִּירָא וְהוֹתֵב הִמּוֹ בְּקִרְיָה דִּי שָׁמְרָיִן וּשְׁאָר עֲבַר נַהֲרָה וּכְעֶנֶת: [עזרא ד, י]

ס) עַד בֹּאִי וְלָקַחְתִּי אֶתְכֶם אֶל אֶרֶץ כְּאַרְצְכֶם אֶרֶץ דָּגָן וְתִירוֹשׁ אֶרֶץ לֶחֶם וּכְרָמִים אֶרֶץ זֵית יִצְהָר וּדְבַשׁ וִחְיוּ וְלֹא תָמֻתוּ וְאַל תִּשְׁמְעוּ אֶל חִזְקִיָּהוּ כִּי יַסִּית אֶתְכֶם לֵאמֹר יְיָ יַצִּילֵנוּ: [מלכים ב' יח, לב]

גליון הש"ס

רש"י ד"ה גיורא וכו' לאו עשירי הוה. ובבחיי פרשת יתרו דעשרה דורות ממצרים בן חם עד יתרו:

ליקוטי רש"י

דאינהו נביאי. שנתנבאו לישראל בשליחותו של מקום והוא לא נשתלח לישראל בשום נבואה. מאי טעמא איבעות. דכתיב בקרא אבל חרדה גדולה נפלה עליהם ויברחו בהחבא [מגילה ג.]. אע"ג דאינהו לא חזו מידי. אע"פ שאדם אינו רואה דבר שהוא נבעת ממנו. מזלייהו. מזלו שברקיע רואהו ולכך נבעת [דניאל י, ז]. שר של כל אדם למעלה. לינשוף. ידלג [מגילה שם]. בוזזי ובזוזי דבזוזי. תרחק הישועה עד שיבאו אויבי' בוזזים אחר בוזזים אחרים ושודדי' אחרי שודדי' ה' בגידות אמורות כאן [ישעיה כד, טז]. שוללים אחר שוללים [כתובות קיב:]. דומה. שומר המתים [חגיגה ה.]. שומר. שומר ישראל. מה מלילה. מה תהא מן הלילה והחשכה הזאת [ישעיה כא, יא]. אמר שומר. הקב"ה. אתא בקר. יש לפני להזריח לעשות בקר לכם [שם, יב]. גאולה לצדיקים [ב"ק ג:]. וגם לילה. מתוקן לעשו לעת קץ [ישעיה שם]. חשך לרשעים אם תשובו בתשובה ותבקשו מחילה בעיו [ב"ק שם]. אם תבעיון בעיו. אם תבקשו בקשתכם למהר הקץ. שובו אתיו. בתשובה [ישעיה שם]. שנעשה חדודים חדודים. נעשה בשרו חדודין חדודין מיצר על איבוד מצרים [שמות יח, ט]. כי ילד יולד לנו. אע"פ שאחז רשע הוא בנו הנולד לו זה כמה שנים להיות לנו תחתיו למלך צדיק יהיה. ותהי המשרה על שכמו. ותהיה משרת הקב"ה ועולו על שכמו שיהיה עוסק בתורה ושומר מצות ויטה שכם למשאו של הקב"ה [ישעיה ט, ה]. אסנפר. סנחריב. רבא ויקירא. שהיה מלך גדול ומכובד שנאמר כה אמר המלך הגדול מלך אשור (ישעיה לו) [עזרא ד, י]. אל ארץ כארצכם. כן דרכי להעביר את האומות ממדינה למדינה. מלך פקח היה. היה לו לומר אל ארץ טובה משלהם שהרי לפתותם בא אלא שידע שיכירו שדבריו שקר [מ"ב יח, לב]. יקד יקוד. ישרף שריפה כשריפת אש. תחת כבודו ולא כבודו ממש. תחת בגדיהם יהיו נשרפין הבגדים הם מכבדים את האדם. ומדרש אגדה כאן פרע לבני שם הכבוד שעשה שם לאביו כשכסה ערות נח אביו שנאמר (בראשי' ט') ויקח שם ויפת וגומר [ישעיה י, טז]. ר' יוחנן משמע ליה תחת כבודו כמו תחת רגליו לשון תחתית וכבודו היינו בגדיו והכי קאמר תחת בגדיהם של חיילותיו של סנחריב יקד יקוד ולא בגדיהם נשרפו [שבת קיג:]. מכבדותי. שמכבדין בעליהן [שם.]. תחת כבודו ממש. ותחת כבודו נשרף ולא כבודו ממש והאי כבודו גופו הוא והלכך כשריפת בני אהרן שריפת נשמה וגוף קיים כדאמרינן בסנהדרין בד' מיתות (נב.) [שם: ועיי"ש היטב].

עוֹלָם – **"Master of the Universe!** וּמַה דָּוִד מֶלֶךְ יִשְׂרָאֵל שֶׁאָמַר כַּמָּה שִׁירוֹת וְתִשְׁבָּחוֹת לְפָנֶיךָ לֹא עֲשִׂיתוֹ מָשִׁיחַ – **If David, King of Israel, who recited multitudes** of **songs and praises before You, You did not make the Messiah,** חִזְקִיָּה שֶׁעָשִׂיתָ לוֹ כָּל הַנִּסִּים הַלָּלוּ וְלֹא אָמַר שִׁירָה לְפָנֶיךָ – then **Chizkiah, for whom You performed all these miracles**[14] **and yet he did** ***not*** **sing songs** of gratitude **before You,** תַּעֲשֵׂהוּ מָשִׁיחַ – **will You** really **make** ***him*** **the Messiah?** This would be an injustice!" Thereupon, God relented and did not bring about the Messianic Era, לְכָךְ נִסְתַּתֵּם – and **because of this, [the letter** ***mem*** **]** in the word *lemarbeh* **was closed.**[15]

The Gemara continues:

מִיָּד פָּתְחָה הָאָרֶץ וְאָמְרָה לְפָנָיו – **At that point, the earth**[16] **interjected and said before [God]:** רִבּוֹנוֹ שֶׁל עוֹלָם – **"Master of the Universe!** אֲנִי אוֹמֶרֶת לְפָנֶיךָ שִׁירָה תַּחַת צַדִּיק זֶה – ***I*** **will recite a song** of praise **to You in this righteous man's [Chizkiah's] stead,** וַעֲשֵׂהוּ מָשִׁיחַ – **only make him Messiah!"**[17] פָּתְחָה וְאָמְרָה שִׁירָה לְפָנָיו – Thereupon, **[the earth] began and recited a song** of praise **to [God],** שֶׁנֶּאֱמַר ,,מִכְּנַף הָאָרֶץ זְמִרֹת שָׁמַעְנוּ צְבִי לַצַּדִּיק וגו׳ " **– as it is written:** ***From the edge of the earth we have heard songs [saying], "[Do] the wish*** **(*tzvi*)** ***of the righteous!"*** **etc.** *[and I said: "It is My secret, it is My secret"].*[18] אָמַר שַׂר הָעוֹלָם לְפָנָיו – This means that **the Minister of the World**[19] **said to [God]:** רִבּוֹנוֹ שֶׁל עוֹלָם צִבְיוֹנוֹ עֲשֵׂה לְצַדִּיק זֶה – **"Master of the Universe! Fulfill the wishes (*tzvi*) of this righteous man!"** I.e. establish Chizkiah as the Messiah. יָצְאָה בַּת קוֹל וְאָמְרָה – **A heavenly voice** then **rang out and proclaimed:** רָזִי־לִי רָזִי־לִי – ***"It is My secret; it is My secret!"***[20] I.e. for reasons known only to Me, I will not make Chizkiah the Messiah.

The Gemara proceeds to expound the second half of the verse from *Isaiah* that was just cited:[21]

אָמַר נָבִיא – Upon hearing that the Messiah's coming was not at hand, **the prophet [Isaiah]** mournfully **exclaimed:** ,,אוֹי לִי" אוֹי לִי עַד מָתַי – ***Woe is to me!*** **Woe is to me; until when** must we wait for the Messiah to arrive? יָצְאָה בַּת קוֹל וְאָמְרָה – **A heavenly voice** then **rang out and proclaimed:** ,,בֹּגְדִים בָּגָדוּ וּבֶגֶד בּוֹגְדִים בָּגָדוּ" – ***Treacherous dealers have dealt treacherously; they have indeed dealt very treacherously;*** וְאָמַר רָבָא וְאִיתֵּימָא רַבִּי יִצְחָק – **and** in explaining this passage, **Rava said, or some say R' Yitzchak** said: עַד דְּאָתוּ בָּזוֹזֵי – The meaning is that the Messiah will not arrive **until plunderers come** upon the Jewish people, וּבָזוֹזֵי דְּבָזוֹזֵי – **and** until they are succeeded by **plunderers of plunderers.**[22]

Another passage from *Isaiah* is expounded to convey a similar idea:

,,מַשָּׂא דּוּמָה אֵלַי קֹרֵא מִשֵּׂעִיר שֹׁמֵר מַה־מִּלַּיְלָה שֹׁמֵר מַה־מִּלֵּיל וגו׳ " – Scripture states:[23] ***The harsh prophecy of Dumah: One calls to me from Seir [saying]:*** ***"Watchman, what of the night? Watchman, what of the night?"*** **etc.** אָמַר רַבִּי יוֹחָנָן – **R' Yochanan said:** אוֹתוֹ מַלְאָךְ הַמְּמוּנֶּה עַל הָרוּחוֹת דּוּמָה שְׁמוֹ – **The angel appointed over spirits, i.e. the souls of the dead, is named Dumah.** נִתְקַבְּצוּ כָּל הָרוּחוֹת אֵצֶל דּוּמָה – And this verse tells that **all the spirits assembled before Dumah,** אָמְרוּ לוֹ – **and they said to him:** ,,שֹׁמֵר מַה־מִּלַּיְלָה שֹׁמֵר מַה־מִּלֵּיל" – ***"Watchman, what of the night? Watchman, what does He say?"***;[24] i.e. when will the Exile end and the Messianic Era begin?

NOTES

14. The reference is to the miraculous salvation of Chizkiah from Sancheiriv's siege [*II Kings* chs. 18-19], and to a subsequent incident in which God prolonged Chizkiah's life by curing him of a terminal illness [see *II Kings* ch. 20] (*Rashi*).

15. *Rashi* offers three ways of explaining the symbolic import of this closed *mem*. (a) It indicates that God's plan to make Chizkiah the Messiah was "closed," i.e. not brought to fruition. (b) The *mem* was closed to indicate that God originally planned to make Chizkiah the Messiah, which would have halted ["closed"] the troubles of the Jewish people. (c) It alludes to the idea that Chizkiah's mouth was "closed," i.e. he failed to sing a song of thanksgiving to God when he was delivered from the Assyrian threat.

Emes LeYaakov (*Yoma* 86b) provides a rationale for the apparent connection between the failure to sing *shirah* – songs of thanksgiving – and the halting of Messianic redemption. The point of singing *shirah* is to give tangible expression to our joy at being miraculously saved by God. When we truly experience this joy, it acts as a powerful catalyst to draw us closer to God, and this in turn can bring about our Redemption. In Chizkiah's case, however, the experience of joy was minimized by the failure to sing *shirah,* and this brought a halt to the redemptive process (cf. *Maharal*).

16. Literally: the land, i.e. the Land of Israel (*Maharsha*).

17. As portrayed here, the Land of Israel desires, so to speak, that the Redemption occur. *Maharsha* explains this by noting that during Chizkiah's reign, the Ten Tribes were exiled (see *II Kings* 17:6), and thus, the Land of Israel "suffered" insofar as the Jewish people had been exiled from it. This being so, the Land of Israel pleaded before God for Chizkiah to be crowned the Messiah, and the exile to be ended. (For further comments on the metaphor of the Land proclaiming *shirah* on behalf of Chizkiah, see *Maharal* and *Toras Chaim.*)

18. *Isaiah* 24:16. According to the plain meaning of the verse, this passage describes the reaction of the prophet Isaiah to the approach of the Messianic Era (*Radak*). The Gemara here, however, relates the verse to the earth's plea to God to crown Chizkiah the Messiah. The message of the song, צְבִי לַצַּדִּיק, is translated as *the wish of the righteous person* rather than its plain meaning, *glory to the righteous* (see *Rashi*).

19. An angel into whose hands the entire world has been given (*Rashi*), [i.e. who serves as God's agent in His providential guidance of everything that happens on earth (see *Ramban* to *Exodus* 12:12; see also *Rambam's* Introduction to this chapter, Fifth Principle).]

20. Ibid. This is the continuation of the verse just cited. In it God proclaims, so to speak: "The time of the Messianic Era is known only to Me, and only I know what is preventing the Messiah's arrival" (*Rashi*).

21. The second half of the verse reads: ,,...אוֹי לִי בֹּגְדִים בָּגָדוּ וּבֶגֶד בּוֹגְדִים בָּגָדוּ, *Woe unto me! Treacherous dealers have dealt treacherously; they have indeed dealt very treacherously.*

22. I.e. successive waves of plunderers must torment the Jewish people before the Messiah comes (*Rashi;* see *Maharal*). *Aruch,* however, takes the Gemara to mean that the first group of plunderers (as well as the Jews themselves) will be plundered by a successive wave of plunderers.

23. *Isaiah* 21:11. This rather cryptic passage is generally interpreted as a prediction of the destruction of Dumah, an Ishmaelite tribe (see *Genesis* 25:14). According to *Radak*, Isaiah is saying that the voice of prophecy called to him, informing him that the destroyer of Dumah will emanate from Seir. Out of fear of the attackers, the people of Dumah will appoint watchmen on the walls of their city, and will ask them: "What is new of the night?" I.e. is the invasion imminent?

The Gemara here interprets the verse differently. Dumah is taken as a reference to the angel Dumah, who has charge of the souls of the dead (see *Shabbos* 152b). Accordingly the phrase מַשָּׂא דּוּמָה would mean *the prophecy uttered by Dumah,* rather than *the harsh prophecy concerning Dumah* (*Rashi*).

24. I.e. what does the Watchman – God, Who watches over us – say of the length of our exile, a phenomenon that can be likened to "night"? (*Rashi*).

[According to *Rashi,* the word מִלֵּיל has a double connotation. On the one hand, it is a verb meaning "to speak"(see, for example, *Genesis* 21:7); on the other hand, it is a noun related to לַיְלָה and it means *from the night.* Thus, שֹׁמֵר מַה־מִּלֵּיל means *what does the watchman say (of the night)?*] Earlier, the verse mentions that the souls call out from Seir. This, too, is an allusion to the Exile, for Seir is the homeland of Esau, the eternal nemesis of the Jews (*Rashi*).

Maharsha explains the connection between this particular exegesis of R' Yochanan and the preceding one concerning Chizkiah's failure to become the Messiah. When it seemed that Chizkiah would be crowned the Messiah, the souls of the dead expected to soon be resurrected. However, once they learned that he would not become the Messiah, they lamented: "How much longer will the exile last; how much longer must we wait to be resurrected?"

א) אינהו עדיפי מיניה ואיהו עדיף מניידהו אינהו עדיפי מיניה דאינהו נביאי ואיהו לאו נביא ואיהו עדיף מניידהו דאיהו חזא ואינהו לא חזו וכי מאחר דלא חזו מאי טעמא איבעות אע"ג דאינהו לא חזו מידי מזלייהו חזי אמר רבינא ש"מ האי מאן דמבעית אף על גב דאיהו לא חזי מזליה חזי מאי תקנתיה ב) לינשוף מדוכתיה ארבעה גרמידי אי נמי ליקרי קרית שמע ואי קאי במקום הטנופת לימא הכי עיזא דבי טבחא שמינא מינאי א) למרבה המשרה ולשלום אין קץ וגו' א"ר תנחום דרש בר קפרא בציפורי מפני מה כל מ"ם שבאמצע תיבה פתוח וזה סתום ביקש הקב"ה לעשות חזקיהו משיח וסנחריב גוג ומגוג אמרה מדת הדין לפני הקב"ה רבש"ע ומה דוד מלך ישראל שאמר כמה שירות ותשבחות לפניך לא עשיתו משיח חזקיה שעשית לו כל הנסים הללו ולא אמר שירה לפניך תעשהו משיח לכך נסתתם מיד פתחה הארץ ואמרה לפניו רבש"ע אני אומרת לפניך שירה תחת צדיק זה ועשהו משיח פתחה ואמרה שירה לפניו שנאמר ב) מכנף הארץ זמירות שמענו צבי לצדיק וגו' אמר שר העולם לפניו רבש"ע צביונו עשה לצדיק זה יצאה בת קול ואמרה רזי לי רזי לי אמר נביא אוי לי אוי לי עד מתי יצאה בת קול ואמרה ב) בוגדים בגדו ובגד בוגדים בגדו ואמר רבא ואיתימא ר' יצחק ג) עד דאתו בוזזי ובוזזי דבוזזי ג) משא דומה אלי קורא משעיר שומר מה מלילה שומר מה מליל וגו' א"ר יוחנן אותו מלאך הממונה על הרוחות דומה שמו נתקבצו כל הרוחות אצל דומה אמרו לו שומר מה מלילה שומר מה מליל [א] ד) אמר שומר אתא בקר וגם לילה אם תבעיון בעיו שובו אתיו תנא משום רבי פפיים גנאי הוא לחזקיה וסייעתו שלא אמרו שירה עד שפתחה הארץ ואמרה שירה שנא' ב) מכנף הארץ זמירות שמענו צבי לצדיק וגו' כיוצא בדבר אתה אומר ה) ויאמר יתרו ברוך ה' אשר הציל אתכם תנא משום רבי פפיים גנאי הוא למשה וששים ריבוא שלא אמרו ברוך עד שבא יתרו ואמר ברוך ה' ו) ויחד יתרו רב ושמואל רב אמר שהעביר חרב חדה על בשרו ושמואל אמר שנעשה חדודים חדודים כל בשרו אמר רב ז) [ב] היינו דאמרי אינשי גיורא עד עשרה דרי לא תבזה ארמאי קמיה ז) לכן ישלח האדון ה' צבאות במשמניו רזון מאי במשמניו רזון אמר הקב"ה יבא חזקיהו שיש לו שמונה שמות ויפרע מסנחריב שיש לו שמונה שמות חזקיה דכתיב ח) כי ילד יולד לנו בן ניתן לנו ותהי המשרה על שכמו ויקרא שמו פלא יועץ אל גבור אבי עד שר שלום והאיכא חזקיה שחזקו יה דבר אחר חזקיה שחיזק את ישראל לאביהם שבשמים סנחריב דכתיב ביה [ג] ט) תגלת פלאסר י) פלנאסר כ) שלמנאסר ל) פול מ) סרגון (סרגין) נ) אסנפר רבא ויקירא והאיכא סנחריב שסיחתו ריב דבר אחר שסח וניחר דברים כלפי מעלה א"ר יוחנן מפני מה זכה אותו רשע לקרותו אסנפר רבא ויקירא מפני שלא סיפר בגנותה של ארץ ישראל שנאמר ס) עד בואי ולקחתי אתכם אל ארץ כארצכם רב ושמואל חד אמר מלך פקח היה וחד אמר מלך טיפש היה למאן דאמר מלך פקח היה אי אמינא להו עדיפא מארעייכו אמרו קא משקרת ומאן דאמר מלך טיפש היה אם כן מאי רבותיה להיכא אגלי להו מר זוטרא אמר לאפריקי ורבי חנינא אמר להרי סלוג אבל ישראל ספרו בגנותה של ארץ ישראל כי מטו שוש אמרי שויא כי ארעין כי מטו עלמין אמרו כעלמין כי מטו שוש תרי אמרי על חד תרין ז) ע) ותחת כבודו [יקד] יקוד כיקוד אש א"ר יוחנן תחת כבודו ולא כבודו ממש י) כי הא דרבי יוחנן קרי ליה למאני מכבדותי י) רבי אלעזר אמר תחת כבודו ממש כשריפת בני אהרן מה להלן ח) שריפת נשמה וגוף קיים אף כאן שריפת נשמה וגוף קיים תנא משמיה דרבי יהושע בן קרחה פרעה שחירף בעצמו נפרע הקב"ה ממנו בעצמו סנחריב שחירף ע"י

אינהו עדיפי מיניה וכו'. איידי דגררא בעלמא קתני הכא ומילתא באפי נפשה היא וברוב ספרים אינה כתובה: מ"ט איבעות. דכתיב אבל חרדה גדולה נפלה עליהם: לנשוף. לדלוג: במקום הטנופת. דלא מצי קרי: לימא הכי. לאש כלומר לך אצל העזים והניחני: מ"ם שבתיבת למרבה המשרה סתום לכך נסתם לומר נסתמו הדברים שעלו במחשבה ולא נעשה ל"א שביקש הקב"ה לסתום צרותיהן של ישראל שבקש לעשותו משיח ומורי רבי פירש לפי שנסתם פיו של חזקיה ולא אמר שירה: כל הנסים הללו. שניצל מסנחריב ונתרפא מחליו: שר העולם. מלאך שכל העולם מסור בידו: שמענו צבי לצדיק. שר העולם שאמר עשה צביונו של צדיק: רזי לי רזי לי. נסתרות שלי הן ואני יודע על מה מעכב: אמר נביא אוי לי עד מתי. יבא משיח: עד דאתי בוזזי ובוזזי דבוזזי. עד שנתבזזו שונאי ישראל כמה פעמים: שר הרוחות. שהנשמות נפקדות אצלו והיינו משא דומה כך אמר דומה אלי קורין הרוחות על עסקי שעיר עשו ואומר לי שומר מה מלילה הקב"ה שהוא שומר מה אומר מן הגלות שהוא כלילה: שומר מה מליל. מה דבר מתי קץ הגאולה מליל זה: אתא בקר. בתמיה ואית ספרים דלא כתיב בהו ונכון אמר להם השר כך אמר שומר הקב"ה אתא בקר גאולה תבא וגם לילה אבל מתחלה תהיה גלות הרבה ל"א שיגאלו ויבנה מקדש שני ויחזרו ויגלו גלות זה ל"א וגם לילה לרשעים וכן תרגומו מוכיח אית אגר לצדיקיא ואית פורענות לרשיעיא: אם תבעיון. אם תבקשו להגאל: בעיו. בקשו רחמים: שובו. בתשובה ואתיו לגאולה: גנאי הוא. דבר מגונה עשו: חרב חדה. שמל את עצמו ונתגייר: חדודין חדודין. קמטין קמטין שהיה מיצר מאד על מפלת מצרים: גיורא עד עשרה דרי. הכי הוא משל בני אדם ומיהו יתרו (ט) לאו עשירי הוה: פלא יועץ אל גבור אבי עד שר שלום: שחיזק ישראל. העוסקין בתורה כדלקמן: תגלת פלאסר. שם אחד הוא דכתיב בימי פקח בן רמליה בא תגלת פלאסר מלך אשור: אסנפר חד רבא חד ויקירא חד: כלפי מעלה. כדלקמן שחירף ע"י מלאך: אל ארץ כארצכם. ולא אמר מוטבת מארצכם: קא משקרת. שהרי אין ארץ מעולה הימנה ולכן לא אמר מוטבת מארצכם: להיכא אגלינהו. סנחריב לעשרת השבטים דכתיב (מלכים ב יח) וינחם בחלח ובחבור נהר גוזן וערי מדי הי ניהו אותן מקומות: אבל ישראל. כי אגלינהו סנחריב ספרו בגנותה של א"י דכי מטו לאותו מקום ששמו שוש אמרו שויא לארעין זאת הארץ שויא לארצנו וכשבאו למקום ששמו עלמין אמרו כי עלמין זה המקום שוה לירושלים שנקראת בית עולמים: כשבאו למקום ששמו שוש תרי אמרו על חד תרין. כלומר זה יפה פי שנים כמקומנו ועל שם כך נקראו כל אותן מקומות כך: ה"ג תחת כבודו ולא כבודו ממש. דכבודו ממש משמע בשרו וגופו תחת כבודו משמע תחת הגוף והבשר כלומר נשמה שבתוך הגוף והשתא אמר תחת כבודו ולא כבודו ממש נשמה שבתוך הגוף אלא האי כבודו היינו בגדיו דתחת בגדיהם נשרפו וכי הא דרבי יוחנן וכו' דכל הגוף נשרף תחת הבגדים ולא גרסי' תחת כבודו ולא תחת כבודו ממש דמשמע דמקרא נפקא לזה דהאי תחת כבודו לא תחת כבודו ממש ומהיכא תיפוק ליה האי אבל השתא דדרשא בעלמא דריש ליה: תחת כבודו ממש. תחת גופו ממש שהגוף קיים ונשמה נשרפת: בעצמו. הוא עצמו ולא ע"י שליח לא היה ביזוי כל כך ולכך הקב"ה כמו כן נפרע ממנו בעצמו ולא נתבייש כל כך דאינו דומה מתבייש מן הגדול למתבייש מן הקטן:

על

אל ארץ כארצכם. כן דרכי להעביר את האומות ממדינה למדינה. מלך פקח היה. היה לו לומר אל ארץ טובה משלהם שהרי לפתותם בא אלא שידע שיכירו שדבריו שקר [מ"ב יח, לב]. יקד יקוד. ישרף שריפה כשריפת אש. תחת כבודו ולא כבודו ממש. תחת בגדיהם יהיו נשרפין הבגדים הם מכבדים את האדם. ומדרש אגדה כאן פרע לבני שם הכבוד שעשה שם לאביו כשכסה ערות נח אביו שנאמר (בראשי' ט') ויקח שם ויפת וגומר [ישעיה י, טז]. ר' יוחנן משמע ליה תחת כבודו כמו תחת רגליו לשון תחתית וכבודו היינו בגדיו והכי קאמר תחת בגדיהם של חיילותיו של סנחריב יקד יקוד ולא בגדיהם נשרפו [שבת קיג:]. מכבדותי. שמכבדין עליהן [שם.]. תחת כבודו ממש. ותחת כבודו נשרף ולא כבודו ממש והאי כבודו גופו הוא והלכך כשריפת בני אהרן שריפת נשמה וגוף קיים כדאמרינן בסנהדרין בד' מיתות (נב.) [שם: ועיי"ש היטב].

מסורת הש"ס

א) [מגילה ג.], ב) [סס ע"ש היט'], ג) [כתובות קיב: פירוש באים שודדים על ארץ ישראל ובאים שודדים אחרים ושודדים המשודדים וישראל עמהן. ערוך בערך בז ד'], ד) ילקוט איתא רב פפא, ה) [שבת קיג.], ו) שבת קיג. ב"ק לח:, ז) [ועי' היטב (תוס') בשבת קיג: תרלה שם בגמרא ובפרש"י דהתם שינויים גדולים בלשון ובגרס' אחרת וצריך ישוב למאד], ח) [לעיל נב. וש"נ].

גליון הש"ס

רש"י ד"ה גיורא וכו' לאו עשירי הוה. ובכתבי פרשת יתרו דעשרה דורות ממצרים בן חס עד יתרו:

ליקוטי רש"י

דאינהו נביאי. שנתנבאו לישראל בשליחותו של מקום והוא לא נשלח לישראל בשום נבואה. מאי טעמא איבעות. דכתיב בקרא אבל חרדה גדולה נפלה עליהם ויברחו בהחבא [מגילה ג.]. אע"ג דאינהו לא חזו מידי. אע"פ שאדם אינו רואה דבר שהוא נבעת ממנו. מזלייהו. מזלו שברקיע רואהו ולכך נבעת [דניאל י, ז]. שר של כל אדם למעלה. לינשוף. ידלג [מגילה שם]. בוזזי ובוזזי דבוזזי. תרחק הישועה עד שיבאו אויבי' בוזזים אחר בוזזים ושודדי' אחרי שודדי' ה' בגידות אמורות כאן [ישעיה כד, טז]. שוללים אחר שוללים [כתובות קיב:]. דומה. שומר המתים [חגיגה ה.]. שומר. שומר ישראל. מה מלילה. מה תהא מן הלילה והחשכה הזאת [ישעיה כא, יא]. אמר שומר. הקב"ה. אתא בקר. יש לפני להזריח לעשות בקר לכם [שם, יב]. גאולה לצדיקים [ב"ק ג:]. וגם לילה. מתוקן לעשו לעת קץ [ישעיה שם]. חשך לרשעים אם תשובו בתשובה ותבקשו מחילה בעיו [ב"ק שם]. אם תבעיון בעיו. אם תבקשו בקשתכם למהר הקץ. שובו אתיו. שובו בתשובה [ישעיה שם]. שנעשה חדודים חדודים. נעשה בשרו חדודין חדודין מיצר על איבוד מצרים [שמות יח, ט]. כי ילד יולד לנו. אע"פ שאחז רשע הוא בנו הנולד לו זה כמה שנים להיות לנו תחתיו למלך צדיק יהיה. ותהי המשרה על שכמו. ותהיה משרת הקב"ה ועולו על שכמו שיהיה עוסק בתורה ושומר מצות ויטה שכם למשאו של הקב"ה [ישעיה ט, ה]. אסנפר. סנחריב. רבא ויקירא. שהיה מלך גדול ומכובד שנאמר כה אמר המלך הגדול מלך אשור (ישעיה לו) [עזרא ד, י].

הגהות הגר"א

[א] גמ' שומר מה מליל. נ"ב לא אתא בוקר. כן גי' רש"י: [ב] שם אמר רב. נ"ב פפא: [ג] שם תגלת פלאסר. נ"ב פלנסר פלנאסר וזה סדרן פול תגלת פלאסר (מ"ב טו) תגלת פלנסר (שם טז) תלגת פלנאסר תלגת פלנסר (דה"א ה) שלמנאסר סרגון אסנפר (ובזה א"ל למה שדחק רש"י בד"ה אסנפר):

תורה אור השלם

א) לְםַרְבֵּה הַמִּשְׂרָה וּלְשָׁלוֹם אֵין קֵץ עַל כִּסֵּא דָוִד וְעַל מַמְלַכְתּוֹ לְהָכִין אֹתָהּ וּלְסַעֲדָהּ בְּמִשְׁפָּט וּבִצְדָקָה מֵעַתָּה וְעַד עוֹלָם קִנְאַת יְיָ צְבָאוֹת תַּעֲשֶׂה זֹּאת: [ישעיה ט, ו]

ב) מִכְּנַף הָאָרֶץ זְמִרֹת שָׁמַעְנוּ צְבִי לַצַּדִּיק וָאֹמַר רָזִי לִי רָזִי לִי אוֹי לִי בֹּגְדִים בָּגָדוּ וּבֶגֶד בּוֹגְדִים בָּגָדוּ: [ישעיה כד, טז]

ג) מַשָּׂא דּוּמָה אֵלַי קֹרֵא מִשֵּׂעִיר שֹׁמֵר מַה מִּלַּיְלָה שֹׁמֵר מַה מִּלֵּיל: [ישעיה כא, יא]

ד) אָמַר שֹׁמֵר אָתָא בֹקֶר וְגַם לָיְלָה אִם תִּבְעָיוּן בְּעָיוּ שֻׁבוּ אֵתָיוּ: [ישעיה כא, יב]

ה) וַיֹּאמֶר יִתְרוֹ בָּרוּךְ יְיָ אֲשֶׁר הִצִּיל אֶתְכֶם מִיַּד מִצְרַיִם וּמִיַּד פַּרְעֹה אֲשֶׁר הִצִּיל אֶת הָעָם מִתַּחַת יַד מִצְרָיִם: [שמות יח, י]

ו) וַיִּחַדְּ יִתְרוֹ עַל כָּל הַטּוֹבָה אֲשֶׁר עָשָׂה יְהוָה לְיִשְׂרָאֵל אֲשֶׁר הִצִּילוֹ מִיַּד מִצְרָיִם: [שמות יח, ט]

ז) לָכֵן יְשַׁלַּח הָאָדוֹן יְיָ צְבָאוֹת בְּמִשְׁמַנָּיו רָזוֹן וְתַחַת כְּבֹדוֹ יֵקַד יְקֹד כִּיקוֹד אֵשׁ: [ישעיה י, טז]

ח) כִּי יֶלֶד יֻלַּד לָנוּ בֵּן נִתַּן לָנוּ וַתְּהִי הַמִּשְׂרָה עַל שִׁכְמוֹ וַיִּקְרָא שְׁמוֹ פֶּלֶא יוֹעֵץ אֵל גִּבּוֹר אֲבִי עַד שַׂר שָׁלוֹם: [ישעיה ט, ה]

ט) בִּימֵי פֶּקַח מֶלֶךְ יִשְׂרָאֵל בָּא תִּגְלַת פִּלְאֶסֶר מֶלֶךְ אַשּׁוּר וַיִּקַּח אֶת עִיּוֹן וְאֶת אָבֵל בֵּית מַעֲכָה וְאֶת יָנוֹחַ וְאֶת קֶדֶשׁ וְאֶת חָצוֹר וְאֶת הַגִּלְעָד וְאֶת הַגָּלִילָה כֹּל אֶרֶץ נַפְתָּלִי וַיַּגְלֵם אַשּׁוּרָה: [מלכים ב' טו, כט]

י) וַיָּבֹא עָלָיו תִּלְּגַת פִּלְנְאֶסֶר מֶלֶךְ אַשּׁוּר וַיָּצַר לוֹ וְלֹא חֲזָקוֹ: [דברי הימים ב' כח, כ]

כ) עָלָיו עָלָה שַׁלְמַנְאֶסֶר מֶלֶךְ אַשּׁוּר וַיְהִי לוֹ הוֹשֵׁעַ עֶבֶד וַיָּשֶׁב לוֹ מִנְחָה: [מלכים ב' יז, ג]

ל) בָּא פוּל מֶלֶךְ אַשּׁוּר עַל הָאָרֶץ וַיִּתֵּן מְנַחֵם לְפוּל אֶלֶף כִּכַּר כָּסֶף לִהְיוֹת יָדָיו אִתּוֹ לְהַחֲזִיק הַמַּמְלָכָה בְּיָדוֹ: [מלכים ב' טו, יט]

מ) בִּשְׁנַת בֹּא תַרְתָּן אַשְׁדּוֹדָה בִּשְׁלֹחַ אֹתוֹ סַרְגוֹן מֶלֶךְ אַשּׁוּר וַיִּלָּחֶם בְּאַשְׁדּוֹד וַיִּלְכְּדָהּ: [ישעיה כ, א]

נ) וּשְׁאָר אֻמַיָּא דִּי הַגְלִי אָסְנַפַּר רַבָּא וְיַקִּירָא וְהוֹתֵב הִמּוֹ בְּקִרְיָה דִּי שָׁמְרָיִן וּשְׁאָר עֲבַר נַהֲרָה וּכְעֶנֶת: [עזרא ד, י]

ס) עַד בֹּאִי וְלָקַחְתִּי אֶתְכֶם אֶל אֶרֶץ כְּאַרְצְכֶם אֶרֶץ דָּגָן וְתִירוֹשׁ אֶרֶץ לֶחֶם וּכְרָמִים אֶרֶץ זֵית יִצְהָר וּדְבַשׁ וִחְיוּ וְלֹא תָמֻתוּ וְאַל תִּשְׁמְעוּ אֶל חִזְקִיָּהוּ כִּי יַסִּית אֶתְכֶם לֵאמֹר יְיָ יַצִּילֵנוּ: [מלכים ב' יח, לב]

,,אָמַר שֹׁמֵר אָתָה בֹקֶר וְגַם־לָיְלָה – The next verse then states: ***The Watchman replied, "Morning comes, and also night;***[25] meaning, the end is not yet at hand. אִם־תִּבְעָיוּן בְּעָיוּ – [However,] ***if you seek*** [to hasten the advent of the Messiah, then] ***seek*** [God's Mercy, and] שֻׁבוּ אֵתָיוּ'' – ***repent;*** [this will] ***bring*** [the Redemption!]"[26]

The Gemara returns to the topic of Chizkiah's failure to sing praises after his miraculous redemption from Sancheiriv:

תָּנָא מִשּׁוּם רַבִּי פַּפְּיָיס – **A Tanna taught in the name of R' Papyas:** גְּנַאי הוּא לְחִזְקִיָּה וְסִיַּיעְתּוֹ שֶׁלֹּא אָמְרוּ שִׁירָה – **It is to the discredit of Chizkiah and his subjects that they did not recite songs** of praise to God עַד שֶׁפָּתְחָה הָאָרֶץ וְאָמְרָה שִׁירָה – **until the earth** itself **interjected and recited** such **a song** in their stead. How, indeed, is it known that the earth recited such a song? שֶׁנֶּאֱמַר – **For it is written:**[27] ,,מִכְּנַף הָאָרֶץ זְמִרֹת שָׁמַעְנוּ – ***From the uttermost part of the earth we have heard songs [saying],*** צְבִי לַצַּדִּיק וגו'" – ***"[Do] the wish (tzvi) of the righteous!"*** **etc.**

The Gemara now sets forth a similar criticism directed at Moses and the generation of Jews who experienced the Exodus:

כַּיּוֹצֵא בַּדָּבָר אַתָּה אוֹמֵר – **You** may **say** the same about this verse: ,,וַיֹּאמֶר יִתְרוֹ בָּרוּךְ ה' אֲשֶׁר הִצִּיל אֶתְכֶם" – ***Yisro said, "Blessed is God, Who rescued you*** *from the hand of Egypt and from the hand of Pharaoh."*[28] תָּנָא מִשּׁוּם רַבִּי פַּפְּיָיס – **A Tanna taught in the name of R' Papyas:** גְּנַאי הוּא לְמֹשֶׁה וְשִׁשִּׁים רִיבּוֹא שֶׁלֹּא אָמְרוּ ,,בָּרוּךְ" – **It is to the discredit of Moses and the six hundred thousand** Jews who experienced the Exodus **that they did not say *"Blessed [is God]"*** upon being saved from the Egyptians, עַד שֶׁבָּא יִתְרוֹ וְאָמַר ,,בָּרוּךְ ה'" – **until Yisro,** who was not born of the Jewish people, **came and said** these words, ***"Blessed is God*** [for having saved you"].[29]

The Gemara probes a further aspect of Yisro's response to the news that the Egyptians had been destroyed:

,,וַיִּחַדְּ יִתְרוֹ" – Scripture states that upon hearing of the Jews' salvation, ***Yisro rejoiced*** *(vayichad).*[30] רַב וּשְׁמוּאֵל – **Rav and Shmuel** disputed the allusion inherent in this: רַב אָמַר שֶׁהֶעֱבִיר חֶרֶב חַדָּה עַל בְּשָׂרוֹ – **Rav said** the verse conveys **that [Yisro] passed a sharp** ***(chadah)*** **sword over his flesh,** i.e. he circumcised himself.[31] וּשְׁמוּאֵל אָמַר שֶׁנַּעֲשָׂה חִדּוּדִים חִדּוּדִים כָּל בְּשָׂרוֹ – **And Shmuel said** it conveys **that [Yisro's] flesh became covered with goose bumps** *(chiddudim)* because of the distress he felt at the downfall of Egypt.[32]

אָמַר רַב – Concerning this latter view, **Rav**[33] **said:** הַיְינוּ דְּאָמְרֵי אִינָשֵׁי – **This** accords with **the popular adage:** גִּיּוֹרָא עַד עֲשָׂרָה דָּרֵי – **"A proselyte unto the tenth generation,**[34] לָא תְּבַזֶּה אֲרַמָּאֵי קַמֵּיהּ – **do not insult an Aramean** [that is, a gentile] **in his presence,"** for he will surely take offense. Although Yisro rejoiced, he still remained sensitive to the misfortunes that befell the Egyptians.

The Gemara resumes its discussion of Chizkiah:

,,לָכֵן יְשַׁלַּח הָאָדוֹן ה' צְבָאוֹת בְּמִשְׁמַנָּיו רָזוֹן" – Scripture states:[35] ***Therefore, the Lord God of Hosts shall send leanness into his fat ones.*** מַאי ,,בְּמִשְׁמַנָּיו רָזוֹן" – **What is the meaning of** ***leanness into his fat ones?*** אָמַר הַקָּדוֹשׁ בָּרוּךְ הוּא – **The Holy One, Blessed is He, said:** יָבֹא חִזְקִיָּהוּ שֶׁיֵּשׁ לוֹ שְׁמוֹנָה שֵׁמוֹת – **Let Chizkiah, who has eight names, come** וְיִפָּרַע מִסַּנְחֵרִיב שֶׁיֵּשׁ לוֹ שְׁמוֹנָה שֵׁמוֹת – **and punish Sancheiriv who** likewise **has eight names.**[36]

The Gemara explains:

חִזְקִיָּה דִּכְתִיב – **Chizkiah** had eight names, **for** in reference to him **it is written:**[37] ,,כִּי־יֶלֶד יֻלַּד־לָנוּ בֵּן נִתַּן־לָנוּ – ***For a child is born to us, a son is given us;*** וַתְּהִי הַמִּשְׂרָה עַל־שִׁכְמוֹ – ***and [God's]*** authority is upon his shoulder; וַיִּקְרָא שְׁמוֹ – ***his name is called:*** פֶּלֶא יוֹעֵץ – ***Wondrous Adviser,*** אֵל גִּבּוֹר – ***Mighty Warrior,***[38]

NOTES

25. I.e. redemption will surely come, but it will not come soon; a long exile (night) will precede it.

Rashi suggests two other possible meanings: (a) *Morning will come:* The Babylonian exile will end and a second Temple will be built, but *night will also come* as well; this second Temple will be destroyed, and another exile will follow. (b) *Morning will come:* Redemption will come for the righteous, but also night; i.e. the wicked shall experience this redemption as a punishment.

This last interpretation is supported by the rendering of *Targum.*

26. These words, אִם־תִּבְעָיוּן בְּעָיוּ שֻׁבוּ אֵתָיוּ, are the final words of *Isaiah* 21:12, the passage the Gemara has been citing. They are interpreted to mean: If you truly seek to repent and thereby end the exile, do so!

27. See note 17.

28. *Exodus* 18:10. The surrounding verses tell that Yisro — the father-in-law of Moses — met Moses in the Wilderness, following the Jews' miraculous salvation from the Egyptians at the Red Sea. After Moses tells of all the miracles God had performed for the Jews in Egypt, Yisro blesses God.

29. A difficulty suggests itself here: The Jewish people *did* sing a song of praise to God after the Egyptians were drowned in the Red Sea. Why, then, are they criticized here for failing to "bless" God in acknowledgment of His miracles?

In dealing with this, *Maharal* points out that the Jews at that time *sang* to God, but they did not *bless* Him. *Maharal* goes on to distinguish between the concepts of song and blessing, asserting that one who blesses God has achieved a higher level of spirituality than one who praises Him in song.

The Gemara elsewhere (*Berachos* 54a) cites Yisro as the source for the obligation to bless God when He performs miracles.

30. *Exodus* 18:9.

31. I.e. when Yisro heard of the miracles surrounding the Exodus, he was moved to convert to Judaism (*Rashi*).

32. *Anaf Yosef* suggests that Rav and Shmuel do not disagree with one another; rather, Yisro experienced *both* these conflicting reactions. He was inspired to convert to Judaism by God's deliverance of the Jewish people from the Egyptian aggressors, but also — as a former gentile himself — he felt a tinge of distress at the destruction of his former brethren.

33. The *Gra* emends the text to read "Rav Pappa" rather than "Rav." The reading of "Rav Pappa" is supported by the fact that throughout the Talmud, Rav Pappa is often one who quotes popular sayings (*Margaliyos HaYam*).

34. I.e. the tenth-generation descendant of a proselyte. [Yisro was a proselyte himself, not the descendant of a proselyte. Nevertheless, the Gemara mentions a descendant because this was the language employed in the adage (*Rashi*). *Rabbeinu Bachya* (cited in *Gilyon HaShas*) suggests that Yisro was a tenth-generation descendant of Mitzraim the son of Ham (the progenitor of the Egyptians). Although he himself was not an Egyptian, it still pained Yisro to hear what had happened to the Egyptians, though he was removed from their line by ten generations. This is the source for the adage (cf. *Yaaros Devash*).]

35. *Isaiah* 10:16. In the verses that precede this one, the prophet states that Israel's oppressor [Sancheiriv] will presume that his successes are due to the superiority of his strategy, rather than to the Hand of Divine Providence. In this verse, Isaiah foretells that God will punish Sancheiriv for this arrogance.

36. The plain meaning of the verse is that God will cause Sancheiriv's officers — "his fat ones" — to become "lean," i.e. weak. Nevertheless, a connection is made between the term *mishmanav* ("fat ones") and the similar sounding word, *shemonah,* eight. The verse is thus taken to also denote the downfall of Sancheiriv himself, who had eight titles (see *Maharsha*).

37. *Isaiah* 9:5.

38. [The power of Chizkiah is described by the use of God's Name אֵל. While it may seem unusual for a human being to be described using the Name of God, there are other examples of this (see for example, *Megillah* 18a, which states that our forefather Jacob was described in such a fashion).]

א) אינהו עדיפי מיניה ואיהו עדיף מנייהו
אינהו עדיפי מיניה דאינהו נביאי ואיהו לאו
נביא ואיהו עדיף מנייהו דאיהו חזא ואינהו
לא חזו וכי מאחר דלא חזו מאי טעמא
איבעות אע"ג דאינהו לא חזו מידי מזלייהו
חזי אמר רבינא ש"מ האי מאן דמבעית
אף על גב דאיהו לא חזי מזליה חזי מאי
תקנתיה ב) לינשוף מדוכתיה ארבעה גרמידי
אי נמי ליקרי קרית שמע ואי קאי במקום
הטנופת לימא הכי עיזא דבי טבחא שמינא
מינאי א) למרבה המשרה ולשלום אין קץ וגו'
א"ר תנחום דרש בר קפרא בציפורי מפני
מה כל מ"ם שבאמצע תיבה פתוח וזה
סתום ביקש הקב"ה לעשות חזקיהו משיח
וסנחריב גוג ומגוג אמרה מדת הדין לפני
הקב"ה רבש"ע ומה דוד מלך ישראל
שאמר כמה שירות ותשבחות לפניך לא
עשיתו משיח חזקיה שעשית לו כל הנסים
הללו ולא אמר שירה לפניך תעשהו משיח
לכך נסתתם מיד פתחה הארץ ואמרה לפניו
רבש"ע אני אומרת לפניך שירה תחת צדיק
זה ועשהו משיח פתחה ואמרה שירה לפניו
שנאמר ב) מכנף הארץ זמירות שמענו צבי
לצדיק וגו' אמר שר העולם לפניו רבש"ע
צביונו עשה לצדיק זה יצאה בת קול ואמרה
רזי לי רזי לי אמר נביא אוי לי אוי לי עד מתי
יצאה בת קול ואמרה ב) בוגדים בגדו ובגד
בוגדים בגדו ואמר רבא ואיתימא ר' יצחק
ג) עד דאתו בוזזי ובזוזי דבזוזי ג) משא דומה
אלי קורא משעיר שומר מה מלילה שומר
מה מליל וגו' א"ר יוחנן אותו מלאך הממונה
על הרוחות דומה שמו נתקבצו כל הרוחות
אצל דומה אמרו לו שומר מה מלילה שומר מה מליל [א] ד) אמר שומר אתא בקר
וגם לילה אם תבעיון בעיו שובו אתיו תנא משום רבי פפיים גנאי הוא לחזקיה
וסייעתו שלא אמרו שירה עד שפתחה הארץ ואמרה שירה שנא' ב) מכנף הארץ זמירות שמענו צבי לצדיק וגו'
כיוצא בדבר אתה אומר ה) ויאמר יתרו ברוך ה' אשר הציל אתכם תנא משום רבי פפיים גנאי הוא למשה
וששים ריבוא שלא אמרו ברוך עד שבא יתרו ואמר ברוך ה' ו) ויחד יתרו רב ושמואל רב אמר שהעביר חרב חדה
על בשרו ושמואל אמר שנעשה חדודים חדודים כל בשרו אמר רב ד) [ב] היינו דאמרי אינשי גיורא עד עשרה דרי
לא תבזה ארמאי קמיה ז) לכן ישלח האדון ה' צבאות במשמניו רזון מאי במשמניו רזון אמר הקב"ה יבא חזקיהו
שיש לו שמונה שמות ויפרע מסנחריב שיש לו שמונה שמות חזקיה דכתיב ח) כי ילד יולד לנו בן ניתן לנו ותהי
המשרה על שכמו ויקרא שמו פלא יועץ אל גבור אבי עד שר שלום והאיכא חזקיה שחזקו יה דבר אחר
חזקיה שחיזק את ישראל לאביהם שבשמים סנחריב דכתיב ביה [ג] ט) תגלת פלאסר י) פלנאסר כ) שלמנאסר
ל) פול מ) סרגון (סרגין) נ) אסנפר רבא ויקירא והאיכא סנחריב שסיחתו ריב דבר אחר שסח וניחר דברים
כלפי מעלה א"ר יוחנן מפני מה זכה אותו רשע לקרותו אסנפר רבא ויקירא מפני שלא סיפר בגנותה
של ארץ ישראל שנאמר ס) עד בואי ולקחתי אתכם אל ארץ כארצכם רב ושמואל חד אמר מלך פקח
היה וחד אמר מלך טיפש היה למאן דאמר מלך פקח היה אי אמינא להו עדיפא מארעייכו אמרו קא
משקרת ומאן דאמר מלך טיפש היה אם כן מאי רבותיה להיכא אגלי להו מר זוטרא אמר לאפריקי
ורבי חנינא אמר להרי סלוג אבל ישראל ספרו בגנותה של ארץ ישראל כי מטו שוש אמרי שויא כי
ארעין כי מטו עלמין אמרו כעלמין כי מטו שוש תרי אמרי על חד תרין ה) ותחת כבודו [יקד] יקוד כיקוד
אש א"ר יוחנן תחת כבודו ולא כבודו ממש ו) כי הא דרבי יוחנן קרי ליה למאני מכבדותי ז) רבי אלעזר
אמר תחת כבודו ממש כשריפת בני אהרן מה להלן ח) שריפת נשמה וגוף קיים אף כאן שריפת נשמה וגוף
קיים תנא משמיה דרבי יהושע בן קרחה פרעה שחירף בעצמו נפרע הקב"ה ממנו בעצמו סנחריב שחירף
ע"י

רש"י

אינהו עדיפי מיניה וכו'. איידי דגררא בעלמא קתני הכא ומילתא באפי נפשה היא וברוב ספרים אינה כתובה: מ"ט איבעות. דכתיב אבל חרדה גדולה נפלה עליהם: לנשוף. לדלוג: במקום הטנופת. דלא מצי קרי: לימא הכי. לאו כלומר לך אצל העזים והניחני: מ"ס שבתיבת למרבה המשרה סתום לכך נסתם לומר נסתמו הדברים שעלו במחשבה ולא נעשה ל"א שביקש הקב"ה לסתום צרותיהן של ישראל שבקש לעשותו משיח ומורי רבי פירש לפי שנסתם פיו של חזקיה ולא אמר שירה: כל הנסים הללו. שניצל מסנחריב ונתרפא מחליו: שר העולם. מלאך שכל העולם מסור בידו: שמענו צבי לצדיק. שר העולם שאמר עשה צביונו של צדיק: רזי לי רזי לי. נסתרות שלי הן ואני יודע על מה מעכב: אמר נביא אוי לי עד מתי. יבא משיח: עד דאתי בוזזי ובוזזי דבוזזי. עד שנתבזזו שונאי ישראל כמה פעמים: שר הרוחות. שהנשמות נפקדות אצלו והיינו משא דומה כך אמר דומה אלי קורין הרוחות על עסקי שעיר עשו ואומר לי שומר מה מלילה הקב"ה שהוא שומר מה אומר מן הגלות שהוא כלילה: שומר מה מליל. מה דבר מתי קץ הגאולה מליל זה: אתא בקר. בתמיה ואית ספרים דלא כתיב בהו ונכון אמר להם השר כך אמר שומר הקב"ה אתא בקר גאולה תבא וגם לילה אבל מתחלה תהיה גלות הרבה ל"א שיגאלו ויבנה מקדש שני ויחזרו ויגלו גלות זה ל"א וגם לילה לרשעים וכן תרגומו מוכיח אית אגר לצדיקיא ואית פורענות לרשיעיא: אם תבעיון. אם תבקשו להגאל: בעיו. בקשו רחמים: שובו. בתשובה ואתיו לגאולה: גנאי הוא. דבר מגונה עשו: חרב חדה. שמל את עצמו ונתגייר: חדודין חדודין. קמטין קמטין שהיה מיצר מאד על מפלת מצרים: גיורא עד עשרה דרי. הכי הוא משל בני אדם ומיהו יתרו [ט] לאו עשירי הוה: פלא יועץ אל גבור אבי עד שר שלום: שחיזק ישראל. העוסקין בתורה כדלקמן: תגלת פלאסר. שם אחד הוא דכתיב בימי פקח בן רמליה בא תגלת פלאסר מלך אשור: אסנפר חד רבא חד ויקירא חד: כלפי מעלה. כדלקמן שחירף ע"י מלאך: אל ארץ כארצכם. ולא אמר מוטבת מארצכם: קא משקרת. שהרי אין ארץ מעולה הימנה ולכן לא אמר מוטבת מארצכם: להיכא אגלינהו. סנחריב לעשרת השבטים דכתיב (מלכים ב יח) וינחם בחלח ובחבור נהר גוזן וערי מדי הי נינהו אותן מקומות: אבל ישראל. כי אגלינהו סנחריב ספרו בגנותה של א"י דכי מטו לאותו מקום ששמו שוש אמרו שוה לארעין זאת הארץ שוה לארצנו וכשבאו למקום ששמו עלמין אמרו כי עלמין זה המקום שוה לירושלים שנקראת בית עולמים: כשבאו למקום ששמו שוש תרי אמרו על חד תרין. כלומר זה יפה פי שנים כמקומנו ועל שם כך נקראו כל אותן מקומות כך: ה"ג תחת כבודו ולא כבודו ממש. דכבודו ממש משמע בשרו וגופו תחת כבודו משמע תחת הגוף והבשר כלומר נשמה שבתוך הגוף והשתא אמר תחת כבודו ולא כבודו ממש נשמה שבתוך הגוף אלא האי כבודו היינו בגדיו דתחת בגדיהם נשרפו וכי הא דרבי יוחנן וכו' דכל הגוף נשרף תחת הבגדים ולא גרסי' תחת כבודו ולא תחת כבודו ממש דמשמע דמקרא נפקא לזה דהאי תחת כבודו לא תחת כבודו ממש ומהיכא תיפוק ליה האי אבל השתא דדרשא בעלמא דריש ליה: תחת כבודו ממש. תחת גופו ממש שהגוף קיים ונשמה נשרפת: בעצמו. הוא עצמו ולא ע"י שליח לא היה ביזוי כל כך ולכך הקב"ה כמו כן נפרע ממנו בעצמו ולא נתבייש כל כך דאינו דומה מתבייש מן הגדול למתבייש מן הקטן:

מסורת הש"ס

א) [מגילה ג.], ב) [שם ע"ש היטב], ג) [כתובות קיב: פירוש באים שודדים על ארץ ישראל ובאים שודדים אחרים ושודדים המשודדים וישראל עמהן. ערוך בערך בז ד'], ד) בילקוט איתא רב פפא, ה) [שבת קיג:], ו) שבת קיג. ב"ק לח., ז) [ועי' היטב (תוס') בשבת קיג: תראה שם בגמרא ובפרש"י דהתם שינויים גדולים בלשון ובגרס' אחרת וצריך ישוב למאד], ח) [לעיל נב. וש"נ].

גליון הש"ס

רש"י ד"ה גיורא וכו' לאו עשירי הוה. ובכמי' פרשת יתרו דעשרה דורות ממצרים בן חם עד יתרו:

ליקוטי רש"י

דאינהו נביאי. שנתנבאו לישראל בשליחותו של מקום והוא לא נשתלח לישראל בשום נבואה. מאי טעמא איבעות. דכתיב בקרא אבל חרדה גדולה נפלה עליהם ויברחו בהחבא [מגילה ג.]. אע"ג דאינהו לא חזו מידי. אע"פ שאדם אינו רואה דבר שהוא נבעת ממנו. מזלייהו. מזלו שברקיע רואהו ולכך נבעת [דניאל י, ז]. שר של כל אדם למעלה. לינשוף. ידלג [מגילה שם]. בוזזי ובוזזי דבוזזי. תרחק הישועה עד שיבאו אויבי' בוזזים אחר בוזזים אחרים ושודדי' אחרי שודדי' ה' בגידות אמורות כאן [ישעיה כד, טז]. שוללים אחר שוללים [כתובות קיב:]. דומה. שומר המתים [חגיגה ה.]. שומר. שומר ישראל. מה מלילה. מה תהא מן הלילה והחשכה הזאת [ישעיה כא, יא]. אמר שומר. הקב"ה. אתא בקר. יש לפני להזריח לעשות בקר לכם [שם, יב]. גאולה לצדיקים [ב"ק ג:]. וגם לילה. מתוקן לעשו לעת קץ [ישעיה שם]. חשך לרשעים אם תשובו בתשובה ותבקשו מחילה בעיו [ב"ק שם]. אם תבעיון בעיו. אם תבקשו בקשתכם למהר הקץ. שובו אתיו. בתשובה [ישעיה שם]. שנעשה חדודים חדודים. נעשה בשרו חדודין חדודין מיצר על איבוד מצרים [שמות יח, ט]. כי ילד יולד לנו. אע"פ שאחז רשע הוא בנו הנולד לו זה כמה שנים להיות לנו תחתיו למלך צדיק יהיה. ותהי המשרה על שכמו. ותהיה משרת הקב"ה ועולו על שכמו שיהיה עוסק בתורה ושומר מצות ויטה שכם למשאו של הקב"ה [ישעיה ט, ה]. אסנפר. סנחריב. רבא ויקירא. שהיה מלך גדול ומכובד שנאמר כה אמר המלך הגדול מלך אשור (ישעיה לו) [עזרא ד, י]. אל ארץ כארצכם. כן דרכי להעביר את האומות ממדינה למדינה. מלך פקח היה. היה לו לומר אל ארץ טובה משלהם שהרי לפתותם בא אלא שידע שיכירו שדבריו שקר [מ"ב יח, לב]. יקד יקוד. ישרף שריפה כשריפת אש. תחת כבודו ולא כבודו ממש. תחת בגדיהם יהיו נשרפין הבגדים הם מכבדים את האדם. ומדרש אגדה כאן פרע לבני שם הכבוד שעשה שם לאביו כשכסה ערות נח אביו שנאמר (בראשי' ט') ויקח שם ויפת וגומר [ישעיה י, טז]. ר' יוחנן משמע ליה תחת כבודו כמו תחת רגליו לשון תחתית וכבודו היינו בגדיו והכי קאמר תחת בגדיהם של חיילותיו של סנחריב יקד יקוד ולא בגדיהם נשרפו [שבת קיג:]. מכבדותי. שמכבדין בעליהן [שם.]. תחת כבודו ממש. ותחת כבודו נשרף ולא כבודו ממש והאי כבודו גופו הוא והלכך כשריפת בני אהרן שריפת נשמה וגוף קיים כדאמרינן בסנהדרין בד' מיתות (נג.) [שם: ועיי"ש היטב].

הגהות הגר"א

[א] גמ' שומר מה מליל. נ"ב לא אתא בוקר. כן גי' רש"י: [ב] שם אמר רב. נ"ב פפא: [ג] שם תגלת פלאסר. נ"ב פלסר פלנסר וזה סדרן פול תגלת פלאסר (מ"ב טו) תגלת פלסר (שם טז) תלגת פלנאסר תלגת פלנסר (דה"א ה) שלמנאסר סרגון אסנפר (ובזה א"ל למה שדחק רש"י בד"ה אסנפר):

תורה אור השלם

א) לְםַרְבֵּה הַמִּשְׂרָה וּלְשָׁלוֹם אֵין קֵץ עַל כִּסֵּא דָוִד וְעַל מַמְלַכְתּוֹ לְהָכִין אֹתָהּ וּלְסַעֲדָהּ בְּמִשְׁפָּט וּבִצְדָקָה מֵעַתָּה וְעַד עוֹלָם קִנְאַת יְיָ צְבָאוֹת תַּעֲשֶׂה זֹּאת: [ישעיה ט, ו]

ב) מִכְּנַף הָאָרֶץ זְמִרֹת שָׁמַעְנוּ צְבִי לַצַּדִּיק וָאֹמַר רָזִי לִי רָזִי לִי אוֹי לִי בֹּגְדִים בָּגָדוּ וּבֶגֶד בּוֹגְדִים בָּגָדוּ: [ישעיה כד, טז]

ג) מַשָּׂא דּוּמָה אֵלַי קֹרֵא מִשֵּׂעִיר שֹׁמֵר מַה מִּלַּיְלָה שֹׁמֵר מַה מִּלֵּיל: [ישעיה כא, יא]

ד) אָמַר שֹׁמֵר אָתָה בֹקֶר וְגַם לָיְלָה אִם תִּבְעָיוּן בְּעָיוּ שֻׁבוּ אֵתָיוּ: [ישעיה כא, יב]

ה) וַיֹּאמֶר יִתְרוֹ בָּרוּךְ יְיָ אֲשֶׁר הִצִּיל אֶתְכֶם מִיַּד מִצְרַיִם וּמִיַּד פַּרְעֹה אֲשֶׁר הִצִּיל אֶת הָעָם מִתַּחַת יַד מִצְרָיִם: [שמות יח, י]

ו) וַיִּחַדְּ יִתְרוֹ עַל כָּל הַטּוֹבָה אֲשֶׁר עָשָׂה יְהוָה לְיִשְׂרָאֵל אֲשֶׁר הִצִּילוֹ מִיַּד מִצְרָיִם: [שמות יח, ט]

ז) לָכֵן יְשַׁלַּח הָאָדוֹן יְיָ צְבָאוֹת בְּמִשְׁמַנָּיו רָזוֹן וְתַחַת כְּבֹדוֹ יֵקַד יְקֹד כִּיקוֹד אֵשׁ: [ישעיה י, טז]

ח) כִּי יֶלֶד יֻלַּד לָנוּ בֵּן נִתַּן לָנוּ וַתְּהִי הַמִּשְׂרָה עַל שִׁכְמוֹ וַיִּקְרָא שְׁמוֹ פֶּלֶא יוֹעֵץ אֵל גִּבּוֹר אֲבִי עַד שַׂר שָׁלוֹם: [ישעיה ט, ה]

ט) בִּימֵי פֶּקַח מֶלֶךְ יִשְׂרָאֵל בָּא תִּגְלַת פִּלְאֶסֶר מֶלֶךְ אַשּׁוּר וַיִּקַּח אֶת עִיּוֹן וְאֶת אָבֵל בֵּית מַעֲכָה וְאֶת יָנוֹחַ וְאֶת קֶדֶשׁ וְאֶת חָצוֹר וְאֶת הַגִּלְעָד וְאֶת הַגָּלִילָה כֹּל אֶרֶץ נַפְתָּלִי וַיַּגְלֵם אַשּׁוּרָה: [מלכים ב' טו, כט]

י) וַיָּבֹא עָלָיו תִּלְגַת פִּלְנְאֶסֶר מֶלֶךְ אַשּׁוּר וַיָּצַר לוֹ וְלֹא חֲזָקוֹ: [דברי הימים ב' כח, כ]

כ) עָלָיו עָלָה שַׁלְמַנְאֶסֶר מֶלֶךְ אַשּׁוּר וַיְהִי לוֹ הוֹשֵׁעַ עֶבֶד וַיָּשֶׁב לוֹ מִנְחָה: [מלכים ב' יז, ג]

ל) בָּא פוּל מֶלֶךְ אַשּׁוּר עַל הָאָרֶץ וַיִּתֵּן מְנַחֵם לְפוּל אֶלֶף כִּכַּר כָּסֶף לִהְיוֹת יָדָיו אִתּוֹ לְהַחֲזִיק הַמַּמְלָכָה בְּיָדוֹ: [מלכים ב' טו, יט]

מ) בִּשְׁנַת בֹּא תַרְתָּן אַשְׁדּוֹדָה בִּשְׁלֹחַ אֹתוֹ סַרְגוֹן מֶלֶךְ אַשּׁוּר וַיִּלָּחֶם בְּאַשְׁדּוֹד וַיִּלְכְּדָהּ: [ישעיה כ, א]

נ) וּשְׁאָר אֻמַּיָּא דִּי הַגְלִי אָסְנַפַּר רַבָּא וְיַקִּירָא וְהוֹתֵב הִמּוֹ בְּקִרְיָה דִּי שָׁמְרָיִן וּשְׁאָר עֲבַר נַהֲרָה וּכְעֶנֶת: [עזרא ד, י]

ס) עַד בֹּאִי וְלָקַחְתִּי אֶתְכֶם אֶל אֶרֶץ כְּאַרְצְכֶם אֶרֶץ דָּגָן וְתִירוֹשׁ אֶרֶץ לֶחֶם וּכְרָמִים אֶרֶץ זֵית יִצְהָר וּדְבַשׁ וִחְיוּ וְלֹא תָמֻתוּ וְאַל תִּשְׁמְעוּ אֶל חִזְקִיָּהוּ כִּי יַסִּית אֶתְכֶם לֵאמֹר יְיָ יַצִּילֵנוּ: [מלכים ב' יח, לב]

אֲבִי עַד – *Everlasting Father,* "שַׂר־שָׁלוֹם" – *Prince of Peace,* eight names in all.[39]

The Gemara asks:

וְהָאִיכָּא חִזְקִיָּה – Did he really have only eight names? **But there is** the name **Chizkiah** itself, which should count as a ninth name! – ? –

The Gemara answers:

שֶׁחִזְּקוֹ יָהּ – The name Chizkiah was merely an appellation indicating **that God strengthened him** *(chizko Yah).* He can thus be said to have had only eight true names.

The Gemara adds:

דָּבָר אַחֵר – **An alternative interpretation:** חִזְקִיָּה שֶׁחִיזֵּק אֶת יִשְׂרָאֵל לַאֲבִיהֶם שֶׁבַּשָּׁמַיִם – The appellation **"Chizkiah"** would denote **that he strengthened** *(chizeik)* **Israel** in their devotion **to their Father in Heaven.**[40]

The Gemara continues:

סַנְחֵרִיב דִּכְתִיב בֵּיהּ – **Sancheiriv** had eight names, **for** in reference to him **it is written:** "תִּגְלַת פִּלְאֶסֶר" – **Tiglas Pileser;**[41] "פִּלְנְאֶסֶר" – **Pilneser;**[42] "שַׁלְמַנְאֶסֶר" – **Shalmaneser;**[43] "פּוּל" – **Pul;**[44] "סַרְגּוֹן" – **Sargon;**[45] "אָסְנַפַּר רַבָּא וְיַקִּירָא" – and **Asnapar, the Great and Venerated.**[46]

The Gemara asks:

וְהָאִיכָּא סַנְחֵרִיב – **But there is** the name **Sancheiriv** itself, which is a ninth name! Why have you said that he had only eight names?

The Gemara answers:

שֶׁסִּיחָתוֹ רִיב – The name Sancheiriv was merely an appellation indicating **that his conversation** *(sicho)* **was contentious** *(riv).*[47]

דָּבָר אַחֵר שֶׁסָּח וְנִיחֵר דְּבָרִים כְּלַפֵּי מַעְלָה – **An alternative interpretation:** It indicates **that he spoke** impudently, **hurling defiance at [God].**[48]

The Gemara discusses Sancheiriv in the context of one of the names just cited:

אָמַר רַבִּי יוֹחָנָן – **R' Yochanan said:** מִפְּנֵי מָה זָכָה אוֹתוֹ רָשָׁע לִקְרוֹתוֹ "אָסְנַפַּר רַבָּא וְיַקִּירָא" – **On what account did that wicked man** [Sancheiriv] **merit to be referred to** in Scripture by an exalted title such as **"Asnapar, the Great and Venerated"?** מִפְּנֵי שֶׁלֹּא סִיפֵּר בִּגְנוּתָהּ שֶׁל אֶרֶץ יִשְׂרָאֵל – **It is because he did not speak derogatorily about Eretz Yisrael,** שֶׁנֶּאֱמַר "עַד־בֹּאִי וְלָקַחְתִּי אֶתְכֶם אֶל־אֶרֶץ כְּאַרְצְכֶם" – **as the verse states:** ***Until I come and take you to a land that is like your land.***[49]

The Gemara relates a dispute between Rav and Shmuel in connection with the verse just cited:

רַב וּשְׁמוּאֵל – **Rav and Shmuel** disputed the implications of this verse: חַד אָמַר מֶלֶךְ פִּקֵּחַ הָיָה – **One said** that Sancheiriv's offer indicates that **he was a clever king,** וְחַד אָמַר מֶלֶךְ טִיפֵּשׁ הָיָה – **and [the other] said** that it indicates that **he was a foolish king.**

The Gemara explains:

לְמַאן דְּאָמַר מֶלֶךְ פִּקֵּחַ הָיָה – **According to the one who said** that Sancheiriv **was a clever king,** אִי אָמֵינָא לְהוּ – Sancheiriv had reasoned to himself: **"If I say to [the Jews]:** עֲדִיפָא מֵאַרְעַיְיכוּ – 'The land to which I will exile you will be **better than your own land,'** אָמְרוּ – **they will say** in response: קָא מְשַׁקְּרַתְּ – **'You are lying!** No land is superior to Eretz Yisrael!' " Thus, Sancheiriv chose a more believable claim – that the land would merely *equal* the quality of Eretz Yisrael – and in so doing, he acted cleverly.[50]

וּמַאן דְּאָמַר מֶלֶךְ טִיפֵּשׁ הָיָה – **But the one who said** that Sancheiriv **was a foolish king** argues: אִם כֵּן מַאי רְבוּתֵיהּ – **If** Sancheiriv offered land that was no better than the land the Jews currently inhabited, **what was its advantage?** I.e. how could the proffered land serve as an inducement to leave Eretz Yisrael? Thus, Sancheiriv acted foolishly, for in saying what he did, he offered a weak inducement to surrender.

While Sancheiriv ultimately failed to conquer Jerusalem and exile the Kingdom of Judah, he did succeed in conquering Israel's Northern Kingdom [the "Ten Tribes"], and exiling them. The Gemara now discusses to which lands the Ten Tribes were dispersed:

לְהֵיכָא אַגְלֵי לְהוּ – **To where did [Sancheiriv] exile [the Ten Tribes]?**[51] מַר זוּטְרָא אָמַר לְאַפְרִיקִי – **Mar Zutra said** that he sent them **to Africa.** וְרַבִּי חֲנִינָא אָמַר לְהָרֵי סְלוּג – **But R' Chanina said** that he sent them **to the Mountains of Selug.**

As we have seen, Sancheiriv did not speak derogatorily of the Land of Israel. The Gemara now shows, though, that the Ten Tribes whom he exiled *were* guilty of this sin:

אֲבָל יִשְׂרָאֵל סִפְּרוּ בִּגְנוּתָהּ שֶׁל אֶרֶץ יִשְׂרָאֵל – **But Israel,** i.e. the Ten Tribes, ***did*** **speak derogatorily about the Land of Israel,** i.e. they felt that their places of exile were worthy replacements of Eretz Yisrael. כִּי מְטוּ שׁוֹשׁ – For **when they came** on their path of exile **to** the land called **Shosh,** אָמְרֵי שָׁוְיָא כִּי אַרְעִין – **they said:** This land is so called because it **is equivalent** (*shaveh*) **to our land,** Eretz Yisrael. כִּי מְטוּ עַלְמִין – And **when they came to**

NOTES

39. Each set of words – *Wondrous Adviser, Mighty Warrior, etc.* – is counted as two names.

[According to the simple explanation of the verse (see *Rashi, Radak* loc cit.), the first six "names" in the verse refer to God, who called Chizkiah the Prince of Peace. Our Gemara, however, expounds all of the names as referring to Chizkiah.]

40. The Gemara below describes exactly how Chizkiah did this (*Rashi*).

41. *II Kings* 15:29. These two words are deemed a single name (*Rashi;* cf. *Hagahos HaGra*). As for why the Gemara assumes that this name denotes Sancheiriv in particular, see below, note 46.

42. *II Chronicles* 28:20.

43. *II Kings* 17:3.

44. Ibid. 15:19.

45. *Isaiah* 20:1.

46. *Ezra* 4:10. Each of these three words is considered a separate name (*Rashi;* cf. *Hagahos HaGra*).

[In the simple meaning of Scripture, each of the names just cited describes a *different* king of Assyria. Nevertheless, our Gemara assumes (presumably, based on tradition) that these were all names of the same king. The *Gra* (in his commentary to *I Chronicles* 5:27, printed at the end of the Warsaw ed. of the *Mikraos Gedolos Tanach*) addresses this problem. He seems to say that each of the kings had *all* eight names (but each was referred to in Scripture by just one of these names; see his comments there).]

47. I.e. he spoke blasphemously; Sancheiriv challenged God Himself to stop him (see *Isaiah* 36:18-20).

Maharsha suggests that the meaning of סִיחָתוֹ רִיב is that Sancheiriv's words provoked contention; i.e. his speech sought to sow discord between Chizkiah and his subjects, so that they would be more likely to surrender. See *Isaiah* 36:14-20.

48. [I.e. he boasted that God could not prevent him from taking Jerusalem.] Under this interpretation, the name סַנְחֵרִיב is a contraction of the words סָח וְנִיחֵר דְּבָרִים.

49. *II Kings* 18:32. After laying siege to Jerusalem, Sancheiriv sent an emissary demanding the surrender of the city. If the city surrendered, Sancheiriv promised, the inhabitants would not be killed, but would be exiled to another land, equal in quality to their native Israel. Sancheiriv did not boast that the new land would be *better* than Eretz Yisrael, and for this reason, he merited the title, "the Great and Venerated"(*Rashi*).

50. By making a reasonable offer, Sancheiriv reasoned that he would be taken at his word, and the Jews would be induced to surrender.

51. Concerning the exile of the Ten Tribes, Scripture states (*II Kings* 18:11): *The king of Assyria carried Israel away into Assyria, and settled them in Halah and in Habor, the Gozan River, and the cities of Media.* The Gemara now seeks to identify these locations.

א) אינהו עדיפי מיניה ואיהו עדיף מנייהו אינהו עדיפי מיניה דאינהו נביאי ואיהו לאו נביא ואיהו עדיף מנייהו דאיהו חזא ואינהו לא חזו וכי מאחר דלא חזו מאי טעמא איבעות אע"ג דאינהו לא חזו מידי מזלייהו חזו אמר רבינא ש"מ האי מאן דמבעית אף על גב דאיהו לא חזי מזליה חזי מאי תקנתיה ב) לינשוף מדוכתיה ארבעה גרמידי אי נמי ליקרי קרית שמע ואי קאי במקום הטנופת לימא הכי עיזא דבי טבחא שמינא מינאי א) למרבה המשרה ולשלום אין קץ וגו' א"ר תנחום דרש בר קפרא בציפורי מפני מה כל מ"ם שבאמצע תיבה פתוח וזה סתום ביקש הקב"ה לעשות חזקיהו משיח וסנחריב גוג ומגוג אמרה מדת הדין לפני הקב"ה רבש"ע ומה דוד מלך ישראל שאמר כמה שירות ותשבחות לפניך לא עשיתו משיח חזקיה שעשית לו כל הנסים הללו ולא אמר שירה לפניך תעשהו משיח לכך נסתתם מיד פתחה הארץ ואמרה לפניו רבש"ע אני אומרת לפניך שירה תחת צדיק זה ועשהו משיח פתחה ואמרה שירה לפניו שנאמר ב) מכנף הארץ זמירות שמענו צבי לצדיק וגו' אמר שר העולם לפניו רבש"ע צביונו עשה לצדיק זה יצאה בת קול ואמרה רזי לי רזי לי אמר נביא אוי לי אוי לי עד מתי יצאה בת קול ואמרה ב) בוגדים בגדו ובגד בוגדים בגדו ואמר רבא ואיתימא ר' יצחק ג) עד דאתו בזוזי ובזוזי דבזוזי ג) משא דומה אלי קורא משעיר שומר מה מלילה שומר מה מליל וגו' א"ר יוחנן אותו מלאך הממונה על הרוחות דומה שמו נתקבצו כל הרוחות אצל דומה אמרו לו שומר מה מלילה שומר מה מליל [א] ד) אמר שומר אתא בקר וגם לילה אם תבעיון בעיו שובו אתיו תנא משום רבי פפיים גנאי הוא לחזקיה וסייעתו שלא אמרו שירה עד שפתחה הארץ ואמרה שירה שנא' ב) מכנף הארץ זמירות שמענו צבי לצדיק וגו' כיוצא בדבר אתה אומר ה) ויאמר יתרו ברוך ה' אשר הציל אתכם תנא משום רבי פפיים גנאי הוא למשה וששים ריבוא שלא אמרו ברוך עד שבא יתרו ואמר ברוך ה' ו) ויחד יתרו רב ושמואל רב אמר שהעביר חרב חדה על בשרו ושמואל אמר שנעשה חדודים חדודים כל בשרו אמר רב ד) [ב] היינו דאמרי אינשי גיורא עד עשרה דרי לא תבזה ארמאי קמיה ז) לכן ישלח האדון ה' צבאות במשמניו רזון מאי במשמניו רזון אמר הקב"ה יבא חזקיהו שיש לו שמונה שמות ויפרע מסנחריב שיש לו שמונה שמות חזקיה דכתיב ח) כי ילד יולד לנו בן ניתן לנו ותהי המשרה על שכמו ויקרא שמו פלא יועץ אל גבור אבי עד שר שלום והאיכא חזקיה שחזקו יה דבר אחר חזקיה שחיזק את ישראל לאביהם שבשמים סנחריב דכתיב ביה [ג] ט) תגלת פלאסר י) פלנאסר כ) שלמנאסר ל) פול מ) סרגון (סרגין) נ) אסנפר רבא ויקירא והאיכא סנחריב שסיחתו ריב דבר אחר שסח וניחר דברים כלפי מעלה א"ר יוחנן מפני מה זכה אותו רשע לקרותו אסנפר רבא ויקירא מפני שלא סיפר בגנותה של ארץ ישראל שנאמר ס) עד בואי ולקחתי אתכם אל ארץ כארצכם רב ושמואל חד אמר מלך פקח היה וחד אמר מלך טיפש היה למאן דאמר מלך פקח היה אי אמינא להו עדיפא מארעייכו אמרו קא משקרת ומאן דאמר מלך טיפש היה אם כן מאי רבותיה להיכא אגלי להו מר זוטרא אמר לאפריקי ורבי חנינא אמר להרי סלוג אבל ישראל ספרו בגנותה של ארץ ישראל כי מטו שוש אמרי שויא כי ארעין כי מטו עלמין אמרו כעלמין כי מטו שוש תרי אמרי על חד תרין ו) ז) ותחת כבודו [יקד] יקוד כיקוד אש א"ר יוחנן תחת כבודו ולא כבודו ממש י) כי הא דרבי יוחנן קרי ליה למאני מכבדותי ז) רבי אלעזר אמר תחת כבודו ממש כשריפת בני אהרן מה להלן ח) שריפת נשמה וגוף קיים אף כאן שריפת נשמה וגוף קיים תנא משמיה דרבי יהושע בן קרחה פרעה שחירף בעצמו נפרע הקב"ה ממנו בעצמו סנחריב שחירף ע"י

אינהו עדיפי מיניה וכו'. איידי דגררא בעלמא קתני הכא ומילתא באפי נפשה היא וברוב ספרים אינה כתובה: מ"ט איבעות. דכתיב אבל חרדה גדולה נפלה עליהם: לנשוף. לדלוג: במקום הטנופת. דלא מצי קרי: לימא הכי. לאם כלומר לך אצל העזים והניחני: מ"ם שבתיבת למרבה המשרה סתום לכך נסתם לומר נסתמו הדברים שעלו במחשבה ולא נעשה לפי שביקש הקב"ה לסתום צרותיהן של ישראל שבקש לעשותו משיח ומורי רבי פירש לפי שנסתם פיו של חזקיה ולא אמר שירה: כל הנסים הללו. שניצל מסנחריב ונתרפא מחליו: שר העולם. מלאך שכל העולם מסור בידו: שמענו צבי לצדיק. שר העולם שאמר עשה צביונו של צדיק: רזי לי רזי לי. נסתרות שלי הן ואני יודע על מה מעכב: אמר נביא אוי לי עד מתי. יבא משיח: עד דאתי בזוזי ובזוזי דבזוזי. עד שנתבזזו שונאי ישראל כמה פעמים: שר הרוחות. שהנשמות נפקדות אצלו והיינו משא דומה כך אמר דומה אלי קורין הרוחות על עסקי שעיר עשו ואומר לי שומר מה מלילה הקב"ה שהוא שומר מה אומר מן הגלות שהוא כלילה: שומר מה מליל. מה דבר מתי קץ הגאולה מליל זה: אתא בקר. בתמיה ואית ספרים דלא כתיב בהו ונכון אמר להם השר כך אמר שומר הקב"ה אתא בקר גאולה תבא וגם לילה אבל מתחלה תהיה גלות הרבה לא שיגאלו ויבנה מקדש שני ויחזרו ויגלו גלות זה לא וגם לילה לרשעים וכן תרגומו מוכיח אית אגר לצדיקיא ואית פורענות לרשיעיא: אם תבעיון. אם תבקשו להגאל: בעיו. בקשו רחמים: שובו. בתשובה ואתיו לגאולה: גנאי הוא. דבר מגונה עשו: חרב חדה. שמל את עצמו ונתגייר: חדודין חדודין. קמטין קמטין שהיה מיצר מאד על מפלת מצרים: גיורא עד עשרה דרי. הכי הוא משל בני אדם ומיהו יתרו ט) לאו עשירי הוה: פלא

יועץ אל גבור אבי עד שר שלום: שחיזק ישראל. העוסקין בתורה כדלקמן: תגלת פלאסר. שם אחד הוא דכתיב בימי פקח בן רמליה בא תגלת פלאסר מלך אשור: אסנפר חד רבא חד ויקירא חד: כלפי מעלה. כדלקמן שחירף ע"י מלאך: אל ארץ כארצכם. ולא אמר מוטבת מארצכם: קא משקרת. שהרי אין ארץ מעולה הימנה ולכן לא אמר מוטבת מארצכם: להיכא אגלינהו. סנחריב לעשרת השבטים דכתיב (מלכים ב יח) וינחם בחלח ובחבור נהר גוזן וערי מדי הי ניניהו אותן מקומות: אבל ישראל. כי אגלינהו סנחריב ספרו בגנותה של א"י דכי מטו לאותו מקום ששמו שוש אמרו שויא לארעין זאת הארץ שויא לארצנו וכשבאו למקום ששמו עלמין אמרו כי עלמין זה המקום שוה לירושלים שנקראת בית עולמים: כשבאו למקום ששמו שוש תרי אמרו על חד תרין. כלומר זה יפה פי שנים כמקומנו ועל שם כך נקראו כל אותן מקומות כך: ה"ג תחת כבודו ולא כבודו ממש. דכבודו ממש משמע בשרו וגופו תחת כבודו משמע תחת הגוף והבשר כלומר נשמה שבתוך הגוף והשתא אמר תחת כבודו ולא כבודו ממש נשמה שבתוך הגוף אלא האי כבודו היינו בגדיו דתחת בגדיהם נשרפו וכי הא דרבי יוחנן וכו' דכל הגוף נשרף תחת הבגדים ולא גרסי' תחת כבודו ולא תחת כבודו ממש דמשמע דמקרא נפקא לזה דהאי תחת כבודו לא תחת כבודו ממש ומהיכא תיפוק ליה האי אבל השתא דדרשא בעלמא דריש ליה: תחת כבודו ממש. תחת גופו ממש שהגוף קיים ונשמה נשרפת: בעצמו. הוא עצמו ולא ע"י שליח לא היה ביזוי כל כך ולכך הקב"ה כמו כן נפרע ממנו בעצמו ולא נתבייש כל כך דאינו דומה מתבייש מן הגדול למתבייש מן הקטן: על

מסורת הש"ס

א) [מגילה ג.], ב) [שם ע"ש היטב], ג) [כתובות קיב: פירוש באים שודדים על ארץ ישראל ובאים שודדים אחרים ושודדים המשודדים וישראל עמהן. ערוך בערך בז ד'], ד) ילקוט איתא רב פפא, ה) [שבת קיג:], ו) שבת קיג. ב"ק לא:, ז) [ועי' היטב (תוס') בשבת קיג: תראה שם בגמרא ובפרש"י דהתם שינויים גדולים בלשון ובגרס' אחרת וצריך ישוב למאד], ח) [לעיל נב. וש"נ].

גליון הש"ס

רש"י ד"ה גיורא וכו' לאו עשירי הוה. ובבחיי פרשת יתרו דעשרה דורות ממצרים בן חם עד יתרו:

ליקוטי רש"י

דאינהו נביאי. שנתנבאו לישראל בשליחותו של מקום והוא לא נשתלח לישראל בשום נבואה. מאי טעמא איבעות. דכתיב בקרא אבל חרדה גדולה נפלה עליהם ויברחו בהחבא [מגילה ג.]. אע"ג דאינהו לא חזו מידי. אע"פ שאדם אינו רואה דבר שהוא נבעת ממנו. מזלייהו. מזלו שברקיע רואהו ולכך נבעת [דניאל י, ז]. שר של כל אדם למעלה. לינשוף. ידלג [מגילה שם]. בזוזי ובזוזי דבזוזי. תרחק הישועה עד שיבאו אויבי' בוזזים אחר בוזזים אחרים ושודדי' אחרי שודדי' ה' בגידות אמורות כאן [ישעיה כד, טז]. שוללים אחר שוללים [כתובות קיב:]. דומה. שומר המתים [חגיגה ה.]. שומר. שומר ישראל. מה מלילה. מה תהא מן הלילה והחשכה הזאת [ישעיה כא, יא]. אמר שומר. הקב"ה. אתא בקר. יש לפני להזריח לעשות בקר לכם [שם, יב]. גאולה לצדיקים [ב"ק ג:]. וגם לילה. מתוקן לעשו לעת קץ [ישעיה שם]. חשך לרשעים אם תשובו בתשובה ותבקשו מחילה בעיו [ב"ק שם]. אם תבעיון בעיו. אם תבקשו בקשתכם למהר הקץ. שובו אתיו. בתשובה [ישעיה שם]. שנעשה חדודים חדודים. נעשה בשרו חדודין חדודין מיצר על איבוד מצרים [שמות יח, ט]. כי ילד יולד לנו. אע"פ שאחז רשע הוא בנו הנולד לו זה כמה שנים להיות לנו תחתיו למלך צדיק יהיה. ותהי המשרה על שכמו. ותהיה משרת הקב"ה ועולו על שכמו שיהיה עוסק בתורה ושומר מצות ויטה שכם למשאו של הקב"ה [ישעיה ט, ה]. אסנפר. סנחריב. רבא ויקירא. שהיה מלך גדול ומכובד שנאמר כה אמר המלך הגדול מלך אשור (ישעיה לו) [עזרא ד, י]. אל ארץ כארצכם. כן דרכי להעביר את האומות ממדינה למדינה. מלך פקח היה. היה לו לומר אל ארץ טובה משלהם שהרי לפתותם בא אלא שידע שיכירו שדבריו שקר [מ"ב יח, לב]. יקד יקוד. ישרף שריפה כשריפת אש. תחת כבודו ולא כבודו ממש. תחת בגדיהם יהיו נשרפין הבגדים הם מכבדים את האדם. ומדרש אגדה כאן פרע לבני שם הכבוד שעשה שם לאביו כשכסה ערות נח אביו שנאמר (בראשי' ט') ויקח שם ויפת וגומר [ישעיה י, טז]. ר' יוחנן משמע ליה תחת כבודו כמו תחת רגליו לשון תחתית וכבודו היינו בגדיו והכי קאמר תחת בגדיהם של חיילותיו של סנחריב יקד יקוד ולא בגדיהם נשרפו [שבת קיג:]. מכבדותי. שמכבדין בעליהן [שם.]. תחת כבודו ממש. ותחת כבודו נשרף ולא כבודו ממש והאי כבודו גופו הוא והלכך כשריפת בני אהרן שריפת נשמה וגוף קיים כדאמרינן בסנהדרין בד' מיתות (נב.) [שם: ועיי"ש היטב].

הגהות הגר"א

[א] גמ' שומר מה מליל. נ"ב לא אתא בוקר. כן גי' רש"י: [ב] שם אמר רב. נ"ב פפא: [ג] שם תגלת פלאסר. נ"ב פלסר פלנסר וזה סדרן פול תגלת פלאסר (מ"ב טו) תגלת פלסר (שם טז) תלגת פלנאסר תלגת פלנסר (דה"א ה) שלמנאסר סרגון אסנפר (ובזה א"ש למה שדחק רש"י בד"ה אסנפר):

תורה אור השלם

א) לְםַרְבֵּה הַמִּשְׂרָה וּלְשָׁלוֹם אֵין קֵץ עַל כִּסֵּא דָוִד וְעַל מַמְלַכְתּוֹ לְהָכִין אֹתָהּ וּלְסַעֲדָהּ בְּמִשְׁפָּט וּבִצְדָקָה מֵעַתָּה וְעַד עוֹלָם קִנְאַת יְיָ צְבָאוֹת תַּעֲשֶׂה זֹּאת: [ישעיה ט, ו]

ב) מִכְּנַף הָאָרֶץ זְמִרֹת שָׁמַעְנוּ צְבִי לַצַּדִּיק וָאֹמַר רָזִי לִי רָזִי לִי אוֹי לִי בֹּגְדִים בָּגָדוּ וּבֶגֶד בּוֹגְדִים בָּגָדוּ: [ישעיה כד, טז]

ג) מַשָּׂא דּוּמָה אֵלַי קֹרֵא מִשֵּׂעִיר שֹׁמֵר מַה מִּלַּיְלָה שֹׁמֵר מַה מִּלֵּיל: [ישעיה כא, יא]

ד) אָמַר שֹׁמֵר אָתָה בֹקֶר וְגַם לָיְלָה אִם תִּבְעָיוּן בְּעָיוּ שֻׁבוּ אֵתָיוּ: [ישעיה כא, יב]

ה) וַיֹּאמֶר יִתְרוֹ בָּרוּךְ יְיָ אֲשֶׁר הִצִּיל אֶתְכֶם מִיַּד מִצְרַיִם וּמִיַּד פַּרְעֹה אֲשֶׁר הִצִּיל אֶת הָעָם מִתַּחַת יַד מִצְרָיִם: [שמות יח, י]

ו) וַיִּחַדְּ יִתְרוֹ עַל כָּל הַטּוֹבָה אֲשֶׁר עָשָׂה יְהוָה לְיִשְׂרָאֵל אֲשֶׁר הִצִּילוֹ מִיַּד מִצְרָיִם: [שמות יח, ט]

ז) לָכֵן יְשַׁלַּח הָאָדוֹן יְיָ צְבָאוֹת בְּמִשְׁמַנָּיו רָזוֹן וְתַחַת כְּבֹדוֹ יֵקַד יְקֹד כִּיקוֹד אֵשׁ: [ישעיה י, טז]

ח) כִּי יֶלֶד יֻלַּד לָנוּ בֵּן נִתַּן לָנוּ וַתְּהִי הַמִּשְׂרָה עַל שִׁכְמוֹ וַיִּקְרָא שְׁמוֹ פֶּלֶא יוֹעֵץ אֵל גִּבּוֹר אֲבִי עַד שַׂר שָׁלוֹם: [ישעיה ט, ה]

ט) בִּימֵי פֶּקַח מֶלֶךְ יִשְׂרָאֵל בָּא תִּגְלַת פִּלְאֶסֶר מֶלֶךְ אַשּׁוּר וַיִּקַּח אֶת עִיּוֹן וְאֶת אָבֵל בֵּית מַעֲכָה וְאֶת יָנוֹחַ וְאֶת קֶדֶשׁ וְאֶת חָצוֹר וְאֶת הַגִּלְעָד וְאֶת הַגָּלִילָה כֹּל אֶרֶץ נַפְתָּלִי וַיַּגְלֵם אַשּׁוּרָה: [מלכים ב' טו, כט]

י) וַיָּבֹא עָלָיו תִּלְּגַת פִּלְנְאֶסֶר מֶלֶךְ אַשּׁוּר וַיָּצַר לוֹ וְלֹא חֲזָקוֹ: [דברי הימים ב' כח, כ]

כ) עָלָיו עָלָה שַׁלְמַנְאֶסֶר מֶלֶךְ אַשּׁוּר וַיְהִי לוֹ הוֹשֵׁעַ עֶבֶד וַיָּשֶׁב לוֹ מִנְחָה: [מלכים ב' יז, ג]

ל) בָּא פוּל מֶלֶךְ אַשּׁוּר עַל הָאָרֶץ וַיִּתֵּן מְנַחֵם לְפוּל אֶלֶף כִּכַּר כָּסֶף לִהְיוֹת יָדָיו אִתּוֹ לְהַחֲזִיק הַמַּמְלָכָה בְּיָדוֹ: [מלכים ב' טו, יט]

מ) בִּשְׁנַת בֹּא תַרְתָּן אַשְׁדּוֹדָה בִּשְׁלֹחַ אֹתוֹ סַרְגוֹן מֶלֶךְ אַשּׁוּר וַיִּלָּחֶם בְּאַשְׁדּוֹד וַיִּלְכְּדָהּ: [ישעיה כ, א]

נ) וּשְׁאָר אֻמַּיָּא דִּי הַגְלִי אָסְנַפַּר רַבָּא וְיַקִּירָא וְהוֹתֵב הִמּוֹ בְּקִרְיָה דִּי שָׁמְרָיִן וּשְׁאָר עֲבַר נַהֲרָה וּכְעֶנֶת: [עזרא ד, י]

ס) עַד בֹּאִי וְלָקַחְתִּי אֶתְכֶם אֶל אֶרֶץ כְּאַרְצְכֶם אֶרֶץ דָּגָן וְתִירוֹשׁ אֶרֶץ לֶחֶם וּכְרָמִים אֶרֶץ זֵית יִצְהָר וּדְבַשׁ וִחְיוּ וְלֹא תָמֻתוּ וְאַל תִּשְׁמְעוּ אֶל חִזְקִיָּהוּ כִּי יַסִּית אֶתְכֶם לֵאמֹר יְיָ יַצִּילֵנוּ: [מלכים ב' יח, לב]

the land called **Almin,** **אָמְרוּ כְּעָלְמִין – they said: [This land] is like our world** (*almin*), i.e. our homeland, Eretz Yisrael.[52] **כִּי מְטוּ שׁוֹשׁ תְּרֵי** – And **when they came to** a land called **Shosh Trei,** **אָמְרֵי עַל חַד תְּרֵין – they said:** This place is so called because it is **twice as good**[53] as Eretz Yisrael.

Earlier, the Gemara expounded the first half of *Isaiah* 10:16 – a verse that describes the destruction of the Assyrian army. The Gemara now expounds the second half of that verse:

"וְתַחַת כְּבֹדוֹ יֵקַד יְקֹד כִּיקוֹד אֵשׁ" – Scripture states:[54] ***And beneath his honor there shall be kindled a flame like the burning of a fire.*** **אָמַר רַבִּי יוֹחָנָן – R' Yochanan said:** **תַּחַת כְּבוֹדוֹ** – Only that which was **beneath his honor** was burned; i.e. only the Assyrian soldiers' bodies were burned, not their clothes.[55]

In the above exposition, R' Yochanan understands the word "honor" as a reference to a person's clothing – hence, that which is *beneath one's "honor"* is his body. The Gemara now explains that this is a deviation from the usual way "honor" is interpreted: **וְלֹא כְּבוֹדוֹ מַמָּשׁ** – **And** R' Yochanan does **not** interpret the word "honor" as a reference to **one's *actual* honor** [i.e. his body]; rather, he interprets it as a reference to clothing.[56] **כִּי הָא דְּרַבִּי יוֹחָנָן קָרֵי לֵיהּ לְמָאנֵי מְכַבְּדוּתַי** – **For** indeed, **R' Yochanan used to refer to his clothes as "those [things] that honor me."**

The Gemara now cites an opposing view:

רַבִּי אֶלְעָזָר אָמַר – But **R' Elazar said:** **תַּחַת כְּבוֹדוֹ מַמָּשׁ** – Scripture means that the fire burned that which was **beneath one's actual honor,** i.e. it burned that which was beneath the soldiers' bodies – meaning, their souls,[57] **כִּשְׂרֵיפַת בְּנֵי אַהֲרֹן** – **just like the burning of the** two **sons of Aaron.**[58] **מַה לְּהַלָּן** – In other words, **just as in that case** [the death of Aaron's sons], **שְׂרֵיפַת נְשָׁמָה וְגוּף קַיָּים – the soul was burned, and the body remained intact,**[59] **אַף כָּאן – so it was here** [in reference to the destruction of Sancheiriv's army]; **שְׂרֵיפַת נְשָׁמָה וְגוּף קַיָּים** – when the Assyrians were killed, **the soul** of each soldier was **burned, while** his **body remained intact.**[60]

The Gemara deals further with the nature of the punishment exacted against Sancheiriv:

תָּנָא מִשְּׁמֵיהּ דְּרַבִּי יְהוֹשֻׁעַ בֶּן קָרְחָה – A Tanna taught in the name of R' Yehoshua ben Korchah: **פַּרְעֹה שֶׁחֵירֵף בְּעַצְמוֹ – Pharaoh, who personally blasphemed against God,**[61] **נִפְרַע הַקָּדוֹשׁ בָּרוּךְ הוּא מִמֶּנּוּ בְּעַצְמוֹ** – merited to have **the Holy One, Blessed is He, personally** punish him.[62] **סַנְחֵרִיב שֶׁחֵירֵף**

NOTES

52. *Rashi* states that *almin* is in particular a reference to Jerusalem, which is referred to in Scripture as בֵּית עוֹלָמִים, *the Eternal House* [the implication is that Jerusalem's sanctity is eternal (see *Shevuos* 16b רש״י ד״ה קדושת עולם; see also *Tos. Yom Tov* to *Zevachim* 14:8)].

53. Literally: for [every] one, two.

54. *Isaiah* 10:16.

Sancheiriv had laid siege to Jerusalem and demanded the city's surrender. In his overwhelming arrogance, Sancheiriv warned that even the Almighty God could not prevent the eventual fall of the city. The besieged, however, led by King Chizkiah and the prophet Isaiah, prayed to God for deliverance. That very night, a heavenly angel destroyed Sancheiriv's army as they slept, killing more than 185,000 men, though sparing Sancheiriv himself (*Isaiah* 37:36-7).

In our passage, Isaiah graphically foretells this destruction of Sancheiriv's army, stating that the Assyrian soldiers will be burned to death.

55. Since the verse states that the burning would be kindled *beneath* their "honor," this indicates that the flames would not touch the soldiers' "honor" itself. As the Gemara proceeds to explain, R' Yochanan interprets "honor" as a reference to clothing.

56. Hence, *beneath his honor* refers to that which is beneath one's garments, namely, his body. Thus, according to R' Yochanan, the verse states that the angel burned the bodies of the Assyrian soldiers, though their garments were miraculously untouched by the fire.

Rashi (*Isaiah* 10:16) quotes a Midrash that explains the reason the clothes of the Assyrians remained untouched. It was because the ancestor of Assyria – Shem – covered Noah when he was naked (see *Genesis* 9:23), and thus, the clothes of Shem's descendants merited special protection.

57. R. Elazar understands the verse as saying that the Assyrians' souls were burned (or destroyed), while their bodies remained intact (*Rashi*; cf. *Shabbos* 113b).

58. At the ceremony inaugurating the Tabernacle in the desert, Aaron's two oldest sons, Nadav and Avihu, performed an inappropriate incense offering. Scripture then states that *a fire came forth from before God and consumed them, and they died before God* (*Leviticus* 10:2). [For a fuller discussion of this enigmatic episode, see ArtScroll *Leviticus* pp. 147-150.]

59. Earlier in our tractate (52a), this same Amora, R' Elazar, expressed the opinion that the bodies of Aaron's children were not burned; rather, only their souls were consumed. See also *Rashi* to *Leviticus* 10:5.

60. [*Be'er Sheva* adds that the comparison here is not meant to be an exact one. In the case of the sons of Aaron, the expression "their souls were burned" simply means that their souls departed from their bodies and they died. In the case of Sancheiriv's troops, however, the expression means that their souls were actually destroyed.]

61. In refusing Moses' request to let the Jews go free, Pharaoh stated: *Who is God that I should obey Him?* (*Exodus* 5:2). The Gemara here notes that he personally expressed these blasphemous words; he did not send an agent to articulate them on his behalf.

62. It was God Himself, not an angel, Who destroyed Pharaoh's army at the Red Sea. Thus, Pharaoh was repaid measure for measure: Since he did not consider it beneath his dignity to personally deliver his blasphemous remarks, God did not, so to speak, consider it beneath His dignity to personally destroy Pharaoh's army. In this sense, Pharaoh salvaged a small measure of dignity, for the more powerful the adversary, the less the dishonor of defeat (*Rashi;* see *Shabbos* 108a and *Yad David* here; cf. *Maharsha*).

א) אינהו עדיפי מיניה ואיהו עדיף מנייהו אינהו עדיפי מיניה דאינהו נביאי ואיהו לאו נביא ואיהו עדיף מנייהו דאיהו חזא ואינהו לא חזו וכי מאחר דלא חזו מאי טעמא איבעות אע"ג דאינהו לא חזו מידי מזלייהו חזי אמר רבינא ש"מ האי מאן דמבעית אף על גב דאיהו לא חזי מזליה חזי מאי תקנתיה ב) לינשוף מדוכתיה ארבעה גרמידי אי נמי ליקרי קרית שמע ואי קאי במקום הטנופת לימא הכי עיזא דבי טבחא שמינא מינאי א) למרבה המשרה ולשלום אין קץ וגו' א"ר תנחום דרש בר קפרא בציפורי מפני מה כל מ"ם שבאמצע תיבה פתוח וזה סתום ביקש הקב"ה לעשות חזקיהו משיח וסנחריב גוג ומגוג אמרה מדת הדין לפני הקב"ה רבש"ע ומה דוד מלך ישראל שאמר כמה שירות ותשבחות לפניך לא עשיתו משיח חזקיה שעשית לו כל הנסים הללו ולא אמר שירה לפניך תעשהו משיח לכך נסתתם מיד פתחה הארץ ואמרה לפניו רבש"ע אני אומרת לפניך שירה תחת צדיק זה ועשהו משיח פתחה ואמרה שירה לפניו שנאמר ב) מכנף הארץ זמירות שמענו צבי לצדיק וגו' אמר שר העולם לפניו רבש"ע צביונו עשה לצדיק זה יצאה בת קול ואמרה רזי לי רזי לי אמר נביא אוי לי אוי לי עד מתי יצאה בת קול ואמרה ב) בוגדים בגדו ובגד בוגדים בגדו ואמר רבא ואיתימא ר' יצחק ג) עד דאתו בוזזי ובוזזי דבוזזי ג) משא דומה אלי קורא משעיר שומר מה מלילה שומר מה מליל וגו' א"ר יוחנן אותו מלאך הממונה על הרוחות דומה שמו נתקבצו כל הרוחות אצל דומה אמרו לו שומר מה מלילה שומר מה מליל [א] ד) אמר שומר אתא בקר וגם לילה אם תבעיון בעיו שובו אתיו תנא משום רבי פפיים גנאי הוא לחזקיה וסייעתו שלא אמרו שירה עד שפתחה הארץ ואמרה שירה שנא' ב) מכנף הארץ זמירות שמענו צבי לצדיק וגו' כיוצא בדבר אתה אומר ה) ויאמר יתרו ברוך ה' אשר הציל אתכם תנא משום רבי פפיים גנאי הוא למשה וששים ריבוא שלא אמרו ברוך עד שבא יתרו ואמר ברוך ה' ו) ויחד יתרו רב ושמואל רב אמר שהעביר חרב חדה על בשרו ושמואל אמר שנעשה חדודים חדודים כל בשרו אמר רב ד) [ב] היינו דאמרי אינשי גיורא עד עשרה דרי לא תבזה ארמאי קמיה ז) לכן ישלח האדון ה' צבאות במשמניו רזון מאי במשמניו רזון אמר הקב"ה יבא חזקיהו שיש לו שמונה שמות ויפרע מסנחריב שיש לו שמונה שמות חזקיה דכתיב ח) כי ילד יולד לנו בן ניתן לנו ותהי המשרה על שכמו ויקרא שמו פלא יועץ אל גבור אבי עד שר שלום והאיכא חזקיה שחזקו יה דבר אחר חזקיה שחיזק את ישראל לאביהם שבשמים סנחריב דכתיב ביה [ג] ט) תגלת פלאסר י) פלנאסר כ) שלמנאסר ל) פול מ) סרגון (סרגין) נ) אסנפר רבא ויקירא והאיכא סנחריב שסיחתו ריב דבר אחר שסח וניחר דברים כלפי מעלה א"ר יוחנן מפני מה זכה אותו רשע לקרותו אסנפר רבא ויקירא מפני שלא סיפר בגנותה של ארץ ישראל שנאמר ס) עד בואי ולקחתי אתכם אל ארץ כארצכם רב ושמואל חד אמר מלך פקח היה וחד אמר מלך טיפש היה למאן דאמר מלך פקח היה אי אמינא להו עדיפא מארעייכו אמרו קא משקרת ומאן דאמר מלך טיפש היה אם כן מאי רבותיה להיכא אגלי להו מר זוטרא אמר לאפריקי ורבי חנינא אמר להרי סלוג אבל ישראל ספרו בגנותה של ארץ ישראל כי מטו שוש אמרי שויא כי ארעין כי מטו עלמין אמרו כעלמין כי מטו שוש תרי אמרי על חד תרין ו) ע) ותחת כבודו [יקד] יקוד כיקוד אש א"ר יוחנן תחת כבודו ולא כבודו ממש ז) כי הא דרבי יוחנן קרי ליה למאני מכבדותי ח) רבי אלעזר אמר תחת כבודו ממש כשריפת בני אהרן מה להלן ט) שריפת נשמה וגוף קיים אף כאן שריפת נשמה וגוף קיים תנא משמיה דרבי יהושע בן קרחה פרעה שחירף בעצמו נפרע הקב"ה ממנו בעצמו סנחריב שחירף ע"י

רש"י

אינהו עדיפי מיניה וכו'. איידי דגררא בעלמא קתני הכא ומילתא באפי נפשה היא וברוב ספרים אינה כתובה: מ"ט איבעות. דכתיב אבל חרדה גדולה נפלה עליהם: לנשוף. לדלוג: במקום הטנופת. דלא מצי קרי: לימא הכי. לאש כלומר לך אצל העזים והניחני: מ"ם שבתיבת למרבה המשרה סתום לכך נסתם לומר נסתמו הדברים שעלו במחשבה ולא נעשה ל"א שביקש הקב"ה לסתום צרותיהן של ישראל שבקש לעשותו משיח ומורי רבי פירש לפי שנסתם פיו של חזקיה ולא אמר שירה: כל הנסים הללו. שניצל מסנחריב ונתרפא מחליו: שר העולם. מלאך שכל העולם מסור בידו: שמענו צבי לצדיק. שר העולם שאמר עשה צביונו של צדיק: רזי לי רזי לי. נסתרות שלי הן ואני יודע על מה מעכב: אמר נביא אוי לי עד מתי. יבא משיח: עד דאתי בוזזי ובוזזי דבוזזי. עד שנתבזזו שונאי ישראל כמה פעמים: שר הרוחות. שהנשמות נפקדות אצלו והיינו משא דומה כך אמר דומה אלי קורין הרוחות על עסקי שעיר עשו ואומר לי שומר מה מלילה הקב"ה שהוא שומר מה אומר מן הגלות שהוא כלילה: שומר מה מליל. מה דבר מתי קץ הגאולה מליל זה: אתא בקר. בתמיה ואית ספרים דלא כתיב בהו וכן אמר להם השר כך אמר שומר הקב"ה אתא בקר גאולה תבא וגם לילה אבל מתחלה תהיה גלות הרבה ל"א שיגאלו ויבנה מקדש שני ויחזרו ויגלו גלות זה ל"א וגם לילה לרשעים וכן תרגומו מוכיח אית אגר לצדיקיא ואית פורענות לרשיעיא: אם תבעיון. אם תבקשו להגאל: בעיו. בקשו רחמים: שובו. בתשובה ואתיו לגאולה: גנאי הוא. דבר מגונה עשו: חרב חדה. שמל את עצמו ונתגייר: חדודין חדודין. קמטין קמטין שהיה מיצר מאד על מפלת מצרים: גיורא עד עשרה דרי. הכי הוא משל בני אדם ומיהו יתרו ט) לאו עשירי הוה: פלא יועץ אל גבור אבי עד שר שלום: שחיזק ישראל. העוסקין בתורה כדלקמן: תגלת פלאסר. שם אחד הוא דכתיב בימי פקח בן רמליה בא תגלת פלאסר מלך אשור: אסנפר חד רבא חד ויקירא חד: כלפי מעלה. כדלקמן שחירף ע"י מלאך: אל ארץ כארצכם. ולא אמר מוטבת מארצכם: קא משקרת. שהרי אין ארץ מעולה הימנה ולכן לא אמר מוטבת מארצכם: להיכא אגלינהו. סנחריב לעשרת השבטים דכתיב (מלכים ב יח) וינחם בחלח ובחבור נהר גוזן וערי מדי הי ניהו אותן מקומות: אבל ישראל. כי אגלינהו סנחריב ספרו בגנותה של א"י דכי מטו לאותו מקום ששמו שוש אמרו שויא לארעין זאת הארץ שויא לארצנו וכשבאו למקום ששמו עלמין אמרו כי עלמין זה המקום שוה לירושלים שנקראת בית עולמים: כשבאו למקום ששמו שוש תרי אמרו על חד תרין. כלומר זה יפה פי שנים כמקומנו ועל שם כך נקראו כל אותן מקומות כך: ה"ג תחת כבודו ולא כבודו ממש. דכבודו ממש משמע בשרו וגופו תחת כבודו משמע תחת הגוף והבשר כלומר נשמה שבתוך הגוף והשתא אמר תחת כבודו ולא כבודו ממש נשמה שבתוך הגוף אלא האי כבודו היינו בגדיו דתחת בגדיהם נשרפו וכי הא דרבי יוחנן וכו' דכל הגוף נשרף תחת הבגדים ולא גרסי' תחת כבודו ולא תחת כבודו ממש דמשמע דמקרא נפקא לזה דהאי תחת כבודו לא תחת כבודו ממש ומהיכא תיפוק ליה האי אבל השתא דדרשא בעלמא דריש ליה: תחת כבודו ממש. תחת גופו ממש שהגוף קיים ונשמה נשרפת: בעצמו. הוא עצמו ולא ע"י שליח לא היה ביזוי כל כך ולכך הקב"ה כמו כן נפרע ממנו בעצמו ולא נתבייש כל כך דאינו דומה מתבייש מן הגדול למתבייש מן הקטן: על

מסורת הש"ס

א) [מגילה ג.], ב) [שם ע"ש היט'], ג) [כתובות קיב: פירוש באים שודדים על ארץ ישראל ובאים שודדים אחרים ושודדים המשודדים וישראל עמהן. ערוך בערך בז ד'], ד) ילקוט איתא רב פפא, ה) [שבת קיג:], ו) שבת קיג. ב"ק נא:, ז) [ועי' היטב (תוס') בשבת קיג: תראה שם בגמרא ובפרש"י דהתם שינויים גדולים בלשון ובגרס' אחרת וצריך ישוב למאד], ח) [לעיל נב. וש"נ].

גליון הש"ס

רש"י ד"ה גיורא וכו' לאו עשירי הוה. ובכמי' פרשת יתרו דעשרה דורות ממצרים בן חם עד יתרו:

ליקוטי רש"י

דאינהו נביאי. שנתנבאו לישראל בשליחותו של מקום והוא לא נשתלח לישראל בשום נבואה. מאי טעמא איבעות. דכתיב בקרא אבל חרדה גדולה נפלה עליהם ויברחו בהחבא [מגילה ג.]. אע"ג דאינהו לא חזו מידי. אע"פ שאדם אינו רואה דבר שהוא נבעת ממנו. מזלייהו. מזלו שברקיע רואהו ולכך נבעת [דניאל י, ז]. שר של כל אדם למעלה. לינשוף. ידלג [מגילה שם]. בוזזי ובוזזי דבוזזי. תרחק הישועה עד שיבאו אויבי' בוזזים אחר בוזזים אחרים ושודדי' אחרי שודדי' ה' בגידות אמורות כאן [ישעיה כד, טז]. שוללים אחר שוללים [כתובות קיב:]. דומה. שומר המתים [חגיגה ה.]. שומר. שומר ישראל. מה מלילה. מה תהא מן הלילה והחשכה הזאת [ישעיה כא, יא]. אמר שומר. הקב"ה. אתא בקר. יש לפני להזריח לעשות בקר לכם [שם, יב]. גאולה לצדיקים [ב"ק ג:]. וגם לילה. מתוקן לעשו לעת קץ [ישעיה שם]. חשך לרשעים אם תשובו בתשובה ותבקשו מחילה בעיו [ב"ק שם]. אם תבעיון בעיו. אם תבקשו בקשתכם למהר הקץ. שובו אתיו. בתשובה [ישעיה שם]. שנעשה חדודים חדודים. נעשה בשרו חדודין מיצר על איבוד מצרים [שמות יח, ט]. כי ילד יולד לנו. אע"פ שאחז רשע הוא בנו הנולד לו זה כמה שנים להיות לנו תחתיו למלך צדיק יהיה. ותהי המשרה על שכמו. ותהיה משרת הקב"ה ועולו על שכמו שיהיה עוסק בתורה ושומר מצות ויטה שכם למשאו של הקב"ה [ישעיה ט, ה]. אסנפר. סנחריב. רבא ויקירא. שהיה מלך גדול ומכובד שנאמר כה אמר המלך הגדול מלך אשור (ישעיה לו) [עזרא ד, י]. אל ארץ כארצכם. כן דרכי להעביר את האומות ממדינה למדינה. מלך פקח היה. היה לו לומר אל ארץ טובה משלכם שהרי לפתותם בא אלא שידע שיכירו שדבריו שקר [מ"ב יח, לב]. יקד יקוד. ישרף שריפה כשריפת אש. תחת כבודו ולא כבודו ממש. תחת בגדיהם יהיו נשרפין הבגדים הם מכבדים את האדם. ומדרש אגדה כאן פרע לבני שם הכבוד שעשה שם לאביו כשכסה ערות נח אביו שנאמר (בראשית ט') ויקח שם ויפת וגומר [ישעיה י, טז]. ר' יוחנן משמע ליה תחת כבודו כמו תחת רגליו לשון תחתיות וכבודו היינו בגדיו והכי קאמר תחת בגדיהם של חיילותיו של סנחריב יקד יקוד ולא בגדיהם נשרפו [שבת קיג:]. מכבדותי. שמכבדין בעליהן [שם]. תחת כבודו ממש. ותחת כבודו כמו כבודו ממש והאי כבודו גופו הוא והלכך כשריפת בני אהרן שריפת נשמה וגוף קיים כדאמרינן בסנהדרין בד' מיתות (נב.) [שם: ועיי"ש היטב].

הגהות הגר"א

[א] גמ' שומר מה מליל. נ"ב לא אתא בוקר. כן גי' רש"י: [ב] שם אמר רב. נ"ב פפא: [ג] שם תגלת פלאסר. נ"ב פלנסר פלנאסר וזה סדרן פול תגלת פלאסר (מ"ב טו) תגלת פלסר (שם טז) תלגת פלנאסר תלגת פלנסר (דה"א ה) שלמנאסר סרגון אסנפר (וכזה א"ל למה שדחק רש"י בד"ה אסנפר):

תורה אור השלם

א) לְםַרְבֵּה הַמִּשְׂרָה וּלְשָׁלוֹם אֵין קֵץ עַל כִּסֵּא דָוִד וְעַל מַמְלַכְתּוֹ לְהָכִין אֹתָהּ וּלְסַעֲדָהּ בְּמִשְׁפָּט וּבִצְדָקָה מֵעַתָּה וְעַד עוֹלָם קִנְאַת יְיָ צְבָאוֹת תַּעֲשֶׂה זֹּאת: [ישעיה ט, ו]

ב) מִכְּנַף הָאָרֶץ זְמִרֹת שָׁמַעְנוּ צְבִי לַצַּדִּיק וָאֹמַר רָזִי לִי רָזִי לִי אוֹי לִי בֹּגְדִים בָּגָדוּ וּבֶגֶד בּוֹגְדִים בָּגָדוּ: [ישעיה כד, טז]

ג) מַשָּׂא דּוּמָה אֵלַי קֹרֵא מִשֵּׂעִיר שֹׁמֵר מַה מִּלַּיְלָה שֹׁמֵר מַה מִּלֵּיל: [ישעיה כא, יא]

ד) אָמַר שֹׁמֵר אָתָה בֹקֶר וְגַם לָיְלָה אִם תִּבְעָיוּן בְּעָיוּ שֻׁבוּ אֵתָיוּ: [ישעיה כא, יב]

ה) וַיֹּאמֶר יִתְרוֹ בָּרוּךְ יְיָ אֲשֶׁר הִצִּיל אֶתְכֶם מִיַּד מִצְרַיִם וּמִיַּד פַּרְעֹה אֲשֶׁר הִצִּיל אֶת הָעָם מִתַּחַת יַד מִצְרָיִם: [שמות יח, י]

ו) וַיִּחַדְּ יִתְרוֹ עַל כָּל הַטּוֹבָה אֲשֶׁר עָשָׂה יְהוָה לְיִשְׂרָאֵל אֲשֶׁר הִצִּילוֹ מִיַּד מִצְרָיִם: [שמות יח, ט]

ז) לָכֵן יְשַׁלַּח הָאָדוֹן יְיָ צְבָאוֹת בְּמִשְׁמַנָּיו רָזוֹן וְתַחַת כְּבֹדוֹ יֵקַד יְקֹד כִּיקוֹד אֵשׁ: [ישעיה י, טז]

ח) כִּי יֶלֶד יֻלַּד לָנוּ בֵּן נִתַּן לָנוּ וַתְּהִי הַמִּשְׂרָה עַל שִׁכְמוֹ וַיִּקְרָא שְׁמוֹ פֶּלֶא יוֹעֵץ אֵל גִּבּוֹר אֲבִי עַד שַׂר שָׁלוֹם: [ישעיה ט, ה]

ט) בִּימֵי פֶּקַח מֶלֶךְ יִשְׂרָאֵל בָּא תִּגְלַת פִּלְאֶסֶר מֶלֶךְ אַשּׁוּר וַיִּקַּח אֶת עִיּוֹן וְאֶת אָבֵל בֵּית מַעֲכָה וְאֶת יָנוֹחַ וְאֶת קֶדֶשׁ וְאֶת חָצוֹר וְאֶת הַגִּלְעָד וְאֶת הַגָּלִילָה כֹּל אֶרֶץ נַפְתָּלִי וַיַּגְלֵם אַשּׁוּרָה: [מלכים ב' טו, כט]

י) וַיָּבֹא עָלָיו תִּלְּגַת פִּלְנְאֶסֶר מֶלֶךְ אַשּׁוּר וַיָּצַר לוֹ וְלֹא חֲזָקוֹ: [דברי הימים ב' כח, כ]

כ) עָלָיו עָלָה שַׁלְמַנְאֶסֶר מֶלֶךְ אַשּׁוּר וַיְהִי לוֹ הוֹשֵׁעַ עֶבֶד וַיָּשֶׁב לוֹ מִנְחָה: [מלכים ב' יז, ג]

ל) בָּא פוּל מֶלֶךְ אַשּׁוּר עַל הָאָרֶץ וַיִּתֵּן מְנַחֵם לְפוּל אֶלֶף כִּכַּר כָּסֶף לִהְיוֹת יָדָיו אִתּוֹ לְהַחֲזִיק הַמַּמְלָכָה בְּיָדוֹ: [מלכים ב' טו, יט]

מ) בִּשְׁנַת בֹּא תַרְתָּן אַשְׁדּוֹדָה בִּשְׁלֹחַ אֹתוֹ סַרְגוֹן מֶלֶךְ אַשּׁוּר וַיִּלָּחֶם בְּאַשְׁדּוֹד וַיִּלְכְּדָהּ: [ישעיה כ, א]

נ) וּשְׁאָר אֻמַיָּא דִּי הַגְלִי אָסְנַפַּר רַבָּא וְיַקִּירָא וְהוֹתֵב הִמּוֹ בְּקִרְיָה דִּי שָׁמְרָיִן וּשְׁאָר עֲבַר נַהֲרָה וּכְעֶנֶת: [עזרא ד, י]

ס) עַד בֹּאִי וְלָקַחְתִּי אֶתְכֶם אֶל אֶרֶץ כְּאַרְצְכֶם אֶרֶץ דָּגָן וְתִירוֹשׁ אֶרֶץ לֶחֶם וּכְרָמִים אֶרֶץ זֵית יִצְהָר וּדְבַשׁ וִחְיוּ וְלֹא תָמֻתוּ וְאַל תִּשְׁמְעוּ אֶל חִזְקִיָּהוּ כִּי יַסִּית אֶתְכֶם לֵאמֹר יְיָ יַצִּילֵנוּ: [מלכים ב' יח, לב]

ע"י שליח נפרע הקב"ה ממנו ע"י שליח פרעה דכתיב ביה (א) מי ה' אשר אשמע בקולו נפרע הקב"ה ממנו בעצמו דכתיב (ב) וינער ה' את מצרים בתוך הים וכתיב (ג) דרכת בים סוסיך וגו' סנחריב דכתיב (ד) ביד מלאכיך חרפת ה' נפרע הקב"ה ממנו ע"י שליח דכתיב (ה) ויצא מלאך ה' ויך במחנה אשור מאה ושמונים וחמשה אלף וגו' ר' חנינא בר פפא רמי כתיב (ו) מרום קיצו וכתיב (ד) מלון קיצו אמר אותו רשע בתחלה אחריב דירה של מטה ואחר כך אחריב דירה של מעלה א"ר יהושע בן לוי מאי דכתיב (ז) עתה המבלעדי ה' עליתי על המקום הזה להשחיתו ה' אמר אלי עלה אל הארץ הזאת והשחיתה מאי היא דשמע לנביא דקאמר (ח) יען כי מאס העם הזה את מי השילוח ההולכים לאט ומשוש את רצין ובן רמליהו אמר רב יוסף אלמלא תרגומא דהאי קרא לא הוה ידענא מאי קאמר חלף דקץ עמא הדין במלכותא דבית דוד דמדבר להון בנייח כמי שילוחא דנגדין בנייח ואיתרעיאו ברצין ובר רמליה א"ר יוחנן מאי דכתיב (ט) מארת ה' בבית רשע ונוה צדיקים יבורך מארת ה' בבית רשע זה פקח בן רמליהו שהיה אוכל מ' סאה גוזלות בקינוח סעודה ונוה צדיקים יבורך זה חזקיה מלך יהודה שהיה אוכל ליטרא ירק בסעודה (י) ולכן הנה ה' מעלה עליהם את מי הנהר העצומים והרבים את מלך אשור וכתיב (כ) וחלף ביהודה שטף ועבר עד צואר יגיע אלא מ"ט איעניש נביא אעשרת השבטים איתנבי איהו יהיב דעתיה על כולה ירושלים בא נביא וא"ל (ל) כי לא מועף לאשר מוצק לה א"ר אלעזר בר ברכיה אין נמסר עם עייף בתורה ביד מי המציק לו מאי (ל) כעת הראשון הקל ארצה זבולון וארצה נפתלי והאחרון הכביד דרך הים עבר הירדן גליל הגוים לא כראשונים שהקלו מעליהם עול תורה אבל אחרונים שהכבידו עליהן עול תורה וראויין הללו לעשות להם נס כעוברי הים וכדורכי הירדן אם חוזר בו מוטב ואם לאו אני אעשה לו גליל בגוים (מ) אחרי הדברים והאמת האלה בא סנחריב מלך אשור ויבא ביהודה ויחן על הערים הבצורות ויאמר לבקעם אליו האי רישנא להאי פרדשנא אחרי הדברים והאמת (אחר מאי) אמר רבינא לאחר שקפץ הקב"ה ונשבע ואמר אי אמינא ליה לחזקיה מייתינא ליה לסנחריב ומסרנא ליה בידך השתא אמר לא הוא בעינא ולא ביעתותיה בעינא מיד קפץ הקב"ה ונשבע דמייתינא ליה שנאמר (נ) נשבע ה' צבאות לאמר אם לא כאשר דמיתי כן היתה וכאשר יעצתי היא תקום לשבור אשור בארצי ועל הרי אבוסנו וסר מעליהם עולו וסבלו מעל שכמו יסור א"ר יוחנן אמר הקב"ה יבא סנחריב וסיעתו ויעשה אבוס לחזקיהו ולסיעתו (ס) והיה ביום ההוא יסור סבלו מעל שכמך ועולו מעל צוארך וחובל עול מפני שמן א"ר יצחק נפחא חובל עול של סנחריב מפני שמנו של חזקיהו שהיה דולק בבתי כנסיות ובבתי מדרשות מה עשה נעץ חרב על פתח בית המדרש ואמר כל מי שאינו עוסק בתורה ידקר בחרב זו בדקו מדן ועד באר שבע ולא מצאו עם הארץ מגבת ועד אנטיפרס ולא מצאו תינוק ותינוקת איש ואשה שלא היו בקיאין בהלכות טומאה וטהרה ועל אותו הדור הוא אומר (ע) והיה ביום ההוא יחיה איש עגלת בקר ושתי צאן וגו' ואומר (פ) והיה ביום ההוא יהיה כל מקום אשר יהיה שם אלף גפן באלף כסף לשמיר ולשית יהיה אע"פ שאלף גפן באלף כסף לשמיר ולשית יהיה (צ) ואוסף שללכם אוסף החסיל אמר להם נביא לישראל אספו שללכם אמרו לו לבזוז או לחלוק אמר להם כאוסף החסיל מה אוסף החסיל כל אחד ואחד לעצמו אף שללכם כל אחד ואחד לעצמו אמרו לו והלא ממון עשרת השבטים מעורב בו אמר להם (צ) כמשק גבים שוקק בו מה גבים הללו מעלין את האדם מטומאה לטהרה אף ממונם של ישראל כיון שנפל ביד עובדי כוכבים מיד טיהר (כדרב פפא דאמר רב פפא עמון ומואב טהרו בסיחון) אמר רב הונא עשר מסעות נסע אותו רשע באותו היום שנאמר (ק) בא על עית עבר במגרון למכמש יפקיד כליו עברו מעברה גבע מלון לנו חרדה הרמה גבעת שאול נסה (ר) צהלי קולך בת גלים הקשיבה לישה עניה ענתות נדדה מדמנה יושבי הגבים העיזו (ש) עוד היום בנוב לעמוד ינופף ידו הר בת ציון גבעת ירושלם) הני טובא הויין צהלי קולך בת גלים נביא הוא דקאמר לה לכנסת ישראל צהלי קולך בת גלים בתו של אברהם יצחק ויעקב שעשו מצות כגלי הים הקשיבה לישה מהאי לא תסתפי אלא איסתפי מנבוכדנצר הרשע דמתיל כאריה שנא' (ת) עלה אריה מסובכו וגו' מאי

עניה

רש"י

על ידי שליח. דהיינו בזוי יותר אף הקב"ה נפרע ע"י שליח ונתבייש יותר: כתיב מרום קצו. בישעיה: וכתיב מלון קיצו. במלכים. מרום קילו משמע דירה של מטה כדכתיב (ירמיה יז) מרום מראשון מקום מקדשנו מלון קילו משמע דירה של מעלה בית מלונו: ה' אמר אלי עלה אל הארץ וגו' מאי היא. היכי אמר לו הקב"ה להשחית: יען כי מאס העם הזה וגו'. ומשוש את רלין ובן רמליהו ואתרעו להשחית' ברלין ובר רמליהו: מארת ה'. שלא נשבע מכל מה שהיה אוכל: ליטרא ירק. במדה: ועלה על כל אפיקיו. שאמר לו הקב"ה עלה והשחת: מ"ט. מאחר שברשות הלך שנביא נתנבא עליו מאי טעמא איענש: בא נביא ואמר לו. כשבא על ירושלים: כי לא מועף לאשר מוצק לה. לא נמסר עמו של חזקיה שהוא עיף בתורה ביד סנחריב המליק לו: כעת הראשון הקל ארצה זבולון וארצה נפתלי וגו' לא כראשונים. עשרת השבטים שהקלו מעליהם עול תורה אבל אחרונים עמו של חזקיה הכבידו עליהם עול תורה והיינו דכתיב האחרון הכביד דרך הים עבר הירדן גליל הגוים ראויין הללו לעשות להם נס כיולאי מלרים שעברו את הים וכדורכי הירדן: אם חוזר בו סנחריב מוטב. ואם לאו אעשה אותו גליל הגוים שמגלגל בחרפה בכל הגוים ל"א גליל לשון גללים. מ"ר: אחרי הדברים והאמת האלה. השתא משמע שהיה מדבר בחזקיהו שהיו עסוקין בתורה בא סנחריב מלך אשור ויבא ביהודה ויחן על הערים ויאמר לבקעם אליו: האי רישנא להאי פרדשנא. וכי מביאין דורון כזה לאדון כזה וכי מפני שהאמת בחזקיהו בא סנחריב: רבינא אמר מאי אחר הדברים והאמת אחר שקפץ הקב"ה ונשבע. להביא סנחריב והיינו אמת שחותמו וקיומו של הקדוש ברוך הוא אמת: ויעשה אבוס. שיהיו כלם פגרים ויאכלו סוסיהם ובהמתם בתוך עצמות הפגרים כעין אבוס: מגבת ועד אנטיפרס. מקומות שבסוף התחומים: אע"פ שאלף גפן באלף כסף. שהן יקרים שאין להם רוב כרמים אפילו הכי לשמיר ולשית יהיה שמניחין אותן לאבוד ומבייריס אותן והיו עוסקין בתורה: לשלל. כל אחד ואחד לעצמו או לחלוק ביחד אותו ממון שנשאר מחיל סנחריב ל"א לחלוק לאחרים מה שאנו שוללים אבל אנו אסורים באותו שלל שממון שבזזו מעשרת השבטים מעורב בו דאיכא משום גזל: כמשק גבים שוקק בו. השקאה של לינורות שמזלפין בהם מים נובעין השקו באותו ממון וטיהרתו דמה לינורות הללו מעלין את האדם מטומאה לטהרה ע"י טבילה אף ממונם וכו' משק שו"ן בלע"ז: בא על עית וגו'. ומתרגמינן ומני רבני משרייתיה: עברו מעברה גבע מלון לנו וגו' יושבי הגבים העיזו. ולא קא חשיב עוד היום בנוב לעמוד דההוא לאו מסע הוא אלא כדאמרינן לקמן אותו היום נשתייר מעונה של נוב: הני טובא הוי. די"ב הוא דאיכא: נביא הוא. קרא דלהלי קולך בת גלים הקשיבי לישה דחשיבנא ביה תלתא בת גלים לישה ענתות הנהו לאו מן חושבנא נינהו דנביא הוא דקאמר להו לישראל וכו': מהאי לא תסתפי. שתנלל מידו היינו דכתיב לחלי קולך אלא אסתפי מנבוכדנלר שנמשל לליש דכתיב ביה עלה אריה מסובכו והיינו דקאמר הקשיבי לישה: החסיל. כאסיפת חסיל שאוסף לו תבואה בקיץ כל א' לעצמו אף כולן יבוזו איש לו. כמשק גבים. כקול מים הנאספים ונופלין בגבים בנהם כן ינהמו הבאים לשלול ולבוז משק ל' נהם כמו (משלי כח) ארי נוהם ודוב שוקק וכן ממשק חרול (צפניה ב) כשהרוח מנשבת בחרולים והם מכים זה על זה נותנים קול וכן בעיר ישוקו (יואל ב). גבים. כמו ולחשוף מים מגבא ורבותינו דרשוהו באגדת חלק בביזת אוכלוסי סנחריב [שם לג, ד]. [המשך בדף צה.]

גליון הש"ס

גמ' בבית רשע זה פקח בן רמליהו. וכן גיטין דף נה ע"ב. אשרי אדם מפחד זה:

תורה אור השלם

א) וַיֹּאמֶר פַּרְעֹה מִי יְיָ אֲשֶׁר אֶשְׁמַע בְּקֹלוֹ לְשַׁלַּח אֶת יִשְׂרָאֵל לֹא יָדַעְתִּי אֶת יְיָ וְגַם אֶת יִשְׂרָאֵל לֹא אֲשַׁלֵּחַ: [שמות ה, ב]

ב) וַיֵּט מֹשֶׁה אֶת יָדוֹ עַל הַיָּם וַיָּשָׁב הַיָּם לִפְנוֹת בֹּקֶר לְאֵיתָנוֹ וּמִצְרַיִם נָסִים לִקְרָאתוֹ וַיְנַעֵר יְיָ אֶת מִצְרַיִם בְּתוֹךְ הַיָּם: [שמות יד, כז]

ג) דָּרַכְתָּ בַיָּם סוּסֶיךָ חֹמֶר מַיִם רַבִּים: [חבקוק ג, טו]

ד) בְּיַד מַלְאָכֶיךָ חֵרַפְתָּ אֲדֹנָי וַתֹּאמֶר בְּרֹב רִכְבִּי אֲנִי עָלִיתִי מְרוֹם הָרִים יַרְכְּתֵי לְבָנוֹן וְאֶכְרֹת קוֹמַת אֲרָזָיו מִבְחוֹר בְּרֹשָׁיו וְאָבוֹאָה מְלוֹן קִצֹּה יַעַר כַּרְמִלּוֹ: [מלכים ב' יט, כג]

ה) וַיְהִי בַּלַּיְלָה הַהוּא וַיֵּצֵא מַלְאַךְ יְיָ וַיַּךְ בְּמַחֲנֵה אַשּׁוּר מֵאָה שְׁמוֹנִים וַחֲמִשָּׁה אָלֶף וַיַּשְׁכִּימוּ בַבֹּקֶר וְהִנֵּה כֻלָּם פְּגָרִים מֵתִים: [מלכים ב' יט, לה]

ו) בְּיַד עֲבָדֶיךָ חֵרַפְתָּ אֲדֹנָי וַתֹּאמֶר בְּרֹב רִכְבִּי אֲנִי עָלִיתִי מְרוֹם הָרִים יַרְכְּתֵי לְבָנוֹן וְאֶכְרֹת קוֹמַת אֲרָזָיו מִבְחַר בְּרֹשָׁיו וְאָבוֹא מְרוֹם קִצּוֹ יַעַר כַּרְמִלּוֹ: [ישעיה לז, כד]

ז) עַתָּה הֲמִבַּלְעֲדֵי יְיָ עָלִיתִי עַל הַמָּקוֹם הַזֶּה לְהַשְׁחִתוֹ יְיָ אָמַר אֵלַי עֲלֵה עַל הָאָרֶץ הַזֹּאת וְהַשְׁחִיתָהּ: [מלכים ב' יח, כה]

ח) יַעַן כִּי מָאַס הָעָם הַזֶּה אֵת מֵי הַשִּׁלֹחַ הַהֹלְכִים לְאַט וּמְשׂוֹשׂ אֶת רְצִין וּבֶן רְמַלְיָהוּ: [ישעיה ח, ו]

ט) מְאֵרַת יְיָ בְּבֵית רָשָׁע וּנְוֵה צַדִּיקִים יְבָרֵךְ: [משלי ג, לג]

י) וְלָכֵן הִנֵּה אֲדֹנָי מַעֲלֶה עֲלֵיהֶם אֶת מֵי הַנָּהָר הָעֲצוּמִים וְהָרַבִּים אֶת מֶלֶךְ אַשּׁוּר וְאֶת כָּל כְּבוֹדוֹ וְעָלָה עַל כָּל אֲפִיקָיו וְהָלַךְ עַל כָּל גְּדוֹתָיו: [ישעיה ח, ז]

כ) וְחָלַף בִּיהוּדָה שָׁטַף וְעָבַר עַד צַוָּאר יַגִּיעַ וְהָיָה מֻטּוֹת כְּנָפָיו מְלֹא רֹחַב אַרְצְךָ עִמָּנוּ אֵל: [ישעיה ח, ח]

ל) כִּי לֹא מוּעָף לַאֲשֶׁר מוּצָק לָהּ כָּעֵת הָרִאשׁוֹן הֵקַל אַרְצָה זְבֻלוּן וְאַרְצָה נַפְתָּלִי וְהָאַחֲרוֹן הִכְבִּיד דֶּרֶךְ הַיָּם עֵבֶר הַיַּרְדֵּן גְּלִיל הַגּוֹיִם: [ישעיה ח, כג]

מ) אַחֲרֵי הַדְּבָרִים וְהָאֱמֶת הָאֵלֶּה בָּא סַנְחֵרִיב מֶלֶךְ אַשּׁוּר וַיָּבֹא בִיהוּדָה וַיִּחַן עַל הֶעָרִים הַבְּצֻרוֹת וַיֹּאמֶר לְבִקְעָם אֵלָיו: [דברי הימים ב' לב, א]

נ) נִשְׁבַּע יְיָ צְבָאוֹת לֵאמֹר אִם לֹא כַּאֲשֶׁר דִּמִּיתִי כֵּן הָיָתָה וְכַאֲשֶׁר יָעַצְתִּי הִיא תָקוּם: לִשְׁבֹּר אַשּׁוּר בְּאַרְצִי וְעַל הָרַי אֲבוּסֶנּוּ וְסָר מֵעֲלֵיהֶם עֻלּוֹ וְסֻבֳּלוֹ מֵעַל שִׁכְמוֹ יָסוּר: [ישעיה יד, כד-כה] ס) וְהָיָה בַּיּוֹם הַהוּא יָסוּר סֻבֳּלוֹ מֵעַל שִׁכְמֶךָ וְעֻלּוֹ מֵעַל צַוָּארֶךָ וְחֻבַּל עֹל מִפְּנֵי שָׁמֶן: [ישעיה י, כז] ע) וְהָיָה בַּיּוֹם הַהוּא יְחַיֶּה אִישׁ עֶגְלַת בָּקָר וּשְׁתֵּי צֹאן: וְהָיָה מֵרֹב עֲשׂוֹת חָלָב יֹאכַל חֶמְאָה כִּי חֶמְאָה וּדְבַשׁ יֹאכֵל כָּל הַנּוֹתָר בְּקֶרֶב הָאָרֶץ: [ישעיה ז, כא-כב] פ) וְהָיָה בַּיּוֹם הַהוּא יִהְיֶה כָל מָקוֹם אֲשֶׁר יִהְיֶה שָׁם אֶלֶף גֶּפֶן בְּאֶלֶף כָּסֶף לַשָּׁמִיר וְלַשַּׁיִת יִהְיֶה: [ישעיה ז, כג] צ) וְאֻסַּף שְׁלַלְכֶם אֹסֶף הֶחָסִיל כְּמַשַּׁק גֵּבִים שׁוֹקֵק בּוֹ: [ישעיה לג, ד] ק) בָּא עַל עַיַּת עָבַר בְּמִגְרוֹן לְמִכְמָשׂ יַפְקִיד כֵּלָיו: עָבְרוּ מַעְבָּרָה גֶּבַע מָלוֹן לָנוּ חָרְדָה הָרָמָה גִּבְעַת שָׁאוּל נָסָה: ר) צַהֲלִי קוֹלֵךְ בַּת גַּלִּים הַקְשִׁיבִי לַיְשָׁה עֲנִיָּה עֲנָתוֹת: נָדְדָה מַדְמֵנָה יֹשְׁבֵי הַגֵּבִים הֵעִיזוּ: [ישעיה י, כח-לא] ש) עוֹד הַיּוֹם בְּנֹב לַעֲמֹד יְנֹפֵף יָדוֹ הַר בַּת צִיּוֹן גִּבְעַת יְרוּשָׁלָיִם: [ישעיה י, לב] ת) עָלָה אַרְיֵה מִסֻּבְּכוֹ וּמַשְׁחִית גּוֹיִם נָסַע יָצָא מִמְּקֹמוֹ לָשׂוּם אַרְצֵךְ לְשַׁמָּה עָרַיִךְ תִּצֶּינָה מֵאֵין יוֹשֵׁב: [ירמיה ד, ז]

מסורת הש"ס

א) [גי' הערוך ערך גל ה' גלילה], ב) גי' הערוך ערך דשן דישנא וכתב המוסיף שהוא בלשון יון מתנה, ג) [צ"ל מאי אחר], ד) ב"ש מ"ז, ה) גיטין לח. חולין ס:, ו) רש"ל מ"ז.

ליקוטי רש"י

את מי השילוח ההולכים לאט. במלכותא דבית דוד דמדבר להון בניח כמי שלוחא דנגדין בניח, שלוח מעין הוא ושמו גיחון ושילוח שרלו להסיר [נ"א, להסב] את מלכות בית דוד בימי אחז לפקח בן רמליהו וכאן ניבא על שבנא וסיעתו שרלו למרוד בחזקיהו שמאסו בו על שראוהו שלא היה בוחר בשולחן מלכים אלא אוכל ליטר' ירק ועוסק בתורה עליו נאמר לדיק אוכל לשובע נפשו (משלי יג) וראו את פקח בן רמליהו אוכל ארבעים סאה גוזלות בקינוח סעודה והיו מליזין על חזקיהו ואומרין זה הגון להיות מלך אין זה מלך אלא רלין ובן רמליהו היו ראויין למלוך בחייהן וזהו ומשוש את רלין וגו' אמר להם הקב"ה אוכלין אתם מתאוי' אני מביא עליכם אוכלין הרבה הנה ה' מעלה עליכם (וגו') את מי הנהר העלומים תחת מי השילוח האטים והנוחים [ישעיה ח, ו]. וחלף ביהודה. באר' יהוד'. שטף. בחזקה. עד צואר. עד עיקר חוזק לואר ות"י עד ירושלם ימטי [שם, ח]. אחרי הדברים והאמת האלה וגו' ויאמר לבקעם. כמו לבקעם כמו (עמוס ב') על מכרם בכסף כמו מוכרם וסמוך ליה (עמוס א') על בקעם הרות הגלעד ופתרונו ודוגמא (ישעיה ז') ונבקיענה ויבקע עלי העולה (בראשית כב) [דה"ב לב, א]. והחבל עול. סנחריב מפני חזקיהו שהיה נוח לדורו כשמן, ורבותינו פירשו מפני שמנו של חזקיהו שהי' דולק בבתי כנסיות ובבתי מדרשות שהעסיקו לעסוק בתורה כענין שנאמר אשר העתיקו אנשי חזקיה וגומר (משלי כה) [ישעיה י, כז]. ולא מצאו עם הארץ. כשנתמנה חזקיהו למלך והוא הושיב תלמידים בכל עיר כדאמרינן בפ' חלק בדקו מדן ועד באר שבע ולא מצאו עם הארץ [משלי כה, א]. ועל אותו הדור וכו'. לא חזקיהו ושב בכל לבבו לדרוש להקב"ה וכל דורו שלימים לא קם דור כישראל כמותם כמו שמפורש בחלק בדקו מדן ועד וכו' [שה"ש ה, י]. והיה ביום ההוא וגו'. כי אותו הדור של חזקיה ישובו אלי לעסוק בתורה ולא לשתות יין וכן היתה כדאמרינן בחלק בדקו מדן ועד באר שבע ולא מצאו איש שלא היה בקי בהלכות איסור והיתר וטומאה וטהרה ועל אותו הדור הוא אומר והיה כל מקום וגומר והוא שנאמר אשר העתיקו אנשי חזקיה מלך יהודה [ישעיה ז, כא]. אלף גפן. אלף כסף. לשמיר ולשית. כי יניחום בעליהם ויהיו מעלות קימושים וחולים ועקרבים [שם, כג]. אוסף גבים שוקק. כקול

עַל יְדֵי שָׁלִיחַ – On the other hand, **Sancheiriv, who blasphemed against God through** the medium of **a messenger,**[1] נִפְרַע הַקָּדוֹשׁ בָּרוּךְ הוּא מִמֶּנּוּ עַל יְדֵי שָׁלִיחַ – suffered the indignity of having **the Holy One, Blessed is He, punish him through a messenger.**[2]

The Gemara explains:

פַּרְעֹה דִּכְתִיב בֵּיהּ ,,מִי ה׳ אֲשֶׁר אֶשְׁמַע בְּקֹלוֹ" – **Pharaoh** blasphemed God directly, **for it is written** that he himself said, ***Who is Hashem that I should heed His voice?***[3] נִפְרַע הַקָּדוֹשׁ בָּרוּךְ הוּא מִמֶּנּוּ בְּעַצְמוֹ – And in return, **the Holy One, Blessed is He, personally punished him,** דִּכְתִיב ,,וַיְנַעֵר ה׳ אֶת־מִצְרַיִם בְּתוֹךְ הַיָּם" – **for it is written:**[4] ***Hashem churned Egypt in the midst of the sea;*** וּכְתִיב ,,דָּרַכְתָּ בַיָּם סוּסֶיךָ" וגו׳ – **and it is** further **written:**[5] ***You have trodden the sea with Your horses, etc.*** סַנְחֵרִיב דִּכְתִיב – **Sancheiriv,** on the other hand, blasphemed God through a messenger, **for it is written:**[6] ,,בְּיַד מַלְאָכֶיךָ חֵרַפְתָּ ה׳" – ***Through your messengers you have blasphemed God.*** נִפְרַע הַקָּדוֹשׁ בָּרוּךְ הוּא מִמֶּנּוּ עַל יְדֵי שָׁלִיחַ – **And in return,** he suffered the indignity of having **the Holy One, Blessed is He, punish him through** a mere **messenger,** דִּכְתִיב ,,וַיֵּצֵא מַלְאַךְ ה׳ וַיַּךְ בְּמַחֲנֵה אַשּׁוּר מֵאָה שְׁמוֹנִים וַחֲמִשָּׁה אָלֶף וגו׳" – **for it is written:**[7] ***An angel of Hashem went out and slew one hundred and eighty-five thousand of the camp of Assyria, etc.***

When Chizkiah and Isaiah prayed to God for deliverance from Sancheiriv, God responded with a message foretelling Sancheiriv's destruction. In this message, God recounted Sancheiriv's boasts and mocked them. God's message is recounted twice in Scripture – once in *Isaiah* ch. 37, and once in *II Kings* ch. 19. The Gemara now discusses a discrepancy between these two versions:

רַבִּי חֲנִינָא בַּר פָּפָּא רָמֵי – **R' Chanina bar Pappa pointed out a contradiction** between the following two verses: כְּתִיב ,,מְרוֹם קִצּוֹ" – In one verse, **it is written** that Sancheiriv boasted: *I will come to **its most remote height;***[8] וּכְתִיב ,,מְלוֹן קִצּוֹ" – **and** yet **it is** also **written:** *I will come to **its most remote lodge.***[9] This apparent contradiction indicates that Sancheiriv actually made *two* boasts. אָמַר אוֹתוֹ רָשָׁע – In other words, **that wicked [Sancheiriv] said:** בַּתְּחִלָּה אַחֲרִיב דִּירָה שֶׁל מַטָּה – **First, I shall destroy [God's] dwelling place below,** i.e. His abode here on earth, וְאַחַר כָּךְ אַחֲרִיב דִּירָה שֶׁל מַעְלָה – **and afterwards I shall destroy [God's] dwelling place above;** i.e. His abode in Heaven.[10]

The Gemara discusses another of Sancheiriv's boasts:

אָמַר רַבִּי יְהוֹשֻׁעַ בֶּן לֵוִי – **R' Yehoshua ben Levi said:** מַאי דִּכְתִיב ,,עַתָּה הֲמִבַּלְעֲדֵי ה׳ עָלִיתִי עַל־הַמָּקוֹם הַזֶּה לְהַשְׁחִתוֹ" – **What is** the meaning of **that which is written:**[11] ***Now, could it be that without Hashem I have come up against this place to destroy it?*** ,,ה׳ אָמַר אֵלַי עֲלֵה עַל־הָאָרֶץ הַזֹּאת וְהַשְׁחִיתָהּ" – ***[Indeed], Hashem has said to me, "Go up against this land and destroy it."*** מַאי הִיא – **What,** indeed, **is** the meaning of **this?** When had God ever told this to the Assyrians?

The Gemara answers that Sancheiriv had deduced that this was God's plan from something the prophet Isaiah had said:

דִּשְׁמַע לְנָבִיא דְּקָאָמַר – Sancheiriv **heard the prophet [Isaiah] say** in God's Name:[12] ,,יַעַן כִּי מָאַס הָעָם הַזֶּה אֵת מֵי הַשִּׁלֹחַ הַהֹלְכִים לְאַט – ***Since this people has rejected the waters of the Shiloach that flow gently,*** וּמְשׂוֹשׂ אֶת־רְצִין וּבֶן־רְמַלְיָהוּ" – ***and [instead] rejoices in Retzin and Ben Remaliahu,*** *therefore, behold; the Lord will bring upon them the mighty and massive waters of the river – the king of Assyria.*

The Gemara explains the cryptic imagery of the verse just cited:

אָמַר רַב יוֹסֵף – **Rav Yosef said:** אִלְמָלֵא תַּרְגּוּמָא דְּהַאי קְרָא לֹא הֲוָה יָדַעְנָא מַאי קָאָמַר – **Were it not for the Targum**[13] **of this verse,** which gives an interpretive translation of the passage, **I would not have known what it meant.** ,,חֲלַף דְּקָץ עַמָּא הָדֵין בְּמַלְכוּתָא דְבֵית דָּוִד – In the Targum, this verse is rendered as follows: ***Since this people has despised the kingship of the Davidic dynasty,*** דִּמְדַבַּר לְהוֹן בְּנַיְיח כְּמֵי שִׁילֹחָא דְּנָגְדִין בְּנַיְיח – ***which leads them gently, like the waters of the Shiloach that flow gently,*** וְאִתְרְעִיאוּ בִּרְצִין וּבַר רְמַלְיָה" – ***and has [instead] preferred [the kingship of] Retzin and the son of Remaliah ...***[14] This translation gives meaning to the words "rejecting the waters of the Shiloach," which otherwise would have been indecipherable.

NOTES

1. Sancheiriv's address to the besieged city of Jerusalem (*Isaiah* 36:13-20), in which he uttered blasphemy against God, was not delivered by Sancheiriv himself. Instead, the Assyrian king sent his servant Ravshakeh to deliver the address. In doing so, Sancheiriv displayed contempt for God, for he evidently considered God a trifling opponent Who did not even warrant Sancheiriv's direct involvement.

2. Sancheiriv was repaid measure for measure: Just as he considered it beneath his dignity to confront God directly, so too, God did not dignify Sancheiriv with His own direct involvement. Rather, God left this task to an angel – His mere servant. Sancheiriv's defeat was thus more humiliating than Pharaoh's (*Rashi;* see *Shabbos* end of 108a; cf. *Maharsha*).

3. *Exodus* 5:2.

4. Ibid. 14:27.

5. *Habakkuk* 3:15. This verse likewise emphasizes God's personal role in the destruction of the Egyptian army.

6. *II Kings* 19:23.

7. Ibid. v. 35.

8. *Isaiah* 37:24. Here, God paraphrases Sancheiriv's boast that he will ascend Mt. Moriah, and reach "its remote height" – i.e. the Holy Temple – whereupon he will destroy it. [Elsewhere in Scripture, the Temple is also referred to as "the height"; see *Jeremiah* 17:12] (*Rashi;* cf. *Maharsha*).

9. *II Kings* 19:23. This verse exactly parallels the verse just cited, with the exception that in this latter verse, Sancheiriv boasts that he will come to "its most remote *lodge*" (rather than *height*). The verses thus appear to contradict one another.

10. That is, the first verse expresses Sancheiriv's desire to destroy the Temple ["the most remote height" of Mt. Moriah]. The second verse, however, refers to Sancheiriv's desire to destroy even His dwelling place [His "lodge"] in Heaven (*Rashi;* see *Maharsha,* however, who interprets the word "lodge" as a reference to the Temple, and "height" as a reference to the Heavens).

11. *II Kings* 18:25. In this verse, Sancheiriv tells the besieged Jews that God Himself has sent the Assyrians to destroy Jerusalem.

12. *Isaiah* 8:6.

13. *Targum* (literally: translation): The Aramaic interpretive translation of Scripture (see *Megillah* 3a).

Be'er Sheva, citing *Ritva,* states that Rav Yosef often quoted *Targum,* for he was blind and was therefore compelled to study Scripture by memory. Rather than recite verses of the Written Torah by heart, which is associated with a prohibition (see *Gittin* 60a), he recited the translation of Scripture embodied in the *Targum* (cf. *Tosafos* to *Bava Kamma* 3b ד״ה כדמתרגם).

14. The Targum explains that "the waters of Shiloach" is a metaphor representing the Davidic dynasty. Chizkiah, the current monarch of this dynasty, had ruled over Judah in a gentle and mild way, comparable to the gentle waters of Shiloach. Opponents of Chizkiah, however, despised him for his modest lifestyle and devotion to Torah, and instead preferred the lavish ways of the wicked king, Pekach ben Remaliahu, leader of the Kingdom of Israel, and his ally, the Aramean king Retzin. In these verses, the prophet chastises the Jews for this, telling them that they are destined to face a tyrannical ruler – Sancheiriv – as punishment for having spurned Chizkiah (*Rashi,* from *Isaiah* 8:6).

ע"י שליח נפרע הקב"ה ממנו ע"י שליח פרעה דכתיב ביה (א) מי ה' אשר אשמע בקולו נפרע הקב"ה ממנו בעצמו דכתיב (ב) וינער ה' את מצרים בתוך הים וכתיב (ג) דרכת בים סוסיך וגו' סנחריב דכתיב (ד) ביד מלאכיך חרפת ה' נפרע הקב"ה ממנו ע"י שליח דכתיב (ה) ויצא מלאך ה' ויך במחנה אשור מאה ושמונים וחמשה אלף וגו' ר' חנינא בר פפא רמי כתיב (ו) מרום קיצו וכתיב (ד) מלון קיצו אמר אותו רשע בתחלה אחריב דירה של מטה ואחר כך אחריב דירה של מעלה א"ר יהושע בן לוי מאי דכתיב (ז) עתה המבלעדי ה' עליתי על המקום הזה להשחיתו ה' אמר אלי עלה אל הארץ הזאת והשחיתה מאי היא דשמע לנביא דקאמר (ח) יען כי מאס העם הזה את מי השילוח ההולכים לאט ומשוש את רצין ובן רמליהו אמר רב יוסף אלמלא תרגומא דהאי קרא לא הוה ידענא מאי קאמר חלף דקץ עמא הדין במלכותא דבית דוד דמדבר להון בנייח כמי שילוחא דנגדין בנייח ואיתרעיאו ברצין ובר רמליה א"ר יוחנן מאי דכתיב (ט) מארת ה' בבית רשע ונוה צדיקים יבורך מארת ה' [°]בבית רשע זה פקח בן רמליהו שהיה אוכל מ' סאה גוזלות בקינוח סעודה ונוה צדיקים יבורך זה חזקיה מלך יהודה שהיה אוכל ליטרא ירק בסעודה (י) ולכן הנה ה' מעלה עליהם את מי הנהר העצומים והרבים את מלך אשור וכתיב (כ) וחלף ביהודה שטף ועבר עד צואר יגיע אלא מ"ט איענשׁ נביא אעשרת השבטים איתנבי איהו יהיב דעתיה על כולה ירושלים בא נביא וא"ל (ל) כי לא מועף לאשר מוצק לה א"ר אלעזר בר ברכיה אין נמסר עם עייף בתורה ביד מי המציק לו מאי (ל) כעת הראשון הקל ארצה זבולון וארצה נפתלי והאחרון הכביד דרך הים עבר הירדן גליל הגוים לא כראשונים שהקלו מעליהם עול תורה אבל אחרונים שהכבידו עליהן עול תורה וראויין הללו לעשות להם נס כעוברי הים וכדורכי הירדן אם חוזר בו מוטב ואם לאו אני אעשה לו [א]גליל בגוים (מ) אחרי הדברים והאמת האלה בא סנחריב מלך אשור ויבא ביהודה ויחן על הערים הבצורות ויאמר לבקעם אליו האי [ב]רישנא להאי פרדשנא אחרי הדברים והאמת [ג](אחר מאי) אמר רבינא לאחר שקפץ הקב"ה ונשבע ואמר אי אמינא ליה לחזקיה מייתינא ליה לסנחריב ומסרנא ליה בידך השתא אמר לא הוא בעינא ולא ביעתותיה בעינא מיד קפץ הקב"ה ונשבע דמייתינא ליה שנאמר (נ) נשבע ה' צבאות לאמר אם לא כאשר דמיתי כן היתה וכאשר יעצתי היא תקום לשבור אשור בארצי ועל הרי אבוסנו וסר מעליהם עולו וסבלו מעל שכמו יסור א"ר יוחנן אמר הקב"ה יבא סנחריב וסיעתו ויעשה אבום לחזקיהו ולסיעתו (ס) והיה ביום ההוא יסור סבלו מעל שכמך ועולו מעל צוארך וחובל עול מפני שמן א"ר יצחק נפחא חובל עול של סנחריב מפני שמנו של חזקיהו שהיה דולק בבתי כנסיות ובבתי מדרשות מה עשה נעץ חרב על פתח בית המדרש ואמר כל מי שאינו עוסק בתורה ידקר בחרב זו בדקו מדן ועד באר שבע ולא מצאו עם הארץ מגבת ועד אנטיפרס ולא מצאו תינוק ותינוקת איש ואשה שלא היו בקיאין בהלכות טומאה וטהרה ועל אותו הדור הוא אומר (ע) והיה ביום ההוא יחיה איש עגלת בקר ושתי צאן וגו' ואומר (פ) והיה ביום ההוא יהיה כל מקום אשר יהיה שם אלף גפן באלף כסף לשמיר ולשית יהיה אע"פ שאלף גפן באלף כסף לשמיר ולשית יהיה (צ) ואוסף שללכם אוסף החסיל אמר להם נביא לישראל אספו שללכם אמרו לו לבזוז או לחלוק אמר להם כאוסף החסיל מה אוסף החסיל כל אחד ואחד לעצמו אף שללכם כל אחד ואחד לעצמו אמרו לו והלא ממון עשרת השבטים מעורב בו אמר להם (צ) כמשק גבים שוקק בו מה גבים הללו מעלין את האדם מטומאה לטהרה אף ממונם של ישראל כיון שנפל ביד עובדי כוכבים מיד טיהר ([ד]כדרב פפא דאמר רב פפא [ה]עמון ומואב טהרו בסיחון) אמר רב הונא עשר מסעות נסע אותו רשע באותו היום שנאמר (ק) בא על עית עבר במגרון למכמש יפקיד כליו עברו מעברה גבע מלון לנו חרדה הרמה גבעת שאול נסה (ר) צהלי קולך בת גלים הקשיבה לישה עניה ענתות נדדה מדמנה יושבי הגבים העיזו ([ו] (ש) עוד היום בנוב לעמוד ינופף ידו הר בת ציון גבעת ירושלם) הני טובא הויין צהלי קולך בת גלים נביא הוא דקאמר לה לכנסת ישראל צהלי קולך בת גלים בתו של אברהם יצחק ויעקב שעשו מצות כגלי הים הקשיבה לישה מהאי לא תסתפי אלא איסתפי מנבוכדנצר הרשע דמתיל כאריה שנא' (ת) עלה אריה מסובכו וגו' מאי

עניה

רש"י

על ידי שליח. דהיינו בזוי יותר אף הקב"ה נפרע ע"י שליח ונתבייש יותר: כתיב מרום קצו. בישעיה: וכתיב מלון קיצו. במלכים. מרום קילו משמע דירה של מטה כדכתיב (ירמיה יז) מרום מראשון מקום מקדשנו מלון קילו משמע דירה של מעלה בית מלונו: ה' אמר אלי עלה אל הארץ וגו' מאי היא. היכי אמר לו הקב"ה להשחית: יען כי מאס העם הזה וגו'. ומשוש את רלין ובן רמליהו ואתרעו להשחית' ברלין ובר רמליהו: מארת ה'. שלא נשבע מכל מה שהיה אוכל: ליטרא ירק. במדה: ועלה על כל אפיקיו. שאמר לו הקב"ה עלה והשחת: מ"ט. מאחר שברשות הלך שנביא נתנבא עליו מאי טעמא איענש: בא נביא ואמר לו. כשבא על ירושלים: כי לא מועף לאשר מוצק לה. לא נמסר עמו של חזקיה שהוא עיף בתורה ביד סנחריב המליק לו: כעת הראשון הקל ארצה זבולון וארצה נפתלי וגו' לא כראשונים. עשרת השבטים שהקלו מעליהם עול תורה אבל אחרונים עמו של חזקיה הכבידו עליהם עול תורה והיינו דכתיב האחרון הכביד דרך הים עבר הירדן גליל הגוים ראויין הללו לעשות להם נס כיוצאי מצרים שעברו את הים וכדורכי הירדן: אם חוזר בו סנחריב מוטב. ואם לאו אעשה אותו גליל הגוים שמגלגל בחרפה בכל הגוים ל"א גליל לשון גללים. מ"ר: אחרי הדברים והאמת האלה. השתא משמע שהיה מדבר בחזקיהו שהיו עסוקין בתורה בא סנחריב מלך אשור ויבא ביהודה ויחן על הערים ויאמר לבקעם אליו: האי רישנא להאי פרדשנא. וכי מביאין דורון כזה לאדון כזה וכי מפני שהאמת בחזקיהו בא סנחריב: רבינא אמר מאי אחר הדברים והאמת אחר שקפץ הקב"ה ונשבע. להביא סנחריב והיינו אמת שחותמו וקיומו של הקדוש ברוך הוא אמת:

ויעשה אבום. שיהיו כלם פגרים ויאכלו סוסיהם ובהמתם בתוך עלמות הפגרים כעין אבוס: מגבת ועד אנטיפרס. מקומות שבסוף התחומים: אע"פ שאלף גפן באלף כסף. שהן יקרים שאין להם רוב כרמים אפילו הכי לשמיר ולשית יהיה שמניחין אותן לאבוד ומבייריס אותן והיו עוסקין בתורה: לשלל. כל אחד ואחד לעצמו או לחלוק ביחד אותו ממון שנשאר מחיל סנחריב ל"א לחלוק לאחרים מה שאנו שוללים אבל אנו אסורים באותו שלל שממון שבזו מעשרת השבטים מעורב בו דאיכא משום גזל: כמשק גבים שוקק בו. השקאה של לינורות שמזלפין בהם מים נובעין השקו באותו ממון וטיהרתו דמה לינורות הללו מעלין את האדם מטומאה לטהרה ע"י טבילה אף ממונם וכו' משק שו"ן בלע"ז: בא על עית וגו'. ומתרגמינן ומני רבני משרייתיה: עברו מעברה גבע מלון לנו וגו' יושבי הגבים העיזו. ולא קא חשיב עוד היום בנוב לעמוד דההוא לאו מסע הוא אלא כדאמרינן לקמן אותו היום נשתייר מעונה של נוב: הני טובא הוי. די"ב הוא דאיכא: נביא הוא. קרא דלהלי קולך בת גלים הקשיבי לישה דחשיבנא ביה תלתא בת גלים לישה ענתות הנהו לאו מן חושבנא נינהו דנביא הוא דקאמר להו לישראל וכו': מהאי לא תסתפי. שתנלל מידו היינו דכתיב להלי קולך אלא אסתפי מנבוכדנלר שנמשל לליש דכתיב ביה עלה אריה מסובכו והיינו דקאמר הקשיבי לישה:

עניה

גליון הש"ס

גמ' בבית רשע זה פקח בן רמליהו. וכן גיטין דף נה ע"ב. אשרי אדם מפחד זה:

תורה אור השלם

א) וַיֹּאמֶר פַּרְעֹה מִי יְיָ אֲשֶׁר אֶשְׁמַע בְּקֹלוֹ לְשַׁלַּח אֶת יִשְׂרָאֵל לֹא יָדַעְתִּי אֶת יְיָ וְגַם אֶת יִשְׂרָאֵל לֹא אֲשַׁלֵּחַ: [שמות ה, ב]

ב) וַיֵּט מֹשֶׁה אֶת יָדוֹ עַל הַיָּם וַיָּשָׁב הַיָּם לִפְנוֹת בֹּקֶר לְאֵיתָנוֹ וּמִצְרַיִם נָסִים לִקְרָאתוֹ וַיְנַעֵר יְיָ אֶת מִצְרַיִם בְּתוֹךְ הַיָּם: [שמות יד, כז]

ג) דָּרַכְתָּ בַיָּם סוּסֶיךָ חֹמֶר מַיִם רַבִּים: [חבקוק ג, טו]

ד) בְּיַד מַלְאָכֶיךָ חֵרַפְתָּ אֲדֹנָי וַתֹּאמֶר בְּרֹב רִכְבִּי אֲנִי עָלִיתִי מְרוֹם הָרִים יַרְכְּתֵי לְבָנוֹן וְאֶכְרֹת קוֹמַת אֲרָזָיו מִבְחוֹר בְּרֹשָׁיו וְאָבוֹאָה מְלוֹן קִצֹּה יַעַר כַּרְמִלּוֹ: [מלכים ב' יט, כג]

ה) וַיְהִי בַּלַּיְלָה הַהוּא וַיֵּצֵא מַלְאַךְ יְיָ וַיַּךְ בְּמַחֲנֵה אַשּׁוּר מֵאָה שְׁמוֹנִים וַחֲמִשָּׁה אָלֶף וַיַּשְׁכִּימוּ בַבֹּקֶר וְהִנֵּה כֻלָּם פְּגָרִים מֵתִים: [מלכים ב' יט, לה]

ו) בְּיַד עֲבָדֶיךָ חֵרַפְתָּ אֲדֹנָי וַתֹּאמֶר בְּרֹב רִכְבִּי אֲנִי עָלִיתִי מְרוֹם הָרִים יַרְכְּתֵי לְבָנוֹן וְאֶכְרֹת קוֹמַת אֲרָזָיו מִבְחַר בְּרֹשָׁיו וְאָבוֹא מְרוֹם קִצּוֹ יַעַר כַּרְמִלּוֹ: [ישעיה לז, כד]

ז) עַתָּה הֲמִבַּלְעֲדֵי יְיָ עָלִיתִי עַל הַמָּקוֹם הַזֶּה לְהַשְׁחִתוֹ יְיָ אָמַר אֵלַי עֲלֵה עַל הָאָרֶץ הַזֹּאת וְהַשְׁחִיתָהּ: [מלכים ב' יח, כה]

ח) יַעַן כִּי מָאַס הָעָם הַזֶּה אֵת מֵי הַשִּׁלֹחַ הַהֹלְכִים לְאַט וּמְשׂוֹשׂ אֶת רְצִין וּבֶן רְמַלְיָהוּ: [ישעיה ח, ו]

ט) מְאֵרַת יְיָ בְּבֵית רָשָׁע וּנְוֵה צַדִּיקִים יְבָרֵךְ: [משלי ג, לג]

י) וְלָכֵן הִנֵּה אֲדֹנָי מַעֲלֶה עֲלֵיהֶם אֶת מֵי הַנָּהָר הָעֲצוּמִים וְהָרַבִּים אֶת מֶלֶךְ אַשּׁוּר וְאֶת כָּל כְּבוֹדוֹ וְעָלָה עַל כָּל אֲפִיקָיו וְהָלַךְ עַל כָּל גְּדוֹתָיו: [ישעיה ח, ז]

כ) וְחָלַף בִּיהוּדָה שָׁטַף וְעָבַר עַד צַוָּאר יַגִּיעַ וְהָיָה מֻטּוֹת כְּנָפָיו מְלֹא רֹחַב אַרְצְךָ עִמָּנוּ אֵל: [ישעיה ח, ח]

ל) כִּי לֹא מוּעָף לַאֲשֶׁר מוּצָק לָהּ כָּעֵת הָרִאשׁוֹן הֵקַל אַרְצָה זְבֻלוּן וְאַרְצָה נַפְתָּלִי וְהָאַחֲרוֹן הִכְבִּיד דֶּרֶךְ הַיָּם עֵבֶר הַיַּרְדֵּן גְּלִיל הַגּוֹיִם: [ישעיה ח, כג]

מ) אַחֲרֵי הַדְּבָרִים וְהָאֱמֶת הָאֵלֶּה בָּא סַנְחֵרִיב מֶלֶךְ אַשּׁוּר וַיָּבֹא בִיהוּדָה וַיִּחַן עַל הֶעָרִים הַבְּצֻרוֹת וַיֹּאמֶר לְבִקְעָם אֵלָיו: [דברי הימים ב' לב, א]

נ) נִשְׁבַּע יְיָ צְבָאוֹת לֵאמֹר אִם לֹא כַּאֲשֶׁר דִּמִּיתִי כֵּן הָיָתָה וְכַאֲשֶׁר יָעַצְתִּי הִיא תָקוּם: לִשְׁבֹּר אַשּׁוּר בְּאַרְצִי וְעַל הָרַי אֲבוּסֶנּוּ וְסָר מֵעֲלֵיהֶם עֻלּוֹ וְסֻבֳּלוֹ מֵעַל שִׁכְמוֹ יָסוּר: [ישעיה יד, כד-כה] ס) וְהָיָה בַּיּוֹם הַהוּא יָסוּר סֻבֳּלוֹ מֵעַל שִׁכְמֶךָ וְעֻלּוֹ מֵעַל צַוָּארֶךָ וְחֻבַּל עֹל מִפְּנֵי שָׁמֶן: [ישעיה י, כז] ע) וְהָיָה בַּיּוֹם הַהוּא יְחַיֶּה אִישׁ עֶגְלַת בָּקָר וּשְׁתֵּי צֹאן: וְהָיָה מֵרֹב עֲשׂוֹת חָלָב יֹאכַל חֶמְאָה כִּי חֶמְאָה וּדְבַשׁ יֹאכַל כָּל הַנּוֹתָר בְּקֶרֶב הָאָרֶץ: [ישעיה ז, כא-כב] פ) וְהָיָה בַּיּוֹם הַהוּא יִהְיֶה כָל מָקוֹם אֲשֶׁר יִהְיֶה שָּׁם אֶלֶף גֶּפֶן בְּאֶלֶף כָּסֶף לַשָּׁמִיר וְלַשַּׁיִת יִהְיֶה: [ישעיה ז, כג] צ) וְאֻסַּף שְׁלַלְכֶם אֹסֶף הֶחָסִיל כְּמַשַּׁק גֵּבִים שֹׁקֵק בּוֹ: [ישעיה לג, ד] ק) בָּא עַל עַיַּת עָבַר בְּמִגְרוֹן לְמִכְמָשׂ יַפְקִיד כֵּלָיו: עָבְרוּ מַעְבָּרָה גֶּבַע מָלוֹן לָנוּ חָרְדָה הָרָמָה גִּבְעַת שָׁאוּל נָסָה: [ישעיה י, כח-כט] ר) צַהֲלִי קוֹלֵךְ בַּת גַּלִּים הַקְשִׁיבִי לַיְשָׁה עֲנִיָּה עֲנָתוֹת: נָדְדָה מַדְמֵנָה יֹשְׁבֵי הַגֵּבִים הֵעִיזוּ: [ישעיה י, ל-לא] ש) עוֹד הַיּוֹם בְּנֹב לַעֲמֹד יְנֹפֵף יָדוֹ הַר בַּת צִיּוֹן גִּבְעַת יְרוּשָׁלִָם: [ישעיה י, לב] ת) עָלָה אַרְיֵה מִסֻּבְּכוֹ וּמַשְׁחִית גּוֹיִם נָסַע יָצָא מִמְּקֹמוֹ לָשׂוּם אַרְצֵךְ לְשַׁמָּה עָרַיִךְ תִּצֶּינָה מֵאֵין יוֹשֵׁב: [ירמיה ד, ז]

מסורת הש"ס

א) [גי' הערוך ערך גל ה' גלילה], ב) גי' הערוך ערך דשן דישנא וכתב המוסיף שהוא בלשון יון מתנה, ג) [צ"ל מאי אחר], ד) ב"ש מ"ז, ה) גיטין לח. חולין ס., ו) רש"ל מ"ז.

ליקוטי רש"י

את מי השילוח ההולכים לאט. במלכותא דבית דוד דמדבר להון בנית כמי שלוחא דנגדין בנית, שלוח מעין הוא ושמו גיחון ושילוח שרצו להסיר [נ"א, להסב] את מלכות בית דוד בימי אחז לפקח בן רמליהו וכאן ניבא על שבנא וסיעתו שרצו למרוד בחזקיהו שמאסו בו על שראוהו שלא היה בוחר בשולחן מלכים אלא אוכל ליטר' ירק ועוסק בתורה עליו נאמר לדיק אוכל לשובע נפשו (משלי יג) וראו את פקח בן רמליהו אוכל ארבעים סאה גוזלות בקינוח סעודה והיו מליזין על חזקיהו ואומרין זה הגון להיות מלך אין זה מלך אלא רלין ובן רמליהו היו ראויין למלוך בחייהן וזהו ומשוש את רלין וגו' אמר להם הקב"ה אוכלין אתם מתאוי' אני מביא עליכם אוכלין הרבה הנה ה' מעלה עליכם (וגו') את מי הנהר העצומים תחת מי השילוח החלשים והנוחים [ישעיה ח, ו]. וחלף ביהודה. בארץ יהוד'. שטף. בחזקה. עד צואר. עד עיקר חוזק לוארם ות"י עד ירושלם ימטי [שם, ח]. אחרי הדברים והאמת האלה וגו' ויאמר לבקעם. כמו לבקעם כמו (עמוס ב') על מכרם בכסף כמו מוכרם וסמוך ליה (עמוס א') על בקעם הרות הגלעד ופתרונו ודוגמא (ישעיה ז') ונבקיענה ויבקע עלי העולה (בראשי' כב) [דה"ב לב, א]. וחובל עול. סנחריב מפני חזקיהו שהיה נוח לדורו כשמן, ורבותינו פירשו מפני שמנו של חזקיהו שהי' דולק בבתי כנסיות ובבתי מדרשות שהשיאם לעסוק בתורה כענין שנאמר אשר העתיקו אנשי חזקיה וגומר (משלי כה) [ישעיה י, כז]. ולא מצאו עם הארץ. כשנתמנה חזקיהו למלך והוא הושיב תלמידים בכל עיר כדאמרינן בפ' חלק בדקו מדן ועד באר שבע ולא מלאו עם הארץ [משלי כה, א]. ועל אותו הדור וכו'. בא חזקיהו ושב בכל לבבו לדרוש להקב"ה וכל דורו שלימים לא קם דור בישראל כמותם כמו שמפורש בחלק בדקו מדן וכו' [שה"ש ה, ז]. ואומר והיה ביום ההוא וכו'. כי אותו הדור של חזקיה ישובו אלי לעסוק בתורה ולא לשתות יין וכן היתה כדאיתא בחלק בדקו מדן ועד באר שבע ולא מלאו איש שלא היה בקי בהלכו' איסור והיתר וטומאה וטהרה ועל אותו הדור הוא אומר והיה כל מקום וגומר הוא שנאמר (משלי כה) אשר העתיקו אנשי חזקיה מלך יהודה [ישעיה ז, כה]. אלף גפן. שוות אלף כסף. לשמיר ולשית. כי יניחום בעליהם וכו' והם מעלות קימשונים ותולעים ועקרבים [שם, כג]. אוסף החסיל. כאסיפת חסיל שאוסף לו תבואה בקיץ כל א' לעצמו אף כולן יבוזו איש לו. כמשק גבים שוקק. כקול נהם מים הנאספים ונופלין בגבים בנהם כן יהמו הבאים לשלול ולבוז משק ל' נהם כמו (משלי כח) ארי נוהם ודוב שוקק וכן ממשק חרול (צפניה ב) כשהרוח מנשבת בחרולים והם מכים זה על זה נותנים קול וכן בעיר ישוקו (יואל ב). גבים. כמו ולחשוף מים מגבא ורבותינו דרשוהו באגדת חלק בביזת אוכלוסי סנחריב [שם לג, ד]. [המשך בדף צה.]

The Gemara elaborates on the contrast between the righteous King Chizkiah of the Davidic dynasty, and the wicked Pekach ben Remaliahu of the Northern Kingdom:

אָמַר רַבִּי יוֹחָנָן – R' Yochanan said: מַאי דִּכְתִיב – **What is** the meaning of **that which is written:**[15] ,,מְאֵרַת ה׳ בְּבֵית רָשָׁע וּנְוֵה צַדִּיקִים יְבָרֵךְ" – ***The curse of Hashem is in the house of the wicked, but [God] shall bless the dwelling of the righteous?*** ,,מְאֵרַת ה׳ בְּבֵית רָשָׁע" זֶה פֶּקַח בֶּן רְמַלְיָהוּ – The first part of the verse, ***the curse of Hashem is in the house of the wicked,* is** a reference **to Pekach ben Remaliahu,** שֶׁהָיָה אוֹכֵל אַרְבָּעִים סְאָה גּוֹזָלוֹת בְּקִינּוּחַ סְעוּדָה – **who,** after finishing a meal, **used to eat forty *se'ahs* of young birds for dessert.**[16] ,,וּנְוֵה צַדִּיקִים יְבָרֵךְ" זֶה חִזְקִיָּה מֶלֶךְ יְהוּדָה – The second part of the verse, ***but [God] shall bless the dwelling of the righteous,* is a reference to Chizkiah, King of Judah,** שֶׁהָיָה אוֹכֵל לִיטְרָא יָרָק בִּסְעוּדָה – **who** by contrast **used to eat a** mere ***litra***[17] **of vegetables for [his]** entire **meal.**

Earlier, the Gemara cited prophetic words that Sancheiriv interpreted as Divine sanction for his attack on Jerusalem. The Gemara now quotes the continuation of this prophecy and examines it:

,,וְלָכֵן הִנֵּה אֲדֹנָי מַעֲלֶה עֲלֵיהֶם אֶת־מֵי הַנָּהָר הָעֲצוּמִים וְהָרַבִּים אֶת־מֶלֶךְ אַשּׁוּר" – The prophet Isaiah stated: ***Therefore, behold the Lord will bring upon them the mighty and massive waters of the river – the king of Assyria.*** וּכְתִיב ,,וְחָלַף בִּיהוּדָה שָׁטַף וְעָבַר עַד־צַוָּאר יַגִּיעַ" – **And it is further written** in the next verse: ***[The river] shall sweep through Judah, overflowing as it passes through; up to the neck will it reach.***[18] This is the rest of the prophecy that Sancheiriv interpreted as foretelling his own invasion of Judah.

The Gemara asks:

אֶלָּא מַאי טַעְמָא אִיעֲנִישׁ – **But why,** then, **was [Sancheiriv] punished?**[19] Since God *did* say that He would send Sancheiriv to invade Judah, what sin did Sancheiriv commit by carrying out God's command?[20]

The Gemara answers:

נָבִיא אַעֲשֶׂרֶת הַשְּׁבָטִים אִיתְנַבֵּי – Actually, in the above-cited verses, **the prophet** Isaiah **was prophesying concerning the** fate of the **Ten Tribes,** not concerning the Kingdom of Judah.[21] אִיהוּ יָהִיב דַּעְתֵּיהּ עַל כּוּלָּהּ יְרוּשָׁלַיִם – **[Sancheiriv],** however, **set his mind on** conquering **all** of **Jerusalem,** and in doing so, he exceeded the limits of the prophecy. בָּא נָבִיא וְאָמַר לֵיהּ – Indeed, **the prophet** Isaiah then **came and** foretold that Sancheiriv would not be successful, **saying to him:** ,,כִּי לֹא מוּעָף לַאֲשֶׁר מוּצָק לָהּ" – ***There is no weariness*** *(muaf)* ***for the one who oppresses her.***[22] אָמַר רַבִּי אֶלְעָזָר בַּר בֶּרֶכְיָה – This was an assurance that Sancheiriv would not, in the end, conquer Jerusalem, as **R' Elazar bar Berechyah said:** אֵין נִמְסַר עַם עָיֵיף בַּתּוֹרָה בְּיַד מִי הַמֵּצִיק לוֹ – The meaning of the verse is: **The nation that is wearied** *(ayef)* **by** intensive study of **Torah,** i.e. the Kingdom of Judah under their righteous king, Chizkiah, **will not be delivered into the hand of the one who oppresses it,** i.e. Sancheiriv.

The Gemara cites and expounds the conclusion of this same verse:

מַאי – **What is** the meaning of the concluding words: ,,כָּעֵת הָרִאשׁוֹן הֵקַל אַרְצָה זְבֻלוּן וְאַרְצָה נַפְתָּלִי – ***The first time he dealt mildly, [exiling only] the land of Zevulun and the land of Naphtali;*** וְהָאַחֲרוֹן הִכְבִּיד דֶּרֶךְ הַיָּם – ***but the last [time] he dealt harshly, [exiling those who lived] by the way of the sea,*** עֵבֶר הַיַּרְדֵּן גְּלִיל הַגּוֹיִם" – ***[in] the Transjordan, [and in] the "attraction of the nations"?***[23] לֹא כָּרִאשׁוֹנִים שֶׁהֵקֵלּוּ מֵעֲלֵיהֶם עוֹל תּוֹרָה – The meaning of this passage is as follows: **[The fate of the Kingdom of Judah] will not resemble** the fate of **the "first ones,"** i.e. the fate of the Ten Tribes, **who "lightened"** *[hakel]* **the yoke of Torah from upon themselves,** and were subsequently exiled.[24] אֲבָל אַחֲרוֹנִים שֶׁהִכְבִּידוּ עֲלֵיהֶן עוֹל תּוֹרָה – **Rather, the "last ones,"** i.e. the Kingdom of Judah under Chizkiah, **who increased** *[hichbid]* **the yoke of Torah upon themselves,** וּרְאוּיִין הַלָּלוּ לַעֲשׂוֹת לָהֶם נֵס – **and are [therefore] worthy of having miracles performed on their behalf,** כְּעוֹבְרֵי הַיָּם וּכְדוֹרְכֵי הַיַּרְדֵּן – miracles **similar** in magnitude to those performed for **the people who crossed the [Red] Sea** *[derech hayam]* **and those who marched across the Jordan** *[ever hayarden],*[25] *these* people I shall save. אִם חוֹזֵר בּוֹ מוּטָב – That is, **if [Sancheiriv] changes his mind** and does not attack Jerusalem, **that is fine;** וְאִם לָאו אֲנִי אֶעֱשֶׂה לוֹ גָּלִיל בַּגּוֹיִם – **but if not, I will make him** the butt of **the nations' mockery,**

NOTES

15. *Proverbs* 3:33.

16. I.e. his curse was that although he used to eat gluttonously, he could never be satiated (*Rashi*).

17. A *litra* is a volume measurement equivalent to a *log,* or six eggs. Chizkiah, in contrast to Pekach, ate sparingly but nevertheless, he was satiated by what he ate.

18. *Isaiah* 8:7-8. In these verses, the prophet foretells that the mighty river, an allusion to Sancheiriv, will reach up to the neck, an allusion to Jerusalem (see *Ramban* to *Genesis* 15:14). Sancheiriv took this to mean that he would ultimately conquer Jerusalem. In fact, however, the prophet only said that the water shall reach *up* to the neck; he never said that the waters shall *cover* the neck. Thus, Sancheiriv never conquered Jerusalem; on the contrary, his army was destroyed there.

19. The Gemara does not mean to question why Sancheiriv *himself* was punished; he was, in fact, punished for his blasphemy (see above). Rather, the question is: For what sin was his *entire* army punished? (*Margaliyos HaYam*).

20. See *Sanhedrei Ketanah* and *Yad David.*

21. It seems difficult to say that the prophecy concerned the Ten Tribes specifically, given the fact that the verse explicitly states: *[The river] shall sweep* ***through Judah.*** (For a possible explanation see *Rif* in *Ein Yaakov*).

22. Ibid. v. 23. The plain meaning of this passage is that Sancheiriv and his army would know no weariness in their campaign against Judah. The Gemara, however, presents an interpretation under which the verse refers to the weariness of *the Jews* – that is, their extraordinary diligence in Torah study, which causes them to become weary. Such sacrifice for the sake of Torah study, says the prophet, will save them from the sword of Sancheiriv.

23. In its plain meaning, this passage discusses the various stages in which the Assyrians exiled the Ten Tribes. First, they would conquer and exile Zevulun and Naphtali (*II Kings* 15:29); later they would conquer and exile the two-and-a-half tribes in Transjordan (*I Chronicles* 5:26) as well as the tribes who lived along the Sea of Galilee (*the way of the sea*); and finally, they would conquer the remaining tribes in central Israel, referred to here as "the attraction of the nations" (*Rashi* to *Isaiah* ibid. and *Radak* ad loc.; see *Gra* to *I Chronicles* 5:27). [For more on the exact chronology of these exiles, see ArtScroll *I Chronicles* pp. 81-83.]

The Gemara here interprets the verse in a completely different vein, as we shall now see.

24. The Gemara interprets the passage as contrasting the fate of the Ten Tribes, who were conquered and exiled by Assyria, with the fate of the people of Judah, who withstood the Assyrian siege. The Ten Tribes had slackened considerably in the areas of Torah study and adherence to its commands. Thus, they were allowed to fall to the Assyrians. Chizkiah, however, had led Judah to enthusiastically embrace the yoke of Torah, and thus, they merited to be saved.

25. The Gemara refers to two occasions where waters miraculously parted and the Jews were allowed to pass on dry land (see *Exodus* 14-15 and *Joshua* 3:16).

גליון הש"ס

גמ' בבית רשע זה פקח בן רמליהו. וכן גיטין דף נח ע"ב, אשרי אדם מפחד זה:

ע"י שליח נפרע הקב"ה ממנו ע"י שליח פרעה דכתיב ביה א) מי ה' אשר אשמע בקולו נפרע הקב"ה ממנו בעצמו דכתיב ב) וינער ה' את מצרים בתוך הים וכתיב ג) דרכת בים סוסיך וגו' סנחריב דכתיב ד) ביד מלאכיך חרפת ה' נפרע הקב"ה ממנו ע"י שליח דכתיב ה) ויצא מלאך ה' ויך במחנה אשור מאה ושמונים וחמשה אלף וגו' ר' חנינא בר פפא רמי כתיב ו) מרום קיצו וכתיב ד) מלון קיצו אמר אותו רשע בתחלה אחריב דירה של מטה ואחר כך אחריב דירה של מעלה א"ר יהושע בן לוי מאי דכתיב ז) עתה המבלעדי ה' עליתי על המקום הזה להשחיתו ה' אמר אלי עלה אל הארץ הזאת והשחיתה מאי היא דשמע לנביא דקאמר ח) יען כי מאס העם הזה את מי השילוח ההולכים לאט ומשוש את רצין ובן רמליהו אמר רב יוסף אלמלא תרגומא דהאי קרא לא הוה ידענא מאי קאמר חלף דקץ עמא הדין במלכותא דבית דוד דמדבר להון בנייח כמי שילוחא דנגדין בנייח ואיתרעיאו ברצין ובר רמליה א"ר יוחנן מאי דכתיב ט) מארת ה' בבית רשע ונוה צדיקים יבורך מארת ה' (א בבית רשע זה פקח בן רמליהו שהיה אוכל מ' סאה גוזלות בקינוח סעודה ונוה צדיקים יבורך זה חזקיה מלך יהודה שהיה אוכל ליטרא ירק בסעודה י) ולכן הנה ה' מעלה עליהם את מי הנהר העצומים והרבים את מלך אשור וכתיב כ) וחלף ביהודה שטף ועבר עד צואר יגיע אלא מ"ט איעניש נביא אעשרת השבטים איתנבי איהו יהיב דעתיה על כולה ירושלים בא נביא וא"ל ל) כי לא מועף לאשר מוצק לה א"ר אלעזר בר ברכיה אין נמסר עם עייף בתורה ביד מי המציק לו מאי ל) כעת הראשון הקל ארצה זבולון וארצה נפתלי והאחרון הכביד דרך הים עבר הירדן גליל הגוים לא כראשונים שהקלו מעליהם עול תורה אבל אחרונים שהכבידו עליהן עול תורה וראויין הללו לעשות להם נס כעוברי הים וכדורכי הירדן אם חוזר בו מוטב ואם לאו אני אעשה לו (ב גליל בגוים מ) אחרי הדברים והאמת האלה בא סנחריב מלך אשור ויבא ביהודה ויחן על הערים הבצורות ויאמר לבקעם אליו האי (ג רישנא להאי פרדשנא אחרי הדברים והאמת (ד (אחר מאי) אמר רבינא לאחר שקפץ הקב"ה ונשבע ואמר אי אמינא ליה לחזקיה מייתינא ליה לסנחריב ומסרנא ליה בידך השתא אמר לא הוא בעינא ולא ביעתותיה בעינא מיד קפץ הקב"ה ונשבע דמייתינא ליה שנאמר נ) נשבע ה' צבאות לאמר אם לא כאשר דמיתי כן היתה וכאשר יעצתי היא תקום לשבור אשור בארצי ועל הרי אבוסנו וסר מעליהם עולו וסבלו מעל שכמו יסור א"ר יוחנן אמר הקב"ה יבא סנחריב וסיעתו ויעשה אבוס לחזקיהו ולסיעתו ס) והיה ביום ההוא יסור סבלו מעל שכמך ועולו מעל צוארך וחובל עול מפני שמן א"ר יצחק נפחא חובל עול של סנחריב מפני שמנו של חזקיהו שהיה דולק בבתי כנסיות ובבתי מדרשות מה עשה נעץ חרב על פתח בית המדרש ואמר כל מי שאינו עוסק בתורה ידקר בחרב זו בדקו מדן ועד באר שבע ולא מצאו עם הארץ מגבת ועד אנטיפרס ולא מצאו תינוק ותינוקת איש ואשה שלא היו בקיאין בהלכות טומאה וטהרה ועל אותו הדור הוא אומר ע) והיה ביום ההוא יחיה איש עגלת בקר ושתי צאן וגו' ואומר פ) והיה ביום ההוא יהיה כל מקום אשר יהיה שם אלף גפן באלף כסף לשמיר ולשית יהיה אע"פ שאלף גפן באלף כסף לשמיר ולשית יהיה צ) ואוסף שללכם אוסף החסיל אמר להם נביא לישראל אספו שללכם אמרו לו לבזוז או לחלוק אמר להם כאוסף החסיל מה אוסף החסיל כל אחד ואחד לעצמו אף שללכם כל אחד ואחד לעצמו אמרו לו והלא ממון עשרת השבטים מעורב בו אמר להם צ) כמשק גבים שוקק בו מה גבים הללו מעלין את האדם מטומאה לטהרה אף ממונם של ישראל כיון שנפל ביד עובדי כוכבים מיד טיהר (ה כדרב פפא דאמר רב פפא (ו עמון ומואב טהרו בסיחון) אמר רב הונא עשר מסעות נסע אותו רשע באותו היום שנאמר ק) בא על עית עבר במגרון למכמש יפקיד כליו עברו מעברה גבע מלון לנו חרדה הרמה גבעת שאול נסה ר) צהלי קולך בת גלים הקשיבה לישה עניה ענתות נדדה מדמנה יושבי הגבים העיזו (ו ש) עוד היום בנוב לעמוד ינופף ידו הר בת ציון גבעת ירושלם) הני טובא הויין צהלי קולך בת גלים נביא הוא דקאמר לה לכנסת ישראל צהלי קולך בת גלים בתו של אברהם יצחק ויעקב שעשו מצות כגלי הים הקשיבה לישה מהאי לא תסתפי אלא איסתפי מנבוכדנצר הרשע דמתיל כאריה שנא' ת) עלה אריה מסובכו וגו' מאי

עניה

על ידי שליח. דהיינו בזוי יותר אף הקב"ה נפרע ע"י שליח ונתבייש יותר: כתיב מרום קצו. בישעיה: וכתיב מלון קיצו. במלכים. מרום קילו משמע דירה של מטה כדכתיב (ירמיה יז) מרום מראשון מקום מקדשנו מלון קילו משמע דירה של מעלה בית מלונו: ה' אמר אלי עלה אל הארץ וגו' מאי היא. היכי אמר לו הקב"ה להשחית: יען כי מאס העם הזה וגו'. ומשוש את רצין ובן רמליהו ואתרעו להשחית' ברצין ובר רמליהו: מארת ה'. שלא נשבע מכל מה שהיה אוכל: ליטרא ירק. בסעודה: ועלה על כל אפיקיו. שאמר לו הקב"ה עלה והשחת: מ"ט. מאחר שברשות הלך שנביא נתנבא עליו מאי טעמא איענש: בא נביא ואמר לו. כשבא על ירושלים: כי לא מועף לאשר מוצק לה. לא נמסר עמו של חזקיה שהוא עיף בתורה ביד סנחריב המציק לו: כעת הראשון הקל ארצה זבולון וארצה נפתלי וגו' לא כראשונים. עשרת השבטים שהקלו מעליהם עול תורה אבל אחרונים עמו של חזקיה הכבידו עליהם עול תורה והיינו דכתיב האחרון הכביד דרך הים עבר הירדן גליל הגוים ראויין הללו לעשות להם נס כיוצאי מצרים שעברו את הים וכדורכי הירדן: אם חוזר בו סנחריב מוטב. ואם לאו אעשה אותו גליל הגוים שמגלגל בחרפה בכל הגוים ל"א גליל לשון גללים. מ"ר: אחרי הדברים והאמת האלה. השתא משמע שהיה מדבר בחזקיהו שהיו עסוקין בתורה בא סנחריב מלך אשור ויבא ביהודה ויחן על הערים ויאמר לבקעם אליו: האי רישנא להאי פרדשנא. וכי מביאין דורון כזה לאדון כזה וכי מפני שהאמת בחזקיהו בא סנחריב: רבינא אמר מאי אחר הדברים והאמת אחר שקפץ הקב"ה ונשבע. להביא סנחריב והיינו אמת שחותמו וקיומו של הקדוש ברוך הוא אמת:

ויעשה אבוס. שיהיו כלם פגרים ויאכלו סוסיהם ובהמתם בתוך עצמות הפגרים כעין אבוס: מגבת ועד אנטיפרס. מקומות שבסוף התחומים: אע"פ שאלף גפן באלף כסף. שהן יקרים שאין להם רוב כרמים אפילו הכי לשמיר ולשית יהיה שמניחין אותן לאבוד ומביירים אותן והיו עוסקין בתורה: לשלל. כל אחד ואחד לעצמו או לחלוק ביחד אותו ממון שנשאר מחיל סנחריב ל"א לחלוק לאחרים מה שאנו שוללים אבל אנו אסורים באותו שלל שממון שבזזו מעשרת השבטים מעורב בו דאיכא משום גזל: כמשק גבים שוקק בו. השקאה של צינורות שמזלפין בהם מים נובעין השקו באותו ממון וטיהרתו דמה צינורות הללו מעלין את האדם מטומאה לטהרה ע"י טבילה אף ממונם וכו' משק שו"ן בלע"ז: בא על עית וגו'. ומתרגמינן ומני רבני משרייתיה: עברו מעברה גבע מלון לנו וגו' יושבי הגבים העיזו. ולא קא חשיב עוד היום בנוב לעמוד דההוא לאו מסע הוא אלא כדאמרינן לקמן אותו היום נשתייר מעונה של נוב: הני טובא הוי. די"ב הוא דאיכא: נביא הוא. קרא דצהלי קולך בת גלים הקשיבי לישה דחשיבנא ביה תלתא בת גלים לישה ענתות הנהו לאו מן חושבנא נינהו דנביא הוא דקאמר להו לישראל וכו': מהאי לא תסתפי. שתנצל מידו היינו דכתיב צהלי קולך אלא אסתפי מנבוכדנצר שנמשל לליש דכתיב ביה עלה אריה מסובכו והיינו דקאמר הקשיבי לישה:

עניה

מסורת הש"ס

א) [גי' הערוך ערך גל ה' גלילה], ב) גי' הערוך ערך דשן דישנא וכתב המוסיף שהוא בלשון יון מתנה, ג) [צ"ל מאי אחר], ד) ב"ש מ"ז, ה) גיטין נח. חולין ס:, ו) רש"ל מ"ז.

ליקוטי רש"י

את מי השילוח ההולכים לאט. במלכותא דבית דוד דמדבר להון בניח כמי שלוחא דנגדין בניח, שלוח מעין הוא ושמו גיחון ושילוח שרצו להסיר [נ"א, להסב] את מלכות בית דוד בימי אחז לפקח בן רמליהו וכאן ניבא על שבנא וסיעתו שרצו למרוד בחזקיהו שמאסו בו על שראוהו שלא היה בוחר בשולחן מלכים אלא אוכל ליטר' ירק ועוסק בתורה עליו נאמר צדיק אוכל לשובע נפשו (משלי יג) וראו את פקח בן רמליהו אוכל ארבעים סאה גוזלות בקינוח סעודה והיו מליזין על חזקיהו ואומרין זה הגון להיות מלך אין זה מלך אלא רצין ובן רמליהו היו ראויין למלוך בחייהן וזהו ומשוש את רצין וגו' אמר להם הקב"ה אוכלין אתם מתאוי' אני מביא עליכם אוכלין הרבה הנה ה' מעלה עליכם (וגו') את מי הנהר העצומים תחת מי השילוח המתאטים והנוחים [ישעיה ח, ו]. וחלף ביהודה. בארץ יהוד'. שטף. בחוזקה. עד צואר. עד עיקר חוזק לואורס ות"י עד ירושלם ימטי [שם, ח]. אחרי הדברים והאמת האלה וגו' ויאמר לבקעם. כמו לבקעם כמו (עמוס ב') על מכרם בכסף כמו מוכרם וסמוך ליה (עמוס א') על בקעם הרות הגלעד ופתרונו ודוגמא (ישעיה ז') ונבקיענה ויבקע עצי העולה (בראשי' כב) [דה"ב לב, א]. וחובל עול. סנחריב מפני חזקיהו שהיה נוח לדורו כשמן, ורבותינו פירשו מפני שמנו של חזקיהו שהי' דולק בבתי כנסיות ובבתי מדרשות שהשיאם לעסוק בתורה כענין שנאמר אשר העתיקו אנשי חזקיה וגומר (משלי כה) [ישעיה י, כז]. ולא מצאו עם הארץ. כשנתמנה חזקיהו למלך והוא הושיב תלמידים בכל עיר כדאמרינן בפ' חלק בדקו מדן ועד באר שבע ולא מצאו עם הארץ [משלי כה, א]. ועל אותו הדור וכו'. בא חזקיהו ושב בכל לבבו לדרוש להקב"ה וכל דורו שלימים לא קם דור בישראל כמותם כמו שמפורש בחלק בדקו מדן וכו' [שה"ש ה, ז]. ואומר והיה ביום ההוא וכו'. כי אותו הדור של חזקיה ישובו אלי לעסוק בתורה ולא לשתות יין וכן היתה כדאיתא בחלק בדקו מדן ועד באר שבע ולא מצאו איש שלא היה בקי בהלכו' איסור והיתר וטומאה וטהרה ועל אותו הדור הוא אומר והיה כל מקום וגומר הוא שנאמר (משלי כה) אשר העתיקו אנשי חזקיה מלך יהודה [ישעיה ז, כה]. אלף גפן. שוות אלף כסף. לשמיר ולשית. כי יניחום בעליהם וכו' והם מעלות קימשונים ותולעים ועקרבים [שם, כג]. אוסף החסיל. כאסיפת חסיל שאוסף לו תבואה בקיץ כל א' לעצמו אף כולן יבוזו איש לו. כמשק גבים שוקק. כקול נהם מים הנאספים ונופלין בגבים בנהם כן ינהמו הבאים לשלול ולבוז משק ל' נהם כמו (משלי כח) ארי נוהם ודוב שוקק וכן ממשק חרול (צפניה ב) כשהרוח מנשבת בחרולים והם מכים זה על זה נותנים קול וכן בעיר ישוקו (יואל ב). גבים. כמו ולחשוף מים מגבא ורבותינו דרשוהו באגדת חלק בביזת אוכלוסי סנחריב [שם לג, ד]. [המשך בדף צה.]

תורה אור השלם

א) וַיֹּאמֶר פַּרְעֹה מִי יְיָ אֲשֶׁר אֶשְׁמַע בְּקֹלוֹ לְשַׁלַּח אֶת יִשְׂרָאֵל לֹא יָדַעְתִּי אֶת יְיָ וְגַם אֶת יִשְׂרָאֵל לֹא אֲשַׁלֵּחַ: [שמות ה, ב]

ב) וַיֵּט מֹשֶׁה אֶת יָדוֹ עַל הַיָּם וַיָּשָׁב הַיָּם לִפְנוֹת בֹּקֶר לְאֵיתָנוֹ וּמִצְרַיִם נָסִים לִקְרָאתוֹ וַיְנַעֵר יְיָ אֶת מִצְרַיִם בְּתוֹךְ הַיָּם: [שמות יד, כז]

ג) דָּרַכְתָּ בַיָּם סוּסֶיךָ חֹמֶר מַיִם רַבִּים: [חבקוק ג, טו]

ד) בְּיַד מַלְאָכֶיךָ חֵרַפְתָּ אֲדֹנָי וַתֹּאמֶר בְּרֹב רִכְבִּי אֲנִי עָלִיתִי מְרוֹם הָרִים יַרְכְּתֵי לְבָנוֹן וְאֶכְרֹת קוֹמַת אֲרָזָיו מִבְחוֹר בְּרֹשָׁיו וְאָבוֹאָה מְלוֹן קִצֹּה יַעַר כַּרְמִלּוֹ: [מלכים ב' יט, כג]

ה) וַיְהִי בַּלַּיְלָה הַהוּא וַיֵּצֵא מַלְאַךְ יְיָ וַיַּךְ בְּמַחֲנֵה אַשּׁוּר מֵאָה שְׁמוֹנִים וַחֲמִשָּׁה אָלֶף וַיַּשְׁכִּימוּ בַבֹּקֶר וְהִנֵּה כֻלָּם פְּגָרִים מֵתִים: [מלכים ב' יט, לה]

ו) בְּיַד עֲבָדֶיךָ חֵרַפְתָּ אֲדֹנָי וַתֹּאמֶר בְּרֹב רִכְבִּי אֲנִי עָלִיתִי מְרוֹם הָרִים יַרְכְּתֵי לְבָנוֹן וְאֶכְרֹת קוֹמַת אֲרָזָיו מִבְחַר בְּרֹשָׁיו וְאָבוֹא מְרוֹם קִצּוֹ יַעַר כַּרְמִלּוֹ: [ישעיה לז, כד]

ז) עַתָּה הֲמִבַּלְעֲדֵי יְיָ עָלִיתִי עַל הַמָּקוֹם הַזֶּה לְהַשְׁחִתוֹ יְיָ אָמַר אֵלַי עֲלֵה עַל הָאָרֶץ הַזֹּאת וְהַשְׁחִיתָהּ: [מלכים ב' יח, כה]

ח) יַעַן כִּי מָאַס הָעָם הַזֶּה אֵת מֵי הַשִּׁלֹחַ הַהֹלְכִים לְאַט וּמְשׂוֹשׂ אֶת רְצִין וּבֶן רְמַלְיָהוּ: [ישעיה ח, ו]

ט) מְאֵרַת יְיָ בְּבֵית רָשָׁע וּנְוֵה צַדִּיקִים יְבָרֵךְ: [משלי ג, לג]

י) וְלָכֵן הִנֵּה אֲדֹנָי מַעֲלֶה עֲלֵיהֶם אֶת מֵי הַנָּהָר הָעֲצוּמִים וְהָרַבִּים אֶת מֶלֶךְ אַשּׁוּר וְאֶת כָּל כְּבוֹדוֹ וְעָלָה עַל כָּל אֲפִיקָיו וְהָלַךְ עַל כָּל גְּדוֹתָיו: [ישעיה ח, ז]

כ) וְחָלַף בִּיהוּדָה שָׁטַף וְעָבַר עַד צַוָּאר יַגִּיעַ וְהָיָה מֻטּוֹת כְּנָפָיו מְלֹא רֹחַב אַרְצְךָ עִמָּנוּ אֵל: [ישעיה ח, ח]

ל) כִּי לֹא מוּעָף לַאֲשֶׁר מוּצָק לָהּ כָּעֵת הָרִאשׁוֹן הֵקַל אַרְצָה זְבֻלוּן וְאַרְצָה נַפְתָּלִי וְהָאַחֲרוֹן הִכְבִּיד דֶּרֶךְ הַיָּם עֵבֶר הַיַּרְדֵּן גְּלִיל הַגּוֹיִם: [ישעיה ח, כג]

מ) אַחֲרֵי הַדְּבָרִים וְהָאֱמֶת הָאֵלֶּה בָּא סַנְחֵרִיב מֶלֶךְ אַשּׁוּר וַיָּבֹא בִיהוּדָה וַיִּחַן עַל הֶעָרִים הַבְּצֻרוֹת וַיֹּאמֶר לְבִקְעָם אֵלָיו: [דברי הימים ב' לב, א]

נ) נִשְׁבַּע יְיָ צְבָאוֹת לֵאמֹר אִם לֹא כַּאֲשֶׁר דִּמִּיתִי כֵּן הָיָתָה וְכַאֲשֶׁר יָעַצְתִּי הִיא תָקוּם: לִשְׁבֹּר אַשּׁוּר בְּאַרְצִי וְעַל הָרַי אֲבוּסֶנּוּ וְסָר מֵעֲלֵיהֶם עֻלּוֹ וְסֻבֳּלוֹ מֵעַל שִׁכְמוֹ יָסוּר: [ישעיה יד, כד-כה] ס) וְהָיָה בַּיּוֹם הַהוּא יָסוּר סֻבֳּלוֹ מֵעַל שִׁכְמֶךָ וְעֻלּוֹ מֵעַל צַוָּארֶךָ וְחֻבַּל עֹל מִפְּנֵי שָׁמֶן: [ישעיה י, כז] ע) וְהָיָה בַּיּוֹם הַהוּא יְחַיֶּה אִישׁ עֶגְלַת בָּקָר וּשְׁתֵּי צֹאן: וְהָיָה מֵרֹב עֲשׂוֹת חָלָב יֹאכַל חֶמְאָה כִּי חֶמְאָה וּדְבַשׁ יֹאכַל כָּל הַנּוֹתָר בְּקֶרֶב הָאָרֶץ: [ישעיה ז, כא-כב] פ) וְהָיָה בַּיּוֹם הַהוּא יִהְיֶה כָל מָקוֹם אֲשֶׁר יִהְיֶה שָׁם אֶלֶף גֶּפֶן בְּאֶלֶף כָּסֶף לַשָּׁמִיר וְלַשַּׁיִת יִהְיֶה: [ישעיה ז, כג] צ) וְאֻסַּף שְׁלַלְכֶם אֹסֶף הֶחָסִיל כְּמַשַּׁק גֵּבִים שֹׁקֵק בּוֹ: [ישעיה לג, ד] ק) בָּא עַל עַיַּת עָבַר בְּמִגְרוֹן לְמִכְמָשׂ יַפְקִיד כֵּלָיו: עָבְרוּ מַעְבָּרָה גֶּבַע מָלוֹן לָנוּ חָרְדָה הָרָמָה גִּבְעַת שָׁאוּל נָסָה: [ישעיה י, כח-כט] ר) צַהֲלִי קוֹלֵךְ בַּת גַּלִּים הַקְשִׁיבִי לַיְשָׁה עֲנִיָּה עֲנָתוֹת: נָדְדָה מַדְמֵנָה יֹשְׁבֵי הַגֵּבִים הֵעִיזוּ: [ישעיה י, ל-לא] ש) עוֹד הַיּוֹם בְּנֹב לַעֲמֹד יְנֹפֵף יָדוֹ הַר בַּת צִיּוֹן גִּבְעַת יְרוּשָׁלָיִם: [ישעיה י, לב] ת) עָלָה אַרְיֵה מִסֻּבְּכוֹ וּמַשְׁחִית גּוֹיִם נָסַע יָצָא מִמְּקֹמוֹ לָשׂוּם אַרְצֵךְ לְשַׁמָּה עָרַיִךְ תִּצֶּינָה מֵאֵין יוֹשֵׁב: [ירמיה ד, ז]

for I will utterly destroy his army.[26]

The Gemara now explores why Chizkiah, a paragon of righteousness, was made to face an Assyrian invasion in the first place:

,,אַחֲרֵי הַדְּבָרִים וְהָאֱמֶת הָאֵלֶּה – Scripture states: ***After these matters and this truth,***[27] בָּא סַנְחֵרִיב מֶלֶךְ־אַשּׁוּר וַיָּבֹא בִיהוּדָה וַיִּחַן עַל הֶעָרִים הַבְּצֻרוֹת – ***Sancheiriv, king of Assyria came, invaded Judah, and set up camps against the fortified cities.*** וַיֹּאמֶר לְבִקְעָם אֵלָיו" – ***He planned to breach them so that he might take them.***[28]

The Gemara asks rhetorically:

הַאי רִישְׁנָא לְהַאי פַּרְדַּשְׁנָא – Now, **this is the reward for this nobleman!?**[29] Did Chizkiah, who labored so diligently on behalf of God, deserve an Assyrian invasion as the reward for his efforts?

The Gemara replies by giving an aggadic interpretation of the verse just cited:

,,אַחֲרֵי הַדְּבָרִים וְהָאֱמֶת" – When the verse states: ***after these matters and this truth,*** אַחַר מַאי – **after what** events, and to what truth, does the verse refer?[30] אָמַר רָבִינָא – **Ravina said** it means as follows: לְאַחַר שֶׁקָּפַץ הַקָּדוֹשׁ בָּרוּךְ הוּא וְנִשְׁבַּע וְאָמַר – **After the Holy One, Blessed is He, resolutely swore** to bring Sancheiriv to Jerusalem and cause his downfall there, that was when Sancheiriv began his campaign against Judah. That is, **[God]**, so to speak, **said** to Himself: אִי אֲמִינָא לֵיהּ לְחִזְקִיָּה – **If I tell Chizkiah:** מַיְיתִינָא לֵיהּ לְסַנְחֵרִיב וּמָסַרְנָא לֵיהּ בְּיָדָךְ – **"I am going to bring Sancheiriv** to Jerusalem, **and** there **I will deliver him into your hand,"** הַשְׁתָּא אָמַר – I know that **[Chizkiah] will reply** to me: לָא הוּא בָּעֵינָא וְלָא בִּיעֲתוּתֵיהּ בָּעֵינָא – **"I want neither him nor his terror,"** i.e. I do not want him to invade Judah, even if I ultimately vanquish him. מִיָּד קָפַץ הַקָּדוֹשׁ בָּרוּךְ הוּא וְנִשְׁבַּע – **Immediately, the Holy One, Blessed is He,** decided he would not consult Chizkiah, and **he swore with alacrity,**[31] דְּמַיְיתִינָא לֵיהּ – **"I will bring [Sancheiriv to Jerusalem]!"** שֶׁנֶּאֱמַר – **For it is written:**[32] ,,נִשְׁבַּע ה׳ צְבָאוֹת לֵאמֹר – *HASHEM the Lord of Hosts swore, saying,* אִם־לֹא כַּאֲשֶׁר דִּמִּיתִי כֵּן הָיָתָה – ***As I have thought, so shall it come to pass,*** וְכַאֲשֶׁר יָעַצְתִּי הִיא תָקוּם – ***and as I have planned, so shall it stand,*** לִשְׁבֹּר אַשּׁוּר בְּאַרְצִי וְעַל־הָרַי אֲבוּסֶנּוּ – ***[namely] to break Assyria in My Land, and upon My mountains will I trample him.*** וְסָר מֵעֲלֵיהֶם עֻלּוֹ וְסֻבֳּלוֹ מֵעַל שִׁכְמוֹ יָסוּר" – ***His yoke shall be removed from upon them, and his burden shall be removed from upon his shoulder."*** Thus, the passage *"after these matters and this truth Sancheiriv came"* does not mean that the invasion of Sancheiriv was Chizkiah's reward for his good deeds; rather, it means that the invasion occurred because God had taken an oath (*truth*) to destroy the Assyrian army in Judah, and to thereby end the Assyrian domination of the Jews.[33]

The Gemara introduces a homiletic interpretation of *Isaiah* 14:25, the last verse cited in the above discussion:

אָמַר רַבִּי יוֹחָנָן – **R' Yochanan said:** אָמַר הַקָּדוֹשׁ בָּרוּךְ הוּא – This verse implies that **the Holy One, Blessed is He, said:** יָבֹא סַנְחֵרִיב וְסִיעָתוֹ – **Let Sancheiriv and his followers come** and attack, וְיֵעָשֶׂה אֵבוּס לְחִזְקִיָּהוּ וּלְסִיעָתוֹ – **and they will become a "trough" for Chizkiah and his followers.**[34]

The Gemara presents further homiletic interpretations of verses from *Isaiah:*

,,וְהָיָה בַּיּוֹם הַהוּא יָסוּר סֻבֳּלוֹ מֵעַל שִׁכְמֶךָ – It is stated in the Book of *Isaiah:*[35] ***It shall come to pass on that day that his burden shall be removed from your shoulder,*** וְעֻלּוֹ מֵעַל צַוָּארֶךָ – ***and his yoke from upon your neck,*** וְחֻבַּל עֹל מִפְּנֵי־שָׁמֶן" – ***and the yoke shall be destroyed because of girth (shamen).***[36] אָמַר רַבִּי יִצְחָק נַפָּחָא – **R' Yitzchak Nafcha said** that the verse implies: חוּבַּל עוֹל שֶׁל סַנְחֵרִיב מִפְּנֵי שַׁמְנוֹ שֶׁל חִזְקִיָּהוּ – **The yoke of Sancheiriv was broken by the oil** (*shemen*) **of Chizkiah,** שֶׁהָיָה דּוֹלֵק בְּבָתֵּי כְנֵסִיּוֹת וּבְבָתֵּי מִדְרָשׁוֹת – **which burned in the synagogues and study halls** of his kingdom to make possible the study of Torah; i.e. the merit of Chizkiah's promotion of Torah study caused the defeat of Sancheiriv.

The Gemara inquires:

מֶה עָשָׂה – **What,** indeed, **did Chizkiah do** to promote Torah study? נָעַץ חֶרֶב עַל פֶּתַח בֵּית הַמִּדְרָשׁ וְאָמַר – **He thrust a sword over the entrance of the study hall, and said:** כָּל מִי שֶׁאֵינוֹ עוֹסֵק בַּתּוֹרָה – **"Whoever does not engage in the study of Torah,** יִדָּקֵר בְּחֶרֶב זוֹ – **shall be pierced by this sword!"**

The Gemara recounts:

בָּדְקוּ מִדָּן וְעַד בְּאֵר שֶׁבַע – In the end, Chizkiah's efforts were so successful that **they searched from Dan to Beersheba,** i.e. from one end of Eretz Yisrael to the other, וְלֹא מָצְאוּ עַם הָאָרֶץ – **and did not find a** single **uneducated person,** i.e. a Jew not versed in the Torah; מִגְּבַת וְעַד אַנְטִיפְּרַס – and they searched **from Gevas to Antipras**[37] וְלֹא מָצְאוּ תִּינוֹק וְתִינוֹקֶת אִישׁ וְאִשָּׁה – **and did not find a boy or girl, man or woman**

NOTES

26. According to *Rashi,* the verse's word גליל is here interpreted as undergoing mockery (see *Bereishis Rabbah* 36:1). If Sancheiriv did not desist from attacking Jerusalem on his own, his defeat would be such that he would become an object of derision throughout the world (see also an alternative interpretation cited by *Rashi* in the name of his teacher; cf. *Aruch* and *Ben Yehoyada*).

27. [Chizkiah's conscientiously undertaken efforts to restore Torah observance to the masses are here referred to as *truth.* See following note.]

28. *II Chronicles* 32:1. When Chizkiah succeeded his wicked father Achaz to the throne, he immediately set about reversing his father's policies. Chizkiah undertook a series of measures which restored Torah study and observance to its former place in Judah. Our verse states that after these praiseworthy achievements, Judah was invaded by Sancheiriv.

29. This translation follows *Rashi* (see also *Maharsha*). For an alternative rendering, see *Aruch* (see also *Megillah* 12b, 13a, and *Avodah Zarah* 71a).

30. In its plain meaning, the words אַחֲרֵי הַדְּבָרִים וְהָאֱמֶת הָאֵלֶּה, would be translated as *after these conscientiously undertaken efforts* [the verse would then refer to the efforts of Chizkiah to restore Torah to his people]. The Gemara, however, will now interpret the word אֱמֶת more literally, as simply *truth.* As such, the word is a euphemism for an oath taken by God – the Being Whose very essence is Truth (*Rashi*).

31. Literally: jumped up and swore.

32. *Isaiah* 14:24-5. The verse explicitly states that God swore to bring the Assyrians to Judah where He would destroy them, and thereby free Judah from Assyrian domination.

33. *Maharsha* explains that God was determined to proceed because the ultimate failure of the Assyrian invasion was destined to serve as a remarkable public demonstration of God's omnipotence.

34. I.e. the Assyrian army will perish, such that the animals of the Jews will eat their corpses as they would eat from a feeding trough (*Rashi*). R' Yochanan connects the verb אֲבוּסֶנּוּ, *I will trample him,* with the term אֵבוּס, *trough.*

35. *Isaiah* 10:27.

36. In this verse, Isaiah prophesies that the yoke of Sancheiriv will be broken by Chizkiah (see *Radak* to *Isaiah* ad loc.). Generally, the word שָׁמֶן that appears in this verse is translated as fat, or girth; the metaphor is thus painted of a yoke around an animal's neck breaking when the neck expands. Our Gemara, however, will interpret שֶׁמֶן in the sense of *oil.* The word is thus an allusion to Torah study at night, an activity which requires the burning of oil to provide light (*Ben Yehoyada*).

37. [Two border towns (*Rashi*) that define the parameters of Judean territory (see *Margaliyos HaYam*).]

ע"י שליח נפרע הקב"ה ממנו ע"י שליח פרעה דכתיב ביה (א) מי ה' אשר אשמע בקולו נפרע הקב"ה ממנו בעצמו דכתיב (ב) וינער ה' את מצרים בתוך הים וכתיב (ג) דרכת בים סוסיך וגו' סנחריב דכתיב (ד) ביד מלאכיך חרפת ה' נפרע הקב"ה ממנו ע"י שליח דכתיב (ה) ויצא מלאך ה' ויך במחנה אשור מאה ושמונים וחמשה אלף וגו' ר' חנינא בר פפא רמי כתיב (ו) מרום קיצו וכתיב (ד) מלון קיצו אמר אותו רשע בתחלה אחריב דירה של מטה ואחר כך אחריב דירה של מעלה א"ר יהושע בן לוי מאי דכתיב (ז) עתה המבלעדי ה' עליתי על המקום הזה להשחיתו ה' אמר אלי עלה אל הארץ הזאת והשחיתה מאי היא דשמע לנביא דקאמר (ח) יען כי מאס העם הזה את מי השילוח ההולכים לאט ומשוש את רצין ובן רמליהו אמר רב יוסף אלמלא תרגומא דהאי קרא לא הוה ידענא מאי קאמר חלף דקץ עמא הדין במלכותא דבית דוד דמדבר להון בנייח כמי שילוחא דנגדין בנייח ואיתרעיאו ברצין ובר רמליה א"ר יוחנן מאי דכתיב (ט) מארת ה' בבית רשע ונוה צדיקים יבורך מארת ה' [ה] בבית רשע זה פקח בן רמליהו שהיה אוכל מ' סאה גוזלות בקינוח סעודה ונוה צדיקים יבורך זה חזקיה מלך יהודה שהיה אוכל ליטרא ירק בסעודה (י) ולכן הנה ה' מעלה עליהם את מי הנהר העצומים והרבים את מלך אשור וכתיב (כ) וחלף ביהודה שטף ועבר עד צואר יגיע אלא מ"ט איעניש נביא אעשרת השבטים איתנבי איהו יהיב דעתיה על כולה ירושלים בא נביא וא"ל (ל) כי לא מועף לאשר מוצק לה א"ר אלעזר בר ברכיה אין נמסר עם עייף בתורה ביד מי המציק לו מאי (ל) כעת הראשון הקל ארצה זבולון וארצה נפתלי והאחרון הכביד דרך הים עבר הירדן גליל הגוים לא כראשונים שהקלו מעליהם עול תורה אבל אחרונים שהכבידו עליהן עול תורה וראויין הללו לעשות להם נס כעוברי הים וכדורכי הירדן אם חוזר בו מוטב ואם לאו אני אעשה לו [א] גליל בגוים (מ) אחרי הדברים והאמת האלה בא סנחריב מלך אשור ויבא ביהודה ויחן על הערים הבצורות ויאמר לבקעם אליו האי [ב] רישנא להאי פרדשנא אחרי הדברים והאמת [ג] (אחר מאי) אמר רבינא לאחר שקפץ הקב"ה ונשבע ואמר אי אמינא ליה לחזקיה מייתינא ליה לסנחריב ומסרנא ליה בידך השתא אמר לא הוא בעינא ולא ביעתותיה בעינא מיד קפץ הקב"ה ונשבע דמייתינא ליה שנאמר (נ) נשבע ה' צבאות לאמר אם לא כאשר דמיתי כן היתה וכאשר יעצתי היא תקום לשבור אשור בארצי ועל הרי אבוסנו וסר מעליהם עולו וסבלו מעל שכמו יסור א"ר יוחנן אמר הקב"ה יבא סנחריב וסיעתו ויעשה אבוס לחזקיהו ולסיעתו (ס) והיה ביום ההוא יסור סבלו מעל שכמך ועולו מעל צוארך וחובל עול מפני שמן א"ר יצחק נפחא חובל עול של סנחריב מפני שמנו של חזקיהו שהיה דולק בבתי כנסיות ובבתי מדרשות מה עשה נעץ חרב על פתח בית המדרש ואמר כל מי שאינו עוסק בתורה ידקר בחרב זו בדקו מדן ועד באר שבע ולא מצאו עם הארץ מגבת ועד אנטיפרס ולא מצאו תינוק ותינוקת איש ואשה שלא היו בקיאין בהלכות טומאה וטהרה ועל אותו הדור הוא אומר (ע) והיה ביום ההוא יחיה איש עגלת בקר ושתי צאן וגו' ואומר (פ) והיה ביום ההוא יהיה כל מקום אשר יהיה שם אלף גפן באלף כסף לשמיר ולשית יהיה אע"פ שאלף גפן באלף כסף לשמיר ולשית יהיה (צ) ואוסף שללכם אוסף החסיל אמר להם נביא לישראל אספו שללכם אמרו לו לבזוז או לחלוק אמר להם כאוסף החסיל מה אוסף החסיל כל אחד ואחד לעצמו אף שללכם כל אחד ואחד לעצמו אמרו לו והלא ממון עשרת השבטים מעורב בו אמר להם (צ) כמשק גבים שוקק בו מה גבים הללו מעלין את האדם מטומאה לטהרה אף ממונם של ישראל כיון שנפל ביד עובדי כוכבים מיד טיהר ([ד] כדרב פפא דאמר רב פפא [ה] עמון ומואב טהרו בסיחון) אמר רב הונא עשר מסעות נסע אותו רשע באותו היום שנאמר (ק) בא על עית עבר במגרון למכמש יפקיד כליו עברו מעברה גבע מלון לנו חרדה הרמה גבעת שאול נסה (ר) צהלי קולך בת גלים הקשיבה לישה עניה ענתות נדדה מדמנה יושבי הגבים העיזו ([ו] (ש) עוד היום בנוב לעמוד ינופף ידו הר בת ציון גבעת ירושלם) הני טובא הויין צהלי קולך בת גלים נביא הוא דקאמר לה לכנסת ישראל צהלי קולך בת גלים בתו של אברהם יצחק ויעקב שעשו מצות כגלי הים הקשיבה לישה מהאי לא תסתפי אלא איסתפי מנבוכדנצר הרשע דמתיל כאריה שנא' (ת) עלה אריה מסובכו וגו' מאי

עניה

על ידי שליח. דהיינו בזוי יותר אף הקב"ה נפרע ע"י שליח ונתבייש יותר: כתיב מרום קצו. בישעיה: וכתיב מלון קיצו. במלכים. מרום קיצו משמע דירה של מטה כדכתיב (ירמיה יז) מרום מראשון מקום מקדשנו מלון קיצו משמע דירה של מעלה בית מלונו: ה' אמר אלי עלה אל הארץ וגו' מאי היא. היכי אמר לו הקב"ה להשחית: יען כי מאס העם הזה וגו'. ומשוש את רצין ובן רמליהו ואתרעו להשחית' ברצין ובר רמליהו: מארת ה'. שלא נשבע מכל מה שהיה אוכל: ליטרא ירק. במדה: ועלה על כל אפיקיו. שאמר לו הקב"ה עלה והשחת: מ"ט. מאחר שברשות הלך שנביא נתנבא עליו מאי טעמא איענש: בא נביא ואמר לו. כשבא על ירושלים: כי לא מועף לאשר מוצק לה. לא נמסר עמו של חזקיה שהוא עיף בתורה ביד סנחריב המציק לו: כעת הראשון הקל ארצה זבולון וארצה נפתלי וגו' לא כראשונים. עשרת השבטים שהקלו מעליהם עול תורה אבל אחרונים עמו של חזקיה הכבידו עליהם עול תורה והיינו דכתיב האחרון הכביד דרך הים עבר הירדן גליל הגוים ראויין הללו לעשות להם נס כיוצאי מצרים שעברו את הים וכדורכי הירדן: אם חוזר בו סנחריב מוטב. ואם לאו אעשה אותו גליל הגוים שמגלגל בחרפה בכל הגוים ל"א גליל לשון גללים. מ"ר: אחרי הדברים והאמת האלה. השתא משמע שהיה מדבר בחזקיהו שהיו עסוקין בתורה בא סנחריב מלך אשור ויבא ביהודה ויחן על הערים ויאמר לבקעם אליו: האי רישנא להאי פרדשנא. וכי מביאין דורון כזה לאדון כזה וכי מפני שהאמת בחזקיהו בא סנחריב: רבינא אמר מאי אחר הדברים והאמת אחר שקפץ הקב"ה ונשבע. להביא סנחריב והיינו אמת שחותמו וקיומו של הקדוש ברוך הוא אמת:

ויעשה אבוס. שיהיו כלם פגרים ויאכלו סוסיהם ובהמתם בתוך עצמות הפגרים כעין אבוס: מגבת ועד אנטיפרס. מקומות שבסוף התחומים: אע"פ שאלף גפן באלף כסף. שהן יקרים שאין להם רוב כרמים אפילו הכי לשמיר ולשית יהיה שמניחין אותן לאבוד ומבייריס אותן והיו עוסקין בתורה: לשלל. כל אחד ואחד לעצמו או לחלוק ביחד אותו ממון שנשאר מחיל סנחריב ל"א לחלוק לאחרים מה שאנו שוללים אבל אנו אסורים באותו שלל שממון שבזזו מעשרת השבטים מעורב בו דאיכא משום גזל: כמשק גבים שוקק בו. השקאה של צינורות שמזלפין בהם מים נובעין השקו באותו ממון וטיהרתו דמה צינורות הללו מעלין את האדם מטומאה לטהרה ע"י טבילה אף ממונם וכו' משק שו"ן בלע"ז: בא על עית וגו'. ומתרגמינן ומני רבני משרייתיה: עברו מעברה גבע מלון לנו וגו' יושבי הגבים העיזו. ולא קא חשיב עוד היום בנוב לעמוד דההוא לאו מסע הוא אלא כדאמרינן לקמן אותו היום נשתייר מעונה של נוב: הני טובא הוי. די"ב הוא דאיכא: נביא הוא. קרא דצהלי קולך בת גלים הקשיבי לישה דחשיבנא ביה תלתא בת גלים לישה ענתות הנהו לאו מן חושבנא נינהו דנביא הוא דקאמר להו לישראל וכו': מהאי לא תסתפי. שתנצל מידו היינו דכתיב צהלי קולך אלא אסתפי מנבוכדנצר שנמשל לליש דכתיב ביה עלה אריה מסובכו והיינו דקאמר הקשיבי לישה:

ענתות

גליון הש"ס

גמ' בבית רשע זה פקח בן רמליהו. וכן גיטין דף נה ע"ב. אשרי אדם מפחד זה:

תורה אור השלם

א) וַיֹּאמֶר פַּרְעֹה מִי יְיָ אֲשֶׁר אֶשְׁמַע בְּקֹלוֹ לְשַׁלַּח אֶת יִשְׂרָאֵל לֹא יָדַעְתִּי אֶת יְיָ וְגַם אֶת יִשְׂרָאֵל לֹא אֲשַׁלֵּחַ: [שמות ה, ב]

ב) וַיֵּט מֹשֶׁה אֶת יָדוֹ עַל הַיָּם וַיָּשָׁב הַיָּם לִפְנוֹת בֹּקֶר לְאֵיתָנוֹ וּמִצְרַיִם נָסִים לִקְרָאתוֹ וַיְנַעֵר יְיָ אֶת מִצְרַיִם בְּתוֹךְ הַיָּם: [שמות יד, כז]

ג) דָּרַכְתָּ בַיָּם סוּסֶיךָ חֹמֶר מַיִם רַבִּים: [חבקוק ג, טו]

ד) בְּיַד מַלְאָכֶיךָ חֵרַפְתָּ אֲדֹנָי וַתֹּאמֶר בְּרֹב רִכְבִּי אֲנִי עָלִיתִי מְרוֹם הָרִים יַרְכְּתֵי לְבָנוֹן וְאֶכְרֹת קוֹמַת אֲרָזָיו מִבְחוֹר בְּרֹשָׁיו וְאָבוֹאָה מְלוֹן קִצֹּה יַעַר כַּרְמִלּוֹ: [מלכים ב' יט, כג]

ה) וַיְהִי בַּלַּיְלָה הַהוּא וַיֵּצֵא מַלְאַךְ יְיָ וַיַּךְ בְּמַחֲנֵה אַשּׁוּר מֵאָה שְׁמוֹנִים וַחֲמִשָּׁה אָלֶף וַיַּשְׁכִּימוּ בַבֹּקֶר וְהִנֵּה כֻלָּם פְּגָרִים מֵתִים: [מלכים ב' יט, לה]

ו) בְּיַד עֲבָדֶיךָ חֵרַפְתָּ אֲדֹנָי וַתֹּאמֶר בְּרֹב רִכְבִּי אֲנִי עָלִיתִי מְרוֹם הָרִים יַרְכְּתֵי לְבָנוֹן וְאֶכְרֹת קוֹמַת אֲרָזָיו מִבְחַר בְּרֹשָׁיו וְאָבוֹא מְרוֹם קִצּוֹ יַעַר כַּרְמִלּוֹ: [ישעיה לז, כד]

ז) עַתָּה הֲמִבַּלְעֲדֵי יְיָ עָלִיתִי עַל הַמָּקוֹם הַזֶּה לְהַשְׁחִתוֹ יְיָ אָמַר אֵלַי עֲלֵה עַל הָאָרֶץ הַזֹּאת וְהַשְׁחִיתָהּ: [מלכים ב' יח, כה]

ח) יַעַן כִּי מָאַס הָעָם הַזֶּה אֵת מֵי הַשִּׁלֹחַ הַהֹלְכִים לְאַט וּמְשׂוֹשׂ אֶת רְצִין וּבֶן רְמַלְיָהוּ: [ישעיה ח, ו]

ט) מְאֵרַת יְיָ בְּבֵית רָשָׁע וּנְוֵה צַדִּיקִים יְבָרֵךְ: [משלי ג, לג]

י) וְלָכֵן הִנֵּה אֲדֹנָי מַעֲלֶה עֲלֵיהֶם אֶת מֵי הַנָּהָר הָעֲצוּמִים וְהָרַבִּים אֶת מֶלֶךְ אַשּׁוּר וְאֶת כָּל כְּבוֹדוֹ וְעָלָה עַל כָּל אֲפִיקָיו וְהָלַךְ עַל כָּל גְּדוֹתָיו: [ישעיה ח, ז]

כ) וְחָלַף בִּיהוּדָה שָׁטַף וְעָבַר עַד צַוָּאר יַגִּיעַ וְהָיָה מֻטּוֹת כְּנָפָיו מְלֹא רֹחַב אַרְצְךָ עִמָּנוּ אֵל: [ישעיה ח, ח]

ל) כִּי לֹא מוּעָף לַאֲשֶׁר מוּצָק לָהּ כָּעֵת הָרִאשׁוֹן הֵקַל אַרְצָה זְבֻלוּן וְאַרְצָה נַפְתָּלִי וְהָאַחֲרוֹן הִכְבִּיד דֶּרֶךְ הַיָּם עֵבֶר הַיַּרְדֵּן גְּלִיל הַגּוֹיִם: [ישעיה ח, כג]

מ) אַחֲרֵי הַדְּבָרִים וְהָאֱמֶת הָאֵלֶּה בָּא סַנְחֵרִיב מֶלֶךְ אַשּׁוּר וַיָּבֹא בִיהוּדָה וַיִּחַן עַל הֶעָרִים הַבְּצֻרוֹת וַיֹּאמֶר לְבִקְעָם אֵלָיו: [דברי הימים ב' לב, א]

נ) נִשְׁבַּע יְיָ צְבָאוֹת לֵאמֹר אִם לֹא כַּאֲשֶׁר דִּמִּיתִי כֵּן הָיָתָה וְכַאֲשֶׁר יָעַצְתִּי הִיא תָקוּם: לִשְׁבֹּר אַשּׁוּר בְּאַרְצִי וְעַל הָרַי אֲבוּסֶנּוּ וְסָר מֵעֲלֵיהֶם עֻלּוֹ וְסֻבֳּלוֹ מֵעַל שִׁכְמוֹ יָסוּר: [ישעיה יד, כד-כה] ס) וְהָיָה בַּיּוֹם הַהוּא יָסוּר סֻבֳּלוֹ מֵעַל שִׁכְמֶךָ וְעֻלּוֹ מֵעַל צַוָּארֶךָ וְחֻבַּל עֹל מִפְּנֵי שָׁמֶן: [ישעיה י, כז] ע) וְהָיָה בַּיּוֹם הַהוּא יְחַיֶּה אִישׁ עֶגְלַת בָּקָר וּשְׁתֵּי צֹאן: וְהָיָה מֵרֹב עֲשׂוֹת חָלָב יֹאכַל חֶמְאָה כִּי חֶמְאָה וּדְבַשׁ יֹאכֵל כָּל הַנּוֹתָר בְּקֶרֶב הָאָרֶץ: [ישעיה ז, כא-כב] פ) וְהָיָה בַּיּוֹם הַהוּא יִהְיֶה כָל מָקוֹם אֲשֶׁר יִהְיֶה שָּׁם אֶלֶף גֶּפֶן בְּאֶלֶף כָּסֶף לַשָּׁמִיר וְלַשַּׁיִת יִהְיֶה: [ישעיה ז, כג] צ) וְאֻסַּף שְׁלַלְכֶם אֹסֶף הֶחָסִיל כְּמַשַּׁק גֵּבִים שֹׁקֵק בּוֹ: [ישעיה לג, ד] ק) בָּא עַל עַיַּת עָבַר בְּמִגְרוֹן לְמִכְמָשׂ יַפְקִיד כֵּלָיו: עָבְרוּ מַעְבָּרָה גֶּבַע מָלוֹן לָנוּ חָרְדָה הָרָמָה גִּבְעַת שָׁאוּל נָסָה: [ישעיה י, כח-כט] ר) צַהֲלִי קוֹלֵךְ בַּת גַּלִּים הַקְשִׁיבִי לַיְשָׁה עֲנִיָּה עֲנָתוֹת: נָדְדָה מַדְמֵנָה יֹשְׁבֵי הַגֵּבִים הֵעִיזוּ: [ישעיה י, ל-לא] ש) עוֹד הַיּוֹם בְּנֹב לַעֲמֹד יְנֹפֵף יָדוֹ הַר בַּת צִיּוֹן גִּבְעַת יְרוּשָׁלִָם: [ישעיה י, לב] ת) עָלָה אַרְיֵה מִסֻּבְּכוֹ וּמַשְׁחִית גּוֹיִם נָסַע יָצָא מִמְּקֹמוֹ לָשׂוּם אַרְצֵךְ לְשַׁמָּה עָרַיִךְ תִּצֶּינָה מֵאֵין יוֹשֵׁב: [ירמיה ד, ז]

מסורת הש"ס

א) [גי' הערוך ערך גל ה' גלילה], ב) גי' הערוך ערך דשן דישנא וכתב המוסיף שהוא בלשון יון מתנה, ג) [נ"ל מאי אחר], ד) ב"ק מ"ז, ה) גיטין לח. חולין ס:, ו) רש"ל מ"ז.

ליקוטי רש"י

את מי השילוח ההולכים לאט. במלכותא דבית דוד דמדבר להון בניח כמי שלוחא דנגדין בניח, שלוח מעין הוא ושמו גיחון ושילוח שרצו להסיר [נ"א, להסב] את מלכות בית דוד בימי אחז לפקח בן רמליהו וכאן ניבא על שבנא וסיעתו שרצו למרוד בחזקיהו שמאסו בו על שראוהו שלא היה בוחר בשולחן מלכים אלא אוכל ליטר' ירק ועוסק בתורה עליו נאמר צדיק אוכל לשובע נפשו (משלי יג) וראו את פקח בן רמליהו אוכל ארבעים סאה גוזלות בקינוח סעודה והיו מליזין על חזקיהו ואומרין זה הגון להיות מלך אין זה מלך אלא רצין ובן רמליהו היו ראויין למלוך בחייהן וזהו ומשוש את רצין וגו' אמר להם הקב"ה אוכלין אתם מתאוי' אני מביא עליכם אוכלין הרבה הנה ה' מעלה עליכם (וגו') את מי הנהר העצומים תחת מי השילוח האטים והנוחים [ישעיה ח, ו]. וחלף ביהודה. בארץ יהוד'. שטף. בחזקה. עד צואר. עד עיקר חוזק צוארם וה"י עד ירושלם ימטי [שם, ח]. אחרי הדברים והאמת האלה וגו' ויאמר לבקעם. כמו לבקעם כמו (עמוס ב') על מכרם בכסף כמו מוכרם וסמוך ליה (עמוס א') על בקעם הרות הגלעד ופתרונו ודוגמא (ישעיה ז') ונבקיענה ויבקע עצי העולה (בראשי' כב) [דה"ב לב, א]. וחובל עול. סנחריב מפני חזקיהו שהיה נוח לדורו כשמן, ורבותינו פירשו מפני שמנו של חזקיהו שהי' דולק בבתי כנסיות ובבתי מדרשות שהשיאם לעסוק בתורה כענין שנאמר אשר העתיקו אנשי חזקיה וגומר (משלי כה) [ישעיה י, כז]. ולא מצאו עם הארץ. כשנתמנה חזקיהו למלך והוא הושיב תלמידים בכל עיר כדאמרינן בפ' חלק בדקו מדן ועד באר שבע ולא מצאו עם הארץ [משלי כה, א]. ועל אותו הדור וכו'. בא חזקיהו ושב בכל לבבו לדרוש להקב"ה וכל דורו שלימים לא קם דור בישראל כמותם כמו שמפורש בחלק בדקו מדן וכו' [שה"ש ה, ז]. ואומר והיה ביום ההוא וכו'. כי אותו הדור של חזקיה ישובו אלי לעסוק בתורה ולא לשתות יין וכן היתה כדאיתא בחלק בדקו מדן ועד באר שבע ולא מצאו איש שלא היה בקי בהלכו' איסור והיתר וטומאה וטהרה ועל אותו הדור הוא אומר והיה כל מקום וגומר הוא שנאמר (משלי כה) אשר העתיקו אנשי חזקיה מלך יהודה [ישעיה ז, כה]. אלף גפן. שוות אלף כסף. לשמיר ולשית. כי יניחום בעליהם וכו' והם מעלות קימשונים ותולעים ועקרבים [שם, כג]. אוסף החסיל. כאסיפת חסיל שאוסף לו תבואה בקיץ כל א' לעצמו אף כולן יבוזו איש לו. כמשק גבים שוקק. כקול נהם מים הנאספים ונופלין בגבים בנהם כן יהמו הבאים לשלול ולבוז משק ל' נהם כמו (משלי כח) ארי נוהם ודוב שוקק וכן ממשק חרול (צפניה ב) כשהרוח מנשבת בחרולים והם מכים זה על זה נותנים קול וכן בעיר ישוקו (יואל ב). גבים. כמו ולחשוף מים מגבא ורבותינו דרשוהו באגדת חלק בביזת אוכלוסי סנחריב [שם לג, ד]. [המשך בדף צה.]

שֶׁלֹּא הָיוּ בְּקִיאִין בְּהִלְכוֹת טוּמְאָה וְטָהֳרָה – **who was not conversant with** even **the** complex **laws of *tumah* and *taharah*.**[38] וְעַל אוֹתוֹ הַדּוֹר הוּא אוֹמֵר – **And** it is **concerning this generation** of Chizkiah **that [Scripture] states:** "וְהָיָה בַּיּוֹם הַהוּא – ***It shall come to pass on that day*** יְחַיֶּה־אִישׁ עֶגְלַת בָּקָר וּשְׁתֵּי־צֹאן" וגו׳ – ***that [every] man will raise a heifer of the herd and two sheep* etc.**[39] וְאוֹמֵר – **And** in that same section of Scripture, **it is** further **written:**[40] "וְהָיָה בַּיּוֹם הַהוּא – ***And it shall come to pass*** יִהְיֶה כָל־מָקוֹם אֲשֶׁר יִהְיֶה־שָׁם אֶלֶף גֶּפֶן בְּאֶלֶף כָּסֶף – ***that every place where there were a thousand vines worth a thousand pieces of silver,*** לַשָּׁמִיר וְלַשַּׁיִת יִהְיֶה" – ***there will be* briers *and thorns.*** אַף עַל פִּי שֶׁאֶלֶף גֶּפֶן בְּאֶלֶף כֶּסֶף – This means that **even though** the Jews will possess land so valuable **that a thousand vines are worth a thousand pieces of silver,** לַשָּׁמִיר וְלַשַּׁיִת יִהְיֶה – **nevertheless, [the land] will be for the briers and the thorns;** i.e. the land will be neglected by its owners, for they will devote themselves exclusively to Torah study. This illustrates the success of Chizkiah's promotion of Torah study throughout the Kingdom of Judah.

The Gemara expounds another verse in Isaiah concerning Sancheiriv's downfall:

"וְאֻסַּף שְׁלַלְכֶם אֹסֶף הֶחָסִיל" – Concerning Sancheiriv, Scripture states:[41] ***Your booty shall be gathered like the gathering of the locusts;*** *like the roar of [water rushing into] pools.* אָמַר לָהֶם נָבִיא לְיִשְׂרָאֵל – The wording of the verse implies that **the prophet** Isaiah **said to Israel:** אִסְפוּ שְׁלַלְכֶם – **Gather your booty** from the Assyrian camp! אָמְרוּ לוֹ – **They replied to him:** לָבוֹז אוֹ לַחֲלוֹק – Are you telling us **to plunder** the camp, or **to divide** it? I.e. should each person keep whatever he personally takes, or should we divide the total booty evenly between us?[42] אָמַר לָהֶם "כְּאֹסֶף הֶחָסִיל" – **[Isaiah] responded to them:** *Your booty shall be gathered* ***like the gathering of the locusts;*** מָה אֹסֶף הֶחָסִיל כָּל אֶחָד וְאֶחָד לְעַצְמוֹ – **just as** when **the locusts gather, each [locust]** takes **for himself** and does not divide it with the others, אַף שְׁלַלְכֶם כָּל אֶחָד וְאֶחָד לְעַצְמוֹ – **so too** when you take **your booty,** let **each person** take **for himself.** אָמְרוּ לוֹ – Upon hearing this, **[the Jews] said to [Isaiah]:** וַהֲלֹא מָמוֹן עֲשֶׂרֶת הַשְּׁבָטִים מְעוֹרָב בּוֹ – **But is not the wealth of the Ten Tribes mixed in** with **[this booty]?** How can we in good conscience plunder it?[43] אָמַר לָהֶם כְּמַשַּׁק גֵּבִים שׁוֹקֵק בּוֹ – **[Isaiah] replied to them:** ***Like the roar of [water rushing into] pools does he roar therein;*** מָה גֵּבִים הַלָּלוּ מַעֲלִין אֶת הָאָדָם מִטּוּמְאָה לְטָהֳרָה – that is, **just as** water rushing into **these pools would transform a person from** a state of ***tumah*** **to** a state of ***taharah,***[44] אַף מָמוֹנָם שֶׁל יִשְׂרָאֵל כֵּיוָן שֶׁנָּפַל בְּיַד עוֹבְדֵי כוֹכָבִים – **so too,** when **money belonging to Jews** is seized by force and **falls into the hands of idolaters,** מִיָּד טִיהֵר – **it immediately becomes cleansed** of any prohibition; i.e. it is no longer viewed as the money of the original owner, and as such, if another Jew later captures it in battle, it is considered a legitimate spoil of war.

The Gemara comments:

(כִּדְרַב פָּפָּא – **This follows the view of Rav Pappa.** דְּאָמַר רַב פָּפָּא – **For Rav Pappa said:** עַמּוֹן וּמוֹאָב טָהֲרוּ בְּסִיחוֹן – The property of **Ammon and Moab was "cleansed" by Sichon.**)[45]

The Gemara examines some other verses in *Isaiah* concerning Sancheiriv's invasion of Judah:

אָמַר רַב הוּנָא – **Rav Huna said:** עֶשֶׂר מַסָּעוֹת נָסַע אוֹתוֹ רָשָׁע בְּאוֹתוֹ הַיּוֹם – **That wicked [Sancheiriv] made ten marches on that day,**[46] i.e. on the day he invaded Judah and traveled toward Jerusalem. שֶׁנֶּאֱמַר – **For Scripture states:**[47] "בָּא עַל־עַיַּת

NOTES

38. The Gemara here speaks of two levels of Torah education. The first idea is that throughout the land, there were no generally ignorant people to be found; the second idea is that there was a widespread knowledge of even the complexities of Torah (e.g. the laws of *tumah* and *taharah*).

[In general, women are exempt from the obligation to study Torah. Nevertheless, *Margaliyos HaYam* (citing *Sefer Chasidim* 313), points to our Gemara as evidence that women must indeed be knowledgeable in all areas of Torah that pertain to them (see also *VaYoel Moshe* pp. 444-447). Indeed, in the days of Chizkiah, observance of the *tumah* and *taharah* laws were a practical daily part of life for both men and women.]

39. *Isaiah* 7:21. This verse is cited to illustrate the life of idyllic simplicity that the generation of Chizkiah merited to experience. The context of the verse is as follows:

During the reign of Achaz, Judah was invaded by the kings of Ephraim and Aram. God then sent Isaiah to assure the wicked Achaz that the invaders would not prevail, and that soon they themselves would be invaded and destroyed by Assyria. Nevertheless, Isaiah warned, Assyria would eventually invade Judah itself and cause much destruction. Isaiah concluded by saying that during the reign of Achaz's son Chizkiah, even the Assyrians would depart, and in that era, the survivors would live modestly but well: Each farmer would raise a single heifer and a pair of sheep, and these would suffice to provide for his family's needs (*Radak*).

In the context of our Gemara, *Gra* sees the verse as describing how the Jews eschewed luxuries, sacrificing material wealth for the pursuit of Torah.

40. Ibid. v. 23. See previous note. The Gemara here interprets the passage to mean that the people will prefer to raise a few animals rather than devote the quantities of time needed to tend to vineyards. In doing so, they will forgo lucrative profits in favor of Torah study.

41. *Isaiah* 33:4. In this prophecy, Isaiah foretells that after Sancheiriv's army is destroyed, the Jews will sack his camp like a plague of locusts. Isaiah further prophesies that the exultant shouts of the Jews will resemble the roar of a waterfall crashing into a pool (*Rashi* ad loc.; see also *Rashi* here).

42. This follows the first interpretation given by *Rashi*. See *Rashi* for an alternative explanation as well.

43. Before the Assyrians invaded Judah, they had conquered the Ten Tribes of the Northern Kingdom, and presumably looted their wealth. As a result, part of the booty the Judeans found in the Assyrian camp was most likely wealth that had been seized from their fellow Jews. Thus, the Jews were hesitant to take the money, for they regarded this as stealing.

[*Aruch LaNer* questions why this objection was raised only now, after Isaiah had said that each man could keep whatever he himself seized. Seemingly, the Jews should have raised this problem earlier, when Isaiah first encouraged them to sack the Assyrian camp. For a possible resolution to this difficulty, see *Aruch LaNer.*]

44. If someone in a state of *tumah* [ritual impurity] immerses himself in a pool fed by a natural spring, that person thereby becomes *tahor* [ritually pure] (see *Mikvaos* 1:8).

45. The Torah recounts that God told the Jews in the Wilderness not to touch the property of the nations of Ammon and Moab (*Deuteronomy* 2:9, 19). Nevertheless, when the Jews subsequently conquered the kingdom of Sichon, they took all its property, despite the fact that Sichon itself had previously conquered part of Ammon and Moab (*Numbers* 21:26). This indicates that once Sichon conquered these nations, the booty it captured ceased to belong to Ammon and Moab, but rather became part of Sichon's property. Thus, the Jews were later permitted to seize it.

Yad Ramah stresses that this general ruling applies only where property is lost in *warfare.* When, for example, an individual Jew loses property or is robbed, we cannot simply assume that the owner gave up hope of ever recovering it – and therefore, the property must indeed be returned to him if a Jew gains control over it (see *Margaliyos HaYam* in detail; see also *Bava Kamma* 114a and *Choshen Mishpat* 259:7).

46. I.e. the journey that should have taken him ten days in fact took him only one day (*Maharsha*; see *Margaliyos HaYam*).

47. *Isaiah* 10:28-32. In these verses, the prophet describes the lightning-like advance of the Assyrian army upon Jerusalem. Each town mentioned was one closer to Sancheiriv's final destination of Jerusalem.

Rashi explains that the last part of the passage – enclosed in our text in parentheses – was not understood by our Gemara as a reference to actual locations. Rather, this part of the passage was understood metaphorically, as will be seen below.

גליון הש"ם

גמ' בבית רשע זה פקח בן רמליהו. וכן גיטין דף נה ע"ב. אשרי אדם מפחד זה:

תורה אור השלם

א) וַיֹּאמֶר פַּרְעֹה מִי יְיָ אֲשֶׁר אֶשְׁמַע בְּקֹלוֹ לְשַׁלַּח אֶת יִשְׂרָאֵל לֹא יָדַעְתִּי אֶת יְיָ וְגַם אֶת יִשְׂרָאֵל לֹא אֲשַׁלֵּחַ: [שמות ה, ב]

ב) וַיֵּט מֹשֶׁה אֶת יָדוֹ עַל הַיָּם וַיָּשָׁב הַיָּם לִפְנוֹת בֹּקֶר לְאֵיתָנוֹ וּמִצְרַיִם נָסִים לִקְרָאתוֹ וַיְנַעֵר יְיָ אֶת מִצְרַיִם בְּתוֹךְ הַיָּם: [שמות יד, כז]

ג) דָּרַכְתָּ בַיָּם סוּסֶיךָ חֹמֶר מַיִם רַבִּים: [חבקוק ג, טו]

ד) בְּיַד מַלְאָכֶיךָ חֵרַפְתָּ אֲדֹנָי וַתֹּאמֶר בְּרֹב רִכְבִּי אֲנִי עָלִיתִי מְרוֹם הָרִים יַרְכְּתֵי לְבָנוֹן וְאֶכְרֹת קוֹמַת אֲרָזָיו מִבְחוֹר בְּרֹשָׁיו וְאָבוֹאָה מְלוֹן קִצֹּה יַעַר כַּרְמִלּוֹ: [מלכים ב' יט, כג]

ה) וַיְהִי בַּלַּיְלָה הַהוּא וַיֵּצֵא מַלְאַךְ יְיָ וַיַּךְ בְּמַחֲנֵה אַשּׁוּר מֵאָה שְׁמוֹנִים וַחֲמִשָּׁה אָלֶף וַיַּשְׁכִּימוּ בַבֹּקֶר וְהִנֵּה כֻלָּם פְּגָרִים מֵתִים: [מלכים ב' יט, לה]

ו) בְּיַד עֲבָדֶיךָ חֵרַפְתָּ אֲדֹנָי וַתֹּאמֶר בְּרֹב רִכְבִּי אֲנִי עָלִיתִי מְרוֹם הָרִים יַרְכְּתֵי לְבָנוֹן וְאֶכְרֹת קוֹמַת אֲרָזָיו מִבְחַר בְּרֹשָׁיו וְאָבוֹא מְרוֹם קִצּוֹ יַעַר כַּרְמִלּוֹ: [ישעיה לז, כד]

ז) עַתָּה הֲמִבַּלְעֲדֵי יְיָ עָלִיתִי עַל הַמָּקוֹם הַזֶּה לְהַשְׁחִתוֹ יְיָ אָמַר אֵלַי עֲלֵה עַל הָאָרֶץ הַזֹּאת וְהַשְׁחִיתָהּ: [מלכים ב' יח, כה]

ח) יַעַן כִּי מָאַס הָעָם הַזֶּה אֵת מֵי הַשִּׁלֹחַ הַהֹלְכִים לְאַט וּמְשׂוֹשׂ אֶת רְצִין וּבֶן רְמַלְיָהוּ: [ישעיה ח, ו]

ט) מְאֵרַת יְיָ בְּבֵית רָשָׁע וּנְוֵה צַדִּיקִים יְבָרֵךְ: [משלי ג, לג]

י) וְלָכֵן הִנֵּה אֲדֹנָי מַעֲלֶה עֲלֵיהֶם אֶת מֵי הַנָּהָר הָעֲצוּמִים וְהָרַבִּים אֶת מֶלֶךְ אַשּׁוּר וְאֶת כָּל כְּבוֹדוֹ וְעָלָה עַל כָּל אֲפִיקָיו וְהָלַךְ עַל כָּל גְּדוֹתָיו: [ישעיה ח, ז]

כ) וְחָלַף בִּיהוּדָה שָׁטַף וְעָבַר עַד צַוָּאר יַגִּיעַ וְהָיָה מֻטּוֹת כְּנָפָיו מְלֹא רֹחַב אַרְצְךָ עִמָּנוּ אֵל: [ישעיה ח, ח]

ל) כִּי לֹא מוּעָף לַאֲשֶׁר מוּצָק לָהּ כָּעֵת הָרִאשׁוֹן הֵקַל אַרְצָה זְבֻלוּן וְאַרְצָה נַפְתָּלִי וְהָאַחֲרוֹן הִכְבִּיד דֶּרֶךְ הַיָּם עֵבֶר הַיַּרְדֵּן גְּלִיל הַגּוֹיִם: [ישעיה ח, כג]

מ) אַחֲרֵי הַדְּבָרִים וְהָאֱמֶת הָאֵלֶּה בָּא סַנְחֵרִיב מֶלֶךְ אַשּׁוּר וַיָּבֹא בִיהוּדָה וַיִּחַן עַל הֶעָרִים הַבְּצֻרוֹת וַיֹּאמֶר לְבִקְעָם אֵלָיו: [דברי הימים ב' לב, א]

עַל יְדֵי שָׁלִיחַ. דהיינו בזוי יותר אף הקב"ה נפרע ע"י שליח ונתבייש יותר: כתיב מרום קצו. בישעיה: וכתיב מלון קיצו. במלכים. מרום קילו משמע דירה של מטה כדכתיב (ירמיה יז) מרום מראשון מקום מקדשנו מלון קילו משמע דירה של מעלה בית מלונו: ה' אמר אלי עלה אל הארץ וגו' מאי היא. היכי אמר לו הקב"ה להשחית: יען כי מאס העם הזה וגו'. ומשוש את רלין ובן רמליהו ואתרעו להשחית' ברלין ובר רמליהו: מארת ה'. שלא נשבע מכל מה שהיה אוכל: ליטרא ירק. במדה: ועלה על כל אפיקיו. שאמר לו הקב"ה עלה והשחת: מ"ט. מאחר שברשות הלך שנביא נתנבא עליו מאי טעמא איענש: בא נביא ואמר לו. כשבא על ירושלים: כי לא מועף לאשר מוצק לה. לא נמסר עמו של חזקיה שהוא עיף בתורה ביד סנחריב המליק לו: כעת הראשון הקל ארצה זבולון וארצה נפתלי וגו' לא כראשונים. עשרת השבטים שהקלו מעליהם עול תורה אבל אחרונים עמו של חזקיה הכבידו עליהם עול תורה והיינו דכתיב האחרון הכביד דרך הים עבר הירדן גליל הגוים ראויין הללו לעשות להם נס כיולאי מלרים שעברו את הים וכדורכי הירדן: אם חוזר בו סנחריב מוטב. ואם לאו אעשה אותו גליל הגוים שמגלגל בחרפה בכל הגוים ל"א גליל לשון גללים. מ"ר: אחרי הדברים והאמת האלה. השתא משמע שהיה מדבר בחזקיהו שהיו עסוקין בתורה בא סנחריב מלך אשור ויבא ביהודה ויחן על הערים ויאמר לבקעם אליו: האי רישנא להאי פרדשנא. וכי מביאין דורון כזה לאדון כזה וכי מפני שהאמת בחזקיהו בא סנחריב: רבינא אמר מאי אחר הדברים והאמת אחר שקפץ הקב"ה ונשבע. להביא סנחריב והיינו אמת שחותמו וקיומו של הקדוש ברוך הוא אמת:

ויעשה אבוס. שיהיו כלם פגרים ויאכלו סוסיהם ובהמתם בתוך עלמות הפגרים כעין אבוס: מגבת ועד אנטיפרס. מקומות שבסוף התחומים: אע"פ שאלף גפן באלף כסף. שהן יקרים שאין להם רוב כרמים אפילו הכי לשמיר ולשית יהיה שמניחין אותן לאבוד ומבויירים אותן והיו עוסקין בתורה: לשלל. כל אחד ואחד לעצמו או לחלוק ביחד אותו ממון שנשאר מחיל סנחריב ל"א לחלוק לאחרים מה שאנו שוללים אבל אנו אסורים באותו שלל שממון שבזזו מעשרת השבטים מעורב בו דאיכא משום גזל: כמשק גבים שוקק בו. השקאה של לינורות שמזלפין בהם מים נובעין השקו באותו ממון וטיהרתו דמה לינורות הללו מעלין את האדם מטומאה לטהרה ע"י טבילה אף ממונם וכו' משק שו"ן בלע"ז: בא על עית וגו'. ומתרגמינן ומני רבני משרייתיה: עברו מעברה גבע מלון לנו וגו' יושבי הגבים העיזו. ולא קא חשיב עוד היום בנוב לעמוד דההוא לאו מסע הוא אלא כדאמרינן לקמן אותו היום נשתייר מעונה של נוב: הני טובא הוי. די"ב הוא דאיכא: נביא הוא. קרא דצהלי קולך בת גלים הקשיבי לישה דחשיבנא ביה תלתא בת גלים לישה ענתות הנהו לאו מן חושבנא נינהו דנביא הוא דקאמר להו לישראל וכו': מהאי לא תסתפי. שתנצל מידו היינו דכתיב צהלי קולך אלא אסתפי מנבוכדנצר שנמשל לליש דכתיב ביה עלה אריה מסובכו והיינו דקאמר הקשיבי לישה:

עניה

ע"י שליח נפרע הקב"ה ממנו ע"י שליח פרעה דכתיב ביה א) מי ה' אשר אשמע בקולו נפרע הקב"ה ממנו בעצמו דכתיב ב) וינער ה' את מצרים בתוך הים וכתיב ג) דרכת בים סוסיך וגו' סנחריב דכתיב ד) ביד מלאכיך חרפת ה' נפרע הקב"ה ממנו ע"י שליח דכתיב ה) ויצא מלאך ה' ויך במחנה אשור מאה ושמונים וחמשה אלף וגו' ר' חנינא בר פפא רמי כתיב ו) מרום קיצו וכתיב ד) מלון קיצו אמר אותו רשע בתחלה אחריב דירה של מטה ואחר כך אחריב דירה של מעלה א"ר יהושע בן לוי מאי דכתיב ז) עתה המבלעדי ה' עליתי על המקום הזה להשחיתו ה' אמר אלי עלה אל הארץ הזאת והשחיתה מאי היא דשמע לנביא דקאמר ח) יען כי מאס העם הזה את מי השילוח ההולכים לאט ומשוש את רצין ובן רמליהו אמר רב יוסף אלמלא תרגומא דהאי קרא לא הוה ידענא מאי קאמר חלף דקץ עמא הדין במלכותא דבית דוד דמדבר להון בנייח כמי שילוחא דנגדין בנייח ואיתרעיאו ברצין ובר רמליה א"ר יוחנן מאי דכתיב ט) מארת ה' בבית רשע ונוה צדיקים יבורך מארת ה' בבית רשע זה פקח בן רמליהו שהיה אוכל מ' סאה גוזלות בקינוח סעודה ונוה צדיקים יבורך זה חזקיה מלך יהודה שהיה אוכל ליטרא ירק בסעודה י) ולכן הנה ה' מעלה עליהם את מי הנהר העצומים והרבים את מלך אשור וכתיב כ) וחלף ביהודה שטף ועבר עד צואר יגיע אלא מ"ט איענש נביא אעשרת השבטים איתנבי איהו יהיב דעתיה על כולה ירושלים בא נביא וא"ל ל) כי לא מועף לאשר מוצק לה א"ר אלעזר בר ברכיה אין נמסר עם עייף בתורה ביד מי המציק לו מאי ל) כעת הראשון הקל ארצה זבולון וארצה נפתלי והאחרון הכביד דרך הים עבר הירדן גליל הגוים לא כראשונים שהקלו מעליהם עול תורה אבל אחרונים שהכבידו עליהן עול תורה וראויין הללו לעשות להם נס כעוברי הים וכדורכי הירדן אם חוזר בו מוטב ואם לאו אני אעשה לו א) גליל בגוים מ) אחרי הדברים והאמת האלה בא סנחריב מלך אשור ויבא ביהודה ויחן על הערים הבצורות ויאמר לבקעם אליו האי ב) רישנא להאי פרדשנא אחרי הדברים והאמת ג) (אחר מאי) אמר רבינא לאחר שקפיץ הקב"ה ונשבע ואמר אי אמינא ליה לחזקיה מייתינא ליה לסנחריב ומסרנא ליה בידך השתא אמר לא הוא בעינא ולא ביעתותיה בעינא מיד קפץ הקב"ה ונשבע דמייתינא ליה שנאמר נ) נשבע ה' צבאות לאמר אם לא כאשר דמיתי כן היתה וכאשר יעצתי היא תקום לשבור אשור בארצי ועל הרי אבוסנו וסר מעליהם עולו וסבלו מעל שכמו יסור א"ר יוחנן אמר הקב"ה יבא סנחריב וסיעתו ויעשה אבוס לחזקיהו ולסיעתו ס) והיה ביום ההוא יסור סבלו מעל שכמך ועולו מעל צוארך וחובל עול מפני שמן א"ר יצחק נפחא חובל עול של סנחריב מפני שמנו של חזקיהו שהיה דולק בבתי כנסיות ובבתי מדרשות מה עשה נעץ חרב על פתח בית המדרש ואמר כל מי שאינו עוסק בתורה ידקר בחרב זו בדקו מדן ועד באר שבע ולא מצאו עם הארץ מגבת ועד אנטיפרס ולא מצאו תינוק ותינוקת איש ואשה שלא היו בקיאין בהלכות טומאה וטהרה ועל אותו הדור הוא אומר ע) והיה ביום ההוא יחיה איש עגלת בקר ושתי צאן וגו' ואומר פ) והיה ביום ההוא יהיה כל מקום אשר יהיה שם אלף גפן באלף כסף לשמיר ולשית יהיה אע"פ שאלף גפן באלף כסף לשמיר ולשית יהיה צ) ואוסף שללכם אוסף החסיל אמר להם נביא לישראל אספו שללכם אמרו לו לבזוז או לחלוק אמר להם כאוסף החסיל מה אוסף החסיל כל אחד ואחד לעצמו אף שללכם כל אחד ואחד לעצמו אמרו לו והלא ממון עשרת השבטים מעורב בו אמר להם צ) כמשק גבים שוקק בו מה גבים הללו מעלין את האדם מטומאה לטהרה אף ממונם של ישראל כיון שנפל ביד עובדי כוכבים מיד טיהר (ד) כדרב פפא דאמר רב פפא ה) עמון ומואב טהרו בסיחון) אמר רב הונא עשר מסעות נסע אותו רשע באותו היום שנאמר ק) בא על עית עבר במגרון למכמש יפקיד כליו עברו מעברה גבע מלון לנו חרדה הרמה גבעת שאול נסה ר) צהלי קולך בת גלים הקשיבה לישה עניה ענתות נדדה מדמנה יושבי הגבים העיזו (ו ש) עוד היום בנוב לעמוד ינופף ידו הר בת ציון גבעת ירושלם) הני טובא הויין צהלי קולך בת גלים נביא הוא דקאמר לה לכנסת ישראל צהלי קולך בת גלים בתו של אברהם יצחק ויעקב שעשו מצות כגלי הים הקשיבה לישה מהאי לא תסתפי אלא איסתפי מנבוכדנצר הרשע דמתיל כאריה שנא' ת) עלה אריה מסובכו וגו' מאי

עניה

מסורת הש"ס

א) [גי' הערוך ערך גל ה' גלילה], ב) גי' הערוך ערך דשן דישנא וכתב המוסיף שהוא בלשון יון מתנה, ג) [נ"ל מאי אחר], ד) ב"ש מ"ז, ה) גיטין לח. חולין ס.:, ו) רש"ל מ"ז.

ליקוטי רש"י

את מי השילוח ההולכים לאט. במלכותא דבית דוד דמדבר להון בניח כמי שלוחא דנגדין בניח, שלוח מעין הוא ושמו גיחון ושילוח שרלו להסיר [נ"א, להסב] את מלכות בית דוד בימי אחז לפקח בן רמליהו וכאן ניבא על שבנא וסיעתו שרלו למרוד בחזקיהו שמאסו בו על שראוהו שלא היה בוחר בשולחן מלכים אלא אוכל ליטר' ירק ועוסק בתורה עליו נאמר לדיק אוכל לשובע נפשו (משלי יג) וראו את פקח בן רמליהו אוכל ארבעים סאה גוזלות בקינוח סעודה והיו מליזין על חזקיהו ואומרין זה הגון להיות מלך אין זה מלך אלא רלין ובן רמליהו היו ראויין למלוך בחייהן וזהו ומשוש את רלין וגו' אמר להם הקב"ה אוכלין אתם מתאוי' אני מביא עליכם אוכלין הרבה הנה ה' מעלה עליכם (וגו') את מי הנהר העצומים תחת מי השילוח האטים והנוחים [ישעיה ח, ו]. וחלף ביהודה. בארץ יהוד'. שטף. בחזקה. עד צואר. עד עיקר חוזק לוארם ות"י עד ירושלם ימטי [שם, ח]. אחרי הדברים והאמת האלה וגו' ויאמר לבקעם. כמו לבקעם כמו (עמוס ב') על מכרם בכסף כמו מוכרם וסמוך ליה (עמוס א') על בקעם הרות הגלעד ופתרונו ודוגמא (ישעיה ז') ונבקיענה ויבקע עלי העולה (בראשי' כב) [דה"ב לב, א]. וחובל עול. סנחריב מפני חזקיהו שהיה נוח לדורו כשמן, ורבותינו פירשו מפני שמנו של חזקיהו שהי' דולק בבתי כנסיות ובבתי מדרשות שהשיאם לעסוק בתורה כענין שנאמר אשר העתיקו אנשי חזקיה וגומר (משלי כה) [ישעיה י, כז]. ולא מצאו עם הארץ. כשנתמנה חזקיהו למלך והוא הושיב תלמידים בכל עיר כדאמרינן בפ' חלק בדקו מדן ועד באר שבע ולא מלאו עם הארץ [משלי כה, א]. ועל אותו הדור וכו'. בא חזקיהו ושב בכל לבבו לדרוש להקב"ה וכל דורו שלימים לא קם דור בישראל כמותם כמו שמפורש בחלק בדקו מדן וכו' [שה"ש ה, ז]. ואומר והיה ביום ההוא וכו'. כי אותו הדור של חזקיה ישובו אלי לעסוק בתורה ולא לשתות יין וכן היתה כדאיתא בחלק בדקו מדן ועד באר שבע ולא מלאו איש שלא היה בקי בהלכו' איסור והיתר וטומאה וטהרה ועל אותו הדור הוא אומר והיה כל מקום וגומר הוא שנאמר (משלי כה) אשר העתיקו אנשי חזקיה מלך יהודה [ישעיה ז, כה]. אלף גפן. שוות אלף כסף. לשמיר ולשית. כי יניחום בעליהם וכו' והם מעלות קימשונים ותולעים ועקרבים [שם, כג]. אוסף החסיל. כאסיפת חסיל שאוסף לו תבואה בקיץ כל א' לעצמו אף כולן יבוזו איש לו. כמשק גבים שוקק. כקול נהם מים הנאספים ונופלין בגבים בנהם כן יהמו הבאים לשלול ולבוז משק ל' נהם כמו (משלי כח) ארי נוהם ודוב שוקק וכן ממשק חרול (צפניה ב) כשהרוח מנשבת בחרולים והם מכים זה על זה נותנים קול וכן בעיר ישוקו (יואל ב). גבים. כמו ולחשוף מים מגבא ורבותינו דרשוהו באגדת חלק בביזת אוכלוסי סנחריב [שם לג, ד]. [המשך בדף צה.].

נ) נִשְׁבַּע יְיָ צְבָאוֹת לֵאמֹר אִם לֹא כַּאֲשֶׁר דִּמִּיתִי כֵּן הָיָתָה וְכַאֲשֶׁר יָעַצְתִּי הִיא תָקוּם: לִשְׁבֹּר אַשּׁוּר בְּאַרְצִי וְעַל הָרַי אֲבוּסֶנּוּ וְסָר מֵעֲלֵיהֶם עֻלּוֹ וְסֻבֳּלוֹ מֵעַל שִׁכְמוֹ יָסוּר: [ישעיה יד, כד-כה] ס) וְהָיָה בַּיּוֹם הַהוּא יָסוּר סֻבֳּלוֹ מֵעַל שִׁכְמֶךָ וְעֻלּוֹ מֵעַל צַוָּארֶךָ וְחֻבַּל עֹל מִפְּנֵי שָׁמֶן: [ישעיה י, כז] ע) וְהָיָה בַּיּוֹם הַהוּא יְחַיֶּה אִישׁ עֶגְלַת בָּקָר וּשְׁתֵּי צֹאן: וְהָיָה מֵרֹב עֲשׂוֹת חָלָב יֹאכַל חֶמְאָה כִּי חֶמְאָה וּדְבַשׁ יֹאכֵל כָּל הַנּוֹתָר בְּקֶרֶב הָאָרֶץ: [ישעיה ז, כא-כב] פ) וְהָיָה בַּיּוֹם הַהוּא יִהְיֶה כָל מָקוֹם אֲשֶׁר יִהְיֶה שָּׁם אֶלֶף גֶּפֶן בְּאֶלֶף כָּסֶף לַשָּׁמִיר וְלַשַּׁיִת יִהְיֶה: [ישעיה ז, כג] צ) וְאֻסַּף שְׁלַלְכֶם אֹסֶף הֶחָסִיל כְּמַשַּׁק גֵּבִים שֹׁקֵק בּוֹ: [ישעיה לג, ד] ק) בָּא עַל עַיַּת עָבַר בְּמִגְרוֹן לְמִכְמָשׂ יַפְקִיד כֵּלָיו: עָבְרוּ מַעְבָּרָה גֶּבַע מָלוֹן לָנוּ חָרְדָה הָרָמָה גִּבְעַת שָׁאוּל נָסָה: [ישעיה י, כח-כט] ר) צַהֲלִי קוֹלֵךְ בַּת גַּלִּים הַקְשִׁיבִי לַיְשָׁה עֲנִיָּה עֲנָתוֹת: נָדְדָה מַדְמֵנָה יֹשְׁבֵי הַגֵּבִים הֵעִיזוּ: [ישעיה י, ל-לא] ש) עוֹד הַיּוֹם בְּנֹב לַעֲמֹד יְנֹפֵף יָדוֹ הַר בַּת צִיּוֹן גִּבְעַת יְרוּשָׁלָיִם: [ישעיה י, לב] ת) עָלָה אַרְיֵה מִסֻּבְּכוֹ וּמַשְׁחִית גּוֹיִם נָסַע יָצָא מִמְּקֹמוֹ לָשׂוּם אַרְצֵךְ לְשַׁמָּה עָרַיִךְ תִּצֶּינָה מֵאֵין יוֹשֵׁב: [ירמיה ד, ז]

[Sancheiriv] has come to Ayas! עָבַר בְּמִגְרוֹן – *He has passed through Migron!* לְמִכְמָשׂ יַפְקִיד כֵּלָיו – *He is placing his tools in Michmash!* עָבְרוּ מַעְבָּרָה – *They have crossed Mabarah!* גֶּבַע מָלוֹן לָנוּ – *They have lodged at Geva!* חָרְדָה הָרָמָה – *Ramah has quaked!* גִּבְעַת שָׁאוּל נָסָה – *Givat Shaul has fled!* צַהֲלִי קוֹלֵךְ בַּת־גַּלִּים הַקְשִׁיבִ(ה)[י] לַיְשָׁה – *Cry out, Bas Galim! Hearken, O Laish!* עֲנִיָּה עֲנָתוֹת – *O you poor Anasos!* נָדְדָה מַדְמֵנָה – *Madmenah has wandered away!* יֹשְׁבֵי הַגֵּבִים הֵעִיזוּ – *The inhabitants of Gevim have gathered together!* (עוֹד הַיּוֹם בְּנֹב לַעֲמֹד – *This very day he intends to stand in Nov,* יְנֹפֵף יָדוֹ הַר בַּת־צִיּוֹן גִּבְעַת יְרוּשָׁלַם" – *waving his hand at the Mount of the Daughter of Zion, the Hill of Jerusalem!)*

The Gemara questions:

הָנֵי טוּבָא הָוְיָין – **This is more** than ten marches; indeed, there are twelve places mentioned in the passage! – ? –

The Gemara replies that not every place mentioned represents a place attacked by Sancheiriv:

"צַהֲלִי קוֹלֵךְ בַּת־גַּלִּים" נָבִיא הוּא דְּקָאָמַר לָהּ לִכְנֶסֶת יִשְׂרָאֵל – In fact, the words, ***Cry out, Bas Galim*** **were said by the prophet [Isaiah]** on his own **to the Congregation of Israel.** That is, Isaiah did not mean these words to represent a particular place Sancheiriv was destined to conquer; "צַהֲלִי קוֹלֵךְ בַּת גַּלִּים" – rather, when he said, ***Cry out, Bas Galim*** [literally, "daughter of the waves"], he meant: בִּתּוֹ שֶׁל אַבְרָהָם יִצְחָק וְיַעֲקֹב – **"Cry out,** O Congregation of Israel, **the daughter of Abraham, Isaac and Jacob,** שֶׁעָשׂוּ מִצְוֹת כְּגַלֵּי הַיָּם – **who performed mitzvos** as mighty **as the waves of the sea!"** Thus, the phrase "Bas Galim" is not a location, but a metaphorical reference to the Jewish people as a whole.

The Gemara continues:

"הַקְשִׁיבִ(ה)[י] לַיְשָׁה" – Likewise, when Isaiah said, ***Hearken, O Laish,*** he was not referring to a place that would be conquered; מֵהַאי לֹא תִּסְתְּפִי – rather, he was saying to the Jews: **Do not be afraid of this one** [i.e. Sancheiriv], for his threat will pass; אֶלָּא אִיסְתְּפִי מִנְּבוּכַדְנֶצַּר הָרָשָׁע דִּמְתִיל כְּאַרְיֵה – **instead, you should be afraid of** a future king who will rise against you – **Nebuchadnezzar, who is compared** in Scripture **to a lion** [*laish*].[48] שֶׁנֶּאֱמַר "עָלָה אַרְיֵה מִסֻּבְּכוֹ" וגו׳ – Indeed, **the verse states** in reference to Nebuchadnezzar:[49] ***A lion has risen from his thicket* etc.**

We thus see that the words *Bas Galim* and *Laish* do not refer to actual locations.[50] The Gemara continues, suggesting that even the next phrase in the verse – *O you poor Anasos* – was not meant as a reference to a place Sancheiriv would conquer:

מַאי

NOTES

48. Accordingly, הַקְשִׁיבִי לַיְשָׁה means: *Listen for the lion.* That is, be wary of Nebuchadnezzar, for unlike Sancheiriv, his threat is real; he is destined to destroy Jerusalem (*Rashi*).

49. *Jeremiah* 4:7.

50. Since *Bas Galim* and *Laish* do not refer to locations, it emerges that there were just ten, not twelve, places that Sancheiriv passed through on his campaign to Jerusalem.

[In the lines that follow, the Gemara will proceed to interpret allegorically even the next part of the verse: *O you poor Anasos.* As such, we will be left with only *nine* places that Sancheiriv marched through. The Gemara later will reconcile this with the earlier statement that there were actually ten such places.]

"עֲנִיָּה עֲנָתוֹת" – **What** did Isaiah mean when he said: ***O you poor Anasos?*** עָתִיד יִרְמְיָה בֶּן חִלְקִיָּה וּמִתְנַבֵּא עֲלָהּ מֵעֲנָתוֹת – He meant that the prophet **Jeremiah the son of Chilkiah is destined to prophesy from** the town of **Anasos concerning [the downfall of Judah and Jerusalem].**[1] דִּכְתִיב "דִּבְרֵי יִרְמְיָהוּ בֶּן־חִלְקִיָּהוּ – **For** indeed, **it is written: *The words of Jeremiah the son of Chilkiah,*** "מִן־הַכֹּהֲנִים אֲשֶׁר בַּעֲנָתוֹת בְּאֶרֶץ בִּנְיָמִן" – ***of the Kohanim who were in Anasos, in the land of Benjamin.***[2] Thus, three of the places mentioned by Isaiah were not meant as places at all, but rather as allegorical representations of future events.[3]

On the previous *amud,* the Gemara expounded Isaiah's mention of *laish* as an allusion to Nebuchadnezzar, the same invader foretold by Jeremiah. The Gemara now objects to this:

מִי דָּמֵי – **Are they** indeed **the same?** הָתָם אֲרִי הָכָא לַיִשׁ – **There,** in Jeremiah's prophecy, the invader is referred to as an ***ari,* whereas here,** in Isaiah's prophecy, he is referred to as a ***laish!***[4] – ? –

R' Yochanan explains that *ari* and *laish* are synonyms:

אָמַר רַבִּי יוֹחָנָן – **R' Yochanan said:** שִׁשָּׁה שֵׁמוֹת יֵשׁ לָאֲרִי – In Scripture, **there are six names** used **to** denote **a lion,** אֵלּוּ הֵן – **and these are they:** אֲרִי כְּפִיר לָבִיא לַיִשׁ שַׁחַל שַׁחַץ – ***Ari, kfir, lavi, laish, shachal,*** and ***shachatz.***[5] Thus, since both prophecies referred to the invader as a lion, they can be understood as referring to the same person – Nebuchadnezzar.

Previously, the Gemara stated that Isaiah had mentioned ten places Sancheiriv passed through en route to Jerusalem. The Gemara now asks:

אִי הָכִי בָּצְרוּ לְהוּ – But **if** it is **so** that we have explained this verse correctly, **there are** in fact **fewer** than ten places![6]

The Gemara answers:

"עָבְרוּ מַעְבָּרָה" תַּרְתֵּי נִינְהוּ – ***Avru Mabarah* is** counted as **two** localities.[7]

Having concluded an exposition of *Isaiah,* verses 10:28-32, the Gemara now expounds the last verse that appears in that passage: "עוֹד הַיּוֹם בְּנֹב לַעֲמֹד" מַאי – **What** is the implication of the verse which states: ***This very day [Sancheiriv] intends to stand in Nov?*** אָמַר רַב הוּנָא – **Rav Huna said:** אוֹתוֹ הַיּוֹם נִשְׁתַּיֵּיר מֵעֲוֹנָהּ שֶׁל נוֹב – It implies: **That day, remained** for the possibility of punishment **for the sin of Nov.**[8] That day thus represented a unique opportunity for Sancheiriv to attack and defeat Jerusalem.

The Gemara explains this in greater detail, reconstructing the events leading up to Sancheiriv's siege:

אָמְרֵי לֵיהּ כַּלְדָּאֵי – When Sancheiriv was still camped far away from Jerusalem, **his astrologers said to him:** אִי אָזְלַתְּ הָאִידָּנָא – **If you go** and attack Jerusalem **today,** יָכְלַתְּ לָהּ – **you will overcome it;** וְאִי לָא – **but if you do not** attack before the day is over, לָא יָכְלַתְּ לָהּ – **you will not overcome it.**[9]

Upon hearing this, Sancheiriv determined to reach Jerusalem that very day. The Gemara relates:

אוֹרְחָא דְּבָעָא לְסַגּוּיֵי בַּעֲשָׂרָה יוֹמֵי – So rapid was his march that **a route which** ordinarily **takes ten days to traverse,** סַגָּא בְּחַד יוֹמָא – **he traversed in a single day.**[10] כִּי מְטוֹ לִירוּשָׁלֵם – **When [the Assyrian army] arrived at** the gates of **Jerusalem,** שַׁדֵּי לֵיהּ בִּיסְתַּרְקֵי – **[Sancheiriv] piled** layers of **rugs** on top of one another, עַד דְּסָלֵיק וְיָתֵיב מֵעִילָּוֵי שׁוּרָה – **until he** created a huge mound, which **he ascended and** was able to **sit higher than the wall** of the city,[11] עַד דְּחַזְיוּהָ לְכוּלָּהּ יְרוּשָׁלֵם – **until he was** able to **see all of Jerusalem.** כִּי חַזְיֵיהּ – **As he gazed upon [the city],** אִיזּוּטַר בְּעֵינֵיהּ – **it appeared small to him.** אָמַר הֲלָא דָא

NOTES

1. *Isaiah* 10:30. The word עֲנִיָּה is here translated as *prophecy.* Thus, the full phrase הַקְשִׁיבִי לַיְשָׁה עֲנִיָּה עֲנָתוֹת means: *Listen for the approach of the lion (Nebuchadnezzar) whose coming is prophesied by Jeremiah, the man from Anasos* (*Rashi*).

2. *Jeremiah* 1:1. This passage explicitly identifies Jeremiah as a native of Anasos. Later in this chapter (vs. 14-15) Jeremiah proceeds to prophesy that Nebuchadnezzar will invade Judah and conquer Jerusalem.

3. See above, 94b note 49.

4. [The Gemara presumes that if Isaiah and Jeremiah each used different terms to describe the invader, they presumably were referring to two different individuals.]

5. The first two terms appear in *Judges* 14:5. The others appear in *Genesis* 49:9, *Psalms* 91:13 and *Job* 28:8 respectively.

6. See above, 94b note 49. The passage in *Isaiah* (10:28-32) listed what appeared to be twelve localities. The Gemara (94b), however, had proceeded to explain that three of these names – *Bas Galim, Laish, and Anasos* – did not represent places at all, but rather were prophetic allusions to future events. This means that there remain only nine actual localities mentioned in the verse, a fact inconsistent with Rav Huna's assertion that Sancheiriv passed through *ten* places on his invasion route.

7. Previously, the phrase עָבְרוּ מַעְבָּרָה was understood to mean: *They have crossed Mabaarah!* The Gemara now asserts, though, that the word עָבְרוּ was not meant as a a verb [*they have crossed*], but was itself the name of a locality. Thus, there are in fact ten places mentioned in the passage (*Rashi;* cf. *Yad Ramah*).

8. I.e. the very day Sancheiriv began his campaign against Jerusalem was the last day the Jewish people were held spiritually culpable for a massacre that took place at Nov centuries earlier. Thus, this particular day was the last day God would allow Judea to be vulnerable to attack. If Sancheiriv succeeded in marshaling his forces against Jerusalem *that day,* the city would indeed fall; but if he delayed, the Jews were destined to survive his siege.

The Massacre at Nov. The story of the massacre at Nov is related in *I Samuel* chs. 21-22. Briefly, it is as follows:

When David was fleeing from the attacks of King Saul, he chanced upon the town of Nov, which housed a settlement of Kohanim. He told Achimelech, the head Kohen, that he was an emissary of King Saul on a royal mission, and Achimelech, believing him, gave him provisions and arms to assist him in his journey. One of Saul's servants, Doeg, witnessed this and subsequently told Saul that the Kohanim had acted traitorously – that they had aided David, although they knew him to be Saul's enemy. Upon hearing this, Saul ordered Doeg to kill all the Kohanim living in Nov, and Doeg did so.

Although the principals responsible for the massacre – Saul and Doeg (and even, to an extent, David) – received various Heavenly punishments for their roles in this tragedy (see 104a note 8), this was not deemed sufficient to fully atone for the crime. Rather, the Heavenly Court also held the entire nation of Israel collectively responsible. This unexpiated guilt of Israel was the spiritual factor that Sancheiriv could have marshaled to his advantage in his campaign against Jerusalem (see *Maharsha* and *Rif* in *Ein Yaakov*).

Maharal explains that the massacre at Nov demonstrated a terrible flaw in the Jewish people: Saul could not have killed the Kohanim of the Mishkan at Nov if the nation had held the sanctuary in proper reverence. That is why, "measure for measure," the Temple in Jerusalem was now endangered.

9. I.e. the astrologers perceived that the Jews were vulnerable to attack only on that day. The reason is that this was the last day the people remained culpable for the sin of Nov (see *Aruch LaNer* for an explanation of why this particular day – which happened to be the day before Passover – was chosen as the last day the sin of Nov held sway; see also *Ben Yehoyada*).

10. These were the ten marches described above; each location represented the end of what should have been a single day's march (*Rashi*).

11. [Sancheiriv wanted to see what the city looked like, but the walls surrounding the city had blocked his view. Thus, he created an artificial mound that was higher than the city's walls to use as a vantage point.]

א) עניה ענתות עתיד ירמיה בן חלקיה ומתנבא עלה מענתות דכתיב ב) דברי ירמיהו בן חלקיהו מן הכהנים אשר בענתות בארץ בנימין מי דמי התם ארי הכא ליש אמר רבי יוחנן ששה שמות יש לארי אלו הן ג) ארי ד) כפיר ג) לביא ה) ליש ו) שחל ז) שחץ אי הכי בצרו להו עברו מעברה תרתי נינהו מאי ח) עוד היום בנוב לעמוד אמר רב הונא אותו היום נשתייר מעונה של נוב אמרי ליה כלדאי אי אזלת האידנא יכלת לה ואי לא לא יכלת לה אורחא דבעא לסגויי בעשרה יומא סגא בחד יומא כי מטו לירושלם שדי ליה ביסתרקי עד דסליק ויתיב מעילוי שורה עד דחזיוה לכולה ירושלם כי חזייה איזוטר בעיניה אמר הלא דא היא קרתא דירושלם דעלה ארגישית כל משיריתי ועלה כבשית כל מדינתא הלא היא זעירא וחלשא מכל כרכי עממיא דכבשית בתקוף ידי עלה וקם ומניד ברישיה מוביל ומייתי בידיה על טור בית מקדשא דבציון ועל עזרתא דבירושלם אמרי נישדי ביה ידא האידנא אמר להו תמהיתו [א] למחר אייתי לי כל חד וחד מינייכו [ג] גולמו הרג מיניה מיד ט) ויהי בלילה ההוא ויצא מלאך ה' ויך במחנה אשור מאה ושמונים וחמשה אלף וישכימו בבקר והנה כלם פגרים מתים אמר רב פפא היינו דאמרי אינשי בת דינא בטל דינא י) וישבי בנוב אשר בילידי הרפה ומשקל קינו שלש מאות משקל נחשת והוא חגור חדשה ויאמר להכות את דוד מאי וישבי בנוב אמר רב יהודה אמר רב איש שבא על עסקי נוב א"ל הקב"ה לדוד עד מתי יהיה עון זה טמון בידך על ידך נהרגה נוב עיר הכהנים ועל ידך נטרד דואג האדומי ועל ידך נהרגו שאול ושלשת בניו רצונך יכלו זרעך או תמסר ביד אויב אמר לפניו רבונו של עולם מוטב אמסר ביד אויב ולא יכלה זרעי יומא חד נפק [ג] לשכור בזאי אתא שטן ואדמי ליה כטביא פתק ביה גירא ולא מטייה משכיה עד דאמטייה לארץ פלשתים כדחזייה ישבי בנוב אמר היינו האי דקטליה לגלית אחי כפתיה קמטיה אותביה ושדייה תותי בי [ד] בדייא אתעביד ליה ניסא מכא ליה ארעא מתותיה היינו דכתיב כ) תרחיב צעדי תחתי ולא מעדו קרסולי ההוא יומא אפניא דמעלי שבתא הוה אבישי בן צרויה קא חייף רישיה בד' גרבי דמיא חזינהו כתמי דמא איכא דאמרי אתא יונה איטריף קמיה [ה] אמר [ו] כנסת ישראל ליונה אימתילא שנאמר ל) כנפי יונה נחפה בכסף שמע מינה דוד מלכא דישראל בצערא שרי אתא לביתיה ולא אשכחיה אמר [ז] תנן אין רוכבין על סוסו ואין יושבין על כסאו ואין משתמשין בשרביטו בשעת הסכנה מאי אתא שאיל בי מדרשא אמרו ליה בשעת הסכנה שפיר דמי רכביה לפרדיה וקם ואזל קפצה ליה ארעא בהדי דקא מסגי חזייה לערפה אמיה דהוות נוולא כי חזיתיה פסקתה לפילכה שדתיה עילויה סברא למקטליה אמרה ליה עלם אייתי לי פלך פתקיה בריש מוחה וקטלה כד חזייה ישבי בנוב אמר השתא הוו בי תרין וקטלין לי פתקיה לדוד לעילא ודץ ליה לרומחיה אמר ניפול עלה ונקטל אמר אבישי שם אוקמיה לדוד בין שמיא לארעא [ח] ונימא ליה איהו אין חבוש מוציא עצמו מבית האסורין א"ל מאי בעית הכא א"ל הכי אמר לי קודשא בריך הוא והכי אהדרי ליה א"ל אפיך צלותיך בר ברך קירא ליזבון ואת לא תצטער א"ל אי הכי סייע בהדן היינו דכתיב מ) ויעזור לו אבישי בן צרויה אמר רב יהודה אמר רב שעזרו בתפלה אמר אבישי שם ואחתיה הוה קא רדיף בתרייהו כי מטא קובי אמרי קום ביה כי מטא בי תרי אמרי בתרי גוריין קטלוה לאריא אמרי ליה זיל אשתכח לערפה אימיך בקיברא כי אדכרו ליה שמא דאימיה כחש חיליה וקטליה היינו דכתיב מ) אז נשבעו אנשי דוד לו לאמר לא תצא עוד אתנו למלחמה ולא תכבה את נר ישראל ת"ר שלשה קפצה להם הארץ אליעזר עבד אברהם ויעקב אבינו ואבישי בן צרויה הא דאמרן אליעזר עבד אברהם דכתיב נ) ואבוא היום אל העין למימרא דההוא יומא נפק יעקב אבינו דכתיב

רש"י

עניה ענתות. כמו עניה כלומר נביאות ירמיה הענתותי היא שעתידה לבא על נבוכד נצר שתמסר ירושלים בידו: ארי כפיר וכו'. ובדוכתא אחריתי מפורש למה נקראו לו כל השמות הללו: אי הכי. דכולי קרא נהלי קולך לא מחושבנא הוא א"כ ליכא אלא תשע מסעות דהא עוד היום לאו מחושבנא [נמי הוא] ומתרך עברו מעברה תרתי אינון עברו חד מעברה חד ואיכא עשר מסעות: אותו היום נשתייר מעונה של נוב. [דמפני עון] שהיה להם לישראל על שנהרגו כהני נוב קבע הקב"ה העונש עד אותו היום ואותו יום בלבד נשתייר מזמן העונש ואילו היה נלחם בירושלים באותו היום היה כובשה והכי משמע קרא עוד היום אותו יום העמידו לסנחריב על ירושלים בעון נוב: סגא בחד יומא. והיינו י' מסעות שנסע אותו היום: שדו ליה. לסנחריב: בסתרקי. תחתיו טפי"ט בלע"ז עד שראה ירושלים כולה: עלה וקם ומניד ברישיה. עליה עמד והיה מניד בראשו: נשדי ביה ידא האידנא. נלחם בה עתה: תמהיתו. תמה הוא להתחיל היום משום חולשא דאורחא ל"א תמהיתו נתיגעתם ודומה ליה [ח] (בסנחריב) איתמה למיתב: גולמו הרג. חתיכה של חומה לשון פרסי אבן רעועה מן החומה ונבקעה: בת דינא בטל דינא. כיון שלן דינא בטל הריב וכן מפני שלא נכבשה בו ביום לא הצליח ממחרת: וישבי בנוב. איידי דאיירי לעיל באותו יום שנשתייר מעונה של נוב נקט הכא וישבי בנוב שבא על עסקי נוב: הרפה. היינו ערפה: משקל קינו. מתרגמינן מתקל סופיניה: והוא חגור חדשה. והוא אסיר איספניקי חדתא: נטרד דואג האדומי. שספר לשון הרע על דוד שנתקנא בו שאול ולפי שקבל אחימלך את דוד בנוב אמר ליה שאול סוב ופגע בכהני ה' נמצא שעל ידך נהרגו ואתה נכשל ובחטא זה נהרג שאול ושלשת בניו במלחמת פלשתים: שכר ביזאי. לשון פרסי קריטא ל"א כפר היא: קמטיה. הכניעו תחת הבד של זיתים ויתיב עלה למעכו: מכא ליה ארעא מתותיה. נתרככה הארץ מתחתיו ולא הזיקו ל"א מכא נשפלת כעין גומא והיתה מגינה עליו: בארבע גריבי דמיא. בארבע סאין של מים ל"א בארבע כורא דמיא בד' [ט] נודות של מים: איטריף קמיה. היתה טורפת ומחבטת עצמה וממרטת כנפיה והומה ומצערת: קפצה ליה ארעא. כמו לא תקפוץ (דברים טו) נתקצרה הארץ והגיע מהרה לארץ פלשתים: לערפה אימיה. דישבי: נוולא. טווה: כד חזיתיה. ערפה לאבישי סברה למקטליה באותו פלך שהיה בידה ולא נגע בו: אמרה ליה. לאבישי אייתי לן ההוא פלך דנפל לפניך: ה"ג פתקיה בריש מוחה וקטלה. השליך אבישי הפלך לראשה ומתה: פתקיה לדוד לעילא. זרקו כלפי מעלה: ודץ ליה. נעץ תחתיו חניתו בקרקע כדי שיפול עליו וימות: ונימא איהו. דוד עצמו לימא שם: אין חבוש. אין דעתו מכוונת לומר השם והשתא ניצל דוד והשליכו השם ברחוק והלכו אבישי ודוד וחזרו להם: אמר ליה. אבישי לדוד: ומאי בעית הכא. למה באת כאן: אמר ליה. הקב"ה אמר לי רצונך שיכלה זרעך או תמסר ביד אויביך והכי אהדרי ליה מוטב שאפול ביד אויב: אמר ליה אפיך צלותיך. הפוך תפלתך ואמור לפניו מוטב יכלה זרעך ולא תמסר ביד אויב דמה לך בצער בניך: בר ברך קירא לזבון ואת לא תצטער. משל הוא שאומרים בני אדם: סייע בהדן. עזור בתפלתך להפכה: והוה קא רדיף בתרייהו. והם בורחין שהיה קרוב לארץ פלשתים: וכי מטו קובי. לאותו כפר ששמו קובי שבין א"י לארץ פלשתים: אמרי קום ביה. אמרו זה לזה עמוד כנגדו ואל תברח ונכנו ולכך נקרא קובי אינהו הוו בקיאי בשמות הכפרים ועדיין היו מפחדין ובורחין: כי מטא בי תרי. שם מקום: אמרו בין תרי גוריין. בתמיהא: בקברא. שהרגנוה: וילא

ליקוטי רש"י

דאמר רב פפא. במסכת גיטין (לח.). עמון ומואב טהרו בסיחון. ע"י סיחון טהרו ארצם לישראל במואב כתיב (במדבר כא) והוא נלחם וגו' ובעמון מפורש בנחלת בני גד בספר יהושע (יג) ויהי להם הגבול יעזר וכל ארץ הגלעד וחצי (ארץ) [ערי] בני עמון וקא חשיב ואזיל וכתיב בסיפיה יתר ממלכות סיחון אלמא סיחון כבש לארץ בני עמון ועוד מצינו במלך בני עמון שאמר למלאכי יפתח (שופטים יא) כי לקח ישראל את ארצי מארנון ועד היבוק אלמא ארץ בני עמון הוא והם מסיחון כבשוה דכתיב בו וירשו את ארצו מארנון ועד היבוק אבל מהנשאר בידם לא לקחו כלום [חולין ס:]. דכתיב (דברים ב) אל תצר את מואב וכן בבני עמון אל תגורם (שם) וכתיב (במדבר כא) כי חשבון עיר סיחון וגו' אלמא טהר מואב בסיחון ובני עמון אשכחן ביפתח (שופטים יא) שאמרו לו מלאכי בני עמון כי לקח ישראל את ארצי בעלותו ממצרים מארנון ועד היבוק ואשכחן כשכבשו את ארץ סיחון ויירש את ארצו מארנון עד יבוק וגו' אלמא מבני עמון כבשה והדור ישראל וכבשו מיניה וטהרה להם על ידו אלמא קנייה בחזקה [גיטין לח.]. בא על עית. מונה והולך מסעות שנסע סנחריב ובא על ערי יהודה לבא ירושלים ביום מפלתו [ישעיה י, כח]. לנו. לשון לינה. נסה. ברחה ברחו כולן מפני חיילותיו [שם, כט]. צהלי קולך. להזיר לעם. הקשיבי לישה. את קול השופר וברחו לכם וכן עניה ענתות [שם, ל]. העיזו. נאספו לברוח [שם, לא] עוד היום בנוב לעמוד. כל הדרך הזה נתלבט כדי לעמוד בעוד היום בנוב לפי שאמרו לו איצטגניניו אם תלא' בה היום תכבשנ' וכשעמד בנוב וראה את ירושלים קטנה לא חש לדברי איצטגניניו והתחיל להניף ידו בגאו' וכי על עיר כזו הרגזתי כל החיילות הללו לינו פה הלילה ולמחר ישליך בה איש אבנו. הר בת ציון. להר בת ציון [שם, לב]. עלה אריה. נבוכדנצר. מסובכו. דרך אריה לישב במארב סבכי היער אשפיישי"ש בלע"ז [ירמיה ד, ז].

[ע"כ שייך לדף צד:].

כפיר. כל כפיר שבמקרא ארי בחור וגבור [יחזקאל יט, ה]. הארי גדול והשחל בינוני והכפיר קטן [איוב ד, י]. עוד היום בנוב לעמוד. כל הדרך הזה נתלבט כדי לעמוד בעוד היום בנוב לפי שאמרו לו איצטגניניו אם תלא' בה היום תכבשנ' וכשעמד בנוב וראה את ירושלים קטנה לא חש לדברי איצטגניניו והתחיל להניף ידו בגאו' וכי על עיר כזו הרגזתי כל החיילות הללו לינו פה הלילה ולמחר ישליך בה איש אבנו [ישעיה י, לב]. ויהי בלילה ההוא. כשבא סנחריב מעל כוש ובא עד נוב שהיתה סמוכה לירושלים. מאה ושמונים וחמשה אלף. כולם ראשי גייסות [מ"ב יט, לה]. בילידי הרפה. כתיב ערפה שם האחת ערפה (רות א) וכתיב הרפה אשר בילידי הרפה והיא ערפה כדאמרי' לקמן שנגזר עליה שיפלו בניה ביד בני רות שנדבקה בשכינה [סוטה מב:]. ומשקל קינו. הוא כמו תיק שבראש בית יד הרומח שקורין ארשטויי"ל בלע"ז ועשוי ככובע, ויש דוגמתו בזבחים (פח:) רמוני המעיל למה הם דומין כמין קולסות שבראשי התינוקות קולסות בלע"ז טז]. קונאות. בוטונ"ש עשוין כמין תיק של נחשת שעושין [בסוף] בית יד הרומח שקורין ארשטייל לשון (ש"ב כא) ומשקל קינו דישבי בנוב והתינוקות תולין אותו בראשי כובעי נלרים שעושין אותו למלחמתן שקורים הילמ"ש [זבחים פח:]. והוא חגור. חגורה חדשה ושמעתי שאותו היום נתחגר לגבוש כלי מלחמה ודרך המתחגרים לעשות נלחון וגבורה ביום חינוכם לכך ויאמר להכות את דוד [ש"ב שם]. על עסקי נוב. שבא עליו על עונש על שאול כמו שפירשו רבותינו כי עון הקב"ה על ידך נטרד דואג האדומי על ידך נהרג שאול ובניו וכו'. פתק ביה. זרק בו. חייף רישיה. פניא. לפנות ערב. ליונה אימתילא. ישראל נמשלה ליונה. ואת יונתי כנפיה מגינות עליה כך ישראל המצות מגינות עליהם [שבת מט.]. כנפי יונה. ומחמדה של תורה ומצות [תהלים סח, יד]. סייע בהדן. והפוך דוד את תפלתו והתפלל שלא יפול ביד אויב. ויעזור לו. עזרו בתפלה [ש"ב כא, יז]. ואבוא היום. היום יצאתי והיום באתי מכאן שקפצה לו הארץ [בראשית כד, מב].

מסורת הש"ס

א) נ"א דאתיתו מאורחא, ב) [בילקוט ישעיה סי' י' איתא קצת בנוסחא אחרת ועי' עוד בערוך ערך גלמסרג], ג) [עי' בערוך ערך שכר בזאי פי' יפה באריכות], ד) נ"א סדייא, ה) [ברכות נג: שבת מט. קל. גיטין מה.], ו) לעיל כב., ז) ברכות ה., ח) רש"ל מ"ז, ט) בורות. רש"ל.

גליון הש"ס

גמ' אמר כנ"י ליונה אימתלי. עיין נ"י סוף פרק ד' מיתות:

תורה אור השלם

א) צַהֲלִי קוֹלֵךְ בַּת גַּלִּים הַקְשִׁיבִי לַיְשָׁה עֲנִיָּה עֲנָתוֹת: [ישעיה י, ל]

ב) דִּבְרֵי יִרְמְיָהוּ בֶּן חִלְקִיָּהוּ מִן הַכֹּהֲנִים אֲשֶׁר בַּעֲנָתוֹת בְּאֶרֶץ בִּנְיָמִן: [ירמיה א, א]

ג) גּוּר אַרְיֵה יְהוּדָה מִטֶּרֶף בְּנִי עָלִיתָ כָּרַע רָבַץ כְּאַרְיֵה וּכְלָבִיא מִי יְקִימֶנּוּ: [בראשית מט, ט]

ד) וַיֵּרֶד שִׁמְשׁוֹן וְאָבִיו וְאִמּוֹ תִּמְנָתָה וַיָּבֹאוּ עַד כַּרְמֵי תִמְנָתָה וְהִנֵּה כְּפִיר אֲרָיוֹת שֹׁאֵג לִקְרָאתוֹ: [שופטים יד, ה]

ה) מַשָּׂא בַּהֲמוֹת נֶגֶב בְּאֶרֶץ צָרָה וְצוּקָה לָבִיא וָלַיִשׁ מֵהֶם אֶפְעֶה וְשָׂרָף מְעוֹפֵף יִשְׂאוּ עַל כֶּתֶף עֲיָרִים חֵילֵהֶם וְעַל דַּבֶּשֶׁת גְּמַלִּים אוֹצְרֹתָם עַל עַם לֹא יוֹעִילוּ: [ישעיה ל, ו]

ו) עַל שַׁחַל וָפֶתֶן תִּדְרֹךְ תִּרְמֹס כְּפִיר וְתַנִּין: [תהלים צא, יג]

ז) לֹא הִדְרִיכֻהוּ בְנֵי שָׁחַץ לֹא עָדָה עָלָיו שָׁחַל: [איוב כח, ח]

ח) עוֹד הַיּוֹם בְּנֹב לַעֲמֹד יְנֹפֵף יָדוֹ הַר בַּת צִיּוֹן גִּבְעַת יְרוּשָׁלָיִם: [ישעיה י, לב]

ט) וַיְהִי בַּלַּיְלָה הַהוּא וַיֵּצֵא מַלְאַךְ יְיָ וַיַּךְ בְּמַחֲנֵה אַשּׁוּר מֵאָה שְׁמוֹנִים וַחֲמִשָּׁה אָלֶף וַיַּשְׁכִּימוּ בַבֹּקֶר וְהִנֵּה כֻלָּם פְּגָרִים מֵתִים: [מלכים ב' יט, לה]

י) וְיִשְׁבִּי בְּנֹב אֲשֶׁר בִּילִידֵי הָרָפָה וּמִשְׁקַל קֵינוֹ שְׁלֹשׁ מֵאוֹת מִשְׁקַל נְחֹשֶׁת וְהוּא חָגוּר חֲדָשָׁה וַיֹּאמֶר לְהַכּוֹת אֶת דָּוִד: [שמואל ב' כא, טז]

כ) תַּרְחִיב צַעֲדִי תַחְתָּי וְלֹא מָעֲדוּ קַרְסֻלָּי: [תהלים יח, לז]

ל) אִם תִּשְׁכְּבוּן בֵּין שְׁפַתָּיִם כַּנְפֵי יוֹנָה נֶחְפָּה בַכֶּסֶף וְאֶבְרוֹתֶיהָ בִּירַקְרַק חָרוּץ: [תהלים סח, יד]

מ) וַיַּעֲזָר לוֹ אֲבִישַׁי בֶּן צְרוּיָה וַיַּךְ אֶת הַפְּלִשְׁתִּי וַיְמִיתֵהוּ אָז נִשְׁבְּעוּ אַנְשֵׁי דָוִד לוֹ לֵאמֹר לֹא תֵצֵא עוֹד אִתָּנוּ לַמִּלְחָמָה וְלֹא תְכַבֶּה אֶת נֵר יִשְׂרָאֵל: [שמואל ב' כא, יז]

נ) וָאָבֹא הַיּוֹם אֶל הָעָיִן וָאֹמַר יְיָ אֱלֹהֵי אֲדֹנִי אַבְרָהָם אִם יֶשְׁךָ נָּא מַצְלִיחַ דַּרְכִּי אֲשֶׁר אָנֹכִי הֹלֵךְ עָלֶיהָ: [בראשית כד, מב]

היא קַרְתָּא דירושלם – He exclaimed, "Is this truly the city of Jerusalem, דַעֲלָהּ אַרְגֵּישִׁית כָּל מַשִּׁירְיָתִי – on whose account I mobilized all my forces, וְעֲלָהּ כְּבָשִׁית כָּל מְדִינָתָא – and for which I conquered all these countries?[12] **הֲלֹא הִיא זְעִירָא מִכָּל כְּרַכֵּי עַמְמַיָּא וַחֲלָשָׁא – Why, it is smaller and weaker דִּכְבָשִׁית בִּתְקוֹף יְדִי – than all the other foreign cities I have conquered with my might!" עֲלָה וְקָם וּמָנִיד בְּרֵישֵׁיהּ – He then arose** from where he was sitting, **and** contemptuously **shook his head; מוֹבִיל וּמַיְיתִי בִּידֵיהּ עַל טוּר בֵּית מִקְדְּשָׁא דִּבְצִיּוֹן – and he waved his hand at the Temple Mount in Zion, וְעַל עֲזָרְתָּא דִּבִירוּשְׁלֵם – and at the Courtyard of the Temple in Jerusalem.**

The Gemara continues:

נִישְׁדֵי בֵּיהּ יָדָא **אָמְרֵי** – Thereupon, **[his soldiers] said** to him: **הָאִידָּנָא** – "Come! **Let us attack** the city **right now!"** אָמַר לְהוּ **– [Sancheiriv] replied to them: תְּמַהִיתוּ – "You are too fatigued**[13] from the day's travels to attack immediately; first, rest this evening, **לְמָחַר אַיְיתִי לִי כָּל חַד וְחַד מִינַיְיכוּ גּוּלְמוֹ הֲרַג מִינֵּיהּ** – and **tomorrow, let each of you bring me a piece of [this city's] walls,** and we shall destroy it."[14]

The Assyrian troops then went to sleep, as their commander had instructed. The Gemara now concludes the story with a citation from the relevant portion of Scripture:

מִיַּד ,,וַיְהִי בַּלַּיְלָה הַהוּא – Thereupon, ***It came to pass on that night*** **וַיֵּצֵא מַלְאַךְ ה׳ –** ***that an angel of God went forth*** **וַיַּךְ בְּמַחֲנֵה אַשּׁוּר מֵאָה שְׁמוֹנִים וַחֲמִשָּׁה אָלֶף –** ***and smote in the Assyrian camp one hundred and eighty-five thousand [men],*** **וַיַּשְׁכִּימוּ בַבֹּקֶר –** ***and when [the survivors] arose in the morning,*** **וְהִנֵּה כֻלָּם פְּגָרִים מֵתִים" –** ***[they looked and] behold, [their fellow soldiers] were all dead corpses.***[15] Sancheiriv's campaign against Jerusalem thus ended in utter defeat, for he delayed his attack until after the culpability for the sin of Nov had expired.

The Gemara presents an adage that reflects this last turn of events:

אָמַר רַב פָּפָּא – Rav Pappa said: הַיְינוּ דְּאָמְרֵי אִינְשֵׁי – This accords with the popular saying: בַּת דִּינָא בָּטַל דִּינָא – Justice delayed is justice canceled;[16] i.e. if action on a case is delayed, the verdict will never, in the end, be carried out. So it was with Sancheiriv and his army: Had they attacked that very day, they would have conquered Jerusalem, for the sin of Nov still weighed upon the Jews. But since they delayed their attack, their opportunity was lost and the Jews were spared.

Having mentioned the massacre of Nov and its consequences, the Gemara relates how King David was punished for his role in precipitating the slaughter:

,,וְיִשְׁבִּי בְּנֹב אֲשֶׁר בִּילִידֵי הָרָפָה – Scripture states: ***And Yishbi of Nov, who was one of the children of Haraphah*** [Orpah], **וּמִשְׁקַל קֵינוֹ שְׁלֹשׁ מֵאוֹת מִשְׁקַל נְחֹשֶׁת –** ***the weight of whose spear-head was three hundred shekels of brass,*** **וְהוּא חָגוּר חֲדָשָׁה –** ***and who was girded with new [armor],*** **וַיֹּאמֶר לְהַכּוֹת אֶת־דָּוִד" –** ***declared [his intent] to kill David.*** *But Avishai the son of Tzeruiah came to his aid. He struck the Philistine and killed him.*[17] **מַאי ,,וְיִשְׁבִּי בְּנֹב" –** Now, **what is** the meaning of the words ***Yishbi B'Nov?*** **אָמַר רַב יְהוּדָה אָמַר רַב – Rav Yehudah said in the name of Rav: אִישׁ שֶׁבָּא עַל עִסְקֵי נוֹב –** It means that David's attacker was **"a man who came** (*ish sheba*) **on account of** the massacre at **Nov."**[18]

The Gemara elaborates with a lengthy narrative detailing the events surrounding Yishbi's attack on King David:

אָמַר לֵיהּ הַקָּדוֹשׁ בָּרוּךְ הוּא לְדָוִד – The Holy One, Blessed is He, said to David: עַד מָתַי יִהְיֶה עָוֹן זֶה טָמוּן בְּיָדְךָ – "How long will this sin remain hidden in your hand?[19] **עַל יָדְךָ נֶהֶרְגָה נוֹב עִיר הַכֹּהֲנִים – It was through you that Nov the city of Kohanim was massacred,**[20] **וְעַל יָדְךָ נִטְרַד דּוֹאֵג הָאֲדוֹמִי – and it was through you that Doeg the Edomite was driven** from the World to Come,[21] **וְעַל יָדְךָ נֶהֶרְגוּ שָׁאוּל וּשְׁלֹשֶׁת בָּנָיו – and it was through you that Saul and his three sons were killed.**[22] **רְצוֹנְךָ – What,** then, **is your choice** of punishments for these things? **יִכְלוּ זַרְעֲךָ אוֹ תִּמָּסֵר בְּיַד אוֹיֵב** – Do you choose to have **your**

NOTES

12. [Presumably, the reference is to the places that lay between Sancheiriv's native Assyria and Jerusalem, which Sancheiriv had to conquer to reach Jerusalem.]

13. Our translation follows *Rashi's* second interpretation of this verb. *Rashi* also presents an alternative interpretation, under which תְּמַהִיתוּ means, "you amaze me"; i.e. I am amazed by your zeal to attack Jerusalem right away, even though you are so fatigued from the day's marches.

14. Sancheiriv contemptuously indicated to his soldiers that their forces were so numerous, and Jerusalem was so small, that they did not need to hurry or to take it by storm. Rather, each soldier could merely pull out a small rock from the city walls, and since there were more soldiers than pieces of mortar, the walls would in effect disappear from before them. The city would then fall into their hands without a fight.

[This explanation follows *Rashi,* who interprets גּוּלְמוֹ הֲרַג מִינֵּיהּ as the Persian phrase for "a piece of a wall" (cf. *Aruch*).]

15. *II Kings* 19:35.

16. Literally: If justice sleeps, justice is canceled. That is, if the adjudication of a pending case is delayed, the two opposing parties will likely resolve their differences in the interim — or new evidence for the defense may turn up — and the case will ultimately be withdrawn or resolved. Similarly, since God's "case" against the Jewish people was not prosecuted by Sancheiriv immediately, his "case" was in effect withdrawn, for the sentence against the Jews expired.

[*Ben Yehoyada* comments that Sancheiriv's fatal delay was itself the origin of this popular adage. Had he pressed his attack against the Jews while the sin of Nov still weighed over them, they would have been vulnerable, and the "sentence" would have been carried out. However, since he allowed action on the case to be delayed (בַּת דִּינָא), the "sentence" was in the end annulled (בָּטַל דִּינָא). From his example, people drew the conclusion that one who delays prosecution of a case lessens his chances of winning it.]

17. *II Samuel* 21:16-17. In the incident described here, King David's life was threatened by a Philistine hero, Yishbi. David, however, was rescued by his servant Avishai, who slew Yishbi.

The plain meaning of the words יִשְׁבִּי בְּנֹב is that Yishbi came from Nov. The Gemara, however, asserts homiletically that Yishbi was not from Nov; rather, he was sent by God to punish David for having played a part in the massacre at Nov (*Maharsha*).

[The Gemara elsewhere identifies הָרָפָה, the mother of Yishbi B'Nov, with Orpah, the sister-in-law of Ruth and an ancestress of Goliath (see *Sotah* 42b). As we shall see later, our Gemara deems Yishbi B'Nov a brother of Goliath.]

18. I.e. The two words of his name, Yishbi B'Nov, are contractions of "*ish sheba al Nov*" (see previous note).

19. I.e. how long will you remain unpunished for your part in causing the massacre at Nov? (See above, note 8).

David obviously did not intend to cause the Kohanim of Nov any harm, but nevertheless, God held him indirectly responsible for their deaths. *Tzemach Tzedek,* quoted by *Margaliyos HaYam* suggests a reason for this: Had David told the Kohanim the truth — that Saul had great enmity towards him, and that he was in fact fleeing from Saul — the Kohanim presumably would not have helped him, and they themselves would never have been harmed (see *Margaliyos HaYam* and *Sanhedrei Ketanah*).

20. See previous note.

21. [Doeg lost his share in the World to Come by telling Saul about the Kohanim's assistance to David. David, by seeking this assistance from the Kohanim, was partially responsible for the events that followed (see *Rashi;* see *Margaliyos HaYam*).]

22. The final chapter in *I Samuel* relates that Saul and his three sons were killed in battle by the Philistines. This was Saul's punishment for having killed the Kohanim at Nov, and to the extent that David was partially responsible for that tragedy, he also bore a share of blame for Saul's death (see *Rashi*).

א) עניה ענתות עתיד ירמיה בן חלקיה ומתנבא עלה מענתות דכתיב ב) דברי ירמיהו בן חלקיהו מן הכהנים אשר בענתות בארץ בנימין מי דמי התם ארי הכא ליש אמר רבי יוחנן ששה שמות יש לארי אלו הן ג) ארי ד) כפיר ג) לביא ה) ליש ו) שחל ז) שחץ אי הכי בצרו להו עברו מעברה תרתי נינהו מאי ח) עוד היום בנוב לעמוד אמר רב הונא אותו היום נשתייר מעונה של נוב אמרי ליה כלדאי אי אזלת האידנא יכלת לה ואי לא לא יכלת לה אורחא דבעא לסגויי בעשרה יומא סגא בחד יומא כי מטו לירושלם שדי ליה ביסתרקי עד דסליק ויתיב מעילוי שורה עד דחזיוה לכולה ירושלם כי חזייה איזוטר בעיניה אמר הלא דא היא קרתא דירושלם דעלה ארגישית כל משיריתי ועלה כבשית כל מדינתא הלא היא זעירא וחלשא מכל כרכי עממיא דכבשית בתקוף ידי עלה וקם ומניד ברישיה מוביל ומייתי בידיה על טור בית מקדשא דבציון ועל עזרתא דבירושלם אמרי נישדי ביה ידא האידנא אמר להו תמהיתו א) למחר אייתי לי כל חד וחד מינייכו ג) גולמו הרג מיניה מיד ט) ויהי בלילה ההוא ויצא מלאך ה' ויך במחנה אשור מאה ושמונים וחמשה אלף וישכימו בבקר והנה כלם פגרים מתים אמר רב פפא היינו דאמרי אינשי בת דינא בטל דינא י) וישבי בנוב אשר בילידי הרפה ומשקל קינו שלש מאות משקל נחשת והוא חגור חדשה ויאמר להכות את דוד מאי וישבי בנוב אמר רב יהודה אמר רב איש שבא על עסקי נוב א"ל הקב"ה לדוד עד מתי יהיה עון זה טמון בידך על ידך נהרגה נוב עיר הכהנים ועל ידך נטרד דואג האדומי ועל ידך נהרגו שאול ושלשת בניו רצונך יכלו זרעך או תמסר ביד אויב אמר לפניו רבונו של עולם מוטב אמסר ביד אויב ולא יכלה זרעי יומא חד נפק ג) לשכור בזאי אתא שטן ואדמי ליה כטביא פתק ביה גירא ולא מטייה משכיה עד דאמטייה לארץ פלשתים כדחזייה ישבי בנוב אמר היינו האי דקטליה לגלית אחי כפתיה קמטיה אותביה ושדייה תותי בי ד) בדייא אתעביד ליה ניסא מכא ליה ארעא מתותיה היינו דכתיב כ) תרחיב צעדי תחתי ולא מעדו קרסולי ההוא יומא אפניא דמעלי שבתא הוה אבישי בן צרויה הוה קא חייף רישיה בד' גרבי דמיא חזינהו כתמי דמא איכא דאמרי אתא יונה איטריף קמיה ה) אמר ו) כנסת ישראל ליונה אימתילא שנאמר ל) כנפי יונה נחפה בכסף שמע מינה דוד מלכא דישראל בצערא שרי אתא לביתיה ולא אשכחיה אמר ו) תנן אין רוכבין על סוסו ואין יושבין על כסאו ואין משתמשין בשרביטו בשעת הסכנה מאי אתא שאיל בי מדרשא אמרו ליה בשעת הסכנה שפיר דמי רכביה לפרדיה וקם ואזל קפצה ליה ארעא בהדי דקא מסגי חזייה לערפה אמיה דהוות נוולא כי חזיתיה פסקתה לפילכה שדתיה עילויה סברא למקטליה אמרה ליה עלם אייתי לי פלך פתקיה בריש מוחה וקטלה כד חזייה ישבי בנוב אמר השתא הוו בי תרין וקטלין לי פתקיה לדוד לעילא ודץ ליה לרומחיה אמר ניפול עלה ונקטל אמר אבישי שם אוקמיה לדוד בין שמיא לארעא ז) ונימא ליה איהו אין חבוש מוציא עצמו מבית האסורין א"ל מאי בעית הכא א"ל הכי אמר לי קודשא בריך הוא והכי אהדרי ליה א"ל אפיך צלותיך בר ברך קירא ליזבון ואת לא תצטער א"ל אי הכי סייע בהדן היינו דכתיב מ) ויעזור לו אבישי בן צרויה אמר רב יהודה אמר רב שעזרו בתפלה אמר אבישי שם ואחתיה הוה קא רדיף בתרייהו כי מטא קובי אמרי קום ביה כי מטא בי תרי אמרי בתרי גוריין קטלוה לאריא אמרי ליה זיל אשתכח לערפה אימיך בקיברא כי אדכרו ליה שמא דאימיה כחש חיליה וקטליה היינו דכתיב מ) אז נשבעו אנשי דוד לו לאמר לא תצא עוד אתנו למלחמה ולא תכבה את נר ישראל ת"ר שלשה קפצה להם הארץ אליעזר עבד אברהם ויעקב אבינו ואבישי בן צרויה הא דאמרן אליעזר עבד אברהם דכתיב נ) ואבוא היום אל העין למימרא דההוא יומא נפק יעקב אבינו דכתיב

עניה ענתות. כמו עניה כלומר נביאות ירמיה הענתותי היא שעתידה לבא על נבוכד נצר שתמסר ירושלים בידו: ארי כפיר וכו'. ובדוכתא אחריתי מפורש למה נקראו לו כל השמות הללו: אי הכי. דכולי קרא נהלי קולך לא מחושבנא הוא א"כ ליכא אלא תשע מסעות דהא עוד היום לאו מחושבנא [נמי הוא] ומתרץ עברו מעברה תרתי אינון עברו חד מעברה חד ואיכא עשר מסעות: אותו היום נשתייר מעונה של נוב. [דמפני עון] שהיה להם לישראל על שנהרגו כהני נוב קבע הקב"ה העונש עד אותו היום ואותו יום בלבד נשתייר מזמן העונש ואילו היה נלחם בירושלים באותו היום היה כובשה והכי משמע קרא עוד היום אותו יום העמידו לסנחריב על ירושלים בעון נוב: סגא בחד יומא. והיינו י' מסעות שנסע אותו היום: שדו ליה. לסנחריב: בסתרקי. תחתיו טפי"ט בלע"ז עד שראה ירושלים כולה: עלה וקם ומניד ברישיה. עליה עמד והיה מניד בראשו: נשדי ביה ידא האידנא. נלחם בה עתה: תמהיתו. תמה הוא להתחיל היום משום חולשא דאורחא ל"א תמהיתו נתיגעתם ודומה ליה ח) (בסנחריב) איתמה למיתב: גולמו הרג. חתיכה של חומה לשון פרסי אבן רעועה מן החומה ונבקעה: בת דינא בטל דינא. כיון שלן דינא בטל הריב וכן מפני שלא נכבשה בו ביום לא הצליח ממחרת: וישבי בנוב. איידי דאיירי לעיל באותו יום שנשתייר מעונה של נוב נקט הכא וישבי בנוב שבא על עסקי נוב: הרפה. היינו ערפה: משקל קינו. מתרגמינן מתקל סופיניה: והוא חגור חדשה. והוא אסיר איספניקי חדתא: נטרד דואג האדומי. שספר לשון הרע על דוד שנתקנא בו שאול ולפי שקבל אחימלך את דוד בנוב אמר ליה שאול סוב ופגע בכהני ה' נמלא שעל ידך נהרגו ואתה נכשל ובחטא זה נהרג שאול ושלשת בניו במלחמת פלשתים: שכר ביזאי. לשון פרסי קריטא ל"א כפר היא: קמטיה. הכניעו תחת הבד של זיתים ויתיב עלה למעכו: מכא ליה ארעא מתותיה. נתרככה הארץ מתחתיו ולא הזיקו ל"א מכא נשפלת כעין גומא והיתה מגינה עליו: בארבע גריבי דמיא. בארבע סאין של מים ל"א בארבע כורא דמיא בד' ט) נודות של מים: איטריף קמיה. היתה טורפת ומחבטת עלמה וממרטת כנפיה והומה ומלערת: קפצה ליה ארעא. כמו לא תקפון (דברים טו) נתקלרה הארץ והגיע מהרה לארץ פלשתים: לערפה אימיה. דישבי: נוולה. טווה: כד חזיתיה. ערפה לאבישי סברה למקטליה באותו פלך שהיה בידה ולא נגע בו: אמרה ליה. לאבישי אייתי לן ההוא פלך דנפל לפניך: ה"ג פתקיה בריש מוחה וקטלה. השליך אבישי הפלך לראשה ומתה: פתקיה לדוד לעילא. זרקו כלפי מעלה: ודץ ליה. נעץ תחתיו חניתו בקרקע כדי שיפול עליו וימות: ונימא איהו. דוד עלמו לימא שם: אין חבוש. אין דעתו מכוונת לומר השם והשתא ניצל דוד והשליכו השם ברחוק והלכו אבישי ודוד וחזרו להם: אמר ליה. אבישי לדוד: ומאי בעית הכא. למה באת כאן: אמר ליה. הקב"ה אמר לי רצונך שיכלה זרעך או תמסר ביד אויביך והכי אהדרי ליה מוטב שאפול ביד אויב: אמר ליה אפיך צלותיך. הפוך תפלתך ואמור לפניו מוטב יכלה זרעך ולא תמסר ביד אויב דמה לך בלער בניך: בר ברך קירא ליזבון ואת לא תצטער. משל הוא שאומרים בני אדם: סייע בהדן. עזור בתפלתך להפכה: והוה קא רדיף בתרייהו. והם בורחין שהיה קרוב לארץ פלשתים: וכי מטו קובי. לאותו כפר ששמו קובי שבין א"י לארץ פלשתים: אמרי קום ביה. אמרו זה לזה עמוד כנגדו ואל תברח ונכנו ולכך נקרא קובי אינהו הוו בקיאי בשמות הכפרים ועדיין היו מפחדין ובורחין: כי מטא בי תרי. שם מקום: אמרו בין תרי גוריון. בתמיהא: בקברא. שהרגנוה: ויצא

א) נ"א דאתיתו מאורחא, ב) [ילקוט ישעיה סי' י' איתא קלא בנוסחא אחרת וע"י עוד בערוך ערך גלמהרג], ג) [עי' בערוך ערך שכר בזאי פי' יפה באריכות], ד) נ"א סדייא, ה) [ברכות נג: שבת מט. קלא. גיטין מה.], ו) לעיל כב., ז) ברכות ה., ח) רש"ל מ"ז, ט) בורות. רש"ל.

גליון הש"ס

גמ' אמר כנ"י ליונה אימתלי. עיין ג"י סוף פרק ד' מיתות:

תורה אור השלם

א) צַהֲלִי קוֹלֵךְ בַּת גַּלִּים הַקְשִׁיבִי לַיְשָׁה עֲנִיָּה עֲנָתוֹת: [ישעיה י, ל]

ב) דִּבְרֵי יִרְמְיָהוּ בֶּן חִלְקִיָּהוּ מִן הַכֹּהֲנִים אֲשֶׁר בַּעֲנָתוֹת בְּאֶרֶץ בִּנְיָמִן: [ירמיה א, א]

ג) גּוּר אַרְיֵה יְהוּדָה מִטֶּרֶף בְּנִי עָלִיתָ כָּרַע רָבַץ כְּאַרְיֵה וּכְלָבִיא מִי יְקִימֶנּוּ: [בראשית מט, ט]

ד) וַיֵּרֶד שִׁמְשׁוֹן וְאָבִיו וְאִמּוֹ תִּמְנָתָה וַיָּבֹאוּ עַד כַּרְמֵי תִמְנָתָה וְהִנֵּה כְּפִיר אֲרָיוֹת שֹׁאֵג לִקְרָאתוֹ: [שופטים יד, ה]

ה) מַשָּׂא בַּהֲמוֹת נֶגֶב בְּאֶרֶץ צָרָה וְצוּקָה לָבִיא וָלַיִשׁ מֵהֶם אֶפְעֶה וְשָׂרָף מְעוֹפֵף יִשְׂאוּ עַל כֶּתֶף עֲיָרִים חֵילֵהֶם וְעַל דַּבֶּשֶׁת גְּמַלִּים אוֹצְרֹתָם עַל עַם לֹא יוֹעִילוּ: [ישעיה ל, ו]

ו) עַל שַׁחַל וָפֶתֶן תִּדְרֹךְ תִּרְמֹס כְּפִיר וְתַנִּין: [תהלים צא, יג]

ז) לֹא הִדְרִיכֻהוּ בְנֵי שָׁחַץ לֹא עָדָה עָלָיו שָׁחַל: [איוב כח, ח]

ח) עוֹד הַיּוֹם בְּנֹב לַעֲמֹד יְנֹפֵף יָדוֹ הַר בַּת צִיּוֹן גִּבְעַת יְרוּשָׁלָיִם: [ישעיה י, לב]

ט) וַיְהִי בַּלַּיְלָה הַהוּא וַיֵּצֵא מַלְאַךְ יְיָ וַיַּךְ בְּמַחֲנֵה אַשּׁוּר מֵאָה שְׁמוֹנִים וַחֲמִשָּׁה אָלֶף וַיַּשְׁכִּימוּ בַבֹּקֶר וְהִנֵּה כֻלָּם פְּגָרִים מֵתִים: [מלכים ב' יט, לה]

י) וְיִשְׁבִּי בְּנֹב אֲשֶׁר בִּילִידֵי הָרָפָה וּמִשְׁקַל קֵינוֹ שְׁלֹשׁ מֵאוֹת מִשְׁקַל נְחֹשֶׁת וְהוּא חָגוּר חֲדָשָׁה וַיֹּאמֶר לְהַכּוֹת אֶת דָּוִד: [שמואל ב' כא, טז]

כ) תַּרְחִיב צַעֲדִי תַחְתָּי וְלֹא מָעֲדוּ קַרְסֻלָּי: [תהלים יח, לז]

ל) אִם תִּשְׁכְּבוּן בֵּין שְׁפַתָּיִם כַּנְפֵי יוֹנָה נֶחְפָּה בַכֶּסֶף וְאֶבְרוֹתֶיהָ בִּירַקְרַק חָרוּץ: [תהלים סח, יד]

מ) וַיַּעֲזָר לוֹ אֲבִישַׁי בֶּן צְרוּיָה וַיַּךְ אֶת הַפְּלִשְׁתִּי וַיְמִיתֵהוּ אָז נִשְׁבְּעוּ אַנְשֵׁי דָוִד לוֹ לֵאמֹר לֹא תֵצֵא עוֹד אִתָּנוּ לַמִּלְחָמָה וְלֹא תְכַבֶּה אֶת נֵר יִשְׂרָאֵל: [שמואל ב' כא, יז]

נ) וָאָבֹא הַיּוֹם אֶל הָעָיִן וָאֹמַר יְיָ אֱלֹהֵי אֲדֹנִי אַבְרָהָם אִם יֶשְׁךָ נָּא מַצְלִיחַ דַּרְכִּי אֲשֶׁר אָנֹכִי הֹלֵךְ עָלֶיהָ: [בראשית כד, מב]

ליקוטי רש"י

דאמר רב פפא. במסכת גיטין (לח.). עמון ומואב טהרו בסיחון. ע"י סיחון טהרו אלים לישראל במואב כתיב (במדבר כא) והוא נלחם וגו' ובעמון מפורש בנחלת בני גד בספר יהושע (יג) ויהי להם הגבול יעזר וכל ארץ הגלעד וחצי (ארץ) [ערי] בני עמון וקא חשיב ואזיל וכתיב בסיפיה יתר ממלכות סיחון אלמא סיחון כבש לארץ בני עמון ועוד מלינו במלך בני עמון שאמר למלאכי יפתח (שופטים יא) כי לקח ישראל את ארלי מארנון ועד היבוק אלמא ארץ בני עמון הוא והם מסיחון כבשוה דכתיב בו וירשו את ארלו מארנון ועד היבוק אבל מהנשאר בידם לא לקחו כלום [חולין ס:]. דכתיב (דברים ב) אל תצר את מואב וכן בבני עמון אל תגורם (שם) וכתיב (במדבר כא) כי חשבון עיר סיחון וגו' אלמא טהר מואב בסיחון ובני עמון אשכחן ביפתח (שופטים יא) שאמרו לו מלאכי בני עמון כי לקח ישראל את ארלי בעלותו ממלרים מארנון ועד היבוק ואשכחן כשכבשו את ארץ סיחון ויירש את ארלו מארנון עד יבוק וגו' אלמא מבני עמון כבשה והדור ישראל וכבשו מיניה וטהרה להם על ידו אלמא קנייה בחזקה [גיטין לח.]. בא על עית. מונה והולך מסעות שנסע סנחריב ובא על ערי יהודה לבא ירושלים ביום מפלתו [ישעיה י, כח]. לנו. לשון לינה. נסה. ברחה ברחו כולן מפני חיילותיו [שם, כט]. צהלי קולך. להזכיר לעם. הקשיבי לישה. את קול השופר וברחו לכם וכן עניה ענתות [שם, ל]. העיזו. נאספו לברוח [שם, לא] עוד היום בנוב לעמוד. כל הדרך הזה נתלבט כדי לעמוד בעוד היום בנוב לפי שאמרו לו איצטגניניו אם תלח' בה היום תכבשנ' וכשעמד בנוב וראה את ירושלים קטנה לא חש לדברי איצטגניניו והתחיל להניף ידו בגאו' וכי על עיר כזו הרגזתי כל החיילות הללו לינו פה הלילה ולמחר ישליך בה איש אבנו. הר בת ציון. להר בת ציון [שם, לב]. עלה אריה. נבוכדנצר. מסובכו. דרך אריה לישב במארב סבכי היער אשפיישי"ש בלע"ז [ירמיה ד, ז].

[ע"כ שייך לדף צד:].

כפיר. כל כפיר שבמקרא ארי בחור וגבור [יחזקאל יט, ה]. הארי גדול והשחל בינוני והכפיר קטן [איוב ד, י]. עוד היום בנוב לעמוד. כל הדרך הזה נתלבט כדי לעמוד בעוד היום בנוב לפי שאמרו לו איצטגניניו אם תלח' בה היום תכבשנ' וכשעמד בנוב וראה את ירושלים קטנה לא חש לדברי איצטגניניו והתחיל להניף ידו בגאו' וכי על עיר כזו הרגזתי כל החיילות הללו לינו פה הלילה ולמחר ישליך בה איש אבנו [ישעיה י, לב]. ויהי בלילה ההוא. כשנב סנחריב מעל כוש ובא עד נוב שהיתה סמוכה לירושלים. מאה ושמונים וחמשה אלף. כולם ראשי גייסות [מ"ב יט, לה]. בילידי הרפה. כתיב ערפה שם האחת ערפה (רות א) וכתיב הרפה אשר בילידי הרפה והיא ערפה כדאמרי' לקמן שנגזר עליה שיפלו בניה בחרב ביד בני רות שדבקה בשכינה [סוטה מב:]. ומשקל קינו. הוא כמו תיק שבראש בית יד הרומח שקורין ארישטויי"ל בלע"ז ועשוי ככובע, ויש דוגמתו בזבחים (פח:) רמוני המעיל למה הם דומין כמין קולסות שבראשי התינוקות קולסות היימלמש בלע"ז [ש"ב כא, טז]. קונאות. כוטונ"ש עשויין כמין תיק של נחשת שעושין [בסוף] בית יד הרומח שקורין ארישטייל לשון (ש"ב כא) ומשקל קינו דישבי בנוב והתינוקות תולין אותו בראשי כובעי נלרים שעושין אותו למלחמתן שקורים הילמ"ש [זבחים פח:]. והוא חגור. חגורה חדשה ושמעתי שאותו היום נתחנך ללבוש כלי מלחמה ודרך המחונכים לעשות נלחון וגבורה ביום חינוכם לקנות שם לכך ויאמר להכות את דוד [ש"ב שם]. על עסקי נוב. שבא עליו על עונשו של שאול כמו שפירשו רבותינו שאמר לו הקב"ה על ידך נטרד דואג האדומי על ידך נהרג שאול ובניו כו' [תהלים ז, א]. פתק ביה. זרק בו [שבועות יח:]. פניא. לפנות ערב [תענית כג:]. חייף רישיה. חופף ראשו [לקמן קיא.]. ליונה אימתילא. כיונה נמשלה [גיטין מה.]. שהיא נמשלת ליונה והמלות ככנפים [שבת מט.]. כנפי יונה. זאת יונתי כנסייתי כנפיה נחפה בכסף ומהו הכסף והחרוץ בפרש שדי וגו' כשפירש הקב"ה לפניהם תורתו אשר המלכים נשלגים ומתלבנים בה בארץ ללמות וחשך אז נחפו כנפיה (כנפי יונה) בכספה ותמדתה של תורה ומלות [תהלים סח, יד]. סייע בהדן. והפך דוד את תפלתו והתפלל שלא יפול בידי אויב [ש"ב שם, יח]. ויעזור לו. שעזרו בתפלה [שם ז, א]. ואבוא היום. היום יצאתי והיום באתי מכאן שקפלה לו הארץ [בראשית כד, מב].

descendants obliterated, or do you choose for **you yourself to be delivered into** your **enemy's hand?"**[23] אָמַר לְפָנָיו – To this, **[David] replied:** רִבּוֹנוֹ שֶׁל עוֹלָם – **"Master of the Universe!** מוּטָב אֶמָּסֵר בְּיַד אוֹיֵב וְלֹא יִכְלֶה זַרְעִי – It is **better that I be delivered to the enemy's hand, and let my children not be obliterated."**

The Gemara relates how David's choice of punishments was eventually actualized:

יוֹמָא חַד נְפַק לְשִׁכּוּר בָּזָאי – **One day, [King David] went hunting.**[24] אֲתָא שָׂטָן וְאִידַּמֵּי לֵיהּ כְּטַבְיָא – when **Satan appeared, disguised as a deer.** פְּתַק בֵּיהּ גִּירָא לֹא מְטְיֵיהּ – **[David] shot an arrow at [the deer],** but **it fell short.** מָשְׁכֵיהּ – David continued chasing the deer, and **[the deer] drew him** further afield, עַד דְּאַמְטְיֵיהּ לְאֶרֶץ פְּלִשְׁתִּים – **until it caused him to reach the land of the Philistines.** כִּדְחַזְיֵיהּ יִשְׁבִּי בְּנוֹב – **When Yishbi B'Nov saw him** there, he recognized him, אָמַר הַיְינוּ הַאי דִּקְטַלֵיהּ לְגָלְיַת אָחִי – and **said, "This is the person who killed my brother Goliath!"**[25] כַּפְתֵּיהּ קַמְטֵיהּ – **[Yishbi]** then **bound [David]** and **doubled him over,** אוֹתְבֵיהּ וְשַׁדְיֵיהּ תּוּתֵי בֵּי בַדְיָא – and **he** then **cast him under an olive press,**[26] sitting on top of it. He thereby hoped to crush David to death. אִתְעֲבִיד לֵיהּ נִיסָּא – However, **a miracle was performed for [David],** מָכָא לֵיהּ אַרְעָא מִתּוֹתֵיהּ – **and the ground under him softened,** enabling him to avoid being crushed. הַיְינוּ דִּכְתִיב – Indeed, **it was in reference to this** miracle **that it is written:** ,,תַּרְחִיב צַעֲדִי תַחְתָּי וְלֹא מָעֲדוּ קַרְסֻלָּי'' – ***You have widened my stride beneath me, and my ankles have not given way.***[27]

Although David was saved from this immediate threat, he remained a prisoner of Yishbi B'Nov, and was therefore still in mortal danger. The Gemara relates how he was eventually saved:

הַהוּא יוֹמָא אַפַּנְיָא דְּמַעֲלֵי שַׁבְּתָא הֲוָה – **Now, the day** David was captured **was Friday, towards evening.** אֲבִישַׁי בֶּן צְרוּיָה הֲוָה קָא חָיֵיף רֵישֵׁיהּ בְּאַרְבְּעָא גַרְבֵי דְמַיָּא – And at that moment, **Avishai the son of Tzeruiah,**[28] one of David's officers, **was** preparing for the Sabbath by **shampooing his head with four measures**[29] **of water.** חֲזִינְהוּ כִּתְמֵי דָמָא – As he was doing so, **he noticed bloodstains** in the water, and this signaled to him that there was great danger abroad. אִיכָּא דְאָמְרֵי אֲתָא יוֹנָה אִיטְרִיף קַמֵּיהּ – **Some say,** though, that he was signaled by **a dove** that **came and began thrashing about in front of him.**[30] אָמַר – Thereupon, [Avishai] **said** to himself: כְּנֶסֶת יִשְׂרָאֵל לְיוֹנָה אִימְתִילָא – **The Congregation of Israel is compared** in Scripture **to a dove,** שֶׁנֶּאֱמַר – **for the verse states:**[31] ,,כַּנְפֵי יוֹנָה נֶחְפָּה בַכֶּסֶף'' – ***[You will be like] the wings of a dove, covered with silver.*** שְׁמַע מִינָּהּ דָּוִד מַלְכָּא דְיִשְׂרָאֵל בְּצַעֲרָא שָׁרֵי – Now, if this dove, the symbol of the people of Israel, is in pain, **I can infer that David, the king of Israel** must be **in distress.**[32] אֲתָא לְבֵיתֵיהּ – **[Avishai]** then **went to [David's] house** to see what was amiss, וְלָא אַשְׁכְּחֵיהּ – **but he did not find him** there.

Avishai was then confronted with a dilemma. His only available means of rapid transportation was David's mule, which was harnessed near his house. But Avishai was not sure whether he was permitted to ride it. The Gemara relates:

אָמַר – **[Avishai]** then **said** to himself: תְּנַן – **We have learned in a Mishnah:**[33] אֵין רוֹכְבִין עַל סוּסוֹ – NO ONE but the king MAY RIDE ON [THE KING'S] HORSE; וְאֵין יוֹשְׁבִין עַל כִּסְאוֹ – NO ONE but the king MAY SIT ON HIS THRONE; וְאֵין מִשְׁתַּמְּשִׁין בְּשַׁרְבִיטוֹ – AND NO ONE but the king MAY USE HIS SCEPTER. בִּשְׁעַת הַסַּכָּנָה מַאי – But **what if it is a time of danger,** and it is necessary to ride on the king's horse to save his life? Is a subject then permitted to do this? אֲתָא שָׁאִיל בֵּי מִדְרְשָׁא – **He went and asked this question** to the Torah scholars **in** a nearby **study hall.** אָמְרוּ לֵיהּ – **They said to him:** בִּשְׁעַת הַסַּכָּנָה שַׁפִּיר דָּמֵי – **If it is a time of danger, it is** indeed **permitted** to ride on the king's horse to save him.

The Gemara continues:

רָכְבֵיהּ לְפִרְדֵּיהּ וְקָם וְאָזַל – **[Avishai]** then **mounted [David's] mule and rode off.** קָפְצָה לֵיהּ אַרְעָא – **The ground** miraculously **contracted under him,** enabling him to reach the land of the Philistines in an extraordinarily short time.[34] בַּהֲדֵי דְּקָא מַסְגֵּי – **As [Avishai] was riding,** חַזְיֵיהּ לְעָרְפָּה אִמֵּיהּ – **he saw Orpah, the mother of [Yishbi B'Nov],**[35] דַּהֲוַות נָוְולָא – and he noticed **that she was spinning** thread. כִּי חֲזִיתֵיהּ – **As soon as she saw [Avishai],** פַּסְקָתָהּ לְפִילְכָּהּ – **she broke** the thread off of **her spindle** שְׁדַתֵּיהּ עִילָּוֵיהּ – **and threw [the spindle] at him** like a dart.[36] סְבָרָא לְמִקְטְלֵיהּ – **She had hoped to kill him** with this, but when she saw that the spindle had failed to hit him, she feigned innocence אָמְרָה לֵיהּ – and **said to [Avishai]:** עֶלֶם – **"Young man!** אַיְיתִי לִי פֶּלֶךְ – **Fetch me [that] spindle** which I accidentally dropped in front of you." פַּתְקֵיהּ בְּרֵישׁ מוֹחָהּ וְקַטְלָהּ – **He threw [the spindle] at the top of her head and killed her.**

NOTES

23. *Maharsha* suggests that the choice David was given reflected his sin: On the one hand, he was given the choice of having his descendants destroyed, for he was a party to the "destruction" of the Kohanim's descendants [i.e. they were never born, since the lives of the Kohanim were cut short]. On the other hand, he was given the choice of falling into the hands of his enemy, for the massacre had been precipitated by David's desire *not* to fall into the hands of Saul (see also *Maharal*).

24. *Aruch* asserts that שְׁכַר בָּזָאי is a Persian phrase which means "to hunt." See *Margaliyos HaYam*.

Alternatively, *Rashi* suggests that the Gemara might be referring to the name of a place.

25. See above, end of note 17.

26. The words אוֹתְבֵיהּ וְשַׁדְיֵיהּ, which literally mean, *he placed him and cast him,* form a redundancy. *Dikdukei Soferim* writes that in some versions of the Gemara's text, the word אוֹתְבֵיהּ does not appear, and in our rendering, we have not translated this word.

It appears from *Rashi's* version of the text that Yishbi subsequently sat on the olive press after casting David beneath it to crush him. See, however, *Maharal.*

27. *Psalms* 18:37.

28. Avishai was David's nephew, and was also the brother of Yoav, David's commander-in-chief. Avishai was one of David's most heroic officers. See *I Chronicles* 11:20.

29. *Rashi* equates a *griva* with the common measure *se'ah.* [It is possible that *Rashi's* text of the Gemara read גְּרִיוֵי, which means *measures,* rather than גַרְבֵי, which is usually translated as *barrels.* Such a reading is indeed found in *Dikdukei Soferim.*]

30. The bird made sounds of distress, and beat itself with its wings until some of its own feathers fell out (*Rashi*).

31. *Psalms* 68:14.

32. Avishai knew that the Jewish people as a whole were not in danger at that moment. Thus, the frightened behavior of the bird must allude to a danger threatening the *representative* of the Jewish people — their king (*Yad Ramah*).

33. *Sanhedrin* 22a. [The Mishnah was of course not formalized yet during the time of David. Nevertheless, the term Mishnah is used here to indicate a law that had been passed down orally, and was later included by R' Yehudah HaNasi in the body of Mishnaic teachings.]

34. Our rendering follows *Rashi,* who asserts that the ground literally contracted. *Yad Ramah,* however, states that this expression is not to be taken literally; rather, it simply means that the mule raced so swiftly that it covered a lengthy distance in an extraordinarily short time. In line with this, *Maharal* explains that Avishai was helped by Divine Providence to reach the land of the Philistines with great speed.

35. See above, note 17.

36. [A spindle is a rod used to twist, wind and hold thread. When thread is hand spun, the spindle that is used tapers toward each end to form a point, and thus, it can conceivably be used as a weapon.]

א) ענֿיה ענתות עתיד ירמיה בן חלקיה ומתנבא עלה מענתות דכתיב ב) דברי ירמיהו בן חלקיהו מן הכהנים אשר בענתות בארץ בנימין מי דמי התם ארי הכא ליש אמר רבי יוחנן ששה שמות יש לארי אלו הן ג) ארי ד) כפיר ה) לביא ה) ליש ו) שחל ז) שחץ אי הכי בצרו להו עברו מעברה תרתי נינהו מאי ח) עוד היום בנוב לעמוד אמר רב הונא אותו היום נשתייר מעונה של נוב כלדאי אמרי ליה אי אזלת האידנא יכלת לה ואי לא לא יכלת לה אורחא דבעא לסגויי בעשרה יומא סגא בחד יומא כי מטו לירושלם שדי ליה ביסתרקי עד דסליק ויתיב מעילוי שורה עד דחזיוה לכולה ירושלם כי חזייה איזוטר בעיניה אמר הלא דא היא קרתא דירושלם דעלה ארגישית כל משיריתי ועלה כבשית כל מדינתא הלא היא זעירא וחלשא מכל כרכי עממיא דכבשית בתקוף ידי עלה וקם ומניד ברישיה מוביל ומייתי בידיה על טור בית מקדשא דבציון ועל עזרתא דבירושלם אמרי נישדי ביה ידא האידנא אמר להו תמהיתו ח) למחר אייתי לי כל חד וחד מינייכו ט) גולמו הרג מיניה מיד ט) ויהי בלילה ההוא ויצא מלאך ה' ויך במחנה אשור מאה ושמונים וחמשה אלף וישכימו בבקר והנה כלם פגרים מתים אמר רב פפא היינו דאמרי אינשי בת דינא בטל דינא י) וישבי בנוב אשר בילידי הרפה ומשקל קינו שלש מאות משקל נחשת והוא חגור חדשה ויאמר להכות את דוד מאי וישבי בנוב אמר רב יהודה אמר רב איש שבא על עסקי נוב אמר ליה הקב"ה לדוד עד מתי יהיה עון זה טמון בידך על ידך נהרגה נוב עיר הכהנים ועל ידך נטרד דואג האדומי ועל ידך נהרגו שאול ושלשת בניו רצונך יכלו זרעך או תמסר ביד אויב אמר לפניו רבונו של עולם מוטב אמסר ביד אויב ולא יכלה זרעי יומא חד נפק ג) לשכור בזאי אתא שטן ואדמי ליה כטביא פתק ביה גירא ולא מטיה משכיה עד דאמטייה לארץ פלשתים כדחזיה ישבי בנוב אמר היינו האי דקטליה לגלית אחי כפתיה קמטיה אותביה ושדייה תותי בי ד) בדייא אתעביד ליה ניסא מכא ליה ארעא מתותיה היינו דכתיב כ) תרחיב צעדי תחתי ולא מעדו קרסולי ההוא יומא מעלי שבתא הוה אבישי בן צרויה הוה קא חייף רישיה בד' גרבי דמיא חזינהו כתמי דמא איכא דאמרי אתא יונה איטריף קמיה אמר ה) כנסת ישראל ליונה אימתילא שנאמר ל) כנפי יונה נחפה בכסף שמע מינה דוד מלכא דישראל בצערא שרי אתא לביתיה ולא אשכחיה אמר ו) תנן אין רוכבין על סוסו ואין יושבין על כסאו ואין משתמשין בשרביטו בשעת הסכנה מאי אתא שאיל בי מדרשא אמרו ליה בשעת הסכנה שפיר דמי רכביה לפרדיה וקם ואזל קפצה ליה ארעא בהדי דקא מסגי חזייה לערפה אמיה דהוות נוולא כי חזיתיה פסקתה לפילכה שדתיה עילויה סברא למקטליה אמרה ליה עלם אייתי לי פלך פתקיה בריש מוחה וקטלה כד חזייה ישבי בנוב אמר השתא הוו בי תרין וקטלין לי פתקיה לדוד לעילא ודץ ליה לרומחיה אמר ניפול עלה ונקטל אמר אבישי שם אוקמיה לדוד בין שמיא לארעא ז) ונימא ליהו איהו אין חבוש מוציא עצמו מבית האסורין א"ל מאי בעית הכא א"ל הכי אמר לי קודשא בריך הוא והכי אהדרי ליה א"ל אפיך צלותיך בר ברך קירא ליזבון ואת לא תצטער א"ל אי הכי סייע בהדן היינו דכתיב מ) ויעזור לו אבישי בן צרויה אמר רב יהודה אמר רב שעזרו בתפלה אמר אבישי שם ואחתיה הוה קא רדיף בתרייהו כי מטא קובי אמרי קום ביה כי מטא בי תרי אמרי בתרי גוריין קטלוה לאריא אמרי ליה זיל אשתכח לערפה אימיך בקיברא כי אדכרו ליה שמא דאמיה כחש חיליה וקטליה היינו דכתיב מ) אז נשבעו אנשי דוד לו לאמר לא תצא עוד אתנו למלחמה ולא תכבה את נר ישראל תנו רבנן שלשה קפצה להם הארץ אליעזר עבד אברהם ויעקב אבינו ואבישי בן צרויה הא דאמרן אליעזר עבד אברהם דכתיב נ) ואבוא היום אל העין למימרא דההוא יומא נפק יעקב אבינו דכתיב

ענֿיה ענתות. כמו עניה כלומר נביאות ירמיה הענתותי היא שעתידה לבא על נבוכד נצר שתמסר ירושלים בידו: ארי כפיר וכו'. ובדוכתא אחריתי מפורש למה נקראו לו כל השמות הללו: אי הכי. דכולי קרא נהלי קולך לא מחושבנא הוא א"כ ליכא אלא תשע מסעות דהא עוד היום לאו מחושבנא [נמי הוא] ומתרץ עברו מעברה תרתי אינון עברו חד מעברה חד ואיכא עשר מסעות: אותו היום נשתייר מעונה של נוב. [דמפני עון] שהיה להם לישראל על שנהרגו כהני נוב קבע הקב"ה העונש עד אותו היום ואותו יום בלבד נשתייר מזמן העונש ואילו היה נלחם בירושלים באותו היום היה כובשה והכי משמע קרא עוד היום אותו יום העמידו לסנחריב על ירושלים בעון נוב: סגא בחד יומא. והיינו י' מסעות שנסע אותו היום: שדו ליה. לסנחריב: בסתרקי. תחתיו טפי"ט בלע"ז עד שראה ירושלים כולה: עלה וקם ומניד ברישיה. עליה עמד והיה מניד בראשו: נשדי ביה ידא האידנא. נלחם בה עתה: תמהיתו. תמה הוא להתחיל היום משום חולשא דאורחא ל"א תמהיתו נתיגעתם ודומה ליה ^(ח) (בסנחריב) איתמה למיתב: גולמו הרג. תתיכה של חומה לשון פרסי אבן רעועה מן החומה ונבקעה: בת דינא בטל דינא. כיון שלן דינא בטל הריב וכן מפני שלא נכבשה בו ביום לא הצליח ממחרת: וישבי בנוב. איידי דאיירי לעיל באותו יום שנשתייר מעונה של נוב נקט הכא וישבי בנוב שבא על עסקי נוב: הרפה. היינו ערפה: משקל קינו. מתרגמינן מתקל סופיניה: והוא חגור חדשה. והוא אסיר איספניקי חדתא: נטרד דואג האדומי. שספר לשון הרע על דוד שנתקנא בו שאול ולפי שקבל אחימלך את דוד בנוב אמר ליה שאול סוב ופגע בכהני ה' נמצא שעל ידך נהרגו ואתה נכשל בחטא זה נהרג שאול ושלשת בניו במלחמת פלשתים: שכר בזאי.

לשון פרסי קריטא ל"א כפר היא: קמטיה. הכניעו תחת הבד של זיתים ויתיב עלה למעכו: מכא ליה ארעא מתותיה. נתרככה הארץ מתחתיו ולא הזיקו ל"א מכא נשפלת כעין גומא והיתה מגינה עליו: בארבע גריבי דמיא. בארבע סאין של מים ל"א בארבע כורא דמיא כד' ^(ט) נודות של מים: איטריף קמיה. היתה טורפת ומחבטת עצמה וממרטת כנפיה והומה ומצערת: קפצה ליה ארעא. כמו לא תקפוץ (דברים טו) נתקצרה הארץ והגיע מהרה לארץ פלשתים: לערפה אימיה. דישבי: נוולה. טווה: כד חזיתיה. ערפה לאבישי סברה למקטליה באותו פלך שהיה בידה ולא נגע בו: אמרה ליה. לאבישי אייתי לן ההוא פלך דנפל לפניך: ה"ג פתקיה בריש מוחה וקטלה. השליך אבישי הפלך לראשה ומתה: פתקיה לדוד לעילא. זרקו כלפי מעלה: ודץ ליה. נעץ תחתיו חניתו בקרקע כדי שיפול עליו וימות: ונימא איהו. דוד עצמו לימא שם: אין חבוש. אין דעתו מכוונת לומר השם והשתא ניצל דוד והשליכו השם ברחוק והלכו אבישי ודוד וחזרו להם: אמר ליה. אבישי לדוד: ומאי בעית הכא. למה באת כאן: אמר ליה. הקב"ה אמר לי רצונך שיכלה זרעך או תמסר ביד אויביך והכי אהדרי ליה מוטב שאפול ביד אויב: אמר ליה אפיך צלותיך. הפוך תפלתך ואמור לפניו מוטב יכלה זרעך ולא תמסר ביד אויב דמה לך בצער בניך: בר ברך קירא לזבון ואת לא תצטער. משל הוא שאומרים בני אדם: סייע בהדן. עזור בתפלתך להפכה: והוה קא רדיף בתרייהו. והם בורחין שהיה קרוב לארץ פלשתים: וכי מטו קובי. לאותו כפר ששמו קובי שבין א"י לארץ פלשתים: אמרי קום ביה. אמרו זה לזה עמוד כנגדו ואל תברח ונכנו ולכך נקרא קובי אינהו הוו בקיאי בשמות הכפרים ועדיין היו מפחדין ובורחין: כי מטא בי תרי. שם מקום: אמרו בין תרי גוריון. בתמיהא: בקברא. שהרגנוה: ויצא

דאמר רב פפא. במסכת גיטין (לח.). עמון ומואב טהרו בסיחון. ע"י סיחון טהרו ארצם לישראל במואב כתיב (במדבר כא) והוא נלחם וגו' ובעמון מפורש בנחלת בני גד בספר יהושע (יג) ויהי להם הגבול יעזר וכל ארץ הגלעד וחצי (ארץ) [ערי] בני עמון וקא חשיב ואזיל וכתיב בסיפיה יתר ממלכות סיחון אלמא סיחון כבש לארץ בני עמון ועוד מצינו במלך בני עמון שאמר למלאכי יפתח (שופטים יא) כי לקח ישראל את ארצי מארנון ועד היבוק אלמא ארץ בני עמון הוא והם מסיחון כבשוה דכתיב בו וירשו את ארצו מארנון ועד היבוק אבל מהנשאר בידם לא לקחו כלום [חולין ס:]. דכתיב (דברים ב) אל תצר את מואב וכן בבני עמון אל תצורם (שם) וכתיב (במדבר כא) כי חשבון עיר סיחון וגו' אלמא טהר מואב בסיחון ובני עמון אשכחן ביפתח (שופטים יא) שאמרו לו מלאכי בני עמון כי לקח ישראל את ארצי בעלותו ממצרים מארנון ועד היבוק ואשכחן כשכבשו את ארץ סיחון ויירש את ארצו מארנון עד יבוק וגו' אלמא מבני עמון כבשה והדור ישראל וכבשו מיניה וטהרה להם על ידו אלמא קנייה בחזקה [גיטין לח.]. בא על עית. מונה והולך מסעות שנסע סנחריב ובא על ערי יהודה לבא ירושלים ביום מפלתו [ישעיה י, כח]. לנו. לשון לינה. נסה. ברחה ברחו כולן מפני חיילותיו [שם, כט]. צהלי קולך. להזהיר לעם. הקשיבי לישה. את קול השופר וברחו לכם וכן עניה ענתות [שם, ל]. העיזו. נאספו לברוח [שם, לא] עוד היום בנוב לעמוד. כל הדרך הזה נתלבט כדי לעמוד בעוד היום בנוב לפי שאמרו לו אילטגניניו אם תלא' בה היום תכבשנ' וכשעמד בנוב וראה את ירושלים קטנה לא חש לדברי אילטגניניו והתחיל להניף ידו בגאו' וכי על עיר כזו הרגזתי כל החיילות הללו לינו פה הלילה ולמחר ישליך בה איש אבנו. הר בת ציון. להר בת ציון [שם, לב]. עלה אריה. נבוכדנצר. מסובכו. דרך אריה לישב במארב סבכי היער אשפיישי"ש בלע"ז [ירמיה ד, ז].

[ע"כ שייך לדף צד:].

כפיר. כל כפיר שבמקרא ארי בחור וגבור [יחזקאל יט, ה]. האריה גדול והשחל בינוני והכפיר קטן [איוב ד, י]. עוד היום בנוב לעמוד. כל הדרך הזה נתלבט כדי לעמוד בעוד היום בנוב לפי שאמרו לו אילטגניניו אם תלא' בה היום תכבשנ' וכשעמד בנוב וראה את ירושלים קטנה לא חש לדברי אילטגניניו והתחיל להניף ידו בגאו' וכי על עיר כזו הרגזתי כל החיילות הללו לינו פה הלילה ולמחר ישליך בה איש אבנו [ישעיה י, לב]. ויהי בלילה ההוא. כשבא סנחריב מעל כוש ובא עד נוב שהיתה סמוכה לירושלים. מאה ושמונים וחמשה אלף. כולם ראשי גייסות [מ"ב יט, לה]. בילידי הרפה. כתיב ערפה שם האחת ערפה (רות א) וכתיב הרפה אשר בילידי הרפה והיא ערפה כדאמרי' לקמן שנגזר עליה שיפלו בניה בחרב ביד בני רות שדבקה בשכינה [סוטה מב:]. ומשקל קינו. הוא כמו תיק שבראש בית יד הרומח שקורין ארשטויי"ל בלע"ז ועשוי ככובע, ויש דוגמתו בזבחים (פח:) רמוני המעיל למה הם דומין כמין קולסות שבראשי התינוקות קולסות היימלמש בלע"ז [ש"ב כא, טז]. קולסות. בוטונ"ש עשויין כמין תיק של נחשת שעושין [בסוף] בית יד הרומח שקורין ארישטייל לשון (ש"ב כא) ומשקל קינו דישבי בנוב והתינוקות תולין אותו בראשי כובעי נכרים שעושין אותו למלחמתן שקורים הילמ"ש [זבחים פח:]. והוא חגור. חגורה חדשה ושמעתי שאותו היום נתחנך ללבוש כלי מלחמה ודרך המתמנים לעשות נצחון וגבורה ביום חינוכם לקנות שם לכך ויאמר להכות את דוד [ש"ב שם]. על עסקי נוב. שבא עליו על עונשו של שאול כמו שפירשו רבותינו שאמר לו הקב"ה על ידך נטרד דואג האדומי על ידך נהרג שאול ובניו כו' [תהלים ז, א]. פתק ביה. זרק בו [שבועות יח:]. פניא. לפנות ערב [תענית כג:]. חייף רישיה. חופף ראשו [לקמן קיא.]. ליונה אימתילא. כיונה נמשלה [גיטין מה.]. שהיא נמשלת ליונה והמצות ככנפים [שבת מט.]. כנפי יונה. זאת יונתי כנסייתי כנפיה נחפה בכסף ומהו הכסף והחרוץ בפרש שדי וגו' כשפירש הקב"ה לפניהם תורתו אשר המלכים נשלגים ומתלבנים בה בארץ ללמות וחשך אז נחפו כנפיה (כנפי יונה) בכספה ותמדתה של תורה ומצות [תהלים סח, יד]. סייע בהדן. והפך דוד את תפלתו והתפלל שלא יפול בידי אויב [ש"ב שם, יח]. ויעזור לו. שעזרו בתפלה [שם ז, א]. ואבוא היום. היום יצאתי והיום באתי מכאן שקפצה לו הארץ [בראשית כד, מב].

מסורת הש"ס

א) נ"א דאתיתו מאורחא, ב) [ילקוט ישעיה סי' י' איתא קלא בנוסחא אחרת ועי' עוד בערוך ערך גלמהרג], ג) [עי' בערוך ערך שכר בזאי פי' יפה באריכות], ד) נ"א סדייא, ה) [ברכות נג: שבת מט. קלא. גיטין מה.], ו) לעיל כב., ז) ברכות ה., ח) רש"ל מ"ז, ט) גורות. רש"ל.

גליון הש"ס

גמ' אמר כנ"י ליונה אימתלי. עיין נ"י סוף פרק ד' מיתות:

תורה אור השלם

א) צַהֲלִי קוֹלֵךְ בַּת גַּלִּים הַקְשִׁיבִי לַיְשָׁה עֲנִיָּה עֲנָתוֹת: [ישעיה י, ל]

ב) דִּבְרֵי יִרְמְיָהוּ בֶּן חִלְקִיָּהוּ מִן הַכֹּהֲנִים אֲשֶׁר בַּעֲנָתוֹת בְּאֶרֶץ בִּנְיָמִן: [ירמיה א, א]

ג) גּוּר אַרְיֵה יְהוּדָה מִטֶּרֶף בְּנִי עָלִיתָ כָּרַע רָבַץ כְּאַרְיֵה וּכְלָבִיא מִי יְקִימֶנּוּ: [בראשית מט, ט]

ד) וַיֵּרֶד שִׁמְשׁוֹן וְאָבִיו וְאִמּוֹ תִּמְנָתָה וַיָּבֹאוּ עַד כַּרְמֵי תִמְנָתָה וְהִנֵּה כְּפִיר אֲרָיוֹת שֹׁאֵג לִקְרָאתוֹ: [שופטים יד, ה]

ה) מַשָּׂא בַּהֲמוֹת נֶגֶב בְּאֶרֶץ צָרָה וְצוּקָה לָבִיא וָלַיִשׁ מֵהֶם אֶפְעֶה וְשָׂרָף מְעוֹפֵף יִשְׂאוּ עַל כֶּתֶף עֲיָרִים חֵילֵהֶם וְעַל דַּבֶּשֶׁת גְּמַלִּים אוֹצְרֹתָם עַל עַם לֹא יוֹעִילוּ: [ישעיה ל, ו]

ו) עַל שַׁחַל וָפֶתֶן תִּדְרֹךְ תִּרְמֹס כְּפִיר וְתַנִּין: [תהלים צא, יג]

ז) לֹא הִדְרִיכֻהוּ בְנֵי שָׁחַץ לֹא עָדָה עָלָיו שָׁחַל: [איוב כח, ח]

ח) עוֹד הַיּוֹם בְּנֹב לַעֲמֹד יְנֹפֵף יָדוֹ הַר בַּת צִיּוֹן גִּבְעַת יְרוּשָׁלָיִם: [ישעיה י, לב]

ט) וַיְהִי בַּלַּיְלָה הַהוּא וַיֵּצֵא מַלְאַךְ יְיָ וַיַּךְ בְּמַחֲנֵה אַשּׁוּר מֵאָה שְׁמוֹנִים וַחֲמִשָּׁה אָלֶף וַיַּשְׁכִּימוּ בַבֹּקֶר וְהִנֵּה כֻלָּם פְּגָרִים מֵתִים: [מלכים ב' יט, לה]

י) וְיִשְׁבִּי בְּנֹב אֲשֶׁר בִּילִידֵי הָרָפָה וּמִשְׁקַל קֵינוֹ שְׁלֹשׁ מֵאוֹת מִשְׁקַל נְחֹשֶׁת וְהוּא חָגוּר חֲדָשָׁה וַיֹּאמֶר לְהַכּוֹת אֶת דָּוִד: [שמואל ב' כא, טז]

כ) תַּרְחִיב צַעֲדִי תַחְתָּי וְלֹא מָעֲדוּ קַרְסֻלָּי: [תהלים יח, לז]

ל) אִם תִּשְׁכְּבוּן בֵּין שְׁפַתָּיִם כַּנְפֵי יוֹנָה נֶחְפָּה בַכֶּסֶף וְאֶבְרוֹתֶיהָ בִּירַקְרַק חָרוּץ: [תהלים סח, יד]

מ) וַיַּעֲזָר לוֹ אֲבִישַׁי בֶּן צְרוּיָה וַיַּךְ אֶת הַפְּלִשְׁתִּי וַיְמִיתֵהוּ אָז נִשְׁבְּעוּ אַנְשֵׁי דָוִד לוֹ לֵאמֹר לֹא תֵצֵא עוֹד אִתָּנוּ לַמִּלְחָמָה וְלֹא תְכַבֶּה אֶת נֵר יִשְׂרָאֵל: [שמואל ב' כא, יז]

נ) וָאָבֹא הַיּוֹם אֶל הָעָיִן וָאֹמַר יְיָ אֱלֹהֵי אֲדֹנִי אַבְרָהָם אִם יֶשְׁךָ נָּא מַצְלִיחַ דַּרְכִּי אֲשֶׁר אָנֹכִי הֹלֵךְ עָלֶיהָ: [בראשית כד, מב]

Avishai then rode on, and came within sight of Yishbi B'Nov. The Gemara continues:

כַּד חֲזְיֵיהּ יִשְׁבִּי בְּנוֹב – **When Yishbi B'Nov saw [Avishai]** approaching him, אָמַר הַשְׁתָּא הֲווּ בֵּי תְרֵין – **he said** to himself: **"Now there will be two** against **me,** וְקָטְלִין לִי – **and they will** overpower me and **kill me!"** He thus attempted to kill David before Avishai could reach them. פַּתְקֵיהּ לְדָוִד לְעֵילָא – **He tossed David up** into the air, וְדָץ לֵיהּ לְרוּמְחֵיהּ – **and planted his spear** in the ground below, אָמַר נִיפּוֹל עֲלַהּ וְנִקְטַל – and **declared: "[David] shall fall on [the spear] and be killed!"**[37] אָמַר אֲבִישַׁי שֵׁם – **Avishai,** seeing that David was about to be killed, **pronounced the Divine Name,** אוֹקְמֵיהּ לְדָוִד בֵּין שְׁמַיָּא לְאַרְעָא – **and David was** miraculously **suspended** in the air **between heaven and earth,** just above the spear.[38]

The Gemara interrupts its narrative with a question:

וְנֵימָא לֵיהּ אִיהוּ – **[David]** ***himself*** **should have pronounced [the Divine Name],** and thereby saved his own life! Why did Avishai have to do this for him?

The Gemara replies by quoting a popular saying:

אֵין חָבוּשׁ מוֹצִיא עַצְמוֹ מִבֵּית הָאֲסוּרִין – **A captive cannot release his own self from prison;**[39] i.e. since David was himself being threatened, he required the assistance of another person, Avishai, to be saved.

The story resumes:

אָמַר לֵיהּ – While David was suspended in mid-air, **[Avishai] said to him:** מַאי בָּעֵית הָכָא – **"What are you doing here?** How did you come to venture all alone in Philistine territory?" אָמַר לֵיהּ – **[David] replied to him:** הָכִי אָמַר לִי קוּדְשָׁא בְּרִיךְ הוּא וְהָכִי אַהֲדְרִי לֵיהּ – **"The Holy One, Blessed is He, said thus-and-thus to me, and I replied thus-and-thus to Him";** i.e. David recounted how he had chosen to fall to the enemy himself, rather than have his children pay for his sin. אָמַר לֵיהּ – **[Avishai]** then **said to [David]:** אַפֵּיךְ צְלוֹתֵיךְ – **"Reverse your prayer,** i.e. pray to God that you prefer your descendants to suffer instead of yourself, as the popular adage has it: בַּר בְּרָךְ קִירָא לִיזְבּוֹן וְאַתְּ לֹא תִּצְטַעַר – **'Let your grandson sell wax** [i.e. be a poor person], **as long as you do not suffer yourself.' "**[40]

David assented to Avishai's plea:

אָמַר לֵיהּ – **[David] responded to him:** אִי הָכִי סַיַּיע בַּהֲדָן – **"If so, help me** escape this threat!"[41] הַיְינוּ דִּכְתִיב ,,וַיַּעֲזָר־לוֹ אֲבִישַׁי בֶּן־צְרוּיָה" – Avishai then did as David asked, for **so it is written in Scripture:**[42] ***And Avishai the son of Tzeruiah helped [David],*** אָמַר רַב יְהוּדָה אָמַר רַב – and the meaning of this is as **Rav Yehudah said in the name of Rav:** שֶׁעֲזָרוֹ בִּתְפִלָּה – **That [Avishai] helped [David] by praying** for him.[43]

The Gemara continues:

אָמַר אֲבִישַׁי שֵׁם וְאַחְתֵיהּ – **Avishai** then **pronounced the Divine Name** a second time, **and** by doing so, **caused [David] to descend** back to the ground, safely out of Yishbi B'Nov's reach.[44] הֲוָה קָא רָדִיף בָּתְרַיְיהוּ – The two immediately fled, but **[Yishbi B'Nov] pursued them.** כִּי מָטָא קוּבִּי – **When [David and Avishai] reached Kubei,** a town that lay on the Philistine-Israelite border, they entertained the possibility of fighting against Yishbi; אָמְרֵי קוּם בֵּיהּ – that is, **they said [to each other]: "Let us take a stand against him!"**[45] כִּי מָטָא בֵּי תְרֵי אָמְרֵי – However, **when they reached** a place called **Bei Trei,** they realized this was futile and **said:** בִּתְרֵי גוּרְיָין קָטְלוּהָ לְאַרְיָא – **"Can two** [*trei*] **whelps kill a** full-grown **lion?** I.e. Yishbi B'Nov is so much stronger than we, that even our combined strength cannot defeat him!"

Having realized that they could not defeat Yishbi in direct combat, David and Avishai tried a different tactic:

אָמְרֵי לֵיהּ – **They said to [Yishbi B'Nov]:** זִיל אִשְׁתַּכַּח לְעָרְפָּה אִימֵּיךְ בְּקִיבְרָא – **"Go and find Orpah your mother in the grave;** we have killed her!" כִּי אַדְכְּרוּ לֵיהּ שְׁמָא דְאִימֵּיהּ – **When they mentioned his mother's name** and said that they had killed her, כָּחַשׁ חֵילֵיהּ – **his strength failed him,** וְקַטְלֵיהּ – **and they killed him.**

This concludes the story of David's miraculous escape from Yishbi. The Gemara now cites the conclusion of the verse in *II Samuel,* and relates it to the above story:

הַיְינוּ דִּכְתִיב – And **this** [i.e. David's narrow escape] explains **that which is written** next in Scripture: ,,אָז נִשְׁבְּעוּ אַנְשֵׁי־דָוִד לוֹ לֵאמֹר – ***Then David's [soldiers] swore to him saying,*** לֹא־תֵצֵא עוֹד אִתָּנוּ לַמִּלְחָמָה – ***"You must no longer go forth with us into battle,*** וְלֹא תְכַבֶּה אֶת־נֵר יִשְׂרָאֵל" – ***so that the light of Israel not be extinguished!"***[46]

Having related how Avishai miraculously traveled a great distance quickly, the Gemara presents a Baraisa that lists other persons for whom similar miracles were performed:

תָּנוּ רַבָּנָן – **The Rabbis taught in a Baraisa:** שְׁלֹשָׁה קָפְצָה לָהֶם הָאָרֶץ – There were THREE PERSONS FOR WHOM THE EARTH

NOTES

37. Yishbi could have killed David by simply stabbing him. Instead, however, he sought to demonstrate his strength to his fellow Philistines by throwing David high in the air and catching his falling body on a spear (*Yad Ramah*).

38. Throughout the Talmud, we find that when an exceedingly righteous person is in a state of mental devotion, and he pronounces the secret and holiest of God's appellations, he is often able to invoke supernatural powers. For more on this, see *Rabbeinu Bachya* to *Exodus* 2:12; see also *Einayim LaMishpat.*

39. [This saying expresses the idea that if one is locked inside a cell, he is not himself in a position to unlock the prison door; only another person on the other side of the wall can open the door from the outside. In our case, *Rashi* says that David, who had been hurled into the air, could not muster the sublime concentration of mind to pronounce the Divine Name and achieve the desired effect (cf. *Margaliyos HaYam* and *Yad David*).]

40. I.e. do not sacrifice the present for the sake of the future.

41. I.e. pray on my behalf that my original prayer indeed be reversed; that is, pray that I *not* be handed over to my enemies (*Rashi;* cf. *Yad Ramah*).

42. *II Samuel* 21:17.

43. I.e. Avishai helped David to pray for the reversal of his earlier acceptance of his doom (*Rashi*; cf. *Yad Ramah* who offers two other explanations).

44. [In the text that we have before us, Avishai pronounces God's name two distinct times – once to arrest David's fall, and then again to bring him safely to earth and out of Yishbi's reach. It appears from *Rashi's* comments (in ד״ה אין), however, that in his text of the Gemara, Avishai pronounced the Name only once (see also *Yad Ramah, Dikdukei Soferim, Rif* in *Ein Yaakov,* and *Margaliyos HaYam*). According to this second version, the ensuing discussion between Avishai and David would relate to further dangers David still faced.

45. The word קוּבִּי is seen as a contraction of קוּם בֵּיהּ, which means: "Let us rise up against him" (*Rashi*).

46. *II Samuel* 21:17. Having seen their king narrowly escape death at the hands of Yishbi, David's soldiers determined that he not expose himself to the enemy again. David's men referred to him as "the light of Israel" because of his great Torah knowledge [Torah is often referred to as light]. Alternatively, it was because as king he was the embodiment of the entire nation of Israel (*Maharsha*).

[The Biblical text itself is very brief on this entire episode involving David and Yishbi. *Maharal* suggests that while it is possible to take the episode literally, as an actual happening, it is more likely meant to be understood as an account of a spiritual battle between David and the forces of impurity, represented by the Philistines. For a complete exposition of the allegorical significance of the many details of this story, see *Maharal.*]

מסורת הש"ס

א) נ"א דאתיתו מאורחא, ב) [ילקוט ישעיה סי' י' איתא קלת בנוסחא אחרת ועי' עוד בערוך ערך גלמהרג], ג) [עי' בערוך ערך שכר בזאי פי' יפה באריכות], ד) נ"א סדריא, ה) [ברכות נג: שבת מט. קלא. גיטין מה.], ו) לעיל כב., ז) ברכות ה., ח) רש"ל מ"ז, ט) בורות. רש"ל.

גליון הש"ס

גמ' אמר כנ"י ליונה אימתלי. עיין נ"י סוף פרק ד' מיתות.

תורה אור השלם

א) צַהֲלִי קוֹלֵךְ בַּת גַּלִּים הַקְשִׁיבִי לַיְשָׁה עֲנִיָּה עֲנָתוֹת: [ישעיה י, ל]

ב) דִּבְרֵי יִרְמְיָהוּ בֶּן חִלְקִיָּהוּ מִן הַכֹּהֲנִים אֲשֶׁר בַּעֲנָתוֹת בְּאֶרֶץ בִּנְיָמִן: [ירמיה א, א]

ג) גּוּר אַרְיֵה יְהוּדָה מִטֶּרֶף בְּנִי עָלִיתָ כָּרַע רָבַץ כְּאַרְיֵה וּכְלָבִיא מִי יְקִימֶנּוּ: [בראשית מט, ט]

ד) וַיֵּרֶד שִׁמְשׁוֹן וְאָבִיו וְאִמּוֹ תִּמְנָתָה וַיָּבֹאוּ עַד כַּרְמֵי תִמְנָתָה וְהִנֵּה כְּפִיר אֲרָיוֹת שֹׁאֵג לִקְרָאתוֹ: [שופטים יד, ה]

ה) מַשָּׂא בַּהֲמוֹת נֶגֶב בְּאֶרֶץ צָרָה וְצוּקָה לָבִיא וָלַיִשׁ מֵהֶם אֶפְעֶה וְשָׂרָף מְעוֹפֵף יִשְׂאוּ עַל כֶּתֶף עֲיָרִים חֵילֵיהֶם וְעַל דַּבֶּשֶׁת גְּמַלִּים אוֹצְרֹתָם עַל עַם לֹא יוֹעִילוּ: [ישעיה ל, ו]

ו) עַל שַׁחַל וָפֶתֶן תִּדְרֹךְ תִּרְמֹס כְּפִיר וְתַנִּין: [תהלים צא, יג]

ז) לֹא הִדְרִיכֻהוּ בְנֵי שָׁחַץ לֹא עָדָה עָלָיו שָׁחַל: [איוב כח, ח]

ח) עוֹד הַיּוֹם בְּנֹב לַעֲמֹד יְנֹפֵף יָדוֹ הַר בַּת צִיּוֹן גִּבְעַת יְרוּשָׁלָיִם: [ישעיה י, לב]

ט) וַיְהִי בַּלַּיְלָה הַהוּא וַיֵּצֵא מַלְאַךְ יְיָ וַיַּךְ בְּמַחֲנֵה אַשּׁוּר מֵאָה שְׁמוֹנִים וַחֲמִשָּׁה אָלֶף וַיַּשְׁכִּימוּ בַבֹּקֶר וְהִנֵּה כֻלָּם פְּגָרִים מֵתִים: [מלכים ב' יט, לה]

י) וְיִשְׁבִּי בְּנֹב אֲשֶׁר בִּילִידֵי הָרָפָה וּמִשְׁקַל קֵינוֹ שְׁלֹשׁ מֵאוֹת מִשְׁקַל נְחֹשֶׁת וְהוּא חָגוּר חֲדָשָׁה וַיֹּאמֶר לְהַכּוֹת אֶת דָּוִד: [שמואל ב' כא, טז]

כ) תַּרְחִיב צַעֲדִי תַחְתָּי וְלֹא מָעֲדוּ קַרְסֻלָּי: [תהלים יח, לז]

ל) אִם תִּשְׁכְּבוּן בֵּין שְׁפַתָּיִם כַּנְפֵי יוֹנָה נֶחְפָּה בַכֶּסֶף וְאֶבְרוֹתֶיהָ בִּירַקְרַק חָרוּץ: [תהלים סח, יד]

מ) וַיַּעֲזָר לוֹ אֲבִישַׁי בֶּן צְרוּיָה וַיַּךְ אֶת הַפְּלִשְׁתִּי וַיְמִיתֵהוּ אָז נִשְׁבְּעוּ אַנְשֵׁי דָוִד לוֹ לֵאמֹר לֹא תֵצֵא עוֹד אִתָּנוּ לַמִּלְחָמָה וְלֹא תְכַבֶּה אֶת נֵר יִשְׂרָאֵל: [שמואל ב' כא, יז]

נ) וָאָבֹא הַיּוֹם אֶל הָעָיִן וָאֹמַר יְיָ אֱלֹהֵי אֲדֹנִי אַבְרָהָם אִם יֶשְׁךָ נָּא מַצְלִיחַ דַּרְכִּי אֲשֶׁר אָנֹכִי הֹלֵךְ עָלֶיהָ: [בראשית כד, מב]

א) עניה ענתות עתיד ירמיה בן חלקיה ומתנבא עלה מענתות דכתיב ב) דברי ירמיהו בן חלקיהו מן הכהנים אשר בענתות בארץ בנימין מי דמי התם ארי הכא ליש אמר רבי יוחנן ששה שמות יש לארי אלו הן ג) ארי ד) כפיר ג) לביא ה) ליש ו) שחל ז) שחץ אי הכי בצרו להו עברו מעברה תרתי נינהו מאי ח) עוד היום בנוב לעמוד אמר רב הונא אותו היום נשתייר מעונה של נוב אמרי ליה כלדאי אי אזלת האידנא יכלת לה ואי לא לא יכלת לה אורחא דבעא לסגויי בעשרה יומא סגא בחד יומא כי מטו לירושלם שדי ליה ביסתרקי עד דסליק ויתיב מעילוי שורה עד דחזיוה לכולה ירושלם כי חזייה איזוטר בעיניה אמר הלא דא היא קרתא דירושלם דעלה ארגישית כל משיריתי ועלה כבשית כל מדינתא הלא היא זעירא וחלשא מכל כרכי עממיא דכבשית בתקוף ידי עלה וקם ומניד ברישיה מוביל ומייתי בידיה על טור בית מקדשא דבציון ועל עזרתא דבירושלם אמרי נישדי ביה ידא האידנא אמר להו תמהיתו א) למחר אייתי לי כל חד וחד מינייכו ב) גולמו הרג מיניה מיד ט) ויהי בלילה ההוא ויצא מלאך ה' ויך במחנה אשור מאה ושמונים וחמשה אלף וישכימו בבקר והנה כלם פגרים מתים אמר רב פפא היינו דאמרי אינשי בת דינא בטל דינא י) וישבי בנוב אשר בילידי הרפה ומשקל קינו שלש מאות משקל נחשת והוא חגור חדשה ויאמר להכות את דוד מאי וישבי בנוב אמר רב יהודה אמר רב איש שבא על עסקי נוב א"ל הקב"ה לדוד עד מתי יהיה עון זה טמון בידך על ידך נהרגה נוב עיר הכהנים ועל ידך נטרד דואג האדומי ועל ידך נהרגו שאול ושלשת בניו רצונך יכלו זרעך או תמסר ביד אויב אמר לפניו רבונו של עולם מוטב אמסר ביד אויב ולא יכלה זרעי יומא חד נפק ג) לשכור בזאי אתא שטן ואדמי ליה כטביא פתק ביה גירא ולא מטייה משכיה עד דאמטייה לארץ פלשתים כדחזייה ישבי בנוב אמר היינו האי דקטליה לגלית אחי כפתיה קמטיה אותביה ושדייה תותי בי ד) בדייא אתעביד ליה ניסא מכא ליה ארעא מתותיה היינו דכתיב כ) תרחיב צעדי תחתי ולא מעדו קרסולי ההוא יומא אפניא דמעלי שבתא הוה אבישי בן צרויה קא חייף רישיה בד' גרבי דמיא חזינהו כתמי דמא איכא דאמרי אתא יונה איטריף קמיה ° אמר ה) כנסת ישראל ליונה אימתילא שנאמר ל) כנפי יונה נחפה בכסף שמע מינה דוד מלכא דישראל בצערא שרי אתא לביתיה ולא אשכחיה אמר ו) תנן אין רוכבין על סוסו ואין יושבין על כסאו ואין משתמשין בשרביטו בשעת הסכנה מאי אתא שאיל בי מדרשא אמרו ליה בשעת הסכנה שפיר דמי רכביה לפרדיה וקם ואזל קפצה ליה ארעא בהדי דקא מסגי חזייה לערפה אמיה דהוות נוולא כי חזיתיה פסקתה לפילכה שדתיה עילויה סברא למקטליה אמרה ליה עלם אייתי לי פלך פתקיה ברישׁ מוחה וקטלה כד חזייה ישבי בנוב אמר השתא הוו בי תרין וקטלין לי פתקיה לדוד לעילא ודץ ליה לרומחיה אמר ניפול עלה ונקטל אמר אבישי שם אוקמיה לדוד בין שמיא לארעא ז) ונימא ליה איהו אין חבוש מוציא עצמו מבית האסורין א"ל מאי בעית הכא א"ל הכי אמר לי קודשא בריך הוא והכי אהדרי ליה א"ל אפיך צלותיך בר ברך קירא ליזבון ואת לא תצטער א"ל אי הכי סייע בהדן היינו דכתיב מ) ויעזור לו אבישי בן צרויה אמר רב יהודה אמר רב שעזרו בתפלה אמר אבישי שם ואחתיה הוה קא רדיף בתרייהו כי מטא קובי אמרי קום ביה כי מטא בי תרי אמרי בתרי גוריין קטלוה לאריא אמרי ליה זיל אשתכח לערפה אימיך בקיברא כי אדכרו ליה שמא דאימיה כחש חיליה וקטליה היינו דכתיב מ) אז נשבעו אנשי דוד לו לאמר לא תצא עוד אתנו למלחמה ולא תכבה את נר ישראל ת"ר שלשה קפצה להם הארץ אליעזר עבד אברהם ויעקב אבינו ואבישי בן צרויה הא דאמרן אליעזר עבד אברהם דכתיב נ) ואבוא היום אל העין למימרא דההוא יומא נפק יעקב אבינו

דכתיב

ענוה ענתות. כמו עניה כלומר נביאות ירמיה הענתותי היא שעתידה לבא על נבוכד נצר שתמסר ירושלים בידו: **ארי כפיר וכו'.** ובדוכתא אחריתי מפורש למה נקראו לו כל השמות הללו: **אי הכי.** דכולי קרא צהלי קולך לא מחושבנא הוא א"כ ליכא אלא תשע מסעות דהא עוד היום לאו מחושבנא [נמי הוא] ומתרץ עברו מעברה תרתי אינון עברו חד מעברה חד ואיכא עשר מסעות: **אותו היום נשתייר מעונה של נוב.** [דמפני עון] שהיה להם לישראל על שנהרגו כהני נוב קבע הקב"ה העונש עד אותו היום ואותו יום בלבד נשתייר מזמן העונש ואילו היה נלחם בירושלים באותו היום היה כובשה והכי משמע קרא עוד היום אותו יום העמידו לסנחריב על ירושלים בעון נוב: **סגא בחד יומא.** והיינו י' מסעות שנסע אותו היום: **שדו ליה.** לסנחריב: **בסתרקי.** תחתיו טפי"ט בלע"ז עד שראה ירושלים כולה: **עלה וקם ומניד ברישיה.** עליה עמד והיה מניד בראשו: **נשדי ביה ידא האידנא.** נלחם בה עתה: **תמהיתו.** תמה הוא להתחיל היום משום חולשא דאורחא ל"א תמהיתו נתיגעתם ודומה ליה ח) (בסנחריב) איתמה למיתב: **גולמו הרג.** חתיכה של חומה לשון פרסי אבן רעועה מן החומה ונבקעה: **בת דינא בטל דינא.** כיון שלן דינא בטל הריב וכן מפני שלא נכבשה בו ביום לא הצליח ממחרת: **וישבי בנוב.** איידי דאיירי לעיל באותו יום שנשתייר מעונה של נוב נקט הכא וישבי בנוב שבא על עסקי נוב: **הרפה.** היינו ערפה: **משקל קינו.** מתרגמינן מתקל סופיניה: **והוא חגור חדשה.** והוא אסיר איספניקי חדתא: **נטרד דואג האדומי.** שספר לשון הרע על דוד שנתקנא בו שאול ולפי שקבל אחימלך את דוד בנוב אמר ליה שאול סוב ופגע בכהני ה' נמלא שעל ידך נהרגו ואתה נכשל ובחטא זה נהרג שאול ושלשת בניו במלחמת פלשתים: **שכר ביזאי.** לשון פרסי קריטא ל"א כפר היא: **קמטיה.** הכניעו תחת הבד של זיתים ויתיב עלה למעכו: **מכא ליה ארעא מתותיה.** נתרככה הארץ מתחתיו ולא הזיקו ל"א מכא נשפלת כעין גומא והיתה מגינה עליו: **בארבע גריבי דמיא.** בארבע סאין של מים ל"א בארבע כורא דמיא בד' ט) נודות של מים: **איטריף קמיה.** היתה טורפת ומחבטת עצמה וממרטת כנפיה והומה ומצערת: **קפצה ליה ארעא.** כמו לא תקפוץ (דברים טו) נתקצרה הארץ והגיע מהרה לארץ פלשתים: **לערפה אימיה.** דישבי: **נוולה.** טווה: **כד חזיתיה.** ערפה לאבישי סברה למקטליה באותו פלך שהיה בידה ולא נגע בו: **אמרה ליה.** לאבישי אייתי לן ההוא פלך דנפל לפניך: ה"ג **פתקיה בריש מוחה וקטלה.** השליך אבישי הפלך לראשה ומתה: **פתקיה לדוד לעילא.** זרקו כלפי מעלה: **ודץ ליה.** נעץ תחתיו חניתו בקרקע כדי שיפול עליו וימות: **ונימא איהו.** דוד עצמו לימא שם: **אין חבוש.** אין דעתו מכוונת לומר השם והשתא ניצל דוד והשליכו השם ברחוק והלכו אבישי ודוד וחזרו להם: **אמר ליה.** אבישי לדוד: **ומאי בעית הכא.** למה באת כאן: **אמר ליה.** הקב"ה אמר לי רצונך שיכלה זרעך או תמסר ביד אויביך והכי אהדרי ליה מוטב שאפול ביד אויב: **אמר ליה אפיך צלותיך.** הפוך תפלתך ואמור לפניו מוטב יכלה זרעך ולא תמסר ביד אויב דמה לך בצער בניך: **בר ברך קירא לזבון ואת לא תצטער.** משל הוא שאומרים בני אדם: **סייע בהדן.** עזור בתפלתך להפכה: **והוה קא רדיף בתרייהו.** והם בורחין שהיה קרוב לארץ פלשתים: **וכי מטו קובי.** לאותו כפר ששמו קובי שבין א"י לארץ פלשתים: **אמרי קום ביה.** אמרו זה לזה עמוד כנגדו ואל תברח ונכנו ולכך נקרא קובי אינהו הוו בקיאי בשמות הכפרים ועדיין היו מפחדין ובורחין: **כי מטא בי תרי.** שם מקום: **אמרו בין תרי גוריין.** בתמיהא: **בקברא.** שהרגנוה: ויצא

ליקוטי רש"י

דאמר רב פפא. במסכת גיטין (לח.). **עמון ומואב טהרו בסיחון.** ע"י סיחון טהרו ארצם לישראל במואב כתיב (במדבר כא) והוא נלחם וגו' ובעמון מפורש בנחלת בני גד בספר יהושע (יג) ויהי להם הגבול יעזר וכל ארץ הגלעד וחצי (ארץ) [ערי] בני עמון וקא חשיב ואזיל וכתיב בסיפיה יתר ממלכות סיחון אלמא סיחון כבש לארץ בני עמון ועוד מלינו במלך בני עמון שאמר למלאכי יפתח (שופטים יא) כי לקח ישראל את ארצי מארנון ועד היבוק אלמא ארץ בני עמון הוא והם מסיחון כבשוה דכתיב בו וירשו את ארצו מארנון ועד היבוק אבל מהנשאר בידם לא לקחו כלום [חולין ס:]. דכתיב (דברים ב) אל תצר את מואב וכן בבני עמון אל תגורם (שם) וכתיב (במדבר כא) כי חשבון עיר סיחון וגו' אלמא טהר מואב בסיחון ובני עמון אשכחן ביפתח (שופטים יא) שאמרו לו מלאכי בני עמון כי לקח ישראל את ארצי בעלותו ממצרים מארנון ועד היבוק ואשכחן כשכבשו את ארץ סיחון ויירש את ארצו מארנון עד יבוק וגו' אלמא מבני עמון כבשה והדור ישראל וכבשו מיניה וטהרה להם על ידו אלמא קנייה בחזקה [גיטין לח.]. **בא על עית.** מונה והולך מסעות שנסע סנחריב ובא על ערי יהודה לבא לירושלים ביום מפלתו [ישעיה י, כח]. **לנו.** לשון לינה. **נסה.** ברחה ברחו כולן מפני חיילותיו [שם, כט]. **צהלי קולך.** להזהיר לעם. **הקשיבי לישה.** את קול השופר וברחו לכם וכן עניה ענתות [שם, ל]. **העיזו.** נאספו לברוח [שם, לא] **עוד היום בנוב לעמוד.** כל הדרך הזה נתלבט כדי לעמוד בעוד היום בנוב לפי שאמרו לו איצטגניניו אם תלח' בה היום תכבשנ' וכשעמד בנוב וראה את ירושלים קטנה לא חש לדברי איצטגניניו והתחיל להניף ידו בגאו' וכי על עיר זו הרגזתי כל החיילות הללו לינו פה הלילה ולמחר ישליך בה איש אבנו. **הר בת ציון.** להר בת ציון [שם, לב]. **עלה אריה.** נבוכדנצר. **מסובכו.** דרך אריה לישב במארב סבכי היער אשפיישי"ש בלע"ז [ירמיה ד, ז].

[ע"כ שייך לדף צד:].

כפיר. כל כפיר שבמקרא ארי בחור וגבור [יחזקאל יט, ה]. הארי גדול והשחל בינוני והכפיר קטן [איוב ד, י]. **עוד היום בנוב לעמוד.** כל הדרך הזה נתלבט כדי לעמוד בעוד היום בנוב לפי שאמרו לו איצטגניניו אם תלח' בה היום תכבשנ' וכשעמד בנוב וראה את ירושלים קטנה לא חש לדברי איצטגניניו והתחיל להניף ידו בגאו' וכי על עיר זו הרגזתי כל החיילות הללו לינו פה הלילה ולמחר ישליך בה איש אבנו [ישעיה י, לב]. **ויהי בלילה ההוא.** כששב סנחריב מעל כוש ובא עד נוב שהיתה סמוכה לירושלים. **מאה ושמונים וחמשה אלף.** כולם ראשי גייסות [מ"ב יט, לה]. **בילידי הרפה.** כתיב ערפה שם האחת ערפה (רות א) וכתיב הרפה אשר בילידי הרפה והיא ערפה כדאמרי' לקמן שנגזר עליה שיפלו בניה בחרב ביד בני רות שדבקה בשכינה [סוטה מב:]. **ומשקל קינו.** הוא כמו תיק שכתב בית יד הרומח שקורין ארישטויי"ל בלע"ז ועשוי ככובע, ויש דוגמתו בזכוכית [פח:] כמו המעיל למה שם לזומין כמין קולסות שבראשי התיתוקות קולסות היימלמש בלע"ז [ש"ב כא, טז]. **קונאות.** בוטונ"ש עשויין כמין תיק של נחשת שעושין [בסוף] בית יד הרומח שקורין ארישטויי"ל לשון (ש"ב כא) ומשקל קינו לישבי בנוב והתיוקות תולין אותו בראשי כובעי נגרים שעושין אותו למלחמתן שקורים הילמ"ש [זבחים פח:]. **והוא חגור.** חגורה חדשה ושמעתי שאותו היום נתחנך ללבוש כלי מלחמה ודרך הממונים לעשות גלמון וגבורה ביום חינוכם לקנות שם לכך ויאמר להכות את דוד [ש"ב שם]. **על עסקי נוב.** שבא עליו על עונשו של שאול כמו שפירשו רבותינו שאמר לו הקב"ה על ידך נטרד דואג האדומי על ידך נהרג שאול ובניו כו' [תהלים ז, א]. **פתק ביה.** זרק בו [שבועות יח:]. **פניא.** לפנות ערב [תענית כג:]. **חייף רישיה.** חופף ראשו [לקמן קיא.]. **ליונה אימתילא.** כיונה נמשלה [גיטין מה.]. שהיא נמשלת ליונה והמצות ככנפים [שבת מט.]. **כנפי יונה.** זאת יונתי כנסייתי כנפיה נחפה בכסף ומהו הכסף והחרוץ בפרש שדי וגו' כשפירש הקב"ה לפניהם תורתו אשר המלכים נשלגים ומתלבנים בה בארץ צלמות וחשך אז נחפו כנפיה (כנפי יונה) בכספה וחמדתה של תורה ומצות [תהלים סח, יד]. **סייע בהדן.** והפך דוד את תפלתו והתפלל שלא יפול בידי אויב [ש"ב שם, יח]. **ויעזור לו.** שעזרו בתפלה [שם ז, א]. **ואבוא היום.** היום יצאתי והיום באתי מכאן שקפצה לו הארץ [בראשית כד, מב].

CONTRACTED to facilitate their quick journey from place to place.[47] These were: אֱלִיעֶזֶר עֶבֶד אַבְרָהָם – ELIEZER, THE SERVANT OF ABRAHAM, וְיַעֲקֹב אָבִינוּ – OUR PATRIARCH JACOB, וַאֲבִישַׁי בֶּן צְרוּיָה – AND AVISHAI THE SON OF TZERUIAH.

The Gemara now elaborates on each of these miracles:

אֲבִישַׁי בֶּן צְרוּיָה הָא דַּאֲמָרָן – In the case of **Avishai ben Tzeruiah,** we know that the earth contracted for him in the episode **we just related.** אֱלִיעֶזֶר עֶבֶד אַבְרָהָם דִּכְתִיב – As for **Eliezer, the servant of Abraham,** the fact that the earth contracted for him can be demonstrated from Scripture, **for it is written:**[48] "וָאָבֹא הַיּוֹם אֶל־הָעָיִן" – ***I came today to the spring,*** לְמֵימְרָא דְּהַהוּא יוֹמָא נְפַק – **which implies that he had departed** Canaan and arrived in Aram **that very** same **day.**[49]

יַעֲקֹב אָבִינוּ – That the earth contracted for **the Patriarch Jacob** can also be seen from Scripture,

NOTES

47. See above, note 34. [Actually we find other instances in which the earth contracted as well. See *Rashi* to *Bamidbar* 13:25; *Margaliyos HaYam* and *Maharal.*]

48. *Genesis* 24:42.

49. Abraham had sent Eliezer on a mission to Aram Naharaim, Abraham's birthplace, to seek a wife for Abraham's son, Isaac. Now, Aram Naharaim was far away from Abraham's residence in Canaan. Nevertheless, when Eliezer arrived in Aram and recounted his mission to the family of Rebecca, he said: *I came today to the spring,* words which imply that the very day Abraham had sent him, Eliezer arrived in Aram. The Tanna thus inferred that Eliezer must have merited to have the earth contract for him, for otherwise, he could not have made such a journey in a single day.

א) עניה ענתות עתיד ירמיה בן חלקיה ומתנבא עלה מענתות דכתיב ב) דברי ירמיהו בן חלקיהו מן הכהנים אשר בענתות בארץ בנימין מי דמי התם ארי הכא ליש אמר רבי יוחנן ששה שמות יש לארי אלו הן ג) ארי ד) כפיר ג) לביא ה) ליש ו) שחל ז) שחץ אי הכי בצרו להו עברו מעברה תרתי נינהו מאי ח) עוד היום בנוב לעמוד אמר רב הונא אותו היום נשתייר מעונה של נוב אמרי ליה כלדאי אי אזלת האידנא יכלת לה ואי לא לא יכלת לה אורחא דבעא לסגויי בעשרה יומא סגא בחד יומא כי מטו לירושלם שדי ליה ביסתרקי עד דסליק ויתיב מעילוי שורה עד דחזיוה לכולה ירושלם כי חזייה איזוטר בעיניה אמר הלא דא היא קרתא דירושלם דעלה ארגישית כל משיריתי ועלה כבשית כל מדינתא הלא היא זעירא וחלשא מכל כרכי עממיא דכבשית בתקוף ידי עלה וקם ומניד ברישיה מוביל ומייתי בידיה על טור בית מקדשא דבציון ועל עזרתא דבירושלם אמרי נישדי ביה ידא האידנא אמר להו תמהיתו למחר אייתי לי כל חד וחד מינייכו גולמו הרג מיניה מיד ט) ויהי בלילה ההוא ויצא מלאך ה' ויך במחנה אשור מאה ושמונים וחמשה אלף וישכימו בבקר והנה כלם פגרים מתים אמר רב פפא היינו דאמרי אינשי בת דינא בטל דינא י) וישבי בנוב אשר בילידי הרפה ומשקל קינו שלש מאות משקל נחשת והוא חגור חדשה ויאמר להכות את דוד מאי וישבי בנוב אמר רב יהודה אמר רב איש שבא על עסקי נוב א"ל הקב"ה לדוד עד מתי יהיה עון זה טמון בידך על ידך נהרגה נוב עיר הכהנים ועל ידך נטרד דואג האדומי ועל ידך נהרגו שאול ושלשת בניו רצונך יכלו זרעך או תמסר ביד אויב אמר לפניו רבונו של עולם מוטב אמסר ביד אויב ולא יכלה זרעי יומא חד נפק לשכור בזאי אתא שטן ואדמי ליה כטביא פתק ביה גירא ולא מטייה משכיה עד דאמטיה לארץ פלשתים כדחזייה ישבי בנוב אמר היינו האי דקטליה לגלית אחי כפתיה קמטיה אותביה ושדייה תותי בי בדייא אתעביד ליה ניסא מכא ליה ארעא מתותיה היינו דכתיב כ) תרחיב צעדי תחתי ולא מעדו קרסולי ההוא יומא אפניא דמעלי שבתא הוה אבישי בן צרויה הוה קא חייף רישיה בד' גרבי דמיא חזינהו כתמי דמא איכא דאמרי אתא יונה איטריף קמיה אמר כנסת ישראל ליונה אימתילא שנאמר ל) כנפי יונה נחפה בכסף שמע מינה דוד מלכא דישראל בצערא שרי אתא לביתיה ולא אשכחיה אמר תנן אין רוכבין על סוסו ואין יושבין על כסאו ואין משתמשין בשרביטו בשעת הסכנה מאי אתא שאיל בי מדרשא אמרו ליה בשעת הסכנה שפיר דמי רכביה לפרדיה וקם ואזל קפצה ליה ארעא בהדי דקא מסגי חזייה לערפה אמיה דהוות נוולא כי חזיתיה פסקתה לפילכה שדתיה עילויה סברא למקטליה אמרה ליה עלם אייתי לי פלך פתקיה בריש מוחה וקטלה כד חזייה ישבי בנוב אמר השתא הוו בי תרין וקטלין לי פתקיה לדוד לעילא ודץ ליה לרומחיה אמר ניפול עלה ונקטל אמר אבישי שם אוקמיה לדוד בין שמיא לארעא ונימא ליה איהו אין חבוש מוציא עצמו מבית האסורין א"ל מאי בעית הכא א"ל הכי אמר לי קודשא בריך הוא והכי אהדרי ליה א"ל אפיך צלותיך בר ברך קירא ליזבון ואת לא תצטער א"ל אי הכי סייע בהדן היינו דכתיב מ) ויעזור לו אבישי בן צרויה אמר רב יהודה אמר רב שעזרו בתפלה אמר אבישי שם ואחתיה הוה קא רדיף בתרייהו כי מטא קובי אמרי קום ביה כי מטא בי תרי אמרי בתרי גוריין קטלוה לאריא אמרי ליה זיל אשתכח לערפה אימיך בקיברא כי אדכרו ליה שמא דאימיה כחש חיליה וקטליה היינו דכתיב מ) אז נשבעו אנשי דוד לו לאמר לא תצא עוד אתנו למלחמה ולא תכבה את נר ישראל ת"ר שלשה קפצה להם הארץ אליעזר עבד אברהם ויעקב אבינו ואבישי בן צרויה הא דאמרן אליעזר עבד אברהם דכתיב נ) ואבוא היום אל העין למימרא דההוא יומא נפק יעקב אבינו דכתיב

רש"י

עניה ענתות. כמו עניה כלומר נביאות ירמיה הענתותי היא שעתידה לבא על נבוכד נצר שתמסר ירושלים בידו: ארי כפיר וכו'. ובדוכתא אחריתי מפורש למה נקראו לו כל השמות הללו: אי הכי. דכולי קרא צהלי קולך לא מחושבנא הוא א"כ ליכא אלא תשע מסעות דהא עוד היום לאו מחושבנא [נמי הוא] ומתרץ עברו מעברה תרתי אינון עברו חד מעברה חד ואיכא עשר מסעות: אותו היום נשתייר מעונה של נוב. [דמפני עון] שהיה להם לישראל על שנהרגו כהני נוב קבע הקב"ה העונש עד אותו היום ואותו יום בלבד נשתייר מזמן העונש ואילו היה נלחם בירושלים באותו היום היה כובשה והכי משמע קרא עוד היום אותו יום העמידו לסנחריב על ירושלים בעון נוב: סגא בחד יומא. והיינו י' מסעות שנסע אותו היום: שדו ליה. לסנחריב: בסתרקי. תחתיו טפי"ט בלע"ז עד שראה ירושלים כולה: עלה וקם ומניד ברישיה. עליה עמד והיה מניד בראשו: נשדי ביה ידא האידנא. נלחם בה עתה: תמהיתו. תמה הוא להתחיל היום משום חולשא דאורחא ל"א תמהיתו נתיגעתם ודומה ליה ח) (בסנחריב) איתמה למיתב: גולמו הרג. חתיכה של חומה לשון פרסי אבן רעועה מן החומה ונבקעה: בת דינא בטל דינא. כיון שלן דינא בטל הריב וכן מפני שלא נכבשה בו ביום לא הצליח ממחרת: וישבי בנוב. איידי דאיירי לעיל באותו יום שנשתייר מעונה של נוב נקט הכא וישבי בנוב שבא על עסקי נוב: הרפה. היינו ערפה: משקל קינו. מתרגמינן מתקל סופיניה: והוא חגור חדשה. והוא אסיר איספניקי חדתא: נטרד דואג האדומי. שספר לשון הרע על דוד שנתקנא בו שאול ולפי שקבל אחימלך את דוד בנוב אמר ליה שאול סוב ופגע בכהני ה' נמצא שעל ידך נהרגו ואתה נכשל ובחטא זה נהרג שאול ושלשת בניו במלחמת פלשתים: שכר ביזאי. לשון פרסי קריטה ל"א כפר היא: קמטיה. הכניעו תחת הבד של זיתים ויתיב עלה למעכו: מכא ליה ארעא מתותיה. נתרככה הארץ מתחתיו ולא הזיקו ל"א מכא נשפלת כעין גומא והיתה מגינה עליו: בארבע גריבי דמיא. בארבע סאין של מים ל"א בארבע כורא דמיא בד' ט) נודות של מים: איטריף קמיה. היתה טורפת ומחבטת עצמה וממרטת כנפיה והומה ומצערת: קפצה ליה ארעא. כמו לא תקפוץ (דברים טו) נתקצרה הארץ והגיע מהרה לארץ פלשתים: לערפה אימיה. דישבי: נוולה. טווה: כד חזיתיה. ערפה לאבישי סברה למקטליה באותו פלך שהיה בידה ולא נגע בו: אמרה ליה. לאבישי אייתי לן ההוא פלך דנפל לפניך: ה"ג פתקיה בריש מוחה וקטלה. השליך אבישי הפלך לראשה ומתה: פתקיה לדוד לעילא. זרקו כלפי מעלה: ודץ ליה. נעץ תחתיו חניתו בקרקע כדי שיפול עליו וימות: ונימא איהו. דוד עצמו לימא שם: אין חבוש. אין דעתו מכוונת לומר השם והשתא ניצל דוד והשליכו השם ברחוק והלכו אבישי ודוד וחזרו להם: אמר ליה. אבישי לדוד: ומאי בעית הכא. למה באת כאן: אמר ליה. הקב"ה אמר לי רצונך שיכלה זרעך או תמסר ביד אויביך והכי אהדרי ליה מוטב שאפול ביד אויב: אמר ליה אפיך צלותיך. הפוך תפלתך ואמור לפניו מוטב יכלה זרעך ולא תמסר ביד אויב דמה לך בצער בניך: בר ברך קירא לזבון ואת לא תצטער. משל הוא שאומרים בני אדם: סייע בהדן. עזור בתפלתך להפכה: והוה קא רדיף בתרייהו. והם בורחין שהיה קרוב לארץ פלשתים: וכי מטו קובי. לאותו כפר ששמו קובי שבין א"י לארץ פלשתים: אמרי קום ביה. אמרו זה לזה עמוד כנגדו ואל תברח וכנו ולכך נקרא קובי אינהו הוו בקיאי בשמות הכפרים ועדיין היו מפחדין ובורחין: כי מטא בי תרי. שם מקום: אמרו בין תרי גורין. בתמיהא: בקברא. שהרגוה:

ויצא

מסורת הש"ס

א) נ"א דאתיתו מאורחא, ב) [ילקוט ישעיה סי' י' איתא קלת בנוסחא אחרת ועי' עוד בערוך ערך גלמהרג], ג) [עי' בערוך ערך שכר בזאי פי' יפה באריכות], ד) נ"א סדייא, ה) [ברכות נג: שבת מט. קלא. גיטין מה.], ו) לעיל כב., ז) ברכות ה., ח) רש"ל מ"ז, ט) בורות. רש"ל.

גליון הש"ס

גמ' אמר כנ"י ליונה אימתלי. עיין ג"י סוף פרק ד' מיתות:

תורה אור השלם

א) צַהֲלִי קוֹלֵךְ בַּת גַּלִּים הַקְשִׁיבִי לַיְשָׁה עֲנִיָּה עֲנָתוֹת: [ישעיה י, ל]

ב) דִּבְרֵי יִרְמְיָהוּ בֶּן חִלְקִיָּהוּ מִן הַכֹּהֲנִים אֲשֶׁר בַּעֲנָתוֹת בְּאֶרֶץ בִּנְיָמִן: [ירמיה א, א]

ג) גּוּר אַרְיֵה יְהוּדָה מִטֶּרֶף בְּנִי עָלִיתָ כָּרַע רָבַץ כְּאַרְיֵה וּכְלָבִיא מִי יְקִימֶנּוּ: [בראשית מט, ט]

ד) וַיֵּרֶד שִׁמְשׁוֹן וְאָבִיו וְאִמּוֹ תִּמְנָתָה וַיָּבֹאוּ עַד כַּרְמֵי תִמְנָתָה וְהִנֵּה כְּפִיר אֲרָיוֹת שֹׁאֵג לִקְרָאתוֹ: [שופטים יד, ה]

ה) מַשָּׂא בַּהֲמוֹת נֶגֶב בְּאֶרֶץ צָרָה וְצוּקָה לָבִיא וָלַיִשׁ מֵהֶם אֶפְעֶה וְשָׂרָף מְעוֹפֵף יִשְׂאוּ עַל כֶּתֶף עֲיָרִים חֵילֵהֶם וְעַל דַּבֶּשֶׁת גְּמַלִּים אוֹצְרֹתָם עַל עַם לֹא יוֹעִילוּ: [ישעיה ל, ו]

ו) עַל שַׁחַל וָפֶתֶן תִּדְרֹךְ תִּרְמֹס כְּפִיר וְתַנִּין: [תהלים צא, יג]

ז) לֹא הִדְרִיכֻהוּ בְנֵי שָׁחַץ לֹא עָדָה עָלָיו שָׁחַל: [איוב כח, ח]

ח) עוֹד הַיּוֹם בְּנֹב לַעֲמֹד יְנֹפֵף יָדוֹ הַר בַּת צִיּוֹן גִּבְעַת יְרוּשָׁלָיִם: [ישעיה י, לב]

ט) וַיְהִי בַּלַּיְלָה הַהוּא וַיֵּצֵא מַלְאַךְ יְיָ וַיַּךְ בְּמַחֲנֵה אַשּׁוּר מֵאָה שְׁמוֹנִים וַחֲמִשָּׁה אָלֶף וַיַּשְׁכִּימוּ בַבֹּקֶר וְהִנֵּה כֻלָּם פְּגָרִים מֵתִים: [מלכים ב' יט, לה]

י) וְיִשְׁבִּי בְּנֹב אֲשֶׁר בִּילִידֵי הָרָפָה וּמִשְׁקַל קֵינוֹ שְׁלֹשׁ מֵאוֹת מִשְׁקַל נְחֹשֶׁת וְהוּא חָגוּר חֲדָשָׁה וַיֹּאמֶר לְהַכּוֹת אֶת דָּוִד: [שמואל ב' כא, טז]

כ) תַּרְחִיב צַעֲדִי תַחְתָּי וְלֹא מָעֲדוּ קַרְסֻלָּי: [תהלים יח, לז]

ל) אִם תִּשְׁכְּבוּן בֵּין שְׁפַתָּיִם כַּנְפֵי יוֹנָה נֶחְפָּה בַכֶּסֶף וְאֶבְרוֹתֶיהָ בִּירַקְרַק חָרוּץ: [תהלים סח, יד]

מ) וַיַּעֲזָר לוֹ אֲבִישַׁי בֶּן צְרוּיָה וַיַּךְ אֶת הַפְּלִשְׁתִּי וַיְמִיתֵהוּ אָז נִשְׁבְּעוּ אַנְשֵׁי דָוִד לוֹ לֵאמֹר לֹא תֵצֵא עוֹד אִתָּנוּ לַמִּלְחָמָה וְלֹא תְכַבֶּה אֶת נֵר יִשְׂרָאֵל: [שמואל ב' כא, יז]

נ) וָאָבֹא הַיּוֹם אֶל הָעָיִן וָאֹמַר יְיָ אֱלֹהֵי אֲדֹנִי אַבְרָהָם אִם יֶשְׁךָ נָּא מַצְלִיחַ דַּרְכִּי אֲשֶׁר אָנֹכִי הֹלֵךְ עָלֶיהָ: [בראשית כד, מב]

ליקוטי רש"י

דאמר רב פפא. במסכת גיטין (לח.). עמון ומואב טהרו בסיחון. ע"י סיחון טהרו ארצם לישראל במואב כתיב (במדבר כא) והוא נלחם וגו' ובעמון מפורש בנחלת בני גד בספר יהושע (יג) ויהי להם הגבול יעזר וכל ארץ הגלעד וחצי (ארץ) [ערי] בני עמון וקא חשיב ואזיל וכתיב בסיפיה יתר ממלכות סיחון אלמא סיחון כבש לארץ בני עמון ועוד מצינו במלך בני עמון שאמר למלאכי יפתח (שופטים יא) כי לקח ישראל את ארצי מארנון ועד היבוק אלמא ארץ בני עמון הוא והם מסיחון כבשוה דכתיב בו ויירשו את ארצו מארנון ועד היבוק אבל מהנשאר בידם לא לקחו כלום [חולין ס:]. דכתיב (דברים ב) אל תצר את מואב וכן בבני עמון אל תגורם (שם) וכתיב (במדבר כא) כי חשבון עיר סיחון וגו' אלמא טהר מואב בסיחון ובני עמון אשכחן ביפתח (שופטים יא) שאמרו לו מלאכי בני עמון כי לקח ישראל את ארצי בעלותו ממצרים מארנון ועד היבוק ואשכחן כשכבשו את ארץ סיחון ויירש את ארצו מארנון עד יבוק וגו' אלמא מבני עמון כבשה והדור ישראל וכבשו מיניה וטהרה להם על ידו אלמא קנייה בחזקה [גיטין לח.]. בא על עית. מונה והולך מסעות שנסע סנחריב ובא על ערי יהודה לבא ירושלים ביום מפלתו [ישעיה י, כח]. לנו. לשון לינה. נסה. ברחה ברחו כולן מפני חיילותיו [שם, כט]. צהלי קולך. להזהיר לעם. הקשיבי לישה. את קול השופר וברחו לכם וכן עניה ענתות [שם, ל]. העיזו. נאספו לברוח [שם, לא] עוד היום בנוב לעמוד. כל הדרך הזה נתלבט כדי לעמוד בעוד היום בנוב לפי שאמרו לו אילטגניניו אם תלח' בה היום תכבשנ' וכשעמד בנוב וראה את ירושלים קטנה לא חש לדברי אילטגניניו והתחיל להניף ידו בגאו' וכי על עיר כזו הרגזתי כל החיילות הללו לינו פה הלילה ולמחר ישליך בה איש אבנו. הר בת ציון. להר בת ציון [שם, לב]. עלה אריה. נבוכדנצר. מסובכו. דרך אריה לישב במארב סבכי היער אשפיישי"ש בלע"ז [ירמיה ד, ז]. [ע"כ שייך לדף צד:].

כפיר. כל כפיר שבמקרא ארי בחור וגבור [יחזקאל יט, ה]. הארי גדול והשחל בינוני והכפיר קטן [איוב ד, י]. עוד היום בנוב לעמוד. כל הדרך הזה נתלבט כדי לעמוד בעוד היום בנוב לפי שאמרו לו אילטגניניו אם תלח' בה היום תכבשנ' וכשעמד בנוב וראה את ירושלים קטנה לא חש לדברי אילטגניניו והתחיל להניף ידו בגאו' וכי על עיר כזו הרגזתי כל החיילות הללו לינו פה הלילה ולמחר ישליך בה איש אבנו [ישעיה י, לב]. ויהי בלילה ההוא. כששב סנחריב מעל כוש ובא עד נוב שהיתה סמוכה לירושלים. מאה ושמונים וחמשה אלף. כולם ראשי גייסות [מ"ב יט, לה]. בילידי הרפה. כתיב ערפה שם האחת ערפה (רות א) וכתיב הרפה אשר בילידי הרפה והיא ערפה כדאמרי' לקמן שנגזר עליה שיפלו בניה בחרב ביד בני רות שדבקה בשכינה [סוטה מב:]. ומשקל קינו. הוא כמו תיק שבראש בית יד הרומח שקורין אריסטויי"ל בלע"ז ועשוי כקובע, ויש דוגמתו בזבחים (פח:) רמוני המעיל למה הם דומין כמין קולסות שבראשי התינוקות קולסות היימלמש בלע"ז [ש"ב כא, טז]. קולסות. בוטונ"ש עשויין כמין תיק של נחשת שעושין [בסוף] בית יד הרומח שקורין אריסטייל לשון (ש"ב כא) ומשקל קינו דישבי בנוב והתינוקות תולין אותו בראשי כובעי נגרים שעושין אותו למלחמתן שקורים הילמ"ש [זבחים פח:]. והוא חגור. חגורה חדשה ושמעתי שאותו היום נתחנך ללבוש כלי מלחמה ודרך המתחנכים לעשות נצחון וגבורה ביום חינוכם לקנות שם לכך ויאמר להכות את דוד [ש"ב שם]. על עסקי נוב. שבא עליו עונשו של שאול כמו שפירשו רבותינו שאמר לו הקב"ה על ידך נטרד דואג האדומי על ידך נהרג שאול ובניו כו' [תהלים ז, א]. פתק ביה. זרק בו [שבועות יח:]. פניא. לפנות ערב [תענית כג:]. חייף רישיה. חופף ראשו [לקמן קיא.]. ליונה אימתילא. כיונה נמשלה [גיטין מה.]. שהיא נמשלת ליונה והמצות ככנפים [שבת מט.]. כנפי יונה. זאת יונתי כנסייתי כנפיה נחפה בכסף ומהו הכסף והחרוץ בפרש שדי וגו' כשפירש הקב"ה לפניהם תורתו אשר המלכים נשלגים ומתלבנים בה בארץ צלמות וחשך אז נחפו כנפיה (כנפי יונה) בכספה ותמדתה של תורה ומצות [תהלים סח, יד]. סייע בהדן. והפך דוד את תפלתו והתפלל שלא יפול בידי אויב [ש"ב שם, יח]. ויעזור לו. שעזרו בתפילה [שם ז, א]. ואבוא היום. היום יצאתי והיום באתי מכאן שקפצה לו הארץ [בראשית כד, מב].

הגהות הגר"א

[א] גמ' ד"א אין פגיעה כו' עד ואל תפגע בי. נמחק: [ב] שם והשאר פרשים. נ"ב ורגלים:

תורה אור השלם

א) וַיֵּצֵא יַעֲקֹב מִבְּאֵר שָׁבַע וַיֵּלֶךְ חָרָנָה: [בראשית כח, י]

ב) וַיִּפְגַּע בַּמָּקוֹם וַיָּלֶן שָׁם כִּי בָא הַשֶּׁמֶשׁ וַיִּקַּח מֵאַבְנֵי הַמָּקוֹם וַיָּשֶׂם מְרַאֲשֹׁתָיו וַיִּשְׁכַּב בַּמָּקוֹם הַהוּא: [בראשית כח, יא]

ג) וְאַתָּה אַל תִּתְפַּלֵּל בְּעַד הָעָם הַזֶּה וְאַל תִּשָּׂא בַעֲדָם רִנָּה וּתְפִלָּה וְאַל תִּפְגַּע בִּי כִּי אֵינֶנִּי שֹׁמֵעַ אֹתָךְ: [ירמיה ז, טז]

ד) וַיִּזְרַח לוֹ הַשֶּׁמֶשׁ כַּאֲשֶׁר עָבַר אֶת פְּנוּאֵל וְהוּא צֹלֵעַ עַל יְרֵכוֹ: [בראשית לב, לא]

ה) וַעֲתַלְיָה אֵם אֲחַזְיָהוּ רָאֲתָה כִּי מֵת בְּנָהּ וַתָּקָם וַתְּאַבֵּד אֵת כָּל זֶרַע הַמַּמְלָכָה: [מלכים ב' יא, א]

ו) וַיִּמָּלֵט בֵּן אֶחָד לַאֲחִימֶלֶךְ בֶּן אֲחִטוּב וּשְׁמוֹ אֶבְיָתָר וַיִּבְרַח אַחֲרֵי דָוִד: [שמואל א' כב, כ]

ז) וְחָלַף בִּיהוּדָה שָׁטַף וְעָבַר עַד צַוָּאר יַגִּיעַ וְהָיָה מֻטּוֹת כְּנָפָיו מְלֹא רֹחַב אַרְצְךָ עִמָּנוּ אֵל: [ישעיה ח, ח]

ח) אֲנִי קַרְתִּי וְשָׁתִיתִי מָיִם וְאַחְרִב בְּכַף פְּעָמַי כֹּל יְאֹרֵי מָצוֹר: [ישעיה לז, כה]

ט) וַיֵּצֵא מַלְאַךְ יְיָ וַיַּכֶּה בְּמַחֲנֵה אַשּׁוּר מֵאָה וּשְׁמֹנִים וַחֲמִשָּׁה אָלֶף וַיַּשְׁכִּימוּ בַבֹּקֶר וְהִנֵּה כֻלָּם פְּגָרִים מֵתִים: [ישעיה לז, לו]

י) לָכֵן יְשַׁלַּח הָאָדוֹן יְיָ צְבָאוֹת בְּמִשְׁמַנָּיו רָזוֹן וְתַחַת כְּבֹדוֹ יֵקַד יְקֹד כִּיקוֹד אֵשׁ: [ישעיה י, טז]

יא) וַיִּשְׁלַח יְיָ מַלְאָךְ וַיַּכְחֵד כָּל גִּבּוֹר חַיִל וְנָגִיד וְשָׂר בְּמַחֲנֵה מֶלֶךְ אַשּׁוּר וַיָּשָׁב בְּבֹשֶׁת פָּנִים לְאַרְצוֹ וַיָּבֹא בֵּית אֱלֹהָיו וּמִיצִיאֵי מֵעָיו שָׁם הִפִּילֻהוּ בֶחָרֶב: [דברי הימים ב' לב, כא]

יב) וַיַּרְא יִשְׂרָאֵל אֶת הַיָּד הַגְּדֹלָה אֲשֶׁר עָשָׂה יְיָ בְּמִצְרַיִם וַיִּירְאוּ הָעָם אֶת יְיָ וַיַּאֲמִינוּ בַּייָ וּבְמֹשֶׁה עַבְדּוֹ: [שמות יד, לא]

יג) וַיֹּאמְרוּ הַחַרְטֻמִּם אֶל פַּרְעֹה אֶצְבַּע אֱלֹהִים הִוא וַיֶּחֱזַק לֵב פַּרְעֹה וְלֹא שָׁמַע אֲלֵהֶם כַּאֲשֶׁר דִּבֶּר יְיָ: [שמות ח, טו]

יד) כִּי מִפְּנֵי חֲרָבוֹת נָדָדוּ מִפְּנֵי חֶרֶב נְטוּשָׁה וּמִפְּנֵי קֶשֶׁת דְּרוּכָה וּמִפְּנֵי כֹּבֶד מִלְחָמָה: [ישעיה כא, טו]

מסורת הש"ס

א) חולין צא:, ב) [ברכות כו: תענית ז: ת. סוטה יד.], ג) [עי' תוס' מגילה כא. ד"ה אלמלא], ד) [נ"ל מפני חרב נטושה וגו'], ה) [עי' תוספות מנחות כט. ד"ה קולי], ו) נ"ל ליה, ז) רש"ל מ"ז.

רש"י

ויצא יעקב מבאר שבע וילך חרנה. אלמא בא לחרן וכתיב ויפגע במקום שעדיין לא הגיע לחרן שהיה עדיין בבית אל: שהתפללו בו אבותי. אברהם ויצחק [ז] (אברהם דכתיב ויעתק משם יצחק אין מקרא בידי): הרהר בדעתיה למהדר. למקום: קפצה ליה ארעא. והיה שם מיד וקרא מוכיח דכתיב ויפגע במקום שהמקום פגעו שקפלה לו הארץ ונתקרב לו המקום: הכי גרסינן ד"א אין פגיעה אלא תפלה. ונראה למורי דהכא לא מיגרסא הך מילתא: בית אל זה ירושלים חרן חוץ לארץ: כי בא השמש. ויבא השמש לא נאמר אלא כי בא השמש דמשמע שהיה דעתו לחזור כי עוד היום גדול כיון שראה כי בא השמש לן: ויזרח לו השמש. משמע השמש שהיה לו כבר שבא בשבילו כבר: ומנ"ל דכלה זרעיה דדוד. כדאפיך ללותיה: התם נמי אשתייר אביתר. מכהני נוב: שגלונות. מלכות: על אברהם. כשנלחם בד' מלכים: בעי אביי. האי חסר חד היכי קאמר אי חסר חד רבוא וכו': ראשונה. כת ראשונה מחיל של סנחריב: עברו בשחי. שטו הסוסים בירדן ונתמעטו המים עד שעברו: אמצעיים בקומה. זקופה ולא היו המים מגיעין אלא עד הצואר יגיע: שחי. כמו שחו: העלו עפר ברגליהם. שלא היה שם מים כל עיקר: קרתי. לשון מקור: ה"ג ויצא מלאך ה' ויך במחנה אשור אמר רבי וכו'. ולא גרסינן והא כתיב ויצא מלאך ה' אלמא כל המחנה אשור אינו אלא קפ"ה אלף ולעיל קתני מאתים וס' רבוא: הללו. קפ"ה אלף ראשי גייסות נגידי החיל שכן עולה לחשבון לכדאמרינן ארבעים וחמשה אלף בני מלכים שמנים אלף גבורים ששים אלף אחוזי חרב הרי קפ"ה אלף אבל האחרים שמתו אין מספר כדאמר והשאר פרשים אין מספר: במה הכם. המלאך: היד הגדולה. יד הגדולה לא נאמר אלא היד דמשמע היד שעתידה וכו': מגלך נטושה. שחוזה מגלך להרוג את אלו: גבריאל. ממונה על בשול הפירות: הזקק לאלו. לחיל סנחריב להרגן: אגב ארחך. כשתלך לדרכך לפי תומך: לבעל דבבך אשתמע. לשונאך התראה והפחידו: נשף. נפח: עשרה. שהנער יכול להטיף טיפה של דיו והיינו יו"ד שנשארו עשרה: ושמואל אמר תשעה. ונשאר בו עוללות כנוקף זית שאין נשארין בו אלא דבר מועט שנים או שלשה גרגרים בראש אמיר כן לא ישתייר במחנהו אלא דבר מועט וכמה ארבעה וחמשה בסעיפיה פוריה ארבעה וחמשה והיינו תשעה: י"ד שנים ושלשה ארבעה וחמשה. ר' יוחנן מקרא לא דייק להו אלא הכי קאמר הללו חמשה נשתיירו מהן סנחריב ושני בניו וקרא משמע כנוקף זית דמשייר מעט בראש ענף שנים או שלשה גרגרים כך ישתייר לו מעט ד' או ה': נבוכדנצר דכתיב. גבי [חנניה] מישאל ועזריה תוארו ורויה די רביעאה דמי לבר אלהין אלמא דחזא גבריאל והכירו בכבשן: סנחריב ושני בניו. דכתיב ויהי הוא משתחוה בית וגו': אי אפשר לאמרו. שהקדוש ב"ה בעצמו גלחו לסנחריב: דאייתיתינהו לבנייהו. כדאמרינן שהביא עמו ארבעים וחמשה אלף בני מלכים: אשני

גמרא

דכתיב א) ויצא יעקב מבאר שבע וילך חרנה וכתיב ב) ויפגע במקום וילן שם כי בא השמש [א] כי מטא לחרן אמר אפשר עברתי על מקום שהתפללו בו אבותי ואני לא התפללתי בו בעי למיהדר כיון דהרהר בדעתיה למיהדר קפצה ליה ארעא מיד ויפגע במקום [א] דבר אחר ב) אין פגיעה אלא תפלה שנאמר ג) ואתה אל תתפלל בעד העם הזה ואל תשא בעדם רנה ותפלה ואל תפגע בי ב) וילן שם כי בא השמש בתר דצלי בעי למיהדר אמר הקב"ה צדיק זה בא לבית מלוני יפטר בלא לינה מיד בא השמש והיינו דכתיב ד) ויזרח לו השמש וכי לו בלבד זרחה והלא לכל העולם כולו זרחה אלא א"ר יצחק שמש שבא בעבורו זרחה בעבורו ומנלן דכלה זרעיה דדוד דכתי' ה) ועתליה אם אחזיהו ראתה כי מת בנה ותקם ותאבד את כל זרע הממלכה והא אשתייר ליה יואש התם נמי אשתייר אביתר דכתיב ו) וימלט בן אחד לאחימלך בן אחיטוב ושמו אביתר אמר רב יהודה אמר רב אלמלא (ג) לא) נשתייר אביתר לאחימלך בן אחיטוב לא נשתייר מזרעו של דוד שריד ופליט אמר רב יהודה אמר רב בא עליהם סנחריב הרשע בארבעים וחמשה אלף איש בני מלכים יושבים בקרונות של זהב ועמהן שגלונות וזונות ובשמנים אלף גבורים לבושי שריון קליפה ובששים אלף אחוזי חרב רצים לפניו [ב] והשאר פרשים וכן באו על אברהם וכן עתידין לבוא עם גוג ומגוג במתניתא תנא אורך מחנהו ארבע מאות פרסי רחב צואר סוסיו ארבעים פרסי סך מחנהו מאתים וששים ריבוא אלפים חסר חד בעי אביי חסר חד ריבויא או חסר חד אלפא או חסר מאה או חסר חד תיקו תנא ראשונים עברו בשחי שנאמר ז) וחלף ביהודה שטף ועבר אמצעיים עברו בקומה שנאמר ז) עד צואר יגיע אחרונים העלו עפר ברגליהם ולא מצאו מים בנהר לשתות עד שהביאו מים ממקום אחר ושתו שנאמר ח) אני קרתי ושתיתי מים וגו' והכתיב ט) ויצא מלאך ה' ויכה במחנה אשור מאה ושמנים וחמשה אלף (ויקומו) [וישכימו] בבקר והנה כלם פגרים מתים אמר ר' אבהו הללו ראשי גייסות הן אמר רב אשי דיקא נמי דכתיב י) במשמניו רזון בשמינים דאית בהו אמר רבינא דיקא נמי דכתיב יא) וישלח ה' מלאך ויכחד כל גבור חיל ונגיד ושר במחנה וגו' ויבא בית אלהיו ומיציאי מעיו שם הפילוהו בחרב שמע מינה במה הכם רבי אליעזר אומר ביד הכם שנאמר יב) וירא ישראל את היד הגדולה היד שעתידה ליפרע מסנחריב רבי יהושע אומר באצבע הכם שנאמר יג) ויאמרו החרטמים אל פרעה אצבע אלהים היא היא אצבע שעתידה ליפרע מסנחריב ר' אליעזר בנו של ר' יוסי הגלילי אומר אמר לו הקב"ה לגבריאל מגלך נטושה אמר לפניו רבונו של עולם נטושה ועומדת מששת ימי בראשית שנאמר יד) מפני חרבות נדדו ד) וגו' ר' שמעון בן יוחי אומר אותו הפרק זמן בישול פירות היה אמר לו הקב"ה לגבריאל כשאתה יוצא לבשל פירות הזקק להם שנאמר טו) מידי עברו יקח אתכם כי בבקר בבקר יעבור ביום ובלילה והיה רק זועה הבין שמועה וגו' אמר רב פפא היינו דאמרי אינשי אגב אורחך לבעל דבבך אישתמע ויש אומרים בחוטמן נשף בהן ומתו שנאמר טז) וגם נשף בהם ויבשו ר' ירמיה בר אבא אמר כפיים ספק להם ומתו שנאמר יז) וגם אני (הכתי) [אכה] כפי אל כפי והניחותי חמתי ר' יצחק נפחא אמר אזנים גלה להם ושמעו שירה מפי חיות ומתו שנאמר יח) מרוממתך נפצו גוים וכמה נשתייר מהם רב אמר ה) עשרה שנאמר יט) ושאר עץ יערו מספר יהיו ונער יכתבם כמה נער יכול לכתוב עשרה ושמואל אמר תשעה שנאמר כ) ונשאר בו עוללות כנוקף זית שנים שלשה גרגרים בראש אמיר ארבעה חמשה בסעיפיה ר' יהושע בן לוי אמר ארבעה עשר שנאמר שנים שלשה [וכו'] ארבעה וחמשה רבי יוחנן אמר חמשה סנחריב ושני בניו נבוכד נצר ונבוזר אדן נבוזר אדן גמרא נבוכד נצר דכתיב כא) ורוה דרביעאה דמי לבר אלהין ואי לאו דחזייה מנא הוה ידע סנחריב ושני בניו דכתיב כב) ויהי הוא משתחוה בית נסרוך אלהיו ואדרמלך ושראצר בניו הכוהו בחרב אמר רבי אבהו אלמלא מקרא כתוב אי אפשר לאמרו דכתיב כג) ביום ההוא יגלח ה' בתער השכירה בעברי נהר במלך אשור את הראש ושער הרגלים וגם את הזקן תספה אתא קודשא בריך הוא ואדמי ליה כגברא סבא א"ל כי אזלת לגבי מלכי מזרח ומערב דאייתיתינהו לבנייהו וקטלתינהו מאי אמרת להו אמר ו) להו ההוא גברא בההוא פחדא נמי יתיב אמר ליה היכי נעביד א"ל זיל ושני

ליקוטי רש"י

וילך חרנה. דמשמע דמטא לחרן והדר כתיב ויפגע במקום דהיינו בית אל דאכתי לא מטא לחרן [חולין צא:]. ויפגע במקום. לא הזכיר הכתוב באיזה מקום אלא במקום הנזכר במקום אחר הוא הר המוריה שנאמר בו (בראשית כב, ד) וירא את המקום מרחוק. ויפגע, כמו (יהושע טז, ז) ופגע ביריחו (שם יט, יא) ופגע בדבשת ורבותינו פירשו לשון תפלה כמו (ירמיה ז, טז) ואל תפגע בי [בראשית כח, יא]. שהתפללו בו אבותי. האי בית אל לאו הסמוך לעי הוא אלא ירושלים ועל שם יהיה בית אלהים קראו בית אל והוא הר המוריה שהתפלל בו אברהם והוא שדה שהתפלל בו יצחק דכתיב (בראשית כד) לשוח בשדה דהכי אמרינן בפסחים (פח.) אל הר ה' ואל בית אלהי יעקב מאי שנא יעקב אלא לא כאברהם שקראו הר דכתיב בהר ה' ולא כיצחק שקראו שדה דכתיב לשוח בשדה אלא כיעקב שקראו בית. קפצה ליה ארעא. לשון (דברים טו) לא תקפוץ את ידך נתקצרה ונתקמצה לו [חולין שם]. וכלפי שאמרו רבותינו שאמר הקב"ה צדיק זה בא לבית מלוני ויפטר בלא לינה ועוד אמרו יעקב קראה לירושלים בית אל וזו לוז היא ולא ירושלים ומהיכן למדו לומר כן אומר אני שנעקר הר המוריה ובא לכאן וזהו היא קפיצת הארץ האמורה בשחיטת חולין (חולין צא:) שבא בית המקדש לקראתו עד בית אל וזהו ויפגע במקום, וא"ת וכשעבר יעקב על בית המקדש מדוע לא עכבו שם איהו לא יהיב לביה להתפלל במקום שהתפללו אבותיו ומן השמים יעכבוהו איהו עד חרן אזל כדאמרינן בפרק גיד הנשה (חולין צא:) וקרא מוכיח וילך חרנה כי מטא לחרן אמר אפשר שעברתי על מקום שהתפללו אבותי ולא התפללתי בו יהב דעתיה למהדר וחזר עד בית אל וקפצה לו הארץ [בראשית שם, יז ועי' במהרש"א בח"א חולין שם ד"ה מקום]. מיד ויפגע במקום. כאדם הפוגע בחבירו שבא כנגדו ודרשינן ליה נמי לשון תפלה כדכתיב (רות א) אל תפגעי בי [חולין שם]. אין פגיעה אלא תפלה. [illegible]

[illegible] ויזרח לו השמש. [illegible] שגלונות. [illegible] שריון קליפה. [illegible] וחלף ביהודה. [illegible] שטף. [illegible] ראשי גייסות. [illegible] ומיציאי

ט) [illegible]

טו) מִדֵּי עָבְרוֹ יִקַּח אֶתְכֶם כִּי בַבֹּקֶר בַּבֹּקֶר יַעֲבֹר בַּיּוֹם וּבַלָּיְלָה וְהָיָה רַק זְוָעָה הָבִין שְׁמוּעָה: [ישעיה כח, יט] טז) אַף בַּל נִטָּעוּ אַף בַּל זֹרָעוּ אַף בַּל שֹׁרֵשׁ בָּאָרֶץ גִּזְעָם וְגַם נָשַׁף בָּהֶם וַיִּבָשׁוּ וּסְעָרָה כַּקַּשׁ תִּשָּׂאֵם: [ישעיה מ, כד] יז) וְגַם אֲנִי אַכֶּה כַפִּי אֶל כַּפִּי וַהֲנִחֹתִי חֲמָתִי אֲנִי יְיָ דִּבַּרְתִּי: [יחזקאל כא, כב] יח) מִקּוֹל הָמוֹן נָדְדוּ עַמִּים מֵרוֹמְמֻתֶךָ נָפְצוּ גּוֹיִם: [ישעיה לג, ג] יט) וּשְׁאָר עֵץ יַעְרוֹ מִסְפָּר יִהְיוּ וְנַעַר יִכְתְּבֵם: [ישעיה י, יט] כ) וְנִשְׁאַר בּוֹ עוֹלֵלֹת כְּנֹקֶף זַיִת שְׁנַיִם שְׁלֹשָׁה גַּרְגְּרִים בְּרֹאשׁ אָמִיר אַרְבָּעָה חֲמִשָּׁה בִּסְעִפֶיהָ פֹּרִיָּה נְאֻם יְיָ אֱלֹהֵי יִשְׂרָאֵל: [ישעיה יז, ו] כא) עָנֵה וְאָמַר הָא אֲנָה חָזֵה גֻּבְרִין אַרְבְּעָה שְׁרַיִן מַהְלְכִין בְּגוֹא נוּרָא וַחֲבָל לָא אִיתַי בְּהוֹן וְרֵוֵהּ דִּי רְבִיעָאָה דָּמֵה לְבַר אֱלָהִין: [דניאל ג, כה] כב) וַיְהִי הוּא מִשְׁתַּחֲוֶה בֵּית נִסְרֹךְ אֱלֹהָיו וְאַדְרַמֶּלֶךְ וְשַׂרְאֶצֶר בָּנָיו הִכֻּהוּ בַחֶרֶב וְהֵמָּה נִמְלְטוּ אֶרֶץ אֲרָרָט וַיִּמְלֹךְ אֵסַר חַדֹּן בְּנוֹ תַּחְתָּיו: [מלכים ב' יט, לז] כג) בַּיּוֹם הַהוּא יְגַלַּח אֲדֹנָי בְּתַעַר הַשְּׂכִירָה בְּעֶבְרֵי נָהָר בְּמֶלֶךְ אַשּׁוּר אֶת הָרֹאשׁ וְשַׂעַר הָרַגְלָיִם וְגַם אֶת הַזָּקָן תִּסְפֶּה: [ישעיה ז, כ]

מעיו. כדכתיב (ישעיה לז) ובניו הכוהו בחרב [דה"ב לב, כא]. מגלך נטושה. כמו לטושה כל אותיות אשר מוצאיהם קרובים להיות ממקום אחד מתחלפות זו בזו נו"ן בלמ"ד כענין שנא' (נחמיה יג) לעשות לו נשכה [illegible] [ישעיה כא, טו]. והיה רק זועה הבין שמועה. זועה לכל השומעים להבין שמועות פורענו' הקשות שאביא עליכם כל השומעים יזועו [שם כח, יט]. [המשך בדף צו.]

דִּכְתִיב – **for it is written:**[1] ,,וַיֵּצֵא יַעֲקֹב מִבְּאֵר שָׁבַע וַיֵּלֶךְ חָרָנָה" – ***Jacob departed from Be'er Sheva and went to Charan.*** וּכְתִיב – **And it is written** further:[2] ,,וַיִּפְגַּע בַּמָּקוֹם וַיָּלֶן שָׁם כִּי־בָא הַשֶּׁמֶשׁ" – ***He encountered the place*** [i.e. Beth El] ***and slept there because the sun had set.*** Now, the two verses seem to contradict each other, for the first verse states that Jacob came to Charan, but the next verse states that he spent the night in Beth El, implying that he did not, in fact, travel as far as Charan![3] – ? –

Because of this apparent contradiction, the Gemara introduces a different understanding of the passage:

כִּי מָטָא לְחָרָן אָמַר – Actually Jacob *did* get as far as Charan; but **once he reached Charan, he said** to himself: אֶפְשָׁר עָבַרְתִּי עַל מָקוֹם שֶׁהִתְפַּלְלוּ בּוֹ אֲבוֹתַי – **Is it possible that I have passed** on my journey **the place where my fathers prayed,** i.e. Beth El,[4] וַאֲנִי לֹא הִתְפַּלַּלְתִּי בּוֹ – **and I did not pray there myself?** I must go back to Beth El, and rectify this oversight! בָּעֵי לְמֵיהְדַר – **He** thus **determined to return** to Eretz Yisrael and pray at Beth El. כֵּיוָן דְּהִרְהֵר בְּדַעְתֵּיהּ לְמֵיהְדַר – And **as soon as he mentally pondered returning** there, קָפְצָה לֵיהּ אַרְעָא – **the ground** between Charan and Beth El miraculously **contracted for him,** and Yaakov found himself instantaneously transported back to Beth El. מִיַּד ,,וַיִּפְגַּע בַּמָּקוֹם" – And this is confirmed by Scripture, for **immediately** after Jacob reached Charan, the verse states: ***He encountered the place*** [i.e. Beth El].[5] Hence, we find that the ground miraculously contracted for the Patriarch Jacob.

The Gemara expounds further on the word וַיִּפְגַּע used in connection with Jacob:

דָּבָר אַחֵר – **Another point:**[6] אֵין פְּגִיעָה אֶלָּא תְּפִלָּה – **The word *pegiah*** found in this verse [i.e. the word *vayifga,* which literally means *he encountered*] **denotes nothing other than prayer,** שֶׁנֶּאֱמַר – **as Scripture states** elsewhere: ,,וְאַתָּה אַל־תִּתְפַּלֵּל בְּעַד־הָעָם הַזֶּה – ***And as for you, do not pray on behalf of this people,*** וְאַל־תִּשָּׂא בַעֲדָם רִנָּה וּתְפִלָּה – ***do not raise any cry or prayer on their behalf*** וְאַל־תִּפְגַּע־בִּי" – ***and do not entreat Me in prayer (tifga).***[7]

The Gemara continues its exposition of the verse:

,,וַיָּלֶן שָׁם כִּי־בָא הַשֶּׁמֶשׁ" בָּתַר דְּצַלֵּי בָּעֵי לְמֵיהְדַר – Now, when Scripture goes on to state that ***[Jacob] slept there because the sun had set,*** it means that **after he prayed** in Beth El **he sought to return** to Charan. אָמַר הַקָּדוֹשׁ בָּרוּךְ הוּא – However, **the Holy One, Blessed is He, declared:** צַדִּיק זֶה בָּא לְבֵית מְלוֹנִי יִפָּטֵר בְּלֹא לִינָה – **This righteous man** [Jacob] **has come to My lodging place.**[8] **Shall he depart without spending a night?** Certainly not! מִיַּד בָּא הַשֶּׁמֶשׁ – Thus, a miracle occurred and **the sun immediately set,** forcing Jacob to spend the night there.[9] וְהַיְינוּ דִּכְתִיב ,,וַיִּזְרַח־לוֹ הַשֶּׁמֶשׁ" – **And this is the meaning** of the cryptic Scriptural passage: ***The sun rose for [Jacob]*** *as he passed Peniel.*[10]

The Gemara explains the difficulty in this passage, and shows how it can be resolved in light of the current discussion:

וְכִי לוֹ בִּלְבַד זָרְחָה – Now, **was it for him alone that the sun rose?** וַהֲלֹא לְכָל הָעוֹלָם כּוּלּוֹ זָרְחָה – **Did it not rise for the whole world?** אֶלָּא אָמַר רַבִּי יִצְחָק – **Rather, said R' Yitzchak,** the verse is implying the following: שֶׁמֶשׁ שֶׁבָּא בַּעֲבוּרוֹ זָרְחָה בַּעֲבוּרוֹ – **The** same **sun that had** prematurely **set on his account** at Beth El, זָרְחָה בַּעֲבוּרוֹ – **now rose** prematurely **on his account** at Peniel.[11]

The Gemara returns to its account of how King David was punished for his role in the massacre at Nov. Earlier, it was stated that David chose to have his own life spared, and to instead allow his descendants to perish in expiation of his sin. The Gemara now elaborates how this punishment eventually came about:

וּמְנָלַן דְּכָלָה זַרְעֵיהּ דְּדָוִד – **And from where** in Scripture **do we know that David's descendants were obliterated?** דִּכְתִיב – **For it is written:**[12] ,,וַעֲתַלְיָה אֵם אֲחַזְיָהוּ רָאֲתָה כִּי מֵת בְּנָהּ – ***Asaliah the mother of Achaziahu saw that her son was dead,*** וַתָּקָם וַתְּאַבֵּד אֵת כָּל־זֶרַע הַמַּמְלָכָה" – ***and she arose and destroyed the entire royal family.***

NOTES

1. *Genesis* 28:10.

2. Ibid. v. 11.

3. Both verses describe Jacob's journey from the Land of Israel to Charan. However, the first verse states that Jacob reached Charan – a land that was far beyond the borders of the Land of Israel – and the next verse states that he came to a place he later named Beth El, which was clearly *within* the borders of Israel. The passages are thus problematic, for if Jacob had already reached Charan, how could he have subsequently stopped in Beth El?

4. Abraham built an altar and prayed to God at Beth El near Ai (see *Genesis* 12:8), and Isaac, too, prayed there (see *Yad Ramah*). [*Rashi* asserts that the place described here as Beth El was actually Jerusalem; see also *Rashi* to *Chullin* 91b ד"ה שהתפללו who states that the place was Mount Moriah.]

5. [The verb פגע connotes a sudden meeting. Thus, the implication is that Jacob encountered Beth El suddenly, for he had only journeyed for a very short time.]

6. [The following point is a digression from the flow of the current discussion, and according to *Rashi's* teacher and *Gra,* it should be deleted from our text.]

7. *Jeremiah* 7:16. In Jeremiah's time, many Jews who lived in Jerusalem believed that they were safe from invasion, for they felt that the presence of God's holy Temple in their midst would protect them. God, however, told Jeremiah that they were in error – that if the people persisted in their evil ways, He would indeed cause Jerusalem and the Temple to be destroyed. In our verse, God tells Jeremiah that it is futile to try and alter His plan by praying [*pegiah*], for if the people did not change their ways, Jerusalem *would* be destroyed.

8. [*Rashi* states that Beth El, the place at which Jacob had prayed, was in fact Mt. Moriah, the future site of the Temple. Thus, the Gemara refers to it as God's "lodging place."]

9. The wording *he spent the night there because the sun had set,* implies that the sun unexpectedly set. [Otherwise, the order should have been reversed to read: "The sun set, so he spent the night there."] That is, Jacob had been planning to travel back to Charan, but he was prevented from doing so by the fact that the sun had set prematurely (*Rashi*).

10. *Genesis* 32:32. While wrestling with an angel in the place called Peniel, Jacob's hip socket became dislocated, causing him to limp in pain. Scripture then states that the sun rose "for Jacob," the meaning of which the Gemara will now explain.

11. I.e. the sun rose prematurely in order to heal Jacob with its warmth (see *Rashi* to *Genesis* 32:32, and *Imrei Binah*). The Gemara's inference comes from the fact that the verse appends the definite article to the word "sun" [הַשֶּׁמֶשׁ, *"the" sun*]. This is taken to imply: The same sun that had earlier set on Jacob's behalf, now rose prematurely on his behalf to heal him (*Rashi*). See also *Yad Ramah.*

12. *II Kings* 11:1. After King Achaziah of Judah was assassinated, the only surviving members of the Davidic dynasty were several very young children (see *II Chronicles* 22:9). At that point, however, Asaliah, Achaziah's mother, saw an opportunity to seize personal control of the throne, and she slew all the surviving members of the royal family and crowned herself ruler of Judah. It is to this massacre that our verse refers. Only one baby, Yoash, survived the slaughter, and he remained the sole link in the Davidic dynasty (see ibid. v. 11).

[*Yad David* points out that not *all* descendants of David were in Asaliah's reach. Rather, the verse means that she killed all the descendants of Solomon, for they alone were heirs to the throne, and they were thus the ones affected by the punishment due David's heirs. See also *Margaliyos HaYam* §6.]

דכתיב (א) ויצא יעקב מבאר שבע וילך חרנה וכתיב (ב) ויפגע במקום וילן שם כי בא השמש (א) כי מטא לחרן אמר אפשר עברתי על מקום שהתפללו בו אבותי ואני לא התפללתי בו בעי למיהדר כיון דהרהר בדעתיה למיהדר קפצה ליה ארעא מיד ויפגע במקום [א] דבר אחר (ב) אין פגיעה אלא תפלה שנאמר (ג) ואתה אל תתפלל בעד העם הזה ואל תשא בעדם רנה ותפלה ואל תפגע בי (ב) וילן שם כי בא השמש בתר דצלי בעי למיהדר אמר הקב"ה צדיק זה בא לבית מלוני יפטר בלא לינה מיד בא השמש והיינו דכתיב (ד) ויזרח לו השמש וכי לו בלבד זרחה והלא לכל העולם כולו זרחה אלא א"ר יצחק שמש שבא בעבורו זרחה בעבורו ומנלן דכלה זרעיה דדוד דכתי' (ה) ועתליה אם אחזיהו ראתה כי מת בנה ותקם ותאבד את כל זרע הממלכה והא אשתייר ליה יואש התם נמי אשתייר אביתר דכתיב (ו) וימלט בן אחד לאחימלך בן אחיטוב ושמו אביתר אמר רב יהודה אמר רב אלמלא (ג) (לא) נשתייר אביתר לאחימלך בן אחיטוב לא נשתייר מזרעו של דוד שריד ופליט אמר רב יהודה אמר רב בא עליהם סנחריב הרשע בארבעים וחמשה אלף איש בני מלכים יושבים בקרונות של זהב ועמהן שגלונות וזונות ובשמנים אלף גבורים לבושי שריון קליפה ובששים אלף אחוזי חרב רצים לפניו [ב] והשאר פרשים וכן באו על אברהם וכן עתידין לבוא עם גוג ומגוג במתניתא תנא אורך מחנהו ארבע מאות פרסי רחב צואר סוסיו ארבעים פרסי סך מחנהו מאתים ושישים ריבוא אלפים חסר חד בעי אביי חסר חד ריבויא או חסר חד אלפא או חסר חד מאה או חסר חד תיקו תנא ראשונים עברו בשחי שנאמר (ז) וחלף ביהודה שטף ועבר אמצעיים עברו בקומה שנאמר (ז) עד צואר יגיע אחרונים העלו עפר ברגליהם ולא מצאו מים בנהר לשתות עד שהביאו מים ממקום אחר ושתו שנאמר (ח) אני קרתי ושתיתי מים וגו' והכתיב (ט) ויצא מלאך ה' ויכה במחנה אשור מאה ושמנים וחמשה אלף (ויקומו) [וישכימו] בבקר והנה כלם פגרים מתים אמר ר' אבהו הללו ראשי גייסות הן אמר רב אשי דיקא נמי דכתיב (י) במשמניו רזון בשמינים דאית בהו אמר רבינא דיקא נמי דכתיב (יא) וישלח ה' מלאך ויכחד כל גבור חיל ונגיד ושר במחנה וגו' ויבא בית אלהיו ומיציאי מעיו שם הפילוהו בחרב שמע מינה במה הכם רבי אליעזר אומר ביד הכם שנאמר (יב) וירא ישראל את היד הגדולה היד שעתידה ליפרע מסנחריב רבי יהושע אומר באצבע הכם שנאמר (יג) ויאמרו החרטמים אל פרעה אצבע אלהים היא היא אצבע שעתידה ליפרע מסנחריב ר' אליעזר בנו של ר' יוסי הגלילי אומר אמר לו הקב"ה לגבריאל מגלך נטושה אמר לפניו רבונו של עולם נטושה ועומדת מששת ימי בראשית שנאמר (יד) מפני חרבות נדדו (ד) וגו' ר' שמעון בן יוחי אומר אותו הפרק זמן בישול פירות היה אמר לו הקב"ה לגבריאל כשאתה יוצא לבשל פירות הזקק להם שנאמר (טו) מידי עברו יקח אתכם כי בבקר בבקר יעבור ביום ובלילה והיה רק זועה הבין שמועה וגו' אמר רב פפא היינו דאמרי אינשי אגב אורחך לבעל דבבך אישתמע ויש אומרים בחוטמן נשף בהן ומתו שנאמר (טז) וגם נשף בהם ויבשו ר' ירמיה בר אבא אמר כפיים ספק להם ומתו שנאמר (יז) וגם אני (הכתי) [אכה] כפי אל כפי והניחותי חמתי ר' יצחק נפחא אמר אזנים גלה להם ושמעו שירה מפי חיות ומתו שנאמר (יח) מרוממתך נפצו גוים וכמה נשתייר מהם רב אמר (ה) עשרה שנאמר (יט) ושאר עץ יערו מספר יהיו ונער יכתבם כמה נער יכול לכתוב עשרה ושמואל אמר תשעה שנאמר (כ) ונשאר בו עוללות כנוקף זית שנים שלשה גרגרים בראש אמיר ארבעה חמשה בסעיפיה ר' יהושע בן לוי אמר ארבעה עשר שנאמר שנים שלשה [וכו'] ארבעה וחמשה רבי יוחנן אמר חמשה סנחריב ושני בניו נבוכד נצר ונבוזר אדן נבוזר אדן גמרא נבוכד נצר דכתיב (כא) ורוה דרביעאה דמי לבר אלהין ואי לאו דחזייה מנא הוה ידע סנחריב ושני בניו דכתיב (כב) ויהי הוא משתחוה בית נסרוך אלהיו ואדרמלך ושראצר בניו הכוהו בחרב אמר רבי אבהו אלמלא מקרא כתוב אי אפשר לאמרו דכתיב (כג) ביום ההוא יגלח ה' בתער השכירה בעברי נהר במלך אשור את הראש ושער הרגלים וגם את הזקן תספה אתא קודשא בריך הוא ואדמי ליה כגברא סבא א"ל כי אזלת לגבי מלכי מזרח ומערב דאייתיתינהו לבנייהו וקטלתינהו מאי אמרת להו אמר (ו) להו ההוא גברא בההוא פחדא נמי יתיב אמר ליה היכי נעביד א"ל זיל

ושני

רש"י

ויצא יעקב מבאר שבע וילך חרנה. אלמא בא לחרן וכתיב ויפגע במקום שעדיין לא הגיע לחרן שהיה עדיין בבית אל: שהתפללו בו אבותי. אברהם ויצחק (ז) (אברהם דכתיב ויעתק משם יצחק אין מקרא בידי): הרהר בדעתיה למהדר. למקום: קפצה ליה ארעא. והיה שם מיד וקרא מוכיח דכתיב ויפגע במקום שהמקום פגעו שקפלה לו הארץ ונתקרב לו המקום: הכי גרסינן ד"א אין פגיעה אלא תפלה. ונראה למורי דהכא לא מיגרסא הך מילתא: בית אל זה ירושלים חרן חוץ לארץ: כי בא השמש. ויבא השמש לא נאמר אלא כי בא השמש דמשמע שהיה דעתו לחזור כי עוד היום גדול כיון שראה כי בא השמש לן: ויזרח לו השמש. משמע השמש שהיה לו כבר שבא בשבילו כבר: ומנ"ל דכלה זרעיה דדוד. כדאפיך צלותיה: התם נמי אשתייר אביתר. מכהני נוב: שגלונות. מלכות: על אברהם. כשנלחם בד' מלכים: בעי אביי. האי חסר חד היכי קאמר אי חסר חד רבוא וכו': ראשונה. כת ראשונה מחיל של סנחריב: עברו בשחי. שטו הסוסים בירדן ונתמעטו המים עד שעברו: אמצעיים בקומה. זקופה ולא היו המים מגיעין אלא עד הצואר יגיע: שחי. כמו שחו: העלו עפר ברגליהם. שלא היה שם מים כל עיקר: קרתי. לשון מקור: ה"ג ויצא מלאך ה' ויך במחנה אשור אמר רבי וכו'. ולא גרסינן והא כתיב ויצא מלאך ה' אלמא כל המחנה אשור אינו אלא קפ"ה אלף ולעיל קתני מאתים וס' רבוא: הללו. קפ"ה אלף ראשי גייסות נגידי החיל שכן עולה לחשבון לכדאמרינן ארבעים וחמשה אלף בני מלכים שמנים אלף גבורים ששים אלף אחוזי חרב הרי קפ"ה אלף אבל האחרים שמתו אין מספר כדאמר והשאר פרשים אין מספר: במה הכם. המלאך: היד הגדולה. יד הגדולה לא נאמר אלא היד דמשמע היד שעתידה וכו': מגלך נטושה. שחוזה מגלך להרוג את אלו: גבריאל. ממונה על בשול הפירות: הזקק לאלו. לחיל סנחריב להרגן: אגב ארחך. כשתלך לדרכך לפי תומך: לבעל דבבך אשתמע. לשונאך התראה והפחידו: נשף. נפח: עשרה. שהנער יכול להטיף טיפה של דיו והיינו יו"ד שנשארו עשרה: ושמואל אמר תשעה. ונשאר בו עוללות כנוקף זית שאין נשארין בו אלא דבר מועט שנים או שלשה גרגרים בראש אמיר כן לא ישתייר במחנהו אלא דבר מועט וכמה ארבעה וחמשה בסעיפיה פוריה ארבעה וחמשה והיינו תשעה: י"ד שנים ושלשה ארבעה וחמשה. ר' יוחנן מקרא לא דייק להו אלא הכי קאמר הללו חמשה נשתיירו מהן סנחריב ושני בניו וקרא משמע כנוקף זית דמשייר מעט בראש ענף שנים או שלשה גרגרים כך ישתייר לו מעט ד' או ה': נבוכדנצר דכתיב. גבי [חנניה] מישאל ועזריה תוארו ורויה די רביעאה דמי לבר אלהין אלמא דחזא גבריאל והכירו בכבשן: סנחריב ושני בניו. דכתיב ויהי הוא משתחוה בית וגו': אי אפשר לאמרו. שהקדוש ב"ה בעצמו גלחו לסנחריב: דאייתיתינהו לבנייהו. כדאמרינן שהביא עמו ארבעים וחמשה אלף בני מלכים: אשני

הגהות הגר"א

[א] גמ' ד"א אין פגיעה כו' עד ואל תפגע בי. נמחק: [ב] שם והשאר פרשים. נ"ב ורגלים:

תורה אור השלם

א) ויצא יעקב מבאר שבע וילך חרנה: [בראשית כח, י]

ב) ויפגע במקום וילן שם כי בא השמש ויקח מאבני המקום וישם מראשתיו וישכב במקום ההוא: [בראשית כח, יא]

ג) ואתה אל תתפלל בעד העם הזה ואל תשא בעדם רנה ותפלה ואל תפגע בי כי אינני שמע אתך: [ירמיה ז, טז]

ד) ויזרח לו השמש כאשר עבר את פנואל והוא צלע על ירכו: [בראשית לב, לא]

ה) ועתליה אם אחזיהו ראתה כי מת בנה ותקם ותאבד את כל זרע הממלכה: [מלכים ב' יא, א]

ו) וימלט בן אחד לאחימלך בן אחטוב ושמו אביתר ויברח אחרי דוד: [שמואל א' כב, כ]

ז) וחלף ביהודה שטף ועבר עד צואר יגיע והיה מטות כנפיו מלא רחב ארצך עמנו אל: [ישעיה ח, ח]

ח) אני קרתי ושתיתי מים ואחרב בכף פעמי כל יארי מצור: [ישעיה לז, כה]

ט) ויצא מלאך יי ויכה במחנה אשור מאה ושמנים וחמשה אלף וישכימו בבקר והנה כלם פגרים מתים: [ישעיה לז, לו]

י) לכן ישלח האדון יי צבאות במשמניו רזון ותחת כבדו יקד יקד כיקוד אש: [ישעיה י, טז]

יא) וישלח יי מלאך ויכחד כל גבור חיל ונגיד ושר במחנה מלך אשור וישב בבשת פנים לארצו ויבא בית אלהיו ומיציאי מעיו שם הפילהו בחרב: [דברי הימים ב' לב, כא]

יב) וירא ישראל את היד הגדלה אשר עשה יי במצרים וייראו העם את יי ויאמינו ביי ובמשה עבדו: [שמות יד, לא]

יג) ויאמרו החרטמם אל פרעה אצבע אלהים הוא ויחזק לב פרעה ולא שמע אלהם כאשר דבר יי: [שמות ח, טו]

יד) כי מפני חרבות נדדו מפני חרב נטושה ומפני קשת דרוכה ומפני כבד מלחמה: [ישעיה כא, טו]

טו) מדי עברו יקח אתכם כי בבקר בבקר יעבר ביום ובלילה והיה רק זועה הבין שמועה: [ישעיה כח, יט]

טז) אף בל נטעו אף בל זרעו אף בל שרש בארץ גזעם וגם נשף בהם ויבשו וסערה כקש תשאם: [ישעיה מ, כד]

יז) וגם אני אכה כפי אל כפי והנחתי חמתי אני יי דברתי: [יחזקאל כא, כב]

יח) מקול המון נדדו עמים מרוממתך נפצו גוים: [ישעיה לג, ג]

יט) ושאר עץ יערו מספר יהיו ונער יכתבם: [ישעיה י, יט]

כ) ונשאר בו עוללת כנקף זית שנים שלשה גרגרים בראש אמיר ארבעה חמשה בסעפיה פריה נאם יי אלהי ישראל: [ישעיה יז, ו]

כא) ענה ואמר הא אנה חזה גברין ארבעה שרין מהלכין בגוא נורא וחבל לא איתי בהון ורוה די רביעאה דמה לבר אלהין: [דניאל ג, כה]

כב) ויהי הוא משתחוה בית נסרך אלהיו ואדרמלך ושראצר בניו הכהו בחרב והמה נמלטו ארץ אררט וימלך אסר חדן בנו תחתיו: [מלכים ב' יט, לז]

כג) ביום ההוא יגלח אדני בתער השכירה בעברי נהר במלך אשור את הראש ושער הרגלים וגם את הזקן תספה: [ישעיה ז, כ]

מסורת הש"ס

א) חולין צא:, ב) [ברכות כו: תענית ז: ת. סוטה יד.], ג) [עי' תוס' מגילה כא. ד"ה אלמלא], ד) [צ"ל מפני חרב נטושה וגר'], ה) [עי' תוספות מנחות כט. ד"ה קולי], ו) צ"ל ליה, ז) רש"ל מ"ז.

ליקוטי רש"י

וילך חרנה. דמשמע דמטא לחרן והדר כתיב ויפגע במקום דהיינו בית אל דאכתי לא מטא לחרן [חולין צא:]. ויפגע במקום. לא הזכיר הכתוב באיזה מקום אלא במקום הנזכר במקום אחר הוא הר המוריה שנאמר בו (בראשית כב, ד) וירא את המקום מרחוק. ויפגע, כמו (יהושע טז, ז) ופגע ביריחו (שם יט, יא) ופגע בדבשת ורבותינו פירשו לשון תפלה כמו (ירמיה ז, טז) ואל תפגע בי [בראשית כח, יא]. שהתפללו בו אבותי. האי בית אל לא הסמוך לעי הוא אלא ירושלים ועל שם יהיה בית אלהים קראו בית אל והוא הר המוריה שהתפלל בו אברהם והוא שדה שהתפלל בו יצחק דכתיב (בראשית כד) לשוח בשדה דהכי אמרינן בפסחים (פח.) אל הר ה' ואל בית אלהי יעקב מאי שנא יעקב אלא לא כאברהם שקראו הר דכתיב בהר ה' ולא כיצחק שקראו שדה דכתיב לשוח בשדה אלא כיעקב שקראו בית. קפצה ליה ארעא. לשון (דברים טו) לא תקפוץ את ידך נתקצרה ונתקמצה לו [חולין שם]. וכלפי שאמרו רבותינו שאמר הקב"ה צדיק זה בא לבית מלוני ויפטר בלא לינה ועוד אמרו יעקב קראה לירושלים בית אל וזו לוז היא ולא ירושלים ומהיכן למדו לומר כן אומר אני שנעקר הר המוריה ובא לכאן וזהו היא קפילת הארץ האמורה בשחיטת חולין (חולין צא:) שבא בית המקדש לקראתו עד בית אל וזהו ויפגע במקום, וא"ת וכשעבר יעקב על בית המקדש מדוע לא עכבו שם איהו לא יהיב לביה להתפלל במקום שהתפללו אבותיו ומן השמים יעכבוהו איהו עד חרן אזל כדאמרינן בפרק גיד הנשה (חולין צא:) וקרא מוכיח וילך חרנה כי מטא לחרן אמר אפשר שעברתי על מקום שהתפללו אבותי ולא התפללתי בו יהב דעתיה למהדר וחזר עד בית אל וקפלה לו הארץ [בראשית שם, יז ועי' במהרש"א בח"א חולין שם ד"ה מקום]. מיד ויפגע במקום. כאדם הפוגע בחבירו שבא כנגדו ודרשינן ליה נמי לשון תפלה כדכתיב (רות א) אל תפגעי בי [חולין שם]. אין פגיעה אלא תפלה. ולמדנו שתקן תפלת ערבית ושנה הכתוב ולא כתב ויתפלל ללמדך שקפלה לו הארץ כמו שמפורש בפרק גיד הנשה (חולין צא:). מיד בא השמש. היה לו לכתוב ויבא השמש וילן שם כי בא השמש משמע ששקעה לו חמה פתאום שלא בעונתה כדי שילין שם [בראשית שם, יא]. כדכתיב וילן שם כי בא השמש למה ליה למיכתב כי בא השמש אלא ללמדנו ששקעה קודם זמנה [חולין שם]. ויזרח לו השמש. לשון בני אדם הוא כשהגענו למקום פלוני האיר לנו השחר זהו פשוטו. ומדרש אגדה ויזרח לו לצרכו לרפאות את צלעתו, כמה דתימא (מלאכי ג, כ) שמש צדקה ומרפא בכנפיה ואותן שעות שמיהרה לשקוע בשבילו כשיצא מבאר שבע מיהרה לזרוח בשבילו [בראשית לב, לב]. שגלונות. שגל, מלכה כמו והשגל יושבת אצלו (דניאל ה) וישתון בהון מלכא ורברבנוהי שגלתיה ולחנתה [תהלים מה, י]. שגלתה, לשון מלכה בלשון ארמי כמו (נחמיה ב) והשגל יושבת אצלו [דניאל ה, ב]. והשגל אשתו המלכה כענין שנאמר (דניאל ה') שגלתיה ולחנתיה שכן נוהג המקרא לכתוב המלכה אצל הפלגש נשיו ופלגשיו כמו מלכות ופלגשים (שה"ש ו') [נחמיה ב, ו]. שריון קליפה. ושריון קשקשים כמין קשקשות דגים עשוין מברזל נופלים על גב השריון (ס"א נקבי השריון) קשקשת לכל נקב [ש"א יז, ה]. יש שריונות שהם עשוין קליפים כענין שנא' (ש"א יז, ה) ושריון קשקשים והקליפים נופלים על נקבי השריון וסותמין אותן [מ"א כב, לד]. וחלף ביהודה. בארץ יהודה. שטף. בחזקה [ישעיה ח, ח]. ראשי גייסות. כולם מלכים קשורי כתרים בראשיהם וקטן שבכולם היה שר על שני אלפים שנאמר (ישעיהו לו) ואתנה לך אלפים סוסים ואיך תשיב את פני פחת אחד וגו' למדנו על קטן שבפחותים שהוא שר על אלפי' איש ונפלו הם וגייסותם [שם לז, לו]. ומיציאי מעיו. כדכתיב (ישעיה לז) ובניו הכוהו בחרב [דה"ב לב, כא]. מגלך נטושה. כמו לטושה כל אותיות אשר מוצאיהם קרובים להיות ממקום אחד מתחלפות זו בזו נו"ן בלמ"ד כענין שנא' (נחמיה יג) לעשות לו נשכה כמו לשכה [שם כא, טו]. והיה רק זועה הבין שמועה. זועה לכל השומעים להבין שמועות פורענו' הקשות שאביא עליכם כל השומעים יזועו [שם כח, יט].

[המשך בדף צו.]

The Gemara objects that Asaliah's massacre should not have sufficed to expiate David's sin:

וְהָא אִשְׁתַּיֵּיר לֵיהּ יוֹאָשׁ – **But Yoash remained** alive **to** perpetuate **[the Davidic dynasty]** even after Asaliah's purge![13] Thus, why was her action deemed a sufficient punishment for David's sin?

The Gemara answers:

הָתָם נַמִּי אִשְׁתַּיֵּיר אֶבְיָתָר – **There, too,** in the case of Nov, a single Kohen named **Evyasar survived,** דִּכְתִיב – **as it is written:** ,,וַיִּמָּלֵט בֵּן־אֶחָד לַאֲחִימֶלֶךְ בֶּן־אֲחִטוּב וּשְׁמוֹ אֶבְיָתָר'' – ***One son of Achimelech ben Achituv escaped, and his name was Evyasar.***[14] Thus, David's punishment exactly corresponded to the crime for which he was punished; just as his negligence had resulted in the death of all but one of the Kohanim of Nov, similarly, all but one of his descendants were put to death by Asaliah.

The Gemara concludes with a final comment on this episode:

אָמַר רַב יְהוּדָה אָמַר רַב – **Rav Yehudah said in the name of Rav:** אִלְמָלֵא (לא) נִשְׁתַּיֵּיר אֶבְיָתָר לַאֲחִימֶלֶךְ בֶּן אֲחִיטוּב – **Had not** at least **one son, Evyasar, been left** alive **to Achimelech ben Achituv** after the massacre, לֹא נִשְׁתַּיֵּיר מִזַּרְעוֹ שֶׁל דָּוִד שָׂרִיד וּפָלִיט – **not a single survivor would have remained of David's progeny.** That is, even Yoash would have been killed in Asaliah's purge, for Divine justice would have demanded that David's punishment correspond exactly to his sin.

Having digressed to discuss the massacre at Nov and its consequences, the Gemara resumes its discussion of Sancheiriv's invasion of Judah:

אָמַר רַב יְהוּדָה אָמַר רַב – **Rav Yehudah said in the name of Rav:** בָּא עֲלֵיהֶם סַנְחֵרִיב הָרָשָׁע – **The wicked Sancheiriv came upon [the Jews]** בְּאַרְבָּעִים וַחֲמִשָּׁה אֶלֶף אִישׁ בְּנֵי מְלָכִים יוֹשְׁבִים בִּקְרוֹנוֹת שֶׁל זָהָב – **with** an army of **forty-five thousand princes seated in golden chariots,** וְעִמָּהֶן שֵׁגְלוֹנוֹת וְזוֹנוֹת – **accompanied by princesses and harlots;**[15] וּבִשְׁמוֹנִים אֶלֶף גִּבּוֹרִים לְבוּשֵׁי שִׁרְיוֹן קְלִיפָּה – **and** he came upon them **with** an additional **eighty thousand mighty warriors clad in coats of mail,** וּבְשִׁשִּׁים אֶלֶף אֲחוּזֵי חֶרֶב רָצִים לְפָנָיו – **and sixty thousand swordsmen running before him.** וְהַשְּׁאָר פָּרָשִׁים – **And the rest** of his troops were **cavalry.**[16]

The Gemara adds that this was not the only time a force so vast was marshaled against the Jews:

וְכֵן בָּאוּ עַל אַבְרָהָם – **And so they came upon Abraham,**[17] וְכֵן עֲתִידִין לָבוֹא עִם גּוֹג וּמָגוֹג – **and so they are destined to come with Gog and Magog** in their apocalyptic war against the Jews.[18]

The Gemara cites a Baraisa in a similar vein:

בְּמַתְנִיתָא תָּנָא – **In a Baraisa it was taught:** אוֹרֶךְ מַחֲנֵהוּ אַרְבַּע מֵאוֹת פַּרְסֵי – Sancheiriv's legions were so numerous that THE LENGTH OF HIS CAMP extended for FOUR HUNDRED *PARSAOS*,[19] רֹחַב צַוַּאר סוּסָיו אַרְבָּעִים פַּרְסֵי – and his horses were so numerous that if they were to stand side by side, THE WIDTH OF all HIS HORSES' NECKS would extend for FORTY *PARSAOS*. סַךְ מַחֲנֵהוּ מָאתַיִם וְשִׁשִּׁים רִיבּוֹא אֲלָפִים חָסֵר חַד – THE TOTAL NUMBER OF troops in HIS CAMP WAS TWO HUNDRED AND SIXTY MYRIAD THOUSANDS [i.e. two billion, six hundred million] MINUS ONE.[20]

The Gemara seeks to clarify the meaning of this last statement:

בָּעֵי אַבָּיֵי – **Abaye inquired:** What is the meaning of "minus one"? חָסֵר חַד רִיבּוֹא – Does it mean **minus one** entire **myriad?** אוֹ חָסֵר חַד אַלְפָּא – **Or** perhaps it means **minus a thousand,** אוֹ חָסֵר מְאָה – **or minus a hundred,** אוֹ חָסֵר חַד – **or minus** just **one** person?

The Gemara responds:

תֵּיקוּ – **[The question] remains unresolved.**[21]

The Gemara recounts how the vast Assyrian army crossed the Jordan River on their way to Judea:

תָּנָא – **It was taught** in a Baraisa: רִאשׁוֹנִים עָבְרוּ בְּשָׂחִי – THE FIRST UNITS of the Assyrian army CROSSED the river SWIMMING,[22] שֶׁנֶּאֱמַר – AS IT IS WRITTEN:[23] ,,וְחָלַף בִּיהוּדָה שָׁטַף וְעָבַר'' – *IT WILL SWEEP INTO JUDAH, OVERFLOWING AND PASSING THROUGH.* אֶמְצָעִיִּים עָבְרוּ בְּקוֹמָה – THE MIDDLE UNITS, however, did not need to swim; rather, THEY MARCHED ERECT across the Jordan,[24] שֶׁנֶּאֱמַר – AS IT IS WRITTEN:[25] ,,עַד־צַוָּאר יַגִּיעַ'' – *IT*

NOTES

13. See previous note.

14. *I Samuel* 22:20. Evyasar was the son of Achimelech ben Achituv, the Kohen who aided David in Nov.

15. Sancheiriv's troops were so certain of an easy victory that they brought their women to the battlefield. In so doing, they displayed contempt for the Jews, implying that their army posed no threat even to defenseless women (*Ben Yehoyada*).

16. [Scripture states that the angel who descended on Sancheiriv's camp killed 185,000 men. It also states, however, that some troops survived the onslaught. Thus, the Gemara first gives the identity of the 185,000 whom Scripture describes as having died – 45,000 princes, 80,000 warriors in coats of mail, and 60,000 swordsman – and then it mentions that "the rest of his troops" were cavalry (*Yad Ramah*).]

17. The Gemara's reference is to Abraham's war against the four kings, mentioned in *Genesis* ch. 14 (see *Rashi;* see also *Bereishis Rabbah* 42:3 and *Pirkei DeRabbi Eliezer* 27; cf. *Margaliyos HaYam*).

18. Scripture indicates that the coming of the Messiah will be connected with the invasion of the Land of Israel by the armies of Magog, led by their king, Gog (see *Ezekiel* chs. 38-39, and *Zechariah* ch. 14); see also above, 94a note 12). Our Gemara asserts that these armies will be as numerous as those of Sancheiriv.

The three enemy forces that are mentioned here – Sancheiriv's army, the armies of the four kings, and Gog and Magog – were all defeated through clearly miraculous circumstances (*Maharsha*). Furthermore, all three wars represent turning points in world history.

19. A *parsah* is a measure of distance equivalent to four *mil.* In modern terms, four hundred *parsaos* would equal approximately one thousand miles.

20. *Ben Yehoyada* says that these numbers are not to be taken literally; rather we have to understand that the Assyrian army was so formidable, so well-disciplined and experienced, that it had the might and overwhelming impact of a force of two-and-a-half billion. Similarly, *Maharal* explains that, while Sancheiriv's forces were vast, the figures given for Sancheiriv's armies should not be taken literally but rather to symbolize the power, authority, and royalty that these armies represented. *Maharal* generally sees numbers as conveying basic concepts (for instance, the number four represents spatial extension in all directions). See *Rashbam, Pesachim* 119a ד"ה משוי שלש מאות, and *Rosh* to *Tamid* 29a ד"ה אמר רבא גוז in regard to the number three hundred; and *R' Avraham ben HaRambam* (*Ma'amar Al HaAggados*) in regard to the number four hundred; see also 96b. [If the numbers are not taken literally, the discussion in the Gemara about the size of the army must be taken as a discussion of just how powerful the army was.]

21. See *Melo HaRo'im* and *Pesach Einayim.*

22. I.e. when the first units crossed the Jordan, the river was too deep to wade across, so the horses actually swam across the river (*Rashi*).

23. *Isaiah* 8:8. This verse describes the Assyrian army sweeping into Judah, overflowing from the Jordan River. The verse speaks of the Jordan as if it had reached a flood stage.

24. [When the first units emerged from the Jordan, they naturally withdrew from the river whatever water had absorbed into their clothing. Thus, the Baraisa means to say that the first units were so numerous that they actually drained the Jordan of a significant amount of water. When *they* were crossing the river had been too deep to wade across, but by the time the middle units crossed, the water reached only to their necks, and the soldiers could wade across.]

25. Ibid.

דכתיב א) ויצא יעקב מבאר שבע וילך חרנה וכתיב ב) ויפגע במקום וילן שם כי בא השמש [א] כי מטא לחרן אמר אפשר עברתי על מקום שהתפללו בו אבותי ואני לא התפללתי בו בעי למיהדר כיון דהרהר בדעתיה למיהדר קפצה ליה ארעא מיד ויפגע במקום [א] דבר אחר [ב] אין פגיעה אלא תפלה שנאמר ג) ואתה אל תתפלל בעד העם הזה ואל תשא בעדם רנה ותפלה ואל תפגע בי ב) וילן שם כי בא השמש בתר דצלי בעי למיהדר אמר הקב"ה צדיק זה בא לבית מלוני יפטר בלא לינה מיד בא השמש והיינו דכתיב ד) ויזרח לו השמש וכי לו בלבד זרחה והלא לכל העולם כולו זרחה אלא א"ר יצחק שמש שבא בעבורו זרחה בעבורו ומנלן דכלה זרעיה דדוד דכתי' ה) ועתליה אם אחזיהו ראתה כי מת בנה ותקם ותאבד את כל זרע הממלכה והא אשתייר ליה יואש התם נמי אשתייר אביתר דכתיב ו) וימלט בן אחד לאחימלך בן אחיטוב ושמו אביתר אמר רב יהודה אמר רב אלמלא (ג) לא) נשתייר אביתר לאחימלך בן אחיטוב לא נשתייר מזרעו של דוד שריד ופליט אמר רב יהודה אמר רב בא עליהם סנחריב הרשע בארבעים וחמשה אלף איש בני מלכים יושבים בקרונות של זהב ועמהן שגלונות וזונות ובשמנים אלף גבורים לבושי שריון קליפה ובששים אלף אחוזי חרב רצים לפניו [ב] והשאר פרשים וכן באו על אברהם וכן עתידין לבוא עם גוג ומגוג במתניתא תנא אורך מחנהו ארבע מאות פרסי רחב צואר סוסיו ארבעים פרסי סך מחנהו מאתים ושישים ריבוא אלפים חסר חד בעי אביי חסר חד ריבויא או חסר חד אלפא או חסר מאה או חסר חד תיקו תנא ראשונים עברו בשחי שנאמר ז) וחלף ביהודה שטף ועבר אמצעיים עברו בקומה שנאמר ז) עד צואר יגיע אחרונים העלו עפר ברגליהם ולא מצאו מים בנהר לשתות עד שהביאו מים ממקום אחר ושתו שנאמר ח) אני קרתי ושתיתי מים וגו' והכתיב ט) ויצא מלאך ה' ויכה במחנה אשור מאה ושמנים וחמשה אלף (ויקומו) [וישכימו] בבקר והנה כלם פגרים מתים אמר ר' אבהו הללו ראשי גייסות הן אמר רב אשי דיקא נמי דכתיב י) במשמניו רזון בשמינים דאית בהו אמר רבינא דיקא נמי דכתיב יא) וישלח ה' מלאך ויכחד כל גבור חיל ונגיד ושר במחנה וגו' ויבא בית אלהיו ומיציאי מעיו שם הפילוהו בחרב שמע מינה במה הכם רבי אליעזר אומר ביד הכם שנאמר יב) וירא ישראל את היד הגדולה היד שעתידה ליפרע מסנחריב רבי יהושע אומר באצבע הכם שנאמר יג) ויאמרו החרטמים אל פרעה אצבע אלהים היא אצבע שעתידה ליפרע מסנחריב ר' אליעזר בנו של ר' יוסי הגלילי אומר אמר לו הקב"ה לגבריאל מגלך נטושה אמר לפניו רבונו של עולם נטושה ועומדת משׁשת ימי בראשית שנאמר יד) מפני חרבות נדדו ד) וגו' ר' שמעון בן יוחי אומר אותו הפרק זמן בישול פירות היה אמר לו הקב"ה לגבריאל כשאתה יוצא לבשל פירות הזקק להם שנאמר טו) מידי עברו יקח אתכם כי בבקר בבקר יעבור ביום ובלילה והיה רק זועה הבין שמועה וגו' אמר רב פפא היינו דאמרי אינשי אגב אורחך לבעל דבבך אישתמע ויש אומרים בחוטמן נשף בהן ומתו שנאמר טז) וגם נשף בהם ויבשו ר' ירמיה בר אבא אמר כפיים ספק להם ומתו שנאמר יז) וגם אני (הכתי) [אכה] כפי אל כפי והניחותי חמתי ר' יצחק נפחא אמר אזנים גלה להם ושמעו שירה מפי חיות ומתו שנאמר יח) מרוממתך נפצו גוים וכמה נשתייר מהם רב אמר ה) עשרה שנאמר יט) ושאר עץ יערו מספר יהיו ונער יכתבם כמה נער יכול לכתוב עשרה ושמואל אמר תשעה שנאמר כ) ונשאר בו עוללות כנוקף זית שנים שלשה גרגרים בראש אמיר ארבעה חמשה בסעיפיה ר' יהושע בן לוי אמר ארבעה עשר שנאמר שנים שלשה [וכו'] ארבעה וחמשה רבי יוחנן אמר חמשה סנחריב ושני בניו נבוכד נצר ונבוזר אדן נבוזר אדן גמרא נבוכד נצר דכתיב כא) ורוה דרביעאה דמי לבר אלהין ואי לאו דחזייה מנא הוה ידע סנחריב ושני בניו דכתיב כב) ויהי הוא משתחוה בית נסרוך אלהיו ואדרמלך ושראצר בניו הכוהו בחרב אמר רבי אבהו אלמלא מקרא כתוב אי אפשר לאמרו דכתיב כג) ביום ההוא יגלח ה' בתער השכירה בעברי נהר במלך אשור את הראש ושער הרגלים וגם את הזקן תספה אתא קודשא בריך הוא ואדמי ליה כגברא סבא א"ל כי אזלת לגבי מלכי מזרח ומערב דאייתיתינהו לבנייהו וקטלתינהו מאי אמרת להו אמר ו) להו ההוא גברא בההוא פחדא נמי יתיב אמר ליה היכי נעביד א"ל זיל ושני

רש"י

ויצא יעקב מבאר שבע וילך חרנה. אלמא בא לחרן וכתיב ויפגע במקום שעדיין לא הגיע לחרן שהיה עדיין בבית אל: שהתפללו בו אבותי. אברהם ויצחק ז) (אברהם דכתיב ויעתק משם יצחק אין מקרא בידי): הרהר בדעתיה למהדר. למקום: קפצה ליה ארעא. והיה שם מיד וקרא מוכיח דכתיב ויפגע במקום שהמקום פגעו שקפלה לו הארץ ונתקרב לו המקום: הכי גרסינן ד"א אין פגיעה אלא תפלה. ונראה למורי דהכא לא מיגרסא הך מילתא: בית אל זה ירושלים חרן חוץ לארץ: כי בא השמש. ויבא השמש לא נאמר אלא כי בא השמש דמשמע שהיה דעתו לחזור כי עוד היום גדול כיון שראה כי בא השמש לן: ויזרח לו השמש. משמע השמש שהיה לו כבר שבא בשבילו כבר: ומנ"ל דכלה זרעיה דדוד. כדאפיך ללותיה: התם נמי אשתייר אביתר. מכהני נוב: שגלונות. מלכות: על אברהם. כשנלחם בד' מלכים: בעי אביי. האי חסר חד היכי קאמר אי חסר חד רבוא וכו': ראשונה. כת ראשונה מחיל של סנחריב: עברו בשחי. שטו הסוסים בירדן ונתמעטו המים עד שעברו: אמצעיים בקומה. זקופה ולא היו המים מגיעין אלא עד הצואר יגיע: שחי. כמו שחו: העלו עפר ברגליהם. שלא היה שם מים כל עיקר: קרתי. לשון מקור: ה"ג ויצא מלאך ה' ויך במחנה אשור אמר רבי וכו'. ולא גרסינן והא כתיב ויצא מלאך ה' אלמא כל המחנה אשור אינו אלא קפ"ה אלף ולעיל קתני מאתים וס' רבוא: הללו. קפ"ה אלף ראשי גייסות נגידי החיל שכן עולה לחשבון לכדאמרינן ארבעים וחמשה אלף בני מלכים שמנים אלף גבורים ששים אלף אחוזי חרב הרי קפ"ה אלף אבל האחרים שמתו אין מספר כדאמר והשאר פרשים אין מספר: במה הכם. המלאך: היד הגדולה. יד הגדולה לא נאמר אלא היד דמשמע היד שעתידה וכו': מגלך נטושה. שחוזה מגלך להרוג את אלו: גבריאל. ממונה על בשול הפירות: הזקק לאלו. לחיל סנחריב להרגן: אגב ארחך. כשתלך לדרכך לפי תומך: לבעל דבבך אשתמע. לשונאך התראה והפחידו: נשף. נפח: עשרה. שהנער יכול להטיף טיפה של דיו והיינו יו"ד שנשארו עשרה: ושמואל אמר תשעה. ונשאר בו עוללות כנוקף זית שאין נשארין בו אלא דבר מועט שנים או שלשה גרגרים בראש אמיר כן לא ישתייר במחנהו אלא דבר מועט וכמה ארבעה וחמשה בסעיפיה פוריה ארבעה וחמשה והיינו תשעה: י"ד שנים ושלשה ארבעה וחמשה. ר' יוחנן מקרא לא דייק להו אלא הכי קאמר הללו חמשה נשתיירו מהן סנחריב ושני בניו וקרא משמע כנוקף זית דמשייר מעט בראש ענף שנים או שלשה גרגרים כך ישתייר לו מעט ד' או ה': נבוכדנצר דכתיב. גבי [חנניה] מישאל ועזריה תואריו ורויה די רביעאה דמי לבר אלהין אלמא דחזא גבריאל והכירו בכבשן: סנחריב ושני בניו. דכתיב ויהי הוא משתחוה בית וגו': אי אפשר לאמרו. שהקדוש ב"ה בעצמו גלחו לסנחריב: דאייתיתינהו לבנייהו. כדאמרינן שהביא עמו ארבעים וחמשה אלף בני מלכים: אשני

הגהות הגר"א

[א] גמ' ד"א אין פגיעה כו' עד ואל תפגע בי. נמחק: [ב] שם והשאר פרשים. נ"ב ורגלים:

תורה אור השלם

א) וַיֵּצֵא יַעֲקֹב מִבְּאֵר שָׁבַע וַיֵּלֶךְ חָרָנָה: [בראשית כח, י]

ב) וַיִּפְגַּע בַּמָּקוֹם וַיָּלֶן שָׁם כִּי בָא הַשֶּׁמֶשׁ וַיִּקַּח מֵאַבְנֵי הַמָּקוֹם וַיָּשֶׂם מְרַאֲשֹׁתָיו וַיִּשְׁכַּב בַּמָּקוֹם הַהוּא: [בראשית כח, יא]

ג) וְאַתָּה אַל תִּתְפַּלֵּל בְּעַד הָעָם הַזֶּה וְאַל תִּשָּׂא בַעֲדָם רִנָּה וּתְפִלָּה וְאַל תִּפְגַּע בִּי כִּי אֵינֶנִּי שֹׁמֵעַ אֹתָךְ: [ירמיה ז, טז]

ד) וַיִּזְרַח לוֹ הַשֶּׁמֶשׁ כַּאֲשֶׁר עָבַר אֶת פְּנוּאֵל וְהוּא צֹלֵעַ עַל יְרֵכוֹ: [בראשית לב, לא]

ה) וַעֲתַלְיָה אֵם אֲחַזְיָהוּ רָאֲתָה כִּי מֵת בְּנָהּ וַתָּקָם וַתְּאַבֵּד אֵת כָּל זֶרַע הַמַּמְלָכָה: [מלכים ב' יא, א]

ו) וַיִּמָּלֵט בֵּן אֶחָד לַאֲחִימֶלֶךְ בֶּן אֲחִטוּב וּשְׁמוֹ אֶבְיָתָר וַיִּבְרַח אַחֲרֵי דָוִד: [שמואל א' כב, כ]

ז) וְחָלַף בִּיהוּדָה שָׁטַף וְעָבַר עַד צַוָּאר יַגִּיעַ וְהָיָה מֻטּוֹת כְּנָפָיו מְלֹא רֹחַב אַרְצְךָ עִמָּנוּ אֵל: [ישעיה ח, ח]

ח) אֲנִי קַרְתִּי וְשָׁתִיתִי מָיִם וְאַחְרִב בְּכַף פְּעָמַי כֹּל יְאֹרֵי מָצוֹר: [ישעיה לז, כה]

ט) וַיֵּצֵא מַלְאַךְ יְיָ וַיַּכֶּה בְּמַחֲנֵה אַשּׁוּר מֵאָה וּשְׁמֹנִים וַחֲמִשָּׁה אָלֶף וַיַּשְׁכִּימוּ בַבֹּקֶר וְהִנֵּה כֻלָּם פְּגָרִים מֵתִים: [ישעיה לז, לו]

י) לָכֵן יְשַׁלַּח הָאָדוֹן יְיָ צְבָאוֹת בְּמִשְׁמַנָּיו רָזוֹן וְתַחַת כְּבֹדוֹ יֵקַד יְקֹד כִּיקוֹד אֵשׁ: [ישעיה י, טז]

יא) וַיִּשְׁלַח יְיָ מַלְאָךְ וַיַּכְחֵד כָּל גִּבּוֹר חַיִל וְנָגִיד וְשָׂר בְּמַחֲנֵה מֶלֶךְ אַשּׁוּר וַיָּשָׁב בְּבֹשֶׁת פָּנִים לְאַרְצוֹ וַיָּבֹא בֵּית אֱלֹהָיו וּמִיצִיאֵי מֵעָיו שָׁם הִפִּילֻהוּ בֶחָרֶב: [דברי הימים ב' לב, כא]

יב) וַיַּרְא יִשְׂרָאֵל אֶת הַיָּד הַגְּדֹלָה אֲשֶׁר עָשָׂה יְיָ בְּמִצְרַיִם וַיִּירְאוּ הָעָם אֶת יְיָ וַיַּאֲמִינוּ בַּייָ וּבְמֹשֶׁה עַבְדּוֹ: [שמות יד, לא]

יג) וַיֹּאמְרוּ הַחַרְטֻמִּם אֶל פַּרְעֹה אֶצְבַּע אֱלֹהִים הִוא וַיֶּחֱזַק לֵב פַּרְעֹה וְלֹא שָׁמַע אֲלֵהֶם כַּאֲשֶׁר דִּבֶּר יְיָ: [שמות ח, טו]

יד) כִּי מִפְּנֵי חֲרָבוֹת נָדָדוּ מִפְּנֵי חֶרֶב נְטוּשָׁה וּמִפְּנֵי קֶשֶׁת דְּרוּכָה וּמִפְּנֵי כֹּבֶד מִלְחָמָה: [ישעיה כא, טו]

טו) מִדֵּי עָבְרוֹ יִקַּח אֶתְכֶם כִּי בַבֹּקֶר בַּבֹּקֶר יַעֲבֹר בַּיּוֹם וּבַלָּיְלָה וְהָיָה רַק זְוָעָה הָבִין שְׁמוּעָה: [ישעיה כח, יט] טז) אַף בַּל נִטָּעוּ אַף בַּל זֹרָעוּ אַף בַּל שֹׁרֵשׁ בָּאָרֶץ גִּזְעָם וְגַם נָשַׁף בָּהֶם וַיִּבָשׁוּ וּסְעָרָה כַּקַּשׁ תִּשָּׂאֵם: [ישעיה מ, כד] יז) וְגַם אֲנִי אַכֶּה כַפִּי אֶל כַּפִּי וַהֲנִחֹתִי חֲמָתִי אֲנִי יְיָ דִּבַּרְתִּי: [יחזקאל כא, כב] יח) מִקּוֹל הָמוֹן נָדְדוּ עַמִּים מֵרוֹמְמֻתֶךָ נָפְצוּ גּוֹיִם: [ישעיה לג, ג] יט) וּשְׁאָר עֵץ יַעְרוֹ מִסְפָּר יִהְיוּ וְנַעַר יִכְתְּבֵם: [ישעיה י, יט] כ) וְנִשְׁאַר בּוֹ עוֹלֵלֹת כְּנֹקֶף זַיִת שְׁנַיִם שְׁלֹשָׁה גַּרְגְּרִים בְּרֹאשׁ אָמִיר אַרְבָּעָה חֲמִשָּׁה בִּסְעִפֶיהָ פֹּרִיָּה נְאֻם יְיָ אֱלֹהֵי יִשְׂרָאֵל: [ישעיה יז, ו] כא) עָנֵה וְאָמַר הָא אֲנָה חָזֵה גֻּבְרִין אַרְבְּעָה שְׁרַיִן מַהְלְכִין בְּגוֹא נוּרָא וַחֲבָל לָא אִיתַי בְּהוֹן וְרֵוֵהּ דִּי רְבִיעָאָה דָּמֵה לְבַר אֱלָהִין: [דניאל ג, כה] כב) וַיְהִי הוּא מִשְׁתַּחֲוֶה בֵּית נִסְרֹךְ אֱלֹהָיו וְאַדְרַמֶּלֶךְ וְשַׂרְאֶצֶר בָּנָיו הִכֻּהוּ בַחֶרֶב וְהֵמָּה נִמְלְטוּ אֶרֶץ אֲרָרָט וַיִּמְלֹךְ אֵסַר חַדֹּן בְּנוֹ תַּחְתָּיו: [מלכים ב' יט, לז] כג) בַּיּוֹם הַהוּא יְגַלַּח אֲדֹנָי בְּתַעַר הַשְּׂכִירָה בְּעֶבְרֵי נָהָר בְּמֶלֶךְ אַשּׁוּר אֶת הָרֹאשׁ וְשַׂעַר הָרַגְלָיִם וְגַם אֶת הַזָּקָן תִּסְפֶּה: [ישעיה ז, כ]

מסורת הש"ס

א) חולין צא:, ב) [ברכות כו: תענית ז: ח. סוטה יד.], ג) [עי' תוס' מגילה כא. ד"ה אלמלא], ד) [צ"ל מפני חרב נטושה וגו'], ה) [עי' תוספות מנחות כט. ד"ה קולין], ו) צ"ל ליה, ז) רש"ל מ"ז.

ליקוטי רש"י

וילך חרנה. דמשמע דמטא לחרן והדר כתיב ויפגע במקום דהיינו בית אל דאכתי לא מטא לחרן [חולין צא:]. ויפגע במקום. לא הזכיר הכתוב באיזה מקום אלא במקום הנזכר במקום אחר הוא הר המוריה שנאמר בו (בראשית כב, ד) וירא את המקום מרחוק. ויפגע, כמו (יהושע טז, ז) ופגע ביריחו (שם יט, יא) ופגע בדבשת ורבותינו פירשו לשון תפלה כמו (ירמיה ז, טז) ואל תפגע בי [בראשית כח, יא]. שהתפללו בו אבותי. האי בית אל לא הסמוך לעי הוא אלא ירושלים ועל שם יהיה בית אלהים קראו בית אל והוא הר המוריה שהתפלל בו אברהם והוא שדה שהתפלל בו יצחק דכתיב (בראשית כד) לשוח בשדה דהכי אמרינן בפסחים (פח.) אל הר ה' ואל בית אלהי יעקב מאי שנא יעקב אלא לא כאברהם שקראו הר דכתיב בהר ה' ולא כיצחק שקראו שדה דכתיב לשוח בשדה אלא כיעקב שקראו בית. קפצה ליה ארעא. לשון (דברים טו) לא תקפוץ את ידך נתקצרה ונתקמצה לו [חולין שם]. וכלפי שאמרו רבותינו שאמר הקב"ה צדיק זה בא לבית מלוני ויפטר בלא לינה ועוד אמרו יעקב קראה לירושלים בית אל וזו לוז היא ולא ירושלים ומהיכן למדו לומר כן אומר אני שנעקר הר המוריה ובא לכאן וזהו היא קפילת הארץ האמורה בשחיטת חולין (חולין צא:) שבא בית המקדש לקראתו עד בית אל וזהו ויפגע במקום, וא"ת וכשעבר יעקב על בית המקדש מדוע לא עכבו שם איהו לא יהיב לביה להתפלל במקום שהתפללו אבותיו ומן השמים יעכבוהו איהו עד חרן אזל כדאמרינן בפרק גיד הנשה (חולין צא:) וקרא מוכיח וילך חרנה כי מטא לחרן אמר אפשר שעברתי על מקום שהתפללו אבותי ולא התפללתי בו יהב דעתיה למהדר וחזר עד בית אל וקפלה לו הארץ [בראשית שם, יז ועי' במהרש"א בח"א חולין שם ד"ה מקום]. מיד ויפגע במקום. כאדם הפוגע בחבירו שבא כנגדו ודרשינן ליה נמי לשון תפלה כדכתיב (רות א) אל תפגעי בי [חולין שם]. אין פגיעה אלא תפלה. ולמדנו שתקן תפלת ערבית ושנה הכתוב ולא כתב ויתפלל ללמדך שקפלה לו הארץ כמו שמפורש בפרק גיד הנשה (חולין צא:). מיד בא השמש. היה לו לכתוב ויבא השמש וילן שם כי בא השמש משמע ששקעה לו חמה פתאום שלא בעונתה כדי שילין שם [בראשית שם, יא]. כדכתיב וילן שם כי בא השמש למה ליה למיכתב כי בא השמש אלא ללמדנו ששקעה קודם זמנה [חולין שם]. ויזרח לו השמש. לשון בני אדם הוא כשהגענו למקום פלוני האיר לנו השחר זהו פשוטו. ומדרש אגדה ויזרח לו לצרכו לרפאות את צלעתו, כמה דתימא (מלאכי ג, כ) שמש צדקה ומרפא בכנפיה ואותן שעות שמיהרה לשקוע בשבילו כשיצא מבאר שבע מיהרה לזרוח בשבילו [בראשית לב, לב]. שגלונות. שגל, מלכה כמו והשגל יושבת אצלו (דניאל ה) וישתון בהון מלכא ורברבנוהי שגלתיה ולחנתה [תהלים מה, י]. שגלתה, לשון מלכה בלשון ארמי כמו (נחמיה ב) והשגל יושבת אצלו [דניאל ה, ב]. והשגל אשתו המלכה כענין שנאמר (דניאל ה') שגלתיה ולחנתיה שכן נוהג המקרא לכתוב המלכה אצל הפלגש נשיו ופלגשיו כמו מלכות ופלגשים (שה"ש ו') [נחמיה ב, ו]. שריון קליפה. ושריון קשקשים כמין קשקשות דגים עשוין מברזל נופלים על גב השריון (ס"א נקבי השריון) קשקשת לכל נקב [ש"א יז, ה]. יש שריונות שהם עשוין קליפים קליפים כענין שנא' (ש"א יז, ה) ושריון קשקשים והקליפים נופלים על נקבי השריון וסותמין אותן [מ"א כב, לד]. וחלף ביהודה. בארץ יהודה. שטף. בחזקה [ישעיה ח, ח]. ראשי גייסות. כולם מלכים קשורי כתרים בראשיהם וקטן שבכולם היה שר על שני אלפים שנאמר (ישעיהו לו) ואתנה לך אלפים סוסים ואיך תשיב את פני פחת אחד וגו' למדנו על קטן שבפחותים שהוא שר על אלפי' איש ונפלו הם וגייסותם [שם לז, לו]. ומיציאי מעיו. כדכתיב (ישעיה לז) ובניו הכוהו בחרב [דה"ב לב, כא]. מגלך נטושה. כמו לטושה כל אותיות אשר מוצאיהם קרובים להיות ממקום אחד מתחלפות זו בזו נו"ן בלמ"ד כענין שנא' (נחמיה יג) לעשות לו נשכה כמו לשכה [ישעיה כא, טו]. והיה רק זועה הבין שמועה. זועה לכל השומעים להבין שמועות פורענו' הקשות שאביא עליכם כל השומעים יזועו [שם כח, יט].

[המשך בדף צו.]

WILL REACH TO THE NECK. אַחֲרוֹנִים הֶעֱלוּ עָפָר בְּרַגְלֵיהֶם – And THE LAST UNITS RAISED CLOUDS OF DUST WITH THEIR FEET as they marched across; וְלֹא מָצְאוּ מַיִם בַּנָּהָר לִשְׁתּוֹת – INDEED, THEY DID NOT even FIND enough WATER left IN THE RIVER TO DRINK,[26] עַד שֶׁהֵבִיאוּ מַיִם מִמָּקוֹם אַחֵר וְשָׁתוּ – and they went thirsty UNTIL THEY finally BROUGHT WATER FROM SOMEWHERE ELSE AND DRANK that water; שֶׁנֶּאֱמַר – FOR IT IS WRITTEN:[27] ,,אֲנִי קַרְתִּי וְשָׁתִיתִי מַיִם" וגו' – *I DUG SPRINGS AND DRANK WATER* etc.; *with the soles of my feet, I cause all the mighty rivers to dry up.*

In the preceding discussion, the Gemara described Sancheiriv's legions as totaling over two million troops. The Gemara now challenges the accuracy of this figure:

וְהָכְתִיב – But in Scripture **it is** explicitly **written:**[28] ,,וַיֵּצֵא מַלְאַךְ ה' וַיַּכֶּה בְּמַחֲנֵה אַשּׁוּר מֵאָה וּשְׁמוֹנִים וַחֲמִשָּׁה אָלֶף – ***And an angel of HASHEM went forth and slew one hundred and eighty-five thousand of the camp of Assyria,*** (ויקומו) וַיַּשְׁכִּימוּ בַבֹּקֶר – ***and they arose in the morning,*** וְהִנֵּה כֻלָּם פְּגָרִים מֵתִים" – ***and behold they were all dead corpses.*** Thus, the verse indicates that the Assyrian troops numbered far less than two billion men![29] – ? –

The Gemara answers:

אָמַר רַבִּי אַבָּהוּ – **R' Abahu said:** הַלָּלוּ רָאשֵׁי גְיָיסוֹת הֵן – **These** one hundred and eighty-five thousand men mentioned by the verse **were** just **the commanders of the legions.**[30] The entire army, however, was much larger.

The Gemara corroborates this explanation:

אָמַר רַב אַשִׁי – **Rav Ashi said:** דַּיְקָא נַמִּי דִּכְתִיב – **A precise reading** of Scripture **also yields this** conclusion, **for it is written:**[31] ,,בְּמִשְׁמַנָּיו רָזוֹן" – *Then the Lord God of Hosts will send* ***leanness into his fat ones,*** בְּשַׁמְנִים דְּאִית בְּהוּ – which implies that Scripture is dealing only with **the "fat ones" among [Sancheiriv's army],** i.e. his commanders.[32]

A similar corroboration:

אָמַר רָבִינָא – **Ravina said:** דַּיְקָא נַמִּי דִּכְתִיב – **A precise reading** of Scripture **also yields this** conclusion, **for it is written:** ,,וַיִּשְׁלַח ה' מַלְאָךְ וַיַּכְחֵד כָּל־גִּבּוֹר חַיִל וְנָגִיד וְשַׂר בְּמַחֲנֵה" וגו' – ***HASHEM sent an angel who destroyed every warrior, commander and officer in the army*** *[of the King of Assyria];* ,,וַיָּבֹא בֵּית אֱלֹהָיו וּמִיצִיאֵי מֵעָיו שָׁם הִפִּילֻהוּ בֶחָרֶב" – *then, [Sancheiriv] returned in humiliation to his own land,* ***and came to his idol's temple, where his own offspring felled him by the sword.***[33] Now, in this verse, Scripture describes those killed by the angel as being officers, not common soldiers. שְׁמַע מִינָּהּ – Thus, **from this you can conclude** that the total troop count of Sancheiriv's army well exceeded one hundred and eighty-five thousand men.

The Gemara presents some opinions as to precisely how the angel smote the Assyrians:

בַּמֶּה הִכָּם – **With what did [the angel] strike them?** רַבִּי אֱלִיעֶזֶר אוֹמֵר – **R' Eliezer says:** בַּיָּד הִכָּם – **[The angel] struck them with** its **hand,**[34] שֶׁנֶּאֱמַר ,,וַיַּרְא יִשְׂרָאֵל אֶת־הַיָּד הַגְּדֹלָה" – **for Scripture states: *Israel saw the great hand,***[35] which implies: הַיָּד שֶׁעֲתִידָה לִיפָּרַע מִסַּנְחֵרִיב – The Jews who witnessed the splitting of the Sea saw **the** same **hand that was destined to punish Sancheiriv.**

רַבִּי יְהוֹשֻׁעַ אוֹמֵר – **R' Yehoshua says:** בְּאֶצְבַּע הִכָּם – The angel **struck them with** its **finger,** שֶׁנֶּאֱמַר ,,וַיֹּאמְרוּ הַחַרְטֻמִּים אֶל־פַּרְעֹה אֶצְבַּע אֱלֹהִים הִוא" – **for Scripture states: *The sorcerers said to Pharaoh, "It is the finger of God!"***[36] implying: הִיא אֶצְבַּע שֶׁעֲתִידָה לִיפָּרַע מִסַּנְחֵרִיב – **It was the same finger that was destined to punish Sancheiriv.**

The Gemara expounds further:

רַבִּי אֱלִיעֶזֶר בְּנוֹ שֶׁל רַבִּי יוֹסֵי הַגְּלִילִי אוֹמֵר – **R' Eliezer the son of R' Yose HaGlili says:** אָמַר לוֹ הַקָּדוֹשׁ בָּרוּךְ הוּא לְגַבְרִיאֵל – Just before the plague descended on the Assyrians, **the Holy One, Blessed is He, said to the** angel **Gabriel:** מַגָּלְךָ נְטוּשָׁה – **Is your scythe sharpened** to begin destroying the Assyrian enemy? אָמַר לְפָנָיו – **[Gabriel]** then **replied [to God]:** רִבּוֹנוֹ שֶׁל עוֹלָם – **"Master of the Universe!** נְטוּשָׁה וְעוֹמֶדֶת מִשֵּׁשֶׁת יְמֵי בְרֵאשִׁית – **It has been sharpened and ready** ever **since the Six Days of Creation!"**[37] שֶׁנֶּאֱמַר ,,מִפְּנֵי חֲרָבוֹת נָדָדוּ" וגו' – **For** indeed,

NOTES

26. I.e. the second units crossed the river in such numbers that they removed all the remaining water in the river, leaving the Jordan completely dry. By the time the last units crossed the Jordan, the riverbed was like dry land, and the trampling of their feet raised clouds of dust (see *Rashi*).

[*Maharsha* suggests that the three waves of invaders that crossed the Jordan corresponded to the three groups of soldiers mentioned earlier: Princes, warriors in coats of mail, and swordsmen.]

27. *Isaiah* 37:25.

28. Ibid. v. 36.

29. [The verse first states that the angel killed one hundred and eighty-five thousand, and then states that when the survivors arose in the morning, they saw that "they were all dead corpses." This implies that for all intents and purposes, the Assyrian force was destroyed. It would thus seem that Sancheiriv's troops numbered only a bit more than one hundred and eighty-five thousand (see *Yad Ramah*).]

30. I.e. the verse mentions only the *officers* killed by the angel. The total number of troops who died, however, was much greater (*Rashi*; cf. *Sanhedrei Ketanah*).

31. Ibid. 10:16. In this verse, the prophet describes how God will punish Sancheiriv for his overwhelming arrogance. The reference is thus to the plague that was destined to decimate the Assyrian army.

32. In other words, the verse describes only the destruction of the *commanders,* while the total number of Assyrian soldiers who were killed actually numbered in the billions (*Rashi*).

33. *II Chronicles* 32:21. This verse recounts the same plague mentioned in *Isaiah* 37:36. It, however, explicitly states that the angel killed *the commanders* of Sancheiriv's army. Thus, we can infer that when the verse in *Isaiah* mentions the decimation of one hundred and eighty-five thousand men, it is referring to the officers alone.

34. *Rashi. Maharal* suggests that when we speak of a blow delivered with the hand, the expression indicates that the blow was massive and final. Such, for example, was the nature of the blow against the Egyptians at the Red Sea, where the entire Egyptian army was destroyed; and such, according to R' Eliezer, was the nature of the blow here, where the vast Assyrian army was similarly decimated. A blow delivered by God's finger, by contrast, is one that is less encompassing and not as destructive. Thus, the ten plagues – which were clearly less destructive than the total decimation of the Egyptian army at the Red Sea – are characterized by Scripture as being the work of God's "finger" (see *Exodus* 8:15).

35. *Exodus* 14:31. The verse describes the crushing defeat of the Egyptian army at the Red Sea. Since Scripture states that the Jews saw ***the** hand* [using the definite article], the implication is that the "hand" the Israelites saw at that moment was the same force they would see again at some other point in their history. Our Gemara states that this second appearance of God's "hand" occurred in the miraculous and all-encompassing defeat of the Assyrians in the days of Chizkiah (*Rashi*).

36. Ibid. 8:15. In this verse, sorcerers tell Pharaoh that the plague of lice was not brought about by sorcery, but was rather a Divine affliction visited upon Egypt. [In this case, the word הוא, which often implies a reference to a *particular* event or thing, alludes to the notion that this was a "particular" finger of God that would reappear elsewhere in history.]

37. The Six Days of Creation are the period during which God established the physical laws that would forever govern the workings of the universe. At this time, however, God also decreed certain exceptions to this order; that is, He stipulated that there would be moments in history when natural law would be suspended, and miracles would occur. This, according to *Maharsha,* is the context in which we must understand Gabriel's response to God here. The collapse of the Assyrian army in the days of Chizkiah was clearly a supernatural event – an overt miracle that was well outside the natural order of things. Thus, Gabriel was

הגהות הגר"א

[א] גמ' ד"א אין פגיעה כו' עד ואל תפגע בי. נמחק: **[ב]** שם והשאר פרשים. נ"ב ורגלים:

ויצא יעקב מבאר שבע וילך חרנה. אלמא בא לחרן וכתיב ויפגע במקום שעדיין לא הגיע לחרן שהיה עדיין בבית אל: **שהתפללו בו אבותי.** אברהם ויצחק [ז](אברהם דכתיב ויעתק משם יצחק אין מקרא בידי): **הרהר בדעתיה למהדר. למקום: קפצה ליה ארעא.** והיה שם מיד וקרא מוכיח דכתיב ויפגע במקום שהמקום פגעו שקפצה לו הארץ ונתקרב לו המקום: **הכי גרסינן ד"א אין פגיעה אלא תפלה.** ונראה למורי דהכא לא מיגרסא הך מילתא: בית אל זה ירושלים חרן חוץ לארץ: **כי בא השמש.** ויבא השמש לא נאמר אלא כי בא השמש דמשמע שהיה דעתו לחזור כי עוד היום גדול כיון שראה כי בא השמש לן: **ויזרח לו השמש.** משמע השמש שהיה לו כבר שבא בשבילו כבר: **ומנ"ל דכלה זרעיה דדוד.** כדאפיך גלותיה: **התם נמי אשתייר אביתר.** מכהני נוב: **שגלונות.** מלכות: **על אברהם.** כשנלחם בד' מלכים: **בעי אביי.** האי חסר חד היכי קאמר אי חסר חד רבוא וכו': **ראשונה.** כת ראשונה מחיל של סנחריב: **עברו בשחי.** שטו הסוסים בירדן ונתמעטו המים עד שעברו: **אמצעיים בקומה.** זקופה ולא היו המים מגיעין אלא עד הצואר יגיע: **שחי.** כמו שחו: **העלו עפר ברגליהם.** שלא היה שם מים כל עיקר: **קרתי.** לשון מקור: **ה"ג ויצא מלאך ה' ויך במחנה אשור אמר רבי וכו'.** ולא גרסינן והא כתיב וילא מלאך ה' אלמא כל המחנה אשור אינו אלא קפ"ה אלף ולעיל קתני מאתים וס' רבוא: **הללו.** קפ"ה אלף ראשי גייסות נגידי החיל שכן עולה לחשבון לכדאמרינן ארבעים וחמשה אלף בני מלכים שמנים אלף גבורים ששים אלף אחוזי חרב הרי קפ"ה אלף אבל האחרים שמתו אין מספר כדאמר והשאר פרשים אין מספר: **במה הכם.** המלאך: **היד הגדולה.** יד הגדולה לא נאמר אלא היד דמשמע היד שעתידה וכו': **מגלך נטושה.** שחוזה מגלך להרוג את אלו: **גבריאל.** ממונה על בשול הפירות: **הזקק לאלו.** לחיל סנחריב להרגן: **אגב ארחך.** כשתלך לדרכך לפי תומך: **לבעל דבבך אשתמע.** לשונאך התראה והפקידו: **נשף.** נפח: **עשרה.** שהנער יכול להטיף טיפה של דיו והיינו יו"ד שנשארו עשרה: **ושמואל אמר תשעה.** ונשאר בו עוללות כנוקף זית שאין נשארין בו אלא דבר מועט שנים או שלשה גרגרים בראש אמיר כן לא ישתייר במחנהו אלא דבר מועט וכמה ארבעה וחמשה בסעיפיה פוריה ארבעה וחמשה והיינו תשעה: **י"ד שנים ושלשה ארבעה וחמשה.** ר' יוחנן מקרא לא דייק להו אלא הכי קאמר הללו חמשה נשתיירו מהן סנחריב ושני בניו וקרא משמע כנוקף זית דמשייר מעט בראש ענף שנים או שלשה גרגרים כך ישתייר לו מעט ד' או ה': **נבוכדנצר דכתיב.** גבי [חנניה] מישאל ועזריה תוארו ורויה די רביעאה דמי לבר אלהין אלמא דחזא גבריאל והכירו בכבשן: **סנחריב ושני בניו.** דכתיב ויהי הוא משתחוה בית וגו': **אי אפשר לאמרו.** שהקדוש ב"ה בעצמו גלחו לסנחריב: **דאייתיתינהו לבנייהו.** כדאמרינן שהביא עמו ארבעים וחמשה אלף בני מלכים: אשני

דכתיב [א] ויצא יעקב מבאר שבע וילך חרנה וכתיב [ב] ויפגע במקום וילן שם כי בא השמש [א] כי מטא לחרן אמר אפשר עברתי על מקום שהתפללו בו אבותי ואני לא התפללתי בו בעי למיהדר כיון דהרהר בדעתיה למיהדר קפצה ליה ארעא מיד ויפגע במקום [א] דבר אחר [ב] אין פגיעה אלא תפלה שנאמר [ג] ואתה אל תתפלל בעד העם הזה ואל תשא בעדם רנה ותפלה ואל תפגע בי [ב] וילן שם כי בא השמש בתר דצלי בעי למיהדר אמר הקב"ה צדיק זה בא לבית מלוני יפטר בלא לינה מיד בא השמש והיינו דכתיב [ד] ויזרח לו השמש וכי לו בלבד זרחה והלא לכל העולם כולו זרחה אלא א"ר יצחק שמש שבא בעבורו זרחה בעבורו ומנלן דכלה זרעיה דדוד דכתי' [ה] ועתליה אם אחזיהו ראתה כי מת בנה ותקם ותאבד את כל זרע הממלכה והא אשתייר ליה יואש התם נמי אשתייר אביתר דכתיב [ו] וימלט בן אחד לאחימלך בן אחיטוב ושמו אביתר אמר רב יהודה אמר רב אלמלא ([ג] לא) נשתייר אביתר לאחימלך בן אחיטוב לא נשתייר מזרעו של דוד שריד ופליט אמר רב יהודה אמר רב בא עליהם סנחריב הרשע בארבעים וחמשה אלף איש בני מלכים יושבים בקרונות של זהב ועמהן שגלונות וזונות ובשמנים אלף גבורים לבושי שריון קליפה ובששים אלף אחוזי חרב רצים לפניו [ב] והשאר פרשים וכן באו על אברהם וכן עתידין לבוא עם גוג ומגוג במתניתא תנא אורך מחנהו ארבע מאות פרסי רחב צואר סוסיו ארבעים פרסי סך מחנהו מאתים וששים ריבוא אלפים חסר חד בעי אביי חסר חד ריבויא או חסר חד אלפא או חסר מאה או חסר חד תיקו תנא ראשונים עברו בשחי שנאמר [ז] וחלף ביהודה שטף ועבר אמצעיים עברו בקומה שנאמר [ז] עד צואר יגיע אחרונים העלו עפר ברגליהם ולא מצאו מים בנהר לשתות עד שהביאו מים ממקום אחר ושתו שנאמר [ח] אני קרתי ושתיתי מים וגו' והכתיב [ט] ויצא מלאך ה' ויכה במחנה אשור מאה ושמנים וחמשה אלף (ויקומו) [וישכימו] בבקר והנה כלם פגרים מתים אמר ר' אבהו הללו ראשי גייסות הן אמר רב אשי דיקא נמי דכתיב [י] במשמניו רזון בשמינים דאית בהו אמר רבינא דיקא נמי דכתיב [יא] וישלח ה' מלאך ויכחד כל גבור חיל ונגיד ושר במחנה וגו' ויבא בית אלהיו ומיציאי מעיו שם הפילוהו בחרב שמע מינה במה הכם רבי אליעזר אומר ביד הכם שנאמר [יב] וירא ישראל את היד הגדולה היד שעתידה ליפרע מסנחריב רבי יהושע אומר באצבע הכם שנאמר [יג] ויאמרו החרטמים אל פרעה אצבע אלהים היא היא אצבע שעתידה ליפרע מסנחריב ר' אליעזר בנו של ר' יוסי הגלילי אומר אמר לו הקב"ה לגבריאל מגלך נטושה אמר לפניו רבונו של עולם נטושה ועומדת משששת ימי בראשית שנאמר [יד] מפני חרבות נדדו [ד] וגו' ר' שמעון בן יוחי אומר אותו הפרק זמן בישול פירות היה אמר לו הקב"ה לגבריאל כשאתה יוצא לבשל פירות הזקק להם שנאמר [טו] מידי עברו יקח אתכם כי בבקר בבקר יעבור ביום ובלילה והיה רק זועה הבין שמועה וגו' אמר רב פפא היינו דאמרי אינשי אגב אורחך לבעל דבבך אישתמע ויש אומרים בחוטמן נשף בהן ומתו שנאמר [טז] וגם נשף בהם ויבשו ר' ירמיה בר אבא אמר כפיים ספק להם ומתו שנאמר [יז] וגם אני (הכתי) [אכה] כפי אל כפי והניחותי חמתי ר' יצחק נפחא אמר אזנים גלה להם ושמעו שירה מפי חיות ומתו שנאמר [יח] מרוממתך נפצו גוים וכמה נשתייר מהם רב אמר [ה] עשרה שנאמר [יט] ושאר עץ יערו מספר יהיו ונער יכתבם כמה נער יכול לכתוב עשרה ושמואל אמר תשעה שנאמר [כ] ונשאר בו עוללות כנוקף זית שנים שלשה גרגרים בראש אמיר ארבעה חמשה בסעיפיה ר' יהושע בן לוי אמר ארבעה עשר שנאמר שנים שלשה [וכו'] ארבעה וחמשה רבי יוחנן אמר חמשה סנחריב ושני בניו נבוכד נצר ונבוזר אדן נבוזר אדן גמרא נבוכד נצר דכתיב [כא] ורוה דרביעאה דמי לבר אלהין ואי לאו דחזייה מנא הוה ידע סנחריב ושני בניו דכתיב [כב] ויהי הוא משתחוה בית נסרוך אלהיו ואדרמלך ושראצר בניו הכוהו בחרב אמר רבי אבהו אלמלא מקרא כתוב אי אפשר לאמרו דכתיב [כג] ביום ההוא יגלח ה' בתער השכירה בעברי נהר במלך אשור את הראש ושער הרגלים וגם את הזקן תספה אתא קודשא בריך הוא ואדמי ליה כגברא סבא א"ל כי אזלת לגבי מלכי מזרח ומערב דאייתיתינהו לבנייהו וקטלתינהו מאי אמרת להו אמר [ו] להו ההוא גברא בההוא פחדא נמי יתיב אמר ליה היכי נעביד א"ל זיל ושני

תורה אור השלם

א) וַיֵּצֵא יַעֲקֹב מִבְּאֵר שָׁבַע וַיֵּלֶךְ חָרָנָה: [בראשית כח, י]

ב) וַיִּפְגַּע בַּמָּקוֹם וַיָּלֶן שָׁם כִּי בָא הַשֶּׁמֶשׁ וַיִּקַּח מֵאַבְנֵי הַמָּקוֹם וַיָּשֶׂם מְרַאֲשֹׁתָיו וַיִּשְׁכַּב בַּמָּקוֹם הַהוּא: [בראשית כח, יא]

ג) וְאַתָּה אַל תִּתְפַּלֵּל בְּעַד הָעָם הַזֶּה וְאַל תִּשָּׂא בַעֲדָם רִנָּה וּתְפִלָּה וְאַל תִּפְגַּע בִּי כִּי אֵינֶנִּי שֹׁמֵעַ אֹתָךְ: [ירמיה ז, טז]

ד) וַיִּזְרַח לוֹ הַשֶּׁמֶשׁ כַּאֲשֶׁר עָבַר אֶת פְּנוּאֵל וְהוּא צֹלֵעַ עַל יְרֵכוֹ: [בראשית לב, לא]

ה) וַעֲתַלְיָה אֵם אֲחַזְיָהוּ רָאֲתָה כִּי מֵת בְּנָהּ וַתָּקָם וַתְּאַבֵּד אֵת כָּל זֶרַע הַמַּמְלָכָה: [מלכים ב' יא, א]

ו) וַיִּמָּלֵט בֵּן אֶחָד לַאֲחִימֶלֶךְ בֶּן אֲחִטוּב וּשְׁמוֹ אֶבְיָתָר וַיִּבְרַח אַחֲרֵי דָוִד: [שמואל א' כב, כ]

ז) וְחָלַף בִּיהוּדָה שָׁטַף וְעָבַר עַד צַוָּאר יַגִּיעַ וְהָיָה מֻטּוֹת כְּנָפָיו מְלֹא רֹחַב אַרְצְךָ עִמָּנוּ אֵל: [ישעיה ח, ח]

ח) אֲנִי קַרְתִּי וְשָׁתִיתִי מָיִם וְאַחְרִב בְּכַף פְּעָמַי כֹּל יְאֹרֵי מָצוֹר: [ישעיה לז, כה]

ט) וַיֵּצֵא מַלְאַךְ יְיָ וַיַּכֶּה בְּמַחֲנֵה אַשּׁוּר מֵאָה וּשְׁמֹנִים וַחֲמִשָּׁה אָלֶף וַיַּשְׁכִּימוּ בַבֹּקֶר וְהִנֵּה כֻלָּם פְּגָרִים מֵתִים: [ישעיה לז, לו]

י) לָכֵן יְשַׁלַּח הָאָדוֹן יְיָ צְבָאוֹת בְּמִשְׁמַנָּיו רָזוֹן וְתַחַת כְּבֹדוֹ יֵקַד יְקֹד כִּיקוֹד אֵשׁ: [ישעיה י, טז]

יא) וַיִּשְׁלַח יְיָ מַלְאָךְ וַיַּכְחֵד כָּל גִּבּוֹר חַיִל וְנָגִיד וְשָׂר בְּמַחֲנֵה מֶלֶךְ אַשּׁוּר וַיָּשָׁב בְּבֹשֶׁת פָּנִים לְאַרְצוֹ וַיָּבֹא בֵּית אֱלֹהָיו וּמִיצִיאֵי מֵעָיו שָׁם הִפִּילֻהוּ בֶחָרֶב: [דברי הימים ב' לב, כא]

יב) וַיַּרְא יִשְׂרָאֵל אֶת הַיָּד הַגְּדֹלָה אֲשֶׁר עָשָׂה יְיָ בְּמִצְרַיִם וַיִּירְאוּ הָעָם אֶת יְיָ וַיַּאֲמִינוּ בַּייָ וּבְמֹשֶׁה עַבְדּוֹ: [שמות יד, לא]

יג) וַיֹּאמְרוּ הַחַרְטֻמִּם אֶל פַּרְעֹה אֶצְבַּע אֱלֹהִים הִוא וַיֶּחֱזַק לֵב פַּרְעֹה וְלֹא שָׁמַע אֲלֵהֶם כַּאֲשֶׁר דִּבֶּר יְיָ: [שמות ח, טו]

יד) כִּי מִפְּנֵי חֲרָבוֹת נָדָדוּ מִפְּנֵי חֶרֶב נְטוּשָׁה וּמִפְּנֵי קֶשֶׁת דְּרוּכָה וּמִפְּנֵי כֹּבֶד מִלְחָמָה: [ישעיה כא, טו]

טו) מִדֵּי עָבְרוֹ יִקַּח אֶתְכֶם כִּי בַבֹּקֶר בַּבֹּקֶר יַעֲבֹר בַּיּוֹם וּבַלָּיְלָה וְהָיָה רַק זְוָעָה הָבִין שְׁמוּעָה: [ישעיה כח, יט] טז) אַף בַּל נִטָּעוּ אַף בַּל זֹרָעוּ אַף בַּל שֹׁרֵשׁ בָּאָרֶץ גִּזְעָם וְגַם נָשַׁף בָּהֶם וַיִּבָשׁוּ וּסְעָרָה כַּקַּשׁ תִּשָּׂאֵם: [ישעיה מ, כד] יז) וְגַם אֲנִי אַכֶּה כַפִּי אֶל כַּפִּי וַהֲנִחֹתִי חֲמָתִי אֲנִי יְיָ דִּבַּרְתִּי: [יחזקאל כא, כב] יח) מִקּוֹל הָמוֹן נָדְדוּ עַמִּים מֵרוֹמְמֻתֶךָ נָפְצוּ גּוֹיִם: [ישעיה לג, ג] יט) וּשְׁאָר עֵץ יַעְרוֹ מִסְפָּר יִהְיוּ וְנַעַר יִכְתְּבֵם: [ישעיה י, יט] כ) וְנִשְׁאַר בּוֹ עוֹלֵלֹת כְּנֹקֶף זַיִת שְׁנַיִם שְׁלֹשָׁה גַרְגְּרִים בְּרֹאשׁ אָמִיר אַרְבָּעָה חֲמִשָּׁה בִּסְעִפֶיהָ פֹּרִיָּה נְאֻם יְיָ אֱלֹהֵי יִשְׂרָאֵל: [ישעיה יז, ו] כא) עָנֵה וְאָמַר הָא אֲנָה חָזֵה גֻּבְרִין אַרְבְּעָה שְׁרַיִן מַהְלְכִין בְּגוֹא נוּרָא וַחֲבָל לָא אִיתַי בְּהוֹן וְרֵוֵהּ דִּי רְבִיעָאָה דָּמֵה לְבַר אֱלָהִין: [דניאל ג, כה] כב) וַיְהִי הוּא מִשְׁתַּחֲוֶה בֵּית נִסְרֹךְ אֱלֹהָיו וְאַדְרַמֶּלֶךְ וְשַׂרְאֶצֶר בָּנָיו הִכֻּהוּ בַחֶרֶב וְהֵמָּה נִמְלְטוּ אֶרֶץ אֲרָרָט וַיִּמְלֹךְ אֵסַר חַדֹּן בְּנוֹ תַּחְתָּיו: [מלכים ב' יט, לז] כג) בַּיּוֹם הַהוּא יְגַלַּח אֲדֹנָי בְּתַעַר הַשְּׂכִירָה בְּעֶבְרֵי נָהָר בְּמֶלֶךְ אַשּׁוּר אֶת הָרֹאשׁ וְשַׂעַר הָרַגְלָיִם וְגַם אֶת הַזָּקָן תִּסְפֶּה: [ישעיה ז, כ]

מסורת הש"ס

א) חולין צא:, ב) [ברכות כו: תענית ז: ח. סוטה יד.], ג) [עי' תוס' מגילה כא. ד"ה אלמלא], ד) [נ"ל מפני חרב נטושה וגו'], ה) [עי' תוספות מנחות כט. ד"ה קולי], ו) נ"ל ליה, ז) רש"ל מ"ז.

ליקוטי רש"י

וילך חרנה. דמשמע דמטא לחרן והדר כתיב ויפגע במקום דהיינו בית אל דאכתי לא מטא לחרן [חולין צא:]. **ויפגע במקום.** לא הזכיר הכתוב באיזה מקום אלא במקום הנזכר במקום אחר הוא הר המוריה שנאמר בו (בראשית כב, ד) וירא את המקום מרחוק. **ויפגע,** כמו (יהושע טז, ז) ופגע ביריחו (שם יט, יא) ופגע בדבשת ורבותינו פירשו לשון תפלה כמו (ירמיה ז, טז) ואל תפגע בי [בראשית כח, יא]. **שהתפללו בו אבותי.** האי בית אל לא הסמוך לעי הוא אלא ירושלים ועל שם יהיה בית אלהים קראו בית אל והוא הר המוריה שהתפלל בו אברהם והוא שדה שהתפלל בו יצחק דכתיב (בראשית כד) לשוח בשדה דהכי אמרינן בפסחים (פח.) אל הר ה' ואל בית אלהי יעקב מאי שנא יעקב אלא לא כאברהם שקראו הר דכתיב בהר ה' ולא כיצחק שקראו שדה דכתיב לשוח בשדה אלא כיעקב שקראו בית. **קפצה ליה ארעא.** לשון (דברים טו) לא תקפוץ את ידך נתקצרה ונתקמצה לו [חולין שם]. וכלפי שאמרו רבותינו שאמר הקב"ה צדיק זה בא לבית מלוני ויפטר בלא לינה ועוד אמרו יעקב קראה לירושלים בית אל וזו לוז היא ולא ירושלים ומהיכן למדו לומר כן אומר אני שנעקר הר המוריה ובא …

… למיכתב כי בא השמש אלא ללמדנו ששקעה קודם זמנה [חולין שם]. **ויזרח לו השמש.** לשון בני א… פלוני האיר לנו השחר זהו פשוטו. ומדרש אגדה ויזרח לו לצרכו לרפאות את צלעתו, כמה דתימא (… ומרפא בכנפיה ואותן שעות שמיהרה לשקוע בשבילו כשיצא מבאר שבע מיהרה לזרוח בשבילו [ברא… שגל, מלכה כמו והשגל יושבת אצלו (נחמיה ב) והשגל יושבת אצלו (דניאל ה) וישתון בהון מלכא ורברבנוהי שגלתיה ולחנתה [תה… מלכה בלשון ארמי כמו (נחמיה ב) והשגל יושבת אצלו [דניאל ה, ב]. והשגל אשתו המלכה כענין שנ… ולחנתיה שכן נוהג המקרא לכתוב המלכה אצל הפלגש נשיו ופלגשיו כמו מלכות ופלגשים (שה"ש … קליפה. ושריון קשקשים כמין קשקשות דגים עשוין מברזל נופלים על גב השריון (ס"א נקבי ה… [ש"א יז, ה]. יש שריונות שהם עשוין קליפים קליפים כענין שנא' (ש"א יז, ה) ושריון קשקשים ו… השריון וסותמין אותן [מ"א כב, לד]. **וחלף ביהודה.** בארץ יהודה. **שטף.** בחזקה [ישעיה ח, ח… מלכים קשורי כתרים בראשיהם וקטן שבכולם היה שר על שני אלפים שנאמר (ישעיהו לו) ואתנ… תשיב את פני פחת אחד וגו' למדנו על קטן שבפחותים שהוא שר על אלפי' איש ונפלו הם וגייסות… **מעיו.** כדכתיב (ישעיה לז) ובניו הכוהו בחרב [דה"ב לב, כא]. **מגלך נטושה.** כמו לטושה כל אותיות אשר מוצאיהם קרובים להיות ממקום אחד מתחלפות זו בזו נו"ן בלמ"ד כענין שנא' (נחמיה יג) לעשות לו נשכה כמ… והיה רק זועה הבין שמועה. זועה לכל השומעים להבין שמועות פורענו' הקשות שאביא עליכם כל השומעים יזועו [שם כח, יט].

[המשך בדף צו.]

Scripture states:[38] ***They fled from the swords* etc.,** *from the sharpened sword.*

A similar homiletical account of Gabriel's destructive mission: רַבִּי שִׁמְעוֹן בֶּן יוֹחַי אוֹמֵר – **R' Shimon ben Yochai says:** אותו הַפֶּרֶק זְמַן בִּישּׁוּל פֵּירוֹת הָיָה – **That season** during which Sancheiriv's army besieged Jerusalem **was the season when the fruits** of Eretz Israel **were due to ripen.** אָמַר לוֹ הַקָּדוֹשׁ בָּרוּךְ הוּא לְגַבְרִיאֵל – At that time, **the Holy One, Blessed is He, said to Gabriel:** כְּשֶׁאַתָּה יוֹצֵא לְבַשֵּׁל פֵּירוֹת – **When you go forth** in the land **to ripen the fruits,** הִזָּקֵק לָהֶם – **engage [the Assyrians]** in battle![39] שֶׁנֶּאֱמַר ,,מִדֵּי עָבְרוֹ יִקַּח אֶתְכֶם – **For it is written:** ***When he passes through he shall take you,*** כִּי־בַבֹּקֶר בַּבֹּקֶר יַעֲבֹר בַּיּוֹם וּבַלָּיְלָה – ***for he shall pass through every morning, by day and by night.*** וְהָיָה רַק־זְוָעָה הָבִין שְׁמוּעָה'' וגו' – ***When [this] message is [truly] understood it shall inspire sheer terror.***[40]

The Gemara adds:

אָמַר רַב פָּפָּא – **Rav Pappa said:** הַיְינוּ דְּאָמְרֵי אִינְשֵׁי – **[Gabriel's actions] are** an example of **the popular adage:** אַגַּב אוֹרְחָךְ לְבַעַל דְּבָבָךְ אִישְׁתַּמַּע – **"As you happen to pass by, make your voice heard to your foe."**[41]

The Gemara proceeds to list several other opinions as to how the Assyrians died:

וְיֵשׁ אוֹמְרִים בְּחוֹטְמָן נָשַׁף בָּהֶן וָמֵתוּ – **And some say: [Gabriel] breathed into their nostrils and they died,** שֶׁנֶּאֱמַר ,,וְגַם נָשַׁף בָּהֶם וַיִּבָשׁוּ'' – **as it is written:**[42] ***When He blows upon them, they wither.*** רַבִּי יִרְמְיָה בַּר אַבָּא אָמַר – **R' Yirmiyah bar Abba said:** כַּפַּיִם סָפַק לָהֶם וָמֵתוּ – **[Gabriel] clapped his hands and they died,**[43] שֶׁנֶּאֱמַר ,,וְגַם־אֲנִי (הכתי) אַכֶּה כַפִּי אֶל־כַּפִּי וַהֲנִחֹתִי חֲמָתִי'' – **as it is written:**[44] ***I too shall pound My hand upon My hand, and I shall [thereby] put My fury to rest.*** רַבִּי יִצְחָק נַפְחָא אָמַר – **R' Yitzchak Nafcha said:** אָזְנַיִם גִּלָּה לָהֶם – **[Gabriel] opened their ears** וְשָׁמְעוּ שִׁירָה מִפִּי חַיּוֹת וָמֵתוּ – **so** that **they heard the** Heavenly **song being sung by the Chayos,**[45] **and** as a result, **they died.**[46] שֶׁנֶּאֱמַר ,,מֵרוֹמְמֻתֶךָ נָפְצוּ גּוֹיִם'' – **For it is written:**[47] ***The nations scattered because of Your exaltedness.***

It is clear from the Scriptural account (*II Kings* 19:35) that at least a small remnant of Sancheiriv's army survived the angel's strike. The Gemara now seeks to determine precisely how many Assyrians survived:

וְכַמָּה נִשְׁתַּיֵּיר מֵהֶם – **And how many of them remained** alive? רַב אָמַר עֲשָׂרָה – **Rav said: Ten** soldiers survived, שֶׁנֶּאֱמַר – **for it is written:** ,,וּשְׁאָר עֵץ יַעְרוֹ מִסְפָּר יִהְיוּ – ***And the remnant of the trees of his forest shall be few,*** וְנַעַר יִכְתְּבֵם'' – ***such that a child can write them down.***[48] כַּמָּה נַעַר יָכוֹל לִכְתּוֹב – Now, **how many** [i.e. what numeral] **is a child able to write down?** עֲשָׂרָה – The numeral **ten.**[49]

A second opinion is offered, based on a different verse:

וּשְׁמוּאֵל אָמַר – **And Shmuel said:** תִּשְׁעָה – **Nine** soldiers survived, שֶׁנֶּאֱמַר – **for it is written:** ,,וְנִשְׁאַר־בּוֹ עֹלֵלוֹת – ***And there shall be left therein small, lone grapes;*** כְּנֹקֶף זַיִת שְׁנַיִם שְׁלֹשָׁה גַּרְגְּרִים בְּרֹאשׁ אָמִיר – ***like one who cuts olives [from a tree] and leaves two or three lone clusters at the top of the highest bough,*** אַרְבָּעָה חֲמִשָּׁה בִּסְעִפֶיהָ'' – ***four or five in its branches.***[50]

A different reading of this verse yields a third opinion:

רַבִּי יְהוֹשֻׁעַ בֶּן לֵוִי אָמַר – **R' Yehoshua ben Levi said:** אַרְבָּעָה עָשָׂר – **Fourteen** soldiers survived, שֶׁנֶּאֱמַר – **as it is written:** ,,שְׁנַיִם (ו)שְׁלֹשָׁה וכו' אַרְבָּעָה חֲמִשָּׁה'' – ***Two and three,* etc.; *four and five.***[51] The total of all these numbers is fourteen.

A final opinion:

רַבִּי יוֹחָנָן אוֹמֵר – **R' Yochanan said:** חֲמִשָּׁה סַנְחֵרִיב וּשְׁנֵי בָנָיו נְבוּכַדְנֶצַּר וּנְבוּזַרְאֲדָן – **Five** Assyrians survived. They were: **Sancheiriv and his two sons,** as well as **Nebuchadnezzar and Nebuzaradan.**[52]

NOTES

prepared to strike the Assyrians "ever since the Days of Creation," for it was during that primordial period that all future exceptions to natural order were decreed (*Maharsha*).

38. *Isaiah* 21:15. [The continuation of the verse states that they fled from a "sharpened" sword, intimating that the sword had been sharpened earlier. See *Toras Chaim.*]

39. Gabriel is the angel whose task it is to oversee the ripening of the fruits (*Rashi*).

40. *Isaiah* 28:19. R' Shimon ben Yochai interprets this verse as referring to the destruction of Sancheiriv's army by Gabriel. As the angel passes by on his daily rounds to ripen the fruits of the land, he will also "take" the Assyrians and destroy them. The implication is that Sancheiriv's mighty forces were so vulnerable before God that His messenger Gabriel did not even need to confront them directly; rather, Gabriel slew the Assyrians offhandedly, almost as an afterthought on his way to ripen the fruits of the land (*Maharsha*).

41. I.e. if in going about your daily business, you pass in the vicinity of your enemy, appear before him to disorient him (see *Rashi*).

42. Ibid. 40:24. The metaphor of execution with breath signifies that even a very slight Divine action – "breathing" – was enough to vanquish Sancheiriv's forces (*Maharsha; Maharal*).

43. Whereas breathing into the nostrils of a foe is a direct action, clapping one's hands to defeat a foe is an *indirect* action. R' Yirmiyah bar Abba thus conveys that the Assyrians were defeated by an even slighter Divine action than breathing (*Maharal*).

44. *Ezekiel* 21:22.

45. *Chayos* are a class of angels mentioned most prominently in the first chapter of *Ezekiel. Rambam* (*Yesodei HaTorah* 2:7) notes that there are ten levels of angels, of which *chayos* are the highest.

46. [Ordinarily, mortals are unable to hear the songs of praise recited by various angels. Indeed, the nature of such songs are so sublime that were a mere mortal to hear them, his soul would depart from his body and he would die. According to R' Yitzchak Nafcha, then, Gabriel killed the Assyrian soldiers by removing their inability to hear angelic songs.]

47. *Isaiah* 33:3. The verse describes the defeat of the Assyrian army (*Ibn Ezra, Radak*). R' Yitzchak Nafcha sees in the words *Your exaltedness* a reference to angelic song – song that was of such a sublime nature that it caused the Assyrians to die when they were allowed to hear it (see *Margaliyos HaYam*).

48. Ibid. 10:19. This verse describes the destruction of the Assyrian army. "Trees" are used as a metaphor for Sancheiriv's soldiers.

49. I.e. he is most easily able to write the letter *yud,* whose numerical equivalent is ten. Even a young child can write a *yud,* for a *yud* is hardly more than a drop of ink placed upon paper (*Rashi;* cf. *Tosafos, Menachos* 29a ד״ה קוצו).

[*Radak* adds that when a child learns to write, he begins with the first letter of the alphabet, *alef* – and when one writes an *alef,* he begins forming the letter by writing a small *yud.*]

50. Ibid. 17:6. In its plain meaning, the verse refers to the small number of Jews who will remain in Israel after the Assyrians exile the Ten Tribes (see *Radak*). Shmuel, however, interprets the verse as referring to the few Assyrian soldiers who will survive the campaign against Jerusalem. These survivors will be as few as the olives that remain on a tree after it has been harvested, or in the words of the verse, *four or five in its branches.* Shmuel thus adds four and five to reach a total of nine (*Rashi*).

[In our number system, the number ten represents a cohesive unit. The number nine, one less than ten, thus represents a group of essentially *isolated* individuals. Thus, Shmuel means to say that only individuals survived; there was no cohesive structure whatsoever left to Sancheiriv's army (*Maharsha*).]

51. Unlike Shmuel, R' Yehoshua ben Levi adds *all* the numbers mentioned in the verse – two, three, four and five – to reach his total.

52. R' Yochanan does not infer from the verse that these particular five people survived. He does, however, interpret *Isaiah* 17:6 as referring to the survivors of Sancheiriv's army. In his view, the verse is saying: Just as there might be only two or three clusters of olives remaining on a tree after its harvest, so too, there would be very few survivors, just four or

דכתיב א) ויצא יעקב מבאר שבע וילך חרנה וכתיב ב) ויפגע במקום וילן שם כי בא השמש [א] כי מטא לחרן אמר אפשר עברתי על מקום שהתפללו בו אבותי ואני לא התפללתי בו בעי למיהדר כיון דהרהר בדעתיה למיהדר קפצה ליה ארעא מיד ויפגע במקום [א] דבר אחר [ב] אין פגיעה אלא תפלה שנאמר ג) ואתה אל תתפלל בעד העם הזה ואל תשא בעדם רנה ותפלה ואל תפגע בי ב) וילן שם כי בא השמש בתר דצלי בעי למיהדר אמר הקב"ה צדיק זה בא לבית מלוני יפטר בלא לינה מיד בא השמש והיינו דכתיב ד) ויזרח לו השמש וכי לו בלבד זרחה והלא לכל העולם כולו זרחה אלא א"ר יצחק שמש שבא בעבורו זרחה בעבורו ומנלן דכלה זרעיה דדוד דכתי' ה) ועתליה אם אחזיהו ראתה כי מת בנה ותקם ותאבד את כל זרע הממלכה והא אשתייר ליה יואש התם נמי אשתייר אביתר דכתיב ו) וימלט בן אחד לאחימלך בן אחיטוב ושמו אביתר אמר רב יהודה אמר רב אלמלא ([ג] לא) נשתייר אביתר לאחימלך בן אחיטוב לא נשתייר מזרעו של דוד שריד ופליט אמר רב יהודה אמר רב בא עליהם סנחריב הרשע בארבעים וחמשה אלף איש בני מלכים יושבים בקרונות של זהב ועמהן שגלונות וזונות ובשמנים אלף גבורים לבושי שריון קליפה ובששים אלף אחוזי חרב רצים לפניו [ב] והשאר פרשים וכן באו על אברהם וכן עתידין לבוא עם גוג ומגוג במתניתא תנא אורך מחנהו ארבע מאות פרסי רחב צואר סוסיו ארבעים פרסי סך מחנהו מאתים וששים ריבוא אלפים חסר חד בעי אביי חסר חד ריבויא או חסר חד אלפא או חסר מאה או חסר חד תיקו תנא ראשונים עברו בשחי שנאמר ז) וחלף ביהודה שטף ועבר אמצעיים עברו בקומה שנאמר ז) עד צואר יגיע אחרונים העלו עפר ברגליהם ולא מצאו מים בנהר לשתות עד שהביאו מים ממקום אחר ושתו שנאמר ח) אני קרתי ושתיתי מים וגו' והכתיב ט) ויצא מלאך ה' ויכה במחנה אשור מאה ושמנים וחמשה אלף (ויקומו) [וישכימו] בבקר והנה כלם פגרים מתים אמר ר' אבהו הללו ראשי גייסות הן אמר רב אשי דיקא נמי דכתיב י) במשמניו רזון בשמינים דאית בהו אמר רבינא דיקא נמי דכתיב יא) וישלח ה' מלאך ויכחד כל גבור חיל ונגיד ושר במחנה וגו' ויבא בית אלהיו ומיציאי מעיו שם הפילוהו בחרב שמע מינה במה הכם רבי אליעזר אומר ביד הכם שנאמר יב) וירא ישראל את היד הגדולה היד שעתידה ליפרע מסנחריב רבי יהושע אומר באצבע הכם שנאמר יג) ויאמרו החרטמים אל פרעה אצבע אלהים היא היא אצבע שעתידה ליפרע מסנחריב ר' אליעזר בנו של ר' יוסי הגלילי אומר אמר לו הקב"ה לגבריאל מגלך נטושה אמר לפניו רבונו של עולם נטושה ועומדת משששת ימי בראשית שנאמר יד) מפני חרבות נדדו [ד] וגו' ר' שמעון בן יוחי אומר אותו הפרק זמן בישול פירות היה אמר לו הקב"ה לגבריאל כשאתה יוצא לבשל פירות הזקק להם שנאמר טו) מידי עברו יקח אתכם כי בבקר בבקר יעבור ביום ובלילה והיה רק זועה הבין שמועה וגו' אמר רב פפא היינו דאמרי אינשי אגב אורחך לבעל דבבך אישתמע ויש אומרים בחוטמן נשף בהן ומתו שנאמר טז) וגם נשף בהם ויבשו ר' ירמיה בר אבא אמר כפיים ספק להם ומתו שנאמר יז) וגם אני (הכתי) [אכה] כפי אל כפי והניחותי חמתי ר' יצחק נפחא אמר אזנים גלה להם ושמעו שירה מפי חיות ומתו שנאמר יח) מרוממתך נפצו גוים וכמה נשתייר מהם רב אמר [ה] עשרה שנאמר יט) ושאר עץ יערו מספר יהיו ונער יכתבם כמה נער יכול לכתוב עשרה ושמואל אמר תשעה שנאמר כ) ונשאר בו עוללות כנוקף זית שנים שלשה גרגרים בראש אמיר ארבעה חמשה בסעיפיה ר' יהושע בן לוי אמר ארבעה עשר שנאמר שנים שלשה [וכו'] ארבעה וחמשה רבי יוחנן אמר חמשה סנחריב ושני בניו נבוכד נצר ונבוזר אדן נבוזר אדן גמרא נבוכד נצר דכתיב כא) ורוה דרביעאה דמי לבר אלהין ואי לאו דחזייה מנא הוה ידע סנחריב ושני בניו דכתיב כב) ויהי הוא משתחוה בית נסרוך אלהיו ואדרמלך ושראצר בניו הכוהו בחרב אמר רבי אבהו אלמלא מקרא כתוב אי אפשר לאומרו דכתיב כג) ביום ההוא יגלח ה' בתער השכירה בעברי נהר במלך אשור את הראש ושער הרגלים וגם את הזקן תספה אתא קודשא בריך הוא ואדמי ליה כגברא סבא א"ל כי אזלת לגבי מלכי מזרח ומערב דאייתיתינהו לבנייהו וקטלתינהו מאי אמרת להו אמר [ו] להו ההוא גברא בההוא פחדא נמי יתיב אמר ליה היכי נעביד א"ל זיל ושני

רש"י

ויצא יעקב מבאר שבע וילך חרנה. אלמא בא לחרן וכתיב ויפגע במקום שעדיין לא הגיע לחרן שהיה עדיין בבית אל: שהתפללו בו אבותי. אברהם ויצחק [ז] (אברהם דכתיב ויעתק משם יצחק אין מקרא בידי): הרהר בדעתיה למהדר. למקום: קפצה ליה ארעא. והיה שם מיד וקרא מוכיח דכתיב ויפגע במקום שהמקום פגעו וקפלה לו הארץ ונתקרב לו המקום: הכי גרסינן ד"א אין פגיעה אלא תפלה. ונראה למורי דהכא לא מיגרסא הך מילתא: בית אל זה ירושלים חרן חוץ לארץ: כי בא השמש. ויבא השמש לא נאמר אלא כי בא השמש דמשמע שהיה דעתו לחזור כי עוד היום גדול כיון שראה כי בא השמש לן: ויזרח לו השמש. משמע השמש שהיה לו כבר שבא בשבילו כבר: ומנ"ל דכלה זרעיה דדוד. כדאפיך גלותיה: התם נמי אשתייר אביתר. מכהני נוב: שגלונות. מלכות: על אברהם. כשנלחם בד' מלכים: בעי אביי. האי חסר חד היכי קאמר אי חסר חד רבוא וכו': ראשונה. כת ראשונה מחיל של סנחריב: עברו בשחי. שטו הסוסים בירדן ונתמעטו המים עד שעברו: אמצעיים בקומה. זקופה ולא היו המים מגיעין אלא עד הצואר יגיע: שחי. כמו שחו: העלו עפר ברגליהם. שלא היה שם מים כל עיקר: קרתי. לשון מקור: ה"ג ויצא מלאך ה' ויך במחנה אשור אמר רבי וכו'. ולא גרסינן והא כתיב ויצא מלאך ה' אלמא כל המחנה אשור אינו אלא קפ"ה אלף ולעיל קתני מאתים וס' רבוא: הללו. קפ"ה אלף ראשי גייסות נגידי החיל שכן עולה לחשבון לכדאמרינן ארבעים וחמשה אלף בני מלכים שמנים אלף גבורים ששים אלף אחוזי חרב הרי קפ"ה אלף אבל האחרים שמתו אין מספר כדאמר והשאר פרשים אין מספר: במה הכם. המלאך: היד הגדולה. יד הגדולה לא נאמר אלא היד דמשמע היד שעתידה וכו': מגלך נטושה. שחוזה מגלך להרוג את אלו: גבריאל. ממונה על בשול הפירות: הזקק לאלו. לחיל סנחריב להרגן: אגב ארחך. כשתלך לדרכך לפי תומך: לבעל דבבך אשתמע. לשונאך התראה והפחידו: נשף. נפח: עשרה. שהנער יכול להטיף טיפה של דיו והיינו יו"ד שנשארו עשרה: ושמואל אמר תשעה. ונשאר בו עוללות כנוקף זית שאין נשארין בו אלא דבר מועט שנים או שלשה גרגרים בראש אמיר כן לא ישתייר במחנהו אלא דבר מועט וכמה ארבעה וחמשה בסעיפיה פוריה ארבעה וחמשה והיינו תשעה: י"ד שנים ושלשה ארבעה וחמשה. ר' יוחנן מקרא לא דייק להו אלא הכי קאמר הללו חמשה נשתיירו מהן סנחריב ושני בניו וקרא משמע כנוקף זית דמשייר מעט בראש ענף שנים או שלשה גרגרים כך ישתייר לו מעט ד' או ה': נבוכדנצר דכתיב. גבי [חנניה] מישאל ועזריה תוארו ורויה די רביעאה דמי לבר אלהין אלמא דחזא גבריאל והכירו בכבשן: סנחריב ושני בניו. דכתיב ויהי הוא משתחוה בית וגו': אי אפשר לאמרו. שהקדוש ב"ה בעצמו גלחו לסנחריב: דאייתיתינהו לבנייהו. כדאמרינן שהביא עמו ארבעים וחמשה אלף בני מלכים: אשני

מסורת הש"ם

א) חולין צא:, ב) [ברכות כו: תענית ז: ח. סוטה יד.], ג) [עי' תוס' מגילה כא. ד"ה אלמלא], ד) [צ"ל מפני חרב נטושה וגו'], ה) [עי' תוספות מנחות כט. ד"ה קולין], ו) צ"ל ליה, ז) רש"ל מ"ז.

ליקוטי רש"י

וילך חרנה. דמשמע דמטא לחרן והדר כתיב ויפגע במקום דהיינו בית אל דאכתי לא מטא לחרן [חולין צא:]. ויפגע במקום. לא הזכיר הכתוב באיזה מקום אלא במקום הנזכר במקום אחר הוא הר המוריה שנאמר בו (בראשית כב, ד) וירא את המקום מרחוק. ויפגע, כמו (יהושע טז, ז) ופגע ביריחו (שם יט, יא) ופגע בדבשת ורבותינו פירשו לשון תפלה כמו (ירמיה ז, טז) ואל תפגע בי [בראשית כח, יא]. שהתפללו בו אבותי. האי בית אל לא הסמוך לעי הוא אלא ירושלים ועל שם יהיה בית אלהים קראו בית אל והוא הר המוריה שהתפלל בו אברהם והוא שדה שהתפלל בו יצחק דכתיב (בראשית כד) לשוח בשדה דהכי אמרינן בפסחים (פח.) אל הר ה' ואל בית אלהי יעקב מאי שנא יעקב אלא לא כאברהם שקראו הר דכתיב בהר ה' ולא כיצחק שקראו שדה דכתיב לשוח בשדה אלא כיעקב שקראו בית. קפצה ליה ארעא. לשון (דברים טו) לא תקפוץ את ידך נתקצרה ונתקמצה לו [חולין שם]. וכלפי שאמרו רבותינו שאמר הקב"ה צדיק זה בא לבית מלוני ויפטר בלא לינה ועוד אמרו יעקב קראה לירושלים בית אל וזו לוז היא ולא ירושלים ומהיכן למדו לומר כן אומר אני שנעקר הר המוריה ובא לכאן וזהו היא קפילת הארץ האמורה בשחיטת חולין (חולין צא:) שבא בית המקדש לקראתו עד בית אל וזהו ויפגע במקום, וא"ת וכשעבר יעקב על בית המקדש מדוע לא עכבו שם איהו לא יהיב לביה להתפלל במקום שהתפללו אבותיו ומן השמים יעכבוהו איהו עד חרן אזל כדאמרינן בפרק גיד הנשה (חולין צא:) וקרא מוכיח וילך חרנה כי מטא לחרן אמר אפשר שעברתי על מקום שהתפללו אבותי ולא התפללתי בו יהב דעתיה למהדר וחזר עד בית אל וקפצה לו הארץ [בראשית שם, יז ועי' במהרש"א בח"א חולין שם ד"ה מקום]. מיד ויפגע במקום. כאדם הפוגע בחבירו שבא כנגדו ודרשינן ליה נמי לשון תפלה כדכתיב (רות א) אל תפגעי בי [חולין שם]. אין פגיעה אלא תפלה. ולמדנו שתקן תפלת ערבית ושנה הכתוב ולא כתב ויתפלל ללמדך שקפצה לו הארץ כמו שמפורש בפרק גיד הנשה (חולין צא:). מיד בא השמש. היה לו לכתוב ויבא השמש וילן שם כי בא השמש משמע ששקעה לו חמה פתאום שלא בעונתה כדי שילין שם [בראשית שם, יא]. כדכתיב וילן שם כי בא השמש למה ליה למיכתב כי בא השמש אלא ללמדנו ששקעה קודם זמנה [חולין שם]. ויזרח לו השמש. לשון בני אדם הוא כשהגענו למקום פלוני האיר לנו השחר זהו פשוטו. ומדרש אגדה ויזרח לו לצרכו לרפאות את צלעתו, כמה דתימא (מלאכי ג, כ) שמש צדקה ומרפא בכנפיה ואותן שעות שמיהרה לשקוע בשבילו כשיצא מבאר שבע מיהרה לזרוח בשבילו [בראשית לב, לב]. שגלונות. שגל, מלכה כמו והשגל יושבת אצלו (דניאל ה) וישתון בהון מלכא ורברבנוהי שגלתיה ולחנתה [תהלים מה, י]. שגלתה, לשון מלכא בלשון ארמי כמו (נחמיה ב) והשגל יושבת אצלו [דניאל ה, ב]. והשגל אשתו המלכה כענין שנאמר (דניאל ה') שגלתיה ולחנתיה שכן נוהג המקרא לכתוב המלכה אצל הפלגש נשיו ופלגשיו כמו מלכות ופלגשים (שה"ש ו') [נחמיה ב, ו]. שריון קליפה. ושריון קשקשים כמין קשקשות דגים עשוין מברזל נופלים על גב השריון (ס"א נקבי השריון) קשקשת לכל נקב [ש"א יז, ה]. יש שריונות שהם עשוין קליפים קליפים כענין שנא' (ש"א יז, ה) ושריון קשקשים והקליפים נופלים על נקבי השריון וסותמין אותן [מ"א כב, לד]. וחלף ביהודה. בארץ יהודה. שטף. בחוזקה [ישעיה ח, ח]. ראשי גייסות. כולם מלכים קשורי כתרים בראשיהם וקטן שבכולם היה שר על שני אלפים שנאמר (ישעיהו לו) ואתנה לך אלפים סוסים ואיך תשיב את פני פחת אחד וגו' למדנו על קטן שבפחותים שהוא שר על אלפי' איש ונפלו הם וגייסותם [שם לז, לו]. ומציאי מעיו. כדכתיב (ישעיה לז) ובניו הכוהו בחרב [דה"ב לב, כא]. מגלך נטושה. כמו לטושה כל אותיות אשר מוצאיהם קרובים להיות ממקום אחד מתחלפות זו בזו נו"ן בלמ"ד כענין שנא' (נחמיה יג) לעשות לו נשכה כמו לשכה [ישעיה כא, טו]. והיה רק זועה הבין שמועה. זועה לכל השומעים להבין שמועות פורענו' הקשות שאביא עליכם כל השומעים יזועו [שם כח, יט]. [המשך בדף צו.]

הגהות הגר"א

[א] גמ' ד"א אין פגיעה כו' עד ואל תפגע בי. נמחק: [ב] שם והשאר פרשים. נ"ב ורגלים:

תורה אור השלם

א) וַיֵּצֵא יַעֲקֹב מִבְּאֵר שָׁבַע וַיֵּלֶךְ חָרָנָה: [בראשית כח, י]

ב) וַיִּפְגַּע בַּמָּקוֹם וַיָּלֶן שָׁם כִּי בָא הַשֶּׁמֶשׁ וַיִּקַּח מֵאַבְנֵי הַמָּקוֹם וַיָּשֶׂם מְרַאֲשֹׁתָיו וַיִּשְׁכַּב בַּמָּקוֹם הַהוּא: [בראשית כח, יא]

ג) וְאַתָּה אַל תִּתְפַּלֵּל בְּעַד הָעָם הַזֶּה וְאַל תִּשָּׂא בַעֲדָם רִנָּה וּתְפִלָּה וְאַל תִּפְגַּע בִּי כִּי אֵינֶנִּי שֹׁמֵעַ אֹתָךְ: [ירמיה ז, טז]

ד) וַיִּזְרַח לוֹ הַשֶּׁמֶשׁ כַּאֲשֶׁר עָבַר אֶת פְּנוּאֵל וְהוּא צֹלֵעַ עַל יְרֵכוֹ: [בראשית לב, לא]

ה) וַעֲתַלְיָה אֵם אֲחַזְיָהוּ רָאֲתָה כִּי מֵת בְּנָהּ וַתָּקָם וַתְּאַבֵּד אֵת כָּל זֶרַע הַמַּמְלָכָה: [מלכים ב' יא, א]

ו) וַיִּמָּלֵט בֵּן אֶחָד לַאֲחִימֶלֶךְ בֶּן אֲחִטוּב וּשְׁמוֹ אֶבְיָתָר וַיִּבְרַח אַחֲרֵי דָוִד: [שמואל א' כב, כ]

ז) וְחָלַף בִּיהוּדָה שָׁטַף וְעָבַר עַד צַוָּאר יַגִּיעַ וְהָיָה מֻטּוֹת כְּנָפָיו מְלֹא רֹחַב אַרְצְךָ עִמָּנוּ אֵל: [ישעיה ח, ח]

ח) אֲנִי קַרְתִּי וְשָׁתִיתִי מָיִם וְאַחְרִב בְּכַף פְּעָמַי כֹּל יְאֹרֵי מָצוֹר: [ישעיה לז, כה]

ט) וַיֵּצֵא מַלְאַךְ יְיָ וַיַּכֶּה בְּמַחֲנֵה אַשּׁוּר מֵאָה וּשְׁמֹנִים וַחֲמִשָּׁה אָלֶף וַיַּשְׁכִּימוּ בַבֹּקֶר וְהִנֵּה כֻלָּם פְּגָרִים מֵתִים: [ישעיה לז, לו]

י) לָכֵן יְשַׁלַּח הָאָדוֹן יְיָ צְבָאוֹת בְּמִשְׁמַנָּיו רָזוֹן וְתַחַת כְּבֹדוֹ יֵקַד יְקֹד כִּיקוֹד אֵשׁ: [ישעיה י, טז]

יא) וַיִּשְׁלַח יְיָ מַלְאָךְ וַיַּכְחֵד כָּל גִּבּוֹר חַיִל וְנָגִיד וְשָׂר בְּמַחֲנֵה מֶלֶךְ אַשּׁוּר וַיָּשָׁב בְּבֹשֶׁת פָּנִים לְאַרְצוֹ וַיָּבֹא בֵּית אֱלֹהָיו וּמִיצִיאֵי מֵעָיו שָׁם הִפִּילֻהוּ בֶחָרֶב: [דברי הימים ב' לב, כא]

יב) וַיַּרְא יִשְׂרָאֵל אֶת הַיָּד הַגְּדֹלָה אֲשֶׁר עָשָׂה יְיָ בְּמִצְרַיִם וַיִּירְאוּ הָעָם אֶת יְיָ וַיַּאֲמִינוּ בַּייָ וּבְמֹשֶׁה עַבְדּוֹ: [שמות יד, לא]

יג) וַיֹּאמְרוּ הַחַרְטֻמִּם אֶל פַּרְעֹה אֶצְבַּע אֱלֹהִים הִוא וַיֶּחֱזַק לֵב פַּרְעֹה וְלֹא שָׁמַע אֲלֵהֶם כַּאֲשֶׁר דִּבֶּר יְיָ: [שמות ח, טו]

יד) כִּי מִפְּנֵי חֲרָבוֹת נָדָדוּ מִפְּנֵי חֶרֶב נְטוּשָׁה וּמִפְּנֵי קֶשֶׁת דְּרוּכָה וּמִפְּנֵי כֹּבֶד מִלְחָמָה: [ישעיה כא, טו]

טו) מִדֵּי עָבְרוֹ יִקַּח אֶתְכֶם כִּי בַבֹּקֶר בַּבֹּקֶר יַעֲבֹר בַּיּוֹם וּבַלָּיְלָה וְהָיָה רַק זְוָעָה הָבִין שְׁמוּעָה: [ישעיה כח, יט] טז) אַף בַּל נִטָּעוּ אַף בַּל זֹרָעוּ אַף בַּל שֹׁרֵשׁ בָּאָרֶץ גִּזְעָם וְגַם נָשַׁף בָּהֶם וַיִּבָשׁוּ וּסְעָרָה כַּקַּשׁ תִּשָּׂאֵם: [ישעיה מ, כד] יז) וְגַם אֲנִי אַכֶּה כַפִּי אֶל כַּפִּי וַהֲנִחֹתִי חֲמָתִי אֲנִי יְיָ דִּבַּרְתִּי: [יחזקאל כא, כב] יח) מִקּוֹל הָמוֹן נָדְדוּ עַמִּים מֵרוֹמְמֻתֶךָ נָפְצוּ גּוֹיִם: [ישעיה לג, ג] יט) וּשְׁאָר עֵץ יַעְרוֹ מִסְפָּר יִהְיוּ וְנַעַר יִכְתְּבֵם: [ישעיה י, יט] כ) וְנִשְׁאַר בּוֹ עוֹלֵלֹת כְּנֹקֶף זַיִת שְׁנַיִם שְׁלֹשָׁה גַרְגְּרִים בְּרֹאשׁ אָמִיר אַרְבָּעָה חֲמִשָּׁה בִּסְעִפֶיהָ פֹּרִיָּה נְאֻם יְיָ אֱלֹהֵי יִשְׂרָאֵל: [ישעיה יז, ו] כא) עָנֵה וְאָמַר הָא אֲנָה חָזֵה גֻּבְרִין אַרְבְּעָה שְׁרַיִן מַהְלְכִין בְּגוֹא נוּרָא וַחֲבָל לָא אִיתַי בְּהוֹן וְרֵוֵהּ דִּי רְבִיעָאָה דָּמֵה לְבַר אֱלָהִין: [דניאל ג, כה] כב) וַיְהִי הוּא מִשְׁתַּחֲוֶה בֵּית נִסְרֹךְ אֱלֹהָיו וְאַדְרַמֶּלֶךְ וְשַׂרְאֶצֶר בָּנָיו הִכֻּהוּ בַחֶרֶב וְהֵמָּה נִמְלְטוּ אֶרֶץ אֲרָרָט וַיִּמְלֹךְ אֵסַר חַדֹּן בְּנוֹ תַּחְתָּיו: [מלכים ב' יט, לז] כג) בַּיּוֹם הַהוּא יְגַלַּח אֲדֹנָי בְּתַעַר הַשְּׂכִירָה בְּעֶבְרֵי נָהָר בְּמֶלֶךְ אַשּׁוּר אֶת הָרֹאשׁ וְשַׂעַר הָרַגְלָיִם וְגַם אֶת הַזָּקָן תִּסְפֶּה: [ישעיה ז, כ]

The Gemara explains how R' Yochanan deduced this:

נְבוּזַרְאֲדָן גְּמָרָא – That **Nebuzaradan** survived is known **through** an **oral tradition.** נְבוּכַדְנֶצַּר דִּכְתִיב ,,וְרֵוֵהּ דִּי רְבִיעָאָה דָּמֵה לְבַר־אֱלָהִין" – And we know that **Nebuchadnezzar** survived, **for it is written** that Nebuchadnezzar said: ***The form of the fourth is like an angel.***[53] וְאִי לָאו דַּחֲזְיֵיהּ מְנָא הֲוָה יָדַע – **Now, if [Nebuchadnezzar] had never seen [an angel]** once before, **how did he know** what one looked like now? Rather, it must be that Nebuchadnezzar *had* seen an angel previously, during the ill-fated siege of Sancheiriv.

R' Yochanan continues:

סַנְחֵרִיב וּשְׁנֵי בָנָיו – And we also know that **Sancheiriv and his two sons** survived the angel's attack, דִּכְתִיב – **for it is written:** ,,וַיְהִי הוּא מִשְׁתַּחֲוֶה בֵּית נִסְרֹךְ אֱלֹהָיו – ***As [Sancheiriv] was prostrating himself in the temple of Nisroch his god,*** וְאַדְרַמֶּלֶךְ וְשַׂרְאֶצֶר בָּנָיו הִכֻּהוּ בַחֶרֶב" – ***his sons Adramelech and Sarezer slew him with a sword.***[54] Since this event took place after Sancheiriv's return from Jerusalem, it is evident that he and his two sons mentioned in the verse survived Gabriel's onslaught.

The Gemara describes how Sancheiriv met his death:

אָמַר רַבִּי אַבָּהוּ – **R' Abahu said:** אִלְמָלֵא מִקְרָא כָּתוּב אִי אֶפְשָׁר לְאָמְרוֹ – **If [the following] were not** actually **written in Scripture, it would be impossible to say it:**[55] דִּכְתִיב – **For it is written:**[56] ,,בַּיּוֹם הַהוּא יְגַלַּח אֲדֹנָי בְּתַעַר הַשְּׂכִירָה בְּעֶבְרֵי נָהָר – ***On that day, the Lord will shave with a hired razor [those who dwell] on the other side of the river,*** בְּמֶלֶךְ אַשּׁוּר – ***[namely] the king of Assyria,*** אֶת־הָרֹאשׁ וְשַׂעַר הָרַגְלָיִם וְגַם אֶת־הַזָּקָן תִּסְפֶּה" – ***[his] head and the hair on [his] legs; [his] beard, too, shall also be destroyed.***

The Gemara proceeds with an aggadic interpretation of the verse:

אֲתָא קוּדְשָׁא בְּרִיךְ הוּא וְאִדַּמֵּי לֵיהּ כְּגַבְרָא סָבָא – It so happened that after Sancheiriv's defeat, **the Holy One, Blessed is He, came** and appeared **to him in the guise of an elderly man.**[57] אָמַר לֵיהּ – **[God]** then **said to [Sancheiriv]:** כִּי אָזְלַת לְגַבֵּי מַלְכֵי מִזְרָח וּמַעֲרָב – **"When you go** back **to** your allies, **the kings of the East and of the West,** דְּאַיְיתִיתִינְהוּ לִבְנַיְיהוּ וְקַטַלְתִּינְהוּ – **whose sons you brought** to Jerusalem **and** then **killed,** i.e. whose death you caused in your utter defeat before Chizkiah,[58] מַאי אָמְרַת לְהוּ – **what will you say to them?** How will you be able to justify your disastrous conduct to them?"

אָמַר לֵיהּ – **[Sancheiriv]** then **replied to [Him]:** הַהוּא גַּבְרָא בְּהַהוּא פַּחְדָּא נַמִּי יָתִיב – **"I myself**[59] **live in** constant **fear of this!"** אָמַר לֵיהּ – **[Sancheiriv then]** continued, **saying to [Him]:** הֵיכִי נַעֲבִיד – **"What,** then, **shall I do?"** אָמַר לֵיהּ זִיל – **[He] replied to Sancheiriv: "Go**

NOTES

five, in Sancheiriv's camp (*Rashi*). See *Yad Ramah,* who discusses how it is known that Sancheiriv's sons went to war along with their father.

53. *Daniel* 3:25. Scripture records that Nebuchadnezzar, a king who reigned over Babylonia some time after Sancheiriv's demise, once decreed that all the people of his kingdom bow before an idol of his making. Three righteous Jews – Chananyah, Mishael, and Azaryah – refused to assent, whereupon Nebuchadnezzar cast them into a fiery furnace as punishment. When, however, Nebuchadnezzar looked into the fiery kiln to witness their demise, he saw the three men standing unharmed, accompanied by a mysterious fourth figure, who in fact was the angel Gabriel (see above, 93a). Nebuchadnezzar identified this person as an angel, leading our Gemara to conclude that he had seen him some place before – presumably, at Sancheiriv's campaign against Jerusalem. It thus follows that Nebuchadnezzar was present at that event (*Rashi*).

54. *II Kings* 19:37. As the preceding verse indicates, Sancheiriv's assassination by his sons took place just after his return from Jerusalem.

55. In the narrative that follows, God is described as appearing to Sancheiriv in the guise of an old man. The Gemara here means that such a grossly anthropomorphic description of God would be considered blasphemous were it not actually stated in Scripture.

As for our Gemara's description, *Rama* (cited in *Anaf Yosef*) stresses that it is not, in fact, meant literally. He suggests various approaches, among them, that the old man did not physically materialize before Sancheiriv, but rather appeared to him in a dream. Alternatively, he suggests that it was an angel that disguised itself as an old man, not God himself (see also *Yad Ramah*).

For a more detailed explanation of the significance of the forthcoming narrative, see below, 96a notes 2 and 5.

56. *Isaiah* 7:20.

57. See above, note 55.

58. The reference is to the forty-five thousand royal princes who served in the invading army (see Gemara above), and who perished along with the other soldiers (*Rashi*).

59. Literally: that man.

וְשַׁנֵּי נַפְשָׁךְ – **and disguise yourself** so that they will not recognize you." בְּמַאי אֱשַׁנֵּי – Sancheiriv then asked: **"How shall I disguise** myself?" אֲמַר לֵיהּ זִיל אַיְיתִי לִי מַסְפַּרְתָּא – **He replied to [Sancheiriv]: "Go** and **bring scissors to me,** וְאֵיגְזְיָיךְ אֲנָא – **and I will shave you."** מֵהֵיכָא אַיְיתִי – Sancheiriv proceeded to ask: **"From where should I bring** these scissors? I.e. where can I find them?" אֲמַר לֵיהּ עוּל לְהַהוּא בֵּיתָא וְאַיְיתִי – **He replied to [Sancheiriv]: "Go to that house,** find scissors there **and bring** them to me." אֲזַל אַשְׁכְּחִינְהוּ – **[Sancheiriv]** then **went** to the house **and found [a pair of scissors],** but this is how he found them:

אָתוּ מַלְאֲכֵי שָׁרֵת – Before Sancheiriv entered the house, some **ministering angels came** there, וְאִידַּמּוּ לֵיהּ כְּגַבְרֵי – **and** when Sancheiriv arrived, **they appeared to him in the guise of men.** וַהֲווּ קָא טָחֲנֵי קַשְׁיָיתָא – **Now, [the angels] had been grinding palm kernels,** אֲמַר לְהוּ הָבוּ לִי מַסְפַּרְתָּא – and **[Sancheiriv],** thinking they were humans, **said to them: "Give me scissors."** אָמְרוּ לֵיהּ – They replied to him: טְחוֹן חַד גְּרִיוָא דְּקַשְׁיָיתָא – "First, **you must grind** for us **a measure of palm kernels;** וְנִיתֵּן לָךְ – **and** afterwards, **we will give you** the scissors."

The Gemara continues relating the story:

טָחַן חַד גְּרִיוָא דְּקַשְׁיָיתָא – **[Sancheiriv]** then **ground a measure of palm kernels,** וְיָהֲבוּ לֵיהּ מַסְפַּרְתָּא – **and [the angels] gave him the scissors.**[1] עַד דְּאָתָא אִיחֲשַׁךְ – But Sancheiriv had spent so much time in the house, that **by the time he came** back with the scissors, **it had grown dark** outside. אֲמַר לֵיהּ – **[God,]** disguised as the elderly man, then **said to [Sancheiriv]:** זִיל אַיְיתִי נוּרָא – "It is too dark to see now; **go bring a fire,** and then I will be able to cut your hair." אֲזַל וְאַיְיתִי נוּרָא – So **[Sancheiriv] went and brought a fire.** בַּהֲדֵי דְּקָא נָפַח לֵיהּ – **As he was blowing on [the fire]** to increase its size, אִתְלֵי בֵּיהּ נוּרָא בִּדְיקְנֵיהּ – **the flame caught hold of his beard;** אֲזַל גַּזְיֵיהּ לְרֵישֵׁיהּ וְדִיקְנֵיהּ – thus, in the end, **he went and shaved** both **his head** ***and*** **his beard,** even though he had not originally planned on cutting the latter.[2] אָמְרוּ הַיְינוּ דִּכְתִיב – And **this, they say, is** the meaning of **that which is written** in Scripture: "וְגַם אֶת־הַזָּקָן תִּסְפֶּה" – ***his beard too shall be destroyed.***[3]

The Gemara interrupts its account of the story with a comment:

אָמַר רַב פַּפָּא – **Rav Pappa said:** הַיְינוּ דְּאָמְרֵי אִינָשֵׁי – **This** story expresses the idea behind **the popular adage:** גְּרִירְתֵּיהּ לַאֲרַמָּאָה וְשַׁפִּיר לֵיהּ – **"If you singe an Aramean** and **he likes it,** אִיתְלִי לֵיהּ נוּרָא בְּדִיקְנֵיהּ – **then you may even set fire to his beard,** וְלָא שָׂבְעַת חוּכָא מִינֵּיהּ – **and still not exhaust** your **amusement from him."**[4]

The Gemara resumes its account:

אֲזַל אַשְׁכַּח דַּפָּא מִתֵּיבוּתָא דְּנֹחַ – After this humiliating episode, **[Sancheiriv] went** and **found a plank from** the remains of **Noah's Ark.** אָמַר – Looking at the plank, **he said** to himself: הַיְינוּ אֱלָהָא רַבָּא דְּשֵׁיזְבֵיהּ לְנֹחַ מִטּוֹפָנָא – **"This** plank must be **the great god that saved Noah from the flood!"**[5] אָמַר – He then addressed the plank, **saying** to it: אִי אָזֵיל הַהוּא גַּבְרָא וּמַצְלַח – "I hereby pledge that **if I go** to war **and prevail,** מְקָרֵב לְהוּ לִתְרֵין בְּנוֹהִי קַמָּךְ – **I will offer my two sons** as a sacrifice **before you!"**[6] שָׁמְעוּ בְּנוֹהִי וְקַטְלוּהוּ – This, then, led to Sancheiriv's death, for **his sons overheard** what he had said, **and they killed him.** הַיְינוּ דִּכְתִיב – And **this,** indeed, **is [the episode]** recorded **in the verse:**[7] "וַיְהִי הוּא מִשְׁתַּחֲוֶה בֵּית נִסְרֹךְ אֱלֹהָיו – ***And it came to pass, as [Sancheiriv] was worshiping in the house of Nisroch his god,*** וְאַדְרַמֶּלֶךְ וְשַׂרְאֶצֶר בָּנָיו הִכֻּהוּ בַחֶרֶב" וגו׳ – ***that Adramelech and Sarezer his sons smote him with the sword,*** **etc.**[8]

Having described how an angel destroyed Sancheiriv's army, the Gemara now discusses another instance in which an angel struck an enemy army:

"וַיֵּחָלֵק עֲלֵיהֶם לַיְלָה הוּא וַעֲבָדָיו וַיַּכֵּם" וגו׳ – With reference to Abraham's war against the four kings, Scripture states: ***And at night (lailah), he and his servants deployed against them and struck them*** **etc.**[9] אָמַר רַבִּי יוֹחָנָן – **R' Yochanan said:** אוֹתוֹ מַלְאָךְ שֶׁנִּזְדַּמֵּן לוֹ לְאַבְרָהָם לַיְלָה שְׁמוֹ – **The angel who was assigned to** aid **Abraham** in this war against the kings **was named** ***lailah*** ("night"), שֶׁנֶּאֱמַר – **for** indeed, **it is written:** "וְהַלַּיְלָה אָמַר הֹרָה גָבֶר" – ***O that the day I was born had perished,*** ***along with lailah, who said,"A male child has been conceived."***[10]

NOTES

1. Thus, Sancheiriv "borrowed" the scissors from the angels. This fulfills the prediction of the verse (*Isaiah* 7:20) that Sancheiriv was to be shaved with *a hired razor.* Also, the same verse mentions the words *the other side of the river,* and in the Gemara's homiletical reading, this refers to Sancheiriv's grinding of palm kernels, an act that is typically done with a millstone alongside a river (*Rashi*).

2. *Maharal* explicates the underlying theme of this narrative: Since Sancheiriv openly mocked God, God saw to it that he himself became an object of derision before he died. *Maharal* then provides an allegorical reading of our Gemara. In this reading *Maharal* sees Sancheiriv's loss of hair as representing his loss of honor following the defeat of his army, and the destruction of Sancheiriv's beard as symbolizing the loss of his kingdom. For a full explication of other details in the story, see *Maharal.*

3. *Isaiah* 7:20. The verse does not state that the beard will be *shaved*, תְּגַלַּח; rather, it states that it will be *destroyed,* תִּסְפֶּה. This, the Gemara understands, implies that the beard was destroyed by fire (*Rashi*).

4. I.e. if a person does not protest when someone else cuts off his beard, then he will likely not react to any other prank played upon him, no matter how outrageous. Thus, he will serve as an endless source of amusement to the prankster (*Aruch*).

5. The Gemara alludes to the idea that Sancheiriv saw himself as another Noah, a sole survivor of a catastrophe, which in Sancheiriv's case was the destruction of his entire army (see *Maharal*). The plank of Noah's Ark reminded him of the deity that had saved Noah, and he sought to propitiate it. (See *Maharal,* who explicates the symbolism of the plank from Noah's Ark.)

6. In doing this, Sancheiriv sought to emulate Noah, who brought sacrifices to God upon emerging safely from the Ark (see *Genesis* 8:20; *Maharal; Maharsha*).

7. *II Kings* 19:37.

8. The Gemara sees *Nisroch,* Sancheiriv's deity, as connected with *neser,* the plank of wood. The verse associates Sancheiriv's worship of this god with his assassination, and in keeping with this, the Gemara concludes that it was because of this worship that he was assassinated (see *Rashi*).

9. *Genesis* 14:15. This passage describes Abraham's successful night attack upon the armies of the four kings, which the Gemara had mentioned earlier.

The Gemara expounds the verse because its sentence structure is unusual. One would have expected the word לַיְלָה, *night,* to have come at the end of the clause [*He and his servants deployed against them at night*]. Instead, however, the word comes in the middle of the clause, in a way that suggests that לַיְלָה is the subject of the verb וַיֵּחָלֵק. Thus, the verse seems to say that someone or something named *lailah* deployed alongside Abraham and his servants in the war against the four kings. This being, R' Yochanan states, was an angel.

10. *Job* 3:3. Bitter over his misfortunes, Job curses the day he was born, as well as the night (*lailah*) he was conceived. If the verse is read literally, however, it suggests that a being named *lailah* announced that a child has been conceived (see also *Niddah* 16b). This being, R' Yochanan concludes, was the same being who joined Abraham's attack on the four kings.

ושני נפשך במאי אישני אמר ליה זיל אייתי לי מספרא ואיגזייך אנא מהיכא אייתי א"ל עול להה־וא ביתא ואייתי אזל אשכחינהו אתו מלאכי שרת ואידמו ליה כגברי והוו קא טחני קשייתא א"ל הבו לי מספרא א"ל טחון חד גריוא דקשייתא וניתן לך טחן חד גריוא דקשייתא ויהבו ליה מספרתא עד דאתא איחשך א"ל זיל אייתי נורא אזל ואייתי נורא בהדי דקא נפח ליה אתלי ביה נורא בדיקניה אזל גזייה לרישיה ודיקניה אמרו היינו דכתיב א) וגם את הזקן תספה אמר רב פפא היינו דאמרי אינשי גרירתיה לארמאה שפיר ליה איתלי ליה נורא בדיקניה ולא שבעת חוכא מיניה אזל אשכח דפא מתיבותא דנח אמר היינו אלהא רבא דשיזביה לנח מטופנא אמר אי אזיל ההוא גברא ומצלח מקרב להו לתרין בנוהי קמך שמעו בנוהי וקטלוהו היינו דכתיב ב) ויהי הוא משתחוה בית נסרוך אלהיו ואדרמלך ושראצר בניו הכהו בחרב וגו' ג) ויחלק עליהם לילה הוא ועבדיו ויכם וגו' אמר רבי יוחנן אותו מלאך שנזדמן לו לאברהם לילה שמו שנאמר ד) והלילה אמר הורה גבר ור' יצחק נפחא אמר שעשה עמו מעשה לילה שנאמר ה) מן שמים נלחמו הכוכבים ממסלותם נלחמו עם סיסרא אמר ריש לקיש טבא דנפחא מדבר נפחא ו) וירדף עד דן אמר רבי יוחנן כיון שבא אותו צדיק עד דן תשש כחו ראה בני בניו שעתידין לעבוד ע"ז בדן שנאמר ז) וישם את האחד בבית אל ואת האחד נתן בדן ואף אותו רשע לא נתגבר עד שהגיע לדן שנאמר ח) מדן נשמע נחרת סוסיו אמר רבי זירא אע"ג דשלח ר' [א] (יהודה בן בתירא מנציבין) [ב] הזהרו בזקן ששכח תלמודו מחמת אונסו והזהרו בוורידין כר' יהודה והזהרו בבני עמי הארץ שמהן תצא תורה כי הא מילתא מודעינן להו ט) צדיק אתה ה' כי אריב אליך אך משפטים אדבר אותך מדוע דרך רשעים צלחה שלו כל בוגדי בגד נטעתם גם שורשו ילכו גם עשו פרי מאי אהדרו ליה י) כי את רגלים רצתה וילאוך ואיך תתחרה את הסוסים ובארץ שלום אתה בוטח ואיך תעשה בגאון הירדן משל לאדם אחד שאמר יכול אני לרוץ ג' פרסאות לפני הסוסים בין בצעי המים נזדמן לו רגלי אחד רץ לפניו ג' מילין ביבשה ונלאה א"ל ומה לפני רגלי כך לפני הסוסים עאכ"ו ומה שלשה מילין כך ג' פרסאות על אחת כמה וכמה ומה ביבשה כך בין בצעי המים על אחת כמה וכמה אף אתה ומה בשכר ארבע פסיעות ששלמתי לאותו רשע שרץ אחר כבודי אתה תמיה כשאני משלם שכר לאברהם יצחק ויעקב שרצו לפני כסוסים עאכ"ו היינו דכתיב כ) לנביאים נשבר לבי בקרבי רחפו כל עצמותי הייתי כאיש שכור וכגבר עברו יין מפני ה' ומפני דברי קדשו הני ד' פסיעות מאי היא דכתיב ל) בעת ההיא שלח מרודך בלאדן בן בלאדן מלך בבל ספרים וגו' משום כי חלה חזקיהו ויחזק שדר ליה ספרים ומנחה (אין) מ) לדרוש (את) המופת אשר היה בארץ דאמר רבי יוחנן אותו היום שמת בו אחז שתי שעות היה וכי חלה חזקיהו ואיתפח אהדרינהו קודשא בריך הוא להנך עשר שעי ניהליה דכתיב נ) הנני משיב את צל המעלות אשר ירדה במעלות אחז בשמש אחורנית עשר מעלות ותשב השמש עשר מעלות במעלות אשר ירדה א"ל מאי האי א"ל חזקיהו חלש ואיתפח אמר איכא גברא כי האי ולא בעינא לשדורי ליה שלמא כתבו ליה שלמא למלכא חזקיה שלם לקרתא דירושלם שלם לאלהא רבא נבוכד נאצר ספריה דבלאדן הוה ההיא שעתא לא הוה התם כי אתא אמר להו היכי כתביתו אמרו ליה הכי כתבינן אמר להו קריתו ליה אלהא רבא וכתביתו ליה לבסוף אמר אלא הכי כתובו שלם לאלהא רבא שלם לקרתא דירושלם שלם למלכא חזקיה אמרי ליה [ג] קריינא דאיגרתא איהו ליהוי פרוונקא רהט בתריה כדרהיט [ד] ארבע פסיעות אתא גבריאל ואוקמיה אמר ר' יוחנן אילמלא [ה] (לא) בא גבריאל והעמידו לא היה תקנה לשונאיהם של ישראל מאי בלאדן בן בלאדן אמרי בלאדן מלכא הוה ואישתני אפיה והוה כי דכלבא הוה יתיב בריה על מלכותא כי הוה כתיב שמיה ושמיה דאבוה בלאדן מלכא היינו דכתיב ס) בן יכבד אב ועבד אדניו בן יכבד אב הא דאמרן ועבד אדוניו דכתי' ע) ובחודש החמישי בעשור לחדש היא שנת תשע עשרה [שנה] למלך נבוכדנאצר מלך בבל בא נבוזראדן רב טבחים עמד לפני מלך בבל בירושלם וישרף את בית ה' ואת בית המלך

ומי

רש"י

אשני נפשך. שנה עלמך כדי שלא יכירוך: ואגזייך אנא. אני אגלחך: קשייתא. גרעיני תמרים: טחון. אלו גרעינין וניתן לך מספרים והיינו דכתיב בתער השכירה על שם שטרח נתנו לו תער לגלח ואיזהו שכר נתנו לו בעברי נהר דברים שדרכן לעשות על ידי נהר דהיינו טחינת ריחים: וגם הזקן תספה. דלא כתיב גלוח אלא הראש אבל אזקן כתיב תספה לשון כלוי על ידי אור שכלתה לגמרי: גרירתיה לארמאה ושפר באפיה. אם אתה מחרך את הארמאי והוטב בעיניו הבער לו אש בזקנו ולא שבעת חוכא מיניה: בית נסרך אלהיו. לשון נסר שהשתחוה לנסר ועשאו אלוה: היינו דכתיב ויהי הוא משתחוה. משמע מפני שמשתחוה לשם הכוהו: ויחלק עליהם. איידי דאיירי במלאכים איירי נמי בהאי קרא דכתיב ויהי בלילה ההוא ויצא מלאך ה' וגו' נקט ויחלק עליהם לילה וגו': מלאך שנזדמן לאברהם לילה שמו. והוא סייעו: מעשה לילה. שנלחמו בשבילו כוכבי לילה כמו שעשו בשביל ברק: טבא מליה דר' יצחק נפחא מדבר נפחא. ר' יוחנן דמקרי בר נפחא בכולא הש"ס כמו (ב"מ דף פה:) מאן עייל בר נפחא נראה למורי דאביו של ר' יוחנן הוי נפחא ולהכי מיקרי בר נפחא ואית דמפרשי בר נפחא על שם יופיו: הזהרו בזקן. אע"פ ששכח תלמודו הואיל ומחמת אונסו הוא: הזהרו בורידין כר' יהודה. דאמר בשחיטת חולין (דף כז.) עד שישחוט את הורידין של עוף הואיל וצולהו כולו כאחד אינו חותכו ומולחו כבשר חיה ובהמה: הזהרו בבני עמי הארץ. שנעשו תלמידי חכמים לעשות להם כבוד שמהם תצא תורה לישראל שהרי יצאו שמעיה ואבטליון מבני בניו של סנחריב ומבני בניו של המן למדו תורה בבני ברק כדלקמן ואע"ג דאמר רבי יהודה הכי הזהרו בבני עמי הארץ:

כי הא מילתא. לקמן מודעינן להו כי היכי דחזינן לקמן דלא זכה נבוכדנצר לאותו כבוד אלא מפני זכות ד' פסיעות כדאמרינן לקמן ה"נ אמרי' לבני עמי הארץ דלא זכו לאותו כבוד אלא מחמת זכות מעט שהיה באביהם מ"ר. ואית דאמרי דרבי זירא אדלעיל קאי אבני סנחריב אע"ג דשלח רבי יהודה הזהרו בבני ע"ה לכבדן שמהם תלא תורה כי היכי דנפקו מסנחריב כי הא מילתא מודיעים להו לבני ע"ה דהא דמוקרין להו לאו משום אביהם אלא משום תורה שבהם שלא תזוח דעתם עליהם ויאמרו אבותיהם לדיקים היו: מדוע דרך רשעים צלחה. מפני מה הצליח נבוכדנצר וכבש ירושלים: אהדרו ליה. לירמיה: בצעי מים. מרש"קו בלעז: ד' פסיעות. מפורש לקמן: על אחת כמה וכמה. שיהו כל אדם יכולין לתמוה על מתן שכר גדול שישתלם עליהם: לנביאים. אברהם יצחק ויעקב: נשבר לבי בקרבי. כלומר תמהתי על מתן שכרן: שתי שעות. כדי שלא יהא פנאי לספדו ולקברו: אתפח. נתרפא: אהדרינהו הקב"ה. להנך שעות לחזקיהו דאותו היום שנתרפא חזקיה היה של כ"ב שעות: רהט בתריה. דשליח: לא היה להם תקנה. שהיה שכרו מרובה והיה לו רשות לאבד שאריתנו: הוה כתיב שמיה ושמיה דאבוה. כדי שיתכבד אביו לכך נקרא שם אביו עליו שנקרא מרודך בלאדן דאי לא כתיב אלא מרודך בן בלאדן לא הוי מיתקרי עליה שמיה דאבוה דהכי כתבי כולהו אינשי פלוני בן פלוני להכי כתיב מרודך בלאדן: בחדש החמישי בעשור לחדש בא נבוזר אדן רב טבחים עמד לפני מלך בבל בירושלם. אלמא נבוכד נצר סליק לירושלם:

גמ' קריינא דאגרתא. בתנחומא פ' תשא איתא דמרודך בלאדן בעלמו נתחרט ורהט בתריה ג' פסיעות:

תורה אור השלם

א) בַּיּוֹם הַהוּא יְגַלַּח אֲדֹנָי בְּתַעַר הַשְּׂכִירָה בְּעֶבְרֵי נָהָר בְּמֶלֶךְ אַשּׁוּר אֶת הָרֹאשׁ וְשַׂעַר הָרַגְלָיִם וְגַם אֶת הַזָּקָן תִּסְפֶּה: [ישעיה ז, כ]

ב) וַיְהִי הוּא מִשְׁתַּחֲוֶה בֵּית נִסְרֹךְ אֱלֹהָיו וְאַדְרַמֶּלֶךְ וְשַׂרְאֶצֶר בָּנָיו הִכֻּהוּ בַחֶרֶב וְהֵמָּה נִמְלְטוּ אֶרֶץ אֲרָרָט וַיִּמְלֹךְ אֵסַר חַדֹּן בְּנוֹ תַּחְתָּיו: [מלכים ב' יט, לז]

ג) וַיֵּחָלֵק עֲלֵיהֶם לַיְלָה הוּא וַעֲבָדָיו וַיַּכֵּם וַיִּרְדְּפֵם עַד חוֹבָה אֲשֶׁר מִשְּׂמֹאל לְדַמָּשֶׂק: [בראשית יד, טו]

ד) יֹאבַד יוֹם אִוָּלֶד בּוֹ וְהַלַּיְלָה אָמַר הֹרָה גָבֶר: [איוב ג, ג]

ה) מִן שָׁמַיִם נִלְחָמוּ הַכּוֹכָבִים מִמְּסִלּוֹתָם נִלְחֲמוּ עִם סִיסְרָא: [שופטים ה, כ]

ו) וַיִּשְׁמַע אַבְרָם כִּי נִשְׁבָּה אָחִיו וַיָּרֶק אֶת חֲנִיכָיו יְלִידֵי בֵיתוֹ שְׁמֹנָה עָשָׂר וּשְׁלֹשׁ מֵאוֹת וַיִּרְדֹּף עַד דָּן: [בראשית יד, יד]

ז) וַיָּשֶׂם אֶת הָאֶחָד בְּבֵית אֵל וְאֶת הָאֶחָד נָתַן בְּדָן: [מלכים א' יב, כט]

ח) מִדָּן נִשְׁמַע נַחְרַת סוּסָיו מִקּוֹל מִצְהֲלוֹת אַבִּירָיו רָעֲשָׁה כָּל הָאָרֶץ וַיָּבוֹאוּ וַיֹּאכְלוּ אֶרֶץ וּמְלוֹאָהּ עִיר וְיֹשְׁבֵי בָהּ: [ירמיה ח, טז]

ט) צַדִּיק אַתָּה יְיָ כִּי אָרִיב אֵלֶיךָ אַךְ מִשְׁפָּטִים אֲדַבֵּר אוֹתָךְ מַדּוּעַ דֶּרֶךְ רְשָׁעִים צָלֵחָה שָׁלוּ כָּל בֹּגְדֵי בָגֶד: נְטַעְתָּם גַּם שֹׁרָשׁוּ יֵלְכוּ גַּם עָשׂוּ פֶרִי קָרוֹב אַתָּה בְּפִיהֶם וְרָחוֹק מִכִּלְיוֹתֵיהֶם: [ירמיה יב, א-ב]

י) כִּי אֶת רַגְלִים רַצְתָּה וַיַּלְאוּךָ וְאֵיךְ תְּתַחֲרֶה אֶת הַסּוּסִים וּבְאֶרֶץ שָׁלוֹם אַתָּה בוֹטֵחַ וְאֵיךְ תַּעֲשֶׂה בִּגְאוֹן הַיַּרְדֵּן: [ירמיה יב, ה]

כ) לַנְּבִאִים נִשְׁבַּר לִבִּי בְקִרְבִּי רָחֲפוּ כָּל עַצְמוֹתַי הָיִיתִי כְּאִישׁ שִׁכּוֹר וּכְגֶבֶר עֲבָרוֹ יָיִן מִפְּנֵי יְיָ וּמִפְּנֵי דִּבְרֵי קָדְשׁוֹ: [ירמיה כג, ט]

ל) בָּעֵת הַהִוא שָׁלַח מְרֹדַךְ בַּלְאֲדָן בֶּן בַּלְאֲדָן מֶלֶךְ בָּבֶל סְפָרִים וּמִנְחָה אֶל חִזְקִיָּהוּ וַיִּשְׁמַע כִּי חָלָה וַיֶּחֱזָק: [ישעיה לט, א]

מ) וְכֵן בִּמְלִיצֵי שָׂרֵי בָבֶל הַמְשַׁלְּחִים עָלָיו לִדְרֹשׁ הַמּוֹפֵת אֲשֶׁר הָיָה בָאָרֶץ עֲזָבוֹ הָאֱלֹהִים לְנַסּוֹתוֹ לָדַעַת כָּל בִּלְבָבוֹ: [דברי הימים ב' לב, לא]

נ) הִנְנִי מֵשִׁיב אֶת צֵל הַמַּעֲלוֹת אֲשֶׁר יָרְדָה בְמַעֲלוֹת אָחָז בַּשֶּׁמֶשׁ אֲחֹרַנִּית עֶשֶׂר מַעֲלוֹת וַתָּשָׁב הַשֶּׁמֶשׁ עֶשֶׂר מַעֲלוֹת בַּמַּעֲלוֹת אֲשֶׁר יָרָדָה: [ישעיה לח, ח] ס) בֵּן יְכַבֵּד אָב וְעֶבֶד אֲדֹנָיו וְאִם אָב אָנִי אַיֵּה כְבוֹדִי וְאִם אֲדוֹנִים אָנִי אַיֵּה מוֹרָאִי אָמַר יְיָ צְבָאוֹת לָכֶם הַכֹּהֲנִים בּוֹזֵי שְׁמִי וַאֲמַרְתֶּם בַּמֶּה בָזִינוּ אֶת שְׁמֶךָ: [מלאכי א, ו] ע) וּבַחֹדֶשׁ הַחֲמִישִׁי בֶּעָשׂוֹר לַחֹדֶשׁ הִיא שְׁנַת תְּשַׁע עֶשְׂרֵה שָׁנָה לַמֶּלֶךְ נְבוּכַדְרֶאצַּר מֶלֶךְ בָּבֶל בָּא נְבוּזַרְאֲדָן רַב טַבָּחִים עָמַד לִפְנֵי מֶלֶךְ בָּבֶל בִּירוּשָׁלָםִ: וַיִּשְׂרֹף אֶת בֵּית יְהוָה וְאֶת בֵּית הַמֶּלֶךְ וְאֵת כָּל בָּתֵּי יְרוּשָׁלַםִ וְאֶת כָּל בֵּית הַגָּדוֹל שָׂרַף בָּאֵשׁ: [ירמיה נב, יב-יג]

מסורת הש"ס

א) ג' ב"ש ריב"ל, ב) ברכות ח:, ג) לעיל דף פב. ב"מ פג:, ד) [במדר' ובילקו' אית' שלש וכ"א ברש"י ירמיה יב פ"ה], ה) [עי' תוס' מגילה כא.].

ליקוטי רש"י

ושאר עץ יערו. הנותרים בחיילותיו. מספר יהיו. נוחים לספור כי מעט הם ונער יוכל לכותבם ואמרו רבותינו עשרה נשאר מהם שאין לך קטן שאינו כותב יו"ד קטנה [שם י, יט]. ונשאר בו. בהמון סנחריב אנשי מעט כנוקף זית. בראש אמיר. בראש הענף. בסעיפיה. בענפיה וכן וכלה סעיפיה (ישעיה כז) וכן מסעף פארה (שם י) [שם יז, ו]. ורוה די רביעאה. ומראו של רביעי. דמה לבר אלהין. דומה למלאך שראיתי בהיותי עם סנחריב כשנשרפו אוכלוסיו שנאמר (שם לז) ויכה במחנה אשור ונבוכדנצר היה שם ונמלט בתוך עשרה שנמלטו מהם [דניאל ג, כה]. בית נסרוך אלהיו. נסר מתיבתו של נח. הכהו בחרב. שמעו אותו שאמר לשוחטן לפניו אם ינלוהו שלא יהרגוהו שרי המלכות שמתו בניהם על ידו [מ"ב יט, לז]. יגלח ה' בתער השכירה. הגדולה וכן גם שכיריה בקרבה (ירמיה מו) ת"י רברבהא יגלח. בעברי נהר. ביושבי עבר הנהר וכמי מן היושבים במלך אשור את הראש יגלח ואת שער הרגלים לפי שהוא דבוק נשתנה לינקד פתח. תספה. תכלה [ישעיה ז, כ]. [ע"כ שייך לדף צה:] בית נסרוך אלהיו. נסר מתיבתו של נח. הכוהו בחרב. שמעו אותו שאמר לשוחטן לפניו אם ינלוהו שלא יהרגוהו שרי המלכות שמתו בניהם על ידו [מ"ב יט, לז]. ויחלק עליהם. לפי פשוטו סרס המקרא ויחלק הוא ועבדיו עליהם לילה כדרך הרודפים שמתפלגים אחר הנרדפים כשבורחים זה לכאן וזה לכאן. לילה. כלומר אחר שחשכה לא נמנעו מלרדפם [בראשית יד, טו ועי' במהרש"א ח"א]. והלילה אמר. ורז"ל אמרו (נדה טז:) מלאך הממונ' על הסריון לילה שמו [איוב ג, ג ועי' מהרש"א בח"א]. תשש כחו. שראה שעתידין בניו להעמיד שם עגל [בראשית שם, יד]. מדן נשמע. על דפלתו לעגלא דבדן. נחרת סוסיו. עטישות נחיריו [ירמיה ח, טז]. מחמת אונסו. שחלה או שנטרד בדוחק מזונות הזהרו בו לכבדו [ברכות ח:]. בוורידין. מוטי הצואר שמקלחין את הדם ובגמרא (חולין כח:) מפרש דאעוף קאי ומשום להוציא את הדם [חולין כז.]. שישחוט את הורידין כדי שיצא כל הדם ולא אמר כן אלא בעוף הואיל וצולהו כולו כאחד [ברכות שם]. צדיק אתה ה' כי אריב אליך. כשאתווכח עמך ידעתי כי תצדק בדבריך אך חפץ אני לדבר משפטים אותך להודיעני דרכך. מדוע דרך רשעים צלחה. שנתת גדולה לנבוכדנצר הרשע ותלליתהו להחריב ביתך. שלו. לשון שלוה [ירמיה יב, א]. ואיך תתחרה את הסוסים. לרוץ את הסוסים וכו' ומדרש רבותינו אם על שכר שלש פסיעות שרץ נבוכדנצר לכבודי בימי מרודך בלאדן אתה תמה שהרביתי גדולתו כל כך מה תתמה עוד כשתראה שילום שכר שאשלם לצדיקים שרצו לפני כסוסים. תתחרה. אאטיר"ש בלע"ז. ובארץ שלום אשר אתה בוטח. שם הלאוך [שם, ה]. הנני משיב. אחורנית עשר מעלות את הצל אשר ירדה. צל המעלות. כמין מדרגות עשויות כנגד החמה לגנון בהם שעות היום כעין אורלוגין שעושין האומנין. אשר ירדה. מיהרה לירד ונתקצר היום י' שעות ביום שמת אחז כדי שלא יהו מספידין אותו ועלו עכשיו לאחוריהם ביום שנתרפא חזקיהו וניתוספו על היום י' שעות [ישעיה לח, ח]. א"ל מאי האי. היה למוד לאכול בשלש שעות וישן עד ט' כיון שחזר גלגל חמה לחזקיהו כשעמד משנתו בט' שעות מלא שהוא שחרית בקש להרוג את כל עבדיו אמר הנחתם אותי ישן יומם ולילה עד הבקר אמרו לו גלגל חמה הוא שחזר אמר להם ומי החזירו אמרו לו אלוהו של חזקיהו כו' כדאיתא בתנחומא ובפסיקתא [שם לט, א]. קריינא דאיגרתא. משל הוא. פרוונקא. שליח [ב"מ פג:]. שליח מוליך ומביא [לעיל לח.].

An alternative interpretation of the verse in *Genesis:* וְרַבִּי יִצְחָק נַפְחָא אָמַר – **And R' Yitzchak Nafcha said:** שֶׁעָשָׂה עִמּוֹ מַעֲשֶׂה לַיְלָה – When the verse mentions *lailah,* the implication is that **"night acts" were performed on behalf of Abraham** [i.e. the very stars in the sky fought on his behalf], שֶׁנֶּאֱמַר – **as it is written** elsewhere: ,,מִן־שָׁמַיִם נִלְחָמוּ הַכּוֹכָבִים מִמְּסִלּוֹתָם נִלְחֲמוּ עִם סִיסְרָא'' – ***They fought from heaven; the stars in their courses fought against Sisera.***[11]

The Gemara indicates a preference for the second of the two explanations just given:

אָמַר רֵישׁ לָקִישׁ – **Reish Lakish said:** טָבָא דְּנַפְחָא מִדְּבַר נַפְחָא – **[The interpretation] of the blacksmith,** i.e. R' Yitzchak Nafcha, **is better than [the interpretation] of the son of the blacksmith,** i.e. R' Yochanan.[12]

Having expounded *Genesis* 14:15, the Gemara now expounds the verse that immediately precedes this:

,,וַיִּרְדֹּף עַד־דָּן'' – In reference to Abraham's war against the four kings, Scripture states:[13] ***[Abraham] pursued them as far as Dan.*** אָמַר רַבִּי יוֹחָנָן – Concerning this, **R' Yochanan said:** כֵּיוָן שֶׁבָּא אוֹתוֹ צַדִּיק עַד דָּן – **When that righteous man** [Abraham] **reached** the territory of **Dan** תָּשַׁשׁ כֹּחוֹ – **his strength faded,** רָאָה בְּנֵי בָנָיו שֶׁעֲתִידִין לַעֲבוֹד עֲבוֹדָה זָרָה בְּדָן – for **he** prophetically **foresaw that his descendants were destined to worship idols in** the territory of **Dan.** שֶׁנֶּאֱמַר – As it is written: ,,וַיָּשֶׂם אֶת־הָאֶחָד בְּבֵית־אֵל וְאֶת־הָאֶחָד נָתַן בְּדָן'' – ***[Yarovam] placed one [of the golden calves] in Beth El, and the other he placed in Dan.***[14] וְאַף אוֹתוֹ רָשָׁע לֹא נִתְגַּבֵּר עַד שֶׁהִגִּיעַ לְדָן – **And** indeed, **even that wicked man [Nebuchadnezzar] did not become overwhelmingly powerful until he reached** the territory of **Dan,** שֶׁנֶּאֱמַר – for it is written: ,,מִדָּן נִשְׁמַע נַחְרַת סוּסָיו'' – ***The snorting of his horses was heard from Dan.***[15]

The Gemara has just referred to Nebuchadnezzar's invasion of Judah – an invasion that ultimately proved successful. The Gemara now begins an extended discussion touching on the question of why God allowed Nebuchadnezzar to succeed where Sancheiriv had failed:

אָמַר רַבִּי זֵירָא – **R' Zeira said:** אַף עַל גַּב דִּשְׁלַח רַבִּי יְהוּדָה בֶּן בְּתֵירָא מִנְּצִיבִין – **Even though R' Yehudah ben Beseira sent** the following message **from** his residence at **Netzivin:** הִזָּהֲרוּ בְּזָקֵן שֶׁשָּׁכַח תַּלְמוּדוֹ מֵחֲמַת אוֹנְסוֹ – **"Be careful** with the honor of **an elderly scholar who has involuntarily forgotten his** Torah **learning;**[16] וְהִזָּהֲרוּ בְּוְרִידִין כְּרַבִּי יְהוּדָה – **and be careful** to sever **the *veridin* in accordance with** the ruling of **R' Yehudah;**[17] וְהִזָּהֲרוּ בִּבְנֵי עַמֵּי הָאָרֶץ – **and be careful with the** honor of **[scholars] who are children of ignorant people,** שֶׁמֵּהֶן תֵּצֵא תּוֹרָה – **for it is from them that Torah** knowledge **shall go forth";**[18] כִּי הָא מִילְּתָא מוֹדְעִינַן לְהוּ – now, even though R' Zeira cautioned us to be careful with the honor of the children of ignorant people, nonetheless, **we *do* tell them something like [the following].**[19]

The Gemara cites a verse in *Jeremiah* as a preface to the lesson it is about to teach:

,,צַדִּיק אַתָּה ה' כִּי אָרִיב אֵלֶיךָ – Scripture states:[20] ***You would prevail, O HASHEM, were I to contend with You,*** אַךְ מִשְׁפָּטִים אֲדַבֵּר אוֹתָךְ – ***yet I will argue with You.*** מַדּוּעַ דֶּרֶךְ רְשָׁעִים צָלֵחָה – ***Why does the way of the wicked prosper?*** שָׁלוּ כָּל־בֹּגְדֵי בָגֶד – ***[Why] do all those who act treacherously enjoy tranquility?*** נְטַעְתָּם גַּם־שֹׁרָשׁוּ – ***You have planted them, and they have taken root;*** יֵלְכוּ גַּם עָשׂוּ פֶרִי'' – ***they grow, they even produce fruit.***

The Gemara inquires:

מַאי אַהְדְּרוּ לֵיהּ – Now, **what did they** [the Heavenly Court] **answer [Jeremiah]?** This answer is given several verses later: ,,כִּי אֶת־רַגְלִים רַצְתָּה וַיַּלְאוּךָ – ***If you raced with foot-runners and they exhausted you,*** וְאֵיךְ תְּתַחֲרֶה אֶת־הַסּוּסִים – ***how then will you compete against horses?*** וּבְאֶרֶץ שָׁלוֹם אַתָּה בוֹטֵחַ – ***If [they exhausted you] in a land of peace, where you placed your trust,*** וְאֵיךְ תַּעֲשֶׂה בִּגְאוֹן הַיַּרְדֵּן'' – ***how will you fare in the heights of the Jordan?***[21]

NOTES

11. *Judges* 5:20.

12. R' Yitzchak was a blacksmith; hence, he was known as R' Yitzchak Nafcha ["R' Yitzchak the blacksmith"]. R' Yochanan, on the other hand, is called "bar Nafcha" ["the blacksmith's son"], for his father had been a blacksmith (*Rashi*). [*Rashi* also quotes another tradition to the effect that "bar Nafcha" means "handsome." Indeed, R' Yochanan was famous for his physical beauty (see *Yerushalmi Avodah Zarah* 3:1; see also *Bava Metzia* 84a).]

13. *Genesis* 14:14. See *Maharsha.*

14. *I Kings* 12:29. The wicked king Yarovam sought to popularize idol worship throughout his kingdom, and to this effect, he set up images of calves for the people to worship.

15. *Jeremiah* 8:16. In describing Nebuchadnezzar's invasion of Judah, the prophet states that the sound of the approaching cavalry could be heard from Dan, the northernmost part of Eretz Yisrael (*Metzudos*). R' Yochanan interprets the verse somewhat differently, as implying that the invasion of Nebuchadnezzar (the snorting of his horses) was destined to be successful once he reached Dan's territory, due to the sin committed there – namely, the Jews' worshiping Yarovam's calf in that place. Yarovam's acts of idolatry were thus so grievous that throughout history they affected the places in which they had been performed (see *Maharsha*).

16. I.e. be careful to give due honor to an elderly scholar who, because of infirmity, has forgotten his Torah knowledge (*Rashi*).

17. There is a Tannaic dispute regarding the proper procedure for slaughtering fowl. The Tanna Kamma of a Mishnah (*Chullin* 27a) maintains that so long as either the bird's trachea or esophagus is pierced, the slaughter is valid. R' Yehudah, however, states that the slaughterer must also sever the *veridin,* the main blood vessels of the neck located on either side of the trachea (see there, 28b, as to when this procedure is necessary). Here, R' Yehudah ben Beseira cautions his disciples to carefully follow R' Yehudah's view (see *Yad David*).

18. I.e. be careful to accord due honor to scholars who descend from unlearned people, for they are destined to be central conduits in the transmission of Torah to Israel. Examples of such important scholars include Shemaya and Avtalyon, who descended from Sancheiriv, and the descendants of Haman, who taught Torah in Bnei Brak (*Rashi;* cf. *Nedarim* 81a; see *Be'er Sheva*).

19. I.e. we tell them something to make them understand that the honor they are now receiving in some way comes to them in their parents' merit. Their parents, although ignorant, evidently performed *some* meritorious deeds – and were it not for these deeds, the children could never have become the Torah scholars they have indeed become. [In this way, the children will place their newfound honor in proper perspective, and will learn not to look down upon their ignorant parents.]

The particular teaching used to convey this message is given by the Gemara in the lines that follow. In brief, its point is that Nebuchadnezzar merited to achieve extraordinary success because of a very small act he once performed that honored God (the four paces he took to retrieve a letter sent to Chizkiah; see below). Thus, this child's parents, although unlearned, may have performed small acts of righteousness, for which they merited to raise scholarly children who would be accorded great honor (*Rashi;* cf. *Yad Ramah* and *Ben Yehoyada;* see *Rashi* for a second, alternative interpretation of our Gemara).

20. Ibid. 12:1-2. Unable to comprehend how God can permit the wicked to prosper – and specifically, why God has permitted Nebuchadnezzar to conquer Jerusalem – the prophet Jeremiah asks God to explain His ways. Although Jeremiah realizes that to contend with God is impossible, he nevertheless puts forward this question, seeking to resolve the perplexities that exist in his own mind (see *Rashi, Radak* to *Jeremiah* ad loc.).

21. Ibid. v. 5. In this verse, God responds to Jeremiah that he, Jeremiah, is but a mortal and cannot hope to comprehend God's ways. That is, Jeremiah was not able to compete against "foot-runners" – he was not

ושני נפשך במאי אישני אמר ליה זיל אייתי לי מספרא ואיגזייך אנא מהיכא אייתי א"ל עול להוא ביתא ואייתי אזל אשכחינהו אתו מלאכי שרת ואידמו ליה כגברי והוו קא טחני קשייתא א"ל הבו לי מספרא א"ל טחון חד גריוא דקשייתא וניתן לך טחן חד גריוא דקשייתא ויהבו ליה מספרתא עד דאתא איחשך א"ל זיל אייתי נורא אזל ואייתי נורא בהדי דקא נפח ליה אתלי ביה נורא בדיקניה אזל גזייה לרישיה ודיקניה אמרו היינו דכתיב א) וגם את הזקן תספה אמר רב פפא היינו דאמרי אינשי גרירתיה לארמאה שפיר ליה איתלי ליה נורא בדיקניה ולא שבעת חוכא מיניה אזל אשכח דפא מתיבותא דנח אמר היינו אלהא רבא דשיזביה לנח מטופנא אמר אי אזיל ההוא גברא ומצלח מקרב להו לתרין בנוהי קמך שמעו בנוהי וקטלוהו היינו דכתיב ב) ויהי הוא משתחוה בית נסרוך אלהיו ואדרמלך ושראצר בניו הכהו בחרב וגו' ג) ויחלק עליהם לילה הוא ועבדיו ויכם וגו' אמר רבי יוחנן אותו מלאך שנזדמן לו לאברהם לילה שמו שנאמר ד) והלילה אמר הורה גבר ור' יצחק נפחא אמר שעשה עמו מעשה לילה שנאמר ה) מן שמים נלחמו הכוכבים ממסלותם נלחמו עם סיסרא אמר ריש לקיש טבא דנפחא מדבר נפחא ו) וירדף עד דן אמר רבי יוחנן כיון שבא אותו צדיק עד דן תשש כחו ראה בני בניו שעתידין לעבוד ע"ז בדן שנאמר ז) וישם את האחד בבית אל ואת האחד נתן בדן ואף אותו רשע לא נתגבר עד שהגיע לדן שנאמר ח) מדן נשמע נחרת סוסיו אמר רבי זירא אע"ג דשלח ר' [א] (יהודה בן בתירא מנציבין) [ב] הזהרו בזקן ששכח תלמודו מחמת אונסו והזהרו בוורידין כר' יהודה והזהרו בבני עמי הארץ שמהן תצא תורה כי הא מילתא מודעינן להו ט) צדיק אתה ה' כי אריב אליך אך משפטים אדבר אותך מדוע דרך רשעים צלחה שלו כל בוגדי בגד נטעתם גם שורשו ילכו גם עשו פרי מאי אהדרו ליה י) כי את רגלים רצתה וילאוך ואיך תתחרה את הסוסים ובארץ שלום אתה בוטח ואיך תעשה בגאון הירדן משל לאדם אחד שאמר יכול אני לרוץ ג' פרסאות לפני הסוסים בין בצעי המים נזדמן לו רגלי אחד רץ לפניו ג' מילין ביבשה ונלאה א"ל ומה לפני רגלי כך לפני הסוסים עאכ"ו ומה שלשת מילין כך ג' פרסאות על אחת כמה וכמה ומה ביבשה כך בין בצעי המים על אחת כמה וכמה אף אתה ומה בשכר ארבע פסיעות ששלמתי לאותו רשע שרץ אחר כבודי אתה תמיה כשאני משלם שכר לאברהם יצחק ויעקב שרצו לפני כסוסים עאכ"ו היינו דכתיב כ) לנביאים נשבר לבי בקרבי רחפו כל עצמותי הייתי כאיש שכור וכגבר עברו יין מפני ה' ומפני דברי קדשו הני ד' פסיעות מאי היא דכתיב ל) בעת ההיא שלח מרודך בלאדן בן בלאדן מלך בבל ספרים וגו' משום כי חלה חזקיהו ויחזק שדר ליה ספרים ומנחה (אין) מ) לדרוש (את) המופת אשר היה בארץ דאמר רבי יוחנן אותו היום שמת בו אחז שתי שעות היה וכי חלה חזקיהו ואיתפח אהדרינהו קודשא בריך הוא להנך עשר שעי ניהליה דכתיב נ) הנני משיב את צל המעלות אשר ירדה במעלות אחז בשמש אחורנית עשר מעלות ותשב השמש עשר מעלות במעלות אשר ירדה א"ל מאי האי א"ל חזקיהו חלש ואיתפח אמר איכא גברא כי האי ולא בעינא לשדורי ליה שלמא כתבו ליה שלמא למלכא חזקיה שלם לקרתא דירושלם שלם לאלהא רבא נבוכד נאצר ספריה דבלאדן הוה ההיא שעתא לא הוה התם כי אתא אמר להו היכי כתביתו אמרו ליה הכי כתבינן אמר להו קריתו ליה אלהא רבא וכתביתו ליה לבסוף אמר אלא הכי כתובו שלם לאלהא רבא שלם לקרתא דירושלם שלם למלכא חזקיה אמרי ליה [ג] קריינא דאיגרתא איהו ליהוי פרוונקא רהט בתריה כדרהיט [ד] ארבע פסיעות אתא גבריאל ואוקמיה אמר ר' יוחנן אילמלא ([ה] לא) בא גבריאל והעמידו לא היה תקנה לשונאיהם של ישראל מאי בלאדן בן בלאדן אמרי בלאדן מלכא הוה ואישתני אפיה והוה כי דכלבא הוה יתיב בריה על מלכותא כי הוה כתיב שמיה ושמיה דאבוה בלאדן מלכא היינו דכתיב ס) בן יכבד אב ועבד אדוניו בן יכבד אב הא דאמרן ועבד אדוניו דכתי' ע) ובחודש החמישי בעשור לחדש היא שנת תשע עשרה [שנה] למלך נבוכדנאצר מלך בבל בא נבוזראדן רב טבחים עמד לפני מלך בבל בירושלם וישרף את בית ה' ואת בית המלך

ומי

רש"י

אשני נפשך. שנה עצמך כדי שלא יכירוך: **ואגזייך אנא.** אני אגלחך: **קשייתא.** גרעיני תמרים: **טחון.** אלו גרעינין וניתן לך מספרים והיינו דכתיב בתער השכירה על שם שטרח נתנו לו תער לגלח ואיזהו שכר נתנו לו בעברי נהר דברים שדרכן לעשות על ידי נהר דהיינו טחינת ריחים: **וגם הזקן תספה.** דלא כתיב גלוח אלא אראש אבל אזקן כתיב תספה לשון כלוי על ידי אור שכלתה לגמרי: **גרירתיה לארמאה ושפר באפיה.** אם אתה מחרך את הארמאי והוטב בעיניו הבער לו את זקנו ולא שבעת חוכא מיניה: **בית נסרך אלהיו.** לשון נסר שהשתחוה לנסר ועשאו אלוה: **היינו דכתיב ויהי הוא משתחוה.** משמע מפני שמשתחוה לשם הכוהו: **ויחלק עליהם.** איידי דאיירי במלאכים איירי נמי בהאי קרא דכתיב ויהי בלילה ההוא ויצא מלאך ה' וגו' נקט ויחלק עליהם לילה וגו': **מלאך שנזדמן לאברהם לילה שמו.** והוא סייעו: **מעשה לילה.** שנלחמו בשבילו כוכבי לילה כמו שעשו בשביל ברק: **טבא מליה דר' יצחק נפחא מדבר נפחא.** ר' יוחנן דמקרי בר נפחא בכולא הש"ס כמו (ב"מ דף פה:) מאן עייל בר נפחא נראה למורי דאביו של ר' יוחנן הוי נפחא ולהכי מיקרי בר נפחא ואית דמפרשי בר נפחא על שם יופיו: **הזהרו בזקן.** אע"פ ששכח תלמודו הואיל ומחמת אונסו הוא: **הזהרו בורידין כר' יהודה.** דאמר בשחיטת חולין (דף כז.) עד שישחוט את הורידין של עוף הואיל וצולהו כולו כאחד אינו חותכו ומולחו כבשר חיה ובהמה: **הזהרו בבני עמי הארץ.** שנעשו תלמידי חכמים לעשות להם כבוד שמהם תצא תורה לישראל שהרי יצאו שמעיה ואבטליון מבני בניו של סנחריב ומבני בניו של המן למדו תורה בבני ברק כדלקמן ואע"ג דאמר רבי יהודה הכי הזהרו בבני עמי הארץ: **כי הא מילתא.** דלקמן מודעינן להו כי היכי דחזינן לקמן דלא זכה נבוכדנצר לאותו כבוד אלא מפני זכות ד' פסיעות כדאמרינן לקמן ה"נ אמרי' לבני עמי הארץ דלא זכו לאותו כבוד אלא מחמת זכות מעט שהיה באביהם מ"ר. ואית דאמרי דרבי זירא אדלעיל קאי אבני סנחריב אע"ג דשלח רבי יהודה הזהרו בבני ע"ה לכבדן שמהם תצא תורה כי היכי דנפקו מסנחריב כי הא מילתא מודיעים להו לבני ע"ה דהא דמוקרין להו לאו משום אביהם אלא משום תורה שבהם שלא תזוח דעתם עליהם ויאמרו אבותיהם לדיקים היו: **מדוע דרך רשעים צלחה.** מפני מה הצליח נבוכדנצר וכבש ירושלים: **אהדרו ליה.** לירמיה: **בצעי מים.** מרש"קו בלעז: **ד' פסיעות.** מפורש לקמן: **על אחת כמה וכמה.** שיהו כל אדם יכולין לתמוה על מתן שכר גדול שישתלם עליהם: **לנביאים.** אברהם יצחק ויעקב: **נשבר לבי בקרבי.** כלומר תמהתי על מתן שכרן: **שתי שעות.** כדי שלא יהא פנאי לספדו ולקברו: **אתפח.** נתרפא: **אהדרינהו הקב"ה.** להנך שעות לחזקיהו דאותו היום שנתרפא חזקיה היה של כ"ב שעות: **רהט בתריה.** דשליח: **לא היה להם תקנה.** שהיה שכרו מרובה והיה לו רשות לאבד שאריתנו: **הוה כתיב שמיה ושמיה דאבוה.** כדי שיתכבד אביו לכך נקרא שם אביו עליו שנקרא מרודך בלאדן דאי לא כתיב אלא מרודך בן בלאדן לא הוי מיתקרי עליה שמיה דאבוה דהכי כתבי כולהו אינשי פלוני בן פלוני להכי כתיב מרודך בלאדן: **בחדש החמישי בעשור לחדש בא נבוזר אדן רב טבחים עמד לפני מלך בבל בירושלם.** אלמא נבוכד נצר סליק לירושלם:

ומי

מסורת הש"ס

א) ג' ב"ש ריב"ל, ב) ברכות ח., ג) לעיל דף פב. ב"מ פג:, ד) [במדר' ובילקו' אית' שליש וכ"א ברש"י ירמיה יב פ"ה], ה) [עי' תוס' מגילה כח.].

ליקוטי רש"י

ושאר עץ יערו. הנותרים בחיילותיו. **מספר יהיו.** נוחים לספור כי מעט הם ונער יוכל לכותבם ואמרו רבותינו עשרה נשאר מהם שאין לך קטן שאינו כותב יו"ד קטנה [שם י, יט]. **ונשאר בו.** בהמון סנחריב אנשי' מעט כנוקף זית. **בראש אמיר.** בראש הענף. **בסעיפיה.** בענפיה וכן וכלה סעיפיה (ישעיה כז) וכן מסעף פארה (שם י) [שם יז, ו]. **ורוה די רביעאה.** ותוארו של רביעי. **דמה לבר אלהין.** דומה למלאך שראיתי בהיותי עם סנחריב כשנשרפו אוכלוסיו שנאמר (שם לז) ויכה במחנה אשור ונבוכדנצר היה שם ונמלט בתוך עשרה שנמלטו מהם [דניאל ג, כה]. **בית נסרוך אלהיו.** נסר מתיבתו של נח. **הכהו בחרב.** שמעו אותו שאמר לשוחטן לפניו אם ילילוהו שלא יהרגוהו שרי המלכות שמתו בניהם על ידו [מ"ב יט, לז]. **יגלח ה' בתער השכירה.** הגדולה וכן גם שכיריה בקרבה (ירמיה מו) פ"י רברבהא יגלח. **בעברי נהר.** ביושבי עבר הנהר ובמי מן היושבים במלך אשור את הראש יגלח ואת שער הרגלים לפי שהוא דבוק נשתנה לינקד פתח. **תספה.** תכלה [ישעיה ז, כ]. [ע"כ שייך לדף צה:] **בית נסרוך אלהיו.** נסר מתיבתו של נח. **הכוהו בחרב.** שמעו אותו שאמר לשוחטן לפניו אם ילילוהו שלא יהרגוהו שרי המלכות שמתו בניהם על ידו [מ"ב יט, לז]. **ויחלק עליהם.** לפי פשוטו סרס המקרא ויחלק הוא ועבדיו עליהם לילה כדרך הרודפים שמתפלגים אחר הנרדפים כשבורחים זה לכאן וזה לכאן. **לילה.** כלומר אחר שחשכה לא נמנעו מלרדפם [בראשית יד, טו ועי' במהרש"א ח"א]. **והלילה אמר.** ורז"ל אמרו (נדה טז:) מלאך הממונ' על ההריון לילה שמו [איוב ג, ג ועי' מהרש"א בח"א]. **תשש כחו.** שראה שעתידין בניו להעמיד שם עגל [בראשית שם, יד]. **מדן נשמע.** על דפלחו לעגלא דבדן. **נחרת סוסיו.** עטישות נחיריו [ירמיה ח, טז]. **מחמת אונסו.** שחלה או שנטרד בדוחק מזונות הזהרו בו לכבדו [ברכות ח:]. **בוורידין.** חוטי הצואר שמקלחין את הדם ובגמרא (חולין כח:) מפרש דלעוף קאי ומשום להוציא את הדם [חולין כז.]. שישחוט את הורידין כדי שיצא כל הדם ולא אמר כן אלא בעוף הואיל וצולהו כולו כאחד [ברכות שם]. **צדיק אתה ה' כי אריב אליך.** כשאתווכח עמך ידעתי כי תצדק בדבריך אך חפץ אני לדבר משפטים אותך להודיעני דרכך. **מדוע דרך רשעים צלחה.** שנתת גדולה לנבוכדנצר הרשע ותצליחהו להחריב ביתך. **שלו.** לשון שלוה [ירמיה יב, א]. **ואיך תתחרה את הסוסים.** לרוץ את הסוסים וכו' ומדרש רבותינו אם על שכר שלש פסיעות שרץ נבוכדנצר לכבודי בימי מרודך בלאדן אתה תמה שהרביתי גדולתו כל כך מה תתמה עוד כשתראה שילום שכר שאשלם לצדיקים שרצו לפני כסוסים. **תתחרה.** אאטיר"ש בלע"ז. **ובארץ שלום אשר אתה בוטח.** שם הלאוך [שם, ה]. **הנני משיב.** אחורנית עשר מעלות את הצל אשר ירדה. **צל המעלות.** כמין מדרגות עשויות כנגד החמה לבחון בהם שעות היום כעין אורלוגין שעושין האומנין. **אשר ירדה.** מיהרה לירד ונתקצר היום י' שעות ביום שמת אחז כדי שלא יהו מספידין אותו ועלו עכשיו לאחוריהם ביום שנתרפא חזקיהו ויתוספו על היום י' שעות [ישעיה לח, ח]. **א"ל מאי האי.** היה למוד לאכול בשלש שעות וישן עד ט' כיון שחזר גלגל חמה לחזקיהו כשעמד משנתו בט' שעות מצא שהוא שחרית בקש להרוג את כל עבדיו אמר הנחתם אותי ישן יומם ולילה עד הבקר אמרו לו גלגל חמה הוא שחזר אמר להם ומי החזירו אמרו לו אלוהו של חזקיהו כו' כדאיתא בתנחומא ובפסיקתא [שם לט, א]. **קריינא דאיגרתא.** משל הוא. **פרוונקא.** שליח [ב"מ פג:]. שליח מוליא ומביא [לעיל לח:].

גליון הש"ס

גמ' **קריינא דאגרתא.** בתנחומא פ' תשא איתא דמרודך בלאדן בעצמו נתחרט ורהט בתריה ג' פסיעות:

תורה אור השלם

א) בַּיּוֹם הַהוּא יְגַלַּח אֲדֹנָי בְּתַעַר הַשְּׂכִירָה בְּעֶבְרֵי נָהָר בְּמֶלֶךְ אַשּׁוּר אֶת הָרֹאשׁ וְשַׂעַר הָרַגְלָיִם וְגַם אֶת הַזָּקָן תִּסְפֶּה: [ישעיה ז, כ]

ב) וַיְהִי הוּא מִשְׁתַּחֲוֶה בֵּית נִסְרֹךְ אֱלֹהָיו וְאַדְרַמֶּלֶךְ וְשַׂרְאֶצֶר בָּנָיו הִכֻּהוּ בַחֶרֶב וְהֵמָּה נִמְלְטוּ אֶרֶץ אֲרָרָט וַיִּמְלֹךְ אֵסַר חַדֹּן בְּנוֹ תַּחְתָּיו: [מלכים ב' יט, לז]

ג) וַיֵּחָלֵק עֲלֵיהֶם לַיְלָה הוּא וַעֲבָדָיו וַיַּכֵּם וַיִּרְדְּפֵם עַד חוֹבָה אֲשֶׁר מִשְּׂמֹאל לְדַמָּשֶׂק: [בראשית יד, טו]

ד) יֹאבַד יוֹם אִוָּלֶד בּוֹ וְהַלַּיְלָה אָמַר הֹרָה גָבֶר: [איוב ג, ג]

ה) מִן שָׁמַיִם נִלְחָמוּ הַכּוֹכָבִים מִמְּסִלּוֹתָם נִלְחֲמוּ עִם סִיסְרָא: [שופטים ה, כ]

ו) וַיִּשְׁמַע אַבְרָם כִּי נִשְׁבָּה אָחִיו וַיָּרֶק אֶת חֲנִיכָיו יְלִידֵי בֵיתוֹ שְׁמֹנָה עָשָׂר וּשְׁלֹשׁ מֵאוֹת וַיִּרְדֹּף עַד דָּן: [בראשית יד, יד]

ז) וַיָּשֶׂם אֶת הָאֶחָד בְּבֵית אֵל וְאֶת הָאֶחָד נָתַן בְּדָן: [מלכים א' יב, כט]

ח) מִדָּן נִשְׁמַע נַחְרַת סוּסָיו מִקּוֹל מִצְהֲלוֹת אַבִּירָיו רָעֲשָׁה כָּל הָאָרֶץ וַיָּבוֹאוּ וַיֹּאכְלוּ אֶרֶץ וּמְלוֹאָהּ עִיר וְיֹשְׁבֵי בָהּ: [ירמיה ח, טז]

ט) צַדִּיק אַתָּה יְיָ כִּי אָרִיב אֵלֶיךָ אַךְ מִשְׁפָּטִים אֲדַבֵּר אוֹתָךְ מַדּוּעַ דֶּרֶךְ רְשָׁעִים צָלֵחָה שָׁלוּ כָּל בֹּגְדֵי בָגֶד: נְטַעְתָּם גַּם שֹׁרָשׁוּ יֵלְכוּ גַּם עָשׂוּ פֶרִי קָרוֹב אַתָּה בְּפִיהֶם וְרָחוֹק מִכִּלְיוֹתֵיהֶם: [ירמיה יב, א-ב]

י) כִּי אֶת רַגְלִים רַצְתָּה וַיַּלְאוּךָ וְאֵיךְ תְּתַחֲרֶה אֶת הַסּוּסִים וּבְאֶרֶץ שָׁלוֹם אַתָּה בוֹטֵחַ וְאֵיךְ תַּעֲשֶׂה בִּגְאוֹן הַיַּרְדֵּן: [ירמיה יב, ה]

כ) לַנְּבִאִים נִשְׁבַּר לִבִּי בְקִרְבִּי רָחֲפוּ כָּל עַצְמוֹתַי הָיִיתִי כְּאִישׁ שִׁכּוֹר וּכְגֶבֶר עֲבָרוֹ יָיִן מִפְּנֵי יְיָ וּמִפְּנֵי דִּבְרֵי קָדְשׁוֹ: [ירמיה כג, ט]

ל) בָּעֵת הַהִוא שָׁלַח מְרֹדַךְ בַּלְאֲדָן בֶּן בַּלְאֲדָן מֶלֶךְ בָּבֶל סְפָרִים וּמִנְחָה אֶל חִזְקִיָּהוּ וַיִּשְׁמַע כִּי חָלָה וַיֶּחֱזָק: [ישעיה לט, א]

מ) וְכֵן בִּמְלִיצֵי שָׂרֵי בָבֶל הַמְשַׁלְּחִים עָלָיו לִדְרֹשׁ הַמּוֹפֵת אֲשֶׁר הָיָה בָאָרֶץ עֲזָבוֹ הָאֱלֹהִים לְנַסּוֹתוֹ לָדַעַת כָּל בִּלְבָבוֹ: [דברי הימים ב' לב, לא]

נ) הִנְנִי מֵשִׁיב אֶת צֵל הַמַּעֲלוֹת אֲשֶׁר יָרְדָה בְמַעֲלוֹת אָחָז בַּשֶּׁמֶשׁ אֲחֹרַנִּית עֶשֶׂר מַעֲלוֹת וַתָּשָׁב הַשֶּׁמֶשׁ עֶשֶׂר מַעֲלוֹת בַּמַּעֲלוֹת אֲשֶׁר יָרָדָה: [ישעיה לח, ח]

ס) בֵּן יְכַבֵּד אָב וְעֶבֶד אֲדֹנָיו וְאִם אָב אָנִי אַיֵּה כְבוֹדִי וְאִם אֲדוֹנִים אָנִי אַיֵּה מוֹרָאִי אָמַר יְיָ צְבָאוֹת לָכֶם הַכֹּהֲנִים בּוֹזֵי שְׁמִי וַאֲמַרְתֶּם בַּמֶּה בָזִינוּ אֶת שְׁמֶךָ: [מלאכי א, ו]

ע) וּבַחֹדֶשׁ הַחֲמִישִׁי בֶּעָשׂוֹר לַחֹדֶשׁ הִיא שְׁנַת תְּשַׁע עֶשְׂרֵה שָׁנָה לַמֶּלֶךְ נְבוּכַדְרֶאצַּר מֶלֶךְ בָּבֶל בָּא נְבוּזַרְאֲדָן רַב טַבָּחִים עָמַד לִפְנֵי מֶלֶךְ בָּבֶל בִּירוּשָׁלָםִ: וַיִּשְׂרֹף אֶת בֵּית יְהוָה וְאֶת בֵּית הַמֶּלֶךְ וְאֵת כָּל בָּתֵּי יְרוּשָׁלַםִ וְאֶת כָּל בֵּית הַגָּדוֹל שָׂרַף בָּאֵשׁ: [ירמיה נב, יב-יג]

God's response is explained by way of analogy: מָשָׁל לְאָדָם אֶחָד שֶׁאָמַר – **This is analogous to a man who said** in boast: יָכוֹל אֲנִי לָרוּץ שָׁלֹשׁ פַּרְסָאוֹת לִפְנֵי הַסּוּסִים – **"I could run before horses** a distance of **three** ***parsaos***[22] and they would not outrace me, בֵּין בִּצְעֵי הַמַּיִם – [even] **on marshy land."** נִזְדַּמֵּן לוֹ רַגְלִי אֶחָד – But then **he chanced upon a person running on foot** רָץ לְפָנָיו שְׁלֹשָׁה מִילִין בַּיַּבָּשָׁה – and seeking to outrace him, **he ran before him** a mere **three** ***mils*** **on dry land,** וְנִלְאָה – **and became exhausted.** אָמְרוּ לוֹ – [People] then **said to him:** וּמָה לִפְנֵי רַגְלִי כָּךְ – **"If this** is what happened when you raced **against a pedestrian,** לִפְנֵי הַסּוּסִים עַל אַחַת כַּמָּה וְכַמָּה – **then how much more** so would you have collapsed attempting to race **against horses!** וּמָה שְׁלֹשֶׁת מִילִין כָּךְ – **If this** is what happened when you ran for a mere **three** ***mils,*** שָׁלֹשׁ פַּרְסָאוֹת עַל אַחַת כַּמָּה וְכַמָּה – **then how much more** so would you have been exhausted had you tried to run **three** *parsaos!* וּמָה בַּיַּבָּשָׁה כָּךְ – **If this** is what happened when you ran **on dry land,** בֵּין בִּצְעֵי הַמַּיִם עַל אַחַת כַּמָּה וְכַמָּה – **then how much more** so would you have been exhausted had you run **on marshlands!"**

The Gemara continues:

אַף אַתָּה – So it was that God said to Jeremiah: **The same** applies **to you:** וּמָה בִּשְׂכַר אַרְבַּע פְּסִיעוֹת שֶׁשִּׁלַּמְתִּי לְאוֹתוֹ רָשָׁע שֶׁרָץ אַחַר כְּבוֹדִי אַתָּה תָּמֵיהַּ – **If you are astonished at the reward I paid to that wicked [Nebuchadnezzar] for the four paces he ran for the sake of My honor,**[23] כְּשֶׁאֲנִי מְשַׁלֵּם שָׂכָר לְאַבְרָהָם יִצְחָק וְיַעֲקֹב – **then when** in the future **I reward Abraham, Isaac and Jacob,** שֶׁרָצוּ לְפָנַי כְּסוּסִים – **who ran before me with** the strength of **horses,**[24] עַל אַחַת כַּמָּה וְכַמָּה – **how much more so** will people be astonished at the magnitude of their reward! הַיְינוּ דִּכְתִיב – **And this,** indeed, **is the meaning of that which is written** in Scripture: "לַנְּבִאִים נִשְׁבַּר לִבִּי בְקִרְבִּי – *[When I think of] the prophets, my heart within me is broken;* רָחֲפוּ כָּל־עַצְמוֹתַי – *all my bones shake;* הָיִיתִי כְּאִישׁ שִׁכּוֹר וּכְגֶבֶר עֲבָרוֹ יָיִן – *I am like a drunken man, like a man overcome by wine;* מִפְּנֵי ה׳ וּמִפְּנֵי דִּבְרֵי קָדְשׁוֹ" – *because of* HASHEM*, and because of His holy words.*[25]

Having mentioned that Nebuchadnezzar was rewarded for taking four steps, the Gemara recounts the full incident:

הָנֵי אַרְבַּע פְּסִיעוֹת – The incident of **those four steps,** מַאי הִיא – **what was it?** דִּכְתִיב "בָּעֵת הַהִיא שָׁלַח מְרֹאדַךְ בַּלְאֲדָן בֶּן־בַּלְאֲדָן מֶלֶךְ־בָּבֶל סְפָרִים" וגו׳ – We find **that it is written:**[26] ***At that time, Merodach Baladan the son of Baladan, king of Babylonia, sent letters* etc.** *[and a gift to Chizkiah, having heard that he* (Chizkiah) *was ill and had recovered].* Now, this verse requires explanation: מִשּׁוּם כִּי חָלָה (חִזְקִיָּהוּ) וַיֶּחֱזַק שָׁדַר לֵיהּ סְפָרִים וּמִנְחָה – **Because he heard that Chizkiah was ill and had recovered, [Merodach Baladan] sent him letters and a gift?!**[27] The Gemara explains the verse: (אִין – **Indeed,**) it was due to Chizkiah's recovery from illness that Merodach Baladan sent him letters and a gift, "לִדְרשׁ (אֶת) הַמּוֹפֵת אֲשֶׁר הָיָה בָאָרֶץ" – for Merodach Baladan wanted ***to find out about the wonder that had happened in the land.***[28] דְּאָמַר רַבִּי יוֹחָנָן – The wonder referred to here is **as R' Yochanan explained:** אוֹתוֹ הַיּוֹם שֶׁמֵּת בּוֹ אָחָז שְׁתֵּי שָׁעוֹת הָיָה – **The day on which Achaz died was** only **two hours** long, i.e. ten hours of daylight were removed from that day,[29] וְכִי חָלָה חִזְקִיָּהוּ וְאִיתְפַּח – **and when Chizkiah fell ill and recovered,** אַהַדְרִינְהוּ קוּדְשָׁא בְּרִיךְ הוּא לְהָנָךְ עֶשֶׂר שָׁעֵי נִיהֲלֵיהּ – **the Holy One, Blessed is He, restored those ten hours to him.** דִּכְתָב "הִנְנִי מֵשִׁיב אֶת־צֵל הַמַּעֲלוֹת אֲשֶׁר יָרְדָה בְמַעֲלוֹת אָחָז בַּשֶּׁמֶשׁ אֲחֹרַנִּית עֶשֶׂר מַעֲלוֹת וַתָּשָׁב הַשֶּׁמֶשׁ עֶשֶׂר מַעֲלוֹת בַּמַּעֲלוֹת אֲשֶׁר יָרָדָה" – This is **as it is written:** ***Behold I will cause the shadow on the sundial***[30] *– **which had descended*** [*speedily*] ***on the sundial of Achaz because of*** [*the hastened progress of*] ***the sun – to recede ten degrees. And the*** [*shadow of the*] ***sun receded ten degrees, the same degrees it had descended.***[31] אָמַר לְהוּ – Bewildered by the extraordinary length of that day, **[Merodach Baladan] said to [his servants]:** מַאי הַאי – **"What is this?"** אָמְרוּ לֵיהּ – **They answered him:** חִזְקִיָּהוּ חָלַשׁ וְאִיתְפַּח – **"Chizkiah** king of Judah **was ill and has recovered."** אָמַר – **[Merodach Baladan] exclaimed:** אִיכָּא גַּבְרָא כִּי הַאי – **"Is there** such **a person as this** וְלָא בָּעֵינָא לְשַׁדּוּרֵי לֵיהּ שְׁלָמָא – **and I am not required to send him greetings?!** כָּתְבוּ לֵיהּ – **[The royal secretaries] wrote** to Chizkiah **for him** (i.e. for Merodach Baladan) as follows: שְׁלָמָא לְמַלְכָּא חִזְקִיָּה – **Greetings to King Chizkiah!** שְׁלָם לְקַרְתָּא דִירוּשְׁלֵם – **Greetings to the city of Jerusalem!** שְׁלָם לֶאֱלָהָא רַבָּא – **Greetings to the great God!"** נְבוּכַדְנֶאצַּר סָפְרֵיהּ דְּבַלְאֲדָן הֲוָה – **Nebuchadnezzar was** Merodach **Baladan's secretary.** הַהִיא שַׁעְתָּא לָא הֲוָה הָתָם – **At that moment, however, [Nebuchanezzar] was not present.** כִּי אֲתָא – **When [Nebuchadnezzar] came** back, אָמַר לְהוּ – **he asked [the other secre-**

NOTES

able to discern the intentions of his own townsmen, who (were it not for God's intervention) would have successfully poisoned him (see ibid. 11:18-23). Thus, how can Jeremiah expect to compete against "horses," i.e. to discern the Divine secrets by which God governs the world? (*Radak;* cf. *Rashi* to *Jeremiah* ad loc.).

[The above is the plain meaning of the verse. Our Gemara, however, interprets the verse as alluding to an actual *explanation* that God gave to Jeremiah of His ways. According to the Gemara, God responded, so to speak, with a rhetorical question: If you are amazed at the reward received by Nebuchadnezzar for seemingly trivial acts of righteousness, how much more so will you be amazed at the reward I am destined to give the Jewish people for the great meritorious acts of their forefathers!]

22. A *parsah* is a measure of distance equivalent to four *mil,* or eight thousand *amos.*

23. The Gemara below will explain these "four paces" in greater detail.

24. I.e. who served Me zealously.

25. *Jeremiah* 23:9. In this verse, Jeremiah proclaims himself awestruck when he contemplates the reward awaiting Abraham, Isaac and Jacob for their meritorious deeds (*Rashi;* cf. *Maharsha*).

R' Yerucham Levovitz (*Daas Chochmah U'Mussar*) explains the allegory as teaching that we must hurry to serve God undeterred by the "swamps" of this world.

26. *Isaiah* 39:1.

27. He was neither a friend nor an acquaintance of Chizkiah!

28. *II Chronicles* 32:31. This verse also speaks of Merodach Baladan's gift to Chizkiah (*Metzudos*).

29. Achaz, the father of Chizkiah, was a terribly wicked king. The day on which he died was shortened to two hours, so that there would be no time to bury him [in a dignified manner (see *Yad Ramah*)] or to eulogize him (*Rashi*).

Maharsha explains that this served to atone for his sins, as the Gemara above (47a) states: "A dead person who was not eulogized . . . this is a good sign for the deceased."

30. Literally: steps or degrees. This word is used idiomatically for a sundial (see *Targum* ad loc.) which shows the time of day by the shadow cast on the degrees marked on its surface. It can also refer to the degrees themselves.

31. *Isaiah* 38:8 (see also *II Kings* 20:8-11). Stricken with a mortal illness, King Chizkiah fervently prayed to God to grant him recovery. God sent the prophet Isaiah to tell Chizkiah that he would indeed recover and live fifteen additional years and, as a sign that the decree of death had been reversed, the sun would reverse its normal course and recede eastward. Isaiah told Chizkiah that after at least ten hours of daylight had passed, the shadow on the sundial would recede ten degrees, indicating that the sun was reversing its course. This meant that the daylight would last an extra ten hours. Those extra ten hours replaced the ten hours that were taken from the day on which Achaz died (see *Rashi* ad loc.).

Maharsha says that the extra hours of sunlight expedited Chizkiah's recovery.

ושני נפשך במאי אישני אמר ליה זיל אייתי לי מספרא ואיגזייך אנא מהיכא אייתי א"ל עול להההוא ביתא ואייתי אזל אשכחינהו אתו מלאכי שרת ואידמו ליה כגברי והוו קא טחני קשייתא א"ל הבו לי מספרא א"ל טחון חד גריוא דקשייתא וניתן לך טחן חד גריוא דקשייתא ויהבו ליה מספרתא עד דאתא איחשך א"ל זיל אייתי נורא אזל ואייתי נורא בהדי דקא נפח ליה אתלי ביה נורא בדיקניה אזל גזייה לרישיה ודיקניה אמרו היינו דכתיב א) וגם את הזקן תספה אמר רב פפא היינו דאמרי אינשי גרירתיה לארמאה שפיר ליה איתלי ליה נורא בדיקניה ולא שבעת חוכא מיניה אזל אשכח דפא מתיבותא דנח אמר היינו אלהא רבא דשיזביה לנח מטופנא אמר אי אזיל ההוא גברא ומצלח מקרב להו לתרין בנוהי קמך שמעו בנוהי וקטלוהו היינו דכתיב ב) ויהי הוא משתחוה בית נסרוך אלהיו ואדרמלך ושראצר בניו הכהו בחרב וגו' ג) ויחלק עליהם לילה הוא ועבדיו ויכם וגו' אמר רבי יוחנן אותו מלאך שנזדמן לו לאברהם לילה שמו שנאמר ד) והלילה אמר הורה גבר ור' יצחק נפחא אמר שעשה עמו מעשה לילה שנאמר ה) מן שמים נלחמו הכוכבים ממסלותם נלחמו עם סיסרא אמר ריש לקיש טבא דנפחא מדבר נפחא ו) וירדף עד דן אמר רבי יוחנן כיון שבא אותו צדיק עד דן תשש כחו ראה בני בניו שעתידין לעבוד ע"ז בדן שנאמר ז) וישם את האחד בבית אל ואת האחד נתן בדן ואף אותו רשע לא נתגבר עד שהגיע לדן שנאמר ח) מדן נשמע נחרת סוסיו אמר רבי זירא אע"ג דשלח ר' [א] (יהודה בן בתירא מנציבין) [ב] הזהרו בזקן ששכח תלמודו מחמת אונסו והזהרו בוורידין כר' יהודה והזהרו בבני עמי הארץ שמהן תצא תורה כי הא מילתא מודעינן להו ט) צדיק אתה ה' כי אריב אליך אך משפטים אדבר אותך מדוע דרך רשעים צלחה שלו כל בוגדי בגד נטעתם גם שורשו ילכו גם עשו פרי מאי אהדרו ליה י) כי את רגלים רצתה וילאוך ואיך תתחרה את הסוסים ובארץ שלום אתה בוטח ואיך תעשה בגאון הירדן משל לאדם אחד שאמר יכול אני לרוץ ג' פרסאות לפני הסוסים בין בצעי המים נזדמן לו רגלי אחד רץ לפניו ג' מילין ביבשה ונלאה א"ל ומה לפני רגלי כך לפני הסוסים עאכ"ו ומה שלשת מילין כך ג' פרסאות על אחת כמה וכמה ומה ביבשה כך בין בצעי המים על אחת כמה וכמה אף אתה ומה בשכר ארבע פסיעות ששלמתי לאותו רשע שרץ אחר כבודי אתה תמיה כשאני משלם שכר לאברהם יצחק ויעקב שרצו לפני כסוסים עאכ"ו היינו דכתיב כ) לנביאים נשבר לבי בקרבי רחפו כל עצמותי הייתי כאיש שכור וכגבר עברו יין מפני ה' ומפני דברי קדשו הני ד' פסיעות מאי היא דכתיב ל) בעת ההיא שלח מרודך בלאדן בן בלאדן מלך בבל ספרים וגו' משום כי חלה חזקיהו ויחזק שדר ליה ספרים ומנחה (אין) מ) לדרוש (את) המופת אשר היה בארץ דאמר רבי יוחנן אותו היום שמת בו אחז שתי שעות היה וכי חלה חזקיהו ואיתפח אהדרינהו קודשא בריך הוא להנך עשר שעי ניהליה דכתיב נ) הנני משיב את צל המעלות אשר ירדה במעלות אחז בשמש אחורנית עשר מעלות ותשב השמש עשר מעלות במעלות אשר ירדה א"ל מאי האי א"ל חזקיהו חלש ואיתפח אמר איכא גברא כי האי ולא בעינא לשדורי ליה שלמא כתבו ליה שלמא למלכא חזקיה שלם לקרתא דירושלם שלם לאלהא רבא נבוכד נאצר ספריה דבלאדן הוה ההיא שעתא לא הוה התם כי אתא אמר להו היכי כתביתו אמרו ליה הכי כתבינן אמר להו קריתו ליה אלהא רבא וכתביתו ליה לבסוף אמר אלא הכי כתובו שלם לאלהא רבא שלם לקרתא דירושלם שלם למלכא חזקיה אמרי ליה [ג] קריינא דאיגרתא איהו ליהוי פרוונקא רהט בתריה כדרהיט ד' ארבע פסיעות אתא גבריאל ואוקמיה אמר ר' יוחנן אילמלא ([ה] לא) בא גבריאל והעמידו לא היה תקנה לשונאיהם של ישראל מאי בלאדן בן בלאדן אמרי בלאדן מלכא הוה ואישתני אפיה והוה כי דכלבא הוה יתיב בריה על מלכותא כי הוה כתיב הוה כתיב שמיה ושמיה דאבוה בלאדן מלכא היינו דכתיב ס) בן יכבד אב ועבד אדוניו בן יכבד אב הא דאמרן ועבד אדוניו דכתי' ע) ובחודש החמישי בעשור לחדש היא שנת תשע עשרה [שנה] למלך נבוכדנאצר מלך בבל בא נבוזראדן רב טבחים עמד לפני מלך בבל בירושלם וישרף את בית ה' ואת בית המלך

ומי

רש"י

אשני נפשך. שנה עצמך כדי שלא יכירוך: ואגזייך אנא. אני אגלחך: קשייתא. גרעיני תמרים: טחון. אלו גרעינין וניתן לך מספרים והיינו דכתיב בתער השכירה על שם שטרח נתנו לו תער לגלח ואיזהו שכר נתנו לו בעברי נהר דברים שדרכן לעשות על ידי נהר דהיינו טחינת ריחים: וגם הזקן תספה. דלא כתיב גלוח אלא אראש אבל אזקן כתיב תספה לשון כלוי על ידי אור שכלתה לגמרי: גרירתיה לארמאה ושפר באפיה. אם אתה מחרך את הארמאי והוטב בעיניו הבער לו אש בזקנו ולא שבעת חוכא מיניה: בית נסרך אלהיו. לשון נסר שהשתחוה לנסר ועשאו אלוה: היינו דכתיב ויהי הוא משתחוה. משמע מפני שמשתחוה לשם הכוהו: ויחלק עליהם. איידי דאיירי במלאכים איירי נמי בהאי קרא דכתיב ויהי בלילה ההוא ויצא מלאך ה' וגו' נקט ויחלק עליהם לילה וגו': מלאך שנזדמן לאברהם לילה שמו. והוא סייעו: מעשה לילה. שנלחמו בשבילו כוכבי לילה כמו שעשו בשביל ברק: טבא מליה דר' יצחק נפחא מדבר נפחא. ר' יוחנן דמקרי בר נפחא בכולא הש"ס כמו (ב"מ דף פה:) מאן עייל בר נפחא נראה למורי דאביו של ר' יוחנן הוי נפחא ולהכי מיקרי בר נפחא ואית דמפרשי בר נפחא על שם יופיו: הזהרו בזקן. אע"פ ששכח תלמודו הואיל ומחמת אונסו הוא: הזהרו בורידין כר' יהודה. דאמר בשחיטת חולין (דף כז.) עד שישחוט את הורידין של עוף הואיל וצולהו כולו כאחד אינו חותכו ומולחו כבשר חיה ובהמה: הזהרו בבני עמי הארץ. שנעשו תלמידי חכמים לעשות להם כבוד שמהם תצא תורה לישראל שהרי יצאו שמעיה ואבטליון מבני בניו של סנחריב ומבני בניו של המן למדו תורה בבני ברק כדלקמן ואע"ג דאמר רבי יהודה הכי הזהרו בבני עמי הארץ:

תוספות

כי הא מילתא. דלקמן מודעינן להו כי היכי דחזינן לקמן דלא זכה נבוכדנצר לאותו כבוד אלא מפני זכות ד' פסיעות כדאמרינן לקמן ה"נ אמרי' לבני עמי הארץ דלא זכו לאותו כבוד אלא מחמת זכות מעט שהיה באביהם מ"ר. ואית דאמרי דרבי זירא אדלעיל קאי אבני סנחריב אע"ג דשלח רבי יהודה הזהרו בבני ע"ה לכבדן שמהם תצא תורה כי היכי דנפקו מסנחריב כי הא מילתא מודיעים להו לבני ע"ה דהא דמוקרין להו לאו משום אביהם אלא משום תורה שבהם שלא תזוח דעתם עליהם ויאמרו אבותיהם לדיקים היו: מדוע דרך רשעים צלחה. מפני מה הצליח נבוכדנצר וכבש ירושלים: אהדרו ליה. לירמיה: בצעי מים. מרש"קו בלעז: ד' פסיעות. מפורש לקמן: על אחת כמה וכמה. שיהו כל אדם יכולין לתמוה על מתן שכר גדול שישתלם עליהם: לנביאים. אברהם יצחק ויעקב: נשבר לבי בקרבי. כלומר תמהתי על מתן שכרן: שתי שעות. כדי שלא יהא פנאי לספדו ולקברו: אתפח. נתרפא: אהדרינהו הקב"ה. להנך שעות לחזקיהו דאותו היום שנתרפא חזקיה היה של כ"ב שעות: רהט בתריה. דשליח: לא היה להם תקנה. שהיה שכרו מרובה והיה לו רשות לאבד שאריתנו: הוה כתיב שמיה ושמיה דאבוה. כדי שיתכבד אביו לכך נקרא שם אביו עליו שנקרא מרודך בלאדן דאי לא כתיב אלא מרודך בן בלאדן לא הוי מיתקרי עליה שמיה דאבוה דהכי כתבי כולהו אינשי פלוני בן פלוני להכי כתיב מרודך בלאדן: בחדש החמישי בעשור לחדש בא נבוזר אדן רב טבחים עמד לפני מלך בבל בירושלם. אלמא נבוכד נצר סליק לירושלם:

רש"י (המשך)

מדוע דרך רשעים צלחה. שנתת גדולה לנבוכדנצר הרשע ותלליתהו להחריב ביתך. שלו. לשון שלוה [ירמיה יב, א]. ואיך תתחרה את הסוסים. לרוץ את הסוסים וכו' ומדרש רבותינו אם על שכר שלש פסיעות שרץ נבוכדנצר לכבודי בימי מרודך בלאדן אתה תמה שהרביתי גדולתו כל כך מה תתמה עוד כשתראה שילום שכר שאשלם לצדיקים שרצו לפני כסוסים. תתחרה. אאטיר"ש בלע"ז. ובארץ שלום אשר אתה בוטח. שם הלאוך [שם, ה]. הנני משיב. אחורנית עשר מעלות את הצל אשר ירדה. צל המעלות. כמין מדרגות עשויות כנגד החמה לבחון בהם שעות היום כעין אורלוגין שעושין האומנין. אשר ירדה. מיהרה לירד ונתקצר היום י' שעות כדי שלא יהו מספידין אותו ועלו עכשיו לאחוריהם ביום שנתרפא חזקיהו ויתוספו על היום י' שעות [ישעיה לח, ח]. א"ל מאי האי. היה למוד לאכול בשלש שעות וישן עד ט' כיון שחזר גלגל חמה לחזקיהו כשעמד משנתו בט' שעות מצא שהוא שחרית בקש להרוג את כל עבדיו אמר הנחתם אותי ישן יומם ולילה עד הבקר אמרו לו גלגל חמה הוא שחזר אמר להם ומי החזירו אמרו לו אלוהו של חזקיהו כו' כדאיתא בתנחומא ובפסיקתא [שם לט, א]. קריינא דאיגרתא. משל הוא. פרוונקא. שליח [ב"מ פג:]. שליח מוליא ומביא [לעיל לח:].

מסורת הש"ס

א) גי' ב"ש ריב"ל, ב) ברכות ח:, ג) לעיל דף פב. ב"מ פג:, ד) [במדר' ובילקו' אית' שלש וכ"א ברש"י ירמיה יב פ"ה], ה) [עי' תוס' מגילה כא.].

ליקוטי רש"י

ושאר עץ יערו. הטותרים בחיילותיו. מספר יהיו. נוחים לספור כי מעט הם ונער יוכל לכותבם ואמרו רבותינו עשרה נשאר מהם שאין לך קטן שאינו כותב יו"ד קטנה [שם י, יט]. ונשאר בו. בהמון סנחריב אנשי' מעט כנוקף זית. בראש אמיר. בראש הענף. בסעיפיה. בענפיה וכן וכלה סעיפיה (ישעיה כז) וכן מסעף פארה (שם י) [שם יז, ו]. ורוה די רביעאה. ותוארו של רביעי. דמה לבר אלהין. דומה למלאך שראיתי בהיותי עם סנחריב כשנשרפו אוכלוסיו שנאמר (שם לז) ויכה במחנה אשור ונבוכדנצר היה שם ונמלט בתוך עשרה שנמלטו מהם [דניאל ג, כה]. בית נסרוך אלהיו. נסר מתיבתו של נח. הכהו בחרב. שמעו אותו שאמר לשוחטן לפניו אם ינצלוהו שלא יהרגוהו שרי המלכות שמתו בניהם על ידו [מ"ב יט, לז]. יגלח ה' בתער השכירה. הגדולה וכן גם שכיריה בקרבה (ירמיה מו) ת"י רברבהא יגלח. בעברי נהר. ביושבי עבר הנהר וכמי מן היושבים במלך אשור את הראש יגלח ואת שער הרגלים לפי שהוא דבוק נשתנה לינקד פתח. תספה. תכלה [ישעיה ז, כ]. [ע"כ שייך לדף צה:]

בית נסרוך אלהיו. נסר מתיבתו של נח. הכוהו בחרב. שמעו אותו שאמר לשוחטן לפניו אם ינצלוהו שלא יהרגוהו שרי המלכות שמתו בניהם על ידו [מ"ב יט, לז]. ויחלק עליהם. לפי פשוטו סרס המקרא ויחלק הוא ועבדיו עליהם לילה כדרך הרודפים שמתפלגים אחר הנרדפים כשבורחים זה לכאן וזה לכאן. לילה. כלומר אחר שחשכה לא נמנעו מלרדפם [בראשית יד, טו ועי' במהרש"א ח"א]. והלילה אמר. ורז"ל אמרו (נדה טז:) מלאך הממונ' על ההריון לילה שמו [איוב ג, ג ועי' מהרש"א בח"א]. תשש כחו. שראה שעתידין בניו להעמיד שם עגל [בראשית שם, יד]. מדן נשמע. על דפלחו לעגלא דבדן. נחרת סוסיו. עטישות נחיריו [ירמיה ח, טז]. מחמת אונסו. שחלה או שנטרד בדוחק מזונות הזהרו בו לכבדו [ברכות ח:]. בוורידין. סוטי הצואר שמקלחין את הדם ובגמרא (חולין כח:) מפרש דלעוף קאי ומשום להוציא את הדם [חולין כז.]. שישחוט את הורידין כדי שיצא כל הדם ולא אמר כן אלא בעוף הואיל וצולהו כולו כאחד [ברכות שם]. צדיק אתה ה' כי אריב אליך. כשאתווכח עמך ידעתי כי תצדק בדבריך אך חפץ אני לדבר משפטים אותך להודיעני דרכך. מדוע דרך רשעים צלחה.

גליון הש"ס

גמ' קריינא דאגרתא. בתנחומא פ' תשא איתא דמרודך בלאדן בעצמו נתחרט ורהט בתריה ג' פסיעות:

תורה אור השלם

א) בַּיּוֹם הַהוּא יְגַלַּח אֲדֹנָי בְּתַעַר הַשְּׂכִירָה בְּעֶבְרֵי נָהָר בְּמֶלֶךְ אַשּׁוּר אֶת הָרֹאשׁ וְשַׂעַר הָרַגְלָיִם וְגַם אֶת הַזָּקָן תִּסְפֶּה: [ישעיה ז, כ]

ב) וַיְהִי הוּא מִשְׁתַּחֲוֶה בֵּית נִסְרֹךְ אֱלֹהָיו וְאַדְרַמֶּלֶךְ וְשַׂרְאֶצֶר בָּנָיו הִכֻּהוּ בַחֶרֶב וְהֵמָּה נִמְלְטוּ אֶרֶץ אֲרָרָט וַיִּמְלֹךְ אֵסַר חַדֹּן בְּנוֹ תַּחְתָּיו: [מלכים ב' יט, לז]

ג) וַיֵּחָלֵק עֲלֵיהֶם לַיְלָה הוּא וַעֲבָדָיו וַיַּכֵּם וַיִּרְדְּפֵם עַד חוֹבָה אֲשֶׁר מִשְּׂמֹאל לְדַמָּשֶׂק: [בראשית יד, טו]

ד) יֹאבַד יוֹם אִוָּלֶד בּוֹ וְהַלַּיְלָה אָמַר הֹרָה גָבֶר: [איוב ג, ג]

ה) מִן שָׁמַיִם נִלְחָמוּ הַכּוֹכָבִים מִמְּסִלּוֹתָם נִלְחֲמוּ עִם סִיסְרָא: [שופטים ה, כ]

ו) וַיִּשְׁמַע אַבְרָם כִּי נִשְׁבָּה אָחִיו וַיָּרֶק אֶת חֲנִיכָיו יְלִידֵי בֵיתוֹ שְׁמֹנָה עָשָׂר וּשְׁלֹשׁ מֵאוֹת וַיִּרְדֹּף עַד דָּן: [בראשית יד, יד]

ז) וַיָּשֶׂם אֶת הָאֶחָד בְּבֵית אֵל וְאֶת הָאֶחָד נָתַן בְּדָן: [מלכים א' יב, כט]

ח) מִדָּן נִשְׁמַע נַחְרַת סוּסָיו מִקּוֹל מִצְהֲלוֹת אַבִּירָיו רָעֲשָׁה כָּל הָאָרֶץ וַיָּבוֹאוּ וַיֹּאכְלוּ אֶרֶץ וּמְלוֹאָהּ עִיר וְיֹשְׁבֵי בָהּ: [ירמיה ח, טז]

ט) צַדִּיק אַתָּה יְיָ כִּי אָרִיב אֵלֶיךָ אַךְ מִשְׁפָּטִים אֲדַבֵּר אוֹתָךְ מַדּוּעַ דֶּרֶךְ רְשָׁעִים צָלֵחָה שָׁלוּ כָּל בֹּגְדֵי בָגֶד: נְטַעְתָּם גַּם שֹׁרָשׁוּ יֵלְכוּ גַּם עָשׂוּ פֶרִי קָרוֹב אַתָּה בְּפִיהֶם וְרָחוֹק מִכִּלְיוֹתֵיהֶם: [ירמיה יב, א-ב]

י) כִּי אֶת רַגְלִים רַצְתָּה וַיַּלְאוּךָ וְאֵיךְ תְּתַחֲרֶה אֶת הַסּוּסִים וּבְאֶרֶץ שָׁלוֹם אַתָּה בוֹטֵחַ וְאֵיךְ תַּעֲשֶׂה בִּגְאוֹן הַיַּרְדֵּן: [ירמיה יב, ה]

כ) לַנְּבִאִים נִשְׁבַּר לִבִּי בְקִרְבִּי רָחֲפוּ כָּל עַצְמוֹתַי הָיִיתִי כְּאִישׁ שִׁכּוֹר וּכְגֶבֶר עֲבָרוֹ יָיִן מִפְּנֵי יְיָ וּמִפְּנֵי דִּבְרֵי קָדְשׁוֹ: [ירמיה כג, ט]

ל) בָּעֵת הַהִוא שָׁלַח מְרֹדַךְ בַּלְאֲדָן בֶּן בַּלְאֲדָן מֶלֶךְ בָּבֶל סְפָרִים וּמִנְחָה אֶל חִזְקִיָּהוּ וַיִּשְׁמַע כִּי חָלָה וַיֶּחֱזָק: [ישעיה לט, א]

מ) וְכֵן בִּמְלִיצֵי שָׂרֵי בָבֶל הַמְשַׁלְּחִים עָלָיו לִדְרֹשׁ הַמּוֹפֵת אֲשֶׁר הָיָה בָאָרֶץ עֲזָבוֹ הָאֱלֹהִים לְנַסּוֹתוֹ לָדַעַת כָּל בִּלְבָבוֹ: [דברי הימים ב' לב, לא]

נ) הִנְנִי מֵשִׁיב אֶת צֵל הַמַּעֲלוֹת אֲשֶׁר יָרְדָה בְמַעֲלוֹת אָחָז בַּשֶּׁמֶשׁ אֲחֹרַנִּית עֶשֶׂר מַעֲלוֹת וַתָּשָׁב הַשֶּׁמֶשׁ עֶשֶׂר מַעֲלוֹת בַּמַּעֲלוֹת אֲשֶׁר יָרָדָה: [ישעיה לח, ח]

ס) בֵּן יְכַבֵּד אָב וְעֶבֶד אֲדֹנָיו וְאִם אָב אָנִי אַיֵּה כְבוֹדִי וְאִם אֲדוֹנִים אָנִי אַיֵּה מוֹרָאִי אָמַר יְיָ צְבָאוֹת לָכֶם הַכֹּהֲנִים בּוֹזֵי שְׁמִי וַאֲמַרְתֶּם בַּמֶּה בָזִינוּ אֶת שְׁמֶךָ: [מלאכי א, ו]

ע) וּבַחֹדֶשׁ הַחֲמִישִׁי בֶּעָשׂוֹר לַחֹדֶשׁ הִיא שְׁנַת תְּשַׁע עֶשְׂרֵה שָׁנָה לַמֶּלֶךְ נְבוּכַדְרֶאצַּר מֶלֶךְ בָּבֶל בָּא נְבוּזַרְאֲדָן רַב טַבָּחִים עָמַד לִפְנֵי מֶלֶךְ בָּבֶל בִּירוּשָׁלָם: וַיִּשְׂרֹף אֶת בֵּית יְהוָה וְאֶת בֵּית הַמֶּלֶךְ וְאֵת כָּל בָּתֵּי יְרוּשָׁלַם וְאֶת כָּל בֵּית הַגָּדוֹל שָׂרַף בָּאֵשׁ: [ירמיה נב, יב-יג]

taries]: הֵיכִי כְּתַבִיתוּ – **"How did you write** the letter?" אָמְרוּ לֵיהּ הָכִי כְּתַבִינַן – **They told him what they had written.**[32] קָרֵיתוּ לֵיהּ אֱלָהָא אָמַר לְהוּ – **[Nebuchadnezzar] said to them:** רַבָּא וְכָתְבִיתוּ לֵיהּ לְבַסּוֹף – **"You call Him 'the great God,' and yet you mention Him last?!"** אָמַר – **He** then **said:** אֶלָּא הָכִי כְּתוּבוּ – **"Rather, write** the letter **as follows:** שְׁלָם לֶאֱלָהָא רַבָּא – **Greetings to the great God!** שְׁלָם לְקַרְתָּא דִירוּשְׁלֵם – **Greetings to the city of Jerusalem!** שְׁלָם לְמַלְכָּא חִזְקִיָּה – **Greetings to King Chizkiah!"**[33] אָמְרֵי לֵיהּ – **They said to [Nebuchadnezzar]:** קַרְיָינָא דְאִיגַּרְתָּא אִיהוּ לֶיהֱוֵי פַּרְוַונְקָא – **"Let the reader of the letter**[34] **be the agent** to carry out its instructions!"[35] רָהַט בַּתְרֵיהּ – **[Nebuchadnezzar] ran after [the messenger]** who had been sent to deliver the letter. כִּדְרָהִיט אַרְבַּע פְּסִיעוֹת – After **[Nebuchadnezzar] had run four**[36] **paces,** אָתָא גַּבְרִיאֵל וְאוֹקְמֵיהּ – the angel **Gabriel came and stopped him.**[37] אָמַר רַבִּי יוֹחָנָן – **R' Yochanan commented:** אִילְמָלֵא (לא) בָּא גַּבְרִיאֵל וְהֶעֱמִידוֹ – **Had Gabriel not come and stopped him,** לֹא הָיָה תַקָּנָה לְשׂוֹנְאֵיהֶם שֶׁל יִשְׂרָאֵל – **there would have been no remedy for the enemies of the Jews.**[38]

In the preceding account, Scripture refers to the king of Babylonia as "Merodach Baladan the son of Baladan." The Gemara asks why one of his names was the same as that of his father:

מַאי "בַּלְאֲדָן בֶּן בַּלְאֲדָן" – **What is** the meaning of ***Baladan the son of Baladan?*** אָמְרֵי – **They said:** בַּלְאֲדָן מַלְכָּא הֲוָה – **Baladan,** the father, **was king,** וְאִישְׁתַּנֵּי אַפֵּיהּ וַהֲוָה כִּי דְּכַלְבָּא – **but his face changed and became like that of a dog.**[39] As a result of this deformity, Baladan was compelled to vacate the throne. הֲוָה יָתִיב בְּרֵיהּ עַל מַלְכוּתָא – **His son,** Merodach, **sat upon the throne** in his stead. כִּי הֲוָה כָּתֵיב – **When [the son] would write,** הֲוָה כָּתֵיב שְׁמֵיהּ וּשְׁמֵיהּ דַּאֲבוּהּ בַּלְאֲדָן מַלְכָּא – **he would write his name and the name of his father, King Baladan,** as a sign of respect.[40] הַיְינוּ דִּכְתִיב "בֵּן יְכַבֵּד אָב וְעֶבֶד אֲדֹנָיו" – **This is** what is meant by **the verse:**[41] ***A son honors his father, and a servant his master.*** "בֵּן יְכַבֵּד אָב" הָא דַּאֲמָרַן – ***A son honors his father*** is exemplified by **that which we said above,** viz. that Merodach adopted his father's name. "וְעֶבֶד אֲדֹנָיו" דִּכְתִיב – ***And a servant his master*** is exemplified by **that which is written** concerning Nebuzaradan:[42] "וּבַחֹדֶשׁ הַחֲמִישִׁי בֶּעָשׂוֹר לַחֹדֶשׁ הִיא שְׁנַת תְּשַׁע־עֶשְׂרֵה שָׁנָה לַמֶּלֶךְ נְבוּכַדְרֶאצַּר מֶלֶךְ־בָּבֶל בָּא נְבוּזַרְאֲדָן רַב־טַבָּחִים עָמַד לִפְנֵי מֶלֶךְ־בָּבֶל בִּירוּשָׁלָם וַיִּשְׂרֹף אֶת־בֵּית־ה׳ וְאֶת־בֵּית הַמֶּלֶךְ" – ***And in the fifth month, in the tenth day of the month – which was the nineteenth year of King Nebuchadnezzar king of Babylonia – Nebuzaradan, captain of the executioners, came; he stood before the king of Babylonia in Jerusalem, and he burned the House of Hashem and the house of the king.***

NOTES

32. Literally: they said to him, "This we wrote."

33. Since you recognize God as superior to all other deities, you should mention Him first (see *Maharsha*).

34. *Yad Ramah;* cf. *Maharsha.*

35. A popular adage which means: Let the person who gave the advice carry it out. If you, Nebuchadnezzar, feel that the letter should have been written differently, overtake the messenger bearing the letter and rewrite it yourself!

36. While the Gemara states that he took four steps, the *Midrash* (*Yalkut Shir HaShirim, Esther Rabbah*) and *Zohar* speak of three steps. This is given as the reason why we take three steps backward after *Shemoneh Esrei*, and beseech God to rebuild the Temple destroyed by Nebuchadnezzar (*Maharsha*).

37. Gabriel took the messenger, who was already far away, and put him in front of Nebuchadnezzar so that Nebuchadnezzar would not have to run any further (*Yad Ramah*).

Ben Yehoyada maintains that Gabriel caused Nebuchadnezzar to stop running so that he was unable to reach the messenger. Nebuchadnezzar had to dispatch someone else to retrieve the letter.

38. [A euphemism for the Jews themselves.] That is to say, had Nebuchadnezzar run more than four steps, his merit would have been so great that it would have enabled him to exterminate the Jewish people (*Rashi*).

39. See *Margaliyos HaYam.*

40. Wishing to show respect to his father, Merodach appended the name Baladan to his own. It would not have sufficed to write "Merodach the son of Baladan," because everyone is called after his father in this way (*Rashi*).

Merodach wanted to demonstrate that although others might regard his father as grotesque, he was not ashamed to identify himself as Baladan's son, as though Baladan were still on the throne (*Maharsha*).

41. *Malachi* 1:6.

42. *Jeremiah* 52:12-13.

ושני נפשך במאי אישני אמר ליה זיל אייתי לי מספרא ואיגזייך אנא מהיכא אייתי א"ל עול לההוא ביתא ואייתי אזל אשכחינהו אתו מלאכי שרת ואידמו ליה כגברי והוו קא טחני קשייתא א"ל הבו לי מספרא א"ל טחון חד גריוא דקשייתא וניתן לך טחן חד גריוא דקשייתא ויהבו ליה מספרתא עד דאתא איחשך א"ל זיל אייתי נורא אזל ואייתי נורא בהדי דקא נפח ליה אתלי ביה נורא בדיקניה אזל גזייה לרישיה ודיקניה אמרו היינו דכתיב (א) וגם את הזקן תספה אמר רב פפא היינו דאמרי אינשי גרירתיה לארמאה שפיר ליה איתלי ליה נורא בדיקניה ולא שבעת חוכא מיניה אזל אשכח דפא מתיבותא דנח אמר היינו אלהא רבא דשיזביה לנח מטופנא אמר אי אזיל ההוא גברא ומצלח מקרב להו לתרין בנוהי קמך שמעו בנוהי וקטלוהו היינו דכתיב (ב) ויהי הוא משתחוה בית נסרוך אלהיו ואדרמלך ושראצר בניו הכהו בחרב וגו' (ג) ויחלק עליהם לילה הוא ועבדיו ויכם וגו' אמר רבי יוחנן אותו מלאך שנזדמן לו לאברהם לילה שמו שנאמר (ד) והלילה אמר הורה גבר ור' יצחק נפחא אמר שעשה עמו מעשה לילה שנאמר (ה) מן שמים נלחמו הכוכבים ממסלותם נלחמו עם סיסרא אמר ריש לקיש טבא דנפחא מדבר נפחא (ו) וירדף עד דן אמר רבי יוחנן כיון שבא אותו צדיק עד דן תשש כחו ראה בני בניו שעתידין לעבוד ע"ז בדן שנאמר (ז) וישם את האחד בבית אל ואת האחד נתן בדן ואף אותו רשע לא נתגבר עד שהגיע לדן שנאמר (ח) מדן נשמע נחרת סוסיו אמר רבי זירא אע"ג דשלח ר' [א] (יהודה בן בתירא מנציבין) [ב] הזהרו בזקן ששכח תלמודו מחמת אונסו והזהרו בוורידין כר' יהודה והזהרו בבני עמי הארץ שמהן תצא תורה כי הא מילתא מודעינן להו (ט) צדיק אתה ה' כי אריב אליך אך משפטים אדבר אותך מדוע דרך רשעים צלחה שלו כל בוגדי בגד נטעתם גם שורשו ילכו גם עשו פרי מאי אהדרו ליה (י) כי את רגלים רצתה וילאוך ואיך תתחרה את הסוסים ובארץ שלום אתה בוטח ואיך תעשה בגאון הירדן משל לאדם אחד שאמר יכול אני לרוץ ג' פרסאות לפני הסוסים בין בצעי המים נזדמן לו רגלי אחד רץ לפניו ג' מילין ביבשה ונלאה א"ל ומה לפני רגלי כך לפני הסוסים עאכ"ו ומה שלשת מילין כך ג' פרסאות על אחת כמה וכמה ומה ביבשה כך בין בצעי המים על אחת כמה וכמה אף אתה ומה בשכר ארבע פסיעות ששלמתי לאותו רשע שרץ אחר כבודי אתה תמיה כשאני משלם שכר לאברהם יצחק ויעקב שרצו לפני כסוסים עאכ"ו היינו דכתיב (כ) לנביאים נשבר לבי בקרבי רחפו כל עצמותי הייתי כאיש שכור וכגבר עברו יין מפני ה' ומפני דברי קדשו הני ד' פסיעות מאי היא דכתיב (ל) בעת ההיא שלח מרודך בלאדן בן בלאדן מלך בבל ספרים וגו' משום כי חלה חזקיהו ויחזק שדר ליה ספרים ומנחה (אין) (מ) לדרוש (את) המופת אשר היה בארץ דאמר רבי יוחנן אותו היום שמת בו אחז שתי שעות היה וכי חלה חזקיהו ואיתפח אהדרינהו קודשא בריך הוא להנך עשר שעי ניהליה דכתיב (נ) הנני משיב את צל המעלות אשר ירדה במעלות אחז בשמש אחורנית עשר מעלות ותשב השמש עשר מעלות במעלות אשר ירדה א"ל מאי האי א"ל חזקיהו חלש ואיתפח אמר איכא גברא כי האי ולא בעינא לשדורי ליה שלמא כתבו ליה שלמא למלכא חזקיה שלם לקרתא דירושלם שלם לאלהא רבא נבוכד נאצר ספריה דבלאדן הוה ההיא שעתא לא הוה התם כי אתא אמר להו היכי כתביתו אמרו ליה הכי כתבינן אמר להו קריתו ליה אלהא רבא וכתביתו ליה לבסוף אמר אלא הכי כתובו שלם לאלהא רבא שלם לקרתא דירושלם שלם למלכא חזקיה אמרי ליה [ג] [ד] קריינא דאיגרתא איהו ליהוי פרוונקא רהט בתריה כדרהיט [ה] ארבע פסיעות אתא גבריאל ואוקמיה אמר ר' יוחנן אילמלא ([ו] לא) בא גבריאל והעמידו לא היה תקנה לשונאיהם של ישראל מאי בלאדן בן בלאדן אמרי בלאדן מלכא הוה ואישתני אפיה והוה כי דכלבא הוה יתיב בריה על מלכותא כי הוה כתיב שמיה ושמיה דאבוה בלאדן מלכא היינו דכתיב (ס) בן יכבד אב ועבד אדניו בן יכבד אב הא דאמרן ועבד אדוניו דכתי' (ע) ובחודש החמישי בעשור לחדש היא שנת תשע עשרה [שנה] למלך נבוכדנאצר מלך בבל בא נבוזראדן רב טבחים עמד לפני מלך בבל בירושלם וישרף את בית ה' ואת בית המלך

ומי

אשני נפשך. שנה עצמך כדי שלא יכירוך: **ואגזייך אנא.** אני אגלחך: **קשייתא.** גרעיני תמרים: **טחון.** אלו גרעינין וניתן לך מספרים והיינו דכתיב בתער השכירה על שם שטרח נתנו לו תער לגלח ואיזהו שכר נתנו לו בעברי נהר דברים שדרכן לעשות על ידי נהר דהיינו טחינת ריחים: **וגם הזקן תספה.** דלא כתיב גלות אלא אראש אבל אזקן כתיב תספה לשון כלוי על ידי אור שכלתה לגמרי: **גרירתיה לארמאה ושפר באפיה.** אם אתה מחרך את הארמאי והוטב בעיניו הבער לו את זקנו ולא שבעת חוכא מיניה: **בית נסרך אלהיו.** לשון נסר שהשתחוה לנסר ועשאו אלוה: **היינו דכתיב ויהי הוא משתחוה.** משמע מפני שמשתחוה לשם הכוהו: **ויחלק עליהם.** איידי דאיירי במלאכים איירי נמי בהאי קרא דכתיב ויהי בלילה ההוא ויצא מלאך ה' וגו' נקט ויחלק עליהם לילה וגו': **מלאך שנזדמן לאברהם לילה שמו.** והוא סייעו: **מעשה לילה.** שנלחמו בשבילו כוכבי לילה כמו שעשו בשביל ברק: **טבא מליה דר' יצחק נפחא מדבר נפחא.** ר' יוחנן דמקרי בר נפחא בכולא הש"ס כמו (ב"מ דף פה:) מאן עייל בר נפחא נראה למורי דאביו של ר' יוחנן הוי נפחא ולהכי מיקרי בר נפחא ואית דמפרשי בר נפחא על שם יופיו: **הזהרו בזקן.** אע"פ ששכח תלמודו הואיל ומחמת אונסו הוא: **הזהרו בורידין כר' יהודה.** דאמר בשחיטת חולין (דף כח.) עד שישחוט את הורידין של עוף הואיל וצולהו כולו כאחד אינו חותכו ומולחו כבשר חיה ובהמה: **הזהרו בבני עמי הארץ.** שנעשו תלמידי חכמים לעשות להם כבוד שמהם תצא תורה לישראל שהרי יצאו שמעיה ואבטליון מבני בניו של סנחריב ומבני בניו של המן למדו תורה בבני ברק כדלקמן ואע"ג דאמר רבי יהודה הכי הזהרו בבני עמי הארץ:

כי הא מילתא. דלקמן מודעינן להו כי היכי דחזינן לקמן דלא זכה נבוכדנצר לאותו כבוד אלא מפני זכות ד' פסיעות כדאמרינן לקמן ה"נ אמרי' לבני עמי הארץ דלא זכו לאותו כבוד אלא מחמת זכות מעט שהיה באביהם מ"ר. ואית דאמרי דרבי זירא אדלעיל קאי אבני סנחריב אע"ג דשלח רבי יהודה הזהרו בבני ע"ה לכבדן שמהם תצא תורה כי היכי דנפקו מסנחריב כי הא מילתא מודיעים להו לבני ע"ה דהא דמוקרין להו לאו משום אביהם אלא משום תורה שבהם שלא תזוח דעתם עליהם ויאמרו אבותיהם לדיקים היו: **מדוע דרך רשעים צלחה.** מפני מה הצליח נבוכדנצר וכבש ירושלים: **אהדרו ליה.** לירמיה: **בצעי מים.** מרש"קו בלעז: **ד' פסיעות.** מפורש לקמן: **על אחת כמה וכמה.** שיהו כל אדם יכולין לתמוה על מתן שכר גדול שישתלם עליהם: **לנביאים.** אברהם יצחק ויעקב: **נשבר לבי בקרבי.** כלומר תמהתי על מתן שכרן: **שתי שעות.** כדי שלא יהא פנאי לספדו ולקברו: **אתפח.** נתרפא: **אהדרינהו הקב"ה.** להנך שעות לחזקיהו דאותו היום שנתרפא חזקיה היה של כ"ב שעות: **רהט בתריה.** דשליח: **לא היה להם תקנה.** שהיה שכרו מרובה והיה לו רשות לאבד שאריתנו: **הוה כתיב שמיה ושמיה דאבוה.** כדי שיתכבד אביו לכך נקרא שם אביו עליו שנקרא מרודך בלאדן דאי לא כתיב אלא מרודך בן בלאדן לא הוי מיתקרי עליה שמיה דאבוה דהכי כתבי כולהו אינשי פלוני בן פלוני להכי כתיב מרודך בלאדן: **בחדש החמישי בעשור לחדש בא נבוזר אדן רב טבחים עמד לפני מלך בבל בירושלם.** אלמא נבוכד נצר סליק לירושלם:

א) ג' ב"ש ריב"ל, ב) ברכות ח., ג) לעיל דף פב. ב"מ פג:, ד) [במדר' ובילק' איתא שלש וכ"א ברש"י ירמיה יב פ"ה], ה) [ע' תוס' מגילה כח.].

ליקוטי רש"י

ושאר עץ יערו. הנותרים בחיילותיו. **מספר יהיו.** נוחים לספור כי מעט הם ונער יוכל לכותבם ואמרו רבותינו עשרה נשאר מהם שאין לך קטן שאינו כותב יו"ד קטנה [שם י, יט]. **ונשאר בו.** בהמון סנחריב אנשי מעט כנוקף בראש הענף. **בסעיפיה.** בענפיה וכן וכלה סעיפיה (ישעיה כז) וכן מסעף פארה [שם י] [שם יז, ו]. **ורוה די רביעאה.** ומראו של רביעי. **דמה לבר אלהין.** דומה למלאך שראיתי בהיותי עם סנחריב כשנשרפו אוכלוסיו שנאמר (שם לז) ויכה במחנה אשור ונבוכדנצר היה שם ונמלט בתוך עשרה שנמלטו מהם [דניאל ג, כה]. **בית נסרך אלהיו.** נסר מתיבתו של נח. **הכהו בחרב.** שמעו אותו שאמר לשוחטן לפניו אם יצליחו שלא יהרגוהו שרי המלכות שמתו בניהם על ידו [מ"ב יט, לז]. **יגלח ה' בתער השכירה.** הגדולה וכן גם שמיה בקרבה (ירמיה מו) ת"י רברבהא יגלח. **בעברי נהר.** ביושבי עבר הנהר ובמי מן היושבים במלך אשור את הראש יגלח ואת שער הרגלים לפי שהוא דבוק נשתנה לינקד פתח. **תספה.** תכלה [ישעיה ז, כ]. [ע"כ שייך לדף צה:] **בית נסרוך אלהיו.** נסר מתיבתו של נח. **הכוהו בחרב.** שמעו אותו שאמר לשוחטן לפניו אם ינלחו שלא יהרגוהו שרי המלכות שמתו בניהם על ידו [מ"ב יט, לז]. **ויחלק עליהם.** לפי פשוטו סרס המקרא ויחלק הוא ועבדיו עליהם לילה כדרך הרודפים שמתפלגים אחר הנרדפים כשבורחים זה לכאן וזה לכאן. **לילה.** כלומר אחר שחשכה לא נמנעו מלרדפם [בראשית יד, טו ועי' במהרש"א ח"א]. **והלילה אמר.** ורז"ל אמרו (נדה טז:) מלאך הממונ' על ההריון לילה שמו [איוב ג, ג ועי' מהרש"א בח"א]. **תשש כחו.** שראה שעתידין בניו להעמיד שם עגל [בראשית שם, יד]. **מדן נשמע.** על דפלחו לעגלא דבדן. **נחרת סוסיו.** עטישות נחיריו [ירמיה ח, טז]. **מחמת אונסו.** שלא זו שנטרד בדוחק מזונות הזהרו בו לכבדו [ברכות ח:]. **בוורידין.** מוטי הצואר שמקלחין את הדם ובגמרא (חולין כח:) מפרש דלאו קאי ומשום להוציא את הדם [חולין כז.]. שישחוט את הורידין כדי שיצא כל הדם ולא אמר כן אלא בעוף הואיל וצולהו כולו כאחד [ברכות שם]. **צדיק אתה ה' כי אריב אליך.** כשאתווכח עמך ידעתי כי תצדק בדבריך אך חפץ אני לדבר משפטים אותך להודיעני דרכך. **מדוע דרך רשעים צלחה.** שנתת גדולה לנבוכדנצר הרשע ותלליתהו להחריב ביתך. **שלו.** לשון שלוה [ירמיה יב, א]. **ואיך תתחרה את הסוסים.** לרוץ את הסוסים וכו' ומדרש רבותינו אם על שכר שלש פסיעות שרץ נבוכדנצר לכבודי בימי מרודך בלאדן אתה תמה שהרביתי גדולתו כל כך מה תתמה עוד כשתראה שלום שכר שאשלם לצדיקים שרצו לפני כסוסים. **תתחרה.** אאטיר"ש בלע"ז. **ובארץ שלום אשר אתה בוטח.** [שם, ה]. **הנני משיב.** אחורנית עשר מעלות את הצל אשר ירדה. **צל המעלות.** כמין מדרגות עשויות כנגד החמה לבחון בהם שעות היום כעין אורלוגין שעושין האומנין. **אשר ירדה.** מיהרה לירד ונתקצר היום י' שעות ביום שמת אחז כדי שלא יהו מספידין אותו ועלו עכשיו לאחוריהם ביום שנתרפא חזקיהו ונתוספו על היום י' שעות [ישעיה לח, ח]. **א"ל מאי האי.** היה למוד לאכול בשלש שעות וישן עד ט' כיון שחזר גלגל חמה לחזקיהו כשעמד משנתו בט' שעות מצא שהוא שחרית בקש להרוג את כל עבדיו אמר הנחתם אותי ישן יומם ולילה עד הבקר אמרו לו גלגל חמה הוא שחזר אמר להם ומי החזירו אמרו לו אלוהו של חזקיהו כו' כדאיתא בתנחומא ובפסיקתא [שם לט, א]. **קריינא דאיגרתא.** משל הוא. **פרוונקא.** שליח [ב"מ פג:]. שליח מוליך ומביא [לעיל לח:].

גמ' **קריינא דאגרתא.** בתנחומא פ' תשא איתא דמרודך בלאדן בעצמו נתחרט ורהט בתריה ג' פסיעות:

תורה אור השלם

א) בַּיּוֹם הַהוּא יְגַלַּח אֲדֹנָי בְּתַעַר הַשְּׂכִירָה בְּעֶבְרֵי נָהָר בְּמֶלֶךְ אַשּׁוּר אֶת הָרֹאשׁ וְשַׂעַר הָרַגְלָיִם וְגַם אֶת הַזָּקָן תִּסְפֶּה: [ישעיה ז, כ]

ב) וַיְהִי הוּא מִשְׁתַּחֲוֶה בֵּית נִסְרֹךְ אֱלֹהָיו וְאַדְרַמֶּלֶךְ וְשַׂרְאֶצֶר בָּנָיו הִכֻּהוּ בַחֶרֶב וְהֵמָּה נִמְלְטוּ אֶרֶץ אֲרָרָט וַיִּמְלֹךְ אֵסַר חַדֹּן בְּנוֹ תַּחְתָּיו: [מלכים ב' יט, לז]

ג) וַיֵּחָלֵק עֲלֵיהֶם לַיְלָה הוּא וַעֲבָדָיו וַיַּכֵּם וַיִּרְדְּפֵם עַד חוֹבָה אֲשֶׁר מִשְּׂמֹאל לְדַמָּשֶׂק: [בראשית יד, טו]

ד) יֹאבַד יוֹם אִוָּלֶד בּוֹ וְהַלַּיְלָה אָמַר הֹרָה גָבֶר: [איוב ג, ג]

ה) מִן שָׁמַיִם נִלְחָמוּ הַכּוֹכָבִים מִמְּסִלּוֹתָם נִלְחֲמוּ עִם סִיסְרָא: [שופטים ה, כ]

ו) וַיִּשְׁמַע אַבְרָם כִּי נִשְׁבָּה אָחִיו וַיָּרֶק אֶת חֲנִיכָיו יְלִידֵי בֵיתוֹ שְׁמֹנָה עָשָׂר וּשְׁלֹשׁ מֵאוֹת וַיִּרְדֹּף עַד דָּן: [בראשית יד, יד]

ז) וַיָּשֶׂם אֶת הָאֶחָד בְּבֵית אֵל וְאֶת הָאֶחָד נָתַן בְּדָן: [מלכים א' יב, כט]

ח) מִדָּן נִשְׁמַע נַחְרַת סוּסָיו מִקּוֹל מִצְהֲלוֹת אַבִּירָיו רָעֲשָׁה כָּל הָאָרֶץ וַיָּבוֹאוּ וַיֹּאכְלוּ אֶרֶץ וּמְלוֹאָהּ עִיר וְיֹשְׁבֵי בָהּ: [ירמיה ח, טז]

ט) צַדִּיק אַתָּה יְיָ כִּי אָרִיב אֵלֶיךָ אַךְ מִשְׁפָּטִים אֲדַבֵּר אוֹתָךְ מַדּוּעַ דֶּרֶךְ רְשָׁעִים צָלֵחָה שָׁלוּ כָּל בֹּגְדֵי בָגֶד: נְטַעְתָּם גַּם שֹׁרָשׁוּ יֵלְכוּ גַּם עָשׂוּ פֶרִי קָרוֹב אַתָּה בְּפִיהֶם וְרָחוֹק מִכִּלְיוֹתֵיהֶם: [ירמיה יב, א-ב]

י) כִּי אֶת רַגְלִים רַצְתָּה וַיַּלְאוּךָ וְאֵיךְ תְּתַחֲרֶה אֶת הַסּוּסִים וּבְאֶרֶץ שָׁלוֹם אַתָּה בוֹטֵחַ וְאֵיךְ תַּעֲשֶׂה בִּגְאוֹן הַיַּרְדֵּן: [ירמיה יב, ה]

כ) לַנְּבִאִים נִשְׁבַּר לִבִּי בְקִרְבִּי רָחֲפוּ כָּל עַצְמוֹתַי הָיִיתִי כְּאִישׁ שִׁכּוֹר וּכְגֶבֶר עֲבָרוֹ יָיִן מִפְּנֵי יְיָ וּמִפְּנֵי דִּבְרֵי קָדְשׁוֹ: [ירמיה כג, ט]

ל) בָּעֵת הַהִוא שָׁלַח מְרֹדַךְ בַּלְאֲדָן בֶּן בַּלְאֲדָן מֶלֶךְ בָּבֶל סְפָרִים וּמִנְחָה אֶל חִזְקִיָּהוּ וַיִּשְׁמַע כִּי חָלָה וַיֶּחֱזָק: [ישעיה לט, א]

מ) וְכֵן בִּמְלִיצֵי שָׂרֵי בָבֶל הַמְשַׁלְּחִים עָלָיו לִדְרֹשׁ הַמּוֹפֵת אֲשֶׁר הָיָה בָאָרֶץ עֲזָבוֹ הָאֱלֹהִים לְנַסּוֹתוֹ לָדַעַת כָּל בִּלְבָבוֹ: [דברי הימים ב' לב, לא]

נ) הִנְנִי מֵשִׁיב אֶת צֵל הַמַּעֲלוֹת אֲשֶׁר יָרְדָה בְמַעֲלוֹת אָחָז בַּשֶּׁמֶשׁ אֲחֹרַנִּית עֶשֶׂר מַעֲלוֹת וַתָּשָׁב הַשֶּׁמֶשׁ עֶשֶׂר מַעֲלוֹת בַּמַּעֲלוֹת אֲשֶׁר יָרָדָה: [ישעיה לח, ח]

ס) בֵּן יְכַבֵּד אָב וְעֶבֶד אֲדֹנָיו וְאִם אָב אָנִי אַיֵּה כְבוֹדִי וְאִם אֲדוֹנִים אָנִי אַיֵּה מוֹרָאִי אָמַר יְיָ צְבָאוֹת לָכֶם הַכֹּהֲנִים בּוֹזֵי שְׁמִי וַאֲמַרְתֶּם בַּמֶּה בָזִינוּ אֶת שְׁמֶךָ: [מלאכי א, ו]

ע) וּבַחֹדֶשׁ הַחֲמִישִׁי בֶּעָשׂוֹר לַחֹדֶשׁ הִיא שְׁנַת תְּשַׁע עֶשְׂרֵה שָׁנָה לַמֶּלֶךְ נְבוּכַדְרֶאצַּר מֶלֶךְ בָּבֶל בָּא נְבוּזַרְאֲדָן רַב טַבָּחִים עָמַד לִפְנֵי מֶלֶךְ בָּבֶל בִּירוּשָׁלָ͏ִם: וַיִּשְׂרֹף אֶת בֵּית יְהוָה וְאֶת בֵּית הַמֶּלֶךְ וְאֵת כָּל בָּתֵּי יְרוּשָׁלַ͏ִם וְאֶת כָּל בֵּית הַגָּדוֹל שָׂרַף בָּאֵשׁ: [ירמיה נב, יב-יג]

ומי סליק נבוכד נצר לירושלים והכתיב א) ויעלו אותו אל מלך בבל רבלתה ואמר ר' אבהו זו אנטוכיא רב חסדא ורב יצחק בר אבודימי חד אמר דמות דיוקנו היתה חקוקה לו על מרכבתו וחד אמר אימה יתירה היתה לו ממנו ודומה כמי שעומד לפניו אמר רבא טעין א) תלת מאה כודנייתא נרגא דפרזלא דשליט בפרזלא שדר ליה נבוכד נצר לנבוזראדן כולהו בלעתינהו חד דשא דירושלם שנאמר ב) פתוחיה יחד בכשיל וכילפות יהלומון בעי למיהדר אמר מסתפינא דלא ליעבדו בי כי היכי דעבדו בסנחריב נפקא קלא ואמר שוור בר שוור נבוזר אדן שוור דמטא זימנא דמקדשא חריב והיכלא מיקלי פש ליה חד נרגא אתא מחייה בקופא ואיפתח שנאמר ג) יודע כמביא למעלה בסבך עץ קרדומות הוה קטיל ואזל עד דמטא להיכלא אדליק ביה נורא גבה היכלא דרכו ביה מן שמיא שנאמר ד) גת דרך ה' לבתולת בת יהודה קא זיחא דעתיה נפקא בת קלא ואמרה ליה עמא קטילא קטלת היכלא קליא קלית קימחא טחינא טחינת שנאמר ה) קחי רחים וטחני קמח גלי צמתך חשפי שובל גלי שוק עברי נהרות חטים לא נאמר אלא קמח ב) חזא דמיה דזכריה דהוה קא רתח אמר להו מאי האי אמרו ליה דם זבחים הוא דאישתפיך אמר להו אייתי ואנסי אי מדמו כסי ולא אידמו אמר להו גלו לי ואי לא סריקנא לבשרייכו במסריקא דפרזלא אמרו ליה האי כהן ונביא הוא דאינבי להו לישראל בחורבנא דירושלם וקטלוהו אמר להו אנא מפייסנא ליה אייתי רבנן קטיל עילויה ולא נח אייתי דרדקי דבי רב קטיל עילויה ולא נח אייתי פרחי כהונה קטיל עילויה ולא נח עד די קטל עילויה תשעין וארבעה ריבוא ולא נח קרב לגביה אמר זכריה זכריה טובים שבהן איבדתים ניחא לך דאיקטלינהו לכולהו מיד נח הרהר תשובה בדעתיה אמר מה הם שלא איבדו אלא נפש אחת כך ההוא גברא מה תיהוי עליה ערק שדר פורטיתא לביתיה ואיתגייר תנו רבנן ג) נעמן גר תושב היה נבוזר אדן גר צדק היה מבני בניו של סיסרא למדו תורה בירושלים מבני בניו של סנחריב לימדו תורה ברבים ומאן נינהו שמעיה ואבטליון מבני בניו של המן למדו תורה בבני ברק ואף מבני בניו של אותו רשע ביקש הקב"ה להכניסן תחת כנפי השכינה אמרו מלאכי השרת לפני הקב"ה רבונו של עולם מי שהחריב את ביתך ושרף את היכלך תכנים תחת כנפי השכינה היינו דכתיב ו) רפינו ד) את בבל ולא נרפתה עולא אמר זה נבוכד נצר רבי שמואל בר נחמני אמר אלו נהרות בבל ותרגמה דצינייתא ה) (צרידתא) דבבלאי אמר עולא ו) עמון ומואב שיבבי בישי דירושלם הוו כיון דשמעינהו לנביאי דקא מיתנבאי לחורבנא דירושלם שלחו לנבוכד נצר פוק ותא אמר מסתפינא דלא ליעבדו לי כדעבדו בקמאי שלחו ליה ז) כי אין האיש בביתו [א] הלך בדרך מרחוק ז) ואין איש אלא הקדוש ברוך הוא שנאמר ח) ה' איש מלחמה שלח להו בקריבא הוא ואתי שלחו ליה הלך בדרך מרחוק שלח להו אית להו צדיקי דבעו רחמי ומייתו ליה שלחו ליה ט) צרור הכסף לקח בידו ואין כסף אלא צדיקים שנאמר י) ואכרה לי בחמשה עשר כסף וחומר שעורים ולתך שעורים שלח להו הדרי רשיעי בתשובה ובעו רחמי ומייתו ליה שלחו ליה כבר קבע להן זמן שנאמר ט) ליום הכסא יבא (ל)ביתו אין כסא אלא זמן שנאמר כ) בכסה ליום חגנו שלח להו סיתווא הוא ולא מצינא דאתי מתלגא וממיטרא שלחו ליה תא אשינא דטורא שנאמר ל) שלחו כר מושל ארץ מסלע מדברה אל הר בת ציון שלח להו אי אתינא לית לי דוכתא דיתיבנא ביה שלחו ליה קברות שלהם מעולין מפלטירין שלך דכתיב מ) בעת ההיא נאום ה' יוציאו את עצמות מלכי יהודה ואת עצמות שריו ואת עצמות הכהנים ואת עצמות הנביאים ואת עצמות יושבי ירושלים מקבריהם ושטחום לשמש ולירח ולכל צבא השמים אשר אהבום ואשר עבדום ואשר הלכו אחריהם אמר ליה רב נחמן לרבי יצחק מי שמיע לך אימת אתי בר נפלי אמר ליה מאן בר נפלי א"ל משיח משיח בר נפלי קרית ליה א"ל אין דכתיב נ) ביום ההוא אקים את

רש"י

ומי סליק כו' והא כתיב. בההיא פרשתא ויעלו לדקיה אל המלך רבלתה אלמא ברבלה הוה: זו אנטוכיא. ואנטוכיא קיימא לן ז) דאינה מארץ ישראל: דמות דיוקנו. של נבוכד נצר: חקוקה לו על מרכבתו. של נבוזר אדן ודומה לו כמו שעומד לפניו ולכך כתיב בא נבוכד נצר והיינו כבוד: טעין תלת מאה כודניית'. משאוי שלש מאות פרדות: נרגא דפרזלא. פטישי ברזל: דשליט' בפרזלא. ברזל חדוד הקוצץ ברזל אחר: בלעתינהו. לא בליעה ממש אלא שיברם שהיו מתפוצצין הפטישים בהכותם בשער לשברה: פתוחיה יחד. משמע על פתח אחד הלמו כל הכשילים וכילפות יחד ולא הועיל כלום: שוור בר שוור. דולג בר דולג קום וכבש ירושלים לנבוזר אדן קאמר ל"א שוור בר שוור מדלג בר מדלג קפלת פעם אחת עם סנחריב ועכשיו פעם שניה: בקופא. מגב הפטיש ולא מחודו כמו קופא דמחטא (ב"מ דף לח:): יודע כמביא למעלה. תפלה היא יודע לפניך אותו סבך עץ קרדומות ששבר בו את ירושלים כאילו הביאו למעלה בכסא הכבוד: גבה היכלא. ובקש לעלות לרקיע: דרכו ביה מן שמיא. והשפילוהו: זחה דעתיה. מתגאה על שהיה מצליח: עמא קטילא. שכבר נגזר עליהם על כך: וטחני קמח. וטחני חטים לא נאמר אלא קמח שאין צריך טחינה: צמתך. מקום שהקלעים צומתין בצד הראש: שובל. קלע הראש שדומין לשבלים: גלי שוק עברי נהרות. פורענות זה היה הקב"ה אומר לישראל לכו וטחנו קמח כלומר טחונים אתם כבר לקמח ותחזרו ותטחן עדיין תגלי קלעי ראשיכם ושוקיכם ותלכו בגלות: אייתו לי ואינסי. ואנסה אם דם זבחים הוא: כסי ולא אידמי. שחט בהמות ולא אידמי הדם: פרטתא. שטר צוואה: ואיתגייר. נבוזראדן: גר תושב. שלא קבל עליו שאר מצות וקבל עליו שלא לעבוד עבודת כוכבים: של אותו רשע. נבוכד נצר: רפינו ולא נרפתה. שהיה הקב"ה מבקש לרפאותו להכניס מבני בניו תחת כנפי השכינה: אלו נהרות בבל. שהם רעים לשתות: צנייתאדבבל. דקלים מרים הם שעומדים בנהרות ל"א צינייתא דבבל דקלים רעים של נהרות בבל שאין נושאים פירות לפי שהמים רעים הן לגדל פירות בסוטה (דף מו:) אמרי' קוסטא הוא דאמריתו הני צנייתא דבבל מששת ימי בראשית איתנהו ונהר שתחת הני צינוייתא מי מרים נינהו: שיבבי. שכנים: פוק תא. צא ממקומך ובא אל ארץ ישראל ותכבשנה: כי אין האיש. מקרא הוא במשלי: בקריבא הוא. בקרוב הוא ויבא בעת דוחקם לפי דרכו של מקרא זה שהם שלחו לו שומעים אנו שהוא אבל מילתא דהוה אמרי ליה הוה משיב דבר זה: צרור הכסף לקח בידו. צדיקים שבהן מתו: ואכרה לי בחמשה עשר כסף. פדיתי אותה במצרים בט"ו בניסן: כסף וחומר שעורים ולתך שעורים. בזכות צדיקים שנקראו כסף חומר שעורים שלשים סאין ולתך חמשה עשר סאין אלו ארבעים וחמשה צדיקים שהעולם מתקיים עליהם ה) בחולין פרק גיד הנשה (דף צב.) פעמים ששלשים כאן וט"ו בארץ ישראל ופעמים שט"ו כאן ושלשים בארץ ישראל ובמסכת חולין היכא דקא מפרש האי קרא בצדיקיא אמרי אין כסף אלא צדיקים וכן הוא אומר צרור הכסף לקח בידו: כבר קבע להם זמן. שלא יבא עד ע' שנה שתשלים גלות בבל: מתלגא וממטרא. מחמת שלגים ומטרים: תא אשינא דטורי. בא דרך תחתית ההרים וההרים יגינו עליך מן השלגים ומן המטרים: שלחו כר מושל ארץ. שלחו שליח אל נבוכד נצר שהיה מושל ארץ שיבא אל הר בת ציון דרך הסלעים וההרים: לית לי דוכתא. לא יהיה לי מקום סביב לירושלים שנוכל אני וחיילי לישב במקום מכוסה מפני הגשמים: קבריהם של ישראל. מערות שלהן סביב לירושלים ובהן אתה וחיילותיך יכולין לישב: יוציאו את עצמות מלכי יהודה. שעתידים להשליך מן הקברים העצמות שבקברים שנאמר בעת ההיא וגו': אימת אתי בר נפלי. איידי דאמרינן צרור הכסף לקח בידו שנתמעטו הצדיקים קא מיירי הא נמי במשיח וקאמ' תלמידים מתמעטין ואיידי דאמרי' ותהי האמת נעדרת אייתי הא דההוא אתרא דשמיה קושטא: את

הגהות הגר"א

[א] גמ' הלך בדרך מרחוק. נמחק:

גליון הש"ס

גמ' עמון ומואב כו'. עי' ברש"י פ"ד מ"ד דידים: רש"י ד"ה כסף וכו'. וכעין זה לעיל לג ע"א ובברכות דף כו ע"א:

ליקוטי רש"י

רבלתה. והיא רבלה ארץ חמת היא אנטוכיא שם נשפט צדקיהו ביד נבוכדנצר כמו שנא' בספר (מ"ב כה) שם שחט את בניו שם נקר את עיניו והיא סוף הגבול שנא' במרגלים ובכמה מקומות עד לבא חמת (במדבר יג) [יחזקאל יא, י]. תלת מאה. לאו דוקא וכן כל שלש מאות שבש"ס [רשב"ם פסחים קיט.]. בכשיל וכילפות. כלי משחית של נגרים הם וקרדומות באו לה תרגום יונתן בכשילא כילפות לשון ערבי הוא כך פירש דונש והוא מכלי הנגרים. יהלומון. האויבים [תהלים עד, ו]. יודע כמביא למעלה בסבך עץ קרדומות. יודע האויב כשהיה מכה בשערי פתחי המקדש שהוא כמביא מכותיו למעלה ברקיע ומנין היה יודע שהרי היה רואה שהיה העץ מסבך ואוחז את הקרדומות ובולען כמו שאמרו רבותינו כולהו בלעתינהו חד תרעא דירושלים בסבך עץ קרדומות לשון נאחז בסבך (בראשית כב) העץ סובך אותם והם נסבכין בו [שם, ה ועי' במהרש"א בח"א]. וטחני קמח. לגדה לדרך גלותך. גלי צמתך. זרועיך ושוקיך דברים המצומת וקשור ומכוסה. חשפי שובל. גלי השבילים מן המים שעליהם כי דרך שם תלאי בגולה או גלי שוקך ועברי נהרות [ישעיה מז, ב]. דמיה דזכריה. בן יהוידע הכהן שהרגוהו שרי יהודה במצות יואש כשהשתחוו לו ליואש ועשאוהו אלוה והרגוהו בעזרה (דה"ב כד). שדר פורטיתא. שטר צוואה שפרט מה תהא על נכסיו. גר תושב היה. שלא קיבל עליו שאר מצות אלא ע"ז שנאמר כי לא יעשה עוד עבדך וגו' (מ"ב ה) [גיטין נז:]. דציניתא דבבלאי. כי ציניתא דבבל מקום הוא ובו דקלים הרבה כמו ציני הר הברזל (סוכה כט:) [סוטה מו: ועי' ברש"י כאן]. פוק ותא. אתרבינהו. מסתפינא. מאלההון [חולין צב.]. כי אין האיש בביתו. ראיתם שסילק הקב"ה שכינתו וכל טוב נתן לעו"ג [משלי ז, יט]. צרור הכסף. הטובים שבהם הרג [שם, כ]. לדיקים שבהם המיתם. ואכרה לי. הקב"ה אומר קניתי לי ישראל בט"ו בניסן בשביל הצדיקים [חולין שם]. ל' סחורה ברגניי"א בלע"ז כמו (בראשית נ) אשר כריתי לי ובכרכי הים קורין למכירה כירה [הושע ג, ב]. ליום הכסא. לזמן המועד הקבוע וכן בכסה ליום חגנו (תהלי' פא) [משלי שם]. בכסה. יום מועד קבוע לכך וכן (משלי ז) ליום הכסא יבוא ביתו למועד הקבוע [תהלים פא, ד]. ושטחום לשמש. והכשדים ישכנו לגור על העיר בקברי השרים שהיו נאים כפלטין [ירמיה ח, ב]. ביום ההוא. אחרי בא עליהם כל אלה יבא יום ההוא המוכן לגאולה ובו אקים סוכת דוד הנופלת י"ת מלכותא דבית דוד [עמוס ט, יא].

מסורת הש"ס

א) [עי' פירוש רשב"ם פסחים קיט. ד"ה שלש מאות], ב) גיטין נז: ע"ש, ג) [שם ע"ש], ד) בקרא רפאנו, ה) [בע"י ליתא וכ"מ מפי' רש"י דלא גריס ליה], ו) [סוטה מב: מח. לעיל לג.], ז) [גיטין מד:].

תורה אור השלם

א) וַיִּתְפְּשׂוּ אֶת הַמֶּלֶךְ וַיַּעֲלוּ אֹתוֹ אֶל מֶלֶךְ בָּבֶל רִבְלָתָה וַיְדַבְּרוּ אִתּוֹ מִשְׁפָּט: [מלכים ב' כה, ו]

ב) וְעַתָּה פִּתּוּחֶיהָ יָּחַד בְּכַשִּׁיל וְכֵילַפֹּת יַהֲלֹמוּן: [תהלים עד, ו]

ג) יִוָּדַע כְּמֵבִיא לְמָעְלָה בִּסְבָךְ עֵץ קַרְדֻּמּוֹת: [תהלים עד, ה]

ד) סִלָּה כָל אַבִּירַי אֲדֹנָי בְּקִרְבִּי קָרָא עָלַי מוֹעֵד לִשְׁבֹּר בַּחוּרָי גַּת דָּרַךְ אֲדֹנָי לִבְתוּלַת בַּת יְהוּדָה: [איכה א, טו]

ה) קְחִי רֵחַיִם וְטַחֲנִי קָמַח גַּלִּי צַמָּתֵךְ חֶשְׂפִּי שֹׁבֶל גַּלִּי שׁוֹק עִבְרִי נְהָרוֹת: [ישעיה מז, ב]

ו) רִפִּאנוּ אֶת בָּבֶל וְלֹא נִרְפָּתָה עִזְבוּהָ וְנֵלֵךְ אִישׁ לְאַרְצוֹ כִּי נָגַע אֶל הַשָּׁמַיִם מִשְׁפָּטָהּ וְנִשָּׂא עַד שְׁחָקִים: [ירמיה נא, ט]

ז) כִּי אֵין הָאִישׁ בְּבֵיתוֹ הָלַךְ בְּדֶרֶךְ מֵרָחוֹק: [משלי ז, יט]

ח) יְיָ אִישׁ מִלְחָמָה יְיָ שְׁמוֹ: [שמות טו, ג]

ט) צְרוֹר הַכֶּסֶף לָקַח בְּיָדוֹ לְיוֹם הַכֶּסֶא יָבֹא בֵיתוֹ: [משלי ז, כ]

י) וָאֶכְּרֶהָ לִּי בַּחֲמִשָּׁה עָשָׂר כָּסֶף וְחֹמֶר שְׂעֹרִים וְלֶתֶךְ שְׂעֹרִים: [הושע ג, ב]

כ) תִּקְעוּ בַחֹדֶשׁ שׁוֹפָר בַּכֶּסֶה לְיוֹם חַגֵּנוּ: [תהלים פא, ד]

ל) שִׁלְחוּ כַר מֹשֵׁל אֶרֶץ מִסֶּלַע מִדְבָּרָה אֶל הַר בַּת צִיּוֹן: [ישעיה טז, א]

מ) בָּעֵת הַהִיא נְאֻם יְיָ יוֹצִיאוּ אֶת עַצְמוֹת מַלְכֵי יְהוּדָה וְאֶת עַצְמוֹת שָׂרָיו וְאֶת עַצְמוֹת הַכֹּהֲנִים וְאֵת עַצְמוֹת הַנְּבִיאִים וְאֵת עַצְמוֹת יוֹשְׁבֵי יְרוּשָׁלָיִם מִקִּבְרֵיהֶם: וּשְׁטָחוּם לַשֶּׁמֶשׁ וְלַיָּרֵחַ וּלְכֹל צְבָא הַשָּׁמַיִם אֲשֶׁר אֲהֵבוּם וַאֲשֶׁר עֲבָדוּם וַאֲשֶׁר הָלְכוּ אַחֲרֵיהֶם וַאֲשֶׁר דְּרָשׁוּם וַאֲשֶׁר הִשְׁתַּחֲווּ לָהֶם לֹא יֵאָסְפוּ וְלֹא יִקָּבֵרוּ לְדֹמֶן עַל פְּנֵי הָאֲדָמָה יִהְיוּ: [ירמיה ח, א-ב]

נ) בַּיּוֹם הַהוּא אָקִים אֶת סֻכַּת דָּוִיד הַנֹּפֶלֶת וְגָדַרְתִּי אֶת פִּרְצֵיהֶן וַהֲרִסֹתָיו אָקִים וּבְנִיתִיהָ כִּימֵי עוֹלָם: [עמוס ט, יא]

The preceding verse alludes to the honor accorded by Nebuzaradan to his master, Nebuchadnezzar. As the first step in demonstrating that this is so, the Gemara questions the verse's statement, "[Nebuzaradan] stood before [Nebuchadnezzar] in Jerusalem," which implies that Nebuchadnezzar was in Jerusalem at that time:

וּמִי סָלֵיק נְבוּכַדְנֶצַּר לִירוּשָׁלַיִם – **But did Nebuchadnezzar** himself **go up to Jerusalem?** וְהָכְתִיב ,,וַיַּעֲלוּ אֹתוֹ אֶל־מֶלֶךְ בָּבֶל רִבְלָתָה" – **Why, it is written:** ***They took him*** [Tzidkiahu] ***up to the king of Babylonia*** [Nebuchadnezzar] ***to Rivlah,***[1] וְאָמַר רַבִּי אַבָּהוּ – **and R' Abahu said** in reference to Rivlah: זוֹ אַנְטוֹכְיָא – **This is** the town of **Antakya.**[2] Thus, Nebuchadnezzar was in Antakya at that time, and not in Jerusalem!

The Gemara explains what the verse means by saying that Nebuzaradan stood before Nebuchadnezzar in Jerusalem:

רַב חִסְדָּא וְרַב יִצְחָק בַּר אֲבוּדִימִי – **Rav Chisda and Rav Yitzchak bar Avudimi** offer different explanations: חַד אָמַר – **One says** that דְּמוּת דְּיוֹקְנוֹ הָיְתָה חֲקוּקָה לוֹ עַל מֶרְכַּבְתּוֹ – **an image of [Nebuchadnezzar's] likeness was engraved on [Nebuzaradan's] chariot.**[3] וְחַד אָמַר – **And** the other **one says** that אֵימָה יְתֵירָה הָיְתָה לוֹ מִמֶּנּוּ – **[Nebuzaradan] was in** such **great awe of [Nebuchadnezzar]** וְדוֹמֶה כְּמִי שֶׁעוֹמֵד לְפָנָיו – **that it seemed** to him **as though he were standing before [Nebuchadnezzar].**[4]

According to either explanation, Nebuzaradan greatly revered his master Nebuchadnezzar. It is to this exemplary devotion that Scripture refers when it says "a servant [honors] his master."

The Gemara describes Nebuzaradan's conquest of Jerusalem: אָמַר רָבָא – **Rava said:** טְעִין תְּלָת מְאָה כּוּדְנְיָיתָא נַרְגָּא דְּפַרְזְלָא דְּשָׁלִיט בְּפַרְזְלָא שַׁדַּר לֵיהּ נְבוּכַדְנֶצַּר לִנְבוּזַרְאֲדָן – **Nebuchadnezzar sent Nebuzaradan three hundred**[5] **mule-loads of iron axes that could prevail over iron.**[6] כּוּלְּהוּ בַּלְעֵתִינְהוּ חַד דַּשָּׁא דִּירוּשָׁלֶם – But **one gate of Jerusalem swallowed them all;** i.e. all the axes shattered when they were used against just one of Jerusalem's gates. שֶׁנֶּאֱמַר ,,פִּתּוּחֶיהָ יָּחַד בְּכַשִּׁיל וְכֵילַפּוֹת יַהֲלֹמוּן" – This is **as it is stated:** [Against one of] ***its entranceways they beat with*** [all their] ***hatchets and axes together*** [but to no avail].[7] בָּעֵי לְמֶיהְדַּר – **[Nebuzaradan] sought to withdraw.** אָמַר – **He said:** מִסְתְּפִינָא דְּלָא לִיעַבְדוּ בִּי כִּי הֵיכִי דְּעָבְדוּ בְּסַנְחֵרִיב – **I am afraid lest they do to me what they did to Sancheiriv.**[8] נְפַקָא קָלָא וְאָמַר – A heavenly **voice**[9] **emanated and said:** שָׁוּור בַּר שָׁוּור – **"O leaper, the son of a leaper!**[10] נְבוּזַרְאֲדָן שָׁוּור – **Nebuzaradan, leap** into battle and conquer Jerusalem! דְּמָטָא זִימְנָא דְּמִקְדְּשָׁא חָרֵיב – **For the time has come for the Temple to be destroyed,** וְהֵיכְלָא מִיקְלֵי – **and for the Sanctuary**[11] **to be burned!"** פָּשׁ לֵיהּ חַד נַרְגָּא – **[Nebuzaradan] had a single axe left over.** אֲתָא מַחְיֵיהּ בְּקוֹפָא וְאִיפְּתַח – **He went** and **struck [the gate] with the** axe's **blunt end,**[12] **and it opened.** שֶׁנֶּאֱמַר ,,יִוָּדַע כְּמֵבִיא לְמָעְלָה בִּסְבָךְ עֵץ־קַרְדֻּמּוֹת" – This is **as it is stated:** ***May*** [that] ***axe of a wooden thicket*** [which the enemy used to breach

NOTES

1. *II Kings* 25:6. When Jerusalem was besieged by the Babylonians, King Tzidkiahu fled the city, but the Babylonians apprehended him and took him to their king's headquarters in Rivlah.

2. Antakya is not in Eretz Yisrael (*Rashi*, from *Gittin* 44b). [Antakya is the ancient town of Antioch, which stands in what today is southern Turkey. Rivlah was the former name of Antakya.]

3. When he stood before this portrait, Nebuzaradan felt as though he were standing before Nebuchadnezzar himself (*Rashi*). This is what the verse means by saying "[Nebuzaradan] stood before [Nebuchadnezzar] in Jerusalem."

This approach can also be used to explain the first verse in that chapter: בָּא נְבֻכַדְנֶאצַּר מֶלֶךְ־בָּבֶל הוּא וְכָל־חֵילוֹ עַל יְרוּשָׁלַם וַיִּחַן עָלֶיהָ, *Nebuchadnezzar the king of Babylonia came, he and all his army, against Jerusalem, and he encamped by it.* Nebuchadnezzar himself did not go to Jerusalem; rather, his portrait was present (*Rashi*, as explained by *Maharsha*; see *Rashash*).

4. [The difference between the two approaches is that according to the first one Nebuzaradan needed a portrait of his king to inspire him to such reverence, while according to the second approach he did not require any external stimulus.]

5. Whenever the number 300 is used [in this type of context], it is not meant literally (*Rashbam* to *Pesachim* 119a ד״ה משוי; see *Eitz Yosef* here).

Certain numbers (e.g. 13, 60, 300, 400) are often used by the Sages in an allegorical sense, to emphasize a point, without their being meant literally (see *Chullin* 90b; *Rashi* to *Shabbos* 90b ד״ה שיתין; ibid. 119a ד״ה תריסר; *Rashi* to *Chullin* 95b ד״ה תריסר; *Tosafos* to *Berachos* 20a ד״ה תליסר; *essay* attributed to *R' Avraham ben HaRambam* recorded in the introductory section of *Ein Yaakov;* see also *Pirkei DeRabbi Eliezer,* ch. 42). Each of these numbers carries a specific esoteric meaning (see *Maharal* here and elsewhere).

Maharal explains the significance of 300 as follows: Three connotes strength, as indicated by the verse (*Ecclesiastes* 4:12): וְהַחוּט הַמְשֻׁלָּשׁ לֹא בִמְהֵרָה יִנָּתֵק, *and the three-ply cord is not readily broken.* A hundred represents the *third* level of magnitude [(1) units; (2) tens; (3) hundreds]. Thus, three hundred (3 x 100) signifies extraordinary strength.

6. The axes were sharp enough to cut through iron (*Rashi*).

7. *Psalms* 74:6. [This chapter of *Psalms* prophetically describes the siege and fall of Jerusalem.] Our elucidation of the verse follows *Rashi;* cf. *Maharsha*. See also note 13 below.

8. Since their God is evidently aiding them in a supernatural manner, I am afraid lest He destroy my army as He destroyed Sancheiriv's army when it attempted to conquer Jerusalem.

9. The Gemara above (11a) states that after the era of prophecy, God delivered messages by means of בַּת קוֹל, literally: the daughter of a voice.

Tosafos (ibid. ד״ה בת קול) explain that the Heavenly voice itself was not heard; rather, something akin to an *echo* of the Heavenly voice was heard. Hence, the term "daughter of a voice." *Tos. Yom Tov* (*Yevamos* 16:6 ד״ה בת קול) suggests that since this form of Divine communication is inferior to prophecy, it is referred to as a "daughter," i.e. a daughter of prophecy (see also *Rif* Responsa §1).

10. The double expression שָׁוּור בַּר שָׁוּור (leaper the son of a leaper) connotes that Nebuzaradan excelled at leaping into battle (*Maharal;* see *Rashi*). Alternatively, it refers to the fact that Nebuzaradan had already leaped enthusiastically to attack Jerusalem once before, with the army of Sancheiriv, and now he is attacking it a second time (*Rashi*).

Toras Chaim maintains that the word שָׁוּור, *leaper*, is used here to signify that Nebuzaradan was impatient. Since he could not destroy Jerusalem immediately, he sought to withdraw rather than wait for a more opportune moment. He acted likewise during Sancheiriv's campaign against Jerusalem, for he was among those who told Sancheiriv to attack Jerusalem immediately: "Let us attack it *today*!" (Gemara above, 95a).

11. The word הֵיכָל, *Sanctuary,* usually refers to the chamber in the Temple that housed the Menorah, the *Shulchan* and the Golden Altar. Sometimes it is used to denote the Temple in its entirety (see *Tos. Yom Tov* to *Midos* 4:6).

Toras Chaim offers two explanations for the double expression: The "destruction of the Temple" connotes the departure of God's presence from the Temple, and the "burning of the Sanctuary" is meant literally. It is only after God's presence has departed that the Temple can be physically destroyed.

Alternatively, the double expression connotes the physical Temple and its Heavenly counterpart. As stated in *Taanis* (5a), God does not reside in His Divine Temple while the earthly Temple is in ruins. Thus, in effect, both Temples were "destroyed" at that time.

12. *Rashi*. Alternatively, the wooden handle (*Yad Ramah*).

Nebuzaradan wished to see whether the gate would be broken by supernatural, Divinely ordained, means. If God had indeed decreed that Jerusalem would fall at this time, then even plain wood would suffice to smash the gate (*Yad Ramah*).

ומי סליק נבוכד נצר לירושלים והכתיב א) ויעלו אותו אל מלך בבל רבלתה ואמר ר' אבהו זו אנטוכיא רב חסדא ורב יצחק בר אבודימי חד אמר דמות דיוקנו היתה חקוקה לו על מרכבתו וחד אמר אימה יתירה היתה לו ממנו ודומה כמי שעומד לפניו אמר רבא טעין א) תלת מאה כודנייתא נרגא דפרזלא דשליט בפרזלא שדר ליה נבוכד נצר לנבוזראדן כולהו בלעתינהו חד דשא דירושלם שנאמר ב) פתוחיה יחד בכשיל וכילפות יהלומון בעי למיהדר אמר מסתפינא דלא ליעבדו בי כי היכי דעבדו בסנחריב נפקא קלא ואמר שוור בר שוור נבוזר אדן שוור דמטא זימנא דמקדשא חריב והיכלא מיקלי פש ליה חד נרגא אתא מחייה בקופא ואיפתח שנאמר ג) יודע כמביא למעלה בסבך עץ קרדומות הוה קטיל ואזל עד דמטא להיכלא אדליק ביה נורא גבה היכלא דרכו ביה מן שמיא שנאמר ד) גת דרך ה' לבתולת בת יהודה קא זיחא דעתיה נפקא בת קלא ואמרה ליה עמא קטילא קטלת היכלא קליא קלית קימחא טחינא טחינת שנאמר ה) קחי רחים וטחני קמח גלי צמתך חשפי שובל גלי שוק עברי נהרות חטים לא נאמר אלא קמח ג) חזא דמיה דזכריה דהוה קא רתח אמר להו מאי האי אמרו ליה דם זבחים הוא דאישתפיך אמר להו אייתי ואנסי אי מדמו כסי ולא אידמו אמר להו גלו לי ואי לא סריקנא לכו לבשרייכו במסריקא דפרזלא אמרו ליה האי כהן ונביא הוא דאינבי להו לישראל בחורבנא דירושלם וקטלוהו אמר להו אנא מפייסנא ליה אייתי רבנן קטיל עילויה ולא נח אייתי דרדקי דבי רב קטיל עילויה ולא נח אייתי פרחי כהונה קטיל עילויה ולא נח עד די קטל עילויה תשעין וארבעה ריבוא ולא נח קרב לגביה אמר זכריה זכריה טובים שבהן איבדתים ניחא לך דאיקטלינהו לכולהו מיד נח הרהר תשובה בדעתיה אמר מה הם שלא איבדו אלא נפש אחת כך ההוא גברא מה תיהוי עליה ערק שדר פורטיתא לביתיה ואיתגייר תנו רבנן ד) נעמן גר תושב היה נבוזר אדן גר צדק היה מבני בניו של סיסרא למדו תורה בירושלים מבני בניו של סנחריב לימדו תורה ברבים ומאן נינהו שמעיה ואבטליון מבני בניו של המן למדו תורה בבני ברק ואף מבני בניו של אותו רשע ביקש הקב"ה להכניסן תחת כנפי השכינה אמרו מלאכי השרת לפני הקב"ה רבונו של עולם מי שהחריב את ביתך ושרף את היכלך תכניס תחת כנפי השכינה היינו דכתיב ו) רפינו ד) את בבל ולא נרפתה עולא אמר זה נבוכד נצר רבי שמואל בר נחמני אמר אלו נהרות בבל ותרגמה דצינייתא (ה) צרידתא) דבבלאי אמר עולא ° עמון ומואב שיבבי בישי דירושלם הוו כיון דשמעינהו לנביאי דקא מיתנבאי לחורבנא דירושלם שלחו לנבוכד נצר פוק ותא אמר מסתפינא דלא ליעבדו לי כדעבדו בקמאי שלחו ליה ז) כי אין האיש בביתו [א] הלך בדרך מרחוק ו) ואין איש אלא הקדוש ברוך הוא שנאמר ח) ה' איש מלחמה שלח להו בקריבא הוא ואתי שלחו ליה הלך בדרך מרחוק שלח להו אית להו צדיקי דבעו רחמי ומייתו ליה שלחו ליה ט) צרור הכסף לקח בידו ואין כסף אלא צדיקים שנאמר י) ואכרה לי בחמשה עשר כסף וחומר שעורים ולתך שעורים שלח להו הדרי רשיעי בתשובה ובעו רחמי ומייתו ליה שלחו ליה כבר קבע להן זמן שנאמר ט) ליום הכסא יבא (ל)ביתו אין כסא אלא זמן שנאמר כ) בכסה ליום חגנו שלח להו סיתווא הוא ולא מצינא דאתי מתלגא וממיטרא שלחו ליה תא אשינא דטורא שנאמר ל) שלחו כר מושל ארץ מסלע מדברה אל הר בת ציון שלח להו אי אתינא לית לי דוכתא דיתיבנא ביה שלחו ליה קברות שלהם מעולין מפלטירין שלך דכתיב מ) בעת ההיא נאום ה' יוציאו את עצמות מלכי יהודה ואת עצמות שריו ואת עצמות הכהנים ואת עצמות הנביאים ואת עצמות יושבי ירושלים מקבריהם ושטחום לשמש ולירח ולכל צבא השמים אשר אהבום ואשר עבדום ואשר הלכו אחריהם אמר ליה רב נחמן לרבי יצחק מי שמיע לך אימת אתי בר נפלי אמר ליה מאן בר נפלי א"ל משיח משיח בר נפלי קרית ליה א"ל אין דכתיב נ) ביום ההוא אקים את

ומי סליק כו' והא כתיב. בההיא פרשתא ויעלו לדקיה אל המלך רבלתה אלמא ברבלה הוה: זו אנטוכיא. ואנטוכיא קיימא לן י) דאינה מארץ ישראל: דמות דיוקנו. של נבוכד נצר: חקוקה לו על מרכבתו. של נבוזר אדן ודומה לו כמו שעומד לפניו ולכך כתיב בא נבוכד נצר והיינו כבוד: טעין תלת מאה כודניית'. משאוי שלש מאות פרדות: נרגא דפרזלא. פטישי ברזל: דשליט' בפרזלא. ברזל חדוד הקוצץ ברזל אחר: בלעתינהו. לא בליעה ממש אלא שיברם שהיו מתפוצצין הפטישים בהכותם בשער לשברה: פתוחיה יחד. משמע על פתח אחד הלמו כל הכשילים וכילפות יחד ולא הועיל כלום: שוור בר שוור. דולג בר דולג קום וכבש ירושלים לנבוזר אדן קאמר ל"א שוור בר שוור מדלג בר מדלג קפלת פעם אחת עם סנחריב ועכשיו פעם שניה: בקופא. מגב הפטיש ולא מחודו כמו קופא דמחטא (ב"מ דף לח:): יודע כמביא למעלה. תפלה היא יודע לפניך אותו סבך עץ קרדומות ששבר בו את ירושלים כאילו הביאו למעלה בכסא הכבוד: גבה היכלא. ובקש לעלות לרקיע: דרכו ביה מן שמיא. והשפילוהו: זחה דעתיה. מתגאה על שהיה מצליח: עמא קטילא. שכבר נגזר עליהם על כך: וטחני קמח. וטחני חטים לא נאמר אלא קמח שאין צריך טחינה: צמתך. מקום שהקלעים צומתין בצד הראש: שובל. קלע הראש שדומין לשבלים: גלי שוק עברי נהרות. פורענות זה היה הקב"ה אומר לישראל לכו וטחנו קמח כלומר טחונים אתם כבר לקמח ותחזרו ותטחן עדיין תגלי קלעי ראשיכם ושוקיכם ותלכו בגלות: אייתו לי ואינסי. ואנסה אם דם זבחים הוא: כסי ולא אידמי. שחט בהמות ולא אידמי הדם: פרטתא. שטר צוואה: ואיתגייר. נבוזראדן: גר תושב. שלא קבל עליו שאר מצות וקבל עליו שלא לעבוד עבודת כוכבים: של אותו רשע. נבוכד נצר: רפינו ולא נרפתה. שהיה הקב"ה מבקש לרפאותו להכניס מבני בניו תחת כנפי השכינה: אלו נהרות בבל. שהם רעים לשתות: צנייתאדבבל.דקליםמריםהםשעומדים בנהרות ל"א צינוייתא דבבל דקלים רעים של נהרות בבל שאין נושאים פירות לפי שהמים רעים הן לגדל פירות בסוטה (דף מו:) אמרי' קוסטא הוא דאמריתו הני צנייתא דבבל מששת ימי בראשית איתנהו ונהר שתחת הני צינוייתא מי מרים נינהו: שיבבי. שכנים: פוק תא. צא ממקומך ובא אל ארץ ישראל ותכבשנה: כי אין האיש. מקרא הוא במשלי: בקריבא הוא. בקרוב הוא ויבא בעת דוחקם לפי דרכו של מקרא זה שהם שלחו לו שומעים אנו שהוא אכל מילתא דהוה אמרי ליה הוה משיב דבר זה: צרור הכסף לקח בידו. צדיקים שבהן מתו: ואכרה לי בחמשה עשר כסף. פדיתי אותה במצרים בט"ו בניסן: כסף וחומר שעורים ולתך שעורים. בזכות צדיקים שנקראו כסף חומר שעורים שלשים סאין ולתך חמשה עשר סאין אלו ארבעים וחמשה צדיקים שהעולם מתקיים עליהם ° בחולין פרק גיד הנשה (דף נב.) פעמים ששלשים כאן וט"ו בארץ ישראל ופעמים שט"ו כאן ושלשים בארץ ישראל ובמסכת חולין היכא דקא מפרש האי קרא בצדיקיא אמרי אין כסף אלא צדיקים וכן הוא אומר צרור הכסף לקח בידו: כבר קבע להם זמן. שלא יבא עד ע' שנה שתשלים גלות בבל: מתלגאוממטרא. מחמת שלגים ומטרים: תא אשינא דטורי. בא דרך תחתית ההרים וההרים יגינו עליך מן השלגים ומן המטרים: שלחו כר מושל ארץ. שלחו שליח אל נבוכד נצר שהיה מושל ארץ שיבא אל הר בת ציון דרך הסלעים וההרים: לית לי דוכתא. לא יהיה לי מקום סביב לירושלים שנוכל אני וחיילי לישב במקום מכוסה מפני הגשמים: קבריהם של ישראל. מערות שלהן סביב לירושלים ובהן אתה וחיילותיך יכולין לישב: יוציאו את עצמות מלכי יהודה. שעתידים להשליך מן הקברים העצמות שבקברים שנאמר בעת ההיא וגו': אימת אתי בר נפלי. איידי דאמרינן צרור הכסף לקח בידו שנתמעטו הצדיקים קא מיירי הא נמי במשיח וקאמ' תלמידים מתמעטין ואיידי דאמרי' ותהי האמת נעדרת אייתי הא דההוא אתרא דשמיה קוסטא:

את

מסורת הש"ס

א) [עי' פירוש רשב"ם פסחים קיט. ד"ה שלש מאות], ב) גיטין נז: ע"ש, ג) [שם ע"ש], ד) בקרא רפאנו, ה) [בע"י ליתא וכ"מ מפי' רש"י דלא גרים ליה], ו) [סוטה מב: מח. לעיל לג.], ז) [גיטין מד:].

תורה אור השלם

א) וַיִּתְפְּשׂוּ אֶת הַמֶּלֶךְ וַיַּעֲלוּ אֹתוֹ אֶל מֶלֶךְ בָּבֶל רִבְלָתָה וַיְדַבְּרוּ אִתּוֹ מִשְׁפָּט: [מלכים ב' כה, ו]

ב) וְעַתָּה פִּתּוּחֶיהָ יָּחַד בְּכַשִּׁיל וְכֵילַפֹּת יַהֲלֹמוּן: [תהלים עד, ו]

ג) יִוָּדַע כְּמֵבִיא לְמָעְלָה בִּסְבָךְ עֵץ קַרְדֻּמּוֹת: [תהלים עד, ה]

ד) סִלָּה כָל אַבִּירַי אֲדֹנָי בְּקִרְבִּי קָרָא עָלַי מוֹעֵד לִשְׁבֹּר בַּחוּרָי גַּת דָּרַךְ אֲדֹנָי לִבְתוּלַת בַּת יְהוּדָה: [איכה א, טו]

ה) קְחִי רֵחַיִם וְטַחֲנִי קָמַח גַּלִּי צַמָּתֵךְ חֶשְׂפִּי שֹׁבֶל גַּלִּי שׁוֹק עִבְרִי נְהָרוֹת: [ישעיה מז, ב]

ו) רִפִּאנוּ אֶת בָּבֶל וְלֹא נִרְפָּתָה עִזְבוּהָ וְנֵלֵךְ אִישׁ לְאַרְצוֹ כִּי נָגַע אֶל הַשָּׁמַיִם מִשְׁפָּטָהּ וְנִשָּׂא עַד שְׁחָקִים: [ירמיה נא, ט]

ז) כִּי אֵין הָאִישׁ בְּבֵיתוֹ הָלַךְ בְּדֶרֶךְ מֵרָחוֹק: [משלי ז, יט]

ח) יְיָ אִישׁ מִלְחָמָה יְיָ שְׁמוֹ: [שמות טו, ג]

ט) צְרוֹר הַכֶּסֶף לָקַח בְּיָדוֹ לְיוֹם הַכֶּסֶא יָבֹא בֵיתוֹ: [משלי ז, כ]

י) וָאֶכְּרֶהָ לִּי בַּחֲמִשָּׁה עָשָׂר כָּסֶף וְחֹמֶר שְׂעֹרִים וְלֶתֶךְ שְׂעֹרִים: [הושע ג, ב]

כ) תִּקְעוּ בַחֹדֶשׁ שׁוֹפָר בַּכֶּסֶה לְיוֹם חַגֵּנוּ: [תהלים פא, ד]

ל) שִׁלְחוּ כַר מֹשֵׁל אֶרֶץ מִסֶּלַע מִדְבָּרָה אֶל הַר בַּת צִיּוֹן: [ישעיה טז, א]

מ) בָּעֵת הַהִיא נְאֻם יְיָ יוֹצִיאוּ אֶת עַצְמוֹת מַלְכֵי יְהוּדָה וְאֶת עַצְמוֹת שָׂרָיו וְאֶת עַצְמוֹת הַכֹּהֲנִים וְאֵת עַצְמוֹת הַנְּבִיאִים וְאֵת עַצְמוֹת יוֹשְׁבֵי יְרוּשָׁלָיִם מִקִּבְרֵיהֶם: וּשְׁטָחוּם לַשֶּׁמֶשׁ וְלַיָּרֵחַ וּלְכֹל צְבָא הַשָּׁמַיִם אֲשֶׁר אֲהֵבוּם וַאֲשֶׁר עֲבָדוּם וַאֲשֶׁר הָלְכוּ אַחֲרֵיהֶם וַאֲשֶׁר דְּרָשׁוּם וַאֲשֶׁר הִשְׁתַּחֲווּ לָהֶם לֹא יֵאָסְפוּ וְלֹא יִקָּבֵרוּ לְדֹמֶן עַל פְּנֵי הָאֲדָמָה יִהְיוּ: [ירמיה ח, א-ב]

נ) בַּיּוֹם הַהוּא אָקִים אֶת סֻכַּת דָּוִיד הַנֹּפֶלֶת וְגָדַרְתִּי אֶת פִּרְצֵיהֶן וַהֲרִסֹתָיו אָקִים וּבְנִיתִיהָ כִּימֵי עוֹלָם: [עמוס ט, יא]

הגהות הגר"א

[א] גמ' הלך בדרך מרחוק. נמחק:

גליון הש"ס

גמ' עמון ומואב כו'. עי' בר"ש פ"ד מ"ד ידים: רש"י ד"ה כסף וכו'. וכעין זה לעיל לג ע"א ובברכות דף כו ע"א:

ליקוטי רש"י

רבלתה. והיא רבלה ארץ חמת היא אנטוכיא שם נשפט צדקיהו ביד נבוכדנצר כמו שנא' בספר (מ"ב כה) שם שחט את בניו שם נקר את עיניו והיא סוף הגבול שנא' במרגלים ובכמה מקומות עד לבא חמת (במדבר יג) [יחזקאל יא, י]. תלת מאה. לאו דוקא וכן כל שלש מאות שבש"ס [רשב"ם פסחים קיט.]. בכשיל וכילפות. כלי משחית של נגרים הם וקרדומות באו לה תרגום יונתן בכשילא כילפות לשון ערבי הוא כך פירש דונש והוא מכלי הנגרים. יהלומון. האויבים [תהלים עד, ו]. יודע כמביא למעלה בסבך עץ קרדומות. יודע האויב כשהיה מכה בשערי פתחי המקדש שהוא כמביא מכותיו למעלה ברקיע ומנין היה יודע שהרי היה רואה שהיה העץ מסבך ואוחז את הקרדומות ובולען כמו שאמרו רבותינו כולהו בלעתינהו חד תרעא דירושלים בסבך עץ קרדומות לשון נאחז בסבך (בראשית כב) העץ סובך אותם והם נסבכין בו [שם, ה ועי' במהרש"א בח"א]. וטחני קמח. לצדה לדרך גלותך. גלי צמתך. זרועיך ושוקיך דברים המצומת וקשור ומכוסה. חשפי שובל. גלי השבילים מן המים שעליהם כי דרך שם תלאי בגולה או גלי שוקך ועברי נהרות [ישעיה מז, ב]. דמיה דזכריה. בן יהוידע הכהן שהרגוהו שרי יהודה במצות יואש כשהשתחוו לו ליואש ועשאוהו אלוה והרגוהו בעזרה (דה"ב כד). שדר פורטיתא. שטר צוואה שפרט מה תהא על נכסיו. גר תושב היה. שלא קיבל עליו שאר מצות אלא ע"ז שנאמר כי לא יעשה עוד עבדך וגו' (מ"ב ה) [גיטין נז:]. דצינייתא דבבלאי. בי ציניתא דבבל מקום הוא וכו דקלים הרבה כמו ציני הר הברזל (סוכה כט:) [סוטה מו: ועי' ברש"י כאן]. פוק ותא. אחרבינהו. מסתפינא. מאלההון [חולין צב.]. כי אין האיש בביתו. ראיתם שסילק הקב"ה שכינתו וכל טוב נתן לעו"ג [משלי ז, יט]. צרור הכסף. הטובים שבהם הרג [שם, כ]. לדיקים שבהם המיתם. ואכרה לי. הקב"ה אומר קניתי לי ישראל בט"ו בניסן בשביל הצדיקים [חולין שם]. ל' סחורה ברגניי"א בלע"ז כמו (בראשית נ) אשר כריתי לי ובכרכי הים קורין למכירה כירה [הושע ג, ב]. ליום הכסא. לזמן המועד הקבוע וכן בכסה ליום חגנו (תהלי' פא) [משלי שם]. בכסה. יום מועד קבוע לכך וכן (משלי ז) ליום הכסא יבוא ביתו למועד הקבוע [תהלים פא, ד]. ושטחום לשמש. והכשדים ישכנו לגור על העיר בקברי השרים שהיו נאים כפלטין [ירמיה ח, ב]. ביום ההוא. אחרי בא עליהם כל אלה יבא יום ההוא המוכן לגאולה וכו אקים סוכת דוד הנופלת י"ת מלכותא דבית דוד [עמוס ט, יא].

Jerusalem] ***be recalled*** [by God] ***as though it were brought Above*** [and laid before the Heavenly Throne].[13] הֲוָה קָטִיל וְאָזִיל עַד דִּמְטָא לְהֵיכְלָא – Nebuzaradan proceeded through the city, **killing as he went, until he reached the Sanctuary.** אַדְלִיק בֵּיהּ נוּרָא – **He set fire to it.** גָּבַהּ הֵיכָלָא – **The Sanctuary ascended** heavenward, דָּרְכוּ בֵּיהּ מִן שְׁמַיָּא – but **they trod on it from Heaven,** pushing it back down.[14] שֶׁנֶּאֱמַר ,,גַּת דָּרַךְ ה׳ לִבְתוּלַת בַּת־יְהוּדָה״ – This is **as it is stated:**[15] [As in] ***a winepress, HASHEM has trodden the virgin daughter of Judah.*** קָא זַיְחָא דַּעְתֵּיהּ – **[Nebuzaradan] became arrogant** in light of his success. נָפְקָא בַּת קָלָא וְאָמְרָה לֵיהּ – **A heavenly voice emanated and said to him:** עַמָּא קְטִילָא קָטְלַת – "It is **a slain nation** that **you slew,**[16] הֵיכָלָא קְלָיָא קָלֵית – it is **a burned Sanctuary** that **you burned,** קִימְחָא טְחִינָא טְחִינַת – it is **ground flour** that **you ground!"** שֶׁנֶּאֱמַר ,,קְחִי רֵחַיִם וְטַחֲנִי קָמַח גַּלִּי צַמָּתֵךְ חֶשְׂפִּי־שֹׁבֶל גַּלִּי־שׁוֹק עִבְרִי נְהָרוֹת״ – This is alluded to in Scripture, **as it is stated:** ***Take millstones and grind flour. Lay bare the side of your head; expose the braids. Lay bare the thigh; wade through the rivers.***[17] חִטִּים לֹא נֶאֱמַר – In this verse, **it is not said: "wheat";** אֶלָּא קֶמַח – **rather, it is said: "flour,"** which is wheat that has already been ground. The verse says "grind *flour*" to teach that Nebuzaradan would crush the Jews only after they had already been "crushed" by Divine decree.

The narrative continues:

חֲזָא דָּמֵיהּ דִּזְכַרְיָה דַּהֲוָה קָא רָתַח – **[Nebuzaradan] saw the blood of Zechariah seething** on the floor of the Temple.[18] אָמַר לְהוּ – **He asked [the Kohanim]:** מַאי הַאי – **"What is this?"** אָמְרוּ לֵיהּ – **They said to him:** דַּם זְבָחִים הוּא דְּאִישְׁתַּפֵּיךְ – **"It is blood of offerings that was spilled."**[19] אָמַר לְהוּ – **[Nebuzaradan] said to them:** אַיְיתוּ וְאֶנְסֵי אִי מִדְמוּ – **"Bring** such blood here, **and I will examine whether they resemble** each other!"[20] בְּסוּ – **They slaughtered** an animal, וְלֹא אִידְמוּ – **and [the bloods] did not resemble** each other. אָמַר לְהוּ – **[Nebuzaradan] said to them:** גַּלּוּ לִי – **"Tell me**[21] what this blood really is. וְאִי לֹא – **And if** you do **not,** סָרֵיקְנָא לְכוּ לְבִשְׂרַיְיכוּ בְּמַסְרֵיקָא דְּפַרְזְלָא – **I will tear your flesh with an iron comb!"** אָמְרוּ לֵיהּ – **They answered him:** הַאי כֹּהֵן וְנָבִיא הוּא – **"This is the blood of a man who was a Kohen and a prophet** דְּאִינַּבֵּי לְהוּ לְיִשְׂרָאֵל בְּחוּרְבָּנָא דִירוּשָׁלַיִם – **who prophesied to Israel about the destruction of Jerusalem,** וְקַטְלוּהוּ – **and they killed him."** אָמַר לְהוּ – **[Nebuzaradan] said to them:** אֲנָא מְפַיֵּיסְנָא לֵיהּ – **"I will appease him."**[22] אַיְיתֵי רַבָּנָן – **He brought rabbinic scholars** קָטִיל עִילָּוֵיהּ – **and slew them over [the blood],** וְלֹא נָח – **but it did not rest.** אַיְיתֵי דַּרְדְּקֵי דְּבֵי רַב – **He brought schoolchildren** קָטִיל עִילָּוֵיהּ – and **slew them over it,** וְלֹא נָח – **but** still **it did not rest.** אַיְיתֵי פִּרְחֵי כְהוּנָּה – **He brought young Kohanim**[23] קָטִיל עִילָּוֵיהּ – and **slew them over it,** וְלֹא נָח – **but** still **it did not rest.** עַד דִּי קְטַל עִילָּוֵיהּ תִּשְׁעִין וְאַרְבָּעָה רִיבּוֹא – Nebuzaradan continued slaying people **until he had killed ninety-four myriads**[24] **over [the blood],** וְלֹא נָח – **but** still **it did not rest.** קָרַב לְגַבֵּיהּ אָמַר – **He approached it** and **exclaimed:** זְכַרְיָה זְכַרְיָה – **"Zechariah! Zechariah!** טוֹבִים שֶׁבָּהֶן אִיבַּדְתִּים – **I have destroyed their best.** נִיחָא לָךְ דְּאִיקְטְלִינְהוּ לְכוּלְּהוּ – **Do you want me to kill them all?"** מִיָּד נָח – **[The blood] immediately rested.** הִרְהֵר תְּשׁוּבָה בְּדַעְתֵּיהּ – At that moment, **thoughts of repentance entered [Nebuzaradan's] mind.** אָמַר– **He said** to himself: מָה הֵם שֶׁלֹּא אִיבְּדוּ אֶלָּא נֶפֶשׁ אַחַת כָּךְ – **If they, who took only one life,** are punished **so** severely, הַהוּא גַּבְרָא מָה תֶּיהֱוֵי עֲלֵיהּ – **then what will become of that man,**[25] who killed all those people! עָרַק – **[Nebuzaradan] ran away.** שְׁדַר פּוּרְטִיתָא לְבֵיתֵיהּ – **He sent a will to his household** וְאִיתְגַּיַּיר – **and he converted to Judaism.**

Having mentioned that Nebuzaradan converted to Judaism, the Gemara cites a Baraisa that enumerates other enemies of Israel who became associated with Judaism:

תָּנוּ רַבָּנָן – **The Rabbis taught in a Baraisa:** נַעֲמָן גֵּר תּוֹשָׁב הָיָה

NOTES

13. *Psalms* 74:5. The Psalmist prays that God will recall the destruction of Jerusalem (see *Rashi;* cf. *Yad Ramah*). [קַרְדֻּמּוֹת literally means axes (plural). For this and other reasons *Maharsha* posits that this verse belongs to the earlier section which describes how the invading army used all their axes against a single gate, whereas the verse cited in that section (*Its entranceways etc.*), which literally speaks of a single axe, belongs here. By error, the verses were reversed. This approach would agree with *Rashi's* commentary to *Psalms* ibid.]

When the Babylonian soldiers pummeled the gate with their many axes, they did not succeed in breaching it. But when the gate was struck with the back of a single axe, it fell open. God performed these miracles in order to show that it is He Who is attacking Israel. Without His assistance, all the enemy's weaponry is useless; with His assistance, their weaponry is unnecessary (*Eitz Yosef*).

Iyun Yaakov maintains that the gate did not open at first because the precise time for Jerusalem's destruction had not yet arrived. Alternatively, God wished to give the people one final chance to repent.

14. God raised the Temple and then thrust it down in order to show Nebuzaradan that the Temple's destruction was being engineered by Heaven (*Yad Ramah's* second explanation; see also *Maharsha, Toras Chaim, Maharal*).

15. *Lamentations* 1:15.

16. Their fate was already decreed by God (*Rashi*). Thus, Nebuzaradan had no grounds for arrogance. He was merely a tool being used by God to implement His decree.

17. *Isaiah* 47:2. [The prophet uses the metaphor of a debased bondwoman to describe the downfall of a people. In context, the reference is to the downfall of Babylonia (see ibid. v. 1). The Gemara, however, interprets the verse as addressing the Jewish people.]

In this verse, God tells Israel the punishment it will suffer. *Go and grind flour* – that is to say, although you have already been "ground to flour," you will be "ground" again. *Lay bare the braids of your head and your legs* – and go into exile (*Rashi;* cf. *Eitz Yosef*).

צַמָּתֵךְ (from the root צמת, *gather*) signifies the sides of the head where the braids are gathered. שֹׁבֶל (related to שִׁבֳּלִים, *ears of wheat*) refers to the braids themselves, which resemble ears of wheat (*Rashi*).

18. Two hundred and fifty-two years earlier, the prophet and Kohen Zechariah ben Yehoyada was murdered in the Temple Courtyard. The aristocrats of Judah, who had been rebuked by Zechariah for treating King Yoash as a deity, slew Zechariah at the king's bidding. As Zechariah died, he said, "*May HASHEM witness and demand an account*" (see *Rashi* to *Gittin* 57b, from *II Chronicles* 24:20-23). Zechariah's blood lay seething on the floor of the Temple. No attempt to cover it with earth and to hide the shameful deed was successful (*Koheles Rabbah* 3:16).

19. [The offerings were recently slaughtered and their blood is still warm.] They did not reveal the truth because they did not want to give Nebuzaradan any excuse for further acts of bloodshed (see the continuation of the Gemara).

20. [Let us slaughter an animal and see whether its blood seethes as does this blood.]

21. Literally: reveal to me.

22. That is, I will avenge his murder. [Zechariah had called for his murder to be avenged (see note 18), and his call had not yet been heeded.]

23. Literally: blossoms of the priesthood. This refers to youths, whose beards have just begun לִפְרֹחַ, *to blossom* (*Rav* to *Yoma* 1:7).

24. 940,000.

25. [Nebuzaradan spoke of himself in the third person, not wishing to incriminate himself directly. It is not proper to speak of oneself being cursed.]

ומי סליק נבוכד נצר לירושלים והכתיב
א) ויעלו אותו אל מלך בבל רבלתה ואמר ר'
אבהו זו אנטוכיא רב חסדא ורב יצחק בר
אבודימי חד אמר דמות דיוקנו היתה חקוקה
לו על מרכבתו וחד אמר אימה יתירה
היתה לו ממנו ודומה כמי שעומד לפניו
אמר רבא טעין [א] תלת מאה כודנייתא נרגא
דפרזלא דשליט בפרזלא שדר ליה נבוכד נצר
לנבוזראדן כולהו בלעתינהו חד דשא
דירושלם שנאמר ב) פתוחיה יחד בכשיל
וכילפות יהלומון בעי למיהדר אמר מסתפינא
דלא ליעבדו בי כי היכי דעבדו בסנחריב
נפקא קלא ואמר שוור בר שוור נבוזר אדן
שוור דמטא זימנא דמקדשא חריב והיכלא
מיקלי פש ליה חד נרגא אתא מחייה בקופא
ואיפתח שנאמר ג) יודע כמביא למעלה בסבך
עץ קרדומות הוה קטיל ואזל עד דמטא
להיכלא אדליק ביה נורא גבה היכלא דרכו
ביה מן שמיא שנאמר ד) גת דרך ה' לבתולת
בת יהודה קא זיחא דעתיה נפקא בת קלא
ואמרה ליה עמא קטילא קטלת היכלא קליא
קלית קימחא טחינא טחינת שנאמר ה) קחי
רחים וטחני קמח גלי צמתך חשפי שובל
גלי שוק עברי נהרות חטים לא נאמר אלא
קמח [ב] חזא דמיה דזכריה דהוה קא רתח אמר
להו מאי האי אמרו ליה דם זבחים הוא
דאישתפיך אמר להו אייתי ואנסי אי מדמו
כסי ולא אידמו אמר להו גלו לי ואי לא
סריקנא לכו לבשרייכו במסריקא דפרזלא
אמרו ליה האי כהן ונביא הוא דאינבי להו
לישראל בחורבנא דירושלם וקטלוהו אמר
להו אנא מפייסנא ליה אייתי רבנן קטיל
עילויה ולא נח אייתי דרדקי דבי רב קטיל
עילויה ולא נח אייתי פרחי כהונה קטיל
עילויה ולא נח עד די קטל עילויה תשעין
וארבעה ריבוא ולא נח קרב לגביה אמר
זכריה זכריה טובים שבהן איבדתים ניחא
לך דאיקטלינהו לכולהו מיד נח הרהר תשובה בדעתיה אמר מה הם שלא איבדו אלא נפש אחת כך
ההוא גברא מה תיהוי עליה ערק שדר פורטיתא לביתיה ואיתגייר תנו רבנן [ג] נעמן גר תושב היה נבוזר אדן
גר צדק היה מבני בניו של סיסרא למדו תורה בירושלים מבני בניו של סנחריב לימדו תורה ברבים ומאן
נינהו שמעיה ואבטליון מבני בניו של המן למדו תורה בבני ברק ואף מבני בניו של אותו רשע ביקש
הקב"ה להכניסן תחת כנפי השכינה אמרו מלאכי השרת לפני הקב"ה רבונו של עולם מי שהחריב את
ביתך ושרף את היכלך תכנים תחת כנפי השכינה היינו דכתיב ו) רפינו [ד] את בבל ולא נרפתה עולא אמר זה
נבוכד נצר רבי שמואל בר נחמני אמר אלו נהרות בבל ותרגמה דציניתא ([ה] צרידתא) דבבלאי אמר עולא
° עמון ומואב שיבבי בישי דירושלם הוו כיון דשמעינהו לנביאי דקא מיתנבאי לחורבנא דירושלם שלחו
לנבוכד נצר פוק ותא אמר מסתפינא דלא ליעבדו לי כדעבדו בקמאי שלחו ליה ז) כי אין האיש בביתו
[א] הלך בדרך מרחוק [ו] ואין איש אלא הקדוש ברוך הוא שנאמר ח) ה' איש מלחמה שלח להו בקריבא
הוא ואתי שלחו ליה הלך בדרך מרחוק שלח להו אית להו צדיקי דבעו רחמי ומייתו ליה שלחו ליה
ט) צרור הכסף לקח בידו ואין כסף אלא צדיקים שנאמר י) ואכרה לי בחמשה עשר כסף וחומר שעורים ולתך
שעורים שלח להו הדרי רשיעי בתשובה ובעו רחמי ומייתו ליה שלחו ליה כבר קבע להן זמן שנאמר
ט) ליום הכסא יבא (ל)ביתו אין כסא אלא זמן שנאמר כ) בכסה ליום חגנו שלח להו סיתווא הוא ולא מצינא
דאתי מתלגא וממיטרא שלחו ליה תא אשינא דטורא שנאמר ל) שלחו כר מושל ארץ מסלע מדברה
אל הר בת ציון שלח להו אי אתינא לית לי דוכתא דיתיבנא ביה שלחו ליה קברות שלהם מעולין
מפלטירין שלך דכתיב מ) בעת ההיא נאום ה' יוציאו את עצמות מלכי יהודה ואת עצמות שריו ואת עצמות
הכהנים ואת עצמות הנביאים ואת עצמות יושבי ירושלים מקבריהם ושטחום לשמש ולירח ולכל צבא
השמים אשר אהבום ואשר עבדום ואשר הלכו אחריהם אמר ליה רב נחמן לרבי יצחק מי שמיע לך אימת
אתי בר נפלי אמר ליה מאן בר נפלי א"ל משיח משיח בר נפלי קרית ליה א"ל אין דכתיב נ) ביום ההוא אקים
את

רש"י

ומי סליק כו' והא כתיב. בההיא פרשתא ויעלו לצדקיה אל המלך רבלתה אלמא ברבלה הוה: זו אנטוכיא. ואנטוכיא קיימא לן [ז] דאינה מארץ ישראל: דמות דיוקנו. של נבוכד נצר: חקוקה לו על מרכבתו. של נבוזר אדן ודומה לו כמו שעומד לפניו ולכך כתיב בא נבוכד נצר והיינו כבוד: טעין תלת מאה כודניית'. משאוי שלש מאות פרדות: נרגא דפרזלא. פטישי ברזל: דשליט' בפרזלא. ברזל חדוד הקוצץ ברזל אחר: בלעתינהו. לא בליעה ממש אלא שיברם שהיו מתפוצצין הפטישים בהכותם בשער לשברה: פתוחיה יחד. משמע על פתח אחד הלמו כל הכשילים וכילפות יחד ולא הועיל כלום: שוור בר שוור. דולג בר דולג קום וכבש ירושלים לנבוזר אדן קאמר ל"א שוור בר שוור מדלג בר מדלג קפלת פעם אחת עם סנחריב ועכשיו פעם שניה: בקופא. מגב הפטיש ולא מחודו כמו קופא דמחטא (ב"מ דף לח:): יודע כמביא למעלה. תפלה היא יודע לפניך אותו סבך עץ קרדומות ששבר בו את ירושלים כאילו הביאו למעלה בכסא הכבוד: גבה היכלא. ובקש לעלות לרקיע: דרכו ביה מן שמיא. והשפילוהו: זחה דעתיה. מתגאה על שהיה מצליח: עמא קטילא. שכבר נגזר עליהם על כך: וטחני קמח. וטחני חטים לא נאמר אלא קמח שאין צריך טחינה: צמתך. מקום שהקלעים צומתין בצד הראש: שובל. קלע הראש שדומין לשבלים: גלי שוק עברי נהרות. פורענות זה היה הקב"ה אומר לישראל לכו וטחנו קמח כלומר טחונים אתם כבר לקמח ותחזרו ותטחן עדיין תגלי קלעי ראשיכם ושוקיכם ותלכו בגלות: אייתו לי ואינסי. ואנסה אם דם זבחים הוא: כסי ולא אידמי. שחט בהמות ולא אידמי הדם: פרטתא. שטר צוואה: ואיתגייר. נבוזראדן: גר תושב. שלא קבל עליו שאר מצות וקבל עליו שלא לעבוד עבודת כוכבים: של אותו רשע. נבוכד נצר: רפינו ולא נרפתה. שהיה הקב"ה מבקש לרפאותו להכניס מבני בניו תחת כנפי השכינה: אלו נהרות בבל. שהם רעים לשתות: צנייתא דבבל. דקלים מרים הם שעומדים בנהרות ל"א ציונייתא דבבל דקלים רעים של נהרות בבל שאין נושאים פירות לפי שהמים רעים הן לגדל פירות בסוטה (דף מו:) אמרי' קוסטא הוא דאמריתו הני צנייתא דבבל מששת ימי בראשית איתנהו ונהר שתחת הני ציונייתא מי מרים נינהו: שיבבי. שכנים: פוק תא. צא ממקומך ובא אל ארץ ישראל ותכבשנה: כי אין האיש. מקרא הוא במשלי: בקריבא הוא. בקרוב הוא ויבא בעת דוחקם לפי דרכו של מקרא זה שהם שלחו לו שומעים אנו שהוא אכל מילתא דהוה אמרי ליה הוה משיב דבר זה: צרור הכסף לקח בידו. צדיקים שבהן מתו: ואכרה לי בחמשה עשר כסף. פדיתי אותה במצרים בט"ו בניסן: כסף וחומר שעורים ולתך שעורים. בזכות צדיקים שנקראו כסף חומר שעורים שלשים סאין ולתך חמשה עשר סאין אלו ארבעים וחמשה צדיקים שהעולם מתקיים עליהם ° בחולין פרק גיד הנשה (דף צב.) פעמים ששלשים כאן וט"ו בארץ ישראל ופעמים שט"ו כאן ושלשים בארץ ישראל ובמסכת חולין היכא דקא מפרש האי קרא בצדיקיא אמרי אין כסף אלא צדיקים וכן הוא אומר צרור הכסף לקח בידו: כבר קבע להם זמן. שלא יבא עד ע' שנה שתשלים גלות בבל: מתלגא וממטרא. מחמת שלגים ומטרים: תא אשינא דטורי. בא דרך תחתית ההרים וההרים יגינו עליך מן השלגים ומן המטרים: שלחו כר מושל ארץ. שלחו שליח אל נבוכד נצר שהיה מושל ארץ שיבא אל הר בת ציון דרך הסלעים וההרים: לית לי דוכתא. לא יהיה לי מקום סביב לירושלים שנוכל אני וחיילי לישב במקום מכוסה מפני הגשמים: קבריהם של ישראל. מערות שלהן סביב לירושלים ובהן אתה וחיילותיך יכולין לישב: יוציאו את עצמות מלכי יהודה. שעתידים להשליך מן הקברים העצמות שבקברים שנאמר בעת ההיא וגו': אימת אתי בר נפלי. איידי דאמרינן צרור הכסף לקח בידו שנתמעטו הצדיקים קא מיירי הא נמי במשיח וקאמ' תלמידים מתמעטין ואיידי דאמרי' ותהי האמת נעדרת אייתי הא דההוא אתרא דשמיה קוסטא:

הגהות הגר"א

[א] גמ' הלך בדרך מרחוק. נמחק:

גליון הש"ס

גמ' עמון ומואב כו'. עי' בר"ש פ"ד מ"ד דידים: רש"י ד"ה כסף וכו'. וכעין זה לעיל לג ע"א ובברכות דף כו ע"א:

ליקוטי רש"י

רבלתה. והיא רבלה ארץ חמת היא אנטוכיא שם נשפט לצדקיהו ביד נבוכדנצר כמו שנא' בספר (מ"ב כה) שם שחט את בניו שם נקר את עיניו והיא סוף הגבול שנא' במרגלים ובכמה מקומות עד לבא חמת (במדבר יג) [יחזקאל יא, י]. תלת מאה. לאו דוקא וכן כל שלש מאות שבש"ס [רשב"ם פסחים קיט.]. בכשיל וכילפות. כלי משחית של נגרים הם ובקרדומות בלא לה תרגום יונתן בכשילא כילפות לשון ערבי הוא כך פירש דונש והוא מכלי הנגרים. יהלומון. הלויים [תהלים עד, ו]. יודע כמביא למעלה בסבך עץ קרדומות. יודע האויב כשהיה מכה בשערי פתחי המקדש שהוא כמביא מכותיו למעלה ברקיע ומנין היה יודע שהרי היה רואה שהיה העץ מסבך ואוחז את הקרדומות ובולען כמו שאמרו רבותינו כולהו בלעתינהו חד תרעא דירושלים בסבך עץ קרדומות לשון נאחז בסבך (בראשית כב) העץ סובך אותם והם נסבכין בו [שם, ה ועי' במהרש"א בח"א]. וטחני קמח. לבא לדרך גלותך. גלי צמתך. זרועיך ושוקיך דברים המלוטות וקשור ומכוסה. חשפי שובל. גלי השבילים מן המים שעליהם כי דרך שם תלאי בגולה או גלי שוקך ועברי נהרות [ישעיה מז, ב]. דמיה דזכריה. בן יהוידע הכהן שהרגוהו שרי יהודה במצות יואש כשהשתחוו לו ליואש ועשאוהו אלוה והרגוהו בעזרה (דה"ב כד). שדר פורטיתא. שטר צוואה שפרט מה תהא על נכסיו. גר תושב היה. שלא קיבל עליו שאר מצות אלא ע"ז שנאמר כי לא יעשה עוד עבדך וגו' (מ"ב ה) [גיטין נז:]. דציניתא דבבלאי. בי ציניתא דבבל מקום הוא ובו דקלים הרבה כמו ציני הר הברזל (סוכה כט:) [סוטה מו: ועי' ברש"י כאן]. פוק ותא. אחריבהו. מסתפינא. מאלהיהון [חולין צב.]. כי אין האיש בביתו. ראיתם שסילק הקב"ה שכינתו וכל טוב נתן לעו"ג [משלי ז, יט]. צרור הכסף. הטובים שבהם הרג [שם, כ]. לצדיקים שבהם המיתם. ואכרה לי. הקב"ה אומר קניתי לי ישראל בט"ו בניסן בשביל הצדיקים [חולין שם]. ל' סחורה ברגניי"א בלע"ז כמו (בראשית נ) אשר כריתי לי ובכרכי הים קורין למכירה כירה [הושע ג, ב]. ליום הכסא. לזמן המועד הקבוע וכן בכסה ליום חגנו (תהלי' פא) [משלי שם]. בכסה. יום מועד קבוע לכך וכן (משלי ז) ליום הכסא יבוא ביתו למועד הקבוע [תהלים פא, ד]. ושטחום לשמש. והכשדים ישכנו לגור על העיר בקברי השרים שהיו נאים כפלטין [ירמיה ח, ב]. ביום ההוא. אחרי בא עליהם כל אלה יבא יום ההוא המוכן לגאולה ובו אקים סוכת דוד הנופלת י"ת מלכותא דבית דוד [עמוס ט, יא].

מסורת הש"ס

א) [עי' פירוש רשב"ם פסחים קיט. ד"ה שלש מאות], ב) גיטין נז: ע"ש, ג) [שם ע"ש], ד) בקרא רפאנו, ה) [בע"י ליתא וכ"מ מפי' רש"י דלא גריס ליה], ו) [סוטה מב: מח. לעיל לג.], ז) [גיטין מד:].

תורה אור השלם

א) וַיִּתְפְּשׂוּ אֶת הַמֶּלֶךְ וַיַּעֲלוּ אֹתוֹ אֶל מֶלֶךְ בָּבֶל רִבְלָתָה וַיְדַבְּרוּ אִתּוֹ מִשְׁפָּט: [מלכים ב' כה, ו]

ב) וְעַתָּה פִּתּוּחֶיהָ יָּחַד בְּכַשִּׁיל וְכֵילַפֹּת יַהֲלֹמוּן: [תהלים עד, ו]

ג) יִוָּדַע כְּמֵבִיא לְמָעְלָה בִּסְבָךְ עֵץ קַרְדֻּמּוֹת: [תהלים עד, ה]

ד) סִלָּה כָל אַבִּירַי אֲדֹנָי בְּקִרְבִּי קָרָא עָלַי מוֹעֵד לִשְׁבֹּר בַּחוּרָי גַּת דָּרַךְ אֲדֹנָי לִבְתוּלַת בַּת יְהוּדָה: [איכה א, טו]

ה) קְחִי רֵחַיִם וְטַחֲנִי קָמַח גַּלִּי צַמָּתֵךְ חֶשְׂפִּי שֹׁבֶל גַּלִּי שׁוֹק עִבְרִי נְהָרוֹת: [ישעיה מז, ב]

ו) רִפִּאנוּ אֶת בָּבֶל וְלֹא נִרְפָּתָה עִזְבוּהָ וְנֵלֵךְ אִישׁ לְאַרְצוֹ כִּי נָגַע אֶל הַשָּׁמַיִם מִשְׁפָּטָהּ וְנִשָּׂא עַד שְׁחָקִים: [ירמיה נא, ט]

ז) כִּי אֵין הָאִישׁ בְּבֵיתוֹ הָלַךְ בְּדֶרֶךְ מֵרָחוֹק: [משלי ז, יט]

ח) יְיָ אִישׁ מִלְחָמָה יְיָ שְׁמוֹ: [שמות טו, ג]

ט) צְרוֹר הַכֶּסֶף לָקַח בְּיָדוֹ לְיוֹם הַכֶּסֶא יָבֹא בֵיתוֹ: [משלי ז, כ]

י) וָאֶכְּרֶהָ לִּי בַּחֲמִשָּׁה עָשָׂר כָּסֶף וְחֹמֶר שְׂעֹרִים וְלֶתֶךְ שְׂעֹרִים: [הושע ג, ב]

כ) תִּקְעוּ בַחֹדֶשׁ שׁוֹפָר בַּכֶּסֶה לְיוֹם חַגֵּנוּ: [תהלים פא, ד]

ל) שִׁלְחוּ כַר מֹשֵׁל אֶרֶץ מִסֶּלַע מִדְבָּרָה אֶל הַר בַּת צִיּוֹן: [ישעיה טז, א]

מ) בָּעֵת הַהִיא נְאֻם יְיָ יוֹצִיאוּ אֶת עַצְמוֹת מַלְכֵי יְהוּדָה וְאֶת עַצְמוֹת שָׂרָיו וְאֶת עַצְמוֹת הַכֹּהֲנִים וְאֵת עַצְמוֹת הַנְּבִיאִים וְאֵת עַצְמוֹת יוֹשְׁבֵי יְרוּשָׁלָיִם מִקִּבְרֵיהֶם: וּשְׁטָחוּם לַשֶּׁמֶשׁ וְלַיָּרֵחַ וּלְכֹל צְבָא הַשָּׁמַיִם אֲשֶׁר אֲהֵבוּם וַאֲשֶׁר עֲבָדוּם וַאֲשֶׁר הָלְכוּ אַחֲרֵיהֶם וַאֲשֶׁר דְּרָשׁוּם וַאֲשֶׁר הִשְׁתַּחֲווּ לָהֶם לֹא יֵאָסְפוּ וְלֹא יִקָּבֵרוּ לְדֹמֶן עַל פְּנֵי הָאֲדָמָה יִהְיוּ: [ירמיה ח, א-ב]

נ) בַּיּוֹם הַהוּא אָקִים אֶת סֻכַּת דָּוִיד הַנֹּפֶלֶת וְגָדַרְתִּי אֶת פִּרְצֵיהֶן וַהֲרִסֹתָיו אָקִים וּבְנִיתִיהָ כִּימֵי עוֹלָם: [עמוס ט, יא]

– NAAMAN WAS A RESIDENT CONVERT.[26] נְבוּזַרְאֲדָן גֵּר צֶדֶק הָיָה – NEBUZARADAN WAS A RIGHTEOUS CONVERT.[27] מִבְּנֵי בָנָיו שֶׁל סִיסְרָא לָמְדוּ תּוֹרָה בִּירוּשָׁלַיִם – DESCENDANTS OF SISERA[28] LEARNED TORAH IN JERUSALEM.[29] מִבְּנֵי בָנָיו שֶׁל סַנְחֵרִיב לִימְּדוּ תּוֹרָה בָּרַבִּים – DESCENDANTS OF SANCHEIRIV TAUGHT TORAH IN PUBLIC.

The Gemara identifies these descendants of Sancheiriv:

וּמַאן נִינְהוּ – **And who were they?** שְׁמַעְיָה וְאַבְטַלְיוֹן – **Shemayah and Avtalyon.**[30]

The Baraisa continues:

מִבְּנֵי בָנָיו שֶׁל הָמָן לָמְדוּ תּוֹרָה בִּבְנֵי בְרַק – DESCENDANTS OF HAMAN[31] TAUGHT TORAH IN BNEI BRAK.[32] וְאַף מִבְּנֵי בָנָיו שֶׁל אוֹתוֹ רָשָׁע – AND there were EVEN DESCENDANTS OF THAT WICKED MAN [Nebuchadnezzar] בִּיקֵּשׁ הַקָּדוֹשׁ בָּרוּךְ הוּא לְהַכְנִיסָן תַּחַת כַּנְפֵי הַשְּׁכִינָה – [WHOM] THE HOLY ONE, BLESSED IS HE, SOUGHT TO BRING UNDER THE WINGS OF THE DIVINE PRESENCE.[33] אָמְרוּ מַלְאֲכֵי הַשָּׁרֵת לִפְנֵי הַקָּדוֹשׁ בָּרוּךְ הוּא – THE MINISTERING ANGELS SAID BEFORE THE HOLY ONE, BLESSED IS HE: רִבּוֹנוֹ שֶׁל עוֹלָם – "MASTER OF THE UNIVERSE! מִי שֶׁהֶחֱרִיב אֶת בֵּיתְךָ – THE ONE WHO DESTROYED YOUR HOUSE וְשָׂרַף אֶת הֵיכָלְךָ – AND BURNED YOUR SANCTUARY, תַּכְנִיס תַּחַת כַּנְפֵי הַשְּׁכִינָה – WILL YOU BRING HIM UNDER THE WINGS OF THE DIVINE PRESENCE?!"[34]

The Gemara provides a Scriptural allusion:

הַיְינוּ דִּכְתִיב ,,רִפִּאנוּ אֶת־בָּבֶל וְלֹא נִרְפָּתָה" – **This is** alluded to by **that which is written:**[35] *We would have healed Babylonia, but she is not healed.* עוּלָּא אָמַר – **Ulla said:** זֶה נְבוּכַדְנֶצַּר – **This is** a reference to **Nebuchadnezzar,** who would have been "cured" through the conversion of his descendants, but they did not convert.

A different interpretation of this verse:

רַבִּי שְׁמוּאֵל בַּר נַחְמָנִי אָמַר – **R' Shmuel bar Nachmani says:** אֵלּוּ נַהֲרוֹת בָּבֶל – **This is** a reference to **the rivers of Babylonia.** וְתַרְגְּמָה דְּצִינְיָיתָא (צרידתא) דְּבַבְלָאֵי – **And he explained it as** referring specifically to **the palms** that grow by the rivers **of the Babylonians.**[36]

The Gemara relates how Nebuchadnezzar was persuaded to attack Jerusalem:

אָמַר עוּלָּא – **Ulla said:** עַמּוֹן וּמוֹאָב שִׁיבְבֵי בִּישֵׁי דִּירוּשָׁלַם הֲווּ – **Ammon and Moab were evil neighbors of Jerusalem.** כֵּיוָן דִּשְׁמַעִינְהוּ לִנְבִיאֵי דְּקָא מִיתְנַבְּאֵי לְחוּרְבָּנָא דִּירוּשָׁלַם – **When they heard** the **prophets** of Israel **prophesying the destruction of Jerusalem,** שַׁלְחוּ לִנְבוּכַדְנֶצַּר – **they sent** the following message **to Nebuchadnezzar:** פּוּק וְתָא – "**Leave** Babylonia **and come** to Eretz Yisrael and conquer it." אָמַר – **[Nebuchadnezzar] replied:** מִסְתְּפִינָא דְּלָא לִיעַבְדוּ לִי כִּדְעָבְדוּ בְּקַמָּאֵי – "**I am afraid lest they do to me what they did to those who came before** me."[37] שַׁלְחוּ לֵיהּ – **They sent him** the following reply: ,,כִּי אֵין הָאִישׁ בְּבֵיתוֹ[38] (הלך בדרך מרחוק)" – "*For the Man is not*

NOTES

26. Naaman, the chief general of Aram, was cured of *tzaraas* by the prophet Elisha. Convinced that the God of Elisha was the true God, Naaman vowed to refrain from idolatry (*II Kings* 5:1-19). But he did not accept upon himself any of the other mitzvos (*Rashi* here and to *Gittin* 57b; *Yad Ramah* here).

The Gemara in *Avodah Zarah* (64b) cites three Tannaic views as to the definition of a גֵּר תּוֹשָׁב, *resident convert*: (a) a gentile who has accepted upon himself to refrain from idolatry; (b) a gentile who has accepted upon himself to observe the seven Noahide laws; (c) a gentile who has accepted upon himself to observe all the Torah's commandments except for the prohibition against eating prohibited foods. [From *Rashi* here it seems that our Baraisa follows the first view (see preceding paragraph); see, however, *Margaliyos HaYam*.]

Such an individual is called a *resident* convert because he is permitted to reside together with the Jewish people in Eretz Yisrael (*Rambam, Hil. Issurei Biah* 14:7; see *Hil. Avodah Zarah* 10:6).

27. I.e. a full convert, as opposed to a resident convert.

28. Sisera was the general of the army of Yavin, king of Canaan. During the "era of the Judges," Sisera oppressed the Jews severely for twenty years. He was eventually defeated by the Jews under the leadership of Barak and Devorah (see *Judges* chs. 4,5).

29. This refers to R' Akiva (see *Margaliyos HaYam*).

30. Shemayah and Avtalyon were two of the greatest sages of the early Tannaic era. They are mentioned in *Pirkei Avos* (1:10) as links in the chain of Torah transmission from Sinai (see *Margaliyos HaYam*).

31. Haman sought the genocide of the entire Jewish people, as related in the Book of *Esther*.

32. This refers to Rav Shmuel bar Shilas (*Ein Yaakov*; see *Yad David*).

The Gemara identifies only the Torah scholars descended from Sancheiriv (namely, Shemayah and Avtalyon), and not those descended from Sisera and Haman. Since Shemayah and Avtalyon openly admitted that they were converts (*Yoma* 71b), there was no reason to hide their ancestry (*Emes LeYaakov*).

33. I.e. some descendants of Nebuchadnezzar thought of converting to Judaism and God wished to give them the opportunity to do so (*Maharsha*; see next note for a different explanation).

34. I.e. Nebuchadnezzar's descendants should not be granted the opportunity to convert because their evil progenitor did not deserve to have progeny that would be part of the Jewish people (*Maharsha*).

[This is puzzling. Why should the wickedness of a grandfather play any role at all in determining whether the righteous inclinations of his grandchildren should be allowed to flower into full conversion? Perhaps the answer is that were they to convert, some merit would accrue to their progenitors. Since Nebuchadnezzar was undeserving of such merit, the angels beseeched God to arrange events in such a way that his descendants would never convert. In the end they did not.]

Maharal, however, explains this Gemara differently. In his view, it was God Himself who sought to bring the descendants of these evildoers to Judaism [בִּיקֵּשׁ הקב״ה לְהַכְנִיסָן וכו׳]. The wicked people listed here were all possessed of extraordinary talents bestowed upon them by Heaven, and it was God's desire that these talents be used to accomplish great things. Though these wicked people corrupted their extraordinary talents in the pursuit of evil ends, it was fitting before God that after the evildoers had been destroyed, those of their progeny who were untainted by the evil should find a way of joining the Jewish people. In this manner, the original blessing of talent would find an outlet for good. In the case of the others, this goal was realized. In the case of Nebuchadnezzar, however, this was not possible. [By destroying the Temple, Nebuchadnezzar had corrupted his potential for good beyond redemption, as the angels argued before God.]

The Gemara, of course, does not mean that God was unaware of this or that He changed His mind. It uses this metaphor to teach that God found nothing worth preserving in Nebuchadnezzar.

35. *Jeremiah* 51:9.

36. The water of the rivers in Babylonia is bad to drink. [As a result,] the dates on the palms growing by these rivers taste bitter. Alternatively, the rivers are not fertile and thus the palms growing at their side are barren (*Rashi*).

According to this interpretation of the verse, the prophet Jeremiah is cursing Babylon by stating that all efforts to purify her putrid waters will fail.

These bitter rivers of Babylonia are referred to in the verse (*Psalms* 137:1): עַל־נַהֲרוֹת בָּבֶל שָׁם יָשַׁבְנוּ גַּם־בָּכִינוּ בְּזָכְרֵנוּ אֶת־צִיּוֹן, *By the rivers of Babylonia – there we sat and also wept when we remembered* [the sweet waters of] *Zion* (*Maharsha*).

Otzar HaGeonim records a text that reads צִירִיתָא – the name of a certain river in Babylonia.

37. Nebuchadnezzar was reluctant to attack the Jews because he had witnessed the miracles God performed on their behalf against Sancheiriv (*Maharsha*).

38. *Gra* deletes the parenthesized words. [It is evident from the continuation of the narrative that these words belong below, rather than here (see *Sanhedrei Ketanah*).]

ומי סליק נבוכד נצר לירושלים והכתיב א) ויעלו אותו אל מלך בבל רבלתה ואמר ר' אבהו זו אנטוכיא רב חסדא ורב יצחק בר אבודימי חד אמר דמות דיוקנו היתה חקוקה לו על מרכבתו וחד אמר אימה יתירה היתה לו ממנו ודומה כמי שעומד לפניו אמר רבא טעין א) תלת מאה כודנייתא נרגא דפרזלא דשליט בפרזלא שדר ליה נבוכד נצר לנבוזראדן כולהו בלעתינהו חד דשא דירושלם שנאמר ב) פתוחיה יחד בכשיל וכילפות יהלומון בעי למיהדר אמר מסתפינא דלא ליעבדו בי כי היכי דעבדו בסנחריב נפקא קלא ואמר שוור בר שוור נבוזר אדן שוור דמטא זימנא דמקדשא חריב והיכלא מיקלי פש ליה חד נרגא אתא מחייה בקופא ואיפתח שנאמר ג) יודע כמביא למעלה בסבך עץ קרדומות הוה קטיל ואזל עד דמטא להיכלא אדליק ביה נורא גבה היכלא דרכו ביה מן שמיא שנאמר ד) גת דרך ה' לבתולת בת יהודה קא זיחא דעתיה נפקא בת קלא ואמרה ליה עמא קטילא קטלת היכלא קליא קלית קימחא טחינא טחינת שנאמר ה) קחי רחים וטחני קמח גלי צמתך חשפי שובל גלי שוק עברי נהרות חטים לא נאמר אלא קמח ב) חזא דמיה דזכריה דהוה קא רתח אמר להו מאי האי אמרו ליה דם זבחים הוא דאישתפיך אמר להו אייתי ואנסי אי מדמו כסי ולא אידמו אמר להו גלו לי ואי לא סריקנא לכו לבשרייכו במסריקא דפרזלא אמרו ליה האי כהן ונביא הוא דאינבי להו לישראל בחורבנא דירושלם וקטלוהו אמר להו אנא מפייסנא ליה אייתי רבנן קטיל עילויה ולא נח אייתי דרדקי דבי רב קטיל עילויה ולא נח אייתי פרחי כהונה קטיל עילויה ולא נח עד די קטל עילויה תשעין וארבעה ריבוא ולא נח קרב לגביה אמר זכריה זכריה טובים שבהן איבדתים ניחא לך דאיקטלינהו לכולהו מיד נח הרהר תשובה בדעתיה אמר מה הם שלא איבדו אלא נפש אחת כך ההוא גברא מה תיהוי עליה ערק שדר פורטיתא לביתיה ואיתגייר תנו רבנן ג) נעמן גר תושב היה נבוזר אדן גר צדק היה מבני בניו של סיסרא למדו תורה בירושלים מבני בניו של סנחריב לימדו תורה ברבים ומאן נינהו שמעיה ואבטליון מבני בניו של המן למדו תורה בבני ברק ואף מבני בניו של אותו רשע ביקש הקב"ה להכניסן תחת כנפי השכינה אמרו מלאכי השרת לפני הקב"ה רבונו של עולם מי שהחריב את ביתך ושרף את היכלך תכנים תחת כנפי השכינה היינו דכתיב ו) רפינו ד) את בבל ולא נרפתה עולא אמר זה נבוכד נצר רבי שמואל בר נחמני אמר אלו נהרות בבל ותרגמה דציניתא (ה) צרידתא) דבבלאי אמר עולא ו) עמון ומואב שיבבי בישי דירושלם הוו כיון דשמעינהו לנביאי דקא מיתנבאי לחורבנא דירושלם שלחו לנבוכד נצר פוק ותא אמר מסתפינא דלא ליעבדו לי כדעבדו בקמאי שלחו ליה ז) כי אין האיש בביתו [א] הלך בדרך מרחוק ו) ואין איש אלא הקדוש ברוך הוא שנאמר ח) ה' איש מלחמה שלח להו בקריבא הוא ואתי שלחו ליה הלך בדרך מרחוק שלח להו אית להו צדיקי דבעו רחמי ומייתו ליה שלחו ליה ט) צרור הכסף לקח בידו ואין כסף אלא צדיקים שנאמר י) ואכרה לי בחמשה עשר כסף וחומר שעורים ולתך שעורים שלח להו הדרי רשיעי בתשובה ובעו רחמי ומייתו ליה שלחו ליה כבר קבע להן זמן שנאמר ט) ליום הכסא יבא (ל)ביתו אין כסא אלא זמן שנאמר כ) בכסה ליום חגנו שלח להו סיתווא הוא ולא מצינא דאתי מתלגא וממיטרא שלחו ליה תא אשינא דטורא שנאמר ל) שלחו כר מושל ארץ מסלע מדברה אל הר בת ציון שלח להו אי אתינא לית לי דוכתא דיתיבנא ביה שלחו ליה קברות שלהם מעולין מפלטירין שלך דכתיב מ) בעת ההיא נאום ה' יוציאו את עצמות מלכי יהודה ואת עצמות שריו ואת עצמות הכהנים ואת עצמות הנביאים ואת עצמות יושבי ירושלים מקבריהם ושטחום לשמש ולירח ולכל צבא השמים אשר אהבום ואשר עבדום ואשר הלכו אחריהם אמר ליה רב נחמן לרבי יצחק מי שמיע לך אימת אתי בר נפלי אמר ליה מאן בר נפלי א"ל משיח בר נפלי א"ל אין דכתיב נ) ביום ההוא אקים את

ומי סליק כו' והא כתיב. בההיא פרשתא ויעלו לדקיה אל המלך רבלתה אלמא ברבלה הוה: זו אנטוכיא. ואנטוכיא קיימא לן דאינה מארץ ישראל: דמות דיוקנו. של נבוכד נצר: חקוקה לו על מרכבתו. של נבוזר אדן ודומה לו כמו שעומד לפניו ולכך כתיב בא נבוכד נצר והיינו כבוד: טעין תלת מאה כודניית'. משאוי שלש מאות פרדות: נרגא דפרזלא. פטישי ברזל: דשליט' בפרזלא. ברזל חדוד הקוצץ ברזל אחר: בלעתינהו. לא בליעה ממש אלא שיברם שהיו מתפוצצין הפטישים בהכותם בשער לשברה: פתוחיה יחד. משמע על פתח אחד הלמו כל הכשילים וכילפות יחד ולא הועיל כלום: שוור בר שוור. דולג בר דולג קום וכבש ירושלים לנבוזר אדן קאמר ל"א שוור בר שוור מדלג בר מדלג קפלת פעם אחת עם סנחריב ועכשיו פעם שניה: בקופא. מגב הפטיש ולא מחודו כמו קופא דמחטא (ב"מ דף לח:): יודע כמביא למעלה. תפלה היא יודע לפניך אותו סבך עץ קרדומות ששבר בו את ירושלים כאילו הביאו למעלה בכסא הכבוד: גבה היכלא. ובקש לעלות לרקיע: דרכו ביה מן שמיא. והשפילוהו: זחה דעתיה. מתגאה על שהיה מצליח: עמא קטילא. שכבר נגזר עליהם על כך: וטחני קמח. וטוחני חטים לא נאמר אלא קמח שאין צריך טחינה: צמתך. מקום שהקלעים צומתין בצד הראש: שובל. קלע הראש שדומין לשבלים: גלי שוק עברי נהרות. פורענות זה היה הקב"ה אומר לישראל לכו וטחנו קמח כלומר טחונים אתם כבר לקמח ותחזרו ותטחן עדיין תגלי קלעי ראשיכם ושוקיכם ותלכו בגלות: אייתו לי ואינסי. ואנסה אם דם זבחים הוא: כסי ולא אידמי. שחט בהמות ולא אידמי הדם: פרטתא. שטר צוואה: ואיתגייר. נבוזראדן: גר תושב. שלא קבל עליו שאר מצות וקבל עליו שלא לעבוד עבודת כוכבים: של אותו רשע. נבוכד נצר: רפינו ולא נרפתה. שהיה הקב"ה מבקש לרפאותו להכניס מבני בניו תחת כנפי השכינה: אלו נהרות בבל. שהם רעים לשתות: צנייתאדבבל. דקלים מרים הם שעומדים בנהרות ל"א ציניתא דבבל דקלים רעים של נהרות בבל שאין נושאים פירות לפי שהמים רעים הן לגדל פירות בסוטה (דף מו:) אמרי' קוסטא הוא דאמריתו הני צנייתא דבבל מששת ימי בראשית איתנהו ונהר שתחת הני ציניתא מי מרים נינהו: שיבבי. שכנים: פוק תא. צא ממקומך ובא אל ארץ ישראל ותכבשנה: כי אין האיש. מקרא הוא במשלי: בקריבא הוא. בקרוב הוא ויבא בעת דוחקם לפי דרכו של מקרא זה שהם שלחו לו שומעים אנו שהוא אבל מילתא דהוה אמרי ליה הוה משיב דבר זה: צרור הכסף לקח בידו. צדיקים שבהן מתו: ואכרה לי בחמשה עשר כסף. פדיתי אותה במצרים בט"ו בניסן: כסף וחומר שעורים ולתך שעורים. בזכות צדיקים שנקראו כסף חומר שעורים שלשים סאין ולתך חמשה עשר סאין אלו ארבעים וחמשה צדיקים שהעולם מתקיים עליהם בחולין פרק גיד הנשה (דף צב.) פעמים שלשים כאן וט"ו בארץ ישראל ופעמים שט"ו כאן ושלשים בארץ ישראל ובמסכת חולין היכא דקא מפרש האי קרא בצדיקיא אמרי אין כסף אלא צדיקים וכן הוא אומר צרור הכסף לקח בידו: כבר קבע להם זמן. שלא יבא עד ע' שנה שתשלים גלות בבל: מתלגאוממטרא. מחמת שלגים ומטרים: תא אשינא דטורי. בא דרך תחתית ההרים וההרים יגינו עליך מן השלגים ומן המטרים: שלחו כר מושל ארץ. שלחו שליח אל נבוכד נצר שהיה מושל ארץ שיבא אל הר בת ציון דרך הסלעים וההרים: לית לי דוכתא. לא יהיה לי מקום סביב לירושלים שנוכל אני וחיילי לישב במקום מכוסה מפני הגשמים: קבריהם של ישראל. מערות שלהן סביב לירושלים ובהן אתה וחיילותיך יכולין לישב: יוציאו את עצמות מלכי יהודה. שעתידים להשליך מן הקברים העצמות שבקברים שנאמר בעת ההיא וגו': אימת אתי בר נפלי. איידי דאמרינן צרור הכסף לקח בידו שנתמעטו הצדיקים קא מיירי הא נמי במשיח וקאמ' תלמידים מתמעטין ואיידי דאמרי' ותהי האמת נעדרת אייתי הא דההוא אתרא דשמיה קוסטא:

א) [עי' פירוש רשב"ם פסחים קיט. ד"ה שלש מאות], ב) גיטין נז: ע"ש, ג) [שם ע"ש], ד) בקרא רפאנו, ה) [בע"י ליתא וכ"מ מפי' רש"י דלא גריס ליה], ו) [סוטה מב: מח. לעיל לג.], ז) [גיטין מד:].

תורה אור השלם

א) וַיִּתְפְּשׂוּ אֶת הַמֶּלֶךְ וַיַּעֲלוּ אֹתוֹ אֶל מֶלֶךְ בָּבֶל רִבְלָתָה וַיְדַבְּרוּ אִתּוֹ מִשְׁפָּט: [מלכים ב' כה, ו]

ב) וְעַתָּה פִּתּוּחֶיהָ יָּחַד בְּכַשִּׁיל וְכֵילַפֹּת יַהֲלֹמוּן: [תהלים עד, ו]

ג) יִוָּדַע כְּמֵבִיא לְמָעְלָה בִּסְבָךְ עֵץ קַרְדֻּמּוֹת: [תהלים עד, ה]

ד) סִלָּה כָל אַבִּירַי אֲדֹנָי בְּקִרְבִּי קָרָא עָלַי מוֹעֵד לִשְׁבֹּר בַּחוּרָי גַּת דָּרַךְ אֲדֹנָי לִבְתוּלַת בַּת יְהוּדָה: [איכה א, טו]

ה) קְחִי רֵחַיִם וְטַחֲנִי קָמַח גַּלִּי צַמָּתֵךְ חֶשְׂפִּי שֹׁבֶל גַּלִּי שׁוֹק עִבְרִי נְהָרוֹת: [ישעיה מז, ב]

ו) רִפִּאנוּ אֶת בָּבֶל וְלֹא נִרְפָּתָה עִזְבוּהָ וְנֵלֵךְ אִישׁ לְאַרְצוֹ כִּי נָגַע אֶל הַשָּׁמַיִם מִשְׁפָּטָהּ וְנִשָּׂא עַד שְׁחָקִים: [ירמיה נא, ט]

ז) כִּי אֵין הָאִישׁ בְּבֵיתוֹ הָלַךְ בְּדֶרֶךְ מֵרָחוֹק: [משלי ז, יט]

ח) יְיָ אִישׁ מִלְחָמָה יְיָ שְׁמוֹ: [שמות טו, ג]

ט) צְרוֹר הַכֶּסֶף לָקַח בְּיָדוֹ לְיוֹם הַכֵּסֶא יָבֹא בֵיתוֹ: [משלי ז, כ]

י) וָאֶכְּרֶהָ לִּי בַּחֲמִשָּׁה עָשָׂר כָּסֶף וְחֹמֶר שְׂעֹרִים וְלֶתֶךְ שְׂעֹרִים: [הושע ג, ב]

כ) תִּקְעוּ בַחֹדֶשׁ שׁוֹפָר בַּכֶּסֶה לְיוֹם חַגֵּנוּ: [תהלים פא, ד]

ל) שִׁלְחוּ כַר מֹשֵׁל אֶרֶץ מִסֶּלַע מִדְבָּרָה אֶל הַר בַּת צִיּוֹן: [ישעיה טז, א]

מ) בָּעֵת הַהִיא נְאֻם יְיָ יוֹצִיאוּ אֶת עַצְמוֹת מַלְכֵי יְהוּדָה וְאֶת עַצְמוֹת שָׂרָיו וְאֶת עַצְמוֹת הַכֹּהֲנִים וְאֵת עַצְמוֹת הַנְּבִיאִים וְאֵת עַצְמוֹת יוֹשְׁבֵי יְרוּשָׁלִָם מִקִּבְרֵיהֶם: וּשְׁטָחוּם לַשֶּׁמֶשׁ וְלַיָּרֵחַ וּלְכֹל צְבָא הַשָּׁמַיִם אֲשֶׁר אֲהֵבוּם וַאֲשֶׁר עֲבָדוּם וַאֲשֶׁר הָלְכוּ אַחֲרֵיהֶם וַאֲשֶׁר דְּרָשׁוּם וַאֲשֶׁר הִשְׁתַּחֲווּ לָהֶם לֹא יֵאָסְפוּ וְלֹא יִקָּבֵרוּ לְדֹמֶן עַל פְּנֵי הָאֲדָמָה יִהְיוּ: [ירמיה ח, א-ב]

נ) בַּיּוֹם הַהוּא אָקִים אֶת סֻכַּת דָּוִיד הַנֹּפֶלֶת וְגָדַרְתִּי אֶת פִּרְצֵיהֶן וַהֲרִסֹתָיו אָקִים וּבְנִיתִיהָ כִּימֵי עוֹלָם: [עמוס ט, יא]

הגהות הגר"א

[א] גמ' הלך בדרך מרחוק. נמחק:

גליון הש"ס

גמ' עמון ומואב כו'. עי' ברש"ש פ"ד מ"ד דידים: רש"י ד"ה כסף וכו'. וכעין זה לעיל לג ע"א ובברכות דף כו ע"א:

ליקוטי רש"י

רבלתה. והיא רבלה ארץ חמת היא אנטוכיא שם נשפט צדקיהו ביד נבוכדנצר כמו שנא' בספר (מ"ב כה) שם שחט את בניו שם נקר את עיניו והיא סוף הגבול שנא' במרגלים וכמה מקומות עד לבא חמת (במדבר יג) [יחזקאל יא, י]. תלת מאה. לאו דוקא וכן כל שלש מאות שבש"ס [רשב"ם פסחים קיט.]. בכשיל וכילפות. כלי משחית של נגרים הם ובקרדומות בא לה תרגום יונתן בכשילא כילפות לשון ערבי הוא כך פירש דונש והוא מכלי הנגרים. יהלומון. הלמו אויבים [תהלים עד, ו]. יודע כמביא למעלה בסבך עץ קרדומות. יודע האויב כשהיה מכה בשערי פתחי המקדש שהוא כמביא מכותיו למעלה ברקיע ומנין היה יודע שהרי היה רואה שהיה העץ מסבך ואוחז את הקרדומות ובולען כמו שאמרו רבותינו כולהו בלעתינהו חד תרעא דירושלים בסבך עץ קרדומות לשון נאחז בסבך (בראשית כב) העץ סובך אותם והם נסבכין בו [שם, ה ועי' במהרש"א בח"א]. וטחני קמח. לצדה לדרך גלותך. גלי צמתך. זרועיך ושוקיך דברים המצומת וקשור ומכוסה. חשפי שובל. גלי השבילים מן המים שעליהם כי דרך שם תלאי בגולה או גלי שוקך ועברי נהרות [ישעיה מז, ב]. דמיה דזכריה. בן יהוידע הכהן שהרגוהו שרי יהודה במצות יואש כשהשתחוו לו ליואש ועשאוהו אלוה והרגוהו בעזרה (דה"ב כד). שדר פורטיתא. שטר צוואה שפרט מה תהא על נכסיו. גר תושב היה. שלא קיבל עליו שאר מצות אלא ע"ז שנאמר כי לא יעשה עוד עבדך וגו' (מ"ב ה) [גיטין נז:]. דציניתא דבבלאי. בי ציניתא דבבל מקום הוא ובו דקלים הרבה כמו ציני הר הברזל (סוכה כט:) [סוטה מו: ועי' ברש"י כאן]. פוק ותא. אחרדינהו. מסתפינא. מאלההון [חולין צב.]. כי אין האיש בביתו. ראיתם שסילק הקב"ה שכינתו וכל טוב נתן לעו"ג [משלי ז, יט]. צרור הכסף. הטובים שבהם הרג [שם, כ]. לצדיקים שבהם המיתם. ואכרה לי. הקב"ה אומר קניתי לי ישראל בט"ו בניסן בשביל הצדיקים [חולין שם]. ל' סחורה ברגניי"א בלע"ז כמו (בראשית נ) אשר כריתי לי ובכרכי הים קורין למכירה כירה [הושע ג, ב]. ליום הכסא. לזמן המועד הקבוע וכן בכסה ליום חגנו (תהלי' פא) [משלי שם]. בכסה. יום מועד קבוע לכך וכן (משלי ז) ליום הכסא יבוא ביתו למועד הקבוע [תהלים פא, ד]. ושטחום לשמש. והכשדים ישכנו לצור על העיר בקברי השרים שהיו נאים כפלטין [ירמיה ח, ב]. ביום ההוא. אחרי בא עליהם כל אלה יבא יום ההוא המוכן לגאולה ובו אקים סוכת דוד הנופלת י"ת מלכותא דבית דוד [עמוס ט, יא].

in His house,"[39] i.e. God has removed His presence from the Jews, and they are no longer under His protection.

The Gemara gives the basis for rendering the word "man" (*ish*) as God:

וְאֵין אִישׁ אֶלָּא הַקָּדוֹשׁ בָּרוּךְ הוּא – And the word **"man"** (*ish*) **is** interpreted here as meaning **nothing other than the Holy One, Blessed is He,** for it is used in this sense elsewhere, **שֶׁנֶּאֱמַר – as it is stated: ,,ה׳ אִישׁ מִלְחָמָה״ – *HASHEM is a Man (ish) of war.*** [40]

The dialogue continues:

שָׁלַח לְהוּ – [Nebuchadnezzar] sent the following message back **to them: בְּקְרִיבָא הוּא וְאָתֵי –** "Maybe **[God] is near, and He will come** to protect the Jews when they need Him."[41]

שָׁלְחוּ לֵיהּ – [Ammon and Moab] sent to him: ,,הָלַךְ בְּדֶרֶךְ מֵרָחוֹק״ – *"He has gone on a distant journey."*[42]

שָׁלַח לְהוּ – [Nebuchadnezzar] sent them the following reply: **אִית לְהוּ צַדִּיקֵי דְּבָעוּ רַחֲמֵי וּמַיְיתוּ לֵיהּ – "They have righteous people who will pray** to God **for mercy and bring Him** back."[43]

שָׁלְחוּ לֵיהּ – [Ammon and Moab] sent to him: ,,צְרוֹר־הַכֶּסֶף לָקַח בְּיָדוֹ״ – *"He has taken the bag of silver coins* (*kesef*) ***with Him,"***[44] i.e. God has taken the souls of the righteous people.[45]

The Gemara gives the basis for interpreting the term "silver coins" (*kesef*) as referring to the righteous:

וְאֵין כֶּסֶף אֶלָּא צַדִּיקִים – And the term **"silver coins"** (*kesef*) **is** interpreted here as meaning **nothing other than the righteous,** for it is used in this sense elsewhere, **שֶׁנֶּאֱמַר – as it is stated: ,,וָאֶכְּרֶהָ לִּי בַּחֲמִשָּׁה עָשָׂר כָּסֶף וְחֹמֶר שְׂעֹרִים וְלֶתֶךְ שְׂעֹרִים״ – *I acquired her for myself with fifteen silver coins (kesef), a* chomer *of barley, and a* lesech *of barley.*** [46]

The dialogue continues:

שָׁלַח לְהוּ – [Nebuchadnezzar] sent the following response **to [Ammon and Moab]: הָדְרֵי רַשִׁיעֵי בִּתְשׁוּבָה – "The wicked** among them **may repent, וּבָעוּ רַחֲמֵי וּמַיְיתוּ לֵיהּ – and** then **they will pray** to God **for mercy and bring Him** back to save them!"

שָׁלְחוּ לֵיהּ – [Ammon and Moab] sent to him: כְּבָר קָבַע לָהֶן זְמַן – "[God] has already set a time for them, before which He will not return,"[47] **שֶׁנֶּאֱמַר – as it is said: ,,לְיוֹם הַכֶּסֶא יָבֹא (לְ)בֵיתוֹ״ – *He will come to His house at the keseh*** (appointed time).[48]

The Gemara gives the basis for rendering *keseh* as appointed time:

אֵין כֶּסֶא אֶלָּא זְמַן – And *keseh* is interpreted here as **meaning nothing other than an** appointed **time,** for it is used in this sense elsewhere, **שֶׁנֶּאֱמַר – as it is stated:**[49] **,,בַּכֶּסֶ(א)[ה] לְיוֹם חַגֵּנוּ״ – *At the time appointed (keseh) for our festive day.***

The dialogue continues:

שָׁלַח לְהוּ – [Nebuchadnezzar] sent to them: סִיתְוָוא הוּא – "It is winter,[50] **וְלָא מָצֵינָא דְּאָתֵי מִתַּלְגָּא וּמִמִּיטְרָא – and I cannot come because of the snow and the rain."**

שָׁלְחוּ לֵיהּ – They sent to him: תָּא אַשִּׁינָּא דְּטוּרָא – "Come by way of **the cliffs of the mountains,"**[51] **שֶׁנֶּאֱמַר – as it is stated: ,,שִׁלְחוּ־כַר מֹשֵׁל אֶרֶץ מִסֶּלַע מִדְבָּרָה אֶל־הַר בַּת צִיּוֹן״ – *Send a messenger*** [*to*] ***the ruler of the world***[52] [*saying*:] ***"By way of the cliffs in the desert,*** [*go*] ***to the mountain of the daughter of Zion."***[53]

שָׁלַח לְהוּ – [Nebuchadnezzar] sent back **to them: אִי אָתֵינָא – "If I come, לֵית לִי דּוּכְתָּא דְּיָתֵיבְנָא בֵּיהּ – I will not have a place where I can stay."**[54]

שָׁלְחוּ לֵיהּ – They sent to him: קִבְרוֹת שֶׁלָּהֶם מְעוּלִּין מִפַּלְטֵירִין שֶׁלְּךָ – "Their graves are better than your palace! There are caves surrounding the city in which they bury their dead, and those caves can accommodate you and your army." **דִּכְתִיב –** It was predicted that the invading army would empty out the graves around Jerusalem, **as it is written:**[55] **,,בָּעֵת הַהִיא נְאֻם־ה׳ יוֹצִיאוּ**

NOTES

39. *Proverbs* 7:19. This chapter in *Proverbs* cautions a person not to fall prey to the seductive wiles of a "strange woman." [This is meant literally, or else it is a metaphor for heresy (see *Rashi* ibid. v. 10).] The "woman" seduces her victim, saying: ,,כִּי אֵין הָאִישׁ בְּבֵיתוֹ הָלַךְ בְּדֶרֶךְ מֵרָחוֹק, *For the man* [my husband] *is not in his house; he has gone on a distant journey* (ibid. v. 19). ,,צְרוֹר־הַכֶּסֶף לָקַח בְּיָדוֹ לְיוֹם הַכֶּסֶא יָבֹא בֵיתוֹ, *He has taken the bag of silver coins with him; he will come* [back] *to his house* [only] *on the appointed day* (ibid. v. 20).

The Gemara proceeds to interpret these verses as though they were spoken by Ammon and Moab to persuade Nebuchadnezzar to come and conquer Jerusalem. [Ammon and Moab did not use these actual words. They merely suggested to Nebuchadnezzar that he should come and they assured him that there was nothing for him to be afraid of. Thus, it was as if they had spoken these words (*Maharal*).]

Scripture frequently uses the metaphor of a husband and wife to describe the relationship between God and Israel (see, for example, note 46). It is on this basis that the Gemara interprets these verses as referring to God's abandonment of the Jewish people prior to the destruction of the Temple because of their sins (see *Maharsha*).

40. *Exodus* 15:3. Thus, the first verse, *The man is not in his house,* conveys that God is not present in his capacity as "Man of war" [i.e. the One Who fights Israel's wars] (*Maharsha*).

41. Perhaps the Jews have not sinned greatly. Although their God has left them, maybe He is still sufficiently close that He will return when they pray for His protection (*Eitz Yosef*). *Maharsha* cites the verse (*Psalms* 145:18): ,,קָרוֹב ה׳ לְכָל־קֹרְאָיו, *HASHEM is close to all who call upon Him*.

42. [See note 38.] They have sinned so greatly that their God has gone far away from them (*Eitz Yosef*). [That is, God will not protect them even when they beseech Him to do so.]

43. Even when God is "far away," he hears the prayers of the righteous (see *Eitz Yosef*).

44. See note 39.

45. The righteous Jews have died out (*Rashi*).

46. *Hosea* 3:2. In that chapter, God describes his relationship with Israel using the metaphor of a man married to an unfaithful wife. In this sense, the verse is interpreted to mean: *I acquired her for Myself on the fifteenth* [of Nissan, when I redeemed the Jewish people from Egypt in the merit of the righteous ones among them who are described as] *silver* (*Rashi*; see *Chullin* 92a; cf. *Yad Ramah*).

The continuation of the verse (*a chomer of barley and a lesech of barley*) also alludes to the righteous. A *chomer* (i.e. a *kor*) is 30 *se'ah,* and a *lesech* is 15 *se'ah*. There are 45 righteous people in whose merit the world is sustained (as signified by the mention of barley), and they are divided into two groups: one of 30 and one of 15. Sometimes 30 of them are in Babylonia and 15 are in Eretz Yisrael, and sometimes vice versa (*Rashi,* from *Chullin* 92a; see *Rashash,* cf. *Rashi* to the verse).

47. God has declared that He will not redeem the Jews until they have been in exile for seventy years [as stated in *Jeremiah* 29:10] (*Rashi*). Even the repentance of sinners will not cause God to return earlier than this preordained time (*Maharsha;* see *Iyun Yaakov*).

48. See note 39.

49. *Psalms* 81:4.

50. Nebuchadnezzar's army initiated the siege of Jerusalem on the tenth of the month of Teves (as stated in *II Kings* 25:1), which is at the height of winter (*Yad Ramah, Maharsha*).

51. That is, travel at the foot of the mountains, and the cliffs of the mountains will protect you from the snow and rain (*Rashi*, *Yad Ramah*). [*Rashi's* version of the text reads טוּרֵי, *mountains* (plural).]

52. Nebuchadnezzar ruled the entire world, as stated in *Megillah* 11a.

53. *Isaiah* 16:1. This is a homiletic interpretation. According to its plain meaning, the verse is addressed to the Moabites, reminding them that they used to pay tribute to Israel: *The ruler of the country* [Moab] *sent fat sheep from* [the city of] *Sela Midbarah to* [the ruler of Israel, who resides on] *the mountain of the daughter of Zion* (*Rashi* ad loc.; cf. *Maharsha*).

54. I will not have a place surrounding Jerusalem where I and my soldiers can stay and be protected from the rain (*Rashi*).

55. *Jeremiah* 8:1,2.

ומי סליק נבוכד נצר לירושלים והכתיב א) ויעלו אותו אל מלך בבל רבלתה ואמר ר' אבהו זו אנטוכיא רב חסדא ורב יצחק בר אבודימי חד אמר דמות דיוקנו היתה חקוקה לו על מרכבתו וחד אמר אימה יתירה היתה לו ממנו ודומה כמי שעומד לפניו אמר רבא טעין א) תלת מאה כודנייתא נרגא דפרזלא דשליט בפרזלא שדר ליה נבוכד נצר לנבוזראדן כולהו בלעתינהו חד דשא דירושלם שנאמר ב) פתוחיה יחד בכשיל וכילפות יהלומון בעי למיהדר אמר מסתפינא דלא ליעבדו בי כי היכי דעבדו בסנחריב נפקא קלא ואמר שוור בר שוור נבוזר אדן שוור דמטא זימנא דמקדשא חריב והיכלא מיקלי פש ליה חד נרגא אתא מחייה בקופא ואיפתח שנאמר ג) יודע כמביא למעלה בסבך עץ קרדומות הוה קטיל ואזל עד דמטא להיכלא אדליק ביה נורא גבה היכלא דרכו ביה מן שמיא שנאמר ד) גת דרך ה' לבתולת בת יהודה קא זיחא דעתיה נפקא בת קלא ואמרה ליה עמא קטילא קטלת היכלא קליא קלית קימחא טחינא טחינת שנאמר ה) קחי רחים וטחני קמח גלי צמתך חשפי שובל גלי שוק עברי נהרות חטים לא נאמר אלא קמח ב) חזא דמיה דזכריה דהוה קא רתח אמר להו מאי האי אמרו ליה דם זבחים הוא דאישתפיך אמר להו אייתי ואנסי אי מדמו כסי ולא אידמו אמר להו גלו לי ואי לא סריקנא לבו לבשרייכו במסריקא דפרזלא אמרו ליה האי כהן ונביא הוא דאינבי להו לישראל בחורבנא דירושלם וקטלוהו אמר להו אנא מפייסנא ליה אייתי רבנן קטיל עילויה ולא נח אייתי דרדקי דבי רב קטיל עילויה ולא נח אייתי פרחי כהונה קטיל עילויה ולא נח עד די קטל עילויה תשעין וארבעה ריבוא ולא נח קרב לגביה אמר זכריה זכריה טובים שבהן איבדתים ניחא לך דאיקטלינהו לכולהו מיד נח הרהר תשובה בדעתיה אמר מה הם שלא איבדו אלא נפש אחת כך ההוא גברא מה תיהוי עליה ערק שדר פורטיתא לביתיה ואיתגייר תנו רבנן ג) נעמן גר תושב היה נבוזר אדן גר צדק היה מבני בניו של סיסרא למדו תורה בירושלים מבני בניו של סנחריב לימדו תורה ברבים ומאן נינהו שמעיה ואבטליון מבני בניו של המן למדו תורה בבני ברק ואף מבני בניו של אותו רשע ביקש הקב"ה להכניסן תחת כנפי השכינה אמרו מלאכי השרת לפני הקב"ה רבונו של עולם מי שהחריב את ביתך ושרף את היכלך תכנים תחת כנפי השכינה היינו דכתיב ו) רפינו ד) את בבל ולא נרפתה עולא אמר זה נבוכד נצר רבי שמואל בר נחמני אמר אלו נהרות בבל ותרגמה דצינייתא (ה) צרידתא) דבבלאי אמר עולא °עמון ומואב שיבבי בישי דירושלם הוו כיון דשמעינהו לנביאי דקא מיתנבאי לחורבנא דירושלם שלחו לנבוכד נצר פוק ותא אמר מסתפינא דלא ליעבדו לי כדעבדו בקמאי שלחו ליה ז) כי אין האיש בביתו [א] הלך בדרך מרחוק ו) ואין איש אלא הקדוש ברוך הוא שנאמר ח) ה' איש מלחמה שלח להו בקריבא הוא ואתי שלחו ליה הלך בדרך מרחוק שלח להו אית להו צדיקי דבעו רחמי ומייתו ליה שלחו ליה ט) צרור הכסף לקח בידו ואין כסף אלא צדיקים שנאמר י) ואכרה לי בחמשה עשר כסף וחומר שעורים ולתך שעורים שלח להו הדרי רשיעי בתשובה ובעו רחמי ומייתו ליה שלחו ליה כבר קבע להן זמן שנאמר ט) ליום הכסא יבא (ל)ביתו אין כסא אלא זמן שנאמר כ) בכסה ליום חגנו שלח להו סיתווא הוא ולא מצינא דאתי מתלגא וממיטרא שלחו ליה תא אשינא דטורא שנאמר ל) שלחו כר מושל ארץ מסלע מדברה אל הר בת ציון שלח להו אי אתינא לית לי דוכתא דיתיבנא ביה שלחו ליה קברות שלהם מעולין מפלטירין שלך דכתיב מ) בעת ההיא נאום ה' יוציאו את עצמות מלכי יהודה ואת עצמות שריו ואת עצמות הכהנים ואת עצמות הנביאים ואת עצמות יושבי ירושלים מקבריהם ושטחום לשמש ולירח ולכל צבא השמים אשר אהבום ואשר עבדום ואשר הלכו אחריהם אמר ליה רב נחמן לרבי יצחק מי שמיע לך אימת אתי בר נפלי אמר ליה מאן בר נפלי א"ל משיח משיח בר נפלי קרית ליה א"ל אין דכתיב נ) ביום ההוא אקים את

רש"י

ומי סליק כו' והא כתיב. בההיא פרשתא ויעלו לדקיה אל המלך רבלתה אלמא ברבלה הוה: זו אנטוכיא. ואנטוכיא קיימא לן ז) דאינה מארץ ישראל: דמות דיוקנו. של נבוכד נצר: חקוקה לו על מרכבתו. של נבוזר אדן ודומה לו כמו שעומד לפניו ולכך כתיב בא נבוכד נצר והיינו כבוד: טעין תלת מאה כודניית'. משאוי שלש מאות פרדות: נרגא דפרזלא. פטישי ברזל: דשליט' בפרזלא. ברזל חדוד הקוצץ ברזל אחר: בלעתינהו. לא בליעה ממש אלא שיברם שהיו מתפוצצין הפטישים בהכותם בשער לשברה: פתוחיה יחד. משמע על פתח אחד הלמו כל הכשילים וכילפות יחד ולא הועיל כלום: שוור בר שוור. דולג בר דולג קום וכבש ירושלים לנבוזר אדן קאמר ל"א שוור בר שוור מדלג בר מדלג קפלת פעם אחת עם סנחריב ועכשיו פעם שניה: בקופא. מגב הפטיש ולא מחודו כמו קופא דמחטא (ב"מ דף לח:): יודע כמביא למעלה. תפלה היא יודע לפניך אותו סבך עץ קרדומות ששבר בו את ירושלים כאילו הביאו למעלה בכסא הכבוד: גבה היכלא. ובקש לעלות לרקיע: דרכו ביה מן שמיא. והשפילוהו: זחה דעתיה. מתגאה על שהיה מצליח: עמא קטילא. שכבר נגזר עליהם על כך: וטחני קמח. וטחני חטים לא נאמר אלא קמח שאין צריך טחינה: צמתך. מקום שהקלעים צומתין בצד הראש: שובל. קלע הראש שדומין לשבלים: גלי שוק עברי נהרות. פורענות זה היה הקב"ה אומר לישראל לכו וטחנו קמח כלומר טחונים אתם כבר לקמח ותחזרו ותטחן עדיין תגלי קלעי ראשיכם ושוקיכם ותלכו בגלות: אייתו לי ואינסי. ואנסה אם דם זבחים הוא: כסי ולא אידמי. שחט בהמות ולא אידמי הדם: פרטתא. שטר צוואה: ואיתגייר. נבוזראדן: גר תושב. שלא קבל עליו שאר מצות וקבל עליו שלא לעבוד עבודת כוכבים: של אותו רשע. נבוכד נצר: רפינו ולא נרפתה. שהיה הקב"ה מבקש לרפאותו להכניס מבני בניו תחת כנפי השכינה: אלו נהרות בבל. שהם רעים לשתות: צנייתא דבבל. דקלים מרים הם שעומדים בנהרות ל"א צינונייתא דבבל דקלים רעים של נהרות בבל שאין נושאים פירות לפי שהמים רעים הן לגדל פירות בסוטה (דף מו:) אמרי' קושטא הוא דאמריתו הני צנייתא דבבל מששת ימי בראשית איתנהו ונהר שתחת הני צינונייתא מי מרים נינהו: שיבבי. שכנים: פוק תא. צא ממקומך ובא אל ארץ ישראל ותכבשנה: כי אין האיש. מקרא הוא במשלי: בקריבא הוא. בקרוב הוא ויבא בעת דוחקם לפי דרכו של מקרא זה שהם שלחו לו שומעים אנו שהוא אכל מילתא דהוה אמרי ליה הוה משיב דבר זה: צרור הכסף לקח בידו. צדיקים שבהן מתו: ואכרה לי בחמשה עשר כסף. פדיתי אותה במצרים בט"ו בניסן: כסף וחומר שעורים ולתך שעורים. בזכות צדיקים שנקראו כסף חומר שעורים שלשים סאין ולתך חמשה עשר סאין אלו ארבעים וחמשה צדיקים שהעולם מתקיים עליהם ° בחולין פרק גיד הנשה (דף צב.) פעמים ששלשים כאן וט"ו בארץ ישראל ופעמים שט"ו כאן ושלשים בארץ ישראל ובמסכת חולין היכא דקא מפרש האי קרא בצדיקיא אמרי אין כסף אלא צדיקים וכן הוא אומר צרור הכסף לקח בידו: כבר קבע להם זמן. שלא יבא עד ע' שנה שתשלים גלות בבל: מתלגא וממטרא. מחמת שלגים ומטרים: תא אשינא דטורי. בא דרך תחתית ההרים וההרים יגינו עליך מן השלגים ומן המטרים: שלחו כר מושל ארץ. שלחו שליח אל נבוכד נצר שהיה מושל ארץ שיבא אל הר בת ציון דרך הסלעים וההרים: לית לי דוכתא. לא יהיה לי מקום סביב לירושלים שנוכל אני וחיילי לישב במקום מכוסה מפני הגשמים: קבריהם של ישראל. מערות שלהן סביב לירושלים ובהן אתה וחיילותיך יכולין לישב: יוציאו את עצמות מלכי יהודה. שעתידים להוליך מן הקברים העצמות שבקברים שנאמר בעת ההיא וגו': אימת אתי בר נפלי. איידי דאמרינן צרור הכסף לקח בידו שנתמעטו הצדיקים קא מיירי הא נמי במשיח וקאמ' תלמידים מתמעטין ואיידי דאמרי' ותהי האמת נעדרת אייתי הא דההוא אתרא דשמיה קושטא: את

הגהות הגר"א

[א] גמ' הלך בדרך מרחוק. נמחק:

גליון הש"ס

גמ' עמון ומואב כו'. עי' בר"ש פ"ד מ"ד דידים: רש"י ד"ה כסף וכו'. וכעין זה לעיל לג ע"א ובברכות דף כו ע"א:

ליקוטי רש"י

רבלתה. והיא רבלה ארץ חמת היא אנטוכיא שם נשפט צדקיהו ביד נבוכדנצר כמו שנא' בספר (מ"ב כה) שם שחט את בניו שם נקר את עיניו והיא סוף הגבול שנא' במרגלים ובכמה מקומות עד לבא חמת (במדבר יג) [יחזקאל יא, י]. תלת מאה. לאו דוקא וכן כל שלש מאות שבש"ס [רשב"ם פסחים קיט.]. בכשיל וכילפות. כלי משחית של נגרים הם וקרדומות באו לה תרגום יונתן בכשילא כילפות לשון ערבי הוא כך פירש דונש והוא מכלי הנגרים. יהלומון. הלמו לה [תהלים עד, ו]. יודע כמביא למעלה בסבך עץ קרדומות. יודע האויב כשהיה מכה בשערי פתחי המקדש שהוא כמביא מכותיו למעלה ברקיע ומנין היה יודע שהרי היה רואה שהיה העץ מסבך ואוחז את הקרדומות ובולען כמו שאמרו רבותינו כולהו בלעתינהו חד דשא דירושלים בסבך עץ קרדומות לשון נאחז בסבך (בראשית כב) העץ סובך אותם והם נסבכין בו [שם, ה ועי' במהרש"א בח"א]. וטחני קמח. לנדה לדרך גלותך. גלי צמתך. קרועיך ושוקיך דברים המצומת וקשור ומכוסה. חשפי שובל. גלי השבילים מן המים שעליהם כי דרך שם תלאי בגולה או גלי שוקך ועברי נהרות [ישעיה מז, ב]. דמיה דזכריה. בן יהוידע הכהן שהרגוהו שרי יהודה במצות יואש כשהשתחוו לו ליואש ועשאוהו אלוה והרגוהו בעזרה (דה"ב כד). שדר פורטיתא. שטר צוואה שפרט מה תהא על נכסיו. גר תושב היה. שלא קיבל עליו שאר מצות אלא ע"ז שנאמר כי לא יעשה עוד עבדך וגו' (מ"ב ה) [גיטין נז:]. דצינייתא דבבלאי. כי צינייתא דבבל מקום הוא וכו דקלים הרבה כמו ציני הר הברזל (סוכה כט:) [סוטה מו: ועי' ברש"י כאן]. פוק ותא. אחרבינהו. מסתפינא. מאלהיהון [חולין צב.]. כי אין האיש בביתו. ראיתם שסילק הקב"ה שכינתו וכל טוב נתן לעו"ג [משלי ז, יט]. צרור הכסף. הטובים שבהם הרג [שם, כ]. לדיקים שבהם המיתם. ואכרה לי. הקב"ה אומר קניתי לי ישראל בט"ו בניסן בשביל הצדיקים [חולין שם]. ל' סחורה ברגניי"א בלע"ז כמו (בראשית נ) אשר כריתי לי ובכרכי הים קורין למכירה כירה [הושע ג, ב]. ליום הכסא. לזמן המועד הקבוע וכן בכסה ליום חגנו (תהלי' פא) [משלי שם]. בכסה. יום מועד קבוע לכך וכן (משלי ז) ליום הכסא יבוא ביתו למועד הקבוע [תהלים פא, ד]. ושטחום לשמש. והכשדים ישכנו לגור על העיר בקברי השרים שהיו נאים כפלטין [ירמיה ח, ב]. ביום ההוא. אחרי בא עליהם כל אלה יבא יום ההוא המוכן לגאולה ובו אקים סוכת דוד הנופלת י"ת מלכותא דבית דוד [עמוס ט, יא].

מסורת הש"ס

א) [עי' פירוש רשב"ם פסחים קיט. ד"ה שלש מאות], ב) גיטין נז: ע"ש, ג) [שם ע"ש], ד) בקרא רפאנו, ה) [בע"י ליתא וכ"מ מפי' רש"י דלא גריס ליה], ו) [סוטה מב: מח. לעיל לג.], ז) [גיטין מד:].

תורה אור השלם

א) וַיִּתְפְּשׂוּ אֶת הַמֶּלֶךְ וַיַּעֲלוּ אֹתוֹ אֶל מֶלֶךְ בָּבֶל רִבְלָתָה וַיְדַבְּרוּ אִתּוֹ מִשְׁפָּט: [מלכים ב' כה, ו]

ב) וְעַתָּה פִּתּוּחֶיהָ יָּחַד בְּכַשִּׁיל וְכֵילַפֹּת יַהֲלֹמוּן: [תהלים עד, ו]

ג) יִוָּדַע כְּמֵבִיא לְמָעְלָה בִּסְבָךְ עֵץ קַרְדֻּמּוֹת: [תהלים עד, ה]

ד) סִלָּה כָל אַבִּירַי אֲדֹנָי בְּקִרְבִּי קָרָא עָלַי מוֹעֵד לִשְׁבֹּר בַּחוּרָי גַּת דָּרַךְ אֲדֹנָי לִבְתוּלַת בַּת יְהוּדָה: [איכה א, טו]

ה) קְחִי רֵחַיִם וְטַחֲנִי קָמַח גַּלִּי צַמָּתֵךְ חֶשְׂפִּי שֹׁבֶל גַּלִּי שׁוֹק עִבְרִי נְהָרוֹת: [ישעיה מז, ב]

ו) רִפִּאנוּ אֶת בָּבֶל וְלֹא נִרְפָּתָה עִזְבוּהָ וְנֵלֵךְ אִישׁ לְאַרְצוֹ כִּי נָגַע אֶל הַשָּׁמַיִם מִשְׁפָּטָהּ וְנִשָּׂא עַד שְׁחָקִים: [ירמיה נא, ט]

ז) כִּי אֵין הָאִישׁ בְּבֵיתוֹ הָלַךְ בְּדֶרֶךְ מֵרָחוֹק: [משלי ז, יט]

ח) יְיָ אִישׁ מִלְחָמָה יְיָ שְׁמוֹ: [שמות טו, ג]

ט) צְרוֹר הַכֶּסֶף לָקַח בְּיָדוֹ לְיוֹם הַכֶּסֶא יָבֹא בֵיתוֹ: [משלי ז, כ]

י) וָאֶכְּרֶהָ לִּי בַּחֲמִשָּׁה עָשָׂר כָּסֶף וְחֹמֶר שְׂעֹרִים וְלֶתֶךְ שְׂעֹרִים: [הושע ג, ב]

כ) תִּקְעוּ בַחֹדֶשׁ שׁוֹפָר בַּכֵּסֶה לְיוֹם חַגֵּנוּ: [תהלים פא, ד]

ל) שִׁלְחוּ כַר מֹשֵׁל אֶרֶץ מִסֶּלַע מִדְבָּרָה אֶל הַר בַּת צִיּוֹן: [ישעיה טז, א]

מ) בָּעֵת הַהִיא נְאֻם יְיָ יוֹצִיאוּ אֶת עַצְמוֹת מַלְכֵי יְהוּדָה וְאֶת עַצְמוֹת שָׂרָיו וְאֶת עַצְמוֹת הַכֹּהֲנִים וְאֵת עַצְמוֹת הַנְּבִיאִים וְאֵת עַצְמוֹת יוֹשְׁבֵי יְרוּשָׁלָיִם מִקִּבְרֵיהֶם: וּשְׁטָחוּם לַשֶּׁמֶשׁ וְלַיָּרֵחַ וּלְכֹל צְבָא הַשָּׁמַיִם אֲשֶׁר אֲהֵבוּם וַאֲשֶׁר עֲבָדוּם וַאֲשֶׁר הָלְכוּ אַחֲרֵיהֶם וַאֲשֶׁר דְּרָשׁוּם וַאֲשֶׁר הִשְׁתַּחֲווּ לָהֶם לֹא יֵאָסְפוּ וְלֹא יִקָּבֵרוּ לְדֹמֶן עַל פְּנֵי הָאֲדָמָה יִהְיוּ: [ירמיה ח, א-ב]

נ) בַּיּוֹם הַהוּא אָקִים אֶת סֻכַּת דָּוִיד הַנֹּפֶלֶת וְגָדַרְתִּי אֶת פִּרְצֵיהֶן וַהֲרִסֹתָיו אָקִים וּבְנִיתִיהָ כִּימֵי עוֹלָם: [עמוס ט, יא]

אֶת־עַצְמוֹת מַלְכֵי־יְהוּדָה – ***At that time, says Hashem, they will remove the bones of the kings of Judah*** וְאֶת־עַצְמוֹת שָׂרָיו וְאֶת־עַצְמוֹת הַכֹּהֲנִים וְאֵת עַצְמוֹת הַנְּבִיאִים וְאֵת עַצְמוֹת יוֹשְׁבֵי־יְרוּשָׁלִַם מִקִּבְרֵיהֶם – ***and the bones of his princes and the bones of the priests and the bones of the prophets and the bones of the inhabitants of Jerusalem from their graves,*** וּשְׁטָחוּם לַשֶּׁמֶשׁ וְלַיָּרֵחַ וּלְכֹל צְבָא הַשָּׁמַיִם אֲשֶׁר אֲהֵבוּם וַאֲשֶׁר עֲבָדוּם וַאֲשֶׁר הָלְכוּ אַחֲרֵיהֶם״ – ***and they will spread them before the sun and the moon and all the host of the heavens, whom they loved and whom they worshiped and whom they followed.***

The Gemara begins a lengthy discussion about the Messiah:[56] אָמַר לֵיהּ רַב נַחְמָן לְרַבִּי יִצְחָק – **Rav Nachman asked R' Yitzchak:** מִי שְׁמִיעַ לָךְ אֵימַת אָתֵי בַּר נַפְלֵי – **"Have you heard when *Bar Nafli* will come?"** אָמַר לֵיהּ – **[R' Yitzchak] said to him:** מַאן בַּר נַפְלֵי – **"Who is *Bar Nafli*?"** אָמַר לֵיהּ – **[Rav Nachman] said to him:** מָשִׁיחַ – **"The Messiah."** מָשִׁיחַ בַּר נַפְלֵי קָרֵית לֵיהּ – R' Yitzchak asked: **"Do you call the Messiah *Bar Nafli*?"** אָמַר לֵיהּ – **[Rav Nachman] answered him:** אִין – "Yes, דִּכְתִיב – **for it is written:** ,,בַּיּוֹם הַהוּא אָקִים״ – ***On that day I will establish***

NOTES

56. This topic is introduced here because the Gemara mentions below (97a) that the number of Torah scholars will diminish prior to the Messiah's arrival, and it was stated above that a similar phenomenon occurred before Nebuchadnezzar conquered Jerusalem [see note 45] (*Rashi*). [The Jewish people are protected in the merit of the righteous people among them. The Temple was destroyed only after the righteous had died. Likewise, the era of travail preceding the Messiah's arrival will occur only when the number of righteous people has diminished (see *Rif* in *Ein Yaakov*).]

Yad Ramah links these two passages as follows: Having mentioned the end of the previous exile (see note 47), the Gemara asks when the Messiah will come and bring an end to the present exile.

The Messiah:

The Jewish people will regain their independence when the Messiah – a descendant of the royal family of David – reestablishes the Davidic dynasty over Israel. Under his leadership, the Temple will be rebuilt, the Jews will return to Eretz Yisrael, and all the laws of the Torah will be restored to their former levels of observance (*Rambam, Hil. Melachim* 11:1).

A sage wiser than Solomon, and a prophet whose greatness approaches that of Moses, the Messianic king will teach the way of God to the world (*Hil. Teshuvah* 9:2). He will inspire all humanity to worship God together (*Hil. Melachim* 11:4).

In the Messianic era there will be neither hunger nor war, neither jealousy nor competition (ibid. 12:5). God will bestow such abundance that it will be possible to procure one's livelihood with minimal effort. Freed from worry and anxiety, people will enjoy long lives (*Rambam's* introduction to *Cheilek*). The occupation of the entire world will be solely that of acquiring knowledge of God (*Hil. Melachim* ibid.).

Belief in the coming of the Messiah:

The books of the Prophets are replete with references to the final Redemption (particularly *Isaiah, Jeremiah, Ezekiel, Obadiah, Zechariah;* see *Ramban, Sefer HaGeulah* ch. 1). Such references are also found in the Torah (e.g. *Deuteronomy* 30:1-10, 32:36-43; see *Ramban Sefer HaGeulah* ibid.; *Rambam, Hil. Melachim* 11:1). Therefore, *Rambam* (ibid.) rules: "Anyone who does not believe in him [the Messiah], or one who does not look foward to his arrival [i.e. he loses hope (*Chafetz Chaim* in *Tzipisa LiShuah* ch. 2)], denies not only the other prophets but [also] the Torah of Moses our teacher, because the Torah attests to him."

Belief in the Messiah's arrival is one of the thirteen articles of faith enumerated by *Rambam* in his introduction to this chapter. In the Siddur, this principle of faith is expressed thus: "I believe with complete faith in the coming of the Messiah, and even though he may delay, nevertheless I long for him each day, [hoping] that he will come."

"אֶת־סֻכַּת דָּוִיד הַנֹּפֶלֶת" – *the booth of David that is fallen* (*hanofeles*).[1]

Having ascertained the meaning of Rav Nachman's question, R' Yitzchak now answers it: **הָכִי אָמַר רַבִּי אָמַר לֵיהּ – [R' Yitzchak] said to [Rav Nachman]: יוֹחָנָן – "This is what R' Yochanan said: דּוֹר שֶׁבֶּן דָּוִד בָּא בּוֹ – In the generation when the son of David** [the Messiah] **will come, תַּלְמִידֵי חֲכָמִים מִתְמַעֲטִים** – the number of **Torah scholars will decrease.**[2] **וְהַשְּׁאָר – And** as for **the rest** of the people, **עֵינֵיהֶם כָּלוֹת בְּיָגוֹן וַאֲנָחָה – their eyes will become worn out**[3] **through grief and anxiety. וְצָרוֹת רַבּוֹת וּגְזֵרוֹת קָשׁוֹת מִתְחַדְּשׁוֹת – Numerous troubles and harsh decrees will be** constantly **appearing anew. שֶׁהָרִאשׁוֹנָה פְּקוּדָה – Before the first [trouble] is over, שְׁנִיָּה מְמַהֶרֶת לָבֹא – a second one will hasten to appear."**[4]

The following Baraisa describes the seven-year cycle[5] preceding the Messiah's arrival:

תָּנוּ רַבָּנַן – The Rabbis taught in a Baraisa: שָׁבוּעַ שֶׁבֶּן דָּוִד בָּא בּוֹ – THE SEVEN-YEAR CYCLE WHEN THE SON OF DAVID WILL COME:[6] **שָׁנָה רִאשׁוֹנָה מִתְקַיֵּים מִקְרָא זֶה** – In **THE FIRST YEAR, THIS VERSE WILL BE FULFILLED: "וְהִמְטַרְתִּי עַל־עִיר אֶחָת וְעַל־עִיר אַחַת לֹא אַמְטִיר" –** ***I WILL BRING RAIN ON ONE TOWN, AND ON ONE TOWN I WILL NOT BRING RAIN,***[7] i.e. there will be a sufficiency in some areas and famine in others. **שְׁנִיָּה חִיצֵּי רָעָב מִשְׁתַּלְּחִים** – In **THE SECOND [YEAR], THE ARROWS OF FAMINE WILL BE SENT FORTH,** i.e. there will be a limited famine in all areas.[8] **שְׁלִישִׁית רָעָב גָּדוֹל –** In **THE THIRD [YEAR]** there will be **A GREAT FAMINE; וּמֵתִים אֲנָשִׁים וְנָשִׁים וְטַף – MEN, WOMEN, AND CHILDREN WILL PERISH, וַחֲסִידִים וְאַנְשֵׁי מַעֲשֶׂה** – and so will **PIOUS PEOPLE AND PEOPLE OF** good **DEEDS;**[9] **וְתוֹרָה מִשְׁתַּכַּחַת מִלּוֹמְדֶיהָ – AND TORAH** knowledge **WILL BE FORGOTTEN BY ITS STUDENTS.**[10] **בָּרְבִיעִית שׂוֹבַע וְאֵינוֹ שׂוֹבַע – IN THE FOURTH [YEAR],** there will be **A SUFFICIENCY BUT NOT A** complete **SUFFICIENCY. בַּחֲמִישִׁית שׂוֹבַע גָּדוֹל – IN THE FIFTH [YEAR]** there will be **A GREAT SUFFICIENCY;**

NOTES

1. *Amos* 9:11. God will send the Messiah to reestablish the fallen Davidic dynasty. Accordingly, the Messiah is called *Bar Nafli* [which means "son of the fallen one"] (*Rashi*).

By giving the Messiah the name of *Bar Nafli* – i.e. son of the fallen kingdom of David – the Gemara stresses the continuity of the Davidic dynasty. The Messiah will not build a new dynasty; rather, he will restore the one that is currently fallen. For this reason, the verse refers to the monarchy of David as a סוּכָּה, *booth*, rather than as a בַּיִת, *house*, which is the more common term for a royal dynasty (see *Sotah* 11b). When a house collapses, the structure is typically ruined and an entirely new one must be built in its stead. But when a booth collapses, the original structure is easily restored to its former state (see *Maharal, Netzach Yisrael* ch. 35). [*Rambam* writes: "The Messianic king will arise and restore the monarchy of David to its *former* state, to its *original* dominion" (*Hil. Melachim* 11:1).]

Anaf Yosef and *Ben Yehoyada* point out that בַּר נַפְלֵי, *Bar Nafli,* has the same numerical value (372) as בֶּן יִשַׁי, *the son of Yishai* (i.e. David).

Aruch LaNer suggests that R' Yitzchak used the term *Bar Nafli* (the fallen one), as opposed to Messiah, because he was not simply asking when the Messiah will come; rather, he was inquiring as to how low the people will have to fall before he can come (see note 4). According to this explanation, Rav Yitzchak's answer that follows is directly appropriate (see *Aruch LaNer* to 96b at length; see also *Maharsha*).

2. The Messiah's arrival will be preceded by terrible suffering (see note 4). The righteous will die beforehand so that they will not have to endure this suffering. Moreover, such troubles cannot be imposed while the righteous are still alive and protecting the people (*Iyun Yaakov;* see 96b note 56).

3. This expression indicates a yearning that extends over a long period of time, but ends in frustration (see *Rashi* to *Leviticus* 26:16 and to *Deuteronomy* 28:32). [In this context, it means that the people will yearn for relief from their suffering, but no relief will be granted.]

4. חֶבְלֵי מָשִׁיחַ, ***The travail preceding the Messiah's arrival:***

The period immediately before the Messiah's arrival is termed by the Sages as חֶבְלֵי מָשִׁיחַ, *the travail of the Messiah.* During this time, the people will undergo suffering analogous to the travail of a woman in childbirth (see 98b notes 5 and 8).

The Gemara below (97b-98a) records a view which maintains that, if necessary, the Jewish people will be "forced" to repent before the Messiah's coming. According to this view, the purpose of the pre-Messianic travail is to force the Jews to realize that their only hope lies with their Father in Heaven and that they must repent to merit His salvation (see *Maharsha* ד״ה עד שירבו).

Some commentators explain that the suffering and pain are symptoms of the world's decline that must necessarily precede the Messianic era. A new order of existence cannot be established before the previous one has deteriorated. (By way of example, *Aruch LaNer* points to a kernel of wheat, which must rot in the ground before it sprouts and brings forth a new stalk.) The Messianic era will be one of profound and comprehensive change. To make way for this new era, the current norms must collapse. This decline will inevitably involve a great deal of suffering (see *Abarbanel, Yeshuos Meshicho, Iyun* 1 ch. 5; *Maharal, Netzach Yisrael* chs. 32, 35; *Aruch LaNer;* see also *Toras Chaim* to 98a ד״ה אף ת״ח).

In line with this approach, *Abarbanel* shows how each of the troubles enumerated in the Gemara is the opposite of a particular phenomenon that will occur after the Messiah's arrival. For instance, when the Messiah comes, מָלְאָה הָאָרֶץ דֵּעָה אֶת־ה׳, *the world will be full of the knowledge of* HASHEM *(Isaiah* 11:9). Thus, in contrast, the pre-Messianic era will necessarily see a dearth of knowledge of God, as the Gemara states above: "[the number of] Torah scholars will decrease." The Messianic era will be one of great joy and happiness (ibid. 55:12, 61:10). In contrast, the period before his coming will be marked by sorrow – "their eyes will become worn out through grief and anxiety."

It has been suggested that "the travail of the Messiah" will occur only in the event that the Messiah comes without our positively meriting him. Should we bring the redemption through studying Torah and performing mitzvos, the Messiah's arrival will not be preceded by suffering (see *Or HaChaim* to *Genesis* 49:11 ד״ה כבס ביין).

Signs indicating the Messiah's arrival:

The Gemara on this *amud* and on 98a-b records several portents of the Messiah's imminent arrival. It is difficult to ascertain the exact meaning of these statements. Many are given widely differing interpretations by the commentators. Our elucidation covers only a fraction of these interpretations, drawing primarily from *Rashi, Yad Ramah* and *Maharsha*.

It should also be noted that any one of several different factors could cause the Messiah to come (see 98a notes 41-44). Depending on the factor, the redemptive process itself may vary (see *Or HaChaim* to *Numbers* 24:17 ד״ה אראנו, cited in 98a note 48). Some of these signs may pertain to one type of redemptive process and some to another.

In a related context, *Rambam* writes (*Hil. Melachim* 12:2): "All these matters and their like, no one will know how they will happen until they happen. For these matters were obscured by the prophets. Also the Sages do not have a clear tradition in these matters, rather [they follow] the probable meanings of the verses, and therefore they have disputes in these matters. At any rate, the order in which these events will occur and their details are not a fundamental principle of faith. A person should not occupy himself with the words of *aggados* nor study at length the *midrashim* dealing with these and similar matters, nor should he regard them as fundamentals. For they lead neither to love nor fear [of God]. . . . Rather, one should wait, and maintain belief in the general fact of the matter . . ."

5. The years follow a seven-year cycle. The Torah commands that every seventh year (*shemittah*) the fields of Eretz Yisrael must lie fallow, and outstanding debts are canceled (see *Rashi*).

6. Actually, the Messiah will come in the year *following* this seven-year period. However, since the eighth year is identified with the preceding cycle (it is called מוֹצָאֵי שְׁבִיעִית, *the aftermath of the seventh*), the Baraisa is justified in saying: "The seven-year cycle *when* the son of David will come" (*Maharsha*).

7. *Amos* 4:7.

8. There will not be an abundance of food anywhere (*Rashi*).

9. See *Rashi* to *Sotah* 49a ד״ה אנשי מעשה.

10. Because they will not have food to eat (*Rashi*).

את סוכת דוד הנופלת א"ל הכי אמר רבי יוחנן דור שבן דוד בא בו תלמידי חכמים מתמעטים והשאר עיניהם כלות ביגון ואנחה וצרות רבות וגזרות קשות מתחדשות עד שהראשונה פקודה שניה ממהרת לבא ת"ר שבוע שבן דוד בא בו שנה ראשונה מתקיים מקרא זה א) והמטרתי על עיר אחת ועל עיר אחת לא אמטיר שניה חיצי רעב משתלחים שלישית רעב גדול ומתים אנשים ונשים וטף חסידים ואנשי מעשה ותורה משתכחת מלומדיה ברביעית שובע ואינו שובע בחמישית שובע גדול ואוכלין ושותין ושמחין ותורה חוזרת ללומדיה א) בששית קולות בשביעית מלחמות במוצאי שביעית בן דוד בא אמר רב יוסף הא כמה שביעית דהוה כן ולא אתא אמר אביי בששית קולות בשביעית מלחמות מי הוה ועוד כסדרן מי הוה [א] ב) ב) (אשר חרפו אויביך ה' אשר חרפו עקבות משיחך) תניא ר' יהודה אומר דור שבן דוד בא בו ג) בית הוועד יהיה לזנות והגליל יחרב והגבלן יאשם [ב] ואנשי גבול יסובבו מעיר לעיר ולא יחוננו וחכמת הסופרים תסרח ויראי חטא ימאסו [ג] ופני הדור כפני כלב והאמת נעדרת שנאמר ג) ותהי האמת נעדרת [ד] ד) (וסר מרע משתולל) מאי ותהי האמת נעדרת אמרי דבי רב מלמד שנעשית עדרים עדרים והולכת לה מאי וסר מרע משתולל אמרי דבי ר' שילא כל מי שסר מרע משתולל על הבריות אמר רבא מריש הוה אמינא ליכא קושטא בעלמא אמר לי ה) ההוא מרבנן ורב טבות שמיה ואמרי לה רב טבומי שמיה דאי הוו יהבי ליה כל חללי דעלמא לא הוה משני בדבוריה זימנא חדא איקלעי לההוא אתרא וקושטא שמיה ולא הוו משני בדיבורייהו ולא הוה מיית איניש מהתם בלא זימניה נסיבי איתתא מינהון והוו לי תרתין בנין מינה יומא חד הוה יתבא דביתהו וקא חייפא רישה אתאי שיבבתה טרפא אדשא ו) סבר לאו אורח ארעא ז) אמר לה ליתא הכא שכיבו ליה תרתין בנין אתו אינשי דאתרא לקמיה אמרו ליה מאי האי אמר להו הכי הוה מעשה א"ל במטותא מינך פוק מאתרין ולא תגרי בהו מותנא בהנך אינשי תניא ר' נהוראי אומר דור שבן דוד בא בו ח) נערים ילבינו פני זקנים וזקנים יעמדו לפני נערים ובת קמה באמה וכלה בחמותה ופני הדור כפני כלב ואין הבן מתבייש מאביו תניא ר' נחמיה אומר דור שבן דוד בא בו העזות תרבה והיוקר יעות והגפן יתן פריו והיין ביוקר ונהפכה כל המלכות למינות ואין תוכחה מסייע ליה לר' יצחק דא"ר יצחק אין בן דוד בא עד שתתהפך כל המלכות למינות אמר רבא מאי קרא ד) כולו הפך לבן טהור הוא ת"ר ה) כי ידין ה' עמו (וגו') כי יראה כי אזלת יד ואפס עצור ועזוב אין בן דוד בא עד שירבו המסורות ד"א עד שיתמעטו התלמידים ד"א עד שתכלה פרוטה מן הכיס ד"א עד שיתיאשו מן הגאולה שנאמר ואפס עצור ועזוב כביכול אין סומך ועוזר לישראל כי הא דר' זירא כי הוה משכח רבנן דמעסקי ביה אמר להו במטותא ט) בעינא מנייכו לא תרחקוה דתנינא ג' באין בהיסח הדעת אלו הן משיח מציאה ועקרב אמר רב קטינא י) שית אלפי שני הוו עלמא וחד חרוב שנאמר ו) ונשגב ה' לבדו ביום ההוא אביי אמר תרי חרוב שנאמר ז) יחיינו מיומים ביום השלישי יקימנו ונחיה לפניו תניא כותיה דרב קטינא כשם שהשביעית משמטת שנה אחת לז' שנים כך העולם משמט אלף שנים לשבעת אלפים שנה שנאמר ונשגב ה' לבדו ביום ההוא ואומר ח) מזמור שיר ליום השבת יום שכולו שבת ואומר ט) כי אלף שנים בעיניך כיום אתמול כי יעבור ל) תנא דבי אליהו ששת אלפים שנה הוי עלמא שני אלפים תוהו שני אלפים תורה שני אלפים ימות המשיח ובעונותינו

רש"י

את סוכת דוד הנופלת. מלכות דוד שנפלה להכי קרי משיח בר נפלי: עד שהראשונה פקודה. עד שלא כלתה צרה ראשונה שניה ממהרת לבא פקודה כמו לא נפקד (במדבר לא): שבוע. שמיטה: והמטרתי על עיר אחת. שיהא מעט מטר ויהא רעב במקום זה ושובע במקום זה: חיצי רעב. רעב מעט שלא יהא שובע בשום מקום: משתכחת מלומדיה. מתוך שאין להם מה לאכול: בששית קולות. יצאו קולות שבן דוד בא ל"א קולות מתקיעת שופר שנאמר יתקע בשופר גדול (ישעיה כז): מלחמות. בין עובדי כוכבים לישראל: דהוה הכי. שנה אחת רעב שנה אחת שובע ואעפ"כ לא בא בן דוד: בששית קולות מי הוה. כלום יצאו קולות שבן דוד בא: ועוד כסדרן מי הוה. כלומר אלו הצרות דקתני הכא כסדרן לא אתרמו בשבוע אחד אבל כי אתרמו אתי משיח: אשר חרפו אויביך ה' אשר חרפו עקבות משיחך. לא אתפרש האי קרא למאי איכתיב הכא דהא לא קא דריש ביה מידי ונראה למורי שכן נכתב בספרים תחלה כמו ששנינו בפ' אחרון דסוטה (דף מט:) בעקבות המשיח חוצפא יסגא וכתבו פירוש זה על בעקבות שהוא לשון סוף כמו אשר חרפו עקבות משיחך: בית הועד. מקום שתלמידי חכמים מתוועדין שם ללמוד תורה: ה"ג והגבלן. מקום ששמו כך ישתומם: ואנשי הגבול. אנשי גבול ארץ ישראל ל"א אנשי גזית סנהדרין: כפני כלב. דדמיין ממש לכלב מ"ר ל"א כפני הכלב שלא יתביישו זה מזה: משתולל על הבריות. כל העולם אומרין עליו שוטה הוא היינו משתולל לשון שטות כמו מוליך יועצים שולל (איוב יב): ליכא קושטא בעלמא. אין אדם בעולם שידבר אמת תמיד: אמר לי ההוא מרבנן דאי הוו יהבי ליה כל חללי דעלמא לא משני בדבוריה. לשקר ואישתעי לי הכי זימנא חדא אקלעי לההוא אתרא וקושטא שמיה: טרפא אבבא. שהיתה שואלת אותה: לאו אורח ארעא. לומר היכן היא הואיל וחייפ' רישה: ה"ג נערים ילבינו פני זקנים. כלומר יחפרו ויביישו אותם: וזקנים יעמדו בפני הנערים. לכבדם והיינו דאמרינן (בסוטה ד' מט:) בעקבות המשיח חוצפא יסגא: בת קמה באמה. לחרפה ולביישה: היוקר יעוות. שלא יכבדו זה את זה יוקר כבוד ל"א היוקר יעות מכובד שבהן יהא עוותן ורמאי. מ"ר: והגפן יתן פריו. ואעפ"כ יהיה היין ביוקר שלא יהיה ברכה בפרי עצמו ל"א שיהיו כולן רודפין אחר היין ומשתכרין ומתייקר היין אע"פ שרוב יין בעולם: כלו הפך לבן טהור הוא. כשפשט הנגע בכל העור כך כשנהפכה כל המלכות למינות תבא גאולה: כי ידין ה' עמו. להביא להם גאולה: כי יראה כי אזלת יד. שתלך ותחזק ידן של מסורות ומלשינין במלשינותן: שיתמעטו התלמידים. שמחזיקין ידי ישראל להחזירן למוטב: שתכלה פרוטה. והיינו אזלת יד שיהו בידים ריקניות: כביכול. כאלו יכולין לומר דבר זה כלפי מעלה: אין עוזר ואין סומך לישראל. שיהיו שפלים למאד ואומר אין עוזר וסומך שיהיו מתייאשין מן הגאולה: דמעסקי ביה. לידע מתי יבא: ועקרב. נושך האדם פתאום: וחד חרוב. שאלף שנה יהיה חרוב חוץ מששת אלפים אלו דהיינו אלף שביעי: תרי. אלפים הוא חרב אלף שביעי ואלף שמיני: יומו של הקב"ה אלף שנה שנאמר כי אלף שנים בעיניך כיום אתמול כי יעבור: משמט. ונעשה חרב: שכולו שבת. שהעולם משמט: הוי עלמא. העולם כך מתקיים: ב' אלפים היה תהו. תחת שלא ניתנה עדיין תורה והיה העולם כתוהו ומאדם הראשון עד שהיה אברהם בן נ"ב שנה איכא אלפים שנה כדמוכחי קראי דכשנשלמו אלפים שנה עסק אברהם בתורה שנאמר (בראשית יב) ואת הנפש אשר עשו בחרן ומתרגמינן דשעבידו לאורייתא בחרן ואמרינן במסכת ע"ז (דף ט.) גמירי דההוא שעתא הוה אברהם בר חמשין ותרתי שנין: ושני אלפים תורה. מן הנפש אשר עשו בחרן עד [אלפים] שנות המשיח ארבעים (ל) ושמנים) שנה עד שנולד יצחק וששים שנה משנולד יצחק עד שנולד יעקב הרי ק"ח וק"ל שהיו ליעקב כשבא למצרים הרי רל"ח ורד"ו שעמדו במצרים הרי תמ"ח ומשיצאו ממצרים עד שנבנה בית ראשון ת"פ דכתיב (מלכים א ו) ויהי בשמנים שנה וארבע מאות שנה לצאת בני ישראל מארץ מצרים וגו' הרי תתקכ"ח ות"י שעמד בית ראשון כדמוכחי קראי על פי חשבון שנות המלכים וע' דגלות בבל ות"כ שעמד בית שני הרי תת"ק ותתקכ"ח הרי אלפים פחות קע"ב וקע"ב קודם השלמת ד' אלפים נחרב הבית ולסוף אותן קע"ב נשלמו שני אלפים תורה ואיידי דאמר שני אלפים תוהו קאמר שני אלפים תורה ולא שתכלה תורה אחר שני אלפים. מ"ר: ושני אלפים שנות המשיח. שלאחר שני אלפים תורה הוה דינו שיבא משיח ותכלה הגלות ויבטל השיעבוד מישראל: אבל

מסורת הש"ס

א) מגילה יז:, ב) רש"ל מ"ז, ג) [סוטה מט:], ד) רש"ל מ"ז, ה) [ב"מ מט. ע"ש], ו) י"ג סברי, ז) י"ג אמרי, ח) סוטה מט:, ט) [בברכות לה: וביומא עב: גם בע"י ליתא מלת בעינא וכן לעיל בסמוך במטותא מינך], י) [ר"ה לא.], כ) ע"ז ט., ל) [צ"ל ושמנה].

הגהות הגר"א

[א] גמ' אשר חרפו. נדפס בגלוי רש"ל מוחק זה נמחק הסג"ה: [ב] שם ואנשי גבול. נמחק תיבת גבול. ונ"ב חול: [ג] שם ופני הדור כפני הכלב. נמחק: [ד] שם וסר מרע משתולל. נדפס בגלוי רש"ל מ"ז נמחק הסג"ה:

תורה אור השלם

א) וְגַם אָנֹכִי מָנַעְתִּי מִכֶּם אֶת הַגֶּשֶׁם בְּעוֹד שְׁלֹשָׁה חֳדָשִׁים לַקָּצִיר וְהִמְטַרְתִּי עַל עִיר אֶחָת וְעַל עִיר אַחַת לֹא אַמְטִיר חֶלְקָה אַחַת תִּמָּטֵר וְחֶלְקָה אֲשֶׁר לֹא תַמְטִיר עָלֶיהָ תִּיבָשׁ: [עמוס ד, ז]

ב) אֲשֶׁר חֵרְפוּ אוֹיְבֶיךָ יְיָ אֲשֶׁר חֵרְפוּ עִקְּבוֹת מְשִׁיחֶךָ: [תהלים פט, נב]

ג) וַתְּהִי הָאֱמֶת נֶעְדֶּרֶת וְסָר מֵרָע מִשְׁתּוֹלֵל וַיַּרְא יְיָ וַיֵּרַע בְּעֵינָיו כִּי אֵין מִשְׁפָּט: [ישעיה נט, טו]

ד) וְרָאָה הַכֹּהֵן וְהִנֵּה כִסְּתָה הַצָּרַעַת אֶת כָּל בְּשָׂרוֹ וְטִהַר אֶת הַנָּגַע כֻּלּוֹ הָפַךְ לָבָן טָהוֹר הוּא: [ויקרא יג, יג]

ה) כִּי יָדִין יְיָ עַמּוֹ וְעַל עֲבָדָיו יִתְנֶחָם כִּי יִרְאֶה כִּי אָזְלַת יָד וְאֶפֶס עָצוּר וְעָזוּב: [דברים לב, לו]

ו) וְשַׁח גַּבְהוּת הָאָדָם וְשָׁפֵל רוּם אֲנָשִׁים וְנִשְׂגַּב יְיָ לְבַדּוֹ בַּיּוֹם הַהוּא: [ישעיה ב, יז]

ז) יְחַיֵּנוּ מִיֹּמָיִם בַּיּוֹם הַשְּׁלִישִׁי יְקִמֵנוּ וְנִחְיֶה לְפָנָיו: [הושע ו, ב]

ח) מִזְמוֹר שִׁיר לְיוֹם הַשַּׁבָּת: [תהלים צב, א]

ט) כִּי אֶלֶף שָׁנִים בְּעֵינֶיךָ כְּיוֹם אֶתְמוֹל כִּי יַעֲבֹר וְאַשְׁמוּרָה בַלָּיְלָה: [תהלים צ, ד]

ליקוטי רש"י

שבוע שבן דוד בא בו. חלוק משאר שנים כדאמרינן בפרק חלק (לז.) שנה ראשונה רעב ולא רעב כו' עד ובשביעית מלחמות ובמוצאי שביעית בן דוד בא [מגילה יז:]. עקבות משיחך. סופי מלך המשיח ולשון משנה הוא בעקבות המשיח חוצפא יסגא [תהלים פט, נב]. בסוף הגלות לפני ביאת משיח [סוטה מט:]. בית הוועד. של חכמים יהיו לבית זונות שכלו החכמים ואין לומד תורה ויהא חרב מאין איש ובעלי זימה מתגודדים שם מפני שחוץ לעיר היו בתי מדרשות שלהם [סוטה שם]. משתולל. מוחזק שוטה על הבריות כמו (מיכה א) אלכה שולל והוא מגזרת שוגג דמתרגמינן שלו וכן (ש"ב ו) על השל [ישעיה נט, טו]. והיין ביוקר. שהכל עוסקין במשתאות. ונהפכה כל המלכות למינות. והמלכות השולטת על רוב העולם תהא למינות נמשכים אחר טעות שלו [ישו] ותלמידיו נקראו מינים [דפו"י]. ואין תוכחה. אין לך אדם שיוכל להוכיח שכולם נכשלים בחטאות וכשמוכיחין אומר לו אתה כמוני [סוטה שם]. כי יראה כי אזלת יד. כשיראה כי יד האויב הולכת וחוזקת מאד עליהם ואפס בהם עצור ועזוב. עצור. נושע על ידי עוצר ומושל שיעצור בהם. עזוב. על ידי עוזב. עוצר הוא המושל העוצר בעם שלא ילכו מפוזרים בצאתם לצבא על האויב. בלשון בלע"ז מיינטינדו"ר עוצר הוא הנושע במעצור המושל עזוב מחוזק כמו (נחמיה ג, ח) ויעזבו את ירושלים עד החומה (ירמיה מט, כה) איך לא עוזבה עיר תהלה עצור מיינטינו"ד עזוב אינפורלדו"ר [דברים לב, לו]. שתכלה פרוטה מן הכים. אין מעות מצויות בכים [לקמן צח.]. שית אלפי שני. נגזר על העולם להתקיים כמנין ימי השבוע וביום השביעי שבת ובשבעת אלפים נוח לעולם [ע"ז ט.]. מזמור שיר. של לוים (נביאים). ליום השבת. שאומרים אותו בשבתות והוא מדבר בענין העולם הבא שכולו שבת [תהלים צב, א]. יום שכולו שבת. שעתיד העולם להיות חרב ואין אדם וכל המלאכות שובתות על אותו יום אומרים שיר של שבת [ר"ה לא.]. שני אלפים. ראשונים נגזר עליו להיות תוהו בלא תורה ושני אלפים תורה בלא ימות המשיח ושני אלפים ימות המשיח. שני אלפים תוהו. לא וחשוב שנות דור ודור שחי כל אחד קודם שנולד בנו דשנים שאחרי כן אתה נותן לבן ותמצא מאדם עד שנולד נח תתרנ"ו שנים ונח חי תק"ב שנים קודם שנולד שם דכתיב (בראשית ה) ויהי נח בן חמש מאות שנה וגו' כשנולד בנו הראשון היה בן ת"ק שנים ויפת הוא הגדול מאם שנה ואם גדול משם שנה הרי תק"ב שנים לנח כשנולד שם כדכתיב (שם, יא) [שם] בן מאת שנה ויולד את ארפכשד שנתים אחר המבול ואם שם לת"ק שנים דנח אתייליד כי מטו שנתים אחר המבול הוה ליה בר ק"ב דהא כתיב (שם, ז) ונח בן שש מאות שנה והמבול היה חשוב תק"ב דנח ומאה דשם עד ארפכשד והוסף על נ"ו של פרט הרי תרנ"ח וארפכשד הוליד את שלח בל"ה הרי תרל"ג ומשלח עד עבר ל' הרי תשכ"ג ומעבר עד פלג ל"ד הרי תשנ"ז ומפלג עד רעו ל' הרי תשפ"ז ומרעו לשרוג ל"ב הרי תתי"ט ומשרוג לנחור ל' הרי תתמ"ט ומנחור לתרח כ"ט הרי תתע"ח ומתרח לאברהם ע' הרי תתקמ"ח על אלף וכו' הוה אברהם בר נ"ב הוסיפם על אלף ותתקמ"ח שהיו בידך כשנולד אברהם הרי אלפים תוהו. שני אלפים תורה. מאברהם עד יצחק ק' הרי אלפים ומ"ח ומיצחק עד מתן תורה ת' שנים כיצד ס' עד שנולד יעקב וכרדתו למצרים כתיב ימי שני מגורי שלשים ומאת שנה הרי ק"ל משנולד יצחק וישראל היו במצרים רד"ו הרי ד' מאות ומ"ח שנים על אלפים לבריאת עולם נמצא ממתן תורה עד ד' אלפים לבריאתו של עולם אלף וחמש מאות וחמשים ושתים. כמה בצירן לך השתא דתורה דתני תנא תמ"ח שנים היו בצירן לך כי מעיינת מואת הנפש אשר עשו עד מתן תורה הכי הוו הוסף אותן על מנין מתן תורה ונמצא אלפים מכוונין מואת הנפש אשר עשו וגו' עד גמר ד' אלפים לבריאת עולם והוא קע"ב שנים לאחר חורבן כיצד הרי מנית עד יציאת מצרים תמ"ח על עודף אלפים וכתיב (מ"א ו) ויהי בשמנים שנה וארבע מאות שנה לצאת בני ישראל עד ויבן שלמה את הבית הרי תתקכ"ח על אלפים כשנבנה הבית וימי בית ראשון ד' מאות ועשר הרי שלשה אלפים ושל"ח שנים וגלות בבל ע' שנים הרי ת"ח וימי בית שני ת"ך הרי תתכ"ח נמצא קע"ב חסרין מד' אלפים והכי תני בסדר עולם [ע"ז שם].

וְאוֹכְלִין וְשׁוֹתִין וּשְׂמֵחִין – [PEOPLE] WILL EAT, DRINK, AND REJOICE, וְתוֹרָה חוֹזֶרֶת לְלוֹמְדֶיהָ – AND TORAH knowledge WILL RETURN TO ITS STUDENTS. בַּשִּׁשִּׁית קוֹלוֹת – IN THE SIXTH [YEAR] there will be SOUNDS.[11] בַּשְּׁבִיעִית מִלְחָמוֹת – IN THE SEVENTH [YEAR] there will be WARS.[12] בְּמוֹצָאֵי שְׁבִיעִית בֶּן דָּוִד בָּא – IN THE AFTERMATH OF THE SEVENTH [YEAR], i.e. the eighth year, THE SON OF DAVID WILL COME.[13]

The Gemara asks:

אָמַר רַב יוֹסֵף – **Rav Yosef said:** הָא כַּמָּה שְׁבִיעִית דַּהֲוָה כֵּן – **But there have been many such seven-year periods,**[14] וְלֹא אָתָא – **and [the Messiah] did not come** after them!

The Gemara answers:

אָמַר אַבַּיֵי – **Abaye said** to Rav Yosef: בַּשִּׁשִּׁית קוֹלוֹת בַּשְּׁבִיעִית מִלְחָמוֹת מִי הֲוָה – **Were there sounds in the sixth [year] and wars in the seventh?** וְעוֹד – **Furthermore,** כְּסִדְרָן מִי הֲוָה – **did** the events to which you refer **occur in** this **order?**

,,אֲשֶׁר חֵרְפוּ אוֹיְבֶיךָ ה׳ אֲשֶׁר חֵרְפוּ עִקְּבוֹת מְשִׁיחֶךָ" – Scripture states: ***That your enemies have taunted, O Hashem, that they have taunted the footsteps of Your Messiah.***[15]

The Gemara cites another Baraisa that describes the pre-Messianic era:

תַּנְיָא – **It was taught in a Baraisa:** רַבִּי יְהוּדָה אוֹמֵר – R' YEHUDAH SAYS: דּוֹר שֶׁבֶּן דָּוִד בָּא בּוֹ – In THE GENERATION WHEN THE SON OF DAVID WILL COME, בֵּית הַוַּועַד יִהְיֶה לִזְנוּת – THE MEETING PLACE WILL BE used FOR LICENTIOUSNESS,[16] וְהַגָּלִיל יֶחֱרַב – THE GALILEE WILL LAY WASTE, וְהַגַּבְלָן יֵאָשֵׁם – AND THE GAVLAN[17] WILL BE DESOLATE. וְאַנְשֵׁי גְבוּל יְסוֹבְבוּ מֵעִיר לְעִיר וְלֹא יְחוֹנָּנוּ – THE PEOPLE OF THE BORDER[18] WILL WANDER FROM TOWN TO TOWN AND NOT BE GRANTED FAVOR. וְחָכְמַת הַסּוֹפְרִים תִּסְרַח – THE WISDOM OF SCHOLARS WILL DECAY, וְיִרְאֵי חֵטְא יִמָּאֲסוּ – THOSE WHO FEAR SIN WILL BE DESPISED, וּפְנֵי הַדּוֹר כִּפְנֵי כֶּלֶב – THE FACE OF THE GENERATION WILL BE LIKE THE FACE OF A DOG,[19] וְהָאֱמֶת נֶעְדֶּרֶת – AND THE TRUTH WILL BE ABSENT, שֶׁנֶּאֱמַר ,,וַתְּהִי הָאֱמֶת נֶעְדֶּרֶת וְסָר מֵרָע מִשְׁתּוֹלֵל" – AS IT IS STATED: *AND THE TRUTH WILL BE ABSENT, AND HE THAT TURNS AWAY FROM EVIL WILL BECOME FOOLISH.*[20]

NOTES

11. Reports that the Messiah is coming. Alternatively, this refers to the sounding of the shofar that will herald the return of the Jews from exile, as prophesied in *Isaiah* (27:13): וְהָיָה בַּיּוֹם הַהוּא יִתָּקַע בְּשׁוֹפָר גָּדוֹל, *On that day a great shofar shall be sounded* (*Rashi;* cf. *Yad Ramah*). [See below, 110b, where this verse is discussed in relation to the redemption. See also *Chasam Sofer,* Responsa vol. 6 §98, who discusses whether the verse refers to a shofar literally or figuratively.]

Maharsha objects to *Rashi's* explanations on the basis of a Baraisa quoted below which states that the Messiah will come when he is not expected. In view of this difficulty, *Maharsha* explains that the "sounds" mentioned here are of a heavenly nature, signifying the judgment of the nations.

[*Rashi* can be defended on the basis of the point made in note 4 that some signs pertain to one type of redemptive process and some to another.]

12. Between the idolatrous nations and the Jews (*Rashi;* see *Maharal*).

13. The inevitable decline required to prepare for the world's renewal (see note 4) will occur in the first part of this seven-year period. Then the trend will be reversed, leading up to the Messiah's arrival in the eighth year (*Maharal*).

See *Maharal* who explains the symbolism of the numbers seven and eight; see also *R' S.R. Hirsch* to *Tehillim* 6:1.

[The Baraisa does not necessarily mean that the Messiah will come *only* in the year following a *shemittah* year. As mentioned in note 4, there are several ways in which the redemption could occur.]

14. I.e. seven-year cycles that included a year of famine and a year of plenty (see *Rashi*).

15. *Psalms* 89:52. The nations mock the delay in the advent of the Messiah to deliver Israel, using this delay as evidence that he will never come (*Radak* ad loc.).

It is not clear why this verse is introduced here, for the Gemara does not expound upon it. Quoting his teacher, *Rashi* suggests that in old manuscripts the text read: בְּעִקְּבוֹת הַמָּשִׁיחַ חוּצְפָּא יִסְגֵּא, *In the footsteps of the Messiah* (i.e. at the end of the pre-Messianic era) *insolence will increase,* as it is said: חֵרְפוּ עִקְּבוֹת מְשִׁיחֶךָ, *They taunt* [during the period of] *the "footsteps of the Messiah."*

Maharsha posits that this verse is connected to the passage below (97b) about the delay in the coming of the Messiah.

Maharshal deletes the verse from the text (see, however, *Hagahos HaGra*).

16. The number of Torah scholars will have decreased to such an extent that their study halls will be desolate. Because these halls are outside residential areas, people will use them for immoral purposes (*Rashi* to *Sotah* 49b).

According to *Yad Ramah,* the Baraisa means that public places will be designated for purposes of prostitution.

17. The name of a place (*Rashi*). [In *Joshua* (13:5) it is stated: וְהָאָרֶץ הַגִּבְלִי, *the land of the Givli*. From the context it appears that this land was in the northeastern part of Eretz Yisrael (see also *I Kings* 5:32). There seems to have also been a place named גְּבָל, *Geval,* near the southern borders of Eretz Yisrael, as suggested by *Psalms* 83:8. *Targum Yonasan* (to *Genesis* 32:4) renders שֵׂעִיר, *Seir,* as גַּבְלָא, *Gavla* (see *Maharsha*).]

According to *Yad Ramah,* the text reads וְהַגְּוִיל, *and the parchment.* The Baraisa means that Torah scrolls will suffer neglect because the number of students will have decreased.

18. I.e. those who were living in any part of Eretz Yisrael that is outside Jerusalem (*Rashi,* as explained by *Maharsha*). [The Talmud often refers to such areas as גְּבוּלִין, literally: borders. In relation to Jerusalem, the other towns of Eretz Yisrael are no more important than border towns (*Maharsha*).]

An alternative version of the text states וְאַנְשֵׁי גָזִית, literally: and the men of hewn stone. This signifies the Upper Sanhedrin [which sat in the לִשְׁכַּת הַגָּזִית, *Chamber of Hewn Stone*] (*Rashi*).

Yad Ramah reads וְאַנְשֵׁי גְוִיל, literally: and the men of parchment, which refers to those who write and sell Torah scrolls. They will wander from town to town trying to earn a livelihood, but they will meet with rejection.

Gra emends the text to read: אַנְשֵׁי חַיִל, *men of worth* (see *Margaliyos HaYam* §5).

19. People will look like dogs (*Rashi* in the name of his teacher; see *Tiferes Yisrael* to *Sotah* 9:15).

Alternatively, like a dog, they will have no shame (*Rashi*). In a similar vein, *Yad Ramah* explains this statement as referring to the trait of brazenness, and *Chida* understands it as connoting insolence. (The Gemara in *Beitzah* 25b describes a dog as the most brazen of creatures.)

Maharsha suggests that the reference is to hypocrisy. In Hebrew, a dog is called כֶּלֶב because it is כּוּלוֹ לֵב, *all heart,* i.e. it is utterly devoted to its master. In the pre-Messianic times, people will appear on their "faces" to be as loyal to their friends as a dog is to its master; but in their hearts they will feel otherwise.

R' Elchonon Wasserman (in *Ikvasa DiMshicha*) cites the following explanation in the name of *R' Yisroel Salanter*: פְּנֵי הַדּוֹר means the heads (i.e. the leaders) of the generation. The behavior of the leaders of the generation will resemble that of dogs. When a dog is walked by its master, it trots ahead and thus appears to be leading. In reality, however, it is the master who chooses the direction in which to go. When the dog comes to a fork in the road, it stops and waits for its master to direct it. In the pre-Messianic era, the leaders will only appear to be leading the nation; in reality they will be following the whims of the masses.

20. *Isaiah* 59:15. The Gemara presently explains this verse. The portion of *Isaiah* in which it appears deals with the advent of the Messiah.

The moral and spiritual decline outlined in this Baraisa is a prerequisite to the religious growth that will be promoted by the Messiah (see note 4). Alternatively, the Messiah may come precisely *because* the people have reached such a degenerate state. If the people are ever in danger of sinking to the level from which it is impossible to return, the Messiah will be sent to save them from spiritual oblivion (see 98a note 43).

[*Yad Ramah* poignantly remarks: "I am in wonderment! According to these signs, why has the son of David not come in this generation of ours?"]

את סוכת דוד הנופלת א"ל הכי אמר רבי יוחנן דור שבן דוד בא בו תלמידי חכמים מתמעטים והשאר עיניהם כלות ביגון ואנחה וצרות רבות וגזרות קשות מתחדשות עד שהראשונה פקודה שניה ממהרת לבא ת"ר שבוע שבן דוד בא בו שנה ראשונה מתקיים מקרא זה (א) והמטרתי על עיר אחת ועל עיר אחת לא אמטיר שניה חיצי רעב משתלחים שלישית רעב גדול ומתים אנשים ונשים וטף חסידים ואנשי מעשה ותורה משתכחת מלומדיה ברביעית שובע ואינו שובע בחמישית שובע גדול ואוכלין ושותין ושמחין ותורה חוזרת ללומדיה (א) בששית קולות בשביעית מלחמות במוצאי שביעית בן דוד בא אמר רב יוסף הא כמה שביעית דהוה כן ולא אתא אמר אביי בששית קולות בשביעית מלחמות מי הוה ועוד כסדרן מי הוה [א] (ב) (ב) (אשר חרפו אויביך ה' אשר חרפו עקבות משיחך) תניא ר' יהודה אומר דור שבן דוד בא בו (ג) בית הוועד יהיה לזנות והגליל יחרב והגבלן יאשם [ב] ואנשי גבול יסובבו מעיר לעיר ולא יחוננו וחכמת הסופרים תסרח ויראי חטא ימאסו [ג] ופני הדור כפני כלב והאמת נעדרת שנאמר (ג) ותהי האמת נעדרת [ד] (ד) (וסר מרע משתולל) מאי ותהי האמת נעדרת אמרי דבי רב מלמד שנעשית עדרים עדרים והולכת לה מאי וסר מרע משתולל אמרי דבי ר' שילא כל מי שסר מרע משתולל על הבריות אמר רבא מריש הוה אמינא ליכא קושטא בעלמא אמר לי (ה) ההוא מרבנן ורב טבות שמיה ואמרי לה רב טביומי שמיה דאי הוו יהבי ליה כל חללי דעלמא לא הוה משני בדבוריה זימנא חדא איקלעי לההוא אתרא וקושטא שמיה ולא הוו משני בדיבורייהו ולא הוה מיית איניש מהתם בלא זימניה נסיבי איתתא מינהון והוו לי תרתין בנין מינה יומא חד הוה יתבא דביתהו וקא חייפא רישה אתאי שיבבתה טרפא אדשא (ו) סבר לאו אורח ארעא (ז) אמר לה ליתא הכא שכיבו ליה תרתין בנין אתו אינשי דאתרא לקמיה אמרו ליה מאי האי אמר להו הכי הוה מעשה א"ל במטותא מינך פוק מאתרין ולא תגרי בהו מותנא בהנך אינשי תניא ר' נהוראי אומר דור שבן דוד בא בו (ח) נערים ילבינו פני זקנים וזקנים יעמדו לפני נערים ובת קמה באמה וכלה בחמותה ופני הדור כפני כלב ואין הבן מתבייש מאביו תניא ר' נחמיה אומר דור שבן דוד בא בו העזות תרבה והיוקר יעות והגפן יתן פריו והיין ביוקר ונהפכה כל המלכות למינות ואין תוכחה מסייע ליה לר' יצחק דא"ר יצחק אין בן דוד בא עד שתתהפך כל המלכות למינות אמר רבא מאי קרא (ד) כולו הפך לבן טהור הוא ת"ר (ה) כי ידין ה' עמו [וגו'] כי יראה כי אזלת יד ואפס עצור ועזוב אין בן דוד בא עד שירבו המסורות ד"א עד שיתמעטו התלמידים ד"א עד שתכלה פרוטה מן הכיס ד"א עד שיתייאשו מן הגאולה שנאמר ואפס עצור ועזוב כביכול אין סומך ועוזר לישראל כי הא דר' זירא כי הוה משכח רבנן דמעסקי ביה אמר להו במטותא (ט) בעינא מנייכו לא תרחקוה דתנינא ג' באין בהיסח הדעת אלו הן משיח מציאה ועקרב אמר רב קטינא (י) שית אלפי שני הוו עלמא וחד חרוב שנאמר (ו) ונשגב ה' לבדו ביום ההוא אביי אמר תרי חרוב שנאמר (ז) יחיינו מיומים ביום השלישי יקימנו ונחיה לפניו תניא כותיה דרב קטינא כשם שהשביעית משמטת שנה אחת לז' שנים כך העולם משמט אלף שנים לשבעת אלפים שנה שנאמר ונשגב ה' לבדו ביום ההוא ואומר (ח) מזמור שיר ליום השבת יום שכולו שבת ואומר (ט) כי אלף שנים בעיניך כיום אתמול כי יעבור (כ) תנא דבי אליהו ששת אלפים שנה הוי עלמא שני אלפים תוהו שני אלפים תורה שני אלפים ימות המשיח ובעונותינו

את סוכת דוד הנופלת. מלכות דוד שנפלה להכי קרי משיח בר נפלי: עד שהראשונה פקודה. עד שלא כלתה צרה ראשונה שניה ממהרת לבא פקודה כמו לא נפקד (במדבר לא): שבוע. שמיטה: והמטרתי על עיר אחת. שיהא מעט מטר ויהא רעב במקום זה ושובע במקום זה: חיצי רעב. רעב מעט שלא יהא שובע בשום מקום: משתכחת מלומדיה. מתוך שאין להם מה לאכול: בששית קולות. יצאו קולות שבן דוד בא ל"א קולות מתקיעת שופר שנאמר יתקע בשופר גדול (ישעיה כז): מלחמות. בין עובדי כוכבים לישראל: דהוה הכי. שנה אחת רעב שנה אחת שובע ואעפ"כ לא בא בן דוד: בששית קולות מי הוה. כלום יצאו קולות שבן דוד בא: ועוד כסדרן מי הוה. כלומר אלו הצרות דקתני הכא כסדרן לא אתרמו בשבוע אחד אבל כי אתרמו אתי משיח: אשר חרפו אויביך ה' אשר חרפו עקבות משיחך. לא אתפרש האי קרא למאי איכתיב הכא דהא לא קא דריש ביה מידי ונראה למורי שכן נכתב בספרים תחלה כמו ששנינו בפ' אחרון דסוטה (דף מט:) בעקבות המשיח חוצפא יסגא וכתבו פירוש זה על בעקבות שהוא לשון סוף כמו אשר חרפו עקבות משיחך: בית הועד. מקום שתלמידי חכמים מתוועדין שם ללמוד תורה: ה"ג והגבלן. מקום ששמו כך ישתומם: ואנשי הגבול. אנשי גבול ארץ ישראל ל"א אנשי גזית סנהדרין: כפני כלב. דדמיין ממש לכלב מ"ר ל"א כפני הכלב שלא יתביישו זה מזה: משתולל על הבריות. כל העולם אומרין עליו שוטה הוא היינו משתולל לשון שטות כמו מוליך יועצים שולל (איוב יב): ליכא קושטא בעלמא. אין אדם בעולם שידבר אמת תמיד: אמר לי ההוא מרבנן דאי הוו יהבי ליה כל חללי דעלמא לא משני בדבוריה. לשקר ואישתעי לי הכי זימנא חדא אקלעי לההוא אתרא וקושטא שמיה: טרפא אבבא. שהיתה שואלת אותה: לאו אורח ארעא. לומר היכן היא הואיל וחייפ' רישה: ה"ג נערים ילבינו פני זקנים. כלומר יחפרו ויביישו אותם: וזקנים יעמדו בפני הנערים. לכבדם והיינו דאמרינן (בסוטה ד' מט:) בעקבות המשיח חוצפא יסגא: בת קמה באמה. לחרפה ולביישה: היוקר יעות. שלא יכבדו זה את זה יקר כבוד ל"א היוקר יעות מכובד שבהן יהא עוותן ורמאי. מ"ר: והגפן יתן פריו. ואעפ"כ יהיה היין ביוקר שלא יהיה ברכה בפרי עצמו ל"א שיהיו כולן רודפין אחר היין ומשתכרין ומתייקר היין אע"פ שרוב יין בעולם: כלו הפך לבן טהור הוא. כשפשט הנגע בכל העור כך כשנהפכה כל המלכות למינות תבא גאולה: כי ידין ה' עמו. להביא להם גאולה: כי יראה כי אזלת יד. שתלך ותחזק ידן של מסורות ומלשינין במלשינותן: שיתמעטו התלמידים. שמחזיקין ידי ישראל להחזירן למוטב: שתכלה פרוטה. והיינו אזלת יד שיהו בידים ריקניות: כביכול. כאלו יכולין לומר דבר זה כלפי מעלה: אין עוזר ואין סומך לישראל. שיהיו שפלים למאד ואומר אין עוזר וסומך שיהיו מתייאשין מן הגאולה: דמעסקי ביה. לידע מתי יבא: ועקרב. נושך האדם פתאום: וחד חרוב. שאלף שנה יהיה חרוב חוץ מששת אלפים אלו דהיינו אלף שביעי: תרי. אלפים הוא חרב אלף שביעי ואלף שמיני: יומו של הקב"ה אלף שנה שנאמר כי אלף שנים בעיניך כיום אתמול כי יעבור: משמט. ונעשה חרב: שכולו שבת. שהעולם משמט: הוי עלמא. העולם כך מתקיים: ב' אלפים היה תהו. תחת שלא ניתנה עדיין תורה והיה העולם כתוהו ומאדם הראשון עד שהיה אברהם בן נ"ב שנה איכא אלפים שנה כדמוכחי קראי דכשנשלמו אלפים שנה עסק אברהם בתורה שנאמר (בראשית יב) ואת הנפש אשר עשו בחרן ומתרגמינן דשעבידו לאורייתא בחרן ואמרינן במסכת ע"ז (דף ט.) גמירי דההוא שעתא הוה אברהם בר חמשין ותרתי שנין: ושני אלפים תורה. מן הנפש אשר עשו בחרן עד [אלפים] שנות המשיח ארבעים ((ל) ושמנים) שנה עד שנולד יצחק וששים שנה משנולד יצחק עד שנולד יעקב הרי ק"ח וק"ל שהיו ליעקב כשבא למצרים הרי רל"ח ורד"ו שעמדו במצרים הרי תמ"ח ומשיצאו ממצרים עד שנבנה בית ראשון ת"פ דכתיב (מלכים א ו) ויהי בשמנים שנה וארבע מאות שנה לצאת בני ישראל מארץ מצרים וגו' הרי תתקכ"ח ות"י שעמד בית ראשון כדמוכחי קראי על פי חשבון שנות המלכים וע' דגלות בבל ות"כ שעמד בית שני הרי תת"ק ותתקכ"ח הרי אלפים פחות קע"ב וקע"ב קודם השלמת ד' אלפים נחרב הבית ולסוף אותן קע"ב נשלמו שני אלפים תורה ואיידי דאמר שני אלפים תוהו קאמר שני אלפים תורה ולא שתכלה תורה אחר שני אלפים. מ"ר: ושני אלפים שנות המשיח. שלאחר שני אלפים תורה הוה דינו שיבא משיח ותכלה הגלות ויבטל השיעבוד מישראל: אבל

מסורת הש"ס

א) מגילה יז:, ב) רש"ל מ"ז, ג) [סוטה מט:], ד) רש"ל מ"ז, ה) [ב"מ מט. ע"ש], ו) י"ג סברי, ז) י"ג אמרי, ח) סוטה מט:, ט) [בברכות לה: וביומא עב: גם בע"י ליתא מלת בעינא וכן לעיל בסמוך במטותא מינך], י) [ר"ה לא.], כ) ע"ז ט., ל) [צ"ל ושמנה].

הגהות הגר"א

[א] גמ' אשר חרפו. נדפס בגלו רש"ל מוחק זה נמחק הסג"ה: [ב] שם ואנשי גבול. נמחק תיבת גבול. ונ"ב חול: [ג] שם ופני הדור כפני הכלב. נמחק: [ד] שם וסר מרע משתולל. נדפס בגלו רש"ל מ"ז נמחק הסג"ה:

תורה אור השלם

א) וְגַם אָנֹכִי מָנַעְתִּי מִכֶּם אֶת הַגֶּשֶׁם בְּעוֹד שְׁלֹשָׁה חֳדָשִׁים לַקָּצִיר וְהִמְטַרְתִּי עַל עִיר אֶחָת וְעַל עִיר אַחַת לֹא אַמְטִיר חֶלְקָה אַחַת תִּמָּטֵר וְחֶלְקָה אֲשֶׁר לֹא תַמְטִיר עָלֶיהָ תִּיבָשׁ: [עמוס ד, ז]

ב) אֲשֶׁר חֵרְפוּ אוֹיְבֶיךָ יְיָ אֲשֶׁר חֵרְפוּ עִקְּבוֹת מְשִׁיחֶךָ: [תהלים פט, נב]

ג) וַתְּהִי הָאֱמֶת נֶעְדֶּרֶת וְסָר מֵרָע מִשְׁתּוֹלֵל וַיַּרְא יְיָ וַיֵּרַע בְּעֵינָיו כִּי אֵין מִשְׁפָּט: [ישעיה נט, טו]

ד) וְרָאָה הַכֹּהֵן וְהִנֵּה כִסְּתָה הַצָּרַעַת אֶת כָּל בְּשָׂרוֹ וְטִהַר אֶת הַנָּגַע כֻּלּוֹ הָפַךְ לָבָן טָהוֹר הוּא: [ויקרא יג, יג]

ה) כִּי יָדִין יְיָ עַמּוֹ וְעַל עֲבָדָיו יִתְנֶחָם כִּי יִרְאֶה כִּי אָזְלַת יָד וְאֶפֶס עָצוּר וְעָזוּב: [דברים לב, לו]

ו) וְשַׁח גַּבְהוּת הָאָדָם וְשָׁפֵל רוּם אֲנָשִׁים וְנִשְׂגַּב יְיָ לְבַדּוֹ בַּיּוֹם הַהוּא: [ישעיה ב, יז]

ז) יְחַיֵּנוּ מִיֹּמָיִם בַּיּוֹם הַשְּׁלִישִׁי יְקִמֵנוּ וְנִחְיֶה לְפָנָיו: [הושע ו, ב]

ח) מִזְמוֹר שִׁיר לְיוֹם הַשַּׁבָּת: [תהלים צב, א]

ט) כִּי אֶלֶף שָׁנִים בְּעֵינֶיךָ כְּיוֹם אֶתְמוֹל כִּי יַעֲבֹר וְאַשְׁמוּרָה בַלָּיְלָה: [תהלים צ, ד]

ליקוטי רש"י

שבוע שבן דוד בא בו. חלוק משאר שנים כדאמרינן בפרק חלק (לז.) שנה ראשונה רעב ולא רעב כו' עד ובשביעית מלחמות ובמוצאי שביעית בן דוד בא [מגילה יז:]. עקבות משיחך. סופי מלך המשיח ולשון משנה הוא בעקבות המשיח חוצפא יסגא [תהלים פט, נב]. בסוף הגלות לפני ביאת משיח [סוטה מט:]. בית הוועד. של חכמים יהיו לבית זנות שכלו החכמים ואין לומד תורה ויהא חרב מאין איש ובעלי זימה מתגודדים שם מפני שחוץ לעיר היו בתי מדרשות שלהם [סוטה שם]. משתולל. מוחזק שוטה על הבריות כמו (מיכה א) אלכה שולל והוא מגזרת שוגג דמתרגמינן שלו וכן (ש"ב ו) על השל [ישעיה נט, טו]. והיין ביוקר. שהכל עוסקין במשתאות. ונהפכה כל המלכות למינות. והמלכות השולטת על רוב העולם תהא למינות נמשכים אחר טעות שלו [ישו] ותלמידיו נקראו מינים [דפו"י]. ואין תוכחה. אין לך אדם שיוכל להוכיח שכולם נכשלים בחטאות וכשמוכיחין אומר לו אתה כמוני [סוטה שם]. כי יראה כי אזלת יד. כשיראה כי יד האויב הולכת וחוזקת מאד עליהם ואפס בהם עצור ועזוב. עצור. נושע על ידי עוצר ומושל שיעצור בהם. עזוב. על ידי עוזב. עוצר הוא המושל העוצר בעם שלא ילכו מפוזרים בצאתם לצבא על האויב. בלשון בלע"ז מיינטינדו"ר עצור הוא הנושע במעצור המושל עזוב מחוזק כמו (נחמיה ג, ח) ויעזבו את ירושלים עד החומה (ירמיה מט, כה) איך לא עוזבה עיר תהלה עצור מיינטינו"ד עזוב אינפורלדו"ר [דברים לב, לו]. שתכלה פרוטה מן הכיס. אין מעות מצויות בכיס [לקמן צח.]. שית אלפי שני. נגזר על העולם להתקיים כמנין ימי השבוע ויום השביעי שבת ובשבעת אלפים נוח לעולם [ע"ז ט.]. מזמור שיר. של לוים (נביאים). ליום השבת. שאומרים אותו בשבתות והוא מדבר בענין העולם הבא שכולו שבת [תהלים צב, א]. יום שכולו שבת. שעתיד העולם להיות חרב ואין אדם וכל המלאכות שובתות על אותו יום אומרים שיר של שבת [ר"ה לא.]. שני אלפים. ראשונים נגזר עליו להיות תוהו בלא תורה ושני אלפים תורה בלא ימות המשיח ושני אלפים ימות המשיח. שני אלפים תוהו. לא וחשוב שנות דור ודור שחי כל אחד קודם שנולד בנו דשנים שאחרי כן אתה נותן לבן ותמצא מאדם עד שנולד נח תתרנ"ו שנים ונח חי תק"ב שנים קודם שנולד שם דכתיב (בראשית ה) ויהי נח בן חמש מאות שנה וגו' כשנולד בנו הראשון היה בן ת"ק שנים ויפת הוא הגדול מחם שנה וחם גדול משם שנה הרי תק"ב שנים לנח כשנולד שם כדכתיב (שם, יא) [שם] בן מאת שנה ויולד את ארפכשד שנתים אחר המבול ואם שם לת"ק שנים דנח אגייליד כי מטו שנתים אחר המבול הוה ליה בר ק"ב דהא כתיב (שם, ז) ונח בן שש מאות שנה והמבול היה חשוב תק"ב דנח ומאה דשם עד ארפכשד והוסף על נ"ו של פרט הרי תרנ"ח וארפכשד הוליד את שלח בל"ה הרי תרצ"ג ומשלח עד עבר ל' הרי תשכ"ג ומעבר עד פלג ל"ד הרי תשנ"ז ומפלג עד רעו ל' הרי תשפ"ז ומרעו לשרוג ל"ב הרי תתי"ט ומשרוג לנחור ל' הרי תתמ"ט ומנחור לתרח כ"ט הרי תתע"ח ומתרח לאברהם ע' הרי תתקמ"ח על אלף וכו' הוה אברהם בר נ"ב הוסיפם על אלף ותתקמ"ח שהיו בידך כשנולד אברהם הרי אלפים תוהו. שני אלפים תורה. מאברהם עד יצחק ק' הרי אלפים ומ"ח ומיצחק עד מתן תורה ת' שנים כיצד ס' עד שנולד יעקב וברדתו למצרים כתיב ימי שני מגורי שלשים ומאת שנה הרי ק"ל משנולד יצחק וישראל היו במצרים רד"ו הרי ד' מאות ומ"ח שנים על אלפים לבריאת עולם נמצא ממתן תורה עד ד' אלפים לבריאתו של עולם אלף וחמש מאות וחמשים ושתים. כמה בצירן לך השתא דתורה דתני תנא תמ"ח שנים היו בצירן לך כי מעיינת מואת הנפש אשר עשו עד מתן תורה הכי הוו הוסף אותן על מנין מתן תורה ונמצא אלפים מכוונין מואת הנפש אשר עשו וגו' עד גמר ד' אלפים לבריאת עולם והוא קע"ב שנים לאחר חורבן כיצד הרי מנית עד יציאת מצרים תמ"ח על עודף אלפים וכתיב (מ"א ו) ויהי בשמנים שנה וארבע מאות שנה לצאת בני ישראל עד ויבן שלמה את הבית הרי תתקכ"ח על אלפים כשנבנה הבית וימי בית ראשון ד' מאות ועשר הרי שלשה אלפים ושל"ח שנים וגלות בבל ע' שנים הרי ת"ח וימי בית שני ת"ך הרי תתכ"ח נמצא קע"ב חסרין מד' אלפים והכי תני בסדר עולם [ע"ז שם].

The Gemara asks:

מַאי ,,וַתְּהִי הָאֱמֶת נֶעְדֶּרֶת״ – **What is** the meaning of: ***and the truth will be absent*** (*nederes*)?[21]

The Gemara answers:

אָמְרֵי דְּבֵי רַב – **In the academy, they said:** מְלַמֵּד שֶׁנַּעֲשֵׂית עֲדָרִים עֲדָרִים וְהוֹלֶכֶת לָהּ – **It teaches that [truth] will be formed into groups** (*adarim*)[22] **and go** away.[23]

The Gemara questions the next part of the verse:

מַאי ,,וְסָר מֵרָע מִשְׁתּוֹלֵל״ – **What** is the meaning of: ***and he that turns away from evil will become foolish?***

The Gemara answers:

אָמְרֵי דְּבֵי רַבִּי שֵׁילָא – **In the academy of R' Shela they said:** כָּל מִי שֶׁסָּר מֵרָע מִשְׁתּוֹלֵל עַל הַבְּרִיּוֹת – This means that **whoever turns away from evil will be** considered **foolish by** the rest of **the people.**

Having mentioned a situation in which truthfulness will be absent, the Gemara digresses to relate a story about people who spoke only the truth:[24]

אָמַר רָבָא – **Rava said:** מֵרֵישׁ הֲוָה אָמֵינָא – **At first I used to say** that לֵיכָּא קוּשְׁטָא בְּעָלְמָא – **there is no truth in the world** (i.e. there is no person who speaks only the truth). אֲמַר לִי הַהוּא מֵרַבָּנַן – But then **one of the rabbis said to me,** וְרַב טָבוּת שְׁמֵיהּ – **and Rav Tavus was his name,** וְאָמְרֵי לָהּ רַב טַבְיוֹמֵי שְׁמֵיהּ – **and some say that Rav Tavyomei was his name,** דְּאִי הֲווּ יָהֲבֵי לֵיהּ כָּל חַלְלֵי דְּעָלְמָא – **that even if they would give him all the riches**[25] **in the world,** לֹא הֲוָה מְשַׁנֵּי בְּדִיבּוּרֵיהּ – **he would not tell a lie.**[26] He related the following story to me: זִימְנָא חֲדָא אִיקְלַעִי לְהַהוּא אַתְרָא – **Once, I visited a certain town** וְקוּשְׁטָא שְׁמֵיהּ – by the **name** of **Kushta**[27] וְלֹא הֲווּ מְשַׁנֵּי בְּדִיבּוּרַיְיהוּ – **[whose inhabitants] would not tell a lie,** וְלֹא הֲוָה מָיֵית אִינִישׁ מֵהָתָם בְּלֹא זִימְנֵיהּ – **and none of the people from there died before his time.**[28] נְסִיבִי אִיתְּתָא מִינַּיְהוּ – **I married a woman from** among **them,** וַהֲווּ לִי תַּרְתֵּין בְּנִין מִינָּהּ – **and I had two sons by her.**

The narrative continues in the third person:

יוֹמָא חַד – **One day,** הֲוָה יָתְבָא דְּבֵיתְהוּ וְקָא חָיְיפָא רֵישָׁא – **his wife**[29] **was sitting and washing her hair.**[30] אֲתַאי שִׁיבַבְתָּהּ טָרְפָא אַדַּשָּׁא – **Her neighbor came** and **knocked on the door,** asking to speak to her. סָבַר לָאו אוֹרַח אַרְעָא – **Thinking** that **it would not be proper** to tell the neighbor that his wife was washing her hair, אֲמַר לָהּ – **he said to [the neighbor]:** לֵיתָא הָכָא – **"She is not here."** שְׁכִיבוּ לֵיהּ תַּרְתֵּין בְּנִין – Subsequently, **his two sons died.** אָתוּ אִינָשֵׁי דְאַתְרָא לְקַמֵּיהּ אָמְרוּ לֵיהּ – **The people of that town came to him** and **asked him:** מַאי הַאי – **"What is** the reason for **this?"** אֲמַר לְהוּ הָכִי הֲוָה מַעֲשֶׂה – **He told them what had happened.**[31] אָמְרוּ לֵיהּ – They said to him: בְּמָטוּתָא מִינָּךְ – **"We beg you,** פּוּק מֵאַתְרִין – **leave our town,** וְלֹא תְּגָרֵי בְּהוּ מוֹתָנָא בְּהָנָךְ אִינָשֵׁי – **and do not incite death against these people!"**[32]

The Gemara resumes its discussion about the pre-Messianic era:

תַּנְיָא – **It was taught in a Baraisa:** רַבִּי נְהוֹרַאי אוֹמֵר – **R' NEHORAI SAYS:** דּוֹר שֶׁבֶּן דָּוִד בָּא בּוֹ – In **THE GENERATION WHEN THE SON OF DAVID WILL COME,** נְעָרִים יַלְבִּינוּ פְּנֵי זְקֵנִים – **YOUNG PEOPLE WILL SHAME THE OLD,** וּזְקֵנִים יַעַמְדוּ לִפְנֵי נְעָרִים – **OLD PEOPLE WILL RISE BEFORE THE YOUNG;**[33] ,,בַּת קָמָה בְאִמָּהּ (ו)כַלָּה בַּחֲמֹתָהּ״ – ***A DAUGHTER WILL STAND AGAINST HER MOTHER,***[34] ***A DAUGHTER-IN-LAW AGAINST HER MOTHER-IN-LAW;***[35] וּפְנֵי הַדּוֹר כִּפְנֵי כֶלֶב – **THE FACE OF THE GENERATION WILL BE LIKE THE FACE OF A DOG;**[36] וְאֵין הַבֵּן מִתְבַּיֵּישׁ מֵאָבִיו – **AND A SON WILL NOT BE ASHAMED BEFORE HIS FATHER.**

Another Baraisa about the pre-Messianic era:

תַּנְיָא – **It was taught in a Baraisa:** רַבִּי נְחֶמְיָה אוֹמֵר – **R' NECHEMIAH SAYS:** דּוֹר שֶׁבֶּן דָּוִד בָּא בּוֹ – In **THE GENERATION WHEN THE SON OF DAVID WILL COME,** הָעַזּוּת תִּרְבֶּה – **INSOLENCE WILL INCREASE,** וְהַיּוֹקֶר יְעַוֵּת – **HONOR WILL DWINDLE,**[37] וְהַגֶּפֶן יִתֵּן פִּרְיוֹ וְהַיַּיִן בְּיוֹקֶר – **THE VINE WILL PRODUCE ITS FRUIT, YET WINE**

NOTES

21. נֶעְדֶּרֶת usually signifies complete lack or absence. However, that cannot be its meaning here, because the Jewish people will never be utterly devoid of Torah scholars, who are devoted to the truth. The Gemara in *Shabbos* (119b) states that even at the time of Jerusalem's fall the Torah scholars did not die out completely (*Maharsha;* cf. *Rif* in *Ein Yaakov*).

22. Literally: flocks [and] flocks. נֶעְדֶּרֶת (absent) shares the same root as עֵדֶר, *flock.*

23. The generation will be so corrupt that the few surviving truthful persons will have to band together in groups and leave the general society (*Maharsha;* see also *Yad Shaul,* cited by *Margaliyos HaYam*).

24. *Rashi* to 96b ד״ה אימת; *Yad Ramah* here.

25. Precious stones and pearls (*Yad Ramah;* cf. *Rashi* to *Shabbos* 77b; see *Maharsha* and *Ben Yehoyada*).

26. Literally: change [the truth] in his speech. Rav Tavus (or Rav Tavyomei) would never lie because he experienced a certain incident which he now proceeds to relate (*Maharsha*).

27. [Literally: and Kushta was its name.] קוּשְׁטָא, *kushta,* is Aramaic for *truth.*

28. A person is allotted a certain number of years at birth. If he is deserving, he will live them all out; if not, his life will be shortened (*Yevamos* 50a). A person who never tells a lie will live his full number of years even if he does not otherwise merit it. Since he kept his word, God will "keep His word" and let him live to the age he was initially assigned (*Iyun Yaakov*).

Maharsha cites the Gemara (above, 64a) which states that the seal of God is truth. It was with this attribute of truth that God created the world. The first three words of the Torah's account of the creation, בְּרֵאשִׁית בָּרָא אֱלֹקִים, end with the letters of the word אֱמֶת, *truth.* Likewise, the last three words, בָּרָא אֱלֹקִים לַעֲשׂוֹת, end with these letters. Thus, one who does not tell the truth undermines the world's existence. Even if he deviates from the truth by only the slightest degree, he brings death to the world. The very word אֱמֶת (truth) contains an allusion to this point. When the letter א, which has the lowest possible numerical value (one), is removed from אֱמֶת, the remaining letters spell מֵת, *dead.*

29. I.e. the wife of Rav Tavus or Rav Tavyomei.

30. Literally: her head.

31. Literally: he said to them, "This was the incident."

32. [I.e. against us.] Actually, it is permitted to lie under certain circumstances (see *Bava Metzia* 23b-24a; see also *Rashi* to *Genesis* 18:13; see also *Michtav MeEliyahu* vol. 1 p. 94). In this case, however, the potential embarrassment was not sufficient to warrant a lie (*Hagahos R' Y. Emden*).

Maharal posits that this narrative is an allegorical tale whose moral is that even in a case where it is correct to lie, the lie has negative repercussions (see note 28).

33. Young people will insult the old, and yet the old will accord honor to the young. This is a manifestation of the statement (cited below and in *Sotah* 49b): בְּעִקְבְתָא דִמְשִׁיחָא חוּצְפָּא יִסְגֵּי, *In the footsteps of the Messiah* (i.e. the pre-Messianic era), *insolence will increase* (*Rashi*).

The social conventions will become inverted to the point that old people, who should by right be respected, will themselves subscribe to the new order, and give reverence to youth (see note 4).

34. To insult and shame her (*Rashi*).

35. *Micah* 7:6.

36. See note 19.

37. People will not respect one another. Alternatively, the most honored people will be corrupt (*Rashi*). [According to the second explanation, וְהַיּוֹקֶר יְעַוֵּת is rendered *and honor will corrupt.*]

Yad Ramah renders הַיָּקָר יְעֻוַּת, *the honored one will be abused.* Those who should be honored will be scorned instead.

את סוכת דוד הנופלת א"ל הכי אמר רבי יוחנן דור שבן דוד בא בו תלמידי חכמים מתמעטים והשאר עיניהם כלות ביגון ואנחה וצרות רבות וגזרות קשות מתחדשות עד שהראשונה פקודה שניה ממהרת לבא ת"ר שבוע שבן דוד בא בו שנה ראשונה מתקיים מקרא זה א) והמטרתי על עיר אחת ועל עיר אחת לא אמטיר שניה חיצי רעב משתלחים שלישית רעב גדול ומתים אנשים ונשים וטף חסידים ואנשי מעשה ותורה משתכחת מלומדיה ברביעית שובע ואינו שובע בחמישית שובע גדול ואוכלין ושותין ושמחין ותורה חוזרת ללומדיה א) בששית קולות בשביעית מלחמות במוצאי שביעית בן דוד בא אמר רב יוסף הא כמה שביעית דהוה כן ולא אתא אמר אביי בששית קולות בשביעית מלחמות מי הוה ועוד כסדרן מי הוה [א] ב) ב) (אשר חרפו אויביך ה' אשר חרפו עקבות משיחך) תניא ר' יהודה אומר דור שבן דוד בא בו ג) בית הוועד יהיה לזנות והגליל יחרב והגבלן יאשם [ב] ואנשי גבול יסובבו מעיר לעיר ולא יחוננו וחכמת הסופרים תסרח ויראי חטא ימאסו [ג] ופני הדור כפני כלב והאמת נעדרת שנאמר ג) ותהי האמת נעדרת [ד] ד) (וסר מרע משתולל) מאי ותהי האמת נעדרת אמרי דבי רב מלמד שנעשית עדרים עדרים והולכת לה מאי וסר מרע משתולל אמרי דבי ר' שילא כל מי שסר מרע משתולל על הבריות אמר רבא מריש הוה אמינא ליכא קושטא בעלמא אמר לי ה) ההוא מרבנן ורב טבות שמיה ואמרי לה רב טביומי שמיה דאי הוו יהבי ליה כל חללי דעלמא לא הוה משני בדבוריה זימנא חדא איקלעי לההוא אתרא וקושטא שמיה ולא הוו משני בדיבורייהו ולא הוה מיית איניש מהתם בלא זימניה נסיבי איתתא מינהון והוו לי תרתין בנין מינה יומא חד הוה יתבא דביתהו וקא חייפא רישה אתאי שיבבתה טרפא אדשא ו) סבר לאו אורח ארעא ז) אמר לה ליתא הכא שכיבו ליה תרתין בנין אתו אינשי דאתרא לקמיה אמרו ליה מאי האי אמר להו הכי הוה מעשה א"ל במטותא מינך פוק מאתרין ולא תגרי בהו מותנא בהנך אינשי תניא ר' נהוראי אומר דור שבן דוד בא בו ח) נערים ילבינו פני זקנים וזקנים יעמדו לפני נערים ובת קמה באמה וכלה בחמותה ופני הדור כפני כלב ואין הבן מתבייש מאביו תניא ר' נחמיה אומר דור שבן דוד בא בו העזות תרבה והיוקר יעות והגפן יתן פריו והיין ביוקר ונהפכה כל המלכות למינות ואין תוכחה מסייע ליה לר' יצחק דא"ר יצחק אין בן דוד בא עד שתתהפך כל המלכות למינות אמר רבא מאי קרא ד) כולו הפך לבן טהור הוא ת"ר ה) כי ידין ה' עמו [וגו'] כי יראה כי אזלת יד ואפס עצור ועזוב אין בן דוד בא עד שירבו המסורות ד"א עד שתכלה פרוטה מן הכיס ד"א עד שיתייאשו מן הגאולה שנאמר ואפס עצור ועזוב כביכול אין סומך ועוזר לישראל כי הא דר' זירא כי הוה משכח רבנן דמעסקי ביה אמר להו במטותא ט) בעינא מנייכו לא תרחקוה דתנינא ג' באין בהיסח הדעת אלו הן משיח מציאה ועקרב אמר רב קטינא י) שית אלפי שני הוו עלמא וחד חרוב שנאמר ו) ונשגב ה' לבדו ביום ההוא אביי אמר תרי חרוב שנאמר ז) יחיינו מיומים ביום השלישי יקימנו ונחיה לפניו תניא כותיה דרב קטינא כשם שהשביעית משמטת שנה אחת לז' שנים כך העולם משמט אלף שנים לשבעת אלפים שנה שנאמר ונשגב ה' לבדו ביום ההוא ואומר ח) מזמור שיר ליום השבת יום שכולו שבת ואומר ט) כי אלף שנים בעיניך כיום אתמול כי יעבור כ) תנא דבי אליהו ששת אלפים שנה הוי עלמא שני אלפים תוהו שני אלפים תורה שני אלפים ימות המשיח ובעונותינו

רש"י

את סוכת דוד הנופלת. מלכות דוד שנפלה להכי קרי משיח בר נפלי: **עד שהראשונה פקודה.** עד שלא כלתה צרה ראשונה שניה ממהרת לבא פקודה כמו לא נפקד (במדבר לא): **שבוע.** שמיטה: **והמטרתי על עיר אחת.** שיהא מעט מטר ויהא רעב במקום זה ושובע במקום זה: **חיצי רעב.** רעב מעט שלא יהא שובע בשום מקום: **משתכחת מלומדיה.** מתוך שאין להם מה לאכול: **בששית קולות.** יצאו קולות שבן דוד בא ל"א קולות מתקיעת שופר שנאמר יתקע בשופר גדול (ישעיה כז): **מלחמות.** בין עובדי כוכבים לישראל: **דהוה הכי.** שנה אחת רעב שנה אחת שובע ואעפ"כ לא בא בן דוד: **בששית קולות מי הוה.** כלום יצאו קולות שבן דוד בא: **ועוד כסדרן מי הוה.** כלומר אלו הצרות דקתני הכא כסדרן לא אתרמו בשבוע אחד אבל כי אתרמו אתי משיח: **אשר חרפו אויביך ה' אשר חרפו עקבות משיחך.** לא אתפרש האי קרא למאי איכתיב הכא דהא לא קא דריש ביה מידי ונראה למורי שכן נכתב בספרים תחלה כמו ששנינו בפ' אחרון דסוטה (דף מט:) בעקבות המשיח חוצפא יסגא וכתבו פירוש זה על בעקבות שהוא לשון סוף כמו אשר חרפו עקבות משיחך: **בית הועד.** מקום שתלמידי חכמים מתוועדין שם ללמוד תורה: **ה"ג והגבלן.** מקום ששמו כך ישתומם: **ואנשי הגבול.** אנשי גבול ארץ ישראל ל"א אנשי גזית סנהדרין: **כפני כלב.** דדמיין ממש לכלב מ"ר ל"א כפני הכלב שלא יתביישו זה מזה: **משתולל על הבריות.** כל העולם אומרין עליו שוטה הוא היינו משתולל לשון שטות כמו מוליך יועצים שולל (איוב יב): **ליכא קושטא בעלמא.** אין אדם בעולם שידבר אמת תמיד: **אמר לי ההוא מרבנן דאי הוו יהבי ליה כל חללי דעלמא לא משני בדבוריה.** לשקר ואישתעי לי הכי זימנא חדא אקלעי לההוא אתרא וקושטא שמיה: **טרפא אבבא.** שהיתה שואלת אותה: **לאו אורח ארעא.** לומר היכן היא הואיל וחייפ' רישה: **ה"ג נערים ילבינו פני זקנים.** כלומר יחפרו ויביישו אותם: **וזקנים יעמדו בפני הנערים.** לכבדם והיינו דאמרינן (בסוטה ד' מט:) בעקבות המשיח חוצפא יסגא: **בת קמה באמה.** לחרפה ולביישה: **היוקר יעות.** שלא יכבדו זה את זה יקר כבוד ל"א היוקר יעות מכובד שבהן יהא עוותן ורמאי. מ"ר: **והגפן יתן פריו.** ואעפ"כ יהיה היין ביוקר שלא יהיה ברכה בפרי עצמו ל"א שיהיו כולן רודפין אחר היין ומשתכרין ומתייקר היין אע"פ שרוב יין בעולם: **כלו הפך לבן טהור הוא.** כשפשט הנגע בכל העור כך כשנהפכה כל המלכות למינות תבא גאולה: **כי ידין ה' עמו.** להביא להם גאולה: **כי יראה כי אזלת יד.** שתלך ותחזק ידן של מסורות ומלשינין במלשינותן: **שיתמעטו התלמידים.** שמחזיקין ידי ישראל להחזירן למוטב: **שתכלה פרוטה.** והיינו אזלת יד שיהו בידים ריקניות: **כביכול.** כאלו יכולין לומר דבר זה כלפי מעלה: **אין עוזר ואין סומך לישראל.** שיהיו שפלים למאד ואומר אין עוזר וסומך שיהיו מתייאשין מן הגאולה: **דמעסקי ביה.** לידע מתי יבא: **ועקרב.** נושך האדם פתאום: **וחד חרוב.** שאלף שנה יהיה חרוב חוץ מששת אלפים אלו דהיינו אלף שביעי: **תרי.** אלפים הוא חרב אלף שביעי ואלף שמיני: יומו של הקב"ה אלף שנה שנאמר כי אלף שנים בעיניך כיום אתמול כי יעבור: **משמט.** ונעשה חרב: **שכולו שבת.** שהעולם משמט: **הוי עלמא.** העולם כך מתקיים: **ב' אלפים היה תהו.** תחת שלא ניתנה עדיין תורה והיה העולם כתוהו ומאדם הראשון עד שהיה אברהם בן נ"ב שנה איכא אלפים שנה כדמוכחי קראי דכשנשלמו אלפים שנה עסק אברהם בתורה שנאמר (בראשית יב) ואת הנפש אשר עשו בחרן ומתרגמינן דשעבידו לאורייתא בחרן ואמרינן במסכת ע"ז (דף ט.) גמירי דההוא שעתא הוה אברהם בר חמשין ותרתי שנין: **ושני אלפים תורה.** מן הנפש אשר עשו בחרן עד [אלפים] שנות המשיח ארבעים (ל) ושמנים) שנה עד שנולד יצחק וששים שנה משנולד יצחק עד שנולד יעקב הרי ק"ח וק"ל שהיו ליעקב כשבא למצרים הרי רל"ח ורד"ו שעמדו במצרים הרי תמ"ח ומשיצאו ממצרים עד שנבנה בית ראשון ת"פ דכתיב (מלכים א ו) ויהי בשמנים שנה וארבע מאות שנה לצאת בני ישראל מארץ מצרים וגו' הרי תתקכ"ח ות"י שעמד בית ראשון כדמוכחי קראי על פי חשבון שנות המלכים וע' דגלות בבל ות"כ שעמד בית שני הרי תת"ק ותתקכ"ח הרי אלפים פחות קע"ב וקע"ב קודם השלמת ד' אלפים נחרב הבית ולסוף אותן קע"ב נשלמו שני אלפים תורה ואיידי דאמר שני אלפים תוהו קאמר שני אלפים תורה ולא שתכלה תורה אחר שני אלפים. מ"ר: **ושני אלפים שנות המשיח.** שלאחר שני אלפים תורה הוה דינו שיבא משיח ותכלה הגלות ויבטל השיעבוד מישראל: אבל

מסורת הש"ס

א) מגילה יז:, ב) רש"ל מ"ז, ג) [סוטה מט:], ד) רש"ל מ"ז, ה) [ב"מ מט. ע"ש], ו) י"ג סברי, ז) י"ג אמרי, ח) סוטה מט:, ט) [בברכות לה: וביומא עב: גם בע"י ליתא מלת **בעינא** וכן לעיל בסמוך **במטותא מינך**], י) [ר"ה לא.], כ) ע"ז ט., ל) [נ"ל ושמנה].

הגהות הגר"א

[א] גמ' **אשר חרפו.** נדפס בגלדו רש"ל מוחק זה נמחק הסג"ה: **[ב]** שם **ואנשי גבול.** נמחק תיבת גבול. ונ"ב חול: **[ג]** שם **ופני הדור כפני הכלב.** נמחק: **[ד]** שם **וסר מרע משתולל.** נדפס בגלדו רש"ל מ"ז נמחק הסג"ה:

תורה אור השלם

א) וְגַם אָנֹכִי מָנַעְתִּי מִכֶּם אֶת הַגֶּשֶׁם בְּעוֹד שְׁלֹשָׁה חֳדָשִׁים לַקָּצִיר וְהִמְטַרְתִּי עַל עִיר אֶחָת וְעַל עִיר אַחַת לֹא אַמְטִיר חֶלְקָה אַחַת תִּמָּטֵר וְחֶלְקָה אֲשֶׁר לֹא תַמְטִיר עָלֶיהָ תִּיבָשׁ: [עמוס ד, ז]

ב) אֲשֶׁר חֵרְפוּ אוֹיְבֶיךָ יְיָ אֲשֶׁר חֵרְפוּ עִקְּבוֹת מְשִׁיחֶךָ: [תהלים פט, נב]

ג) וַתְּהִי הָאֱמֶת נֶעְדֶּרֶת וְסָר מֵרָע מִשְׁתּוֹלֵל וַיַּרְא יְיָ וַיֵּרַע בְּעֵינָיו כִּי אֵין מִשְׁפָּט: [ישעיה נט, טו]

ד) וְרָאָה הַכֹּהֵן וְהִנֵּה כִסְּתָה הַצָּרַעַת אֶת כָּל בְּשָׂרוֹ וְטִהַר אֶת הַנָּגַע כֻּלּוֹ הָפַךְ לָבָן טָהוֹר הוּא: [ויקרא יג, יג]

ה) כִּי יָדִין יְיָ עַמּוֹ וְעַל עֲבָדָיו יִתְנֶחָם כִּי יִרְאֶה כִּי אָזְלַת יָד וְאֶפֶס עָצוּר וְעָזוּב: [דברים לב, לו]

ו) וְשַׁח גַּבְהוּת הָאָדָם וְשָׁפֵל רוּם אֲנָשִׁים וְנִשְׂגַּב יְיָ לְבַדּוֹ בַּיּוֹם הַהוּא: [ישעיה ב, יז]

ז) יְחַיֵּנוּ מִיֹּמָיִם בַּיּוֹם הַשְּׁלִישִׁי יְקִמֵנוּ וְנִחְיֶה לְפָנָיו: [הושע ו, ב]

ח) מִזְמוֹר שִׁיר לְיוֹם הַשַּׁבָּת: [תהלים צב, א]

ט) כִּי אֶלֶף שָׁנִים בְּעֵינֶיךָ כְּיוֹם אֶתְמוֹל כִּי יַעֲבֹר וְאַשְׁמוּרָה בַלָּיְלָה: [תהלים צ, ד]

ליקוטי רש"י

שבוע שבן דוד בא בו. חלוק משאר שנים כדאמרינן בפרק חלק (לז.) שנה ראשונה רעב ולא רעב כו' עד ובשביעית מלחמות ובמוצאי שביעית בן דוד בא [מגילה יז:]. **עקבות משיחך.** סופי מלך המשיח ולשון משנה הוא בעקבות המשיח חוצפא יסגא [תהלים פט, נב]. בסוף הגלות לפני ביאת משיח [סוטה מט:]. **בית הוועד.** של חכמים יהיו לבית זונות שכלו החכמים ואין לומד תורה ויהא חרב מאין איש ובעלי זימה מתגודדים שם מפני שחוץ לעיר היו בתי מדרשות שלהם [סוטה שם]. **משתולל.** מוחזק שוטה על הבריות כמו (מיכה א) אלכה שולל והוא מגזרת שוגג דמתרגמינן שלו וכן (ש"ב ו) על השל [ישעיה נט, טו]. **והיין ביוקר.** שהכל עוסקין במשתאות. **ונהפכה כל המלכות למינות.** והמלכות השולטת על רוב העולם תהא למינות נמשכים אחר טעות שלו [ישו] ותלמידיו נקראו מינים [דפו"י]. **ואין תוכחה.** אין לך אדם שיוכל להוכיח שכולם נכשלים בחטאות וכשמוכיחין אומר לו אתה כמוני [סוטה שם]. **כי יראה כי אזלת יד.** כשיראה כי יד האויב הולכת וחוזקת מאד עליהם ואפס בהם עצור ועזוב. **עצור.** נושע על ידי עוצר ומושל שיעצור בהם. **עזוב.** על ידי עוזב. עוצר הוא המושל העוצר בעם שלא ילכו מפוזרים בצאתם לצבא על האויב. בלשון בלע"ז מיינטינדו"ר עצור הוא הנושע במעצור המושל עזוב מחוזק כמו (נחמיה ג, ח) ויעזבו את ירושלים עד החומה (ירמיה מט, כה) איך לא עזבה עיר תהלה עצור מיינטינו"ד עזוב אינפורצדו"ר [דברים לב, לו]. **שתכלה פרוטה מן הכיס.** אין מעות מצויות בכיס [לקמן צח.]. **שית אלפי שני.** נגזר על העולם להתקיים כמנין ימי השבוע וביום השביעי שבת ובשבעת אלפים נוח לעולם [ע"ז ט.]. **מזמור שיר.** של לוים (נביאים). **ליום השבת.** שאומרים אותו בשבתות והוא מדבר בענין העולם הבא שכולו שבת [תהלים צב, א]. **יום שכולו שבת.** שעתיד העולם להיות חרב ואין אדם וכל המלאכות שובתות על אותו יום אומרים שיר של שבת [ר"ה לא.]. **שני אלפים.** ראשונים נגזר עליו להיות תוהו בלא תורה ושני אלפים תורה בלא ימות המשיח ושני אלפים ימות המשיח. **שני אלפים תוהו.** צא וחשוב שנות דור ודור שמי כל אחד קודם שנולד בנו דשנים שאחרי כן אתה נותן לבן ותמצא מאדם עד שנולד נח תתרנ"ו שנים ונח חי תק"ב שנים קודם שנולד שם דכתיב (בראשית ה) ויהי נח בן חמש מאות שנה וגו' כשנולד בנו הראשון היה בן ת"ק שנים ויפת הוא הגדול מחם שנה וחם גדול משם שנה הרי תק"ב שנים לנח כשנולד שם כדכתיב (שם, יא) [שם] בן מאת שנה ויולד את ארפכשד שנתים אחר המבול ואם שם לת"ק שנים דנח אתייליד כי מטו שנתים אחר המבול הוה ליה בר ק"ב דהא כתיב (שם, ז) ונח בן שש מאות שנה והמבול היה חשוב תק"ב דנח ומאה דשם עד ארפכשד והוסף על נ"ו של פרט הרי תרנ"ח וארפכשד הוליד את שלח בל"ה הרי תרצ"ג ומשלח עד עבר ל' הרי תשכ"ג ומעבר עד פלג ל"ד הרי תשנ"ז ומפלג עד רעו ל' הרי תשפ"ז ומרעו לשרוג ל"ב הרי תתי"ט ומשרוג לנחור ל' הרי תתמ"ט ומנחור לתרח כ"ט הרי תתע"ח ומתרח לאברהם ע' הרי תתקמ"ח על אלף וכו' הוה אברהם בר נ"ב הוסיפם על אלף ותתקמ"ח שהיו בידך כשנולד אברהם הרי אלפים תוהו. **שני אלפים תורה.** מאברהם עד יצחק ק' הרי אלפים ומ"ח ומיצחק עד מתן תורה ת' שנים כיצד ס' עד שנולד יעקב וברדתו למצרים כתיב ימי שני מגורי שלשים ומאת שנה הרי ק"צ משנולד יצחק וישראל היו במצרים רד"ו הרי ד' מאות ומ"ח שנים על אלפים לבריאת עולם נמצא ממתן תורה עד ד' אלפים לבריאתו של עולם אלף ותשע מאות וחמשים ושתים. כמה בצירן לך השתא דתורה דתני תנא תמ"ח שנים היו בצירן לך כי מעיינת מואת הנפש אשר עשו עד מתן תורה הכי הוו הוסף אותן על מנין מתן תורה ונמצא אלפים מכוונין מואת הנפש אשר עשו וגו' עד גמר ד' אלפים לבריאת עולם והוא קע"ב שנים לאחר חורבן כיצד הרי מנית עד יציאת מצרים תמ"ח על עודף אלפים וכתיב (מ"א ו) ויהי בשמנים שנה וארבע מאות שנה לצאת בני ישראל עד ויבן שלמה את הבית הרי תתקכ"ח על אלפים כשנבנה הבית וימי בית ראשון ד' מאות ועשר הרי שלשה אלפים ושל"ח שנים וגלות בבל ע' שנים הרי ת"ח וימי בית שני ת"ך הרי תתכ"ח נמצא קע"ב חסרין מד' אלפים והכי תני בסדר עולם [ע"ז שם].

WILL BE EXPENSIVE,[38] וְנֶהְפְּכָה כָּל הַמַּלְכוּת לְמִינוּת – THE ENTIRE KINGDOM WILL CONVERT TO HERESY,[39] וְאֵין תּוֹכֵחָה – AND THERE WILL BE NO REBUKE.[40]

The Gemara notes that this Baraisa supports a certain Amoraic view:

מְסַיֵּיעַ לֵיהּ לְרַבִּי יִצְחָק – It supports the statement of **R' Yitzchak,** **דְּאָמַר רַבִּי יִצְחָק – for R' Yitzchak said:** **אֵין בֶּן דָּוִד בָּא עַד שֶׁתִּתְהַפֵּךְ כָּל הַמַּלְכוּת לְמִינוּת – The son of David will not come until the entire kingdom converts to heresy.**

The Gemara provides a Scriptural allusion to this point:

אָמַר רָבָא – Rava said: **מַאי קְרָא – What is the verse?** **"כֻּלּוֹ הָפַךְ לָבָן טָהוֹר הוּא" – *All of it has turned white, it is pure.***[41]

The following Baraisa interprets a verse that refers to the redemption:

תָּנוּ רַבָּנָן – The Rabbis taught in a Baraisa: "כִּי־יָדִין ה׳ עַמּוֹ וגו׳ כִּי יִרְאֶה כִּי־אָזְלַת יָד וְאֶפֶס עָצוּר וְעָזוּב" – Scripture states:[42] *FOR HASHEM WILL JUDGE HIS PEOPLE* ETC. (i.e. He will bring the redemption) *WHEN HE SEES THAT THE HAND IS GOING*[43] *AND NO ONE IS BEING PROTECTED OR HELPED.*

אֵין בֶּן דָּוִד בָּא עַד שֶׁיִּרְבּוּ הַמָּסוֹרוֹת – This verse teaches that THE SON OF DAVID WILL NOT COME UNTIL THE INFORMERS HAVE BECOME NUMEROUS.[44]

דָּבָר אַחֵר – ANOTHER EXPLANATION: עַד שֶׁיִּתְמַעֲטוּ הַתַּלְמִידִים – He will not come UNTIL THE STUDENTS OF TORAH HAVE BECOME FEW.[45]

דָּבָר אַחֵר – ANOTHER EXPLANATION: עַד שֶׁתִּכְלֶה פְּרוּטָה מִן הַכִּיס – He will not come UNTIL the *PERUTAH* HAS GONE FROM THE PURSE.[46]

דָּבָר אַחֵר – ANOTHER EXPLANATION: עַד שֶׁיִּתְיָיאֲשׁוּ מִן הַגְּאוּלָּה – He will not come UNTIL [THE JEWS] DESPAIR OF THE REDEMPTION, שֶׁנֶּאֱמַר "וְאֶפֶס עָצוּר וְעָזוּב" – AS IT IS STATED in that verse: *AND NO ONE IS BEING PROTECTED OR HELPED,* כִּבְיָכוֹל אֵין סוֹמֵךְ וְעוֹזֵר לְיִשְׂרָאֵל – which implies that, AS IT WERE, THERE IS NO SUPPORTER OR HELPER OF ISRAEL.[47]

The Gemara records an incident:

כִּי הָא דְּרַבִּי זֵירָא – This last point is **related to that which R' Zeira said.** **כִּי הֲוָה מַשְׁכַּח רַבָּנָן דְּמַעַסְקֵי בֵּיהּ – When [R' Zeira] found the Rabbis dealing with [this matter],**[48] **אָמַר לְהוּ – he said to them:** **בְּמָטוּתָא בָּעֵינָא מִנַּיְיכוּ לָא תְרַחֲקוּהָ – "Please! I beg you not to delay [the coming of the Messiah],** **דִּתְנִינָא – for we have learned in a Baraisa:** **שְׁלֹשָׁה בָּאִין בְּהֶיסֵּחַ הַדַּעַת** – THREE THINGS COME WHEN they are NOT EXPECTED.[49] אֵלּוּ הֵן – THEY ARE: מָשִׁיחַ מְצִיאָה וְעַקְרָב – THE MESSIAH, A FIND,[50] AND A SCORPION."[51]

The Gemara discusses a related topic:

אָמַר רַב קְטִינָא – Rav Katina said: **שִׁית אַלְפֵי שְׁנֵי הָווּ עָלְמָא –** For **six thousand years will the world exist,** **וְחַד חָרוּב – and** for **one** thousand years[52] it will be **destroyed,** **שֶׁנֶּאֱמַר "וְנִשְׂגַּב ה׳ לְבַדּוֹ בַּיּוֹם הַהוּא" – as it is stated: *HASHEM alone will be exalted on that day.***[53]

A dissenting view:

אַבַּיֵי אָמַר – Abaye says: **תְּרֵי חָרוּב –** For **two** thousand years it will be **destroyed,** **שֶׁנֶּאֱמַר "יְחַיֵּנוּ מִיֹּמָיִם בַּיּוֹם הַשְּׁלִישִׁי יְקִמֵנוּ וְנִחְיֶה לְפָנָיו" – as it is stated: *After two days He will revive us; on the third day He will raise us up and we will live in His presence.***[54]

NOTES

38. Grapes will not yield their normal amount of juice. Hence, although grapes will be abundant, wine will be scarce (*Rashi*).

An alternative explanation: Drunkenness will be so rampant that even a plentiful supply of wine will not satisfy the demand (*Rashi, Yad Ramah*).

39. The world's dominant power will be drawn after the false beliefs of the heretics (*Meleches Shlomo* to *Sotah* 9:15). It will propagate the heresy (*Tiferes Yisrael* ibid. §90).

This wave of heresy has a beneficial aspect. If people no longer remain entrenched in their ancestral beliefs, they will be open to the Messiah's call to turn to God (see *Yeshuos Meshicho Iyun* 1 ch. 5; see also *Rambam, Hil. Melachim* end of ch. 11 [original version]).

40. One will not be able to rebuke another, because all will be sinners. Upon being rebuked, a person will retort, "You are no better than I am!" (*Rashi* to *Sotah* 49b).

Alternatively, this point is connected to the previous one. There will be no Jew capable of engaging the heretics in debate and driving their false beliefs from their minds (*Yeshuos Meshicho* ibid.; *Eitz Yosef*).

41. *Leviticus* 13:13. When *tzaraas* (a certain type of skin affliction) covers part of a person's body, he is impure (see ibid. chs. 13,14). But when it covers his *entire* body, he is pure. Likewise, when heresy spreads across the entire world, the time for redemption has come (*Rashi*).

42. *Deuteronomy* 32:36. In this passage, God predicts that the Jews will sin and He will send a foreign nation to vanquish them. When the oppression of the Jews becomes so severe that their very existence is threatened, God will relent and rescue them by bringing the Messiah.

43. This phrase is interpreted below in various ways.

44. The phrase אָזְלַת יָד is translated "the power is going up" (i.e. it is growing), and it refers to those who inform against the Jews to foreign authorities. When these informers become too successful, God will bring the redemption (*Rashi*).

45. The source of Israel's power is its Torah scholars, who lead the people onto the right path (*Rashi*). When this power fades (i.e. the number of Torah scholars decreases), God will bring the redemption. According to this explanation, the phrase אָזְלַת יָד means "the power is going away" (i.e. it is diminishing). The verb אזל is used in this sense in *I Samuel* 9:7.

46. That is, the people are reduced to destitution. אָזְלַת יָד means: "the hands [of the people] will go [empty]" (*Rashi*).

[In Talmudic times, a *perutah* was the coin of the lowest denomination.]

47. The Jews will be in such an abysmal state that they will think God has forsaken them, and they will despair of being redeemed (*Rashi*; see *Maharsha*).

48. They were attempting to predict when the Messiah will come (*Rashi, Yad Ramah*).

49. Literally: when [there is] diversion of the mind.

50. [A person typically finds a lost article through happenstance. One who deliberately searches for such articles is often unsuccessful.]

51. A scorpion bites a person suddenly [i.e. without warning] (*Rashi*).

The Baraisa mentions the Messiah together with a find and a scorpion to teach the following lesson: If one is meritorious, the unexpected arrival of the Messiah will be like finding a lost article, which is a joyful experience. If one is not meritorious, the Messiah's unexpected arrival will be to him like being bitten by a scorpion (*Maharsha*).

[R' Zeira was certainly not opposed to expecting the Messiah's arrival. It is an obligation to await the Messiah every day! (see 96b note 56). Rather, R' Zeira was opposed to predicting the date when the Messiah will come (see note 48). His reason is that when the predicted date arrives, people will expect the Messiah to come specifically at that time. It is this specific degree of expectation that could delay the advent of the Messiah.] (See the novel explanation offered by *Emes LeYaakov.*)

52. I.e. the seventh millennium (*Rashi* et al.; see note 59 below).

53. *Isaiah* 2:11. A "day of God" equals a thousand years, as it is stated (*Psalms* 90:4): כִּי אֶלֶף שָׁנִים בְּעֵינֶיךָ כְּיוֹם אֶתְמוֹל כִּי יַעֲבֹר, *For a thousand years in Your eyes are like a bygone yesterday* (*Rashi,* from Gemara below).

[Of course, God is above time. The meaning is merely that when man is told about "God's day," it carries the connotation of a thousand years (*Yefeh To'ar*).]

54. *Hosea* 6:2. Each day mentioned in this verse equals a thousand years (see the beginning of note 53). According to Abaye, the world will be destroyed during the seventh and eighth millennia (*Rashi*).

"On the third day" – i.e. the ninth millennia – God will raise us up

את סוכת דוד הנופלת א"ל הכי אמר רבי יוחנן דור שבן דוד בא בו תלמידי חכמים מתמעטים והשאר עיניהם כלות ביגון ואנחה וצרות רבות וגזרות קשות מתחדשות עד שהראשונה פקודה שניה ממהרת לבא ת"ר שבוע שבן דוד בא בו שנה ראשונה מתקיים מקרא זה [א] והמטרתי על עיר אחת ועל עיר אחת לא אמטיר שניה חיצי רעב משתלחים שלישית רעב גדול ומתים אנשים ונשים וטף חסידים ואנשי מעשה ותורה משתכחת מלומדיה ברביעית שובע ואינו שובע בחמישית שובע גדול ואוכלין ושותין ושמחין ותורה חוזרת ללומדיה [א] בששית קולות בשביעית מלחמות במוצאי שביעית בן דוד בא אמר רב יוסף הא כמה שביעית דהוה כן ולא אתא אמר אביי בששית קולות בשביעית מלחמות מי הוה ועוד כסדרן מי הוה [א] [ב] [ג] (אשר חרפו אויביך ה' אשר חרפו עקבות משיחך) תניא ר' יהודה אומר דור שבן דוד בא בו [ג] בית הוועד יהיה לזנות והגליל יחרב והגבלן יאשם [ב] ואנשי גבול יסובבו מעיר לעיר ולא יחוננו וחכמת הסופרים תסרח ויראי חטא ימאסו [ג] ופני הדור כפני כלב והאמת נעדרת שנאמר [ג] ותהי האמת נעדרת [ד] [ז] (וסר מרע משתולל) מאי ותהי האמת נעדרת אמרי דבי רב מלמד שנעשית עדרים עדרים והולכת לה מאי וסר מרע משתולל אמרי דבי ר' שילא כל מי שסר מרע משתולל על הבריות אמר רבא מריש הוה אמינא ליכא קושטא בעלמא אמר לי [ה] ההוא מרבנן ורב טבות שמיה ואמרי לה רב טביומי שמיה דאי הוו יהבי ליה כל חללי דעלמא לא הוה משני בדבוריה זימנא חדא איקלעי לההוא אתרא וקושטא שמיה ולא הוו משני בדיבורייהו ולא הוה מיית איניש מהתם בלא זימניה נסיבי איתתא מינהון והוו לי תרתין בנין מינה יומא חד הוה יתבא דביתהו וקא חייפא רישה אתאי שיבבתה טרפא אדשא [ו] סבר לאו אורח ארעא [י] אמר לה ליתא הכא שכיבו ליה תרתין בנין אתו אינשי דאתרא לקמיה אמרו ליה מאי האי אמר להו הכי הוה מעשה א"ל במטותא מינך פוק מאתרין ולא תגרי בהו מותנא בהנך אינשי תניא ר' נהוראי אומר דור שבן דוד בא בו [ח] נערים ילבינו פני זקנים וזקנים יעמדו לפני נערים ובת קמה באמה וכלה בחמותה ופני הדור כפני כלב ואין הבן מתבייש מאביו תניא ר' נחמיה אומר דור שבן דוד בא בו העזות תרבה והיוקר יעות והגפן יתן פריו והיין ביוקר ונהפכה כל המלכות למינות ואין תוכחה מסייע ליה לר' יצחק דא"ר יצחק אין בן דוד בא עד שתתהפך כל המלכות למינות אמר רבא מאי קרא [ד] כולו הפך לבן טהור הוא ת"ר [ה] כי ידין ה' עמו [וגו'] כי יראה כי אזלת יד ואפס עצור ועזוב אין בן דוד בא עד שירבו המסורות ד"א עד שיתמעטו התלמידים ד"א עד שתכלה פרוטה מן הכיס ד"א עד שיתייאשו מן הגאולה שנאמר ואפס עצור ועזוב כביכול אין סומך ועוזר לישראל כי הא דר' זירא כי הוה משכח רבנן דמעסקי ביה אמר להו במטותא [ט] בעינא מנייכו לא תרחקוה דתנינא ג' באין בהיסח הדעת אלו הן משיח מציאה ועקרב אמר רב קטינא [י] שית אלפי שני הוו עלמא וחד חרוב שנאמר [ו] ונשגב ה' לבדו ביום ההוא אביי אמר תרי חרוב שנאמר [ז] יחיינו מיומים ביום השלישי יקימנו ונחיה לפניו תניא כותיה דרב קטינא כשם שהשביעית משמטת שנה אחת לז' שנים כך העולם משמט אלף שנים לשבעת אלפים שנה שנאמר ונשגב ה' לבדו ביום ההוא ואומר [ח] מזמור שיר ליום השבת יום שכולו שבת ואומר [ט] כי אלף שנים בעיניך כיום אתמול כי יעבור [כ] תנא דבי אליהו ששת אלפים שנה הוי עלמא שני אלפים תוהו שני אלפים תורה שני אלפים ימות המשיח ובעונותינו

רש"י

את סוכת דוד הנופלת. מלכות דוד שנפלה להכי קרי משיח בר נפלי: עד שהראשונה פקודה. עד שלא כלתה צרה ראשונה שניה ממהרת לבא פקודה כמו לא נפקד (במדבר לא): שבוע. שמיטה: והמטרתי על עיר אחת. שיהא מעט מטר ויהא רעב במקום זה ושובע במקום זה: חיצי רעב. רעב מעט שלא יהא שובע בשום מקום: משתכחת מלומדיה. מתוך שאין להם מה לאכול: בששית קולות. יצאו קולות שבן דוד בא ל"א קולות מתקיעת שופר שנאמר יתקע בשופר גדול (ישעיה כז): מלחמות. בין עובדי כוכבים לישראל: דהוה הכי. שנה אחת רעב שנה אחת שובע ואעפ"כ לא בא בן דוד: בששית קולות מי הוה. כלום יצאו קולות שבן דוד בא: ועוד כסדרן מי הוה. כלומר אלו הצרות דקתני הכא כסדרן לא אתרמו בשבוע אחד אבל כי אתרמו אתי משיח: אשר חרפו אויביך ה' אשר חרפו עקבות משיחך. לא אתפרש האי קרא למאי איכתיב הכא דהא לא קא דריש ביה מידי ונראה למורי שכן נכתב בספרים תחלה כמו ששנינו בפ' אחרון דסוטה (דף מט:) בעקבות המשיח חוצפא יסגא וכתבו פירוש זה על בעקבות שהוא לשון סוף כמו אשר חרפו עקבות משיחך: בית הועד. מקום שתלמידי חכמים מתוועדין שם ללמוד תורה: ה"ג והגבלן. מקום ששמו כך ישתומם: ואנשי הגבול. אנשי גבול ארץ ישראל ל"א אנשי גזית סנהדרין: כפני כלב. דדמיין ממש לכלב מ"ר ל"א כפני הכלב שלא יתביישו זה מזה: משתולל על הבריות. כל העולם אומרין עליו שוטה הוא היינו משתולל לשון שטות כמו מוליך יועצים שולל (איוב יב): ליכא קושטא בעלמא. אין אדם בעולם שידבר אמת תמיד: אמר לי ההוא מרבנן דאי הוו יהבי ליה כל חללי דעלמא לא משני בדבוריה. לשקר ואישתעי לי הכי זימנא חדא אקלעי לההוא אתרא וקושטא שמיה: טרפא אבבא. שהיתה שואלת אותה: לאו אורח ארעא. לומר היכן היא הואיל וחייפ' רישה: ה"ג נערים ילבינו פני זקנים. כלומר יחפרו ויביישו אותם: וזקנים יעמדו בפני הנערים. לכבדם והיינו דאמרינן (בסוטה ד' מט:) בעקבות המשיח חוצפא יסגא: בת קמה באמה. לחרפה ולביישה: היוקר יעות. שלא יכבדו זה את זה יקר כבוד ל"א היוקר יעות מכובד שבהן יהא עוותן ורמאי. מ"ר: והגפן יתן פריו. ואעפ"כ יהיה היין ביוקר שלא יהיה ברכה בפרי עצמו ל"א שיהיו כולן רודפין אחר היין ומשתכרין ומתייקר היין אע"פ שרוב יין בעולם: כלו הפך לבן טהור הוא. כשפשט הנגע בכל העור כך כשנהפכה כל המלכות למינות תבא גאולה: כי ידין ה' עמו. להביא להם גאולה: כי יראה כי אזלת יד. שתלך ותחזק ידן של מסורות ומלשינין במלשינותן: שיתמעטו התלמידים. שמחזיקין ידי ישראל להחזירן למוטב: שתכלה פרוטה. והיינו אזלת יד שיהו בידים ריקניות: כביכול. כאלו יכולין לומר דבר זה כלפי מעלה: אין עוזר ואין סומך לישראל. שיהיו שפלים למאד ואומר אין עוזר וסומך שיהיו מתייאשין מן הגאולה: דמעסקי ביה. לידע מתי יבא: ועקרב. נושך האדם פתאום: וחד חרוב. שאלף שנה יהיה חרוב חוץ מששת אלפים אלו דהיינו אלף שביעי: תרי. אלפים הוא חרב אלף שביעי ואלף שמיני: יומו של הקב"ה אלף שנה שנאמר כי אלף שנים בעיניך כיום אתמול כי יעבור: משמט. ונעשה חרב: שכולו שבת. שהעולם משמט: הוי עלמא. העולם כך מתקיים: ב' אלפים היה תהו. תחת שלא ניתנה עדיין תורה והיה העולם כתוהו ומאדם הראשון עד שהיה אברהם בן נ"ב שנה איכא אלפים שנה כדמוכחי קראי דכשנשלמו אלפים שנה עסק אברהם בתורה שנאמר (בראשית יב) ואת הנפש אשר עשו בחרן ומתרגמינן דשעבידו לאורייתא בחרן ואמרינן במסכת ע"ז (דף ט.) גמירי דההוא שעתא הוה אברהם בר חמשין ותרתי שנין: ושני אלפים תורה. מן הנפש אשר עשו בחרן עד [אלפים] שנות המשיח ארבעים ([ל] ושמנים) שנה עד שנולד יצחק וששים שנה משנולד יצחק עד שנולד יעקב הרי ק"ח וק"ל שהיו ליעקב כשבא למצרים הרי רל"ח ורד"ו שעמדו במצרים הרי תמ"ח ומשיצאו ממצרים עד שנבנה בית ראשון ת"פ דכתיב (מלכים א ו) ויהי בשמנים שנה וארבע מאות שנה לצאת בני ישראל מארץ מצרים וגו' הרי תתקכ"ח ות"י שעמד בית ראשון כדמוכחי קראי על פי חשבון שנות המלכים וע' דגלות בבל ות"כ שעמד בית שני הרי תת"ק ותתקכ"ח הרי אלפים פחות קע"ב וקע"ב קודם השלמת ד' אלפים נחרב הבית ולסוף אותן קע"ב נשלמו שני אלפים תורה ואיידי דאמר שני אלפים תוהו קאמר שני אלפים תורה ולא שתכלה תורה אחר שני אלפים. מ"ר: ושני אלפים שנות המשיח. שלאחר שני אלפים תורה הוה דינו שיבא משיח ותכלה הגלות ויבטל השיעבוד מישראל: אבל

מסורת הש"ס

א) מגילה יז:, ב) רש"ל מ"ז, ג) [סוטה מט:], ד) רש"ל מ"ז, ה) [ב"מ מט. ע"ש], ו) י"ג סברי, ז) י"ג אמרי, ח) סוטה מט:, ט) [בברכות לה: וביומא עב: גם בע"י ליתא מלת בעינא וכן לעיל בסמוך במטותא מינך], י) [ר"ה לא.], כ) ע"ז ט., ל) [צ"ל ושמנה].

הגהות הגר"א

[א] גמ' אשר חרפו. נדפס בלדו רש"ל מוחק זה נמחק הסג"ה: [ב] שם ואנשי גבול. נמחק תיבת גבול. ונ"ב חול: [ג] שם ופני הדור כפני הכלב. נמחק: [ד] שם וסר מרע משתולל. נדפס בלדו רש"ל מ"ז נמחק הסג"ה:

תורה אור השלם

א) וְגַם אָנֹכִי מָנַעְתִּי מִכֶּם אֶת הַגֶּשֶׁם בְּעוֹד שְׁלֹשָׁה חֳדָשִׁים לַקָּצִיר וְהִמְטַרְתִּי עַל עִיר אֶחָת וְעַל עִיר אַחַת לֹא אַמְטִיר חֶלְקָה אַחַת תִּמָּטֵר וְחֶלְקָה אֲשֶׁר לֹא תַמְטִיר עָלֶיהָ תִּיבָשׁ: [עמוס ד, ז]

ב) אֲשֶׁר חֵרְפוּ אוֹיְבֶיךָ יְיָ אֲשֶׁר חֵרְפוּ עִקְּבוֹת מְשִׁיחֶךָ: [תהלים פט, נב]

ג) וַתְּהִי הָאֱמֶת נֶעְדֶּרֶת וְסָר מֵרָע מִשְׁתּוֹלֵל וַיַּרְא יְיָ וַיֵּרַע בְּעֵינָיו כִּי אֵין מִשְׁפָּט: [ישעיה נט, טו]

ד) וְרָאָה הַכֹּהֵן וְהִנֵּה כִסְּתָה הַצָּרַעַת אֶת כָּל בְּשָׂרוֹ וְטִהַר אֶת הַנָּגַע כֻּלּוֹ הָפַךְ לָבָן טָהוֹר הוּא: [ויקרא יג, יג]

ה) כִּי יָדִין יְיָ עַמּוֹ וְעַל עֲבָדָיו יִתְנֶחָם כִּי יִרְאֶה כִּי אָזְלַת יָד וְאֶפֶס עָצוּר וְעָזוּב: [דברים לב, לו]

ו) וְשַׁח גַּבְהוּת הָאָדָם וְשָׁפֵל רוּם אֲנָשִׁים וְנִשְׂגַּב יְיָ לְבַדּוֹ בַּיּוֹם הַהוּא: [ישעיה ב, יז]

ז) יְחַיֵּנוּ מִיֹּמָיִם בַּיּוֹם הַשְּׁלִישִׁי יְקִמֵנוּ וְנִחְיֶה לְפָנָיו: [הושע ו, ב]

ח) מִזְמוֹר שִׁיר לְיוֹם הַשַּׁבָּת: [תהלים צב, א]

ט) כִּי אֶלֶף שָׁנִים בְּעֵינֶיךָ כְּיוֹם אֶתְמוֹל כִּי יַעֲבֹר וְאַשְׁמוּרָה בַלָּיְלָה: [תהלים צ, ד]

ליקוטי רש"י

שבוע שבן דוד בא בו. חלוק משאר שנים כדאמרינן בפרק חלק (לז.) שנה ראשונה רעב ולא רעב כו' עד ובשביעית מלחמות ובמוצאי שביעית בן דוד בא [מגילה יז:]. עקבות משיחך. סופי מלך המשיח ולשון משנה הוא בעקבות המשיח חוצפא יסגא [תהלים פט, נב]. בסוף הגלות לפני ביאת משיח [סוטה מט:]. בית הוועד. של חכמים יהיו לבית זונות שכלו החכמים ואין לומד תורה ויהא חרב מאין איש ובעלי זימה מתגודדים שם מפני שחוץ לעיר היו בתי מדרשות שלהם [סוטה שם]. משתולל. מוחזק שוטה על הבריות כמו (מיכה א) אלכה שולל והוא מגזרת שוגג דמתרגמינן שלו וכן (ש"ב ו) על השל [ישעיה נט, טו]. והיין ביוקר. שהכל עוסקין במשתאות. ונהפכה כל המלכות למינות. והמלכות השולטת על רוב העולם תהא למינות נמשכים אחר טעות שלו [ישו] ותלמידיו נקראו מינים [דפו"י]. ואין תוכחה. אין לך אדם שיוכל להוכיח שכולם נכשלים בחטאות וכשמוכיחין אומר לו אתה כמוני [סוטה שם]. כי יראה כי אזלת יד. כשיראה כי יד האויב הולכת וחוזקת מאד עליהם ואפס בהם עצור ועזוב. עצור. נושע על ידי עוצר ומושל שיעצור בהם. עזוב. על ידי עוזב. עוצר הוא המושל העוצר בעם שלא ילכו מפוזרים בצאתם לצבא על האויב. בלשון בלע"ז מיינטינדו"ר עצור הוא הנושע במעצור המושל עזוב מחוזק כמו (נחמיה ג, ח) ויעזבו את ירושלים עד החומה (ירמיה מט, כה) איך לא עוזבה עיר תהלה עצור מיינטינו"ד עזוב אינפורלדו"ר [דברים לב, לו]. שתכלה פרוטה מן הכיס. אין מעות מצויות בכיס [לקמן צח.]. שית אלפי שני. נגזר על העולם להתקיים כמנין ימי השבוע וביום השביעי שבת ובשבעת אלפים נוח לעולם [ע"ז ט.]. מזמור שיר. של לוים (נביאים). ליום השבת. שאומרים אותו בשבתות והוא מדבר בענין העולם הבא שכולו שבת [תהלים צב, א]. יום שכולו שבת. שעתיד העולם להיות חרב ואין אדם וכל המלאכות שובתות על אותו יום אומרים שיר של שבת [ר"ה לא.]. שני אלפים. ראשונים נגזר עליו להיות תוהו בלא תורה ושני אלפים תורה בלא ימות המשיח ושני אלפים ימות המשיח. שני אלפים תוהו. לא וחשוב שנות דור ודור שמי כל אחד קודם שנולד בנו דשנים שאחרי כן אתה נותן לבן ותמצא מאדם עד שנולד נח תתרנ"ו שנים ונח חי תק"ב שנים קודם שנולד שם דכתיב (בראשית ה) ויהי נח בן חמש מאות שנה וגו' כשנולד בנו הראשון היה בן ת"ק שנים ויפת הוא הגדול מחם שנה וחם גדול משם שנה הרי תק"ב שנים לנח כשנולד שם כדכתיב (שם, יא) [שם] בן מאת שנה ויולד את ארפכשד שנתים אחר המבול ואם שם לת"ק שנים דנח אתייליד כי מטו שנתים אחר המבול הוה ליה בר ק"ב דהא כתיב (שם, ז) ונח בן שש מאות שנה והמבול היה חשוב תק"ב דנח ומאה דשם עד ארפכשד והוסף על נ"ו של פרט הרי תרנ"ח וארפכשד הוליד את שלח בל"ה הרי תרל"ג ומשלח עד עבר ל' הרי תשכ"ג ומעבר עד פלג ל"ד הרי תשנ"ז ומפלג עד רעו ל' הרי תשפ"ז ומרעו לשרוג ל"ב הרי תתי"ט ומשרוג לנחור ל' הרי תתמ"ט ומנחור לתרח כ"ט הרי תתע"ח ומתרח לאברהם ע' הרי תתקמ"ח על אלף ותתקמ"ח שהיו בידך כשנולד אברהם הרי אלפים תוהו. שני אלפים תורה. מאברהם עד שנולד יצחק ק' הרי אלפים ומ"ח ומיצחק עד מתן תורה ת' שנים כיצד ס' עד שנולד יעקב וכרדתו למצרים כתיב ימי שני מגורי שלשים ומאת שנה הרי ק"ל משנולד יצחק וישראל היו במצרים רד"ו הרי ד' מאות ומ"ח שנים על אלפים לבריאת עולם נמצא ממתן תורה עד ד' אלפים לבריאתו של עולם אלף וחמש מאות וחמשים ושתים. כמה בצירן לך השתא דתורה דתני תנא תמ"ח שנים היו בצירן לך כי מעיינת מואת הנפש אשר עשו עד מתן תורה הכי הוו הוסף אותן על מנין מתן תורה ונמצא אלפים מכוונין מואת הנפש אשר עשו וגו' עד גמר ד' אלפים לבריאת עולם והוא קע"ב שנים לאחר חורבן כיצד הרי מנית עד יציאת מצרים תמ"ח על עודף אלפים וכתיב (מ"א ו) ויהי בשמנים שנה וארבע מאות שנה לצאת בני ישראל עד ויבן שלמה את הבית הרי תתקכ"ח על אלפים כשנבנה הבית וימי בית ראשון ד' מאות ועשר הרי שלשה אלפים ושל"ח שנים וגלות בבל ע' שנים הרי ת"ח וימי בית שני ת"ך הרי תתכ"ח נמצא קע"ב חסרין מד' אלפים והכי תני בסדר עולם [ע"ז שם].

The Gemara cites support for Rav Katina's view:

תַּנְיָא כְּוָתֵיהּ דְּרַב קְטִינָא – **It was taught in a Baraisa in accordance with** the opinion of **Rav Katina:** כְּשֵׁם שֶׁהַשְּׁבִיעִית מְשַׁמֶּטֶת שָׁנָה אַחַת לְשֶׁבַע שָׁנִים – JUST AS THE SABBATICAL YEAR CAUSES CESSATION[55] ONE YEAR OUT OF SEVEN YEARS, כָּךְ הָעוֹלָם מְשַׁמֵּט אֶלֶף שָׁנִים לְשִׁבְעַת אֲלָפִים שָׁנָה – SO TOO THE WORLD CEASES[56] ONE MILLENNIUM OUT OF SEVEN MILLENNIA, שֶׁנֶּאֱמַר ,,וְנִשְׂגַּב ה' לְבַדּוֹ בַּיּוֹם הַהוּא'' – AS IT IS STATED: *HASHEM ALONE WILL BE EXALTED ON THAT DAY,* which indicates that there will be a "day" when the world is desolate. וְאוֹמֵר ,,מִזְמוֹר שִׁיר לְיוֹם הַשַּׁבָּת'' יוֹם שֶׁכּוּלּוֹ שַׁבָּת – AND further IT SAYS:[57] *A PSALM, A SONG FOR THE DAY OF THE SABBATH,* which is interpreted as meaning A "DAY" THAT IS COMPLETELY A SABBATH.[58] וְאוֹמֵר ,,כִּי אֶלֶף שָׁנִים בְּעֵינֶיךָ כְּיוֹם אֶתְמוֹל כִּי יַעֲבֹר'' – AND IT SAYS: *FOR A THOUSAND YEARS IN YOUR EYES ARE LIKE A BYGONE YESTERDAY*, which indicates that the "day" referred to in the previous two verses is a millennium.[59]

The following Baraisa gives the earliest possible date of the Messiah's arrival:[60]

תָּנָא דְּבֵי אֵלִיָּהוּ – **The academy of Eliyahu**[61] **taught the following Baraisa:** שֵׁשֶׁת אֲלָפִים שָׁנָה הֲוֵי עָלְמָא – THE WORLD IS destined to exist for SIX THOUSAND YEARS: שְׁנֵי אֲלָפִים תוֹהוּ – The first TWO THOUSAND years were OF NOTHINGNESS;[62]

NOTES

in a new world and we shall live before him (*Maharsha*). [This apparently refers to the World to Come (see note 59).]

[The plain meaning of the verse is that God will give us the strength to survive two periods of tragedy – the destruction of the First and Second Temples. When the third Temple is built, the presence of God will once again reside among us (see *Rashi* ad loc.).]

55. The land lies fallow (see note 5).

56. It is laid waste (*Rashi*).

57. *Psalms* 92:1. The plain meaning of the verse refers to the weekly Sabbath.

58. שַׁבָּת (Sabbath) means cessation of activity. [The Gemara's exposition is apparently based on the word יוֹם, *day,* which seems to be superfluous.]

59. *Psalms* 90:4. [The first verse (*Hashem alone* etc.) teaches only that there will be an era when the world is desolate. The second verse (*A song for the day of the Sabbath*) indicates that this era will last for a seventh of the world's existence, just as the Sabbath day is a seventh of each week. The third verse (*A thousand years* etc.) conveys that it will last one thousand years.]

The thousand years of destruction: The simple meaning of Rav Katina's statement is that world history, from Creation to the end of the Messianic era, will last six millennia, after which the world as we know it will be destroyed. This destruction will follow the Messianic era (*Yad Ramah;* see also *Rashi* at the end of 92a and the beginning of 92b), the Resurrection of the Dead (see *Rashi* ibid.) and the great Day of Judgment (*Daas Tevunos* pp. 90-94). The period of destruction will last for one thousand years, after which the world will be reconstructed on a much higher spiritual level. The Gemara above, 92b, states that during the thousand years of destruction (see *Rashi* ibid., *Maharsha* here) the righteous will be given "wings like eagles and they will float above the water." During this period, they will undergo a process of progressive purification until the last traces of their physical nature have been removed and they attain a level of pure spirituality (*Ramchal, Maamar HaIkkarim*, section 8, "On the *Geulah*"; as elaborated by *Michtav MeEliyahu* IV, pp. 150-156). This straightforward interpretation of Rav Katina's statement is the view of many commentators. However, there are dissenting views as well. We present therefore a brief summary of the basic issues and opinions:

(a) *The nature of the destruction.* In the opinion of most Rishonim, the destruction referred to by Rav Katina is literal. The entire world will be utterly destroyed; it will return to the state of absolute nothingness that prevailed before the Creation. (*Raavad* to *Hil. Teshuvah* 8:8; *Ramban, Derashah al Divrei Koheles* [*Kisvei HaRamban,* Chavel ed. vol. 1 pg. 188]; *Rashba* Responsa vol. 1 §9 [cited in *Perushei HaHagados* to *Bava Basra* 74b]; cf. *Abarbanel, Yeshuos Meshicho, Iyun* 1 ch. 1 ד״ה ואומר).

In the opinion of others, the destruction will be less than total. *Rabbeinu Bachya* writes that the world will only be partially destroyed in the seventh millennium. This partial destruction will recur every seven millennia, until the fiftieth millennium, when the world will be completely destroyed. This 50,000-year cycle will then repeat itself many times (see *Rabbeinu Bachya* to *Numbers* 10:35).

Some Rishonim suggest that Rav Katina's statement is meant figuratively (one possibility suggested by *Rambam* in *Moreh Nevuchim* 2:29). In line with this, *Meiri* posits that Rav Katina refers to a millennium of terrible persecution of the Jewish people. According to this approach, Rav Katina refers to the *sixth* millennium, not the seventh. Thus, Rav Katina's statement is to be understood to mean that the world will run for six millennia of which the sixth will be the millennium of "destruction" (see *Meiri's* introduction to *Pirkei Avos*).

In an alternative interpretation, *Meiri* (ibid.) suggests that the destruction refers to the destruction of the יֵצֶר הָרַע, *evil inclination*. Thus, Rav Katina means that in the seventh millennium it will be easier for man to gain mastery over his evil inclination (see also *Akeidas Yitzchak* cited by *Margaliyos HaYam*; *R' Yosef Karo* in *Maggid Mesharim, Behar* and *Vayakhel; Recanti* to *Leviticus* 25:8).

(b) *The sequence of events*: As stated above, the view of *Rashi, Yad Ramah* and others is that the thousand years of destruction will follow the Messianic era and lead up to the World to Come.

According to *Meiri's* first approach, the period of destruction will precede the Messianic era. According to *Meiri's* second approach, however, there is no clear indication of the sequence. The Messianic era could occur either before or during this period.

(c) *Is Rav Katina's statement universally accepted*? Our Gemara does not record anyone disputing Rav Katina's statement. Indeed, *Rashba* (Responsa ibid.) states that no Tanna or Amora disputes Rav Katina's statement (except Abaye in regard to the duration of the period). *Rambam,* however, contends that Rav Katina's view is not accepted by other Talmudic sages, and that Rav Katina himself may have meant it only figuratively (*Moreh Nevuchim* 2:29; see also *Raavad's* criticism of *Rambam* in *Hil. Teshuvah* 8:8, and see *Kesef Mishneh* there). *Abarbanel* explains that *Rambam's* view is based on the Gemara below (99a) which records various opinions that give a specific length for the Messianic era (see *Mifalos Elokim* 7:3; see also 99a note 26).

60. **The Date of the Redemption:**

In discussing the advent of the Messiah, two dates must be considered – the earliest and the latest dates. The exile following the destruction of the Second Temple was decreed to last a certain minimum number of years, and the Messiah will not come during that period under any circumstances. The end of that era is the earliest date for the redemption. From then on, the Messiah will come whenever the people have sufficient merit. The latest date (the קֵץ, *End*) is the Divinely preordained deadline by which the exile will certainly have ended (see *Abarbanel* in *Yeshuos Meshicho*).

Between these two dates there are several times that are particularly suited for the redemption. *Ramban* states that "many dates were preordained for our future redemption," but since we continued to act in our usual manner at those times, the opportunity was lost and the redemption did not materialize (*Sefer HaGeulah* ch. 4, Chavel ed. vol. I p. 292). This concept is echoed by *Gra,* who writes that each generation has its own appointed "End" depending upon the unique forms of merit and repentance expected of it (*Even Sheleimah* 11:9).

61. See 92a note 57. [*Yad Ramah* evidently maintains that this Baraisa was taught by the prophet Elijah (see below, 97b note 6).]

62. That is, the world was without Torah (*Rashi* here and to *Avodah Zarah* 9a).

It is evident from Scripture that two thousand years after the creation of Adam, Abraham was fifty-two years old. (The calculation is given by *Rashi* to *Avodah Zarah* ibid.) Tradition teaches that at that age Abraham began to spread the message of the Torah and to influence people to follow its ways, as the verse states (*Genesis* 12:5): וְאֶת־הַנֶּפֶשׁ אֲשֶׁר־עָשׂוּ בְחָרָן, *and the souls they had made in Charan,* which the Targum renders: וְיָת נַפְשָׁתָא דְשַׁעְבִּידוּ לְאוֹרַיְתָא בְּחָרָן, *and the souls they had subjected to the Torah in Charan* (*Rashi*).

חלק פרק אחד עשר סנהדרין

את סוכת דוד הנופלת א"ל הכי אמר רבי יוחנן דור שבן דוד בא בו תלמידי חכמים מתמעטים והשאר עיניהם כלות ביגון ואנחה וצרות רבות וגזרות קשות מתחדשות עד שהראשונה פקודה שניה ממהרת לבא ת"ר שבוע שבן דוד בא בו שנה ראשונה מתקיים מקרא זה א) והמטרתי על עיר אחת ועל עיר אחת לא אמטיר שניה חיצי רעב משתלחים שלישית רעב גדול ומתים אנשים ונשים וטף חסידים ואנשי מעשה ותורה משתכחת מלומדיה ברביעית שובע ואינו שובע בחמישית שובע גדול ואוכלין ושותין ושמחין ותורה חוזרת ללומדיה א) בששית קולות בשביעית מלחמות במוצאי שביעית בן דוד בא אמר רב יוסף הא כמה שביעית דהוה כן ולא אתא אמר אביי בששית קולות בשביעית מלחמות מי הוה ועוד כסדרן מי הוה [א] ב) ב) (אשר חרפו אויביך ה' אשר חרפו עקבות משיחך) תניא ר' יהודה אומר דור שבן דוד בא בו ג) בית הוועד יהיה לזנות והגליל יחרב והגבלן יאשם [ב] ואנשי גבול יסובבו מעיר לעיר ולא יחוננו וחכמת הסופרים תסרח ויראי חטא ימאסו [ג] ופני הדור כפני כלב והאמת נעדרת שנאמר ג) ותהי האמת נעדרת [ד] ד) (וסר מרע משתולל) מאי ותהי האמת נעדרת אמרי דבי רב מלמד שנעשית עדרים עדרים והולכת לה מאי וסר מרע משתולל אמרי דבי ר' שילא כל מי שסר מרע משתולל על הבריות אמר רבא מריש הוה אמינא ליכא קושטא בעלמא אמר לי ה) ההוא מרבנן ורב טבות שמיה ואמרי לה רב טביומי שמיה דאי הוו יהבי ליה כל חללי דעלמא לא הוה משני בדבוריה זימנא חדא איקלעי להההוא אתרא וקושטא שמיה ולא הוו משני בדיבורייהו ולא הוה מיית איניש מהתם בלא זימניה נסיבי איתתא מינהון והוו לי תרתין בנין מינה יומא חד הוה יתבא דביתהו וקא חייפא רישה אתאי שיבבתה טרפא אדשא ו) סבר לאו אורח ארעא ז) אמר לה ליתא הכא שכיבו ליה תרתין בנין אתו אינשי דאתרא לקמיה אמרו ליה מאי האי אמר להו הכי הוה מעשה א"ל במטותא מינך פוק מאתרין ולא תגרי בהו מותנא בהנך אינשי תניא ר' נהוראי אומר דור שבן דוד בא בו ח) נערים ילבינו פני זקנים וזקנים יעמדו לפני נערים ובת קמה באמה וכלה בחמותה ופני הדור כפני כלב ואין הבן מתבייש מאביו תניא ר' נחמיה אומר דור שבן דוד בא בו העזות תרבה והיוקר יעות והגפן יתן פריו והיין ביוקר ונהפכה כל המלכות למינות ואין תוכחה מסייע ליה לר' יצחק דא"ר יצחק אין בן דוד בא עד שתתהפך כל המלכות למינות אמר רבא מאי קרא ד) כולו הפך לבן טהור הוא ת"ר ה) כי ידין ה' עמו [וגו'] כי יראה כי אזלת יד ואפס עצור ועזוב אין בן דוד בא עד שירבו המסורות ד"א עד שיתמעטו התלמידים ד"א עד שתכלה פרוטה מן הכיס ד"א עד שיתייאשו מן הגאולה שנאמר ואפס עצור ועזוב כביכול אין סומך ועוזר לישראל כי הא דר' זירא כי הוה משכח רבנן דמעסקי ביה אמר להו במטותא ט) בעינא מנייכו לא תרחקוה דתנינא ג' באין בהיסח הדעת אלו הן משיח מציאה ועקרב אמר רב קטינא י) שית אלפי שני הוו עלמא וחד חרוב שנאמר ו) ונשגב ה' לבדו ביום ההוא אביי אמר תרי חרוב שנאמר ז) יחיינו מיומים ביום השלישי יקימנו ונחיה לפניו תניא כותיה דרב קטינא כשם שהשביעית משמטת שנה אחת לז' שנים כך העולם משמט אלף שנים לשבעת אלפים שנה שנאמר ונשגב ה' לבדו ביום ההוא ואומר ח) מזמור שיר ליום השבת יום שכולו שבת ואומר ט) כי אלף שנים בעיניך כיום אתמול כי יעבור כ) תנא דבי אליהו ששת אלפים שנה הוי עלמא שני אלפים תוהו שני אלפים תורה שני אלפים ימות המשיח ובעוונותינו

רש"י

את סוכת דוד הנופלת. מלכות דוד שנפלה להכי קרי משיח בר נפלי: עד שהראשונה פקודה. עד שלא כלתה צרה ראשונה שניה ממהרת לבא פקודה כמו לא נפקד (במדבר לא): שבוע. שמיטה: והמטרתי על עיר אחת. שיהא מעט מטר ויהא רעב במקום זה ושובע במקום זה: חיצי רעב. רעב מעט שלא יהא שובע בשום מקום: משתכחת מלומדיה. מתוך שאין להם מה לאכול: בששית קולות. יצאו קולות שבן דוד בא ל"א קולות מתקיעת שופר שנאמר יתקע בשופר גדול (ישעיה כז): מלחמות. בין עובדי כוכבים לישראל: דהוה הכי. שנה אחת רעב שנה אחת שובע ואעפ"כ לא בא בן דוד: בששית קולות מי הוה. כלום יצאו קולות שבן דוד בא: ועוד כסדרן מי הוה. כלומר אלו הצרות דקתני הכא כסדרן לא אתרמו בשבוע אחד אבל כי אתרמו אתי משיח: אשר חרפו אויביך ה' אשר חרפו עקבות משיחך. לא אתפרש האי קרא למאי איכתיב הכא דהא לא קא דריש ביה מידי ונראה למורי שכן נכתב בספרים תחלה כמו ששנינו בפ' אחרון דסוטה (דף מט:) בעקבות המשיח חוצפא יסגא וכתבו פירוש זה על בעקבות שהוא לשון סוף כמו אשר חרפו עקבות משיחך: בית הועד. מקום שתלמידי חכמים מתוועדין שם ללמוד תורה: ה"ג והגבלן. מקום ששמו כך ישתומם: ואנשי הגבול. אנשי גבול ארץ ישראל ל"א אנשי גזית סנהדרין: כפני כלב. דדמיין ממש לכלב מ"ר ל"א כפני הכלב שלא יתביישו זה מזה: משתולל על הבריות. כל העולם אומרין עליו שוטה הוא היינו משתולל לשון שטות כמו מוליך יועצים שולל (איוב יב): ליכא קושטא בעלמא. אין אדם בעולם שידבר אמת תמיד: אמר לי ההוא מרבנן דאי הוו יהבי ליה כל חללי דעלמא לא משני בדבוריה. לשקר ואישתעי לי הכי זימנא חדא אקלעי לההוא אתרא וקושטא שמיה: טרפא אבבא. שהיתה שואלת אותה: לאו אורח ארעא. לומר היכן היא הואיל וחייפ' רישה: ה"ג נערים ילבינו פני זקנים. כלומר יחפרו ויביישו אותם: וזקנים יעמדו בפני הנערים. לכבדם והיינו דאמרינן (בסוטה ד' מט:) בעקבות המשיח חוצפא יסגא: בת קמה באמה. לחרפה ולביישה: היוקר יעות. שלא יכבדו זה את זה יקר כבוד ל"א היוקר יעות מכובד שבהן יהא עוותן ורמאי. מ"ר: והגפן יתן פריו. ואעפ"כ יהיה היין ביוקר שלא יהיה ברכה בפרי עצמו לפי שיהיו כולן רודפין אחר היין ומשתכרין ומתייקר היין אע"פ שרוב יין בעולם: כלו הפך לבן טהור הוא. כשפשט הנגע בכל העור כך כשנהפכה כל המלכות למינות תבא גאולה: כי ידין ה' עמו. להביא להם גאולה: כי יראה כי אזלת יד. שתלך ותחזק ידן של מסורות ומצליחין במלשינותן: שיתמעטו התלמידים. שמחזיקין ידי ישראל להחזירן למוטב: שתכלה פרוטה. והיינו אזלת יד שיהו בידים ריקניות: כביכול. כאלו יכולין לומר דבר זה כלפי מעלה: אין עוזר ואין סומך לישראל. שיהיו שפלים למאד ואומר אין עוזר וסומך שיהיו מתייאשין מן הגאולה: דמעסקי ביה. לידע מתי יבא: ועקרב. נושך האדם פתאום: וחד חרוב. שאלף שנה יהיה חרוב חוץ מששת אלפים אלו דהיינו אלף שביעי: תרי. אלפים הוא חרב אלף שביעי ואלף שמיני: יומו של הקב"ה אלף שנה שנאמר כי אלף שנים בעיניך כיום אתמול כי יעבור: משמט. ונעשה חרב: שכולו שבת. שהעולם משמט: הוי עלמא. העולם כך מתקיים: ב' אלפים היה תהו. תחת שלא ניתנה עדיין תורה והיה העולם כתוהו ומאדם הראשון עד שהיה אברהם בן נ"ב שנה איכא אלפים שנה כדמוכחי קראי דכשנשלמו אלפים שנה עסק אברהם בתורה שנאמר (בראשית יב) ואת הנפש אשר עשו בחרן ומתרגמינן דשעבידו לאורייתא בחרן ואמרינן במסכת ע"ז (דף ט.) גמירי דההוא שעתא הוה אברהם בר חמשין ותרתי שנין: ושני אלפים תורה. מן הנפש אשר עשו בחרן עד [אלפים] שנות המשיח ארבעים (ל) ושמנים) שנה עד שנולד יצחק וששים שנה משנולד יצחק עד שנולד יעקב הרי ק"ח וק"ל שהיו ליעקב כשבא למצרים הרי רל"ח ורד"ו שעמדו במצרים הרי תמ"ח ומשיצאו ממצרים עד שנבנה בית ראשון ת"פ דכתיב (מלכים א ו) ויהי בשמנים שנה וארבע מאות שנה לצאת בני ישראל מארץ מצרים וגו' הרי תתקכ"ח ות"י שעמד בית ראשון כדמוכחי קראי על פי חשבון שנות המלכים וע' דגלות בבל ות"כ שעמד בית שני הרי תת"ק ותתקכ"ח הרי אלפים פחות קע"ב וקע"ב קודם השלמת ד' אלפים נחרב הבית ולסוף אותן קע"ב נשלמו שני אלפים תורה ואיידי דאמר שני אלפים תוהו קאמר שני אלפים תורה ולא שתכלה תורה אחר שני אלפים. מ"ר: ושני אלפים שנות המשיח. שלאחר שני אלפים תורה הוה דינו שיבא משיח ותכלה הגלות ויבטל השיעבוד מישראל: אבל

(שם, ז) ונח בן שש מאות שנה והמבול היה חשוב תק"ב דנח ומאה דשם עד ארפכשד והוסף על נ"ו של פרט הרי תרנ"ח וארפכשד הוליד את שלח בל"ה הרי תרל"ג ומשלח עד עבר ל' הרי תשכ"ג ומעבר עד פלג ל"ד הרי תשנ"ז ומפלג עד רעו ל' הרי תשפ"ז ומרעו לשרוג ל"ב הרי תתי"ט ומשרוג לנחור ל' הרי תתמ"ט ומנחור לתרח כ"ט הרי תתע"ח ומתרח לאברהם ע' הרי תתקמ"ח על אלף וכו' הוה אברהם בר נ"ב הוסיפם על אלף ותתקמ"ח שהיו בידך כשנולד אברהם הרי אלפים תוהו. שני אלפים תורה. [illegible] אלפים ומ"ח ומיצחק עד מתן תורה ת' שנים כילד ס' עד שנולד יעקב וכרדתו למצרים כתיב ימי שני מגורי שלשים ומאת שנה הרי ק"ל משנולד יצחק וישראל היו במצרים רד"ו הרי ד' מאות ומ"ח שנים על אלפים לבריאת עולם נמצא בריאתו של עולם אלף וחמש מאות וחמשים ושתים. כמה בצירן לך השתא דתורה דתני תנא תמ"ח שנים היו בצירן לך כי מעיינת מואת הנפש אשר עשו עד מתן תורה הכי הוו הוסף אותן על מנין מתן תורה ונמצא אלפים מכוונין מואת לד' אלפים לבריאת עולם והוא קע"ב שנים לאחר חורבן כילד הרי מנית עד יציאת מצרים תמ"ח על עודף אלפים וכתיב (מ"א ו) ויהי בשמנים שנה וארבע מאות שנה לצאת בני ישראל עד ויבן שלמה את הבית הרי תתקכ"ח על אלפים כשנבנה הבית וימי בית ראשון ד' מאות ועשר הרי שלשה אלפים ושל"ח שנים וגלות בבל ע' שנים הרי ת"ח וימי בית שני ת"ך הרי תתכ"ח נמצא קע"ב חסרין מד' אלפים והכי תני בסדר עולם [ע"ז שם].

מסורת הש"ס

א) מגילה יז:, ב) רש"ל מ"ז, ג) [סוטה מט:], ד) רש"ל מ"ז, ה) [ב"מ מט. ע"ש], ו) י"ג סברי, ז) י"ג אמרי, ח) סוטה מט:, ט) [ברכות לה: ויומא עב: גם בע"י ליתא מלת בעינא וכן לעיל בסמוך במטותא מינך], י) [ר"ה לא.], כ) ע"ז ט., ל) [צ"ל ושמנים].

הגהות הגר"א

[א] גמ' אשר חרפו. נדפס בגלו רש"ל מוחק זה נמחק הסג"ה: [ב] שם ואנשי גבול. נמחק תיבת גבול. וג"ב חול: [ג] שם ופני הדור כפני הכלב. נמחק: [ד] שם וסר מרע משתולל. נדפס בגלו רש"ל מ"ז נמחק הסג"ה:

תורה אור השלם

א) וְגַם אָנֹכִי מָנַעְתִּי מִכֶּם אֶת הַגֶּשֶׁם בְּעוֹד שְׁלֹשָׁה חֳדָשִׁים לַקָּצִיר וְהִמְטַרְתִּי עַל עִיר אֶחָת וְעַל עִיר אַחַת לֹא אַמְטִיר חֶלְקָה אַחַת תִּמָּטֵר וְחֶלְקָה אֲשֶׁר לֹא תַמְטִיר עָלֶיהָ תִּיבָשׁ: [עמוס ד, ז]

ב) אֲשֶׁר חֵרְפוּ אוֹיְבֶיךָ יְיָ אֲשֶׁר חֵרְפוּ עִקְּבוֹת מְשִׁיחֶךָ: [תהלים פט, נב]

ג) וַתְּהִי הָאֱמֶת נֶעְדֶּרֶת וְסָר מֵרָע מִשְׁתּוֹלֵל וַיַּרְא יְיָ וַיֵּרַע בְּעֵינָיו כִּי אֵין מִשְׁפָּט: [ישעיה נט, טו]

ד) וְרָאָה הַכֹּהֵן וְהִנֵּה כִסְּתָה הַצָּרַעַת אֶת כָּל בְּשָׂרוֹ וְטִהַר אֶת הַנָּגַע כֻּלּוֹ הָפַךְ לָבָן טָהוֹר הוּא: [ויקרא יג, יג]

ה) כִּי יָדִין יְיָ עַמּוֹ וְעַל עֲבָדָיו יִתְנֶחָם כִּי יִרְאֶה כִּי אָזְלַת יָד וְאֶפֶס עָצוּר וְעָזוּב: [דברים לב, לו]

ו) וְשַׁח גַּבְהוּת הָאָדָם וְשָׁפֵל רוּם אֲנָשִׁים וְנִשְׂגַּב יְיָ לְבַדּוֹ בַּיּוֹם הַהוּא: [ישעיה ב, יז]

ז) יְחַיֵּנוּ מִיֹּמָיִם בַּיּוֹם הַשְּׁלִישִׁי יְקִמֵנוּ וְנִחְיֶה לְפָנָיו: [הושע ו, ב]

ח) מִזְמוֹר שִׁיר לְיוֹם הַשַּׁבָּת: [תהלים צב, א]

ט) כִּי אֶלֶף שָׁנִים בְּעֵינֶיךָ כְּיוֹם אֶתְמוֹל כִּי יַעֲבֹר וְאַשְׁמוּרָה בַלָּיְלָה: [תהלים צ, ד]

ליקוטי רש"י

שבוע שבן דוד בא בו. חלוק משאר שנים כדאמרינן בפרק חלק (לז.) שנה ראשונה רעב ולא רעב כו' עד ובשביעית מלחמות ובמוצאי שביעית בן דוד בא [מגילה יז:]. עקבות משיחך. סופי מלך המשיח ולשון משנה הוא בעקבות המשיח חוצפא יסגא [תהלים פט, נב]. בסוף הגלות לפני ביאת משיח [סוטה מט:]. בית הוועד. של חכמים יהיו לבית זנות שכלו החכמים ואין לומד תורה ויהא חרב מאין איש ובעלי זימה מתגודדים שם מפני שחוץ לעיר היו בתי מדרשות שלהם [סוטה שם]. משתולל. מוחזק שוטה על הבריות כמו (מיכה א) אלכה שולל והוא מגזרת שוגג דמתרגמינן שלו וכן (ש"ב ו) על השל [ישעיה נט, טו]. והיין ביוקר. שהכל עוסקין במשתאות. ונהפכה כל המלכות למינות. והמלכות השולטת על רוב העולם תהא למינות נמשכים אחר טעות שלו [ישו] ותלמידיו נקראו מינים [דפו"י]. ואין תוכחה. אין לך אדם שיוכל להוכיח שכולם נכשלים בחטאות וכשמוכיחין אומר לו אתה כמוני [סוטה שם]. כי יראה כי אזלת יד. כשיראה כי יד האויב הולכת וחוזקת מאד עליהם ואפס בהם עצור ועזוב. עצור. נושע על ידי עוצר ומושל שיעצור בהם. עזוב. על ידי עוזב. עוצר הוא המושל העוצר בעם שלא ילכו מפוזרים בצאתם לצבא על האויב. בלשון בלע"ז מיינטינדו"ר עצור הוא הנושע במעצור המושל עזוב מחוזק כמו (נחמיה ג, ח) ויעזבו את ירושלים עד החומה (ירמיה מט, כה) איך לא עזבה עיר תהלה עזור מיינטינו"ד עזוב אינפורלדו"ר [דברים לב, לו]. שתכלה פרוטה מן הכיס. אין מעות מצויות בכיס [לקמן צח.]. שית אלפי שני. נגזר על העולם להתקיים כמנין ימי השבוע וביום השביעי שבת ובשבעת אלפים נוח לעולם [ע"ז ט.]. מזמור שיר. של לוים (נביאים). ליום השבת. שאומרים אותו בשבתות והוא מדבר בענין העולם הבא שכולו שבת [תהלים צב, א]. יום שכולו שבת. שעתיד העולם להיות חרב ואין אדם וכל המלאכות שובתות על אותו יום אומרים שיר של שבת [ר"ה לא.]. שני אלפים. ראשונים נגזר עליו להיות תוהו בלא תורה ושני אלפים תורה בלא ימות המשיח ושני אלפים ימות המשיח. שני אלפים תוהו. צא וחשוב שנות דור ודור שחי כל אחד קודם שנולד בנו דשנים שאחרי כן אתה נותן לבן ותמצא מאדם עד שנולד נח תתרנ"ו שנים ונח חי תק"ב שנים קודם שנולד שם דכתיב (בראשית ה) ויהי נח בן חמש מאות שנה וגו' כשנולד בנו הראשון היה בן ת"ק שנים ויפת הוא הגדול מחם שנה וחם גדול משם שנה הרי תק"ב שנים לנח כשנולד שם כדכתיב (שם, יא) [שם] בן מאת שנה ויולד את ארפכשד שנתים אחר המבול ואם שם לת"ק שנים דנח אתייליד כי מטו שנתים אחר המבול הוה ליה בר ק"ב דהא כתיב

שְׁנֵי אֲלָפִים תּוֹרָה – the second TWO THOUSAND years were OF TORAH;[63] שְׁנֵי אֲלָפִים יְמוֹת הַמָּשִׁיחַ – the third TWO THOUSAND years should have been THE DAYS OF THE MESSIAH,[64]

NOTES

63. As stated in the previous note, the two millennia of Torah began when Abraham was fifty-two years old. The following two thousand years can be calculated as follows:

– 48 years later, Isaac was born.
– When Isaac was 60, Jacob was born.
– Jacob was 130 when he and his family went down to Egypt.
– The Egyptian exile lasted 210 years.
– The First Temple was built 480 years after the Exodus from Egypt (*I Kings* 6:1).
– The First Temple stood for 410 years. (This can be calculated on the basis of the kings' reigns.)
– The Second Temple was built 70 years after the destruction of the first.
– The Second Temple stood for 420 years.

This yields a total of 1,828 years. Thus, the 2,000 years of Torah ended 172 years after the destruction of the Second Temple (*Rashi*).

The Baraisa does not mean that Torah came to an end after four millennia. It uses the term "two thousand years of Torah" for the sake of contrast with the preceding phrase "two thousand years of nothingness [i.e. no Torah]" (*Rashi*). When the Baraisa says "Torah," it means "Torah *before* the Messianic era" as opposed to "Torah *during* the Messianic era" (see *Rashi* to *Avodah Zarah* 9a).

According to *Maharsha,* however, the Baraisa means that Torah *flourished* during those two thousand years. One hundred and seventy-two years after the destruction of the Second Temple, the study of Torah deteriorated significantly. Following the death of Rebbi [in the year 3,952 (*Halevi*)], which marked the end of the Tannaic era, the tribulations of the exile grew more severe, and the centers of Torah study declined (*Maharsha*; see also *Hagahos Yavetz*).

64. The Messiah was supposed to come at the end of the first four millennia (*Rashi*).

Yad Ramah explains that the Messiah could not possibly have come before the year 4,000, because the exile was decreed to last at least 172 years (see note 60). From that date on, the Messiah could come; but our sins have prevented him from doing so.

Maharsha maintains that the final two millennia are the חֶבְלֵי מָשִׁיחַ, *travail of the Messiah* (see above, note 4). At any time during this period it is possible for the Messiah to come and bring an end to our suffering.

The commentators draw an analogy between these six millennia and the six days of creation. The trends of each millennium are foretold by the events of the corresponding day of creation (see *Ramban* to *Genesis* 2:3; *Rabbeinu Bachya* ibid.; *Abarbanel, Yeshuos Meshicho, Iyun* 1 ch. 1; see also *Beur HaGra* to *Tamid* 7:4).

את סוכת דוד הנופלת א"ל הכי אמר רבי יוחנן דור שבן דוד בא בו תלמידי חכמים מתמעטים והשאר עיניהם כלות ביגון ואנחה וצרות רבות וגזרות קשות מתחדשות עד שהראשונה פקודה שניה ממהרת לבא ת"ר שבוע שבן דוד בא בו שנה ראשונה מתקיים מקרא זה א) והמטרתי על עיר אחת ועל עיר אחת לא אמטיר שניה חיצי רעב משתלחים שלישית רעב גדול ומתים אנשים ונשים וטף חסידים ואנשי מעשה ותורה משתכחת מלומדיה ברביעית שובע ואינו שובע בחמישית שובע גדול ואוכלין ושותין ושמחין ותורה חוזרת ללומדיה א) בששית קולות בשביעית מלחמות במוצאי שביעית בן דוד בא אמר רב יוסף הא כמה שביעית דהוה כן ולא אתא אמר אביי בששית קולות בשביעית מלחמות מי הוה ועוד כסדרן מי הוה [א] ב) ב) (אשר חרפו אויביך ה' אשר חרפו עקבות משיחך) תניא ר' יהודה אומר דור שבן דוד בא בו ג) בית הוועד יהיה לזנות והגליל יחרב והגבלן יאשם [ב] ואנשי גבול יסובבו מעיר לעיר ולא יחוננו וחכמת הסופרים תסרח ויראי חטא ימאסו [ג] ופני הדור כפני כלב והאמת נעדרת שנאמר ג) ותהי האמת נעדרת [ד] ד) (וסר מרע משתולל) מאי ותהי האמת נעדרת אמרי דבי רב מלמד שנעשית עדרים עדרים והולכת לה מאי וסר מרע משתולל אמרי דבי ר' שילא כל מי שסר מרע משתולל על הבריות אמר רבא מריש הוה אמינא ליכא קושטא בעלמא אמר לי ה) ההוא מרבנן ורב טבות שמיה ואמרי לה רב טביומי שמיה דאי הוו יהבי ליה כל חללי דעלמא לא הוה משני בדבוריה זימנא חדא איקלעי לההוא אתרא וקושטא שמיה ולא הוו משני בדיבורייהו ולא הוה מיית איניש מהתם בלא זימניה נסיבי איתתא מינהון והוו לי תרתין בנין מינה יומא חד הוה יתבא דביתהו וקא חייפא רישה אתאי שיבבתה טרפא אדשא ו) סבר לאו אורח ארעא ז) אמר לה ליתא הכא שכיבו ליה תרתין בנין אתו אינשי דאתרא לקמיה אמרו ליה מאי האי אמר להו הכי הוה מעשה א"ל במטותא מינך פוק מאתרין ולא תגרי בהו מותנא בהנך אינשי תניא ר' נהוראי אומר דור שבן דוד בא בו ח) נערים ילבינו פני זקנים וזקנים יעמדו לפני נערים ובת קמה באמה וכלה בחמותה ופני הדור כפני כלב ואין הבן מתבייש מאביו תניא ר' נחמיה אומר דור שבן דוד בא בו העזות תרבה והיוקר יעות והגפן יתן פריו והיין ביוקר ונהפכה כל המלכות למינות ואין תוכחה מסייע ליה לר' יצחק דא"ר יצחק אין בן דוד בא עד שתתהפך כל המלכות למינות אמר רבא מאי קרא ד) כולו הפך לבן טהור הוא ת"ר ה) כי ידין ה' עמו [וגו'] כי יראה כי אזלת יד ואפס עצור ועזוב אין בן דוד בא עד שירבו המסורות ד"א עד שיתמעטו התלמידים ד"א עד שתכלה פרוטה מן הכיס ד"א עד שיתייאשו מן הגאולה שנאמר ואפס עצור ועזוב כביכול אין סומך ועוזר לישראל כי הא דר' זירא כי הוה משכח רבנן דמעסקי ביה אמר להו במטותא ט) בעינא מנייכו לא תרחקוה דתנינא ג' באין בהיסח הדעת אלו הן משיח מציאה ועקרב אמר רב קטינא י) שית אלפי שני הוו עלמא וחד חרוב שנאמר ו) ונשגב ה' לבדו ביום ההוא אביי אמר תרי חרוב שנאמר ז) יחיינו מיומים ביום השלישי יקימנו ונחיה לפניו תניא כותיה דרב קטינא כשם שהשביעית משמטת שנה אחת לז' שנים כך העולם משמט אלף שנים לשבעת אלפים שנה שנאמר ונשגב ה' לבדו ביום ההוא ואומר ח) מזמור שיר ליום השבת יום שכולו שבת ואומר ט) כי אלף שנים בעיניך כיום אתמול כי יעבור כ) תנא דבי אליהו ששת אלפים שנה הוי עלמא שני אלפים תוהו שני אלפים תורה שני אלפים ימות המשיח

ובעונותינו

רש"י

את סוכת דוד הנופלת. מלכות דוד שנפלה להכי קרי משיח בר נפלי: עד שהראשונה פקודה. עד שלא כלתה צרה ראשונה שניה ממהרת לבא פקודה כמו לא נפקד (במדבר לא): שבוע. שמיטה: והמטרתי על עיר אחת. שיהא מעט מטר ויהא רעב במקום זה ושובע במקום זה: חיצי רעב. רעב מעט שלא יהא שובע בשום מקום: משתכחת מלומדיה. מתוך שאין להם מה לאכול: בששית קולות. יצאו קולות שבן דוד בא ל"א קולות מתקיעת שופר שנאמר יתקע בשופר גדול (ישעיה כז): מלחמות. בין עובדי כוכבים לישראל: דהוה הכי. שנה אחת רעב שנה אחת שובע ואעפ"כ לא בא בן דוד: בששית קולות מי הוה. כלום יצאו קולות שבן דוד בא: ועוד כסדרן מי הוה. כלומר אלו הצרות דקתני הכא כסדרן לא אתרמו בשבוע אחד אבל כי אתרמו אתי משיח: אשר חרפו אויביך ה' אשר חרפו עקבות משיחך. לא אתפרש האי קרא למאי איכתיב הכא דהא לא קא דריש ביה מידי ונראה למורי שכן נכתב בספרים תחלה כמו ששנינו בפ' אחרון דסוטה (דף מט:) בעקבות המשיח חוצפא יסגא וכתבו פירוש זה על בעקבות שהוא לשון סוף כמו אשר חרפו עקבות משיחך: בית הועד. מקום שתלמידי חכמים מתוועדין שם ללמוד תורה: ה"ג והגבלן. מקום ששמו כך ישתומם: ואנשי הגבול. אנשי גבול ארץ ישראל ל"א אנשי גזית סנהדרין: כפני כלב. דדמיין ממש לכלב מ"ר ל"א כפני הכלב שלא יתביישו זה מזה: משתולל על הבריות. כל העולם אומרין עליו שוטה הוא היינו משתולל לשון שטות כמו מוליך יועצים שולל (איוב יב): ליכא קושטא בעלמא. אין אדם בעולם שידבר אמת תמיד: אמר לי ההוא מרבנן דאי הוו יהבי ליה כל חללי דעלמא לא משני בדבוריה. לשקר ואישתעי לי הכי זימנא חדא אקלעי לההוא אתרא וקושטא שמיה: טרפא אבבא. שהיתה שואלת אותה: לאו אורח ארעא. לומר היכן היא הואיל וחייפ' רישה: ה"ג נערים ילבינו פני זקנים. כלומר יחפרו ויביישו אותם: וזקנים יעמדו בפני הנערים. לכבדם והיינו דאמרינן (בסוטה ד' מט:) בעקבות המשיח חוצפא יסגא: בת קמה באמה. לחרפה ולביישה: היוקר יעות. שלא יכבדו זה את זה יקר כבוד ל"א היוקר יעות מכובד שבהן יהא עוותן ורמאי. מ"ר: והגפן יתן פריו. ואעפ"כ יהיה היין ביוקר שלא יהיה ברכה בפרי עצמו ל"א שיהיו כולן רודפין אחר היין ומשתכרין ומתייקר היין אע"פ שרוב יין בעולם: כלו הפך לבן טהור הוא. כשפשט הנגע בכל העור כך כשנהפכה כל המלכות למינות תבא גאולה: כי ידין ה' עמו. להביא להם גאולה: כי יראה כי אזלת יד. שתלך ותחזק ידן של מסורות ומצליחין במלשינותן: שיתמעטו התלמידים. שמחזיקין ידי ישראל להחזירן למוטב: שתכלה פרוטה. והיינו אזלת יד שיהו בידים ריקניות: כביכול. כאלו יכולין לומר דבר זה כלפי מעלה: אין עוזר ואין סומך לישראל. שיהיו שפלים למאד ואומר אין עוזר וסומך שיהיו מתייאשין מן הגאולה: דמעסקי ביה. לידע מתי יבא: ועקרב. נושך האדם פתאום: וחד חרוב. שאלף שנה יהיה חרוב חוץ מששת אלפים אלו דהיינו אלף שביעי: תרי. אלפים הוא חרב אלף שביעי ואלף שמיני: יומו של הקב"ה אלף שנה שנאמר כי אלף שנים בעיניך כיום אתמול כי יעבור: משמט. ונעשה חרב: שכולו שבת. שהעולם משמט: הוי עלמא. העולם כך מתקיים: ב' אלפים היה תהו. תחת שלא ניתנה עדיין תורה והיה העולם כתוהו ומאדם הראשון עד שהיה אברהם בן נ"ב שנה איכא אלפים שנה כדמוכחי קראי דכשנשלמו אלפים שנה עסק אברהם בתורה שנאמר (בראשית יב) ואת הנפש אשר עשו בחרן ומתרגמינן דשעבידו לאורייתא בחרן ואמרינן במסכת ע"ז (דף ט.) גמירי דההוא שעתא הוה אברהם בר חמשין ותרתי שנין: ושני אלפים תורה. מן הנפש אשר עשו בחרן עד [אלפים] שנות המשיח ארבעים (ל) ושמנים) שנה עד שנולד יצחק וששים שנה משנולד יצחק עד שנולד יעקב הרי ק"ח וק"ל שהיו ליעקב כשבא למצרים הרי רל"ח ורד"ו שעמדו במצרים הרי תמ"ח ומשיצאו ממצרים עד שנבנה בית ראשון ת"פ דכתיב (מלכים א ו) ויהי בשמנים שנה וארבע מאות שנה לצאת בני ישראל מארץ מצרים וגו' הרי תתקכ"ח ות"י שעמד בית ראשון כדמוכחי קראי על פי חשבון שנות המלכים וע' דגלות בבל ות"כ שעמד בית שני הרי תת"ק ותתקכ"ח הרי אלפים פחות קע"ב וקע"ב קודם השלמת ד' אלפים נחרב הבית ולסוף אותן קע"ב נשלמו שני אלפים תורה ואיידי דאמר שני אלפים תוהו קאמר שני אלפים תורה ולא שתכלה תורה אחר שני אלפים. מ"ר: ושני אלפים שנות המשיח. שלאחר שני אלפים תורה הוה דינו שיבא משיח ותכלה הגלות ויבטל השיעבוד מישראל:

אבל

ליקוטי רש"י

שבוע שבן דוד בא בו. חלוק משאר שנים כדאמרינן בפרק חלק (לז.) שנה ראשונה רעב ולא רעב כו' עד ובשביעית מלחמות ובמוצאי שביעית בן דוד בא [מגילה יז:]. עקבות משיחך. סופי מלך המשיח ולשון משנה הוא בעקבות המשיח חוצפא יסגא [תהלים פט, נב]. בסוף הגלות לפני ביאת משיח [סוטה מט:]. בית הוועד. של חכמים יהיו לבית זנות שכלו החכמים ואין לומד תורה ויהא חרב מאין איש ובעלי זימה מתגודדים שם מפני שחוץ לעיר היו בתי מדרשות שלהם [סוטה שם]. משתולל. מוחזק שוטה על הבריות כמו (מיכה א) אלכה שולל והוא מגזרת שוגג דמתרגמינן שלו וכן (ש"ב ו) על השל [ישעיה נט, טו]. והיין ביוקר. שהכל עוסקין במשתאות. ונהפכה כל המלכות למינות. והמלכות השולטת על רוב העולם תהא למינות נמשכים אחר טעות שלו [ישו] ותלמידיו נקראו מינים [דפו"י]. ואין תוכחה. אין לך אדם שיוכל להוכיח שכולם נכשלים בחטאות וכשמוכיחין אומר לו אתה כמוני [סוטה שם]. כי יראה כי אזלת יד. כשיראה כי יד האויב הולכת וחוזקת מאד עליהם ואפס בהם עצור ועזוב. עצור. נושע על ידי עוצר ומושל שיעצור בהם. עזוב. על ידי עוזב. עוצר הוא המושל העוצר בעם שלא ילכו מפוזרים בצאתם לצבא על האויב. בלשון בלע"ז מיינטינדו"ר עצור הוא הנושע במעצור המושל עזוב מחוזק כמו (נחמיה ג, ח) ויעזבו את ירושלים עד החומה (ירמיה מט, כה) איך לא עוזבה עיר תהלה עצור מיינטינו"ד עזוב אינפורלדו"ר [דברים לב, לו]. שתכלה פרוטה מן הכיס. אין מעות מצויות בכיס [לקמן צח.]. שית אלפי שני. נגזר על העולם להתקיים כמנין ימי השבוע וביום השביעי שבת ובשבעת אלפים נוח לעולם [ע"ז ט.]. מזמור שיר. של לוים (נביאים). ליום השבת. שאומרים אותו בשבתות והוא מדבר בענין העולם הבא שכולו שבת [תהלים צב, א]. יום שכולו שבת. שעתיד העולם להיות חרב ואין אדם וכל המלאכות שובתות על אותו יום אומרים שיר של שבת [ר"ה לא.]. שני אלפים. ראשונים נגזר עליו להיות תוהו בלא תורה ושני אלפים תורה בלא ימות המשיח ושני אלפים ימות המשיח. שני אלפים תוהו. צא וחשוב שנות דור ודור שחי כל אחד קודם שנולד בנו דשנים שאחרי כן אתה נותן לבן ותמצא מאדם עד שנולד נח תתרנ"ו שנים ונח חי תק"ב שנים קודם שנולד שם דכתיב (בראשית ה) ויהי נח בן חמש מאות שנה וגו' כשנולד בנו הראשון היה בן ת"ק שנים ויפת הוא הגדול מחם שנה וחם גדול משם שנה הרי תק"ב שנים לנח כשנולד שם כדכתיב (שם, יא) [שם] בן מאת שנה ויולד את ארפכשד שנתים אחר המבול ואם שם לת"ק שנים דנח אתייליד כי מטו שנתים אחר המבול הוה ליה בר ק"ב דהא כתיב (שם, ז) ונח בן שש מאות שנה והמבול היה חשוב תק"ב דנח ומאה דשם עד ארפכשד והוסף על נ"ו של פרט הרי תרנ"ח וארפכשד הוליד את שלח בל"ה הרי תרצ"ג ומשלח עד עבר ל' הרי תשכ"ג ומעבר עד פלג ל"ד הרי תשנ"ז ומפלג עד רעו ל' הרי תשפ"ז ומרעו לשרוג ל"ב הרי תתי"ט ומשרוג לנחור ל' הרי תתמ"ט ומנחור לתרח כ"ט הרי תתע"ח ומתרח לאברהם ע' הרי תתקמ"ח על אלף וכו' הוה אברהם בר נ"ב הוסיפם על אלף ותתקמ"ח שהיו בידך כשנולד אברהם הרי אלפים תוהו. **שני אלפים תורה.** מאברהם עד יצחק ק' הרי אלפים ומ"ח ומיצחק עד מתן תורה ת' שנים כיצד ס' עד שנולד יעקב וכשירדו למצרים כתיב ימי שני מגורי שלשים ומאת שנה הרי ק"ל משנולד יצחק וישראל היו במצרים רד"ו הרי ד' מאות ומ"ח שנים על אלפים לבריאת עולם נמצא ממתן תורה עד ד' אלפים לבריאתו של עולם אלף וחמש מאות וחמשים ושתים. כמה בצירן לך השתא דתורה דתני תנא תמ"ח שנים היו בצירן לך כי מעיינת מואת הנפש אשר עשו עד מתן תורה הכי הוו הוסף אותן על מנין מתן תורה ונמצא אלפים מכוונין מואת הנפש אשר עשו וגו' עד גמר ד' אלפים לבריאת עולם והוא קע"ב שנים לאחר חורבן כיצד הרי מנית עד יציאת מצרים תמ"ח על עודף אלפים וכתיב (מ"א ו) ויהי בשמנים שנה וארבע מאות שנה לצאת בני ישראל עד ויבן שלמה את הבית הרי תתקכ"ח על אלפים כשנבנה הבית וימי בית ראשון ד' מאות ועשר הרי שלשה אלפים ושל"ח שנים וגלות בבל ע' שנים הרי ת"ח וימי בית שני ת"ך הרי תתכ"ח נמצא קע"ב חסרין מד' אלפים והכי תני בסדר עולם [ע"ז שם].

מסורת הש"ס

א) מגילה יז:, ב) רש"ל מ"ז, ג) [סוטה מט:], ד) רש"ל מ"ז, ה) [ב"מ מט. ע"ש], ו) י"ג סברי, ז) י"ג אמרי, ח) סוטה מט:, ט) [בברכות לה: וביומא עב: גם בע"י ליתא מלת בעינא וכן לעיל בסמוך במטותא מינך], י) [ר"ה לא.], כ) ע"ז ט., ל) [צ"ל ושמנים].

הגהות הגר"א

[א] גמ' אשר חרפו. נדפס בגלוי רש"ל מוחק זה נמחק הסג"ה: [ב] שם ואנשי גבול. נמחק תיבת גבול. וצ"ל חול: [ג] שם ופני הדור כפני הכלב. נמחק: [ד] שם וסר מרע משתולל. נדפס בגלוי רש"ל מ"ז נמחק הסג"ה:

תורה אור השלם

א) וְגַם אָנֹכִי מָנַעְתִּי מִכֶּם אֶת הַגֶּשֶׁם בְּעוֹד שְׁלֹשָׁה חֳדָשִׁים לַקָּצִיר וְהִמְטַרְתִּי עַל עִיר אֶחָת וְעַל עִיר אַחַת לֹא אַמְטִיר חֶלְקָה אַחַת תִּמָּטֵר וְחֶלְקָה אֲשֶׁר לֹא תַמְטִיר עָלֶיהָ תִּיבָשׁ: [עמוס ד, ז]

ב) אֲשֶׁר חֵרְפוּ אוֹיְבֶיךָ יְיָ אֲשֶׁר חֵרְפוּ עִקְּבוֹת מְשִׁיחֶךָ: [תהלים פט, נב]

ג) וַתְּהִי הָאֱמֶת נֶעְדֶּרֶת וְסָר מֵרָע מִשְׁתּוֹלֵל וַיַּרְא יְיָ וַיֵּרַע בְּעֵינָיו כִּי אֵין מִשְׁפָּט: [ישעיה נט, טו]

ד) וְרָאָה הַכֹּהֵן וְהִנֵּה כִסְּתָה הַצָּרַעַת אֶת כָּל בְּשָׂרוֹ וְטִהַר אֶת הַנָּגַע כֻּלּוֹ הָפַךְ לָבָן טָהוֹר הוּא: [ויקרא יג, יג]

ה) כִּי יָדִין יְיָ עַמּוֹ וְעַל עֲבָדָיו יִתְנֶחָם כִּי יִרְאֶה כִּי אָזְלַת יָד וְאֶפֶס עָצוּר וְעָזוּב: [דברים לב, לו]

ו) וְשַׁח גַּבְהוּת הָאָדָם וְשָׁפֵל רוּם אֲנָשִׁים וְנִשְׂגַּב יְיָ לְבַדּוֹ בַּיּוֹם הַהוּא: [ישעיה ב, יז]

ז) יְחַיֵּנוּ מִיֹּמָיִם בַּיּוֹם הַשְּׁלִישִׁי יְקִמֵנוּ וְנִחְיֶה לְפָנָיו: [הושע ו, ב]

ח) מִזְמוֹר שִׁיר לְיוֹם הַשַּׁבָּת: [תהלים צב, א]

ט) כִּי אֶלֶף שָׁנִים בְּעֵינֶיךָ כְּיוֹם אֶתְמוֹל כִּי יַעֲבֹר וְאַשְׁמוּרָה בַלָּיְלָה: [תהלים צ, ד]

ובעונותינו שרבו יצאו מהם מה שיצאו אמר ליה אליהו לרב יהודה אחוה דרב סלא חסידא אין העולם פחות משמונים וחמשה יובלות וביובל האחרון בן דוד בא אמר ליה בתחילתו או בסופו אמר ליה איני יודע כלה או אינו כלה אמר ליה איני יודע רב אשי אמר הכי א"ל עד הכא לא תיסתכי ליה מכאן ואילך איסתכי ליה שלח ליה רב חנן בר תחליפא לרב יוסף מצאתי אדם אחד ובידו מגילה אחת כתובה אשורית ולשון קדש אמרתי לו זו מניין לך אמר לי לחיילות של רומי נשכרתי ובין גינזי רומי מצאתיה וכתוב בה לאחר ד' אלפים ומאתים [א] ותשעים ואחד שנה לבריאתו של עולם העולם יתום מהן מלחמות תנינים מהן מלחמות גוג ומגוג ושאר ימות המשיח ואין הקב"ה מחדש את עולמו אלא לאחר שבעת אלפים שנה רב אחא בריה דרבא אמר לאחר חמשת אלפים שנה איתמר תניא רבי נתן אומר מקרא זה נוקב ויורד עד תהום א) כי עוד חזון למועד ויפח לקץ ולא יכזב אם יתמהמה חכה לו כי בא יבא לא יאחר לא כרבותינו שהיו דורשין ב) עד עידן עידנין ופלג עידן ולא כר' שמלאי שהיה דורש ג) האכלתם לחם דמעה ותשקמו בדמעות שליש ולא כרבי עקיבא שהיה דורש ד) עוד אחת מעט היא ואני מרעיש את השמים ואת הארץ אלא מלכות ראשון שבעים שנה מלכות שניה חמשים ושתים ומלכות בן כוזיבא שתי שנים ומחצה מאי ויפח לקץ ולא יכזב אמר רבי שמואל בר נחמני אמר ר' יונתן תיפח עצמן של מחשבי קיצין שהיו אומרים כיון שהגיע את הקץ ולא בא שוב אינו בא אלא חכה לו שנאמר אם יתמהמה חכה לו שמא תאמר אנו מחכין והוא אינו מחכה ת"ל ה) לכן יחכה ה' לחננכם ולכן ירום לרחמכם וכי מאחר שאנו מחכים והוא מחכה מי מעכב מדת הדין מעכבת וכי מאחר שמדת הדין מעכבת אנו למה מחכין לקבל שכר שנאמר ה) אשרי כל חוכי לו אמר אביי א) לא פחות עלמא מתלתין ושיתא צדיקי דמקבלי אפי שכינה בכל דרא שנאמר אשרי כל חוכי לו לו בגימטריא תלתין ושיתא הוו איני והאמר רבא דרא דקמי קודשא בריך הוא תמני סרי אלפי [פרסא] הואי שנאמר ו) סביב שמנה עשר אלף לא קשיא הא דמסתכלי באיספקלריא המאירה הא דמסתכלי באיספקלריא שאינה מאירה ומי נפישי כולי האי ב) והאמר חזקיה א"ר ירמיה משום רשב"י ראיתי בני עלייה והן מועטין אם אלף הם אני ובני מהם אם מאה הם אני ובני מהם אם שנים הם אני ובני הם לא קשיא הא דעיילי בבר הא דעיילי בלא בר אמר רב כלו כל הקיצין ואין הדבר תלוי אלא בתשובה ומעשים טובים ושמואל אמר דיו לאבל שיעמוד באבלו כתנאי ר' אליעזר אומר אם ישראל עושין תשובה נגאלין ואם לאו אין נגאלין אמר ליה רבי יהושע אם אין עושין תשובה אין נגאלין ג) אלא הקב"ה מעמיד להן מלך שגזרותיו קשות כהמן וישראל עושין תשובה ומחזירן למוטב תניא אידך ר' אליעזר אומר אם ישראל עושין תשובה נגאלין שנאמר ז) שובו בנים שובבים ארפא משובותיכם אמר לו רבי יהושע והלא כבר נאמר ח) חנם נמכרתם ולא בכסף תגאלו חנם נמכרתם בעבודת כוכבים ולא בכסף תגאלו לא בתשובה ומעשים טובים אמר לו רבי אליעזר לר' יהושע והלא כבר נאמר ט) שובו אלי ואשובה אליכם אמר ליה רבי יהושע והלא כבר נאמר י) כי אנכי בעלתי בכם ולקחתי אתכם אחד מעיר ושנים ממשפחה והבאתי אתכם ציון אמר לו ר' אליעזר והלא כבר נאמר כ) בשובה ונחת תושעון אמר לו ר' יהושע לרבי אליעזר והלא כבר נאמר ל) כה אמר ה' גואל ישראל וקדושו לבזה נפש למתעב גוי לעבד מושלים מלכים

אבל בשביל עונותינו שרבו. לא בא משיח לסוף ד' אלפים ויצאו מה שיצאו שעדיין הוא מעוכב לבא: **שמנים וחמשה יובלין.** היינו ד' אלפים מאתים וחמשים [שנה]: **בתחלת.** היובל האחרון הוא בא או בסופו: **כלה.** זמן הזה קודם שיבא משיח או אינו כלה דבתוך היובל בסופו הוא בא: **עד הכא לא תיסתכי ליה.** עד יובל האחרון לא תצפה לו דודאי לא יבא קודם הזמן הזה: **איסתכי ליה.** חכה לו שיבא: **אשורית.** כתב שלנו אשורית שבא מאשור כדאמר באידך פירקין (ד' כב.): **לחיילות של רומי נשכרתי.** שהייתי גולייר לאחד מהם: **תנינים.** דגים: **והשאר ימות המשיח.** שכלה השעבוד ומשיח בא: **מחדש עולמו.** לברוא עולם חדש: **נוקב ויורד עד התהום.** מה תהום אין לו קץ וסוף כך אין אדם יכול לעמוד על סוף פסוק זה ד) (וכי קא מפרש אימת קאמר אם) יתמהמה חכה לו דאין לו סוף: **לא כרבותינו.** אל תצפו לאותו קץ שהיו רבותינו דורשין: **עד עידן עידנין ופלג עידן.** עידן כעידן הגלות של מצרים והיינו ד' מאות ב' עידנין ח' מאות היינו י"ב מאות ופלג עידן ב' מאות סך הכל אלף וד' מאות: **ותשקמו בדמעות שליש.** כלומר השקה אותם הקב"ה בין גלות מצרים לגלות בבל שליש גלות אדום כי קץ גלות אדום זה יהיה לסוף ג' פעמים ת' שנים וג' פעמים ע' שנה כנגד גלות בבל דהיינו לסוף אלף וארבע מאות ועשר שנים [ב] כבר עברו ולא היה כך מצאתי כתוב בשם הרב רבי שמואל בר דוד ז"ל: **עוד אחת מעט היא.** בנבואת חגי כתיב שהיה מתנבא כשיצאו ישראל מגלות בבל ויבנה בית המקדש והיינו עוד אחת מעט היא מעט כבוד אתן להם לישראל ואני מרעיש את השמים ואת הארץ והבאתי כל חמדת גוים לירושלים ור"ע דריש ליה לימות המשיח ולאחר חורבן והכי דריש ליה [עוד אחת מעט היא מעט כבוד אתן לישראל ואח"כ יבא המשיח ודרשה זו אינה אלא קרא אלפני הבית קאי וה"ק] עוד אחת מעט היא מעט כבוד אתן להם לישראל ושוב לא אתן להם כל ימות בית אחרון וכן היה דמלכות ראשונה של מלכות חשמונאי נתקיימה שבעים שנה ואע"ג דאמרינן בסדר עולם דמלכות בית חשמונאי מאה ושלש ומלכות הורדוס מאה ושלש עיקר כבודם ופארם שלא שלטה בהם אומה לא נתקיים כל כך ומלכות שניה של הורדוס נ"ב שנה ומלכות בן כוזיבא ב' שנים ומחצה ושוב לא היה להם מלך מ"ר. וכל הנך דרשות לאו משנה ולאו ברייתא. ל"א עוד אחת מעט היא מעט מלכות אתן להם לישראל לאחר חורבן ולאחר אותו מלכות הנני מרעיש שמים וארץ ויבא משיח. ואין דרשה זו כלום שהרי ראינו כמה מלכיות לישראל לאחר חורבן ואעפ"כ לא בא משיח שהמלכות הראשונה שהיתה להם לישראל לאחר חורבן שבעים שנה הורדוס נ"ב בן כוזיבא ב' ומחצה ומצינו בסדר עולם מפולמוס של אספסיאנוס עד פולמוס של טיטוס שתים עשרה שנה ומפולמוס של טיטוס עד מלכות בן כוזיבא י"ז שנים ומלכות בן כוזיבא ב' שנים ומחצה: [בן כוזיבא מלך בביתר]: **ויפח לקץ.** תיפח נפשו של מחשב הקץ שלא היה לו לכזב ולומר כיון שהגיע וכו': **יחכה ה'.** הוא עצמו מחכה ומתאוה שיבא משיח: **סביב י"ח אלף.** בירושלים של מעלה משתעי קרא בסוף יחזקאל: **באספקלריא המאירה.** בחוזק נגהו של הקב"ה אין מסתכלין אלא תלתין ושית אבל בקלישות הנוגה לצדדין מרחוק מסתכלין כתות הרבה: **ומי נפישי כולי האי.** דלהוי בריר לן תלתין ושיתא הוו ולא פחות: **והא רבי שמעון בן יוחאי.** לא הוה ידע אם אלף הם אם מאה הם אם שנים הם: **הא דעיילי בבר.** שצריכין ליטול רשות כשנכנסין להסתכל באספקלריא המאירה בהנהו לא פחיתי מתלתין ושית אבל אותן הנכנסין בלא רשות ברוב צדקם הנהו מספקא לן כמה הוו: **בתשובה.** אם כל ישראל חוזרין בתשובה יבא ואם לאו לא יבא: **דיו לאבל שעומד באבלו.** דיו להקב"ה שעומד כמה ימים וימינו אחור כלומר אם לא יעשו תשובה אינו עומד באבלו כל הימים אלא ודאי קץ לדבר ל"א דיו לאבל דיין לישראל לער גלות אפילו בלא תשובה נגאלין: **לא בכסף.** לא בתשובה ומעשים טובים דאפילו אין עושין תשובה נגאלין משום דאמר חנם נמכרתם קרי כסף בלשון תשובה: **בעלתי אתכם.** משמע בעל כרחכם בלא תשובה: **אחד מעיר.** אברור הצדיקים ואביאם לציון אע"פ שאין כולם חוזרין: **כה אמר ה' לבזה נפש למתעב גוי.** אותן הבזויין והמתועבין בעבירות אעפ"כ יגאלו מלכים יראו וקמו:

כי

עין משפט נר מצוה

י א מיי' פי"ב מהלכות מלכים ומלחמותיהם הלכה ב:

יא ב מיי' פ"ז מהל' תשובה הלכה ה:

גליון הש"ס

גמ' לא פחות עלמא. ועי' במ"ר בראשית פ' ל"ה שם איתא לא פחות מתלתין צדיקי ועיין במ"ר במדבר פ' ג':

ליקוטי רש"י

ובעונותינו שרבו יצאו. משני אלפים אחרונים מה שיצאו ומשיח לא בא [ע"ז ט.]. **עד עידן עידנין ופלג עידן.** קץ סתום הוא זה כאשר נאמר לדניאל סתום הדברים וחתום ודרשוהו הראשונים איש לפי דעתו וכלו הקצים ויש לנו לפותרו עוד כאשר ראיתי כתוב בשם רב סעדיה הם אלף וג' מאות ול"ה שנים האמור בסוף הספר אשרי המחכה וגו' ופי' המועד עד עת שני עתים וחצי עת ואמר שהעתים הם ד' מאות ופ' שמיום לאתם ממצרים עד שנבנה הבית וד' מאות ועשר ימי מקדש ראשון הרי תת"ץ ועוד חצי העת הזה תמ"ה הרי אלף של"ה את אלה חשוב מעת הוסר התמיד עד שוב זבח התמיד אל מקומו והוא הוסר שש שנים לפני החורבן ויש קצת ראיה בספר זה ועוד יש מביאין ראיה לחשבון זה הסתר אסתיר פני הסתר אסתיר בגי' אלף ושל"ה [דניאל ז, כה]. **אשרי כל חוכי לו.** לנחמות אשר הבטיח כי לא יפול דבר [ישעיה ל, יח]. **אמר אביי כו' אשרי כל חוכי לו.** המחכים לכת שהוא כמנין לו. **סביב שמנה עשר אלף.** סיפיה דקרא ה' שמה דאף על גב דבירושלים שלעתיד לבא כתיב קרא דרשינן ליה נמי להכי דמקום ששכינה שמה סובבין אותו שמנה עשר אלף והם הצדיקים הנתונים לפנים ממלאכי השרת שנאמר (במדבר כג) כעת יאמר ליעקב ולישראל מה פעל אל ואומר (ישעיה כג) ליושבים לפני ה' יהיה סחרה ואומר (שם ל) והיו עיניך רואות את מוריך. **איספקלריא.** מחילה שחוצצת ביניהם לשכינה. **המאירה.** כמראה זו שרואין בה ויש צדיקים שאין מאירה להם כל כך ואין יכולין לראות ממש. **ראיתי בני עלייה והן מועטין.** רואה אני לפי מעשה הבריות שבני עלייה כת המקבלין פני שכינה מועטים הם. **בבר.** ברשות. **דעיילי בלא בר.** בלא רשות מועטים הן ובהנהו קאמר אני ובני מהם [סוכה מה:]. **שובבים.** אנווישי"ר בלע"ז שסובבתם דרככם מרוב כל שהייתם בשלוה ועונג כמו שהוא אומר הפורטים על פי הנבל (עמוס ו) השותים במזרקי יין (שם) [ירמיה ג, יד]. לשון משובה נערו' וילדות אינווייזור"א בלע"ז וכן בנים שובבים (ירמיה ג) הבת השובבה (שם לא) [הושע ו, יא]. משמע מזידים ופרהסיא [שובב] לשון מרד וגאוה כמו וילך שובב בדרך לבו (ישעיה נז) [ע"ז ז:]. **כי אנכי בעלתי בכם.** ונקראתם בשמי שאני אדון לכם ואין כבודי להניח אתכם ביד אויבי [ירמיה שם]. **בשובה ונחת.** תהיה לכם תשועה בלא שום טורח אם תשמעו לי. **בשובה.** לשון ישוב ומרגוע וכן שובה ה' רבבות אלפי ישראל (במדבר י) [ישעיה ל, טו]. **לבזה נפש.** נפש בזויה לישראל שהם בזוים [שם מט, ז]. לישראל הבזוים ומתועבים [תענית טו.]. **למתעב גוי.** למי שהגוי מתעבו [ישעיה שם]. **לעבד מושלים.** ועבדים מושלין בהן [תענית שם].

מסורת הש"ס

א) סוכה מה: ע"ש, ב) ג"ז שם., ג) בירושלמי הגי' א"ל ר"א, ד) ס"א שאין קץ למשיח אלא אם.

הגהות הגר"א

[א] גמ' ותשעים. נמחק ונ"ב שלשים (עי' בע"ז ט' ב' ובתוס' ד"ה לאחר): [ב] רש"י ד"ה ותשקמו כו' עשר שנים. עשה כאן נקודות להפסיק ותיבת וכבר עברו וכו' עד בר דוד ז"ל נמחק:

תורה אור השלם

א) כִּי עוֹד חָזוֹן לַמּוֹעֵד וְיָפֵחַ לַקֵּץ וְלֹא יְכַזֵּב אִם יִתְמַהְמָהּ חַכֵּה לוֹ כִּי בֹא יָבֹא לֹא יְאַחֵר: [חבקוק ב, ג]

ב) וּמִלִּין לְצַד עִלָּאָה יְמַלִּל וּלְקַדִּישֵׁי עֶלְיוֹנִין יְבַלֵּא וְיִסְבַּר לְהַשְׁנָיָה זִמְנִין וְדָת וְיִתְיַהֲבוּן בִּידֵהּ עַד עִדָּן וְעִדָּנִין וּפְלַג עִדָּן: [דניאל ז, כה]

ג) הֶאֱכַלְתָּם לֶחֶם דִּמְעָה וַתַּשְׁקֵמוֹ בִּדְמָעוֹת שָׁלִישׁ: [תהלים פ, ו]

ד) כִּי כֹה אָמַר יְיָ צְבָאוֹת עוֹד אַחַת מְעַט הִיא וַאֲנִי מַרְעִישׁ אֶת הַשָּׁמַיִם וְאֶת הָאָרֶץ וְאֶת הַיָּם וְאֶת הֶחָרָבָה: [חגי ב, ו]

ה) וְלָכֵן יְחַכֶּה יְיָ לַחֲנַנְכֶם וְלָכֵן יָרוּם לְרַחֶמְכֶם כִּי אֱלֹהֵי מִשְׁפָּט יְיָ אַשְׁרֵי כָּל חוֹכֵי לוֹ: [ישעיה ל, יח]

ו) סָבִיב שְׁמֹנָה עָשָׂר אָלֶף וְשֵׁם הָעִיר מִיּוֹם יְיָ שָׁמָּה: [יחזקאל מח, לה]

ז) שׁוּבוּ בָּנִים שׁוֹבָבִים אֶרְפָּה מְשׁוּבֹתֵיכֶם הִנְנוּ אָתָנוּ לָךְ כִּי אַתָּה יְיָ אֱלֹהֵינוּ: [ירמיה ג, כב]

ח) כִּי כֹה אָמַר יְיָ חִנָּם נִמְכַּרְתֶּם וְלֹא בְכֶסֶף תִּגָּאֵלוּ: [ישעיה נב, ג]

ט) לְמִימֵי אֲבֹתֵיכֶם סַרְתֶּם מֵחֻקַּי וְלֹא שְׁמַרְתֶּם שׁוּבוּ אֵלַי וְאָשׁוּבָה אֲלֵיכֶם אָמַר יְיָ צְבָאוֹת וַאֲמַרְתֶּם בַּמֶּה נָשׁוּב: [מלאכי ג, ז]

י) שׁוּבוּ בָנִים שׁוֹבָבִים נְאֻם יְיָ כִּי אָנֹכִי בָּעַלְתִּי בָכֶם וְלָקַחְתִּי אֶתְכֶם אֶחָד מֵעִיר וּשְׁנַיִם מִמִּשְׁפָּחָה וְהֵבֵאתִי אֶתְכֶם צִיּוֹן: [ירמיה ג, יד]

כ) כִּי כֹה אָמַר אֲדֹנָי אֱלֹהִים קְדוֹשׁ יִשְׂרָאֵל בְּשׁוּבָה וָנַחַת תִּוָּשֵׁעוּן בְּהַשְׁקֵט וּבְבִטְחָה תִּהְיֶה גְּבוּרַתְכֶם וְלֹא אֲבִיתֶם: [ישעיה ל, טו]

ל) כֹּה אָמַר יְיָ גֹּאֵל יִשְׂרָאֵל קְדוֹשׁוֹ לִבְזֹה נֶפֶשׁ לִמְתָעֵב גּוֹי לְעֶבֶד מֹשְׁלִים מְלָכִים יִרְאוּ וָקָמוּ שָׂרִים וְיִשְׁתַּחֲווּ לְמַעַן יְיָ אֲשֶׁר נֶאֱמָן קְדֹשׁ יִשְׂרָאֵל וַיִּבְחָרֶךָּ: [ישעיה מט, ז]

וּבַעֲוֹנוֹתֵינוּ שֶׁרַבּוּ – BUT BECAUSE OF OUR SINS, WHICH ARE NUMEROUS, יָצְאוּ מֵהֶם מַה שֶׁיָּצְאוּ – [THE YEARS] THAT HAVE GONE FROM [THE MESSIANIC ERA] HAVE GONE.[1]

The prophet Elijah reveals a date for the Messiah's arrival: אָמַר לֵיהּ אֵלִיָּהוּ לְרַב יְהוּדָה אֲחוּהּ דְּרַב סַלָּא חֲסִידָא – **Elijah said to Rav Yehudah the brother of Rav Salla the Pious:** אֵין הָעוֹלָם פָּחוֹת מִשְּׁמוֹנִים וַחֲמִשָּׁה יוֹבְלוֹת – **"The world is** destined to exist for **not less than eighty-five jubilee cycles.** וּבַיּוֹבֵל הָאַחֲרוֹן בֶּן דָּוִד בָּא – **In the final jubilee cycle, the son of David will come."**[2] אָמַר לֵיהּ – **[Rav Yehudah] asked [Elijah]:** בִּתְחִילָּתוֹ אוֹ בְסוֹפוֹ – "Will he come **at the beginning of [the last jubilee cycle] or at its end?"** אָמַר לֵיהּ – **[Elijah] answered him:** אֵינִי יוֹדֵעַ – **"I do not know."**[3] כָּלֶה אוֹ אֵינוֹ כָּלֶה – Rav Yehudah then asked Elijah: **"Will [the final jubilee cycle] have ended** by the time the Messiah comes, **or will it not have ended?"**[4] אָמַר לֵיהּ – **[Elijah] answered him:** אֵינִי יוֹדֵעַ – **"I do not know."**[5]

The Gemara cites a different version of Elijah's last reply: רַב אַשִׁי אָמַר – **Rav Ashi says:** הָכִי אָמַר לֵיהּ – **This is what [Elijah] answered [Rav Yehudah]:** עַד הָכָא לָא תִּיסְתְּכֵי לֵיהּ – **"Until then, do not expect [the Messiah].** מִכָּאן וְאֵילָךְ אִיסְתְּכֵי לֵיהּ – **From then on, expect him."**[6]

The Gemara cites another prediction concerning the redemption:

שְׁלַח לֵיהּ רַב חָנָן בַּר תַּחֲלִיפָא לְרַב יוֹסֵף – **Rav Chanan bar Tachalifa sent** the following message **to Rav Yosef:** מָצָאתִי אָדָם אֶחָד – **I met a man** וּבְיָדוֹ מְגִילָּה אַחַת כְּתוּבָה אַשּׁוּרִית וּלְשׁוֹן קֹדֶשׁ – **in whose hand there was a scroll, written** in **Ashuri** script[7] **and** in **the Holy Tongue.**[8] אָמַרְתִּי לוֹ – **I asked him:** זוֹ מִנַּיִן לְךָ – **"From where did you get this** scroll?" אָמַר לִי – **He answered me:** לְחַיָּילוֹת שֶׁל רוֹמִי נִשְׂכַּרְתִּי – **"I was hired** as an aid **to** one of **the soldiers of Rome,** וּבֵין גִּינְזֵי רוֹמִי מְצָאתִיהָ – **and I found it among the hidden treasures of Rome."**[9] וְכָתוּב בָּהּ – **And in it was written:** לְאַחַר אַרְבַּעַת אֲלָפִים וּמָאתַיִם וְתִשְׁעִים וְאֶחָד שָׁנָה לִבְרִיאָתוֹ שֶׁל עוֹלָם – **"After four thousand two hundred and ninety**[10]**-one years from the world's creation,** הָעוֹלָם יָתוֹם – **the world will end.**[11] מֵהֶן מִלְחֲמוֹת תַּנִּינִים – During some **of them**[12] there will be **the wars of the great sea creatures.**[13] מֵהֶן מִלְחֲמוֹת גּוֹג וּמָגוֹג – During some **of them** there will be **the wars of Gog and Magog.**[14] וּשְׁאָר יְמוֹת הַמָּשִׁיחַ – **And the rest**[15] **will be the days of the Messiah.**[16]

NOTES

1. Because of our sins the Messiah did not come at the end of the fourth millennium. The final two millennia, which were supposed to have been the Messianic era, have turned out differently, for the Messiah has still not come (*Rashi*).

2. A jubilee cycle is fifty years long. Hence, eighty-five jubilee cycles amount to 4,250 years (*Rashi*).

The Gemara below discusses whether Elijah was referring to the earliest or the latest date for the Messiah's arrival (see 97a note 60).

An allusion to Elijah's prediction is found in the Torah. In *Numbers* 10:35-36, Moses prays that God will rise and disperse His enemies (i.e. the enemies of Israel [*Rashi* ad loc.]) and that He will reside among the Jewish people. These verses are separated from the rest of the Torah by means of an inverted letter *nun* before and after them. Since these two verses are set off from the rest of the Torah, the Gemara in *Shabbos* (115b-116a) speaks of them as a separate "book," indicating that it has a message of its own. These verses contain exactly eighty-five letters. The letter *nun* has a numerical value of fifty – the number of years in a jubilee cycle. The Torah thus indicates that in the eighty-fifth jubilee cycle an era will begin during which God will arise, disperse the enemies of the Jewish people, and reside among His people (*Abarbanel* ibid.).

3. A different version of the Gemara's text records Elijah as answering that the Messiah will come at the *end* of the last jubilee cycle (*Dikdukei Sofrim*). This version is followed by *Yad Ramah* and *Abarbanel* (ibid.).

4. Will the Messiah come *after* the final jubilee cycle has ended, or *during* (i.e. at the end of) the cycle? (*Rashi*).

Since Elijah already said that he did not know whether the Messiah will come at the beginning or the end of the final jubilee cycle, it is difficult to understand why Rav Yehudah subsequently asked him this question. [This difficulty obviously does not arise according to the version of the text cited in the previous note.]

Maharsha raises a different problem: Elijah said explicitly that the Messiah will come "in (i.e. during) the final jubilee cycle." How, then, could Rav Yehudah ask whether he might come *after* this cycle has ended? *Maharsha* explains, therefore, that Rav Yehudah was asking whether the date predicted by Elijah was the *earliest* date for the coming of the Messiah or the *latest* date (see 97a note 60). Rav Yehudah's words are interpreted thus: כָּלֶה – *Will [this cycle] certainly end* after his arrival (i.e. he will certainly have come by this date), אוֹ אֵינוֹ כָּלֶה – *or will it not necessarily end* after his arrival (i.e. he will come only after this date)? [According to this explanation, Rav Ashi's version of the response given by Elijah directly answers Rav Yehudah's question (see the continuation of the Gemara).]

5. *Yad Ramah* asserts that Elijah certainly knew the preordained date for the redemption. See there for an explanation of Elijah's doubt.

6. That is, the year 4,250 is the earliest possible date for the Messiah's arrival (see end of note 4).

Yad Ramah points out a contradiction between two teachings of Elijah. It was recorded above in the name of Elijah that the Messiah could come any time during the final two millennia (which began in the year 4,000), whereas here it is stated that Elijah told Rav Yehudah not to expect the Messiah before the year 4,250 (see 97a note 61).

Yad Ramah answers that in fact the date is 4,250. Hence, the period during which the Messiah could come is actually less than two millennia (1,750 years). The Baraisa above defined this period as two millennia because it treats the majority of a millennium as a complete millennium.

7. There are two Hebrew scripts: *Ashuri* and *Ivri*. [*Ashuri* is our standard square script; *Ivri* is the script found on coins dating from Temple times.] In those times, *Ashuri* was reserved for sacred purposes, whereas *Ivri* was the commonly used script (see above, 21b-22a; *Rabbeinu Chananel* ibid. 21b; *Ramban* in an appendix to his commentary on *Chumash* regarding the weights of Biblical coins; *Ritva* to *Megillah* 2b; see *Torah Sheleimah* for a complete treatment of this topic).

The *Ashuri* script is called by this name because it came from Ashur [Assyria] (*Rashi*). [That is, its use became more widespread among the Jews when they were in Assyria (see *HaMikra VeHaMesorah*).]

Rashi cites only one of two Tannaic views on this matter. According to the opposing view, *Ashuri* means choicest (from the root אשר, *praise*). *Rabbeinu Chananel* (ibid.) accepts the latter view as authoritative.

8. [I.e. the Hebrew language.] The fact that the scroll was written in the *Ashuri* script *and* in the Hebrew language proved that it was of Jewish origin (*Yad Ramah; see Maharsha*).

9. The Romans had confiscated it when they pillaged Jerusalem (*Yad Ramah*).

10. *Gra* emends the text to read שְׁלֹשִׁים, *thirty* (see *Avodah Zarah* 9a).

11. [I.e. the world in its current state will end. A new era will commence in which events will move in the direction leading to the advent of the Messiah.]

Alternatively, יָתוֹם means orphan. Like children without a father to control them, the nations will war against each other (*Yad Ramah*).

12. I.e. during the years that follow the first 4,291 years (*Yad Ramah;* cf. *Abarbanel* in *Yeshuos Meshicho, Iyun* 1 end of ch. 1).

13. A תַּנִּין is some type of gigantic sea creature (see *Rashi* and *Ramban* to *Genesis* 1:21). In the present context, this word is used allegorically for kings whose dominion includes seas or other major bodies of water [see *Ezekiel* 29:3] (*Yad Ramah*).

Alternatively, this is a general reference to the nations of the world, who will fight against each other before the war of Gog and Magog breaks out (*Abarbanel, Yeshuos Meshicho* ibid.; *Maharsha*). *Abarbanel* (ibid.) also suggests that this term signifies the nations that have persecuted the Jews, or the false messiahs [whose claims led to wars of religion].

14. Gog, the king of Magog, will lead the nations in a cataclysmic war against the Jews in Eretz Yisrael, as described in *Ezekiel* chs. 38-39. This subject is dealt with above – see 94a note 12.

15. [I.e. the years remaining before the year 6,000 (see note 17).]

16. The Jews will no longer be under foreign domination and the Messiah will have come (*Rashi*).

ובעונותינו שרבו יצאו מהם מה שיצאו אמר ליה אליהו לרב יהודה אחוה דרב סלא חסידא אין העולם פחות משמונים וחמשה יובלות וביובל האחרון בן דוד בא אמר ליה בתחילתו או בסופו אמר ליה איני יודע כלה או אינו כלה אמר ליה איני יודע רב אשי אמר הכי א"ל עד הכא לא תיסתכי ליה מכאן ואילך איסתכי ליה שלח ליה רב חנן בר תחליפא לרב יוסף מצאתי אדם אחד ובידו מגילה אחת כתובה אשורית ולשון קדש אמרתי לו זו מניין לך אמר לי לחיילות של רומי נשכרתי ובין גינזי רומי מצאתיה וכתוב בה לאחר ד' אלפים ומאתים [א] ותשעים ואחד שנה לבריאתו של עולם העולם יתום מהן מלחמות תנינים מהן מלחמות גוג ומגוג ושאר ימות המשיח ואין הקב"ה מחדש את עולמו אלא לאחר שבעת אלפים שנה רב אחא בריה דרבא אמר לאחר חמשת אלפים שנה איתמר תניא רבי נתן אומר מקרא זה נוקב ויורד עד תהום א) כי עוד חזון למועד ויפח לקץ ולא יכזב אם יתמהמה חכה לו כי בא יבא לא יאחר לא כרבותינו שהיו דורשין ב) עד עידן עידנין ופלג עידן ולא כר' שמלאי שהיה דורש ג) האכלתם לחם דמעה ותשקמו בדמעות שליש ולא כרבי עקיבא שהיה דורש ד) עוד אחת מעט היא ואני מרעיש את השמים ואת הארץ אלא מלכות ראשון שבעים שנה מלכות שניה חמשים ושתים ומלכות בן כוזיבא שתי שנים ומחצה מאי ויפח לקץ ולא יכזב א"ר שמואל בר נחמני אמר ר' יונתן א) תיפח עצמן של מחשבי קיצין שהיו אומרים כיון שהגיע את הקץ ולא בא שוב אינו בא אלא חכה לו שנאמר אם יתמהמה חכה לו שמא תאמר אנו מחכין והוא אינו מחכה ת"ל ה) לכן יחכה ה' לחננכם ולכן ירום לרחמכם וכי מאחר שאנו מחכים והוא מחכה מי מעכב מדת הדין מעכבת וכי מאחר שמדת הדין מעכבת אנו למה מחכין לקבל שכר שנאמר ה) אשרי כל חוכי לו ב) אמר אביי ב) לא פחות עלמא מתלתין ושיתא צדיקי דמקבלי אפי שכינה בכל דרא שנאמר אשרי כל חוכי לו לו בגימטריא תלתין ושיתא הוו איני והאמר רבא דרא דקמי קודשא בריך הוא תמני סרי אלפי [פרסא] הואי שנאמר ו) סביב שמונה עשר אלף לא קשיא הא דמסתכלי באיספקלריא המאירה הא דמסתכלי באיספקלריא שאינה מאירה ומי נפישי כולי האי ג) והאמר חזקיה א"ר ירמיה משום רשב"י ראיתי בני עלייה והן מועטין אם אלף הם אני ובני מהם אם מאה הם אני ובני מהם אם שנים הם אני ובני הם לא קשיא הא דעיילי בבר הא דעיילי בלא בר אמר רב כלו כל הקיצין ואין הדבר תלוי אלא בתשובה ומעשים טובים ושמואל אמר דיו לאבל שיעמוד באבלו כתנאי ר' אליעזר אומר אם ישראל עושין תשובה נגאלין ואם לאו אין נגאלין אמר ליה רבי יהושע אם אין עושין תשובה אין נגאלין ד) אלא הקב"ה מעמיד להן מלך שגזרותיו קשות כהמן ה) וישראל עושין תשובה ומחזירן למוטב תניא אידך ר' אליעזר אומר אם ישראל עושין תשובה נגאלין שנאמר ז) שובו בנים שובבים ארפא משובותיכם אמר לו רבי יהושע והלא כבר נאמר ח) חנם נמכרתם ולא בכסף תגאלו חנם נמכרתם בעבודת כוכבים ולא בכסף תגאלו לא בתשובה ומעשים טובים אמר לו רבי אליעזר לר' יהושע והלא כבר נאמר ט) שובו אלי ואשובה אליכם אמר ליה רבי יהושע והלא כבר נאמר י) כי אנכי בעלתי בכם ולקחתי אתכם אחד מעיר ושנים ממשפחה והבאתי אתכם ציון אמר לו ר' אליעזר והלא כבר נאמר כ) בשובה ונחת תושעון אמר לו ר' יהושע לרבי אליעזר והלא כבר נאמר ל) כה אמר ה' גואל ישראל וקדושו לבזה נפש למתעב גוי לעבד מושלים מלכים

אבל בשביל עונותינו שרבו. לא בא משיח לסוף ד' אלפים ויצאו מה שיצאו שעדיין הוא מעוכב לבא: שמנים וחמשה יובלין. היינו ד' אלפים מאתים וחמשים [שנה]: בתחלת. היובל האחרון הוא בא או בסופו: כלה. זמן הזה קודם שיבא משיח או אינו כלה דבתוך היובל בסופו הוא בא: עד הכא לא תיסתכי ליה. עד יובל האחרון לא תצפה לו דודאי לא יבא קודם הזמן הזה: איסתכי ליה. חכה לו שיבא: אשורית. כתב שלנו אשורית שבא מאשור כדאמר באידך פירקין (ד' כב.): לחיילות של רומי נשכרתי. שהייתי גולייר לאחד מהם: תנינים. דגים: והשאר ימות המשיח. שכלה השעבוד ומשיח בא: מחדש עולמו. לברוא עולם חדש: נוקב ויורד עד התהום. מה תהום אין לו קץ וסוף כך אין אדם יכול לעמוד על סוף פסוק זה ז) (וכי קא מפרש אימת קאמר אם) יתמהמה חכה לו דאין לו סוף: לא כרבותינו. אל תצפו לאותו קץ שהיו רבותינו דורשין: עד עידן עידנין ופלג עידן. עידן כעידן הגלות של מצרים והיינו ד' מאות ב' עידנין ח' מאות היינו י"ב מאות ופלג עידן ב' מאות סך הכל אלף וד' מאות: ותשקמו בדמעות שליש. כלומר השקה אותם הקב"ה בין גלות מצרים לגלות בבל שליש גלות אדום כי קץ גלות אדום זה יהיה לסוף ג' פעמים ת' שנים וג' פעמים ע' שנה כנגד גלות בבל דהיינו לסוף אלף וארבע מאות ועשר שנים [ב] כבר עברו ולא היה כך מצאתי כתוב בשם הרב רבי שמואל בר דוד ז"ל: עוד אחת מעט היא. בנבואת חגי כתיב שהיה מתנבא כשיצאו ישראל מגלות בבל ויבנה בית המקדש והיינו עוד אחת מעט היא מעט כבוד אתן להם לישראל ואני מרעיש את השמים ואת הארץ והבאתי כל חמדת גוים לירושלים ור"ע דריש ליה לימות המשיח ולאחר חורבן והכי דריש ליה [עוד אחת מעט היא מעט כבוד אתן לישראל ואח"כ יבא המשיח ודרשה זו אינה אלא קרא אלפני הבית קאי וה"ק] עוד אחת מעט היא מעט כבוד אתן להם לישראל ושוב לא אתן להם כל ימות בית אחרון וכן היה דמלכות ראשונה של מלכות חשמונאי נתקיימה שבעים שנה ואע"ג דאמרינן בסדר עולם דמלכות בית חשמונאי מאה ושלש ומלכות הורדוס מאה ושלש עיקר כבודם ופארם שלא שלטה בהם אומה לא נתקיים כל כך ומלכות שניה של הורדוס נ"ב שנה ומלכות בן כוזיבא ב' שנים ומחצה ושוב לא היה להם מלך מ"ר. וכל הנך דרשות לאו משנה ולאו ברייתא. ל"א עוד אחת מעט היא מעט מלכות אתן להם לישראל לאחר חורבן ולאחר אותו מלכות הנני מרעיש שמים וארץ ויבא משיח. ואין דרשה זו כלום שהרי ראינו כמה מלכיות לישראל לאחר חורבן ואעפ"כ לא בא משיח שהמלכות הראשונה שהיתה להם לישראל לאחר חורבן שבעים שנה הורדוס נ"ב בן כוזיבא ב' ומחצה ומצינו בסדר עולם מפולמוס של אספסיאנוס עד פולמוס של טיטוס שתים עשרה שנה ומפולמוס של טיטוס עד מלכות בן כוזיבא י"ז שנים ומלכות בן כוזיבא ב' שנים ומחצה: [בן כוזיבא מלך בביתר]: ויפח לקץ. תיפח נפשו של מחשב הקץ שלא היה לו לכזב ולומר כיון שהגיע וכו': יחכה ה'. הוא עצמו מחכה ומתאוה שיבא משיח: סביב י"ח אלף. בירושלים של מעלה משתעי קרא בסוף יחזקאל: באספקלריא המאירה. בחוזק נגהו של הקב"ה אין מסתכלין אלא תלתין ושית אבל בקלישות הנוגה לצדדין מרחוק מסתכלין כמות הרבה: ומי נפישי כולי האי. דלהוי בריר לן תלתין ושיתא הוו ולא פחות: והא רבי שמעון בן יוחאי. לא הוה ידע אם אלף הם אם מאה הם אם שנים הם: הא דעיילי בבר. שצריכין ליטול רשות כשנכנסין להסתכל באספקלריא המאירה בהנהו לא פחיתי מתלתין ושית אבל אותן הנכנסין בלא רשות ברוב צדקם הנהו מספקא לן כמה הוו: בתשובה. אם כל ישראל חוזרין בתשובה יבא ואם לאו לא יבא: דיו לאבל שעומד באבלו. דיו להקב"ה שעומד כמה ימים וימינו אחור כלומר אם לא יעשו תשובה אינו עומד באבלו כל הימים אלא ודאי קץ לדבר ל"א דיו לאבל דיין לישראל צער גלות אפילו בלא תשובה נגאלין: לא בכסף. לא בתשובה ומעשים טובים דאפילו אין עושין תשובה נגאלין משום דאמר חנם נמכרתם קרי כסף בלשון תשובה: בעלתי אתכם. משמע בעל כרחכם בלא תשובה: אחד מעיר. אברור הצדיקים ואביאם לציון אע"פ שאין כולם חוזרין: כה אמר ה' לבזה נפש למתעב גוי. אותן הבזויין ומתועבין בעבירות אעפ"כ יגאלו מלכים יראו וקמו: כי

עין משפט
נר מצוה

י א מיי' פי"ב מהלכות מלכים ומלחמותיהם הלכה ב:
יא ב מיי' פ"ז מהל' תשובה הלכה ה:

גליון הש"ס

גמ' לא פחות עלמא. ועי' במ"ר בראשית פ' ל"ה שם איתא לא פחות מתלתין צדיקי ועיין במ"ר במדבר פ' ג':

ליקוטי רש"י

ובעונותינו שרבו יצאו. משני אלפים אחרונים מה שיצאו ומשיח לא בא [ע"ז ט.]. עד עידן עידנין ופלג עידן. קץ סתום הוא זה כאשר נאמר לדניאל סתום הדברים וחתום ודרשוהו הראשונים איש לפי דעתו וכלו הקצים ויש לנו לפותרו עוד כאשר ראיתי כתוב בשם רב סעדיה הם אלף וג' מאות ול"ה שנים האמור בסוף הספר אשרי המחכה וגו' ופי' המועד עד עת שני עתים וחצי עת ואמר שהעתים הם ד' מאות ופי' שמיום צאתם ממצרים עד שנבנה הבית וד' מאות ועשר ימי מקדש ראשון הרי תת"ן ועוד חצי העת הזה תמ"ה הרי אלף של"ה את אלה חשוב מעת הוסר התמיד עד שוב זבח התמיד אל מקומו והוא הוסר שש שנים לפני החורבן ויש קצת ראיה בספר זה ועוד יש מביאין ראיה לחשבון זה הסתר אסתיר פני הסתר אסתיר בגי' אלף ושל"ה [דניאל ז, כה]. אשרי כל חוכי לו. לנחמות אשר הבטיח כי לא יפול דבר [ישעיה ל, יח]. אמר אביי כו' אשרי כל חוכי לו. המחכים לכת שהוא כמנין לו. סביב שמנה עשר אלף. סיפיה דקרא ה' שמה דקאי על גב דירושלים שלעתיד לבא כתיב קרא דרשינן ליה נמי להכי דמקום ששכינה שמה סובבין אותו שמנה עשר אלף והם הצדיקים הנתונים לפנים ממלאכי השרת שנאמר (במדבר כג) כעת יאמר ליעקב ולישראל מה פעל אל ואומר (ישעיה כג) ליושבים לפני ה' יהיה סחרה ואומר (שם ל) והיו עיניך רואות את מוריך. איספקלריא. מחילה שחוצצת ביניהם לשכינה. המאירה. כמראה זו שרואין בה ויש לצדיקים שאין מאירה להם כל כך ואין יכולין לראות ממש. ראיתי בני עלייה והן מועטין. רואה אני לפי מעשה הבריות שבני עלייה כת המקבלין פני שכינה מועטים הם. בבר. ברשות. דעיילי בלא בר. בלא רשות מועטים הן ובהנהו קאמר אני ובני מהם [סוכה מה:]. שובבים. אנוויש"ר בלע"ז שסובבתם דרככם מרוב כל שהייתם בשלוה ועונג כמו שהוא אומר הפורטים על פי הנבל (עמוס ו) השותים במזרקי יין (שם) [ירמיה ג, יד]. לשון משובה נערו' ויולדות איטווייזור"א בלע"ז וכן בנים שובבים (ירמיה ג) הבת השובבה (שם לא) [הושע ו, יא]. משמע מזידים ופרהסיא [שובב] לשון מרד וגאוה כמו וילך שובב בדרך לבו (ישעיה נז) [ע"ז ז:]. כי אנכי בעלתי בכם. ונקראתם בשמי שאני אדון לכם ואין כבודי להניח אתכם ביד אויבי [ירמיה שם]. בשובה ונחת. תהיה לכם תשועה בלא שום טורח אם תשמעו לי. בשובה. לשון ישוב ומרגוע וכן שובה ה' רבבות אלפי ישראל (במדבר י) [ישעיה ל, טו]. לבזה נפש. נפש בזויה לישראל שהם בזוים [שם מט, ז]. לישראל הבזוים ומתועבים [תענית טו.]. למתעב גוי. למי שהגוי מתעבו [ישעיה שם]. לעבד מושלים. ועבדים מושלין בהן [תענית שם].

מסורת הש"ס

א) סוכה מה: ע"ש, ב) ג"ז שם:, ג) בירושלמי הגי' א"ל ר"א, ד) ס"א שאין קץ למשיח אלא אם.

הגהות הגר"א

[א] גמ' ותשעים. נמחק וג"ב שלשים (עי' בע"ז ט' ב' ובתום' ד"ה לאחר): [ב] רש"י ד"ה ותשקמו כו' עשר שנים. עשה כאן נקודות להפסיק ותיבת וכבר עברו וכו' עד בר דוד ז"ל נמחק:

תורה אור השלם

א) כִּי עוֹד חָזוֹן לַמּוֹעֵד וְיָפֵחַ לַקֵּץ וְלֹא יְכַזֵּב אִם יִתְמַהְמָהּ חַכֵּה לוֹ כִּי בֹא יָבֹא לֹא יְאַחֵר: [חבקוק ב, ג]

ב) וּמִלִּין לְצַד עִלָּאָה יְמַלִּל וּלְקַדִּישֵׁי עֶלְיוֹנִין יְבַלֵּא וְיִסְבַּר לְהַשְׁנָיָה זִמְנִין וְדָת וְיִתְיַהֲבוּן בִּידֵהּ עַד עִדָּן וְעִדָּנִין וּפְלַג עִדָּן: [דניאל ז, כה]

ג) הֶאֱכַלְתָּם לֶחֶם דִּמְעָה וַתַּשְׁקֵמוֹ בִּדְמָעוֹת שָׁלִישׁ: [תהלים פ, ו]

ד) כִּי כֹה אָמַר יְיָ צְבָאוֹת עוֹד אַחַת מְעַט הִיא וַאֲנִי מַרְעִישׁ אֶת הַשָּׁמַיִם וְאֶת הָאָרֶץ וְאֶת הַיָּם וְאֶת הֶחָרָבָה: [חגי ב, ו]

ה) וְלָכֵן יְחַכֶּה יְיָ לַחֲנַנְכֶם וְלָכֵן יָרוּם לְרַחֶמְכֶם כִּי אֱלֹהֵי מִשְׁפָּט יְיָ אַשְׁרֵי כָּל חוֹכֵי לוֹ: [ישעיה ל, יח]

ו) סָבִיב שְׁמֹנָה עָשָׂר אָלֶף וְשֵׁם הָעִיר מִיּוֹם יְיָ שָׁמָּה: [יחזקאל מח, לה]

ז) שׁוּבוּ בָּנִים שׁוֹבָבִים אֶרְפָּה מְשׁוּבֹתֵיכֶם הִנְנוּ אָתָנוּ לָךְ כִּי אַתָּה יְיָ אֱלֹהֵינוּ: [ירמיה ג, כב]

ח) כִּי כֹה אָמַר יְיָ חִנָּם נִמְכַּרְתֶּם וְלֹא בְכֶסֶף תִּגָּאֵלוּ: [ישעיה נב, ג]

ט) לְמִימֵי אֲבֹתֵיכֶם סַרְתֶּם מֵחֻקַּי וְלֹא שְׁמַרְתֶּם שׁוּבוּ אֵלַי וְאָשׁוּבָה אֲלֵיכֶם אָמַר יְיָ צְבָאוֹת וַאֲמַרְתֶּם בַּמֶּה נָשׁוּב: [מלאכי ג, ז]

י) שׁוּבוּ בָנִים שׁוֹבָבִים נְאֻם יְיָ כִּי אָנֹכִי בָּעַלְתִּי בָכֶם וְלָקַחְתִּי אֶתְכֶם אֶחָד מֵעִיר וּשְׁנַיִם מִמִּשְׁפָּחָה וְהֵבֵאתִי אֶתְכֶם צִיּוֹן: [ירמיה ג, יד]

כ) כִּי כֹה אָמַר אֲדֹנָי אֱלֹהִים קְדוֹשׁ יִשְׂרָאֵל בְּשׁוּבָה וָנַחַת תִּוָּשֵׁעוּן בְּהַשְׁקֵט וּבְבִטְחָה תִּהְיֶה גְּבוּרַתְכֶם וְלֹא אֲבִיתֶם: [ישעיה ל, טו]

ל) כֹּה אָמַר יְיָ גֹּאֵל יִשְׂרָאֵל קְדוֹשׁוֹ לִבְזֹה נֶפֶשׁ לִמְתָעֵב גּוֹי לְעֶבֶד מֹשְׁלִים מְלָכִים יִרְאוּ וָקָמוּ שָׂרִים וְיִשְׁתַּחֲווּ לְמַעַן יְיָ אֲשֶׁר נֶאֱמָן קְדֹשׁ יִשְׂרָאֵל וַיִּבְחָרֶךָּ: [ישעיה מט, ז]

וְאֵין הַקָּדוֹשׁ בָּרוּךְ הוּא מְחַדֵּשׁ אֶת עוֹלָמוֹ אֶלָּא לְאַחַר שִׁבְעַת אֲלָפִים שָׁנָה – **And the Holy One, Blessed is He, will not renew His world until after seven thousand years."**[17]

The Gemara records a different version of the scroll's text:

רַב אַחָא בְּרֵיהּ דְּרָבָא אָמַר – **Rav Acha the son of Rava said:** לְאַחַר חֲמֵשֶׁת אֲלָפִים שָׁנָה אִיתְמַר – **"After five thousand years"** is what **was stated** in the scroll.[18]

The following Baraisa underscores the futility of attempting to predict the date of the redemption:

תַּנְיָא – **It was taught in a Baraisa:** רַבִּי נָתָן אוֹמֵר – R' NASSAN SAYS: מִקְרָא זֶה נוֹקֵב וְיוֹרֵד עַד תְּהוֹם – THIS VERSE PIERCES AND PLUMMETS TO THE DEPTHS![19] "כִּי עוֹד חָזוֹן לַמּוֹעֵד וְיָפֵחַ לַקֵּץ וְלֹא יְכַזֵּב – *FOR THERE IS ANOTHER VISION OF THE APPOINTED TIME; IT SHALL SPEAK OF THE "END," AND IT SHALL NOT LIE.* אִם־יִתְמַהְמַהּ חַכֵּה־לוֹ כִּי־בֹא יָבֹא לֹא יְאַחֵר" – *IF IT TARRIES, WAIT FOR IT, BECAUSE IT WILL SURELY COME; IT WILL NOT DELAY.*[20] This verse implies that the date of the redemption is concealed from us.[21] לֹא כְּרַבּוֹתֵינוּ שֶׁהָיוּ דּוֹרְשִׁין "עַד־עִדָּן וְעִדָּנִין וּפְלַג עִדָּן" – Thus, it is CONTRARY TO OUR SAGES WHO EXPOUNDED the verse: *UNTIL A TIME, AND TIMES, AND HALF A TIME,* to determine the date of the redemption;[22] וְלֹא כְּרַבִּי שִׂמְלַאי שֶׁהָיָה דּוֹרֵשׁ "הֶאֱכַלְתָּם לֶחֶם דִּמְעָה וַתַּשְׁקֵמוֹ בִּדְמָעוֹת שָׁלִישׁ" – it is also CONTRARY TO R' SIMLAI, WHO EXPOUNDED the verse: *YOU FED THEM BREAD OF TEARS; YOU MADE THEM DRINK TEARS for A THIRD*, to determine the date of the redemption;[23] וְלֹא כְּרַבִּי עֲקִיבָא שֶׁהָיָה דּוֹרֵשׁ "עוֹד אַחַת מְעַט הִיא וַאֲנִי מַרְעִישׁ אֶת־הַשָּׁמַיִם וְאֶת־הָאָרֶץ" – and it is CONTRARY TO R' AKIVA WHO EXPOUNDED the verse: *There shall be ANOTHER ONE, IT SHALL BE SLIGHT, AND then I WILL SHAKE THE HEAVENS AND THE EARTH*, to determine the date of the redemption.[24] אֶלָּא – IN FACT, the verse expounded by R' Akiva refers to a different matter altogether[25] – namely, that after the second Temple is built, מַלְכוּת רִאשׁוֹן שִׁבְעִים שָׁנָה – THE FIRST Jewish KINGDOM will last SEVENTY YEARS, מַלְכוּת שְׁנִיָּה חֲמִשִּׁים וּשְׁתַּיִם – THE SECOND Jewish KINGDOM will last FIFTY-TWO YEARS, וּמַלְכוּת בֶּן כּוֹזִיבָא שְׁתֵּי שָׁנִים וּמֶחֱצָה – AND THE KINGDOM OF BEN KOZIVA will last TWO AND A HALF YEARS.[26]

The Gemara discusses the verse cited at the beginning of the Baraisa:

מַאי "וְיָפֵחַ לַקֵּץ וְלֹא יְכַזֵּב" – **What is** the meaning of: ***It shall speak of the End, and it shall not lie?***[27]

The Gemara answers:

אָמַר רַבִּי שְׁמוּאֵל בַּר נַחְמָנִי אָמַר רַבִּי יוֹנָתָן – **R' Shmuel Bar Nachmani said in the name of R' Yonasan:** תִּיפַּח עַצְמָן שֶׁל מְחַשְּׁבֵי קִיצִין – **May the very essence of those who calculate "Ends" suffer agony!**[28] שֶׁהָיוּ אוֹמְרִים – **For they say:** כֵּיוָן שֶׁהִגִּיעַ אֶת הַקֵּץ וְלֹא בָא – **"Since the** date of the **End** that we

NOTES

17. This accords with Rav Katina's teaching (above, 97a) that the world will be destroyed after six thousand years (*Yad Ramah*). Then, after a thousand years of destruction, God will renew the world (*Abarbanel;* see 97a note 59).

18. Instead of saying 4,291 years, the scroll said 5,000 years (*Yad Ramah*).

According to *Abarbanel* and *Toras Chaim,* Rav Acha was correcting only the first digit – the date recorded in the scroll was not 4,291, but 5,291.

19. I.e. this verse is as unfathomable as the ocean. Just as it is impossible to measure the depth of the ocean, so too it is impossible to determine the "End" to which this verse alludes (*Rashi*).

Yad Ramah explains R' Nassan's exclamation as follows: Even if the exile is as long as the ocean is deep, the following verse will always provide hope to the Jews ("it will descend [with them] to the depths"), for it assures them that the redemption will ultimately come.

20. *Habakkuk* 2:3.

The verse refers to the *latest* date for the redemption (see 97a note 60). It is understood thus: וְלֹא יְכַזֵּב, *and [that date] shall not lie* (i.e. it will not pass without the redemption). אִם־יִתְמַהְמַהּ חַכֵּה־לוֹ, *If it tarries* (i.e. the date seems long in arriving), *wait for it,* כִּי־בֹא יָבֹא לֹא יְאַחֵר, *because* once it arrives *[the Messiah] will certainly come and will not delay* (*Abarbanel, Yeshuos Meshicho, Cheilek* §1 pg. 18).

[*Rashi* and *Radak* ad loc. explain the verse as referring to the end of the Babylonian exile. The Gemara, however, interprets it as alluding to the final redemption.]

21. For in stating when the Messiah will come, the verse only says: *If he tarries, wait for him.* This implies that we cannot know the date of his arrival – all we can do is wait for him (see *Rashi*).

Alternatively, the proof is from the words עוֹד חָזוֹן לַמּוֹעֵד, *there is another vision of the appointed time.* This means that whatever appointed time for the redemption is alluded to in this verse, there is more to it than meets the eye (*Maharal*; see also *Maharsha*). R' Nassan infers from here that any Scriptural allusion to the "End" is too enigmatic for its meaning to be discernible.

22. *Daniel* 7:25. R' Nassan warns us not to rely on the date projected by those Sages (*Rashi*).

These Sages understand that "time" signifies the length of the Egyptian exile, which was 400 years (see *Genesis* 15:13). The verse mentions three and a half such "times" – *a time* (1), *and times* (2), *and half a time* (1/2). This yields a total of 1,400 [3 1/2 x 400] years (*Rashi*). [*Rashi* does not say whether these 1,400 years are counted from the destruction of the first Temple or from the destruction of the Second Temple (see *Yad Ramah*).]

Many diverse calculations based on this verse have been offered (see, for example, *Rashi* ad loc. in the name of *Rav Saadiah Gaon,* and *Yad Ramah*). *Rashi* (ad loc.) comments: "The early Sages interpreted this verse, each according to his understanding, but the 'Ends' [that they predicted] have passed."

23. *Psalms* 80:6. According to R' Simlai, *You made them drink tears* [for] *a third* means that God made the Jewish people drink the bitter waters of exile – first in Egypt and subsequently in Babylonia – for a period equal to one-third of the final exile. Since the Egyptian exile lasted 400 years (see previous note) and the Babylonian exile 70 years (*Jeremiah* 29:10), it follows that the final exile will last 1,410 [3 x 470] years (*Rashi*).

24. *Haggai* 2:6. R' Akiva interpreted this verse as teaching that after the destruction of the Second Temple, the Jews will enjoy another period of limited glory – *Another one, it shall be slight.* Then the Messiah will come – *I will shake the heavens and the earth* (see *Rashi*).

According to *Maharsha,* however, R' Akiva understood the verse as meaning that there will be another *exile,* but it will be slight, and then the Messiah will come. In R' Akiva's view, this prophecy referred to Bar Koziva, who led a revolt against Rome approximately fifty-three years after the Second Temple's destruction. R' Akiva considered Bar Koziva to be the Messiah (see Midrash *Eichah Rabbasi; Yerushalmi Taanis* 4:4; Gemara above, 93b and note 22 there; *Rambam, Hil Melachim* 11:3; *Doros HaRishonim* vol. 4 §621).

25. Unlike the verses expounded by the Sages and R' Simlai, which indeed speak of the final redemption, the verse expounded by R' Akiva refers to a different topic (*Yad Ramah*).

26. The verse expounded by R' Akiva does not refer to the period *after* the Second Temple was destroyed. Rather, it means that *during* the Second Temple era, the Jews will enjoy a relatively short period of sovereignty. For the rest of that era, they will be ruled by foreign powers. This is indeed what happened. The Second Temple stood for 420 years, but the Jewish people enjoyed complete independence for only the 70 years of the Hasmonean dynasty and the 52 years of the Herodian dynasty. (Although it is stated in *Seder Olam Rabbah* ch. 30 [and *Avodah Zarah* 9a] that the Hasmonean and Herodian dynasties each lasted 103 years, they were fully independent for only 70 and 52 years respectively.) Several years after the destruction of the Second Temple, the Jews enjoyed a short period of independence during the two-and-a-half years of Bar Koziva's reign in Jerusalem [3,886-9] (*Rashi*).

27. Why does the verse use the verb נפח to signify speaking?

28. The Gemara is answering that the verb נפח is used to allude to this curse.

[The Gemara in *Rosh Hashanah* (31a; see *Hagahos HaBach* ibid. §7) and *Kesubos* (105b) records a slightly different version of this curse: תִּיפַּח נַפְשָׁן, *May their soul suffer agony* (see *Rashi* here; cf. *Kiddushin* 29b). A

ובעונותינו שרבו יצאו מהם מה שיצאו
אמר ליה אליהו לרב יהודה אחוה דרב סלא
חסידא אין העולם פחות משמונים וחמשה
יובלות וביובל האחרון בן דוד בא אמר ליה
בתחילתו או בסופו אמר ליה איני יודע כלה
או אינו כלה אמר ליה איני יודע רב אשי
אמר הכי א"ל עד הכא לא תיסתכי ליה מכאן
ואילך איסתכי ליה שלח ליה רב חנן בר
תחליפא לרב יוסף מצאתי אדם אחד ובידו
מגילה אחת כתובה אשורית ולשון קדש
אמרתי לו זו מניין לך אמר לי לחיילות של
רומי נשכרתי ובין גינזי רומי מצאתיה וכתוב
בה לאחר ד' אלפים ומאתים [א] ותשעים ואחד
שנה לבריאתו של עולם העולם יתום מהן
מלחמות תנינים מהן מלחמות גוג ומגוג
ושאר ימות המשיח ואין הקב"ה מחדש את
עולמו אלא לאחר שבעת אלפים שנה רב
אחא בריה דרבא אמר לאחר חמשת אלפים
שנה איתמר תניא רבי נתן אומר מקרא זה
נוקב ויורד עד תהום (א) כי עוד חזון למועד
ויפח לקץ ולא יכזב אם יתמהמה חכה לו
כי בא יבא לא יאחר לא כרבותינו שהיו
דורשין (ב) עד עידן עידנין ופלג עידן ולא כר'
שמלאי שהיה דורש (ג) האכלתם לחם דמעה
ותשקמו בדמעות שליש ולא כרבי עקיבא
שהיה דורש (ד) עוד אחת מעט היא ואני
מרעיש את השמים ואת הארץ אלא מלכות
ראשון שבעים שנה מלכות שניה חמשים
ושתים ומלכות בן כוזיבא שתי שנים ומחצה
מאי ויפח לקץ ולא יכזב אמר רבי שמואל בר
נחמני אמר ר' יונתן (א) תיפח עצמן של מחשבי
קיצין שהיו אומרים כיון שהגיע את הקץ
ולא בא שוב אינו בא אלא חכה לו שנאמר
אם יתמהמה חכה לו שמא תאמר אנו
מחכין והוא אינו מחכה ת"ל (ה) לכן יחכה ה'
לחננכם ולכן ירום לרחמכם וכי מאחר שאנו
מחכים והוא מחכה מי מעכב מדת הדין
מעכבת וכי מאחר שמדת הדין מעכבת אנו
למה מחכין לקבל שכר שנאמר (ה) אשרי כל
חוכי לו (ב) אמר אביי לא פחות עלמא מתלתין
ושיתא צדיקי דמקבלי אפי שכינה בכל דרא
שנאמר אשרי כל חוכי לו לו בגימטריא תלתין ושיתא הוו איני והאמר רבא
דרא דקמי קודשא בריך הוא תמני סרי אלפי [פרסא] הואי שנאמר (ו) סביב
שמנה עשר אלף לא קשיא הא דמסתכלי באיספקלריא המאירה הא
דמסתכלי באיספקלריא שאינה מאירה ומי נפישי כולי האי (ג) והאמר חזקיה א"ר ירמיה משום רשב"י
ראיתי בני עלייה והן מועטין אם אלף הם אני ובני מהם אם מאה הם אני ובני מהם אם שנים הם אני ובני
הם לא קשיא הא דעיילי בבר הא דעיילי בלא בר כלו כל הקיצין ואין הדבר תלוי אלא בתשובה
ומעשים טובים ושמואל אמר דיו לאבל שיעמוד באבלו כתנאי ר' אליעזר אומר אם ישראל עושין תשובה
נגאלין ואם לאו אין נגאלין אמר ליה רבי יהושע אם אין עושין תשובה אין נגאלין (ג) אלא הקב"ה
מעמיד להן מלך שגזרותיו קשות כהמן (ד) וישראל עושין תשובה ומחזירן למוטב תניא אידך ר' אליעזר
אומר אם ישראל עושין תשובה נגאלין שנאמר (ז) שובו בנים שובבים ארפא משובותיכם אמר לו רבי
יהושע והלא כבר נאמר (ח) חנם נמכרתם ולא בכסף תגאלו חנם נמכרתם בעבודת כוכבים ולא בכסף תגאלו לא
בתשובה ומעשים טובים אמר לו רבי אליעזר לר' יהושע והלא כבר נאמר (ט) שובו אלי ואשובה אליכם
אמר ליה רבי יהושע והלא כבר נאמר (י) כי אנכי בעלתי בכם ולקחתי אתכם אחד מעיר ושנים
ממשפחה והבאתי אתכם ציון אמר לו ר' אליעזר והלא כבר נאמר (כ) בשובה ונחת תושעון אמר לו ר' יהושע
לרבי אליעזר והלא כבר נאמר (ל) כה אמר ה' גואל ישראל וקדושו לבזה נפש למתעב גוי לעבד מושלים
מלכים

רש"י

אבל בשביל עונותינו שרבו. לא בא משיח לסוף ד' אלפים ויצאו מה שיצאו שעדיין הוא מעוכב לבא: **שמנים וחמשה יובלין.** היינו ד' אלפים מאתים וחמשים [שנה]: **בתחלת.** היובל האחרון הוא בא או בסופו: **כלה.** זמן הזה קודם שיבא משיח או אינו כלה דבתוך היובל בסופו הוא בא: **עד הכא לא תיסתכי ליה.** עד יובל האחרון לא תצפה לו דודאי לא יבא קודם הזמן הזה: **איסתכי ליה.** חכה לו שיבא: **אשורית.** כתב שלנו אשורית שבא מאשור כדאמר באידך פירקין (ד' כב.): **לחיילות של רומי נשכרתי.** שהייתי גולייר לאחד מהם: **תנינים.** דגים: **והשאר ימות המשיח.** שכלה השעבוד ומשיח בא: **מחדש עולמו.** לברוא עולם חדש: **נוקב ויורד עד התהום.** מה תהום אין לו קץ וסוף כך אין אדם יכול לעמוד על סוף פסוק זה [7] (וכי קא מפרש אימת קאמר אם) יתמהמה חכה לו דאין לו סוף: **לא כרבותינו.** אל תצפו לאותו קץ שהיו רבותינו דורשין: **עד עידן עידנין ופלג עידן.** עידן כעידן הגלות של מצרים והיינו ד' מאות ב' עידנין ח' מאות היינו י"ב מאות ופלג עידן ב' מאות סך הכל אלף וד' מאות: **ותשקמו בדמעות שליש.** כלומר השקה אותם הקב"ה בין גלות מצרים לגלות בבל שליש גלות אדום כי קץ גלות אדום זה יהיה לסוף ג' פעמים ת' שנים וג' פעמים ע' שנה כנגד גלות בבל דהיינו לסוף אלף וארבע מאות ועשר שנים [ב] כבר עברו ולא היה כך מצאתי כתוב בשם הרב רבי שמואל בר דוד ז"ל: **עוד אחת מעט היא.** בנבואת חגי כתיב שהיה מתנבא כשיצאו ישראל מגלות בבל ויבנה בית המקדש והיינו עוד אחת מעט היא מעט כבוד אתן להם לישראל ואני מרעיש את השמים ואת הארץ והבאתי כל חמדת גוים לירושלים ור"ע דריש ליה לימות המשיח ולאחר חורבן והכי דריש ליה [עוד אחת מעט היא מעט כבוד אתן לישראל ואח"כ יבא המשיח ודרשה זו אינה אלא קרא אלפני הבית קאי וה"ק] עוד אחת מעט היא מעט כבוד אתן להם לישראל ושוב לא אתן להם כל ימות בית אחרון וכן היה דמלכות ראשונה של מלכות חשמונאי נתקיימה שבעים שנה ואע"ג דאמרינן בסדר עולם דמלכות בית חשמונאי מאה ושלש ומלכות הורדוס מאה ושלש עיקר כבודם ופארם שלא שלטה בהם אומה לא נתקיים כל כך ומלכות שניה של הורדוס נ"ב שנה ומלכות בן כוזיבא ב' שנים ומחצה ושוב לא היה להם מלך מ"ר. וכל הנך דרשות לאו משנה ולאו ברייתא. ל"א עוד אחת מעט היא מעט מלכות אתן להם לישראל לאחר חורבן ולאחר אותו מלכות הנני מרעיש שמים וארץ ויבא משיח. ואין דרשה זו כלום שהרי ראינו כמה מלכיות לישראל לאחר חורבן ואעפ"כ לא בא משיח שהמלכות הראשונה שהיתה להם לישראל לאחר חורבן שבעים שנה הורדוס נ"ב בן כוזיבא ב' ומחצה ומצינו בסדר עולם מפולמוס של אספסיאנוס עד פולמוס של טיטוס שתים עשרה שנה ומפולמוס של טיטוס עד מלכות בן כוזיבא י"ז שנים ומלכות בן כוזיבא ב' שנים ומחצה: [בן כוזיבא מלך בביתר]: **ויפח לקץ.** תיפח נפשו של מחשב הקץ שלא היה לו לכזב ולומר כיון שהגיע וכו': **יחכה ה'.** הוא עצמו מחכה ומתאוה שיבא משיח: **סביב י"ח אלף.** בירושלים של מעלה משתעי קרא בסוף יחזקאל: **באספקלריא המאירה.** בחוזק נגהו של הקב"ה אין מסתכלין אלא תלתין ושית אבל בקלישות הנוגה לצדדין מרחוק מסתכלין כתות הרבה: **ומי נפישי כולי האי.** דלהוי בריר לן תלתין ושיתא הוו ולא פחות: **והא רבי שמעון בן יוחאי.** לא הוה ידע אם אלף הם אם מאה הם אם שנים הם: **הא דעיילי בבר.** שצריכין ליטול רשות כשנכנסין להסתכל באספקלריא המאירה בהנהו לא פחיתי מתלתין ושית אבל אותן הנכנסין בלא רשות ברוב צדקם הנהו מספקא לן כמה הוו: **בתשובה.** אם כל ישראל חוזרין בתשובה יבא ואם לאו לא יבא: **דיו לאבל שעומד באבלו.** דיו להקב"ה שעומד כמה ימים וימינו אחור כלומר אם לא יעשו תשובה אינו עומד באבלו כל הימים אלא ודאי קץ לדבר ל"א דיו לאבל דיין לישראל צער גלות אפילו בלא תשובה נגאלין: **לא בכסף.** לא בתשובה ומעשים טובים דאפילו אין עושין תשובה נגאלין משום דאמר חנם נמכרתם קרי כסף בלשון תשובה: **בעלתי אתכם.** משמע בעל כרחכם בלא תשובה: **אחד מעיר.** אברור הצדיקים ואביאם לציון אע"פ שאין כולם חוזרין: **כה אמר ה' לבזה נפש למתעב גוי.** אותן הבזויין ומתועבין בעבירות אעפ"כ יגאלו מלכים יראו וקמו:

עין משפט נר מצוה

י א מיי' פי"ב מהלכות מלכים ומלחמותיהם הלכה ב:

יא ב מיי' פ"ז מהל' תשובה הלכה ה:

גליון הש"ס

גמ' **לא פחות עלמא.** ועי' במ"ר בראשית פ' ל"ה שם איתא לא פחות מתלתין לדיקי ועיין במ"ר במדבר פ' ג':

ליקוטי רש"י

ובעונותינו שרבו יצאו. משני אלפים אחרונים מה שיצאו ומשיח לא בא [ע"ז ט.]. **עד עידן עידנין ופלג עידן.** קץ סתום הוא זה כאשר נאמר לדניאל סתום הדברים וחתום ודרשוהו הראשונים איש לפי דעתו וכלו הקצים ויש לנו לפותרו עוד כאשר ראיתי כתוב בשם רב סעדיה הם אלף וג' מאות ול"ה שנים האמור בסוף הספר אשרי המחכה וגו' ופי' המועד עד עת שני עתים וחצי עת ואמר שהעתים הם ד' מאות ופ' שמיום צאתם ממצרים עד שנבנה הבית וד' מאות ועשר ימי מקדש ראשון הרי תת"ן ועוד חצי העת הזה תמ"ה הרי אלף של"ה את אלה חשוב מעת הוסר התמיד עד שוב זבח התמיד אל מקומו והוא הוסר שש שנים לפני החורבן ויש קצת ראיה בספר זה ועוד יש מביאין ראיה לחשבון זה הסתר אסתיר פני הסתר אסתיר בגי' אלף ושל"ה [דניאל ז, כה]. **אשרי כל חוכי לו.** לנחמות אשר הבטיח כי לא יפול דבר [ישעיה ל, יח]. **אמר אביי כו' אשרי כל חוכי לו.** המחכים לכת שהוא כמנין לו. **סביב שמנה עשר אלף.** סיפיה דקרא ה' שמה דאף על גב דבירושלים שלעתיד לבא כתיב קרא דרשינן ליה נמי להכי דמקום ששכינה שמה סובבין אותו שמנה עשר אלף והם הצדיקים הנתונים לפנים ממלאכי השרת שנאמר (במדבר כג) כעת יאמר ליעקב ולישראל מה פעל אל ואומר (ישעיה כג) ליושבים לפני ה' יהיה סחרה ואומר (שם ל) והיו עיניך רואות את מוריך. **איספקלריא.** מחילה שחוצצת ביניהם לשכינה. **המאירה.** כמראה זו שרואין בה ויש צדיקים שאין מאירה להם כל כך ואין יכולין לראות ממש. **ראיתי בני עלייה והן מועטין.** רואה אני לפי מעשה הבריות שבני עלייה כת המקבלין פני שכינה מועטים הם. **בבר.** ברשות. **דעיילי בלא בר.** בלא רשות מועטים הן ובהנהו קאמר אני ובני מהם [סוכה מה:]. **שובבים.** אנויישי"ר בלע"ז ששובבתם דרככם מרוב כל שהייתם בשלוה ועונג כמו שהוא אומר הפורטים על פי הנבל (עמוס ו) השותים במזרקי יין (שם) [ירמיה ג, יד]. לשון משובה נערו' ויולדות אינוויזור"א בלע"ז וכן בנים שובבים (ירמיה ג) הבת השובבה (שם לא) [הושע ו, יא]. משמע מזידים ופרהסיא [שובב] לשון מרד וגאוה כמו וילך שובב בדרך לבו (ישעיה נז) [ע"ז ז:]. **כי אנכי בעלתי בכם.** ונקראתם בשמי שאני אדון לכם ואין כבודי להניח אתכם ביד אויבי [ירמיה שם]. **בשובה ונחת.** תהיה לכם תשועה בלא שום טורח אם תשמעו לי. **בשובה.** לשון ישוב ומרגוע וכן שובה ה' רבבות אלפי ישראל (במדבר י) [ישעיה ל, טו]. **לבזה נפש.** נפש בזויה לישראל שהם בזוים [שם מט, ז]. לישראל הבזוים ומתועבים [תענית טו.]. **למתעב גוי.** למי שהגוי מתעבו [ישעיה שם]. **לעבד מושלים.** ועבדים מושלין בהן [תענית שם].

מסורת הש"ס

א) סוכה מה: ע"ש, ב) ג"ז שם., ג) בירושלמי הגי' א"ל ר"א, ד) ס"א שאין קץ למשיח אלא אם.

הגהות הגר"א

[א] גמ' ותשעים. נמחק וג"ב שלשים (עי' בע"ז ט' ב' ובתוס' ד"ה לאחר): **[ב]** רש"י ד"ה ותשקמו כו' עשר שנים. עשה כאן נקודות להפסיק ותיבת וכבר עברו וכו' עד בר דוד ז"ל נמחק:

תורה אור השלם

א) כִּי עוֹד חָזוֹן לַמּוֹעֵד וְיָפֵחַ לַקֵּץ וְלֹא יְכַזֵּב אִם יִתְמַהְמָהּ חַכֵּה לוֹ כִּי בֹא יָבֹא לֹא יְאַחֵר: [חבקוק ב, ג]

ב) וּמִלִּין לְצַד עִלָּאָה יְמַלִּל וּלְקַדִּישֵׁי עֶלְיוֹנִין יְבַלֵּא וְיִסְבַּר לְהַשְׁנָיָה זִמְנִין וְדָת וְיִתְיַהֲבוּן בִּידֵהּ עַד עִדָּן וְעִדָּנִין וּפְלַג עִדָּן: [דניאל ז, כה]

ג) הֶאֱכַלְתָּם לֶחֶם דִּמְעָה וַתַּשְׁקֵמוֹ בִּדְמָעוֹת שָׁלִישׁ: [תהלים פ, ו]

ד) כִּי כֹה אָמַר יְיָ צְבָאוֹת עוֹד אַחַת מְעַט הִיא וַאֲנִי מַרְעִישׁ אֶת הַשָּׁמַיִם וְאֶת הָאָרֶץ וְאֶת הַיָּם וְאֶת הֶחָרָבָה: [חגי ב, ו]

ה) וְלָכֵן יְחַכֶּה יְיָ לַחֲנַנְכֶם וְלָכֵן יָרוּם לְרַחֶמְכֶם כִּי אֱלֹהֵי מִשְׁפָּט יְיָ אַשְׁרֵי כָּל חוֹכֵי לוֹ: [ישעיה ל, יח]

ו) סָבִיב שְׁמֹנָה עָשָׂר אָלֶף וְשֵׁם הָעִיר מִיּוֹם יְיָ שָׁמָּה: [יחזקאל מח, לה]

ז) שׁוּבוּ בָּנִים שׁוֹבָבִים אֶרְפָּה מְשׁוּבֹתֵיכֶם הִנְנוּ אָתָנוּ לָךְ כִּי אַתָּה יְיָ אֱלֹהֵינוּ: [ירמיה ג, כב]

ח) כִּי כֹה אָמַר יְיָ חִנָּם נִמְכַּרְתֶּם וְלֹא בְכֶסֶף תִּגָּאֵלוּ: [ישעיה נב, ג]

ט) לְמִימֵי אֲבֹתֵיכֶם סַרְתֶּם מֵחֻקַּי וְלֹא שְׁמַרְתֶּם שׁוּבוּ אֵלַי וְאָשׁוּבָה אֲלֵיכֶם אָמַר יְיָ צְבָאוֹת וַאֲמַרְתֶּם בַּמֶּה נָשׁוּב: [מלאכי ג, ז]

י) שׁוּבוּ בָנִים שׁוֹבָבִים נְאֻם יְיָ כִּי אָנֹכִי בָּעַלְתִּי בָכֶם וְלָקַחְתִּי אֶתְכֶם אֶחָד מֵעִיר וּשְׁנַיִם מִמִּשְׁפָּחָה וְהֵבֵאתִי אֶתְכֶם צִיּוֹן: [ירמיה ג, יד]

כ) כִּי כֹה אָמַר אֲדֹנָי אֱלֹהִים קְדוֹשׁ יִשְׂרָאֵל בְּשׁוּבָה וָנַחַת תִּוָּשֵׁעוּן בְּהַשְׁקֵט וּבְבִטְחָה תִּהְיֶה גְּבוּרַתְכֶם וְלֹא אֲבִיתֶם: [ישעיה ל, טו]

ל) כֹּה אָמַר יְיָ גֹּאֵל יִשְׂרָאֵל קְדוֹשׁוֹ לִבְזֹה נֶפֶשׁ לִמְתָעֵב גּוֹי לְעֶבֶד מֹשְׁלִים מְלָכִים יִרְאוּ וָקָמוּ שָׂרִים וְיִשְׁתַּחֲווּ לְמַעַן יְיָ אֲשֶׁר נֶאֱמָן קְדֹשׁ יִשְׂרָאֵל וַיִּבְחָרֶךָּ: [ישעיה מט, ז]

calculated **has arrived and [the Messiah] did not come,** שוּב אֵינוֹ בָא – **he will never come!"**[29] אֶלָּא חַכֵּה לוֹ – **Rather,** one should **wait for him,** שֶׁנֶּאֱמַר ,,אִם יִתְמַהְמָהּ חַכֵּה־לוֹ" – **as it is said:** ***if he tarries, wait for him.***[30] שֶׁמָּא תֹּאמַר – **Lest you counter** that אָנוּ מְחַכִּין וְהוּא אֵינוֹ מְחַכֶּה – **we are awaiting** the Messiah, **but [God] is not awaiting** him,[31] תַּלְמוּד לוֹמַר – **Scripture therefore states:** ,,וְלָכֵן יְחַכֶּה ה׳ לַחֲנַנְכֶם וְלָכֵן יָרוּם לְרַחֶמְכֶם" – ***And therefore* Hashem *waits***[32] – ***to grant you favor; and therefore He is exalted – to grant you mercy.***[33] וְכִי מֵאַחַר שֶׁאָנוּ מְחַכִּים – And if you ask that **since we are awaiting** the Messiah וְהוּא מְחַכֶּה – **and God is awaiting** him, מִי מְעַכֵּב – **who is preventing** his arrival – מִדַּת הַדִּין מְעַכֶּבֶת – the answer is that **the Divine Attribute of Justice is preventing** him from coming.[34] וְכִי מֵאַחַר שֶׁמִּדַּת הַדִּין מְעַכֶּבֶת אָנוּ לָמָּה מְחַכִּין – **And** if you ask that **since the Divine Attribute of Justice prevents** him from coming, **why do we await** him[35] – לְקַבֵּל שָׂכָר – the answer is that we await him **in order to receive reward,**[36] שֶׁנֶּאֱמַר ,,אַשְׁרֵי כָּל־חוֹכֵי לוֹ" – **as it is stated:** ***Fortunate are all who wait for him.***[37]

The Gemara digresses to record another teaching based on this verse:

אָמַר אַבַּיֵי – **Abaye said:** לֹא פָּחוּת עָלְמָא מִתְּלָתִין וְשִׁיתָּא צַדִּיקֵי דִּמְקַבְּלֵי אַפֵּי שְׁכִינָה בְּכָל דָּרָא – **The world is comprised of not less than thirty-six righteous people in each generation who receive the countenance of the Divine Presence,**[38] שֶׁנֶּאֱמַר ,,אַשְׁרֵי כָּל־חוֹכֵי לוֹ" – **as it is stated:** ***Fortunate are all who wait for Him,*** לוֹ בְּגִימַטְרִיָּא תְּלָתִין וְשִׁיתָּא הָווּ – and the word לוֹ (*for Him*) **has the numerical value of thirty-six.**[39]

The Gemara challenges Abaye's teaching:

אֵינִי – **Is this so?** וְהָאָמַר רָבָא דָּרָא דְּקַמֵּי קוּדְשָׁא בְּרִיךְ הוּא תַּמְנֵי סְרֵי אַלְפֵי [פרסא] הֲוַאי – **Why, Rava has said that the row before the Holy One, Blessed is He, is** comprised of **eighteen thousand,** שֶׁנֶּאֱמַר ,,סָבִיב שְׁמֹנָה עָשָׂר אָלֶף" – **as it is said:** ***Surrounding are eighteen thousand.***[40] – ? –

NOTES

similar expression appears in *Jeremiah* (15:9): נָפְחָה נַפְשָׁהּ, which *Rashi* (ad loc.) relates to the verse in *Deuteronomy* (28:65): דַּאֲבוֹן נָפֶשׁ, *agony of the soul* (see also *Job* 11:20 and 31:39; *Shabbos* 127b and *Rashi* ibid. ד״ה בפחי נפש).]

29. **Calculating the date of the Redemption:**

The Gemara apparently forbids any attempt to calculate when the Messiah will come. This prohibition is codified by *Rambam* in *Hil. Melachim* 12:2. Yet, throughout the generations, great sages have predicted and announced such dates (see *Margaliyos HaYam* §10, who cites several examples). *Rambam* deals with this problem in *Iggeres Teiman,* where he is hard put to explain *Rav Saadiah Gaon's* calculation of the "End." The only justification he finds is that in the Gaon's generation there was a need to strengthen the faith in the coming of the Messiah and so he offered a possible "End" in the near future. [This is presumably the reason why *Rambam* himself advanced a date.]

Ramban and *Abarbanel* give broader grounds for permitting the search for the "End." In their view, the prohibition is only against making a *definite* prediction, which, if proven wrong, could cause people to lose their faith. These commentators point out that after expressing the prohibition, the Gemara adds, in explanation: *For they say, "Since the End came and [the Messiah] did not come, he will never come."* Therefore, if one advances an interpretation of these verses only as a possible meaning, not as a definite conclusion, it is permitted (*Sefer HaGeulah* ch. 4; *Mayanei HaYeshuah* 1:2; see *Rashi* ד״ה ויפח).

Ramban (ibid.) also suggests that the Sages, being close to the destruction of the Temple, knew that the redemption was still far off. Therefore, they forbade all investigation of the "End" so as not to discourage the people with the length of the bitter exile. This, he maintains, is no longer applicable in his times, 1,200 years into the exile.

Rashi apparently follows the lenient approach. After explaining a passage dealing with the "End" (*Daniel* 8:14), *Rashi* concludes: "We await the fulfillment of God's promise to redeem us, even though one [predicted] "End" after another has passed. If the "End" predicted by a commentator passes, then we know that he erred, and whoever comes after him should search and interpret otherwise."

In explaining how great sages (including even Tannaim) erred in their calculations, *Ramban* (ibid.) states that it was God's will that the "End" be concealed (see also *Rashi* to *Daniel* 11:35; *Ibn Ezra,* end of commentary to v. 30 ibid.).

However, these sages did not necessarily err in the conventional sense of the word. As mentioned above (97a note 60), there are many times suited for the redemption, when the Messiah would have come if only the generation had been worthy. The various predictions made by our great sages were for those propitious times (see *Ramban* ibid.; see also *Maharal, Netzach Yisrael* end of ch. 44; *Bnei Yisaschar,* cited by *Margaliyos HaYam* end of §10).

30. *Habakkuk* 2:3. That is, *if he tarries* after the time when you thought he would come, *wait for him* (*Maharsha;* see *Rambam, Iggeres Teiman,* beginning of ch. 3; *Tzipisa LiShuah* ch. 2).

31. [I.e. God does not want to bring the Messiah.] Why should God want to benefit us when we have sinned before Him? (*Maharsha*).

32. God Himself eagerly awaits the Messiah's arrival (*Rashi*).

33. *Isaiah* 30:18.That passage speaks of a time when the nation had sinned. Yet, even at such a time, God longs for the opportunity to benefit us (*Maharsha;* cf. *Rashi* ad loc.). [This is a sign of His exalted level.]

The Gemara proceeds to interpret this verse, phrase by phrase. The entire verse reads: וְלָכֵן יְחַכֶּה ה׳ לַחֲנַנְכֶם וְלָכֵן יָרוּם לְרַחֶמְכֶם כִּי־אֱלֹהֵי מִשְׁפָּט ה׳ אַשְׁרֵי כָּל־חוֹכֵי לוֹ, *And therefore* Hashem *waits – to grant you favor; and therefore He is exalted – to grant you mercy. For* Hashem *is a God of justice. Fortunate are all who wait for him.*

34. As the verse continues, *For* Hashem *is a God of Justice* (see previous note). Because the Jews have sinned, God's Attribute of Justice does not allow them to be redeemed before the final "End" (see *Yad Ramah, Maharsha, Maharal*).

35. Since we do not know when the Messiah will come, perhaps it is better not to pine for him. Pining for something over an extended period without knowing when it will occur can make one heartsick.

An alternative explanation: By awaiting the Messiah, we could postpone his coming, because (as stated above, 97a) the Messiah will come when attention is diverted from him (*Maharsha*).

36. Indeed, pining for the Messiah is harmful, and could even delay his coming (see previous note). Thus, our reward for doing so is all the greater (see *Maharsha*).

[Alternatively, the teaching that the Messiah will come when he is not expected does not rule out longing for him; rather, it is directed against calculating when he will come (see 97a note 51).]

37. See note 33.

38. That is, in every generation in this world there are no less than thirty-six people who are so righteous that they will merit to perceive the *Shechinah* when they enter the World to Come (*Yad Ramah's* second explanation). [The reference is to a particularly elevated level in the World to Come (see continuation of the Gemara).]

[In the parallel passage in *Succah* (45b), the text reads בְּכָל יוֹם, *every day,* instead of בְּכָל דָּרָא, *in every generation.* According to this version, Abaye possibly means that thirty-six is the total number of righteous people from all the generations who will merit to perceive the *Shechinah* to this degree (see *Yad Ramah* here).]

39. [ל = 30; ו = 6.] The verse thus means: *Fortunate are all who expect* [to join] *the* [group of] *thirty-six* (see *Rashi* to *Succah* ibid. ד״ה אשרי).

The word לוֹ, *for Him,* is apparently superfluous, because the verse could have said אַשְׁרֵי כָּל חוֹכָיו. Hence, it may be interpreted in this manner (*Maharsha*).

40. *Ezekiel* 48:35 (the last verse in *Ezekiel*). Eighteen thousand righteous people are closer to the *Shechinah* than are the ministering angels (see *Rashi* to *Succah* ibid.).

This contradicts Abaye's teaching because if, as Abaye maintains, there are only thirty-six completely righteous people in each generation, then even in the course of 6,000 years, the total number of such people would not reach 18,000 (see *Yad Ramah*). [Although Abaye said "not less" than thirty-six, he did not mean to imply that there could be *more* than this number (see *Maharsha* ד״ה ודקאמר ל״ק; cf. *Aruch LaNer*).]

According to its plain meaning, the verse gives the circumference of Jerusalem in the Messianic era. The figure 18,000 refers to rods that

ובעוונותינו שרבו יצאו מהם מה שיצאו אמר ליה אליהו לרב יהודה אחוה דרב סלא חסידא אין העולם פחות משמונים וחמשה יובלות וביובל האחרון בן דוד בא אמר ליה בתחילתו או בסופו אמר ליה איני יודע כלה או אינו כלה אמר ליה איני יודע רב אשי אמר הכי א"ל עד הכא לא תיסתכי ליה מכאן ואילך איסתכי ליה שלח ליה רב חנן בר תחליפא לרב יוסף מצאתי אדם אחד ובידו מגילה אחת כתובה אשורית ולשון קדש אמרתי לו זו מניין לך אמר לי לחיילות של רומי נשכרתי ובין גינזי רומי מצאתיה וכתוב בה לאחר ד' אלפים ומאתים [א] ותשעים ואחד שנה לבריאתו של עולם יתום מהן מלחמות תנינים מהן מלחמות גוג ומגוג ושאר ימות המשיח ואין הקב"ה מחדש את עולמו אלא לאחר שבעת אלפים שנה רב אחא בריה דרבא אמר לאחר חמשת אלפים שנה איתמר תניא רבי נתן אומר מקרא זה נוקב ויורד עד תהום א) כי עוד חזון למועד ויפח לקץ ולא יכזב אם יתמהמה חכה לו כי בא יבא לא יאחר לא כרבותינו שהיו דורשין ב) עד עידן עידנין ופלג עידן ולא כר' שמלאי שהיה דורש ג) האכלתם לחם דמעה ותשקמו בדמעות שליש ולא כרבי עקיבא שהיה דורש ד) עוד אחת מעט היא ואני מרעיש את השמים ואת הארץ אלא מלכות ראשון שבעים שנה מלכות שניה חמשים ושתים ומלכות בן כוזיבא שתי שנים ומחצה מאי ויפח לקץ ולא יכזב א"ר שמואל בר נחמני אמר ר' יונתן תיפח עצמן של מחשבי קיצין שהיו אומרים כיון שהגיע את הקץ ולא בא שוב אינו בא אלא חכה לו שנאמר אם יתמהמה חכה לו שמא תאמר אנו מחכין והוא אינו מחכה ת"ל ה) לכן יחכה ה' לחננכם ולכן ירום לרחמכם וכי מאחר שאנו מחכים והוא מחכה מי מעכב מדת הדין מעכבת וכי מאחר שמדת הדין מעכבת אנו למה מחכין לקבל שכר שנאמר ה) אשרי כל חוכי לו אמר אביי לא פחות עלמא מתלתין ושיתא צדיקי דמקבלי אפי שכינה בכל דרא שנאמר אשרי כל חוכי לו לו בגימטריא תלתין ושיתא הוו איני והאמר רבא דרא דקמי קודשא בריך הוא תמני סרי אלפי [פרסא] הואי שנאמר ו) סביב שמנה עשר אלף לא קשיא הא דמסתכלי באיספקלריא המאירה הא דמסתכלי באיספקלריא שאינה מאירה ומי נפישי כולי האי והאמר חזקיה א"ר ירמיה משום רשב"י ראיתי בני עליה והן מועטין אם אלף הם אני ובני מהם אם מאה הם אני ובני מהם אם שנים הם אני ובני הם לא קשיא הא דעיילי בבר הא דעיילי בלא בר אמר רב כלו כל הקיצין ואין הדבר תלוי אלא בתשובה ומעשים טובים ושמואל אמר דיו לאבל שיעמוד באבלו כתנאי ר' אליעזר אומר אם ישראל עושין תשובה נגאלין ואם לאו אין נגאלין אמר ליה רבי יהושע אם אין עושין תשובה אין נגאלין אלא הקב"ה מעמיד להן מלך שגזרותיו קשות כהמן וישראל עושין תשובה ומחזירן למוטב תניא אידך ר' אליעזר אומר אם ישראל עושין תשובה נגאלין שנאמר ז) שובו בנים שובבים ארפא משובותיכם אמר לו רבי יהושע והלא כבר נאמר ח) חנם נמכרתם ולא בכסף תגאלו חנם נמכרתם בעבודת כוכבים ולא בכסף תגאלו לא בתשובה ומעשים טובים אמר לו רבי אליעזר לר' יהושע והלא כבר נאמר ט) שובו אלי ואשובה אליכם אמר ליה רבי יהושע והלא כבר נאמר י) כי אנכי בעלתי בכם ולקחתי אתכם אחד מעיר ושנים ממשפחה והבאתי אתכם ציון אמר לו ר' אליעזר והלא כבר נאמר כ) בשובה ונחת תושעון אמר לו ר' יהושע לרבי אליעזר והלא כבר נאמר ל) כה אמר ה' גואל ישראל וקדושו לבזה נפש למתעב גוי לעבד מושלים מלכים

רש"י

אבל בשביל עונותינו שרבו. לא בא משיח לסוף ד' אלפים ויצאו מה שיצאו שעדיין הוא מעוכב לבא: **שמנים וחמשה יובלין.** היינו ד' אלפים מאתים וחמשים [שנה]: **בתחלת.** היובל האחרון הוא בא או בסופו: **כלה.** זמן הזה קודש שיבא משיח או אינו כלה דבתוך היובל בסופו הוא בא: **עד הכא לא תיסתכי ליה.** עד יובל האחרון לא תצפה לו דודאי לא יבא קודם הזמן הזה: **איסתכי ליה.** חכה לו שיבא: **אשורית.** כתב שלנו אשורית שבא מאשור כדאמר באידך פירקין (ד' כב.): **לחיילות של רומי נשכרתי.** שהייתי גולייר לאחד מהם: **תנינים.** דגים: **והשאר ימות המשיח.** שכלה השעבוד ומשיח בא: **מחדש עולמו.** לברוא עולם חדש: **נוקב ויורד עד התהום.** מה תהום אין לו קץ וסוף כך אין אדם יכול לעמוד על סוף פסוק זה [ז] (וכי קא מפרש אימת קאמר אם) יתמהמה חכה לו דאין לו סוף: **לא כרבותינו.** אל תצפו לאותו קץ שהיו רבותינו דורשין: **עד עידן עידנין ופלג עידן.** עידן כעידן הגלות של מצרים והיינו ד' מאות ב' עידנין ח' מאות היינו י"ב מאות ופלג עידן ב' מאות סך הכל אלף וד' מאות: **ותשקמו בדמעות שליש.** כלומר השקה אותם הקב"ה בין גלות מצרים לגלות בבל שליש גלות אדום כי קץ גלות אדום זה יהיה לסוף ג' פעמים ת' שנים וג' פעמים ע' שנה כנגד גלות בבל דהיינו לסוף אלף וארבע מאות ועשר שנים [ב] כבר עברו ולא היה כך מצאתי כתוב בשם הרב רבי שמואל בר דוד ז"ל: **עוד אחת מעט היא.** בנבואת חגי כתיב שהיה מתנבא כשיצאו ישראל מגלות בבל ויבנה בית המקדש והיינו עוד אחת מעט היא מעט כבוד אתן להם לישראל ואני מרעיש את השמים ואת הארץ והבאתי כל חמדת גוים לירושלים ור"ע דריש ליה לימות המשיח ולאחר חורבן והכי דריש ליה [עוד אחת מעט היא מעט כבוד אתן לישראל ואח"כ יבא המשיח ודרשה זו אינה אלא קרא אלפני הבית קאי וה"ק] עוד אחת מעט היא מעט כבוד אתן להם לישראל ושוב לא אתן להם כל ימות בית אחרון וכן היה דמלכות ראשונה של מלכות חשמונאי נתקיימה שבעים שנה ואע"ג דאמרינן בסדר עולם דמלכות בית חשמונאי מאה ושלש ומלכות הורדוס מאה ושלש עיקר כבודם ופארם שלא שלטה בהם אומה לא נתקיים כל כך ומלכות שניה

תוספות

של הורדוס נ"ב שנה ומלכות בן כוזיבא ב' שנים ומחצה ושוב לא היה להם מלך מ"ר. וכל הנך דרשות לאו משנה ולאו ברייתא. ל"א עוד אחת מעט היא מעט מלכות אתן להם לישראל לאחר חורבן ולאחר אותו מלכות הנני מרעיש שמים וארץ ויבא משיח. ואין דרשה זו כלום שהרי ראינו כמה מלכיות לישראל לאחר חורבן ואעפ"כ לא בא משיח שהמלכות הראשונה שהיתה להם לישראל לאחר חורבן שבעים שנה הורדוס נ"ב בן כוזיבא ב' ומחצה ומצינו בסדר עולם מפולמוס של אספסיאנוס עד פולמוס של טיטוס שתים עשרה שנה ומפולמוס של טיטוס עד מלכות בן כוזיבא י"ז שנים ומלכות בן כוזיבא ב' שנים ומחצה: [בן כוזיבא מלך בביתר]: **ויפח לקץ.** תיפח נפשו של מחשב הקץ שלא היה לו לכזב ולומר כיון שהגיע וכו': **יחכה ה'.** הוא עצמו מחכה ומתאוה שיבא משיח: **סביב י"ח אלף.** בירושלים של מעלה משתעי קרא בסוף יחזקאל: **באספקלריא המאירה.** בחוזק נגהו של הקב"ה אין מסתכלין אלא תלתין ושית אבל בקלישות הנוגה לצדדין מרחוק מסתכלין כתות הרבה: **ומי נפישי כולי האי.** דלהוי בריר לן תלתין ושיתא הוו ולא פחות: **והא רבי שמעון בן יוחאי.** לא הוה ידע אם אלף הם אם מאה הם אם שנים הם: **הא דעיילי בבר.** שצריכין ליטול רשות כשנכנסין להסתכל באספקלריא המאירה בהנהו לא פחיתי מתלתין ושית אבל אותן הנכנסין בלא רשות ברוב צדקם הנהו מספקא לן כמה הוו: **בתשובה.** אם כל ישראל חוזרין בתשובה יבא ואם לאו לא יבא: **דיו לאבל שעומד באבלו.** דיו להקב"ה שעומד כמה ימים וימינו אחור כלומר אם לא יעשו תשובה אינו עומד באבלו כל הימים אלא ודאי קץ לדבר ל"א דיו לאבל דיין לישראל צער גלות אפילו בלא תשובה נגאלין: **לא בכסף.** לא בתשובה ומעשים טובים דאפילו אין עושין תשובה נגאלין משום דאמר חנם נמכרתם קרי כסף בלשון תשובה: **בעלתי אתכם.** משמע בעל כרחכם בלא תשובה: **אחד מעיר.** אברור הצדיקים ואביאם לציון אע"פ שאין כולם חוזרין: **כה אמר ה' לבזה נפש למתעב גוי.** אותן הבזויין ומתועבין בעבירות אעפ"כ יגאלו מלכים יראו וקמו:

כי

(ישעיה נז) [ע"ז ז:]. **כי אנכי בעלתי בכם.** ונקראתם בשמי שאני אדון לכם ואין כבודי להניח אתכם ביד אויבי [ירמיה שם]. **בשובה ונחת.** תהיה לכם תשועה בלא שום טורח אם תשמעו לי. **בשובה.** לשון ישוב ומרגוע וכן שובה ה' רבבות אלפי ישראל (במדבר י) [ישעיה ל, טו]. **לבזה נפש.** נפש בזויה לישראל שהם בזוים [שם מט, ז]. לישראל הבזוים ומתועבים [תענית טו.]. **למתעב גוי.** למי שהגוי מתעבו [ישעיה שם]. **לעבד מושלים.** ועבדים מושלין בהן [תענית שם].

עין משפט נר מצוה

י א מיי' פי"ב מהלכות מלכים ומלחמותיהם הלכה ב:

יא ב מיי' פ"ז מהל' תשובה הלכה ה:

גליון הש"ס

גמ' **לא פחות עלמא.** ועי' במ"ר בראשית פ' ל"ה שם איתא לא פחות מתלתין לדיקי ועיין במ"ר במדבר פ' ג':

ליקוטי רש"י

ובעוונותינו שרבו יצאו. משני אלפים אחרונים מה שיצאו ומשיח לא בא [ע"ז ט.]. **עד עידן עידנין ופלג עידן.** קץ סתום הוא זה כאשר נאמר לדניאל סתום הדברים וחתום ודרשוהו הראשונים איש לפי דעתו וכלו הקצים ויש לנו לפותרו עוד כאשר ראיתי כתוב בשם רב סעדיה הם אלף וג' מאות ול"ה שנים האמור בסוף הספר אשרי המחכה וגו' ופי' המועד עד עת שני עתים וחצי עת ואמר שהעתים הם ד' מאות ופ' שמיום לאתם ממצרים עד שנבנה הבית וד' מאות ועשר ימי מקדש ראשון הרי תת"ן ועוד חצי העת הזה תמ"ה הרי אלף של"ה את אלה חשוב מעת הוסר התמיד עד שוב זבח התמיד אל מקומו והוא הוסר שש שנים לפני החורבן ויש קצת ראיה בספר זה ועוד יש מביאין ראיה לחשבון זה הסתר אסתיר פני הסתר אסתיר בגי' אלף ושל"ה [דניאל ז, כה]. **אשרי כל חוכי לו.** לנחמות אשר הבטיח כי לא יפול דבר [ישעיה ל, יח]. **אמר אביי כו' אשרי כל חוכי לו.** המחכים לכת שהוא כמנין לו. **סביב שמנה עשר אלף.** סיפיה דקרא ה' שמה דאף על גב דבירושלים שלעתיד לבא כתיב קרא דרשינן ליה נמי להכי דמקום ששכינה שמה סובבין אותו שמנה עשר אלף והם הצדיקים הנתונים לפנים ממלאכי השרת שנאמר (במדבר כג) כעת יאמר ליעקב ולישראל מה פעל אל ואומר (ישעיה כג) ליושבים לפני ה' יהיה סחרה ואומר (שם ל) והיו עיניך רואות את מוריך. **איספקלריא.** מחילה שחוללת ביניהם לשכינה. **המאירה.** כמראה זו שרואין בה ויש לדיקים שאין מאירה להם כל כך ואין יכולין לראות ממש. **ראיתי בני עלייה והן מועטין.** רואה אני לפי מעשה הבריות שבני עלייה כת המקבלין פני שכינה מועטים הם. **בבר.** ברשות. **דעיילי בלא בר.** בלא רשות מועטים הן ובהנהו קאמר אני ובני מהם [סוכה מה:]. **שובבים.** אנויש"ר בלע"ז ששובבתם דרככם מרוב כל שהייתם בשלוה ועונג כמו שהוא אומר הפורטים על פי הנבל (עמוס ו) השותים במזרקי יין (שם) [ירמיה ג, יד]. לשון משובה נערו' וילדות אינוויזור"א בלע"ז וכן בנים שובבים (ירמיה ג) הבת השובבה (שם לא) [הושע ו, יא]. משמע מזידים ופרהסיא [שובב] לשון מרד וגאוה כמו וילך שובב בדרך לבו

מסורת הש"ס

א) סוכה מה: ע"ש, ב) ג"ז שם., ג) בירושלמי הגי' א"ל ר"א, ד) ס"א שאין קץ למשיח אלא אם.

הגהות הגר"א

[א] גמ' ותשעים. נמחק ונ"ב שלשים (עי' בע"ז ט' ב' ובתוס' ד"ה לאחר): **[ב]** רש"י ד"ה ותשקמו כו' עשר שנים. עשה כאן נקודות להפסיק ותיבת וכבר עברו וכו' עד בר דוד ז"ל נמחק:

תורה אור השלם

א) כִּי עוֹד חָזוֹן לַמּוֹעֵד וְיָפֵחַ לַקֵּץ וְלֹא יְכַזֵּב אִם יִתְמַהְמָהּ חַכֵּה לוֹ כִּי בֹא יָבֹא לֹא יְאַחֵר: [חבקוק ב, ג]

ב) וּמִלִּין לְצַד עִלָּאָה יְמַלִּל וּלְקַדִּישֵׁי עֶלְיוֹנִין יְבַלֵּא וְיִסְבַּר לְהַשְׁנָיָה זִמְנִין וְדָת וְיִתְיַהֲבוּן בִּידֵהּ עַד עִדָּן וְעִדָּנִין וּפְלַג עִדָּן: [דניאל ז, כה]

ג) הֶאֱכַלְתָּם לֶחֶם דִּמְעָה וַתַּשְׁקֵמוֹ בִּדְמָעוֹת שָׁלִישׁ: [תהלים פ, ו]

ד) כִּי כֹה אָמַר יְיָ צְבָאוֹת עוֹד אַחַת מְעַט הִיא וַאֲנִי מַרְעִישׁ אֶת הַשָּׁמַיִם וְאֶת הָאָרֶץ וְאֶת הַיָּם וְאֶת הֶחָרָבָה: [חגי ב, ו]

ה) וְלָכֵן יְחַכֶּה יְיָ לַחֲנַנְכֶם וְלָכֵן יָרוּם לְרַחֶמְכֶם כִּי אֱלֹהֵי מִשְׁפָּט יְיָ אַשְׁרֵי כָּל חוֹכֵי לוֹ: [ישעיה ל, יח]

ו) סָבִיב שְׁמֹנָה עָשָׂר אָלֶף וְשֵׁם הָעִיר מִיּוֹם יְיָ שָׁמָּה: [יחזקאל מח, לה]

ז) שׁוּבוּ בָּנִים שׁוֹבָבִים אֶרְפָּה מְשׁוּבֹתֵיכֶם הִנְנוּ אָתָנוּ לָךְ כִּי אַתָּה יְיָ אֱלֹהֵינוּ: [ירמיה ג, כב]

ח) כִּי כֹה אָמַר יְיָ חִנָּם נִמְכַּרְתֶּם וְלֹא בְכֶסֶף תִּגָּאֵלוּ: [ישעיה נב, ג]

ט) לְמִימֵי אֲבֹתֵיכֶם סַרְתֶּם מֵחֻקַּי וְלֹא שְׁמַרְתֶּם שׁוּבוּ אֵלַי וְאָשׁוּבָה אֲלֵיכֶם אָמַר יְיָ צְבָאוֹת וַאֲמַרְתֶּם בַּמֶּה נָשׁוּב: [מלאכי ג, ז]

י) שׁוּבוּ בָנִים שׁוֹבָבִים נְאֻם יְיָ כִּי אָנֹכִי בָּעַלְתִּי בָכֶם וְלָקַחְתִּי אֶתְכֶם אֶחָד מֵעִיר וּשְׁנַיִם מִמִּשְׁפָּחָה וְהֵבֵאתִי אֶתְכֶם צִיּוֹן: [ירמיה ג, יד]

כ) כִּי כֹה אָמַר אֲדֹנָי אֱלֹהִים קְדוֹשׁ יִשְׂרָאֵל בְּשׁוּבָה וָנַחַת תִּוָּשֵׁעוּן בְּהַשְׁקֵט וּבְבִטְחָה תִּהְיֶה גְּבוּרַתְכֶם וְלֹא אֲבִיתֶם: [ישעיה ל, טו]

ל) כֹּה אָמַר יְיָ גֹּאֵל יִשְׂרָאֵל קְדוֹשׁוֹ לִבְזֹה נֶפֶשׁ לִמְתָעֵב גּוֹי לְעֶבֶד מֹשְׁלִים מְלָכִים יִרְאוּ וָקָמוּ שָׂרִים וְיִשְׁתַּחֲווּ לְמַעַן יְיָ אֲשֶׁר נֶאֱמָן קְדֹשׁ יִשְׂרָאֵל וַיִּבְחָרֶךָּ: [ישעיה מט, ז]

The Gemara answers:

לֹא קַשְׁיָא – This is **not a difficulty.** **הָא דְּמִסְתַּכְּלֵי בְּאִיסְפַּקְלַרְיָא הַמְּאִירָה** – **This** [Abaye's teaching] refers to persons **who view** the Divine Presence as though **through a clear screen;** **הָא דְּמִסְתַּכְּלֵי בְּאִיסְפַּקְלַרְיָא שֶׁאֵינָהּ מְאִירָה** – **whereas this** [Rava's teaching] refers to persons **who view** the Divine Presence as though **through an opaque screen.**[41]

The Gemara raises another difficulty with Abaye's teaching: **וּמִי נְפִישֵׁי כּוּלֵּי הַאי** – **But are there so many** who view the Divine Presence clearly? **וְהָאָמַר חִזְקִיָּה אָמַר רַבִּי יִרְמְיָה מִשּׁוּם רַבִּי שִׁמְעוֹן בֶּן יוֹחַי** – **Why, Chizkiyah has said that R' Yirmiyah said in the name of R' Shimon ben Yochai:** **רָאִיתִי בְּנֵי עֲלִיָּיה וְהֵן מוּעָטִין** – **I have seen the people of the highest level,**[42] **and they are few.** **אִם אֶלֶף הֵם אֲנִי וּבְנִי מֵהֶם** – **If they are a thousand, I and my son are among them.** **אִם מֵאָה הֵם אֲנִי וּבְנִי מֵהֶם** – **If they are a hundred, I and my son are among them.** **אִם שְׁנַיִם הֵם אֲנִי וּבְנִי הֵם** – **If they are two, they are myself and my son.**[43] R' Shimon ben Yochai considered it possible that only two people were of this supreme level. How, then, could Abaye be certain that there are never less than thirty-six?

The Gemara answers:

לֹא קַשְׁיָא – This is **not a difficulty.** **הָא דְּעָיְילֵי בְּבַר** – **This** [Abaye's teaching] refers to those **who may enter** only **with permission;** **הָא דְּעָיְילֵי בְּלֹא בַּר** – whereas **this** [R' Shimon ben Yochai's statement] refers to those **who may enter without permission.**[44]

The Gemara resumes its discussion about the advent of the Messiah:

אָמַר רַב – **Rav said:** **כָּלוּ כָּל הַקִּיצִּין** – **All the "Ends" have passed,**[45] **וְאֵין הַדָּבָר תָּלוּי אֶלָּא בִּתְשׁוּבָה וּמַעֲשִׂים טוֹבִים** – **and the matter** of the Messiah's arrival **depends only on repentance and good deeds.**[46]

A dissenting view:

וּשְׁמוּאֵל אָמַר – **But Shmuel says:** **דַּיּוֹ לָאָבֵל שֶׁיַּעֲמוֹד בְּאֶבְלוֹ** – **It is enough for the mourner to endure his** period of **mourning.**[47]

The Gemara notes that this issue has been debated by Tannaim: **כְּתַנָּאֵי** – This dispute between Rav and Shmuel is **parallel to** the

NOTES

measure six *amos* each (see *Tosafos* to *Succah* ibid.). [For this reason *Tosafos* delete the word פרסא from the Gemara's text (cf. *Yad Ramah* here and *Rabbeinu Chananel* ibid.).] However, the verse ends with the words, ה׳ שָׁמָּה, *HASHEM is there,* which allude to the "place" of the *Shechinah.* Thus, when the verse says, *surrounding are eighteen thousand,* it also means that eighteen thousand righteous people surround the *Shechinah* (*Rashi* ibid.; see *Maharsha* ibid.).

Rashi (here) writes that the verse speaks of the celestial Jerusalem (see *Rashi* to *Tehillim* 122:3). This is the same as "the place of the *Shechinah*" that Rashi mentions in *Succah* (*Maharsha* ibid; see, however, *Yad Ramah* here; see also *Tos. Yom Tov* in his *Tzuras HaBayis*).

41. The number of those who perceive the full radiance of the *Shechinah* is only thirty-six. Many more perceive the *Shechinah* to a lesser extent (see *Rashi, Yad Ramah;* see *Rambam, Shemonah Perakim* ch. 7, for an elaboration). [See *Maharsha* (based on *Yevamos* 49) who writes that Moses was the only person who ever perceived the full radiance of the *Shechinah* through the medium of *prophecy.*]

An אִסְפַּקְלַרְיָא is an opaque screen through which objects appear distorted. The word is a contraction of סָפֵק רְאִיָּה, *doubtful* (i.e. unclear) *vision.* A screen that is perfectly transparent (e.g. one of clear glass) is called an אִסְפַּקְלַרְיָא מְאִירָה, literally: an illuminating screen (*Rambam,* Commentary to *Keilim* 30:1; *Yad Ramah;* see *Rashi* to *Succah* ibid.).

Alternatively, אִסְפַּקְלַרְיָא means mirror [as in the Latin *specularia*] (*Rav* to *Keilim* ibid.; see *Tos. Yom Tov* and *Tiferes Yisrael, Boaz* §1).

According to either explanation, the term is used here as a metaphor for perception of the *Shechinah,* which cannot be "viewed" directly, but only through a screen or as a reflected image.

42. There are many different levels of reward for the righteous. עֲלִיָּה signifies the highest level (*Yad Ramah* in the name of *Rav Hai Gaon*).

Alternatively, בְּנֵי עֲלִיָּה is translated as people of ascent, i.e. those who are fit to ascend to Heaven (*Rabbeinu Chananel* to *Succah* ibid.; *Maharsha* ibid.).

43. Based upon his assessment of peoples' deeds, R' Shimon ben Yochai concluded that the group of people who fully perceive the Divine Presence is small (*Rashi* ibid.; cf. *Rabbeinu Chananel* ibid.; cf. *Yad Ramah* here).

R' Shimon ben Yochai had been Divinely assured that he and his son were members of this supreme group. Hence, although there were many prophets who were greater than R' Shimon ben Yochai, he was sure that he and his son belonged to this group regardless of its size (*Yad Ramah*).

Yad Ramah implies that R' Shimon ben Yochai's statement applies to all the generations. *Rabbeinu Chananel,* however, states (*Succah* ibid.) that he was referring only to his own generation.

44. They are of such eminence that they may approach the *Shechinah* without first asking permission of the angels appointed for this purpose (*Rashi,* as explained by *Rabbeinu Chananel* to *Succah* ibid.). [The analogy is drawn to a royal household. Only the king's family members and those servants who attend to him at all times may enter his chambers without permission (*Eitz Yosef*).]

Alternatively, בַּר is translated here as *son.* R' Shimon ben Yochai was speaking of righteous people who merit to receive the supreme reward together with their sons. Of these, there are very few (*Yad Ramah* in the name of *Rav Hai Gaon; Rabbeinu Chananel* ibid.; *Aruch*).

Maharsha raises the following difficulty: Abaye said that only thirty-six people fully perceive the Divine Presence (see note 40), whereas R' Shimon ben Yochai entertained the possibility that there are as many as a thousand such people. (See the answers given by *Maharsha* and *Aruch LaNer.*) This problem can be solved with *Yad Ramah's* approach that R' Shimon was referring to the righteous of all the generations (see end of note 43). Abaye, on the other hand, was speaking of each generation individually.

[See *Maharsha,* who contrasts Abaye's teaching with the Gemara in *Chullin* 92a, which states that in every generation there are *forty-five* righteous people in whose merit the world is sustained (see 96b note 46).]

45. That is to say, there is no preordained date for the end of the exile (*Maharsha;* see the following note).

Alternatively, Rav means that all the various times predicted by the Sages as suited for the redemption have passed (see end of note 29). Therefore, the only obstacle now preventing the Messiah's immediate arrival is our failure to repent (*Maharal*).

46. If all the Jewish people repent, the Messiah will come. Otherwise, he will not come (*Rashi*).

Rav maintains that there is no preordained date for the redemption (*Maharsha;* this would also seem to be *Rashi's* understanding of Rav's position). As shall be proven below from Scripture, the redemption will occur only when the people merit it through their repentance and good deeds. Since repentance is dependent on man's free will, the date of the redemption cannot be predetermined (*Maharsha*).

Alternatively, Rav agrees that there is a preordained "End." However, even at that date, the redemption will not occur unless the people are deserving of it. God will prolong the exile until the people repent (*Ramban, Sefer HaGeulah* ch. 2).

Rav certainly agrees that the redemption will eventually occur. The Torah's prophecies of redemption will not go unfulfilled, as the Gemara in *Berachos* (7a) states: "Every single statement expressed by God that is for the good (i.e. it conveys reward), even if it was conditional, will eventually be fulfilled" (*Ramban, Sefer HaGeulah* ibid.). *Maharal* writes that since the goal of Creation can be attained only through the redemption, it is axiomatic that the people will eventually repent (see *Netzach Yisrael* ch. 31).

47. The mourner is God who has been "unable" to bring the redemption all these years. Alternatively, the mourner is the Jewish people who have had to suffer the exile. According to either explanation, Shmuel's point is that just as a period of mourning eventually comes to an end, the same is true of the exile. Even if the people do not repent, the redemption will occur at its preordained time (*Rashi;* see note 50 for further elaboration on Shmuel's view).

Shmuel's reasoning is that the very suffering of the exile atones for the Jews. Hence, repentance is not a prerequisite (*Yad Ramah;* see *Ben Yehoyada*).

ובעוונותינו שרבו יצאו מהם מה שיצאו אמר ליה אליהו לרב יהודה אחוה דרב סלא חסידא אין העולם פחות משמונים וחמשה יובלות וביובל האחרון בן דוד בא אמר ליה בתחילתו או בסופו אמר ליה איני יודע כלה או אינו כלה אמר ליה איני יודע רב אשי אמר הכי א"ל עד הכא לא תיסתכי ליה מכאן ואילך איסתכי ליה שלח ליה רב חנן בר תחליפא לרב יוסף מצאתי אדם אחד ובידו מגילה אחת כתובה אשורית ולשון קודש אמרתי לו זו מניין לך אמר לי לחיילות של רומי נשכרתי ובין גינזי רומי מצאתיה וכתוב בה לאחר ד' אלפים ומאתים [א] ותשעים ואחד שנה לבריאתו של עולם העולם יתום מהן מלחמות תנינים מהן מלחמות גוג ומגוג ושאר ימות המשיח ואין הקב"ה מחדש את עולמו אלא לאחר שבעת אלפים שנה רב אחא בריה דרבא אמר לאחר חמשת אלפים שנה איתמר תניא רבי נתן אומר מקרא זה נוקב ויורד עד התהום [א] כי עוד חזון למועד ויפח לקץ ולא יכזב אם יתמהמה חכה לו כי בא יבא לא יאחר לא כרבותינו שהיו דורשין [ב] עד עידן עידנין ופלג עידן ולא כר' שמלאי שהיה דורש [ג] האכלתם לחם דמעה ותשקמו בדמעות שליש ולא כרבי עקיבא שהיה דורש [ד] עוד אחת מעט היא ואני מרעיש את השמים ואת הארץ אלא מלכות ראשון שבעים שנה מלכות שניה חמשים ושתים ומלכות בן כוזיבא שתי שנים ומחצה מאי ויפח לקץ ולא יכזב א"ר שמואל בר נחמני אמר ר' יונתן [א] תיפח עצמן של מחשבי קיצין שהיו אומרים כיון שהגיע את הקץ ולא בא שוב אינו בא אלא חכה לו שנאמר אם יתמהמה חכה לו שמא תאמר אנו מחכין והוא אינו מחכה ת"ל [ה] לכן יחכה ה' לחננכם ולכן ירום לרחמכם וכי מאחר שאנו מחכים והוא מחכה מי מעכב מדת הדין מעכבת וכי מאחר שמדת הדין מעכבת אנו למה מחכין לקבל שכר שנאמר [ה] אשרי כל חוכי לו [ב] אמר אביי לא פחות עלמא מתלתין ושיתא צדיקי דמקבלי אפי שכינה בכל דרא שנאמר אשרי כל חוכי לו לו בגימטריא תלתין ושיתא הוו איני והאמר רבא דרא דקמי קודשא בריך הוא תמני סרי אלפי [פרסא] הואי שנאמר [ו] סביב שמנה עשר אלף לא קשיא הא דמסתכלי באיספקלריא המאירה הא דמסתכלי באיספקלריא שאינה מאירה ומי נפישי כולי האי [ג] והאמר חזקיה א"ר ירמיה משום רשב"י ראיתי בני עליה והן מועטין אם אלף הם אני ובני מהם אם מאה הם אני ובני מהם אם שנים הם אני ובני הם לא קשיא הא דעיילי בבר הא דעיילי בלא בר אמר רב כלו כל הקיצין ואין הדבר תלוי אלא בתשובה ומעשים טובים ושמואל אמר דיו לאבל שיעמוד באבלו כתנאי ר' אליעזר אומר אם ישראל עושין תשובה נגאלין ואם לאו אין נגאלין אמר ליה רבי יהושע אם אין עושין תשובה אין נגאלין [ג] אלא הקב"ה מעמיד להן מלך שגזרותיו קשות כהמן [ב] וישראל עושין תשובה ומחזירן למוטב תניא אידך ר' אליעזר אומר אם ישראל עושין תשובה נגאלין שנאמר [ז] שובו בנים שובבים ארפא משובותיכם אמר לו רבי יהושע והלא כבר נאמר [ח] חנם נמכרתם ולא בכסף תגאלו חנם נמכרתם בעבודת כוכבים ולא בכסף תגאלו לא בתשובה ומעשים טובים אמר לו רבי אליעזר לר' יהושע והלא כבר נאמר [ט] שובו אלי ואשובה אליכם אמר ליה רבי יהושע והלא כבר נאמר [י] כי אנכי בעלתי בכם ולקחתי אתכם אחד מעיר ושנים ממשפחה והבאתי אתכם ציון אמר לו ר' אליעזר והלא כבר נאמר [כ] בשובה ונחת תושעון אמר לו ר' יהושע לרבי אליעזר והלא כבר נאמר [ל] כה אמר ה' גואל ישראל וקדושו לבזה נפש למתעב גוי לעבד מושלים מלכים

רש"י

אבל בשביל עונותינו שרבו. לא בא משיח לסוף ד' אלפים ויצאו מה שיצאו שעדיין הוא מעוכב לבא: שמנים וחמשה יובלין. היינו ד' אלפים מאתים וחמשים [שנה]: בתחלת. היובל האחרון הוא בא או בסופו: כלה. זמן הזה קודם שיבא משיח או אינו כלה דבתוך היובל בסופו הוא בא: עד הכא לא תיסתכי ליה. עד יובל האחרון לא תצפה לו דודאי לא יבא קודם הזמן הזה: איסתכי ליה. חכה לו שיבא: אשורית. כתב שלנו אשורית שבא מאשור כדאמר באידך פירקין (ד' כב.): לחיילות של רומי נשכרתי. שהייתי גולייר לאחד מהם: תנינים. דגים: והשאר ימות המשיח. שכלה השעבוד ומשיח בא: מחדש עולמו. לברוא עולם חדש: נוקב ויורד עד התהום. מה תהום אין לו קץ וסוף כך אין אדם יכול לעמוד על סוף פסוק זה [ד] (וכי קא מפרש אימת קאמר אם) יתמהמה חכה לו דאין לו סוף: לא כרבותינו. אל תצפו לאותו קץ שהיו רבותינו דורשין: עד עידן עידנין ופלג עידן. עידן כעידן הגלות של מצרים והיינו ד' מאות ב' עידנין ח' מאות היינו י"ב מאות ופלג עידן ב' מאות סך הכל אלף וד' מאות: ותשקמו בדמעות שליש. כלומר השקה אותם הקב"ה בין גלות מצרים לגלות בבל שליש גלות אדום כי קץ גלות אדום זה יהיה לסוף ג' פעמים ת' שנים וג' פעמים ע' שנה כנגד גלות בבל דהיינו לסוף אלף וארבע מאות ועשר שנים [ב] כבר עברו ולא היה כך מצאתי כתוב בשם הרב רבי שמואל בר דוד ז"ל: עוד אחת מעט היא. בנבואת חגי כתיב שהיה מתנבא כשיצאו ישראל מגלות בבל ויבנה בית המקדש והיינו עוד אחת מעט היא מעט כבוד אתן להם לישראל ואני מרעיש את השמים ואת הארץ והבאתי כל חמדת גוים לירושלים ור"ע דריש ליה לימות המשיח ולאחר חורבן והכי דריש ליה [עוד אחת מעט היא מעט כבוד אתן לישראל ואח"כ יבא המשיח ודרשה זו אינה אלא קרא אלפני הבית קאי וה"ק] עוד אחת מעט היא מעט כבוד אתן להם לישראל ושוב לא אתן להם כל ימות בית אחרון וכן היה דמלכות ראשונה של מלכות חשמונאי נתקיימה שבעים שנה ואע"ג דאמרינן בסדר עולם דמלכות בית חשמונאי מאה ושלש ומלכות הורדוס מאה ושלש עיקר כבודם ופארם שלא שלטה בהם אומה לא נתקיים כל כך ומלכות שניה של הורדוס נ"ב שנה ומלכות בן כוזיבא ב' שנים ומחצה ושוב לא היה להם מלך מ"ר. וכל הנך דרשות לאו משנה ולאו ברייתא. ל"א עוד אחת מעט היא מעט מלכות אתן להם לישראל לאחר חורבן ולאחר אותו מלכות הנני מרעיש שמים וארץ ויבא משיח. ואין דרשה זו כלום שהרי ראינו כמה מלכיות לישראל לאחר חורבן ואעפ"כ לא בא משיח שהמלכות הראשונה שהיתה להם לישראל לאחר חורבן שבעים שנה הורדוס נ"ב בן כוזיבא ב' ומחצה ומצינו בסדר עולם מפולמוס של אספסיאנוס עד פולמוס של טיטוס שתים עשרה שנה ומפולמוס של טיטוס עד מלכות בן כוזיבא י"ז שנים ומלכות בן כוזיבא ב' שנים ומחצה: [בן כוזיבא מלך בביתר]: ויפח לקץ. תיפח נפשו של מחשב הקץ שלא היה לו לכזב ולומר כיון שהגיע וכו': יחכה ה'. הוא עצמו מחכה ומתאוה שיבא משיח: סביב י"ח אלף. בירושלים של מעלה משתעי קרא בסוף יחזקאל: באספקלריא המאירה. בחוזק נגהו של הקב"ה אין מסתכלין אלא תלתין ושית אבל בקלישות הנוגה לצדדין מרחוק מסתכלין כתות הרבה: ומי נפישי כולי האי. דלהוי בריר לן תלתין ושיתא הוו ולא פחות: והא רבי שמעון בן יוחאי. לא הוה ידע אם אלף הם אם מאה הם אם שנים הם: הא דעיילי בבר. שצריכין ליטול רשות כשנכנסין להסתכל באספקלריא המאירה בהנהו לא פחיתי מתלתין ושית אבל אותן הנכנסין בלא רשות ברוב צדקם הנהו מספקא לן כמה הוו: בתשובה. אם כל ישראל חוזרין בתשובה יבא ואם לאו לא יבא: דיו לאבל שעומד באבלו. דיו להקב"ה שעומד כמה ימים וימינו אחור כלומר אם לא יעשו תשובה אינו עומד באבלו כל הימים אלא ודאי קץ לדבר ל"א דיו לאבל דיין לישראל צער גלות אפילו בלא תשובה נגאלין: לא בכסף. לא בתשובה ומעשים טובים דאפילו אין עושין תשובה נגאלין משום דאמר חנם נמכרתם קרי כסף בלשון תשובה: בעלתי אתכם. משמע בעל כרחכם בלא תשובה: אחד מעיר. אברור הצדיקים ואביאם לציון אע"פ שאין כולם חוזרין: כה אמר ה' לבזה נפש למתעב גוי. אותן הבזויין ומתועבין בעבירות אעפ"כ יגאלו מלכים יראו וקמו: כי

עין משפט נר מצוה

י א מיי' פי"ב מהלכות מלכים ומלחמותיהם הלכה ב:

יא ב מיי' פ"ז מהל' תשובה הלכה ה:

גליון הש"ס

גמ' לא פחות עלמא. ועי' במ"ר בראשית פ' ל"ה שם איתא לא פחות מתלתין צדיקי ועיין במ"ר במדבר פ' ג':

ליקוטי רש"י

ובעונותינו שרבו יצאו. משני אלפים אחרונים מה שיצאו ומשיח לא בא [ע"ז ט.]. עד עידן עידנין ופלג עידן. קץ סתום הוא זה כאשר נאמר לדניאל סתום הדברים וחתום ודרשוהו הראשונים איש לפי דעתו וכלו הקצים ויש לנו לפותרו עוד כאשר ראיתי כתוב בשם רב סעדיה הם אלף וג' מאות ול"ה שנים האמור בסוף הספר אשרי המחכה וגו' ופי' המועד עד עת שני עתים וחצי עת ואמר שהעתים הם ד' מאות ופ' שמיום לאתם ממצרים עד שנבנה הבית וד' מאות ועשר ימי מקדש ראשון הרי תת"ן ועוד חצי העת הזה תמ"ה הרי אלף של"ה את אלה חשוב מעת הוסר התמיד עד שוב זבח התמיד אל מקומו והוא הוסר שש שנים לפני החורבן ויש קצת ראיה בספר זה ועוד יש מביאין ראיה לחשבון זה הסתר אסתיר פני הסתר אסתיר בגי' אלף ושל"ה [דניאל ז, כה]. אשרי כל חוכי לו. לנחמות אשר הבטיח כי לא יפול דבר [ישעיה ל, יח]. אמר אביי כו' אשרי כל חוכי לו. המחכים לכת שהוא כמנין לו. סביב שמנה עשר אלף. סיפיה דקרא ה' שמה דאף על גב דבירושלים שלעתיד לבא כתיב קרא דרשינן ליה נמי להכי דמקום ששכינה שמה סובבין אותו שמנה עשר אלף והם הצדיקים הנתונים לפנים ממלאכי השרת שנאמר (במדבר כג) כעת יאמר ליעקב ולישראל מה פעל אל ואומר (ישעיה כג) ליושבים לפני ה' יהיה סחרה ואומר (שם ל) והיו עיניך רואות את מוריך. איספקלריא. מחילה שחוללת ביניהם לשכינה. המאירה. כמראה זו שרואין בה ויש לצדיקים שאין מאירה להם כל כך ואין יכולין לראות ממש. ראיתי בני עלייה והן מועטין. רואה אני לפי מעשה הבריות שבני עלייה כת המקבלין פני שכינה מועטים הם. בבר. ברשות. דעיילי בלא בר. בלא רשות מועטים הן ובהנהו קאמר אני ובני מהם [סוכה מה:]. שובבים. אנויישי"ר בלע"ז ששובבתם דרככם מרוב כל שהייתם בשלוה ועונג כמו שהוא אומר הפורטים על פי הנבל (עמוס ו) השותים במזרקי יין (שם) [ירמיה ג, יד]. לשון משובה נערו' ויולדות אינווייזור"א בלע"ז וכן בנים שובבים (ירמיה ג) הבת השובבה (שם לא) [הושע ו, יא]. משמע מזידים ופרהסיא [שובב] לשון מרד וגאוה כמו וילך שובב בדרך לבו (ישעיה נז) [ע"ז ז:]. כי אנכי בעלתי בכם. ונקראתם בשמי שאני אדון לכם ואין כבודי להניח אתכם ביד אויבי [ירמיה שם]. בשובה ונחת. תהיה לכם תשועה בלא שום טורח אם תשמעו לי. בשובה. לשון ישוב ומרגוע וכן שובה ה' רבבות אלפי ישראל (במדבר י) [ישעיה ל, טו]. לבזה נפש. נפש בזויה לישראל שהם בזוים [שם מט, ז]. למתעב גוי. למי שהגוי מתעבו [ישעיה שם]. לעבד מושלים. ועבדים מושלין בכן [תענית שם].

מסורת הש"ס

א) סוכה מה: ע"ש, ב) ג"ז שם., ג) בירושלמי הגי' א"ר ר"א, ד) ס"א שאין קץ למשיח אלא אם.

הגהות הגר"א

[א] גמ' ותשעים. נמחק וני"ב שלשים (עי' בע"ז ט' ב' ובתוס' ד"ה לאחר): [ב] רש"י ד"ה ותשקמו כו' עשר שנים. עשה כאן נקודות להפסיק ותיבת וכבר עברו וכו' עד בר דוד ז"ל נמחק:

תורה אור השלם

א) כי עוד חזון למועד ויפח לקץ ולא יכזב אם יתמהמה חכה לו כי בא יבא לא יאחר: [חבקוק ב, ג]

ב) ומלין לצד עלאה ימלל ולקדישי עליונין יבלא ויסבר להשניה זמנין ודת ויתיהבון בידה עד עדן ועדנין ופלג עדן: [דניאל ז, כה]

ג) האכלתם לחם דמעה ותשקמו בדמעות שליש: [תהלים פ, ו]

ד) כי כה אמר יי צבאות עוד אחת מעט היא ואני מרעיש את השמים ואת הארץ ואת הים ואת החרבה: [חגי ב, ו]

ה) ולכן יחכה יי לחננכם ולכן ירום לרחמכם כי אלהי משפט יי אשרי כל חוכי לו: [ישעיה ל, יח]

ו) סביב שמנה עשר אלף ושם העיר מיום יי שמה: [יחזקאל מח, לה]

ז) שובו בנים שובבים ארפה משובתיכם הננו אתנו לך כי אתה יי אלהינו: [ירמיה ג, כב]

ח) כי כה אמר יי חנם נמכרתם ולא בכסף תגאלו: [ישעיה נב, ג]

ט) למימי אבתיכם סרתם מחקי ולא שמרתם שובו אלי ואשובה אליכם אמר יי צבאות ואמרתם במה נשוב: [מלאכי ג, ז]

י) שובו בנים שובבים נאם יי כי אנכי בעלתי בכם ולקחתי אתכם אחד מעיר ושנים ממשפחה והבאתי אתכם ציון: [ירמיה ג, יד]

כ) כי כה אמר אדני אלהים קדוש ישראל בשובה ונחת תושעון בהשקט ובבטחה תהיה גבורתכם ולא אביתם: [ישעיה ל, טו]

ל) כה אמר יי גאל ישראל קדושו לבזה נפש למתעב גוי לעבד משלים מלכים יראו וקמו שרים וישתחוו למען יי אשר נאמן קדש ישראל ויבחרך: [ישעיה מט, ז]

following dispute between **Tannaim:** רַבִּי אֱלִיעֶזֶר אוֹמֵר – **R' ELIEZER SAYS:** אִם יִשְׂרָאֵל עוֹשִׂין תְּשׁוּבָה נִגְאָלִין – **IF THE JEWISH PEOPLE REPENT, THEY WILL BE REDEEMED;** וְאִם לָאו אֵין נִגְאָלִין – **AND IF NOT, THEY WILL NOT BE REDEEMED.**[48]

אָמַר לֵיהּ רַבִּי יְהוֹשֻׁעַ – **R' YEHOSHUA SAID TO [R' ELIEZER]:** אִם אֵין עוֹשִׂין תְּשׁוּבָה אֵין נִגְאָלִין – **IF THEY DO NOT REPENT, THEY WILL NOT BE REDEEMED?!** אֶלָּא הַקָּדוֹשׁ בָּרוּךְ הוּא מַעֲמִיד לָהֶן מֶלֶךְ שֶׁגְּזֵרוֹתָיו קָשׁוֹת כְּהָמָן – **RATHER, THE HOLY ONE, BLESSED IS HE, WILL APPOINT A KING OVER THEM WHOSE DECREES WILL BE AS HARSH AS** those of **HAMAN,**[49] וְיִשְׂרָאֵל עוֹשִׂין תְּשׁוּבָה – **AND THE JEWISH PEOPLE WILL REPENT.** וּמַחֲזִירָן לְמוּטָב – **AND** in this way **[GOD] WILL BRING THEM BACK TO THE RIGHT** path.[50]

The Gemara cites a Baraisa in which these Tannaim debate the issue:

תַּנְיָא אִידָךְ – **It was taught in another Baraisa:** רַבִּי אֱלִיעֶזֶר אוֹמֵר – **R' ELIEZER SAYS:** אִם יִשְׂרָאֵל עוֹשִׂין תְּשׁוּבָה נִגְאָלִין – **IF THE JEWISH PEOPLE REPENT, THEY WILL BE REDEEMED,** שֶׁנֶּאֱמַר ,,שׁוּבוּ בָּנִים שׁוֹבָבִים אֶרְפָּה מְשׁוּבֹתֵיכֶם" – **AS IT IS STATED:** ***REPENT, O WAYWARD CHILDREN, I WILL CURE YOU OF YOUR WAYWARDNESS.***[51] אָמַר לוֹ רַבִּי יְהוֹשֻׁעַ – **R' YEHOSHUA SAID TO HIM:** וַהֲלֹא כְּבָר נֶאֱמַר – **BUT IS IT NOT ALREADY STATED:** ,,חִנָּם נִמְכַּרְתֶּם וְלֹא בְכֶסֶף תִּגָּאֵלוּ" – ***FOR NOTHING WERE YOU SOLD, AND WITHOUT MONEY SHALL YOU BE REDEEMED?***[52] ,,חִנָּם נִמְכַּרְתֶּם" בַּעֲבוֹדַת כּוֹכָבִים – The first clause, ***FOR NOTHING WERE YOU SOLD,*** means that you were exiled **BECAUSE** you committed **IDOLATRY,** which has no value. ,,וְלֹא בְכֶסֶף תִּגָּאֵלוּ" לֹא בִּתְשׁוּבָה וּמַעֲשִׂים טוֹבִים – The second clause, ***AND WITHOUT MONEY SHALL YOU BE REDEEMED,*** means that you will be redeemed even **WITHOUT REPENTANCE OR GOOD DEEDS.**[53]

אָמַר לוֹ רַבִּי אֱלִיעֶזֶר לְרַבִּי יְהוֹשֻׁעַ – **R' ELIEZER SAID TO R' YEHOSHUA:** וַהֲלֹא כְּבָר נֶאֱמַר – **BUT IS IT NOT ALREADY STATED:** ,,שׁוּבוּ אֵלַי וְאָשׁוּבָה אֲלֵיכֶם" – ***RETURN TO ME, AND I WILL RETURN TO YOU?***[54] אָמַר לֵיהּ רַבִּי יְהוֹשֻׁעַ – **R' YEHOSHUA SAID TO [R' ELIEZER]:** וַהֲלֹא כְּבָר נֶאֱמַר – **BUT IS IT NOT ALREADY STATED:** ,,כִּי אָנֹכִי בָּעַלְתִּי בָכֶם וְלָקַחְתִּי אֶתְכֶם אֶחָד מֵעִיר וּשְׁנַיִם מִמִּשְׁפָּחָה וְהֵבֵאתִי אֶתְכֶם צִיּוֹן" – ***FOR I MADE MYSELF MASTER OVER YOU, AND I WILL TAKE YOU, ONE FROM A CITY AND TWO FROM A FAMILY, AND I WILL BRING YOU TO ZION?***[55] אָמַר לוֹ רַבִּי אֱלִיעֶזֶר – **R' ELIEZER SAID TO [R' YEHOSHUA]:** וַהֲלֹא כְּבָר נֶאֱמַר – **BUT IS IT NOT ALREADY STATED:** ,,בְּשׁוּבָה וָנַחַת תִּוָּשֵׁעוּן" – ***IN REPOSE AND CALM SHALL YOU BE REDEEMED?***[56]

אָמַר לוֹ רַבִּי יְהוֹשֻׁעַ לְרַבִּי אֱלִיעֶזֶר – **R' YEHOSHUA SAID TO [R' ELIEZER]:** וַהֲלֹא כְּבָר נֶאֱמַר – **BUT IS IT NOT ALREADY STATED:** ,,כֹּה אָמַר־ה׳ גֹּאֵל יִשְׂרָאֵל קְדוֹשׁוֹ לִבְזֹה־נֶפֶשׁ לִמְתָעֵב גּוֹי לְעֶבֶד מֹשְׁלִים – ***THUS SAYS HASHEM — THE REDEEMER OF ISRAEL, HIS HOLY ONE — TO ONE WHO IS DESPISED BY MEN, ABHORRED BY NATIONS, AND WHO IS A SLAVE OF RULERS:***

NOTES

48. R' Eliezer's opinion corresponds to that of Rav (see note 46).

49. Haman sought the extermination of the entire Jewish nation, as related in the Book of *Esther.*

50. Faced with no other option, the people will come to realize that their only hope lies with their Father in Heaven and that they must repent to merit His salvation. [This is indeed what happened in the case of Haman (see *Esther* ch. 4; Gemara *Megillah* 14a).]

The following difficulty must be addressed: From this statement of R' Yehoshua it is evident that even he agrees that repentance is a prerequisite for redemption. Yet the Gemara draws a parallel between R' Yehoshua's view and that of Shmuel, who maintains that redemption can occur even without repentance (see note 47).

Maharsha resolves this difficulty by asserting that even according to Shmuel some measure of repentance is required. Shmuel's words ("it is enough for the mourner etc.") mean that it is sufficient for the Jewish people to repent as a result of their mourning – i.e. in order to escape a king's harsh decrees. God can "force" this type of repentance by creating conditions in which the people will realize that they have no other option. It is possible, therefore, for God to engineer such repentance at a given date as part of a preordained redemptive process. This is in contrast to the opinion of Rav and R' Eliezer which maintains that since the necessary repentance must be self-motivated, God cannot "force" it to occur at a preordained date (*Maharsha).* [*Rashi* does not necessarily disagree with *Maharsha's* approach. Although *Rashi* wrote that according to Shmuel the people will be redeemed even without repentance (see note 47), he possibly means that if the people have not yet repented of their own accord, God will set the redemptive process – including "forced" repentance – into motion.]

[It should be noted that this problem does not arise according to the *Yerushalmi's* version of the text (*Taanis* 4:4), which reads א״ל (abbreviation of אָמַר לֵיהּ, *he said to him*) in place of אֶלָּא (*rather*). According to this version, the words that follow – הַקָּדוֹשׁ בָּרוּךְ הוּא מַעֲמִיד לָהֶן מֶלֶךְ וכו׳, *The Holy One, Blessed is He, will appoint a king over them etc.* – were said not by R' Yehoshua, but by R' Eliezer. The major commentators, however, accept our version of the text (see *Yad Ramah, Abarbanel, Maharsha, Maharal* et al.).]

51. *Jeremiah* 3:22. The first clause sets forth a prerequisite for the fulfillment of the second clause: *If* the people repent, God will cure (i.e. redeem) them. The verse thus proves that repentance is necessary for redemption.

52. *Isaiah* 52:3.

53. Since the first part of the verse (חִנָּם נִמְכַּרְתֶּם, *For nothing were you sold*) refers to a lack of value in the spiritual sense, the second part of the verse (וְלֹא בְכֶסֶף תִּגָּאֵלוּ, *and without money shall you be redeemed*) should be interpreted likewise. It is evident, therefore, that "money" is used here as a metaphor for repentance and good deeds (*Rashi;* see 96b and note 46 there; cf. *Maharsha*).

How does R' Yehoshua explain the verse cited by R' Eliezer (שׁוּבוּ בָּנִים שׁוֹבָבִים, *Repent, O wayward children*), which indicates that the people must repent to merit redemption? *Maharsha* answers that according to R' Yehoshua the verse speaks of "forced" repentance (see note 50).

54. *Malachi* 3:7. First the people must turn to God in repentance, and then God will turn to them and redeem them.

This verse (שׁוּבוּ אֵלַי, *Return to Me*) is a stronger proof than the verse R' Eliezer already cited (שׁוּבוּ בָּנִים שׁוֹבָבִים, *Return, O wayward children*) because it is a request [rather than an exhortation]. Thus, it more readily connotes self-motivated repentance (as opposed to forced repentance) than the other verse does (*Maharsha*).

As for the verse cited by R' Yehoshua (וְלֹא בְכֶסֶף תִּגָּאֵלוּ, *And without money shall you be redeemed*), R' Eliezer could take it literally to mean that money will not buy you redemption, only repentance will (based on *Rashi* and *Radak* ad loc., cited by *Maharsha*).

55. *Jeremiah* 3:14. The phrase בָּעַלְתִּי בָכֶם, *I made Myself master over you,* implies that God will bring the redemption even against the people's will, i.e. even though they have not all repented. God will select the few righteous individuals – "one from a city, two from a family" – and bring them to Zion (*Rashi*).

As explained above, R' Yehoshua maintains that if the people have not repented of their own accord, God will "force" them to repent by subjecting them to terrible calamities. The few who survive those calamities and repent as a result of them ("one from a city etc.") will merit to return to Eretz Yisrael (see *Maharsha;* see Gemara below, 111a, where this verse is discussed further).

With regard to the verse cited by R' Eliezer (שׁוּבוּ אֵלַי, *Return to Me*), R' Yehoshua agrees that it refers to self-motivated repentance. He contends, however, that God requested this form of repentance only as an ideal. If the Jewish people do not reach that level, God will bring the redemption in any event (see *Maharsha*).

56. *Isaiah* 30:15. The redemption will occur in conditions of peace and tranquility. This proves that the redemption will be effected by self-motivated repentance, rather than by "forced" repentance, which is based on a desire to escape suffering and tribulation (*Maharsha*).

As for the verse, בָּעַלְתִּי בָכֶם, *I made Myself master over you,* R' Eliezer could explain it as teaching that the Jewish people are *servants* of God, as opposed to His *children.* Therefore, unlike children, who can gain their father's favor without repentance, the Jewish people must repent to merit redemption (*Rif* in *Ein Yaakov*).

,,מְלָכִים יִרְאוּ וָקָמוּ שָׂרִים וְיִשְׁתַּחֲווּ'' – *"KINGS SHALL SEE AND RISE; PRINCES ALSO SHALL PROSTRATE THEMSELVES"?*[1]

וַהֲלֹא אָמַר לוֹ רַבִּי אֱלִיעֶזֶר – R' ELIEZER SAID TO [R' YEHOSHUA]: כְּבָר נֶאֱמַר – BUT IS IT NOT ALREADY STATED: ,,אִם־תָּשׁוּב יִשְׂרָאֵל נְאֻם־ה' אֵלַי תָּשׁוּב'' – *IF YOU RETURN, O ISRAEL, SAYS HASHEM, YOU SHALL RETURN TO ME?*[2]

וַהֲלֹא אָמַר לוֹ רַבִּי יְהוֹשֻׁעַ – R' YEHOSHUA SAID TO [R' ELIEZER]: כְּבָר נֶאֱמַר – BUT IS IT NOT ALREADY STATED:[3] ,,וָאֶשְׁמַע אֶת־הָאִישׁ לְבוּשׁ הַבַּדִּים אֲשֶׁר מִמַּעַל לְמֵימֵי הַיְאֹר – *I HEARD THE MAN CLOTHED IN LINEN, WHO WAS ABOVE THE WATERS OF THE RIVER*. וַיָּרֶם יְמִינוֹ וּשְׂמֹאלוֹ אֶל־הַשָּׁמַיִם – *HE LIFTED HIS RIGHT HAND AND HIS LEFT HAND HEAVENWARD* וַיִּשָּׁבַע בְּחֵי הָעוֹלָם – *AND HE SWORE BY THE LIFE OF THE WORLD* כִּי לְמוֹעֵד מוֹעֲדִים וָחֵצִי וּכְכַלּוֹת נַפֵּץ יַד־עַם־קֹדֶשׁ תִּכְלֶינָה כָל־אֵלֶּה'' וגו' – *THAT IN A TIME, TIMES, AND A HALF, AND UPON THE CESSATION OF THE POWER*[4] *OF THE HOLY PEOPLE, ALL THESE SHALL CEASE,* etc.[5]

The Baraisa concludes:

וְשָׁתַק רַבִּי אֱלִיעֶזֶר – AND R' ELIEZER WAS SILENT.[6]

The Gemara records further signs indicating the Messiah's arrival:[7]

וְאָמַר רַבִּי אַבָּא – And R' Abba said: אֵין לְךָ קֵץ מְגוּלֶּה מִזֶּה – **There is no clearer indication of the "End" than this,** שֶׁנֶּאֱמַר – **as it is stated:** ,,וְאַתֶּם הָרֵי יִשְׂרָאֵל עַנְפְּכֶם תִּתֵּנוּ וּפֶרְיְכֶם תִּשְׂאוּ לְעַמִּי יִשְׂרָאֵל וגו' '' – ***But you, O mountains of Israel, you shall shoot forth your branches and bear your fruit for My people Israel,* etc.** *[when they are about to come]*.[8]

רַבִּי (אליעזר) [אֶלְעָזָר] אוֹמֵר – **R' Elazar says:** אַף מִזֶּה – There is **also** no clearer indication of the "End" **than this,**[9] שֶׁנֶּאֱמַר – **as it is stated:** ,,כִּי לִפְנֵי הַיָּמִים (האלה) [הָהֵם] שְׂכַר הָאָדָם לֹא נִהְיָה וּשְׂכַר הַבְּהֵמָה אֵינֶנָּה – ***For before those days, there was no wage for man and no wage for animals,*** וְלַיּוֹצֵא וְלַבָּא אֵין־שָׁלוֹם מִן־הַצָּר'' – ***and to him that leaves or enters there was no peace from the adversary.***[10]

NOTES

1. *Isaiah* 49:7. [The Jewish people, who were hated and despised while in exile, will be held in the highest esteem after their redemption.]

R' Yehoshua understands the verse as meaning that the people will be despicable and abhorrent in a spiritual sense, because of their sins. Nonetheless, they will be redeemed, and "kings will rise before them" (*Rashi*). The verse thus proves that repentance is not a prerequisite for redemption.

According to *Yad Ramah,* however, R' Yehoshua takes the verse literally (i.e. the Jews will be despised and abhorred by the nations prior to their redemption). R' Yehoshua deduces that since the verse mentions only the degradation of the Jews as a reason for redemption, it implies that repentance is not necessary (see 97b note 47 second paragraph).

In *Maharsha's* view, R' Yehoshua interprets the verse as teaching that because the Jews will be despised and abhorred in exile, they will repent in order to escape their dreadful conditions, and then they will be redeemed. Hence, the verse indicates that "forced" repentance suffices to bring the redemption.

As for the verse בְּשׁוּבָה וָנַחַת תִּוָּשֵׁעוּן, *in* [a state of] *repose and calm shall you be redeemed,* R' Yehoshua could explain it as referring to the conditions that will prevail *after* the redemption (*Maharsha;* cf. *Rif* in *Ein Yaakov*).

2. *Jeremiah* 4:1. This verse is the strongest proof R' Eliezer has adduced until now for his position that the people must repent of their own accord to merit redemption. The word "if" in the phrase, *If you return,* implies that it is questionable whether the people will repent. Hence, it must refer to self-motivated repentance, which cannot be preordained, rather than to "forced" repentance, which is a product of Divinely arranged circumstances (*Maharsha; Rif* in *Ein Yaakov*).

3. *Daniel* 12:7. Daniel beheld a vision in which one angel asked another when the exile will end. This verse describes the second angel's response.

4. Literally: spreading of the hand (see *Rashi*).

5. When the power of the Jewish people has utterly ceased and they are at the end of their tether, their troubles will finally cease and the Messiah will come. This verse reflects the one discussed on 97a: כִּי־יָדִין ה' עַמּוֹ וגו' כִּי יִרְאֶה כִּי־אָזְלַת יָד, *For HASHEM will judge His people* etc. (i.e. He will bring the redemption [*Rashi* ibid.]) *when He sees that [their] power has gone* (*Rashi*).

The verse gives a preordained date for the redemption: לְמוֹעֵד מוֹעֲדִים וָחֵצִי, *in a time, times, and a half*. [This is a Hebrew version of the Aramaic phrase quoted on 97b: עַד־עִדָּן וְעִידָּנִין וּפְלַג עִדָּן, *until a time, and times, and half a time*.] It thus refutes R' Eliezer's view that the redemption is contingent upon repentance alone and has no fixed date (see *Rashi, Yad Ramah;* cf. *Maharsha*).

As for the verse אִם־תָּשׁוּב, *If you return,* which seems to support R' Eliezer's view (see note 2), R' Yehoshua could translate it, *When can you return*. It is evident from several sources (e.g. *Exodus* 22:24) that אִם can also be translated as *when (Maharsha)*.

6. R' Eliezer conceded that R' Yehoshua was right (*Yad Ramah, Maharal*).

Rambam (*Hil. Teshuvah* 7:5) declares: "The Jewish people will not be redeemed except through repentance. The Torah promises that the Jewish people will eventually repent at the end of their exile, and then they will be redeemed immediately, as it is said (*Deuteronomy* 30:1-3): *It will be that when all these things come upon you . . . you will return to HASHEM, your God . . . Then HASHEM, your God, will bring back your captivity and have mercy upon you, and He will gather you in from all the peoples to which HASHEM your God had scattered you."* [Although R' Eliezer apparently conceded to R' Yehoshua, *Rambam* rules that repentance is a prerequisite for redemption, because even R' Yehoshua agrees that some form of repentance is required, as explained above (97b note 50; see *Haggadah Simchas Yaabetz* by *R' Dovid Cohen* pp. 20-21 for an elaboration of *Rambam's* ruling).]

7. *Rashi, Yad Ramah* (second explanation), *Maharsha.* Alternatively, *Yad Ramah* views the next passage as a continuation of the preceding one (see notes 8 and 10).

8. *Ezekiel* 36:8. [God tells the Land of Israel to resume producing fruit in preparation for the return of the Jewish people (*Metzudos*).]

Eretz Yisrael will yield fruit in abundance shortly before the redemption. This is the clearest sign of all that the exile is about to end (*Rashi*).

Maharsha explains that when Eretz Yisrael is not inhabited by the Jewish people, the land does not produce fruit to its usual degree. Thus, when it resumes producing fruit, this is a clear sign that the time is approaching for the Jewish people's return to their land.

Alternatively, *Maharsha* explains the verse as referring to the phenomenon described in *Shabbos* 30b [and *Kesubos* 111b] that in the Future World trees will produce fruit every day. The Gemara assumes that this will begin shortly *before* the Messiah's arrival. Since this phenomenon is of a miraculous nature, it is a clear sign of the approaching redemption.

Yad Ramah (first explanation) connects this statement to the dispute between R' Eliezer and R' Yehoshua. The end of the verse, כִּי קָרְבוּ לָבוֹא, *when they are about to come,* implies that there is a preordained date for the redemption, for otherwise the people's coming could not be predicted beforehand (see *Targum* ad loc.). It thus supports R' Yehoshua's contention that there is such a date. R' Abba's statement, "There is no clearer indication of the 'End' than this," means that this verse is the strongest proof of all that the exile has a definite end.

9. That is to say: The following portent of the Messiah's imminent arrival is as clear as the one offered above by R' Abba.

10. *Zechariah* 8:10. The verse speaks of a time in which economic conditions are so severe that people cannot find jobs, animals are not being leased for work on the land and it is unsafe to travel from one town to another. When such conditions prevail, one can expect the Messiah's imminent arrival. This echoes the Tannaic opinion above (97a) which states that the Messiah will not come "until the *perutah* is gone from the purse" (*Rashi;* see *Maharsha*; see also *Chafetz Chaim* in *Likkutei Halachos*, Introduction p. 3). [Although the verse actually refers to the period before the building of the Second Temple, the Gemara assumes that the same conditions will apply before the final redemption.]

In line with his approach to the previous teaching, *Yad Ramah* explains that the words *before those days* (which imply particular days) prove that there is a preordained date for the redemption (see end of note 8).

מלכים יראו וקמו שרים וישתחוו אמר לו רבי אליעזר והלא כבר נאמר [א] אם תשוב ישראל נאום ה' אלי תשוב אמר לו רבי יהושע והלא כבר נאמר [ב] ואשמע את האיש לבוש הבדים אשר ממעל למימי היאור וירם ימינו ושמאלו אל השמים וישבע בחי העולם כי למועד מועדים וחצי וככלות נפץ יד עם קדש תכלינה כל אלה וגו' ושתק רבי אליעזר ואמר רבי אבא אין לך קץ מגולה מזה שנאמר [ג] ואתם הרי ישראל ענפכם תתנו ופריכם תשאו לעמי ישראל וגו' רבי ([א] אליעזר) אומר אף מזה שנאמר [ד] כי לפני הימים (האלה) [ההם] שכר האדם לא נהיה ושכר הבהמה איננה וליוצא ולבא אין שלום מן הצר [ג] מאי ליוצא ולבא אין שלום מן הצר רב אמר אף תלמידי חכמים שכתוב בהם שלום דכתיב [ה] שלום רב לאהבי תורתך אין שלום מפני צר ושמואל אמר עד שיהיו כל השערים כולן שקולין אמר רבי חנינא אין בן דוד בא עד שיתבקש דג לחולה ולא ימצא שנאמר [ו] אז אשקיע מימיהם ונהרותם כשמן אוליך וכתב ([ג] בתריה) [ז] ביום ההוא אצמיח קרן לבית ישראל אמר רבי חמא בר חנינא אין בן דוד בא עד שתכלה מלכות הזלה מישראל שנאמר [ח] וכרת הזלזלים במזמרות [א] וכתיב בתריה [ט] בעת ההיא יובל שי לה' צבאות עם ממשך ומורט אמר זעירי אמר רבי חנינא אין בן דוד בא עד שיכלו גסי הרוח מישראל שנאמר [י] כי אז אסיר מקרבך עליזי גאותך וכתיב [יא] והשארתי בקרבך עם עני ודל וחסו בשם ה' אמר רבי שמלאי משום רבי אלעזר בר"ש [ד] אין בן דוד בא עד שיכלו כל שופטים ושוטרים מישראל שנאמר [יב] ואשיבה ידי עליך ואצרוף כבור סיגיך וגו' ואשיבה שופטיך [ה] אמר עולא אין [ו] ירושלים נפדית אלא בצדקה שנאמר [יג] ציון במשפט תפדה ושביה בצדקה אמר רב פפא אי בטלי יהירי בטלי אמגושי אי בטלי דייני בטלי [ז] גזירפטי אי בטלי יהירי בטלי אמגושי דכתיב [יב] ואצרוף כבור סיגיך ואסירה כל בדיליך ואי בטלי דייני בטלי גזירפטי דכתיב [יד] הסיר ה' משפטיך פנה אויבך אמר ר' יוחנן אם ראית דור שמתמעט והולך חכה לו שנאמר [טו] ואת עם עני תושיע וגו' אמר רבי יוחנן אם ראית דור שצרות רבות באות עליו כנהר חכה לו שנאמר [טז] כי יבא כנהר צר (ו)רוח ה' נוססה בו וסמיך ליה ובא לציון גואל ואמר רבי יוחנן אין בן דוד בא אלא בדור שכולו זכאי או כולו חייב בדור שכולו זכאי דכתיב [יז] ועמך כולם צדיקים לעולם יירשו ארץ בדור שכולו חייב דכתיב [יח] וירא כי אין איש וישתומם כי אין מפגיע וכתיב [יט] למעני אעשה אמר רבי אלכסנדרי רבי יהושע בן לוי רמי כתיב [כ] בעתה וכתיב אחישנה זכו אחישנה לא זכו בעתה אמר רבי אלכסנדרי רבי יהושע בן לוי רמי כתיב [כא] וארו עם ענני שמיא כבר אינש אתה וכתיב [כב] עני ורוכב על חמור זכו עם ענני שמיא לא זכו עני רוכב על חמור אמר ליה שבור מלכא לשמואל אמריתו משיח על חמרא אתי אישדר ליה סוסיא [ח] ברקא דאית לי אמר ליה מי אית לך בר חיור גווני ר' יהושע בן לוי אשכח לאליהו דהוי קיימי אפיתחא דמערתא דרבי שמעון בן יוחאי אמר ליה אתינא לעלמא דאתי אמר ליה אם ירצה אדון הזה אמר רבי יהושע בן לוי שנים ראיתי וקול ג' שמעתי אמר ליה אימת אתי משיח אמר ליה זיל שייליה לדידיה והיכא יתיב אפיתחא [א] דקרתא ומאי סימניה יתיב ביני עניי סובלי חלאים וכולן שרו ואסירי בחד זימנא איהו שרי חד ואסיר חד אמר דילמא מבעינא דלא איעכב אזל לגביה אמר ליה שלום עליך רבי ומורי אמר ליה שלום עליך בר ליואי א"ל לאימת אתי מר א"ל היום אתא לגבי אליהו א"ל מאי אמר לך א"ל שלום עליך בר ליואי א"ל אבטחך לך ולאבוך לעלמא דאתי א"ל שקורי קא שקר בי דאמר לי היום אתינא ולא אתא א"ל הכי אמר לך [כג] היום אם בקולו תשמעו שאלו תלמידיו את רבי יוסי בן קיסמא אימתי בן דוד בא אמר מתיירא אני שמא תבקשו ממני אות אמרו לו אין אנו מבקשין ממך אות א"ל לכשיפול השער הזה ויבנה ויפול ויבנה ויפול ואין מספיקין לבנותו עד שבן דוד בא אמרו לו רבינו תן לנו אות אמר להם ולא כך אמרתם לי שאין אתם מבקשין ממני אות אמרו לו ואף על פי כן אמר להם אם כך יהפכו מי מערת פמייס לדם ונהפכו לדם בשעת פטירתו אמר להן העמיקו לי ארוני שאין

רש"י

כי למועד מועדים. אלמא יש קץ בדבר: וככלות נפץ יד עם קדש. כשתכלה תקומתם וחוזק ידיהם שהיתה נפולה אילך ואילך גבורה ותועלת לפשוט אנה ואנה ואחר שתכלה גבורתם שיהיו שפלים למאד: תכלינה. אלו הצרות ויבא משיח כדאמרינן כי אזלת יד: מגולה מזה. כשתתן ארץ ישראל פריה בעין יפה אז יקרב הקץ ואין לך קץ מגולה יותר: ר' אליעזר אומר מזה. הפסוק כשתראה דאין שום אדם משתכר ואף שכר הבהמה לא נהיה והיינו כדאמרן עד שתכלה פרוטה מן הכיס אין מעות מצויות בכיס: שכר בהמה. עבודת האדמה שהיא על ידי בהמה איננה: וליוצא ולבא אין שלום. אז יבא משיח: [שלום רב]. והיינו וליוצא ולבא אלו תלמידי חכמים אותם שהיה דינם לצאת ולבא בשלום כדכתיב שלום רב לאוהבי תורתך אפילו להנהו אין שלום: מן הצר. מרוב הצרות ל"א מיצר הרע: שקולין. שוין שער התבואה ויין רווחי' כדאמרן חמישית שובע גדול ל"א שקולין שוין שכולן יקרין: כשמן אוליך. שיהיו כולן קפויין וכיון שהם קפויין אין דגים נמצאין בתוכה: עד שתכלה מלכות הזלה. שלא תהא להם שום שולטנות לישראל אפילו שולטנות קלה ודלה: נטישותיו. ענפים קטנים כלומר השרים והשופטים: וחסו בשם השם. כלומר שתבא להם גאולה ויחסו בצל שדי: סיגיך. תערובות שבך: בדיליך. המובדלים לראשי עם: יהירי. גסי רוח מישראל: אמגושי. פרסיים מכשפין שמצערין ישראל במס' שבת (דף עה.) פלוגתא איכא למאן דאמר אמגושי חרשי ואיכא מ"ד גדופי עובדי כוכבים: גזירפטי. שופטים עובדי כוכבים החובטין את ישראל במקלות: ואצרוף כבור סיגיך. רבים וגדולים בגסותם כשאצרוף ואסלקם ממך אזי אסירה כל בדיליך: אמגושי. הבדלים מיראת המקום: סיגיך. כמו רב דמתרגמינן סגי: משפטיך. כמו [ב] (צפניה ג) שופטיך: פנה אויבך. גזירפטי: נוססה. כמו (ישעיה י) כמסוס נוסס וכמו (שם נא) יאכלם סס רוח המקום נוקבת ומתרבת אותן עם הצרות הבאות שאף הוא מתכוין להשמידם: יירשו ארץ. היינו גאולה: עם ענני שמיא כבר אינש אתי. במהירות: וכתיב עני ורוכב על החמור. כעני הבא על חמורו בעצלות: סוסי ברקא. סוס מסורק [ט] ומכוון ונאה שיש לי דגנאי הוא שיבא על חמור מלגלג היה ל"א סוסיא בדקא סוס בדוק לרוץ: בר חיור גווני. כלום יש לך סוס בר מאה גוונין שחמור שלו כן הוא במלתא בעלמא דחייה: חיור. מאה בלשון פרסי: האדון הזה. שכינה היתה עמהם: קול שלשה. דשכינה הוה בהדייהו: לדידיה. למשיח: בפתחא ([י] דקרתא). נראה למורי לא בפתח העיר ממש אלא גן עדן הוא כנגד כל העולם וקאמר ליה דבאותו צד של גן עדן שכנגד פתח העיר משיח שרוי: סובלי חלאים. מנוגעים והוא נמי מנוגע דכתיב (ישעיה נג) והוא מחולל מפשעינו וכתיב (שם) חליינו הוא נשא: כולהו. מי שיש לו ארבע וחמש נגעים: אסרי להו ושרו בחדא זימנא. מתירין כל נגעתן ביחד ומקנחין אותן וחוזרין וקושרין אותן: ואיהו. משיח: שרי חד. נגע ומקנחו וקושרו ואח"כ מתיר האחר ועושה כן ואינו מתיר שני נגעים יחד דסבר אי בעי לי לצאת וליגאל את ישראל לא איתעכב כדי קשירת שני נגעים: אמר ליה. ר' יהושע למשיח לאימת אתי מר אמר ליה היום: אבטחך לך ולאביך לעולם הבא. דאי לאו צדיקים גמורין אתם לא הוה יהיב לך שלמא ולא הוה מדכר שמיה דאבוך: היום אם בקולו. של הקב"ה תשמעו: השער הזה. של עיר רומי שבעיר רומי היה אותו שער: ואין מספיקין לבנותו. פעם שלישית: מי פמיים. שירדן נובע ממנו כדתניא בבכורות (דף נה.) דן יוצא ממערת פמייס ומפרש התם שפיר: העמיקו ארוני. עשו לי קבר בקרקע עמוק: שאין

מסורת הש"ס

א) [צ"ל אליעזר] ב) [חגיגה י. ע"ש וע"ע] ג) עיין רש"א בח"א ד) [שבת קלט. ע"ש] ה) שבת דף קלט. ו) [הרמב"ם פרק י מהלכות מתנות עניים וכן בטור י"ד סי' רמז איתא ישראל וכצ"ל לקמן ושביה בצדקה ולא כמ"ש רש"א בח"א שנדחק בזה טובא בד"ה עד שיכלו שופטים מישראל וכו' ע"ש ברש"י לנוסחא שהיה עדים נאמנים הרמב"ם וטור אחר לשפיר] ז) [גי' הערוך גזוי דפאטי פי' פריסים ושוטרי השרים] ח) [ע' פרש"י דע"ז ל. ד"ה מי בחלב וכו' בחלב לשון פרק משונה כמו סוסי בחלב בחלק ע"ש] ט) ע"ן ומלוין רש"ל, י) נ"ל דרומי.

ליקוטי רש"י

מלכים יראו. אותו וקמו [ישעיה מט, ז]. וקמו. לקראת ישראל לעמוד לפניהם [תענית טו.]. אם תשוב ישראל. בתשובה זו אלי. תשוב. לכבודך הראשון תשוב [ירמיה ד, א]. וככלות נפץ יד עם קדש. כשתכלה כח ישראל כי אזלת יד ואפס עצור ועזוב (דברים לב) [דניאל יב, ז]. וכרת. הגפן הם הזמורות והשריגים. במזמרות. [הנטישות]. הם עיקרי הגפנים שקורין ציפ"ש בלע"ז [ישעיה יח, ה]. עם עני ודל. עם עניו ומקבל עלבון [צפניה ג, יב]. ואשיבה ידי עליך. מכה אחר מכה עד כלות הפושעים. כבור. ל' בורית סבו"ן בלע"ז ולשונו ל' נקיון כמו ובר לבב (תהלים כד) שהוא מנקה הכתם. סיגיך. כמו כספך היה לסיגים האמור למעלה (ישעיה א, כב) תערובות נחשת בכסף קרוי סיג על כן תערובת רשעים עם הכשרים אני אכלה הפושעים. בדיליך. בדיל המעורב בכסף כלומר הרשעים שבך [ישעיה א, כה]. במשפט תפדה. ע"י שיהיו בה עושה משפט. תפדה. מעונותיה. ושביה. עושי תשובה שבתוכה. בצדקה. [במצדיקים עצמם משפט וצדקה] [שם, כז]. ואשיבה שופטיך. אעמיד לכם שופטים כשרים [שם, כו]. ואחר כך יקרא לך עיר הצדק לשרות בה שכינה [ע"ש]. אי בטלי יהירי. מתייהרים בגלותם ובמלבושי יהירות כפרסים הללו. בטלי אמגושי. מסיתים ומדיחים [דפ"י, המינים גלחים] המשעבדים אותנו. סיגיך. הם גסי הרוח שמבדלין אותם לשון שגא מאד (איוב ח) ואסירה כל בדיליך אלו אותם המבדלים שחולקים עם הקדוש ברוך הוא בשקריהם ובכפירותם. בטלי דייני. בטלו משפטים דין. בטלי. מעל ישראל. גזירפטי. וגם שוטרי עובדי כוכבים [שבת קלט.]. נוססה בו. נפלאות בו ג"ם ד"א נוססה בו אוכלת בו כתולעת בעץ כמו (ישעיה י) והיה כמסוס נוסס [ישעיה נט, יט]. וירא כי אין איש. כשהקב"ה רואה על הרעה לעמו רואה כי אין איש צדיק לעמוד בפרץ. וישתומם. ויחרש לראות אם יש מפגיע בעדם ואין מפגיע וישתומם ל' אדם העומד ותוהא ושותק בתמהונו ותי"ו וישתומם כתי"ו של משתולל שניהם משמשות לשון מתפעל וכן דרך התיבה שיסודה הלשון שי"ן או סמ"ך כשהיא נהפכת ללשון מתפעל נתפעל ויתפעל בא התי"ו באמצע אותיות שורש התיבה כגון לשון שממון שמו שמים (ירמיה ב) משמים בתוכם (יחזקאל ג) נשמו אחרונים (איוב יח) ל' תמהון [שם, טז]. למעני. ולמען שמי הקדוש [שם מח, יא]. כבר אינש אתה. הוא מלך המשיח [דניאל ז, יג]. עני. ענותן. ורוכב על חמור. מדת ענוה היא [זכריה ט, ט]. שבור מלכא. מלך פרס היה [סוכה נג.]. עובד כוכבים היה [ע"ז עו:]. פמיים. שמשם ירדן יוצא כדאמר מר ירדן יוצא ממערת פמייס (בכורות נה.) [מגילה ו.].

הגהות הגר"א

[א] גמ' אפתחא דקרתא. נמחק תיבת דקרתא וג"כ דרומי: [ב] רש"י ד"ה משפטיך כמו (צפניה ג). נמחק לפניה ג:

הגהות מהר"ב רנשבורג

א] גמ' שנאמר וכרת הזלזלים במזמרות ואת הנטישות הסר. כצ"ל:

תורה אור השלם

א) אִם תָּשׁוּב יִשְׂרָאֵל נְאֻם יְיָ אֵלַי תָּשׁוּב וְאִם תָּסִיר שִׁקּוּצֶיךָ מִפָּנַי וְלֹא תָנוּד: [ירמיה ד, א]

ב) וָאֶשְׁמַע אֶת הָאִישׁ לְבוּשׁ הַבַּדִּים אֲשֶׁר מִמַּעַל לְמֵימֵי הַיְאֹר וַיָּרֶם יְמִינוֹ וּשְׂמֹאלוֹ אֶל הַשָּׁמַיִם וַיִּשָּׁבַע בְּחֵי הָעוֹלָם כִּי לְמוֹעֵד מוֹעֲדִים וָחֵצִי וּכְכַלּוֹת נַפֵּץ יַד עַם קֹדֶשׁ תִּכְלֶינָה כָל אֵלֶּה: [דניאל יב, ז]

ג) וְאַתֶּם הָרֵי יִשְׂרָאֵל עַנְפְּכֶם תִּתֵּנוּ וּפֶרְיְכֶם תִּשְׂאוּ לְעַמִּי יִשְׂרָאֵל כִּי קֵרְבוּ לָבוֹא: [יחזקאל לו, ח]

ד) כִּי לִפְנֵי הַיָּמִים הָהֵם שְׂכַר הָאָדָם לֹא נִהְיָה וּשְׂכַר הַבְּהֵמָה אֵינֶנָּה וְלַיּוֹצֵא וְלַבָּא אֵין שָׁלוֹם מִן הַצָּר וַאֲשַׁלַּח אֶת כָּל הָאָדָם אִישׁ בְּרֵעֵהוּ: [זכריה ח, י]

ה) שָׁלוֹם רָב לְאֹהֲבֵי תוֹרָתֶךָ וְאֵין לָמוֹ מִכְשׁוֹל: [תהלים קיט, קסה]

ו) אָז אַשְׁקִיעַ מֵימֵיהֶם וְנַהֲרוֹתָם כַּשֶּׁמֶן אוֹלִיךְ נְאֻם אֲדֹנָי אֱלֹהִים: [יחזקאל לב, יד]

ז) בַּיּוֹם הַהוּא אַצְמִיחַ קֶרֶן לְבֵית יִשְׂרָאֵל וּלְךָ אֶתֵּן פִּתְחוֹן פֶּה בְּתוֹכָם וְיָדְעוּ כִּי אֲנִי יְיָ: [יחזקאל כט, כא]

ח) כִּי לִפְנֵי קָצִיר כְּתָם פֶּרַח וּבֹסֶר גֹּמֵל יִהְיֶה נִצָּה וְכָרַת הַזַּלְזַלִּים בַּמַּזְמֵרוֹת וְאֶת הַנְּטִישׁוֹת הֵסִיר הֵתַז: [ישעיה יח, ה]

ט) בָּעֵת הַהִיא יוּבַל שַׁי לַייָ צְבָאוֹת עַם מְמֻשָּׁךְ וּמוֹרָט וּמֵעַם נוֹרָא מִן הוּא וָהָלְאָה גּוֹי קַו קָו וּמְבוּסָה אֲשֶׁר בָּזְאוּ נְהָרִים אַרְצוֹ אֶל מְקוֹם שֵׁם יְיָ צְבָאוֹת הַר צִיּוֹן: [ישעיה יח, ז]

י) בַּיּוֹם הַהוּא לֹא תֵבוֹשִׁי מִכֹּל עֲלִילֹתַיִךְ אֲשֶׁר פָּשַׁעַתְּ בִּי כִּי אָז אָסִיר מִקִּרְבֵּךְ עַלִּיזֵי גַּאֲוָתֵךְ וְלֹא תוֹסִפִי לְגָבְהָה עוֹד בְּהַר קָדְשִׁי: [צפניה ג, יא]

יא) וְהִשְׁאַרְתִּי בְקִרְבֵּךְ עַם עָנִי וָדָל וְחָסוּ בְּשֵׁם יְיָ: [צפניה ג, יב]

יב) וְאָשִׁיבָה יָדִי עָלַיִךְ וְאֶצְרֹף כַּבֹּר סִיגָיִךְ וְאָסִירָה כָּל בְּדִילָיִךְ: וְאָשִׁיבָה שֹׁפְטַיִךְ כְּבָרִאשֹׁנָה וְיֹעֲצַיִךְ כְּבַתְּחִלָּה אַחֲרֵי כֵן יִקָּרֵא לָךְ עִיר הַצֶּדֶק קִרְיָה נֶאֱמָנָה: [ישעיה א, כה-כו] יג) צִיּוֹן בְּמִשְׁפָּט תִּפָּדֶה וְשָׁבֶיהָ בִּצְדָקָה: [ישעיה א, כז] יד) הֵסִיר יְיָ מִשְׁפָּטַיִךְ פִּנָּה אֹיְבֵךְ מֶלֶךְ יִשְׂרָאֵל יְיָ בְּקִרְבֵּךְ לֹא תִירְאִי רָע עוֹד: [צפניה ג, טו] טו) וְאֶת עַם עָנִי תּוֹשִׁיעַ וְעֵינֶיךָ עַל רָמִים תַּשְׁפִּיל: [שמואל ב' כב, כח] טז) וְיִירְאוּ מִמַּעֲרָב אֶת שֵׁם יְיָ וּמִמִּזְרַח שֶׁמֶשׁ אֶת כְּבוֹדוֹ כִּי יָבוֹא כַנָּהָר צָר רוּחַ יְיָ נֹסְסָה בוֹ: וּבָא לְצִיּוֹן גּוֹאֵל וּלְשָׁבֵי פֶשַׁע בְּיַעֲקֹב נְאֻם יְיָ: [ישעיה נט, יט-כ] יז) וְעַמֵּךְ כֻּלָּם צַדִּיקִים לְעוֹלָם יִירְשׁוּ אָרֶץ נֵצֶר מַטָּעַי מַעֲשֵׂה יָדַי לְהִתְפָּאֵר: [ישעיה ס, כא] יח) וַיַּרְא כִּי אֵין אִישׁ וַיִּשְׁתּוֹמֵם כִּי אֵין מַפְגִּיעַ וַתּוֹשַׁע לוֹ זְרֹעוֹ וְצִדְקָתוֹ הִיא סְמָכָתְהוּ: [ישעיה נט, טז] יט) לְמַעֲנִי לְמַעֲנִי אֶעֱשֶׂה כִּי אֵיךְ יֵחָל וּכְבוֹדִי לְאַחֵר לֹא אֶתֵּן: [ישעיה מח, יא] כ) הַקָּטֹן יִהְיֶה לָאֶלֶף וְהַצָּעִיר לְגוֹי עָצוּם אֲנִי יְיָ בְּעִתָּהּ אֲחִישֶׁנָּה: [ישעיה ס, כב] כא) חָזֵה הֲוֵית בְּחֶזְוֵי לֵילְיָא וַאֲרוּ עִם עֲנָנֵי שְׁמַיָּא כְּבַר אֱנָשׁ אָתֵה הֲוָה וְעַד עַתִּיק יוֹמַיָּא מְטָה וּקְדָמוֹהִי הַקְרְבוּהִי: [דניאל ז, יג] כב) גִּילִי מְאֹד בַּת צִיּוֹן הָרִיעִי בַּת יְרוּשָׁלִַם הִנֵּה מַלְכֵּךְ יָבוֹא לָךְ צַדִּיק וְנוֹשָׁע הוּא עָנִי וְרֹכֵב עַל חֲמוֹר וְעַל עַיִר בֶּן אֲתֹנוֹת: [זכריה ט, ט] כג) כִּי הוּא אֱלֹהֵינוּ וַאֲנַחְנוּ עַם מַרְעִיתוֹ וְצֹאן יָדוֹ הַיּוֹם אִם בְּקֹלוֹ תִשְׁמָעוּ: [תהלים צה, ז]

The Gemara interprets the end of the verse:

מאי ,,לַיּוֹצֵא וְלַבָּא אֵין־שָׁלוֹם מִן־הַצָּר" – **What is** the meaning of ***and to him that leaves or enters there was no peace from the adversary?***

The Gemara offers two explanations:

רַב אָמַר – **Rav says:** אַף תַּלְמִידֵי חֲכָמִים – **Even Torah scholars,** שֶׁכָּתוּב בָּהֶם שָׁלוֹם דִּכְתִיב ,,שָׁלוֹם רָב לְאֹהֲבֵי תוֹרָתֶךָ" – **concerning whom it is written** that they shall enjoy **peace, as it is written:**[11] ***There is abundant peace for the lovers of your Torah,*** אֵין שָׁלוֹם מִפְּנֵי צַר – will have **no peace from** the **adversary.**[12]

An alternative explanation:

וּשְׁמוּאֵל אָמַר – **But Shmuel says:** עַד שֶׁיִּהְיוּ כָּל הַשְּׁעָרִים כּוּלָּן שְׁקוּלִין – The verse teaches that the Messiah will not come **until all the prices are equal.**[13]

The Gemara enumerates further signs of the Messiah's imminent arrival:

אָמַר רַבִּי חֲנִינָא – **R' Chanina said:** אֵין בֶּן דָּוִד בָּא – **The son of David will not come** עַד שֶׁיִּתְבַּקֵּשׁ דָּג לְחוֹלֶה וְלֹא יִמָּצֵא – **until a fish will be sought for a sick person, and it will not be found,**[14] שֶׁנֶּאֱמַר ,,אָז אַשְׁקִיעַ מֵימֵיהֶם וְנַהֲרוֹתָם כַּשֶּׁמֶן אוֹלִיךְ" – **as it is stated:** ***Then I will make their waters settle and cause their rivers to flow like oil,***[15] וּכְתִיב (בַּתְרֵיהּ) ,,בַּיּוֹם הַהוּא אַצְמִיחַ קֶרֶן לְבֵית יִשְׂרָאֵל" – **and (after that) it is written: *On that day I will cause power to sprout for the House of Israel.***[16]

אָמַר רַבִּי חָמָא בַּר חֲנִינָא – **R' Chama bar Chanina said:** אֵין בֶּן דָּוִד בָּא – **The son of David will not come** עַד שֶׁתִּכְלֶה מַלְכוּת הַזֵּלָה מִיִּשְׂרָאֵל – **until the petty government has ceased from Israel,**[17] שֶׁנֶּאֱמַר ,,וְכָרַת הַזַּלְזַלִּים בַּמַּזְמֵרוֹת" – **as it is stated:** ***He will cut off the shoots with shears,***[18] וּכְתִיב בַּתְרֵיהּ ,,בָּעֵת הַהִיא יוּבַל־שַׁי לַה׳ צְבָאוֹת עַם מְמֻשָּׁךְ וּמוֹרָט" – **and after that it is written:** ***At that time, a gift shall be brought to the Lord of Hosts – a people pulled and torn.***[19]

אָמַר זְעִירִי אָמַר רַבִּי חֲנִינָא – **Zeiri said in the name of R' Chanina:** אֵין בֶּן דָּוִד בָּא – **The son of David will not come** עַד שֶׁיִּכְלוּ גַּסֵּי הָרוּחַ מִיִּשְׂרָאֵל – **until the arrogant are eliminated from Israel,** שֶׁנֶּאֱמַר ,,כִּי־אָז אָסִיר מִקִּרְבֵּךְ עַלִּיזֵי גַּאֲוָתֵךְ" – **as it is stated:** ***For then I will remove from your midst those who delight in your arrogance,***[20] וּכְתִיב ,,וְהִשְׁאַרְתִּי בְקִרְבֵּךְ עַם עָנִי וָדָל וְחָסוּ בְּשֵׁם ה׳" – **and** in the next verse **it is written:** ***I will leave in your midst a humble and forbearing people, and they will take refuge in the Name of HASHEM.***[21]

אָמַר רַבִּי שִׂמְלַאי מִשּׁוּם רַבִּי אֶלְעָזָר בְּרַבִּי שִׁמְעוֹן – **R' Simlai said in the name of R' Elazar the son of R' Shimon:** אֵין בֶּן דָּוִד בָּא – **The son of David will not come** עַד שֶׁיִּכְלוּ כָּל שׁוֹפְטִים וְשׁוֹטְרִים מִיִּשְׂרָאֵל – **until all judges and officers**[22] **cease from Israel,**[23]

NOTES

11. *Psalms* 119:165.

12. The verse thus means that even those who deserve to go to and fro in peace (i.e. the Torah scholars) will not enjoy peace because of the multitude of troubles. Alternatively, they will have no peace from the evil inclination (*Rashi*).

In line with *Rashi's* second approach (viz. that the reference is to the evil inclination), *Maharsha* interprets the verse as follows: Even the Torah scholars who used to go and come in peace – i.e. they used to thrust and parry in Talmudic debate peaceably – will not enjoy peace between themselves, for they will be overcome by the evil inclination. This reflects the Gemara in *Kesubos* (112b) which states: "In the generation when the son of David comes there will be denunciation among the Torah scholars."

13. That is, the prices of different commodities (e.g. grain, wine) will be equally low. Following the economic depression described above, there will be such an abundance that all foodstuffs will be cheap. This dramatic upswing corresponds to that outlined in the Baraisa on 97a: "The seven-year cycle when the son of David will come . . . in the third year there will be a great famine . . . in the fifth year there will be a great sufficiency."

Alternatively, the Gemara means that all prices will be equally high (*Rashi*).

It is difficult to see how *Rashi's* explanations are implied by the words of the verse, *and to him that leaves* etc. (*Maharsha*). *Chafetz Chaim* explains that *to him that leaves or enters* refers to merchants who buy cheaply in one place and sell at a higher price in another. In the pre-Messianic era these merchants will lose their means of livelihood because all prices will be the same everywhere (*Likkutei Halachos,* Introduction p. 3; see also *Yad Ramah* and *Ben Yehoyada*).

14. This demonstrates the severity of the food shortage. Normally, a sick person is given meat, rather than fish. Furthermore, even during a famine, it is usually possible to procure fish at minimal cost, by catching one in a sea or river. In those days, however, food will be so scarce that even a sick person will be unable to obtain even fish (*Ben Yehoyada*).

The Gemara is teaching that the world's decline prior to the redemption [see 97a note 4] will be so comprehensive that it will affect even aquatic creatures, which dwell in a completely different environment than that of man (*Maharal's* second explanation; see also *Kiddushin* end of 13a).

15. *Ezekiel* 32:14. All waters will congeal and thus become unable to support aquatic life (*Rashi*).

[The plain meaning of the verse refers to the Nile after Egypt has been defeated by the Babylonians (see *Rashi* ad loc.; see also *Maharsha*).]

16. Ibid. 29:21. I.e. the Messiah will reign.

[The word בַּתְרֵיהּ, *after that,* is problematic because this verse actually appears *before* the one cited above (see *Maharsha;* cf. *Margaliyos HaYam*).]

17. The Jewish people will not have even minimal autonomy (*Rashi;* cf. *Maharsha,* cited in note 19).

This point is found in the verse discussed on 97a: כִּי יִרְאֶה כִּי־אָזְלַת יָד, *when He sees that [their] power is gone,* and also in the verse quoted above: וּכְכַלּוֹת נַפֵּץ יַד־עַם קֹדֶשׁ, *and upon the cessation of the power of the holy people* (*Yad Ramah*; see note 5).

18. *Isaiah* 18:5. Basing itself on the similarity between זַלְזַלִּים, *zalzalim* (shoots), and זַלָּה, *zalah* (petty), the Gemara interprets the verse as teaching that God will eradicate even the most petty vestige of the Jewish people's autonomy (see previous note; cf. *Rashi* and *Radak* ad loc.).

The verse continues וְאֶת־הַנְּטִישׁוֹת הֵסִיר, *and the twigs He removed.* This refers to the elimination of officials and judges (*Rashi;* see *Hagahos R' Ronsburg*).

19. Ibid. v. 7. When their adversaries (Gog and Magog) have been defeated, the Jewish people – "a people pulled and torn" – will be restored to God's benevolent care.

The proximity of these two verses teaches that the Jewish people will be stripped of all autonomy shortly before the Messianic era.

Maharsha interprets מַלְכוּת הַזֵּלָה as referring to Rome, which is considered a corrupt and debased kingdom. [In *Maharsha's* view, זַלָּה is used here to mean debased, rather than petty.] The Messiah will not come until Rome has ceased to dominate the Jewish people (see below, note 65).The first verse is interpreted as follows: וְכָרַת הַזַּלְזַלִּים, *He will cut off the debased ones,* i.e. the kingdom of Rome, בַּמַּזְמֵרוֹת, *with the songs,* i.e. because of the psalms (many of which begin מִזְמוֹר, *song*) recited in prayer by the Jewish people.

20. *Zephaniah* 3:11.

21. That is to say: Once they have been redeemed, they will be protected under the wing of the Almighty (*Rashi*; see *Maharsha*).

The Gemara in *Sotah* (5a) teaches that arrogance pushes the *Shechinah* away. Therefore, the *Shechinah* will return to the Jewish people only when arrogant people are no longer among them (*Iyun Yaakov*; see *Maharsha*).

22. Officials who enforce the law at the bidding of the judges (see *Rashi* to *Deuteronomy* 16:18 ד״ה ושוטרים).

23. No one will enforce the law and a state of anarchy will prevail (*Yad Ramah; cf. Ben Yehoyada*).

Yad Ramah intimates that the Gemara refers to all judges. *Maharsha,* however, implies that the reference is only to corrupt or ignorant judges, for he draws a parallel between our Gemara and the Gemara in *Shabbos*

מסורת הש"ס

א) [צ"ל אלעזר], ב) [חגיגה י. ע"ש וצ"ע], ג) עיין רש"א בח"א, ד) [שבת קלט. ע"ש], ה) שבת דף קלט., ו) [הרמב"ם פרק י מהלכות מתנות עניים וכן בטור י"ד סי' רמז איתא ישראל וכצ"ל למוכן ושביה בצדקה ודלא כמ"ש רש"א בח"א שנדחק בזה טובא בד"ה עד שילא שופטים מישראל וכו' ע"ש ברם לנוסחא שניה עדים נאמנים הרמב"ם וטור אתי' לשפיר], ז) [גיר' הערוך גאזי דפאטי פי' פריסי ושוטרי השרים], ח) [עי' ברש"י דהכא ועי' ברש"י דע"ז ל. ד"ה מי בארג וכו' בארג לשון פרס משובח כמו סוסי בארג בחלק ע"ש], ט) ומצוין רש"ל, י) צ"ל דרומי.

רש"י

כי למועד מועדים. אלמא יש קץ בדבר: וככלות נפץ יד עם קדש. כשתכלה תקומתם וחוזק ידיהם שהיתה נפוצה אילך ואילך גבורה ותועלת לפשוט אנה ואנה ואחר שתכלה גבורתם שיהיו שפלים למאד: תכלינה. אלו הצרות ויבא משיח כדאמרינן כי אזלת יד: מגולה מזה. כשתתן ארץ ישראל פריה בעין יפה אז יקרב הקץ ואין לך קץ מגולה יותר: ר' אליעזר אומר מזה. הפסוק כשתראה דאין שום אדם משתכר ואף שכר הבהמה לא נהיה והיינו כדאמרן עד שתכלה פרוטה מן הכיס אין מעות מצויות בכיס: שכר בהמה. עבודת האדמה שהיא על ידי בהמה איננה: וליוצא ולבא אין שלום. אז יבא משיח: [שלום רב]. והיינו ליוצא ולבא אלו תלמידי חכמים אותם שהיה דינם לצאת ולבא בשלום כדכתיב שלום רב לאוהבי תורתך אפילו להנהו אין שלום: מן הצר. מרוב הצרות ל"א מיצר הרע: שקולין. שוין שער התבואה ויין רווחי' כדאמרן חמישית שובע גדול ל"א שקולין שוין שכולן יקרין: כשמן אוליך. שיהיו כולן קפויין וכיון שהם קפויין אין דגים נמצאין בהכה: עד שתכלה מלכות הזלה. שלא תהא להם שום שולטנות לישראל אפילו שולטנות קלה ודלה: נטישותיו. ענפים קטנים כלומר השרים והשופטים: וחסו בשם השם. כלומר שתבא להם גאולה ויחסו בצל שדי: סיגיך. תערובות שבך: בדיליך. המובדלים לראשי עם: יהירי. גסי רוח מישראל: אמגושי. פרסיים מכשפין שמצערין ישראל במס' שבת (דף עה.) פלוגתא איכא למאן דאמר אמגושי חרשי ואיכא מ"ד גדופי עובדי כוכבים: גזירפטי. שופטים עובדי כוכבים החובטין את ישראל במקלות: ואצרוף כבור סיגיך. רבים וגדולים בגסותם כשאצרוף ואסלקם ממך אזי אסירה כל בדיליך: אמגושי. הבדלים מיראת המקום: סיגיך. כמו רב דמתרגמינן סגי: משפטיך. כמו [ב] (צפניה ג) שופטיך: פנה אויבך. גזירפטי: נוספה. כמו (ישעיה י) כמסוס נוסס וכמו (שם נא) יאכלם סס רוח המקום נוקבת ומחרבת אותן עם הצרות הבאות שאף הוא מתכוין להשמידם: יירשו ארץ. היינו גאולה: עם ענני שמיא כבר אינש אתי. במהירות: וכתיב עני ורוכב על החמור. כעני הבא על חמורו בעצלות: סוסי ברקא. סוס מסורק ט) ומכוון ונאה שיש לי דגנאי הוא שיבא על חמור מלגלג היה ל"א סוסיא בדקא סוס בדוק לרוץ: בר חיור גווני. כלום יש לך סוס בר מאה גוונין שחמור שלו כן הוא במלתא בעלמא דחייה: חיור. מאה בלשון פרסי: האדון הזה. שכינה היתה עמהם: קול שלשה. דשכינה הוה בהדייהו: לדידיה. למשיח: בפתחא (י) דקרתא). נראה למורי לא בפתח העיר ממש אלא גן עדן הוא כנגד כל העולם וקאמר ליה דבאותו לד של גן עדן שכנגד פתח העיר משיח שרוי: סובלי חלאים. מנוגעים והוא נמי מנוגע דכתיב (ישעיה נג) והוא מחולל מפשעינו וכתיב (שם) חליינו הוא נשא: כולהו. מי שיש לו ארבע וחמש נגעים: אסרי להו ושרו בחדא זימנא. מתירין כל נגעתן ביחד ומקנחין אותן וחוזרין וקושרין אותן: ואיהו. משיח: שרי חד. נגע ומקנחו וקושרו ואח"כ מתיר האחר ועושה כן ואינו מתיר שני נגעים יחד דסבר אי בעי לי לצאת וליגאל את ישראל לא איתעכב כדי קשירת שני נגעים: אמר ליה. ר' יהושע למשיח לאימת אתי מר אמר ליה היום: אבטחך לך ולאביך לעולם הבא. דאי לאו לדיקים גמורין אתם לא הוה יהיב לך שלמא ולא הוה מדכר שמיה דאבוך: היום אם בקולו. של הקב"ה תשמעו: השער הזה. של עיר רומי שבעיר רומי היה אותו שער: ואין מספיקין לבנותו. פעם שלישית: מי פמיים. שירדן נובע ממנו כדתניא בבכורות (דף נה.) דן יוצא ממערת פמיים ומפרש התם שפיר: העמיקו ארוני. עשו לי קבר בקרקע עמוק:

גמרא

מלכים יראו וקמו שרים וישתחוו אמר לו רבי אליעזר והלא כבר נאמר א) אם תשוב ישראל נאום ה' אלי תשוב אמר לו רבי יהושע והלא כבר נאמר ב) ואשמע את האיש לבוש הבדים אשר ממעל למימי היאור וירם ימינו ושמאלו אל השמים וישבע בחי העולם כי למועד מועדים וחצי וככלות נפץ יד עם קדש תכלינה כל אלה וגו' ושתק רבי אליעזר ואמר רבי אבא אין לך קץ מגולה מזה שנאמר ג) ואתם הרי ישראל ענפכם תתנו ופריכם תשאו לעמי ישראל וגו' רבי (א) אליעזר) אומר אף מזה שנאמר ד) כי לפני הימים (האלה) [ההם] שכר האדם לא נהיה ושכר הבהמה איננה וליוצא ולבא אין שלום מן הצר ב) מאי ליוצא ולבא אין שלום מן הצר רב אמר אף תלמידי חכמים שכתוב בהם שלום דכתיב ה) שלום רב לאהבי תורתך אין שלום מפני צר ושמואל אמר עד שיהיו כל השערים כולן שקולין אמר רבי חנינא אין בן דוד בא עד שיתבקש דג לחולה ולא ימצא שנאמר ו) אז אשקיע מימיהם ונהרותם כשמן אוליך וכתב (ג) בתריה) ז) ביום ההוא אצמיח קרן לבית ישראל אמר רבי חמא בר חנינא אין בן דוד בא עד שתכלה מלכות הזלה מישראל שנאמר ח) וכרת הזלזלים במזמרות א] וכתיב בתריה ט) בעת ההיא יובל שי לה' צבאות עם ממשך ומורט אמר זעירי אמר רבי חנינא אין בן דוד בא עד שיכלו גסי הרוח מישראל שנאמר י) כי אז אסיר מקרבך עליזי גאותך וכתיב יא) והשארתי בקרבך עם עני ודל וחסו בשם ה' אמר רבי שמלאי משום רבי אלעזר בר"ש ד) אין בן דוד בא עד שיכלו כל שופטים ושוטרים מישראל שנאמר יב) ואשיבה ידי עליך ואצרוף כבור סיגיך וגו' ואשיבה שופטיך ה) אמר עולא אין ו) ירושלים נפדית אלא בצדקה שנאמר יג) ציון במשפט תפדה ושביה בצדקה אמר רב פפא אי בטלי יהירי בטלי אמגושי אי בטלי דייני בטלי ז) גזירפטי אי בטלי יהירי בטלי אמגושי דכתיב יב) ואצרוף כבור סיגיך ואסירה כל בדיליך ואי בטלי דייני בטלי גזירפטי דכתיב יד) הסיר ה' משפטיך פנה אויבך אמר ר' יוחנן אם ראית דור שמתמעט והולך חכה לו שנאמר טו) ואת עם עני תושיע וגו' אמר רבי יוחנן אם ראית דור שצרות רבות באות עליו כנהר חכה לו שנאמר טז) כי יבא כנהר צר (ו)רוח ה' נוססה בו וסמיך ליה ובא לציון גואל ואמר רבי יוחנן אין בן דוד בא אלא בדור שכולו זכאי או כולו חייב בדור שכולו זכאי דכתיב יז) ועמך כולם צדיקים לעולם יירשו ארץ בדור שכולו חייב דכתיב יח) וירא כי אין איש וישתומם כי אין מפגיע וכתיב יט) למעני אעשה אמר רבי אלכסנדרי רבי יהושע בן לוי רמי כתיב כ) בעתה וכתיב אחישנה זכו אחישנה לא זכו בעתה אמר רבי אלכסנדרי רבי יהושע בן לוי רמי כתיב כא) וארו עם ענני שמיא כבר אינש אתה וכתיב כב) עני ורוכב על חמור זכו עם ענני שמיא לא זכו עני רוכב על חמור אמר ליה שבור מלכא לשמואל אמריתו משיח על חמרא אתי אישדר ליה סוסיא ח) ברקא דאית לי אמר ליה מי אית לך בר חיור גווני ר' יהושע בן לוי אשכח לאליהו דהוי קיימי אפיתחא דמערתא דרבי שמעון בן יוחאי אמר ליה אתינא לעלמא דאתי אמר ליה אם ירצה אדון הזה אמר רבי יהושע בן לוי שנים ראיתי וקול ג' שמעתי אמר ליה אימת אתי משיח אמר ליה זיל שייליה לדידיה והיכא יתיב אפיתחא [א] דקרתא ומאי סימניה יתיב ביני עניי סובלי חלאים וכולן שרו ואסירי בחד זימנא איהו שרי חד ואסיר חד אמר דילמא מבעינא דלא איעכב אזל לגביה אמר ליה שלום עליך רבי ומורי אמר ליה שלום עליך בר ליואי א"ל לאימת אתי מר א"ל היום אתא לגבי אליהו א"ל מאי אמר לך א"ל שלום עליך בר ליואי א"ל אבטחך לך ולאבוך לעלמא דאתי א"ל שקורי קא שקר בי דאמר לי היום אתינא ולא אתא א"ל הכי אמר לך כג) היום אם בקולו תשמעו שאלו תלמידיו את רבי יוסי בן קיסמא אימתי בן דוד בא אמר מתיירא אני שמא תבקשו ממני אות אמרו לו אין אנו מבקשין ממך אות א"ל לכשיפול השער הזה ויבנה ויפול ויבנה ויפול ואין מספיקין לבנותו עד שבן דוד בא אמרו לו רבינו תן לנו אות אמר להם ולא כך אמרתם לי שאין אתם מבקשין ממני אות אמרו לו ואף על פי כן אמר להם אם כך יהפכו מי מערת פמיים לדם ונהפכו לדם בשעת פטירתו אמר להן העמיקו לי ארוני

שאין

הגהות הגר"א

[א] גמ' אפתחא דקרתא. נמחק תיבת דקרתא וכ"ב דרומי: [ב] רש"י ד"ה משפטיך כמו (צפניה ג). נמחק לפניה ג:

הגהות מהר"ב רנשבורג

א] גמ' שנאמר וכרת הזלזלים במזמרות ואת הנטישות הסר. כצ"ל:

תורה אור השלם

א) אִם תָּשׁוּב יִשְׂרָאֵל נְאֻם יְיָ אֵלַי תָּשׁוּב וְאִם תָּסִיר שִׁקּוּצֶיךָ מִפָּנַי וְלֹא תָנוּד: [ירמיה ד, א]

ב) וָאֶשְׁמַע אֶת הָאִישׁ לְבוּשׁ הַבַּדִּים אֲשֶׁר מִמַּעַל לְמֵימֵי הַיְאֹר וַיָּרֶם יְמִינוֹ וּשְׂמֹאלוֹ אֶל הַשָּׁמַיִם וַיִּשָּׁבַע בְּחֵי הָעוֹלָם כִּי לְמוֹעֵד מוֹעֲדִים וָחֵצִי וּכְכַלּוֹת נַפֵּץ יַד עַם קֹדֶשׁ תִּכְלֶינָה כָל אֵלֶּה: [דניאל יב, ז]

ג) וְאַתֶּם הָרֵי יִשְׂרָאֵל עַנְפְּכֶם תִּתֵּנוּ וּפֶרְיְכֶם תִּשְׂאוּ לְעַמִּי יִשְׂרָאֵל כִּי קֵרְבוּ לָבוֹא: [יחזקאל לו, ח]

ד) כִּי לִפְנֵי הַיָּמִים הָהֵם שְׂכַר הָאָדָם לֹא נִהְיָה וּשְׂכַר הַבְּהֵמָה אֵינֶנָּה וְלַיּוֹצֵא וְלַבָּא אֵין שָׁלוֹם מִן הַצָּר וַאֲשַׁלַּח אֶת כָּל הָאָדָם אִישׁ בְּרֵעֵהוּ: [זכריה ח, י]

ה) שָׁלוֹם רָב לְאֹהֲבֵי תוֹרָתֶךָ וְאֵין לָמוֹ מִכְשׁוֹל: [תהלים קיט, קסה]

ו) אָז אַשְׁקִיעַ מֵימֵיהֶם וְנַהֲרוֹתָם כַּשֶּׁמֶן אוֹלִיךְ נְאֻם אֲדֹנָי אֱלֹהִים: [יחזקאל לב, יד]

ז) בַּיּוֹם הַהוּא אַצְמִיחַ קֶרֶן לְבֵית יִשְׂרָאֵל וּלְךָ אֶתֵּן פִּתְחוֹן פֶּה בְּתוֹכָם וְיָדְעוּ כִּי אֲנִי יְיָ: [יחזקאל כט, כא]

ח) כִּי לִפְנֵי קָצִיר כְּתָם פֶּרַח וּבֹסֶר גֹּמֵל יִהְיֶה נִצָּה וְכָרַת הַזַּלְזַלִּים בַּמַּזְמֵרוֹת וְאֶת הַנְּטִישׁוֹת הֵסִיר הֵתַז: [ישעיה יח, ה]

ט) בָּעֵת הַהִיא יוּבַל שַׁי לַייָ צְבָאוֹת עַם מְמֻשָּׁךְ וּמוֹרָט וּמֵעַם נוֹרָא מִן הוּא וָהָלְאָה גּוֹי קַו קָו וּמְבוּסָה אֲשֶׁר בָּזְאוּ נְהָרִים אַרְצוֹ אֶל מְקוֹם שֵׁם יְיָ צְבָאוֹת הַר צִיּוֹן: [ישעיה יח, ז]

י) בַּיּוֹם הַהוּא לֹא תֵבוֹשִׁי מִכֹּל עֲלִילֹתַיִךְ אֲשֶׁר פָּשַׁעַתְּ בִּי כִּי אָז אָסִיר מִקִּרְבֵּךְ עַלִּיזֵי גַּאֲוָתֵךְ וְלֹא תוֹסִפִי לְגָבְהָה עוֹד בְּהַר קָדְשִׁי: [צפניה ג, יא]

יא) וְהִשְׁאַרְתִּי בְקִרְבֵּךְ עַם עָנִי וָדָל וְחָסוּ בְּשֵׁם יְיָ: [צפניה ג, יב]

יב) וְאָשִׁיבָה יָדִי עָלַיִךְ וְאֶצְרֹף כַּבֹּר סִיגָיִךְ וְאָסִירָה כָּל בְּדִילָיִךְ: וְאָשִׁיבָה שֹׁפְטַיִךְ כְּבָרִאשֹׁנָה וְיֹעֲצַיִךְ כְּבַתְּחִלָּה אַחֲרֵי כֵן יִקָּרֵא לָךְ עִיר הַצֶּדֶק קִרְיָה נֶאֱמָנָה: [ישעיה א, כה-כו]

יג) צִיּוֹן בְּמִשְׁפָּט תִּפָּדֶה וְשָׁבֶיהָ בִּצְדָקָה: [ישעיה א, כז]

יד) הֵסִיר יְיָ מִשְׁפָּטַיִךְ פִּנָּה אֹיְבֵךְ מֶלֶךְ יִשְׂרָאֵל יְיָ בְּקִרְבֵּךְ לֹא תִירְאִי רָע עוֹד: [צפניה ג, טו]

טו) וְאֶת עַם עָנִי תּוֹשִׁיעַ וְעֵינֶיךָ עַל רָמִים תַּשְׁפִּיל: [שמואל ב' כב, כח]

טז) וְיִירְאוּ מִמַּעֲרָב אֶת שֵׁם יְיָ וּמִמִּזְרַח שֶׁמֶשׁ אֶת כְּבוֹדוֹ כִּי יָבוֹא כַנָּהָר צָר רוּחַ יְיָ נֹסְסָה בוֹ: וּבָא לְצִיּוֹן גּוֹאֵל וּלְשָׁבֵי פֶשַׁע בְּיַעֲקֹב נְאֻם יְיָ: [ישעיה נט, יט-כ]

יז) וְעַמֵּךְ כֻּלָּם צַדִּיקִים לְעוֹלָם יִירְשׁוּ אָרֶץ נֵצֶר מַטָּעַי מַעֲשֵׂה יָדַי לְהִתְפָּאֵר: [ישעיה ס, כא]

יח) וַיַּרְא כִּי אֵין אִישׁ וַיִּשְׁתּוֹמֵם כִּי אֵין מַפְגִּיעַ וַתּוֹשַׁע לוֹ זְרֹעוֹ וְצִדְקָתוֹ הִיא סְמָכָתְהוּ: [ישעיה נט, טז]

יט) לְמַעֲנִי לְמַעֲנִי אֶעֱשֶׂה כִּי אֵיךְ יֵחָל וּכְבוֹדִי לְאַחֵר לֹא אֶתֵּן: [ישעיה מח, יא]

כ) הַקָּטֹן יִהְיֶה לָאֶלֶף וְהַצָּעִיר לְגוֹי עָצוּם אֲנִי יְיָ בְּעִתָּהּ אֲחִישֶׁנָּה: [ישעיה ס, כב]

כא) חָזֵה הֲוֵית בְּחֶזְוֵי לֵילְיָא וַאֲרוּ עִם עֲנָנֵי שְׁמַיָּא כְּבַר אֱנָשׁ אָתֵה הֲוָה וְעַד עַתִּיק יוֹמַיָּא מְטָה וּקְדָמוֹהִי הַקְרְבוּהִי: [דניאל ז, יג]

כב) גִּילִי מְאֹד בַּת צִיּוֹן הָרִיעִי בַּת יְרוּשָׁלַיִם הִנֵּה מַלְכֵּךְ יָבוֹא לָךְ צַדִּיק וְנוֹשָׁע הוּא עָנִי וְרֹכֵב עַל חֲמוֹר וְעַל עַיִר בֶּן אֲתֹנוֹת: [זכריה ט, ט]

כג) כִּי הוּא אֱלֹהֵינוּ וַאֲנַחְנוּ עַם מַרְעִיתוֹ וְצֹאן יָדוֹ הַיּוֹם אִם בְּקֹלוֹ תִשְׁמָעוּ: [תהלים צה, ז]

ליקוטי רש"י

מלכים יראו. אותו וקמו [ישעיה מט, ז]. וקמו. לקראת ישראל לעתיד לבא [תענית טו.]. אם תשוב ישראל. בתשובה זו אלי תשוב. לכבודך ולגדולך הראשונה [ירמיה ד, א]. וככלות נפץ יד עם קדש. כשתכלה כח ישראל כי אזלת יד ואפס עצור ועזוב [דברים לב] [דניאל יב, ז]. וכרת. הכורת את זלזלי הגפן הם הזמורות והשריגים. במזמרות. שרפ"ש בלע"ז. [הנטישות]. הם עיקרי הגפנים שקורין ליפ"ש בלע"ז [ישעיה יח, ה]. עם עני ודל. עם ענוותן ומקבל עולבן [צפניה ג, יב]. ואשיבה ידי עליך. מכה אחר מכה עד כלות הפושעים. כבור. ל' בורית סבון ... סיגיך. כלומר הרשעים ... בדיליך. בדיל לשון ... במשפט תפדה. ע"י שיהיו בה עושי משפט. תפדה. מעונותיה. ושביה. עושי תשובה. בצדקה. [בשלמים] עוסקים במשפט ובצדקה [שם, כז]. ואשיבה שופטיך. כמו שהיו בראשונה ... בטלי יהירי. ... בטלי אמגושי. ... סיגיך. הם גסי הרוח שמגדלין ... בדיליך. ... בטלי דייני. רשעים שופטי ישראל. בטלי גזירפטי. ... שוטרי עובדי כוכבים [שבת קלט.].

נוספה בו. נפלות בו ל' גם ד"א נוספה בו אוכלת בו כתולעת בעץ כמו (ישעיה י) והיה כמסוס נוסס [ישעיה נט, יט]. וירא כי אין איש. ועתה בהנחמו על הרעה לעמו רואה כי אין איש צדיק לעמוד בפרץ. וישתומם. ויחרש לראות אם יש מפגיע בעדם ואין מפגיע וישתומם ל' אדם העומד ותוהא ושותק בתמהונו ותי"ו וישתומם כתי"ו של משתולל שניהם משמשות לשון מתפעל ובן דרך התיבה שתחלת יסוד התיבה הראשון שי"ן או סמ"ך כשהיא נהפכת ללשון מתפעל נתפעל ויתפעל בא התי"ו באמצע אותיות שורש התיבה כגון וישתומם לשון שמו שמים (ירמיה ב) משמים בתוכם (יחזקאל ג) נשמו אחרונים (איוב יח) ל' תמהון [שם, טז]. למעני. למען שמי הקדוש [שם מח, יא]. כבר אינש אתה. הוא מלך המשיח [דניאל ז, יג]. עני. ענותן. ורוכב על חמור. מלך עני רוכב היה [זכריה ט, ט]. שבור מלכא. מלך פרס היה [סוכה נג.]. עובד כוכבים היה [ע"ז עו:]. פמיים. שמשם ירדן יוצא כדאמר מר ירדן יוצא ממערת פמיים (בכורות נה.) [מגילה ו.].

The Gemara resumes its discussion about the advent of the Messiah with a series of three teachings by R' Yochanan:

אָמַר רַבִּי יוֹחָנָן – **R' Yochanan said:** אִם רָאִיתָ דּוֹר שֶׁמִּתְמַעֵט וְהוֹלֵךְ חַכֵּה לוֹ – **If you see a generation that is dwindling,**[35] **expect [the Messiah],** שֶׁנֶּאֱמַר ,,וְאֶת־עַם עָנִי תּוֹשִׁיעַ וגו׳ ״ – **as it is stated:** ***And the impoverished nation shall you save,*** **etc.**[36]

אָמַר רַבִּי יוֹחָנָן – **R' Yochanan said:** אִם רָאִיתָ דּוֹר שֶׁצָּרוֹת רַבּוֹת בָּאוֹת עָלָיו כְּנָהָר חַכֵּה לוֹ – **If you see a generation upon which numerous troubles come like a river,**[37] **expect [the Messiah],** שֶׁנֶּאֱמַר ,,כִּי־יָבֹא כַנָּהָר צָר (ו)רוּחַ ה׳ נֹסְסָה בוֹ״ – **as it is stated:** ***For distress shall come like a river [with] the spirit of HASHEM devouring within it,***[38] וּסְמִיךְ לֵיהּ ,,וּבָא לְצִיּוֹן גּוֹאֵל״ – **and next to [that verse] it is written:** ***A redeemer shall come to Zion.***[39]

וְאָמַר רַבִּי יוֹחָנָן – **And R' Yochanan said:** אֵין בֶּן דָּוִד בָּא אֶלָּא בְּדוֹר שֶׁכּוּלּוֹ זַכַּאי אוֹ כוּלּוֹ חַיָּיב – **The son of David will come only in a generation that is** either **entirely virtuous or entirely guilty.**[40]

The Scriptural sources:

בְּדוֹר שֶׁכּוּלּוֹ זַכַּאי – He will come **in a generation that is entirely virtuous,** דִּכְתִיב ,,וְעַמֵּךְ כֻּלָּם צַדִּיקִים לְעוֹלָם יִירְשׁוּ אָרֶץ״ – as it is written: ***And Your people are all righteous, they shall inherit the land forever.***[41] בְּדוֹר שֶׁכּוּלּוֹ חַיָּיב – He will come **in a generation that is entirely guilty,** דִּכְתִיב ,,וַיַּרְא כִּי־אֵין אִישׁ וַיִּשְׁתּוֹמֵם כִּי אֵין מַפְגִּיעַ״ – **as it is written:** ***He saw that there was no man,***

שֶׁנֶּאֱמַר ,,וְאָשִׁיבָה יָדִי עָלַיִךְ וְאֶצְרֹף כַּבֹּר סִיגָיִךְ וגו׳ – **as it is stated:** ***I will turn My hand against you, clean away your dross as though with soap,* etc.** ,,וְאָשִׁיבָה שֹׁפְטַיִךְ״ – ***Then I will restore your judges.***[24]

The Gemara cites a teaching based on the next verse:

אָמַר עוּלָּא – **Ulla said:** אֵין יְרוּשָׁלַיִם נִפְדֵּית אֶלָּא בִּצְדָקָה – **Jerusalem**[25] **will not be redeemed except through charity,**[26] שֶׁנֶּאֱמַר ,,צִיּוֹן בְּמִשְׁפָּט תִּפָּדֶה וְשָׁבֶיהָ בִּצְדָקָה״ – **as it is stated:** ***Zion shall be redeemed through justice and her returnees through charity.***[27]

Having mentioned the elimination of judges, the Gemara digresses on this point:[28]

אָמַר רַב פָּפָּא – **Rav Pappa said:** אִי בָּטְלֵי יְהִירֵי – **If the arrogant disappear,** בָּטְלֵי אַמְגּוּשֵׁי – **the** ***amgushei***[29] **will disappear.**[30] אִי בָּטְלֵי דַּיָּינֵי – **If the judges disappear,** בָּטְלֵי גַּזִירְפָּטֵי – **the** ***gazirpatei***[31] **will disappear.**[32]

The Scriptural allusions to these teachings:

אִי בָּטְלֵי יְהִירֵי בָּטְלֵי אַמְגּוּשֵׁי – **If the arrogant disappear, the** ***amgushei*** **will disappear,** דִּכְתִיב ,,וְאֶצְרֹף כַּבֹּר סִיגָיִךְ וְאָסִירָה כָּל־בְּדִילָיִךְ״ – **as it is written:** ***I will clean away your dross as though with soap, and I will remove all your tin.***[33]

וְאִי בָּטְלֵי דַּיָּינֵי בָּטְלֵי גַּזִירְפָּטֵי – **If the judges disappear, the** ***gazirpatei*** **will disappear,** דִּכְתִיב ,,הֵסִיר ה׳ מִשְׁפָּטַיִךְ פִּנָּה אֹיְבֵךְ״ – **as it is written:** ***God has removed your judgments; He has turned away your enemy.***[34]

NOTES

(139a) which teaches: "God will not rest His *Shechinah* on Israel until the bad judges have been eliminated" (see also *Iyun Yaakov*).

24. *Isaiah* 1:25,26. The exposition is based on the continuation of verse 25: וְאָסִירָה כָּל־בְּדִילָיִךְ, *and I will remove all your tin* (i.e. I will remove the inferior metals from the silver). The word בְּדִיל (tin), which is similar to מוּבְדָּל, *distinguished*, alludes to those who are distinguished from the people by virtue of their office — e.g. judges. The phrase thus means: *I will remove all your judges* (see *Rashi*).

Alternatively, the derivation is from verse 26: By stating "I will *restore* your judges," the verse implies that the Messiah will come after a period in which judges were absent (*Yad Ramah*).

25. The text used by *Rambam* (*Hil. Matnos Aniyim* 10:1) and *Tur* (*Yoreh Deah* 247:1) reads יִשְׂרָאֵל, *Israel* (see note 27).

26. This means that Jerusalem will be rebuilt in the merit of the mitzvah of charity (*Metzudos* to *Isaiah* 1:27). [Alternatively, it means that God will employ the attribute of רַחֲמִים, *mercy* or *charity* (as opposed to דין, *justice*), to allow for the rebuilding of Jerusalem.]

27. Ibid. v. 27.

Maharsha raises the following difficulty: The verse states that Zion [Jerusalem] itself will be redeemed with *justice* (only its returnees will be redeemed with charity). How, then, can the Gemara infer from it that Jerusalem itself will be redeemed with charity? See *Maharsha* for his solution to this difficulty; see also *Haggadah Simchas Yaabetz* by *R' Dovid Cohen,* pp. 143-4. [This problem does not arise according to the text quoted in note 25.]

28. *Yad Ramah.*

29. The Gemara in *Shabbos* (75a) cites a dispute as to whether the *amgushei* were sorcerers or fanatical idol worshipers (*Rashi*). [Some relate the *amgushei* to the magi — a priestly caste in ancient Persia.]

30. Our translation of יְהִירֵי as arrogant people follows *Rashi.* According to *Yad Ramah* and *Maharsha,* however, the reference is to hypocrites — wicked Jews who portray themselves as God fearing. *Yad Ramah* explains that it was at the request of these hypocrites, who would not attack other Jews openly, that the *amgushei* would engage in their machinations against the Jews. Hence, if these Jewish hypocrites would be eliminated, the attacks of the *amgushei* would cease.

31. Idolatrous judges who used physical force against the Jews (*Rashi*).

32. If there will be no corrupt Jewish judges, there will be no hostile gentile judges. This is a manifestation of מִדָּה כְּנֶגֶד מִדָּה, *measure for measure* — a deed is rewarded or punished in a manner that resembles and is commensurate with it (*Maharsha*; cf. *Yad Ramah*).

33. *Isaiah* 1:25. In Aramaic, סַגִּי means big. Thus, סִגָּיִךְ (your dross) is interpreted as referring to big-headed, arrogant people. בְּדִיל (tin), which is similar to מוּבְדָּל, *separate,* alludes to the *amgushei,* who are separate (i.e. estranged) from the fear of God. The verse thus means: *When I clean away your arrogant ones* etc., *I will remove all the amgushei* (*Rashi*).

34. *Zephaniah* 3:15. מִשְׁפָּטַיִךְ (your judgments) resembles שֹׁפְטַיִךְ, *your judges.* אֹיְבֵךְ, *your enemy,* signifies the *gazirpatei* (*Rashi*). Hence, the verse is interpreted: *When HASHEM removes your* [corrupt] *judges, He will remove the gazirpatei.*

35. I.e. it is becoming increasingly impoverished (*Maharsha*).

36. *II Samuel* 22:28.

37. That is, the troubles constantly grow, like a river which constantly flows without ever stopping (*Maharsha*).

38. *Isaiah* 59:19. [It will seem as though] God Himself intends to destroy them (*Rashi*).

39. Ibid. v. 20.

40. This teaching is explained in the following notes.

41. Ibid. 60:21. The phrase, *they will inherit the land,* signifies the redemption (*Rashi*).

The commentators understand the Gemara to mean that if the people possess sufficient merit, they will be redeemed even *before* the preordained date for the redemption.

In line with his approach to the passage above (97b-98a), *Maharsha* explains that if the people repent willingly, and not merely because they want to be rescued from their dire conditions, the Messiah will come to redeem them. Both R' Eliezer and R' Yehoshua agree with this (*Maharsha*; *Sanhedrei Ketanah* to 97b; see Gemara below and note 64).

The merit of Torah study is paramount in this context. See the Gemara below (99b) and in *Bava Basra* (8a) where it is taught that Torah study can hasten the redemption. In fact, the *Vilna Gaon* maintains that we can bring the redemption *only* through the study of Torah (*Even Sheleimah* 11:3; see also *Chomas HaDas* by *Chafetz Chaim*, ch. 14; *Beis HaLevi* to *Parshas Bo* עה״פ ויאמר ה׳ וגו׳ זאת חקת הפסח; *Otzros Acharis HaYamim* ch. 4).

Chafetz Chaim asserts that the combined merit of *all* the generations accumulates until it suffices to warrant the redemption. When that moment arrives, the Messiah will come immediately even if the generation extant at that time is relatively inferior (*Chafetz Chaim al HaTorah, Deuteronomy* 30:3).

מלכים יראו וקמו שרים וישתחוו אמר לו רבי אליעזר והלא כבר נאמר א) אם תשוב ישראל נאום ה' אלי תשוב אמר לו רבי יהושע והלא כבר נאמר ב) ואשמע את האיש לבוש הבדים אשר ממעל למימי היאור וירם ימינו ושמאלו אל השמים וישבע בחי העולם כי למועד מועדים וחצי וככלות נפץ יד עם קדש תכלינה כל אלה וגו' ושתק רבי אליעזר ואמר רבי אבא אין לך קץ מגולה מזה שנאמר ג) ואתם הרי ישראל ענפכם תתנו ופריכם תשאו לעמי ישראל וגו' רבי (א) אליעזר) אומר אף מזה שנאמר ד) כי לפני הימים (האלה) [ההם] שכר האדם לא נהיה ושכר הבהמה איננה וליוצא ולבא אין שלום מן הצר ג) מאי ליוצא ולבא אין שלום מן הצר רב אמר אף תלמידי חכמים שכתוב בהם שלום דכתיב ה) שלום רב לאהבי תורתך אין שלום מפני צר ושמואל אמר עד שיהיו כל השערים כולן שקולין אמר רבי חנינא אין בן דוד בא עד שיתבקש דג לחולה ולא ימצא שנאמר ו) אז אשקיע מימיהם ונהרותם כשמן אוליך וכתב (ד בתריה) ז) ביום ההוא אצמיח קרן לבית ישראל אמר רבי חמא בר חנינא אין בן דוד בא עד שתכלה מלכות הזלה מישראל שנאמר ח) וכרת הזלזלים במזמרות א) וכתיב בתריה ט) בעת ההיא יובל שי לה' צבאות עם ממשך ומורט אמר זעירי אמר רבי חנינא אין בן דוד בא עד שיכלו גסי הרוח מישראל שנאמר י) כי אז אסיר מקרבך עליזי גאותך וכתיב יא) והשארתי בקרבך עם עני ודל וחסו בשם ה' אמר רבי שמלאי משום רבי אלעזר בר"ש ו) אין בן דוד בא עד שיכלו כל שופטים ושוטרים מישראל שנאמר יב) ואשיבה ידי עליך ואצרוף כבור סיגיך וגו' ואשיבה שופטיך ז) אמר עולא אין ירושלים נפדית אלא בצדקה שנאמר יג) ציון במשפט תפדה ושביה בצדקה אמר רב פפא אי בטלי יהירי בטלי אמגושי אי בטלי דייני בטלי ז) גזירפטי אי בטלי יהירי בטלי אמגושי דכתיב יב) ואצרוף כבור סיגיך ואסירה כל בדיליך ואי בטלי דייני בטלי גזירפטי דכתיב יד) הסיר ה' משפטיך פנה אויבך אמר ר' יוחנן אם ראית דור שמתמעט והולך חכה לו שנאמר טו) ואת עם עני תושיע וגו' אמר רבי יוחנן אם ראית דור שצרות רבות באות עליו כנהר חכה לו שנאמר טז) כי יבא כנהר צר (ו)רוח ה' נוססה בו וסמיך ליה ובא לציון גואל ואמר רבי יוחנן אין בן דוד בא אלא בדור שכולו זכאי או כולו חייב בדור שכולו זכאי דכתיב יז) ועמך כולם צדיקים לעולם יירשו ארץ בדור שכולו חייב דכתיב יח) וירא כי אין איש וישתומם כי אין מפגיע וכתיב יט) למעני אעשה אמר רבי אלכסנדרי רבי יהושע בן לוי רמי כתיב כ) בעתה וכתיב אחישנה זכו אחישנה לא זכו בעתה אמר רבי אלכסנדרי רבי יהושע בן לוי רמי כתיב כא) וארו עם ענני שמיא כבר אינש אתה וכתיב כב) עני ורוכב על חמור זכו עם ענני שמיא לא זכו עני רוכב על חמור אמר ליה שבור מלכא לשמואל אמריתו משיח על חמרא אתי אישדר ליה סוסיא ח) ברקא דאית לי אמר ליה מי אית לך בר חיור גווני ר' יהושע בן לוי אשכח לאליהו דהוי קיימי אפיתחא דמערתא דרבי שמעון בן יוחאי אמר ליה אתינא לעלמא דאתי אמר ליה אם ירצה אדון הזה אמר רבי יהושע בן לוי שנים ראיתי וקול ג' שמעתי אמר ליה אימת אתי משיח אמר ליה זיל שייליה לדידיה והיכא יתיב אפיתחא [א] דקרתא ומאי סימניה יתיב ביני עניי סובלי חלאים וכולן שרו ואסירי בחד זימנא איהו שרי חד ואסיר חד אמר דילמא מבעינא דלא איעכב אזל לגביה אמר ליה שלום עליך רבי ומורי אמר ליה שלום עליך בר ליואי א"ל לאימת אתי מר א"ל היום אתא לגבי אליהו א"ל מאי אמר לך א"ל שלום עליך בר ליואי א"ל אבטחך לך ולאבוך לעלמא דאתי א"ל שקורי קא שקר בי דאמר לי היום אתינא ולא אתא א"ל הכי אמר לך כג) היום אם בקולו תשמעו שאלו תלמידיו את רבי יוסי בן קיסמא אימתי בן דוד בא אמר מתיירא אני שמא תבקשו ממני אות אמרו לו אין אנו מבקשין ממך אות א"ל לכשיפול השער הזה ויבנה ויפול ויבנה ויפול ואין מספיקין לבנותו עד שבן דוד בא אמרו לו רבינו תן לנו אות אמר להם ולא כך אמרתם לי שאין אתם מבקשין ממני אות אמרו לו ואף על פי כן אמר להם אם כך יהפכו מי מערת פמייס לדם ונהפכו לדם בשעת פטירתו אמר להן העמיקו לי ארוני שאין

כי למועד מועדים. אלמא יש קץ בדבר: וככלות נפץ יד עם קדש. כשתכלה תקומתם וחוזק ידיהם שהיתה נפולה אילך ואילך גבורה ותועלת לפשוט אנה ואנה ואחר שתכלה גבורתם שיהיו שפלים למאד: תכלינה. אלו הצרות ויבא משיח כדאמרינן כי אזלת יד: מגולה מזה. כשתתן ארץ ישראל פריה בעין יפה אז יקרב הקץ ואין לך קץ מגולה יותר: ר' אליעזר אומר מזה. הפסוק כשתראה דאין שום אדם משתכר ואף שכר הבהמה לא נהיה והיינו כדאמרן עד שתכלה פרוטה מן הכיס אין מעות מצויות בכיס: שכר בהמה. עבודת האדמה שהיא על ידי בהמה איננה: וליוצא ולבא אין שלום. אז יבא משיח: [שלום רב]. והיינו ליוצא ולבא אלו תלמידי חכמים אותם שהיה דינם לצאת ולבא בשלום כדכתיב שלום רב לאוהבי תורתך אפילו להנהו אין שלום: מן הצר. מרוב הצרות לא מיצר הרע: שקולין. שוין שער התבואה ויין רווחי' כדאמרן חמישית שובע גדול ל"א שקולין שוין שכולן יקרין: כשמן אוליך. שיהיו כולן קפויין וכיון שהם קפויין אין דגים נמצאין בחכה: עד שתכלה מלכות הזלה. שלא תהא להם שום שולטנות לישראל אפילו שולטנות קלה ודלה: נטישותיו. ענפים קטנים כלומר השרים והשופטים: וחסו בשם השם. כלומר שתבא להם גאולה ויחסו בצל שדי: סיגיך. תערובות שבך: בדיליך. המובדלים לראשי עם: יהירי. גסי רוח מישראל: אמגושי. פרסיים מכשפין שמלערין ישראל במס' שבת (דף עה.) פלוגתא איכא למאן דאמר אמגושי חרשי ואיכא מ"ד גדופי עובדי כוכבים: גזירפטי. שופטים עובדי כוכבים החובטין את ישראל במקלות: ואצרוף כבור סיגיך. רבים וגדולים בגסותם כשאצרוף ואסלקם ממך אזי אסירה כל בדיליך: אמגושי. הבדלים מיראת המקום: סיגיך. כמו רב דמתרגמינן סגי: משפטיך. כמו [ב] (צפניה ג) שופטיך: פנה אויבך. גזירפטי: נוססה.

כמו (ישעיה י) כמסוס נוסס וכמו (שם נט) יאכלם סס רוח המקום נוקבת ומחרבת אותן עם הצרות הבאות שאף הוא מתכוין להשמידם: יירשו ארץ. היינו גאולה: עם ענני שמיא כבר אינש אתי. במהירות: וכתיב עני ורוכב על החמור. כעני הבא על חמורו בעצלות: סוסי ברקא. סוס מסורק ט) ומכוון ונאה שיש לי דגנאי הוא שיבא על חמור מלגלג היה ל"א סוסיא בדקא סוס בדוק לרוץ: בר חיור גווני. כלום יש לך סוס בר מאה גוונין שחמור שלו כן הוא במלתא בעלמא דחייה: חיור. מאה בלשון פרסי: האדון הזה. שכינה היתה עמהם: קול שלשה. דשכינה הוה בהדייהו: לדידיה. למשיח: בפתחא (י) דקרתא). נראה למורי לא בפתח העיר ממש אלא גן עדן הוא כנגד כל העולם וקאמר ליה דבאותו לד של גן עדן שכנגד פתח העיר משיח שרוי: סובלי חלאים. מנוגעים והוא נמי מנוגע דכתיב (ישעיה נג) והוא מחולל מפשעינו וכתיב (שם) חליינו הוא נשא: כולהו. מי שיש לו ארבע וחמש נגעים: אסרי להו ושרו בחדא זימנא. מתירין כל נגעתן ביחד ומקנחין אותן וחוזרין וקושרין אותן: ואיהו. משיח: שרי חד. נגע ומקנחו וקושרו ואח"כ מתיר האחר ועושה כן ואינו מתיר שני נגעים יחד דסבר אי בעי לי לצאת וליגאל את ישראל לא איתעכב כדי קשירת שני נגעים: אמר ליה. ר' יהושע למשיח לאימת אתי מר אמר ליה היום: אבטחך לך ולאביך לעולם הבא. דאי לאו צדיקים גמורין אתם לא הוה יהיב לך שלמא ולא הוה מדכר שמיה דאבוך: היום אם בקולו. של הקב"ה תשמעו: השער הזה. של עיר רומי שבעיר רומי היה אותו שער: ואין מספיקין לבנותו. פעם שלישית: מי פמייס. שירדן נובע ממנו כדתניא בבכורות (דף נה.) דן יוצא ממערת פמייס ומפרש התם ספיר: העמיקו ארוני. עשו לי קבר בקרקע עמוק: שאין

נוססה בו. נפלאות בו ל' נס ד"א נוססה בו אוכלת בו כתולעת בעץ כמו (ישעיה י) והיה כמסוס נוסס [ישעיה נט, יט]. וירא כי אין איש. ועתה בהנחמו על הרעה לעמו רואה כי אין איש צדיק לעמוד בפרץ. וישתומם. ויחרש לראות אם יש מפגיע בעדם ואין מפגיע וישתומם ל' אדם העומד ותוהא ושותק בתמהונו ותי"ו וישתומם כתי"ו של משתולל שניהם משמשות לשון מתפעל וכן דרך התיבה שיסודה הראשון שי"ן או סמ"ך כשהיא נהפכת ללשון מתפעל נתפעל ויתפעל בא התי"ו באמצע אותיות שורש התיבה נמצא וישתומם לשון שמו שמים (ירמיה ב) משמים בתוכם (יחזקאל ג) נשמו אחרונים (איוב יח) ל' תמהון [שם, טז]. למעני. ולמען שמי הקדוש [שם מח, יא]. כבר אינש אתה. הוא מלך המשיח [דניאל ז, יג]. עני. ענותן. ורוכב על חמור. מדת ענוה היא [זכריה ט, ט]. שבור מלכא. מלך פרס היה [סוכה נג.]. עובד כוכבים היה [ע"ז עו:]. פמיים. שמשם ירדן יוצא כדאמר מר ירדן יוצא ממערת פמייס (בכורות נה.) [מגילה ו.].

מסורת הש"ס

א) [נ"ל אלעזר], ב) [חגיגה י. ע"ש ול"ע], ג) עיין רש"א בח"א, ד) [שבת קלט. ע"ש], ה) שבת דף קלט., ו) [הרמב"ם פרק י מהלכות מתנות עניים וכן בטור י"ד סי' רמז איתא ישראל וכל"ל למובן ושביה בצדקה ודלא כמ"ש רש"א בח"א שנדחק בזה טובא כד"ה עד שיכלו שופטים מישראל וכו' ע"ש ברם לנוסחא שניה עדים נאמנים הרמב"ם וטור אתי' לשפיר], ז) [גיר' הערוך גאזי דפאטי פי' סריסי ושוטרי השרים], ח) [עי' ברש"י דהכא ועי' ברש"י דע"ז ל. ד"ה מי בארג וכו' בארג לשון פרס משובח כמו סוסי בארג בחלק ע"ש], ט) ומלויין רש"ל, י) נ"ל דרומי.

הגהות הגר"א

[א] גמ' אפתחא דקרתא. נמחק תיבת דקרתא וכ"ב דרומי: [ב] רש"י ד"ה משפטיך כמו (צפניה ג). נמחק לפניה ג:

הגהות מהר"ב רנשבורג

א] גמ' שנאמר וכרת הזלזלים במזמרות ואת הנטישות הסר. כצ"ל:

תורה אור השלם

א) אִם תָּשׁוּב יִשְׂרָאֵל נְאֻם יְיָ אֵלַי תָּשׁוּב וְאִם תָּסִיר שִׁקּוּצֶיךָ מִפָּנַי וְלֹא תָנוּד: [ירמיה ד, א]

ב) וָאֶשְׁמַע אֶת הָאִישׁ לְבוּשׁ הַבַּדִּים אֲשֶׁר מִמַּעַל לְמֵימֵי הַיְאֹר וַיָּרֶם יְמִינוֹ וּשְׂמֹאלוֹ אֶל הַשָּׁמַיִם וַיִּשָּׁבַע בְּחֵי הָעוֹלָם כִּי לְמוֹעֵד מוֹעֲדִים וָחֵצִי וּכְכַלּוֹת נַפֵּץ יַד עַם קֹדֶשׁ תִּכְלֶינָה כָל אֵלֶּה: [דניאל יב, ז]

ג) וְאַתֶּם הָרֵי יִשְׂרָאֵל עַנְפְּכֶם תִּתֵּנוּ וּפֶרְיְכֶם תִּשְׂאוּ לְעַמִּי יִשְׂרָאֵל כִּי קֵרְבוּ לָבוֹא: [יחזקאל לו, ח]

ד) כִּי לִפְנֵי הַיָּמִים הָהֵם שְׂכַר הָאָדָם לֹא נִהְיָה וּשְׂכַר הַבְּהֵמָה אֵינֶנָּה וְלַיּוֹצֵא וְלַבָּא אֵין שָׁלוֹם מִן הַצָּר וַאֲשַׁלַּח אֶת כָּל הָאָדָם אִישׁ בְּרֵעֵהוּ: [זכריה ח, י]

ה) שָׁלוֹם רָב לְאֹהֲבֵי תוֹרָתֶךָ וְאֵין לָמוֹ מִכְשׁוֹל: [תהלים קיט, קסה]

ו) אָז אַשְׁקִיעַ מֵימֵיהֶם וְנַהֲרוֹתָם כַּשֶּׁמֶן אוֹלִיךְ נְאֻם אֲדֹנָי אֱלֹהִים: [יחזקאל לב, יד]

ז) בַּיּוֹם הַהוּא אַצְמִיחַ קֶרֶן לְבֵית יִשְׂרָאֵל וּלְךָ אֶתֵּן פִּתְחוֹן פֶּה בְּתוֹכָם וְיָדְעוּ כִּי אֲנִי יְיָ: [יחזקאל כט, כא]

ח) כִּי לִפְנֵי קָצִיר כְּתָם פֶּרַח וּבֹסֶר גֹּמֵל יִהְיֶה נִצָּה וְכָרַת הַזַּלְזַלִּים בַּמַּזְמֵרוֹת וְאֶת הַנְּטִישׁוֹת הֵסִיר הֵתַז: [ישעיה יח, ה]

ט) בָּעֵת הַהִיא יוּבַל שַׁי לַייָ צְבָאוֹת עַם מְמֻשָּׁךְ וּמוֹרָט וּמֵעַם נוֹרָא מִן הוּא וָהָלְאָה גּוֹי קַו קָו וּמְבוּסָה אֲשֶׁר בָּזְאוּ נְהָרִים אַרְצוֹ אֶל מְקוֹם שֵׁם יְיָ צְבָאוֹת הַר צִיּוֹן: [ישעיה יח, ז]

י) בַּיּוֹם הַהוּא לֹא תֵבוֹשִׁי מִכֹּל עֲלִילֹתַיִךְ אֲשֶׁר פָּשַׁעַתְּ בִּי כִּי אָז אָסִיר מִקִּרְבֵּךְ עַלִּיזֵי גַּאֲוָתֵךְ וְלֹא תוֹסִפִי לְגָבְהָה עוֹד בְּהַר קָדְשִׁי: [צפניה ג, יא]

יא) וְהִשְׁאַרְתִּי בְקִרְבֵּךְ עַם עָנִי וָדָל וְחָסוּ בְּשֵׁם יְיָ: [צפניה ג, יב]

יב) וְאָשִׁיבָה יָדִי עָלַיִךְ וְאֶצְרֹף כַּבֹּר סִיגָיִךְ וְאָסִירָה כָּל בְּדִילָיִךְ: וְאָשִׁיבָה שֹׁפְטַיִךְ כְּבָרִאשֹׁנָה וְיֹעֲצַיִךְ כְּבַתְּחִלָּה אַחֲרֵי כֵן יִקָּרֵא לָךְ עִיר הַצֶּדֶק קִרְיָה נֶאֱמָנָה: [ישעיה א, כה-כו] יג) צִיּוֹן בְּמִשְׁפָּט תִּפָּדֶה וְשָׁבֶיהָ בִּצְדָקָה: [ישעיה א, כז] יד) הֵסִיר יְיָ מִשְׁפָּטַיִךְ פִּנָּה אֹיְבֵךְ מֶלֶךְ יִשְׂרָאֵל יְיָ בְּקִרְבֵּךְ לֹא תִירְאִי רָע עוֹד: [צפניה ג, טו] טו) וְאֶת עַם עָנִי תּוֹשִׁיעַ וְעֵינֶיךָ עַל רָמִים תַּשְׁפִּיל: [שמואל ב' כב, כח] טז) וְיִירְאוּ מִמַּעֲרָב אֶת שֵׁם יְיָ וּמִמִּזְרַח שֶׁמֶשׁ אֶת כְּבוֹדוֹ כִּי יָבוֹא כַנָּהָר צָר רוּחַ יְיָ נֹסְסָה בוֹ: וּבָא לְצִיּוֹן גּוֹאֵל וּלְשָׁבֵי פֶשַׁע בְּיַעֲקֹב נְאֻם יְיָ: [ישעיה נט, יט-כ] יז) וְעַמֵּךְ כֻּלָּם צַדִּיקִים לְעוֹלָם יִירְשׁוּ אָרֶץ נֵצֶר מַטָּעַי מַעֲשֵׂה יָדַי לְהִתְפָּאֵר: [ישעיה ס, כא] יח) וַיַּרְא כִּי אֵין אִישׁ וַיִּשְׁתּוֹמֵם כִּי אֵין מַפְגִּיעַ וַתּוֹשַׁע לוֹ זְרֹעוֹ וְצִדְקָתוֹ הִיא סְמָכָתְהוּ: [ישעיה נט, טז] יט) לְמַעֲנִי לְמַעֲנִי אֶעֱשֶׂה כִּי אֵיךְ יֵחָל וּכְבוֹדִי לְאַחֵר לֹא אֶתֵּן: [ישעיה מח, יא] כ) הַקָּטֹן יִהְיֶה לָאֶלֶף וְהַצָּעִיר לְגוֹי עָצוּם אֲנִי יְיָ בְּעִתָּהּ אֲחִישֶׁנָּה: [ישעיה ס, כב] כא) חָזֵה הֲוֵית בְּחֶזְוֵי לֵילְיָא וַאֲרוּ עִם עֲנָנֵי שְׁמַיָּא כְּבַר אֱנָשׁ אָתֵה הֲוָה וְעַד עַתִּיק יוֹמַיָּא מְטָה וּקְדָמוֹהִי הַקְרְבוּהִי: [דניאל ז, יג] כב) גִּילִי מְאֹד בַּת צִיּוֹן הָרִיעִי בַּת יְרוּשָׁלַיִם הִנֵּה מַלְכֵּךְ יָבוֹא לָךְ צַדִּיק וְנוֹשָׁע הוּא עָנִי וְרֹכֵב עַל חֲמוֹר וְעַל עַיִר בֶּן אֲתֹנוֹת: [זכריה ט, ט] כג) כִּי הוּא אֱלֹהֵינוּ וַאֲנַחְנוּ עַם מַרְעִיתוֹ וְצֹאן יָדוֹ הַיּוֹם אִם בְּקֹלוֹ תִשְׁמָעוּ: [תהלים צה, ז]

ליקוטי רש"י

מלכים יראו. אותו וקמו [ישעיה מט, ז]. וקמו. לקראת ישראל לעתיד לבא [תענית טו.]. אם תשוב ישראל. בתשובה זו אלי. תשוב. לכבודך וגדולתך הראשונה [ירמיה ד, א]. וככלות נפץ יד עם קדש. כשתכלה כח ישראל כי אזלת יד ואפס עצור ועזוב (דברים לב) [דניאל יב, ז]. וכרת. הכורת את זלזלי הגפן הם הזמורות והשריגים. במזמרות. שרפ"ש בלע"ז. [הנטישות]. הם עיקרי הגפנים שקורין ליפ"ש בלע"ז [ישעיה יח, ה]. עם עני ודל. עם ענותן ומקבל עולבן [צפניה ג, יב]. ואשיבה ידי עליך. מכה אחר מכה עד כלות הפושעים. כבור. ל' בורית סבו"ן בלע"ז ולשונו ל' נקיון כמו ובר לבב (תהלים כד) ע"ש שהוא מנקה הבגד מכתמיו. סיגיך. כמו כספך היה לסיגים האמור למעלה (ישעיה א, כב) תערובת נחשת בכסף קרוי סיג אף כאן תערוב' רשעים עם הכשרים אני אכלה הפושעי' שהם הסיג. כל בדיליך. בדיל המעורב בכסף כלומר הרשעים שבך בדיל אשטיי"ם בלע"ז [ישעיה א, כה]. במשפט תפדה. ע"י שיהיו בה עושה משפט. תפדה. מעונותיה. ושביה. עושי תשובה שבתוכה. בצדקה. [במצדיקים עצמם במשפט ובצדק' שבתוכה] [שם, כז]. ואשיבה שופטיך. אעמיד לכם שופטים כשרים [שם, כו]. ואחר כך יקרא לך עיר הצדק לשרות בה שכינה [ע"ש]. אי בטלי יהירי. ישראל מתייהרים בצלורית ובמלבושי יהירות כפרסים הללו. בטלי אמגושי. יבטלו מסיתים ומדיחים [דפ"י, המינים גלחים] המשניאים אותנו. סיגיך. הם גסי הרוח שמגדלין עצמן לשון ישגה מאד (איוב ח) ואחר כך ואסירה כל בדיליך אלו אותם המבדילים שונאי ישראל מן הקדוש ברוך הוא בשקריהם ובפחזותם. בטלי דייני. רשעים מישראל שמטין דין. בטלי. מעל ישראל. גזירפטי. נוגשי שוטרי עובדי כוכבים [שבת קלט.].

and He was amazed that there was no intercessor.[42] **וּכְתִיב „לְמַעֲנִי אֶעֱשֶׂה”** – **And** also **it is written: *For My sake I will act.***[43]

The Gemara discusses a verse that refers to the redemption – אֲנִי ה׳ בְּעִתָּהּ אֲחִישֶׁנָּה, *I, HASHEM, in its time I will hasten it* (*Isaiah* 60:22):

אָמַר רַבִּי אֲלֶכְּסַנְדְּרִי – **R' Alexandri said: רַבִּי יְהוֹשֻׁעַ בֶּן לֵוִי רָמֵי** – **R' Yehoshua ben Levi noted a contradiction: כְּתִיב „בְּעִתָּהּ”** – On the one hand **it is written: *in its time,*** which implies that the redemption will occur in its preordained time. **וּכְתִיב „אֲחִישֶׁנָּה”** – **But** on the other hand **it is written: *I will hasten it,*** which implies that God will bring the redemption before its preordained time! R' Yehoshua ben Levi resolved this contradiction as follows: **זָכוּ „אֲחִישֶׁנָּה”** – **If [the Jews] are deserving, *I will hasten it.*** **לֹא זָכוּ „בְּעִתָּהּ”** – **If they are not deserving,** the redemption will come ***in its time.***[44]

Another contradiction posed by R' Yehoshua ben Levi: **אָמַר רַבִּי אֲלֶכְּסַנְדְּרִי** – **R' Alexandri said: רַבִּי יְהוֹשֻׁעַ בֶּן לֵוִי רָמֵי** – **R' Yehoshua ben Levi noted a contradiction: כְּתִיב „וַאֲרוּ עִם־עֲנָנֵי שְׁמַיָּא כְּבַר אֱנָשׁ אָתֵה”** – On the one hand **it is written: *And behold! With the clouds of Heaven, one like a man came,***[45] which implies that the Messiah will come swiftly. **וּכְתִיב „עָנִי וְרֹכֵב עַל־חֲמוֹר”** – **But** on the other hand **it is written: *a humble man, riding on a donkey,***[46] which implies that the Messiah will come sluggishly. R' Yehoshua ben Levi resolved this contradiction as follows: **זָכוּ „עִם־עֲנָנֵי שְׁמַיָּא”** – **If [the Jews] are deserving,**[47] the Messiah will arrive ***with the clouds of Heaven.*** **לֹא זָכוּ „עָנִי וְרוֹכֵב עַל חֲמוֹר”** – **If they are not deserving,** he will come as ***a humble man, riding on a donkey.***[48]

NOTES

42. *Isaiah* 59:16. The passage continues (v. 20): וּבָא לְצִיּוֹן גּוֹאֵל, *A redeemer shall come to Zion.*

There was no man means that no righteous person was present to shore up the breach in the people's spiritual standing. מַפְגִּיעַ, *intercessor,* signifies one who prays on their behalf [see *Taanis* 8a] (*Rashi* ad loc.).

Radak explains that the verse cannot mean that every single Jew will be undeserving of redemption. The Jewish people will never sink to such an abysmal state! Rather, the meaning is that *most* of the people will not deserve to be redeemed, and the few righteous ones will not possess sufficient merit to bring the redemption on behalf of their brethren.

43. Ibid. 48:11. The verse continues, כִּי אֵיךְ יֵחָל, *for how could it be profaned*, i.e. how could God let His Name be profaned by letting the Jewish people fall into oblivion? God will bring the redemption even if the generation is undeserving, so that those who worship other gods will not be able to say, "The God of the Jews is powerless to save His people" (see *Rashi* and *Radak* ad loc.).

Redemption of a generation that is entirely guilty:

Abarbanel (*Yeshuos Meshicho* p.19) asks: "How could it even enter one's mind that the Messiah will come [because] the generation is entirely guilty, wicked and sinful?!"

Abarbanel interprets the Gemara to mean that when the preordained date for the redemption arrives, the Messiah will come *even* if the generation is entirely guilty (see *Or HaChaim* to *Leviticus* 25:28).

Maharsha, too, understands the Gemara as referring to the final "End." It reflects the view of R' Yehoshua, who maintains that the Messiah will come at that time even if the people have not yet repented of their own accord. In those circumstances, God will compel the people to repent by "appointing a king over them whose decrees are as harsh as those of Haman" (Baraisa, 97b).

Along these lines, *Radak* (*Isaiah* loc. cit.) explains that if the redemption must come at a time when the people are not entirely deserving (see previous note), the redemptive process itself will elevate the people to the necessary level. For when the people see that the redemption is imminent, they will repent and thus become deserving of redemption. The Jewish people will then leave their lands of exile. Those who had repented will reach Eretz Yisrael, whereas those who had not repented will perish on the way.

The *Vilna Gaon* states that when the final "End" arrives, even if the people have not repented, God will bring the redemption out of kindness, as it is written, *For my sake I will act,* and also in the merit of the Patriarchs. This is the meaning of the words in the *Shemoneh Esrei:* וְזוֹכֵר חַסְדֵי אָבוֹת וּמֵבִיא גוֹאֵל לִבְנֵי בְנֵיהֶם לְמַעַן שְׁמוֹ, *Who recalls the kindnesses of the Patriarchs and brings a Redeemer to their children's children, for His Name's sake* (*Even Sheleimah* 11:9).

Some later commentators, however, have proposed that the very sinfulness of a generation could indeed *cause* the Messiah to come:

In *Tzipisa LiYeshuah* (ch. 1), *Chafetz Chaim* woefully portrays an era in which the young rebel against the old (see 97a note 33), and parents and teachers are unable to transmit the fundamentals of the faith to the next generation. In such circumstances, if the exile would continue, our tradition could be lost, God forbid. To prevent this from happening, God will hasten the redemption.

Following this approach, *R' Elchonon Wasserman* (*Beurei Aggados*) draws an analogy to the redemption from the Egyptian exile. Before the Exodus from Egypt, the spiritual state of the people had sunk almost to the point of no return. Had they not been redeemed at that time, they would have assimilated without trace, and redemption would no longer have been possible (see *Beis HaLevi* to *Parshas Bo* ד״ה והנה בהגדה). The same applies to the final redemption. The people will be redeemed from exile when it becomes untenable for them to remain in exile.

In explanation of this Gemara, *R' E.E. Dessler* observes that a person who is somewhat virtuous, but not completely so, is unlikely to repent because he is inclined to focus only on his good attributes and ignore the bad. On the other hand, a person who completely lacks virtue, and thus has no grounds for self-deception, is open to the realization that he must repent and merit God's redemption, lest he be doomed forever. Hence, it is only a person who is either entirely virtuous or entirely sinful that is ready for the redemption (*Michtav MeEliyahu* vol. 3 p. 222; see also the explanation given by *Noda BiYehudah* [cited by *Margaliyos HaYam*] which implies this approach).

44. See note 41 for a discussion of the merits that could warrant an early redemption.

In conclusion:

(a) There is a specific preordained date for the advent of the Messiah (see *Ramban, Sefer HaGeulah* ch. 2; cf. *Rashi* and *Maharsha* in explanation of R' Eliezer; see 97b note 46). This date is unknown to man (*Rambam, Iggeres Teiman* beginning of ch. 3).

(b) Tannaim debated whether the people must repent [of their own accord] for the redemption to come. R' Eliezer eventually conceded to R' Yehoshua (see above, note 6) who maintained that if the people have not repented by the preordained date, God will force them to do so by "appointing a king over them whose decrees are as harsh as those of Haman" (text of the Talmud *Bavli;* cf. *Yerushalmi;* see 97b note 50).

(c) Both R' Eliezer and R' Yehoshua agree that if the people possess sufficient merit, the Messiah will come even before the preordained date (see note 41). [See also note 43 where it was suggested that factors other than merit could hasten the redemption.]

45. *Daniel* 7:13. Daniel beheld a vision of the Messiah (*Rashi* ad loc.).

46. *Zechariah* 9:9. Because of his humility, the Messiah will choose to ride on a donkey [as opposed to a more stately animal, such as a horse] (see *Rashi* and *Radak* ad loc.; see also note 48).

47. I.e. they repent without being "forced" to do so (*Maharsha;* see also note 41).

48. As explained above (notes 41-44), there are various circumstances that could bring about the advent of the Messiah. The Gemara teaches here that depending on these circumstances the redemption will differ not only in date but even in process. If the redemption is effected through the merit of the Jewish people, the Messiah's arrival will be of a miraculous nature – *with the clouds of Heaven.* Otherwise, it will be of a different nature – *a humble man, riding on a donkey* (see *Or HaChaim* to *Numbers* 24:17 ד״ה אראנו; *Haggadah Simchas Yaabetz* by *R' Dovid Cohen* p. 214; see also note 64 below, and 99a note 20).

The donkey symbolizes that the Messiah is coming for some reason other than the people's merit. As a beast of burden, it signifies that the Messiah is coming as a result of the harsh and heavy burden of exile.

מלכים יראו וקמו שרים וישתחוו אמר לו רבי אליעזר והלא כבר נאמר א) אם תשוב ישראל נאום ה' אלי תשוב אמר לו רבי יהושע והלא כבר נאמר ב) ואשמע את האיש לבוש הבדים אשר ממעל למימי היאור וירם ימינו ושמאלו אל השמים וישבע בחי העולם כי למועד מועדים וחצי וככלות נפץ יד עם קדש תכלינה כל אלה וגו' ושתק רבי אליעזר ואמר רבי אבא אין לך קץ מגולה מזה שנאמר ג) ואתם הרי ישראל ענפכם תתנו ופריכם תשאו לעמי ישראל וגו' רבי (א) אליעזר) אומר אף מזה שנאמר ד) כי לפני הימים (האלה) [ההם] שכר האדם לא נהיה ושכר הבהמה איננה וליוצא ולבא אין שלום מן הצר ג) מאי ליוצא ולבא אין שלום מן הצר רב אמר אף תלמידי חכמים שכתוב בהם שלום דכתיב ה) שלום רב לאהבי תורתך אין שלום מפני צר ושמואל אמר עד שיהיו כל השערים כולן שקולין אמר רבי חנינא אין בן דוד בא עד שיתבקש דג לחולה ולא ימצא שנאמר ו) אז אשקיע מימיהם ונהרותם כשמן אוליך וכתב (ג) בתריה) ז) ביום ההוא אצמיח קרן לבית ישראל אמר רבי חמא בר חנינא אין בן דוד בא עד שתכלה מלכות הזלה מישראל שנאמר ח) וכרת הזלזלים במזמרות [א] וכתיב בתריה ט) בעת ההיא יובל שי לה' צבאות עם ממשך ומורט אמר זעירי אמר רבי חנינא אין בן דוד בא עד שיכלו גסי הרוח מישראל שנאמר י) כי אז אסיר מקרבך עליזי גאותך וכתיב יא) והשארתי בקרבך עם עני ודל וחסו בשם ה' אמר רבי שמלאי משום רבי אלעזר בר"ש ד) אין בן דוד בא עד שיכלו כל שופטים ושוטרים מישראל שנאמר יב) ואשיבה ידי עליך ואצרוף כבור סיגיך וגו' ואשיבה שופטיך ה) אמר עולא אין ו) ירושלים נפדית אלא בצדקה שנאמר יג) ציון במשפט תפדה ושביה בצדקה אמר רב פפא אי בטלי יהירי בטלי אמגושי אי בטלי דייני בטלי ז) גזירפטי אי בטלי יהירי בטלי אמגושי דכתיב יב) ואצרוף כבור סיגיך ואסירה כל בדיליך ואי בטלי דייני בטלי גזירפטי דכתיב יד) הסיר ה' משפטיך פנה אויבך אמר ר' יוחנן אם ראית דור שמתמעט והולך חכה לו שנאמר טו) ואת עם עני תושיע וגו' אמר רבי יוחנן אם ראית דור שצרות רבות באות עליו כנהר חכה לו שנאמר טז) כי יבא כנהר צר (ו)רוח ה' נוססה בו וסמיך ליה ובא לציון גואל ואמר רבי יוחנן אין בן דוד בא אלא בדור שכולו זכאי או כולו חייב בדור שכולו זכאי דכתיב יז) ועמך כולם צדיקים לעולם יירשו ארץ בדור שכולו חייב דכתיב יח) וירא כי אין איש וישתומם כי אין מפגיע וכתיב יט) למעני אעשה אמר רבי אלכסנדרי רבי יהושע בן לוי רמי כתיב כ) בעתה וכתיב אחישנה זכו אחישנה לא זכו בעתה אמר רבי אלכסנדרי רבי יהושע בן לוי רמי כתיב כא) וארו עם ענני שמיא כבר אינש אתה וכתיב כב) עני ורוכב על חמור זכו עם ענני שמיא לא זכו עני רוכב על חמור אמר ליה שבור מלכא לשמואל אמריתו משיח על חמרא אתי אישדר ליה סוסיא ח) ברקא דאית לי אמר ליה מי אית לך בר חיור גווני ר' יהושע בן לוי אשכח לאליהו דהוי קיימי אפיתחא דמערתא דרבי שמעון בן יוחאי אמר ליה אתינא לעלמא דאתי אמר ליה אם ירצה אדון הזה אמר רבי יהושע בן לוי שנים ראיתי וקול ג' שמעתי אמר ליה אימת אתי משיח אמר ליה זיל שייליה לדידיה והיכא יתיב אפיתחא [א] דקרתא ומאי סימניה יתיב ביני עניי סובלי חלאים וכולן שרו ואסירי בחד זימנא איהו שרי חד ואסיר חד אמר דילמא מבעינא דלא איעכב אזל לגביה אמר ליה שלום עליך רבי ומורי אמר ליה שלום עליך בר ליואי א"ל לאימת אתי מר א"ל היום אתא לגבי אליהו א"ל מאי אמר לך א"ל שלום עליך בר ליואי א"ל אבטחך לך ולאבוך לעלמא דאתי א"ל שקורי קא שקר בי דאמר לי היום אתינא ולא אתא א"ל הכי אמר לך כג) היום אם בקולו תשמעו שאלו תלמידיו את רבי יוסי בן קיסמא אימתי בן דוד בא אמר מתיירא אני שמא תבקשו ממני אות אמרו לו אין אנו מבקשין ממך אות א"ל לכשיפול השער הזה ויבנה ויפול ויבנה ויפול ואין מספיקין לבנותו עד שבן דוד בא אמרו לו רבינו תן לנו אות אמר להם ולא כך אמרתם לי שאין אתם מבקשין ממני אות אמרו לו ואף על פי כן אמר להם אם כך יהפכו מי מערת פמיים לדם ונהפכו לדם בשעת פטירתו אמר להן העמיקו לי ארוני

שאין

רש"י

כי למועד מועדים. אלמא יש קץ בדבר: וככלות נפץ יד עם קדש. כשתכלה תקומתם וחוזק ידיהם שהיתה נפולה אילך ואילך גבורה ותועלת לפשוט אנה ואנה ואחר שתכלה גבורתם שיהיו שפלים למאד: תכלינה. אלו הצרות ויבא משיח כדאמרינן כי אזלת יד: מגולה מזה. כשתתן ארץ ישראל פריה בעין יפה אז יקרב הקץ ואין לך קץ מגולה יותר: ר' אליעזר אומר מזה. הפסוק כשתראה דאין שום אדם משתכר ואף שכר הבהמה לא נהיה והיינו כדאמרן עד שתכלה פרוטה מן הכיס אין מעות מצויות בכיס: שכר בהמה. עבודת האדמה שהיא על ידי בהמה איננה: וליוצא ולבא אין שלום. אז יבא משיח: [שלום רב]. והיינו וליוצא ולבא אלו תלמידי חכמים אותם שהיה דינם לצאת ולבא בשלום כדכתיב שלום רב לאוהבי תורתך אפילו להנהו אין שלום: מן הצר. מרוב הצרות ל"א מיצר הרע: שקולין. שוין שער התבואה ויין רווחי' כדאמרן חמישית שובע גדול ל"א שקולין שוין שכולן יקרין: כשמן אוליך. שיהיו כולן קפויין וכיון שהם קפויין אין דגים נמצאין בהכה: עד שתכלה מלכות הזלה. שלא תהא להם שום שולטנות לישראל אפילו שולטנות קלה ודלה: נטישותיו. ענפים קטנים כלומר השרים והשופטים: וחסו בשם השם. כלומר שתבא להם גאולה ויחסו בצל שדי: סיגיך. תערובות שבך: בדיליך. המובדלים לראשי עם: יהירי. גסי רוח מישראל: אמגושי. פרסיים מכשפין שמצערין ישראל במס' שבת (דף עה.) פלוגתא איכא למאן דאמר אמגושי חרשי ואיכא מ"ד גדופי עובדי כוכבים: גזירפטי. שופטים עובדי כוכבים החובטין את ישראל במקלות: ואצרוף כבור סיגיך. רבים וגדולים בגסותם כשאצרוף ואסלקם ממך אזי אסירה כל בדיליך: אמגושי. הבדלים מיראת המקום: סיגיך. כמו רב דמתרגמינן סגי: משפטיך. כמו [ב] (צפניה ג) שופטיך: פנה אויבך. גזירפטי: נוססה. כמו (ישעיה י) כמסוס נוסס וכמו (שם נא) יאכלם סס רוח המקום נוקבת ומחרבת אותן עם הצרות הבאות שאף הוא מתכוין להשמידם: יירשו ארץ. היינו גאולה: עם ענני שמיא כבר אינש אתי. במהירות: וכתיב עני ורוכב על החמור. כעני הבא על חמורו בעצלות: סוסי ברקא. סוס מסורק ט) ומכוון ונאה שיש לי דגנאי הוא שיבא על חמור מלגלג היה ל"א סוסיא בדקא סוס בדוק לרוץ: בר חיור גווני. כלום יש לך סוס בר מאה גוונין שחמור שלו כן הוא במלתא בעלמא דחייה: חיור. מאה בלשון פרסי: האדון הזה. שכינה היתה עמהם: קול שלשה. דשכינה הוה בהדייהו: לדידיה. למשיח: בפתחא (י) דקרתא). נראה למורי לא בפתח העיר ממש אלא גן עדן הוא כנגד כל העולם וקאמר ליה דבאותו לד של גן עדן שכנגד פתח העיר משיח שרוי: סובלי חלאים. מנוגעים והוא נמי מנוגע דכתיב (ישעיה נג) והוא מחולל מפשעינו וכתיב (שם) חליינו הוא נשא: כולהו. מי שיש לו ארבע וחמש נגעים: אסרי להו ושרו בחדא זימנא. מתירין כל נגעתן ביחד ומקנחין אותן וחוזרין וקושרין אותן: ואיהו. משיח: שרי חד. נגע ומקנחו וקושרו ואח"כ מתיר האחר ועושה כן ואינו מתיר שני נגעים יחד דסבר אי בעי לי לצאת וליגאל את ישראל לא איתעכב כדי קשירת שני נגעים: אמר ליה. ר' יהושע למשיח לאימת אתי מר אמר ליה היום: אבטחך לך ולאביך לעולם הבא. דאי לאו צדיקים גמורין אתם לא הוה יהיב לך שלמא ולא הוה מדכר שמיה דאבוך: היום אם בקולו. של הקב"ה תשמעו: השער הזה. של עיר רומי שבעיר רומי היה אותו שער: ואין מספיקין לבנותו. פעם שלישית: מי פמיים. שירדן נובע ממנו כדתניא בבכורות (דף נה.) דן יוצא ממערת פמיים ומפרש התם שפיר: העמיקו ארוני. עשו לי קבר בקרקע עמוק:

שאין

א) [צ"ל אליעזר], ב) [חגיגה י. ע"ש וצ"ע], ג) עיין רש"א בח"א, ד) [שבת קלט. ע"ש], ה) שבת דף קלט., ו) [הרמב"ם פרק י מהלכות מתנות עניים וכן בטור י"ד סי' רמז איתא ישראל וכצ"ל למובן ושביה בצדקה ודלא כמ"ש רש"א בח"א שנדחק בזה טובא בד"ה עד שיכלו שופטים מישראל וכו' ע"ש ברם לנוסחא שניה עדים נאמנים הרמב"ם וטור אחי' לשפיר], ז) [גיר' הערוך גאזי דפאטי פי' סריסי ושוטרי השרים], ח) [עי' ברש"י דהכא ועי' ברש"י דע"ז ל. ד"ה מי בארג וכו' בארג לשון פרס משובח כמו סוסי בארג בחלק ע"ש], ט) ומצויין רש"ל, י) צ"ל דרומי.

ליקוטי רש"י

מלכים יראו. אותו וקמו [ישעיה מט, ז]. וקמו. לקראת ישראל לעתיד לבא [תענית טו.]. אם תשוב ישראל. בתשובה זו אלי. תשוב. לכבודך וגדולתך הראשונה [ירמיה ד, א]. וככלות נפץ יד עם קדש. כשתכלה כח ישראל כי אזלת יד ואפס עצור ועזוב (דברים לב) [דניאל יב, ז]. וכרת. הכורת את זלזלי הגפן הם הזמורות והשריגים. במזמרות. שרפ"ש בלע"ז. [הנטישות]. הם עיקרי הגפנים שקורין ליפ"ש בלע"ז [ישעיה יח, ה]. עם עני ודל. עם ענוותן ומקבל עולבן [צפניה ג, יב]. ואשיבה ידי עליך. מכה אחר מכה עד כלות הפושעים. כבור. ל' בורית סבו"ן בלע"ז ולשונו ל' נקיון כמו ובר לבב (תהלים כד) ע"ש שהוא מנקה הבגד מכתמיו. סיגיך. כמו כספך היה לסיגים האמור למעלה (ישעיה א, כב) תערובת נחשת בכסף קרוי סיג אף כאן תערוב' רשעים עם הכשרים אני אכלה הפושעי' שהם הסיג. כל בדיליך. בדיל המעורב בכסף כלומר הרשעים שביך בדיל אשטיי"ם בלע"ז [ישעיה א, כה]. במשפט תפדה. ע"י שיהיו בה עושה משפט. תפדה. מעונותיה. ושביה. עושי תשובה שבתוכה. בצדקה. [במצדיקים עצמם במשפט ובצדק' שבתוכה] [שם, כז]. ואשיבה שופטיך. אעמיד לכם שופטים כשרים [שם, כו]. ואחר כך יקרא לך עיר הצדק לשרות בה שכינה [ע"ש]. אי בטלי יהירי. ישראל מתייהרים בבלורית ובמלבושי יהירות כפרסים הללו. בטלי אמגושי. יבטלו מסיתים ומדיחים [דפ"י, המינים גלחים] המשניאים אותנו. סיגיך. הם גסי הרוח שמגדלין עצמן לשון ישגה מאד (איוב ח) ואחר כך ואסירה כל בדיליך אלו אותם המבדילים שונאי ישראל מן הקדוש ברוך הוא בשקריהם ובפחזותם. בטלי דייני. רשעים מישראל שמטין דין. בטלי. מעל ישראל. גזירפטי. נוגשי שוטרי עובדי כוכבים [שבת קלט.]. נוססה בו. נפלאות בו ל' נס ד"א נוססה בו אוכלת בו כתולעת בעץ כמו (ישעיה י) והיה כמסוס נוסס [ישעיה נט, יט]. וירא כי אין איש. ועתה בהנחמו על הרעה לעמו רואה כי אין איש צדיק לעמוד בפרץ. וישתומם. ויחרש לראות אם יש מפגיע בעדם ואין מפגיע וישתומם ל' אדם העומד ותוהא ושותק בתמהונו ותי"ו וישתומם כתי"ו של משתולל שניהם משמשות לשון מתפעל וכן דרך התיבה שיסודה הראשון שי"ן או סמ"ך כשהיא נהפכת ללשון מתפעל נתפעל ויתפעל בא התי"ו באמצע אותיות שורש התיבה נמצא וישתומם לשון שמו שמים (ירמיה ב) משמים בתוכם (יחזקאל ג) נשמו אחרונים (איוב יח) ל' תמהון [שם, טז]. למעני. ולמען שמי הקדוש [שם מח, יא]. כבר אינש אתה. הוא מלך המשיח [דניאל ז, יג]. עני. ענותן. ורוכב על חמור. מלת עניה היא [זכריה ט, ט]. שבור מלכא. מלך פרס היה [סוכה נג.]. עובד כוכבים היה [ע"ז עו:]. פמיים. שמשם ירדן יוצא כדאמר מר ירדן יוצא ממערת פמיים (בכורות נה.) [מגילה ו.].

הגהות הגר"א

[א] גמ' אפתחא דקרתא. נמחק תיבת דקרתא ונ"ב דרומי: [ב] רש"י ד"ה משפטיך כמו (צפניה ג). נמחק לפניה ג:

הגהות מהר"ב רנשבורג

א] גמ' שנאמר וכרת הזלזלים במזמרות ואת הנטישות הסר. כצ"ל:

תורה אור השלם

א) אִם תָּשׁוּב יִשְׂרָאֵל נְאֻם יְיָ אֵלַי תָּשׁוּב וְאִם תָּסִיר שִׁקּוּצֶיךָ מִפָּנַי וְלֹא תָנוּד: [ירמיה ד, א]

ב) וָאֶשְׁמַע אֶת הָאִישׁ לְבוּשׁ הַבַּדִּים אֲשֶׁר מִמַּעַל לְמֵימֵי הַיְאֹר וַיָּרֶם יְמִינוֹ וּשְׂמֹאלוֹ אֶל הַשָּׁמַיִם וַיִּשָּׁבַע בְּחֵי הָעוֹלָם כִּי לְמוֹעֵד מוֹעֲדִים וָחֵצִי וּכְכַלּוֹת נַפֵּץ יַד עַם קֹדֶשׁ תִּכְלֶינָה כָל אֵלֶּה: [דניאל יב, ז]

ג) וְאַתֶּם הָרֵי יִשְׂרָאֵל עַנְפְּכֶם תִּתֵּנוּ וּפֶרְיְכֶם תִּשְׂאוּ לְעַמִּי יִשְׂרָאֵל כִּי קֵרְבוּ לָבוֹא: [יחזקאל לו, ח]

ד) כִּי לִפְנֵי הַיָּמִים הָהֵם שְׂכַר הָאָדָם לֹא נִהְיָה וּשְׂכַר הַבְּהֵמָה אֵינֶנָּה וְלַיּוֹצֵא וְלַבָּא אֵין שָׁלוֹם מִן הַצָּר וַאֲשַׁלַּח אֶת כָּל הָאָדָם אִישׁ בְּרֵעֵהוּ: [זכריה ח, י]

ה) שָׁלוֹם רָב לְאֹהֲבֵי תוֹרָתֶךָ וְאֵין לָמוֹ מִכְשׁוֹל: [תהלים קיט, קסה]

ו) אָז אַשְׁקִיעַ מֵימֵיהֶם וְנַהֲרוֹתָם כַּשֶּׁמֶן אוֹלִיךְ נְאֻם אֲדֹנָי אֱלֹהִים: [יחזקאל לב, יד]

ז) בַּיּוֹם הַהוּא אַצְמִיחַ קֶרֶן לְבֵית יִשְׂרָאֵל וּלְךָ אֶתֵּן פִּתְחוֹן פֶּה בְּתוֹכָם וְיָדְעוּ כִּי אֲנִי יְיָ: [יחזקאל כט, כא]

ח) כִּי לִפְנֵי קָצִיר כְּתָם פֶּרַח וּבֹסֶר גֹּמֵל יִהְיֶה נִצָּה וְכָרַת הַזַּלְזַלִּים בַּמַּזְמֵרוֹת וְאֶת הַנְּטִישׁוֹת הֵסִיר הֵתַז: [ישעיה יח, ה]

ט) בָּעֵת הַהִיא יוּבַל שַׁי לַייָ צְבָאוֹת עַם מְמֻשָּׁךְ וּמוֹרָט וּמֵעַם נוֹרָא מִן הוּא וָהָלְאָה גּוֹי קַו קָו וּמְבוּסָה אֲשֶׁר בָּזְאוּ נְהָרִים אַרְצוֹ אֶל מְקוֹם שֵׁם יְיָ צְבָאוֹת הַר צִיּוֹן: [ישעיה יח, ז]

י) בַּיּוֹם הַהוּא לֹא תֵבוֹשִׁי מִכֹּל עֲלִילֹתַיִךְ אֲשֶׁר פָּשַׁעַתְּ בִּי כִּי אָז אָסִיר מִקִּרְבֵּךְ עַלִּיזֵי גַּאֲוָתֵךְ וְלֹא תוֹסִפִי לְגָבְהָה עוֹד בְּהַר קָדְשִׁי: [צפניה ג, יא]

יא) וְהִשְׁאַרְתִּי בְקִרְבֵּךְ עַם עָנִי וָדָל וְחָסוּ בְּשֵׁם יְיָ: [צפניה ג, יב]

יב) וְאָשִׁיבָה יָדִי עָלַיִךְ וְאֶצְרֹף כַּבֹּר סִיגָיִךְ וְאָסִירָה כָּל בְּדִילָיִךְ: וְאָשִׁיבָה שֹׁפְטַיִךְ כְּבָרִאשֹׁנָה וְיֹעֲצַיִךְ כְּבַתְּחִלָּה אַחֲרֵי כֵן יִקָּרֵא לָךְ עִיר הַצֶּדֶק קִרְיָה נֶאֱמָנָה: [ישעיה א, כה-כו]

יג) צִיּוֹן בְּמִשְׁפָּט תִּפָּדֶה וְשָׁבֶיהָ בִּצְדָקָה: [ישעיה א, כז]

יד) הֵסִיר יְיָ מִשְׁפָּטַיִךְ פִּנָּה אֹיְבֵךְ מֶלֶךְ יִשְׂרָאֵל יְיָ בְּקִרְבֵּךְ לֹא תִירְאִי רָע עוֹד: [צפניה ג, טו]

טו) וְאֶת עַם עָנִי תּוֹשִׁיעַ וְעֵינֶיךָ עַל רָמִים תַּשְׁפִּיל: [שמואל ב' כב, כח]

טז) וְיִירְאוּ מִמַּעֲרָב אֶת שֵׁם יְיָ וּמִמִּזְרַח שֶׁמֶשׁ אֶת כְּבוֹדוֹ כִּי יָבוֹא כַנָּהָר צָר רוּחַ יְיָ נֹסְסָה בוֹ: וּבָא לְצִיּוֹן גּוֹאֵל וּלְשָׁבֵי פֶשַׁע בְּיַעֲקֹב נְאֻם יְיָ: [ישעיה נט, יט-כ]

יז) וְעַמֵּךְ כֻּלָּם צַדִּיקִים לְעוֹלָם יִירְשׁוּ אָרֶץ נֵצֶר מַטָּעַי מַעֲשֵׂה יָדַי לְהִתְפָּאֵר: [ישעיה ס, כא]

יח) וַיַּרְא כִּי אֵין אִישׁ וַיִּשְׁתּוֹמֵם כִּי אֵין מַפְגִּיעַ וַתּוֹשַׁע לוֹ זְרֹעוֹ וְצִדְקָתוֹ הִיא סְמָכָתְהוּ: [ישעיה נט, טז]

יט) לְמַעֲנִי לְמַעֲנִי אֶעֱשֶׂה כִּי אֵיךְ יֵחָל וּכְבוֹדִי לְאַחֵר לֹא אֶתֵּן: [ישעיה מח, יא]

כ) הַקָּטֹן יִהְיֶה לָאֶלֶף וְהַצָּעִיר לְגוֹי עָצוּם אֲנִי יְיָ בְּעִתָּהּ אֲחִישֶׁנָּה: [ישעיה ס, כב]

כא) חָזֵה הֲוֵית בְּחֶזְוֵי לֵילְיָא וַאֲרוּ עִם עֲנָנֵי שְׁמַיָּא כְּבַר אֱנָשׁ אָתֵה הֲוָה וְעַד עַתִּיק יוֹמַיָּא מְטָה וּקְדָמוֹהִי הַקְרְבוּהִי: [דניאל ז, יג]

כב) גִּילִי מְאֹד בַּת צִיּוֹן הָרִיעִי בַּת יְרוּשָׁלַםִ הִנֵּה מַלְכֵּךְ יָבוֹא לָךְ צַדִּיק וְנוֹשָׁע הוּא עָנִי וְרֹכֵב עַל חֲמוֹר וְעַל עַיִר בֶּן אֲתֹנוֹת: [זכריה ט, ט]

כג) כִּי הוּא אֱלֹהֵינוּ וַאֲנַחְנוּ עַם מַרְעִיתוֹ וְצֹאן יָדוֹ הַיּוֹם אִם בְּקֹלוֹ תִשְׁמָעוּ: [תהלים צה, ז]

The Gemara cites a related exchange:

אָמַר לֵיהּ שָׁבוּר מַלְכָּא לִשְׁמוּאֵל – King Shapur said to Shmuel:[49] **אָמְרִיתוּ מָשִׁיחַ עַל חֲמָרָא אָתֵי – "You say** that **the Messiah will come on a donkey?! אִישַׁדַּר לֵיהּ סוּסְיָא בִּרְקָא דְּאִית לִי – I will send him my finest**[50] **horse!"**[51] **אָמַר לֵיהּ – [Shmuel] retorted to him: מִי אִית לָךְ בַּר חִיוַּר גַּוְונֵי – "Do you have [a horse] of a hundred colors?"**[52]

A third teaching from R' Yehoshua ben Levi:

רַבִּי יְהוֹשֻׁעַ בֶּן לֵוִי אַשְׁכַּח לְאֵלִיָּהוּ – R' Yehoshua ben Levi met the prophet **Elijah דַּהֲוֵי קָיְימִי אַפִּיתְחָא דִּמְעַרְתָּא דְּרַבִּי שִׁמְעוֹן בֶּן יוֹחַאי – who was standing at the entrance of the cave of R' Shimon ben Yochai.**[53] **אָמַר לֵיהּ – [R' Yehoshua ben Levi] asked [Elijah]: אָתֵינָא לְעָלְמָא דְּאָתֵי – "Will I enter the World to Come?"**[54] **אָמַר לֵיהּ – [Elijah] answered him: אִם יִרְצֶה אָדוֹן הַזֶּה – "If this Lord wishes it."**[55] **אָמַר רַבִּי יְהוֹשֻׁעַ בֶּן לֵוִי – R' Yehoshua ben Levi said: שְׁנַיִם רָאִיתִי – I saw two people, וְקוֹל שְׁלֹשָׁה שָׁמַעְתִּי – but I heard the voice of three.**[56] **אָמַר לֵיהּ – [R' Yehoshua ben Levi] asked [Elijah]: אֵימַת אָתֵי מָשִׁיחַ – "When will the Messiah come?" אָמַר לֵיהּ – [Elijah] answered him: זִיל שַׁיְילֵיהּ לְדִידֵיהּ – "Go and ask [the Messiah] himself!" וְהֵיכָא יָתִיב** – R' Yehoshua ben Levi asked: **"And where is he sitting?" אַפִּיתְחָא דְּקַרְתָּא** – Elijah responded: **"At the gate of the city."**[57] **וּמַאי סִימָנֵיהּ** – R' Yehoshua ben Levi asked: **"And what is his distinguishing feature?"**[58] **יָתִיב בֵּינֵי עֲנִיֵּי סוֹבְלֵי חֳלָאִים** – Elijah responded: **"He is sitting among paupers afflicted with disease.**[59] **וְכוּלָּן שָׁרוּ וְאָסִירֵי בְּחַד זִימְנָא – All of them**[60] **untie and tie** all their bandages **at the same time. אִיהוּ שָׁרֵי חַד וְאָסִיר חַד** – But **he unties and ties** his bandages **one by one,**[61] **אָמַר** – for **he says: דִּילְמָא מִבָּעֵינָא – I might be needed** at any moment; **דְּלָא אִיעַכֵּב** – therefore, I deal with my bandages in this way so **that I will not be delayed."**[62] **אֲזַל לְגַבֵּיהּ – [R' Yehoshua ben Levi] went to [the Messiah]. אָמַר לֵיהּ – He said to him: שָׁלוֹם עָלֶיךָ רַבִּי וּמוֹרִי – "Peace be upon you, my master and teacher!" אָמַר לֵיהּ – [The Messiah] said to [R' Yehoshua ben Levi]: שָׁלוֹם עָלֶיךָ בַּר לֵיוָאֵי – "Peace be upon you, son of Levi." אָמַר לֵיהּ – [R' Yehoshua ben Levi] asked him: לְאֵימַת אָתֵי מָר – "When is master coming?" אָמַר לֵיהּ – [The Messiah] answered him: הַיּוֹם – "Today!" אֲתָא לְגַבֵּי אֵלִיָּהוּ – [R' Yehoshua ben Levi] went** back **to Elijah. אָמַר לֵיהּ – [Elijah] asked him: מַאי אָמַר לָךְ – "What did he say to you?" אָמַר לֵיהּ – [R' Yehoshua**

NOTES

Alternatively, it shows that the Messiah is coming in the merit of our father Abraham, about whom Scripture states (*Genesis* 22:3): *He saddled his donkey* [to obey God's command to sacrifice his son, Isaac] (*Iyun Yaakov*).

Maharal explains that the word חֲמוֹר (donkey) is derived from חוֹמֶר — *raw material,* which lacks final form and finish. This is the opposite of spirituality, because spirituality is the ultimate in final form and finish. One who rides an animal is seen as totally separated from it, but yet in control of it. Thus, the Messiah, as a rider of a donkey, is portrayed in complete opposition to חוֹמֶר, *gross physicality*. He is the closest among men to pure spirituality. At the same time, he is in control of physicality — he rules it, and adapts it to its spiritual purpose.

A cloud is created from water, which has no shape of its own. [Water automatically assumes the shape of its receptacle.] Thus, a cloud too denotes raw physicality. However, a cloud differs from a donkey in that, being a heavenly body, a cloud represents physicality of a heavenly level. If the Jews are deserving, the Messiah will "ride the clouds" — an altogether more sublime level than that signified by a rider of a donkey (*Chidushei Aggados;* see *Gevuras Hashem* ch. 29 at length; see also *Rashi* to *Exodus* 4:20 and *Gur Aryeh* ibid.).

49. Several exchanges between Shmuel and Shapur [Shapur I, king of Persia, 241-272 C.E.] are recorded in the Talmud (e.g. *Berachos* 56a).

50. An alternative version of the text reads בְּדָקָא, *tested.* According to this version, the reference is to a horse that has been tested and found to be fast (*Rashi*).

51. Shapur was poking fun: It does not behoove the exalted Messiah to ride a donkey. Surely, a fine steed would be more appropriate! (*Rashi*).

Alternatively, סוּסְיָא בִּרְקָא means a horse that runs as fast as lightning (בִּרְקָא is from בָּרָק, *lightning*). According to this translation, Shapur meant: Perhaps the Messiah has not yet come because he has to ride a slow donkey. If he would ride my fastest horse, he might arrive sooner! (*Yad Ramah;* see *Maharsha* for another explanation).

52. [That is to say: Your finest horse is not as splendid as the Messiah's donkey.] Shmuel did not mean this seriously; he said it only to brush off Shapur's mockery by responding in kind (*Rashi;* cf. *Maharal;* see also *Maharsha*).

53. R' Shimon ben Yochai and his son hid in a cave for twelve years to avoid arrest by the Romans. During that time they were sustained in a miraculous fashion and their sole occupation was studying Torah (see *Shabbos* 33b).

54. In fact, all Jews have a share in the World to Come, as stated in the Mishnah on 90a. R' Yehoshua ben Levi was asking whether he would enter the World to Come directly, without prior judgment and suffering (see *Tosafos* to *Kesubos* 103b ד״ה מזומן).

55. The *Shechinah* [the Divine Presence] was with them (*Rashi*).

56. He saw only Elijah and himself, but he also heard the voice of the *Shechinah* [lamenting the length of the exile (see *Maharsha*)] (see *Rashi;* cf. *Yad Ramah*, *Maharsha*).

57. *Gra* emends the text to read: אַפִּתְחָא דְּרוֹמִי, *the gate of Rome* (cf. *Maharsha,* who translates *the southern gate*). This was the text of *Yad Ramah, Abarbanel, Maharsha* et al. (see *Dikdukei Sofrim*).

Elijah did not literally mean that the Messiah was at the gate of the city. Rather, he meant that the Messiah was in the part of Gan Eden that faces the city (*Rashi,* in the name of his teacher; cf. *Maharsha*).

The Midrash states that the Messiah was born when the Temple was destroyed and was subsequently taken to Gan Eden (*Maharsha*).

This should not be understood to mean that the Messiah is not a natural-born human being. Rather, in every generation since the destruction of the Temple there has lived a person of outstanding piety, ready to be invested with the spirit of the Messiah when the time for the redemption comes. As was the case with Moses, this person will not know that he is destined to be the Messiah, until the time is ready (*Chasam Sofer* Responsa vol. 6 §98; *R' Chaim Vital*, cited by *Margaliyos HaYam*).

58. How will it be possible to identify him?

59. They were afflicted with *tzaraas* — a disease whose symptoms include discolored patches on the skin (see *Leviticus* ch. 13). The Messiah himself is likewise afflicted, as stated in *Isaiah* (53:4): אָכֵן חֳלָיֵנוּ הוּא נָשָׂא וּמַכְאֹבֵינוּ סְבָלָם וַאֲנַחְנוּ חֲשַׁבְנֻהוּ נָגוּעַ מֻכֵּה אֱלֹהִים וּמְעֻנֶּה, *Indeed, it was our diseases that he bore and our pains that he endured, whereas we considered him plagued* (i.e. suffering *tzaraas* [see 98b note 39]), *smitten by God, and afflicted.* This verse teaches that the diseases that the people ought to have suffered because of their sins are borne instead by the Messiah (see *Rashi, Yad Ramah;* see also *Anaf Yosef, Maharal*).

It is difficult to explain the presence in Gan Eden of the other sickly paupers (*Maharsha;* see *Yeshuos Meshicho Iyun* 1, beginning of ch. 2). In light of this difficulty, *Abarbanel* shows that this story is a parable.

60. That is, all those who have several sores (*Rashi*).

61. [Literally: he unties one and ties one.] Each of the others unties all his bandages at the same time, cleans all his sores, and then reties all the bandages. The Messiah, however, unties only one bandage at a time; he cleans that sore and reties the bandage before proceeding to the next one. He does not allow two sores to be exposed at the same time (*Rashi*).

62. He does not want to delay even the amount of time it takes to tie two bandages (*Rashi*).

When the moment of redemption comes it must be grasped at once, before Israel's Heavenly accusers have an opportunity to issue new denunciations and postpone the redemption. The redemption from Egypt was "in haste" (*Exodus* 12:11) for the same reason (*Toras Chaim*).

מלכים יראו וקמו שרים וישתחוו אמר לו רבי אליעזר והלא כבר נאמר (א) אם תשוב ישראל נאום ה' אלי תשוב אמר לו רבי יהושע והלא כבר נאמר (ב) ואשמע את האיש לבוש הבדים אשר ממעל למימי היאור וירם ימינו ושמאלו אל השמים וישבע בחי העולם כי למועד מועדים וחצי וככלות נפץ יד עם קדש תכלינה כל אלה וגו' ושתק רבי אליעזר ואמר רבי אבא אין לך קץ מגולה מזה שנאמר (ג) ואתם הרי ישראל ענפכם תתנו ופריכם תשאו לעמי ישראל וגו' רבי (א) (אליעזר) אומר אף מזה שנאמר (ד) כי לפני הימים (האלה) [ההם] שכר האדם לא נהיה ושכר הבהמה איננה וליוצא ולבא אין שלום מן הצר (ב) מאי ליוצא ולבא אין שלום מן הצר רב אמר אף תלמידי חכמים שכתוב בהם שלום דכתיב (ה) שלום רב לאהבי תורתך אין שלום מפני צר ושמואל אמר עד שיהיו כל השערים כולן שקולין אמר רבי חנינא אין בן דוד בא עד שיתבקש דג לחולה ולא ימצא שנאמר (ו) אז אשקיע מימיהם ונהרותם כשמן אוליך וכתב (ג) (בתריה) (ז) ביום ההוא אצמיח קרן לבית ישראל אמר רבי חמא בר חנינא אין בן דוד בא עד שתכלה מלכות הזלה מישראל שנאמר (ח) וכרת הזלזלים במזמרות [א] וכתיב בתריה (ט) בעת ההיא יובל שי לה' צבאות עם ממשך ומורט אמר זעירי אמר רבי חנינא אין בן דוד בא עד שיכלו גסי הרוח מישראל שנאמר (י) כי אז אסיר מקרבך עליזי גאותך וכתיב (יא) והשארתי בקרבך עם עני ודל וחסו בשם ה' אמר רבי שמלאי משום רבי אלעזר בר"ש (ד) אין בן דוד בא עד שיכלו כל שופטים ושוטרים מישראל שנאמר (יב) ואשיבה ידי עליך ואצרוף כבור סיגיך וגו' ואשיבה שופטיך (ה) אמר עולא אין (ו) ירושלים נפדית אלא בצדקה שנאמר (יג) ציון במשפט תפדה ושביה בצדקה אמר רב פפא אי בטלי יהירי בטלי אמגושי אי בטלי דייני בטלי (ז) גזירפטי אי בטלי יהירי בטלי אמגושי דכתיב (יב) ואצרוף כבור סיגיך ואסירה כל בדיליך ואי בטלי דייני בטלי גזירפטי דכתיב (יד) הסיר ה' משפטיך פנה אויבך אמר ר' יוחנן אם ראית דור שמתמעט והולך חכה לו שנאמר (טו) ואת עם עני תושיע וגו' אמר רבי יוחנן אם ראית דור שצרות רבות באות עליו כנהר חכה לו שנאמר (טז) כי יבא כנהר צר (ו)רוח ה' נוססה בו וסמיך ליה ובא לציון גואל ואמר רבי יוחנן אין בן דוד בא אלא בדור שכולו זכאי או כולו חייב בדור שכולו זכאי דכתיב (יז) ועמך כולם צדיקים לעולם יירשו ארץ בדור שכולו חייב דכתיב (יח) וירא כי אין איש וישתומם כי אין מפגיע וכתיב (יט) למעני אעשה אמר רבי אלכסנדרי רבי יהושע בן לוי רמי כתיב (כ) בעתה וכתיב אחישנה זכו אחישנה לא זכו בעתה אמר רבי אלכסנדרי רבי יהושע בן לוי רמי כתיב (כא) וארו עם ענני שמיא כבר אינש אתה וכתיב (כב) עני ורוכב על חמור זכו עם ענני שמיא לא זכו עני רוכב על חמור אמר ליה שבור מלכא לשמואל אמריתו משיח על חמרא אתי אישדר ליה סוסיא (ח) ברקא דאית לי אמר ליה מי אית לך בר חיור גווני ר' יהושע בן לוי אשכח לאליהו דהוי קיימי אפיתחא דמערתא דרבי שמעון בן יוחאי אמר ליה אתינא לעלמא דאתי אמר ליה אם ירצה אדון הזה אמר רבי יהושע בן לוי שנים ראיתי וקול ג' שמעתי אמר ליה אימת אתי משיח אמר ליה זיל שייליה לדידיה והיכא יתיב אפיתחא [א] דקרתא ומאי סימניה יתיב ביני עניי סובלי חלאים וכולן שרו ואסירי בחד זימנא איהו שרי חד ואסיר חד אמר דילמא מבעינא דלא איעכב אזל לגביה אמר ליה שלום עליך רבי ומורי אמר ליה שלום עליך בר ליואי א"ל לאימת אתי מר א"ל היום אתא לגבי אליהו א"ל מאי אמר לך א"ל שלום עליך בר ליואי א"ל אבטחך לך ולאבוך לעלמא דאתי א"ל שקורי קא שקר בי דאמר לי היום אתינא ולא אתא א"ל הכי אמר לך (כג) היום אם בקולו תשמעו שאלו תלמידיו את רבי יוסי בן קיסמא אימתי בן דוד בא אמר מתיירא אני שמא תבקשו ממני אות אמרו לו אין אנו מבקשין ממך אות א"ל לכשיפול השער הזה ויבנה ויפול ויבנה ויפול ואין מספיקין לבנותו עד שבן דוד בא אמרו לו רבינו תן לנו אות אמר להם ולא כך אמרתם לי שאין אתם מבקשין ממני אות אמרו לו ואף על פי כן אמר להם אם כך יהפכו מי מערת פמיים לדם ונהפכו לדם בשעת פטירתו אמר להן העמיקו לי ארוני שאין

רש"י

כי למועד מועדים. אלמא יש קץ בדבר: וככלות נפץ יד עם קדש. כשתכלה תקומתם וחוזק ידיהם שהיתה נפולה אילך ואילך גבורה ותועלת לפשוט אנה ואנה ואחר שתכלה גבורתם שיהיו שפלים למאד: תכלינה. אלו הצרות ויבא משיח כדאמרינן כי אזלת יד: מגולה מזה. כשתתן ארץ ישראל פריה בעין יפה אז יקרב הקץ ואין לך קץ מגולה יותר: ר' אליעזר אומר מזה. הפסוק כשתראה דאין שום אדם משתכר ואף שכר הבהמה לא נהיה והיינו כדאמרן עד שתכלה פרוטה מן הכיס אין מעות מצויות בכיס: שכר בהמה. עבודת האדמה שהיא על ידי בהמה איננה: וליוצא ולבא אין שלום. אז יבא משיח: [שלום רב]. והיינו וליוצא ולבא אלו תלמידי חכמים אותם שהיה דינם לצאת ולבא בשלום כדכתיב שלום רב לאוהבי תורתך אפילו להנהו אין שלום: מן הצר. מרוב הצרות ל"א מיצר הרע: שקולין. שוין שער התבואה ויין רווחי' כדאמרן חמישית שובע גדול ל"א שקולין שוין שכולן יקרין: כשמן אוליך. שיהיו כולן קפויין וכיון שהם קפויין אין דגים נמצאין בתוכה: עד שתכלה מלכות הזלה. שלא תהא להם שום שולטנות לישראל אפילו שולטנות קלה ודלה: נטישותיו. ענפים קטנים כלומר השרים והשופטים: וחסו בשם השם. כלומר שתבא להם גאולה ויחסו בצל שדי: סיגיך. תערובות שבך: בדיליך. המובדלים לראשי עם: יהירי. גסי רוח מישראל: אמגושי. פרסיים מכשפין שמצערין ישראל במס' שבת (דף עה.) פלוגתא איכא למאן דאמר אמגושי חרשי ואיכא מ"ד גדופי עובדי כוכבים: גזירפטי. שופטים עובדי כוכבים החובטין את ישראל במקלות: ואצרוף כבור סיגיך. רבים וגדולים בגסותם כשאצרוף ואסלקם ממך אזי אסירה כל בדיליך: אמגושי. הבדלים מיראת המקום: סיגיך. כמו רב דמתרגמינן סגי: משפטיך. כמו [ב] (צפניה ג) שופטיך: פנה אויבך. גזירפטי: נוססה. כמו (ישעיה י) כמסוס נוסס וכמו (שם נא) יאכלם סס רוח המקום נוקבת ומחרבת אותן עם הצרות הבאות שאף הוא מתכוין להשמידם: יירשו ארץ. היינו גאולה: עם ענני שמיא כבר אינש אתי. במהירות: וכתיב עני ורוכב על החמור. כעני הבא על חמורו בעצלות: סוסי ברקא. סוס מסורק (ט) ומכוון ונאה שיש לי דגנאי הוא שיבא על חמור מלגלג היה ל"א סוסיא בדקא סוס בדוק לרוץ: בר חיור גווני. כלום יש לך סוס בר מאה גוונין שחמור שלו כן הוא במלתא בעלמא דחייה: חיור. מאה בלשון פרסי: האדון הזה. שכינה היתה עמהם: קול שלשה. דשכינה הוה בהדייהו: לדידיה. למשיח: בפתחא (י) דקרתא). נראה למורי לא בפתח העיר ממש אלא גן עדן הוא כנגד כל העולם וקאמר ליה דבאותו צד של גן עדן שכנגד פתח העיר משיח שרוי: סובלי חלאים. מנוגעים והוא נמי מנוגע דכתיב (ישעיה נג) והוא מחולל מפשעינו וכתיב (שם) חליינו הוא נשא: כולהו. מי שיש לו ארבע וחמש נגעים: אסרי להו ושרו בחדא זימנא. מתירין כל נגעתן ביחד ומקנחין אותן וחוזרין וקושרין אותן: ואיהו. משיח: שרי חד. נגע ומקנחו וקושרו ואח"כ מתיר האחר ועושה כן ואינו מתיר שני נגעים יחד דסבר אי בעי לי לצאת וליגאל את ישראל לא איתעכב כדי קשירת שני נגעים: אמר ליה. ר' יהושע למשיח לאימת אתי מר אמר ליה היום: אבטחך לך ולאביך לעולם הבא. דאי לאו צדיקים גמורין אתם לא הוה יהיב לך שלמא ולא הוה מדכר שמיה דאבוך: היום אם בקולו. של הקב"ה תשמעו: השער הזה. של עיר רומי שבעיר רומי היה אותו שער: ואין מספיקין לבנותו. פעם שלישית: מי פמיים. שירדן נובע ממנו כדתניא בבכורות (דף נה.) דן יוצא ממערת פמיים ומפרש התם שפיר: העמיקו ארוני. עשו לי קבר בקרקע עמוק: שאין

מסורת הש"ס

א) [נ"ל אלעזר], ב) [חגיגה י. ע"ש וצ"ע], ג) עיין רש"א בח"א, ד) [שבת קלט. ע"ש], ה) שבת דף קלט., ו) [הרמב"ם פרק י מהלכות מתנות עניים וכן בטור י"ד סי' רמז איתא ישראל וכצ"ל למובן ושביה בצדקה ודלא כמ"ש רש"א בח"א שנדחק בזה טובא בד"ה עד שיכלו שופטים מישראל וכו' ע"ש ברם לנוסחא שניה עדים נאמנים הרמב"ם וטור אחי' לספיר], ז) [גיר' הערוך גאזי דפאטי פי' פריסי ושוטרי השרים], ח) [עי' ברש"י דהכא ועי' ברש"י דע"ז ל. ד"ה מי בארג וכו' בארג לשון פרס משובח כמו סוסי בארג בחלק ע"ש], ט) ומלוין רש"ל, י) נ"ל דרומי.

ליקוטי רש"י

מלכים יראו. אותו וקמו [ישעיה מט, ז]. וקמו. לקראת ישראל לעתיד לבא [תענית טו.]. אם תשוב ישראל. בתשובה זו אלי. תשוב. לכבודך וגדולתך הראשונה [ירמיה ד, א]. וככלות נפץ יד עם קדש. כשתכלה כח ישראל כי אזלת יד ואפס עצור ועזוב (דברים לב) [דניאל יב, ז]. וכרת. הכורת את זלזלי הגפן הם הזמורות והשריגים. במזמרות. סרפ"ש בלע"ז. [הנטישות]. הם עיקרי הגפנים שקורין ליפ"ש בלע"ז [ישעיה יח, ה]. עם עני ודל. עם ענוותן ומקבל עולבן [צפניה ג, יב]. ואשיבה ידי עליך. מכה אחר מכה עד כלות הפושעים. כבור. ל' בורית סבו"ן בלע"ז ולשונו ל' נקיון כמו ובר לבב (תהלים כד) ע"ש שהוא מנקה הבגד מכתמיו. סיגיך. כמו כספך היה לסיגים האמור למעלה (ישעיה א, כב) תערובת נחשת בכסף קרוי סיג אף כאן תערוב' רשעים עם הכשרים אני אכלה הפושעי' שהם הסיג. כל בדיליך. בדיל המעורב בכסף כלומר הרשעים שבך בדיל אשטיי"ם בלע"ז [ישעיה א, כה]. במשפט תפדה. ע"י שיהיו בה עושה משפט. תפדה. מעוונותיה. ושביה. עושי תשובה שבתוכה. בצדקה. [במצדיקים עצמם במשפט ובצדק' שבתוכה] [שם, כז]. ואשיבה שופטיך. אעמיד לכם שופטים כשרים [שם, כו]. ואחר כך יקרא לך עיר הצדק לשרות בה שכינה [ע"ש]. אי בטלי יהירי. ישראל מתייהרים בבגדים וכמלבושי יהירות כפרסיים הללו. בטלי אמגושי. יבטלו מסיתים ומדיחים [דפ"י, המינים גלחים] המשניאים אותנו. סיגיך. הם גסי הרוח שמגדלין עצמן לשון ישגה מאד (איוב ח) ואחר כך ואסירה כל בדיליך אלו אותם המבדילים שונאי ישראל מן הקדוש ברוך הוא בשקריהם ובפחזותם. בטלי דייני. רשעים מישראל שמטין דין. בטלי. מעל ישראל. גזירפטי. נוגשי שוטרי עובדי כוכבים [שבת קלט.].
נוססה בו. נפלאות בו ל' נס [illegible] [ישעיה נט, יט]. וירא כי אין איש. ועתה בהנחמו על הרעה [illegible] ואין מפגיע וישתומם ל' אדם העומד [illegible] למעני. ולמען שמי הקדוש [שם מח, יא]. [illegible] מדת ענוה היא [זכריה ט, ט]. שבור מלכא. [illegible] פמיים. [illegible] כדאמר מר ירדן יוצא ממערת פמיים (בכורות נה.) [מגילה ו.].

הגהות הגר"א

[א] גמ' אפתחא דקרתא. נמחק תיבת דקרתא וצ"ב דרומי: [ב] רש"י ד"ה משפטיך כמו (צפניה ג). נמחק לפניה ג:

הגהות מהר"ב רנשבורג

א] גמ' שנאמר וכרת הזלזלים במזמרות ואת הנטישות הסר. כצ"ל:

תורה אור השלם

א) אִם תָּשׁוּב יִשְׂרָאֵל נְאֻם יְיָ אֵלַי תָּשׁוּב וְאִם תָּסִיר שִׁקּוּצֶיךָ מִפָּנַי וְלֹא תָנוּד: [ירמיה ד, א]
ב) וָאֶשְׁמַע אֶת הָאִישׁ לְבוּשׁ הַבַּדִּים אֲשֶׁר מִמַּעַל לְמֵימֵי הַיְאֹר וַיָּרֶם יְמִינוֹ וּשְׂמֹאלוֹ אֶל הַשָּׁמַיִם וַיִּשָּׁבַע בְּחֵי הָעוֹלָם כִּי לְמוֹעֵד מוֹעֲדִים וָחֵצִי וּכְכַלּוֹת נַפֵּץ יַד עַם קֹדֶשׁ תִּכְלֶינָה כָל אֵלֶּה: [דניאל יב, ז]
ג) וְאַתֶּם הָרֵי יִשְׂרָאֵל עַנְפְּכֶם תִּתֵּנוּ וּפֶרְיְכֶם תִּשְׂאוּ לְעַמִּי יִשְׂרָאֵל כִּי קֵרְבוּ לָבוֹא: [יחזקאל לו, ח]
ד) כִּי לִפְנֵי הַיָּמִים הָהֵם שְׂכַר הָאָדָם לֹא נִהְיָה וּשְׂכַר הַבְּהֵמָה אֵינֶנָּה וְלַיּוֹצֵא וְלַבָּא אֵין שָׁלוֹם מִן הַצָּר וַאֲשַׁלַּח אֶת כָּל הָאָדָם אִישׁ בְּרֵעֵהוּ: [זכריה ח, י]
ה) שָׁלוֹם רָב לְאֹהֲבֵי תוֹרָתֶךָ וְאֵין לָמוֹ מִכְשׁוֹל: [תהלים קיט, קסה]
ו) אָז אַשְׁקִיעַ מֵימֵיהֶם וְנַהֲרוֹתָם כַּשֶּׁמֶן אוֹלִיךְ נְאֻם אֲדֹנָי אֱלֹהִים: [יחזקאל לב, יד]
ז) בַּיּוֹם הַהוּא אַצְמִיחַ קֶרֶן לְבֵית יִשְׂרָאֵל וּלְךָ אֶתֵּן פִּתְחוֹן פֶּה בְּתוֹכָם וְיָדְעוּ כִּי אֲנִי יְיָ: [יחזקאל כט, כא]
ח) כִּי לִפְנֵי קָצִיר כְּתָם פֶּרַח וּבֹסֶר גֹּמֵל יִהְיֶה נִצָּה וְכָרַת הַזַּלְזַלִּים בַּמַּזְמֵרוֹת וְאֶת הַנְּטִישׁוֹת הֵסִיר הֵתַז: [ישעיה יח, ה]
ט) בָּעֵת הַהִיא יוּבַל שַׁי לַייָ צְבָאוֹת עַם מְמֻשָּׁךְ וּמוֹרָט וּמֵעַם נוֹרָא מִן הוּא וָהָלְאָה גּוֹי קַו קָו וּמְבוּסָה אֲשֶׁר בָּזְאוּ נְהָרִים אַרְצוֹ אֶל מְקוֹם שֵׁם יְיָ צְבָאוֹת הַר צִיּוֹן: [ישעיה יח, ז]
י) בַּיּוֹם הַהוּא לֹא תֵבוֹשִׁי מִכֹּל עֲלִילֹתַיִךְ אֲשֶׁר פָּשַׁעַתְּ בִּי כִּי אָז אָסִיר מִקִּרְבֵּךְ עַלִּיזֵי גַּאֲוָתֵךְ וְלֹא תוֹסִפִי לְגָבְהָה עוֹד בְּהַר קָדְשִׁי: [צפניה ג, יא]
יא) וְהִשְׁאַרְתִּי בְקִרְבֵּךְ עַם עָנִי וָדָל וְחָסוּ בְּשֵׁם יְיָ: [צפניה ג, יב]
יב) וְאָשִׁיבָה יָדִי עָלַיִךְ וְאֶצְרֹף כַּבֹּר סִיגָיִךְ וְאָסִירָה כָּל בְּדִילָיִךְ: וְאָשִׁיבָה שֹׁפְטַיִךְ כְּבָרִאשֹׁנָה וְיֹעֲצַיִךְ כְּבַתְּחִלָּה אַחֲרֵי כֵן יִקָּרֵא לָךְ עִיר הַצֶּדֶק קִרְיָה נֶאֱמָנָה: [ישעיה א, כה-כו]
יג) צִיּוֹן בְּמִשְׁפָּט תִּפָּדֶה וְשָׁבֶיהָ בִּצְדָקָה: [ישעיה א, כז]
יד) הֵסִיר יְיָ מִשְׁפָּטַיִךְ פִּנָּה אֹיְבֵךְ מֶלֶךְ יִשְׂרָאֵל יְיָ בְּקִרְבֵּךְ לֹא תִירְאִי רָע עוֹד: [צפניה ג, טו]
טו) וְאֶת עַם עָנִי תּוֹשִׁיעַ וְעֵינֶיךָ עַל רָמִים תַּשְׁפִּיל: [שמואל ב כב, כח]
טז) וְיִירְאוּ מִמַּעֲרָב אֶת שֵׁם יְיָ וּמִמִּזְרַח שֶׁמֶשׁ אֶת כְּבוֹדוֹ כִּי יָבוֹא כַנָּהָר צָר רוּחַ יְיָ נֹסְסָה בוֹ: וּבָא לְצִיּוֹן גּוֹאֵל וּלְשָׁבֵי פֶשַׁע בְּיַעֲקֹב נְאֻם יְיָ: [ישעיה נט, יט-כ]
יז) וְעַמֵּךְ כֻּלָּם צַדִּיקִים לְעוֹלָם יִירְשׁוּ אָרֶץ נֵצֶר מַטָּעַי מַעֲשֵׂה יָדַי לְהִתְפָּאֵר: [ישעיה ס, כא]
יח) וַיַּרְא כִּי אֵין אִישׁ וַיִּשְׁתּוֹמֵם כִּי אֵין מַפְגִּיעַ וַתּוֹשַׁע לוֹ זְרֹעוֹ וְצִדְקָתוֹ הִיא סְמָכָתְהוּ: [ישעיה נט, טז]
יט) לְמַעֲנִי לְמַעֲנִי אֶעֱשֶׂה כִּי אֵיךְ יֵחָל וּכְבוֹדִי לְאַחֵר לֹא אֶתֵּן: [ישעיה מח, יא]
כ) הַקָּטֹן יִהְיֶה לָאֶלֶף וְהַצָּעִיר לְגוֹי עָצוּם אֲנִי יְיָ בְּעִתָּהּ אֲחִישֶׁנָּה: [ישעיה ס, כב]
כא) חָזֵה הֲוֵית בְּחֶזְוֵי לֵילְיָא וַאֲרוּ עִם עֲנָנֵי שְׁמַיָּא כְּבַר אֱנָשׁ אָתֵה הֲוָה וְעַד עַתִּיק יוֹמַיָּא מְטָה וּקְדָמוֹהִי הַקְרְבוּהִי: [דניאל ז, יג]
כב) גִּילִי מְאֹד בַּת צִיּוֹן הָרִיעִי בַּת יְרוּשָׁלַיִם הִנֵּה מַלְכֵּךְ יָבוֹא לָךְ צַדִּיק וְנוֹשָׁע הוּא עָנִי וְרֹכֵב עַל חֲמוֹר וְעַל עַיִר בֶּן אֲתֹנוֹת: [זכריה ט, ט]
כג) כִּי הוּא אֱלֹהֵינוּ וַאֲנַחְנוּ עַם מַרְעִיתוֹ וְצֹאן יָדוֹ הַיּוֹם אִם בְּקֹלוֹ תִשְׁמָעוּ: [תהלים צה, ז]

ben Levi] answered [Elijah]: שָׁלוֹם עָלֶיךָ בַּר לִיוָאֵי – "He said, **'Peace be upon you, son of Levi.'** " אֲמַר לֵיהּ – **[Elijah] said to [R' Yehoshua ben Levi]:** אַבְטְחָךְ לָךְ וְלַאֲבוּךְ לְעָלְמָא דְאָתֵי – **"He has assured you and your father** that you are both destined **to** enter **the World to Come."**[63] אֲמַר לֵיהּ – **[R' Yehoshua ben Levi]** then **said to [Elijah]:** שַׁקּוּרֵי קָא שַׁקַּר בִּי – **"He lied to me,** דַּאֲמַר לִי הַיּוֹם אָתֵינָא – **for he said to me, 'I am coming today,'** וְלֹא אָתָא – **and he has not come!"** אֲמַר לֵיהּ – **[Elijah] said to [R' Yehoshua ben Levi]:** הָכִי אֲמַר לָךְ – **"This is what he was saying to you:** "הַיּוֹם אִם־בְּקֹלוֹ תִשְׁמָעוּ" – ***Today, if you heed His voice!*"**[64] [65]

The Gemara relates another exchange concerning the time of Messiah's arrival:

שָׁאֲלוּ תַּלְמִידָיו אֶת רַבִּי יוֹסֵי בֶּן קִיסְמָא – **R' Yose ben Kisma was asked by his students:** אֵימָתַי בֶּן דָּוִיד בָּא – **"When will the son of David come?"** אָמַר – **He answered:** מִתְיָירֵא אֲנִי שֶׁמָּא תְּבַקְשׁוּ מִמֶּנִּי אוֹת – **"I am afraid lest you ask me for a sign."**[66] אָמְרוּ לוֹ – **They said to him:** אֵין אָנוּ מְבַקְשִׁין מִמְּךָ אוֹת – **"We will not ask you for a sign."** אָמַר לָהֶם – **He said to them:** לִכְשֶׁיִּפּוֹל הַשַּׁעַר הַזֶּה וְיִבָּנֶה – **"When this gate**[67] **falls and is rebuilt,** וְיִפּוֹל וְיִבָּנֶה – **and** then **falls** a second time **and is rebuilt** וְיִפּוֹל – **and** then **falls** a third time, וְאֵין מַסְפִּיקִין לִבְנוֹתוֹ עַד שֶׁבֶּן דָּוִד בָּא – **they will not have a chance to rebuild it before the son of David comes."** אָמְרוּ לוֹ – **They said to him:** רַבֵּינוּ תֵּן לָנוּ אוֹת – **"Our teacher! Give us a sign!"** אָמַר לָהֶם – **He said to them:** וְלֹא כָּךְ אֲמַרְתֶּם לִי שֶׁאֵין אַתֶּם מְבַקְשִׁים מִמֶּנִּי אוֹת – **"But did you not tell me that you would not ask me for a sign?"** אָמְרוּ לוֹ – **They said to him:** וְאַף עַל פִּי כֵן – **"Even so."** אָמַר לָהֶם – **He said to them:** אִם כָּךְ יֵהָפְכוּ מֵי מְעָרַת פַּמְיָיס לְדָם – **"If so,**[68] **may the waters of the cave of Pame'as**[69] **turn into blood!"** וְנֶהֶפְכוּ לְדָם – **And** indeed **they turned into blood.**

R' Yose ben Kisma gives another prediction concerning the advent of the Messianic era:

בִּשְׁעַת פְּטִירָתוֹ אָמַר לָהֶן – **At the time of his death he said to [those present]:** הַעֲמִיקוּ לִי אֲרוֹנִי – **"Put my coffin deep** in the ground,

NOTES

63. Unless you are both completely righteous he would not have greeted you and mentioned your father's name (*Rashi*).

64. *Psalms* 95:7. The redemption will come before its fixed time, *if* the people "heed God's voice" — i.e. they repent and perform virtuous deeds (*Maharsha*).

Maharsha raises the following difficulty: The Gemara in *Eruvin* 43b states that Elijah will appear to the people the day before the Messiah arrives. In this narrative, it is clear Elijah had not yet come. Therefore, how could the Messiah suggest that it was possible for him to arrive that very day?

In view of this difficulty, *Maharsha* concludes that when the Messiah said "today" he did not mean it literally [rather, he meant the earliest possible opportunity].

However, if this is so, why did the Messiah prepare himself to come to redeem the Jews at just a moment's notice?

Some commentators resolve both of these difficulties by asserting that Elijah will precede the Messiah only if the redemption occurs in its preordained time. In the event of an early redemption, they will arrive together. The reference here is to an early redemption, as is evident from the Messiah's remark that he will come "today" (*Otzar Balum* on *Ein Yaakov;* see *Chasam Sofer* Responsa vol. 6 §98; see also note 48).

65. *Maharal* explains this episode as an allegory in line with his general approach that the Sages expressed profound spiritual concepts in simple terms. The following are some of his points in brief:

R' Yehoshua ben Levi met Elijah: The appearance of Elijah is not necessarily a visual matter. It may involve the reception in one's mind of a thought implanted there by Elijah.

Ask the Messiah himself: Asking the Messiah means dwelling upon the concept of the Messiah.

He sits at the gate of Rome: When Rome falls, the Messianic Kingdom will rise.

He sits among sickly paupers: The natural world is hostile to him because his role is to bring the supernatural redemption.

[See also *Abarbanel* (*Yeshuos Meshicho, Iyun* 1 ch. 2) who shows that this narrative is allegorical (see note 59), and presents two interpretations of it.]

66. I.e. a supernatural sign that will attest to the truth of my prediction (*Maharsha*).

67. I.e. the gate of Rome (see notes 19 and 65). R' Yose ben Kisma was visiting Rome at that time (*Rashi* in *Ein Yaakov;* cf. *Maharsha, Maharal, Ben Yehoyada*).

68. That is to say: Since you insist on a sign, I will give you one.

[See *Ben Yehoyada,* who explains the students' behavior and why R' Yose ben Kisma eventually acquiesced and gave them a sign.]

69. The source of the Jordan (*Rashi,* from *Bechoros* 55a). [פַּמְיָיס, *Pame'as,* is the modern Banias, a town in Upper Galilee on the southern slope of Mt. Hermon. In ancient times it was rebuilt by Herod's son Phillipus, who named the town Caesarea.]

מלכים יראו וקמו שרים וישתחוו אמר לו רבי אליעזר והלא כבר נאמר א) אם תשוב ישראל נאום ה' אלי תשוב אמר לו רבי יהושע והלא כבר נאמר ב) ואשמע את האיש לבוש הבדים אשר ממעל למימי היאור וירם ימינו ושמאלו אל השמים וישבע בחי העולם כי למועד מועדים וחצי וככלות נפץ יד עם קדש תכלינה כל אלה וגו' ושתק רבי אליעזר ואמר רבי אבא אין לך קץ מגולה מזה שנאמר ג) ואתם הרי ישראל ענפכם תתנו ופריכם תשאו לעמי ישראל וגו' רבי (א) אליעזר) אומר אף מזה שנאמר ד) כי לפני הימים (האלה) [ההם] שכר האדם לא נהיה ושכר הבהמה איננה וליוצא ולבא אין שלום מן הצר ב) מאי ליוצא ולבא אין שלום מן הצר רב אמר אף תלמידי חכמים שכתוב בהם שלום דכתיב ה) שלום רב לאהבי תורתך אין שלום מפני צר ושמואל אמר עד שיהיו כל השערים כולן שקולין אמר רבי חנינא אין בן דוד בא עד שיתבקש דג לחולה ולא ימצא שנאמר ו) אז אשקיע מימיהם ונהרותם כשמן אוליך וכתב (ג) בתריה) ז) ביום ההוא אצמיח קרן לבית ישראל אמר רבי חמא בר חנינא אין בן דוד בא עד שתכלה מלכות הזלה מישראל שנאמר ח) וכרת הזלזלים במזמרות א] וכתיב בתריה ט) בעת ההיא יובל שי לה' צבאות עם ממשך ומורט אמר זעירי אמר רבי חנינא אין בן דוד בא עד שיכלו גסי הרוח מישראל שנאמר י) כי אז אסיר מקרבך עליזי גאותך וכתיב יא) והשארתי בקרבך עם עני ודל וחסו בשם ה' אמר רבי שמלאי משום רבי אלעזר בר"ש ד) אין בן דוד בא עד שיכלו כל שופטים ושוטרים מישראל שנאמר יב) ואשיבה ידי עליך ואצרוף כבור סיגיך וגו' ואשיבה שופטיך ה) אמר עולא אין ו) ירושלים נפדית אלא בצדקה שנאמר יג) ציון במשפט תפדה ושביה בצדקה אמר רב פפא אי בטלי יהירי בטלי אמגושי אי בטלי דייני בטלי ז) גזירפטי אי בטלי יהירי בטלי אמגושי דכתיב יב) ואצרוף כבור סיגיך ואסירה כל בדיליך ואי בטלי דייני בטלי גזירפטי דכתיב יד) הסיר ה' משפטיך פנה אויבך אמר ר' יוחנן אם ראית דור שמתמעט והולך חכה לו שנאמר טו) ואת עם עני תושיע וגו' אמר רבי יוחנן אם ראית דור שצרות רבות באות עליו כנהר חכה לו שנאמר טז) כי יבא כנהר צר (ו)רוח ה' נוססה בו וסמיך ליה ובא לציון גואל ואמר רבי יוחנן אין בן דוד בא אלא בדור שכולו זכאי או כולו חייב בדור שכולו זכאי דכתיב יז) ועמך כולם צדיקים לעולם יירשו ארץ בדור שכולו חייב דכתיב יח) וירא כי אין איש וישתומם כי אין מפגיע וכתיב יט) למעני אעשה אמר רבי אלכסנדרי רבי יהושע בן לוי רמי כתיב כ) בעתה וכתיב אחישנה זכו אחישנה לא זכו בעתה אמר רבי אלכסנדרי רבי יהושע בן לוי רמי כתיב כא) וארו עם ענני שמיא כבר אינש אתה וכתיב כב) עני ורוכב על חמור זכו עם ענני שמיא לא זכו עני רוכב על חמור אמר ליה שבור מלכא לשמואל אמריתו משיח על חמרא אתי אישדר ליה סוסיא ח) ברקא דאית לי אמר ליה מי אית לך בר חיור גווני ר' יהושע בן לוי אשכח לאליהו דהוי קיימי אפיתחא דמערתא דרבי שמעון בן יוחאי אמר ליה אתינא לעלמא דאתי אמר ליה אם ירצה אדון הזה אמר רבי יהושע בן לוי שנים ראיתי וקול ג' שמעתי אמר ליה אימת אתי משיח אמר ליה זיל שייליה לדידיה והיכא יתיב אפיתחא א] דקרתא ומאי סימניה יתיב ביני עניי סובלי חלאים וכולן שרו ואסירי בחד זימנא איהו שרי חד ואסיר חד אמר דילמא מבעינא דלא איעכב אזל לגביה אמר ליה שלום עליך רבי ומורי אמר ליה שלום עליך בר ליואי א"ל לאימת אתי מר א"ל היום אתא לגבי אליהו א"ל מאי אמר לך א"ל שלום עליך בר ליואי א"ל אבטחך לך ולאבוך לעלמא דאתי א"ל שקורי קא שקר בי דאמר לי היום אתינא ולא אתא א"ל הכי אמר לך כג) היום אם בקולו תשמעו שאלו תלמידיו את רבי יוסי בן קיסמא אימתי בן דוד בא אמר מתיירא אני שמא תבקשו ממני אות אמרו לו אין אנו מבקשין ממך אות א"ל לכשיפול השער הזה ויבנה ויפול ויבנה ויפול ואין מספיקין לבנותו עד שבן דוד בא אמרו לו רבינו תן לנו אות אמר להם ולא כך אמרתם לי שאין אתם מבקשין ממני אות אמרו לו ואף על פי כן אמר להם אם כך יהפכו מי מערת פמיים לדם ונהפכו לדם בשעת פטירתו אמר להן העמיקו לי ארוני שאין

רש"י

כי למועד מועדים. אלמא יש קץ בדבר: וככלות נפץ יד עם קדש. כשתכלה תקומתם וחוזק ידיהם שהיתה נפולה אילך ואילך גבורה ותועלת לפשוט אנה ואנה ואחר שתכלה גבורתם שיהיו שפלים למאד: תכלינה. אלו הצרות ויבא משיח כדאמרינן כי אזלת יד: מגולה מזה. כשתתן ארץ ישראל פריה בעין יפה אז יקרב הקץ ואין לך קץ מגולה יותר: ר' אליעזר אומר מזה. הפסוק כשתראה דאין שום אדם משתכר ואף שכר הבהמה לא נהיה והיינו כדאמרן עד שתכלה פרוטה מן הכיס אין מעות מצויות בכיס: שכר בהמה. עבודת האדמה שהיא על ידי בהמה איננה: וליוצא ולבא אין שלום. אז יבא משיח: [שלום רב]. והיינו וליוצא ולבא אלו תלמידי חכמים אותם שהיה דינם לצאת ולבא בשלום כדכתיב שלום רב לאוהבי תורתך אפילו להנהו אין שלום: מן הצר. מרוב הצרות ל"א מיצר הרע: שקולין. שוין שער התבואה ויין רוחי' כדאמרן חמישית שובע גדול ל"א שקולין שוין שכולן יקרין: כשמן אוליך. שיהיו כולן קפויין וכיון שהם קפויין אין דגים נמצאין בתוכה: עד שתכלה מלכות הזלה. שלא תהא להם שום שולטנות לישראל אפילו שולטנות קלה ודלה: נטישותיו. ענפים קטנים כלומר השרים והשופטים: וחסו בשם השם. כלומר שתבא להם גאולה ויחסו בצל שדי: סיגיך. תערובות שבך: בדיליך. המובדלים לראשי עם: יהירי. גסי רוח מישראל: אמגושי. פרסיים מכשפין שמצערין ישראל במס' שבת (דף עה.) פלוגתא איכא למאן דאמר אמגושי חרשי ואיכא מ"ד גדופי עובדי כוכבים: גזירפטי. שופטים עובדי כוכבים השוטטין את ישראל במקלות: ואצרוף כבור סיגיך. רבים וגדולים בגסותם כשאצרוף ואסלקם ממך אזי אסירה כל בדיליך: אמגושי. הבדלים מיראת המקום: סיגיך. כמו רב דמתרגמינן סגי: משפטיך. כמו [ב] (צפניה ג) שופטיך: פנה אויבך. גזירפטי: נוססה. כמו (ישעיה י) כמסוס נוסס וכמו (שם נט) יאכלם סס רוח המקום נוקבת ומחרבת אותן עם הצרות הבאות שאף הוא מתכוין להשמידם: יירשו ארץ. היינו גאולה: עם ענני שמיא כבר אינש אתי. במהירות: וכתיב עני ורוכב על החמור. כעני הבא על חמורו בעצלות: סוסי ברקא. סוס מסורק ט) ומכוון ונאה שיש לי דגנאי הוא שיבא על חמור מלגלג היה ל"א סוסיא בדקא סוס בדוק לרוץ: בר חיור גווני. כלום יש לך סוס בר מאה גוונין שחמור שלו כן הוא במלתא בעלמא דחייה: חיור. מאה בלשון פרסי: האדון הזה. שכינה היתה עמהם: קול שלשה. דשכינה הוה בהדייהו: לדידיה. למשיח: בפתחא (י) דקרתא). נראה למורי לא בפתח העיר ממש אלא גן עדן הוא כנגד כל העולם וקאמר ליה דבאותו צד של גן עדן שכנגד פתח העיר משיח שרוי: סובלי חלאים. מנוגעים והוא נמי מנוגע דכתיב (ישעיה נג) והוא מחולל מפשעינו וכתיב (שם) חליינו הוא נשא: כולהו. מי שיש לו ארבע וחמש נגעים: אסרי להו ושרו בחדא זימנא. מתירין כל נגעתן ביחד ומקנחין אותן וחוזרין וקושרין אותן: ואיהו. משיח: שרי חד. נגע ומקנחו וקושרו ואח"כ מתיר האחר ועושה כן ואינו מתיר שני נגעים יחד דסבר אי בעי לי לצאת וליגאל את ישראל לא איתעכב כדי קשירת שני נגעים: אמר ליה. ר' יהושע למשיח לאימת אתי מר אמר ליה היום: אבטחך לך ולאביך לעולם הבא. דאי לאו לדיקים גמורין אתם לא הוה יהיב לך שלמא ולא הוה מדכר שמיה דאבוך: היום אם בקולו. של הקב"ה תשמעו: השער הזה. של עיר רומי שבעיר רומי היה אותו שער: ואין מספיקין לבנותו. פעם שלישית: מי פמיים. שירדן נובע ממנו כדתניא בבכורות (דף נה.) דן יוצא ממערת פמיים ומפרש התם שפיר: העמיקו ארוני. עשו לי קבר בקרקע עמוק:

מסורת הש"ס

א) [נ"ל אלעזר], ב) [חגיגה י. ע"ש ונ"ע], ג) עיין רש"א בח"א, ד) [שבת קלט. ע"ש], ה) שבת דף קלט., ו) [הרמב"ם פרק י מהלכות מתנות עניים וכן בטור י"ד סי' רמז איתא ישראל וכנ"ל למובן ושביה בצדקה ודלא כמ"ש רש"א בח"א שנדחק בזה טובא בד"ה עד שילא שופטים מישראל וכו' ע"ש ברם לנוסחא שניה עדים נאמנים הרמב"ם וטור אתי' לשפיר], ז) [גיר' הערוך גאזי דפאטי פי' סריסי ושוטרי השרים], ח) [עי' ברש"י דהכא ועי' ברש"י דע"ז ל. ד"ה מי באנג וכו' באנג לשון פרס משובח כמו סוסי באנג בחלק ע"ש], ט) ומצויין רש"ל, י) נ"ל דרומי.

ליקוטי רש"י

מלכים יראו. אותו וקמו [ישעיה מט, ז]. וקמו. לקראת ישראל לעתיד לבא [תענית טו.]. אם תשוב ישראל. בתשובה זו אלי. תשוב. לכבודך וגדולתך הראשונה [ירמיה ד, א]. וככלות נפץ יד עם קדש. כשתכלה כח ישראל כי אזלת יד ואפס עצור ועזוב (דברים לב) [דניאל יב, ז]. וכרת. הכורת את זלזלי הגפן הם הזמורות והשריגים. במזמרות. שרפ"ש בלע"ז. [הנטישות]. הם עיקרי הגפנים שקורין ליפ"ש בלע"ז [ישעיה יח, ה]. עם עני ודל. עם ענותן ומקבל עולבן [צפניה ג, יב]. ואשיבה ידי עליך. מכה אחר מכה עד כלות הפושעים. כבור. ל' בורית סבו"ן בלע"ז ולשונו ל' נקיון כמו ובר לבב (תהלים כד) ע"ש שהוא מנקה הבגד מכתמיו. סיגיך. כמו כספך היה לסיגים האמור למעלה (ישעיה א, כב) תערובת נחשת בכסף קרוי סיג אף כאן תערוב' רשעים עם הכשרים אני אכלה הפושעי' שהם הסיג. כל בדיליך. בדיל המעורב בכסף כלומר הרשעים שבך בדיל אסטיי"ם בלע"ז [ישעיה א, כה]. במשפט תפדה. ע"י שיהיו בה עושה משפט. תפדה. מעונותיה. ושביה. עושי תשובה שבתוכה. בצדקה. [במצדיקים עצמם במשפט ובצדק' שבתוכה] [שם, כז]. ואשיבה שופטיך. אעמיד לכם שופטים כשרים [שם, כו]. ואחר כן יקרא לך עיר הצדק לשרות בה שכינה [שם, כז]. אי בטלי יהירי. ישראל מתיהרים בבלורית ומלבושי יהירות כפרסים הללו. בטלי אמגושי. יבטלו חכמים ומדיחים [דף' המינים גלחים] המתעתעים אותם. סיגיך. הם גסי הרוח שמגדלין עצמן כלשון ישגא מאד (איוב ח) ואמר כך ואסירה כל בדיליך אלו אותם המבדלים שונאי ישראל מן הקדוש ברוך הוא בשקריהם ובפתוייהם. בטלי דייני. רשעים מישראל שמטין דין. בטלי. מעל ישראל. גזירפטי. נוגשי שוטרי עובדי כוכבים [שבת קלט.]. נוספה בו. נפלאות בו ל' נס ד"א נוספה בו אוכלת בו כתולעת בעץ כמו (ישעיה י) והיה כמסוס נוסס [ישעיה נט, יט]. וירא כי אין איש. ועתה בהנחמו על הרעה לעמו רואה כי אין איש צדיק לעמוד בפרץ. וישתומם. ויתרעם לראות אם יש מפגיע בעדם ואין מפגיע וישתומם ל' אדם העומד ותוהא ושותק בתמהונו ותי"ו וישתומם כתי"ו של משתולל שניהם משמשות לשון מתפעל וכן דרך התיבה שיסודה הראשון שי"ן או סמ"ך כשהיא נהפכת ללשון מתפעל נתפעל ויתפעל בא התי"ו באמצע אותיות שורש התיבה נמצא וישתומם לשון שמו שמים (ירמיה ב) משמים בתוכם (יחזקאל ג) נשמו אחרונים (איוב יח) ל' תמהון [שם, טז]. למעני. ולמען שמי הקדוש [שם מח, יא]. כבר אינש אתה. הוא מלך המשיח [דניאל ז, יג]. עני. ענותן. ורוכב על חמור. מדת ענוה היא [זכריה ט, ט]. שבור מלכא. מלך פרס היה [סוכה נג.]. עובד כוכבים היה [ע"ז עו:]. פמיים. שמשם ירדן יוצא כדאמר מר ירדן יוצא ממערת פמיים (בכורות נה.) [מגילה ו.].

הגהות הגר"א

[א] גמ' אפתחא דקרתא. נמחק תיבת דקרתא ונ"ב דרומי: [ב] רש"י ד"ה משפטיך כמו (צפניה ג). נמחק לפניה ג:

הגהות מהר"ב רנשבורג

א] גמ' שנאמר וכרת הזלזלים במזמרות ואת הנטישות הסר. כנ"ל:

תורה אור השלם

א) אם תשוב ישראל נאם יי אלי תשוב ואם תסיר שקוציך מפני ולא תנוד: [ירמיה ד, א]

ב) ואשמע את האיש לבוש הבדים אשר ממעל למימי היאר וירם ימינו ושמאלו אל השמים וישבע בחי העולם כי למועד מועדים וחצי וככלות נפץ יד עם קדש תכלינה כל אלה: [דניאל יב, ז]

ג) ואתם הרי ישראל ענפכם תתנו ופריכם תשאו לעמי ישראל כי קרבו לבוא: [יחזקאל לו, ח]

ד) כי לפני הימים ההם שכר האדם לא נהיה ושכר הבהמה איננה וליוצא ולבא אין שלום מן הצר ואשלח את כל האדם איש ברעהו: [זכריה ח, י]

ה) שלום רב לאהבי תורתך ואין למו מכשול: [תהלים קיט, קסה]

ו) אז אשקיע מימיהם ונהרותם כשמן אוליך נאם אדני אלהים: [יחזקאל לב, יד]

ז) ביום ההוא אצמיח קרן לבית ישראל ולך אתן פתחון פה בתוכם וידעו כי אני יי: [יחזקאל כט, כא]

ח) כי לפני קציר כתם פרח ובסר גמל יהיה נצה וכרת הזלזלים במזמרות ואת הנטישות הסיר התז: [ישעיה יח, ה]

ט) בעת ההיא יובל שי ליי צבאות עם ממשך ומורט ומעם נורא מן הוא והלאה גוי קו קו ומבוסה אשר בזאו נהרים ארצו אל מקום שם יי צבאות הר ציון: [ישעיה יח, ז]

י) ביום ההוא לא תבושי מכל עלילתיך אשר פשעת בי כי אז אסיר מקרבך עליזי גאותך ולא תוספי לגבהה עוד בהר קדשי: [צפניה ג, יא]

יא) והשארתי בקרבך עם עני ודל וחסו בשם יי: [צפניה ג, יב]

יב) ואשיבה ידי עליך ואצרף כבר סיגיך ואסירה כל בדיליך: ואשיבה שפטיך כבראשנה ויעציך כבתחלה אחרי כן יקרא לך עיר הצדק קריה נאמנה: [ישעיה א, כה-כו]

יג) ציון במשפט תפדה ושביה בצדקה: [ישעיה א, כז]

יד) הסיר יי משפטיך פנה איבך מלך ישראל יי בקרבך לא תיראי רע עוד: [צפניה ג, טו]

טו) ואת עם עני תושיע ועיניך על רמים תשפיל: [שמואל ב' כב, כח]

טז) וייראו ממערב את שם יי וממזרח שמש את כבודו כי יבוא כנהר צר רוח יי נססה בו: ובא לציון גואל ולשבי פשע ביעקב נאם יי: [ישעיה נט, יט-כ]

יז) ועמך כלם צדיקים לעולם ירשו ארץ נצר מטעי מעשה ידי להתפאר: [ישעיה ס, כא]

יח) וירא כי אין איש וישתומם כי אין מפגיע ותושע לו זרעו וצדקתו היא סמכתהו: [ישעיה נט, טז]

יט) למעני למעני אעשה כי איך יחל וכבודי לאחר לא אתן: [ישעיה מח, יא]

כ) הקטן יהיה לאלף והצעיר לגוי עצום אני יי בעתה אחישנה: [ישעיה ס, כב]

כא) חזה הוית בחזוי ליליא וארו עם ענני שמיא כבר אנש אתה הוה ועד עתיק יומיא מטה וקדמוהי הקרבוהי: [דניאל ז, יג]

כב) גילי מאד בת ציון הריעי בת ירושלים הנה מלכך יבוא לך צדיק ונושע הוא עני ורכב על חמור ועל עיר בן אתנות: [זכריה ט, ט]

כג) כי הוא אלהינו ואנחנו עם מרעיתו וצאן ידו היום אם בקלו תשמעו: [תהלים צה, ז]

שאין כל דקל ודקל שבבבל שאין סוס של פרסיים נקשר בו ואין לך כל ארון וארון שבארץ ישראל שאין סוס מדי אוכל בו תבן [א] אמר רב אין בן דוד בא עד שתתפשט המלכות [ב] על ישראל תשעה חדשים שנאמר [א] לכן יתנם עד עת יולדה ילדה ויתר אחיו ישובון על בני ישראל אמר עולא ייתי ולא איחמיניה וכן אמר [[ג] רבה] ייתי ולא איחמיניה רב יוסף אמר ייתי ואזכי דאיתיב בטולא דכופיתא דחמריה אמר ליה אביי (לרבא) [[ד] לרבה] מאי טעמא אילימא משום חבלו של משיח והתניא שאלו תלמידיו את רבי אלעזר מה יעשה אדם וינצל מחבלו של משיח יעסוק בתורה ובגמילות חסדים ומר הא תורה והא גמילות חסדים אמר [ליה] שמא יגרום החטא כדר' יעקב בר אידי [ה] דר' יעקב בר אידי רמי כתיב [ב] הנה אנכי עמך ושמרתיך בכל אשר תלך וכתיב [ג] ויירא יעקב מאד וייצר לו שהיה מתיירא שמא [ו] יגרום החטא כדתניא [ד] עד יעבור עמך ה' זו ביאה ראשונה עד יעבור עם זו קנית זו ביאה שניה אמור מעתה ראויים היו ישראל לעשות להם נס בביאה שניה כביאה ראשונה אלא שגרם החטא וכן אמר ר' יוחנן ייתי ולא איחמיניה א"ל ריש לקיש מ"ט אילימא משום דכתיב [ה] כאשר ינוס איש מפני הארי ופגעו הדוב [ובא הבית] וסמך ידו אל הקיר ונשכו נחש בא ואראך דוגמתו בעולם הזה בזמן שאדם יוצא לשדה ופגע בו סנטר דומה כמי שפגע בו ארי נכנס לעיר פגע בו גבאי דומה כמי שפגעו דוב נכנס לביתו ומצא בניו ובנותיו מוטלין ברעב דומה כמי שנשכו נחש אלא משום דכתיב [ו] שאלו נא וראו אם ילד זכר מדוע ראיתי כל גבר ידיו על חלציו כיולדה ונהפכו כל פנים לירקון מאי ראיתי כל גבר אמר רבא בר יצחק אמר רב מי שכל גבורה שלו ומאי ונהפכו כל פנים לירקון אמר רבי יוחנן פמליא של מעלה ופמליא של מטה בשעה שאמר הקב"ה הללו מעשה ידי והללו מעשה ידי היאך אאבד אלו מפני אלו אמר רב פפא היינו דאמרי אינשי רהיט ונפל תורא ואזיל ושדי ליה סוסיא באורייה אמר רב גידל אמר רב עתידין ישראל דאכלי שני משיח אמר רב יוסף פשיטא ואלא מאן אכיל להו חילק ובילק אכלי להו לאפוקי [ז] מדרבי הילל דאמר אין משיח לישראל שכבר אכלוהו בימי חזקיה אמר רב לא אברי עלמא אלא לדוד ושמואל אמר למשה ורבי יוחנן אמר למשיח מה שמו דבי רבי שילא אמרי שילה שמו שנאמר [ז] עד כי יבא שילה דבי רבי ינאי אמרי ינון שמו שנאמר [ח] יהי שמו לעולם לפני שמש ינון שמו דבי רבי חנינה אמר חנינה שמו שנאמר [ט] אשר לא אתן לכם חנינה ויש אומרים מנחם בן חזקיה שמו שנאמר [י] כי רחק ממני מנחם משיב נפשי ורבנן אמרי חיוורא דבי רבי שמו שנאמר [כ] אכן חליינו הוא נשא ומכאובינו סבלם ואנחנו חשבנוהו נגוע מוכה אלהים ומעונה אמר רב נחמן אי מן חייא הוא כגון אנא שנאמר [ל] והיה אדירו ממנו ומושלו מקרבו יצא אמר רב אי מן חייא הוא כגון רבינו הקדוש אי מן מתיא הוא כגון דניאל איש חמודות אמר רב יהודה אמר רב עתיד הקדוש ברוך הוא להעמיד להם דוד אחר שנאמר [מ] ועבדו את ה' אלהיהם ואת דוד מלכם אשר אקים להם הקים לא נאמר אלא אקים א"ל רב פפא לאביי והכתיב [נ] ודוד עבדי נשיא להם לעולם כגון קיסר ופלגי קיסר דרש רבי שמלאי מאי דכתיב [ס] הוי המתאוים את יום ה' למה זה לכם יום ה' הוא חשך ולא אור משל לתרנגול ועטלף שהיו מצפין לאור א"ל תרנגול לעטלף אני מצפה לאורה שאורה שלי היא ואתה למה לך אורה והיינו

שאין סוס מדי אוכל בו תבן. שמוליכין הארונות חוץ לקרקע ועושין מהן אבוסים במלחמת גוג ומגוג: שאין כל דקל וכו'. כלומר עתידין פרס ומדי לבא על בבל וללכדה ונתמלאה כל ארץ בבל חיילות פרסיים וסוסיהם ומשם באים לא"י ולוכדים אותה: עד שתפשוט מלכות על ישראל ט' חדשים שנאמר לכן יתנם לישראל עד עת יולדה ילדה. היינו ט' חדשים כדמתרגמינן בכן יתמסרון כעידן דילדתא למילד וכתיב (מיכה ה) ועמד ורעה בעוז ה' וגו' וישבו כי עתה יגדל ומתרגמינן ויתיבון מביני גלוותהון: על בני ישראל. היינו כל העולם שישראל מפוזרים בו: ייתי. משיח ולא אחמיניה: בטולא דכופיתא דחמריה. בצל הרעי של חמורו כלומר אפילו בכך אני רוצה ובלבד שאראנו: כופיתא. רעי כמו רמא כופת' וסכר ירדנא בבבא בתרא (ד' עג:): מאי טעמא. אמר לא אחמיניה: חבלו של משיח. גורלו ולקמן בעי מאי היא ל"א חבלו פחדים וחבלים שיהיו בימיו מחיל העובדי כוכבים: לעשות להם נס. לעלות בזרוע על כרחם של מלכי פרס: בביאה שניה. בימי עזרא כביאה ראשונה בימי יהושע מדהקישן הכתוב: מאי טעמא. איזו צרה באה בארץ בימיו שאתה אומר לא אחמיניה: סנטר. מפרש בב"ב (דף סח.) בר מחוזניתא שיודע מיצרי השדות וגבוליהן עד כאן של פלוני מכאן ואילך של פלוני ובידו לרבות לאחד ולמעט לאחר וכשפוגעו אותו סנטר רוצה למדוד שדותיו לקצר מיצרי השדות ודומה כמי שפגע בו ארי: גבאי. גובה מס המלך: מי שכל הגבורה שלו. הקב"ה מצטער בעצמו כיולדה ואומר בשעה שמעביר העובדי כוכבים מפני ישראל היאך אאביד אלו מפני אלו: פמליא של מעלה ושל מטה. מלאכים וישראל: אפילו הגרים לא גרסינן: רהיט ונפיל תורא ואזיל ושדי סוסיא באורייה. כשרץ השור ונפל מעמידין סוס במקומו באבוסו מה שלא היה רוצה לעשות קודם מפלתו של שור שהיה חביב עליו שורו ביותר וכשמתרפא השור היום או למחר ממפלתו קשה לו להוציא סוסו מפני השור לאחר שהעמידו שם כך הקב"ה כיון שרואה מפלתן של ישראל נותן גדולתו לעובדי כוכבים וכשחוזרים ישראל בתשובה ונגאלין קשה לו לאבד עובדי כוכבים מפני ישראל: אורייה. כמו (מלכים א ה) ארוות סוסים: דאכלי שני משיח. שובע שיהיה באותן הימים לישראל יהיה: אלא חילק ובילק אכלי להו. כך היו רגילין לומר כאדם שאומר וכי שדים ושדות יאכלוהו ובמסכת חולין (דף יט.) לא חילק ידענא ולא בילק ידענא ולי נראה דמשמעות לשון חילק ובילק לשון חורבה כמו בוקה ומבוקה ומבולקה (נחום ב) ואמרינן בחולין (שם) לא חילק דרבנן דמצריכין לחלק הסימן שמצריכין לחלק כל הטבעת ולשייר על פני כולו ולא בילק לרבי יוסי שמחריב הסימן שחותך קצת בתוך הטבעת והשאר חוץ לטבעת ונראה למורי דאין לו משמעות לא הכא ולא התם ל"א חילק ובילק ב' דייני סדום שהיו שמותיהן כך: אין משיח לישראל. שחזקיה היה משיח ועליו נאמרו כל הנבואות אצמיח קרן לבית ישראל ועמד ורעה בעוז ה' [ח]: אלא לדוד. בזכות דוד שהיה עתיד לומר כמה שירות ותושבחות: למשה. בשביל משה שהיה עתיד לקבל את התורה: מה שמו. של משיח: ינון שמו. כמו ינאי כל אחד היה דורש אחר שמו: לפני שמש. עד שלא נברא היה שמו ינון והיינו אחד [ט] מז' דברים שעלו במחשבה ליבראות: ולא אתן להם חנינה. עדיין לא יבא משיח: מנחם. בן חזקיה: חיוורא דבי רבי. מצורע של בית רבי: אי מן חייא הוא כגון רבינו הקדוש. אם משיח מאותן שחיים עכשיו ודאי היינו רבינו הקדוש דסובל תחלואים וחסיד גמור הוה כדאמרינן בבבא מציעא (דף פה.) ואם היה מאותן שמתו כבר היה דניאל איש חמודות שנדון ביסורין בגוב אריות וחסיד גמור היה והאי כגון לאו דווקא ל"א כגון רבינו הקדוש כלומר אם יש דוגמתו בחיים היינו רבינו הקדוש ואם דוגמא הוא למתים היינו כגון דניאל איש חמודות: דוד אחר. שעתיד למלוך עליהם: אקים. הקים לא נאמר אלא אקים: כגון קיסר ופלגי קיסר. מלך ושני לו כן דוד החדש מלך כדכתיב ודוד מלכם אשר אקים ודוד המלך שני לו כדכתיב נשיא להם ולא כתוב מלך: עטלף. קלבא שורי"ך בלע"ז ואין לה עינים: שאורה שלי הוא. שיש לי עינים לראות ונמצאתי נהנית בה כך ישראל מצפין לגאולה שיום ה' יהיה להם אור אבל העובדי כוכבים למה מקוים אותו הרי הוא להם חשך ולא אור:

ה"ג

ליקוטי רש"י

לכן יתנם עד עת יולדה. יתנם ביד אויביהם עד בא העת אשר חלה וילדה ציון את בניה, ציון אשר החזיקה עתה חיל כיולדה ועכשיו היא קרויה יולדת ורבותינו אמרו מכאן אין בן דוד בא עד שתפשוט המלכות הרשעה ט' חדשים על כל העולם כולו אך לפי פשוטו זהו הלצה שפירשתי. ויתר אחיו. של מלך יהודה, כלומר שאר שבט יהודה. ישובון על בית ישראל. יתחברו עם שאר השבטים ויהיו לממלכה אחת ולא יחצו עוד לשתי ממלכות [מיכה ה, ב]. אנכי עמך. לפי שהיה ירא מעשו ומלבן [בראשית כח, טו]. שמא יגרום החטא. קטנתי מכל החסדים. נתמעטו זכיותי על ידי החסדים והאמת שעשית עמי לכך אני ירא שמא משהבטחתני נתלכלכתי בחטא ויגרום לי להמסר ביד עשו [בראשית לב, יא]. ויירא יעקב. שמא אחר הבטחה חטאתי וכדתניא שהחטא גורם שאין ההבטחה מתקיימת. ביאה ראשונה. שבאו בימי יהושע. ביאה שניה. כשעלו מגלות בבל בימי עזרא. ראויים היו ליעשות להם נס. לבוא ביד רמה. אלא שגרם החטא. ולא הלכו אלא ברשות כורש, וכל ימי מלכי פרס נשתעבדו להם, לכורש ולאחשורוש ולדריוש האחרון [ברכות ד.]. ליעשות להם נס. לעלות בזרוע ולא יהיו משתעבדים למלכות אלא שגרם חטאם של ישראל בימי בית ראשון ונגזר עליהם שלא יעלו אלא ברשות כדכתיב מי בכם מכל עמו (עזרא א) [סוטה לו.]. סנטר. מפרש בבבא בתרא (דף סח) בר מחוזיא זקן הממונה להיות בקי בנחלת גבול שדה כל איש ואיש [גיטין פ:]. אם יולד זכר. אם דרך לזכרים ללדת שיאחוז חבלים כיולדה. חלציו. כמו מתניו [ירמיהו ל, ו]. עד כי יבא שילה. מלך המשיח שהמלוכה שלו וכן תרגם אנקלוס ומדרש אגדה שילו שי לו שנאמר (תהלים עו, יב) יובילו שי למורא [בראשית מט, י]. לפני שמש ינון שמו. כל ימי השמש יגדל שמו ינון לשון מלכות ושררה כמו (משלי כ"ט) ואחריתו יהיה מנון, ולניני, השליט על נכסי אחרים, אמרו בלבם נינם יחד (תהלים ע"ד) מלכיהם יחד [תהלים עב, יז]. אכן חליינו הוא נשא. אכן לשון אבל בכל מקום אבל עתה אנו רואים שלא מחמ' שפלותו בא לו אלא מיוסר היה ביסורין. ואנחנו חשבנוהו. אנו היינו סבורים שהוא שנאוי למקום והוא לא היה כן אלא מחולל היה מפשעינו ומדוכא מעונותינו [ישעיהו נג, ד]. אדירו. שר שלו [ירמיהו ל, כא].

מסורת הש"ס

א) [יומא י. ע"ש], ב) [שם איתא בכל העולם כולו וכן הוא גיר' תוס' בע"ז ב: ד"ה משכא וכו'], ג) ב"ש, ד) [עי' תוס' ר"ה יח. ד"ה רבה ותוס' יבמות קה. ד"ה רבא], ה) ברכות ד., ו) ג"ז שם סוטה לו., ז) [לקמן לט. וע"ש פירש"י ד"ה אין להם], ח) [מיכה ה], ט) [פסחים נד. נדרים לט:].

תורה אור השלם

א) לָכֵן יִתְּנֵם עַד עֵת יוֹלֵדָה יָלָדָה וְיֶתֶר אֶחָיו יְשׁוּבוּן עַל בְּנֵי יִשְׂרָאֵל: [מיכה ה, ב]

ב) וְהִנֵּה אָנֹכִי עִמָּךְ וּשְׁמַרְתִּיךָ בְּכֹל אֲשֶׁר תֵּלֵךְ וַהֲשִׁבֹתִיךָ אֶל הָאֲדָמָה הַזֹּאת כִּי לֹא אֶעֱזָבְךָ עַד אֲשֶׁר אִם עָשִׂיתִי אֵת אֲשֶׁר דִּבַּרְתִּי לָךְ: [בראשית כח, טו]

ג) וַיִּירָא יַעֲקֹב מְאֹד וַיֵּצֶר לוֹ וַיַּחַץ אֶת הָעָם אֲשֶׁר אִתּוֹ וְאֶת הַצֹּאן וְאֶת הַבָּקָר וְהַגְּמַלִּים לִשְׁנֵי מַחֲנוֹת: [בראשית לב, ח]

ד) תִּפֹּל עֲלֵיהֶם אֵימָתָה וָפַחַד בִּגְדֹל זְרוֹעֲךָ יִדְּמוּ כָּאָבֶן עַד יַעֲבֹר עַמְּךָ יְיָ עַד יַעֲבֹר עַם זוּ קָנִיתָ: [שמות טו, טז]

ה) כַּאֲשֶׁר יָנוּס אִישׁ מִפְּנֵי הָאֲרִי וּפְגָעוֹ הַדֹּב וּבָא הַבַּיִת וְסָמַךְ יָדוֹ עַל הַקִּיר וּנְשָׁכוֹ הַנָּחָשׁ: [עמוס ה, יט]

ו) שַׁאֲלוּ נָא וּרְאוּ אִם יֹלֵד זָכָר מַדּוּעַ רָאִיתִי כָל גֶּבֶר יָדָיו עַל חֲלָצָיו כַּיּוֹלֵדָה וְנֶהֶפְכוּ כָל פָּנִים לְיֵרָקוֹן: [ירמיה ל, ו]

ז) לֹא יָסוּר שֵׁבֶט מִיהוּדָה וּמְחֹקֵק מִבֵּין רַגְלָיו עַד כִּי יָבֹא שִׁילֹה וְלוֹ יִקְּהַת עַמִּים: [בראשית מט, י]

ח) יְהִי שְׁמוֹ לְעוֹלָם לִפְנֵי שֶׁמֶשׁ יִנּוֹן שְׁמוֹ וְיִתְבָּרְכוּ בוֹ כָּל גּוֹיִם יְאַשְּׁרוּהוּ: [תהלים עב, יז]

ט) וְהֵטַלְתִּי אֶתְכֶם מֵעַל הָאָרֶץ הַזֹּאת עַל הָאָרֶץ אֲשֶׁר לֹא יְדַעְתֶּם אַתֶּם וַאֲבוֹתֵיכֶם וַעֲבַדְתֶּם שָׁם אֶת אֱלֹהִים אֲחֵרִים יוֹמָם וָלַיְלָה אֲשֶׁר לֹא אֶתֵּן לָכֶם חֲנִינָה: [ירמיה טז, יג]

י) עַל אֵלֶּה אֲנִי בוֹכִיָּה עֵינִי עֵינִי יֹרְדָה מַּיִם כִּי רָחַק מִמֶּנִּי מְנַחֵם מֵשִׁיב נַפְשִׁי הָיוּ בָנַי שׁוֹמֵמִים כִּי גָבַר אוֹיֵב: [איכה א, טז]

כ) אָכֵן חֳלָיֵנוּ הוּא נָשָׂא וּמַכְאֹבֵינוּ סְבָלָם וַאֲנַחְנוּ חֲשַׁבְנֻהוּ נָגוּעַ מֻכֵּה אֱלֹהִים וּמְעֻנֶּה: [ישעיה נג, ד]

ל) וְהָיָה אַדִּירוֹ מִמֶּנּוּ וּמֹשְׁלוֹ מִקִּרְבּוֹ יֵצֵא וְהִקְרַבְתִּיו וְנִגַּשׁ אֵלָי כִּי מִי הוּא זֶה עָרַב אֶת לִבּוֹ לָגֶשֶׁת אֵלַי נְאֻם יְיָ: [ירמיה ל, כא]

מ) וְעָבְדוּ אֵת יְיָ אֱלֹהֵיהֶם וְאֵת דָּוִד מַלְכָּם אֲשֶׁר אָקִים לָהֶם: [ירמיה ל, ט] נ) וְיָשְׁבוּ עַל הָאָרֶץ אֲשֶׁר נָתַתִּי לְעַבְדִּי לְיַעֲקֹב אֲשֶׁר יָשְׁבוּ בָהּ אֲבוֹתֵיכֶם וְיָשְׁבוּ עָלֶיהָ הֵמָּה וּבְנֵיהֶם וּבְנֵי בְנֵיהֶם עַד עוֹלָם וְדָוִד עַבְדִּי נָשִׂיא לָהֶם לְעוֹלָם: [יחזקאל לז, כה] ס) הוֹי הַמִּתְאַוִּים אֶת יוֹם יְיָ לָמָּה זֶּה לָכֶם יוֹם יְיָ הוּא חֹשֶׁךְ וְלֹא אוֹר: [עמוס ה, יח]

שֶׁאֵין כָּל דֶּקֶל וְדֶקֶל שֶׁבְּבָבֶל – **because there will not be a single palm in Babylonia** שֶׁאֵין סוּס שֶׁל פָּרְסִיִּים נִקְשָׁר בּוֹ – **to which a horse of the Persians will not be tethered,** וְאֵין לְךָ כָּל אָרוֹן – **and there will not be a single coffin in** וְאָרוֹן שֶׁבְּאֶרֶץ יִשְׂרָאֵל **Eretz Yisrael** שֶׁאֵין סוּס מָדִי אוֹכֵל בּוֹ תֶּבֶן – **out of which a horse of the Medes will not be eating straw."**[1]

The Gemara discusses the period known as חֶבְלֵי מָשִׁיחַ, *the travail of the Messiah*:[2]

אָמַר רַב – **Rav said:** אֵין בֶּן דָּוִד בָּא – **The son of David will not come** עַד שֶׁתִּתְפַּשֵּׁט הַמַּלְכוּת עַל יִשְׂרָאֵל תִּשְׁעָה חֳדָשִׁים – **until the kingdom**[3] **has extended its dominion over Israel**[4] **for nine months,** שֶׁנֶּאֱמַר – **as it is stated:** "לָכֵן יִתְּנֵם עַד־עֵת יוֹלֵדָה יָלָדָה וְיֶתֶר אֶחָיו יְשׁוּבוּן עַל־בְּנֵי יִשְׂרָאֵל" – ***Therefore, He will surrender them until the time that one who gives birth has given birth; then the rest of his brothers will return with the Children of Israel.***[5]

The Gemara quotes statements made by Amoraim regarding "the travail of the Messiah":

אָמַר עוּלָּא – **Ulla said:** יֵיתֵי וְלֹא אִיחְמִינֵיהּ – **May he** [the Messiah] **come, but may I not see him!**[6]

וְכֵן אָמַר רַבָּה – **And so said Rabbah:** יֵיתֵי וְלֹא אִיחְמִינֵיהּ – **May he come, but may I not see him!**

רַב יוֹסֵף אָמַר – But **Rav Yosef says:** יֵיתֵי – **May he come,** וְאֶזְכֵּי דְּאֵיתִיב בְּטוּלָּא דְּכוּפִיתָא דַּחֲמָרֵיהּ – **and may I merit to sit in the shadow of his donkey's dung!**[7]

Abaye challenges Rabbah:

אָמַר לֵיהּ אַבַּיֵי (לרבא) [לְרַבָּה] – **Abaye asked Rabbah:** מַאי טַעְמָא – **"Why** do you not want to see the Messiah's arrival? אִילֵימָא מִשּׁוּם חֶבְלוֹ שֶׁל מָשִׁיחַ – **Is it because** you fear **the travail of the Messiah?**[8] וְהָתַנְיָא – **But it was taught in a Baraisa:** שֶׁאֲלוּ תַּלְמִידָיו אֶת רַבִּי אֶלְעָזָר – R' ELAZAR WAS ASKED BY HIS STUDENTS: מַה יַּעֲשֶׂה אָדָם וְיִנָּצֵל מֵחֶבְלוֹ שֶׁל מָשִׁיחַ – WHAT CAN A PERSON DO TO BE SPARED THE TRAVAIL OF THE MESSIAH? יַעֲסוֹק בַּתּוֹרָה וּבִגְמִילוּת חֲסָדִים – And he responded: ONE SHOULD OCCUPY HIMSELF IN the study of TORAH AND IN ACTS OF KINDNESS.[9] וּמָר הָא תּוֹרָה וְהָא גְּמִילוּת חֲסָדִים – **And master** [Rabbah] **is the** personification of both **Torah and kindness!"**

Rabbah replies:

אָמַר [לֵיהּ] – **He answered him:** שֶׁמָּא יִגְרוֹם הַחֵטְא – "I am afraid **lest a sin cause** me to lose whatever protection I have earned."[10]

Having mentioned that sin could cause a person to lose earned reward, the Gemara cites two sources for this concept:

כִּדְרַבִּי יַעֲקֹב בַּר אִידִי – This **accords with [the teaching] of R' Yaakov bar Idi,** דְּרַבִּי יַעֲקֹב בַּר אִידִי רָמֵי – **for R' Yaakov bar Idi pointed out a contradiction:** כְּתִיב – On the one hand **it is written** that God promised Jacob:[11] "וְהִנֵּה אָנֹכִי עִמָּךְ וּשְׁמַרְתִּיךָ בְּכֹל אֲשֶׁר־תֵּלֵךְ" – ***Behold, I am with you and will guard you wherever you go.*** וּכְתִיב – **But** on the other hand **it is written:**[12] "וַיִּירָא יַעֲקֹב מְאֹד וַיֵּצֶר לוֹ" – ***Jacob became very frightened and it distressed him***. Jacob was frightened despite God's promise to protect him, שֶׁהָיָה מִתְיָירֵא שֶׁמָּא יִגְרוֹם הַחֵטְא – **because he was afraid lest a sin cause** him to lose this protection.

The second source for this concept is based on the verse: *Until Your people passes, HASHEM; until this people You have acquired passes.*[13] The following Baraisa interprets this double expression:

כִּדְתַנְיָא – It also **accords with what has been taught in a Baraisa:** "עַד־יַעֲבֹר עַמְּךָ ה'" – *UNTIL YOUR PEOPLE PASSES, HASHEM:* זוֹ בִּיאָה רִאשׁוֹנָה – THIS IS a reference to THE FIRST ENTERING of the Jewish people into Eretz Yisrael.[14]

NOTES

1. The army of Persia and Media will vanquish Babylonia before proceeding to conquer Eretz Yisrael in the war of Gog and Magog. Their cavalry will be so immense that it will fill the entire country of Babylonia. In Eretz Yisrael, coffins will be dug out of the ground for use as feeding troughs for their horses (*Rashi*).

2. The period of suffering that will occur at the dawn of the Messianic Era. The word חֵבֶל, *travail,* connotes the pain of a woman in childbirth (*Rashi* to *Shabbos* 118a; see notes 5 and 8).

3. The Roman empire, representing Edom, the power of evil in the world (see end of note 5).

4. I.e. its dominion has extended over all those parts of the world to which the Jews are dispersed (*Rashi*; see end of note 5).

5. *Micah* 5:2. God will surrender the Jewish people to their enemies for the length of time that a woman bears a child – nine months. Then the rest of the Messiah's brothers (i.e. the rest of the tribe of Judah) will join the other tribes of Israel and form a unified kingdom in Eretz Yisrael (see *Rashi* ad loc.).

The pain of a woman in childbirth is frequently used as a metaphor for the suffering that will accompany the birth of the Messianic Era (see for example, the verse cited below, note 21). For nine months – corresponding to the nine months of pregnancy – the anguish will be particularly acute. During that time, the entire Jewish people will be under the domination of a single government, and thus will have no avenue of escape (*Maharsha;* see *Beur HaGra* to *Bechoros* 8b [printed in *The Juggler and the King* by *R' Aharon Feldman*]).

The Gemara in *Yoma* (10a) records a slightly different version of this teaching: "Rav Yehudah said in the name of Rav: The son of David will not come until the wicked kingdom of Rome has spread over the entire world for nine months, as it is said: *Therefore, He will surrender them,* etc."

6. Although Ulla prays for the Messiah's arrival (*Yad Ramah*), he would rather not witness this event than endure the suffering that will accompany it.

7. Rav Yosef was prepared to suffer the worst degradation in order to be present at the advent of the Messianic era (*Rashi;* see *Maharal* and *Iyun Yaakov*).

8. *Rashi* (*Shabbos* 118a), *Yad Ramah* and *Maharsha* relate this term to חֶבְלֵי לֵידָה, *pangs of childbirth. Rashi* here (second explanation) writes that this refers to the anguish that will be caused by the foreign army destined to invade Eretz Yisrael when the Messiah comes.

Alternatively, *Rashi* here translates חֶבְלוֹ שֶׁל מָשִׁיחַ as *the lot of the Messiah.*

9. By studying Torah, which is the ultimate good in the spiritual realm, and bestowing kindness, which is the ultimate good in the material realm, a person is completely protected against the evil of the "travail of the Messiah" (*Maharal;* see also *Berachos* 5b and *Chafetz Chaim al HaTorah, Exodus* 15:13).

R' Elazar could also have answered that one should eat three meals on the Sabbath. The Gemara in *Shabbos* (118a) states: "Whoever fulfills [the mitzvah of eating] three meals on the Sabbath is saved from three punishments – the travail of the Messiah, the retribution of Gehinnom and the war of Gog and Magog" (*Maharsha;* see *Mishnah Berurah* 291:1).

10. Even if someone has been promised a certain benefit by God, or has earned it through his deeds, he could lose the reward should he subsequently sin.

The commentators point out that this is apparently contradicted by the Gemara in *Berachos* (7a): "Every single statement expressed by God that is for the good (i.e. it conveys reward), even if it was conditional, will eventually be fulfilled." *Rambam* resolves this difficulty by asserting that the Gemara in *Berachos* refers only to promises that God instructed a prophet to convey to the people (*Rambam's Introduction to the Mishnah* באד"ה והחלק השני בענין הנביא; cf. *Lechem Mishneh* to *Hil. Yesodei HaTorah* 10:4; *Maharsha* to *Berachos* 4a).

11. *Genesis* 28:15.

12. Ibid. 32:8. Jacob was told that Esau was marching toward him with an army of four hundred men.

13. *Exodus* 15:16. This verse is from the *Shirah* – the song that the people sang upon being saved from the Egyptian army at the Red Sea.

14. In the days of Joshua.

שאין כל דקל ודקל שבבבל שאין סוס של פרסיים נקשר בו ואין לך כל ארון וארון שבארץ ישראל שאין סוס מדי אוכל בו תבן [א] אמר רב אין בן דוד בא עד שתתפשט המלכות [ב] על ישראל תשעה חדשים שנאמר א) לכן יתנם עד עת יולדה ילדה ויתר אחיו ישובון על בני ישראל אמר עולא ייתי ולא איחמיניה וכן אמר [ג] רבה] ייתי ולא איחמיניה רב יוסף אמר ייתי ואזכי דאיתיב בטולא דכופיתא דחמריה אמר ליה אביי (לרבא) [ד] לרבה] מאי טעמא אילימא משום חבלו של משיח והתניא שאלו תלמידיו את רבי אלעזר מה יעשה אדם וינצל מחבלו של משיח יעסוק בתורה ובגמילות חסדים ומר הא תורה והא גמילות חסדים אמר [ליה] שמא יגרום החטא כדר' יעקב בר אידי [ה] דר' יעקב בר אידי רמי כתיב ב) הנה אנכי עמך ושמרתיך בכל אשר תלך וכתיב ג) ויירא יעקב מאד ויצר לו שהיה מתיירא שמא [ו] יגרום החטא כדתניא ד) עד יעבור עמך ה' זו ביאה ראשונה עד יעבור עם זו קנית זו ביאה שניה אמור מעתה ראויים היו ישראל לעשות להם נס בביאה שניה כביאה ראשונה אלא שגרם החטא וכן אמר ר' יוחנן ייתי ולא איחמיניה א"ל ריש לקיש מ"ט אילימא משום דכתיב ה) כאשר ינוס איש מפני הארי ופגעו הדוב [ובא הבית] וסמך ידו אל הקיר ונשכו נחש בא ואראך דוגמתו בעולם הזה בזמן שאדם יוצא לשדה ופגע בו סנטר דומה כמי שפגע בו ארי נכנס לעיר פגע בו גבאי דומה כמי שפגעו דוב נכנס לביתו ומצא בניו ובנותיו מוטלין ברעב דומה כמי שנשכו נחש אלא משום דכתיב ו) שאלו נא וראו אם ילד זכר מדוע ראיתי כל גבר ידיו על חלציו כיולדה ונהפכו כל פנים לירקון מאי ראיתי כל גבר אמר רבא בר יצחק אמר רב מי שכל גבורה שלו ומאי ונהפכו כל פנים לירקון אמר רבי יוחנן פמליא של מעלה ופמליא של מטה בשעה שאמר הקב"ה הללו מעשה ידי והללו מעשה ידי היאך אאבד אלו מפני אלו אמר רב פפא היינו דאמרי אינשי רהיט ונפל תורא ואזיל ושדי ליה סוסיא באורייה אמר רב גידל אמר רב עתידין ישראל דאכלי שני משיח אמר רב יוסף פשיטא ואלא מאן אכיל להו חילק ובילק אכלי להו לאפוקי [ז] מדרבי הילל דאמר אין משיח לישראל שכבר אכלוהו בימי חזקיה אמר רב לא אברי עלמא אלא לדוד ושמואל אמר למשה ורבי יוחנן אמר למשיח מה שמו דבי רבי שילא אמרי שילה שמו שנאמר ז) עד כי יבא שילה דבי רבי ינאי אמרי ינון שמו שנאמר ח) יהי שמו לעולם לפני שמש ינון שמו דבי רבי חנינה אמר חנינה שמו שנאמר ט) אשר לא אתן לכם חנינה ויש אומרים מנחם בן חזקיה שמו שנאמר י) כי רחק ממני מנחם משיב נפשי ורבנן אמרי חיוורא דבי רבי שמו שנאמר כ) אכן חליינו הוא נשא ומכאובינו סבלם ואנחנו חשבנוהו נגוע מוכה אלהים ומעונה אמר רב נחמן אי מן חייא הוא כגון אנא שנאמר ל) והיה אדירו ממנו ומושלו מקרבו יצא אמר רב אי מן חייא הוא כגון רבינו הקדוש אי מן מתיא הוא כגון דניאל איש חמודות אמר רב יהודה אמר רב עתיד הקדוש ברוך הוא להעמיד להם דוד אחר שנאמר מ) ועבדו את ה' אלהיהם ואת דוד מלכם אשר אקים להם הקים לא נאמר אלא אקים א"ל רב פפא לאביי והכתיב נ) ודוד עבדי נשיא להם לעולם כגון קיסר ופלגי קיסר דרש רבי שמלאי מאי דכתיב ס) הוי המתאוים את יום ה' למה זה לכם יום ה' הוא חשך ולא אור משל לתרנגול ועטלף שהיו מצפין לאור א"ל תרנגול לעטלף אני מצפה לאורה שאורה שלי היא ואתה למה לך אורה

והיינו

רש"י

שאין סוס מדי אוכל בו תבן. שמוציאין הארונות חוץ לקרקע ועושין מהן אבוסים במלחמת גוג ומגוג: שאין כל דקל וכו'. כלומר עתידין פרס ומדי לבא על בבל וללכדה ונתמלאה כל ארץ בבל חיילות פרסיים וסוסיהם ומשם באים לא"י ולוכדים אותה: עד שתפשוט מלכות על ישראל ט' חדשים שנאמר לכן יתנם לישראל עד עת יולדה ילדה. היינו ט' חדשים כדמתרגמינן בכן יתמסרון כעידן דילדתא למילד וכתיב (מיכה ה) ועמד ורעה בעוז ה' וגו' וישבו כי עתה יגדל ומתרגמינן ויתיבון מביני גלוותהון: על בני ישראל. היינו כל העולם שישראל מפוזרים בו: ייתי. משיח ולא אחמיניה: בטולא דכופיתא דחמריה. בצל הרעי של חמורו כלומר אפילו בכך אני רוצה ובלבד שאראנו: כופיתא. רעי כמו רמא כופת' וסכר ירדנא בבבא בתרא (ד' עג:): מאי טעמא. אמר לא אחמיניה: חבלו של משיח. גורלו ולקמן בעי מאי היא ל"א חבלו פחדים וחבלים שיהיו בימיו מחיל העובדי כוכבים: לעשות להם נס. לעלות בזרוע על כרחם של מלכי פרס: בביאה שניה. בימי עזרא כביאה ראשונה בימי יהושע מדהקישן הכתוב: מאי טעמא. איזו צרה באה בארץ בימיו שאתה אומר לא אחמיניה: סנטר. מפרש בב"ב (דף סח.) בר מחוזנייתא שיודע מיצרי השדות וגבוליהן עד כאן של פלוני מכאן ואילך של פלוני ובידו לרבות לאחד ולמעט לאחר וכשפוגעו אותו סנטר רוצה למדוד שדותיו לקצר מיצרי השדות ודומה כמי שפגע בו ארי: גבאי. גובה מס המלך: מי שכל הגבורה שלו. הקב"ה מצטער בעצמו כיולדה ואומר בשעה שמעביר העובדי כוכבים מפני ישראל היאך אאביד אלו מפני אלו: פמליא של מעלה ושל מטה. מלאכים וישראל: אפילו הגרים לא גרסינן: רהיט ונפיל תורא ואזיל ושדי סוסיא באורייה. כשרץ השור ונפל מעמידין סוס במקומו באבוסו מה שלא היה רוצה לעשות קודם מפלתו של שור שהיה חביב עליו שורו ביותר וכשמתרפא השור היום או למחר ממפלתו קשה לו להוציא סוסו מפני השור לאחר שהעמידו שם כך הקב"ה כיון שראה מפלתן של ישראל נותן גדולתו לעובדי כוכבים וכשחוזרים ישראל בתשובה ונגאלין קשה לו לאבד עובדי כוכבים מפני ישראל: אורייה. כמו (מלכים א ה) ארוות סוסים: דאכלי שני משיח. שובע שיהיה באותן הימים לישראל יהיה: אלא חילק ובילק אכלי להו. כך היו רגילין לומר כאדם שאומר וכי שדים ושדות יאכלוהו ובמסכת חולין (דף יט.) לא חילק ידענא ולא בילק ידענא ולי נראה דמשמעות לשון חילק ובילק לשון חורבה כמו בוקה ומבוקה ומבולקה (נחום ב) ואמרינן בחולין (שם) לא חילק דרבנן דמצריכין לחלק הסימן שמצריכין לחלק כל הטבעת ולשייר על פני כולו ולא בילק לרבי יוסי שמחריב הסימן שחותך קצת בתוך הטבעת והשאר חוץ לטבעת ונראה למורי דאין לו משמעות לא הכא ולא התם ל"א חילק ובילק ב' דייני סדום שהיו שמותיהן כך: אין משיח לישראל. שחזקיה היה משיח ועליו נאמרו כל הנבואות אצמיח קרן לבית ישראל ועמד ורעה בעוז ה' [ח]: אלא לדוד. בזכות דוד שהיה עתיד לומר כמה שירות ותושבחות: למשה. בשביל משה שהיה עתיד לקבל את התורה: מה שמו. של משיח: ינון שמו. כמו ינאי כל אחד היה דורש אחר שמו: לפני שמש. עד שלא נברא היה שמו ינון והיינו אחד [ט] מז' דברים שעלו במחשבה ליבראות: ולא אתן להם חנינה. עדיין לא יבא משיח: מנחם. בן חזקיה: חיוורא דבי רבי. מצורע של בית רבי: אי מן חייא הוא כגון רבינו הקדוש. אם משיח מאותן שחיים עכשיו ודאי היינו רבינו הקדוש דסובל תחלואים וחסיד גמור הוה כדאמרינן בבבא מציעא (דף פה.) ואם היה מאותן שמתו כבר היה דניאל איש חמודות שנדון ביסורין בגוב אריות וחסיד גמור היה והאי כגון לאו דווקא ל"א כגון רבינו הקדוש כלומר אם יש דוגמתו בחיים היינו רבינו הקדוש ואם דוגמא הוא למתים היינו כגון דניאל איש חמודות: דוד אחר. שעתיד למלוך עליהם: אקים. הקים לא נאמר אלא אקים: כגון קיסר ופלגי קיסר. מלך ושני לו כן דוד החדש מלך כדכתיב ודוד מלכם אשר אקים ודוד המלך שני לו כדכתיב נשיא להם ולא כתוב מלך: עטלף. קלבא שורי"ץ בלע"ז ואין לה עינים: שאורה שלי הוא. שיש לי עינים לראות ונמצאתי נהנית בה כך ישראל מצפין לגאולה שיום ה' יהיה להם אור אבל העובדי כוכבים למה מקוים אותו הרי הוא להם חשך ולא אור:

ה"ג

ליקוטי רש"י

לכן יתנם עד עת יולדה. יתנם ביד אויביהם עד בא העת אשר חלה וילדה ציון את בניה, ציון אשר החזיקה עתה חיל כיולדה ועכשיו היא קרויה יולדת ורבותינו אמרו מכאן אין בן דוד בא עד שתפשוט המלכות הרשעה ט' חדשים על כל העולם כולו אך לפי פשוטו זהו הלעה שפירשתי. ויתר אחיו. של מלך יהודה, כלומר שאר שבט יהודה. ישובון על בית ישראל. יתחברו עם שאר השבטים ויהיו לממלכה אחת ולא יחלו עוד לשתי ממלכות [מיכה ה, ב]. אנכי עמך. לפי שהיה ירא מעשו ומלבן [בראשית כח, טו]. שמא יגרום החטא. קטנתי מכל החסדים. נתמעטו זכיותי על ידי החסדים והאמת שעשית עמי לכך אני ירא שמא משהבטחתני נתלכלכתי בחטא ויגרום לי להמסר ביד עשו [בראשית לב, יא]. ויירא יעקב. שמא אחר הבטחה חטאתי וכדתניא שהחטא גורם שאין הבטחה מתקיימת. ביאה ראשונה. שבאו בימי יהושע. ביאה שניה. כשעלו מגלות בבל בימי עזרא. ראויים היו ליעשות להם נס. לבוא ביד רמה. אלא שגרם החטא. ולא הלכו אלא ברשות כורש, וכל ימי מלכי פרס נשתעבדו להם, לכורש ולאחשורוש ולדריוש האחרון [ברכות ד.]. ליעשות להם נס. לעלות בזרוע ולא יהיו משתעבדים למלכות אלא שגרם חטאם של ישראל בימי בית ראשון ונגזר עליהם שלא יעלו אלא ברשות כדכתיב מי בכם מכל עמו (עזרא א) [סוטה לו.]. סנטר. מפרש בבבא בתרא (דף סח) בר מחוזיא זקן הממונה להיות בקי בנחלת גבול שדה כל איש ואיש [גיטין פ:]. אם יולד זכר. אם דרך לזכרים ללדת שיאחזום חבלים כיולדה. חלציו. כמו מתניו [ירמיהו ל, ו]. עד כי יבא שילה. מלך המשיח שהמלוכה שלו וכן תרגם אנקלוס ומדרש אגדה שילו שי לו שנאמר (תהלים עו, יב) יובילו שי למורא [בראשית מט, י]. לפני שמש ינון שמו. כל ימי השמש יגדל שמו ינון לשון מלכות ושררה כמו (משלי כ"ט) ואחריתו יהיה מנון, ולניני, השליט על נכסי אחרים, אמרו בלבם נינם יחד (תהלים ע"ד) מלכיהם יחד [תהלים עב, יז]. אכן חליינו הוא נשא. אכן לשון אבל בכל מקום אבל עתה אנו רואים שלא מחמ' שפלותו בא לו אלא מיוסר היה ביסורין. ואנחנו חשבנוהו. אנו היינו סבורים שהוא שנאוי למקום והוא לא היה כן אלא מחולל היה מפשעינו ומדוכא מעונותינו [ישעיהו נג, ד]. אדירו. שר שלו [ירמיהו ל, כא].

מסורת הש"ס

א) [יומא י. ע"ש], ב) [שם איתא בכל העולם כולו וכן הוא גיר' תוס' בע"ז ב: ד"ה משכא וכו'], ג) ב"ש, ד) [עי' תוס' ר"ה יח. ד"ה רבה ותוס' יבמות קה. ד"ה רבא], ה) ברכות ד., ו) ג"ז שם סוטה לו., ז) [לקמן צט. וע"ש פירש"י ד"ה אין להם], ח) [מיכה ה], ט) [פסחים נד. נדרים לט:].

תורה אור השלם

א) לָכֵן יִתְּנֵם עַד עֵת יוֹלֵדָה יָלָדָה וְיֶתֶר אֶחָיו יְשׁוּבוּן עַל בְּנֵי יִשְׂרָאֵל: [מיכה ה, ב]

ב) וְהִנֵּה אָנֹכִי עִמָּךְ וּשְׁמַרְתִּיךָ בְּכֹל אֲשֶׁר תֵּלֵךְ וַהֲשִׁבֹתִיךָ אֶל הָאֲדָמָה הַזֹּאת כִּי לֹא אֶעֱזָבְךָ עַד אֲשֶׁר אִם עָשִׂיתִי אֵת אֲשֶׁר דִּבַּרְתִּי לָךְ: [בראשית כח, טו]

ג) וַיִּירָא יַעֲקֹב מְאֹד וַיֵּצֶר לוֹ וַיַּחַץ אֶת הָעָם אֲשֶׁר אִתּוֹ וְאֶת הַצֹּאן וְאֶת הַבָּקָר וְהַגְּמַלִּים לִשְׁנֵי מַחֲנוֹת: [בראשית לב, ח]

ד) תִּפֹּל עֲלֵיהֶם אֵימָתָה וָפַחַד בִּגְדֹל זְרוֹעֲךָ יִדְּמוּ כָּאָבֶן עַד יַעֲבֹר עַמְּךָ יְיָ עַד יַעֲבֹר עַם זוּ קָנִיתָ: [שמות טו, טז]

ה) כַּאֲשֶׁר יָנוּס אִישׁ מִפְּנֵי הָאֲרִי וּפְגָעוֹ הַדֹּב וּבָא הַבַּיִת וְסָמַךְ יָדוֹ עַל הַקִּיר וּנְשָׁכוֹ הַנָּחָשׁ: [עמוס ה, יט]

ו) שַׁאֲלוּ נָא וּרְאוּ אִם יֹלֵד זָכָר מַדּוּעַ רָאִיתִי כָל גֶּבֶר יָדָיו עַל חֲלָצָיו כַּיּוֹלֵדָה וְנֶהֶפְכוּ כָל פָּנִים לְיֵרָקוֹן: [ירמיה ל, ו]

ז) לֹא יָסוּר שֵׁבֶט מִיהוּדָה וּמְחֹקֵק מִבֵּין רַגְלָיו עַד כִּי יָבֹא שִׁילֹה וְלוֹ יִקְּהַת עַמִּים: [בראשית מט, י]

ח) יְהִי שְׁמוֹ לְעוֹלָם לִפְנֵי שֶׁמֶשׁ יִנּוֹן שְׁמוֹ וְיִתְבָּרְכוּ בוֹ כָּל גּוֹיִם יְאַשְּׁרוּהוּ: [תהלים עב, יז]

ט) וְהֵטַלְתִּי אֶתְכֶם מֵעַל הָאָרֶץ הַזֹּאת עַל הָאָרֶץ אֲשֶׁר לֹא יְדַעְתֶּם אַתֶּם וַאֲבוֹתֵיכֶם וַעֲבַדְתֶּם שָׁם אֶת אֱלֹהִים אֲחֵרִים יוֹמָם וָלַיְלָה אֲשֶׁר לֹא אֶתֵּן לָכֶם חֲנִינָה: [ירמיה טז, יג]

י) עַל אֵלֶּה אֲנִי בוֹכִיָּה עֵינִי עֵינִי יֹרְדָה מַּיִם כִּי רָחַק מִמֶּנִּי מְנַחֵם מֵשִׁיב נַפְשִׁי הָיוּ בָנַי שׁוֹמֵמִים כִּי גָבַר אוֹיֵב: [איכה א, טז]

כ) אָכֵן חֳלָיֵנוּ הוּא נָשָׂא וּמַכְאֹבֵינוּ סְבָלָם וַאֲנַחְנוּ חֲשַׁבְנֻהוּ נָגוּעַ מֻכֵּה אֱלֹהִים וּמְעֻנֶּה: [ישעיה נג, ד]

ל) וְהָיָה אַדִּירוֹ מִמֶּנּוּ וּמשְׁלוֹ מִקִּרְבּוֹ יֵצֵא וְהִקְרַבְתִּיו וְנִגַּשׁ אֵלָי כִּי מִי הוּא זֶה עָרַב אֶת לִבּוֹ לָגֶשֶׁת אֵלַי נְאֻם יְיָ: [ירמיה ל, כא]

מ) וְעָבְדוּ אֵת יְיָ אֱלֹהֵיהֶם וְאֵת דָּוִד מַלְכָּם אֲשֶׁר אָקִים לָהֶם: [ירמיה ל, ט] נ) וְיָשְׁבוּ עַל הָאָרֶץ אֲשֶׁר נָתַתִּי לְעַבְדִּי לְיַעֲקֹב אֲשֶׁר יָשְׁבוּ בָהּ אֲבוֹתֵיכֶם וְיָשְׁבוּ עָלֶיהָ הֵמָּה וּבְנֵיהֶם וּבְנֵי בְנֵיהֶם עַד עוֹלָם וְדָוִד עַבְדִּי נָשִׂיא לָהֶם לְעוֹלָם: [יחזקאל לז, כה] ס) הוֹי הַמִּתְאַוִּים אֶת יוֹם יְיָ לָמָּה זֶּה לָכֶם יוֹם יְיָ הוּא חֹשֶׁךְ וְלֹא אוֹר: [עמוס ה, יח]

"עַד־יַעֲבֹר עַם־זוּ קָנִיתָ" – *UNTIL THIS PEOPLE YOU HAVE ACQUIRED PASSES:* זוּ בִּיאָה שְׁנִיָּה – THIS IS a reference to THE SECOND ENTERING.[15] אֱמוֹר מֵעַתָּה – SAY THEN that since both enterings are alluded to in the same verse, they share the following characteristic: רְאוּיִים הָיוּ יִשְׂרָאֵל לַעֲשׂוֹת לָהֶם נֵס בְּבִיאָה שְׁנִיָּה – THE JEWISH PEOPLE DESERVED THAT A MIRACLE BE PERFORMED FOR THEM IN THE SECOND ENTERING כְּבִיאָה רִאשׁוֹנָה – just AS it was IN THE FIRST ENTERING.[16] אֶלָּא שֶׁגָּרַם הַחֵטְא – HOWEVER, that did not happen BECAUSE SIN CAUSED them to lose this reward.[17]

The Gemara resumes its previous discussion:

וְכֵן אָמַר רַבִּי יוֹחָנָן – **And so said R' Yochanan:** יֵיתֵי וְלָא אִיחְמִינֵיהּ – **May he** [the Messiah] **come, but may I not see him!** אֲמַר לֵיהּ רֵישׁ לָקִישׁ – **Reish Lakish asked [R' Yochanan]:** מַאי טַעְמָא – **Why** do you not want to see the Messiah's arrival? אִילֵימָא מִשּׁוּם דִּכְתִיב – **Is it because it is written** in reference to that period: "כַּאֲשֶׁר יָנוּס אִישׁ מִפְּנֵי הָאֲרִי וּפְגָעוֹ הַדֹּב וּבָא הַבַּיִת וְסָמַךְ יָדוֹ עַל־הַקִּיר וּנְשָׁכוֹ הַנָּחָשׁ" – ***When a man flees from a lion, and a bear meets him, and, entering his house, he leans his hand on the wall and a snake bites him?***[18] בֹּא וְאַרְאֲךָ דּוּגְמָתוֹ בָּעוֹלָם הַזֶּה – **Come and I will show you an example of this in this world:** בִּזְמַן שֶׁאָדָם יוֹצֵא לַשָּׂדֶה – **When a man goes out to** his **field** וּפָגַע בּוֹ סַנְטֵר – **and a** ***santeir*** **approaches him,**[19] דּוֹמֶה כְּמִי שֶׁפָּגַע בּוֹ אֲרִי – **it is as though he had been approached by a lion.** נִכְנַס לָעִיר – When **he enters the town** פָּגַע בּוֹ גַּבַּאי – **and a tax collector approaches him,** דּוֹמֶה כְּמִי שֶׁפְּגָעוֹ דֹּב – **it is as though he had been approached by a bear.** נִכְנַס לְבֵיתוֹ – When **he comes home** וּמָצָא בָּנָיו וּבְנוֹתָיו מוּטָּלִין בָּרָעָב – **and finds his sons and daughters lying in hunger,** דּוֹמֶה כְּמִי שֶׁנְּשָׁכוֹ נָחָשׁ – **it is as though he had been bitten by a snake.**[20]

Having rejected the preceding reason for R' Yochanan's unwillingness to witness the Messiah's arrival, the Gemara suggests a different reason:

אֶלָּא מִשּׁוּם דִּכְתִיב – **Rather,** he was afraid **because of that which is written:** "שַׁאֲלוּ־נָא וּרְאוּ אִם־יֹלֵד זָכָר מַדּוּעַ רָאִיתִי כָל־גֶּבֶר יָדָיו עַל־חֲלָצָיו כַּיּוֹלֵדָה וְנֶהֶפְכוּ כָל־פָּנִים לְיֵרָקוֹן" – ***Ask now and see whether a man gives birth! Why do I see every man with his hands on his loins like a woman in labor, and all faces have turned pale?***[21]

The Gemara interprets this verse:

מַאי "רָאִיתִי כָל־גֶּבֶר" – **What is** the meaning of ***I see every man*** *(kal gever)*? אָמַר רָבָא בַּר יִצְחָק אָמַר רַב – **Rava bar Yitzchak said in the name of Rav:** מִי שֶׁכָּל גְּבוּרָה שֶׁלּוֹ – This refers to **the One to Whom all power** (*kal gevurah*) **belongs.**[22]

וּמַאי "וְנֶהֶפְכוּ כָל־פָּנִים לְיֵרָקוֹן" – **And what is** the meaning of ***all faces have turned pale?*** אָמַר רַבִּי יוֹחָנָן – **R' Yochanan said:** פָּמַלְיָא שֶׁל מַעְלָה וּפָמַלְיָא שֶׁל מַטָּה – It means that the faces of the **host above** [the angels] **and the host below** [the Jewish people][23] will all turn pale from fright בְּשָׁעָה שֶׁאָמַר הַקָּדוֹשׁ בָּרוּךְ הוּא – **when the Holy One, Blessed is He, will say:** הַלָּלוּ מַעֲשֵׂה יָדַי וְהַלָּלוּ מַעֲשֵׂה יָדַי – **"These are My handiwork, and these are My handiwork!** הֵיאַךְ אֲאַבֵּד אֵלּוּ מִפְּנֵי אֵלּוּ – **How can I destroy these for the sake of these?"**[24]

אָמַר רַב פָּפָּא – **Rav Pappa said:** הַיְינוּ דְּאָמְרֵי אִינְשֵׁי – **This is** reflected in the adage **that people say:** רָהִיט וְנָפֵל תּוֹרָא – **"An ox runs and falls,** וְאָזִיל וְשָׁדֵי לֵיהּ סוּסְיָא בְּאוּרְיֵיהּ – **and [its master] goes and puts a horse at its trough."**[25]

The Gemara begins a discussion about the identity and character of the Messiah:

אָמַר רַב גִּידֵּל אָמַר רַב – **Rav Gidel said in the name of Rav:** עֲתִידִין יִשְׂרָאֵל דְּאָכְלֵי שְׁנֵי מָשִׁיחַ – **The Jewish people is destined**

NOTES

15. When they ascended from Babylonia under the leadership of Ezra.

16. The Jordan split, the walls of Jericho fell and several other miracles were performed for the Jewish people when they entered Eretz Yisrael under Joshua. In the second entering, too, they should have gone up from exile in a miraculous fashion, defying the will and might of their rulers.

[They earned these rewards when they demonstrated their faith in God by following Him into the Wilderness and crossing the Red Sea.]

17. The Jews were unable to return to Eretz Yisrael from Babylonia until their rulers allowed them to do so. God decreed it thus because of the sins they had committed during the First Temple era (*Rashi* to *Sotah* 36a).

18. *Amos* 5:19. That is to say, a person will escape from one trouble only to encounter another (*Radak, Ibn Ezra;* cf. *Maharsha*).

19. [Literally: and a *santeir* meets him.] A *santeir* was an official responsible for recording the boundaries of private holdings. He had the authority to expand or diminish a person's property should he deem it necessary. A landowner would be greatly disturbed to find a *santeir* surveying his field, lest the *santeir* decide to diminish his property (*Rashi;* see *Yad Ramah*).

20. Reish Lakish's point is that the troubles attributed to the pre-Messianic era are not necessarily more severe than those commonly found in current times. Hence, this is not a sufficient reason for wishing to avoid the Messiah's arrival.

21. *Jeremiah* 30:6. Men do not give birth. Why, then, is every man in agony as though he were in the travail of childbirth?

22. The verse teaches that, anthropomorphically speaking, God will suffer like a woman giving birth. The reason for this distress is the need to destroy other nations (*Rashi;* see note 24), or the suffering of the Jewish people (*Maharsha*). [The word כָּל, *every,* is apparently superfluous. Therefore, this expression (כָּל־גֶּבֶר) is interpreted as meaning מִי שֶׁכָּל גְּבוּרָה שֶׁלּוֹ, *the One to Whom all power belongs* – i.e. God (*Maharsha*).]

Yad Ramah strongly objects to this interpretation. In his view, מִי שֶׁכָּל גְּבוּרָה שֶׁלּוֹ means the mightiest of men. Even the mightiest warriors will be reduced to agony during the pre-Messianic travail (see also *Iyun Yaakov*, *Ben Yehoyada*).

23. The word כָּל, *all,* seems to be unnecessary (*Maharsha*). It is therefore interpreted as referring to both the earthly and the heavenly host (*Rashi;* cf. *Maharsha*).

24. All human beings are God's creatures. Therefore, anthropomorphically speaking, it will be difficult for God to overthrow the pagan nations to make way for the rise of the Messianic kingdom (*Rashi*). [Because of this "difficulty," it might appear at some point as though God will let the pagan nations hold sway. It was this moment, the darkest and most terrifying of all, that R' Yochanan sought to avoid.]

Yad Ramah rejects this explanation, because it implies that God will be in a state of doubt. Rather, the Gemara is stressing the favor that God will show His people – He will destroy even His own handiwork for their sake! The Gemara should be understood thus: "These are My handiwork, and these are My handiwork. Therefore, it should amaze you: How can I destroy these because of these?!"

25. The analogy is drawn to a farmer who owned an ox and a horse. The farmer cherished the ox, and he gave it a feeding trough of its own. One day, the ox ran and fell. While the ox recovered from its injuries, the farmer let the horse use the ox's feeding trough. When the ox returned, the farmer was faced with a dilemma: How could he remove the horse, which he himself had put at the trough, to make way for the ox?

Likewise, when God sees the Jewish people fall [in sin], He transfers their eminence to the idolatrous nations. Then, when the Jewish people repent and are redeemed, it will be "difficult" for God to overthrow the idolatrous nations and restore the Jews to their former position (*Rashi*).

In line with his objection to the preceding approach (see note 24), *Yad Ramah* explains the metaphor differently: רָהִיט וְנָפֵל תּוֹרָא וְאָזִיל וְשָׁדֵי לֵיהּ סוּסְיָא בְּאוּרְיֵיהּ, *An ox runs and falls, but it will go and hurl the horse into its trough.* An ox is awkward and stumbles when it runs. Therefore, when an ox fights a horse, the horse will repeatedly escape the ox's charges. Eventually, however, the ox will corner the horse and hurl it to its death. This is a metaphor for God's treatment of the nations that oppressed the Jews. It may seem as though He is letting them escape justice. In the end, though, the punishment they deserve will catch up with them (see also *Ben Yehoyada*).

שאין כל דקל ודקל שבבבל שאין סוס של פרסיים נקשר בו ואין לך כל ארון וארון שבארץ ישראל שאין סוס מדי אוכל בו תבן [א] אמר רב אין בן דוד בא עד שתתפשט המלכות [ב] על ישראל תשעה חדשים שנאמר [א] לכן יתנם עד עת יולדה ילדה ויתר אחיו ישובון על בני ישראל אמר עולא ייתי ולא איחמיניה וכן אמר [[ג] רבה] ייתי ולא איחמיניה רב יוסף אמר ייתי ואזכי דאיתיב בטולא דכופיתא דחמריה אמר ליה אביי (לרבא) [[ד] לרבה] מאי טעמא אילימא משום חבלו של משיח והתניא שאלו תלמידיו את רבי אלעזר מה יעשה אדם וינצל מחבלו של משיח יעסוק בתורה ובגמילות חסדים ומר הא תורה והא גמילות חסדים אמר [ליה] שמא יגרום החטא כדר' יעקב בר אידי [ה] דר' יעקב בר אידי רמי כתיב [ב] הנה אנכי עמך ושמרתיך בכל אשר תלך וכתיב [ג] ויירא יעקב מאד ויצר לו שהיה מתיירא שמא [ו] יגרום החטא כדתניא [ד] עד יעבור עמך ה' זו ביאה ראשונה עד יעבור עם זו קנית זו ביאה שניה אמור מעתה ראויים היו ישראל לעשות להם נס בביאה שניה כביאה ראשונה אלא שגרם החטא וכן אמר ר' יוחנן ייתי ולא איחמיניה א"ל ריש לקיש מ"ט אילימא משום דכתיב [ה] כאשר ינוס איש מפני הארי ופגעו הדוב [ובא הבית] וסמך ידו אל הקיר ונשכו נחש בא ואראך דוגמתו בעולם הזה בזמן שאדם יוצא לשדה ופגע בו סנטר דומה כמי שפגע בו ארי נכנס לעיר פגע בו גבאי דומה כמי שפגעו דוב נכנס לביתו ומצא בניו ובנותיו מוטלין ברעב דומה כמי שנשכו נחש אלא משום דכתיב [ו] שאלו נא וראו אם ילד זכר מדוע ראיתי כל גבר ידיו על חלציו כיולדה ונהפכו כל פנים לירקון מאי ראיתי כל גבר אמר רבא בר יצחק אמר רב מי שכל גבורה שלו ומאי ונהפכו כל פנים לירקון אמר רבי יוחנן פמליא של מעלה ופמליא של מטה בשעה שאמר הקב"ה הללו מעשה ידי והללו מעשה ידי היאך אאבד אלו מפני אלו אמר רב פפא היינו דאמרי אינשי רהיט ונפל תורא ואזיל ושדי ליה סוסיא באורייה אמר רב גידל אמר רב עתידין ישראל דאכלי שני משיח אמר רב יוסף פשיטא ואלא מאן אכיל להו חילק ובילק אכלי להו לאפוקי [ז] מדרבי הילל דאמר אין משיח לישראל שכבר אכלוהו בימי חזקיה אמר רב לא אברי עלמא אלא לדוד ושמואל אמר למשה ורבי יוחנן אמר למשיח מה שמו דבי רבי שילא אמרי שילה שמו שנאמר [ז] עד כי יבא שילה דבי רבי ינאי אמרי ינון שמו שנאמר [ח] יהי שמו לעולם לפני שמש ינון שמו דבי רבי חנינה אמר חנינה שמו שנאמר [ט] אשר לא אתן לכם חנינה ויש אומרים מנחם בן חזקיה שמו שנאמר [י] כי רחק ממני מנחם משיב נפשי ורבנן אמרי חיוורא דבי רבי שמו שנאמר [כ] אכן חליינו הוא נשא ומכאובינו סבלם ואנחנו חשבנוהו נגוע מוכה אלהים ומעונה אמר רב נחמן אי מן חייא הוא כגון אנא שנאמר [ל] והיה אדירו ממנו ומושלו מקרבו יצא אמר רב אי מן חייא הוא כגון רבינו הקדוש אי מן מתיא הוא כגון דניאל איש חמודות אמר רב יהודה אמר רב עתיד הקדוש ברוך הוא להעמיד להם דוד אחר שנאמר [מ] ועבדו את ה' אלהיהם ואת דוד מלכם אשר אקים להם הקים לא נאמר אלא אקים א"ל רב פפא לאביי והכתיב [נ] ודוד עבדי נשיא להם לעולם כגון קיסר ופלגי קיסר דרש רבי שמלאי מאי דכתיב [ס] הוי המתאוים את יום ה' למה זה לכם יום ה' הוא חשך ולא אור משל לתרנגול ועטלף שהיו מצפין לאור א"ל תרנגול לעטלף אני מצפה לאורה שאורה שלי היא ואתה למה לך אורה והיינו

שאין סוס מדי אוכל בו תבן. שמוליכין הארונות חוץ לקרקע ועושין מהן אבוסים במלחמת גוג ומגוג: שאין כל דקל וכו'. כלומר עתידין פרס ומדי לבא על בבל וללכדה ונתמלאה כל ארץ בבל חיילות פרסיים וסוסיהם ומשם באים לא"י ולוכדים אותה: עד שתפשוט מלכות על ישראל ט' חדשים שנאמר לכן יתנם לישראל עד עת יולדה ילדה. היינו ט' חדשים כדמתרגמינן בכן יתמסרון כעידן דילדתא למילד וכתיב (מיכה ה) ועמד ורעה בעוז ה' וגו' וישבו כי עתה יגדל ומתרגמינן ויתיבון מביני גלוותהון: על בני ישראל. היינו כל העולם שישראל מפוזרים בו: ייתי. משיח ולא אחמיניה: בטולא דכופיתא דחמריה. בצל הרעי של חמורו כלומר אפילו בכך אני רוצה ובלבד שאראנו: כופיתא. רעי כמו רמא כופת' וסכר ירדנא בבבא בתרא (ד' עג:): מאי טעמא. אמר לא אחמיניה: חבלו של משיח. גורלו ולקמן בעי מאי היא ל"א חבלו פחדים וחבלים שיהיו בימיו מחיל העובדי כוכבים: לעשות להם נס. לעלות בזרוע על כרחם של מלכי פרס: בביאה שניה. בימי עזרא כביאה ראשונה בימי יהושע מדהקישן הכתוב: מאי טעמא. איזו צרה באה בארץ בימיו שאתה אומר לא אחמיניה: סנטר. מפרש בב"ב (דף סח.) בר מחוזנייתא שיודע מיצרי השדות וגבוליהן עד כאן של פלוני מכאן ואילך של פלוני ובידו לרבות לאחד ולמעט לאחר וכשפוגעו אותו סנטר רוצה למדוד שדותיו לקצר מיצרי השדות ודומה כמי שפגע בו ארי: גבאי. גובה מס המלך: מי שכל הגבורה שלו. הקב"ה מצטער בעצמו כיולדה ואומר בשעה שמעביר העובדי כוכבים מפני ישראל היאך אאביד אלו מפני אלו: פמליא של מעלה ושל מטה. מלאכים וישראל: אפילו הגרים לא גרסינן: רהיט ונפיל תורא ואזיל ושדי סוסיא באורייה. כשרץ השור ונפל מעמידין סוס במקומו באבוסו מה שלא היה רוצה לעשות קודם מפלתו של שור שהיה חביב עליו שורו ביותר וכשמתרפא השור היום או למחר ממפלתו קשה לו להוציא סוסו מפני השור לאחר שהעמידו שם כך הקב"ה כיון שראה מפלתן של ישראל נותן גדולתו לעובדי כוכבים וכשחוזרים ישראל בתשובה ונגאלין קשה לו לאבד עובדי כוכבים מפני ישראל: אורייה. כמו (מלכים א ה) ארוות סוסים: דאכלי שני משיח. שובע שיהיה באותן הימים לישראל יהיה: אלא חילק ובילק אכלי להו. כך היו רגילין לומר כאדם שאומר וכי שדים ושדתות יאכלוהו ובמסכת חולין (דף יט.) לא חילק ידענא ולא בילק ידענא ולי נראה דמשמעות לשון חילק ובילק לשון חורבה כמו בוקה ומבוקה ומבולקה (נחום ב) ואמרינן בחולין (שם) לא חילק דרבנן דמצריכין לחלק הסימן שמצריכין לחלק כל הטבעת ולשייר על פני כולו ולא בילק לרבי יוסי שמחריב הסימן שחותך קצת בתוך הטבעת והשאר חוץ לטבעת ונראה למורי דאין לו משמעות לא הכא ולא התם ל"א חילק ובילק ב' דייני סדום שהיו שמותיהן כך: אין משיח לישראל. שחזקיה היה משיח ועליו נאמרו כל הנבואות אצמיח קרן לבית ישראל ועמד ורעה בעוז ה' [ח]: אלא לדוד. בזכות דוד שהיה עתיד לומר כמה שירות ותושבחות: למשה. בשביל משה שהיה עתיד לקבל את התורה: מה שמו. של משיח: ינון שמו. כמו ינאי כל אחד היה דורש אחר שמו: לפני שמש. עד שלא נברא היה שמו ינון והיינו אחד [ט] מז' דברים שעלו במחשבה ליבראות: ולא אתן להם חנינה. עדיין לא יבא משיח: מנחם. בן חזקיה: חיוורא דבי רבי. מצורע של בית רבי: אי מן חייא הוא כגון רבינו הקדוש. אם משיח מאותן שחיים עכשיו ודאי היינו רבינו הקדוש דסובל תחלואים וחסיד גמור הוה כדאמרינן בבבא מציעא (דף פה.) ואם היה מאותן שמתו כבר היה דניאל איש חמודות שנדון ביסורין בגוב אריות וחסיד גמור היה והאי כגון לאו דווקא ל"א כגון רבינו הקדוש כלומר אם יש דוגמתו בחיים היינו רבינו הקדוש ואם דוגמא הוא למתים היינו כגון דניאל איש חמודות: דוד אחר. שעתיד למלוך עליהם: אקים. הקים לא נאמר אלא אקים: כגון קיסר ופלגי קיסר. מלך ושני לו כן דוד החדש מלך כדכתיב ודוד מלכם אשר אקים ודוד המלך שני לו כדכתיב נשיא להם ולא כתוב מלך: עטלף. קלבא שורי"ך בלע"ז ואין לה עינים: שאורה שלי הוא. שיש לי עינים לראות ונמלאתי נהנית בה כך ישראל מצפין לגאולה שיום ה' יהיה להם אור אבל העובדי כוכבים למה מקוים אותו הרי הוא להם חשך ולא אור: ה"ג

ליקוטי רש"י

לכן יתנם עד עת יולדה. יתנם ביד אויביהם עד בא העת אשר חלה וילדה ציון את בניה, ציון אשר החזיקה עתה חיל כיולדה ועכשיו היא קרויה יולדת ורבותינו אמרו מכאן אין בן דוד בא עד שתפשוט המלכות הרשעה ט' חדשים על כל העולם כולו אך לפי פשוטו זהו הלעה שפירשתי. ויתר אחיו. של מלך יהודה, כלומר שאר שבט יהודה. ישובון על בית ישראל. יתחברו עם שאר השבטים ויהיו לממלכה אחת ולא יחלו עוד לשתי ממלכות [מיכה ה, ב]. אנכי עמך. לפי שהיה ירא מעשו ומלבן [בראשית כח, טו]. שמא יגרום החטא. קטנתי מכל החסדים. נתמעטו זכיותי על ידי החסדים והאמת שעשית עמי לכך אני ירא שמא משהבטחתני נתלכלכתי בחטא ויגרום לי להמסר ביד עשו [בראשית לב, יא]. ויירא יעקב. שמא אחר הבטחה חטאתי וכדתניא שהחטא גורם שאין ההבטחה מתקיימת. ביאה ראשונה. שבאו בימי יהושע. ביאה שניה. כשעלו מגלות בבל בימי עזרא. ראויים היו ליעשות להם נס. לבוא ביד רמה. אלא שגרם החטא. ולא הלכו אלא ברשות כורש, וכל ימי מלכי פרס נשתעבדו להם, לכורש ולאחשורוש ולדריוש האחרון [ברכות ד.]. ליעשות להם נס. לעלות בזרוע ולא יהיו משתעבדים למלכות אלא שגרם חטאם של ישראל בימי בית ראשון ונגזר עליהם שלא יעלו אלא ברשות כדכתיב מי בכם מכל עמו (עזרא א) [סוטה לו.]. סנטר. מפרש בבבא בתרא (דף סח) בר מחוזיא זקן הממונה להיות בקי בנחלת גבול שדה כל איש ואיש [גיטין פ:]. אם יולד זכר. אם דרך לזכרים ללדת שיאחזום חבלים כיולדה. חלציו. כמו מתניו [ירמיהו ל, ו]. עד כי יבא שילה. מלך המשיח שהמלוכה שלו וכן תרגם אנקלוס ומדרש אגדה שילו שי לו שנאמר (תהלים עו, יב) יובילו שי למורא [בראשית מט, י]. לפני שמש ינון שמו. כל ימי השמש יגדל שמו ינון לשון מלכות ושררה כמו (משלי כ"ט) ואחריתו יהיה מנון, ולנייני, השליט על נכסי אחרים, אמרו בלבם נינם יחד (תהלים ע"ד) מלכיהם יחד [תהלים עב, יז]. אכן חליינו הוא נשא. אכן לשון אבל בכל מקום אבל עתה אנו רואים שלא מחמ' שפלותו בא לו אלא מיוסר היה ביסורין. ואנחנו חשבנוהו. אנו היינו סבורים שהוא שנאוי למקום והוא לא היה כן אלא מחולל היה מפשעינו ומדוכא מעונותינו [ישעיהו נג, ד]. אדירו. שר שלו [ירמיהו ל, כא].

מסורת הש"ס

א) [יומא י. ע"ש], ב) [שם איתא בכל העולם כולו וכן הוא גיר' תוס' בע"ז ב: ד"ה משכא וכו'], ג) ב"ש, ד) [עי' תוס' ר"ה יח. ד"ה רבה ותוס' יבמות קה. ד"ה רבא], ה) ברכות ד., ו) ג"ז שם סוטה לו., ז) [לקמן צט. וע"ש פירש"י ד"ה אין להם], ח) [מיכה ה], ט) [פסחים נד. נדרים לט:].

תורה אור השלם

א) לָכֵן יִתְּנֵם עַד עֵת יוֹלֵדָה יָלָדָה וְיֶתֶר אֶחָיו יְשׁוּבוּן עַל בְּנֵי יִשְׂרָאֵל: [מיכה ה, ב]

ב) וְהִנֵּה אָנֹכִי עִמָּךְ וּשְׁמַרְתִּיךָ בְּכֹל אֲשֶׁר תֵּלֵךְ וַהֲשִׁבֹתִיךָ אֶל הָאֲדָמָה הַזֹּאת כִּי לֹא אֶעֱזָבְךָ עַד אֲשֶׁר אִם עָשִׂיתִי אֵת אֲשֶׁר דִּבַּרְתִּי לָךְ: [בראשית כח, טו]

ג) וַיִּירָא יַעֲקֹב מְאֹד וַיֵּצֶר לוֹ וַיַּחַץ אֶת הָעָם אֲשֶׁר אִתּוֹ וְאֶת הַצֹּאן וְאֶת הַבָּקָר וְהַגְּמַלִּים לִשְׁנֵי מַחֲנוֹת: [בראשית לב, ח]

ד) תִּפֹּל עֲלֵיהֶם אֵימָתָה וָפַחַד בִּגְדֹל זְרוֹעֲךָ יִדְּמוּ כָּאָבֶן עַד יַעֲבֹר עַמְּךָ יְיָ עַד יַעֲבֹר עַם זוּ קָנִיתָ: [שמות טו, טז]

ה) כַּאֲשֶׁר יָנוּס אִישׁ מִפְּנֵי הָאֲרִי וּפְגָעוֹ הַדֹּב וּבָא הַבַּיִת וְסָמַךְ יָדוֹ עַל הַקִּיר וּנְשָׁכוֹ הַנָּחָשׁ: [עמוס ה, יט]

ו) שַׁאֲלוּ נָא וּרְאוּ אִם יֹלֵד זָכָר מַדּוּעַ רָאִיתִי כָל גֶּבֶר יָדָיו עַל חֲלָצָיו כַּיּוֹלֵדָה וְנֶהֶפְכוּ כָל פָּנִים לְיֵרָקוֹן: [ירמיה ל, ו]

ז) לֹא יָסוּר שֵׁבֶט מִיהוּדָה וּמְחֹקֵק מִבֵּין רַגְלָיו עַד כִּי יָבֹא שִׁילֹה וְלוֹ יִקְּהַת עַמִּים: [בראשית מט, י]

ח) יְהִי שְׁמוֹ לְעוֹלָם לִפְנֵי שֶׁמֶשׁ יִנּוֹן שְׁמוֹ וְיִתְבָּרְכוּ בוֹ כָּל גּוֹיִם יְאַשְּׁרוּהוּ: [תהלים עב, יז]

ט) וְהֵטַלְתִּי אֶתְכֶם מֵעַל הָאָרֶץ הַזֹּאת עַל הָאָרֶץ אֲשֶׁר לֹא יְדַעְתֶּם אַתֶּם וַאֲבוֹתֵיכֶם וַעֲבַדְתֶּם שָׁם אֶת אֱלֹהִים אֲחֵרִים יוֹמָם וָלַיְלָה אֲשֶׁר לֹא אֶתֵּן לָכֶם חֲנִינָה: [ירמיה טז, יג]

י) עַל אֵלֶּה אֲנִי בוֹכִיָּה עֵינִי עֵינִי יֹרְדָה מַּיִם כִּי רָחַק מִמֶּנִּי מְנַחֵם מֵשִׁיב נַפְשִׁי הָיוּ בָנַי שׁוֹמֵמִים כִּי גָבַר אוֹיֵב: [איכה א, טז]

כ) אָכֵן חֳלָיֵנוּ הוּא נָשָׂא וּמַכְאֹבֵינוּ סְבָלָם וַאֲנַחְנוּ חֲשַׁבְנֻהוּ נָגוּעַ מֻכֵּה אֱלֹהִים וּמְעֻנֶּה: [ישעיה נג, ד]

ל) וְהָיָה אַדִּירוֹ מִמֶּנּוּ וּמֹשְׁלוֹ מִקִּרְבּוֹ יֵצֵא וְהִקְרַבְתִּיו וְנִגַּשׁ אֵלָי כִּי מִי הוּא זֶה עָרַב אֶת לִבּוֹ לָגֶשֶׁת אֵלַי נְאֻם יְיָ: [ירמיה ל, כא]

מ) וְעָבְדוּ אֵת יְיָ אֱלֹהֵיהֶם וְאֵת דָּוִד מַלְכָּם אֲשֶׁר אָקִים לָהֶם: [ירמיה ל, ט] נ) וְיָשְׁבוּ עַל הָאָרֶץ אֲשֶׁר נָתַתִּי לְעַבְדִּי לְיַעֲקֹב אֲשֶׁר יָשְׁבוּ בָהּ אֲבוֹתֵיכֶם וְיָשְׁבוּ עָלֶיהָ הֵמָּה וּבְנֵיהֶם וּבְנֵי בְנֵיהֶם עַד עוֹלָם וְדָוִד עַבְדִּי נָשִׂיא לָהֶם לְעוֹלָם: [יחזקאל לז, כה] ס) הוֹי הַמִּתְאַוִּים אֶת יוֹם יְיָ לָמָּה זֶּה לָכֶם יוֹם יְיָ הוּא חֹשֶׁךְ וְלֹא אוֹר: [עמוס ה, יח]

to enjoy the years of the Messiah.[26]

The Gemara exclaims:

אָמַר רַב יוֹסֵף – Rav Yosef said: פְּשִׁיטָא – That is **obvious!** וְאֶלָּא מַאן אָכִיל לְהוּ – **Who will enjoy [the years of the Messiah]** if not the Jews? חִילְק וּבִילְק אָכְלֵי לְהוּ – **Chillak and Billak will enjoy them?!**[27]

The Gemara explains why Rav's teaching is necessary:

לְאַפּוּקֵי מִדְּרַבִּי הִילֵּל – It serves **to exclude** the opinion of **R' Hillel,** דְּאָמַר אֵין מָשִׁיחַ לְיִשְׂרָאֵל – **who said** that **there will be no Messiah for the Jewish people,** שֶׁכְּבָר אֲכָלוּהוּ בִּימֵי חִזְקִיָּה – **because they already enjoyed [the years of the Messiah] in the days of Chizkiah.**[28]

The Gemara cites a dispute that concerns the Messiah:

אָמַר רַב – **Rav said:** לֹא אִבְּרֵי עָלְמָא אֶלָּא לְדָוִד – **The world was created only for David.**[29]

וּשְׁמוּאֵל אָמַר – **But Shmuel says:** לְמֹשֶׁה – It was created only **for Moses.**[30]

וְרַבִּי יוֹחָנָן אָמַר – **And R' Yochanan says:** לַמָּשִׁיחַ – It was created only **for the Messiah.**[31]

The Gemara discusses the name of the Messiah:

מַה שְּׁמוֹ – **What is his name?** דְּבֵי רַבִּי שִׁילָא אָמְרֵי – **The school of R' Shela say:** שִׁילֹה שְׁמוֹ – **Shiloh is his name,** שֶׁנֶּאֱמַר ,,עַד כִּי־יָבֹא שִׁילֹה" – **as it is stated:** ***until Shiloh comes.***[32]

דְּבֵי רַבִּי יַנַּאי אָמְרֵי – **The school of R' Yannai say:** יִנּוֹן שְׁמוֹ – **Yinon**[33] **is his name,** שֶׁנֶּאֱמַר ,,יְהִי שְׁמוֹ לְעוֹלָם לִפְנֵי־שֶׁמֶשׁ יִנּוֹן שְׁמוֹ" – **as it is stated:** ***May his name endure forever; for as long as the sun may his name continue*** (*yinon*).[34]

דְּבֵי רַבִּי חֲנִינָה אָמַר – **The school of R' Chaninah says:** חֲנִינָה שְׁמוֹ – **Chaninah is his name,** שֶׁנֶּאֱמַר ,,אֲשֶׁר לֹא־אֶתֵּן לָכֶם חֲנִינָה" – **as it is stated:** ***For I will not give you mercy*** (*chaninah*).[35]

וְיֵשׁ אוֹמְרִים – **And some say:** מְנַחֵם בֶּן חִזְקִיָּה שְׁמוֹ – **Menachem ben Chizkiah is his name,** שֶׁנֶּאֱמַר ,,כִּי־רָחַק מִמֶּנִּי מְנַחֵם מֵשִׁיב נַפְשִׁי" – **as it is stated:** ***because a comforter*** (*menachem*) ***to revive my spirit is far from me.***[36]

וְרַבָּנָן אָמְרֵי – **And the Rabbis say:** חִיוָּורָא דְּבֵי רַבִּי שְׁמוֹ – ***Metzora***[37] **of the House of Rebbi is his name,**[38] שֶׁנֶּאֱמַר ,,אָכֵן חֳלָיֵנוּ הוּא נָשָׂא וּמַכְאֹבֵינוּ סְבָלָם וַאֲנַחְנוּ חֲשַׁבְנֻהוּ נָגוּעַ מֻכֵּה אֱלֹהִים וּמְעֻנֶּה" – **as it is stated:** ***Indeed, it was our diseases that he bore and our pains that he endured, whereas we considered him plagued, smitten by God and afflicted.***[39]

NOTES

26. The abundance of those years will be Israel's (*Rashi*).

27. Chillak and Billak were names used to connote fictitious figures of an undesirable nature. *Rashi* suggests that they derive from roots signifying destruction (see *Nahum* 2:11 and *Chullin* 19a). Alternatively, they were the names of two judges from Sodom. In the name of his teacher, *Rashi* writes that these names carry no meaning at all (see the commentaries to *Chullin* ibid.; see also *Ben Yehoyada* here).

28. R' Hillel maintains that King Chizkiah was the Messiah and all the prophecies about the Messiah (e.g. *Ezekiel* 29:21, *Micah* 5:3) were stated in reference to him (see above, 94a with notes 12 and 15). R' Hillel's view is elaborated below, 99a note 13.

When Rav said "the Jewish people will enjoy the years of the Messiah" his intent was not to exclude other peoples. Rather, it was to stress that, contrary to R' Hillel's view, there *will* be a Messiah (*Yad Ramah*).

29. The world was created in the merit of David who was destined to offer many songs and praises to God (*Rashi*).

30. Who was destined to receive the Torah (*Rashi*).

31. Whose greatness is supreme (*Yad Ramah*).

Ran explains that these Sages are debating the question of which period in the world's existence is the most blessed in terms of physical benefit. According to Shmuel, the greatest physical blessings were experienced in the era of Moses [when the people ate the manna and were protected by the Clouds of Glory etc.]. Rav holds that the generation of David enjoyed the greatest blessings [when the people lived prosperously in Eretz Yisrael, united under one king]. R' Yochanan opines that the world will reach its physical zenith in the Messianic era. These three views are recorded in contrast to that of R' Hillel, who maintains that the greatest physical blessings were enjoyed during the reign of King Chizkiah (*Ran* to 99a; see 99a note 13).

According to *Maharsha,* the point of the Gemara is that the achievements of these three personalities — the Davidic dynasty, the Torah, the redemption — will endure forever in this world.

32. *Genesis* 49:10. שִׁילֹה, *Shiloh,* is interpreted as referring to the Messiah on the basis of the verse: יוּבַל־שַׁי לַה׳, *a gift shall be offered to Hashem* (*Isaiah* 18:7), which the Midrash (*Yalkut Shimoni, Genesis* §160) renders: *All the nations are destined to bring a gift to Israel and the Messianic king.* שִׁילֹה, *Shiloh,* is formed from the two words, שַׁי, *shai* [a gift] and לוֹ, *lo* [to him] (*Maharsha;* cf. *Rashi* to *Genesis* 49:10).

Jacob blessed his sons before he died. In this verse, Jacob promises Judah that the kings of the Jewish people will emerge exclusively from his tribe, until the advent of the Messiah [who will rule not only over the Jewish people, but over all the other nations of the world as well] (*Ramban* ad loc.; see *Anaf Yosef*).

33. יִנּוֹן, *Yinon,* is similar to יַנַּאי, *Yannai* (*Rashi;* see note 35).

34. *Psalms* 72:17. David prays for the success of his descendant, the Messiah.

The verse is interpreted here to mean: לִפְנֵי־שֶׁמֶשׁ יִנּוֹן שְׁמוֹ, *before the sun* [was created] *Yinon was his name.* The name of the Messiah was one of seven things that God created before the world (*Rashi,* from *Pesachim* 54a).

35. *Jeremiah* 16:13.

Each one of these sages (R' Shela, R' Yannai and R' Chaninah) derived from Scripture that the Messiah's name is similar to his own (*Rashi*).

It was not the intent of each sage that the Messiah will definitely bear this name. Rather, each sage meant that the name he specified is suited for the Messiah because he found an allusion to it in Scripture (*Ben Yehoyada*).

Maharal explains that the character of the Messiah encompasses the virtues of every human being. Hence, one who studies the Messiah will naturally be drawn to seeing his own personality. For this reason, when these sages attempted to determine the Messiah's name (i.e. the name that describes his personality [see note 39]), they concluded that it was the same as their own. There is no dispute whatsoever between these sages. Each one is simply stressing the aspect of the Messiah's personality with which he is most familiar (see *Netzach Yisrael* ch. 41).

36. *Lamentations* 1:16. Jeremiah weeps over the destruction of Jerusalem.

The verse mentions only מְנַחֵם, *Menachem.* A tradition taught that his father's name is Chizkiah (*Maharsha*).

37. A *metzora* is one afflicted with the disease of *tzaraas,* which is described in *Leviticus* ch. 13.

38. He will be a *metzora* and a descendant of Rebbi. The verse that follows is cited to prove the first point (*Yad Ramah*).

Alternatively, דְּבֵי רַבִּי means "of the *school* of Rebbi." The Gemara in *Bava Metzia* (85a) relates that Rebbi endured agonizing disease for many years. Like Rebbi, the Messiah will also undergo terrible suffering [see 98a note 59 and below, note 42] (*Maharsha*).

According to *Maharal,* the Gemara does not mean that the Messiah will actually be afflicted with *tzaraas.* He is allegorically described in this way, because *tzaraas*, which involves the decay of the physical body, is an apt metaphor for a person whose spiritual aspect is so sublime that he seems to be the antithesis of the physical.

39. *Isaiah* 53:4. The word נָגוּעַ, *plagued,* is used to connote *tzaraas,* as in *Leviticus* 13:22.

The commentators stress that the names given here are descriptive, rather than real, and all of them are applicable to the Messiah. (Compare to Moses who also had several descriptive names [*Megillah* 13a].) The name שִׁילֹה, *Shiloh,* is related to the Midrash which states: *All the nations are destined to bring a gift* [shai] *to Israel and the Messianic king* (see note 32). [It thus connotes the Messiah's dominion over the nations.] יִנּוֹן, *Yinon,* signifies authority and majesty (see *Rashi* to *Psalms* 72:17). חֲנִינָה, *Chaninah,* means mercy, and מְנַחֵם, *Menachem,*

שאין כל דקל ודקל שבבבל שאין סוס של פרסיים נקשר בו ואין לך כל ארון וארון שבארץ ישראל שאין סוס מדי אוכל בו תבן [א] אמר רב אין בן דוד בא עד שתתפשט המלכות [ב] על ישראל תשעה חדשים שנאמר [א] לכן יתנם עד עת יולדה ילדה ויתר אחיו ישובון על בני ישראל אמר עולא ייתי ולא איחמיניה וכן אמר [ג] רבה] ייתי ולא איחמיניה רב יוסף אמר ייתי ואזכי דאיתיב בטולא דכופיתא דחמריה אמר ליה אביי (לרבא) [ד] לרבה] מאי טעמא אילימא משום חבלו של משיח והתניא שאלו תלמידיו את רבי אלעזר מה יעשה אדם וינצל מחבלו של משיח יעסוק בתורה ובגמילות חסדים ומר הא תורה והא גמילות חסדים אמר [ליה] שמא יגרום החטא כדר' יעקב בר אידי [ה] דר' יעקב בר אידי רמי כתיב [ב] הנה אנכי עמך ושמרתיך בכל אשר תלך וכתיב [ג] ויירא יעקב מאד וייצר לו שהיה מתירא שמא [ו] יגרום החטא כדתניא [ד] עד יעבור עמך ה' זו ביאה ראשונה עד יעבור עם זו קנית זו ביאה שניה אמור מעתה ראויים היו ישראל לעשות להם נס בביאה שניה כביאה ראשונה אלא שגרם החטא וכן אמר ר' יוחנן ייתי ולא איחמיניה א"ל ריש לקיש מ"ט אילימא משום דכתיב [ה] כאשר ינוס איש מפני הארי ופגעו הדוב [ובא הבית] וסמך ידו אל הקיר ונשכו נחש בא ואראך דוגמתו בעולם הזה בזמן שאדם יוצא לשדה ופגע בו סנטר דומה כמי שפגע בו ארי נכנס לעיר פגע בו גבאי דומה כמי שפגעו דוב נכנס לביתו ומצא בניו ובנותיו מוטלין ברעב דומה כמי שנשכו נחש אלא משום דכתיב [ו] שאלו נא וראו אם ילד זכר מדוע ראיתי כל גבר ידיו על חלציו כיולדה ונהפכו כל פנים לירקון מאי ראיתי כל גבר אמר רבא בר יצחק אמר רב מי שכל גבורה שלו ומאי ונהפכו כל פנים לירקון אמר רבי יוחנן פמליא של מעלה ופמליא של מטה בשעה שאמר הקב"ה הללו מעשה ידי והללו מעשה ידי היאך אאבד אלו מפני אלו אמר רב פפא היינו דאמרי אינשי רהיט ונפל תורא ואזיל ושדי ליה סוסיא באורייה אמר רב גידל אמר רב עתידין ישראל דאכלי שני משיח אמר רב יוסף פשיטא ואלא מאן אכיל להו חילק ובילק אכלי להו לאפוקי [ז] מדרבי הילל דאמר אין משיח לישראל שכבר אכלוהו בימי חזקיה אמר רב לא אברי עלמא אלא לדוד ושמואל אמר למשה ורבי יוחנן אמר למשיח מה שמו דבי רבי שילא אמרי שילה שמו שנאמר [ז] עד כי יבא שילה דבי רבי ינאי אמרי ינון שמו שנאמר [ח] יהי שמו לעולם לפני שמש ינון שמו דבי רבי חנינה אמר חנינה שמו שנאמר [ט] אשר לא אתן לכם חנינה ויש אומרים מנחם בן חזקיה שמו שנאמר [י] כי רחק ממני מנחם משיב נפשי ורבנן אמרי חיוורא דבי רבי שמו שנאמר [כ] אכן חליינו הוא נשא ומכאובינו סבלם ואנחנו חשבנוהו נגוע מוכה אלהים ומעונה אמר רב נחמן אי מן חייא הוא כגון אנא שנאמר [ל] והיה אדירו ממנו ומושלו מקרבו יצא אמר רב אי מן חייא הוא כגון רבינו הקדוש אי מן מתיא הוא כגון דניאל איש חמודות אמר רב יהודה אמר רב עתיד הקדוש ברוך הוא להעמיד להם דוד אחר שנאמר [מ] ועבדו את ה' אלהיהם ואת דוד מלכם אשר אקים להם הקים לא נאמר אלא אקים א"ל רב פפא לאביי והכתיב [נ] ודוד עבדי נשיא להם לעולם כגון קיסר ופלגי קיסר דרש רבי שמלאי מאי דכתיב [ס] הוי המתאוים את יום ה' למה זה לכם יום ה' הוא חשך ולא אור משל לתרנגול ועטלף שהיו מצפין לאור א"ל תרנגול לעטלף אני מצפה לאורה שאורה שלי היא ואתה למה לך אורה והיינו

רש"י

שאין סוס מדי אוכל בו תבן. שמוליכין הארונות חוץ לקרקע ועושין מהן אבוסים במלחמת גוג ומגוג: שאין כל דקל וכו'. כלומר עתידין פרס ומדי לבא על בבל וללכדה ונתמלאה כל ארץ בבל חיילות פרסיים וסוסיהם ומשם באים לא"י ולוכדים אותה: עד שתפשוט מלכות על ישראל ט' חדשים שנאמר לכן יתנם לישראל עד עת יולדה ילדה. היינו ט' חדשים כדמתרגמינן בכן יתמסרון כעידן דילדתא למילד וכתיב (מיכה ה) ועמד ורעה בעוז ה' וגו' וישבו כי עתה יגדל ומתרגמינן ויתיבון מביני גלוותהון: על בני ישראל. היינו כל העולם שישראל מפוזרים בו: ייתי. משיח ולא אחמיניה: בטולא דכופיתא דחמריה. בצל הרעי של חמורו כלומר אפילו בכך אני רוצה ובלבד שאראנו: כופיתא. רעי כמו רמא כופת' וסכר ירדנא בבבא בתרא (ד' עג:): מאי טעמא. אמר לא אחמיניה: חבלו של משיח. גורלו ולקמן בעי מאי היא ל"א חבלו פחדים וחבלים שיהיו בימיו מחיל העובדי כוכבים: לעשות להם נס. לעלות בזרוע על כרחם של מלכי פרס: בביאה שניה. בימי עזרא כביאה ראשונה בימי יהושע מדהקישן הכתוב: מאי טעמא. איזו צרה באה בארץ בימיו שאתה אומר לא אחמיניה: סנטר. מפרש בב"ב (דף סח.) בר מחוזניתא שיודע מיצרי השדות וגבוליהן עד כאן של פלוני מכאן ואילך של פלוני ובידו לרבות לאחד ולמעט לאחר וכשפוגעו אותו סנטר רוצה למדוד שדותיו לקצר מיצרי השדות ודומה כמי שפגע בו ארי: גבאי. גובה מס המלך: מי שכל הגבורה שלו. הקב"ה מצטער בעצמו כיולדה ואומר בשעה שמעביר העובדי כוכבים מפני ישראל היאך אאביד אלו מפני אלו: פמליא של מעלה ושל מטה. מלאכים וישראל: אפילו הגרים לא גרסינן: רהיט ונפיל תורא ואזיל ושדי סוסיא באורייה. כשרץ השור ונפל מעמידין סוס במקומו באבוסו מה שלא היה רוצה לעשות קודם מפלתו של שור שהיה חביב עליו שורו ביותר וכשמתרפא השור היום או למחר ממפלתו קשה לו להוציא סוסו מפני השור לאחר שהעמידו שם כך הקב"ה כיון שראה מפלתן של ישראל נותן גדולתו לעובדי כוכבים וכשחוזרים ישראל בתשובה ונגאלין קשה לו לאבד עובדי כוכבים מפני ישראל: אורייה. כמו (מלכים א ה) ארוות סוסים: דאכלי שני משיח. שובע שיהיה באותן הימים לישראל יהיה: אלא חילק ובילק אכלי להו. כך היו רגילין לומר כאדם שאומר וכי שדים ושדות יאכלוהו ובמסכת חולין (דף יט.) לא חילק ידענא ולא בילק ידענא ולי נראה דמשמעות לשון חילק ובילק לשון חורבה כמו בוקה ומבוקה ומבולקה (נחום ב) ואמרינן בחולין (שם) לא חילק דרבנן דמצריכין לחלק הסימן שמצריכין לחלק כל הטבעת ולשייר על פני כולו ולא בילק לרבי יוסי שמחריב הסימן שחותך קצת בתוך הטבעת והשאר חוץ לטבעת ונראה למורי דאין לו משמעות לא הכא ולא התם ל"א חילק ובילק ב' דייני סדום שהיו שמותיהן כך: אין משיח לישראל. שחזקיה היה משיח ועליו נאמרו כל הנבואות אצמיח קרן לבית ישראל ועמד ורעה בעוז ה' [ח]: אלא לדוד. בזכות דוד שהיה עתיד לומר כמה שירות ותושבחות: למשה. בשביל משה שהיה עתיד לקבל את התורה: מה שמו. של משיח: ינון שמו. כמו ינאי כל אחד היה דורש אחר שמו: לפני שמש. עד שלא נברא היה שמו ינון והיינו אחד [ט] מז' דברים שעלו במחשבה ליבראות: ולא אתן להם חנינה. עדיין לא יבא משיח: מנחם. בן חזקיה: חיוורא דבי רבי. מצורע של בית רבי: אי מן חייא הוא כגון רבינו הקדוש. אם משיח מאותן שחיים עכשיו ודאי היינו רבינו הקדוש דסובל תחלואים וחסיד גמור הוה כדאמרינן בבבא מציעא (דף פה.) ואם היה מאותן שמתו כבר היה דניאל איש חמודות שנדון ביסורין בגוב אריות וחסיד גמור היה והאי כגון לאו דווקא ל"א כגון רבינו הקדוש כלומר אם יש דוגמתו בחיים היינו רבינו הקדוש ואם דוגמא הוא למתים היינו כגון דניאל איש חמודות: דוד אחר. שעתיד למלוך עליהם: אקים. הקים לא נאמר אלא אקים: כגון קיסר ופלגי קיסר. מלך ושני לו כן דוד החדש מלך כדכתיב ודוד מלכם אשר אקים ודוד המלך שני לו כדכתיב נשיא להם ולא כתוב מלך: עטלף. קלבא שורי"ץ בלע"ז ואין לה עינים: שאורה שלי הוא. שיש לי עינים לראות ונמצאתי נהנית בה כך ישראל מצפין לגאולה שיום ה' יהיה להם אור אבל העובדי כוכבים למה מקוים אותו הרי הוא להם חשך ולא אור:

ה"ג

ליקוטי רש"י

לכן יתנם עד עת יולדה. יתנם ביד אויביהם עד בא העת אשר חלה וילדה ציון את בניה, ציון אשר החזיקה עתה חיל כיולדה ועכשיו היא קרויה יולדת ורבותינו אמרו מכאן אין בן דוד בא עד שתפשוט המלכות הרשעה ט' חדשים על כל העולם כולו אך לפי פשוטו זהו הצעה שפירשתי. ויתר אחיו. של מלך יהודה, כלומר שאר שבט יהודה. ישובון על בית ישראל. יתחברו עם שאר השבטים ויהיו לממלכה אחת ולא יחלו עוד לשתי ממלכות [מיכה ה, ב]. אנכי עמך. לפי שהיה ירא מעשו ומלבן [בראשית כח, טו]. שמא יגרום החטא. קטנתי מכל החסדים. נתמעטו זכיותי על ידי החסדים והאמת שעשית עמי לכך אני ירא שמא משהבטחתני נתלכלכתי בחטא ויגרום לי להמסר ביד עשו [בראשית לב, יא]. ויירא יעקב. שמא אחר הבטחה חטאתי וכדתניא שהחטא גורם שאין ההבטחה מתקיימת. ביאה ראשונה. שבאו בימי יהושע. ביאה שניה. כשעלו מגלות בבל בימי עזרא. ראויים היו ליעשות להם נס. לבוא ביד רמה. אלא שגרם החטא. ולא הלכו אלא ברשות כורש, וכל ימי מלכי פרס נשתעבדו להם, לכורש ולאחשורוש ולדריוש האחרון [ברכות ד.]. ליעשות להם נס. לעלות בזרוע ולא יהיו משתעבדים למלכות אלא שגרם חטאם של ישראל בימי בית ראשון ונגזר עליהם שלא יעלו אלא ברשות כדכתיב מי בכם מכל עמו (עזרא א) [סוטה לו.]. סנטר. מפרש בבבא בתרא (דף סח) בר מחווניא זקן הממונה להיות בקי בנחלת גבול שדה כל איש ואיש [גיטין פ:]. אם יולד זכר. אם דרך לזכרים ללדת שיאחזום חבלים כיולדה. חלציו. כמו מתניו [ירמיהו ל, ו]. עד כי יבא שילה. מלך המשיח שהמלוכה שלו וכן תרגם אנקלוס ומדרש אגדה שילו שי לו שנאמר (תהלים עו, יב) יובילו שי למורא [בראשית מט, י]. לפני שמש ינון שמו. כל ימי השמש יגדל שמו ינון לשון מלכות ושררה כמו (משלי כ"ט) ואחריתו יהיה מנון, ולניני, השליט על נכסי אחרים, אמרו בלבם נינם יחד (תהלים ע"ד) מלכיהם יחד [תהלים עב, יז]. אכן חליינו הוא נשא. אכן לשון אבל בכל מקום אבל עתה אנו רואים שלא מחמ' שפלותו בא לו אלא מיוסר היה ביסורין. ואנחנו חשבנוהו. אנו היינו סבורים שהוא שנאוי למקום והוא לא היה כן אלא מחולל היה מפשעינו ומדוכא מעונותינו [ישעיהו נג, ד]. אדירו. שר שלו [ירמיהו ל, כא].

מסורת הש"ס

א) [יומא י. ע"ש], ב) [שם איתא בכל העולם כולו וכן הוא גיר' תוס' בע"ז ב: ד"ה משכא וכו'], ג) כ"ש, ד) [עי' תוס' ר"ה יח. ד"ה רבה ותוס' יבמות קה. ד"ה רבא], ה) ברכות ד., ו) ג"ז שם סוטה לו., ז) [לקמן לט. וע"ש פירש"י ד"ה אין להם], ח) [מיכה ה], ט) [פסחים נד. נדרים לט:].

תורה אור השלם

א) לָכֵן יִתְּנֵם עַד עֵת יוֹלֵדָה יָלָדָה וְיֶתֶר אֶחָיו יְשׁוּבוּן עַל בְּנֵי יִשְׂרָאֵל: [מיכה ה, ב]

ב) וְהִנֵּה אָנֹכִי עִמָּךְ וּשְׁמַרְתִּיךָ בְּכֹל אֲשֶׁר תֵּלֵךְ וַהֲשִׁבֹתִיךָ אֶל הָאֲדָמָה הַזֹּאת כִּי לֹא אֶעֱזָבְךָ עַד אֲשֶׁר אִם עָשִׂיתִי אֵת אֲשֶׁר דִּבַּרְתִּי לָךְ: [בראשית כח, טו]

ג) וַיִּירָא יַעֲקֹב מְאֹד וַיֵּצֶר לוֹ וַיַּחַץ אֶת הָעָם אֲשֶׁר אִתּוֹ וְאֶת הַצֹּאן וְאֶת הַבָּקָר וְהַגְּמַלִּים לִשְׁנֵי מַחֲנוֹת: [בראשית לב, ח]

ד) תִּפֹּל עֲלֵיהֶם אֵימָתָה וָפַחַד בִּגְדֹל זְרוֹעֲךָ יִדְּמוּ כָּאָבֶן עַד יַעֲבֹר עַמְּךָ יְיָ עַד יַעֲבֹר עַם זוּ קָנִיתָ: [שמות טו, טז]

ה) כַּאֲשֶׁר יָנוּס אִישׁ מִפְּנֵי הָאֲרִי וּפְגָעוֹ הַדֹּב וּבָא הַבַּיִת וְסָמַךְ יָדוֹ עַל הַקִּיר וּנְשָׁכוֹ הַנָּחָשׁ: [עמוס ה, יט]

ו) שַׁאֲלוּ נָא וּרְאוּ אִם יֹלֵד זָכָר מַדּוּעַ רָאִיתִי כָל גֶּבֶר יָדָיו עַל חֲלָצָיו כַּיּוֹלֵדָה וְנֶהֶפְכוּ כָל פָּנִים לְיֵרָקוֹן: [ירמיה ל, ו]

ז) לֹא יָסוּר שֵׁבֶט מִיהוּדָה וּמְחֹקֵק מִבֵּין רַגְלָיו עַד כִּי יָבֹא שִׁילֹה וְלוֹ יִקְּהַת עַמִּים: [בראשית מט, י]

ח) יְהִי שְׁמוֹ לְעוֹלָם לִפְנֵי שֶׁמֶשׁ יִנּוֹן שְׁמוֹ וְיִתְבָּרְכוּ בוֹ כָּל גּוֹיִם יְאַשְּׁרוּהוּ: [תהלים עב, יז]

ט) וְהֵטַלְתִּי אֶתְכֶם מֵעַל הָאָרֶץ הַזֹּאת עַל הָאָרֶץ אֲשֶׁר לֹא יְדַעְתֶּם אַתֶּם וַאֲבוֹתֵיכֶם וַעֲבַדְתֶּם שָׁם אֶת אֱלֹהִים אֲחֵרִים יוֹמָם וָלַיְלָה אֲשֶׁר לֹא אֶתֵּן לָכֶם חֲנִינָה: [ירמיה טז, יג]

י) עַל אֵלֶּה אֲנִי בוֹכִיָּה עֵינִי עֵינִי יֹרְדָה מַּיִם כִּי רָחַק מִמֶּנִּי מְנַחֵם מֵשִׁיב נַפְשִׁי הָיוּ בָנַי שׁוֹמֵמִים כִּי גָבַר אוֹיֵב: [איכה א, טז]

כ) אָכֵן חֳלָיֵנוּ הוּא נָשָׂא וּמַכְאֹבֵינוּ סְבָלָם וַאֲנַחְנוּ חֲשַׁבְנֻהוּ נָגוּעַ מֻכֵּה אֱלֹהִים וּמְעֻנֶּה: [ישעיה נג, ד]

ל) וְהָיָה אַדִּירוֹ מִמֶּנּוּ וּמֹשְׁלוֹ מִקִּרְבּוֹ יֵצֵא וְהִקְרַבְתִּיו וְנִגַּשׁ אֵלָי כִּי מִי הוּא זֶה עָרַב אֶת לִבּוֹ לָגֶשֶׁת אֵלַי נְאֻם יְיָ: [ירמיה ל, כא]

מ) וְעָבְדוּ אֵת יְיָ אֱלֹהֵיהֶם וְאֵת דָּוִד מַלְכָּם אֲשֶׁר אָקִים לָהֶם: [ירמיה ל, ט]

נ) וְיָשְׁבוּ עַל הָאָרֶץ אֲשֶׁר נָתַתִּי לְעַבְדִּי לְיַעֲקֹב אֲשֶׁר יָשְׁבוּ בָהּ אֲבוֹתֵיכֶם וְיָשְׁבוּ עָלֶיהָ הֵמָּה וּבְנֵיהֶם וּבְנֵי בְנֵיהֶם עַד עוֹלָם וְדָוִד עַבְדִּי נָשִׂיא לָהֶם לְעוֹלָם: [יחזקאל לז, כה]

ס) הוֹי הַמִּתְאַוִּים אֶת יוֹם יְיָ לָמָּה זֶּה לָכֶם יוֹם יְיָ הוּא חֹשֶׁךְ וְלֹא אוֹר: [עמוס ה, יח]

אָמַר רַב נַחְמָן – **Rav Nachman said:** אִי מִן חַיַּיָא הוּא – **If [the Messiah] is among the living,** כְּגוֹן אֲנָא – **he is** someone **like me,** שֶׁנֶּאֱמַר ,,וְהָיָה אַדִּירוֹ מִמֶּנּוּ וּמשְׁלוֹ מִקִּרְבּוֹ יֵצֵא" – **as it is stated:** ***And their prince shall be one of their own, and their ruler shall emerge from their midst.***[40]

אָמַר רַב – **Rav said:** אִי מִן חַיַּיָא הוּא – **If [the Messiah] is among the living,** כְּגוֹן רַבֵּינוּ הַקָּדוֹשׁ – **he is** someone **like Rabbeinu HaKadosh.**[41] אִי מִן מֵתַיָּא הוּא – **If he is among the dead,** כְּגוֹן דָּנִיֵּאל אִישׁ חֲמוּדוֹת – **he is** someone **like Daniel the Greatly Beloved.**[42]

אָמַר רַב יְהוּדָה אָמַר רַב – **Rav Yehudah said in the name of Rav:** עָתִיד הַקָּדוֹשׁ בָּרוּךְ הוּא לְהַעֲמִיד לָהֶם דָּוִד אַחֵר – **The Holy One, Blessed is He, is destined to raise another David**[43] **for them** [the Jewish people], שֶׁנֶּאֱמַר ,,וְעָבְדוּ אֵת ה' אֱלֹהֵיהֶם וְאֵת דָּוִד מַלְכָּם אֲשֶׁר אָקִים לָהֶם" – **as it is stated:** ***They will serve Hashem their God and David their king, whom I will raise up for them.***[44] ,,הֵקִים" לֹא נֶאֱמַר – The verse does not say: ***He raised*** (past),[45] which would connote the return of the original David to his throne; אֶלָּא ,,אָקִים" – **rather,** it says: ***I will raise*** (future), which connotes the rise of someone else.

The Gemara asks:

אָמַר לֵיהּ רַב פַּפָּא לְאַבַּיֵי – **Rav Pappa said to Abaye:** וְהָכְתִיב ,,וְדָוִד עַבְדִּי נָשִׂיא לָהֶם לְעוֹלָם" – **But it is written:** ***My servant David*** *will be* ***a prince over them forever,***[46] which indicates that it is the original David who will reign over the Jews in the future!

The Gemara answers:

כְּגוֹן קֵיסָר וּפַלְגֵי קֵיסָר – The two Davids will be **like an emperor and a half-emperor.**[47]

The Gemara cites a Tannaic teaching:

דָּרַשׁ רַבִּי שִׂמְלַאי – **R' Simlai expounded:** מַאי דִּכְתִיב – **What is** the meaning of **that which is written:** ,,הוֹי הַמִּתְאַוִּים אֶת־יוֹם ה' לָמָּה־זֶּה לָכֶם יוֹם ה' הוּא־חֹשֶׁךְ וְלֹא אוֹר" – ***Woe unto those who yearn for the day of Hashem! Why should you want the day of Hashem? It is darkness, and not light.***[48] מָשָׁל לְתַרְנְגוֹל וַעֲטַלֵּף – **An analogy** is drawn **to a rooster and a bat** שֶׁהָיוּ מְצַפִּין לָאוֹר – **who were awaiting the light** of dawn. אָמַר לֵיהּ תַּרְנְגוֹל לַעֲטַלֵּף – **The rooster said to the bat,** אֲנִי מְצַפֶּה לְאוֹרָה – **"I am awaiting the light,** שֶׁאוֹרָה שֶׁלִּי הִיא – **because the light is mine.**[49] וְאַתָּה לָמָּה לְךָ אוֹרָה – **But you, why do you want the light?"**[50]

NOTES

means comforter. חִיוָּרָא דְּבֵי רַבִּי, *Metzora of the House of Rebbi,* signifies the Messiah's suffering, as explained above. Each of these attributes will be found in the Messiah (*Maharsha; see Maharal, Netzach Yisrael,* ch. 41, who explains the Gemara along similar lines; see also *Michtav MeEliyahu* vol. 4 p. 144).

The word מָשִׁיחַ (M-SH-Y-CH), *Messiah,* is an acronym for מְנַחֵם, ***Menachem,*** שִׁילֹה, ***Shiloh,*** יִנּוֹן, ***Yinon,*** חֲנִינָה, ***Chaninah*** (*Gra, Kol Eliyahu* p. 93). [It thus demonstrates that the Messiah will have all of the virtues signified by these names.]

Maharsha also cites the Gemara in *Bava Basra* (75b), "The Messiah is called by the Name of the Holy One, Blessed is He," and demonstrates how the names יִנּוֹן, *Yinon,* and חֲנִינָה, *Chaninah,* are forms of God's Specific Name (*yud, kei, vav, kei*).

40. *Jeremiah* 30:21. This verse teaches that the Messiah will be a powerful ruler who is a member of the Jewish royal family (i.e. the family of David). Rav Nachman possessed both of these qualities. His father-in-law, the Exilarch, was a scion of the Davidic dynasty. (The Exilarchs perpetuated the Davidic dynasty in Babylonia [see *Rashi* to *Genesis* 49:10].) It is reasonable to assume, therefore, that Rav Nachman himself was descended from David. Furthermore, as son-in-law of the Exilarch, Rav Nachman was in a position of authority. Rav Nachman states that the Messiah will be someone like him insofar as he meets the qualifications outlined in this verse (see *Maharsha* and *Be'er Sheva*).

According to *Maharal,* Rav Nachman is teaching that although the Messiah will be a greatly exalted figure, he will not be divorced from contact with his subjects. Rather, he will be like Rav Nachman himself who was directly involved in communal matters.

41. I.e. R' Yehudah HaNasi (Rebbi).

42. I.e. the prophet Daniel. In *Daniel* 10:11, he is called דָּנִיֵּאל אִישׁ־חֲמֻדוֹת, *Daniel the Greatly Beloved.* [This translation is based on *Radak* (*Shorashim* ד"ה חמד) and *Metzudos*; cf. *Rashi* ad loc.]

Rashi offers two explanations of Rav's statement:

(a) If the Messiah is currently alive, he is certainly Rebbi. If the Messiah is someone who has already died, he is Daniel. [*Abarbanel* explains that it is possible for the Messiah to be among the resurrected (*Yeshuos Meshicho Iyun* 2 ch. 1).] According to this approach, the word כְּגוֹן does not carry its usual meaning of "like" (see *Sdei Chemed* ד"ה כגון).

(b) If the person who most closely *resembles* the Messiah is alive, it is Rebbi. If that person is among the dead, it is Daniel.

Rebbi and Daniel exemplified the Messiah insofar as they endured suffering [Rebbi suffered agonizing disease (*Bava Metzia* 85a); Daniel was cast into a den of lions (*Daniel* ch. 6)] and each was perfectly devout (*Rashi*).

Maharsha points out that Rebbi and Daniel enjoyed positions of authority, which is one of the Messiah's qualifications (see note 40). Rebbi was the leader (*nasi*) of the community in Eretz Yisrael; Daniel was an advisor to kings of Babylonia and Persia.

It should be noted that *Rambam* writes: "[Before the Messiah arises] you will not be able to say that he is the son of So-and-so and from such and such a family. Rather, a man will arise who was not known before he revealed himself" (*Iggeres Teiman* ch. 4). This man himself will not know that he is to be the Messiah until God calls upon him (*Chasam Sofer* Responsa vol. 6 §98; see 98a note 57).

43. I.e. the Messiah, who will be a descendant of David (*Ben Yehoyada*).

44. *Jeremiah* 30:9. This verse speaks of the Messianic era.

45. [See *Maharsha* who explains why the Gemara shifted from first person to third.]

46. *Ezekiel* 37:25.

47. The new David, whom the verse calls מֶלֶךְ, *king,* will be the supreme ruler. The original David, who is referred to as נָשִׂיא, *prince,* will be subordinate to him (*Rashi; cf. Aruch*).

Maharal understands the Gemara as teaching that the Messiah will be so exalted that even his subordinate will be as great as King David.

Yad Ramah concludes his commentary to this passage with a prayer: "We do not have even a partial understanding of these matters . . . May the One Who knows their true meaning teach it to us clearly and not enigmatically, for the sake of His great Name." [See the passage from *Rambam* cited in 97a end of note 4.]

48. *Amos* 5:18. In *Isaiah* (5:19) the prophet speaks of people who, after being warned that God will punish them for their sins, respond mockingly: *Let Him be speedy, Let Him hasten what he will do*! It is in reference to such people that Amos exhorts: *Woe unto those who yearn for the day of* H*ASHEM* etc. (*Rashi* and *Radak* to *Amos* ibid.).

[The Gemara, however, seeks a different meaning of the verse, because it describes a *day,* when light typically reigns, as *darkness and not light.*]

49. It benefits from the light (*Rashi*).

50. The bat, which does not have eyes, has no use for light (*Rashi*).

The Jewish people await the day of Hashem (i.e. the redemption) because it will bring them light. The idolaters, however, have no reason to await this day — to them it will be *darkness and not light* (*Rashi;* see *Anaf Yosef*).

וְהַיְינוּ דְּאָמַר לֵיהּ הַהוּא מִינָא לְרַבִּי אַבָּהוּ – And it was for **this reason that** when **a certain heretic asked R' Abahu: אֵימָתַי אָתֵי מָשִׁיחַ – "When will the Messiah come?" אָמַר לֵיהּ – [R' Abahu] answered him: לְכִי חָפֵי לְהוּ חֲשׁוֹכָא לְהָנְהוּ אִינָשֵׁי – "When darkness covers those people!"**[1] **אָמַר לֵיהּ – The heretic** then **exclaimed to [R' Abahu]: מֵילַט קָא לָיְיטַת לִי – "You are cursing me!"**[2] **אָמַר לֵיהּ – [R' Abahu] said to him: קְרָא כְּתִיב – "**Why, it is **a verse written** in Scripture: ,,כִּי־הִנֵּה הַחֹשֶׁךְ יְכַסֶּה־אֶרֶץ וַעֲרָפֶל לְאֻמִּים וְעָלַיִךְ יִזְרַח ה' וּכְבוֹדוֹ עָלַיִךְ יֵרָאֶה'' – ***For behold! Darkness will cover the earth, and thick clouds the peoples; but upon you HASHEM will shine, and upon you will His glory be seen.***"[3]

The Gemara begins a discussion about the length of the Messianic Era:

תַּנְיָא – It was taught in a Baraisa: רַבִּי אֱלִיעֶזֶר אוֹמֵר – R' ELIEZER[4] SAYS: יְמוֹת הַמָּשִׁיחַ אַרְבָּעִים שָׁנָה – THE MESSIANIC ERA WILL LAST FORTY YEARS,[5] שֶׁנֶּאֱמַר ,,אַרְבָּעִים שָׁנָה אָקוּט בְּדוֹר'' – AS IT IS STATED: *FOR FORTY YEARS I SHALL TAKE A GENERATION.*[6] רַבִּי אֶלְעָזָר בֶּן עֲזַרְיָה אוֹמֵר – R' ELAZAR BEN AZARIAH SAYS: שִׁבְעִים שָׁנָה – The Messianic Era will last SEVENTY YEARS, שֶׁנֶּאֱמַר ,,וְהָיָה בַּיּוֹם הַהוּא וְנִשְׁכַּחַת צֹר שִׁבְעִים שָׁנָה כִּימֵי מֶלֶךְ אֶחָד'' – AS IT IS STATED: *IT SHALL COME TO PASS ON THAT DAY THAT TYRE SHALL REMAIN FORGOTTEN FOR SEVENTY YEARS, WHICH CORRESPOND TO THE DAYS OF ONE KING.*[7] אֵיזֶהוּ מֶלֶךְ מְיוּחָד – Now, to WHICH UNIQUE KING does the verse refer?[8] הֱוֵי אוֹמֵר זֶה מָשִׁיחַ – ONE WOULD SAY that THIS IS THE MESSIAH.[9] רַבִּי אוֹמֵר – REBBI SAYS: שְׁלֹשָׁה דוֹרוֹת – The Messianic Era will last THREE GENERATIONS,[10] שֶׁנֶּאֱמַר ,,יִירָאוּךָ עִם־שָׁמֶשׁ וְלִפְנֵי יָרֵחַ דּוֹר דּוֹרִים'' – AS IT IS STATED: *MAY THEY FEAR YOU AS LONG AS THE SUN AND THE MOON ENDURE, FOR A GENERATION AND GENERATIONS.*[11] רַבִּי הִילֵּל אוֹמֵר – R' HILLEL[12] SAYS: אֵין לָהֶם מָשִׁיחַ לְיִשְׂרָאֵל – THERE WILL BE NO MESSIAH FOR THE JEWISH PEOPLE, שֶׁכְּבָר אֲכָלוּהוּ בִּימֵי חִזְקִיָּה – BECAUSE THEY ALREADY ENJOYED [THE MESSIANIC ERA] IN THE DAYS OF CHIZKIAH.[13]

The Gemara refutes R' Hillel's view:

אָמַר רַב יוֹסֵף – Rav Yosef said: שָׁרָא לֵיהּ מָרֵיהּ לְרַבִּי הִילֵּל – May his Master forgive R' Hillel![14] **חִזְקִיָּה אֵימַת הֲוָה – When did**

NOTES

1. I.e. you and your fellow heretics. R' Abahu spoke in the third person lest he give the impression that he was cursing the heretic (see *Maharsha*).

2. Although you spoke in the third person, your *intent* was to curse me (*Maharsha*).

3. *Isaiah* 60:2. R' Abahu answered that he was simply quoting a verse in response to the heretic's question, and it was not his intent to curse him (*Maharsha*).

4. An alternative version of the text reads ר' אֶלְעָזָר, *R' Elazar* (see note 20).

5. R' Eliezer is not diminishing the glory of Israel. On the contrary, he is increasing it! The Messianic Era serves as a period of preparation for the Resurrection of the Dead. R' Eliezer maintains that after only forty years the people will be ready for this lofty spiritual level (*Ran;* see *Maharal*).

6. *Psalms* 95:10. This interpretation relates אָקוּט to the Aramaic root נקט, *take.* The verse thus means: I will *take* the generation as my subjects and reign over them (*Rashi*; cf. *Yad Ramah*). By specifying a particular generation, the verse implies that it refers to a generation different from any other. Presumably, this is the generation of the Messiah (see *Rashi*).

According to its plain meaning, the verse refers to the generation that wandered in the Wilderness for forty years. However, since the verb אָקוּט, *I will take,* is in the future tense, it is understood as alluding to a future generation as well (*Rashi, Yad Ramah*).

Maharsha maintains that the verse's *plain* meaning deals with the Messianic Era. He derives this from verse 7: הַיּוֹם אִם־בְּקֹלוֹ תִשְׁמָעוּ, *Today, if you heed his voice*, which the Gemara above understood as referring to the Messiah's arrival (see 98a with note 64). In verses 8 and 9, the generation of the Messiah is warned not to behave stubbornly and test God as the generation of the Wilderness did.

7. *Isaiah* 23:15. [King Hiram of Tyre made a peace treaty with King David; but after the death of Solomon, Tyre attacked Israel mercilessly. The verse warns that in retribution Tyre will lie desolate for seventy years. According to its plain meaning, "one king" refers to David (see *Rashi* and *Radak* ad loc.).]

8. By stating "one king," the verse implies a reference to a quintessential king, whose eminence is unsurpassed (see *Rashi*).

Maharsha maintains that "one king" connotes a king who will be the only one in the world.

9. Hence, when the verse says "seventy years which correspond to the days of one king," it teaches that the Messiah will reign for seventy years.

10. In contrast to the original Davidic dynasty which reigned over the entire country for only two generations (following Solomon's death the country was split into two kingdoms), the Messianic dynasty will last three generations (*Maharsha*).

In his introduction to this chapter *Rambam* writes that after a lengthy reign the Messiah will die, and he will be succeeded by a son and then a grandson. By specifying these three generations, *Rambam* implies that the Messianic dynasty will not endure any longer than that before the Era of the Resurrection begins (*Margaliyos HaYam*).

11. *Psalms* 72:5. In this psalm, David prays for his son Solomon, and also for his more distant descendant, the Messiah.

The word "sun" alludes to the Messiah, concerning whom it is written in this very psalm (v. 17): לִפְנֵי־שֶׁמֶשׁ יִנּוֹן שְׁמוֹ, *As long as the sun lasts may his name continue* (see 98b note 34). The moon is a metaphor for the Davidic dynasty, as it is written elsewhere (*Psalms* 89:38): כְּיָרֵחַ יִכּוֹן עוֹלָם, *Like the moon it shall be established forever* (see *Rosh Hashanah* 25a and *Rashi* there). Accordingly, the verse is interpreted: יִירָאוּךָ עִם־שֶׁמֶשׁ וְלִפְנֵי יָרֵחַ דּוֹר דּוֹרִים, *May they — with the Messiah and the Davidic monarchy — fear You for a generation and generations.* "Generation" (singular) connotes one generation, while "generations" (plural) connotes two. The verse thus refers to a total of three generations (*Rashi*).

12. This was not Hillel the Elder, but a descendant, who was a grandson of Rebbi (*Toldos Tannaim V'Amoraim* p. 374).

13. R' Hillel maintains that King Chizkiah was the Messiah and that all the prophecies about a Messianic king were fulfilled in him (*Rashi* to 98b ד"ה אין משיח לישראל). R' Hillel does not dispute that the Jews will be redeemed from exile. Rather, he maintains that the redemption will be wrought not by a human messiah, but by God Himself (*Rashi*).

Yad Ramah rejects this explanation of R' Hillel's view by pointing out that R' Hillel says, "They already enjoyed [the Messianic Era] in the days of Chizkiah," which implies that the redemption and the Messianic Era have already come to pass. According to *Yad Ramah,* R' Hillel maintains that the redemption promised in the Torah occurred when God saved the Jews from Sancheiriv in the time of Chizkiah.

Ran, however, argues that the righteous R' Hillel could not possibly have meant that the Jews will remain in exile forever and become lost among the nations. The Torah explicitly promises and attests: וְשָׁב וְקִבֶּצְךָ מִכָּל־הָעַמִּים וגו', *[God] will return and gather you in from all the peoples* etc. (*Deuteronomy* 30:3). Indeed, that entire passage (vs. 1-10) speaks of this matter and so does chapter 32 (vs. 36-43). Rather, R' Hillel certainly agrees that we will be redeemed from exile. He maintains, however, that as soon as God has redeemed us, He will resurrect the dead and they will benefit from the radiance of His presence. There will be no period of physical utopia intervening between the redemption and the resurrection, for that period already came to pass during the reign of Chizkiah. When R' Hillel said, "they already enjoyed [the Messianic Era] in the days of Chizkiah," he was referring only to the *physical* aspect of the Messianic era (see 98b note 31) — the *spiritual* aspect is yet to be fulfilled.

[For another approach, see *Toras HaOlah* (cited by *Anaf Yosef*) and *Bartenura* to *Ruth.* See also *Ben Yehoyada* and *Yad David.*]

14. That is to say: May God forgive R' Hillel for making this statement (see *Berachos* 25a and *Succah* 32b). Alternatively, this is a facetious expression, meaning that God must have permitted R' Hillel to say it [for otherwise he would not have dared to do so]. The latter usage is found in *Yoma* 86a (*Yad Ramah;* see *Rabbeinu Yehonasan* to *Yoma* ibid.).

והיינו דא"ל ההוא מינא לרבי אבהו אימתי אתי משיח א"ל לכי חפי להו חשוכא להנהו אינשי א"ל מילט קא לייטת לי א"ל קרא כתיב א) כי הנה החשך יכסה ארץ וערפל לאומים ועליך יזרח ה' וכבודו עליך יראה תניא ר' אליעזר אומר ימות המשיח ארבעים שנה שנאמר ב) ארבעים שנה אקוט בדור רבי אלעזר בן עזריה אומר שבעים שנה שנאמר ג) והיה ביום ההוא ונשכחת צור שבעים שנה כימי מלך אחד איזהו מלך מיוחד הוי אומר זה משיח רבי אומר שלשה דורות שנאמר ד) ייראוך עם שמש ולפני ירח דור דורים [א] ר' הילל אומר אין להם משיח לישראל שכבר אכלוהו בימי חזקיה אמר רב יוסף שרא ליה מריה לרבי הילל חזקיה אימת הוה בבית ראשון ואילו זכריה קא מתנבי בבית שני ואמר ה) גילי מאד בת ציון הריעי בת ירושלים הנה מלכך יבא לך צדיק ונושע הוא עני ורוכב על חמור ועל עיר בן אתונות תניא אידך ר' אליעזר אומר ימות המשיח ארבעים שנה כתיב הכא ו) ויענך וירעיבך ויאכילך וכתיב התם ז) שמחנו כימות עניתנו שנות ראינו רעה רבי דוסא אומר ד' מאות שנה כתיב הכא ח) ועבדום וענו אותם ארבע מאות שנה וכתיב התם שמחנו כימות עניתנו רבי אומר ג' מאות וששים וחמש שנה כמנין ימות החמה שנאמר ט) כי יום נקם בלבי ושנת גאולי באה מאי יום נקם בלבי אמר ר' יוחנן ללבי גליתי לאבריי לא גליתי ר"ש בן לקיש אמר ללבי גליתי למלאכי השרת לא גליתי תני אבימי בריה דרבי אבהו ימות המשיח לישראל שבעת אלפים שנה שנאמר י) ומשוש חתן על כלה (כן) ישיש עליך (ה') אלהיך אמר רב יהודה אמר שמואל ימות המשיח כמיום שנברא העולם ועד עכשיו שנאמר כ) כימי השמים על הארץ רב נחמן בר יצחק אמר כימי נח עד עכשיו שנאמר ל) כי מי נח זאת לי אשר נשבעתי [ב] אמר רבי חייא בר אבא א"ר יוחנן [א] כל הנביאים כולן לא נתנבאו אלא לימות המשיח אבל לעולם הבא מ) עין לא ראתה אלהים זולתך (אלהים) יעשה למחכה לו ופליגא דשמואל דאמר שמואל [ג] אין בין העולם הזה לימות המשיח אלא שעבוד מלכיות בלבד ואמר רבי חייא בר אבא א"ר יוחנן כל הנביאים לא נתנבאו אלא לבעלי תשובה אבל צדיקים גמורים עין לא ראתה אלהים זולתך ופליגא דרבי אבהו דא"ר אבהו (ד) א"ר) [ב] מקום שבעלי תשובה עומדין שם צדיקים אינן עומדין שם שנאמר נ) שלום שלום לרחוק ולקרוב ברישא רחוק והדר קרוב מאי רחוק רחוק דמעיקרא ומאי קרוב קרוב דמעיקרא ודהשתא ורבי יוחנן אמר לרחוק שהוא רחוק מעבירה קרוב שהוא קרוב מעבירה ונתרחק ממנה וא"ר חייא בר אבא [ה] א"ר יוחנן כל הנביאים כולן לא נתנבאו אלא למשיא בתו לתלמיד חכם ולעושה פרקמטיא לתלמיד חכם ולמהנה תלמיד חכם מנכסיו אבל תלמידי חכמים עצמן עין לא ראתה אלהים זולתך [ו] מאי עין לא ראתה אמר רבי יהושע בן לוי זה יין המשומר בענביו מששת ימי בראשית [ז] ר"ל אמר זה עדן לא ראתה עין מעולם וא"ת אדם היכן דר בגן ואם תאמר גן הוא עדן תלמוד לומר ס) ונהר יוצא מעדן להשקות את הגן: והאומר אין תורה מן השמים וכו': תנו רבנן ע) כי דבר ה' בזה [ח] ומצותו הפר הכרת תכרת זה האומר אין תורה מן השמים ד"א [ט] כי דבר ה' בזה זה אפיקורוס ד"א כי דבר ה' בזה זה המגלה פנים בתורה ואת מצותו הפר זה המפר ברית בשר הכרת תכרת הכרת בעולם הזה תכרת לעולם הבא מכאן אמר [י] רבי אליעזר המודעי [ג] המחלל את הקדשים והמבזה את המועדות והמפר בריתו של אברהם אבינו והמגלה פנים בתורה שלא כהלכה והמלבין פני חבירו ברבים אף על פי שיש בידו תורה ומעשים טובים אין לו חלק לעולם הבא תניא אידך כי דבר ה' בזה זה האומר אין תורה מן השמים [ד] ואפילו אמר כל התורה כולה מן השמים חוץ מפסוק זה שלא אמרו הקדוש ברוך הוא אלא משה מפי עצמו זהו כי דבר ה' בזה ואפילו אמר כל התורה כולה מן השמים חוץ מדקדוק זה מקל וחומר זה מגזרה שוה זו זה הוא כי דבר ה' בזה תניא היה רבי מאיר אומר הלומד תורה ואינו מלמדה זה הוא דבר ה' בזה רבי נתן אומר כל מי שאינו משגיח על המשנה ר' נהוראי אומר [ה] כל שאפשר לעסוק בתורה ואינו עוסק רבי ישמעאל אומר זה העובד עבודת כוכבים מאי משמעה דתנא דבי ר' ישמעאל כי דבר ה' בזה זה המבזה דבור שנאמר [א] לו למשה מסיני פ) אנכי ה' אלהיך לא יהיה לך אלהים אחרים וגו' [כ] רבי יהושע בן קרחה אומר כל הלומד תורה ואינו חוזר עליה דומה לאדם שזורע ואינו קוצר רבי יהושע אומר כל הלומד תורה ומשכחה דומה לאשה שיולדת וקוברת רבי עקיבא אומר

זמר

ס) וְנָהָר יֹצֵא מֵעֵדֶן לְהַשְׁקוֹת אֶת הַגָּן וּמִשָּׁם יִפָּרֵד וְהָיָה לְאַרְבָּעָה רָאשִׁים: [בראשית ב, י] ע) כִּי דְבַר יְיָ בָּזָה וְאֶת מִצְוָתוֹ הֵפַר הִכָּרֵת תִּכָּרֵת הַנֶּפֶשׁ הַהִוא עֲוֹנָה בָהּ: [במדבר טו, לא] פ) אָנֹכִי יְיָ אֱלֹהֶיךָ אֲשֶׁר הוֹצֵאתִיךָ מֵאֶרֶץ מִצְרַיִם מִבֵּית עֲבָדִים: לֹא יִהְיֶה לְךָ אֱלֹהִים אֲחֵרִים עַל פָּנָי: [שמות כ, ב-ג]

רש"י

ה"ג היינו דאמר ליה ההוא מינא לרבי אבהו וכו': אקוט בדור. אקוט ישראל ואמלוך עליהם כמו נקטיה ארבעים שנה אקוט בדור בדור קטן של ארבעים שנה שהוא משונה מדורות שלפניו ומסתמא היינו משיח שסימן גדולים יהיו בדורו ופשטיה דקרא מיהא גבי מתי מדבר אבל מדכתיב אקוט משמע אף להבא היה מתנבא: מיוחד. חשוב: ה"ג רבי אומר ג' דורות שנאמר ייראוך עם שמש. כלומר בהדי משיח שכתב בו (תהלים עב) לפני שמש ינון שמו ייראוך ישראל ולפני ירח לפני מלכות בית דוד שנמשל כירח כדכתיב (שם פט) כירח יכון עולם וגו' כמו כן ייראוך דור דורים דור אחד דורים ב' הרי ג': אין להם משיח לישראל. אלא הקב"ה ימלוך בעצמו ויגאלם לבדו: שרי ליה מריה. ימחול לו הקב"ה שאמר דברים אשר לא כן: ואלו זכריה מיהא מתנבא על משיח בבית שני. דכתיב בתרי עשר הנה מלכך יבא לך וגו' ולאו היינו זכריה בן יהוידע הכהן שניבא בבית ראשון אלא זכריה בן ברכיה שהיה במלכות דריוש: רבי אומר שס"ה כמנין ימות החמה דכתיב כי יום נקם בלבי ושנת גאולי באה. [ליום נקם של מרגלים ארבעים יום מה יום נקם של מרגלים] שנה אחת בכל יום כדכתיב (במדבר יד) יום לשנה יום לשנה וגו' כך שנת גאולי באה שנה ליום שנה לכל יום ויום של שנה זו הכתובה שנת גאולי במקרא זה נותנים שנה אחת ואית דגרסי רבי אומר שס"ה אלפים שנה דכתיב שנת גאולי באה ושנה של הקב"ה הכי הוי דכתיב (תהלים צ) כי אלף שנים בעיניך כיום: ועד עכשיו. ימות המשיח: לאיברי לא גליתי. שלא הוצאתי דבר מפי שהיו איברי יכולין לשמוע אבל בלבי היה טמון הדבר: למען ירבו ימיכם כימי השמים על הארץ. ולא עמדו בארצם כל כך אבל עתידין לעמוד כשיבא משיח: כמשוש חתן. שבעת ימי המשתה כן ישיש עליך שבעת ימים ויומו של הקב"ה אלף שנה: כי מי נח. כמו כימי נח כחשבון השנים שנמלא בידו לאותו זמן שנשבע ה' מעבור מי נח עוד על הארץ כן נשבעתי כפי אותו חשבון נשבעתי מקצף עליך ומגער בך שלא אחריב את עולמי לאחר שיבא משיח עד שיכלה זה הזמן: לא נתנבאו. טובה לישראל: עין לא ראתה. דאין קץ לדבר: צדיקים אינן עומדין. דגדול כחן של בעלי תשובה שאין בריה יכולה לעמוד (לפניהם) [במחילתם]: ברישא לרחוק. שנתרחק מן הקב"ה ואח"כ שב אליו בתשובה והדר שלום לקרוב מעיקרא לצדיק גמור דגדול כחן של בעלי תשובה: שהיה רחוק מן העבירה. כל ימיו דהיינו לצדיק גמור: אפיקורוס ומגלה פנים. מפורש לקמן: ברית בשר. מילה: מכאן. מן הפסוק הזה שכתוב כי דבר ה' בזה (אמר ר"א וכו' מחלל את הקדשים דמחלל קדשים ומבזה מועדות ומגלה פנים כו' היינו דבר ה' בזה) דבזיון הוא: מפר ברית. היינו את בריתי הפר: מועדות. חולו של מועד: דקדוק זה. חסרות ויתרות: מק"ו [זה] ומגזירה שוה [זו]. [ושא"ל רבו גזירה שוה] לא גמר מרבו: המשנה. זה שעושה כמו שאינה עיקר: זה העובד ע"ז. היינו דבר ה' דבור שדבר הקב"ה בעצמו לישראל דאנכי ולא יהיה לך מפי הגבורה שמענום: חוזר. לשנותה:

מסורת הש"ס

א) [לעיל לח:], ב) ברכות לד: שבת סג., ג) ברכות לד: שבת סג. קנא: פסחים סח: לעיל לא., ד) [בברכו' ליתא], ה) ברכות לד., ו) [שם], ז) [בברכו' איתא ר"ש בר נחמני], ח) [ל"ל ואת מצותו], ט) [שבועות יג. ע"ש], י) אבות פ"ג משנה יא, כ) [תוספתא דפרה פ"ג ותוספתא דאהלות פט"ז].

תורה אור השלם

א) כִּי הִנֵּה הַחֹשֶׁךְ יְכַסֶּה אֶרֶץ וַעֲרָפֶל לְאֻמִּים וְעָלַיִךְ יִזְרַח יְיָ וּכְבוֹדוֹ עָלַיִךְ יֵרָאֶה: [ישעיה ס, ב]

ב) אַרְבָּעִים שָׁנָה אָקוּט בְּדוֹר וָאֹמַר עַם תֹּעֵי לֵבָב הֵם וְהֵם לֹא יָדְעוּ דְרָכָי: [תהלים צה, י]

ג) וְהָיָה בַּיּוֹם הַהוּא וְנִשְׁכַּחַת צֹר שִׁבְעִים שָׁנָה כִּימֵי מֶלֶךְ אֶחָד מִקֵּץ שִׁבְעִים שָׁנָה יִהְיֶה לְצֹר כְּשִׁירַת הַזּוֹנָה: [ישעיה כג, טו]

ד) יִירָאוּךָ עִם שָׁמֶשׁ וְלִפְנֵי יָרֵחַ דּוֹר דּוֹרִים: [תהלים עב, ה]

ה) גִּילִי מְאֹד בַּת צִיּוֹן הָרִיעִי בַּת יְרוּשָׁלִַם הִנֵּה מַלְכֵּךְ יָבוֹא לָךְ צַדִּיק וְנוֹשָׁע הוּא עָנִי וְרֹכֵב עַל חֲמוֹר וְעַל עַיִר בֶּן אֲתֹנוֹת: [זכריה ט, ט]

ו) וַיְעַנְּךָ וַיַּרְעִבֶךָ וַיַּאֲכִלְךָ אֶת הַמָּן אֲשֶׁר לֹא יָדַעְתָּ וְלֹא יָדְעוּן אֲבֹתֶיךָ לְמַעַן הוֹדִיעֲךָ כִּי לֹא עַל הַלֶּחֶם לְבַדּוֹ יִחְיֶה הָאָדָם כִּי עַל כָּל מוֹצָא פִי יְיָ יִחְיֶה הָאָדָם: [דברים ח, ג]

ז) שַׂמְּחֵנוּ כִּימוֹת עִנִּיתָנוּ שְׁנוֹת רָאִינוּ רָעָה: [תהלים צ, טו]

ח) וַיֹּאמֶר לְאַבְרָם יָדֹעַ תֵּדַע כִּי גֵר יִהְיֶה זַרְעֲךָ בְּאֶרֶץ לֹא לָהֶם וַעֲבָדוּם וְעִנּוּ אֹתָם אַרְבַּע מֵאוֹת שָׁנָה: [בראשית טו, יג]

ט) כִּי יוֹם נָקָם בְּלִבִּי וּשְׁנַת גְּאוּלַי בָּאָה: [ישעיה סג, ד]

י) כִּי יִבְעַל בָּחוּר בְּתוּלָה יִבְעָלוּךְ בָּנָיִךְ וּמְשׂוֹשׂ חָתָן עַל כַּלָּה יָשִׂישׂ עָלַיִךְ אֱלֹהָיִךְ: [ישעיה סב, ה]

כ) לְמַעַן יִרְבּוּ יְמֵיכֶם וִימֵי בְנֵיכֶם עַל הָאֲדָמָה אֲשֶׁר נִשְׁבַּע יְיָ לַאֲבֹתֵיכֶם לָתֵת לָהֶם כִּימֵי הַשָּׁמַיִם עַל הָאָרֶץ: [דברים יא, כא]

ל) כִּי מֵי נֹחַ זֹאת לִי אֲשֶׁר נִשְׁבַּעְתִּי מֵעֲבֹר מֵי נֹחַ עוֹד עַל הָאָרֶץ כֵּן נִשְׁבַּעְתִּי מִקְּצֹף עָלַיִךְ וּמִגְּעָר בָּךְ: [ישעיה נד, ט]

מ) וּמֵעוֹלָם לֹא שָׁמְעוּ לֹא הֶאֱזִינוּ עַיִן לֹא רָאָתָה אֱלֹהִים זוּלָתְךָ יַעֲשֶׂה לִמְחַכֵּה לוֹ: [ישעיה סד, ג]

נ) בּוֹרֵא נִיב שְׂפָתָיִם שָׁלוֹם שָׁלוֹם לָרָחוֹק וְלַקָּרוֹב אָמַר יְיָ וּרְפָאתִיו: [ישעיה נז, יט]

עין משפט נר מצוה

יב א מיי' פ"ח מהל' תשובה הלכה ז וע"ש בכ"מ:
יג ב מיי' שם פ"ז הלכה ד:
יד ג מיי' שם פ"ג הלכה יד:
טו ד מיי' שם הלכה ח:
טז ה מיי' פ"ג מהל' ת"ת הלכה יג סמג עשין יב טוש"ע י"ד סי' רמו סעיף כה:

הגהות הגר"א

[א] גמ' זה המבזה דיבור שנא' לו למשה. נמחק ב' תיבות לו למשה וכ"ב להם לישראל:

ליקוטי רש"י

ונשכחת צור. לפי שמזכירה בלשון גנאי לשון זונה אמר ונשכחת, כזונה ששכחוה אוהביה, אף היא תשכח מאין סוחרים ותגרים פונים אליה לפי שתהיה חריבה. כימי מלך אחד. ימי דוד שבעים שנה היו ואיני יודע מהו הסימן הזה הניתן כאן [ישעיהו כג, טו]. הנה מלכך יבוא לך. אי אפשר לפותרו אלא על מלך המשיח שנאמר בו ומשלו מים ועד ים ולא מצינו מושל לישראל כזה בימי בית שני. צדיק ונושע. כה'. עני. ענותן. ורוכב על חמור. מדת ענוה היא. ועל עיר. כמו ועירים עשרה (בראשית לב) [זכריה ט, ט]. שמחנו כימות עניתנו. שמחנו לימות משיחנו כמנין ימות שעניתנו בגליות וכמנין שנות אשר ראינו רעה [תהלים צ, טו]. כי יבעל וגו'. הרי כמה דמתיישב עולם עם בתולה כן יתייתבין בגוייכי בנייכי [ישעיהו סב, ה]. עין לא ראתה אלהים אחר זולתך אשר יעשה האלהים למחכה לו מה שעשית אתה למחכה לך כך שמעתי מר' יוסי והנאני, אבל רבותינו שאמרו כל הנביאים כולם לא נתנבאו אלא לימות המשיח אבל לעולם הבא עין לא ראתה וגו' משמעו עין שום נביא לא ראתה את אשר יעשה הקב"ה למחכה לו זולתי עיניך אתה אלהים [ישעיהו סד, ג]. לרחוק ולקרוב. שניהם שוין מי שנתיישן והורגל בתורתי ועבודתי מנעוריו ומי שנתקרב עתה מקרוב לשוב מדרכו הרעה. אמר ה' ורפאתיו. מחליו ומחטאיו [ישעיהו נז, יט]. לא נתנבאו. דברי נחמות שלהן. עין לא ראתה. עין של נביאים לא שלטה לראותו [שבת סג.]. מגלה פנים. בא על דברי תורה בחוצפא ובגלוי עזות פניו כגון (סנהדרין דף צט:) מנשה שהיה יושב ודורש באגדות של דופי לא היה למשה לכתוב אלא ותמנע היתה פלגש וילך ראובן בימי קציר חטים (בראשית ל) [שבועות יג.]. דורש באגדות של דופי כגון מנשה שהיה אומר מה היה לו למשה לומר ותמנע היתה פילגש [כריתות ז.]. זה המיפר ברית בבשר. שהיא מלוה יחידי [שבועות יג.]. את המועדות. חולו של מועד [מכות כג.].

Chizkiah live? בְּבַיִת רִאשׁוֹן – **During the First Temple Era!** וְאִילּוּ זְכַרְיָה קָא מִתְנַבֵּי בְּבַיִת שֵׁנִי וְאָמַר – **Now Zechariah,** who was **prophesying during the Second Temple Era, said:** ,,גִּילִי מְאֹד בַּת-צִיּוֹן הָרִיעִי בַּת יְרוּשָׁלַם הִנֵּה מַלְכֵּךְ יָבוֹא לָךְ צַדִּיק וְנוֹשָׁע הוּא עָנִי וְרֹכֵב עַל-חֲמוֹר וְעַל-עַיִר בֶּן-אֲתֹנוֹת" – ***Rejoice greatly, O Daughter of Zion! Shout, O Daughter of Jerusalem! Behold, your king is coming to you. He is righteous and victorious, yet humble, riding on a donkey – upon a colt, the foal of an ass.***[15] Zechariah, who lived long after Chizkiah, predicted the Messiah's arrival. It is evident, therefore, that Chizkiah was not the Messiah.[16]

The Gemara cites another Baraisa that discusses the length of the Messianic Era:

תַּנְיָא אִידָךְ – **It was taught in another Baraisa:** רַבִּי אֱלִיעֶזֶר אוֹמֵר – R' ELIEZER SAYS: יְמוֹת הַמָּשִׁיחַ אַרְבָּעִים שָׁנָה – THE MESSIANIC ERA WILL LAST FORTY YEARS. This is derived as follows: כְּתִיב הָכָא – HERE, in reference to the generation that wandered in the Wilderness, IT IS WRITTEN: ,,וַיְעַנְּךָ וַיַּרְעִבֶךָ וַיַּאֲכִלְךָ" – *HE AFFLICTED YOU AND LET YOU GO HUNGRY, AND HE FED YOU the manna.*[17] וּכְתִיב הָתָם – AND THERE, in reference to the Messianic Era, IT IS WRITTEN: ,,שַׂמְּחֵנוּ כִּימוֹת עִנִּיתָנוּ שְׁנוֹת רָאִינוּ רָעָה" – *GLADDEN US ACCORDING TO THE DAYS YOU AFFLICTED US, THE YEARS WHEN WE SAW HARM.*[18] The second verse teaches that the Messianic Era will last as long as "the days you *afflicted* us," which refers to the years in the Wilderness, concerning which it is stated, "He *afflicted* you." Therefore, like the wandering in the Wilderness, the Messianic Era will last forty years.

רַבִּי דּוֹסָא אוֹמֵר – R' DOSA SAYS: אַרְבַּע מֵאוֹת שָׁנָה – The Messianic Era will last FOUR HUNDRED YEARS. This is derived as follows: כְּתִיב הָכָא – HERE, in reference to the Egyptian exile, IT IS WRITTEN: ,,וַעֲבָדוּם וְעִנּוּ אֹתָם אַרְבַּע מֵאוֹת שָׁנָה" – *THEY WILL SERVE THEM, AND THEY WILL AFFLICT THEM FOUR HUNDRED YEARS.*[19] וּכְתִיב הָתָם – AND THERE, in reference to the Messianic Era, IT IS WRITTEN: ,,שַׂמְּחֵנוּ כִּימוֹת עִנִּיתָנוּ" – *GLADDEN US ACCORDING TO THE DAYS YOU AFFLICTED US.* R' Dosa relates "the days you *afflicted* us" to the Egyptian exile, concerning which it is written, "they will *afflict* them." Therefore, like the Egyptian exile, the Messianic Era will last four hundred years.[20]

רַבִּי אוֹמֵר – REBBI SAYS: שְׁלֹשׁ מֵאוֹת וְשִׁשִּׁים וְחָמֵשׁ שָׁנָה – The Messianic Era will last THREE HUNDRED AND SIXTY-FIVE YEARS, כְּמִנְיַן יְמוֹת הַחַמָּה – CORRESPONDING TO THE NUMBER OF DAYS IN A SOLAR YEAR, שֶׁנֶּאֱמַר ,,כִּי יוֹם נָקָם בְּלִבִּי וּשְׁנַת גְּאוּלַי בָּאָה" – AS IT IS STATED: *FOR THE DAY OF VENGEANCE IS IN MY HEART, AND THE YEAR*[21] *OF MY PEOPLE'S REDEMPTION*[22] *IS COME.*[23]

The Gemara interprets this verse:

מַאי ,,יוֹם נָקָם בְּלִבִּי" – **What is** the meaning of ***the day of vengeance is in My heart?*** אָמַר רַבִּי יוֹחָנָן – **R' Yochanan said:** לְלִבִּי גִּלִּיתִי לְאֵבָרַיי לֹא גִּלִּיתִי – **I have revealed** the date of the redemption **to My heart; I have not revealed** it **to my limbs.**[24]

A different interpretation:

רַבִּי שִׁמְעוֹן בֶּן לָקִישׁ אָמַר – **R' Shimon ben Lakish says:** לְלִבִּי גִּלִּיתִי לְמַלְאֲכֵי הַשָּׁרֵת לֹא גִּלִּיתִי – **I have revealed** the date of the redemption **to My heart; I have not revealed** it **to the Ministering Angels.**[25]

NOTES

15. *Zechariah* 9:9. The author of the Book of *Zechariah* was Zechariah the son of Berechiah, who lived during the reign of King Darius [at the end of the Babylonian exile], as stated in *Zechariah* 1:1 (see *Yad Ramah*). He is not to be confused with Zechariah the son of Yehoyada, who prophesied during the First Temple era [see above, 96b] (*Rashi*).

16. According to many Rishonim, R' Hillel agrees that there will be a redemption (see note 13). It is therefore understood why Rav Yosef did not refute R' Hillel's view with one of the many verses about the redemption. He specifically used this verse, which refers to the Messiah himself (*Maharsha;* see *Anaf Yosef*).

Sefer HaIkkarim (1:1) infers from this Gemara that belief in the Messiah is not a fundamental article of faith, because, if it were, R' Hillel would be deemed a heretic and have no share in the World to Come! *Rambam*, however, does consider it an article of faith (see 96b note 56). *Abarbanel* defends *Rambam's* view by arguing that since R' Hillel does not diminish the promised reward of the Messianic Era (on the contrary, he increases it by asserting that God Himself will redeem us), he cannot be considered a non-believer in this principle (see *Rosh Amanah* 10:14).

Nevertheless, it is improper to follow R' Hillel's view. One who does so denies the law of the Torah which states that the majority view is accepted as authoritative (*Anaf Yosef;* see *Chasam Sofer* Responsa *Yoreh Deah* §356).

17. *Deuteronomy* 8:3. Moses reminds the people of their experiences in the Wilderness.

God *afflicted you* with the hardship of travel and *let you hunger* by not affording you extraneous pleasures (*Ibn Ezra*). Even the miraculous manna was a test for the people because they had no prior experience with anything like it, and they did not know whether human beings could subsist for long on such food (*Ramban* ad loc.). [Although this period was extraordinarily blessed (see 98b note 31), it also involved much distress and anguish.]

18. *Psalms* 90:15. Moses prays that God will gladden the Jews in the Messianic Era for the same length as a certain period of time during which He had afflicted them. [This period is identified presently.]

19. *Genesis* 15:13. God tells Abraham that his descendants will be in exile for four hundred years (see *Rashi* ad loc. and *Maharal*).

20. In *Yad Ramah's* version of the text, this opinion is the first recorded in the Baraisa and it is attributed to R' Eliezer. Hence, *Yad Ramah* poses a contradiction between this statement of R' Eliezer (viz. that the Messianic Era will last four hundred years), and the statement of R' Eliezer recorded in the first Baraisa in this passage (viz. that it will last only forty years). *Yad Ramah* resolves the contradiction by explaining that if the people are worthy, the Messianic Era will last four hundred years; if they are not worthy, it will last only forty years.

21. A "year" signifies a solar year unless the context indicates otherwise. A solar year is a natural unit, for it represents a complete orbit of the earth around the sun. [This is in contrast to a lunar year, which is merely a sequence of twelve lunar cycles] (see *Yad Ramah;* cf. *Rashash*; see also *Maharal*).

22. Literally: the year of my redeemed ones (see *Ibn Ezra*).

23. *Isaiah* 63:4. The "day of vengeance" refers to the punishment meted out to Israel for believing the false report of the Spies (*Rashi;* cf. *Maharsha*). For every day that the Spies spent in Eretz Yisrael (a total of forty days), the Jews had to spend one year wandering in the Wilderness (*Numbers* 14:34). The same formula applies to the "year of redemption" mentioned at the end of the verse. For every day in the year (a total of 365 days), the Jews will enjoy a year of redemption. Thus, the Messianic Era will last 365 years (*Rashi*).

An alternative version of the text reads: 365,000 years. This version is explained as follows: it was taught above (97a) that a "day of God" equals one thousand years. Hence a "year of God" (365 days) amounts to 365,000 years (*Rashi*). [According to this version, the "day of vengeance" refers not to the punishment of the Spies, but to the time when God will avenge Himself on the idolatrous nations (*Yad Ramah*).]

24. God did not express the date of the redemption. He kept it hidden in His "heart" and did not say it aloud so that His "limbs" could hear it (*Rashi;* see following note).

25. Unlike R' Yochanan, Reish Lakish maintains that God *did* put this thought into words. However, God did not communicate it to the angels (*Yad Ramah's* first explanation).

Alternatively, Reish Lakish agrees that God did not express this thought. Reish Lakish's point is that God did not reveal this secret even to the angels, with whom He communicates without "speech" (*Yad Ramah's* second explanation). [*Yad Ramah* stresses that God is infinite and does not possess a physical body. The Gemara uses the body only as a metaphor to allow people to understand the concept under discussion.]

The Vilna Gaon interprets God's "Heart" as symbolizing the

והיינו דא"ל ההוא מינא לרבי אבהו אימתי אתי משיח א"ל לכי חפי להו חשוכא להנהו אינשי א"ל מילט קא לייטת לי א"ל קרא כתיב א) כי הנה החשך יכסה ארץ וערפל לאומים ועליך יזרח ה' וכבודו עליך יראה תניא ר' אליעזר אומר ימות המשיח ארבעים שנה שנאמר ב) ארבעים שנה אקוט בדור רבי אלעזר בן עזריה אומר שבעים שנה שנאמר ג) והיה ביום ההוא ונשכחת צור שבעים שנה כימי מלך אחד איזהו מלך מיוחד הוי אומר זה משיח רבי אומר שלשה דורות שנאמר ד) ייראוך עם שמש ולפני ירח דור דורים [א] ר' הילל אומר אין להם משיח לישראל שכבר אכלוהו בימי חזקיה אמר רב יוסף שרא ליה מריה לרבי הילל חזקיה אימת הוה בבית ראשון ואילו זכריה קא מתנבי בבית שני ואמר ה) גילי מאד בת ציון הריעי בת ירושלים הנה מלכך יבא לך צדיק ונושע הוא עני ורוכב על חמור ועל עיר בן אתונות תניא אידך ר' אליעזר אומר ימות המשיח ארבעים שנה כתיב הכא ו) ויענך וירעיבך ויאכילך וכתיב התם ז) שמחנו כימות עניתנו שנות ראינו רעה רבי דוסא אומר ד' מאות שנה כתיב הכא ח) ועבדום וענו אותם ארבע מאות שנה וכתיב התם שמחנו כימות עניתנו רבי אומר ג' מאות וששים וחמש שנה כמנין ימות החמה שנאמר ט) כי יום נקם בלבי ושנת גאולי באה מאי יום נקם בלבי א"ר יוחנן ללבי גליתי לאבריי לא גליתי ר"ש בן לקיש אמר ללבי גליתי למלאכי השרת לא גליתי תני אבימי בריה דרבי אבהו ימות המשיח לישראל שבעת אלפים שנה שנאמר י) ומשוש חתן על כלה (כן) ישיש עליך (ה') אלהיך אמר רב יהודה אמר שמואל ימות המשיח כמיום שנברא העולם ועד עכשיו שנאמר כ) כימי השמים על הארץ רב נחמן בר יצחק אמר כימי נח עד עכשיו שנאמר ל) כי מי נח זאת לי אשר נשבעתי [ג] אמר רבי חייא בר אבא א"ר יוחנן [א] כל הנביאים כולן לא נתנבאו אלא לימות המשיח אבל לעולם הבא מ) עין לא ראתה אלהים זולתך (אלהים) יעשה למחכה לו ופליגא דשמואל דאמר שמואל [ג] אין בין העולם הזה לימות המשיח אלא שעבוד מלכיות בלבד ואמר רבי חייא בר אבא א"ר יוחנן כל הנביאים לא נתנבאו אלא לבעלי תשובה אבל צדיקים גמורים עין לא ראתה אלהים זולתך ופליגא דרבי אבהו דא"ר אבהו (ד) א"ר) [ב] מקום שבעלי תשובה עומדין שם צדיקים אינן עומדין שם שנאמר נ) שלום שלום לרחוק ולקרוב ברישא רחוק והדר קרוב מאי רחוק רחוק דמעיקרא ומאי קרוב קרוב דמעיקרא ודהשתא ורבי יוחנן אמר לרחוק שהוא רחוק מעבירה קרוב שהוא קרוב מעבירה ונתרחק ממנה וא"ר חייא בר אבא [ה] א"ר יוחנן כל הנביאים כולן לא נתנבאו אלא למשיא בתו לתלמיד חכם ולעושה פרקמטיא לתלמיד חכם ולמהנה תלמיד חכם מנכסיו אבל תלמידי חכמים עצמן עין לא ראתה אלהים זולתך [י] מאי עין לא ראתה אמר רבי יהושע בן לוי זה יין המשומר בענביו מששת ימי בראשית [ז] ר"ל אמר זה עדן לא ראתה עין מעולם וא"ת אדם היכן דר בגן ואם תאמר גן הוא עדן תלמוד לומר ס) ונהר יוצא מעדן להשקות את הגן: והאומר אין תורה מן השמים וכו': תנו רבנן ע) כי דבר ה' בזה [ח] ומצותו הפר הכרת תכרת זה האומר אין תורה מן השמים ד"א [ט] כי דבר ה' בזה זה אפיקורוס ד"א כי דבר ה' בזה זה המגלה פנים בתורה ואת מצותו הפר זה המפר ברית בשר הכרת תכרת הכרת בעולם הזה תכרת לעולם הבא מכאן אמר [י] רבי אליעזר המודעי [ג] המחלל את הקדשים והמבזה את המועדות והמפר בריתו של אברהם אבינו והמגלה פנים בתורה שלא כהלכה והמלבין פני חבירו ברבים אף על פי שיש בידו תורה ומעשים טובים אין לו חלק לעולם הבא תניא אידך כי דבר ה' בזה זה האומר אין תורה מן השמים [ד] ואפילו אמר כל התורה כולה מן השמים חוץ מפסוק זה שלא אמרו הקדוש ברוך הוא אלא משה מפי עצמו זהו כי דבר ה' בזה ואפילו אמר כל התורה כולה מן השמים חוץ מדקדוק זה מקל וחומר זה מגזרה שוה זו זה הוא כי דבר ה' בזה תניא היה רבי מאיר אומר הלומד תורה ואינו מלמדה זה הוא דבר ה' בזה רבי נתן אומר כל מי שאינו משגיח על המשנה ר' נהוראי אומר [ה] כל שאפשר לעסוק בתורה ואינו עוסק רבי ישמעאל אומר זה העובד עבודת כוכבים מאי משמעה דתנא דבי ר' ישמעאל כי דבר ה' בזה זה המבזה דבור שנאמר [א] לו למשה מסיני פ) אנכי ה' אלהיך לא יהיה לך אלהים אחרים וגו' [כ] רבי יהושע בן קרחה אומר כל הלומד תורה ואינו חוזר עליה דומה לאדם שזורע ואינו קוצר רבי יהושע אומר כל הלומד תורה ומשכחה דומה לאשה שיולדת וקוברת רבי עקיבא אומר

זמר

רש"י

ה"ג היינו דאמר ליה ההוא מינא לרבי אבהו וכו': אקוט בדור. אקוט ישראל ואמלוך עליהם כמו נקטיה ארבעים שנה אקוט בדור בדור קטן של ארבעים שנה שהוא משונה מדורות שלפניו ומסתמא היינו משיח ששינוין גדולים יהיו בדורו ופשטיה דקרא מיהא גבי מתי מדבר אבל מדכתיב אקוט משמע אף להבא היה מתנבא: מיוחד. חשוב: ה"ג רבי אומר ג' דורות שנאמר ייראוך עם שמש. כלומר בהדי משיח שכתב בו (תהלים עב) לפני שמש ינון שמו ייראוך ישראל ולפני ירח לפני מלכות בית דוד שנמשל כירח כדכתיב (שם פט) כירח יכון עולם וגו' כמו כן ייראוך דור דורים דור אחד דורים ב' הרי ג': אין להם משיח לישראל. אלא הקב"ה ימלוך בעצמו ויגאלם לבדו: שרי ליה מריה. ימחול לו הקב"ה שאמר דברים אשר לא כן: ואלו זכריה מיהא מתנבא על משיח בבית שני. דכתיב בתרי עשר הנה מלכך יבא לך וגו' ולאו היינו זכריה בן יהוידע הכהן שניבא בבית ראשון אלא זכריה בן ברכיה שהיה במלכות דריוש: רבי אומר שס"ה כמנין ימות החמה דכתיב כי יום נקם בלבי ושנת גאולי באה. [ליום נקם של מרגלים ארבעים יום מה יום נקם של מרגלים] שנה אחת בכל יום כדכתיב (במדבר יד) יום לשנה יום לשנה וגו' כך שנת גאולי באה שנה ליום שנה ליום שלכל יום ויום של שנה זו הכתובה שנת גאולי במקרא זה נותנים שנה אחת ואית דגרסי רבי אומר שס"ה אלפים שנה דכתיב שנת גאולי באה ושנה של הקב"ה הכי הוי דכתיב (תהלים צ) כי אלף שנים בעיניך כיום: ועד עכשיו. ימות המשיח: לאיברי לא גליתי. שלא הוצאתי דבר מפי שהיו איברי יכולין לשמוע אבל בלבי היה טמון הדבר: למען ירבו ימיכם כימי השמים על הארץ. ולא עמדו בארצם כל כך אבל עתידין לעמוד כשיבא משיח: כמשוש חתן. שבעת ימי המשתה כן ישיש עליך שבעת ימים ויומו של הקב"ה אלף שנה: כי מי נח. כמו כימי נח כחשבון השנים שנמלא בידו לאותו זמן שנשבע ה' מעבור מי נח עוד על הארץ כן נשבעתי כפי אותו חשבון נשבעתי מקצף עליך ומגער בך שלא אחריב את עולמי לאחר שיבא משיח עד שיכלה זה הזמן: לא נתנבאו. טובה לישראל: עין לא ראתה. דאין קץ לדבר: צדיקים אינן עומדין. דגדול כחן של בעלי תשובה שאין בריה יכולה לעמוד (לפניהם) [במחיצתם]: ברישא לרחוק. שנתרחק מן הקב"ה ואח"כ שב אליו בתשובה והדר שלום לקרוב מעיקרא לצדיק גמור דגדול כחן של בעלי תשובה: שהיה רחוק מן העבירה. כל ימיו דהיינו צדיק גמור: אפיקורוס ומגלה פנים. מפורש לקמן: ברית בשר. מילה: מכאן. מן הפסוק הזה שכתוב כי דבר ה' בזה (אמר ר"א וכו' מחלל את הקדשים דמחלל קדשים ומבזה מועדות ומגלה פנים כו' היינו דבר ה' בזה) דבזיון הוא: מפר ברית. היינו את בריתי הפר: מועדות. חולו של מועד: דקדוק זה. חסרות ויתרות: מק"ו [זה] ומגזירה שוה [זו]. [ושא"ל רבו גזירה שוה] לא גמר מרבו: המשנה. זה שעושה כמו שאינה עיקר: זה העובד ע"ז. היינו דבר ה' דבור שדבר הקב"ה בעצמו לישראל דאנכי ולא יהיה לך מפי הגבורה שמענום: חוזר. לשנותה:

זמר

מסורת הש"ס

א) [לעיל לח:], ב) ברכות לד: שבת סג., ג) ברכות לד: שבת סג. קנא: פסחים סח: לעיל לא., ד) [בברכו' ליתא], ה) ברכות לד., ו) [שם], ז) [בברכו' איתא ר"ש בר נחמני], ח) [נ"ל ואת מצותו], ט) [שבועות יג. ע"ש], י) אבות פ"ג משנה יא, כ) [תוספתא דפרה פ"ג ותוספתא דאהלות פט"ז].

תורה אור השלם

א) כִּי הִנֵּה הַחֹשֶׁךְ יְכַסֶּה אֶרֶץ וַעֲרָפֶל לְאֻמִּים וְעָלַיִךְ יִזְרַח יְיָ וּכְבוֹדוֹ עָלַיִךְ יֵרָאֶה: [ישעיה ס, ב]

ב) אַרְבָּעִים שָׁנָה אָקוּט בְּדוֹר וָאֹמַר עַם תֹּעֵי לֵבָב הֵם וְהֵם לֹא יָדְעוּ דְרָכָי: [תהלים צה, י]

ג) וְהָיָה בַּיּוֹם הַהוּא וְנִשְׁכַּחַת צֹר שִׁבְעִים שָׁנָה כִּימֵי מֶלֶךְ אֶחָד מִקֵּץ שִׁבְעִים שָׁנָה יִהְיֶה לְצֹר כְּשִׁירַת הַזּוֹנָה: [ישעיה כג, טו]

ד) יִירָאוּךָ עִם שָׁמֶשׁ וְלִפְנֵי יָרֵחַ דּוֹר דּוֹרִים: [תהלים עב, ה]

ה) גִּילִי מְאֹד בַּת צִיּוֹן הָרִיעִי בַּת יְרוּשָׁלַיִם הִנֵּה מַלְכֵּךְ יָבוֹא לָךְ צַדִּיק וְנוֹשָׁע הוּא עָנִי וְרֹכֵב עַל חֲמוֹר וְעַל עַיִר בֶּן אֲתֹנוֹת: [זכריה ט, ט]

ו) וַיְעַנְּךָ וַיַּרְעִבֶךָ וַיַּאֲכִלְךָ אֶת הַמָּן אֲשֶׁר לֹא יָדַעְתָּ וְלֹא יָדְעוּן אֲבֹתֶיךָ לְמַעַן הוֹדִיעֲךָ כִּי לֹא עַל הַלֶּחֶם לְבַדּוֹ יִחְיֶה הָאָדָם כִּי עַל כָּל מוֹצָא פִי יְיָ יִחְיֶה הָאָדָם: [דברים ח, ג]

ז) שַׂמְּחֵנוּ כִּימוֹת עִנִּיתָנוּ שְׁנוֹת רָאִינוּ רָעָה: [תהלים צ, טו]

ח) וַיֹּאמֶר לְאַבְרָם יָדֹעַ תֵּדַע כִּי גֵר יִהְיֶה זַרְעֲךָ בְּאֶרֶץ לֹא לָהֶם וַעֲבָדוּם וְעִנּוּ אֹתָם אַרְבַּע מֵאוֹת שָׁנָה: [בראשית טו, יג]

ט) כִּי יוֹם נָקָם בְּלִבִּי וּשְׁנַת גְּאוּלַי בָּאָה: [ישעיה סג, ד]

י) כִּי יִבְעַל בָּחוּר בְּתוּלָה יִבְעָלוּךְ בָּנָיִךְ וּמְשׂוֹשׂ חָתָן עַל כַּלָּה יָשִׂישׂ עָלַיִךְ אֱלֹהָיִךְ: [ישעיה סב, ה]

כ) לְמַעַן יִרְבּוּ יְמֵיכֶם וִימֵי בְנֵיכֶם עַל הָאֲדָמָה אֲשֶׁר נִשְׁבַּע יְיָ לַאֲבֹתֵיכֶם לָתֵת לָהֶם כִּימֵי הַשָּׁמַיִם עַל הָאָרֶץ: [דברים יא, כא]

ל) כִּי מֵי נֹחַ זֹאת לִי אֲשֶׁר נִשְׁבַּעְתִּי מֵעֲבֹר מֵי נֹחַ עוֹד עַל הָאָרֶץ כֵּן נִשְׁבַּעְתִּי מִקְּצֹף עָלַיִךְ וּמִגְּעָר בָּךְ: [ישעיה נד, ט]

מ) וּמֵעוֹלָם לֹא שָׁמְעוּ לֹא הֶאֱזִינוּ עַיִן לֹא רָאָתָה אֱלֹהִים זוּלָתְךָ יַעֲשֶׂה לִמְחַכֵּה לוֹ: [ישעיה סד, ג]

נ) בּוֹרֵא נִיב שְׂפָתָיִם שָׁלוֹם שָׁלוֹם לָרָחוֹק וְלַקָּרוֹב אָמַר יְיָ וּרְפָאתִיו: [ישעיה נז, יט]

ס) וְנָהָר יֹצֵא מֵעֵדֶן לְהַשְׁקוֹת אֶת הַגָּן וּמִשָּׁם יִפָּרֵד וְהָיָה לְאַרְבָּעָה רָאשִׁים: [בראשית ב, י] ע) כִּי דְבַר יְיָ בָּזָה וְאֶת מִצְוָתוֹ הֵפַר הִכָּרֵת תִּכָּרֵת הַנֶּפֶשׁ הַהִוא עֲוֹנָה בָהּ: [במדבר טו, לא] פ) אָנֹכִי יְיָ אֱלֹהֶיךָ אֲשֶׁר הוֹצֵאתִיךָ מֵאֶרֶץ מִצְרַיִם מִבֵּית עֲבָדִים: לֹא יִהְיֶה לְךָ אֱלֹהִים אֲחֵרִים עַל פָּנָי: [שמות כ, ב-ג]

עין משפט נר מצוה

יב א מיי' פ"ח מהל' תשובה הלכה ז וע"ש בכ"מ:

יג ב מיי' שם פ"ז הלכה ד:

יד ג מיי' שם פ"ג הלכה יד:

טו ד מיי' שם הלכה ח:

טז ה מיי' פ"ג מהל' ת"ת הלכה יג סמג עשין יב טוש"ע י"ד סי' רמו סעיף כה:

הגהות הגר"א

[א] גמ' זה המבזה דיבור שנא' לו למשה. נמחק ב' תיבות לו למשה ונ"ב להם לישראל:

ליקוטי רש"י

ונשכחת צור. לפי שמזכירה בלשון גנאי לשון זונה אמר ונשכחת, כזונה ששכחוה אוהביה, אף היא תשכח מאין סוחרים ותגרים פונים אליה לפי שתהיה חריבה. כימי מלך אחד. ימי דוד שבעים שנה היו ואיני יודע מהו הסימן הזה הניתן כאן [ישעיהו כג, טו]. הנה מלכך יבוא לך. אי אפשר לפותרו אלא על מלך המשיח שנאמר בו ומשלו מים ועד ים ולא מצינו מושל לישראל כזה בימי בית שני. צדיק ונושע. כה'. עני. ענותן. ורוכב על חמור. מדת ענוה היא. ועל עיר. כמו ועירים עשרה (בראשית לב) [זכריה ט, ט]. שמחנו כימות עניתנו. שמחנו לימות משיחנו כמנין ימות שעניתנו בגליות וכמנין שנות אשר ראינו רעה [תהלים צ, טו]. כי יבעל וגו'. ארי כמה דמתיתב עולם עם בתולתא כן יתייתבון בגווייכי בנייכי [ישעיהו סב, ה]. עין לא ראתה אלהים אחר זולתך אשר יעשה האלהים למחכה לו מה שעשית אתה למחכה לך כך שמעתי מר' יוסי והנאני, אבל רבותינו שאמרו כל הנביאים כולם לא נתנבאו אלא לימות המשיח אבל לעולם הבא עין לא ראתה וגו' משמעו עין שום נביא לא ראתה את אשר יעשה הקב"ה למחכה לו זולתי עייך אתה אלהים [ישעיהו סד, ג]. לרחוק ולקרוב. שניהם שוין מי שנתיישן והורגל בתורתי ועבודתי מנעוריו ומי שנתקרב עתה מקרוב לשוב מדרכו הרעה. אמר ה' ורפאתיו. מחליו ומחטאיו [ישעיהו נז, יט]. לא נתנבאו. דברי נחמות שלהן. עין לא ראתה. עין של נביאים לא שלטה לראותו [שבת סג.]. מגלה פנים. בא על דברי תורה בחוצפא ובגלוי עזות פניו כגון (סנהדרין דף צט:) מנשה שהיה יושב ודורש באגדות של דופי לא היה למשה לכתוב אלא ותמנע היתה פלגש וילך ראובן בימי קציר חטים (בראשית ל) [שבועות יג.]. דורש באגדות של דופי כגון מנשה שהיה אומר מה היה לו למשה לומר ותמנע היתה פילגש [כריתות ז.]. זה המיפר ברית בבשר. שהיא מלוה יחידי [שבועות יג.]. את המועדות. חולו של מועד [מכות כג.].

The Gemara continues its discussion about the length of the Messianic Era:

תָּנֵי אֲבִימִי בְּרֵיהּ דְּרַבִּי אַבָּהוּ – **Avimi the son of R' Abahu taught** the following Baraisa: יְמוֹת הַמָּשִׁיחַ לְיִשְׂרָאֵל שִׁבְעַת אֲלָפִים שָׁנָה – **THE MESSIANIC ERA WILL LAST SEVEN THOUSAND YEARS FOR ISRAEL,**[26] "שֶׁנֶּאֱמַר ,,וּמְשׂוֹשׂ חָתָן עַל־כַּלָּה כֵּן יָשִׂישׂ עָלַיִךְ ה' אֱלֹהָיִךְ" – **AS IT IS STATED:** ***AS A BRIDEGROOM REJOICES OVER A BRIDE, SO WILL HASHEM YOUR GOD REJOICE OVER YOU.***[27]

The Gemara cites two Amoraic opinions:

אָמַר רַב יְהוּדָה אָמַר שְׁמוּאֵל – **Rav Yehudah said in the name of Shmuel:** יְמוֹת הַמָּשִׁיחַ כְּמִיּוֹם שֶׁנִּבְרָא הָעוֹלָם וְעַד עַכְשָׁיו – **The Messianic Era** will last **as** long as the time that has elapsed **since the day the world was created until now,**[28] "שֶׁנֶּאֱמַר ,,כִּימֵי הַשָּׁמַיִם עַל־הָאָרֶץ" – **as it is stated:** ***like the days of the heaven on the earth.***[29]

רַב נַחְמָן בַּר יִצְחָק אָמַר – **Rav Nachman bar Yitzchak says:** כִּימֵי נֹחַ עַד עַכְשָׁיו – The Messianic Era will last **as** long as the time that has elapsed since **the days of Noah until now,** שֶׁנֶּאֱמַר ,,כִּי מֵי־נֹחַ "זֹאת לִי אֲשֶׁר נִשְׁבַּעְתִּי" – **as it is stated:** ***This is like the waters of Noah to me, regarding which I swore*** etc.[30]

The Gemara presents a series of three teachings reported by R' Chiya bar Abba in the name of R' Yochanan:

אָמַר רַבִּי חִיָּיא בַּר אַבָּא אָמַר רַבִּי יוֹחָנָן – **R' Chiya bar Abba said in the name of R' Yochanan:** כָּל הַנְּבִיאִים כּוּלָּן לֹא נִתְנַבְּאוּ אֶלָּא לִימוֹת הַמָּשִׁיחַ – **All the prophets prophesied only about the Messianic Era;** "אֲבָל לָעוֹלָם הַבָּא ,,עַיִן לֹא־רָאָתָה אֱלֹהִים זוּלָתְךָ יַעֲשֶׂה לִמְחַכֵּה־לוֹ" – **but as for the World to Come:** ***No eye except Yours, O God, has seen [that which] He will do for one who awaits Him.***[31]

A dissenting view:

וּפְלִיגָא דִּשְׁמוּאֵל – **And he** [R' Yochanan] **disagrees with Shmuel,** דְּאָמַר שְׁמוּאֵל – **for Shmuel said:** אֵין בֵּין הָעוֹלָם הַזֶּה לִימוֹת הַמָּשִׁיחַ אֶלָּא שִׁעְבּוּד מַלְכֻיּוֹת בִּלְבַד – **There is no difference between this world and** that of **the Messianic Era except for** Jewish independence from **the dominion of** foreign **kingdoms.**[32]

NOTES

Patriarchs and Moses (*Even Sheleimah* 11:9). According to this approach R' Yochanan teaches that God revealed the date of the redemption only to the Patriarchs and Moses, while Reish Lakish apparently maintains that God revealed it to other prophets as well.

The Midrash (*Bereishis Rabbah* 98:2) states that two people knew the "End" – Jacob and Daniel – but it was later hidden from them (see *Pesachim* 56a; see *Maharal, Netzach Yisrael* ch. 44).

26. This Tanna disagrees with Rav Katina who said that the world will last 6,000 years (*Yad Ramah;* see 97a note 59). [The same is seemingly true of Rebbi, according to the version of his opinion which sets the length of the Messianic Era at 365,000 years (see note 23). Furthermore, the two Amoraic views that follow are also inconsistent with Rav Katina's position (see *Emes LeYaakov* to 90a).]

27. *Isaiah* 62:5. The verse compares the joy of the Messianic Era to the joy of a bridegroom and bride, which is celebrated for seven days (*Yerushalmi, Kesubos* 1:1). Since, a "day of God" equals one thousand years (Gemara, 97a), this verse teaches that the Messianic Era will last 7,000 years (*Rashi;* see *Maharsha*).

28. I.e. the beginning of the Messianic Era (*Rashi, Yad Ramah, Maharsha*). To sound an encouraging note, Shmuel refers to the redemption as occurring "now" (*Yad Ramah*).

29. *Deuteronomy* 11:21. The entire verse reads: לְמַעַן יִרְבּוּ יְמֵיכֶם וִימֵי בְנֵיכֶם עַל הָאֲדָמָה אֲשֶׁר נִשְׁבַּע ה' לַאֲבֹתֵיכֶם לָתֵת לָהֶם כִּימֵי הַשָּׁמַיִם עַל־הָאָרֶץ, *In order to prolong your days and the days of your children upon the land that* HASHEM *has sworn to your ancestors to give them, like the days of the heaven on the earth.* God promises the Jewish people that they will live in Eretz Yisrael for a period of time that equals the *rest* of the world's duration ["the days of the heaven on the earth"] (see *Yad Ramah*).

This promise was not fulfilled in the past. [When the Second Temple was destroyed in the year 3,828, the Jews had been in their land for only 1,270 years.] Hence, this promise must refer to the Messianic Era (*Rashi;* cf. *Maharsha*).

30. *Isaiah* 54:9. The entire verse reads: כִּי־מֵי נֹחַ זֹאת לִי אֲשֶׁר נִשְׁבַּעְתִּי מֵעֲבֹר מֵי־נֹחַ עוֹד עַל־הָאָרֶץ כֵּן נִשְׁבַּעְתִּי מִקְּצֹף עָלַיִךְ וּמִגְּעָר־בָּךְ, *This is like the waters of Noah to Me, regarding which I swore that the waters of Noah shall not pass again over the earth, so have I sworn not to be angry with you or rebuke you.* Just as God swore not to bring another flood (see *Shevuos* 36a), so too he swears that there will be a time (i.e. the Messianic Era) when he will never be angry with His people.

Rav Nachman bar Yitzchak reads the words כִּי־מֵי (like the waters of) as though they were combined into one word כִּימֵי, *like the days of* (see *Radak* ad loc.). The verse thus teaches that *like the days* during which God's oath not to bring a flood applied (i.e. from the time of the Flood until the redemption), so too will his oath not to destroy the world *after* the redemption apply (*Rashi*).

Shmuel and Rav Nachman bar Yitzchak agree that since the Messianic Era is a world in its own right, it should endure for as long as this world (*Maharal;* see *Maharsha*). Shmuel reckons this world's duration from the Creation, whereas Rav Nachman reckons it from the Flood, when the world was renewed (*Maharal*).

31. Ibid. 64:3. The Books of the *Prophets* contain many descriptions of a utopian reward designated for the Jewish people. R' Yochanan maintains that these prophecies refer to the Messianic Era. They cannot refer to the World to Come, because no prophet has ever perceived the reward of the World to Come due to its infinite nature (see *Rashi* here and to *Shabbos* 63a).

Rambam writes: "A human being does not have the capacity to properly comprehend the goodness of the World to Come. No one knows its glory, beauty and potency except God Himself. All the benefits that the prophets predicted for Israel are only physical matters, which the Jewish people will enjoy in the Messianic Era, when their sovereignty is restored. The goodness of the life of the World to Come is immeasurable and utterly beyond comparison. The prophets did not describe it by means of analogy lest they cheapen it by doing so . . . The Sages said: *All the prophets prophesied only about the Messianic Era; but as for the World to Come: No eye except yours, O God, has seen" (Hil. Teshuvah* 8:7).

32. According to Shmuel, the natural laws and even the basic norms of society will not change in the Messianic Era. In *Berachos* 34b, Shmuel cites the following verse as proof: *Poor people will not cease to exist within the land* (*Deuteronomy* 15:11). The only major difference will be that in the Messianic Era the Jewish people will enjoy independence from foreign rule. The prophecies that describe a supernatural existence refer not to the Messianic Era, but to the World to Come (*Yad Ramah*). [Thus, Shmuel disagrees with R' Yochanan who maintains that these prophecies apply to the Messianic Era.]

Shmuel's view is apparently adopted by *Rambam*, who writes: "Do not think that in the Messianic Era any of the current norms will cease or that there will be a change in the natural order. Rather, the world will function in its normal manner. That which is said in *Isaiah* (11:6), *The wolf shall dwell with the lamb, and the leopard shall lie down with the kid,* is merely a metaphor whose point is that the Jewish people will live securely with the wicked nations . . . all of whom will return to the true religion, and they will not steal or destroy; rather, they will eat that which is permitted in harmony with Israel . . . All such things stated about the Messiah are metaphors . . . The Sages said: *There is no difference between this world and that of the Messianic Era except foreign domination*" (*Hil. Melachim* 12:1,2; see *Hil. Teshuvah* 9:2).

Rambam cites the views of both Shmuel (above) and R' Yochanan (see note 31). The Gemara, however, states that R' Yochanan disagrees with Shmuel! *Kesef Mishneh* (*Hil. Teshuvah* ibid.) raises this problem and concludes that the matter requires further study (see also *Kesef Mishneh* to *Hil. Melachim* 12:1).

Lechem Mishneh (*Hil. Teshuvah* ibid.) suggests that R' Yochanan also agrees that natural laws will not change. R' Yochanan's point of contention with Shmuel is that he maintains that human society will rise to a utopian level of peace and cooperation, whereas Shmuel holds that the current norms of society will continue (as is evidenced by Shmuel's proof text: *Poor people will not cease to exist* etc.) According to this approach, *Rambam's* rulings are entirely consistent with R' Yochanan's view. When *Rambam* cited Shmuel's words, "There is no difference between this world and the Messianic Era except for foreign dominion" (*Hil. Teshuvah* 9:2, *Hil. Melachim* 12:2), he did so only to support his

והיינו דא"ל ההוא מינא לרבי אבהו אימתי אתי משיח א"ל לכי חפי להו חשוכא להנהו אינשי א"ל מילט קא לייטת לי א"ל קרא כתיב א) כי הנה החשך יכסה ארץ וערפל לאומים ועליך יזרח ה' וכבודו עליך יראה תניא ר' אליעזר אומר ימות המשיח ארבעים שנה שנאמר ב) ארבעים שנה אקוט בדור רבי אלעזר בן עזריה אומר שבעים שנה שנאמר ג) והיה ביום ההוא ונשכחת צור שבעים שנה כימי מלך אחד איזהו מלך מיוחד הוי אומר זה משיח רבי אומר שלשה דורות שנאמר ד) ייראוך עם שמש ולפני ירח דור דורים א) ר' הילל אומר אין להם משיח לישראל שכבר אכלוהו בימי חזקיה אמר רב יוסף שרא ליה מריה לרבי הילל חזקיה אימת הוה בבית ראשון ואילו זכריה קא מתנבי בבית שני ואמר ה) גילי מאד בת ציון הריעי בת ירושלים הנה מלכך יבא לך צדיק ונושע הוא עני ורוכב על חמור ועל עיר בן אתונות תניא אידך ר' אליעזר אומר ימות המשיח ארבעים שנה כתיב הכא ו) ויענך וירעיבך ויאכילך וכתיב התם ז) שמחנו כימות עניתנו שנות ראינו רעה רבי דוסא אומר ד' מאות שנה כתיב הכא ח) ועבדום וענו אותם ארבע מאות שנה וכתיב התם שמחנו כימות עניתנו רבי אומר ג' מאות וששים וחמש שנה כמנין ימות החמה שנאמר ט) כי יום נקם בלבי ושנת גאולי באה מאי יום נקם בלבי

א"ר יוחנן ללבי גליתי לאבריי לא גליתי ר"ש בן לקיש אמר ללבי גליתי למלאכי השרת לא גליתי תני אבימי בריה דרבי אבהו ימות המשיח לישראל שבעת אלפים שנה שנאמר י) ומשוש חתן על כלה (כן) ישיש עליך (ה') אלהיך אמר רב יהודה אמר שמואל ימות המשיח כמיום שנברא העולם ועד עכשיו שנאמר כ) כימי השמים על הארץ רב נחמן בר יצחק אמר כימי נח עד עכשיו שנאמר ל) כי מי נח זאת לי אשר נשבעתי ב) אמר רבי חייא בר אבא א"ר יוחנן א) כל הנביאים כולן לא נתנבאו אלא לימות המשיח אבל לעולם הבא מ) עין לא ראתה אלהים זולתך (אלהים) יעשה למחכה לו ופליגא דשמואל דאמר שמואל ג) אין בין העולם הזה לימות המשיח אלא שעבוד מלכיות בלבד ואמר רבי חייא בר אבא א"ר יוחנן כל הנביאים לא נתנבאו אלא לבעלי תשובה אבל צדיקים גמורים עין לא ראתה אלהים זולתך ופליגא דרבי אבהו דא"ר אבהו (ד) א"ר) ב) מקום שבעלי תשובה עומדין שם צדיקים אינן עומדין שנאמר נ) שלום שלום לרחוק ולקרוב ברישא רחוק והדר קרוב מאי רחוק רחוק דמעיקרא ומאי קרוב קרוב דמעיקרא ודהשתא ורבי יוחנן אמר לרחוק שהוא רחוק מעבירה קרוב שהוא קרוב מעבירה ונתרחק ממנה וא"ר חייא בר אבא ה) א"ר יוחנן כל הנביאים כולן לא נתנבאו אלא למשיא בתו לתלמיד חכם ולעושה פרקמטיא לתלמיד חכם ולמהנה תלמיד חכם מנכסיו אבל תלמידי חכמים עצמן עין לא ראתה אלהים זולתך ו) מאי עין לא ראתה אמר רבי יהושע בן לוי זה יין המשומר בענביו מששת ימי בראשית ז) ר"ל אמר זה עדן לא ראתה עין מעולם וא"ת אדם היכן דר בגן ואם תאמר גן הוא עדן תלמוד לומר ס) ונהר יוצא מעדן להשקות את הגן: והאומר אין תורה מן השמים וכו': תנו רבנן ע) כי דבר ה' בזה ח) ומצותו הפר הכרת תכרת זה האומר אין תורה מן השמים ד"א ט) כי דבר ה' בזה זה אפיקורוס ד"א כי דבר ה' בזה זה המגלה פנים בתורה ואת מצותו הפר זה המפר ברית בשר הכרת תכרת הכרת בעולם הזה תכרת לעולם הבא מכאן אמר י) רבי אליעזר המודעי ג) המחלל את הקדשים והמבזה את המועדות והמפר בריתו של אברהם אבינו והמגלה פנים בתורה שלא כהלכה והמלבין פני חבירו ברבים אף על פי שיש בידו תורה ומעשים טובים אין לו חלק לעולם הבא תניא אידך כי דבר ה' בזה זה האומר אין תורה מן השמים ד) ואפילו אמר כל התורה כולה מן השמים חוץ מפסוק זה שלא אמרו הקדוש ברוך הוא אלא משה מפי עצמו זהו כי דבר ה' בזה ואפילו אמר כל התורה כולה מן השמים חוץ מדקדוק זה מקל וחומר זה מגזרה שוה זו זה הוא כי דבר ה' בזה תניא היה רבי מאיר אומר הלומד תורה ואינו מלמדה זה הוא דבר ה' בזה רבי נתן אומר כל מי שאינו משגיח על המשנה ר' נהוראי אומר ה) כל שאפשר לעסוק בתורה ואינו עוסק רבי ישמעאל אומר זה העובד עבודת כוכבים מאי משמעה דתנא דבי ר' ישמעאל כי דבר ה' בזה זה המבזה דבור שנאמר [א] לו למשה מסיני פ) אנכי ה' אלהיך לא יהיה לך אלהים אחרים וגו' כ) רבי יהושע בן קרחה אומר כל הלומד תורה ואינו חוזר עליה דומה לאדם שזורע ואינו קוצר רבי יהושע אומר כל הלומד תורה ומשכחה דומה לאשה שיולדת וקוברת רבי עקיבא אומר

זמר

רש"י

ה"ג היינו דאמר ליה ההוא מינא לרבי אבהו וכו': אקוט בדור. אקת ישראל ואמלוך עליהם כמו נקטיה ארבעים שנה אקוט בדור בדור קטן של ארבעים שנה שהוא משונה מדורות שלפניו ומסתמא היינו משיח שעינוין גדולים יהיו בדורו ופשטיה דקרא מיהא גבי מתי מדבר אבל מדכתיב אקוט משמע אף להבא היה מתנבא: מיוחד. חשוב: ה"ג רבי אומר ג' דורות שנאמר ייראוך עם שמש. כלומר בהדי משיח שכתב בו (תהלים עב) לפני שמש ינון שמו ייראוך ישראל ולפני ירח לפני מלכות בית דוד שנמשל כירח כדכתיב (שם פט) כירח יכון עולם וגו' כמו כן ייראוך דור דורים דור אחד דורים ב' הרי ג': אין להם משיח לישראל. אלא הקב"ה ימלוך בעצמו ויגאלם לבדו: שרי ליה מריה. ימחול לו הקב"ה שאמר דברים אשר לא כן: ואלו זכריה מיהא מתנבא על משיח בבית שני. דכתיב בתרי עשר הנה מלכך יבא לך וגו' ולאו היינו זכריה בן יהוידע הכהן שניבא בבית ראשון אלא זכריה בן ברכיה שהיה במלכות דריוש: רבי אומר שס"ה כמנין ימות החמה דכתיב כי יום נקם בלבי ושנת גאולי באה. [ליום נקם של מרגלים ארבעים יום מה יום נקם של מרגלים] שנה אחת בכל יום כדכתיב (במדבר יד) יום לשנה יום לשנה וגו' כך שנת גאולי באה שנה ליום שנה ליום שלכל יום ויום של שנה זו הכתובה שנת גאולי במקרא זה נותנים שנה אחת ואית דגרסי רבי אומר שס"ה אלפים שנה דכתיב שנת גאולי באה ושנה של הקב"ה הכי הוי דכתיב (תהלים צ) כי אלף שנים בעיניך כיום: ועד עכשיו. ימות המשיח:

תוספות

לאיברי לא גליתי. שלא הוצאתי דבר מפי שהיו איברי יכולין לשמוע אבל בלבי היה טמון הדבר: למען ירבו ימיכם כימי השמים על הארץ. ולא עמדו בארצם כל כך אבל עתידין לעמוד כשיבא משיח: כמשוש חתן. שבעת ימי המשתה כן ישיש עליך שבעת ימים ויומו של הקב"ה אלף שנה: כי מי נח. כמו כימי נח כחשבון השנים שנמלא בידו לאותו זמן שנשבע ה' מעבור מי נח עוד על הארץ כן נשבעתי כפי אותו חשבון נשבעתי מקצף עליך ומגער בך שלא אחריב את עולמי לאחר שיבא משיח עד שיכלה זה הזמן: לא נתנבאו. טובה לישראל: עין לא ראתה. דאין קץ לדבר: צדיקים אינן עומדין. דגדול כחן של בעלי תשובה שאין בריה יכולה לעמוד (לפניהם) [במחילתם]: ברישא לרחוק. שנתרחק מן הקב"ה ואח"כ שב אליו בתשובה והדר שלום לקרוב מעיקרא לדיק גמור דגדול כחן של בעלי תשובה: שהיה רחוק מן העבירה. כל ימיו דהיינו לדיק גמור: אפיקורוס ומגלה פנים. מפורש לקמן: ברית בשר. מילה: מכאן. מן הפסוק הזה שכתוב כי דבר ה' בזה (אמר ר"א וכו' מחלל את הקדשים דמחלל קדשים ומבזה מועדות ומגלה פנים כו' היינו דבר ה' בזה) דבזיון הוא: מפר ברית. היינו את בריתי הפר: מועדות. חולו של מועד: דקדוק זה. חסרות ויתרות: מק"ו [זה] ומגזירה שוה [זו]. [ושא"ל רבו גזירה שוה] לא גמר מרבו: המשנה. זה שעושה כמו שאינה עיקר: זה העובד ע"ז. היינו דבר ה' דבור שדבר הקב"ה בעצמו לישראל דאנכי ולא יהיה לך מפי הגבורה שמענום: חוזר. לשנותה:

זמר

מסורת הש"ס

א) [לעיל לח:], ב) ברכות לד: שבת סג., ג) ברכות לד: שבת סג. קנא: פסחים סח: לעיל לא:, ד) [בברכו' ליתא], ה) ברכות לד., ו) [שם], ז) [בברכו' איתא ר"ש בר נחמני], ח) [נ"ל ואת מצותו], ט) [שבועות יג. ע"ש], י) אבות פ"ג משנה יא, כ) [תוספתא דפרה פ"ג ותוספתא דאהלות פט"ז].

תורה אור השלם

א) כִּי הִנֵּה הַחֹשֶׁךְ יְכַסֶּה אֶרֶץ וַעֲרָפֶל לְאֻמִּים וְעָלַיִךְ יִזְרַח יְיָ וּכְבוֹדוֹ עָלַיִךְ יֵרָאֶה: [ישעיה ס, ב]

ב) אַרְבָּעִים שָׁנָה אָקוּט בְּדוֹר וָאֹמַר עַם תֹּעֵי לֵבָב הֵם וְהֵם לֹא יָדְעוּ דְרָכָי: [תהלים צה, י]

ג) וְהָיָה בַּיּוֹם הַהוּא וְנִשְׁכַּחַת צֹר שִׁבְעִים שָׁנָה כִּימֵי מֶלֶךְ אֶחָד מִקֵּץ שִׁבְעִים שָׁנָה יִהְיֶה לְצֹר כְּשִׁירַת הַזּוֹנָה: [ישעיה כג, טו]

ד) יִירָאוּךָ עִם שָׁמֶשׁ וְלִפְנֵי יָרֵחַ דּוֹר דּוֹרִים: [תהלים עב, ה]

ה) גִּילִי מְאֹד בַּת צִיּוֹן הָרִיעִי בַּת יְרוּשָׁלַםִ הִנֵּה מַלְכֵּךְ יָבוֹא לָךְ צַדִּיק וְנוֹשָׁע הוּא עָנִי וְרֹכֵב עַל חֲמוֹר וְעַל עַיִר בֶּן אֲתֹנוֹת: [זכריה ט, ט]

ו) וַיְעַנְּךָ וַיַּרְעִבֶךָ וַיַּאֲכִלְךָ אֶת הַמָּן אֲשֶׁר לֹא יָדַעְתָּ וְלֹא יָדְעוּן אֲבֹתֶיךָ לְמַעַן הוֹדִיעֲךָ כִּי לֹא עַל הַלֶּחֶם לְבַדּוֹ יִחְיֶה הָאָדָם כִּי עַל כָּל מוֹצָא פִי יְיָ יִחְיֶה הָאָדָם: [דברים ח, ג]

ז) שַׂמְּחֵנוּ כִּימוֹת עִנִּיתָנוּ שְׁנוֹת רָאִינוּ רָעָה: [תהלים צ, טו]

ח) וַיֹּאמֶר לְאַבְרָם יָדֹעַ תֵּדַע כִּי גֵר יִהְיֶה זַרְעֲךָ בְּאֶרֶץ לֹא לָהֶם וַעֲבָדוּם וְעִנּוּ אֹתָם אַרְבַּע מֵאוֹת שָׁנָה: [בראשית טו, יג]

ט) כִּי יוֹם נָקָם בְּלִבִּי וּשְׁנַת גְּאוּלַי בָּאָה: [ישעיה סג, ד]

י) כִּי יִבְעַל בָּחוּר בְּתוּלָה יִבְעָלוּךְ בָּנָיִךְ וּמְשׂוֹשׂ חָתָן עַל כַּלָּה יָשִׂישׂ עָלַיִךְ אֱלֹהָיִךְ: [ישעיה סב, ה]

כ) לְמַעַן יִרְבּוּ יְמֵיכֶם וִימֵי בְנֵיכֶם עַל הָאֲדָמָה אֲשֶׁר נִשְׁבַּע יְיָ לַאֲבֹתֵיכֶם לָתֵת לָהֶם כִּימֵי הַשָּׁמַיִם עַל הָאָרֶץ: [דברים יא, כא]

ל) כִּי מֵי נֹחַ זֹאת לִי אֲשֶׁר נִשְׁבַּעְתִּי מֵעֲבֹר מֵי נֹחַ עוֹד עַל הָאָרֶץ כֵּן נִשְׁבַּעְתִּי מִקְּצֹף עָלַיִךְ וּמִגְּעָר בָּךְ: [ישעיה נד, ט]

מ) וּמֵעוֹלָם לֹא שָׁמְעוּ לֹא הֶאֱזִינוּ עַיִן לֹא רָאָתָה אֱלֹהִים זוּלָתְךָ יַעֲשֶׂה לִמְחַכֵּה לוֹ: [ישעיה סד, ג]

נ) בּוֹרֵא נִיב שְׂפָתָיִם שָׁלוֹם שָׁלוֹם לָרָחוֹק וְלַקָּרוֹב אָמַר יְיָ וּרְפָאתִיו: [ישעיה נז, יט]

ס) וְנָהָר יֹצֵא מֵעֵדֶן לְהַשְׁקוֹת אֶת הַגָּן וּמִשָּׁם יִפָּרֵד וְהָיָה לְאַרְבָּעָה רָאשִׁים: [בראשית ב, י] ע) כִּי דְבַר יְיָ בָּזָה וְאֶת מִצְוָתוֹ הֵפַר הִכָּרֵת תִּכָּרֵת הַנֶּפֶשׁ הַהִוא עֲוֹנָה בָהּ: [במדבר טו, לא] פ) אָנֹכִי יְיָ אֱלֹהֶיךָ אֲשֶׁר הוֹצֵאתִיךָ מֵאֶרֶץ מִצְרַיִם מִבֵּית עֲבָדִים: לֹא יִהְיֶה לְךָ אֱלֹהִים אֲחֵרִים עַל פָּנָי: [שמות כ, ב-ג]

עין משפט נר מצוה

יב א מיי' פ"ח מהל' תשובה הלכה ז וע"ש בכ"מ:
יג ב מיי' שם פ"ז הלכה ד:
יד ג מיי' שם פ"ג הלכה יד:
טו ד מיי' שם הלכה ח:
טז ה מיי' פ"ג מהל' ת"ת הלכה יג סמג עשין יג טוש"ע י"ד סי' רמו סעיף כה:

הגהות הגר"א

[א] גמ' זה המבזה דיבור שנא' לו למשה. נמחק ב' תיבות לו למשה וכ"ב להם לישראל:

ליקוטי רש"י

ונשכחת צור. לפי שמזכירה בלשון גנאי לשון זונה אמר ונשכחת, כזונה ששכחוה אוהביה, אף היא תשכח מאין סוחרים ותגרים פונים אליה לפי שתהיה חריבה. כימי מלך אחד. ימי דוד שבעים שנה היו ואיני יודע מהו הסימן הזה הניתן כאן [ישעיהו כג, טו]. הנה מלכך יבוא לך. אי אפשר לפותרו אלא על מלך המשיח שנאמר בו ומשלו מים ועד ים ולא מלינו מושל לישראל כזה בימי בית שני. צדיק ונושע. כמ'. עני. ענותן. ורוכב על חמור. מדת ענוה היא. ועל עיר. כמו ועירים עשרה (בראשית לב) [זכריה ט, ט]. שמחנו כימות עניתנו. שמחנו לימות משיחנו כמנין ימות שעניתנו בגליות וכמנין שנות אשר ראינו רעה [תהלים צ, טו]. כי יבעל וגו'. ארי כמה דמתיתב עולם עם בתולתא כן יתייתבין בגוייכי בנייכי [ישעיהו סב, ה]. עין לא ראתה אלהים אחר זולתך אשר יעשה האלהים למחכה לו מה שעשית אתה למחכה לך כך שמעתי מר' יוסי והגאני, אבל רבותינו שאמרו כל הנביאים כולם לא נתנבאו אלא לימות המשיח אבל לעולם הבא עין לא ראתה וגו' משמעו עין שום נביא לא ראתה את אשר יעשה הקב"ה למחכה לו זולתי עייך אתה אלהים [ישעיהו סד, ג]. לרחוק ולקרוב. שניהם שוין מי שנתיישן והורגל בתורתי ועבודתי מנעוריו ומי שנתקרב עתה מקרוב לשוב מדרכו הרעה. אמר ה' ורפאתיו. מחליו ומחטאיו [ישעיהו נז, יט]. לא נתנבאו. דברי נחמות שלהן. עין לא ראתה. עין של נביאים לא שלטה לראותו [שבת סג.]. מגלה פנים. בא על דברי תורה בחוצפא ובגלוי עזות פניו כגון (סנהדרין דף לט:) מנשה שהיה יושב ודורש באגדות של דופי לא היה למשה לכתוב אלא ותמנע היתה פלגש וילך ראובן בימי קציר חטים (בראשית ל) [שבועות יג.]. דורש באגדות של דופי כגון מנשה שהיה אומר מה היה לו למשה לומר ותמנע היתה פילגש [כריתות ז.]. זה המיפר ברית בבשר. שהיא מלוה יחידי [שבועות יג.]. את המועדות. חולו של מועד [מכות כג.].

The second teaching reported by R' Chiya bar Abba in the name of R' Yochanan:

וְאָמַר רַבִּי חִיָּיא בַּר אַבָּא אָמַר רַבִּי יוֹחָנָן – **And R' Chiya bar Abba said in the name of R' Yochanan:** כָּל הַנְּבִיאִים לֹא נִתְנַבְּאוּ אֶלָּא לְבַעֲלֵי תְשׁוּבָה – **All the prophets prophesied only** about the reward **for penitents;** אֲבָל צַדִּיקִים גְּמוּרִים ,,עַיִן לֹא־רָאָתָה אֱלֹהִים זוּלָתְךָ" – **but** the reward for **the completely righteous,** ***no eye except yours, O God, has seen.***

A dissenting view:

וּפְלִיגָא דְּרַבִּי אַבָּהוּ – **And he** [R' Yochanan] **disagrees with R' Abahu,** דְּאָמַר רַבִּי אַבָּהוּ אָמַר רַב – **for R' Abahu said in the name of Rav:** מָקוֹם שֶׁבַּעֲלֵי תְשׁוּבָה עוֹמְדִין שָׁם – **Where penitents stand,** צַדִּיקִים אֵינָן עוֹמְדִין שָׁם – **there the righteous do not stand,**[33] שֶׁנֶּאֱמַר ,,שָׁלוֹם שָׁלוֹם לָרָחוֹק וְלַקָּרוֹב" – **as it is stated:** ***Peace, peace, to the far and to the near.***[34] בְּרֵישָׁא רָחוֹק וְהָדַר קָרוֹב – God's greetings are extended **first** to the **far and then** to the **near.** מַאי ,,רָחוֹק" – **What is** the meaning of ***far?*** רָחוֹק דְּמֵעִיקָּרָא – One who was far from God **before,** i.e. one who repented. וּמַאי ,,קָרוֹב" – **And what is** the meaning of ***near?*** קָרוֹב דְּמֵעִיקָּרָא וּדְהַשְׁתָּא – One who was **near** to God both **before and now,** i.e. one who was always righteous.

The Gemara now explains how R' Yochanan, who disagrees with R' Abahu, explains the verse that R' Abahu cited :

וְרַבִּי יוֹחָנָן אָמַר – **But R' Yochanan says:** ,,לָרָחוֹק" שֶׁהוּא רָחוֹק מֵעֲבֵירָה – ***To the far*** refers to one **who was** always **far from sin,** ,,קָרוֹב" שֶׁהוּא קָרוֹב מֵעֲבֵירָה וְנִתְרַחֵק מִמֶּנָּה – and the ***near*** signifies one **who was near sin and** subsequently **drew far away from it.**[35]

The third teaching reported by R' Chiya bar Abba in the name of R' Yochanan:

וְאָמַר רַבִּי חִיָּיא בַּר אַבָּא אָמַר רַבִּי יוֹחָנָן – **And R' Chiya bar Abba said in the name of R' Yochanan:** כָּל הַנְּבִיאִים כּוּלָּן לֹא נִתְנַבְּאוּ אֶלָּא לְמַשִּׂיא בִּתּוֹ לְתַלְמִיד חָכָם – **All the prophets prophesied only** about the reward **for one who marries his daughter to a Torah scholar,** וּלְעוֹשֶׂה פְּרַקְמַטְיָא לְתַלְמִיד חָכָם – **and for one who engages in business on behalf of a Torah scholar,**[36] וְלִמְהַנֶּה תַּלְמִיד חָכָם מִנְּכָסָיו – **and for one who benefits a Torah scholar with his possessions;**[37] אֲבָל תַּלְמִידֵי חֲכָמִים עַצְמָן ,,עַיִן לֹא־רָאָתָה אֱלֹהִים זוּלָתְךָ" – **but** the reward for **Torah scholars themselves,** ***no eye except yours, O God, has seen.***[38]

The Gemara discusses this infinite reward:

מַאי ,,עַיִן לֹא־רָאָתָה" – **What is** that which ***no eye has seen?*** אָמַר רַבִּי יְהוֹשֻׁעַ בֶּן לֵוִי – **R' Yehoshua ben Levi said:** זֶה יַיִן הַמְשׁוּמָּר בַּעֲנָבָיו מִשֵּׁשֶׁת יְמֵי בְרֵאשִׁית – **This is wine preserved in its grapes since the six days of Creation.**[39] רֵישׁ לָקִישׁ אָמַר – **Reish Lakish says:** זֶה עֵדֶן – **This is Eden,** לֹא רָאֲתָה עַיִן מֵעוֹלָם – which **no eye has ever seen.** וְאִם תֹּאמַר – **And if you ask:** אָדָם הֵיכָן דָּר – **Where did Adam live** if not in Eden[40] – בַּגַּן – the answer is that Adam lived **in the Garden.** וְאִם תֹּאמַר גַּן הוּא עֵדֶן – **And if you ask:** But **the Garden is Eden** – תַּלְמוּד לוֹמַר ,,וְנָהָר יֹצֵא מֵעֵדֶן לְהַשְׁקוֹת אֶת־הַגָּן" – **Scripture therefore states:** ***A river issues from Eden to water the Garden,***[41] which indicates that Eden and the Garden are different places.[42]

The Gemara has just concluded its extended discussion of the Messiah and the Messianic Era, a discussion engendered by the Mishnah's having listed a person who denies resurrection as the first case of one who has no portion in the World to Come. The Gemara now discusses the second person listed there – namely, one who denies the Divine origin of the Torah, as the Mishnah stated:

וְהָאוֹמֵר אֵין תּוֹרָה מִן הַשָּׁמַיִם וכו' – **AND HE WHO SAYS** that **THE TORAH IS NOT FROM HEAVEN.**

A Baraisa identifies the source of this ruling:

תָּנוּ רַבָּנָן – **The Rabbis taught** in a Baraisa: ,,כִּי דְבַר־ה' בָּזָה [וְאֶת] (וּ)מִצְוָתוֹ הֵפַר הִכָּרֵת תִּכָּרֵת" – Scripture states:[43] ***FOR HE***

NOTES

point that the laws of nature will remain in effect, and not because he adopts the view of Shmuel. [This approach is apparently borne out by *Rambam's* several descriptions of the Messianic Era in which he stresses that the world will continue to function in its normal manner, but human society will be so exalted that "there will be no war or hunger, no jealousy or competition" (*Hil. Melachim* 12:5; see 96b note 56).]

[Also see the solution forwarded by *R' E. E. Dessler* (*Michtav MeEliyahu* III pp. 353-4) which distinguishes between various levels of redemption.]

33. The level of penitents is so exalted that no one else can stand in their division [in Gan Eden] (*Rashi*).

Penitents are superior because it is harder for them to control their evil inclination than it is for the perfectly righteous, who never became accustomed to sin (*Yad Ramah; Rambam, Hil. Teshuvah* 7:4).

In addition to the preceding reason, *Sama DeChayei* (cited by *Yad Yosef* to *Berachos* 34b) offers two others: The Gemara in *Yoma* (86b) states that if one repents out of love for God, even his sinful deeds are treated as meritorious. Furthermore, a penitent has fulfilled the mitzvah of repentance (which *Rambam* counts as one of the 613 Scriptural mitzvos), whereas one who was always righteous lacks this mitzvah. (See also *Maharsha* to *Berachos* ibid.; *Beur HaGra* to *Orach Chaim* 53:5; *Michtav MeEliyahu* III p. 353.)

34. *Isaiah* 57:19.

35. According to this interpretation, the verse gives precedence to a person who was always righteous.

36. He engages in business using a Torah scholar's capital and awards the profit to the scholar, who is thereby left free to devote himself to his studies (*Rashi* to *Kesubos* 111b).

37. The Gemara in *Kesubos* (111b) states: "*To love Hashem your God . . . and to cleave to Him* (*Deuteronomy* 30:20). Now is it possible for a human being to cleave to the *Shechinah*?! Rather, whoever marries off his daughter to a Torah scholar, or does business for a Torah scholar, or benefits a Torah scholar with his possessions is regarded by Scripture as though he cleaves to the *Shechinah*."

On the basis of this teaching, *Rambam* rules that it is a positive commandment of the Torah to associate with Torah scholars in every way possible in order to learn from their behavior (*Hil. De'os* 6:2, *Kesef Mishneh* ibid; see *Meshech Chochmah* to *Leviticus* 26:6, and *Maharsha* to *Berachos* 34b).

38. It emerges from these three teachings reported by R' Chiya bar Abba in the name of R' Yochanan that Torah scholars and those who were always righteous will enjoy the infinite reward (referred to by the verse, *No eye has seen* etc.) even in the Messianic Era. All others (i.e. penitents and those who merely benefited Torah scholars) will enjoy this reward only in the World to Come (*Iyun Yaakov* to *Berachos* ibid.; see *Maharsha* ibid.).

39. This reward is allegorically portrayed as wine, because nothing gladdens a person's heart in this world more than wine does. It is described as "preserved in its grapes since the Creation" to convey that no human being has ever perceived it, just as no one has touched wine that is still within its grapes (*Yad Ramah* to 90a ד״ה והא דגרסינן).

"Wine preserved in its grapes since the Creation" is a metaphor for secret Torah wisdom which has not been made known to man. This wisdom will be revealed to the righteous in the World to Come (*Midrash HaNe'elam,* cited by *Margaliyos HaYam*; *Even Sheleimah* 11:11; see also *Maharsha* [*Berachos* ibid.] and *Maharal*).

40. Therefore, how can it be said that "no eye has seen" this reward?

41. *Genesis* 2:10.

42. Eden is the World to Come, about which it is said (*Berachos* 17a) "there is no eating or drinking . . . rather, the righteous sit with their crowns on their heads and delight in the radiance of the Divine Presence" (*Maharsha* to *Berachos* 34a; see *Eitz Yosef* for an explanation of the difference between the Garden and Eden).

[See *Maharal,* who explains the difference between the answers given by R' Yochanan and Reish Lakish.]

43. *Numbers* 15:31.

והיינו דא"ל ההוא מינא לרבי אבהו אימתי אתי משיח א"ל לכי חפי להו חשוכא להנהו אינשי א"ל מילט קא לייטת לי א"ל קרא כתיב א) כי הנה החשך יכסה ארץ וערפל לאומים ועליך יזרח ה' וכבודו עליך יראה תניא ר' אליעזר אומר ימות המשיח ארבעים שנה שנאמר ב) ארבעים שנה אקוט בדור רבי אלעזר בן עזריה אומר שבעים שנה שנאמר ג) והיה ביום ההוא ונשכחת צור שבעים שנה כימי מלך אחד איזהו מלך מיוחד הוי אומר זה משיח רבי אומר שלשה דורות שנאמר ד) ייראוך עם שמש ולפני ירח דור דורים א) ר' הילל אומר אין להם משיח לישראל שכבר אכלוהו בימי חזקיה אמר רב יוסף שרא ליה מריה לרבי הילל חזקיה אימת הוה בבית ראשון ואילו זכריה קא מתנבי בבית שני ואמר ה) גילי מאד בת ציון הריעי בת ירושלים הנה מלכך יבא לך צדיק ונושע הוא עני ורוכב על חמור ועל עיר בן אתונות תניא אידך ר' אליעזר אומר ימות המשיח ארבעים שנה כתיב הכא ו) ויענך וירעיבך ויאכילך וכתיב התם ז) שמחנו כימות עניתנו שנות ראינו רעה רבי דוסא אומר ד' מאות שנה כתיב הכא ח) ועבדום וענו אותם ארבע מאות שנה וכתיב התם שמחנו כימות עניתנו רבי אומר ג' מאות וששים וחמש שנה כמנין ימות החמה שנאמר ט) כי יום נקם בלבי ושנת גאולי באה מאי יום נקם בלבי א"ר יוחנן ללבי גליתי לאברי לא גליתי ר"ש בן לקיש אמר ללבי גליתי למלאכי השרת לא גליתי תני אבימי בריה דרבי אבהו ימות המשיח לישראל שבעת אלפים שנה שנאמר י) ומשוש חתן על כלה (כן) ישיש עליך (ה') אלהיך אמר רב יהודה אמר שמואל ימות המשיח כמיום שנברא העולם ועד עכשיו שנאמר כ) כימי השמים על הארץ רב נחמן בר יצחק אמר כימי נח עד עכשיו שנאמר ל) כי מי נח זאת לי אשר נשבעתי ב) אמר רבי חייא בר אבא א"ר יוחנן ג) כל הנביאים כולן לא נתנבאו אלא לימות המשיח אבל לעולם הבא מ) עין לא ראתה אלהים זולתך (אלהים) יעשה למחכה לו ופליגא דשמואל דאמר שמואל ג) אין בין העולם הזה לימות המשיח אלא שעבוד מלכיות בלבד ואמר רבי חייא בר אבא א"ר יוחנן כל הנביאים לא נתנבאו אלא לבעלי תשובה אבל צדיקים גמורים עין לא ראתה אלהים זולתך ופליגא דרבי אבהו דא"ר אבהו (ד) א"ר) ב) מקום שבעלי תשובה עומדין שם צדיקים אינן עומדין שם שנאמר נ) שלום שלום לרחוק ולקרוב ברישא רחוק והדר קרוב מאי רחוק רחוק דמעיקרא ומאי קרוב קרוב דמעיקרא ודהשתא ורבי יוחנן אמר לרחוק שהוא רחוק מעבירה קרוב שהוא קרוב מעבירה ונתרחק ממנה וא"ר חייא בר אבא ה) א"ר יוחנן כל הנביאים כולן לא נתנבאו אלא למשיא בתו לתלמיד חכם ולעושה פרקמטיא לתלמיד חכם ולמהנה תלמיד חכם מנכסיו אבל תלמידי חכמים עצמן עין לא ראתה אלהים זולתך ו) מאי עין לא ראתה אמר רבי יהושע בן לוי זה יין המשומר בענביו מששת ימי בראשית ז) ר"ל אמר זה עדן לא ראתה עין מעולם וא"ת אדם היכן דר בגן ואם תאמר גן הוא עדן תלמוד לומר ס) ונהר יוצא מעדן להשקות את הגן: והאומר אין תורה מן השמים וכו': תנו רבנן ע) כי דבר ה' בזה ח) ומצותו הפר הכרת תכרת זה האומר אין תורה מן השמים ד"א ט) כי דבר ה' בזה זה אפיקורוס ד"א כי דבר ה' בזה זה המגלה פנים בתורה ואת מצותו הפר זה המפר ברית בשר הכרת תכרת הכרת בעולם הזה תכרת לעולם הבא מכאן אמר י) רבי אליעזר המודעי ג) המחלל את הקדשים והמבזה את המועדות והמפר בריתו של אברהם אבינו והמגלה פנים בתורה שלא כהלכה והמלבין פני חבירו ברבים אף על פי שיש בידו תורה ומעשים טובים אין לו חלק לעולם הבא תניא אידך כי דבר ה' בזה זה האומר אין תורה מן השמים ד) ואפילו אמר כל התורה כולה מן השמים חוץ מפסוק זה שלא אמרו הקדוש ברוך הוא אלא משה מפי עצמו זהו כי דבר ה' בזה ואפילו אמר כל התורה כולה מן השמים חוץ מדקדוק זה מקל וחומר זה מגזרה שוה זו זה הוא כי דבר ה' בזה תניא היה רבי מאיר אומר הלומד תורה ואינו מלמדה זה הוא דבר ה' בזה רבי נתן אומר כל מי שאינו משגיח על המשנה ר' נהוראי אומר ה) כל שאפשר לעסוק בתורה ואינו עוסק רבי ישמעאל אומר זה העובד עבודת כוכבים מאי משמעה דתנא דבי ר' ישמעאל כי דבר ה' בזה זה המבזה דבור שנאמר [א] לו למשה מסיני פ) אנכי ה' אלהיך לא יהיה לך אלהים אחרים וגו' כ) רבי יהושע בן קרחה אומר כל הלומד תורה ואינו חוזר עליה דומה לאדם שזורע ואינו קוצר רבי יהושע אומר כל הלומד תורה ומשכחה דומה לאשה שיולדת וקוברת רבי עקיבא אומר

זמר

ה"ג היינו דאמר ליה ההוא מינא לרבי אבהו וכו': אקוט בדור. אקח ישראל ואמלוך עליהם כמו נקטיה ארבעים שנה אקוט בדור בדור קטן של ארבעים שנה שהוא משונה מדורות שלפניו ומסתמא היינו משיח שעינון גדולים יהיו בדורו ופשטיה דקרא מיהא גבי מתי מדבר אבל מדכתיב אקוט משמע אף להבא היה מתנבא: מיוחד. חשוב: ה"ג רבי אומר ג' דורות שנאמר ייראוך עם שמש. כלומר בהדי משיח שכתב בו (תהלים עב) לפני שמש ינון שמו ייראוך ישראל ולפני ירח לפני מלכות בית דוד שנמשל כירח כדכתיב (שם פט) כירח יכון עולם וגו' כמו כן ייראוך דור דורים דור אחד דורים ב' הרי ג': אין להם משיח לישראל. אלא הקב"ה ימלוך בעצמו ויגאלם לבדו: שרי ליה מריה. ימחול לו הקב"ה שאמר דברים אשר לא כן: ואלו זכריה מיהא מתנבא על משיח בבית שני. דכתיב בתרי עשר הנה מלכך יבא לך וגו' ולאו היינו זכריה בן יהוידע הכהן שניבא בבית ראשון אלא זכריה בן ברכיה שהיה במלכות דריוש: רבי אומר שס"ה כמנין ימות החמה דכתיב כי יום נקם בלבי ושנת גאולי באה. [ליום נקם של מרגלים ארבעים יום מה יום נקם של מרגלים] שנה אחת בכל יום כדכתיב (במדבר יד) יום לשנה יום לשנה וגו' כך שנת גאולי באה שנה ליום שנה ליום שלכל יום ויום של שנה זו הכתובה שנת גאולי במקרא זה נותנים שנה אחת ואית דגרסי רבי אומר שס"ה אלפים שנה דכתיב שנת גאולי באה ושנה של הקב"ה הכי הוי דכתיב (תהלים צ) כי אלף שנים בעיניך כיום: ועד עכשיו. ימות המשיח: לאיברי לא גליתי. שלא הוצאתי דבר מפי שהיו איברי יכולין לשמוע אבל בלבי היה טמון הדבר: למען ירבו ימיכם כימי השמים על הארץ. ולא עמדו בארץ כל כך אבל עתידין לעמוד כשיבא משיח: כמשוש חתן. שבעת ימי המשתה כן ישיש עליך שבעת ימים ויומו של הקב"ה אלף שנה: כי מי נח. כמו כימי נח כחשבון השנים שנמלא בידו לאותו זמן שנשבע ה' מעבור מי נח עוד על הארץ כן נשבעתי כפי אותו חשבון נשבעתי מקצף עליך ומגער בך שלא אחריב את עולמי לאחר שיבא משיח עד שיכלה זה הזמן: לא נתנבאו. טובה לישראל: עין לא ראתה. דאין קץ לדבר: צדיקים אינן עומדין. דגדול כחן של בעלי תשובה שאין בריה יכולה לעמוד (לפניהם) [במחיצתם]: ברישא לרחוק. שנתרחק מן הקב"ה ואח"כ שב אליו בתשובה והדר שלום לקרוב מעיקרא לדיק גמור דגדול כחן של בעלי תשובה: שהיה רחוק מן העבירה. כל ימיו דהיינו לדיק גמור: אפיקורום ומגלה פנים. מפורש לקמן: ברית בשר. מילה: מכאן. מן הפסוק הזה שכתוב כי דבר ה' בזה (אמר ר"א וכו' מחלל את הקדשים דמחלל קדשים ומבזה מועדות ומגלה פנים כו' היינו דבר ה' בזה) דבזיון הוא: מפר ברית. היינו את בריתי הפר: מועדות. חולו של מועד: דקדוק זה. חסרות ויתרות: מק"ו [זה] ומגזירה שוה [זו]. [ושא"ל רבו גזירה שוה] לא גמר מרבו: המשנה. זה שעושה כמו שאינה עיקר: זה העובד ע"ז. היינו דבר ה' דבור שדבר הקב"ה בעצמו לישראל דאנכי ולא יהיה לך מפי הגבורה שמענום: חוזר. לשונתה:

זמר

מסורת הש"ס

א) [לעיל לח:], ב) ברכות לד: שבת סג., ג) ברכות לד: שבת סג. קנא: פסחים סח: לעיל לא., ד) [בברכו' ליתא], ה) ברכות לד., ו) [שם], ז) [בברכו' איתא ר"ש בר נחמני], ח) [נ"ל ואת מצותו], ט) [שבועות יג. ע"ש], י) אבות פ"ג משנה יא, כ) [תוספתא דפרה פ"ג ותוספתא דאהלות פט"ז].

תורה אור השלם

א) כִּי הִנֵּה הַחֹשֶׁךְ יְכַסֶּה אֶרֶץ וַעֲרָפֶל לְאֻמִּים וְעָלַיִךְ יִזְרַח יְיָ וּכְבוֹדוֹ עָלַיִךְ יֵרָאֶה: [ישעיה ס, ב]

ב) אַרְבָּעִים שָׁנָה אָקוּט בְּדוֹר וָאֹמַר עַם תֹּעֵי לֵבָב הֵם וְהֵם לֹא יָדְעוּ דְרָכָי: [תהלים צה, י]

ג) וְהָיָה בַּיּוֹם הַהוּא וְנִשְׁכַּחַת צֹר שִׁבְעִים שָׁנָה כִּימֵי מֶלֶךְ אֶחָד מִקֵּץ שִׁבְעִים שָׁנָה יִהְיֶה לְצֹר כְּשִׁירַת הַזּוֹנָה: [ישעיה כג, טו]

ד) יִירָאוּךָ עִם שָׁמֶשׁ וְלִפְנֵי יָרֵחַ דּוֹר דּוֹרִים: [תהלים עב, ה]

ה) גִּילִי מְאֹד בַּת צִיּוֹן הָרִיעִי בַּת יְרוּשָׁלִַם הִנֵּה מַלְכֵּךְ יָבוֹא לָךְ צַדִּיק וְנוֹשָׁע הוּא עָנִי וְרֹכֵב עַל חֲמוֹר וְעַל עַיִר בֶּן אֲתֹנוֹת: [זכריה ט, ט]

ו) וַיְעַנְּךָ וַיַּרְעִבֶךָ וַיַּאֲכִלְךָ אֶת הַמָּן אֲשֶׁר לֹא יָדַעְתָּ וְלֹא יָדְעוּן אֲבֹתֶיךָ לְמַעַן הוֹדִיעֲךָ כִּי לֹא עַל הַלֶּחֶם לְבַדּוֹ יִחְיֶה הָאָדָם כִּי עַל כָּל מוֹצָא פִי יְיָ יִחְיֶה הָאָדָם: [דברים ח, ג]

ז) שַׂמְּחֵנוּ כִּימוֹת עִנִּיתָנוּ שְׁנוֹת רָאִינוּ רָעָה: [תהלים צ, טו]

ח) וַיֹּאמֶר לְאַבְרָם יָדֹעַ תֵּדַע כִּי גֵר יִהְיֶה זַרְעֲךָ בְּאֶרֶץ לֹא לָהֶם וַעֲבָדוּם וְעִנּוּ אֹתָם אַרְבַּע מֵאוֹת שָׁנָה: [בראשית טו, יג]

ט) כִּי יוֹם נָקָם בְּלִבִּי וּשְׁנַת גְּאוּלַי בָּאָה: [ישעיה סג, ד]

י) כִּי יִבְעַל בָּחוּר בְּתוּלָה יִבְעָלוּךְ בָּנָיִךְ וּמְשׂוֹשׂ חָתָן עַל כַּלָּה יָשִׂישׂ עָלַיִךְ אֱלֹהָיִךְ: [ישעיה סב, ה]

כ) לְמַעַן יִרְבּוּ יְמֵיכֶם וִימֵי בְנֵיכֶם עַל הָאֲדָמָה אֲשֶׁר נִשְׁבַּע יְיָ לַאֲבֹתֵיכֶם לָתֵת לָהֶם כִּימֵי הַשָּׁמַיִם עַל הָאָרֶץ: [דברים יא, כא]

ל) כִּי מֵי נֹחַ זֹאת לִי אֲשֶׁר נִשְׁבַּעְתִּי מֵעֲבֹר מֵי נֹחַ עוֹד עַל הָאָרֶץ כֵּן נִשְׁבַּעְתִּי מִקְּצֹף עָלַיִךְ וּמִגְּעָר בָּךְ: [ישעיה נד, ט]

מ) וּמֵעוֹלָם לֹא שָׁמְעוּ לֹא הֶאֱזִינוּ עַיִן לֹא רָאָתָה אֱלֹהִים זוּלָתְךָ יַעֲשֶׂה לִמְחַכֵּה לוֹ: [ישעיה סד, ג]

נ) בּוֹרֵא נִיב שְׂפָתָיִם שָׁלוֹם שָׁלוֹם לָרָחוֹק וְלַקָּרוֹב אָמַר יְיָ וּרְפָאתִיו: [ישעיה נז, יט]

ס) וְנָהָר יֹצֵא מֵעֵדֶן לְהַשְׁקוֹת אֶת הַגָּן וּמִשָּׁם יִפָּרֵד וְהָיָה לְאַרְבָּעָה רָאשִׁים: [בראשית ב, י] ע) כִּי דְבַר יְיָ בָּזָה וְאֶת מִצְוָתוֹ הֵפַר הִכָּרֵת תִּכָּרֵת הַנֶּפֶשׁ הַהִוא עֲוֹנָה בָהּ: [במדבר טו, לא] פ) אָנֹכִי יְיָ אֱלֹהֶיךָ אֲשֶׁר הוֹצֵאתִיךָ מֵאֶרֶץ מִצְרַיִם מִבֵּית עֲבָדִים: לֹא יִהְיֶה לְךָ אֱלֹהִים אֲחֵרִים עַל פָּנָי: [שמות כ, ב-ג]

עין משפט נר מצוה

יב א מיי' פ"ח מהל' תשובה הלכה ז וע"ש בכ"מ:

יג ב מיי' שם פ"ז הלכה ד:

יד ג מיי' שם פ"ג הלכה יד:

טו ד מיי' שם הלכה ח:

טז ה מיי' פ"ג מהל' ת"ת הלכה יג סמג עשין יב טוש"ע י"ד סי' רמו סעיף כה:

הגהות הגר"א

[א] גמ' זה המבזה דיבור שנא' לו למשה. נמחק ב' תיבות לו למשה ונ"ב להם לישראל:

ליקוטי רש"י

ונשכחת צור. לפי שמזכירה בלשון גנאי לשון זונה אמר ונשכחת, כזונה ששכחוה אוהביה, אף היא תשכח מאין סוחרים ותגרים פונים אליה לפי שתהיה חריבה. כימי מלך אחד. ימי דוד שבעים שנה היו ואיני יודע מהו הסימן הזה הניתן כאן [ישעיהו כג, טו]. הנה מלכך יבוא לך. אי אפשר לפותרו אלא על מלך המשיח שנאמר בו ומשלו מים ועד ים ולא מצינו מושל לישראל כזה בימי בית שני. צדיק ונושע. כה'. עני. ענותן. ורוכב על חמור. מדת ענוה היא. ועל עיר. כמו ועירים עשרה (בראשית לב) [זכריה ט, ט]. שמחנו כימות עניתנו. שמחנו לימות משיחנו כמנין ימות שעניתנו בגליות וכמנין שנות אשר ראינו רעה [תהלים צ, טו]. כי יבעל וגו'. ארי כמה דמתיתב עולם עם בתולא כן יתייתבן בגוייכי בנייכי [ישעיהו סב, ה]. עין לא ראתה אלהים אחר זולתך אשר יעשה האלהים למחכה לו מה שעשית אתה למחכה לך כך שמעתי מר' יוסי והנאי, אבל רבותינו שאמרו כל הנביאים כולם לא נתנבאו אלא לימות המשיח אבל לעולם הבא עין לא ראתה וגו' משמעו עין שום נביא לא ראתה את אשר יעשה הקב"ה למחכה לו זולתי עיניך אתה אלהים [ישעיהו סד, ג]. לרחוק ולקרוב. שניהם שוין מי שנתיישן והורגל בתורתי ועבודתי מנעוריו ומי שנתקרב עתה מקרוב לשוב מדרכו הרעה. אמר ה' ורפאתיו. מחליו ומחטאיו [ישעיהו נז, יט]. לא נתנבאו. דברי נחמות שלהן. עין לא ראתה. עין של נביאים לא שלטה לראותו [שבת סג.]. מגלה פנים. בא על דברי תורה בחוצפא ובגלוי עזות פניו כגון (סנהדרין דף לט:) מנשה שהיה יושב ודורש באגדות של דופי לא היה למשה לכתוב אלא ותמנע היתה פלגש וילך ראובן בימי קציר חטים (בראשית ל) [שבועות יג.]. דורש באגדות של דופי כגון מנשה שהיה אומר מה היה לו למשה לומר ותמנע היתה פילגש [כריתות ז.]. זה המיפר ברית בבשר. שהיא מלוה יחידי [שבועות יג.]. את המועדות. חולו של מועד [מכות כג.].

DESPISED THE WORD OF HASHEM, AND HAS VIOLATED HIS COMMANDMENT; that soul SHALL BE UTTERLY CUT OFF. זֶה הָאוֹמֵר אֵין תּוֹרָה מִן הַשָּׁמַיִם – THIS refers to ONE WHO SAYS that THE TORAH IS NOT FROM HEAVEN.[44] דָּבָר אַחֵר – ANOTHER [INTERPRETATION] of this verse: ,,כִּי דְבַר־ה׳ בָּזָה" זֶה אַפִּיקוֹרוֹס – *FOR HE DESPISED THE WORD OF HASHEM* – THIS refers to AN *APIKOROS.*[45] דָּבָר אַחֵר – ANOTHER [INTERPRETATION] of this verse:[46] ,,כִּי דְבַר־ה׳ בָּזָה" זֶה הַמְגַלֶּה פָּנִים בַּתּוֹרָה – *FOR HE DESPISED THE WORD OF HASHEM* – THIS refers to ONE WHO ACTS INSOLENTLY WITH REGARD TO THE TORAH.[45]

The Baraisa expounds upon the next part of the verse: ,,וְאֶת מִצְוָתוֹ הֵפַר" זֶה הַמֵּפֵר בְּרִית בָּשָׂר – *AND HAS VIOLATED HIS COMMANDMENT* – THIS refers to ONE WHO VIOLATES THE COVENANT OF THE FLESH (e.g. he refuses to circumcise himself).[47]

The Baraisa expounds upon the final part of the verse: ,,הִכָּרֵת תִּכָּרֵת" – . . . *that soul SHALL BE UTTERLY CUT OFF* – the repetitive Hebrew expression, הִכָּרֵת תִּכָּרֵת[48] indicates that the sinner will be "cut off" twice: ,,הִכָּרֵת" בָּעוֹלָם הַזֶּה – He shall be *CUT OFF* from life IN THIS WORLD (i.e. he will die prematurely), ,,תִּכָּרֵת" לָעוֹלָם הַבָּא – and his soul *SHALL BE CUT OFF* from life IN THE WORLD TO COME (i.e. he will have no portion in the World to Come).[49] מִכַּאן אָמַר רַבִּי אֶלְעָזָר הַמּוֹדָעִי – BASED ON what is stated HERE in this verse, viz. that one who despises or acts contemptuously with regard to any of God's laws will be cut off from life in this world and in the World to Come, R' ELAZAR HAMODA'I SAID: הַמְחַלֵּל אֶת הַקֳּדָשִׁים – Regarding ONE WHO DESECRATES SACRED PROPERTY,[50] וְהַמְבַזֶּה אֶת הַמּוֹעֲדוֹת – OR DISGRACES THE FESTIVALS,[51] וְהַמֵּפֵר בְּרִיתוֹ שֶׁל אַבְרָהָם אָבִינוּ – OR VIOLATES THE COVENANT OF OUR FOREFATHER ABRAHAM,[52] וְהַמְגַלֶּה פָּנִים בַּתּוֹרָה שֶׁלֹּא כַהֲלָכָה – OR ACTS INSOLENTLY WITH REGARD TO THE TORAH, CONTRARY TO THE LAW,[53] וְהַמַּלְבִּין פְּנֵי חֲבֵירוֹ בָּרַבִּים – OR HUMILIATES HIS FELLOW IN PUBLIC,[54] אַף עַל פִּי שֶׁיֵּשׁ בְּיָדוֹ תּוֹרָה וּמַעֲשִׂים טוֹבִים – EVEN THOUGH HE MAY HAVE IN HIS HAND TORAH AND GOOD DEEDS, אֵין לוֹ חֵלֶק לָעוֹלָם הַבָּא – HE HAS NO PORTION IN THE WORLD TO COME, so severe are these sins.[55]

A Baraisa elaborates on the case of one who denies the Divine origin of the Torah:

תַּנְיָא אִידָךְ – **It was taught in another Baraisa:** ,,כִּי דְבַר־ה׳ בָּזָה" – Scripture states: *FOR HE DESPISED THE WORD OF HASHEM* – זֶה הָאוֹמֵר אֵין תּוֹרָה מִן הַשָּׁמַיִם – THIS refers to ONE WHO SAYS that THE TORAH IS NOT FROM HEAVEN. וַאֲפִילוּ אָמַר כָּל הַתּוֹרָה כּוּלָּהּ מִן הַשָּׁמַיִם – AND EVEN IF HE SAID that THE ENTIRE TORAH IS FROM HEAVEN חוּץ מִפָּסוּק זֶה – WITH THE EXCEPTION OF THIS VERSE, שֶׁלֹּא אֲמָרוֹ הַקָּדוֹשׁ בָּרוּךְ הוּא – WHICH WAS STATED NOT BY THE HOLY ONE, BLESSED IS HE, אֶלָּא מֹשֶׁה מִפִּי עַצְמוֹ – BUT BY MOSES ON HIS OWN, זֶהוּ ,,כִּי דְבַר־ה׳ בָּזָה" – THIS, too, IS an instance of *FOR HE DESPISED THE WORD OF HASHEM.*[56] וַאֲפִילוּ אָמַר כָּל הַתּוֹרָה כּוּלָּהּ מִן הַשָּׁמַיִם – AND, moreover, EVEN IF HE SAID that THE ENTIRE TORAH IS FROM HEAVEN חוּץ מִדִּקְדּוּק זֶה – WITH THE EXCEPTION OF THIS SUBTLETY,[57] מִקַּל וָחֹמֶר זֶה – or OF THIS *KAL VACHOMER,*[58] מִגְּזֵרָה שָׁוָה זוֹ – or OF THIS *GEZEIRAH*

NOTES

44. One despises the Torah by saying that it is not *the word of Hashem* – i.e. that it is not from Heaven (*Maharsha*).

45. The Gemara will discuss the meaning of this term below (99b).

46. See *Dikdukei Soferim,* who derives from *Rashi* below (99b ד״ה איכא) that the text from this point (דָּבָר אַחֵר) until "*Based on . . . here*" etc. (מכאן אמר וכו׳) should be deleted.

47. The Baraisa understands *His commandment,* since it is written in the singular, as referring to circumcision, which was the single commandment imposed upon the patriarch Abraham (*Rashi* to *Shevuos* 13a ד״ה זה המיפר, as interpreted by *Ritva* there; see *Ritva* ibid. for a different interpretation). See *Yad Ramah* here.

48. Which literally means, *cut off,* [*that soul*] *shall be cut off.*

49. See *Ramban* to *Leviticus* 18:29, where he discusses the various aspects of *kares.*

50. I.e. he causes holy objects such as Temple offerings to become profaned and thereby lose their sacred status. When, for example, a person who is *tamei* eats *terumah,* he fails to adhere to the stringent requirements the Torah prescribes, thereby displaying an attitude that indicates that *he despised the word of Hashem* (*Yad Ramah;* cf. *Maharsha* and *Be'er Sheva* here, and *Gra* to *Avos* 3:11, who maintain that this and the following case are not derived from *he despised the word of Hashem*).

51. I.e. he violates the laws of Chol HaMoed, i.e. the Torah's restrictions on work during the Intermediate days of the Passover and Succos Festivals. Since the restrictions on these days are not as severe as those that apply on the first and last days of Passover and Succos, he is lax in complying with them; hence, his attitude indicates that *he despises the word of Hashem* (*Rashi* ibid.; see also *Rashi* here, with *Be'er Sheva*).

However, *Rambam (Hil. Yom Tov* 6:16; see also *Tosafos* to *Chagigah* 18a) understands "the festivals" as referring to Yom Tov itself, and R' Elazar HaModa'i as referring to one who does not honor the Yomim Tovim with special festive meals, indicating his lack of proper respect for these holy days. *Rambam* and *Tosafos* differ from *Rashi* because (unlike *Rashi*) they hold that the prohibition against work during Chol HaMoed is only Rabbinic, and therefore would not carry the harsh punishment specified here (*Be'er Sheva*).

52. I.e. he refuses to circumcise himself, or else attempts to undo his circumcision. This case is indicated by the middle part of our verse: *and has violated His commandment* (*Yad Ramah;* cf. *Rabbeinu Yonah* to *Avos* ibid.).

53. The Gemara will explain this case below (99b). [See *Dikdukei Soferim,* who notes that some commentators delete the words, "contrary to the law," from the text.]

54. Literally: causes his fellow's face to turn white. He embarrasses his fellow so severely that the blood drains from that person's face (*Bava Metzia* 58b).

Rashi (*Avos* ibid.) questions how this last sin could be derived from our verse, and *Rif* and *Ashri* actually delete it from R' Elazar's dictum. See *Be'er Sheva,* who discusses this.

55. *Rambam* writes: *There are certain sins . . . that our Sages have said cause the person accustomed to committing them to lose his share in the World to Come. One ought therefore to distance himself from them and to beware of them. They include . . . one who humiliates his friend in public, one who disgraces the festivals, and one who profanes sacred things. When do we say that these [people] lose their share in the World to Come? If the sinner dies without repenting. However, if he does repent his evil deed and dies a penitent, he is one of those who will enter the World to Come, for nothing can withstand the power of repentance (Hil. Teshuvah 3:14).*

56. In stating דְבַר־ה׳ (*the word of Hashem*) in the singular, and not דִּבְרֵי ה׳ (*the words of Hashem*) in the plural, the Torah teaches that one who denies the Divine origin of even a single verse has committed the sin of despising the Torah (*Maharsha*).

57. I.e. an ostensibly missing or extra letter in the Scriptural text [from which the Rabbis expound a new teaching] (*Rashi, Yad Ramah*).

Maharal explains that the Torah is regarded as a single textual entity, for even one imperfectly written letter disqualifies an entire Torah scroll. Hence, if one denigrates even one textual subtlety (e.g. one apparently extraneous letter), it is as if he denigrates the entire Torah.

58. [The *kal vachomer,* or *a fortiori* argument, is one of the thirteen rules of Biblical exegesis. In this interpretation, inference of a stringency is drawn from a lenient case (*kal*) to a strict case (*chomer*), and inference of a leniency is drawn from a strict case to a lenient one.] Since *kal vachomer* interpretations are not explicitly written in the Torah, but were taught *orally* (בְּדִיבּוּר) by the Sages, they are aptly encompassed by our verse, which speaks of one who *despises the* ***word*** (דְּבַר) *of Hashem* (*Maharsha*).

Margaliyos HaYam points out a problem in our text: Since a *kal vachomer* argument is based on logic rather than tradition, why, indeed, is one not permitted to take issue with it, and argue that a particular *kal vachomer* is not reasonable? Such an argument is not heretical; indeed,

והיינו דא"ל ההוא מינא לרבי אבהו אימתי אתי משיח א"ל לכי חפי להו חשוכא להנהו אינשי א"ל מילט קא לייטת לי א"ל קרא כתיב א) כי הנה החשך יכסה ארץ וערפל לאומים ועליך יזרח ה' וכבודו עליך יראה תניא ר' אליעזר אומר ימות המשיח ארבעים שנה שנאמר ב) ארבעים שנה אקוט בדור רבי אלעזר בן עזריה אומר שבעים שנה שנאמר ג) והיה ביום ההוא ונשכחת צור שבעים שנה כימי מלך אחד איזהו מלך מיוחד הוי אומר זה משיח רבי אומר שלשה דורות שנאמר ד) ייראוך עם שמש ולפני ירח דור דורים א) ר' הילל אומר אין להם משיח לישראל שכבר אכלוהו בימי חזקיה אמר רב יוסף שרא ליה מריה לרבי הילל חזקיה אימת הוה בבית ראשון ואילו זכריה קא מתנבי בבית שני ואמר ה) גילי מאד בת ציון הריעי בת ירושלים הנה מלכך יבא לך צדיק ונושע הוא עני ורוכב על חמור ועל עיר בן אתונות תניא אידך ר' אליעזר אומר ימות המשיח ארבעים שנה כתיב הכא ו) ויענך וירעיבך ויאכילך וכתיב התם ז) שמחנו כימות עניתנו שנות ראינו רעה רבי דוסא אומר ד' מאות שנה כתיב הכא ח) ועבדום וענו אותם ארבע מאות שנה וכתיב התם שמחנו כימות עניתנו רבי אומר ג' מאות וששים וחמש שנה כמנין ימות החמה שנאמר ט) כי יום נקם בלבי ושנת גאולי באה מאי יום נקם בלבי

א"ר יוחנן ללבי גליתי לאבריי לא גליתי ר"ש בן לקיש אמר ללבי גליתי למלאכי השרת לא גליתי תני אבימי בריה דרבי אבהו ימות המשיח לישראל שבעת אלפים שנה שנאמר י) ומשוש חתן על כלה (כן) ישיש עליך (ה') אלהיך אמר רב יהודה אמר שמואל ימות המשיח כמיום שנברא העולם ועד עכשיו שנאמר כ) כימי השמים על הארץ רב נחמן בר יצחק אמר כימי נח עד עכשיו שנאמר ל) כי מי נח זאת לי אשר נשבעתי ב) אמר רבי חייא בר אבא א"ר יוחנן א) כל הנביאים כולן לא נתנבאו אלא לימות המשיח אבל לעולם הבא מ) עין לא ראתה אלהים זולתך (אלהים) יעשה למחכה לו ופליגא דשמואל דאמר שמואל ג) אין בין העולם הזה לימות המשיח אלא שעבוד מלכיות בלבד ואמר רבי חייא בר אבא א"ר יוחנן כל הנביאים לא נתנבאו אלא לבעלי תשובה אבל צדיקים גמורים עין לא ראתה אלהים זולתך ופליגא דרבי אבהו דא"ר אבהו (ד) א"ר) ב) מקום שבעלי תשובה עומדין שם צדיקים אינן עומדין שנאמר נ) שלום שלום לרחוק ולקרוב ברישא רחוק והדר קרוב מאי רחוק רחוק דמעיקרא ומאי קרוב קרוב דמעיקרא ודהשתא ורבי יוחנן אמר לרחוק שהוא רחוק מעבירה קרוב שהוא קרוב מעבירה ונתרחק ממנה וא"ר חייא בר אבא ה) א"ר יוחנן כל הנביאים כולן לא נתנבאו אלא למשיא בתו לתלמיד חכם ולעושה פרקמטיא לתלמיד חכם ולמהנה תלמיד חכם מנכסיו אבל תלמידי חכמים עצמן עין לא ראתה אלהים זולתך ו) מאי עין לא ראתה אמר רבי יהושע בן לוי זה יין המשומר בענביו מששת ימי בראשית ז) ר"ל אמר זה עדן לא ראתה עין מעולם וא"ת אדם היכן דר בגן ואם תאמר גן הוא עדן תלמוד לומר ס) ונהר יוצא מעדן להשקות את הגן: והאומר אין תורה מן השמים וכו': תנו רבנן ע) כי דבר ה' בזה פ) ומצותו הפר הכרת תכרת זה האומר אין תורה מן השמים ד"א ט) כי דבר ה' בזה זה אפיקורוס ד"א כי דבר ה' בזה זה המגלה פנים בתורה ואת מצותו הפר זה המפר ברית בשר הכרת תכרת הכרת בעולם הזה תכרת לעולם הבא מכאן אמר י) רבי אליעזר המודעי ג) המחלל את הקדשים והמבזה את המועדות והמפר בריתו של אברהם אבינו והמגלה פנים בתורה שלא כהלכה והמלבין פני חבירו ברבים אף על פי שיש בידו תורה ומעשים טובים אין לו חלק לעולם הבא תניא אידך כי דבר ה' בזה זה האומר אין תורה מן השמים ד) ואפילו אמר כל התורה כולה מן השמים חוץ מפסוק זה שלא אמרו הקדוש ברוך הוא אלא משה מפי עצמו זהו כי דבר ה' בזה ואפילו אמר כל התורה כולה מן השמים חוץ מדקדוק זה מקל וחומר זה מגזרה שוה זו זה הוא כי דבר ה' בזה תניא היה רבי מאיר אומר הלומד תורה ואינו מלמדה זה הוא דבר ה' בזה רבי נתן אומר כל מי שאינו משגיח על המשנה ר' נהוראי אומר ה) כל שאפשר לעסוק בתורה ואינו עוסק רבי ישמעאל אומר זה העובד עבודת כוכבים מאי משמעה דתנא דבי ר' ישמעאל כי דבר ה' בזה זה המבזה דבור שנאמר [א] לו למשה מסיני פ) אנכי ה' אלהיך לא יהיה לך אלהים אחרים וגו' כ) רבי יהושע בן קרחה אומר כל הלומד תורה ואינו חוזר עליה דומה לאדם שזורע ואינו קוצר רבי יהושע אומר כל הלומד תורה ומשכחה דומה לאשה שיולדת וקוברת רבי עקיבא אומר

זמר

רש"י

ה"ג היינו דאמר ליה ההוא מינא לרבי אבהו וכו': אקוט בדור. אקוט ישראל ואמלוך עליהם כמו נקטיה ארבעים שנה אקוט בדור בדור קטן של ארבעים שנה שהוא משונה מדורות שלפניו ומסתמא היינו משיח ששינוין גדולים יהיו בדורו ופשטיה דקרא מיהא גבי מתי מדבר אבל מדכתיב אקוט משמע אף להבא היה מתנבא: מיוחד. חשוב: ה"ג רבי אומר ג' דורות שנאמר ייראוך עם שמש. כלומר בהדי משיח שכתב בו (תהלים עב) לפני שמש ינון שמו ייראוך ישראל ולפני ירח לפני מלכות בית דוד שנמשל כירח כדכתיב (שם פט) כירח יכון עולם וגו' כמו כן ייראוך דור דורים דור אחד דורים ב' הרי ג': אין להם משיח לישראל. אלא הקב"ה ימלוך בעצמו ויגאלם לבדו: שרי ליה מריה. ימחול לו הקב"ה שאמר דברים אשר לא כן: ואלו זכריה מיהא מתנבא על משיח בבית שני. דכתיב בתרי עשר הנה מלכך יבא לך וגו' ולאו היינו זכריה בן יהוידע הכהן שניבא בבית ראשון אלא זכריה בן ברכיה שהיה במלכות דריוש: רבי אומר שס"ה כמנין ימות החמה דכתיב כי יום נקם בלבי ושנת גאולי באה. [ליום נקם של מרגלים ארבעים יום מה יום נקם של מרגלים] שנה אחת בכל יום כדכתיב (במדבר יד) יום לשנה יום לשנה וגו' כך שנת גאולי באה שנה ליום שנה לכל יום ויום של שנה זו הכתובה שנת גאולי במקרא זה נותנים שנה אחת ואית דגרסי רבי אומר שס"ה אלפים שנה דכתיב שנת גאולי באה ושנה של הקב"ה הכי הוי דכתיב (תהלים צ) כי אלף שנים בעיניך כיום: ועד עכשיו. ימות המשיח:

לאיברי לא גליתי. שלא הוצאתי דבר מפי שהיו איברי יכולין לשמוע אבל בלבי היה טמון הדבר: למען ירבו ימיכם כימי השמים על הארץ. ולא עמדו בארץ כל כך אבל עתידין לעמוד כשיבא משיח: כמשוש חתן. שבעת ימי המשתה כן ישיש עליך שבעת ימים ויומו של הקב"ה אלף שנה: כי מי נח. כמו כימי נח כחשבון השנים שנמלא בידו לאותו זמן שנשבע ה' מעבור מי נח עוד על הארץ כן נשבעתי כפי אותו חשבון נשבעתי מקצף עליך ומגער בך שלא אחריב את עולמי לאחר שיבא משיח עד שיכלה זה הזמן: לא נתנבאו. טובה לישראל: עין לא ראתה. דאין קץ לדבר: צדיקים אינן עומדין. דגדול כחן של בעלי תשובה שאין בריה יכולה לעמוד (לפניהם) [במחילתם]: ברישא לרחוק. שנתרחק מן הקב"ה ואח"כ שב אליו בתשובה והדר שלום לקרוב מעיקרא לדיק גמור דגדול כחן של בעלי תשובה: שהיה רחוק מן העבירה. כל ימיו דהיינו לדיק גמור: אפיקורוס ומגלה פנים. מפורש לקמן: ברית בשר. מילה: מכאן. מן הפסוק הזה שכתוב כי דבר ה' בזה (אמר ר"א וכו' מחלל את הקדשים דמחלל קדשים ומבזה מועדות ומגלה פנים כו' היינו דבר ה' בזה) דבזיון הוא: מפר ברית. היינו את בריתי הפר: מועדות. חולו של מועד: דקדוק זה. חסרות ויתרות: מק"ו [זה] ומגזירה שוה [זו]. [וסא"ל רבו גזירה שוה] לא גמר מרבו: המשנה. זה שעושה כמו שאינה עיקר: זה העובד ע"ז. היינו דבר ה' דבור שדבר הקב"ה בעצמו לישראל דאנכי ולא יהיה לך מפי הגבורה שמענום: חוזר. לשנותה:

א) [לעיל לח:], ב) ברכות לד: שבת סג., ג) ברכות לד: שבת סג. קנא: פסחים סח: לעיל לא., ד) [בברכו' ליתא], ה) ברכות לד., ו) [שם], ז) [בברכו' איתא ר"ש בר נחמני], ח) [ל"ל ואת מצותו], ט) [שבועות יג. ע"ש], י) אבות פ"ג משנה יא, כ) [תוספתא דפרה פ"ג ותוספתא דאהלות פט"ז].

תורה אור השלם

א) כִּי הִנֵּה הַחֹשֶׁךְ יְכַסֶּה אֶרֶץ וַעֲרָפֶל לְאֻמִּים וְעָלַיִךְ יִזְרַח יְיָ וּכְבוֹדוֹ עָלַיִךְ יֵרָאֶה: [ישעיה ס, ב]

ב) אַרְבָּעִים שָׁנָה אָקוּט בְּדוֹר וָאֹמַר עַם תֹּעֵי לֵבָב הֵם וְהֵם לֹא יָדְעוּ דְרָכָי: [תהלים צה, י]

ג) וְהָיָה בַּיּוֹם הַהוּא וְנִשְׁכַּחַת צֹר שִׁבְעִים שָׁנָה כִּימֵי מֶלֶךְ אֶחָד מִקֵּץ שִׁבְעִים שָׁנָה יִהְיֶה לְצֹר כְּשִׁירַת הַזּוֹנָה: [ישעיה כג, טו]

ד) יִירָאוּךָ עִם שָׁמֶשׁ וְלִפְנֵי יָרֵחַ דּוֹר דּוֹרִים: [תהלים עב, ה]

ה) גִּילִי מְאֹד בַּת צִיּוֹן הָרִיעִי בַּת יְרוּשָׁלַיִם הִנֵּה מַלְכֵּךְ יָבוֹא לָךְ צַדִּיק וְנוֹשָׁע הוּא עָנִי וְרֹכֵב עַל חֲמוֹר וְעַל עַיִר בֶּן אֲתֹנוֹת: [זכריה ט, ט]

ו) וַיְעַנְּךָ וַיַּרְעִבֶךָ וַיַּאֲכִלְךָ אֶת הַמָּן אֲשֶׁר לֹא יָדַעְתָּ וְלֹא יָדְעוּן אֲבֹתֶיךָ לְמַעַן הוֹדִיעֲךָ כִּי לֹא עַל הַלֶּחֶם לְבַדּוֹ יִחְיֶה הָאָדָם כִּי עַל כָּל מוֹצָא פִי יְיָ יִחְיֶה הָאָדָם: [דברים ח, ג]

ז) שַׂמְּחֵנוּ כִּימוֹת עִנִּיתָנוּ שְׁנוֹת רָאִינוּ רָעָה: [תהלים צ, טו]

ח) וַיֹּאמֶר לְאַבְרָם יָדֹעַ תֵּדַע כִּי גֵר יִהְיֶה זַרְעֲךָ בְּאֶרֶץ לֹא לָהֶם וַעֲבָדוּם וְעִנּוּ אֹתָם אַרְבַּע מֵאוֹת שָׁנָה: [בראשית טו, יג]

ט) כִּי יוֹם נָקָם בְּלִבִּי וּשְׁנַת גְּאוּלַי בָּאָה: [ישעיה סג, ד]

י) כִּי יִבְעַל בָּחוּר בְּתוּלָה יִבְעָלוּךְ בָּנָיִךְ וּמְשׂוֹשׂ חָתָן עַל כַּלָּה יָשִׂישׂ עָלַיִךְ אֱלֹהָיִךְ: [ישעיה סב, ה]

כ) לְמַעַן יִרְבּוּ יְמֵיכֶם וִימֵי בְנֵיכֶם עַל הָאֲדָמָה אֲשֶׁר נִשְׁבַּע יְיָ לַאֲבֹתֵיכֶם לָתֵת לָהֶם כִּימֵי הַשָּׁמַיִם עַל הָאָרֶץ: [דברים יא, כא]

ל) כִּי מֵי נֹחַ זֹאת לִי אֲשֶׁר נִשְׁבַּעְתִּי מֵעֲבֹר מֵי נֹחַ עוֹד עַל הָאָרֶץ כֵּן נִשְׁבַּעְתִּי מִקְּצֹף עָלַיִךְ וּמִגְּעָר בָּךְ: [ישעיה נד, ט]

מ) וּמֵעוֹלָם לֹא שָׁמְעוּ לֹא הֶאֱזִינוּ עַיִן לֹא רָאָתָה אֱלֹהִים זוּלָתְךָ יַעֲשֶׂה לִמְחַכֵּה לוֹ: [ישעיה סד, ג]

נ) בּוֹרֵא נִיב שְׂפָתָיִם שָׁלוֹם שָׁלוֹם לָרָחוֹק וְלַקָּרוֹב אָמַר יְיָ וּרְפָאתִיו: [ישעיה נז, יט]

ס) וְנָהָר יֹצֵא מֵעֵדֶן לְהַשְׁקוֹת אֶת הַגָּן וּמִשָּׁם יִפָּרֵד וְהָיָה לְאַרְבָּעָה רָאשִׁים: [בראשית ב, י] ע) כִּי דְבַר יְיָ בָּזָה וְאֶת מִצְוָתוֹ הֵפַר הִכָּרֵת תִּכָּרֵת הַנֶּפֶשׁ הַהִוא עֲוֹנָה בָהּ: [במדבר טו, לא] פ) אָנֹכִי יְיָ אֱלֹהֶיךָ אֲשֶׁר הוֹצֵאתִיךָ מֵאֶרֶץ מִצְרַיִם מִבֵּית עֲבָדִים: לֹא יִהְיֶה לְךָ אֱלֹהִים אֲחֵרִים עַל פָּנָי: [שמות כ, ב-ג]

עין משפט נר מצוה

יב א מיי' פ"ח מהל' תשובה הלכה ז וע"ש בכ"מ:
יג ב מיי' שם פ"ז הלכה ד:
יד ג מיי' שם פ"ג הלכה יד:
טו ד מיי' שם הלכה ח:
טז ה מיי' פ"ג מהל' ת"ת הלכה יג סמג עשין יב טוש"ע י"ד סי' רמו סעיף כה:

הגהות הגר"א

[א] גמ' זה המבזה דיבור שנא' לו למשה. נמחק ב' תיבות לו למשה וצ"ב להם לישראל:

ליקוטי רש"י

ונשכחת צור. לפי שמזכירה בלשון גנאי לשון זונה אמר ונשכחת, כזונה ששכחוה אוהביה, אף היא תשכח מאין סוחרים ותגרים פונים אליה לפי שתהיה חריבה. כימי מלך אחד. ימי דוד שבעים שנה היו ואיני יודע מהו הסימן הזה הניתן כאן [ישעיהו כג, טו]. הנה מלכך יבוא לך. אי אפשר לפותרו אלא על מלך המשיח שנאמר בו ומשלו מים ועד ים ולא מצינו מושל לישראל כזה בימי בית שני. צדיק ונושע. בה'. עני. ענותן. ורוכב על חמור. מדת ענוה היא. ועל עיר. כמו ועירים עשרה (בראשית לב) [זכריה ט, ט]. שמחנו כימות עניתנו. שמחנו לימות משיחנו כמנין ימות שעניתנו בגליות וכמנין שנות אשר ראינו רעה [תהלים צ, טו]. כי יבעל וגו'. ארי כמה דמתיתב עולם עם בתולתא כן יתייתבין בגוייכי בנייכי [ישעיהו סב, ה]. עין לא ראתה אלהים אחר זולתך אשר יעשה האלהים למחכה לו מה שעשית אתה למחכה לך כך שמעתי מר' יוסי והגאוני, אבל רבותינו שאמרו כל הנביאים כולם לא נתנבאו אלא לימות המשיח אבל לעולם הבא עין לא ראתה וגו' משמעו עין שום נביא לא ראתה את אשר יעשה הקב"ה למחכה לו זולתי עיניך אתה אלהים [ישעיהו סד, ג]. לרחוק ולקרוב. שניהם שוין מי שנתיישן והורגל בתורתי ועבודתי מנעוריו ומי שנתקרב עתה מקרוב לשוב מדרכו הרעה. אמר ה' ורפאתיו. מחליו ומחטאיו [ישעיהו נז, יט]. לא נתנבאו. דברי נחמות שלהן. עין לא ראתה. עין של נביאים לא שלטה לראותו [שבת סג.]. מגלה פנים. בא על דברי תורה בחוצפה ובגלוי עזות פניו כגון (סנהדרין דף לט:) מנשה שהיה יושב ודורש באגדות של דופי לא היה למשה לכתוב אלא ותמנע היתה פלגש וילך ראובן בימי קציר חטים (בראשית ל) [שבועות יג.]. דורש באגדות של דופי כגון מנשה שהיה אומר מה היה לו למשה לומר ותמנע היתה פילגש [כריתות ז.]. זה המיפר ברית בבשר. שהיא מלוה יחידי [שבועות יג.]. את המועדות. חולו של מועד [מכות כג.].

SHAVAH,[59] זֶה הוּא ,,כִּי דְבַר־ה׳ בָּזָה'' – **THIS**, too, **IS** an instance of ***FOR HE DESPISED THE WORD OF HASHEM.***

Another Baraisa applies our verse to different sins:

תַּנְיָא – It was taught in a Baraisa: **הָיָה רַבִּי מֵאִיר אוֹמֵר – R' MEIR WAS WONT TO SAY:** **הַלּוֹמֵד תּוֹרָה וְאֵינוֹ מְלַמְּדָהּ** – Regarding **ONE WHO LEARNS TORAH BUT DOES NOT TEACH IT** to others, **זֶה הוּא ,,דְבַר־ה׳ בָּזָה''** – **THIS IS** an instance of ***FOR HE DESPISED THE WORD OF HASHEM.***[60] **רַבִּי נָתָן אוֹמֵר – R' NASSAN SAYS:** **כָּל מִי שֶׁאֵינוֹ מַשְׁגִּיחַ עַל הַמִּשְׁנָה** – Our verse refers to **ANYONE WHO DOES NOT HEED THE MISHNAH.**[61] **רַבִּי נְהוֹרַאי אוֹמֵר – R' NEHORAI SAYS:** **כָּל שֶׁאֶפְשָׁר לַעֲסוֹק בַּתּוֹרָה וְאֵינוֹ עוֹסֵק** – The verse refers to **ANYONE WHO IS ABLE TO ENGAGE IN TORAH** study **AND DOES NOT ENGAGE** in it.[62] **רַבִּי יִשְׁמָעֵאל אוֹמֵר – R' YISHMAEL SAYS:** **זֶה הָעוֹבֵד עֲבוֹדַת כּוֹכָבִים** – **THIS** verse refers to **ONE WHO WORSHIPS IDOLS.** **מַאי מַשְׁמָעָהּ – HOW IS [IDOLATRY] INDICATED** in the verse? **דְּתָנָא דְּבֵי רַבִּי יִשְׁמָעֵאל** – It is indicated in accordance with that **WHICH** one **OF** the sages from **THE ACADEMY OF R' YISHMAEL TAUGHT:** **,,כִּי דְבַר־ה׳ בָּזָה''** – Scripture states, ***FOR HE DESPISED THE WORD OF HASHEM,*** **זֶה הַמְבַזֶּה דִּבּוּר שֶׁנֶּאֱמַר לוֹ לְמֹשֶׁה מִסִּינַי** – and **THIS** refers to **ONE WHO DESPISES THE UTTERANCE SPOKEN** by God **TO MOSES**[63] **ON** Mt. **SINAI:**[64] **,,אָנֹכִי ה׳ אֱלֹהֶיךָ . . . לֹא־יִהְיֶה לְךָ אֱלֹהִים אֲחֵרִים וגו׳ ''** – ***I AM HASHEM, YOUR GOD . . . YOU SHALL NOT RECOGNIZE THE GODS OF OTHERS*** **etc.**[65]

Having cited three Sages who condemned those who do not learn Torah properly, the Gemara now presents three other Sages who evaluate various methods of Torah study:

רַבִּי יְהוֹשֻׁעַ בֶּן קָרְחָה אוֹמֵר – It was taught in the *Tosefta:*[66] **R' YEHOSHUA BEN KARCHAH SAYS:** **כָּל הַלּוֹמֵד תּוֹרָה וְאֵינוֹ חוֹזֵר עָלֶיהָ – WHOEVER LEARNS TORAH BUT DOES NOT REVIEW [HIS LEARNING]** **דּוֹמֶה לְאָדָם שֶׁזּוֹרֵעַ וְאֵינוֹ קוֹצֵר – IS LIKE A PERSON WHO PLANTS BUT DOES NOT HARVEST.**[67] **רַבִּי יְהוֹשֻׁעַ אוֹמֵר – R' YEHOSHUA SAYS:** **כָּל הַלּוֹמֵד תּוֹרָה וּמְשַׁכְּחָהּ – WHOEVER LEARNS TORAH AND** then **FORGETS [HIS LEARNING]** **דּוֹמֶה לְאִשָּׁה שֶׁיּוֹלֶדֶת וְקוֹבֶרֶת – IS LIKE A WOMAN WHO GIVES BIRTH AND** then **BURIES** the child.[68] **רַבִּי עֲקִיבָא אוֹמֵר – R' AKIVA SAYS:**

NOTES

there are many such opinions in the Gemara. *Margaliyos HaYam* therefore contends that the word זֶה, *this*, was mistakenly inserted in the text (indeed the word is missing in older editions of the Gemara; see *Dikdukei Soferim,* note 8). Accordingly, the Baraisa refers to one who denies the very rule of *kal vachomer,* falsely claiming that no law may be derived through this hermeneutical method because it was not given by God to Moses on Mt. Sinai. Denying this tradition is indeed a denigration of the Torah.

[*Talmud Yerushalmi* states, however, that the Baraisa does not speak of the denial of a *kal vachomer* argument taught by oral tradition, but of the denial of a *kal vachomer* explicitly written in the Torah (e.g. *Genesis* 4:24), which is clearly a rejection of God's word.]

59. This is another of the thirteen rules of Biblical exegesis. If a similar word or phrase occurs in two otherwise unrelated passages in the Torah, the principle of *gezeirah shavah* teaches that these passages are linked to one another, and the laws of one passage are applied to the other. However, only certain specific words, related by God to Moses on Mt. Sinai, serve as the basis for a *gezeirah shavah.* The Baraisa speaks of one who, upon being taught a *gezeirah shavah,* denies that God related such words to Moses (*Rashi;* cf. *Margaliyos HaYam,* and see previous note), and thus denies a fundamental aspect of the **oral** tradition. Such a transgression is certainly alluded to by our verse, which speaks of one who *despises the* ***word*** *of Hashem* (see *Maharsha*).

60. One enhances the honor of the Torah by disseminating its teachings to others. Hence, one who refuses to impart what he has learned demonstrates that he despises the Torah, *the word of Hashem,* for he refrains from contributing to its glorification (*Maharal;* see *Maharsha*).

61. I.e. he does not regard the Mishnah as being the authoritative exposition of Scripture (*Rashi, Yad Ramah*).

Alternatively, the Mishnah, because it delineates the mitzvos of the Torah, is considered "the word of Hashem." *Pilpul* (Talmudic debate that is not based on the Written Law), is not "the word of Hashem" because it emanates from the rational human mind. Hence, one who engages in excessive *pilpul* and ignores the study of Mishnah is viewed as a person who *despises the word of Hashem* (*Maharal*).

Alternatively, the Mishnah is the explanation of the Written Law. One who does not scrutinize it [demonstrates that he does not care to know Hashem's word] – a denigration thereof (*Maharsha*).

According to *Margaliyos HaYam,* the word "Mishnah" as it appears in the Baraisa does not refer to the Mishnah of R' Yehudah HaNasi; rather, it means repetition. Thus, R' Nassan is criticizing the person who does not review his studies, for he will surely forget what he learned.

62. One who is free to engage in Torah study and instead involves himself with idle pursuits demonstrates his disrespect for the Torah (*Maharsha*).

63. *Hagahos HaGra* emends לוֹ לְמֹשֶׁה ("to Moses") to לָהֶם לְיִשְׂרָאֵל ("to Israel"), for the first two of the ten Commandments were spoken to the entire Jewish people by God Himself.

64. *Exodus* 20:2,3 and *Deuteronomy* 5:6,7. The following verses are the first two of the Ten Commandments.

65. An idolater *denigrates* what was literally *Hashem's word,* for the first two of the Ten Commandments, which teach belief in God and prohibit idolatry, were told to the Jews by God Himself [see *Makkos* 24a and *Shavuos* 20b] (*Rashi*).

66. *Oholos* 16:4 and *Parah* 4:4.

67. One who fails to harvest what he has planted has nothing to show for his efforts. Studying of a Torah subject only once will prove similarly futile and fruitless (*Maharsha*). *Maharal* explains that when one harvests a crop he separates it from the earth to which it had been attached. Similarly, when one reviews his studies he refines the information in his mind, separating the information from the "materiality" of distortion and misperception. One who does not review his studies will not fully grasp the material he has learned.

68. Forgetting is likened to death. Hence, just as in the latter case it is as if the child was never born, so in the former case it is as if the Torah subject was never learned (*Maharsha*). Forgetting one's learning, then, is worse than not reviewing it, for one can review belatedly (just as a farmer can harvest belatedly). Once knowledge has been completely forgotten, however, it is gone, as is a child who died (*Rif* in *Ein Yaakov*). See *Ahavas Ayson* for a different explanation of the relationship between the two Talmudic statements.

Forgetting one's learning is indeed a serious matter, as it may in certain circumstances involve transgressing a prohibition of the Torah; see *Avos* 3:8 and *Menachos* 99b. In any case, its being compared to the death of a child intimates that forgetting Torah is tantamount to losing one's life, for it is only through Torah that a person is linked to eternity and merits the World to Come (*Chofetz Chaim al HaTorah, Deuteronomy* 4:11).

והיינו דא"ל ההוא מינא לרבי אבהו אימתי אתי משיח א"ל לכי חפי להו חשוכא להנהו אינשי א"ל מילט קא לייטת לי א"ל קרא כתיב (א) כי הנה החשך יכסה ארץ וערפל לאומים ועליך יזרח ה' וכבודו עליך יראה תניא ר' אליעזר אומר ימות המשיח ארבעים שנה שנאמר (ב) ארבעים שנה אקוט בדור רבי אלעזר בן עזריה אומר שבעים שנה שנאמר (ג) והיה ביום ההוא ונשכחת צור שבעים שנה כימי מלך אחד איזהו מלך מיוחד הוי אומר זה משיח רבי אומר שלשה דורות שנאמר (ד) ייראוך עם שמש ולפני ירח דור דורים [א] ר' הילל אומר אין להם משיח לישראל שכבר אכלוהו בימי חזקיה אמר רב יוסף שרא ליה מריה לרבי הילל חזקיה אימת הוה בבית ראשון ואילו זכריה קא מתנבי בבית שני ואמר (ה) גילי מאד בת ציון הריעי בת ירושלים הנה מלכך יבא לך צדיק ונושע הוא עני ורוכב על חמור ועל עיר בן אתונות תניא אידך ר' אליעזר אומר ימות המשיח ארבעים שנה כתיב הכא (ו) ויענך וירעיבך ויאכילך וכתיב התם (ז) שמחנו כימות עניתנו שנות ראינו רעה רבי דוסא אומר ד' מאות שנה כתיב הכא (ח) ועבדום וענו אותם ארבע מאות שנה וכתיב התם שמחנו כימות עניתנו רבי אומר ג' מאות וששים וחמש שנה כמנין ימות החמה שנאמר (ט) כי יום נקם בלבי ושנת גאולי באה מאי יום נקם בלבי א"ר יוחנן ללבי גליתי לאבריי לא גליתי ר"ש בן לקיש אמר ללבי גליתי למלאכי השרת לא גליתי תני אבימי בריה דרבי אבהו ימות המשיח לישראל שבעת אלפים שנה שנאמר (י) ומשוש חתן על כלה (כן) ישיש עליך (ה') אלהיך אמר רב יהודה אמר שמואל ימות המשיח כמיום שנברא העולם ועד עכשיו שנאמר (כ) כימי השמים על הארץ רב נחמן בר יצחק אמר כימי נח עד עכשיו שנאמר (ל) כי מי נח זאת לי אשר נשבעתי [ג] אמר רבי חייא בר אבא א"ר יוחנן [א] כל הנביאים כולן לא נתנבאו אלא לימות המשיח אבל לעולם הבא (מ) עין לא ראתה אלהים זולתך (אלהים) יעשה למחכה לו ופליגא דשמואל דאמר שמואל [ג] אין בין העולם הזה לימות המשיח אלא שעבוד מלכיות בלבד ואמר רבי חייא בר אבא א"ר יוחנן כל הנביאים לא נתנבאו אלא לבעלי תשובה אבל צדיקים גמורים עין לא ראתה אלהים זולתך ופליגא דרבי אבהו דא"ר אבהו (ד) א"ר) [ב] מקום שבעלי תשובה עומדין שם צדיקים אינן עומדין שנאמר (נ) שלום שלום לרחוק ולקרוב ברישא רחוק והדר קרוב מאי רחוק רחוק דמעיקרא ומאי קרוב קרוב דמעיקרא ודהשתא ורבי יוחנן אמר לרחוק שהוא רחוק מעבירה קרוב שהוא קרוב מעבירה ונתרחק ממנה וא"ר חייא בר אבא [ה] א"ר יוחנן כל הנביאים כולן לא נתנבאו אלא למשיא בתו לתלמיד חכם ולעושה פרקמטיא לתלמיד חכם ולמהנה תלמיד חכם מנכסיו אבל תלמידי חכמים עצמן עין לא ראתה אלהים זולתך [י] מאי עין לא ראתה אמר רבי יהושע בן לוי זה יין המשומר בענביו מששת ימי בראשית [י] ר"ל אמר זה עדן לא ראתה עין מעולם וא"ת אדם היכן דר בגן ואם תאמר גן הוא עדן תלמוד לומר (ס) ונהר יוצא מעדן להשקות את הגן: והאומר אין תורה מן השמים וכו': תנו רבנן (ע) כי דבר ה' בזה (פ) ומצותו הפר הכרת תכרת זה האומר אין תורה מן השמים ד"א (ט) כי דבר ה' בזה זה אפיקורוס ד"א כי דבר ה' בזה זה המגלה פנים בתורה ואת מצותו הפר זה המפר ברית בשר הכרת תכרת הכרת בעולם הזה תכרת לעולם הבא מכאן אמר [י] רבי אליעזר המודעי [ג] המחלל את הקדשים והמבזה את המועדות והמפר בריתו של אברהם אבינו והמגלה פנים בתורה שלא כהלכה והמלבין פני חבירו ברבים אף על פי שיש בידו תורה ומעשים טובים אין לו חלק לעולם הבא תניא אידך כי דבר ה' בזה זה האומר אין תורה מן השמים [ד] ואפילו אמר כל התורה כולה מן השמים חוץ מפסוק זה שלא אמרו הקדוש ברוך הוא אלא משה מפי עצמו זהו כי דבר ה' בזה ואפילו אמר כל התורה כולה מן השמים חוץ מדקדוק זה מקל וחומר זה מגזרה שוה זו זה הוא כי דבר ה' בזה תניא היה רבי מאיר אומר הלומד תורה ואינו מלמדה זה הוא דבר ה' בזה רבי נתן אומר כל מי שאינו משגיח על המשנה ר' נהוראי אומר [ה] כל שאפשר לעסוק בתורה ואינו עוסק רבי ישמעאל אומר זה העובד עבודת כוכבים מאי משמעה דתנא דבי ר' ישמעאל כי דבר ה' בזה זה המבזה דבור שנאמר [א] לו למשה מסיני (פ) אנכי ה' אלהיך לא יהיה לך אלהים אחרים וגו' [כ] רבי יהושע בן קרחה אומר כל הלומד תורה ואינו חוזר עליה דומה לאדם שזורע ואינו קוצר רבי יהושע אומר כל הלומד תורה ומשכחה דומה לאשה שיולדת וקוברת רבי עקיבא אומר

זמר

רש"י

ה"ג היינו דאמר ליה ההוא מינא לרבי אבהו וכו': אקוט בדור. אקח ישראל ואמלוך עליהם כמו נקטיה ארבעים שנה אקוט בדור בדור קטן של ארבעים שנה שהוא משונה מדורות שלפניו ומסתמא היינו משיח ששינוין גדולים יהיו בדורו ופשטיה דקרא מיהא גבי מתי מדבר אבל מדכתיב אקוט משמע אף להבא היה מתנבא: מיוחד. חשוב: ה"ג רבי אומר ג' דורות שנאמר ייראוך עם שמש. כלומר בהדי משיח שכתב בו (תהלים עב) לפני שמש ינון שמו ייראוך ישראל ולפני ירח לפני מלכות בית דוד שנמשל כירח כדכתיב (שם פט) כירח יכון עולם וגו' כמו כן ייראוך דור דורים דור אחד דורים ב' הרי ג': אין להם משיח לישראל. אלא הקב"ה ימלוך בעצמו ויגאלם לבדו: שרי ליה מריה. ימחול לו הקב"ה שאמר דברים אשר לא כן: ואלו זכריה מיהא מתנבא על משיח בבית שני. דכתיב בתרי עשר הנה מלכך יבא לך וגו' ולאו היינו זכריה בן יהוידע הכהן שניבא בבית ראשון אלא זכריה בן ברכיה שהיה במלכות דריוש: רבי אומר שס"ה כמנין ימות החמה דכתיב כי יום נקם בלבי ושנת גאולי באה. [ליום נקם של מרגלים ארבעים יום מה יום נקם של מרגלים] שנה אחת בכל יום כדכתיב (במדבר יד) יום לשנה יום לשנה וגו' כך שנת גאולי באה שנה ליום שנה ליום שלכל יום ויום של שנה זו הכתובה שנת גאולי במקרא זה נותנים שנה אחת ואית דגרסי רבי אומר שס"ה אלפים שנה דכתיב שנת גאולי באה ושנה של הקב"ה הכי הוי דכתיב (תהלים צ) כי אלף שנים בעיניך כיום: ועד עכשיו. ימות המשיח: לאיברי לא גליתי. שלא הוצאתי דבר מפי שהיו איברי יכולין לשמוע אבל בלבי היה טמון הדבר: למען ירבו ימיכם כימי השמים על הארץ. ולא עמדו בארצם כל כך אבל עתידין לעמוד כשיבא משיח: כמשוש חתן. שבעת ימי המשתה כן ישיש עליך שבעת ימים ויומו של הקב"ה אלף שנה: כי מי נח. כמו כימי נח כחשבון השנים שנמלא בידו לאותו זמן שנשבע ה' מעבור מי נח עוד על הארץ כן נשבעתי כפי אותו חשבון נשבעתי מקצף עליך ומגער בך שלא אחריב את עולמי לאחר שיבא משיח עד שיכלה זה הזמן: לא נתנבאו. טובה לישראל: עין לא ראתה. דאין קץ לדבר: צדיקים אינן עומדין. דגדול כחן של בעלי תשובה שאין בריה יכולה לעמוד (לפניהם) [במחילתם]: ברישא לרחוק. שנתרחק מן הקב"ה ואח"כ שב אליו בתשובה והדר שלום לקרוב מעיקרא לצדיק גמור דגדול כחן של בעלי תשובה: שהיה רחוק מן העבירה. כל ימיו דהיינו לצדיק גמור: אפיקורוס ומגלה פנים. מפורש לקמן: ברית בשר. מילה: מכאן. מן הפסוק הזה שכתוב כי דבר ה' בזה (אמר ר"א וכו' מחלל את הקדשים דמחלל קדשים ומבזה מועדות ומגלה פנים כו' היינו דבר ה' בזה) דבזיון הוא: מפר ברית. היינו את בריתי הפר: מועדות. חולו של מועד: דקדוק זה. חסרות ויתרות: מק"ו [זה] ומגזירה שוה [זו]. [ושא"ל רבו גזירה שוה] לא גמר מרבו: המשנה. זה שעושה כמו שאינה עיקר: זה העובד ע"ז. היינו דבר ה' דבור שדבר הקב"ה בעצמו לישראל דאנכי ולא יהיה לך מפי הגבורה שמענום: חוזר. לשנותה:

זמר

מסורת הש"ס

א) [לעיל לח:], ב) ברכות לד: שבת סג., ג) ברכות לד: שבת סג. קנא: פסחים סח: לעיל לא:, ד) [בברכו' ליתא], ה) ברכות לד., ו) [שם], ז) [בברכו' איתא ר"ש בר נחמני], ח) [נ"ל ואת מצותו], ט) [שבועות יג. ע"ש], י) אבות פ"ג משנה יא, כ) [תוספתא דפרה פ"ג ותוספתא דאהלות פט"ז].

תורה אור השלם

א) כִּי הִנֵּה הַחֹשֶׁךְ יְכַסֶּה אֶרֶץ וַעֲרָפֶל לְאֻמִּים וְעָלַיִךְ יִזְרַח יְיָ וּכְבוֹדוֹ עָלַיִךְ יֵרָאֶה: [ישעיה ס, ב]

ב) אַרְבָּעִים שָׁנָה אָקוּט בְּדוֹר וָאֹמַר עַם תֹּעֵי לֵבָב הֵם וְהֵם לֹא יָדְעוּ דְרָכָי: [תהלים צה, י]

ג) וְהָיָה בַּיּוֹם הַהוּא וְנִשְׁכַּחַת צֹר שִׁבְעִים שָׁנָה כִּימֵי מֶלֶךְ אֶחָד מִקֵּץ שִׁבְעִים שָׁנָה יִהְיֶה לְצֹר כְּשִׁירַת הַזּוֹנָה: [ישעיה כג, טו]

ד) יִירָאוּךָ עִם שָׁמֶשׁ וְלִפְנֵי יָרֵחַ דּוֹר דּוֹרִים: [תהלים עב, ה]

ה) גִּילִי מְאֹד בַּת צִיּוֹן הָרִיעִי בַּת יְרוּשָׁלַיִם הִנֵּה מַלְכֵּךְ יָבוֹא לָךְ צַדִּיק וְנוֹשָׁע הוּא עָנִי וְרֹכֵב עַל חֲמוֹר וְעַל עַיִר בֶּן אֲתֹנוֹת: [זכריה ט, ט]

ו) וַיְעַנְּךָ וַיַּרְעִבֶךָ וַיַּאֲכִלְךָ אֶת הַמָּן אֲשֶׁר לֹא יָדַעְתָּ וְלֹא יָדְעוּן אֲבֹתֶיךָ לְמַעַן הוֹדִיעֲךָ כִּי לֹא עַל הַלֶּחֶם לְבַדּוֹ יִחְיֶה הָאָדָם כִּי עַל כָּל מוֹצָא פִי יְיָ יִחְיֶה הָאָדָם: [דברים ח, ג]

ז) שַׂמְּחֵנוּ כִּימוֹת עִנִּיתָנוּ שְׁנוֹת רָאִינוּ רָעָה: [תהלים צ, טו]

ח) וַיֹּאמֶר לְאַבְרָם יָדֹעַ תֵּדַע כִּי גֵר יִהְיֶה זַרְעֲךָ בְּאֶרֶץ לֹא לָהֶם וַעֲבָדוּם וְעִנּוּ אֹתָם אַרְבַּע מֵאוֹת שָׁנָה: [בראשית טו, יג]

ט) כִּי יוֹם נָקָם בְּלִבִּי וּשְׁנַת גְּאוּלַי בָּאָה: [ישעיה סג, ד]

י) כִּי יִבְעַל בָּחוּר בְּתוּלָה יִבְעָלוּךְ בָּנָיִךְ וּמְשׂוֹשׂ חָתָן עַל כַּלָּה יָשִׂישׂ עָלַיִךְ אֱלֹהָיִךְ: [ישעיה סב, ה]

כ) לְמַעַן יִרְבּוּ יְמֵיכֶם וִימֵי בְנֵיכֶם עַל הָאֲדָמָה אֲשֶׁר נִשְׁבַּע יְיָ לַאֲבֹתֵיכֶם לָתֵת לָהֶם כִּימֵי הַשָּׁמַיִם עַל הָאָרֶץ: [דברים יא, כא]

ל) כִּי מֵי נֹחַ זֹאת לִי אֲשֶׁר נִשְׁבַּעְתִּי מֵעֲבֹר מֵי נֹחַ עוֹד עַל הָאָרֶץ כֵּן נִשְׁבַּעְתִּי מִקְּצֹף עָלַיִךְ וּמִגְּעָר בָּךְ: [ישעיה נד, ט]

מ) וּמֵעוֹלָם לֹא שָׁמְעוּ לֹא הֶאֱזִינוּ עַיִן לֹא רָאָתָה אֱלֹהִים זוּלָתְךָ יַעֲשֶׂה לִמְחַכֵּה לוֹ: [ישעיה סד, ג]

נ) בּוֹרֵא נִיב שְׂפָתָיִם שָׁלוֹם שָׁלוֹם לָרָחוֹק וְלַקָּרוֹב אָמַר יְיָ וּרְפָאתִיו: [ישעיה נז, יט]

ס) וְנָהָר יֹצֵא מֵעֵדֶן לְהַשְׁקוֹת אֶת הַגָּן וּמִשָּׁם יִפָּרֵד וְהָיָה לְאַרְבָּעָה רָאשִׁים: [בראשית ב, י] ע) כִּי דְבַר יְיָ בָּזָה וְאֶת מִצְוָתוֹ הֵפַר הִכָּרֵת תִּכָּרֵת הַנֶּפֶשׁ הַהִוא עֲוֹנָה בָהּ: [במדבר טו, לא] פ) אָנֹכִי יְיָ אֱלֹהֶיךָ אֲשֶׁר הוֹצֵאתִיךָ מֵאֶרֶץ מִצְרַיִם מִבֵּית עֲבָדִים: לֹא יִהְיֶה לְךָ אֱלֹהִים אֲחֵרִים עַל פָּנָי: [שמות כ, ב-ג]

עין משפט נר מצוה

יב א מיי' פ"ח מהל' תשובה הלכה ז וע"ש בכ"מ:

יג ב מיי' שם פ"ז הלכה ד:

יד ג מיי' שם פ"ג הלכה יד:

טו ד מיי' שם הלכה ח:

טז ה מיי' פ"ג מהל' ת"ת הלכה יג סמג עשין יב טוש"ע י"ד סי' רמו סעיף כה:

הגהות הגר"א

[א] גמ' זה המבזה דיבור שנא' לו למשה. נמחק ב' תיבות לו למשה ונ"ב להם לישראל:

ליקוטי רש"י

ונשכחת צור. לפי שמזכירה בלשון גנאי לשון זונה אמר ונשכחת, כזונה ששכחוה אוהביה, אף היא תשכח מאין סוחרים ותגרים פונים אליה לפי שתהיה חריבה. כימי מלך אחד. ימי דוד שבעים שנה היו ואיני יודע מהו הסימן הזה הניתן כאן [ישעיהו כג, טו]. הנה מלכך יבוא לך. אי אפשר לפותרו אלא על מלך המשיח שנאמר בו ומשלו מים ועד ים ולא מצינו מושל לישראל כזה בימי בית שני. צדיק ונושע. כה'. עני. ענותן. ורוכב על חמור. מדת ענוה היא. ועל עיר. כמו ועירים עשרה (בראשית לב) [זכריה ט, ט]. שמחנו כימות עניתנו. שמחנו לימות משיחנו כמנין ימות שעניתנו בגליות וכמנין שנות אשר ראינו רעה [תהלים צ, טו]. כי יבעל וגו'. אדי כמה דמתיתב עולם עם בתולתא כן יתייתבון בגוייכי בנייכי [ישעיהו סב, ה]. עין לא ראתה אלהים אחר זולתך אשר יעשה האלהים למחכה לו מה שעשית אתה למחכה לך כך שמעתי מר' יוסי והנלאי, אבל רבותינו שאמרו כל הנביאים כולם לא נתנבאו אלא לימות המשיח אבל לעולם הבא עין לא ראתה וגו' משמעו עין שום נביא לא ראתה את אשר יעשה הקב"ה למחכה לו זולתי עיניך אתה אלהים [ישעיהו סד, ג]. לרחוק ולקרוב. שניהם שוין מי שנתיישן והורגל בתורתי ועבודתי מנעוריו ומי שנתקרב עתה מקרוב לשוב מדרכו הרעה. אמר ה' ורפאתיו. מחליו ומחטאיו [ישעיהו נז, יט]. לא נתנבאו. דברי נחמות שלהן. עין לא ראתה. עין של נביאים לא שלטה לראותו [שבת סג.]. מגלה פנים. בא על דברי תורה בחוצפא ובגלוי עזות פניו כגון (סנהדרין דף לט:) מנשה שהיה יושב ודורש באגדות של דופי לא היה למשה לכתוב אלא ותמנע היתה פלגש וילך ראובן בימי קציר חטים (בראשית ל) [שבועות יג.]. דורש באגדות של דופי כגון מנשה שהיה אומר מה היה לו למשה לומר ותמנע היתה פילגש [כריתות ז.]. זה המיפר ברית בבשר. שהיא מצוה יחידי [שבועות יג.]. את המועדות. חולו של מועד [מכות כג.].

עין משפט
נר מצוה

יז א מיי' פ"ג מהלכות תשובה הלכה יד ע' בכ"מ:
יח ב מיי' שם הלכה יא:

זמר בכל יום זמר בכל יום אמר רב יצחק בר אבודימי מאי קרא שנאמר א) נפש עמל עמלה לו כי אכף עליו פיהו הוא עמל במקום זה ותורתו עומלת לו במקום אחר אמר רבי אלעזר א) כל אדם לעמל נברא שנאמר ב) כי אדם לעמל יולד איני יודע אם לעמל פה נברא אם לעמל מלאכה נברא כשהוא אומר כי אכף עליו פיהו הוי אומר לעמל פה נברא ועדיין איני יודע אם לעמל תורה אם לעמל שיחה כשהוא אומר ג) לא ימוש ספר התורה הזה מפיך הוי אומר לעמל תורה נברא והיינו דאמר רבא כולהו גופי דרופתקי נינהו טובי לדזכי דהוי דרופתקי דאורייתא ד) ונואף אשה חסר לב אמר [א] ריש לקיש זה הלומד תורה לפרקים שנאמר ה) כי נעים כי תשמרם בבטנך יכונו יחדיו על שפתיך ת"ר ו) והנפש אשר תעשה ביד רמה זה מנשה בן חזקיה שהיה יושב ודורש בהגדות של דופי אמר וכי לא היה לו למשה לכתוב אלא ז) ואחות לוטן תמנע ח) ותמנע היתה פלגש לאליפז ט) וילך ראובן בימי קציר חטים וימצא דודאים בשדה יצאה ב"ק ואמרה לו י) תשב באחיך תדבר בבן אמך תתן דופי אלה עשית והחרשתי דמית היות אהיה כמוך אוכיחך ואערכה לעיניך ועליו מפורש בקבלה כ) הוי מושכי העון בחבלי השוא וכעבות העגלה חטאה מאי כעבות העגלה ג) א"ר אסי יצר הרע בתחלה דומה לחוט של ג) כוביא ולבסוף דומה לעבות העגלה דאתן עלה מיהת אחות לוטן תמנע מאי היא תמנע בת מלכים הואי דכתיב ל) אלוף לוטן מ) אלוף תמנע וכל אלוף ד) מלכותא בלא תאגא היא בעיא לאיגיורי באתה אצל אברהם יצחק ויעקב ולא קבלוה הלכה והיתה פילגש לאליפז בן עשו אמרה מוטב תהא שפחה לאומה זו ולא תהא גבירה לאומה אחרת נפק מינה עמלק דצערינהו לישראל מאי טעמא דלא איבעי להו לרחקה וילך ראובן בימי קציר חטים אמר רבא בר' יצחק אמר רב מכאן לצדיקים ה) שאין פושטין ידיהן בגזל וימצא דודאים בשדה מאי דודאים אמר רב יברוחי לוי אמר סיגלי ר' יונתן אמר (סיבסוך) [סביסקי]: א"ר אלכסנדרי כל העוסק בתורה לשמה משים שלום בפמליא של מעלה ובפמליא של מטה שנאמר נ) או יחזק במעוזי יעשה שלום לי שלום יעשה לי: רב אמר כאילו בנה פלטרין של מעלה ושל מטה שנאמר ס) ואשים דברי בפיך ובצל ידי כסיתיך לנטוע שמים וליסד ארץ (אמר ריש לקיש) [רבי יוחנן אמר] אף מגין על כל העולם כולו שנאמר ובצל ידי כסיתיך ולוי אמר אף מקרב את הגאולה שנאמר ס) ולאמר לציון עמי אתה אמר ריש לקיש ו) כל המלמד את בן חבירו תורה מעלה עליו הכתוב כאילו עשאו שנאמר ע) ואת הנפש אשר עשו בחרן ר' [ב] (ז) אליעזר) אומר כאילו עשאן לדברי תורה שנאמר פ) ושמרתם את דברי הברית הזאת ועשיתם אותם רבא אמר [ג] כאילו עשאו לעצמו שנאמר ועשיתם אותם אל תקרי אותם אלא אתם אמר רבי אבהו [ד] כל המעשה את חבירו לדבר מצוה מעלה עליו הכתוב (א) כאילו עשאה שנאמר צ) ומטך אשר הכית בו את היאר וכי משה הכהו והלא אהרן הכהו אלא לומר לך כל המעשה את חבירו לדבר מצוה מעלה עליו הכתוב כאילו עשאה: אפיקורוס: רב ור' חנינא אמרי תרוייהו זה א) המבזה ת"ח רבי יוחנן ור' יהושע בן לוי אמרי זה המבזה חבירו בפני ת"ח בשלמא למ"ד המבזה חבירו בפני ת"ח אפיקורוס הוי מבזה תלמיד חכם עצמו מגלה פנים בתורה שלא כהלכה הוי אלא למ"ד מבזה תלמיד חכם עצמו אפיקורוס הוי מגלה פנים בתורה כגון מאי ב) כגון מנשה בן חזקיה ואיכא דמתני לה אסיפא מגלה פנים בתורה רב ור' חנינא אמרי זה המבזה ת"ח רבי יוחנן וריב"ל אמרי זה המבזה את חבירו בפני תלמיד חכם בשלמא למ"ד המבזה תלמיד חכם עצמו מגלה פנים בתורה הוי מבזה חבירו בפני ת"ח אפיקורוס הוי אלא למ"ד מבזה חבירו בפני תלמיד חכם מגלה פנים בתורה הוי אפיקורוס כגון מאן אמר רב יוסף כגון הני דאמרי מאי אהנו לן רבנן לדידהו קרו לדידהו תנו אמר ליה אביי האי מגלה פנים בתורה נמי הוא דכתיב ק) אם לא בריתי יומם ולילה חקות שמים וארץ לא שמתי אמר רב נחמן בר יצחק מהכא נמי שמע מינה שנאמר ר) ונשאתי לכל המקום בעבורם אלא כגון דיתיב קמיה רביה ונפלה ליה שמעתא בדוכתא אחריתי ואמר הכי אמרינן התם ולא אמר הכי אמר מר רבא אמר כגון הני דבי בנימין אסיא דאמרי מאי אהני לן רבנן מעולם

לא

זמר בכל יום. היה מסדר למודך אע"פ שסדור בפיך כזמר והוא יגרום לך שתהא לעולם הבא בשמחה ובשירים: נפש עמל עמלה לו. מפני שעמל בתורה תורה עומלת לו: כי אכף עליו פיהו. מפני שהוא משים דברים בפיו תמיד כאוכף שעל החמור לישנא אחרינא זמר כלומר שעוסק בשירים ובזמירות תדיר תדיר נעשה זמר כך החוזר על התורה נעשה לו סדורה בפיו: תורה עומלת לו. שמחזרת עליו ומבקשת מאת קונה למסור לו טעמי תורה וסדריה וכל כך למה מפני שאכף שכפף פיהו על דברי תורה: דרופתקי. טרחנין כלומר כל הגופין לעמל נבראו: טוביה לדזכי. אשריו למי שזכה והיה עמלו וטרחו בתורה לשון אחר דרפתקי כיס ארוך שמשימין בו מעות כל הגופין נרתקין הם לקבל ולהכניס דברים אשריו למי שזכה ונעשה נרתק לתורה: לומד תורה לפרקים. ואינו לומד תדיר כמי שאין לו אשה ובועל פעמים זו פעמים זו: שנאמר כי נעים כי תשמרם. אימתי תשמרם בבטנך [בזמן] שיכונו יחדיו על שפתיך: לא היה לו למשה לכתוב אלא ואחות לוטן תמנע. בתמיה דבר שאינו צריך הוא וכן היה מלגלג ואומר שכתבו משה שלא לצורך ולקמיה מפרש דהיינו מגלה פנים בתורה: וילך ראובן וגו'. והיינו נמי שלא לצורך: בחבלי השוא. בחנם בלא שום הנאה היה חוטא: מלכותא בלא תגא. שר גדול אלא שאינו מעוטר וכיון דתמנע היתה אחות מלך ודאי בת מלך היא: מוטב שאהיה שפחה לאומה זו. לבני אברהם יצחק (ויעקב) שהן יראי שמים ולא אהיה גברת לאומה אחרת ולכך נעשית פילגש לאליפז בן עשו שהיה מזרע יצחק: לרחקה. מתחת כנפי השכינה שהיה להם לגיירה: בימי קציר חטים. לאחר שקצרו השדה שהכל רשאין ליכנס בתוך שדה חבריהן: יברוחי. כדמתרגמינן ולא איתפרש מאי היא: סיגלי וסביסקי [וסבסוך]. מינין אחרים סיגלי עיקרי עשבים והוא ממיני בשמים ואמהות של אותן עשבים קרי סגלי (וסבסך) [וסביסקי] נמי מין בשמים: מעוזי. תורה: שלום שלום. תרתי זימני אחד למעלה ואחד למטה: פלטירין של מעלה ושלמטה. כדכתיב לנטוע שמים וליסוד ארץ: אשר עשו בחרן. דמתרגמינן דשעבידו לאורייתא בחרן וקרי להו עשייה: כאילו עשאו. לאותו דבר מצוה: והלא אהרן הכה. דכתיב (שמות ז) ח) (ויאמר) אל אהרן קח מטך ונטה ידך: מגלה פנים בתורה. מעיז פנים כלפי עוסקי תורה מגלה פנים משתמע לן דחמיר מאפיקורוס דאפיקורוס היינו דאית ביה אפקירותא בעלמא: אלא למ"ד מבזה תלמידי חכמים עצמן אפיקורוס הוי. כ"ש דמבזה חברו בפני תלמידי חכמים לאו מגלה פנים הוא והשתא מאי ניהו מגלה פנים בתורה: מנשה בן חזקיה. שהיה דורש באגדות של דופי: איכא דמתני לה אסיפא. ט) דברייתא דקתני מכאן אמר רבי אלעזר וכו' המגלה פנים בתורה רב ור' חנינא וכו': מאי אהני לן. והם אינן יודעין שעולם מתקיים עליהם: מגלה פנים בתורה הוא. שכופר במה שכתוב בתורה: אם לא בריתי יומם ולילה וגו'. שמהנין לעולם ומקיימין [אותו] והוא אומר דלא מהני מידי: מהכא נמי שמעינן. שהצדיקים מהנין לאחרים:

לא

מסורת הש"ס

א) [כל המאמר הזה יפה נדרש בשל"ה סוף דף עש"ה, ע"ש פי' נאה ומתוקן], ב) [סוטה נב.], ג) [בסוכה איתא כוביא ובערוך גר' בוביא ובסוכה פירש"י בוכיא עכביש], ד) [לקמן קה.], ה) [סוטה יב. חולין נא.], ו) [עי' בילקוט עה"ש], ז) [ג"ל אלעזר], ח) [ג"ל אמורך], ט) [היינו משנה דלעיל עמוד א].

הגהות הב"ח

(א) גמ' כאילו עשאו שנאמר ומטך וכו' כאילו עשאו:

הגהות הגר"א

[א] גמ' אמר ריש לקיש. נרשם עליו אות ג: [ב] שם רבי אלעזר. נרשם עליו אות ד: [ג] שם רבא אמר. נרשם עליו אות ג: [ד] שם א"ר אבהו. נרשם עליו אות ז:

תורה אור השלם

א) נֶפֶשׁ עָמֵל עָמְלָה לּוֹ כִּי אָכַף עָלָיו פִּיהוּ: [משלי טז, כו]
ב) כִּי אָדָם לְעָמָל יוּלָּד וּבְנֵי רֶשֶׁף יַגְבִּיהוּ עוּף: [איוב ה, ז]
ג) לֹא יָמוּשׁ סֵפֶר הַתּוֹרָה הַזֶּה מִפִּיךָ וְהָגִיתָ בּוֹ יוֹמָם וָלַיְלָה לְמַעַן תִּשְׁמֹר לַעֲשׂוֹת כְּכָל הַכָּתוּב בּוֹ כִּי אָז תַּצְלִיחַ אֶת דְּרָכֶךָ וְאָז תַּשְׂכִּיל: [יהושע א, ח]
ד) נֹאֵף אִשָּׁה חֲסַר לֵב מַשְׁחִית נַפְשׁוֹ הוּא יַעֲשֶׂנָּה: [משלי ו, לב]
ה) כִּי נָעִים כִּי תִשְׁמְרֵם בְּבִטְנֶךָ יִכֹּנוּ יַחְדָּו עַל שְׂפָתֶיךָ: [משלי כב, יח]
ו) וְהַנֶּפֶשׁ אֲשֶׁר תַּעֲשֶׂה בְּיָד רָמָה מִן הָאֶזְרָח וּמִן הַגֵּר אֶת יְיָ הוּא מְגַדֵּף וְנִכְרְתָה הַנֶּפֶשׁ הַהִוא מִקֶּרֶב עַמָּהּ: [במדבר טו, ל]
ז) וַיִּהְיוּ בְנֵי לוֹטָן חֹרִי וְהֵימָם וַאֲחוֹת לוֹטָן תִּמְנָע: [בראשית לו, כב]
ח) וְתִמְנַע הָיְתָה פִילֶגֶשׁ לֶאֱלִיפַז בֶּן עֵשָׂו וַתֵּלֶד לֶאֱלִיפַז אֶת עֲמָלֵק אֵלֶּה בְּנֵי עָדָה אֵשֶׁת עֵשָׂו: [בראשית לו, יב]
ט) וַיֵּלֶךְ רְאוּבֵן בִּימֵי קְצִיר חִטִּים וַיִּמְצָא דוּדָאִים בַּשָּׂדֶה וַיָּבֵא אֹתָם אֶל לֵאָה אִמּוֹ וַתֹּאמֶר רָחֵל אֶל לֵאָה תְּנִי נָא לִי מִדּוּדָאֵי בְּנֵךְ: [בראשית ל, יד]
י) תֵּשֵׁב בְּאָחִיךָ תְדַבֵּר בְּבֶן אִמְּךָ תִּתֶּן דֹּפִי: אֵלֶּה עָשִׂיתָ וְהֶחֱרַשְׁתִּי דִּמִּיתָ הֱיוֹת אֶהְיֶה כָמוֹךָ אוֹכִיחֲךָ וְאֶעֶרְכָה לְעֵינֶיךָ: [תהלים נ, כ-כא]
כ) הוֹי מֹשְׁכֵי הֶעָוֹן בְּחַבְלֵי הַשָּׁוְא וְכַעֲבוֹת הָעֲגָלָה חַטָּאָה: [ישעיה ה, יח]
ל) אֵלֶּה אַלּוּפֵי הַחֹרִי אַלּוּף לוֹטָן אַלּוּף שׁוֹבָל אַלּוּף צִבְעוֹן אַלּוּף עֲנָה: [בראשית לו, כט] מ) וְאֵלֶּה שְׁמוֹת אַלּוּפֵי עֵשָׂו לְמִשְׁפְּחֹתָם לִמְקֹמֹתָם בִּשְׁמֹתָם אַלּוּף תִּמְנָע אַלּוּף עַלְוָה אַלּוּף יְתֵת: [בראשית לו, מ] נ) אוֹ יַחֲזֵק בְּמָעוּזִּי יַעֲשֶׂה שָׁלוֹם לִי שָׁלוֹם יַעֲשֶׂה לִּי: [ישעיה כז, ה] ס) וָאָשִׂים דְּבָרַי בְּפִיךָ וּבְצֵל יָדִי כִּסִּיתִיךָ לִנְטֹעַ שָׁמַיִם וְלִיסֹד אָרֶץ וְלֵאמֹר לְצִיּוֹן עַמִּי אָתָּה: [ישעיה נא, טז] ע) וַיִּקַּח אַבְרָם אֶת שָׂרַי אִשְׁתּוֹ וְאֶת לוֹט בֶּן אָחִיו וְאֶת כָּל רְכוּשָׁם אֲשֶׁר רָכָשׁוּ וְאֶת הַנֶּפֶשׁ אֲשֶׁר עָשׂוּ בְחָרָן וַיֵּצְאוּ לָלֶכֶת אַרְצָה כְּנַעַן וַיָּבֹאוּ אַרְצָה כְּנָעַן: [בראשית יב, ה] פ) וּשְׁמַרְתֶּם אֶת דִּבְרֵי הַבְּרִית הַזֹּאת וַעֲשִׂיתֶם אֹתָם לְמַעַן תַּשְׂכִּילוּ אֵת כָּל אֲשֶׁר תַּעֲשׂוּן: [דברים כט, ח] צ) וַיֹּאמֶר יְיָ אֶל מֹשֶׁה עֲבֹר לִפְנֵי הָעָם וְקַח אִתְּךָ מִזִּקְנֵי יִשְׂרָאֵל וּמַטְּךָ אֲשֶׁר הִכִּיתָ בּוֹ אֶת הַיְאֹר קַח בְּיָדְךָ וְהָלָכְתָּ: [שמות יז, ה] ק) כֹּה אָמַר יְיָ אִם לֹא בְרִיתִי יוֹמָם וָלָיְלָה חֻקּוֹת שָׁמַיִם וָאָרֶץ לֹא שָׂמְתִּי: [ירמיה לג, כה] ר) וַיֹּאמֶר יְיָ אִם אֶמְצָא בִסְדֹם חֲמִשִּׁים צַדִּיקִם בְּתוֹךְ הָעִיר וְנָשָׂאתִי לְכָל הַמָּקוֹם בַּעֲבוּרָם: [בראשית יח, כו]

ליקוטי רש"י

כי נעים. יהי לך לאחר זמן אם תשמרם ותצפנם בבטנך שלא תשכחם ואימתי יהיו שמורים בלבך בזמן שיכונו על שפתיך כאשר תוציאם בפיך [משלי כב, יח]. ותמנע היתה פילגש לאליפז. להודיע גדולתו של אברהם כמה היו תאבים לידבק בזרעו תמנע זו בת אלופים היתה, שנאמר (פסוק כב) ואחות לוטן תמנע, ולוטן מאלופי יושבי שעיר היה, מן החורים שישבו בה לפנים, אמרה איני זוכה להנשא לך, הלואי ואהיה פילגש. ובדברי הימים מונה אותה (דברי הימים א' א לו) בבניו של אליפז, מלמד שבא על אשתו של שעיר וילאה תמנע מביניהם, וכשגדלה נעשית פילגשו, וזהו ואחות לוטן תמנע, ולא מנאה עם בני שעיר שהיתה אחותו מן האם ולא מן האב [בראשית לו, יב]. בימי קציר חטים. להגיד שבחן של שבטים שעת הקציר היה ולא פשט ידו בגזל להביא חטים ושעורים אלא דבר ההפקר שאין אדם מקפיד בו. דודאים. סיגלי, עשב הוא ובלשון ישמעאל יסמי"ן [שם ל, יד]. דמית. סבור אתה שאהיה כמוך להתרצו' במעשיך הרעים, (וי"מ דמית כי אינני יודע הנסתרות) [תהלים נ, כא]. הוי מושכי העון. גוררים יצר הרע עליהם מעט מעט בתחלה בחבלי השוא כחוט של קורי עכביש ומשנתגרה בהם מתגבר והולך עד שעושה כעבות העגלה שקושרין בו את הקרון למשוך. השוא. דבר שאין בו ממש. חטאה. חטא [ישעיהו ה, יח]. מלכותא בלא תגא. כלומר שררה גדולה ואינו חסר אלא כתר מלכות [לקמן קה.]. או יחזק במעוזי. או לשון אם, כמו או נודע כי שור נגח הוא (שמות כא) אם יחזק עמי במעוזי שלא יבקש אותי אלא מעוזי אז יעשה שלום לי להנית דעתי ואפי' שלום יעשה לי שלא ימצא בו שום צד קטרוג [ישעיהו כז, ה]. אשר עשו בחרן. שהכניסן תחת כנפי השכינה אברהם מגייר את האנשים ושרה מגיירת הנשים ומעלה עליהם הכתוב כאלו עשאום ופשוטו של מקרא עבדים ושפחות שקנו להם כמו (שם לא א) עשה את כל הכבוד הזה (במדבר כד יח) וישראל עושה חיל לשון קונה וכונס [בראשית יב, ה]. המלמד את בן חבירו. ואלה תולדת אהרן ומשה, ואינו מזכיר אלא בני אהרן ונקראו תולדות משה לפי שלמדן תורה מלמד שכל המלמד את בן חבירו תורה מעלה עליו הכתוב כאלו ילדו [במדבר ג, א]. אם לא בריתי וגו'. אי אפשר שלא יתקיים הברית שכרתי ליום ולילה להיות בעתם ואי אפשר לחוקות שמים וארץ ליבטל כאילו לא שמתים גם זרע יעקב וגו' ורבותינו דרשוהו לענין ברית התורה ללמוד מכאן שבשביל התורה נבראו שמים וארץ אך אין המדרש מיושב על סדר המקראות [ירמיהו לג, כה].

זַמֵּר בְּכָל יוֹם זַמֵּר בְּכָל יוֹם – SING EVERY DAY, SING EVERY DAY.[1]

The Gemara asks:

אָמַר רַב יִצְחָק בַּר אֲבוּדִימִי – **Rav Yitzchak bar Avudimi said:** מַאי קְרָא – **What** is the **verse** that teaches about the reward for constant Torah study and review?[2]

The Gemara answers:

שֶׁנֶּאֱמַר ,,נֶפֶשׁ עָמֵל עָמְלָה לוֹ כִּי־אָכַף עָלָיו פִּיהוּ" – It is that **which states:**[3] ***[If] a person toils*** [i.e. in the study of Torah], ***[the Torah] will toil for him, for he saddled his mouth to it.***[4] הוּא עָמֵל בְּמָקוֹם זֶה – This verse teaches that **[a person] toils** in the study of Torah **in this place,** i.e. in this world, וְתוֹרָתוֹ עוֹמֶלֶת לוֹ בְּמָקוֹם אַחֵר – **and his Torah,** i.e. the Torah knowledge he learned and constantly reviewed, **toils on his behalf in another place,** i.e. before the Almighty.[5]

The Gemara uses the aforecited verse to clarify another, related verse:

אָמַר רַבִּי אֶלְעָזָר – **R' Elazar said:** כָּל אָדָם לְעָמָל נִבְרָא – **Every man is created for toil,** שֶׁנֶּאֱמַר ,,כִּי־אָדָם לְעָמָל יוּלָּד" – **as it is stated:**[6] ***But man is born for toil.*** אֵינִי יוֹדֵעַ אִם לַעֲמַל פֶּה נִבְרָא – Now, **I do not know** from the verse itself **whether he is created for verbal toil,** אִם לַעֲמַל מְלָאכָה נִבְרָא – or **whether he is created for the toil of** physical **labor.**[7] כְּשֶׁהוּא אוֹמֵר ,,כִּי־אָכַף עָלָיו פִּיהוּ" – **When,** however, **[Scripture] states,** ***for he saddled his mouth to it,*** which clearly refers to the ceaseless talk to which man is so attached, הֱוֵי אוֹמֵר לַעֲמַל פֶּה נִבְרָא – **you have to say** that **[man] is created for verbal toil.** וַעֲדַיִין אֵינִי יוֹדֵעַ אִם לַעֲמַל תּוֹרָה – **However, I still do not know** with certainty **whether** he is created **for** the verbal **toil of Torah** study, אִם לַעֲמַל שִׂיחָה – or **whether** he is created **for** the verbal **toil of conversation** about other matters.[8] כְּשֶׁהוּא אוֹמֵר ,,לֹא־יָמוּשׁ סֵפֶר הַתּוֹרָה הַזֶּה מִפִּיךָ" – **When,** however, **[Scripture] states,** ***This Book of the Torah is not to leave your mouth,***[9] הֱוֵי אוֹמֵר לַעֲמַל תּוֹרָה נִבְרָא – **you have to say** that **[man] is created for** the verbal **toil of Torah** study, i.e. the ceaseless oral review of one's learning.[10] וְהַיְינוּ דְּאָמַר רָבָא – **And this is** the meaning of that **which Rava said:** כּוּלְּהוּ גּוּפֵי דְּרוּפְתְּקֵי נִינְהוּ – **All bodies are instruments of toil** (i.e. they are created for toil); טוּבֵי לִדְזָכֵי דַּהֲוֵי דְּרוּפְתְּקֵי דְּאוֹרַיְיתָא – **fortunate are those who merit to be toilers in Torah** study, and not toilers in other endeavors.[11]

The Gemara censures those who do not regularly review their Torah studies:

,,נֹאֵף אִשָּׁה חֲסַר־לֵב" – Scripture states:[12] ***He who philanders with a woman is devoid of sense.*** אָמַר רֵישׁ לָקִישׁ – **Reish Lakish said:** זֶה הַלּוֹמֵד תּוֹרָה לִפְרָקִים – **This** refers to **one who learns Torah** only **occasionally,**[13] שֶׁנֶּאֱמַר ,,כִּי־נָעִים כִּי־תִשְׁמְרֵם בְּבִטְנֶךָ יִכֹּנוּ יַחְדָּו עַל־שְׂפָתֶיךָ" – **for it says:** ***For it is a pleasant***

NOTES

1. Even though one is fluent in the subject he is learning as if it were a familiar song, he should nonetheless constantly review it (as implied by the first "sing every day"). By doing so he will merit to sing for joy in the World to Come, which is implied by the second "sing every day" (*Rashi,* first interpretation).

Alternatively, the word זמר is vowelized זַמָּר, which means *a singer.* One who learns many songs and practices them constantly ("every day... every day") will become an accomplished singer. Similarly, one who constantly reviews his Torah learning will know it well [and will become an accomplished Torah scholar] (*Rashi,* second interpretation).

There are those who constantly sing old and familiar songs simply because they love the melodies. Similarly, one should daily review his Torah learning by singing it, not merely for purposes of memorization, but out of love for the Torah knowledge he has acquired (*Yad Ramah*).

Maharal understands R' Akiva to mean that it is not sufficient to obtain knowledge of Torah and to cogitate upon it, just as it is insufficient merely to know the lyrics of a song. Rather, a song is fully realized only when it is sung. Similarly, Torah thoughts must be given oral expression before they are fully actualized.

2. See *Maharsha.*

3. *Proverbs* 16:26.

4. I.e. he constantly places the words of Torah in his mouth (*Rashi;* see following note).

5. The very Torah the person has learned beseeches God to grant him a special insight into its deeper meanings and secrets (*Rashi*).

In his interpretation Rav Yitzchak bar Avudimi relates the word אָכַף to אוּכָף, *a saddle.* Scripture thus intimates that through constant review a person ensures that the Torah knowledge he has acquired becomes "saddled"; that is, it becomes attached to him in the sense that he does not forget it, as a saddle is strapped onto a donkey. As a reward, the Torah will exert itself on that person's behalf, as explained above (*Rashi*).

Thus, this verse extols the virtue of continually reviewing aloud one's Torah learning in order to ensure that it will not be forgotten.

6. *Job* 5:7.

7. R' Elazar queries whether the ideal life is one of verbal toil (i.e. engaging exclusively in Torah study and teaching), or whether the ideal life involves also physical toil, whereby one supports himself with his own labor while setting aside fixed times for Torah study (*Maharsha;* see *Berachos* 35b).

According to *R' Yonasan Eibschutz* the question is: Which is superior – verbal toil, i.e. those commandments whose performance involves speech alone (such as Torah study and prayer), or physical toil, i.e. those commandments whose performance involves physical action (such as building a succah) [*Yaaros Dvash*]? In *Kuntres Kedushas HaShabbos* 1:3, R' Tzadok HaKohen writes that "physical toil" refers specifically to performing acts of kindness.

8. Pursuant to the explanation cited in the previous note, *Yaaros Dvash* understands "conversation" to mean prayer; see *Genesis* 24:63 [R' Tzadok HaKohen, ibid. 1:4, concurs with this interpretation]. *Maharsha* explains, however, that any permitted conversation is meant, since speech is the distinguishing characteristic of man, who is called a מְדַבֵּר, *speaker* (see *Targum Onkelos* to *Genesis* 2:7). [The reference here may be to the discretionary conversation of a Torah scholar, which itself requires study; see *Avodah Zarah* 19b, *Succah* 21b (*Iyun Yaakov*).]

9. *Joshua* 1:8. Here Scripture unequivocally states that one is obligated to devote himself constantly to Torah study.

10. One who reviews his Torah learning 101 times is called "God's servant" (*Chagigah* 9b), and this is the toil of Torah study, as the verse, *for he saddled his mouth to it* (כִּי־אָכַף עָלָיו פִּיהוּ), intimates. That is, the *gematria* of both אָכַף (*he saddled*) and פִּיהוּ (*his mouth*) is 101 (see *Margaliyos HaYam*).

11. This is *Rashi*'s first interpretation, in which דְּרוּפְתְּקֵי means a laboring entity. In *Rashi's* second interpretation the term is translated to mean a "long purse," into which coins are placed. According to this interpretation, Rava states as follows: All human beings are like purses (i.e. they receive and retain many things and ideas); fortunate are those who merit to become purses (i.e. receptacles) for Torah.

Maharal stresses that because man is a physical being, his potential is unrealized, and so he can never be at rest. Rather, he must constantly toil to attain perfection. A person should not think, however, that he was created for physical toil, or for toil through speech (a higher level of toil); rather, he was created to toil with his intellect in the study of Torah, which is the highest level of perfection.

12. *Proverbs* 6:32.

13. Reish Lakish compares a philanderer, who occasionally frequents this woman and occasionally that one and does not conform to a normal married lifestyle, to one who does not study Torah constantly, but only when he is inclined to do so (*Rashi*). [As to how women, who are physical entities, can serve as a metaphor for the supernal Torah, see *Ben Yehoyada.*]

Just as a philanderer is devoid of sense, for he has nothing to show for his fleeting affairs (for when the affair is over he is left with a feeling of emptiness), so one who engages only occasionally in Torah study will have nothing to show for his efforts. Since he did not constantly review what he learned, he will forget everything (see *Yad Ramah, Maharsha*).

זמר בכל יום זמר בכל יום אמר רב יצחק בר אבודימי מאי קרא שנאמר א) נפש עמל עמלה לו כי אכף עליו פיהו הוא עמל במקום זה ותורתו עומלת לו במקום אחר אמר רבי אלעזר א) כל אדם לעמל נברא שנאמר ב) כי אדם לעמל יולד איני יודע אם לעמל פה נברא אם לעמל מלאכה נברא כשהוא אומר כי אכף עליו פיהו הוי אומר לעמל פה נברא ועדיין איני יודע אם לעמל תורה אם לעמל שיחה כשהוא אומר ג) לא ימוש ספר התורה הזה מפיך הוי אומר לעמל תורה נברא והיינו דאמר רבא כולהו גופי דרופתקי נינהו טובי לדזכי דהוי דרופתקי דאורייתא ד) ונואף אשה חסר לב אמר [א] ריש לקיש זה הלומד תורה לפרקים שנאמר ה) כי נעים כי תשמרם בבטנך יכונו יחדיו על שפתיך ת"ר ו) והנפש אשר תעשה ביד רמה זה מנשה בן חזקיה שהיה יושב ודורש בהגדות של דופי אמר וכי לא היה לו למשה לכתוב אלא ז) ואחות לוטן תמנע ח) ותמנע היתה פלגש לאליפז ט) וילך ראובן בימי קציר חטים וימצא דודאים בשדה יצאה ב"ק ואמרה לו י) תשב באחיך תדבר בבן אמך תתן דופי אלה עשית והחרשתי דמית היות אהיה כמוך אוכיחך ואערכה לעיניך ועליו מפורש בקבלה כ) הוי מושכי העון בחבלי השוא וכעבות העגלה חטאה מאי כעבות העגלה ב) א"ר אסי יצר הרע בתחלה דומה לחוט של ג) כוביא ולבסוף דומה לעבות העגלה דאתן עלה מיהת אחות לוטן תמנע מאי היא תמנע בת מלכים הואי דכתיב ל) אלוף לוטן מ) אלוף תמנע וכל אלוף ד) מלכותא בלא תאגא היא בעיא לאיגיורי באתה אצל אברהם יצחק ויעקב ולא קבלוה הלכה והיתה פילגש לאליפז בן עשו אמרה מוטב תהא שפחה לאומה זו ולא תהא גבירה לאומה אחרת נפק מינה עמלק דצערינהו לישראל מאי טעמא דלא איבעי להו לרחקה וילך ראובן בימי קציר חטים אמר רבא בר' יצחק אמר רב מכאן לצדיקים ה) שאין פושטין ידיהן בגזל וימצא דודאים בשדה מאי דודאים אמר רב יברוחי לוי אמר סיגלי ר' יונתן אמר (סיבסוך) [סביסקי]: א"ר אלכסנדרי כל העוסק בתורה לשמה משים שלום בפמליא של מעלה ובפמליא של מטה שנאמר נ) או יחזק במעוזי יעשה שלום לי שלום יעשה לי: רב אמר כאילו בנה פלטרין של מעלה ושל מטה שנאמר ס) ואשים דברי בפיך ובצל ידי כסיתיך לנטוע שמים וליסד ארץ (אמר ריש לקיש) [רבי יוחנן אמר] אף מגין על כל העולם כולו שנאמר ובצל ידי כסיתיך ולוי אמר אף מקרב את הגאולה שנאמר ס) ולאמר לציון עמי אתה אמר ריש לקיש ו) כל המלמד את בן חבירו תורה מעלה עליו הכתוב כאילו עשאו שנאמר ע) ואת הנפש אשר עשו בחרן ר' [ב] (ז) אליעזר) אומר כאילו עשאן לדברי תורה שנאמר פ) ושמרתם את דברי הברית הזאת ועשיתם אותם רבא אמר [ג] כאילו עשאו לעצמו שנאמר ועשיתם אותם אל תקרי אותם אלא אתם אמר רבי אבהו [ד] כל המעשה את חבירו לדבר מצוה מעלה עליו הכתוב (א) כאילו עשאה שנאמר צ) ומטך אשר הכית בו את היאר וכי משה הכהו והלא אהרן הכהו אלא לומר לך כל המעשה את חבירו לדבר מצוה מעלה עליו הכתוב כאילו עשאה: אפיקורוס: רב ור' חנינא אמרי תרוייהו זה ח) המבזה ת"ח רבי יוחנן ור' יהושע בן לוי אמרי זה המבזה חבירו בפני ת"ח בשלמא למ"ד המבזה חבירו בפני ת"ח אפיקורוס הוי מבזה תלמיד חכם עצמו מגלה פנים בתורה שלא כהלכה הוי אלא למ"ד מבזה תלמיד חכם עצמו אפיקורוס הוי מגלה פנים בתורה כגון מאי ט) כגון מנשה בן חזקיה ואיכא דמתני לה אסיפא מגלה פנים בתורה רב ור' חנינא אמרי זה המבזה ת"ח רבי יוחנן וריב"ל אמרי זה המבזה את חבירו בפני תלמיד חכם בשלמא למ"ד המבזה תלמיד חכם מגלה פנים בתורה הוי מבזה חבירו בפני ת"ח אפיקורוס הוי אלא למ"ד מבזה חבירו בפני תלמיד חכם מגלה פנים בתורה הוי אפיקורוס כגון מאן אמר רב יוסף כגון הני דאמרי מאי אהנו לן רבנן לדידהו קרו לדידהו תנו אמר ליה אביי האי מגלה פנים בתורה נמי הוא דכתיב ק) אם לא בריתי יומם ולילה חקות שמים וארץ לא שמתי אמר רב נחמן בר יצחק מהכא נמי שמע מינה שנאמר ר) ונשאתי לכל המקום בעבורם אלא כגון דיתיב קמיה רביה ונפלה ליה שמעתא בדוכתא אחריתי ואמר הכי אמרינן התם ולא אמר הכי אמר מר רבא אמר כגון הני דבי בנימין אסיא דאמרי מאי אהני לן רבנן מעולם
לא

זמר בכל יום. היה מסדר למודך אע"פ שסדור בפיך כזמר והוא יגרום לך שתהא לעולם הבא בשמחה ובשירים: נפש עמל עמלה לו. מפני שעמל בתורה תורה עומלת לו: כי אכף עליו פיהו. מפני שהוא משים דברים בפיו תמיד כאוכף שעל החמור לישנא אחרינא זמר כלומר שעוסק בשירים ובזמירות תדיר תדיר נעשה זמר כך החוזר על התורה נעשה לו סדורה בפיו: תורה עומלת לו. שמחזרת עליו ומבקשת מאת קונה למסור לו טעמי תורה וסדריה וכל כך למה מפני שאכף שכפף פיהו על דברי תורה: דרופתקי. טרחנין כלומר כל הגופין לעמל נבראו: טוביה לדזכי. אשריו למי שזכה והיה עמלו וטרחו בתורה לשון אחר דרפתקי כיס ארוך שמשימין בו מעות כל הגופין נרתקין הם לקבל ולהכניס דברים אשריו למי שזכה ונעשה נרתק לתורה: לומד תורה לפרקים. ואינו לומד תדיר כמי שאין לו אשה ובועל פעמים זו פעמים זו: שנאמר כי נעים כי תשמרם. אימתי תשמרם בבטנך [בזמן] שיכונו יחדיו על שפתיך: לא היה לו למשה לכתוב אלא ואחות לוטן תמנע. בתמיה דבר שאינו צריך הוא וכן היה מלגלג ואומר שכתבו משה שלא לצורך ולקמיה מפרש דהיינו מגלה פנים בתורה: וילך ראובן וגו'. והיינו נמי שלא לצורך: בחבלי השוא. בחנם בלא שום הנאה היה חוטא: מלכותא בלא תגא. שר גדול אלא שאינו מעוטר וכיון דתמנע היתה אחות מלך ודאי בת מלך היא: מוטב שאהיה שפחה לאומה זו. לבני אברהם יצחק (ויעקב) שהן יראי שמים ולא אהיה גברת לאומה אחרת ולכך נעשית פילגש לאליפז בן עשו שהיה מזרע יצחק: לרחקה. מתחת כנפי השכינה שהיה להם לגיירה: בימי קציר חטים. לאחר שקצרו השדה שהכל רשאין ליכנס בתוך שדה חבריהן: יברוחי. כדמתרגמינן ולא איתפרש מאי היא: סיגלי וסביסקי [וסבסוך]. מינין אחרים סיגלי עיקרי עשבים והוא ממיני בשמים ואמהות של אותן עשבים קרי סגלי (וסבסך) [וסביסקי] נמי מין בשמים: מעוזי. תורה: שלום שלום. תרתי זימני אחד למעלה ואחד למטה: פלטירין של מעלה ושלמטה. כדכתיב לנטוע שמים וליסוד ארץ: אשר עשו בחרן. דמתרגמינן דשעבידו לאורייתא בחרן וקרי להו עשייה: כאילו עשאו. לאותו דבר מצוה: והלא אהרן הכה. דכתיב (שמות ז) ח) (ויאמר) אל אהרן קח מטך ונטה ידך: מגלה פנים בתורה. מעיז פנים כלפי עוסקי תורה מגלה פנים משתמע לן דחמיר מאפיקורוס דאפיקורוס היינו דאית ביה אפקירותא בעלמא: אלא למ"ד מבזה תלמידי חכמים עצמן אפיקורוס הוי. כ"ש דמבזה חברו בפני תלמידי חכמים לאו מגלה פנים הוא והשתא מאי ניהו מגלה פנים בתורה: מנשה בן חזקיה. שהיה דורש באגדות של דופי: איכא דמתני לה אסיפא. ט) דברייתא דקתני מכאן אמר רבי אלעזר וכו' המגלה פנים בתורה רב ור' חנינא וכו': מאי אהני לן. והם אינן יודעין שעולם מתקיים עליהם: מגלה פנים בתורה הוא. שכופר במה שכתוב בתורה: אם לא בריתי יומם ולילה וגו'. שמהנין לעולם ומקיימין [אותו] והוא אומר דלא מהני מידי: מהכא נמי שמעינן. שהצדיקים מהנין לאחרים:
לא

עין משפט
נר מצוה

יז א מיי' פ"ג מהלכות תשובה הלכה יד ע' בכ"מ:
יח ב מיי' שם הלכה יא:

ליקוטי רש"י

כי נעים. יהי לך לאחר זמן אם תשמרם ותצפנם בבטנך שלא תשכחם ואימתי יהיו שמורים בלבך בזמן שיכונו על שפתיך כאשר תוציאם בפיך [משלי כב, יח]. ותמנע היתה פילגש לאליפז. להודיע גדולתו של אברהם כמה היו תאבים לידבק בזרעו תמנע זו בת אלופים היתה, שנאמר (פסוק כב) ואחות לוטן תמנע, ולוטן מאלופי יושבי שעיר היה, מן החורים שישבו בה לפנים, אמרה איני זוכה להנשא לך, הלואי ואהיה פילגש. ובדברי הימים מונה אותה (דברי הימים א' א לו) בבניו של אליפז, מלמד שבא על אשתו של שעיר וילדה תמנע מביניהם, וכשגדלה נעשית פילגשו, וזהו ואחות לוטן תמנע, ולא מנאה עם בני שעיר שהיתה אחותו מן האם ולא מן האב [בראשית לו, יב]. בימי קציר חטים. להגיד שבחן של שבטים שעת הקציר היה ולא פשט ידו בגזל להביא חטים ושעורים אלא דבר ההפקר שאין אדם מקפיד בו. דודאים. סיגלי, עשב הוא ובלשון ישמעאל יסמי"ן [שם ל, יד]. דמית. סבור אתה שאהיה כמוך להתרצו' במעשיך הרעים, (וי"מ דמית כי אינני יודע הנסתרות) [תהלים נ, כא]. הוי מושכי העון. גוררים יצר הרע עליהם מעט מעט בתחלה בחבלי השוא כחוט של קורי עכביש ומשנתגרה בהם מתגבר והולך עד שנעשה כעבות העגלה שקושרין בו את הקרון למשוך. השוא. דבר שאין בו ממש. חטאה. חטא [ישעיהו ה, יח]. מלכותא בלא תגא. כלומר שררה גדולה ואינו חסר אלא כתר מלכות [לקמן קה.]. או יחזק במעוזי. או לשון אם, כמו או נודע כי שור נגח הוא (שמות כא) או יחזק עמי במעוזי שלא יבקש מעוז אלא מעוזי אז יעשה שלום לי להניח דעתי ואפי שמתקשקשת בי על שאיני נוקם בצרי ואנקם בהם. שלום יעשה לי. ממדת הדין שלא יוכל לקטרג ולומר מה נשתנו אלו מאלו [ישעיהו כז, ה]. אשר עשו בחרן. שהכניסן תחת כנפי השכינה אברהם מגייר את האנשים ושרה מגיירת הנשים ומעלה עליהם הכתוב כאלו עשאום ופשוטו של מקרא עבדים ושפחות שקנו להם כמו (שם לא א) עשה את כל הכבוד הזה (במדבר כד יח) וישראל עושה חיל לשון קונה וכונס [בראשית יב, ה]. המלמד את בן חבירו. ואלה תולדת אהרן ומשה, ואינו מזכיר אלא בני אהרן ונקראו תולדות משה לפי שלמדן תורה מלמד שכל המלמד את בן חבירו תורה מעלה עליו הכתוב כאלו ילדו [במדבר ג, א]. אם לא בריתי וגו'. אי אפשר שלא יתקיים הברית שכרתי ליום ולילה להיות בעתם ואי אפשר לחוקות שמים וארץ ליבטל כאילו לא שמתים גם זרע יעקב וגו' ורבותינו דרשוהו לענין ברית התורה ללמוד מכאן שבשביל התורה נבראו שמים וארץ אך אין המדרש מיושב על סדר המקראות [ירמיהו לג, כה].

מסורת הש"ס

א) [כל המאמר הזה יפה נדרש בשל"ה סוף דף שע"ה: ע"ש פי' נאה ומתוקן], ב) [סוכה נב.], ג) [בסוכה איתא בוביא ובערוך גר' כוביא ובסוכה פירש"י בוכיא עכביש], ד) [לקמן קה.], ה) [סוטה יב. חולין לא.], ו) [לעיל יט: ע"ש], ז) [צ"ל אלעזר], ח) [צ"ל אמור], ט) [היינו משנה דאבות לעיל עמוד א].

הגהות הב"ח

(א) גמ' כאילו עשאו שנאמר ומטך וכו' כאילו עשאו:

הגהות הגר"א

[א] גמ' אמר ריש לקיש. נרשם עליו אות ג: [ב] שם רבי אלעזר. נרשם עליו אות א: [ג] שם רבא אמר. נרשם עליו אות ב: [ד] שם א"ר אבהו. נרשם עליו אות ד:

תורה אור השלם

א) נֶפֶשׁ עָמֵל עָמְלָה לּוֹ כִּי אָכַף עָלָיו פִּיהוּ: [משלי טז, כו]
ב) כִּי אָדָם לְעָמָל יוּלָּד וּבְנֵי רֶשֶׁף יַגְבִּיהוּ עוּף: [איוב ה, ז]
ג) לֹא יָמוּשׁ סֵפֶר הַתּוֹרָה הַזֶּה מִפִּיךָ וְהָגִיתָ בּוֹ יוֹמָם וָלַיְלָה לְמַעַן תִּשְׁמֹר לַעֲשׂוֹת כְּכָל הַכָּתוּב בּוֹ כִּי אָז תַּצְלִיחַ אֶת דְּרָכֶךָ וְאָז תַּשְׂכִּיל: [יהושע א, ח]
ד) נֹאֵף אִשָּׁה חֲסַר לֵב מַשְׁחִית נַפְשׁוֹ הוּא יַעֲשֶׂנָּה: [משלי ו, לב]
ה) כִּי נָעִים כִּי תִשְׁמְרֵם בְּבִטְנֶךָ יִכֹּנוּ יַחְדָּו עַל שְׂפָתֶיךָ: [משלי כב, יח]
ו) וְהַנֶּפֶשׁ אֲשֶׁר תַּעֲשֶׂה בְּיָד רָמָה מִן הָאֶזְרָח וּמִן הַגֵּר אֶת יְיָ הוּא מְגַדֵּף וְנִכְרְתָה הַנֶּפֶשׁ הַהִוא מִקֶּרֶב עַמָּהּ: [במדבר טו, ל]
ז) וַיִּהְיוּ בְנֵי לוֹטָן חֹרִי וְהֵימָם וַאֲחוֹת לוֹטָן תִּמְנָע: [בראשית לו, כב]
ח) וְתִמְנַע הָיְתָה פִילֶגֶשׁ לֶאֱלִיפַז בֶּן עֵשָׂו וַתֵּלֶד לֶאֱלִיפַז אֶת עֲמָלֵק אֵלֶּה בְּנֵי עָדָה אֵשֶׁת עֵשָׂו: [בראשית לו, יב]
ט) וַיֵּלֶךְ רְאוּבֵן בִּימֵי קְצִיר חִטִּים וַיִּמְצָא דוּדָאִים בַּשָּׂדֶה וַיָּבֵא אֹתָם אֶל לֵאָה אִמּוֹ וַתֹּאמֶר רָחֵל אֶל לֵאָה תְּנִי נָא לִי מִדּוּדָאֵי בְּנֵךְ: [בראשית ל, יד]
י) תֵּשֵׁב בְּאָחִיךָ תְדַבֵּר בְּבֶן אִמְּךָ תִּתֶּן דֹּפִי: אֵלֶּה עָשִׂיתָ וְהֶחֱרַשְׁתִּי דִּמִּיתָ הֱיוֹת אֶהְיֶה כָמוֹךָ אוֹכִיחֲךָ וְאֶעֶרְכָה לְעֵינֶיךָ: [תהלים נ, כ-כא]
כ) הוֹי מֹשְׁכֵי הֶעָוֹן בְּחַבְלֵי הַשָּׁוְא וְכַעֲבוֹת הָעֲגָלָה חַטָּאָה: [ישעיה ה, יח]
ל) אֵלֶּה אַלּוּפֵי הַחֹרִי אַלּוּף לוֹטָן אַלּוּף שׁוֹבָל אַלּוּף צִבְעוֹן אַלּוּף עֲנָה: [בראשית לו, כט]
מ) וְאֵלֶּה שְׁמוֹת אַלּוּפֵי עֵשָׂו לְמִשְׁפְּחֹתָם לִמְקֹמֹתָם בִּשְׁמֹתָם אַלּוּף תִּמְנָע אַלּוּף עַלְוָה אַלּוּף יְתֵת: [בראשית לו, מ]
נ) אוֹ יַחֲזֵק בְּמָעוּזִּי יַעֲשֶׂה שָׁלוֹם לִי שָׁלוֹם יַעֲשֶׂה לִּי: [ישעיה כז, ה]
ס) וָאָשִׂים דְּבָרַי בְּפִיךָ וּבְצֵל יָדִי כִּסִּיתִיךָ לִנְטֹעַ שָׁמַיִם וְלִיסֹד אָרֶץ וְלֵאמֹר לְצִיּוֹן עַמִּי אָתָּה: [ישעיה נא, טז]
ע) וַיִּקַּח אַבְרָם אֶת שָׂרַי אִשְׁתּוֹ וְאֶת לוֹט בֶּן אָחִיו וְאֶת כָּל רְכוּשָׁם אֲשֶׁר רָכָשׁוּ וְאֶת הַנֶּפֶשׁ אֲשֶׁר עָשׂוּ בְחָרָן וַיֵּצְאוּ לָלֶכֶת אַרְצָה כְּנַעַן וַיָּבֹאוּ אַרְצָה כְּנָעַן: [בראשית יב, ה]
פ) וּשְׁמַרְתֶּם אֶת דִּבְרֵי הַבְּרִית הַזֹּאת וַעֲשִׂיתֶם אֹתָם לְמַעַן תַּשְׂכִּילוּ אֵת כָּל אֲשֶׁר תַּעֲשׂוּן: [דברים כט, ח]
צ) וַיֹּאמֶר יְיָ אֶל מֹשֶׁה עֲבֹר לִפְנֵי הָעָם וְקַח אִתְּךָ מִזִּקְנֵי יִשְׂרָאֵל וּמַטְּךָ אֲשֶׁר הִכִּיתָ בּוֹ אֶת הַיְאֹר קַח בְּיָדְךָ וְהָלָכְתָּ: [שמות יז, ה]
ק) כֹּה אָמַר יְיָ אִם לֹא בְרִיתִי יוֹמָם וָלָיְלָה חֻקּוֹת שָׁמַיִם וָאָרֶץ לֹא שָׂמְתִּי: [ירמיה לג, כה]
ר) וַיֹּאמֶר יְיָ אִם אֶמְצָא בִסְדֹם חֲמִשִּׁים צַדִּיקִם בְּתוֹךְ הָעִיר וְנָשָׂאתִי לְכָל הַמָּקוֹם בַּעֲבוּרָם: [בראשית יח, כו]

thing if you keep them within you; let them be established altogether on your lips.[14]

Having expounded *Numbers* 15:31 as referring to one who denies the divine origin of the Torah, the Gemara now expounds the preceding verse, *Numbers* 15:30, as referring to one who actually ridicules the Torah's contents:

תָּנוּ רַבָּנָן – **The Rabbis taught** in a Baraisa: ,,וְהַנֶּפֶשׁ אֲשֶׁר־תַּעֲשֶׂה בְּיָד רָמָה" – Scripture states: *A PERSON WHO SHALL ACT HIGH-HANDEDLY... it is God Whom he blasphemes* – זֶה מְנַשֶּׁה בֶּן חִזְקִיָּה – THIS refers to MENASHEH THE SON OF CHIZKIAH,[15] שֶׁהָיָה יוֹשֵׁב וְדוֹרֵשׁ בְּהַגָּדוֹת שֶׁל דּוֹפִי – WHO USED TO SIT AND EXPOUND ON THE Scriptural NARRATIVES IN A RIDICULING FASHION. אָמַר – HE SAID: "וְכִי לֹא הָיָה לוֹ לְמֹשֶׁה לִכְתּוֹב אֶלָּא ,,וַאֲחוֹת לוֹטָן תִּמְנָע" – "DID MOSES HAVE NOTHING TO WRITE in the Torah OTHER THAN such useless trivia as *LOTAN'S SISTER WAS TIMNA,*[16] ,,וְתִמְנַע הָיְתָה פִילֶגֶשׁ לֶאֱלִיפַז" – and *TIMNA WAS A CONCUBINE OF ELIPHAZ,*[17] ,,וַיֵּלֶךְ רְאוּבֵן בִּימֵי קְצִיר־חִטִּים וַיִּמְצָא דוּדָאִים בַּשָּׂדֶה" – or *REUVEN WENT OUT IN THE DAYS OF THE WHEAT HARVEST; HE FOUND DUDAIM IN THE FIELD?*"[18] יָצְאָה בַּת קוֹל וְאָמְרָה לוֹ – A HEAVENLY VOICE thereupon ISSUED FORTH AND SAID TO [MENASHEH]:[19] ,,תֵּשֵׁב בְּאָחִיךָ תְדַבֵּר בְּבֶן־אִמְּךָ תִּתֶּן־דֹּפִי אֵלֶּה עָשִׂיתָ וְהֶחֱרַשְׁתִּי דִּמִּיתָ הֱיוֹת־אֶהְיֶה כָמוֹךָ אוֹכִיחֲךָ וְאֶעֶרְכָה לְעֵינֶיךָ" – *YOU SIT AND SPEAK AGAINST YOUR BROTHER, YOUR MOTHER'S SON YOU RIDICULE. IF YOU DO THESE THINGS AND I REMAIN SILENT, YOU WILL THINK THAT I AM LIKE YOU.*[20] *WELL, I WILL REBUKE YOU AND EXPOSE [YOUR SINS] BEFORE YOUR VERY EYES!*[21] וְעָלָיו מְפוֹרָשׁ בַּקַּבָּלָה – AND CONCERNING [MENASHEH] IT WAS STATED IN THE TRADITION:[22] ,,הוֹי מֹשְׁכֵי הֶעָוֹן בְּחַבְלֵי הַשָּׁוְא וְכַעֲבוֹת הָעֲגָלָה חַטָּאָה" – *WOE UNTO THOSE WHO DRAW INIQUITY WITH CORDS OF NOTHINGNESS, AND SIN AS WITH A CART ROPE!*[23]

The Gemara queries regarding the last verse quoted by the Baraisa:

מַאי ,,כַּעֲבוֹת הָעֲגָלָה" – **What is** meant by *AS WITH A CART ROPE?*[24]

The Gemara explains:

אָמַר רַבִּי אַסִּי – **R' Assi said:** יֵצֶר הָרַע – The verse is actually speaking about two aspects of **the Evil Inclination.** בַּתְּחִלָּה דּוֹמֶה לְחוּט שֶׁל כּוּבְיָא – **Initially, [the Evil Inclination] resembles a spider's thread,** וּלְבַסּוֹף דּוֹמֶה לַעֲבוֹת הָעֲגָלָה – **but ultimately it resembles a cart rope.**[25]

The Gemara now discusses the first two verses Menasheh quoted in order to ridicule that which he found irrelevant and useless. The Gemara demonstrates that the verses actually contain an important message:

דְּאָתָן עֲלָהּ מֵיהַת ,,אֲחוֹת לוֹטָן תִּמְנָע" – Now, **however, that we have come upon [the verse],** ***Lotan's sister was Timna,*** מַאי הִיא – **what,** in fact, **is its** deeper significance?

The Gemara explains:

תִּמְנָע בַּת מְלָכִים הֲוַאי – **Timna was a daughter of kings,** i.e. a member of a royal family, דִּכְתִיב ,,אַלּוּף לוֹטָן... אַלּוּף תִּמְנָע" – **for it is written,** ***Chief Lotan***[26] ... ***Chief Timna,***[27] וְכָל אַלּוּף מַלְכוּתָא בְּלֹא תָּאגָא הִיא – **and every** mention of the word ***Chief*** in Scripture refers to **kingship without** a royal **diadem,** i.e. a ruler one degree less exalted than a crowned king. Since Lotan was such a ruler and Timna was his sister, she was perforce a member of a royal family.[28]

NOTES

14. *Proverbs* 22:18. This verse is found in a passage that describes the proper method of Torah study (compare the preceding verse: *Incline your ear and listen to the words of the Sages . . .*). Reish Lakish points to the last half of the verse, *let them be established altogether on your lips,* which teaches that one must study Torah constantly, as part of one's daily schedule, and not occasionally or haphazardly. Only then will *you keep them within you* – will you retain what you learned (*Rashi*).

15. The wicked Menasheh reigned as king of Judah for fifty-five years; see *II Kings* 21:1.

16. *Genesis* 36:22. This verse is found in a passage that delineates the genealogy of the Horites, a people that inhabited the land of Seir before it was conquered by Esau and to whom Timna, the concubine of Eliphaz, belonged. To Menasheh the entire passage seemed dryly academic. Of what concern is the lineage of Timna, a mere concubine? If Scripture contains only matters of eternal importance and relevance, why does it include such a passage? Menasheh thus ridiculed Moses for including this material in the Chumash (*Maharsha*).

17. Ibid. v. 12. The inclusion of this verse was not ridiculed by Menasheh, for generally the Torah does list the wives of Esau's family (*Maharsha*). [The Gemara cites it because Menasheh quoted this verse to underscore the fact that Timna was merely a concubine, whose lineage should be of no concern.]

18. Ibid. 30:14. The essentials of the episode involving the *dudaim,* a fertility-inducing plant whose exact identity the Gemara will discuss below, are that Reuven gave them to his mother Leah, who then gave them to her sister Rachel in exchange for the latter's night with Jacob. The result of that union was the birth of Issachar, the progenitor of one of the twelve tribes of Israel. The fact that Reuven found the *dudaim* at the time of the wheat harvest is but a minor detail. Once again, Menasheh argued, the inclusion of such unnecessary information indicates Moses' inadequacy as the writer of the Pentateuch (see *Rashi*).

19. *Psalms* 50:20-21. This verse is found in a passage that is addressed to the wicked (see v. 16: *But to the wicked man God said, "To what purpose do you recount My decrees . . ."*). The Baraisa applies the verse to Menasheh, who held up his own heritage in order to ridicule and malign Moses, whom the Psalmist calls *your brother* (see *Maharsha*).

20. Our translation follows *Maharsha,* who explains that Menasheh was told that if God did not react to his heresy, he might think that God was in accord with it; hence, it was necessary to rebuke Menasheh for his sin.

21. *Rambam* writes: "There is no difference between verses such as *And Timna was a concubine etc. . . . Lotan's sister was Timna,* on the one hand, and *I am HASHEM, your God,* or *Hear O Israel, HASHEM is our God, HASHEM the one and only,* on the other . . . All issued from the Almighty and all are God's perfect Torah – pure, holy and true" (*Introduction to Cheilek, Eighth Article of Faith*).

Rambam elaborates on this point in his *Moreh Nevuchim* (*Guide for the Perplexed* III:50). There he stresses that seemingly irrelevant verses such as those cited by our Gemara actually "contain secrets of the Torah . . . Many have stumbled over them, and it is necessary to explain them, for these are stories concerning which many think there is no purpose in their inclusion [in the Torah] . . . I will tell you one rule before turning to details: Know that every story you find in the Torah has an indispensable purpose . . ."

22. I.e. the "Prophets" portion of Scripture.

23. *Isaiah* 5:18. *Cords of nothingness* is a metaphor for Menasheh's ridiculing Scripture, as he derived no personal gain from doing so (*Rashi*). *Rashi* to *Berachos* 24b (ד״ה בחבלי השוא) explains the term to mean cords that are weak and are easily snapped, and this interpretation accords with R' Assi's metaphor below (see note 25 below).

24. The verse describes Menasheh's act of sinning with conflicting metaphors – *cords of nothingness* (i.e. thin ropes) and *a cart rope* (i.e. a thick rope). The Gemara questions how both metaphors can be valid (*Maharsha*).

25. The first time a person is tempted to commit a particular sin, it is not difficult to resist that temptation. However, once the person becomes accustomed to committing that sin, he discovers that he is addicted to it and it is extremely difficult to resist the temptation to repeat the sin. This, then, is R' Assi's metaphor: Initially, the Evil Inclination pulls one to sin with a spider's thread, which is very weak and easily broken. Once the person becomes addicted to the sin but wants to stop, he discovers that he is bound to that sin with a cart rope, which is very thick and almost unbreakable (*Rashi* to *Succah* 52a ד״ה ולבסוף).

26. *Genesis* 36:29.

27. Ibid. v. 40. [Note that these two verses are widely separated and are recorded in different passages.]

28. The proof that Timna was "a daughter of kings" derives from her being a sister of Lotan, here mentioned as a ruler, a position that presumably he inherited from his father (*Rashi*). According to this

עין משפט
נר מצוה

יז א מיי' פ"ג מהלכות תשובה הלכה יד ועי' בכ"מ:
יח ב מיי' שם הלכה יא:

ליקוטי רש"י

כי נעים. יהי לך לאחר זמן אם תשמרם ותצפנם בבטנך שלא תשכחם ואימתי יהיו שמורים בלבך בזמן שיכונו על שפתיך כאשר תוציאם בפיך [משלי כב, יח]. ותמנע היתה פילגש לאליפז. להודיע גדולתו של אברהם כמה היו תאבים לידבק בזרעו תמנע זו בת אלופים היתה, שנאמר (פסוק כב) ואחות לוטן תמנע, ולוטן מאלופי יושבי שעיר היה, מן החורים שישבו בה לפנים, אמרה איני זוכה להנשא לך, הלואי ואהיה פילגש. ובדברי הימים מונה אותה (דברי הימים א' א לו) בבניו של אליפז, מלמד שבא על אשתו של שעיר ויצאה תמנע מביניהם, וכשגדלה נעשית פילגשו, וזהו ואחות לוטן תמנע, ולא מנאה עם בני שעיר שהיתה אחותו מן האם ולא מן האב [בראשית לו, יב]. בימי קציר חטים. להגיד שבחן של שבטים שעת הקציר היה ולא פשט ידו בגזל להביא חטים ושעורים אלא דבר ההפקר שאין אדם מקפיד בו. דודאים. סיגלי, עשב הוא ובלשון ישמעאל יסמי"ן [שם ל, יד]. דמית. סבור אתה שאהיה כמוך להתרצו' במעשיך הרעים, (וי"מ דמית כי אינני יודע הנסתרות) [תהלים נ, כא]. הוי מושכי העון. גוררים יצר הרע עליהם מעט מעט בתחלה בחבלי השוא כחוט של קורי עכביש ומשנתגרה בהם מתגבר והולך עד שנעשה כעבות העגלה שקושרין בו את הקרון למשוך. השוא. דבר שאין בו ממש. חטאה. חטא [ישעיהו ה, יח]. מלכותא בלא תגא. כלומר שררה גדולה ואינו חסר אלא כתר מלכות [לקמן קה.]. או יחזק במעוזי. או לשון אם, כמו או נודע כי שור נגח הוא (שמות כא) או יחזק עמי במעוזי שלא יבקש מעוז אלא מעוזי אז יעשה שלום לי להניח דעתי ואפי שמתקשקשת בי על שאיני נוקם בצרי ואנקם בהם. שלום יעשה לי. ממדת הדין שלא יוכל לקטרג ולומר מה נשתנו אלו מאלו [ישעיהו כז, ה]. אשר עשו בחרן. שהכניסן תחת כנפי השכינה אברהם מגייר את האנשים ושרה מגיירת הנשים ומעלה עליהם הכתוב כאלו עשאום ופשוטו של מקרא עבדים ושפחות שקנו להם כמו (שם לא א) עשה את כל הכבוד הזה (במדבר כד יח) וישראל עושה חיל לשון קונה וכונס [בראשית יב, ה]. המלמד את בן חבירו. ואלה תולדת אהרן ומשה, ואינו מזכיר אלא בני אהרן ונקראו תולדות משה לפי שלמדן תורה מלמד שכל המלמד את בן חבירו תורה מעלה עליו הכתוב כאלו ילדו [במדבר ג, א]. אם לא בריתי וגו'. אי אפשר שלא יתקיים הברית שכרתי ליום ולילה להיות בעתם ואי אפשר לחוקות שמים וארץ ליבטל כאילו לא שמתים גם זרע יעקב וגו' ורבותינו דרשוהו לענין ברית התורה ללמוד מכאן שבשביל התורה נבראו שמים וארץ אך אין המדרש מיושב על סדר המקראות [ירמיהו לג, כה].

זמר בכל יום. היה מסדר למודך אע"פ שסדור בפיך כזמר והוא יגרוס לך שתהא לעולם הבא בשמחה ובשירים: נפש עמל עמלה לו. מפני שעמל בתורה תורה עומלת לו: כי אכף עליו פיהו. מפני שהוא משים דברים בפיו תמיד כאוכף שעל החמור לישנא אחרינא זמר כלומר שעוסק בשירים ובזמירות תדיר תדיר נעשה זמר כך החוזר על התורה נעשה לו סדורה בפיו: תורה עומלת לו. שמחזרת עליו ומבקשת מאת קונה למסור לו טעמי תורה וסדריה וכל כך למה מפני שאכף שכפף פיהו על דברי תורה: דרופתקי. טרחנין כלומר כל הגופין לעמל נבראו: טוביה לדזכי. אשריו למי שזכה והיה עמלו וטרחו בתורה לשון אחר דרפתקי כיס ארוך שמשימין בו מעות כל הגופין נרתקין הם לקבל ולהכניס דברים אשריו למי שזכה ונעשה נרתק לתורה: לומד תורה לפרקים. ואינו לומד תדיר תדיר כמי שאין לו אשה ובועל פעמים זו פעמים זו: שנאמר כי נעים כי תשמרם. אימתי תשמרם בבטנך [בזמן] שיכונו יחדיו על שפתיך: לא היה לו למשה לכתוב אלא ואחות לוטן תמנע. בתמיה דבר שאינו צריך הוא וכן היה מלגלג ואומר שכתבו משה שלא לצורך ולקמיה מפרש דהיינו מגלה פנים בתורה: וילך ראובן וגו'. והיינו נמי שלא לצורך: בחבלי השוא. בחנם בלא שום הנאה היה חוטא: מלכותא בלא תגא. שר גדול אלא שאינו מעוטר וכיון דתמנע היתה אחות מלך ודאי בת מלך היא: מוטב שאהיה שפחה לאומה זו. לבני אברהם יצחק (ויעקב) שהן יראי שמים ולא אהיה גברת לאומה אחרת ולכך נעשית פילגש לאליפז בן עשו שהיה מזרע יצחק: לרחקה. מתחת כנפי השכינה שהיה להם לגיירה: בימי קציר חטים. לאחר שקצרו השדה שהכל רשאין ליכנס בתוך שדה חבריהן: יברוחי. כדמתרגמינן ולא איתפרש מאי היא: סיגלי וסביסקי [וסבסוך]. מינין אחרים סיגלי עיקרי עשבים והוא ממיני בשמים ואמהות של אותן עשבים קרי סגלי (וסבסך) [וסביסקי] נמי מין בשמים: מעוזי. תורה: שלום שלום. תרתי זימני אחד למעלה ואחד למטה: פלטירין של מעלה ושלמטה. כדכתיב לנטוע שמים וליסוד ארץ: אשר עשו בחרן. דמתרגמינן דשעבידו לאורייתא בחרן וקרי להו עשייה: כאילו עשאו. לאותו דבר מצוה: והלא אהרן הכה. דכתיב (שמות ז) [ח] (ויאמר) אל אהרן קח מטך ונטה ידך: מגלה פנים בתורה. מעיז פנים כלפי עוסקי תורה מגלה פנים משתמע לן דחמיר מאפיקורוס דאפיקורוס היינו דאית ביה אפקירותא בעלמא: אלא למ"ד מבזה תלמידי חכמים עצמן אפיקורוס הוי. כ"ש דמבזה חברו בפני תלמידי חכמים לאו מגלה פנים הוא והשתא מאי ניניהו מגלה פנים בתורה: מנשה בן חזקיה. שהיה דורש באגדות של דופי: איכא דמתני לה אסיפא. [ט] דברייתא דקתני מכאן אמר רבי אלעזר וכו' המגלה פנים בתורה רב ור' חנינא וכו': מאי אהני לן. והם אינן יודעין שעולם מתקיים עליהם: מגלה פנים בתורה הוא. שכופר במה שכתוב בתורה: אם לא בריתי יומם ולילה וגו'. שמהנין לעולם ומקיימין [אותו] והוא אומר דלא מהני מידי: מהכא נמי שמעינן. שהצדיקים מהנין לאחרים:

זמר בכל יום זמר בכל יום אמר רב יצחק בר אבודימי מאי קרא שנאמר [א] נפש עמל עמלה לו כי אכף עליו פיהו הוא עמל במקום זה ותורתו עומלת לו במקום אחר אמר רבי אלעזר [א] כל אדם לעמל נברא שנאמר [ב] כי אדם לעמל יולד איני יודע אם לעמל פה נברא אם לעמל מלאכה נברא כשהוא אומר כי אכף עליו פיהו הוי אומר לעמל פה נברא ועדיין איני יודע אם לעמל תורה אם לעמל שיחה כשהוא אומר [ג] לא ימוש ספר התורה הזה מפיך הוי אומר לעמל תורה נברא והיינו דאמר רבא כולהו גופי דרופתקי נינהו טובי לדזכי דהוי דרופתקי דאורייתא [ד] ונואף אשה חסר לב אמר [א] ריש לקיש זה הלומד תורה לפרקים שנאמר [ה] כי נעים כי תשמרם בבטנך יכונו יחדיו על שפתיך ת"ר [ו] והנפש אשר תעשה ביד רמה זה מנשה בן חזקיה שהיה יושב ודורש בהגדות של דופי אמר וכי לא היה לו למשה לכתוב אלא [ז] ואחות לוטן תמנע [ח] ותמנע היתה פלגש לאליפז [ט] וילך ראובן בימי קציר חטים וימצא דודאים בשדה יצאה ב"ק ואמרה לו [י] תשב באחיך תדבר בבן אמך תתן דופי אלה עשית והחרשתי דמית היות אהיה כמוך אוכיחך ואערכה לעיניך ועליו מפורש בקבלה [כ] הוי מושכי העון בחבלי השוא וכעבות העגלה חטאה מאי כעבות העגלה [ג] א"ר אסי יצר הרע בתחלה דומה לחוט של [ג] כוביא ולבסוף דומה לעבות העגלה דאתן עלה מיהת אחות לוטן תמנע מאי היא תמנע בת מלכים הואי דכתיב [ל] אלוף לוטן [מ] אלוף תמנע וכל אלוף [ד] מלכותא בלא תאגא היא בעיא לאיגיורי באתה אצל אברהם יצחק ויעקב ולא קבלוה הלכה והיתה פילגש לאליפז בן עשו אמרה מוטב תהא שפחה לאומה זו ולא תהא גבירה לאומה אחרת נפק מינה עמלק דצערינהו לישראל מאי טעמא דלא איבעי להו לרחקה וילך ראובן בימי קציר חטים אמר רבא בר' יצחק אמר רב מכאן לצדיקים [ה] שאין פושטין ידיהן בגזל וימצא דודאים בשדה מאי דודאים אמר רב יברוחי לוי אמר סיגלי ר' יונתן אמר (סיבסוך) [סביסקי]: א"ר אלכסנדרי כל העוסק בתורה לשמה משים שלום בפמליא של מעלה ובפמליא של מטה שנאמר [נ] או יחזק במעוזי יעשה שלום לי שלום יעשה לי: רב אמר כאילו בנה פלטרין של מעלה ושל מטה שנאמר [ס] ואשים דברי בפיך ובצל ידי כסיתיך לנטוע שמים וליסד ארץ (אמר ריש לקיש) [רבי יוחנן אמר] אף מגין על כל העולם כולו שנאמר ובצל ידי כסיתיך ולוי אמר אף מקרב את הגאולה שנאמר [ס] ולאמר לציון עמי אתה אמר ריש לקיש [ו] כל המלמד את בן חבירו תורה מעלה עליו הכתוב כאילו עשאו שנאמר [ע] ואת הנפש אשר עשו בחרן ר' [ב] ([ז] אליעזר) אומר כאילו עשאן לדברי תורה שנאמר [פ] ושמרתם את דברי הברית הזאת ועשיתם אותם רבא אמר [ג] כאילו עשאו לעצמו שנאמר ועשיתם אותם אל תקרי אותם אלא אתם אמר רבי אבהו [ד] כל המעשה את חבירו לדבר מצוה מעלה עליו הכתוב (א) כאילו עשאה שנאמר [צ] ומטך אשר הכית בו את היאר וכי משה הכהו והלא אהרן הכהו אלא לומר לך כל המעשה את חבירו לדבר מצוה מעלה עליו הכתוב כאילו עשאה: אפיקורוס: רב ור' חנינא אמרי תרוייהו זה [א] המבזה ת"ח רבי יוחנן ור' יהושע בן לוי אמרי זה המבזה חבירו בפני ת"ח בשלמא למ"ד המבזה חבירו בפני ת"ח אפיקורוס הוי מבזה תלמיד חכם עצמו מגלה פנים בתורה שלא כהלכה הוי אלא למ"ד מבזה תלמיד חכם עצמו אפיקורוס הוי מגלה פנים בתורה כגון מאי [ב] כגון מנשה בן חזקיה ואיכא דמתני לה אסיפא מגלה פנים בתורה רב ור' חנינא אמרי זה המבזה ת"ח רבי יוחנן וריב"ל אמרי זה המבזה את חבירו בפני תלמיד חכם בשלמא למ"ד המבזה תלמיד חכם עצמו מגלה פנים בתורה הוי מבזה חבירו בפני ת"ח אפיקורוס הוי אלא למ"ד מבזה חבירו בפני תלמיד חכם מגלה פנים בתורה הוי אפיקורוס כגון מאן אמר רב יוסף כגון הני דאמרי מאי אהנו לן רבנן לדידהו קרו לדידהו תנו אמר ליה אביי האי מגלה פנים בתורה נמי הוא דכתיב [ק] אם לא בריתי יומם ולילה חקות שמים וארץ לא שמתי אמר רב נחמן בר יצחק מהכא נמי שמע מינה שנאמר [ר] ונשאתי לכל המקום בעבורם אלא כגון דיתיב קמיה רביה ונפלה ליה שמעתא בדוכתא אחריתי ואמר הכי אמרינן התם ולא אמר הכי אמר מר רבא אמר כגון הני דבי בנימין אסיא דאמרי מאי אהני לן רבנן מעולם לא

מסורת הש"ס

א) [כל המאמר הזה יפה נדרש בשל"ה סוף דף שע"ה: ע"ש פי' נאה ומתוקן], ב) [סוכה נב.], ג) [בסוכה איתא בוביא ובערוך גר' כוביא ובסוכה פירש"י בוכיא עכבים], ד) [לקמן קה.], ה) [סוטה יב. חולין לא.], ו) [לעיל יט: ע"ש], ז) [צ"ל אלעזר], ח) [צ"ל אמור], ט) [היינו משנה דאבות לעיל עמוד א].

הגהות הב"ח

(א) גמ' כאילו עשאו שנאמר ומטך וכו' כאילו עשאו:

הגהות הגר"א

[א] גמ' אמר ריש לקיש. נרשם עליו אות ג: [ב] שם רבי אלעזר. נרשם עליו אות א: [ג] שם רבא אמר. נרשם עליו אות ב: [ד] שם א"ר אבהו. נרשם עליו אות ד:

תורה אור השלם

א) נֶפֶשׁ עָמֵל עָמְלָה לּוֹ כִּי אָכַף עָלָיו פִּיהוּ: [משלי טז, כו]

ב) כִּי אָדָם לְעָמָל יוּלָּד וּבְנֵי רֶשֶׁף יַגְבִּיהוּ עוּף: [איוב ה, ז]

ג) לֹא יָמוּשׁ סֵפֶר הַתּוֹרָה הַזֶּה מִפִּיךָ וְהָגִיתָ בּוֹ יוֹמָם וָלַיְלָה לְמַעַן תִּשְׁמֹר לַעֲשׂוֹת כְּכָל הַכָּתוּב בּוֹ כִּי אָז תַּצְלִיחַ אֶת דְּרָכֶךָ וְאָז תַּשְׂכִּיל: [יהושע א, ח]

ד) נֹאֵף אִשָּׁה חֲסַר לֵב מַשְׁחִית נַפְשׁוֹ הוּא יַעֲשֶׂנָּה: [משלי ו, לב]

ה) כִּי נָעִים כִּי תִשְׁמְרֵם בְּבִטְנֶךָ יִכֹּנוּ יַחְדָּו עַל שְׂפָתֶיךָ: [משלי כב, יח]

ו) וְהַנֶּפֶשׁ אֲשֶׁר תַּעֲשֶׂה בְּיָד רָמָה מִן הָאֶזְרָח וּמִן הַגֵּר אֶת יְיָ הוּא מְגַדֵּף וְנִכְרְתָה הַנֶּפֶשׁ הַהִוא מִקֶּרֶב עַמָּהּ: [במדבר טו, ל]

ז) וַיִּהְיוּ בְנֵי לוֹטָן חֹרִי וְהֵימָם וַאֲחוֹת לוֹטָן תִּמְנָע: [בראשית לו, כב]

ח) וְתִמְנַע הָיְתָה פִילֶגֶשׁ לֶאֱלִיפַז בֶּן עֵשָׂו וַתֵּלֶד לֶאֱלִיפַז אֶת עֲמָלֵק אֵלֶּה בְּנֵי עָדָה אֵשֶׁת עֵשָׂו: [בראשית לו, יב]

ט) וַיֵּלֶךְ רְאוּבֵן בִּימֵי קְצִיר חִטִּים וַיִּמְצָא דוּדָאִים בַּשָּׂדֶה וַיָּבֵא אֹתָם אֶל לֵאָה אִמּוֹ וַתֹּאמֶר רָחֵל אֶל לֵאָה תְּנִי נָא לִי מִדּוּדָאֵי בְּנֵךְ: [בראשית ל, יד]

י) תֵּשֵׁב בְּאָחִיךָ תְדַבֵּר בְּבֶן אִמְּךָ תִּתֶּן דֹּפִי: אֵלֶּה עָשִׂיתָ וְהֶחֱרַשְׁתִּי דִּמִּיתָ הֱיוֹת אֶהְיֶה כָמוֹךָ אוֹכִיחֲךָ וְאֶעֶרְכָה לְעֵינֶיךָ: [תהלים נ, כ-כא]

כ) הוֹי מֹשְׁכֵי הֶעָוֹן בְּחַבְלֵי הַשָּׁוְא וְכַעֲבוֹת הָעֲגָלָה חַטָּאָה: [ישעיה ה, יח]

ל) אֵלֶּה אַלּוּפֵי הַחֹרִי אַלּוּף לוֹטָן אַלּוּף שׁוֹבָל אַלּוּף צִבְעוֹן אַלּוּף עֲנָה: [בראשית לו, כט] מ) וְאֵלֶּה שְׁמוֹת אַלּוּפֵי עֵשָׂו לְמִשְׁפְּחֹתָם לִמְקֹמֹתָם בִּשְׁמֹתָם אַלּוּף תִּמְנָע אַלּוּף עַלְוָה אַלּוּף יְתֵת: [בראשית לו, מ] נ) אוֹ יַחֲזֵק בְּמָעוּזִּי יַעֲשֶׂה שָׁלוֹם לִי שָׁלוֹם יַעֲשֶׂה לִּי: [ישעיה כז, ה] ס) וָאָשִׂים דְּבָרַי בְּפִיךָ וּבְצֵל יָדִי כִּסִּיתִיךָ לִנְטֹעַ שָׁמַיִם וְלִיסֹד אָרֶץ וְלֵאמֹר לְצִיּוֹן עַמִּי אָתָּה: [ישעיה נא, טז] ע) וַיִּקַּח אַבְרָם אֶת שָׂרַי אִשְׁתּוֹ וְאֶת לוֹט בֶּן אָחִיו וְאֶת כָּל רְכוּשָׁם אֲשֶׁר רָכָשׁוּ וְאֶת הַנֶּפֶשׁ אֲשֶׁר עָשׂוּ בְחָרָן וַיֵּצְאוּ לָלֶכֶת אַרְצָה כְּנַעַן וַיָּבֹאוּ אַרְצָה כְּנָעַן: [בראשית יב, ה] פ) וּשְׁמַרְתֶּם אֶת דִּבְרֵי הַבְּרִית הַזֹּאת וַעֲשִׂיתֶם אֹתָם לְמַעַן תַּשְׂכִּילוּ אֵת כָּל אֲשֶׁר תַּעֲשׂוּן: [דברים כט, ח] צ) וַיֹּאמֶר יְיָ אֶל מֹשֶׁה עֲבֹר לִפְנֵי הָעָם וְקַח אִתְּךָ מִזִּקְנֵי יִשְׂרָאֵל וּמַטְּךָ אֲשֶׁר הִכִּיתָ בּוֹ אֶת הַיְאֹר קַח בְּיָדְךָ וְהָלָכְתָּ: [שמות יז, ה] ק) כֹּה אָמַר יְיָ אִם לֹא בְרִיתִי יוֹמָם וָלָיְלָה חֻקּוֹת שָׁמַיִם וָאָרֶץ לֹא שָׂמְתִּי: [ירמיה לג, כה] ר) וַיֹּאמֶר יְיָ אִם אֶמְצָא בִסְדֹם חֲמִשִּׁים צַדִּיקִם בְּתוֹךְ הָעִיר וְנָשָׂאתִי לְכָל הַמָּקוֹם בַּעֲבוּרָם: [בראשית יח, כו]

The Gemara continues with the story of Timna:

בָּעֲיָא לְאִיגַּיּוֹרֵי – **[Timna] sought to convert** to the faith of Abraham, בָּאתָה אֵצֶל אַבְרָהָם יִצְחָק וְיַעֲקֹב – and **came to Abraham, Isaac and Jacob** for that purpose,[29] וְלֹא קִבְּלוּהָ – **but they did not accept her** as a convert. הָלְכָה וְהָיְתָה פִּילֶגֶשׁ לֶאֱלִיפַז בֶּן עֵשָׂו – **She** thereupon **went and became a concubine of Eliphaz, the son of Esau,** אָמְרָה מוּטָב תְּהֵא שִׁפְחָה לְאוּמָּה זוּ – **saying** in explanation, **"It is better to be a maidservant to this nation** וְלֹא תְּהֵא גְבִירָה לְאוּמָּה אַחֶרֶת – **than to be a princess to** any **other nation!"**[30] נְפַק מִינָּהּ עֲמָלֵק – **From her issued Amalek,** דְּצַעֲרִינְהוּ לְיִשְׂרָאֵל – **who distressed Israel** so greatly. מַאי טַעְמָא – For **what reason** was Amalek able to cause Israel so much anguish and pain? What sin did the Jews commit that caused them to suffer so greatly at the hands of Amalek and his descendants? דְּלֹא אִיבְּעֵי לְהוּ לְרַחֲקָהּ – It was **because [Abraham, Isaac and Jacob] should not have rejected [Timna].** Because the Patriarchs refused to accept her as a convert, God caused their descendants to suffer at the hands of her descendants.[31] Thus, this verse, which was ridiculed by Menasheh as irrelevant and trivial, in fact teaches us in what great esteem Abraham's family, including even Esau, was held by the most aristocratic families of that era.

The Gemara now reveals the message of the second verse that Menasheh ridiculed:

"וַיֵּלֶךְ רְאוּבֵן בִּימֵי קְצִיר־חִטִּים" – Scripture states: ***Reuven went out in the days of the wheat harvest.*** אָמַר רָבָא בְּרַבִּי יִצְחָק אָמַר רַב – **Rava, the son of R' Yitzchak, said in the name of Rav:** מִכָּאן לַצַּדִּיקִים שֶׁאֵין פּוֹשְׁטִין יְדֵיהֶן בְּגָזֵל – **From here** we learn that **righteous people** are careful **not to stretch forth their hands in** acts of **robbery.**[32]

The Gemara now explains what *dudaim* are, citing three opinions:

"וַיִּמְצָא דוּדָאִים בַּשָּׂדֶה" – Scripture states: ***He found* dudaim *in the field.*** מַאי דוּדָאִים – **What is** the meaning of the word ***dudaim?*** אָמַר רַב יַבְרוּחֵי – **Rav said** that *dudaim* are ***yavruchei;***[33] לֵוִי אָמַר סִיגְלֵי – **Levi said** that *dudaim* are ***siglei;***[34] רַבִּי יוֹנָתָן אָמַר (סיבסוך) [סְבִיסְקֵי] – **R' Yonasan said** that *dudaim* are ***seviskei.***[35]

The Gemara interrupted its evaluation of various methods of Torah study to discuss the wicked King Menasheh, who mocked the Torah. The Gemara now returns to its original subject, quoting four sages who describe the power of Torah study לִשְׁמָהּ, *for its own sake:*

אָמַר רַבִּי אֲלֶכְּסַנְדְּרִי – **R' Alexandri said:** כָּל הָעוֹסֵק בַּתּוֹרָה לִשְׁמָהּ – **Whoever engages in Torah** study **for its own sake**[36] מֵשִׂים שָׁלוֹם בְּפָמַלְיָא שֶׁל מַעְלָה וּבְפָמַלְיָא שֶׁל מַטָּה – **promotes peace among the** heavenly **host above, and among the host below** on earth,[37] שֶׁנֶּאֱמַר "אוֹ יַחֲזֵק בְּמָעֻזִּי יַעֲשֶׂה שָׁלוֹם לִי שָׁלוֹם יַעֲשֶׂה־לִּי" – **as it is**

NOTES

explanation, it is unnecessary for the Gemara to quote the second verse, *Chief Timna.* Indeed, *Bereishis Rabbah* 82:14, cited by *Margaliyos HaYam*, deletes it from the Gemara, and many commentators understand that the verse refers not to Lotan's sister, but to one of Eliphaz's sons (see *Even Ezra* to *Genesis* 36:40 and *Rashbam* ibid. v. 12). See also commentaries to *I Chronicles* 1:36. Cf. *Yad Ramah,* who cites an opinion that *Chief Timna* refers to Timna herself.

29. [It would seem impossible that Timna actually came to Abraham, inasmuch as she was Eliphaz's daughter (see *Rashi* to *Genesis* 36:12), Eliphaz was Esau's son, and Esau was only fifteen years old when Abraham died. Rather, the Gemara means to say that Timna sought to attach herself to the *descendants* of Abraham, Isaac and Jacob by converting to Judaism.]

30. Timna felt that it was better to marry into the family of the Patriarchs, a God-fearing people, than to retain her royal status in another nation. She therefore accepted the lowly rank of concubine (which she euphemistically called "a maidservant") to Eliphaz, since he was Isaac's grandson (*Rashi*).

31. Why did the Patriarchs reject Timna, after having converted so many other idolaters? *Rif* (in *Ein Yaakov*) explains that Timna was illegitimate (a *mamzeress*), born of an adulterous union between the wife of Seir and Eliphaz (see *Rashi* to *Genesis* 36:12). The Patriarchs therefore refused to accept Timna as a convert because a *mamzer* is forbidden to marry an ordinary Jew. But if the Patriarchs acted so wisely and prudently, why were their descendants punished? *Rif* explains that even though our forebears could never sanction Timna's marrying an ordinary Jew, they should have allowed her to come closer to God by joining His people.

Yalkut HaMeiri (by Rabbi Abraham Meir Israel) suggests that the Patriarchs were aware that Timna was primarily motivated by her desire to marry into Abraham's family. However, Jewish law rejects those who wish to convert in order to marry a Jew (*Yoreh Deah* 268:12; see also *Hagahos Yavetz*).

32. Scripture teaches us that Reuven did not go out to collect *dudaim* until after the crops had been harvested and the farmers no longer cared whether anyone entered their fields. Had he taken the *dudaim* before or during the harvest, Reuven would have committed an act of robbery (*Rashi, Yad Ramah*). *Be'er Sheva* finds this interpretation difficult, and contends that it was authored by one of *Rashi's* students, who misunderstood his master's words. He argues that the language, *in the days of the wheat harvest,* implies just that – i.e. Reuven went out while the harvest was underway, and not after its completion. *Be'er Sheva* therefore interprets the Gemara to mean that although Reuven went out to collect at the time of the harvest, he did not steal the farmers' wheat, but took only that which was considered ownerless, the *dudaim.* Indeed, *Be'er Sheva* cites *Rashi* to *Chumash* (*Genesis* 30:14), who interprets the verse in this very manner!

33. *Yavruchei* are a type of plant, but it is unclear exactly which (*Rashi*). It is commonly conjectured that *yavruchei* are mandrakes; see ArtScroll *Bereishis* pp. 1300-2.

34. *Rashi* (*Berachos* 43b) translates *siglei* as violets, as does *Orach Chaim* 216:8. *Aruch* identifies them as cypress, and *Mussaf HaAruch* as a narcissus plant. See also *Mizrachi* ad loc. and *Maharsha* here. See also *Ibn Ezra* on the verse.

35. These are a certain type of spice (*Rashi*).

36. There are various explanations of this concept. We present three that are presented by Rishonim: (a) to study without hope of reward or fear of punishment, but solely because Torah is truth (*Rambam, Introduction* to *Cheilek*); (b) to study with the intent to practice (*Sefer Chasidim*, §544 Margolios ed. or §17 Lewin-Epstein ed.); (c) to study Torah "for the Torah's sake" – i.e. simply to know and understand its contents and to extrapolate therefrom, and not for the purposes of enhancing one's stature or vexing others with one's knowledge (*Rosh* to *Nedarim* 62a, *Nefesh HaChaim* 4:3).

37. God has two worlds, the heavenly and the earthly. Conflict erupts in both when Jews do not learn Torah for its own sake. The angelic forces reproach God for giving the holy Torah to earthly beings: [You] who *places your majesty on the heavens . . . What is man that you should remember him?* (*Psalms* 8:2,5). On earth itself God must take issue with man for accepting the Torah and then learning it for personal gain. When Torah is studied in the correct manner, however, peace will reign in heaven and on earth (*Rif* in *Ein Yaakov*).

Yad Ramah explains R' Alexandri's dictum as follows: When one studies Torah for its own sake, he is worthy of reward, not punishment. Since it is the unpleasant duty of the heavenly host to administer punishment to errant man, these celestial beings are happy when they are not summoned to their appointed task. This is the meaning of the first part of R' Alexandri's statement, "Torah study for its own sake promotes peace among the heavenly host." In addition, in the merit of such pure Torah study the entire world is protected (as R' Yochanan explicitly states below), and this is what is meant by the second part of R' Alexandri's statement, ". . . and among the host below."

Maharal translates R' Alexandri's dictum as follows: [He] promotes peace between the host above and the host below. *Maharal* explains that the Torah, divine in origin yet given to mortal man, is the bridge between the heavenly and earthly realms. One who is purely motivated

זמר בכל יום אמר רב יצחק בר אבודימי מאי קרא שנאמר א) נפש עמל עמלה לו כי אכף עליו פיהו הוא עמל במקום זה ותורתו עומלת לו במקום אחר אמר רבי אלעזר א) כל אדם לעמל נברא שנאמר ב) כי אדם לעמל יולד איני יודע אם לעמל פה נברא אם לעמל מלאכה נברא כשהוא אומר כי אכף עליו פיהו הוי אומר לעמל פה נברא ועדיין איני יודע אם לעמל תורה אם לעמל שיחה כשהוא אומר ג) לא ימוש ספר התורה הזה מפיך הוי אומר לעמל תורה נברא והיינו דאמר רבא כולהו גופי דרופתקי נינהו טובי לדזכי דהוי דרופתקי דאורייתא ד) ונואף אשה חסר לב אמר [א] ריש לקיש זה הלומד תורה לפרקים שנאמר ה) כי נעים כי תשמרם בבטנך יכונו יחדיו על שפתיך ת"ר ו) והנפש אשר תעשה ביד רמה זה מנשה בן חזקיה שהיה יושב ודורש בהגדות של דופי אמר וכי לא היה לו למשה לכתוב אלא ז) ואחות לוטן תמנע ח) ותמנע היתה פלגש לאליפז ט) וילך ראובן בימי קציר חטים וימצא דודאים בשדה יצאה ב"ק ואמרה לו י) תשב באחיך תדבר בבן אמך תתן דופי אלה עשית והחרשתי דמית היות אהיה כמוך אוכיחך ואערכה לעיניך ועליו מפורש בקבלה כ) הוי מושכי העון בחבלי השוא וכעבות העגלה חטאה מאי כעבות העגלה ג) א"ר אסי יצר הרע בתחלה דומה לחוט של ג) כוביא ולבסוף דומה לעבות העגלה דאתן עלה מיהת אחות לוטן תמנע מאי היא תמנע בת מלכים הואי דכתיב ל) אלוף לוטן מ) אלוף תמנע וכל אלוף ד) מלכותא בלא תאגא היא בעיא לאיגיורי באתה אצל אברהם יצחק ויעקב ולא קבלוה הלכה והיתה פילגש לאליפז בן עשו אמרה מוטב תהא שפחה לאומה זו ולא תהא גבירה לאומה אחרת נפק מינה עמלק דצערינהו לישראל מאי טעמא דלא איבעי להו לרחקה וילך ראובן בימי קציר חטים אמר רבא בר' יצחק אמר רב מכאן לצדיקים ה) שאין פושטין ידיהן בגזל וימצא דודאים בשדה מאי דודאים אמר רב יברוחי לוי אמר סיגלי ר' יונתן אמר (סיבסוך) [סביסקי]: א"ר אלכסנדרי כל העוסק בתורה לשמה משים שלום בפמליא של מעלה ובפמליא של מטה שנאמר נ) או יחזק במעוזי יעשה שלום לי שלום יעשה לי: רב אמר כאילו בנה פלטרין של מעלה ושל מטה שנאמר ס) ואשים דברי בפיך ובצל ידי כסיתיך לנטוע שמים וליסד ארץ (אמר ריש לקיש) [רבי יוחנן אמר] אף מגין על כל העולם כולו שנאמר ובצל ידי כסיתיך ולוי אמר אף מקרב את הגאולה שנאמר ס) ולאמר לציון עמי אתה אמר ריש לקיש ו) כל המלמד את בן חבירו תורה מעלה עליו הכתוב כאילו עשאו שנאמר ע) ואת הנפש אשר עשו בחרן ר' [ב] (ז) אליעזר) אומר כאילו עשאן לדברי תורה שנאמר פ) ושמרתם את דברי הברית הזאת ועשיתם אותם רבא אמר [ג] כאילו עשאו לעצמו שנאמר ועשיתם אותם אל תקרי אותם אלא אתם אמר רבי אבהו [ד] כל המעשה את חבירו לדבר מצוה מעלה עליו הכתוב (א) כאילו עשאה שנאמר צ) ומטך אשר הכית בו את היאר וכי משה הכהו והלא אהרן הכהו אלא לומר לך כל המעשה את חבירו לדבר מצוה מעלה עליו הכתוב כאילו עשאה: אפיקורוס: רב ור' חנינא אמרי תרוייהו זה ח) המבזה ת"ח רבי יוחנן ור' יהושע בן לוי אמרי זה המבזה חבירו בפני ת"ח בשלמא למ"ד המבזה חבירו בפני ת"ח אפיקורוס הוי מבזה תלמיד חכם עצמו מגלה פנים בתורה שלא כהלכה הוי אלא למ"ד מבזה תלמיד חכם עצמו אפיקורוס הוי מגלה פנים בתורה כגון מאי ט) כגון מנשה בן חזקיה ואיכא דמתני לה אסיפא מגלה פנים בתורה רב ור' חנינא אמרי זה המבזה ת"ח רבי יוחנן וריב"ל אמרי זה המבזה את חבירו בפני תלמיד חכם בשלמא למ"ד המבזה תלמיד חכם עצמו מגלה פנים בתורה הוי מבזה חבירו בפני ת"ח אפיקורוס הוי אלא למ"ד מבזה חבירו בפני תלמיד חכם מגלה פנים בתורה הוי אפיקורוס כגון מאן אמר רב יוסף כגון הני דאמרי מאי אהנו לן רבנן לדידהו קרו לדידהו תנו אמר ליה אביי האי מגלה פנים בתורה נמי הוא דכתיב ק) אם לא בריתי יומם ולילה חקות שמים וארץ לא שמתי אמר רב נחמן בר יצחק מהכא נמי שמע מינה שנאמר ר) ונשאתי לכל המקום בעבורם אלא כגון דיתיב קמיה רביה ונפלה ליה שמעתא בדוכתא אחריתי ואמר הכי אמרינן התם ולא אמר הכי אמר מר רבא אמר כגון הני דבי בנימין אסיא דאמרי מאי אהני לן רבנן מעולם

לא

רש"י

זמר בכל יום. היה מסדר למודך אע"פ שסדור בפיך כזמר והוא יגרוס לך שתהא לעולם הבא בשמחה ובשירים: נפש עמל עמלה לו. מפני שעמל בתורה תורה עומלת לו: כי אכף עליו פיהו. מפני שהוא משים דברים בפיו תמיד כאוכף שעל החמור לישנא אחרינא זמר כלומר שעוסק בשירים ובזמירות תדיר תדיר נעשה זמר כך החוזר על התורה נעשה לו סדורה בפיו: תורה עומלת לו. שמחזרת עליו ומבקשת מאת קונה למסור לו טעמי תורה וסדריה וכל כך למה מפני שאכף שכפף פיהו על דברי תורה: דרופתקי. טרחנין כלומר כל הגופין לעמל נבראו: טוביה לדזכי. אשריו למי שזכה והיה עמלו וטרחו בתורה לשון אחר דרפתקי כיס ארוך שמשימין בו מעות כל הגופין נרתקין הם לקבל ולהכניס דברים אשריו למי שזכה ונעשה נרתק לתורה: לומד תורה לפרקים. ואינו לומד תדיר כמי שאין לו אשה ובועל פעמים זו פעמים זו: שנאמר כי נעים כי תשמרם. אימתי תשמרם בבטנך [בזמן] שיכונו יחדיו על שפתיך: לא היה לו למשה לכתוב אלא ואחות לוטן תמנע. בתמיה דבר שאינו צריך הוא וכן היה מלגלג ואומר שכתבו משה שלא לצורך ולקמיה מפרש דהיינו מגלה פנים בתורה: וילך ראובן וגו'. והיינו נמי שלא לצורך: בחבלי השוא. בחנם בלא שום הנאה היה חוטא: מלכותא בלא תגא. שר גדול אלא שאינו מעוטר וכיון דתמנע היתה אחות מלך ודאי בת מלך היא: מוטב שאהיה שפחה לאומה זו. לבני אברהם יצחק (ויעקב) שהן יראי שמים ולא אהיה גברת לאומה אחרת ולכך נעשית פילגש לאליפז בן עשו שהיה מזרע יצחק: לרחקה. מתחת כנפי השכינה שהיה להם לגיירה: בימי קציר חטים. לאחר שקצרו השדה שהכל רשאין ליכנס בתוך שדה חבריהן: יברוחי. כדמתרגמינן ולא איתפרש מאי היא: סיגלי וסביסקי [וסבסוך]. מינין אחרים סיגלי עיקרי עשבים והוא ממיני בשמים ואמהות של אותן עשבים קרי סגלי (וסבסך) [וסביסקי] נמי מין בשמים: מעוזי. תורה: שלום שלום. תרתי זימני אחד למעלה ואחד למטה: פלטירין של מעלה ושלמטה. כדכתיב לנטוע שמים וליסוד ארץ: אשר עשו בחרן. דמתרגמינן דשעבידו לאורייתא בחרן וקרי להו עשייה: כאילו עשאו. לאותו דבר מצוה: והלא אהרן הכה. דכתיב (שמות ז) ט) (ויאמר) אל אהרן קח מטך ונטה ידך: מגלה פנים בתורה. מעיז פנים כלפי עוסקי תורה מגלה פנים משתמע לן דחמיר מאפיקורוס דאפיקורוס היינו דאית ביה אפקירותא בעלמא: אלא למ"ד מבזה תלמידי חכמים עצמן אפיקורוס הוי. כ"ש דמבזה חברו בפני תלמידי חכמים לאו מגלה פנים הוא והשתא מאי נינהו מגלה פנים בתורה: מנשה בן חזקיה. שהיה דורש באגדות של דופי: איכא דמתני לה אסיפא. ט) דברייתא דקתני מכאן אמר רבי אלעזר וכו' המגלה פנים בתורה רב ור' חנינא וכו': מאי אהני לן. והם אינן יודעין שעולם מתקיים עליהם: מגלה פנים בתורה הוא. שכופר במה שכתוב בתורה: אם לא בריתי יומם ולילה וגו'. שמהנין לעולם ומקיימין [אותו] והוא אומר דלא מהני מידי: מהכא נמי שמעינן. שהצדיקים מהנין לאחרים:

לא

עין משפט נר מצוה

יז א מיי' פ"ג מהלכות תשובה הלכה יד עי' בכ"מ:

יח ב מיי' שם הלכה יא:

ליקוטי רש"י

כי נעים. יהי לך לאחר זמן אם תשמרם ותצפנם בבטנך שלא תשכחם ואימתי יהיו שמורים בלבך בזמן שיכונו על שפתיך כאשר תוציאם בפיך [משלי כב, יח]. ותמנע היתה פילגש לאליפז. להודיע גדולתו של אברהם כמה היו תאבים לידבק בזרעו תמנע זו בת אלופים היתה, שנאמר (פסוק כב) ואחות לוטן תמנע, ולוטן מאלופי יושבי שעיר היה, מן החורים שישבו בה לפנים, אמרה איני זוכה להנשא לך, הלואי ואהיה פילגש. ובדברי הימים מונה אותה (דברי הימים א' א לו) בבניו של אליפז, מלמד שבא על אשתו של שעיר ויצאה תמנע מביניהם, וכשגדלה נעשית פילגשו, וזהו ואחות לוטן תמנע, ולא מנאה עם בני שעיר שהיתה אחותו מן האם ולא מן האב [בראשית לו, יב]. בימי קציר חטים. להגיד שבחן של שבטים שעת הקציר היה ולא פשט ידו בגזל להביא חטים ושעורים אלא דבר ההפקר שאין אדם מקפיד בו. דודאים. סיגלי, עשב הוא ובלשון ישמעאל יסמי"ן [שם ל, יד]. דמית. סבור אתה שאהיה כמוך להתרצו' במעשיך הרעים, (וי"מ דמית כי אינני יודע הנסתרות) [תהלים נ, כא]. הוי מושכי העון. גוררים יצר הרע עליהם מעט מעט בתחלה בחבלי השוא כחוט של קורי עכבים ומשנתגרה בהם מתגבר והולך עד שנעשה כעבות העגלה שקושרין בו את הקרון למשוך. השוא. דבר שאין בו ממש. חטאה. חטא [ישעיהו ה, יח]. מלכותא בלא תגא. כלומר שררה גדולה ואינו חסר אלא כתר מלכות [לקמן קה.]. או יחזק במעוזי. או לשון אם, כמו או נודע כי שור נגח הוא (שמות כא) או יחזק עמי במעוזי שלא יבקש מעוז אלא מעוזי אז יעשה שלום לי להניח דעתי ואפי' שמתקשקשת בי על שאיני נוקם בצרי ואנקם בהם. שלום יעשה לי. ממדת הדין שלא יוכל לקטרג ולומר מה נשתנו אלו מאלו [ישעיהו כז, ה]. אשר עשו בחרן. שהכניסן תחת כנפי השכינה אברהם מגייר את האנשים ושרה מגיירת הנשים ומעלה עליהם הכתוב כאלו עשאום ופשוטו של מקרא עבדים ושפחות שקנו להם כמו (שם לא א) עשה את כל הכבוד הזה (במדבר כד יח) וישראל עושה חיל לשון קונה וכונס [בראשית יב, ה]. המלמד את בן חבירו. ואלה תולדת אהרן ומשה, ואינו מזכיר אלא בני אהרן ונקראו תולדות משה לפי שלמדן תורה מלמד שכל המלמד את בן חבירו תורה מעלה עליו הכתוב כאלו ילדו [במדבר ג, א]. אם לא בריתי וגו'. אי אפשר שלא יתקיים הברית שכרתי ליום ולילה להיות בעתם ואי אפשר לחוקות שמים וארץ ליבטל כאילו לא שמתים גם זרע יעקב וגו' ורבותינו דרשוהו לענין ברית התורה ללמוד מכאן שבשביל התורה נבראו שמים וארץ אך אין המדרש מיושב על סדר המקראות [ירמיהו לג, כה].

מסורת הש"ס

א) [כל המאמר הזה יפה נדרש בשל"ה סוף דף שע"ה: ע"ש פי' נאה ומתוקן], ב) [סוכה נב.], ג) [בסוכה איתא בוכיא ובערוך גר' כוכיא ובסוכה פירש"י בוכיא עכבים], ד) [לקמן קה.], ה) [סוטה יב. חולין לא.], ו) [לעיל יט: ע"ש], ז) [צ"ל אלעזר], ח) [צ"ל אמור], ט) [היינו משנה דאבות לעיל עמוד א].

הגהות הב"ח

(א) גמ' כאילו עשאו שנאמר ומטך וכו' כאילו עשאו:

הגהות הגר"א

[א] גמ' אמר ריש לקיש. נרשם עליו אות ג: [ב] שם רבי אלעזר. נרשם עליו אות א: [ג] שם רבא אמר. נרשם עליו אות ב: [ד] שם א"ר אבהו. נרשם עליו אות ד:

תורה אור השלם

א) נֶפֶשׁ עָמֵל עָמְלָה לּוֹ כִּי אָכַף עָלָיו פִּיהוּ: [משלי טז, כו]

ב) כִּי אָדָם לְעָמָל יוּלָּד וּבְנֵי רֶשֶׁף יַגְבִּיהוּ עוּף: [איוב ה, ז]

ג) לֹא יָמוּשׁ סֵפֶר הַתּוֹרָה הַזֶּה מִפִּיךָ וְהָגִיתָ בּוֹ יוֹמָם וָלַיְלָה לְמַעַן תִּשְׁמֹר לַעֲשׂוֹת כְּכָל הַכָּתוּב בּוֹ כִּי אָז תַּצְלִיחַ אֶת דְּרָכֶךָ וְאָז תַּשְׂכִּיל: [יהושע א, ח]

ד) נֹאֵף אִשָּׁה חֲסַר לֵב מַשְׁחִית נַפְשׁוֹ הוּא יַעֲשֶׂנָּה: [משלי ו, לב]

ה) כִּי נָעִים כִּי תִשְׁמְרֵם בְּבִטְנֶךָ יִכֹּנוּ יַחְדָּו עַל שְׂפָתֶיךָ: [משלי כב, יח]

ו) וְהַנֶּפֶשׁ אֲשֶׁר תַּעֲשֶׂה בְּיָד רָמָה מִן הָאֶזְרָח וּמִן הַגֵּר אֶת יְיָ הוּא מְגַדֵּף וְנִכְרְתָה הַנֶּפֶשׁ הַהִוא מִקֶּרֶב עַמָּהּ: [במדבר טו, ל]

ז) וַיִּהְיוּ בְנֵי לוֹטָן חֹרִי וְהֵימָם וַאֲחוֹת לוֹטָן תִּמְנָע: [בראשית לו, כב]

ח) וְתִמְנַע הָיְתָה פִילֶגֶשׁ לֶאֱלִיפַז בֶּן עֵשָׂו וַתֵּלֶד לֶאֱלִיפַז אֶת עֲמָלֵק אֵלֶּה בְּנֵי עָדָה אֵשֶׁת עֵשָׂו: [בראשית לו, יב]

ט) וַיֵּלֶךְ רְאוּבֵן בִּימֵי קְצִיר חִטִּים וַיִּמְצָא דוּדָאִים בַּשָּׂדֶה וַיָּבֵא אֹתָם אֶל לֵאָה אִמּוֹ וַתֹּאמֶר רָחֵל אֶל לֵאָה תְּנִי נָא לִי מִדּוּדָאֵי בְּנֵךְ: [בראשית ל, יד]

י) תֵּשֵׁב בְּאָחִיךָ תְדַבֵּר בְּבֶן אִמְּךָ תִּתֶּן דֹּפִי: אֵלֶּה עָשִׂיתָ וְהֶחֱרַשְׁתִּי דִּמִּיתָ הֱיוֹת אֶהְיֶה כָמוֹךָ אוֹכִיחֲךָ וְאֶעֶרְכָה לְעֵינֶיךָ: [תהלים נ, כ-כא]

כ) הוֹי מֹשְׁכֵי הֶעָוֹן בְּחַבְלֵי הַשָּׁוְא וְכַעֲבוֹת הָעֲגָלָה חַטָּאָה: [ישעיה ה, יח]

ל) אֵלֶּה אַלּוּפֵי הַחֹרִי אַלּוּף לוֹטָן אַלּוּף שׁוֹבָל אַלּוּף צִבְעוֹן אַלּוּף עֲנָה: [בראשית לו, כט] מ) וְאֵלֶּה שְׁמוֹת אַלּוּפֵי עֵשָׂו לְמִשְׁפְּחֹתָם לִמְקֹמֹתָם בִּשְׁמֹתָם אַלּוּף תִּמְנָע אַלּוּף עַלְוָה אַלּוּף יְתֵת: [בראשית לו, מ] נ) אוֹ יַחֲזֵק בְּמָעֻזִּי יַעֲשֶׂה שָׁלוֹם לִי שָׁלוֹם יַעֲשֶׂה לִּי: [ישעיה כז, ה] ס) וָאָשִׂים דְּבָרַי בְּפִיךָ וּבְצֵל יָדִי כִּסִּיתִיךָ לִנְטֹעַ שָׁמַיִם וְלִיסֹד אָרֶץ וְלֵאמֹר לְצִיּוֹן עַמִּי אָתָּה: [ישעיה נא, טז] ע) וַיִּקַּח אַבְרָם אֶת שָׂרַי אִשְׁתּוֹ וְאֶת לוֹט בֶּן אָחִיו וְאֶת כָּל רְכוּשָׁם אֲשֶׁר רָכָשׁוּ וְאֶת הַנֶּפֶשׁ אֲשֶׁר עָשׂוּ בְחָרָן וַיֵּצְאוּ לָלֶכֶת אַרְצָה כְּנַעַן וַיָּבֹאוּ אַרְצָה כְּנָעַן: [בראשית יב, ה] פ) וּשְׁמַרְתֶּם אֶת דִּבְרֵי הַבְּרִית הַזֹּאת וַעֲשִׂיתֶם אֹתָם לְמַעַן תַּשְׂכִּילוּ אֵת כָּל אֲשֶׁר תַּעֲשׂוּן: [דברים כט, ח]

צ) וַיֹּאמֶר יְיָ אֶל מֹשֶׁה עֲבֹר לִפְנֵי הָעָם וְקַח אִתְּךָ מִזִּקְנֵי יִשְׂרָאֵל וּמַטְּךָ אֲשֶׁר הִכִּיתָ בּוֹ אֶת הַיְאֹר קַח בְּיָדְךָ וְהָלָכְתָּ: [שמות יז, ה] ק) כֹּה אָמַר יְיָ אִם לֹא בְרִיתִי יוֹמָם וָלָיְלָה חֻקּוֹת שָׁמַיִם וָאָרֶץ לֹא שָׂמְתִּי: [ירמיה לג, כה]

ר) וַיֹּאמֶר יְיָ אִם אֶמְצָא בִסְדֹם חֲמִשִּׁים צַדִּיקִם בְּתוֹךְ הָעִיר וְנָשָׂאתִי לְכָל הַמָּקוֹם בַּעֲבוּרָם: [בראשית יח, כו]

stated: ***Or let him take hold of My strength, that he may make peace with Me; yea, let him make peace with Me.***[38] רַב אָמַר – **Rav said:** כְּאִילּוּ בָּנָה פַּלְטֵרִין שֶׁל מַעְלָה וְשֶׁל מַטָּה – When one studies Torah for its own sake, it is **as if he built the palace above and the palace below,** שֶׁנֶּאֱמַר ,,וָאָשִׂם דְּבָרַי בְּפִיךָ וּבְצֵל יָדִי כִּסִּיתִיךָ לִנְטֹעַ שָׁמַיִם וְלִיסֹד אָרֶץ" – **as it is stated:** ***I have put My words in your mouth and have covered you with the shadow of My hand, to plant the heavens and lay the foundations of the earth.***[39] (אָמַר רֵישׁ לָקִישׁ) [רַבִּי יוֹחָנָן אָמַר] – **(Reish Lakish said) R' Yochanan said:** אַף מֵגֵין עַל כָּל הָעוֹלָם כּוּלּוֹ – When a person studies Torah for its own sake, **he also provides protection for the entire world,** שֶׁנֶּאֱמַר ,,וּבְצֵל יָדִי כִּסִּיתִיךָ" – **as it is stated:** ***I covered you with the shadow of My hand,*** which implies that God protects the world on his account. וְלֵוִי אָמַר – **And Levi said:** אַף מְקָרֵב אֶת הַגְּאוּלָּה – **[Such a person] even brings the Final Redemption closer,** שֶׁנֶּאֱמַר ,,וְלֵאמֹר לְצִיּוֹן עַמִּי־אָתָּה" – **as it is stated:** ***And to say to Zion, "You are My people."***[40]

Three sages reveal the significance of teaching Torah to another person's son:

אָמַר רֵישׁ לָקִישׁ – **Reish Lakish said:** כָּל הַמְלַמֵּד אֶת בֶּן חֲבֵירוֹ תּוֹרָה – **Whoever teaches his fellow's son Torah** מַעֲלֶה עָלָיו הַכָּתוּב כְּאִילּוּ עֲשָׂאוֹ – **is regarded by Scripture as if he "made" [that son],** שֶׁנֶּאֱמַר ,,וְאֶת־הַנֶּפֶשׁ אֲשֶׁר־עָשׂוּ בְחָרָן" – **as it is stated:** ***and the people they made in Charan.***[41] רַבִּי אֶלְעָזָר אוֹמֵר – **R' Elazar says:** כְּאִילּוּ עֲשָׂאָן לְדִבְרֵי תוֹרָה – He is regarded by Scripture **as if he "made" the words of the Torah,** שֶׁנֶּאֱמַר ,,וּשְׁמַרְתֶּם אֶת־דִּבְרֵי הַבְּרִית הַזֹּאת וַעֲשִׂיתֶם אֹתָם" – **as it is stated:** ***If you preserve the words of this covenant, you will make them.***[42] רָבָא אָמַר – **Rava said:** כְּאִילּוּ עֲשָׂאוֹ לְעַצְמוֹ – He is regarded by Scripture **as if he "made"** (i.e. created) **himself,** שֶׁנֶּאֱמַר ,,וַעֲשִׂיתֶם אֹתָם" – **as it is stated:** ***you will make them:*** That is, אַל תִּקְרֵי ,,אֹתָם" – **do not read** the last word of the verse as ***them*** (*osam*), אֶלָּא אַתֶּם – **but** as ***you*** (*atem*).[43]

The Gemara reveals the significance of inspiring another person to perform mitzvos:

אָמַר רַבִּי אַבָּהוּ – **R' Abahu said:** כָּל הַמְעַשֶּׂה אֶת חֲבֵירוֹ לִדְבַר מִצְוָה – **Whoever causes his fellow to perform a mitzvah** מַעֲלֶה עָלָיו הַכָּתוּב כְּאִילּוּ עֲשָׂאָהּ – **is regarded by Scripture as if he performed it** himself, שֶׁנֶּאֱמַר ,,וּמַטְּךָ אֲשֶׁר הִכִּיתָ בּוֹ אֶת־הַיְאֹר" – **as it is stated** concerning Moses' staff:[44] ***and your staff, with which you struck the river*** [i.e. to initiate the first of the Ten Plagues]. וְכִי מֹשֶׁה הִכָּהוּ – **Now, did Moses** himself **strike [the river]?** וַהֲלֹא אַהֲרֹן הִכָּהוּ – **Was it not Aaron who struck it?** Why, then, does Scripture state that Moses struck it? אֶלָּא לוֹמַר לְךָ כָּל הַמְעַשֶּׂה אֶת חֲבֵירוֹ לִדְבַר מִצְוָה – **Rather,** it is **to tell you that whoever causes his fellow to perform a mitzvah** מַעֲלֶה עָלָיו הַכָּתוּב כְּאִילּוּ עֲשָׂאָהּ – **is regarded by Scripture as if he performed it** himself.[45]

The Gemara has concluded its discussion of one who denies the divine origin of the Torah, the Mishnah's second case of one who has no portion in the World to Come. The Gemara now discusses the third case mentioned there – the *apikoros* – and cites a dispute concerning the meaning of that term:

,,אַפִּיקוֹרוֹס" – The Baraisa[46] stated: AN *APIKOROS*.[47] רַב וְרַבִּי

NOTES

to study Torah actualizes this bridge and thereby unites ("promotes peace" between) the two realms.

38. *Isaiah* 27:5. In this verse *strength* symbolizes Torah; "taking hold of God's strength" is a metaphor for studying Torah for its own sake. Scripture thus teaches that one who does this *makes peace with Me,* i.e. in My world, among the heavenly host. The repetitive *yea, let him make peace with Me* intimates that such a person also promotes peace among the host below (*Yad Ramah*).

39. Ibid. 51:16. The ongoing existence of heaven and earth depends upon purely motivated Torah study below. Scripture thus indicates that when one studies Torah for its own sake (*I have put My words in your mouth*), his merit is so great that it is as if he has sustained heaven (*to plant the heavens*) and earth (*and lay the foundations of the earth*) [see *Rif*].

40. This is the conclusion of the previously quoted verse. Scripture intimates that by becoming distinguished (מְצוּיָן, related to צִיּוֹן, *Zion*) in Torah study – that is, by reaching the level of Torah study *for its own sake* – the Jews will merit to be called *My people*, a title that is associated with redemption (see *Hosea* 1:9 and 2:25) [*Maharsha*]. *Rif* points out that the prophet Malachi admonishes the Jews to remember the Torah (3:22), and then predicts the coming of the Prophet Elijah (v. 23), thereby intimating a connection between Torah study and redemption.

41. *Genesis* 12:5. This verse describes the people who accompanied Abraham when he left his birthplace and journeyed to the land of Canaan. In that company were, in addition to Abraham's wife and nephew, *the people they made in Charan,* which Onkelos translates: וְיָת נַפְשָׁתָא דְשַׁעְבִּידוּ לְאוֹרַיְתָא בְחָרָן, *the people [Abraham and Sarah] made subject to the Torah in Charan* (by converting them to Abraham's faith). Thus, we see that when one person offers another religious instruction and forms him into a Torah-observant Jew, the instructor is regarded as having "made" – that is, as having spiritually created – his student (*Rashi*).

Maharsha explains that a person who has not learned Torah is no different from other living creatures. Through knowledge of Torah, however, he is elevated to the status of "man," which is the purpose of his creation.

The Gemara speaks of teaching "his fellow's son" rather than "another man." According to *Toras Chaim,* the Gemara is intimating that one is considered his parents' son only insofar as his physical existence is concerned. However, his soul comes from God, and if it is properly nurtured by a teacher, the teacher becomes the child's spiritual father.

42. *Deuteronomy* 29:8. Our Sages teach that while a person learns much from his teachers and even more from his colleagues, he learns the most from his students (*Taanis* 7a, *Makkos* 10a), for in the course of transmitting his knowledge and answering their questions he gains many new insights and ideas. Hence, the verse teaches that *if you preserve the words of this covenant* (i.e. the words of Torah) in your mouth, to impart them to your fellow's son, then *you will make them* – i.e. you will create new words of Torah, the new perceptions you have brought into the world as a result of your teaching (*Maharsha*). [In the simple meaning of the verse, the words וַעֲשִׂיתֶם אֹתָם refer to the *fulfillment* of the words of the covenant.]

43. The word אתם can be vowelized in more than one way. According to authoritative Masoretic tradition, the word was vowelized at Sinai as אֹתָם. Nevertheless, when alternative vowelizations yield other Hebrew words, those words are viewed as being alluded to in the Torah. Hence, Rava is adding that by teaching the Torah to the son of one's fellow, it is possible to create oneself. That is, perhaps when a person commenced teaching he had not attained the status of "man" (see note 41 above). However, as a result of teaching the child his wisdom increased (see previous note), and eventually he did attain that desired status (*Maharsha*). This lesson is indicated by vowelizing אתם as אַתֶּם – *you will make yourselves* – i.e. into "men."

According to *Haamek Davar* (on *Deuteronomy* 29:8), the three sages are here referring to those historical periods when yeshivos were destroyed and the very future of Torah study itself was threatened (see *Yevamos* 62b). Under such circumstances those who undertake to teach Torah to others are actually effectuating the survival of the Torah and the spiritual survival of those whom they teach. In that sense they "make" the Torah and their students, while simultaneously ensuring their own growth.

44. *Exodus* 17:5.

45. Pursuant to God's command, Moses instructed Aaron to strike the Nile river with Moses' staff (see *Exodus* 7:19), and Aaron did so (v. 20). Because Moses was responsible for Aaron's striking the river, Scripture attributes the act to Moses. Similarly, one who induces another to perform a mitzvah is also credited with performing that mitzvah (*Rashi;* see *Rif*).

46. Above, 99a; see *Yad Ramah, Rashi* below ד"ה איכא דמתני לה אסיפא.

47. *Yad Ramah* notes that the word *apikoros* (אַפִּיקוֹרוֹס) is related to the word הֶפְקֵר, for this person has *declared* himself *free* of the Torah's

עין משפט נר מצוה

יז א מיי' פ"ג מהלכות תשובה הלכה יד ע' בכ"מ:
יח ב מיי' שם הלכה יא:

ליקוטי רש"י

כי נעים. יהי לך לאחר זמן אם תשמרם ותצפנם בבטנך שלא תשכחם ואימתי יהיו שמורים בלבך בזמן שיכונו על שפתיך כאשר תוציאם בפיך [משלי כב, יח]. **ותמנע היתה פילגש לאליפז.** להודיע גדולתו של אברהם כמה היו תאבים לידבק בזרעו תמנע זו בת אלופים היתה, שנאמר (פסוק כב) ואחות לוטן תמנע, ולוטן מאלופי יושבי שעיר היה, מן החורים שישבו בה לפנים, אמרה איני זוכה להנשא לך, הלואי ואהיה פילגש. ובדברי הימים מונה אותה (דברי הימים א' א לו) בבניו של אליפז, מלמד שבא על אשתו של שעיר ויצאה תמנע מביניהם, וכשגדלה נעשית פילגשו, וזהו ואחות לוטן תמנע, ולא מנאה עם בני שעיר שהיתה אחותו מן האם ולא מן האב [בראשית לו, יב]. **בימי קציר חטים.** להגיד שבחן של שבטים שעת הקציר היה ולא פשט ידו בגזל להביא חטים ושעורים אלא דבר ההפקר שאין אדם מקפיד בו. **דודאים.** סיגלי, עשב הוא ובלשון ישמעאל יסמי"ן [שם ל, יד]. **דמית.** סבור אתה שאהיה כמוך להתרצו' במעשיך הרעים, (וי"מ דמית כי אינני יודע הנסתרות) [תהלים נ, כא]. **הוי מושכי העון.** גוררים יצר הרע עליהם מעט מעט בתחלה בחבלי השוא כחוט של קורי עכבים ומשנתגרה בהם מתגבר והולך עד שנעשה כעבות העגלה שקושרין בו את הקרון למשוך. **השוא.** דבר שאין בו ממש. **חטאה.** חטא [ישעיהו ה, יח]. **מלכותא בלא תגא.** כלומר שררה גדולה ואינו חסר אלא כתר מלכות [לקמן קה.]. **או יחזק במעוזי.** או לשון אם, כמו או נודע כי שור נגח הוא (שמות כא) או יחזק עמי במעוזי שלא יבקש מעוז אלא מעוזי אז יעשה שלום לי להניח דעתי ואפי שמתקשקשת בי על שאיני נוקם בצרי ואנקם בהם. **שלום יעשה לי.** ממדת הדין שלא יוכל לקטרג ולומר מה נשתנו אלו מאלו [ישעיהו כז, ה]. **אשר עשו בחרן.** שהכניסן תחת כנפי השכינה אברהם מגייר את האנשים ושרה מגיירת הנשים ומעלה עליהם הכתוב כאלו עשאום ופשוטו של מקרא עבדים ושפחות שקנו להם כמו (שם לא א) עשה את כל הכבוד הזה (במדבר כד יח) וישראל עושה חיל לשון קונה וכונס [בראשית יב, ה]. **המלמד את בן חבירו.** ואלה תולדת אהרן ומשה, ואינו מזכיר אלא בני אהרן ונקראו תולדות משה לפי שלמדן תורה מלמד שכל המלמד את בן חבירו תורה מעלה עליו הכתוב כאלו ילדו [במדבר ג, א]. **אם לא בריתי וגו'.** אי אפשר שלא יתקיים הברית שכרתי ליום ולילה להיות בעתם ואי אפשר לחוקות שמים וארץ ליבטל כאילו לא שמתים גם זרע יעקב וגו' ורבותינו דרשוהו לענין ברית התורה ללמוד מכאן שבשביל התורה נבראו שמים וארץ אך אין המדרש מיושב על סדר המקראות [ירמיהו לג, כה].

זמר בכל יום זמר בכל יום אמר רב יצחק בר אבודימי מאי קרא שנאמר א) נפש עמל עמלה לו כי אכף עליו פיהו הוא עמל במקום זה ותורתו עומלת לו במקום אחר אמר רבי אלעזר ז) כל אדם לעמל נברא שנאמר ב) כי אדם לעמל יולד איני יודע אם לעמל פה נברא אם לעמל מלאכה נברא כשהוא אומר כי אכף עליו פיהו הוי אומר לעמל פה נברא ועדיין איני יודע אם לעמל תורה אם לעמל שיחה כשהוא אומר ג) לא ימוש ספר התורה הזה מפיך הוי אומר לעמל תורה נברא והיינו דאמר רבא כולהו גופי דרופתקי נינהו טובי לדזכי דהוי דרופתקי דאורייתא ד) ונואף אשה חסר לב אמר [א] ריש לקיש זה הלומד תורה לפרקים שנאמר ה) כי נעים כי תשמרם בבטנך יכונו יחדיו על שפתיך ת"ר ו) והנפש אשר תעשה ביד רמה זה מנשה בן חזקיה שהיה יושב ודורש בהגדות של דופי אמר וכי לא היה לו למשה לכתוב אלא ז) ואחות לוטן תמנע ח) ותמנע היתה פלגש לאליפז ט) וילך ראובן בימי קציר חטים וימצא דודאים בשדה יצאה ב"ק ואמרה לו י) תשב באחיך תדבר בבן אמך תתן דופי אלה עשית והחרשתי דמית היות אהיה כמוך אוכיחך ואערכה לעיניך ועליו מפורש בקבלה כ) הוי מושכי העון בחבלי השוא וכעבות העגלה חטאה מאי כעבות העגלה ו) א"ר אסי יצר הרע בתחלה דומה לחוט של ג) כוביא ולבסוף דומה לעבות העגלה דאתן עלה מיהת אחות לוטן תמנע מאי היא תמנע בת מלכים הואי דכתיב ל) אלוף לוטן מ) אלוף תמנע וכל אלוף ד) מלכותא בלא תאגא היא בעיא לאיגיורי באתה אצל אברהם יצחק ויעקב ולא קבלוה הלכה והיתה פילגש לאליפז בן עשו אמרה מוטב תהא שפחה לאומה זו ולא תהא גבירה לאומה אחרת נפק מינה עמלק דצערינהו לישראל מאי טעמא דלא איבעי להו לרחקה וילך ראובן בימי קציר חטים אמר רבא בר' יצחק אמר רב מכאן לצדיקים ה) שאין פושטין ידיהן בגזל וימצא דודאים בשדה מאי דודאים אמר רב יברוחי לוי אמר סיגלי ר' יונתן אמר (סיבסוך) [סביסקי]: א"ר אלכסנדרי כל העוסק בתורה לשמה משים שלום בפמליא של מעלה ובפמליא של מטה שנאמר נ) או יחזק במעוזי יעשה שלום לי שלום יעשה לי: רב אמר כאילו בנה פלטרין של מעלה ושל מטה שנאמר ס) ואשים דברי בפיך ובצל ידי כסיתיך לנטוע שמים וליסד ארץ (אמר ריש לקיש) [רבי יוחנן אמר] אף מגין על כל העולם כולו שנאמר ובצל ידי כסיתיך ולוי אמר אף מקרב את הגאולה שנאמר ס) ולאמר לציון עמי אתה אמר ריש לקיש ו) כל המלמד את בן חבירו תורה מעלה עליו הכתוב כאילו עשאו שנאמר ע) ואת הנפש אשר עשו בחרן ר' [ב] (ז) אליעזר) אומר כאילו עשאן לדברי תורה שנאמר פ) ושמרתם את דברי הברית הזאת ועשיתם אותם רבא אמר [ג] כאילו עשאו לעצמו שנאמר ועשיתם אותם אל תקרי אותם אלא אתם אמר רבי אבהו [ד] כל המעשה את חבירו לדבר מצוה מעלה עליו הכתוב (א) כאילו עשאה שנאמר צ) ומטך אשר הכית בו את היאר וכי משה הכהו והלא אהרן הכהו אלא לומר לך כל המעשה את חבירו לדבר מצוה מעלה עליו הכתוב כאילו עשאה: אפיקורוס: רב ור' חנינא אמרי תרווייהו זה [א] המבזה ת"ח רבי יוחנן ור' יהושע בן לוי אמרי זה המבזה חבירו בפני ת"ח בשלמא למ"ד המבזה חבירו בפני ת"ח אפיקורוס הוי מבזה תלמיד חכם עצמו מגלה פנים בתורה שלא כהלכה הוי אלא למ"ד מבזה תלמיד חכם עצמו אפיקורוס הוי מגלה פנים בתורה כגון מאי [ב] כגון מנשה בן חזקיה ואיכא דמתני לה אסיפא מגלה פנים בתורה רב ור' חנינא אמרי זה המבזה ת"ח רבי יוחנן וריב"ל אמרי זה המבזה את חבירו בפני תלמיד חכם בשלמא למ"ד המבזה תלמיד חכם עצמו מגלה פנים בתורה הוי מבזה חבירו בפני ת"ח אפיקורוס הוי אלא למ"ד מבזה חבירו בפני תלמיד חכם מגלה פנים בתורה הוי אפיקורוס כגון מאן אמר רב יוסף כגון הני דאמרי מאי אהנו לן רבנן לדידהו קרו לדידהו תנו אמר ליה אביי האי מגלה פנים בתורה נמי הוא דכתיב ק) אם לא בריתי יומם ולילה חקות שמים וארץ לא שמתי אמר רב נחמן בר יצחק מהכא נמי שמע מינה שנאמר ר) ונשאתי לכל המקום בעבורם אלא כגון דיתיב קמיה רביה ונפלה ליה שמעתא בדוכתא אחריתי ואמר הכי אמרינן התם ולא אמר הכי אמר מר רבא אמר כגון הני דבי בנימין אסיא דאמרי מאי אהני לן רבנן מעולם

לא

רש"י

זמר בכל יום. היה מסדר למודך אע"פ שסדור בפיך כזמר והוא יגרוס לך שתהא לעולם הבא בשמחה ובשירים: נפש עמל עמלה לו. מפני שעמל בתורה תורה עומלת לו: כי אכף עליו פיהו. מפני שהוא משים דברים בפיו תמיד כאוכף שעל החמור לישנא אחרינא זמר כלומר שעוסק בשירים ובזמירות תדיר תדיר נעשה זמר כך החוזר על התורה נעשה לו סדורה בפיו: תורה עומלת לו. שמחזרת עליו ומבקשת מאת קונה למסור לו טעמי תורה וסדריה וכל כך למה מפני שאכף שכפף פיהו על דברי תורה: דרופתקי. טרחנין כלומר כל הגופין לעמל נבראו: טוביה לדזכי. אשריו למי שזכה והיה עמלו וטרחו בתורה לשון אחר דרפתקי כיס ארוך שמשימין בו מעות כל הגופין נרתקין הם לקבל ולהכניס דברים אשריו למי שזכה ונעשה נרתק לתורה: לומד תורה לפרקים. ואינו לומד תדיר כמי שאין לו אשה ובועל פעמים זו פעמים זו: שנאמר כי נעים כי תשמרם. אימתי תשמרם בבטנך [בזמן] שיכונו יחדיו על שפתיך: לא היה לו למשה לכתוב אלא ואחות לוטן תמנע. בתמיה דבר שאינו צריך הוא וכן היה מלגלג ואומר שכתבו משה שלא לצורך ולקמיה מפרש דהיינו מגלה פנים בתורה: וילך ראובן וגו'. והיינו נמי שלא לצורך: בחבלי השוא. בחנם בלא שום הנאה היה חוטא: מלכותא בלא תגא. שר גדול אלא שאינו מעוטר וכיון דתמנע היתה אחות מלך ודאי בת מלך היא: מוטב שאהיה שפחה לאומה זו. לבני אברהם יצחק (ויעקב) שהן יראי שמים ולא אהיה גברת לאומה אחרת ולכך נעשית פילגש לאליפז בן עשו שהיה מזרע יצחק: לרחקה. מתחת כנפי השכינה שהיה להם לגיירה: בימי קציר חטים. לאחר שקצרו השדה שהכל רשאין ליכנס בתוך שדה חבריהן: יברוחי. כדמתרגמינן ולא איתפרש מאי היא: סיגלי וסביסקי [וסבסוך]. מינין אחרים סיגלי עיקרי עשבים והוא ממיני בשמים ואמהות של אותן עשבים קרי סגלי (וסבסך) [וסביסקי] נמי מין בשמים: מעוזי. תורה: שלום שלום. תרתי זימני אחד למעלה ואחד למטה: פלטירין של מעלה ושלמטה. כדכתיב לנטוע שמים וליסוד ארץ: אשר עשו בחרן. דמתרגמינן דשעבידו לאורייתא בחרן וקרי להו עשייה: כאילו עשאו. לאותו דבר מצוה: והלא אהרן הכה. דכתיב (שמות ז) ח) (ויאמר) אל אהרן קח מטך ונטה ידך: מגלה פנים בתורה. מעיז פנים כלפי עוסקי תורה מגלה פנים משתמע לן דחמיר מאפיקורוס דאפיקורוס היינו דאית ביה אפקירותא בעלמא: אלא למ"ד מבזה תלמידי חכמים עצמן אפיקורוס הוי. כ"ש דמבזה חברו בפני תלמידי חכמים לאו מגלה פנים הוא והשתא מאי ניהו מגלה פנים בתורה: מנשה בן חזקיה. שהיה דורש באגדות של דופי: איכא דמתני לה אסיפא. ט) דברייתא דקתני מכאן אמר רבי אלעזר וכו' המגלה פנים בתורה רב ור' חנינא וכו': מאי אהני לן. והם אינן יודעין שעולם מתקיים עליהם: מגלה פנים בתורה הוא. שכופר במה שכתוב בתורה: אם לא בריתי יומם ולילה וגו'. שמהנין לעולם ומקיימין [אותו] והוא אומר דלא מהני מידי: מהכא נמי שמעינן. שהצדיקים מהנין לאחרים:

לא

מסורת הש"ס

א) [כל המאמר הזה יפה נדרש בשל"ה סוף דף שע"ה: ע"ש פי' נאה ומתוקן], ב) [סוכה נב.], ג) [בסוכה איתא בוביא ובערוך גר' כוביא ובסוכה פירש"י בוכיא עכבים], ד) [לקמן קה.], ה) [סוטה יב. חולין נא.], ו) [לעיל יט: ע"ש], ז) [צ"ל אלעזר], ח) [צ"ל אמור], ט) [היינו משנה דלאבות לעיל עמוד א].

הגהות הב"ח

(א) גמ' כאילו עשאו שנאמר ומטך וכו' כאילו עשאו:

הגהות הגר"א

[א] גמ' אמר ריש לקיש. נרשם עליו אות ג: [ב] שם רבי אליעזר. נרשם עליו אות א: [ג] שם רבא אמר. נרשם עליו אות ב: [ד] שם א"ר אבהו. נרשם עליו אות ד:

תורה אור השלם

א) נֶפֶשׁ עָמֵל עָמְלָה לּוֹ כִּי אָכַף עָלָיו פִּיהוּ: [משלי טז, כו]
ב) כִּי אָדָם לְעָמָל יוּלָּד וּבְנֵי רֶשֶׁף יַגְבִּיהוּ עוּף: [איוב ה, ז]
ג) לֹא יָמוּשׁ סֵפֶר הַתּוֹרָה הַזֶּה מִפִּיךָ וְהָגִיתָ בּוֹ יוֹמָם וָלַיְלָה לְמַעַן תִּשְׁמֹר לַעֲשׂוֹת כְּכָל הַכָּתוּב בּוֹ כִּי אָז תַּצְלִיחַ אֶת דְּרָכֶךָ וְאָז תַּשְׂכִּיל: [יהושע א, ח]
ד) נֹאֵף אִשָּׁה חֲסַר לֵב מַשְׁחִית נַפְשׁוֹ הוּא יַעֲשֶׂנָּה: [משלי ו, לב]
ה) כִּי נָעִים כִּי תִשְׁמְרֵם בְּבִטְנֶךָ יִכֹּנוּ יַחְדָּו עַל שְׂפָתֶיךָ: [משלי כב, יח]
ו) וְהַנֶּפֶשׁ אֲשֶׁר תַּעֲשֶׂה בְּיָד רָמָה מִן הָאֶזְרָח וּמִן הַגֵּר אֶת יְיָ הוּא מְגַדֵּף וְנִכְרְתָה הַנֶּפֶשׁ הַהִוא מִקֶּרֶב עַמָּהּ: [במדבר טו, ל]
ז) וַיִּהְיוּ בְנֵי לוֹטָן חֹרִי וְהֵימָם וַאֲחוֹת לוֹטָן תִּמְנָע: [בראשית לו, כב]
ח) וְתִמְנַע הָיְתָה פִילֶגֶשׁ לֶאֱלִיפַז בֶּן עֵשָׂו וַתֵּלֶד לֶאֱלִיפַז אֶת עֲמָלֵק אֵלֶּה בְּנֵי עָדָה אֵשֶׁת עֵשָׂו: [בראשית לו, יב]
ט) וַיֵּלֶךְ רְאוּבֵן בִּימֵי קְצִיר חִטִּים וַיִּמְצָא דוּדָאִים בַּשָּׂדֶה וַיָּבֵא אֹתָם אֶל לֵאָה אִמּוֹ וַתֹּאמֶר רָחֵל אֶל לֵאָה תְּנִי נָא לִי מִדּוּדָאֵי בְּנֵךְ: [בראשית ל, יד]
י) תֵּשֵׁב בְּאָחִיךָ תְדַבֵּר בְּבֶן אִמְּךָ תִּתֶּן דֹּפִי: אֵלֶּה עָשִׂיתָ וְהֶחֱרַשְׁתִּי דִּמִּיתָ הֱיוֹת אֶהְיֶה כָמוֹךָ אוֹכִיחֲךָ וְאֶעֶרְכָה לְעֵינֶיךָ: [תהלים נ, כ-כא]
כ) הוֹי מֹשְׁכֵי הֶעָוֹן בְּחַבְלֵי הַשָּׁוְא וְכַעֲבוֹת הָעֲגָלָה חַטָּאָה: [ישעיה ה, יח]
ל) אֵלֶּה אַלּוּפֵי הַחֹרִי אַלּוּף לוֹטָן אַלּוּף שׁוֹבָל אַלּוּף צִבְעוֹן אַלּוּף עֲנָה: [בראשית לו, כט]
מ) וְאֵלֶּה שְׁמוֹת אַלּוּפֵי עֵשָׂו לְמִשְׁפְּחֹתָם לִמְקֹמֹתָם בִּשְׁמֹתָם אַלּוּף תִּמְנָע אַלּוּף עַלְוָה אַלּוּף יְתֵת: [בראשית לו, מ]
נ) אוֹ יַחֲזֵק בְּמָעוּזִּי יַעֲשֶׂה שָׁלוֹם לִי שָׁלוֹם יַעֲשֶׂה לִּי: [ישעיה כז, ה]
ס) וָאָשִׂים דְּבָרַי בְּפִיךָ וּבְצֵל יָדִי כִּסִּיתִיךָ לִנְטֹעַ שָׁמַיִם וְלִיסֹד אָרֶץ וְלֵאמֹר לְצִיּוֹן עַמִּי אָתָּה: [ישעיה נא, טז]
ע) וַיִּקַּח אַבְרָם אֶת שָׂרַי אִשְׁתּוֹ וְאֶת לוֹט בֶּן אָחִיו וְאֶת כָּל רְכוּשָׁם אֲשֶׁר רָכָשׁוּ וְאֶת הַנֶּפֶשׁ אֲשֶׁר עָשׂוּ בְחָרָן וַיֵּצְאוּ לָלֶכֶת אַרְצָה כְּנַעַן וַיָּבֹאוּ אַרְצָה כְּנָעַן: [בראשית יב, ה]
פ) וּשְׁמַרְתֶּם אֶת דִּבְרֵי הַבְּרִית הַזֹּאת וַעֲשִׂיתֶם אֹתָם לְמַעַן תַּשְׂכִּילוּ אֵת כָּל אֲשֶׁר תַּעֲשׂוּן: [דברים כט, ח]
צ) וַיֹּאמֶר יְיָ אֶל מֹשֶׁה עֲבֹר לִפְנֵי הָעָם וְקַח אִתְּךָ מִזִּקְנֵי יִשְׂרָאֵל וּמַטְּךָ אֲשֶׁר הִכִּיתָ בּוֹ אֶת הַיְאֹר קַח בְּיָדְךָ וְהָלָכְתָּ: [שמות יז, ה]
ק) כֹּה אָמַר יְיָ אִם לֹא בְרִיתִי יוֹמָם וָלָיְלָה חֻקּוֹת שָׁמַיִם וָאָרֶץ לֹא שָׂמְתִּי: [ירמיה לג, כה]
ר) וַיֹּאמֶר יְיָ אִם אֶמְצָא בִסְדֹם חֲמִשִּׁים צַדִּיקִם בְּתוֹךְ הָעִיר וְנָשָׂאתִי לְכָל הַמָּקוֹם בַּעֲבוּרָם: [בראשית יח, כו]

רַב וְרַבִּי חֲנִינָא אָמְרֵי תַּרְוַיְיהוּ – Rav and R' Chanina both said: זֶה הַמְבַזֶּה תַּלְמִיד חָכָם – This refers to one who denigrates a Torah scholar. רַבִּי יוֹחָנָן וְרַבִּי יְהוֹשֻׁעַ בֶּן לֵוִי אָמְרֵי – R' Yochanan and R' Yehoshua ben Levi said: זֶה הַמְבַזֶּה חֲבֵירוֹ בִּפְנֵי תַלְמִיד חָכָם – This refers to one who denigrates his fellow in the presence of a Torah scholar.[48]

The Gemara analyzes this dispute:

בִּשְׁלָמָא לְמַאן דְּאָמַר הַמְבַזֶּה חֲבֵירוֹ בִּפְנֵי תַלְמִיד חָכָם אַפִּיקוֹרוֹס הָוֵי – Now, it is reasonable according to the one (i.e. R' Yochanan and R' Yehoshua ben Levi) who says that one who denigrates his fellow in the presence of a Torah scholar is considered an *apikoros,* מְבַזֶּה תַלְמִיד חָכָם עַצְמוֹ – for then one who denigrates a Torah scholar himself, which is a more brazen and thus more reprehensible act, מְגַלֶּה פָנִים בַּתּוֹרָה (שֶׁלֹּא כַהֲלָכָה)[49] הָוֵי – may be considered one who acts insolently toward the Torah.[50] אֶלָּא לְמַאן דְּאָמַר מְבַזֶּה תַלְמִיד חָכָם עַצְמוֹ אַפִּיקוֹרוֹס הָוֵי – However, according to the one (i.e. Rav and R' Chanina) who says that one who denigrates a Torah scholar himself is considered an *apikoros,* מְגַלֶּה פָנִים בַּתּוֹרָה כְּגוֹן מַאי – what type of case can one who acts insolently toward the Torah be? What could be worse than denigrating a Torah scholar?

The Gemara answers:

כְּגוֹן מְנַשֶּׁה בֶּן חִזְקִיָּה – Rav and R' Chanina had in mind a case like that of Menasheh the son of Chizkiah, who denigrated Scripture itself.

The Gemara presents a different tradition regarding the aforecited Amoraic dispute:

וְאִיכָּא דְּמַתְנֵי לָהּ אַסֵּיפָא – And there are those who teach [this Amoraic dispute] as referring to the last part of the Baraisa,[51] which states: מְגַלֶּה פָנִים בַּתּוֹרָה – Scripture states: *For he despised the word of* HASHEM. This refers to ONE WHO ACTS INSOLENTLY TOWARD THE TORAH. רַב וְרַבִּי חֲנִינָא אָמְרֵי זֶה הַמְבַזֶּה תַּלְמִיד חָכָם – Rav and R' Chanina say that this is one who denigrates a Torah scholar. רַבִּי יוֹחָנָן וְרַבִּי יְהוֹשֻׁעַ בֶּן לֵוִי אָמְרֵי זֶה הַמְבַזֶּה אֶת חֲבֵירוֹ בִּפְנֵי תַלְמִיד חָכָם – R' Yochanan and R' Yehoshua ben Levi say that this is one who denigrates his fellow in the presence of a Torah scholar. בִּשְׁלָמָא לְמַאן דְּאָמַר הַמְבַזֶּה תַּלְמִיד חָכָם עַצְמוֹ מְגַלֶּה פָנִים בַּתּוֹרָה הָוֵי – Now, it is reasonable according to the one (i.e. Rav and R' Chanina) who says that one who denigrates a Torah scholar himself is considered [a person] who acts insolently toward the Torah, מְבַזֶּה חֲבֵירוֹ בִּפְנֵי תַלְמִיד חָכָם אַפִּיקוֹרוֹס הָוֵי – for then one who denigrates his fellow in the presence of a Torah scholar, which is not as brazen an act, may be considered an *apikoros,* a less reprehensible type of sinner. אֶלָּא לְמַאן דְּאָמַר מְבַזֶּה חֲבֵירוֹ בִּפְנֵי תַלְמִיד חָכָם – However, according to the one (R' Yochanan and R' Yehoshua ben Levi) who says that one who denigrates his fellow in the presence of a Torah scholar, which would not seem to be so brazen an act, מְגַלֶּה פָנִים בַּתּוֹרָה הָוֵי – is nevertheless considered one who acts insolently toward the Torah, אַפִּיקוֹרוֹס כְּגוֹן מַאן – what sort of person is considered only an *apikoros?*

The Gemara answers:

אָמַר רַב יוֹסֵף – Rav Yosef said: כְּגוֹן הָנֵי דְּאָמְרֵי מַאי אַהֲנוּ לָן רַבָּנַן – R' Yochanan and R' Yehoshua ben Levi had in mind a case like those who say, "Of what use to us are the Rabbis? לְדִידְהוּ קְרוֹ – They study Scripture only for themselves, לְדִידְהוּ תְּנוֹ – and they study [Oral Law] only for themselves, and we derive no benefit from their learning!"[52]

The Gemara challenges Rav Yosef's opinion:

אָמַר לֵיהּ אַבַּיֵי – Abaye said to [Rav Yosef]: Not so! הַאי מְגַלֶּה פָנִים בַּתּוֹרָה נַמִּי הוּא – This person, whom you erroneously classify as an *apikoros,* is also a case of *one who acts insolently toward the Torah,*[53] דִּכְתִיב ,,אִם־לֹא בְרִיתִי יוֹמָם וָלָיְלָה חֻקּוֹת שָׁמַיִם וָאָרֶץ לֹא־שָׂמְתִּי'' – for it is written:[54] *If not for My covenant* [i.e. the Torah] *day and night, I would not have established the statutes of heaven and earth.* This verse clearly states that the existence of the world depends upon the Torah study of the Rabbis. Those who claim that they do not benefit from the Rabbis' Torah study thus deny an explicit Scriptural passage, and should be included in the category of one who acts insolently toward the Torah.

The Gemara adds:

אָמַר רַב נַחְמָן בַּר יִצְחָק – Rav Nachman bar Yitzchak said: מֵהָכָא נַמִּי שְׁמַע מִינָּהּ – That the righteous of the world benefit others may be learned from here [the following verse] as well, שֶׁנֶּאֱמַר ,,וְנָשָׂאתִי לְכָל־הַמָּקוֹם בַּעֲבוּרָם'' – for it is stated: *I would spare the entire place on their account.*[55]

Abaye offers his own definition of the term *apikoros:*

אֶלָּא כְּגוֹן דְּיָתִיב קַמֵּיהּ רַבֵּיהּ – Rather, the case of an *apikoros* is one who sits before his teacher while the latter is delivering a Torah lecture וְנָפְלָה לֵיהּ שְׁמַעְתָּא בְּדוּכְתָּא אַחֲרִיתִי – and, when he recalls a teaching[56] from a place in the Torah other than where the teacher is expounding, וְאָמַר הָכִי אָמְרִינַן הָתָם – says, "We said thus there," וְלֹא אָמַר הָכִי אָמַר מָר – instead of saying, "Master said thus."[57]

Rava offers a different definition:

רָבָא אָמַר – Rava said: כְּגוֹן הָנֵי דְּבֵי בִנְיָמִין אַסְיָא – The case of an *apikoros* is like those members of the household of Benjamin the physician, דְּאָמְרֵי מַאי אַהֲנֵי לָן רַבָּנַן – who say, "Of what use to us are the Rabbis? מֵעוֹלָם –

NOTES

strictures (cf. *Maharsha*; see *Aruch*).

Rambam (*Commentary*) writes that an *apikoros* is one who denigrates the Torah or Torah scholars. Hence, *apikorsus* is a general term for not believing in any of the fundamentals of Torah or for any manner of denigrating a Torah scholar. *Rashi* here (סוד"ה מגלה) and to *Moed Katan* 16a and *Eruvin* 63a defines it as אַפְקָרוּתָא, *disrespect.*

48. Denigrating any individual in the presence of the Torah scholar is, in fact, an act of disrespect for the Torah scholar himself.

49. It is apparent from the commentary of *Rashi* and *Yad Ramah* that the words שֶׁלֹּא כַהֲלָכָה (*contrary to the law*) do not belong in the text, and we have deleted them in our translation. Indeed, these words are incomprehensible in the context of this passage. See *Dikdukei Soferim.*

50. מְגַלֶּה פָנִים בַּתּוֹרָה is then interpreted as one who acts insolently toward [those who engage in] Torah [study]. This act of brazenness is a more serious transgression than that committed by the *apikoros,* who merely acts irreverently (*Rashi*).

51. Cited above, 99a (*Rashi*). [From the fact that *Rashi* identifies "the last part" of the Baraisa as beginning with *"Based on"* and not with *"Another interpretation," Dikdukei Soferim* concludes that a section of the Baraisa did not appear in *Rashi's* text of the Gemara (see above, 99a note 46).

52. Such people do not realize that the ongoing existence of the world depends upon the Rabbis' Torah study (*Rashi*).

53. For he denies what is explicitly written in the Torah, as the Gemara explains (*Rashi*).

54. *Jeremiah* 33:25.

55. *Genesis* 18:26. God told Abraham that although the wicked city of Sodom deserved to be destroyed, He would nevertheless spare it if a few righteous people lived there. Scripture thus indicates that the deeds of the righteous protect and benefit not only themselves, but others as well (see *Rashi*).

56. Literally: a [Torah] teaching fell to him.

57. *Maharsha* explains that even though the particular teaching emerged from a discussion between this disciple and the teacher, he should not have stated "we said," but "Master said." He should have quoted the teaching in his mentor's name out of respect for the teacher. The fact that he failed to display the proper respect and veneration for his Torah teacher defines him, according to Abaye, as an *apikoros* (see also *Yad Ramah*).

לֹא שָׁרוּ לָן עוֹרְבָא – **They have never permitted us** to eat **a raven** וְלֹא אָסְרוּ לָן יוֹנָה – **or forbidden us** to eat **a dove!"**[1] Apropos of this incidence of *apikorsus* the Gemara relates a story involving Rava: רָבָא כִּי הֲווּ מַיְיתֵי טְרֵיפְתָּא דְּבֵי בִנְיָמִין קַמֵּיהּ – **When they would bring a** suspected ***tereifah***[2] **from the house of Benjamin before Rava** for inspection, כִּי הֲוָה חָזֵי בָּהּ טַעְמָא לְהֶיתֵּירָא – **if he detected in [the creature]** a valid **reason for permitting** its consumption, אָמַר לְהוּ – **he would say to them:** תֶּחֱזוּ דְּקָא שָׁרֵינָא לְכוּ עוֹרְבָא – **"Take note that I am permitting a raven for you!"**[3] כִּי הֲוָה חָזֵי לָהּ טַעְמָא לְאִיסּוּרָא – And **if he detected a** valid **reason for prohibiting** the creature's consumption, אָמַר לְהוּ – **he would say to them:** תֶּחֱזוּ דְּקָא אָסַרְנָא לְכוּ יוֹנָה – **"Take note that I am prohibiting a dove to you!** My ability to determine the true halachic status of your animal was acquired by the many years of Torah study that you so disparage."

Another definition of an *apikoros*:

רַב פָּפָּא אָמַר – **Rav Pappa said:** כְּגוֹן דְּאָמַר הָנֵי רַבָּנָן – **The case** of an *apikoros* is one **who says, "Those Rabbis!"**[4] רַב פָּפָּא אִישְׁתְּלֵי – **Rav Pappa** once **forgot** himself וְאָמַר כְּגוֹן הָנֵי רַבָּנָן – **and said** in the course of a conversation, **". . . like those Rabbis!"** וְאִיתֵּיב בְּתַעֲנִיתָא – When he realized what he had said, he had such remorse that **he fasted** to atone for his improper choice of words.

Rav Yehudah's definition of an *apikoros*:

לֵוִי בַּר שְׁמוּאֵל וְרַב הוּנָא בַּר חִיָּיא הֲווּ קָא מְתַקְּנֵי מִטְפְּחוֹת סִפְרֵי דְּבֵי רַב יְהוּדָה – **Levi bar Shmuel and Rav Huna bar Chiya were** once **repairing the mantles of the** various **scrolls [owned by] the academy of Rav Yehudah.** כִּי מָטוּ מְגִילַּת אֶסְתֵּר – **When they came to a scroll** containing the Book **of Esther,** אָמְרֵי – **they said** to Rav Yehudah: הָא מְגִילַּת אֶסְתֵּר לֹא בָּעֵי מִטְפַּחַת – **"This scroll of Esther** is not as sacred as the other scrolls; it **does not need a mantle,** does it?" אָמַר לְהוּ – **[Rav Yehudah] said to them:** כִּי הַאי גַּוְונָא נַמִּי מִיחֲזֵי כִּי אַפְקִירוּתָא – "Addressing your teacher **in this manner also seems like irreverence."**[5]

Rav Nachman's definition of an *apikoros*:

רַב נַחְמָן אָמַר – **Rav Nachman said:** זֶה הַקּוֹרֵא רַבּוֹ בִּשְׁמוֹ – **This** *apikoros* **is one who calls his teacher by his name** instead of using a respectful title, such as "My teacher, Rabbi So-and-so," דְּאָמַר רַבִּי יוֹחָנָן – **for R' Yochanan said:** מִפְּנֵי מָה נֶעֱנַשׁ גֵּיחֲזִי – **Why was Geichazi,** the servant of the prophet Elisha, **punished?**[6] מִפְּנֵי שֶׁקָּרָא לְרַבּוֹ בִּשְׁמוֹ – **Because he called his master by his name,** שֶׁנֶּאֱמַר ,,וַיֹּאמֶר גֵּחֲזִי אֲדֹנִי הַמֶּלֶךְ זֹאת הָאִשָּׁה וְזֶה־בְּנָהּ אֲשֶׁר־הֶחֱיָה אֱלִישָׁע'' – **as it is stated:**[7] ***Geichazi said, "My lord the king! This is the woman, and this is her son, whom Elisha restored to life."***[8]

The Gemara discusses other possible examples of *apikorsus:*

יָתִיב רַבִּי יִרְמְיָה קַמֵּיהּ דְּרַבִּי זֵירָא – **R' Yirmiyah was** once **sitting before R' Zeira,** וְיָתִיב וְקָאָמַר – **and he sat and said:**[9] עָתִיד הַקָּדוֹשׁ בָּרוּךְ הוּא לְהוֹצִיא נַחַל מִבֵּית קָדְשֵׁי הַקֳּדָשִׁים – **In the future the**

NOTES

1. For all their studying, the Rabbis have never revealed to us anything we did not already know. After all, *Leviticus* 11:15 expressly states that a raven may not be eaten, and everyone knows that any bird not similarly (i.e. explicitly) prohibited in *Leviticus* is permitted (*Chullin* 63b) [see *Rashi*].

The Gemara specifies the raven and the dove because the former is inherently unchaste [it defied God's command and copulated in Noah's ark], while the latter is naturally faithful to its mate. Hence, throughout Torah literature the raven and dove appear as symbols for spiritual impurity and purity, respectively. The members of Benjamin's household therefore argued: Of what use to us are the Rabbis? They have never prohibited anything that appeared *tahor* like a dove, nor permitted anything that appeared *tamei* like a raven [i.e. they exhibit no special insight or expertise when judging the halachic status of such creatures] (*Maharsha*).

It is understandable that people are considered *apikorsim* if they complain that the Rabbis are of no use to them, since they do not find ways to permit that which is clearly forbidden. But what is wrong if they complain that the Rabbis do not forbid the permitted? Such a complaint appears to be no more than harmless, though misguided, piety. However, *Emes L'Yaakov* points out that this is not so. What seems to be piety is in reality an effort to undermine the authority of the Rabbis, for once the case is made that they are not sufficiently stringent and can therefore be ignored, it can then be claimed even when they are stringent that they can likewise be ignored.

2. An animal or bird with one of eighteen specific defects that will certainly cause its death. Any of these defects renders the animal or bird unfit for consumption even if it was ritually slaughtered (see *Chullin* ch. 3).

3. Rava was able to apply a Biblical leniency found in the Oral Law to permit the suspected *tereifah.* Because the leniency does not appear in the Written Law (the Scriptures), it was unknown to Benjamin's household, and so – Rava was telling them – from their perspective the creature could have been prohibited to them just as a raven is (*Rashi;* cf. *Maharsha*).

4. "Those Rabbis" is an expression of contempt. A more proper reference would have been, "Our teachers in such-and-such place." Alternatively, use of the adjective הָנֵי in this context is insulting. A more respectful choice would have been הַנְהוּ (*Rashi*).

[*Margaliyos HaYam* suggests that Rav Pappa's unfortunate statement is the one quoted in *Bava Metzia* 73b.]

5. By presuming to know the answer and merely asking Rav Yehudah in a pro forma way, Levi and Rav Huna insulted their teacher. They should have asked him directly, "Does this scroll require a mantle, or does it not?" (*Rashi*). [*Maharsha* explains that Levi and Rav Huna held that a scroll of *Esther* does not require a mantle because it does not render one's hands *tamei,* since *Esther* was not composed under the influence of the Divine Spirit (רוּחַ הַקֹּדֶשׁ) for purposes of being recorded and included in the Holy Scriptures (see *Megillah* 7a); see *Maharsha* for different explanations of their sin.] Cf. *Yad Ramah,* who explains that their use of the adjective הָא ("*this* scroll") was insulting (see previous note). [According to *Yad Ramah,* the insult was directed to the *scroll,* whereas according to *Rashi* it was directed to the teacher.]

6. R' Yochanan does not refer to Geichazi's being stricken with *tzaraas,* as recorded in *II Kings* 5:27, for Geichazi was already a *metzora* when he mentioned Elisha in a disrespectful manner; moreover, Scripture specifically attributes his leprosy to his having taken Naaman's gifts. Rather, R' Yochanan was referring to Geichazi's being denied a portion in the World to Come, as stated in our Mishnah (*Yad Ramah, Maharsha*).

Maharal explains that R' Yochanan was seeking to understand how the great prophet Elisha could have a disciple so unworthy that he even forfeits his portion in the World to Come. R' Yochanan's explanation is that Geichazi was not a true disciple of Elisha, for if he were he would not have referred to Elisha so irreverently.

According to *Ben Yehoyada,* R' Yochanan sought to explain why Elisha did not cure Geichazi of his *tzaraas,* but instead repudiated him. R' Yochanan explains that Elisha refused to forgive and pray for Geichazi because the latter's disrespectful attitude toward him demonstrated his unworthiness.

7. *II Kings* 8:5. The background of this incident is related in the preceding verse: *Now the king* (Jehoram) *was talking to Geichazi, the servant of the man of God* (Elisha), *and he said, "Tell me all the wonderful things that Elisha has done." While [Geichazi] was telling the king how [Elisha] had revived a dead person, the woman whose son he had revived entered . . .*

8. *Shulchan Aruch* states: A student may not call his teacher by the latter's name, even if the teacher is no longer living. If his teacher has an uncommon name, the student may not call someone else who has the same name by that name. If the name is not uncommon, the student may call someone else by that name so long as the teacher himself is not present. One may, however, call his teacher by the latter's name if one attaches to the teacher's name some title of respect, such as "Rabbi" (*Yoreh Deah* 242:15, with *Rama;* cf. *Shach*).

9. R' Yirmiyah was sitting in the study hall of his teacher, R' Zeira. When he wanted to say something, he rose out of respect for his teacher and requested the teacher's permission to speak; when he received it, he took

לא שרו לן עורבא ולא אסרו לן יונה רבא כי הוו מייתי טריפתא דבי בנימין קמיה כי הוה חזי בה טעמא להיתירא אמר להו תחזו דקא שרינא לכו עורבא כי הוה חזי לה טעמא לאיסורא אמר להו תחזו דקא אסרנא לכו יונה רב פפא אמר כגון דאמר הני רבנן רב פפא אישתלי ואמר כגון הני רבנן ואיתיב בתעניתא לוי בר שמואל ורב הונא בר חייא הוו קא מתקני מטפחות ספרי דבי רב יהודה כי מטו מגילת אסתר אמרי הא [מגילת אסתר] לא בעי מטפחת אמר להו כי האי גוונא נמי מיחזי כי אפקירותא רב נחמן אמר °זה [א]הקורא רבו בשמו דאמר רבי יוחנן מפני מה נענש גיחזי מפני שקרא לרבו בשמו שנאמר א) ויאמר גחזי אדני המלך זאת האשה וזה בנה אשר החיה אלישע יתיב רבי ירמיה קמיה דרבי זירא ויתיב וקאמר עתיד הקב"ה להוציא נחל מבית קדשי הקדשים ועליו כל מיני מגדים שנאמר ב) ועל הנחל יעלה על שפתו מזה ומזה כל עץ מאכל לא יבול עלהו ולא יתם פריו לחדשיו יבכר כי מימיו מן המקדש [המה] יוצאים והיה פריו למאכל ועלהו לתרופה א"ל ההוא סבא יישר וכן אמר ר' יוחנן [א] (יישר) אמר ליה ר' ירמיה לרבי זירא כי האי גונא מיחזי אפקרותא אמר ליה הא [האי] סיועי קא מסייע (ליה) [לך] אלא אי שמיע לך הא שמיע לך כי הא דיתיב רבי יוחנן וקא דריש עתיד הקב"ה להביא אבנים טובות ומרגליות שהן שלשים על שלשים אמות וחוקק בהם עשר ברום עשרים ומעמידן בשערי ירושלים שנאמר ג) ושמתי כדכוד שמשותיך ושעריך לאבני אקדח וגו' לגלג עליו אותו תלמיד אמר השתא כביעתא דצילצלא לא משכחינן כולי האי משכחינן לימים הפליגה ספינתו בים חזינהו למלאכי השרת דקא מנסרי אבנים טובות ומרגליות אמר להו הני למאן אמרי עתיד הקב"ה להעמידן בשערי ירושלים כי הדר אשכחיה לר' יוחנן דיתיב וקא דריש א"ל רבי דרוש ולך נאה לדרוש כשם שאמרת כך ראיתי אמר לו ריקה אם לא ראית לא האמנת מלגלג על דברי חכמים אתה יהב ביה עיניה ועשאו גל של עצמות מיתיבי ד) ואולך אתכם קוממיות ר"מ אומר מאתים אמה כשתי קומות של אדם הראשון רבי יהודה אומר ק' אמה כנגד היכל וכותליו שנאמר ה) אשר בנינו כנטיעים מגודלים בנעוריהם בנותינו כזויות מחוטבות תבנית היכל וגו' כי קאמר ר' יוחנן לכוי דבי זיקא מאי ועלהו לתרופה ר' יצחק בר אבודימי ורב חסדא חד אמר להתיר פה של מעלה וחד אמר להתיר פה של מטה איתמר (נמי) חזקיה אמר להתיר פה אילמין בר קפרא אמר להתיר פה עקרות ר' יוחנן אמר לתרופה ממש מאי לתרופה ר' שמואל בר נחמני אמר לתואר פנים של בעלי הפה דרש ר' יהודה ברבי סימון כל המשחיר פניו על דברי תורה בעולם הזה הקב"ה מבהיק זיוו לעולם הבא שנאמר ו) מראהו כלבנון בחור כארזים אמר ר' תנחום בר' חנילאי כל המרעיב עצמו על דברי תורה בעולם הזה הקב"ה משביעו לעולם הבא שנאמר ז) ירוין מדשן ביתך ונחל עדניך תשקם כי אתא רב דימי אמר עתיד הקב"ה ליתן לכל צדיק וצדיק מלא עומסו שנאמר ח) ברוך ה' יום יום יעמס לנו האל ישועתנו סלה א"ל אביי וכי אפשר לומר כן והלא כבר נאמר ט) מי מדד בשעלו מים ושמים בזרת תכן אמר מאי טעמא לא שכיחת באגדתא דאמרי במערבא משמיה דרבא בר מרי עתיד הקב"ה ליתן לכל צדיק וצדיק ג' מאות ועשרה עולמות שנא' י) להנחיל אוהבי יש ואוצרותיהם אמלא יש בגימטריא תלת מאה ועשרה הוי תניא ר' מאיר אומר במדה שאדם מודד מודדין לו דכתיב כ) בסאסאה בשלחה תריבנה אמר ר' [ב] יהושע וכי אפשר לומר כן אדם נותן מלא עומסו לעני בעולם הזה הקב"ה נותן לו מלא עומסו לעולם הבא והכתיב ט) שמים בזרת תכן [ג] ואתה אי אומר כן איזו היא מדה מרובה מדת טובה מרובה או מדת פורענות הוי

רש"י

לא שרו לן עורבא. לא אמרו לנו שום חידוש שלא מצינו בתורה (דשרינן עורבא): [דקא שרינא לכו עורבא]. שהיתר זה אינו מלוי בתורה אלא סופרים אמרוהו: כגון דאמר הנהו רבנן. כאדם שאומר אותו ת"ח דלשון בזוי הוא זה שהיה לו לומר רבותינו שבמקום פלוני ל"א כגון דאמר הני רבנן דכשהוא מספר שום דבר מרבנן אומר הני ולשון גנאי הוא הני אבל הנהו רבנן אינו גנאי: כי מטו מגלת אסתר. לתקן לה מטפחת אמרי הא מגלת אסתר לא בעיא מטפחת כלומר בלשון בעיא א"ל לרב יהודה הא ודאי לא צריכא מטפחת כגון האחרות ולשון גנאי הוא דהוה להו למימר לרבם בלשון שאלה כך צריכה או אינה צריכה: מעיין בית ה'. יצא והשקה את נחל שטים (יואל ד): מגדים. דינטר"ש בלע"ז כל מיני פירות מתוקים: יבכר. בכל חדש וחדש יתבשלו בו פירות: בשמו. שאומר פלוני ואינו אומר מורי רבי פלוני: א"ל ההוא סבא יישר וכן אמר רבי יוחנן. כדברך ור' יוחנן נמי הכי קאמר כדאמרת מ"ר ולא גרסינן וכן אמר רבי יוחנן יישר: כי האי גוונא. מי מיחזי כאפקרותא: אלא אי שמיע לך מידי הא שמיע לך: לגלג עליו אותו תלמיד. אדרבי יוחנן דהיינו אפקירותא: כדכד. אבן טובה וכך שמה: שמשותיך. חלונות שהשמש זורח בהם [ד] כמו (תהלים פד) שמש ומגן היינו שמש ממש (ל"א) לאבני אקדח שהקב"ה חוקקן כבמקדח עד שחוקק בהם עשר ברום עשרים: צילצלתא. עוף קטן: גל של עצמות. שמת לאדם שמת נעשה גל של עצמות: קוממיות. שתי קומות של אדם הראשון כדאמרינן בחגיגה (דף יב.) שמיעטו הקב"ה והעמידו על מאה אמה שנאמר ותשת עלי כפך כף בגימטריא הכי הוי: כנגד היכל וכותליו. שכך היה אורך כל ההיכל עם הכותלים דכתיב (מלכים א ו) והבית אשר בנה המלך שלמה לה' ששים אמה ארכו וכותל מזרח שש אמות וכותל מערב שש אמות ואמה אחת טרקסין הרי י"ג אמות ואולם עשר אמה רוחב וכותל האולם שש הרי כ"ט ומאחורי האולם תא אחד רחבו שש וכתלו ה' הרי מ' וס' אמה של אורך הבית הרי מאה והיאך יכולין לכוף קומתן וליכנס בפתח שאין לו אלא רום עשרים כדאמרת: אשר בנינו. כלומר בנים שלנו יהיו לעתיד כאילנות גבוהין מגודלים: ובנותינו. ובנות שלנו כזויות המחוטבות לתבנית היכל כלומר ככותל ההיכל מחוטבות כמו (דברים כט) מחוטב עציך לישנא אחרינא אהיכל דבית שני קאמר דקים לן היכל ס' אורך ברום מאה הוא: לכוי דבי זיקא. לחלונות שהשמש והאור נכנסין בהן אבל השערים גבוהים יותר: [להתיר פה של מטה]. להתיר פה אלמים שיהו מדברים: להתיר פה של מטה. רחם של העקרות האוכלות מן העלין נפקדות: איתמר נמי חזקיה וכו'. והיינו הך דלעיל לתרופה: מראהו כלבנון. וכתיב לעיל מיניה שחורות כעורב וסמיך ליה חכו ממתקים: ירוין מדשן ביתך. אמר לי רבי דלעיל מינה מהאי קרא איירי ענינא דמרעיב את עצמו וקאמר ירוין מדשן ביתך שהקב"ה משביען לעוה"ב: מלא עומסו. מלא חופנו של הקב"ה טובה: וכי אפשר לומר כן. היאך אדם יכול לקבל מלא עומסו של הקב"ה והרי אין לו מקום ליתן דכל העולם כולו אינו אלא כמזרת ועוד אגודל: באותן עולמות יתן לצדיק את העומס: במדה שאדם מודד. אם מדד ונתן צדקה לעני מלא חפניו הקב"ה מודד בחפניו ונותן לו: וכי אפשר לומר כן. שיהא הקב"ה נותן לאדם מלא חפניו והלא אינו יכול לסבול כל כך:

עין משפט נר מצוה

יט א מיי' פ"ה מהלכות ת"ת הלכה ה סמג עשין עד טוש"ע י"ד סי' רמב סעיף ט:

מסורת הש"ס

א) [ברכות מב: וש"נ], ב) [טעות הדפוס], ג) ב"ב עה., ד) [ב"ב עה. ע"ש שבת לד. ברכות נח.], ה) [מנחות דף לח. ע"ש], ו) [במנחו' ליתא], ז) [משנה סוף עוקלים ול"ע ועי' בים סדר למשנה ישוב נכון על זה], ח) [סוטה ח: ושם אית' רבי אומר אמנם שם טו: דמסיק דשמעי' לר"מ כו' משמע דגי' דהכא עיקר וע"ש ברש"י וכן איתא ג"כ בתוספתא שם פ"ג], ט) [נ"א יהודה], י) צ"ל למעלה, כ) [עי' רש"י מנחות לח.], ל) [עי' רש"י שם], מ) צ"ל שלש מאות באותן וכו'.

הגהות הגר"א

[א] גמ' יישר. נמחק: [ב] שם יהושע. נמחק: [ג] שם בזרת תכן ואתה. נ"ב א"ל ר"י ואתה: [ד] רש"י ד"ה שמשותיך כו' זורח בהם. נ"ב עי' רש"י בע"י:

גליון הש"ס

גמ' זה הקורא רבו בשמו. עי' יבמות נז ע"ב תד"ה אמר:

תורה אור השלם

א) וַיְהִי הוּא מְסַפֵּר לַמֶּלֶךְ אֵת אֲשֶׁר הֶחֱיָה אֶת הַמֵּת וְהִנֵּה הָאִשָּׁה אֲשֶׁר הֶחֱיָה אֶת בְּנָהּ צֹעֶקֶת אֶל הַמֶּלֶךְ עַל בֵּיתָהּ וְעַל שָׂדָהּ וַיֹּאמֶר גֵּחֲזִי אֲדֹנִי הַמֶּלֶךְ זֹאת הָאִשָּׁה וְזֶה בְּנָהּ אֲשֶׁר הֶחֱיָה אֱלִישָׁע: [מלכים ב' ח, ה]

ב) וְעַל הַנַּחַל יַעֲלֶה עַל שְׂפָתוֹ מִזֶּה וּמִזֶּה כָּל עֵץ מַאֲכָל לֹא יִבּוֹל עָלֵהוּ וְלֹא יִתֹּם פִּרְיוֹ לָחֳדָשָׁיו יְבַכֵּר כִּי מֵימָיו מִן הַמִּקְדָּשׁ הֵמָּה יוֹצְאִים וְהָיָה פִרְיוֹ לְמַאֲכָל וְעָלֵהוּ לִתְרוּפָה: [יחזקאל מז, יב]

ג) וְשַׂמְתִּי כַּדְכֹד שִׁמְשֹׁתַיִךְ וּשְׁעָרַיִךְ לְאַבְנֵי אֶקְדָּח וְכָל גְּבוּלֵךְ לְאַבְנֵי חֵפֶץ: [ישעיה נד, יב]

ד) אֲנִי יְיָ אֱלֹהֵיכֶם אֲשֶׁר הוֹצֵאתִי אֶתְכֶם מֵאֶרֶץ מִצְרַיִם מִהְיֹת לָהֶם עֲבָדִים וָאֶשְׁבֹּר מֹטֹת עֻלְּכֶם וָאוֹלֵךְ אֶתְכֶם קוֹמְמִיּוּת: [ויקרא כו, יג]

ה) אֲשֶׁר בָּנֵינוּ כִּנְטִעִים מְגֻדָּלִים בִּנְעוּרֵיהֶם בְּנוֹתֵינוּ כְזָוִיֹּת מְחֻטָּבוֹת תַּבְנִית הֵיכָל: [תהלים קמד, יב]

ו) שׁוֹקָיו עַמּוּדֵי שֵׁשׁ מְיֻסָּדִים עַל אַדְנֵי פָז מַרְאֵהוּ כַּלְּבָנוֹן בָּחוּר כָּאֲרָזִים: [שיר השירים ה, טו]

ז) יִרְוְיֻן מִדֶּשֶׁן בֵּיתֶךָ וְנַחַל עֲדָנֶיךָ תַשְׁקֵם: [תהלים לו, ט]

ח) בָּרוּךְ אֲדֹנָי יוֹם יוֹם יַעֲמָס לָנוּ הָאֵל יְשׁוּעָתֵנוּ סֶלָה: [תהלים סח, כ]

ט) מִי מָדַד בְּשָׁעֳלוֹ מַיִם וְשָׁמַיִם בַּזֶּרֶת תִּכֵּן וְכָל בַּשָּׁלִשׁ עֲפַר הָאָרֶץ וְשָׁקַל בַּפֶּלֶס הָרִים וּגְבָעוֹת בְּמֹאזְנָיִם: [ישעיה מ, יב]

י) לְהַנְחִיל אֹהֲבַי יֵשׁ וְאֹצְרֹתֵיהֶם אֲמַלֵּא: [משלי ח, כא]

כ) בְּסַאסְּאָה בְּשַׁלְחָהּ תְּרִיבֶנָּה הָגָה בְּרוּחוֹ הַקָּשָׁה בְּיוֹם קָדִים: [ישעיה כז, ח]

ליקוטי רש"י

לתרופה. פירשו רבותינו ז"ל להתיר פה אלמים ופה עקרות ומשמעו ל' רפואה כמו (ירמיה ו) וירפאו את שבר עמי על נקלה וכן חברו מנחם [יחזקאל מז, יב]. כדכד. מין אבן טובה. שמשותיך י"ת אמך ומנחם חברו עם ישמשוניה ויש פותרין ל' שמש חלונות שחמה זורחת בהן ועושין כנגדו מחילה במיני זכוכית צבעים לנוי ומדרש תהלים פותר שמשותיך ושמש ומגן (תהלים פד) שיני החומה. לאבני אקדח. י"ת לאבני גמר גומרין תרגום גחלים פתר אקדח לשון קדחי אש והם מין אבנים טובות בוערות כלפידי' והוא קרבונקל"א לשון גחלת ויש פותרין ל' מקדח אבנים גדולות שכל חלל הפתח קדוח בתוכו והמזוזות והמפתן והסף כולן מתוך האבן הם. לאבני חפץ. לאבני רצון [ישעיהו נד, יב]. וחוקק עשר. של רוחב ברום עשרים והיינו אקדח לשון קודח שחוקק בהם ומשמע נמי אבן טובה שמאירה כאש קודחת כמו קודחי אש (ישעיהו ג). אקדח. קרבונקל"א בלע"ז ובתרגום יונתן אבני גומרא. כביעתא דצילצלתא. ביצת עוף קטן ששמו תאציל. קוממיות. שתי קומות שני ממי"ן דריש. כשתי קומות של אדם הראשון. שמיעטו עד ק' אמה במסכת חגיגה (דף יב). ההיכל. של בית שני שהיה רום מאה אמה ולפי קומתן צריך שערים גבוהים וקשיא לר' יוחנן דאמר רום עשרים. לכווי דבי זיקא. לחלונות העשויין לאויר והיינו שעריך דקרא חלונות החומה [ב"ב עה.]. גל של עצמות. גל מעצמות, כמת שנרקב בשרו ונפל מזמן הרבה [שבת לד.]. מאי ועלהו לתרופה. גבי מעיין שעתיד לצאת מבית קדשי הקדשים קאי ועל שפת הנחל יעלה מזה ומזה כל [עץ] (עלה) מאכל והיה פריו למאכל ועלהו לתרופה וכו' וקדריש נוטריקון לתרופה. להתיר פה שלמעלה. פה אלמים שכל אלם האוכל ממנו נרפא. פה שלמטה. פה רחם של עקרות. חזקיה ובר קפרא. מפרשא מילתייהו טפי והיא היא [מנחות צח.]. בחור כארזים. נבחר בין הבנים כארז בין שאר עצים [שה"ש ה, טו]. יעמס לנו. יתן לנו ישועה רבה מכל עומס ככל אשר נוכל שאת [תהלים סח, כ]. בשעלו. בהליכתו שנא' דרכת בים סוסיך (חבקוק ג), בשעלו כמו (במדבר כב) במשעול הכרמים שביל, ד"א שעל שם כלי הוא וכן בשעלי שעורים (יחזקאל יג). תכן. אמולאי"ר בלע"ז ל' מדה ומנין כמו ותוכן לבנים תתנו (שמות ה) [ישעיהו מ, יב]. להנחיל אוהבי יש. יש אחי נחלה רבה [משלי ח, כא]. בסאסאה. באותה מדה. בשלחה תריבנה. כששלחה מצרים את ישראל תריבנה המדה בסאה סאה [ישעיהו כז, ח]. בסאסאה. בתוך אותה סאה עצמה כשאתה משלחה לאבדון תריבנה [סוטה שם]. מדה טובה. רבה על חברתה מדה טובה מרובה על הרעה חמש מאות בה שבמדה טובה נאמר (שמות לד) נוצר חסד לאלפים ובמדת פורענות הוא אומר על שלשים ועל רבעים אף כאן מדת הטוב של ירידת המן רבתה על ירידת המבול במדת פורענות הוא אומר וארובות השמים, לא ירד מבול אלא דרך שתי ארובות ובמדה טובה הוא אומר דלתי שמים פתח ותנא כמה ארובות יש באורך דלת ארבע הרי לשתי דלתות שמונה ארובות ואחרי ששתי ארובות הורידו גשמים גובה חמש עשרה אמה שמונה ארובות הורידו מן ששים אמות שהרי אמרת מדה טובה מרובה על של פורעניות וכל שכן שלענין נמנועות סימנה [יומא עו.]. דמדה טובה מרובה ממדת פורענות אחד מחמש מאות דבמדת פורענות כתיב (שמות כ) פוקד עון אבות על בנים על שלשים ועל רבעים ובמדה טובה כתיב (שמות כ) עושה חסד לאלפים ומתרגמינן לאלפין דרי ארבעה דורות כנגד אלפים דורות היינו אחד מחמש מאות מיעוט לאלפים אינו פחות משני אלפים וכל שכן אם כפשוטו דמשמע אלפים עד סוף כל הדורות [מכות כג.].

Holy One, Blessed is He, will bring forth a stream from the chamber of the Holy of Holies, וְעָלָיו כָּל מִינֵי מְגָדִים – **and along** the banks of [**the stream**] there will be **all kinds of delicious fruits,** שֶׁנֶּאֱמַר ,,וְעַל־הַנַּחַל יַעֲלֶה עַל־שְׂפָתוֹ מִזֶּה וּמִזֶּה כָּל־עֵץ־מַאֲכָל לֹא־יִבּוֹל עָלֵהוּ וְלֹא־יִתֹּם פִּרְיוֹ לֶחֳדָשָׁיו יְבַכֵּר כִּי מֵימָיו מִן־הַמִּקְדָּשׁ הֵמָּה יוֹצְאִים וְהָיָה פִרְיוֹ לְמַאֲכָל וְעָלֵהוּ לִתְרוּפָה" – **as it is stated:** ***By the stream there will rise along its bank**, on this side and that, **every manner of food tree**; its leaf will not wither, nor will its fruit give out; every month it will yield new fruit, for its waters emanate from the Sanctuary. So its fruit will be for food and its leaf for healing.*[10] אָמַר לֵיהּ הַהוּא סָבָא – **A certain elderly man** who happened to be there **said to [R' Yirmiyah]:** יִישַׁר וְכֵן אָמַר רַבִּי יוֹחָנָן (ויישר) – **Well spoken!**[11] **R' Yochanan has** also **said thus.** אָמַר לֵיהּ רַבִּי יִרְמְיָה לְרַבִּי זֵירָא – Upon hearing the old man's approbation **R' Yirmiyah said to** his teacher, **R' Zeira:** כִּי הַאי גַּוְונָא מִיחְזֵי אַפִּקְרוּתָא – Does remarking upon a Torah scholar's teaching **in this manner appear to be irreverence** (*apikorsus*)?[12]

R' Zeira's reply:

הָא [הַאי] סִיוּעֵי קָא אָמַר לֵיהּ – [**R' Zeira**] **said to** [**R' Yirmiyah**]: מְסַיֵּיעַ (ליה) לָךְ – **But this** old man was not disparaging you when he voiced his approval and cited R' Yochanan; rather, he **was supporting you,** both personally and in the name of another sage. אֶלָּא אִי שְׁמִיעַ לָךְ – **However, if you have heard** of this sort of *apikorsus,* הָא שְׁמִיעַ לָךְ כִּי – **this** is the case **you heard about,** הָא דְּיָתֵיב רַבִּי יוֹחָנָן וְקָא דָרֵישׁ – **as when R' Yochanan was sitting and expounding:** עָתִיד הַקָּדוֹשׁ בָּרוּךְ הוּא לְהָבִיא אֲבָנִים טוֹבוֹת וּמַרְגָּלִיּוֹת – **In the future the Holy One, Blessed is He, will bring precious stones and pearls** שֶׁהֵן שְׁלֹשִׁים עַל שְׁלֹשִׁים אַמּוֹת – **that are thirty** *amos* **by thirty** ***amos*** וְחוֹקֵק בָּהֶם עֶשֶׂר בְּרוּם עֶשְׂרִים – **and will cut out from** each of **them** an opening **ten** *amos* wide **by twenty** *amos* **high,** וּמַעֲמִידָן בְּשַׁעֲרֵי יְרוּשָׁלַיִם – **and He will install them at the gates of Jerusalem,** to be the gateways of the city, שֶׁנֶּאֱמַר ,,וְשַׂמְתִּי כַּדְכֹד שִׁמְשֹׁתַיִךְ וּשְׁעָרַיִךְ לְאַבְנֵי אֶקְדָּח" וגו' – **as it is stated:**[13] ***I will make your windows***[14] ***out of kadkod stone***[15] ***and your gates out of hewn stones***[16] **etc.** לְגַלֵּג עָלָיו אוֹתוֹ תַּלְמִיד – **A certain student** who was present **mocked [R' Yochanan]** for discussing such incredible occurrences.[17] אָמַר – **[The student] said:** הַשְׁתָּא כְּבֵיעֲתָא דְּצִילְצְלָא לֹא מַשְׁכְּחִינַן – **Now, we cannot find** precious stones and pearls even **the size of an egg of a small dove;**[18] כּוּלֵּי הַאי מַשְׁכְּחִינַן – **shall we** ever **find** stones **of such magnitude** as you describe?! לְיָמִים הִפְלִיגָה סְפִינָתוֹ בַּיָּם – **After a time [the student's] ship set sail upon the sea,** חֲזֵינְהוּ דְּקָא מְנַסְּרֵי – **and he saw ministering angels** לְמַלְאֲכֵי הַשָּׁרֵת אֲבָנִים טוֹבוֹת וּמַרְגָּלִיּוֹת – **who were sawing precious stones and pearls** as large as R' Yochanan had described.[19] אָמַר לְהוּ – **He said to [the angels]:** הָנֵי לְמַאן – **For whom are these** stones? אָמְרֵי – **They said** to him: עָתִיד הַקָּדוֹשׁ בָּרוּךְ הוּא לְהַעֲמִידָן בְּשַׁעֲרֵי יְרוּשָׁלַיִם – **In the future the Holy One, Blessed is He, will install them in the gates of Jerusalem.** כִּי הֲדַר – **When [the student] returned** home, אַשְׁכְּחֵיהּ לְרַבִּי יוֹחָנָן דְּיָתֵיב וְקָא דָרֵישׁ – **he found R' Yochanan sitting and expounding.** אָמַר לֵיהּ – **[The student] said to [R' Yochanan]:** רַבִּי דְּרוֹשׁ – **My master!** Continue to **expound!** וּלְךָ נָאֶה לִדְרוֹשׁ – **For you it is fitting to expound!** כְּשֵׁם שֶׁאָמַרְתָּ כָּךְ רָאִיתִי – **Just as you said, so did I see!** אָמַר לוֹ – **[R' Yochanan] said to him:** רֵיקָה – You **empty person!** אִם לֹא רָאִיתָ לֹא הֶאֱמַנְתָּ – **If you had not seen** it yourself, **you would not have believed** it?! Do you think that I would teach an untruth? מְלַגְלֵג עַל דִּבְרֵי חֲכָמִים אַתָּה – **You are one who mocks the words of the Sages.** יָהַב בֵּיהּ עֵינֵיהּ – **[R' Yochanan] set his eyes upon [the student]** וְנַעֲשָׂה גַּל שֶׁל עֲצָמוֹת – **and turned him into a heap of bones.**[20] Thus, when R' Yirmiyah heard about a student who was an *apikoros,* it was this student about whom he had heard.

R' Yochanan had stated that in the Messianic future God would make the gates of Jerusalem twenty *amos* high. The Gemara now cites a Baraisa that seems to contradict this teaching:

מֵיתִיבֵי – **They raised an objection** from the following Baraisa: ,,וָאוֹלֵךְ אֶתְכֶם קוֹמְמִיּוּת" – Scripture states: *I WILL LEAD YOU VERY*

NOTES

his seat once again and began speaking (*Mishnas Chachamim,* cited by *Margaliyos HaYam*). Hence, our Gemara mentions twice that "he sat."

10. *Ezekiel* 47:12. In a prophetic vision Ezekiel was shown a stream emanating from the Holy of Holies and gradually widening until it became a river that flowed from the Temple southward to the Dead Sea. Since it came from the Sanctuary, this stream of water would have the power to sweeten the waters of the Dead Sea and to grow into a river containing a copious supply of fish. The abundant waters would cause all manner of fruit trees and other edible vegetation to grow along its banks. Thus, the desert between Jerusalem and the Dead Sea would be transformed into a veritable paradise. It was to this stream that R' Yirmiyah was referring, and although he appears to add nothing to the plain meaning of the verse, *Maharsha* explains that R' Yirmiyah merely intended to stress that the verse should be understood literally. *Rif* in *Ein Yaakov* explains, however, that without R' Yirmiyah's clarification we would think that the stream and its miraculous productivity did not actually materialize in the Holy of Holies, but just outside of it, since the verse is silent on that point.

11. Literally: be strong!

12. [R' Yirmiyah evidently objected to the fact that the old man presumed to approve of and offer support for his statement. Although the text of our Gemara does not indicate that he expressed this objection in the form of a question, we are following Rashi's interpretation.] Cf. *Yad Ramah,* who bases his interpretation on a variant text, and *Maharsha.*

13. *Isaiah* 54:12. This verse describes the rebuilt Jerusalem in the Messianic era.

14. The word שִׁמְשֹׁתַיִךְ derives from שֶׁמֶשׁ, *sun,* and thus means *windows,* since the sun shines through them (*Rashi;* cf. *Rashbam* to *Bava Basra* 75a, who renders it *walls*).

15. The Gemara (*Bava Basra* ibid.) cites a dispute as to the meaning of *kadkod.* One opinion maintains that it is *shoham* (variously translated as *beryl* and *onyx*), and the other holds that it is jasper. The Gemara's conclusion is that the rebuilt windows (or walls) of Jerusalem will be composed of both types of stone.

16. I.e. the stones will be so massive that the entire gate – lintel, sideposts and threshold – will be hewn out of a single stone, as R' Yochanan expounded (see *Rashi* to *Isaiah* ibid.).

17. This is the act of *apikorsus* (irreverence) to which R' Zeira referred (*Rashi*).

18. The translation of צִילְצְלָא as *small dove* follows *Aruch* ד״ה דייציפי and ד״ה צצלא. *Rashi* describes it simply as a small bird.

19. I.e. he saw the angels sawing blocks of precious stone, each measuring thirty *amos* by thirty *amos,* and cutting out openings in each block measuring ten *amos* wide and twenty *amos* high (*Bava Basra* 75a).

20. See *Eruvin* 21b, where it is taught that whoever transgresses or mocks the words of the Sages is liable to the death penalty for breaching their authority [See also *Rashash.*]

"He became a heap of bones" means that his flesh started rotting off his bones, like the body of a person who died long ago (*Rashi* to *Shabbos* 34a). The student of our story was a wicked person. The Gemara (*Berachos* 18b) teaches that the wicked are regarded as dead even during their lifetimes. To demonstrate this, he became a heap of bones (*Maharsha* to *Bava Basra* 75a; cf. *Ohr HaChaim* to *Exodus* 11:5).

Maharal (*Netzach Yisrael*) explains the profound lesson of this story. The student mocked R' Yochanan because he did not perceive the difference between the conditions today and the World to Come. However, when he "embarked on a sea journey" – i.e. when he gave due consideration to the "wisdom that is wider than the sea" – he realized that the angels indeed cut such stones (i.e. ordained such extraordinary phenomena). Because he did not believe R' Yochanan and had to arrive at his own conclusions, the student was punished (cf. *R' Chaim Shmulevitz, Kovetz Sichos Mussar*).

לא שרו לן עורבא ולא אסרו לן יונה רבא כי הוו מייתי טריפתא דבי בנימין קמיה כי הוה חזי בה טעמא להיתירא אמר להו תחזו דקא שרינא לכו עורבא כי הוה חזי לה טעמא לאיסורא אמר להו תחזו דקא אסרנא לכו יונה רב פפא אמר כגון דאמר הני רבנן רב פפא אישתלי ואמר כגון הני רבנן ואיתיב בתעניתא לוי בר שמואל ורב הונא בר חייא הוו קא מתקני מטפחות ספרי דבי רב יהודה כי מטו מגילת אסתר אמרי הא [מגילת אסתר] לא בעי מטפחת אמר להו כי האי גוונא נמי מיחזי כי אפקירותא רב נחמן אמר זה [א]הקורא רבו בשמו דאמר רבי יוחנן מפני מה נענש גיחזי מפני שקרא לרבו בשמו שנאמר א) ויאמר גחזי אדני המלך זאת האשה וזה בנה אשר החיה אלישע יתיב רבי ירמיה קמיה דרבי זירא ויתיב וקאמר עתיד הקב"ה להוציא נחל מבית קדשי הקדשים ועליו כל מיני מגדים שנאמר ב) ועל הנחל יעלה על שפתו מזה ומזה כל עץ מאכל לא יבול עלהו ולא יתם פריו לחדשיו יבכר כי מימיו מן המקדש [המה] יוצאים והיה פריו למאכל ועלהו לתרופה א"ל ההוא סבא [א]יישר וכן אמר ר' יוחנן [א] ([ב]יישר) אמר ליה ר' ירמיה לרבי זירא כי האי גונא מיחזי אפקרותא אמר ליה הא [האי] סיועי קא מסייע (ליה) [לך] אלא אי שמיע לך הא שמיע לך כי הא [ג]דיתיב רבי יוחנן וקא דריש עתיד הקב"ה להביא אבנים טובות ומרגליות שהן שלשים על שלשים אמות וחוקק בהם עשר ברום עשרים ומעמידן בשערי ירושלים שנאמר ג) ושמתי כדכוד שמשותיך ושעריך לאבני אקדה וגו' לגלג עליו אותו תלמיד אמר השתא כביעתא דצילצלא לא משכחינן כולי האי משכחינן לימים הפליגה ספינתו בים חזינהו למלאכי השרת דקא מנסרי אבנים טובות ומרגליות אמר להו הני למאן אמרי עתיד הקב"ה להעמידן בשערי ירושלים כי הדר אשכחיה לר' יוחנן דיתיב וקא דריש א"ל רבי דרוש ולך נאה לדרוש כשם שאמרת כך ראיתי אמר לו ריקה אם לא ראית לא האמנת מלגלג על דברי חכמים אתה [ד]יהב ביה עיניה ועשאו גל של עצמות מיתיבי ד) ואולך אתכם קוממיות ר"מ אומר מאתים אמה כשתי קומות של אדם הראשון רבי יהודה אומר ק' אמה כנגד היכל וכותליו שנאמר ה) אשר בנינו כנטיעים מגודלים בנעוריהם בנותינו כזויות מחוטבות תבנית היכל וגו' כי קאמר ר' יוחנן לכוי דבי זיקא מאי [ה]ועלהו לתרופה ר' יצחק בר אבודימי ורב חסדא חד אמר להתיר פה של מעלה וחד אמר להתיר פה של מטה איתמר ([ו]נמי) חזקיה אמר להתיר פה אילמין בר קפרא אמר להתיר פה עקרות ר' יוחנן אמר לתרופה ממש מאי לתרופה ר' שמואל בר נחמני אמר לתואר פנים של בעלי הפה דרש ר' יהודה ברבי סימון כל המשחיר פניו על דברי תורה בעולם הזה הקב"ה מבהיק זיוו לעולם הבא שנאמר ו) מראהו כלבנון בחור כארזים אמר ר' תנחום בר' חנילאי כל המרעיב עצמו על דברי תורה בעולם הזה הקב"ה משביעו לעולם הבא שנאמר ז) ירוין מדשן ביתך ונחל עדניך תשקם כי אתא רב דימי אמר עתיד הקב"ה ליתן לכל צדיק וצדיק מלא עומסו שנאמר ח) ברוך ה' יום יום יעמס לנו האל ישועתנו סלה א"ל אביי וכי אפשר לומר כן והלא כבר נאמר ט) מי מדד בשעלו מים ושמים בזרת תכן אמר מאי טעמא לא שכיחת באגדתא דאמרי במערבא משמיה דרבא בר מרי [ז]עתיד הקב"ה ליתן לכל צדיק וצדיק ג' מאות ועשרה עולמות שנא' י) להנחיל אוהבי יש ואוצרותיהם אמלא יש בגימטריא תלת מאה ועשרה הוי תניא [ח]ר' מאיר אומר במדה שאדם מודד מודדין לו דכתיב כ) בסאסאה בשלחה תריבנה אמר ר' [ב] [ט]יהושע וכי אפשר לומר כן אדם נותן מלא עומסו לעני בעולם הזה הקב"ה נותן לו מלא עומסו לעולם הבא והכתיב ט) שמים בזרת תכן [ג] ואתה אי אומר כן איזו היא מדה מרובה מדת טובה מרובה או מדת פורענות

הוי

רש"י

לא שרו לן עורבא. לא אמרו לנו שום חידוש שלא מצינו בתורה (דשרינן עורבא): [דקא שרינא לכו עורבא]. שהיתר זה אינו מלוי בתורה אלא סופרים אמרוהו: כגון דאמר הנהו רבנן. כאדם שאומר אותו ת"ח דלשון בזוי הוא זה שהיה לו לומר רבותינו שבמקום פלוני ל"א כגון דאמר הני רבנן דכשהוא מספר שום דבר מרבנן אומר הני ולשון גנאי הוא הני אבל הנהו רבנן אינו גנאי: כי מטו מגלת אסתר. לתקן לה מטפחת אמרי הא מגלת אסתר לא בעיא מטפחת כלומר בלשון בעיא א"ל לרב יהודה הא ודאי לא צריכא מטפחת כגון האחרות ולשון גנאי הוא דהוה להו למימר לרבם בלשון שאלה כך צריכה או אינה צריכה: מעיין בית ה'. יצא והשקה את נחל שטים (יואל ד): מגדים. דינטר"ש בלע"ז כל מיני פירות מתוקים: יבכר. בכל חדש וחדש יתבשלו בו פירות: בשמו. שאומר פלוני ואינו אומר מורי רבי פלוני: א"ל ההוא סבא יישר וכן אמר רבי יוחנן. כדבריך ור' יוחנן נמי הכי קאמר כדאמרת מ"ר ולא גרסינן וכן אמר רבי יוחנן יישר: כי האי גוונא. מי מיחזי כאפקרותא: אלא אי שמיע לך מידי הא שמיע לך: לגלג עליו אותו תלמיד. אדרבי יוחנן דהיינו אפקירותא: כדכד. אבן טובה וכך שמה: שמשותיך. חלונות שהשמש זורח בהם [ד] כמו (תהלים פד) שמש ומגן היינו שמש ממש (ל"א) לאבני אקדח שהקב"ה חוקקן כבמקדח עד שחוקק בהם עשר ברום עשרים: צילצלתא. עוף קטן: גל של עצמות. שמת דאדם שמת נעשה גל של עצמות: קוממיות. שתי קומות של אדם הראשון כדאמרינן בחגיגה (דף יב.) שמיעטו הקב"ה והעמידו על מאה אמה שנאמר ותשת עלי כפך כף בגימטריא הכי הוי: כנגד היכל וכותליו. שכך היה אורך כל ההיכל עם הכותלים דכתיב (מלכים א ו) והבית אשר בנה המלך שלמה לה' ששים אמה ארכו וכותל מזרח שש אמות וכותל מערב שש אמות ואמה אחת טרקסין הרי י"ג אמות ואולם עשר אמה רוחב וכותל האולם שש הרי כ"ט ומאחורי האולם תא אחד רחבו שש וכתלו ה' הרי מ' וס' אמה של אורך הבית הרי מאה והיאך יכולין לכוף קומתן וליכנס בפתח שאין לו אלא רום עשרים כדאמרת: אשר בנינו. כלומר בנים שלנו יהיו לעתיד כאילנות גבוהין מגודלים: ובנותינו. ובנות שלנו כזויות המחוטבות לתבנית היכל כלומר ככותל ההיכל מחוטבות כמו (דברים כט) מחוטב עציך לישנא אחרינא אהיכל דבית שני קאמר דקים לן היכל ס' אורך ברום מאה הוא: לכוי דבי זיקא. לחלונות שהשמש והאור נכנסין בהן אבל השערים גבוהים יותר: [להתיר פה של [י]מטה]. להתיר [כ]פה אלמים שיהו מדברים: להתיר פה של מטה. רחם של העקרות האוכלות מן העלין נפקדות [ל]: איתמר נמי חזקיה וכו'. והיינו הך דלעיל לתרופה: מראהו כלבנון. וכתיב לעיל מיניה שחורות כעורב וסמיך ליה חכו ממתקים: ירוין מדשן ביתך. אמר לי רבי דלעיל מינה מהאי קרא מיירי עניינא דמרעיב את עצמו וקאמר ירוין מדשן ביתך שהקב"ה משביען לעוה"ב: מלא עומסו. מלא חופנו של הקב"ה טובה: וכי אפשר לומר כן. היאך אדם יכול לקבל מלא עומסו של הקב"ה והרי אין לו מקום ליתן דכל העולם כולו אינו אלא כמזרת ועד אגודל: [מ]באותן עולמות יתן לצדיק את העומס: במדה שאדם מודד. אם מדד ונתן לדקה לעני מלא חפניו הקב"ה מודד בחפניו ונותן לו: וכי אפשר לומר כן. שיהא הקב"ה נותן לאדם מלא חפניו והלא אינו יכול לסבול כל כך:

הוי

עין משפט נר מצוה

יט א מיי' פ"ה מהלכות ת"ת הלכה ה סמג עשין עד טוש"ע י"ד סי' רמב סעיף ט:

ליקוטי רש"י

לתרופה. פירשו רבותינו ז"ל להתיר פה אלמים ופה עקרות ומשמעו ל' רפואה כמו (ירמיה ו) וירפאו את שבר עמי על נקלה וכן חברו מנחם [יחזקאל מז, יב]. כדכד. מין אבן טובה. שמשותיך י"ת אמך ומנחם חברו עם ישמשוניה ויש פותרין ל' שמש חלונות שחמה זורחת בהן ועושין כנגדו מחילה במיני זכוכית לבעים לנוי ומדרש תהלים פותר שמשותיך ושמש ומגן (תהלים פד) שיני החומה. לאבני אקדח. י"ת לאבני גמר גומרין תרגום גחלים פתר אקדח לשון קדחי אש והם מין אבנים טובות בוערות כלפידי' והוא קרבונקל"א לשון גחלת ויש פותרין ל' מקדח אבנים גדולות שכל חלל הפתח קדוח בתוכו והמזוזות והמפתן והסף כולן מתוך האבן הם. לאבני חפץ. לאבני רצון [ישעיהו נד, יב]. וחוקק עשר. של רוחב ברום עשרים והיינו אקדח לשון קודח שחוקק בהם ומשמע נמי אבן טובה שמאירה כאש קודחת כמו קודחי אש (ישעיהו נ). אקדח. קרבונקל"א בלע"ז ובתרגום יונתן אבני גומרא. כביעתא דצילצלתא. ביצת עוף קטן ששמו תאליל. קוממיות. שתי קומות שני ממי"ן דריש. כשתי קומות של אדם הראשון. שמיעטו עד ק' אמה במסכת חגיגה (דף יב). ההיכל. של בית שני שהיה רום מאה אמה ולפי קומתן צריך שערים גבוהים וקשיא לר' יוחנן דאמר רום עשרים. לכווי דבי זיקא. לחלונות העשויין לאויר והיינו שעריך דקרא חלונות החומה [ב"ב עה.]. גל של עצמות. גל מעצמות, כמת שנרקב בשרו ונפל מזמן הרבה [שבת לד.]. מאי ועלהו לתרופה. גבי מעיין שעתיד לצאת מבית קדשי הקדשים קאי ועל שפת הנחל יעלה מזה ומזה כל [עץ] (עלה) מאכל והיה פריו למאכל ועלהו לתרופה וכו' וקדריש נוטריקון לתרופה. להתיר פה שלמעלה. פה אלמים שכל אלם האוכל ממנו נרפא. פה שלמטה. פה רחם של עקרות. חזקיה ובר קפרא. מפרשא מילתייהו טפי והיא היא [מנחות צח.]. בחור כארזים. נבחר בין הבנים כארז בין שאר עצים [שה"ש ה, טו]. יעמס לנו. יתן לנו ישועה רבה מכל עומס ככל אשר נוכל שאת [תהלים סח, כ]. בשעלו. בהליכתו שנא' דרכת בים סוסיך (חבקוק ג), בשעלו כמו (במדבר כב) במשעול הכרמים שביל, ד"א שעל שם כלי הוא וכן בשעלי שעורים (יחזקאל יג). תכן. אמולאי"ר בלע"ז ל' מדה ומנין כמו ותוכן לבנים תתנו (שמות ה) [ישעיהו מ, יב]. להנחיל אוהבי יש. יש אתי נחלה רבה [משלי ח, כא]. בסאסאה. באותה מדה. בשלחה תריבנה. כששלחה מצרים את ישראל תריבנה המדה בסאה שלה [ישעיהו כז, ח]. בסאסאה. בתוך אותה סאה עצמה כשאתה משלחה לאבדון תריבנה [סוטה שם]. מדה טובה. רבה על מכרתה מדה טובה מרובה על הרעה חמש מאות בה שבמדה טובה נאמר (שמות לד) נוצר חסד לאלפים ובמדת פורענות הוא אומר על שלשים ועל רבעים אף כאן מדת הטוב של ירידת המן רבתה על ירידת המבול במדת פורענות הוא אומר וארובות השמים, לא ירד מבול אלא דרך שתי ארובות ובמדה טובה הוא אומר דלתי שמים פתח ותנא כמה ארובות יש באורך דלת ארבע הרי לשתי דלתות שמונה ארובות ואחרי ששתי ארובות הורידו גשמים גובה חמש עשרה אמה שמונה ארובות הורידו מן ששים אמות שהרי אמרת מדה טובה מרובה על של פורענות וכל שכן שאינה ממועטת הימנה [יומא עו.]. דמדה טובה מרובה ממדת פורענות אחד מחמש מאות דבמדת פורענות כתיב (שמות כ) פוקד עון אבות על בנים על שלשים ועל רבעים ובמדה טובה כתיב (שמות כ) עושה חסד לאלפים ומתרגמינן לאלפין דרי ארבעה דורות כנגד אלפים דורות היינו אחד מחמש מאות מיעוט לאלפים אינו פחות משני אלפים וכל שכן אם כפשוטו דמשמע אלפים עד סוף כל הדורות [מכות כג.].

מסורת הש"ס

א) [ברכות מב: וש"נ], ב) [טעות הדפוס], ג) ב"ב עה., ד) [ב"ב עה. ע"ש שבת לד. ברכות נח.], ה) [מנחות דף לח. ע"ש], ו) [במנחו' ליתא], ז) [משנה סוף עוקצים ול"ע ועי' בים סדר למשנה ישוב נכון על זה], ח) [סוטה ח: ושם אית' רבי אומר אמנם שם טו: דמסיק דשמעי' לר"מ כו' משמע דגי' דהכא עיקר וע"ש ברש"י וכן איתא ג"כ בתוספתא שם פ"ג], ט) [נ"א יהודה], י) צ"ל למעלה, כ) [עי' רש"י מנחות לח.], ל) [עי' רש"י שם], מ) צ"ל שלש מאות באותן וכו'.

הגהות הגר"א

[א] גמ' יישר. נמחק: [ב] שם יהושע. נמחק: [ג] שם בזרת תכן ואתה. נ"ב א"ל ר"י ואתה: [ד] רש"י ד"ה שמשותיך כו' זורח בהם. נ"ב עי' רש"י בע"י:

גליון הש"ס

גמ' זה הקורא רבו בשמו. עי' יבמות נז ע"ב תד"ה אמר:

תורה אור השלם

א) וַיְהִי הוּא מְסַפֵּר לַמֶּלֶךְ אֵת אֲשֶׁר הֶחֱיָה אֶת הַמֵּת וְהִנֵּה הָאִשָּׁה אֲשֶׁר הֶחֱיָה אֶת בְּנָהּ צֹעֶקֶת אֶל הַמֶּלֶךְ עַל בֵּיתָהּ וְעַל שָׂדָהּ וַיֹּאמֶר גֵּחֲזִי אֲדֹנִי הַמֶּלֶךְ זֹאת הָאִשָּׁה וְזֶה בְּנָהּ אֲשֶׁר הֶחֱיָה אֱלִישָׁע: [מלכים ב' ח, ה]

ב) וְעַל הַנַּחַל יַעֲלֶה עַל שְׂפָתוֹ מִזֶּה וּמִזֶּה כָּל עֵץ מַאֲכָל לֹא יִבּוֹל עָלֵהוּ וְלֹא יִתֹּם פִּרְיוֹ לֶחֳדָשָׁיו יְבַכֵּר כִּי מֵימָיו מִן הַמִּקְדָּשׁ הֵמָּה יוֹצְאִים וְהָיָה פִרְיוֹ לְמַאֲכָל וְעָלֵהוּ לִתְרוּפָה: [יחזקאל מז, יב]

ג) וְשַׂמְתִּי כַּדְכֹד שִׁמְשֹׁתַיִךְ וּשְׁעָרַיִךְ לְאַבְנֵי אֶקְדָּח וְכָל גְּבוּלֵךְ לְאַבְנֵי חֵפֶץ: [ישעיה נד, יב]

ד) אֲנִי יְיָ אֱלֹהֵיכֶם אֲשֶׁר הוֹצֵאתִי אֶתְכֶם מֵאֶרֶץ מִצְרַיִם מִהְיֹת לָהֶם עֲבָדִים וָאֶשְׁבֹּר מֹטֹת עֻלְּכֶם וָאוֹלֵךְ אֶתְכֶם קוֹמְמִיּוּת: [ויקרא כו, יג]

ה) אֲשֶׁר בָּנֵינוּ כִּנְטִעִים מְגֻדָּלִים בִּנְעוּרֵיהֶם בְּנוֹתֵינוּ כְזָוִיֹּת מְחֻטָּבוֹת תַּבְנִית הֵיכָל: [תהלים קמד, יב]

ו) שׁוֹקָיו עַמּוּדֵי שֵׁשׁ מְיֻסָּדִים עַל אַדְנֵי פָז מַרְאֵהוּ כַּלְּבָנוֹן בָּחוּר כָּאֲרָזִים: [שיר השירים ה, טו]

ז) יִרְוְיֻן מִדֶּשֶׁן בֵּיתֶךָ וְנַחַל עֲדָנֶיךָ תַשְׁקֵם: [תהלים לו, ט]

ח) בָּרוּךְ אֲדֹנָי יוֹם יוֹם יַעֲמָס לָנוּ הָאֵל יְשׁוּעָתֵנוּ סֶלָה: [תהלים סח, כ]

ט) מִי מָדַד בְּשָׁעֳלוֹ מַיִם וְשָׁמַיִם בַּזֶּרֶת תִּכֵּן וְכָל בַּשָּׁלִשׁ עֲפַר הָאָרֶץ וְשָׁקַל בַּפֶּלֶס הָרִים וּגְבָעוֹת בְּמֹאזְנָיִם: [ישעיה מ, יב]

י) לְהַנְחִיל אֹהֲבַי יֵשׁ וְאֹצְרֹתֵיהֶם אֲמַלֵּא: [משלי ח, כא]

כ) בְּסַאסְּאָה בְּשַׁלְחָהּ תְּרִיבֶנָּה הָגָה בְּרוּחוֹ הַקָּשָׁה בְּיוֹם קָדִים: [ישעיה כז, ח]

HIGH.[21] How high will we be? רַבִּי מֵאִיר אוֹמֵר – R' MEIR SAYS: מָאתַיִם אַמָּה – TWO HUNDRED *AMOS,* which is כִּשְׁתֵּי קוֹמוֹת שֶׁל אָדָם הָרִאשׁוֹן – TWICE THE HEIGHT OF ADAM, THE FIRST human being.[22] רַבִּי יְהוּדָה אוֹמֵר – R' YEHUDAH SAYS: מֵאָה אַמָּה – ONE HUNDRED *AMOS,* כְּנֶגֶד הֵיכָל וְכוֹתָלָיו – CORRESPONDING TO the length of THE *HEICHAL* AND ITS WALLS,[23] שֶׁנֶּאֱמַר ,,אֲשֶׁר בָּנֵינוּ כִּנְטִעִים מְגֻדָּלִים בִּנְעוּרֵיהֶם – AS IT IS STATED: *FOR OUR SONS SHALL BE LIKE SAPLINGS NURTURED FROM THEIR YOUTHS,* בְּנוֹתֵינוּ כְזָוִיֹּת מְחֻטָּבוֹת תַּבְנִית הֵיכָל וגו׳" – *OUR DAUGHTERS LIKE CORNERSTONES CRAFTED IN THE FORM OF THE HEICHAL* etc.[24] Now, according to R' Yochanan the gateways of the rebuilt Jerusalem are to be twenty *amos* high. However, according to both opinions in the Baraisa, such gateways would be much too low for the immensely tall inhabitants of the future! – ? –

The Gemara reinterprets R' Yochanan's statement:

כִּי קָאָמַר רַבִּי יוֹחָנָן – **When R' Yochanan said** that God will cut out openings in the precious stones twenty *amos* high, לְכַוֵּי דְּבֵי זִיקָא – he was referring **to apertures for air,** not to the gateways themselves.[25]

Three sages describe the curative powers of the leaf mentioned in the verse expounded above by R' Yirmiyah:

מַאי ,,וְעָלֵהוּ לִתְרוּפָה" – **What is** the meaning of ***its leaf shall be for healing?*** רַבִּי יִצְחָק בַּר אֲבוּדִימִי וְרַב חִסְדָּא – **R' Yitzchak bar Avudimi and Rav Chisda** dispute the meaning of this verse. חַד אָמַר – **One said** לְהַתִּיר פֶּה שֶׁל מַעְלָה – that when eaten the leaf will have the power **to open**[26] **the upper mouth,** i.e. to cure the mute and allow them to speak. וְחַד אָמַר – **And one said** לְהַתִּיר פֶּה שֶׁל מַטָּה – that the leaf will have the power **to open**[26] **the lower mouth,**[27] i.e. to cure barren women so that they may conceive. אִיתְּמַר (נַמִּי) – **It was stated (also)** by others: חִזְקִיָּה אָמַר לְהַתִּיר פֶּה אִילְּמִין – **Chizkiah said:** When eaten the leaf will have the power **to open the mouths of the mute.** בַּר קַפָּרָא אָמַר לְהַתִּיר פֶּה עֲקָרוֹת – **Bar Kappara said:** It will have the power **to open the [wombs] of the barren.**[28]

The opinion of the third sage:

רַבִּי יוֹחָנָן אָמַר לִתְרוּפָה מַמָּשׁ – **R' Yochanan said:** The verse means **"for actual medicine."**[29]

The Gemara asks:

מַאי ,,לִתְרוּפָה" – **What,** then, **is** the point of stating ***lisrufah?***[30]

The Gemara answers:

רַבִּי שְׁמוּאֵל בַּר נַחְמָנִי אָמַר – **R' Shmuel bar Nachmani said:** לְתוֹאַר פָּנִים שֶׁל בַּעֲלֵי הַפֶּה – The word *lisrufah* is actually an acrostic for: **for brightening the countenance of the speakers.**[31] דָּרַשׁ רַבִּי יְהוּדָה בְּרַבִּי סִימוֹן – Along similar lines **R' Yehudah the son of R' Simon expounded:** כָּל הַמַּשְׁחִיר פָּנָיו עַל דִּבְרֵי תוֹרָה בָּעוֹלָם הַזֶּה – **Whoever blackens his face for the words of Torah in this world,**[32] הַקָּדוֹשׁ בָּרוּךְ הוּא מַבְהִיק זִיוָיו לָעוֹלָם הַבָּא – **the Holy One, Blessed is He, causes his countenance to shine brightly in the World to Come,** i.e. that person receives great reward for his selfless Torah study, שֶׁנֶּאֱמַר ,,מַרְאֵהוּ כַּלְּבָנוֹן בָּחוּר כָּאֲרָזִים" – **as it is stated: *His appearance is like Lebanon, excellent as the cedars.***[33] אָמַר רַבִּי תַּנְחוּם בְּרַבִּי חֲנִילַאי – And in the same vein **R' Tanchum the son of R' Chanilai said:** כָּל הַמַּרְעִיב עַצְמוֹ עַל דִּבְרֵי תוֹרָה בָּעוֹלָם הַזֶּה – **Whoever starves himself for the words of Torah in this world,** i.e. studies so assiduously that he neglects to eat, הַקָּדוֹשׁ בָּרוּךְ הוּא מַשְׂבִּיעוֹ לָעוֹלָם הַבָּא – **the Holy One, Blessed is He, will satiate him in the World to Come,** שֶׁנֶּאֱמַר ,,יִרְוְיֻן מִדֶּשֶׁן בֵּיתֶךָ וְנַחַל עֲדָנֶיךָ תַשְׁקֵם" – **as it is stated: *They will be sated from the abundance of Your house; and from the stream of Your delights You will give them to drink.***[34]

NOTES

21. *Leviticus* 26:13. קוֹמְמִיּוּת (with a double *mem*) is the dual form of קוֹמָה, *height.* It is a reference to the spiritual [and physical] heights which we will merit in the World to Come (see *Chasam Sofer* to *Bava Basra* ibid.).

22. Adam's height was one hundred *amos* (*Rashi,* from *Chagigah* 12a). In the World to Come, God will recreate the human being. Since the word קוֹמְמִיּוּת is a dual form, R' Meir interprets it to mean twice the height that man was at his original creation (see *Maharsha* to *Bava Basra* ibid.). *Maharal* explains that "100 *amos*" represents the restoration of mankind to Adam's state before he sinned, and "200 *amos*" represents mankind's supernatural elevation beyond this state (see also *Eitz Yosef* and *Michtav MeEliyahu* II, p. 137).

23. The entire length of the *Heichal,* the central building of the Temple, was one hundred *amos. Rashi* establishes this measurement as follows: Proceeding east to west, the doorway of the *Ulam* (Hall) was six *amos* thick; the *Ulam* itself was ten *amos* long; the wall separating the *Ulam* and the *Heichal* was six *amos* thick; the *Kodesh* part of the *Heichal* was forty *amos* long; the *amah traksin,* a wall separating the rest of the *Heichal* from the Holy of Holies, was one *amah* thick; the Holy of Holies was twenty *amos* long; the wall behind the Holy of Holies was six *amos* thick; behind that wall was a chamber six *amos* long; behind that chamber was a wall five *amos* thick. This wall was the very end of the building. Thus, the *Heichal* was one hundred *amos* long from end to end (*Rashi*). [These are the measurements of the First Temple. See *Middos* 4:7, which states that the entire *Heichal* of the Second Temple was likewise one hundred *amos* long.]

This measurement of one hundred *amos* is equal to a height of two stories (see *Middos* 4:6). Thus, according to R' Yehudah, the dual form of קוֹמְמִיּוּת alludes to the two stories (*Rashash* to *Bava Basra* ibid.).

24. *Psalms* 144:12. The latter part of the verse, *our daughters shall be like cornerstones crafted in the form of the Heichal,* likens the children of the future to the hewn cornerstones of the First Temple, which stood one hundred *amos* apart along the length of the *Heichal.* The verse thus teaches that in the World to Come our height will equal the length of the *Heichal* (see *Rashi*).

25. The twenty-*amah* dimension given by R' Yochanan corresponds to the height of the ventilation holes in the gates. The gateways were much higher (*Rashi,* as emended by *Rashash*).

26. Literally: loosen, untie. [Both R' Yitzchak and Rav Chisda interpret the word לִתְרוּפָה as an acrostic (לתרו/פה) for לְהַתִּיר פֶּה, *to loosen* (i.e. open) *the mouth.*]

27. A euphemism for the womb (*Rashi*).

28. *Maharal* explains that it is not only the mute and the barren who will be cured. Rather, the "upper mouth" represents mankind, who are speaking beings, and the "lower mouth" symbolizes the world itself, which is the arena for creativity. The Sages thus teach that in the Messianic future both mankind and the rest of creation will realize their total spiritual and physical potentials. Cf. *Ben Yehoyada,* and see *Yerushalmi Shekalim* 6:2 and *Devarim Rabbah* 1.

29. I.e. Scripture teaches that the leaves will be taken as medicine to cure physical illnesses.

30. I.e. how does R' Yochanan interpret לִתְרוּפָה as an acrostic for "for actual medicine"? See note 26 above, and cf. *Ben Yehoyada* and *Rif* in *Ein Yaakov.*

31. I.e. for Torah scholars, who engage in the verbal toil of Torah study (see Gemara above, 99b).

The letters of *lisrufah* (ל,ת,ר,פ,ה) form an acrostic for לְתוֹאַר פָּנִים שֶׁל בַּעֲלֵי הַפֶּה. According to this new interpretation, the leaves will serve as medicine not for physical illnesses, as previously understood, but for the darkened countenances of dedicated Torah scholars, as the Gemara now explains (*Ben Yehoyada*).

32. I.e. he studies Torah with such intensity and single-mindedness that he neglects his physical well-being.

33. *Song of Songs* 5:15. This verse appears in a passage that describes the Torah scholar, as is evidenced by the following verse: *The words of his palate are sweet and all sheer delight,* a reference to the words of Torah. However, earlier in the passage (v. 11) the scholar is described as being *black as a raven* (i.e. from hunger, as a result of his total immersion in his studies). How, then, can Scripture subsequently describe him as being handsome like a cedar of Lebanon? The answer is that the second verse describes his appearance in the World to Come, where his countenance will shine brilliantly (*Rashi;* cf. *Maharsha;* see *Maharal*).

34. *Psalms* 36:9. See *Maharsha,* who explains that which *Rashi* says – viz. that the preceding verse describes a person who subjects himself to

מסורת הש"ס

א) [ברכות מב: וש"נ], ב) [טעות הדפוס], ג) ב"ב עה., ד) [ב"ב עה. ע"ש שבת לד. ברכות נח.], ה) [מנחות דף לב. ע"ש], ו) [במנחו' ליתא], ז) [משנה סוף עוקלים ול"ע ועי' ב"ש סדר למשנה ישוב נכון על זה], ח) [סוטה ח: וש"נ], ט) [עי' רבי אומר אמנם שם טו: דמסיק דשמעי' לר"מ כו' משמע דגי' דהכא עיקר וע"ש ברש"י וכן איתא בתוספתא שם פ"ג], י) [ל"א יהודה], ל) נ"ל למעלה, מ) [עי' רש"י מנחות לג.], נ) [עי' רש"י שם], ס) נ"ל שלש מאות באותן וכו'.

הגהות הגר"א

[א] גמ' יישר. נמחק: [ב] שם יהושע. נמחק: [ג] שם בזרת תכן ואתה. נ"ב ל"ל ר"ה ולפתח: [ד] רש"י ד"ה שמשותיך כו' זורח בהם. נ"ב ע' רש"י בע"י.

גליון הש"ס

גמ' זה הקורא רבו בשמו. ע' יבמות נו ע"ב תד"ה אמר:

תורה אור השלם

א) וַיְהִי הוּא מְסַפֵּר לַמֶּלֶךְ אֵת אֲשֶׁר הֶחֱיָה אֶת הַמֵּת וְהִנֵּה הָאִשָּׁה אֲשֶׁר הֶחֱיָה אֶת בְּנָהּ צֹעֶקֶת אֶל הַמֶּלֶךְ עַל בֵּיתָהּ וְעַל שָׂדָהּ וַיֹּאמֶר גֵּחֲזִי אֲדֹנִי הַמֶּלֶךְ זֹאת הָאִשָּׁה וְזֶה בְּנָהּ אֲשֶׁר הֶחֱיָה אֱלִישָׁע: [מלכים ב ח, ה]

ב) וְעַל הַנַּחַל יַעֲלֶה עַל שְׂפָתוֹ מִזֶּה וּמִזֶּה כָּל עֵץ מַאֲכָל לֹא יִבּוֹל עָלֵהוּ וְלֹא יִתֹּם פִּרְיוֹ לָחֳדָשָׁיו יְבַכֵּר כִּי מֵימָיו מִן הַמִּקְדָּשׁ הֵמָּה יוֹצְאִים וְהָיָה פִרְיוֹ לְמַאֲכָל וְעָלֵהוּ לִתְרוּפָה: [יחזקאל מז, יב]

ג) וְשַׂמְתִּי כַּדְכֹד שִׁמְשֹׁתַיִךְ וּשְׁעָרַיִךְ לְאַבְנֵי אֶקְדָּח וְכָל גְּבוּלֵךְ לְאַבְנֵי חֵפֶץ: [ישעיה נד, יב]

ד) אֲנִי יְיָ אֱלֹהֵיכֶם אֲשֶׁר הוֹצֵאתִי אֶתְכֶם מֵאֶרֶץ מִצְרַיִם מִהְיֹת לָהֶם עֲבָדִים וָאֶשְׁבֹּר מֹטֹת עֻלְּכֶם וָאוֹלֵךְ אֶתְכֶם קוֹמְמִיּוּת: [ויקרא כו, יג]

ה) אֲשֶׁר בָּנֵינוּ כִּנְטִעִים מְגֻדָּלִים בִּנְעוּרֵיהֶם בְּנוֹתֵינוּ כְזָוִיֹּת מְחֻטָּבוֹת תַּבְנִית הֵיכָל: [תהלים קמד, יב]

ו) שׁוֹקָיו עַמּוּדֵי שֵׁשׁ מְיֻסָּדִים עַל אַדְנֵי פָז מַרְאֵהוּ כַּלְּבָנוֹן בָּחוּר כָּאֲרָזִים: [שיר השירים ה, טו]

ז) יִרְוְיֻן מִדֶּשֶׁן בֵּיתֶךָ וְנַחַל עֲדָנֶיךָ תַשְׁקֵם: [תהלים לו, ט] ח) בָּרוּךְ אֲדֹנָי יוֹם יוֹם יַעֲמָס לָנוּ הָאֵל יְשׁוּעָתֵנוּ סֶלָה: [תהלים סח, כ] ט) מִי מָדַד בְּשָׁעֳלוֹ מַיִם וְשָׁמַיִם בַּזֶּרֶת תִּכֵּן וְכָל בַּשָּׁלִשׁ עֲפַר הָאָרֶץ וְשָׁקַל בַּפֶּלֶס הָרִים וּגְבָעוֹת בְּמֹאזְנָיִם: [ישעיה מ, יב] י) לְהַנְחִיל אֹהֲבַי יֵשׁ וְאֹצְרֹתֵיהֶם אֲמַלֵּא: [משלי ח, כא] כ) בְּסַאסְּאָה בְּשַׁלְחָהּ תְּרִיבֶנָּה הָגָה בְּרוּחוֹ הַקָּשָׁה בְּיוֹם קָדִים: [ישעיה כז, ח]

לא שרו לן עורבא ולא אסרו לן יונה רבא כי הוו מייתי טריפתא דבי בנימין קמיה כי הוה חזי בה טעמא להיתירא אמר להו תחזו דקא שרינא לכו עורבא כי הוה חזי לה טעמא לאיסורא אמר להו תחזו דקא אסרנא לכו יונה רב פפא אמר כגון דאמר הני רבנן רב פפא אישתלי ואמר כגון הני רבנן ואיתיב בתעניתא לוי בר שמואל ורב הונא בר חייא הוו קא מתקני מטפחות ספרי דבי רב יהודה כי מטו מגילת אסתר אמרי הא [מגילת אסתר] לא בעי מטפחת אמר להו כי האי גוונא נמי מיחזי כי אפקירותא רב נחמן אמר זה [א]הקורא רבו בשמו דאמר רבי יוחנן מפני מה נענש גיחזי מפני שקרא לרבו בשמו שנאמר א) ויאמר גחזי אדני המלך זאת האשה וזה בנה אשר החיה אלישע יתיב רבי ירמיה קמיה דרבי זירא ויתיב וקאמר עתיד הקב"ה להוציא נחל מבית קדשי הקדשים ועליו כל מיני מגדים שנאמר ב) ועל הנחל יעלה על שפתו מזה ומזה כל עץ מאכל לא יבול עלהו ולא יתם פריו לחדשיו יבכר כי מימיו מן המקדש [המה] יוצאים והיה פריו למאכל ועלהו לתרופה א"ל ההוא סבא יישר וכן אמר ר' יוחנן [א] (יישר) אמר ליה ר' ירמיה לרבי זירא כי האי גונא מיחזי אפקרותא אמר ליה הא [האי] סיועי קא מסייע (ליה) [לך] אלא אי שמיע לך הא שמיע לך כי הא דיתיב רבי יוחנן וקא דריש עתיד הקב"ה להביא אבנים טובות ומרגליות שהן שלשים על שלשים אמות וחוקק בהם עשר ברום עשרים ומעמידן בשערי ירושלים שנאמר ג) ושמתי כדכוד שמשותיך ושעריך לאבני אקדח וגו' לגלג עליו אותו תלמיד אמר השתא כביעתא דצילצלא לא משכחינן כולי האי משכחינן לימים הפליגה ספינתו בים חזינהו למלאכי השרת דקא מנסרי אבנים טובות ומרגליות אמר להו הני למאן אמרי עתיד הקב"ה להעמידן בשערי ירושלים כי הדר אשכחיה לר' יוחנן דיתיב וקא דריש א"ל רבי דרוש ולך נאה לדרוש כשם שאמרת כך ראיתי אמר לו ריקה אם לא ראית לא האמנת מלגלג על דברי חכמים אתה יהב ביה עיניה ועשאו גל של עצמות מיתיבי ד) ואולך אתכם קוממיות ר"מ אומר מאתים אמה כשתי קומות של אדם הראשון רבי יהודה אומר ק' אמה כנגד היכל וכותליו שנאמר ה) אשר בנינו כנטעים מגודלים בנעוריהם בנותינו כזויות מחוטבות תבנית היכל וגו' כי קאמר ר' יוחנן לכוי דבי זיקא מאי ועלהו לתרופה ר' יצחק בר אבודימי ורב חסדא חד אמר להתיר פה של מעלה וחד אמר להתיר פה של מטה איתמר (נמי) חזקיה אמר להתיר פה אילמין בר קפרא אמר להתיר פה עקרות ר' יוחנן אמר לתרופה ממש מאי לתרופה ר' שמואל בר נחמני אמר לתואר פנים של בעלי הפה דרש ר' יהודה ברבי סימון כל המשחיר פניו על דברי תורה בעולם הזה הקב"ה מבהיק זיוו לעולם הבא שנאמר ו) מראהו כלבנון בחור כארזים אמר ר' תנחום בר' חנילאי כל המרעיב עצמו על דברי תורה בעולם הזה הקב"ה משביעו לעולם הבא שנאמר ז) ירויון מדשן ביתך ונחל עדניך תשקם כי אתא רב דימי אמר עתיד הקב"ה ליתן לכל צדיק וצדיק מלא עומסו שנאמר ח) ברוך ה' יום יום יעמס לנו האל ישועתנו סלה א"ל אביי וכי אפשר לומר כן והלא כבר נאמר ט) מי מדד בשעלו מים ושמים בזרת תכן אמר מאי טעמא לא שכיחת באגדתא דאמרי במערבא משמיה דרבא בר מרי עתיד הקב"ה ליתן לכל צדיק וצדיק ג' מאות ועשרה עולמות שנא' י) להנחיל אוהבי יש ואוצרותיהם אמלא יש בגימטריא תלת מאה ועשרה הוי תניא ר' מאיר אומר במדה שאדם מודד מודדין לו דכתיב כ) בסאסאה בשלחה תריבנה אמר ר' [ב] יהושע וכי אפשר לומר כן אדם נותן מלא עומסו לעני בעולם הזה הקב"ה נותן לו מלא עומסו לעולם הבא והכתיב ט) שמים בזרת תכן [ג] ואתה אי אומר כן איזו היא מדה מרובה מדת טובה מרובה או מדת פורענות

הוי

לא שרו לן עורבא. לא אמרו לנו שום חידוש שלא מצינו בתורה (דשרין עורבא): [דקא שרינא לכו עורבא]. שהיתר זה אינו מלוי בתורה אלא סופרים אמרוהו: כגון דאמר הנהו רבנן. כאדם שאומר אותו מ"ת דלשון בזוי הוא זה שהיה לו לומר רבותינו שבמקום פלוני ל"א כגון דאמר הני רבנן דכשהוא מספר שום דבר מרבנן אומר הני ולשון גנאי הוא הני אבל הנהו רבנן אינו גנאי: כי מטו מגלת אסתר. לתקן לה מטפחת אמרי הא מגלת אסתר לא בעיא מטפחת כלומר בלשון בעיא א"ל לרב יהודה הא ודאי לא צריכא מטפחת כגון האחרות ולשון גנאי הוא דהוה להו למימר לרבם בלשון שאלה כך צריכה או אינה צריכה: מעיין בית ה'. יצא והשקה את נחל שטים (יואל ד): מגדים. דינטר"ש בלע"ז כל מיני פירות מתוקים: יבכר. בכל חדש וחדש יתבשלו בו פירות: בשמו. שאומר פלוני ואינו אומר מורי רבי פלוני: א"ל ההוא סבא יישר וכן אמר רבי יוחנן. כדבריך ור' יוחנן נמי הכי קאמר כדאמרת מ"ר ולא גרסינן וכן אמר רבי יוחנן יישר: כי האי גוונא. מי מיחזי כאפקרותא: אלא אי שמיע לך מידי הא שמיע לך: לגלג עליו אותו תלמיד. אדרבי יוחנן דהיינו אפקירותא: כדכד. אבן טובה וכך שמה: שמשותיך. חלונות שהשמש זורח בהם [ד] כמו (תהלים פד) שמש ומגן היינו שמש ממש (ל"א) לאבני אקדח שהקב"ה מוקקן כבמקדח עד שחוקק בהם עשר ברום עשרים: צילצלתא. עוף קטן: גל של עצמות. שמת לאדם שמת נעשה גל של עצמות: קוממיות. שתי קומות של אדם הראשון כדאמרינן בחגיגה (דף יב.) שמיעטו הקב"ה והעמידו על מאה אמה שנאמר ותשת עלי כפך כף בגימטריא הכי הוי: כנגד היכל וכותליו. שכך היה אורך כל ההיכל עם הכותלים דכתיב (מלכים א ו) והבית אשר בנה המלך שלמה לה' ששים אמה ארכו וכותל מזרח שש אמות וכותל מערב שש אמות ואמה אחת טרקסין הרי י"ג אמות ואולם עשר אמה רוחב וכותל האולם שש הרי כ"ט ומאחורי האולם תא אחד רחבו שש וכתלו ה' הרי מ' וס' אמה של אורך הבית הרי מאה והיאך יכולין לכוף קומתן וליכנס בפתח שאין לו אלא רום עשרים כדאמרת: אשר בנינו. כלומר בנים שלנו יהיו לעתיד כאילנות גבוהין מגודלים: ובנותינו. ובנות שלנו כזויות המחוטבות לתבנית היכל כלומר ככותל ההיכל מחוטבות כמו (דברים כט) מחוטב עציך לישנא אחרינא אהיכל דבית שני קאמר דקים לן היכל ס' אורך ברום מאה הוא: לכוי דבי זיקא. לחלונות שהשמש והאור נכנסין בהן אבל השערים גבוהים יותר: [להתיר פה של מטה]. להתיר פה אלמים שיהו מדברים: להתיר פה של מטה. רחם של העקרות האוכלות מן העלין נפקדות: איתמר נמי חזקיה וכו'. והיינו הך דלעיל לתרופה: מראהו כלבנון. וכתיב לעיל מיניה שחורות כעורב וסמיך ליה חכו ממתקים: ירויון מדשן ביתך. אמר לי רבי דלעיל מינה מהאי קרא איירי ענינא דמרעיב את עצמו וקאמר ירויון מדשן ביתך שהקב"ה משביען לעוה"ב: מלא עומסו. מלא חופנו של הקב"ה טובה: וכי אפשר לומר כן. היאך אדם יכול לקבל מלא עומסו של הקב"ה והרי אין לו מקום ליתן דכל העולם כולו אינו אלא כמזרת ועד אגודל: באותן עולמות יתן לצדיק את העומס: במדה שאדם מודד. אם מדד ונתן צדקה לעני מלא חפניו הקב"ה מודד בחפניו ונותן לו: וכי אפשר לומר כן. שיהא הקב"ה נותן לאדם מלא חפניו והלא אינו יכול לסבול כל כך:

הוי

עין משפט נר מצוה

יט א מיי' פ"ה מהלכות ת"ת הלכה ה סמג עשין יג טוש"ע י"ד סי' רמב סעיף טו:

ליקוטי רש"י

לתרופה. פירשו רבותינו ז"ל להתיר פה אלמים ופה עקרות ומשמעו ל' רפואה כמו (ירמיה ו) וירפאו את שבר עמי על נקלה וכן חברו מנחם [יחזקאל מז, יב]. כדכד. מין אבן טובה. שמשותיך י"מ אמך ומנחם חברו עם ישמשוניה ויש פותרין ל' שמש חלונות שחמה זורחת בהן ועושין כנגדו מחילה במיני זכוכית לצבעים לנוי ומדרש תהלים פותר שמשותיך ושמש ומגן (תהלים פד) שיני החומה. לאבני אקדח. י"מ לאבני גמר גומרין תרגום גחלים פחר אקדח לשון קדחי אש והם מין אבנים טובות בוערות כלפידי' והוא קרבונקל"א לשון גחלת ויש פותרין ל' מקדח אבנים גדולות שכל חלל הפתח קדוח בתוכו והמזוזות והמפתן והסף כולן מתוך האבן הם. לאבני חפץ. לאבני צרוך [ישעיהו נד, יב]. וחוקק עשר. של רוחב ברום עשרים והיינו אקדח לשון קודח שחוקק בהם ומשמע נמי אבן טובה שמאירה כאש קודחת כמו קודחי אש (ישעיהו נ). אקדח. קרבונקל"א בלע"ז ובתרגום יונתן אבני גומרא. כביעתא דצילצלתא. בילת עוף קטן ששמו תאליל. קוממיות. שתי קומות שני ממי"ן דריש. כשתי קומות של אדם הראשון. שמיעטו עד ק' אמה במסכת חגיגה (דף יב). ההיכל. של בית שני שהיה רום מאה אמה ולפי קומתן צריך שערים גבוהים וקשיא לר' יוחנן דאמר רום עשרים. לכווי דבי זיקא. לחלונות העשויין לאויר והיינו שעריך דקרא חלונות החומה [ב"ב עה.]. גל של עצמות. גל מעצמות, כמת שנרקב בשרו ונפל מזמן הרבה [שבת לד.]. מאי ועלהו לתרופה. גבי מעיין שעתיד לצאת מבית קדשי הקדשים קאי ועל שפת הנחל יעלה מזה ומזה כל [עץ] (עלה) מאכל והיה פריו למאכל ועלהו לתרופה וכו' וקדריס נוטריקון לתרופה. להתיר פה שלמעלה. פה אלמים שכל אלם האוכל ממנו נרפא. פה שלמטה. פה רחם של עקרות. חזקיה ובר קפרא. מפרשא מילתייהו טפי והיא היא [מנחות צח.]. בחור כארזים. נבחר בין הבנים כארז בין שאר עצים [שה"ש ה, טו]. יעמס לנו. יתן לנו ישועה רבה מכל עומס ככל אשר נוכל שאת [תהלים סח, כ]. בשעלו. בהליכתו שנא' דרכת בים סוסיך (חבקוק ג), בשעלו כמו (במדבר כב) במשעול הכרמים שביל, ד"א שעל שם כלי הוא וכן בשעלי שעורים (יחזקאל יג). תכן. אמולאי"ר בלע"ז ל' מדה ומנין כמו ותוכן לבנים תתנו (שמות ה) [ישעיהו מ, יב]. להנחיל אוהבי יש. יש אתי נחלה רבה [משלי ח, כא]. בסאסאה. באותה מדה. בשלחה תריבנה. כששילחה מצרים את ישראל תריבנה המדה בסאה שלה [ישעיהו כז, ח]. בסאסאה. בתוך אותה סאה עצמה כשאתה משלחה לאבדון תריבנה [סוטה שם]. מדה טובה. רבה על חברתה מדה טובה מרובה על הרעה חמש מאות בה שבמדה טובה נאמר (שמות לד) נוצר חסד לאלפים ובמדת פורענות הוא אומר על שלשים ועל רבעים אף כאן מדת הטוב של ירידת המן כנגדה על ירידת המבול במדת פורענות הוא אומר וארובות השמים, לא ירד מבול אלא דרך שתי ארובות ובמדה טובה הוא אומר דלתי שמים פתח ותנא כמה ארובות יש באורך דלת ארבע הרי לשתי דלתות שמונה ארובות ואמרי שתי ארובות הורידו גשמים גובה חמש עשרה אמה שמונה ארובות הורידו מן ששים אמות שהרי אמרת מדה טובה מרובה על של פורענות וכל שכן שאינה ממועטת הימנה [יומא עו.]. דמדה טובה מרובה (שמות כ) פוקד עון אבות על בנים על שלשים ועל רבעים ובמדה טובה כתיב (שמות כ) עושה חסד לאלפים ומתרגמינן לאלפין דרי ארבעה דורות כנגד אלפים דורות היינו אחד מחמש מאות מיעוט אלפים אינו פחות משני אלפים וכל שכן אם כפשוטו דמשמע אלפים עד סוף כל הדורות [מכות כג.].

The Gemara discusses the reward awaiting the righteous in the World to Come:

כִּי אֲתָא רַב דִּימִי אָמַר – **When Rav Dimi came** to Babylonia from Eretz Yisrael **he said:** עָתִיד הַקָּדוֹשׁ בָּרוּךְ הוּא לִיתֵּן לְכָל צַדִּיק וְצַדִּיק מְלֹא עוֹמְסוֹ – **In the future the Holy One, Blessed is He, will give to every righteous person** a reward that **fills the hollow of His hand,** שֶׁנֶּאֱמַר ,,בָּרוּךְ ה׳ יוֹם יוֹם יַעֲמָס־לָנוּ הָאֵל יְשׁוּעָתֵנוּ סֶלָה״ – **as it is stated:** ***Blessed is the Lord; day by day He burdens us, the God of our salvation, Selah.***[35]

Rav Dimi's interpretation is challenged:

אָמַר לֵיהּ אַבָּיֵי – **Abaye said to him:** וְכִי אֶפְשָׁר לוֹמַר כֵּן – **Is it possible to say so?!** וַהֲלֹא כְּבָר נֶאֱמַר ,,מִי־מָדַד בְּשָׁעֳלוֹ מַיִם וְשָׁמַיִם בַּזֶּרֶת תִּכֵּן״ – **Has it not already been stated:**[36] ***Who measured the waters with the hollow of His hand, and gauged the skies with a span?***[37]

Rav Dimi responds:

אָמַר – **[Rav Dimi] said** to Abaye: מַאי טַעְמָא לָא שְׁכִיחַתְּ בְּאַגַּדְתָּא – For **what reason are you not familiar with the** ***Aggadata?***[38] דְּאָמְרֵי בְּמַעֲרְבָא מִשְּׁמֵיהּ דְּרָבָא בַּר מָרִי – **For they say in the West** (Eretz Yisrael) **in the name of Rava bar Mari** the following homiletic exposition: עָתִיד הַקָּדוֹשׁ בָּרוּךְ הוּא לִיתֵּן לְכָל צַדִּיק וְצַדִּיק שְׁלֹשׁ מֵאוֹת וַעֲשָׂרָה עוֹלָמוֹת – **In the future the Holy One, Blessed is He, will give to every righteous person three hundred and ten worlds,** שֶׁנֶּאֱמַר ,,לְהַנְחִיל אֹהֲבַי יֵשׁ וְאֹצְרֹתֵיהֶם אֲמַלֵּא״ – **as it is stated:** ***That I may grant to those who love me substance, and that I may fill their treasuries.***[39] ,,יֵשׁ״ בְּגִימַטְרִיָּא תְּלָת מְאָה וַעֲשָׂרָה הָוֵי – Now, **the numerical value of** the Hebrew word ***yesh*** ("substance") **is three hundred and ten,**[40] which indicates that the "substance" promised to the righteous consists of three hundred and ten worlds.[41] From here we see that the righteous will be able to receive the enormous reward contained in the hollow of God's hand, for they will each receive three hundred and ten worlds as a storehouse for it.

The Gemara offers support for Rav Dimi's explanation:

תַּנְיָא – Along similar lines **it was taught in a Baraisa:** רַבִּי מֵאִיר אוֹמֵר – **R' MEIR SAYS:** בְּמִדָּה שֶׁאָדָם מוֹדֵד מוֹדְדִין לוֹ – **WITH THE MEASURE THAT A MAN MEASURES** for others, **THEY** (the Heavenly tribunal) **MEASURE FOR HIM,**[42] דִּכְתִיב ,,בְּסַאסְּאָה בְּשַׁלְּחָהּ תְּרִיבֶנָּה״ – **AS IT IS WRITTEN:** ***WITH A PRECISE MEASURE YOU SHALL CONTEND WITH HER WHEN YOU SEND HER AWAY.***[43] אָמַר רַבִּי יְהוֹשֻׁעַ – **R' YEHOSHUA SAID** to R' Meir in reply: וְכִי אֶפְשָׁר לוֹמַר כֵּן – **IS IT POSSIBLE TO SAY SO?!** אָדָם נוֹתֵן מְלֹא עוֹמְסוֹ לֶעָנִי בָּעוֹלָם הַזֶּה – **If A MAN GIVES TO A PAUPER A HANDFUL** of food or other necessities **IN THIS WORLD,** הַקָּדוֹשׁ בָּרוּךְ הוּא נוֹתֵן לוֹ מְלֹא עוֹמְסוֹ לָעוֹלָם הַבָּא – **DOES THE HOLY ONE, BLESSED IS HE, GIVE TO [THE DONOR] A HANDFUL** of reward **IN THE WORLD TO COME?!** וְהָכְתִיב ,,שָׁמַיִם בַּזֶּרֶת תִּכֵּן״ – **BUT IT IS WRITTEN:**[44] ***[GOD] GAUGED THE SKIES WITH A SPAN,*** which indicates that God's hand is larger than the entire world.[45] How, then, can you say that the charitable man will be bestowed with blessings that are measured out in the hollow of God's hand when such an amount far exceeds what man is capable of receiving? וְאַתָּה אִי אוֹמֵר כֵּן – R' Meir retorted to R' Yehoshua: **BUT DO YOU NOT SAY THE SAME THING?** אֵיזוֹ הִיא מִדָּה מְרוּבָּה – Indeed, **WHICH IS THE GREATER MEASURE** – מִדַּת טוֹבָה מְרוּבָּה אוֹ מִדַּת פּוּרְעָנוּת – **IS [GOD'S] MEASURE OF BENEFICENCE GREATER, OR IS [HIS] MEASURE OF RETRIBUTION** greater?

NOTES

privation in order to study Torah.

35. *Psalms* 68:20. *He burdens* (יַעֲמָס) and "the hollow of His hand" (עומסו) derive from the same root. The Psalmist thus teaches that in the World to Come God *burdens* the righteous, who during their lifetime studied Torah *day by day* (יום יום), with a *handful* of His blessings, which is an enormous amount — a thousand years' worth for each day (see *Rashi, Iyun Yaakov*).

36. *Isaiah* 40:12.

37. That is, how can man receive what is contained in God's hand? Indeed, he has no place to receive it, since the entire world is only, figuratively speaking, the size of God's span (the distance from the little finger to the thumb of a spread hand) [*Rashi*].

38. The homiletical teachings of the Sages and all non-halachic Rabbinic literature found in the Talmud.

39. *Proverbs* 8:21. This verse belongs to a passage in which Wisdom (i.e. the Torah) delivers a speech and promises to reward with much substance those who live by its precepts.

40. *Gematria* is a method of Biblical interpretation, listed among the 32 Rules of R' Eliezer bar R' Yose HaGlili, in which each letter of the Hebrew alphabet is assigned a numerical value. In our case of יֵשׁ, י=10 and ש=300, totaling 310. See *Toras Chaim*.

41. *Rambam* (*Commentary* to *Uktzin* 3:12) explains this to mean that the reward in the World to Come is three hundred and ten times all the conceivable pleasures of this world. However, in contradistinction to the pleasures of this world, which are transitory in nature, the reward in the World to Come will be everlasting, for the soul of the righteous person who enters the World to Come will remain there for all eternity.

Rambam concludes: *This is merely an expression to describe how awesome is the reward destined for the righteous. In reality, however, just as there can be no comparison between the finite and the infinite, similarly there can be no comparison between the pleasures of this world and those of the World to Come.*

Noda BiYehudah (*II Yoreh Deah* 161) was asked: How is it possible that Abaye could be unfamiliar with the homiletic teaching cited by Rava bar Mari, when in fact it was taken from the last Mishnah in *Uktzin*?! It is inconceivable that Abaye was unfamiliar with a Mishnah! *Noda BiYehudah* explains that Rava bar Mari's teaching and the Mishnah in *Uktzin* are not identical: The Mishnah states that God will *grant* (לְהַנְחִיל) each righteous person 310 worlds, whereas Rava bar Mari stated that God will *give* (לִיתֵּן) them. Abaye could have interpreted the homily to mean that one could be granted more reward than he was capable of receiving; he would enjoy what he could and the remainder would accrue to his descendants, even if they themselves were unworthy. According to this understanding, the righteous person himself would not enjoy more than he was capable of receiving. To dispel such a misconception Rav Dimi adduced Rava bar Mari's dictum as evidence that God will indeed miraculously endow the righteous person himself with the capacity to enjoy unlimited blessings, for the word לִיתֵּן (*give*) implies that the blessings will actually be received by the righteous person. See, however, *Meleches Shlomo,* who answers *Noda BiYehudah's* question by explaining that the statement (of Rabbi Yehudah ben Levi) in *Uktzin* is not part of the Mishnah, but was added later (this view is not held by *Rambam,* but appears to be that of *Rash* and *Rosh;* see also *Margaliyos HaYam*). For further discussion of R' Dimi's statement, see *Tos. Yom Tov* and *Tiferes Yisrael in Uktzin*; see *Maharal* and *Emes L'Yaakov*.

42. E.g. if a person measures out a handful of gold coins and gives them as a charitable donation to a pauper, the Holy One will, as it were, measure out His own handful of reward and give it to the donor (*Rashi*).

43. *Isaiah* 27:8. The plain meaning of the verse is that God admonishes an angel — who is to serve as His instrument to punish the Jewish people by driving them from Eretz Yisrael — not to exceed specific limits; that is, not to cause the total destruction of the Jewish people. Rather, the angel should take care that their punishment corresponds exactly to their sins. The word בְּסַאסְּאָה derives from סְאָה, *se'ah,* which is a dry measurement. *Rashi* ad loc. interprets this passage as follows: With the very measure of punishment that was applied to Egypt when she expelled the Jews, *you shall contend with her.* That is, just as the Egyptians were punished in a manner that was commensurate with their crimes, so should the Jews, when it is necessary to punish them, be afflicted in a manner that is commensurate with, but does not exceed, their sins.

44. *Isaiah* 40:12. See note 37 above.

45. [In truth, God is infinite. These measurements are written only because the numbers are codes for theological lessons, as we often find in the works of *Maharal.*]

לא שרו לן עורבא ולא אסרו לן יונה רבא כי הוו מייתי טריפתא דבי בנימין קמיה כי הוה חזי בה טעמא להיתירא אמר להו תחזו דקא שרינא לכו עורבא כי הוה חזי לה טעמא לאיסורא אמר להו תחזו דקא אסרנא לכו יונה רב פפא אמר כגון דאמר הני רבנן רב פפא אישתלי ואמר כגון הני רבנן ואיתיב בתעניתא לוי בר שמואל ורב הונא בר חייא הוו קא מתקני מטפחות ספרי דבי רב יהודה כי מטו מגילת אסתר אמרי הא [מגילת אסתר] לא בעי מטפחת אמר להו כי האי גוונא נמי מיחזי כי אפקירותא רב נחמן אמר ◦זה א) הקורא רבו בשמו דאמר רבי יוחנן מפני מה נענש גיחזי מפני שקרא לרבו בשמו שנאמר א) ויאמר גחזי אדני המלך זאת האשה וזה בנה אשר החיה אלישע יתיב רבי ירמיה קמיה דרבי זירא ויתיב וקאמר עתיד הקב"ה להוציא נחל מבית קדשי הקדשים ועליו כל מיני מגדים שנאמר ב) ועל הנחל יעלה על שפתו מזה ומזה כל עץ מאכל לא יבול עלהו ולא יתם פריו לחדשיו יבכר כי מימיו מן המקדש [המה] יוצאים והיה פריו למאכל ועלהו לתרופה א"ל ההוא סבא ה) יישר וכן אמר ר' יוחנן [א] (ו) יישר) אמר ליה ר' ירמיה לרבי זירא כי האי גונא מיחזי אפקרותא אמר ליה הא [האי] סיועי קא מסייע (ליה) [לך] אלא אי שמיע לך הא שמיע לך כי הא ג) דיתיב רבי יוחנן וקא דריש עתיד הקב"ה להביא אבנים טובות ומרגליות שהן שלשים על שלשים אמות וחוקק בהם עשר ברום עשרים ומעמידן בשערי ירושלים שנאמר ג) ושמתי כדכוד שמשותיך ושעריך לאבני אקדח וגו' לגלג עליו אותו תלמיד אמר השתא כביעתא דצילצלא לא משכחינן כולי האי משכחינן לימים הפליגה ספינתו בים חזינהו למלאכי השרת דקא מנסרי אבנים טובות ומרגליות אמר להו הני למאן אמרי עתיד הקב"ה להעמידן בשערי ירושלים כי הדר אשכחיה לר' יוחנן דיתיב וקא דריש א"ל רבי דרוש ולך נאה לדרוש כשם שאמרת כך ראיתי אמר לו ריקה אם לא ראית לא האמנת מלגלג על דברי חכמים אתה ד) יהב ביה עיניה ועשאו גל של עצמות מיתיבי ד) ואולך אתכם קוממיות ר"מ אומר מאתים אמה כשתי קומות של אדם הראשון רבי יהודה אומר ק' אמה כנגד היכל וכותליו שנאמר ה) אשר בנינו כנטיעים מגודלים בנעוריהם בנותינו כזויות מחוטבות תבנית היכל וגו' כי קאמר ר' יוחנן לכוי דבי זיקא מאי ה) ועלהו לתרופה ר' יצחק בר אבודימי ורב חסדא חד אמר להתיר פה של מעלה וחד אמר להתיר פה של מטה איתמר (ו) נמי) חזקיה אמר להתיר פה אילמין בר קפרא אמר להתיר פה עקרות ר' יוחנן אמר לתרופה ממש מאי לתרופה ר' שמואל בר נחמני אמר לתואר פנים של בעלי הפה דרש ר' יהודה ברבי סימון כל המשחיר פניו על דברי תורה בעולם הזה הקב"ה מבהיק זיוו לעולם הבא שנאמר ו) מראהו כלבנון בחור כארזים אמר ר' תנחום בר' חנילאי כל המרעיב עצמו על דברי תורה בעולם הזה הקב"ה משביעו לעולם הבא שנאמר ז) ירויון מדשן ביתך ונחל עדניך תשקם כי אתא רב דימי אמר עתיד הקב"ה ליתן לכל צדיק וצדיק מלא עומסו שנאמר ח) ברוך ה' יום יום יעמס לנו האל ישועתנו סלה א"ל אביי וכי אפשר לומר כן והלא כבר נאמר ט) מי מדד בשעלו מים ושמים בזרת תכן אמר מאי טעמא לא שכיחת באגדתא דאמרי במערבא משמיה דרבא בר מרי ז) עתיד הקב"ה ליתן לכל צדיק וצדיק ג' מאות ועשרה עולמות שנא' י) להנחיל אוהבי יש ואוצרותיהם אמלא יש בגימטריא תלת מאה ועשרה הוי תניא ח) ר' מאיר אומר במדה שאדם מודד מודדין לו דכתיב כ) בסאסאה בשלחה תריבנה אמר ר' [ב] ט) יהושע וכי אפשר לומר כן אדם נותן מלא עומסו לעני בעולם הזה הקב"ה נותן לו מלא עומסו לעולם הבא והכתיב ט) שמים בזרת תכן [ג] ואתה אי אומר כן איזו היא מדה מרובה מדת טובה מרובה או מדת פורענות

הוי

רש"י

לא שרו לן עורבא. לא אמרו לנו שום חידוש שלא מצינו בתורה (דשרינן עורבא): **[דקא שרינא לכו עורבא].** שהיתר זה אינו מצוי בתורה אלא סופרים אמרוהו: **כגון דאמר הנהו רבנן.** כאדם שאומר אותו ת"ח דלשון בזוי הוא זה שהיה לו לומר רבותינו שבמקום פלוני ל"א כגון דאמר הני רבנן דכשהוא מספר שום דבר מרבנן אומר הני ולשון גנאי הוא הני אבל הנהו רבנן אינו גנאי: **כי מטו מגלת אסתר.** לתקן לה מטפחת אמרי הא מגלת אסתר לא בעיא מטפחת כלומר בלשון בעיא א"ל לרב יהודה הא ודאי לא צריכא מטפחת כגון האחרות ולשון גנאי הוא דהוה להו למימר לרבם בלשון שאלה כך צריכה או אינה צריכה: **מעיין בית ה'.** יצא והשקה את נחל שטים (יואל ד): **מגדים.** דינטר"ש בלע"ז כל מיני פירות מתוקים: **יבכר.** בכל חדש וחדש יתבשלו בו פירות: **בשמו.** שאומר פלוני ואינו אומר מורי רבי פלוני: **א"ל ההוא סבא יישר וכן אמר רבי יוחנן.** כדבריך ור' יוחנן נמי הכי קאמר כדאמרת מ"ר ולא גרסינן וכן אמר רבי יוחנן יישר: **כי האי גוונא.** מי מיחזי כאפקרותא: **אלא אי שמיע לך** מידי הא שמיע לך: **לגלג עליו אותו תלמיד.** אדרבי יוחנן דהיינו אפקירותא: **כדכד.** אבן טובה וכך שמה: **שמשותיך.** חלונות שהשמש זורח בהם [ד] כמו (תהלים פד) שמש ומגן היינו שמש ממש (ל"א) לאבני אקדח שהקב"ה חוקקן כבמקדח עד שחוקק בהם עשר ברום עשרים: **צילצלתא.** עוף קטן: **גל של עצמות.** שמת לאדם שמת נעשה גל של עצמות: **קוממיות.** שתי קומות של אדם הראשון כדאמרינן בחגיגה (דף יב.) שמיעטו הקב"ה והעמידו על מאה אמה שנאמר ותשת עלי כפך כף בגימטריא הכי הוי: **כנגד היכל וכותליו.** שכך היה אורך כל ההיכל עם הכותלים דכתיב (מלכים א ו) והבית אשר בנה המלך שלמה לה' ששים אמה ארכו וכותל מזרח שש אמות וכותל מערב שש אמות ואמה אחת טרקסין הרי י"ג אמות ואולם עשר אמה רוחב וכותל האולם שש הרי כ"ט ומאחורי האולם תא אחד רחבו שש וכתלו ה' הרי מ' וס' אמה של אורך הבית הרי מאה והיאך יכולין לכוף קומתן וליכנס בפתח שאין לו אלא רום עשרים כדאמרת: **אשר בנינו.** כלומר בנים שלנו יהיו לעתיד כאילנות גבוהין מגודלים: **ובנותינו.** ובנות שלנו כזויות המחוטבות לתבנית היכל כלומר ככותל ההיכל מחוטבות כמו (דברים כט) מחוטב עציך לישנא אחרינא אהיכל דבית שני קאמר דקים לן היכל ס' אורך ברום מאה הוא: **לכוי דבי זיקא.** לחלונות שהשמש והאור נכנסין בהן אבל השערים גבוהים יותר: **[להתיר פה של י) מטה].** להתיר כ) פה אלמים שיהו מדברים: **להתיר פה של מטה.** רחם של העקרות האוכלות מן העלין נפקדות ל): **איתמר נמי חזקיה וכו'.** והיינו הך דלעיל לתרופה: **מראהו כלבנון.** וכתיב לעיל מיניה שחורות כעורב וסמיך ליה חכו ממתקים: **ירויון מדשן ביתך.** אמר לי רבי דלעיל מינה מהאי קרא מיירי עניינא דמרעיב את עצמו וקאמר ירויון מדשן ביתך שהקב"ה משביען לעוה"ב: **מלא עומסו.** מלא חופנו של הקב"ה טובה: **וכי אפשר לומר כן.** היאך אדם יכול לקבל מלא עומסו של הקב"ה והרי אין לו מקום ליתן דכל העולם כולו אינו אלא כמזרת ועד אגודל: מ) באותן עולמות יתן לצדיק את העומס: **במדה שאדם מודד.** אם מדד ונתן צדקה לעני מלא חפניו הקב"ה מודד בחפניו ונותן לו: **וכי אפשר לומר כן.** שיהא הקב"ה נותן לאדם מלא חפניו והלא אינו יכול לסבול כל כך: שביל, ד"א שעל שם כלי הוא וכן בשעלי שעורים (יחזקאל יג). **תכן.** אמולאי"ר בלע"ז ל' מדה ומנין כמו ותוכן לבנים תתנו (שמות ה) [ישעיהו מ, יב]. **להנחיל אוהבי יש.** יש אתי נחלה רבה [משלי ח, כא]. **בסאסאה.** באותה מדה. **בשלחה תריבנה.** כששילחה מצרים את ישראל תריבנה המדה בסאה שלה [ישעיהו כז, ח]. **בסאסאה.** בתוך אותה סאה עצמה כשאתה משלחה לאבדון תריבנה [סוטה שם]. **מדה טובה.** רבה על חברתה מדה טובה מרובה על הרעה חמש מאות בה שבמדה טובה נאמר (שמות לד) נוצר חסד לאלפים ובמדת פורענות הוא אומר על שלשים ועל רבעים אף כאן

מדת הטוב של ירידת המן רבתה על ירידת המבול במדת פורענות הוא אומר וארובות השמים, לא ירד מבול אלא דרך שתי ארובות ובמדה טובה הוא אומר דלתי שמים פתח ותנא כמה ארובות יש באורך דלת ארבע הרי לשתי דלתות שמונה ארובות ואחרי ששתי ארובות הורידו גשמים גובה חמש עשרה אמה שמונה ארובות הורידו מן ששים אמות שהרי אמרת מדה טובה מרובה על של פורענות וכל שכן שאינה ממועטת הימנה [יומא עו.]. דמדה טובה מרובה ממדת פורענות אחד מחמש מאות דבמדת פורענות כתיב (שמות כ) פוקד עון אבות על בנים ועל שלשים ועל רבעים ובמדה טובה כתיב (שמות כ) עושה חסד לאלפים ומתרגמינן לאלפין דרי ארבעה דורות כנגד אלפים דורות היינו אחד מחמש מאות מיעוט לאלפים אינו פחות משני אלפים וכל שכן אם כפשוטו דמשמע אלפים עד סוף כל הדורות [מכות כג.].

מסורת הש"ס

א) [ברכות מב: וש"נ], ב) [טעות הדפוס], ג) ב"ב עה., ד) [ב"ב עה. ע"ש שבת לד. ברכות נח.], ה) [מנחות דף לח. ע"ש], ו) [במנחו' ליתא], ז) [משנה סוף עוקצים ול"ע ועי' ביש סדר למשנה ישוב נכון על זה], ח) [סוטה ח: ושם אית' רבי אומר אמנם שם טו: דמסיק דשמעי' לר"מ כו' משמע דגי' דהכא עיקר וע"ש ברש"י וכן איתא ג"כ בתוספתא שם פ"ג], ט) [נ"א יהודה], י) צ"ל למעלה, כ) [עי' רש"י מנחות לח.], ל) [עי' רש"י שם], מ) צ"ל שלש מאות באותן וכו'.

הגהות הגר"א

[א] גמ' יישר. נמחק: [ב] שם יהושע. נמחק: [ג] שם בזרת תכן ואתה. נ"ב א"ל ר' ואתה: [ד] רש"י ד"ה שמשותיך כו' זורח בהם. נ"ב עי' רש"י בע"י:

גליון הש"ס

גמ' זה הקורא רבו בשמו. עי' יבמות נז ע"ב תד"ה אמר:

תורה אור השלם

א) וַיְהִי הוּא מְסַפֵּר לַמֶּלֶךְ אֵת אֲשֶׁר הֶחֱיָה אֶת הַמֵּת וְהִנֵּה הָאִשָּׁה אֲשֶׁר הֶחֱיָה אֶת בְּנָהּ צֹעֶקֶת אֶל הַמֶּלֶךְ עַל בֵּיתָהּ וְעַל שָׂדָהּ וַיֹּאמֶר גֵּחֲזִי אֲדֹנִי הַמֶּלֶךְ זֹאת הָאִשָּׁה וְזֶה בְּנָהּ אֲשֶׁר הֶחֱיָה אֱלִישָׁע: [מלכים ב' ח, ה]

ב) וְעַל הַנַּחַל יַעֲלֶה עַל שְׂפָתוֹ מִזֶּה וּמִזֶּה כָּל עֵץ מַאֲכָל לֹא יִבּוֹל עָלֵהוּ וְלֹא יִתֹּם פִּרְיוֹ לָחֳדָשָׁיו יְבַכֵּר כִּי מֵימָיו מִן הַמִּקְדָּשׁ הֵמָּה יוֹצְאִים וְהָיָה פִרְיוֹ לְמַאֲכָל וְעָלֵהוּ לִתְרוּפָה: [יחזקאל מז, יב]

ג) וְשַׂמְתִּי כַּדְכֹד שִׁמְשֹׁתַיִךְ וּשְׁעָרַיִךְ לְאַבְנֵי אֶקְדָּח וְכָל גְּבוּלֵךְ לְאַבְנֵי חֵפֶץ: [ישעיה נד, יב]

ד) אֲנִי יְיָ אֱלֹהֵיכֶם אֲשֶׁר הוֹצֵאתִי אֶתְכֶם מֵאֶרֶץ מִצְרַיִם מִהְיֹת לָהֶם עֲבָדִים וָאֶשְׁבֹּר מֹטֹת עֻלְּכֶם וָאוֹלֵךְ אֶתְכֶם קוֹמְמִיּוּת: [ויקרא כו, יג]

ה) אֲשֶׁר בָּנֵינוּ כִּנְטִעִים מְגֻדָּלִים בִּנְעוּרֵיהֶם בְּנוֹתֵינוּ כְזָוִיֹּת מְחֻטָּבוֹת תַּבְנִית הֵיכָל: [תהלים קמד, יב]

ו) שׁוֹקָיו עַמּוּדֵי שֵׁשׁ מְיֻסָּדִים עַל אַדְנֵי פָז מַרְאֵהוּ כַּלְּבָנוֹן בָּחוּר כָּאֲרָזִים: [שיר השירים ה, טו]

ז) יִרְוְיֻן מִדֶּשֶׁן בֵּיתֶךָ וְנַחַל עֲדָנֶיךָ תַשְׁקֵם: [תהלים לו, ט]

ח) בָּרוּךְ אֲדֹנָי יוֹם יוֹם יַעֲמָס לָנוּ הָאֵל יְשׁוּעָתֵנוּ סֶלָה: [תהלים סח, כ]

ט) מִי מָדַד בְּשָׁעֳלוֹ מַיִם וְשָׁמַיִם בַּזֶּרֶת תִּכֵּן וְכָל בַּשָּׁלִשׁ עֲפַר הָאָרֶץ וְשָׁקַל בַּפֶּלֶס הָרִים וּגְבָעוֹת בְּמֹאזְנָיִם: [ישעיה מ, יב]

י) לְהַנְחִיל אֹהֲבַי יֵשׁ וְאֹצְרֹתֵיהֶם אֲמַלֵּא: [משלי ח, כא]

כ) בְּסַאסְּאָה בְּשַׁלְחָהּ תְּרִיבֶנָּה הָגָה בְּרוּחוֹ הַקָּשָׁה בְּיוֹם קָדִים: [ישעיה כז, ח]

עין משפט נר מצוה

יט א מיי' פ"ה מהלכות ת"ת הלכה ה סמג עשין עד טוש"ע י"ד סי' רמב סעיף ט:

ליקוטי רש"י

לתרופה. פירשו רבותינו ז"ל להתיר פה אלמים ופה עקרות ומשמעו ל' רפואה כמו (ירמיה ו) וירפאו את שבר עמי על נקלה וכן חברו מנחם [יחזקאל מז, יב]. **כדכד.** מין אבן טובה. **שמשותיך** י"מ אמך ומנחם חברו עם ישמשוניה ויש פותרין ל' שמש חלונות שחמה זורחת בהן ועושין כנגדו מחילה במיני זכוכית לבעים לנוי ומדרש תהלים פותר שמשותיך ושמש ומגן (תהלים פד) שיני החומה. **לאבני אקדח.** י"מ לאבני גמר גומרין תרגום גחלים פתר אקדח לשון קדחי אש והם מין אבנים טובות בוערות כלפידי' והוא קרבונקל"א לשון גחלת ויש פותרין ל' מקדח אבנים גדולות שכל חלל הפתח קדוח בתוכו והמזוזות והמפתן והסף כולן מתוך האבן הם. **לאבני חפץ.** לאבני לרוך [ישעיהו נד, יב]. **וחוקק עשר.** של רוחב ברום עשרים והיינו אקדח לשון קודח שחוקק בהם ומשמע נמי אבן טובה שמאירה כאש קודחת כמו קודחי אש (ישעיהו נ). **אקדח.** קרבונקל"א בלע"ז ובתרגום יונתן אבני גומרא. **כביעתא דצילצלתא.** בילת עוף קטן ששמו תאליל. **קוממיות.** שתי קומות שני ממי"ן דריש. **כשתי קומות של אדם הראשון.** שמיעטו עד ק' אמה במסכת חגיגה (דף יב). **ההיכל.** של בית שני שהיה רום מאה אמה ולפי קומתן לריך שערים גבוהים וקשיא לר' יוחנן דאמר רום עשרים. **לכווי דבי זיקא.** לחלונות העשויין לאויר והיינו שעריך דקרא חלונות החומה [ב"ב עה.]. **גל של עצמות.** גל מעצמות, כמת שנרקב בשרו ונפל מזמן הרבה [שבת לד.]. **מאי ועלהו לתרופה.** גבי מעיין שעתיד לצאת מבית קדשי הקדשים קאי ועל שפת הנחל יעלה מזה ומזה כל [עץ] (עלה) מאכל והיה פריו למאכל ועלהו לתרופה וכו' וקדריש נוטריקון לתרופה. **להתיר פה שלמעלה.** פה אלמים שכל אלם האוכל ממנו נרפא. **פה שלמטה.** פה רחם של עקרות. **חזקיה ובר קפרא.** מפרשא מילתייהו טפי והיא היא [מנחות צח.]. **בחור כארזים.** נבחר בין הבנים כארז בין שאר עצים [שה"ש ה, טו]. **יעמס לנו.** יתן לנו ישועה רבה מלא עומס ככל אשר נוכל שאת [תהלים סח, כ]. **בשעלו.** בהליכתו שנא' דרכת בים סוסיך (חבקוק ג), בשעלו כמו (במדבר כב) במשעול הכרמים

עין משפט נר מצוה

כ א מיי' פ"ב מהל' עכו"ם הלכה ב:

מסורת הש"ס

א) יומא עו. [סוטה יא. וע' מ"ש תוס' שם ד"ה ולעולם], ב) [ע' ברי"ף וברא"ש], ג) ב"ב עג: קידושין פב: [פסחים סה.], ד) יומא עה: סוטה מב., ה) [ברכות סג.], ו) [יבמות סג: ע"ש], ז) כתובות קי: [ב"ב קמו.], ח) ב"ב קמה:, ט) [נדה ז:].

(א) הוי אומר מדה טובה מרובה ממדת פורענות במדה טובה כתיב (א) ויצו שחקים ממעל ודלתי שמים פתח וימטר עליהם מן לאכול ובמידת פורענות הוא אומר (ב) וארובות השמים נפתחו במידת פורענות כתיב (ג) ויצאו וראו בפגרי האנשים הפושעים בי כי תולעתם לא תמות ואשם לא תכבה והיו דראון לכל בשר והלא אדם מושיט אצבעו באור בעולם הזה מיד נכוה אלא כשם שנותן הקב"ה כח ברשעים לקבל פורענותם כך נותן הקב"ה כח בצדיקים לקבל טובתן: רבי עקיבא אומר (א) אף הקורא בספרים החיצונים וכו': תנא בספרי צדוקים (ב) רב יוסף אמר בספר בן סירא נמי אסור למיקרי א"ל אביי מאי טעמא אילימא משום דכתב [ביה] לא תינטוש גילדנא מאודניה דלא ליזיל משכיה לחבלא אלא צלי יתיה בנורא ואיכול ביה תרתין גריצים אי מפשטיה באורייתא נמי כתב (ד) לא תשחית את עצה אי מדרשא אורח ארעא קמ"ל דלא ליבעול שלא כדרכה ואלא משום דכתיב בת לאביה מטמונת שוא מפחדה לא יישן בלילה בקטנותה שמא תתפתה בנערותה שמא תזנה בגרה שמא לא תינשא נישאת שמא לא יהיו לה בנים הזקינה שמא תעשה כשפים הא רבנן נמי אמרוה (ג) אי אפשר לעולם בלא זכרים ובלא נקבות אשרי מי שבניו זכרים אוי לו למי שבניו נקבות אלא משום דכתיב לא תעיל דויא בלבך דגברי גיברין קטל דויא הא שלמה אמרה (ה) דאגה בלב איש ישחנה (ד) ר' אמי ור' אסי חד אמר ישיחנה מדעתו וחד אמר ישיחנה לאחרים ואלא משום דכתיב מנע רבים מתוך ביתך ולא הכל תביא אל ביתך והא רבי נמי אמרה דתניא (ה) רבי אומר לעולם לא ירבה אדם רעים בתוך ביתו שנאמר (ו) איש רעים להתרועע אלא משום דכתיב זלדקן קורטמן עבדקן סכסן דנפח בכסיה לא צחי אמר במאי איכול לחמא סב מיניה מאן דאית ליה מעברתא בדיקני' כולי עלמא לא יכלי ליה אמר רב יוסף מילי מעלייתא דאית ביה דרשינן להו (ו) אשה טובה מתנה טובה בחיק ירא אלהים תנתן אשה רעה צרעת לבעלה מאי תקנתיה יגרשנה מביתו ויתרפא מצרעתו אשה יפה אשרי בעלה מספר ימיו כפלים העלם עיניך מאשת חן פן תלכד במצודתה אל תט אצל בעלה למסוך עמו יין ושכר כי בתואר אשה יפה רבים הושחתו ועצומים כל הרוגיה רבים היו פצעי רוכל המרגילים לדבר ערוה כניצוץ מבעיר גחלת (ז) ככלוב מלא עוף כן בתיהם מלאים מרמה מנע רבים מתוך ביתך ולא הכל תביא ביתך רבים יהיו דורשי שלומך גלה סודך לאחד מאלף (ח) משוכבת חיקך שמור פתחי פיך אל תצר צרת מחר (ט) כי לא תדע מה ילד יום שמא למחר איננו ונמצא מצטער על עולם שאינו שלו (י) כל ימי עני רעים בן סירא אומר אף לילות בשפל גגים גגו ובמרום הרים כרמו ממטר גגים לגגו ומעפר כרמו לכרמים [סימן זיר"א רב"א משרשי"א חנינ"א טובי"ה ינא"י יפ"ה יוחנ"ן מרח"ם יהוש"ע מקצ"ר] (ז) אמר ר' זירא אמר רב מאי דכתיב (י) כל ימי עני רעים אלו בעלי תלמוד וטוב לב משתה תמיד אלו בעלי משנה רבא אמר איפכא והיינו דאמר רב משרשיא משמיה דרבא מאי דכתיב (כ) מסיע אבנים יעצב בהם אלו בעלי משנה (כ) ובוקע עצים יסכן בם אלו בעלי תלמוד רבי חנינא אומר כל ימי עני רעים זה מי שיש לו אשה רעה וטוב לב משתה תמיד זה שיש לו אשה טובה רבי ינאי אומר כל ימי עני רעים זה אסטנים וטוב לב משתה תמיד זה שדעתו יפה רבי יוחנן אמר כל ימי עני רעים זה רחמני וטוב לב משתה תמיד זה אכזרי רבי יהושע בן לוי אמר כל ימי עני רעים זה

שדעתו

הוי אומר מדה טובה מרובה ממדת פורענות. דבמידה טובה כתיב דלתות ובמדת פורענות כתיב ארובות ודלת גדול מארובה דד' ארובות יש בדלת במסכת יומא בפרק יום הכפורים (דף עו.) אלמא מדה טובה מרובה ומעכשיו אין לתמוה היאך יש באדם כח לקבל שכר כל כך שהרי למדת פורענות נותן הקב"ה כח באדם לקבלו כל שכן שנותן כח באדם לקבל מדה טובה: צדוקים. [שכופרין בהא חי]: רב יוסף אמר אף בספר בן סירא. שיש בו דברי הבאי ובא עליהם לידי ביטול תורה: לא תיפשוט גילדנא מאודניה. כלומר לא תטול עורו של דג אפילו מעל אזנו מפני שאתה מפסיד העור דאזיל משכיה לחבלא להפסידא אלא צלי יתיה בנורא ואכול ביה תרתין גריצין שאתה יכול לצלות עור הדג עמו ולאכול בו שתי חלות דהוי לפתן לשתי חלות: גלדנא. שם הדג ל"א להכי נקט מאודניה שדרכו של דג להתחיל הפשטו מאזנו: אי מפשטיה. אי ממשמעותיה קא מתמהת באורייתא נמי כתיב: דלא לבעול שלא כדרכה. דאין הגון לאדם לשנות את דרכו והיינו דקאמר מאודניה: לא יישן. אינו יכול לישן: קטנה. קודם שהביאה שתי שערות: נערה. משהביאה שתי שערות עד שירבה שחור על הלבן הרי היא בוגרת: בנערותה שמא תזנה. משבגרה ראויה היא לנישואין להכי אמר שלא תנשא: דויא. דאגה: מנע רבים. אותם שאין לך עסק עמהם מנעם מתוך ביתך: ולא הכל תביא ביתך. אפילו אותם שאתה מתעסק עמהם לא תביאם תדיר לביתך אלא מבחוץ תדבר עמהם: איש רעים. שיש לו רעים הרבה: להתרועע. לסוף מריעים לו שמתקוטט עמהם: זלדקן. מי שזקנו דקה וחלושה: קורטמן. תדע שחכם וחריף הוא ביותר: עבדקן סכסן. מי שזקנו עבה שוטה הוא: סכסן. כמו כל בר בר חנא סכסא בבבא בתרא (דף עד.): נפח בכסיה. מי שנופח אופיא שבכוסו: לא צחי. בידוע שאינו צמא: אמר במאי איכול לחמא. האומר באיזה לפתן אוכל פת זה: סב לחמא מיניה. בידוע שאינו רעב וקח הלחם מידו שאילו היה רעב היה אוכל: מאן דאית ליה מעברתא בדקניה. שזקנו מחולק ומפוצל ויש בין שני שבילות כמין מעבר: כולי עלמא לא יכלי ליה. בערמימותיה דמתוך שחשב כל ימיו בערמות הוא משים ידו לזקנו ומושך כאדם שמחשב עד שנקרחה ל"א גרסינן הכרתא מי שיש לו היכר בזקנו שסעד כולי עלמא שלא סעדו אין יכולין להגיע לכחו ל"א גורתא והוא לשון קרחה וכל הני דברי רוח ולכך אין קורין בו: דרשינן. כלומר אמרינן להו בפרקא ומשמעינן להו לכולי עלמא כגון כל הני אשה טובה כו' אשה רעה צרעת לבעלה מה תקנתו יגרשנה מביתו כך הלשון של ספר בן סירא. אשה רעה מתנה רעה ל"ג: כפליים. מרוב הנאה חשובין ככפליים: אל תט אצל בעלה. למסוך עמו יין ושכר: רבים היו פצעי רוכל. כמה וכמה מכות מקבל רוכל המחזיר בעיר [ונושא] תכשיטי נשים ועסקו עמהם שפעמים שמוצאו בעלה עמה מתיחד עם אשתו ומכהו ופוצעו: המרגילים לדבר עבירה. ניאוף הרי הן כניצוץ מבעיר גחלת כשביב המבעיר את הפחם כך כל אשר להם כלה והולך: גחלת. אקרי פחם שאינו בוער כדאמרינן (ברכות דף נג:) גחלים עוממות. מ"ר: ככלוב. דירה של עופות: רבים יהיו דורשי שלומך. שתהא מתאהב עם הכל ואף על פי כן לא תגלה סודך לכולם אלא לאחד מני אלף: מה ילד יום. מה אירע היום שמא למחר איננו שמת הוא היום: ונמצא. שמיצר על יום שאינו עתיד לראות והיינו עולם שאינו שלו שהוא מצטער עליו ודואג על חנם מיום המחרת שלא תבא עליו צרה: כל ימי עני רעים וטוב לב משתה. פסוק הוא במשלי (טו): בשפל גגים גגו. שעני הוא ואינו יכול להגביהו לפיכך ממטר גגים לגגו שיורד מטר הגגים הגבוהים לגגו ומזלפים עליו הגשמים ואין לו מנוחה אפילו בלילות: במרום הרים כרמו. שאין לו השגת יד לקנות כרם בשפלה בדמים יקרים וקונה לו באחד מן ההרים בזול וכל עפר שהוא מוציא לזבל (ולדייר) מוליך הרוח מן ההר לשאר כרמים שבבקעה ונמצא העני נפסד: בעלי תלמוד. שקשה ללמוד מרוב קושיות וסוגיות שיש בו: משנה. נוחה ללמוד: רבא אמר איפכא. דבעלי תלמוד נהנין מיגיעו שידעו להורות איסור והיתר אבל בעלי משנה שונה ואינו יודע מהו אומר דאין (ט) מורין הלכה מתוך משנה: יסכן. יתחמם:

שדעתו

ליקוטי רש"י

תולעתם. רמה האוכלת את בשרם. ואשם. בגיהנם. דראון. לשון בזיון, וי"ת כמין שתי תיבות די ראייה, עד דיימרון עליהון צדיקיא מיסת חזינא [ישעיהו ו, כד]. גילדנא. שם דג קטן [ב"ב עג:]. גריצין. ככרות עבים [ביצה כא:]. דאגה. פחד שדואג על הפסד שום דבר פן יבואהו [יומא עה.]. כל דאגה שבמקרא לשון יראה הוא כמו אני דואג את היהודים דצדקיהו [יהושע כב, כד]. כל לשון דאגה לשון יראה דוטי"ר בלע"ז [ש"א י, ב]. איינס"א בלע"ז ובלשונינו טרוא"ר בלע"ז [יחזקאל ד, טז]. דאגה בלב איש ישחנה. ישיחנה מדעתו. ודבר טוב ישמחנה, יעסוק בתורה והיא תשמח את הדאגה שבלבו ותצילנו ממנה, ולדברי האומר ישיחנה לאחרי' כך סופו של מקרא ודבר טוב שינחמנו חבירו ישמח את הדאג' [משלי יב, כה]. ישיחנה לאחרים. שמא ישיאוהו עצה [יומא עה.]. להתרועע. להתרוצץ [ברכות סג.]. מספר ימיו כפלים. כלומר שמח בחלקו ודומה לו כאילו ימיו כפלים. מאשת חן. של אחרים. רוכל. המוכר בשמים לנשים להתקשט בהן ומצוי בו ניאוף ובא בעלה ופצעו. מבעיר גחלת. כן יצרו מבעירו. ככלוב. קן עופות. שמא למחר איננו. ואיננו בעולם ולא יראה אותה דאגה שהוא מיצר וירא ודואג עליה ונמצא שנצטער אתמול על עולם שאין שלו [יבמות סג:]. ככלוב. הוא מקום שמפטמין בו עופות וכן תרגמו יונתן כבית פיטמא ובלעז פרנ"ק [ירמיהו ה, כז]. כל ימי עני רעים. ואפילו שבתות וי"ט דאמר שמואל שנוי וסת תחלת חולי מעים [משלי טו, טו]. בן סירא אומר. שלמה כתב כל ימי עני רעים אבל בלילות כשישן יש לו מנוחה ובן סירא אומר אף הלילות אין לו מנוחה כי בשפל גגים גגו ונמצא דלף טורדו ביום סגריר. מעפר כרמו לכרמים. זבל ואשפה שהביא לכרמו נשפך לכרמים אחרים שהוא במקום רעוע בהרים ובסלעים במקום שאין עשיר חפץ בו נופל למטה בכרמים של עשירים שהם במקום טוב ומדרון ונוח לעסוק בהן [ב"ב קמו.]. במרום הרים כרמו. שאין בידו ממון לקנות במקום טוב וקונה בראש ההר וכל זבלים שהוא מוציא לו נופל וזב לכרמים שתחתיו [כתובות קי:]. זה בעלי תלמוד. סוגיית גמרא ותרוצי משניות וברייתות וזהו עיקר הגמרא שאם לא הגמרא אין למדין הלכה מתוך משנה כדאמרינן התנאים מבלי עולם (סוטה דף כב). כל ימי עני רעים אלו בעלי תלמוד. שממית עצמו לכוין הלכות ולתרץ הוויות. רבא אמר איפכא. כל ימי עני רעים זה בעל משנה שאינו יכול להורות הלכה מתוך משנתו וגם כי כשחולקות זו על זו אינו יכול לתרץ וטוב לב זה בעל הגמרא שיודע משניות על עיקרם ובקי בטעמיהם ויש בידו כח להורות הלכה למעשה. יעצב. לשון בעצבון תאכלנה (בראשית ג). זה בעל משנה. ששונה משניות כל היום ואין לו אלא צער שמתקשה בטעמיהן ואינו יודע לפרש. יסכן. לשון תמימות כמו ותהי למלך סוכנת (מלכים א א) ... מהן. זה איסטנים. מי שדעתו קצה ולבו נמאס בכל דבר מגונה שהוא רואה. יפה. שסובל הכל דאינו מזיק לו שום לכלוך ושום דבר מיאוס. זה רחמני. כמה עניים הוא רואה וכמה מאורעות שלבו בוכה תדיר עליהן [ב"ב קמה:]. יעצב בהם. מסיע אבנים ממחצבתם בהרים מתיגע להם. יעצב. לשון יגיעה כמו (בראשית ג) בעצבון תאכלנה כלומר כל אדם לפי מלאכתו עצבונו אף עושה רעה לפי זריעתו יקצור. יסכן בם. יתחמם בם כמו (מלכים א א) ... העוסק בתורה ובמצות סופו ליהנות מהם [קהלת י, ט]. מסיע אבנים יעצב בם אלו בעלי משנה. לא שימש תלמידי חכמים ללמוד סברת הגמרא בטעמי המשנה מה הם רשע הוא שאין תורתו על בורייה ואין ללמוד הימנו ... חילוק באיסור והיתר ובדיני ממונות לזכות ולחייב ובטהרות לטמא ולטהר כדאמר בכמה דוכתי מ"ט אמר מר הכי ומר הכי ואמר מאי בינייהו איכא בינייהו כך וכך וערום הוא שהשומע את קולו שונה משניותיו כסבור הוא שבקי ... בו כבוד כתלמידי חכמים [סוטה כב.]. ובוקע עצים יסכן בם אלו בעלי תלמוד. סברת טעמי המשניות שממנו יוצאה הוראה אבל המורים הוראה מן המשנה נקראו מבלי העולם במסכת סוטה (דף כ"ב א) [ברכות ה.]. עיקר תורה שממנו הוראה יוצאה גמרא היינו סברת טעמי משנה ותירוצי משניות הסותרות זו את זו וחסורי מחסרא [שם יא.]. לתת סברא להבין בטעמי המשנה והלכה כדברי מי [סוטה מד.].

תורה אור השלם

א) ויצו שחקים ממעל ודלתי שמים פתח: וימטר עליהם מן לאכל ודגן שמים נתן למו: [תהלים עח, כג-כד]

ב) בשנת שש מאות שנה לחיי נח בחדש השני בשבעה עשר יום לחדש ביום הזה נבקעו כל מעינות תהום רבה וארבת השמים נפתחו: [בראשית ז, יא]

ג) ויצאו וראו בפגרי האנשים הפשעים בי כי תולעתם לא תמות ואשם לא תכבה והיו דראון לכל בשר: [ישעיה סו, כד]

ד) כי תצור אל עיר ימים רבים להלחם עליה לתפשה לא תשחית את עצה לנדח עליו גרזן כי ממנו תאכל ואתו לא תכרת כי האדם עץ השדה לבא מפניך במצור: [דברים כ, יט]

ה) דאגה בלב איש ישחנה ודבר טוב ישמחנה: [משלי יב, כה]

ו) איש רעים להתרעע ויש אהב דבק מאח: [משלי יח, כד]

ז) ככלוב מלא עוף כן בתיהם מלאים מרמה על כן גדלו ויעשירו: [ירמיה ה, כז]

ח) אל תאמינו ברע אל תבטחו באלוף משכבת חיקך שמר פתחי פיך: [מיכה ז, ה]

ט) אל תתהלל ביום מחר כי לא תדע מה ילד יום: [משלי כז, א]

י) כל ימי עני רעים וטוב לב משתה תמיד: [משלי טו, טו]

כ) מסיע אבנים יעצב בהם בוקע עצים יסכן בם: [קהלת י, ט]

הֱוֵי אוֹמֵר מִדָּה טוֹבָה מְרוּבָּה מִמִּדַּת פּוּרְעָנוּת – YOU MUST SAY THAT [HIS] MEASURE OF BENEFICENCE IS GREATER THAN [HIS] MEASURE OF RETRIBUTION, בְּמִדָּה טוֹבָה כְּתִיב – for CONCERNING [HIS] MEASURE OF BENEFICENCE IT IS WRITTEN: ,,וַיְצַו שְׁחָקִים מִמָּעַל וְדַלְתֵי שָׁמַיִם פָּתָח וַיַּמְטֵר עֲלֵיהֶם מָן לֶאֱכֹל'' – *HE COMMANDED THE SKIES ABOVE, AND THE DOORS OF HEAVEN HE OPENED, AND RAINED UPON THEM MANNA TO EAT,*[1] וּבְמִידַּת פּוּרְעָנוּת הוּא אוֹמֵר – WHEREAS CONCERNING [HIS] MEASURE OF RETRIBUTION IT SAYS: ,,וַאֲרֻבֹּת הַשָּׁמַיִם נִפְתָּחוּ'' – *THE WINDOWS OF THE HEAVENS WERE OPENED.*[2] בְּמִידַּת פּוּרְעָנוּת כְּתִיב – Now, CONCERNING [GOD'S] MEASURE OF RETRIBUTION IT IS WRITTEN: ,,וְיָצְאוּ וְרָאוּ בְּפִגְרֵי הָאֲנָשִׁים הַפֹּשְׁעִים בִּי כִּי תוֹלַעְתָּם לֹא תָמוּת וְאִשָּׁם לֹא תִכְבֶּה וְהָיוּ דֵרָאוֹן לְכָל־בָּשָׂר'' – *AND THEY SHALL GO FORTH AND LOOK UPON THE CORPSES OF THE MEN WHO HAVE SINNED AGAINST ME; FOR THEIR WORMS SHALL NOT DIE, NEITHER SHALL THEIR FIRE BE QUENCHED, AND THEY SHALL BE AN ABHORRENCE TO ALL FLESH.*[3] וַהֲלֹא אָדָם מוֹשִׁיט אֶצְבָּעוֹ בָּאוּר בָּעוֹלָם הַזֶּה מִיָּד נִכְוֶה – Now, IS IT NOT [TRUE] THAT WHEN A PERSON EXTENDS HIS FINGER INTO A FLAME IN THIS WORLD IT IS IMMEDIATELY BURNT, because fire destroys human flesh? How, then, is it possible for the corpses to burn continually without being consumed? אֶלָּא כְּשֵׁם שֶׁנּוֹתֵן הַקָּדוֹשׁ בָּרוּךְ הוּא כֹּחַ בָּרְשָׁעִים לְקַבֵּל פּוּרְעָנוּתָם – RATHER, JUST AS THE HOLY ONE, BLESSED IS HE, GIVES THE WICKED THE CAPACITY TO RECEIVE THEIR PUNISHMENT, for Scripture assures us that God will miraculously endow the corpses of the armies of Gog and Magog with the power to remain intact and receive their punishment, כָּךְ נוֹתֵן הַקָּדוֹשׁ בָּרוּךְ הוּא כֹּחַ בַּצַּדִּיקִים לְקַבֵּל טוֹבָתָן – SO THE HOLY ONE, BLESSED IS HE, GIVES THE RIGHTEOUS THE CAPACITY TO RECEIVE THEIR REWARD, however enormous it may be.

The Gemara now discusses the Mishnah's fourth case of one who has no share in the World to Come – namely, the person who reads "external" books. The Mishnah stated:

רַבִּי עֲקִיבָא אוֹמֵר אַף הַקּוֹרֵא בִּסְפָרִים הַחִיצוֹנִים וכו׳ – R' AKIVA SAYS: ALSO ONE WHO READS EXTERNAL BOOKS **etc.**[4]

The Gemara elucidates this statement:

תָּנָא – **[A Tanna] taught:** בִּסְפְרֵי מִינִים – R' Akiva was referring to one who reads THE BOOKS OF THE HERETICS.[5]

The Gemara discusses whether it is forbidden to read the *Book of Ben Sira*:

רַב יוֹסֵף אָמַר – **Rav Yosef said:** בְּסֵפֶר בֶּן סִירָא נַמִּי אָסוּר לְמִיקְרֵי – **It is also forbidden to read the *Book of Ben Sira*.**[6]

This ruling is questioned:

אָמַר לֵיהּ אַבָּיֵי – **Abaye said to [Rav Yosef]:** מַאי טַעְמָא – **What is the reason** for prohibiting the reading of *Ben Sira*? אִילֵימָא מִשּׁוּם דִּכְתַב בֵּיהּ – **If you say** it is **because he wrote in it,** ,,לֹא תִינְטוֹשׁ גִּילְדָנָא מֵאוּדְנֵיהּ – **Do not strip a gildana,**[7] even **from its**

NOTES

1. *Psalms* 78:23-24. These verses describe how God sustained the Children of Israel during their forty-year sojourn in the desert.

2. *Genesis* 7:11, which speaks of the great Flood that God visited upon errant mankind. In these verses God's beneficence is described as issuing through *doors,* whereas His retribution is described as issuing through *windows.* The Gemara (*Yoma* 76a) notes that in Talmudic times doors contained four panels (two at the top, two at the bottom), any of which could be converted into a window. Hence, just as these doors were much larger than those windows, so does God's measure of beneficence exceed His measure of retribution (*Rashi*).

3. *Isaiah* 66:24. This verse describes how after the defeat of Gog and Magog in the Messianic era all the nations will come to worship Hashem in the Temple in Jerusalem, after which they will exit Jerusalem and descend into the nearby Valley of Jehosaphat to view the corpses of the army of Gog and Magog. Although the Jews will eventually bury their fallen enemy in order to purify the land (*Ezekiel* 39:12), the nations will be able to view the corpses for seven months prior to burial (*Radak*).

The relevant point of this verse is that the corpses will not rot, but will, during the pre-burial period, continually burn and suffer worm infestation, all in violation of the laws of nature. Hence, these bodies will be subjected to punishments that exceed a corpse's natural capacity to endure.

4. The three sins mentioned by R' Akiva and Abba Shaul all involve disrespect for or misuse of God's Torah. The World to Come is gained through Torah, as the Sages have taught. One who denigrates the Torah and its Giver cannot, therefore, aspire to a share in the World to Come.

5. In the Talmud the words סִפְרֵי צְדוֹקִים (*books of the Sadducees*) appear in the text of the Gemara as well as in the texts of *Rashi* and *Rosh;* however, older versions read: סִפְרֵי מִינִים, *books of the heretics* (see *Yad Ramah* and *Dikdukei Soferim;* censors frequently substituted "Sadducees" for "heretics"). *Rif, Rosh* and *Yad Ramah* explain that the books referred to here are commentaries on Scripture that are not based on the interpretation of the Sages. Since these books contain heretical ideas alongside correct ones, a reader may acquire false beliefs that will cause him to lose his share in the World to Come. Therefore, reading these books is forbidden. *Meiri* states that the prohibition applies only when the reader intends to follow the books' teachings; however, if one wishes only to ascertain their contents and to teach others to avoid them, reading is permitted (see *Deuteronomy* 18:9 and *Rashi* ad loc.).

According to *Margaliyos HaYam, Talmud Yerushalmi* understands that by "external books" R' Akiva meant the Apocrypha and Pseudepigrapha. These books are outside the Biblical Canon, which was closed by the Men of the Great Assembly, including the last prophets; hence, they are "external." Some were not accepted simply because they were not written with Divine inspiration (*ruach haKodesh*). If people were allowed to read them, they could be mistaken for authentic Holy Writings. Others of the Apocrypha, particularly those composed in the later years of the Second Temple, were written by sectarians and promoted heretical ideas. Still others were of the so-called "wisdom literature" genre, and often harbored ideas inimical to Torah or contained suggestive material. Since a reader was in grave danger of absorbing false and heretical ideas, our Sages proscribed these books on the grounds that reading them could cause a person to lose his share in the World to Come (see *Yad David* and *Margaliyos HaYam*).

Yerushalmi states here that in contrast to these works, purely secular books, such as chronicles and Homer's works, may be read (cf. *Tiferes Yisrael,* who writes that Homer is objectionable), and some authorities are lenient in this matter so long as the reader's Torah study is not disrupted. [*Yerushalmi's* mention of Homer's works poses a problem; see *Korban HaEidah* and *Rav Hai Gaon. Be'er Sheva* therefore suggests emending the *Yerushalmi's* statement.] Others rule, however, that many secular works fall into the category of "external books" (see *Be'er Sheva, Rav* and *Tos. Yom Tov* to our Mishnah).

6. Ben Sira was a writer who flourished in Temple times, whom legend suggests was a son of the prophet Jeremiah (see *Chelkas Mechokeik* to *Even HaEzer* 1:8 and *Mishneh LaMelech, Hil. Ishus* 15:4). The *Book of Ben Sira,* a collection of proverbs, is one of the books of the Apocrypha. [Many of the passages cited by the Gemara from the *Book of Ben Sira* do not appear in the Apocryphal *Ben Sira.* However, the original Hebrew version of the book was lost over the course of centuries (although parts have been rediscovered in the last century), and the version included in the Apocrypha is based on the Greek translation of the original by Ben Sira's grandson, who lived in Egypt. For further discussion of this issue, see *Binu Shenos Dor VaDor* by R' Nosson David Rabinowitz.] According to *Rashi* and others, Rav Yosef did not mean to equate *Ben Sira* with the books proscribed by R' Akiva. Rather, Rav Yosef objects to the reading of *Ben Sira* only on the grounds that it contains worthless and vain notions that can cause a disruption of Torah study (see also *Rif* and *Rosh*). Hence, *Ritva* (to *Bava Basra* 98b) permits looking into it occasionally. According to *Yad Ramah* and *Rif,* however, Rav Yosef is adding *Ben Sira* to the group of books proscribed by R' Akiva, for although it does not contain outright heresy, it can cause people not to rely on God [and ultimately lose their share in the World to Come]. Indeed, *Yerushalmi* mentions *Ben Sira* as an example of the books forbidden by R' Akiva. [*Be'er Sheva,* however, suggests emending this *Yerushalmi* to reflect *Ritva's* view.]

7. This is the name of a certain type of fish (*Rashi;* see *Yad Ramah*).

עין משפט
נר מצוה

כ א מיי' פ"ב מהל' עכו"ם הלכה ב:

ליקוטי רש"י

תולעתם. רמה האוכלת את בשרם. ואשם. בגיהנם. דראון. לשון בזיון, וי"א כמין שתי תיבות די ראייה, עד דיימרון עליהון לדיקיא מיסת חזוא [ישעיהו ו, כד]. גילדנא. שם דג קטן [ב"ב עג:]. גריצין. ככרות עבים [ביצה כא:]. דאגה. פחד שדואג על הפסד שום דבר פן יבואהו [יומא עה.]. כל דאגה שבמקרא לשון יראה הוא כמו אני דואג את היהודים דלדקיהו [יהושע כב,כד]. כל לשון דאגה לשון יראה דוטשי"ר בלע"ז [ש"א י, ב]. איינש"א בלע"ז ובלשונינו טרוא"ר בלע"ז [יחזקאל ד, טז]. דאגה בלב איש ישחנה. ישיחנה מדעתו. ודבר טוב ישמחנה, יעסוק בתורה והיא תשמח את הדאגה שבלבו ותגילנו ממנה, ולדברי האומר ישיחנה לאחרי' כך סופו של מקרא ודבר טוב שינחמנו חבירו ישמח את הדאג' [משלי יב, כה]. ישיחנה לאחרים. שמא ישיאוהו עצה [יומא עה.]. להתרועע. להתרוצץ [ברכות סג.]. מספר ימיו כפלים. כלומר שמח בחלקו ודומה לו כאילו ימיו כפלים. מאשת חן. של אחרים. רוכל. המוכר בשמים לנשים להתקשט בהן ומצוי בו ניאוף ובא בעלה ופלעו. מבעיר גחלת. כן יצרו מבעירו. ככלוב. קן עופות. שמא למחר איננו. ואיננו בעולם ולא יראה אותה דאגה שהוא מיצר וירא ודואג עליה ונמצא שנצטער אתמול על עולם שאין שלו [יבמות סג:]. ככלוב. הוא מקום שמפטמין בו עופות וכן תרגמו יונתן כבית פיטמא ובלעז פרנ"ק [ירמיהו ה, כז]. כל ימי עני רעים. ואפילו שבתות וי"ט דאמר שמואל שנוי וסת תחלת חולי מעים [משלי טו, טו]. בן סירא אומר. שלמה כתב כל ימי עני רעים אבל בלילות כשישן יש לו מנוחה ובן סירא אומר אף הלילות אין לו מנוחה כי בשפל גגים גגו ונמצא דלף טורדו ביום סגריר. מעפר כרמו לכרמים. זבל ואשפה שהביא לכרמו נשפך לכרמים אחרים שהוא במקום רעוע בהרים ובסלעים במקום שאין עשיר חפץ בו נופל למטה בכרמים של עשירים שהם במקום טוב ומדרון וגות לעסוק בהן [ב"ב קמו.]. במרום הרים כרמו. שאין בידו ממון לקנות במקום טוב וקונה בראש ההר וכל זבלים שהוא מוליך לו נופל חוץ לכרמים שתחתיו [כתובות קי:]. זה בעלי תלמוד. סוגיית גמרא ותרוצי משניות ובריייתות וזהו עיקר הגמרא שאם לא הגמרא אין למדין הלכה מתוך משנה כדאמרינן התנאים מבלי עולם (סוטה דף כב). כל ימי עני רעים אלו בעלי תלמוד. שממית עצמו לכוין הלכות ולתרץ הוויות. רבא אמר איפכא. כל ימי עני רעים זה בעל משנה שאינו יכול להורות הלכה מתוך משנתו וגם כי כשחולקות זו על זו אינו יכול לתרץ וטוב לב זה בעל הגמרא שיודע משניות על עיקרם ובקי בטעמיהם ויש בידו כח להורות הלכה למעשה. יעצב. לשון בעצבון תאכלנה (בראשית ג). זה בעל משנה. ששונה משניות כל היום ואין לו אלא צער שמתקשה בטעמיהן ואינו יודע לפרש. יסכן. לשון תמימות כמו ותהי למלך סוכנת (מלכים א א) כלומר שנהנה מהן. זה איסטנים. מי שדעתו קצה ולבו נמאס בכל דבר מגונה שהוא רואה. יפה. שסובל הכל דאינו מזיק לו שום לכלוך ושום דבר מיאוס. זה רחמני. כמה עניים הוא רואה וכמה מאורעות שלבו בוכה תדיר עליהן [ב"ב קמה:]. מסיע אבנים יעצב בהם. מסיע אבנים ממחצבתם בהרים מתיגע להם. יעצב. לשון יגיעה כמו (בראשית ג) בעצבון תאכלנה כלומר כל אדם לפי מלאכתו עצבונו אף עושה רעה לפי זריעתו יקצור. יסכן בם. יתחמם בם כמו (מלכים א א) ותהי לו סוכנת אף העוסק בתורה ובמצות סופו ליהנות מהם [קהלת י, ט]. מסיע אבנים יעצב בם אלו בעלי משנה. לא שימש תלמידי חכמים ללמוד סברת הגמרא בטעמי המשנה מה הם רשע הוא שאין תורתו על בורייה ואין ללמוד הימנו שע"י הטעמים יש חילוק באיסור והיתר ובדיני ממונות לזכות ולחייב ובטהרות לטמא ולטהר כדאמר בכמה דוכתי מ"ט אמר מר הכי ומר הכי ואמר מאי בינייהו איכא בינייהו כך וכך וערום הוא שהשומע את קולו שונה משניותיו כסבור הוא שבקי בטעמיהם ונוהגין בו כבוד כתלמידי חכמים [סוטה כב.]. ובוקע עצים יסכן בם אלו בעלי תלמוד. סברת טעמי המשניות שממנו יוצאה הוראה אבל המורים הוראה מן המשנה נקראו מבלי העולם במסכת סוטה (דף כ"ב א) [ברכות ה.]. עיקר התורה שממנו הוראה יוצאה גמרא היינו סברת טעמי משנה ותירוצי משניות הסותרות זו את זו וחסורי מחסרא [שם יא.]. לתת סברא להבין בטעמי המשנה והלכה כדברי מי [סוטה מד.].

א) הוי אומר מדה טובה מרובה ממדת פורענות במדה טובה כתיב א) ויצו שחקים ממעל ודלתי שמים פתח וימטר עליהם מן לאכול ובמידת פורענות הוא אומר ב) וארובות השמים נפתחו במידת פורענות כתיב ג) ויצאו וראו בפגרי האנשים הפושעים בי כי תולעתם לא תמות ואשם לא תכבה והיו דראון לכל בשר והלא אדם מושיט אצבעו באור בעולם הזה מיד נכוה אלא כשם שנותן הקב"ה כח ברשעים לקבל פורענותם כך נותן הקב"ה כח בצדיקים לקבל טובתן: רבי עקיבא אומר אף הקורא בספרים החיצונים וכו': תנא בספרי צדוקים ב) רב יוסף אמר בספר בן סירא נמי אסור למיקרי א"ל אביי מאי טעמא אילימא משום דכתב [ביה] לא תינטוש גילדנא מאודניה דלא ליזיל משכיה לחבלא אלא צלי יתיה בנורא ואיכול ביה תרתין גריצים אי מפשטיה באורייתא נמי כתב ד) לא תשחית את עצה אי מדרשא אורח ארעא קמ"ל דלא ליבעול שלא כדרכה ואלא משום דכתיב בת לאביה מטמונת שוא מפחדה לא יישן בלילה בקטנותה שמא תתפתה בנערותה שמא תזנה בגרה שמא לא תינשא נישאת שמא לא יהיו לה בנים הזקינה שמא תעשה כשפים הא רבנן נמי אמרוה ג) אי אפשר לעולם בלא זכרים ובלא נקבות אשרי מי שבניו זכרים אוי לו למי שבניו נקבות אלא משום דכתיב לא תעיל דויא בלבך דגברי גיברין קטל דויא הא שלמה אמרה ה) דאגה בלב איש ישחנה ד) ר' אמי ור' אסי חד אמר ישיחנה מדעתו וחד אמר ישיחנה לאחרים ואלא משום דכתיב מנע רבים מתוך ביתך ולא הכל תביא אל ביתך והא רבי נמי אמרה דתניא ה) רבי אומר לעולם לא ירבה אדם רעים בתוך ביתו שנאמר ו) איש רעים להתרועע אלא משום דכתיב זלדקן קורטמן עבדקן סכסן דנפח בכסיה לא צחי אמר במאי איכול לחמא לחמא סב מיניה מאן דאית ליה מעברתא בדיקני' כולי עלמא לא יכלי ליה אמר רב יוסף מילי מעלייתא דאית ביה דרשינן להו ו) אשה טובה מתנה טובה בחיק ירא אלהים תנתן אשה רעה צרעת לבעלה מאי תקנתיה יגרשנה מביתו ויתרפא מצרעתו אשה יפה אשרי בעלה מספר ימיו כפלים העלם עיניך מאשת חן פן תלכד במצודתה אל תט אצל בעלה למסוך עמו יין ושכר כי בתואר אשה יפיה רבים הושחתו ועצומים כל הרוגיה רבים היו פצעי רוכל המרגילים לדבר ערוה כניצוץ מבעיר גחלת ז) ככלוב מלא עוף כן בתיהם מלאים מרמה מנע רבים מתוך ביתך ולא הכל תביא ביתך רבים יהיו דורשי שלומך גלה סודך לאחד מאלף ח) משוכבת חיקך שמור פתחי פיך אל תצר צרת מחר ט) כי לא תדע מה ילד יום שמא למחר איננו ונמצא מצטער על עולם שאינו שלו י) כל ימי עני רעים בן סירא אומר אף לילות בשפל גגים גגו ובמרום הרים כרמו ממטר גגים לגגו ומעפר כרמו לכרמים [סימן זיר"א רב"א משרשי"א חנינ"א טובי"ה ינא"י יפ"ה יוחנ"ן מרח"ם יהוש"ע מקצ"ר] ז) אמר ר' זירא אמר רב מאי דכתיב י) כל ימי עני רעים אלו בעלי תלמוד וטוב לב משתה תמיד אלו בעלי משנה רבא אמר איפכא והיינו דאמר רב משרשיא משמיה דרבא מאי דכתיב כ) מסיע אבנים יעצב בהם אלו בעלי משנה כ) ובוקע עצים יסכן בם אלו בעלי תלמוד רבי חנינא אומר כל ימי עני רעים זה מי שיש לו אשה רעה וטוב לב משתה תמיד זה שיש לו אשה טובה רבי ינאי אומר כל ימי עני רעים זה אסטנים וטוב לב משתה תמיד זה שדעתו יפה רבי יוחנן אמר כל ימי עני רעים זה רחמני וטוב לב משתה תמיד זה אכזרי רבי יהושע בן לוי אמר כל ימי עני רעים זה שדעתו

הוי אומר מדה טובה מרובה ממדת פורענות. דבמידה טובה כתיב דלתות ובמדת פורענות כתיב ארובות ודלת גדול מארובה דד' ארובות יש בדלת במסכת יומא בפרק יום הכפורים (דף עו.) אלמא מדה טובה מרובה ומעכשיו אין לתמוה היאך יש באדם כח לקבל שכר כל כך שהרי למדת פורענות נותן הקב"ה כח באדם לקבלו כל שכן שנותן כח באדם לקבל מדה טובה: צדוקים. [שכופרין באל חי]: רב יוסף אמר אף בספר בן סירא. שיש בו דברי הבאי ובא עליהם לידי ביטול תורה: לא תיפשוט גילדנא מאודניה. כלומר לא תטול עורו של דג אפילו מעל אזנו מפני שאתה מפסיד העור דאזיל משכיה לחבלא להפסידא אלא צלי יתיה בנורא ואכול ביה תרתין גרילין שאתה יכול לצלות עור הדג עמו ולאכול בו שתי חלות דהוי לפתן לשתי חלות: גלדנא. שם הדג ל"א להכי נקט מאודניה שדרכו של דג להתחיל הפשטו מאזנו: אי מפשטיה. אי ממשמעותיה קא מתמהת באורייתא נמי כתיב: דלא לבעול שלא כדרכה. דאין הגון לאדם לשנות את דרכו והיינו דקאמר מאודניה: לא יישן. אינו יכול לישן: קטנה. קודם שהביאה שתי שערות: נערה. משהביאה שתי שערות עד שירבה שחור על הלבן הרי היא בוגרת: בנערותה שמא תזנה. משבגרה ראויה היא לנישואין להכי אמר שלא תנשא: דויא. דאגה: מנע רבים. אותם שאין לך עסק עמהם מנעם מתוך ביתך: ולא הכל תביא ביתך. אפילו אותם שאתה מתעסק עמהם לא תביאם תדיר לביתך אלא מבחוץ תדבר עמהם: איש רעים. שיש לו רעים הרבה: להתרועע. לסוף מריעים לו שמתקוטט עמהם: זלדקן. מי שזקנו דקה וחלושה: קורטמן. תדע שחכם וחריף הוא ביותר: עבדקן סכסן. מי שזקנו עבה שוטה הוא: סכסן. כמו כל בר בר חנא סכסא בבבא בתרא (דף עד.): נפח בכסיה. מי שנופח אופיא שבכוסו: לא צחי. בידוע שאינו צמא: אמר במאי איכול לחמא. האומר באיזה לפתן אוכל פת זה: סב לחמא מיניה. בידוע שאינו רעב וקח הלחם מידו שאילו היה רעב היה אוכל: מאן דאית ליה מעברתא בדקניה. שזקנו מחולק ומפוצל ויש בין שני שבילות כמין מעבר: כולי עלמא לא יכלי ליה. בערמימותיה דמתוך שחשב כל ימיו בערמות הוא משים ידו לזקנו ומושך כאדם שמחשב עד שנקרחה ל"א גרסינן הכרתא מי שיש לו היכר בזקנו שסעד כולי עלמא שלא סעדו אין יכולין להגיע לכחו ל"א גורתא והוא לשון קרחה וכל הני דברי רוח ולכך אין קורין בו: דרשינן. כלומר אמרינן להו בפרקא ומשמעינן להו לכולי עלמא כגון כל הני אשה טובה כו' אשה רעה צרעת לבעלה מה תקנתו יגרשנה מביתו כך הלשון של ספר בן סירא. אשה רעה מתנה רעה ל"ג: כפליים. מרוב הנאה חשובין ככפליים: אל תט אצל בעלה. למסוך עמו יין ושכר: רבים היו פצעי רוכל. כמה וכמה מכות מקבל רוכל המחזיר בעיר [ונושא] תכשיטי נשים ועסקו עמהם שפעמים שמוצאו בעלה עמה מתיחד עם אשתו ומכהו ופוצעו: המרגילים לדבר עבירה. ניאוף הרי הן כניצוץ מבעיר גחלת כשביב המבעיר את הפחם כך כל אשר להם כלה והולך: גחלת. אקרי פחם שאינו בוער כדאמרינן (ברכות דף נג:) גחלים עוממות. מ"ר: ככלוב. דירה של עופות: רבים יהיו דורשי שלומך. שתהא מתאהב עם הכל ואף על פי כן לא תגלה סודך לכולם אלא לאחד מני אלף: מה ילד יום. מה אירע היום שמא למחר איננו שמת הוא היום: ונמצא. שמיצר על יום שאינו עתיד לראות והיינו עולם שאינו שלו שהוא מצטער עליו ודואג על חנם מיום המחרת שלא תבא עליו צרה: כל ימי עני רעים וטוב לב משתה. פסוק הוא במשלי (טו): בשפל גגים גגו. שעני הוא ואינו יכול להגביהו לפיכך ממטר גגים לגגו שיורד מטר הגגים הגבוהים לגגו ומזלפים עליו הגשמים ואין לו מנוחה אפילו בלילות: במרום הרים כרמו. שאין לו השגת יד לקנות כרם בשפלה בדמים יקרים וקונה לו באחד מן ההרים בזול וכל עפר שהוא מוליא לזבל (ולדייר) מוליך הרוח מן ההר לשאר כרמים שבבקעה ונמצא העני נפסד: בעלי תלמוד. שקשה ללמוד מרוב קושיות וסוגיות שיש בו: משנה. נוחה ללמוד: רבא אמר איפכא. דבעלי תלמוד נהנין מיגיעו שידעו להורות איסור והיתר אבל בעלי משנה שונה ואינו יודע מהו אומר דאין ט) מורין הלכה מתוך משנה: יסכן. יתחמם: שדעתו

מסורת הש"ס

א) יומא עו. [סוטה יא. וע' מ"ש תוס' שם ד"ה ולעולם], ב) [עי' ברי"ף וברא"ש], ג) ב"ב טז: קידושין פב: [פסחים סה.], ד) יומא עה: סוטה מב., ה) [ברכות סג.], ו) [יבמות סג: ע"ש], ז) כתובות קי: [ב"ב קמו.], ח) ב"ב קמה:, ט) [נדה ז:].

תורה אור השלם

א) וַיְצַו שְׁחָקִים מִמָּעַל וְדַלְתֵי שָׁמַיִם פָּתָח: וַיַּמְטֵר עֲלֵיהֶם מָן לֶאֱכֹל וּדְגַן שָׁמַיִם נָתַן לָמוֹ: [תהלים עח, כג-כד]

ב) בִּשְׁנַת שֵׁשׁ מֵאוֹת שָׁנָה לְחַיֵּי נֹחַ בַּחֹדֶשׁ הַשֵּׁנִי בְּשִׁבְעָה עָשָׂר יוֹם לַחֹדֶשׁ בַּיּוֹם הַזֶּה נִבְקְעוּ כָּל מַעְיְנוֹת תְּהוֹם רַבָּה וַאֲרֻבֹּת הַשָּׁמַיִם נִפְתָּחוּ: [בראשית ז, יא]

ג) וְיָצְאוּ וְרָאוּ בְּפִגְרֵי הָאֲנָשִׁים הַפֹּשְׁעִים בִּי כִּי תוֹלַעְתָּם לֹא תָמוּת וְאִשָּׁם לֹא תִכְבֶּה וְהָיוּ דֵרָאוֹן לְכָל בָּשָׂר: [ישעיה סו, כד]

ד) כִּי תָצוּר אֶל עִיר יָמִים רַבִּים לְהִלָּחֵם עָלֶיהָ לְתָפְשָׂהּ לֹא תַשְׁחִית אֶת עֵצָהּ לִנְדֹּחַ עָלָיו גַּרְזֶן כִּי מִמֶּנּוּ תֹאכֵל וְאֹתוֹ לֹא תִכְרֹת כִּי הָאָדָם עֵץ הַשָּׂדֶה לָבֹא מִפָּנֶיךָ בַּמָּצוֹר: [דברים כ, יט]

ה) דְּאָגָה בְלֶב אִישׁ יַשְׁחֶנָּה וְדָבָר טוֹב יְשַׂמְּחֶנָּה: [משלי יב, כה]

ו) אִישׁ רֵעִים לְהִתְרֹעֵעַ וְיֵשׁ אֹהֵב דָּבֵק מֵאָח: [משלי יח, כד]

ז) כִּכְלוּב מָלֵא עוֹף כֵּן בָּתֵּיהֶם מְלֵאִים מִרְמָה עַל כֵּן גָּדְלוּ וַיַּעֲשִׁירוּ: [ירמיה ה, כז]

ח) אַל תַּאֲמִינוּ בְרֵעַ אַל תִּבְטְחוּ בְּאַלּוּף מִשֹּׁכֶבֶת חֵיקֶךָ שְׁמֹר פִּתְחֵי פִיךָ: [מיכה ז, ה]

ט) אַל תִּתְהַלֵּל בְּיוֹם מָחָר כִּי לֹא תֵדַע מַה יֵּלֶד יוֹם: [משלי כז, א]

י) כָּל יְמֵי עָנִי רָעִים וְטוֹב לֵב מִשְׁתֶּה תָמִיד: [משלי טו, טו]

כ) מַסִּיעַ אֲבָנִים יֵעָצֵב בָּהֶם בּוֹקֵעַ עֵצִים יִסָּכֶן בָּם: [קהלת י, ט]

gill,[8] דְּלֹא לֵיזוּל מַשְׁכֵּיהּ לְחַבְלָא – **lest its skin go to ruin;** אֶלָּא וְאֵיכוֹל בֵּיהּ – **rather, roast it** with its skin **in fire** צְלֵי יָתֵיהּ בְּנוּרָא – **and eat with it two cakes** of bread[9] – what is objectionable about that passage? תַּרְתֵּין גְּרִיצִים" – **If** you object to **its plain meaning,**[10] that one should not let the fish's skin go to waste, but should eat it along with its meat, אִי מִפְּשְׁטֵיהּ – **in the Torah, too, it is written:** ***You shall not destroy its trees,***[11] which likewise forbids the gratuitous destruction of anything that can be eaten. Thus, this passage in *Ben Sira,* far from being empty and worthless, actually articulates a Torah principle. בְּאוֹרַיְיתָא נַמִּי כְּתַב ,,לֹא־תַשְׁחִית אֶת־עֵצָהּ" – And **if** you object to its exegetical **interpretation,** אִי מִדְּרָשָׁא – this also is valuable, for **it teaches us proper behavior,**[12] אוֹרַח אַרְעָא קָא מַשְׁמַע לָן – viz. **that one should not cohabit in an unnatural manner.**[13] דְּלֹא לִיבְעוֹל שֶׁלֹּא כְּדַרְכָּהּ Hence, there is nothing about this passage that justifies prohibiting the reading of *Ben Sira.*

Abaye examines a second potentially objectionable passage: וְאֶלָּא מִשּׁוּם דִּכְתִיב ,,בַּת לְאָבִיהָ מַטְמוֹנֶת שָׁוְא – **Rather,** was the prohibition issued **because it is written: A daughter is a false treasure for her father;**[14] מִפַּחְדָּהּ לֹא יִישַׁן בַּלַּיְלָה – **from worrying about her he [cannot] sleep at night:** בִּקְטַנּוּתָהּ שֶׁמָּא תִּתְפַּתֶּה – **in her childhood**[15] **[he worries] that she may be seduced;** בְּנַעֲרוּתָהּ שֶׁמָּא תִּזְנֶה – **in her puberty**[16] **[he worries] that she may behave promiscuously;**[17] בָּגְרָה שֶׁמָּא לֹא תִינָּשֵׂא – **[when] she reaches maturity**[18] **[he worries] that she may not marry;** נִישֵּׂאת שֶׁמָּא לֹא יִהְיוּ לָהּ בָּנִים – **[when] she marries [he worries] that she may not have children;**[19] הִזְקִינָה שֶׁמָּא תַּעֲשֶׂה כְשָׁפִים" – **[when] she grows old [he worries] that she may practice sorcery?**[20] הָא רַבָּנָן נַמִּי אֲמָרוּהָ – You cannot dismiss the above as a specious maxim, for **the Rabbis also have expressed [such sentiments],** for they said:[21] אִי אֶפְשָׁר לָעוֹלָם בְּלֹא זְכָרִים וּבְלֹא נְקֵבוֹת – **It is impossible for the world** to exist **without both males and females.** אַשְׁרֵי מִי שֶׁבָּנָיו זְכָרִים – Nevertheless, **fortunate is he whose children are male,** אוֹי לוֹ לְמִי שֶׁבָּנָיו נְקֵבוֹת – and **woe to him whose children are female.**[22] Hence, this passage of *Ben Sira* also makes a valid and illuminating point.

Abaye examines a third potentially objectionable passage: אֶלָּא מִשּׁוּם דִּכְתִיב ,,לָא תָעֵיל דַּוְיָא בְּלִבָּךְ דִּגְבַרֵי גִיבָּרִין קְטַל דַּוְיָא" – **Rather,** was the prohibition issued **because it is written: Do not allow sorrow into your heart, for sorrow has killed mighty men?** הָא שְׁלֹמֹה אֲמָרָהּ – But this, too, cannot be dismissed as a specious maxim, for King **Solomon** himself **has said it:**[23] ,,דְּאָגָה בְלֶב־אִישׁ יַשְׁחֶנָּה" – ***[If] there is anxiety in a man's heart, let him quash it (yashchenah),*** רַבִּי אַמִּי וְרַבִּי אַסִּי – and the meaning of the word *yashchenah* is disputed by **R' Ami and R' Assi.** חַד אָמַר יְשִׂיחֶנָּה מִדַּעְתּוֹ – **One said** it means that **he should uproot**[24] **[the worry] from his mind** by thinking about other matters, וְחַד אָמַר יְשִׂיחֶנָּה לַאֲחֵרִים – **and one said** it means that **he should tell [his concerns] to others,** for they may be able to advise him how to find solace.[25] Hence, this passage as well imparts a valid and illuminating message.

Abaye examines yet another potentially objectionable passage: וְאֶלָּא מִשּׁוּם דִּכְתִיב ,,מְנַע רַבִּים מִתּוֹךְ בֵּיתָךְ וְלֹא הַכֹּל תָּבִיא אֶל בֵּיתָךְ" – **Rather,** was the prohibition issued **because it is written: Prevent the public from [coming] into your house;**[26] **do not bring everyone into your house?**[27] וְהָא רַבִּי נַמִּי אֲמָרָהּ – But this, too, cannot be dismissed as a false maxim, for **Rebbi also said it,** דְּתַנְיָא – **as was taught in a Baraisa:**[28] רַבִּי אוֹמֵר – REBBI SAYS: לְעוֹלָם לֹא יַרְבֶּה אָדָם רֵעִים בְּתוֹךְ בֵּיתוֹ – A MAN SHOULD NEVER [INVITE] MANY FRIENDS INTO HIS HOUSE, שֶׁנֶּאֱמַר ,,אִישׁ רֵעִים לְהִתְרוֹעֵעַ" – AS IT IS STATED: *A MAN WITH MANY FRIENDS [IS DESTINED] TO BE HARMED.*[29] Hence, this passage as well teaches a valid and valuable lesson.

The objectionable passages are finally discovered: אֶלָּא מִשּׁוּם דִּכְתִיב ,,זַלְדְּקָן קוּרְטְמָן – **Rather,** the prohibition against reading Ben Sira was issued **because it is written** therein: **A thin-bearded man is,** presumably, **exceedingly wise;** עַבְדְּקָן סַכְסָן" – **a thick-bearded man is,** presumably, **a fool.** ,,דִּנְפַח בְּכַסֵּיהּ לֹא צָחֵי" – He **who blows** away the froth **in his mug** of beer **is not thirsty.**[30]

NOTES

8. The skin around the gills is the most inferior on the fish, and you might think its being discarded is no loss (*Rashi;* cf. *Yad Ramah*).

9. I.e. an amount of relish that would normally be eaten with two cakes of bread (*Rashi*).

10. I.e. on the grounds that the statement is worthless and unnecessary (*Rashi;* cf. *Yad Ramah*).

11. *Deuteronomy* 20:19, which prohibits the destruction of fruit-bearing trees.

12. Literally: the way of the land.

13. *Ben Sira* speaks euphemistically of deviant forms of cohabitation (*Rashi*).

14. A person might think that he derives greater financial benefit from the birth of a daughter than he does from the birth of a son, since he is entitled to sell his young daughter as a Hebrew maidservant, to betroth her for money, or to receive her earnings — none of which is possible in the case of a son. However, such a "treasure" is not all that it seems to be, since the aforementioned financial advantages are offset by emotional disadvantages, as the passage now explains (*Maharsha*).

15. I.e. before she sprouts two pubic hairs (*Rashi*).

16. I.e. from the time she sprouts two pubic hairs until a majority of the pubic area is covered with hair (*Rashi*).

17. See *Ben Yehoyada.*

18. And it is time to marry (*Rashi;* cf. *Maharsha, Ben Yehoyada*).

19. One of a woman's primary purposes in life is to bear and raise children (see *Maharsha;* cf. *Ben Yehoyada*).

20. If she is married many years without children, she may employ sorcery to retain her husband's love and to prevent him from acquiring another wife (*Ben Yehoyada*).

21. See *Bava Basra* 16b.

22. [For a daughter is a constant source of worry to her father, as explained in *Ben Sira.*]

23. *Proverbs* 12:25.

24. When the שׁ in the word יַשְׁחֶנָּה is interchanged with שׂ, we get the word יַשְׂחֶנָּה; and when the שׂ is further interchanged with the letter ס (*samech*), the result is יַסְחֶנָּה, which connotes עֲקִירָה: *uproot it* (see *Rashi* to *Deuteronomy* 28:63).

[*Rashi* to *Proverbs* (12:25) writes that he should uproot the worry by engaging in Torah study.]

25. *Maharsha.* Alternatively, *Sfas Emes* (*Likkutei Yehudah* to *Proverbs* ibid.) explains that since the listeners will be distressed by the man's troubles, God may eliminate those troubles in order to spare the listeners any undeserved suffering.

26. I.e. do not allow those people with whom you have no dealings to enter your house (*Rashi*).

27. I.e. you should not invite even those with whom you do have dealings into your home on a regular basis; rather, speak to them outside (*Rashi*).

28. *Berachos* 63a.

29. *Proverbs* 18:24. This verse is usually translated: *A man [acquires] friends in order to fraternize,* with the word לְהִתְרוֹעֵעַ deriving from רֵעִים, *friendship* or *companionship.* Rebbi here interprets לְהִתְרוֹעֵעַ as deriving from רַע, *evil.* Thus, the meaning of the verse is that if one has many friends, sooner or later he will quarrel with them and he will thereby suffer at their hands (*Rashi*).

30. If he were truly thirsty he would hasten to drink, and would not be concerned about removing the froth on the surface of the beverage (*Yad Ramah*).

עין משפט נר מצוה

כ א מיי' פ"ב מהל' עכו"ם הלכה ב:

[א] הוי אומר מדה טובה מרובה ממדת פורענות במדה טובה כתיב [א] ויצו שחקים ממעל ודלתי שמים פתח וימטר עליהם מן לאכול ובמידת פורענות הוא אומר [ב] וארובות השמים נפתחו במידת פורענות כתיב [ג] ויצאו וראו בפגרי האנשים הפושעים בי כי תולעתם לא תמות ואשם לא תכבה והיו דראון לכל בשר והלא אדם מושיט אצבעו באור בעולם הזה מיד נכוה אלא כשם שנותן הקב"ה כח ברשעים לקבל פורענותם כך נותן הקב"ה כח בצדיקים לקבל טובתן: רבי עקיבא אומר [א] אף הקורא בספרים החיצונים וכו': תנא בספרי צדוקים [ג] רב יוסף אמר בספר בן סירא נמי אסור למיקרי א"ל אביי מאי טעמא אילימא משום דכתב [ביה] לא תינטוש גילדנא מאודניה דלא ליזיל משכיה לחבלא אלא צלי יתיה בנורא ואיכול ביה תרתין גריצים אי מפשטיה באורייתא נמי כתב [ד] לא תשחית את עצה אי מדרשא אורח ארעא קמ"ל דלא ליבעול שלא כדרכה ואלא משום דכתיב בת לאביה מטמונת שוא מפחדה לא יישן בלילה בקטנותה שמא תתפתה בנערותה שמא תזנה בגרה שמא לא תינשא נישאת שמא לא יהיו לה בנים הזקינה שמא תעשה כשפים הא רבנן נמי אמרוה [ג] אי אפשר לעולם בלא זכרים ובלא נקבות אשרי מי שבניו זכרים אוי לו למי שבניו נקבות אלא משום דכתיב לא תעיל דויא בלבך דגברי גיברין קטל דויא הא שלמה אמרה [ה] דאגה בלב איש ישחנה [ד] ר' אמי ור' אסי חד אמר ישיחנה מדעתו וחד אמר ישיחנה לאחרים ואלא משום דכתיב מנע רבים מתוך ביתך ולא הכל תביא אל ביתך והא רבי נמי אמרה דתניא [ה] רבי אומר לעולם לא ירבה אדם רעים בתוך ביתו שנאמר [ו] איש רעים להתרועע אלא משום דכתיב זלדקן קורטמן עבדקן סכסן דנפח בכסיה לא צחי אמר במאי איכול לחמא לחמא סב מיניה מאן דאית ליה מעברתא בדיקני' כולי עלמא לא יכלי ליה אמר רב יוסף מילי מעלייתא דאית ביה דרשינן להו [ו] אשה טובה מתנה טובה בחיק ירא אלהים תנתן אשה רעה צרעת לבעלה מאי תקנתיה יגרשנה מביתו ויתרפא מצרעתו אשה יפה אשרי בעלה מספר ימיו כפלים העלם עיניך מאשת חן פן תלכד במצודתה אל תט אצל בעלה למסוך עמו יין ושכר כי בתואר אשה יפיה רבים הושחתו ועצומים כל הרוגיה רבים היו פצעי רוכל המרגילים לדבר ערוה כניצוץ מבעיר גחלת [ז] ככלוב מלא עוף כן בתיהם מלאים מרמה מנע רבים מתוך ביתך ולא הכל תביא ביתך רבים יהיו דורשי שלומך גלה סודך לאחד מאלף [ח] משוכבת חיקך שמור פתחי פיך אל תצר צרת מחר [ט] כי לא תדע מה ילד יום שמא למחר איננו ונמצא מצטער על עולם שאינו שלו [י] כל ימי עני רעים בן סירא אומר אף לילות בשפל גגים גגו ובמרום הרים כרמו ממטר גגים לגגו ומעפר כרמו לכרמים [סימן זיר"א רב"א משרשי"א חנינ"א טובי"ה ינא"י יפ"ה יוחנ"ן מרח"ם יהוש"ע מקצ"ר] [ז] אמר ר' זירא אמר רב מאי דכתיב [י] כל ימי עני רעים אלו בעלי תלמוד וטוב לב משתה תמיד אלו בעלי משנה רבא אמר איפכא והיינו דאמר רב משרשיא משמיה דרבא מאי דכתיב [כ] מסיע אבנים יעצב בהם אלו בעלי משנה [כ] ובוקע עצים יסכן בם אלו בעלי תלמוד רבי חנינא אומר כל ימי עני רעים זה מי שיש לו אשה רעה וטוב לב משתה תמיד זה שיש לו אשה טובה רבי ינאי אומר כל ימי עני רעים זה אסטנים וטוב לב משתה תמיד זה שדעתו יפה רבי יוחנן אמר כל ימי עני רעים זה רחמני וטוב לב משתה תמיד זה אכזרי רבי יהושע בן לוי אמר כל ימי עני רעים זה שדעתו

הוי אומר מדה טובה מרובה ממדת פורענות. דבמדה טובה כתיב דלתות ובמדת פורענות כתיב ארובות ודלת גדול מארובה דד' ארובות יש בדלת במסכת יומא בפרק יום הכפורים (דף עו.) אלמא מדה טובה מרובה ומעכשיו אין לתמוה היאך יש באדם כח לקבל שכר כל כך שהרי למדת פורענות נותן הקב"ה כח באדם לקבלו כל שכן שנותן כח באדם לקבל מדה טובה: **צדוקים.** [שכופרין בא"ל חי]: **רב יוסף אמר אף בספר בן סירא.** שיש בו דברי הבאי ובא עליהם לידי ביטול תורה: **לא תיפשוט גילדנא מאודניה.** כלומר לא תטול עורו של דג אפילו מעל אזנו מפני שאתה מפסיד העור דאזיל משכיה לחבלא להפסידא אלא צלי יתיה בנורא ואכול ביה תרתין גרילין שאתה יכול לצלות עור הדג עמו ולאכול בו שתי חלות דהוי לפתן לשתי חלות: **גלדנא.** שם הדג ל"א להכי נקט מאודניה שדרכו של דג להתחיל הפשטו מאזנו: **אי מפשטיה.** אי ממשמעותיה קא מתמהת באורייתא נמי כתיב: **דלא לבעול שלא כדרכה.** דאין הגון לאדם לשנות את דרכו והיינו דקאמר מאודניה: **לא יישן.** אינו יכול לישן: **קטנה.** קודם שהביאה שתי שערות: **נערה.** משהביאה שתי שערות עד שירבה שחור על הלבן הרי היא בוגרת: **בנערותה שמא תזנה.** משבגרה ראויה היא לנישואין להכי אמר שלא תנשא: **דויא.** דאגה: **מנע רבים.** אותם שאין לך עסק עמהם מנעם מתוך ביתך: **ולא הכל תביא ביתך.** אפילו אותם שאתה מתעסק עמהם לא תביאם תדיר לביתך אלא מבחוץ תדבר עמהם: **איש רעים.** שיש לו רעים הרבה: **להתרועע.** לסוף מריעים לו שמתקוטט עמהם: **זלדקן.** מי שזקנו דקה וחלושה: **קורטמן.** תלע שחכם וחריף הוא ביותר: **עבדקן סכסן.** מי שזקנו עבה שוטה הוא: **סכסן.** כמו כל בר בר חנא סכסא בבבא בתרא (דף עד.): **נפח בכסיה.** מי שנופח אופיא שבכוסו: **לא צחי.** בידוע שאינו צמא: **אמר במאי איכול לחמא.** האומר באיזה לפתן אוכל פת זה: **סב לחמא מיניה.** בידוע שאינו רעב וקח הלחם מידו שאילו היה רעב היה אוכל: **מאן דאית ליה מעברתא בדקניה.** שזקנו מחולק ומפולל ויש בין שני שבילות כמין מעבר: **כולי עלמא לא יכלי ליה.** בערמימותיה דמתוך שחשב כל ימיו בערמות הוא משים ידו לזקנו ומושך כאדם שמחשב עד שנקרחה ל"א גרסינן הכרתא מי שיש לו היכר בזקנו שסעד כולי עלמא שלא סעדו אין יכולין להגיע לכחו ל"א גוורתא והוא לשון קרחה וכל הני דברי רוח ולכך אין קורין בו: **דרשינן.** כלומר אמרינן להו בפרקא ומשמעינן להו לכולי עלמא כגון כל הני אשה טובה כו' אשה רעה צרעת לבעלה מה תקנתו יגרשנה מביתו כך הלשון של ספר בן סירא. אשה רעה מתנה רעה ל"ג: **כפליים.** מרוב הנאה חשובין ככפליים: **אל תט אצל בעלה.** למסוך עמו יין ושכר: **רבים היו פצעי רוכל.** כמה וכמה מכות מקבל רוכל המחזיר בעיר [ונושא] תכשיטי נשים ועסקו עמהם שפעמים שמוצאו בעלה עמה מתיחד עם אשתו ומכהו ופוצעו: **המרגילים לדבר עבירה.** ניאוף הרי הן כניצוץ מבעיר גחלת כשביב המבעיר את הפחם כך כל אשר להם כלה והולך: **גחלת.** אקרי פחם שאינו בוער כדאמרינן (ברכות דף נג:) גחלים עוממות. מ"ר: **ככלוב.** דירה של עופות: **רבים יהיו דורשי שלומך.** שתהא מתאהב עם הכל ואף על פי כן לא תגלה סודך לכולם אלא לאחד מני אלף: **מה ילד יום.** מה אירע היום שמא למחר איננו שמת הוא היום: **ונמצא.** שמיצר על יום שאינו עתיד לראות והיינו עולם שאינו שלו שהוא מצטער עליו ודואג על חנם מיום המחרת שלא תבא עליו צרה: **כל ימי עני רעים וטוב לב משתה.** פסוק הוא במשלי (טו): **בשפל גגים גגו.** שעני הוא ואינו יכול להגביהו לפיכך ממטר גגים לגגו שיורד מטר הגגים הגבוהים לגגו ומזלפים עליו הגשמים ואין לו מנוחה אפילו בלילות: **במרום הרים כרמו.** שאין לו השגת יד לקנות כרם בשפלה בדמים יקרים וקונה לו באחד מן ההרים בזול וכל עפר שהוא מוליא לזבל (ולדייר) מוליך הרוח מן ההר לשאר כרמים שבבקעה ונמצא העני נפסד: **בעלי תלמוד.** שקשה ללמוד מרוב קושיות וסוגיות שיש בו: **משנה.** נוחה ללמוד: **רבא אמר איפכא.** דבעלי תלמוד נהנין מיגיעו שידעו להורות איסור והיתר אבל בעלי משנה שונה ואינו יודע מהו אומר דאין [ט] מורין הלכה מתוך משנה: **יסכן.** יתחמם: **שדעתו**

ליקוטי רש"י

תולעתם. רמה האוכלת את בשרם. **ואשם.** בגיהנם. **דראון.** לשון בזיון, וי"ת כמין שתי תיבות די ראייה, עד דיימרון עליהון לדיקיא מיסת חזינא [ישעיהו ו, כד]. **גילדנא.** שם דג קטן [ב"ב עג:]. **גריצין.** ככרות עבים [ביצה כא:]. **דאגה.** פחד שדואג על הפסד שום דבר פן יבואהו [יומא עה.]. כל דאגה שבמקרא לשון יראה הוא כמו אני דואג את היהודים דלדקיהו [יהושע כב, כד]. כל לשון דאגה לשון יראה דוטטי"ר בלע"ז [ש"א י, ב]. איינס"א בלע"ז ובלשונינו טרוא"ר בלע"ז [יחזקאל ד, טז]. **דאגה בלב איש ישחנה.** ישיחנה מדעתו. ודבר טוב ישמחנה, יעסוק בתורה והיא תשמח את הדאגה שבלבו ותצילנו ממנה, ולדברי האומר ישיחנה לאחרי' כך סופו של מקרא ודבר טוב שינחמנו חבירו ישמח את הדאג' [משלי יב, כה]. **ישיחנה לאחרים.** שמא ישיאוהו עלה [יומא עה.]. **להתרועע.** להתרוצץ [ברכות סג.]. **מספר ימיו כפלים.** כלומר שמח בחלקו ודומה לו כאילו ימיו כפלים. **מאשת חן.** של אחרים. **רוכל.** המוכר בשמים לנשים להתקשט בהן ומלוי בו ניאוף ובא בעלה ופלעו. **מבעיר גחלת.** כן ילרו מבעירו. **ככלוב.** קן עופות. **שמא למחר איננו.** ואיננו בעולם ולא יראה אותה דאגה שהוא מיצר וירא ודואג עליה ונמצא שנצטער אמתול על עולם שאין שלו [יבמות סג:]. **בכלוב.** הוא מקום שמשימין בו עופות וכן תרגמו יונתן כבית פיטמא וכלוב מלא עוף [ירמיה ה, כז]. **כל ימי עני רעים.** ואפילו שבתות וי"ט דאמר מר שמואל שינוי וסת תחלת חולי מעים [משלי טו, טו]. **בן סירא אומר.** שלמה כתב כל ימי עני רעים אבל בן סירא אומר אף הלילות כששוכב אין לו מנוחה כי בשפל גגים גגו ונמצא לגג עודפי גשם ספגיר. **ומעפר כרמו לכרמים.** זבל ואשפה שהביא לכרמו נספך לכרמים אחרים שהוא במקום רועץ בהרים וכשגשמים במקום שאין עשיר חפץ בו נופל למטה לכרמים של עשירים שהם במקום טוב ומדרון וגוח לעסוק בהם [ב"ב קמה:]. **במרום הרים כרמו.** שאין בידו ממון לקנות במקום טוב וקונה בראש ההר וכל זבלים שהוא מוליא לו נופל וזב לכרמים שתחתיו [כתובות קי:]. **זה בעלי תלמוד.** סוגית גמרא ותגלי משניות וברייתות וזהו עיקר הגמרא שאם לא הגמרא אין למדין הלכה מתוך משנה כדאמרינן התנאים מבלי עולם (סוטה דף כב). **כל ימי עני רעים אלו בעלי תלמוד.** שממית עלמו לכוין הלכות ולתרץ הוויות. **רבא אמר איפכא.** כל ימי עני רעים זה בעל משנה שאינו יכול להורות הלכה מתוך משנתו וגם כי כשחולקות זו על זו אינו יכול לתרץ וטוב לב זה בעל הגמרא שיודע משניות על עיקרם ובקי בטעמיהם ויש בידו כח להורות הלכה למעשה. **יעצב.** לשון בעצבון תאכלנה (בראשית ג). **זה בעל משנה.** ששונה משניות כל היום ואין לו אלא צער שמתקשה בטעמיהן ואינו יודע לפרש. **יסכן.** לשון תמימות כמו ותהי למלך סוכנת (מלכים א א) כלומר שנהנה מהן. **זה איסטנים.** מי שדעתו קלה ולבו נמאס בכל דבר מגונה שהוא רואה. **יפה.** שסובל הכל דאינו מזיק לו שום לכלוך ושום דבר מיאוס. **זה רחמני.** כמה עניים הוא רואה וכמה מאורעות שלבו בוכה תדיר עליהן [ב"ב קמה:]. **מסיע אבנים יעצב בהם.** מסיע אבנים ממחצבתם בהרים מתיגע להם. **יעצב.** לשון יגיעה כמו (בראשית ג) בעצבון תאכלנה כלומר כל אדם לפי מלאכתו עצבונו אף עושה רעה לפי זריעתו יקצור. **יסכן בם.** יתחמם בם כמו (מלכים א א) ותהי לו סוכנת אף העוסק בתורה ובמצות סופו ליהנות מהם [קהלת י, ט]. **מסיע אבנים יעצב בם אלו בעלי משנה.** לא שימש תלמידי חכמים ללמוד סברת הגמרא בטעמי המשנה מה הם רשע הוא שאין תורתו על בורייה ואין ללמוד הימנו סילוק באיסור והיתר ובדיני ממונות לזכות ולחייב ובטהרות לטמא ולטהר כדאמר בכמה דוכתי מ"ט אמר מר הכי ומר הכי ואמר מאי בינייהו איכא בינייהו כך וכך וערום הוא שהשומע את קולו שונה משניותיו כסבור הוא שבקי בהן ונוהגין בו כבוד כתלמידי חכמים [סוטה כב.]. **ובוקע עצים יסכן בם אלו בעלי תלמוד.** סברת טעמי המשניות שממנו יוצאה הוראה אבל המורים הוראה מן המשנה נקראו מבלי העולם במסכת סוטה (דף כ"ב א) [ברכות ה.]. עיקר התורה שממנו הוראה יוצאה גמרא היינו סברת טעמי משנה ותירולי משניות הסותרות זו את זו וחסורי מחסרא [שם יא.]. לתת סברא להבין בטעמי המשנה והלכה כדברי מי [סוטה מד.].

מסורת הש"ס

א) יומא עו. [סוטה יא. וע' מ"ש תוס' שם ד"ה ולעולם], ב) [ע' ברי"ף ובר"ש], ג) ב"ב טו: קידושין פב: [פסחים סה.], ד) יומא עה: סוטה מב., ה) [ברכות סג. ע"ש], ו) יבמות סג: ע"ש, ז) כתובות קי: [ב"ב קמה.], ח) ב"ב קמה:, ט) [נדה ז:].

תורה אור השלם

א) וַיְצַו שְׁחָקִים מִמָּעַל וְדַלְתֵי שָׁמַיִם פָּתָח: וַיַּמְטֵר עֲלֵיהֶם מָן לֶאֱכֹל וּדְגַן שָׁמַיִם נָתַן לָמוֹ: [תהלים עח, כג-כד]

ב) בִּשְׁנַת שֵׁשׁ מֵאוֹת שָׁנָה לְחַיֵּי נֹחַ בַּחֹדֶשׁ הַשֵּׁנִי בְּשִׁבְעָה עָשָׂר יוֹם לַחֹדֶשׁ בַּיּוֹם הַזֶּה נִבְקְעוּ כָּל מַעְיְנוֹת תְּהוֹם רַבָּה וַאֲרֻבֹּת הַשָּׁמַיִם נִפְתָּחוּ: [בראשית ז, יא]

ג) וְיָצְאוּ וְרָאוּ בְּפִגְרֵי הָאֲנָשִׁים הַפֹּשְׁעִים בִּי כִּי תוֹלַעְתָּם לֹא תָמוּת וְאִשָּׁם לֹא תִכְבֶּה וְהָיוּ דֵרָאוֹן לְכָל בָּשָׂר: [ישעיה סו, כד]

ד) כִּי תָצוּר אֶל עִיר יָמִים רַבִּים לְהִלָּחֵם עָלֶיהָ לְתָפְשָׂהּ לֹא תַשְׁחִית אֶת עֵצָהּ לִנְדֹּחַ עָלָיו גַּרְזֶן כִּי מִמֶּנּוּ תֹאכֵל וְאֹתוֹ לֹא תִכְרֹת כִּי הָאָדָם עֵץ הַשָּׂדֶה לָבֹא מִפָּנֶיךָ בַּמָּצוֹר: [דברים כ, יט]

ה) דְּאָגָה בְלֶב אִישׁ יַשְׁחֶנָּה וְדָבָר טוֹב יְשַׂמְּחֶנָּה: [משלי יב, כה]

ו) אִישׁ רֵעִים לְהִתְרֹעֵעַ וְיֵשׁ אֹהֵב דָּבֵק מֵאָח: [משלי יח, כד]

ז) כִּכְלוּב מָלֵא עוֹף כֵּן בָּתֵּיהֶם מְלֵאִים מִרְמָה עַל כֵּן גָּדְלוּ וַיַּעֲשִׁירוּ: [ירמיה ה, כז]

ח) אַל תַּאֲמִינוּ בְרֵעַ אַל תִּבְטְחוּ בְּאַלּוּף מִשֹּׁכֶבֶת חֵיקֶךָ שְׁמֹר פִּתְחֵי פִיךָ: [מיכה ז, ה]

ט) אַל תִּתְהַלֵּל בְּיוֹם מָחָר כִּי לֹא תֵדַע מַה יֵּלֶד יוֹם: [משלי כז, א]

י) כָּל יְמֵי עָנִי רָעִים וְטוֹב לֵב מִשְׁתֶּה תָמִיד: [משלי טו, טו]

כ) מַסִּיעַ אֲבָנִים יֵעָצֵב בָּהֶם בּוֹקֵעַ עֵצִים יִסָּכֶן בָּם: [קהלת י, ט]

,,אָמַר בְּמַאי אֵיכוּל לַחְמָא – If **one said, "With what** relish **shall I eat my bread?"** ,,לַחְמָא סַב מִינֵּיהּ – **take the bread away from him.**[31]

,,מַאן דְּאִית לֵיהּ מַעְבַּרְתָּא בְּדִיקְנֵיהּ – **One who has a part in his beard** – ,,כּוּלֵי עָלְמָא לָא יָכְלֵי לֵיהּ – **the entire world cannot defeat him.**[32] These aphorisms are frivolous and devoid of any redeeming value. It was because the *Book of Ben Sira* contains such worthless passages that Rav Yosef forbade people to read it.[33]

Rav Yosef cites a number of maxims from the *Book of Ben Sira* that may be quoted:

אָמַר רַב יוֹסֵף – **Rav Yosef said:** מִילֵי מְעַלְיָיתָא דְּאִית בֵּיהּ דָּרְשִׁינַן לְהוּ – Even though *an individual* is forbidden to read *Ben Sira* because it contains a number of frivolous passages, nevertheless, **the good things in it** (i.e. those passages that are insightful and edifying) **we may expound upon** in public lectures and widely publicize.[34] Such passages include: ,,אִשָּׁה טוֹבָה מַתָּנָה טוֹבָה בְּחֵיק יְרֵא אֱלֹהִים תִּנָּתֵן" – **A good wife is a precious gift; she is given into the embrace of a God-fearing man.**[35] ,,אִשָּׁה רָעָה צָרַעַת לְבַעְלָהּ – **A bad wife is leprosy to her husband.** מַאי תַּקַּנְתֵּיהּ – **What is his remedy?** ,,יְגָרְשֶׁנָּה מִבֵּיתוֹ וְיִתְרַפֵּא מִצָּרַעְתּוֹ" – **He should expel her from his house** (i.e. divorce her), **and he will** thereby **be cured of his leprosy.**[36]

,,אִשָּׁה יָפָה אַשְׁרֵי בַּעְלָהּ – **A beautiful wife – fortunate is her husband;** ,,מִסְפַּר יָמָיו כִּפְלַיִם" – **the number of his days is doubled.**[37]

,,הַעְלֵם עֵינֶיךָ מֵאֵשֶׁת חֵן פֶּן תִּלָּכֵד בִּמְצוּדָתָהּ – **Conceal your eyes from a woman of charm, lest you be caught in her trap.**[38] אַל תֵּט אֵצֶל בַּעְלָהּ לִמְסוֹךְ עִמּוֹ יַיִן וְשֵׁכָר – **Do not turn to her husband to share**[39] **wine and strong drink with him,**[40] כִּי בְתוֹאַר אִשָּׁה יָפָה רַבִּים הוּשְׁחָתוּ – **for many have been destroyed by the countenance of a beautiful woman,**[41] ,,וַעֲצוּמִים כָּל הֲרוּגֶיהָ" – **and numerous are her victims.**[42]

,,רַבִּים הָיוּ פִּצְעֵי רוֹכֵל" – **Many are the blows [sustained by] peddlers.**[43]

,,הַמַּרְגִּילִים לִדְבַר עֶרְוָה כְּנִיצוֹץ מַבְעִיר גַּחֶלֶת – **Those who habituate** others **to immorality are like a spark that ignites a coal;**[44] ,,כִּכְלוּב מָלֵא עוֹף כֵּן בָּתֵּיהֶם מְלֵאִים מִרְמָה" – **as a coop is full of birds, so are their houses full of deceit.**[45]

,,מְנַע רַבִּים מִתּוֹךְ בֵּיתְךָ וְלֹא הַכֹּל תָּבִיא בֵּיתְךָ" – **Prevent the public from [coming] into your house; do not bring everyone** into **your house.**[46]

,,רַבִּים יִהְיוּ דּוֹרְשֵׁי שְׁלוֹמְךָ גַּלֵּה סוֹדְךָ לְאֶחָד מֵאֶלֶף" – **Many should inquire after your welfare;** nevertheless, **reveal your secret to one in a thousand.**[47] ,,מִשּׁוֹכֶבֶת חֵיקְךָ שְׁמוֹר פִּתְחֵי פִיךָ" – Indeed, **guard your words**[48] even **from the one who lies in your embrace.**[49]

NOTES

31. If he were truly hungry he would not spend time deliberating about a condiment; he would simply eat the bread. Since he does not really need the bread, you may take it from him (see *Rashi, Yad Ramah*).

32. The bald streak resembling a part in the middle of his beard was caused by constant stroking, the action of a man who spends all of his time plotting and calculating. Such a person will outwit all his opponents (*Rashi*).

33. We have followed *Rashi's* explanation throughout the Gemara's discussion of the passages from *Ben Sira.* However, according to *Yad Ramah,* who holds that Rav Yosef equates *Ben Sira* with the heretical books banned by R' Akiva (see above, note 6), many of these passages are objectionable (in potential or in fact) because they teach a kind of determinism. To take the last passage as an example: No matter what one does, he will not be able to overcome the man with the parted beard. In truth, all is in God's hands, and the proper thing to do is to pray to God for protection from him or any other man.

34. From this statement as well as from the fact that *Ben Sira* is quoted twice in the Talmud, *Ritva* concludes that the prohibition against reading *Ben Sira* applies only to studying it as if it were part of the Torah and it contained Divine wisdom. However, it is perfectly acceptable to peruse the book in order to acquaint oneself with its contents, which include much that is useful (*Ritva* to *Bava Basra* 98b; see note 6 above). [The above accords with the first interpretation of Rav Yosef's previous statement (see note 6 above). However, according to the second interpretation, in which Rav Yosef absolutely forbids the reading of *Ben Sira,* his ruling there appears to contradict his ruling here (unless we follow *Meiri's* opinion, cited above in note 5).]

Yad Ramah, however, quotes a variant text of the Gemara, which removes the above difficulty: אִי לָאו דְּגָנְזוּהָ רַבָּנָן לְהַאי סִיפְרָא הֲוָה דָּרְשִׁינַן לְהוּ הָנֵי מִילֵּי מְעַלְיָיתָא דְּאִית בֵּיהּ, *If not for the fact that the Rabbis banned this book* (*Ben Sira*), *we would expound its edifying passages [to the public].* According to this version, *Ben Sira* may never be read.

35. *Maharsha* explains: *A good* (i.e. pious) *wife is a precious gift* to the one designated by Heaven, forty days before conception, to be her husband [whether he is worthy of her or not; see above, 22a, *Moed Katan* 18b, *Sotah* 2a]. However, through prayer it is possible to change the decree, so that *she is given into the embrace of a God-fearing man.*

36. Just as leprosy is a vileness that is attached to a person's body, so a wicked wife is a vileness that is attached by the bond of marriage to her husband. The only way to sever that attachment is to divorce her and physically banish her from his house (*Maharsha*).

37. His lifetime is not actually doubled; rather, the great pleasure he derives from her makes it seem as if he lived twice as long (*Rashi*).

Maharsha explains: Fortunate is the man whose wife is beautiful, whether physically or in her deeds, for she prevents him from sinning with other married women, an iniquity whose punishment is *kares* (excision). Hence, *the number of his days is doubled* — that is, he will live a full life in this world, and an eternal one in the World to Come.

38. Though she may not be beautiful, a married woman is endowed with charm by the Evil Inclination. One who does not avoid her may thus be ensnared in the Evil Inclination's trap (*Maharsha*).

39. Literally: to dilute. In Talmudic times these beverages were thick and syrupy, and were drunk only after being diluted with water.

40. For perforce you will frequent her company as well (*Yad Ramah*).

41. In this world (*Maharsha*).

42. They descend to Gehinnom in the World to Come (ibid.).

43. I.e. peddlers of ladies' adornments. It is the nature of their work to deal directly with women, and it often happens that when a husband comes home he finds his wife alone with the peddler. Suspecting the couple of adultery, the husband thrashes the peddler (*Rashi*).

44. Just as a spark causes a smoldering coal to burst into flame, so one who advances the cause of adultery ignites a fire that will destroy all that he possesses (*Rashi*).

45. [This last phrase corresponds to *Jeremiah* 5:27.] Just as feathers of birds in a crowded coop invariably protrude from the coop and are noticeable from the outside, so the houses of these adulterers and panderers are full of deceit, which is obvious to all outsiders (*Maharsha*).

Our elucidation has followed *Rashi,* who interprets *Many are the blows* etc. and *Those who habituate* etc. as two separate maxims. *Yad Ramah* interprets these passages, however, as one continuous maxim, as follows: *Many are the blows* inflicted by *peddlers* of ladies' adornments, which cause women to become haughty and which *habituate* people *to* commit acts of *immorality,* just *as a spark causes a coal to burst into flame.* Indeed, *as a coop is full of birds, so are the houses* of these peddlers *full of deceit* — that is, the adornments they sell transform what is as repulsive as a coop full of birds (a metaphor for adultery) into something attractive, and deceive people into straying after it.

46. See above, notes 26 and 27.

47. Gain the friendship of as many people as you can; however, do not share your secrets with them. Restrict your confidences to the closest and most discreet of your associates (*Rashi*).

48. Literally: the openings of your mouth.

49. I.e. do not share your secrets even with your wife, for she may inadvertently divulge them (see *Maharsha*).

עין משפט
נר מצוה

כ א מיי׳ פ״ב מהל׳ עכו״ם הלכה ב:

הוי אומר מדה טובה מרובה ממדת פורעניות במדה טובה כתיב א) ויצו שחקים ממעל ודלתי שמים פתח וימטר עליהם מן לאכול ובמידת פורענות הוא אומר ב) וארובות השמים נפתחו במידת פורענות כתיב ג) ויצאו וראו בפגרי האנשים הפושעים בי כי תולעתם לא תמות ואשם לא תכבה והיו דראון לכל בשר והלא אדם מושיט אצבעו באור בעולם הזה מיד נכוה אלא כשם שנותן הקב״ה כח ברשעים לקבל פורענותם כך נותן הקב״ה כח בצדיקים לקבל טובתן: רבי עקיבא אומר אף הקורא בספרים החיצונים וכו׳: תנא בספרי צדוקים רב יוסף אמר בספר בן סירא נמי אסור למיקרי א״ל אביי מאי טעמא אילימא משום דכתב [ביה] לא תינטוש גילדנא מאודניה דלא ליזיל משכיה לחבלא אלא צלי יתיה בנורא ואיכול ביה תרתין גריצים אי מפשטיה באורייתא נמי כתב ד) לא תשחית את עצה אי מדרשא אורח ארעא קמ״ל דלא ליבעול שלא כדרכה ואלא משום דכתיב בת לאביה מטמונת שוא מפחדה לא יישן בלילה בקטנותה שמא תתפתה בנערותה שמא תזנה בגרה שמא לא תינשא נישאת שמא לא יהיו לה בנים הזקינה שמא תעשה כשפים הא רבנן נמי אמרוה אי אפשר לעולם בלא זכרים ובלא נקבות אשרי מי שבניו זכרים אוי לו למי שבניו נקבות אלא משום דכתיב לא תעיל דויא בלבך דגברי גיברין קטל דויא הא שלמה אמרה ה) דאגה בלב איש ישחנה ר׳ אמי ור׳ אסי חד אמר ישיחנה מדעתו וחד אמר ישיחנה לאחרים ואלא משום דכתיב מנע רבים מתוך ביתך ולא הכל תביא אל ביתך והא רבי נמי אמרה דתניא רבי אומר לעולם לא ירבה אדם רעים בתוך ביתו שנאמר ו) איש רעים להתרועע אלא משום דכתיב זלדקן קורטמן עבדקן סכסן דנפח בכסיה לא צחי אמר במאי איכול לחמא לחמא סב מיניה מאן דאית ליה מעברתא בדיקני׳ כולי עלמא לא יכלי ליה אמר רב יוסף מילי מעלייתא דאית ביה דרשינן להו אשה טובה מתנה טובה בחיק ירא אלהים תנתן אשה רעה צרעת לבעלה מאי תקנתיה יגרשנה מביתו ויתרפא מצרעתו אשה יפה אשרי בעלה מספר ימיו כפלים העלם עיניך מאשת חן פן תלכד במצודתה אל תט אצל בעלה למסוך עמו יין ושכר כי בתואר אשה יפיה רבים הושחתו ועצומים כל הרוגיה רבים היו פצעי רוכל המרגילים לדבר ערוה כניצוץ מבעיר גחלת ז) ככלוב מלא עוף כן בתיהם מלאים מרמה מנע רבים מתוך ביתך ולא הכל תביא ביתך רבים יהיו דורשי שלומך גלה סודך לאחד מאלף ח) משוכבת חיקך שמור פתחי פיך אל תצר צרת מחר ט) כי לא תדע מה ילד יום שמא למחר איננו ונמצא מצטער על עולם שאינו שלו י) כל ימי עני רעים בן סירא אומר אף לילות בשפל גגים גגו ובמרום הרים כרמו ממטר גגים לגגו ומעפר כרמו לכרמים [סימן זיר״א רב״א משרשי״א חנינ״א טובי״ה ינא״י יפ״ה יוחנ״ן מרח״ם יהוש״ע מקצ״ר] אמר ר׳ זירא אמר רב מאי דכתיב י) כל ימי עני רעים אלו בעלי תלמוד וטוב לב משתה תמיד אלו בעלי משנה רבא אמר איפכא והיינו דאמר רב משרשיא משמיה דרבא מאי דכתיב כ) מסיע אבנים יעצב בהם אלו בעלי משנה ובוקע עצים יסכן בם אלו בעלי תלמוד רבי חנינא אומר כל ימי עני רעים זה מי שיש לו אשה רעה וטוב לב משתה תמיד זה שיש לו אשה טובה רבי ינאי אומר כל ימי עני רעים זה אסטנים וטוב לב משתה תמיד זה שדעתו יפה רבי יוחנן אמר כל ימי עני רעים זה רחמני וטוב לב משתה תמיד זה אכזרי רבי יהושע בן לוי אמר כל ימי עני רעים זה שדעתו

הוי אומר מדה טובה מרובה ממדת פורעניות. דבמידה טובה כתיב דלתות ובמדת פורענות כתיב ארובות ודלת גדול מארובה דד׳ ארובות יש בדלת במסכת יומא בפרק יום הכפורים (דף עו.) אלמא מדה טובה מרובה ומעכשיו אין לתמוה היאך יש באדם כח לקבל שכר כל כך שהרי למדת פורענות נותן הקב״ה כח באדם לקבלו כל שכן שנותן כח באדם לקבל מדה טובה: צדוקים. [שכופרין באל חי]: רב יוסף אמר אף בספר בן סירא. שיש בו דברי הבאי ובא עליהם לידי ביטול תורה: לא תיפשוט גילדנא מאודניה. כלומר לא תטול עורו של דג אפילו מעל אזנו מפני שאתה מפסיד העור דאזיל משכיה לחבלא להפסידא אלא צלי יתיה בנורא ואכול ביה תרתין גריצין שאתה יכול ללוות עור הדג עמו ולאכול בו שתי חלות דהוי לפתן לשתי חלות: גלדנא. שם הדג ל״א להכי נקט מאודניה שדרכו של דג להתחיל הפשטו מאזנו: אי מפשטיה. אי ממשמעותיה קא מתמהת באורייתא נמי כתיב: דלא לבעול שלא כדרכה. דאין הגון לאדם לשנות את דרכו והיינו דקאמר מאודניה: לא יישן. אינו יכול לישן: קטנה. קודם שהביאה שתי שערות: נערה. משהביאה שתי שערות עד שירבה שחור על הלבן הרי היא בוגרת: בנערותה שמא תזנה. משבגרה ראויה היא לנישואין להכי אמר שלא תנשא: דויא. דאגה: מנע רבים. אותם שאין לך עסק עמהם מנעם מתוך ביתך: ולא הכל תביא ביתך. אפילו אותם שאתה מתעסק עמהם לא תביאם תדיר לביתך אלא מבחוץ תדבר עמהם: איש רעים. שיש לו רעים הרבה: להתרועע. לסוף מריעים לו שמתקוטט עמהם: זלדקן. מי שזקנו דקה ומלושה: קורטמן. תדע שחכם וחריף הוא ביותר: עבדקן סכסן. מי שזקנו עבה שוטה הוא: סכסן. כמו כל בר בר חנא סכסא בבבא בתרא (דף עד.): נפח בכסיה. מי שנופח אופיא שבכוסו: לא צחי. בידוע שאינו צמא: אמר במאי איכול לחמא. האומר באיזה לפתן אוכל פת זה: סב לחמא מיניה. בידוע שאינו רעב וקח הלחם מידו שאילו היה רעב היה אוכל: מאן דאית ליה מעברתא בדקניה. שזקנו מחולק ומפולל ויש בין שני שבילות כמין מעבר: כולי עלמא לא יכלי ליה. בערמימותיה דמתוך שחשב כל ימיו בערמות הוא משים ידו לזקנו ומושך כאדם שמחשב עד שנקרחה ל״א גרסינן הכרתא מי שיש לו היכר בזקנו שסעד כולי עלמא שלא סעדו אין יכולין להגיע לכחו ל״א גוורתא והוא לשון קרחה וכל הני דברי רוח ולכך אין קורין בו: דרשינן. כלומר אמרינן להו בפרקא ומשמעינן להו לכולי עלמא כגון כל הני אשה טובה כו׳ אשה רעה לרעת לבעלה מה תקנתו יגרשנה מביתו כך הלשון של ספר בן סירא. אשה רעה מתנה רעה ל״ג: כפליים. מרוב הנאה חשובין ככפליים: אל תט אצל בעלה. למסוך עמו יין ושכר: רבים היו פצעי רוכל. כמה וכמה מכות מקבל רוכל המחזיר בעיר [ונושא] תכשיטי נשים ועסקו עמהם שפעמים שמוצאו בעלה עמה מתיחד עם אשתו ומכהו ופוצעו: המרגילים לדבר עבירה. ניאוף הרי הן כניצוץ מבעיר גחלת כשביב המבעיר את הפחם כך כל אשר להם כלה והולך: גחלת. אקרי פחם שאינו בוער כדאמרינן (ברכות דף נג:) גחלים עוממות. מ״ר: ככלוב. דירה של עופות: רבים יהיו דורשי שלומך. שתהא מתאהב עם הכל ואף על פי כן לא תגלה סודך לכולם אלא לאחד מני אלף: מה ילד יום. מה אירע היום שמא למחר איננו שמת הוא היום: ונמצא. שמיצר על יום שאינו עתיד לראות והיינו עולם שאינו שלו שהוא מצטער עליו ודואג על חנם מיום המחרת שלא תבא עליו צרה: כל ימי עני רעים וטוב לב משתה. פסוק הוא במשלי (טו): בשפל גגים גגו. שעני הוא ואינו יכול להגביהו לפיכך ממטר גגים לגגו שיורד מטר הגגים הגבוהים לגגו ומזלפים עליו הגשמים ואין לו מנוחה אפילו בלילות: במרום הרים כרמו. שאין לו השגת יד לקנות כרם בשפלה בדמים יקרים וקונה לו באחד מן ההרים בזול וכל עפר שהוא מוליא לזבל (ולדייר) מוליך הרוח מן ההר לשאר כרמים שבבקעה ונמצא העני נפסד: בעלי תלמוד. שקשה ללמוד מרוב קושיות וסוגיות שיש בו: משנה. נוחה ללמוד: רבא אמר איפכא. דבעלי תלמוד נהנין מיגיעו שידעו להורות איסור והיתר אבל בעלי משנה שונה ואינו יודע מהו אומר דאין מורין הלכה מתוך משנה: יסכן. יתחמם:

שדעתו

מסורת הש״ס

א) יומא עו. [סוטה יא. וע׳ מ״ש תוס׳ שם ד״ה ולעולם], ב) [ע׳ ברי״ף וברא״ש], ג) ב״ב טז: קידושין פב: [פסחים סה.], ד) יומא עה: סוטה מב., ה) [ברכות סג.], ו) [יבמות סג: ע״ש], ז) כתובות קי: [ב״ב קמו.], ח) ב״ב קמה:, ט) [נדה ז:].

תורה אור השלם

א) וַיְצַו שְׁחָקִים מִמָּעַל וְדַלְתֵי שָׁמַיִם פָּתָח: וַיַּמְטֵר עֲלֵיהֶם מָן לֶאֱכֹל וּדְגַן שָׁמַיִם נָתַן לָמוֹ: [תהלים עח, כג-כד]

ב) בִּשְׁנַת שֵׁשׁ מֵאוֹת שָׁנָה לְחַיֵּי נֹחַ בַּחֹדֶשׁ הַשֵּׁנִי בְּשִׁבְעָה עָשָׂר יוֹם לַחֹדֶשׁ בַּיּוֹם הַזֶּה נִבְקְעוּ כָּל מַעְיְנוֹת תְּהוֹם רַבָּה וַאֲרֻבֹּת הַשָּׁמַיִם נִפְתָּחוּ: [בראשית ז, יא]

ג) וְיָצְאוּ וְרָאוּ בְּפִגְרֵי הָאֲנָשִׁים הַפֹּשְׁעִים בִּי כִּי תוֹלַעְתָּם לֹא תָמוּת וְאִשָּׁם לֹא תִכְבֶּה וְהָיוּ דֵרָאוֹן לְכָל בָּשָׂר: [ישעיה סו, כד]

ד) כִּי תָצוּר אֶל עִיר יָמִים רַבִּים לְהִלָּחֵם עָלֶיהָ לְתָפְשָׂהּ לֹא תַשְׁחִית אֶת עֵצָהּ לִנְדֹּחַ עָלָיו גַּרְזֶן כִּי מִמֶּנּוּ תֹאכֵל וְאֹתוֹ לֹא תִכְרֹת כִּי הָאָדָם עֵץ הַשָּׂדֶה לָבֹא מִפָּנֶיךָ בַּמָּצוֹר: [דברים כ, יט]

ה) דְּאָגָה בְלֶב אִישׁ יַשְׁחֶנָּה וְדָבָר טוֹב יְשַׂמְּחֶנָּה: [משלי יב, כה]

ו) אִישׁ רֵעִים לְהִתְרֹעֵעַ וְיֵשׁ אֹהֵב דָּבֵק מֵאָח: [משלי יח, כד]

ז) כִּכְלוּב מָלֵא עוֹף כֵּן בָּתֵּיהֶם מְלֵאִים מִרְמָה עַל כֵּן גָּדְלוּ וַיַּעֲשִׁירוּ: [ירמיה ה, כז]

ח) אַל תַּאֲמִינוּ בְרֵעַ אַל תִּבְטְחוּ בְּאַלּוּף מִשֹּׁכֶבֶת חֵיקֶךָ שְׁמֹר פִּתְחֵי פִיךָ: [מיכה ז, ה]

ט) אַל תִּתְהַלֵּל בְּיוֹם מָחָר כִּי לֹא תֵדַע מַה יֵּלֶד יוֹם: [משלי כז, א]

י) כָּל יְמֵי עָנִי רָעִים וְטוֹב לֵב מִשְׁתֶּה תָמִיד: [משלי טו, טו]

כ) מַסִּיעַ אֲבָנִים יֵעָצֵב בָּהֶם בּוֹקֵעַ עֵצִים יִסָּכֶן בָּם: [קהלת י, ט]

ליקוטי רש״י

תולעתם. רמה האוכלת את בשרם. ואשם. בגיהנם. דראון. לשון בזיון, וי״ת כמין שתי תיבות די ראייה, עד דיימרון עליהון לדיקיא מיסת חזינא [ישעיהו ו, כד]. גילדנא. שם דג קטן [ב״ב עג:]. גריצין. ככרות עבים [ביצה כא:]. דאגה. פחד שדואג על הפסד שום דבר פן יבואהו [יומא עה.]. כל דאגה שבמקרא לשון יראה הוא כמו אני דואג את היהודים דלדקיהו [יהושע כב,כד]. כל לשון דאגה לשון יראה דוסטי״ר בלע״ז [ש״א י, ב]. איינס״א בלע״ז ובלשונינו טרוא״ר בלע״ז [יחזקאל ד, טז]. דאגה בלב איש ישחנה. ישיחנה מדעתו. ודבר טוב ישמחנה, יעסוק בתורה והיא תשמח את הדאגה שבלבו ותצילנו ממנה, ולדברי האומר ישיחנה לאחרי׳ כך סופו של מקרא ודבר טוב שינחמנו חבירו ישמח את הדאג׳ [משלי יב, כה]. ישיחנה לאחרים. שמא ישיאוהו עלה [יומא עה.]. להתרועע. להתרוצץ [ברכות סג.]. מספר ימיו כפלים. כלומר שמח בחלקו ודומה לו כאילו ימיו כפלים. מאשת חן. של אחרים. רוכל. המוכר בשמים לנשים להתקשט בהן ומצוי בו ניאוף ובא בעלה ופצעו. מבעיר גחלת. כן יצרו מבעירו. ככלוב. קן עופות. שמא למחר איננו. ואיננו בעולם ולא יראה אותה דאגה שהוא מיצר וירא ודואג עליה ונמצא שנצטער אתמול על עולם שאין שלו [יבמות סג:]. ככלוב. הוא מקום שמפטמין בו עופות וכן תרגמו יונתן כבית פיטמא ובלעז פרנ״ק [ירמיהו ה, כז]. כל ימי עני רעים. ואפילו שבתות וי״ט דאמר שמואל שנוי וסת תחלת חולי מעים [משלי טו, ט]. בן סירא אומר. שלמה כתב כל ימי עני רעים אבל בלילות כשישן יש לו מנוחה ובן סירא אומר אף הלילות אין לו מנוחה כי בשפל גגים גגו ונמצא דלף טורדו ביום סגריר. מעפר כרמו לכרמים. זבל ואשפה שהביא לכרמו נשפך לכרמים אחרים שהוא במקום רעוע בהרים ובסלעים במקום שאין עשיר חפץ בו נופל למטה בכרמים של עשירים שהם במקום טוב ומדרון ונוח לעסוק בהן [ב״ב קמו.]. במרום הרים כרמו. שאין בידו ממון לקנות במקום טוב וקונה בראש ההר וכל זבלים שהוא מוציא לו נופל וזב לכרמים שתחתיו [כתובות קי:]. זה בעלי תלמוד. סוגיית גמרא ותרוצי משניות וברייתות וזהו עיקר הגמרא שאם לא הגמרא אין למדין הלכה מתוך משנה כדאמרינן התנאים מבלי עולם (סוטה דף כב). כל ימי עני רעים אלו בעלי תלמוד. שממית עצמו לכוין הלכות ולתרץ הוויות. רבא אמר איפכא. כל ימי עני רעים זה בעל משנה שאינו יכול להורות הלכה מתוך משנתו וגם כי כשחולקות זו על זו אינו יכול לתרץ וטוב לב זה בעל הגמרא שיודע משניות על עיקרם ובקי בטעמיהם ויש בידו כח להורות הלכה למעשה. יעצב. לשון בעצבון תאכלנה (בראשית ג). זה בעל משנה. ששונה משניות כל היום ואין לו אלא צער שמתקשה בטעמיהן ואינו יודע לפרש. יסכן. לשון תמימות כמו ותהי למלך סוכנת (מלכים א א) כלומר שנהנה מהן. זה איסטנים. מי שדעתו קצה ולבו נמאס בכל דבר מגונה שהוא רואה. יפה. שסובל הכל דאינו מזיק לו שום לכלוך ושום דבר מיאוס. זה רחמני. כמה עניים הוא רואה וכמה מאורעות שלבו בוכה תדיר עליהן [ב״ב קמה:]. מסיע אבנים יעצב בהם. מסיע אבנים ממחצבתם בהרים מתיגע בהם. יעצב. לשון יגיעה כמו (בראשית ג) בעצבון תאכלנה כלומר כל אדם לפי מלאכתו עצבונו אף עושה רעה לפי זריעתו יקצור. יסכן בם. יתחמם בם כמו (מלכים א א) ותהי לו סוכנת אף העוסק בתורה ובמצות סופו ליהנות מהם [קהלת י, ט]. מסיע אבנים יעצב בם אלו בעלי משנה. לא שימש תלמידי חכמים ללמוד סברת הגמרא בטעמי המשנה מה הם רשע הוא שאין תורתו על בורייה ואין ללמוד הימנו שע״י הטעמים יש חילוק באיסור והיתר ובדיני ממונות לזכות ולחייב ובטהרות לטמא ולטהר כדאמר בכמה דוכתי מ״ט אמר מר הכי ומר הכי ואמר מאי בינייהו איכא בינייהו כך וכך וערום הוא שהשומע את קולו שונה משניותיו כסבור הוא שבקי בטעמיהם ונוהגין בו כבוד כתלמידי חכמים [סוטה כב.]. ובוקע עצים יסכן בם אלו בעלי תלמוד. סברת טעמי המשניות שממנו יוצאה הוראה אבל המורים הוראה מן המשנה נקראו מבלי העולם במסכת סוטה (דף כ״ב א) [ברכות ה.]. עיקר התורה שממנו הוראה יוצאה גמרא היינו סברת טעמי משנה ותירוצי משניות הסותרות זו את זו וחסורי מחסרא [שם יא.]. לתת סברא להבין בטעמי המשנה והלכה כדברי מי [סוטה מד.].

"אַל תֵּצַר צָרַת מָחָר כִּי לֹא תֵדַע מַה יֵּלֶד יוֹם" – **Do not be distressed by tomorrow's troubles, for you do not know what will happen today;** שֶׁמָּא לְמָחָר אֵינֶנּוּ – **perhaps by tomorrow one will not be** alive,[50] וְנִמְצָא מִצְטַעֵר עַל עוֹלָם שֶׁאֵינוֹ שֶׁלּוֹ" – **and it turns out that he was grieving over a world that was not his.**[51]

"כָּל־יְמֵי עָנִי רָעִים" – Scripture states:[52] ***All the days of a pauper are bad,*** בֶּן סִירָא אוֹמֵר, "אַף לֵילוֹת – **and Ben Sira states: Even the nights** are bad, בִּשְׁפַל גַּגִּים גַּגּוֹ – **for at the base of** other **roofs is his roof**[53] וּבִמְרוֹם הָרִים כַּרְמוֹ – **and at the height of mountains is his vineyard.**[54] מִמְּטַר גַּגִּים לְגַגּוֹ – Thus, **rain from** the higher **roofs runs off onto his roof,**[55] וּמֵעֲפַר כַּרְמוֹ לִכְרָמִים" – **and the soil of his vineyard** is blown **onto** the **vineyards** below.[56]

Six sages apply the aforecited verse from *Proverbs* (15:15) to various types of people:

[סִימָן זֵירָ"א רָבָ"א מְשַׁרְשִׁיָּ"א חֲנִינָ"א טוֹבִיָּ"ה יַנַּא"י יָפֶ"ה יוֹחָנָ"ן מְרַחֵ"ם יְהוֹשֻׁ"עַ מְקַצֵּ"ר] – **[A mnemonic: Zeira, Rava, Mesharshiya, Chanina *Toviyah,* Yannai *Yafeh,* Yochanan *Merachem,* Yehoshua *Mekatzeir.*]**[57] אָמַר רַבִּי זֵירָא אָמַר רַב – **R' Zeira said in the name of Rav:** מַאי דִּכְתִיב "כָּל־יְמֵי עָנִי רָעִים" – **What is** the meaning of that **which is written: *All the days of a pauper are bad?*** אֵלּוּ בַּעֲלֵי תַלְמוּד – **These are the masters of Talmud.**[58] "וְטוֹב־לֵב מִשְׁתֶּה תָמִיד" – And what is the meaning of the second half of that verse: ***But he of a good heart has a continual feast?*** אֵלּוּ בַּעֲלֵי מִשְׁנָה – **These are the masters of Mishnah.**[59] רָבָא אָמַר אִיפְּכָא – **Rava said the opposite,**[60] וְהַיְינוּ דְּאָמַר רַב מְשַׁרְשִׁיָּא מִשְּׁמֵיהּ דְּרָבָא – **and this is what Rav Mesharshiya said in the name of Rava:** מַאי דִּכְתִיב "מַסִּיעַ אֲבָנִים יֵעָצֵב בָּהֶם" – **What is** the meaning of that **which is written** in Scripture:[61] ***He who quarries stones will be aggrieved by them?*** אֵלּוּ בַּעֲלֵי מִשְׁנָה – **These are the masters of Mishnah.** "וּבוֹקֵעַ עֵצִים יִסָּכֶן בָּם" – **And** what is the meaning of the second half of that verse: ***He who fells trees will be warmed by them?*** אֵלּוּ בַּעֲלֵי תַלְמוּד – **These are the masters of Talmud.**[62]

The Gemara cites other interpretations of the verse:

רַבִּי חֲנִינָא אוֹמֵר – **R' Chanina says:** "כָּל־יְמֵי עָנִי רָעִים" זֶה מִי שֶׁיֵּשׁ לוֹ אִשָּׁה רָעָה – ***All the days of a pauper are bad*** – **this** refers to **one who has a bad wife;** "וְטוֹב־לֵב מִשְׁתֶּה תָמִיד" זֶה שֶׁיֵּשׁ לוֹ אִשָּׁה טוֹבָה – ***but he of a good heart has a continual feast*** – **this** refers to **one who has a good wife.** רַבִּי יַנַּאי אוֹמֵר – **R' Yannai says:** "כָּל־יְמֵי עָנִי רָעִים" זֶה אִסְטְנִיס – ***All the days of a pauper are bad*** – **this** refers to **one who is squeamish;**[63] "וְטוֹב־לֵב מִשְׁתֶּה תָמִיד" זֶה שֶׁדַּעְתּוֹ יָפָה – ***but he of a good heart has a continual feast*** – **this** refers to **one who is tolerant.**[64] רַבִּי יוֹחָנָן אָמַר – **R' Yochanan said:** "כָּל־יְמֵי עָנִי רָעִים" זֶה רַחֲמָנִי – ***All the days of a pauper are bad*** – **this** refers to **one who is compassionate;**[65] "וְטוֹב־לֵב מִשְׁתֶּה תָמִיד" זֶה אַכְזָרִי – ***but he of a good heart has a continual feast*** – **this** refers to **one who is callous.**[66] רַבִּי יְהוֹשֻׁעַ בֶּן לֵוִי אָמַר – **R' Yehoshua ben Levi said:** "כָּל־יְמֵי עָנִי רָעִים" זֶה – ***All the days of a pauper are bad*** – **this** refers to

NOTES

50. I.e. perhaps he will die today (*Rashi*). Ben Sira changes from the familiar second-person to the impersonal third-person because he does not want to curse the reader (*Maharsha;* see there for another explanation).

51. I.e. a day he will not see. That is, he suffered and worried about tomorrow's troubles for naught, since he never lived to see that day (*Rashi*).

52. *Proverbs* 15:15.

53. Because he cannot afford to build a higher roof (*Rashi*).

54. The more expensive plots for vineyards are located in the valley, and he cannot afford to buy one (*Rashi*).

55. King Solomon (the author of *Proverbs*) bemoans only the daytime existence of the poor. But at night, when they sleep peacefully, the poor are contented. However, Ben Sira considers even the nights of the poor to be times of suffering, for on rainy nights their sleep is disturbed by the constant runoff beating down on their roofs from the roofs of the higher dwellings of the more prosperous (see *Rashi*).

56. The pauper fertilizes his exposed hilltop vineyard at considerable expense, but the wind sweeps the enriched topsoil onto the vineyards of the wealthier people below, thus causing the pauper a financial loss (*Rashi*). [Since the wind is active at all hours, this represents a second way in which the poor suffer even at night.]

57. The first three words of the mnemonic are the names of Amoraim who apply the verse to Torah scholars. The next two words of the mnemonic, חֲנִינָא טוֹבִיָּה, refer to R' Chanina who applies the verse to different types of wives (one of which is טוֹבָה, *good*). The last six words of the mnemonic, יַנַּאי יָפֶה יוֹחָנָן מְרַחֵם יְהוֹשֻׁעַ מְקַצֵּר, refer to R' Yannai, R' Yochanan and R' Yehoshua, who apply the verse to people with different temperaments (יָפֶה, מְרַחֵם and מְקַצֵּר, respectively).

58. Their days are "bad" in the sense that they are involved in an arduous field of study, for the Gemara contains many difficulties that must be resolved and many discussions that must be mastered (*Rashi*).

59. The study of Mishnah is a relatively easy pursuit (*Rashi*), since it involves little analytic effort. Hence, the study of Mishnah is not a burden – but a veritable "continual feast."

60. Rava reversed the interpretation of the verse, on the grounds that there is more satisfaction in studying Gemara than in studying Mishnah. Although Mishnah is easier to understand, its students do not gain the expertise to decide practical questions of law (see *Sotah* 22a). On the other hand, although Talmud study is difficult, those who persevere gain the clear understanding and the ability to apply their learning to practical legal problems (*Rashi*; cf. *Yad Ramah*).

61. *Ecclesiastes* 10:9.

62. [The Gemara understands *stones* as a metaphor for Mishnah, and *trees* as a metaphor for Gemara. According to Rava, the verse is describing one who is cold and seeks fuel with which to warm himself. The person who quarries rocks for fuel will experience only frustration. Similarly, one who studies Mishnah exclusively will in the end be unable to render a proper ruling in a practical question of law, as was explained above. However, one who procures wood for fuel will be warmed as a result of his efforts. Similarly, one who studies Gemara will gain the ability to decide practical questions of law.]

63. I.e. one who is sickened by the sight of anything repulsive (*Rashbam* to *Bava Basra* 145b ד"ה זה איסטניס).

64. I.e. one who can endure without ill effect anything coarse or repulsive (*Rashbam* ibid. ד"ה יפה).

65. A compassionate person emotionally experiences the distress and misfortunes of others, pities all who suffer, and as a result is constantly sad of heart (see *Rashbam* ibid. ד"ה זה רחמן).

66. [A callous person is not affected by the suffering of others; hence, as long as he prospers, life for him is *a continual feast.*]

שֶׁדַּעְתּוֹ קְצָרָה – **one who is short-tempered;** ,,וְטוֹב־לֵב מִשְׁתֶּה תָּמִיד" זֶה שֶׁדַּעְתּוֹ רְחָבָה – ***but he of a good heart has a continual feast*** – **this** refers to **one who is forbearing.**[1]

The final Amoraic interpretation of the verse:

וְאָמַר רַבִּי יְהוֹשֻׁעַ בֶּן לֵוִי – **And R' Yehoshua ben Levi said:** ,,כָּל־יְמֵי עָנִי רָעִים" – Can it be that ***all the days of a pauper are bad*** – i.e. without exception? וְהָאִיכָּא שַׁבָּתוֹת וְיָמִים טוֹבִים – **But there are the Sabbaths and festivals,** which are times of happiness?![2] כִּדְשְׁמוּאֵל – It may be explained **according to** the teaching **of Shmuel,** דְּאָמַר שְׁמוּאֵל – **for Shmuel said:** שִׁינּוּי וֶסֶת תְּחִלַּת חוֹלִי מֵעַיִים – **A change of routine** with respect to diet **is the beginning of stomach illness.**[3]

A Baraisa discusses disrespectful conduct toward the Torah:

תָּנוּ רַבָּנָן – **The Rabbis taught** in a Baraisa: הַקּוֹרֵא פָּסוּק שֶׁל שִׁיר הַשִּׁירִים – ONE WHO RECITES A VERSE OF *THE SONG OF SONGS* וְעוֹשֶׂה אוֹתוֹ כְּמִין זֶמֶר – AND RENDERS IT A KIND OF SONG by singing it with a common melody[4] וְהַקּוֹרֵא פָּסוּק בְּבֵית מִשְׁתָּאוֹת בְּלֹא זְמַנּוֹ – AND ONE WHO RECITES A [SCRIPTURAL] VERSE IN A BANQUET HALL AT AN INAPPROPRIATE TIME[5] מֵבִיא רָעָה לָעוֹלָם – BRINGS MISFORTUNE TO THE WORLD, מִפְּנֵי שֶׁהַתּוֹרָה חוֹגֶרֶת שַׂק – FOR then THE TORAH DONS SACKCLOTH, וְעוֹמֶדֶת לִפְנֵי הַקָּדוֹשׁ בָּרוּךְ הוּא – STANDS BEFORE THE HOLY ONE, BLESSED IS HE, וְאוֹמֶרֶת לְפָנָיו – AND SAYS,[6] רִבּוֹנוֹ שֶׁל עוֹלָם – "MASTER OF THE UNIVERSE! עֲשָׂאוּנִי בָּנֶיךָ כְּכִנּוֹר שֶׁמְּנַגְּנִין בּוֹ לֵצִים – YOUR CHILDREN HAVE TREATED ME LIKE A LUTE UPON WHICH SCOFFERS PLAY!"[7] אָמַר לָהּ – [GOD] SAID TO [THE TORAH] in reply: בִּתִּי – "MY DAUGHTER! בְּשָׁעָה שֶׁאוֹכְלִין וְשׁוֹתִין בַּמֶּה יִתְעַסְּקוּ – IN WHAT activity, then, SHOULD THEY BE ENGAGED WHEN THEY ARE EATING AND DRINKING?"[8] אָמְרָה לְפָנָיו – [THE TORAH] SAID BEFORE [GOD] in reply: רִבּוֹנוֹ שֶׁל עוֹלָם – "MASTER OF THE UNIVERSE! אִם בַּעֲלֵי מִקְרָא הֵן – IF THEY ARE STUDENTS OF SCRIPTURE, יַעַסְקוּ בְּתוֹרָה וּבִנְבִיאִים וּבִכְתוּבִים – LET THEM ENGAGE IN the study of PENTATEUCH, THE PROPHETS, AND THE WRITINGS;[9] אִם בַּעֲלֵי מִשְׁנָה הֵן – IF THEY ARE STUDENTS OF MISHNAH, יַעַסְקוּ בְּמִשְׁנָה בַּהֲלָכוֹת וּבַהַגָּדוֹת – LET THEM ENGAGE IN the study of MISHNAH, LAWS, AND AGGADOS;[10] וְאִם בַּעֲלֵי תַלְמוּד הֵן – AND IF THEY ARE STUDENTS OF TALMUD, יַעַסְקוּ בְּהִלְכוֹת פֶּסַח בְּפֶסַח – LET THEM ENGAGE IN the study of THE LAWS OF PASSOVER ON PASSOVER, בְּהִלְכוֹת עֲצֶרֶת בָּעֲצֶרֶת – IN the study of THE LAWS OF SHAVUOS[11] ON SHAVUOS, בְּהִלְכוֹת חַג בֶּחָג – AND IN the study of THE LAWS OF SUCCOS[12] ON SUCCOS, and let them not occupy themselves with irreverent singing!"[13]

The Gemara discusses the effect of properly reciting Scriptural verses at a banquet:

הֵעִיד רַבִּי שִׁמְעוֹן בֶּן אֶלְעָזָר מִשּׁוּם רַבִּי שִׁמְעוֹן בֶּן חֲנַנְיָא – **R' Shimon ben Elazar testified in the name of R' Shimon ben Chananya:** כָּל הַקּוֹרֵא פָּסוּק בִּזְמַנּוֹ – **Whoever recites a** Scriptural **verse at the appropriate time**[14] מֵבִיא טוֹבָה לָעוֹלָם – **brings good fortune to the world,** שֶׁנֶּאֱמַר ,,וְדָבָר בְּעִתּוֹ מַה־טּוֹב" – **as it is stated:**[15] ***A word spoken in due season, how good it is!***

The Gemara now discusses the Mishnah's fifth case of one who has no share in the World to Come – namely, the person who incants a Scriptural verse[16] over a wound in order to heal it. The Mishnah stated:

וְהַלּוֹחֵשׁ עַל הַמַּכָּה וכו׳ – **AND ONE WHO INCANTS OVER A WOUND etc.**

The Gemara cites three interpretations of this ruling:

אָמַר רַבִּי יוֹחָנָן – **R' Yochanan said:** וּבְרוֹקֵק בָּהּ – The Mishnah speaks **of one who expectorates on [the wound]** before reciting the verse, לְפִי שֶׁאֵין מַזְכִּירִין שֵׁם שָׁמַיִם עַל הָרְקִיקָה – **for one may**

NOTES

1. This follows *Rashi's* second interpretation. He also defines דַּעְתּוֹ קְצָרָה as an obsessive worrier, and דַּעְתּוֹ רְחָבָה as one who more calmly faces the future (cf. *Rashbam* to *Bava Basra* 145b ד״ה קצרה).

2. [R' Yehoshua ben Levi returns to the simple meaning of the verse, that the poor suffer constant privation.] But do they suffer privation every day? Why, on the eves of each Sabbath and festival day every Jewish community saw to it that the needy were supplied with ample food and delicacies! (*Yad Ramah*). The Sabbath and festival days, then, were oases of respite for the poor. How can the verse state that *all* the days of the poor are bad? (*Rashi*).

3. A poor man is accustomed to eating meager fare during the week. On the Sabbaths and festivals he eats larger amounts of richer foods. As a result of the abrupt change in diet, however, he suffers from stomach ailments. Hence, even the Sabbaths and festivals are considered "bad days" for the poor (see *Rashi*).

4. I.e. any melody other than that indicated by the traditional notes of cantillation. The point is that one ought not think that since the verse is from *The Song of Songs,* whose essence is song, one may sing it as a profane song; rather, it is a part of Scripture and must be recited with the same reverence and attention to tradition with which one recites any other part of the Torah (*Rashi*). *Maharal* explains that when one sings Scriptural verses with his own melody, he concentrates on the musical recital of the verses rather than on their profound intellectual content. This constitutes a negation of the Torah, whose essence is the wisdom it contains.

Yad Ramah suggests that the prohibition applies only if one sings the verses for his own enjoyment. However, if one's intent is to praise God with his song, perhaps using one's own melody is permitted. See also *Yad David* and *Sdei Chemed* (*Asifas Dinim, Zayin* §12).

5. I.e. as he is reclining over his cup of wine he recites Scripture aloud for the amusement of the guests (*Rashi*). Alternatively, he recites verses containing the names of distinguished guests for the purpose of praising those guests (*Ben Yehoyada*). However, if one raises his cup at a festive Yom Tov meal and recites passages from Scripture and Aggadah that pertain to the holy day, he brings blessing to the world, as the Gemara explains below (*Rashi*).

Maharsha explains that "an inappropriate time" refers to any banquet that is not tendered for a religious reason. At such occasions Scripture may not be recited.

6. This, of course, is an allegory; the Torah is not an animate being. Rather, God responds to people's actions on behalf of the Torah (*Yad Ramah*).

7. I.e. I am recited for their amusement, as if I were a musical instrument played at banquets for the amusement of the guests (see *Maharsha*).

8. Since they should not sing Scriptural verses for their enjoyment, and are not permitted to sing secular songs (*Orach Chaim* 560:3), what should they do at their banquets that are not religious occasions? (*Maharsha;* see *Eitz Yosef* and *Mishnah Berurah* 560:14 and 670:8,9).

9. Instead of putting Scriptural verses to music, diners should discuss and analyze them, for they are part of the Torah (*Maharsha*). The Sages teach (*Avos* 3:4): *If three have eaten at the same table and have not spoken words of Torah there, it is as if they have eaten of offerings to the dead idols . . . But if three have eaten at the same table and have spoken words of Torah there, it is as if they have eaten from the table of the Omnipresent.*

10. I.e. Midrash, as well as passages in the Mishnah (and Gemara) that contain stories, parables, and other non-legal matters.

11. In Rabbinic literature the Yom Tov of Shavuos is sometimes called עֲצֶרֶת, *assembly* (see Mishnah *Succah* 5:7, *Rosh Hashanah* 1:2, *Megillah* 3:5, *Bikkurim* 1:3,10).

12. The Torah (*Leviticus* 23:41) refers to the Yom Tov of Succos as חַג לַה׳, *a festival for God,* and the Sages often called it simply הֶחָג, *the festival;* see *Succah* 5:2,5,6; *Rosh Hashanah* 1:2; *Taanis* 1:1,2,3; *Megillah* 3:5 et al.

13. See *Rif* here and to *Berachos* (21b in pages of *Rif*), and *Kallah Rabbasi* §1, for different versions of the Torah's response to God's question.

14. See note 5 above.

15. *Proverbs* 15:23.

16. Such as: כָּל־הַמַּחֲלָה אֲשֶׁר־שַׂמְתִּי בְמִצְרַיִם לֹא־אָשִׂים עָלֶיךָ כִּי אֲנִי ה׳ רֹפְאֶךָ, *All the diseases that I placed upon Egypt, I will not place upon you, for I am* Hashem, *your Healer* (*Exodus* 15:26).

שדעתו קצרה וטוב לב משתה תמיד זה שדעתו רחבה א) ואמר ר' יהושע בן לוי כל ימי עני רעים והאיכא שבתות וימים טובים כדשמואל ב) דאמר שמואל שינוי וסת תחלת חולי מעיים תנו רבנן ג) הקורא פסוק של שיר השירים ועושה אותו כמין זמר והקורא פסוק בבית משתאות בלא זמנו מביא רעה לעולם מפני שהתורה חוגרת שק ועומדת לפני הקב"ה ואומרת לפניו רבונו של עולם עשאוני בניך ככנור שמנגנין בו לצים אמר לה בתי בשעה שאוכלין ושותין במה יתעסקו אמרה לפניו רבונו של עולם אם בעלי מקרא הן יעסקו בתורה ובנביאים ובכתובים אם בעלי משנה הן יעסקו במשנה בהלכות ובהגדות ואם בעלי תלמוד הן יעסקו בהלכות פסח בפסח בהלכות עצרת בעצרת בהלכות חג בחג העיד רבי שמעון בן אלעזר משום רבי ד) שמעון בן חנניא כל הקורא פסוק בזמנו מביא טובה לעולם שנאמר א) ודבר בעתו מה טוב: א והלוחש על המכה וכו': ה) אמר ר' יוחנן ב וברוקק בה לפי שאין מזכירין שם שמים על הרקיקה איתמר רב אמר אפילו נגע צרעת ר' חנינא אמר אפילו ויקרא אל משה תנו רבנן סכין וממשמשין בבני מעיים בשבת ג ולוחשין לחישת נחשים ועקרבים בשבת ד ומעבירין כלי על גב העין בשבת אמר רשב"ג ה במה דברים אמורים בכלי הניטל אבל בכלי שאינו ניטל אסור ואין שואלין בדבר שדים בשבת רבי יוסי אומר אף בחול אסור אמר רב הונא [א] ו (ו) אין) הלכה כר' יוסי ואף רבי יוסי לא אמרה אלא משום סכנה כי הא דרב יצחק בר יוסף דאיבלע בארזא ואתעביד ליה ניסא פקע ארזא ופלטיה ז) ת"ר סכין ז וממשמשין בבני מעיים בשבת ובלבד שלא יעשה כדרך שהוא עושה בחול היכי עביד רבי חמא ברבי חנינא אמר סך ואחר כך ממשמש רבי יוחנן אמר ח סך וממשמש בבת אחת תנו רבנן שרי שמן ושרי ביצים מותרין לשאול בהן [ב] ח) אלא מפני שמכזבין לוחשין על שמן שבכלי ואין לוחשין על שמן שביד לפיכך סכין משמן שביד ואין סכין משמן שבכלי רב יצחק בר שמואל בר מרתא איקלע להאוא אושפיזא אייתי ליה מישחא במנא שף נפקן ליה צימחי באפיה נפק לשוק חזיתיה ההיא איתתא אמרה זיקא דחמת קא חזינא הכא עבדא ליה מלתא ואיתסי אמר ליה ר' אבא לרבה בר מרי כתיב ב) כל המחלה אשר שמתי במצרים לא אשים עליך כי אני ה' רופאך וכי מאחר שלא שם רפואה למה אמר ליה הכי אמר ר' יוחנן מקרא זה מעצמו נדרש שנאמר ב) ויאמר אם שמוע תשמע לקול ה' אלהיך אם תשמע לא אשים ואם לא תשמע אשים אעפ"כ כי אני ה' רופאך אמר רבה בר בר חנה כשחלה ר' אליעזר נכנסו תלמידיו לבקרו אמר להן חמה עזה יש בעולם התחילו הן בוכין ורבי עקיבא משחק אמרו לו למה אתה משחק אמר להן וכי מפני מה אתם בוכים אמרו לו אפשר ספר תורה שרוי בצער ולא נבכה אמר להן לכך אני משחק כל זמן שאני רואה רבי שאין יינו מחמיץ ואין פשתנו לוקה ואין שמנו מבאיש ואין דובשנו מדביש אמרתי שמא חס ושלום קיבל רבי עולמו ועכשיו שאני רואה רבי בצער אני שמח אמר לו עקיבא כלום חיסרתי מן התורה כולה אמר לו ט) לימדתנו רבינו ג) כי אדם אין צדיק בארץ אשר יעשה טוב ולא יחטא ת"ר כשחלה ר' אליעזר נכנסו ארבעה זקנים לבקרו ר' טרפון ור' יהושע ור' אלעזר בן עזריה ור' עקיבא נענה ר' טרפון ואמר טוב אתה לישראל מטיפה של גשמים שטיפה של גשמים בעולם הזה ורבי בעולם הזה ובעולם הבא נענה ר' יהושע ואמר טוב אתה לישראל יותר מגלגל חמה שגלגל חמה בעולם הזה ורבי בעולם הזה ובעולם הבא נענה רבי אלעזר בן עזריה ואמר טוב אתה לישראל יותר מאב ואם שאב ואם בעולם הזה ורבי בעולם הזה ובעולם הבא נענה רבי עקיבא ואמר חביבין יסורין אמר להם סמכוני ואשמעה דברי עקיבא תלמידי שאמר חביבין יסורין אמר לו עקיבא זו מנין לך אמר מקרא אני דורש ד) בן שתים עשרה שנה מנשה במלכו וחמשים וחמש שנה מלך בירושלים [וגו'] ויעש הרע בעיני ה' וכתיב

גם

שדעתו קצרה. משים ללבו כל דאגות חבירו ודואג על כל מה שעתיד לבא עליו: רחבה. ואינו משים ללבו דאגה כל כך ל"א דעתו קצרה רגזן: והא איכא שבתות וימים טובים. שאין לך עני בישראל שאין לו מעדנים: שנוי וסת. משנה וסת ואוכל יותר שאינו רגיל לאכול היינו תחילת חולי מעיים לפיכך אפילו שבתות ויו"ט רעים לו: ה"ג הקורא שיר השירים ועושה אותו כמין זמר. שקורא בנגינה אחרת שאינו נקוד בה ועושה אותה כמין שיר אע"פ שמשיר השירים הוא ועיקרו שיר אסור לעשותו כמין שיר אלא בקריאתו: הקורא פסוק בבית המשתאות בלא זמנו. במיסב על יינו עושה שחיקותיו בדברי תורה וקורא פסוקים בקול רם לשחק בהם בני המשתה אבל אם אומרו בזמנו על המשתה כגון שהוא יום טוב ונוטל כוס בידו ואומר עליו דברי הגדה ופסוקים מענינו של יום מביא טובה לעולם: וברוקק. שכן דרך מלחשים לרקק קודם הלחש ואסור להזכיר פסוק על הלחישה ויש לחשים שדרכן לרקק אחריהם ואומר אותן בלשון לעז ומזכירין להם שם בלשון לעז וא"ל רבי דמותר דאין אסור אלא לוחש אחר הרקיקה דנראה שמזכיר השם על הרקיקה ועוד לא נאסר אלא בלשון הקודש אבל בלעז לא: אפילו נגע צרעת. אפילו לוחש (אחרי האי) קרא דלית ביה שם שמים על הרקיקה שקורא נגע צרעת כי תהיה באדם והובא אל הכהן (ויקרא יג) לשם רפואה אין לו חלק לעולם הבא: ואפילו ויקרא אל משה. שאין בו לא חולי ולא נגע דאין ראוי ללחשו על המכה ואין מזכירו לשם רפואה אלא כסבור הוא להנצל בזכות דברי תורה שהוא הזכיר אסור ללוחשו: וממשמשין במעיים. של חולה בשבת ואין בכך משום רפואה דסיכה איתקש לשתיה: ולוחשין על נחשים ועל עקרבים בשבת. בשביל שלא יזיקו ואין בכך

משום לידה: כלי על העין. שכן דרך ליתן כלי מתכות על העין כדי לקרר העין. א"נ כגון שעושין לאדם שחש בעינו מקיפים עינו בטבעת: כלי הניטל. כגון מפתח סכין וטבעת: בדבר שדים. שכן עושין כשאובדין שום דבר שואלין במעשה שדים והם מגידים להם ואסור לעשות בשבת משום ממצוא חפצך (ישעיה נח): אף בחול אסור. לשאול בשדים כדמפרש לקמן משום סכנה: כי הא דרב יצחק. היה שואל במעשה שדים ובקש השד להזיקו ונעשה לו נס ט) ובלעו הארז: סך ואחר כך ממשמש. הוי שנוי דבחול דרך למשמש ואח"כ לסוך: שרי שמן. יש מעשה שדים ששואלין על ידי שמן וקרי להו שרי שמן והיינו שרי בוהן ויש ששואלין בשפופרת של ביצה וקרי להו שרי ביצים: אלא שמכזבין. לכך נמנעו מלשאול בהן: לוחשים על שמן שבכלי. אותן העושין מעשה שדים דרכן ללחוש על שמן שבכלי ואין דרכן ללחוש על שמן שביד שאינו מועיל לפיכך אדם יכול לסוך על ידו משמן שביד ואין לחוש שמא נעשה בו מעשה שדים ואין בו סכנת השד: שף. סך שמן בפניו: צמחין. אבעבועות מלנ"ץ: זיקא דחמת. רוח של אותו שד ששמו חמת אני רואה בפניך שאחזתך: חמה עזה יש בעולם. על עצמו היה אומר שכעס עליו המקום והכביד חוליו: שכל זמן שהייתי רואה את רבי שאין יינו מחמיץ וכו'. כלומר שהיתה הצלחה בכל מעשיו: אמרתי קבל רבי את עולמו. כל שכרו: רואה רבי בצער. ושכרו משתמר להבא לכך אני שמח: מדביש י). מתקלקל ונעשה צלול מחמת חמימות: כלום חסרתי. שאתה אומר אני סובל עונותי: שגלגל חמה בעולם הזה. ולא לעתיד שמאורות מתחדשות: חביבין יסורין. שמכפרין עליך:

גס

מסורת הש"ס

א) כתובות קי: (נדרים לז) ב"ב קמו., ב) [נדרים לז: וש"נ], ג) [מס' כלה], ד) [ברב אלפס איתא ר' יהושע], ה) שבועות טו:, ו) ס"א ל"ג, ז) שבת קמז:, ח) [עי' ריב"ש בתשובה ל"ב גירס' הנכונה], ט) אולי צ"ל ופלטו הארז, י) [ועפרש"י שבת קנד: ד"ה כשהדביש ובפירש"י ב"מ לח. ד"ה הדביש מאריך קצת ע"ש].

ליקוטי רש"י

קצרה. כמו צרן וקפדן עינו רעה בשלו ובשל אחרים [ב"ב קמה:]. ואמר ר' יהושע בן לוי. כתיב כל ימי עני רעים והא איכא שבתות וימים טובים שיש לו מנות ומזונות שהיו מחלקין לעניים מערב שבת לערב שבת אלא כשמואל אתא קרא לאשמועי' וכולה ר' יהושע קאמר לה. שינוי ווסת. חוק כמו עני שכל ימות החול אוכל פת חריבה ובשבת אוכל בשר הכי גרסי' תחלת חולי מתוך כך מתחיל לחלות ואית דגרסי חולי מעיים [ב"ב קמו.]. אפילו לטובה [כתובות קי:]. הלוחש על המכה. ואומר כל המחלה אשר שמתי במצרים וגו' (שמות טו). וברוקק בה. ברוקק ואחר כך לוחש. שאין מזכירין שם שמים כו'. והכא קאמר כי אני ה' רופאך [שבועות טו:]. לא אשים עליך. ואם אשים הרי היא כלא הושמה, כי אני ה' רופאך זהו מדרשו ולפי פשוטו כי אני ה' רופאך ומלמדך תורה ומצות למען תנצל מהם, כרופא הזה האומר לאדם אל תאכל [דבר זה פן יביאך לידי חולי זה] וכן הוא אומר (משלי ג ח) רפאות תהי לשרך [שמות טו, כו]. ואין דובשנו מדביש. הדביש. יצא טעם דובשנו והחמיץ אשמלי"ר בלעז כמו (איוב לא) ובכל תבואתי תשרש תעקר שרשיה וכמו עד לא ירתק חבל הכסף (קהלת יב) יפתחו רתוקות עבותיה [ב"מ לח.]. קיבל רבי עולמו. כל מנוחתו לעתיד [ערכין טז:]. כי אדם אין צדיק בארץ. לפיכך צריך לפשפש במעשיו [קהלת ז, כ].

עין משפט נר מצוה

כא א מיי' פי"א מהל' עכו"ם הלכה יב סמג עשין ד טוש"ע י"ד סי' קעט סעיף ח:
כב ב מיי' שם טוש"ע שם ועיין בכ"מ:
כג ג מיי' שם הלכה יא וסמג שם טוש"ע שם סעיף ז וטוש"ע א"ח סי' שכח סעיף מו [וברב אלפס עוד במכילתין דף רעו. וגם סמוך לסוף פכ"ב בשבת סט:]:
כד ד ה טוש"ע א"ח סי' שכח סעיף מו [וברב אלפס שם]:
כה ו טוש"ע י"ד סי' קעט סעיף טו [וברב אלפס שם]:
כו ז ח מיי' פכ"א מהל' שבת הלכה כא סמג לאוין סה טוש"ע א"ח סי' שכז סעיף ב:

הגהות הגר"א

[א] גמ' אין הלכה. נמחק תיבת אין: [ב] שם אלא מפני. נמחק תיבת אלא וכ"ב הרא"ש לא גריס לה:

גליון הש"ס

גמ' למדתנו רבינו כי אדם אין צדיק. עי' שבת נה ע"ב תוס' ד"ה ארבעה ובדרשות הרא"ן ח פרשה בא:

תורה אור השלם

א) שִׂמְחָה לָאִישׁ בְּמַעֲנֵה פִיו וְדָבָר בְּעִתּוֹ מַה טּוֹב: [משלי טו, כג]
ב) וַיֹּאמֶר אִם שָׁמוֹעַ תִּשְׁמַע לְקוֹל יְיָ אֱלֹהֶיךָ וְהַיָּשָׁר בְּעֵינָיו תַּעֲשֶׂה וְהַאֲזַנְתָּ לְמִצְוֹתָיו וְשָׁמַרְתָּ כָּל חֻקָּיו כָּל הַמַּחֲלָה אֲשֶׁר שַׂמְתִּי בְמִצְרַיִם לֹא אָשִׂים עָלֶיךָ כִּי אֲנִי יְיָ רֹפְאֶךָ: [שמות טו, כו]
ג) כִּי אָדָם אֵין צַדִּיק בָּאָרֶץ אֲשֶׁר יַעֲשֶׂה טּוֹב וְלֹא יֶחֱטָא: [קהלת ז, כ]
ד) בֶּן שְׁתֵּים עֶשְׂרֵה שָׁנָה מְנַשֶּׁה בְמָלְכוֹ וַחֲמִשִּׁים וְחָמֵשׁ שָׁנָה מָלַךְ בִּירוּשָׁלָיִם וְשֵׁם אִמּוֹ חֶפְצִי בָהּ: וַיַּעַשׂ הָרַע בְּעֵינֵי יְיָ כְּתוֹעֲבֹת הַגּוֹיִם אֲשֶׁר הוֹרִישׁ יְיָ מִפְּנֵי בְּנֵי יִשְׂרָאֵל: [מלכים ב' כא, א-ב]

not mention the name of Heaven over spittle.[17] אִיתְּמַר – In connection with this ruling **it was stated:** רַב אָמַר אֲפִילּוּ ,,נֶגַע צָרַעַת" – **Rav said** that the Mishnah's ruling applies **even** when the incantation does not contain the Name of God – such as when the verse,[18] *If the plague of tzaraas is in a man, he should be brought to the Kohen,* is recited.[19] רַבִּי חֲנִינָא אָמַר אֲפִילּוּ ,,וַיִּקְרָא אֶל־מֹשֶׁה" – And **R' Chanina said** that **even** a verse such as ***And He called to Moses,***[20] which contains neither the Name of God nor any reference to illness or healing, is included in the Mishnah's ruling.[21]

Having discussed prohibited incantations, the Gemara cites a Baraisa that mentions a permitted incantation:

תָּנוּ רַבָּנָן – **The Rabbis taught** in a Baraisa: סָכִין וּמְמַשְׁמְשִׁין בִּבְנֵי מֵעַיִים בַּשַּׁבָּת – WE MAY ANOINT AND MASSAGE THE STOMACH of an ill person ON THE SABBATH,[22] וְלוֹחֲשִׁין לְחִישַׁת נְחָשִׁים וְעַקְרַבִּים בַּשַּׁבָּת – AND WE MAY RECITE ON THE SABBATH INCANTATIONS that ward off SNAKES AND SCORPIONS,[23] וּמַעֲבִירִין כְּלִי עַל גַּב הָעַיִן בַּשַּׁבָּת – AND WE MAY ON THE SABBATH PLACE A UTENSIL ON THE EYELID of one whose eye troubles him.[24] אָמַר רַבָּן שִׁמְעוֹן בֶּן גַּמְלִיאֵל – RABBAN SHIMON BEN GAMLIEL SAID: בַּמֶּה דְבָרִים אֲמוּרִים – UNDER WHAT circumstances IS [THIS LAST RULING] SAID? בִּכְלִי הַנִּיטָּל – WHEN THE UTENSIL is of the type THAT MAY BE HANDLED on the Sabbath;[25] אֲבָל בִּכְלִי שֶׁאֵינוֹ נִיטָּל אָסוּר – HOWEVER, WHEN THE UTENSIL is of the type THAT MAY NOT BE HANDLED on the Sabbath, IT IS FORBIDDEN to place it on the sufferer's eyelid.[26] וְאֵין שׁוֹאֲלִין בְּדָבָר שֵׁדִים בַּשַּׁבָּת – AND WE MAY NOT INQUIRE OF DEMONS ON THE SABBATH;[27] רַבִּי יוֹסֵי אוֹמֵר אַף בַּחוֹל אָסוּר – R' YOSE SAYS: EVEN ON WEEKDAYS IT IS FORBIDDEN to inquire of demons.[28]

The Gemara comments on this last ruling:

אָמַר רַב הוּנָא – **Rav Huna said:** (אֵין) הֲלָכָה כְּרַבִּי יוֹסֵי – **The law does (not)**[29] **accord with R' Yose's** ruling, וְאַף רַבִּי יוֹסֵי לֹא אֲמָרָהּ אֶלָּא מִשּׁוּם סַכָּנָה – **and even R' Yose did not state it except because of** the **danger** that an inquirer will be harmed by the demons,[30] כִּי הָא דְּרַב יִצְחָק בַּר יוֹסֵף – **as** in **this case of Rav Yitzchak bar Yosef,** דְּאִיבְּלַע בְּאַרְזָא – **who was swallowed up in a cedar** tree through the machinations of demons who wished to harm him, וְאִתְעֲבִיד לֵיהּ נִיסָּא – **and** then **a miracle was performed on his behalf:** פָּקַע אַרְזָא וּפַלְטֵיהּ – **the cedar split and discharged him.**[31]

NOTES

17. It was the custom of incantation healers to expectorate on the wound before uttering their incantations. The Mishnah teaches that if in such a case one incants a verse containing the Name of God (such as the verse cited in the Mishnah; see previous note), he loses his share in the World to Come [for such an act is extremely disrespectful]. However, the above ruling does not apply if the incantation was recited in a language other than Hebrew, or if the healer expectorated *after* incanting (*Rashi;* see *Rama* to *Yoreh Deah* 179:8).

18. *Leviticus* 13:9.

19. Rav disputes R' Yochanan's interpretation, holding that even if the verse incanted over spittle for purposes of healing does not contain God's Name, the incantation healer nonetheless forfeits his portion in the World to Come (*Rashi*).

20. *Leviticus* 1:1.

21. Such a verse is not suitable to be recited for healing, since it mentions neither illness nor affliction. Hence, the incantation healer does not intend that the verse itself should effect a cure, but that a cure should come in the merit of his reciting words of Torah. Even so, holds R' Chanina, one who recites such a verse loses his portion in the World to Come (*Rashi*).

Rif, Rosh and *Yad Ramah* all rule that the halachah accords with R' Yochanan's interpretation of the Mishnah. Hence, one forfeits his portion in the World to Come only if he incants over spittle a verse that contains God's Name. Citing *Shevuos* 15b, *Rif* and *Rosh* rule that it is nonetheless prohibited to effect a healing "with words of Torah" even if the verse does not contain God's Name and even if it is not incanted over spittle. It is permissible, however, for a healthy person to recite verses for protection against threats to his health, and for a dangerously ill person to employ any method of incantation (see also *Yoreh Deah* 179:8).

22. Even though this is done for healing purposes, and in the absence of a grave health risk healing procedures may not be performed on the Sabbath (by Rabbinic decree, lest one perform the forbidden labor of *grinding* while preparing medicines), this procedure is permitted so long as it is performed in an unusual manner (see below). *Rashi* and *Yad Ramah* explain that the law is lenient here because anointing is likened to drinking (see *Rashi* to *Yevamos* 74a ד״ה שמותר, and *Orach Chaim* 327:2).

23. Although the incantation prevents these dangerous creatures from causing injury, this is not considered an act of *trapping,* which is one of the thirty-nine labors prohibited on the Sabbath (*Rashi*). See *Be'er Sheva,* who takes issue with *Rashi's* interpretation, and argues that the Baraisa's point is that incanting in this situation is not considered a proscribed act of *healing.*

Rambam (Hil. Avodas Kochavim 11:11) understands that the Baraisa speaks of where someone has already been bitten by a snake or scorpion. Although incanting over the wound would be futile (and thus could constitute "idle talk," which is forbidden on the Sabbath; see *Isaiah* 58:13), the Baraisa nonetheless permits it, since it serves the purpose of alleviating the victim's mental distress (see *Kesef Mishneh* there, and *Be'er Sheva*).

24. We may place a cold metal utensil on an aching eye in order to cool and soothe it, or encircle the eye with a ring or other utensil in order to prevent any swelling from spreading (*Rashi;* see *Orach Chaim* 328:46 with *Mishnah Berurah* 144). The Baraisa's point is that since these treatments are accomplished with whole metal objects and not with crushed herbs, the Rabbis were not compelled to proscribe them to prevent people from inadvertently performing the forbidden labor of *grinding* (*Yad Ramah*).

25. For example, when he uses a key, a knife or a ring [which are not *muktzeh* (forbidden to move on the Sabbath – see Glossary)] (*Rashi*).

26. The procedure is prohibited in this instance because the utensil is *muktzeh* (see *Orach Chaim* 328:46; cf. *Pri Megadim*).

27. It was an ancient practice of those who lost property to inquire of demons as to the whereabouts of the missing articles. However, the prophet declared that we are to honor the Sabbath by *not doing your ways, nor pursuing your business, nor speaking thereof (Isaiah* 58:13). It is therefore improper to inquire after one's lost article (*pursuing your business*) on the Sabbath day (*Rashi*). The Tanna Kamma's statement implies that otherwise it is proper to inquire of demons. See below.

28. R' Yose's reasoning will be explained below.

29. *Hagahos HaGra* deletes the word אין (*not*), and it does not appear in the texts of *Rif, Rosh* and *Ramban*; see *Margaliyos HaYam.*

30. Sometimes the demon becomes angered when compelled to disclose information, and it wishes to kill the inquirer (*Yad Ramah*).

Although the Torah prohibits performing acts of sorcery (see *Exodus* 22:17), *Ramban* questions whether the act of conjuring demons is included in the prohibition. If it is not (on the grounds that they are different activities), then certainly consulting demons is permitted. And even if conjuring is forbidden, it is nonetheless permitted to consult demons conjured by a non-Jew (*Teshuvos Rashba HaMeyuchasos LeRamban* §283; *Teshuvas Rivash* §92; cf. *Radvaz* I:485).

31. [Our translation follows the text of *Rashash* and *Mesoras HaShas. Rashi* apparently had a different text, in which the demons sought to harm Rav Yitzchak and a miracle was performed on his behalf – he was swallowed up in a cedar tree, and saved.]

When Rav Yitzchak bar Yosef consulted a demon, the demon wanted to harm him, but a miracle was performed to save him (*Rashi; Yad Ramah*).

Yad Ramah explains that although God could just as easily have saved Rav Yitzchak by dispatching the demon, He wanted to show Rav Yitzchak a great miracle.

שדעתו קצרה וטוב לב משתה תמיד זה שדעתו רחבה (א) ואמר ר' יהושע בן לוי כל ימי עני רעים והאיכא שבתות וימים טובים כדשמואל (ב) דאמר שמואל שינוי וסת תחלת חולי מעיים תנו רבנן (ג) הקורא פסוק של שיר השירים ועושה אותו כמין זמר והקורא פסוק בבית משתאות בלא זמנו מביא רעה לעולם מפני שהתורה חוגרת שק ועומדת לפני הקב"ה ואומרת לפניו רבונו של עולם עשאוני בניך ככנור שמנגנין בו לצים אמר לה בתי בשעה שאוכלין ושותין במה יתעסקו אמרה לפניו רבונו של עולם אם בעלי מקרא הן יעסקו בתורה ובנביאים ובכתובים אם בעלי משנה הן יעסקו במשנה בהלכות ובהגדות ואם בעלי תלמוד הן יעסקו בהלכות פסח בפסח בהלכות עצרת בעצרת בהלכות חג בחג העיד רבי שמעון בן אלעזר משום רבי (ד) שמעון בן חנניא כל הקורא פסוק בזמנו מביא טובה לעולם שנאמר (א) ודבר בעתו מה טוב: א והלוחש על המכה וכו': (ה) אמר ר' יוחנן ב וברוקק בה לפי שאין מזכירין שם שמים על הרקיקה איתמר רב אמר אפילו נגע צרעת ר' חנינא אמר אפילו ויקרא אל משה תנו רבנן סכין וממשמשין בבני מעיים בשבת ג ולוחשין לחישת נחשים ועקרבים בשבת ד ומעבירין כלי על גב העין בשבת אמר רשב"ג ה במה דברים אמורים בכלי הניטל אבל בכלי שאינו ניטל אסור ואין שואלין בדבר שדים בשבת רבי יוסי אומר אף בחול אסור אמר רב הונא [א] ו ((ו) אין) הלכה כר' יוסי ואף רבי יוסי לא אמרה אלא משום סכנה כי הא דרב יצחק בר יוסף דאיבלע בארזא ואתעביד ליה ניסא פקע ארזא ופלטיה (ז) ת"ר סכין ז וממשמשין בבני מעיים בשבת ובלבד שלא יעשה כדרך שהוא עושה בחול היכי עביד רבי חמא ברבי חנינא אמר סך ואחר כך ממשמש רבי יוחנן אמר ח סך וממשמש בבת אחת תנו רבנן שרי שמן ושרי ביצים מותרין לשאול בהן [ב] (ח) אלא מפני שמכזבין לוחשין על שמן שבכלי ואין לוחשין על שמן שביד לפיכך סכין משמן שביד ואין סכין משמן שבכלי רב יצחק בר שמואל בר מרתא איקלע להההוא אושפיזא אייתי ליה מישחא במנא שף נפקן ליה צימחי באפיה נפק לשוק חזיתיה ההיא איתתא אמרה זיקא דחמת קא חזינא הכא עבדא ליה מלתא ואיתסי אמר ליה ר' אבא לרבה בר מרי כתיב (ב) כל המחלה אשר שמתי במצרים לא אשים עליך כי אני ה' רופאך וכי מאחר שלא שם רפואה למה אמר ליה הכי אמר ר' יוחנן מקרא זה מעצמו נדרש שנאמר (ב) ויאמר אם שמוע תשמע לקול ה' אלהיך אם תשמע לא אשים ואם לא תשמע אשים אעפ"כ כי אני ה' רופאך אמר רבה בר בר חנה כשחלה ר' אליעזר נכנסו תלמידיו לבקרו אמר להן חמה עזה יש בעולם התחילו הן בוכין ורבי עקיבא משחק אמרו לו למה אתה משחק אמר להן וכי מפני מה אתם בוכים אמרו לו אפשר ספר תורה שרוי בצער ולא נבכה אמר להן לכך אני משחק כל זמן שאני רואה רבי שאין יינו מחמיץ ואין פשתנו לוקה ואין שמנו מבאיש ואין דובשנו מדביש אמרתי שמא חס ושלום קיבל רבי עולמו ועכשיו שאני רואה רבי בצער אני שמח אמר לו עקיבא כלום חיסרתי מן התורה כולה אמר לו ° לימדתנו רבינו (ג) כי אדם אין צדיק בארץ אשר יעשה טוב ולא יחטא ת"ר כשחלה ר' אליעזר נכנסו ארבעה זקנים לבקרו ר' טרפון ור' יהושע ור' אלעזר בן עזריה ור' עקיבא נענה ר' טרפון ואמר טוב אתה לישראל מטיפה של גשמים שטיפה של גשמים בעולם הזה ורבי בעולם הזה ובעולם הבא נענה ר' יהושע ואמר טוב אתה לישראל יותר מגלגל חמה שגלגל חמה בעולם הזה ורבי בעולם הזה ובעולם הבא נענה רבי אלעזר בן עזריה ואמר טוב אתה לישראל יותר מאב ואם שאב ואם בעולם הזה ורבי בעולם הזה ובעולם הבא נענה רבי עקיבא ואמר חביבין יסורין אמר להם סמכוני ואשמעה דברי עקיבא תלמידי שאמר חביבין יסורין אמר לו עקיבא זו מנין לך אמר מקרא אני דורש (ד) בן שתים עשרה שנה מנשה במלכו וחמשים וחמש שנה מלך בירושלים [וגו'] ויעש הרע בעיני ה' וכתיב

גם

שדעתו קצרה. מסים ללבו כל דאגות חבירו ודואג על כל מה שעתיד לבא עליו: רחבה. ואינו מסים ללבו דאגה כל כך ל"א דעתו קצרה רגזן: והא איכא שבתות וימים טובים. שאין לך עני בישראל שאין לו מעדנים: שנוי וסת. משנה וסת ואוכל יותר שאינו רגיל לאכול היינו תחילת חולי מעיים לפיכך אפילו שבתות ויו"ט רעים לו: ה"ג הקורא שיר השירים ועושה אותו כמין זמר. שקורא בנגינה אחרת שאינו נקוד בה ועושה אותה כמין שיר אע"פ שמשיר השירים הוא ועיקרו שיר אסור לעשותו כמין שיר אלא בקריאתו: הקורא פסוק בבית המשתאות בלא זמנו. במיסב על יינו עושה שחיקותיו בדברי תורה וקורא פסוקים בקול רם לשחק בהם בני המשתה אבל אם אומרו בזמנו על המשתה כגון שהוא יום טוב ונוטל כוס בידו ואומר עליו דברי הגדה ופסוקים מעניינו של יום מביא טובה לעולם: וברוקק. שכן דרך מלחשים לרקק קודם הלחש ואסור להזכיר פסוק על הלחישה ויש לחשים שדרכן לרקק אחריהם ואומר אותן בלשון לעז ומזכירין להם שם בלשון לעז וא"ל רבי דמותר דאין אסור אלא לוחש אחר הרקיקה דנראה שמזכיר השם על הרקיקה ועוד לא נאסר אלא בלשון הקודש אבל בלעז לא: אפילו נגע צרעת. אפילו לוחש (אחרי האי) קרא דלית ביה שם שמים על הרקיקה שקורא נגע צרעת כי תהיה באדם והובא אל הכהן (ויקרא יג) לשם רפואה אין לו חלק לעולם הבא: ואפילו ויקרא אל משה. שאין בו לא חולי ולא נגע דאין ראוי ללחשו על המכה ואין מזכירו לשם רפואה אלא כסבור הוא להנצל בזכות דברי תורה שהוא הזכיר אסור ללוחשו: וממשמשין במעיים. של חולה בשבת ואין בכך משום רפואה דסיכה איתקש לשתיה: ולוחשין על נחשים ועל עקרבים בשבת. בשביל שלא יזיקו ואין בכך משום לידה: כלי על העין. שכן דרך ליתן כלי מתכות על העין כדי לקרר העין. א"נ כגון שעושין לאדם שחש בעינו מקיפים עינו בטבעת: כלי הניטל. כגון מפתח סכין וטבעת: בדבר שדים. שכן עושין כשאובדין שום דבר שואלין במעשה שדים והם מגידים להם ואסור לעשות בשבת משום ממצוא חפצך (ישעיה נח): אף בחול אסור. לשאול בשדים כדמפרש לקמן משום סכנה: כי הא דרב יצחק. היה שואל במעשה שדים ובקש השד להזיקו ונעשה לו נס (ט) ובלעו הארז: סך ואחר כך ממשמש. הוי שנוי דבחול דרך למשמש ואח"כ לסוך: שרי שמן. יש מעשה שדים ששואלין על ידי שמן וקרי להו שרי שמן והיינו שרי בוהן ויש ששואלין בשפופרת של ביצה וקרי להו שרי ביצים: אלא שמכזבין. לכך נמנעו מלשאול בהן: לוחשים על שמן שבכלי. אותן העושין מעשה שדים דרכן ללחוש על שמן שבכלי ואין דרכן ללחוש על שמן שביד שאינו מועיל לפיכך אדם יכול לסוך על ידו משמן שביד ואין לחוש שמא נעשה בו מעשה שדים ואין בו סכנת השד: שף. סך שמן בפניו: צמחין. אבעבועות מלנ"ך: זיקא דחמת. רוח של אותו שד ששמו חמת אני רואה בפניך שאחזתך: חמה עזה יש בעולם. על עצמו היה אומר שכעס עליו המקום והכביד חוליו: שכל זמן שהייתי רואה את רבי שאין יינו מחמיץ וכו'. כלומר שהיתה הצלחה בכל מעשיו: אמרתי קבל רבי את עולמו. כל שכרו: רואה רבי בצער. ושכרו משתמר להבא לכך אני שמח: מדביש (י). מתקלקל ונעשה נלול מחמת חמימות: כלום חסרתי. שאתה אומר אני סובל עונותי: שגלגל חמה בעולם הזה. ולא לעתיד שמאורות מתחדשות: חביבין יסורין. שמכפרין עליך:

גם

מסורת הש"ס

א) כתובות קי: (נדרים לז) ב"ב קמו., ב) [נדרים לז: וש"נ], ג) [מס' כלה], ד) [ברב אלפס איתא ר' יהושע], ה) שבועות טו:, ו) ס"א ל"ג, ז) שבת קמז:, ח) [עי' ריב"ש בתשובה ל"ב גירס' הנכונה], ט) אולי צ"ל ופלטו הארז, י) [ועפרש"י שבת קנד: ד"ה כשהדבים ובפירש"י ב"מ לח. ד"ה הדבים מאריך קצת ע"ש].

ליקוטי רש"י

קצרה. כמו עצרן וקפדן עינו רעה בשלו ובשל אחרים [ב"ב קמה:]. ואמר ר' יהושע בן לוי. כתיב כל ימי עני רעים והא איכא שבתות וימים טובים שיש לו מנות ומזונות שהיו מתקנין לעניים מערב שבת לערב שבת אלא כשמואל אתא קרא לאשמועי' וכולה ר' יהושע קאמר לה. שינוי וסת. חוק כמו עני שכל ימות החול אוכל פת חריבה ובשבת אוכל בשר הכי גרסי' תחלת חולי מתוך כך מתחיל לחלות ואית דגרסי חולי מעיים [ב"ב קמו.]. אפילו לטובה [כתובות קי:]. הלוחש על המכה. ואומר כל המחלה אשר שמתי במצרים וגו' (שמות טו). וברוקק בה. ברוקק ואחר כך לוחש. שאין מזכירין שם שמים כו'. והכא קאמר כי אני ה' רופאך [שבועות טו:]. לא אשים עליך. ואם אשים הרי היא כלא הושמה, כי אני ה' רופאך זהו מדרשו ולפי פשוטו כי אני ה' רופאך ומלמדך תורה ומצות למען תנצל מהם, כרופא הזה האומר לאדם אל תאכל [דבר זה פן יביאך לידי חולי זה] וכן הוא אומר (משלי ג ח) רפאות תהי לשרך [שמות טו, כו]. ואין דובשנו מדביש. הדבש. יצא טעם דובשו והחמיץ אשמלי"ר בלעז כמו (איוב לא) ובכל תבואתי תשרש תעקר שרשיה וכמו עד לא ירתק חבל הכסף (קהלת יב) יפתחו רתוקות עבותיה [ב"מ לח.]. קיבל רבי עולמו. כל מנוחתו לעתיד [ערכין טז:]. כי אדם אין צדיק בארץ. לפיכך צריך לפשפש במעשיו [קהלת ז, כ].

עין משפט
נר מצוה

כא א מיי' פי"א מהל' עכו"ם הלכה יב סמג עשין ד טוש"ע י"ד סי' קעט סעיף ח:
כב ב מיי' שם טוש"ע שם ועיין בכ"מ:
כג ג מיי' שם הלכה יא וסמג שם טוש"ע שם סעיף ז וטוש"ע א"ח סי' שכח סעיף מו [וברב אלפס עוד במכילתין דף רעו. וגם סמוך לסוף פכ"ב בשבת סט:]:
כד ד ה טוש"ע א"ח סי' שכח סעיף מו [וברב אלפס שם]:
כה ו טוש"ע י"ד סי' קעט סעיף טו [וברב אלפס שם]:
כו ז ח מיי' פכ"א מהל' שבת הלכה כא סמג לאוין פה טוש"ע א"ח סי' שכז סעיף ב:

הגהות הגר"א

[א] גמ' אין הלכה. נמחק תיבת אין: [ב] שם אלא מפני. נמחק תיבת אלא וכ"ב הרא"ש לא גרים לה:

גליון הש"ס

גמ' למדתנו רבינו כי אדם אין צדיק. עי' שבת נה ע"ב תוס' ד"ה ארבעה ובדרשות הרא"ח פרשה כא:

תורה אור השלם

א) שִׂמְחָה לָאִישׁ בְּמַעֲנֵה פִיו וְדָבָר בְּעִתּוֹ מַה טּוֹב: [משלי טו, כג]

ב) וַיֹּאמֶר אִם שָׁמוֹעַ תִּשְׁמַע לְקוֹל יְיָ אֱלֹהֶיךָ וְהַיָּשָׁר בְּעֵינָיו תַּעֲשֶׂה וְהַאֲזַנְתָּ לְמִצְוֹתָיו וְשָׁמַרְתָּ כָּל חֻקָּיו כָּל הַמַּחֲלָה אֲשֶׁר שַׂמְתִּי בְמִצְרַיִם לֹא אָשִׂים עָלֶיךָ כִּי אֲנִי יְיָ רֹפְאֶךָ: [שמות טו, כו]

ג) כִּי אָדָם אֵין צַדִּיק בָּאָרֶץ אֲשֶׁר יַעֲשֶׂה טּוֹב וְלֹא יֶחֱטָא: [קהלת ז, כ]

ד) בֶּן שְׁתֵּים עֶשְׂרֵה שָׁנָה מְנַשֶּׁה בְמָלְכוֹ וַחֲמִשִּׁים וְחָמֵשׁ שָׁנָה מָלַךְ בִּירוּשָׁלָיִם וְשֵׁם אִמּוֹ חֶפְצִי בָהּ: וַיַּעַשׂ הָרַע בְּעֵינֵי יְיָ כְּתוֹעֲבֹת הַגּוֹיִם אֲשֶׁר הוֹרִישׁ יְיָ מִפְּנֵי בְּנֵי יִשְׂרָאֵל: [מלכים ב' כא, א-ב]

Continuing the previous discussion, the Gemara cites a Baraisa that discusses anointing and massaging oneself on the Sabbath: תָּנוּ רַבָּנָן – **The Rabbis taught** in a Baraisa: סָכִין וּמְמַשְׁמְשִׁין בִּבְנֵי מֵעַיִים בְּשַׁבָּת – WE MAY ANOINT AND MASSAGE THE STOMACH ON THE SABBATH וּבִלְבַד שֶׁלֹּא יַעֲשֶׂה כְּדֶרֶךְ שֶׁהוּא עוֹשֶׂה בַּחוֹל – PROVIDED THAT ONE DOES NOT DO so IN THE MANNER THAT HE DOES it ON A WEEKDAY.

The Gemara asks:

הֵיכִי עָבִיד – **How,** then, **should he perform** this treatment? רַבִּי חָמָא בְּרַבִּי חֲנִינָא אָמַר – **R' Chama the son of R' Chanina said:** סָךְ וְאַחַר כָּךְ מְמַשְׁמֵשׁ – One should first **anoint** the stomach **and afterward massage** it, for this is the reverse of the normal, weekday procedure. רַבִּי יוֹחָנָן אָמַר – **R' Yochanan said:** סָךְ וּמְמַשְׁמֵשׁ בְּבַת אַחַת – One should **anoint and massage** the stomach **simultaneously,** for this is a change from the normal, weekday procedure.[32]

The Gemara returns to the subject of consulting demons:

תָּנוּ רַבָּנָן – **The Rabbis taught** in a Baraisa: שָׂרֵי שֶׁמֶן וְשָׂרֵי בֵיצִים מוּתָּרִין לִשְׁאוֹל בָּהֶן – IT IS PERMITTED TO INQUIRE OF OIL-DEMONS AND EGG-DEMONS;[33] אֶלָּא מִפְּנֵי שֶׁמְּכַזְּבִין – HOWEVER, this is not common practice, BECAUSE [THE DEMONS] LIE.[34] לוֹחֲשִׁין עַל שֶׁמֶן שֶׁבִּכְלִי – Those who consult demons UTTER INCANTATIONS OVER OIL IN A VESSEL, for this method is effective, וְאֵין לוֹחֲשִׁין עַל שֶׁמֶן שֶׁבְּיָד – BUT DO NOT UTTER INCANTATIONS OVER OIL IN A HAND, for this method is ineffective. לְפִיכָךְ סָכִין מִשֶּׁמֶן שֶׁבְּיָד – THEREFORE, WE MAY ANOINT the body WITH OIL FROM [SOMEONE'S] HAND, for we may be certain that it was not used for consulting demons, and so is harmless, וְאֵין סָכִין מִשֶּׁמֶן שֶׁבִּכְלִי – BUT WE MAY NOT ANOINT the body WITH OIL FROM A VESSEL, for it may have been used for consulting demons, and is therefore dangerous.

The Gemara illustrates this ruling with the following incident:

רַב יִצְחָק בַּר שְׁמוּאֵל בַּר מָרְתָא אִיקְלַע לְהַהוּא אוּשְׁפִּיזָא – **Rav Yitzchak bar Shmuel bar Marsa** once **came to a certain inn.** אַיְיתִי לֵיהּ מִישְׁחָא בְּמָנָא – **They brought him oil in a vessel.** שָׁף – **He anointed** himself with it, and נָפְקָן לֵיהּ צִימְחֵי בְּאַפֵּיהּ – **boils** subsequently **erupted on his face.** נָפַק לַשּׁוּק – Thus blemished, **he went out to the marketplace.** חֲזִיתֵיהּ הַהִיא אִיתְּתָא – **A certain woman**[35] **saw him,** אָמְרָה – and **said** to him: זִיקָא דַּחֲמַת קָא חָזֵינָא הָכָא – **"I see the spirit of** the demon named **Chamas**[36] **here** on your face!" עָבְדָא לֵיהּ מִלְּתָא וְאִיתַּסִּי – Whereupon **she did something for him,** i.e. she recited the appropriate incantation, **and he was healed.** Thus, we see how harmful it is to anoint oneself with oil that has been used for incantations.

Since the Gemara is discussing that part of the Mishnah which mentions *Exodus* 15:26, the Gemara expounds that verse:

אָמַר לֵיהּ רַבִּי אַבָּא לְרַבָּה בַּר מָרִי – **R' Abba said to Rabbah bar Mari:** כְּתִיב ,,כָּל־הַמַּחֲלָה אֲשֶׁר־שַׂמְתִּי בְמִצְרַיִם לֹא־אָשִׂים עָלֶיךָ כִּי אֲנִי ה׳ רֹפְאֶךָ" – **It is written:**[37] *Any of the diseases that I placed upon Egypt I shall not place upon you, for I am* HASHEM, *your Healer*. וְכִי מֵאַחַר שֶׁלֹּא שָׂם – Now, **inasmuch as** God has promised **that He will not place** any disease upon us, i.e. that we never become ill in the first place, רְפוּאָה לָמָּה – **why** is there a need for His **healing?** אָמַר לֵיהּ – **[Rabbah bar Mari] said to [R' Abba]** in reply: הָכִי אָמַר רַבִּי יוֹחָנָן – **R' Yochanan said thus** concerning that verse: מִקְרָא זֶה מֵעַצְמוֹ נִדְרָשׁ – **This verse is self-explanatory,**[38] שֶׁנֶּאֱמַר ,,וַיֹּאמֶר אִם־שָׁמוֹעַ תִּשְׁמַע לְקוֹל ה׳ אֱלֹהֶיךָ" – **for it is stated** earlier in that verse: *And [*HASHEM*] said, "If you hearken diligently to the voice of* HASHEM, *your God . . ."* אִם תִּשְׁמַע לֹא אָשִׂים – In this verse God explicitly states that *if you hearken* to Me and faithfully observe My commandments, *I shall not place* any disease upon you, וְאִם לֹא תִשְׁמַע אָשִׂים – **and** He thereby implies: **If you do not hearken** to Me, **I shall place** the diseases of Egypt upon you; אַף עַל פִּי כֵן ,,כִּי אֲנִי ה׳ רֹפְאֶךָ" – **nevertheless,** I shall eventually cure you, *for I am* HASHEM, *your Healer*.[39] This is the meaning of the seemingly contradictory language of the latter part of this verse.

From this discussion of illness the Gemara proceeds to a narrative about the illness of R' Eliezer ben Hyrkanos:[40]

אָמַר רַבָּה בַּר בַּר חָנָה – **Rabbah bar bar Chanah said:** כְּשֶׁחָלָה רַבִּי אֱלִיעֶזֶר – **When R' Eliezer took ill,** נִכְנְסוּ תַלְמִידָיו לְבַקְּרוֹ – **his students came in to visit him.** אָמַר לָהֶן – **[R' Eliezer] said to them:** חֵמָה עַזָּה יֵשׁ בָּעוֹלָם – **"There is great anger in the world!"**[41] הִתְחִילוּ הֵן בּוֹכִין – **[All but one of the students] began to weep,** וְרַבִּי עֲקִיבָא מְשַׂחֵק – **but R' Akiva laughed.** אָמְרוּ לוֹ – **[The other students] said to him:** לָמָּה אַתָּה מְשַׂחֵק – **"Why do you laugh?"** אָמַר לָהֶן – **[R' Akiva] said to them:** וְכִי מִפְּנֵי מָה אַתֶּם בּוֹכִים – **"But why are you weeping?"** אָמְרוּ לוֹ – **They said to him:** אֶפְשָׁר סֵפֶר תּוֹרָה שָׁרוּי בְּצַעַר וְלֹא נִבְכֶּה – **"Is it possible that a Torah scroll**[42] **dwells in pain and we do not weep?"**

NOTES

32. See *Orach Chaim* 372:2.

33. I.e. demons who are consulted through the medium of oil or egg-shells (*Rashi*).

34. This is *Rashi's* reading of the Gemara. Others, however, have a variant text, which contains the word בְּשַׁבָּת (*on the Sabbath*) and omits the word אֶלָּא (*however*). According to this version, the reason the Baraisa permits making inquiries of these demons even on the Sabbath is because they lie; that is, one cannot obtain reliable information from them. Hence, consulting such demons is not a violation of the prohibition against *pursuing your business* on the Sabbath day; see note 27 above (*Yad Ramah, Ramban* ibid., *Rivash* 92). For a different approach, see *Rif, Rosh* and *Meiri*.

The explanations of *Rashi* and *Yad Ramah* follow the opinion of the Rabbis who disagreed with R' Yose and permitted the consultation of demons on weekdays (see *Yad Ramah*). That being so, the Baraisa would appear to refute Rav Huna, who ruled above that the law accords with R' Yose (according to the text possessed by many Rishonim; see note 29 above). See *Be'er Sheva*.

35. Who was knowledgeable about incantations (*Yad Ramah*).

36. This follows *Rashi.* According to the second interpretation in *Yad Ramah,* "Chamas" was the name of a sorcerer. Accordingly, the woman exclaims that she sees in Rav Yitzchak's face an evil spirit conjured up by the sorcerer Chamas. See there for a variant text.

37. *Exodus* 15:26.

38. Literally: is expounded by itself. That is, the passage in question can be understood when read together with the first part of the verse.

39. *Eitz Yosef* explains that the purpose of these afflictions is to cure the Jews of the spiritual malaise that caused them to sin in the first place. Hence, the afflictions are remedial, not punitive. All this is indicated by what is written: *If you hearken . . . I shall not place,* because *I am . . . your Healer* – hence, if you obey Me you need no spiritual healing. See *Targum Yonasan* ad loc. Cf. *Rashi* ad loc., and *Maharsha*.

40. Known as R' Eliezer *HaGadol* (the Great), he was one of the main disciples of R' Yochanan ben Zakkai. He compiled the volume of Baraisos entitled *Pirkei DeRabbi Eliezer*.

41. R' Eliezer was speaking of himself, indicating to his disciples that God was angry at him, and thus caused him to suffer a severe illness (*Rashi*). *Maharsha* objects to this interpretation, since R' Eliezer stated that there was anger "in the world." He understands R' Eliezer to mean that God's anger was directed at these students (see there). Still others interpret that R' Eliezer believed that he was suffering for the sins of his generation (*Rif* to *Ein Yaakov*, *Iyun Yaakov*).

42. In *Sotah* (49b), too, R' Eliezer is compared to a Torah scroll, whereas his students R' Yehoshua and R' Akiva are called "well-springs of wisdom." *Margaliyos HaYam* explains that, unlike the latter two, R' Eliezer never said anything that his teacher had not taught

שדעתו קצרה וטוב לב משתה תמיד זה שדעתו רחבה [א] ואמר ר' יהושע בן לוי כל ימי עני רעים והאיכא שבתות וימים טובים כדשמואל [ב] דאמר שמואל שינוי וסת תחלת חולי מעיים תנו רבנן [ג] הקורא פסוק של שיר השירים ועושה אותו כמין זמר והקורא פסוק בבית משתאות בלא זמנו מביא רעה לעולם מפני שהתורה חוגרת שק ועומדת לפני הקב"ה ואומרת לפניו רבונו של עולם עשאוני בניך ככנור שמנגנין בו לצים אמר לה בתי בשעה שאוכלין ושותין במה יתעסקו אמרה לפניו רבונו של עולם אם בעלי מקרא הן יעסקו בתורה ובנביאים ובכתובים אם בעלי משנה הן יעסקו במשנה בהלכות ובהגדות ואם בעלי תלמוד הן יעסקו בהלכות פסח בפסח בהלכות עצרת בעצרת בהלכות חג בחג העיד רבי שמעון בן אלעזר משום רבי [ד] שמעון בן חנניא כל הקורא פסוק בזמנו מביא טובה לעולם שנאמר (א) ודבר בעתו מה טוב: א והלוחש על המכה וכו': [ה] אמר ר' יוחנן ב וברוקק בה לפי שאין מזכירין שם שמים על הרקיקה איתמר רב אמר אפילו נגע צרעת ר' חנינא אמר אפילו ויקרא אל משה תנו רבנן סכין וממשמשין בבני מעיים בשבת ג ולוחשין לחישת נחשים ועקרבים בשבת ד ומעבירין כלי על גב העין בשבת אמר רשב"ג ה במה דברים אמורים בכלי הניטל אבל בכלי שאינו ניטל אסור ואין שואלין בדבר שדים בשבת רבי יוסי אומר אף בחול אסור אמר רב הונא [א] ו ([ו] אין) הלכה כר' יוסי ואף רבי יוסי לא אמרה אלא משום סכנה כי הא דרב יצחק בר יוסף דאיבלע בארזא ואתעביד ליה ניסא פקע ארזא ופלטיה [ז] ת"ר סכין ז וממשמשין בבני מעיים בשבת ובלבד שלא יעשה כדרך שהוא עושה בחול היכי עביד רבי חמא ברבי חנינא אמר סך ואחר כך ממשמש רבי יוחנן אמר ח סך וממשמש בבת אחת תנו רבנן שרי שמן ושרי ביצים מותרין לשאול בהן [ב] [ח] אלא מפני שמכזבין לוחשין על שמן שבכלי ואין לוחשין על שמן שביד לפיכך סכין משמן שביד ואין סכין משמן שבכלי רב יצחק בר שמואל בר מרתא איקלע להההוא אושפיזא אייתי ליה מישחא במנא שף נפקן ליה צימחי באפיה נפק לשוק חזיתיה ההיא איתתא אמרה זיקא דחמת קא חזינא הכא עבדא ליה מלתא ואיתסי אמר ליה ר' אבא לרבה בר מרי כתיב (ב) כל המחלה אשר שמתי במצרים לא אשים עליך כי אני ה' רופאך וכי מאחר שלא שם רפואה למה אמר ליה הכי אמר ר' יוחנן מקרא זה מעצמו נדרש שנאמר (ב) ויאמר אם שמוע תשמע לקול ה' אלהיך אם תשמע לא אשים ואם לא תשמע אשים אעפ"כ כי אני ה' רופאך אמר רבה בר בר חנה כשחלה ר' אליעזר נכנסו תלמידיו לבקרו אמר להן חמה עזה יש בעולם התחילו הן בוכין ורבי עקיבא משחק אמרו לו למה אתה משחק אמר להן וכי מפני מה אתם בוכים אמרו לו אפשר ספר תורה שרוי בצער ולא נבכה אמר להן לכך אני משחק כל זמן שאני רואה רבי שאין יינו מחמיץ ואין פשתנו לוקה ואין שמנו מבאיש ואין דובשנו מדביש אמרתי שמא חס ושלום קיבל רבי עולמו ועכשיו שאני רואה רבי בצער אני שמח אמר לו עקיבא כלום חיסרתי מן התורה כולה אמר לו [ט] לימדתנו רבינו (ג) כי אדם אין צדיק בארץ אשר יעשה טוב ולא יחטא ת"ר כשחלה ר' אליעזר נכנסו ארבעה זקנים לבקרו ר' טרפון ור' יהושע ור' אלעזר בן עזריה ור' עקיבא נענה ר' טרפון ואמר טוב אתה לישראל מטיפה של גשמים שטיפה של גשמים בעולם הזה ורבי בעולם הזה ובעולם הבא נענה ר' יהושע ואמר טוב אתה לישראל יותר מגלגל חמה שגלגל חמה בעולם הזה ורבי בעולם הזה ובעולם הבא נענה רבי אלעזר בן עזריה ואמר טוב אתה לישראל יותר מאב ואם שאב ואם בעולם הזה ורבי בעולם הזה ובעולם הבא נענה רבי עקיבא ואמר חביבין יסורין אמר להם סמכוני ואשמעה דברי עקיבא תלמידי שאמר חביבין יסורין אמר לו עקיבא זו מנין לך אמר מקרא אני דורש (ד) בן שתים עשרה שנה מנשה במלכו וחמשים וחמש שנה מלך בירושלים [וגו'] ויעש הרע בעיני ה' וכתיב

גם

שדעתו קצרה. משים ללבו כל דאגות חבירו ודואג על כל מה שעתיד לבא עליו: רחבה. ואינו משים ללבו דאגה כל כך ל"א דעתו קצרה רגזן: והא איכא שבתות וימים טובים. שאין לך עני בישראל שאין לו מעדנים: שנוי וסת. משנה וסת ואוכל יותר שאינו רגיל לאכול היינו תחילת חולי מעיים לפיכך אפילו שבתות ויו"ט רעים לו: ה"ג הקורא שיר השירים ועושה אותו כמין זמר. שקורא בנגינה אחרת שאינו נקוד בה ועושה אותה כמין שיר אע"פ שמשיר השירים הוא ועיקרו שיר אסור לעשותו כמין שיר אלא בקריאתו: הקורא פסוק בבית המשתאות בלא זמנו. במיסב על יינו עושה שחיקותיו בדברי תורה וקורא פסוקים בקול רם לשחק בהם בני המשתה אבל אם אומרו בזמנו על המשתה כגון שהוא יום טוב ונוטל כוס בידו ואומר עליו דברי הגדה ופסוקים מענינו של יום מביא טובה לעולם: וברוקק. שכן דרך מלחשים לרקק קודם הלחש ואסור להזכיר פסוק על הלחישה ויש לחשים שדרכן לרקק אחריהם ואומר אותן בלשון לעז ומזכירין להם שם בלשון לעז וא"ל רבי דמותר דאין אסור אלא לוחש אחר הרקיקה דנראה שמזכיר השם על הרקיקה ועוד לא נאסר אלא בלשון הקודש אבל בלעז לא: אפילו נגע צרעת. אפילו לוחש (אחרי האי) קרא דלית ביה שם שמים על הרקיקה שקורא נגע צרעת כי תהיה באדם והובא אל הכהן (ויקרא יג) לשם רפואה אין לו חלק לעולם הבא: ואפילו ויקרא אל משה. שאין בו לא חולי ולא נגע דאין ראוי ללחשו על המכה ואין מזכירו לשם רפואה אלא כסבור הוא להנצל בזכות דברי תורה שהוא הזכיר אסור ללוחשו: וממשמשין במעיים. של חולה בשבת ואין בכך משום רפואה דסיכה איתקש לשתיה: ולוחשין על נחשים ועל עקרבים בשבת. בשביל שלא יזיקו ואין בכך משום צידה: כלי על העין. שכן דרך ליתן כלי מתכות על העין כדי לקרר העין. א"נ כגון שעושין לאדם שחש בעיניו מקיפים עינו בטבעת: כלי הניטל. כגון מפתח סכין וטבעת: בדבר שדים. שכן עושין כשאובדין שום דבר שואלין במעשה שדים והם מגידים להם ואסור לעשות בשבת משום ממצוא חפצך (ישעיה נח): אף בחול אסור. לשאול בשדים כדמפרש לקמן משום סכנה: כי הא דרב יצחק. היה שואל במעשה שדים ובקש השד להזיקו ונעשה לו נס [ט] ובלעו הארז: סך ואחר כך ממשמש. הוי שנוי דבחול דרך למשמש ואח"כ לסוך: שרי שמן. יש מעשה שדים ששואלין על ידי שמן וקרי להו שרי שמן והיינו שרי בוהן ויש ששואלין בשפופרת של ביצה וקרי להו שרי ביצים: אלא שמכזבין. לכך נמנעו מלשאול בהן: לוחשים על שמן שבכלי. אותן העושין מעשה שדים דרכן ללחוש על שמן שבכלי ואין דרכן ללחוש על שמן שביד שאינו מועיל לפיכך אדם יכול לסוך על ידו משמן שביד ואין לחוש שמא נעשה בו מעשה שדים ואין בו סכנת השד: שף. סך שמן בפניו: צמחין. אבעבועות מלנ"ץ: זיקא דחמת. רוח של אותו שד ששמו חמת אני רואה בפניך שאחזתך: חמה עזה יש בעולם. על עצמו היה אומר שכעס עליו המקום והכביד חוליו: שכל זמן שהייתי רואה את רבי שאין יינו מחמיץ וכו'. כלומר שהיתה הצלחה בכל מעשיו: אמרתי קבל רבי את עולמו. כל שכרו: רואה רבי בצער. ושכרו משתמר להבא לכך אני שמח: מדביש [י]. מתקלקל ונעשה גלול מחמת חמימות: כלום חסרתי. שאתה אומר אני סובל עונותי: שגלגל חמה בעולם הזה. ולא לעתיד שמאורות מתחדשות: חביבין יסורין. שמכפרין עליך:

גם

מסורת הש"ם

א) כתובות קי: (נדרים לז) ב"ב קמו., ב) [נדרים לז: וש"נ], ג) [מס' כלה], ד) [ברב אלפס איתא ר' יהושע], ה) שבועות טו:, ו) ס"א ל"ג, ז) שבת קמז:, ח) [עי' ריב"ש בתשובה ל"ב גירס' הנכונה], ט) אולי צ"ל ופלטו הארז, י) [ועפרש"י שבת קנד: ד"ה כשהדביש ובפירש"י ב"מ לח. ד"ה הדביש מאריך קצת ע"ש].

ליקוטי רש"י

קצרה. כמו עצרן וקפדן עינו רעה בשלו ובשל אחרים [ב"ב קמה:]. ואמר ר' יהושע בן לוי. כתיב כל ימי עני רעים והא איכא שבתות וימים טובים שיש לו מנות ומזונות שהיו מחלקין לעניים מערב שבת לערב שבת אלא כשמואל אתא קרא לאשמועי' וכולה ר' יהושע קאמר לה. שינוי וסת. חוק כמו עני שכל ימות החול אוכל פת חריבה ובשבת אוכל בשר הכי גרסי' תחלת חולי מתוך כך מתחיל לחלות ואית דגרסי חולי מעיים [ב"ב קמו.]. אפילו לטובה [כתובות קי:]. הלוחש על המכה. ואומר כל המחלה אשר שמתי במצרים וגו' (שמות טו). וברוקק בה. ברוקק ואחר כך לוחש. שאין מזכירין שם שמים כו'. והכא קאמר כי אני ה' רופאך [שבועות טו:]. לא אשים עליך. ואם אשים הרי היא כלא הושמה, כי אני ה' רופאך זהו מדרשו ולפי פשוטו כי אני ה' רופאך ומלמדך תורה ומצות למען תנצל מהם, כרופא הזה האומר לאדם אל תאכל [דבר זה פן יביאך לידי חולי זה] וכן הוא אומר (משלי ג ח) רפאות תהי לשרך [שמות טו, כו]. ואין דובשנו מדביש. הדביש. יצא טעם דובשנו והחמיץ אשמלי"ר בלעז כמו (איוב לא) ובכל תבואתי תשרש תעקר שרשיה וכמו עד לא ירתק חבל הכסף (קהלת יב) יפתחו רתוקות עבותיה [ב"מ לח.]. קיבל רבי עולמו. כל מנוחתו לעתיד [ערכין טז:]. כי אדם אין צדיק בארץ. לפיכך צריך לפשפש במעשיו [קהלת ז, כ].

עין משפט נר מצוה

כא א מיי' פי"א מהל' עכו"ם הלכה יב סמג עשין ד טוש"ע י"ד סי' קעט סעיף ח:

כב ב מיי' שם טוש"ע שם ועיין בכ"מ:

כג ג מיי' שם הלכה יא וסמג שם טוש"ע שם סעיף ז וטוש"ע א"ח סי' שכח סעיף מו [וברב אלפס עוד במכילתין דף רעו. וגם סמוך לסוף פכ"ב בשבת סט:]:

כד ד ה טוש"ע א"ח סי' שכח סעיף מו [וברב אלפס שם]:

כה ו טוש"ע י"ד סי' קעט סעיף טז [וברב אלפס שם]:

כו ז ח מיי' פכ"א מהל' שבת הלכה כא סמג לאוין סה טוש"ע א"ח סי' שכז סעיף ב:

הגהות הגר"א

[א] גמ' אין הלכה. נמחק תיבת אין: [ב] שם אלא מפני. נמחק תיבת אלא וכ"ב הרא"ש לא גרים לה:

גליון הש"ס

גמ' למדתנו רבינו כי אדם אין צדיק. עי' שבת נה ע"ב תוס' ד"ה ארבעה ובדרשות הרא"ן פרשה בא:

תורה אור השלם

א) שִׂמְחָה לָאִישׁ בְּמַעֲנֵה פִיו וְדָבָר בְּעִתּוֹ מַה טּוֹב: [משלי טו, כג]

ב) וַיֹּאמֶר אִם שָׁמוֹעַ תִּשְׁמַע לְקוֹל יְיָ אֱלֹהֶיךָ וְהַיָּשָׁר בְּעֵינָיו תַּעֲשֶׂה וְהַאֲזַנְתָּ לְמִצְוֹתָיו וְשָׁמַרְתָּ כָּל חֻקָּיו כָּל הַמַּחֲלָה אֲשֶׁר שַׂמְתִּי בְמִצְרַיִם לֹא אָשִׂים עָלֶיךָ כִּי אֲנִי יְיָ רֹפְאֶךָ: [שמות טו, כו]

ג) כִּי אָדָם אֵין צַדִּיק בָּאָרֶץ אֲשֶׁר יַעֲשֶׂה טּוֹב וְלֹא יֶחֱטָא: [קהלת ז, כ]

ד) בֶּן שְׁתֵּים עֶשְׂרֵה שָׁנָה מְנַשֶּׁה בְמָלְכוֹ וַחֲמִשִּׁים וְחָמֵשׁ שָׁנָה מָלַךְ בִּירוּשָׁלָיִם וְשֵׁם אִמּוֹ חֶפְצִי בָהּ: וַיַּעַשׂ הָרַע בְּעֵינֵי יְיָ כְּתוֹעֲבֹת הַגּוֹיִם אֲשֶׁר הוֹרִישׁ יְיָ מִפְּנֵי בְּנֵי יִשְׂרָאֵל: [מלכים ב' כא, א-ב]

לְכָךְ אֲנִי אָמַר לָהֶן – [R' Akiva] said to [the other students]: כָּל זְמַן שֶׁאֲנִי מְשַׂחֵק – "For that [very reason] I am laughing! רוֹאֶה רַבִּי – Indeed, as long as I saw my master, R' Eliezer, prospering – שֶׁאֵין יֵינוֹ מַחְמִיץ – for his wine does not ferment and turn into vinegar, וְאֵין פִּשְׁתָּנוֹ לוֹקֶה – his flax is not smitten by hail or blight, וְאֵין שַׁמְנוֹ מַבְאִישׁ – his oil does not turn rancid, וְאֵין דּוּבְשָׁנוֹ מַדְבִּישׁ – and his honey does not spoil – אָמַרְתִּי שֶׁמָּא חַס וְשָׁלוֹם קִיבֵּל רַבִּי עוֹלָמוֹ – I said to myself, 'Perhaps, God forbid, my master has already received his world' (i.e. the full measure of reward for his righteous deeds in this world). וְעַכְשָׁיו שֶׁאֲנִי רוֹאֶה רַבִּי בְּצַעַר – But now that I see my master in pain, אֲנִי שָׂמֵחַ – I rejoice."[43] אָמַר לוֹ – [R' Eliezer] then said to [R' Akiva]: עֲקִיבָא כְּלוּם חִיסַּרְתִּי מִן הַתּוֹרָה כּוּלָּהּ – "Akiva! Is there any precept that I have omitted, i.e. failed to fulfill, from the entire Torah?! Why do you assume that my suffering is due to my sins? What sins have I committed?" אָמַר לוֹ – [R' Akiva] said to [R' Eliezer] in reply: לִימַּדְתָּנוּ רַבֵּינוּ ,,כִּי אָדָם אֵין צַדִּיק בָּאָרֶץ אֲשֶׁר יַעֲשֶׂה־טּוֹב וְלֹא יֶחֱטָא'' – Our master (i.e. R' Eliezer) has taught us the verse:[44] ***For there is not a righteous man on earth who has done good and never sinned;*** hence, you must have some imperfection for which you are now suffering."[45]

Another narrative about R' Eliezer's illness:

תָּנוּ רַבָּנָן – The Rabbis taught in a Baraisa: כְּשֶׁחָלָה רַבִּי אֱלִיעֶזֶר – WHEN R' ELIEZER TOOK ILL, נִכְנְסוּ אַרְבָּעָה זְקֵנִים לְבַקְּרוֹ – FOUR ELDERS, i.e. sages, CAME IN TO VISIT HIM. רַבִּי טַרְפוֹן וְרַבִּי יְהוֹשֻׁעַ וְרַבִּי אֶלְעָזָר בֶּן עֲזַרְיָה וְרַבִּי עֲקִיבָא – They were R' TARFON, R' YEHOSHUA,[46] R' ELAZAR BEN AZARIAH AND R' AKIVA. נַעֲנָה רַבִּי טַרְפוֹן וְאָמַר – R' TARFON SPOKE UP AND SAID to R' Eliezer: טוֹב אַתָּה לְיִשְׂרָאֵל מִטִּיפָּה שֶׁל גְּשָׁמִים – YOU ARE BETTER FOR ISRAEL THAN A DROP OF RAIN, שֶׁטִּיפָּה שֶׁל גְּשָׁמִים בָּעוֹלָם הַזֶּה – FOR A DROP OF RAIN is beneficial IN THIS WORLD, וְרַבִּי בָּעוֹלָם הַזֶּה וּבָעוֹלָם הַבָּא – WHEREAS MY MASTER, by teaching Torah, benefits us both IN THIS WORLD AND IN THE WORLD TO COME! נַעֲנָה רַבִּי יְהוֹשֻׁעַ וְאָמַר – Then R' YEHOSHUA SPOKE UP AND SAID to R' Eliezer: טוֹב אַתָּה לְיִשְׂרָאֵל יוֹתֵר מִגַּלְגַּל חַמָּה – YOU ARE BETTER FOR ISRAEL THAN THE VERY ORB OF THE SUN, שֶׁגַּלְגַּל חַמָּה בָּעוֹלָם הַזֶּה – FOR THE ORB OF THE SUN provides light IN THIS WORLD,[47] וְרַבִּי בָּעוֹלָם הַזֶּה וּבָעוֹלָם הַבָּא – WHEREAS MY MASTER provides light both IN THIS WORLD AND IN THE WORLD TO COME. נַעֲנָה רַבִּי אֶלְעָזָר בֶּן עֲזַרְיָה וְאָמַר – Then R' ELAZAR BEN AZARIAH SPOKE UP AND SAID: טוֹב אַתָּה לְיִשְׂרָאֵל יוֹתֵר מֵאָב וָאֵם – YOU ARE BETTER FOR ISRAEL THAN A FATHER AND MOTHER, שֶׁאָב וָאֵם בָּעוֹלָם הַזֶּה – FOR A FATHER AND MOTHER create life IN THIS WORLD, וְרַבִּי בָּעוֹלָם הַזֶּה וּבָעוֹלָם הַבָּא – WHEREAS MY MASTER creates life both IN THIS WORLD AND IN THE WORLD TO COME.[48] נַעֲנָה רַבִּי עֲקִיבָא וְאָמַר – Whereupon R' AKIVA SPOKE UP AND SAID to R' Eliezer: חֲבִיבִין יִסּוּרִין – PRECIOUS ARE SUFFERINGS, for they effect atonement for you![49] אָמַר לָהֶם – [R' ELIEZER] then SAID TO [THE OTHERS]: סַמְּכוּנִי וְאֶשְׁמְעָה דִּבְרֵי עֲקִיבָא תַּלְמִידִי שֶׁאָמַר חֲבִיבִין יִסּוּרִין – SUPPORT ME,[50] AND I SHALL HEAR THE WORDS OF AKIVA MY STUDENT, WHO SAID, "PRECIOUS ARE SUFFERINGS." אָמַר לוֹ – [R' ELIEZER] thereupon SAID TO [R' AKIVA]: עֲקִיבָא זוּ מִנַּיִן לְךָ – AKIVA, FROM WHERE do YOU derive THIS opinion? אָמַר – [R' AKIVA] SAID in reply: מִקְרָא אֲנִי דּוֹרֵשׁ – I EXPOUND A BIBLICAL VERSE, which states:[51] ,,בֶּן־שְׁתֵּים עֶשְׂרֵה שָׁנָה מְנַשֶּׁה בְמָלְכוֹ וַחֲמִשִּׁים וְחָמֵשׁ שָׁנָה מָלַךְ בִּירוּשָׁלָם [וגו'] וַיַּעַשׂ הָרַע בְּעֵינֵי ה''' – ***MENASHEH WAS TWELVE YEARS OLD WHEN HE BECAME KING, AND HE REIGNED FIFTY-FIVE YEARS IN JERUSALEM ... AND HE DID EVIL IN THE EYES OF HASHEM.*** וּכְתִיב – AND IT IS WRITTEN elsewhere:

NOTES

him (see *Yoma* 66b, *Succah* 27b). See also *Sanhedrin* 68a, where R' Eliezer compares his arms to two Torah scrolls.

43. R' Akiva had thought that the uninterrupted prosperity and success R' Eliezer was enjoying in his lifetime so exceeded the ordinary that it could be explained only as a special Divine gift. Since R' Akiva understood that no person is perfect (see below), he was sure that such a gift could be obtained only at the cost of losing one's reward in the World to Come, and thus only punishment for shortcomings would await the recipient there (see *Arachin* 16b, which states that anyone who experiences absolutely no suffering during a forty-day period has already received his Heavenly reward). However, when R' Akiva saw R' Eliezer suffering, he rejoiced, for he knew that his master was experiencing atonement for his shortcomings in this world, and would receive the full reward for his righteous deeds in the World to Come (see *Be'er Sheva*).

44. *Ecclesiastes* 7:20.

45. *Nefesh HaChaim* (1:6, in the gloss beginning וזה היה) states that while there are people who commit no sins, there are none who "do good and never sin." That is, some flaw invariably creeps into and adulterates their good deeds. [Hence, R' Eliezer may have correctly thought that he committed no sins; however, in some good deed of his there must have been an imperfection.]

46. Some commentators substitute "R' Yose HaGlili" for "R' Yehoshua" (see *Margaliyos HaYam*).

47. However, our sun will not provide light in the World to Come, since light is destined to be recreated (*Rashi;* see above, 91b, and *Pesachim* 68a).

48. These three sages were not merely praising R' Eliezer; rather, they meant to stress his importance to the world and thus to prevail upon God to send him a full recovery (*Rabbi Chaim Shmulevitz*, *Kovetz Sichos Mussar*).

According to *Maharal,* R' Tarfon compares R' Eliezer to a raindrop because rain prepares the earth to yield its fruit. Similarly, through his teachings and his exhortations, R' Eliezer prepares Israel to perform good deeds, which are called "the fruit" of their labors and which gain them entry into the World to Come. R' Yehoshua, however, took exception to this analogy, arguing that the greatest sage of the generation does more than *prepare* Israel for the World to Come. Rather, he actually causes them to realize their potential, for just as by its light the sun allows man to utilize his power of vision, so by his teachings and reproofs a great sage allows Israel to actualize their potential to achieve all that is good and holy. R' Elazar ben Azariah then argued that even this analogy is inadequate to describe R' Eliezer's value, for a great sage does more than inspire his generation to reach their perfection. Like a father and mother who bring a child into the world, a great sage and teacher is regarded as having sired his generation. See also *Ben Yehoyada* and *Einayim LaMishpat.*

49. [Suffering is good for a person, since the pain one feels constitutes punishment for his sins. Thus, when a person suffers he knows that he will not be punished for that sin in the World to Come, where the punishment would be infinitely greater.]

The statements of the first three sages are consistent with their opinion, expressed in the previous narrative, that R' Eliezer had never sinned and that he suffered only to protect the Jewish people. R' Akiva, in turn, is consistent with his point – viz. that it was impossible for R' Eliezer not to have some imperfection (*Iyun Yaakov*).

50. I.e. help me to sit up.

51. *II Kings* 21:1-2.

שדעתו קצרה וטוב לב משתה תמיד זה שדעתו רחבה (א) ואמר ר' יהושע בן לוי כל ימי עני רעים והאיכא שבתות וימים טובים כדשמואל (ב) דאמר שמואל שינוי וסת תחלת חולי מעיים תנו רבנן (ג) הקורא פסוק של שיר השירים ועושה אותו כמין זמר והקורא פסוק בבית משתאות בלא זמנו מביא רעה לעולם מפני שהתורה חוגרת שק ועומדת לפני הקב"ה ואומרת לפניו רבונו של עולם עשאוני בניך ככנור שמנגנין בו לצים אמר לה בתי בשעה שאוכלין ושותין במה יתעסקו אמרה לפניו רבונו של עולם אם בעלי מקרא הן יעסקו בתורה ובנביאים ובכתובים אם בעלי משנה הן יעסקו במשנה בהלכות ובהגדות ואם בעלי תלמוד הן יעסקו בהלכות פסח בפסח בהלכות עצרת בעצרת בהלכות חג בחג העיד רבי שמעון בן אלעזר משום רבי (ד) שמעון בן חנניא כל הקורא פסוק בזמנו מביא טובה לעולם שנאמר (א) ודבר בעתו מה טוב: א והלוחש על המכה וכו': (ה) אמר ר' יוחנן ב וברוקק בה לפי שאין מזכירין שם שמים על הרקיקה איתמר רב אמר אפילו נגע צרעת ר' חנינא אמר אפילו ויקרא אל משה תנו רבנן סכין וממשמשין בבני מעיים בשבת ג ולוחשין לחישת נחשים ועקרבים בשבת ד ומעבירין כלי על גב העין בשבת אמר רשב"ג ה במה דברים אמורים בכלי הניטל אבל בכלי שאינו ניטל אסור ואין שואלין בדבר שדים בשבת רבי יוסי אומר אף בחול אסור אמר רב הונא [א] ו (ו) אין) הלכה כר' יוסי ואף רבי יוסי לא אמרה אלא משום סכנה כי הא דרב יצחק בר יוסף דאיבלע בארזא ואתעביד ליה ניסא פקע ארזא ופלטיה (ז) ת"ר סכין ז וממשמשין בבני מעיים בשבת ובלבד שלא יעשה כדרך שהוא עושה בחול היכי עביד רבי חמא ברבי חנינא אמר סך ואחר כך ממשמש רבי יוחנן אמר ח סך וממשמש בבת אחת תנו רבנן שרי שמן ושרי ביצים מותרין לשאול בהן [ב] (ט) אלא מפני שמכזבין לוחשין על שמן שבכלי ואין לוחשין על שמן שביד לפיכך סכין משמן שביד ואין סכין משמן שבכלי רב יצחק בר שמואל בר מרתא איקלע להוא אושפיזא אייתי ליה מישחא במנא שף נפקן ליה צימחי באפיה נפק לשוק חזיתיה ההיא איתתא אמרה זיקא דחמת קא חזינא הכא עבדא ליה מלתא ואיתסי אמר ליה ר' אבא לרבה בר מרי כתיב (ב) כל המחלה אשר שמתי במצרים לא אשים עליך כי אני ה' רופאך וכי מאחר שלא שם רפואה למה אמר ליה הכי אמר ר' יוחנן מקרא זה מעצמו נדרש שנאמר (ב) ויאמר אם שמוע תשמע לקול ה' אלהיך אם תשמע לא אשים ואם לא תשמע אשים אעפ"כ כי אני ה' רופאך אמר רבה בר בר חנה כשחלה ר' אליעזר נכנסו תלמידיו לבקרו אמר להן חמה עזה יש בעולם התחילו הן בוכין ורבי עקיבא משחק אמרו לו למה אתה משחק אמר להן וכי מפני מה אתם בוכים אמרו לו אפשר ספר תורה שרוי בצער ולא נבכה אמר להן לכך אני משחק כל זמן שאני רואה רבי שאין יינו מחמיץ ואין פשתנו לוקה ואין שמנו מבאיש ואין דובשנו מדביש אמרתי שמא ח"ס ושלום קיבל רבי עולמו ועכשיו שאני רואה רבי בצער אני שמח אמר לו עקיבא כלום חיסרתי מן התורה כולה אמר לו (י) לימדתנו רבינו (ג) כי אדם אין צדיק בארץ אשר יעשה טוב ולא יחטא ת"ר כשחלה ר' אליעזר נכנסו ארבעה זקנים לבקרו ר' טרפון ור' יהושע ור' אלעזר בן עזריה ור' עקיבא נענה ר' טרפון ואמר טוב אתה לישראל מטיפה של גשמים שטיפה של גשמים בעולם הזה ורבי בעולם הזה ובעולם הבא נענה ר' יהושע ואמר טוב אתה לישראל יותר מגלגל חמה שגלגל חמה בעולם הזה ורבי בעולם הזה ובעולם הבא נענה רבי אלעזר בן עזריה ואמר טוב אתה לישראל יותר מאב ואם שאב ואם בעולם הזה ורבי בעולם הזה ובעולם הבא נענה רבי עקיבא ואמר חביבין יסורין אמר להם סמכוני ואשמעה דברי עקיבא תלמידי שאמר חביבין יסורין אמר לו עקיבא זו מנין לך אמר מקרא אני דורש (ד) בן שתים עשרה שנה מנשה במלכו וחמשים וחמש שנה מלך בירושלים [וגו'] ויעש הרע בעיני ה' וכתיב

גם

שדעתו קצרה. משים ללבו כל דאגות חבירו ודואג על כל מה שעתיד לבא עליו: רחבה. ואינו משים ללבו דאגה כל כך ל"א דעתו קצרה רגזן: והא איכא שבתות וימים טובים. שאין לך עני בישראל שאין לו מעדנים: שנוי וסת. משנה וסת ואוכל יותר שאינו רגיל לאכול היינו תחילת חולי מעיים לפיכך אפילו שבתות ויו"ט רעים לו: ה"ג הקורא שיר השירים ועושה אותו כמין זמר. שקורא בנגינה אחרת שאינו נקוד בה ועושה אותה כמין שיר אע"פ שמשיר השירים הוא ועיקרו שיר אסור לעשותו כמין שיר אלא בקריאתו: הקורא פסוק בבית המשתאות בלא זמנו. במיסב על יינו עושה שחיקותיו בדברי תורה וקורא פסוקים בקול רם לשחק בהם בני המשתה אבל אם אומרו בזמנו על המשתה כגון שהוא יום טוב ונוטל כוס בידו ואומר עליו דברי הגדה ופסוקים מענינו של יום מביא טובה לעולם: וברוקק. שכן דרך מלחשים לרקק קודם הלחש ואסור להזכיר פסוק על הלחישה ויש לחשים שדרכן לרקק אחריהם ואומר אותן בלשון לעז ומזכירין להם שם בלשון לעז וא"ל רבי דמותר דאין אסור אלא לוחש אחר הרקיקה דנראה שמזכיר השם על הרקיקה ועוד לא נאסר אלא בלשון הקודש אבל בלעז לא: אפילו נגע צרעת. אפילו לוחש (אחרי הא׳) קרא דלית ביה שם שמים על הרקיקה שקורא נגע צרעת כי תהיה באדם והובא אל הכהן (ויקרא יג) לשם רפואה אין לו חלק לעולם הבא: ואפילו ויקרא אל משה. שאין בו לא חולי ולא נגע דאין ראוי ללחשו על המכה ואין מזכירו לשם רפואה אלא כסבור הוא להנצל בזכות דברי תורה שהוא הזכיר אסור ללוחשו: וממשמשין במעיים. של חולה בשבת ואין בכך משום רפואה דסיכה איתקש לשתיה: ולוחשין על נחשים ועל עקרבים בשבת. בשביל שלא יזיקו ואין בכך משום צידה: כלי על העין. שכן דרך ליתן כלי מתכות על העין כדי לקרר העין. א"נ כגון שעושין לאדם שחש בעינו מקיפים עינו בטבעת: כלי הניטל. כגון מפתח סכין וטבעת: בדבר שדים. שכן עושין כשאובדין שום דבר שואלין במעשה שדים והם מגידים להם ואסור לעשות בשבת משום ממצוא חפצך (ישעיה נח): אף בחול אסור. לשאול בשדים כדמפרש לקמן משום סכנה: כי הא דרב יצחק. היה שואל במעשה שדים ובקש השד להזיקו ונעשה לו נס (ט) ובלעו הארז: סך ואחר כך ממשמש. הוי שנוי דבחול דרך למשמש ואח"כ לסוך: שרי שמן. יש מעשה שדים ששואלין על ידי שמן וקרי להו שרי שמן והיינו שרי בוהן ויש ששואלין בשפופרת של ביצה וקרי להו שרי ביצים: אלא שמכזבין. לכך נמנעו מלשאול בהן: לוחשים על שמן שבכלי. אותן העושין מעשה שדים דרכן ללחוש על שמן שבכלי ואין דרכן ללחוש על שמן שביד שאינו מועיל לפיכך אדם יכול לסוך על ידו משמן שביד ואין לחוש שמא נעשה בו מעשה שדים ואין בו סכנת השד: שף. סך שמן בפניו: צמחין. אבעבועות מלנ"ך: זיקא דחמת. רוח של אותו שד ששמו חמת אני רואה בפניך שאחזתך: חמה עזה יש בעולם. על עצמו היה אומר שכעס עליו המקום והכביד חוליו: שכל זמן שהייתי רואה את רבי שאין יינו מחמיץ וכו'. כלומר שהיתה הצלחה בכל מעשיו: אמרתי קבל רבי את עולמו. כל שכרו: רואה רבי בצער. ושכרו משתמר להבא לכך אני שמח: מדביש (י). מתקלקל ונעשה צלול מחמת חמימות: כלום חסרתי. שאתה אומר אני סובל עונותי: שגלגל חמה בעולם הזה. ולא לעתיד שמאורות מתחדשות: חביבין יסורין. שמכפרין עליך:

גם

מסורת הש"ם

א) כתובות קי: (נדרים לז) ב"ב קמו., ב) [נדרים לז: וש"נ], ג) [מס' כלה], ד) [ברכ אלפס איתא ר' יהושע], ה) שבועות טו:, ו) ס"א ל"ג, ז) שבת קמז:, ח) [עי' ריב"ש בתשובה ל"ב גירס' הנכונה], ט) אולי צ"ל ופלטו הארז, י) [ועפרש"י שבת קנד: ד"ה כשהדבש ופירש"י ב"מ לח. ד"ה הדבש מאריך קצת ע"ש].

ליקוטי רש"י

קצרה. כמו עצרן וקפדן עינו רעה בשלו ובשל אחרים [ב"ב קמה:]. ואמר ר' יהושע בן לוי. כתיב כל ימי עני רעים והא איכא שבתות וימים טובים שיש לו מנות ומזונות שהיו מחלקין לעניים מערב שבת לערב שבת אלא כשמואל אתא קרא לאשמועי' וכולה ר' יהושע קאמר לה. שינוי וסת. חוק כמו עני שכל ימות החול אוכל פת חריבה ובשבת אוכל בשר הכי גרסי' תחלת חולי מתוך כך מתחיל לחלות ואית דגרסי חולי מעיים [ב"ב קמו.]. אפילו לטובה [כתובות קי:]. הלוחש על המכה. ואומר כל המחלה אשר שמתי במצרים וגו' (שמות טו). וברוקק בה. ברוקק ואחר כך לוחש. שאין מזכירין שם שמים כו'. והכא קאמר כי אני ה' רופאך [שבועות טו:]. לא אשים עליך. ואם אשים הרי היא כלא הושמה, כי אני ה' רופאך זהו מדרשו ולפי פשוטו כי אני ה' רופאך ומלמדך תורה ומצות למען תנצל מהם, כרופא הזה האומר לאדם אל תאכל [דבר זה פן יביאך לידי חולי זה] וכן הוא אומר (משלי ג ח) רפאות תהי לשרך [שמות טו, כו]. ואין דובשנו מדביש. הדבש. יצא טעם דובשנו והחמיץ אשמלי"ר בלעז כמו (איוב לא) ובכל תבואתי תשרש תעקר שרשיה וכמו עד לא ירתק חבל הכסף (קהלת יב) יפתחו רתוקות עבותיה [ב"מ לח.]. קיבל רבי עולמו. כל מנוחתו לעתיד [ערכין טז:]. כי אדם אין צדיק בארץ. לפיכך צריך לפשפש במעשיו [קהלת ז, כ].

עין משפט נר מצוה

כא א מיי' פי"א מהל' עכו"ם הלכה יב סמג עשין ד טוש"ע י"ד סי' קעט סעיף ח:

כב ב מיי' שם טוש"ע שם ועיין בכ"מ:

כג ג מיי' שם הלכה יא וסמג שם טוש"ע שם סעיף ז וטוש"ע א"ח סי' שכח סעיף מו [וברב אלפס עוד במכילתין דף רעו. וגם סמוך לסוף פכ"ב בשבת סט:]:

כד ד ה טוש"ע א"ח סי' שכח סעיף מו [וברב אלפס שם]:

כה ו טוש"ע י"ד סי' קעט סעיף טז [וברב אלפס שם]:

כו ז ח מיי' פכ"א מהל' שבת הלכה כח סמג לאוין סה טוש"ע א"ח סי' שכז סעיף ב:

הגהות הגר"א

[א] גמ' אין הלכה. נמחק תיבת אין: [ב] שם אלא מפני. נמחק תיבת אלא וכ"ב הרא"ש לא גריס לה:

גליון הש"ם

גמ' למדתנו רבינו כי אדם אין צדיק. עי' שבת נה ע"ב תוס' ד"ה ארבעה ובדרשות הרא"ח פרשה כא:

תורה אור השלם

א) שִׂמְחָה לָאִישׁ בְּמַעֲנֵה פִיו וְדָבָר בְּעִתּוֹ מַה טּוֹב: [משלי טו, כג]

ב) וַיֹּאמֶר אִם שָׁמוֹעַ תִּשְׁמַע לְקוֹל יְיָ אֱלֹהֶיךָ וְהַיָּשָׁר בְּעֵינָיו תַּעֲשֶׂה וְהַאֲזַנְתָּ לְמִצְוֹתָיו וְשָׁמַרְתָּ כָּל חֻקָּיו כָּל הַמַּחֲלָה אֲשֶׁר שַׂמְתִּי בְמִצְרַיִם לֹא אָשִׂים עָלֶיךָ כִּי אֲנִי יְיָ רֹפְאֶךָ: [שמות טו, כו]

ג) כִּי אָדָם אֵין צַדִּיק בָּאָרֶץ אֲשֶׁר יַעֲשֶׂה טּוֹב וְלֹא יֶחֱטָא: [קהלת ז, כ]

ד) בֶּן שְׁתֵּים עֶשְׂרֵה שָׁנָה מְנַשֶּׁה בְמָלְכוֹ וַחֲמִשִּׁים וְחָמֵשׁ שָׁנָה מָלַךְ בִּירוּשָׁלָיִם וְשֵׁם אִמּוֹ חֶפְצִי בָהּ: וַיַּעַשׂ הָרַע בְּעֵינֵי יְיָ כְּתוֹעֲבֹת הַגּוֹיִם אֲשֶׁר הוֹרִישׁ יְיָ מִפְּנֵי בְּנֵי יִשְׂרָאֵל: [מלכים ב' כא, א-ב]

גם אלה משלי שלמה אשר העתיקו אנשי חזקיה מלך יהודה וכי חזקיה מלך יהודה לכל העולם כולו לימד תורה ולמנשה בנו לא לימד תורה אלא מכל טורח שטרח בו ומכל עמל שעמל בו לא העלהו למוטב אלא יסורין שנאמר [ב] וידבר ה' אל מנשה ואל עמו ולא הקשיבו ויבא ה' עליהם את שרי הצבא אשר למלך אשור וילכדו את מנשה בחוחים ויאסרוהו בנחשתים ויוליכהו בבלה וכתיב [א] [ג] ובהיצר לו חילה את פני ה' אלהיו ויכנע מאד מלפני (ה') אלהי אבותיו ויתפלל אליו ויעתר לו וישמע תחינתו וישיבהו ירושלים למלכותו וידע מנשה כי ה' הוא האלהים הא למדת שחביבין יסורין ת"ר שלשה באו בעלילה אלו הן קין עשו ומנשה קין דכתיב [ד] גדול עוני מנשוא אמר לפניו רבונו של עולם כלום גדול עוני משישים ריבוא שעתידין לחטוא לפניך ואתה סולח להם עשו דכתיב [ה] הברכה אחת היא לך אבי מנשה בתחילה קרא לאלוהות הרבה ולבסוף קרא לאלהי אבותיו[ב]: אבא שאול אומר אף ההוגה את השם באותיותיו וכו': תנא ובגבולין ובלשון עגה: שלשה מלכים וארבעה הדיוטות וכו': ת"ר ירבעם שריבע עם ד"א ירבעם שעשה מריבה בעם דבר אחר ירבעם שעשה מריבה בין ישראל לאביהם שבשמים בן נבט בן שניבט ולא ראה תנא הוא נבט הוא מיכה הוא שבע בן בכרי נבט שניבט ולא ראה מיכה שנתמכמך בבנין ומה שמו שבע בן בכרי שמו תנו רבנן שלשה ניבטו ולא ראו ואלו הן נבט ואחיתופל ואיצטגניני פרעה נבט ראה אש שיוצאת מאמתו הוא סבר איהו מליך ולא היא ירבעם הוא דנפק מיניה אחיתופל ראה צרעת שזרחה לו על אמתו הוא סבר איהו מלך ולא היא בת שבע בתו הוא דנפקא מינה שלמה איצטגניני פרעה[ג] דאמר רבי חמא ברבי חנינא מאי דכתיב [ו] המה מי מריבה המה שראו איצטגניני פרעה וטעו ראו שמושיען של ישראל במים הוא לוקה אמר [ז] כל הבן הילוד היאורה תשליכוהו והן לא ידעו שעל עסקי מי מריבה לוקה ומנא לן דלא אתי לעלמא דאתי דכתיב [ח] ויהי בדבר הזה לחטאת בית ירבעם ולהכחיד ולהשמיד מעל פני אדמה להכחיד בעולם הזה ולהשמיד לעולם הבא אמר רבי יוחנן מפני מה זכה ירבעם למלכות מפני שהוכיח את שלמה ומפני מה נענש מפני שהוכיחו ברבים שנאמר [ט] וזה הדבר אשר הרים יד במלך שלמה בנה את המלוא סגר את פרץ עיר דוד אביו אמר לו דוד אביך פרץ פרצות בחומה כדי שיעלו ישראל לרגל ואתה גדרת אותם כדי לעשות אנגריא לבת פרעה ומאי וזה אשר הרים יד במלך אמר רב נחמן שחלץ תפיליו בפניו אמר רב נחמן גסות הרוח שהיה בו בירבעם טרדתו מן העולם שנאמר [י] ויאמר ירבעם בלבו עתה תשוב הממלכה לבית דוד אם יעלה העם הזה לעשות זבחים בבית ה' בירושלים ושב לב העם הזה אל אדוניהם אל רחבעם מלך יהודה והרגוני ושבו אל רחבעם מלך יהודה אמר[ד] גמירי [א]דאין ישיבה בעזרה אלא למלכי בית יהודה בלבד כיון דחזו ליה לרחבעם דיתיב ואנא קאימנא סברי הא מלכא והא עבדא ואי יתיבנא מורד במלכות הואי וקטלין לי ואזלו בתריה מיד [כ] ויועץ המלך ויעש שני עגלי זהב ויאמר אליהם רב לכם מעלות ירושלים הנה אלהיך ישראל אשר העלוך מארץ מצרים וישם את האחד בבית אל ואת האחד נתן בדן מאי ויועץ אמר רבי יהודה שהושיב רשע אצל צדיק אמר להו חתמיתו על כל דעבידנא אמרו ליה הין אמר להו מלכא בעינא למיהוי אמרו ליה הין כל דאמינא לכו עבידתו אמרו ליה הין אפילו למפלח לעבודת כוכבים אמר ליה צדיק ח"ו אמר ליה רשע לצדיק ס"ד דגברא כירבעם פלח לעבודת כוכבים אלא למינסינהו הוא דקא בעי אי קבליתו למימריה

ואף

רש"י

גם אלה משלי שלמה אשר העתיקו אנשי חזקיה. היינו תלמידי חזקיה כדקיימא לן בהשותפין בבבא בתרא (דף טו.) חזקיה וסיעתו כתבו משלי מכלל דחזקיה היה מלמד לכל וכדאמרן (לעיל דף לד.) נעץ חרב על פתח בית המדרש וכל שכן שלמנשה בנו לימד: מכל טורח שטרח בו. ללמדו: שבאו בעלילה. שלא באו לבקש לפני הקב"ה בתפלה אלא באו בעלילה שאמרו דברים של נצחון שאין להם תשובה: הברכה אחת היא. וכי אין לך ברכה יותר תשובה נצחת השיבו ועלתה לו: מנשה. בא בעלילה שלא להתפלל למקום אלא לבסוף אם לא תושיעני מה הועיל לי שקראתי לך יותר משאר אלהות והיינו דכתיב ויכנע[ה] לפני (ה') אלהי אבותיו מכלל דעד השתא לפני אלוהות אחרים נכנע: תנא. כי אמרינן דהוגה את השם באותיותיו אין לו חלק לעולם הבא בגבולין אבל במקדש לא שהרי בשם היו מברכין: ובלשון עגה. אפילו במקדש לא לשון עגה לעז שאינו הוגה באותיותיו בלשון הקדש שלנו אלא שאר לועזין עגה לשון בלעגי שפה (ישעיה כח) מ"ר ל"א עגה לשון עוגה מקום שיש בו חבורת בני אדם שמדברין דברי חול גבולין קרי חוץ למקדש ואסור לפרש שם בן ארבעים ושתים בלשון עגה חוץ למקדש ואי עבד אין לו חלק אבל בלשון קדש אינו נענש כל כך ובמקדש הואיל ונהגו להזכיר פירושו אינו נענש: שריבע עם. שריבץ את ישראל והשפילם: עשה מריבה בעם. הריבם אלו עם אלו בעסק עבודת כוכבים זה עובד וזה מוחה בידו ובאו לידי מחלוקת: שניבט ולא ראה. היה סבור להביט יפה ולעמוד על דבר עיקר ולא ראה שטעה כדאמרינן לקמן ראה אש יוצאה מאמתו וכו': נתמכמך בבנין. של מצרים שנתנוהו בבנין במקום לבנה כדמפרש באגדה שאמר לו משה להקב"ה אתה הרעות לעם הזה שעכשיו אם אין להם לבנים משימין בניהם של ישראל בבנין אמר לו הקב"ה קוצים הם מכלין שגלוי לפני אילו הם חיים היו רשעים [גמורים] ואם תרצה תנסה והוציא אחד מהן הלך והוציא את מיכה. ל"א נתמכמך עסק בבנין עד שנעשה מך כדאמרינן (סוטה דף יא.) כל העוסק בבנין מתמסכן: הוא סבר איהו מליך. ולכן נתאמן שבע בן בכרי וקבץ כל ישראל אליו והיה רוצה למלוך כדכתיב במקרא: איהו מליך. ולכך נעשה יועץ לאבשלום כדי שתשוב המלוכה מדוד לאבשלום ובין כך ובין כך יתגלגל הדבר ותשוב אליו: על מי מריבה. שבעון שאמר שמעו נא המורים נענש ולא נכנס לארץ ישראל: ומנא לן דלא אתי. ירבעם לעלמא דאתי והכי נמי מפרש לקמן בכלהו שלשה מלכים וארבעה הדיוטות: הוכיח את שלמה. כדמפרש ואזיל דאמר דוד אביך וכו': ומפני מה נענש שהוכיחו ברבים. לביישו: פרץ פרצות בחומה כדי שיעלו. (וירדו) [ויכנסו] בריוח: ואתה גדרת אותם כדי לעשות אנגריא. כדי שיכנסו בשערים לידע מי נכנס כדי לגבות מס לבת פרעה מ"ר ל"א שסגר השערים ועשה מגדל לבת פרעה על אחד מן השערים וכולם עוברים דרך שם כדי שיהיו מלווין עמה לכבדה ולעבדה כל עבודת בית המלך קרי אנגריא ל"א שהיה רגיל שלמה לסגור דלתות העזרה ומצניע מפתחות בידו ודרכו של מלך לישן ג' שעות ביום וישראל עומדין על העזרה עד שיעמוד המלך ואמר לו ירבעם אתה רוצה שיתנו לך אנגריא לבת פרעה אשתך שתתן להם מפתחות: (בית) [את] המלוא. אחת מן הפרצות גדר ומלאו לכותל החומה ובנה שם מגדל לבת פרעה ולאנשים שעובדין לה לעיל מהאי קרא כתיב וירם יד במלך כלומר קם בדברים כנגד המלך ומרד בו: שחלץ תפילין בפניו. שהיה לו לפנות לצד אחר מפני אימת מלכותו ולחלוץ שלא בפניו ל"א חולץ תפילין בפניו לבא להתרים כנגדו בחזקה: חליץ תפילין. אין נכון להיות בגלוי ראש לפני המלך [והוא התחיל במרד בכך להראות ולומר לו שאינו נוהג כמלך]: גמירי דאין ישיבה. הלכה למשה מסיני ולא מקרא: שהושיב רשע אצל צדיק. ואומר להם להעמיד להם צלם אחד בבית אל ואחד בדן הסכימו עמו: אמר לו רשע לצדיק. סלקא דעתך גברא כירבעם פלח לעבודת כוכבים אלא לנסיונהו בעי אם דעתנו שלם עמו נתרצה בדבר וכך היה מטעה רשע לצדיק עד שהיו כולן חתומים שהן היו רוצים ושוב לא היו יכולים לחזור בהן:

ואף

עין משפט נר מצוה

כז א מיי' פ"ז מהלכות בית הבחירה הלכה ו ופי"ד מהל' סנהדרין הלכה יב ופ"ב מהל' מלכים הלכה ד:

ליקוטי רש"י

הברכה אחת. ה"א זו משמשת לשון תמיה כמו (במדבר יג, יט) הבמחנים (במדבר יג, כ) השמנה היא (ש"ב ג, לג) הכמות נבל [בראשית כז, לח]. מיכה שנתמכמך בבנין. עגל מסכה, יש אומרים מיכה היה שם שיצא מתוך דמוסי בנין שנתמעך בו במצרים והיה בידו שם וטס שכתב בו משה עלה שור עלה שור להעלות ארונו של יוסף מתוך נילוס והשליכו לתוך הכור ויצא העגל [שמות לב, ד וער' רש"י כאן]. אחיתופל. נתן עיניו במלוכה כדאמר בחלק ראה אש יוצא מאמתו וכסבור שעתיד למלוך ומה שבידו נטלו הימנו לא יחצו ימיהם [סוטה ט: וצ"ע מגירסא המובא כאן]. איצטגניני. איצטגנינות דכל התלמוד לשון מזלות וחוזים בכוכבים [לעיל מט:]. איצטגניני פרעה. כך דרך איצטגנינין אין רואין אלא סימן אבל לא פירושו של כל דבר. ראו. אצטגניני פרעה. שמושיען של ישראל כו'. וכדרבי אלעזר דאמר שאין יודעים מה הוגין הילכך ראו המצרים ולא ידעו מה ראו [סוטה יב:]. יום שנולד משה אמרו לו אצטגניניו היום נולד מושיען ואין אנו יודעין אם ממצרים אם מישראל ורואין אנו שסופו ללקות במים לפיכך גזר אותו היום אף על המצרים שנאמר כל הבן הילוד ולא נאמר הילוד לעברים והם לא היו יודעים שסופו ללקות על מי מריבה [שמות א, כב]. המה מי מריבה. הם הנזכרים במקום אחר את אלו ראו אצטגניני פרעה שמושיען של ישראל לוקה במים לכך גזרו (שמות א, כב) כל הבן הילוד היאורה תשליכוהו [במדבר כ, יג]. וזה הדבר. אשר הוכיחו עליו. שלמה בנה את המלוא. ובנין זה סגר את פרץ העיר דוד שהיה הפרץ אחורי המלוא אמר לו אביך פרץ פרצות בחומה ליכנס בו עולי רגלים ואתה גדרת אותה לעשות אנגריא לבת פרעה להושיב שם עבדיה ומשרתיה [מ"א יא, יז]. אם יעלה העם הזה וגו'. אין ישיבה בעזרה אלא למלכי בית דוד בלבד ויהיה הוא יושב ואני עומד ובמוצאי שביעית בזמן הקהל יקרא את פרשת המלך שהוא ראש במדינתו ואני כשאר העם נמצאתי בזוי [מ"א יב, כז]. אין ישיבה בעזרה. שנאמר (דברים פרק יח) לעמוד לשרת העומדים שם לפני ה'. אלא למלכי בית דוד. שמצינו בהן ישיבה, שנאמר (שמואל ב פרק ז) ויבא המלך דוד וישב לפני ה' ויאמר מי אנכי ומי ביתי וגו' [יומא כה.]. אין ישיבה בעזרה. דכתיב לעמוד לשרת (דברים יח) העומדים שם לפני ה' (דברים יח) ולא מצינו בה ישיבה אלא למלכי בית דוד שנאמר ויבא המלך דוד וישב וגו' כשאמר לו נתן הנביא אתה לא תבנה הבית כי ימלאו ימיך וגו' [שם סט:]. אין ישיבה בעזרה, דאין כבוד שמים בכך ואפי' מלאכי השרת אין להם שם ישיבה דכתיב (ישעיהו ו) עומדים ממעל לו [וקרבת] על חד מן קאמיא (דניאל ז). אלא למלכי בית דוד, שמלך להם המקום כבוד להראות שמלכותו שלימה [סוטה מ:].

מסורת הש"ס

א) בקרא וכהצר, ב) [עי' הגירסא בע"י וגיר' הערוך ערך אפיא אמר קמי' רבון דעלמא אי ענית לי ענית אי לא אמינא הא כל אפיא שוין], ג) [סוטה יב:], ד) סוטה מ: מח: יומא כה. סט: קידושין עח. תמיד כז., ה) בקרא מאד מלפני.

תורה אור השלם

א) גַּם אֵלֶּה מִשְׁלֵי שְׁלֹמֹה אֲשֶׁר הֶעְתִּיקוּ אַנְשֵׁי חִזְקִיָּה מֶלֶךְ יְהוּדָה: [משלי כה, א]

ב) וַיְדַבֵּר יְיָ אֶל מְנַשֶּׁה וְאֶל עַמּוֹ וְלֹא הִקְשִׁיבוּ: וַיָּבֵא יְיָ עֲלֵיהֶם אֶת שָׂרֵי הַצָּבָא אֲשֶׁר לְמֶלֶךְ אַשּׁוּר וַיִּלְכְּדוּ אֶת מְנַשֶּׁה בַּחֹחִים וַיַּאַסְרֻהוּ בַּנְחֻשְׁתַּיִם וַיּוֹלִיכֻהוּ בָּבֶלָה: [דברי הימים ב' לג, י-יא]

ג) וּכְהָצֵר לוֹ חִלָּה אֶת פְּנֵי יְיָ אֱלֹהָיו וַיִּכָּנַע מְאֹד מִלִּפְנֵי אֱלֹהֵי אֲבֹתָיו: וַיִּתְפַּלֵּל אֵלָיו וַיֵּעָתֶר לוֹ וַיִּשְׁמַע תְּחִנָּתוֹ וַיְשִׁיבֵהוּ יְרוּשָׁלַיִם לְמַלְכוּתוֹ וַיֵּדַע מְנַשֶּׁה כִּי יְיָ הוּא הָאֱלֹהִים: [דברי הימים ב' לג, יב-יג]

ד) וַיֹּאמֶר קַיִן אֶל יְיָ גָּדוֹל עֲוֹנִי מִנְּשֹׂא: [בראשית ד, יג]

ה) וַיֹּאמֶר עֵשָׂו אֶל אָבִיו הַבְרָכָה אַחַת הִוא לְךָ אָבִי בָּרְכֵנִי גַם אָנִי אָבִי וַיִּשָּׂא עֵשָׂו קֹלוֹ וַיֵּבְךְּ: [בראשית כז, לח]

ו) הֵמָּה מֵי מְרִיבָה אֲשֶׁר רָבוּ בְנֵי יִשְׂרָאֵל אֶת יְיָ וַיִּקָּדֵשׁ בָּם: [במדבר כ, יג]

ז) וַיְצַו פַּרְעֹה לְכָל עַמּוֹ לֵאמֹר כָּל הַבֵּן הַיִּלּוֹד הַיְאֹרָה תַּשְׁלִיכֻהוּ וְכָל הַבַּת תְּחַיּוּן: [שמות א, כב]

ח) וַיְהִי בַּדָּבָר הַזֶּה לְחַטַּאת בֵּית יָרָבְעָם וּלְהַכְחִיד וּלְהַשְׁמִיד מֵעַל פְּנֵי הָאֲדָמָה: [מלכים א' יג, לד]

ט) וְזֶה הַדָּבָר אֲשֶׁר הֵרִים יָד בַּמֶּלֶךְ שְׁלֹמֹה בָּנָה אֶת הַמִּלּוֹא סָגַר אֶת פֶּרֶץ עִיר דָּוִד אָבִיו: [מלכים א' יא, כז]

י) וַיֹּאמֶר יָרָבְעָם בְּלִבּוֹ עַתָּה תָּשׁוּב הַמַּמְלָכָה לְבֵית דָּוִד: אִם יַעֲלֶה הָעָם הַזֶּה לַעֲשׂוֹת זְבָחִים בְּבֵית יְיָ בִּירוּשָׁלַיִם וְשָׁב לֵב הָעָם הַזֶּה אֶל אֲדֹנֵיהֶם אֶל רְחַבְעָם מֶלֶךְ יְהוּדָה וַהֲרָגֻנִי וְשָׁבוּ אֶל רְחַבְעָם מֶלֶךְ יְהוּדָה: [מלכים א' יב, כו-כז]

כ) וַיִּוָּעַץ הַמֶּלֶךְ וַיַּעַשׂ שְׁנֵי עֶגְלֵי זָהָב וַיֹּאמֶר אֲלֵהֶם רַב לָכֶם מֵעֲלוֹת יְרוּשָׁלַיִם הִנֵּה אֱלֹהֶיךָ יִשְׂרָאֵל אֲשֶׁר הֶעֱלוּךָ מֵאֶרֶץ מִצְרָיִם: וַיָּשֶׂם אֶת הָאֶחָד בְּבֵית אֵל וְאֶת הָאֶחָד נָתַן בְּדָן: [מלכים א' יב, כח-כט]

,,גַּם־אֵלֶּה מִשְׁלֵי שְׁלֹמֹה אֲשֶׁר הֶעְתִּיקוּ אַנְשֵׁי חִזְקִיָּה מֶלֶךְ־יְהוּדָה" – ***THESE, TOO, ARE THE PROVERBS OF SOLOMON, WHICH THE MEN OF CHIZKIAH, KING OF JUDAH, WROTE DOWN,***[1] which indicates how zealously King Chizkiah, Menasheh's father, spread Torah knowledge. וְכִי חִזְקִיָּה מֶלֶךְ יְהוּדָה לְכָל הָעוֹלָם כּוּלּוֹ לִימֵּד תּוֹרָה – Now, is it possible that **CHIZKIAH, THE KING OF JUDAH, TAUGHT TORAH TO THE ENTIRE WORLD,** וְלִמְנַשֶּׁה בְּנוֹ לֹא לִימֵּד תּוֹרָה – **YET DID NOT TEACH TORAH TO MENASHEH, HIS SON?** Certainly not! אֶלָּא מִכָּל טוֹרַח שֶׁטָּרַח בּוֹ – **RATHER, FOR ALL THE TROUBLE CHIZKIAH TOOK WITH [MENASHEH]** to teach him the paths of righteousness, וּמִכָּל עָמָל שֶׁעָמַל בּוֹ – **AND FOR ALL THE EFFORT HE PUT INTO [MENASHEH],** לֹא הֶעֱלָהוּ לְמוּטָב אֶלָּא יִסּוּרִין – in the end **IT WAS ONLY SUFFERINGS THAT ELEVATED [MENASHEH] TO** the path of **PROPER CONDUCT,** שֶׁנֶּאֱמַר ,,וַיְדַבֵּר ה׳ אֶל־מְנַשֶּׁה וְאֶל־עַמּוֹ וְלֹא הִקְשִׁיבוּ וַיָּבֵא ה׳ עֲלֵיהֶם אֶת־שָׂרֵי הַצָּבָא אֲשֶׁר לְמֶלֶךְ אַשּׁוּר וַיִּלְכְּדוּ אֶת־מְנַשֶּׁה בַּחֹחִים וַיַּאַסְרֻהוּ בַּנְחֻשְׁתַּיִם וַיּוֹלִיכֻהוּ בָּבֶלָה" – **AS IT IS STATED:**[2] ***HASHEM SPOKE TO MENASHEH AND TO HIS PEOPLE, BUT THEY DID NOT PAY HEED. SO HASHEM BROUGHT UPON THEM THE COMMANDERS OF THE KING OF ASSYRIA, AND THEY CAPTURED MENASHEH WITH HOOKS, BOUND HIM WITH COPPER FETTERS, AND TRANSPORTED HIM TO BABYLONIA.*** וּכְתִיב ,,וּכְהָצֵר לוֹ חִלָּה אֶת־פְּנֵי ה׳ אֱלֹהָיו וַיִּכָּנַע מְאֹד מִלִּפְנֵי אֱלֹהֵי אֲבֹתָיו וַיִּתְפַּלֵּל אֵלָיו וַיֵּעָתֶר לוֹ וַיִּשְׁמַע תְּחִנָּתוֹ וַיְשִׁיבֵהוּ יְרוּשָׁלַם לְמַלְכוּתוֹ וַיֵּדַע מְנַשֶּׁה כִּי ה׳ הוּא הָאֱלֹהִים" – **AND** in the very next verses **IT IS WRITTEN:** ***AND WHEN [MENASHEH] WAS IN DISTRESS HE ENTREATED HASHEM HIS GOD, AND HUMBLED HIMSELF GREATLY BEFORE THE GOD OF HIS FATHERS. AND HE PRAYED TO HIM, AND [HASHEM] WAS ENTREATED OF HIM AND HEARD HIS SUPPLICATION, AND RETURNED HIM TO JERUSALEM, TO HIS KINGDOM; THEN MENASHEH KNEW THAT HASHEM IS THE LORD.*** הָא לָמַדְתָּ שֶׁחֲבִיבִין יִסּוּרִין – From here, concluded R' Akiva, **YOU LEARN THAT SUFFERINGS ARE PRECIOUS,** for it was his afflictions,[3] not the Torah studies of his youth, that inspired Menasheh to turn to God in sincere repentance and thereby regain his throne.

A Baraisa describes Menasheh's reluctant repentance: תָּנוּ רַבָּנַן – **The Rabbis taught** in a Baraisa: שְׁלֹשָׁה בָּאוּ בַּעֲלִילָה – **THREE** persons **CAME WITH CRAFTINESS,**[4] אֵלּוּ הֵן קַיִן עֵשָׂו וּמְנַשֶּׁה – and **THESE ARE THEY: CAIN, ESAU AND MENASHEH.** קַיִן דִּכְתִיב ,,גָּדוֹל עֲוֹנִי מִנְּשׂוֹא" – **CAIN – AS IT IS WRITTEN:** ***IS MY INIQUITY TOO GREAT TO BE BORNE?***[5] אָמַר לְפָנָיו רִבּוֹנוֹ שֶׁל עוֹלָם – **[CAIN] SAID BEFORE [GOD]: MASTER OF THE UNIVERSE!** כְּלוּם גָּדוֹל עֲוֹנִי מִשִּׁשִּׁים רִיבּוֹא שֶׁעֲתִידִין לַחֲטוֹא לְפָנֶיךָ – **IS MY INIQUITY GREATER THAN** that of **THE SIX HUNDRED THOUSAND WHO WILL SIN AGAINST YOU IN THE FUTURE,** וְאַתָּה סוֹלֵחַ לָהֶם – **AND WHOM YOU** nevertheless **WILL FORGIVE?!**[6] עֵשָׂו דִּכְתִיב ,,הַבְרָכָה אַחַת [הוא־] לְךָ אָבִי" – **ESAU – AS IT IS WRITTEN:** ***HAVE YOU BUT ONE BLESSING, FATHER?***[7] מְנַשֶּׁה בַּתְּחִילָּה קָרָא לֶאֱלוֹהוֹת הַרְבֵּה – **MENASHEH – AT FIRST HE CALLED UPON NUMEROUS** pagan **DEITIES** to free him from his captivity and restore him to his throne,[8] וּלְבַסּוֹף קָרָא לֵאלֹהֵי אֲבוֹתָיו – **AND IN THE END HE CALLED UPON THE GOD OF HIS FATHERS.**[9]

The Gemara discusses the Mishnah's sixth case of one who has no share in the World to Come – namely, the person who utters the Name of God according to its letters. The Mishnah stated: אַבָּא שָׁאוּל אוֹמֵר – **ABBA SHAUL SAYS:** אַף הַהוֹגֶה אֶת הַשֵּׁם בְּאוֹתִיּוֹתָיו וכו׳ – **ALSO ONE WHO UTTERS THE NAME** of God **ACCORDING TO ITS LETTERS,**[10] **etc.**

The Gemara clarifies this ruling:

תָּנָא – **[A Tanna] taught:** וּבַגְּבוּלִין – This refers to one who utters the Name of God **OUTSIDE OF THE TEMPLE**[11] וּבִלְשׁוֹן עֲגָה – **AND IN A FOREIGN TONGUE.**[12]

NOTES

1. *Proverbs* 25:1. King Chizkiah and his disciples compiled the Book of *Proverbs* (see *Bava Basra* 15a). Also, see above, 94a, where it is related how the king vigorously strengthened Torah study among the Jewish people (*Rashi*).

2. *II Chronicles* 33:10-11.

3. As it states: *And [when] Menasheh was in distress, he prayed to Hashem.*

4. Rather than beseech God with sincere prayer to attain their objectives, they each employed an irrefutable argument (*Rashi*). [It would seem from *Rashi's* comments that their "craftiness" lay in their self-reliant approach to attaining their objective, not in the arguments themselves, which were sound. According to *Maharsha's* understanding of *Rashi,* however, "craftiness" refers to the speciousness of their arguments. He writes that although, in truth, each argument could have been refuted, all three proponents were convinced of their rightness, and had God not acceded to each, they would have questioned His conduct of human affairs.]

5. *Genesis* 4:13. After murdering his brother Abel, Cain was told by God that he would spend the rest of his life as a wanderer. To this Cain responded: *Is my sin too great to be forgiven?*

6. [See *Exodus* 32 and *Numbers* 14, where God forgave the Children of Israel for the sin of the Golden Calf and for the sin of the Spies.] Cain argued that certainly the sin of an entire nation is greater than that of an individual; alternatively, that he sinned only against his fellow, whereas the Children of Israel will sin against God Himself [and nonetheless will be forgiven] (*Maharsha*).

Sefer HaIkkarim (IV, 21) explains Cain's question – "Is my sin too great to bear?" – as a challenge to God: Can it be that my power to sin is greater than God's power to forgive? (*Margaliyos HaYam*).

Cain's argument was accepted and, indeed, God forgave him, as stated in *Genesis* 4:15 (see *Bereishis Rabbah* 22:12-13).

How did Cain know what would happen in the distant future? *Yavetz* explains that he was a prophet, as we indeed find instances of God speaking to him. *Eitz Yosef* suggests that he knew this because Adam was shown every generation and its leaders (see also *Toras Chaim*).

7. *Genesis* 27:38. Isaac had promised to bless Esau when the latter brought him food. While Esau was away, Jacob disguised himself as his brother and received the blessing in Esau's stead. When he returned and discovered what had transpired in his absence, Esau appealed to Isaac for a blessing of his own, saying: *Have you but one blessing, Father?* This was a reasonable request, one which Isaac was compelled to grant (see vs. 39-40). [According to *Maharsha,* Esau was in essence arguing: "Have you only one blessing from God to bestow? If He is truly Omnipotent He possesses all the blessings, and will entrust to you all that you need to bestow!"]

8. This is indicated by the verse, *and when he was in distress . . . he humbled himself greatly before the God of his fathers,* which implies that until that moment he had humbled himself before pagan deities (*Rashi*).

9. By first supplicating all the pagan deities Menasheh cleverly ensured, as it were, that God would save him, for had God not done so, it would have seemed that He was as powerless as the idols (*Rashi;* the full text of this episode is found in *Ein Yaakov*).

10. According to *Rashi*, Abba Shaul refers to one who utters the *Shem HaMeforash,* the forty-two-letter Name that was uttered only in the Temple. According to *Yad Ramah*, Abba Shaul refers to one who utters the Tetragrammaton (*yud, kei, vav, kei*) according to the way it is written – as opposed to the way we commonly pronounce it ("Adonoy"). This is also *Tosafos'* position in *Avodah Zarah* (18a ד״ה הוגה); see note 12 below. See also *Yad David.*

11. Literally: within the borders [of Eretz Yisrael]. The law is less severe inside the Temple, for there God's Name was pronounced when they blessed (*Rashi*). [*Rashi* is apparently referring to the priestly blessing (*Birkas Kohanim*); see *Sotah* 38a and *Yoma* 39b. However, cf. *Rav* to Mishnah *Taanis* 2:5 and *Kuntres Acharon* to *Afikei Yam* II:3.] See following note.

12. The word עֲגָה has several interpretations. We have translated it according to the first one found in *Rashi,* who relates עֲגָה to the verse בְּלַעֲגֵי שָׂפָה, *with a foreign tongue (Isaiah 28:11).* According to *Rashi's* second explanation, the word עֲגָה is related to עוּגָה (literally "a circle"), a place where people congregate and speak of profane matters. Hence, the word refers to the type of conversation that occurs in "common circles."

According to Rashi's first explanation, the Tanna's words, וּבִלְשׁוֹן עֲגָה, are translated: "*or* in a foreign tongue." That is, the Tanna's intent is that one loses his portion in the World to Come if either one of the two

עין משפט
נר מצוה

כז א מיי׳ פ״ז מהלכות בית הבחירה הלכה ו ופי״ד מהל׳ סנהדרין הלכה יב ופ״ב מהל׳ מלכים הלכה ד:

ליקוטי רש״י

הברכה אחת. ה״א זו משמשת לשון תמיה כמו (במדבר יג, יט) הבמחנים (במדבר יג, כ) השמנה היא (ש״ב ג, לג) הכמות נבל [בראשית כז, לח]. **מיכה שנתמכמך בבנין.** עגל מסכה, יש אומרים מיכה היה שם שילא מתוך דמוסי בנין שנתמעך בו במצרים והיה בידו שם וטס שכתב בו משה עלה שור עלה שור להעלות ארונו של יוסף מתוך נילוס והשליכו לתוך הכור וילא העגל [שמות לב, ד ועי׳ רש״י כאן]. **אחיתופל.** נתן עיניו במלוכה כדאמר בחלק ראה אש יוצא מאמתו וכסבור שעתיד למלוך ומה שבידו נטלו הימנו לא יחלו ימיהם [סוטה ט: רצ״ע מגירסא המובא כאן]. **איצטגניני.** אילטגנינות דכל התלמוד לשון מזלות וחוזים בכוכבים [לעיל מט:]. **איצטגניני פרעה.** כך דרך אילטגנינין אינן רואין אלא סימן אבל לא פירושו של כל דבר. **ראו.** אלטגניני פרעה. **שמושיען של ישראל כו׳.** וכדרבי אלעזר דאמר שאין יודעים מה הוגין הילכך ראו המלרים ולא ידעו מה ראו [סוטה יב:]. יום שנולד משה אמרו לו אלטגניניו היום נולד מושיען ואין אנו יודעין אם ממלרים אם מישראל ורואין אנו שסופו ללקות במים לפיכך גזר אותו היום אף על המלרים שנאמר כל הבן הילוד ולא נאמר הילוד לעברים והם לא היו יודעים שסופו ללקות על מי מריבה [שמות א, כב]. **המה מי מריבה.** הם הנזכרים במקום אחר את אלו ראו אלטגניני פרעה שמושיען של ישראל לוקה במים לכך גזרו (שמות א, כב) כל הבן הילוד היאורה תשליכוהו [במדבר כ, יג]. **וזה הדבר.** אשר הוכיחו עליו. **שלמה בנה את המלוא.** ובבנין זה סגר את פרץ העיר דוד שהיה הפרץ אחורי המלוא אמר לו אביך פרץ פרלות בחומה ליכנס בו עולי רגלים ואתה גדרת אותה לעשות אנגריא לבת פרעה להושיב שם עבדיה ומשרתיה [מ״א יא, כז]. **אם יעלה העם הזה וגו׳.** אין ישיבה בעזרה אלא למלכי בית דוד בלבד ויהיה הוא יושב ואני עומד ובמולאי שביעית בזמן הקהל יקרא את פרשת המלך שהוא ראש במדינתו ואני כשאר העם נמלאתי בזוי [מ״א יב, כז]. **אין ישיבה בעזרה.** שנאמר (דברים פרק יח) לעמוד לשרת העומדים שם לפני ה׳. **אלא למלכי בית דוד.** שמלינו בהן ישיבה, שנאמר (שמואל ב פרק ז) ויבא המלך דוד וישב לפני ה׳ ויאמר מי אנכי ומי ביתי וגו׳ [יומא כה.]. **אין ישיבה בעזרה.** דכתיב לעמוד לשרת (דברים יח) העומדים שם לפני ה׳ (דברים יח) ולא מלינו בה ישיבה אלא למלכי בית דוד שנאמר ויבא המלך דוד וישב וגו׳ כשאמר לו נתן הנביא אתה לא תבנה הבית כי ימלאו ימיך וגו׳ [שם שם:]. אין ישיבה בעזרה, דאין כבוד שמים בכך ואפי׳ מלאכי השרת אין להם שם ישיבה דכתיב (ישעיה ו) עומדים ממעל לו [קרבת] על חד מן קאמיא (דניאל ז). אלא למלכי בית דוד, שחלק להם המקום כבוד להראות שמלכותו קיימת [סוטה מ:].

גם אלה משלי שלמה אשר העתיקו אנשי חזקיה. היינו תלמידי חזקיה כדקיימא לן בהשותפין בבבא בתרא (דף טו.) חזקיה וסיעתו כתבו משלי מכלל דחזקיה היה מלמד לכל וכדאמרן (לעיל דף לד.) נעץ חרב על פתח בית המדרש וכל שכן שלמנשה בנו לימד: **מכל טורח שטרח בו.** ללמדו: **שבאו בעלילה.** שלא באו לבקש לפני הקב״ה בתפלה אלא באו בעלילה שאמרו דברים של נלחון שאין להם תשובה: **הברכה אחת היא.** וכי אין לך ברכה יותר תשובה נילחת השיבו ועלתה לו: **מנשה.** בא בעלילה שלא להתפלל למקום אלא לבסוף אם לא תושיעני מה הועיל לי שקראתי לך יותר משאר אלהות והיינו דכתיב ויכנע ה) לפני (ה׳) אלהי אבותיו מכלל דעד השתא לפני אלוהות אחרים נכנע: **תנא.** כי אמרינן דהוגה את השם באותיותיו אין לו חלק לעולם הבא בגבולין אבל במקדש לא שהרי בשם היו מברכין: **ובלשון עגה.** אפילו במקדש לא לשון עגה לעז שאינו הוגה באותיותיו בלשון הקדש שלנו אלא שאר לועזין עגה לשון בלעגי שפה (ישעיה כח) מ״ר ל״א עגה לשון עוגה מקום שיש בו חבורת בני אדם שמדברין דברי חול גבולין קרי חוץ למקדש ואסור לפרש שם בן ארבעים ושתים בלשון עגה חוץ למקדש ואי עבד אין לו חלק אבל בלשון קדש אינו נענש כל כך ובמקדש הואיל ונהגו להזכיר פירושו אינו נענש: **שריבע עם.** שריבך את ישראל והשפילם: **עשה מריבה בעם.** הריבם אלו עם אלו בעסק עבודת כוכבים זה עובד וזה מוחה בידו ובאו לידי מחלוקת: **שניבט ולא ראה.** היה סבור להביט יפה ולעמוד על דבר עיקר ולא ראה שטעה כדאמרינן לקמן ראה אש יוצאה מאמתו וכו׳: **נתמכמך בבנין.** של מצרים שנתנוהו בבנין במקום לבנה כדמפרש באגדה שאמר לו משה להקב״ה אתה הרעות לעם הזה שעכשיו אם אין להם לבנים משימין בניהם של ישראל בבנין אמר לו הקב״ה קוצים הם מכלין שגלוי לפני אילו הם חיים היו רשעים [גמורים] ואם תרצה תנסה והוציא אחד מהן הלך והוציא את מיכה. ל״א נתמכמך עסק בבנין עד שנעשה מך כדאמרינן (סוטה דף יא.) כל העוסק בבנין מתמסכן: **הוא סבר איהו מליך.** ולכן נתאמץ שבע בן בכרי וקבץ כל ישראל אליו והיה רוצה למלוך כדכתיב במקרא: **איהו מליך.** ולכך נעשה יועץ לאבשלום כדי שתשוב המלוכה מדוד לאבשלום ובין כך ובין כך יתגלגל הדבר ותשוב אליו: **על מי מריבה.** שבעון שאמר שמעו נא המורים נענש ולא נכנס לארץ ישראל: **ומנא לן דלא אתי.** ירבעם לעלמא דאתי והכי נמי מפרש לקמן בכלהו שלשה מלכים וארבעה הדיוטות: **הוכיח את שלמה.** כדמפרש ואזיל דאמר דוד אביך וכו׳: **ומפני מה נענש שהוכיחו ברבים.** לביישו: **פרץ פרצות בחומה כדי שיעלו.** (וילדו) [ויכנסו] בריוח: **ואתה גדרת אותם כדי לעשות אנגריא.** כדי שיכנסו בשערים לידע מי נכנס כדי לגבות מס לבת פרעה מ״ר ל״א שסגר השערים ועשה מגדל לבת פרעה על אחד מן השערים וכולם עוברים דרך שם כדי שיהיו מלויין עמה לכבדה ולעבדה כל עבודת בית המלך קרי אנגריא ל״א שהיה רגיל שלמה לסגור דלתות העזרה ומלניע מפתחות בידו ודרכו של מלך לישן ג׳ שעות ביום וישראל עומדין על העזרה עד שיעמוד המלך ואמר לו ירבעם אתה רוצה שיתנו לך אנגריא לבת פרעה אשתך שתתן להם מפתחות: **(בית) [את] המלוא.** אחת מן הפרלות גדר ומלאו לכותל החומה ובנה שם מגדל לבת פרעה ולאנשים שעובדין לה לעיל מהאי קרא כתיב וירם יד במלך כלומר קם בדברים כנגד המלך ומרד בו: **שחלץ תפילין בפניו.** שהיה לו לפנות לצד אחר מפני אימת מלכותו ולחלוץ שלא בפניו ל״א חולץ תפילין בפניו לבא להתריס כנגדו בחזקה: **חלץ תפילין.** אין נכון להיות בגלוי ראש לפני המלך [והוא התחיל במרד בכך להראות ולומר לו שאינו נוהג כמלך]: **גמירי דאין ישיבה.** הלכה למשה מסיני ולא מקרא: **שהושיב רשע אצל צדיק.** ואומר להם להעמיד להם צלם אחד בבית אל ואחד בדן הסכימו עמו: **אמר לו רשע לצדיק.** סלקא דעתך גברא כירבעם פלח לעבודת כוכבים אלא לנסיונהו בעי אם דעתנו שלם עמו נתרלה בדבר וכך היה מטעה רשע לצדיק עד שהיו כולן חתומים שהן היו רוצים ושוב לא היו יכולים לחזור בהן: ואף

א) גם אלה משלי שלמה אשר העתיקו אנשי חזקיה מלך יהודה וכי חזקיה מלך יהודה לכל העולם כולו לימד תורה ולמנשה בנו לא לימד תורה אלא מכל טורח שטרח בו ומכל עמל שעמל בו לא העלהו למוטב אלא יסורין שנאמר ב) וידבר ה׳ אל מנשה ואל עמו ולא הקשיבו ויבא ה׳ עליהם את שרי הצבא אשר למלך אשור וילכדו את מנשה בחוחים ויאסרוהו בנחשתים ויוליכהו בבלה וכתיב ה) ג) ובהיצר לו חילה את פני ה׳ אלהיו ויכנע מאד מלפני (ה׳) אלהי אבותיו ויתפלל אליו ויעתר לו וישמע תחינתו וישיבהו ירושלים למלכותו וידע מנשה כי ה׳ הוא האלהים הא למדת שחביבין יסורין ת״ר שלשה באו בעלילה אלו הן קין עשו ומנשה קין דכתיב ד) גדול עוני מנשוא אמר לפניו רבונו של עולם כלום גדול עוני משישים ריבוא שעתידין לחטוא לפניך ואתה סולח להם עשו דכתיב ה) הברכה אחת היא לך אבי מנשה בתחילה קרא לאלוהות הרבה ולבסוף קרא לאלהי אבותיו: ו) אבא שאול אומר אף ההוגה את השם באותיותיו וכו׳: תנא ובגבולין ובלשון עגה: שלשה מלכים וארבעה הדיוטות וכו׳: ת״ר ירבעם שריבע עם ד״א ירבעם שעשה מריבה בעם דבר אחר ירבעם שעשה מריבה בין ישראל לאביהם שבשמים בן נבט בן שניבט ולא ראה תנא הוא נבט הוא מיכה הוא שבע בן בכרי נבט שניבט ולא ראה מיכה שנתמכמך בבנין ומה שמו שבע בן בכרי שמו תנו רבנן שלשה ניבטו ולא ראו ואלו הן נבט ואחיתופל ואיצטגניני פרעה נבט ראה אש שיוצאת מאמתו הוא סבר איהו מליך ולא היא ירבעם הוא דנפק מיניה אחיתופל ראה צרעת שזרחה לו על אמתו הוא סבר איהו מליך ולא היא בת שבע בתו הוא דנפקא מינה שלמה איצטגניני פרעה ז) דאמר רבי חמא ברבי חנינא מאי דכתיב ו) המה מי מריבה המה שראו איצטגניני פרעה וטעו ראו שמושיען של ישראל במים הוא לוקה אמר ז) כל הבן הילוד היאורה תשליכוהו והן לא ידעו שעל עסקי מי מריבה לוקה ומנא לן דלא אתי לעלמא דאתי דכתיב ח) ויהי בדבר הזה לחטאת בית ירבעם ולהכחיד ולהשמיד מעל פני אדמה להכחיד בעולם הזה ולהשמיד לעולם הבא אמר רבי יוחנן מפני מה זכה ירבעם למלכות מפני שהוכיח את שלמה ומפני מה נענש מפני שהוכיחו ברבים שנאמר ט) וזה הדבר אשר הרים יד במלך שלמה בנה את המלוא סגר את פרץ עיר דוד אביו אמר לו דוד אביך פרץ פרצות בחומה כדי שיעלו ישראל לרגל ואתה גדרת אותם כדי לעשות אנגריא לבת פרעה ומאי וזה אשר הרים יד במלך אמר רב נחמן שחלץ תפיליו בפניו אמר רב נחמן גסות הרוח שהיה בו בירבעם טרדתו מן העולם שנאמר י) ויאמר ירבעם בלבו עתה תשוב הממלכה לבית דוד אם יעלה העם הזה לעשות זבחים בבית ה׳ בירושלים ושב לב העם הזה אל אדוניהם אל רחבעם מלך יהודה והרגוני ושבו אל רחבעם מלך יהודה אמר ז) גמירי דאין ישיבה בעזרה אלא למלכי בית יהודה בלבד כיון דחזו ליה לרחבעם דיתיב ואנא קאימנא סברי הא מלכא והא עבדא ואי יתיבנא מורד במלכות הואי וקטלין לי ואזלו בתריה מיד כ) ויועץ המלך ויעש שני עגלי זהב ויאמר אליהם רב לכם מעלות ירושלים הנה אלהיך ישראל אשר העלוך מארץ מצרים וישם את האחד בבית אל ואת האחד נתן בדן מאי ויועץ אמר רבי יהודה שהושיב רשע אצל צדיק אמר להו חתמיתו על כל דעבידנא אמרו ליה הין אמר להו מלכא בעינא למיהוי אמרו ליה הין כל דאמינא לכו עבידתו אמרו ליה הין אפילו למפלח לעבודת כוכבים אמר ליה צדיק ח״ו אמר ליה רשע לצדיק ס״ד דגברא כירבעם פלח לעבודת כוכבים אלא למינסינהו הוא דקא בעי אי קבליתו למימריה ואף

מסורת הש״ס

א) בקרא וכהצר, ב) [עי׳ הגירסא בע״י וגיר׳ הערוך ערך אפיא **אמר קמי׳ רבון דעלמא אי ענית לי ענית אי לא אמינא הא כל אפיא שוין**], ג) [סוטה יב:], ד) סוטה מ: מא: יומא כה. סט: קידושין עח. תמיד כז., ה) בקרא מאד מלפני.

תורה אור השלם

א) גַּם אֵלֶּה מִשְׁלֵי שְׁלֹמֹה אֲשֶׁר הֶעְתִּיקוּ אַנְשֵׁי חִזְקִיָּה מֶלֶךְ יְהוּדָה: [משלי כה, א]

ב) וַיְדַבֵּר יְיָ אֶל מְנַשֶּׁה וְאֶל עַמּוֹ וְלֹא הִקְשִׁיבוּ: וַיָּבֵא יְיָ עֲלֵיהֶם אֶת שָׂרֵי הַצָּבָא אֲשֶׁר לְמֶלֶךְ אַשּׁוּר וַיִּלְכְּדוּ אֶת מְנַשֶּׁה בַּחֹחִים וַיַּאַסְרֻהוּ בַּנְחֻשְׁתַּיִם וַיּוֹלִיכֻהוּ בָּבֶלָה: [דברי הימים ב׳ לג, י-יא]

ג) וּכְהָצֵר לוֹ חִלָּה אֶת פְּנֵי יְיָ אֱלֹהָיו וַיִּכָּנַע מְאֹד מִלִּפְנֵי אֱלֹהֵי אֲבֹתָיו: וַיִּתְפַּלֵּל אֵלָיו וַיֵּעָתֶר לוֹ וַיִּשְׁמַע תְּחִנָּתוֹ וַיְשִׁיבֵהוּ יְרוּשָׁלַיִם לְמַלְכוּתוֹ וַיֵּדַע מְנַשֶּׁה כִּי יְיָ הוּא הָאֱלֹהִים: [דברי הימים ב׳ לג, יב-יג]

ד) וַיֹּאמֶר קַיִן אֶל יְיָ גָּדוֹל עֲוֹנִי מִנְּשֹׂא: [בראשית ד, יג]

ה) וַיֹּאמֶר עֵשָׂו אֶל אָבִיו הַבְרָכָה אַחַת הִוא לְךָ אָבִי בָּרְכֵנִי גַם אָנִי אָבִי וַיִּשָּׂא עֵשָׂו קֹלוֹ וַיֵּבְךְּ: [בראשית כז, לח]

ו) הֵמָּה מֵי מְרִיבָה אֲשֶׁר רָבוּ בְנֵי יִשְׂרָאֵל אֶת יְיָ וַיִּקָּדֵשׁ בָּם: [במדבר כ, יג]

ז) וַיְצַו פַּרְעֹה לְכָל עַמּוֹ לֵאמֹר כָּל הַבֵּן הַיִּלּוֹד הַיְאֹרָה תַּשְׁלִיכֻהוּ וְכָל הַבַּת תְּחַיּוּן: [שמות א, כב]

ח) וַיְהִי בַּדָּבָר הַזֶּה לְחַטַּאת בֵּית יָרָבְעָם וּלְהַכְחִיד וּלְהַשְׁמִיד מֵעַל פְּנֵי הָאֲדָמָה: [מלכים א׳ יג, לד]

ט) וְזֶה הַדָּבָר אֲשֶׁר הֵרִים יָד בַּמֶּלֶךְ שְׁלֹמֹה בָּנָה אֶת הַמִּלּוֹא סָגַר אֶת פֶּרֶץ עִיר דָּוִד אָבִיו: [מלכים א׳ יא, כז]

י) וַיֹּאמֶר יָרָבְעָם בְּלִבּוֹ עַתָּה תָּשׁוּב הַמַּמְלָכָה לְבֵית דָּוִד: אִם יַעֲלֶה הָעָם הַזֶּה לַעֲשׂוֹת זְבָחִים בְּבֵית יְיָ בִּירוּשָׁלַיִם וְשָׁב לֵב הָעָם הַזֶּה אֶל אֲדֹנֵיהֶם אֶל רְחַבְעָם מֶלֶךְ יְהוּדָה וַהֲרָגֻנִי וְשָׁבוּ אֶל רְחַבְעָם מֶלֶךְ יְהוּדָה: [מלכים א׳ יב, כו-כז]

כ) וַיִּוָּעַץ הַמֶּלֶךְ וַיַּעַשׂ שְׁנֵי עֶגְלֵי זָהָב וַיֹּאמֶר אֲלֵהֶם רַב לָכֶם מֵעֲלוֹת יְרוּשָׁלַיִם הִנֵּה אֱלֹהֶיךָ יִשְׂרָאֵל אֲשֶׁר הֶעֱלוּךָ מֵאֶרֶץ מִצְרָיִם: וַיָּשֶׂם אֶת הָאֶחָד בְּבֵית אֵל וְאֶת הָאֶחָד נָתַן בְּדָן: [מלכים א׳ יב, כח-כט]

The Gemara proceeds to the next segment of the Mishnah: שְׁלֹשָׁה מְלָכִים וְאַרְבָּעָה הֶדְיוֹטוֹת וכו׳ – **THREE KINGS AND FOUR COMMONERS, etc.** [do not have a share in the World to Come].

The first of these three kings is Yarovam ben Nevat.[13] The Gemara expounds upon this name:[14]

תָּנוּ רַבָּנָן – **The Rabbis taught in a Baraisa:** יָרָבְעָם שֶׁרִיבֵּע עָם – **YAROVAM** was so called **BECAUSE HE LAID LOW THE** Jewish **PEOPLE** *(riba am)*.[15] דָּבָר אַחֵר – **ALTERNATIVELY:** יָרָבְעָם שֶׁעָשָׂה מְרִיבָה בָּעָם – **YAROVAM** was so called **BECAUSE HE CREATED DISCORD AMONG THE** Jewish **PEOPLE** *(merivah ba'am)*.[16] דָּבָר אַחֵר – **ALTERNATIVELY:** יָרָבְעָם שֶׁעָשָׂה מְרִיבָה בֵּין יִשְׂרָאֵל לַאֲבִיהֶם שֶׁבַּשָּׁמַיִם – **YAROVAM** was so called **BECAUSE** by introducing idol worship **HE CREATED DISCORD** *(merivah)* **BETWEEN ISRAEL AND THEIR FATHER** *(avihem)* **IN HEAVEN.**

The Gemara expounds the name of Yarovam's father:

בֶּן־נְבָט בֶּן שֶׁנִּיבַּט וְלֹא רָאָה – Yarovam was **THE SON OF NEVAT.** Nevat was so called because he was **A PERSON WHO BEHELD** *(nibbat)* **BUT DID NOT SEE.**[17]

The Gemara digresses to discuss Nevat:

תָּנָא – **A Tanna taught:** הוּא נְבָט הוּא מִיכָה הוּא שֶׁבַע בֶּן בִּכְרִי – **NEVAT IS THE SAME** person **AS MICHAH**[18] **AND THE SAME** person **AS SHEVA BEN BICHRI.**[19] נְבָט שֶׁנִּיבַּט וְלֹא רָאָה – He was called **NEVAT BECAUSE HE BEHELD** *(nibbat)* **BUT DID NOT SEE;**[20] מִיכָה שֶׁנִּתְמַכְמֵךְ בַּבִּנְיָן – he was called **MICHAH BECAUSE HE WAS CRUSHED** *(nismachmech)* **IN THE BUILDING;**[21] וּמַה שְּׁמוֹ – **AND WHAT WAS HIS** true **NAME?** שֶׁבַע בֶּן בִּכְרִי שְׁמוֹ – **HIS** true **NAME WAS SHEVA BEN BICHRI.**

The Gemara relates how Sheva ben Bichri, alias Nevat, came to revolt against King David:

תָּנוּ רַבָּנָן – **The Rabbis taught in a Baraisa:** שְׁלֹשָׁה נִיבְּטוּ וְלֹא רָאוּ – **THREE PERSONS BEHELD BUT DID NOT SEE;** i.e. they beheld an omen but did not interpret it correctly, וְאֵלּוּ הֵן נְבָט וַאֲחִיתוֹפֶל וְאִיצְטַגְנִינֵי פַּרְעֹה – **AND THESE ARE THEY: NEVAT, ACHITHOPEL,**[22] **AND THE ASTROLOGERS OF PHARAOH.**

The Gemara explains these references one by one.

נְבָט רָאָה אֵשׁ שֶׁיּוֹצֵאת מֵאַמָּתוֹ – **Nevat saw fire issue from his member.** הוּא סָבַר אִיהוּ מָלֵיךְ – **He thought** it meant that **he would** one day **be king.** וְלֹא הִיא – **However, it was not so,** i.e.

NOTES

conditions is met: (a) He utters the Name outside of the Temple, even if he does so in Hebrew, *or* (b) he utters the Name in a foreign tongue, even in the Temple.

According to *Rashi's* second explanation, וּבִלְשׁוֹן עֲגָה means "in common circles," and the prefix *vav* means *and.* Hence, the Tanna's intent is that one incurs the severe penalty only if *both* conditions are met: (a) He utters the Name outside of the Temple, *and* (b) the Name is mentioned in common circles, i.e. in a discussion of profane (rather than holy) matters. One who utters this Name in holy conversation is not subject to this penalty even if he does so outside the Temple. [When *Rashi* uses the phrase לְשׁוֹן קֹדֶשׁ at the end of this second explanation, he means by it *sacred matters* in contrast to דִּבְרֵי חוֹל, *profane matters,* of which he spoke earlier. (Note that *Rashi* does not say לְשׁוֹן הַקֹּדֶשׁ, the usual phrase for Hebrew.)]

Aruch and *Ibn Janach* explain עֲגָה to refer to pronouncing God's Name in a joking or denigrating manner. In *Avodah Zarah* 18a, *Tosafos* explain that the Mishnah refers to one who pronounces the Tetragrammaton as it is written (see above, note 10); this pronunciation is reserved for the World to Come (see *Pesachim* 50a). *Yerushalmi* likewise understands עֲגָה as referring to the practice of the Samaritans, who in their pronunciation recited the Tetragrammaton in its written form (see *Margaliyos HaYam*; see also *Yad Ramah* and *Meiri*).

13. See 90a note 13.

14. In the pages that follow, the Gemara discovers in the names of certain Biblical personages allusions to their wicked deeds. It seems obvious that when their parents named them, they did not foresee the uncomplimentary interpretations expounded here. Rather, they probably had noble intentions in choosing these names, and were unaware of their evil portent. More importantly, the portentous nature of these names in no way inclined their bearers to lives of wickedness. Rather, every name had an equal potential as an augury of good; had these people chosen to act righteously, they would have invested their names with other, propitious meanings. For example, in his position as king, Achav (Ahab) could have guided the nation in the service of God with brotherly love and fatherly devotion. The Gemara would then have interpreted the name Achav (אַחְאָב) as a compound of the words a *brother* (אח) and *father* (אב) – i.e. as portending that Achav would be a devoted brother and father to his people. It is only *after* Achav chose to cleave to idolatry that the Gemara could look back and declare (below, 102b) that the name "Achav" portended wickedness (*R' Avigdor Miller*; see also *Maharal, Berachos* 7b and *Yoma* 83b; see also *R' Moshe Chaim Luzzatto* in *Maamar al HaAggados* cited in 106b note 6).

Alternatively, these personages were possibly known to their generations by *other* names. The names used in Scripture were applied to these people *because* of their deeds (*R' Dovid Cohen*). [For a fuller discussion of names in Scripture, see Overview to ArtScroll *I Divrei HaYamim.*]

15. יָרָבְעָם is a compound of the words רִבַּע עָם, *he laid low the people.* [The two interpretations that follow are likewise compounds.] That is, by inducing the people [i.e. the Ten Tribes] to worship idols (*I Kings* 12:28-33), Yarovam started them on a downhill course of sin that eventually led God to expel them from the Land (ibid. 14:15-16, *II Kings* 17:21-23). See also *Maharsha.* Cf. *Maharal.*

16. By introducing idolatry into Israel, Yarovam caused discord between the adherents and the opponents of idolatry (*Rashi*).

Alternatively, Yarovam led the Ten Tribes in their secession from the House of David, which led to civil war; see *I Kings* 14:30 (*Maharsha*).

17. I.e. he beheld an omen but misunderstood its intent; see note 23 (*Rashi*).

18. Michah lived during the early era of the Judges, in the portion of Ephraim. He set up a forbidden image in his house. See *Judges* Ch. 17.

19. Sheva ben Bichri led an unsuccessful revolt against King David – see *II Samuel* 20.

The commentators (see *Radak, I Kings* 11:26) puzzle over the Gemara's identifying Nevat as Sheva ben Bichri, for Nevat was from the tribe of Ephraim (ibid.), while Scripture refers to Sheva ben Bichri as a Benjamite (*II Samuel* 20:1). *Maharsha* suggests that perhaps Sheva in fact was not a Benjamite, but was so labeled by Scripture because he opposed King David. Since David's main opposition came from the tribe of Benjamin (they viewed David as a usurper of the throne from their fellow tribesman Saul), anyone who opposed David was called a "Benjamite." See *Ben Yehoyada* in the name of *Chida* for an alternative explanation based on kabbalistic concepts.

20. As the Gemara will explain shortly.

21. *Rashi* explains with the following Midrash: When God sent Moses to demand that Pharaoh allow the Hebrews to leave, Pharaoh responded by intensifying the work load and requiring the Hebrews to supply straw themselves for the manufacture of the bricks, without diminishing their output. Thereupon Moses complained to God: "Why have You dealt badly with this people by sending me on this mission? Now, when the Hebrews fall short of their quotas, the Egyptians immure the Hebrew babies in the walls in lieu of the missing bricks!" God replied, "The Egyptians are merely ridding the nation of thorns; i.e., if allowed to live, these babies would grow up to be sinners. If you wish, you may test My word and take one of the babies out of the wall." Moses did so, and the child grew up to be Michah the idolater. He was called מִיכָה because he had been נִתְמַכְמֵךְ (*crushed*) into the wall (see *Midrash Tanchuma, Ki Sissa* 19). It is noteworthy that Moses' own grandson later became a priest for Michah's idol, as related in *Bava Basra* 110a (*R' Dovid Cohen*).]

[*Yad Ramah* wonders how such a wicked person as Michah merited to live for so many centuries (i.e. from the time of the Exodus till the post-Judges' period of David and Solomon). *Maharal* suggests, however, that in fact Michah did not live so long. Rather, the Gemara means that Michah was Nevat's ancestor, and Nevat inherited Michah's evil qualities. See along similar lines *Abarbanel* to *I Kings* 11:26 and *Margaliyos HaYam.* See also *Ben Yehoyada* in name of *Chida.*]

Alternatively, *Rashi* translates נִתְמַכְמֵךְ בַּבִּנְיָן to mean *he was impoverished by [the cost of] building* (presumably, the shrine for his image).

22. Achithopel was King David's advisor, who sided with David's son Absalom in his revolt against his father – see *II Samuel* 15.

א) גם אלה משלי שלמה אשר העתיקו אנשי חזקיה מלך יהודה וכי חזקיה מלך יהודה לכל העולם כולו לימד תורה ולמנשה בנו לא לימד תורה אלא מכל טורח שטרח בו ומכל עמל שעמל בו לא העלהו למוטב אלא יסורין שנאמר ב) וידבר ה' אל מנשה ואל עמו ולא הקשיבו ויבא ה' עליהם את שרי הצבא אשר למלך אשור וילכדו את מנשה בחוחים ויאסרוהו בנחשתים ויוליכהו בבלה וכתיב א) ג) ובהיצר לו חילה את פני ה' אלהיו ויכנע מאד מלפני (ה') אלהי אבותיו ויתפלל אליו ויעתר לו וישמע תחינתו וישיבהו ירושלים למלכותו וידע מנשה כי ה' הוא האלהים הא למדת שחביבין יסורין ת"ר שלשה באו בעלילה אלו הן קין עשו ומנשה קין דכתיב ד) גדול עוני מנשוא אמר לפניו רבונו של עולם כלום גדול עוני משששים ריבוא שעתידין לחטוא לפניך ואתה סולח להם עשו דכתיב ה) הברכה אחת היא לך אבי מנשה בתחילה קרא לאלוהות הרבה ולבסוף קרא לאלהי אבותיו ב): אבא שאול אומר אף ההוגה את השם באותיותיו וכו': תנא ובגבולין ובלשון עגה: שלשה מלכים וארבעה הדיוטות וכו': ת"ר ירבעם שריבע עם ד"א ירבעם שעשה מריבה בעם דבר אחר ירבעם שעשה מריבה בין ישראל לאביהם שבשמים בן נבט בן שניבט ולא ראה תנא הוא נבט הוא מיכה הוא שבע בן בכרי נבט שניבט ולא ראה מיכה שנתמכמך בבנין ומה שמו שבע בן בכרי שמו תנו רבנן שלשה ניבטו ולא ראו ואלו הן נבט ואחיתופל ואיצטגניני פרעה נבט ראה אש שיוצאת מאמתו הוא סבר איהו מליך ולא היא ירבעם הוא דנפק מיניה אחיתופל ראה צרעת שזרחה לו על אמתו הוא סבר איהו מלך ולא היא בת שבע בתו הוא דנפקא מינה שלמה איצטגניני פרעה ג) דאמר רבי חמא ברבי חנינא מאי דכתיב ו) המה מי מריבה שראו איצטגניני פרעה וטעו ראו שמושיען של ישראל במים הוא לוקה אמר ז) כל הבן הילוד היאורה תשליכוהו והן לא ידעו שעל עסקי מי מריבה לוקה ומנא לן דלא אתי לעלמא דאתי דכתיב ח) ויהי בדבר הזה לחטאת בית ירבעם ולהכחיד ולהשמיד מעל פני אדמה להכחיד בעולם הזה ולהשמיד לעולם הבא אמר רבי יוחנן מפני מה זכה ירבעם למלכות מפני שהוכיח את שלמה ומפני מה נענש מפני שהוכיחו ברבים שנאמר ט) וזה הדבר אשר הרים יד במלך שלמה בנה את המלוא סגר את פרץ עיר דוד אביו אמר לו דוד אביך פרץ פרצות בחומה כדי שיעלו ישראל לרגל ואתה גדרת אותם כדי לעשות אנגריא לבת פרעה ומאי וזה אשר הרים יד במלך אמר רב נחמן שחלץ תפיליו בפניו אמר רב נחמן גסות הרוח שהיה בו בירבעם טרדתו מן העולם שנאמר י) ויאמר ירבעם בלבו עתה תשוב הממלכה לבית דוד אם יעלה העם הזה לעשות זבחים בבית ה' בירושלים ושב לב העם הזה אל אדוניהם אל רחבעם מלך יהודה והרגוני ושבו אל רחבעם מלך יהודה אמר ד) גמירי א) דאין ישיבה בעזרה אלא למלכי בית יהודה בלבד כיון דחזו ליה לרחבעם דיתיב ואנא קאימנא סברי הא מלכא והא עבדא ואי יתיבנא מורד במלכות הואי וקטלין לי ואזלו בתריה מיד כ) ויועץ המלך ויעש שני עגלי זהב ויאמר אליהם רב לכם מעלות ירושלים הנה אלהיך ישראל אשר העלוך מארץ מצרים וישם את האחד בבית אל ואת האחד נתן בדן מאי ויועץ אמר רבי יהודה שהושיב רשע אצל צדיק אמר להו חתמיתו על כל דעבידנא אמרו ליה הין אמר להו מלכא בעינא למיהוי אמרו ליה הין כל דאמינא לכו עבידתו אמרו ליה הין אפילו למפלח לעבודת כוכבים אמר ליה צדיק ח"ו אמר ליה רשע לצדיק ס"ד דגברא כירבעם פלח לעבודת כוכבים אלא למינסינהו הוא דקא בעי אי קבליתו למימריה

ואף

גם אלה משלי שלמה אשר העתיקו אנשי חזקיה. היינו תלמידי חזקיה כדקיימא לן בהשותפין בבבא בתרא (דף טו.) חזקיה וסיעתו כתבו משלי מכלל דחזקיה היה מלמד לכל וכדאמרן (לעיל דף צד:) נעץ חרב על פתח בית המדרש וכל שכן שלמנשה בנו לימד: מכל טורח שטרח בו. ללמדו: שבאו בעלילה. שלא באו לבקש לפני הקב"ה בתפלה אלא באו בעלילה שאמרו דברים של נצחון שאין להם תשובה: הברכה אחת היא. וכי אין לך ברכה יותר תשובה נילחת השיבו ועלתה לו: מנשה. בא בעלילה שלא להתפלל למקום אלא לבסוף אם לא תושיעני מה הועיל לי שקראתי לך יותר משאר אלהות והיינו דכתיב ויכנע ה) לפני (ה') אלהי אבותיו מכלל דעד השתא לפני אלוהות אחרים נכנע: תנא. כי אמרינן דהוגה את השם באותיותיו אין לו חלק לעולם הבא בגבולין אבל במקדש לא שהרי בשם היו מברכין: ובלשון עגה. אפילו במקדש לא לשון עגה לעז שאינו הוגה באותיותיו בלשון הקדש שלנו אלא שאר לועזין עגה לשון בלעגי שפה (ישעיה כח) מ"ר ל"א עגה לשון עוגה מקום שיש בו חבורת בני אדם שמדברין דברי חול גבולין קרי חוץ למקדש ואסור לפרש שם בן ארבעים ושתים בלשון עגה חוץ למקדש ואי עבד אין לו חלק אבל בלשון קדש אינו נענש כל כך ובמקדש הואיל ונהגו להזכיר פירושו אינו נענש: שריבע עם. שריבץ את ישראל והשפילם: עשה מריבה בעם. הרידם אלו עם אלו בעסק עבודת כוכבים זה עובד וזה מוחה בידו ובאו לידי מחלוקת: שניבט ולא ראה. היה סבור להביט יפה ולעמוד על דבר עיקר ולא ראה שטעה כדאמרינן לקמן ראה אש יוצאה מאמתו וכו': נתמכמך בבנין. של מצרים שנתנוהו בבנין במקום לבנה כדמפרש באגדה שאמר לו משה להקב"ה אתה הרעות לעם הזה שעכשיו אם אין להם לבנים משימין בניהם של ישראל בבנין אמר לו הקב"ה קוצים הם מכלין שגלוי לפני אילו הם חיים היו רשעים [גמורים] ואם תרצה תנסה והוציא אחד מהן הלך והוציא את מיכה. ל"א נתמכמך עסק בבנין עד שנעשה מך כדאמרינן (סוטה דף יא.) כל העוסק בבנין מתמסכן: הוא סבר איהו מליך. ולכן נתאמץ שבע בן בכרי וקבץ כל ישראל אליו והיה רוצה למלוך כדכתיב במקרא: איהו מליך. ולכך נעשה יועץ לאבשלום כדי שתשוב המלוכה מדוד לאבשלום ובין כך ובין כך יתגלגל הדבר ותשוב אליו: על מי מריבה. שבעון שאמר שמעו נא המורים נענש ולא נכנס לארץ ישראל: ומנא לן דלא אתי. ירבעם לעלמא דאתי והכי נמי מפרש לקמן בכלהו שלשה מלכים וארבעה הדיוטות: הוכיח את שלמה. כדמפרש ואזיל דאמר דוד אביך וכו': ומפני מה נענש שהוכיחו ברבים. לביישו: פרץ פרצות בחומה כדי שיעלו. (וירדו) [ויכנסו] בריוח: ואתה גדרת אותם כדי לעשות אנגריא. כדי שיכנסו בשערים לידע מי נכנס כדי לגבות מס לבת פרעה מ"ר ל"א שסגר השערים ועשה מגדל לבת פרעה על אחד מן השערים וכולם עוברים דרך שם כדי שיהיו מלויין עמה לכבדה ולעבדה כל עבודת בית המלך קרי אנגריא ל"א שהיה רגיל שלמה לסגור דלתות העזרה ומצניע מפתחות בידו ודרכו של מלך לישן ג' שעות ביום וישראל עומדין על העזרה עד שיעמוד המלך ואמר לו ירבעם אתה רוצה שיתנו לך אנגריא לבת פרעה אשתך שתתן להם מפתחות: (בית) [את] המלוא. אחת מן הפרצות גדר ומלאו לכותל החומה ובנה שם מגדל לבת פרעה ולאנשים שעובדין לה לעיל מהאי קרא כתיב וירם יד במלך כלומר קם בדברים כנגד המלך ומרד בו: שחלץ תפילין בפניו. שהיה לו לפנות לצד אחר מפני אימת מלכותו ולחלוץ שלא בפניו ל"א חולץ תפילין בפניו לבא להתריס כנגדו בחזקה: חלץ תפילין. אין נכון להיות בגלוי ראש לפני המלך [והוא התחיל במרד בכך להראות ולומר לו שאינו נוהג כמלך]: גמירי דאין ישיבה. הלכה למשה מסיני ולא מקרא: שהושיב רשע אצל צדיק. ואומר להם להעמיד להם צלם אחד בבית אל ואחד בדן הסכימו עמו: אמר לו רשע לצדיק. סלקא דעתך גברא כירבעם פלח לעבודת כוכבים אלא לנסיונהו בעי אם דעתנו שלם עמו נתרצה בדבר וכך היה מטעה רשע לצדיק עד שהיו כולן חתומים שהן היו רוצים ושוב לא היו יכולים לחזור בהן:

ואף

עין משפט
נר מצוה

כז א מיי' פ"ז מהלכות בית הבחירה הלכה ו ופי"ד מהל' סנהדרין הלכה יב ופ"ב מהל' מלכים הלכה ז:

ליקוטי רש"י

הברכה אחת. ה"א זו משמשת לשון תמיה כמו (במדבר יג, יט) הבמחנים (במדבר יג, כ) השמנה היא (ש"ב ג, לג) הכמות נבל [בראשית כז, לח]. מיכה שנתמכמך בבנין. עגל מסכה, יש אומרים מיכה היה שם שיצא מתוך דמוסי בנין שנתמעך בו במצרים והיה בידו שם וטס שכתב בו משה עלה שור עלה שור להעלות ארונו של יוסף מתוך נילוס והשליכו לתוך הכור ויצא העגל [שמות לב, ד ועי' רש"י כאן]. אחיתופל. נתן עיניו במלוכה כדאמר בחלק ראה אש יוצא מאמתו וכסבור שעתיד למלוך ומה שבידו נטלו הימנו לא יחצו ימיהם [סוטה ט: וצ"ע מגירסא המובא כאן]. איצטגניני. אצטגנינות דכל התלמוד לשון מזלות וחוזים בכוכבים [לעיל מט:]. איצטגניני פרעה. כך דרך אצטגנינין אין רואין אלא סימן אבל לא פירושו של כל דבר. ראו. אצטגניני פרעה. שמושיען של ישראל כו'. וכדרבי אלעזר דאמר שאין יודעים מה הוגין הילכך ראו המצרים ולא ידעו מה ראו [סוטה יב:]. יום שנולד משה אמרו לו אצטגניניו היום נולד מושיען ואין אנו יודעין אם ממצרים אם מישראל ורואין אנו שסופו ללקות במים לפיכך גזר אותו היום אף על המצרים שנאמר כל הבן הילוד ולא נאמר הילוד לעברים והם לא היו יודעים שסופו ללקות על מי מריבה [שמות א, כב]. המה מי מריבה. הם הנזכרים במקום אחר את אלו ראו אצטגניני פרעה שמושיען של ישראל לוקה במים לכך גזרו (שמות א, כב) כל הבן הילוד היאורה תשליכוהו [במדבר כ, יג]. וזה הדבר. אשר הוכיחו עליו. שלמה בנה את המלוא. ובבנין זה סגר את פרץ העיר דוד שהיה הפרץ אחורי המלוא אמר לו אביך פרץ פרצות בחומה ליכנס בו עולי רגלים ואתה גדרת אותה לעשות אנגריא לבת פרעה להושיב שם עבדיה ומשרתיה [מ"א יא, כז]. אם יעלה העם הזה וגו'. אין ישיבה בעזרה אלא למלכי בית דוד בלבד ויהיה הוא יושב ואני עומד ובמוצאי שביעית בזמן הקהל יקרא את פרשת המלך שהוא ראש במדינתו ואני כשאר העם נמצאתי בזוי [מ"א יב, כז]. אין ישיבה בעזרה. שנאמר (דברים פרק יח) לעמוד לשרת העומדים שם לפני ה'. אלא למלכי בית דוד. שמצינו בהן ישיבה, שנאמר (שמואל ב פרק ז) ויבא המלך דוד וישב לפני ה' ויאמר מי אנכי ומי ביתי וגו' [יומא כה.]. אין ישיבה בעזרה. דכתיב לעמוד לשרת (דברים יח) העומדים שם לפני ה' (דברים יח) ולא מצינו בה ישיבה אלא למלכי בית דוד שנאמר ויבא המלך דוד וישב וגו' כשאמר לו נתן הנביא אתה לא תבנה הבית כי ימלאו ימיך וגו' [שם סט:]. אין ישיבה בעזרה, דאין כבוד שמים בכך ואפי' מלאכי השרת אין להם שם ישיבה דכתיב (ישעיהו ו) עומדים ממעל לו [וקרבת] על חד מן קאמיא (דניאל ז). אלא למלכי בית דוד, שחלק להם המקום כבוד להראות שמלכותו שלימה [סוטה מ:].

מסורת הש"ס

א) בקרא וכהצר, ב) [עי' הגירסא בע"י וגיר' הערוך ערך אפיא אמר קמי' רבון דעלמא אי ענית לי ענית אי לא אמינא הא כל אפיא שוין], ג) [סוטה יב:], ד) סוטה מ: מא: יומא כה. סט: קידושין עח. תמיד כז., ה) בקרא מאד מלפני.

תורה אור השלם

א) גַּם אֵלֶּה מִשְׁלֵי שְׁלֹמֹה אֲשֶׁר הֶעְתִּיקוּ אַנְשֵׁי חִזְקִיָּה מֶלֶךְ יְהוּדָה: [משלי כה, א]

ב) וַיְדַבֵּר יְיָ אֶל מְנַשֶּׁה וְאֶל עַמּוֹ וְלֹא הִקְשִׁיבוּ: וַיָּבֵא יְיָ עֲלֵיהֶם אֶת שָׂרֵי הַצָּבָא אֲשֶׁר לְמֶלֶךְ אַשּׁוּר וַיִּלְכְּדוּ אֶת מְנַשֶּׁה בַּחֹחִים וַיַּאַסְרֻהוּ בַּנְחֻשְׁתַּיִם וַיּוֹלִיכֻהוּ בָּבֶלָה: [דברי הימים ב' לג, י-יא]

ג) וּכְהָצֵר לוֹ חִלָּה אֶת פְּנֵי יְיָ אֱלֹהָיו וַיִּכָּנַע מְאֹד מִלִּפְנֵי אֱלֹהֵי אֲבֹתָיו: וַיִּתְפַּלֵּל אֵלָיו וַיֵּעָתֶר לוֹ וַיִּשְׁמַע תְּחִנָּתוֹ וַיְשִׁיבֵהוּ יְרוּשָׁלַיִם לְמַלְכוּתוֹ וַיֵּדַע מְנַשֶּׁה כִּי יְיָ הוּא הָאֱלֹהִים: [דברי הימים ב' לג, יב-יג]

ד) וַיֹּאמֶר קַיִן אֶל יְיָ גָּדוֹל עֲוֹנִי מִנְּשֹׂא: [בראשית ד, יג]

ה) וַיֹּאמֶר עֵשָׂו אֶל אָבִיו הַבְרָכָה אַחַת הִוא לְךָ אָבִי בָּרֲכֵנִי גַם אָנִי אָבִי וַיִּשָּׂא עֵשָׂו קֹלוֹ וַיֵּבְךְּ: [בראשית כז, לח]

ו) הֵמָּה מֵי מְרִיבָה אֲשֶׁר רָבוּ בְנֵי יִשְׂרָאֵל אֶת יְיָ וַיִּקָּדֵשׁ בָּם: [במדבר כ, יג]

ז) וַיְצַו פַּרְעֹה לְכָל עַמּוֹ לֵאמֹר כָּל הַבֵּן הַיִּלּוֹד הַיְאֹרָה תַּשְׁלִיכֻהוּ וְכָל הַבַּת תְּחַיּוּן: [שמות א, כב]

ח) וַיְהִי בַּדָּבָר הַזֶּה לְחַטַּאת בֵּית יָרָבְעָם וּלְהַכְחִיד וּלְהַשְׁמִיד מֵעַל פְּנֵי הָאֲדָמָה: [מלכים א' יג, לד]

ט) וְזֶה הַדָּבָר אֲשֶׁר הֵרִים יָד בַּמֶּלֶךְ שְׁלֹמֹה בָּנָה אֶת הַמִּלּוֹא סָגַר אֶת פֶּרֶץ עִיר דָּוִד אָבִיו: [מלכים א' יא, כז]

י) וַיֹּאמֶר יָרָבְעָם בְּלִבּוֹ עַתָּה תָּשׁוּב הַמַּמְלָכָה לְבֵית דָּוִד: אִם יַעֲלֶה הָעָם הַזֶּה לַעֲשׂוֹת זְבָחִים בְּבֵית יְיָ בִּירוּשָׁלַיִם וְשָׁב לֵב הָעָם הַזֶּה אֶל אֲדֹנֵיהֶם אֶל רְחַבְעָם מֶלֶךְ יְהוּדָה וַהֲרָגֻנִי וְשָׁבוּ אֶל רְחַבְעָם מֶלֶךְ יְהוּדָה: [מלכים א' יב, כו-כז]

כ) וַיִּוָּעַץ הַמֶּלֶךְ וַיַּעַשׂ שְׁנֵי עֶגְלֵי זָהָב וַיֹּאמֶר אֲלֵהֶם רַב לָכֶם מֵעֲלוֹת יְרוּשָׁלַיִם הִנֵּה אֱלֹהֶיךָ יִשְׂרָאֵל אֲשֶׁר הֶעֱלוּךָ מֵאֶרֶץ מִצְרָיִם: וַיָּשֶׂם אֶת הָאֶחָד בְּבֵית אֵל וְאֶת הָאֶחָד נָתַן בְּדָן: [מלכים א' יב, כח-כט]

he misinterpreted the omen, יָרָבְעָם הוּא דְּנָפַק מִינֵּיהּ – for **it was Yarovam, who issued from him,** who was indicated.[23] אֲחִיתוֹפֶל רָאָה צָרַעַת שֶׁזָּרְחָה לוֹ עַל אַמָּתוֹ – **Achithopel saw** *tzaraas* **break out on his member.** הוּא סָבַר אִיהוּ מָלֵךְ – **He thought** it meant that **he would** one day **be king.** וְלֹא הִיא – **However, it was not so,** i.e. he misinterpreted the omen, בַּת שֶׁבַע בִּתּוֹ הוּא – for **it was his** grand**daughter Bathsheba** who was indicated, דְּנַפְקָא מִינָּהּ שְׁלֹמֹה – **from whom issued Solomon,** who indeed became a king.[24]

אִיצְטַגְנִינֵי פַּרְעֹה דְּאָמַר רַבִּי חָמָא בְּרַבִּי חֲנִינָא – **The astrologers of Pharaoh – as R' Chama son of R' Chanina said:** מַאי דִּכְתִיב ,,הֵמָּה מֵי מְרִיבָה" – **What is the meaning of that which is written:** ***these are the waters of strife?***[25] הֵמָּה שֶׁרָאוּ אִיצְטַגְנִינֵי פַּרְעֹה וְטָעוּ – **It was these** waters **which the astrologers of Pharaoh saw and** about whose interpretation they **erred.** רָאוּ שֶׁמּוֹשִׁיעָן שֶׁל יִשְׂרָאֵל בְּמַיִם הוּא לוֹקֶה – **They saw** in the stars **that the savior of Israel** (Moses) **would be smitten through water.** אָמַר ,,כָּל־הַבֵּן הַיִּלּוֹד הַיְאֹרָה תַּשְׁלִיכֻהוּ" – They therefore advised Pharaoh accordingly, and, hoping to kill the Jewish savior, **[Pharaoh] declared:** ***"Every son that will be born – into the river shall you throw him!"***[26] וְהֵן לֹא יָדְעוּ שֶׁעַל עִסְקֵי מֵי מְרִיבָה לוֹקֶה – **They did not realize, however, that it was** not literally by water but rather **on account of the matter of the waters of strife that he would be smitten.** Thus, the astrologers saw the omen that Moses would be undone by water, but they misinterpreted it.

The Gemara returns to discuss the Mishnah's statement regarding Yarovam's fate:

וּמְנָא לָן דְּלָא אָתֵי לְעָלְמָא דְּאָתֵי – **And from where do we know that Yarovam will not come to the World to Come?** דִּכְתִיב ,,וַיְהִי בַּדָּבָר הַזֶּה לְחַטַּאת בֵּית יָרָבְעָם וּלְהַכְחִיד וּלְהַשְׁמִיד מֵעַל פְּנֵי [הָ]אֲדָמָה" – **For it is written:** ***Thereby the House of Yarovam incurred guilt, which led to their being obliterated and utterly destroyed from the face of the earth.***[27] ,,לְהַכְחִיד" בָּעוֹלָם הַזֶּה – ***Being obliterated*** refers to exclusion **from this world,** i.e. dying; ,,וּלְהַשְׁמִיד" לָעוֹלָם הַבָּא – ***and utterly destroyed*** refers to exclusion **from the World to Come.**

The Gemara continues discussing Yarovam:

מִפְּנֵי מַה זָּכָה יָרָבְעָם לְמַלְכוּת – אָמַר רַבִּי יוֹחָנָן – **R' Yochanan said: Why did Yarovam merit kingship?** מִפְּנֵי שֶׁהוֹכִיחַ אֶת שְׁלֹמֹה – It was **because he rebuked** King **Solomon.**[28] וּמִפְּנֵי מַה נֶּעֱנַשׁ – **And why was** he subsequently **punished?**[29] מִפְּנֵי שֶׁהוֹכִיחוֹ בָּרַבִּים – **Because he rebuked [Solomon] in public,**[30] שֶׁנֶּאֱמַר ,,וְזֶה הַדָּבָר אֲשֶׁר־הֵרִים יָד בַּמֶּלֶךְ שְׁלֹמֹה בָּנָה אֶת־הַמִּלּוֹא סָגַר אֶת־פֶּרֶץ עִיר דָּוִד אָבִיו" – **as it is stated:**[31] ***And this was the matter that he raised a hand against the king: Solomon had built up the Millo and closed up the breach of the City of David his father.*** אָמַר לוֹ – **[Yarovam] said to [Solomon]:** דָּוִד אָבִיךָ פָּרַץ פְּרָצוֹת בַּחוֹמָה כְּדֵי שֶׁיַּעֲלוּ יִשְׂרָאֵל לָרֶגֶל – **"Your father David made breaches in the wall so that Israel might come up** to Jerusalem **for the Festivals** and enter the city with ease. וְאַתָּה גָּדַרְתָּ אוֹתָם כְּדֵי לַעֲשׂוֹת אַנְגַּרְיָא לְבַת פַּרְעֹה – **You, on the other hand, closed up [the breaches] in order to levy a toll for Pharaoh's daughter!"**[32]

NOTES

23. Nevat, alias Sheva ben Bichri, saw this omen in a dream (*Aruch* ע׳ נבט [ג], *Yad Ramah*). Seeing fire coming from his member (which symbolized to him his manhood and therefore his power – *Maharal*), he wrongly assumed that he would become king; for that reason he launched a revolt against King David (*Rashi*). In reality, however, the omen meant that his seed, Yarovam, would come to rule, the fire presaging the "fire of contention" kindled by Yarovam when he led the Ten Tribes in their break from the Davidic dynasty (*Maharsha*).

24. Here, too, a dream omen was misunderstood, and led Achithopel to join Absalom's rebellion against David. Achithopel planned to use Absalom to remove David; subsequently Achithopel hoped that the throne would pass to him, in fulfillment of what he mistakenly thought was his own destiny (*Rashi*). To Achithopel's mind, the *tzaraas* spot indicated kingship, for just as a *metzora* is set apart from others, so is a king in a class by himself (*Maharal,* second explanation). Actually, however, it was Solomon, the son of his granddaughter Bathsheba, who was meant to become king. [The word בִּתּוֹ, *his daughter,* is imprecise, for above (69b) the Gemara states that Bathsheba was a *granddaughter* of Achithopel (see *R' Yaakov Emden* and *Rashash*).]

[*Rashi* is not specific about how Achithopel hoped to gain the throne after Absalom became king. The Midrash, however, relates that Achithopel had a diabolic plan: Scripture relates (*II Samuel* 16:21-22) that when David fled Jerusalem at the time of Absalom's rebellion, Achithopel advised Absalom to consort with David's concubines, whom David had left behind, and to do so in such a way that his deed would become known to all. This act, Achithopel told Absalom, would serve to allay any apprehension on the part of the public to side with Absalom, for fear that Absalom might subsequently make peace with his father, thereby causing anyone who had previously followed Absalom to be regarded as an enemy of the crown. By performing the brazen act of consorting with his father's concubines, Achithopel argued, Absalom would convince everyone that there was no hope of his becoming reconciled with his father. In truth, however, Achithopel's scheme was to subsequently try Absalom for this capital crime, and have him put to death. He (Achithopel) would then become king (*Maharshal* from *Yalkut Shimoni, II Samuel* ch. 16).]

25. *Numbers* 20:13. When, after the death of Miriam, the Jews in the Wilderness complained that they were thirsty, Moses, at the behest of God, assembled them before a certain rock to cause it to give forth water for them. Before doing so, however, he addressed them [angrily] and began, "Listen now, O rebels!" For his sin he was punished by God by not being allowed to enter the Land of Israel (see *Rashi* here and to *Deuteronomy* 33:8; *Rambam* in Introduction to Tractate *Avos* [*Shemonah Perakim*], ch. 4; cf. *Rashi* to *Numbers* 20:12).

The narrative of this incident in Scripture concludes with the words: *These are the waters of strife.* The expression "these are" intimates that some earlier allusion had been made to these waters (*Torah Temimah* to *Numbers* ibid.). To what allusion does Scripture refer?

26. *Exodus* 1:22.

27. *I Kings* 13:34. The preceding verse states: *After this matter Yarovam did not turn back from his evil way; he kept on appointing priests for the altars from among the people. Whoever wished would consecrate himself and become [one of the] priests of the altars.* The verse cited by the Gemara goes on to say that due to this sin his entire family was *obliterated* and *utterly destroyed.*

28. As the Gemara will explain shortly (*Rashi*).

29. Actually, Scripture states openly that he was punished for spreading idolatry – see note 27. The Gemara must therefore be understood to ask: Why did Yarovam's good deeds not protect him from succumbing to the temptation to worship idols? (*Yad Ramah*; see also *Maharsha*).

30. The bold act of rebuking King Solomon was in and of itself meritorious, and one for which he was rewarded by God. However, because he delivered the rebuke in public in order to shame Solomon (*Rashi*), the merit of his deed did not protect him from the temptation of idolatry (*Yad Ramah*). Additionally, the arrogance displayed by his public rebuke was a precursor to the arrogance that led to his introduction of the golden calves – see Rav Nachman below and note 37 (*Maharsha*).

31. *I Kings* 11:27. The previous verse states that Yarovam "raised a hand against the king (Solomon)." The present verse goes on to elaborate (*Rashi* ד״ה את המלוא).

32. When Solomon married Pharaoh's daughter, he installed her in the part of Jerusalem known as the City of David (*I Kings* 3:1). Subsequently, he removed her from there and installed her in a palace in a different part of the city (*II Chronicles* 8:11). In the process, he expropriated a large plaza, know as the Millo, and built her palace on that spot, thereby depriving the public of its use (*Radak* to *I Kings* 11:27). Furthermore, in building the palace he also closed up the breach in the wall opposite the plaza (*Rashi* here ד״ה את המלוא and to *I Kings* 11:27). This led to Yarovam's rebuke.

Rashi presents three alternative explanations as to the exact nature of Yarovam's complaint: (a) Solomon closed up all the breaches in the walls of Jerusalem. As a result, anyone who wished to enter the city had to do so through one of the officially controlled gates, where a toll was

גם אלה משלי שלמה אשר העתיקו אנשי חזקיה. היינו תלמידי חזקיה כדקיימא לן בהשותפין בבבא בתרא (דף טו.) חזקיה וסיעתו כתבו משלי מכלל דחזקיה היה מלמד לכל וכדאמרן (לעיל דף לד.) נעץ חרב על פתח בית המדרש וכל שכן שלמנשה בנו לימד: מכל טורח שטרח בו. ללמדו: שבאו בעלילה. שלא באו לבקש לפני הקב"ה בתפלה אלא באו בעלילה שאמרו דברים של נלחון שאין להם תשובה: הברכה אחת היא. וכי אין לך ברכה יותר תשובה ניצחת השיבו ועלתה לו: מנשה. בא בעלילה שלא להתפלל למקום אלא לבסוף אם לא תושיעני מה הועיל לי שקראתי לך יותר משאר אלהות והיינו דכתיב ויכנע ה) לפני (ה') אלהי אבותיו מכלל דעד השתא לפני אלוהות אחרים נכנע: תנא. כי אמרינן דהוגה את השם באותיותיו אין לו חלק לעולם הבא בגבולין אבל במקדש לא שהרי בשם היו מברכין: ובלשון עגה. אפילו במקדש לא לשון עגה לעז שאינו הוגה באותיותיו בלשון הקדש שלנו אלא שאר לועזין עגה לשון בלעגי שפה (ישעיה כח) מ"ר ל"א עגה לשון עוגה מקום שיש בו חבורת בני אדם שמדברין דברי חול גבולין קרי חוץ למקדש ואסור לפרש שם בן ארבעים ושתים בלשון עגה חוץ למקדש ואי עבד אין לו חלק אבל בלשון קדש אינו נענש כל כך ובמקדש הואיל ונהגו להזכיר פירושו אינו נענש: שריבע עם. שריבן את ישראל והשפילם: עשה מריבה בעם. הריבם אלו עם אלו בעסק עבודת כוכבים זה עובד וזה מוחה בידו ובאו לידי מחלוקת: שניבט ולא ראה. היה סבור להביט יפה ולעמוד על דבר עיקר ולא ראה שטעה כדאמרינן לקמן ראה אש יוצאה מאמתו וכו': נתמכמך בבנין. של מצרים שנתנוהו בבנין במקום לבנה כדמפרש באגדה שאמר לו משה להקב"ה אתה הרעות לעם הזה שעכשיו אם אין להם לבנים משימין בניהם של ישראל בבנין אמר לו הקב"ה קוצים הם מכלין שגלוי לפני אילו הם חיים היו רשעים [גמורים] ואם תרצה תנסה והוציא אחד מהן הלך והוציא את מיכה. ל"א נתמכמך עסק בבנין עד שנעשה מך כדאמרינן (סוטה דף יא.) כל העוסק בבנין מתמסכן: הוא סבר איהו מליך. ולכן נתאמץ שבע בן בכרי וקבץ כל ישראל אליו והיה רוצה למלוך כדכתיב במקרא: איהו מליך. ולכן נעשה יועץ לאבשלום כדי שתשוב המלוכה מדוד לאבשלום ובין כך ובין כך יתגלגל הדבר ותשוב אליו: על מי מריבה. שבשעה שאמר שמעו נא המורים נענש ולא נכנס לארץ ישראל: ומנא לן דלא אתי. ירבעם לעלמא דאתי והכי נמי מפרש לקמן בכלהו שלשה מלכים וארבעה הדיוטות: הוכיח את שלמה. כדמפרש ואזיל דאמר דוד אביך וכו': ומפני מה נענש שהוכיחו ברבים. לבייש: פרץ פרצות בחומה כדי שיעלו. (וירדו) [ויכנסו] בריוח: ואתה גדרת אותם כדי לעשות אנגריא. כדי שיכנסו בשערים לידע מי נכנס כדי לגבות מס לבת פרעה מ"ר ל"א שסגר השערים ועשה מגדל לבת פרעה על אחד מן השערים וכולם עוברים דרך שם כדי שיהיו מלויין עמה לכבדה ולעבדה כל עבודת בית המלך קרי אנגריא ל"א שהיה רגיל שלמה לסגור דלתות העזרה ומניע מפתחות בידו ודרכו של מלך לישן ג' שעות ביום וישראל עומדין על העזרה עד שיעמוד המלך ואמר לו ירבעם אתה רוצה שיתנו לך אנגריא לבת פרעה אשתך שתתן להם מפתחות: (בית) [את] המלוא. אחת מן הפרצות גדר ומלאו לכותל החומה ובנה שם מגדל לבת פרעה ולאנשים שעובדין לה לעיל מהאי קרא כתיב וירם יד במלך כלומר קם בדברים כנגד המלך ומרד בו: שחלץ תפילין בפניו. שהיה לו לפנות לצד אחר מפני אימת מלכותו ולחלוץ שלא בפניו ל"א חולץ תפילין בפניו לבא להתריס כנגדו בחוזקה: חלץ תפילין. אין נכון להיות בגלוי ראש לפני המלך [והוא התחיל במרד בכך להראות ולומר לו שאינו נוהג כמלך]: גמירי דאין ישיבה. הלכה למשה מסיני ולא מקרא: שהושיב רשע אצל צדיק. ואומר להם להעמיד להם צלם אחד בבית אל ואחד בדן הסכימו עמו: אמר לו רשע לצדיק. סלקא דעתך גברא כירבעם פלח לעבודת כוכבים אלא לנסיונהו בעי אם דעתו שלם עמו או נתרצה בדבר וכך היה מטעה רשע לצדיק עד שהיו כולן תמומים שכן היו רוצים ושוב לא היו יכולים לחזור בהן: ואף

א) גם אלה משלי שלמה אשר העתיקו אנשי חזקיה מלך יהודה וכי חזקיה מלך יהודה לכל העולם כולו לימד תורה ולמנשה בנו לא לימד תורה אלא מכל טורח שטרח בו ומכל עמל שעמל בו לא העלהו למוטב אלא יסורין שנאמר ב) וידבר ה' אל מנשה ואל עמו ולא הקשיבו ויבא ה' עליהם את שרי הצבא אשר למלך אשור וילכדו את מנשה בחוחים ויאסרוהו בנחשתים ויוליכהו בבלה וכתיב ג) ובהיצר לו חילה את פני ה' אלהיו ויכנע מאד מלפני (ה') אלהי אבותיו ויתפלל אליו ויעתר לו וישמע תחינתו וישיבהו ירושלים למלכותו וידע מנשה כי ה' הוא האלהים הא למדת שחביבין יסורין ת"ר שלשה באו בעלילה אלו הן קין עשו ומנשה קין דכתיב ד) גדול עוני מנשוא אמר לפניו רבונו של עולם כלום גדול עוני משישים ריבוא שעתידין לחטוא לפניך ואתה סולח להם עשו דכתיב ה) הברכה אחת היא לך אבי מנשה בתחילה קרא לאלוהות הרבה ולבסוף קרא לאלהי אבותיו: אבא שאול אומר אף ההוגה את השם באותיותיו וכו': תנא ובגבולין ובלשון עגה: שלשה מלכים וארבעה הדיוטות וכו': ת"ר ירבעם שריבע עם ד"א ירבעם שעשה מריבה בעם דבר אחר ירבעם שעשה מריבה בין ישראל לאביהם שבשמים בן נבט בן שניבט ולא ראה תנא הוא נבט הוא מיכה הוא שבע בן בכרי נבט שניבט ולא ראה מיכה שנתמכמך בבנין ומה שמו שבע בן בכרי שמו תנו רבנן שלשה ניבטו ולא ראו ואלו הן נבט ואחיתופל ואיצטגניני פרעה נבט ראה אש שיוצאת מאמתו הוא סבר איהו מליך ולא היא ירבעם הוא דנפק מיניה אחיתופל ראה צרעת שזרחה לו על אמתו הוא סבר איהו מלך ולא היא בת שבע בתו הוא דנפקא מינה שלמה איצטגניני פרעה דאמר רבי חמא ברבי חנינא מאי דכתיב ו) המה מי מריבה המה שראו איצטגניני פרעה וטעו ראו שמושיען של ישראל במים הוא לוקה אמר ז) כל הבן הילוד היאורה תשליכוהו והן לא ידעו שעל עסקי מי מריבה לוקה ומנא לן דלא אתי לעלמא דאתי דכתיב ח) ויהי בדבר הזה לחטאת בית ירבעם ולהכחיד ולהשמיד מעל פני אדמה להכחיד בעולם הזה ולהשמיד לעולם הבא אמר רבי יוחנן מפני מה זכה ירבעם למלכות מפני שהוכיח את שלמה ומפני מה נענש מפני שהוכיחו ברבים שנאמר ט) וזה הדבר אשר הרים יד במלך שלמה בנה את המלוא סגר את פרץ עיר דוד אביו אמר לו דוד אביך פרץ פרצות בחומה כדי שיעלו ישראל לרגל ואתה גדרת אותם כדי לעשות אנגריא לבת פרעה ומאי וזה אשר הרים יד במלך אמר רב נחמן שחלץ תפיליו בפניו אמר רב נחמן גסות הרוח שהיה בו בירבעם טרדתו מן העולם שנאמר י) ויאמר ירבעם בלבו עתה תשוב הממלכה לבית דוד אם יעלה העם הזה לעשות זבחים בבית ה' בירושלים ושב לב העם הזה אל אדוניהם אל רחבעם מלך יהודה והרגוני ושבו אל רחבעם מלך יהודה אמר גמירי דאין ישיבה בעזרה אלא למלכי בית דוד בלבד כיון דחזו ליה לרחבעם דיתיב ואנא קאימנא סברי הא מלכא והא עבדא ואי יתיבנא מורד במלכות הואי וקטלין לי ואזלו בתריה מיד כ) ויועץ המלך ויעש שני עגלי זהב ויאמר אליהם רב לכם מעלות ירושלים הנה אלהיך ישראל אשר העלוך מארץ מצרים וישם את האחד בבית אל ואת האחד נתן בדן מאי ויועץ אמר רבי יהודה שהושיב רשע אצל צדיק אמר להו חתמיתו על כל דעבידנא אמרו ליה הין אמר להו מלכא בעינא למיהוי אמרו ליה הין כל דאמינא לכו עבידתו אמרו ליה הין אפילו למפלח לעבודת כוכבים אמר ליה צדיק ח"ו אמר ליה רשע לצדיק ס"ד דגברא כירבעם פלח לעבודת כוכבים אלא למינסינהו הוא דקא בעי אי קבליתו למימריה ואף

עין משפט נר מצוה

כז א מיי' פ"ז מהלכות בית הבחירה הלכה ו ופי"ד מהל' סנהדרין הלכה יב ופ"ב מהל' מלכים הלכה ז:

ליקוטי רש"י

הברכה אחת. ה"א זו משמשת לשון תמיה כמו (במדבר יג, יט) הבמחנים (במדבר יג, כ) השמנה היא (ש"ב ג, לג) הכמות נבל [בראשית כז, לח]. מיכה שנתמכמך בבנין. עגל מסכה, יש אומרים מיכה היה שם שיצא מתוך דמוסי בנין שנתמעך בו במצרים והיה בידו שם וטס שכתב בו משה עלה שור עלה שור להעלות ארונו של יוסף מתוך נילוס והשליכו לתוך הכור ויצא העגל [שמות לב, ד ועי' רש"י כאן]. אחיתופל. נתן עיניו במלוכה כדאמר בחלק ראה אש יוצא מאמתו וכסבור שעתיד למלוך ומה שבידו נטלו הימנו לא יחצו ימיהם [סוטה ט: וצ"ע מגירסא המובא כאן]. איצטגניני. אילטגניגות דכל התלמוד לשון מזלות וחוזים בכוכבים [לעיל מט:]. איצטגניני פרעה. כך דרך אילטגנינין אינן רואין אלא סימן אבל לא פירושו של כל דבר. ראו. אלטגניני פרעה. שמושיען של ישראל כו'. וכדרבי אלעזר דאמר שאין יודעים מה הוגין הילכך ראו המצרים ולא ידעו מה ראו [סוטה יב:]. יום שנולד משה אמרו לו אלטגניניו היום נולד מושיען ואין אנו יודעין אם ממצרים אם מישראל ורואין אנו שסופו ללקות במים לפיכך גזר אותו היום אף על המצרים שנאמר כל הבן הילוד ולא נאמר הילוד לעברים והם לא היו יודעים שסופו ללקות על מי מריבה [שמות א, כב]. המה מי מריבה. הם הנזכרים במקום אחר אם אלו ראו אלטגניני פרעה שמושיען של ישראל לוקה במים לכך גזרו (שמות א, כב) כל הבן הילוד היאורה תשליכוהו [במדבר כ, יג]. וזה הדבר. אשר הוכיחו עליו. שלמה בנה את המלוא. ובבנין זה סגר את פרץ העיר דוד שהיה הפרץ אחורי המלוא אמר לו אביך פרץ פרצות בחומה ליכנס בו עולי רגלים ואתה גדרת אותה לעשות אנגריא לבת פרעה להושיב שם עבדיה ומשרתיה [מ"א יא, יז]. אם יעלה העם הזה וגו'. אין ישיבה בעזרה אלא למלכי בית דוד בלבד ויהיה הוא יושב ואני עומד ובמוצאי שביעית בזמן הקהל יקרא את פרשת המלך שהוא ראש במדינתו ואני כשאר העם נמצאתי בזוי [מ"א יב, כז]. אין ישיבה בעזרה. שנאמר (דברים פרק יח) לעמוד לשרת העומדים שם לפני ה'. אלא למלכי בית דוד. שמצינו בהן ישיבה, שנאמר (שמואל ב פרק ז) ויבא המלך דוד וישב לפני ה' ויאמר מי אנכי ומי ביתי וגו' [יומא כה.]. אין ישיבה בעזרה. דכתיב לעמוד לשרת (דברים יח) העומדים שם לפני ה' (דברים יח) ולא מצינו בה ישיבה אלא למלכי בית דוד שנאמר ויבא המלך דוד וישב וגו' כשאמר לו נתן הנביא אתה לא תבנה הבית כי ימלאו ימיך וגו' [שם סט:]. אין ישיבה בעזרה, דאין כבוד שמים בכך ואפי' מלאכי השרת אין להם שם ישיבה דכתיב (ישעיהו ו) עומדים ממעל לו [קרבת] על חד מן קאמיא (דניאל ז). אלא למלכי בית דוד, שחלק להם המקום כבוד להראות שמלכותו שלימה [סוטה מ:].

מסורת הש"ס

א) בקרא וכהצר, ב) [עי' הגירסא בע"י וגיר' הערוך ערך אפיא אמר קמי' רבון דעלמא אי ענית לי ענית אי לא אמינא הא כל אפיא שוין], ג) [סוטה יב:], ד) סוטה מ: מא: יומא כה. סט: קידושין עח. תמיד כז., ה) בקרא מאד מלפני.

תורה אור השלם

א) גַּם אֵלֶּה מִשְׁלֵי שְׁלֹמֹה אֲשֶׁר הֶעְתִּיקוּ אַנְשֵׁי חִזְקִיָּה מֶלֶךְ יְהוּדָה: [משלי כה, א]

ב) וַיְדַבֵּר יְיָ אֶל מְנַשֶּׁה וְאֶל עַמּוֹ וְלֹא הִקְשִׁיבוּ: וַיָּבֵא יְיָ עֲלֵיהֶם אֶת שָׂרֵי הַצָּבָא אֲשֶׁר לְמֶלֶךְ אַשּׁוּר וַיִּלְכְּדוּ אֶת מְנַשֶּׁה בַּחֹחִים וַיַּאַסְרֻהוּ בַּנְחֻשְׁתַּיִם וַיּוֹלִיכֻהוּ בָּבֶלָה: [דברי הימים ב' לג, י-יא]

ג) וּכְהָצֵר לוֹ חִלָּה אֶת פְּנֵי יְיָ אֱלֹהָיו וַיִּכָּנַע מְאֹד מִלִּפְנֵי אֱלֹהֵי אֲבֹתָיו: וַיִּתְפַּלֵּל אֵלָיו וַיֵּעָתֶר לוֹ וַיִּשְׁמַע תְּחִנָּתוֹ וַיְשִׁיבֵהוּ יְרוּשָׁלִַם לְמַלְכוּתוֹ וַיֵּדַע מְנַשֶּׁה כִּי יְיָ הוּא הָאֱלֹהִים: [דברי הימים ב' לג, יב-יג]

ד) וַיֹּאמֶר קַיִן אֶל יְיָ גָּדוֹל עֲוֹנִי מִנְּשֹׂא: [בראשית ד, יג]

ה) וַיֹּאמֶר עֵשָׂו אֶל אָבִיו הַבְרָכָה אַחַת הִוא לְךָ אָבִי בָּרְכֵנִי גַם אָנִי אָבִי וַיִּשָּׂא עֵשָׂו קֹלוֹ וַיֵּבְךְּ: [בראשית כז, לח]

ו) הֵמָּה מֵי מְרִיבָה אֲשֶׁר רָבוּ בְנֵי יִשְׂרָאֵל אֶת יְיָ וַיִּקָּדֵשׁ בָּם: [במדבר כ, יג]

ז) וַיְצַו פַּרְעֹה לְכָל עַמּוֹ לֵאמֹר כָּל הַבֵּן הַיִּלּוֹד הַיְאֹרָה תַּשְׁלִיכֻהוּ וְכָל הַבַּת תְּחַיּוּן: [שמות א, כב]

ח) וַיְהִי בַּדָּבָר הַזֶּה לְחַטַּאת בֵּית יָרָבְעָם וּלְהַכְחִיד וּלְהַשְׁמִיד מֵעַל פְּנֵי הָאֲדָמָה: [מלכים א' יג, לד]

ט) וְזֶה הַדָּבָר אֲשֶׁר הֵרִים יָד בַּמֶּלֶךְ שְׁלֹמֹה בָּנָה אֶת הַמִּלּוֹא סָגַר אֶת פֶּרֶץ עִיר דָּוִד אָבִיו: [מלכים א' יא, כז]

י) וַיֹּאמֶר יָרָבְעָם בְּלִבּוֹ עַתָּה תָּשׁוּב הַמַּמְלָכָה לְבֵית דָּוִד: אִם יַעֲלֶה הָעָם הַזֶּה לַעֲשׂוֹת זְבָחִים בְּבֵית יְיָ בִּירוּשָׁלִַם וְשָׁב לֵב הָעָם הַזֶּה אֶל אֲדֹנֵיהֶם אֶל רְחַבְעָם מֶלֶךְ יְהוּדָה וַהֲרָגֻנִי וְשָׁבוּ אֶל רְחַבְעָם מֶלֶךְ יְהוּדָה: [מלכים א' יב, כו-כז]

כ) וַיִּוָּעַץ הַמֶּלֶךְ וַיַּעַשׂ שְׁנֵי עֶגְלֵי זָהָב וַיֹּאמֶר אֲלֵהֶם רַב לָכֶם מֵעֲלוֹת יְרוּשָׁלִַם הִנֵּה אֱלֹהֶיךָ יִשְׂרָאֵל אֲשֶׁר הֶעֱלוּךָ מֵאֶרֶץ מִצְרָיִם: וַיָּשֶׂם אֶת הָאֶחָד בְּבֵית אֵל וְאֶת הָאֶחָד נָתַן בְּדָן: [מלכים א' יב, כח-כט]

וּמַאי ,,וְזֶה. . . אֲשֶׁר־הֵרִים יָד בַּמֶּלֶךְ״ – **And what is the meaning of:** ***And this . . . that he raised a hand against the king*****?**[33] אָמַר רַב נַחְמָן – **Rav Nachman said:** שֶׁחָלַץ תְּפִילָּיו בְּפָנָיו – This means **that [Yarovam] removed his tefillin in [Solomon's] presence.**[34]

The Gemara comments further about Yarovam:

אָמַר רַב נַחְמָן – **Rav Nachman said:** גַּסּוּת הָרוּחַ שֶׁהָיָה בּוֹ בְּיָרָבְעָם טְרָדַתּוּ מִן הָעוֹלָם – **The arrogance that was in Yarovam banished him from the World** to Come, שֶׁנֶּאֱמַר ,,וַיֹּאמֶר יָרָבְעָם בְּלִבּוֹ עַתָּה תָּשׁוּב הַמַּמְלָכָה לְבֵית־דָּוִד אִם־יַעֲלֶה הָעָם הַזֶּה לַעֲשׂוֹת זְבָחִים בְּבֵית־ה׳ בִּירוּשָׁלַם וְשָׁב לֵב הָעָם הַזֶּה אֶל־אֲדֹנֵיהֶם אֶל רְחַבְעָם מֶלֶךְ יְהוּדָה וַהֲרָגֻנִי וְשָׁבוּ אֶל־רְחַבְעָם מֶלֶךְ־יְהוּדָה״ – **as it is stated:** ***Yarovam said to himself, "Now the kingdom may well revert to the House of David; if these people will go up to offer sacrifices at the House of*** H**ASHEM** ***in Jerusalem, the heart of the people will turn back to their master, to Rechavam king of Judah; they will kill me and return to Rechavam king of Judah."***[35] אָמַר – **[Yarovam] said:** גְּמִירֵי דְּאֵין יְשִׁיבָה בָּעֲזָרָה אֶלָּא לְמַלְכֵי בֵית יְהוּדָה בִּלְבַד – **There is a tradition** from Sinai[36] **that there is no sitting** permitted **in the Temple Courtyard by anyone other than the kings of the House of Judah.** כֵּיוָן דְּחָזוּ לֵיהּ לִרְחַבְעָם דְּיָתִיב – **When [the people] see Rechavam sitting** there וַאֲנָא קָאֵימְנָא – **while I,** who am not from Judah, **stand,** סָבְרֵי – **they will think:** הָא מַלְכָּא וְהָא עַבְדָּא – **This one** [Rechavam], **is the king, whereas that one** [Yarovam], **must be the servant** (i.e. the subject). וְאִי יָתִיבְנָא – **And if I,** too, **sit,** מוֹרֵד בַּמַּלְכוּת הֲוַאי – **I will be** regarded as **a rebel against the** Davidic **monarchy,** i.e. as a usurper of that prerogative that Sinaitic tradition has assigned exclusively to kings descended from the tribe of Judah, וְקָטְלִין לִי – **and they will kill me** וְאָזְלוּ בָּתְרֵיהּ – **and follow him** [Rechavam].[37] מִיָּד ,,וַיִּוָּעַץ הַמֶּלֶךְ וַיַּעַשׂ שְׁנֵי עֶגְלֵי זָהָב וַיֹּאמֶר אֲלֵהֶם רַב־לָכֶם מֵעֲלוֹת יְרוּשָׁלַם הִנֵּה אֱלֹהֶיךָ יִשְׂרָאֵל אֲשֶׁר הֶעֱלוּךָ מֵאֶרֶץ מִצְרָיִם וַיָּשֶׂם אֶת־הָאֶחָד בְּבֵית־אֵל וְאֶת־הָאֶחָד נָתַן בְּדָן״ – **Thereupon,** ***The king*** (Yarovam) ***took counsel and made two golden calves. He said to [the people], "You have been going up to Jerusalem long enough! This is your god, O Israel, who brought you up from the land of Egypt!" He set up one in Beth El and the other he placed in Dan.***[38] מַאי ,,וַיִּוָּעַץ״ – **What is the meaning of "he took counsel"?** אָמַר רַבִּי יְהוּדָה שֶׁהוֹשִׁיב רָשָׁע אֵצֶל צַדִּיק – **R' Yehudah said:** It means **that [Yarovam] seated a wicked man by the side of a righteous man** in the royal council-chamber.[39] אָמַר לְהוּ – [Yarovam] then **said to [his counselors]:** חָתְמִיתוּ עַל כָּל דְּעָבִידְנָא – **"Will you sign** your approval **to all that I am going to do?"** אָמְרוּ לֵיהּ הֵין – **"Yes," they said.** אָמַר לְהוּ – **He said to them:** מַלְכָּא בְּעֵינָא לְמֶיהֱוֵי – **"I wish to become king."** אָמְרוּ לֵיהּ הֵין – **They said, "Yes,** we approve." כָּל דְּאָמֵינָא לְכוּ עָבִידְתּוּ – **"Will you do all that I tell you** as your king?" אָמְרוּ לֵיהּ הֵין – **"Yes," they said.** אֲפִילּוּ לְמִפְלַח לַעֲבוֹדַת כּוֹכָבִים – **"Even** if I command you **to worship idols?"** אָמַר לֵיהּ צַדִּיק – At that, **the righteous** member of the council **said to [Yarovam]:** חַס וְחָלִילָה – **"Heaven forbid!"** אָמַר לֵיהּ רָשָׁע לְצַדִּיק – **The wicked** member of the council thereupon **said to the righteous one:** סַלְקָא דַּעְתָּךְ דְּגַבְרָא כְּיָרָבְעָם פָּלַח לַעֲבוֹדַת כּוֹכָבִים – **"Do you really think that a** righteous **man like Yarovam would worship idols?!** Of course not![40] אֶלָּא לְמִינַסִּינְהוּ הוּא דְּקָא בָּעֵי – **Rather, it is merely to test us that he asks** this, אִי קַבְּלִיתוּ לְמֵימְרֵיהּ – to see **whether** or not **we accept his commands."** Convinced that Yarovam's written decree establishing the two idols was not intended to be actually implemented, the righteous members of the council signed. When it became clear later that Yarovam actually intended to institute idol worship, they could no longer retract.[41]

NOTES

levied. The revenue was earmarked for the upkeep of the household of Pharaoh's daughter. (b) Solomon closed up all the gates of the city with the exception of one. Over this gate he built a tower attached to Pharaoh's daughter's palace; she thus controlled all ingress and egress to and from the city. In this way servants and maids were always available to do her bidding. Also, anyone entering or leaving Jerusalem was compelled to do so through this passageway and would have to pay gifts and homage to her. (This is also the interpretation of *Aruch* ע׳ אנגריא.) (c) Solomon used to lock the doors of the Temple court and keep the keys. Since it was customary for kings to sleep until three hours after daybreak (*Berachos* 9b), the Jews would have to wait until Solomon awoke in order to commence the Temple service. Yarovam accused him of doing this so that the Jews would have to pay tribute to Pharaoh's daughter in order to obtain the keys of the Temple court.

Yad Ramah points out that in truth Yarovam's accusation was incorrect, for it is inconceivable that the righteous Solomon could have had this intention. Moreover, Solomon was so exceedingly wealthy (see *I Kings* 10:14-29) that he certainly could have supported Pharaoh's daughter in grand style without recourse to the extra revenue a toll or tribute would bring in. Rather, Yarovam merely used these accusations as a rallying point for his rebellion.

33. Since the previous verse already stated that "he raised a hand against the king" (see note 31), which is interpreted to mean a verbal assault, what does the following verse mean to add by repeating this phrase?

34. I.e. Yarovam *raised his hand* and removed his tefillin. This was a demonstrative act *against the king,* for in removing the tefillin from his head he had of necessity to bare his head, even if only for a moment; and it is considered disrespectful to appear even for a moment before the royal presence with uncovered head (*Rashi*; see *Beis Yosef* to *Tur Orach Chaim* §38 ד״ה אמר רבא).

According to an alternate interpretation, Yarovam removed his tefillin threatening to assault Solomon; thus, although he evidently was prevented from actually doing so, nevertheless, when he removed his tefillin he was *raising his hand against the king* (see *Yad Ramah;* it is unclear from *Rashi's* second explanation if the reference is to a physical assault or merely to a verbal one).

[A third interpretation cited by *Yad Ramah* is that Yarovam was actually going to remove his tefillin anyway because he needed to relieve himself (see *Shulchan Aruch Orach Chaim* 38:1). Out of respect for the royal dignity, Yarovam ought to have discreetly exited Solomon's presence and only then removed his tefillin and proceeded to the privy. Instead, Yarovam removed his tefillin in Solomon's presence, publicly indicating what he was going to do and thereby displaying contempt for the king.]

35. *I Kings* 12:26-27.

36. *Rashi* (cf. *Rashi* to *Yoma* 25a and 69b ד״ה אין; see also *Be'er Sheva* here and *Mishneh LaMelech, Hil. Beis HaBechirah* 7:6; *Teshuvos Chavos Yair* 192).

37. Yarovam's concern that he would be viewed as inferior to Rechavam indicates his arrogance (*Maharsha, Toras Chaim*). Moreover, his reputation was so important to him that he would have been willing to violate the law and sit if not for fear of being killed (*Maharsha*).

[That these were Yarovam's two concerns (that he would be regarded as inferior if he stood or would be killed if he sat down) is hinted to by the repetitiveness of the verse: *the heart of the people will turn back to Rechavam . . . they will kill me and return to Rechavam* (*Toras Chaim*).]

38. Ibid. 28-29.

39. [I.e. he followed this arrangement throughout the chamber, alternately seating a wicked man and a righteous man.]

40. Yarovam was beyond suspicion, because he had already established his piety by reproaching Solomon (*Maharsha*). Furthermore, as we will learn below, Yarovam was a preeminent Torah scholar.

41. Yarovam used the document to "prove" to the populace that his innovation was endorsed by the righteous men (*Yad Ramah*).

וְאַף אֲחִיָּה הַשִּׁילוֹנִי טָעָה וְחָתַם – **And even** the righteous prophet **Achiyah the Shilonite erred,** i.e. was misled, **and signed.**[1] דְּהָא יֵהוּא צַדִּיקָא רַבָּה הֲוָה – How is this evident? **For Yehu**[2] **was a very righteous person,** שֶׁנֶּאֱמַר ,,וַיֹּאמֶר ה׳ אֶל־יֵהוּא יַעַן אֲשֶׁר־הֱטִיבֹתָ לַעֲשׂוֹת הַיָּשָׁר בְּעֵינַי כְּכֹל אֲשֶׁר בִּלְבָבִי עָשִׂיתָ לְבֵית אַחְאָב בְּנֵי רְבִעִים יֵשְׁבוּ לְךָ עַל־כִּסֵּא יִשְׂרָאֵל״ – **as it is stated:**[3] ***Hashem said to Yehu: "Because you have acted well and done what was right in My eyes, having carried out all that I desired upon the house of Ahab, four generations of your descendants shall occupy the throne of Israel."*** וּכְתִיב ,,וְיֵהוּא לֹא שָׁמַר לָלֶכֶת בְּתוֹרַת־ה׳ אֱלֹהֵי־יִשְׂרָאֵל בְּכָל־לְבָבוֹ לֹא סָר מֵעַל חַטֹּאות יָרָבְעָם אֲשֶׁר הֶחֱטִיא אֶת־יִשְׂרָאֵל״ – **Yet it is** subsequently **written:** ***But Yehu was not careful to follow the teachings of Hashem the God of Israel with all his heart. He did not turn away from the sins that Yarovam had caused Israel to commit.***[4] מַאי גְּרַמָא לֵיהּ – Now **what caused** an apparently righteous man like [**Yehu**] to permit the worship of the golden calves to continue unmolested during his reign? אָמַר אַבַּיֵי – **Abaye said:** בְּרִית כְּרוּתָה לִשְׂפָתַיִם – **A covenant has been made with the lips;** i.e. whatever is pronounced with the lips, even insincerely, comes to pass, שֶׁנֶּאֱמַר ,,אַחְאָב עָבַד אֶת־הַבַּעַל מְעָט יֵהוּא יַעַבְדֶנּוּ הַרְבֵּה״ – **as it is stated:** Yehu proclaimed: ***"Ahab served Baal little; Yehu shall serve him much!"***[5] רָבָא אָמַר – **Rava said:** חוֹתָמוֹ שֶׁל אֲחִיָּה הַשִּׁילוֹנִי רָאָה – [**Yehu**] **saw the seal of Achiyah the Shilonite** on Yarovam's decree establishing the cult of the golden calves, וְטָעָה – **and** [**Yehu**] therefore **erred** and thought that the prophet Achiyah had actually approved the cult of the golden calves, and that it therefore could not be something evil. Yehu himself therefore became an adherent of the cult.

From Rava's explanation we see that Achiyah the Shilonite was also tricked into signing Yarovam's decree.[6]

In addition to setting up the golden calves, Yarovam also forbade the populace, under pain of death, from performing the thrice-yearly pilgrimage to Jerusalem on the Festivals, and he posted guards on the roads to enforce this decree. The kings that succeeded Yarovam continued this practice. The Gemara cites a statement by the prophet Hosea regarding this:

[ד]כְּתִיב[7] ,,וְשַׁחֲטָה שֵׂטִים הֶעְמִיקוּ וַאֲנִי מוּסָר לְכֻלָּם״ – **It is written:** ***And [in the matter of] slaughtering, the strayers went deeper; I [will bring] chastisement to them all.***[8] אָמַר רַבִּי יוֹחָנָן – **R' Yochanan said** that the meaning of this passage is: אָמַר הַקָּדוֹשׁ בָּרוּךְ הוּא – **The Holy One, Blessed is He, said:** הֵם הֶעֱמִיקוּ מִשֶּׁלִּי – **They went beyond**[9] **My** laws, i.e. their laws enforcing slaughtering to the golden calves were more stringent than the laws of the Torah, אֲנִי אָמַרְתִּי כָּל שֶׁאֵינוֹ עוֹלֶה לָרֶגֶל עוֹבֵר בַּעֲשֵׂה – for **I said** in the Torah **that whoever does not go on the pilgrimage** to the Temple to slaughter animals on the Festivals merely **transgresses a positive commandment** and is only lightly punished,[10] וְהֵם אָמְרוּ – **while they said,** כָּל הָעוֹלֶה לָרֶגֶל יִדָּקֵר בַּחֶרֶב – **that whoever** abandons the golden calves and **goes on the pilgrimage** to the Temple **shall be pierced with the sword,** i.e. shall be killed.

The Gemara discusses the fateful meeting at which Achiyah the Shilonite informed Yarovam that he would become king:

,,וַיְהִי בָּעֵת הַהִיא וְיָרָבְעָם יָצָא מִירוּשָׁלִָם וַיִּמְצָא אֹתוֹ אֲחִיָּה הַשִּׁילֹנִי הַנָּבִיא בַּדֶּרֶךְ וְהוּא מִתְכַּסֶּה בְּשַׂלְמָה חֲדָשָׁה״ – Scripture states: ***It was at that time that Yarovam went out of Jerusalem, and the prophet Achiyah the Shilonite found him on the way, and he***

NOTES

1. Achiyah the Shilonite was the old, venerated prophet [he was among those who left Egypt and heard words of Torah from Moses – see *Bava Basra* 121b and *Rambam's Introduction to Mishneh Torah*] sent by God to inform Yarovam that he would be given rulership over ten tribes, as punishment to the House of David for Solomon's misdeeds (*I Kings* 11:29-39). The Gemara states that Achiyah, too, was present at the above council meeting, and he too signed the document, thinking that Yarovam was merely testing the loyalty of his counselors (*Rashi*).

Yad Ramah argues vehemently, however, that it is inconceivable that a prophet such as Achiyah could have lent his signature to a decree legalizing paganism, no matter what pretense was used. Rather, Achiyah, who was concerned with protecting the authority of the king chosen by God, signed a statement which said simply that he would obey Yarovam's commands as the rightful king of Israel. His error was that he should have inserted in the document a proviso to the effect that his endorsement did not include commands contrary to the Torah. However, it never occurred to Achiyah that Yarovam would actually proclaim paganism, and Achiyah of course never meant his statement to be so construed, although it was so understood by Yehu – see below.

2. Yehu was the tenth king of the northern kingdom of Israel, the kingdom of the ten tribes, see *II Kings* chs. 9-10.

3. *II Kings* 10:30. Yehu, a general in the Israelite army, was anointed king by a prophet and ordered to exterminate the wicked dynasty of Ahab. Yehu did so zealously, killing the king (Ahab's grandson) and engineering the execution of Ahab's seventy other sons. In addition, he killed all practitioners of Ahab's Baal cult (see below, note 6), destroyed all monuments to Baal, and converted the temple of Baal into a public latrine. Through a prophet, God commended Yehu for his zeal.

4. Ibid. v. 31. Although Yehu did exterminate the dynasty of Ahab and the worship of Baal, he did not put an end to the worship of the golden calves which Yarovam had instituted.

5. Ibid. v. 18. In order to eradicate the worship of Baal from Israel, Yehu devised a ruse to kill all the worshipers of Baal with one blow. He pretended that he himself was an enthusiastic adherent of the Baal cult, more devoted to it than even the wicked Ahab had been, and announced that he would outdo Ahab ("*Ahab served Baal little; Yehu shall serve him much!*"). He invited all Baal worshipers to a great ceremony to be held in the temple of Baal. Deceived, the Baal worshipers came to the temple. Yehu then had the temple surrounded and proceeded to kill everyone inside. Thus, at one stroke he wiped out this pagan cult.

Although he made his declaration of loyalty to Baal purely to deceive the others, Abaye holds that Yehu erred in this; one should never allow himself to pronounce any sinful statement, for any statement, once it leaves one's lips, may come to pass (even if in a modified sense). Yehu said that he would serve Baal much; it eventually came to pass that he indeed worshiped idols, namely, the golden calves of Yarovam. See *Margaliyos HaYam* for other examples of this principle.

6. To explain the apparent paradox of Yehu so zealously eradicating the worship of Baal while at the same time allowing the calves of Yarovam to continue, it is informative to cite the words of *Kuzari* (4:14):

"It is necessary to make a great distinction between the party of Yarovam and the party of Ahab. The worshipers of the Baal were absolute idolaters (i.e. they intended to worship other gods) . . . [whereas] all the deeds of Yarovam's party were [intended] for the God of Israel, and whatever prophets they had [claimed to be] prophets of God. But the prophets of Ahab were prophets of the Baal. Yehu ben Nimshi arose to wipe out the work of Ahab . . . until he wiped out the Baal entirely, although he did nothing against the calves (of Yarovam). Those who made the first calf, the company of Yarovam, . . . intended *solely the worship of the God of Israel* (i.e. the calf was a symbol of the true God), albeit through transgressions punishable by death" [i.e. though the worship of the calves was punishable by death as idolatry, the worshipers' intent was for a form of worship of God]. See also *Radak, I Kings* 21:25, who makes the same point. For a full treatment of this issue see *Doros HaRishonim* vol. 6 ch. 5.

7. Emendation follows *Bach*.

8. *Hosea* 5:2.

9. Literally: went deeper.

10. Scripture states: *Three times a year shall all your males appear before the Presence of the Lord Hashem* (*Exodus* 23:17). This constitutes a positive commandment to make a pilgrimage to Jerusalem on the Festivals. For neglecting to perform a positive commandment, one does not incur lashes, and certainly not the death penalty. Hence, in the verse: *I [will bring] chastisement to them all,* God says: I merely chastise them, that is, mildly punish them when they fail to follow My commandment to make the pilgrimage (*Rashi; Yad Ramah*).

ואף אחיה השילוני טעה וחתם דהא יהוא צדיקא רבה הוה שנאמר א) ויאמר ה' אל יהוא יען אשר הטיבות לעשות הישר בעיני ככל אשר בלבבי עשית לבית אחאב בני רביעים ישבו לך על כסא ישראל וכתיב ב) ויהוא לא שמר ללכת בתורת ה' אלהי ישראל בכל לבבו לא סר מעל חטאת ירבעם אשר החטיא את ישראל מאי גרמא ליה אמר אביי א) ברית כרותה לשפתים שנאמר ג) אחאב עבד הבעל מעט יהוא יעבדנו הרבה רבא אמר חותמו של אחיה השילוני ראה וטעה (א) [א] דכתיב ד) ושחטה שטים העמיקו ואני מוסר לכולם אמר רבי יוחנן אמר הקב"ה הם העמיקו משלי אני אמרתי א כל שאינו עולה לרגל עובר בעשה והם אמרו כל העולה לרגל ידקר בחרב ה) ויהי בעת ההיא וירבעם יצא מירושלם וימצא אותו אחיה השילוני הנביא בדרך והוא מתכסה בשלמה חדשה תנא משום רבי יוסי עת היא מזומנת לפורענות ו) בעת פקודתם יאבדו תנא משום רבי יוסי עת מזומנת לפורענות ז) בעת רצון עניתיך תנא משום ר' יוסי עת מזומנת לטובה ח) וביום פקדי ופקדתי עליהם חטאתם תנא משום רבי יוסי עת היא מזומנת לפורענות ט) ויהי בעת ההיא וירד יהודה מאת אחיו תנא משום ר' יוסי עת מזומנת לפורענות י) וילך רחבעם שכם כי שכם בא כל ישראל להמליך אותו תנא משום ר' יוסי מקום מזומן לפורענות בשכם עינו את דינה בשכם מכרו אחיו את יוסף בשכם נחלקה מלכות בית דוד ה) וירבעם יצא מירושלים אמר ר' חנינא בר פפא שיצא מפיתקה של ירושלים ה) וימצא אותו אחיה השילוני הנביא בדרך והוא מתכסה בשלמה חדשה ושניהם לבדם בשדה מאי בשלמה חדשה אמר רב נחמן כשלמה חדשה מה שלמה חדשה אין בה שום דופי אף תורתו של ירבעם לא היה בה שום דופי ד"א שלמה חדשה שחידשו דברים שלא שמעה אזן מעולם מאי ושניהם לבדם בשדה אמר רב יהודה אמר רב שכל תלמידי חכמים דומין לפניהם כעשבי השדה ואיכא דאמר שכל טעמי תורה מגולין להם כשדה כ) לכן תתני שלוחים על מורשת גת בתי אכזיב לאכזב למלכי ישראל אמר ר' חנינא בר פפא יצאה בת קול ואמרה להן מי שהרג את הפלשתי והוריש אתכם גת תתנו שילוחים לבניו בתי אכזיב לאכזב למלכי ישראל ב) אמר רב חיננא בר פפא כל הנהנה מן העולם הזה בלא ברכה כאילו גוזל להקב"ה וכנסת ישראל שנאמר ל) גוזל אביו ואמו ואומר אין פשע חבר הוא לאיש משחית ואין אביו אלא הקב"ה שנאמר מ) הלא הוא אביך קנך ואין אמו אלא כנסת ישראל שנאמר נ) שמע בני מוסר אביך ואל תטוש תורת אמך מאי חבר הוא לאיש משחית חבר הוא לירבעם בן נבט שהשחית ישראל לאביהם שבשמים ס) וידח ירבעם (בן נבט) את ישראל מאחרי ה' והחטיאם חטאה גדולה אמר רבי חנין כשתי מקלות המתחיות זו את זו ע) ודי זהב ג) אמרו דבי ר' ינאי אמר משה לפני הקב"ה רבונו של עולם בשביל כסף וזהב שהשפעת להן לישראל עד שיאמרו דיי גרם להם לעשות להם אלהי זהב משל אין ארי דורס ונוהם מתוך קופה של תבן אלא מתוך קופה של בשר אמר ר' אושעיא עד ירבעם היו ישראל יונקים מעגל אחד מכאן ואילך משנים ושלשה עגלים אמר ר' יצחק אין לך כל פורענות ופורענות שבאה לעולם שאין בה אחד מעשרים וארבעה בהכרע ליטרא של עגל הראשון שנאמר ח) וביום פקדי ופקדתי עליהם חטאתם אמר רבי חנינא לאחר עשרים וארבעה דורות נגבה פסוק זה שנאמר פ) ויקרא באזני קול גדול לאמר קרבו פקדות העיר ואיש כלי משחתו בידו צ) אחר הדבר הזה לא שב ירבעם מדרכו הרעה מאי אחר אמר ר' אבא אחר שתפשו הקב"ה לירבעם בבגדו ואמר לו חזור בך ואני ואתה ובן ישי נטייל בגן עדן אמר לו מי בראש בן ישי בראש אי הכי לא בעינא ר' אבהו הוה רגיל דהוה קא דריש בשלשה מלכים חלש קביל עליה דלא דריש כיון דאיתפח

ואף אחיה השילוני טעה בדבר. דסבר לנסוייהו אתי וחתם בלאותו מעשה: שנאמר ויאמר ה' אל יהוא וגו' לעשות הישר וכתיב ויהוא לא שמר ללכת בתורת ה'. ואמרינן מאי גרמא ליה ואמר רבא חותמו של אחיה השילוני ראה וטעה מכלל דהוא טעה: ושחטה שטים העמיקו. שטים עובדי כוכבים על שם ששטים אחריה לשחוט לעבודת כוכבים: העמיקו. והחמירו שאמרו שכל מי שעולה לרגל ידקר בחרב כדי שילכו וישחטו לפני העגלים: ואני מוסר לכולם. כלומר אנכי לא חשתי כל כך לכבוד עצמי לומר כל מי שאינו עולה לרגל ידקר בחרב כמו שחשו הם לכבוד עבודת כוכבים אלא יסורין בעלמא יסרתים כלומר דעבר בעשה ל"א שטים כלומר שטיות שלהם שסרו מאחרי העמיקו עד שחיטה שחייבו מיתה כל מי שעולה לרגל ומניח את העגלים. ושחטה לשון שחיטה: מזומנת לפורענות. ששם נחלקה מלכות ישראל דסמיך ליה ויקח את השלמה ויקרעה לשנים עשר קרעים וגו': וביום פקדי. בתשעה באב שבכל השנה מאותן מ' שנה שעמדו במדבר יום מזומן לפורענות בו חזרו מרגלים בו נחרב הבית בראשונה ובשניה: ויהי בעת ההיא וירד יהודה. מזומנת לפורענות שתמר נתחייבה שריפה ומתו שני בניו: בשכם מכרו אחיו את יוסף. כדכתיב (בראשית לז) הלא אחיך רועים בשכם ודותן דכתיב בקרא היינו כפר הסמוך לשכם ונקראת על שם שכם אי נמי כמדרשו שהיו דנין עליו להרגו: בשכם נחלקה מלכות בית דוד. כדכתיב במלכים (א יב): מפתקה של ירושלים. מכללה שלא לחזור בה לעולם ולא ליטול חלק בעבודה: מפתקה. כגון (ב"מ דף פו.) נפל פתקה מרקיעא כלומר מחזקת של ירושלים הכתוב וחתום בה: שום דופי. גימגום בגמ': שחדשו. דרשו דברי תורה בין ירבעם לאחיה: יצתה בת קול ואמרה. כשהמליכו את ירבעם: מי שהרג. דוד: את הפלשתי. וע"י כן היה מוריש לכם גת לכן תתנו שלוחים לבניו שתעזבו מלכות בית דוד ותמליכו אחרים: בתי אכזיב לאכזב. למלכי בית דוד אתם מכזבים והלכתם אחר מלכי ישראל לפיכך תהיו נמסרין לאכזב ביד עובדי כוכבים שהן סטי כזב: אין אביו אלא הקב"ה שנאמר וכו'. ואין גזילה כלפי מעלה וכלפי כנסת ישראל אלא זו בלבד שמונע מלברך כנסת ישראל הוא גוזל להקב"ה שחכמים תקנו על כל דבר ודבר ברכה כדאמר התם (ברכות דף לה.) כל הטועם ואינו מברך נקרא גזלן שנאמר לה' הארץ ומלואה: כשתי מקלות המתיזות זו את זו. כאדם שיש בידו מקל א' ומכה בו מקל אחר ומתיזו ומשליכו ברחוק כך הדיח ירבעם את ישראל מאחרי ה' בעל כרחם: ודי זהב. איידי דאיירי עד השתא בעגלים של ירבעם מפרש האי קרא: מתוך קופה של בשר. כשיש לו הרבה לאכול הוא נוהם: עד ירבעם היו ישראל יונקים מעגל אחד. לוקין על חטא עגל אחד שעשו במדבר: ה"ג מכאן ואילך היו יונקין משלשה עגלים. שנים מירבעם ושלישי של המדבר ולפי מה שכתוב בספרים שנים ושלשה עגלים ניחא כלומר משנים שעשה ירבעם ושלישי שנעשה במדבר ושלשה היינו שלישי כמו (משלי ל) שלשה המה נפלאו ממני וארבעה לא ידעתים: אחד מעשרים וארבעה בהכרע ליטרא. לאו דוקא אלא כלומר דבר מועט מאד כמה שכף המשקל נוטה לצד זה יותר מצד זה בב"ב (דף פט.) כמה הוי הכרע ליטרא: לאחר כ"ד דורות. למעשה העגל: פסוק זה. דכתיב בעגל וביום פקדי והכא בימי צדקיה כשחרב הבית כתוב קרבו פקודות העיר קרב אותו מעשה שנאמר וביום פקדי וממעשה העגל עד צדקיה כ"ד דורות דבימי נחשון נעשה העגל צא וחשוב כמה דורות מנחשון עד צדקיה נחשון שלמון בנו בועז בנו עובד בנו ישי בנו דוד בנו שלמה בנו רחבעם בנו אביה בנו אסא בנו יהושפט בנו יורם בנו אחזיה בנו יואש בנו אמציה בנו עוזיה בנו יותם בנו אחז בנו חזקיה בנו מנשה בנו אמון בנו יאשיה בנו יהואחז ויהויקים בניו ומלכו זה אחר זה ודור אחד הם יהויכין בנו של יהויקים הרי כ"ד ד) יהויקים לא סיים מלכותו שהוגלה לבבל עם החרש והמסגר והמליכו צדקיהו דודו במקומו והלכך לא קא חשיב צדקיה דור באפיה נפשיה דהוא מלך בדור כ"ד: דהוה דריש בשלשה מלכים. דהוה קאי במתני' דשלשה מלכים אין להם חלק: איתפח

כח א מיי' פ"א מהל' חגיגה הלכה ז:

ליקוטי רש"י

בני רבעים. ארבע דורות תחת שהשמדת את בן אחאב שמלכו ארבע דורות עמרי ואחאב ואחזיה ויהורם [מ"ב י, ל]. **ושחטה שטים העמיקו.** משך שטיות' העמיקו אני אמרתי כל שאינו עולה לרגל עובר בעשה והם גזרו כל העול' לרגל יהרג הרי שהעמיקו יותר ממני ושחטה לשון זהב שחוט (מלכים א י) נמשך ונטוה וי"ת ל' שחיטת זבחים לעכו"ם. **ואני מוסר לכולם.** ואף אני אייסרם ביסורין אכין מוסר לכולן [הושע ה, ב]. **בעת פקודתם.** כשיפקוד הקב"ה עליהם ועל עובדיהם [ירמיהו נח, יא]. **מקום מזומן לפורענות.** ויצא שכמה, מקום מוכן לפורענות שם קלקלו השבטים שם ענו את דינה שם נחלקה מלכות בית דוד שנאמר (מ"א י"ב, א) וילך רחבעם שכמה וגו' [בראשית לז, יד]. **לכן תתני שלוחים על מורשת גת.** על אשר תתני שלוחים על מלכות דוד אשר הוריש אתכם גת כענין שנאמר (דה"א יח) ויקח דוד את גת מיד פלשתים ואתם מואסים בו כמו שנאמר (ישעיה ח) יען אשר מאס העם הזה את מי השלוח וגומר לפיכך בתי אכזיב שהיתה מארץ יהודה ונמשכו אחר פקח בן רמליהו סופן להיות לאכזב למלכי ישראל שיהרג פקח בן רמליהו ויכזבו הנסמכים עליו ובימי אחז נתנבאת נבואה זו. **לכן תתני שלוחים.** פי' לכן כמו על אשר כמו (ישעיה יז) על כן תטעי נטעי נעמנים על אשר נטעתיך נטעי נעמנים ואת נהפכת לזמורות זר. **בתי אכזיב לאכזב.** ל' נופל על הלשון מאגדת חלק למדתי מדרש מקרא זה כך [מיכה א, יד]. **גוזל להקדוש ברוך הוא.** את ברכתו. **וכנסת ישראל.** שכשחטאו הפירות לוקין. **אין פשע.** ולפי שהוא מיקל רואים האחרים ולמדין ממנו לעשות כן ליהנות מן העולם בלא ברכה ולכך נקרא זה המיקל חבר לאיש משחית. **לירבעם בן נבט.** שחטא והחטיא את ישראל כך הוא חוטא ומחטיא [ברכות לה:]. **גוזל אביו.** הקב"ה. **ואמו.** כנסת ישראל המחטיא את הרבי' שגוזל הקב"ה מפריד ממנו בניו וגוזל מהם טובה. **משחית.** ירבעם [משלי כח, כד]. **הלא הוא אביך קנך.** שקנאך שקנך בקן הסלעים ובארץ חזקה, שתקנך בכל מיני תקנה [דברים לב, ו]. **שמע בני מוסר אביך.** מה שנתן הקב"ה למשה בכתב ועל פה. **אמך.** אומתך כנסת ישראל כמו (יחזקאל יט) מה אמך לביאה והם דברי סופרים שחדשו והוסיפו ועשו סייגים לתורה [משלי א, ח]. **ודי זהב.** הוכיחן על העגל שעשו בשביל רוב זהב שהיה להם שנאמר (הושע ב י) וכסף הרביתי לה וזהב עשו לבעל [דברים א, א]. **אמרו דבי רבי ינאי.** לא הזכיר העון אלא למעטו ולומר אתה גרמת להם משל לאדם שהיה לו בן נאה ומאכילו ומשקו ותולה לו כיס של דינרין בצוארו והושיבו בפתח זונות מה יעשה שלא יחטא [יומא פו:]. **אין ארי דורס ונוהם.** שמח ומשתגע ומזיק [ברכות לב.]. **קרבו פקודות העיר.** הקריבו את הפקודים אשר הפקדתי לשחת את העיר [יחזקאל ט, א]. **אחר הדבר הזה.** שראה את המופת הזה ושמע את דברי הנביא ואף על פי כן לא שב ורבותינו דרשו אחר שתפסו הקב"ה בבגדו ואמר לו חזור בך ואני ואתה ובן ישי נטייל בגן עדן [מ"א יג, לג].

מסורת הש"ס

א) [מו"ק יח. ע"ש], ב) ברכות לה:, ג) ברכות לב. יומא פו:, ד) [צ"ל יהויכין כי כך מבואר בסוף מלכים ב דיהויכין הוגלה עם החרש והמסגר וכן לעיל בגמ' לח. אבל יהויקים מת בירושלים ולא הוגלה כלל].

הגהות הב"ח

(א) גמ' וטעה כתיב ושחטה. כצ"ל ואות ד נמחק:

הגהות הגר"א

[א] גמ' ראה וטעה דכתיב. נמחק תיבת דכתיב:

תורה אור השלם

א) וַיֹּאמֶר יְיָ אֶל יֵהוּא יַעַן אֲשֶׁר הֱטִיבֹתָ לַעֲשׂוֹת הַיָּשָׁר בְּעֵינַי כְּכֹל אֲשֶׁר בִּלְבָבִי עָשִׂיתָ לְבֵית אַחְאָב בְּנֵי רְבִעִים יֵשְׁבוּ לְךָ עַל כִּסֵּא יִשְׂרָאֵל: [מלכים ב' י, ל]

ב) וְיֵהוּא לֹא שָׁמַר לָלֶכֶת בְּתוֹרַת יְיָ אֱלֹהֵי יִשְׂרָאֵל בְּכָל לְבָבוֹ לֹא סָר מֵעַל חַטֹּאות יָרָבְעָם אֲשֶׁר הֶחֱטִיא אֶת יִשְׂרָאֵל: [מלכים ב' י, לא]

ג) וַיִּקְבֹּץ יֵהוּא אֶת כָּל הָעָם וַיֹּאמֶר אֲלֵהֶם אַחְאָב עָבַד אֶת הַבַּעַל מְעָט יֵהוּא יַעַבְדֶנּוּ הַרְבֵּה: [מלכים ב' י, יח]

ד) וְשַׁחֲטָה שֵׂטִים הֶעְמִיקוּ וַאֲנִי מוּסָר לְכֻלָּם: [הושע ה, ב]

ה) וַיְהִי בָּעֵת הַהִיא וְיָרָבְעָם יָצָא מִירוּשָׁלָיִם וַיִּמְצָא אֹתוֹ אֲחִיָּה הַשִּׁילֹנִי הַנָּבִיא בַּדֶּרֶךְ וְהוּא מִתְכַּסֶּה בְּשַׂלְמָה חֲדָשָׁה וּשְׁנֵיהֶם לְבַדָּם בַּשָּׂדֶה: [מלכים א' יא, כט]

ו) הֶבֶל הֵמָּה מַעֲשֵׂה תַּעְתֻּעִים בְּעֵת פְּקֻדָּתָם יֹאבֵדוּ: [ירמיה נא, יח]

ז) כֹּה אָמַר יְיָ בְּעֵת רָצוֹן עֲנִיתִיךָ וּבְיוֹם יְשׁוּעָה עֲזַרְתִּיךָ וְאֶצָּרְךָ וְאֶתֶּנְךָ לִבְרִית עָם לְהָקִים אֶרֶץ לְהַנְחִיל נְחָלוֹת שֹׁמֵמוֹת: [ישעיה מט, ח]

ח) וְעַתָּה לֵךְ נְחֵה אֶת הָעָם אֶל אֲשֶׁר דִּבַּרְתִּי לָךְ הִנֵּה מַלְאָכִי יֵלֵךְ לְפָנֶיךָ וּבְיוֹם פָּקְדִי וּפָקַדְתִּי עֲלֵהֶם חַטָּאתָם: [שמות לב, לד]

ט) וַיְהִי בָּעֵת הַהִוא וַיֵּרֶד יְהוּדָה מֵאֵת אֶחָיו וַיֵּט עַד אִישׁ עֲדֻלָּמִי וּשְׁמוֹ חִירָה: [בראשית לח, א]

י) וַיֵּלֶךְ רְחַבְעָם שְׁכֶם כִּי שְׁכֶם בָּא כָל יִשְׂרָאֵל לְהַמְלִיךְ אֹתוֹ: [מלכים א יב, א]

כ) לָכֵן תִּתְּנִי שִׁלּוּחִים עַל מוֹרֶשֶׁת גַּת בָּתֵּי אַכְזִיב לְאַכְזָב לְמַלְכֵי יִשְׂרָאֵל: [מיכה א, יד]

ל) גּוֹזֵל אָבִיו וְאִמּוֹ וְאֹמֵר אֵין פָּשַׁע חָבֵר הוּא לְאִישׁ מַשְׁחִית: [משלי כח, כד] מ) הַלְיְיָ תִּגְמְלוּ זֹאת עַם נָבָל וְלֹא חָכָם הֲלוֹא הוּא אָבִיךָ קָּנֶךָ הוּא עָשְׂךָ וַיְכֹנְנֶךָ: [דברים לב, ו] נ) שְׁמַע בְּנִי מוּסַר אָבִיךָ וְאַל תִּטֹּשׁ תּוֹרַת אִמֶּךָ: [משלי א, ח] ס) כִּי קָרַע יִשְׂרָאֵל מֵעַל בֵּית דָּוִד וַיַּמְלִיכוּ אֶת יָרָבְעָם בֶּן נְבָט וַיַּדַּח יָרָבְעָם אֶת יִשְׂרָאֵל מֵאַחֲרֵי יְיָ וְהֶחֱטִיאָם חֲטָאָה גְדוֹלָה: [מלכים ב' יז, כא] ע) אֵלֶּה הַדְּבָרִים אֲשֶׁר דִּבֶּר מֹשֶׁה אֶל כָּל יִשְׂרָאֵל בְּעֵבֶר הַיַּרְדֵּן בַּמִּדְבָּר בָּעֲרָבָה מוֹל סוּף בֵּין פָּארָן וּבֵין תֹּפֶל וְלָבָן וַחֲצֵרֹת וְדִי זָהָב: [דברים א, א] פ) וַיִּקְרָא בְאָזְנַי קוֹל גָּדוֹל לֵאמֹר קָרְבוּ פְּקֻדּוֹת הָעִיר וְאִישׁ כְּלִי מַשְׁחֵתוֹ בְּיָדוֹ: [יחזקאל ט, א] צ) אַחַר הַדָּבָר הַזֶּה לֹא שָׁב יָרָבְעָם מִדַּרְכּוֹ הָרָעָה וַיָּשָׁב וַיַּעַשׂ מִקְצוֹת הָעָם כֹּהֲנֵי בָמוֹת הֶחָפֵץ יְמַלֵּא אֶת יָדוֹ וִיהִי כֹּהֲנֵי בָמוֹת: [מלכים א' יג, לג]

was cloaked in a new robe.[11] תָּנָא מִשּׁוּם רַבִּי יוֹסֵי – Concerning this encounter, **a Tanna taught in the name of R' Yose:** עֵת הִיא מְזוּמֶּנֶת לְפוּרְעָנוּת – IT WAS A MOMENT in history PREDESTINED FOR MISFORTUNE.[12]

Having cited the teaching of R' Yose regarding the fateful moment of the split of the Jewish kingdom, the Gemara cites parallel teachings of R' Yose in regard to other fateful moments mentioned in Scripture:[13]

,,בְּעֵת פְּקֻדָּתָם יֹאבֵדוּ" – Similarly, concerning the verse: ***In their hour of visitation they shall go lost,***[14] תָּנָא מִשּׁוּם רַבִּי יוֹסֵי עֵת מְזוּמֶּנֶת לְפוּרְעָנוּת – **a Tanna taught in the name of R' Yose:** It was A MOMENT PREDESTINED FOR MISFORTUNE.

,,בְּעֵת רָצוֹן עֲנִיתִיךָ" – Similarly, concerning the verse: ***In an hour of favor, I will answer you,***[15] תָּנָא מִשּׁוּם רַבִּי יוֹסֵי – **a Tanna taught in the name of R' Yose:** עֵת מְזוּמֶּנֶת לְטוֹבָה – It is A MOMENT PREDESTINED FOR GOOD.

,,וּבְיוֹם פָּקְדִי וּפָקַדְתִּי עֲלֵהֶם חַטָּאתָם" – Similarly, concerning the verse: ***On the day I make My account, I shall bring their sin to account against them,***[16] תָּנָא מִשּׁוּם רַבִּי יוֹסֵי עֵת הִיא מְזוּמֶּנֶת לְפוּרְעָנוּת – **a Tanna taught in the name of R' Yose:** It is A MOMENT PREDESTINED FOR MISFORTUNE.

,,וַיְהִי בָּעֵת הַהִוא וַיֵּרֶד יְהוּדָה מֵאֵת אֶחָיו" – Similarly, concerning the verse: ***It was at that time that Judah went down from his brothers,***[17] תָּנָא מִשּׁוּם רַבִּי יוֹסֵי – **a Tanna taught in the name of R' Yose:** עֵת מְזוּמֶּנֶת לְפוּרְעָנוּת – It was A MOMENT PREDESTINED FOR MISFORTUNE.

The Gemara cites a parallel teaching of R' Yose concerning a fateful *place*:

,,וַיֵּלֶךְ רְחַבְעָם שְׁכֶם כִּי שְׁכֶם בָּא כָל־יִשְׂרָאֵל לְהַמְלִיךְ אֹתוֹ" – Similarly, concerning the verse: ***Rechavam went to Shechem, for to Shechem all Israel had come to coronate him,***[18] תָּנָא מִשּׁוּם רַבִּי יוֹסֵי – **a Tanna taught in the name of R' Yose:** מָקוֹם מְזוּמָּן לְפוּרְעָנוּת – Shechem was A PLACE PREDESTINED from earliest times FOR MISFORTUNE: בִּשְׁכֶם עִינּוּ אֶת דִּינָה – IN SHECHEM THEY VIOLATED DINAH;[19] בִּשְׁכֶם מְכָרוּ אֶחָיו אֶת יוֹסֵף – IN SHECHEM THE BROTHERS SOLD JOSEPH;[20] בִּשְׁכֶם נֶחְלְקָה מַלְכוּת בֵּית דָּוִד – IN SHECHEM THE KINGDOM OF THE HOUSE OF DAVID, i.e. the united kingdom of the Jews, WAS SPLIT.

The Gemara expounds *I Kings* 11:29, cited above:

,,וְיָרָבְעָם יָצָא מִירוּשָׁלַםִ" – ***Yarovam departed Jerusalem*** – אָמַר רַבִּי חֲנִינָא בַּר פַּפָּא – **R' Chanina bar Pappa said:** שֶׁיָּצָא מִפִּיתְקָהּ שֶׁל יְרוּשָׁלַיִם – This means **that [Yarovam] departed,** i.e. withdrew, **from the** city **rolls of Jerusalem.**[21] ,,וַיִּמְצָא אֹתוֹ אֲחִיָּה הַשִּׁילֹנִי הַנָּבִיא בַּדֶּרֶךְ וְהוּא מִתְכַּסֶּה בְּשַׂלְמָה חֲדָשָׁה וּשְׁנֵיהֶם לְבַדָּם בַּשָּׂדֶה" – ***And the prophet Achiyah the Shilonite found him on the way, and he was cloaked in a new robe, and the two of them were alone in the field.*** מַאי ,,בְּשַׂלְמָה חֲדָשָׁה" – **What is the meaning of** ***a new robe***? אָמַר רַב נַחְמָן – **Rav Nachman said:** כְּשַׂלְמָה חֲדָשָׁה – It is a metaphor for Yarovam's Torah knowledge, which was **like a new robe:** מָה שַׂלְמָה חֲדָשָׁה אֵין בָּהּ שׁוּם דּוֹפִי – **Just as a new robe has no defect,** אַף תּוֹרָתוֹ שֶׁל יָרָבְעָם לֹא הָיָה בָּהּ שׁוּם דּוֹפִי – **so, too, Yarovam's Torah knowledge had no defect.**[22] דָּבָר אַחֵר – **An alternate explanation:** ,,שַׂלְמָה חֲדָשָׁה" שֶׁחִידְּשׁוּ דְּבָרִים שֶׁלֹּא שָׁמְעָה אֹזֶן מֵעוֹלָם – ***A new robe*** – Yarovam and Achiyah were such outstanding Torah scholars that in the course of the Torah discussion that ensued between them, **they innovated things,** i.e. Torah insights, **no ear had ever before heard.**[23] מַאי ,,וּשְׁנֵיהֶם לְבַדָּם בַּשָּׂדֶה" – What is the

NOTES

11\. . . . *Achiyah took hold of the new robe that was upon him and tore it into twelve pieces. He said to Yarovam, "Take for yourself ten pieces, for thus said HASHEM the God of Israel: 'I am going to tear the kingdom from Solomon's hand, and I will give you ten tribes' "* (*I Kings* 11:29-31). [*Ruth Rabbah* 7:12 cites an Amoraic dispute whether it was Achiyah's new robe or Yarovam's, and most commentators to *I Kings* 11:29 follow the view that it was Achiyah's. However, the Gemara below clearly assumes the view that it was Yarovam's robe.]

12\. I.e. that occasion, when the prophet announced that the united kingdom of the Jews would be split into two, had been preordained by God to be a tragic moment in Jewish history (*Rashi*). R' Yose explains that the expression בָּעֵת הַהִיא, *at that time,* is indicative of a moment predestined by Divine Providence (*Yad Ramah*).

13\. In each of the following verses, the expression בְּעֵת, *at a time* (or hour) or בְּיוֹם, *on a day,* is used. R' Yose teaches that these expressions always indicate a moment specifically predestined by God (*Yad Ramah*).

14\. *Jeremiah* 10:15 and 51:18. In its plain context this passage is a reference to idols and their worshipers; *Yad Ramah,* however, explains that in the context of our Gemara it refers to the conquering of the Land of Israel and the subsequent destruction of the Temple on the Ninth of Av. See also note 16 below.

15\. *Isaiah* 49:8. In this passage God assures the Jewish people of their future redemption.

16\. *Exodus* 32:34. In this passage God says that He will one day punish the Jews for the sin of the Golden Calf. That day is the Ninth of Av, on which so many misfortunes occurred – see Mishnah *Taanis* 26a-b (*Rashi, Yad Ramah*).

Maharsha questions the foregoing explanation of *Rashi,* arguing that the Ninth of Av marks the date of the sin of the spies (*meraglim*), not the sin of the Golden Calf, to which the verse cited by the Gemara is referring. *Maharsha* therefore explains the Gemara to refer to the seventeenth of Tammuz, the day on which Moses beheld the Golden Calf and smashed the Tablets of the Law. This day was designated for misfortune, for numerous tragedies subsequently occurred on the seventeenth of Tammuz (Mishnah in *Taanis* ibid.).

It seems, however, that *Rashi's* explanation follows his comment in *Numbers* 14:33 that God had planned the punishment of wandering forty years in the Wilderness (which is mentioned in Scripture as the punishment for the sin of the spies) from the time the Jews sinned with the Golden Calf, but had deferred its implementation until Israel's "measure of sin became full" after the incident of the spies. Thus, the Ninth of Av was indeed the day ordained for punishment for the Golden Calf (see *Mitzpeh Eisan*).

17\. *Genesis* 38:1. This verse is the beginning of the account of the misfortunes that struck Judah's family, including the deaths of his two sons Er and Onan as well as the near execution of his daughter-in-law Tamar (*Rashi*).

18\. *I Kings* 12:1. The verse is the beginning of the tragic account of how the united kingdom of the Jews split in two.

19\. *Genesis* 34:1-2. Dinah, daughter of the Patriarch Jacob, was violated by the son of the prince of Shechem, in whose territory her family was residing at the time (ibid. 33:18-34:2).

20\. Ibid. 37:12-28. Actually, Scripture states that Joseph was sold at Dosan, a hamlet near Shechem; however, it is viewed by R' Yose as part of the territory of Shechem. Alternatively, the Gemara follows the Aggadic exposition that Dosan (דֹּתָן) is not the name of a place, but a reference to the fact that the brothers sought דָּתוֹת, *laws,* i.e. legal grounds, for their action against Joseph [see *Rashi* ibid. v. 17 and *Rashi* to *Sotah* 13b ד״ה משכם] (*Rashi*).

21\. I.e. Yarovam left Jerusalem for good. As Solomon's servant (*I Kings* 11:26), he had resided in Jerusalem; he now left the city determined never to return, so as to disassociate himself from the Temple service performed there (*Rashi*; cf. *Gilyonei HaShas*). See also *Maharal.*

Alternatively, *Aruch* (ע׳ פתק [א]) translates מִפִּיתְקָהּ שֶׁל יְרוּשָׁלַיִם as: *from that which was written concerning Jerusalem*; i.e. from the glorious reward foretold by Isaiah as being in store for the righteous in Jerusalem in the era of the Redemption: וְהָיָה הַנִּשְׁאָר בְּצִיּוֹן וְהַנּוֹתָר בִּירוּשָׁלַםִ קָדוֹשׁ יֵאָמֶר לוֹ כָּל־הַכָּתוּב לַחַיִּים בִּירוּשָׁלָםִ, *And it shall come to pass that those who remain in Zion and are left in Jerusalem – all who are inscribed for life in Jerusalem – shall be called holy* (*Isaiah* 4:3).

22\. There was no confusion or unclarity in his Torah knowledge (*Rashi*). [At the time of his appointment, Yarovam was worthy of it (*Maharsha*).]

23\. *Rashi.* Alternatively, "matters that no ear had ever before heard" refers to Yaravam's future kingship (*Yad Ramah*).

ואף אחיה השילוני טעה וחתם דהא יהוא צדיקא רבה הוה שנאמר א) ויאמר ה' אל יהוא יען אשר הטיבות לעשות הישר בעיני ככל אשר בלבבי עשית לבית אחאב בני רביעים ישבו לך על כסא ישראל וכתיב ב) ויהוא לא שמר ללכת בתורת ה' אלהי ישראל בכל לבבו לא סר מעל חטאת ירבעם אשר החטיא את ישראל מאי גרמא ליה אמר אביי א) ברית כרותה לשפתים שנאמר ג) אחאב עבד הבעל מעט יהוא יעבדנו הרבה רבא אמר חותמו של אחיה השילוני ראה וטעה (א) [א] דכתיב ד) ושחטה שטים העמיקו ואני מוסר לכולם אמר רבי יוחנן אמר הקב"ה הם העמיקו משלי אני אמרתי א כל שאינו עולה לרגל עובר בעשה והם אמרו כל העולה לרגל ידקר בחרב ה) ויהי בעת ההיא וירבעם יצא מירושלם וימצא אותו אחיה השילוני הנביא בדרך והוא מתכסה בשלמה חדשה תנא משום רבי יוסי עת היא מזומנת לפורענות ו) בעת פקודתם יאבדו תנא משום רבי יוסי עת מזומנת לפורענות ז) בעת רצון עניתיך תנא משום ר' יוסי עת מזומנת לטובה ח) וביום פקדי ופקדתי עליהם חטאתם תנא משום רבי יוסי עת היא מזומנת לפורענות ט) ויהי בעת ההיא וירד יהודה מאת אחיו תנא משום ר' יוסי עת מזומנת לפורענות י) וילך רחבעם שכם כי שכם בא כל ישראל להמליך אותו תנא משום ר' יוסי מקום מזומן לפורענות בשכם עינו את דינה בשכם מכרו אחיו את יוסף בשכם נחלקה מלכות בית דוד ה) וירבעם יצא מירושלים אמר ר' חנינא בר פפא שיצא מפיתקה של ירושלים ה) וימצא אותו אחיה השילוני הנביא בדרך והוא מתכסה בשלמה חדשה ושניהם לבדם בשדה מאי בשלמה חדשה אמר רב נחמן כשלמה חדשה מה שלמה חדשה אין בה שום דופי אף תורתו של ירבעם לא היה בה שום דופי ד"א שלמה חדשה שחידשו דברים שלא שמעה אזן מעולם מאי ושניהם לבדם בשדה אמר רב יהודה אמר רב שכל תלמידי חכמים דומין לפניהם כעשבי השדה ואיכא דאמר שכל טעמי תורה מגולין להם כשדה כ) לכן תתני שלוחים על מורשת גת בתי אכזיב לאכזב למלכי ישראל אמר ר' חנינא בר פפא יצאה בת קול ואמרה להן מי שהרג את הפלשתי והוריש אתכם גת תתנו שילוחים לבניו בתי אכזיב לאכזב למלכי ישראל ג) אמר רב חיננא בר פפא כל הנהנה מן העולם הזה בלא ברכה כאילו גוזל להקב"ה וכנסת ישראל שנאמר ל) גוזל אביו ואמו ואומר אין פשע חבר הוא לאיש משחית ואין אביו אלא הקב"ה שנאמר מ) הלא הוא אביך קנך ואין אמו אלא כנסת ישראל שנאמר נ) שמע בני מוסר אביך ואל תטוש תורת אמך מאי חבר הוא לאיש משחית חבר הוא לירבעם בן נבט שהשחית ישראל לאביהם שבשמים ס) וידח ירבעם (בן נבט) את ישראל מאחרי ה' והחטיאם חטאה גדולה אמר רבי חנין כשתי מקלות המתיזות זו את זו ע) ודי זהב ג) אמרו דבי ר' ינאי אמר משה לפני הקב"ה רבונו של עולם בשביל כסף וזהב שהשפעת להן לישראל עד שיאמרו דיי גרם להם לעשות להם אלהי זהב משל אין ארי דורס ונוהם מתוך קופה של תבן אלא מתוך קופה של בשר אמר ר' אושעיא עד ירבעם היו ישראל יונקים מעגל אחד מכאן ואילך משנים ושלשה עגלים אמר ר' יצחק אין לך כל פורענות ופורענות שבאה לעולם שאין בה אחד מעשרים וארבעה בהכרע ליטרא של עגל הראשון שנאמר ח) וביום פקדי ופקדתי עליהם חטאתם אמר רבי חנינא לאחר עשרים וארבעה דורות נגבה פסוק זה שנאמר פ) ויקרא באזני קול גדול לאמר קרבו פקדות העיר ואיש כלי משחתו בידו צ) אחר הדבר הזה לא שב ירבעם מדרכו הרעה מאי אחר אמר ר' אבא אחר שתפשו הקב"ה לירבעם בבגדו ואמר לו חזור בך ואני ואתה ובן ישי נטייל בגן עדן אמר לו מי בראש בן ישי בראש אי הכי לא בעינא ר' אבהו הוה רגיל דהוה קא דריש בשלשה מלכים חלש קביל עליה דלא דריש כיון

דאיתפח

ואף אחיה השילוני טעה בדבר. דסבר לנסויינהו אתי וחתם באותו מעשה: שנאמר ויאמר ה' אל יהוא וגו' לעשות הישר וכתיב ויהוא לא שמר ללכת בתורת ה'. ואמרינן מאי גרמא ליה ואמר רבא חותמו של אחיה השילוני ראה וטעה מכלל דהוא טעה: ושחטה שטים העמיקו. שטים עובדי כוכבים על שם שסטים אחריה לשוט לעבודת כוכבים: העמיקו. והחמירו שאמרו שכל מי שעולה לרגל ידקר בחרב כדי שילכו וישתחוו לפני העגלים: ואני מוסר לכולם. כלומר אנכי לא חשתי כל כך לכבוד עצמי לומר כל מי שאינו עולה לרגל ידקר בחרב כמו שחשו הם לכבוד עבודת כוכבים אלא יסורין בעלמא יסרתים כלומר דעבר בעשה ל"א שטים כלומר שטיות שלהם שסרו מאחרי העמיקו עד שחיטה שחייבו מיתה כל מי שעולה לרגל ומניח את העגלים. ושחטה לשון שחיטה: מזומנת לפורענות. שבה נחלקה מלכות ישראל דסמיך ליה ויקח את השלמה ויקרעה לשנים עשר קרעים וגו': וביום פקדי. בתשעה באב שבכל השנה מאותן מ' שנה שעמדו במדבר יום מזומן לפורענות בו חזרו מרגלים בו נחרב הבית בראשונה ובשניה: ויהי בעת ההיא וירד יהודה. מזומנת לפורענות שתמר נתחייבה שריפה ומתו שני בניו: בשכם מכרו אחיו את יוסף. כדכתיב (בראשית לז) הלא אחיך רועים בשכם ודותן דכתיב בקרא היינו כפר הסמוך לשכם ונקראת על שם שכם אי נמי כמדרשו שהיו דנין עליו להרגו: בשכם נחלקה מלכות בית דוד. כדכתיב במלכים (א יב): מפתקה של ירושלים. מכללה שלא לחזור בה לעולם ולא ליטול חלק בעבודה: מפתקה. כגון (ב"מ דף פו.) נפל פתקה מרקיעא כלומר מחזקת של ירושלים הכתוב ותפוס בה: שום דופי. גימגום בגמ': שחדשו. דרשו דברי תורה בין ירבעם לאחיה: יצתה בת קול ואמרה. כשהמליכו את ירבעם: מי שהרג. דוד: את הפלשתי. וע"י כן היה מוריש לכם גת לכן תתנו שלוחים לבניו שתעזבו מלכות בית דוד ותמליכו אחרים: בתי אכזיב לאכזב. למלכי בית דוד אתם מכזבים והלכתם אחר מלכי ישראל לפיכך תהיו נמסרין לאכזב ביד עובדי כוכבים שהן שטי כזב: אין אביו אלא הקב"ה שנאמר

וכו'. ואין גזילה כלפי מעלה וכלפי כנסת ישראל אלא זו בלבד שמונע מלברך כנסת ישראל הוא גוזל להקב"ה שחכמים תקנו על כל דבר ודבר ברכה כדאמר התם (ברכות דף לה.) כל הטועם ואינו מברך נקרא גזלן שנאמר לה' הארץ ומלואה: כשתי מקלות המתיזות זו את זו. כאדם שיש בידו מקל א' ומכה בו מקל אחר ומתיזו ומשליכו ברחוק כך הדיח ירבעם את ישראל מאחרי ה' בעל כרחם: ודי זהב. איידי דאיירי עד השתא בעגלים של ירבעם מפרש האי קרא: מתוך קופה של בשר. כשיש לו הרבה לאכול הוא נוהם: עד ירבעם היו ישראל יונקים מעגל אחד. לוקין על חטא עגל אחד שעשו במדבר: ה"ג מכאן ואילך היו יונקין משלשה עגלים. שנים מירבעם ושלישי של המדבר ולפי מה שכתוב בספרים שנים ושלשה עגלים ניחא כלומר משנים שעשה ירבעם ושלישי שנעשה במדבר ושלשה היינו שלישי כמו (משלי ל) שלשה המה נפלאו ממני וארבעה לא ידעתים: אחד מעשרים וארבעה בהכרע ליטרא. לאו דוקא אלא כלומר דבר מועט מאד כמה שכף המשקל נוטה לצד זה יותר מצד זה בב"ב (דף פט.) כמה הוי הכרע ליטרא: לאחר כ"ד דורות. למעשה העגל: פסוק זה. דכתיב בעגל וביום פקדי והכא בימי צדקיה כשחרב הבית כתוב קרבו פקודות העיר קרב אותו מעשה שנאמר וביום פקדי וממעשה העגל עד צדקיה כ"ד דורות דבימי נחשון נעשה העגל צא וחשוב כמה דורות מנחשון עד צדקיה נחשון שלמון בנו בועז בנו עובד בנו ישי בנו דוד בנו שלמה בנו רחבעם בנו אביה בנו אסא בנו יהושפט בנו יורם בנו אחזיה בנו יואש בנו אמציה בנו עוזיה בנו יותם בנו אחז בנו חזקיה בנו מנשה בנו אמון בנו יאשיה בנו יהואחז ויהויקים בניו ומלכו זה אחר זה ודור אחד הם יהויכין בנו של יהויקים הרי כ"ד [7] יהויקים לא סיים מלכותו שהוגלה לבבל עם החרש והמסגר והמליכו לצדקיהו דודו במקומו והלכך לא קא חשיב לצדקיה דור באפיה נפשיה דהוא מלך בדור כ"ד: דהוה דריש בשלשה מלכים. דהוה קאי במתני' דשלשה מלכים אין להם חלק:

איתפח

מסורת הש"ס

א) [מו"ק יח. ע"ש], ב) ברכות לה:, ג) ברכות לב. יומא פו:, ד) [צ"ל יהויכין כי כך מבואר בסוף מלכים ב דיהויכין הוגלה עם החרש והמסגר וכן לעיל בגמ' לח. אבל יהויקים מת בירושלים ולא הוגלה כלל].

הגהות הב"ח

(א) גמ' וטעה כתיב ושחטה. כצ"ל ואות ד נמחק:

הגהות הגר"א

[א] גמ' ראה וטעה דכתיב. נמחק תיבת דכתיב:

תורה אור השלם

א) וַיֹּאמֶר יְיָ אֶל יֵהוּא יַעַן אֲשֶׁר הֱטִיבֹתָ לַעֲשׂוֹת הַיָּשָׁר בְּעֵינַי כְּכֹל אֲשֶׁר בִּלְבָבִי עָשִׂיתָ לְבֵית אַחְאָב בְּנֵי רְבִעִים יֵשְׁבוּ לְךָ עַל כִּסֵּא יִשְׂרָאֵל: [מלכים ב' י, ל]

ב) וְיֵהוּא לֹא שָׁמַר לָלֶכֶת בְּתוֹרַת יְיָ אֱלֹהֵי יִשְׂרָאֵל בְּכָל לְבָבוֹ לֹא סָר מֵעַל חַטֹּאות יָרָבְעָם אֲשֶׁר הֶחֱטִיא אֶת יִשְׂרָאֵל: [מלכים ב' י, לא]

ג) וַיִּקְבֹּץ יֵהוּא אֶת כָּל הָעָם וַיֹּאמֶר אֲלֵהֶם אַחְאָב עָבַד אֶת הַבַּעַל מְעָט יֵהוּא יַעַבְדֶנּוּ הַרְבֵּה: [מלכים ב' י, יח]

ד) וְשַׁחֲטָה שֵׂטִים הֶעְמִיקוּ וַאֲנִי מוּסָר לְכֻלָּם: [הושע ה, ב]

ה) וַיְהִי בָּעֵת הַהִיא וְיָרָבְעָם יָצָא מִירוּשָׁלָ͏ִם וַיִּמְצָא אֹתוֹ אֲחִיָּה הַשִּׁילֹנִי הַנָּבִיא בַּדֶּרֶךְ וְהוּא מִתְכַּסֶּה בְּשַׂלְמָה חֲדָשָׁה וּשְׁנֵיהֶם לְבַדָּם בַּשָּׂדֶה: [מלכים א' יא, כט]

ו) הֶבֶל הֵמָּה מַעֲשֵׂה תַּעְתֻּעִים בְּעֵת פְּקֻדָּתָם יֹאבֵדוּ: [ירמיה נא, יח]

ז) כֹּה אָמַר יְיָ בְּעֵת רָצוֹן עֲנִיתִיךָ וּבְיוֹם יְשׁוּעָה עֲזַרְתִּיךָ וְאֶצָּרְךָ וְאֶתֶּנְךָ לִבְרִית עָם לְהָקִים אֶרֶץ לְהַנְחִיל נְחָלוֹת שֹׁמֵמוֹת: [ישעיה מט, ח]

ח) וְעַתָּה לֵךְ נְחֵה אֶת הָעָם אֶל אֲשֶׁר דִּבַּרְתִּי לָךְ הִנֵּה מַלְאָכִי יֵלֵךְ לְפָנֶיךָ וּבְיוֹם פָּקְדִי וּפָקַדְתִּי עֲלֵיהֶם חַטָּאתָם: [שמות לב, לד]

ט) וַיְהִי בָּעֵת הַהִוא וַיֵּרֶד יְהוּדָה מֵאֵת אֶחָיו וַיֵּט עַד אִישׁ עֲדֻלָּמִי וּשְׁמוֹ חִירָה: [בראשית לח, א]

י) וַיֵּלֶךְ רְחַבְעָם שְׁכֶם כִּי שְׁכֶם בָּא כָל יִשְׂרָאֵל לְהַמְלִיךְ אֹתוֹ: [מלכים א יב, א]

כ) לָכֵן תִּתְּנִי שִׁלּוּחִים עַל מוֹרֶשֶׁת גַּת בָּתֵּי אַכְזִיב לְאַכְזָב לְמַלְכֵי יִשְׂרָאֵל: [מיכה א, יד]

ל) גּוֹזֵל אָבִיו וְאִמּוֹ וְאֹמֵר אֵין פָּשַׁע חָבֵר הוּא לְאִישׁ מַשְׁחִית: [משלי כח, כד]

מ) הַלַיְיָ תִּגְמְלוּ זֹאת עַם נָבָל וְלֹא חָכָם הֲלוֹא הוּא אָבִיךָ קָּנֶךָ הוּא עָשְׂךָ וַיְכֹנְנֶךָ: [דברים לב, ו]

נ) שְׁמַע בְּנִי מוּסַר אָבִיךָ וְאַל תִּטֹּשׁ תּוֹרַת אִמֶּךָ: [משלי א, ח]

ס) כִּי קָרַע יִשְׂרָאֵל מֵעַל בֵּית דָּוִד וַיַּמְלִיכוּ אֶת יָרָבְעָם בֶּן נְבָט וַיַּדַּח יָרָבְעָם אֶת יִשְׂרָאֵל מֵאַחֲרֵי יְיָ וְהֶחֱטִיאָם חֲטָאָה גְדוֹלָה: [מלכים ב' יז, כא]

ע) אֵלֶּה הַדְּבָרִים אֲשֶׁר דִּבֶּר מֹשֶׁה אֶל כָּל יִשְׂרָאֵל בְּעֵבֶר הַיַּרְדֵּן בַּמִּדְבָּר בָּעֲרָבָה מוֹל סוּף בֵּין פָּארָן וּבֵין תֹּפֶל וְלָבָן וַחֲצֵרֹת וְדִי זָהָב: [דברים א, א]

פ) וַיִּקְרָא בְאָזְנַי קוֹל גָּדוֹל לֵאמֹר קָרְבוּ פְּקֻדּוֹת הָעִיר וְאִישׁ כְּלִי מַשְׁחֵתוֹ בְּיָדוֹ: [יחזקאל ט, א]

צ) אַחַר הַדָּבָר הַזֶּה לֹא שָׁב יָרָבְעָם מִדַּרְכּוֹ הָרָעָה וַיָּשָׁב וַיַּעַשׂ מִקְצוֹת הָעָם כֹּהֲנֵי בָמוֹת הֶחָפֵץ יְמַלֵּא אֶת יָדוֹ וִיהִי כֹּהֲנֵי בָמוֹת: [מלכים א' יג, לג]

עין משפט נר מצוה

כח א מיי' פ"א מהל' חגיגה הלכה ז:

ליקוטי רש"י

בני רבעים. ארבע דורות תחת שהשמדת את בן אחאב שמלכו ארבע דורות עמרי ואחאב ואחזיהו ויהורם [מ"ב י, ל]. ושחטה שטים העמיקו. משך שטיות העמיקו אני אמרתי כל שאינו עולה לרגל עובר בעשה והם גזרו כל העולה לרגל יהרג הרי שהעמיקו יותר ממני ושחטה לשון זהב שחוט (מלכים א י) נמשך ונטוה וי"מ ל' שחיטת זבחים לעכו"ם. ואני מוסר לכולם. ואף אני אייסרם ביסורין אכין מוסר לכולן [הושע ה, ב]. בעת פקודתם. כשיפקוד הקב"ה עליהם ועל עונותיהם [ירמיהו נא, יח]. מקום מזומן לפורענות. מקום מוכן לפורענות שם קלקלו השבטים שם ענו את דינה שם נחלקה מלכות בית דוד שנאמר (מ"א י"ב, א) וילך רחבעם שכמה וגו' [בראשית לז, יד]. לכן תתני שלוחים על מורשת גת. על אשר תתני שלוחים על מלכות דוד אשר הוריש אתכם גת כענין שנאמר (דה"א יח) ויקח דוד את גת מיד פלשתים ואתם מואסים בו כמו שנאמר (ישעיה ח) יען אשר מאס העם הזה את מי השלוח וגומר לפיכך בתי אכזיב שהיא מלכות יהודה ונמשכו אחר פקח בן רמליהו סופן להיות לאכזב למלכי ישראל שיהרג פקח בן רמליהו ויכזבו הנסמכים עליו ובימי אחז נתנבאת נבואה זו. לכן תתני שלוחים. פי' לכן כמו על אשר כמו (ישעיה יז) על כן תטעי נטעי נעמנים על אשר נטעתיך נטעי נעמנים ואת נהפכת לזמורות זר. בתי אכזיב לאכזב. ל' נופל על הלשון מאגדת מלך למדתי מדרש מקרא זה כך [מיכה א, יד]. גוזל להקדוש ברוך הוא. את ברכתו. וכנסת ישראל. שבשחטאתו הפירות לוקין. אין פשע. ולפי שהוא מיקל רואה האחרים ולמדין ממנו לעשות כן ליהנות מן העולם בלא ברכה ולכך נקרא זה המיקל חבר לאיש משחית. לירבעם בן נבט. שחטא והחטיא את ישראל כך הוא חוטא ומחטיא [ברכות לה:]. גוזל אביו. הקב"ה. ואמו. כנסת ישראל. המחטיא את הרבים גוזל הקב"ה מפריש ממנו בניו וגוזל מהם טובה. משחית. ירבעם [משלי כח, כד]. הלא הוא אביך קנך. שקנאך שקננך בקן הסלעים ובארץ חזקה, שתקנך בכל מיני תקנה [דברים לב, ו]. שמע בני מוסר אביך. מה שנתן הקב"ה למשה בכתב ועל פה. אמך. אומתך כנסת ישראל כמו (יחזקאל יט) מה אמך לביאה והם דברי סופרים שחדשו והוסיפו ועשו סייגים לתורה [משלי א, ח]. ודי זהב. הוכיחן על העגל שעשו בשביל רוב זהב שהיה להם שנאמר (הושע ב ז) וכסף הרביתי לה וזהב עשו לבעל [דברים א, א]. אמרו דבי רבי ינאי. לא הזכיר העון אלא למעטו ולומר אתה גרמת להם משל לאדם שהיה לו בן נאה ומאכילו ומשקהו ותולה לו כיס של דינרין בצוארו והושיבו בפתח זונות מה יעשה שלא יחטא [יומא פו:]. אין ארי דורס ונוהם. שמח ומשתגע ומזיק [ברכות לב.]. קרבו פקדות העיר. הקריבו את הפקודים אשר הפקדתי לשחת את העיר [יחזקאל ט, א]. אחר הדבר הזה. שראה את המופת הזה ושמע את דברי הנביא ואף על פי כן לא שב ורבותינו דרשו אחר שתפשו הקב"ה בבגדו ואמר לו חזור בך ואני ואתה ובן ישי נטייל בגן עדן [מ"א יג, לג].

meaning of *and the two of them were alone in the field*? אָמַר רַב יְהוּדָה אָמַר רַב – **Rav Yehudah said in the name of Rav:** שֶׁכָּל תַּלְמִידֵי חֲכָמִים דּוֹמִין לִפְנֵיהֶם כְּעִשְׂבֵי הַשָּׂדֶה – It means **that all the** other **Torah scholars were like grass in the field,** i.e. insignificant, **compared to them.** וְאִיכָּא דְּאָמַר – **And some say:** שֶׁכָּל טַעֲמֵי תוֹרָה מְגוּלִּין לָהֶם כְּשָׂדֶה – It means that they were such accomplished Torah scholars **that all the reasons for** the commandments of **the Torah were as revealed to them as an open field** is to an onlooker.

The Ten Tribes are castigated for abandoning the Davidic dynasty in favor of Yarovam:[24]

,,לָכֵן תִּתְּנִי שִׁלּוּחִים עַל מוֹרֶשֶׁת גַּת בָּתֵּי אַכְזִיב לְאַכְזָב לְמַלְכֵי יִשְׂרָאֵל" – Scripture states: ***Because you gave discharges to Moreshes Gath, [therefore] the houses of Achziv shall be a disappointment*** (*achzav*) ***for the kings of Israel.***[25] אָמַר רַבִּי חֲנִינָא בַּר פָּפָּא – **R' Chanina bar Pappa said:** יָצְאָה בַּת קוֹל וְאָמְרָה לָהֶן – When Yarovam was proclaimed king by the tribes of Israel, **a heavenly voice rang out and said to them:** מִי שֶׁהָרַג אֶת הַפְּלִשְׁתִּי וְהוֹרִישׁ אֶתְכֶם גַּת תִּתְּנוּ שִׁילּוּחִים לְבָנָיו – Is this how you show your gratitude to David? **He who slew the Philistine** (Goliath) **and bequeathed** the Philistine city of **Gath to you,** i.e. David, **will you give discharge to his descendants!?**[26] ,,בָּתֵּי אַכְזִיב לְאַכְזָב לְמַלְכֵי יִשְׂרָאֵל" – ***The houses of falseness*** *(Achziv),* i.e. the Ten Tribes, who betrayed their allegiance to the House of David and followed Yarovam, ***[will fall] to those who stray after falsehood*** (*achzav*), i.e. gentile idolaters, ***[because]*** those tribes abandoned David's heirs in favor ***of the kings of Israel.***[27]

Yarovam is cited as the man who damaged the relationship between God and the people of Israel:

כָּל הַנֶּהֱנֶה – אָמַר רַב חִינָנָא בַּר פָּפָּא – **Rav Chinena bar Pappa said:** מִן הָעוֹלָם הַזֶּה בְּלֹא בְרָכָה – **Whoever derives pleasure from this world without** first reciting **a blessing** כְּאִילּוּ גּוֹזֵל לְהַקָּדוֹשׁ בָּרוּךְ הוּא וּכְנֶסֶת יִשְׂרָאֵל – **is considered as if he robs God as well as the Assembly of Israel,**[28] שֶׁנֶּאֱמַר ,,גּוֹזֵל אָבִיו וְאִמּוֹ וְאֹמֵר אֵין־פָּשַׁע חָבֵר הוּא לְאִישׁ מַשְׁחִית" – **as it is stated:**[29] ***He who robs his father and his mother and says, "It is no crime," is a companion to a destructive person,*** וְאֵין ,,אָבִיו" אֶלָּא הַקָּדוֹשׁ בָּרוּךְ הוּא – ***his father*** **being none other than the Holy One, Blessed is He,** שֶׁנֶּאֱמַר ,,הֲלוֹא־הוּא אָבִיךָ קָּנֶךָ" – **as it is stated:** ***Is He not your Father, your Master?***[30] וְאֵין אִמּוֹ אֶלָּא כְּנֶסֶת יִשְׂרָאֵל – **and** ***his mother*** **being none other than the Assembly of Israel,** i.e. the Jewish people, שֶׁנֶּאֱמַר ,,שְׁמַע בְּנִי מוּסַר אָבִיךָ וְאַל־תִּטֹּשׁ תּוֹרַת אִמֶּךָ" – **as it is stated:** ***Heed, my son, the discipline of your father, and do not forsake the instruction of your mother.***[31] מַאי ,,חָבֵר הוּא לְאִישׁ מַשְׁחִית" – **What** is the meaning of ***he is a companion to a destructive person***? חָבֵר הוּא לְיָרָבְעָם בֶּן נְבָט – It means that **he is a companion to Yarovam ben Nevat,** שֶׁהִשְׁחִית יִשְׂרָאֵל לַאֲבִיהֶם שֶׁבַּשָּׁמַיִם – **who destroyed** the bond that tied **Israel to their Father in Heaven.**[32]

The Gemara expounds another verse along these same lines: ,,וַיַּדַּח יָרָבְעָם אֶת־יִשְׂרָאֵל מֵאַחֲרֵי ה' וְהֶחֱטִיאָם חֲטָאָה גְדוֹלָה" – ***And Yarovam pushed Israel away from Hashem; he caused them to commit a great sin.***[33] אָמַר רַבִּי חָנִין – **R' Chanin said:** כִּשְׁתֵּי מַקְלוֹת הַמַּתִּיזוֹת זוֹ אֶת זוֹ – **Like two sticks** that are knocked together, **one sending the other flying.**[34]

Having discussed the golden calves set up by Yarovam, the Gemara now discusses the original Golden Calf of *Exodus* 32: ,,וְדִי זָהָב" – Scripture states: ***And Di-zahav.***[35] אָמְרוּ דְּבֵי

NOTES

24. Even though Yarovam was chosen by God to be king over Israel, as the prophet Achiyah stated, this fact was communicated to Yarovam only in private, and was not known to the tribes. Thus, they could be held responsible for their disloyalty to David's family (*Ben Yehoyada*). Additionally, at the time of the communication, Achiyah stated that Yarovam's rulership was conditional upon his following the Torah as meticulously as did David (*I Kings* 11:38), and even then it was only temporary [ibid. v. 39] (*Hagahos Yavetz*). Moreover, even if the Ten Tribes knew of Achiyah's mission, they acted toward the House of David with a contempt which was a sin in itself (*Yad David*).

25. *Micah* 1:14. This obscure verse, here literally translated, is variously interpreted by the commentators ad loc. R' Chanina bar Pappa will presently give an original translation, in accordance with his exegesis of the verse.

26. I.e. is this how you repay David for his slaying of Goliath of Gath (*I Samuel* 17:49-50), whereby the Jews became masters of Gath (*Rashi*)?

[Actually, the Jews did not become masters of Gath at the time David killed Goliath; rather, this occurred a number of years later when David, as king, conquered Gath (*I Chronicles* 18:1). Perhaps *Rashi* refers to the terms under which the duel between David and Goliath was fought: Goliath proposed that he would represent the Philistines, and that the Jews would send someone to represent themselves; if the Jew would triumph, the Philistines would be servants of the Jews, and if he, Goliath, would be victorious, the Jews would become slaves to the Philistines. Based on these terms, by killing Goliath David won for Israel mastery over the Philistines (and, by extension, over their principal city Gath). Thus, when David subsequently attacked and subjugated Gath, he was merely taking for Israel what they were entitled to under the terms of the duel. (See also *Rashi* to *Samuel* 21:12 where it is evident that even the Philistines recognized the validity of these terms.)]

27. אַכְזָב refers to idolaters, who in *Psalms* 40:5 are called שָׂטֵי כָזָב, *strayers after falseness* (see *Rashi;* cf. *Yad Ramah*).

28. I.e. such a person robs God of the blessing due Him as the One Who provided the pleasure (*Rashi*); alternatively, he robs God of the *food,* for before a blessing is pronounced, the food belongs to God (see *Berachos* 35a and *Marasha* there). Additionally, he robs the Jewish people, because his ingratitude calls down God's wrath upon the Land of Israel; as a result the crops fail and the Jewish people suffer famine (*Rashi* to *Berachos* 35b).

29. *Proverbs* 28:24.

30. *Deuteronomy* 32:6. The verse in its entirety reads: *Is it to Hashem that you do this, O vile and unwise people? Is He not your Father, your Master, Has He not created you and firmed you?*

31. *Proverbs* 1:8. [The Torah, which *Deuteronomy* 33:4 calls *the heritage of the Congregation of Jacob* (the entire Jewish nation), is here referred to as *the instruction of your mother*; thus, *mother* is a metaphor for the Jewish nation, *the Assembly of Israel.*]

32. Just as Yarovam led Israel astray by inducing them to worship idols, so does one who eats without pronouncing a blessing lead others astray, for others learn from his negative example to make light of reciting blessings (*Rashi* to *Berachos* ibid. ד"ה אין פשע). In both cases, the Divine blessings Israel could have received are lost.

33. *II Kings* 17:21.

34. R' Chanin describes Yarovam's causing Israel to sin by comparing it to a person who took a stick, swung it with great force at another stick, and thereby caused that other stick to fly a great distance away. [The second stick flies not because of its own power, but solely due to the force of the first stick.] So, too, by his fostering of idolatry, Yarovam gave the Jews a "violent push" away from God against their will (*Rashi*). [This is stated as a למוד זכות, an argument in defense of the Jews (*R' Avigdor Miller*).]

Alternatively, the two sticks here represent not Yarovam and Israel but Judah and Israel, following the metaphor of *Ezekiel* 37:16: *Now you, son of man, take yourself one wooden stick and write upon it, "For Judah and the Children of Israel, his comrades," and take another wooden stick and write upon it, "For Joseph, the wooden stick of Ephraim, and all the Children of Israel his comrades"* (see also *Zechariah* 11:7-14). That is, Yarovam's secession led to clashes between the kingdom of Ephraim (i.e. the Ten Tribes) and the kingdom of Judah (*Margaliyos HaYam*).

35. *Deuteronomy* 1:1. In its entirety, the verse reads: *These are the words that Moses spoke to all Israel, on the other side of the Jordan, in the Wilderness, in the Arabah, opposite the Sea of Reeds, between Paran and Tophel, and Laban, and Hazeroth, and Di-zahav.* The Sages interpreted the various place-names as reminders of sins done in the Wilderness. Here the interpretation of Di-zahav is given.

ואף אחיה השילוני טעה וחתם דהא יהוא צדיקא רבה הוה שנאמר [א] ויאמר ה' אל יהוא יען אשר הטיבות לעשות הישר בעיני ככל אשר בלבבי עשית לבית אחאב בני רביעים ישבו לך על כסא ישראל וכתיב [ב] ויהוא לא שמר ללכת בתורת ה' אלהי ישראל בכל לבבו לא סר מעל חטאת ירבעם אשר החטיא את ישראל מאי גרמא ליה אמר אביי ברית כרותה לשפתים שנאמר [ג] אחאב עבד הבעל מעט יהוא יעבדנו הרבה רבא אמר חותמו של אחיה השילוני ראה וטעה (א) [א] דכתיב [ד] ושחטה שטים העמיקו ואני מוסר לכולם אמר רבי יוחנן אמר הקב"ה הם העמיקו משלי אני אמרתי כל שאינו עולה לרגל עובר בעשה והם אמרו כל העולה לרגל ידקר בחרב [ה] ויהי בעת ההיא וירבעם יצא מירושלם וימצא אותו אחיה השילוני הנביא בדרך והוא מתכסה בשלמה חדשה תנא משום רבי יוסי עת היא מזומנת לפורענות [ו] בעת פקודתם יאבדו תנא משום רבי יוסי עת מזומנת לפורענות [ז] בעת רצון עניתיך תנא משום ר' יוסי עת מזומנת לטובה [ח] וביום פקדי ופקדתי עליהם חטאתם תנא משום רבי יוסי עת היא מזומנת לפורענות [ט] ויהי בעת ההיא וירד יהודה מאת אחיו תנא משום ר' יוסי עת מזומנת לפורענות [י] וילך רחבעם שכם כי שכם בא כל ישראל להמליך אותו תנא משום ר' יוסי מקום מזומן לפורענות בשכם עינו את דינה בשכם מכרו אחיו את יוסף בשכם נחלקה מלכות בית דוד [ה] וירבעם יצא מירושלים אמר ר' חנינא בר פפא שיצא מפיתקה של ירושלים [ה] וימצא אותו אחיה השילוני הנביא בדרך והוא מתכסה בשלמה חדשה ושניהם לבדם בשדה מאי בשלמה חדשה אמר רב נחמן כשלמה חדשה מה שלמה חדשה אין בה שום דופי אף תורתו של ירבעם לא היה בה שום דופי ד"א שלמה חדשה שחידשו דברים שלא שמעה אזן מעולם מאי ושניהם לבדם בשדה אמר רב יהודה אמר רב שכל תלמידי חכמים דומין לפניהם כעשבי השדה ואיכא דאמר שכל טעמי תורה מגולין להם כשדה [כ] לכן תתני שלוחים על מורשת גת בתי אכזיב לאכזב למלכי ישראל אמר ר' חנינא בר פפא יצאה בת קול ואמרה להן מי שהרג את הפלשתי והוריש אתכם גת תתנו שילוחים לבניו בתי אכזיב לאכזב למלכי ישראל [ג] אמר רב חיננא בר פפא כל הנהנה מן העולם הזה בלא ברכה כאילו גוזל להקב"ה וכנסת ישראל שנאמר [ל] גוזל אביו ואמו ואומר אין פשע חבר הוא לאיש משחית ואין אביו אלא הקב"ה שנאמר [מ] הלא הוא אביך קנך ואין אמו אלא כנסת ישראל שנאמר [נ] שמע בני מוסר אביך ואל תטוש תורת אמך מאי חבר הוא לאיש משחית חבר הוא לירבעם בן נבט שהשחית ישראל לאביהם שבשמים [ס] וידח ירבעם (בן נבט) את ישראל מאחרי ה' והחטיאם חטאה גדולה אמר רבי חנין כשתי מקלות המתיזות זו את זו [ע] ודי זהב [ג] אמרו דבי ר' ינאי אמר משה לפני הקב"ה רבונו של עולם בשביל כסף וזהב שהשפעת להן לישראל עד שיאמרו דיי גרם להם לעשות להם אלהי זהב משל אין ארי דורס ונוהם מתוך קופה של תבן אלא מתוך קופה של בשר אמר ר' אושעיא עד ירבעם היו ישראל יונקים מעגל אחד מכאן ואילך משנים ושלשה עגלים אמר ר' יצחק אין לך כל פורענות ופורענות שבאה לעולם שאין בה אחד מעשרים וארבעה בהכרע ליטרא של עגל הראשון שנאמר [ח] וביום פקדי ופקדתי עליהם חטאתם אמר רבי חנינא לאחר עשרים וארבעה דורות נגבה פסוק זה שנאמר [פ] ויקרא באזני קול גדול לאמר קרבו פקדות העיר ואיש כלי משחתו בידו [צ] אחר הדבר הזה לא שב ירבעם מדרכו הרעה מאי אחר אמר ר' אבא אחר שתפסו הקב"ה לירבעם בבגדו ואמר לו חזור בך ואני ואתה ובן ישי נטייל בגן עדן אמר לו מי בראש בן ישי בראש אי הכי לא בעינא ר' אבהו הוה רגיל דהוה קא דריש בשלשה מלכים חלש קביל עליה דלא דריש כיון

דאיתפח

רש"י

ואף אחיה השילוני טעה בדבר. דסבר לנסוייהו אתי ותפס באותו מעשה: שנאמר ויאמר ה' אל יהוא וגו' לעשות הישר וכתיב ויהוא לא שמר ללכת בתורת ה'. ואמרינן מאי גרמא ליה ואמר רבא חותמו של אחיה השילוני ראה וטעה מכלל דהוא טעה: ושחטה שטים העמיקו. שטים עובדי כוכבים על שם שסטים אחריה לשחוט לעבודת כוכבים: העמיקו. והחמירו שאמרו שכל מי שעולה לרגל ידקר בחרב כדי שילכו וישחטו לפני העגלים: ואני מוסר לכולם. כלומר אנכי לא חשתי כל כך לכבוד עצמי לומר כל מי שאינו עולה לרגל ידקר בחרב כמו שחשו הם לכבוד עבודת כוכבים אלא יסורין בעלמא יסרתים כלומר דעבר בעשה ל"א שטים כלומר שטיות שלהם שסרו מאחרי העמיקו עד שחיטה שחייבו מיתה כל מי שעולה לרגל ומניח את העגלים. ושחטה לשון שחיטה: מזומנת לפורענות. שאז נחלקה מלכות ישראל דסמיך ליה ויקח את השלמה ויקרעה לשנים עשר קרעים וגו': וביום פקדי. בתשעה באב שבכל השנה מאותן מ' שנה שעמדו במדבר יום מזומן לפורענות בו חזרו מרגלים בו נחרב הבית בראשונה ובשניה: ויהי בעת ההיא וירד יהודה. מזומנת לפורענות שתמר נתחייבה שריפה ומתו שני בניו: בשכם מכרו אחיו את יוסף. כדכתיב (בראשית לז) הלא אחיך רועים בשכם ודותן דכתיב בקרא היינו כפר הסמוך לשכם ונקראת על שם שכם אי נמי כמדרשו שהיו דנין עליו להרגו: בשכם נחלקה מלכות בית דוד. כדכתיב במלכים (א יב): מפתקה של ירושלים. מכללה שלא לחזור בה לעולם ולא ליטול חלק בעבודה: מפתקה. כגון (ב"מ דף פו.) נפל פתקה מרקיעא כלומר מחזקת של ירושלים הכתוב וחתום בה: שום דופי. גימגום בגמ': שחדשו. דרשו דברי תורה בין ירבעם לאחיה: יצתה בת קול ואמרה. כשהמליכו את ירבעם: מי שהרג. דוד: את הפלשתי. וע"י כן היה מוריש לכם גת לכן תתנו שלוחים לבניו שתעזבו מלכות בית דוד ותמליכו אחרים: בתי אכזיב לאכזב. למלכי בית דוד אתם מכזבים והלכתם אחר מלכי ישראל לפיכך תהיו נמסרין לאכזב ביד עובדי כוכבים שהן שטי כזב: אין אביו אלא הקב"ה שנאמר וכו'. ואין גזילה כלפי מעלה וכלפי כנסת ישראל אלא זו בלבד שמונע מלברך כנסת ישראל הוא גוזל להקב"ה שחכמים תקנו על כל דבר ודבר ברכה כדאמר התם (ברכות דף לה.) כל הטועם ואינו מברך נקרא גזלן שנאמר לה' הארץ ומלואה: כשתי מקלות המתיזות זו את זו. כאדם שיש בידו מקל א' ומכה בו מקל אחר ומתיזו ומשליכו ברחוק כך הדיח ירבעם את ישראל מאחרי ה' בעל כרחם: ודי זהב. איידי דאיירי עד השתא בעגלים של ירבעם מפרש האי קרא: מתוך קופה של בשר. כשיש לו הרבה לאכול הוא נוהם: עד ירבעם היו ישראל יונקים מעגל אחד. לוקין על חטא עגל אחד שעשו במדבר: ה"ג מכאן ואילך היו יונקין משלשה עגלים. שנים מירבעם ושלישי של המדבר ולפי מה שכתוב בספרים שנים ושלשה עגלים ניחא כלומר משנים שעשה ירבעם ושלישי שנעשה במדבר ושלשה היינו שלישי כמו (משלי ל) שלשה המה נפלאו ממני וארבעה לא ידעתים: אחד מעשרים וארבעה בהכרע ליטרא. לאו דוקא אלא כלומר דבר מועט מאד כמה שכף המשקל נוטה לצד זה יותר מצד זה בב"ב (דף פט.) כמה הוי הכרע ליטרא: לאחר כ"ד דורות. למעשה העגל: פסוק זה. דכתיב בעגל וביום פקדי והכא בימי צדקיה כשחרב הבית כתוב קרבו פקודות העיר קרב אותו מעשה שנאמר וביום פקדי וממעשה העגל עד צדקיה כ"ד דורות דבימי נחשון נעשה העגל לא וחשוב כמה דורות מנחשון עד צדקיה נחשון שלמון בנו בועז בנו עובד בנו ישי בנו דוד בנו שלמה בנו רחבעם בנו אביה בנו אסא בנו יהושפט בנו יורם בנו אחזיה בנו יואש בנו אמציה בנו עוזיה בנו יותם בנו אחז בנו חזקיה בנו מנשה בנו אמון בנו יאשיה בנו יהואחז ויהויקים בניו ומלכו זה אחר זה ודור אחד הם יהויכין בנו של יהויקים הרי כ"ד [ד] יהויקים לא סיים מלכותו שהוגלה לבבל עם החרש והמסגר והמליכו לצדקיהו דודו במקומו והלכך לא קא חשיב לצדקיה דור באפיה נפשיה דהוא מלך בדור כ"ד: דהוה דריש בשלשה מלכים. דהוה קאי במתני' דשלשה מלכים אין להם חלק:

איתפח

עין משפט נר מצוה

כח א מיי' פ"א מהל' חגיגה הלכה ז:

ליקוטי רש"י

בני רבעים. ארבע דורות תחת שהשמדת את בן אחאב שמלכו ארבע דורות עמרי ואחאב ואחזיה ויהורם [מ"ב י, ל]. ושחטה שטים העמיקו. משך שטיות' העמיקו אני אמרתי כל שאינו עולה לרגל עובר בעשה והם גזרו כל העול' לרגל יהרג הרי שהעמיקו יותר ממני ושחטה לשון זהב שחוט (מלכים א י) נמשך ונטוה וי"ת ל' שחיטת זבחים לעכו"ם. ואני מוסר לכולם. ואף אני אייסרם ביסורין אכין מוסר לכולן [הושע ה, ב]. בעת פקודתם. כשיפקוד הקב"ה עליהם ועל עובדיהם [ירמיהו נח, יא]. מקום מזומן לפורענות. ויצא שכמה, מקום מוכן לפורענות שם קלקלו השבטים שם ענו את דינה שם נחלקה מלכות בית דוד שנאמר (מ"א י"ב, א) וילך רחבעם שכמה וגו' [בראשית לז, יד]. לכן תתני שלוחים על מורשת גת. על אשר תתני שלוחים על מלכות דוד אשר הוריש אתכם גת כענין שנאמר (דה"א יח) ויקח דוד את גת מיד פלשתים ואתם מואסים בו כמו שנאמר (ישעיה ח) יען אשר מאס העם הזה את מי השלוח וגומר לפיכך בתי אכזיב שהיתה מארץ יהודה ונמשכו אחר פקח בן רמליהו סופן להיות לאכזב למלכי ישראל שיהרג פקח בן רמליהו ויכזבו הנסמכים עליו ובימי אחז נתנבאת נבואה זו. לכן תתני שלוחים. פי' לכן כמו על אשר כמו (ישעיה יז) על כן תטעי נטעי נעמנים על אשר נטעתיך נטעי נעמנים ואת נהפכת לזמורות זר. בתי אכזיב לאכזב. ל' נופל על הלשון מאגדת חלק למדתי מדרש מקרא זה כך [מיכה א, יד]. גוזל להקדוש ברוך הוא. את ברכתו. וכנסת ישראל. שכשחטאו הפירות לוקין. אין פשע. ולפי שהוא מיקל רואים האחרים ולמדין ממנו לעשות כן ליהנות מן העולם בלא ברכה ולכך נקרא זה המיקל חבר לאיש משחית. לירבעם בן נבט. שחטא והחטיא את ישראל כך הוא חוטא ומחטיא [ברכות לה:]. גוזל אביו. הקב"ה. ואמו. כנסת ישראל המחטיא את הרבי' שגוזל הקב"ה מפריד ממנו בניו וגוזל מהם טובה. משחית. ירבעם [משלי כח, כד]. הלא הוא אביך קנך. שקנאך שקננך בקן הסלעים ובארץ חזקה, שתקנך בכל מיני תקנה [דברים לב, ו]. שמע בני מוסר אביך. מה שנתן הקב"ה למשה בכתב ועל פה. אמך. אומתך כנסת ישראל כמו (יחזקאל יט) מה אמך לביאה והם דברי סופרים שחדשו והוסיפו ועשו סייגים לתורה [משלי א, ח]. ודי זהב. הוכיחן על העגל שעשו בשביל רוב זהב שהיה להם שנאמר (הושע ב י) וכסף הרביתי לה וזהב עשו לבעל [דברים א, א]. אמרו דבי רבי ינאי. לא הזכיר העון אלא למעטו ולומר אתה גרמת להם משל לאדם שהיה לו בן נאה ומאכילו ומשקהו ותולה לו כיס של דינרין בצוארו והושיבו בפתח זונות מה יעשה שלא יחטא [יומא פו:]. אין ארי דורס ונוהם. שמח ומשתגע ומזיק [ברכות לב.]. קרבו פקודות העיר. הקריבו את הפקודים אשר הפקדתי לשחת את העיר [יחזקאל ט, א]. אחר הדבר הזה. שראה את המופת הזה ושמע את דברי הנביא ואף על פי כן לא שב ורבותינו דרשו אחר שתפסו הקב"ה בבגדו ואמר לו חזור בך ואני ואתה ובן ישי נטייל בגן עדן [מ"א יג, לג].

מסורת הש"ס

א) [מו"ק יח. ע"ש], ב) ברכות לה:, ג) ברכות לב. יומא פו:, ד) [צ"ל יהויכין כי כך מבואר בסוף מלכים ב דיהויכין הוגלה עם החרש והמסגר וכן לעיל בגמ' לח. אבן יהויקים מת בירושלים ולא הוגלה כלל].

הגהות הב"ח

(א) גמ' וטעה כתיב ושחטה. כצ"ל ואות ד נמחק:

הגהות הגר"א

[א] גמ' ראה וטעה דכתיב. נמחק תיבת דכתיב:

תורה אור השלם

א) וַיֹּאמֶר יְיָ אֶל יֵהוּא יַעַן אֲשֶׁר הֱטִיבֹתָ לַעֲשׂוֹת הַיָּשָׁר בְּעֵינַי כְּכֹל אֲשֶׁר בִּלְבָבִי עָשִׂיתָ לְבֵית אַחְאָב בְּנֵי רְבִעִים יֵשְׁבוּ לְךָ עַל כִּסֵּא יִשְׂרָאֵל: [מלכים ב' י, ל]

ב) וְיֵהוּא לֹא שָׁמַר לָלֶכֶת בְּתוֹרַת יְיָ אֱלֹהֵי יִשְׂרָאֵל בְּכָל לְבָבוֹ לֹא סָר מֵעַל חַטֹּאות יָרָבְעָם אֲשֶׁר הֶחֱטִיא אֶת יִשְׂרָאֵל: [מלכים ב' י, לא]

ג) וַיִּקְבֹּץ יֵהוּא אֶת כָּל הָעָם וַיֹּאמֶר אֲלֵהֶם אַחְאָב עָבַד אֶת הַבַּעַל מְעָט יֵהוּא יַעַבְדֶנּוּ הַרְבֵּה: [מלכים ב' י, יח]

ד) וְשַׁחֲטָה שֵׂטִים הֶעְמִיקוּ וַאֲנִי מוּסָר לְכֻלָּם: [הושע ה, ב]

ה) וַיְהִי בָּעֵת הַהִיא וְיָרָבְעָם יָצָא מִירוּשָׁלָיִם וַיִּמְצָא אֹתוֹ אֲחִיָּה הַשִּׁילֹנִי הַנָּבִיא בַּדֶּרֶךְ וְהוּא מִתְכַּסֶּה בְּשַׂלְמָה חֲדָשָׁה וּשְׁנֵיהֶם לְבַדָּם בַּשָּׂדֶה: [מלכים א' יא, כט]

ו) הֶבֶל הֵמָּה מַעֲשֵׂה תַּעְתֻּעִים בְּעֵת פְּקֻדָּתָם יֹאבֵדוּ: [ירמיה נא, יח]

ז) כֹּה אָמַר יְיָ בְּעֵת רָצוֹן עֲנִיתִיךָ וּבְיוֹם יְשׁוּעָה עֲזַרְתִּיךָ וְאֶצָּרְךָ וְאֶתֶּנְךָ לִבְרִית עָם לְהָקִים אֶרֶץ לְהַנְחִיל נְחָלוֹת שֹׁמֵמוֹת: [ישעיה מט, ח]

ח) וְעַתָּה לֵךְ נְחֵה אֶת הָעָם אֶל אֲשֶׁר דִּבַּרְתִּי לָךְ הִנֵּה מַלְאָכִי יֵלֵךְ לְפָנֶיךָ וּבְיוֹם פָּקְדִי וּפָקַדְתִּי עֲלֵהֶם חַטָּאתָם: [שמות לב, לד]

ט) וַיְהִי בָּעֵת הַהִוא וַיֵּרֶד יְהוּדָה מֵאֵת אֶחָיו וַיֵּט עַד אִישׁ עֲדֻלָּמִי וּשְׁמוֹ חִירָה: [בראשית לח, א]

י) וַיֵּלֶךְ רְחַבְעָם שְׁכֶם כִּי שְׁכֶם בָּא כָל יִשְׂרָאֵל לְהַמְלִיךְ אֹתוֹ: [מלכים א יב, א]

כ) לָכֵן תִּתְּנִי שִׁלּוּחִים עַל מוֹרֶשֶׁת גַּת בָּתֵּי אַכְזִיב לְאַכְזָב לְמַלְכֵי יִשְׂרָאֵל: [מיכה א, יד]

ל) גּוֹזֵל אָבִיו וְאִמּוֹ וְאֹמֵר אֵין פָּשַׁע חָבֵר הוּא לְאִישׁ מַשְׁחִית: [משלי כח, כד] מ) הֲלַיְיָ תִּגְמְלוּ זֹאת עַם נָבָל וְלֹא חָכָם הֲלוֹא הוּא אָבִיךָ קָּנֶךָ הוּא עָשְׂךָ וַיְכֹנְנֶךָ: [דברים לב, ו] נ) שְׁמַע בְּנִי מוּסַר אָבִיךָ וְאַל תִּטֹּשׁ תּוֹרַת אִמֶּךָ: [משלי א, ח] ס) כִּי קָרַע יִשְׂרָאֵל מֵעַל בֵּית דָּוִד וַיַּמְלִיכוּ אֶת יָרָבְעָם בֶּן נְבָט וַיַּדַּח יָרָבְעָם אֶת יִשְׂרָאֵל מֵאַחֲרֵי יְיָ וְהֶחֱטִיאָם חֲטָאָה גְדוֹלָה: [מלכים ב' יז, כא] ע) אֵלֶּה הַדְּבָרִים אֲשֶׁר דִּבֶּר מֹשֶׁה אֶל כָּל יִשְׂרָאֵל בְּעֵבֶר הַיַּרְדֵּן בַּמִּדְבָּר בָּעֲרָבָה מוֹל סוּף בֵּין פָּארָן וּבֵין תֹּפֶל וְלָבָן וַחֲצֵרֹת וְדִי זָהָב: [דברים א, א] פ) וַיִּקְרָא בְאָזְנַי קוֹל גָּדוֹל לֵאמֹר קָרְבוּ פְּקֻדּוֹת הָעִיר וְאִישׁ כְּלִי מַשְׁחֵתוֹ בְּיָדוֹ: [יחזקאל ט, א] צ) אַחַר הַדָּבָר הַזֶּה לֹא שָׁב יָרָבְעָם מִדַּרְכּוֹ הָרָעָה וַיָּשָׁב וַיַּעַשׂ מִקְצוֹת הָעָם כֹּהֲנֵי בָמוֹת הֶחָפֵץ יְמַלֵּא אֶת יָדוֹ וִיהִי כֹּהֲנֵי בָמוֹת: [מלכים א' יג, לג]

אָמַר רַבִּי יַנַּאי – A Tanna **of the academy of R' Yannai said:** **מֹשֶׁה לִפְנֵי הַקָּדוֹשׁ בָּרוּךְ הוּא** – **Moses said to the Holy One, Blessed is He:** **רִבּוֹנוֹ שֶׁל עוֹלָם** – **"Master of the universe!** **בִּשְׁבִיל כֶּסֶף וְזָהָב שֶׁהִשְׁפַּעְתָּ לָהֶן לְיִשְׂרָאֵל עַד שֶׁיֹּאמְרוּ דַּי** – **It was the gold and silver that You lavished upon Israel until they said, 'Enough!'** – **גָּרַם לָהֶם לַעֲשׂוֹת לָהֶם אֱלֹהֵי זָהָב** – **that caused them to make themselves gods of gold!"**[36] **מָשָׁל אֵין אֲרִי דּוֹרֵס וְנוֹהֵם מִתּוֹךְ קוּפָּה שֶׁל תֶּבֶן** – As the **parable** puts it: **A lion does not claw and roar due to** having **a basket of straw,** **אֶלָּא מִתּוֹךְ קוּפָּה שֶׁל בָּשָׂר** – **but rather due to** having **a basket of meat.**[37]

אָמַר רַבִּי אוֹשַׁעְיָא – **R' Oshaya said:** **עַד יָרָבְעָם הָיוּ יִשְׂרָאֵל יוֹנְקִים מֵעֵגֶל אֶחָד** – **Until** the time of **Yarovam, Israel suckled from one calf;** **מִכָּאן וְאֵילָךְ מִשְּׁנַיִם וּשְׁלֹשָׁה עֲגָלִים** – **from then on, from two calves plus the third,** original one.[38]

אָמַר רַבִּי יִצְחָק – **R' Yitzchak said:** **אֵין לְךָ כָּל פּוּרְעָנוּת וּפוּרְעָנוּת שֶׁבָּאָה לָעוֹלָם** – **There is not a single punishment that comes to the world** (i.e. Israel) **שֶׁאֵין בָּהּ אֶחָד מֵעֶשְׂרִים וְאַרְבָּעָה בְּהֶכְרֵעַ לִיטְרָא שֶׁל עֵגֶל הָרִאשׁוֹן** – **that does not contain one twenty-fourth of the overbalance of a** ***litra*** **of the first** Golden **Calf,**[39] **שֶׁנֶּאֱמַר "וּבְיוֹם פָּקְדִי וּפָקַדְתִּי עֲלֵהֶם חַטָּאתָם"** – **as it is stated:** ***On the day I make My account, I shall bring their sin to account against them.***[40] **אָמַר רַבִּי חֲנִינָא** – **R' Chanina said:** **לְאַחַר עֶשְׂרִים וְאַרְבָּעָה דּוֹרוֹת נִגְבָּה פָּסוּק זֶה** – **After twenty-four generations** the account referred to in **this verse was paid up,** **שֶׁנֶּאֱמַר "וַיִּקְרָא בְאָזְנַי קוֹל גָּדוֹל לֵאמֹר קָרְבוּ פְּקֻדּוֹת הָעִיר וְאִישׁ כְּלִי מַשְׁחֵתוֹ בְּיָדוֹ"** – **as it is stated:** ***He called in my ears with a loud voice, saying, "The city's accounts*** *(pekudos)* ***draw near, each man with his weapon of destruction in his hand."***[41]

Yarovam spurns God's summons to repentance:

"אַחַר הַדָּבָר הַזֶּה לֹא־שָׁב יָרָבְעָם מִדַּרְכּוֹ הָרָעָה" – Scripture states:[42] ***After this thing, Yarovam did not turn back from his evil way.*** **מַאי "אַחַר"** – **What is** the meaning of ***after*** *this thing*?[43] **אָמַר רַבִּי אַבָּא** – **R' Abba said:** **אַחַר שֶׁתְּפָשׂוֹ הַקָּדוֹשׁ בָּרוּךְ הוּא לְיָרָבְעָם בְּבִגְדוֹ** – **After the Holy One, Blessed is He, seized Yarovam by his garment** **וְאָמַר לוֹ חֲזוֹר בָּךְ** – **and said to him, "Return!** i.e. repent, **וַאֲנִי וְאַתָּה וּבֶן יִשַׁי נְטַיֵּיל בְּגַן עֵדֶן** – **and I, you and the son of Jesse** (David) **will stroll** together **in the Garden of Eden!"** **אָמַר לוֹ** – [Yarovam] thereupon **said to [God]:** **מִי בָּרֹאשׁ** – **"Who will be at the head?"** **בֶּן יִשַׁי בָּרֹאשׁ** – God replied, **"The son of Jesse** will be **at the head."** **אִי הָכִי לֹא בָּעֵינָא** – **"If so,"** Yarovam replied, **"I do not desire** it.**"**[44]

NOTES

36. דַּי זָהָב is expounded to mean דַּי זָהָב, *enough gold.* That is, the Jews in the Wilderness would never have been able to make a golden calf had they not possessed the large quantity of gold that God had instructed them to take from the Egyptians at the time of the Exodus. Thus, Moses argued that God Himself was, as it were, partly to blame for the sin of the Golden Calf, and He ought therefore show mercy to the Jewish people and not destroy them for this sin.

37. When a lion has an abundance of meat to eat, it becomes wild with euphoria, roaring and attacking the animals around it (*Rashi* to *Berachos* 32a ד״ה אין ארי and *Yad Ramah* here). However, a lion does not become excited on a diet of straw, for lions do not eat straw.

Similarly, the Jewish people would never have "clawed and roared," that is, would never have disobeyed God and made the Golden Calf, if they had not been given so much "meat," that is, if they had not been surfeited with an abundance of gold and silver.

38. I.e. until Yarovam, the Jews were subjected to punishment for the Golden Calf they had made in the Wilderness, as is stated in the next words of the Gemara. Yarovam made two more golden calves and persuaded the Jews to worship them. From that time on, the Jewish people have been subjected to punishment for three golden calves: the two made by Yarovam, and the third, original golden calf, made by the Jews in the Wilderness (*Rashi*).

39. As explained in *Bava Basra* 88b, *Deuteronomy* 25:15 requires a seller to allow the side of the scale that contains the produce being sold to sink lower than the side of the scale holding the weight. This is to ensure the righteousness of the seller's measure by adding a little extra to the amount stipulated (see *Shulchan Aruch Choshen Mishpat* 231:14). When weighing at least a *litra* of merchandise, the side holding the produce must sink a *tefach* lower than the side holding the weight (*Rashbam* ibid. ד״ה וחייב; cf. *Yad Ramah* here). This amount of overbalance is slight, and one twenty-fourth of that overbalance represents a very small amount indeed. R' Yitzchak says that a similarly small part of every punishment that God has ever inflicted upon the Jewish people since the sin of the Golden Calf is due to that sin. In other words, whenever the Jews sin, God inflicts a punishment upon them equal to the offense committed, plus an additional minute amount of punishment to collect what was left owing for the sin of the Golden Calf.

The phrase *one twenty-fourth of the overbalance* is not meant to be taken literally; it merely denotes a very small amount (*Rashi*).

Maharal explains that there is not a single punishment in which the sin of the Golden Calf did not play some role, that is, did not make some slight contribution. Since the Golden Calf was made at a formative period in the history of the Jewish people, immediately after they received the Torah, it contributed an element of sin and rebelliousness which reasserts itself in the subsequent sins of the people.

40. *Exodus* 32:34. God tells Moses that He will not destroy the Jewish people as punishment for their worship of the Golden Calf; however, whenever they would sin in the future, God would remember, so to speak, the sin of the Golden Calf, and would punish them then on that account as well. *Maharsha* stresses that just as in a scale the overbalance tips the scale to one side if the two sides were level before, so too, whenever the sins and merits of the Jewish people are evenly balanced, the sin of the Golden Calf tips the scale.

41. *Ezekiel* 9:1. During the reign of King Tzidkiah, six years before the destruction of the First Temple, Ezekiel was transported in a prophetic vision from Babylonia to Jerusalem, where God showed him the sins of the people of the city which were going to lead to Jerusalem's destruction and their own deaths. In our verse, Ezekiel heard God call to the destroyers of Jerusalem to come attack and destroy the city: קָרְבוּ פְּקֻדּוֹת הָעִיר, *Bring near those appointed over the city* (*Rashi, Radak* ad loc.). Our Gemara, however, connects the word פְּקֻדּוֹת to the similar expression regarding the Golden Calf: וּבְיוֹם פָּקְדִי וּפָקַדְתִּי, *on the day I make My account, I shall bring to account,* thus taking our verse to mean that God declared, "*The city's accounts draw near*"; i.e. the time has come to settle the long-standing account for the sin of the Golden Calf (*Rashi*). [*Maharsha* adds that the plural form פְּקֻדּוֹת, *accounts,* hints at the fact that *two* accounts were being settled: the one of the generation, and the previous account of the Calf.]

Thus, the destruction of Jerusalem and the Temple was going to be the last punishment inflicted on the Jews for the sin of the Golden Calf. With the destruction of the city, the account was to be closed, for the Jews would have paid the full price for their sin (see *Eichah Rabbah* 2:3). R' Chanina points out that this final punishment took place twenty-four generations after the sin of the Golden Calf. *Rashi* enumerates the twenty-four generations from the generation of the Golden Calf to the generation of Jehoiachin and Tzidkiah, the last kings of Judah, in whose time the city was destroyed.

It would appear that this statement of R' Chanina – that the account of the sin of the Golden Calf was finally settled – disputes the statement by R' Yitzchak cited previously by the Gemara that every punishment that comes upon Israel always contains a small amount of the retribution for the Golden Calf (*Yefei Anaf* to *Eichah Rabbah* 2:3).

42. *I Kings* 13:33.

43. I.e. what is the *thing* the verse refers to as having failed to move Yarovam to *turn back from his evil way*? (See *Maharsha* for further elaboration of the forthcoming exposition.)

44. This anthropomorphic account, as well as others in this chapter, are not meant to be taken literally. *Yad Ramah* explains that a person can be shown things in prophetic visions or dreams that are meant to convey ideas in a figurative manner. Thus, God's "pulling at Yarovam's garment" means that Yarovam dreamt that a prophet or some other messenger of God had come to him and urged him to repent. When he refused to do so, the messenger entreated him again and again so

מסורת הש"ס

א) [מו"ק יח. ע"ש], ב) ברכות לה:, ג) ברכות לב. יומא פו:, ד) [נ"ל יהויכין כי כך מבואר בפסוק מלכים ב דיהויכין הוגלה עם החרש והמסגר וכן לעיל בגמ' לח. אכן יהויקים מת בירושלים ולא הוגלה כלל].

הגהות הב"ח

(א) גמ' וטעה כתיב ושחטה. כצ"ל ואות ד נמחק:

הגהות הגר"א

[א] גמ' ראה וטעה דכתיב. נמחק תיבת דכתיב:

תורה אור השלם

א) וַיֹּאמֶר יְיָ אֶל יֵהוּא יַעַן אֲשֶׁר הֱטִיבֹתָ לַעֲשׂוֹת הַיָּשָׁר בְּעֵינַי כְּכֹל אֲשֶׁר בִּלְבָבִי עָשִׂיתָ לְבֵית אַחְאָב בְּנֵי רְבִעִים יֵשְׁבוּ לְךָ עַל כִּסֵּא יִשְׂרָאֵל: [מלכים ב' י, ל]

ב) וְיֵהוּא לֹא שָׁמַר לָלֶכֶת בְּתוֹרַת יְיָ אֱלֹהֵי יִשְׂרָאֵל בְּכָל לְבָבוֹ לֹא סָר מֵעַל חַטֹּאות יָרָבְעָם אֲשֶׁר הֶחֱטִיא אֶת יִשְׂרָאֵל: [מלכים ב' י, לא]

ג) וַיִּקְבֹּץ יֵהוּא אֶת כָּל הָעָם וַיֹּאמֶר אֲלֵהֶם אַחְאָב עָבַד אֶת הַבַּעַל מְעָט יֵהוּא יַעַבְדֶנּוּ הַרְבֵּה: [מלכים ב' י, יח]

ד) וְשַׁחֲטָה שֵׂטִים הֶעְמִיקוּ וַאֲנִי מוּסָר לְכֻלָּם: [הושע ה, ב]

ה) וַיְהִי בָּעֵת הַהִיא וְיָרָבְעָם יָצָא מִירוּשָׁלָםִ וַיִּמְצָא אֹתוֹ אֲחִיָּה הַשִּׁילֹנִי הַנָּבִיא בַּדֶּרֶךְ וְהוּא מִתְכַּסֶּה בְּשַׂלְמָה חֲדָשָׁה וּשְׁנֵיהֶם לְבַדָּם בַּשָּׂדֶה: [מלכים א' יא, כט]

ו) הֶבֶל הֵמָּה מַעֲשֵׂה תַּעְתֻּעִים בְּעֵת פְּקֻדָּתָם יֹאבֵדוּ: [ירמיה נא, יח]

ז) כֹּה אָמַר יְיָ בְּעֵת רָצוֹן עֲנִיתִיךָ וּבְיוֹם יְשׁוּעָה עֲזַרְתִּיךָ וְאֶצָּרְךָ וְאֶתֶּנְךָ לִבְרִית עָם לְהָקִים אֶרֶץ לְהַנְחִיל נְחָלוֹת שֹׁמֵמוֹת: [ישעיה מט, ח]

ח) וְעַתָּה לֵךְ נְחֵה אֶת הָעָם אֶל אֲשֶׁר דִּבַּרְתִּי לָךְ הִנֵּה מַלְאָכִי יֵלֵךְ לְפָנֶיךָ וּבְיוֹם פָּקְדִי וּפָקַדְתִּי עֲלֵיהֶם חַטָּאתָם: [שמות לב, לד]

ט) וַיְהִי בָּעֵת הַהִוא וַיֵּרֶד יְהוּדָה מֵאֵת אֶחָיו וַיֵּט עַד אִישׁ עֲדֻלָּמִי וּשְׁמוֹ חִירָה: [בראשית לח, א]

י) וַיֵּלֶךְ רְחַבְעָם שְׁכֶם כִּי שְׁכֶם בָּא כָל יִשְׂרָאֵל לְהַמְלִיךְ אֹתוֹ: [מלכים א' יב, א]

כ) לָכֵן תִּתְּנִי שִׁלּוּחִים עַל מוֹרֶשֶׁת גַּת בָּתֵּי אַכְזִיב לְאַכְזָב לְמַלְכֵי יִשְׂרָאֵל: [מיכה א, יד]

ל) גּוֹזֵל אָבִיו וְאִמּוֹ וְאֹמֵר אֵין פָּשַׁע חָבֵר הוּא לְאִישׁ מַשְׁחִית: [משלי כח, כד]

מ) הַלַיְיָ תִּגְמְלוּ זֹאת עַם נָבָל וְלֹא חָכָם הֲלוֹא הוּא אָבִיךָ קָּנֶךָ הוּא עָשְׂךָ וַיְכֹנְנֶךָ: [דברים לב, ו]

נ) שְׁמַע בְּנִי מוּסַר אָבִיךָ וְאַל תִּטֹּשׁ תּוֹרַת אִמֶּךָ: [משלי א, ח]

ס) כִּי קָרַע יִשְׂרָאֵל מֵעַל בֵּית דָּוִד וַיַּמְלִיכוּ אֶת יָרָבְעָם בֶּן נְבָט וַיַּדַּח יָרָבְעָם אֶת יִשְׂרָאֵל מֵאַחֲרֵי יְיָ וְהֶחֱטִיאָם חֲטָאָה גְדוֹלָה: [מלכים ב' יז, כא]

ע) אֵלֶּה הַדְּבָרִים אֲשֶׁר דִּבֶּר מֹשֶׁה אֶל כָּל יִשְׂרָאֵל בְּעֵבֶר הַיַּרְדֵּן בַּמִּדְבָּר בָּעֲרָבָה מוֹל סוּף בֵּין פָּארָן וּבֵין תֹּפֶל וְלָבָן וַחֲצֵרֹת וְדִי זָהָב: [דברים א, א]

פ) וַיִּקְרָא בְאָזְנַי קוֹל גָּדוֹל לֵאמֹר קָרְבוּ פְּקֻדּוֹת הָעִיר וְאִישׁ כְּלִי מַשְׁחֵתוֹ בְּיָדוֹ: [יחזקאל ט, א]

צ) אַחַר הַדָּבָר הַזֶּה לֹא שָׁב יָרָבְעָם מִדַּרְכּוֹ הָרָעָה וַיָּשָׁב וַיַּעַשׂ מִקְצוֹת הָעָם כֹּהֲנֵי בָמוֹת הֶחָפֵץ יְמַלֵּא אֶת יָדוֹ וִיהִי כֹּהֲנֵי בָמוֹת: [מלכים א' יג, לג]

ואף אחיה השילוני טעה וחתם דהא יהוא צדיקא רבה הוה שנאמר א) ויאמר ה' אל יהוא יען אשר הטיבות לעשות הישר בעיני ככל אשר בלבבי עשית לבית אחאב בני רביעים ישבו לך על כסא ישראל וכתיב ב) ויהוא לא שמר ללכת בתורת ה' אלהי ישראל בכל לבבו לא סר מעל חטאת ירבעם אשר החטיא את ישראל מאי גרמא ליה אמר אביי (א) ברית כרותה לשפתים שנאמר ג) אחאב עבד הבעל מעט יהוא יעבדנו הרבה רבא אמר חותמו של אחיה השילוני ראה וטעה (א) [א] דכתיב ד) ושחטה שטים העמיקו ואני מוסר לכולם אמר רבי יוחנן אמר הקב"ה הם העמיקו משלי אני אמרתי א כל שאינו עולה לרגל עובר בעשה והם אמרו כל העולה לרגל ידקר בחרב ה) ויהי בעת ההיא וירבעם יצא מירושלם וימצא אותו אחיה השילוני הנביא בדרך והוא מתכסה בשלמה חדשה תנא משום רבי יוסי עת היא מזומנת לפורענות ו) בעת פקודתם יאבדו תנא משום רבי יוסי עת מזומנת לפורענות ז) בעת רצון עניתיך תנא משום ר' יוסי עת מזומנת לטובה ח) וביום פקדי ופקדתי עליהם חטאתם תנא משום רבי יוסי עת היא מזומנת לפורענות ט) ויהי בעת ההיא וירד יהודה מאת אחיו תנא משום ר' יוסי עת מזומנת לפורענות י) וילך רחבעם שכם כי שכם בא כל ישראל להמליך אותו תנא משום ר' יוסי מקום מזומן לפורענות בשכם עינו את דינה בשכם מכרו אחיו את יוסף בשכם נחלקה מלכות בית דוד ה) וירבעם יצא מירושלים אמר ר' חנינא בר פפא שיצא מפיתקה של ירושלים ה) וימצא אותו אחיה השילוני הנביא בדרך והוא מתכסה בשלמה חדשה ושניהם לבדם בשדה מאי בשלמה חדשה אמר רב נחמן כשלמה חדשה מה שלמה חדשה אין בה שום דופי אף תורתו של ירבעם לא היה בה שום דופי ד"א שלמה חדשה שחידשו דברים שלא שמעה אזן מעולם מאי ושניהם לבדם בשדה אמר רב יהודה אמר רב שכל תלמידי חכמים דומין לפניהם כעשבי השדה ואיכא דאמר שכל טעמי תורה מגולין להם כשדה כ) לכן תתני שלוחים על מורשת גת בתי אכזיב לאכזב למלכי ישראל אמר ר' חנינא בר פפא יצאה בת קול ואמרה להן מי שהרג את הפלשתי והוריש אתכם גת תתנו שילוחים לבניו בתי אכזיב לאכזב למלכי ישראל ב אמר רב חיננא בר פפא כל הנהנה מן העולם הזה בלא ברכה כאילו גוזל להקב"ה וכנסת ישראל שנאמר ל) גוזל אביו ואמו ואומר אין פשע חבר הוא לאיש משחית ואין אביו אלא הקב"ה שנאמר מ) הלא הוא אביך קנך ואין אמו אלא כנסת ישראל שנאמר נ) שמע בני מוסר אביך ואל תטוש תורת אמך מאי חבר הוא לאיש משחית חבר הוא לירבעם בן נבט שהשחית ישראל לאביהם שבשמים ס) וידח ירבעם (בן נבט) את ישראל מאחרי ה' והחטיאם חטאה גדולה אמר רבי חנין כשתי מקלות המתיזות זו את זו ע) ודי זהב ג אמרו דבי ר' ינאי אמר משה לפני הקב"ה רבונו של עולם בשביל כסף וזהב שהשפעת להן לישראל עד שיאמרו דיי גרם להם לעשות להם אלהי זהב משל אין ארי דורס ונוהם מתוך קופה של תבן אלא מתוך קופה של בשר אמר ר' אושעיא עד ירבעם היו ישראל יונקים מעגל אחד מכאן ואילך משנים ושלשה עגלים אמר ר' יצחק אין לך כל פורענות ופורענות שבאה לעולם שאין בה אחד מעשרים וארבעה בהכרע ליטרא של עגל הראשון שנאמר ח) וביום פקדי ופקדתי עליהם חטאתם אמר רבי חנינא לאחר עשרים וארבעה דורות נגבה פסוק זה שנאמר פ) ויקרא באזני קול גדול לאמר קרבו פקדות העיר ואיש כלי משחתו בידו צ) אחר הדבר הזה לא שב ירבעם מדרכו הרעה מאי אחר אמר ר' אבא אחר שתפשו הקב"ה לירבעם בבגדו ואמר לו חזור בך ואני ואתה ובן ישי נטייל בגן עדן אמר לו מי בראש בן ישי בראש אי הכי לא בעינא ר' אבהו הוה רגיל דהוה קא דריש בשלשה מלכים חלש קביל עליה דלא דריש כיון

דאיתפח

ואף אחיה השילוני טעה בדבר. דסבר לנסויינהו אתי וחתם באותו מעשה: שנאמר ויאמר ה' אל יהוא וגו' לעשות הישר וכתיב ויהוא לא שמר ללכת בתורת ה'. ואמרינן מאי גרמא ליה ואמר רבא חותמו של אחיה השילוני ראה וטעה מכלל דהוא טעה: ושחטה שטים העמיקו. שטים עובדי כוכבים על שם שסטים אחריה לשחוט לעבודת כוכבים: העמיקו. והחמירו שאמרו שכל מי שעולה לרגל ידקר בחרב כדי שילכו וישחטו לפני העגלים: ואני מוסר לכולם. כלומר אנכי לא חשתי כל כך לכבוד עצמי לומר כל מי שאינו עולה לרגל ידקר בחרב כמו שחשו הם לכבוד עבודת כוכבים אלא יסורין בעלמא יסרתים כלומר דעבר בעשה ל"א שטים כלומר שטיות שלהם שסרו מאחרי העמיקו עד שחיטה שחייבו מיתה כל מי שעולה לרגל ומניח את העגלים. ושחטה לשון שחיטה: מזומנת לפורענות. שהם נחלקה מלכות ישראל דסמיך ליה ויקח את השלמה ויקרעה לשנים עשר קרעים וגו': וביום פקדי. בתשעה באב שבכל השנה מאותן מ' שנה שעמדו במדבר יום מזומן לפורענות בו חזרו מרגלים בו נחרב הבית בראשונה ובשניה: ויהי בעת ההיא וירד יהודה. מזומנת לפורענות שתמר נתחייבה שריפה ומתו שני בניו: בשכם מכרו אחיו את יוסף. כדכתיב (בראשית לז) הלא אחיך רועים בשכם ודותן דכתיב בקרא היינו כפר הסמוך לשכם ונקראת על שם שכם אי נמי כמדרשו שהיו דנין עליו להרגו: בשכם נחלקה מלכות בית דוד. כדכתיב במלכים (א יב): מפתקה של ירושלים. מכללה שלא לחזור בה לעולם ולא ליטול חלק בעבודה: מפתקה. כגון (ב"מ דף פו.) נפל פתקה מרקיעא כלומר מחזקת של ירושלים הכתוב יחתום בה: שום דופי. גימגום בגמ': שחדשו. דרשו דברי תורה בין ירבעם לאחיה: יצתה בת קול ואמרה. כשהמליכו את ירבעם: מי שהרג. דוד: את הפלשתי. וע"י כן היה מוריש לכם גת לכן תתנו שלוחים לבניו שתעזבו מלכות בית דוד ותמליכו אחרים: בתי אכזיב לאכזב. למלכי בית דוד אתם מכזבים והלכתם אחר מלכי ישראל לפיכך תהיו נמסרין לאכזב ביד עובדי כוכבים שהן שטי כזב: אין אביו אלא הקב"ה שנאמר וכו'. ואין גזילה כלפי מעלה וכלפי כנסת ישראל אלא זו בלבד שמונע מלברך כנסת ישראל הוא גוזל להקב"ה שחכמים תקנו על כל דבר ודבר ברכה כדאמר התם (ברכות דף לה.) כל הטועם ואינו מברך נקרא גזלן שנאמר לה' הארץ ומלואה: כשתי מקלות המתיזות זו את זו. כאדם שיש בידו מקל א' ומכה בו מקל אחר ומתיזו ומשליכו ברחוק כך הדיח ירבעם את ישראל מאחרי ה' בעגל כרסם: ודי זהב. איידי דאיירי עד השתא בעגלים של ירבעם מפרש האי קרא: מתוך קופה של בשר. כשיש לו הרבה לאכול הוא נוהם: עד ירבעם היו ישראל יונקים מעגל אחד. לוקין על חטא עגל אחד שעשו במדבר: ה"ג מכאן ואילך היו יונקין משלשה עגלים. שנים מירבעם ושלישי של המדבר ולפי מה שכתוב בספרים שנים ושלשה עגלים ניחא כלומר משנים שעשה ירבעם ושלישי שנעשה במדבר ושלשה היינו שלישי כמו (משלי ל) שלשה המה נפלאו ממני וארבעה לא ידעתים: אחד מעשרים וארבעה בהכרע ליטרא. לאו דוקא אלא כלומר דבר מועט מאד כמה שכף המשקל נוטה לצד זה יותר מצד זה בב"ב (דף פט.) כמה הוי הכרע ליטרא: לאחר כ"ד דורות. למעשה העגל: פסוק זה. דכתיב בעגל וביום פקדי והכא בימי צדקיה כשחרב הבית כתוב קרבו פקודות העיר קרב אותו מעשה שנאמר וביום פקדי וממעשה העגל עד צדקיה כ"ד דורות דבימי נחשון נעשה העגל צא וחשוב כמה דורות מנחשון עד צדקיה נחשון שלמון בנו בועז בנו עובד בנו ישי בנו דוד בנו שלמה בנו רחבעם בנו אביה בנו אסא בנו יהושפט בנו יורם בנו אחזיה בנו יואש בנו אמציה בנו עוזיה בנו יותם בנו אחז בנו חזקיה בנו מנשה בנו אמון בנו יאשיה בנו יהואחז ויהויקים בניו ומלכו זה אחר זה ודור אחד הם יהויכין בנו של יהויקים הרי כ"ד ד) יהויקים לא סיים מלכותו שהוגלה לבבל עם החרש והמסגר והמליכו צדקיהו דודו במקומו והלכך לא קא חשיב צדקיה דור באפיה נפשיה דהוא מלך בדור כ"ד: דהוה דריש בשלשה מלכים. דהוה קאי במתני' דשלשה מלכים אין להם חלק:

איתפח

כח א מיי' פ"א מהל' חגיגה הלכה ז:

ליקוטי רש"י

בני רבעים. ארבע דורות תחת שהשמדת את בן אחאב שמלכו ארבע דורות עמרי ואחאב ואחזיה ויהורם [מ"ב י, ל]. ושחטה שטים העמיקו. משך שטות' העמיקו אני אמרתי כל שאינו עולה לרגל עובר בעשה והם גזרו כל העול' לרגל יהרג הרי שהעמיקו יותר ממני ושחטה לשון זהב שחוט (מלכים א י) נמשך ונטוה וי"מ ל' שחיטת זבחים לעכו"ם. ואני מוסר לכולם. ואף אני אייסרם ביסורין אכין מוסר לכולן [הושע ה, ב]. בעת פקודתם. כשיפקוד הקב"ה עליהם ועל עובדיהם [ירמיהו נא, יא]. מקום מזומן לפורענות. ויצא שכמה, מקום מוכן לפורענות שם קלקלו השבטים שם ענו את דינה שם נחלקה מלכות בית דוד שנאמר (מ"א י"ב, א) וילך רחבעם שכמה וגו' [בראשית לז, יד]. לכן תתני שלוחים על מורשת גת. על אשר תתני שלוחים על מלכות דוד אשר הוריש אתכם גת כענין שנאמר (דה"א יח) ויקח דוד את גת מיד פלשתים ואתם מואסים בו כמו שנאמר (ישעיה ח) יען אשר מאס העם הזה את מי השלוח וגומר לפיכך בתי אכזיב שהיתה מארץ יהודה ונמשכו אחר פקח בן רמליהו סופן להיות לאכזב למלכי ישראל שיהרג פקח בן רמליהו ויכזבו הנסמכים עליו ובימי אחז נתנבאת נבואה זו. לכן תתני שלוחים. פי' לכן כמו על אשר כמו (ישעיה יז) על כן תטעי נטעי נעמנים על אשר נטעתיך נטעי נעמנים ואת נהפכת לזמורות זר. בתי אכזיב לאכזב. ל' נופל על הלשון מאגדת חלק למדתי מדרש מקרא זה כך [מיכה א, יד]. גוזל להקדוש ברוך הוא. את ברכתו. וכנסת ישראל. שכשחטאו הפירות לוקין. אין פשע. ולפי שהוא מיקל רואים האחרים ולמדין ממנו לעשות כן ליהנות מן העולם בלא ברכה ולכך נקרא זה המיקל חבר לאיש משחית. לירבעם בן נבט. שחטא והחטיא את ישראל כך הוא חוטא ומחטיא [ברכות לה:]. גוזל אביו. הקב"ה. ואמו. כנסת ישראל המחטיא את הרבי' שגוזל הקב"ה מפריד ממנו בניו וגוזל מהם טובה. משחית. ירבעם [משלי כח, כד]. הלא הוא אביך קנך. שקנאך שקנך בקן הסלעים ובארץ חזקה, שתקנך בכל מיני תקנה [דברים לב, ו]. שמע בני מוסר אביך. מה שנתן הקב"ה למשה בכתב ועל פה. אמך. אומתך כנסת ישראל כמו (יחזקאל יט) מה אמך לביאה והם דברי סופרים שחדשו והוסיפו ועשו סייגים לתורה [משלי א, ח]. ודי זהב. הוכיחן על העגל שעשו בשביל רוב זהב שהיה להם שנאמר (הושע ב י) וכסף הרביתי לה וזהב עשו לבעל [דברים א, א]. אמרו דבי רבי ינאי. לא הזכיר העון אלא למעטו ולומר אתה גרמת להם משל לאדם שהיה לו בן נאה ומאכילו ומשקהו ותולה לו כיס של דינרין בצוארו והושיבו בפתח זונות מה יעשה שלא יחטא [יומא פו:]. אין ארי דורס ונוהם. שמח ומשתגע ומזיק [ברכות לב.]. קרבו פקודות העיר. הקריבו את הפקודים אשר הפקדתי לשחת את העיר [יחזקאל ט, א]. אחר הדבר הזה. שראה את המופת הזה ושמע את דברי הנביא ואף על פי כן לא שב ורבותינו דרשו אחר שתפסו הקב"ה בבגדו ואמר לו חזור בך ואני ואתה ובן ישי נטייל בגן עדן [מ"א יג, לג].

The Gemara presents two stories that illustrate the fact that although Yarovam and the other two kings were guilty of sins that cost them their share in the World to Come, they were nevertheless great personalities who ought not to be viewed with contempt:

רַבִּי אַבָּהוּ הֲוָה רָגִיל דַּהֲוָה קָא דָרִישׁ בִּשְׁלֹשָׁה מְלָכִים – R' Abahu used to deliver Torah lectures on the subject of **the three kings** listed in our Mishnah as not having any portion in the World to Come. **חָלַשׁ – It happened once that he fell ill.**[45] **קַבֵּיל עֲלֵיהּ דְּלָא דָרִישׁ –** Assuming that he was being punished for lecturing about the sins of the three kings, **he undertook not to lecture** on this subject ever again. **כֵּיוָן – Once**

NOTES

persistently, that it was akin to someone grabbing hold of a person's garment and refusing to let go until he acceded to his request.

Others see in this expression a reference to *I Kings* 11:30-31, where the prophet Achiyah tore Yarovam's garment into twelve strips and gave ten of them to Yarovam, symbolizing his kingship over ten tribes. It was these strips, the prophetic symbol of his kingship, that God, so to speak, "grabbed," warning Yarovam that unless he repented he would lose them (*Metzudas David* cited in *Margaliyos HaYam*).

Still others see Yarovam's garment as symbolizing his great Torah knowledge, described above as *his new robe.* Even though Yarovam had sinned grievously by setting up the Golden Calves and interdicting the people's pilgrimages to the Temple in Jerusalem, in the merit of his greatness in Torah, God still offered him a chance to repent. Though our Sages stress that one who causes others to sin is not given the opportunity to repent, an exception was made with Yarovam because of all the Torah he had once learned so assiduously (*Iyun Yaakov, Aruch LaNer*).

Along similar lines, *R' Yaakov Emden* translates the word בְּבִגְדוֹ as *betrayal* or *treason* (cf. *Exodus* 21:8). Thus, God summoned Yarovam to repentance in spite of Yarovam's betrayal of God's trust, because it was God – through the prophet Achiyah – who had raised him to the kingship.

Nachalas Yaakov (quoted in *Anaf Yosef*) understands the Gemara here to be recounting the thought process of Yarovam (not his dream). As often happens with people, he experienced a moment of inspiration to repentance. (This is referred to as "God taking hold of him by his garment.") At that point, he began to consider the consequences of his repentance. On the one hand, he was sure that he surpassed David and his descendants in true greatness. Thus, were he to repent, it would only be proper for him to be held in higher esteem than David. (That is, he should "walk with God in the Garden of Eden ahead of David.") At the same time, he realized that if he were to repent, he would have to join all of Israel in the thrice-yearly pilgrimage to the Temple in Jerusalem, which would lead to the eventual restoration of the Davidic throne over all of Israel. In the end, therefore, his repentance would lead to his subservience to the House of David. ("The son of Jesse would be at the head.") Recognizing the inevitability of this outcome, he refused to pursue his inspiration to repentance. ("If so, I do not desire it.")

R' Chaim Soloveitchik explains that our Gemara actually illuminates the point of our Sages that somebody who causes others to sin is not given the opportunity to repent. There are three ways to influence a person to change for the better: threats, logical arguments, and inducements. God used all three of them with Yarovam: He "shook Yarovam by his garments" (threat), tried persuading him to return (logic), and held out a reward to him (inducement). Yet in the end, Yarovam did not repent – because as the one who caused the Ten Tribes to sin, he was beyond repentance (quoted by the *Brisker Rav*).

Commentators note that King David was a famous penitent, following the incident with Bathsheba (*II Samuel* ch. 12). For this reason, God listed him in the trio who would "stroll together in the Garden of Eden." God now summoned Yarovam to imitate David and repent; he, too, would then be a penitent like David and would earn a similar reward (*Rif* in *Ein Yaakov*; *Iyun Yaakov*).

Of course, the expression to "stroll with God in the Garden of Eden" is not meant literally; it refers to an enhanced ability to perceive the Divine Presence, the greatest gift to which a person can aspire (*Yad Ramah;* see *Berachos* 17a).

The question is asked: Why was Yarovam told that David would go first? After all, God in his initial offer had mentioned Yarovam *before* David!

It is possible that Yarovam was indeed meant to go first (as indicated in God's initial words). But when he asked specifically whether he would be first, he thereby forfeited that honor, because it showed the weakness of his character. God wanted him to repent out of love, without consideration of reward; had he done so, he would indeed have merited to go first. But when he showed that his repentance was for the sake of reward, he lost this chance (*Aruch LaNer*).

This raises the question, however, of why Yarovam asked the question. Had he not heard God say that he, Yarovam, would walk ahead of David with God?

R' Chaim Shmulevitz (*Sichos Mussar,* 5732:29) explains that conceited people hanker to hear others relate their praise. Hence, although Yarovam certainly picked up the intimation that he would be first, due to his conceit he desired to hear God enunciate this fact openly and clearly. It was this very character flaw that caused God to reply that David would walk first. "If so," Yarovam responded, "I do not want it."

45. I.e. he became critically ill and was near death (*Yad Ramah*).

ואף אחיה השילוני טעה וחתם דהא יהוא צדיקא רבה הוה שנאמר א) ויאמר ה' אל יהוא יען אשר הטיבות לעשות הישר בעיני ככל אשר בלבבי עשית לבית אחאב בני רביעים ישבו לך על כסא ישראל וכתיב ב) ויהוא לא שמר ללכת בתורת ה' אלהי ישראל בכל לבבו לא סר מעל חטאת ירבעם אשר החטיא את ישראל מאי גרמא ליה אמר אביי א) ברית כרותה לשפתים שנאמר ג) אחאב עבד הבעל מעט יהוא יעבדנו הרבה רבא אמר חותמו של אחיה השילוני ראה וטעה (א) [א] דכתיב ד) ושחטה שטים העמיקו ואני מוסר לכולם אמר רבי יוחנן אמר הקב"ה הם העמיקו משלי אני אמרתי *כל שאינו עולה לרגל עובר בעשה והם אמרו כל העולה לרגל ידקר בחרב ה) ויהי בעת ההיא וירבעם יצא מירושלם וימצא אותו אחיה השילוני הנביא בדרך והוא מתכסה בשלמה חדשה תנא משום רבי יוסי עת היא מזומנת לפורענות ו) בעת פקודתם יאבדו תנא משום רבי יוסי עת מזומנת לפורענות ז) בעת רצון עניתיך תנא משום ר' יוסי עת מזומנת לטובה ח) וביום פקדי ופקדתי עליהם חטאתם תנא משום רבי יוסי עת היא מזומנת לפורענות ט) ויהי בעת ההיא וירד יהודה מאת אחיו תנא משום ר' יוסי עת מזומנת לפורענות י) וילך רחבעם שכם כי שכם בא כל ישראל להמליך אותו תנא משום ר' יוסי מקום מזומן לפורענות בשכם עינו את דינה בשכם מכרו אחיו את יוסף בשכם נחלקה מלכות בית דוד ה) וירבעם יצא מירושלים אמר ר' חנינא בר פפא שיצא מפיתקה של ירושלים ה) וימצא אותו אחיה השילוני הנביא בדרך והוא מתכסה בשלמה חדשה ושניהם לבדם בשדה מאי בשלמה חדשה אמר רב נחמן כשלמה חדשה מה שלמה חדשה אין בה שום דופי אף תורתו של ירבעם לא היה בה שום דופי ד"א שלמה חדשה שחידשו דברים שלא שמעה אזן מעולם מאי ושניהם לבדם בשדה אמר רב יהודה אמר רב שכל תלמידי חכמים דומין לפניהם כעשבי השדה ואיכא דאמר שכל טעמי תורה מגולין להם כשדה כ) לכן תתני שלוחים על מורשת גת בתי אכזיב לאכזב למלכי ישראל אמר ר' חנינא בר פפא יצאה בת קול ואמרה להן מי שהרג את הפלשתי והוריש אתכם גת תתנו שלוחים לבניו בתי אכזיב לאכזב למלכי ישראל ג) אמר רב חנינא בר פפא כל הנהנה מן העולם הזה בלא ברכה כאילו גוזל להקב"ה וכנסת ישראל שנאמר ל) גוזל אביו ואמו ואומר אין פשע חבר הוא לאיש משחית ואין אביו אלא הקב"ה שנאמר מ) הלא הוא אביך קנך ואין אמו אלא כנסת ישראל שנאמר נ) שמע בני מוסר אביך ואל תטוש תורת אמך מאי חבר הוא לאיש משחית חבר הוא לירבעם בן נבט שהשחית ישראל לאביהם שבשמים ס) וידח ירבעם (בן נבט) את ישראל מאחרי ה' והחטיאם חטאה גדולה אמר רבי חנין כשתי מקלות המתיזות זו את זו ע) ודי זהב אמרו דבי ר' ינאי אמר משה לפני הקב"ה רבונו של עולם בשביל כסף וזהב שהשפעת להן לישראל עד שיאמרו דיי גרם להם לעשות להם אלהי זהב משל אין ארי דורס ונוהם מתוך קופה של תבן אלא מתוך קופה של בשר אמר ר' אושעיא עד ירבעם היו ישראל יונקים מעגל אחד מכאן ואילך משנים ושלשה עגלים אמר ר' יצחק אין לך כל פורענות ופורענות שבאה לעולם שאין בה אחד מעשרים וארבעה בהכרע ליטרא של עגל הראשון שנאמר ח) וביום פקדי ופקדתי עליהם חטאתם אמר רבי חנינא לאחר עשרים וארבעה דורות נגבה פסוק זה שנאמר פ) ויקרא באזני קול גדול לאמר קרבו פקדות העיר ואיש כלי משחתו בידו צ) אחר הדבר הזה לא שב ירבעם מדרכו הרעה מאי אחר אמר ר' אבא אחר שתפשו הקב"ה לירבעם בבגדו ואמר לו חזור בך ואני ואתה ובן ישי נטייל בגן עדן אמר לו מי בראש בן ישי בראש אי הכי לא בעינא ר' אבהו הוה רגיל דהוה קא דריש בשלשה מלכים חלש קביל עליה דלא דריש כיון דאיתפח

ואף אחיה השילוני טעה בדבר. דסבר לנסוייהו אתי ותפס באותו מעשה: שנאמר ויאמר ה' אל יהוא וגו' לעשות הישר וכתיב ויהוא לא שמר ללכת בתורת ה'. ואמרינן מאי גרמא ליה ואמר רבא חותמו של אחיה השילוני ראה וטעה מכלל דהוא טעה: ושחטה שטים העמיקו. שטים עובדי כוכבים על שם שסטים אחריה לשחוט לעבודת כוכבים: העמיקו. והחמירו שאמרו שכל מי שעולה לרגל ידקר בחרב כדי שילכו וישחטו לפני העגלים: ואני מוסר לכולם. כלומר אנכי לא חשתי כל כך לכבוד עצמי לומר כל מי שאינו עולה לרגל ידקר בחרב כמו שחשו הם לכבוד עבודת כוכבים אלא יסורין בעלמא יסרתים כלומר דעבר בעשה ל"א שטים כלומר שטיות שלהם שסרו מאחרי העמיקו עד שחיטה שחייבו מיתה כל מי שעולה לרגל ומניח את העגלים. ושחטה לשון שחיטה: מזומנת לפורענות. שבו נחלקה מלכות ישראל דסמיך ליה ויקח את השלמה ויקרעה לשנים עשר קרעים וגו': וביום פקדי. בתשעה באב שבכל השנה מאותן מ' שנה שעמדו במדבר יום מזומן לפורענות בו חזרו מרגלים בו נחרב הבית בראשונה ובשניה: ויהי בעת ההיא וירד יהודה. מזומנת לפורענות שתמר נתחייבה שריפה ומתו שני בניו: בשכם מכרו אחיו את יוסף. כדכתיב (בראשית לז) הלא אחיך רועים בשכם ודותן דכתיב בקרא היינו כפר הסמוך לשכם ונקראת על שם שכם אי נמי כמדרשו שהיו דנין עליו להרגו: בשכם נחלקה מלכות בית דוד. כדכתיב במלכים (א יב): מפתקה של ירושלים. מכללה שלא לחזור בה לעולם ולא ליטול חלק בעבודה: מפתקה. כגון (ב"מ דף פו.) נפל פתקה מרקיעא כלומר מחזקת של ירושלים הכתוב וחתום בה: שום דופי. גימגום בגמ': שחדשו. דרשו דברי תורה בין ירבעם לאחיה: יצתה בת קול ואמרה. כשהמליכו את ירבעם: מי שהרג. דוד: את הפלשתי. וע"י כן היה מוריש לכם גת לכן תתנו שלוחים לבניו שתעזבו מלכות בית דוד ותמליכו אחרים: בתי אכזיב לאכזב. למלכי בית דוד אתם מכזבים והלכתם אחר מלכי ישראל לפיכך תהיו נמסרין לאכזב ביד עובדי כוכבים שהן שטי כזב: אין אביו אלא הקב"ה שנאמר וכו'. ואין גזילה כלפי מעלה וכלפי כנסת ישראל אלא זו בלבד שמונע מלברך כנסת ישראל הוא גוזל להקב"ה שחכמים תקנו על כל דבר ודבר ברכה כדאמר התם (ברכות דף לה.) כל הטועם ואינו מברך נקרא גזלן שנאמר לה' הארץ ומלואה: כשתי מקלות המתיזות זו את זו. כאדם שיש בידו מקל א' ומכה בו מקל אחר ומתיזו ומשליכו ברחוק כך הדיח ירבעם את ישראל מאחרי ה' בעל כרחם: ודי זהב. איידי דאיירי עד השתא בעגלים של ירבעם מפרש האי קרא: מתוך קופה של בשר. כשיש לו הרבה לאכול הוא נוהם: עד ירבעם היו ישראל יונקים מעגל אחד. לוקין על חטא עגל אחד שעשו במדבר: ה"ג מכאן ואילך היו יונקין משלשה עגלים. שנים מירבעם ושלישי של המדבר ולפי מה שכתוב בספרים שנים ושלשה עגלים ניחא כלומר משנים שעשה ירבעם ושלישי שנעשה במדבר ושלשה היינו שלישי כמו (משלי ל) שלשה המה נפלאו ממני וארבעה לא ידעתים: אחד מעשרים וארבעה בהכרע ליטרא. לאו דוקא אלא כלומר דבר מועט מאד כמה שכף המשקל נוטה לצד זה יותר מצד זה בב"ב (דף פט.) כמה הוי הכרע ליטרא: לאחר כ"ד דורות. למעשה העגל: פסוק זה. דכתיב בעגל וביום פקדי והכא בימי צדקיה כשחרב הבית כתוב קרבו פקודות העיר קרב אותו מעשה שנאמר וביום פקדי וממעשה העגל עד צדקיה כ"ד דורות דבימי נחשון נעשה העגל צא וחשוב כמה דורות מנחשון עד צדקיה נחשון שלמון בנו בועז בנו עובד בנו ישי בנו דוד בנו שלמה בנו רחבעם בנו אביה בנו אסא בנו יהושפט בנו יורם בנו אחזיה בנו יואש בנו אמציה בנו עוזיה בנו יותם בנו אחז בנו חזקיה בנו מנשה בנו אמון בנו יאשיה בנו יהואחז ויהויקים בניו ומלכו זה אחר זה ודור אחד הם יהויכין בנו של יהויקים הרי כ"ד ד) יהויקים לא סיים מלכותו שהוגלה לבבל עם החרש והמסגר והמליכו לצדקיהו דודו במקומו והלכך לא קא חשיב לצדקיה דור באפיה נפשיה דהוא מלך בדור כ"ד: דהוה דריש בשלשה מלכים. דהוה קאי במתני' דשלשה מלכים אין להם חלק:

מסורת הש"ס

א) [מו"ק יח. ע"ש], ב) ברכות לה:, ג) ברכות לב. יומא פו:, ד) [צ"ל יהויכין כי כך מבואר בסוף מלכים ב דיהויכין הוגלה עם החרש והמסגר וכן לעיל בגמ' לח. אבל יהויקים מת בירושלים ולא הוגלה כלל].

הגהות הב"ח

(א) גמ' וטעה כתיב ושחטה. כצ"ל ואות ד נמחק:

הגהות הגר"א

[א] גמ' ראה וטעה דכתיב. נמחק תיבת דכתיב:

תורה אור השלם

א) ויאמר יי אל יהוא יען אשר הטיבת לעשות הישר בעיני ככל אשר בלבבי עשית לבית אחאב בני רבעים ישבו לך על כסא ישראל: [מלכים ב' י, ל]

ב) ויהוא לא שמר ללכת בתורת יי אלהי ישראל בכל לבבו לא סר מעל חטאות ירבעם אשר החטיא את ישראל: [מלכים ב' י, לא]

ג) ויקבץ יהוא את כל העם ויאמר אלהם אחאב עבד את הבעל מעט יהוא יעבדנו הרבה: [מלכים ב' י, יח]

ד) ושחטה שטים העמיקו ואני מוסר לכלם: [הושע ה, ב]

ה) ויהי בעת ההיא וירבעם יצא מירושלים וימצא אתו אחיה השילני הנביא בדרך והוא מתכסה בשלמה חדשה ושניהם לבדם בשדה: [מלכים א' יא, כט]

ו) הבל המה מעשה תעתעים בעת פקדתם יאבדו: [ירמיה נא, יח]

ז) כה אמר יי בעת רצון עניתיך וביום ישועה עזרתיך ואצרך ואתנך לברית עם להקים ארץ להנחיל נחלות שממות: [ישעיה מט, ח]

ח) ועתה לך נחה את העם אל אשר דברתי לך הנה מלאכי ילך לפניך וביום פקדי ופקדתי עליהם חטאתם: [שמות לב, לד]

ט) ויהי בעת ההוא וירד יהודה מאת אחיו ויט עד איש עדלמי ושמו חירה: [בראשית לח, א]

י) וילך רחבעם שכם כי שכם בא כל ישראל להמליך אתו: [מלכים א יב, א]

כ) לכן תתני שלוחים על מורשת גת בתי אכזיב לאכזב למלכי ישראל: [מיכה א, יד]

ל) גוזל אביו ואמו ואמר אין פשע חבר הוא לאיש משחית: [משלי כח, כד] מ) הליי תגמלו זאת עם נבל ולא חכם הלוא הוא אביך קנך הוא עשך ויכננך: [דברים לב, ו] נ) שמע בני מוסר אביך ואל תטש תורת אמך: [משלי א, ח] ס) כי קרע ישראל מעל בית דוד וימליכו את ירבעם בן נבט וידח ירבעם את ישראל מאחרי יי והחטיאם חטאה גדולה: [מלכים ב' יז, כא] ע) אלה הדברים אשר דבר משה אל כל ישראל בעבר הירדן במדבר בערבה מול סוף בין פארן ובין תפל ולבן וחצרת ודי זהב: [דברים א, א] פ) ויקרא באזני קול גדול לאמר קרבו פקדות העיר ואיש כלי משחתו בידו: [יחזקאל ט, א] צ) אחר הדבר הזה לא שב ירבעם מדרכו הרעה וישב ויעש מקצות העם כהני במות החפץ ימלא את ידו ויהי כהני במות: [מלכים א' יג, לג]

עין משפט נר מצוה

כח א מיי' פ"א מהל' חגיגה הלכה ז:

ליקוטי רש"י

בני רבעים. ארבע דורות תחת שהשמדת את בן אחאב שמלכו ארבע דורות עמרי ואחאב ואחזיה ויהורם [מ"ב י, ל]. ושחטה שטים העמיקו. משך שטיות' העמיקו אני אמרתי כל שאינו עולה לרגל עובר בעשה והם גזרו כל העול' לרגל יהרג הרי שהעמיקו יותר ממני ושחטה לשון זהב שחוט (מלכים א י) נמשך ונטוה וי"ת ל' שחיטת זבחים לעכו"ם. ואני מוסר לכולם. ואף אני אייסרם ביסורין אכין מוסר לכולן [הושע ה, ב]. בעת פקודתם. כשיפקוד הקב"ה עליהם ועל עובדיהם [ירמיהו נח, יא]. מקום מזומן לפורענות. ויצא שכמה, מקום מוכן לפורענות שם קלקלו השבטים שם ענו את דינה שם נחלקה מלכות בית דוד שנאמר (מ"א י"ב, א) וילך רחבעם שכמה וגו' [בראשית לז, יד]. לכן תתני שלוחים על מורשת גת. על אשר תתני שלוחים על מלכות דוד אשר הוריש אתכם גת כענין שנאמר (דה"א יח) ויקח דוד את גת מיד פלשתים ואתם מואסים בו כמו שנאמר (ישעיה ח) יען אשר מאס העם הזה את מי השלוח וגומר לפיכך בתי אכזיב שהיתה מארץ יהודה ונמשכו אחר פקח בן רמליהו סופן להיות לאכזב למלכי ישראל שיהרג פקח בן רמליהו ויכזבו הנסמכים עליו ובימי אחז נתנבאת נבואה זו. לכן תתני שלוחים. פי' לכן כמו על אשר כמו (ישעיה יז) על כן תטעי נטעי נעמנים על אשר נטעתיך נטעי נעמנים ואת נהפכת לזמורות זר. בתי אכזיב לאכזב. ל' נופל על הלשון מאגדת חלק למדתי מדרש מקרא זה כך [מיכה א, יד]. גוזל להקדוש ברוך הוא. את ברכתו. וכנסת ישראל. שכשחטאו הפירות לוקין. אין פשע. ולפי שהוא מיקל רואים האחרים ולמדין ממנו לעשות כן ליהנות מן העולם בלא ברכה ולכך נקרא זה המיקל חבר לאיש משחית. לירבעם בן נבט. שחטא והחטיא את ישראל כך הוא חוטא ומחטיא [ברכות לה:]. גוזל אביו. הקב"ה. ואמו. כנסת ישראל המחטיא את הרבי' שגוזל הקב"ה מפריד ממנו בניו וגוזל מהם טובה. משחית. ירבעם [משלי כח, כד]. הלא הוא אביך קנך. שקנאך שקנך בקן הסלעים ובארץ חזקה, שתקנך בכל מיני תקנה [דברים לב, ו]. שמע בני מוסר אביך. מה שנתן הקב"ה למשה בכתב ועל פה. אמך. אומתך כנסת ישראל כמו (יחזקאל יט) מה אמך לביאה והם דברי סופרים שחדשו והוסיפו ועשו סייגים לתורה [משלי א, ח]. ודי זהב. הוכיחן על העגל שעשו בשביל רוב זהב שהיה להם שנאמר (הושע ב י) וכסף הרביתי לה וזהב עשו לבעל [דברים א, א]. אמרו דבי רבי ינאי. לא הזכיר העון אלא למעטו ולומר אתה גרמת להם משל לאדם שהיה לו בן נאה ומאכילו ומשקהו ותולה לו כיס של דינרין בצוארו והושיבו בפתח זונות מה יעשה שלא יחטא [יומא פו:]. אין ארי דורס ונוהם. [ברכות לב.]. קרבו פקדות העיר. הקריבו את הפקודים אשר הפקדתי לשחת את העיר [יחזקאל ט, א]. אחר הדבר הזה. שראה את המופת הזה ושמע את דברי הנביא ואף על פי כן לא שב ורבותינו דרשו אחר שתפשו הקב"ה בבגדו ואמר לו חזור בך ואני ואתה ובן ישי נטייל בגן עדן [מ"א יג, לג].

דאיתפח הדר קא דריש אמרי לא קבילת עלך דלא דרשת בהו אמר אינהו מי הדרו בהו דאנא אהדר בי רב אשי אוקי אשלשה מלכים אמר למחר נפתח בחברין אתא מנשה איתחזי ליה בחלמיה אמר חברך וחבירי דאבוך קרית לן מהיכא בעית למישרא המוציא אמר ליה לא ידענא א"ל מהיכא דבעית למישרא המוציא לא גמירת וחברך קרית לן א"ל אגמריה לי ולמחר דרישנא ליה משמך בפירקא א"ל [א]מהיכא דקרים בישולא א"ל מאחר דחכימתו כולי האי מאי טעמא קא פלחיתו לעבודת כוכבים א"ל אי הות התם הות א) נקיטנא בשיפולי גלימא ורהטת אבתראי למחר אמר להו לרבנן נפתח ברבוותא אחאב אח לשמים אב לעבודת כוכבים אח לשמים דכתיב א) אח לצרה יולד אב לעבודת כוכבים דכתיב ב) כרחם אב על בנים ג) ויהי הנקל לכתו בחטאת ירבעם בן נבט אמר ר' יוחנן קלות שעשה אחאב כחמורות שעשה ירבעם ומפני מה תלה הכתוב בירבעם מפני שהוא היה תחילה לקלקלה ד) גם מזבחותם כגלים על תלמי שדי א"ר יוחנן אין לך ב) כל תלם ותלם בא"י שלא העמיד עליו אחאב עבודת כוכבים והשתחוה לו ומנא לן דלא אתי לעלמא דאתי דכתיב ה) והכרתי לאחאב משתין בקיר ועצור ועזוב בישראל עצור בעוה"ז ועזוב לעוה"ב א"ר יוחנן מפני מה זכה עמרי למלכות מפני שהוסיף כרך אחד בארץ ישראל שנאמר ו) ויקן את ההר שמרון מאת שמר בככרים כסף ויבן את ההר ויקרא [את] שם העיר אשר בנה על שם שמר אדני ההר שמרון א"ר יוחנן מפני מה זכה אחאב למלכות כ"ב שנה מפני שכיבד את התורה שניתנה בכ"ב אותיות שנאמר ז) וישלח מלאכים אל אחאב מלך ישראל העירה ויאמר לו כה אמר בן הדד כספך וזהבך לי הוא ונשיך ובניך הטובים לי הם כי אם כעת מחר אשלח את עבדי אליך וחפשו את ביתך ואת בתי עבדיך והיה כל מחמד עיניך ישימו בידם ולקחו ויאמר למלאכי בן הדד אמרו לאדוני המלך כל אשר שלחת (לעבדך) [אל עבדך] בראשונה אעשה והדבר הזה לא אוכל לעשות מאי מחמד עיניך לאו ס"ת דילמא עבודת כוכבים לא ס"ד דכתיב ח) ויאמרו אליו כל הזקנים וכל העם (ג) לא תאבה ולא תשמע) ודילמא סבי דבהתא הוו מי לא כתיב ט) ויישר הדבר בעיני אבשלום (והזקנים) [ובעיני כל זקני ישראל] ואמר רב יוסף סבי דבהתא התם לא כתיב וכל העם הכא כתיב וכל העם דאי אפשר דלא הוו בהון צדיקי וכתיב י) והשארתי בישראל שבעת אלפים כל הברכים אשר לא כרעו לבעל וכל הפה אשר לא נשק לו אמר ר"נ אחאב שקול היה שנאמר כ) ויאמר ה' מי יפתה את אחאב ויעל ויפול ברמות גלעד ויאמר זה בכה וזה אומר בכה מתקיף לה רב יוסף מאן דכתב ביה ל) רק לא היה כאחאב אשר התמכר לעשות הרע בעיני ה' אשר הסתה אותו איזבל אשתו ותנינא בכל יום היתה שוקלת שקלי זהב לעבודת כוכבים ואת אמרת שקול היה אלא אחאב וותרן בממונו היה ומתוך ד) שההנה תלמידי חכמים מנכסיו כיפרו לו מחצה מ) ויצא הרוח ויעמד לפני ה' ויאמר אני אפתנו ויאמר ה' אליו במה ויאמר אצא והייתי רוח שקר בפי כל נביאיו ויאמר תפתה וגם תוכל צא ועשה כן ה) מאי רוח א"ר יוחנן רוחו של נבות היזרעאלי מאי צא אמר רבינא צא ממחיצתי שכן כתיב נ) דובר שקרים לא יכון לנגד עיני אמר רב פפא היינו דאמרי אינשי דפרע קיניה מחריב ביתיה ס) ויעש אחאב את האשרה ויוסף אחאב לעשות להכעים את ה' אלהי ישראל מכל מלכי ישראל אשר היו לפניו א"ר יוחנן שכתב על דלתות שמרון אחאב כפר באלהי ישראל לפיכך אין לו חלק באלהי ישראל ע) ויבקש את אחזיהו וילכדהו והוא מתחבא בשמרון א"ר לוי שהיה קודר אזכרות וכותב עבודת כוכבים תחתיהן מנשה שנשה יה ד"א מנשה שהנשי את ישראל לאביהם שבשמים ומנלן דלא אתי לעלמא דאתי דכתיב פ) בן שתים עשרה שנה מנשה במלכו וחמשים וחמש שנה מלך בירושלים צ) ויעש (הרע) [אשרה] (בעיני ה') כאשר עשה אחאב מלך ישראל מה אחאב אין לו חלק לעוה"ב אף מנשה אין לו חלק לעוה"ב: רבי יהודה אומר מנשה יש לו חלק לעוה"ב שנאמר ו) ק) ויתפלל מנשה אל ה' ויעתר לו וכו': א"ר יוחנן ושניהם מקרא אחד דרשו שנאמר ר) ונתתים לזועה לכל ממלכות הארץ בגלל מנשה בן יחזקיהו מר סבר בגלל מנשה שעשה תשובה ואינהו לא עבוד ומר סבר בגלל

רש"י

איתפח. נתרפא: אמרו לו. תלמידיו לא קבלת עילווך וכו': אמר אינהו מי הדרו בהו. מדרכם הרעה דאנא אהדר לי מלדרוש: אוקי אשלשה מלכים. אוקי סיום הך פירקא עד שהגיעו לג' מלכים: אמר למחר נפתח בחברין. נדרוש בחברינו שהיו תלמידי חכמים כמותנו ואין להם חלק לעתיד: א"ל. מנשה בחלום חברך וחברא דאביך אנן. כלומר וכי סבור אתה שנהיה חבירך וחבירי דאבוך: מהיכא בעית למשרא המוציא. אינך יודע מאיזה מקום בפת אתה צריך לבצוע המוציא: וחבירך קרית לן. ואתה קורא אותנו חבירך: מהיכא דקרים בשולא. דרפתא ממקום שנקרמין פניה של פת בתנור דהיינו מלמעלה או מסביבות הפת או משוליו אבל באמצע לא שאם הביאו לפניו פרוסה של לחם לא יהא בוצע ומברך אלא משולי הפת ולא מאמצעיתו ל"א מהיכא דקדים כלומר מהיכא שמקדים לאפות והיינו הך ל"א מהיכא דגמר בשולא ממקום שהלחם אפוי יפה ולא מאותו מקום שקורין בשו"ל ורא[ש]ון נראה: הוית נקוט שיפולי גלימך. היית מגבה שפת חלוקך מבין רגליך כדי שתהא קל לרוץ והיית רץ לשם מפני יצר עבודת כוכבים שהיה שולט: נפתח ברבוותא. נתחיל לדרוש ברבותינו ולא אמר בחבירינו: אח לשמים. רע לשמים כדאמרינן (מגילה דף יא.) באחשורוש אח וראש: דכתיב ואח לצרה יולד. [ווי לצרה] אלמא אח [°]לשון רעה ווי: אב לעבודת כוכבים. שהיה אוהבה ביותר דכתיב כרחם אב אלמא אב מרחם והני קראי בכדי נקט להו: ויהי הנקל. באחאב כתוב [כלומר קלות היו לאחאב כל חטאותיו של ירבעם]: מפני מה תלה הכתוב בירבעם. דבכמה מקומות כתיב לא סר מכל חטאת ירבעם ולא כתיב אחאב אע"פ שהיה רשע ממנו: תחלה לקלקלה. שהיה מלך ראשון שהקדים את תבשילו: גם מזבחותם. הכי רישיה דקרא בגלגל שוורים זבחו גם מזבחותם כגלים על תלמי שדי: משתין בקיר. ת"ח משית בקירות לבו: ומניין שכבד את התורה דכתיב והיה כל מחמד עיניך ישימו בידם והיינו ספר תורה ועל זה השיבו את הדבר הזה לא אוכל לעשות: ודילמא. מחמד עיניו היינו עבודת כוכבים: לא ס"ד. מדקאמרי ליה זקנים לא תשמע ולא תאבה ואי עבודת כוכבים מי הוו אמרו ליה הכי: סבי דבהתא. זקנים שפלים שהיו רשעים כמו שמצינו באבשלום דקרי ליה לסבי דבהתא זקנים: שקול היה. מחצה עונות ומחצה זכיות מדמהדרי כולי האי מי יפתה את אחאב משמע דבקושי גדול נענש: רוחו של נבות. שלפי שהוא הרג נבות היה רוחו מחזר לפתותו ולהפילו: דפרע קיניה. קנאה הפורע נוקם חמתו וקנאתו מחריב ביתיה כרוח של נבות שנקם כעסו מאחאב ויצא ממחיצתו של הקב"ה: קודר אזכרות. מוחק שמות שבתורה: וכותב שם עבודת כוכבים תחתיהן. לפיכך היה מתחבא שאילו היה עושה בפרהסיא לא היו מניחין [אותו] לעשות כן. קודר כמו (ערכין נח.) מקדרין בהרים ל' (נוקב) [מחטט ונוקר]: שנשה יה. ששכח הקב"ה: שהנשי. השכיח: מה אחאב אין לו חלק. כדאמרן עזוב לעולם הבא: ושניהם. רבי יהודה דאמר יש לו חלק ורבנן דאמרי אין לו חלק: בגלל

עין משפט נר מצוה

כט א מיי' פ"ז מהלכות ברכות הלכה ג סמג עשין כז טוש"ע א"ח סי' קסז סעיף א [ובהרי"ף פ"ז דברכות לח.]:

מסורת הש"ס

א) נ"ל נקוט, ב) [לקמן קיג.], ג) [נ"ל אל תשמע ואל תאבה], ד) נ"א שהיה מהנה, ה) [לעיל פט.] שבת קמט:, ו) [נ"ל ויתפלל אליו ויעתר].

תורה אור השלם

א) בְּכָל עֵת אֹהֵב הָרֵעַ וְאָח לְצָרָה יִוָּלֵד: [משלי יז, יז]

ב) כְּרַחֵם אָב עַל בָּנִים רִחַם יְיָ עַל יְרֵאָיו: [תהלים קג, יג]

ג) וַיְהִי הֲנָקֵל לֶכְתּוֹ בְּחַטֹּאות יָרָבְעָם בֶּן נְבָט וַיִּקַּח אִשָּׁה אֶת אִיזֶבֶל בַּת אֶתְבַּעַל מֶלֶךְ צִידֹנִים וַיֵּלֶךְ וַיַּעֲבֹד אֶת הַבַּעַל וַיִּשְׁתַּחוּ לוֹ: [מלכים א' טז, לא]

ד) אִם גִּלְעָד אָוֶן אַךְ שָׁוְא הָיוּ בַּגִּלְגָּל שְׁוָרִים זִבֵּחוּ גַּם מִזְבְּחוֹתָם כְּגַלִּים עַל תַּלְמֵי שָׂדָי: [הושע יב, יב]

ה) הִנְנִי מֵבִיא אֵלֶיךָ רָעָה וּבִעַרְתִּי אַחֲרֶיךָ וְהִכְרַתִּי לְאַחְאָב מַשְׁתִּין בְּקִיר וְעָצוּר וְעָזוּב בְּיִשְׂרָאֵל: [מלכים א' כא, כא]

ו) וַיִּקֶן אֶת הָהָר שֹׁמְרוֹן מֵאֶת שֶׁמֶר בְּכִכְּרַיִם כָּסֶף וַיִּבֶן אֶת הָהָר וַיִּקְרָא אֶת שֵׁם הָעִיר אֲשֶׁר בָּנָה עַל שֶׁם שֶׁמֶר אֲדֹנֵי הָהָר שֹׁמְרוֹן: [מלכים א' טז, כד]

ז) וַיִּשְׁלַח מַלְאָכִים אֶל אַחְאָב מֶלֶךְ יִשְׂרָאֵל הָעִירָה: וַיֹּאמֶר לוֹ כֹּה אָמַר בֶּן הֲדַד כַּסְפְּךָ וּזְהָבְךָ לִי הוּא וְנָשֶׁיךָ וּבָנֶיךָ הַטּוֹבִים לִי הֵם: כִּי אִם כָּעֵת מָחָר אֶשְׁלַח אֶת עֲבָדַי אֵלֶיךָ וְחִפְּשׂוּ אֶת בֵּיתְךָ וְאֵת בָּתֵּי עֲבָדֶיךָ וְהָיָה כָּל מַחְמַד עֵינֶיךָ יָשִׂימוּ בְיָדָם וְלָקָחוּ: וַיֹּאמֶר לְמַלְאֲכֵי בֶן הֲדַד אִמְרוּ לַאדֹנִי הַמֶּלֶךְ כֹּל אֲשֶׁר שָׁלַחְתָּ אֶל עַבְדְּךָ בָרִאשֹׁנָה אֶעֱשֶׂה וְהַדָּבָר הַזֶּה לֹא אוּכַל לַעֲשׂוֹת וַיֵּלְכוּ הַמַּלְאָכִים וַיְשִׁבֻהוּ דָּבָר: [מלכים א' כ, ב,ג,ו,ט]

ח) וַיֹּאמְרוּ אֵלָיו כָּל הַזְּקֵנִים וְכָל הָעָם אַל תִּשְׁמַע וְלוֹא תֹאבֶה: [מלכים א' כ, ח]

ט) וַיִּישַׁר הַדָּבָר בְּעֵינֵי אַבְשָׁלֹם וּבְעֵינֵי כָּל זִקְנֵי יִשְׂרָאֵל: [שמואל ב' יז, ד]

י) וְהִשְׁאַרְתִּי בְיִשְׂרָאֵל שִׁבְעַת אֲלָפִים כָּל הַבִּרְכַּיִם אֲשֶׁר לֹא כָרְעוּ לַבַּעַל וְכָל הַפֶּה אֲשֶׁר לֹא נָשַׁק לוֹ: [מלכים א' יט, יח]

כ) וַיֹּאמֶר יְיָ מִי יְפַתֶּה אֶת אַחְאָב וְיַעַל וְיִפֹּל בְּרָמֹת גִּלְעָד וַיֹּאמֶר זֶה בְּכֹה וְזֶה אֹמֵר בְּכֹה: [מלכים א' כב, כ]

ל) רַק לֹא הָיָה כְאַחְאָב אֲשֶׁר הִתְמַכֵּר לַעֲשׂוֹת הָרַע בְּעֵינֵי יְיָ אֲשֶׁר הֵסַתָּה אֹתוֹ אִיזֶבֶל אִשְׁתּוֹ: [מלכים א' כא, כה]

מ) וַיֵּצֵא הָרוּחַ וַיַּעֲמֹד לִפְנֵי יְיָ וַיֹּאמֶר אֲנִי אֲפַתֶּנּוּ וַיֹּאמֶר יְיָ אֵלָיו בַּמָּה: וַיֹּאמֶר אֵצֵא וְהָיִיתִי רוּחַ שֶׁקֶר בְּפִי כָּל נְבִיאָיו וַיֹּאמֶר תְּפַתֶּה וְגַם תּוּכָל צֵא וַעֲשֵׂה כֵן: [מלכים א' כב, כא-כב]

נ) לֹא יֵשֵׁב בְּקֶרֶב בֵּיתִי עֹשֵׂה רְמִיָּה דֹּבֵר שְׁקָרִים לֹא יִכּוֹן לְנֶגֶד עֵינָי: [תהלים קא, ז]

ס) וַיַּעַשׂ אַחְאָב אֶת הָאֲשֵׁרָה וַיּוֹסֶף אַחְאָב לַעֲשׂוֹת לְהַכְעִיס אֶת יְיָ אֱלֹהֵי יִשְׂרָאֵל מִכֹּל מַלְכֵי יִשְׂרָאֵל אֲשֶׁר הָיוּ לְפָנָיו: [מלכים א' טז, לג]

ע) וַיְבַקֵּשׁ אֶת אֲחַזְיָהוּ וַיִּלְכְּדֻהוּ וְהוּא מִתְחַבֵּא בְשֹׁמְרוֹן וַיְבִאֻהוּ אֶל יֵהוּא וַיְמִתֻהוּ וַיִּקְבְּרֻהוּ כִּי אָמְרוּ בֶּן יְהוֹשָׁפָט הוּא אֲשֶׁר דָּרַשׁ אֶת יְיָ בְּכָל לְבָבוֹ וְאֵין לְבֵית אֲחַזְיָהוּ לַעְצֹר כֹּחַ לְמַמְלָכָה: [דברי הימים ב' כב, ט]

פ) בֶּן שְׁתֵּים עֶשְׂרֵה שָׁנָה מְנַשֶּׁה בְמָלְכוֹ וַחֲמִשִּׁים וְחָמֵשׁ שָׁנָה מָלַךְ בִּירוּשָׁלָיִם: [דברי הימים ב' לג, א]

צ) וַיָּשָׁב וַיִּבֶן אֶת הַבָּמוֹת אֲשֶׁר אִבַּד חִזְקִיָּהוּ אָבִיו וַיָּקֶם מִזְבְּחֹת לַבַּעַל וַיַּעַשׂ אֲשֵׁרָה כַּאֲשֶׁר עָשָׂה אַחְאָב מֶלֶךְ יִשְׂרָאֵל וַיִּשְׁתַּחוּ לְכָל צְבָא הַשָּׁמַיִם וַיַּעֲבֹד אֹתָם: [מלכים ב' כא, ג]

ק) וַיִּתְפַּלֵּל אֵלָיו וַיֵּעָתֶר לוֹ וַיִּשְׁמַע תְּחִנָּתוֹ וַיְשִׁיבֵהוּ יְרוּשָׁלַיִם לְמַלְכוּתוֹ וַיֵּדַע מְנַשֶּׁה כִּי יְיָ הוּא הָאֱלֹהִים: [דברי הימים ב' לג, יג]

ר) וּנְתַתִּים לְזַעֲוָה לְכֹל מַמְלְכוֹת הָאָרֶץ בִּגְלַל מְנַשֶּׁה בֶן יְחִזְקִיָּהוּ מֶלֶךְ יְהוּדָה עַל אֲשֶׁר עָשָׂה בִּירוּשָׁלָיִם: [ירמיה טו, ד]

גליון הש"ס

רש"י ד"ה דכתיב. לשון רעה ווי. עי' ברש"י הושע יג טו:

ליקוטי רש"י

גם מזבחותם. רבים כגלים שעל תלמי שדי תלמי שדי היא מענית המחרישה קרויה תלם [הושע יב, יב]. כל מחמד עיניך ישימו בידם ולקחו. והלא כל הראשונים דברי חמד' הם אלא מהו מחמד עיניך חמדה מתוך חמדה זה ספר תורה שנאמר בו הנחמדי' מזהב ומפז רב (תהלים י"ט י"א) אמר אחאב בלבו דבר גדול זה מבקש אין זה שלי לבדי של זקני ישראל היא לפיכך ויקרא לכל זקני הארץ אע"פ שהיו עובדין ע"ג היו מכבדין את התורה [מ"א כ, ו]. ובעיני זקני ישראל. זקני אשמאי [ש"ב יז, ד]. רק לא היה כאחאב. הכתוב מעיד עליו שלא היה במלכים כמותו שירבעם וכל אשר אחריו עבדו את העגלים מיראה אם יעלה העם ירושלים תשוב הממלכה לבית דוד וזה הוסיף הבעל והאשרה להכעיס. התמכר. נמכר לע"ג ראיתי בירושלמי היאל בית האלי שושבינו היה ובכל יום שם דמיו ונתן לע"ג [מ"א כא, כה]. ויצא הרוח. פתרון ויצא המלאך שהרי אומר לעיל וכל צבא השמים וגו' ועתה יצא אחד מן המלאכים ויאמר אני אפתנו כדאמר (תהלים קד) עושה מלאכיו רוחות ולפיכך קדם ואמר לעיל וכל צבא השמים עומדים שאל תתמה כשתאמר ויצא הרוח מי הוא ומהיכן יצא וכשאמר וכל צבא השמים עומדים כדי להודיע מהיכן יצא משאר הרוחות העומדים עליו ורבותינו פירשו זהו רוחו של נבות [דה"ב יח, כ]. אשרה. אילן נעבד [מ"א טז, לג]. לזעוה. מגזרת לא קם ולא זע (אסתר ה) וכמוהו גאוה מגזרת גא מאד (ישעיה טו). לכל ממלכות הארץ. כל השומע רעה שבאה עליהם יזוע [ירמיהו טו, ד].

דְּאִיתְּפַח – **he recovered,** however, הֲדַר קָא דָרֵישׁ – **he resumed lecturing.** אָמְרֵי – **[His students] said to him:** לֹא קַבֵּילְתְּ עֲלָךְ דְּלָא דָּרְשַׁתְּ בְּהוּ – **"Did you not undertake not to lecture about them?"** אָמַר – **[R' Abahu] said** to them: אִינְהוּ מִי הֲדַרוּ בְּהוּ דַּאֲנָא אֶהְדַּר בִּי – **"Did they repent that I should repent?"**[1]

A similar story involving King Menasheh and Rav Ashi:

רַב אַשִׁי אוֹקִי אַשְׁלֹשָׁה מְלָכִים – It once happened that **Rav Ashi concluded** his lecture when he came to **the three kings.**[2] אָמַר – **He said** to his students: לְמָחָר נִפְתַּח בְּחַבְרִין – **"Tomorrow we shall commence** our studies **with** the Mishnah concerning **our colleagues,** i.e. the three kings."[3] אָתָא מְנַשֶּׁה אִיתְחֲזֵי לֵיהּ בְּחֶלְמֵיהּ – That night, **Menasheh came** and **appeared to [Rav Ashi] in his dream.** אָמַר – **[Menasheh] said:** חַבְרָךְ וַחֲבֵירֵי דַּאֲבוּךְ קָרֵית לָן – **"You refer to us,** i.e. regard us, **as 'your colleagues' and 'the colleagues of your father'?!** Answer me, then, this question of Jewish law: מֵהֵיכָא בָּעֵית לְמִישְׁרָא הַמּוֹצִיא – **From where are you supposed to break** the loaf of bread over which you recite **the *hamotzi*?"**[4] אָמַר לֵיהּ לֹא יָדַעְנָא – **[Rav Ashi] said to [Menasheh]: "I do not know."** אָמַר לֵיהּ – **[Menasheh] said to [Rav Ashi]:** מֵהֵיכָא דְּבָעֵית לְמִישְׁרָא הַמּוֹצִיא לֹא גְמִירַתְּ – **"You have not learned** a simple law as **from where you are supposed to break** the bread for **the *hamotzi,*** וְחַבְרָךְ קָרֵית לָן – **yet you refer to us as your colleagues?!"** אָמַר לֵיהּ – **[Rav Ashi] said to [Menasheh]:** אַגְמְרֵיהּ לִי – **"Teach me [this rule],** וּלְמָחָר דְּרִישְׁנָא לֵיהּ מִשְּׁמָךְ בְּפִירְקָא – **and tomorrow** I promise that **I will teach it in your name in the lecture."** אָמַר לֵיהּ – **[Menasheh] said to [Rav Ashi]:** מֵהֵיכָא דְּקָרִים בִּישׁוּלָא – **"From the part that is baked into a crust."**[5] אָמַר לֵיהּ – **[Rav Ashi] said to [Menasheh]:** מֵאַחַר דְּחַכִּימִתוּ כּוּלֵּי הַאי – **"Since you are so learned,** מַאי טַעְמָא קָא פָּלְחִיתוּ לַעֲבוֹדַת כּוֹכָבִים – **why did you worship idols?"** אָמַר לֵיהּ – **[Menasheh] said to [Rav Ashi]:** אִי הֲוַת הָתָם – **"Had you been there,** i.e. had you been living when I was alive, הֲוַת נְקִיטְנָא בְּשִׁיפּוּלֵי גְלִימָא וּרְהַטַתְּ אַבַּתְרַאי – **you would have lifted the bottom of your garment and run after me!"**[6] לְמָחָר אָמַר לְהוּ לְרַבָּנָן – **The next day, Rav Ashi said to the Rabbis** as he began his lecture: נִפְתַּח בְּרַבְּוָותָא – **"We will commence** today's lecture **with our teachers."**[7]

The Gemara continues with a discussion of Ahab, the next of the three kings listed in our Mishnah as having no share in the World to Come:[8]

אַחְאָב אָח לַשָּׁמַיִם אָב לַעֲבוֹדַת כּוֹכָבִים – The name **Ahab** means **"woe** *(ach)* **to heaven"** and **"father** *(av)* **to idolatry,"** i.e. Ahab was a thoroughly wicked king.[9] אָח לַשָּׁמַיִם דִּכְתִיב ,,אָח לְצָרָה יִוָּלֵד" – **"Woe to heaven" – as it is written: *woe (ach) the trouble that will be born!***[10] אָב לַעֲבוֹדַת כּוֹכָבִים דִּכְתִיב ,,כְּרַחֵם אָב עַל־בָּנִים" – **"Father to idolatry" – as it is written: *As a father has compassion for his children,*** *so* HASHEM *has compassion for those who fear Him.* [11]

,,וַיְהִי הֲנָקֵל לֶכְתּוֹ בְּחַטֹּאות יָרָבְעָם בֶּן־נְבָט" – Scripture states concerning Ahab:[12] ***His most trivial deed was to follow the sins of Yarovam the son of Nevat.*** אָמַר רַבִּי יוֹחָנָן – **R' Yochanan said:** קַלּוֹת שֶׁעָשָׂה אַחְאָב כַּחֲמוּרוֹת שֶׁעָשָׂה יָרָבְעָם – This means that **the light sins committed by Ahab were equal to the severest sins committed by Yarovam.**[13] וּמִפְּנֵי מָה תָּלָה הַכָּתוּב

NOTES

1. I.e. I thought about it and came to the conclusion that since the three kings did not repent their evil ways, I need not repent speaking ill of them in my lectures (*Rashi*). Just as they all had experiences that should have made them rethink their ways but they did not, so too my sickness should not be viewed as a reason for my reevaluating my remarks concerning them (*Maharsha*; see *Iyun Yaakov*; see also *Chida, Maris Ayin*).

2. Rav Ashi would deliver a daily lecture to his students. On this day, he concluded the Mishnah preceding our Mishnah, which discusses the three kings (*Rashi*). He planned to study this Mishnah on the following day.

3. By referring to them as "our colleagues," Rav Ashi meant: Although they were our peers in Torah scholarship, they have no share in the World to Come (*Rashi*). Cf. *Maharsha*. [See above, 102a and below, 103b, regarding the great scholarship of these three kings.]

4. The law is that upon reciting a blessing over bread, one should break off and eat his first bite from the choicest part of the loaf. Rav Ashi certainly knew this law. Menasheh, however, asked him if he knew *which* section of the loaf is considered the choicest part (*Yad Ramah*).

5. I.e. if one has before him a cut loaf rather than a whole one, he should recite the blessing and break off a piece from the crust rather than from the center (*Rashi*). Alternatively, the text reads מֵהֵיכָא דְּגָמִיר בִּישׁוּלָא, *from where it is most well baked* (*Rashi,* third explanation; *Yad Ramah; Rambam, Hil. Berachos* 7:3). This is considered the tastiest part of the bread (*Yad Ramah*), and is therefore the most appropriate piece on which to recite the blessing.

As simply understood, Menasheh chose to test Rav Ashi with a relatively minor law, as if to say: You do not even know a simple law as where one breaks the bread for *hamotzi,* and you call me your colleague?

Chida adds that Menasheh was upset that Rav Ashi considered himself, in contrast to the three kings, a *chassid* (pious person); therefore, he challenged him concerning a blessing, for the Sages declare that a *chassid* is one who is meticulous in the laws of blessings (*Bava Kamma* 30a). [Other, more analytical interpretations of Menasheh's question can be found in *Akeidas Yitzchak* to *Parashas Beshalach* (beginning of chapter 40), *Maharal, Maharsha, Toras Chaim* and *Iyun Yaakov*.]

6. I.e. the desire to worship idols in my time was so strong that had you lived then, you would have lifted up your garment so that it should not impede you in your headlong rush to the place of idolatry (*Rashi*). In other words, you cannot understand how powerful the temptation to worship idols was during my lifetime.

Menasheh's words show that idolatry, which to us appears so absurd, was as tempting in his age as other sins still are today. If we do not feel the same way today, it is because the Men of the Great Assembly beseeched God to banish the Evil Inclination for idolatry (see *Yoma* 69b), while we still have the urge for other sins. If we were totally free of the Evil Inclination, all sins would appear to us equally ludicrous (*R' Chaim Shmulevitz, Sichos Mussar* 5733:7 and 12, and see *Michtav MeEliyahu IV* p. 134).

7. Rav Ashi no longer referred to the three kings as his colleagues; instead he referred to them as his masters in Torah learning (*Rashi*), that is, as persons whose Torah knowledge was worthy of respect, despite the tragic fact that their sins had led them to lose their portions in the World to Come.

8. See 90a note 14.

9. [This follows *Rashi,* who translates the word *ach* as an onomatopoeia, an expression of anguish. Others understand *ach* to mean brother. According to them, the phrase is translated: *a brother to heaven and a father to idolatry,* i.e. Ahab was a person who displayed contradictory character traits; in certain respects he was good, particularly when he was in trouble, while in other respects, particularly when he prospered, he was an idolater (*Maharsha*), as is evident from his reaction to the demand of Ben Hadad, see below (*Rif* in *Ein Yaakov*). Cf. *Maharal.*]

10. *Proverbs* 17:17. Thus, *ach* means "woe!"

[This follows *Rashi,* who understands *ach* as an exclamation of lament, see preceding note. According to *Maharsha,* who understands *ach* to mean brother, the meaning of the Scriptural passage is *a brother is born to share adversity.* (This is indeed how the verse is translated by most commentators ad loc.)]

11. *Psalms* 103:13. It is thus evident that a father symbolizes love and compassion. So too, Ahab loved idol worship as deeply as a father loves a child (*Rashi*). See also *Maharsha* and *Maharal.*

The Gemara cites the verses superfluously, because the connotations of "*ach*" and "father" are self-evident (*Rashi*).

12. *I Kings* 16:31.

13. In addition to the golden calves, Ahab instituted the worship of Baal and Asheirah (*Maharsha*). See comment of *Kuzari* above, 102a note 6.

דאיתפח הדר קא דריש אמרי לא קבילת עלך דלא דרשת בהו אמר אינהו מי הדרו בהו דאנא אהדר בי רב אשי אוקי אשלשה מלכים אמר למחר נפתח בחברין אתא מנשה איתחזי ליה בחלמיה אמר חברך וחבירי דאבוך קרית לן מהיכא בעית למישרא המוציא אמר ליה לא ידענא א"ל מהיכא דבעית למישרא המוציא לא גמירת וחברך קרית לן א"ל אגמריה לי ולמחר דרישנא ליה משמך בפירקא א"ל [א]מהיכא דקרים בישולא א"ל מאחר דחכימתו כולי האי מאי טעמא קא פלחיתו לעבודת כוכבים א"ל אי הות התם הות [א]נקיטנא בשיפולי גלימא ורהטת אבתראי למחר אמר להו לרבנן נפתח ברבוותא אחאב אח לשמים אב לעבודת כוכבים אח לשמים דכתיב [א]אח לצרה יולד אב לעבודת כוכבים דכתיב [ב]כרחם אב על בנים [ג]ויהי הנקל לכתו בחטאת ירבעם בן נבט אמר ר' יוחנן קלות שעשה אחאב כחמורות שעשה ירבעם ומפני מה תלה הכתוב בירבעם מפני שהוא היה תחילה לקלקלה [ד]גם מזבחותם כגלים על תלמי שדי א"ר יוחנן אין לך [ב]כל תלם ותלם בא"י שלא העמיד עליו אחאב עבודת כוכבים והשתחוה לו ומנא לן דלא אתי לעלמא דאתי דכתיב [ה]והכרתי לאחאב משתין בקיר ועצור ועזוב בישראל עצור בעוה"ז ועזוב לעוה"ב א"ר יוחנן מפני מה זכה עמרי למלכות מפני שהוסיף כרך אחד בארץ ישראל שנאמר [ו]ויקן את ההר שמרון מאת שמר בככרים כסף ויבן את ההר ויקרא [את] שם העיר אשר בנה על שם שמר אדני ההר שמרון א"ר יוחנן מפני מה זכה אחאב למלכות כ"ב שנה מפני שכיבד את התורה שניתנה בכ"ב אותיות שנאמר [ז]וישלח מלאכים אל אחאב מלך ישראל העירה ויאמר לו כה אמר בן הדד כספך וזהבך לי הוא ונשיך ובניך הטובים לי הם כי אם כעת מחר אשלח את עבדי אליך וחפשו את ביתך ואת בתי עבדיך והיה כל מחמד עיניך ישימו בידם ולקחו ויאמר למלאכי בן הדד אמרו לאדוני המלך כל אשר שלחת (לעבדך) [אל עבדך] בראשונה אעשה והדבר הזה לא אוכל לעשות מאי מחמד עיניך לאו ס"ת דילמא עבודת כוכבים לא ס"ד דכתיב [ח]ויאמרו אליו כל הזקנים וכל העם ([ג]לא תאבה ולא תשמע) ודילמא סבי דבהתא הוו מי לא כתיב [ט]ויישר הדבר בעיני אבשלום (והזקנים) [ובעיני כל זקני ישראל] ואמר רב יוסף סבי דבהתא התם לא כתיב וכל העם הכא כתיב וכל העם דאי אפשר דלא הוו בהון צדיקי וכתיב [י]והשארתי בישראל שבעת אלפים כל הברכים אשר לא כרעו לבעל וכל הפה אשר לא נשק לו אמר ר"נ אחאב שקול היה שנאמר [כ]ויאמר ה' מי יפתה את אחאב ויעל ויפול ברמות גלעד ויאמר זה בכה וזה אומר בכה מתקיף לה רב יוסף מאן דכתב ביה [ל]רק לא היה כאחאב אשר התמכר לעשות הרע בעיני ה' אשר הסתה אותו איזבל אשתו ותנינא בכל יום היתה שוקלת שקלי זהב לעבודת כוכבים ואת אמרת שקול היה אלא אחאב וותרן בממונו היה ומתוך [ד]שההנה תלמידי חכמים מנכסיו כיפרו לו מחצה [מ]ויצא הרוח ויעמד לפני ה' ויאמר אני אפתנו ויאמר ה' אליו במה ויאמר אצא והייתי רוח שקר בפי כל נביאיו ויאמר תפתה וגם תוכל צא ועשה כן [ה]מאי רוח א"ר יוחנן רוחו של נבות היזרעאלי מאי צא אמר רבינא צא ממחיצתי שכן כתיב [נ]דובר שקרים לא יכון לנגד עיני אמר רב פפא היינו דאמרי אינשי דפרע קיניה מחריב ביתיה [ס]ויעש אחאב את האשרה ויוסף אחאב לעשות להכעיס את ה' אלהי ישראל מכל מלכי ישראל אשר היו לפניו א"ר יוחנן שכתב על דלתות שמרון אחאב כפר באלהי ישראל לפיכך אין לו חלק באלהי ישראל [ע]ויבקש את אחזיהו וילכדהו והוא מתחבא בשמרון א"ר לוי שהיה קודר אזכרות וכותב עבודת כוכבים תחתיהן מנשה שנשה יה ד"א מנשה שהנשי את ישראל לאביהם שבשמים ומנלן דלא אתי לעלמא דאתי דכתיב [פ]בן שתים עשרה שנה מנשה במלכו וחמשים וחמש שנה מלך בירושלים [צ]ויעש (הרע) [אשרה] (בעיני ה') כאשר עשה אחאב מלך ישראל מה אחאב אין לו חלק לעוה"ב אף מנשה אין לו חלק לעוה"ב: רבי יהודה אומר מנשה יש לו חלק לעוה"ב שנאמר [ו][ק]ויתפלל מנשה אל ה' ויעתר לו וכו': א"ר יוחנן ושניהם מקרא אחד דרשו שנאמר [ר]ונתתים לזועה לכל ממלכות הארץ בגלל מנשה בן יחזקיהו מר סבר בגלל מנשה שעשה תשובה ואינהו לא עבוד ומר סבר בגלל

רש"י

איתפח. נתרפא: אמרו לו. תלמידיו לא קבלת עילווך וכו': אמר אינהו מי הדרו בהו. מדרכם הרעה דאנא אהדר לי מלדרוש: אוקי אשלשה מלכים. אוקי סיום הך פירקא עד שהגיעו לג' מלכים: אמר למחר נפתח בחברין. נדרוש בחברינו שהיו תלמידי חכמים כמותנו ואין להם חלק לעתיד: א"ל. מנשה בחלום חברך וחברא דאביך אנן. כלומר וכי סבור אתה שנהיה חבירך וחבירי דאבוך: מהיכא בעית למשרא המוציא. אינך יודע מאיזה מקום בפת אתה צריך לבצוע המוציא: וחבירך קרית לן. ואתה קורא אותנו חבירך: מהיכא דקרים בשולא. דרפתא ממקום שנקרמין פניה של פת בתנור דהיינו מלמעלה או מסביבות הפת או משוליו אבל באמצע לא שאם הביאו לפניו פרוסה של לחם לא יהא בוצע ומברך אלא משולי הפת ולא מאמצעיתו ל"א מהיכא דקדים כלומר מהיכא שמקדים לאפות והיינו הך ל"א מהיכא דגמר בשולא ממקום שהלחם אפוי יפה ולא מאותו מקום שקורין בשו"ל ולשון נראה: הוית נקוט שיפולי גלימך. היית מגבה שפת חלוקך מבין רגליך כדי שתהא קל לרוץ והיית רץ לשם מפני יצר עבודת כוכבים שהיה שולט: נפתח ברבוותא. נתחיל לדרוש ברבותינו ולא אמר בחבירינו: אח לשמים. רע לשמים כדאמרינן (מגילה דף יא.) באחשורוש אח וראש: דכתיב ואח לצרה יולד. [ווי לצרה] אלמא אח [ה]לשון רעה ווי: אב לעבודת כוכבים. שהיה אוהבה ביותר דכתיב כרחם אב אלמא אב מרחם והני קראי בכדי נקט להו: ויהי הנקל. באחאב כתוב [כלומר קלות היו לאחאב כל חטאותיו של ירבעם]: מפני מה תלה הכתוב בירבעם. דבכמה מקומות כתיב לא סר מכל חטאת ירבעם ולא כתיב אחאב אע"פ שהיה רשע ממנו: תחלה לקלקלה. שהיה מלך ראשון שהקדים את תבשילו: גם מזבחותם. הכי רישיה דקרא בגלגל שוורים זבחו גם מזבחותם כגלים על תלמי שדי: משתין בקיר. ת"ח משית בקירות לבו: ומניין שכבד את התורה דכתיב והיה כל מחמד עיניך ישימו בידם והיינו ספר תורה ועל זה השיבו את הדבר הזה לא אוכל לעשות: ודילמא. מחמד עיניו היינו עבודת כוכבים: לא ס"ד. מדקאמרי ליה זקנים לא תשמע ולא תאבה ואי עבודת כוכבים מי הוו אמרו ליה הכי: סבי דבהתא. זקנים שפלים שהיו רשעים כמו שמצינו באבשלום דקרי ליה לסבי דבהתא זקנים: שקול היה. מחצה עונות ומחצה זכיות מדמהדרי כולי האי מי יפתה את אחאב משמע דבקושי גדול נענש: רוחו של נבות. שלפי שהוא הרג נבות היה רוחו מחזר לפתותו ולהפילו: דפרע קיניה. קנאה הפורע נוקם חמתו וקנאתו מחריב ביתיה כרוח של נבות שנקם כעסו מאחאב ויצא ממחילתו של הקב"ה: קודר אזכרות. מוחק שמות שבתורה: וכותב שם עבודת כוכבים תחתיהן. לפיכך היה מתחבא שאילו היה עושה בפרהסיא לא היו מניחין [אותו] לעשות כן. קודר כמו (עירובין נח.) מקדרין בהרים ל' (נוקב) [מחטט ונוקר]: שנשה יה. ששכח הקב"ה: שהנשי. השכיח: מה אחאב אין לו חלק. כדאמרן עזוב לעולם הבא: ושניהם. רבי יהודה דאמר יש לו חלק ורבנן דאמרי אין לו חלק: בגלל

כט א מיי' פ"ז מהלכות ברכות הלכה ג סמג עשין כז טוש"ע א"ח סי' קסז סעיף א [וברי"ף פ"ז דברכות לח.]:

גליון הש"ס

רש"י ד"ה דכתיב. לשון רעה ווי. עי' ברש"י הושע יג טו:

ליקוטי רש"י

גם מזבחותם. רבים כגלים שעל תלמי שדי תלמי שדי היא מענית המחרישה קרויה תלם [הושע יב, יב]. כל מחמד עיניך ישימו בידם ולקחו. והלא כל הראשונים דברי חמד' הם אלא מהו מחמד עיניך חמדה מתוך חמדה זה ספר תורה שנאמר בו הנחמדי' מזהב ומפז רב (תהלים י"ט י"א) אמר אחאב בלבו דבר גדול זה מבקש אין זה שלי לבדי של זקני ישראל היא לפיכך ויקרא לכל זקני הארץ אע"פ שהיו עובדין ע"ג היו מכבדין את התורה [מ"א כ, ו]. ובעיני זקני ישראל. זקני אשמאי [ש"ב יז, ד]. רק לא היה כאחאב. הכתוב מעיד עליו שלא היה במלכים כמותו שירבעם וכל אשר אחריו עבדו את העגלים מיראה אם יעלה העם ירושלים תשוב הממלכה לבית דוד וזה הוסיף הבעל והאשרה להכעים. התמכר. נמכר לע"ג ראיתי בירושלמי חיאל בית האלי שושבינו היה ובכל יום שם דמיו ונתן לע"ג [מ"א כא, כה]. ויצא הרוח. פתרון ויצא המלאך שהרי אומר לעיל וכל צבא השמים וגו' ועתה יצא אחד מן המלאכים ויאמר אני אפתנו כדאמר (תהלים קד) עושה מלאכיו רוחות ולפיכך קדם ואמר לעיל וכל צבא השמים עומדים שאל תתמה כשתאמר ויצא הרוח מי הוא ומהיכן יצא וכשאמר וכל צבא השמים עומדים כדי להודיע מהיכן יצא משאר הרוחות העומדים עליו ורבותינו פירשו זהו רוחו של נבות [דה"ב יח, כ]. אשרה. אילן נעבד [מ"א טז, לג]. לזעוה. מגורת לא קם ולא זע (אסתר ה) וכמוהו גאוה מגורת גא מאד (ישעיה טז). לכל ממלכות הארץ. כל השומע רעה שבאה עליהם יזוע [ירמיהו טו, ד].

מסורת הש"ס

א) נ"ל נקוט, ב) [לקמן קיג.], ג) [נ"ל אל תשמע ואל תאבה], ד) נ"א שהיה מהנה, ה) [לעיל פט.] שבת קמט:, ו) [נ"ל ויתפלל אליו ויעתר].

תורה אור השלם

א) בְּכָל עֵת אֹהֵב הָרֵעַ וְאָח לְצָרָה יִוָּלֵד: [משלי יז, יז]

ב) כְּרַחֵם אָב עַל בָּנִים רִחַם יְיָ עַל יְרֵאָיו: [תהלים קג, יג]

ג) וַיְהִי הֲנָקֵל לֶכְתּוֹ בְּחַטֹּאות יָרָבְעָם בֶּן נְבָט וַיִּקַּח אִשָּׁה אֶת אִיזֶבֶל בַּת אֶתְבַּעַל מֶלֶךְ צִידֹנִים וַיֵּלֶךְ וַיַּעֲבֹד אֶת הַבַּעַל וַיִּשְׁתַּחוּ לוֹ: [מלכים א' טז, לא]

ד) אִם גִּלְעָד אָוֶן אַךְ שָׁוְא הָיוּ בַּגִּלְגָּל שְׁוָרִים זִבֵּחוּ גַּם מִזְבְּחוֹתָם כְּגַלִּים עַל תַּלְמֵי שָׂדָי: [הושע יב, יב]

ה) הִנְנִי מֵבִיא אֵלֶיךָ רָעָה וּבִעַרְתִּי אַחֲרֶיךָ וְהִכְרַתִּי לְאַחְאָב מַשְׁתִּין בְּקִיר וְעָצוּר וְעָזוּב בְּיִשְׂרָאֵל: [מלכים א' כא, כא]

ו) וַיִּקֶן אֶת הָהָר שֹׁמְרוֹן מֵאֶת שֶׁמֶר בְּכִכְּרַיִם כָּסֶף וַיִּבֶן אֶת הָהָר וַיִּקְרָא אֶת שֵׁם הָעִיר אֲשֶׁר בָּנָה עַל שֶׁם שֶׁמֶר אֲדֹנֵי הָהָר שֹׁמְרוֹן: [מלכים א' טז, כד]

ז) וַיִּשְׁלַח מַלְאָכִים אֶל אַחְאָב מֶלֶךְ יִשְׂרָאֵל הָעִירָה: וַיֹּאמֶר לוֹ כֹּה אָמַר בֶּן הֲדַד כַּסְפְּךָ וּזְהָבְךָ לִי הוּא וְנָשֶׁיךָ וּבָנֶיךָ הַטּוֹבִים לִי הֵם: כִּי אִם כָּעֵת מָחָר אֶשְׁלַח אֶת עֲבָדַי אֵלֶיךָ וְחִפְּשׂוּ אֶת בֵּיתְךָ וְאֵת בָּתֵּי עֲבָדֶיךָ וְהָיָה כָּל מַחְמַד עֵינֶיךָ יָשִׂימוּ בְיָדָם וְלָקָחוּ: וַיֹּאמֶר לְמַלְאֲכֵי בֶן הֲדַד אִמְרוּ לַאדֹנִי הַמֶּלֶךְ כֹּל אֲשֶׁר שָׁלַחְתָּ אֶל עַבְדְּךָ בָרִאשֹׁנָה אֶעֱשֶׂה וְהַדָּבָר הַזֶּה לֹא אוּכַל לַעֲשׂוֹת וַיֵּלְכוּ הַמַּלְאָכִים וַיְשִׁבֻהוּ דָּבָר: [מלכים א' כ, ב,ג,ו,ט]

ח) וַיֹּאמְרוּ אֵלָיו כָּל הַזְּקֵנִים וְכָל הָעָם אַל תִּשְׁמַע וְלוֹא תֹאבֶה: [מלכים א' כ, ח]

ט) וַיִּישַׁר הַדָּבָר בְּעֵינֵי אַבְשָׁלֹם וּבְעֵינֵי כָּל זִקְנֵי יִשְׂרָאֵל: [שמואל ב' יז, ד]

י) וְהִשְׁאַרְתִּי בְיִשְׂרָאֵל שִׁבְעַת אֲלָפִים כָּל הַבִּרְכַּיִם אֲשֶׁר לֹא כָרְעוּ לַבַּעַל וְכָל הַפֶּה אֲשֶׁר לֹא נָשַׁק לוֹ: [מלכים א' יט, יח]

כ) וַיֹּאמֶר יְיָ מִי יְפַתֶּה אֶת אַחְאָב וְיַעַל וְיִפֹּל בְּרָמֹת גִּלְעָד וַיֹּאמֶר זֶה בְּכֹה וְזֶה אֹמֵר בְּכֹה: [מלכים א' כב, כ]

ל) רַק לֹא הָיָה כְאַחְאָב אֲשֶׁר הִתְמַכֵּר לַעֲשׂוֹת הָרַע בְּעֵינֵי יְיָ אֲשֶׁר הֵסַתָּה אֹתוֹ אִיזֶבֶל אִשְׁתּוֹ: [מלכים א' כא, כה]

מ) וַיֵּצֵא הָרוּחַ וַיַּעֲמֹד לִפְנֵי יְיָ וַיֹּאמֶר אֲנִי אֲפַתֶּנּוּ וַיֹּאמֶר יְיָ אֵלָיו בַּמָּה: וַיֹּאמֶר אֵצֵא וְהָיִיתִי רוּחַ שֶׁקֶר בְּפִי כָּל נְבִיאָיו וַיֹּאמֶר תְּפַתֶּה וְגַם תּוּכָל צֵא וַעֲשֵׂה כֵן: [מלכים א' כב, כא-כב]

נ) לֹא יֵשֵׁב בְּקֶרֶב בֵּיתִי עֹשֵׂה רְמִיָּה דֹּבֵר שְׁקָרִים לֹא יִכּוֹן לְנֶגֶד עֵינָי: [תהלים קא, ז]

ס) וַיַּעַשׂ אַחְאָב אֶת הָאֲשֵׁרָה וַיּוֹסֶף אַחְאָב לַעֲשׂוֹת לְהַכְעִיס אֶת יְיָ אֱלֹהֵי יִשְׂרָאֵל מִכֹּל מַלְכֵי יִשְׂרָאֵל אֲשֶׁר הָיוּ לְפָנָיו: [מלכים א' טז, לג]

ע) וַיְבַקֵּשׁ אֶת אֲחַזְיָהוּ וַיִּלְכְּדֻהוּ וְהוּא מִתְחַבֵּא בְשֹׁמְרוֹן וַיְבִאֻהוּ אֶל יֵהוּא וַיְמִתֻהוּ וַיִּקְבְּרֻהוּ כִּי אָמְרוּ בֶּן יְהוֹשָׁפָט הוּא אֲשֶׁר דָּרַשׁ אֶת יְיָ בְּכָל לְבָבוֹ וְאֵין לְבֵית אֲחַזְיָהוּ לַעְצֹר כֹּחַ לְמַמְלָכָה: [דברי הימים ב' כב, ט]

פ) בֶּן שְׁתֵּים עֶשְׂרֵה שָׁנָה מְנַשֶּׁה בְמָלְכוֹ וַחֲמִשִּׁים וְחָמֵשׁ שָׁנָה מָלַךְ בִּירוּשָׁלָיִם: [דברי הימים ב' לג, א]

צ) וַיָּשָׁב וַיִּבֶן אֶת הַבָּמוֹת אֲשֶׁר אִבַּד חִזְקִיָּהוּ אָבִיו וַיָּקֶם מִזְבְּחֹת לַבַּעַל וַיַּעַשׂ אֲשֵׁרָה כַּאֲשֶׁר עָשָׂה אַחְאָב מֶלֶךְ יִשְׂרָאֵל וַיִּשְׁתַּחוּ לְכָל צְבָא הַשָּׁמַיִם וַיַּעֲבֹד אֹתָם: [מלכים ב' כא, ג]

ק) וַיִּתְפַּלֵּל אֵלָיו וַיֵּעָתֶר לוֹ וַיִּשְׁמַע תְּחִנָּתוֹ וַיְשִׁיבֵהוּ יְרוּשָׁלַיִם לְמַלְכוּתוֹ וַיֵּדַע מְנַשֶּׁה כִּי יְיָ הוּא הָאֱלֹהִים: [דברי הימים ב' לג, יג]

ר) וּנְתַתִּים לְזַעֲוָה לְכֹל מַמְלְכוֹת הָאָרֶץ בִּגְלַל מְנַשֶּׁה בֶן יְחִזְקִיָּהוּ מֶלֶךְ יְהוּדָה עַל אֲשֶׁר עָשָׂה בִּירוּשָׁלָיִם: [ירמיה טו, ד]

בְּיָרָבְעָם – **Why, then, did Scripture hang** the guilt **on Yarovam?**[14] מִפְּנֵי שֶׁהוּא הָיָה תְּחִילָּה לְקַלְקָלָה – **Because he** (Yarovam) **was the beginning of the ruination;** i.e. he was the first king to go bad.

,,גַּם מִזְבְּחוֹתָם כְּגַלִּים עַל תַּלְמֵי שָׂדָי" – Scripture states: ***Their altars, too, are like heaps on the furrows of the field.***[15] אָמַר רַבִּי יוֹחָנָן **– R' Yochanan said:** אֵין לְךָ כָּל תֶּלֶם וְתֶלֶם בְּאֶרֶץ יִשְׂרָאֵל – **There is not a single furrow in Israel** שֶׁלֹּא הֶעֱמִיד עָלָיו אַחְאָב עֲבוֹדַת כּוֹכָבִים וְהִשְׁתַּחֲוָה לוֹ – **on which Ahab did not set up an idol and bow to it.** וּמְנָא לָן דְּלֹא אָתֵי לְעָלְמָא דְּאָתֵי – **And from where do we know that [Ahab] will not enter to the World to Come?** דִּכְתִיב – **As it is written:** ,,וְהִכְרַתִּי לְאַחְאָב מַשְׁתִּין בְּקִיר וְעָצוּר וְעָזוּב בְּיִשְׂרָאֵל" ***I will cut off from** the house of **Ahab every one that possesses knowledge, and [Ahab will be] withheld and abandoned in Israel;***[16] ,,עָצוּר" בָּעוֹלָם הַזֶּה – ***withheld*** **in this world,** ,,וְעָזוּב" לָעוֹלָם הַבָּא – ***and abandoned*** **in the World to Come.**

R' Yochanan explains how the two idolatrous kings Omri and his son Ahab became kings of Israel and enjoyed a relatively long reign: אָמַר רַבִּי יוֹחָנָן – **R' Yochanan said:** מִפְּנֵי מָה זָכָה עָמְרִי לְמַלְכוּת – **Why did Omri merit kingship?**[17] מִפְּנֵי שֶׁהוֹסִיף כְּרַךְ אֶחָד בְּאֶרֶץ יִשְׂרָאֵל – **Because he added one fortified city to Eretz Yisrael,** שֶׁנֶּאֱמַר ,,וַיִּקֶן אֶת־הָהָר שֹׁמְרוֹן מֵאֵת שֶׁמֶר בְּכִכְּרַיִם כָּסֶף וַיִּבֶן אֶת־הָהָר וַיִּקְרָא אֶת־שֵׁם הָעִיר אֲשֶׁר בָּנָה עַל שֶׁם־שֶׁמֶר אֲדֹנֵי הָהָר שֹׁמְרוֹן" – **as it is stated: *[Omri] purchased the mountain of Samaria*** (*Shomron*) ***from Shemer for two talents of silver; he built [a city on] the mountain, and he called the name of the city that he built Shomron*** (*Samaria*) ***after Shemer the lord of the mountain.***[18]

אָמַר רַבִּי יוֹחָנָן – **R' Yochanan said:** מִפְּנֵי מָה זָכָה אַחְאָב לְמַלְכוּת עֶשְׂרִים וּשְׁתַּיִם שָׁנָה – **Why did Ahab merit kingship for twenty-two years?** מִפְּנֵי שֶׁכִּיבֵּד אֶת הַתּוֹרָה שֶׁנִּיתְּנָה בְּעֶשְׂרִים וּשְׁתַּיִם אוֹתִיּוֹת – **Because he honored the Torah, which was given** to the Jewish people **through** the medium of the **twenty-two letters** of the Hebrew alphabet.[19] שֶׁנֶּאֱמַר ,,וַיִּשְׁלַח מַלְאָכִים אֶל־אַחְאָב מֶלֶךְ־יִשְׂרָאֵל הָעִירָה – **As it is stated:**[20] ***[Ben Hadad] sent messengers to Ahab king of Israel to the city,*** וַיֹּאמֶר לוֹ כֹּה אָמַר בֶּן־הֲדַד כַּסְפְּךָ וּזְהָבְךָ לִי־הוּא וְנָשֶׁיךָ וּבָנֶיךָ הַטּוֹבִים לִי־הֵם – ***and he said to him, "Your silver and your gold are mine, and your finest wives and children are mine." The king of Israel replied, "As you say, my lord king: I and all I have are yours." Then the messengers came again and said, "Thus said Ben Hadad: When I sent you the order to give me your silver and gold, and your wives and children,*** כִּי אִם־כָּעֵת מָחָר אֶשְׁלַח אֶת־עֲבָדַי אֵלֶיךָ וְחִפְּשׂוּ אֶת־בֵּיתְךָ וְאֵת בָּתֵּי עֲבָדֶיךָ – ***[I meant] that tomorrow at this time I will send my servants to you and they will search your house and the houses of your servants*** וְהָיָה כָּל־מַחְמַד עֵינֶיךָ יָשִׂימוּ בְיָדָם וְלָקָחוּ – ***and seize everything that is precious to you and take it away."*** וַיֹּאמֶר לְמַלְאֲכֵי בֶן־הֲדַד – ***. . . and [Ahab] said to the messengers of Ben Hadad:*** אִמְרוּ לַאדֹנִי הַמֶּלֶךְ כֹּל אֲשֶׁר־שָׁלַחְתָּ אֶל־עַבְדְּךָ בָרִאשֹׁנָה אֶעֱשֶׂה וְהַדָּבָר הַזֶּה לֹא אוּכַל לַעֲשׂוֹת" – ***"Say to my lord the king: 'All that you [first] demanded of your servant I shall do, but this thing I cannot do.' "*** מַאי ,,מַחְמַד עֵינֶיךָ" – **What is** the meaning of ***[that which is] precious to you?*** לָאו סֵפֶר תּוֹרָה – **Is it not the Torah scroll?**[21] Thus, we see that Ahab showed greater respect for his Torah scroll, which he was unwilling to relinquish under any circumstances, than for his own wives and children, whom he was willing to surrender.

The Gemara asks:

דִּילְמָא עֲבוֹדַת כּוֹכָבִים – How do we know that *[that which is] precious to you* refers to his Torah scroll? **Maybe** it refers to his **idol. – ? –**

The Gemara answers:

לֹא סָלְקָא דַּעְתָּךְ – **Do not think so,** דִּכְתִיב ,,וַיֹּאמְרוּ אֵלָיו כָּל־הַזְּקֵנִים וְכָל־הָעָם אַל־תִּשְׁמַע וְלוֹא תֹאבֶה" – **for it is written: *All the elders and all the people said to [Ahab], "Do not consent and do not obey!"***[22]

The Gemara asks:

וְדִילְמָא סָבֵי דְּבַהֲתָא הֲווּ – **But perhaps they were shameful elders,** who would counsel the king to fight for an idol. מִי לֹא כְּתִיב ,,וַיִּישַׁר הַדָּבָר בְּעֵינֵי אַבְשָׁלֹם וּבְעֵינֵי כָּל־זִקְנֵי יִשְׂרָאֵל" – **Is it not written** elsewhere:[23] ***The thing seemed right in the eyes of Absalom and in the eyes of all the elders of Israel,*** וְאָמַר רַב יוֹסֵף סָבֵי דְּבַהֲתָא – **and Rav Yosef said** that these elders who plotted against King David were **shameful elders?**[24] Perhaps,

NOTES

14. Why is it that whenever Scripture refers to subsequent idolatrous kings of Israel, it always states that those idolatrous kings followed the "sinful ways of Yarovam" (*II Kings* 10:31; 13:2, 11; 14:24; 15:9, 18; 15:24, 28). Why does it not say that they followed the sinful ways of Ahab, inasmuch as Ahab was more wicked and a greater idolater than Yarovam? (*Rashi*).

[It is not clear why the Gemara considers this a question, for perhaps the kings who reigned subsequent to Yehu's wiping out of the Baal cult followed only in Yarovam's footsteps and served the golden calves, but did not reinstitute Baal worship. Possibly the Gemara refers to the Asheirah trees, which are not mentioned as having been destroyed by Yehu. Alternatively, in *II Kings* ch. 17, Scripture summarizes the sins that led to the exile of the Ten Tribes, and mentions Baal and general idol worship as having been among the causes. Perhaps this is understood by the Gemara as indicating that the later kings also worshiped Baal and other idols.]

15. *Hosea* 12:12. The preceding words of the verse are: *In Gilgal they sacrificed oxen,* which is understood as a reference to idolatrous sacrifices (*Rashi*).

16. *I Kings* 21:21. The last part of the verse is usually understood as referring to the extermination of Ahab's family (see *Radak* ad loc.). Here, the Gemara understands it to refer to Ahab himself.

[The translation of מַשְׁתִּין בְּקִיר as *one that possesses knowledge* follows *Rashi* here and to *I Kings* 14:10. Other commentators there translate it differently.]

17. About Ahab's father Omri it is written: *Omri did what was bad in the eyes of Hashem; he was worse than all those who preceded him* (*I Kings* 16:25). In spite of his wickedness, Omri founded one of the longer-lasting dynasties in the history of the kingdom of Israel. Why did he merit this? (*Maharsha,* from *Yalkut Shimoni* to *I Kings* 16:24).

18. *I Kings* 16:24. *Ben Yehoyada* explains that the fact that Omri did not name the city after himself indicates that he did not build the city for his own aggrandizement, but for the sake of Eretz Yisrael and the nation. It was this unselfish deed that led God to make him king.

19. [This appears to be the plain meaning of the Gemara. Interestingly, however, *Radak* to *I Kings* 20:4 translates עֶשְׂרִים וּשְׁתַּיִם אוֹתִיּוֹת to mean "twenty-two *words*" (not *letters*), and interprets the Gemara to mean that verse 9, which is the proof that Ahab honored the Torah (see below), contains twenty-two words (assuming that בֶּן־הֲדַד is counted as a single word).]

20. Ibid. 20:2-9. King Ben Hadad of Aram invaded Israel and besieged the capital city of Samaria. The Gemara cites the ultimatum he gave Ahab.

21. As is written in *Psalms* (19:11) in regard to the Torah's commandments: הַנֶּחֱמָדִים מִזָּהָב, *they are more precious than gold* (*Rashi* to *I Kings,* from *Tanchuma Parashas Shemos* 29).

22. *I Kings* 20:8. It is inconceivable that the elders, who were presumably righteous (for such is usually the connotation of the word "elders") would encourage Ahab to fight to retain a pagan deity (*Rashi*).

23. *II Samuel* 17:4. King David's son Absalom launched a rebellion against his father, aided by Achithophel. After seizing Jerusalem and forcing David to flee with a few men, Achithophel advised Absalom to pursue David without delay, overtake and kill him before he had time to gather his own forces. The verse cited by the Gemara describes the reaction of Absalom and his men to this plan.

24. Although the word "elders" usually refers to righteous men, here it refers to elders of low character.

דאיתפח הדר קא דריש אמרי לא קבילת עלך דלא דרשת בהו אמר אינהו מי הדרו בהו דאנא אהדר בי רב אשי אוקי אשלשה מלכים אמר למחר נפתח בחברין אתא מנשה איתחזי ליה בחלמיה אמר חברך וחבירי דאבוך קרית לן מהיכא בעית למישרא המוציא אמר ליה לא ידענא א"ל מהיכא דבעית למישרא המוציא לא גמירת וחברך קרית לן א"ל אגמריה לי ולמחר דרישנא ליה משמך בפירקא א"ל [א]מהיכא דקרים בישולא א"ל מאחר דחכימתו כולי האי מאי טעמא קא פלחיתו לעבודת כוכבים א"ל אי הות התם הות [א]נקיטנא בשיפולי גלימא ורהטת אבתראי למחר אמר להו לרבנן נפתח ברבוותא אחאב אח לשמים אב לעבודת כוכבים אח לשמים דכתיב א) אח לצרה יולד אב לעבודת כוכבים דכתיב ב) כרחם אב על בנים ג) ויהי הנקל לכתו בחטאת ירבעם בן נבט אמר ר' יוחנן קלות שעשה אחאב כחמורות שעשה ירבעם ומפני מה תלה הכתוב בירבעם מפני שהוא היה תחילה לקלקלה ד) גם מזבחותם כגלים על תלמי שדי א"ר יוחנן אין לך [ג]כל תלם ותלם בא"י שלא העמיד עליו אחאב עבודת כוכבים והשתחוה לו ומנא לן דלא אתי לעלמא דאתי דכתיב ה) והכרתי לאחאב משתין בקיר ועצור ועזוב בישראל עצור בעוה"ז ועזוב לעוה"ב א"ר יוחנן מפני מה זכה עמרי למלכות מפני שהוסיף כרך אחד בארץ ישראל שנאמר ו) ויקן את ההר שמרון מאת שמר בככרים כסף ויבן את ההר ויקרא [את] שם העיר אשר בנה על שם שמר אדני ההר שמרון א"ר יוחנן מפני מה זכה אחאב למלכות כ"ב שנה מפני שכיבד את התורה שניתנה בכ"ב אותיות שנאמר ז) וישלח מלאכים אל אחאב מלך ישראל העירה ויאמר לו כה אמר בן הדד כספך וזהבך לי הוא ונשיך ובניך הטובים לי הם כי אם כעת מחר אשלח את עבדי אליך וחפשו את ביתך ואת בתי עבדיך והיה כל מחמד עיניך ישימו בידם ולקחו ויאמר למלאכי בן הדד אמרו לאדוני המלך כל אשר שלחת (לעבדך) [אל עבדך] בראשונה אעשה והדבר הזה לא אוכל לעשות מאי מחמד עיניך לאו ס"ת דילמא עבודת כוכבים לא ס"ד דכתיב ח) ויאמרו אליו כל הזקנים וכל העם ([ג]לא תאבה ולא תשמע) ודילמא סבי דבהתא הוו מי לא כתיב ט) ויישר הדבר בעיני אבשלום (והזקנים) [ובעיני כל זקני ישראל] ואמר רב יוסף סבי דבהתא התם לא כתיב וכל העם הכא כתיב וכל העם דאי אפשר דלא הוו בהון צדיקי וכתיב י) והשארתי בישראל שבעת אלפים כל הברכים אשר לא כרעו לבעל וכל הפה אשר לא נשק לו אמר ר"נ אחאב שקול היה שנאמר כ) ויאמר ה' מי יפתה את אחאב ויעל ויפול ברמות גלעד ויאמר זה בכה וזה אומר בכה מתקיף לה רב יוסף מאן דכתב ביה ל) רק לא היה כאחאב אשר התמכר לעשות הרע בעיני ה' אשר הסתה אותו איזבל אשתו ותנינא בכל יום היתה שוקלת שקלי זהב לעבודת כוכבים ואת אמרת שקול היה אלא אחאב וותרן בממונו היה ומתוך [ד]שההנה תלמידי חכמים מנכסיו כיפרו לו מחצה מ) ויצא הרוח ויעמד לפני ה' ויאמר אני אפתנו ויאמר ה' אליו במה ויאמר אצא והייתי רוח שקר בפי כל נביאיו ויאמר תפתה וגם תוכל צא ועשה כן [ה]מאי רוח א"ר יוחנן רוחו של נבות היזרעאלי מאי צא אמר רבינא צא ממחיצתי שכן כתיב נ) דובר שקרים לא יכון לנגד עיני אמר רב פפא היינו דאמרי אינשי דפרע קיניה מחריב ביתיה ס) ויעש אחאב את האשרה ויוסף אחאב לעשות להכעיס את ה' אלהי ישראל מכל מלכי ישראל אשר היו לפניו א"ר יוחנן שכתב על דלתות שמרון אחאב כפר באלהי ישראל לפיכך אין לו חלק באלהי ישראל ע) ויבקש את אחזיהו וילכדהו והוא מתחבא בשמרון א"ר לוי שהיה קודר אזכרות וכותב עבודת כוכבים תחתיהן מנשה שנשה יה ד"א מנשה שהנשי את ישראל לאביהם שבשמים ומנלן דלא אתי לעלמא דאתי דכתיב פ) בן שתים עשרה שנה מנשה במלכו וחמשים וחמש שנה מלך בירושלים צ) ויעש (הרע) [אשרה] (בעיני ה') כאשר עשה אחאב מלך ישראל מה אחאב אין לו חלק לעוה"ב אף מנשה אין לו חלק לעוה"ב: רבי יהודה אומר מנשה יש לו חלק לעוה"ב שנאמר [ו]ק) ויתפלל מנשה אל ה' ויעתר לו וכו': א"ר יוחנן ושניהם מקרא אחד דרשו שנאמר ר) ונתתים לזועה לכל ממלכות הארץ בגלל מנשה בן יחזקיהו מר סבר בגלל מנשה שעשה תשובה ואינהו לא עבוד ומר סבר בגלל

איתפח. נתרפא: אמרו לו. תלמידיו לא קבלת עילווך וכו': אמר אינהו מי הדרו בהו. מדרכם הרעה דאנא אהדר לי מלדרוש: אוקי אשלשה מלכים. אוקי סיום הך פירקא עד שהגיעו לג' מלכים: אמר למחר נפתח בחברין. נדרוש בחברינו שהיו תלמידי חכמים כמותנו ואין להם חלק לעתיד: א"ל. מנשה בחלום חברך וחברא דאביך אנן. כלומר וכי סבור אתה שנהיה חבירך וחבירי דאבוך: מהיכא בעית למשרא המוציא. איך יודע מאיזה מקום בפת אתה צריך לבצוע המוציא: וחבירך קרית לן. ואתה קורא אותנו חבירך: מהיכא דקרים בשולא. דרפתא ממקום שנקרמין פניה של פת בתנור דהיינו מלמעלה או מסביבות הפת או משוליו אבל באמצע לא שאם הביאו לפניו פרוסה של לחם לא יהא בוצע ומברך אלא משולי הפת ולא מאמצעיתו ל"א מהיכא דקדים כלומר מהיכא שמקדים לאפות והיינו הך ל"א מהיכא דגמר בשולא ממקום שהלחם אפוי יפה ולא מאותו מקום שקורין בשו"ל ולשון נראה: הוית נקוט שיפולי גלימך. היית מגבה שפת חלוקך מבין רגליך כדי שתהא קל לרוץ והיית רץ לשם מפני יצר עבודת כוכבים שהיה שולט: נפתח ברבוותא. נתחיל לדרוש ברבותינו ולא אמר בחבירינו: אח לשמים. רע לשמים כדאמרינן (מגילה דף יא.) באחשורוש אח ורשע: דכתיב ואח לצרה יולד. [ווי לצרה] אלמא אח °לשון רעה ווי: אב לעבודת כוכבים. שהיה אוהבה ביותר דכתיב כרחם אב אלמא אב מרחם והני קראי בכדי נקט להו: ויהי הנקל. באחאב כתוב [כלומר קלות היו לאחאב כל חטאותיו של ירבעם]: מפני מה תלה הכתוב בירבעם. דבכמה מקומות כתיב לא סר מכל חטאת ירבעם ולא כתיב אחאב אע"פ שהיה רשע ממנו: תחלה לקלקלה. שהיה מלך ראשון שהקדיח את תבשילו: גם מזבחותם. הכי רישיה דקרא בגלגל שוורים זבחו גם מזבחותם כגלים על תלמי שדי: משתין בקיר. ת"ח משית בקירות לבו: ומניין שכבד את התורה דכתיב והיה כל מחמד עיניך ישימו בידם והיינו ספר תורה ועל זה השיבו את הדבר הזה לא אוכל לעשות: ודילמא. מחמד עיניו היינו עבודת כוכבים: לא ס"ד. מדקאמרי ליה זקנים לא תשמע ולא תאבה ואי עבודת כוכבים מי הוו אמרו ליה הכי: סבי דבהתא. זקנים שפלים שהיו רשעים כמו שמצינו באבשלום דקרי ליה לסבי דבהתא זקנים: שקול היה. מחלה עונות ומחלה זכיות מדמהדרי כולי האי מי יפתה את אחאב משמע דבקושי גדול נענש: רוחו של נבות. שלפי שהוא הרג נבות היה רוחו מחזר לפתותו ולהפילו: דפרע קיניה. קנאה הפורע נוקם חמתו וקנאתו מחריב ביתיה כרוח של נבות שנקם כעסו מאחאב ויצא ממחילתו של הקב"ה: קודר אזכרות. מוחק שמות שבתורה: וכותב שם עבודת כוכבים תחתיהן. לפיכך היה מתחבא שאילו היה עושה בפרהסיא לא היו מניחין [אותו] לעשות כן. קודר כמו (עירובין נח.) מקדרין בהרים ל' (נוקב) [מחטט ונוקר]: שנשה יה. ששכח הקב"ה: שהנשי. השכיח: מה אחאב אין לו חלק. כדאמרן עזוב לעולם הבא: ושניהם. רבי יהודה דאמר יש לו חלק ורבנן דאמרי אין לו חלק: בגלל

עין משפט
נר מצוה

כט א מיי' פ"ז מהלכות ברכות הלכה ג סמג עשין כז טוש"ע א"ח סי' קסז סעיף א [וברי"ף פ"ז דברכות לח.]:

גליון הש"ס

רש"י ד"ה דכתיב. לשון רעה ווי. עי' ברש"י הושע יג טו:

ליקוטי רש"י

גם מזבחותם. רבים כגלים שעל תלמי שדי תלמי שדי היא מענית המחרישה קרויה תלם [הושע יב, יב]. כל מחמד עיניך ישימו בידם ולקחו. והלא כל הראשונים דברי חמד' הם אלא מהו מחמד עיניך חמדה מתוך חמדה זה ספר תורה שנאמר בו הנחמדי' מזהב ומפז רב (תהלים י"ט י"א) אמר אחאב בלבו דבר גדול זה מבקש אין זה שלי לבדי של זקני ישראל היא לפיכך ויקרא לכל זקני הארץ אע"פ שהיו עובדין ע"ג היו מכבדין את התורה [מ"א כ, ו]. ובעיני זקני ישראל. זקני אשמאי [ש"ב יז, ד]. רק לא היה כאחאב. הכתוב מעיד עליו שלא היה במלכים כמותו שירבעם וכל אשר אחריו עבדו את העגלים מיראה אם יעלה העם ירושלים תשוב הממלכה לבית דוד וזה הוסיף הבעל והאשרה להכעים. התמכר. נמכר לע"ג ראיתי בירושלמי חיאל בית האלי שושבינו היה ובכל יום שם דמיו ונתן לע"ג [מ"א כא, כה]. ויצא הרוח. פתרון ויצא המלאך שהרי אומר לעיל וכל צבא השמים וגו' ועתה יצא אחד מן המלאכים ויאמר אני אפתנו כדאמר (תהלים קד) עושה מלאכיו רוחות ולפיכך קדם ואמר לעיל וכל צבא השמים עומדים שלא תתמה כשתאמר ויצא הרוח מי הוא ומהיכן יצא וכשאמר וכל צבא השמים עומדים כדי להודיע מהיכן יצא משאר הרוחות העומדים עליו ורבותינו פירשו זהו רוחו של נבות [דה"ב יח, כ]. אשרה. אילן נעבד [מ"א טז, לג]. לזעוה. מגורת לא קם ולא זע (אסתר ה) וכמוהו גאוה מגורת גא מאד (ישעיה טו). לכל ממלכות הארץ. כל השומע רעה שבאה עליהם יזוע [ירמיהו טו, ד].

מסורת הש"ס

א) נ"ל נקוט, ב) [לקמן קיג.], ג) [נ"ל אל תשמע ואל תאבה], ד) נ"א שהיה מהנה, ה) [לעיל פט.] שבת קמט:, ו) [נ"ל ויתפלל אליו ויעתר].

תורה אור השלם

א) בְּכָל עֵת אֹהֵב הָרֵעַ וְאָח לְצָרָה יִוָּלֵד: [משלי יז, יז]

ב) כְּרַחֵם אָב עַל בָּנִים רִחַם יְיָ עַל יְרֵאָיו: [תהלים קג, יג]

ג) וַיְהִי הֲנָקֵל לֶכְתּוֹ בְּחַטֹּאות יָרָבְעָם בֶּן נְבָט וַיִּקַּח אִשָּׁה אֶת אִיזֶבֶל בַּת אֶתְבַּעַל מֶלֶךְ צִידֹנִים וַיֵּלֶךְ וַיַּעֲבֹד אֶת הַבַּעַל וַיִּשְׁתַּחוּ לוֹ: [מלכים א' טז, לא]

ד) אִם גִּלְעָד אָוֶן אַךְ שָׁוְא הָיוּ בַּגִּלְגָּל שְׁוָרִים זִבֵּחוּ גַּם מִזְבְּחוֹתָם כְּגַלִּים עַל תַּלְמֵי שָׂדָי: [הושע יב, יב]

ה) הִנְנִי מֵבִיא אֵלֶיךָ רָעָה וּבִעַרְתִּי אַחֲרֶיךָ וְהִכְרַתִּי לְאַחְאָב מַשְׁתִּין בְּקִיר וְעָצוּר וְעָזוּב בְּיִשְׂרָאֵל: [מלכים א' כא, כא]

ו) וַיִּקֶן אֶת הָהָר שֹׁמְרוֹן מֵאֶת שֶׁמֶר בְּכִכְּרַיִם כָּסֶף וַיִּבֶן אֶת הָהָר וַיִּקְרָא אֶת שֵׁם הָעִיר אֲשֶׁר בָּנָה עַל שֶׁם שֶׁמֶר אֲדֹנֵי הָהָר שֹׁמְרוֹן: [מלכים א' טז, כד]

ז) וַיִּשְׁלַח מַלְאָכִים אֶל אַחְאָב מֶלֶךְ יִשְׂרָאֵל הָעִירָה: וַיֹּאמֶר לוֹ כֹּה אָמַר בֶּן הֲדַד כַּסְפְּךָ וּזְהָבְךָ לִי הוּא וְנָשֶׁיךָ וּבָנֶיךָ הַטּוֹבִים לִי הֵם: כִּי אִם כָּעֵת מָחָר אֶשְׁלַח אֶת עֲבָדַי אֵלֶיךָ וְחִפְּשׂוּ אֶת בֵּיתְךָ וְאֵת בָּתֵּי עֲבָדֶיךָ וְהָיָה כָּל מַחְמַד עֵינֶיךָ יָשִׂימוּ בְיָדָם וְלָקָחוּ: וַיֹּאמֶר לְמַלְאֲכֵי בֶן הֲדַד אִמְרוּ לַאדֹנִי הַמֶּלֶךְ כֹּל אֲשֶׁר שָׁלַחְתָּ אֶל עַבְדְּךָ בָרִאשֹׁנָה אֶעֱשֶׂה וְהַדָּבָר הַזֶּה לֹא אוּכַל לַעֲשׂוֹת וַיֵּלְכוּ הַמַּלְאָכִים וַיְשִׁבֻהוּ דָּבָר: [מלכים א' כ, ב,ג,ו,ט]

ח) וַיֹּאמְרוּ אֵלָיו כָּל הַזְּקֵנִים וְכָל הָעָם אַל תִּשְׁמַע וְלוֹא תֹאבֶה: [מלכים א' כ, ח]

ט) וַיִּישַׁר הַדָּבָר בְּעֵינֵי אַבְשָׁלֹם וּבְעֵינֵי כָּל זִקְנֵי יִשְׂרָאֵל: [שמואל ב' יז, ד]

י) וְהִשְׁאַרְתִּי בְיִשְׂרָאֵל שִׁבְעַת אֲלָפִים כָּל הַבִּרְכַּיִם אֲשֶׁר לֹא כָרְעוּ לַבַּעַל וְכָל הַפֶּה אֲשֶׁר לֹא נָשַׁק לוֹ: [מלכים א' יט, יח]

כ) וַיֹּאמֶר יְיָ מִי יְפַתֶּה אֶת אַחְאָב וְיַעַל וְיִפֹּל בְּרָמֹת גִּלְעָד וַיֹּאמֶר זֶה בְּכֹה וְזֶה אֹמֵר בְּכֹה: [מלכים א' כב, כ]

ל) רַק לֹא הָיָה כְאַחְאָב אֲשֶׁר הִתְמַכֵּר לַעֲשׂוֹת הָרַע בְּעֵינֵי יְיָ אֲשֶׁר הֵסַתָּה אֹתוֹ אִיזֶבֶל אִשְׁתּוֹ: [מלכים א' כא, כה] מ) וַיֵּצֵא הָרוּחַ וַיַּעֲמֹד לִפְנֵי יְיָ וַיֹּאמֶר אֲנִי אֲפַתֶּנּוּ וַיֹּאמֶר יְיָ אֵלָיו בַּמָּה: וַיֹּאמֶר אֵצֵא וְהָיִיתִי רוּחַ שֶׁקֶר בְּפִי כָּל נְבִיאָיו וַיֹּאמֶר תְּפַתֶּה וְגַם תּוּכָל צֵא וַעֲשֵׂה כֵן: [מלכים א' כב, כא-כב]
נ) לֹא יֵשֵׁב בְּקֶרֶב בֵּיתִי עֹשֵׂה רְמִיָּה דֹּבֵר שְׁקָרִים לֹא יִכּוֹן לְנֶגֶד עֵינָי: [תהלים קא, ז] ס) וַיַּעַשׂ אַחְאָב אֶת הָאֲשֵׁרָה וַיּוֹסֶף אַחְאָב לַעֲשׂוֹת לְהַכְעִיס אֶת יְיָ אֱלֹהֵי יִשְׂרָאֵל מִכֹּל מַלְכֵי יִשְׂרָאֵל אֲשֶׁר הָיוּ לְפָנָיו: [מלכים א' טז, לג]
ע) וַיְבַקֵּשׁ אֶת אֲחַזְיָהוּ וַיִּלְכְּדֻהוּ וְהוּא מִתְחַבֵּא בְשֹׁמְרוֹן וַיְבִאֻהוּ אֶל יֵהוּא וַיְמִתֻהוּ וַיִּקְבְּרֻהוּ כִּי אָמְרוּ בֶּן יְהוֹשָׁפָט הוּא אֲשֶׁר דָּרַשׁ אֶת יְיָ בְּכָל לְבָבוֹ וְאֵין לְבֵית אֲחַזְיָהוּ לַעְצֹר כֹּחַ לְמַמְלָכָה: [דברי הימים ב' כב, ט] פ) בֶּן שְׁתֵּים עֶשְׂרֵה שָׁנָה מְנַשֶּׁה בְמָלְכוֹ וַחֲמִשִּׁים וְחָמֵשׁ שָׁנָה מָלַךְ בִּירוּשָׁלָיִם: [דברי הימים ב' לג, א] צ) וַיָּשָׁב וַיִּבֶן אֶת הַבָּמוֹת אֲשֶׁר אִבַּד חִזְקִיָּהוּ אָבִיו וַיָּקֶם מִזְבְּחֹת לַבַּעַל וַיַּעַשׂ אֲשֵׁרָה כַּאֲשֶׁר עָשָׂה אַחְאָב מֶלֶךְ יִשְׂרָאֵל וַיִּשְׁתַּחוּ לְכָל צְבָא הַשָּׁמַיִם וַיַּעֲבֹד אֹתָם: [מלכים ב' כא, ג] ק) וַיִּתְפַּלֵּל אֵלָיו וַיֵּעָתֶר לוֹ וַיִּשְׁמַע תְּחִנָּתוֹ וַיְשִׁיבֵהוּ יְרוּשָׁלַיִם לְמַלְכוּתוֹ וַיֵּדַע מְנַשֶּׁה כִּי יְיָ הוּא הָאֱלֹהִים: [דברי הימים ב' לג, יג] ר) וּנְתַתִּים לְזַעֲוָה לְכֹל מַמְלְכוֹת הָאָרֶץ בִּגְלַל מְנַשֶּׁה בֶן יְחִזְקִיָּהוּ מֶלֶךְ יְהוּדָה עַל אֲשֶׁר עָשָׂה בִּירוּשָׁלָיִם: [ירמיה טו, ד]

then, the elders who advised Ahab to fight were likewise such elders. – ? –

The Gemara answers:

הָתָם לֹא כְּתִיב ,,וְכָל הָעָם'' – **There,** in the verse describing those who counseled Absalom, **it is not written:** ***and all the people;*** הָכָא כְּתִיב ,,וְכָל הָעָם'' – however, **here,** in the verse concerning those who counseled Ahab, **it is written:** ***and all the people.*** דְּאִי אֶפְשָׁר דְּלֹא הֲווּ בְּהוֹן צַדִּיקֵי – Thus, it cannot mean that they counseled him to fight for his idol, **because it is impossible that there were no righteous persons among [the people of Samaria],** וּכְתִיב ,,וְהִשְׁאַרְתִּי בְיִשְׂרָאֵל שִׁבְעַת אֲלָפִים כָּל־הַבִּרְכַּיִם אֲשֶׁר לֹא־כָרְעוּ לַבַּעַל וְכָל־הַפֶּה אֲשֶׁר לֹא־נָשַׁק לוֹ'' – **for**[25] **it is written:** ***I will leave in Israel seven thousand – every knee that has not bent to Baal and every mouth that has not kissed him,***[26] from which it is evident that there were at least seven thousand righteous persons there. These righteous persons would certainly never have counseled Ahab to wage war on behalf of his idol. Therefore, it must have been his Torah scroll for which they counseled him to fight.

The Gemara discusses Ahab's character:

אָמַר רַב נַחְמָן – **Rav Nachman said:** אַחְאָב שָׁקוּל הָיָה – **Ahab was equally balanced** in his actions, i.e. his good deeds and his bad deeds were equal, שֶׁנֶּאֱמַר ,,וַיֹּאמֶר ה׳ מִי יְפַתֶּה אֶת־אַחְאָב וְיַעַל וְיִפֹּל בְּרָמֹת גִּלְעָד'' – **as it is stated:** ***and Hashem said, "Who will entice Ahab so that he go up and fall at Ramos Gilead?"*** ,,וַיֹּאמֶר זֶה בְּכֹה וְזֶה אֹמֵר בְּכֹה'' – ***One said thus, and another said thus.***[27]

This interpretation is challenged:

מַתְקִיף לָהּ רַב יוֹסֵף – **Rav Yosef objected to this:** מַאן דִּכְתַב בֵּיהּ ,,רַק לֹא־הָיָה כְאַחְאָב אֲשֶׁר הִתְמַכֵּר לַעֲשׂוֹת הָרַע בְּעֵינֵי ה׳ אֲשֶׁר־הֵסַתָּה אֹתוֹ אִיזֶבֶל אִשְׁתּוֹ'' – **Someone regarding whom it is written:** ***Indeed there never was anyone like Ahab, who sold himself to do what was evil in the eyes of Hashem, his wife Jezebel instigating him,***[28] וּתְנִינָא בְּכָל יוֹם הָיְתָה שׁוֹקֶלֶת שִׁקְלֵי זָהָב לַעֲבוֹדַת כּוֹכָבִים – **and we have learned in a Baraisa** in explanation of this: EVERY DAY [JEZEBEL] USED TO WEIGH OUT GOLD SHEKELS and use them FOR IDOLATROUS PURPOSES,[29] וְאַתְּ אָמְרַתְּ שָׁקוּל הָיָה – **will you say that he was equally balanced?!** He was clearly thoroughly wicked! – ? –

Rav Yosef offers an alternate explanation of why Ahab's fate was the subject of debate:

אֶלָּא אַחְאָב וַוִּתְּרָן בְּמָמוֹנוֹ הָיָה – Rather, **Ahab was liberal with his money,** וּמִתּוֹךְ שֶׁהֶהֱנָה תַּלְמִידֵי חֲכָמִים מִנְּכָסָיו – **and because he benefited Torah scholars from his wealth,** כִּיפְּרוּ לוֹ מֶחֱצָה – **half his sins were forgiven.**[30]

The Gemara expands upon the Heavenly proceedings concerning Ahab:

,,וַיֵּצֵא הָרוּחַ וַיַּעֲמֹד לִפְנֵי ה׳ וַיֹּאמֶר אֲנִי אֲפַתֶּנּוּ וַיֹּאמֶר ה׳ אֵלָיו בַּמָּה וַיֹּאמֶר אֵצֵא וְהָיִיתִי רוּחַ שֶׁקֶר בְּפִי כָּל־נְבִיאָיו וַיֹּאמֶר תְּפַתֶּה וְגַם־תּוּכָל צֵא וַעֲשֵׂה־כֵן'' – Scripture states: ***And the spirit came forth and stood before Hashem and said, "I will entice him." Hashem said to him, "How?" [The spirit] said, "I will go forth and be a lying spirit in the mouth of all [Ahab's] prophets." [Hashem] said, "You will entice and also prevail. Go out and do so."***[31] מַאי ,,רוּחַ'' – **What is** ***the spirit*** of which the verse speaks? אָמַר רַבִּי יוֹחָנָן – **R' Yochanan said:** רוּחוֹ שֶׁל נָבוֹת הַיִּזְרְעֵאלִי – It refers to **the spirit of Navos the Yizraelite.**[32] מַאי ,,צֵא'' – **What is** the meaning of ***Go out?***[33] אָמַר רָבִינָא – **Ravina said:** צֵא מִמְּחִיצָּתִי – God said: **"Leave My environs!"** שֶׁכֵּן כְּתִיב ,,דֹּבֵר שְׁקָרִים לֹא־יִכּוֹן לְנֶגֶד עֵינָי'' – **for thus is it written:**[34] *One*

NOTES

25. [Translation follows texts cited by *Dikdukei Soferim* which read דִּכְתִיב.]

26. *I Kings* 19:18. Threatened with death by Ahab's wife Jezebel, the prophet Elijah fled the country and went to Mount Horeb. There, God told him to anoint the Aramean general Chazael as king of Aram, the Israelite general Yehu as king of Israel, and Elisha as Elijah's own successor as prophet. Between the three of them, God told Elijah, all Jews who had ever worshiped Baal would be killed, leaving behind seven thousand survivors who had never worshiped that pagan deity. This proves that there were seven thousand Jews who were righteous.

27. Ibid. 22:20. Ahab resolved to go to war against Aram at a place called Ramos Gilead. The prophet Michayhu advised against it, describing a prophetic vision he had had in which God was consulting the Heavenly Host, asking them how best to bring about the death of Ahab in battle at Ramos Gilead. The Heavenly Host offered various suggestions. Eventually it was decided to entice Ahab to war by means of false prophets. Ahab ultimately went to war there and was mortally wounded in battle.

The point is: Why was it necessary to hold a Heavenly council to discover a way to bring about Ahab's undoing? This indicates that it was not a simple matter to bring about Ahab's punishment, for although Ahab committed many grave sins, he also performed many good deeds (*Rashi*).

Alternatively, the proof that Ahab was equally balanced is indicated by the verse *one said thus and one said thus;* i.e. the Heavenly Host advanced arguments both for and against Ahab (*Maharsha*). See also *Rashi* to *Bereishis* 1:26.

28. *I Kings* 21:25.

29. That is, she used to donate Ahab's value to the shrine of the idol each day, as if he had been sold anew to the shrine each day and it was necessary to redeem him from its possessions (*Maharsha*).

30. The Gemara does not cite a Scriptural basis for the statement that Ahab was liberal with his money. Apparently, the Gemara had a tradition that this was so. Alternatively, the Gemara's statement that Ahab benefited Torah scholars is a reference to the banquet he made for King Yehoshafat of Judea and his men [mentioned in *II Chronicles* 18:2], who were all righteous people [see *Chullin* 4b] (*Maharsha*).

Ben Yehoyada suggests that Ahab did not consciously support Torah scholars. Rather, during times of famine he distributed his money to the needy without discriminating between ordinary people and Torah scholars.

31. *I Kings* 22:21-22.

32. Navos owned a vineyard adjacent to Ahab's palace. Ahab wished to purchase the vineyard, but Navos refused to sell it for any price. Finally, Jezebel hired witnesses who falsely testified that Navos had cursed God and the king, a crime punishable by death and confiscation of property. Navos was executed and the vineyard automatically became the property of the crown (*I Kings* ch. 21). It was the spirit of the murdered Navos who sought to bring about Ahab's death and offered to entice him (*Rashi*). For an explanation of how the Gemara knows that the spirit was Navos', see above, 89a note 41.

"Although there are worse crimes than bloodshed, none causes such destruction to civilized society as bloodshed. Even idolatry, and certainly immorality or desecration of the Sabbath, is not the equal of bloodshed. For these crimes are between man and God, while bloodshed is a crime between man and man. Anyone who has on his record this crime is deemed wholly wicked, and all the meritorious acts he has performed during his lifetime cannot outweigh this crime nor save him from judgment . . . . A lesson may be taken from Ahab the idolater, of whom it is said, *Indeed, there never was anyone like Ahab* (*I Kings* 22:21). Yet when his sins and his merits were set in array before the God of All Spirits, the one sin that brought on him the doom of extermination and the weightiest of all his crimes was the blood of Navos. For Scripture relates: *A spirit came forward and stood before Hashem*; this was the spirit of Navos, who was told, *"You will entice and also prevail."* Now consider: The wicked Ahab did not commit murder himself but only brought it about. How much greater, then, is the crime of one who commits murder with his own hand!" (*Rambam, Hil. Rotzeach* 4:9).

33. It would have sufficed for God to say, *"Do so,"* for it is obvious that the spirit would have to go out in order to accomplish its mission (*Yad Ramah*).

34. *Psalms* 101:7.

דאיתפח הדר קא דריש אמרי לא קבילת עלך דלא דרשת בהו אמר אינהו מי הדרו בהו דאנא אהדר בי רב אשי אוקי אשלשה מלכים אמר למחר נפתח בחברין אתא מנשה איתחזי ליה בחלמיה אמר חברך וחבירי דאבוך קרית לן מהיכא בעית למישרא המוציא אמר ליה לא ידענא א"ל מהיכא דבעית למישרא המוציא לא גמירת וחברך קרית לן א"ל אגמריה לי ולמחר דרישנא ליה משמך בפירקא א"ל [א]מהיכא דקרים בישולא א"ל מאחר דחכימתו כולי האי מאי טעמא קא פלחיתו לעבודת כוכבים א"ל אי הות התם הות [א)]נקיטנא בשיפולי גלימא ורהטת אבתראי למחר אמר להו לרבנן נפתח ברבוותא אחאב אח לשמים אב לעבודת כוכבים אח לשמים דכתיב [א)]אח לצרה יולד אב לעבודת כוכבים דכתיב [ב)]כרחם אב על בנים [ג)]ויהי הנקל לכתו בחטאת ירבעם בן נבט אמר ר' יוחנן קלות שעשה אחאב כחמורות שעשה ירבעם ומפני מה תלה הכתוב בירבעם מפני שהוא היה תחילה לקלקלה [ד)]גם מזבחותם כגלים על תלמי שדי א"ר יוחנן אין לך [ב)]כל תלם ותלם בא"י שלא העמיד עליו אחאב עבודת כוכבים והשתחוה לו ומנא לן דלא אתי לעלמא דאתי דכתיב [ה)]והכרתי לאחאב משתין בקיר ועצור ועזוב בישראל עצור בעוה"ז ועזוב לעוה"ב א"ר יוחנן מפני מה זכה עמרי למלכות מפני שהוסיף כרך אחד בארץ ישראל שנאמר [ו)]ויקן את ההר שמרון מאת שמר בככרים כסף ויבן את ההר ויקרא [את] שם העיר אשר בנה על שם שמר אדני ההר שמרון א"ר יוחנן מפני מה זכה אחאב למלכות כ"ב שנה מפני שכיבד את התורה שניתנה בכ"ב אותיות שנאמר [ז)]וישלח מלאכים אל אחאב מלך ישראל העירה ויאמר לו כה אמר בן הדד כספך וזהבך לי הוא ונשיך ובניך הטובים לי הם כי אם כעת מחר אשלח את עבדי אליך וחפשו את ביתך ואת בתי עבדיך והיה כל מחמד עיניך ישימו בידם ולקחו ויאמר למלאכי בן הדד אמרו לאדוני המלך כל אשר שלחת (לעבדך) [אל עבדך] בראשונה אעשה והדבר הזה לא אוכל לעשות מאי מחמד עיניך לאו ס"ת דילמא עבודת כוכבים לא ס"ד דכתיב [ח)]ויאמרו אליו כל הזקנים וכל העם ([ג)]לא תאבה ולא תשמע) ודילמא סבי דבהתא הוו מי לא כתיב [ט)]ויישר הדבר בעיני אבשלום (והזקנים) [ובעיני כל זקני ישראל] ואמר רב יוסף סבי דבהתא התם לא כתיב וכל העם הכא כתיב וכל העם דאי אפשר דלא הוו בהון צדיקי וכתיב [י)]והשארתי בישראל שבעת אלפים כל הברכים אשר לא כרעו לבעל וכל הפה אשר לא נשק לו אמר ר"נ אחאב שקול היה שנאמר [כ)]ויאמר ה' מי יפתה את אחאב ויעל ויפול ברמות גלעד ויאמר זה בכה וזה אומר בכה מתקיף לה רב יוסף מאן דכתב ביה [ל)]רק לא היה כאחאב אשר התמכר לעשות הרע בעיני ה' אשר הסתה אותו איזבל אשתו ותנינא בכל יום היתה שוקלת שקלי זהב לעבודת כוכבים ואת אמרת שקול היה אלא אחאב וותרן בממונו היה ומתוך [ד)]שההנה תלמידי חכמים מנכסיו כיפרו לו מחצה [מ)]ויצא הרוח ויעמד לפני ה' ויאמר אני אפתנו ויאמר ה' אליו במה ויאמר אצא והייתי רוח שקר בפי כל נביאיו ויאמר תפתה וגם תוכל צא ועשה כן [ה)]מאי רוח א"ר יוחנן רוחו של נבות היזרעאלי מאי צא אמר רבינא צא ממחיצתי שכן כתיב [נ)]דובר שקרים לא יכון לנגד עיני אמר רב פפא היינו דאמרי אינשי דפרע קיניה מחריב ביתיה [ס)]ויעש אחאב את האשרה ויוסף אחאב לעשות להכעיס את ה' אלהי ישראל מכל מלכי ישראל אשר היו לפניו א"ר יוחנן שכתב על דלתות שמרון אחאב כפר באלהי ישראל לפיכך אין לו חלק באלהי ישראל [ע)]ויבקש את אחזיהו וילכדהו והוא מתחבא בשמרון א"ר לוי שהיה קודר אזכרות וכותב עבודת כוכבים תחתיהן מנשה שנשה יה ד"א מנשה שהנשי את ישראל לאביהם שבשמים ומנלן דלא אתי לעלמא דאתי דכתיב [פ)]בן שתים עשרה שנה מנשה במלכו וחמשים וחמש שנה מלך בירושלים [צ)]ויעש (הרע) [אשרה] (בעיני ה') כאשר עשה אחאב מלך ישראל מה אחאב אין לו חלק לעוה"ב אף מנשה אין לו חלק לעוה"ב: רבי יהודה אומר מנשה יש לו חלק לעוה"ב שנאמר [ו)] [ק)]ויתפלל מנשה אל ה' ויעתר לו וכו': א"ר יוחנן ושניהם מקרא אחד דרשו שנאמר [ר)]ונתתים לזועה לכל ממלכות הארץ בגלל מנשה בן יחזקיהו מר סבר בגלל מנשה שעשה תשובה ואינהו לא עבוד ומר סבר בגלל

רש"י

איתפח. נתרפא: אמרו לו. תלמידיו לא קבלת עילווך וכו': אמר אינהו מי הדרו בהו. מדרכם הרעה דאנא אהדר לי מלדרוש: אוקי אשלשה מלכים. אוקי סיום הך פירקא עד שהגיעו לג' מלכים: אמר למחר נפתח בחברין. נדרוש בחברינו שהיו תלמידי חכמים כמותנו ואין להם חלק לעתיד: א"ל. מנשה בחלום חברך וחברא דאביך אנן. כלומר וכי סבור אתה שנהיה חבירך וחבירי לאבוך: מהיכא בעית למשרא המוציא. אינך יודע מאיזה מקום בפת אתה צריך לבצוע המוציא: וחבירך קרית לן. ואתה קורא אותנו חבירך: מהיכא דקרים בשולא. דרפתא ממקום שנקרמין פניה של פת בתנור דהיינו מלמעלה או מסביבות הפת או משוליו אבל באמצע לא שאם הביאו לפניו פרוסה של לחם לא יהא בוצע ומברך אלא משולי הפת ולא מאמצעיתו ל"א מהיכא דקדים כלומר מהיכא שמקדים לאפות והיינו הך ל"א מהיכא דגמר בשולא ממקום שהלחם אפוי יפה ולא מאותו מקום שקורין בשו"ל ורא' נראה: הוית נקוט שיפולי גלימך. היית מגבה שפת חלוקך מבין רגליך כדי שתהא קל לרוץ והיית רץ לשם מפני יצר עבודת כוכבים שהיה שולט: נפתח ברבוותא. נתחיל לדרוש ברבותינו ולא אמר בחבירינו: אח לשמים. רע לשמים כדאמרינן (מגילה דף יא.) באחשורוש אח וראש: דכתיב ואח לצרה יולד. [ווי לצרה] אלמא אח [ט]לשון רעה ווי: אב לעבודת כוכבים. שהיה אוהבה ביותר דכתיב כרחם אב אלמא אב מרחם והכי קראי בכדי נקט להו: ויהי הנקל. באחאב כתוב [כלומר קלות היו לאחאב כל חטאותיו של ירבעם]: מפני מה תלה הכתוב בירבעם. דבכמה מקומות כתיב לא סר מכל חטאת ירבעם ולא כתיב אחאב אע"פ שהיה רשע ממנו: תחלה לקלקלה. שהיה מלך ראשון שהקדיח את תבשילו: גם מזבחותם. הכי רישיה דקרא בגלגל שוורים זבחו גם מזבחותם כגלים על תלמי שדי: משתין בקיר. ת"ח משית בקירות לבו: ומניין שכבד את התורה דכתיב והיה כל מחמד עיניך ישימו בידם והיינו ספר תורה ועל זה השיבו את הדבר הזה לא אוכל לעשות: ודילמא. מחמד עיניו היינו עבודת כוכבים: לא ס"ד. מדקאמרי ליה זקנים לא תשמע ולא תאבה ואי עבודת כוכבים מי הוו אמרו ליה הכי: סבי דבהתא. זקנים שפלים שהיו רשעים כמו שמצינו באבשלום דקרי ליה לסבי דבהתא זקנים: שקול היה. מחצה עונות ומחצה זכיות מדמהדרי כולי האי מי יפתה את אחאב משמע דבקושי גדול נענש: רוחו של נבות. שלפי שהוא הרג נבות היה רוחו מחזר לפתותו ולהפילו: דפרע קיניה. קנאה הפורע נוקם חמתו וקנאתו מחריב ביתיה כרוח של נבות שנקם כעסו מאחאב ויצא ממחיצתו של הקב"ה: קודר אזכרות. מוחק שמות שבתורה: וכותב שם עבודת כוכבים תחתיהן. לפיכך היה מתחבא שאילו היה עושה בפרהסיא לא היו מניחין [אותו] לעשות כן. קודר כמו (עירובין נח.) מקדרין בהרים ל' (נוקב) [מחטט ונוקר]: שנשה יה. ששכח הקב"ה: שהנשי. השכיח: מה אחאב אין לו חלק. כדאמרן עזוב לעולם הבא: ושניהם. רבי יהודה דאמר יש לו חלק ורבנן דאמרי אין לו חלק: בגלל

עין משפט נר מצוה

כט א מיי' פ"ז מהלכות ברכות הלכה ג סמג עשין כז טוש"ע א"ח סי' קסז סעיף א [וברי"ף פ"ז דברכות לח.]:

גליון הש"ס

רש"י ד"ה דכתיב. לשון רעה ווי. עי' ברש"י הושע יג טו:

ליקוטי רש"י

גם מזבחותם. רבים כגלים שעל תלמי שדי תלמי שדי היא מענית המחרישה קרויה תלם [הושע יב, יב]. כל מחמד עיניך ישימו בידם ולקחו. והלא כל הראשונים דברי חמד' הם אלא מהו מחמד עיניך חמדה מתוך חמדה זה ספר תורה שנאמר בו הנחמדי' מזהב ומפז רב (תהלים י"ט י"א) אמר אחאב בלבו דבר גדול זה מבקש אין זה שלי לבדי של זקני ישראל היא לפיכך ויקרא לכל זקני הארץ אע"פ שהיו עובדין ע"ג היו מכבדין את התורה [מ"א כ, ו]. ובעיני זקני ישראל. זקני אשמאי [ש"ב יז, ד]. רק לא היה כאחאב. הכתוב מעיד עליו שלא היה במלכים כמותו שירבעם וכל אשר אחריו עבדו את העגלים מיראה אם יעלה העם ירושלים תשוב הממלכה לבית דוד וזה הוסיף הבעל והאשרה להכעים. התמכר. נמכר לע"ג ראיתי בירושלמי חיאל בית האלי שושבינו היה ובכל יום שם דמיו ונתן לע"ג [מ"א כא, כה]. ויצא הרוח. פתרון ויצא המלאך שהרי אומר לעיל וכל צבא השמים וגו' ועתה יצא אחד מן המלאכים ויאמר אני אפתנו כדאמר (תהלים קד) עושה מלאכיו רוחות ולפיכך קדם ואמר לעיל וכל צבא השמים עומדים שאל תתמה כשתאמר ויצא הרוח מי הוא ומהיכן יצא וכשאמר וכל צבא השמים עומדים כדי להודיע מהיכן יצא משאר הרוחות העומדים עליו ורבותינו פירשו זהו רוחו של נבות [דה"ב יח, כ]. אשרה. אילן נעבד [מ"א טז, לג]. לזעוה. מגורת לא קם ולא זע (אסתר ה) וכמוהו גאוה מגורת גא מאד (ישעיה טז). לכל ממלכות הארץ. כל השומע רעה שבאה עליהם יזוע [ירמיהו טו, ד].

מסורת הש"ס

א) נ"ל נקוט, ב) [לקמן קיג.], ג) [נ"ל אל תשמע ואל תאבה], ד) נ"א שהיה מהנה, ה) [לעיל פט.] שבת קמט:, ו) [נ"ל ויתפלל אליו ויעתר].

תורה אור השלם

א) בְּכָל עֵת אֹהֵב הָרֵעַ וְאָח לְצָרָה יִוָּלֵד: [משלי יז, יז]

ב) כְּרַחֵם אָב עַל בָּנִים רִחַם יְיָ עַל יְרֵאָיו: [תהלים קג, יג]

ג) וַיְהִי הֲנָקֵל לֶכְתּוֹ בְּחַטֹּאות יָרָבְעָם בֶּן נְבָט וַיִּקַּח אִשָּׁה אֶת אִיזֶבֶל בַּת אֶתְבַּעַל מֶלֶךְ צִידֹנִים וַיֵּלֶךְ וַיַּעֲבֹד אֶת הַבַּעַל וַיִּשְׁתַּחוּ לוֹ: [מלכים א' טז, לא]

ד) אִם גִּלְעָד אָוֶן אַךְ שָׁוְא הָיוּ בַּגִּלְגָּל שְׁוָרִים זִבֵּחוּ גַּם מִזְבְּחוֹתָם כְּגַלִּים עַל תַּלְמֵי שָׂדָי: [הושע יב, יב]

ה) הִנְנִי מֵבִיא אֵלֶיךָ רָעָה וּבִעַרְתִּי אַחֲרֶיךָ וְהִכְרַתִּי לְאַחְאָב מַשְׁתִּין בְּקִיר וְעָצוּר וְעָזוּב בְּיִשְׂרָאֵל: [מלכים א' כא, כא]

ו) וַיִּקֶן אֶת הָהָר שֹׁמְרוֹן מֵאֶת שֶׁמֶר בְּכִכְּרַיִם כָּסֶף וַיִּבֶן אֶת הָהָר וַיִּקְרָא אֶת שֵׁם הָעִיר אֲשֶׁר בָּנָה עַל שֶׁם שֶׁמֶר אֲדֹנֵי הָהָר שֹׁמְרוֹן: [מלכים א' טז, כד]

ז) וַיִּשְׁלַח מַלְאָכִים אֶל אַחְאָב מֶלֶךְ יִשְׂרָאֵל הָעִירָה: וַיֹּאמֶר לוֹ כֹּה אָמַר בֶּן הֲדַד כַּסְפְּךָ וּזְהָבְךָ לִי הוּא וְנָשֶׁיךָ וּבָנֶיךָ הַטּוֹבִים לִי הֵם: כִּי אִם כָּעֵת מָחָר אֶשְׁלַח אֶת עֲבָדַי אֵלֶיךָ וְחִפְּשׂוּ אֶת בֵּיתְךָ וְאֵת בָּתֵּי עֲבָדֶיךָ וְהָיָה כָּל מַחְמַד עֵינֶיךָ יָשִׂימוּ בְיָדָם וְלָקָחוּ: וַיֹּאמֶר לְמַלְאֲכֵי בֶן הֲדַד אִמְרוּ לַאדֹנִי הַמֶּלֶךְ כֹּל אֲשֶׁר שָׁלַחְתָּ אֶל עַבְדְּךָ בָרִאשֹׁנָה אֶעֱשֶׂה וְהַדָּבָר הַזֶּה לֹא אוּכַל לַעֲשׂוֹת וַיֵּלְכוּ הַמַּלְאָכִים וַיְשִׁבֻהוּ דָּבָר: [מלכים א' כ, ב,ג,ו,ט]

ח) וַיֹּאמְרוּ אֵלָיו כָּל הַזְּקֵנִים וְכָל הָעָם אַל תִּשְׁמַע וְלוֹא תֹאבֶה: [מלכים א' כ, ח]

ט) וַיִּישַׁר הַדָּבָר בְּעֵינֵי אַבְשָׁלֹם וּבְעֵינֵי כָּל זִקְנֵי יִשְׂרָאֵל: [שמואל ב' יז, ד]

י) וְהִשְׁאַרְתִּי בְיִשְׂרָאֵל שִׁבְעַת אֲלָפִים כָּל הַבִּרְכַּיִם אֲשֶׁר לֹא כָרְעוּ לַבַּעַל וְכָל הַפֶּה אֲשֶׁר לֹא נָשַׁק לוֹ: [מלכים א' יט, יח]

כ) וַיֹּאמֶר יְיָ מִי יְפַתֶּה אֶת אַחְאָב וְיַעַל וְיִפֹּל בְּרָמֹת גִּלְעָד וַיֹּאמֶר זֶה בְּכֹה וְזֶה אֹמֵר בְּכֹה: [מלכים א' כב, כ]

ל) רַק לֹא הָיָה כְאַחְאָב אֲשֶׁר הִתְמַכֵּר לַעֲשׂוֹת הָרַע בְּעֵינֵי יְיָ אֲשֶׁר הֵסַתָּה אֹתוֹ אִיזֶבֶל אִשְׁתּוֹ: [מלכים א' כא, כה]

מ) וַיֵּצֵא הָרוּחַ וַיַּעֲמֹד לִפְנֵי יְיָ וַיֹּאמֶר אֲנִי אֲפַתֶּנּוּ וַיֹּאמֶר יְיָ אֵלָיו בַּמָּה: וַיֹּאמֶר אֵצֵא וְהָיִיתִי רוּחַ שֶׁקֶר בְּפִי כָּל נְבִיאָיו וַיֹּאמֶר תְּפַתֶּה וְגַם תּוּכָל צֵא וַעֲשֵׂה כֵן: [מלכים א' כב, כא-כב]

נ) לֹא יֵשֵׁב בְּקֶרֶב בֵּיתִי עֹשֵׂה רְמִיָּה דֹּבֵר שְׁקָרִים לֹא יִכּוֹן לְנֶגֶד עֵינָי: [תהלים קא, ז]

ס) וַיַּעַשׂ אַחְאָב אֶת הָאֲשֵׁרָה וַיּוֹסֶף אַחְאָב לַעֲשׂוֹת לְהַכְעִיס אֶת יְיָ אֱלֹהֵי יִשְׂרָאֵל מִכֹּל מַלְכֵי יִשְׂרָאֵל אֲשֶׁר הָיוּ לְפָנָיו: [מלכים א' טז, לג]

ע) וַיְבַקֵּשׁ אֶת אֲחַזְיָהוּ וַיִּלְכְּדֻהוּ וְהוּא מִתְחַבֵּא בְשֹׁמְרוֹן וַיְבִאֻהוּ אֶל יֵהוּא וַיְמִתֻהוּ וַיִּקְבְּרֻהוּ כִּי אָמְרוּ בֶּן יְהוֹשָׁפָט הוּא אֲשֶׁר דָּרַשׁ אֶת יְיָ בְּכָל לְבָבוֹ וְאֵין לְבֵית אֲחַזְיָהוּ לַעְצֹר כֹּחַ לְמַמְלָכָה: [דברי הימים ב' כב, ט]

פ) בֶּן שְׁתֵּים עֶשְׂרֵה שָׁנָה מְנַשֶּׁה בְמָלְכוֹ וַחֲמִשִּׁים וְחָמֵשׁ שָׁנָה מָלַךְ בִּירוּשָׁלָיִם: [דברי הימים ב' לג, א]

צ) וַיָּשָׁב וַיִּבֶן אֶת הַבָּמוֹת אֲשֶׁר אִבַּד חִזְקִיָּהוּ אָבִיו וַיָּקֶם מִזְבְּחֹת לַבַּעַל וַיַּעַשׂ אֲשֵׁרָה כַּאֲשֶׁר עָשָׂה אַחְאָב מֶלֶךְ יִשְׂרָאֵל וַיִּשְׁתַּחוּ לְכָל צְבָא הַשָּׁמַיִם וַיַּעֲבֹד אֹתָם: [מלכים ב' כא, ג]

ק) וַיִּתְפַּלֵּל אֵלָיו וַיֵּעָתֶר לוֹ וַיִּשְׁמַע תְּחִנָּתוֹ וַיְשִׁיבֵהוּ יְרוּשָׁלַיִם לְמַלְכוּתוֹ וַיֵּדַע מְנַשֶּׁה כִּי יְיָ הוּא הָאֱלֹהִים: [דברי הימים ב' לג, יג]

ר) וּנְתַתִּים לְזַעֲוָה לְכֹל מַמְלְכוֹת הָאָרֶץ בִּגְלַל מְנַשֶּׁה בֶן יְחִזְקִיָּהוּ מֶלֶךְ יְהוּדָה עַל אֲשֶׁר עָשָׂה בִּירוּשָׁלָיִם: [ירמיה טו, ד]

who tells lies shall not be established before My eyes, i.e. God, Who is the essence of truth, cannot abide falsehood being uttered in His presence in any form. Since the spirit of Navos said that it would become ***a lying spirit,*** it was expelled from God's Presence.[35] אָמַר רַב פָּפָּא – **Rav Pappa said:** הַיְינוּ דְּאָמְרֵי אִינְשֵׁי – **This is the meaning of the popular adage:**[36] דְּפָרַע קִינֵיהּ מַחֲרִיב בֵּיתֵיהּ – **"He who gives vent to his desire for vengeance destroys his** own **house,"** for as a result of his determination to bring about Ahab's death, the spirit of Navos was banished from God's Presence.

The Gemara concludes its discussion of Ahab with a verse which indicates why he has no share in the World to Come:

,,וַיַּעַשׂ אַחְאָב אֶת־הָאֲשֵׁרָה וַיּוֹסֶף אַחְאָב לַעֲשׂוֹת לְהַכְעִיס אֶת־ה׳ אֱלֹהֵי יִשְׂרָאֵל מִכֹּל מַלְכֵי יִשְׂרָאֵל אֲשֶׁר הָיוּ לְפָנָיו'' – Scripture states:[37] ***Ahab made an asheirah,***[38] ***and Ahab did more to anger Hashem the God of Israel than all the kings of Israel who preceded him.*** אָמַר רַבִּי יוֹחָנָן – **R' Yochanan said:** שֶׁכָּתַב עַל דַּלְתוֹת שֹׁמְרוֹן – This means **that [Ahab] wrote on the doors of Samaria,** his capital city, the following inscription: אַחְאָב כָּפַר בֵּאלֹהֵי יִשְׂרָאֵל – **"Ahab has denied the God of Israel."** לְפִיכָךְ אֵין לוֹ חֵלֶק בֵּאלֹהֵי יִשְׂרָאֵל – **Therefore, he has no portion in the God of Israel,** i.e. he is cut off from the World to Come.[39]

R' Levi discusses the wickedness of Ahab's grandson, King Achaziahu of Judah:

,,וַיְבַקֵּשׁ אֶת־אֲחַזְיָהוּ וַיִּלְכְּדֻהוּ וְהוּא מִתְחַבֵּא בְשֹׁמְרוֹן'' – Scripture states: ***[Yehu] sought out Achaziahu and captured him, and he had been hiding in Samaria.***[40] אָמַר רַבִּי לֵוִי – **R' Levi said:** שֶׁהָיָה קוֹדֵר אַזְכָּרוֹת – This means **that [Achaziahu] would scratch out**[41] **the mention** of God's name from Torah scrolls וְכוֹתֵב עֲבוֹדַת כּוֹכָבִים תַּחְתֵּיהֶן – **and write** the names of **pagan deities in their place.**[42]

The Gemara resumes its discussion of King Menasheh of Judah, the last of the three wicked kings listed in our Mishnah as having no portion in the World to Come:

מְנַשֶּׁה שֶׁנָּשָׁה יָהּ – **Menasheh** was so named **because he forgot God** (*nashah Yah*). דָּבָר אַחֵר – **An alternate explanation:** מְנַשֶּׁה שֶׁהִנְשִׁי אֶת יִשְׂרָאֵל לַאֲבִיהֶם שֶׁבַּשָּׁמַיִם – He was named **Menasheh because he caused Israel to be forgotten,** as it were, **by their Father in Heaven** (*hinshi Yah*).

וּמִנַּלָן דְּלָא אָתֵי לְעָלְמָא דְּאָתֵי – **And from where do we know that he does not come to the World to Come,** as the Tanna Kamma in the Mishnah claims? דִּכְתִיב ,,בֶּן־שְׁתֵּים עֶשְׂרֵה שָׁנָה מְנַשֶּׁה בְמָלְכוֹ וַחֲמִשִּׁים וְחָמֵשׁ שָׁנָה מָלַךְ בִּירוּשָׁלָם ... וַיַּעַשׂ הָרַע בְּעֵינֵי ה׳ ... וַיַּעַשׂ אֲשֵׁרָה כַּאֲשֶׁר עָשָׂה אַחְאָב מֶלֶךְ יִשְׂרָאֵל'' – **For it is written:**[43] ***Menasheh was twelve years old when he became king, and he reigned fifty-five years in Jerusalem ... He did what was wicked in the eyes of Hashem ... and he made an asheirah just as Ahab King of Israel had done.*** מָה אַחְאָב אֵין לוֹ חֵלֶק לָעוֹלָם הַבָּא – From the fact that Menasheh is compared here to Ahab, we learn that **just as Ahab has no portion in the World to Come,** as mentioned above, אַף מְנַשֶּׁה אֵין לוֹ חֵלֶק לָעוֹלָם הַבָּא – **so too Menasheh has no portion in the World to Come.**

The Mishnah cites the opposing view of R' Yehudah:

רַבִּי יְהוּדָה אוֹמֵר מְנַשֶּׁה יֵשׁ לוֹ חֵלֶק לָעוֹלָם הַבָּא – **R' YEHUDAH SAYS: MENASHEH DOES HAVE A PORTION IN THE WORLD TO COME,** שֶׁנֶּאֱמַר ,,וַיִּתְפַּלֵּל אֵלָיו וַיֵּעָתֶר לוֹ וגו׳'' – **AS IT IS STATED:**[44] ***HE PRAYED TO [HASHEM] AND [HASHEM] GRANTED HIS PLEA,*** **etc.**

The Gemara gives the basis for the dispute between the Tanna Kamma and R' Yehudah:

אָמַר רַבִּי יוֹחָנָן – **R' Yochanan said:** וּשְׁנֵיהֶם מִקְרָא אֶחָד דָּרְשׁוּ – **Both of them expounded the** very **same verse,** שֶׁנֶּאֱמַר ,,וּנְתַתִּים לְזַעֲוָה לְכֹל מַמְלְכוֹת הָאָרֶץ בִּגְלַל מְנַשֶּׁה בֶן־יְחִזְקִיָּהוּ'' – **as it is stated:**[45] ***I will make [the people of Judah] a shuddering for all the kingdoms of the earth, on account of Menasheh son of Chizkiah.*** מַר סָבַר בִּגְלַל מְנַשֶּׁה שֶׁעָשָׂה תְּשׁוּבָה – One **master** [R' Yehudah] **is of the opinion** that the verse means thus: **on account of Menasheh, who did repent,** וְאִינְהוּ לֹא עָבוּד – **whereas they,** i.e. the rest of the sinful people of Judah, **did not repent.**[46] וּמַר סָבַר – **And** the other **master** [the Tanna Kamma] **maintains**

NOTES

35. Although God consented to allow the spirit to carry out its suggestion, He banished it from His presence. True, the task of being the spirit of untruth in the mouths of Ahab's prophets had to be accomplished somehow, but one should not volunteer on his own to be the instrument of any act that involves lying. The fact that Navos' spirit was eager to fulfill this mission was a character flaw (*Yad Ramah*).

36. Literally: so people say. [Rav Pappa was in the habit of quoting popular sayings to highlight a particular teaching or lesson. See also above, 95a and 98b, and below, 103a and 106a.]

37. *I Kings* 16:33.

38. A tree that is worshiped is called an *asheirah* – see *Avodah Zarah* 48a.

39. [This does not necessarily mean that Ahab inscribed these very words on the gates. The Gemara may mean that Ahab inscribed words that were *tantamount* to a proclamation denying God; for example, he may have inscribed that the city of Samaria was dedicated to Baal (*R' Avigdor Miller*).]

40. *II Chronicles* 22:9. As related above (102a note 3), Yehu was sent by a prophet to exterminate the family of Ahab. At this juncture, the royal families of Israel and Judea were related: Achaziahu, king of Judea, was a grandson of Ahab (his father having married Ahab's daughter). Thus, besides killing the king of Israel, who was Ahab's son, Yehu also killed Achaziahu.

Now, the plain meaning of the verse cited by the Gemara would seem to be that Achaziahu was in hiding in order to avoid being killed by Yehu. However, from *II Kings* 9:27 it is clear that Yehu killed Achaziahu before Achaziahu even had a chance to hide. The Gemara therefore explains the verse in *Chronicles* to mean that Achaziahu had *previously* been hiding for a *totally different* reason (*Rashi* to *II Kings* 9:27; cf. *Maharal, Maharsha*).

41. Literally: cut out.

42. He did this in secret, for the public would never have sanctioned this atrocity (*Rashi*). Furthermore, he did this in Samaria, where idolaters held sway, rather than in his home capital of Jerusalem; he feared doing it in Jerusalem, where the government officials abhorred foreign gods (*Rashi* to *II Kings* ibid.).

43. *II Kings* 21:1-3.

44. *II Chronicles* 33:13.

45. *Jeremiah* 15:4.

46. That is, they should have learned from Menasheh's good example and repented, but they did not. It is for this, the prophet says, that they will be punished (*Maharsha*; see also *Targum Yonasan* ad loc.).

בִּגְלַל מְנַשֶּׁה דְּלָא עֲבַד תְּשׁוּבָה – that the verse means thus: **on account of Menasheh, who did not repent,** and who drew the people of Judah into sin after him.[1]

R' Yochanan asserts that Menasheh was a true penitent: אָמַר רַבִּי יוֹחָנָן – **R' Yochanan said:** כָּל הָאוֹמֵר מְנַשֶּׁה אֵין לוֹ חֵלֶק לָעוֹלָם הַבָּא – **Whoever says that Menasheh has no portion in the World to Come** מְרַפֶּה יְדֵיהֶן שֶׁל בַּעֲלֵי תְשׁוּבָה – **weakens the hands,** i.e. the resolve, **of** potential **penitents,** for they will hesitate to repent when they reflect upon the fact that although Menasheh was a penitent for such a long period of time, it did him no good, for he was nevertheless excluded from the World to Come. דְּתָנֵי תַּנָּא קַמֵּיהּ דְּרַבִּי יוֹחָנָן – **For a teacher of Baraisos taught the** following **Baraisa before R' Yochanan:** מְנַשֶּׁה עָשָׂה תְּשׁוּבָה (ל)שְׁלֹשִׁים וְשָׁלֹשׁ שָׁנִים – MENASHEH REPENTED for the last THIRTY-THREE YEARS of his life, דִּכְתִיב ,,בֶּן־שְׁתֵּים עֶשְׂרֵה שָׁנָה מְנַשֶּׁה בְמָלְכוֹ וַחֲמִשִּׁים וְחָמֵשׁ שָׁנָה מָלַךְ בִּירוּשָׁלַם . . . וַיַּעַשׂ (הרע) אֲשֵׁרָה כַּאֲשֶׁר עָשָׂה אַחְאָב מֶלֶךְ יִשְׂרָאֵל'' – AS IT IS WRITTEN: *"MENASHEH WAS TWELVE YEARS OLD WHEN HE BECAME KING, AND HE REIGNED FIFTY-FIVE YEARS IN JERUSALEM . . . HE MADE AN ASHEIRA," JUST AS AHAB KING OF ISRAEL HAD DONE.*[2] This last phrase implies that Menasheh was wicked for a length of time equal to Ahab's reign. כַּמָּה מָלַךְ אַחְאָב – Now, HOW LONG DID AHAB REIGN? עֶשְׂרִין וְתַרְתֵּין שְׁנִין – TWENTY-TWO YEARS. מְנַשֶּׁה כַּמָּה מָלַךְ – HOW LONG DID MENASHEH REIGN? חֲמִשִּׁים וְחָמֵשׁ – FIFTY-FIVE YEARS. דַּל מִינַּיְיהוּ עֶשְׂרִים וְתַרְתֵּין – SUBTRACT FROM THESE TWENTY-TWO פָּשׁוּ לְהוּ תְּלָתִין וּתְלָת – AND THERE REMAIN THIRTY-THREE. Thus we see that for the last thirty-three years of his reign Menasheh was a penitent.

In connection with its discussion of Menasheh, the Gemara now presents an exegesis of *II Chronicles* 33:13, the first of four interpretations of unusual Scriptural words or phrases relating to various kings of Judah, by R' Yochanan in the name of R' Shimon ben Yochai:

אָמַר רַבִּי יוֹחָנָן מִשּׁוּם רַבִּי שִׁמְעוֹן בֶּן יוֹחַי – **R' Yochanan reported in the name of R' Shimon ben Yochai:** מַאי דִּכְתִיב ,,וַיִּשְׁמַע אֵלָיו וַיֵּחָתֵר לוֹ'' – **What is** the meaning of **that which is written** concerning Menasheh: ***God hearkened unto him "vayeichaser lo"?*** ,,וַיֵּעָתֵר לוֹ'' מִיבְּעֵי לֵיהּ – Why does the verse use the verb *vayeichaser*? ***Vayei'aser lo*** **is what it should have said!**[3] מְלַמֵּד שֶׁעָשָׂה לוֹ הַקָּדוֹשׁ בָּרוּךְ הוּא כְּמִין מַחְתֶּרֶת בָּרָקִיעַ כְּדֵי לְקַבְּלוֹ בִּתְשׁוּבָה – **This teaches that the Holy One, Blessed is He, made for [Menasheh] a type of** secret **tunnel** *(machteres)* **in the firmament in order to** surreptitiously **receive him in penitence,** מִפְּנֵי מִדַּת הַדִּין – **on account of the** opposition to Menasheh's admittance on the part of **the Attribute of Strict Justice.**[4]

The second of the four interpretations:

וְאָמַר רַבִּי יוֹחָנָן מִשּׁוּם רַבִּי שִׁמְעוֹן בֶּן יוֹחַי – **And R' Yochanan said** further **in the name of R' Shimon ben Yochai:** מַאי דִּכְתִיב ,,בְּרֵאשִׁית מַמְלְכוּת יְהוֹיָקִים בֶּן־יֹאשִׁיָּהוּ'' – **What is the meaning of that which is written:**[5] ***In the beginning*** *(bereishis)* ***of the reign of Yehoiakim the son of Yoshiahu,*** וּכְתִיב ,,בְּרֵאשִׁית מַמְלֶכֶת צִדְקִיָּה'' – **and** of that which **is written:** ***In the***

NOTES

1. The verse thus blames the punishment that befell the people on Menasheh's lack of repentance.

This opinion — that Menasheh did not repent — seems difficult, for *II Chronicles* ch. 33 discusses the fact of Menasheh's repentance openly and at length (vs. 11-19, 23). However, the Gemara reflects the fact that Menasheh was one of the three who "came to God with craftiness" — see above, 101b. Thus, his repentance may have been insincere (*Tiferes Yisrael* to Mishnah — see Midrash cited in note 4) or was insufficient, for he did not exert himself sufficiently to also bring back the people he had previously led astray (*R' Avigdor Miller*).

2. *II Kings* 21:1-3.

3. The verse obviously intends to state that God accepted Menasheh's prayer. The correct Hebrew verb denoting acceptance of prayer is וַיֵּעָתֵר (*vayei'aser*), *and He allowed Himself to be entreated*, and indeed this is the קְרִי, the way tradition tells us the word is *pronounced*. But the כְּתִיב, the way it is *written* in Scripture, is וַיֵּחָתֵר (*vayeichaser*), *and He was undermined* (i.e. tunneled under). What does Scripture mean to indicate with this peculiar expression? (see *Rashi,* who concludes, "This is the explanation I have heard"; see also *Yad Ramah* סוף ד"ה פיסקא).

In point of fact, our texts of Scripture have the verb *vayei'aser,* not *vayeichaser,* and there is no *keri* and *kesiv* at all. At first glance, it would appear that the Gemara had a different textual version than our Scripture, but, *Yad Malachi* 283 argues that except for יְתֵרוֹת וַחֲסֵרוֹת (cases where words are written *plene* or not), we do not find actual textual variants. He lists and provides explanations for various apparent instances of such variants. The Gemara and commentators do indeed quote verses which do not appear in that form in our Scriptures; however, this is due to the fact that very often they quote what is an abbreviated or paraphrased version of the actual verse.

Now, we find in various Midrashim and *Yerushalmi* (*Sanhedrin* 51b) the following version of the Gemara's present exposition: וַיֵּעָתֵר לוֹ וַיֵּחָתֵר לוֹ מְלַמֵּד וכו'. That is, the verse is expounded *as if* it read וַיֵּחָתֵר, for as the Midrash (*Vayikra Rabbah* 30:3) and *Yerushalmi* (ibid.) explain, in Arabic a tunnel, חֲתִירְתָּא, is called עֲתִירְתָּא.

Alternatively, the Gemara means that the words וַיֵּעָתֵר לוֹ are superfluous, for Scripture could have simply stated וַיִּשְׁמַע תְּחִנָּתוֹ. We therefore expound וַיֵּעָתֵר as if it read וַיֵּחָתֵר, employing the exegetical device that allows the guttural letters ח and ע to be interchanged (*Yad Ramah*; see also commentary of *R' Samson Raphael Hirsch* to *Genesis* 25:21).

On the basis of all this, many commentators suggest that our Gemara did not, in fact, have a variant text at all and that Rabbi Yochanan's statement originally read like the text in the Midrashim. Our Gemara texts, however, became corrupted through the inadvertent deletion of the word *vayei'aser,* leading to our present Gemara text (see *Minchas Shai* ad loc.; *Yefei Einayim* and *Mitzpeh Eisan* here, *Yad Malachi* ibid.).

4. This is an allegory. It means: By all standards of justice, Menasheh's sins were too grievous to allow him to be accepted in repentance. Nevertheless, God in His great mercy chose to accept him. This is figuratively expressed here in the following manner: God realized that the Attribute of Strict Justice, which stands at the entrance to Heaven and denies admittance to the repentence of those sinners who do not deserve it, would deny entry to Menasheh's penitence. God, however, wished to accept Menasheh's penitence, so He prepared a second, secret entrance into Heaven, a tunnel unknown to the Attribute of Strict Justice (the secrecy hinting to the unfathomable depth of God's mercy). Menasheh's penitence was thus surreptitiously able to enter Heaven through this tunnel. The purpose of this allegory is to teach that God's willingness to accept true penitence transcends the Attribute of Strict Justice (*Yad Ramah,* first explanation).

The Midrash, however — alluded to in brief by the Gemara on 101b — provides some additional background information and an expanded allegory, which puts our Gemara's statement in a somewhat different light: *"So God brought upon them the officers of the army of the king of Ashur and they captured Menasheh in hooks, and bound him in copper chains and brought him to Babylonia* (*II Chronicles* 33:10-11). They made for him a copper vessel, under which they began to kindle a fire . . . At that time, Menasheh cried out to all the gods in the world to whom he was accustomed to sacrifice, but not one answered him . . . When Menasheh realized his bitter straits, he began crying to the Holy One, Blessed is He. He said, 'Master of the universe! I have called to all the gods in the world, and I [now] realize that they are without power. Master of the universe! . . . If You do not answer me, I will say, "They are all the same! (i.e. God is no different than the idols)." God replied, 'Wicked one! By right I should not answer you, for you have angered me. But in order not to close the door to penitents, so that they do not say that Menasheh sought to repent but he was not accepted, I will answer you.' . . .. However, the angels began shutting the windows to Heaven to block out his prayers. What did God do? He excavated a tunnel in Heaven beneath the Throne of Glory and accepted his prayers" (*Devarim Rabbah* 2:20; see also *Yerushalmi Sanhedrin* 51b).

5. *Jeremiah* 26:1; see also 27:1.

בגלל מנשה דלא עבד תשובה א"ר יוחנן כל האומר מנשה אין לו חלק לעוה"ב מרפה ידיהן של בעלי תשובה דתני תנא קמיה דר' יוחנן מנשה עשה תשובה (ל)שלשים ושלש שנים דכתיב א) בן שתים עשרה שנה מנשה במלכו וחמשים וחמש שנה מלך בירושלים ויעש (הרע) [אשרה] כאשר עשה אחאב מלך ישראל כמה מלך אחאב עשרין ותרתין שנין מנשה כמה מלך חמשים וחמש דל מינייהו עשרים ותרתין פשו להו תלתין ותלת א"ר יוחנן משום רשב"י מאי דכתי' ב) וישמע אליו א) ויחתר לו ויעתר לו מיבעי ליה מלמד שעשה לו הקב"ה כמין מחתרת ברקיע כדי לקבלו בתשובה מפני מדת הדין ב) וא"ר יוחנן משום רשב"י מאי דכתיב ג) בראשית ממלכות יהויקים בן יאשיהו וכתיב ד) בראשית ממלכת צדקיה וכי עד האידנא לא הוו מלכי אלא בקש הקב"ה להחזיר את העולם כולו לתוהו ובוהו בשביל יהויקים נסתכל בדורו ונתקררה דעתו בקש הקב"ה להחזיר את העולם כולו לתוהו ובוהו בשביל דורו של צדקיה נסתכל בצדקיה ונתקררה דעתו בצדקיה נמי כתיב ה) ויעש הרע בעיני ה' שהיה בידו למחות ולא מיחה וא"ר יוחנן משום רשב"י מאי דכתיב ו) איש חכם נשפט את איש אויל ורגז ושחק ואין נחת אמר הקב"ה כעסתי על אחז ונתתיו ביד מלכי דמשק זיבח וקיטר [לאלהיהם] שנאמר ז) ויזבח לאלהי דרמשק המכים בו ויאמר [כי] אלהי מלכי ארם הם מעזרים אותם להם אזבח ויעזרוני והם היו [לו] להכשילו ולכל ישראל שחקתי עם אמציה ונתתי מלכי אדום בידו הביא אלהיהם והשתחוה להם שנאמר ח) ויהי אחרי (כן) בא אמציה מהכות את אדומים ויבא את אלהי בני שעיר ויעמידם [לו] לאלהים ולפניהם ישתחוה ולהם יקטר אמר רב פפא היינו דאמרי אינשי בכיי ליה למר דלא ידע חייכי למר דלא ידע ווי ליה ג) למר דלא ידע בין טב לביש ט) ויבאו כל [שרי] מלך בבל (ויבאו) [וישבו] בשער התוך א"ר יוחנן משום רשב"י מקום שמחתכין בו הלכות אמר רב פפא היינו ד) דאמרי אינשי באתרא דמריה תלא ליה זייניה תמן קולבא רעיא קולתיה תלא (סימן על שדה בתים לא תאונה) אמר רב חסדא אמר רבי ירמיה בר אבא מאי דכתיב י) על שדה איש עצל עברתי ועל כרם אדם חסר לב והנה עלה כולו קמשונים כסו פניו חרולים וגדר אבניו נהרסה על שדה איש עצל עברתי זה אחז ועל כרם אדם חסר לב זה מנשה והנה עלה כולו קמשונים זה אמון כסו פניו חרולים זה יהויקים וגדר אבניו נהרסה זה צדקיהו שנחרב בית המקדש בימיו ה) ואמר רב חסדא אמר רבי ירמיה בר אבא ארבע כיתות אין מקבלות פני שכינה כת לצים כת שקרנים כת חניפים כת מספרי לשון הרע כת לצים דכתיב כ) משך ידו את לוצצים כת שקרנים דכתיב ל) דובר שקרים לא יכון לנגד עיני כת חניפים דכתיב מ) כי לא לפניו חנף יבוא כת מספרי לשון הרע דכתיב נ) כי לא אל חפץ רשע אתה לא יגורך רע ו) צדיק אתה ולא יהיה במגורך רע ז) ואמר רב חסדא אמר רבי ירמיה בר אבא מאי דכתיב ס) לא תאונה אליך רעה ונגע לא יקרב באהלך לא תאונה אליך רעה שלא ישלוט ח) בהן יצר הרע ונגע לא יקרב באהלך ט) שלא תמצא אשתך ספק נדה בשעה שתבא מן הדרך דבר אחר לא תאונה אליך רעה שלא יבעתוך חלומות רעים והרהורים רעים ונגע לא יקרב באהלך שלא יהא לך בן או תלמיד שמקדיח תבשילו ברבים עד כאן ברכו אביו מכאן ואילך ברכתו אמו ע) כי מלאכיו יצוה לך לשמרך בכל דרכיך על כפים ישאונך וגו' על שחל ופתן תדרוך וגו' עד כאן ברכתו אמו מכאן ואילך ברכתו שמים

כי

ל) לא ישב בקרב ביתי עשה רמיה דבר שקרים לא יכון לנגד עיני: [תהלים קא, ז] מ) גם הוא לי לישועה כי לא לפניו חנף יבוא: [איוב יג, טז] נ) כי לא אל חפץ רשע אתה לא יגרך רע: [תהלים ה, ה] ס) לא תאנה אליך רעה ונגע לא יקרב באהלך: [תהלים צא, י] ע) כי מלאכיו יצוה לך לשמרך בכל דרכיך: על כפים ישאונך פן תגף באבן רגלך: על שחל ופתן תדרך תרמס כפיר ותנין: [תהלים צא, יא-יג]

בגלל מנשה דלא עשה תשובה. והמשיכן כולן אחריו: כאשר עשה אחאב. דמשמע כשיעור השנים שחטא אחאב במלכו חטא מנשה והיינו כ"ב שנה שחטא בהם כנגד כ"ב שנים שמלך אחאב: פשו להו ל"ג. שעשה תשובה: וישמע אליו ויחתר לו. ומבחוץ כתיב ויעתר לו כך שמעתי: מדת הדין. היתה מעכבת שלא להקביל פני מנשה בתשובה ועשה הקב"ה מחתרת ברקיע ופשט ידו וקבלו בלא ידיעת מדת הדין: מאי דכתיב בראשית ממלכות יהויקים ובראשית ממלכת צדקיה. מ"ט כתיב בהני בראשית יותר מאחריני: וכי עד האידנא לא הוו מלכי. ואי משום תחלת ממלכתו קאמר ה"ל למכתב בשנה ראשונה למלכותו אלא להכי שני קרא בדיבוריה וכתיב בראשית ללמדך מעשה בראשית היה בימי יהויקים שבקש הקב"ה להחזיר את עולמו לתהו ובהו כמו שהיה מבראשית: כיון שנסתכל בדורו. של יהויקים שהיו צדיקים שעדיין לא גלו החרש והמסגר: דורו של צדקיהו. היו רשעים שכל הצדיקים הגלו כבר עם יהויכין: איש חכם נשפט. זה הקב"ה שנקרא ה' איש מלחמה (שמות טו) איש אויל אלו מלכים שבסמוך אחז ואמציה ורגז ושחק ואין נחת בין שהוא כועס עמהם בין שהוא שוחק עמהם אינן יראין מלפניו ואינם חתים לחזור למוטב: בכי ליה למר כו'. לאו דוקא נקט מר אלא משום דהכי מילי דאינשי כשהוא חכם כשהוא רוצה להישפט ולהתווכח עמהן בין שהוא שוחק עליהם בין שהוא כועס עמהן אינם יראים מלפניו ואינם חתים לחזור למוטב: מקום שהיו מחתכין בו. ודורשין הלכות נהפך למושב לגיס של שרי מלך בבל: בשער התוך. לשון חותך והיינו בהר הבית ובעזרה ששם היו יושבים סנהדרין וכדאמר בעלמא (לעיל דף פו:) ג' בתי דינין היו שם אחד בלשכת הגזית ואחד על פתח העזרה ואחד על פתח הר הבית: קולתיה תלא. כלומר במקום שהיו חותכין הלכות בו דנין שרי בבל דינים שלהם: באתרא דמריה תלא זייניה. מקום שהאדון תולה כליו: קולבא רעיא (א). נבל רועה: קולתיה תלא. כדו תלה לשם כמו (בראשית כד) כדה דמתרגמינן קולתא. ל"א קודתיה מקדתו כמו (סוטה דף ט.) מקדה של חרס: והנה עלה כולו קמשונים זה אמון. שהעלה שממית ע"ג המזבח לקמן: כסו פניו חרולים זה יהויקים. שכסה פניו מאורו של הקב"ה כדאמר לקמן כלום אנו צריכים אלא לאורו יטול אורו: על שדה איש עצל עברתי זה אחז. ולהכי קרי ליה עצל שחתם את התורה ובטל את העבודה לקמן: ועל כרם אדם חסר לב זה מנשה. שקדר אזכרות והרס את המזבח (ל"א) חרולים אורטיג"ש: זה צדקיה. שהיה צדיק ונהרס בית המקדש בימיו: משך ידו את לוצצים. משך הקב"ה את ידיו מן הלוצצים שלא להתקרב אצלם: לא יגורך רע. היינו מספרי לשון הרע דכתיב בתריה תאבד דוברי כזב איש דמים וגו' ועוד דכתיב בתריה קברם הוות קבר פתוח גרונם וגו': שלא תמצא אשתך ספק נדה וכו'. והיינו באהלך באשתך כדאמרי' י) אין אהלו אלא אשה כ) ובשעה שאדם בא מן הדרך קשה לו כשימצא את אשתו ספק נדה יותר מנדה ודאית שעל ספק הוא מיצר ויצרו תקפו ואומר טהורה היא ועל חנם אני מונע: עד כאן ברכו אביו. דוד אביו לשלמה בנו מסתמא לפי ענין הברכות יש לידע סדור ברכות שכן דרך האב בדברים האלו בספק נדה ובילה"ר ובהרהורים רעים ובבנים ותלמידים שלא יקדיחו תבשילם ברבים אבל אשה אינה נותנת דעת בכך אלא מהמרכת הלב שיש לה מתפללת על בנה שינצל מאבן נגף ומרוחין ושדין לפיכך קא דריש לפי הענין שאלו ברכות ברכתו אמו כי מלאכיו יצוה לך מ"ר ועוד משום דכתיב כי מלאכיו משמע ליה דסליק ענין אחד דברכה ומכי מלאכיו עד כי בי חשק סליק חד ענין הלכך מוקים דמי לדמי דע"כ ברכו אביו וכו'. מ"ר:

מסורת הש"ס

א) [בפסוק כתיב ויעתר וכן העתיק לעיל קא: ואפשר דבדברי הימים שהיה לפני רשב"י היה כתוב ויחתר לו עמ"ש תוס' בשבת נה: ד"ה מעבירין כו' וכן מצינו בירושלמי כו' ע"ש], ב) [ערכין יז. ע"ש], ג) למאן רש"ל, ד) ב"מ פד:, ה) סוטה מב. ע"ש, ו) [שבת קמט: חגיגה יב: סוטה מב.], ז) [ברכות נה: ע"ש קל"ע], ח) [נ"ל בך], ט) [ב"מ קז.], י) בד"י אין אהלו אלא אשתו, כ) [מועד קטן ז:].

ליקוטי רש"י

מאי דכתיב. ביהויקים ולדקיהו בראשית לפי שביקש הקב"ה להפוך מעשה בראשית בימיהם [ערכין יז.]. איש חכם נשפט. מתוכח עם האויל. ואין נחת. בין מראה לו פנים זעופו' בין שמראהו פנים שוחקו' אין נחת לא בזו ולא בזו אינו מולא קורת רוח מצינו באמציה שהראה לו הקב"ה פנים שוחקות ומסר בידו אדום ובשובו מהכות (דה"ב כה) ויבא את אלהיהם ולהם השתחוה לאחז הראה הקב"ה פנים זועפות ומסרו ביד מלכי ארם ויזבח לאלהי דמשק כי אמר אלהי ארם מעזרים להם [משלי כט, ט]. באתרא דמריה תלא זייניה כולבא רעיא קולתיה תלא. יתד שהיה הגבור רגיל לתלות בו כלי זיינו הנבל הרועה תרמילו תלה בולז"א בלעז [ב"מ פד:]. קמשונים. קוצים. כסו. נכסו. חרלים. גדולי' מקמשונים והרי הם חדים כקולים [משלי כד, לא]. משך ידו. הקב"ה מהיות את לוצצים. לא יגורך רע. לא יגור עמך רע וגבי מספרי לשון הרע כתיב דכתיב בההוא פרשתא כי אין בפיהו נכונה וגו' [סוטה מב.]. חנף. המסית חבירו בדרך רע [משלי יא, ט]. לא תאנה. לא תקרה וכן והאלהי' אנה לידו (שמות כא) [תהלים צא, י].

הגהות הב"ח

(א) רש"י ד"ה קולבא רעיא. נ"ב ובב"מ פרק הפועלים גרסינן כלבא רעיא בכ':

תורה אור השלם

א) בֶּן שְׁתֵּים עֶשְׂרֵה שָׁנָה מְנַשֶּׁה בְמָלְכוֹ וַחֲמִשִּׁים וְחָמֵשׁ שָׁנָה מָלַךְ בִּירוּשָׁלָיִם וְשֵׁם אִמּוֹ חֶפְצִי בָהּ: וַיָּשָׁב וַיִּבֶן אֶת הַבָּמוֹת אֲשֶׁר אִבַּד חִזְקִיָּהוּ אָבִיו וַיָּקֶם מִזְבְּחֹת לַבַּעַל וַיַּעַשׂ אֲשֵׁרָה כַּאֲשֶׁר עָשָׂה אַחְאָב מֶלֶךְ יִשְׂרָאֵל וַיִּשְׁתַּחוּ לְכָל צְבָא הַשָּׁמַיִם וַיַּעֲבֹד אֹתָם: [מלכים ב' כא, א,ג]

ב) וַיִּתְפַּלֵּל אֵלָיו וַיֵּעָתֶר לוֹ וַיִּשְׁמַע תְּחִנָּתוֹ וַיְשִׁיבֵהוּ יְרוּשָׁלַיִם לְמַלְכוּתוֹ וַיֵּדַע מְנַשֶּׁה כִּי יְיָ הוּא הָאֱלֹהִים: [דברי הימים ב' לג, יג]

ג) בְּרֵאשִׁית מַמְלְכוּת יְהוֹיָקִים בֶּן יֹאשִׁיָּהוּ מֶלֶךְ יְהוּדָה הָיָה הַדָּבָר הַזֶּה מֵאֵת יְיָ לֵאמֹר: [ירמיה כו, א]

ד) וַיְהִי בַּשָּׁנָה הַהִיא בְּרֵאשִׁית מַמְלֶכֶת צִדְקִיָּה מֶלֶךְ יְהוּדָה בַּשָּׁנָה הָרְבִעִית בַּחֹדֶשׁ הַחֲמִישִׁי אָמַר אֵלַי חֲנַנְיָה בֶן עַזּוּר הַנָּבִיא אֲשֶׁר מִגִּבְעוֹן בְּבֵית יְיָ לְעֵינֵי הַכֹּהֲנִים וְכָל הָעָם לֵאמֹר: [ירמיה כח, א]

ה) וַיַּעַשׂ הָרַע בְּעֵינֵי יְיָ כְּכֹל אֲשֶׁר עָשָׂה יְהוֹיָקִים: [מלכים ב' כד, יט]

ו) אִישׁ חָכָם נִשְׁפָּט אֶת אִישׁ אֱוִיל וְרָגַז וְשָׂחַק וְאֵין נָחַת: [משלי כט, ט]

ז) וַיִּזְבַּח לֵאלֹהֵי דַרְמֶשֶׂק הַמַּכִּים בּוֹ וַיֹּאמֶר כִּי אֱלֹהֵי מַלְכֵי אֲרָם הֵם מַעְזְרִים אוֹתָם לָהֶם אֲזַבֵּחַ וְיַעְזְרוּנִי וְהֵם הָיוּ לוֹ לְהַכְשִׁילוֹ וּלְכָל יִשְׂרָאֵל: [דברי הימים ב' כח, כג]

ח) וַיְהִי אַחֲרֵי בוֹא אֲמַצְיָהוּ מֵהַכּוֹת אֶת אֲדוֹמִים וַיָּבֵא אֶת אֱלֹהֵי בְּנֵי שֵׂעִיר וַיַּעֲמִידֵם לוֹ לֵאלֹהִים וְלִפְנֵיהֶם יִשְׁתַּחֲוֶה וְלָהֶם יְקַטֵּר: [דברי הימים ב' כה, יד]

ט) וַיָּבֹאוּ כֹּל שָׂרֵי מֶלֶךְ בָּבֶל וַיֵּשְׁבוּ בְּשַׁעַר הַתָּוֶךְ נֵרְגַל שַׂר אֶצֶר סַמְגַּר נְבוּ שַׂר סְכִים רַב סָרִים נֵרְגַל שַׂר אֶצֶר רַב מָג וְכָל שְׁאֵרִית שָׂרֵי מֶלֶךְ בָּבֶל: [ירמיה לט, ג]

י) עַל שְׂדֵה אִישׁ עָצֵל עָבַרְתִּי וְעַל כֶּרֶם אָדָם חֲסַר לֵב: וְהִנֵּה עָלָה כֻלּוֹ קִמְּשֹׂנִים כָּסּוּ פָנָיו חֲרֻלִּים וְגֶדֶר אֲבָנָיו נֶהֱרָסָה: [משלי כד, ל-לא]

כ) יוֹם מַלְכֵּנוּ הֶחֱלוּ שָׂרִים חֲמַת מִיָּיִן מָשַׁךְ יָדוֹ אֶת לֹצְצִים: [הושע ז, ה]

beginning** (bereishis) **of the reign of Tzidkiah?[6] וְכִי עַד הָאִידְנָא לֹא הֲווּ מַלְכֵי – **Why, until this time were there not** already **kings?**[7] אֶלָּא בִּקֵּשׁ הַקָּדוֹשׁ בָּרוּךְ הוּא לְהַחֲזִיר אֶת הָעוֹלָם כּוּלּוֹ לְתוֹהוּ וָבוֹהוּ – **Rather,** the phrase *in the beginning* is reminiscent of Creation, and indicates that **the Holy One, Blessed is He, sought to restore the world to** its primordial **formlessness and emptiness,** i.e. to destroy the world, בִּשְׁבִיל יְהוֹיָקִים – **on account of** the wickedness of **Yehoiakim.**[8] נִסְתַּכֵּל בְּדוֹרוֹ – **However, [God] looked at** the people of **[Yehoiakim's] generation** וְנִתְקָרְרָה דַּעְתּוֹ – **and His anger abated.**[9] בִּקֵּשׁ הַקָּדוֹשׁ בָּרוּךְ הוּא לְהַחֲזִיר אֶת הָעוֹלָם כּוּלּוֹ לְתוֹהוּ וָבוֹהוּ בִּשְׁבִיל דּוֹרוֹ שֶׁל צִדְקִיָּה – Similarly, **the Holy One, Blessed is He, sought to restore the world to** its primordial **formlessness and emptiness,** i.e. to destroy the world, **on account of** the wickedness of **the generation of Tzidkiah.** נִסְתַּכֵּל בְּצִדְקִיָּה וְנִתְקָרְרָה דַּעְתּוֹ – However, **[God] looked at Tzidkiah** himself **and His anger abated.**[10]

The Gemara challenges the assertion that Tzidkiah was a righteous king:

בְּצִדְקִיָּה נַמִּי כְּתִיב ,,וַיַּעַשׂ הָרַע בְּעֵינֵי ה׳״ – But **of Tzidkiah too it is written:**[11] ***He did what was evil in the eyes of God.*** Why do you say that he was righteous?

The Gemara answers:

שֶׁהָיָה בְּיָדוֹ לִמְחוֹת וְלֹא מִיחָה – Tzidkiah's sin lay in the fact **that it was in his power to protest** the wicked deeds of his subjects, **yet he did not protest.** As far as his own deeds were concerned, however, he was righteous.

The third of the four interpretations:

וְאָמַר רַבִּי יוֹחָנָן מִשּׁוּם רַבִּי שִׁמְעוֹן בֶּן יוֹחַי – **And R' Yochanan said** further **in the name of R' Shimon ben Yochai:** מַאי דִּכְתִיב ,,אִישׁ־חָכָם נִשְׁפָּט אֶת־אִישׁ אֱוִיל וְרָגַז וְשָׂחַק וְאֵין נָחַת״ – **What is the meaning of that which is written: *The wise man contends with the fool; he rages and smiles, yet there is no fear?***[12] אָמַר הַקָּדוֹשׁ בָּרוּךְ הוּא – It means that **the Holy One, Blessed is He,** complained and **said:** כָּעַסְתִּי עַל אָחָז – **I became angry at** the wicked King **Achaz** of Judah וּנְתַתִּיו בְּיַד מַלְכֵי דַמֶּשֶׂק – **and delivered him into the hand of the kings of Damascus,** hoping that his defeat at their hands would convince him of the evil of his ways and cause him to repent. זִיבֵּחַ וְקִיטֵּר לֵאלֹהֵיהֶם – Instead, **he sacrificed and offered incense to their gods!** שֶׁנֶּאֱמַר ,,וַיִּזְבַּח לֵאלֹהֵי דַרְמֶשֶׂק הַמַּכִּים בּוֹ וַיֹּאמֶר כִּי אֱלֹהֵי מַלְכֵי־אֲרָם הֵם מַעְזְרִים אֹתָם לָהֶם אֲזַבֵּחַ וְיַעְזְרוּנִי וְהֵם הָיוּ־לוֹ לְהַכְשִׁילוֹ וּלְכָל־יִשְׂרָאֵל״ – **As it is stated:**[13] ***[Achaz] sacrificed to the gods of Darmesek who smote him;*** – ***he said, "Because the gods of the kings of Aram help them,*** – ***to them shall I sacrifice that they may help me."*** – ***But they were the ruin of him and of all Israel.*** שָׂחַקְתִּי עִם אֲמַצְיָה – **I smiled,** i.e. bestowed good fortune, **upon** King **Amatziah** of Judah, וְנָתַתִּי מַלְכֵי אֱדוֹם בְּיָדוֹ – **and I delivered the kings of Edom into his hand,** hoping that this victory would prove to him that My power was greater than that of the pagan deities worshiped by the Edomites. הֵבִיא אֱלֹהֵיהֶם וְהִשְׁתַּחֲוָה לָהֶם – **Instead, he brought their gods** back to Judah **and bowed down to them!** שֶׁנֶּאֱמַר ,,וַיְהִי אַחֲרֵי בוֹא אֲמַצְיָהוּ מֵהַכּוֹת אֶת־אֲדוֹמִים וַיָּבֵא אֶת־אֱלֹהֵי בְּנֵי שֵׂעִיר וַיַּעֲמִידֵם לוֹ לֵאלֹהִים וְלִפְנֵיהֶם יִשְׁתַּחֲוֶה וְלָהֶם יְקַטֵּר״ – **As it says:** ***Now it was after Amatziahu returned from smiting the Edomites,*** – ***that he brought the idols of the Seirites*** – ***and installed them as his gods;*** – ***before them he prostrated himself, and to them he made sacrifice.***[14] אָמַר רַב פָּפָּא – **Rav Pappa said:** הַיְינוּ דְּאָמְרֵי אִינָשֵׁי – **This is the meaning of the popular adage:**[15] בָּכֵיי לֵיהּ לְמָר דְּלָא יָדַע – **"I cried to the master, but he did not realize it;** חָיִיכֵי לְמָר דְּלָא יָדַע – **I smiled at the master, but he did not realize it;**[16] וַוי לֵיהּ לְמָר דְּלָא יָדַע בֵּין טָב לְבִישׁ – **woe to a master who does not realize** what is happening, **whether** that happening is **good or bad!"**

The last of the four interpretations, dealing with the fall of Jerusalem at the time of Tzidkiah:

,,וַיָּבֹאוּ כֹּל שָׂרֵי מֶלֶךְ־בָּבֶל וַיֵּשְׁבוּ בְּשַׁעַר הַתָּוֶךְ״ – Scripture states: ***All the officers of the king of Babylon entered [Jerusalem] and sat***

NOTES

6. Ibid. 28:1; see also 49:34.

Ordinarily, Scripture describes the beginning of a reign by saying "In the first year of King So-and-so." Why in regard to these two kings does Scripture depart from its normal usage and employ the word בְּרֵאשִׁית, the same term used in *Genesis* 1:1 in describing the creation of the world? (*Rashi*). [In fact, the *only* occurrences of the word בְּרֵאשִׁית in Scripture other than in *Genesis* are in connection with these two kings. Moreover, the use of the word בְּרֵאשִׁית is even more strange in the case of Tzidkiah in that it does not indicate the actual beginning of the reign, for the end of that verse clearly states that the incident described there occurred in the *fourth* year of Tzidkiah's reign.]

7. The use of the word בְּרֵאשִׁית could indicate *the very inception* of kingship, just as it indicates in *Genesis* the very beginning of Creation. But the institution of kingship certainly predated Yehoiakim and Tzidkiah! (*Maharsha*).

8. I.e. the word בְּרֵאשִׁית indicates that Yehoiakim was so wicked that God wanted to "go back to the Beginning"; that is, to destroy the world and return it to its pre-Creation state (*Rashi*).

9. Literally: His mind cooled.

Yehoiakim succeeded his father Yoshiahu as king of Judah. Yoshiahu had been a very righteous king, and had influenced his subjects to follow his example. Yehoiakim, by contrast, promoted idolatry and persecuted the true prophets. In addition, Yehoiakim rebelled against King Nebuchadnezzar of Babylonia, who thereupon besieged Jerusalem and compelled its capitulation. Yehoiakim was captured and died in captivity, and a few months later the elite of the kingdom, including the Sanhedrin and the leading Torah scholars (referred to as "the craftsmen and the locksmiths" in *II Kings* 24:14), were exiled to Babylonia together with Yehoiakim's son, Yehoiachin (ibid ch. 24). The removal of these Torah scholars had a disastrous effect upon the spiritual state of the populace, and in the subsequent ten last years of its existence, during the reign of King Tzidkiah, the people of the Kingdom of Judah deteriorated into idolatry.

The point is that during Yehoiakim's reign, due to the influence of the Torah scholars, the populace remained faithful to the Torah. Because of this, although God was very angry because of Yehoiakim's sins, He did not unleash His anger (see *Rashi*).

10. Whereas during the reign of Yehoiakim it was the king who was wicked and the people were righteous, during the reign of Tzidkiah, after the exile of the Torah scholars, the situation was reversed – the people were wicked and the king, Tzidkiah himself, was righteous. It was on Tzidkiah's account that God did not unleash His anger upon the land (*Rashi*).

11. *II Kings* 24:19.

12. *Proverbs* 29:9. [The translation of נַחַת as "fear" follows *Rashi* here. *Rashi* ad loc., however, translates it as "satisfaction." See also *Yad Ramah*.]

13. *II Chronicles* 28:23.

14. Ibid. 25:14. Thus, these kings were incorrigible; no matter what God did to move them to repentance, they persisted in their idolatry. This is the meaning of the verse in *Proverbs* quoted by R' Yochanan in the name of R' Shimon ben Yochai: *When a wise man* (God, who is called "a man" in *Exodus* 15:3 – *God is a Man of war*) *contends with a fool*, such as Achaz and Amatziah, *He may rage* at him, as He did at Achaz, who was wicked, causing him to be defeated by Damascus, *or He may smile* at him, as He did upon Amatziah, who was a good king and to whom He therefore granted victory over Edom, *yet there will be no fear,* for Achaz did not repent and Amatziah turned to idolatry; neither of them learned from their experience (*Rashi*; *Maharsha*).

15. Literally: what people say.

16. [Translation follows text found in *Ein Yaakov*, which has וְלָא in place of דְּלָא.]

בגלל מנשה דלא עבד תשובה א"ר יוחנן כל האומר מנשה אין לו חלק לעוה"ב מרפה ידיהן של בעלי תשובה דתני תנא קמיה דר' יוחנן מנשה עשה תשובה (ל)שלשים ושלש שנים דכתיב א) בן שתים עשרה שנה מנשה במלכו וחמשים וחמש שנה מלך בירושלים ויעש (הרע) [אשרה] כאשר עשה אחאב מלך ישראל כמה מלך אחאב עשרין ותרתין שנין מנשה כמה מלך חמשים וחמש דל מינייהו עשרים ותרתין פשו להו תלתין ותלת א"ר יוחנן משום רשב"י מאי דכתי' ב) וישמע אליו [א] ויחתר לו ויעתר לו מיבעי ליה מלמד שעשה לו הקב"ה כמין מחתרת ברקיע כדי לקבלו בתשובה מפני מדת הדין ג) וא"ר יוחנן משום רשב"י מאי דכתיב ג) בראשית ממלכות יהויקים בן יאשיהו וכתיב ד) בראשית ממלכת צדקיה וכי עד האידנא לא הוו מלכי אלא בקש הקב"ה להחזיר את העולם כולו לתוהו ובוהו בשביל יהויקים נסתכל בדורו ונתקררה דעתו בקש הקב"ה להחזיר את העולם כולו לתוהו ובוהו בשביל דורו של צדקיה נסתכל בצדקיה ונתקררה דעתו בצדקיה נמי כתיב ה) ויעש הרע בעיני ה' שהיה בידו למחות ולא מיחה וא"ר יוחנן משום רשב"י מאי דכתיב ו) איש חכם נשפט את איש אויל ורגז ושחק ואין נחת אמר הקב"ה כעסתי על אחז ונתתיו ביד מלכי דמשק זיבח וקיטר [לאלהיהם] שנאמר ז) ויזבח לאלהי דרמשק המכים בו ויאמר [כי] אלהי מלכי ארם הם מעזרים אותם להם אזבח ויעזרוני והם היו [לו] להכשילו ולכל ישראל שחקתי עם אמציה ונתתי מלכי אדום בידו הביא אלהיהם והשתחוה להם שנאמר ח) ויהי אחרי (כן) בא אמציה מהכות את אדומים ויבא את אלהי בני שעיר ויעמידם [לו] לאלהים ולפניהם ישתחוה ולהם יקטר אמר רב פפא היינו דאמרי אינשי בכיי ליה למר דלא ידע חייכי למר דלא ידע ווי ליה ג) למר דלא ידע בין טב לביש ט) ויבאו כל [שרי] מלך בבל (ויבאו) [וישבו] בשער התוך א"ר יוחנן משום רשב"י מקום שמחתכין בו הלכות אמר רב פפא היינו ד) דאמרי אינשי באתרא דמריה תלא ליה זייניה תמן קולבא רעיא קולתיה תלא (סימן על שדה בתים לא תאונה) אמר רב חסדא אמר רבי ירמיה בר אבא מאי דכתיב י) על שדה איש עצל עברתי ועל כרם אדם חסר לב והנה עלה כולו קמשונים כסו פניו חרולים וגדר אבניו נהרסה על שדה איש עצל עברתי זה אחז ועל כרם אדם חסר לב זה מנשה והנה עלה כולו קמשונים זה אמון כסו פניו חרולים זה יהויקים וגדר אבניו נהרסה זה צדקיהו שנחרב בית המקדש בימיו ו) ואמר רב חסדא אמר רבי ירמיה בר אבא ארבע כיתות אין מקבלות פני שכינה כת לצים כת שקרנים כת חניפים כת מספרי לשון הרע כת לצים דכתיב כ) משך ידו את לוצצים כת שקרנים דכתיב ל) דובר שקרים לא יכון לנגד עיני כת חניפים דכתיב מ) כי לא לפניו חנף יבוא כת מספרי לשון הרע דכתיב נ) כי לא אל חפץ רשע אתה לא יגורך רע ז) צדיק אתה ולא יהיה במגורך רע ז) ואמר רב חסדא אמר רבי ירמיה בר אבא מאי דכתיב ס) לא תאונה אליך רעה ונגע לא יקרב באהלך לא תאונה אליך רעה שלא ישלוט ח) בהן יצר הרע ונגע לא יקרב באהלך ט) שלא תמצא אשתך ספק נדה בשעה שתבא מן הדרך דבר אחר לא תאונה אליך רעה שלא יבעתוך חלומות רעים והרהורים רעים ונגע לא יקרב באהלך שלא יהא לך בן או תלמיד שמקדיח תבשילו ברבים עד כאן ברכו אביו מכאן ואילך ברכתו אמו ע) כי מלאכיו יצוה לך לשמרך בכל דרכיך על כפים ישאונך וגו' על שחל ופתן תדרוך וגו' עד כאן ברכתו אמו מכאן ואילך ברכתו שמים

כי

רש"י

בגלל מנשה דלא עשה תשובה. והמשיכן כולן אחריו: כאשר עשה אחאב. דמשמע כשיעור השנים שחטא אחאב במלכו חטא מנשה והיינו כ"ב שנה שחטא בהם כנגד כ"ב שנים שמלך אחאב: פשו להו ל"ג. שעשה תשובה: וישמע אליו ויחתר לו. ומבחוץ כתיב ויעתר לו כך שמעתי: מדת הדין. היתה מעכבת שלא להקביל פני מנשה בתשובה ועשה הקב"ה מחתרת ברקיע ופשט ידו וקבלו בלא ידיעת מדת הדין: מאי דכתיב בראשית ממלכות יהויקים ובראשית ממלכת צדקיה. מ"ט כתיב בהני בראשית יותר מאחריני: וכי עד האידנא לא הוו מלכי. ואי משום תחלת ממלכתו קאמר ה"ל למכתב בשנה ראשונה למלכותו אלא להכי שני קרא בדיבוריה וכתיב בראשית ללמדך מעשה בראשית היה בימי יהויקים שבקש הקב"ה להחזיר את עולמו לתהו ובהו כמו שהיה מבראשית: כיון שנסתכל בדורו. של יהויקים שהיו צדיקים שעדיין לא גלו החרש והמסגר: דורו של צדקיהו. היו רשעים שכל הצדיקים הגלו כבר עם יהויכין: איש חכם נשפט. זה הקב"ה שנקרא ה' איש מלחמה (שמות טו) איש אויל אלו מלכים שבסמוך אחז ואמציה ורגז ושחק ואין נחת בין שהוא כועס עמהם בין שהוא שוחק עמהם אינן יראין מלפניו ואינם חתים לחזור למוטב: בכי ליה למר כו'. לאו דוקא נקט מר אלא משום דהכי מילי דאינשי כשהוא חכם כשהוא רוצה להישפט ולהתווכח עמהן בין שהוא שותק עליהם בין שהוא כועס עמהן אינם יראים מלפניו ואינם חתים לחזור למוטב: מקום שהיו מחתכין בו. ודורשין הלכות נהפך למושב לצים של שרי מלך בבל: בשער התוך. לשון חותך והיינו בהר הבית ובעזרה ששם היו יושבים סנהדרין וכדאמר בעלמא (לעיל דף פו:) ג' בתי דינין היו שם אחד בלשכת הגזית ואחד על פתח העזרה ואחד על פתח הר הבית: קולתיה תלא. כלומר במקום שהיו חותכין הלכות בו דנין שרי בבל דינים שלהם: באתרא דמריה תלא זייניה. מקום שהאדון תולה כליו: קולבא רעיא (א). נבל רועה: קולתיה תלא. כדו תלה לשם כמו (בראשית כד) כדה דמתרגמינן קולתא. ל"א קודתיה מקדתו כמו (סוטה דף ט.) מקדה של חרס: והנה עלה כולו קמשונים זה אמון. שהעלה שממית ע"ג המזבח לקמן: כסו פניו חרולים זה יהויקים. שכסה פניו מאורו של הקב"ה כדאמר לקמן כלום אנו צריכים אלא לאורו יטול אורו: על שדה איש עצל עברתי זה אחז. ולהכי קרי ליה עצל שחתם את התורה ובטל את העבודה לקמן: ועל כרם אדם חסר לב זה מנשה. שקדר אזכרות והרס את המזבח (ל"א) חרולים אורטיג"ש: זה צדקיה. שהיה צדיק ונהרס בית המקדש בימיו: משך ידו את לוצצים. משך הקב"ה את ידיו מן הלוצצים שלא להתקרב אצלם: לא יגורך רע. היינו מספרי לשון הרע דכתיב בתריה תאבד דוברי כזב איש דמים וגו' ועוד דכתיב בתריה קרבם הוות קבר פתוח גרונם וגו': שלא תמצא אשתך ספק נדה וכו'. והיינו באהלך באשתך כדאמרי' ל) אין אהלו אלא אשה ס) ובשעה שאדם בא מן הדרך קשה לו כשימצא את אשתו ספק נדה יותר מנדה ודאית שעל ספק הוא מיצר ויצרו תקפו ואומר טהורה היא ועל חנם אני מונע: עד כאן ברכו אביו. דוד אביו לשלמה בנו מסתמא לפי ענין הברכות יש לידע סדור ברכות שכן דרך האב בדברים האלו בספק נדה ובילה"ר ובהרהורים רעים ובבנים ותלמידים שלא יקדיחו תבשילם ברבים אבל אשה אינה נותנת דעת בכך אלא מהמרכת הלב שיש לה מתפללת על בנה שינצל מאבן נגף ומרוחין ושדין לפיכך קא דריש לפי הענין שאלו ברכות ברכתו אמו כי מלאכיו יצוה לך מ"ר ועוד משום דכתיב כי מלאכיו משמע ליה דסליק ענין אחד דברכה ומכי מלאכיו עד כי בי חשק סליק חד ענין הלכך מוקים דמי לדמי דע"כ ברכו אביו וכו'. מ"ר:

מסורת הש"ס

א) [בפסוק כתיב ויעתר וכן העתיק לעיל קא: ואפשר דבדברי הימים שהיה לפני רשב"י היה כתוב ויחתר לו עמ"ש תוס' בשבת נה: ד"ה מעבירין כו' וכן מצינו בירושלמי כו' ע"ש], ב) [ערכין יז. ע"ש], ג) למאן רש"ל, ד) ב"מ פד., ה) סוטה מב. ע"ש, ו) [שבת קמט: חגיגה יב: סוטה מב.], ז) [ברכות נה: ע"ש קל"ע], ח) [נ"ל בך], ט) [ב"מ קז.], י) בד"י אין אהלו אלא אשתו, כ) [מועד קטן ז:].

ליקוטי רש"י

מאי דכתיב. ביהויקים ולדקיהו בראשית לפי שביקש הקב"ה להפוך מעשה בראשית בימיהם [ערכין יז.]. איש חכם נשפט. מתוכח עם האויל. ואין נחת. בין מראה לו פנים זועפו' בין שמראהו פנים שוחקו' אין נחת לא בזו ולא בזו אינו מולא קורת רוח מלינו באמליה שהראה לו הקב"ה פנים שוחקות ומסר בידו אדום ובשובו מהכות (דה"ב כה) ויבא את אלהיהם ולהם השתחוה לאחז הראה הקב"ה פנים זועפות ומסרו ביד מלכי ארם ויזבח לאלהי דמשק כי אמר אלהי ארם מעוזרים להם [משלי כט, ט]. באתרא דמריה תלא זייניה כולבא רעיא קולתיה תלא. יתד שהיה הגבור רגיל לתלות בו כלי זיינו הנבל הרועה תרמילו תלה בו[ל"א] בלעז [ב"מ פד:]. קמשונים. קוצים. כסו. נכסו. חרלים. גדולי' מקמשונים והרי הם חדים כקוצים [משלי כד, לא]. משך ידו. הקב"ה מהיות את לוצצים. לא יגורך רע. לא יגור עמך רע וגבי מספרי לשון הרע כתיב דכתיב בההוא פרשתא כי אין בפיהו נכונה וגו' [סוטה מב.]. חנף. המסית חבירו לדרך רע [משלי יא, ט]. לא תאונה. לא תקרה וכן והאלהי' אנה לידו (שמות כא) [תהלים צא, י].

הגהות הב"ח

(א) רש"י ד"ה קולבא רעיא. נ"ב ובב"מ פרק הפועלים גרסינן כלבא רעיא בכ':

תורה אור השלם

א) בֶּן שְׁתֵּים עֶשְׂרֵה שָׁנָה מְנַשֶּׁה בְמָלְכוֹ וַחֲמִשִּׁים וְחָמֵשׁ שָׁנָה מָלַךְ בִּירוּשָׁלָיִם וְשֵׁם אִמּוֹ חֶפְצִי בָהּ: וַיָּשָׁב וַיִּבֶן אֶת הַבָּמוֹת אֲשֶׁר אִבַּד חִזְקִיָּהוּ אָבִיו וַיָּקֶם מִזְבְּחֹת לַבַּעַל וַיַּעַשׂ אֲשֵׁרָה כַּאֲשֶׁר עָשָׂה אַחְאָב מֶלֶךְ יִשְׂרָאֵל וַיִּשְׁתַּחוּ לְכָל צְבָא הַשָּׁמַיִם וַיַּעֲבֹד אֹתָם: [מלכים ב' כא, א,ג]

ב) וַיִּתְפַּלֵּל אֵלָיו וַיֵּעָתֶר לוֹ וַיִּשְׁמַע תְּחִנָּתוֹ וַיְשִׁיבֵהוּ יְרוּשָׁלַיִם לְמַלְכוּתוֹ וַיֵּדַע מְנַשֶּׁה כִּי יְיָ הוּא הָאֱלֹהִים: [דברי הימים ב' לג, יג]

ג) בְּרֵאשִׁית מַמְלְכוּת יְהוֹיָקִים בֶּן יֹאשִׁיָּהוּ מֶלֶךְ יְהוּדָה הָיָה הַדָּבָר הַזֶּה מֵאֵת יְיָ לֵאמֹר: [ירמיה כו, א]

ד) וַיְהִי בַּשָּׁנָה הַהִיא בְּרֵאשִׁית מַמְלֶכֶת צִדְקִיָּה מֶלֶךְ יְהוּדָה בַּשָּׁנָה הָרְבִעִית בַּחֹדֶשׁ הַחֲמִישִׁי אָמַר אֵלַי חֲנַנְיָה בֶן עַזּוּר הַנָּבִיא אֲשֶׁר מִגִּבְעוֹן בְּבֵית יְיָ לְעֵינֵי הַכֹּהֲנִים וְכָל הָעָם לֵאמֹר: [ירמיה כח, א]

ה) וַיַּעַשׂ הָרַע בְּעֵינֵי יְיָ כְּכֹל אֲשֶׁר עָשָׂה יְהוֹיָקִים: [מלכים ב' כד, יט]

ו) אִישׁ חָכָם נִשְׁפָּט אֶת אִישׁ אֱוִיל וְרָגַז וְשָׂחַק וְאֵין נָחַת: [משלי כט, ט]

ז) וַיִּזְבַּח לֵאלֹהֵי דַרְמֶשֶׂק הַמַּכִּים בּוֹ וַיֹּאמֶר כִּי אֱלֹהֵי מַלְכֵי אֲרָם הֵם מַעְזְרִים אוֹתָם לָהֶם אֲזַבֵּחַ וְיַעְזְרוּנִי וְהֵם הָיוּ לוֹ לְהַכְשִׁילוֹ וּלְכָל יִשְׂרָאֵל: [דברי הימים ב' כח, כג]

ח) וַיְהִי אַחֲרֵי בוֹא אֲמַצְיָהוּ מֵהַכּוֹת אֶת אֲדוֹמִים וַיָּבֵא אֶת אֱלֹהֵי בְּנֵי שֵׂעִיר וַיַּעֲמִידֵם לוֹ לֵאלֹהִים וְלִפְנֵיהֶם יִשְׁתַּחֲוֶה וְלָהֶם יְקַטֵּר: [דברי הימים ב' כה, יד]

ט) וַיָּבֹאוּ כֹּל שָׂרֵי מֶלֶךְ בָּבֶל וַיֵּשְׁבוּ בְּשַׁעַר הַתָּוֶךְ נֵרְגַל שַׂר אֶצֶר סַמְגַּר נְבוּ שַׂר סְכִים רַב סָרִיס נֵרְגַל שַׂר אֶצֶר רַב מָג וְכָל שְׁאֵרִית שָׂרֵי מֶלֶךְ בָּבֶל: [ירמיה לט, ג]

י) עַל שְׂדֵה אִישׁ עָצֵל עָבַרְתִּי וְעַל כֶּרֶם אָדָם חֲסַר לֵב: וְהִנֵּה עָלָה כֻלּוֹ קִמְּשֹׂנִים כָּסּוּ פָנָיו חֲרֻלִּים וְגֶדֶר אֲבָנָיו נֶהֱרָסָה: [משלי כד, ל-לא]

כ) יוֹם מַלְכֵּנוּ הֶחֱלוּ שָׂרִים חֲמַת מִיָּיִן מָשַׁךְ יָדוֹ אֶת לֹצְצִים: [הושע ז, ה]

ל) לֹא יֵשֵׁב בְּקֶרֶב בֵּיתִי עֹשֵׂה רְמִיָּה דֹּבֵר שְׁקָרִים לֹא יִכּוֹן לְנֶגֶד עֵינָי: [תהלים קא, ז] מ) גַּם הוּא לִי לִישׁוּעָה כִּי לֹא לְפָנָיו חָנֵף יָבוֹא: [איוב יג, טז] נ) כִּי לֹא אֵל חָפֵץ רֶשַׁע אָתָּה לֹא יְגֻרְךָ רָע: [תהלים ה, ה] ס) לֹא תְאֻנֶּה אֵלֶיךָ רָעָה וְנֶגַע לֹא יִקְרַב בְּאָהֳלֶךָ: [תהלים צא, י] ע) כִּי מַלְאָכָיו יְצַוֶּה לָּךְ לִשְׁמָרְךָ בְּכָל דְּרָכֶיךָ: עַל כַּפַּיִם יִשָּׂאוּנְךָ פֶּן תִּגֹּף בָּאֶבֶן רַגְלֶךָ: עַל שַׁחַל וָפֶתֶן תִּדְרֹךְ תִּרְמֹס כְּפִיר וְתַנִּין: [תהלים צא, יא-יג]

down at the "tavech" gate.[17] אָמַר רַבִּי יוֹחָנָן מִשּׁוּם רַבִּי שִׁמְעוֹן בֶּן יוֹחַי – **R' Yochanan said in the name of R' Shimon ben Yochai:** מָקוֹם שֶׁמְּחַתְּכִין בּוֹ הֲלָכוֹת – The "tavech gate" was **a place where they decide (*mechatchin*) the laws,** i.e. the meeting-place of the Sanhedrin.[18] אָמַר רַב פָּפָּא – **Rav Pappa said:** הַיְינוּ דְּאָמְרֵי אִינְשֵׁי – **This is an example of the popular adage:** בְּאַתְרָא דְּמָרֵיהּ תָּלָא לֵיהּ זַיְינֵיהּ – **"On the spot where the master** formerly **hung his weapon,** תַּמָּן קוּלְבָּא רַעְיָא קוּלְתֵיהּ תָּלָא – **there the base shepherd** now **hangs his jug."**[19]

In connection with its discussion of the wicked kings of Judah, the Gemara now presents an exegesis of *Proverbs* 24:30-31, the first of three interpretations of Scriptural passages by Rav Chisda in the name of R' Yirmiyah bar Abba:

(סִימָן עַל שְׂדֵה בָּתִּים לֹא תְאוּנֶּה) – **A mnemonic: By the field of houses there shall not befall.)**[20] אָמַר רַב חִסְדָּא אָמַר רַבִּי יִרְמְיָה בַּר אַבָּא – **Rav Chisda said in the name of R' Yirmiyah bar Abba:** מַאי דִּכְתִיב ,,עַל־שְׂדֵה אִישׁ־עָצֵל עָבַרְתִּי – **What is the meaning of that which is written:**[21] ***I passed by the field of a lazy man,*** וְעַל־כֶּרֶם אָדָם חֲסַר־לֵב – ***by the vineyard of a man who lacks sense.*** וְהִנֵּה עָלָה כֻלּוֹ קִמְּשׂוֹנִים – ***It was all overgrown with thorns;*** כָּסּוּ פָנָיו חֲרֻלִּים – ***its face was covered with nettles,*** וְגֶדֶר אֲבָנָיו נֶהֱרָסָה" – ***and its stone fence lay in ruins?*** ,,עַל־שְׂדֵה אִישׁ־עָצֵל עָבַרְתִּי" זֶה אָחָז – ***I passed by the field of a lazy man*** **– this refers to Achaz;**[22] ,,וְעַל־כֶּרֶם אָדָם חֲסַר־לֵב" זֶה מְנַשֶּׁה – ***by the vineyard of a man who lacks sense*** **– this refers to Menasheh;**[23] ,,וְהִנֵּה עָלָה כֻלּוֹ קִמְּשׂוֹנִים" זֶה אָמוֹן – ***it was all overgrown with thorns*** **– this refers to Amon,** the wicked son and successor of Menasheh;[24] ,,כָּסּוּ פָנָיו חֲרֻלִּים" זֶה יְהוֹיָקִים – ***its face was covered with nettles*** **– this refers to Yehoiakim;**[25] ,,וְגֶדֶר אֲבָנָיו נֶהֱרָסָה" זֶה צִדְקִיָּהוּ – ***and its stone fence lay in ruins*** **– this refers to Tzidkiahu,** שֶׁנֶּחֱרַב בֵּית הַמִּקְדָּשׁ בְּיָמָיו – **in whose days the Temple** (the *stone fence*) **was destroyed.**[26]

The second of the three interpretations:

וְאָמַר רַב חִסְדָּא אָמַר רַבִּי יִרְמְיָה בַּר אַבָּא – **And Rav Chisda said in the name of R' Yirmiyah bar Abba:** אַרְבַּע כִּיתּוֹת אֵין מְקַבְּלוֹת פְּנֵי שְׁכִינָה – **Four classes of sinners do not receive the Divine Presence:**[27] כַּת לֵצִים – **the class of scoffers,** כַּת שַׁקְרָנִים – **the class of liars,** כַּת חֲנֵיפִים – **the class of flatterers,**[28] כַּת מְסַפְּרֵי לָשׁוֹן הָרָע – **and the class of those who speak *lashon hara.***[29] כַּת לֵצִים דִּכְתִיב ,,מָשַׁךְ יָדוֹ אֶת־לֹצְצִים" – **The class of scoffers – as it is written: *He withdrew His hand from scoffers;***[30] כַּת שַׁקְרָנִים דִּכְתִיב ,,דֹּבֵר שְׁקָרִים לֹא־יִכּוֹן לְנֶגֶד עֵינָי" – **the class of liars – as it is written:**[31] ***One who tells lies shall not be established before My eyes;*** כַּת חֲנֵיפִים דִּכְתִיב ,,כִּי־לֹא לְפָנָיו חָנֵף יָבוֹא" – **the class of flatterers – as it is written:**[32] ***For before Him no flatterer shall come;*** כַּת מְסַפְּרֵי לָשׁוֹן הָרָע דִּכְתִיב ,,כִּי לֹא אֵל־חָפֵץ רֶשַׁע אָתָּה לֹא יְגֻרְךָ רָע" – **the class of those who speak *lashon hara* – as it is written:**[33] ***For You are not a God who desires wickedness; evil cannot abide with You,*** צַדִּיק אַתָּה וְלֹא יִהְיֶה בִּמְגוּרְךָ רָע – which means: **You,** God, **are righteous; therefore, an evil one,** i.e. one who speaks evil, **shall not be** allowed **in Your abode.**[34]

The last of the three interpretations:

וְאָמַר רַב חִסְדָּא אָמַר רַבִּי יִרְמְיָה בַּר אַבָּא – **And Rav Chisda said in the name of R' Yirmiyah bar Abba:** מַאי דִּכְתִיב ,,לֹא־תְאֻנֶּה אֵלֶיךָ רָעָה וְנֶגַע לֹא־יִקְרַב בְּאָהֳלֶךָ" – **What is the meaning of that which is written:**[35] ***No evil will befall you, nor will any plague come near your tent?*** ,,לֹא־תְאֻנֶּה אֵלֶיךָ רָעָה" שֶׁלֹּא יִשְׁלוֹט בָּהֶן יֵצֶר הָרָע – ***No evil will befall you*** – this means: **May the Evil Inclination not rule over you.**[36] ,,וְנֶגַע לֹא־יִקְרַב בְּאָהֳלֶךָ" שֶׁלֹּא תִּמְצָא אִשְׁתְּךָ סָפֵק נִדָּה בְּשָׁעָה שֶׁתָּבֹא מִן הַדֶּרֶךְ – ***Nor will any plague come***

NOTES

17. *Jeremiah* 39:3. The verse describes an incident during the Babylonian siege of Jerusalem: The city wall was breached on the ninth of Tammuz and the Babylonian generals established their headquarters inside the city, at a place called שַׁעַר הַתָּוֶךְ, which *Targum Yonasan* translates as *the middle gate*. R' Yochanan here interprets the word *tavech* differently.

18. I.e. the Scriptural word הַתָּוֶךְ is interpreted by R' Yochanan to read חתוך (the letter *ches* is similar in sound to the letter *hei*), which means *cutting,* or, in the judicial or legislative sense, deciding the law. This is an obvious reference to the Sanhedrin, the supreme judicial and legislative body. Thus, the verse states that the Babylonian generals established themselves not at one of the gates of Jerusalem, but rather in the precincts of the three Sanhedrins that had offices on the Temple Mount (see *Rashi*).

19. An expression of sad irony: The place once used for honorable purposes is now put to vulgar use. Similarly, the former headquarters of the sublime Sanhedrin is now the site of the Babylonian army camp.

20. It is unclear how the word בָּתִּים, *houses,* stands for the second interpretation (the four classes). Some editions of the Gemara cited by *Dikdukei Soferim* omit the entire mnemonic.

21. *Proverbs* 24:30-31.

22. See 103b note 28.

23. See ibid. note 29.

24. See ibid. note 30.

25. See ibid. note 37.

26. *Maharal* and *Maharsha* explain that the verse describing the ruined farmstead is to be understood as describing a process of progressive decline. The laziness of the farmer led him to neglect the vineyard and allow the walls to become covered with nettles and eventually to crumble. A similar process of progressive decline and of cause-and-effect is discernible among the kings of Judah. Achaz's sabotaging of Torah learning formed the basis for Menasheh's desecrations of Torah scrolls and the Temple Altar, which in turn formed the basis for Amon's still more reprehensible depravities, which in turn made possible Yehoiakim's open blasphemies — all of which are described below — which ultimately led to the Destruction which took place in the reign of Tzidkiah.

27. I.e. even if one has learned much Torah and has performed many good deeds and therefore merits admittance into the World to Come, nevertheless, if he is guilty of any of these four sins he will not be privileged to behold the Divine Presence through the אַסְפַּקְלַרְיָא הַמְּאִירָה, *the clear screen* (*Yad Ramah*). [For a definition of this term see 97b note 41.]

Maharsha (*Sotah* 42a) notes that the four classes of people enumerated here have in common the misuse of language.

See *Shaarei Teshuvah* III:172-231, where each of these four classes is subdivided into various categories and is analyzed at length.

28. The term "flatterer" refers to one who attempts to curry favor with wrongdoers by praising or otherwise showing approval of them or their deeds, or refrains from rebuking such people (see *Shaarei Teshuvah* 3:187-199). It does not include one who flatters good people either to encourage them in their ways or to boost their self-image.

29. *Lashon hara* (evil speech) is the term used for disparaging statements made about another person.

30. *Hosea* 7:5.

31. *Psalms* 101:7.

32. *Job* 13:16.

33. *Psalms* 5:5.

34. I.e. the last part of the verse, *evil cannot abide with You,* is understood here to refer to those who speak *lashon hara*. This is borne out by the subsequent passages in this psalm (v. 7): *May You doom the speakers of deception, a bloodthirsty and deceitful man . . .,* and (v. 10): *For there is no sincerity on their lips . . . their throat is an open grave; their tongue slippery* (*Rashi;* see also *Yad Ramah* and *Margaliyos HaYam.*).

35. Ibid. 91:10. As will be seen below, Rav Chisda takes the verse to be a record of David's fatherly blessings to his son Solomon.

36. Translation follows *Mesoras HaShas* who emends בָּהֶן to בְּךָ.

בגלל מנשה דלא עבד תשובה א"ר יוחנן כל האומר מנשה אין לו חלק לעוה"ב מרפה ידיהן של בעלי תשובה דתני תנא קמיה דר' יוחנן מנשה עשה תשובה (ל)שלשים ושלש שנים דכתיב א) בן שתים עשרה שנה מנשה במלכו וחמשים וחמש שנה מלך בירושלים ויעש (הרע) [אשרה] כאשר עשה אחאב מלך ישראל כמה מלך אחאב עשרין ותרתין שנין מנשה כמה מלך חמשים וחמש דל מינייהו עשרים ותרתין פשו להו תלתין ותלת א"ר יוחנן משום רשב"י מאי דכתי' ב) וישמע אליו א) ויחתר לו ויעתר לו מיבעי ליה מלמד שעשה לו הקב"ה כמין מחתרת ברקיע כדי לקבלו בתשובה מפני מדת הדין ג) וא"ר יוחנן משום רשב"י מאי דכתיב ג) בראשית ממלכות יהויקים בן יאשיהו וכתיב ד) בראשית ממלכת צדקיה וכי עד האידנא לא הוו מלכי אלא בקש הקב"ה להחזיר את העולם כולו לתוהו ובוהו בשביל יהויקים נסתכל בדורו ונתקררה דעתו בקש הקב"ה להחזיר את העולם כולו לתוהו ובוהו בשביל דורו של צדקיה נסתכל בצדקיה ונתקררה דעתו בצדקיה נמי כתיב ה) ויעש הרע בעיני ה' שהיה בידו למחות ולא מיחה וא"ר יוחנן משום רשב"י מאי דכתיב ו) איש חכם נשפט את איש אויל ורגז ושחק ואין נחת אמר הקב"ה כעסתי על אחז ונתתיו ביד מלכי דמשק זיבח וקיטר [לאלהיהם] שנאמר ז) ויזבח לאלהי דרמשק המכים בו ויאמר [כי] אלהי מלכי ארם הם מעזרים אותם להם אזבח ויעזרוני והם היו [לו] להכשילו ולכל ישראל שחקתי עם אמציה ונתתי מלכי אדום בידו הביא אלהיהם והשתחוה להם שנאמר ח) ויהי אחרי (כן) בא אמציה מהכות את אדומים ויבא את אלהי בני שעיר ויעמידם [לו] לאלהים ולפניהם ישתחוה ולהם יקטר אמר רב פפא היינו דאמרי אינשי בכיי ליה למר דלא ידע חייכי למר דלא ידע ווי ליה ד) למר דלא ידע בין טב לביש ט) ויבאו כל [שרי] מלך בבל (ויבאו) [וישבו] בשער התוך א"ר יוחנן משום רשב"י מקום שמחתכין בו הלכות אמר רב פפא היינו ז) דאמרי אינשי באתרא דמריה תלא ליה זייניה תמן קולבא רעיא קולתיה תלא (סימן על שדה בתים לא תאונה) אמר רב חסדא אמר רבי ירמיה בר אבא מאי דכתיב י) על שדה איש עצל עברתי ועל כרם אדם חסר לב והנה עלה כולו קמשונים כסו פניו חרולים וגדר אבניו נהרסה על שדה איש עצל עברתי זה אחז ועל כרם אדם חסר לב זה מנשה והנה עלה כולו קמשונים זה אמון כסו פניו חרולים זה יהויקים וגדר אבניו נהרסה זה צדקיהו שנחרב בית המקדש בימיו ח) ואמר רב חסדא אמר רבי ירמיה בר אבא ארבע כיתות אין מקבלות פני שכינה כת לצים כת שקרנים כת חניפים כת מספרי לשון הרע כת לצים דכתיב כ) משך ידו את לוצצים כת שקרנים דכתיב ל) דובר שקרים לא יכון לנגד עיני כת חניפים דכתיב מ) כי לא לפניו חנף יבוא כת מספרי לשון הרע דכתיב נ) כי לא אל חפץ רשע אתה לא יגורך רע ט) צדיק אתה ולא יהיה במגורך רע י) ואמר רב חסדא אמר רבי ירמיה בר אבא מאי דכתיב ס) לא תאונה אליך רעה ונגע לא יקרב באהלך לא תאונה אליך רעה שלא ישלוט כ) בהן יצר הרע ונגע לא יקרב באהלך ט) שלא תמצא אשתך ספק נדה בשעה שתבא מן הדרך דבר אחר לא תאונה אליך רעה שלא יבעתוך חלומות רעים והרהורים רעים ונגע לא יקרב באהלך שלא יהא לך בן או תלמיד שמקדיח תבשילו ברבים עד כאן ברכו אביו מכאן ואילך ברכתו אמו ע) כי מלאכיו יצוה לך לשמרך בכל דרכיך על כפים ישאונך וגו' על שחל ופתן תדרוך וגו' עד כאן ברכתו אמו מכאן ואילך ברכתו שמים

כי

רש"י

בגלל מנשה דלא עשה תשובה. והמשיכן כולן אחריו: כאשר עשה אחאב. דמשמע כשיעור השנים שחטא אחאב במלכו חטא מנשה והיינו כ"ב שנה שחטא בהם כנגד כ"ב שנים שמלך אחאב: פשו להו ל"ג. שעשה תשובה: וישמע אליו ויחתר לו. ומבחוץ כתיב ויעתר לו כך שמעתי: מדת הדין. היתה מעכבת שלא להקביל פני מנשה בתשובה ועשה הקב"ה מחתרת ברקיע ופשט ידו וקבלו בלא ידיעת מדת הדין: מאי דכתיב בראשית ממלכות יהויקים ובראשית ממלכת צדקיה. מ"ט כתיב בהני בראשית יותר מאחריני: וכי עד האידנא לא הוו מלכי. ואי משום תחלת ממלכתו קאמר ה"ל למכתב בשנה ראשונה למלכותו אלא להכי שני קרא בדיבוריה וכתיב בראשית ללמדך מעשה בראשית היה בימי יהויקים שבקש הקב"ה להחזיר את עולמו לתהו ובהו כמו שהיה מבראשית: כיון שנסתכל בדורו. של יהויקים שהיו צדיקים שעדיין לא גלו החרש והמסגר: דורו של צדקיהו. היו רשעים שכל הצדיקים הגלו כבר עם יהויכין: איש חכם נשפט. זה הקב"ה שנקרא ה' איש מלחמה (שמות טו) איש אויל אלו מלכים שבסמוך אחז ואמציה ורגז ושחק ואין נחת בין שהוא כועס עמהם בין שהוא שוחק עמהם אינן יראין מלפניו ואינם חתים לחזור למוטב: בכי ליה למר כו'. לאו דוקא נקט מר אלא משום דהכי מילי דאינשי כשהוא חכם כשהוא רוצה להשפט ולהתווכח עמהן בין שהוא שוחק עליהם בין שהוא כועס עמהן אינם יראים מלפניו ואינם חתים לחזור למוטב: מקום שהיו מחתכין בו. ודורשין הלכות נהפך למושב לגיס של שרי מלך בבל: בשער התוך. לשון חותך והיינו בהר הבית ובעזרה ששם היו יושבים סנהדרין וכדאמר בעלמא (לעיל דף פו:) ג' בתי דינין היו שם אחד בלשכת הגזית ואחד על פתח העזרה ואחד על פתח הר הבית: קולתיה תלא. כלומר במקום שהיו חותכין הלכות בו דנין שרי בבל דינים שלהם: באתרא דמריה תלא זייניה. מקום שהאדון תולה כליו: קולבא רעיא (א). נבל רועה: קולתיה תלא. כדו תלה לשם כמו (בראשית כד) כדה דמתרגמינן קולתא. ל"א קודתיה מקדתו כמו (סוטה דף ט.) מקדה של חרס: והנה עלה כולו קמשונים זה אמון. שהעלה שממית ע"ג המזבח לקמן: כסו פניו חרולים זה יהויקים. שכסה פניו מאורו של הקב"ה כדאמר לקמן כלום אנו צריכים אלא לאורו יטול אורו: על שדה איש עצל עברתי זה אחז. ולהכי קרי ליה עצל שחתם את התורה ובטל את העבודה לקמן: ועל כרם אדם חסר לב זה מנשה. שקדר אזכרות והרס את המזבח (ל"א) חרולים אורטיג"ש: זה צדקיה. שהיה צדיק ונהרס בית המקדש בימיו: משך ידו את לוצצים. משך הקב"ה את ידיו מן הלוצצים שלא להתקרב אצלם: לא יגורך רע. היינו מספרי לשון הרע דכתיב בתריה תאבד דוברי כזב איש דמים וגו' ועוד דכתיב בתריה קבר פתוח גרונם וגו': שלא תמצא אשתך ספק נדה וכו'. והיינו באהלך באשתך כדאמרי' י) אין אהלו אלא אשה כ) ובשעה שאדם בא מן הדרך קשה לו כשימצא את אשתו ספק נדה יותר מנדה ודאית שעל ספק הוא מיצר ויצרו תקפו ואומר טהורה היא ועל אנס אני מוגע: עד כאן ברכו אביו. דוד אביו לשלמה בנו מסתמא לפי ענין הברכות יש לידע סדור ברכות שכן דרך האב בדברים האלו בספק נדה ובילה"ר ובהרהורים רעים ובבנים ותלמידים שלא יקדיחו תבשילם ברבים אבל אשה אינה נותנת דעת בכך אלא מהמרכת הלב שיש לה מתפללת על בנה שינצל מאבן נגף ומרוחין ושדין לפיכך קא דריש לפי הענין שאלו ברכות ברכתו אמו כי מלאכיו יצוה לך מ"ר ועוד משום דכתיב כי מלאכיו משמע ליה דסליק ענין אחד דברכה ומכי מלאכיו עד כי כי חשק סליק חד ענין הלכך מוקים דמי לדמי דע"כ ברכו אביו וכו'. מ"ר:

מסורת הש"ס

א) [בפסוק כתיב ויעתר וכן העתיק לעיל קא: ואפשר דבדברי הימים שהיה לפני רשב"י היה כתוב ויחתר לו עמ"ש תוס' בשבת נה: ד"ה מעבירין כו' וכן מצינו בירושלמי כו' ע"ש], ב) [ערכין יז. ע"ש], ג) למאן רש"ל, ד) ב"מ פד:, ה) סוטה מב. ע"ש, ו) [שבת קמט: חגיגה יב: סוטה מב.], ז) [ברכות נה: ע"ש קל"ע], ח) [צ"ל בך], ט) [ב"מ קז.], י) בד"י אין אהלו אלא אשתו, כ) [מועד קטן ז:].

ליקוטי רש"י

מאי דכתיב. ביהויקים ולדקיהו בראשית לפי שביקש הקב"ה להפוך מעשה בראשית בימיהם [ערכין יז.]. איש חכם נשפט. מתוכח עם האויל. ואין נחת. בין מראהו לו פנים זעופו' בין שמראהו פנים שוחקו' אין נחת לא בזו ולא בזו אינו מוצא קורת רוח מצינו באמציה שהראה לו הקב"ה פנים שוחקות ומסר בידו אדום ובשובו מהכות (דה"ב כה) ויבא את אלהיהם ולהם השתחוה לאחז הראה הקב"ה פנים זועפות ומסרו ביד מלכי ארם ויזבח לאלהי דמשק כי אמר אלהי ארם מעזרים להם [משלי כט, ט]. באתרא דמריה תלא זייניה כולבא רעיא קולתיה תלא. יתד שהיה הגבור רגיל לתלות בו כלי זיינו הנבל הרועה תרמילו תלה בולז"א בלעז [ב"מ פד:]. קמשונים. קוצים. כסו. נכסו. חרלים. גדולי' מקמשונים והרי הם חדים כקוצים [משלי כד, לא]. משך ידו. הקב"ה מהיות את לוצצים. לא יגורך רע. לא יגור עמך רע וגבי מספרי לשון הרע כתיב דכתיב בההוא פרשתא כי אין בפיהו נכונה וגו' [סוטה מב.]. חנף. המסית חבירו בדרך רע [משלי יא, ט]. לא תאנה. לא תקרה וכן והאלהי' אנה לידו (שמות כא) [תהלים צא, י].

הגהות הב"ח

(א) רש"י ד"ה קולבא רעיא. נ"ב ובב"מ פרק הפועלים גרסינן כלבא רעיא בכ':

תורה אור השלם

א) בֶּן שְׁתֵּים עֶשְׂרֵה שָׁנָה מְנַשֶּׁה בְמָלְכוֹ וַחֲמִשִּׁים וְחָמֵשׁ שָׁנָה מָלַךְ בִּירוּשָׁלָיִם וְשֵׁם אִמּוֹ חֶפְצִי בָהּ: וַיָּשָׁב וַיִּבֶן אֶת הַבָּמוֹת אֲשֶׁר אִבַּד חִזְקִיָּהוּ אָבִיו וַיָּקֶם מִזְבְּחֹת לַבַּעַל וַיַּעַשׂ אֲשֵׁרָה כַּאֲשֶׁר עָשָׂה אַחְאָב מֶלֶךְ יִשְׂרָאֵל וַיִּשְׁתַּחוּ לְכָל צְבָא הַשָּׁמַיִם וַיַּעֲבֹד אֹתָם: [מלכים ב' כא, א,ג]

ב) וַיִּתְפַּלֵּל אֵלָיו וַיֵּעָתֶר לוֹ וַיִּשְׁמַע תְּחִנָּתוֹ וַיְשִׁיבֵהוּ יְרוּשָׁלַיִם לְמַלְכוּתוֹ וַיֵּדַע מְנַשֶּׁה כִּי יְיָ הוּא הָאֱלֹהִים: [דברי הימים ב' לג, יג]

ג) בְּרֵאשִׁית מַמְלְכוּת יְהוֹיָקִים בֶּן יֹאשִׁיָּהוּ מֶלֶךְ יְהוּדָה הָיָה הַדָּבָר הַזֶּה מֵאֵת יְיָ לֵאמֹר: [ירמיה כו, א]

ד) וַיְהִי בַּשָּׁנָה הַהִיא בְּרֵאשִׁית מַמְלֶכֶת צִדְקִיָּה מֶלֶךְ יְהוּדָה בַּשָּׁנָה הָרְבִעִית בַּחֹדֶשׁ הַחֲמִישִׁי אָמַר אֵלַי חֲנַנְיָה בֶן עַזּוּר הַנָּבִיא אֲשֶׁר מִגִּבְעוֹן בְּבֵית יְיָ לְעֵינֵי הַכֹּהֲנִים וְכָל הָעָם לֵאמֹר: [ירמיה כח, א]

ה) וַיַּעַשׂ הָרַע בְּעֵינֵי יְיָ כְּכֹל אֲשֶׁר עָשָׂה יְהוֹיָקִים: [מלכים ב' כד, יט]

ו) אִישׁ חָכָם נִשְׁפָּט אֶת אִישׁ אֱוִיל וְרָגַז וְשָׂחַק וְאֵין נָחַת: [משלי כט, ט]

ז) וַיִּזְבַּח לֵאלֹהֵי דַרְמֶשֶׂק הַמַּכִּים בּוֹ וַיֹּאמֶר כִּי אֱלֹהֵי מַלְכֵי אֲרָם הֵם מַעְזְרִים אוֹתָם לָהֶם אֲזַבֵּחַ וְיַעְזְרוּנִי וְהֵם הָיוּ לוֹ לְהַכְשִׁילוֹ וּלְכָל יִשְׂרָאֵל: [דברי הימים ב' כח, כג]

ח) וַיְהִי אַחֲרֵי בוֹא אֲמַצְיָהוּ מֵהַכּוֹת אֶת אֲדוֹמִים וַיָּבֵא אֶת אֱלֹהֵי בְּנֵי שֵׂעִיר וַיַּעֲמִידֵם לוֹ לֵאלֹהִים וְלִפְנֵיהֶם יִשְׁתַּחֲוֶה וְלָהֶם יְקַטֵּר: [דברי הימים ב' כה, יד]

ט) וַיָּבֹאוּ כֹּל שָׂרֵי מֶלֶךְ בָּבֶל וַיֵּשְׁבוּ בְּשַׁעַר הַתָּוֶךְ נֵרְגַל שַׂר אֶצֶר סַמְגַּר נְבוּ שַׂר סְכִים רַב סָרִיס נֵרְגַל שַׂר אֶצֶר רַב מָג וְכָל שְׁאֵרִית שָׂרֵי מֶלֶךְ בָּבֶל: [ירמיה לט, ג]

י) עַל שְׂדֵה אִישׁ עָצֵל עָבַרְתִּי וְעַל כֶּרֶם אָדָם חֲסַר לֵב: וְהִנֵּה עָלָה כֻלּוֹ קִמְּשֹׂנִים כָּסּוּ פָנָיו חֲרֻלִּים וְגֶדֶר אֲבָנָיו נֶהֱרָסָה: [משלי כד, ל-לא]

כ) יוֹם מַלְכֵּנוּ הֶחֱלוּ שָׂרִים חֲמַת מִיָּיִן מָשַׁךְ יָדוֹ אֶת לֹצְצִים: [הושע ז, ה]

ל) לֹא יֵשֵׁב בְּקֶרֶב בֵּיתִי עֹשֵׂה רְמִיָּה דֹּבֵר שְׁקָרִים לֹא יִכּוֹן לְנֶגֶד עֵינָי: [תהלים קא, ז] מ) גַּם הוּא לִי לִישׁוּעָה כִּי לֹא לְפָנָיו חָנֵף יָבוֹא: [איוב יג, טז] נ) כִּי לֹא אֵל חָפֵץ רֶשַׁע אָתָּה לֹא יְגֻרְךָ רָע: [תהלים ה, ה] ס) לֹא תְאֻנֶּה אֵלֶיךָ רָעָה וְנֶגַע לֹא יִקְרַב בְּאָהֳלֶךָ: [תהלים צא, י] ע) כִּי מַלְאָכָיו יְצַוֶּה לָּךְ לִשְׁמָרְךָ בְּכָל דְּרָכֶיךָ: עַל כַּפַּיִם יִשָּׂאוּנְךָ פֶּן תִּגֹּף בָּאֶבֶן רַגְלֶךָ: עַל שַׁחַל וָפֶתֶן תִּדְרֹךְ תִּרְמֹס כְּפִיר וְתַנִּין: [תהלים צא, יא-יג]

near your tent – this means: **May you not find your wife in a doubtful state of *niddah* when you come** home **from** a long journey on **the road.**[37] דָּבָר אַחֵר – **An alternate explanation:** ,,לֹא־תְאֻנֶּה אֵלֶיךָ רָעָה" שֶׁלֹּא יְבַעֲתוּךָ חֲלוֹמוֹת רָעִים וְהִרְהוּרִים רָעִים – ***No evil will befall you*** – this means: **May no bad dreams or bad thoughts terrify you;** ,,וְנֶגַע לֹא־יִקְרַב בְּאָהֳלֶךָ" שֶׁלֹּא יְהֵא לְךָ בֵּן אוֹ תַּלְמִיד שֶׁמַּקְדִּיחַ תַּבְשִׁילוֹ בָּרַבִּים – ***nor will any plague come near your tent*** – this means: **May you not have a son or student who "burns his dish" in public.**[38] עַד כָּאן בֵּרְכוֹ אָבִיו – **Up to this point [Solomon's] father blessed him;** מִכָּאן וְאֵילָךְ בֵּרְכַתּוּ אִמּוֹ – **from this point on his mother blessed him:**[39] ,,כִּי מַלְאָכָיו יְצַוֶּה־לָּךְ לִשְׁמָרְךָ בְּכָל־דְּרָכֶיךָ עַל־כַּפַּיִם יִשָּׂאוּנְךָ וגו׳ עַל־שַׁחַל וָפֶתֶן תִּדְרֹךְ וגו׳ " – ***For [God] will charge His angels for you, to guard you in all your ways. On palms they will carry you,*** *lest you strike your foot against a rock.* ***Upon the lion and the viper you will tread,*** *you will trample the young lion and the serpent.*[40] עַד כָּאן בֵּרְכַתּוּ אִמּוֹ – **Up to this point his mother blessed him;** מִכָּאן וְאֵילָךְ בֵּרְכַתּוּ שָׁמַיִם – **from this point on Heaven** (God) **blessed him.**

NOTES

37. *Your tent* signifies your wife, who is the mainstay of the household, the "tent."

The Torah prohibits marital relations with a *niddah,* a menstruant (*Leviticus* 18:19). When a man returns home from a long journey, and naturally looks forward to being maritally reunited with his wife, he is more distressed to find his wife in a doubtful state of *niddah* than in a definite state: If she were a definite *niddah,* he would resign himself to the fact. But in the case of a doubtful *niddah,* he must abstain from relations because of the possibility that she is in fact a *niddah,* yet he is tempted by his Evil Inclination which argues that in truth she is not a *niddah* and that he is abstaining unnecessarily (*Rashi*; cf. *Rashi* to *Bava Metzia* 107a ד״ה ספק נדה; see also *Pesach Einayim [Chida]*). See also *Maharal.*

38. I.e. a son or student whose public conduct is disreputable. Such a person brings shame to those who bore him and taught him.

The allusion to sons and students is seen in the word אָהֳלֶךָ, *your tent* – i.e. the tent of study [אֹהֶל שֶׁל תּוֹרָה] (*Maharsha*).

39. The blessing found in *Psalms* 91:10, the one just expounded by the Gemara, expresses the wish that Solomon be spared the domination of his Evil Inclination, that he enjoy a wholesome family life, that he be free from impure thought, and that he raise good children and students. Such a blessing, judging by its content, is evidently a fatherly blessing. The content of verses 11-13, by contrast, shows that they are a motherly blessing (*Rashi*), uttered by Solomon's mother Bathsheba.

40. See preceding note. These tender prayers for Solomon's physical safety and comfort are characteristic of a mother's blessing (*Rashi*).

בגלל מנשה דלא עבד תשובה א"ר יוחנן כל האומר מנשה אין לו חלק לעוה"ב מרפה ידיהן של בעלי תשובה דתני תנא קמיה דר' יוחנן מנשה עשה תשובה (ל)שלשים ושלש שנים דכתיב [א] בן שתים עשרה שנה מנשה במלכו וחמשים וחמש שנה מלך בירושלים ויעש (הרע) [אשרה] כאשר עשה אחאב מלך ישראל כמה מלך אחאב עשרין ותרתין שנין מנשה כמה מלך חמשים וחמש דל מינייהו עשרים ותרתין פשו להו תלתין ותלת א"ר יוחנן משום רשב"י מאי דכתי' [ב] וישמע אליו [א] ויחתר לו ויעתר לו מיבעי ליה מלמד שעשה לו הקב"ה כמין מחתרת ברקיע כדי לקבלו בתשובה מפני מדת הדין [ב] וא"ר יוחנן משום רשב"י מאי דכתיב [ג] בראשית ממלכות יהויקים בן יאשיהו וכתיב [ד] בראשית ממלכת צדקיה וכי עד האידנא לא הוו מלכי אלא בקש הקב"ה להחזיר את העולם כולו לתוהו ובוהו בשביל יהויקים נסתכל בדורו ונתקררה דעתו בקש הקב"ה להחזיר את העולם כולו לתוהו ובוהו בשביל דורו של צדקיה נסתכל בצדקיה ונתקררה דעתו בצדקיה נמי כתיב [ה] ויעש הרע בעיני ה' שהיה בידו למחות ולא מיחה וא"ר יוחנן משום רשב"י מאי דכתיב [ו] איש חכם נשפט את איש אויל ורגז ושחק ואין נחת אמר הקב"ה כעסתי על אחז ונתתיו ביד מלכי דמשק זיבח וקיטר [לאלהיהם] שנאמר [ז] ויזבח לאלהי דרמשק המכים בו ויאמר [כי] אלהי מלכי ארם הם מעזרים אותם להם אזבח ויעזרוני והם היו [לו] להכשילו ולכל ישראל שחקתי עם אמציה ונתתי מלכי אדום בידו הביא אלהיהם והשתחוה להם שנאמר [ח] ויהי אחרי (כן) בא אמציה מהכות את אדומים ויבא את אלהי בני שעיר ויעמידם [לו] לאלהים ולפניהם ישתחוה ולהם יקטר אמר רב פפא היינו דאמרי אינשי בכיי ליה למר דלא ידע חייכי למר דלא ידע ווי ליה [ג] למר דלא ידע בין טב לביש [ט] ויבאו כל [שרי] מלך בבל (ויבאו) [וישבו] בשער התוך א"ר יוחנן משום רשב"י מקום שמחתכין בו הלכות אמר רב פפא היינו [ד] דאמרי אינשי באתרא דמריה תלא ליה זייניה תמן קולבא רעיא קולתיה תלא (סימן על שדה בתים לא תאונה) אמר רב חסדא אמר רבי ירמיה בר אבא מאי דכתיב [י] על שדה איש עצל עברתי ועל כרם אדם חסר לב והנה עלה כולו קמשונים כסו פניו חרולים וגדר אבניו נהרסה על שדה איש עצל עברתי זה אחז ועל כרם אדם חסר לב זה מנשה והנה עלה כולו קמשונים זה אמון כסו פניו חרולים זה יהויקים וגדר אבניו נהרסה זה צדקיהו שנחרב בית המקדש בימיו [ה] ואמר רב חסדא אמר רבי ירמיה בר אבא ארבע כיתות אין מקבלות פני שכינה כת לצים כת שקרנים כת חניפים כת מספרי לשון הרע כת לצים דכתיב [כ] משך ידו את לוצצים כת שקרנים דכתיב [ל] דובר שקרים לא יכון לנגד עיני כת חניפים דכתיב [מ] כי לא לפניו חנף יבוא כת מספרי לשון הרע דכתיב [נ] כי לא אל חפץ רשע אתה לא יגורך רע [ו] צדיק אתה ולא יהיה במגורך רע [ז] ואמר רב חסדא אמר רבי ירמיה בר אבא מאי דכתיב [ס] לא תאונה אליך רעה ונגע לא יקרב באהלך לא תאונה אליך רעה שלא ישלוט [ח] בהן יצר הרע ונגע לא יקרב באהלך [ט] שלא תמצא אשתך ספק נדה בשעה שתבא מן הדרך דבר אחר לא תאונה אליך רעה שלא יבעתוך חלומות רעים והרהורים רעים ונגע לא יקרב באהלך שלא יהא לך בן או תלמיד שמקדיח תבשילו ברבים עד כאן ברכו אביו מכאן ואילך ברכתו אמו [ע] כי מלאכיו יצוה לך לשמרך בכל דרכיך על כפים ישאונך וגו' על שחל ופתן תדרוך וגו' עד כאן ברכתו אמו מכאן ואילך ברכתו שמים

כי

רש"י

בגלל מנשה דלא עשה תשובה. והמשיכן כולן אחריו: כאשר עשה אחאב. דמשמע כשיעור השנים שחטא אחאב במלכו חטא מנשה והיינו כ"ב שנה שחטא בהם כנגד כ"ב שנים שמלך אחאב: פשו להו ל"ג. שעשה תשובה: וישמע אליו ויחתר לו. ומבחוץ כתיב ויעתר לו כך שמעתי: מדת הדין. היתה מעכבת שלא להקביל פני מנשה בתשובה ועשה הקב"ה מחתרת ברקיע ופשט ידו וקבלו בלא ידיעת מדת הדין: מאי דכתיב בראשית ממלכות יהויקים ובראשית ממלכת צדקיה. מ"ט כתיב בהני בראשית יותר מאחריני: וכי עד האידנא לא הוו מלכי. ואי משום תחלת ממלכתו קאמר ה"ל למכתב בשנה ראשונה למלכותו אלא להכי שני קרא בדיבוריה וכתיב בראשית ללמדך מעשה בראשית היה בימי יהויקים שבקש הקב"ה להחזיר את עולמו לתהו ובהו כמו שהיה מבראשית: כיון שנסתכל בדורו. של יהויקים שהיו צדיקים שעדיין לא גלו החרש והמסגר: דורו של צדקיהו. היו רשעים שכל הצדיקים הגלו כבר עם יהויכין: איש חכם נשפט. זה הקב"ה שנקרא ה' איש מלחמה (שמות טו) איש אויל אלו מלכים שבסמוך אחז ואמציה ורגז ושחק ואין נחת בין שהוא כועס עמהם בין שהוא שוחק עמהם אינן יראין מלפניו ואינם חוזרים למוטב: בכי ליה למר כו'. לאו דוקא נקט מר אלא משום דהכי מילי דאינשי כשהוא חכם כשהוא רוצה להשפט ולהתווכח עמהן בין שהוא שוחק עליהם בין שהוא כועס עמהן אינם יראים מלפניו ואינם חוזרים לחזור למוטב: מקום שהיו מחתכין בו. ודורשין הלכות נהפך למושב לצים של שרי מלך בבל: בשער התוך. לשון חותך והיינו בהר הבית ובעזרה ששם היו יושבים סנהדרין וכדאמר בעלמא (לעיל דף פו:) ג' בתי דינין היו שם אחד בלשכת הגזית ואחד על פתח העזרה ואחד על פתח הר הבית: קולתיה תלא. כלומר במקום שהיו חותכין הלכות בו דנין שרי בבל דינים שלהם: באתרא דמריה תלא זייניה. מקום שהאדון תולה כליו: קולבא רעיא (א). נבל רועה: קולתיה תלא. כדו תלה לשם כמו (בראשית כד) כדה דמתרגמינן קולתא. ל"א קודתיה מקדתו כמו (סוטה דף ט.) מקדה של חרס: והנה עלה כולו קמשונים זה אמון. שהעלה שממית ע"ג המזבח לקמן: כסו פניו חרולים זה יהויקים. שכסה פניו מאורו של הקב"ה כדאמר לקמן כלום אנו צריכים אלא לאורו יטול אורו: על שדה איש עצל עברתי זה אחז. ולהכי קרי ליה עצל שחתם את התורה ובטל את העבודה לקמן: ועל כרם אדם חסר לב זה מנשה. שקדר אזכרות והרס את המזבח (ל"א) חרולים אורטיג"ש: זה צדקיה. שהיה צדיק ונהרס בית המקדש בימיו: משך ידו את לוצצים. משך הקב"ה את ידיו מן הלוצצים שלא להתקרב אצלם: לא יגורך רע. היינו מספרי לשון הרע דכתיב בתריה תאבד דוברי כזב איש דמים וגו' ועוד דכתיב בתריה קבר פתוח גרונם וגו': שלא תמצא אשתך ספק נדה וכו'. והיינו באהלך באשתך כדאמרי' [י] אין אהלו אלא אשה [כ] ובשעה שאדם בא מן הדרך קשה לו כשימצא את אשתו ספק נדה יותר מנדה ודאית שעל ספק הוא מיצר ויצרו תקפו ואומר טהורה היא ועל חנם אני מונע: עד כאן ברכו אביו. דוד אביו לשלמה בנו מסתמא לפי ענין הברכות יש לידע סדור ברכות שכן דרך האב בדברים האלו בספק נדה ובילה"ר ובהרהורים רעים ובבנים ותלמידים שלא יקדיחו תבשילם ברבים אבל אשה אינה נותנת דעת בכך אלא מהמרכת הלב שיש לה מתפללת על בנה שינצל מאבן נגף ומרוחין ושדין לפיכך קא דריש לפי הענין שאלו ברכות ברכתו אמו כי מלאכיו יצוה לך מ"ר ועוד משום דכתיב כי מלאכיו משמע ליה דסליק ענין אחד דברכה ומכי מלאכיו עד כי בי חשק סליק חד ענין הלכך מוקים דמי לדמי דע"כ ברכו אביו וכו'. מ"ר:

מסורת הש"ס

א) [בפסוק כתיב ויעתר וכן העתיק לעיל קא: ואפשר דבדברי הימים שהיה לפני רשב"י היה כתוב ויחתר לו עמ"ש תוס' בשבת נה: ד"ה מעבירין כו' וכן מלינו בירושלמי כו' ע"ש], ב) [ערכין יז. ע"ש], ג) למאן רש"ל, ד) ב"מ פד:, ה) סוטה מב. ע"ש, ו) [שבת קמט: חגיגה יב: סוטה מב:], ז) [ברכות נה: ע"ש קל"ע], ח) [נ"ל בך], ט) [ב"מ קז.], י) כד"י אין אהלו אלא אשתו, כ) [מועד קטן ז:].

ליקוטי רש"י

מאי דכתיב. ביהויקים ולדקיהו בראשית לפי שביקש הקב"ה להפוך מעשה בראשית בימיהם [ערכין יז.]. איש חכם נשפט. מתוכח עם האויל. ואין נחת. בין מראה לו פנים זעופו' בין שמראהו פנים שוחקו' אין נחת לא בזו ולא בזו אינו מוצא קורת רוח מלינו באמציה שהראה לו הקב"ה פנים שוחקות ומסר בידו אדום ובשובו מהכות (דה"ב כה) ויבא את אלהיהם ולהם השתחוה לאחז הראה הקב"ה פנים זועפות ומסרו ביד מלכי ארם ויזבח לאלהי דמשק כי אמר אלהי ארם מעזרים להם [משלי כט, ט]. באתרא דמריה תלא זייניה כולבא רעיא קולתיה תלא. יתד שהיה הגבור רגיל לתלות בו כלי זיינו הנבל הרועה תרמילו תלה בולז"א בלעז [ב"מ פד:]. קמשונים. קוצים. כסו. נכסו. חרלים. גדולי' מקמשונים והרי הם חדים כקולים [משלי כד, לא]. משך ידו. הקב"ה מהיות את לוצצים. לא יגורך רע. לא יגור עמך רע וגבי מספרי לשון הרע כתיב דכתיב בההוא פרשתא כי אין בפיהו נכונה וגו' [סוטה מב.]. חנף. המסית חבירו בדרך רע [משלי יא, ט]. לא תאנה. לא תקרה וכן והאלהי' אנה לידו (שמות כא) [תהלים צא, י].

הגהות הב"ח

(א) רש"י ד"ה קולבא רעיא. נ"ב ובב"מ פרק הפועלים גרסינן כלבא רעיא בכ':

תורה אור השלם

א) בֶּן שְׁתֵּים עֶשְׂרֵה שָׁנָה מְנַשֶּׁה בְמָלְכוֹ וַחֲמִשִּׁים וְחָמֵשׁ שָׁנָה מָלַךְ בִּירוּשָׁלָיִם וְשֵׁם אִמּוֹ חֶפְצִי בָהּ: וַיָּשָׁב וַיִּבֶן אֶת הַבָּמוֹת אֲשֶׁר אִבַּד חִזְקִיָּהוּ אָבִיו וַיָּקֶם מִזְבְּחֹת לַבַּעַל וַיַּעַשׂ אֲשֵׁרָה כַּאֲשֶׁר עָשָׂה אַחְאָב מֶלֶךְ יִשְׂרָאֵל וַיִּשְׁתַּחוּ לְכָל צְבָא הַשָּׁמַיִם וַיַּעֲבֹד אֹתָם: [מלכים ב' כא, א,ג]

ב) וַיִּתְפַּלֵּל אֵלָיו וַיֵּעָתֶר לוֹ וַיִּשְׁמַע תְּחִנָּתוֹ וַיְשִׁיבֵהוּ יְרוּשָׁלַיִם לְמַלְכוּתוֹ וַיֵּדַע מְנַשֶּׁה כִּי יְיָ הוּא הָאֱלֹהִים: [דברי הימים ב' לג, יג]

ג) בְּרֵאשִׁית מַמְלְכוּת יְהוֹיָקִים בֶּן יֹאשִׁיָּהוּ מֶלֶךְ יְהוּדָה הָיָה הַדָּבָר הַזֶּה מֵאֵת יְיָ לֵאמֹר: [ירמיה כו, א]

ד) וַיְהִי בַּשָּׁנָה הַהִיא בְּרֵאשִׁית מַמְלֶכֶת צִדְקִיָּה מֶלֶךְ יְהוּדָה בַּשָּׁנָה הָרְבִעִית בַּחֹדֶשׁ הַחֲמִישִׁי אָמַר אֵלַי חֲנַנְיָה בֶן עַזּוּר הַנָּבִיא אֲשֶׁר מִגִּבְעוֹן בְּבֵית יְיָ לְעֵינֵי הַכֹּהֲנִים וְכָל הָעָם לֵאמֹר: [ירמיה כח, א]

ה) וַיַּעַשׂ הָרַע בְּעֵינֵי יְיָ כְּכֹל אֲשֶׁר עָשָׂה יְהוֹיָקִים: [מלכים ב' כד, יט]

ו) אִישׁ חָכָם נִשְׁפָּט אֶת אִישׁ אֱוִיל וְרָגַז וְשָׂחַק וְאֵין נָחַת: [משלי כט, ט]

ז) וַיִּזְבַּח לֵאלֹהֵי דַרְמֶשֶׂק הַמַּכִּים בּוֹ וַיֹּאמֶר כִּי אֱלֹהֵי מַלְכֵי אֲרָם הֵם מַעְזְרִים אוֹתָם לָהֶם אֲזַבֵּחַ וְיַעְזְרוּנִי וְהֵם הָיוּ לוֹ לְהַכְשִׁילוֹ וּלְכָל יִשְׂרָאֵל: [דברי הימים ב' כח, כג]

ח) וַיְהִי אַחֲרֵי בוֹא אֲמַצְיָהוּ מֵהַכּוֹת אֶת אֲדוֹמִים וַיָּבֵא אֶת אֱלֹהֵי בְּנֵי שֵׂעִיר וַיַּעֲמִידֵם לוֹ לֵאלֹהִים וְלִפְנֵיהֶם יִשְׁתַּחֲוֶה וְלָהֶם יְקַטֵּר: [דברי הימים ב' כה, יד]

ט) וַיָּבֹאוּ כֹּל שָׂרֵי מֶלֶךְ בָּבֶל וַיֵּשְׁבוּ בְּשַׁעַר הַתָּוֶךְ נֵרְגַל שַׂר אֶצֶר סַמְגַּר נְבוּ שַׂר סְכִים רַב סָרִיס נֵרְגַל שַׂר אֶצֶר רַב מָג וְכָל שְׁאֵרִית שָׂרֵי מֶלֶךְ בָּבֶל: [ירמיה לט, ג]

י) עַל שְׂדֵה אִישׁ עָצֵל עָבַרְתִּי וְעַל כֶּרֶם אָדָם חֲסַר לֵב: וְהִנֵּה עָלָה כֻלּוֹ קִמְּשֹׂנִים כָּסּוּ פָנָיו חֲרֻלִּים וְגֶדֶר אֲבָנָיו נֶהֱרָסָה: [משלי כד, ל-לא]

כ) יוֹם מַלְכֵּנוּ הֶחֱלוּ שָׂרִים חֲמַת מִיָּיִן מָשַׁךְ יָדוֹ אֶת לֹצְצִים: [הושע ז, ה]

ל) לֹא יֵשֵׁב בְּקֶרֶב בֵּיתִי עֹשֵׂה רְמִיָּה דֹּבֵר שְׁקָרִים לֹא יִכּוֹן לְנֶגֶד עֵינָי: [תהלים קא, ז] מ) גַּם הוּא לִי לִישׁוּעָה כִּי לֹא לְפָנָיו חָנֵף יָבוֹא: [איוב יג, טז] נ) כִּי לֹא אֵל חָפֵץ רֶשַׁע אָתָּה לֹא יְגֻרְךָ רָע: [תהלים ה, ה] ס) לֹא תְאֻנֶּה אֵלֶיךָ רָעָה וְנֶגַע לֹא יִקְרַב בְּאָהֳלֶךָ: [תהלים צא, י] ע) כִּי מַלְאָכָיו יְצַוֶּה לָּךְ לִשְׁמָרְךָ בְּכָל דְּרָכֶיךָ: עַל כַּפַּיִם יִשָּׂאוּנְךָ פֶּן תִּגֹּף בָּאֶבֶן רַגְלֶךָ: עַל שַׁחַל וָפֶתֶן תִּדְרֹךְ תִּרְמֹס כְּפִיר וְתַנִּין: [תהלים צא, יא-יג]

א) כי בי חשק ואפלטהו אשגבהו כי ידע שמי יקראני ואענהו עמו אנכי בצרה אחלצהו ואכבדהו אורך ימים אשביעהו ואראהו בישועתי אמר ר"ש בן לקיש מאי דכתיב ב) וימנע מרשעים אורם וזרוע רמה תשבר מפני מה עי"ן של רשעים תלויה כיון שנעשה אדם רש מלמטה נעשה רש מלמעלה ולא נכתביה כלל ר' יוחנן ור"א חד אמר מפני כבודו של דוד וחד אמר משום כבודו של נחמיה בן חכליה תנו רבנן מנשה היה שונה חמשים וחמשה פנים בתורת כהנים כנגד שני מלכותו אחאב שמנים וחמשה ירבעם מאה ושלשה תניא היה ר"מ אומר אבשלום אין לו חלק לעוה"ב שנאמר ג) ויכו את אבשלום וימיתוהו ויכוהו בעוה"ז וימיתוהו לעוה"ב תניא ר"ש בן אלעזר אומר משום ר"מ אחז ואחזיה וכל מלכי ישראל שכתוב בהן ויעש הרע בעיני ה' לא חיין ולא נידונין ד) וגם דם נקי שפך מנשה הרבה מאד עד אשר מלא את ירושלים פה לפה לבד מחטאתו אשר החטיא את יהודה לעשות הרע בעיני ה' הכא א) תרגימו שהרג ישעיה במערבא אמרי שעשה צלם משאוי אלף בני אדם ובכל יום ויום הורג (את) כולם כמאן אזלא הא דאמר רבה בר בר חנה שקולה נשמה של צדיק אחד כנגד כל העולם כולו כמ"ד ישעיה הרג כתיב ה) פסל וכתיב ו) פסילים א"ר יוחנן בתחלה עשה לו פרצוף אחד ולבסוף עשה לו ארבעה פרצופים כדי שתראה שכינה ותכעוס אחז העמידו בעלייה שנאמר ז) ואת המזבחות אשר על הגג עליית אחז וגו' מנשה העמידו בהיכל שנאמר ח) וישם את פסל האשרה אשר עשה בבית אשר אמר ה' אל דוד ואל שלמה [בנו] בבית הזה ובירושלים אשר בחרתי מכל שבטי ישראל אשים את שמי לעולם אמון הכניסו לבית קדשי הקדשים שנאמר ט) כי קצר המצע מהשתרע והמסכה צרה כהתכנס מאי כי קצר המצע מהשתרע אמר ב) רבי שמואל בר נחמני אמר רבי יונתן [כי] קצר המצע זה מלהשתרר עליו שני רעים כאחד מאי והמסכה צרה וגו' אמר רבי שמואל בר נחמני רבי יונתן כי הוה מטי להאי קרא הוה קא בכי מי שכתב בו י) כונס כנד מי הים תעשה לו מסכה צרה [אחז בטל את העבודה] וחתם את התורה שנאמר כ) צור תעודה חתום תורה בלמודי מנשה ג) קדר את האזכרות והרס את המזבח אמון [שרף את התורה] והעלה שממית על גבי המזבח אחז התיר את הערוה מנשה בא על אחותו אמון בא על אמו שנאמר ל) כי הוא אמון הרבה אשמה רבי יוחנן ור"א חד אמר ששרף את התורה וחד אמר שבא על אמו אמרה לו אמו כלום יש לך הנאה ממקום שיצאת ממנו א"ל כלום אני עושה אלא להכעיס את בוראי כי אתא יהויקים אמר קמאי לא ידעי לארגוזי כלום אנו צריכין אלא לאורו יש לנו זהב פרויים שאנו משתמשין בו יטול אורו אמרו לו והלא כסף וזהב שלו הוא שנאמר מ) לי הכסף ולי הזהב נאם ה' צבאות אמר להם כבר נתנו לנו שנאמר נ) השמים שמים לה' והארץ נתן לבני האדם א"ל רבא לרבה בר מרי מפני מה לא מנו את יהויקים משום דכתיב ביה ס) ויתר דברי יהויקים ותועבותיו אשר עשה והנמצא עליו מאי והנמצא עליו רבי יוחנן ור"א חד אמר שחקק שם עבודת כוכבים על אמתו וחד אמר שחקק שם שמים על אמתו א"ל במלכים לא שמעתי בהדיוטות שמעתי מפני מה לא מנו את מיכה מפני שפתו מצויה לעוברי דרכים שנאמר ד) כל העובר ושב אל הלוים ע) ועבר בים צרה והכה בים גלים א"ר יוחנן זה פסלו של מיכה תניא רבי נתן אומר מגרב לשילה ג' מילין והיה עשן המערכה ועשן פסל מיכה מתערבין זה בזה בקשו מלאכי השרת לדוחפו אמר להן הקב"ה הניחו לו שפתו מצויה לעוברי דרכים ועל דבר זה נענשו אנשי פלגש בגבעה אמר להן הקב"ה ה) בכבודי לא מחיתם על כבודו של בשר ודם מחיתם א"ר יוחנן משום רבי יוסי בן ו) קסמא גדולה לגימה שהרחיקה שתי משפחות מישראל שנאמר פ) על דבר אשר לא קדמו אתכם בלחם ובמים ורבי יוחנן דידיה אמר מרחקת את הקרובים ומקרבת את הרחוקים ומעלמת עינים מן הרשעים ומשרה שכינה על נביאי הבעל ז) ושגגתו עולה זדון מרחקת את הקרובים

מעמון

רש"י

כי בי חשק. לא שייך אלא ברבונא דעלמא כלומר אותו שחפץ בי ובירלאתי אפלטהו: ע' שברשעים תלויה. שאינה כתובה בשיטת אותיות התיבה אלא תלויה היא למעלה ונראה ככתוב רשים: כיון שנעשה אדם רש מלמטה. שיש לו שונאין ואין רוח הבריות נוחה הימנו: נעשה רש מלמעלה. בידוע ששונאין אותו מלמעלה להכי כתוב רשים שני מיני רשות: ולא נכתביה. לעי"ן כלל: משום כבודו של דוד. שאין הדבר נוהג בצדיקים ודוד היו לו שונאים הרבה: ונחמיה בן חכליה. שהיו לו שונאים הרבה מנכרים שמבקשין להרגו על שהיה בונה בית המקדש כדכתיב בעזרא (נחמיה ד) ואחת מחזקת השלח וגו' ל"א היו לו קנאים מישראל דכתיב (שם ז) רבים ביהודה בעלי שבועה לו כי הוא חתן לשכניה בן ארח שהיו מבזין אותו. בקדושין (דף ע.) מפרש להאי קרא ולהכי איכתבא לומר שברשעים אמרינן ולא בצדיקים: היה שונה חמשים וחמשה פנים בתורת כהנים. ספר ויקרא היה מחדש בו כל שנה ושנה ודורשו מפלפולו: לא חיין. לא יחיו לעולם הבא עם הצדיקים ואין נדונין נמי בגיהנם ודוקא קאמר מלכי ישראל אבל שלמה וצדקיה מבית דוד אתו ואף על גב דכתיב בהו ויעש הרע חיין הן לעתיד: אחז ואחזיה. ממלכי יהודה וקים להו שהיו רשעים ואמון ויהויקים לא חשיב ואף על גב דהוו רשעים מאד כדלקמן בהנהו קים להו דחיין: הורג את כולן. שהיו נבקעין בכובד המשאוי: כמ"ד שהרג ישעיה. והאי קאמר קרא מלא את ירושלים פה לפה שנשמתו של צדיק שקולה כמו שמלא את ירושלים חללים: כתוב. (במלכים) [דה"ב לג] וישם את פסל הסמל אשר עשה בבית האלהים: וכתיב והעמיד את האשרים והפסילים בד"ה (שם): ולבסוף עשה. מנשה לאותו דמות ד' פרצופים: כדי שתראה שכינה מכל צד. שתכנס להיכל תראה פרצוף כנגדו ותכעוס: מלהשתרר עליו שני רעים. שכינה ודמות הפרצוף: מצע. בית המקדש: תעשה לו מסכה צרה. כאשה שנעשית צרה לחברתה: העלה שממית. קורי עכבים שבטל עבודה מכל וכל עד שארגו עכבים קוריהן ע"ג המזבח: היתר. נעשה לו כהיתר: ממקום שיצאת משם. מקום שאדם יוצא ממנו שבע הוא ממנו ואינו מתאוה להנאת אותו מקום: קמאי לא ידעי לארגוזי. מלכים ראשונים שלפנינו לא היו יודעים להכעיס המקום כמו שהוא חרף ואמר כלום אנו צריכין אלא לאורו שמאיר לנו השמש יצא ויטול אורו: שאנו משתמשין בו. שמאיר ביותר: אמרו לו. בני דורו והלא כסף וכו' דבני דורו צדיקים היו כדאמרן נסתכל בדורו של יהויקים ונתקררה דעתו: מפני מה לא מנו את יהויקים. בהדי הנך שאין להם חלק לעולם הבא: משום דכתיב ויתר דברי יהויקים. בתמיהה משום דכתיב ביה רשע כזה לא מנאוהו: שם עבודת כוכבים על גופו. מתוך שהיה אדוק בה: שם שמים. משום בזיון: במלכים לא שמעתי. מפני מה לא מנו את יהויקים: בהדיוטות שמעתי. מפני מה לא מנו מיכה בהדי ארבעה הדיוטות דמתניתין: פתו מצויה לעוברי דרכים. שהיו כל העולם מתארחין אצלו כדכתיב (במקרא) כל העובר ושב אל הלוים זה מיכה: זה פסלו של מיכה. כשכתב משה את השם והשליכו על נילוס להעלות ארונו של יוסף בא מיכה ונטלו בהחבא והיינו דכתיב ועבר בים צרה כשהעביר הקדוש ברוך הוא לישראל עבר מיכה עמהם שבידו השם לעשות העגל ל"א מיכה עשה פסל והביאו עמו כשעברו ישראל הים: גרב. מקומו של מיכה בגרב הוה פסלו של מיכה קבוע ובשילה היה המשכן: לדוחפו. למיכה: ועל דבר זה. על פסלו של מיכה שלא מיחו ישראל בידו נענשו אנשי פילגש בגבעה שנפלו ביד בנימין והרגו מהם ארבעים אלף: לגימה. אכילה שמאכילין אורחים: שתי משפחות. עמון ומואב שלפי שלא קדמו ישראל בלחם ובמים נכתב שלא יבאו בקהל: מעלמת עינים מן הרשעים. מעלמת מעיני המקום שלא להביט ברשעו לשלם לו כדרכו הרעה אלא עושה כאילו אינו רואה במעשיו:

עמון

גליון הש"ס

גמרא אבשלום אין לו חלק לעוה"ב. עי' סוטה דף י ע"ב תוספות ד"ה דקרב: שם ר"י ור"א חד אמר. עי' מדרש רבה ויקרא סוף פ' מצורע:

תורה אור השלם

א) כִּי בִי חָשַׁק וַאֲפַלְּטֵהוּ אֲשַׂגְּבֵהוּ כִּי יָדַע שְׁמִי: יִקְרָאֵנִי וְאֶעֱנֵהוּ עִמּוֹ אָנֹכִי בְצָרָה אֲחַלְּצֵהוּ וַאֲכַבְּדֵהוּ: אֹרֶךְ יָמִים אַשְׂבִּיעֵהוּ וְאַרְאֵהוּ בִּישׁוּעָתִי: [תהלים צא, יד-טז]

ב) וְיִמָּנַע מֵרְשָׁעִים אוֹרָם וּזְרוֹעַ רָמָה תִּשָּׁבֵר: [איוב לח, טו]

ג) וַיָּסֹבּוּ עֲשָׂרָה נְעָרִים נֹשְׂאֵי כְּלֵי יוֹאָב וַיַּכּוּ אֶת אַבְשָׁלוֹם וַיְמִיתֻהוּ: [שמואל ב' יח, טו]

ד) וְגַם דָּם נָקִי שָׁפַךְ מְנַשֶּׁה הַרְבֵּה מְאֹד עַד אֲשֶׁר מִלֵּא אֶת יְרוּשָׁלַיִם פֶּה לָפֶה לְבַד מֵחַטָּאתוֹ אֲשֶׁר הֶחֱטִיא אֶת יְהוּדָה לַעֲשׂוֹת הָרַע בְּעֵינֵי יְיָ: [מלכים ב' כא, טז]

ה) וַיָּשֶׂם אֶת פֶּסֶל הַסֶּמֶל אֲשֶׁר עָשָׂה בְּבֵית הָאֱלֹהִים אֲשֶׁר אָמַר אֱלֹהִים אֶל דָּוִיד וְאֶל שְׁלֹמֹה בְנוֹ בַּבַּיִת הַזֶּה וּבִירוּשָׁלַיִם אֲשֶׁר בָּחַרְתִּי מִכֹּל שִׁבְטֵי יִשְׂרָאֵל אָשִׂים אֶת שְׁמִי לְעֵילוֹם: [דברי הימים ב' לג, ז]

ו) וּתְפִלָּתוֹ וְהֵעָתֶר לוֹ וְכָל חַטָּאתוֹ וּמַעְלוֹ וְהַמְּקֹמוֹת אֲשֶׁר בָּנָה בָהֶם בָּמוֹת וְהֶעֱמִיד הָאֲשֵׁרִים וְהַפְּסִלִים לִפְנֵי הִכָּנְעוֹ הִנָּם כְּתוּבִים עַל דִּבְרֵי חוֹזָי: [דברי הימים ב' לג, יט]

ז) וְאֶת הַמִּזְבְּחוֹת אֲשֶׁר עַל הַגָּג עֲלִיַּת אָחָז אֲשֶׁר עָשׂוּ מַלְכֵי יְהוּדָה וְאֶת הַמִּזְבְּחוֹת אֲשֶׁר עָשָׂה מְנַשֶּׁה בִּשְׁתֵּי חַצְרוֹת בֵּית יְיָ נָתַץ הַמֶּלֶךְ וַיָּרָץ מִשָּׁם וְהִשְׁלִיךְ אֶת עֲפָרָם אֶל נַחַל קִדְרוֹן: [מלכים ב' כג, יב]

ח) וַיָּשֶׂם אֶת פֶּסֶל הָאֲשֵׁרָה אֲשֶׁר עָשָׂה בַּבַּיִת אֲשֶׁר אָמַר יְיָ אֶל דָּוִד וְאֶל שְׁלֹמֹה בְנוֹ בַּבַּיִת הַזֶּה וּבִירוּשָׁלַיִם אֲשֶׁר בָּחַרְתִּי מִכֹּל שִׁבְטֵי יִשְׂרָאֵל אָשִׂים אֶת שְׁמִי לְעוֹלָם: [מלכים ב' כא, ז]

ט) כִּי קָצַר הַמַּצָּע מֵהִשְׂתָּרֵעַ וְהַמַּסֵּכָה צָרָה כְּהִתְכַּנֵּס: [ישעיה כח, כ]

י) כֹּנֵס כַּנֵּד מֵי הַיָּם נֹתֵן בְּאֹצָרוֹת תְּהוֹמוֹת: [תהלים לג, ז]

כ) צוֹר תְּעוּדָה חֲתוֹם תּוֹרָה בְּלִמֻּדָי: [ישעיה ח, טז]

ל) וְלֹא נִכְנַע מִלִּפְנֵי יְיָ כְּהִכָּנַע מְנַשֶּׁה אָבִיו כִּי הוּא אָמוֹן הִרְבָּה אַשְׁמָה: [דברי הימים ב' לג, כג]

מ) לִי הַכֶּסֶף וְלִי הַזָּהָב נְאֻם יְיָ צְבָאוֹת: [חגי ב, ח]

נ) הַשָּׁמַיִם שָׁמַיִם לַייָ וְהָאָרֶץ נָתַן לִבְנֵי אָדָם: [תהלים קטו, טז]

ס) וְיֶתֶר דִּבְרֵי יְהוֹיָקִים וְתֹעֲבֹתָיו אֲשֶׁר עָשָׂה וְהַנִּמְצָא עָלָיו הִנָּם כְּתוּבִים עַל סֵפֶר מַלְכֵי יִשְׂרָאֵל וִיהוּדָה וַיִּמְלֹךְ יְהוֹיָכִין בְּנוֹ תַּחְתָּיו: [דברי הימים ב' לו, ח]

ע) וְעָבַר בַּיָּם צָרָה וְהִכָּה בַיָּם גַּלִּים וְהֹבִישׁוּ כֹּל מְצוּלוֹת יְאֹר וְהוּרַד גְּאוֹן אַשּׁוּר וְשֵׁבֶט מִצְרַיִם יָסוּר: [זכריה י, יא]

פ) עַל דְּבַר אֲשֶׁר לֹא קִדְּמוּ אֶתְכֶם בַּלֶּחֶם וּבַמַּיִם בַּדֶּרֶךְ בְּצֵאתְכֶם מִמִּצְרָיִם וַאֲשֶׁר שָׂכַר עָלֶיךָ אֶת בִּלְעָם בֶּן בְּעוֹר מִפְּתוֹר אֲרַם נַהֲרַיִם לְקַלְלֶךָּ: [דברים כג, ה]

מסורת הש"ס

א) [יבמות מט:], ב) יומא ט: ע"ש, ג) [גירסת הערוך קדר], ד) לא נמצא מקרא [גם בע"י ליתא להך קרא עיין חידושי אגדות שם], ה) [לקמן קי. נדרים לט:], ו) [בשאילתות סימן ל"ט פ' שמות איתא קצרתא], ז) [ב"מ לג:].

ליקוטי רש"י

כי קצר המצע מהשתרע. כי אביא עליכם שונא דוחק אתכם אשר לא תוכלו להספיק עבודתו כשיגיע מלעו עליכם יקצר לו מהשתרע השוכב עליו מהשתרע מהשתטח להאריך איבריו אישטנדליי"ר בלע"ז. והמסכה צרה. הנסיך שימשול עליכם יהיה מקומכם דחוק לו בהתכנסו לתוכו ורבותינו דרשוהו על עכו"ם שהכניס מנשה להיכל קצר המצע הזה מהשתרע מהשתרר עליו שני רעים ואני פרשתיו לפי פשוטו ובדרך זה ת"י ואף מדרש רבותינו יש לישבו על אופן הדבור כלומר למה אני מביא עליכם פורענות זו לפי שקצר המצע מהשתרע אני לבדי עליו שנאמר (מ"א ח) הנה השמים לא יכלכלוך וכל שכן בהכניסכם מסכה עמי כביכול צר לנו המקום [ישעיהו כח, כ]. לי הכסף ולי הזהב. ובידי להביא לאשר חפצתי בו [חגי ב, ח]. ותועבתיו שבא על אמו. והנמצא עליו. כתובת קעקע [דה"ב לו, ח].

,,כִּי בִי חָשַׁק וַאֲפַלְּטֵהוּ אֲשַׂגְּבֵהוּ כִּי־יָדַע שְׁמִי יִקְרָאֵנִי וְאֶעֱנֵהוּ עִמּוֹ־אָנֹכִי בְצָרָה אֲחַלְּצֵהוּ וַאֲכַבְּדֵהוּ אֹרֶךְ יָמִים אַשְׂבִּיעֵהוּ וְאַרְאֵהוּ בִּישׁוּעָתִי'' – ***For he has yearned for Me and I will deliver him; I will elevate him because he knows My Name. He will call upon Me and I will answer him. I am with him in distress, I will release him and I will honor him. I will satiate him with long life and I will show him My salvation.***[1]

Returning to its discussion of the wicked kings of Judah, the Gemara presents an exegesis of R' Shimon ben Lakish concerning wicked people in general:

אָמַר רַבִּי שִׁמְעוֹן בֶּן לָקִישׁ – **R' Shimon ben Lakish said:** מַאי דִּכְתִיב ,,וְיִמָּנַע מֵרְשָׁעִים אוֹרָם וּזְרוֹעַ רָמָה תִּשָּׁבֵר'' – **What** is meant by what **is written:**[2] ***And from the wicked will be withheld their light; the high arm will be broken;*** מִפְּנֵי מָה עי"ן שֶׁל רְשָׁעִים תְּלוּיָה – specifically, **why is the** letter ***ayin*** **in** the word ***reshaim*** (*the wicked*) **suspended** higher than the other letters in that word?[3] כֵּיוָן שֶׁנַּעֲשָׂה אָדָם רָשׁ מִלְּמַטָּה – It is to teach you that **once a person becomes destitute** of friends **below,** i.e. in this world, נַעֲשָׂה רָשׁ מִלְמַעְלָה – it is an indication that **he has become** similarly **destitute Above,** i.e. in Heaven.[4]

The Gemara asks:

וְלֹא נִכְתְּבֵיהּ כְּלָל – **But** if this is the point of the verse, **let [the *ayin*] not be written at all. – ? –**

The Gemara answers:

רַבִּי יוֹחָנָן וְרַבִּי אֶלְעָזָר – **R' Yochanan and R' Elazar** each offer an answer to this question. חַד אָמַר מִפְּנֵי כְבוֹדוֹ שֶׁל דָּוִד – **One says** that the *ayin* is retained **because of the honor of David,**[5] וְחַד אָמַר מִשּׁוּם כְּבוֹדוֹ שֶׁל נְחֶמְיָה בֶּן חֲכַלְיָה – **and one says** the *ayin* is retained **because of the honor of Nehemiah the son of Chachaliah.**[6]

The Gemara presents three Baraisos concerning wicked personages in Scripture:

תָּנוּ רַבָּנַן – **The Rabbis taught in a Baraisa:** מְנַשֶּׁה הָיָה שׁוֹנֶה חֲמִשִּׁים וַחֲמִשָּׁה פָּנִים בְּתוֹרַת כֹּהֲנִים – MENASHEH USED TO STUDY, i.e. expound, FIFTY-FIVE different FACETS of meaning IN THE BOOK OF *LEVITICUS,*[7] כְּנֶגֶד שְׁנֵי מַלְכוּתוֹ – CORRESPONDING TO THE number of YEARS OF HIS REIGN;[8] אַחְאָב שְׁמֹנִים וַחֲמִשָּׁה – AHAB, EIGHTY-FIVE facets; יָרָבְעָם מֵאָה וּשְׁלֹשָׁה – YAROVAM, ONE HUNDRED AND THREE facets.[9]

The second Baraisa:

תַּנְיָא – **It was taught in a Baraisa:** הָיָה רַבִּי מֵאִיר אוֹמֵר – R' MEIR USED TO SAY: אַבְשָׁלוֹם אֵין לוֹ חֵלֶק לָעוֹלָם הַבָּא – ABSALOM HAS NO PORTION IN THE WORLD TO COME, שֶׁנֶּאֱמַר ,,וַיַּכּוּ אֶת־אַבְשָׁלוֹם וַיְמִיתֻהוּ'' – AS IT IS STATED: *THEY STRUCK ABSALOM AND THEY CAUSED HIM TO DIE;*[10] ,,וַיַּכּוּהוּ'' בָּעוֹלָם הַזֶּה – *THEY STRUCK HIM* – this refers to his death IN THIS WORLD; ,,וַיְמִיתֻהוּ'' לָעוֹלָם הַבָּא – *AND THEY CAUSED HIM TO DIE* – this refers to his losing his share IN THE WORLD TO COME.

The third Baraisa:

תַּנְיָא – **It was taught in a Baraisa:** רַבִּי שִׁמְעוֹן בֶּן אֶלְעָזָר אוֹמֵר מִשּׁוּם רַבִּי מֵאִיר – R' SHIMON BEN ELAZAR SAID IN THE NAME OF R' MEIR: אָחָז וַאֲחַזְיָה וְכָל מַלְכֵי יִשְׂרָאֵל שֶׁכָּתוּב בָּהֶן ,,וַיַּעַשׂ הָרַע בְּעֵינֵי ה' '' – ACHAZ AND ACHAZIAH among the kings of Judah, AS WELL AS ANY KING OF ISRAEL OF WHOM IT IS WRITTEN: *HE DID WHAT WAS EVIL IN THE EYES OF HASHEM,*[11] לֹא חַיִּין וְלֹא נִידּוֹנִין – WILL NOT COME TO LIFE at the time of the Resurrection; BUT NEITHER ARE

NOTES

1. These verses (*Psalms* 91:14-16) [which speak in the first person] are obviously not a prayer but are spoken by God; they are God's blessing bestowed upon Solomon (*Rashi*).

2. *Job* 38:15.

3. In the masoretic text the letter *ayin* in the word *reshaim* is not written on the same line as the other letters of that word, but rather slightly higher (רְשָׁעִים). The visual effect of this variation is that the word may be read as if the letter *ayin* were missing, with the resulting word being רָשִׁים, *poor persons* (*Rashi*).

4. I.e. if a person is hated by people, it is a sign that God, too, hates him. This is indicated by the plural, רָשִׁים; i.e. he is subjected to two forms of poverty; he is poor in friends both on earth and in Heaven (*Rashi; cf. Yad Ramah, Iyun Yaakov*).

This same thought is expressed in a maxim cited in *Avos* 3:10: *If the spirit of one's fellows is not pleased with him, the spirit of the Omnipresent is not pleased with him.*

This teaching can have two meanings: (a) When someone is hated by the broad spectrum of the populace, both great and small alike, it is a sign that God, for good reason, has implanted hatred toward him in people's hearts. God would not do this to one He loves. People's feelings toward him are thus a *barometer* for God's feelings toward him (see *Chovos HaLevavos* 5:5 בד"ה וראוי שנבאר עתה). (b) A Jew who acts in a way that causes people to hate him brings disrepute to the Torah. God hates him for this. Thus, people's hatred of him is the *cause* of God's hating him (see *Rabbeinu Yonah* to *Avos* ibid.).

5. I.e. David had many enemies (*Rashi*), as is related in the Book of *Samuel* and as he himself states many times in *Psalms*. The inclusion of the *ayin* teaches that the principle that one who is hated below is also hated Above applies only to the wicked, not to someone like David, who was hated simply because of jealousy.

6. The righteous Nehemiah had many gentile enemies who attempted to kill him for rebuilding the wall around Jerusalem (*Nehemiah* chs. 2-6). Alternatively, he had many Jewish enemies among those who had intermarried with influential gentile families (ibid 6:1-19). For the sake of Nehemiah, the verse emphasizes that the principle that a person who is hated below is hated Above applies only to the wicked (*Rashi*).

7. Literally: the Law of the Kohanim.

8. I.e. Menasheh used to study the Book of *Leviticus* every year of his fifty-five-year reign, and each time he would offer profound, original insights, a monumental feat of Torah scholarship (see *Rashi*). Due to its numerous and detailed laws, *Leviticus* in particular lends itself to many interpretations and insights (*Haamek Davar,* Introduction to *Leviticus*).

Yad Ramah strongly objects to *Rashi's* interpretation, for it is inconceivable that the same idolatrous Menasheh who murdered and blasphemed so extensively should at the same time have devoted so much time and effort to intensive Torah study. Rather the meaning is that in his youth, before he became wicked, Menasheh expounded *Leviticus* fifty-five times, and it was in that merit that he reigned fifty-five years.

9. *Maharsha* explains the Baraisa's point to be that these three kings did not lose their portion in the World to Come out of ignorance. On the contrary, they knew full well the consequences of their sins; they were expert in the requirements of the Torah, particularly in the area of the Temple service, which is the subject of *Leviticus.* In spite of this, they chose of their own free will to scorn God and His Torah. They therefore fully deserved their punishment. (*Rambam* in his *Commentary to the Mishnah* makes this same point.)

10. *II Samuel* 18:15. Absalom, King David's rebel son and would-be parricide, was wounded in battle by David's general Yoav. Yoav's servants then surrounded Absalom and killed him. R' Meir is bothered by the apparent superfluity of the word וַיְמִיתֻהוּ, *and they caused him to die,* for the verses following this one state that the soldiers tossed Absalom's body into a pit. Clearly, their blows had killed him. Why, then, does Scripture need to mention this fact? (*Maharsha*).

[See *Tosafos* to *Yoma* 66b ד"ה פלוני and *Tosafos* to *Sotah* 10b ד"ה דקרב for further discussion of Absalom's sin and his punishment.]

11. This includes every king of Israel aside from Yehu (*Yad Ramah*).

By stressing "the kings of *Israel*," the Baraisa excludes certain kings of Judah – specifically Solomon and Tzidkiah – concerning whom it is also written: *He did what was evil in the eyes of HASHEM* (*I Kings* 11:6, *II Kings* 24:19). In spite of this, they do have a share in the World to Come (*Rashi*).

א) כי בי חשק ואפלטהו אשגבהו כי ידע שמי יקראני ואענהו עמו אנכי בצרה אחלצהו ואכבדהו אורך ימים אשביעהו ואראהו בישועתי אמר ר"ש בן לקיש מאי דכתיב ב) וימנע מרשעים אורם וזרוע רמה תשבר מפני מה עי"ן של רשעים תלויה כיון שנעשה אדם רש מלמטה נעשה רש מלמעלה ולא נכתביה כלל ר' יוחנן ור"א חד אמר מפני כבודו של דוד וחד אמר משום כבודו של נחמיה בן חכליה תנו רבנן מנשה היה שונה חמשים וחמשה פנים בתורת כהנים כנגד שני מלכותו אחאב שמנים וחמשה ירבעם מאה ושלשה תניא היה ר"מ אומר °אבשלום אין לו חלק לעוה"ב שנאמר ג) ויכו את אבשלום וימיתוהו ויכוהו בעוה"ז וימיתוהו לעוה"ב תניא ר"ש בן אלעזר אומר משום ר"מ אחז ואחזיה וכל מלכי ישראל שכתוב בהן ויעש הרע בעיני ה' לא חיין ולא נידונין ד) וגם דם נקי שפך מנשה הרבה מאד עד אשר מלא את ירושלים פה לפה לבד מחטאתו אשר החטיא את יהודה לעשות הרע בעיני ה' הכא א) תרגימו שהרג ישעיה במערבא אמרי שעשה צלם משאוי אלף בני אדם ובכל יום ויום הורג (את) כולם כמאן אזלא הא דאמר רבה בר בר חנה שקולה נשמה של צדיק אחד כנגד כל העולם כולו כמ"ד ישעיה הרג כתיב ה) פסל וכתיב ו) פסילים א"ר יוחנן בתחלה עשה לו פרצוף אחד ולבסוף עשה לו ארבעה פרצופים כדי שתראה שכינה ותכעוס אחז העמידו בעלייה שנאמר ז) ואת המזבחות אשר על הגג עליית אחז וגו' מנשה העמידו בהיכל שנאמר ח) וישם את פסל האשרה אשר עשה בבית אשר אמר ה' אל דוד ואל שלמה [בנו] בבית הזה ובירושלים אשר בחרתי מכל שבטי ישראל אשים את שמי לעולם אמון הכניסו לבית קדשי הקדשים שנאמר ט) כי קצר המצע מהשתרע והמסכה צרה כהתכנס מאי כי קצר המצע מהשתרע אמר ב) רבי שמואל בר נחמני אמר רבי יונתן [כי] קצר המצע זה מלהשתרר עליו שני רעים כאחד מאי והמסכה צרה וגו' אמר רבי שמואל בר נחמני רבי יונתן כי הוה מטי להאי קרא הוה קא בכי מי שכתב בו י) כונס כנד מי הים תעשה לו מסכה צרה [אחז בטל את העבודה] וחתם את התורה שנאמר כ) צור תעודה חתום תורה בלמודי מנשה ג) קדר את האזכרות והרס את המזבח אמון [שרף את התורה] והעלה שממית על גבי המזבח אחז התיר את הערוה מנשה בא על אחותו אמון בא על אמו שנאמר ל) כי הוא אמון הרבה אשמה °רבי יוחנן ור"א חד אמר ששרף את התורה וחד אמר שבא על אמו אמרה לו אמו כלום יש לך הנאה ממקום שיצאת ממנו א"ל כלום אני עושה אלא להכעיס את בוראי כי אתא יהויקים אמר קמאי לא ידעי לארגוזי כלום אנו צריכין אלא לאורו יש לנו זהב פרויים שאנו משתמשין בו יטול אורו אמרו לו והלא כסף וזהב שלו הוא שנאמר מ) לי הכסף ולי הזהב נאם ה' צבאות אמר להם כבר נתנו לנו שנאמר נ) השמים שמים לה' והארץ נתן לבני האדם א"ל רבא לרבה בר מרי מפני מה לא מנו את יהויקים משום דכתיב ביה ס) ויתר דברי יהויקים ותועבותיו אשר עשה והנמצא עליו מאי והנמצא עליו רבי יוחנן ור"א חד אמר שחקק שם עבודת כוכבים על אמתו וחד אמר שחקק שם שמים על אמתו א"ל במלכים לא שמעתי מפני מה לא מנו את מיכה מפני שפתו מצויה לעוברי דרכים שנאמר ד) כל העובר ושב אל הלוים ע) ועבר בים צרה והכה בים גלים א"ר יוחנן זה פסלו של מיכה תניא רבי נתן אומר מגרב לשילה ג' מילין והיה עשן המערכה ועשן פסל מיכה מתערבין זה בזה בקשו מלאכי השרת לדוחפו אמר להן הקב"ה הניחו לו שפתו מצויה לעוברי דרכים ועל דבר זה נענשו אנשי פלגש בגבעה אמר להן הקב"ה ה) בכבודי לא מחיתם על כבודו של בשר ודם מחיתם א"ר יוחנן משום רבי יוסי בן ו) קסמא גדולה לגימה שהרחיקה שתי משפחות מישראל שנאמר פ) על דבר אשר לא קדמו אתכם בלחם ובמים ורבי יוחנן דידיה אמר מרחקת את הקרובים ומקרבת את הרחוקים ומעלמת עינים מן הרשעים ומשרה שכינה על נביאי הבעל ז) ושגגתו עולה זדון מרחקת את הקרובים מעמון

כי בי חשק. לא שייך אלא ברבונא דעלמא כלומר אותו שחפץ בי ובירלאתי אפלטהו: ע' שברשעים תלויה. שאינה כתובה בשיטת אותיות התיבה אלא תלויה היא למעלה ונראה ככתוב רשים: כיון שנעשה אדם רש מלמטה. שיש לו שונאין ואין רוח הבריות נוחה הימנו: נעשה רש מלמעלה. בידוע ששונאין אותו מלמעלה להכי כתוב רשים שני מיני רשות: ולא נכתביה. לעי"ן כלל: משום כבודו של דוד. שאין הדבר נוהג בצדיקים ודוד היו לו שונאים הרבה: ונחמיה בן חכליה. שהיו לו שונאים הרבה מנכרים שמבקשין להרגו על שהיה בונה בית המקדש כדכתיב בעזרא (נחמיה ד) ואחת מחזקת השלח וגו' נ"א היו לו קנאים מישראל דכתיב (שם ו) רבים ביהודה בעלי שבועה לו כי הוא חתן לשכניה בן ארח שהיו מבזין אותו. בקדושין (דף ע.) מפרש להאי קרא ולהכי איכתבא לומר שברשעים אמרינן ולא בצדיקים: היה שונה חמשים וחמשה פנים בתורת כהנים. ספר ויקרא היה מחדש בו כל שנה ושנה ודורשו מפלפולו: לא חיין. לא יחיו לעולם הבא עם הצדיקים ואין נדונין נמי בגיהנם ודוקא קאמר מלכי ישראל אבל שלמה וצדקיה מבית דוד אתו ואף על גב דכתיב בהו ויעש הרע חיין הן לעתיד: אחז ואחזיה. ממלכי יהודה וקים להו שהיו רשעים ואמון ויהויקים לא חשיב ואף על גב דהוו רשעים מאד כדלקמן בהנהו קים להו דחיין: הורג את כולן. שהיו נבקעין בכובד המשאוי: כמ"ד שהרג ישעיה. והא קאמר קרא מלא את ירושלים פה לפה שנשמתו של צדיק שקולה כמו שמלא את ירושלים חללים: כתוב. (במלכים) [דה"ב לג] וישם את פסל הסמל אשר עשה בבית האלהים: וכתיב והעמיד את האשרים והפסילים בד"ה (שם): ולבסוף עשה. מנשה לאותו דמות ד' פרצופים: כדי שתראה שכינה מכל צד. שתכנס להיכל תראה פרצוף כנגדו ותכעוס: מלהשתרר עליו שני רעים. שכינה ודמות הפרצוף: מצע. בית המקדש: תעשה לו מסכה צרה. כאשה שנעשית צרה לחברתה: העלה שממית. קורי עכביש שבטל עבודה מכל וכל עד שארגו עכבים קוריהן ע"ג המזבח: היתר. נעשה לו כהיתר: ממקום שיצאת משם. מקום שאדם יוצא ממנו שבע הוא ממנו ואינו מתאוה להנאת אותו מקום: קמאי לא ידעי לארגוזי. מלכים ראשונים שלפנינו לא היו יודעים להכעיס המקום כמו שהוא חרף ואמר כלום אנו צריכין אלא לאורו שמאיר לנו השמש יצא ויטול אורו: שאנו משתמשין בו. שמאיר ביותר: אמרו לו. בני דורו והלא כסף וכו' דבני דורו צדיקים היו כדאמרן נסתכל בדורו של יהויקים ונתקררה דעתו: מפני מה לא מנו את יהויקים. בהדי הנך שאין להם חלק לעולם הבא: משום דכתיב ויתר דברי יהויקים. בתמיהה משום דכתיב ביה רשע כזה לא מנאוהו: שם עבודת כוכבים על גופו. מתוך שהיה אדוק בה: שם שמים. משום בזיון: במלכים לא שמעתי. מפני מה לא מנו את יהויקים: בהדיוטות שמעתי. מפני מה לא מנו מיכה בהדי ארבעה הדיוטות דמתניתין: פתו מצויה לעוברי דרכים. שהיו כל העולם מתארחין אצלו כדכתיב (במקרא) כל העובר ושב אל הלוים זה מיכה: זה פסלו של מיכה. כשכתב משה את השם והשליכו על נילוס להעלות ארונו של יוסף בא מיכה ונטלו בהחבא והיינו דכתיב ועבר בים צרה כשהעביר הקדוש ברוך הוא לישראל עבר מיכה עמהם שבידו השם לעשות העגל נ"א מיכה עשה פסל והביאו עמו כשעברו ישראל הים: גרב. מקומו של מיכה בגרב הוה פסלו של מיכה קבוע ובשילה היה המשכן: לדוחפו. למיכה: ועל דבר זה. על פסלו של מיכה שלא מיחו ישראל בידו נענשו אנשי פילגש בגבעה שנפלו ביד בנימין והרגו מהם ארבעים אלף: לגימה. אכילה שמאכילין אורחים: שתי משפחות. עמון ומואב שלפי שלא קדמו ישראל בלחם ובמים נכתב שלא יבאו בקהל: מעלמת עינים מן הרשעים. מעלמת מעיני המקום שלא להביט ברשעו לשלם לו כדרכו הרעה אלא עושה כאילו אינו רואה במעשיו:

גליון הש"ס

גמרא אבשלום אין לו חלק לעוה"ב. עי' סוטה דף י ע"ב תוספות ד"ה דקרב: שם ר"י ור"א חד אמר. עי' מדרש רבה ויקרא סוף פ' מצורע:

תורה אור השלם

א) כִּי בִי חָשַׁק וַאֲפַלְּטֵהוּ אֲשַׂגְּבֵהוּ כִּי יָדַע שְׁמִי: יִקְרָאֵנִי וְאֶעֱנֵהוּ עִמּוֹ אָנֹכִי בְצָרָה אֲחַלְּצֵהוּ וַאֲכַבְּדֵהוּ: אֹרֶךְ יָמִים אַשְׂבִּיעֵהוּ וְאַרְאֵהוּ בִּישׁוּעָתִי: [תהלים צא, יד-טז]

ב) וְיִמָּנַע מֵרְשָׁעִים אוֹרָם וּזְרוֹעַ רָמָה תִּשָּׁבֵר: [איוב לח, טו]

ג) וַיָּסֹבּוּ עֲשָׂרָה נְעָרִים נֹשְׂאֵי כְּלֵי יוֹאָב וַיַּכּוּ אֶת אַבְשָׁלוֹם וַיְמִיתֻהוּ: [שמואל ב' יח, טו]

ד) וְגַם דָּם נָקִי שָׁפַךְ מְנַשֶּׁה הַרְבֵּה מְאֹד עַד אֲשֶׁר מִלֵּא אֶת יְרוּשָׁלַיִם פֶּה לָפֶה לְבַד מֵחַטָּאתוֹ אֲשֶׁר הֶחֱטִיא אֶת יְהוּדָה לַעֲשׂוֹת הָרַע בְּעֵינֵי יְיָ: [מלכים ב' כא, טז]

ה) וַיָּשֶׂם אֶת פֶּסֶל הַסֶּמֶל אֲשֶׁר עָשָׂה בְּבֵית הָאֱלֹהִים אֲשֶׁר אָמַר אֱלֹהִים אֶל דָּוִיד וְאֶל שְׁלֹמֹה בְנוֹ בַּבַּיִת הַזֶּה וּבִירוּשָׁלַיִם אֲשֶׁר בָּחַרְתִּי מִכֹּל שִׁבְטֵי יִשְׂרָאֵל אָשִׂים אֶת שְׁמִי לְעֵילוֹם: [דברי הימים ב' לג, ז]

ו) וּתְפִלָּתוֹ וְהֵעָתֶר לוֹ וְכָל חַטָּאתוֹ וּמַעְלוֹ וְהַמְּקֹמוֹת אֲשֶׁר בָּנָה בָהֶם בָּמוֹת וְהֶעֱמִיד הָאֲשֵׁרִים וְהַפְּסִלִים לִפְנֵי הִכָּנְעוֹ הִנָּם כְּתוּבִים עַל דִּבְרֵי חוֹזָי: [דברי הימים ב' לג, יט]

ז) וְאֶת הַמִּזְבְּחוֹת אֲשֶׁר עַל הַגָּג עֲלִיַּת אָחָז אֲשֶׁר עָשׂוּ מַלְכֵי יְהוּדָה וְאֶת הַמִּזְבְּחוֹת אֲשֶׁר עָשָׂה מְנַשֶּׁה בִּשְׁתֵּי חַצְרוֹת בֵּית יְיָ נָתַץ הַמֶּלֶךְ וַיָּרָץ מִשָּׁם וְהִשְׁלִיךְ אֶת עֲפָרָם אֶל נַחַל קִדְרוֹן: [מלכים ב' כג, יב]

ח) וַיָּשֶׂם אֶת פֶּסֶל הָאֲשֵׁרָה אֲשֶׁר עָשָׂה בַּבַּיִת אֲשֶׁר אָמַר יְיָ אֶל דָּוִד וְאֶל שְׁלֹמֹה בְנוֹ בַּבַּיִת הַזֶּה וּבִירוּשָׁלַיִם אֲשֶׁר בָּחַרְתִּי מִכֹּל שִׁבְטֵי יִשְׂרָאֵל אָשִׂים אֶת שְׁמִי לְעוֹלָם: [מלכים ב' כא, ז]

ט) כִּי קָצַר הַמַּצָּע מֵהִשְׂתָּרֵעַ וְהַמַּסֵּכָה צָרָה כְּהִתְכַּנֵּס: [ישעיה כח, כ]

י) כֹּנֵס כַּנֵּד מֵי הַיָּם נֹתֵן בְּאֹצָרוֹת תְּהוֹמוֹת: [תהלים לג, ז]

כ) צוֹר תְּעוּדָה חֲתוֹם תּוֹרָה בְּלִמֻּדָי: [ישעיה ח, טז]

ל) וְלֹא נִכְנַע מִלִּפְנֵי יְיָ כְּהִכָּנַע מְנַשֶּׁה אָבִיו כִּי הוּא אָמוֹן הִרְבָּה אַשְׁמָה: [דברי הימים ב' לג, כג]

מ) לִי הַכֶּסֶף וְלִי הַזָּהָב נְאֻם יְיָ צְבָאוֹת: [חגי ב, ח]

נ) הַשָּׁמַיִם שָׁמַיִם לַייָ וְהָאָרֶץ נָתַן לִבְנֵי אָדָם: [תהלים קטו, טז] ס) וְיֶתֶר דִּבְרֵי יְהוֹיָקִים וְתֹעֲבֹתָיו אֲשֶׁר עָשָׂה וְהַנִּמְצָא עָלָיו הִנָּם כְּתוּבִים עַל סֵפֶר מַלְכֵי יִשְׂרָאֵל וִיהוּדָה וַיִּמְלֹךְ יְהוֹיָכִין בְּנוֹ תַּחְתָּיו: [דברי הימים ב' לו, ח]

ע) וְעָבַר בַּיָּם צָרָה וְהִכָּה בַיָּם גַּלִּים וְהֹבִישׁוּ כֹּל מְצוּלוֹת יְאֹר וְהוּרַד גְּאוֹן אַשּׁוּר וְשֵׁבֶט מִצְרַיִם יָסוּר: [זכריה י, יא] פ) עַל דְּבַר אֲשֶׁר לֹא קִדְּמוּ אֶתְכֶם בַּלֶּחֶם וּבַמַּיִם בַּדֶּרֶךְ בְּצֵאתְכֶם מִמִּצְרָיִם וַאֲשֶׁר שָׂכַר עָלֶיךָ אֶת בִּלְעָם בֶּן בְּעוֹר מִפְּתוֹר אֲרַם נַהֲרַיִם לְקַלְלֶךָּ: [דברים כג, ה]

מסורת הש"ס

א) [יבמות מט:], ב) יומא ט: ע"ש, ג) [גירסת הערוך קדדך], ד) לא נמצא מקרא [גם בע"י ליתא להך קרא עיין חידושי אגדות שם], ה) [לקמן קי. נדרים לט:], ו) [בשאילתות סימן ל"ט פ' שמות איתא קצרתא], ז) [ב"מ לג:].

ליקוטי רש"י

כי קצר המצע מהשתרע. כי אביא עליכם שונא דוחק אתכם אשר לא תוכלו להספיק עבודתו כשיליע מלעו עליכם יקצר לו מהשתרע השוכב עליו מהשתרע מהשתטח להאריך איבריו איסטנדליי"ר בלע"ז. והמסכה צרה. הנסיך שימשול עליכם יהיה מקומכם דחוק לו בהתכנסו לתוכו ורבותינו דרשוהו על עכו"ם שהכניס מנשה להיכל קצר המצע הזה מהשתרע מהשתרר עליו שני רעים ואני פרשתיו לפי פשוטו ובדרך זה ת"י ואף מדרש רבותינו יש לישבו על אופן הדבור כלומר למה אני מביא עליכם פורענות זו לפי שקצר המצע מהשתרע אני לבדי עליו שנאמר (מ"א ח) הנה השמים לא יכלכלוך וכל שכן בהכניסכם מסכה עמי כביכול צר לנו המקום [ישעיהו כח, כ]. לי הכסף ולי הזהב. ובידי להביא לאשר חפצתי בו [חגי ב, ח]. ותועבתיו שבא על אמו. והנמצא עליו. כתובת קעקע [דה"ב לו, ח].

THEY CONDEMNED to Gehinnom for their sins.[12]

The Gemara discusses the crimes of Menasheh:

,,וְגַם דָּם נָקִי שָׁפַךְ מְנַשֶּׁה הַרְבֵּה מְאֹד עַד אֲשֶׁר־מִלֵּא אֶת־יְרוּשָׁלַםִ פֶּה לָפֶה – Scripture states:[13] ***Moreover, Menasheh shed very much innocent blood, until he filled Jerusalem with blood from end to end,*** לְבַד מֵחַטָּאתוֹ אֲשֶׁר הֶחֱטִיא אֶת־יְהוּדָה לַעֲשׂוֹת הָרַע בְּעֵינֵי ה׳ '' – ***besides for the sin he committed in causing Judah to do that which was evil in the eyes of HASHEM.*** What is the meaning of *from end to end?*[14] הָכָא תַּרְגִּימוּ שֶׁהָרַג יְשַׁעְיָה – **Here,** in Babylonia, **they explain** it to mean **that [Menasheh] killed Isaiah.**[15] בְּמַעַרְבָא אָמְרֵי – **In the West** (the Land of Israel) **they say** it means שֶׁעָשָׂה צֶלֶם מַשּׂאוֹי אֶלֶף בְּנֵי אָדָם – **that every day [Menasheh] made an idol which was so heavy that it required a thousand men** to carry it, וּבְכָל יוֹם וָיוֹם הוֹרֵג אֶת כּוּלָּם – **and every day** he would make them carry this crushingly heavy idol about and **it would kill them all,** for it was too heavy for them.[16]

The Gemara interjects:

כְּמַאן אָזְלָא הָא דְּאָמַר רַבָּה בַּר בַּר חָנָה – **Whose opinion reflects that which Rabbah bar bar Chanah said:** שְׁקוּלָה נִשְׁמָה שֶׁל צַדִּיק אֶחָד כְּנֶגֶד כָּל הָעוֹלָם כּוּלּוֹ – **The soul of a single righteous person is equal to an entire world?** כְּמַאן דְּאָמַר יְשַׁעְיָה הָרַג – **It reflects the opinion of the one who said that [Menasheh] killed Isaiah.**[17]

The Gemara continues with its subject:

כְּתִיב ,,פֶּסֶל'' – **It is written** that Menasheh made ***a graven image*** (singular),[18] וּכְתִיב ,,פְּסִלִים'' – **and it is** also **written** that he made ***graven images*** (plural).[19] The two statements seem contradictory. אָמַר רַבִּי יוֹחָנָן – **R' Yochanan said:** בַּתְּחִלָּה עָשָׂה לוֹ פַּרְצוּף אֶחָד – **At first he made [a graven image] that had one visage,** וּלְבַסּוֹף עָשָׂה לוֹ אַרְבָּעָה פַּרְצוּפִים – **and in the end he made it with four visages,** כְּדֵי שֶׁתִּרְאֶה שְׁכִינָה וְתִכְעוֹס – **so that** from whichever direction **the Divine Presence** would enter the Temple, it **would see it and become enraged.**[20]

The Gemara discusses a progression of sin in the royal Davidic line of Achaz, Menasheh and Amon:

אָחָז הֶעֱמִידוֹ בָּעֲלִיָּיה – **Achaz installed [an idol] in the upper chamber** of the Temple, שֶׁנֶּאֱמַר ,,וְאֶת־הַמִּזְבְּחוֹת אֲשֶׁר עַל־הַגָּג עֲלִיַּת אָחָז וגו׳ '' – **as it is stated:** ***And the altars that were on the roof of Achaz's upper chamber* etc.**[21] מְנַשֶּׁה הֶעֱמִידוֹ בַּהֵיכָל – **Menasheh** went further and **installed [an image] in the Sanctuary** itself,[22] שֶׁנֶּאֱמַר ,,וַיָּשֶׂם אֶת־פֶּסֶל הָאֲשֵׁרָה אֲשֶׁר עָשָׂה – **as it is stated:**[23] ***And [Menasheh] placed the graven image of Asheirah that he made*** בַּבַּיִת אֲשֶׁר אָמַר ה׳ אֶל־דָּוִד וְאֶל־שְׁלֹמֹה בְנוֹ – ***in the House concerning which HASHEM had said to David and to Solomon his son,*** בַּבַּיִת הַזֶּה וּבִירוּשָׁלַםִ אֲשֶׁר בָּחַרְתִּי מִכֹּל שִׁבְטֵי יִשְׂרָאֵל אָשִׂים אֶת־שְׁמִי לְעוֹלָם'' – ***"In this House and in Jerusalem, which I chose out of all the tribes of Israel, I will establish My Name forever."*** אָמוֹן הִכְנִיסוֹ לְבֵית קָדְשֵׁי הַקֳּדָשִׁים – **Amon** outdid his wicked predecessors and **introduced [his idol] into the** very **Holy of Holies,** שֶׁנֶּאֱמַר ,,כִּי־קָצַר הַמַּצָּע מֵהִשְׂתָּרֵעַ וְהַמַּסֵּכָה צָרָה כְּהִתְכַּנֵּס'' – **as it is stated:** ***For the couch is too short for stretching out, and the cover too narrow for curling up.***[24] מַאי ,,כִּי־קָצַר הַמַּצָּע מֵהִשְׂתָּרֵעַ'' – **What is the meaning of** ***For the couch is too short for stretching out*** *(meihistareia)*? אָמַר רַבִּי שְׁמוּאֵל בַּר נַחְמָנִי אָמַר רַבִּי יוֹנָתָן – **R' Shmuel bar Nachmani said in the name of R' Yonasan:** [כִּי] קָצַר הַמַּצָּע זֶה מִלְּהִשְׁתָּרֵר עָלָיו שְׁנֵי רֵעִים כְּאֶחָד – **For this couch** (the Temple) **is too short for two companions to have dominion over it at one time,** i.e. the Temple cannot house the Divine Presence and an idol at the same time; one or the other must go.[25] מַאי ,,וְהַמַּסֵּכָה צָרָה וגו׳ '' – **What is the meaning of** ***and the cover is too narrow* etc.** for curling up (*kehiskaneis*)? אָמַר רַבִּי שְׁמוּאֵל בַּר נַחְמָנִי – **R' Shmuel bar Nachmani said:** רַבִּי יוֹנָתָן כִּי הֲוָה מָטֵי לְהַאי קְרָא – **R' Yonasan, whenever he would come to this verse,** הֲוָה קָא בָּכֵי – **would weep** and say: מִי שֶׁכָּתַב בּוֹ ,,כֹּנֵס כַּנֵּד מֵי הַיָּם'' – **"He of whom it is written:**[26] ***He gathers (koneis) like a mound the waters of the sea,*** i.e. God, תֵּעָשֶׂה לוֹ מַסֵּכָה צָרָה – **shall an idol** (*maseichah*) now **become a rival** (*tzarah*) **to Him?**[27]

More crimes by Achaz, Menasheh, and Amon:

[אָחָז בִּטֵּל אֶת הָעֲבוֹדָה] – **Achaz abolished the Temple Service**

NOTES

12. Rather, their souls will wander aimlessly through the world, neither enjoying the bliss of the World to Come nor suffering the tortures of Gehinnom. [However, it is reasonable to assume that they will suffer anguish at being prevented from returning to their source in the World to Come] (*Yad Ramah*).

The sparing of these kings from Gehinnom is in exchange for their constant efforts to protect the lives of their subjects, including the terribly difficult wars they were compelled to wage and the genuine empathy they displayed when their subjects were suffering (ibid.).

The other wicked kings of Judah, [such as] Amon and Yehoiakim, are not mentioned here because they will be resurrected (*Rashi*) after suffering in Gehinnom for their sins (see *Yad Ramah*).

All these matters were apparently known to the Sages via tradition.

13. *II Kings* 21:16.

14. I.e. can one person possibly fill Jerusalem from end to end with blood? (*Yalkut Shimoni* ad loc.).

15. I.e. Menasheh's murder of the prophet Isaiah was a crime so heinous that it was as if he had filled Jerusalem with blood from end to end (*Rashi*). The expression פֶּה לָפֶה hints at Isaiah who, in his generation, was the equivalent of Moses, of whom it says in *Numbers* 12:8: פֶּה אֶל־פֶּה אֲדַבֶּר־בּוֹ (*Iyun Yaakov* from *Yalkut Shimoni* ibid.; cf. *Maharsha*).

See *Yevamos* 49b for a full account of Menasheh's killing of Isaiah.

16. *Maharal* suggests that this was the idol's mode of worship, namely, to compel this very heavy idol to be carried by an insufficient number of men, thereby assuring the death of those men, a fiendish form of human sacrifice.

17. I.e. the fact that Scripture describes the murder of the righteous Isaiah by saying that "Menasheh filled Jerusalem with blood from end to end" indicates that the murder of one righteous man is equivalent to filling an entire city with murder victims (*Rashi*).

18. *II Chronicles* 33:7. *And he placed the graven image that he made in the House of God*.

19. Ibid. v. 19. *And the places . . . at which he placed . . . graven images.*

20. I.e. it would be confronted by one of the four visages of the graven image (*Rashi*). Alternatively, the four faces of the idol were a crude imitation of God's throne, which has four faces (*Maharsha*).

21. *II Kings* 23:12. This verse describes the efforts of Menasheh's grandson, the righteous King Yoshiah, to cleanse Judea of idolatry. Among the other idols he destroyed is listed the one Achaz installed in the upper chamber, which the Gemara here understands as referring to the upper chamber of the Temple.

22. That is, in the Holy, the room just outside the Holy of Holies.

23. *II Kings* 21:7.

24. *Isaiah* 28:20.

25. The word מֵהִשְׂתָּרֵעַ is expounded as a mnemonic for מֵהִשְׂתָּרֵר רֵיעַ, *for the dominion of a companion* (*Rashi* to *Yoma* 9b ד״ה מהשתרע). Alternatively, מֵהִשְׂתָּרֵעַ is a mnemonic for מִשְּׁתֵּי רֵעִים, *for two companions* (*Rashash* ibid.).

26. *Psalms* 33:7.

27. I.e. shall the One Who pushes back the powerful seas to make room for the dry land now feel constrained by the presence of a lifeless idol? Alas, such is the sad consequence of Israel's sins! (*Maharsha,* first explanation; cf. second explanation there and in *Toras Chaim*).

The plain translation of וְהַמַּסֵּכָה צָרָה כְּהִתְכַּנֵּס is *and the cover too narrow for curling up,* the word מַסֵּכָה meaning *cover* and צָרָה meaning *narrow.* However, the Gemara presently translates מַסֵּכָה as *idol* and צָרָה as *rival*, translating the phrase: *the idol is a rival when it is brought in* (see *Yad Ramah*; cf. *Rashi* ad loc.).

גליון הש"ס

גמרא אבשלום אין לו חלק לעוה"ב. ע' סוטה דף י ע"ב תוספות ד"ה דקרב: שם ר"י ור"א חד אמר. ע' מדרש רבה ויקרא סוף פ' מצורע:

תורה אור השלם

א) כִּי בִי חָשַׁק וַאֲפַלְּטֵהוּ אֲשַׂגְּבֵהוּ כִּי יָדַע שְׁמִי: יִקְרָאֵנִי וְאֶעֱנֵהוּ עִמּוֹ אָנֹכִי בְצָרָה אֲחַלְּצֵהוּ וַאֲכַבְּדֵהוּ: אֹרֶךְ יָמִים אַשְׂבִּיעֵהוּ וְאַרְאֵהוּ בִּישׁוּעָתִי: [תהלים צא, יד-טז]

ב) וְיִמָּנַע מֵרְשָׁעִים אוֹרָם וּזְרוֹעַ רָמָה תִּשָּׁבֵר: [איוב לח, טו]

ג) וַיָּסֹבּוּ עֲשָׂרָה נְעָרִים נֹשְׂאֵי כְּלֵי יוֹאָב וַיַּכּוּ אֶת אַבְשָׁלוֹם וַיְמִיתֻהוּ: [שמואל ב' יח, טו]

ד) וְגַם דָּם נָקִי שָׁפַךְ מְנַשֶּׁה הַרְבֵּה מְאֹד עַד אֲשֶׁר מִלֵּא אֶת יְרוּשָׁלִַם פֶּה לָפֶה לְבַד מֵחַטָּאתוֹ אֲשֶׁר הֶחֱטִיא אֶת יְהוּדָה לַעֲשׂוֹת הָרַע בְּעֵינֵי יְיָ: [מלכים ב' כא, טז]

ה) וַיָּשֶׂם אֶת פֶּסֶל הַסֶּמֶל אֲשֶׁר עָשָׂה בְּבֵית הָאֱלֹהִים אֲשֶׁר אָמַר אֱלֹהִים אֶל דָּוִיד וְאֶל שְׁלֹמֹה בְנוֹ בַּבַּיִת הַזֶּה וּבִירוּשָׁלִַם אֲשֶׁר בָּחַרְתִּי מִכֹּל שִׁבְטֵי יִשְׂרָאֵל אָשִׂים אֶת שְׁמִי לְעֵילוֹם: [דברי הימים ב' לג, ז]

ו) וּתְפִלָּתוֹ וְהֵעָתֶר לוֹ וְכָל חַטָּאתוֹ וּמַעְלוֹ וְהַמְּקֹמוֹת אֲשֶׁר בָּנָה בָהֶם בָּמוֹת וְהֶעֱמִיד הָאֲשֵׁרִים וְהַפְּסִלִים לִפְנֵי הִכָּנְעוֹ הִנָּם כְּתוּבִים עַל דִּבְרֵי חוֹזָי: [דברי הימים ב' לג, יט]

ז) וְאֶת הַמִּזְבְּחוֹת אֲשֶׁר עַל הַגָּג עֲלִיַּת אָחָז אֲשֶׁר עָשׂוּ מַלְכֵי יְהוּדָה וְאֶת הַמִּזְבְּחוֹת אֲשֶׁר עָשָׂה מְנַשֶּׁה בִּשְׁתֵּי חַצְרוֹת בֵּית יְיָ נָתַץ הַמֶּלֶךְ וַיָּרָץ מִשָּׁם וְהִשְׁלִיךְ אֶת עֲפָרָם אֶל נַחַל קִדְרוֹן: [מלכים ב' כג, יב]

ח) וַיָּשֶׂם אֶת פֶּסֶל הָאֲשֵׁרָה אֲשֶׁר עָשָׂה בַּבַּיִת אֲשֶׁר אָמַר יְיָ אֶל דָּוִד וְאֶל שְׁלֹמֹה בְנוֹ בַּבַּיִת הַזֶּה וּבִירוּשָׁלִַם אֲשֶׁר בָּחַרְתִּי מִכֹּל שִׁבְטֵי יִשְׂרָאֵל אָשִׂים אֶת שְׁמִי לְעוֹלָם: [מלכים ב' כא, ז]

ט) כִּי קָצַר הַמַּצָּע מֵהִשְׂתָּרֵעַ וְהַמַּסֵּכָה צָרָה כְּהִתְכַּנֵּס: [ישעיה כח, כ]

י) כֹּנֵס כַּנֵּד מֵי הַיָּם נֹתֵן בְּאֹצָרוֹת תְּהוֹמוֹת: [תהלים לג, ז]

כ) צוֹר תְּעוּדָה חֲתוֹם תּוֹרָה בְּלִמֻּדָי: [ישעיה ח, טז]

ל) וְלֹא נִכְנַע מִלִּפְנֵי יְיָ כְּהִכָּנַע מְנַשֶּׁה אָבִיו כִּי הוּא אָמוֹן הִרְבָּה אַשְׁמָה: [דברי הימים ב' לג, כג]

מ) לִי הַכֶּסֶף וְלִי הַזָּהָב נְאֻם יְיָ צְבָאוֹת: [חגי ב, ח]

א) כי בי חשק ואפלטהו אשגבהו כי ידע שמי יקראני ואענהו עמו אנכי בצרה אחלצהו ואכבדהו אורך ימים אשביעהו ואראהו בישועתי אמר ר"ש בן לקיש מאי דכתיב ב) וימנע מרשעים אורם וזרוע רמה תשבר מפני מה עי"ן של רשעים תלויה כיון שנעשה אדם רש מלמטה נעשה רש מלמעלה ולא נכתביה כלל ר' יוחנן ור"א חד אמר מפני כבודו של דוד וחד אמר משום כבודו של נחמיה בן חכליה תנו רבנן מנשה היה שונה חמשים וחמשה פנים בתורת כהנים כנגד שני מלכותו אחאב שמנים וחמשה ירבעם מאה ושלשה תניא היה ר"מ אומר °אבשלום אין לו חלק לעוה"ב שנאמר ג) ויכו את אבשלום וימיתוהו ויכוהו בעוה"ז וימיתוהו לעוה"ב תניא ר"ש בן אלעזר אומר משום ר"מ אחז ואחזיה וכל מלכי ישראל שכתוב בהן ויעש הרע בעיני ה' לא חיין ולא נידונין ד) וגם דם נקי שפך מנשה הרבה מאד עד אשר מלא את ירושלים פה לפה לבד מחטאתו אשר החטיא את יהודה לעשות הרע בעיני ה' הכא א) תרגימו שהרג ישעיה במערבא אמרי שעשה צלם משאוי אלף בני אדם ובכל יום ויום הורג (את) כולם כמאן אזלא הא דאמר רבה בר בר חנה שקולה נשמה של צדיק אחד כנגד כל העולם כולו כמ"ד ישעיה הרג כתיב ה) פסל וכתיב ו) פסילים א"ר יוחנן בתחלה עשה לו פרצוף אחד ולבסוף עשה לו ארבעה פרצופים כדי שתראה שכינה ותכעוס אחז העמידו בעלייה שנאמר ז) ואת המזבחות אשר על הגג עליית אחז וגו' מנשה העמידו בהיכל שנאמר ח) וישם את פסל האשרה אשר עשה בבית אשר אמר ה' אל דוד ואל שלמה [בנו] בבית הזה ובירושלים אשר בחרתי מכל שבטי ישראל אשים את שמי לעולם אמון הכניסו לבית קדשי הקדשים שנאמר ט) כי קצר המצע מהשתרע והמסכה צרה כהתכנס מאי כי קצר המצע מהשתרע אמר ב) רבי שמואל בר נחמני אמר רבי יונתן [כי] קצר המצע זה מלהשתרר עליו שני רעים כאחד מאי והמסכה צרה וגו' אמר רבי שמואל בר נחמני רבי יונתן כי הוה מטי להאי קרא הוה קא בכי מי שכתב בו י) כונס כנד מי הים תעשה לו מסכה צרה [אחז בטל את העבודה] וחתם את התורה שנאמר כ) צור תעודה חתום תורה בלמודי ג) מנשה קדר את האזכרות והרס את המזבח אמון [שרף את התורה] והעלה שממית על גבי המזבח אחז התיר את הערוה מנשה בא על אחותו אמון בא על אמו שנאמר ל) כי הוא אמון הרבה אשמה °רבי יוחנן ור"א חד אמר ששרף את התורה וחד אמר שבא על אמו אמרה לו אמו כלום יש לך הנאה ממקום שיצאת ממנו א"ל כלום אני עושה אלא להכעיס את בוראי כי אתא יהויקים אמר קמאי לא ידעי לארגוזי כלום אנו צריכין אלא לאורו יש לנו זהב פרויים שאנו משתמשין בו יטול אורו אמרו לו והלא כסף וזהב שלו הוא שנאמר מ) לי הכסף ולי הזהב נאם ה' צבאות אמר להם כבר נתנו לנו שנאמר נ) השמים שמים לה' והארץ נתן לבני האדם א"ל רבא לרבה בר מרי מפני מה לא מנו את יהויקים משום דכתיב ביה ס) ויתר דברי יהויקים ותועבותיו אשר עשה והנמצא עליו מאי והנמצא עליו רבי יוחנן ור"א חד אמר שחקק שם עבודת כוכבים על אמתו וחד אמר שחקק שם שמים על אמתו א"ל במלכים לא שמעתי מפני מה לא מנו את מיכה מפני שפתו מצויה לעוברי דרכים שנאמר ד) כל העובר ושב אל הלוים ע) ועבר בים צרה והכה בים גלים א"ר יוחנן זה פסלו של מיכה תניא רבי נתן אומר מגרב לשילה ג' מילין והיה עשן המערכה ועשן פסל מיכה מתערבין זה בזה בקשו מלאכי השרת לדוחפו אמר להן הקב"ה הניחו לו שפתו מצויה לעוברי דרכים ועל דבר זה נענשו אנשי פלגש בגבעה אמר להן הקב"ה ה) בכבודי לא מחיתם על כבודו של בשר ודם מחיתם א"ר יוחנן משום רבי יוסי בן ו) קסמא גדולה לגימה שהרחיקה שתי משפחות מישראל שנאמר פ) על דבר אשר לא קדמו אתכם בלחם ובמים ורבי יוחנן דידיה אמר מרחקת את הקרובים ומקרבת את הרחוקים ומעלמת עינים מן הרשעים ומשרה שכינה על נביאי הבעל ז) ושגגתו עולה זדון מרחקת את הקרובים
מעמון

רש"י

כי בי חשק. לא שייך אלא ברבונא דעלמא כלומר אותו שחפץ בי וכיראתי אפלטהו: ע' שברשעים תלויה. שאינה כתובה בשיטת אותיות התיבה אלא תלויה היא למעלה ונראה ככתוב רשים: כיון שנעשה אדם רש מלמטה. שיש לו שונאין ואין רוח הבריות נוחה הימנו: נעשה רש מלמעלה. בידוע ששונאין אותו מלמעלה להכי כתוב רשים שני מיני רשות: ולא נכתביה. לעי"ן כלל: משום כבודו של דוד. שאין הדבר נוהג בצדיקים ודוד היו לו שונאים הרבה: ונחמיה בן חכליה. שהיו לו שונאים הרבה מנכרים שמבקשין להרגו על שהיה בונה בית המקדש כדכתיב בעזרא (נחמיה ד) ואחת מחזקת השלח וגו' ל"א היו לו קנאים מישראל דכתיב (שם ו) רבים ביהודה בעלי שבועה לו כי הוא חתן לשכניה בן ארח שהיו מבזין אותו. בקדושין (דף ע.) מפרש להאי קרא ולהכי איכתבא לומר שברשעים אמרינן ולא בצדיקים: היה שונה חמשים וחמשה פנים בתורת כהנים. ספר ויקרא היה מחדש בו כל שנה ושנה ודורשו מפלפולו: לא חיין. לא יחיו לעולם הבא עם הצדיקים ואין נדונין נמי בגיהנם ודוקא קאמר מלכי ישראל אבל שלמה וצדקיה מבית דוד אתו ואף על גב דכתיב בהו ויעש הרע חיין הן לעתיד: אחז ואחזיה. ממלכי יהודה וקים להו שהיו רשעים ואמון ויהויקים לא חשיב ואף על גב דהוו רשעים מאד כדלקמן בהנהו קים להו דחיין: הורג את כולן. שהיו נבקעין בכובד המשאוי: כמ"ד שהרג ישעיה. והאי קאמר קרא מלא את ירושלים פה לפה שנשמתו של צדיק שקולה כמו שמלא את ירושלים חללים: כתוב. (במלכים) [דה"ב לג] ויסם את פסל הסמל אשר עשה בבית האלהים: וכתיב והעמיד את האשרים והפסילים בד"ה (שם): ולבסוף עשה. מנשה לאותו דמות ד' פרצופים: כדי שתראה שכינה מכל צד. שתכנס להיכל תראה פרצוף כנגדו ותכעוס: מלהשתרר עליו שני רעים. שכינה ודמות הפרצוף: מצע. בית המקדש: תעשה לו מסכה צרה. כאשה שנעשית צרה לחברתה: העלה שממית. קורי עכבים שבטל עבודה מכל וכל עד שארגו עכבים קוריהן ע"ג המזבח: היתר. נעשה לו כהיתר: ממקום שיצאת משם. מקום שאדם יוצא ממנו שבע הוא ממנו ואינו מתאוה להנאת אותו מקום: קמאי לא ידעי לארגוזי. מלכים ראשונים שלפנינו לא היו יודעים להכעיס המקום כמו שהוא חרף ואמר כלום אנו צריכין אלא לאורו שמאיר לנו השמש יצא ויטול אורו: שאנו משתמשין בו. שמאיר ביותר: אמרו לו. בני דורו והלא כסף וכו' דבני דורו צדיקים היו כדאמרן נסתכל בדורו של יהויקים ונתקררה דעתו: מפני מה לא מנו את יהויקים. בהדי הנך שאין להם חלק לעולם הבא: משום דכתיב ויתר דברי יהויקים. בתמיהה משום דכתיב ביה רשע כזה לא מנאוהו: שם עבודת כוכבים על גופו. מתוך שהיה אדוק בה: שם שמים. משום בזיון: במלכים לא שמעתי. מפני מה לא מנו את יהויקים: בהדיוטות שמעתי. מפני מה לא מנו מיכה בהדי ארבעה הדיוטות דמתניתין: פתו מצויה לעוברי דרכים. שהיו כל העולם מתארחין אצלו כדכתיב (במקרא) כל העובר ושב אל הלוים זה מיכה: זה פסלו של מיכה. כשכתב משה את השם והשליכו על נילוס להעלות ארונו של יוסף בא מיכה ונטלו בהחבא והיינו דכתיב ועבר בים צרה כשהעביר הקדוש ברוך הוא לישראל עבר מיכה עמהם שבידו השם לעשות העגל ל"א מיכה עשה פסל והביאו עמו כשעברו ישראל הים: גרב. מקומו של מיכה בגרב הוה פסלו של מיכה קבוע ובשילה היה המשכן: לדוחפו. למיכה: ועל דבר זה. על פסלו של מיכה שלא מיחו ישראל בידו נענשו אנשי פילגש בגבעה שנפלו ביד בנימין והרגו מהם ארבעים אלף: לגימה. אכילה שמאכילין אורחים: שתי משפחות. עמון ומואב שלפי שלא קדמו ישראל בלחם ובמים נכתב שלא יבאו בקהל: מעלמת עינים מן הרשעים. מעלמת מעיני המקום שלא להביט ברשעו לשלם לו כדרכו הרעה אלא עושה כאילו אינו רואה במעשיו:
עמון

מסורת הש"ס

א) [יבמות מט:], ב) יומא ט: ע"ש, ג) [גירסת הערוך קדר], ד) לא נמצא מקרא [גם בע"י ליתא להך קרא עיין חידושי אגדות שם], ה) [לקמן קי. נדרים לט:], ו) [בשאלתות סימן ל"ט פ' שמות איתא קצרתא], ז) [ב"מ לג:].

ליקוטי רש"י

כי קצר המצע מהשתרע. כי אביא עליכם שונא דוחק אתכם אשר לא תוכלו להספיק עבודתו כשיגיע מלעו עליכם יקצר לו מהשתרע השוכב עליו מהשתרע מהשתטח להאריך איבריו אישטנדליי"ר בלע"ז. והמסכה צרה. הנסיך שימשול עליכם יהיה מקומכם דחוק לו בהתכנסו לתוכו ורבותינו דרשוהו על עכו"ם שהכניס מנשה להיכל קצר המצע הזה מהשתרע מהשתרר עליו שני רעים ואני פרשתיו לפי פשוטו ובדרך זה ת"י ואף מדרש רבותינו יש לישבו על אופן הדבור כלומר למה אני מביא עליכם פורענות זו לפי שקצר המצע מהשתרע אני לבדי עליו שנאמר (מ"א ח) הנה השמים לא יכלכלוך וכל שכן בהכניסכם מסכה עמי כביכול צר לנו המקום [ישעיהו כח, כ]. לי הכסף ולי הזהב. ובידי להביא לאשר חפלתי בו [חגי ב, ח]. ותועבותיו שבא על אמו. והנמצא עליו. כתובת קעקע [דה"ב לו, ח].

נ) הַשָּׁמַיִם שָׁמַיִם לַיְיָ וְהָאָרֶץ נָתַן לִבְנֵי אָדָם: [תהלים קטו, טז] ס) וְיֶתֶר דִּבְרֵי יְהוֹיָקִים וְתֹעֲבֹתָיו אֲשֶׁר עָשָׂה וְהַנִּמְצָא עָלָיו הִנָּם כְּתוּבִים עַל סֵפֶר מַלְכֵי יִשְׂרָאֵל וִיהוּדָה וַיִּמְלֹךְ יְהוֹיָכִין בְּנוֹ תַּחְתָּיו: [דברי הימים ב' לו, ח]
ע) וְעָבַר בַּיָּם צָרָה וְהִכָּה בַיָּם גַּלִּים וְהֹבִישׁוּ כֹּל מְצוּלוֹת יְאֹר וְהוּרַד גְּאוֹן אַשּׁוּר וְשֵׁבֶט מִצְרַיִם יָסוּר: [זכריה י, יא] פ) עַל דְּבַר אֲשֶׁר לֹא קִדְּמוּ אֶתְכֶם בַּלֶּחֶם וּבַמַּיִם בַּדֶּרֶךְ בְּצֵאתְכֶם מִמִּצְרָיִם וַאֲשֶׁר שָׂכַר עָלֶיךָ אֶת בִּלְעָם בֶּן בְּעוֹר מִפְּתוֹר אֲרַם נַהֲרַיִם לְקַלְלֶךָּ: [דברים כג, ה]

וְחָתַם אֶת הַתּוֹרָה – and "sealed off" the Torah, שֶׁנֶּאֱמַר ,,צוֹר תְּעוּדָה חֲתוֹם תּוֹרָה בְּלִמֻּדָי" – as it is stated: ***Bind up the testimony, seal the instruction with My disciples.***[28] מְנַשֶּׁה קָדַר אֶת הָאַזְכָּרוֹת – **Menasheh scratched out the mention** of God's Name from Torah scrolls וְהָרַס אֶת הַמִּזְבֵּחַ – **and tore down the Altar** in the Temple.[29] אָמוֹן [שָׂרַף אֶת הַתּוֹרָה] – **Amon burned the Torah** וְהֶעֱלָה שְׂמָמִית עַל גַּבֵּי הַמִּזְבֵּחַ – **and caused cobwebs to grow on the Altar,** i.e. he prohibited the bringing of sacrifices, which resulted in the Altar's falling into neglect.[30] אָחָז הִתִּיר אֶת הָעֶרְוָה – **Achaz permitted,** i.e. was totally unrestrained, in the matter of **forbidden sexual relationships;**[31] מְנַשֶּׁה בָּא עַל אֲחוֹתוֹ – **Menasheh had relations with his** own **sister;** אָמוֹן בָּא עַל אִמּוֹ – **Amon had relations with his** own **mother,** שֶׁנֶּאֱמַר ,,כִּי הוּא אָמוֹן הִרְבָּה אַשְׁמָה" – **as it is stated: *For he was the Amon who did ever more evil.***[32] רַבִּי יוֹחָנָן וְרַבִּי אֶלְעָזָר – **R' Yochanan and R' Elazar** dispute the meaning of this verse: חַד אָמַר שֶׁשָּׂרַף אֶת הַתּוֹרָה – **One said** that it means **that [Amon] burned the Torah,** וְחַד אָמַר שֶׁבָּא עַל אִמּוֹ – **and one said** that it means **that [Amon] had relations with his mother.** אָמְרָה לוֹ אִמּוֹ – **His mother said to him:** כְּלוּם יֵשׁ לְךָ הֲנָאָה מִמָּקוֹם שֶׁיָּצָאתָ מִמֶּנּוּ – **"Can you have any pleasure from the source from which you issued?"**[33] אָמַר לָהּ – **[Amon] said to her:** כְּלוּם אֲנִי עוֹשֶׂה אֶלָּא לְהַכְעִיס אֶת בּוֹרְאִי – **"Am I doing this for any purpose other than to vex my Creator?"**

But Yehoiakim outdid his predecessors:

כִּי אָתָא יְהוֹיָקִים – **When Yehoiakim came along,** אָמַר – **he said:** קַמָּאֵי לֹא יָדְעֵי לְאַרְגּוּזֵי – **"The earlier ones,** i.e. my predecessors, **did not know how to anger** God." Thereupon, he proceeded to blaspheme and declared: כְּלוּם אָנוּ צְרִיכִין אֶלָּא לְאוֹרוֹ – **"Do we need** God for **anything other than His light,** i.e. the light of the sun? יֵשׁ לָנוּ זָהָב פַּרְוַיִים שֶׁאָנוּ מִשְׁתַּמְּשִׁין בּוֹ – **We have** brilliant **Parvaim gold,** which provides sufficient illumination, and **which we** already **use.** יִטּוֹל אוֹרוֹ – **Let Him take His light** and keep it for Himself. We do not need it!" אָמְרוּ לוֹ – **[His subjects],** who were righteous,[34] **said to him:** וַהֲלֹא כֶּסֶף וְזָהָב שֶׁלּוֹ הוּא – **"Are not** all **gold and silver His,** שֶׁנֶּאֱמַר ,,לִי הַכֶּסֶף וְלִי הַזָּהָב נְאֻם ה' צְבָאוֹת" – **as it is stated:**[35] ***'Mine is the silver and Mine is the gold,' says Hashem of Hosts?"*** אָמַר לָהֶם – **[Yehoiakim] said to them:** כְּבָר נְתָנוֹ לָנוּ – **"He has already given it to us,** שֶׁנֶּאֱמַר ,,הַשָּׁמַיִם שָׁמַיִם לַה' וְהָאָרֶץ נָתַן לִבְנֵי־אָדָם" – **as it is stated:**[36] ***As for the heavens – the heavens are Hashem's, but the earth He has given to the sons of man."***[37]

Having described the extreme sinfulness of Yehoiakim, the Gemara discusses why our Mishnah fails to include Yehoiakim or any other very wicked king or commoner among those who have no share in the World to Come:

אָמַר לֵיהּ רָבָא לְרַבָּה בַּר מָרִי – **Rava said to Rabbah bar Mari:** מִפְּנֵי מָה לֹא מָנוּ אֶת יְהוֹיָקִים – **Why did they not list Yehoiakim** in our Mishnah among the kings who have no portion in the World to Come? מִשּׁוּם דִּכְתִיב בֵּיהּ ,,וְיֶתֶר דִּבְרֵי יְהוֹיָקִים וְתֹעֲבֹתָיו אֲשֶׁר־עָשָׂה וְהַנִּמְצָא עָלָיו" – **Is it because it is written concerning him:**[38] ***Now the rest of the matters of Yehoiakim and the abomina-***

NOTES

28. *Isaiah* 8:16. The Gemara interprets this verse as representing the command of Achaz to end the Temple Service and Torah study: *Bind up the testimony,* i.e. cease the Temple Service, which is the testimony that the Divine Presence rests with Israel; *seal the instruction with my disciples,* i.e. let the study of the Torah cease (*Maharsha*).

Elsewhere, we are told that Achaz undertook a campaign to drive the Divine Presence from Israel. He reasoned: "If the children do not study Torah, there will in time be no Torah scholars. Without Torah scholars, no prophets can develop. And without prophets, the Divine Presence will not rest in Israel." He therefore sealed the synagogues and study halls so that children could not be taught Torah (see *Maharsha, Yerushalmi Sanhedrin* 51a, *Bereishis Rabbah* 42:3).

It was to these crimes of Achaz that the verse cited by Rav Chisda on 103a applies: *I passed by the field of a lazy man* (*Rashi* there ד"ה על שדה), for by sabotaging the Temple service and educational system, Achaz sought to make the people too "lazy" to offer sacrifices or study Torah (*Yad Ramah* ibid.).

29. This is evident from *II Chronicles* 33:16, where it is recounted that after Menasheh changed his evil ways, *he built the Altar of Hashem.* This implies that the Altar had been torn down (*Maharsha*).

It is to these crimes of Menasheh that the verse cited by Rav Chisda on 103a refers: *by the vineyard of a man who lacks sense* (*Rashi* ibid. ד"ה ועל כרם), for Menasheh's crimes were senseless, since he could not cause God any harm by scratching out His Name or by tearing down His Altar (*Yad Ramah* ibid.).

According to one interpretation, the reference here is not to the actual destruction of the Altar, but to the resulting eradication of the Heavenly fire which descended from heaven onto the Altar during Solomon's reign and which remained there for centuries until Menasheh removed it by destroying the Altar, as stated in *Zevachim* 61b (see *Rashi* to *II Kings* 16:14 and ArtScroll edition of *II Chronicles* p. 437).

30. This follows *Rashi.* Others translate שְׂמָמִית as a lizard (*Aruch*), a type of bird (*Yad Ramah*) or a monkey (*Ibn Ezra* to *Proverbs* 30:28). According to these translations, Amon sacrificed these unclean animals on the Altar. In so doing he exceeded the depredations of his predecessor Menasheh, who did not go so far as to pollute the Altar with such sacrifices, but was satisfied to tear the Altar down (*Margaliyos HaYam*). Likewise, Amon went beyond his predecessors in the suppression of the Torah learning by burning the Torah scrolls.

It is to this crime of Amon's that the verse cited by Rav Chisda on 103a refers: *It was all overgrown with thorns* (*Rashi* ibid. ד"ה והנה עלה).

31. Achaz was so depraved that he lost all sense of right and wrong and came to view such relationships as perfectly permissible (see *Rashi*).

Maharsha explains that the sexual excesses of Achaz and Menasheh are indicated by the Biblical statements (*II Chronicles* 28:3, 33:2) that they imitated the abominations of the Canaanite peoples, whose sexual perversions are warned against in the Torah (*Leviticus* 18:27).

32. *II Chronicles* 33:23. The verse states that Amon went beyond the sins of his predecessors, indicating that in all respects, including sexual misconduct, he exceeded his predecessors (*Maharsha*).

33. Incest with one's mother is so unnatural that one does not lust after it (*Rashi*).

[This would seem to contradict the Gemara above, 64a, that it was through the efforts of the Men of the Great Assembly that the impulse for relations with relatives (such as one's mother or sister [*Rashi* there]) was eliminated (*Margaliyos HaYam* to 64a). See *Igros Moshe Even HaEzer* IV 64:1.]

34. *Rashi;* see 103a note 10.

35. *Haggai* 2:8.

36. *Psalms* 115:16.

37. I.e. it is to this blasphemy of Yehoiakim's that the verse cited by Rav Chisda on 103a refers: *its face was covered with nettles*, for Yehoiakim "covered his face" from God's sunlight (*Rashi* ibid. ד"ה כסו).

Toras Chaim suggests that by this statement Yehoiakim meant: God has created the earth to be self-sufficient, except for the fact that we need the sunlight, which streams to earth from the heavens beyond. But we have developed artificial means of light. Let Him therefore take His sun and be gone – we can manage on our own. See also *Maharsha*.

R' Chaim Shmulevitz asserts that the desire of these kings to provoke God with deeds that gave them no personal pleasure indicates that they recognized God's existence, but that they could not resist the urge for idolatry. This can only be understood in light of the fact already mentioned on 102b, that in ancient times idolatry possessed a lure which it no longer possesses today. Apparently, as a result of the lure of idol worship there was a certain pleasure derived from rebelling against God (*Sichos Mussar* 5733:7).

38. *II Chronicles* 36:8.

א) כי בי חשק ואפלטהו אשגבהו כי ידע שמי יקראני ואענהו עמו אנכי בצרה אחלצהו ואכבדהו אורך ימים אשביעהו ואראהו בישועתי אמר ר"ש בן לקיש מאי דכתיב ב) וימנע מרשעים אורם וזרוע רמה תשבר מפני מה עי"ן של רשעים תלויה כיון שנעשה אדם רש מלמטה נעשה רש מלמעלה ולא נכתביה כלל ר' יוחנן ור"א חד אמר מפני כבודו של דוד וחד אמר משום כבודו של נחמיה בן חכליה תנו רבנן מנשה היה שונה חמשים וחמשה פנים בתורת כהנים כנגד שני מלכותו אחאב שמנים וחמשה ירבעם מאה ושלשה תניא היה ר"מ אומר °אבשלום אין לו חלק לעוה"ב שנאמר ג) ויכו את אבשלום וימיתוהו ויכוהו בעוה"ז וימיתוהו לעוה"ב תניא ר"ש בן אלעזר אומר משום ר"מ אחז ואחזיה וכל מלכי ישראל שכתוב בהן ויעש הרע בעיני ה' לא חיין ולא נידונין ד) וגם דם נקי שפך מנשה הרבה מאד עד אשר מלא את ירושלים פה לפה לבד מחטאתו אשר החטיא את יהודה לעשות הרע בעיני ה' הכא א) תרגימו שהרג ישעיה במערבא אמרי שעשה צלם משאוי אלף בני אדם ובכל יום ויום הורג (את) כולם כמאן אזלא הא דאמר רבה בר בר חנה שקולה נשמה של צדיק אחד כנגד כל העולם כולו כמ"ד ישעיה הרג כתיב ה) פסל וכתיב ו) פסילים א"ר יוחנן בתחלה עשה לו פרצוף אחד ולבסוף עשה לו ארבעה פרצופים כדי שתראה שכינה ותכעוס אחז העמידו בעלייה שנאמר ז) ואת המזבחות אשר על הגג עליית אחז וגו' מנשה העמידו בהיכל שנאמר ח) וישם את פסל האשרה אשר עשה בבית אשר אמר ה' אל דוד ואל שלמה [בנו] בבית הזה ובירושלים אשר בחרתי מכל שבטי ישראל אשים את שמי לעולם אמון הכניסו לבית קדשי הקדשים שנאמר ט) כי קצר המצע מהשתרע והמסכה צרה כהתכנס מאי כי קצר המצע מהשתרע אמר ב) רבי שמואל בר נחמני אמר רבי יונתן [כי] קצר המצע זה מלהשתרר עליו שני רעים כאחד מאי והמסכה צרה וגו' אמר רבי שמואל בר נחמני רבי יונתן כי הוה מטי להאי קרא הוה קא בכי מי שכתב בו י) כונס כנד מי הים תעשה לו מסכה צרה [אחז בטל את העבודה] וחתם את התורה שנאמר כ) צור תעודה חתום תורה בלמודי מנשה ג) קדר את האזכרות והרס את המזבח אמון [שרף את התורה] והעלה שממית על גבי המזבח אחז התיר את הערוה מנשה בא על אחותו אמון בא על אמו שנאמר ל) כי הוא אמון הרבה אשמה °רבי יוחנן ור"א חד אמר ששרף את התורה וחד אמר שבא על אמו אמרה לו אמו כלום יש לך הנאה ממקום שיצאת ממנו א"ל כלום אני עושה אלא להכעיס את בוראי כי אתא יהויקים אמר קמאי לא ידעי לארגוזי כלום אנו צריכין אלא לאורו יש לנו זהב פרויים שאנו משתמשין בו יטול אורו אמרו לו והלא כסף וזהב שלו הוא שנאמר מ) לי הכסף ולי הזהב נאם ה' צבאות אמר להם כבר נתנו לנו שנאמר נ) השמים שמים לה' והארץ נתן לבני האדם א"ל רבא לרבה בר מרי מפני מה לא מנו את יהויקים משום דכתיב ביה ס) ויתר דברי יהויקים ותועבותיו אשר עשה והנמצא עליו מאי והנמצא עליו רבי יוחנן ור"א חד אמר שחקק שם עבודת כוכבים על אמתו וחד אמר שחקק שם שמים על אמתו א"ל במלכים לא שמעתי בהדיוטות שמעתי מפני מה לא מנו את מיכה מפני שפתו מצויה לעוברי דרכים שנאמר ד) כל העובר ושב אל הלוים ע) ועבר בים צרה והכה בים גלים א"ר יוחנן זה פסלו של מיכה תניא רבי נתן אומר מגרב לשילה ג' מילין והיה עשן המערכה ועשן פסל מיכה מתערבין זה בזה בקשו מלאכי השרת לדוחפו אמר להן הקב"ה הניחו לו שפתו מצויה לעוברי דרכים ועל דבר זה נענשו אנשי פלגש בגבעה אמר להן הקב"ה ה) בכבודי לא מחיתם על כבודו של בשר ודם מחיתם א"ר יוחנן משום רבי יוסי בן ו) קסמא גדולה לגימה שהרחיקה שתי משפחות מישראל שנאמר פ) על דבר אשר לא קדמו אתכם בלחם ובמים ורבי יוחנן דידיה אמר מרחקת את הקרובים ומקרבת את הרחוקים ומעלמת עינים מן הרשעים ומשרה שכינה על נביאי הבעל ז) ושגגתו עולה זדון מרחקת את הקרובים
מעמון

כי בי חשק. לא שייך אלא ברבונא דעלמא כלומר אותו שחפץ בי ובירא(ו)תי אפלטהו: ע' שברשעים תלויה. שאינה כתובה בשיטת אותיות התיבה אלא תלויה היא למעלה ונראה ככתוב רשים: כיון שנעשה אדם רש מלמטה. שיש לו שונאין ואין רוח הבריות נוחה הימנו: נעשה רש מלמעלה. בידוע ששונאין אותו מלמעלה להכי כתוב רשים שני מיני רשות: ולא נכתביה. לעי"ן כלל: משום כבודו של דוד. שאין הדבר נוהג בצדיקים ודוד היו לו שונאים הרבה: ונחמיה בן חכליה. שהיו לו שונאים הרבה מנכרים שמבקשין להרגו על שהיה בונה בית המקדש כדכתיב בעזרא (נחמיה ד) ואחת מחזקת השלח וגו' נ"א היו לו קנאים מישראל דכתיב (שם ו) רבים ביהודה בעלי שבועה לו כי הוא חתן לשכניה בן ארח שהיו מבזין אותו. בקדושין (דף ע.) מפרש להאי קרא ולהכי איכתבא לומר שברשעים אמרינן ולא בצדיקים: היה שונה חמשים וחמשה פנים בתורת כהנים. ספר ויקרא היה מחדש בו כל שנה ושנה ודורשו מפלפולו: לא חיין. לא יחיו לעולם הבא עם הצדיקים ואין נדונין נמי בגיהנם ודוקא קאמר מלכי ישראל אבל שלמה וצדקיה מבית דוד אתו ואף על גב דכתיב בהו ויעש הרע חיין הן לעתיד: אחז ואחזיה. ממלכי יהודה וקים להו שהיו רשעים ואמון ויהויקים לא חשיב ואף על גב דהוו רשעים מאד כדלקמן בהנהו קים להו דחיין: הורג את כולן. שהיו נבקעין בכובד המשאוי: כמ"ד שהרג ישעיה. והאי קאמר קרא מלא את ירושלים פה לפה שנשמתו של צדיק שקולה כמו שמלא את ירושלים חללים: כתוב. (במלכים) [דה"ב לג] וישם את פסל הסמל אשר עשה בבית האלהים: וכתיב והעמיד את האשרים והפסילים בד"ה (שם): ולבסוף עשה. מנשה לאותו דמות ד' פרצופים: כדי שתראה שכינה מכל צד. שתכנס להיכל תראה פרצוף כנגדו ותכעוס: מלהשתרר עליו שני רעים. שכינה ודמות הפרצוף: מצע. בית המקדש: תעשה לו מסכה צרה. כאשה שנעשית צרה לחברתה: העלה שממית. קורי עכבים שבטל עבודה מכל וכל עד שארגו עכבים קוריהן ע"ג המזבח: היתר. נעשה לו כהיתר: ממקום שיצאת משם. מקום שאדם יוצא ממנו שבע הוא ממנו ואינו מתאוה להנאת אותו מקום: קמאי לא ידעי לארגוזי. מלכים ראשונים שלפנינו לא היו יודעים להכעיס המקום כמו שהוא חרף ואמר כלום אנו צריכין אלא לאורו שמאיר לנו השמש יצא ויטול אורו: שאנו משתמשין בו. שמאיר ביותר: אמרו לו. בני דורו והלא כסף וכו' דבני דורו צדיקים היו כדאמרן נסתכל בדורו של יהויקים ונתקררה דעתו: מפני מה לא מנו את יהויקים. בהדי הנך שאין להם חלק לעולם הבא: משום דכתיב ויתר דברי יהויקים. בתמיהה משום דכתיב ביה רשע כזה לא מנאוהו: שם עבודת כוכבים על גופו. מתוך שהיה אדוק בה: שם שמים. משום בזיון: במלכים לא שמעתי. מפני מה לא מנו את יהויקים: בהדיוטות שמעתי. מפני מה לא מנו מיכה בהדי ארבעה הדיוטות דמתניתין: פתו מצויה לעוברי דרכים. שהיו כל העולם מתארחין אצלו כדכתיב (במקרא) כל העובר ושב אל הלוים זה מיכה: זה פסלו של מיכה. כשכתב משה את השם והשליכו על נילוס להעלות ארונו של יוסף בא מיכה ונטלו בהחבא והיינו דכתיב ועבר בים צרה כשהעביר הקדוש ברוך הוא לישראל עבר מיכה עמהם שבידו השם לעשות העגל נ"א מיכה עשה פסל והביאו עמו כשעברו ישראל הים: גרב. מקומו של מיכה בגרב הוה פסלו של מיכה קבוע ובשילה היה המשכן: לדוחפו. למיכה: ועל דבר זה. על פסלו של מיכה שלא מיחו ישראל בידו נענשו אנשי פילגש בגבעה שנפלו ביד בנימין והרגו מהם ארבעים אלף: לגימה. אכילה שמאכילין אורחים: שתי משפחות. עמון ומואב שלפי שלא קדמו ישראל בלחם ובמים נכתב שלא יבאו בקהל: מעלמת עינים מן הרשעים. מעלמת מעיני המקום שלא להביט ברשעו לשלם לו כדרכו הרעה אלא עושה כאילו אינו רואה במעשיו:
עמון

מסורת הש"ס

א) [יבמות מט:], ב) יומא ט: ע"ש, ג) [גירסת הערוך קדד], ד) לא נמצא מקרא [גם בע"י ליתא להך קרא עיין חידושי אגדות שם], ה) [לקמן קי. נדרים לט:], ו) [בשאילתות סימן ל"ט פ' שמות איתא קצרתא], ז) [ב"מ לג:].

ליקוטי רש"י

כי קצר המצע מהשתרע. כי אביא עליכם שונא דוחק אתכם אשר לא תוכלו להספיק עבודתו כשיליע מלעו עליכם יקצר לו מהשתרע השוכב עליו מהשתרע מהשתטח להאריך איבריו אישטנדליי"ר בלע"ז. והמסכה צרה. הנסיך שימשול עליכם יהיה מקומכם דחוק לו בהתכנסו לתוכו ורבותינו דרשוהו על עכו"ם שהכניס מנשה להיכל קצר המצע הזה מהשתרע מהשתרר עליו שני רעים ואני פרשתיו לפי פשוטו ובדרך זה ת"י ואף מדרש רבותינו יש לישבו על אופן הדבור כלומר למה אני מביא עליכם פורענות זו לפי שקצר המצע מהשתרע אני לבדי עליו שנאמר (מ"א ח) הנה השמים לא יכלכלוך וכל שכן בהכניסכם מסכה עמי כביכול צר לנו המקום [ישעיהו כח, כ]. לי הכסף ולי הזהב. ובידי להביא לאשר חפצתי בו [חגי ב, ח]. ותועבתיו שבא על אמו. והנמצא עליו. כתובת קעקע [דה"ב לו, ח].

גליון הש"ס

גמרא אבשלום אין לו חלק לעוה"ב. עי' סוטה דף י ע"ב תוספות ד"ה דקרב: שם ר"י ור"א חד אמר. עי' מדרש רבה ויקרא סוף פ' מצורע:

תורה אור השלם

א) כִּי בִי חָשַׁק וַאֲפַלְּטֵהוּ אֲשַׂגְּבֵהוּ כִּי יָדַע שְׁמִי: יִקְרָאֵנִי וְאֶעֱנֵהוּ עִמּוֹ אָנֹכִי בְצָרָה אֲחַלְּצֵהוּ וַאֲכַבְּדֵהוּ: אֹרֶךְ יָמִים אַשְׂבִּיעֵהוּ וְאַרְאֵהוּ בִּישׁוּעָתִי: [תהלים צא, יד-טז]

ב) וְיִמָּנַע מֵרְשָׁעִים אוֹרָם וּזְרוֹעַ רָמָה תִּשָּׁבֵר: [איוב לח, טו]

ג) וַיָּסֹבּוּ עֲשָׂרָה נְעָרִים נֹשְׂאֵי כְּלֵי יוֹאָב וַיַּכּוּ אֶת אַבְשָׁלוֹם וַיְמִיתֻהוּ: [שמואל ב' יח, טו]

ד) וְגַם דָּם נָקִי שָׁפַךְ מְנַשֶּׁה הַרְבֵּה מְאֹד עַד אֲשֶׁר מִלֵּא אֶת יְרוּשָׁלַיִם פֶּה לָפֶה לְבַד מֵחַטָּאתוֹ אֲשֶׁר הֶחֱטִיא אֶת יְהוּדָה לַעֲשׂוֹת הָרַע בְּעֵינֵי יְיָ: [מלכים ב' כא, טז]

ה) וַיָּשֶׂם אֶת פֶּסֶל הַסֶּמֶל אֲשֶׁר עָשָׂה בְּבֵית הָאֱלֹהִים אֲשֶׁר אָמַר אֱלֹהִים אֶל דָּוִיד וְאֶל שְׁלֹמֹה בְנוֹ בַּבַּיִת הַזֶּה וּבִירוּשָׁלַיִם אֲשֶׁר בָּחַרְתִּי מִכֹּל שִׁבְטֵי יִשְׂרָאֵל אָשִׂים אֶת שְׁמִי לְעֵילוֹם: [דברי הימים ב' לג, ז]

ו) וּתְפִלָּתוֹ וְהֵעָתֶר לוֹ וְכָל חַטָּאתוֹ וּמַעְלוֹ וְהַמְּקֹמוֹת אֲשֶׁר בָּנָה בָהֶם בָּמוֹת וְהֶעֱמִיד הָאֲשֵׁרִים וְהַפְּסִלִים לִפְנֵי הִכָּנְעוֹ הִנָּם כְּתוּבִים עַל דִּבְרֵי חוֹזָי: [דברי הימים ב' לג, יט]

ז) וְאֶת הַמִּזְבְּחוֹת אֲשֶׁר עַל הַגָּג עֲלִיַּת אָחָז אֲשֶׁר עָשׂוּ מַלְכֵי יְהוּדָה וְאֶת הַמִּזְבְּחוֹת אֲשֶׁר עָשָׂה מְנַשֶּׁה בִּשְׁתֵּי חַצְרוֹת בֵּית יְיָ נָתַץ הַמֶּלֶךְ וַיָּרָץ מִשָּׁם וְהִשְׁלִיךְ אֶת עֲפָרָם אֶל נַחַל קִדְרוֹן: [מלכים ב' כג, יב]

ח) וַיָּשֶׂם אֶת פֶּסֶל הָאֲשֵׁרָה אֲשֶׁר עָשָׂה בַּבַּיִת אֲשֶׁר אָמַר יְיָ אֶל דָּוִד וְאֶל שְׁלֹמֹה בְנוֹ בַּבַּיִת הַזֶּה וּבִירוּשָׁלַיִם אֲשֶׁר בָּחַרְתִּי מִכֹּל שִׁבְטֵי יִשְׂרָאֵל אָשִׂים אֶת שְׁמִי לְעוֹלָם: [מלכים ב' כא, ז]

ט) כִּי קָצַר הַמַּצָּע מֵהִשְׂתָּרֵעַ וְהַמַּסֵּכָה צָרָה כְּהִתְכַּנֵּס: [ישעיה כח, כ]

י) כֹּנֵס כַּנֵּד מֵי הַיָּם נֹתֵן בְּאֹצָרוֹת תְּהוֹמוֹת: [תהלים לג, ז]

כ) צוֹר תְּעוּדָה חֲתוֹם תּוֹרָה בְּלִמֻּדָי: [ישעיה ח, טז]

ל) וְלֹא נִכְנַע מִלִּפְנֵי יְיָ כְּהִכָּנַע מְנַשֶּׁה אָבִיו כִּי הוּא אָמוֹן הִרְבָּה אַשְׁמָה: [דברי הימים ב' לג, כג]

מ) לִי הַכֶּסֶף וְלִי הַזָּהָב נְאֻם יְיָ צְבָאוֹת: [חגי ב, ח]

נ) הַשָּׁמַיִם שָׁמַיִם לַייָ וְהָאָרֶץ נָתַן לִבְנֵי אָדָם: [תהלים קטו, טז] ס) וְיֶתֶר דִּבְרֵי יְהוֹיָקִים וְתֹעֲבֹתָיו אֲשֶׁר עָשָׂה וְהַנִּמְצָא עָלָיו הִנָּם כְּתוּבִים עַל סֵפֶר מַלְכֵי יִשְׂרָאֵל וִיהוּדָה וַיִּמְלֹךְ יְהוֹיָכִין בְּנוֹ תַּחְתָּיו: [דברי הימים ב' לו, ח]

ע) וְעָבַר בַּיָּם צָרָה וְהִכָּה בַיָּם גַּלִּים וְהֹבִישׁוּ כֹּל מְצוּלוֹת יְאֹר וְהוּרַד גְּאוֹן אַשּׁוּר וְשֵׁבֶט מִצְרַיִם יָסוּר: [זכריה י, יא] פ) עַל דְּבַר אֲשֶׁר לֹא קִדְּמוּ אֶתְכֶם בַּלֶּחֶם וּבַמַּיִם בַּדֶּרֶךְ בְּצֵאתְכֶם מִמִּצְרָיִם וַאֲשֶׁר שָׂכַר עָלֶיךָ אֶת בִּלְעָם בֶּן בְּעוֹר מִפְּתוֹר אֲרַם נַהֲרַיִם לְקַלְלֶךָּ: [דברים כג, ה]

tions which he committed and that which was found on him? Certainly not![39] – ? –

The Gemara interjects:

מַאי ,,וְהַנִּמְצָא עָלָיו״ – And **what is the meaning of** ***and that which was found on him?*** רַבִּי יוֹחָנָן וְרַבִּי אֶלְעָזָר – **R' Yochanan and R' Elazar** dispute the matter: חַד אָמַר שֶׁחָקַק שֵׁם עֲבוֹדַת כּוֹכָבִים עַל אַמָּתוֹ – **One says that** it means that **he tattooed the name of a pagan deity on his male organ,** וְחַד אָמַר שֶׁחָקַק שֵׁם שָׁמַיִם עַל אַמָּתוֹ – **and one says that** it means that **he tattooed the Name of God on his male organ.**[40]

The Gemara returns to Rava's question:

אָמַר לֵיהּ – **[Rabbah bar Mari] said to [Rava]:** בִּמְלָכִים לֹא שָׁמַעְתִּי – **As far as kings are concerned, I have not heard** why Yehoiakim was not included in our Mishnah as having no portion in the World to Come.[41] בְּהֶדְיוֹטוֹת שָׁמַעְתִּי – **However, concerning commoners, I have heard** why a certain sinful commoner was not listed. For I have heard the following teaching: מִפְּנֵי מָה לֹא מָנוּ אֶת מִיכָה – **Why** in our Mishnah **did they not list Michah** among the commoners who have no portion in the World to Come?[42] מִפְּנֵי שֶׁפִּתּוֹ מְצוּיָה לְעוֹבְרֵי דְרָכִים – **It is because his bread was always available for wayfarers,** שֶׁנֶּאֱמַר ,,כָּל הָעוֹבֵר וְשָׁב אֶל הַלְוִיִּם״ – **as it is stated:** ***all who traveled to and fro to the Levites.*** [43]

More about Michah:

,,וְעָבַר בַּיָּם צָרָה וְהִכָּה בַיָּם גַּלִּים״ – Scripture states:[44] ***The rival (tzarah) shall pass through the sea, and it shall strike waves in the sea.*** אָמַר רַבִּי יוֹחָנָן – **R' Yochanan said:** זֶה פִּסְלוֹ שֶׁל מִיכָה – **This refers to Michah's graven image.**[45] תַּנְיָא – **It was taught in a Baraisa:** רַבִּי נָתָן אוֹמֵר – R' NASSAN SAYS: מִגָּרֵב לְשִׁילֹה שְׁלֹשָׁה מִילִין – FROM GERAV TO SHILOH WAS a distance of only THREE MILS.[46] וְהָיָה עֲשַׁן הַמַּעֲרָכָה וַעֲשַׁן פֶּסֶל מִיכָה מִתְעָרְבִין זֶה בָּזֶה – As a result of this proximity, THE SMOKE OF THE TABERNACLE FIRE[47] AND THE SMOKE FROM the sacrifices offered to MICHAH'S IDOL rose and INTERMINGLED. בִּקְשׁוּ מַלְאֲכֵי הַשָּׁרֵת לְדוֹחֲפוֹ – Enraged at this sacrilege, THE MINISTERING ANGELS SOUGHT TO DRIVE [MICHAH] from the world, i.e. to kill him and thereby end his cult.[48] אָמַר לָהֶן הַקָּדוֹשׁ בָּרוּךְ הוּא – Thereupon THE HOLY ONE, BLESSED IS HE, SAID TO [THE MINISTERING ANGELS]: הַנִּיחוּ לוֹ – "LEAVE HIM ALONE, שֶׁפִּתּוֹ מְצוּיָה לְעוֹבְרֵי דְרָכִים – AS HIS BREAD IS always AVAILABLE TO WAYFARERS." וְעַל דָּבָר זֶה נֶעֶנְשׁוּ אַנְשֵׁי פִּלֶגֶשׁ בַּגִּבְעָה – AND IT WAS ON ACCOUNT OF THIS idol of Michah THAT THE PEOPLE OF THE era of the incident of the CONCUBINE OF GIVAH WERE PUNISHED,[49] אָמַר לָהֶן הַקָּדוֹשׁ בָּרוּךְ הוּא – for THE HOLY ONE, BLESSED IS HE, SAID TO THEM [the people of that era]: בִּכְבוֹדִי לֹא מְחִיתֶם – AT the affront to MY HONOR, i.e. when Michah's idol was set up, YOU DID NOT PROTEST. עַל כְּבוֹדוֹ שֶׁל בָּשָׂר וָדָם מְחִיתֶם – However, AT the affront to THE HONOR OF FLESH AND BLOOD, i.e. the rape of the concubine at Givah, YOU DID PROTEST![50]

NOTES

39. Rava concluded rhetorically: Could the reason that Yehoiakim is not listed be that he was so wicked?! Of course not! (*Rashi;* cf. *Yad Ramah* for a different interpretation of the entire passage).

40. I.e. when the verse mentions *that which was found on him,* it refers to a physical mark which was found literally *on him,* i.e. inscribed on his body. According to the first opinion, Yehoiakim tattooed the name of a pagan deity on his organ as a sign of his great attachment to paganism (*Rashi*), or in the hope that his offspring would grow up as followers of paganism (*Yad Ramah*). According to the other view, Yehoiakim tattooed the Name of God on his organ as an obscene gesture of contempt and ridicule (*Rashi*). [*Rashash* notes that *Rashi's* text of the Gemara apparently read that he tattooed the name of a pagan deity עַל גּוּפוֹ, *on his body,* rather than עַל אַמָּתוֹ, *on his organ.*]

41. Rabbah bar Mari meant: Yehoiakim does in fact have a share in the World to Come, but I have not heard why this is so (see *Rashi* above ד״ה אחד).

Alternatively he meant: He certainly does not have a share in the World to Come, but I do not know why he was not listed (*Yad Ramah*).

42. *Judges* 17 relates how Michah, an Ephraimite, fashioned an idol out of silver and set up a shrine to it in his house, to which people came to worship. Later, the idol was taken by a group of Danites who wished to worship it in Dan: *They set up Michah's graven image which he had made, and maintained it throughout the time that the House of God was in Shiloh* (ibid. 18:31). See above, 101b note 18.

Thus, Michah caused many Jews to worship an idol, just as Yarovam did. Why, then, is Michah not listed as one of those who have no share in the World to Come?

43. There is in fact no such verse in Scripture, and indeed in the text of the Gemara in *Ein Yaakov* this "verse" does not appear (*Mesoras HaShas*). It is, however, evident from *Judges* 17:8 and 18:2 that Michah's house was open to wayfarers (*Eitz Yosef*).

Ben Yehoyada explains the great merit of Michah's hospitality to wayfarers: There were a number of poor righteous persons among those wayfarers who had no food. Had they not found food at Michah's house they would have starved to death. Because Michah was responsible for preserving their lives, he shared the reward they earned through all the good deeds they were able to perform.

Alternatively, in truth Michah has no share in the World to Come. The Gemara means merely that on account of his hospitality, this embarrassing fact was not publicized in the Mishnah (*Yad Ramah*).

44. *Zechariah* 10:11. This obscure verse is variously translated by the commentators ad loc. The translation given here follows R' Yochanan's exegesis.

45. At the time of the Exodus, Moses searched for Joseph's body in order to take it up for burial in the Land of Israel, but he was told that the Egyptians had placed Joseph's bones in a metal coffin and had sunk it in the Nile (*Sotah* 13a). Moses thereupon wrote the Divine Name on a plate and cast it into the Nile, thereby raising the coffin. Michah surreptitiously retrieved this Divine Name from the Nile and carried it with him at the time he crossed the Reed Sea along with the rest of the Jewish people. Subsequently, he used this Name to create the Golden Calf in the desert (cf. *Rashi* to *Exodus* 32:4 from *Tanchuma Ki Sisa* 19). Alternatively, the Gemara means that Michah actually fashioned an idol and carried it with him across the Reed Sea. It is to Michah's presence (or the presence of the idol) at the crossing of the Reed Sea that the verse refers (*Rashi*). [This idol was evidently not the same one discussed in *Judges* 17, which was made by Michah many years later] Cf. *Yad Ramah*.

Others explain that it was not Michah's idol at all that crossed the Reed Sea, but the *roots* of this sin in the hearts of certain individuals. In due course, these produced their evil fruit (*Gra* in *Aderes Eliyahu* to *Deuteronomy* 29:17).

46. Gerav was the location of Michah's idol; Shiloh was the location of the Tabernacle (*Rashi*).

47. Literally: the smoke from the [wood] arrangement.

48. This follows *Rashi.* According to *Maharsha,* the angels sought to drive away the smoke emitting from Michah's idol.

49. *Judges* 19 relates the story of a concubine who fled from her angry husband to her father's house. Subsequently, the couple reconciled and he came to her father's house to take her home. On their way home they spent the night in the Benjamite town of Givah, where a group of evil Benjamites besieged the couple and eventually violated the concubine, who subsequently died. This set off a chain of events which resulted in bloody civil war between the tribe of Benjamin, which refused to punish the perpetrators, and the rest of the Jewish people. In our Baraisa, R' Nassan states that this tragic episode, which claimed forty thousand lives on the side of the allied tribes alone, was a Divine punishment to the Jewish people.

50. I.e. there was no public outcry when Michah set up his idol. Although the idol was in the vicinity of the very Tabernacle itself, no effort was made to remove it. On the other hand, when the concubine was violated and she died, it was seen as such an intolerable stain on the nation's honor that the tribes of Israel were determined that the perpetrators be punished, even if it resulted in civil war. Evidently, the Jews were more outraged by the crime against the concubine, which they perceived as an affront to their honor as a decent law-abiding nation, than at the erection of an idolatrous shrine. This

אִ) כי בי חשק ואפלטהו אשגבהו כי ידע שמי יקראני ואענהו עמו אנכי בצרה אחלצהו ואכבדהו אורך ימים אשביעהו ואראהו בישועתי אמר ר"ש בן לקיש מאי דכתיב בִ) וימנע מרשעים אורם וזרוע רמה תשבר מפני מה עי"ן של רשעים תלויה כיון שנעשה אדם רש מלמטה נעשה רש מלמעלה ולא נכתביה כלל ר' יוחנן ור"א חד אמר מפני כבודו של דוד וחד אמר משום כבודו של נחמיה בן חכליה תנו רבנן מנשה היה שונה חמשים וחמשה פנים בתורת כהנים כנגד שני מלכותו אחאב שמנים וחמשה ירבעם מאה ושלשה תניא היה ר"מ אומר ° אבשלום אין לו חלק לעוה"ב שנאמר גִ) ויכו את אבשלום וימיתוהו ויכוהו בעוה"ז וימיתוהו לעוה"ב תניא ר"ש בן אלעזר אומר משום ר"מ אחז ואחזיה וכל מלכי ישראל שכתוב בהן ויעש הרע בעיני ה' לא חיין ולא נידונין דִ) וגם דם נקי שפך מנשה הרבה מאד עד אשר מלא את ירושלים פה לפה לבד מחטאתו אשר החטיא את יהודה לעשות הרע בעיני ה' הכא אִ) תרגימו שהרג ישעיה במערבא אמרי שעשה צלם משאוי אלף בני אדם ובכל יום ויום הורג (את) כולם כמאן אזלא הא דאמר רבה בר בר חנה שקולה נשמה של צדיק אחד כנגד כל העולם כולו כמ"ד ישעיה הרג כתיב הִ) פסל וכתיב וִ) פסילים א"ר יוחנן בתחלה עשה לו פרצוף אחד ולבסוף עשה לו ארבעה פרצופים כדי שתראה שכינה ותכעוס אחז העמידו בעלייה שנאמר זִ) ואת המזבחות אשר על הגג עליית אחז וגו' מנשה העמידו בהיכל שנאמר חִ) וישם את פסל האשרה אשר עשה בבית אשר אמר ה' אל דוד ואל שלמה [בנו] בבית הזה ובירושלים אשר בחרתי מכל שבטי ישראל אשים את שמי לעולם אמון הכניסו לבית קדשי הקדשים שנאמר טִ) כי קצר המצע מהשתרע והמסכה צרה כהתכנס מאי כי קצר המצע מהשתרע אמר בִ) רבי שמואל בר נחמני אמר רבי יונתן [כי] קצר המצע זה מלהשתרר עליו שני רעים כאחד מאי והמסכה צרה וגו' אמר רבי שמואל בר נחמני רבי יונתן כי הוה מטי להאי קרא הוה קא בכי מי שכתב בו יִ) כונס כנד מי הים תעשה לו מסכה צרה [אחז בטל את העבודה] וחתם את התורה שנאמר כִ) צור תעודה חתום תורה בלמודי מנשה גִ) קדר את האזכרות והרס את המזבח אמון [שרף את התורה] והעלה שממית על גבי המזבח אחז התיר את הערוה מנשה בא על אחותו אמון בא על אמו שנאמר לִ) כי הוא אמון הרבה אשמה ° רבי יוחנן ור"א חד אמר ששרף את התורה וחד אמר שבא על אמו אמרה לו אמו כלום יש לך הנאה ממקום שיצאת ממנו א"ל כלום אני עושה אלא להכעיס את בוראי כי אתא יהויקים אמר קמאי לא ידעי לארגוזי כלום אנו צריכין אלא לאורו יש לנו זהב פרויים שאנו משתמשין בו יטול אורו אמרו לו והלא כסף וזהב שלו הוא שנאמר מִ) לי הכסף ולי הזהב נאם ה' צבאות אמר להם כבר נתנו לנו שנאמר נִ) השמים שמים לה' והארץ נתן לבני האדם א"ל רבא לרבה בר מרי מפני מה לא מנו את יהויקים משום דכתיב ביה סִ) ויתר דברי יהויקים ותועבותיו אשר עשה והנמצא עליו מאי והנמצא עליו רבי יוחנן ור"א חד אמר שחקק שם עבודת כוכבים על אמתו וחד אמר שחקק שם שמים על אמתו א"ל במלכים לא שמעתי מפני מה לא מנו את מיכה מפני שפתו מצויה לעוברי דרכים שנאמר דִ) כל העובר ושב אל הלוים עִ) ועבר בים צרה והכה בים גלים א"ר יוחנן זה פסלו של מיכה תניא רבי נתן אומר מגרב לשילה ג' מילין והיה עשן המערכה ועשן פסל מיכה מתערבין זה בזה בקשו מלאכי השרת לדוחפו אמר להן הקב"ה הניחו לו שפתו מצויה לעוברי דרכים ועל דבר זה נענשו אנשי פלגש בגבעה אמר להן הקב"ה הִ) בכבודי לא מחיתם על כבודו של בשר ודם מחיתם א"ר יוחנן משום רבי יוסי בן וִ) קסמא גדולה לגימה שהרחיקה שתי משפחות מישראל שנאמר פִ) על דבר אשר לא קדמו אתכם בלחם ובמים ורבי יוחנן דידיה אמר מרחקת את הקרובים ומקרבת את הרחוקים ומעלמת עינים מן הרשעים ומשרה שכינה על נביאי הבעל וִ) ושגגתו עולה זדון מרחקת את הקרובים

מעמון

רש"י

כי בי חשק. לא שייך אלא ברבונא דעלמא כלומר אותו שחפץ בי ובירלאתי אפלטהו: ע' שברשעים תלויה. שאינה כתובה בשיטת אותיות התיבה אלא תלויה היא למעלה ונראה ככתוב רשים: כיון שנעשה אדם רש מלמטה. שיש לו שונאין ואין רוח הבריות נוחה הימנו: נעשה רש מלמעלה. בידוע ששונאין אותו מלמעלה להכי כתוב רשים שני מיני רשות: ולא נכתביה. לעי"ן כלל: משום כבודו של דוד. שאין הדבר נוהג בצדיקים ודוד היו לו שונאים הרבה: ונחמיה בן חכליה. שהיו לו שונאים הרבה מנכרים שמבקשין להרגו על שהיה בונה בית המקדש כדכתיב בעזרא (נחמיה ד) ואחת מחזקת השלח וגו' ל"א היו לו קנאים מישראל דכתיב (שם ו) רבים ביהודה בעלי שבועה לו כי הוא חתן לשכניה בן ארח שהיו מבזין אותו. בקדושין (דף ע.) מפרש להאי קרא ולהכי איכתבא לומר שברשעים אמרינן ולא בצדיקים: היה שונה חמשים וחמשה פנים בתורת כהנים. ספר ויקרא היה מחדש בו כל שנה ושנה ודורשו מפלפולו: לא חיין. לא יחיו לעולם הבא עם הצדיקים ואין נדונין נמי בגיהנם ודוקא קאמר מלכי ישראל אבל שלמה וצדקיה מבית דוד אתו ואף על גב דכתיב בהו ויעש הרע חיין הן לעתיד: אחז ואחזיה. ממלכי יהודה וקים להו שהיו רשעים ואמון ויהויקים לא חשיב ואף על גב דהוו רשעים מאד כדלקמן בהנהו קים להו דחיין: הורג את כולן. שהיו נבקעין בכובד המשאוי: כמ"ד שהרג ישעיה. והאי קאמר קרא מלא את ירושלים פה לפה שנשמתו של צדיק שקולה כמו שמלא את ירושלים חללים: כתוב. (במלכים) [דה"ב לג] וישם את פסל הסמל אשר עשה בבית האלהים: וכתיב והעמיד את האשרים והפסילים בד"ה (שם): ולבסוף עשה. מנשה לאותו דמות ד' פרצופים: כדי שתראה שכינה מכל צד. שתכנס להיכל תראה פרצוף כנגדו ותכעוס: מלהשתרר עליו שני רעים. שכינה ודמות הפרצוף: מצע. בית המקדש: תעשה לו מסכה צרה. כאשה שנעשית צרה לחברתה: העלה שממית. קורי עכבים שבטל עבודה מכל וכל עד שהרגו עכבים קוריהן ע"ג המזבח: היתר. נעשה לו כהיתר: ממקום שיצאת משם. מקום שאדם יוצא ממנו שבע הוא ממנו ואינו מתאוה להנאת אותו מקום: קמאי לא ידעי לארגוזי. מלכים ראשונים שלפנינו לא היו יודעים להכעיס המקום כמו שהוא חרף ואמר כלום אנו צריכין אלא לאורו שמאיר לנו השמש יצא ויטול אורו: שאנו משתמשין בו. שמאיר ביותר: אמרו לו. בני דורו והלא כסף וכו' דבני דורו צדיקים היו כדאמרן נסתכל בדורו של יהויקים ונתקררה דעתו: מפני מה לא מנו את יהויקים. בהדי הנך שאין להם חלק לעולם הבא: משום דכתיב ויתר דברי יהויקים. בתמיהה משום דכתיב ביה רשע כזה לא מנאוהו: שם עבודת כוכבים על גופו. מתוך שהיה אדוק בה: שם שמים. משום בזיון: במלכים לא שמעתי. מפני מה לא מנו את יהויקים: בהדיוטות שמעתי. מפני מה לא מנו מיכה בהדי ארבעה הדיוטות דמתניתין: פתו מצויה לעוברי דרכים. שהיו כל העולם מתארחין אצלו כדכתיב (במקרא) כל העובר ושב אל הלוים זה מיכה: זה פסלו של מיכה. כשכתב משה את השם והשליכו על נילוס להעלות ארונו של יוסף בא מיכה ונטלו בהחבא והיינו דכתיב ועבר בים צרה כשהעביר הקדוש ברוך הוא לישראל עבר מיכה עמהם שבידו השם לעשות העגל ל"א מיכה עשה פסל והביאו עמו כשעברו ישראל הים: גרב. מקומו של מיכה בגרב הוה פסלו של מיכה קבוע ובשילה היה המשכן: לדוחפו. למיכה: ועל דבר זה. על פסלו של מיכה שלא מיחו ישראל בידו נענשו אנשי פילגש בגבעה שנפלו ביד בנימין והרגו מהם ארבעים אלף: לגימה. אכילה שמאכילין אורחים: שתי משפחות. עמון ומואב שלפי שלא קדמו ישראל בלחם ובמים נכתב שלא יבאו בקהל: מעלמת עינים מן הרשעים. מעלמת מעיני המקום שלא להביט ברשעו לשלם לו כדרכו הרעה אלא עושה כאילו אינו רואה במעשיו:

עמון

גליון הש"ס

גמרא אבשלום אין לו חלק לעוה"ב. עי' סוטה דף י ע"ב תוספות ד"ה דקרב: שם ר"י ור"א חד אמר. עי' מדרש רבה ויקרא סוף פ' מצורע:

תורה אור השלם

א) כִּי בִי חָשַׁק וַאֲפַלְּטֵהוּ אֲשַׂגְּבֵהוּ כִּי יָדַע שְׁמִי: יִקְרָאֵנִי וְאֶעֱנֵהוּ עִמּוֹ אָנֹכִי בְצָרָה אֲחַלְּצֵהוּ וַאֲכַבְּדֵהוּ: אֹרֶךְ יָמִים אַשְׂבִּיעֵהוּ וְאַרְאֵהוּ בִּישׁוּעָתִי: [תהלים צא, יד-טז]

ב) וְיִמָּנַע מֵרְשָׁעִים אוֹרָם וּזְרוֹעַ רָמָה תִּשָּׁבֵר: [איוב לח, טו]

ג) וַיָּסֹבּוּ עֲשָׂרָה נְעָרִים נֹשְׂאֵי כְּלֵי יוֹאָב וַיַּכּוּ אֶת אַבְשָׁלוֹם וַיְמִיתֻהוּ: [שמואל ב' יח, טו]

ד) וְגַם דָּם נָקִי שָׁפַךְ מְנַשֶּׁה הַרְבֵּה מְאֹד עַד אֲשֶׁר מִלֵּא אֶת יְרוּשָׁלַיִם פֶּה לָפֶה לְבַד מֵחַטָּאתוֹ אֲשֶׁר הֶחֱטִיא אֶת יְהוּדָה לַעֲשׂוֹת הָרַע בְּעֵינֵי יְיָ: [מלכים ב' כא, טז]

ה) וַיָּשֶׂם אֶת פֶּסֶל הַסֶּמֶל אֲשֶׁר עָשָׂה בְּבֵית הָאֱלֹהִים אֲשֶׁר אָמַר אֱלֹהִים אֶל דָּוִיד וְאֶל שְׁלֹמֹה בְנוֹ בַּבַּיִת הַזֶּה וּבִירוּשָׁלַיִם אֲשֶׁר בָּחַרְתִּי מִכֹּל שִׁבְטֵי יִשְׂרָאֵל אָשִׂים אֶת שְׁמִי לְעֵילוֹם: [דברי הימים ב' לג, ז]

ו) וּתְפִלָּתוֹ וְהֵעָתֶר לוֹ וְכָל חַטָּאתוֹ וּמַעְלוֹ וְהַמְּקֹמוֹת אֲשֶׁר בָּנָה בָהֶם בָּמוֹת וְהֶעֱמִיד הָאֲשֵׁרִים וְהַפְּסִלִים לִפְנֵי הִכָּנְעוֹ הִנָּם כְּתוּבִים עַל דִּבְרֵי חוֹזָי: [דברי הימים ב' לג, יט]

ז) וְאֶת הַמִּזְבְּחוֹת אֲשֶׁר עַל הַגָּג עֲלִיַּת אָחָז אֲשֶׁר עָשׂוּ מַלְכֵי יְהוּדָה וְאֶת הַמִּזְבְּחוֹת אֲשֶׁר עָשָׂה מְנַשֶּׁה בִּשְׁתֵּי חַצְרוֹת בֵּית יְיָ נָתַץ הַמֶּלֶךְ וַיָּרָץ מִשָּׁם וְהִשְׁלִיךְ אֶת עֲפָרָם אֶל נַחַל קִדְרוֹן: [מלכים ב' כג, יב]

ח) וַיָּשֶׂם אֶת פֶּסֶל הָאֲשֵׁרָה אֲשֶׁר עָשָׂה בַּבַּיִת אֲשֶׁר אָמַר יְיָ אֶל דָּוִד וְאֶל שְׁלֹמֹה בְנוֹ בַּבַּיִת הַזֶּה וּבִירוּשָׁלַיִם אֲשֶׁר בָּחַרְתִּי מִכֹּל שִׁבְטֵי יִשְׂרָאֵל אָשִׂים אֶת שְׁמִי לְעוֹלָם: [מלכים ב' כא, ז]

ט) כִּי קָצַר הַמַּצָּע מֵהִשְׂתָּרֵעַ וְהַמַּסֵּכָה צָרָה כְּהִתְכַּנֵּס: [ישעיה כח, כ]

י) כֹּנֵס כַּנֵּד מֵי הַיָּם נֹתֵן בְּאֹצָרוֹת תְּהוֹמוֹת: [תהלים לג, ז]

כ) צוֹר תְּעוּדָה חֲתוֹם תּוֹרָה בְּלִמֻּדָי: [ישעיה ח, טז]

ל) וְלֹא נִכְנַע מִלִּפְנֵי יְיָ כְּהִכָּנַע מְנַשֶּׁה אָבִיו כִּי הוּא אָמוֹן הִרְבָּה אַשְׁמָה: [דברי הימים ב' לג, כג]

מ) לִי הַכֶּסֶף וְלִי הַזָּהָב נְאֻם יְיָ צְבָאוֹת: [חגי ב, ח]

נ) הַשָּׁמַיִם שָׁמַיִם לַייָ וְהָאָרֶץ נָתַן לִבְנֵי אָדָם: [תהלים קטו, טז]

ס) וְיֶתֶר דִּבְרֵי יְהוֹיָקִים וְתֹעֲבֹתָיו אֲשֶׁר עָשָׂה וְהַנִּמְצָא עָלָיו הִנָּם כְּתוּבִים עַל סֵפֶר מַלְכֵי יִשְׂרָאֵל וִיהוּדָה וַיִּמְלֹךְ יְהוֹיָכִין בְּנוֹ תַּחְתָּיו: [דברי הימים ב' לו, ח]

ע) וְעָבַר בַּיָּם צָרָה וְהִכָּה בַיָּם גַּלִּים וְהֹבִישׁוּ כֹּל מְצוּלוֹת יְאֹר וְהוּרַד גְּאוֹן אַשּׁוּר וְשֵׁבֶט מִצְרַיִם יָסוּר: [זכריה י, יא]

פ) עַל דְּבַר אֲשֶׁר לֹא קִדְּמוּ אֶתְכֶם בַּלֶּחֶם וּבַמַּיִם בַּדֶּרֶךְ בְּצֵאתְכֶם מִמִּצְרָיִם וַאֲשֶׁר שָׂכַר עָלֶיךָ אֶת בִּלְעָם בֶּן בְּעוֹר מִפְּתוֹר אֲרַם נַהֲרַיִם לְקַלְלֶךָּ: [דברים כג, ה]

מסורת הש"ס

א) [יבמות מט:], ב) יומא ט: ע"ש, ג) [גירסת הערוך קדר], ד) לא נמצא מקרא [גם בעי' ליתא להך קרא עיין חידושי אגדות שם], ה) [לקמן קי. נדרים לט:], ו) [בשאילתות סימן ל"ט פ' שמות איתא קצרתא], ז) [ב"מ לג:].

ליקוטי רש"י

כי קצר המצע מהשתרע. כי אביא עליכם שונא דוחק אתכם אשר לא תוכלו להספיק עבודתו כשיגיע מלעו עליכם יקצר לו מהשתרע השוכב עליו מהשתרע מהשתטח להאריך איבריו אישטנדלי"ר בלע"ז. והמסכה צרה. הנסיך שימשול עליכם יהיה מקומכם דחוק לו בהתכנסו לתוכו ורבותינו דרשוהו על עכו"ם שהכניס מנשה להיכל קצר המצע הזה מהשתרע מהשתרר עליו שני רעים ואני פרשתיו לפי פשוטו ובדרך זה ת"י ואף מדרש רבותינו יש לישבו על אופן הדבור כלומר למה אני מביא עליכם פורענות זו לפי שקצר המצע מהשתרע אני לבדי עליו שנאמר (מ"א ח) הנה השמים לא יכלכלוך וכל שכן בהכניסכם מסכה עמי כביכול צר לנו המקום [ישעיהו כח, כ]. לי הכסף ולי הזהב. ובידי להביא לאשר חפצתי בו [חגי ב, ח]. ותועבותיו שבא על אמו. והנמצא עליו. כתובת קעקע [דה"ב לו, ח].

The Gemara discusses the importance of hospitality to wayfarers:

אָמַר רַבִּי יוֹחָנָן מִשּׁוּם רַבִּי יוֹסֵי בֶּן קִסְמָא – **R' Yochanan said in the name of R' Yose ben Kisma:** גְּדוֹלָה לְגִימָה – **Great** indeed **is** the deed of providing **food** to travelers and guests, שֶׁהִרְחִיקָה שְׁתֵּי מִשְׁפָּחוֹת מִיִּשְׂרָאֵל – **for [the failure to do so] repulsed two families,** i.e. nations, **from Israel,** שֶׁנֶּאֱמַר ,,עַל דְּבַר אֲשֶׁר לֹא־קִדְּמוּ אֶתְכֶם בַּלֶּחֶם וּבַמַּיִם'' – **as it is stated:** *An Ammonite and a Moabite may not enter the Congregation of* HASHEM, *even their tenth generation shall not enter the Congregation of* HASHEM, *to eternity. **This is because they did not greet you with bread and water** on the road when you were leaving Egypt.*[51] וְרַבִּי יוֹחָנָן דִּידֵיהּ אָמַר – **And R' Yochanan said in his own name:** מַרְחֶקֶת אֶת הַקְּרוֹבִים – **It** [i.e. failure to display hospitality] **repulses those** who would otherwise be **near,** וּמְקָרֶבֶת אֶת הָרְחוֹקִים – **while it** [i.e. timely hospitality] **draws near those** who would otherwise be **far away,** וּמַעֲלֶמֶת עֵינַיִם מִן הָרְשָׁעִים – **and causes the eyes** of God **to look away from the wicked,** i.e. wins the wicked reprieve for their sins, וּמַשְׁרָה שְׁכִינָה עַל נְבִיאֵי הַבַּעַל – **and causes the Divine Spirit to descend upon the prophets of Baal,** i.e. grants pagan prophets genuine prophecies from God; וְשִׁגְגָתוֹ עוֹלָה זָדוֹן – **furthermore, [one's] inadvertent failure** to display proper hospitality **is accounted** by God **as willful** failure to do so.

R' Yochanan explains each of his five points, one by one:

מַרְחֶקֶת אֶת הַקְּרוֹבִים – **"It repulses those** who would otherwise be **near"** –

NOTES

betrayed a lack of zeal for God's honor, which was a grievous failing. As a result, the avenging of the concubine's treatment led to a disastrous civil war, which almost wiped out an entire tribe in Israel.

In an excursus on the incident of the Concubine at Givah, *Ramban* to *Genesis* 19:8 explains that for all its depravity, the rape was not a capital crime, for the woman was only a concubine, not a married woman. Furthermore, the assailants had not intended to kill the woman, and she died only as an indirect result of their deed. The worship of Michah's idol, on the other hand, was a sin deserving of the death penalty. The nation's decision to prosecute the attackers while ignoring the idolaters was therefore considered a severe sin.

51. *Deuteronomy* 23:4-5. Thus, the refusal of the Ammonites and the Moabites to provide food and drink to the traveling Children of Israel (in contrast to the hospitality displayed by Michah) led to their being eternally excluded from intermarriage with any Jew. This is the meaning of R' Yochanan's statement: "Great indeed is the providing of food to wayfarers," that is, great is the power of the merit earned by hospitality to wayfarers, and great is the penalty for failing to display such hospitality.

[It is apparent from this Gemara that both the Ammonites *and* the Moabites did not offer food to the Israelites. This stands in contradiction to *Ramban* to this verse, who asserts that only the Ammonites are blamed for this lack of hospitality but not the Moabites. See *Maharsha* and *Be'er Sheva* for a discussion of this question.]

מֵעַמּוֹן וּמוֹאָב – as is evident **from** what happened to **Ammon and Moab.**[1]

וּמְקָרֶבֶת אֶת הָרְחוֹקִים מִיִּתְרוֹ – **"And draws near those** who would otherwise be **far"** – as may be seen **from** what happened to **Yisro,** דְּאָמַר רַבִּי יוֹחָנָן – **for R' Yochanan said:** בִּשְׂכַר ,,קִרְאֶן לוֹ וְיֹאכַל לָחֶם" – **As a reward for** Yisro's saying: ***Call him and let him eat bread,***[2] זָכוּ בְּנֵי בָנָיו וְיָשְׁבוּ בְּלִשְׁכַּת הַגָּזִית – **his descendants merited to sit in the Chamber of Hewn Stone,**[3] שֶׁנֶּאֱמַר ,,וּמִשְׁפְּחוֹת סֹפְרִים יֹשְׁבֵי יַעְבֵּץ תִּרְעָתִים שִׁמְעָתִים שׂוּכָתִים הֵמָּה הַקִּינִים הַבָּאִים מֵחַמַּת אֲבִי בֵית־רֵכָב" – **as it is stated:** ***The families of scribes, dwellers in Yabetz – the Tirathites, the Shimathites, and the Suchatites; they are the Kenites who are descended from Chammath, father of Beth Rechav.***[4] וּכְתִיב הָתָם ,,וּבְנֵי קֵינִי חֹתֵן מֹשֶׁה עָלוּ מֵעִיר הַתְּמָרִים אֶת־בְּנֵי יְהוּדָה מִדְבַּר יְהוּדָה אֲשֶׁר בְּנֶגֶב עֲרָד וַיֵּלֶךְ וַיֵּשֶׁב אֶת־הָעָם" – **And it is written elsewhere:**[5] ***The children of the Kenite, Moses' father-in-law, went up out of the city of palm trees with the children of Judah into the wilderness of Judah, which is south of Arad; they went and dwelt with the people.*** In these two verses the Kenites are identified both as *the families of scribes,* that is, members of the Sanhedrin, and as the descendants of *Moses' father-in-law,* i.e. Yisro. Thus, Yisro's descendants were members of the Sanhedrin who sat in the Chamber of Hewn Stone. The reason they reached such positions, says R' Yochanan, was the hospitality to Moses displayed by Yisro.

וּמְעַלֶּמֶת עֵינַיִם מִן הָרְשָׁעִים מִמִּיכָה – **"And closes [God's] eyes to the wicked"** – as may be seen **from** what happened to **Michah.**[6]

וּמַשְׁרָה שְׁכִינָה עַל נְבִיאֵי הַבַּעַל מֵחֲבֵירוֹ שֶׁל עִדּוֹ הַנָּבִיא – **"And causes the Divine Spirit to rest upon the prophets of Baal"** – as may be seen **from** what happened to **the friend of Iddo the Prophet,** דִּכְתִיב ,,וַיְהִי הֵם יֹשְׁבִים אֶל־הַשֻּׁלְחָן וַיְהִי דְּבַר־ה׳ אֶל־הַנָּבִיא אֲשֶׁר הֱשִׁיבוֹ" – **as it is written:** ***While they were sitting at the table, the word of Hashem came to the prophet who had brought him back.***[7]

וְשִׁגְגָתָהּ עוֹלָה זָדוֹן דְּאָמַר רַב יְהוּדָה אָמַר רַב – **"[And one's] inadvertent failure** to display proper hospitality **is accounted** by God **as willful"** – **for Rav Yehudah said in the name of Rav:** אִלְמָלֵי הִלְוָוהוּ יְהוֹנָתָן לְדָוִד שְׁתֵּי כִּכְּרוֹת לֶחֶם – **If only Jonathan had escorted,** i.e. supplied, **David with two loaves of bread** for his flight, לֹא נֶהֶרְגָה נוֹב עִיר הַכֹּהֲנִים – the people of **Nov, the city of the Kohanim, would not have been killed,** וְלֹא נִטְרַד דּוֹאֵג הָאֲדוֹמִי – **Doeg the Edomite would not have been banished** from the World to Come, וְלֹא נֶהֱרַג שָׁאוּל וּשְׁלֹשֶׁת בָּנָיו – **and Saul and his three sons would not have been killed.**[8]

The Gemara returns to the topic of why the Mishnah did not list certain very wicked kings among those have no share in the World to Come:[9]

וּמִפְּנֵי מָה לֹא מָנוּ אֶת אָחָז – **And why did they not list Achaz** in our Mishnah as one of the kings who have no portion in the World to Come?

Two explanations are advanced:

אָמַר רַבִּי יִרְמְיָה בַּר אַבָּא – **R' Yirmiyah bar Abba said:** מִפְּנֵי שֶׁמּוּטָל בֵּין שְׁנֵי צַדִּיקִים – **It was because [Achaz] was placed between two righteous men,** בֵּין יוֹתָם לְחִזְקִיָּהוּ – **between Yosam and Chizkiah,** i.e. Achaz was the son of the righteous King Yosam and the father of the righteous King Chizkiah.[10]

רַב יוֹסֵף אָמַר – **Rav Yosef said:** מִפְּנֵי שֶׁהָיָה לוֹ בֹּשֶׁת פָּנִים מִישַׁעְיָהוּ

NOTES

1. The nations of Ammon and Moab were "near" in that their territories were close to the Land of Israel (see *Rashi;* cf. *Maharsha*).

2. *Exodus* 2:20. After killing an Egyptian, Moses was compelled to flee for his life to Midian. There, alone and a fugitive from Pharaoh, he aided the daughters of Yisro, the priest of Midian. Upon hearing of this, Yisro instructed his daughters to invite Moses to dine. Moses came, and eventually married one of Yisro's daughters.

3. This was the room in the Temple area that was the seat of the Great Sanhedrin (High Court) of seventy-one judges. Thus, Yisro's descendants were members of the Great Sanhedrin. See below, 106a and *Maharsha* here.

4. *I Chronicles* 2:55. These "families of scribes" are identified by *Sifri* to *Numbers* 10:29 as being a group of converts to Judaism who became great Torah scholars and ultimately sat on the Sanhedrin (see *Rashi*).

5. *Judges* 1:16.

6. I.e. who, on account of the hospitality he displayed to wayfarers, merited to have God overlook his sins (*Rashi* to 103b ד״ה מעלמת).

7. *I Kings* 13:20. Scripture tells there of a certain prophet – unnamed in Scripture but identified here as Iddo – who was ordered by God to proceed to Bethel, rebuke King Yarovam for his idolatry, and then return home, taking care not to retrace his steps, but rather to return home by a different route than the one he had taken to Bethel. In addition, the prophet was warned not to eat or drink anything until he had returned home. Iddo carried out his mission and was returning home when he was overtaken by another prophet who told him that God had countermanded His original order and had instructed him, the second prophet, to bring Iddo to his (the second prophet's) house in Bethel and provide him with food and drink. This was a lie. The second prophet was in reality a false prophet, identified here as a prophet of Baal. Believing the false prophet, Iddo accompanied him to his home, where he ate a meal. During the meal, the false prophet suddenly received a genuine prophetic communication from God. He was told to tell Iddo that Iddo was going to die for disobeying God's instructions. Shortly thereafter Iddo was killed by a lion (see above, 89b). See *Maharal.*

The point here is that despite being a false prophet, the second prophet was privileged to receive a genuine prophetic communication from God in the merit of the refreshment he provided Iddo. This indicates the immense merit one earns when he shows hospitality (*Rashi*; see *Shabbos* 151b, and *Maharal* here).

8. See *I Samuel* 20-22 for the story of the massacre of Nov: Saul, the king of Israel, suspected David of plotting to take his throne and sought to kill David. David was warned by Saul's son, Jonathan, who was David's close friend. Thus alerted, David fled to Nov, a city inhabited by Kohanim. David told Achimelech, the head Kohen, that he was on a secret mission on behalf of King Saul, and that he, David, required food. Not suspecting that David's story was a fabrication, Achimelech provided David with bread as well as the sword of the slain Goliath, and David went on his way. Doeg, one of Saul's courtiers, had been present at Nov at the time of this incident. He went to Saul and accused the Kohanim of knowingly aiding an enemy of the king, an act of treason punishable by death. At the king's instructions, Doeg proceeded to kill all the Kohanim. This was a terrible crime, both the slander against the Kohanim as well as the actual massacre. Saul ultimately paid the price for this crime, for at the Battle of Gilboa, Saul, Jonathan, and two of Jonathan's brothers all fell in battle (see *Maharsha*). As for Doeg, although Scripture does not describe his end, our Mishnah states that he was forever excluded from the World to Come (see below, 106b).

In our Gemara, Rav observes that the entire tragic chain of events occurred because David had been in desperate need of food. Had Jonathan supplied David with sufficient food at the time he warned David to flee, David would never have gone to Nov, the Kohanim would never have been accused of aiding him and would never have been killed for it, Doeg would not have lost his share in the World to Come and Saul would never have been punished by falling in battle (*Rashi*).

Thus, Jonathan's inadvertent failure to provide David with food led to his own death, a punishment usually associated with a deliberate sin.

9. Although there were numerous wicked kings, the Gemara asks its question only regarding those who were mentioned above as having been *exceedingly* wicked (*Rashi* ד״ה משום).

10. *Maharal* explains that being bracketed between two righteous generations – i.e. being the son of one righteous person and the father of another – is a sign that one is still part of the Jewish people and a participant in the World to Come.

מעמון ומואב ומקרבת את הרחוקים מיתרו דאמר ר' יוחנן בשכר א) קראן לו ויאכל לחם א) זכו בני בניו וישבו בלשכת הגזית שנאמר ב) וממשפחות סופרים יושבי יעבץ תרעתים שמעתים סוכתים המה הקינים הבאים מחמת אבי בית רכב וכתיב התם ג) ובני קיני חותן משה עלו מעיר התמרים את בני יהודה מדבר יהודה אשר בנגב ערד וילך וישב את העם ומעלמת עינים מן הרשעים ממיכה ומשרה שכינה על נביאי הבעל מחבירו של עדו הנביא דכתיב ד) ויהי הם יושבים אל השלחן ויהי דבר ה' אל הנביא אשר השיבו ושגגתה עולה זדון דאמר רב יהודה אמר רב אלמלי הלווהו יהונתן לדוד שתי ככרות לחם לא נהרגה נוב עיר הכהנים ולא נטרד דואג האדומי ולא נהרג שאול ושלשת בניו ומפני מה לא מנו את אחז אמר ר' ירמיה בר אבא מפני שמוטל בין שני צדיקים בין יותם לחזקיהו רב יוסף אמר מפני שהיה לו בשת פנים מישעיהו שנאמר ה) ויאמר ה' אל ישעיהו צא נא לקראת אחז אתה ושאר ישוב בנך אל קצה תעלת הברכה העליונה אל מסלת שדה כובס מאי כובס איכא דאמרי דכבשינהו לאפיה וחלף ואיכא דאמרי ב) אוכלא דקצרי סחף ארישיה וחלף מפני מה לא מנו את אמון מפני כבודו של יאשיהו מנשה נמי לא נמני מפני כבודו של חזקיהו ברא מזכי ג) אבא אבא לא מזכי ברא דכתיב ו) ואין מידי מציל [*] אין אברהם מציל את ישמעאל אין יצחק מציל את עשו השתא דאתית להכי אחז נמי לא אימני משום כבודו של חזקיהו ומפני מה לא מנו את יהויקים משום דר' חייא בר' אבויה ד) דאמר ר' חייא בר' אבויה כתיב על גולגלתו [של] יהויקים זאת ועוד אחרת זקינו דרבי פרידא אשכח גולגלתא דהוה קא שדיא בשערי ירושלים וכתיב בה זאת ועוד אחרת קברה ולא איקברא קברה ולא איקברא אמר גולגלתו של יהויקים היא דכתיב ביה ז) קבורת חמור יקבר סחוב והשלך וגו' אמר מלכא הוא ולא איכשר לזלזולי ביה כרכה בשיראי ואותבה בסיפתא ה) חזיתא דביתהו סברא הא דאיתתא קמייתא הוה דהא לא קא מנשי לה שגרא תנורא וקלתה היינו דכתיב זאת ועוד אחרת תניא אמר רבי שמעון בן אלעזר בשביל ח) הטוב בעיניך עשיתי ט) מה אות נכרים אכלו על שולחנו בשביל שנכרים אכלו על שולחנו גרם גלות לבניו מסייע ליה לחזקיה דאמר חזקיה כל המזמן עובד כוכבים לתוך ביתו ומשמש עליו גורם גלות לבניו שנאמר י) ובניך אשר יצאו ממך [אשר תוליד] יקחו והיו סריסים בהיכל מלך בבל כ) וישמח עליהם חזקיה ויראם את (כל) בית נכתה את הכסף ואת הזהב ואת הבשמים ואת השמן הטוב וגו' אמר רב מאי בית נכתה אשתו השקתה עליהם ושמואל אמר בית גנזיו הראה להם ור' יוחנן אמר זין אוכל זין הראה להן ל) איכה ישבה בדד אמר ו) רבא אמר רבי יוחנן מפני מה לקו ישראל באיכה מפני שעברו על שלשים ושש כריתות שבתורה אמר רבי יוחנן מפני מה לקו באל"ף בי"ת מפני שעברו על התורה שניתנה באל"ף בי"ת ישבה בדד אמר ז) רבא אמר רבי יוחנן אמר הקב"ה אני אמרתי מ) וישכן ישראל בטח בדד עין יעקב אל ארץ דגן ותירוש אף שמיו יערפו טל עכשיו יהיה בדד מושבם ל) העיר רבתי עם אמר ט) רבא אמר רבי יוחנן שהיו משיאין קטנה לגדול וגדולה לקטן כדי שיהו להם בנים הרבה ל) היתה כאלמנה י) אמר רב יהודה אמר רב כאלמנה ולא אלמנה ממש אלא כאשה שהלך בעלה למדינת הים ודעתו לחזור אליה ל) רבתי בגוים שרתי במדינות אמר כ) רבא אמר רבי יוחנן כל מקום שהן הולכין נעשין שרים לאדוניהן ת"ר מעשה בשני בני אדם שנשבו בהר הכרמל והיה שבאי מהלך אחריהם

א"ל

רש"י

עמון ומואב. קרובין לישראל שבאו מלוט בן אחי אברהם ורחקן המקום שלא יבאו בקהל ל"א קרובין ממש ליכא למימר דהא מדין מבני קטורה היו בני אברהם וקרובים היו בני מדין לישראל יותר מעמון ומואב שהם בני אברהם אלא עמון ומואב שכנים וקרובים היו לארץ ישראל ומדין רחוקים להם היו: **וישבו בלשכת הגזית.** ממשפחות סופרים והאי קרא מפרש ליה כולי בסיפרי בפרשת ויאמר משה לחובב: **המה הקינים הבאים מחמת אבי בית רכב.** וקינים אלו בניו של יתרו דכתיב ובני קיני חותן משה ובניו של יתרו הן הן בניו של רכב דכתיב הקינים הבאים מחמת אבי בית רכב וכתיב (ירמיה לה) ולבית הרכבים אמר ירמיהו כי כה אמר ה' [וגו'] יען אשר שמעתם [על] מצות [יהונדב] אביכם [וגו'] לא יכרת איש ליונדב בן רכב [עומד] לפני כל הימים ואמרינן בסיפרי אפשר נכרים הם ונכנסין להיכל והרי כל ישראל לא נכנסו להיכל אלא שהיו יושבין בסנהדרין ומורין בדברי תורה. מ"ר: **ממיכה.** דאמרינן לעיל הניחו לו שפתו מצויה לעוברי דרכים: **ומשרה שכינה על נביאי הבעל מחברו של עדו הנביא.** דעדו הנביא נתנבא על מזבח בית אל שיחרב מפני שהעמיד בו ירבעם צלמים דכתיב (במ"א יג) והנה איש האלהים בא מיהודה וגו' ויאמר מזבח מזבח ומפרש בסדר עולם דהיינו עדו הנביא ובא נביא השקר והטעהו לעדו והשיבו לבית אל והעבירו על מצות הקב"ה שאמר לו לא תשוב לבית אל והאכילו ובזכות שהאכילו שרתה עליו שכינה שנאמר ויהי דבר ה' אל האיש הנביא אשר השיבו להאכילו אללו: **ושגגתה עולה זדון.** שהרי מצינו ביהונתן ששגג ולא הלוהו לדוד שתי ככרות ונענש דאמר רב יהודה וכו': **לווהו.** לשון לויה: **לא נהרגה נוב.** שלא היה צריך דוד לשאול לחם מכהני נוב ולא היה דואג מלשין עליהם: **ולא היה שאול נהרג.** על אותו עון: **שמוטל.** דאביו יותם ובנו חזקיה: **ושאר** מישראל ששבו להיות בניך ותלמידיך וכל מי שישוב לביתך דהיינו תלמידיו כדמתרגמינן ושאר' דלא חטאו ודתבו חטיאי תלמידוהי: **מאי כובס דכבשינהו לאפיה.** שכבש את פניו והיה מתבייש מפני ישעיה: **כובס.** כמו כובש: **אוכלא דקצרי סחף ארישיה.** כלי מנוקב של כובסין שמזלפין בו מים על הבגדים ואותו כלי הפך אחז על ראשו כדי שלא יכירו ישעיה שהיה מתבייש [ממנו]: **יאשיהו. בן אמון:** חזקיהו. אבי מנשה: [**ברא מזכה אבא וכו'**]. יאשיה מזכה אמון אביו ולא חזקיה מנשה בנו דכתיב אין מידי מציל ודרשינן ליה בהגדה אין אברהם מציל וכו': **השתא דאתית להכי.** דברא מזכה לאבא: **אחז נמי.** לא תימא דכבשינהו [לאפיה] אלא מפני כבודו של חזקיה לא מנאוהו: **מפני מה לא מנו את יהויקים.** באותן שאין להם חלק [לעוה"ב]: **משום דר' חייא בר אבויה.** שנתכפר על שלא ניתן לקבורה וכל הני מפני מה לא מנו לא בעי אלא מהנך דהוו רשעים גמורים כדחשיבנא להו לעיל אחז חתם את התורה וכו': [**זאת ועוד כו'.** נקמה נעשית בה כבר ועוד אחרת תעשה בה]: **פרידא.** כך שמו: **סיפתא.** ארגז: **בשביל הטוב מה אות.** בשביל חזקיה [שסיבח את] עצמו דאמר הטוב בעיניך עשיתי גרם לו שאמר מה אות כי אעלה בית ה' ששאל אות מהקב"ה שעבירה גוררת עבירה: **אכלו נכרים על שולחנו.** אותם ששלח לו מרודך בלאדן ספרים ומנחה על ידם: **ומשמש עליו.** כגון חזקיה דאמרינן לקמן אשתו השקתה עליהם: **גורם גלות.** דכתיב וישמח עליהם חזקיהו ויראם את (כל) בית נכתה וכתיב בתריה ומבניך אשר יצאו ממך יקחו והיו סריסים בהיכל מלך בבל: **אשתו השקתה עליהם.** היא עצמה מוזגת להם והיינו בית נכתה לשון מנכה על שם צלע שנפחתה מן האדם וממנה נבראת אשה: **בית גנזיו.** והכי מתרגמינן בית גניזוהי ומנחם פתר במחברתו לשון סממנים כמו (בראשית לז) נכאת וצרי ולוט: **זין אוכל זין.** כגון פרזלא דשליט בפרזלא ל): **איכה.** ל"ו בגימטריא: ל"ו כריתות. בכריתות (דף ב.) חשיב להו: **לקו בא"ב.** שכל מגילת איכה סדורה באלפא ביתא: **בטח בדד.** שיושבין יחידים ואינן מתיראין לא מן הנכרים ולא מן חיות רעות: **רבתי עם.** עם שמתרבה והולך יותר משאר עם: **קטנה לגדול.** ש"ז של קטן אינו מבושל ואינו מזריע מהר כשל גדול וכן רחם של קטנה אינה קולטת מהר כשל גדולה לפיכך משיאין גדולה לקטן כדי לכשתהא זרעו [מבושל] קולט מהר וקטנה לגדול כדי שיהא שכבת זרעו קולט מהר ולא קטנה לקטן ששוין להוליד ולא קטן וקטנה ממש אלא שעומדין על פרקן וראוין הם להוליד ומיהו אין זרע שלהם מבושל כל כך:

אחד

מסורת הש"ס

א) [לקמן קו. ע"ש סוטה יא. ע"ש], ב) [גירסת ערוך בערך אבל אובלא וכתיב על צד שני פירושים ע"ש], ג) [עי' תוספות סוטה י: ד"ה דאתי'], ד) לעיל פב. ע"ש, ה) נ"א אתיא דביתהו חזיתא נפקא אמרה להו לשיבבתה אמרי לה ההיא כו', ו) [במלכים איתא וישמע ובישעיה לט כתיב וישמח], ז) [נ"ל רבה], ח) [נ"ל רבה], ט) [נ"ל רבה], י) [תענית כ.], כ) [נ"ל רבה], ל) [לעיל צו:].

ליקוטי רש"י

מעיר התמרים. היא יריחו שניתן להם דושנה של יריחו לאוכלה עד שיבנה בית המקדש ומי שיבנה בית הבחירה בחלקו יטלנה כדי שיהא לכל ישראל חלק בבית הבחירה ונתנוה לבני יתרו ת"מ שנה והתלמידים שבהם הניחוה והלכו אצל עתניאל בן קנז הוא יעבץ במדבר יהודה אשר בנגב ערד ללמוד תורה. **וישב את העם.** עם התלמידים היושבים לפניו הוא בקש מאת הקב"ה שיזמין לו תלמידים הגונים שנאמר ויקרא יעבץ לאלהים וגו' וזימן לו החסידים הללו [שופטים א, טז]. **אל הנביא.** נביא השקר אשר השיבו לאיש האלהים מכאן אמרו גדולה לגימא שמשרה שכינה על נביאי הבעל [מ"א יג, כ]. **שדה כובם.** שדה שהכובסים שוטחים שם בגדים לנגבם כך תירגם יונתן ורבותינו דרשו נכנע אחז לפני ישעיהו ושם על ראשו אוכלא דקצרי כפה עליו כלי פי' כלי מנוקב של כובסים שמזלפין בו מים על הבגדים [ישעיהו ז, ג]. **אוכלא דקצרי.** כלי נחושת העשוי כנפה נקבים נקבים והוא של כובסים ונותנו על הבגדים ומזלף בו המים עליהן ויש מפרשים שמגמרין מוגמר מתחתיו והבגדים מונחין עליו ומתגמרין דרך הנקבים [שבת קכג:]. כלי של כובסין שהוא מנוקב ומזלפין בו מים על הבגדים [לעיל צב.]. **זאת ועוד אחרת** נקמה נעשית בה כבר ועוד אחרת תעשה בה. **זקינו דר' פרידא.** הוא ר' חייא בר אבויה והכי אמרינן בחלק. **קברה ולא איקברא.** בגבלה ויצאה מקבורתה. **קבורת חמור.** מושלך ברחובות. **בסיפתא.** ארגז. **דלא קא מנשי לה.** אינה נשכחת מלבו. **שגרא לתנורא.** הסיקה את התנור [שם פב.]. **בית נכתה.** בית גנזי בשמיו כמו נכאת וצרי ולוט (בראשית ל"ז כ"ד). **ואת השמן הטוב.** יש פותרין שמן המשחה ויש פותרים שמן אפרסמון (בלסמון) שהוא מצוי בא"י שנאמר (ביחזקאל כז י"ז) יהודה וישראל המה רוכליך בחטי מנית ופנג וראיתי בס' יוסיפון פנג הוא אפרסמון וגדל בירחו ועל שם הריח נקרא יריחו. [מ"ב כ, יג]. **בטח בדד.** כל יחיד ויחיד איש תחת גפנו ותחת תאנתו מפוזרין ואין צריכים להתאסף ולישב יחד מפני האויב [דברים לג, כח]. **רבתי עם.** יו"ד יתירה כמו רבת עם שהיתה עמה רב יש מדרשי אגדה הרבה ואני באתי לפרש לשון המקרא כמשמעו [איכה א, א]. **ולא אלמנה ממש.** דהא לא כתיב אלמנה אלא היתה כאלמנה כאשה העומדת באלמנות חיות על בעלה שהלך ועתיד לחזור [תענית כ.].

גליון הש"ס

גמ' **אין אברהם מציל.** עי' יומא לח ע"ב בתוס' ד"ה מעשה:

תורה אור השלם

א) וַיֹּאמֶר אֶל בְּנֹתָיו וְאַיּוֹ לָמָּה זֶּה עֲזַבְתֶּן אֶת הָאִישׁ קִרְאֶן לוֹ וְיֹאכַל לָחֶם: [שמות ב, כ]

ב) וּמִשְׁפְּחוֹת סֹפְרִים יֹשְׁבֵי יַעְבֵּץ תִּרְעָתִים שִׁמְעָתִים שׂוּכָתִים הֵמָּה הַקִּינִים הַבָּאִים מֵחַמַּת אֲבִי בֵית רֵכָב: [דברי הימים א' ב, נה]

ג) וּבְנֵי קֵינִי חֹתֵן מֹשֶׁה עָלוּ מֵעִיר הַתְּמָרִים אֶת בְּנֵי יְהוּדָה מִדְבַּר יְהוּדָה אֲשֶׁר בְּנֶגֶב עֲרָד וַיֵּלֶךְ וַיֵּשֶׁב אֶת הָעָם: [שופטים א, טז]

ד) וַיְהִי הֵם יֹשְׁבִים אֶל הַשֻּׁלְחָן וַיְהִי דְּבַר יְיָ אֶל הַנָּבִיא אֲשֶׁר הֱשִׁיבוֹ: [מלכים א' יג, כ]

ה) וַיֹּאמֶר יְיָ אֶל יְשַׁעְיָהוּ צֵא נָא לִקְרַאת אָחָז אַתָּה וּשְׁאָר יָשׁוּב בְּנֶךָ אֶל קְצֵה תְּעָלַת הַבְּרֵכָה הָעֶלְיוֹנָה אֶל מְסִלַּת שְׂדֵה כוֹבֵס: [ישעיה ז, ג]

ו) רְאוּ עַתָּה כִּי אֲנִי אֲנִי הוּא וְאֵין אֱלֹהִים עִמָּדִי אֲנִי אָמִית וַאֲחַיֶּה מָחַצְתִּי וַאֲנִי אֶרְפָּא וְאֵין מִיָּדִי מַצִּיל: [דברים לב, לט]

ז) קְבוּרַת חֲמוֹר יִקָּבֵר סָחוֹב וְהַשְׁלֵךְ מֵהָלְאָה לְשַׁעֲרֵי יְרוּשָׁלָםִ: [ירמיה כב, יט]

ח) אָנָּה יְיָ זְכָר נָא אֵת אֲשֶׁר הִתְהַלַּכְתִּי לְפָנֶיךָ בֶּאֱמֶת וּבְלֵבָב שָׁלֵם וְהַטּוֹב בְּעֵינֶיךָ עָשִׂיתִי וַיֵּבְךְּ חִזְקִיָּהוּ בְּכִי גָדוֹל: [מלכים ב' כ, ג]

ט) וַיֹּאמֶר חִזְקִיָּהוּ אֶל יְשַׁעְיָהוּ מָה אוֹת כִּי יִרְפָּא יְיָ לִי וְעָלִיתִי בַּיּוֹם הַשְּׁלִישִׁי בֵּית יְיָ: [מלכים ב' כ, ח]

י) וּמִבָּנֶיךָ אֲשֶׁר יֵצְאוּ מִמְּךָ אֲשֶׁר תּוֹלִיד יִקָּחוּ וְהָיוּ סָרִיסִים בְּהֵיכַל מֶלֶךְ בָּבֶל: [מלכים ב' כ, יח]

כ) וַיִּשְׁמַע עֲלֵיהֶם חִזְקִיָּהוּ וַיַּרְאֵם אֶת כָּל בֵּית נְכֹתֹה אֶת הַכֶּסֶף וְאֶת הַזָּהָב וְאֶת הַבְּשָׂמִים וְאֵת שֶׁמֶן הַטּוֹב וְאֵת בֵּית כֵּלָיו וְאֵת כָּל אֲשֶׁר נִמְצָא בְּאוֹצְרֹתָיו לֹא הָיָה דָבָר אֲשֶׁר לֹא הֶרְאָם חִזְקִיָּהוּ בְּבֵיתוֹ וּבְכָל מֶמְשַׁלְתּוֹ: [מלכים ב' כ, יג] וַיִּשְׂמַח עֲלֵיהֶם חִזְקִיָּהוּ וַיַּרְאֵם אֶת בֵּית נְכֹתֹה אֶת הַכֶּסֶף וְאֶת הַזָּהָב וְאֶת הַבְּשָׂמִים וְאֵת הַשֶּׁמֶן הַטּוֹב וְאֵת כָּל בֵּית כֵּלָיו וְאֵת כָּל אֲשֶׁר נִמְצָא בְּאוֹצְרֹתָיו לֹא הָיָה דָבָר אֲשֶׁר לֹא הֶרְאָם חִזְקִיָּהוּ בְּבֵיתוֹ וּבְכָל מֶמְשַׁלְתּוֹ: [ישעיה לט, ב]

ל) אֵיכָה יָשְׁבָה בָדָד הָעִיר רַבָּתִי עָם הָיְתָה כְּאַלְמָנָה רַבָּתִי בַגּוֹיִם שָׂרָתִי בַּמְּדִינוֹת הָיְתָה לָמַס: [איכה א, א]

מ) וַיִּשְׁכֹּן יִשְׂרָאֵל בֶּטַח בָּדָד עֵין יַעֲקֹב אֶל אֶרֶץ דָּגָן וְתִירוֹשׁ אַף שָׁמָיו יַעַרְפוּ טָל: [דברים לג, כח]

– It was because [Achaz] felt shamefaced in the presence of Isaiah, שֶׁנֶּאֱמַר ,,וַיֹּאמֶר ה׳ אֶל־יְשַׁעְיָהוּ צֵא־נָא לִקְרַאת אָחָז אַתָּה וּשְׁאָר יָשׁוּב בְּנֶךָ אֶל־קְצֵה תְּעָלַת הַבְּרֵכָה הָעֶלְיוֹנָה אֶל־מְסִלַּת שְׂדֵה כוֹבֵס״ **– as it is stated:** ***And Hashem said to Isaiah, "Go out now towards Achaz, you and She'ar Yashuv your son, to the edge of the conduit of the upper pool, to the road of the field of the koveis."***[11] מַאי ,,כּוֹבֵס״ **– What is the meaning of** the word ***koveis*****?** אִיכָּא דְּאָמְרֵי דִּכְבְשִׁינְהוּ לְאַפֵּיהּ וְחָלַף **– Some say that [Achaz] hid** (*kavash*) **his face and turned away,**[12] וְאִיכָּא דְּאָמְרֵי אוּכְלָא דְּקַצְרֵי סָחַף אַרֵישֵׁיהּ וְחָלַף **– and some say** that **[Achaz] inverted a perforated washer's trough over his head and turned away.**[13]

The Gemara explains the Mishnah's omission of Amon:

מִפְּנֵי מָה לֹא מָנוּ אֶת אָמוֹן **– Why did they not list Amon** in our Mishnah as one of the kings who have no portion in the World to Come? מִפְּנֵי כְּבוֹדוֹ שֶׁל יֹאשִׁיָּהוּ **– Because of the honor of** his righteous son **Yoshiahu.**

The Gemara asks:

מְנַשֶּׁה נַמִּי לֹא נִמְנֵי מִפְּנֵי כְּבוֹדוֹ שֶׁל חִזְקִיָּהוּ – But if this is the reason, **let them also not list Menasheh, because of the honor** of his father **Chizkiah. – ? –**

The Gemara answers:

בְּרָא מְזַכֵּי אַבָּא **– A** righteous **son can earn merit for a** wicked **father;** אַבָּא לֹא מְזַכֵּי בְּרָא **–** however, **a** righteous **father cannot earn merit for a** wicked **son,** דִּכְתִיב ,,וְאֵין מִיָּדִי מַצִּיל״ **– as it is written:**[14] ***there is no rescuer from My hand,*** and this is explained by *Sifri* as follows: אֵין אַבְרָהָם מַצִּיל אֶת יִשְׁמָעֵאל **–** ABRAHAM CANNOT SAVE his wicked son ISHMAEL from Divine punishment; אֵין יִצְחָק מַצִּיל אֶת עֵשָׂו **–** ISAAC CANNOT SAVE his wicked son ESAU from Divine punishment. Similarly, Chizkiah could not save Menasheh from Divine punishment, and Menasheh is accordingly listed in our Mishnah as having no portion in the World to Come.[15]

In light of the above, the Gemara says:

הַשְׁתָּא דְּאָתֵית לְהָכִי **– Now that you have arrived at this** conclusion that a righteous son earns merit for a wicked father, אָחָז נַמִּי לֹא אִימְנֵי מִשּׁוּם כְּבוֹדוֹ שֶׁל חִזְקִיָּהוּ **–** you can explain that **Achaz as well is not listed out of concern for the honor of** his righteous son **Chizkiah.**[16]

The Gemara returns to the question of the Mishnah's omission of Yehoiakim:

וּמִפְּנֵי מָה לֹא מָנוּ אֶת יְהוֹיָקִים **– And why did they not list Yehoiakim?**[17] מִשּׁוּם דְּרַבִּי חִיָּיא בְּרַבִּי אֲבוּיָה **– Because** he gained atonement through the fact that his body was never buried, as was taught **by R' Chiya the son of R' Avuyah.** דְּאָמַר רַבִּי חִיָּיא בְּרַבִּי אֲבוּיָה **– For R' Chiya the son of R' Avuyah said:** כְּתִיב עַל גּוּלְגָּלְתּוֹ [שֶׁל] יְהוֹיָקִים ,,זֹאת וְעוֹד אַחֶרֶת״ **– It was written on the skull of Yehoiakim: "This and still another";** i.e. *this* retribution you have already received *and still another* retribution is due you.

NOTES

11. *Isaiah* 7:3. [See *Rashi* for an alternative translation of the words שְׁאָר יָשׁוּב.]

12. I.e. as soon as Achaz saw Isaiah, he hid his face, because he was ashamed of his sins. This was a praiseworthy characteristic.

The word *koveis* is interpreted as *koveish*, which means to press or cover (one's face) (*Rashi*).

13. The word *koveis* is translated as a washer, which is indeed the usual translation of the word.

Akeidas Yitzchak (*Parashas Beshalach*, ch. 40) explains that Achaz's embarrassment indicated that the sins he committed were due to momentary impulses rather than to deliberate attempts to defy God. Therefore, despite the truly terrible sins he committed, Achaz was not in the same category as the three kings listed in the Mishnah, who sinned in order to deliberately display their contempt for God and His Torah. See also *Berachos* 12b on the merits of being embarrassed by one's sins; see also *Maharal*.

14. *Deuteronomy* 32:39.

15. This phenomenon of a son rescuing a father, but not a father a son, is explained by *Rashba* as follows: Since it is the parents who are the cause of the child's existence in this world, they may be said to live on through their progeny. Thus, if the child performs righteous deeds, it means that the parents too are performing those deeds through their child. The reverse, however, is not true: The existence of the parents is not due to the child. Thus, there is no way that the righteous deeds of the parents may be viewed as having been performed by their child (*Responsa* V, 49; see, however, *Tosafos* to *Sotah* 10b).

Other commentators add that a child is molded by the instruction of its parents. In most cases, the child of wicked parents would never grow up to be righteous if his parents had not instructed and encouraged, or at least permitted him to be righteous. Thus, the righteousness of the child is due to his parents, whose own righteousness reveals itself in the person of their child, even if it did not reveal itself in the parents themselves. For this reason, parents whose children were righteous are not included in the same category as the thoroughly wicked persons listed in our Mishnah (see *Sefer Chasidim* 1171; *Maharsha; Iyun Yaakov*; see also *Tosafos* to *Sotah* 10b).

The commentators raise the question that the Gemara's statement that a father's merit cannot benefit the son seems to contradict the principle of זְכוּת אָבוֹת, i.e. that the reward for the deeds of the righteous accrues to the benefit of their descendants – see *Exodus* 20:6. As a case in point, did not Moses at the time of the sin of the Golden Calf invoke the merit of the Patriarchs for the sake of their descendants (ibid. 32:13)?

Rashba (ibid.) answers that the principle of זְכוּת אָבוֹת applies only to reward in *this* world. As long as the son lives, he can be the beneficiary of the righteous deeds performed by his predecessors. Once he passes on, however, his reward depends solely on his own merits (see *Yoma* 87a; see also *Rif* in *Ein Yaakov* and *Margaliyos HaYam*).

[It should be noted that the Baraisa's statement that Abraham's deeds could not save Yishmael from punishment apparently takes the position that Yishmael died a wicked man. This disputes the more well-known opinion mentioned in *Bava Basra* 16b and cited by *Rashi* to *Genesis* 25:9 that Yishmael repented in his later years (*Bereishis Rabbah* 45:9; *Tosefos Yeshanim* to *Yoma* 38b ד״ה מעשה, cited by *R' Akiva Eiger*).]

16. It is no longer necessary to say that the reason Achaz was not listed is that he was ashamed before Isaiah. Rather, it is because of the honor of Chizkiah (*Rashi*). [*Rashi* does not explain that it is also no longer necessary to say that Achaz was not listed because he was sandwiched between two righteous men. See *Metzudos David* cited in *Margaliyos HaYam*. See also *Ahavas Eisan* in *Ein Yaakov*.]

[In concluding the discussion regarding Achaz's status vis-a-vis the World to Come, it should be pointed out that the various statements of the Gemara on this matter do not appear to be consistent. The implication of the statement that Achaz was not listed "because of the honor of Chizkiah" would seem to be that Achaz in fact has no share in the World to Come, but that this fact was purposely suppressed by the Mishnah due to Chizkiah's honor. However, the Gemara goes on to explain the reason for this by saying that "a son earns merit for his father." This principle is more than just a reason for not publicizing the father's status; it is a statement that a righteous son can actually save his father from punishment in the Afterworld – see *Rashba* and commentaries cited in the preceding note. It is therefore clear that the Gemara means that Achaz was not listed in the Mishnah because he in fact has a share in the World to Come.

On the other hand, the Gemara on 103b cited a Baraisa in the name of R' Meir that Achaz, among other kings, will not be resurrected. Assuming that resurrection is synonymous with the World to Come (see Chapter Introduction), our Gemara and the Baraisa on 103b contradict one another.

It may be that this reflects a dispute among Tannaim. For while our Mishnah omits Achaz and lists only three kings as having no share in the World to Come, the *Tosefta* (12:5) in fact lists Achaz, adding his name to those of the three kings enumerated by the Mishnah. Perhaps, then, our Gemara, which comes to explain the Mishnah, takes the position that Achaz received a portion in the World to Come, while the Baraisa on 103b accords with the *Tosefta* that Achaz does not receive a portion.]

17. This question was asked earlier but was not answered (see 103b).

מעמון ומואב ומקרבת את הרחוקים מיתרו
דאמר ר' יוחנן בשכר (א) קראן לו ויאכל לחם
(א) זכו בני בניו וישבו בלשכת הגזית שנאמר
(ב) וממשפחות סופרים יושבי יעבץ תרעתים
שמעתים סוכתים המה הקינים הבאים
מחמת אבי בית רכב וכתיב התם (ג) ובני קיני
חותן משה עלו מעיר התמרים את בני יהודה
מדבר יהודה אשר בנגב ערד וילך וישב
את העם ומעלמת עינים מן הרשעים ממיכה
ומשרה שכינה על נביאי הבעל מחבירו
של עדו הנביא דכתיב (ד) ויהי הם יושבים
אל השלחן ויהי דבר ה' אל הנביא אשר
השיבו ושגגתה עולה זדון דאמר רב יהודה
אמר רב אלמלי הלווהו יהונתן לדוד שתי
ככרות לחם לא נהרגה נוב עיר הכהנים
ולא נטרד דואג האדומי ולא נהרג שאול
ושלשת בניו ומפני מה לא מנו את אחז אמר
ר' ירמיה בר אבא מפני שמוטל בין שני
צדיקים בין יותם לחזקיהו רב יוסף אמר
מפני שהיה לו בשת פנים מישעיהו שנאמר
(ה) ויאמר ה' אל ישעיהו צא נא לקראת אחז
אתה ושאר ישוב בנך אל קצה תעלת
הברכה העליונה אל מסלת שדה כובס
מאי כובס איכא דאמרי דכבשינהו לאפיה
וחלף ואיכא דאמרי (ג) אוכלא דקצרי סחף
ארישיה וחלף מפני מה לא מנו את אמון
מפני כבודו של יאשיהו מנשה נמי לא נמני
מפני כבודו של חזקיהו ברא מזכי (ג) אבא אבא
לא מזכי ברא דכתיב (ו) ואין מידי מציל (*) אין
אברהם מציל את ישמעאל אין יצחק מציל
את עשו השתא דאתית להכי אחז נמי לא
אימני משום כבודו של חזקיהו ומפני מה לא
מנו את יהויקים משום דר' חייא בר' אבויה
(ד) דאמר ר' חייא בר' אבויה כתיב על גולגלתו
[של] יהויקים זאת ועוד אחרת זקינו דרבי
פרידא אשכח גולגלתא דהוה קא שדיא
בשערי ירושלים וכתיב בה זאת ועוד אחרת
קברה ולא איקברא קברה ולא איקברא אמר
גולגלתו של יהויקים היא דכתיב ביה (ז) קבורת
חמור יקבר סחוב והשלך וגו' אמר מלכא
הוא ולא איכשר לזלזולי ביה כרכה בשיראי
ואותבה בסיפתא (ה) חזיתא דביתהו סברא
הא דאיתתא קמייתא הוה דהא לא קא
מנשי לה שגרא תנורא וקלתה היינו דכתיב
זאת ועוד אחרת תניא אמר רבי שמעון בן אלעזר בשביל (ח) הטוב
בעיניך עשיתי מה אות בשביל (ט) מה אות נכרים אכלו על שולחנו בשביל
שנכרים אכלו על שולחנו גרם גלות לבניו מסייע ליה לחזקיה דאמר
חזקיה כל המזמן עובד כוכבים לתוך ביתו ומשמש עליו גורם גלות לבניו שנאמר (י) ובניך אשר יצאו ממך
[אשר תוליד] יקחו והיו סריסים בהיכל מלך בבל (כ) (ו) וישמח עליהם חזקיה ויראם את (כל) בית נכתה
את הכסף ואת הזהב ואת הבשמים ואת השמן הטוב וגו' אמר רב מאי בית נכתה אשתו השקתה
עליהם ושמואל אמר בית גנזיו הראה להם ור' יוחנן אמר זין אוכל זין הראה להן (ל) איכה ישבה בדד אמר (ז) רבא
אמר רבי יוחנן מפני מה לקו ישראל באיכה מפני שעברו על שלשים ושש כריתות שבתורה אמר רבי יוחנן
מפני מה לקו באל"ף בי"ת מפני שעברו על התורה שניתנה באל"ף בי"ת ישבה בדד אמר (ח) רבא אמר רבי
יוחנן אמר הקב"ה אני אמרתי (מ) וישכן ישראל בטח בדד עין יעקב אל ארץ דגן ותירוש אף שמיו יערפו טל
עכשיו יהיה בדד מושבם (ל) העיר רבתי עם אמר (ט) רבא אמר רבי יוחנן שהיו משיאין קטנה לגדול וגדולה לקטן
כדי שיהיו להם בנים הרבה (ל) היתה כאלמנה (י) אמר רב יהודה אמר רב כאלמנה ולא אלמנה ממש אלא כאשה
שהלך בעלה למדינת הים ודעתו לחזור אליה (ל) רבתי בגוים שרתי במדינות אמר (כ) רבא אמר רבי יוחנן כל מקום
שהן הולכין נעשין שרים לאדוניהן ת"ר מעשה בשני בני אדם שנשבו בהר הכרמל והיה שבאי מהלך אחריהם
א"ל

רש"י

עמון ומואב. קרובין לישראל שבאו מלוט בן אחי אברהם ורחקן המקום שלא יבאו בקהל ל"א קרובין ממש ליכא למימר דהא מדין מבני קטורה היו בני אברהם וקרובים היו בני מדין לישראל יותר מעמון ומואב שהם בני אברהם אלא עמון ומואב שכנים וקרובים היו לארץ ישראל ומדין רחוקים להם היו: וישבו בלשכת הגזית. ממשפחות סופרים והאי קרא מפרש ליה כולי בסיפרי בפרשת ויאמר משה לחובב: המה הקינים הבאים מחמת אבי בית רכב. וקינים אלו בניו של יתרו דכתיב ובני קיני חותן משה ובניו של יתרו הן הן בניו של רכב דכתיב הקינים הבאים מחמת אבי בית רכב וכתיב (ירמיה לה) ולבית הרכבים אמר ירמיהו כי כה אמר ה' [וגו'] יען אשר שמעתם [על] מצות [יהונדב] אביכם [וגו'] לא יכרת איש ליונדב בן רכב [עומד] לפני כל הימים ואמרינן בסיפרי אפשר נכרים הם ונכנסין להיכל והרי כל ישראל לא נכנסו להיכל אלא שהיו יושבין בסנהדרין ומורין בדברי תורה. מ"ר: ממיכה. דאמרינן לעיל הניחו לו שפתו מצויה לעוברי דרכים: ומשרה שכינה על נביאי הבעל מחברו של עדו הנביא. דעדו הנביא נתנבא על מזבח בית אל שיחרב מפני שהעמיד בו ירבעם צלמים דכתיב (במ"א יג) והנה איש האלהים בא מיהודה וגו' ויאמר מזבח מזבח ומפרש בסדר עולם דהיינו עדו הנביא ובא נביא השקר והטעהו לעדו והשיבו לבית אל והעבירו על מצות הקב"ה שאמר לו לא תשוב לבית אל והאכילו ובזכות שהאכילו שרתה עליו שכינה שנאמר ויהי דבר ה' אל האיש הנביא אשר השיבו להאכילו אצלו: ושגגתה עולה זדון. שהרי מצינו ביהונתן ששגג ולא הלוהו לדוד שתי ככרות ונענש דאמר רב יהודה וכו': לוֹוהו. לשון לויה: לא נהרגה נוב. שלא היה צריך דוד לשאול לחם מכהני נוב ולא היה דואג מלשין עליהם: ולא היה שאול נהרג. על אותו עון: שמוטל. דאביו יותם ובנו חזקיה: ושאר מישראל ששבו להיות בניך ותלמידיך וכל מי שישוב לביתך דהיינו תלמידיו כדמתרגמינן ושאר' דלא חטאו ודתבו חטיאי תלמידוהי: מאי כובס דכבשינהו לאפיה. שכבש את פניו והיה מתבייש מפני ישעיה: כובס. כמו כובש: אוכלא דקצרי סחף ארישיה. כלי מנוקב של כובסין שמזלפין בו מים על הבגדים ואותו כלי הפך אחז על ראשו כדי שלא יכירו ישעיה שהיה מתבייש [ממנו]: יאשיהו. בן אמון: חזקיהו. אבי מנשה: [ברא מזכה אבא וכו']. יאשיה מזכה אמון אביו ולא חזקיה מנשה בנו דכתיב אין מידי מציל ודרשינן ליה בהגדה אין אברהם מציל וכו': השתא דאתית להכי. דברא מזכה לאבא: אחז נמי. לא תימא דכבשינהו [לאפיה] אלא מפני כבודו של חזקיה לא מנאוהו: מפני מה לא מנו את יהויקים. באותן שאין להם חלק [לעוה"ב]: משום דר' חייא בר אבויה. שנתכפר על שלא ניתן לקבורה וכל הני מפני מה לא מנו לא בעי אלא מהנך דהוו רשעים גמורים כדחשיבנא להו לעיל אחז חתם את התורה וכו': [זאת ועוד כו'. נקמה נעשית בה כבר ועוד אחרת תעשה בה]: פרידא. כך שמו: סיפתא. ארגז: בשביל הטוב מה אות. בשביל חזקיה [ששיבח את עצמו דאמר הטוב בעיניך עשיתי גרם לו שאמר מה אות כי אעלה בית ה' ששאל אות מהקב"ה שעבירה גוררת עבירה: אכלו נכרים על שולחנו. אותם ששלח לו מרודך בלאדן ספרים ומנחה על ידם: ומשמש עליו. כגון חזקיה דאמרינן לקמן אשתו השקתה עליהם: גורם גלות. דכתיב וישמח עליהם חזקיהו ויראם את (כל) בית נכתה וכתיב בתריה ומבניך אשר יצאו ממך יקחו והיו סריסים בהיכל מלך בבל: אשתו השקתה עליהם. היא עצמה מוזגת להם והיינו בית נכתה לשון מנכה על שם צלע שנפחתה מן האדם וממנה נבראת אשה: בית גנזיו. והכי מתרגמינן בית גניזוהי ומנחם פתר במחברתו לשון סממנים כמו (בראשית לז) נכאת וצרי ולוט: זין אוכל זין. כגון פרזלא דשליט בפרזלא (ל): איכה. ל"ו בגימטריא: ל"ו כריתות. בכריתות (דף ב.) חשיב להו: לקו בא"ב. שכל מגילת איכה סדורה באלפא ביתא: בטח בדד. שיושבין יחידים ואינן מתיראין לא מן הנכרים ולא מן חיות רעות: רבתי עם. עם שמתרבה והולך יותר משאר עם: קטנה לגדול. ש"ז של קטן אינו מבושל ואינו מזריע מהר כשל גדול וכן רחם של קטנה אינה קולטת מהר כשל גדולה לפיכך משיאין גדולה לקטן כדי לכשתהא זרעו [מבושל] קולט מהר וקטנה לגדול כדי שיהא שכבת זרעו קולט מהר ולא קטנה לקטן שושין להוליד ולא קטן וקטנה ממש אלא שעומדין על פרקן וראויין הם להוליד ומיהו אין זרע שלהם מבושל כל כך:
אחד

מסורת הש"ס

א) [לקמן קו. ע"ש סוטה יא. ע"ש], ב) [גירסת ערוך בערך אבל **אובלא** וכתיב על זה שני פירושים ע"ש], ג) [עי' תוספות סוטה י: ד"ה דאתי'], ד) לעיל פב. ע"ש, ה) נ"א **אתיא דביתהו חזיתא נפקא אמרה להו לשיבבתה אמרי לה ההיא** כו', ו) [במלכים איתא וישמע ובישעיה לט כתיב וישמח], ז) [נ"ל רבה], ח) [נ"ל רבה], ט) [נ"ל רבה], י) [תענית כ.], כ) [נ"ל רבה], ל) [לעיל נו:].

ליקוטי רש"י

מעיר התמרים. היא יריחו שניתן להם דושנה של יריחו לאוכלה עד שיבנה בית המקדש ומי שיבנה בית הבחירה בחלקו יטלנה כדי שיהא לכל ישראל חלק בבית הבחירה ונתנוה לבני יתרו ת"מ שנה והתלמידים שבהם הניחוה והלכו אצל עתניאל בן קנז הוא יעבץ במדבר יהודה אשר בנגב ערד ללמוד תורה. **וישב את העם.** עם התלמידים היושבים לפניו הוא בקש מאת הקב"ה שיזמין לו תלמידים הגונים שנאמר ויקרא יעבץ לאלהים וגו' וזימן לו החסידים הללו [שופטים א, טז]. **אל הנביא.** נביא השקר אשר השיבו לאיש האלהים מכאן אמרו גדולה לגימא שמשרה שכינה על נביאי הבעל [מ"א יג, כ]. **שדה כובס.** שדה שהכובסים שוטחים שם בגדים לנגבם כך תירגם יונתן ורבותינו דרשו נכנע אחז לפני ישעיהו ושם על ראשו אוכלא דקצרי כפה עליו כלי פי' כלי מנוקב של כובסים שמזלפין בו מים על הבגדים [ישעיהו ז, ג]. **אוכלא דקצרי.** כלי נחושת העשוי כנפה נקבים נקבים והוא של כובסים ונותנו על הבגדים ומזלף בו המים עליהן ויש מפרשים שמגמרין מוגמר מתחתיו והבגדים מונחין עליו ומתגמרין דרך הנקבים [שבת קכג:]. כלי של כובסין שהוא מנוקב ומזלפין בו מים על הבגדים [לעיל צב.]. **זאת ועוד אחרת.** נקמה נעשית בה כבר ועוד אחרת תעשה בה. **זקינו דר' פרידא.** הוא ר' חייא בר אבויה והכי אמרינן בחלק. **קברה ולא איקברא.** בגללה ויצאה מקבורתה. **קבורת חמור.** מושלך ברחובות. **בסיפתא.** ארגז. **דלא קא מנשי לה.** אינה נשכחת מלבו. **שגרא לתנורא.** הסיקה את התנור [שם פב.]. **בית נכתה.** בית גנזי בשמיו כמו נכאת וצרי ולוט (בראשית ל"ז כ"ד). **ואת השמן הטוב.** יש פותרין שמן המשחה ויש פותרים שמן אפרסמון (בלסמון) שהוא מצוי בא"י שנאמר (יחזקאל כז י"ז) יהודה וישראל המה רוכליך בחטי מנית ופנג וראיתי בס' יוסיפון פנג הוא אפרסמון וגדל בירחו ועל שם הריח נקרא ירחו. [מ"ב כ, יג]. **בטח בדד.** כל יחיד ויחיד איש תחת גפנו ותחת תאנתו מפוזרין ואין צריכים להתאסף ולישב יחד מפני האויב [דברים לג, כח]. **רבתי עם.** יו"ד יתירה כמו רבת עם שהיתה עמה רב יש מדרשי אגדה הרבה ואני באתי לפרש לשון המקרא כמשמעו [איכה א, א]. **ולא אלמנה ממש.** דהא לא כתיב אלמנה אלא היתה כאלמנה כאשה העומדת באלמנות חיות על בעלה שהלך ועתיד לחזור [תענית כ.].

גליון הש"ס

גמ' **אין אברהם מציל.** עי' יומא לח ע"ב בתוס' ד"ה מעשה:

תורה אור השלם

א) וַיֹּאמֶר אֶל בְּנֹתָיו וְאַיּוֹ לָמָּה זֶּה עֲזַבְתֶּן אֶת הָאִישׁ קִרְאֶן לוֹ וְיֹאכַל לָחֶם: [שמות ב, כ]

ב) וּמִשְׁפְּחוֹת סֹפְרִים יֹשְׁבֵי יַעְבֵּץ תִּרְעָתִים שִׁמְעָתִים שׂוּכָתִים הֵמָּה הַקִּינִים הַבָּאִים מֵחַמַּת אֲבִי בֵית רֵכָב: [דברי הימים א' ב, נה]

ג) וּבְנֵי קֵינִי חֹתֵן מֹשֶׁה עָלוּ מֵעִיר הַתְּמָרִים אֶת בְּנֵי יְהוּדָה מִדְבַּר יְהוּדָה אֲשֶׁר בְּנֶגֶב עֲרָד וַיֵּלֶךְ וַיֵּשֶׁב אֶת הָעָם: [שופטים א, טז]

ד) וַיְהִי הֵם יֹשְׁבִים אֶל הַשֻּׁלְחָן וַיְהִי דְּבַר יְיָ אֶל הַנָּבִיא אֲשֶׁר הֱשִׁיבוֹ: [מלכים א' יג, כ]

ה) וַיֹּאמֶר יְיָ אֶל יְשַׁעְיָהוּ צֵא נָא לִקְרַאת אָחָז אַתָּה וּשְׁאָר יָשׁוּב בְּנֶךָ אֶל קְצֵה תְּעָלַת הַבְּרֵכָה הָעֶלְיוֹנָה אֶל מְסִלַּת שְׂדֵה כוֹבֵס: [ישעיה ז, ג]

ו) רְאוּ עַתָּה כִּי אֲנִי אֲנִי הוּא וְאֵין אֱלֹהִים עִמָּדִי אֲנִי אָמִית וַאֲחַיֶּה מָחַצְתִּי וַאֲנִי אֶרְפָּא וְאֵין מִיָּדִי מַצִּיל: [דברים לב, לט]

ז) קְבוּרַת חֲמוֹר יִקָּבֵר סָחוֹב וְהַשְׁלֵךְ מֵהָלְאָה לְשַׁעֲרֵי יְרוּשָׁלִָם: [ירמיה כב, יט]

ח) אָנָּה יְיָ זְכָר נָא אֵת אֲשֶׁר הִתְהַלַּכְתִּי לְפָנֶיךָ בֶּאֱמֶת וּבְלֵבָב שָׁלֵם וְהַטּוֹב בְּעֵינֶיךָ עָשִׂיתִי וַיֵּבְךְּ חִזְקִיָּהוּ בְּכִי גָדוֹל: [מלכים ב' כ, ג]

ט) וַיֹּאמֶר חִזְקִיָּהוּ אֶל יְשַׁעְיָהוּ מָה אוֹת כִּי יִרְפָּא יְיָ לִי וְעָלִיתִי בַּיּוֹם הַשְּׁלִישִׁי בֵּית יְיָ: [מלכים ב' כ, ח]

י) וּמִבָּנֶיךָ אֲשֶׁר יֵצְאוּ מִמְּךָ אֲשֶׁר תּוֹלִיד יִקָּחוּ וְהָיוּ סָרִיסִים בְּהֵיכַל מֶלֶךְ בָּבֶל: [מלכים ב' כ, יח]

כ) וַיִּשְׁמַע עֲלֵיהֶם חִזְקִיָּהוּ וַיַּרְאֵם אֶת כָּל בֵּית נְכֹתֹה אֶת הַכֶּסֶף וְאֶת הַזָּהָב וְאֶת הַבְּשָׂמִים וְאֵת שֶׁמֶן הַטּוֹב וְאֵת בֵּית כֵּלָיו וְאֵת כָּל אֲשֶׁר נִמְצָא בְּאוֹצְרֹתָיו לֹא הָיָה דָבָר אֲשֶׁר לֹא הֶרְאָם חִזְקִיָּהוּ בְּבֵיתוֹ וּבְכָל מֶמְשַׁלְתּוֹ: [מלכים ב' כ, יג] וַיִּשְׂמַח עֲלֵיהֶם חִזְקִיָּהוּ וַיַּרְאֵם אֶת בֵּית נְכֹתוֹ אֶת הַכֶּסֶף וְאֶת הַזָּהָב וְאֶת הַבְּשָׂמִים וְאֵת הַשֶּׁמֶן הַטּוֹב וְאֵת כָּל בֵּית כֵּלָיו וְאֵת כָּל אֲשֶׁר נִמְצָא בְּאוֹצְרֹתָיו לֹא הָיָה דָבָר אֲשֶׁר לֹא הֶרְאָם חִזְקִיָּהוּ בְּבֵיתוֹ וּבְכָל מֶמְשַׁלְתּוֹ: [ישעיה לט, ב]

ל) אֵיכָה יָשְׁבָה בָדָד הָעִיר רַבָּתִי עָם הָיְתָה כְּאַלְמָנָה רַבָּתִי בַגּוֹיִם שָׂרָתִי בַּמְּדִינוֹת הָיְתָה לָמַס: [איכה א, א]

מ) וַיִּשְׁכֹּן יִשְׂרָאֵל בֶּטַח בָּדָד עֵין יַעֲקֹב אֶל אֶרֶץ דָּגָן וְתִירוֹשׁ אַף שָׁמָיו יַעַרְפוּ טָל: [דברים לג, כח]

The Gemara relates a story that clarifies this enigmatic inscription:

זְקִינוֹ דְּרַבִּי פְּרִידָא אַשְׁכַּח גּוּלְגָּלְתָּא דַּהֲוָה קָא שַׁדְיָא בְּשַׁעֲרֵי יְרוּשָׁלַיִם – **The grandfather of R' Pereida found a skull that was cast down at the gates of Jerusalem,** וּכְתִיב בָּהּ ,,זֹאת וְעוֹד אַחֶרֶת" – **and upon it was written "This and still another."** קְבָרָהּ וְלֹא אִיקַּבְרָא – **He buried it, but it would not stay buried,** i.e. it reemerged from the ground. קְבָרָהּ וְלֹא אִיקַּבְרָא – Again **he buried it, but** again **it would not stay buried.** אָמַר – Thereupon **he said:** גּוּלְגָּלְתּוֹ שֶׁל יְהוֹיָקִים הִיא – **It is the skull of Yehoiakim,** דִּכְתִיב בֵּיהּ ,,קְבוּרַת חֲמוֹר יִקָּבֵר סָחוֹב וְהַשְׁלֵךְ וגו' " – **concerning whom it is written:** ***He shall be buried with the burial of a donkey, dragged and cast*** **etc.** [*beyond the gates of Jerusalem*].[18] אָמַר מַלְכָּא הוּא – **He said** to himself: [Yehoiakim] **was** nonetheless **a king,** וְלֹא אִיכַּשַׁר לְזַלְזוּלֵי בֵּיהּ – **and it is not proper to treat [his skull] irreverently.** כְּרָכָהּ בְּשִׁירָאֵי וְאוֹתְבָהּ בְּסִיפְתָּא – So **he wrapped [the skull] in silk and placed it in a chest.** חֲזִיתָא דְּבֵיתְהוּ – Later, **his wife saw [the skull].** סָבְרָא – **She thought:** הָא דְּאִיתְתָא קַמַּיְיתָא הֲוָה דְּהָא לֹא קָא מִנְשֵׁי לָהּ – **This is** surely the skull **of** my husband's **first wife,** whom he cannot forget! שַׁגְרָא תַּנּוּרָא וְקַלְתָהּ – So **she fired up the oven and burned [the skull].** הַיְינוּ דִּכְתִיב ,,זֹאת וְעוֹד אַחֶרֶת" – **This is** the meaning of **what was written** on the skull: **"This and still another."** I.e. the words foretold that Yehoiakim was destined to suffer a twofold retribution: *this* – the casting of the skull into the streets, *and still another* – its being consumed by fire.[19]

This punishment atoned for Yehoiakim's sins. For that reason, he was not listed in our Mishnah along with the kings who have no portion in the World to Come.

Having extolled the merits of hospitality, the Gemara points out that hospitality can sometimes be misplaced:

תַּנְיָא – **It was taught in a Baraisa:** אָמַר רַבִּי שִׁמְעוֹן בֶּן אֶלְעָזָר – R' SHIMON BEN ELAZAR SAID: בִּשְׁבִיל ,,וְהַטּוֹב בְּעֵינֶיךָ עָשִׂיתִי" – BECAUSE Chizkiah sinned and said: *I HAVE DONE THAT WHICH WAS GOOD IN YOUR EYES,* ,,מָה אוֹת" – he was led to sin again and came to say *WHAT SHALL BE THE SIGN?*[20] בִּשְׁבִיל ,,מָה אוֹת" – BECAUSE he said: *WHAT SHALL BE THE SIGN?* נָכְרִים אָכְלוּ עַל שׁוּלְחָנוֹ – he sinned again and FOREIGNERS (i.e. idolaters) ATE AT HIS TABLE.[21] בִּשְׁבִיל שֶׁנָּכְרִים אָכְלוּ עַל שׁוּלְחָנוֹ – BECAUSE FOREIGNERS ATE AT HIS TABLE, גָּרַם גָּלוּת לְבָנָיו – HE CAUSED HIS DESCENDANTS TO GO INTO EXILE in Babylon. מְסַיֵּיע לֵיהּ לְחִזְקִיָּה – **This supports** a teaching by the Amora **Chizkiah,** דְּאָמַר חִזְקִיָּה – **for Chizkiah said:** כָּל הַמְזַמֵּן עוֹבֵד כּוֹכָבִים לְתוֹךְ בֵּיתוֹ וּמְשַׁמְּשׁוֹ עָלָיו גּוֹרֵם גָּלוּת לְבָנָיו – **Whoever invites a worshiper of idols into his house and waits on him causes his descendants to go into exile,** שֶׁנֶּאֱמַר ,,וּמִבָּנֶיךָ אֲשֶׁר יֵצְאוּ מִמְּךָ אֲשֶׁר תּוֹלִיד יִקָּח וְהָיוּ סָרִיסִים בְּהֵיכַל מֶלֶךְ בָּבֶל" – **as it is stated:** ***And some of your sons, your own issue whom you will have fathered, will be taken, and they will be stewards in the palace of the king of Babylon.***[22]

The Gemara details the extent of Chizkiah's hospitality to the idolaters:

,,וַיִּשְׂמַח עֲלֵיהֶם חִזְקִיָּהוּ וַיַּרְאֵם אֶת־בֵּית נְכֹתֹה אֶת־הַכֶּסֶף וְאֶת־הַזָּהָב וְאֶת־הַבְּשָׂמִים וְאֵת הַשֶּׁמֶן הַטּוֹב וגו' " – Scripture states:[23] ***Chizkiah rejoiced over them, and he showed them his beis nechos, the silver, the gold, the spices, the fragrant oil,*** **etc.** אָמַר רַב – **Rav said:** מַאי ,,בֵּית נְכֹתֹה" – **What is the meaning of** ***his beis nechos?*** אִשְׁתּוֹ הִשְׁקָתָה עֲלֵיהֶם – It means that **[Chizkiah's]** own **wife poured them drinks.**[24] וּשְׁמוּאֵל אָמַר – **And Shmuel said:** בֵּית גְּנָזָיו הֶרְאָה לָהֶם – It means that **[Chizkiah] showed them his treasure house.**[25] וְרַבִּי יוֹחָנָן אָמַר – **And R' Yochanan said:** זַיִן אוֹכֵל זַיִן הֶרְאָה לָהֶן – **He showed them weapons that destroy other weapons.**[26]

Having discussed the sins of the kings of Judah which led to the destruction of Jerusalem, the Gemara now commences an explication of selections from the Book of *Lamentations,* which describes that destruction, beginning with the opening verse:

,,אֵיכָה יָשְׁבָה בָדָד" – Scripture states: ***Alas*** (*eichah*) ***– she sits in***

NOTES

18. *Jeremiah* 22:19. I.e. his corpse will be discarded like the corpse of a donkey, i.e. he will not be accorded burial (*Radak* ad loc.; see also *Jeremiah* 36:30). Thus, his skull refuses to stay buried, in fulfillment of this prophecy.

19. *Maharsha* points out that Yehoiakim's two punishments exactly matched his two outstanding sins cited on 103b: (a) He inscribed obscenities and blasphemies on his own body, and the earth refused to accept that body in burial. (b) He claimed that God's light could be replaced by man-made means of illumination, and his own body was consumed in fire (see also *Iyun Yaakov*).

[*Rashi* to 82a (ד"ה זקינו) identifies the grandfather of R' Pereida as R' Chiyah the son of Avuyah, the sage just mentioned as having made the statement about the inscription on Yehoiakim's skull.]

20. When Chizkiah was dangerously ill, he prayed to God and said: *Please, O HASHEM, remember how I have walked before You sincerely and wholeheartedly, how I have done that which was good in your eyes* (*II Kings* 20:3). In other words, Chizkiah claimed that he was so righteous that he deserved to be healed by God. This was an immodest statement.

Based on the dictum that "one sin leads to another" (see *Avos* 4:2), R' Shimon ben Elazar states that this sin led Chizkiah to an even greater sin. When the prophet Isaiah came to Chizkiah to inform him that God had heard his prayer and would grant him fifteen more years of life, Chizkiah asked (*II Kings* 20:8): *What shall be the sign that HASHEM will heal me?* (*Rashi*). In asking this question, Chizkiah betrayed a lack of faith in God (*Yad Ramah*; but see *Maharsha*).

21. I.e. a few verses later, Scripture relates how the envoys of the king of Babylon, Merodach Baladan, came to visit Chizkiah, having become aware of his miraculous recovery [see above, 96a, where the story is related in detail]. Chizkiah hosted these guests in an overly regal fashion. This was a sin, as the Gemara will explain below.

22. *II Kings* 20:18. Ibid. v. 18. In this passage, the prophet Isaiah rebuked Chizkiah for entertaining the messengers of the king of Babylon and for arrogantly showing them his treasures (see *Maharal* and *Yalkut Shimoni* to *Genesis* §77). Isaiah foretold that one day the Babylonians would return to sack Jerusalem and carry off those treasures. In addition, they would enslave members of the royal family, Chizkiah's descendants, and carry them off to Babylon, where they would be made into stewards to serve in the royal palace of their conquerors. This prophecy came true when Daniel, a descendant of Chizkiah (and possibly also Chananiah, Mishael and Azariah – see above, 93b), was made a steward in Nebuchadnezzar's palace.

For explanations of the connection between the various sins of Chizkiah, see *Maharsha, Maharal, Toras Chaim,* and *Ben Yehoyada.*

23. *Isaiah* 39:2. *Isaiah* contains a parallel account of Chizkiah's reception of the Babylonian ambassadors recorded in *Kings.*

24. Rav relates the word נְכֹתֹה to the Aramaic word meaning "subtraction," which signifies a wife, for the first wife, Eve, was created from a rib of Adam's body that was removed or "subtracted" from him (*Rashi*). Alternatively, Rav derives his interpretation from the word בֵּית, *house,* for the wife is referred to as a man's "house" in *Leviticus* 16:11 (*Yad Ramah*).

According to *Maharsha,* Rav agrees with Shmuel (cited immediately below) that בֵּית נְכֹתֹה means a treasure house. A man's wife is his main treasure and ought to be treated as such, not as something to be displayed to every stranger.

25. This translation follows *Targum Yonasan* ad loc. Alternatively, *Rashi* cites *Menachem ben Seruk* (a tenth-century grammarian) who translates בֵּית נְכֹתֹה as "spice treasury" (see *Genesis* 37:25).

26. Literally: weapons that eat other weapons, i.e. weapons made of the strongest metals, which could shatter other metals (*Rashi*; see *Ben Yohoyada*).

עמון ומואב. קרובין לישראל שבאו מלוט בן אחי אברהם ורחקן המקום שלא יבאו בקהל ל"א קרובין ממש ליכא למימר דהא מדין מבני קטורה היו בני אברהם וקרובים היו בני מדין לישראל יותר מעמון ומואב שהם בני אברהם אלא עמון ומואב שכנים וקרובים היו לארץ ישראל ומדין רחוקים להם היו: וישבו בלשכת הגזית. ממשפחות סופרים והאי קרא מפרש ליה כולי בסיפרי בפרשת ויאמר משה לחובב: המה הקינים הבאים מחמת אבי בית רכב. וקינים אלו בניו של יתרו דכתיב ובני קיני חותן משה ובניו של יתרו הן הן בניו של רכב דכתיב הקינים הבאים מחמת אבי בית רכב וכתיב (ירמיה לה) ולבית הרכבים אמר ירמיהו כי כה אמר ה' [וגו'] יען אשר שמעתם [על] מצות [יהונדב] אביכם [וגו'] לא יכרת איש ליונדב בן רכב [עומד] לפני כל הימים ואמרינן בסיפרי אפשר נכרים הם ונכנסין להיכל והרי כל ישראל לא נכנסו להיכל אלא שהיו יושבין בסנהדרין ומורין בדברי תורה. מ"ר: ממיכה. דאמרינן לעיל הניחו לו שפתו מצויה לעוברי דרכים: ומשרה שכינה על נביאי הבעל מחברו של עדו הנביא. דעדו הנביא נתנבא על מזבח בית אל שיחרב מפני שהעמיד בו ירבעם צלמים דכתיב (במ"א יג) והנה איש האלהים בא מיהודה וגו' ויאמר מזבח מזבח ומפרש בסדר עולם דהיינו עדו הנביא ובא נביא השקר והטעהו לעדו והשיבו לבית אל והעבירו על מצות הקב"ה שאמר לו לא תשוב לבית אל והאכילו ובזכות שהאכילו שרתה עליו שכינה שנאמר ויהי דבר ה' אל האיש הנביא אשר השיבו להאכילו אכלו: ושגגתה עולה זדון. שהרי מלינו ביהונתן ששגג ולא הלוהו לדוד שתי ככרות ונענש דאמר רב יהודה וכו': לווהו. לשון לויה: לא נהרגה נוב. שלא היה צריך דוד לשאול לחם מכהני נוב ולא היה דואג מלשין עליהם: ולא היה שאול נהרג. על אותו עון: שמוטל. דאביו יותם ובנו חזקיה: ושאר מישראל ששבו להיות בניך ותלמידיך וכל מי שישוב לביתך דהיינו תלמידיו כדמתרגמינן ושאר' דלא חטאו ודתבו חטיאי תלמידוהי: מאי כובס דכבשינהו לאפיה. שכבש את פניו והיה מתבייש מפני ישעיה: כובס. כמו כובש: אוכלא דקצרי סחף ארישיה. כלי מנוקב של כובסין שמזלפין בו מים על הבגדים ואותו כלי הפך אחז על ראשו כדי שלא יכירו ישעיה שהיה מתבייש [ממנו]: יאשיהו. בן אמון: חזקיהו. אבי מנשה: [ברא מזכה אבא וכו']. יאשיה מזכה אמון אביו ולא חזקיה מנשה בנו דכתיב אין מידי מציל ודרשינן ליה בהגדה אין אברהם מציל וכו': השתא דאתית להכי. דברא מזכה לאבא: אחז נמי. לא תימא דכבשינהו [לאפיה] אלא מפני כבודו של חזקיה לא מנאוהו: מפני מה לא מנו את יהויקים. באותן שאין להם חלק [לעוה"ב]: משום דר' חייא בר אבויה. שנתכפר על שלא ניתן לקבורה וכל הני מפני מה לא מנו לא בעי אלא מהנך דהוו רשעים גמורים כדחשיבנא להו לעיל אחז חתם את התורה וכו': [זאת ועוד כו'. נקמה נעשית בה כבר ועוד אחרת תעשה בה]: פרידא. כך שמו: סיפתא. ארגז: בשביל הטוב מה אות. בשביל חזקיה [שתיבח את עצמו דאמר הטוב בעיניך עשיתי גרם לו שאמר מה אות כי אעלה בית ה' ששאל אות מהקב"ה שעבירה גוררת עבירה: אכלו נכרים על שולחנו. אותם ששלח לו מרודך בלאדן ספרים ומנחה על ידם: ומשמש עליו. כגון חזקיה דאמרינן לקמן אשתו השקתה עליהם: גורם גלות. דכתיב וישמח עליהם חזקיהו ויראם את (כל) בית נכתה וכתיב בתריה ומבניך אשר יצאו ממך יקחו והיו סריסים בהיכל מלך בבל: אשתו השקתה עליהם. היא עצמה מוזגת להם והיינו בית נכתה לשון מנכה על שם צלע שנפחתה מן האדם וממנה נבראת אשה: בית גנזיו. והכי מתרגמינן בית גניזוהי ומנחם פתר במחברתו לשון סממנים כמו (בראשית לז) נכאת וצרי ולוט: זין אוכל זין. כגון פרזלא דשליט בפרזלא[ל]: איכה. ל"ו בגימטריא: ל"ו כריתות. בכריתות (דף ב.) חשיב להו: לקו בא"ב. שכל מגילת איכה סדורה באלפא ביתא: בטח בדד. שיושבין יחידים ואינן מתיראין לא מן הנכרים ולא מן חיות רעות: רבתי עם. עם שמתרבה והולך יותר משאר עם: קטנה לגדול. ש"ז של קטן אינו מבושל ואינו מזריע מהר כשל גדול וכן רחם של קטנה אינה קולטת מהר כשל גדולה לפיכך משיאין גדולה לקטן כדי לכשתהא זרעו [מבושל] קולט מהר וקטנה לגדול כדי שיהא שכבת זרעו קולט מהר ולא קטנה לקטן שווהין להוליד ולא קטן וקטנה ממש אלא שעומדין על פרקן ורואין הם להוליד ומיהו אין זרע שלהם מבושל כל כך:

אחד

מעמון ומואב ומקרבת את הרחוקים מיתרו דאמר ר' יוחנן בשכר [א] קראן לו ויאכל לחם [א] זכו בני בניו וישבו בלשכת הגזית שנאמר [ב] וממשפחות סופרים יושבי יעבץ תרעתים שמעתים סוכתים המה הקינים הבאים מחמת אבי בית רכב וכתיב התם [ג] ובני קיני חותן משה עלו מעיר התמרים את בני יהודה מדבר יהודה אשר בנגב ערד וילך וישב את העם ומעלמת עינים מן הרשעים ממיכה ומשרה שכינה על נביאי הבעל מחבירו של עדו הנביא דכתיב [ד] ויהי הם יושבים אל השלחן ויהי דבר ה' אל הנביא אשר השיבו ושגגתה עולה זדון דאמר רב יהודה אמר רב אלמלי הלווהו יהונתן לדוד שתי ככרות לחם לא נהרגה נוב עיר הכהנים ולא נטרד דואג האדומי ולא נהרג שאול ושלשת בניו ומפני מה לא מנו את אחז אמר ר' ירמיה בר אבא מפני שמוטל בין שני צדיקים בין יותם לחזקיהו רב יוסף אמר מפני שהיה לו בשת פנים מישעיהו שנאמר [ה] ויאמר ה' אל ישעיהו צא נא לקראת אחז אתה ושאר ישוב בנך אל קצה תעלת הברכה העליונה אל מסלת שדה כובס מאי כובס איכא דאמרי דכבשינהו לאפיה וחלף ואיכא דאמרי [ב] אוכלא דקצרי סחף ארישיה וחלף מפני מה לא מנו את אמון מפני כבודו של יאשיהו מנשה נמי לא נמני מפני כבודו של חזקיהו ברא מזכי [ג] אבא אבא לא מזכי ברא דכתיב [ו] ואין מידי מציל [ה] אין אברהם מציל את ישמעאל אין יצחק מציל את עשו השתא דאתית להכי אחז נמי לא אימני משום כבודו של חזקיהו ומפני מה לא מנו את יהויקים משום דר' חייא בר' אבויה [ד] דאמר ר' חייא בר' אבויה כתיב על גולגלתו [של] יהויקים זאת ועוד אחרת זקינו דרבי פרידא אשכח גולגלתא דהוה קא שדיא בשערי ירושלים וכתיב בה זאת ועוד אחרת קברה ולא איקברא קברה ולא איקברא אמר גולגלתו של יהויקים היא דכתיב ביה [ז] קבורת חמור יקבר סחוב והשלך וגו' אמר מלכא הוא ולא איכשר לזלזולי ביה כרכה בשיראי ואותבה בסיפתא [ה] חזיתא דביתהו סברא הא דאיתתא קמייתא הוה דהא לא קא מנשי לה שגרא תנורא וקלתה היינו דכתיב זאת ועוד אחרת תניא אמר רבי שמעון בן אלעזר בשביל [ח] הטוב בעיניך עשיתי מה אות בשביל [ט] מה אות נכרים אכלו על שולחנו בשביל שנכרים אכלו על שולחנו גרם גלות לבניו מסייע ליה לחזקיה דאמר חזקיה כל המזמן עובד כוכבים לתוך ביתו ומשמש עליו גורם גלות לבניו שנאמר [י] ובניך אשר יצאו ממך [אשר תוליד] יקחו והיו סריסים בהיכל מלך בבל [ו] [כ] וישמח עליהם חזקיה ויראם את (כל) בית נכתה את הכסף ואת הזהב ואת הבשמים ואת השמן הטוב וגו' אמר רב מאי בית נכתה אשתו השקתה עליהם ושמואל אמר בית גנזיו הראה להם ור' יוחנן אמר זין אוכל זין הראה להן [ל] איכה ישבה בדד אמר [ז] רבא אמר רבי יוחנן מפני מה לקו ישראל באיכה מפני שעברו על שלשים ושש כריתות שבתורה אמר רבי יוחנן מפני מה לקו באל"ף בי"ת מפני שעברו על התורה שניתנה באל"ף בי"ת ישבה בדד אמר [ח] רבא אמר רבי יוחנן אמר הקב"ה אני אמרתי [מ] וישכן ישראל בטח בדד עין יעקב אל ארץ דגן ותירוש אף שמיו יערפו טל עכשיו יהיה בדד מושבם [ל] העיר רבתי עם אמר [ט] רבא אמר רבי יוחנן שהיו משיאין קטנה לגדול וגדולה לקטן כדי שיהו להם בנים הרבה [ל] היתה כאלמנה [י] אמר רב יהודה אמר רב כאלמנה ולא אלמנה ממש אלא כאשה שהלך בעלה למדינת הים ודעתו לחזור אליה [ל] רבתי בגוים שרתי במדינות אמר [כ] רבא אמר רבי יוחנן כל מקום שהן הולכין נעשין שרים לאדוניהן ת"ר מעשה בשני בני אדם שנשבו בהר הכרמל והיה שבאי מהלך אחריהם

א"ל

מסורת הש"ס

א) [לקמן קו. ע"ש סוטה יא. ע"ש], ב) [גירסת ערוך בערך אבל אובלא וכתיב על לב שני פירושים ע"ש], ג) [עי' תוספות סוטה י: ד"ה דאתי'], ד) לעיל פב. ע"ש, ה) נ"א אתיא דביתהו חזיתא נפקא אמרה להו לשיבבתה אמרי לה ההיא כו', ו) [במלכים איתא וישמע ובישעיה לט כתיב וישמח], ז) [צ"ל רבה], ח) [צ"ל רבה], ט) [צ"ל רבה], י) [תענית כ.], כ) [צ"ל רבה], ל) [לעיל צו:].

ליקוטי רש"י

מעיר התמרים. היא יריחו שניתן להם דושנה של יריחו לאוכלה עד שיבנה בית המקדש ומי שיבנה בית הבחירה בחלקו יטלנה כדי שיהא לכל ישראל חלק בבית הבחירה ונתנוה לבני יתרו ת"מ שנה והתלמידים שבהם הניחוה והלכו אצל עתניאל בן קנז הוא יעבץ במדבר יהודה אשר בנגב ערד ללמוד תורה. וישב את העם. עם התלמידים היושבים לפניו הוא בקש מאת הקב"ה שיזמין לו תלמידים הגונים שנאמר ויקרא יעבץ לאלהים וגו' ויזמן לו התמידים הללו [שופטים א, טז]. אל הנביא. נביא השקר אשר השיבו לאיש האלהים מכאן אמרו גדולה לגימא שמשרה שכינה על נביאי הבעל [מ"א יג, כ]. שדה כובס. שדה שהכובסים שוטחים שם בגדים לנגבם כך תירגם יונתן ורבותינו דרשו נכנע אחז לפני ישעיהו ושם על ראשו אוכלא דקצרי כפה עליו כלי פי' כלי מנוקב של כובסים שמזלפין בו מים על הבגדים [ישעיהו ז, ג]. אוכלא דקצרי. כלי נחושת העשוי כנפה נקבים נקבים והוא של כובסים ונותנו על הבגדים ומזלף בו המים עליהן ויש מפרשים שמגמרין מוגמר מתחתיו והבגדים מונחין עליו ומתגמרין דרך הנקבים [שבת קכג:]. כלי של כובסין שהוא מנוקב ומזלפין בו מים על הבגדים [לעיל צב.]. זאת ועוד אחרת. נקמה נעשית בה כבר ועוד אחרת תעשה בה. זקינו דר' פרידא. הוא ר' חייא בר אבויה והכי אמרינן בחלק. קברה ולא איקברא. בגלגלה ולאחר מקבורתה. קבורת חמור. מושלך ברחובות. בסיפתא. ארגז. דלא קא מנשי לה. אינה נשכחת מלבו. שגרא לתנורא. הסיקה את התנור [שם פב.]. בית נכתה. בית גנזי בשמיו כמו נכאת וצרי ולוט (בראשית ל"ז כ"ד). ואת השמן הטוב. יש פותרין שמן המשחה ויש פותרים שמן אפרסמון (בלסמון) שהוא מצוי בא"י שנאמר (יחזקאל כז י"ז) יהודה וישראל המה רוכליך בחטי מנית ופנג וראיתי בס' יוסיפון פנג הוא אפרסמון וגדל בירחו ועל שם הריח נקרא יריחו. [מ"ב כ, יג]. בטח בדד. כל יחיד ויחיד איש תחת גפנו ותחת תאנתו מפוזרין ואין צריכים להתאסף ולישב יחד מפני האויב [דברים לג, כח]. רבתי עם. יו"ד יתירה כמו רבת עם שהיתה עמה רב יש מדרשי אגדה הרבה ואני באתי לפרש לשון המקרא כמשמעו [איכה א, א]. ולא אלמנה ממש. דהא לא כתיב אלמנה אלא היתה כאלמנה כאשה העומדת באלמנות חיות על בעלה שהלך ועתיד לחזור [תענית כ.].

גליון הש"ס

גמ' אין אברהם מציל. עי' יומא לח ע"ב בתוס' ישנים ד"ה מעשה:

תורה אור השלם

א) וַיֹּאמֶר אֶל בְּנֹתָיו וְאַיּוֹ לָמָּה זֶּה עֲזַבְתֶּן אֶת הָאִישׁ קִרְאֶן לוֹ וְיֹאכַל לָחֶם: [שמות ב, כ]

ב) וּמִשְׁפְּחוֹת סֹפְרִים יֹשְׁבֵי יַעְבֵּץ תִּרְעָתִים שִׁמְעָתִים שׂוּכָתִים הֵמָּה הַקִּינִים הַבָּאִים מֵחַמַּת אֲבִי בֵית רֵכָב: [דברי הימים א' ב, נה]

ג) וּבְנֵי קֵינִי חֹתֵן מֹשֶׁה עָלוּ מֵעִיר הַתְּמָרִים אֶת בְּנֵי יְהוּדָה מִדְבַּר יְהוּדָה אֲשֶׁר בְּנֶגֶב עֲרָד וַיֵּלֶךְ וַיֵּשֶׁב אֶת הָעָם: [שופטים א, טז]

ד) וַיְהִי הֵם יֹשְׁבִים אֶל הַשֻּׁלְחָן וַיְהִי דְּבַר יְיָ אֶל הַנָּבִיא אֲשֶׁר הֱשִׁיבוֹ: [מלכים א' יג, כ]

ה) וַיֹּאמֶר יְיָ אֶל יְשַׁעְיָהוּ צֵא נָא לִקְרַאת אָחָז אַתָּה וּשְׁאָר יָשׁוּב בְּנֶךָ אֶל קְצֵה תְּעָלַת הַבְּרֵכָה הָעֶלְיוֹנָה אֶל מְסִלַּת שְׂדֵה כוֹבֵס: [ישעיה ז, ג]

ו) רְאוּ עַתָּה כִּי אֲנִי אֲנִי הוּא וְאֵין אֱלֹהִים עִמָּדִי אֲנִי אָמִית וַאֲחַיֶּה מָחַצְתִּי וַאֲנִי אֶרְפָּא וְאֵין מִיָּדִי מַצִּיל: [דברים לב, לט]

ז) קְבוּרַת חֲמוֹר יִקָּבֵר סָחוֹב וְהַשְׁלֵךְ מֵהָלְאָה לְשַׁעֲרֵי יְרוּשָׁלָיִם: [ירמיה כב, יט]

ח) אָנָּה יְיָ זְכָר נָא אֵת אֲשֶׁר הִתְהַלַּכְתִּי לְפָנֶיךָ בֶּאֱמֶת וּבְלֵבָב שָׁלֵם וְהַטּוֹב בְּעֵינֶיךָ עָשִׂיתִי וַיֵּבְךְּ חִזְקִיָּהוּ בְּכִי גָדוֹל: [מלכים ב' כ, ג]

ט) וַיֹּאמֶר חִזְקִיָּהוּ אֶל יְשַׁעְיָהוּ מָה אוֹת כִּי יִרְפָּא יְיָ לִי וְעָלִיתִי בַּיּוֹם הַשְּׁלִישִׁי בֵּית יְיָ: [מלכים ב' כ, ח]

י) וּמִבָּנֶיךָ אֲשֶׁר יֵצְאוּ מִמְּךָ אֲשֶׁר תּוֹלִיד יִקָּחוּ וְהָיוּ סָרִיסִים בְּהֵיכַל מֶלֶךְ בָּבֶל: [מלכים ב' כ, יח]

כ) וַיִּשְׁמַע עֲלֵיהֶם חִזְקִיָּהוּ וַיַּרְאֵם אֶת כָּל בֵּית נְכֹתֹה אֶת הַכֶּסֶף וְאֶת הַזָּהָב וְאֶת הַבְּשָׂמִים וְאֵת שֶׁמֶן הַטּוֹב וְאֵת בֵּית כֵּלָיו וְאֵת כָּל אֲשֶׁר נִמְצָא בְּאוֹצְרֹתָיו לֹא הָיָה דָבָר אֲשֶׁר לֹא הֶרְאָם חִזְקִיָּהוּ בְּבֵיתוֹ וּבְכָל מֶמְשַׁלְתּוֹ: [מלכים ב' כ, יג] וַיִּשְׂמַח עֲלֵיהֶם חִזְקִיָּהוּ וַיַּרְאֵם אֶת בֵּית נְכֹתֹה אֶת הַכֶּסֶף וְאֶת הַזָּהָב וְאֶת הַבְּשָׂמִים וְאֵת הַשֶּׁמֶן הַטּוֹב וְאֵת כָּל בֵּית כֵּלָיו וְאֵת כָּל אֲשֶׁר נִמְצָא בְּאֹצְרֹתָיו לֹא הָיָה דָבָר אֲשֶׁר לֹא הֶרְאָם חִזְקִיָּהוּ בְּבֵיתוֹ וּבְכָל מֶמְשַׁלְתּוֹ: [ישעיה לט, ב]

ל) אֵיכָה יָשְׁבָה בָדָד הָעִיר רַבָּתִי עָם הָיְתָה כְּאַלְמָנָה רַבָּתִי בַגּוֹיִם שָׂרָתִי בַּמְּדִינוֹת הָיְתָה לָמַס: [איכה א, א]

מ) וַיִּשְׁכֹּן יִשְׂרָאֵל בֶּטַח בָּדָד עֵין יַעֲקֹב אֶל אֶרֶץ דָּגָן וְתִירוֹשׁ אַף שָׁמָיו יַעַרְפוּ טָל: [דברים לג, כח]

solitude![27] אָמַר רָבָא אָמַר רַבִּי יוֹחָנָן – **Rava**[28] **said in the name of R' Yochanan:** "מִפְּנֵי מָה לָקוּ יִשְׂרָאֵל בְּ,,אֵיכָה – **Why was Israel stricken with *eichah*,** i.e. why was the word *eichah* used to describe Israel's fallen state?[29] מִפְּנֵי שֶׁעָבְרוּ עַל שְׁלֹשִׁים וָשֵׁשׁ כְּרִיתוֹת שֶׁבַּתּוֹרָה – **It was because** the numerical value of the word *eichah* is thirty-six, and **[the Jews] transgressed** all **thirty-six sins mentioned in the Torah that carry the penalty of *kares*.**[30] אָמַר רַבִּי יוֹחָנָן – **R' Yochanan said:** מִפְּנֵי מָה לָקוּ בְּאל״ף בי״ת – **Why were they stricken with the letters of the Hebrew alphabet,** i.e. why was the destruction of Jerusalem described in the Book of *Lamentations* in alphabetical acrostics? מִפְּנֵי שֶׁעָבְרוּ עַל הַתּוֹרָה – **It was because they transgressed** the commands of **the Torah,** שֶׁנִּיתְּנָה בְּאל״ף בי״ת – **which was given to them through** the medium of **the alphabet.**[31]

Another part of the opening verse of *Lamentations*:

"יָשְׁבָה בָדָד,, – ***She sits in solitude.*** אָמַר רָבָא אָמַר רַבִּי יוֹחָנָן – **Rava said in the name of R' Yochanan:** אָמַר הַקָּדוֹשׁ בָּרוּךְ הוּא – **The Holy One, Blessed is He, said:** "אֲנִי אָמַרְתִּי ,,וַיִּשְׁכֹּן יִשְׂרָאֵל בֶּטַח בָּדָד עֵין יַעֲקֹב אֶל־אֶרֶץ דָּגָן וְתִירוֹשׁ אַף־שָׁמָיו יַעַרְפוּ טָל – **I said:**[32] ***Israel shall dwell securely, alone, in a land of grain and wine, just like Jacob. Even its heavens shall drip with dew.*** עַכְשָׁיו יִהְיֶה בָּדָד מוֹשָׁבָם – **Now their dwelling shall be alone.**[33]

Another part of that opening verse:

"הָעִיר רַבָּתִי עָם,, – ***The city that was great with people.*** אָמַר רָבָא אָמַר רַבִּי יוֹחָנָן – **Rava said in the name of R' Yochanan:** שֶׁהָיוּ מַשִּׂיאִין קְטַנָּה לְגָדוֹל – This indicates that **they used to marry a young girl to an adult man,** וּגְדוֹלָה לְקָטָן – **and an adult woman to a young boy,** כְּדֵי שֶׁיְּהוּ לָהֶם בָּנִים הַרְבֵּה – **so that they should have many children.**[34]

Another part of that opening verse:

"הָיְתָה כְּאַלְמָנָה,, – ***She*** (Jerusalem) ***has become like a widow.*** אָמַר רַב יְהוּדָה אָמַר רַב – **Rav Yehudah said in the name of Rav:** "כְּאַלְמָנָה,, וְלֹא אַלְמָנָה מַמָּשׁ – Jerusalem has merely become ***like*** **a widow, but not truly a widow.** אֶלָּא כְּאִשָּׁה שֶׁהָלַךְ בַּעְלָהּ לִמְדִינַת הַיָּם – Rather, she is **like a woman whose husband has gone overseas,** וְדַעְתּוֹ לַחֲזוֹר אֵלֶיהָ – **but his intention is to return to her.** Similarly, Jerusalem is not permanently estranged from God, but will one day be reunited with Him.[35]

Another part of the opening verse:

"רַבָּתִי בַגּוֹיִם שָׂרָתִי בַּמְּדִינוֹת,, – ***The greatest among nations, the princess among provinces.*** אָמַר רָבָא אָמַר רַבִּי יוֹחָנָן – **Rava said in the name of R' Yochanan:** כָּל מָקוֹם שֶׁהֵן הוֹלְכִין – This means that **wherever they go** in their exiles נַעֲשִׂין שָׂרִים לַאֲדוֹנֵיהֶן – **they become the princes of their masters,** i.e. prized for their intellect.

A Baraisa illustrating Rava's interpretation:

תָּנוּ רַבָּנָן – **The Rabbis taught in a Baraisa:** מַעֲשֶׂה בִּשְׁנֵי בְנֵי אָדָם שֶׁנִּשְׁבּוּ בְּהַר הַכַּרְמֶל – There is **A STORY CONCERNING TWO MEN WHO WERE TAKEN CAPTIVE ON MOUNT CARMEL,** וְהָיָה שַׁבַּאי מְהַלֵּךְ אַחֲרֵיהֶם – **AND THEIR CAPTOR WAS WALKING BEHIND THEM.**

NOTES

27. *Lamentations* 1:1. The verse describes Jerusalem at the time of her destruction.

28. [*Mesoras HaShas* emends the name רָבָא (Rava) in the various attributions אָמַר רָבָא אָמַר רַבִּי יוֹחָנָן appearing on this page and the next, to read רַבָּה (Rabbah).]

29. *Maharsha* explains that the three original chapters of *Lamentations* (1,2 and 4) all begin with the word אֵיכָה (the Book of *Lamentations* was written in two stages – see *Jeremiah* 36:32 and *Rashi* there). This is striking, because although each of these chapters follows an alphabetical acrostic, only the *aleph* verse in each case begins with the same word.

30. These are enumerated in *Kereisos* 2a.

31. I.e. they violated the entire Torah, "from *aleph* to *tav*" (*Torah Temimah* ad loc.). See ArtScroll *The Wisdom in the Hebrew Alphabet* pp. 34-35.

32. *Deuteronomy* 33:28.

33. I.e. R' Yochanan contrasts two types of isolation. God originally planned that the Jews would enjoy a splendid isolation in Eretz Yisrael, free of all outside influences or threats (see *Rashi*). Instead, because of their sins, Israel was conquered and was condemned to a wretched isolation in which they were shunned by everyone (see *Maharsha*).

Netziv explains the meaning of this passage differently. It was God's plan for the Jews that they dwell by themselves in Eretz Yisrael, apart from the negative influences of the gentiles and their culture. But the Jews strove for the reverse, doing their utmost to emulate the gentiles and merge with them. God therefore enforced his policy of isolationism in a different manner: He caused the gentiles to despise and reject the Jews. In the final analysis, God's plan of Jewish isolation was fulfilled, but rather than it being done through honor and tranquility, it occurred through persecution and humiliation. This was Jeremiah's lament (*Meishiv Davar* I:44; *Haamek Davar* to *Deuteronomy* 33:28).

34. I.e. they used to marry off young teenagers to older spouses. This was done to promote a higher birthrate, for extreme youth was viewed as a biological impediment to the capacity for procreation. If both spouses were very young, this impediment would be aggravated. If one spouse was older, on the other hand, it would attenuate the impediment (see *Rashi*).

35. When the nations of the world fall, their decline is forever. In contrast, even when the Jewish people suffer exile, it is not a permanent rejection, for God will take them back (see *Maharsha*). Moreover, says *Iyun Yaakov,* as long as the marriage relationship still exists, the husband (in most cases) has obligations of support, and God indeed assured the Jewish people that even when they are in exile, He will not totally reject them (*Leviticus* 26:44).

מעמון ומואב ומקרבת את הרחוקים מיתרו
דאמר ר' יוחנן בשכר א) קראן לו ויאכל לחם
א) זכו בני בניו וישבו בלשכת הגזית שנאמר
ב) וממשפחות סופרים יושבי יעבץ תרעתים
שמעתים סוכתים המה הקינים הבאים
מחמת אבי בית רכב וכתיב התם ג) ובני קיני
חותן משה עלו מעיר התמרים את בני יהודה
מדבר יהודה אשר בנגב ערד וילך וישב
את העם ומעלמת עינים מן הרשעים ממיכה
ומשרה שכינה על נביאי הבעל מחבירו
של עדו הנביא דכתיב ד) ויהי הם יושבים
אל השלחן ויהי דבר ה' אל הנביא אשר
השיבו ושגגתה עולה זדון דאמר רב יהודה
אמר רב אלמלי הלווהו יהונתן לדוד שתי
ככרות לחם לא נהרגה נוב עיר הכהנים
ולא נטרד דואג האדומי ולא נהרג שאול
ושלשת בניו ומפני מה לא מנו את אחז אמר
ר' ירמיה בר אבא מפני שמוטל בין שני
צדיקים בין יותם לחזקיהו רב יוסף אמר
מפני שהיה לו בשת פנים מישעיהו שנאמר
ה) ויאמר ה' אל ישעיהו צא נא לקראת אחז
אתה ושאר ישוב בנך אל קצה תעלת
הברכה העליונה אל מסלת שדה כובס
מאי כובס איכא דאמרי דכבשינהו לאפיה
וחלף ואיכא דאמרי ב) אוכלא דקצרי סחף
ארישיה וחלף מפני מה לא מנו את אמון
מפני כבודו של יאשיהו מנשה נמי לא נמני
מפני כבודו של חזקיהו ברא מזכי ג) אבא אבא
לא מזכי ברא דכתיב ו) ואין מידי מציל *אין
אברהם מציל את ישמעאל אין יצחק מציל
את עשו השתא דאתית להכי אחז נמי לא
אימני משום כבודו של חזקיהו ומפני מה לא
מנו את יהויקים משום דר' חייא בר' אבויה
ד) דאמר ר' חייא בר' אבויה כתיב על גולגלתו
[של] יהויקים זאת ועוד אחרת זקינו דרבי
פרידא אשכח גולגלתא דהוה קא שדיא
בשערי ירושלים וכתיב בה זאת ועוד אחרת
קברה ולא איקברא קברה ולא איקברא אמר
גולגלתו של יהויקים היא דכתיב ביה ז) קבורת
חמור יקבר סחוב והשלך וגו' אמר מלכא
הוא ולאו איכשר לזלזולי ביה כרכה בשיראי
ואותבה בסיפתא ה) חזיתא דביתהו סברה
הא דאיתתא קמייתא הוה דהא לא קא
מנשי לה שגרא תנורא וקלתה היינו דכתיב
זאת ועוד אחרת תניא אמר רבי שמעון בן אלעזר בשביל ח) הטוב
בעיניך עשיתי מה אות בשביל ט) מה אות נכרים אכלו על שולחנו בשביל
שנכרים אכלו על שולחנו גרם גלות לבניו מסייע ליה לחזקיה דאמר
חזקיה כל המזמן עובד כוכבים לתוך ביתו ומשמש עליו גורם גלות לבניו שנאמר י) ובניך אשר יצאו ממך
[אשר תוליד] יקחו והיו סריסים בהיכל מלך בבל כ) וישמח עליהם חזקיה ויראם את (כל) בית נכתה
את הכסף ואת הזהב ואת הבשמים ואת השמן הטוב וגו' אמר רב מאי בית נכתה אשתו השקתה
עליהם ושמואל אמר בית גנזיו הראה להם ור' יוחנן אמר זין אוכל זין הראה להן ל) איכה ישבה בדד אמר ו) רבא
אמר רבי יוחנן מפני מה לקו ישראל באיכה מפני שעברו על שלשים ושש כריתות שבתורה אמר רבי יוחנן
מפני מה לקו באל"ף בי"ת מפני שעברו על התורה שניתנה באל"ף בי"ת ישבה בדד אמר ז) רבא אמר רבי
יוחנן אמר הקב"ה אני אמרתי מ) וישכן ישראל בטח בדד עין יעקב אל ארץ דגן ותירוש אף שמיו יערפו טל
עכשיו יהיה בדד מושבם ח) העיר רבתי עם אמר ט) רבא אמר רבי יוחנן שהיו משיאין קטנה לגדול וגדולה לקטן
כדי שיהו להם בנים הרבה י) היתה כאלמנה אמר רב יהודה אמר רב כאלמנה ולא אלמנה ממש אלא כאשה
שהלך בעלה למדינת הים ודעתו לחזור אליה כ) רבתי בגוים שרתי במדינות אמר ל) רבא אמר רבי יוחנן כל מקום
שהן הולכין נעשין שרים לאדוניהן ת"ר מעשה בשני בני אדם שנשבו בהר הכרמל והיה שבאי מהלך אחריהם
א"ל

רש"י

עמון ומואב. קרובין לישראל שבאו מלוט בן אחי אברהם ורחקן המקום שלא יבאו בקהל ל"א קרובין ממש ליכא למימר דהא מדין מבני קטורה היו בני אברהם וקרובים היו בני מדין לישראל יותר מעמון ומואב שהם בני אברהם אלא עמון ומואב שכנים וקרובים היו לארץ ישראל ומדין רחוקים להם היו: וישבו בלשכת הגזית. ממשפחות סופרים והאי קרא מפרש ליה כולי בסיפרי בפרשת ויאמר משה לחובב: המה הקינים הבאים מחמת אבי בית רכב. וקינים אלו בניו של יתרו דכתיב ובני קיני חותן משה ובניו של יתרו הן הן בניו של רכב דכתיב הקינים הבאים מחמת אבי בית רכב וכתיב (ירמיה לה) ולבית הרכבים אמר ירמיהו כי כה אמר ה' [וגו'] יען אשר שמעתם [על] מצות [יהונדב] אביכם [וגו'] לא יכרת איש ליונדב בן רכב [עומד] לפני כל הימים ואמרינן בסיפרי אפשר נכרים הם ונכנסין להיכל והרי כל ישראל לא נכנסו להיכל אלא שהיו יושבין בסנהדרין ומורין בדברי תורה. מ"ר: ממיכה. דאמרינן לעיל הניחו לו שפתו מצויה לעוברי דרכים: ומשרה שכינה על נביאי הבעל מחברו של עדו הנביא. דעדו הנביא נתנבא על מזבח בית אל שיחרב מפני שהעמיד בו ירבעם צלמים דכתיב (במ"א יג) והנה איש האלהים בא מיהודה וגו' ויאמר מזבח מזבח ומפרש בסדר עולם דהיינו עדו הנביא ובא נביא השקר והטעהו לעדו והשיבו לבית אל והעבירו על מצות הקב"ה שאמר לו לא תשוב לבית אל והאכילו ובזכות שהאכילו שרתה עליו שכינה שנאמר ויהי דבר ה' אל האיש הנביא אשר השיבו להאכילו אללו: ושגגתה עולה זדון. שהרי מלינו ביהונתן ששגג ולא הלוהו לדוד שתי ככרות ונענש דאמר רב יהודה וכו': לווהו. לשון לויה: לא נהרגה נוב. שלא היה צריך דוד לשאול לחם מכהני נוב ולא היה דואג מלשין עליהם: ולא היה שאול נהרג. על אותו עון: שמוטל. דאביו יותם ובנו חזקיה: ושאר מישראל ששבו להיות בניך ותלמידיך וכל מי שישוב לביתך דהיינו תלמידיו כדמתרגמינן ושאר' דלא חטאו ודתבו חטיאי תלמידוהי: מאי כובס דכבשינהו לאפיה. שכבש את פניו והיה מתבייש מפני ישעיה: כובס. כמו כובש: אוכלא דקצרי סחף ארישיה. כלי מנוקב של כובסין שמזלפין בו מים על הבגדים ואותו כלי הפך אחז על ראשו כדי שלא יכירו ישעיה שהיה מתבייש [ממנו]: יאשיהו. בן אמון: חזקיהו. אבי מנשה: [ברא מזכה אבא וכו']. יאשיה מזכה אמון אביו ולא חזקיה מנשה בנו דכתיב אין מידי מציל ודרשינן ליה בהגדה אין אברהם מציל וכו': השתא דאתית להכי. דברא מזכה לאבא: אחז נמי. לא תימא דכבשינהו [לאפיה] אלא מפני כבודו של חזקיה לא מנאוהו: מפני מה לא מנו את יהויקים. באותן שאין להם חלק [לעוה"ב]: משום דר' חייא בר אבויה. שנתכפר על שלא ניתן לקבורה וכל הני מפני מה לא מנו לא בעי אלא מהנך דהוו רשעים גמורים כדחשיבנא להו לעיל אחז חתם את התורה וכו': [זאת ועוד כו'. נקמה נעשית בה כבר ועוד אחרת תעשה בה]: פרידא. כך שמו: סיפתא. ארגז: בשביל הטוב מה אות. בשביל חזקיה [ששיבח את] עצמו דאמר הטוב בעיניך עשיתי גרם לו שאמר מה אות כי אעלה בית ה' ששאל אות מהקב"ה שעבירה גוררת עבירה: אכלו נכרים על שולחנו. אותם ששלח לו מרודך בלאדן ספרים ומנחה על ידם: ומשמש עליו. כגון חזקיה דאמרינן לקמן אשתו השקתה עליהם: גורם גלות. דכתיב וישמח עליהם חזקיהו ויראם את (כל) בית נכתה וכתיב בתריה ומבניך אשר יצאו ממך יקחו והיו סריסים בהיכל מלך בבל: אשתו השקתה עליהם. היא עצמה מוזגת להם והיינו בית נכתה לשון מנכה על שם נלע שנפחתה מן האדם וממנה נבראת אשה: בית גנזיו. והכי מתרגמינן בית גניזוהי ומנחם פתר במחברתו לשון סממנים כמו (בראשית לז) נכאת וצרי ולוט: זין אוכל זין. כגון פרזלא דשליט בפרזלא ל): איכה. ל"ו בגימטריא: ל"ו כריתות. בכריתות (דף ב.) חשיב להו: לקו בא"ב. שכל מגילת איכה סדורה באלפא ביתא: בטח בדד. שיושבין יחידים ואינן מתיראין לא מן הנכרים ולא מן חיות רעות: רבתי עם. עם שמתרבה והולך יותר משאר עם: קטנה לגדול. ש"ז של קטן אינו מבושל ואינו מזריע מהר כשל גדול וכן רחם של קטנה אינה קולטת מהר כשל גדולה לפיכך משיאין גדולה לקטן כדי לכשתהא זרעו [מבושל] קולט מהר וקטנה לגדול כדי שיהא שכבת זרעו קולט מהר ולא קטנה לקטן ששוהין להוליד ולא קטן וקטנה ממש אלא שעומדין על פרקן וראויין הם להוליד ומיהו אין זרע שלהם מבושל כל כך:

אחד

מסורת הש"ס

א) [לקמן קו. ע"ש סוטה יא. ע"ש], ב) [גירסת ערוך בערך אבל אובלא וכתיב על גד שני פירושים ע"ש], ג) [עי' תוספות סוטה י: ד"ה דאתי'], ד) לעיל פב. ע"ש, ה) נ"א אתיא דביתהו חזיתא נפקא אמרה להו לשיבבתה אמרי לה ההיא כו', ו) [במלכים איתא וישמע ובישעיה לא כתיב וישמח], ז) [צ"ל רבה], ח) [צ"ל רבה], ט) [צ"ל רבה], י) [תענית כ.], כ) [צ"ל רבה], ל) [לעיל נו:].

ליקוטי רש"י

מעיר התמרים. היא יריחו שניתן להם דושנה של יריחו לאוכלה עד שיבנה בית המקדש ומי שיבנה בית הבחירה בחלקו יטלנה כדי שיהא לכל ישראל חלק בבית הבחירה ונתנוה לבני יתרו ת"מ שנה והתלמידים שבהם הניחוה והלכו אצל עתניאל בן קנז הוא יעבץ במדבר יהודה אשר בנגב ערד ללמוד תורה. וישב את העם. עם התלמידים היושבים לפניו הוא בקש מאת הקב"ה שיזמין לו תלמידים הגונים שנאמר ויקרא יעבץ לאלהים וגו' וזימן לו התקידים הללו [שופטים א, טז]. אל הנביא. נביא השקר אשר השיבו לאיש האלהים מכאן אמרו גדולה לגימא שמשרה שכינה על נביאי הבעל [מ"א יג, כ]. שדה כובס. שדה שהכובסים שוטחים שם בגדים לנגבם כך תירגם יונתן ורבותינו דרשו נכנע אחז לפני ישעיהו ושם על ראשו אוכלא דקצרי כפה עליו כלי פי' כלי מנוקב של כובסים שמזלפין בו מים על הבגדים [ישעיהו ז, ג]. אוכלא דקצרי. כלי נחושת העשוי כנפה נקבים נקבים והוא של כובסים ונותנו על הבגדים ומזלף בו המים עליהן ויש מפרשים שמגמרין מוגמר מתחתיו והבגדים מונחין עליו ומתגמרין דרך הנקבים [שבת קכג:]. כלי של כובסין שהוא מנוקב ומזלפין בו מים על הבגדים [לעיל צב.]. זאת ועוד אחרת נקמה נעשית בה כבר ועוד אחרת תעשה בה. זקינו דר' פרידא. הוא ר' חייא בר אבויה והכי אמרינן בחלק. קברה ולא איקברא. בזיזה ולאה מקבורתה. קבורת חמור. מושלך ברחובות. בסיפתא. ארגז. דלא קא מנשי לה. אינה נשכחת מלבו. שגרא לתנורא. הסיקה את התנור [שם פב.]. בית נכתה. בית גנזי בשמיו כמו נכאת וצרי ולוט (בראשית ל"ז כ"ד). ואת השמן הטוב. יש פותרין שמן המשחה ויש פותרים שמן אפרסמון (בלסמון) שהוא מצוי בא"י שנאמר (ביחזקאל כז י"ז) יהודה וישראל המה רוכליך בחטי מנית ופנג וראיתי בס' יוסיפון פנג הוא אפרסמון וגדל בירחו ועל שם הריח נקרא ירחו. [מ"ב כ, יג]. בטח בדד. כל יחיד ויחיד איש תחת גפנו ותחת תאנתו מפוזרין ואין צריכים להתאסף ולישב יחד מפני האויב [דברים לג, כח]. רבתי עם. יו"ד יתירה כמו רבת עם שהיתה עמה רב יש מדרשי אגדה הרבה ואני באתי לפרש לשון המקרא כמשמעו [איכה א, א]. ולא אלמנה ממש. דהא לא כתיב אלמנה אלא היתה כאלמנה כאשה העומדת באלמנות חיות על בעלה שהלך ועתיד לחזור [תענית כ.].

גליון הש"ס

גמ' אין אברהם מציל. עי' יומא לח ע"ב בתוס' ישנים ד"ה מעשה:

תורה אור השלם

א) וַיֹּאמֶר אֶל בְּנֹתָיו וְאַיּוֹ לָמָּה זֶּה עֲזַבְתֶּן אֶת הָאִישׁ קִרְאֶן לוֹ וְיֹאכַל לָחֶם: [שמות ב, כ]

ב) וּמִשְׁפְּחוֹת סֹפְרִים יֹשְׁבֵי יַעְבֵּץ תִּרְעָתִים שִׁמְעָתִים שׂוּכָתִים הֵמָּה הַקִּינִים הַבָּאִים מֵחַמַּת אֲבִי בֵית רֵכָב: [דברי הימים א' ב, נה]

ג) וּבְנֵי קֵינִי חֹתֵן מֹשֶׁה עָלוּ מֵעִיר הַתְּמָרִים אֶת בְּנֵי יְהוּדָה מִדְבַּר יְהוּדָה אֲשֶׁר בְּנֶגֶב עֲרָד וַיֵּלֶךְ וַיֵּשֶׁב אֶת הָעָם: [שופטים א, טז]

ד) וַיְהִי הֵם יֹשְׁבִים אֶל הַשֻּׁלְחָן וַיְהִי דְּבַר יְיָ אֶל הַנָּבִיא אֲשֶׁר הֱשִׁיבוֹ: [מלכים א' יג, כ]

ה) וַיֹּאמֶר יְיָ אֶל יְשַׁעְיָהוּ צֵא נָא לִקְרַאת אָחָז אַתָּה וּשְׁאָר יָשׁוּב בְּנֶךָ אֶל קְצֵה תְּעָלַת הַבְּרֵכָה הָעֶלְיוֹנָה אֶל מְסִלַּת שְׂדֵה כוֹבֵס: [ישעיה ז, ג]

ו) רְאוּ עַתָּה כִּי אֲנִי אֲנִי הוּא וְאֵין אֱלֹהִים עִמָּדִי אֲנִי אָמִית וַאֲחַיֶּה מָחַצְתִּי וַאֲנִי אֶרְפָּא וְאֵין מִיָּדִי מַצִּיל: [דברים לב, לט]

ז) קְבוּרַת חֲמוֹר יִקָּבֵר סָחוֹב וְהַשְׁלֵךְ מֵהָלְאָה לְשַׁעֲרֵי יְרוּשָׁלָיִם: [ירמיה כב, יט]

ח) אָנָּה יְיָ זְכָר נָא אֵת אֲשֶׁר הִתְהַלַּכְתִּי לְפָנֶיךָ בֶּאֱמֶת וּבְלֵבָב שָׁלֵם וְהַטּוֹב בְּעֵינֶיךָ עָשִׂיתִי וַיֵּבְךְּ חִזְקִיָּהוּ בְּכִי גָדוֹל: [מלכים ב' כ, ג]

ט) וַיֹּאמֶר חִזְקִיָּהוּ אֶל יְשַׁעְיָהוּ מָה אוֹת כִּי יִרְפָּא יְיָ לִי וְעָלִיתִי בַּיּוֹם הַשְּׁלִישִׁי בֵּית יְיָ: [מלכים ב' כ, ח]

י) וּמִבָּנֶיךָ אֲשֶׁר יֵצְאוּ מִמְּךָ אֲשֶׁר תּוֹלִיד יִקָּחוּ וְהָיוּ סָרִיסִים בְּהֵיכַל מֶלֶךְ בָּבֶל: [מלכים ב' כ, יח]

כ) וַיִּשְׁמַע עֲלֵיהֶם חִזְקִיָּהוּ וַיַּרְאֵם אֶת כָּל בֵּית נְכֹתֹה אֶת הַכֶּסֶף וְאֶת הַזָּהָב וְאֶת הַבְּשָׂמִים וְאֵת שֶׁמֶן הַטּוֹב וְאֵת בֵּית כֵּלָיו וְאֵת כָּל אֲשֶׁר נִמְצָא בְּאוֹצְרֹתָיו לֹא הָיָה דָבָר אֲשֶׁר לֹא הֶרְאָם חִזְקִיָּהוּ בְּבֵיתוֹ וּבְכָל מֶמְשַׁלְתּוֹ: [מלכים ב' כ, יג] וַיִּשְׂמַח עֲלֵיהֶם חִזְקִיָּהוּ וַיַּרְאֵם אֶת בֵּית נְכֹתֹה אֶת הַכֶּסֶף וְאֶת הַזָּהָב וְאֶת הַבְּשָׂמִים וְאֵת הַשֶּׁמֶן הַטּוֹב וְאֵת כָּל בֵּית כֵּלָיו וְאֵת כָּל אֲשֶׁר נִמְצָא בְּאֹצְרֹתָיו לֹא הָיָה דָבָר אֲשֶׁר לֹא הֶרְאָם חִזְקִיָּהוּ בְּבֵיתוֹ וּבְכָל מֶמְשַׁלְתּוֹ: [ישעיה לט, ב]

ל) אֵיכָה יָשְׁבָה בָדָד הָעִיר רַבָּתִי עָם הָיְתָה כְּאַלְמָנָה רַבָּתִי בַגּוֹיִם שָׂרָתִי בַּמְּדִינוֹת הָיְתָה לָמַס: [איכה א, א]

מ) וַיִּשְׁכֹּן יִשְׂרָאֵל בֶּטַח בָּדָד עֵין יַעֲקֹב אֶל אֶרֶץ דָּגָן וְתִירוֹשׁ אַף שָׁמָיו יַעַרְפוּ טָל: [דברים לג, כח]

א"ל אחד מהם לחבירו גמל שמהלכת לפנינו סומא באחת מעיניה וטעונה שתי נודות אחת של יין ואחת של שמן ושני בני אדם המנהיגים אותה אחד ישראל ואחד נכרי אמר להן [שבאי] עם קשה עורף מאין אתם יודעין אמרו לו גמל מעשבים שלפניה מצד שרואה אוכלת מצד שאינה רואה אינה אוכלת וטעונה שתי נודות אחת של יין ואחת של שמן של יין מטפטף ושוקע ושל שמן מטפטף וצף ושני בני אדם המנהיגים אותה אחד נכרי ואחד ישראל נכרי נפנה (א) לדרך וישראל נפנה לצדדין רדף אחריהם ומצא כדבריהם בא ונשקן על ראשן והביאן לביתו ועשה להן סעודה גדולה והיה מרקד לפניהם ואמר ברוך שבחר בזרעו של אברהם ונתן להם מחכמתו ובכל מקום שהן הולכים נעשין שרים לאדוניהם ופטרן [והלכו] לבתיהם לשלום (א) בכה תבכה בלילה שתי בכיות הללו למה אמר רבה אמר רבי יוחנן אחד על מקדש ראשון ואחד על מקדש שני בלילה על עסקי לילה שנאמר (ב) ותשא כל העדה ויתנו את קולם ויבכו העם בלילה ההוא (ג) אמר רבה א"ר יוחנן אותו (ג)(היום) ליל ט' באב היה אמר להן הקב"ה לישראל אתם בכיתם בכיה של חנם ואני אקבע לכם בכיה לדורות ד"א בלילה שכל הבוכה בלילה קולו נשמע ד"א בלילה שכל הבוכה בלילה כוכבים ומזלות בוכין עמו ד"א בלילה שכל הבוכה בלילה השומע קולו בוכה כנגדו מעשה באשה אחת שכנתו של רבן גמליאל שמת בנה והיתה בוכה עליו בלילה שמע רבן גמליאל קולה ובכה כנגדה עד שנשרו ריסי עיניו למחר הכירו בו תלמידיו והוציאוה משכונתו (א) ודמעתה על לחיה אמר (ד) רבא אמר ר' יוחנן כאשה שבוכה על בעל נעוריה שנאמר (ג) אלי כבתולה חגורת שק על בעל נעוריה (ד) היו צריה לראש אמר (ה) רבא אמר רבי יוחנן [א] (ו) כל המיצר לישראל נעשה ראש שנאמר [א] (ה) כי לא מועף לאשר מוצק לה כעת הראשון הקל ארצה זבולון וארצה נפתלי והאחרון הכביד דרך הים עבר הירדן גליל הגוים אמר (י) רבא אמר ר' יוחנן כל המציק לישראל אינו עיף (ו) לא אליכם כל עוברי דרך אמר (כ) רבא אמר ר' יוחנן מכאן לקובלנא מן התורה כל עוברי דרך אמר רב עמרם אמר רב עשאוני כעוברי על דת דאילו בסדום כתיב (ז) וה' המטיר על סדום ואילו בירושלים כתיב (ח) ממרום שלח אש בעצמותי וירדנה וגו' [ב] (ט) וכתיב ויגדל עון בת עמי מחטאת סדום וכי משוא פנים יש בדבר אמר (ט) רבא אמר ר' יוחנן מדה יתירה היתה בירושלים שלא היתה בסדום דאילו בסדום כתיב (י) הנה זה היה עון סדום אחותך גאון שבעת לחם ויד עני ואביון לא החזיקה וגו' ואילו בירושלים כתיב (כ) ידי נשים רחמניות בשלו ילדיהן (ל) סלה כל אבירי ה' בקרבי כאדם שאומר לחבירו נפסלה מטבע זו (מ) פצו עליך פיהם אמר (י) רבא אמר רבי יוחנן בשביל מה הקדים פ"א לעי"ן בשביל מרגלים שאמרו בפיהם מה שלא ראו בעיניהם (נ) אוכלי עמי אכלו לחם ה' לא קראו אמר (כ) רבא אמר ר' יוחנן כל האוכל מלחמן של ישראל טועם טעם לחם ושאינו אוכל מלחמן של ישראל אינו טועם טעם לחם ה' לא קראו רב אמר אלו הדיינין ושמואל אמר אלו מלמדי תינוקות מי מנאן אמר רב אשי אנשי כנסת הגדולה מנאום אמר רב יהודה אמר רב בקשו עוד למנות אחד באה (ל) דמות דיוקנו של אביו (א) ונשטחה לפניהם ולא השגיחו עליה באה אש מן השמים ולחכה אש בספסליהם ולא השגיחו עליה יצאה בת קול ואמרה להם (ס) חזית איש מהיר במלאכתו לפני מלכים יתיצב בל יתיצב לפני חשוכים מי שהקדים ביתי לביתו ולא עוד אלא שביתי בנה בשבע שנים וביתו בנה בשלש עשרה שנה לפני מלכים יתיצב [בל יתיצב] לפני חשוכים ולא השגיח עליה יצאה בת קול ואמרה (ע) המעמך ישלמנה כי מאסת כי אתה תבחר ולא אני וגו' (מ) דורשי רשומות היו אומרים כולן באין לעולם הבא שנאמר (פ) לי גלעד ולי מנשה ואפרים מעוז ראשי יהודה מחוקקי מואב סיר רחצי על אדום אשליך נעלי עלי פלשת התרועעי לי גלעד [ג] (נ) (ולי מנשה) זה אחאב שנפל ברמות גלעד מנשה כמשמעו אפרים מעוז ראשי זה ירבעם דקאתי מאפרים יהודה מחוקקי זה אחיתופל דקאתי

אחד. מן הנשבים לחבירו: גמל. זו שמהלכת לפנינו סומא וכו': [מצד שרואה. שאינה אוכלת פעמים מצד ימין ופעמים מצד שמאל כבהמה הרואה שאוכלת מכאן ומכאן אלא מצד שרואה אוכלת]: יין מטפטף ושוקע. בקרקע ורואין אנו בין רגלינו הטיפין שנפלו כשעברה הגמל במקום זה מצד אחד שקועין ומצד אחר הטיפין של שמן שצפים: נפנה לצדדין. שכן דרך ישראל להיותו צנוע: רדף. השבאי דרך הגמל והמנהיג ומצא כדבריהם ואמרו (ס) אותם יהודים על אותו שבאי אדוניהם שהוא בן קלסתר מלך אשקנ"ק בלע"ז שהיה דיוקנו דומה למגמת פניו של אותו קלסתר של מלך שבזנות הולידו: על עסקי לילה. לפי שבכו אותו לילה בכיית חנם: קולו נשמע יותר מביום. כדאמרינן בעלמא (יומא דף כ.) מפני מה אין הקול נשמע ביום כבלילה מפני גלגל חמה המנסר ברקיע והיינו דכתיב בכה תבכה בלילה כדי שיהא קולה נשמע וירחמו עליה ואף על פי כן אין מנחם לה: כוכבים ומזלות בוכים. שנכמרו רחמים עליו: בוכה כנגדו. מתוך שנשמע בהדיא מרכך לבו של אדם השומע קולו לבכות עמו: ריסי עיניו. שער שבגבת העין היה נופל ונכפל על העין מרוב דמעות: אלי. קוננו קינה מתרגמינן איליא: על בעל נעוריה. שבוכה תמיד ומלויה דמעות: על לחיה. לשון לחות ונערות כגון לח ויבש: מכאן לקובלנא מן התורה. כשאדם מודיע צערו לאחר צריך שיאמר לו לא תבא זאת לך כמו שבאה אלי כי קשה הוא לשמוע שפעמים חוזרת עליו והמקפיד על כך אין בו משום ניחוש. ל"א לקובלנא כשיש לו צרה יודיענה לרבים קובלנא צעקה ל"א נגד דמתרגמינן קבל כאדם שאומר לחבירו לא כנגדך אני אומר: וירדנה. ושרף אותה והיינו עשאוני כעוברי דת שדנני באש כסדום: לא אליכם. נביא היה מתנודד על החורבן כאילו באה עליו צרה ומהפכה לאחרים ואומר להם לישראל לא תהא לכם צרה כזו כמדומה לי נביא היה מדבר כנגד בני משה או כנגד י' השבטים שלא הגלה נבוכדנצר: וירדנה. לשון שבירה כמו (במדבר כד) וירד מיעקב כאדם המושל בחבירו להלקותו ולשברו: הכי גרסינן ויגדל עון בת עמי מחטאת סדום וכי משוא פנים יש בדבר והואיל וישראל רעים יותר מסדום למה לא נהפכו כסדום לשון אחר וכי משוא פנים יש בדבר דהתם כתיב וה' המטיר הוא בעצמו והכא כתיב שלח על ידי שליח: מדה יתירה לטובה. דבירושלים כתיב ידי נשים רחמניות בשלו ילדיהן היו לברות למו שהיתה מזמנת חברתה ואוכלת בנה אלמא רחמניות היו ואילו בסדום כתיב יד עני ואביון לא החזיקה ומדה זו כפרה עליהם שלא נהפכו לשון אחר מדה יתירה פורענות גדולה היתה בירושלים שילדיהם היו אוכלות זו עם זו דכתיב היו לברות למו ואילו בסדום כתיב גאון שבעת לחם שלא טעמו טעם עוני הא למדת גדול פורענות ירושלים מפורענות סדום ולא היה משוא פנים בדבר: סלה. לשון מסלה כלומר כל האבירים פסלם הקב"ה ועשאם פסולים וכבושים כמסלה זו והיינו דמיא למטבע שנפסל ואין לו תקנה: מפני מה הקדים פ"א לעי"ן. ברוב האלפא ביתא שבאיכה: מפני מרגלים. שהקדימו מאמר פיהם עד שלא ראו בעין: טועם טעם לחם. שהכותים מואסים טעמם בלחמם של ישראל שהנאה הוא להם כשגוזלין אותן: אלו הדיינין. מטה משפט בשביל עונותיהם היו לחם עמי למאכל אויביו: מלמדי תינוקות. שעושין מלאכתן רמיה: מי מנאן. להנך מלכים והדיוטות דקתני במתני' אין להם חלק: עוד אחד. שלמה: דיוקנו. של דוד אביו נשתטח לפניהם שלא למנותו עמהם: בל יתיצב לפני חשוכים. בגיהנם: לפני מלכים יתיצב. בגן עדן ולא לפני חשוכים: המעמך ישלמנה. וכי עליכם לשלם תשלומי עונשו לאדם שאתם נמאסים בו בשלמה לומר שאין לו חלק לעולם הבא: כי אתה תבחר ולא אני. וכי הבחירה בכם תלויה ולא די לומר מי שיש לו חלק ומי אין לו חלק הלא בי הדבר תלוי: דורשי רשומות. דורשי פסוקים כדכתיב (דניאל י) את הרשום בכתב אמת היו אומרים שלכולם יש להם חלק אפילו למנשה וירבעם ולאחאב: לי גלעד ולי מנשה. עלי לסבול עונם כדי שיהו הם זוכים: מנשה כמשמעו. מנשה בן חזקיהו: דקא

הגהות מהר"ב רנשבורג

א] בגמרא כל המיצר לישראל נעשה ראש שנא'. מלת שנאמר נמחק:

תורה אור השלם

א) בָּכוֹ תִבְכֶּה בַּלַּיְלָה וְדִמְעָתָהּ עַל לֶחֱיָהּ אֵין לָהּ מְנַחֵם מִכָּל אֹהֲבֶיהָ כָּל רֵעֶיהָ בָּגְדוּ בָהּ הָיוּ לָהּ לְאֹיְבִים: [איכה א, ב]

ב) וַתִּשָּׂא כָּל הָעֵדָה וַיִּתְּנוּ אֶת קוֹלָם וַיִּבְכּוּ הָעָם בַּלַּיְלָה הַהוּא: [במדבר יד, א]

ג) אֱלִי כִּבְתוּלָה חֲגֻרַת שַׂק עַל בַּעַל נְעוּרֶיהָ: [יואל א, ח]

ד) הָיוּ צָרֶיהָ לְרֹאשׁ אֹיְבֶיהָ שָׁלוּ כִּי יְיָ הוֹגָהּ עַל רֹב פְּשָׁעֶיהָ עוֹלָלֶיהָ הָלְכוּ שְׁבִי לִפְנֵי צָר: [איכה א, ה]

ה) כִּי לֹא מוּעָף לַאֲשֶׁר מוּצָק לָהּ כָּעֵת הָרִאשׁוֹן הֵקַל אַרְצָה זְבֻלוּן וְאַרְצָה נַפְתָּלִי וְהָאַחֲרוֹן הִכְבִּיד דֶּרֶךְ הַיָּם עֵבֶר הַיַּרְדֵּן גְּלִיל הַגּוֹיִם: [ישעיה ח, כג]

ו) לוֹא אֲלֵיכֶם כָּל עֹבְרֵי דֶרֶךְ הַבִּיטוּ וּרְאוּ אִם יֵשׁ מַכְאוֹב כְּמַכְאֹבִי אֲשֶׁר עוֹלַל לִי אֲשֶׁר הוֹגָה יְיָ בְּיוֹם חֲרוֹן אַפּוֹ: [איכה א, יב]

ז) וַייָ הִמְטִיר עַל סְדֹם וְעַל עֲמֹרָה גָּפְרִית וָאֵשׁ מֵאֵת יְיָ מִן הַשָּׁמָיִם: [בראשית יט, כד]

ח) מִמָּרוֹם שָׁלַח אֵשׁ בְּעַצְמֹתַי וַיִּרְדֶּנָּה פָּרַשׂ רֶשֶׁת לְרַגְלַי הֱשִׁיבַנִי אָחוֹר נְתָנַנִי שֹׁמֵמָה כָּל הַיּוֹם דָּוָה: [איכה א, יג]

ט) וַיִּגְדַּל עֲוֺן בַּת עַמִּי מֵחַטַּאת סְדֹם הַהֲפוּכָה כְמוֹ רָגַע וְלֹא חָלוּ בָהּ יָדָיִם: [איכה ד, ו]

י) הִנֵּה זֶה הָיָה עֲוֺן סְדֹם אֲחוֹתֵךְ גָּאוֹן שִׂבְעַת לֶחֶם וְשַׁלְוַת הַשְׁקֵט הָיָה לָהּ וְלִבְנוֹתֶיהָ וְיַד עָנִי וְאֶבְיוֹן לֹא הֶחֱזִיקָה: [יחזקאל טז, מט]

כ) יְדֵי נָשִׁים רַחֲמָנִיּוֹת בִּשְּׁלוּ יַלְדֵיהֶן הָיוּ לְבָרוֹת לָמוֹ בְּשֶׁבֶר בַּת עַמִּי: [איכה ד, י]

ל) סִלָּה כָל אַבִּירַי אֲדֹנָי בְּקִרְבִּי קָרָא עָלַי מוֹעֵד לִשְׁבֹּר בַּחוּרָי גַּת דָּרַךְ אֲדֹנָי לִבְתוּלַת בַּת יְהוּדָה: [איכה א, טו]

מ) פָּצוּ עָלַיִךְ פִּיהֶם כָּל אוֹיְבַיִךְ שָׁרְקוּ וַיַּחַרְקוּ שֵׁן אָמְרוּ בִּלָּעְנוּ אַךְ זֶה הַיּוֹם שֶׁקִּוִּינֻהוּ מָצָאנוּ רָאִינוּ: [איכה ב, טז]

נ) הֲלֹא יָדְעוּ כָּל פֹּעֲלֵי אָוֶן אֹכְלֵי עַמִּי אָכְלוּ לֶחֶם יְיָ לֹא קָרָאוּ: [תהלים יד, ד]

ס) חָזִיתָ אִישׁ מָהִיר בִּמְלַאכְתּוֹ לִפְנֵי מְלָכִים יִתְיַצָּב בַּל יִתְיַצֵּב לִפְנֵי חֲשֻׁכִּים: [משלי כב, כט]

ע) הֲמֵעִמְּךָ יְשַׁלְמֶנָּה כִּי מָאַסְתָּ כִּי אַתָּה תִבְחַר וְלֹא אָנִי וּמַה יָּדַעְתָּ דַבֵּר: [איוב לד, לג]

פ) לִי גִלְעָד וְלִי מְנַשֶּׁה וְאֶפְרַיִם מָעוֹז רֹאשִׁי יְהוּדָה מְחֹקְקִי: מוֹאָב סִיר רַחְצִי עַל אֱדוֹם אַשְׁלִיךְ נַעֲלִי עָלַי פְּלֶשֶׁת הִתְרֹעָעִי: [תהלים ס, ט-י]

מסורת הש"ס

א) [פי' שהנכרי נפנה בדרך אצל בהמתו וישראל מסתלק לצדדים כך איתא בפי' הר"ש טהרות פ"ד מ"ה], ב) [תענית כט. סוטה לה.], ג) [צ"ל הלילה], ד) [צ"ל רבה], ה) [צ"ל רבה], ו) גיטין נו: ע"ש [עי' תוספות חגיגה יג: ד"ה שלא יאמרו ביד אומה שפילה מסר את בניו כלומר קודם שמילר כבר נעשה ראש], ז) [צ"ל רבה], ח) [צ"ל רבה], ט) [צ"ל רבה], י) [צ"ל רבה], כ) [צ"ל רבה], ל) [פי' נכון במאמר הלזה תמצא בשל"ה למסכת פסחים קעב.], מ) [עי' פירש"י ברכות כד. ד"ה דורשי וכו'], נ) [בע"י ליתא וכצ"ל], ס) [עי' בערוך ערך קלסטרא א' איתא הגירסא שהיא לפנינו בגמרא דהכא ואז תבין דברי רש"י הללו].

הגהות הב"ח

(א) גמרא דיוקנו של אביו. ונשתטחה לפניהם:

הגהות הגר"א

[א] גמ' שנא' כי לא מועף. נמחק תיבת שנאמר: [ב] שם וכתיב ויגדל. נמחק תיבת וכתיב: [ג] שם בסוף ולי מנשה. נמחקו ב' תיבות הללו:

ליקוטי רש"י

בכו תבכה. שתי בכיות על שתי חורבנין. בלילה. שהמקדש נשרף בלילה דאמר מר לעת ערב הציתו בו את האור דבר אחר בלילה לילה של בכיית מרגלים בתשעה באב גרמה להם, דבר אחר בלילה שכל הבוכה בלילה השומע קולו בוכה עמו [איכה א, ב]. אתם בכיתם בכיה של חים. ולהפיל זרעם בגוים. מאותו שעה נגזר עליהם חורבן הבית שהרי ליל ט' באב בכו ואמר הקב"ה הם בכו בכיה של חנם ואני אקבע להם בכיה לדורות [תהלים קו, כז]. קרא עלי מועד. במסכת תענית (דף כט) תמוז דההיא שתא מלא שנה השניה ליציאת מצרים שנשתלחו בה מרגלים בעשרים ותשעה בסיון מלויי מליוהו לתמוז לפיכך אירע בו יום חזרת מרגלים בשמונה באב ויבכו העם בלילה ההוא בתשעה באב בכו בכיה של חנם והוקבעה להם בכיה לדורות [שבועות י.]. כי לא מועף לאשר מוצק לה. כי מלך אשור אשר ניתן למוצק ולהצר לה לארצכם אינו עיף ואינו עצל מלבא עליהם עד שלש פעמים [ישעיהו ח, כג]. לא אליכם. לא תהא כצרה הזאת עוד לכל עוברי על דת אמרו חכמים מכאן לקובלנא מן התורה ראו מה עשה לי הביטו וראו וגומר [איכה א, יב]. וירדנה. וירדה אותה וישבר אותה וישבר אותה ע"י רידוי ויסורין לכן הנו"ן דגושה לפותרו בלשון יחידית כמו יעשנה יכרסמנה ירעגה שהעצם ל' נקבה כמו דאת אומר (יחזקאל לו) העצמות היבשות שבר כל אחת ואחת, ד"א וירדנה כמו (שופטים יד) וירדהו אל כפיו הריק את המוות גורר ורודה המוות מתוכו [שם יב]. ויגדל עון וגו'. פורענותם מוכיח עליהם שגדול עונש משל סדום [שם ד, ו]. סלה. רמס ורפס לשון (ישעיה סב) סולו סולו המסילה [שם א, טו]. ה' לא קראו. לא חשבוהו ולא זכרו נפלאותיו ונוראותיו במשתיהם ונשתמשו בכליו ורבותינו פירשו כל שלא היה גוזל את ישראל לא היה טועם טעם ערב במאכלו אוכלי עמי נדמה להם כאוכלי לחם שטעמו טעם מאכל ערב [תהלים יד, ד]. המעמך ישלמנה כי מאסת וגו'. כך אמר אליהו לאיוב המעמך היה לו להקב"ה להימלך בפירעון תשלומין ממך. כי מאסת. לאמר מאסתי לא לעולם אחיה (איוב ז) יתר ידו ויבלעני (איוב ו) סבור אתה שיגבה ממך לפי דעתך ורצונך ואתה תבחר התשלומין ולא אני במקום הקב"ה דבר אליהו בתמיה [איוב לד, לג]. דורשי רשומות. קשרים וסתומים הכלולים בתורה דורשי חמורות גרסינן והיא היא [ברכות כד.].

אָמַר לו אֶחָד מֵהֶם לַחֲבֵירו – SAID ONE OF THEM TO HIS FELLOW: גָּמָל שֶׁמְּהַלֶּכֶת לְפָנֵינו סוּמָא בְּאַחַת מֵעֵינֶיהָ – "THE CAMEL WALKING IN FRONT OF US IS BLIND IN ONE EYE וּטְעוּנָה שְׁתֵּי נוּדוֹת – AND IS LADEN WITH TWO FLASKS, אַחַת שֶׁל יַיִן וְאַחַת שֶׁל שֶׁמֶן – ONE CONTAINING WINE AND ONE CONTAINING OIL. וּשְׁנֵי בְּנֵי אָדָם הַמַּנְהִיגִים אוֹתָהּ – AND of THE TWO MEN LEADING [THE CAMEL] אֶחָד יִשְׂרָאֵל וְאֶחָד נָכְרִי – ONE IS A JEW AND ONE IS A GENTILE." אָמַר לָהֶן [שַׁבַּאי] – Overhearing this remark, THE CAPTOR SAID TO THEM: עַם קְשֵׁה עוֹרֶף – "STIFF-NECKED PEOPLE! מֵאַיִן אַתֶּם יוֹדְעִין – FROM WHERE DO YOU KNOW this?"[1] אָמְרוּ לוֹ – THEY SAID TO HIM: גָּמָל מֵעֲשָׂבִים שֶׁלְּפָנֶיהָ – "We can ascertain that THE CAMEL is blind in one eye BY THE GRASS on the ground IN FRONT OF IT: מִצַּד שֶׁרוֹאָה אוֹכֶלֶת – ON THE SIDE IT CAN SEE, IT EATS. מִצַּד שֶׁאֵינָהּ רוֹאָה אֵינָהּ אוֹכֶלֶת – ON THE SIDE IT CANNOT SEE, IT DOES NOT EAT, i.e. from the fact that it only eats the grass on one side, we can tell that it cannot see the grass on the other side. וּטְעוּנָה שְׁתֵּי נוּדוֹת – We can ascertain that IT IS LADEN WITH TWO FLASKS, אַחַת שֶׁל יַיִן וְאַחַת שֶׁל שֶׁמֶן – ONE CONTAINING WINE AND ONE CONTAINING OIL, שֶׁל יַיִן מְטַפְטֵף וְשׁוֹקֵעַ – because we know that WINE DRIPS AND SINKS into the ground וְשֶׁל שֶׁמֶן מְטַפְטֵף וְצָף – WHEREAS OIL DRIPS AND FLOATS on the earth's surface and does not become absorbed into the ground. From the fact that the contents of one flask dripped and was absorbed into the ground, while the contents of the other flask dripped but would not sink into the ground, we were able to ascertain that one flask contained wine, while the other contained oil. וּשְׁנֵי בְּנֵי אָדָם הַמַּנְהִיגִים אוֹתָהּ אֶחָד נָכְרִי וְאֶחָד יִשְׂרָאֵל – We could ascertain that of THE TWO MEN LEADING [THE CAMEL], ONE IS GENTILE AND ONE IS JEWISH נָכְרִי נִפְנֶה לַדֶּרֶךְ – because A GENTILE RELIEVES HIMSELF ON THE ROAD וְיִשְׂרָאֵל נִפְנֶה לַצְּדָדִין – whereas A JEW RELIEVES HIMSELF ON THE SIDES of the road, out of a sense of modesty. Thus, when we observed what remained after they relieved themselves and noticed that some was in the middle of the road and some was off on the sides,[2] we deduced that one driver was an idolater and the other was a Jew." רָדַף אַחֲרֵיהֶם וּמָצָא כְּדִבְרֵיהֶם – [THE CAPTOR] CHASED AFTER [THE CAMELEERS], AND HE FOUND THAT IT WAS AS [THE CAPTIVES] HAD SAID. בָּא וּנְשָׁקָן עַל רֹאשָׁן – HE CAME AND KISSED THEM ON THEIR HEADS, וֶהֱבִיאָן לְבֵיתָן – BROUGHT THEM TO HIS HOUSE,[3] וְעָשָׂה לָהֶן סְעוּדָה גְּדוֹלָה – MADE THEM A GREAT FEAST, וְהָיָה מְרַקֵּד לִפְנֵיהֶם – AND DANCED BEFORE THEM, וְאָמַר בָּרוּךְ שֶׁבָּחַר בְּזַרְעוֹ שֶׁל אַבְרָהָם וְנָתַן לָהֶם מֵחָכְמָתוֹ – SAYING, "BLESSED IS HE WHO CHOSE THE SEED OF ABRAHAM AND GAVE THEM OF HIS WISDOM; וּבְכָל מָקוֹם שֶׁהֵן הוֹלְכִים נַעֲשִׂין שָׂרִים לַאֲדוֹנֵיהֶם – WHEREVER THEY GO THEY BECOME THE PRINCES OF THEIR MASTERS!" וּפְטָרָן [וְהָלְכוּ] לְבָתֵּיהֶם לְשָׁלוֹם – AND HE RELEASED THEM AND THEY WENT TO THEIR HOMES IN PEACE.[4]

The second verse in the Book of *Lamentations*:

שְׁתֵּי ,,בָּכ(ה)[וֹ] תִבְכֶּה בַּלַּיְלָה'' – ***She weeps, weeps in the night.*** שְׁתֵּי בְּכִיּוֹת הַלָּלוּ לָמָּה – **Why these two weepings?** אָמַר רַבָּה אָמַר רַבִּי יוֹחָנָן – **Rabbah said in the name of R' Yochanan:** אֶחָד עַל מִקְדָּשׁ רִאשׁוֹן וְאֶחָד עַל מִקְדָּשׁ שֵׁנִי – **One** weeping **for the** destruction of the **First Temple and one for** the destruction of **the Second Temple.**[5] ,,בַּלַּיְלָה'' – And what is the significance of ***in the night?*** עַל עִסְקֵי לַיְלָה – It indicates that the Temple was destroyed **because of matters that occurred at night,** שֶׁנֶּאֱמַר ,,וַתִּשָּׂא כָּל־הָעֵדָה וַיִּתְּנוּ אֶת־קוֹלָם וַיִּבְכּוּ הָעָם בַּלַּיְלָה הַהוּא'' – **as it is stated** in connection with the incident of the Spies: ***All the congregation raised up their voices and cried out, and the people wept on that night,***[6] אָמַר רַבָּה אָמַר רַבִּי יוֹחָנָן – and **Rabbah said in the name of R' Yochanan:** אוֹתוֹ הַיּוֹם לֵיל תִּשְׁעָה בְּאָב הָיָה – **That date was the night of the Ninth of Av.** אָמַר לָהֶן הַקָּדוֹשׁ בָּרוּךְ הוּא לְיִשְׂרָאֵל – **The Holy One, Blessed is He, said to Israel:** אַתֶּם בְּכִיתֶם בְּכִיָּה שֶׁל חִנָּם – **You wept a weeping without cause;** וַאֲנִי אֶקְבַּע לָכֶם בְּכִיָּה לְדוֹרוֹת – **therefore, I shall establish** this day **for you** as **a** day of **weeping for generations** to come, i.e. I will give you good reason to weep on this day, for both Temples will be destroyed on the ninth of Av.[7] דָּבָר אַחֵר – **An alternate explanation:** ,,בַּלַּיְלָה'' שֶׁכָּל הַבּוֹכֶה בַּלַּיְלָה קוֹלוֹ נִשְׁמָע – ***In the***

NOTES

1. In calling his captives "stiff-necked," the captor meant: You stubbornly refuse to humble yourselves in captivity, but even in this wretched state comport yourself as wise men or prophets, for how else could you claim to know these things? (*Maharsha*).

2. *Yad Ramah.*

3. [The translation follows the text appearing in *Ein Yaakov*, which has לְבֵיתוֹ in place of לְבֵיתָן. See also *Rashash.*]

4. As noted by *Mesoras HaShas,* it seems that *Rashi* had before him an expanded version of this story which appears in some early editions of the Gemara, but which, for some unknown reason, was omitted from the Vilna edition. We quote the expanded version here, from *Dikdukei Sofrim.*

They said to [their captor], "It appears to us that our master here is the son of the king's cupbearer" [for his facial features resemble those of the cupbearer, who must have fathered him adulterously – *Rashi*]. He went and asked his mother and said to her, "If you reveal [the matter] to me, fine; if not, I will command that you be killed." She said to him, "At the time of her (i.e. my) wedding, her (my) husband left [the room] and the king's cupbearer entered and cohabited with her (me) and she (I) became pregnant with you."

He then served [the captives] meat. They said to him, "This meat has in it the taste of a dog." He went and asked his mother. He said, "If you reveal [the matter] to me, fine; if not, I will kill you." She said to him, "There was a lamb, and its mother died. They therefore had it nurse from a dog."

He served them wine. They said to him, "This wine has the taste of a corpse." He went and asked his mother. He said, "If you reveal [the matter] fine; if not, I will kill you." She said to him, "This wine comes from a vine that rests on your father's grave."

[Thereupon] he stood up and kissed them on their heads and said, "Blessed is He. . . ."

[The translation of the word קַלְסְתַּר in *Rashi* as "cupbearer" follows *Targum HaLaaz al HaShas* by Dayan I. Gukovitzki. *Aruch,* however, (ע' קלסטרא [א']) translates it as "executioner."]

5. Jeremiah, who composed *Lamentations* at the time of the destruction of the First Temple, prophetically hinted at the destruction of the Second Temple as well, which was destined to be destroyed on the very same date (*Maharsha*).

6. *Numbers* 14:1. This verse describes how the Israelites in the Wilderness bemoaned their fate when they heard the report of the Spies who were sent by Moses. They were convinced that they would never be able to conquer the Land of Israel, though God had assured them that they would. This was a grievous sin. [See *Taanis* 29a.]

7. *Maharal* explains why the people's sinful reaction to the Spies' report led to the exile from the Land. God's plan was that the Exodus from Egypt be eternal. It was through being taken out of Egypt that we became God's people, and so we remain till this very day. Had the entry into the Land flowed naturally from the Exodus, i.e. had the same generation that left Egypt entered the Land, the Exodus and the entry into the Land would have all been part of one continuous process. Consequently, just as the Exodus was eternal, so the entry into the Land would have been eternal. But because the Jews wept needlessly, showing that they were not yet spiritually ready, they caused God to swear that the generation would not enter the Land; thereby the entry into the Land became severed from the act of the Exodus. It thus lost its quality of eternality. See also explanation of *Malbim (Torah Or* to *Numbers* 14).

[In his commentary to *Numbers* 14:1, *Ramban* makes the observation that in addition to being *hinted at* by the Torah, the idea that the future exile of Israel was the direct result of the sin of the Spies is stated *openly* in *Psalms* 106:24-27: "And they despised the desirable Land, they had no faith in His word. They murmured in their tents, they did not heed the voice of HASHEM. So He lifted up His hand [in an oath] against them, to throw them down in the Wilderness, *and to throw down their descendants among the peoples and to scatter them among the lands.*"]

א"ל אחד מהם לחבירו גמל שמהלכת לפנינו סומא באחת מעיניה וטעונה שתי נודות אחת של יין ואחת של שמן ושני בני אדם המנהיגים אותה אחד ישראל ואחד נכרי אמר להן [שבאי] עם קשה עורף מאין אתם יודעין אמרו לו גמל מעשבים שלפניה מצד שרואה אוכלת מצד שאינה רואה אינה אוכלת וטעונה שתי נודות אחת של יין ואחת של שמן של יין מטפטף ושוקע ושל שמן מטפטף וצף ושני בני אדם המנהיגים אותה אחד נכרי ואחד ישראל נכרי נפנה א) לדרך וישראל נפנה לצדדין רדף אחריהם ומצא כדבריהם בא ונשקן על ראשן והביאן לביתן ועשה להן סעודה גדולה והיה מרקד לפניהם ואמר ברוך שבחר בזרעו של אברהם ונתן להם מחכמתו ובכל מקום שהן הולכים נעשין שרים לאדוניהם ופטרן [והלכו] לבתיהם לשלום א) בכה תבכה בלילה שתי בכיות הללו למה אמר רבה אמר רבי יוחנן אחד על מקדש ראשון ואחד על מקדש שני בלילה על עסקי לילה שנאמר ב) ותשא כל העדה ויתנו את קולם ויבכו העם בלילה ההוא ב) אמר רבה א"ר יוחנן אותו (ג) היום) ליל ט' באב היה אמר להן הקב"ה לישראל אתם בכיתם בכיה של חנם ואני אקבע לכם בכיה לדורות ד"א בלילה שכל הבוכה בלילה קולו נשמע ד"א בלילה שכל הבוכה בלילה כוכבים ומזלות בוכין עמו ד"א בלילה שכל הבוכה בלילה השומע קולו בוכה כנגדו מעשה באשה אחת שכנתו של רבן גמליאל שמת בנה והיתה בוכה עליו בלילה שמע רבן גמליאל קולה ובכה כנגדה עד שנשרו ריסי עיניו למחר הכירו בו תלמידיו והוציאוה משכונתו א) ודמעתה על לחיה אמר ד) רבא אמר ר' יוחנן כאשה שבוכה על בעל נעוריה שנאמר ג) אלי כבתולה חגורת שק על בעל נעוריה ד) היו צריה לראש אמר ה) רבא אמר רבי יוחנן [א] ו) כל המיצר לישראל נעשה ראש שנאמר [א] ה) כי לא מועף לאשר מוצק לה כעת הראשון הקל ארצה זבולון וארצה נפתלי והאחרון הכביד דרך הים עבר הירדן גליל הגוים אמר ז) רבא אמר ר' יוחנן כל המציק לישראל אינו עיף ו) לא אליכם כל עוברי דרך אמר ח) רבא אמר ר' יוחנן מכאן לקובלנא מן התורה כל עוברי דרך אמר רב עמרם אמר רב עשאוני כעוברי על דת דאילו בסדום כתיב ז) וה' המטיר על סדום ואילו בירושלים כתיב ח) ממרום שלח אש בעצמותי וירדנה וגו' [ב] וכתיב ט) ויגדל עון בת עמי מחטאת סדום וכי משוא פנים יש בדבר אמר ט) רבא אמר ר' יוחנן מדה יתירה היתה בירושלים שלא היתה בסדום דאילו בסדום כתיב י) הנה זה היה עון סדום אחותך גאון שבעת לחם ויד עני ואביון לא החזיקה וגו' ואילו בירושלים כתיב כ) ידי נשים רחמניות בשלו ילדיהן ל) סלה כל אבירי ה' בקרבי כאדם שאומר לחברו נפסלה מטבע זו מ) פצו עליך פיהם אמר י) רבא אמר רבי יוחנן בשביל מה הקדים פ"א לעי"ן בשביל מרגלים שאמרו בפיהם מה שלא ראו בעיניהם נ) אוכלי עמי אכלו לחם ה' לא קראו אמר כ) רבא אמר ר' יוחנן כל האוכל מלחמן של ישראל טועם טעם לחם ושאינו אוכל מלחמן של ישראל אינו טועם טעם לחם ה' לא קראו רב אמר אלו הדיינין ושמואל אמר אלו מלמדי תינוקות מי מנאן אמר רב אשי אנשי כנסת הגדולה מנאום אמר רב יהודה אמר רב בקשו עוד למנות אחד באה ל) דמות דיוקנו של אביו (א) ונשטחה לפניהם ולא השגיחו עליה באה אש מן השמים ולחכה אש בספסליהם ולא השגיחו עליה יצאה בת קול ואמרה להם ס) חזית איש מהיר במלאכתו לפני מלכים יתיצב בל יתיצב לפני חשוכים מי שהקדים ביתי לביתו ולא עוד אלא שביתי בנה בשבע שנים וביתו בנה בשלש עשרה שנה לפני מלכים יתיצב [בל יתיצב] לפני חשוכים ולא השגיח עליה יצאה בת קול ואמרה ע) המעמך ישלמנה כי מאסת כי אתה תבחר ולא אני וגו' מ) דורשי רשומות היו אומרים כולן באין לעולם הבא שנאמר פ) לי גלעד ולי מנשה ואפרים מעוז ראשי יהודה מחוקקי מואב סיר רחצי על אדום אשליך נעלי עלי פלשת התרועעי לי גלעד [ג] נ) (ולי מנשה) זה אחאב שנפל ברמות גלעד מנשה כמשמעו אפרים מעוז ראשי זה ירבעם דקאתי מאפרים יהודה מחוקקי זה אחיתופל דקאתי

אחד. מן הנשבים לחברו: גמל. זו שמהלכת לפנינו סומא וכו': [מצד שרואה. שאינה אוכלת פעמים מצד ימין ופעמים מצד שמאל כבהמה הרואה שאוכלת מכאן ומכאן אלא מצד שרואה אוכלת]: יין מטפטף ושוקע. בקרקע ורואין אנו בין רגלינו הטיפין שנפלו כשעברה הגמל במקום זה מצד אחד שקועין ומצד אחר הטיפין של שמן שצפים: נפנה לצדדין. שכן דרך ישראל להיותו צנוע: רדף. השבאי דרך הגמל והמנהיג ומצא כדבריהם ואמרו ס) אותם יהודים על אותו שבאי אדוניהם שהוא בן קלסתר מלך אשקנ"ק בלע"ז שהיה דיוקנו דומה למגמת פניו של אותו קלסתר של מלך שבזנות הולידו: על עסקי לילה. לפי שבכו אותו לילה בכיית חנם: קולו נשמע יותר מביום. כדאמרינן בעלמא (יומא דף כ.) מפני מה אין הקול נשמע ביום כבלילה מפני גלגל חמה המנסר ברקיע והיינו דכתיב בכה תבכה בלילה כדי שיהא קולה נשמע וירחמו עליה ואף על פי כן אין מנחם לה: כוכבים ומזלות בוכים. שנכמרו רחמים עליו: בוכה כנגדו. מתוך שנשמע בהדיא מרכך לבו של אדם השומע קולו לבכות עמו: ריסי עיניו. שער שבגבת העין היה נופל ונכפל על העין מרוב דמעות: אלי. קוננו קינה מתרגמינן איליא: על בעל נעוריה. שבוכה תמיד ומלויה דמעות: על לחיה. לשון לחות ונערות כגון לח ויבש: מכאן לקובלנא מן התורה. כשאדם מודיע צערו לאחר צריך שיאמר לו לא תבא זאת לך כמו שבאה אלי כי קשה הוא לשמוע שפעמים חוזרת עליו והמקפיד על כך אין בו משום ניחוש. ל"א לקובלנא כשיש לו צרה יודיענה לרבים קובלנא צעקה ל"א נגד דמתרגמינן קבל כאדם שאומר לחברו לא כנגדך אני אומר: וירדנה. ושרף אותה והיינו עשאוני כעוברי דת שדנני באש כסדום: לא אליכם. נביא היה מתנודד על החורבן כאילו באה עליו צרה ומהפכה לאחרים ואומר להם לישראל לא תהא לכם צרה כזו כמדומה לי נביא היה מדבר כנגד בני משה או כנגד י' השבטים שלא הגלה נבוכדנצר: וירדנה. לשון שבירה כמו (במדבר כד) וירד מיעקב כאדם המושל בחברו להלקותו ולשברו: הכי גרסינן ויגדל עון בת עמי מחטאת סדום וכי משוא פנים יש בדבר והואיל וישראל רעים יותר מסדום למה לא נהפכו כסדום לשון אחר וכי משוא פנים יש בדבר דהתם כתיב וה' המטיר הוא בעצמו והכא כתיב שלח על ידי שליח: מדה יתירה לטובה. דבירושלים כתיב ידי נשים רחמניות בשלו ילדיהן היו לברות למו שהיתה מזומנת חברתה ואוכלת בנה אלמא רחמניות היו ואילו בסדום כתיב יד עני ואביון לא החזיקה ומדה זו כפרה עליהם שלא נהפכו לשון אחר מדה יתירה פורענות גדולה היתה בירושלים שילדיהם היו אוכלות זו עם זו דכתיב היו לברות למו ואילו בסדום כתיב גאון שבעת לחם שלא טעמו טעם עוני הא למדת גדול פורענות ירושלים מפורענות סדום ולא היה משוא פנים בדבר: סלה. לשון מסלה כלומר כל האבירים פסלם הקב"ה ועשאם פסולים וכבושים כמסלה זו והיינו דמיא למטבע שנפסל ואין לו תקנה: מפני מה הקדים פ"א לעי"ן. ברוב האלפא ביתא שבאיכה: מפני מרגלים. שהקדימו מאמר פיהם עד שלא ראו בעין: טועם טעם לחם. שהכותים מולאים טעמם בלחמם של ישראל שהנאה הוא להם כשגוזלין אותן: אלו הדיינין. מטה משפט בשביל עונותיהם היו לחם עמי למאכל אויביו: מלמדי תינוקות. שעושין מלאכתן רמיה: מי מנאן. להנך מלכים והדיוטות דקתני במתני' אין להם חלק: עוד אחד. שלמה: דיוקנו. של דוד אביו נשתטח לפניהם שלא למנותו עמהם: בל יתיצב לפני חשוכים. בגיהנם: לפני מלכים יתיצב. בגן עדן ולא לפני חשוכים: המעמך ישלמנה. וכי עליכם לשלם תשלומי עונשו לאדם שאתם נמאסים בו בשלמה לומר שאין לו חלק לעולם הבא: כי אתה תבחר ולא אני. וכי הבחירה בכם תלויה ולא די לומר מי שיש לו חלק ומי אין לו חלק הלא בי הדבר תלוי: דורשי רשומות. דורשי פסוקים כדכתיב (דניאל י) את הרשום בכתב אמת היו אומרים שלכולם יש להם חלק אפילו למנשה וירבעם ולאחאב: לי גלעד ולי מנשה. עלי לסבול עונם כדי שיהו הם זוכים: מנשה כמשמעו. מנשה בן חזקיהו: דקא

הגהות מהר"ב רנשבורג

א] בגמרא כל המיצר לישראל נעשה ראש שנא'. מלת שנאמר נמחק:

תורה אור השלם

א) בָּכוֹ תִבְכֶּה בַּלַּיְלָה וְדִמְעָתָהּ עַל לֶחֱיָהּ אֵין לָהּ מְנַחֵם מִכָּל אֹהֲבֶיהָ כָּל רֵעֶיהָ בָּגְדוּ בָהּ הָיוּ לָהּ לְאֹיְבִים: [איכה א, ב]
ב) וַתִּשָּׂא כָּל הָעֵדָה וַיִּתְּנוּ אֶת קוֹלָם וַיִּבְכּוּ הָעָם בַּלַּיְלָה הַהוּא: [במדבר יד, א]
ג) אֱלִי כִּבְתוּלָה חֲגֻרַת שַׂק עַל בַּעַל נְעוּרֶיהָ: [יואל א, ח]
ד) הָיוּ צָרֶיהָ לְרֹאשׁ אֹיְבֶיהָ שָׁלוּ כִּי יְיָ הוֹגָהּ עַל רֹב פְּשָׁעֶיהָ עוֹלָלֶיהָ הָלְכוּ שְׁבִי לִפְנֵי צָר: [איכה א, ה]
ה) כִּי לֹא מוּעָף לַאֲשֶׁר מוּצָק לָהּ כָּעֵת הָרִאשׁוֹן הֵקַל אַרְצָה זְבֻלוּן וְאַרְצָה נַפְתָּלִי וְהָאַחֲרוֹן הִכְבִּיד דֶּרֶךְ הַיָּם עֵבֶר הַיַּרְדֵּן גְּלִיל הַגּוֹיִם: [ישעיה ח, כג]
ו) לוֹא אֲלֵיכֶם כָּל עֹבְרֵי דֶרֶךְ הַבִּיטוּ וּרְאוּ אִם יֵשׁ מַכְאוֹב כְּמַכְאֹבִי אֲשֶׁר עוֹלַל לִי אֲשֶׁר הוֹגָה יְיָ בְּיוֹם חֲרוֹן אַפּוֹ: [איכה א, יב]
ז) וַייָ הִמְטִיר עַל סְדֹם וְעַל עֲמֹרָה גָּפְרִית וָאֵשׁ מֵאֵת יְיָ מִן הַשָּׁמָיִם: [בראשית יט, כד]
ח) מִמָּרוֹם שָׁלַח אֵשׁ בְּעַצְמֹתַי וַיִּרְדֶּנָּה פָּרַשׂ רֶשֶׁת לְרַגְלַי הֱשִׁיבַנִי אָחוֹר נְתָנַנִי שֹׁמֵמָה כָּל הַיּוֹם דָּוָה: [איכה א, יג]
ט) וַיִּגְדַּל עֲוֹן בַּת עַמִּי מֵחַטַּאת סְדֹם הַהֲפוּכָה כְמוֹ רָגַע וְלֹא חָלוּ בָהּ יָדָיִם: [איכה ד, ו]
י) הִנֵּה זֶה הָיָה עֲוֹן סְדֹם אֲחוֹתֵךְ גָּאוֹן שִׂבְעַת לֶחֶם וְשַׁלְוַת הַשְׁקֵט הָיָה לָהּ וְלִבְנוֹתֶיהָ וְיַד עָנִי וְאֶבְיוֹן לֹא הֶחֱזִיקָה: [יחזקאל טז, מט]
כ) יְדֵי נָשִׁים רַחֲמָנִיּוֹת בִּשְּׁלוּ יַלְדֵיהֶן הָיוּ לְבָרוֹת לָמוֹ בְּשֶׁבֶר בַּת עַמִּי: [איכה ד, י]
ל) סִלָּה כָל אַבִּירַי אֲדֹנָי בְּקִרְבִּי קָרָא עָלַי מוֹעֵד לִשְׁבֹּר בַּחוּרָי גַּת דָּרַךְ אֲדֹנָי לִבְתוּלַת בַּת יְהוּדָה: [איכה א, טו]
מ) פָּצוּ עָלַיִךְ פִּיהֶם כָּל אוֹיְבַיִךְ שָׁרְקוּ וַיַּחַרְקוּ שֵׁן אָמְרוּ בִּלָּעְנוּ אַךְ זֶה הַיּוֹם שֶׁקִּוִּינֻהוּ מָצָאנוּ רָאִינוּ: [איכה ב, טז]
נ) הֲלֹא יָדְעוּ כָּל פֹּעֲלֵי אָוֶן אֹכְלֵי עַמִּי אָכְלוּ לֶחֶם יְיָ לֹא קָרָאוּ: [תהלים יד, ד]
ס) חָזִיתָ אִישׁ מָהִיר בִּמְלַאכְתּוֹ לִפְנֵי מְלָכִים יִתְיַצָּב בַּל יִתְיַצֵּב לִפְנֵי חֲשֻׁכִּים: [משלי כב, כט]
ע) הֲמֵעִמְּךָ יְשַׁלְּמֶנָּה כִּי מָאַסְתָּ כִּי אַתָּה תִבְחַר וְלֹא אָנִי וּמַה יָּדַעְתָּ דַבֵּר: [איוב לד, לג]
פ) לִי גִלְעָד וְלִי מְנַשֶּׁה וְאֶפְרַיִם מָעוֹז רֹאשִׁי יְהוּדָה מְחֹקְקִי: מוֹאָב סִיר רַחְצִי עַל אֱדוֹם אַשְׁלִיךְ נַעֲלִי עָלַי פְּלֶשֶׁת הִתְרֹעָעִי: [תהלים ס, ט-י]

מסורת הש"ס

א) [פי' שהנכרי נפנה בדרך אצל בהמתו וישראל מסתלק לצדדים כך איתא בפי' הר"ש טהרות פ"ד מ"ה], ב) [תענית כט. סוטה לה.], ג) [צ"ל הלילה], ד) [צ"ל רבה], ה) [צ"ל רבה], ו) גיטין נו: ע"ש [עי' תוספות חגיגה יג: ד"ה שלא יאמרו ביד אומה שפילה מסר את בניו כלומר קודם שמילך כבר נעשה ראש], ז) [צ"ל רבה], ח) [צ"ל רבה], ט) [צ"ל רבה], י) [צ"ל רבה], כ) [צ"ל רבה], ל) [פי' נכון במאמר הלזה תמצא בשל"ה למסכת פסחים קעב.], מ) [עי' פירש"י ברכות כד. ד"ה דורשי וכו'], נ) [בע"י ליתא וכצ"ל], ס) [עי' בערוך ערך קלסטרא א' איתא הגירסא שהיא לפנינו בגמרא דהכא ואז תבין דברי רש"י הללו].

הגהות הב"ח

(א) גמרא דיוקנו של אביו. ונשתטחה לפניהם:

הגהות הגר"א

[א] גמ' שנא' כי לא מועף. נמחק תיבת שנאמר: **[ב]** שם וכתיב ויגדל. נמחק תיבת וכתיב: **[ג]** שם בסוף ולי מנשה. נמחקו ב' תיבות הללו:

ליקוטי רש"י

בכו תבכה. שתי בכיות על שתי חורבנין. **בלילה.** שהמקדש נשרף בלילה דאמר מר לעת ערב הציתו בו את האור דבר אחר בלילה לילה של בכיית מרגלים בתשעה באב גרמה להם, דבר אחר בלילה שכל הבוכה בלילה השומע קולו בוכה עמו [איכה א, ב]. **אתם בכיתם בכיה של חנם.** והפיל זרעם בגוים. מאותו שעה נגזר עליהם חורבן הבית שהרי ליל ט' באב בכו ואמר הקב"ה הם בכו בכיה של חנם ואני אקבע להם בכיה לדורות [תהלים קו, כז]. קרא עלי מועד. במסכת תענית (דף כט) תמוז דהשיא שתא של שנה השניה ליציאת מצרים שנשתלחו בה מרגלים בעשרים ותשעה בסיון מלויי מליוהו לתמוז לפיכך אירע בו יום חזרת מרגלים בשמונה באב ויבכו העם בלילה ההוא בתשעה באב בכו בכיה של חנם והוקבעה להם בכיה לדורות [שבועות י.]. **כי לא מועף לאשר מוצק לה.** כי מלך אשור אשר ניתן למוצק ולהצר לה לארצכם אינו עיף ואינו עצל מלבא עליהם עד שלש פעמים [ישעיהו ח, כג]. **לא אליכם.** לא תהא כצרה הזאת עוד לכל עוברי על דת אמרו חכמים מכאן לקובלנא מן התורה ראו מה עשה לי הביטו וראו וגומר [איכה א, יב]. **וירדנה.** וירדה אותה וישבר אותה וישבר אותה ע"י רידוי ויסורין לכן הנו"ן דגושה לפותרו בלשון יחידית כמו יעשנה יכרסמנה ירענה שהעלם ל' נקבה כמו דאת אומר (יחזקאל לז) העצמות היבשות שבר כל אחת ואחת, ד"א וירדנה כמו (שופטים יד) וירדהו אל כפיו הריק את המות גורר ורודה המות מתוכו [שם יב]. **ויגדל עון וגו'.** פורענותם מוכיח עליהם שגדול עונם משל סדום [שם ד, ו]. **סלה.** רמס ורפס לשון (ישעיה סב) סולו סולו המסילה [שם א, טו]. **ה' לא קראו.** לא חשבוהו ולא זכרו נפלאותיו ונוראותיו במשתיהם ונשתמשו בכליו ורבותינו פירשו כל שלא היה גוזל את ישראל לא היה טועם טעם ערב במאכלו אוכלי עמי נדמה להם כאוכלי לחם שטעמו טעם מאכל ערב [תהלים יד, ד]. **המעמך ישלמנה כי מאסת וגו'.** כך אמר אליהו לאיוב המעמך היה לו להקב"ה להימלך בפירעון תשלומין ממך. **כי מאסת.** לאמר מאסתי לא לעולם אחיה (איוב ז) יתר ידו ויבלעני (איוב ו) סבור אתה שיגבה ממך לפי דעתך ורצונך ואתה תבחר התשלומין ולא אני במקום הקב"ה דבר אליהו בתמיה [איוב לד, לג]. **דורשי רשומות.** קשרים וסתומים הכלולים בתורה דורשי חמורות גרסינן והיא היא [ברכות כד.].

***night* – for when one weeps at night, his voice is heard** more readily than in the day.[8] דָּבָר אַחֵר – **An alternate explanation:** ,,בַּלַּיְלָה'' שֶׁכָּל הַבּוֹכֶה בַּלַּיְלָה כּוֹכָבִים וּמַזָּלוֹת בּוֹכִין עִמּוֹ – ***In the night* – for when one weeps at night, the stars and constellations weep along with him.**[9] דָּבָר אַחֵר – **An alternate explanation:** ,,בַּלַּיְלָה'' שֶׁכָּל הַבּוֹכֶה בַּלַּיְלָה הַשּׁוֹמֵעַ קוֹלוֹ בּוֹכֶה כְּנֶגְדּוֹ – ***In the night* – for when one weeps at night, whoever hears his voice weeps along with him.**[10]

The Gemara illustrates this last point:

מַעֲשֶׂה בְּאִשָּׁה אַחַת – **The story** is told **of a woman,** שְׁכֶנְתּוֹ שֶׁל רַבָּן גַּמְלִיאֵל – **the neighbor of Rabban Gamliel,** שֶׁמֵּת בְּנָהּ – **whose son died.** וְהָיְתָה בּוֹכָה עָלָיו בַּלַּיְלָה – **She would weep for [her dead son] at night.** שָׁמַע רַבָּן גַּמְלִיאֵל קוֹלָהּ וּבָכָה כְּנֶגְדָּהּ – **Rabban Gamliel heard her voice and cried with her** עַד שֶׁנָּשְׁרוּ רִיסֵי עֵינָיו – **until his eyelashes fell out**, i.e. drooped over his eyes.[11] לְמָחָר הִכִּירוּ בּוֹ תַּלְמִידָיו – **The next day his students noticed [the change in his facial appearance]** וְהוֹצִיאוּהָ מִשְּׁכוּנָתוֹ – **and,** fearing that such constant emotional distress would damage their teacher's health, **they removed her from his neighborhood.**

More on the second verse of *Lamentations*:

,,וְדִמְעָתָהּ עַל לֶחֱיָהּ'' – ***And her tears are on her cheeks.*** אָמַר רָבָא אָמַר רַבִּי יוֹחָנָן – **Rava said in the name of R' Yochanan:** כְּאִשָּׁה שֶׁבּוֹכָה עַל בַּעַל נְעוּרֶיהָ – **Like a woman who cries over** the death of **the husband of her youth,** that is, her tears are constantly on her cheeks because she ceaselessly mourns the husband of her youth,[12] שֶׁנֶּאֱמַר ,,אֱלִי כִּבְתוּלָה חֲגֻרַת־שַׂק עַל־בַּעַל נְעוּרֶיהָ'' – **as it is stated:** ***Lament – like a virgin girded with sackcloth for the husband of her youth!***[13]

Lamentations 1:5:

,,הָיוּ צָרֶיהָ לְרֹאשׁ'' – ***Her persecutors have become leaders.*** אָמַר רָבָא אָמַר רַבִּי יוֹחָנָן – **Rava said in the name of R' Yochanan:** כָּל הַמֵּיצֵר לְיִשְׂרָאֵל נַעֲשֶׂה רֹאשׁ – **Whoever persecutes Israel becomes a leader.**[14]

A similar interpretation of another verse by Rava in the name of R' Yochanan:

[שנאמר][15] ,,כִּי לֹא מוּעָף לַאֲשֶׁר מוּצָק לָהּ כָּעֵת הָרִאשׁוֹן הֵקַל אַרְצָה זְבֻלוּן וְאַרְצָה נַפְתָּלִי וְהָאַחֲרוֹן הִכְבִּיד דֶּרֶךְ הַיָּם עֵבֶר הַיַּרְדֵּן גְּלִיל הַגּוֹיִם'' – ***For there is no weariness (muaf) to the one who oppresses (mutzak) her.*** *[The second time will be]* ***like the first time,*** *[in which]* ***he dealt mildly,*** *[exiling only]* ***the land of Zevulun and the land of Naphtali, but the last*** *[time]* ***he will deal harshly.*** *[In all three stages he will have exiled, in turn, those who lived]* ***by the way of the sea, on the other side of the Jordan,*** *[and in]* ***the attraction of the nations.***[16] אָמַר רָבָא אָמַר רַבִּי יוֹחָנָן – **Rava said in the name of R' Yochanan:** כָּל הַמֵּצִיק לְיִשְׂרָאֵל אֵינוֹ עָיֵף – **Whoever oppresses** *(meitzik)* **Israel does not become weary** *(ayef)*.[17]

Lamentations 1:12:

,,לוֹא אֲלֵיכֶם כָּל־עֹבְרֵי דֶרֶךְ'' – ***May it not befall you – all who pass by the road.*** אָמַר רָבָא אָמַר רַבִּי יוֹחָנָן – **Rava said in the name of R' Yochanan:** מִכָּאן לְקוּבְלָנָא מִן הַתּוֹרָה – **From here** we have a source for ***kuvlana*** **from the** Written **Torah.**[18]

Another interpretation of that verse:

,,כָּל־עֹבְרֵי דֶרֶךְ'' – ***All who pass by the road.*** אָמַר רַב עַמְרָם אָמַר רַב – **Rav Amram said in the name of Rav:** עֲשָׂאוּנִי כְּעוֹבְרֵי עַל דָּת – Jerusalem declared: **They have made me like transgressors of the law,**[19] דְּאִילּוּ בִּסְדוֹם כְּתִיב ,,וַה׳ הִמְטִיר עַל־סְדֹם'' – **for regarding** the destruction of **Sodom it is written:**[20] ***And***

NOTES

8. When one wishes to evoke pity and mercy through crying, night is the best time, because sound travels farther at night than during the day when, as stated in *Yoma* 20b, "the noise of the sun in orbit sawing through the sky" weakens other sounds (*Rashi*).

Alternatively, the sound of crying is more harrowing in the still of the night than in the daytime bustle (*Yad Ramah*).

Yet despite all this, the verse continues, אֵין־לָהּ מְנַחֵם, *she* [Jerusalem] *finds no one to comfort her (Rashi)*.

9. For they are moved at his plight (*Rashi*). See *Rambam, Hil. Yesodei HaTorah* 3:9.

Maharal explains that while the light of day elicits happiness and joy, the darkness of night sets the mood for one who is grieving, and the stars that appear at nighttime further this mood (see also next note). In so doing, they are said to "weep along" with the weeper.

Torah Temimah (ad loc.) explains this passage somewhat similarly: When one weeps unrestrainedly at night, it seems to him as if the very stars weep along with him.

10. Literally: weeps opposite him. This is because the darkness of night has a melancholy effect upon a person that renders him particularly susceptible to tears, including the tears of others (*Maharal*).

11. *Rashi.* Rabban Gamliel was reminded by her tears of the destruction of the Temple (*Maharsha* from *Eichah Rabbah* 1:24).

12. Rava translates the word לֶחֱיָהּ as *freshness* or *youth,* from the Hebrew לַח, meaning *wet* or *fresh.* According to Rava, the verse is translated as follows: *Her tears are over her youth* (*Rashi*).

13. *Joel* 1:8.

Iyun Yaakov points out that this ceaseless grief is actually a source of hope for Israel. Usually, one becomes consoled for the death of a loved one sooner or later. The exception is when the loved one is not actually dead (as in the case of Jacob's mourning for Joseph – see *Rashi* to *Genesis* 37:34). Thus, if Jerusalem does not stop mourning over the loss of her spouse – i.e. the Divine Presence – it is because that spouse is destined to return one day, as was stated above: Jerusalem was like a widow, but not truly a widow.

14. I.e. in order that it not be said that the Jews were vanquished by a lowly and contemptible person, God arranges that whoever is destined to vanquish the Jews rises to greatness beforehand (*Tosafos* to *Chagigah* 13b ד״ה שלא). Thus, shame is not added to Jewish distress, for there is no shame in defeat at the hand of a powerful foe.

Iyun Yaakov (*Gittin* 56b) suggests that the oppressor does God's work to bring the Jews to repentance. Therefore, he is entitled to a reward.

15. *Gra* deletes this word.

16. *Isaiah* 8:23. This verse describes the Assyrian invasions of Israel and Judah; see above, 94b. These invasions and their concomitant exiles came in three stages. Isaiah prophesied between the first and second stages, foretelling that the second stage would be relatively mild, like the first stage, involving the exile of only a few tribes, but the third stage would be severe, involving all the remnants of the Ten Tribes. The "attraction of the nations" refers to the balance of Eretz Yisrael that would be conquered in the third invasion. It is called the "attraction of the nations" because all the nations are drawn to it (*Rashi* to *Isaiah*).

17. I.e. the oppression of the Jews is a supernatural, Divinely ordained phenomenon, for when Jews are oppressed it is in punishment for their sins. Since such oppression is not the result of normal political events, it is not surprising that anyone chosen by God to be their oppressor should not tire as other men do, but should be possessed of superhuman energy in order to carry out the Divinely ordained punishment (*Maharsha*).

18. *Kuvlana* derives from the Aramaic word קבל, meaning *toward.* When recounting one's misfortune to another, the speaker should add, "May my misfortune never befall you," so that the listener not be stricken by that misfortune as well, as if the recounting were directed toward him. R' Yochanan here observes that since Jeremiah in our verse uses such an expression when speaking to the passersby, we learn that the custom is appropriate, not superstitious.

Alternatively, *kuvlana* means "outcry"; that is, from our verse we learn that it is proper to make known one's misfortune to others so that they should pray for him (*Rashi*), and it is not viewed as questioning God's judgment (*Chamra VeChayei*). [According to this explanation, this teaching is derived from the *end* of the verse (not cited by the Gemara): הַבִּיטוּ וּרְאוּ אִם־יֵשׁ מַכְאוֹב כְּמַכְאֹבִי, *look and see if there is any pain like my pain* (see *Rashi* to *Eichah* and *Maharsha* here).]

19. I have been punished like the Sodomites, who violated the "laws" of basic decency and reason (*Maharsha*).

20. *Genesis* 19:24.

א"ל אחד מהם לחבירו גמל שמהלכת לפנינו סומא באחת מעיניה וטעונה שתי נודות אחת של יין ואחת של שמן ושני בני אדם המנהיגים אותה אחד ישראל ואחד נכרי אמר להן [שבאי] עם קשה עורף מאין אתם יודעין אמרו לו גמל מעשבים שלפניה מצד שרואה אוכלת מצד שאינה רואה אינה אוכלת וטעונה שתי נודות אחת של יין ואחת של שמן של יין מטפטף ושוקע ושל שמן מטפטף וצף ושני בני אדם המנהיגים אותה אחד נכרי ואחד ישראל נכרי נפנה [א] לדרך וישראל נפנה לצדדין רדף אחריהם ומצא כדבריהם בא ונשקן על ראשן והביאן לביתן ועשה להן סעודה גדולה והיה מרקד לפניהם ואמר ברוך שבחר בזרעו של אברהם ונתן להם מחכמתו ובכל מקום שהן הולכים נעשין שרים לאדוניהם ופטרן [והלכו] לבתיהם לשלום (א) בכה תבכה בלילה שתי בכיות הללו למה אמר רבה אמר רבי יוחנן אחד על מקדש ראשון ואחד על מקדש שני בלילה על עסקי לילה שנאמר (ב) ותשא כל העדה ויתנו את קולם ויבכו העם בלילה ההוא [ג] אמר רבה א"ר יוחנן אותו ([ג] היום) ליל ט' באב היה אמר להן הקב"ה לישראל אתם בכיתם בכיה של חנם ואני אקבע לכם בכיה לדורות ד"א בלילה שכל הבוכה בלילה קולו נשמע ד"א בלילה שכל הבוכה בלילה כוכבים ומזלות בוכין עמו ד"א בלילה שכל הבוכה בלילה השומע קולו בוכה כנגדו מעשה באשה אחת שכנתו של רבן גמליאל שמת בנה והיתה בוכה עליו בלילה שמע רבן גמליאל קולה ובכה כנגדה עד שנשרו ריסי עיניו למחר הכירו בו תלמידיו והוציאוה משכונתו (א) ודמעתה על לחיה אמר [ד] רבא אמר ר' יוחנן כאשה שבוכה על בעל נעוריה שנאמר (ג) אלי כבתולה חגורת שק על בעל נעוריה (ד) היו צריה לראש אמר [ה] רבא אמר רבי יוחנן א] [ו] כל המיצר לישראל נעשה ראש שנאמר [א] (ה) כי לא מועף לאשר מוצק לה כעת הראשון הקל ארצה זבולון וארצה נפתלי והאחרון הכביד דרך הים עבר הירדן גליל הגוים אמר [ו] רבא אמר ר' יוחנן כל המציק לישראל אינו עיף (ו) לא אליכם כל עוברי דרך אמר [ח] רבא אמר ר' יוחנן מכאן לקובלנא מן התורה כל עוברי דרך אמר רב עמרם אמר רב עשאוני כעוברי על דת דאילו בסדום כתיב (ז) וה' המטיר על סדום ואילו בירושלים כתיב (ח) ממרום שלח אש בעצמותי וירדנה וגו' [ב] וכתיב (ט) ויגדל עון בת עמי מחטאת סדום וכי משוא פנים יש בדבר אמר [ט] רבא אמר ר' יוחנן מדה יתירה היתה בירושלים שלא היתה בסדום דאילו בסדום כתיב (י) הנה זה היה עון סדום אחותך גאון שבעת לחם ויד עני ואביון לא החזיקה וגו' ואילו בירושלים כתיב (כ) ידי נשים רחמניות בשלו ילדיהן (ל) סלה כל אבירי ה' בקרבי כאדם שאומר לחברו נפסלה מטבע זו (מ) פצו עליך פיהם אמר [י] רבא אמר רבי יוחנן בשביל מה הקדים פ"א לעי"ן בשביל מרגלים שאמרו בפיהם מה שלא ראו בעיניהם (נ) אוכלי עמי אכלו לחם ה' לא קראו אמר [כ] רבא אמר ר' יוחנן כל האוכל מלחמן של ישראל טועם טעם לחם ושאינו אוכל מלחמן של ישראל אינו טועם טעם לחם ה' לא קראו רב אמר אלו הדיינין ושמואל אמר אלו מלמדי תינוקות מי מנאן אמר רב אשי אנשי כנסת הגדולה מנאום אמר רב יהודה אמר רב בקשו עוד למנות אחד באה [ל] דמות דיוקנו של אביו (א) ונשטחה לפניהם ולא השגיחו עליה באה אש מן השמים ולחכה אש בספסליהם ולא השגיחו עליה יצאה בת קול ואמרה להם (ס) חזית איש מהיר במלאכתו לפני מלכים יתיצב בל יתיצב לפני חשוכים מי שהקדים ביתי לביתו ולא עוד אלא שביתי בנה בשבע שנים וביתו בנה בשלש עשרה שנה לפני מלכים יתיצב [בל יתיצב] לפני חשוכים ולא השגיח עליה יצאה בת קול ואמרה (ע) המעמך ישלמנה כי מאסת כי אתה תבחר ולא אני וגו' [מ] דורשי רשומות היו אומרים כולן באין לעולם הבא שנאמר (פ) לי גלעד ולי מנשה ואפרים מעוז ראשי יהודה מחוקקי מואב סיר רחצי על אדום אשליך נעלי עלי פלשת התרועעי לי גלעד [ג] [נ] (ולי מנשה) זה אחאב שנפל ברמות גלעד מנשה כמשמעו אפרים מעוז ראשי זה ירבעם דקאתי מאפרים יהודה מחוקקי זה אחיתופל דקאתי

רש"י

אחד. מן הנשבים לחברו: גמל. זו שמהלכת לפנינו סומא וכו': [מצד שרואה. שאינה אוכלת פעמים מצד ימין ופעמים מצד שמאל כבהמה הרואה שאוכלת מכאן ומכאן אלא מצד שרואה אוכלת]: יין מטפטף ושוקע. בקרקע ורואין אנו בין רגלינו הטיפין שנפלו כשעברה הגמל במקום זה מצד אחד שקועין ומצד אחר הטיפין של שמן שצפים: נפנה לצדדין. שכן דרך ישראל להיותו צנוע: רדף. השבאי דרך הגמל והמנהיג ומצא כדבריהם ואמרו [ס] אותם יהודים על אותו שבאי אדוניהם שהוא בן קלסתר מלך אשקנ"ק בלע"ז שהיה דיוקנו דומה למגמת פניו של אותו קלסתר של מלך שבזנות הולידו: על עסקי לילה. לפי שבכו אותו לילה בכיית חנם: קולו נשמע יותר מביום. כדאמרינן בעלמא (יומא דף כ.) מפני מה אין הקול נשמע ביום כבלילה מפני גלגל חמה המנסר ברקיע והיינו דכתיב בכה תבכה בלילה כדי שיהא קולה נשמע וירחמו עליה ואף על פי כן אין מנחם לה: כוכבים ומזלות בוכים. שנכמרו רחמים עליו: בוכה כנגדו. מתוך שנשמע בהדיא מרכך לבו של אדם השומע קולו לבכות עמו: ריסי עיניו. שער שבגבת העין היה נופל ונכפל על העין מרוב דמעות: אלי. קוננו קינה מתרגמינן איליא: על בעל נעוריה. שבוכה תמיד ומלויה דמעות: על לחיה. לשון לחות ונערות כגון לח ויבש: מכאן לקובלנא מן התורה. כשאדם מודיע צערו לאחר צריך שיאמר לו לא תבא זאת לך כמו שבאה אלי כי קשה הוא לשמוע שפעמים חוזרת עליו והמקפיד על כך אין בו משום ניחוש. ל"א לקובלנא כשיש לו צרה יודיענה לרבים קובלנא צעקה ל"א נגד דמתרגמינן קבל כאדם שאומר לחברו לא כנגדך אני אומר: וירדנה. ושרף אותה והיינו עשאוני כעוברי דת שדנני באש כסדום: לא אליכם. נביא היה מתנודד על החורבן כאילו באה עליו צרה ומהפכה לאחרים ואומר להם לישראל לא תהא לכם צרה כזו כמדומה לי נביא היה מדבר כנגד בני משה או כנגד י' השבטים שלא הגלה נבוכדנצר: וירדנה. לשון שבירה כמו (במדבר כד) וירד מיעקב כאדם המושל בחברו להלקותו ולשברו: הכי גרסינן ויגדל עון בת עמי מחטאת סדום וכי משוא פנים יש בדבר והואיל וישראל רעים יותר מסדום למה לא נהפכו כסדום לשון אחר וכי משוא פנים יש בדבר דהתם כתיב וה' המטיר הוא בעצמו והכא כתיב שלא על ידי שליח: מדה יתירה לטובה. דבירושלים כתיב ידי נשים רחמניות בשלו ילדיהן היו לברות למו שהיתה מזמנת חברתה ואוכלת בנה אלמא רחמניות היו ואילו בסדום כתיב יד עני ואביון לא החזיקה ומדה זו כפרה עליהם שלא נהפכו לשון אחר מדה יתירה פורענות גדולה היתה בירושלים שילדיהם היו אוכלות זו עם זו דכתיב היו לברות למו ואילו בסדום כתיב גאון שבעת לחם שלא טעמו טעם עוני הא למדת גדול פורענות ירושלים מפורענות סדום ולא היה משוא פנים בדבר: סלה. לשון מסלה כלומר כל האבירים פסלם הקב"ה ועשאם פסולים וכבושים כמסלה זו והיינו דמיא למטבע שנפסל ואין לו תקנה: מפני מה הקדים פ"א לעי"ן. ברוב האלפא ביתא שבאיכה: מפני מרגלים. שהקדימו מאמר פיהם עד שלא ראו בעין: טועם טעם לחם. שהכותים מואסים טעמם בלחמם של ישראל שהנאה הוא להם כשגוזלין אותן: אלו הדיינין. מטה משפט בשביל עונותיהם היו לחם עמי למאכל אויביו: מלמדי תינוקות. שעושין מלאכתן רמיה: מי מנאן. להנך מלכים והדיוטות דקתני במתני' אין להם חלק: עוד אחד. שלמה: דיוקנו. של דוד אביו נשטח לפניהם שלא למנותו עמהם: בל יתיצב לפני חשוכים. בגיהנם: לפני מלכים יתיצב. בגן עדן ולא לפני חשוכים: המעמך ישלמנה. וכי עליכם לשלם תשלומי עונשו לאדם שאתם נמאסים בו בשלמה לומר שאין לו חלק לעולם הבא: כי אתה תבחר ולא אני. וכי הבחירה בכם תלויה ולא בי לומר מי שיש לו חלק ומי אין לו חלק הלא בי הדבר תלוי: דורשי רשומות. דורשי פסוקים כדכתיב (דניאל י) את הרשום בכתב אמת היו אומרים שלכולם יש להם חלק אפילו למנשה וירבעם ולאחאב: לי גלעד ולי מנשה. עלי לסבול עונם כדי שיהו הם זוכים: מנשה כמשמעו. מנשה בן חזקיהו: דקא

הגהות מהר"ב רנשבורג

א] בגמרא כל המיצר לישראל נעשה ראש שנא'. מלת שנאמר נמחק:

תורה אור השלם

א) בָּכוֹ תִבְכֶּה בַּלַּיְלָה וְדִמְעָתָהּ עַל לֶחֱיָהּ אֵין לָהּ מְנַחֵם מִכָּל אֹהֲבֶיהָ כָּל רֵעֶיהָ בָּגְדוּ בָהּ הָיוּ לָהּ לְאֹיְבִים: [איכה א, ב]

ב) וַתִּשָּׂא כָּל הָעֵדָה וַיִּתְּנוּ אֶת קוֹלָם וַיִּבְכּוּ הָעָם בַּלַּיְלָה הַהוּא: [במדבר יד, א]

ג) אֱלִי כִּבְתוּלָה חֲגֻרַת שַׂק עַל בַּעַל נְעוּרֶיהָ: [יואל א, ח]

ד) הָיוּ צָרֶיהָ לְרֹאשׁ אֹיְבֶיהָ שָׁלוּ כִּי יְיָ הוֹגָהּ עַל רֹב פְּשָׁעֶיהָ עוֹלָלֶיהָ הָלְכוּ שְׁבִי לִפְנֵי צָר: [איכה א, ה]

ה) כִּי לֹא מוּעָף לַאֲשֶׁר מוּצָק לָהּ כָּעֵת הָרִאשׁוֹן הֵקַל אַרְצָה זְבֻלוּן וְאַרְצָה נַפְתָּלִי וְהָאַחֲרוֹן הִכְבִּיד דֶּרֶךְ הַיָּם עֵבֶר הַיַּרְדֵּן גְּלִיל הַגּוֹיִם: [ישעיה ח, כג]

ו) לוֹא אֲלֵיכֶם כָּל עֹבְרֵי דֶרֶךְ הַבִּיטוּ וּרְאוּ אִם יֵשׁ מַכְאוֹב כְּמַכְאֹבִי אֲשֶׁר עוֹלַל לִי אֲשֶׁר הוֹגָה יְיָ בְּיוֹם חֲרוֹן אַפּוֹ: [איכה א, יב]

ז) וַיְיָ הִמְטִיר עַל סְדֹם וְעַל עֲמֹרָה גָּפְרִית וָאֵשׁ מֵאֵת יְיָ מִן הַשָּׁמָיִם: [בראשית יט, כד]

ח) מִמָּרוֹם שָׁלַח אֵשׁ בְּעַצְמֹתַי וַיִּרְדֶּנָּה פָּרַשׂ רֶשֶׁת לְרַגְלַי הֱשִׁיבַנִי אָחוֹר נְתָנַנִי שֹׁמֵמָה כָּל הַיּוֹם דָּוָה: [איכה א, יג]

ט) וַיִּגְדַּל עֲוֹן בַּת עַמִּי מֵחַטַּאת סְדֹם הַהֲפוּכָה כְמוֹ רָגַע וְלֹא חָלוּ בָהּ יָדָיִם: [איכה ד, ו]

י) הִנֵּה זֶה הָיָה עֲוֹן סְדֹם אֲחוֹתֵךְ גָּאוֹן שִׂבְעַת לֶחֶם וְשַׁלְוַת הַשְׁקֵט הָיָה לָהּ וְלִבְנוֹתֶיהָ וְיַד עָנִי וְאֶבְיוֹן לֹא הֶחֱזִיקָה: [יחזקאל טז, מט]

כ) יְדֵי נָשִׁים רַחֲמָנִיּוֹת בִּשְּׁלוּ יַלְדֵיהֶן הָיוּ לְבָרוֹת לָמוֹ בְּשֶׁבֶר בַּת עַמִּי: [איכה ד, י]

ל) סִלָּה כָל אַבִּירַי אֲדֹנָי בְּקִרְבִּי קָרָא עָלַי מוֹעֵד לִשְׁבֹּר בַּחוּרָי גַּת דָּרַךְ אֲדֹנָי לִבְתוּלַת בַּת יְהוּדָה: [איכה א, טו]

מ) פָּצוּ עָלַיִךְ פִּיהֶם כָּל אוֹיְבַיִךְ שָׁרְקוּ וַיַּחַרְקוּ שֵׁן אָמְרוּ בִּלָּעְנוּ אַךְ זֶה הַיּוֹם שֶׁקִּוִּינֻהוּ מָצָאנוּ רָאִינוּ: [איכה ב, טז]

נ) הֲלֹא יָדְעוּ כָּל פֹּעֲלֵי אָוֶן אֹכְלֵי עַמִּי אָכְלוּ לֶחֶם יְיָ לֹא קָרָאוּ: [תהלים יד, ד]

ס) חָזִיתָ אִישׁ מָהִיר בִּמְלַאכְתּוֹ לִפְנֵי מְלָכִים יִתְיַצָּב בַּל יִתְיַצֵּב לִפְנֵי חֲשֻׁכִּים: [משלי כב, כט]

ע) הֲמֵעִמְּךָ יְשַׁלְּמֶנָּה כִּי מָאַסְתָּ כִּי אַתָּה תִבְחַר וְלֹא אָנִי וּמַה יָּדַעְתָּ דַבֵּר: [איוב לד, לג]

פ) לִי גִלְעָד וְלִי מְנַשֶּׁה וְאֶפְרַיִם מָעוֹז רֹאשִׁי יְהוּדָה מְחֹקְקִי: מוֹאָב סִיר רַחְצִי עַל אֱדוֹם אַשְׁלִיךְ נַעֲלִי עָלַי פְּלֶשֶׁת הִתְרֹעָעִי: [תהלים ס, ט-י]

מסורת הש"ס

א) [פי' שהנכרי נפנה בדרך אלא בהמתו וישראל מסתלק לצדדים כך איתא בפי' הר"ש טהרות פ"ד מ"ה], ב) [תענית כט. סוטה לה.], ג) [צ"ל הלילה], ד) [צ"ל רבה], ה) [צ"ל רבה], ו) גיטין נו: ע"ש [עי' תוספות חגיגה יג: ד"ה שלא יאמרו ביד אומה שפילה מסר את בניו כלומר קודם שמילך כבר נעשה ראש], ז) [צ"ל רבה], ח) [צ"ל רבה], ט) [צ"ל רבה], י) [צ"ל רבה], כ) [צ"ל רבה], ל) [פי' נכון במאמר הלזה תמצא בשל"ה למסכת פסחים קעב.], מ) [עי' פירש"י ברכות כד. ד"ה דורשי וכו'], נ) [בע"י ליתא וכל"ל], ס) [עי' בערוך ערך קלסטרא א' איתא הגירסא שהיא לפנינו בגמרא דהכא ואז תבין דברי רש"י הללו].

הגהות הב"ח

(א) גמרא דיוקנו של אביו. ונשטחה לפניהם:

הגהות הגר"א

[א] גמ' שנא' כי לא מועף. נמחק תיבת שנאמר: **[ב]** שם וכתיב ויגדל. נמחק תיבת וכתיב: **[ג]** שם בסוף ולי מנשה. נמחקו ב' תיבות הללו:

ליקוטי רש"י

בכו תבכה. שתי בכיות על שתי חורבנין. **בלילה.** שהמקדש נשרף בלילה דאמר מר לעת ערב הציתו בו את האור דבר אחר בלילה לילה של בכיית מרגלים בתשעה באב גרמה להם, דבר אחר בלילה שכל הבוכה בלילה השומע קולו בוכה עמו [איכה א, ב]. **אתם בכיתם בכיה של חנם.** ולהפיל זרעם בגוים. מאותו שעה נגזר עליהם חורבן הבית שהרי ליל ט' באב בכו ואמר הקב"ה הם בכו בכיה של חנם ואני אקבע להם בכיה לדורות [תהלים קו, כז]. קרא עלי מועד. במסכת תענית (דף כט) תמוז דההיא שתא של שנה השניה ליציאת מצרים שנשתלחו בה מרגלים בעשרים ותשעה בסיון מלויי מליוהו לתמוז לפיכך אירע בו יום חזרת מרגלים בשמונה באב ויבכו העם בלילה ההוא בתשעה באב בכו בכיה של חנם והוקבעה להם בכיה לדורות [שבועות י.]. **כי לא מועף לאשר מוצק לה.** כי מלך אשור אשר ניתן למוצק ולהצר לה לארצכם אינו עיף ואינו עצל מלבא עליהם עד שלש פעמים [ישעיהו ח, כג]. **לא אליכם.** לא תהא כצרה הזאת עוד לכל עוברי על דת אמרו חכמים מכאן לקובלנא מן התורה ראו מה עשה לי הביטו וראו וגומר [איכה א, יב]. **וירדנה.** וירדה אותה וישבר אותה וישבר אותה ע"י רידוי ויסורין לכן הנו"ן דגושה לפותרו בלשון יחידית כמו יעשנה יכרסמנה ירענה שהעצם ל' נקבה כמו דאת אומר (יחזקאל לו) העצמות היבשות שבר כל אחת ואחת, ד"א וירדנה כמו (שופטים יד) וירדהו אל כפיו הריק את המוח גורר ורודה המוח מתוכו [שם יב]. **ויגדל עון וגו'.** פורענותם מוכיח עליהם שגדול עונש משל סדום [שם ד, ו]. **סלה.** רמס ורפס לשון (ישעיה סב) סולו סולו המסילה [שם א, טו]. **ה' לא קראו.** לא חשבוהו ולא זכרו נפלאותיו ונוראותיו במשתיהם ונשתמשו בכליו ורבותינו פירשו כל שלא היה גוזל את ישראל לא היה טועם טעם ערב במאכלו אוכלי עמי נדמה להם כאוכלי לחם שטעמו טעם מאכל ערב [תהלים יד, ד]. **המעמך ישלמנה כי מאסת וגו'.** כך אמר אליהו לאיוב המעמך היה לו להקב"ה להימלך בפירעון תשלומין ממך. **כי מאסת.** לאמר מאחי לא לעולם אחיה (איוב ז) יתר ידו ויבלעני (איוב ו) סבור אתה שיגבה ממך לפי דעתך ורצונך ואתה תבחר התשלומין ולא אני במקום הקב"ה דבר אליהו בתמיה [איוב לד, לג]. **דורשי רשומות.** קשרים וסתומים הכלולים בתורה דורשי חמורות גרסינן והיא היא [ברכות כד.].

***HASHEM* rained down upon Sodom** *sulfur and fire,* וְאִילּוּ בִּירוּשָׁלַיִם כְּתִיב ,,מִמָּרוֹם שָׁלַח־אֵשׁ בְּעַצְמֹתַי וַיִּרְדֶּנָּה וגו׳ ״ – while **regarding** the destruction of **Jerusalem it is written:**[21] ***From on high He sent a fire into my bones, and it crushed them,* etc.** Thus, Jerusalem declared: I was punished through fire, just like Sodom.

Having likened Jerusalem's punishment to that of Sodom, the Gemara cites a verse that compares the sins of these two cities: וּכְתִיב ,,וַיִּגְדַּל עֲוֹן בַּת־עַמִּי מֵחַטַּאת סְדֹם״ – **And it is written:**[22] ***The iniquity of the daughter of my people was greater than the sin of Sodom.***

The verse states that Jerusalem's sins surpassed those of Sodom. The Gemara asks:

וְכִי מַשּׂוֹא פָּנִים יֵשׁ בַּדָּבָר – **Now** if Jerusalem was more wicked than Sodom, **should favoritism be shown in the matter?** Why was Jerusalem not completely overturned as was Sodom?[23]

The Gemara answers:

אָמַר רָבָא אָמַר רַבִּי יוֹחָנָן – **Rava said in the name of R' Yochanan:** מִדָּה יְתֵירָה הָיְתָה בִּירוּשָׁלַיִם שֶׁלֹּא הָיְתָה בִסְדוֹם – **There was an extra measure in Jerusalem that was not present in Sodom,** i.e. Jerusalem had something in its favor that Sodom did not have, דְּאִילּוּ בִסְדוֹם כְּתִיב ,,הִנֵּה־זֶה הָיָה עֲוֹן סְדֹם אֲחוֹתֵךְ גָּאוֹן שִׂבְעַת־לֶחֶם. . .וְיַד־עָנִי וְאֶבְיוֹן לֹא הֶחֱזִיקָה וגו׳ ״ – **for regarding Sodom it is written:**[24] ***See! This was the sin of Sodom your sister: pride, surfeit of bread, and undisturbed peace were hers and her daughter's, but the hand of the poor and the needy they did not support,* etc.,** וְאִילּוּ בִּירוּשָׁלַיִם כְּתִיב ,,יְדֵי נָשִׁים רַחֲמָנִיּוֹת בִּשְּׁלוּ יַלְדֵיהֶן״ – **whereas regarding Jerusalem it is written: *The hands of compassionate women boiled their own children.***[25] I.e. the women of Jerusalem, even in their most desperate straits, were compassionate,[26] whereas the inhabitants of Sodom, although blessed with prosperity and an abundance of food, did not share any of it with the needy. It was this compassion that spared Jerusalem the total obliteration that befell Sodom.[27]

Lamentations 1:15:

,,סִלָּה כָל־אַבִּירַי ה׳ בְּקִרְבִּי״ – ***The Lord has trampled* (*silah*) *all my mighty ones in my midst.*** כְּאָדָם שֶׁאוֹמֵר לַחֲבֵרוֹ – **Like a man who says to his friend:** נִפְסְלָה מַטְבֵּעַ זוֹ – **This coin has become worthless** (*nifsilah*).[28]

Lamentations 2:16:

,,פָּצוּ עָלַיִךְ פִּיהֶם״ – ***They jeered at you.*** אָמַר רָבָא אָמַר רַבִּי יוֹחָנָן – **Rava said in the name of R' Yochanan:** בִּשְׁבִיל מָה הִקְדִּים פ״א לְעי״ן – **Why did [Jeremiah],** the author of *Lamentations,* **place the *pei* before the *ayin*?**[29] בִּשְׁבִיל מְרַגְּלִים – It was **because of the Spies,** שֶׁאָמְרוּ בְּפִיהֶם מַה שֶּׁלֹּא רָאוּ בְעֵינֵיהֶם – **who spoke with their mouths** (*peh*) **what they had not seen with their eyes** (*ayin*).[30]

Another interpretation of a verse describing the destruction of Israel by vicious foes:

,,אֹכְלֵי עַמִּי אָכְלוּ לֶחֶם ה׳ לֹא קָרָאוּ״ – ***They who devour my people devour bread, they who call not upon HASHEM.***[31] אָמַר רָבָא אָמַר רַבִּי יוֹחָנָן – **Rava said in the name of R' Yochanan:** כָּל הָאוֹכֵל מִלַּחְמָן שֶׁל יִשְׂרָאֵל טוֹעֵם טַעַם לֶחֶם – **Whoever eats the bread of Israel tastes the** true **taste of bread,** וְשֶׁאֵינוֹ אוֹכֵל מִלַּחְמָן שֶׁל יִשְׂרָאֵל אֵינוֹ טוֹעֵם טַעַם לֶחֶם – **and whoever does not eat the bread of Israel does not taste the** true **taste of bread.**[32] ,,ה׳ לֹא קָרָאוּ״ – ***They who call not upon HASHEM.*** רַב אָמַר – **Rav said:** אֵלּוּ הַדַּיָּינִין – **These are the** corrupt Jewish **judges.** וּשְׁמוּאֵל אָמַר – **And Shmuel said:** אֵלּוּ מְלַמְּדֵי תִינוֹקוֹת – **These are teachers of young children,** who do not perform their work honestly. It is due to such persons that the bread of the Jewish people is devoured by their foes.[33]

The Gemara now returns to its discussion of our Mishnah, which enumerates three kings and four commoners who have no portion in the World to Come:

מִי מְנָאָן – **Who enumerated them?** אָמַר רַב אַשִׁי – **Rav Ashi said:** אַנְשֵׁי כְּנֶסֶת הַגְּדוֹלָה מְנָאוּם – **The Men of the Great**

NOTES

21. *Lamentations* 1:13.

22. Ibid. 4:6.

23. This follows *Rashi's* first explanation.

Rashi suggests an alternate interpretation: In the case of Sodom, Scripture states that God Himself rained down fire upon Sodom, that is, God personally destroyed the city. In describing the destruction of Jerusalem, on the other hand, Scripture states: "He *sent* a fire," implying that God personally did not destroy the city, but did it through the medium of a messenger. Thus, the Gemara's question is: If Jerusalem was more wicked than Sodom, why was Jerusalem not destroyed by God Himself?

24. *Ezekiel* 16:49.

25. *Lamentations* 4:10. This verse describes the horrors of the siege of Jerusalem. Ordinarily compassionate mothers were so crazed with hunger that they killed and ate their own children.

26. When eating their "meal" of the flesh of their children, they still evinced their compassionate nature and invited their starving neighbors to partake (*Rashi*).

27. According to an alternate interpretation given by *Rashi*, the phrase, *there was an extra measure in Jerusalem that was not present in Sodom,* refers to the *suffering* endured by the two cities. In the case of Sodom, there was no prolonged suffering. They were suddenly destroyed in the midst of their prosperity. In the case of Jerusalem, however, the inhabitants suffered so horribly that parents were reduced to eating their own children. The extra suffering endured by the inhabitants of Jerusalem more than made up for the increased amount of sin. For that reason, although Jerusalem was not completely obliterated, it paid for its extra sin through extra suffering.

28. I.e. the word *silah* means trodding or trampling, as in *mesilah*, which means a trodden path. In this verse *silah* connotes trampling something until it is completely crushed and rendered useless, as in the case of a coin which loses its value when the image stamped on it is effaced (*nifsilah*). The meaning of the verse is that God rendered all the mighty men useless during the siege of Jerusalem (*Rashi;* see also *Ben Yehoyada*).

29. I.e. in the first four chapters of *Lamentations*, the verses follow each other in alphabetical order, but in this chapter (2), and also in chapters 3 and 4, the verses beginning with פ, *pei*, precede those of ע, *ayin* (*Rashi*). [In the first chapter the order is the customary one, to show that Jeremiah did not generally follow a different order of the *aleph-beis* (*Maharsha*).]

30. The word for mouth is *peh,* and the word for eye is *ayin.* The Spies put their *peh* before their *ayin*, for they reported things to the Israelites that they had not actually seen. Therefore, the author of *Lamentations* did likewise, to indicate the connection between the destruction of Jerusalem and the sin of the Spies (see *Rashi*).

Alternatively, in stating that the Spies put their mouth before their eyes, R' Yochanan accords with his view in *Sotah* 35a that even before setting out on their mission to reconnoiter the Land, the Spies collaborated amongst themselves to deliver a derogatory report (see *Eitz Yosef*).

31. *Psalms* 14:4.

32. I.e. the idol worshipers take so much pleasure in robbing Jews that the bread they seize from a Jew tastes better to them than their own (*Rashi*).

Toras Chaim explains that the persecutors of the Jews are granted by God a special enjoyment of the bread they steal, so they will continue to do so with enthusiasm, thus punishing the Jews for their sins.

33. Teachers of Torah and judges have a higher calling, namely, to teach and execute the laws of the Torah. They ought to be the ones who *call to God,* that is, they ought to carry out their greater responsibilities honestly, mindful of God, Whose representatives they are (*Yad Ramah*).

א"ל אחד מהם לחבירו גמל שמהלכת לפנינו סומא באחת מעיניה וטעונה שתי נודות אחת של יין ואחת של שמן ושני בני אדם המנהיגים אותה אחד ישראל ואחד נכרי אמר להן [שבאי] עם קשה עורף מאין אתם יודעין אמרו לו גמל מעשבים שלפניה מצד שרואה אוכלת מצד שאינה רואה אינה אוכלת וטעונה שתי נודות אחת של יין ואחת של שמן של יין מטפטף ושוקע ושל שמן מטפטף וצף ושני בני אדם המנהיגים אותה אחד נכרי ואחד ישראל נכרי נפנה [א] לדרך וישראל נפנה לצדדין רדף אחריהם ומצא כדבריהם בא ונשקן על ראשן והביאן לביתן ועשה להן סעודה גדולה והיה מרקד לפניהם ואמר ברוך שבחר בזרעו של אברהם ונתן להם מחכמתו ובכל מקום שהן הולכים נעשין שרים לאדוניהם ופטרן [והלכו] לבתיהם לשלום (א) בכה תבכה בלילה שתי בכיות הללו למה אמר רבה אמר רבי יוחנן אחד על מקדש ראשון ואחד על מקדש שני בלילה על עסקי לילה שנאמר (ב) ותשא כל העדה ויתנו את קולם ויבכו העם בלילה ההוא [ג] אמר רבה א"ר יוחנן אותו (ג היום) ליל ט' באב היה אמר להן הקב"ה לישראל אתם בכיתם בכיה של חנם ואני אקבע לכם בכיה לדורות ד"א בלילה שכל הבוכה בלילה קולו נשמע ד"א בלילה שכל הבוכה בלילה כוכבים ומזלות בוכין עמו ד"א בלילה שכל הבוכה בלילה השומע קולו בוכה כנגדו מעשה באשה אחת שכנתו של רבן גמליאל שמת בנה והיתה בוכה עליו בלילה שמע רבן גמליאל קולה ובכה כנגדה עד שנשרו ריסי עיניו למחר הכירו בו תלמידיו והוציאוה משכונתו (א) ודמעתה על לחיה אמר [ד] רבא אמר ר' יוחנן כאשה שבוכה על בעל נעוריה שנאמר (ג) אלי כבתולה חגורת שק על בעל נעוריה (ד) היו צריה לראש אמר [ה] רבא אמר רבי יוחנן [א] [ו] כל המיצר לישראל נעשה ראש שנאמר [א] (ה) כי לא מועף לאשר מוצק לה כעת הראשון הקל ארצה זבולון וארצה נפתלי והאחרון הכביד דרך הים עבר הירדן גליל הגוים אמר [ז] רבא אמר ר' יוחנן כל המציק לישראל אינו עיף (ו) לא אליכם כל עוברי דרך אמר [ח] רבא אמר ר' יוחנן מכאן לקובלנא מן התורה כל עוברי דרך אמר רב עמרם אמר רב עשאוני כעוברי על דת דאילו בסדום כתיב (ז) וה' המטיר על סדום ואילו בירושלים כתיב (ח) ממרום שלח אש בעצמותי וירדנה וגו' [ב] וכתיב (ט) ויגדל עון בת עמי מחטאת סדום וכי משוא פנים יש בדבר אמר [ט] רבא אמר ר' יוחנן מדה יתירה היתה בירושלים שלא היתה בסדום דאילו בסדום כתיב (י) הנה זה היה עון סדום אחותך גאון שבעת לחם ויד עני ואביון לא החזיקה וגו' ואילו בירושלים כתיב (כ) ידי נשים רחמניות בשלו ילדיהן (ל) סלה כל אבירי ה' בקרבי כאדם שאומר לחברו נפסלה מטבע זו (מ) פצו עליך פיהם אמר [י] רבא אמר רבי יוחנן בשביל מה הקדים פ"א לעי"ן בשביל מרגלים שאמרו בפיהם מה שלא ראו בעיניהם (נ) אוכלי עמי אכלו לחם ה' לא קראו אמר [כ] רבא אמר ר' יוחנן כל האוכל מלחמן של ישראל טועם טעם לחם ושאינו אוכל מלחמן של ישראל אינו טועם טעם לחם ה' לא קראו רב אמר אלו הדיינין ושמואל אמר אלו מלמדי תינוקות מי מנאן אמר רב אשי אנשי כנסת הגדולה מנאום אמר רב יהודה אמר רב בקשו עוד למנות אחד באה [ל] דמות דיוקנו של אביו (א) ונשטחה לפניהם ולא השגיחו עליה באה אש מן השמים ולחכה אש בספסליהם ולא השגיחו עליה יצאה בת קול ואמרה להם (ס) חזית איש מהיר במלאכתו לפני מלכים יתיצב בל יתיצב לפני חשוכים מי שהקדים ביתי לביתו ולא עוד אלא שביתי בנה בשבע שנים וביתו בנה בשלש עשרה שנה לפני מלכים יתיצב [בל יתיצב] לפני חשוכים ולא השגיח עליה יצאה בת קול ואמרה (ע) המעמך ישלמנה כי מאסת כי אתה תבחר ולא אני וגו' [מ] דורשי רשומות היו אומרים כולן באין לעולם הבא שנאמר (פ) לי גלעד ולי מנשה ואפרים מעוז ראשי יהודה מחוקקי מואב סיר רחצי על אדום אשליך נעלי עלי פלשת התרועעי לי גלעד [ג] [ס] (ולי מנשה) זה אחאב שנפל ברמות גלעד מנשה כמשמעו אפרים מעוז ראשי זה ירבעם דקאתי מאפרים יהודה מחוקקי זה אחיתופל דקאתי

רש"י

אחד. מן הנשבים לחברו: גמל. זו שמהלכת לפנינו סומא וכו': [מצד שרואה. שאינה אוכלת פעמים מצד ימין ופעמים מצד שמאל כבהמה הרואה שאוכלת מכאן ומכאן אלא מצד שרואה אוכלת]: יין מטפטף ושוקע. בקרקע ורואין אנו בין רגלינו הטיפין שנפלו כשעברה הגמל במקום זה מצד אחד שקוע ומצד אחר הטיפין של שמן שצפים: נפנה לצדדין. שכן דרך ישראל להיותו צנוע: רדף. השבאי דרך הגמל והמנהיג ומצא כדבריהם ואמרו [ס] אותם יהודים על אותו שבאי אדוניהם שהוא בן קלסתר מלך אשקנ"ק בלע"ז שהיה דיוקנו דומה למגמת פניו של אותו קלסתר של מלך שבזנות הולידו: על עסקי לילה. לפי שבכו אותו לילה בכיית חנם: קולו נשמע יותר מביום. כדאמרינן בעלמא (יומא דף כ.) מפני מה אין הקול נשמע ביום כבלילה מפני גלגל חמה המנסר ברקיע והיינו דכתיב בכה תבכה בלילה כדי שיהא קולה נשמע וירחמו עליה ואף על פי כן אין מנחם לה: כוכבים ומזלות בוכים. שנכמרו רחמים עליו: בוכה כנגדו. מתוך שנשמע בהדיא מרכך לבו של אדם השומע קולו לבכות עמו: ריסי עיניו. שער שבגבת העין היה נופל ונכפל על העין מרוב דמעות: אלי. קונו קינה מתרגמינן אילא: על בעל נעוריה. שבוכה תמיד ומלויה דמעות: על לחיה. לשון לחות ונערות כגון לא ויבש: מכאן לקובלנא מן התורה. כשאדם מודיע צערו לאחר צריך שיאמר לו לא תבא זאת לך כמו שבאה אלי כי קשה הוא לשמוע שפעמים חוזרת עליו והמקפיד על כך אין בו משום ניחוש. ל"א לקובלנא כשיש לו צרה יודיענה לרבים קובלנא צעקה ל"א נגד דמתרגמינן קבל כאדם שאומר לחברו לא כנגדך אני אומר: וירדנה. ושרף אותה והיינו עשאוני כעוברי דת שדנני באש כסדום: לא אליכם. נביא היה מתנודד על החורבן כאילו באה עליו צרה ומהפכה לאחרים ואומר להם לישראל לא תהא לכם צרה כזו כמדומה לי נביא היה מדבר כנגד בני משה או כנגד י' השבטים שלא הגלה נבוכדנצר: וירדנה. לשון שבירה כמו (במדבר כד) וירד מיעקב כאדם המושל בחברו להלקותו ולשברו: הכי גרסינן ויגדל עון בת עמי מחטאת סדום וכי משוא פנים יש בדבר והואיל וישראל רעים יותר מסדום למה לא נהפכו כסדום לשון אחר וכי משוא פנים יש בדבר דהתם כתיב וה' המטיר הוא בעצמו והכא כתיב שלא על ידי שליח: מדה יתירה לטובה. דבירושלים כתיב ידי נשים רחמניות בשלו ילדיהן היו לברות למו שהיתה מזמנת חברתה ואוכלת בנה אלמא רחמניות היו ואילו בסדום כתיב יד עני ואביון לא החזיקה ומדה זו כפרה עליהם שלא נהפכו לשון אחר מדה יתירה פורענות גדולה היתה בירושלים שילדיהם היו אוכלות זו עם זו דכתיב היו לברות למו ואילו בסדום כתיב גאון שבעת לחם שלא טעמו טעם עוני הא למדת גדול פורענות ירושלים מפורענות סדום ולא היה משוא פנים בדבר: סלה. לשון מסלה כלומר כל האבירים פסלם הקב"ה ועשאם פסולים וכבושים כמסלה זו והיינו דמיא למטבע שנפסל ואין לו תקנה: מפני מה הקדים פ"א לעי"ן. ברוב האלפא ביתא שבאיכה: מפני מרגלים. שהקדימו מאמר פיהם עד שלא ראו בעין: טועם טעם לחם. שהכותים מולאים טעמם בלחמם של ישראל שהנאה הוא להם כשגוזלין אותן: אלו הדיינין. מטה משפטו בשביל עונותיהם היו לחם עמי למאכל אויביו: מלמדי תינוקות. שעושין מלאכתן רמיה: מי מנאן. להנך מלכים והדיוטות דקתני במתני' אין להם חלק: עוד אחד. שלמה: דיוקנו. של דוד אביו נשתטח לפניהם שלא למנותו עמהם: בל יתיצב לפני חשוכים. בגיהנם: לפני מלכים יתיצב. בגן עדן ולא לפני חשוכים: המעמך ישלמנה. וכי עליכם לשלם תשלומי עונשו לאדם שאתם נמאסים בו בשלמה לומר שאין לו חלק לעולם הבא: כי אתה תבחר ולא אני. וכי הבחירה בכם תלויה ולא בי לומר מי שיש לו חלק ומי אין לו חלק הלא בי הדבר תלוי: דורשי רשומות. דורשי פסוקים כדכתיב (דניאל י) את הרשום בכתב אמת היו אומרים שלכולם יש להם חלק אפילו למנשה וירבעם ולאחאב: לי גלעד ולי מנשה. עלי לסבול עונם כדי שיהו הם זוכים: מנשה כמשמעו. מנשה בן חזקיהו: דקא

תורה אור השלם

א) בָּכוֹ תִבְכֶּה בַּלַּיְלָה וְדִמְעָתָהּ עַל לֶחֱיָהּ אֵין לָהּ מְנַחֵם מִכָּל אֹהֲבֶיהָ כָּל רֵעֶיהָ בָּגְדוּ בָהּ הָיוּ לָהּ לְאֹיְבִים: [איכה א, ב]

ב) וַתִּשָּׂא כָּל הָעֵדָה וַיִּתְּנוּ אֶת קוֹלָם וַיִּבְכּוּ הָעָם בַּלַּיְלָה הַהוּא: [במדבר יד, א]

ג) אֱלִי כִּבְתוּלָה חֲגֻרַת שַׂק עַל בַּעַל נְעוּרֶיהָ: [יואל א, ח]

ד) הָיוּ צָרֶיהָ לְרֹאשׁ אֹיְבֶיהָ שָׁלוּ כִּי יְיָ הוֹגָהּ עַל רֹב פְּשָׁעֶיהָ עוֹלָלֶיהָ הָלְכוּ שְׁבִי לִפְנֵי צָר: [איכה א, ה]

ה) כִּי לֹא מוּעָף לַאֲשֶׁר מוּצָק לָהּ כָּעֵת הָרִאשׁוֹן הֵקַל אַרְצָה זְבֻלוּן וְאַרְצָה נַפְתָּלִי וְהָאַחֲרוֹן הִכְבִּיד דֶּרֶךְ הַיָּם עֵבֶר הַיַּרְדֵּן גְּלִיל הַגּוֹיִם: [ישעיה ח, כג]

ו) לוֹא אֲלֵיכֶם כָּל עֹבְרֵי דֶרֶךְ הַבִּיטוּ וּרְאוּ אִם יֵשׁ מַכְאוֹב כְּמַכְאֹבִי אֲשֶׁר עוֹלַל לִי אֲשֶׁר הוֹגָה יְיָ בְּיוֹם חֲרוֹן אַפּוֹ: [איכה א, יב]

ז) וַיְיָ הִמְטִיר עַל סְדֹם וְעַל עֲמֹרָה גָּפְרִית וָאֵשׁ מֵאֵת יְיָ מִן הַשָּׁמָיִם: [בראשית יט, כד]

ח) מִמָּרוֹם שָׁלַח אֵשׁ בְּעַצְמֹתַי וַיִּרְדֶּנָּה פָּרַשׂ רֶשֶׁת לְרַגְלַי הֱשִׁיבַנִי אָחוֹר נְתָנַנִי שֹׁמֵמָה כָּל הַיּוֹם דָּוָה: [איכה א, יג]

ט) וַיִּגְדַּל עֲוֹן בַּת עַמִּי מֵחַטַּאת סְדֹם הַהֲפוּכָה כְמוֹ רָגַע וְלֹא חָלוּ בָהּ יָדָיִם: [איכה ד, ו]

י) הִנֵּה זֶה הָיָה עֲוֹן סְדֹם אֲחוֹתֵךְ גָּאוֹן שִׂבְעַת לֶחֶם וְשַׁלְוַת הַשְׁקֵט הָיָה לָהּ וְלִבְנוֹתֶיהָ וְיַד עָנִי וְאֶבְיוֹן לֹא הֶחֱזִיקָה: [יחזקאל טז, מט]

כ) יְדֵי נָשִׁים רַחֲמָנִיּוֹת בִּשְּׁלוּ יַלְדֵיהֶן הָיוּ לְבָרוֹת לָמוֹ בְּשֶׁבֶר בַּת עַמִּי: [איכה ד, י]

ל) סִלָּה כָל אַבִּירַי אֲדֹנָי בְּקִרְבִּי קָרָא עָלַי מוֹעֵד לִשְׁבֹּר בַּחוּרָי גַּת דָּרַךְ אֲדֹנָי לִבְתוּלַת בַּת יְהוּדָה: [איכה א, טו]

מ) פָּצוּ עָלַיִךְ פִּיהֶם כָּל אוֹיְבַיִךְ שָׁרְקוּ וַיַּחַרְקוּ שֵׁן אָמְרוּ בִּלָּעְנוּ אַךְ זֶה הַיּוֹם שֶׁקִּוִּינֻהוּ מָצָאנוּ רָאִינוּ: [איכה ב, טז]

נ) הֲלֹא יָדְעוּ כָּל פֹּעֲלֵי אָוֶן אֹכְלֵי עַמִּי אָכְלוּ לֶחֶם יְיָ לֹא קָרָאוּ: [תהלים יד, ד]

ס) חָזִיתָ אִישׁ מָהִיר בִּמְלַאכְתּוֹ לִפְנֵי מְלָכִים יִתְיַצָּב בַּל יִתְיַצֵּב לִפְנֵי חֲשֻׁכִּים: [משלי כב, כט]

ע) הַמֵעִמְּךָ יְשַׁלְּמֶנָּה כִּי מָאַסְתָּ כִּי אַתָּה תִבְחַר וְלֹא אָנִי וּמַה יָּדַעְתָּ דַבֵּר: [איוב לד, לג]

פ) לִי גִלְעָד וְלִי מְנַשֶּׁה וְאֶפְרַיִם מָעוֹז רֹאשִׁי יְהוּדָה מְחֹקְקִי: מוֹאָב סִיר רַחְצִי עַל אֱדוֹם אַשְׁלִיךְ נַעֲלִי עָלַי פְּלֶשֶׁת הִתְרֹעָעִי: [תהלים ס, ט-י]

הגהות מהר"ב רנשבורג

א] בגמרא כל המיצר לישראל נעשה ראש שנא'. מלת שנאמר נמחק:

מסורת הש"ס

א) [פי' שהנכרי נפנה בדרך אצל בהמתו וישראל מסתלק לצדדים כך איתא בפי' הר"ש טהרות פ"ד מ"ה], ב) [תענית כט. סוטה לה.], ג) [צ"ל הלילה], ד) [צ"ל רבה], ה) [צ"ל רבה], ו) גיטין נו: ע"ש [עי' תוספות חגיגה יג: ד"ה שלא יאמרו ביד אומה שפילה מסר את בניו כלומר קודם שמילך כבר נעשה ראש], ז) [צ"ל רבה], ח) [צ"ל רבה], ט) [צ"ל רבה], י) [צ"ל רבה], כ) [צ"ל רבה], ל) [פי' נכון במאמר הלזה תמצא בשל"ה למסכת פסחים קעב.], מ) [עי' פירש"י ברכות כד. ד"ה דורשי וכו'], נ) [בע"י ליתא וכצ"ל], ס) [עי' בערוך ערך קלסטרא א' איתא הגירסא שהיא לפנינו בגמרא דהכא ואז תבין דברי רש"י הללו].

הגהות הב"ח

(א) גמרא דיוקנו של אביו. ונשתטחה לפניהם:

הגהות הגר"א

[א] גמ' שנא' כי לא מועף. נמחק תיבת שנאמר: [ב] שם וכתיב ויגדל. נמחק תיבת וכתיב: [ג] שם בסוף ולי מנשה. נמחקו ב' תיבות הללו:

ליקוטי רש"י

בכו תבכה. שתי בכיות על שתי חורבנין. בלילה. שהמקדש נשרף בלילה דאמר מר לעת ערב הציתו בו את האור דבר אחר בלילה לילה של בכיית מרגלים בתשעה באב גרמה להם, דבר אחר בלילה שכל הבוכה בלילה השומע קולו בוכה עמו [איכה א, ב]. אתם בכיתם בכיה של חנם. ולהפיל זרעם בגוים. מאותו שעה נגזר עליהם חורבן הבית שהרי ליל ט' באב בכו ואמר הקב"ה הם בכו בכיה של חנם ואני אקבע להם בכיה לדורות [תהלים קו, כז]. קרא עלי מועד. במסכת תענית (דף כט) תמוז דהשנה שתא של שנה השניה ליציאת מצרים שנשתלחו בה מרגלים בעשרים ותשעה בסיון מלויי מליוהו לתמוז לפיכך אירע בו יום חזרת מרגלים בשמונה באב ויבכו העם בלילה ההוא בתשעה באב בכו בכיה של חנם והוקבעה להם בכיה לדורות [שבועות י.]. כי לא מועף לאשר מוצק לה. כי מלך אשור אשר ניתן למוצק ולהצר לה לארצכם אינו עיף ואינו עצל מלבא עליהם עד שלש פעמים [ישעיהו ח, כג]. לא אליכם. לא תהא כצרה הזאת עוד לכל עוברי על דת אמרו חכמים מכאן לקובלנא מן התורה ראו מה עשה לי הביטו וראו וגומר [איכה א, יב]. וירדנה. וירדה אותה וישבר אותה וישבר אותה ע"י רידוי ויסורין לכן הנו"ן דגושה לפותרו בלשון יחידית כמו יעשנה יכרסמנה ירענה שהעלם נ' נקבה כמו דאת אומר (יחזקאל לו) העצמות היבשות שבר כל אחת ואחת, ד"א וירדנה כמו (שופטים יד) וירדהו אל כפיו הריק את המות גורר ורודה המות מתוכו [שם יג]. ויגדל עון וגו'. פורענותם מוכיח עליהם שגדול עונם משל סדום [שם ד, ו]. סלה. רמס ורפס לשון (ישעיה סב) סולו סולו המסילה [שם א, טו]. ה' לא קראו. לא חשבוהו ולא זכרו נפלאותיו ונוראותיו במשתיהם ונשתמשו בכליו ורבותינו פירשו כל שלא היה גוזל את ישראל לא היה טועם טעם ערב במאכלו אוכלי עמי נדמה להם כאוכלי לחם שטעמו טעם מאכל ערב [תהלים יד, ד]. המעמך ישלמנה כי מאסת וגו'. כך אמר אליהו לאיוב המעמך היה לו להקב"ה להימלך בפירעון תשלומין ממך. כי מאסת. לאמר מאסתי לא לעולם אחיה (איוב ז) יתר ידו ויבלעני (איוב ו) סבור אתה שיגבה ממך לפי דעתך ורצונך ואתה תבחר התשלומין ולא אני במקום הקב"ה דבר אליהו במיה [איוב לד, לג]. דורשי רשומות. קשרים וסתומים הכלולים בתורה דורשי תמורות גרסינן והיא היא [ברכות כד.].

Assembly enumerated them.[34]

The Gemara recounts an incident that took place at the time of the Great Assembly's deliberations:

אָמַר רַב יְהוּדָה אָמַר רַב – **Rav Yehudah said in the name of Rav:** בִּקְשׁוּ עוֹד לִמְנוֹת אֶחָד – **They sought to enumerate one more** king, i.e. Solomon.[35] בָּאָה דְמוּת דְּיוֹקְנוֹ שֶׁל אָבִיו וְנִשְׁתַּטְּחָה לִפְנֵיהֶם – At that moment **the image of his father** David **came and prostrated itself** in supplication **before [the Men of the Great Assembly],** entreating them not to include Solomon's name in the list, וְלֹא הִשְׁגִּיחוּ עָלֶיהָ – **but they did not pay attention to it.** בָּאָה אֵשׁ מִן הַשָּׁמַיִם וְלִחֲכָה אֵשׁ בְּסַפְסְלֵיהֶם – **A fire came** down **from heaven and the flames licked their benches,** וְלֹא הִשְׁגִּיחוּ עָלֶיהָ – **yet they would not pay attention to it.** יָצְאָה בַּת קוֹל וְאָמְרָה לָהֶם – **A heavenly voice rang out and said to them:** ,,חָזִיתָ אִישׁ מָהִיר בִּמְלַאכְתּוֹ לִפְנֵי־מְלָכִים יִתְיַצָּב בַּל־יִתְיַצֵּב לִפְנֵי חֲשֻׁכִּים'' – ***Do you see a man diligent at his work? He shall stand before kings; he shall not stand before darkened ones.***[36] מִי שֶׁהִקְדִּים בֵּיתִי לְבֵיתוֹ – **He who built My House** [the Temple] **before his own house,**[37] וְלֹא עוֹד – **and not only that,** אֶלָּא שֶׁבֵּיתִי בָּנָה בְּשֶׁבַע שָׁנִים – **but My House he built in seven years** וּבֵיתוֹ בָּנָה בִּשְׁלֹשׁ עֶשְׂרֵה שָׁנָה – **while his house he built in thirteen years,**[38] ,,לִפְנֵי־מְלָכִים יִתְיַצָּב [בַּל־יִתְיַצֵּב] לִפְנֵי חֲשֻׁכִּים'' – *[such a man]* ***shall stand before kings; he shall not stand before darkened ones,*** i.e. he shall be in the company of the righteous kings in Gan Eden, not with the wicked kings in Gehinnom. וְלֹא הִשְׁגִּיחַ עָלֶיהָ – **Still, [the Men of the Great Assembly] would not pay attention to [the voice].** יָצְאָה בַּת קוֹל וְאָמְרָה ,,הֲמֵעִמְּךָ יְשַׁלְּמֶנָּה כִּי־מָאַסְתָּ כִּי־אַתָּה תִבְחַר וְלֹא־אָנִי וגו'' – Thereupon **a** second **heavenly voice rang out and said:** ***Is it from you that [punishment] is meted out, that you despise [him]? Shall you choose and not I* etc.?**[39] At this, the Men of the Great Assembly desisted.[40]

Having shown that God alone decides who is included or excluded from the World to Come, the Gemara cites an opinion that even the wicked persons cited in our Mishnah enter the World to Come:

דּוֹרְשֵׁי רְשׁוּמוֹת הָיוּ אוֹמְרִים – **The Interpreters of Verses**[41] **used to say:** כּוּלָּן בָּאִין לָעוֹלָם הַבָּא – **All of them,** i.e. the persons listed in our Mishnah, **enter the World to Come,** שֶׁנֶּאֱמַר ,,לִי גִלְעָד וְלִי מְנַשֶּׁה וְאֶפְרַיִם מָעוֹז רֹאשִׁי יְהוּדָה מְחֹקְקִי מוֹאָב סִיר רַחְצִי עַל־אֱדוֹם אַשְׁלִיךְ נַעֲלִי עָלַי פְּלֶשֶׁת הִתְרוֹעָעִי'' – **as it is stated:** ***Gilead is mine, Menasheh is mine; Ephraim is the stronghold of my head; Judah is my lawgiver. Moab is my washbasin, upon Edom I will cast my lock – Philistia will make overtures of friendship to me.***[42] ,,לִי גִלְעָד'' (ולי מנשה) זֶה אַחְאָב – ***Gilead is mine*** – **this is** a reference to **Ahab,** שֶׁנָּפַל בְּרָמוֹת גִּלְעָד – **who fell** in battle **at Ramos Gilead.**[43] ,,מְנַשֶּׁה'' כְּמַשְׁמָעוֹ – ***Menasheh*** – **this is** a reference to King Menasheh, **as the name indicates.** ,,אֶפְרַיִם מָעוֹז רֹאשִׁי'' זֶה יָרָבְעָם – ***Ephraim is the stronghold of my head*** – **this is** a reference to **Yarovam** דְּקָאָתֵי מֵאֶפְרַיִם – **who was descended from** the tribe of **Ephraim.**[44] ,,יְהוּדָה מְחֹקְקִי'' זֶה אֲחִיתוֹפֶל – ***Judah is My lawgiver*** – **this is** a reference to **Achithophel,**[45]

NOTES

34. The Gemara means to ask: Who could possibly have declared the fates of these people in the Afterworld, a matter that is seemingly beyond the ken of mortals? The Gemara answers that it was the Men of the Great Assembly, who were possessed of the Divine Spirit, and among whom there were a number of prophets (*Be'er Sheva*).

35. Out of deference to Solomon, the Gemara does not refer to him by name, but says merely that they sought to enumerate "one more" (*R' Avigdor Miller*).

The reason for this attempted inclusion was Scripture's description of Solomon's later years (*I Kings* 11:4-5): *And it came to pass at the time of Solomon's old age, his wives turned his heart after other gods, and his heart was not complete with HASHEM as the heart of his father David. And Solomon went after Ashtores the god of the Zidonians and after Milkom the abomination of the Ammonites. And Solomon did that which was bad in the eyes of HASHEM, and he did not follow wholeheartedly after HASHEM like David his father (Maharsha).*

It must be noted, however, that the Gemara in *Shabbos* (56b) proves that this does not mean that Solomon actually worshiped idols. From the fact that Scripture states that *his heart was not complete with HASHEM as the heart of his father David,* it is clear that his sin consisted merely of not living up to the example of his father, not that he actually worshiped idols. Rather, since he did not prevent his wives from worshiping idols, Scripture considers it as if he himself had done so.

36. *Proverbs* 22:29.

37. Solomon began building the Temple in the fourth year of his reign and concluded it in the eleventh, as is stated in *I Kings* 6:36-37. In the following verse, it states that he began to build his palace. From this it is understood that he did not commence to build his palace until after the Temple was completed.

38. Ibid. 7:1.

39. *Job* 34:33. This verse, spoken by Elihu to Iyov, is here used to express God's harsh response to the Men of the Great Assembly: Do you have the power to punish the dead, that you despise Solomon (*Is it from you that it is meted out, that you despise*)? Is the choice as to who gets a share in the World to Come up to you and not Me (*Shall you choose and not I*)? Certainly not – that is My exclusive prerogative! (*Rashi*; cf. *Maharsha*).

40. As a general principle, God accords with the decisions of the great Torah sages in each generation. Accordingly, David feared that if Solomon were included in the Mishnah's list, he would indeed lose his share in the World to Come. Moreover, following the principle that the final say in Torah matters was left to the considered opinion of the Sages, the Men of the Great Assembly ignored David's entreaties, the supernatural fire and even the first Heavenly voice (*R' Avigdor Miller*). Only when the second voice informed them that the matter was beyond their jurisdiction did they desist. [Compare the similar incident recorded in *Bava Metzia* 59b.] See further, *Maharsha* and *Shelah, Maseches Pesachim* p. 172.

41. Literally: *inscriptions* (see *Rashi;* cf. *Rashi* to *Berachos* 24a ד"ה דורשי).

Alternatively, *R' Tzadok HaKohen* translates דּוֹרְשֵׁי רְשׁוּמוֹת as *those who seek out the traces (reshumos)*; e.g. those scholars who uncovered the traces of holiness in the souls of even the greatest sinners, thus ensuring *all* Jews a share in the World to Come (*Machsheves Charutz,* p. 89 col. 1).

42. *Psalms* 60:9-10 (see also ibid. 108:9-10). This Psalm was composed by David during one of his wars. He states that he had been promised by God that he would conquer all of Israel's surrounding enemy nations. According to the interpretation of the Interpreters of Verses, these two verses are not spoken by David, but by God, and the entire verse is a reference to the three kings and three Jewish commoners (i.e. Bilam excluded) enumerated in our Mishnah.

God says *Gilead is Mine, Menasheh is Mine,* etc.; that is, the sins of these persons are My burden and Mine alone, and I shall find a way to tolerate their sins so as to admit them into the World to Come (*Rashi*).

43. *I Kings* 22:29-37.

Ahab's death in battle atoned for his sins and gained him entry into the World to Come (*Maharsha*).

44. In the merit of Yarovam's being the "stronghold of my head" – i.e. the first king of the Ten Tribes and one appointed by a prophet – he ought not be consigned to Gehinnom (*Maharsha*).

[*Maharsha* notes that Menasheh is the only one of the kings or commoners mentioned in the verse by name. This is because the others gained entry to the World to Come for the particular reason hinted at by the verse's allusion to them (e.g. Ahab because he fell at Ramos Gilead, Yarovam because he was "my stronghold," i.e. the first king of the Ten Tribes, etc.). However, as far as their essence, represented by their names, they deserved to be excluded. Menasheh, by contrast, repented. He thereby gained a share in the World to Come based on his name, i.e. his essence.]

45. [Achithophel was the erstwhile advisor of King David, who deserted him and assisted the rebellion of Absalom (see *II Samuel* ch. 17).]

דְּקָאָתֵי מִיהוּדָה – who was descended from the tribe of **Judah.**[1] **,,מוֹאָב סִיר רַחְצִי" זֶה גֵּחֲזִי שֶׁלָּקָה עַל עִסְקֵי רְחִיצָה** – ***Moab is my washbasin*** – **this is** a reference to **Geichazi, who was smitten** with leprosy **on account of matters involving washing.**[2] **,,עַל־אֱדוֹם אַשְׁלִיךְ נַעֲלִי" זֶה דּוֹאֵג הָאֲדוֹמִי** – ***Upon Edom I will cast my lock*** – **this is** a reference to **Doeg the Edomite.**[3] **,,עָלַי פְּלֶשֶׁת הִתְרוֹעָעִי" אָמְרוּ מַלְאֲכֵי הַשָּׁרֵת לִפְנֵי הַקָּדוֹשׁ בָּרוּךְ הוּא** – ***Philistia will make overtures of friendship to me*** – **the ministering angels said to the Holy One, Blessed is He: רִבּוֹנוֹ שֶׁל עוֹלָם – Master of the Universe! אִם יָבֹא דָּוִד שֶׁהָרַג אֶת הַפְּלִשְׁתִּי וְהוֹרִישׁ אֶת בָּנֶיךָ גַּת – If David, who slew the Philistine** (Goliath) **and who gave possession of** the Philistine city of **Gath to Your children,**[4] **will come** and object that You have allowed his enemies Doeg and Achithophel into the World to Come, **מָה אַתָּה עוֹשֶׂה לוֹ – what will you do,** i.e. say, **to him? אָמַר לָהֶן – [God] said to [the ministering angels]: עָלַי לַעֲשׂוֹתָן רֵיעִים זֶה לָזֶה – It is** incumbent **upon Me to make them friends** *(rei'im)* **with each other.**[5]

Concluding its discussion of the three kings of the First Temple era who have no portion in the World to Come, the Gemara points out that these kings were not alone in their wickedness. Their subjects, the Jews of that era, likewise refused to repent, and hurled clever, impudent rejoinders at the prophets who sought to rebuke them and move them to repentance. The Gemara cites three examples of such behavior, starting with that given by Rav: **,,מַדּוּעַ שׁוֹבְבָה הָעָם הַזֶּה יְרוּשָׁלַםִ מְשֻׁבָה נִצַּחַת וגו'"** – Scripture states: ***Why is this people – Jerusalem – rebellious with a persistent rebellion*** **etc.?**[6] **אָמַר רַב – Rav said: תְּשׁוּבָה נִצַּחַת הֵשִׁיבָה כְּנֶסֶת יִשְׂרָאֵל לַנָּבִיא** – The verse indicates that **the Assembly of Israel** (the Jewish people), instead of accepting the prophet Zechariah's summons to repentance, **responded to the prophet with a defiant rejoinder.**[7] **אָמַר לָהֶן נָבִיא יִשְׂרָאֵל חִזְרוּ בִּתְשׁוּבָה – The prophet said to Israel: "Repent! אֲבוֹתֵיכֶם שֶׁחָטְאוּ הֵיכָן הֵם** – Consider: **Your ancestors who sinned, where are they** now? Dead!" **אָמְרוּ לָהֶן – [The Jews] said to [Zechariah]:**[8] **וּנְבִיאֵיכֶם שֶׁלֹּא חָטְאוּ הֵיכָן הֵם – "And your prophets, who did not sin, where are they** now? Also dead!" **שֶׁנֶּאֱמַר ,,אֲבוֹתֵיכֶם אַיֵּה־הֵם וְהַנְּבִאִים הַלְעוֹלָם יִחְיוּ" – As it is stated:** ***Your ancestors, where are they? And the prophets, do they live forever?***[9] **אָמַר לָהֶן – [The prophet Zechariah] said to [the Assembly of Israel]: (אֲבוֹתֵיכֶם) חָזְרוּ וְהוֹדוּ – "Your ancestors repented and confessed** their sins, **שֶׁנֶּאֱמַר ,,אַךְ דְּבָרַי וְחֻקַּי אֲשֶׁר צִוִּיתִי אֶת־עֲבָדַי הַנְּבִיאִים וגו'" – as it is stated** in the next verse: ***But the warnings and the decrees with which I charged my servants the prophets*** **etc.** *overtook your ancestors – did they not? – and in the end [those ancestors] had to admit: 'God has dealt with us according to our ways and our deeds, just as He purposed.'* " Thus, it behooves you to profit from the experience of your ancestors and repent before punishment befalls you as it befell them.[10]

It was to this defiance, this refusal to accept prophetic rebuke, that the verse in *Jeremiah* referred when it stated: *Why is this people – Jerusalem – rebellious with a persistent rebellion?*

Shmuel's example of the Jews' defiance of prophetic rebuke: **שְׁמוּאֵל אָמַר – Shmuel said: בָּאוּ עֲשָׂרָה בְּנֵי אָדָם וְיָשְׁבוּ לְפָנָיו** – The verse is referring to a different incident: **Ten persons came and**

NOTES

1. As is evident from David's description of Achithophel in *Psalms* 55:14 as *my kinsman,* which indicates that Achithophel, like David, was a member of the tribe of Judah (*Rashi*). See also *II Samuel* 15:12, where Achithophel is called *the man from Giloh,* a town located within the territory of the tribe of Judah (*Joshua* 15:51) (*Maharzu* to *Bamidbar Rabbah* 14:1).

As the Gemara teaches below (106b), Achithophel was originally a Torah teacher of David. Thus, God is saying that in the merit of Achithophel's being David's "lawgiver," i.e. teacher, Achithophel merits the Afterworld (*Maharsha* to 104b).

2. Geichazi was the servant of the prophet Elisha. Once, the Aramean general Naaman was stricken with leprosy and came to Elisha to be cured. Elisha told him to bathe seven times in the Jordan River and the leprosy would disappear. When this actually happened, Naaman wished to reward Elisha, but the latter steadfastly refused any compensation and sent Naaman on his way. Without telling Elisha, Geichazi ran after Naaman and told him that Elisha had changed his mind and would accept a gift after all. Naaman gladly complied and gave Geichazi silver and clothing. When Geichazi returned, Elisha sternly rebuked him for his conduct and informed him that he and his descendants would henceforth be stricken with leprosy (*II Kings* ch. 5; see 107b).

Thus, the *washbasin* is understood as a reference to Geichazi, who was punished because of his conduct after the bathing or washing of Naaman. However, his punishment through leprosy gained him forgiveness, returning to him his share in the World to Come (*Maharsha*).

The word *Moab* seems out of place here, for it has no connection to Geichazi. *Maharsha* (to 104b, in explanation of *Rashi* to 105a ד"ה מואב) suggests that it belongs to the preceding exegesis: *Judah is my lawgiver,* [*says David, who was descended from*] *Moab.*

3. *Upon Edom I will cast my lock* is understood here in a positive sense: Doeg will eventually be "locked up" in *Gan Eden* (*Rashi*).

In this explanation, *Rashi* is consistent with his commentary to *Psalms,* in which he renders נַעֲלִי as *my lock* (from מַנְעוּל). *Maharsha,* however, following most other commentaries ad loc. (and *Rashi* himself to *Psalms* 108:10) translates נַעֲלִי as *my shoe.* He explains that Doeg regained his share in the World to Come because his ashes were scattered in the synagogues (see below, 106b), and David trod on them; this was sufficient punishment for him.

4. See 102a note 26.

5. The phrase עָלַי פְּלֶשֶׁת הִתְרוֹעָעִי is thus translated: *It is incumbent upon me to make the conqueror of the Philistines (David) friends* with Doeg and Achithophel (*Rashi*).

David is referred to here in connection with the slaying of Goliath because it was when David fought Goliath that Doeg, as advisor to King Saul, cast aspersions upon David's ancestry (see *Yevamos* 76b). Subsequently, Doeg slandered David when the latter was given the sword of the slain Goliath by the Kohanim at Nov (see *I Samuel* 22:9-22). These aspersions and slanders were the chief causes of David's hostility to Doeg (*Maharsha; Toras Chaim*).

[According to this explanation, the main question raised by the ministering angels, and to which God addressed his reply, was the schism between David and Doeg, not between David and Achithophel (*Maharsha*). Indeed, the Gemara below, 106b, records a dialogue between God and David as to whether Doeg should be allowed entry into the World to Come.]

The view of the Interpreters of Verses is given as a dissenting opinion to the Mishnah's. The accepted view, however, is the Mishnah's – that all the above individuals are excluded from the World to Come (*Yad Ramah*). [See, however, *Ben Yehoyada* to the Mishnah (90a) and *Margaliyos HaYam* to 104b §18.]

6. *Jeremiah* 8:5. This is the usual translation. Rav, however, interprets the words שׁוֹבְבָה and מְשֻׁבָה as *responses* or *rejoinders.* Thus the verse is translated: *Why does this people – Jerusalem – respond with defiant responses?*

7. Literally: a victorious retort (from the Hebrew verb נצח, *to be victorious*), which usually refers to a successful riposte which leaves no room for counterargument. Our translation, *a defiant rejoinder*, focuses on their unwillingness to humbly accept prophetic rebuke.

8. [The translation follows *Maharshal,* who emends אָמְרוּ לָהֶן to אָמְרוּ לוֹ.]

9. *Zechariah* 1:5. This verse is interpreted here as a dialogue: The prophet says: *Your ancestors, where are they?* and the Jewish people rejoin: *And the prophets, do they live forever?*

10. [Our elucidation has followed the textual version of *Maharshal,* and is the one appearing in the Vilna edition. *Dikdukei Soferim* states, however, that most earlier prints omit the words אָמַר לָהֶן אֲבוֹתֵיכֶם. According to these versions, the Gemara's words חָזְרוּ וְהוֹדוּ refer to the Jews debating Zechariah. That is, in the end the Jews repented and admitted to the prophet their error, as the conclusion of v. 6 states: *and they responded and said*: *God has dealt with us according to our deeds* (see *Iyun Yaakov;* cf. *Maharsha*).]

דקאתי מיהודה מואב סיר רחצי זה גחזי שלקה על עסקי רחיצה על אדום אשליך נעלי זה דואג האדומי עלי פלשת התרועעי אמרו מלאכי השרת לפני הקב"ה רבש"ע אם יבא דוד שהרג את הפלשתי והוריש את בניך גת מה אתה עושה לו אמר להן עלי לעשותן ריעים זה לזה א) מדוע שובבה העם הזה ירושלים משובה נצחת וגו' אמר רב תשובה נצחת השיבה כנסת ישראל לנביא אמר להן נביא לישראל חזרו בתשובה אבותיכם שחטאו היכן הם אמרו להן ונביאיכם שלא חטאו היכן הם שנאמר ב) אבותיכם איה הם והנביאים הלעולם יחיו אמר להן (אבותיכם) חזרו והודו שנאמר ג) אך דברי וחוקי אשר צויתי את עבדי הנביאים וגו' שמואל אמר באו עשרה בני אדם וישבו לפניו אמר להן חזרו בתשובה אמרו לו עבד שמכרו רבו ואשה שגרשה בעלה כלום יש לזה על זה כלום אמר לו הקב"ה לנביא לך אמור להן ד) איזה ספר כריתות אמכם אשר שלחתיה או מי מנושי אשר מכרתי אתכם לו הן בעונותיכם נמכרתם ובפשעכם שלחה אמכם והיינו דאמר ריש לקיש מאי דכתיב ה) דוד עבדי ו) נבוכדנצר עבדי גלוי וידוע לפני מי שאמר והיה העולם שעתידין ישראל לומר כך לפיכך הקדים הקב"ה וקראו עבדו א) עבד שקנה נכסים עבד למי נכסים למי ז) והעולה על רוחכם היה לא תהיה אשר אתם אומרים נהיה כגוים כמשפחות הארצות לשרת עץ ואבן חי אני נאם ה' אלהים אם לא ביד חזקה ובזרוע נטויה ובחימה שפוכה אמלוך עליכם ב) אמר רב נחמן כל כי האי ריתחא לירתח רחמנא עלן ולפרוקינן ח) ויסרו למשפט אלהיו יורנו אמר רבה בר בר חנה אמר להן נביא לישראל חזרו בתשובה אמרו לו אין אנו יכולין יצר הרע שולט בנו אמר להם יסרו יצריכם אמרו לו אלהיו יורנו: ארבעה הדיוטות בלעם ודואג ואחיתופל וגחזי: בלעם ג) בלא עם דבר אחר בלעם שבלה עם בן בעור שבא על בעיר תנא הוא בעור הוא כושן רשעתים הוא לבן הארמי בעור שבא על בעיר כושן רשעתים דעבד שתי רשעיות בישראל אחת בימי יעקב ואחת בימי שפוט השופטים ומה שמו לבן הארמי שמו כתיב ט) בן בעור וכתיב י) בנו בעור אמר רבי יוחנן אביו בנו הוא לו בנביאות בלעם הוא דלא אתי לעלמא דאתי הא אחריני אתו מתניתין מני רבי יהושע היא דתניא ד) ר"א אומר יא) ישובו רשעים לשאולה כל גוים שכחי אלהים ישובו רשעים לשאולה אלו פושעי ישראל כל גוים שכחי אלהים אלו פושעי עובדי כוכבים דברי ר"א [א] אמר לו ר' יהושע וכי נאמר ה) בכל גוים והלא לא נאמר אלא כל גוים שכחי אלהים אלא ישובו רשעים לשאולה מאן נינהו כל גוים שכחי אלהים ואף אותו רשע נתן סימן בעצמו אמר יב) תמות נפשי מות ישרים אם תמות נפשי מות ישרים תהא אחריתי כמוהו ואם לאו יג) הנני הולך לעמי יד) וילכו זקני מואב וזקני מדין תנא מדין ומואב לא היה להם שלום מעולם משל לשני כלבים שהיו בעדר והיו צהובין זה לזה בא זאב על האחד אמר האחד אם איני עוזרו היום הורג אותו ולמחר בא עלי הלכו שניהם והרגו הזאב אמר רב פפא היינו דאמרי אינשי כרכושתא ושונרא עבדו הלולא מתרבא דביש גדא טו) וישבו שרי מואב עם בלעם ושרי מדין להיכן אזול כיון דאמר להו טו) לינו פה הלילה והשבותי אתכם דבר אמרו כלום יש אב ששונא את בנו אמר רב נחמן חוצפא אפילו כלפי שמיא מהני מעיקרא כתיב טז) לא תלך עמהם ולבסוף כתיב יז) קום לך אתם אמר רב ששת חוצפא ו) מלכותא בלא תאגא היא דכתיב יח) ואנכי היום רך ומשוח מלך והאנשים האלה בני צרויה קשים ממני וגו' א"ר יוחנן בלעם ז) חיגר ברגלו אחת היה שנאמר יט) וילך שפי שמשון בשתי רגליו שנאמר כ) שפיפון עלי אורח הנושך עקבי סוס בלעם סומא באחת מעיניו היה שנאמר י) שתום העין קוסם באמתו היה כתיב הכא כא) נופל וגלוי עינים וכתיב התם כב) והנה המן נופל על המטה וגו' איתמר מר זוטרא אמר קוסם באמתו היה מר בריה דרבינא אמר שבא על אתונו מ"ד קוסם באמתו היה כדאמרן ומ"ד בא על אתונו היה כתיב הכא ח) [א] כג) כרע שכב וכתיב התם כד) בין רגליה כרע

דקא אתי מיהודה. דקאמר לו דוד ואתה אנוש כערכי אלופי ומיודעי שהיה קורא לאחיתופל מיודעי קרובי שהיה משבט יהודה כדוד: מואב סיר רחצי. דוד דקא אתי ממואב: סיר רחצי. גחזי שסר ונצטרע על עסקי רחיצה: על אדום אשליך נעלי. אנעיל אותם בגן עדן: אם יבא דוד שהרג את הפלשתי. ויצעק לפניך על שאתה נותן חלק לדואג ואחיתופל לעוה"ב מה אתה עושה להפיס דעתו שהם היו שונאין אותו: אמר להם. עלי לפייסן ולעשותן ריעים ואהובים זה לזה והיינו התרועעי לשון ריעות: ושמואל אמר מאי תשובה נצחת כה"ג [באו] עשרה בני אדם וכו': עבד שמכרו רבו. ומאחר שמכרנו הקב"ה לנבוכדנצר וגרשנו מעליו יש לו עלינו כלום: מאי דכתיב ודוד עבדי נבוכדנצר עבדי. שקראו לאותו רשע עבד כמו שקראו לדוד דכתיב בסוף ירמיה (מג) הנני שולח ולקחתי את נבוכדנצר עבדי לא מפני שדומה זה לזה אלא גלוי וידוע לפני מי שאמר והיה העולם שעתידין ישראל לומר כבר מכרנו הקב"ה לנבוכדנצר לפיכך הקדים הקב"ה וקרא עבדי לנבוכדנצר כדי להחזיר להן תשובה: עבד למי נכסים למי. כלומר נבוכדנצר עבדי הוא וכל מה שקנה לי הוא ועדיין לא יצאתם מרשותי: והעולה על רוחכם היה לא תהיה. כל מה שאתם סבורים לא יהיה: כל כי האי ריתחא. מי יתן ויבא לנו זה הכעס בחימה שפוכה אמלוך עליכם שיגאלנו בעל כרחנו וימלוך עלינו: א"ר אבא בר כהנא. היינו תשובה נצחת דאמרו ליה אלהים יורנו שאין אנו יכולין ליסר אותו: בלא עם. שאין לו חלק עם עם: שבלה עם. שבלבל ישראל בעצתו שהשיאו לבלק כדבעינן למימר לקמן והפיל מהם כ"ד אלפים: בעור שבא על בעיר. שבא על אתונו כמו בהמה דמתרגמינן בעיר: תנא הוא בעור. אביו של בלעם הוא כושן רשעתים הוא לבן הארמי: אחת בימי יעקב. שרדף אחריו ובקש לעקור הכל: ואחת בימי שופטים. לאחר מיתת יהושע דכתיב (שופטים ג) ויחר אף ה' בישראל ויתנם ביד כושן רשעתים: בנו בעור. משמע בעור בנו של בלעם היה: בנו הוא. לבלעם בנביאות שבלעם גדול מאביו היה בנביאות: הא שאר נכרים אתו. כלומר מדקא חשיב תנא דמתניתין דבלעם שהיה נכרי בהדי הדיוטות וקאמר דאין לו חלק מכלל דשאר נכרים יש להם חלק: מתניתין מני וכו'. א"ל ר' יהושע אלו נאמר ישובו רשעים לשאולה ט) בכל הגוים משמע כדקאמרת השתא דכתיב כל גוים שכחי אלהים לא משמע אלא אותן השוכחים אלוה כגון בלעם [ושכמותו] אבל אחריני אתו כדאמרינן בריש פרקין (דף צא:) ורעו זרים צאנכם ובני נכר אכריכם לעולם הבא: מאי נינהו כל גוים שכחי אלהים. דמשום הכי בורר הקב"ה הרשעים שבהם ונותן אותם בגיהנם ואין להם חלק לעתיד אבל השאר יש להם חלק: ואף אותו רשע נתן סימן בעצמו. שאין לו חלק לעתיד: תמות נפשי מות ישרים. אם ימות מיתת עצמו תהא אחריתי כמוהו דודאי יש לו חלק עמהם: ואם לאו. דלא ימות אלא יהרג הנני הולך לעמי לגיהנם: לא היה להם שלום. דכתיב המכה את מדין בשדה מואב: צהובין. כעוסין כאדם שכועס פניו צהובין: כרכושתא. חולדה: כרכושתא ושונרא. אין להם שלום מעולם: ביש גדא. מזל רע: כלום יש אב ששונא את בנו. שהוא סבור שיאמר לו הקב"ה קלל את בני דקאמר בלעם לינו פה [הלילה]: חוצפא אפילו כלפי שמיא מהני. דאהני ליה מה שהחציף פניו לומר לשלוחי בלק י) לינו פה שאמר לו הקב"ה בתחילה לא תלך והדר אמר לך: מלכותא בלא תגא. כלומר שררה גדולה ואינו חסר אלא כתר מלכות: אנכי היום רך ומשוח מלך והאנשים האלה קשים ממני. כלומר איני גדול מהם אלא משיחת מלכות: שפי. כמו (חולין דף נד:) בוקא דאטמא דשף מדוכתיה: שפיפון. משמעו שתים: שתום העין. סתום פתוח כמו שתומו ניכר כ) כלומר עינו אחת פתוחה מכלל דהאחרת סתומה והכי נמי מתרגמינן דשפיר חזי אית דמפרשי סתום כמו סתום ולאו מילתא היא: קוסם באמתו. כגון מעלה בזכורו: כרע

מסורת הש"ס

א) [לעיל צא. מגילה טו.], ב) ר"ה לב:, ג) [גיר' הערוך בלע עם פי' שיעץ עצות לבלע עם ישראל ד"א בלעם בלא עם פי' שאין לו חלק עם ישראל. ערך בלע], ד) [תוספ' פי"ג], ה) [בילקוט ליתא אכן בע"י איתא בכל וגיר' זו נראה נכונה ודע דבתוספתא פרק י"ג תניא להך פלוגתא דר"א ור' יהושע בנוסחא אחריני ע"ש על נכון], ו) [לעיל לט:], ז) [סוטה י.], ח) [כל העובר על הפסוקים יראה דהך קרא כרע שכב דכתיב בפרשת בלק כ"ד פסוק ט' כרע שכב כארי וכלביא מי יקימנו בשבח לישראל נאמרה כדמפרש בתרגום ורש"י וכן בברכות יב: וע"ש דאין לענין כרע שכב שום שייכות לבלעם כלל ומצוה לתקן ולהסביר ועמ"ש בתקוני כלי שרת], ט) [צ"ל בכל], י) [בקרא דהכא לא כתיב כך ואולי כוונת רש"י על המכוון דכתיב כ"ב פסוק י"ט שבו גם בזה גם אתם הלילה], כ) [ע"ז סט: וע"ש ברש"י סט. ד"ה ותיגוב].

תורה אור השלם

א) מַדּוּעַ שׁוֹבְבָה הָעָם הַזֶּה יְרוּשָׁלַםִ מְשֻׁבָה נִצַּחַת הֶחֱזִיקוּ בַּתַּרְמִית מֵאֲנוּ לָשׁוּב: [ירמיה ח, ה]

ב) אֲבוֹתֵיכֶם אַיֵּה הֵם וְהַנְּבִאִים הַלְעוֹלָם יִחְיוּ: [זכריה א, ה]

ג) אַךְ דְּבָרַי וְחֻקַּי אֲשֶׁר צִוִּיתִי אֶת עֲבָדַי הַנְּבִיאִים הֲלוֹא הִשִּׂיגוּ אֲבֹתֵיכֶם וַיָּשׁוּבוּ וַיֹּאמְרוּ כַּאֲשֶׁר זָמַם יְיָ צְבָאוֹת לַעֲשׂוֹת לָנוּ כִּדְרָכֵינוּ וּכְמַעֲלָלֵינוּ כֵּן עָשָׂה אִתָּנוּ: [זכריה א, ו]

ד) כֹּה אָמַר יְיָ אֵי זֶה סֵפֶר כְּרִיתוּת אִמְּכֶם אֲשֶׁר שִׁלַּחְתִּיהָ אוֹ מִי מִנּוֹשַׁי אֲשֶׁר מָכַרְתִּי אֶתְכֶם לוֹ הֵן בַּעֲוֹנֹתֵיכֶם נִמְכַּרְתֶּם וּבְפִשְׁעֵיכֶם שֻׁלְּחָה אִמְּכֶם: [ישעיה נ, א]

ה) וְעַתָּה עֲשׂוּ כִּי יְיָ אָמַר אֶל דָּוִד לֵאמֹר בְּיַד דָּוִד עַבְדִּי הוֹשִׁיעַ אֶת עַמִּי יִשְׂרָאֵל מִיַּד פְּלִשְׁתִּים וּמִיַּד כָּל אֹיְבֵיהֶם: [שמואל ב' ג, יח]

ו) וְאָמַרְתָּ אֲלֵיהֶם כֹּה אָמַר יְיָ צְבָאוֹת אֱלֹהֵי יִשְׂרָאֵל הִנְנִי שֹׁלֵחַ וְלָקַחְתִּי אֶת נְבוּכַדְרֶאצַּר מֶלֶךְ בָּבֶל עַבְדִּי וְשַׂמְתִּי כִסְאוֹ מִמַּעַל לָאֲבָנִים הָאֵלֶּה אֲשֶׁר טָמָנְתִּי וְנָטָה אֶת שַׁפְרִירוֹ עֲלֵיהֶם: [ירמיה מג, י]

ז) וְהָעֹלָה עַל רוּחֲכֶם הָיוֹ לֹא תִהְיֶה אֲשֶׁר אַתֶּם אֹמְרִים נִהְיֶה כַגּוֹיִם כְּמִשְׁפְּחוֹת הָאֲרָצוֹת לְשָׁרֵת עֵץ וָאָבֶן: חַי אָנִי נְאֻם אֲדֹנָי אֱלֹהִים אִם לֹא בְּיָד חֲזָקָה וּבִזְרוֹעַ נְטוּיָה וּבְחֵמָה שְׁפוּכָה אֶמְלוֹךְ עֲלֵיכֶם: [יחזקאל כ, לב-לג]

ח) וְיִסְּרוֹ לַמִּשְׁפָּט אֱלֹהָיו יוֹרֶנּוּ: [ישעיה כח, כו]

ט) וַיִּשְׁלַח מַלְאָכִים אֶל בִּלְעָם בֶּן בְּעוֹר פְּתוֹרָה אֲשֶׁר עַל הַנָּהָר אֶרֶץ בְּנֵי עַמּוֹ לִקְרֹא לוֹ לֵאמֹר הִנֵּה עַם יָצָא מִמִּצְרַיִם הִנֵּה כִסָּה אֶת עֵין הָאָרֶץ וְהוּא יֹשֵׁב מִמֻּלִי: [במדבר כב, ה] י) וַיִּשָּׂא מְשָׁלוֹ וַיֹּאמַר נְאֻם בִּלְעָם בְּנוֹ בְעֹר וּנְאֻם הַגֶּבֶר שְׁתֻם הָעָיִן: [במדבר כד, ג] יא) יָשׁוּבוּ רְשָׁעִים לִשְׁאוֹלָה כָּל גּוֹיִם שְׁכֵחֵי אֱלֹהִים: [תהלים ט, יח] יב) מִי מָנָה עֲפַר יַעֲקֹב וּמִסְפָּר אֶת רֹבַע יִשְׂרָאֵל תָּמֹת נַפְשִׁי מוֹת יְשָׁרִים וּתְהִי אַחֲרִיתִי כָּמֹהוּ: [במדבר כג, י] יג) וְעַתָּה הִנְנִי הוֹלֵךְ לְעַמִּי לְכָה אִיעָצְךָ אֲשֶׁר יַעֲשֶׂה הָעָם הַזֶּה לְעַמְּךָ בְּאַחֲרִית הַיָּמִים: [במדבר כד, יד] יד) וַיֵּלְכוּ זִקְנֵי מוֹאָב וְזִקְנֵי מִדְיָן וּקְסָמִים בְּיָדָם וַיָּבֹאוּ אֶל בִּלְעָם וַיְדַבְּרוּ אֵלָיו דִּבְרֵי בָלָק: [במדבר כב, ז] טו) וַיֹּאמֶר אֲלֵיהֶם לִינוּ פֹה הַלַּיְלָה וַהֲשִׁבֹתִי אֶתְכֶם דָּבָר כַּאֲשֶׁר יְדַבֵּר יְיָ אֵלָי וַיֵּשְׁבוּ שָׂרֵי מוֹאָב עִם בִּלְעָם: [במדבר כב, ח] טז) וַיֹּאמֶר אֱלֹהִים אֶל בִּלְעָם לֹא תֵלֵךְ עִמָּהֶם לֹא תָאֹר אֶת הָעָם כִּי בָרוּךְ הוּא: [במדבר כב, יב] יז) וַיָּבֹא אֱלֹהִים אֶל בִּלְעָם לַיְלָה וַיֹּאמֶר לוֹ אִם לִקְרֹא לְךָ בָּאוּ הָאֲנָשִׁים קוּם לֵךְ אִתָּם וְאַךְ אֶת הַדָּבָר אֲשֶׁר אֲדַבֵּר אֵלֶיךָ אֹתוֹ תַעֲשֶׂה: [במדבר כב, כ] יח) וְאָנֹכִי הַיּוֹם רַךְ וּמָשׁוּחַ מֶלֶךְ וְהָאֲנָשִׁים הָאֵלֶּה בְּנֵי צְרוּיָה קָשִׁים מִמֶּנִּי יְשַׁלֵּם יְיָ לְעֹשֵׂה הָרָעָה כְּרָעָתוֹ: [שמואל ב' ג, לט] יט) וַיֹּאמֶר בִּלְעָם לְבָלָק הִתְיַצֵּב עַל עֹלָתֶךָ וְאֵלְכָה אוּלַי יִקָּרֵה יְיָ לִקְרָאתִי וּדְבַר מַה יַּרְאֵנִי וְהִגַּדְתִּי לָךְ וַיֵּלֶךְ שֶׁפִי: [במדבר כג, ג] כ) יְהִי דָן נָחָשׁ עֲלֵי דֶרֶךְ שְׁפִיפֹן עֲלֵי אֹרַח הַנֹּשֵׁךְ עִקְּבֵי סוּס וַיִּפֹּל רֹכְבוֹ אָחוֹר: [בראשית מט, יז] כא) נְאֻם שֹׁמֵעַ אִמְרֵי אֵל וְיֹדֵעַ דַּעַת עֶלְיוֹן מַחֲזֵה שַׁדַּי יֶחֱזֶה נֹפֵל וּגְלוּי עֵינָיִם: [במדבר כד, טז] כב) וְהַמֶּלֶךְ שָׁב מִגִּנַּת הַבִּיתָן אֶל בֵּית מִשְׁתֵּה הַיַּיִן וְהָמָן נֹפֵל עַל הַמִּטָּה אֲשֶׁר אֶסְתֵּר עָלֶיהָ וַיֹּאמֶר הַמֶּלֶךְ הֲגַם לִכְבּוֹשׁ אֶת הַמַּלְכָּה עִמִּי בַּבָּיִת הַדָּבָר יָצָא מִפִּי הַמֶּלֶךְ וּפְנֵי הָמָן חָפוּ: [אסתר ז, ח] כג) כָּרַע שָׁכַב כַּאֲרִי וּכְלָבִיא מִי יְקִימֶנּוּ מְבָרְכֶיךָ בָרוּךְ וְאֹרְרֶיךָ אָרוּר: [במדבר כד, ט] כד) בֵּין רַגְלֶיהָ כָּרַע נָפַל שָׁכָב בֵּין רַגְלֶיהָ כָּרַע נָפָל בַּאֲשֶׁר כָּרַע שָׁם נָפַל שָׁדוּד: [שופטים ה, כז]

[א מיי' פ' י"א מהלכות עדות דין י ופ"ג מהל' תשובה דין ה]:

הגהות הגר"א

[א] גמ' כתיב הכא כרע שכב. נמחק ב' תיבות כרע שכב וג"ב נופל:

ליקוטי רש"י

אבותיכם איה הם. ראו שלקו מכה רעה ברעב בחרב ובשבי. והנביאים הלעולם יחיו. וא"ת אף הנביאים איה הם הרי מתו אני משיב לכם וכי הנביאים היה להם לעולם לחיות אך סופן מוכיח כי אמת היה דבריהם שכל דברי וחוקי גזירות פורענותי אשר צויתי את עבדי הנביאים עליכם הלא השיגו אבותיכם [זכריה א, ה]. באו עשרה בני אדם וישבו לפניו. ויהי בשנה השביעית בחמישי בעשור לחודש באו אנשים מזקני ישראל לדרוש את ה' וישבו לפני. לדרוש את ה' על צרכיהם ואם אינו שומע לנו גם אנו לא נענש על עבירות שבידנו שהרי כבר מכרנו ואין לו עלינו כלום עבד שמכרו רבו ואשה שגרשה בעלה כלום יש לזה על זה כלום ומסוף הענין אתה למד מחשבה שהשיבו והעולה על רוחכם וגו' [יחזקאל כ, א]. והעולה על רוחכם. שעולה על דעתכם. נהיה כגוים. נפרוק עולו מעל צוארנו מאחר שהוציאנו מעליו. היו לא תהיה. כי כבר קבלתם עליכם מדעתכם בימי יהושע כמו שנאמר (יהושע כד) ויאסוף יהושע את כל שבטי ישראל וכל הענין [יחזקאל כ, לב]. זו מדה טובה לישראל שכל זמן שיהיו אומרים הואיל וגלינו בין האומות נעשה כמעשיהם אני איני מניחם אלא מעמיד אני את נביאי ומחזירם לתחת כנפי שנאמר (יחזקאל כ, לב) והעולה על רוחכם היו לא תהיה וגו' חי אני וגו' אם לא ביד חזקה וגו' [ויקרא כו, מא]. בימי שפוט השופטים. לפני מלוך מלך שאול שהיו הדורות מתפרנסים על ידי שופטים ובימי אבצן היה שאמרו רבותינו אבצן זה בועז [רות א, א]. בנו בעור. כמו למעינו מים (תהלים קיד, ח). ומדרש אגדה שניהם היו גדולים מאבותיהם בלק בנו צפור אביו בנו הוא במלכות ובלעם גדול מאביו בנביאות מנה בן פרס היה [במדבר כד, ג]. זקני מואב וזקני מדין. והלא מעולם היו שונאים זה את זה שנאמר (בראשית לו, לה) המכה את מדין בשדה מואב שבאו מדין על מואב למלחמה אלא מיראתן של ישראל עשו שלום ביניהם [במדבר כב, ד]. המכה את מדין בשדה מואב. שבא מדין על מואב למלחמה והלך מלך אדום לעזור את מואב ומכאן אנו למדים שהיו מדין ומואב מריבים זה עם זה ובימי בלעם עשו שלום להתקשר על ישראל [בראשית לו, לה]. מלכותא בלא תגא. שר גדול שאינו מעוטר [לעיל צט.]. שפי. אשלוייש"ה כמו דשף מדוכתיה [חולין דף נד:]. שפיפון. שפייה כפולה [סוטה י.]. שתם העין. עינו נקורה ומוצאת לחוץ וחור שלה נראה פתוח ולשון משנה הוא כדי שישתום ויסתום ויגוב (ע"ז סט.) ורבותינו אמרו לפי שאמר ומספר את רובע ישראל שהקב"ה יושב ומונה רביעיותיהן של ישראל מתי תבא טפה שנולד הצדיק ממנה אמר בלבו מי שהוא קדוש ומשרתיו קדושים יסתכל בדברים הללו ועל דבר זה נסמת עינו של בלעם ויש מפרשים שתום העין פתוח העין כמו שתרגם אונקלוס ועל שאמר שתום העין ולא אמר שתום העינים למדנו שסומא באחת מעיניו היה [במדבר כד, ג].

sat down before [the prophet Ezekiel]. אָמַר לָהֶן חִזְרוּ בִּתְשׁוּבָה – **[Ezekiel] said to them: "Repent!"** אָמְרוּ לוֹ – **They said to him:** עֶבֶד שֶׁמְּכָרוֹ רַבּוֹ וְאִשָּׁה שֶׁגֵּרְשָׁהּ בַּעְלָהּ – **"A slave whose master has sold him, or a wife whose husband has divorced her,** כְּלוּם יֵשׁ לָזֶה עַל זֶה כְּלוּם – **do they have any [claim] on each other** any longer?" Of course not! I.e. by the same token, God, Who has allowed us to be conquered and enslaved by the king of Babylon, has thereby sold us and divorced Himself from us. Since we no longer belong to Him but to the king of Babylon, God no longer has any claims on us and cannot by right demand our repentance.[11] אָמַר לוֹ הַקָּדוֹשׁ בָּרוּךְ הוּא לַנָּבִיא – Thereupon, **the Holy One, Blessed is He, said to the prophet:** לֵךְ אֱמוֹר לָהֶן ,,אֵי זֶה סֵפֶר כְּרִיתוּת אִמְּכֶם אֲשֶׁר שִׁלַּחְתִּיהָ אוֹ מִי מִנּוֹשַׁי אֲשֶׁר־מָכַרְתִּי אֶתְכֶם לוֹ – **"Go say to them** the words I spoke to the prophet Isaiah: ***Where is the divorce document of your mother whom I dismissed? And which of My creditors was it to whom I sold you off?*** הֵן בַּעֲוֹנֹתֵיכֶם נִמְכַּרְתֶּם וּבְפִשְׁעֵיכֶם שֻׁלְּחָה אִמְּכֶם" – ***It was for your sins that you were sold off, and your mother was dismissed for your crimes."***[12]

The Gemara adds:

וְהַיְינוּ דְּאָמַר רֵישׁ לָקִישׁ – **And this is what Reish Lakish** meant when he **said:** מַאי דִּכְתִיב ,,דָּוִד עַבְדִּי" ,,נְבוּכַדְנֶצַּר . . . עַבְדִּי" – **What is** the meaning of **that which is written:** ***My servant David*** and ***My servant Nebuchadnezzar*?**[13] That is, why did God refer to the wicked Nebuchadnezzar by the same term, *My servant,* as he did to the righteous David? גָּלוּי וְיָדוּעַ לִפְנֵי מִי שֶׁאָמַר וְהָיָה הָעוֹלָם – For **it was clearly known** beforehand **to Him Who spoke and thereby brought the world into being,** i.e. God, שֶׁעֲתִידִין יִשְׂרָאֵל לוֹמַר כָּךְ – **that in the future the Jews would say this,** i.e. that after their conquest by Nebuchadnezzar they would claim that they were no longer God's subjects but Nebuchadnezzar's. לְפִיכָךְ הִקְדִּים הַקָּדוֹשׁ בָּרוּךְ הוּא וּקְרָאוֹ עַבְדּוֹ – **Therefore the Holy One, Blessed is He, anticipated** them **and referred to [Nebuchadnezzar] as His servant.** עֶבֶד שֶׁקָּנָה נְכָסִים עֶבֶד לְמִי נְכָסִים לְמִי – For **a servant who acquires property, to whom does the servant belong and to whom does the property belong?** Certainly to the master! Therefore, even though the Jews were conquered by Nebuchadnezzar they still belonged to God, for Nebuchadnezzar was God's servant; thus everything he conquered belonged to God.

It was this refusal to listen to Ezekiel, this claim that God no longer had the right to make demands of them, to which the verse in *Jeremiah* referred when it stated: *Why is this people — Jerusalem — rebellious with a persistent rebellion?*

As we have seen, the Jews of Ezekiel's time claimed that they no longer had any connection with God, that they belonged to their conquerors and as such were no longer obligated to obey the Torah. This claim was strongly rejected by God. The Gemara now presents the Scriptural passage where this objection is explicitly stated, *Ezekiel* 20:32-33, and Rav Nachman's comment on it:

,,וְהָעֹלָה עַל־רוּחֲכֶם הָיוֹ לֹא תִהְיֶה – ***What you have in mind shall never come to pass!*** אֲשֶׁר אַתֶּם אֹמְרִים נִהְיֶה כַגּוֹיִם כְּמִשְׁפְּחוֹת הָאֲרָצוֹת לְשָׁרֵת עֵץ וָאָבֶן – ***that which you say, "We will be like the nations, like the families of the lands, to worship wood and stone."*** חַי־אָנִי נְאֻם ה׳ אֱלֹהִים אִם־לֹא בְּיָד חֲזָקָה וּבִזְרוֹעַ נְטוּיָה וּבְחֵמָה שְׁפוּכָה אֶמְלוֹךְ עֲלֵיכֶם" – ***As I live — declares my Lord Hashem/Elohim — with a strong hand and an outstretched arm and with outpoured fury will I rule over you!*** אָמַר רַב נַחְמָן – **Rav Nachman said:** כָּל כִּי הַאי רִיתְחָא לִירְתַּח רַחֲמָנָא עֲלַן וְלִפְרוֹקִינַן – **O that the Merciful One would bring all this wrath upon us and redeem us!**[14]

Rabbah bar bar Chanah's example of the Jews' defiance of prophetic rebuke:

,,וְיִסְּרוֹ לַמִּשְׁפָּט אֱלֹהָיו יוֹרֶנּוּ" – Scripture states: ***Let him chastise it to [compel it to do what is] right. Let its God instruct it.***[15] אָמַר רַבָּה בַּר בַּר חָנָה – **Rabbah bar bar Chanah said:** אָמַר לָהֶן נָבִיא לְיִשְׂרָאֵל – **The prophet** Isaiah **said to Israel:** חִזְרוּ בִּתְשׁוּבָה – **"Repent!"** אָמְרוּ לוֹ – **They said to him:** אֵין אָנוּ יְכוֹלִין – **"We are not able** to do so. יֵצֶר הָרַע שׁוֹלֵט בָּנוּ – Our **Evil Inclination** is so powerful that it **controls us."** אָמַר לָהֶם – **[Isaiah] said to them:** יַסְּרוּ יִצְרֵיכֶם – **"Chastise,** i.e. overcome, **your Inclination** and repent." אָמְרוּ לוֹ ,,אֱלֹהָיו יוֹרֶנּוּ" – **They said to [Isaiah]: "Let its God,** Who created it [the Evil Inclination], **instruct it** not to seduce us." I.e. if God will not do so, then we are not to blame for following its urgings.

Thus, instead of heeding the prophet Isaiah's call to repentance, the Jews responded with counterarguments.[16]

The Gemara's discussion of the three kings who have no share in the World to Come is concluded. The Gemara now proceeds to the next part of our Mishnah, the four commoners who have no share in the World to Come:

אַרְבָּעָה הֶדְיוֹטוֹת בִּלְעָם וְדוֹאֵג וַאֲחִיתוֹפֶל וְגֵחֲזִי – **FOUR COMMONERS: BILAM, DOEG, ACHITHOPHEL, AND GEICHAZI.**

The Gemara analyzes the name "Bilam":

בִּלְעָם ,,בְּלֹא עַם" – **Bilam** was so called because he was a man **without a people** *(belo am).*[17] דָּבָר אַחֵר – **An alternate explanation:** בִּלְעָם שֶׁ,,בִּלָּה עַם" – **Bilam** was so called **because he confused the people** *(bilah am)* of Israel.[18]

NOTES

11. In *Ezekiel* 20:1, Scripture tells of *a group of men from among the elders of Israel* who came to Ezekiel to *inquire of Hashem.* However, neither the identity of these men nor the nature of their inquiry is revealed there. Shmuel teaches that these were a group of ten men who came to ask Ezekiel to pray to God on their behalf. They declared: If God answers us favorably, fine. However, if he does not, but rather leaves us in the hands of Nebuchadnezzar, then He has no right to punish us for our sins, for a husband who has divorced his wife or a master who has sold his servant no longer has a claim of loyalty upon them (*Rashi* to *Ezekiel* 20:1).

12. *Isaiah* 50:1. I.e. you were not actually divorced or sold, for you have no bill of divorce and I have no creditors. Rather, our separation is a temporary estrangement due to your sins, and when your sins will ultimately be expiated I will take you back (see *Radak* ad loc.).

13. See *II Samuel* 3:18 and *Jeremiah* 43:10. [The verse in *Jeremiah* uses the alternate name נְבוּכַדְרֶאצַּר common in this book.]

14. The verse states that the House of Israel yearned to be like the pagan nations of the world, but that God responded that He would force His rulership upon them. To this Rav Nachman exclaimed: Would that God indeed pour out upon us all the fury mentioned here and thereby bring about the redemption and rule over us, even against our wishes! (*Rashi*).

15. *Isaiah* 28:26. This difficult verse is variously translated and interpreted. Our translation reflects Rabbah bar bar Chanah's interpretation of the verse as a dialogue; see below.

16. The argument of the Jews was, of course, absurd. God created man with free will. Had the Jews chosen to resist the Evil Inclination they certainly could have done so. In reality they did not want to stop sinning, so they sought to defend their actions on philosophical grounds, in effect blaming God for their sins (*Yad Ramah*).

17. He had no connection with any particular people (*Rashi;* see *Pesach Einayim* for what this might mean; see also *Maharal*).

Alternatively, he had no connection with the Jewish people (*Aruch* ע׳ בלעם). [Presumably this refers to sharing their lot in the World to Come.]

18. I.e. through his devious counsel, Bilam confused the Jews and led them to sin.

After repeated unsuccessful attempts to curse the Jewish people, Bilam advised King Balak of Moab that it was useless to try to curse the

דקאתי מיהודה מואב סיר רחצי זה גחזי שלקה על עסקי רחיצה על אדום אשליך נעלי זה דואג האדומי עלי פלשת התרועעי אמרו מלאכי השרת לפני הקב"ה רבש"ע אם יבא דוד שהרג את הפלשתי והוריש את בניך גת מה אתה עושה לו אמר להן עלי לעשותן ריעים זה לזה א) מדוע שובבה העם הזה ירושלים משובה נצחת וגו' אמר רב תשובה נצחת השיבה כנסת ישראל לנביא אמר להן נביא לישראל חזרו בתשובה אבותיכם שחטאו היכן הם אמרו להן ונביאיכם שלא חטאו היכן הם שנאמר ב) אבותיכם איה הם והנביאים הלעולם יחיו אמר להן (אבותיכם) חזרו והודו שנאמר ג) אך דברי וחוקי אשר צויתי את עבדי הנביאים וגו' שמואל אמר באו עשרה בני אדם וישבו לפניו אמר להן חזרו בתשובה אמרו לו עבד שמכרו רבו ואשה שגרשה בעלה כלום יש לזה על זה כלום אמר לו הקב"ה לנביא לך אמור להן ד) איזה ספר כריתות אמכם אשר שלחתיה או מי מנושי אשר מכרתי אתכם לו הן בעונותיכם נמכרתם ובפשעכם שלחה אמכם והיינו דאמר ריש לקיש מאי דכתיב ה) דוד עבדי ו) נבוכדנצר עבדי גלוי וידוע לפני מי שאמר והיה העולם שעתידין ישראל לומר כך לפיכך הקדים הקב"ה וקראו עבדו א) עבד שקנה נכסים עבד למי נכסים למי ז) והעולה על רוחכם היה לא תהיה אשר אתם אומרים נהיה כגוים כמשפחות הארצות לשרת עץ ואבן חי אני נאם ה' אלהים אם לא ביד חזקה ובזרוע נטויה ובחימה שפוכה אמלוך עליכם ב) אמר רב נחמן כל כי האי ריתחא לירתח רחמנא עלן ולפרוקינן ח) ויסרו למשפט אלהיו יורנו אמר רבה בר בר חנה אמר להן נביא לישראל חזרו בתשובה אמרו לו אין אנו יכולין יצר הרע שולט בנו אמר להם יסרו יצריכם אמרו לו אלהיו יורנו: ארבעה הדיוטות בלעם ודואג ואחיתופל וגחזי: בלעם ג) בלא עם דבר אחר בלעם שבלה עם בן בעור שבא על בעיר תנא הוא בעור הוא כושן רשעתים הוא לבן הארמי בעור שבא על בעיר כושן רשעתים דעבד שתי רשעיות בישראל אחת בימי יעקב ואחת בימי שפוט השופטים ומה שמו לבן הארמי שמו כתיב ט) בן בעור וכתיב י) בנו בעור אמר רבי יוחנן אביו בנו הוא לו בנביאות בלעם הוא דלא אתי לעלמא דאתי הא אחריני אתו מתניתין מני רבי יהושע היא דתניא ד) ר"א אומר יא) ישובו רשעים לשאולה כל גוים שכחי אלהים ישובו רשעים לשאולה אלו פושעי ישראל כל גוים שכחי אלהים אלו פושעי עובדי כוכבים דברי ר"א [א] אמר לו ר' יהושע וכי נאמר ה) בכל גוים והלא לא נאמר אלא כל גוים שכחי אלהים אלא ישובו רשעים לשאולה מאן נינהו כל גוים שכחי אלהים ואף אותו רשע נתן סימן בעצמו אמר יב) תמות נפשי מות ישרים אם תמות נפשי מות ישרים תהא אחריתי כמוהו ואם לאו יג) הנני הולך לעמי יד) וילכו זקני מואב וזקני מדין תנא מדין ומואב לא היה להם שלום מעולם משל לשני כלבים שהיו בעדר והיו צהובין זה לזה בא זאב על האחד אמר האחד אם איני עוזרו היום הורג אותו ולמחר בא עלי הלכו שניהם והרגו הזאב אמר רב פפא היינו דאמרי אינשי כרכושתא ושונרא עבדו הלולא מתרבא דביש גדא טו) וישבו שרי מואב עם בלעם ושרי מדין להיכן אזול כיון דאמר להו טו) לינו פה הלילה והשבותי אתכם דבר אמרו כלום יש אב ששונא את בנו אמר רב נחמן חוצפא אפילו כלפי שמיא מהני מעיקרא כתיב טז) לא תלך עמהם ולבסוף כתיב יז) קום לך אתם אמר רב ששת חוצפא ו) מלכותא בלא תאגא היא דכתיב יח) ואנכי היום רך ומשוח מלך והאנשים האלה בני צרויה קשים ממני וגו' א"ר יוחנן בלעם ז) חיגר ברגלו אחת היה שנאמר יט) וילך שפי שמשון בשתי רגליו שנאמר כ) שפיפון עלי אורח הנושך עקבי סוס בלעם סומא באחת מעיניו היה שנאמר י) שתום העין קוסם באמתו היה כתיב הכא כא) נופל וגלוי עינים וכתיב התם כב) והנה המן נופל על המטה וגו' איתמר מר זוטרא אמר קוסם באמתו היה מר בריה דרבינא אמר שבא על אתונו מ"ד קוסם באמתו היה כדאמרן ומ"ד בא על אתונו היה כתיב הכא ח) [א] כג) כרע שכב וכתיב התם כד) בין רגליה כרע

רש"י

דקא אתי מיהודה. דקאמר לו דוד ואתה אנוש כערכי אלופי ומיודעי שהיה קורא לאחיתופל מיודעי קרובי שהיה משבט יהודה כדוד: מואב סיר רחצי. דוד דקא אתי ממואב: סיר רחצי. גחזי שסר ונצטרע על עסקי רחילה: על אדום אשליך נעלי. אנעיל אותם בגן עדן: אם יבא דוד שהרג את הפלשתי. ויצעק לפניך על שאתה נותן חלק לדואג ואחיתופל לעוה"ב מה אתה עושה להפיס דעתו שהם היו שונאין אותו: אמר להם. עלי לפייסן ולעשותן ריעים ואהובים זה לזה והיינו התרועעי לשון ריעות: ושמואל אמר מאי תשובה נצחת כה"ג [באו] עשרה בני אדם וכו': עבד שמכרו רבו. ומאחר שמכרנו הקב"ה לנבוכדנצר וגרשנו מעליו יש לו עלינו כלום: מאי דכתיב ודוד עבדי נבוכדנצר עבדי. שקראו לאותו רשע עבד כמו שקראו לדוד דכתיב בסוף ירמיה (מג) הנני שולח ולקחתי את נבוכדנצר עבדי לא מפני שדומה זה לזה אלא גלוי וידוע לפני מי שאמר והיה העולם שעתידין ישראל לומר כבר מכרנו הקב"ה לנבוכדנצר לפיכך הקדים הקב"ה וקרא עבדי לנבוכדנצר כדי להחזיר להן תשובה: עבד למי נכסים למי. כלומר נבוכדנצר עבדי הוא וכל מה שקנה לי הוא ועדיין לא יצאתם מרשותי: והעולה על רוחכם היה לא תהיה. כל מה שאתם סבורים לא יהיה: כל כי האי ריתחא. מי יתן ויבא לנו זה הכעס בחימה שפוכה אמלוך עליכם שיגאלנו בעל כרחנו וימלוך עלינו: א"ר אבא בר כהנא. היינו תשובה נצחת דאמרו ליה אלהים יורנו שאין אנו יכולין ליסר אותו: בלא עם. שאין לו חלק עם עם: שבלה עם. שבלבל ישראל בעצתו שהשיאו לבלק כדבעינן למימר לקמן והפיל מהם כ"ד אלפים: בעור שבא על בעיר. שבא על אתונו כמו בהמה דמתרגמינן בעיר: תנא הוא בעור. אביו של בלעם הוא כושן רשעתים הוא לבן הארמי: אחת בימי יעקב. שרדף אחריו ובקש לעקור הכל: ואחת בימי שופטים. לאחר מיתת יהושע דכתיב (שופטים ג) ויחר אף ה' בישראל ויתנם ביד כושן רשעתים: בנו בעור. משמע בעור בנו של בלעם היה: בנו הוא. לבלעם בנביאות שבלעם גדול מאביו היה בנביאות: הא שאר נכרים אתו. כלומר מדקא חשיב תנא דמתניתין דבלעם שהיה נכרי בהדי הדיוטות וקאמר דאין לו חלק מכלל דשאר נכרים יש להם חלק: מתניתין מני וכו'. א"ל ר' יהושע אלו נאמר ישובו רשעים לשאולה ט) בכל הגוים משמע כדקאמרת השתא דכתיב כל גוים שכחי אלהים לא משמע אלא אותן השוכחים אלוה כגון בלעם [ושכמותו] אבל אחריני אתו כדאמרינן בריש פרקין (דף צא:) ורעו זרים צאנכם ובני נכר אכריכם לעולם הבא: מאי נינהו כל גוים שכחי אלהים. דמשום הכי בורר הקב"ה הרשעים שבהם ונותן אותם בגיהנם ואין להם חלק לעתיד אבל השאר יש להם חלק: ואף אותו רשע נתן סימן בעצמו. שאין לו חלק לעתיד: תמות נפשי מות ישרים. אם ימות מיתת עצמו תהא אחריתי כמוהו דודאי יש לו חלק עמהם: ואם לאו. דלא ימות אלא יהרג הנני הולך לעמי לגיהנם: לא היה להם שלום. דכתיב המכה את מדין בשדה מואב: צהובין. כעוסין כאדם שכועס פניו צהובין: כרכושתא. חולדה: כרכושתא ושונרא. אין להם שלום מעולם: ביש גדא. מזל רע: כלום יש אב ששונא את בנו. שהוא סבור שיאמר לו הקב"ה קלל את בני דקאמר בלעם לינו פה [הלילה]: חוצפא אפילו כלפי שמיא מהני. דאהני ליה מה שהחציף פניו לומר לשלוחי בלק י) לינו פה שאמר לו הקב"ה בתחילה לא תלך והדר אמר לך: מלכותא בלא תגא. כלומר שררה גדולה ואינו חסר אלא כתר מלכות: אנכי היום רך ומשוח מלך והאנשים האלה קשים ממני. כלומר איני גדול מהם אלא משיחת מלכות: שפי. כמו (חולין דף נד:) בוקא דאטמא דשף מדוכתיה: שפיפון. משמעו שתים: שתום העין. שתום פתוח כמו שתומו ניכר כ) כלומר עינו אחת פתוחה מכלל דהאחרת סתומה והכי נמי מתרגמינן דשפיר חזי אית דמפרשי שתום כמו סתום ולאו מילתא היא: קוסם באמתו. כגון מעלה בזכורו: כרע

עין משפט נר מצוה

[א מיי' פ' י"א מהלכות עדות דין י ופ"ג מהל' תשובה דין ה]:

הגהות הגר"א

[א] גמ' כתיב הכא כרע שכב. נמחק ב' תיבות כרע שכב וצ"ל נופל:

ליקוטי רש"י

אבותיכם איה הם. ראו שלקו מכה רעה ברעב בחרב ובשבי. והנביאי' הלעולם יחיו. ואע"פ אף הנביאים איה הם הרי מתו אני משיב לכם וכי הנביאים היה להם לעולם לחיות אך סופן מוכיח כי אמת היה דבריהם שכל דברי וחוקי גזירות פורענותי אשר צויתי את עבדי הנביאים עליכם הלא השיגו אבותיכם [זכריה א, ה]. באו עשרה בני אדם וישבו לפניו. ויהי בשנה השביעית בחמישי בעשור לחודש באו אנשים מזקני ישראל לדרוש את ידוד וישבו לפני. לדרוש את ה' על צרכיהם ואם אינו שומע לנו גם אנו לא נענש על עבירות שבידנו שהרי כבר מכרנו ואין לו עלינו כלום עבד שמכרו רבו ואשה שגרשה בעלה כלום יש לזה על זה כלום ומסוף הענין אתה למד מתשובה שהשיבם והעולה על רוחכם וגו' [יחזקאל כ, א]. העולה על רוחכם. שעולה על דעתכם. נהיה כגוים. נפרוק עולו מעל צוארנו מאחר ששלח מעליו. היו לא תהיה. כי כבר קבלתם עליכם מדעתכ' בימי יהושע כמו שנאמר (יהושע כד) ויאסוף יהושע את כל שבטי ישראל וכל הענין [יחזקאל כ, לב]. זו מדה טובה לישראל שלא יהיו אומרים הואיל וגלינו בין האומות נעשה כמעשיהם אני איני מניחם אלא מעמיד אני את נביאי ומחזירן לתחת כנפי שנאמר (יחזקאל כ, לג) והעולה על רוחכם היו לא תהיה וגו' חי אני וגו' אם לא ביד חזקה וגו' [ויקרא כו, מא]. בימי שפוט השופטים. לפני מלוך מלך שאול שהיו הדורות מתפרנסים על ידי שופטים ובימי אבצן היה שאמרו רבותינו אבצן זה בועז [רות א, א]. בנו בעור. כמו למעינו מים (תהלים קיד, ח). ומדרש אגדה שניהם היו גדולים מאבותיהם בלק בנו לצפור אביו בנו הוא במלכות ובלעם גדול מאביו בנביאות מנה בן פרס היה [במדבר כד, ג]. זקני מואב וזקני מדין. אל זקני מדין. והלא מעולם היו שונאים זה את זה שנאמר (בראשית לו, לה) המכה את מדין בשדה מואב שבאו מדין על מואב למלחמה אלא מיראתן של ישראל עשו שלום ביניהם [במדבר כב, ד]. המכה את מדין בשדה מואב. שבא מדין על מואב למלחמה והלך מלך אדום לעזור את מואב ומכאן אנו למדים שהיו מדין ומואב מריבים זה עם זה ובימי בלעם עשו שלום להתקשר על ישראל [בראשית לו, לה]. מלכותא בלא תגא. שר גדול אלא שאינו מעוטר [לעיל צט:]. שפי. אשלוייש"ם כמו דשף מדוכתיה (חולין דף מג:). שפיפון. שפייה כפולה [סוטה י.]. שתם העין. עינו נקורה ומוצאת לחוץ וחור שלה נראה פתוח ולשון משנה הוא כדי שישתום ויסתום ויגוב (ע"ז סט.) ורבותינו אמרו לפי שאמר ומספר את רובע ישראל שהקב"ה יושב ומונה רביעותיהן של ישראל מתי תבא טפה שנולד הצדיק ממנה אמר בלבו מי שהוא קדוש ומשרתיו קדושים יסתכל בדברים הללו ועל דבר זה נסמית עינו של בלעם ויש מפרשים שתום העין פתוח העין כמו שתרגם אונקלוס ועל שאמר שתום העין ולא אמר שתום העינים למדנו שסומא באחת מעיניו היה [במדבר כד, ג].

מסורת הש"ס

א) [לעיל לא. מגילה טז.], ב) ר"ה לב:, ג) [גיר' הערוך בלע עם פי' שיען עלות לבלע עם ישראל ד"א בלעם בלא עם פי' שאין לו חלק עם ישראל. ערך בלע], ד) [תוספ' פי"ג], ה) [בילקוט ליתא אכן בע"י איתא בכל וגיר' זו נראה נכונה ודע דבתוספתא פרק י"ג תניא להך פלוגתא דר"א ור' יהושע בנוסחא אחריני ע"ש על נכון], ו) [לעיל לט:], ז) [סוטה י.], ח) [כל העובר על הפסוקים יראה דהך קרא כרע שכב דכתיב בפרשת בלק כ"ד פסוק ט' כרע שכב כארי וכלביא מי יקימנו בשבח לישראל נאמרה כדמפרש בתרגום ורש"י וכן בברכות יב: וע"ש דאין לענין כרע שכב שום שייכות לבלעם כלל ומצוה לתקן ולהסביר ועמ"ש בתקוני כלי שרת], ט) [צ"ל בכל], י) [בקרא דהכא לא כתיב כך ואולי כוונת רש"י על המכוון דכתיב כ"ב פסוק י"ט שבו נא בזה גם אתם הלילה], כ) [ע"ז סט: וע"ש ברש"י סט. ד"ה ותיגוב].

תורה אור השלם

א) מַדּוּעַ שׁוֹבְבָה הָעָם הַזֶּה יְרוּשָׁלַיִם מְשֻׁבָה נִצַּחַת הֶחֱזִיקוּ בַּתַּרְמִית מֵאֲנוּ לָשׁוּב: [ירמיה ח, ה]

ב) אֲבוֹתֵיכֶם אַיֵּה הֵם וְהַנְּבִאִים הַלְעוֹלָם יִחְיוּ: [זכריה א, ה]

ג) אַךְ דְּבָרַי וְחֻקַּי אֲשֶׁר צִוִּיתִי אֶת עֲבָדַי הַנְּבִיאִים הֲלוֹא הִשִּׂיגוּ אֲבֹתֵיכֶם וַיָּשׁוּבוּ וַיֹּאמְרוּ כַּאֲשֶׁר זָמַם יְיָ צְבָאוֹת לַעֲשׂוֹת לָנוּ כִּדְרָכֵינוּ וּכְמַעֲלָלֵינוּ כֵּן עָשָׂה אִתָּנוּ: [זכריה א, ו]

ד) כֹּה אָמַר יְיָ אֵי זֶה סֵפֶר כְּרִיתוּת אִמְּכֶם אֲשֶׁר שִׁלַּחְתִּיהָ אוֹ מִי מִנּוֹשַׁי אֲשֶׁר מָכַרְתִּי אֶתְכֶם לוֹ הֵן בַּעֲוֹנֹתֵיכֶם נִמְכַּרְתֶּם וּבְפִשְׁעֵיכֶם שֻׁלְּחָה אִמְּכֶם: [ישעיה נ, א]

ה) וְעַתָּה עֲשׂוּ כִּי יְיָ אָמַר אֶל דָּוִד לֵאמֹר בְּיַד דָּוִד עַבְדִּי הוֹשִׁיעַ אֶת עַמִּי יִשְׂרָאֵל מִיַּד פְּלִשְׁתִּים וּמִיַּד כָּל אֹיְבֵיהֶם: [שמואל ב' ג, יח]

ו) וְאָמַרְתָּ אֲלֵיהֶם כֹּה אָמַר יְיָ צְבָאוֹת אֱלֹהֵי יִשְׂרָאֵל הִנְנִי שֹׁלֵחַ וְלָקַחְתִּי אֶת נְבוּכַדְרֶאצַּר מֶלֶךְ בָּבֶל עַבְדִּי וְשַׂמְתִּי כִסְאוֹ מִמַּעַל לָאֲבָנִים הָאֵלֶּה אֲשֶׁר טָמָנְתִּי וְנָטָה אֶת שַׁפְרִירוֹ עֲלֵיהֶם: [ירמיה מג, י]

ז) וְהָעֹלָה עַל רוּחֲכֶם הָיוֹ לֹא תִהְיֶה אֲשֶׁר אַתֶּם אֹמְרִים נִהְיֶה כַגּוֹיִם כְּמִשְׁפְּחוֹת הָאֲרָצוֹת לְשָׁרֵת עֵץ וָאָבֶן: חַי אָנִי נְאֻם אֲדֹנָי אֱלֹהִים אִם לֹא בְּיָד חֲזָקָה וּבִזְרוֹעַ נְטוּיָה וּבְחֵמָה שְׁפוּכָה אֶמְלוֹךְ עֲלֵיכֶם: [יחזקאל כ, לב-לג]

ח) וְיִסְּרוֹ לַמִּשְׁפָּט אֱלֹהָיו יוֹרֶנּוּ: [ישעיה כח, כו]

ט) וַיִּשְׁלַח מַלְאָכִים אֶל בִּלְעָם בֶּן בְּעוֹר פְּתוֹרָה אֲשֶׁר עַל הַנָּהָר אֶרֶץ בְּנֵי עַמּוֹ לִקְרֹא לוֹ לֵאמֹר הִנֵּה עַם יָצָא מִמִּצְרַיִם הִנֵּה כִסָּה אֶת עֵין הָאָרֶץ וְהוּא יֹשֵׁב מִמֻּלִי: [במדבר כב, ה]

י) וַיִּשָּׂא מְשָׁלוֹ וַיֹּאמַר נְאֻם בִּלְעָם בְּנוֹ בְעֹר וּנְאֻם הַגֶּבֶר שְׁתֻם הָעָיִן: [במדבר כד, ג]

יא) יָשׁוּבוּ רְשָׁעִים לִשְׁאוֹלָה כָּל גּוֹיִם שְׁכֵחֵי אֱלֹהִים: [תהלים ט, יח]

יב) מִי מָנָה עֲפַר יַעֲקֹב וּמִסְפָּר אֶת רֹבַע יִשְׂרָאֵל תָּמֹת נַפְשִׁי מוֹת יְשָׁרִים וּתְהִי אַחֲרִיתִי כָּמֹהוּ: [במדבר כג, י]

יג) וְעַתָּה הִנְנִי הוֹלֵךְ לְעַמִּי לְכָה אִיעָצְךָ אֲשֶׁר יַעֲשֶׂה הָעָם הַזֶּה לְעַמְּךָ בְּאַחֲרִית הַיָּמִים: [במדבר כד, יד]

יד) וַיֵּלְכוּ זִקְנֵי מוֹאָב וְזִקְנֵי מִדְיָן וּקְסָמִים בְּיָדָם וַיָּבֹאוּ אֶל בִּלְעָם וַיְדַבְּרוּ אֵלָיו דִּבְרֵי בָלָק: [במדבר כב, ז]

טו) וַיֹּאמֶר אֲלֵיהֶם לִינוּ פֹה הַלַּיְלָה וַהֲשִׁבֹתִי אֶתְכֶם דָּבָר כַּאֲשֶׁר יְדַבֵּר יְיָ אֵלָי וַיֵּשְׁבוּ שָׂרֵי מוֹאָב עִם בִּלְעָם: [במדבר כב, ח]

טז) וַיֹּאמֶר אֱלֹהִים אֶל בִּלְעָם לֹא תֵלֵךְ עִמָּהֶם לֹא תָאֹר אֶת הָעָם כִּי בָרוּךְ הוּא: [במדבר כב, יב]

יז) וַיָּבֹא אֱלֹהִים אֶל בִּלְעָם לַיְלָה וַיֹּאמֶר לוֹ אִם לִקְרֹא לְךָ בָּאוּ הָאֲנָשִׁים קוּם לֵךְ אִתָּם וְאַךְ אֶת הַדָּבָר אֲשֶׁר אֲדַבֵּר אֵלֶיךָ אֹתוֹ תַעֲשֶׂה: [במדבר כב, כ]

יח) וְאָנֹכִי הַיּוֹם רַךְ וּמָשׁוּחַ מֶלֶךְ וְהָאֲנָשִׁים הָאֵלֶּה בְּנֵי צְרוּיָה קָשִׁים מִמֶּנִּי יְשַׁלֵּם יְיָ לְעֹשֵׂה הָרָעָה כְּרָעָתוֹ: [שמואל ב' ג, לט]

יט) וַיֹּאמֶר בִּלְעָם לְבָלָק הִתְיַצֵּב עַל עֹלָתֶךָ וְאֵלְכָה אוּלַי יִקָּרֵה יְיָ לִקְרָאתִי וּדְבַר מַה יַּרְאֵנִי וְהִגַּדְתִּי לָךְ וַיֵּלֶךְ שֶׁפִי: [במדבר כג, ג]

כ) יְהִי דָן נָחָשׁ עֲלֵי דֶרֶךְ שְׁפִיפֹן עֲלֵי אֹרַח הַנֹּשֵׁךְ עִקְּבֵי סוּס וַיִּפֹּל רֹכְבוֹ אָחוֹר: [בראשית מט, יז]

כא) נְאֻם שֹׁמֵעַ אִמְרֵי אֵל וְיֹדֵעַ דַּעַת עֶלְיוֹן מַחֲזֵה שַׁדַּי יֶחֱזֶה נֹפֵל וּגְלוּי עֵינָיִם: [במדבר כד, טז]

כב) וְהַמֶּלֶךְ שָׁב מִגִּנַּת הַבִּיתָן אֶל בֵּית מִשְׁתֵּה הַיַּיִן וְהָמָן נֹפֵל עַל הַמִּטָּה אֲשֶׁר אֶסְתֵּר עָלֶיהָ וַיֹּאמֶר הַמֶּלֶךְ הֲגַם לִכְבּוֹשׁ אֶת הַמַּלְכָּה עִמִּי בַּבָּיִת הַדָּבָר יָצָא מִפִּי הַמֶּלֶךְ וּפְנֵי הָמָן חָפוּ: [אסתר ז, ח]

כג) כָּרַע שָׁכַב כַּאֲרִי וּכְלָבִיא מִי יְקִימֶנּוּ מְבָרֲכֶיךָ בָרוּךְ וְאֹרְרֶיךָ אָרוּר: [במדבר כד, ט]

כד) בֵּין רַגְלֶיהָ כָּרַע נָפַל שָׁכָב בֵּין רַגְלֶיהָ כָּרַע נָפָל בַּאֲשֶׁר כָּרַע שָׁם נָפַל שָׁדוּד: [שופטים ה, כז]

The Gemara analyzes Bilam's father's name:

,,בֶּן בְּעוֹר״ שֶׁבָּא עַל בְּעִיר – Bilam was **the son of Beor.** Beor was so called **because he copulated with a beast** *(be'ir)*.[19]

More about Beor:

תָּנָא – **A Tanna taught:** הוּא בְּעוֹר הוּא כּוּשַׁן רִשְׁעָתַיִם הוּא לָבָן הָאֲרַמִּי – BEOR IS the same person as KUSHAN RISHASAIM AND the same person as LABAN THE ARAMEAN.[20] בְּעוֹר שֶׁבָּא עַל בְּעִיר – He was called BEOR BECAUSE HE COPULATED WITH A BEAST *(be'ir)*; כּוּשַׁן רִשְׁעָתַיִם דְּעָבַד שְׁתֵּי רִשְׁעִיּוֹת בְּיִשְׂרָאֵל – he was called KUSHAN RISHASAIM BECAUSE HE PERPETRATED TWO EVILS UPON ISRAEL:[21] אַחַת בִּימֵי יַעֲקֹב וְאַחַת בִּימֵי שְׁפוֹט הַשּׁוֹפְטִים – ONE IN THE DAYS OF JACOB AND ONE IN THE DAYS WHEN THE JUDGES JUDGED.[22] וּמָה שְׁמוֹ – AND WHAT WAS HIS real NAME? לָבָן הָאֲרַמִּי שְׁמוֹ – LABAN THE ARAMEAN WAS HIS NAME.[23]

The Gemara notes and explains an inconsistency concerning the Torah's description of Bilam's relationship to Beor:

כְּתִיב ,,בֶּן־בְּעוֹר״ וּכְתִיב ,,בְּנוֹ בְעֹר״ – **It is written** that Bilam was ***the son of Beor,*** **yet it is** also **written:** ***his son was Beor,***[24] implying that Bilam was the father, not the son, of Beor. How is this to be explained? אָמַר רַבִּי יוֹחָנָן – **R' Yochanan said:** אָבִיו בְּנוֹ הוּא לוֹ בִּנְבִיאוּת – **[Bilam's] father was his "son" in prophecy,** i.e. when Scripture states that Beor was Bilam's son, it means that he was inferior to Bilam in prophetic powers. In fact, however, Beor was Bilam's biological father.[25]

Among those wicked individuals who have no share in the World to Come, the Mishnah lists the gentile Bilam. The Gemara draws an inference from this:

בִּלְעָם הוּא דְּלֹא אָתֵי לְעָלְמָא דְּאָתֵי – **It is** the wicked gentile **Bilam who** the Mishnah states **will not come to the World to Come.** הָא אַחֲרִינֵי אָתוּ – **This implies that other** gentiles, who are not wicked, **will come** there. מַתְנִיתִין מַנִּי – **Whose opinion does our Mishnah follow?** רַבִּי יְהוֹשֻׁעַ הִיא – **It follows** the opinion of **R' Yehoshua,** דְּתַנְיָא – **for it was taught in a Baraisa:** רַבִּי אֱלִיעֶזֶר אוֹמֵר – R' ELIEZER SAYS: ,,יָשׁוּבוּ רְשָׁעִים לִשְׁאוֹלָה כָּל־גּוֹיִם שְׁכֵחֵי אֱלֹהִים״ – Scripture states: *THE WICKED WILL RETURN TO THE GRAVE, ALL PEOPLES WHO ARE FORGETFUL OF GOD.*[26] ,,יָשׁוּבוּ רְשָׁעִים לִשְׁאוֹלָה״ אֵלּוּ פּוֹשְׁעֵי יִשְׂרָאֵל – *THE WICKED WILL RETURN TO THE GRAVE* – THESE ARE THE SINFUL JEWS. ,,כָּל־גּוֹיִם שְׁכֵחֵי אֱלֹהִים״ אֵלּוּ [פּוֹשְׁעֵי][27] עוֹבְדֵי כּוֹכָבִים – *ALL PEOPLES WHO ARE FORGETFUL OF GOD* – THESE ARE THE GENTILES, i.e. gentiles in general, both sinful and otherwise. דִּבְרֵי רַבִּי אֱלִיעֶזֶר – These are THE WORDS OF R' ELIEZER.[28] אָמַר לוֹ רַבִּי יְהוֹשֻׁעַ – R' YEHOSHUA SAID TO HIM: וְכִי נֶאֱמַר ,,[בבכל] וְכָל גּוֹיִם״[29] – BUT DOES [THE VERSE] SAY: *"AND" ALL PEOPLES who are forgetful of God,* which would imply that it refers to a second group of people? וַהֲלֹא לֹא נֶאֱמַר אֶלָּא ,,כָּל־גּוֹיִם שְׁכֵחֵי אֱלֹהִים״ – WHY, IT STATES ONLY: *ALL PEOPLES WHO ARE FORGETFUL OF GOD,* without the word "and." אֶלָּא – **Rather,** the verse refers to only one group of people, as follows: ,,יָשׁוּבוּ רְשָׁעִים לִשְׁאוֹלָה״ מַאן נִינְהוּ ,,כָּל־גּוֹיִם שְׁכֵחֵי אֱלֹהִים״ – ***The wicked will return to the grave*** – and **who are these [wicked persons]?** – ***All peoples who are forgetful of God.***[30]

NOTES

Jews as long as they followed the Torah. Instead, Bilam counseled Balak to catch the Jews off guard (*confuse the people*) and entice the Jewish men into debauchery. God would then become angry at them and would punish them Himself. This plan worked all too well; see below, 106a (*Rashi*).

Aruch (ibid.) records an alternate reading: בָּלַע עָם, *He devoured the people,* or: בִּלַּע עָם, *destroyed the people.* That is, he caused thousands of the people of Israel to die as a result of his sinister plot.

19. I.e. he copulated with his she-donkey. *Be'ir* is the Aramaic word for בְּהֵמָה, *beast* (*Rashi*).

Our explanation takes the approach that in saying "he copulated with a beast," the Gemara refers to Bilam's father Beor, not to Bilam himself. This would appear to be *Rashi's* understanding – see *Rashi* ד״ה תנא. [However, see *Melo HaRoim* in the name of *Shelah*.]

Alternatively, the Gemara means that it was Bilam who copulated with his beast. According to this interpretation, the word בֶּן in the phrase בֶּן־בְּעוֹר is understood as meaning "man of" [as in בֶּן תּוֹרָה or בַּר מִצְוָה] (*Yad Ramah*).

[According to this explanation, the following Gemara as well refers to Bilam (see *Eitz Yosef*).]

20. All three are described in Scripture as being from Aram Naharaim: (a) Concerning Beor it is written: . . . *he hired against you Bilam the son of Beor, of Pesor in Aram Naharaim, to curse you* (*Deuteronomy* 23:5); (b) concerning Kushan Rishasaim, who oppressed the Jews during the era of the Judges, it is written: *And HASHEM became incensed at Israel and surrendered them to Kushan Rishasaim King of Aram Naharaim* (*Judges* 3:8); (c) concerning Laban it is written: . . . *[Eliezer] made his way to Aram Naharaim to the city of Nachor . . . Laban ran to the man, outside to the spring* (*Genesis* 24:10,29).

21. *Rishasaim* means "two evils."

22. One as Laban, who pursued Jacob with intent to kill him (*Genesis* 31:23-29), and one as Kushan Rishasaim, who oppressed the Jews [*Judges* 3:8] (*Rashi*).

23.The statement of the Gemara that these three individuals were the same person is apparently not intended in a literal sense, for Laban and Kushan Rishasaim lived many centuries apart. Rather, it means that they were of the same family (*Torah Temimah* to *Numbers* 22:5) or that they exhibited similar behaviors (see *Ibn Ezra* to *Genesis* 36:32). Accordingly, when the Gemara says, "His real name was Laban," it means that it was Laban whose teachings formed the basis of the ideology of the others (*R' Avigdor Miller*). See also *Ben Yehoyada* in the name of *Ari z"l* for an explanation based on kabbalistic teachings; see also above, 101b note 19, concerning Michah.

24. *Numbers* 22:5 and 24:3 respectively.

25. [*Toras Chaim* adds that for this reason the expression בְּנוֹ בְעֹר is used only when Bilam was actually uttering a prophecy (*Numbers* 24:3 and 15). At all other times, he is referred to as בֶּן־בְּעוֹר (see *Toras Chaim*).]

26. *Psalms* 9:18.

27. The word פּוֹשְׁעֵי that appears in the Vilna Shas is an interpolation by government censors and does not appear in early prints of the Gemara (*Dikdukei Soferim*).

28. R' Eliezer expounds the redundancy of the verse as indicating two different groups of people. *The wicked will return to the grave* refers to wicked Jews, teaching that they have no share in the World to Come. *All peoples who are forgetful of God* refers to all other peoples, sinful or otherwise, and teaches that gentiles in general have no share in the World to Come, for gentiles in general are forgetful of God.

[The phrase *all peoples who are forgetful of God* cannot be understood as indicating that only those gentiles who forget God are excluded from the World to Come, but that those gentiles who are mindful of God are not excluded, for then Scripture would have simply omitted this phrase, and the verse's first phrase, *the wicked will return to the grave,* would have been understood to include *all* wicked people, both Jew and gentile alike. The fact that Scripture writes the second phrase indicates, therefore, that the words *who are forgetful of God* must be read not as limiting *which* peoples will return to the grave, but as an appositional phrase *explaining* the previous one: *all [other] peoples, who [in general] are forgetful of God* (see *Yad Ramah*).]

29. The word בְּכָל found in the Vilna Shas appears to be an error. We have followed the version of *Yad Ramah,* which substitutes the word וְכָל. See also *Rif* in *Ein Yaakov*. Cf. *Mesoras HaShas* and *Tosefta* 13:1.

30. I.e. the second phrase of the verse is in apposition to the first and comes to explain it; in other words, when the verse condemns the wicked to the grave, implying exclusion from the World to Come, it refers specifically to those who forget God. Those gentiles who do not forget God do in fact have a share in the World to Come, as the Gemara explains above on 91b (*Rashi*).

The Gemara thus states that our Mishnah, which specifies the gentile Bilam as having no share in the World to Come, follows the opinion of R' Yehoshua that other gentiles do merit the Afterworld. This is also *Rambam's* well-known ruling: *Any gentile who accepts the seven Noahide commandments and observes them scrupulously is considered among the righteous gentiles and has a portion in the World to Come* (see *Hil. Melachim* 8:11).

דקאתי מיהודה מואב סיר רחצי זה גחזי שלקה על עסקי רחיצה על אדום אשליך נעלי זה דואג האדומי עלי פלשת התרועעי אמרו מלאכי השרת לפני הקב"ה רבש"ע אם יבא דוד שהרג את הפלשתי והוריש את בניך גת מה אתה עושה לו אמר להן עלי לעשותן ריעים זה לזה א) מדוע שובבה העם הזה ירושלים משובה נצחת וגו' אמר רב תשובה נצחת השיבה כנסת ישראל לנביא אמר להן נביא לישראל חזרו בתשובה אבותיכם שחטאו היכן הם אמרו להן ונביאיכם שלא חטאו היכן הם שנאמר ב) אבותיכם איה הם והנביאים הלעולם יחיו אמר להן (אבותיכם) חזרו והודו שנאמר ג) אך דברי וחוקי אשר צויתי את עבדי הנביאים וגו' שמואל אמר באו עשרה בני אדם וישבו לפניו אמר להן חזרו בתשובה אמרו לו עבד שמכרו רבו ואשה שגרשה בעלה כלום יש לזה על זה כלום אמר לו הקב"ה לנביא לך אמור להן ד) איזה ספר כריתות אמכם אשר שלחתיה או מי מנושי אשר מכרתי אתכם לו הן בעונותיכם נמכרתם ובפשעכם שלחה אמכם והיינו דאמר ריש לקיש מאי דכתיב ה) דוד עבדי ו) נבוכדנצר עבדי גלוי וידוע לפני מי שאמר והיה העולם שעתידין ישראל לומר כך לפיכך הקדים הקב"ה וקראו עבדו [א] עבד שקנה נכסים עבד למי נכסים למי ז) והעולה על רוחכם היה לא תהיה אשר אתם אומרים נהיה כגוים כמשפחות הארצות לשרת עץ ואבן חי אני נאם ה' אלהים אם לא ביד חזקה ובזרוע נטויה ובחימה שפוכה אמלוך עליכם [ב] אמר רב נחמן כל כי האי ריתחא לירתח רחמנא עלן ולפרוקינן ח) ויסרו למשפט אלהיו יורנו אמר רבה בר בר חנה אמר להן נביא לישראל חזרו בתשובה אמרו לו אין אנו יכולין יצר הרע שולט בנו אמר להם יסרו יצריכם אמרו לו אלהיו יורנו: ארבעה הדיוטות בלעם ודואג ואחיתופל וגחזי: בלעם [ג] בלא עם דבר אחר בלעם שבלה עם בן בעור שבא על בעיר תנא הוא בעור הוא כושן רשעתים הוא לבן הארמי בעור שבא על בעיר כושן רשעתים דעבד שתי רשעיות בישראל אחת בימי יעקב ואחת בימי שפוט השופטים ומה שמו לבן הארמי שמו כתיב ט) בן בעור וכתיב י) בנו בעור אמר רבי יוחנן אביו בנו הוא לו בנביאות בלעם הוא דלא אתי לעלמא דאתי הא אחריני אתו מתניתין מני רבי יהושע היא דתניא [ד] ר"א אומר יא) ישובו רשעים לשאולה כל גוים שכחי אלהים ישובו רשעים לשאולה אלו פושעי ישראל כל גוים שכחי אלהים אלו פושעי עובדי כוכבים דברי ר"א [א] אמר לו ר' יהושע וכי נאמר [ה] בכל גוים והלא לא נאמר אלא כל גוים שכחי אלהים אלא ישובו רשעים לשאולה מאן נינהו כל גוים שכחי אלהים ואף אותו רשע נתן סימן בעצמו אמר יב) תמות נפשי מות ישרים אם תמות נפשי מות ישרים תהא אחריתי כמוהו ואם לאו יג) הנני הולך לעמי יד) וילכו זקני מואב וזקני מדין תנא מדין ומואב לא היה להם שלום מעולם משל לשני כלבים שהיו בעדר והיו צהובין זה לזה בא זאב על האחד אמר האחד אם איני עוזרו היום הורג אותו ולמחר בא עלי הלכו שניהם והרגו הזאב אמר רב פפא היינו דאמרי אינשי כרכושתא ושונרא עבדו הלולא מתרבא דביש גדא טו) וישבו שרי מואב עם בלעם ושרי מדין להיכן אזול כיון דאמר להו טו) לינו פה הלילה והשבותי אתכם דבר אמרו כלום יש אב ששונא את בנו אמר רב נחמן חוצפא אפילו כלפי שמיא מהני מעיקרא כתיב טז) לא תלך עמהם ולבסוף כתיב יז) קום לך אתם אמר רב ששת חוצפא [ו] מלכותא בלא תאגא היא דכתיב יח) ואנכי היום רך ומשוח מלך והאנשים האלה בני צרויה קשים ממני וגו' א"ר יוחנן בלעם [ז] חיגר ברגלו אחת היה שנאמר יט) וילך שפי שמשון בשתי רגליו שנאמר כ) שפיפון עלי אורח הנושך עקבי סוס בלעם סומא באחת מעיניו היה שנאמר [ח] שתום העין קוסם באמתו היה כתיב הכא כא) נופל וגלוי עינים וכתיב התם כב) והנה המן נופל על המטה וגו' איתמר מר זוטרא אמר קוסם באמתו היה מר בריה דרבינא אמר שבא על אתונו מ"ד קוסם באמתו היה כדאמרן ומ"ד בא על אתונו היה כתיב הכא [ט] [א] כג) כרע שכב וכתיב התם כד) בין רגליה כרע

רש"י

דקא אתי מיהודה. דקאמר לו דוד ואתה אנוש כערכי אלופי ומיודעי שהיה קורא לאחיתופל מיודעי קרובי שהיה משבט יהודה כדוד: מואב סיר רחצי. דוד דקא אתי ממואב: סיר רחצי. גחזי שסר ונצטרע על עסקי רחיצה: על אדום אשליך נעלי. אנעיל אותם בגן עדן: אם יבא דוד שהרג את הפלשתי. ויצעק לפניך על שאתה נותן חלק לדואג ואחיתופל לעוה"ב מה אתה עושה להפיס דעתו שהם היו שונאין אותו: אמר להם. עלי לפייסן ולעשותן ריעים ואהובים זה לזה והיינו התרועעי לשון ריעות: ושמואל אמר מאי תשובה נצחת כה"ג [באו] עשרה בני אדם וכו': עבד שמכרו רבו. ומאחר שמכרנו הקב"ה לנבוכדנצר וגרשנו מעליו יש לו עלינו כלום: מאי דכתיב ודוד עבדי נבוכדנצר עבדי. שקראו לאותו רשע עבד כמו שקראו לדוד דכתיב בסוף ירמיה (מג) הנני שולח ולקחתי את נבוכדנצר עבדי לא מפני שדומה זה לזה אלא גלוי וידוע לפני מי שאמר והיה העולם שעתידין ישראל לומר כבר מכרנו הקב"ה לנבוכדנצר לפיכך הקדים הקב"ה וקרא עבדי לנבוכדנצר כדי להחזיר להן תשובה: עבד למי נכסים למי. כלומר נבוכדנצר עבדי הוא וכל מה שקנה לי הוא ועדיין לא יצאתם מרשותי: והעולה על רוחכם היה לא תהיה. כל מה שאתם סבורים לא יהיה: כל כי האי ריתחא. מי יתן ויבא לנו זה הכעס בחימה שפוכה אמלוך עליכם שיגאלנו בעל כרחנו וימלוך עלינו: א"ר אבא בר כהנא. היינו תשובה נצחת דאמרו ליה אלהים יורנו שאין אנו יכולין ליסר אותו: בלא עם. שאין לו חלק עם עם: שבלה עם. שבלבל ישראל בעצתו שהשיאו לבלק כדבעינן למימר לקמן והפיל מהם כ"ד אלפים: בעור שבא על בעיר. שבא על אתונו כמו בהמה דמתרגמינן בעיר: תנא הוא בעור. אביו של בלעם הוא כושן רשעתים הוא לבן הארמי: אחת בימי יעקב. שרדף אחריו ובקש לעקור הכל: ואחת בימי שופטים. לאחר מיתת יהושע דכתיב (שופטים ג) ויחר אף ה' בישראל ויתנם ביד כושן רשעתים: בנו בעור. משמע בעור בנו של בלעם היה: בנו הוא. לבלעם בנביאות שבלעם גדול מאביו היה בנביאות: הא שאר נכרים אתו. כלומר מדקא חשיב תנא דמתניתין דבלעם שהיה נכרי בהדי הדיוטות וקאמר דאין לו חלק מכלל דשאר נכרים יש להם חלק: מתניתין מני וכו'. א"ל ר' יהושע אלו נאמר ישובו רשעים לשאולה [ט] בכל הגוים משמע כדקאמרת השתא דכתיב כל גוים שכחי אלהים לא משמע אלא אותן השוכחים אלוה כגון בלעם [ושכמותו] אבל אחריני אתו כדאמרינן בריש פרקין (דף צא:) ורעו זרים צאנכם ובני נכר אכריכם לעולם הבא: מאי נינהו כל גוים שכחי אלהים. דמשום הכי בורר הקב"ה הרשעים שבהם ונותן אותם בגיהנם ואין להם חלק לעתיד אבל השאר יש להם חלק: ואף אותו רשע נתן סימן בעצמו. שאין לו חלק לעתיד: תמות נפשי מות ישרים. אם ימות מיתת עצמו תהא אחריתי כמוהו דודאי יש לו חלק עמהם: ואם לאו. דלא ימות אלא יהרג הנני הולך לעמי לגיהנם: לא היה להם שלום. דכתיב המכה את מדין בשדה מואב: צהובין. כעוסין כאדם שכועס פניו להובין: כרכושתא. חולדה: כרכושתא ושונרא. אין להם שלום מעולם: ביש גדא. מזל רע: כלום יש אב ששונא את בנו. שהוא סבור שיאמר לו הקב"ה קלל את בני דקאמר בלעם לינו פה [הלילה]: חוצפא אפילו כלפי שמיא מהני. דאהני ליה מה שהחציף פניו לומר לשלוחי בלק [י] לינו פה שאמר לו הקב"ה בתחילה לא תלך והדר אמר לך: מלכותא בלא תגא. כלומר שררה גדולה ואינו חסר אלא כתר מלכות: אנכי היום רך ומשוח מלך והאנשים האלה קשים ממני. כלומר איני גדול מהם אלא משיחת מלכות: שפי. כמו (חולין דף נד:) בוקא דאטמא דשף מדוכתיה: שפיפון. משמעו שתים: שתום העין. שתום פתוח כמו שתומו ניכר [כ] כלומר עינו אחת פתוחה מכלל דהאחרת סתומה והכי נמי מתרגמינן דשפיר חזי אית דמפרשי שתום כמו סתום ולאו מילתא היא: קוסם באמתו. כגון מעלה בזכורו:

[א מיי' פ' י"א מהלכות עדות דין י ופ"ג מהל' תשובה דין ה]:

הגהות הגר"א

[א] גמ' כתיב הכא כרע שכב. נמחק ב' תיבות כרע שכב ונ"ב נופל:

ליקוטי רש"י

אבותיכם איה הם. ראו שלקו מכה רעה ברעב בחרב ובשבי. והנביא' הלעולם יחיו. וא"ת אף הנביאים איה הם הרי מתו אני משיב לכם וכי הנביאים היה להם לעולם לחיות אך סופן מוכיח כי אמת היה דבריהם שכל דברי וחוקי גזירות פורענותי אשר צויתי את עבדי הנביאים עליכם הלא השיגו אבותיכם [זכריה א, ה]. באו עשרה בני אדם וישבו לפניו. ויהי בשנה השביעית בחמישי בעשור לחודש באו אנשים מזקני ישראל לדרוש את ידוד וישבו לפני. לדרוש את ה' על צרכיהם ואם אינו שומע לנו גם אנו לא נענש על עבירות שבידנו שהרי כבר מכרנו ואין לו עלינו כלום עבד שמכרו רבו ואשה שגרשה בעלה כלום יש לזה על זה כלום ומסוף הענין אתה למד מתשובה שהשיבם והעולה על רוחכם וגו' [יחזקאל כ, א]. העולה על רוחכם. שעולה על דעתכם. נהיה כגוים. נפרוק עולו מעל צוארנו מאחר ששלח מעליו. היו לא תהיה. כי כבר קבלתם עליכם מדעתכ' בימי יהושע כמו שנאמר (יהושע כד) ויאסוף יהושע את כל שבטי ישראל וכל הענין [יחזקאל כ, לב]. זו מדה טובה לישראל שלא יהיו אומרים הואיל וגלינו בין האומות נעשה כמעשיהם אני איני מניחם אלא מעמיד אני את נביאי ומחזירן לתחת כנפי שנאמר (יחזקאל כ, לג) והעולה על רוחכם היו לא תהיה וגו' חי אני וגו' אם לא ביד חזקה וגו' [ויקרא כו, מא]. בימי שפוט השופטים. לפני מלוך מלך שאול שהיו הדורות מתפרנסים על ידי שופטים ובימי אבצן היה שאמרו רבותינו אבצן זה בועז [רות א, א]. בנו בעור. כמו למעינו מים (תהלים קיד, ח). ומדרש אגדה שניהם היו גדולים מאבותיהם בלק בנו צפור אביו בנו הוא במלכות ובלעם גדול מאביו בנביאות מנה בן פרס היה [במדבר כד, ג]. זקני מואב וזקני מדין. או זקני מדין. והלא מעולם היו שונאים זה את זה שנאמר (בראשית לו, לה) המכה את מדין בשדה מואב שבאו מדין על מואב למלחמה אלא מיראתן של ישראל עשו שלום ביניהם [במדבר כב, ד]. המכה את מדין בשדה מואב. שבא מדין על מואב למלחמה והלך מלך אדום לעזור את מואב ומכאן אנו למדים שהיו מדין ומואב מריבים זה עם זה ובימי בלעם עשו שלום להתקשר על ישראל [בראשית לו, לה]. מלכותא בלא תגא. שר גדול אלא שאינו מעוטר [לעיל צט:]. שפי. אשלוייש"ש כמו דשף מדוכתיה (חולין דף מב:). שפיפון. שפייה כפולה [סוטה י.]. שתם העין. עינו נקורה ומוצאת לחוץ וחור שלה נראה פתוח ולשון משנה הוא כדי שישתום ויסתום ויגוב (ע"ז סט.) ורבותינו אמרו לפי שאמר ומספר את רובע ישראל שהקב"ה יושב ומונה רביעיותיהן של ישראל מתי תבא טפה שנולד הצדיק ממנה אמר בלבו מי שהוא קדוש ומשרתיו קדושים יסתכל בדברים הללו ועל דבר זה נסמת עינו של בלעם ויש מפרשים שתום העין פתוח העין כמו שתרגם אונקלוס ועל שאמר שתום העין ולא אמר שתום העינים למדנו שסומא באחת מעיניו היה [במדבר כד, ג].

א) [לעיל לא. מגילה טו.], ב) ר"ה לב:, ג) [גיר' הערוך בלע עם פי' שיען עלות לבלע עם ישראל ד"א בלעם בלא עם פי' שאין לו חלק עם ישראל. ערך בלע], ד) [תוספ' פי"ג], ה) [בילקוט ליתא אכן בע"י איתא בכל וגיר' זו נראה נכונה ודע דבתוספתא פרק י"ג תניא להך פלוגתא דר"א ור' יהושע בנוסחא אחריני ע"ש על נכון], ו) [לעיל לט:], ז) [סוטה י.], ח) [כל העובר על הפסוקים יראה דהך קרא כרע שכב דכתיב בפרשת בלק כ"ד פסוק ט' כרע שכב כארי וכלביא מי יקימנו בשבח לישראל נאמרה כדמפרש בתרגום ורש"י וכן בברכות יב: וע"ש דאין לענין כרע שכב שום שייכות לבלעם כלל ומלוה לתקן ולהסביר ועמ"ש בתקוני כלי שרת], ט) [צ"ל ככל], י) [בקרא דהכא לא כתיב כך ואולי כוונת רש"י על המכוון דכתיב כ"ב פסוק י"ט שבו נא בזה גם אתם הלילה], כ) [ע"ז סט: וע"ש ברש"י סט. ד"ה ותיגוב].

תורה אור השלם

א) מַדּוּעַ שׁוֹבְבָה הָעָם הַזֶּה יְרוּשָׁלַם מְשֻׁבָה נִצַּחַת הֶחֱזִיקוּ בַּתַּרְמִית מֵאֲנוּ לָשׁוּב: [ירמיה ח, ה]

ב) אֲבוֹתֵיכֶם אַיֵּה הֵם וְהַנְּבִאִים הַלְעוֹלָם יִחְיוּ: [זכריה א, ה]

ג) אַךְ דְּבָרַי וְחֻקַּי אֲשֶׁר צִוִּיתִי אֶת עֲבָדַי הַנְּבִיאִים הֲלוֹא הִשִּׂיגוּ אֲבֹתֵיכֶם וַיָּשׁוּבוּ וַיֹּאמְרוּ כַּאֲשֶׁר זָמַם יְיָ צְבָאוֹת לַעֲשׂוֹת לָנוּ כִּדְרָכֵינוּ וּכְמַעֲלָלֵינוּ כֵּן עָשָׂה אִתָּנוּ: [זכריה א, ו]

ד) כֹּה אָמַר יְיָ אֵי זֶה סֵפֶר כְּרִיתוּת אִמְּכֶם אֲשֶׁר שִׁלַּחְתִּיהָ אוֹ מִי מִנּוֹשַׁי אֲשֶׁר מָכַרְתִּי אֶתְכֶם לוֹ הֵן בַּעֲוֹנֹתֵיכֶם נִמְכַּרְתֶּם וּבְפִשְׁעֵיכֶם שֻׁלְּחָה אִמְּכֶם: [ישעיה נ, א]

ה) וְעַתָּה עֲשׂוּ כִּי יְיָ אָמַר אֶל דָּוִד לֵאמֹר בְּיַד דָּוִד עַבְדִּי הוֹשִׁיעַ אֶת עַמִּי יִשְׂרָאֵל מִיַּד פְּלִשְׁתִּים וּמִיַּד כָּל אֹיְבֵיהֶם: [שמואל ב' ג, יח]

ו) וְאָמַרְתָּ אֲלֵיהֶם כֹּה אָמַר יְיָ צְבָאוֹת אֱלֹהֵי יִשְׂרָאֵל הִנְנִי שֹׁלֵחַ וְלָקַחְתִּי אֶת נְבוּכַדְרֶאצַּר מֶלֶךְ בָּבֶל עַבְדִּי וְשַׂמְתִּי כִסְאוֹ מִמַּעַל לָאֲבָנִים הָאֵלֶּה אֲשֶׁר טָמָנְתִּי וְנָטָה אֶת שַׁפְרִירוֹ עֲלֵיהֶם: [ירמיה מג, י]

ז) וְהָעֹלָה עַל רוּחֲכֶם הָיוֹ לֹא תִהְיֶה אֲשֶׁר אַתֶּם אֹמְרִים נִהְיֶה כַגּוֹיִם כְּמִשְׁפְּחוֹת הָאֲרָצוֹת לְשָׁרֵת עֵץ וָאָבֶן: חַי אָנִי נְאֻם אֲדֹנָי אֱלֹהִים אִם לֹא בְּיָד חֲזָקָה וּבִזְרוֹעַ נְטוּיָה וּבְחֵמָה שְׁפוּכָה אֶמְלוֹךְ עֲלֵיכֶם: [יחזקאל כ, לב-לג]

ח) וְיִסְּרוֹ לַמִּשְׁפָּט אֱלֹהָיו יוֹרֶנּוּ: [ישעיה כח, כו]

ט) וַיִּשְׁלַח מַלְאָכִים אֶל בִּלְעָם בֶּן בְּעוֹר פְּתוֹרָה אֲשֶׁר עַל הַנָּהָר אֶרֶץ בְּנֵי עַמּוֹ לִקְרֹא לוֹ לֵאמֹר הִנֵּה עַם יָצָא מִמִּצְרַיִם הִנֵּה כִסָּה אֶת עֵין הָאָרֶץ וְהוּא יֹשֵׁב מִמֻּלִי: [במדבר כב, ה] י) וַיִּשָּׂא מְשָׁלוֹ וַיֹּאמַר נְאֻם בִּלְעָם בְּנוֹ בְעֹר וּנְאֻם הַגֶּבֶר שְׁתֻם הָעָיִן: [במדבר כד, ג] יא) יָשׁוּבוּ רְשָׁעִים לִשְׁאוֹלָה כָּל גּוֹיִם שְׁכֵחֵי אֱלֹהִים: [תהלים ט, יח] יב) מִי מָנָה עֲפַר יַעֲקֹב וּמִסְפָּר אֶת רֹבַע יִשְׂרָאֵל תָּמֹת נַפְשִׁי מוֹת יְשָׁרִים וּתְהִי אַחֲרִיתִי כָּמֹהוּ: [במדבר כג, י] יג) וְעַתָּה הִנְנִי הוֹלֵךְ לְעַמִּי לְכָה אִיעָצְךָ אֲשֶׁר יַעֲשֶׂה הָעָם הַזֶּה לְעַמְּךָ בְּאַחֲרִית הַיָּמִים: [במדבר כד, יד] יד) וַיֵּלְכוּ זִקְנֵי מוֹאָב וְזִקְנֵי מִדְיָן וּקְסָמִים בְּיָדָם וַיָּבֹאוּ אֶל בִּלְעָם וַיְדַבְּרוּ אֵלָיו דִּבְרֵי בָלָק: [במדבר כב, ז] טו) וַיֹּאמֶר אֲלֵיהֶם לִינוּ פֹה הַלַּיְלָה וַהֲשִׁבֹתִי אֶתְכֶם דָּבָר כַּאֲשֶׁר יְדַבֵּר יְיָ אֵלָי וַיֵּשְׁבוּ שָׂרֵי מוֹאָב עִם בִּלְעָם: [במדבר כב, ח] טז) וַיֹּאמֶר אֱלֹהִים אֶל בִּלְעָם לֹא תֵלֵךְ עִמָּהֶם לֹא תָאֹר אֶת הָעָם כִּי בָרוּךְ הוּא: [במדבר כב, יב] יז) וַיָּבֹא אֱלֹהִים אֶל בִּלְעָם לַיְלָה וַיֹּאמֶר לוֹ אִם לִקְרֹא לְךָ בָּאוּ הָאֲנָשִׁים קוּם לֵךְ אִתָּם וְאַךְ אֶת הַדָּבָר אֲשֶׁר אֲדַבֵּר אֵלֶיךָ אֹתוֹ תַעֲשֶׂה: [במדבר כב, כ] יח) וְאָנֹכִי הַיּוֹם רַךְ וּמָשׁוּחַ מֶלֶךְ וְהָאֲנָשִׁים הָאֵלֶּה בְּנֵי צְרוּיָה קָשִׁים מִמֶּנִּי יְשַׁלֵּם יְיָ לְעֹשֵׂה הָרָעָה כְּרָעָתוֹ: [שמואל ב' ג, לט] יט) וַיֹּאמֶר בִּלְעָם לְבָלָק הִתְיַצֵּב עַל עֹלָתֶךָ וְאֵלְכָה אוּלַי יִקָּרֵה יְיָ לִקְרָאתִי וּדְבַר מַה יַּרְאֵנִי וְהִגַּדְתִּי לָךְ וַיֵּלֶךְ שֶׁפִי: [במדבר כג, ג] כ) יְהִי דָן נָחָשׁ עֲלֵי דֶרֶךְ שְׁפִיפֹן עֲלֵי אֹרַח הַנֹּשֵׁךְ עִקְּבֵי סוּס וַיִּפֹּל רֹכְבוֹ אָחוֹר: [בראשית מט, יז] כא) נְאֻם שֹׁמֵעַ אִמְרֵי אֵל וְיֹדֵעַ דַּעַת עֶלְיוֹן מַחֲזֵה שַׁדַּי יֶחֱזֶה נֹפֵל וּגְלוּי עֵינָיִם: [במדבר כד, טז] כב) וְהַמֶּלֶךְ שָׁב מִגִּנַּת הַבִּיתָן אֶל בֵּית מִשְׁתֵּה הַיַּיִן וְהָמָן נֹפֵל עַל הַמִּטָּה אֲשֶׁר אֶסְתֵּר עָלֶיהָ וַיֹּאמֶר הַמֶּלֶךְ הֲגַם לִכְבּוֹשׁ אֶת הַמַּלְכָּה עִמִּי בַּבָּיִת הַדָּבָר יָצָא מִפִּי הַמֶּלֶךְ וּפְנֵי הָמָן חָפוּ: [אסתר ז, ח] כג) כָּרַע שָׁכַב כַּאֲרִי וּכְלָבִיא מִי יְקִימֶנּוּ מְבָרְכֶיךָ בָרוּךְ וְאֹרְרֶיךָ אָרוּר: [במדבר כד, ט] כד) בֵּין רַגְלֶיהָ כָּרַע נָפַל שָׁכָב בֵּין רַגְלֶיהָ כָּרַע נָפָל בַּאֲשֶׁר כָּרַע שָׁם נָפַל שָׁדוּד: [שופטים ה, כז]

The Gemara notes that the source for the Mishnah's teaching that Bilam has no share in the World to Come is a statement by Bilam himself:

וְאַף אוֹתוֹ רָשָׁע נָתַן סִימָן בְּעַצְמוֹ – **And even that wicked one** [Bilam] **set a sign for himself** whereby it is derived that he has no share in the World to Come. אָמַר ,,תָּמֹת נַפְשִׁי מוֹת יְשָׁרִים'' – **He said:**[31] ***May my soul die the death of the upright,*** *and my end will be like his.* This implies: אִם תָּמוּת נַפְשִׁי מוֹת יְשָׁרִים – **If my soul,** i.e. I, **die the death of the upright,** i.e. a natural death, ,,תְּהֵא אַחֲרִיתִי כָּמֹהוּ'' – then ***my end* will be *like his,*** i.e. my fate will be like that of the Jewish people, who are admitted to the World to Come, וְאִם לַאו – **but if not,** i.e. if I do not die a natural death, ,,הִנְנִי הוֹלֵךְ לְעַמִּי'' – then ***Behold, I go to my people,*** i.e. it will indicate that I go to join my wicked compatriots in Gehinnom.[32]

Bilam is invited to curse the Jews by Moab and Midian, two traditional enemies:

,,וַיֵּלְכוּ זִקְנֵי מוֹאָב וְזִקְנֵי מִדְיָן'' – Scripture states:[33] ***The elders of Moab and the elders of Midian went . . .*** *they came to Bilam and spoke to him the words of Balak.* תָּנָא – **A Tanna taught:** מִדְיָן וּמוֹאָב לֹא הָיָה לָהֶם שָׁלוֹם מֵעוֹלָם – **MIDIAN AND MOAB HAD NEVER BEEN AT PEACE WITH EACH OTHER.**[34] Why did they now suddenly unite? מָשָׁל לִשְׁנֵי כְּלָבִים שֶׁהָיוּ בָעֵדֶר – This can be explained by **A PARABLE OF TWO WATCHDOGS WHO WERE WITH A FLOCK** of sheep, וְהָיוּ צְהוּבִין זֶה לָזֶה – **AND [THE DOGS] WERE FIERCELY HOSTILE TO EACH OTHER.**[35] בָּא זְאֵב עַל הָאֶחָד – **A WOLF CAME AGAINST ONE** of the dogs. אָמַר הָאֶחָד – **THE** other **ONE SAID:** אִם אֵינִי עוֹזְרוֹ – **IF I DO NOT HELP [MY FELLOW],** הַיּוֹם הוֹרֵג אוֹתוֹ וּלְמָחָר בָּא עָלַי – **TODAY [THE WOLF] WILL KILL HIM, AND TOMORROW HE WILL COME AGAINST ME.** הָלְכוּ שְׁנֵיהֶם וְהָרְגוּ הַזְּאֵב – So **THE TWO OF THEM WENT AND** together **KILLED THE WOLF.** אָמַר רַב פָּפָּא – **Rav Pappa said:** הַיְינוּ דְּאָמְרֵי אִינְשֵׁי – **This is the meaning of the popular adage:**[36] כַּרְכּוּשְׁתָּא וְשׁוּנְרָא עֲבָדוּ הִלּוּלָא מִתַּרְבָּא דְּבִישׁ גַּדָּא – **"The weasel and the cat made a wedding feast from the fat of an unlucky** victim."[37]

The reaction to Bilam's initial response:

,,וַיֵּשְׁבוּ שָׂרֵי־מוֹאָב עִם־בִּלְעָם'' – ***The officers of Moab stayed with Bilam.***[38] וְשָׂרֵי מִדְיָן לְהֵיכָן אָזוּל – **And where did the officers of Midian go?**[39] כֵּיוָן דְּאָמַר לְהוּ ,,לִינוּ פֹה הַלַּיְלָה וַהֲשִׁבֹתִי אֶתְכֶם דָּבָר'' – **Once [Bilam] said to [the Moabite and Midianite emissaries]:** ***Spend the night here and I shall give you a response,*** אָמְרוּ – **[the Midianites] said:** כְּלוּם יֵשׁ אָב שֶׁשּׂוֹנֵא אֶת בְּנוֹ – **Is there any father that hates his own son?** Of course not![40]

The Gemara derives a lesson from the incident of Bilam:

אָמַר רַב נַחְמָן – **Rav Nachman said:** חוּצְפָּא אֲפִילוּ כְּלַפֵּי שְׁמַיָּא מְהַנֵּי – **Audacity prevails even against** the opposition of **Heaven,** מֵעִיקָּרָא כְּתִיב ,,לֹא תֵלֵךְ עִמָּהֶם'' – **for at first it is written:**[41] ***Do not go with them,*** וּלְבַסּוֹף כְּתִיב ,,קוּם לֵךְ אִתָּם'' – **and at the end it is written:** ***Arise, go with them.***[42]

A similar thought along the same vein:

אָמַר רַב שֵׁשֶׁת – **Rav Sheishess said:** חוּצְפָּא מַלְכוּתָא בְּלֹא תָּאגָא הִיא – **Audacity is "kingship without a crown,"**[43] דִּכְתִיב ,,וְאָנֹכִי הַיּוֹם רַךְ וּמָשׁוּחַ מֶלֶךְ וְהָאֲנָשִׁים הָאֵלֶּה בְּנֵי צְרוּיָה קָשִׁים מִמֶּנִּי וגו' '' – **as it is written:** ***And I am this day weak and have just been anointed king, and these men, the sons of Zeruiah, are too harsh for me,* etc.**[44]

R' Yochanan describes Bilam's deformities and depravities:

אָמַר רַבִּי יוֹחָנָן – **R' Yochanan said:** בִּלְעָם חִיגֵּר בְּרַגְלוֹ אַחַת הָיָה – **Bilam was lame in one of his feet,** שֶׁנֶּאֱמַר ,,וַיֵּלֶךְ שֶׁפִי'' – **as it is stated:** ***He walked limping*** *(shefi).*[45] שִׁמְשׁוֹן בִּשְׁתֵּי רַגְלָיו –

NOTES

31. *Numbers* 23:10.

32. Ibid. 24:14. As it happened, Bilam did not die a natural death, for he was killed by the sword (ibid. 31:8). It is therefore evident from his own words that he did not enter the World to Come, but instead descended to Gehinnom (*Rashi*; cf. *Yad Ramah*).

33. Ibid. 22:7.

34. As it states (*Genesis* 36:35): *And after him there reigned Hadad son of Bedad, who defeats the Midianites in the field of Moab* (*Rashi* from *Sifri, Parashas Mattos* 157; see *Rashi* to *Genesis* ad loc.). Although this refers to an incident that occurred long before the advent of Balak and Bilam, Scripture's use of the present tense (*defeats* instead of *defeated*) indicates that the feud between Midian and Moab was ongoing (*Sifsei Chachamim* to *Numbers* 22:4).

35. Literally: golden or glowing toward each other (see *Torah Temimah Numbers* 6:25 §146). When a man becomes angry, his face glows with rage (*Rashi*).

36. Literally: so people say.

37. I.e. the cat and the weasel are natural enemies. Nevertheless, they are prepared to bond together when it is in their interest to do so. When the opportunity arises, both cat and weasel will abstain from attacking each other and instead unite to attack and devour a victim. Similarly, Moab and Midian, although centuries-old foes, were prepared to unite against the common threat of the Jews.

38. *Numbers* 22:8.

39. The previous verse states that the emissaries of both Midian and Moab came to speak to Bilam. Yet our verse makes no mention of the Midianite officers. Where did they go?

40. I.e. Bilam did not give an immediate reply to the request of the Midianites and Moabites to come and curse the Jews. Instead, he told them that he would ascertain whether God would permit him to comply with their request. At this, the Midianites despaired of Bilam's compliance, for they reasoned that God [Who referred to Himself as the Father of the Jews (*Exodus* 4:22; *Deuteronomy* 14:1)] would never consent to His children being cursed, for it would be unnatural for any father to agree to this (*Rashi*; cf. *Rashi* to *Numbers* 22:7).

41. Ibid. v. 12.

42. Ibid. v. 20. I.e. when Bilam first asked God whether he had permission to accept the Moabite invitation, God replied: *Do not go with them.* Yet when the Moabites sent a second mission to invite Bilam, he asked God a second time whether he might accept. This time God replied: *Arise, go with them.*

Bilam's asking a second time after he saw that God disapproved of his going was an act of audacity. The fact that God eventually permitted him to go with the Moabites indicates that his audacity was rewarded with success. Thus, we learn that audacity prevails even against Heavenly opposition (*Rashi*). [For explanations as to why indeed God agreed to let Bilam go after initially denying his request, see commentaries ad loc.]

43. I.e. the power of audacity is vast. Through it, a person can often overawe his fellow man and dominate him. Indeed, in his domination of people he is a king; all he lacks is a crown (*Rashi; Yad Ramah;* cf. *Maharsha*).

44. *II Samuel* 3:39. Seeking to end a civil war, David and Avner, the two leaders of the opposing sides, came to terms, with Avner agreeing to support David as king over all the tribes of Israel. However, David's general Yoav, the son of Zeruiah, hated Avner and blamed him for the death of Yoav's brother Asael. In spite of the fact that Avner had come to David's headquarters in Hebron in peace, Yoav killed Avner there. Shocked at the killing, David cursed Yoav and ordered him and his men to participate in honoring Avner at the latter's funeral. However, David did not otherwise punish Yoav for the killing. In our verse he explained why: *I am this day weak and have just been anointed king, and these men, the sons of Zeruiah, are too harsh for me;* in other words, the only advantage I have over them is the fact that I was anointed. In terms of power, however, they are stronger than I.

Thus we see that David gave greater weight to their boldness and audacity than to his own sovereignty. This confirms Rav Sheishess' observation that an audacious person is also a kind of king (*Rashi*).

45. *Numbers* 23:3. The word שֶׁפִי (*shefi*), normally translated *alone,* is translated by R' Yochanan as *limping,* from the word שָׁף, meaning *slipped* or *disjointed.*

Maharsha suggests that this refers to the fact that Bilam's leg had been crushed when his donkey had pressed it against a wall on the road

דקאתי מיהודה מואב סיר רחצי זה גחזי שלקה על עסקי רחיצה על אדום אשליך נעלי זה דואג האדומי עלי פלשת התרועעי אמרו מלאכי השרת לפני הקב"ה רבש"ע אם יבא דוד שהרג את הפלשתי והוריש את בניך גת מה אתה עושה לו אמר להן עלי לעשותן ריעים זה לזה א) מדוע שובבה העם הזה ירושלים משובה נצחת וגו' אמר רב תשובה נצחת השיבה כנסת ישראל לנביא אמר להן נביא לישראל חזרו בתשובה אבותיכם שחטאו היכן הם אמרו להן ונביאיכם שלא חטאו היכן הם שנאמר ב) אבותיכם איה הם והנביאים הלעולם יחיו אמר להן (אבותיכם) חזרו והודו שנאמר ג) אך דברי וחוקי אשר צויתי את עבדי הנביאים וגו' שמואל אמר באו עשרה בני אדם וישבו לפניו אמר להן חזרו בתשובה אמרו לו עבד שמכרו רבו ואשה שגרשה בעלה כלום יש לזה על זה כלום אמר לו הקב"ה לנביא לך אמור להן ד) איזה ספר כריתות אמכם אשר שלחתיה או מי מנושי אשר מכרתי אתכם לו הן בעונותיכם נמכרתם ובפשעכם שלחה אמכם והיינו דאמר ריש לקיש מאי דכתיב ה) דוד עבדי ו) נבוכדנצר עבדי גלוי וידוע לפני מי שאמר והיה העולם שעתידין ישראל לומר כך לפיכך הקדים הקב"ה וקראו עבדו א) עבד שקנה נכסים עבד למי נכסים למי ז) והעולה על רוחכם היה לא תהיה אשר אתם אומרים נהיה כגוים כמשפחות הארצות לשרת עץ ואבן חי אני נאם ה' אלהים אם לא ביד חזקה ובזרוע נטויה ובחימה שפוכה אמלוך עליכם ב) אמר רב נחמן כל כי האי ריתחא לירתח רחמנא עלן ולפרוקינן ח) ויסרו למשפט אלהיו יורנו אמר רבה בר בר חנה אמר להן נביא לישראל חזרו בתשובה אמרו לו אין אנו יכולין יצר הרע שולט בנו אמר להם יסרו יצריכם אמרו לו אלהיו יורנו: ארבעה הדיוטות בלעם ודואג ואחיתופל וגחזי: בלעם ג) בלא עם דבר אחר בלעם שבלה עם בן בעור שבא על בעיר תנא הוא בעור הוא כושן רשעתים הוא לבן הארמי בעור שבא על בעיר כושן רשעתים דעבד שתי רשעיות בישראל אחת בימי יעקב ואחת בימי שפוט השופטים ומה שמו לבן הארמי שמו כתיב ט) בן בעור וכתיב י) בנו בעור אמר רבי יוחנן אביו בנו הוא לו בנביאות בלעם הוא דלא אתי לעלמא דאתי הא אחריני אתו מתניתין מני רבי יהושע היא דתניא ד) ר"א אומר יא) ישובו רשעים לשאולה כל גוים שכחי אלהים ישובו רשעים לשאולה אלו פושעי ישראל כל גוים שכחי אלהים אלו פושעי עובדי כוכבים דברי ר"א [א] אמר לו ר' יהושע וכי נאמר ה) בכל גוים והלא לא נאמר אלא כל גוים שכחי אלהים אלא ישובו רשעים לשאולה מאן נינהו כל גוים שכחי אלהים ואף אותו רשע נתן סימן בעצמו אמר יב) תמות נפשי מות ישרים אם תמות נפשי מות ישרים תהא אחריתי כמוהו ואם לאו יג) הנני הולך לעמי יד) וילכו זקני מואב וזקני מדין תנא מדין ומואב לא היה להם שלום מעולם משל לשני כלבים שהיו בעדר והיו צהובין זה לזה בא זאב על האחד אמר האחד אם איני עוזרו היום הורג אותו ולמחר בא עלי הלכו שניהם והרגו הזאב אמר רב פפא היינו דאמרי אינשי כרכושתא ושונרא עבדו הלולא מתרבא דביש גדא טו) וישבו שרי מואב עם בלעם ושרי מדין להיכן אזול כיון דאמר להו טו) לינו פה הלילה והשבותי אתכם דבר אמרו כלום יש אב ששונא את בנו אמר רב נחמן חוצפא אפילו כלפי שמיא מהני מעיקרא כתיב טז) לא תלך עמהם ולבסוף כתיב יז) קום לך אתם אמר רב ששת חוצפא ו) מלכותא בלא תאגא היא דכתיב יח) ואנכי היום רך ומשוח מלך והאנשים האלה בני צרויה קשים ממני וגו' א"ר יוחנן בלעם ז) חיגר ברגלו אחת היה שנאמר יט) וילך שפי שמשון בשתי רגליו שנאמר כ) שפיפון עלי אורח הנושך עקבי סוס בלעם סומא באחת מעיניו היה שנאמר ז) שתום העין קוסם באמתו היה כתיב הכא כא) נופל וגלוי עינים וכתיב התם כב) והנה המן נופל על המטה וגו' איתמר מר זוטרא אמר קוסם באמתו היה מר בריה דרבינא אמר שבא על אתונו מ"ד קוסם באמתו היה כדאמרן ומ"ד בא על אתונו היה כתיב הכא ח) [א] כג) כרע שכב וכתיב התם כד) בין רגליה כרע

דקא אתי מיהודה. דקאמר לו דוד ואתה אנוש כערכי אלופי ומיודעי שהיה קורא לאחיתופל מיודעי קרובי שהיה משבט יהודה כדוד: מואב סיר רחצי. דוד דקא אתי ממואב: סיר רחצי. גחזי שסר ונצטרע על עסקי רחילה: על אדום אשליך נעלי. אנעיל אותם בגן עדן: אם יבא דוד שהרג את הפלשתי. ויצעק לפניך על שאתה נותן חלק לדואג ואחיתופל לעוה"ב מה אתה עושה להפיס דעתו שהם היו שונאין אותו: אמר להם. עלי לפייסן ולעשותן ריעים ואהובים זה לזה והיינו התרועעי לשון ריעות: ושמואל אמר מאי תשובה נלחת כה"ג [באו] עשרה בני אדם וכו': עבד שמכרו רבו. ומאחר שמכרנו הקב"ה לנבוכדנצר וגרשנו מעליו יש לו עלינו כלום: מאי דכתיב ודוד עבדי נבוכדנצר עבדי. שקראו לאותו רשע עבד כמו שקראו לדוד דכתיב בסוף ירמיה (מג) הנני שולח ולקחתי את נבוכדנצר עבדי לא מפני שדומה זה לזה אלא גלוי וידוע לפני מי שאמר והיה העולם שעתידין ישראל לומר כבר מכרנו הקב"ה לנבוכדנצר לפיכך הקדים הקב"ה וקרא עבדי לנבוכדנצר כדי להחזיר להן תשובה: עבד למי נכסים למי. כלומר נבוכדנצר עבדי הוא וכל מה שקנה לי הוא ועדיין לא יצאתם מרשותי: והעולה על רוחכם היה לא תהיה. כל מה שאתם סבורים לא יהיה: כל כי האי ריתחא. מי יתן ויבא לנו זה הכעס בחימה שפוכה אמלוך עליכם שיגאלנו בעל כרחנו וימלוך עלינו: א"ר אבא בר כהנא. היינו תשובה נלחת דאמרו ליה אלהים יורנו שאין אנו יכולין ליסר אותו: בלא עם. שאין לו חלק עם עם: שבלה עם. שבלבל ישראל בעצתו שהשיאו לבלק כדבעינן למימר לקמן והפיל מהם כ"ד אלפים: בעור שבא על בעיר. שבא על אתונו כמו בהמה דמתרגמינן בעיר: תנא הוא בעור. אביו של בלעם הוא כושן רשעתים הוא לבן הארמי: אחת בימי יעקב. שרדף אחריו ובקש לעקור הכל: ואחת בימי שופטים. לאחר מיתת יהושע דכתיב (שופטים ג) ויחר אף ה' בישראל ויתנם ביד כושן רשעתים: בנו בעור. משמע בעור בנו של בלעם היה: בנו הוא. לבלעם בנביאות שבלעם גדול מאביו היה בנביאות: הא שאר נכרים אתו. כלומר מדקא חשיב תנא דמתניתין דבלעם שהיה נכרי בהדי הדיוטות וקאמר דאין לו חלק מכלל דשאר נכרים יש להם חלק: מתניתין מני וכו'. א"ל ר' יהושע אלו נאמר ישובו רשעים לשאולה ט) בכל הגוים משמע כדקאמרת השתא דכתיב כל גוים שכחי אלהים לא משמע אלא אותן השוכחים אלוה כגון בלעם [ושכמותו] אבל אחריני אתו כדאמרינן בריש פרקין (דף נא:) ורעו זרים צאנכם ובני נכר אכריכם לעולם הבא: מאי נינהו כל גוים שכחי אלהים. דמשום הכי בורר הקב"ה הרשעים שבהם ונותן אותם בגיהנם ואין להם חלק לעתיד אבל השאר יש להם חלק: ואף אותו רשע נתן סימן בעצמו. שאין לו חלק לעתיד: תמות נפשי מות ישרים. אם ימות מיתת עצמו תהא אחריתי כמוהו דודאי יש לו חלק עמהם: ואם לאו. דלא ימות אלא יהרג הנני הולך לעמי לגיהנם: לא היה להם שלום. דכתיב המכה את מדין בשדה מואב: צהובין. כעוסין כאדם שכועס פניו להובין: כרכושתא. חולדה: כרכושתא ושונרא. אין להם שלום מעולם: ביש גדא. מזל רע: כלום יש אב ששונא את בנו. שהוא סבור שיאמר לו הקב"ה קלל את בני דקאמר בלעם לינו פה [הלילה]: חוצפא אפילו כלפי שמיא מהני. דאהני ליה מה שהאליף פניו לומר לשלוחי בלק י) לינו פה שאמר לו הקב"ה בתחילה לא תלך והדר אמר לך: מלכותא בלא תגא. כלומר שררה גדולה ואינו חסר אלא כתר מלכות: אנכי היום רך ומשוח מלך והאנשים האלה קשים ממני. כלומר איני גדול מהם אלא משיחת מלכות: שפי. כמו (חולין דף נד:) בוקא דאטמא דשף מדוכתיה: שפיפון. משמעו שתים: שתום העין. שתום פתוח כמו שתומו ניכר כ) כלומר עינו אחת פתוחה מכלל דהאחרת סתומה והכי נמי מתרגמינן דשפיר חזי אית דמפרשי שתום כמו סתום ולאו מילתא היא: קוסם באמתו. כגון מעלה בזכורו:

כרע

א) [לעיל לא. מגילה טז.], ב) ר"ה לב:, ג) [גיר' הערוך בלע עם פי' שיצן עצות לבלע עם ישראל ד"א בלעם בלא עם פי' שאין לו חלק עם ישראל. ערך בלע], ד) [תוספ' פי"ג], ה) [בילקוט ליתא אכן בע"י איתא בכל וגיר' זו נראה נכונה ודע דבתוספתא פרק י"ג תניא להך פלוגתא דר"א ור' יהושע בנוסחא אחריני ע"ש על נכון], ו) [לעיל לט:], ז) [סוטה י.], ח) [כל העובר על הפסוקים יראה דהך קרא כרע שכב דכתיב בפרשת בלק כ"ד פסוק ט' כרע שכב כארי וכלביא מי יקימנו בשבח לישראל נאמרה כדמפרש בתרגום ורש"י וכן בברכות יב: וע"ש דאין לענין כרע שכב שום שייכות לבלעם כלל ומלוה לתקן ולהסביר ועמ"ש בתקוני כלי שרת], ט) [נ"ל ככל], י) [בקרא דהכא לא כתיב כך ואולי כוונת רש"י על המכוון דכתיב כ"ב פסוק י"ט שבו נא בזה גם אתם הלילה], כ) [ע"ז סט: וע"ש ברש"י סט. ד"ה ותיגוב].

תורה אור השלם

א) מַדּוּעַ שׁוֹבְבָה הָעָם הַזֶּה יְרוּשָׁלַםִ מְשֻׁבָה נִצַּחַת הֶחֱזִיקוּ בַּתַּרְמִית מֵאֲנוּ לָשׁוּב: [ירמיה ח, ה]

ב) אֲבוֹתֵיכֶם אַיֵּה הֵם וְהַנְּבִאִים הַלְעוֹלָם יִחְיוּ: [זכריה א, ה]

ג) אַךְ דְּבָרַי וְחֻקַּי אֲשֶׁר צִוִּיתִי אֶת עֲבָדַי הַנְּבִיאִים הֲלוֹא הִשִּׂיגוּ אֲבֹתֵיכֶם וַיָּשׁוּבוּ וַיֹּאמְרוּ כַּאֲשֶׁר זָמַם יְיָ צְבָאוֹת לַעֲשׂוֹת לָנוּ כִּדְרָכֵינוּ וּכְמַעֲלָלֵינוּ כֵּן עָשָׂה אִתָּנוּ: [זכריה א, ו]

ד) כֹּה אָמַר יְיָ אֵי זֶה סֵפֶר כְּרִיתוּת אִמְּכֶם אֲשֶׁר שִׁלַּחְתִּיהָ אוֹ מִי מִנּוֹשַׁי אֲשֶׁר מָכַרְתִּי אֶתְכֶם לוֹ הֵן בַּעֲוֹנֹתֵיכֶם נִמְכַּרְתֶּם וּבְפִשְׁעֵיכֶם שֻׁלְּחָה אִמְּכֶם: [ישעיה נ, א]

ה) וְעַתָּה עֲשׂוּ כִּי יְיָ אָמַר אֶל דָּוִד לֵאמֹר בְּיַד דָּוִד עַבְדִּי הוֹשִׁיעַ אֶת עַמִּי יִשְׂרָאֵל מִיַּד פְּלִשְׁתִּים וּמִיַּד כָּל אֹיְבֵיהֶם: [שמואל ב' ג, יח]

ו) וְאָמַרְתָּ אֲלֵיהֶם כֹּה אָמַר יְיָ צְבָאוֹת אֱלֹהֵי יִשְׂרָאֵל הִנְנִי שֹׁלֵחַ וְלָקַחְתִּי אֶת נְבוּכַדְרֶאצַּר מֶלֶךְ בָּבֶל עַבְדִּי וְשַׂמְתִּי כִסְאוֹ מִמַּעַל לָאֲבָנִים הָאֵלֶּה אֲשֶׁר טָמָנְתִּי וְנָטָה אֶת שַׁפְרִירוֹ עֲלֵיהֶם: [ירמיה מג, י]

ז) וְהָעֹלָה עַל רוּחֲכֶם הָיוֹ לֹא תִהְיֶה אֲשֶׁר אַתֶּם אֹמְרִים נִהְיֶה כַגּוֹיִם כְּמִשְׁפְּחוֹת הָאֲרָצוֹת לְשָׁרֵת עֵץ וָאָבֶן: חַי אָנִי נְאֻם אֲדֹנָי אֱלֹהִים אִם לֹא בְּיָד חֲזָקָה וּבִזְרוֹעַ נְטוּיָה וּבְחֵמָה שְׁפוּכָה אֶמְלוֹךְ עֲלֵיכֶם: [יחזקאל כ, לב-לג]

ח) וְיִסְּרוֹ לַמִּשְׁפָּט אֱלֹהָיו יוֹרֶנּוּ: [ישעיה כח, כו]

ט) וַיִּשְׁלַח מַלְאָכִים אֶל בִּלְעָם בֶּן בְּעוֹר פְּתוֹרָה אֲשֶׁר עַל הַנָּהָר אֶרֶץ בְּנֵי עַמּוֹ לִקְרֹא לוֹ לֵאמֹר הִנֵּה עַם יָצָא מִמִּצְרַיִם הִנֵּה כִסָּה אֶת עֵין הָאָרֶץ וְהוּא יֹשֵׁב מִמֻּלִי: [במדבר כב, ה] י) וַיִּשָּׂא מְשָׁלוֹ וַיֹּאמַר נְאֻם בִּלְעָם בְּנוֹ בְעֹר וּנְאֻם הַגֶּבֶר שְׁתֻם הָעָיִן: [במדבר כד, ג] יא) יָשׁוּבוּ רְשָׁעִים לִשְׁאוֹלָה כָּל גּוֹיִם שְׁכֵחֵי אֱלֹהִים: [תהלים ט, יח] יב) מִי מָנָה עֲפַר יַעֲקֹב וּמִסְפָּר אֶת רֹבַע יִשְׂרָאֵל תָּמֹת נַפְשִׁי מוֹת יְשָׁרִים וּתְהִי אַחֲרִיתִי כָּמֹהוּ: [במדבר כג, י] יג) וְעַתָּה הִנְנִי הוֹלֵךְ לְעַמִּי לְכָה אִיעָצְךָ אֲשֶׁר יַעֲשֶׂה הָעָם הַזֶּה לְעַמְּךָ בְּאַחֲרִית הַיָּמִים: [במדבר כד, יד] יד) וַיֵּלְכוּ זִקְנֵי מוֹאָב וְזִקְנֵי מִדְיָן וּקְסָמִים בְּיָדָם וַיָּבֹאוּ אֶל בִּלְעָם וַיְדַבְּרוּ אֵלָיו דִּבְרֵי בָלָק: [במדבר כב, ז] טו) וַיֹּאמֶר אֲלֵיהֶם לִינוּ פֹה הַלַּיְלָה וַהֲשִׁבֹתִי אֶתְכֶם דָּבָר כַּאֲשֶׁר יְדַבֵּר יְיָ אֵלָי וַיֵּשְׁבוּ שָׂרֵי מוֹאָב עִם בִּלְעָם: [במדבר כב, ח] טז) וַיֹּאמֶר אֱלֹהִים אֶל בִּלְעָם לֹא תֵלֵךְ עִמָּהֶם לֹא תָאֹר אֶת הָעָם כִּי בָרוּךְ הוּא: [במדבר כב, יב] יז) וַיָּבֹא אֱלֹהִים אֶל בִּלְעָם לַיְלָה וַיֹּאמֶר לוֹ אִם לִקְרֹא לְךָ בָּאוּ הָאֲנָשִׁים קוּם לֵךְ אִתָּם וְאַךְ אֶת הַדָּבָר אֲשֶׁר אֲדַבֵּר אֵלֶיךָ אֹתוֹ תַעֲשֶׂה: [במדבר כב, כ] יח) וְאָנֹכִי הַיּוֹם רַךְ וּמָשׁוּחַ מֶלֶךְ וְהָאֲנָשִׁים הָאֵלֶּה בְּנֵי צְרוּיָה קָשִׁים מִמֶּנִּי יְשַׁלֵּם יְיָ לְעֹשֵׂה הָרָעָה כְּרָעָתוֹ: [שמואל ב' ג, לט] יט) וַיֹּאמֶר בִּלְעָם לְבָלָק הִתְיַצֵּב עַל עֹלָתֶךָ וְאֵלְכָה אוּלַי יִקָּרֶה יְיָ לִקְרָאתִי וּדְבַר מַה יַּרְאֵנִי וְהִגַּדְתִּי לָךְ וַיֵּלֶךְ שֶׁפִי: [במדבר כג, ג] כ) יְהִי דָן נָחָשׁ עֲלֵי דֶרֶךְ שְׁפִיפֹן עֲלֵי אֹרַח הַנֹּשֵׁךְ עִקְּבֵי סוּס וַיִּפֹּל רֹכְבוֹ אָחוֹר: [בראשית מט, יז] כא) נְאֻם שֹׁמֵעַ אִמְרֵי אֵל וְיֹדֵעַ דַּעַת עֶלְיוֹן מַחֲזֵה שַׁדַּי יֶחֱזֶה נֹפֵל וּגְלוּי עֵינָיִם: [במדבר כד, טז] כב) וְהַמֶּלֶךְ שָׁב מִגִּנַּת הַבִּיתָן אֶל בֵּית מִשְׁתֵּה הַיַּיִן וְהָמָן נֹפֵל עַל הַמִּטָּה אֲשֶׁר אֶסְתֵּר עָלֶיהָ וַיֹּאמֶר הַמֶּלֶךְ הֲגַם לִכְבּוֹשׁ אֶת הַמַּלְכָּה עִמִּי בַּבָּיִת הַדָּבָר יָצָא מִפִּי הַמֶּלֶךְ וּפְנֵי הָמָן חָפוּ: [אסתר ז, ח] כג) כָּרַע שָׁכַב כַּאֲרִי וּכְלָבִיא מִי יְקִימֶנּוּ מְבָרְכֶיךָ בָרוּךְ וְאֹרְרֶיךָ אָרוּר: [במדבר כד, ט] כד) בֵּין רַגְלֶיהָ כָּרַע נָפַל שָׁכָב בֵּין רַגְלֶיהָ כָּרַע נָפָל בַּאֲשֶׁר כָּרַע שָׁם נָפַל שָׁדוּד: [שופטים ה, כז]

עין משפט
נר מצוה

[א מיי' פ' י"א מהלכות עדות דין י ופ"ג מהל' תשובה דין ה]:

הגהות הגר"א

[א] גמ' כתיב הכא כרע שכב. נמחק ב' תיבות כרע שכב ונ"ב נופל:

ליקוטי רש"י

אבותיכם איה הם. ראו שלקו מכה רעה ברעב בחרב ובשבי. והנביאי' הלעולם יחיו. וא"ת אף הנביאים איה הם הרי מתו אני משיב לכם וכי הנביאים היה להם לעולם לחיות אך סופן מוכיח כי אמת היה דבריהם שכל דברי וחוקי גזירות פורענותי אשר צויתי את עבדי הנביאים עליכם הלא השיגו אבותיכם [זכריה א, ה]. באו עשרה בני אדם וישבו לפניו. ויהי בשנה השביעית בחמישי בעשור לחודש באו אנשים מזקני ישראל לדרוש את ידוד וישבו לפני. לדרוש את ה' על צרכיהם ואם אינו שומע לנו גם אנו לא נענש על עבירות שבידנו שהרי כבר מכרנו ואין לו עלינו כלום עבד שמכרו רבו ואשה שגרשה בעלה כלום יש לזה על זה כלום ומסוף הענין אתה למד מתשובה שהשיבם והעולה על רוחכם וגו' [יחזקאל כ, א]. העולה על רוחכם. שעולה על דעתכם. נהיה כגוים. נפרוק עולו מעל צוארנו מאחר ששלח מעליו. היו לא תהיה. כי כבר קבלתם עליכם מדעתכ' בימי יהושע כמו שנאמר (יהושע כד) ויאסוף יהושע את כל שבטי ישראל וכל הענין [יחזקאל כ, לב]. זו מדה טובה לישראל שלא יהיו אומרים הואיל וגלינו בין האומות נעשה כמעשיהם אני איני מניחם אלא מעמיד אני את נביאי ומחזירן לתחת כנפי שנאמר (יחזקאל כ, לג) והעולה על רוחכם היו לא תהיה וגו' חי אני וגו' אם לא ביד חזקה וגו' [ויקרא כו, מא]. בימי שפוט השופטים. לפני מלוך מלך שאול שהיו הדורות מתפרנסים על ידי שופטים ובימי אבצן היה שאמרו רבותינו אבצן זה בועז [רות א, א]. בנו בעור. כמו למעינו מים (תהלים קיד, ח). ומדרש אגדה שניהם היו גדולים מאבותיהם בלק בנו צפור אביו בנו הוא במלכות ובלעם גדול מאביו בנביאות מנה בן פרס היה [במדבר כד, ג]. זקני מואב וזקני מדין. אל זקני מדין. והלא מעולם היו שונאים זה את זה שנאמר (בראשית לו, לה) המכה את מדין בשדה מואב שבאו מדין על מואב למלחמה אלא מיראתן של ישראל עשו שלום ביניהם [במדבר כב, ד]. המכה את מדין בשדה מואב. שבא מדין על מואב למלחמה והלך מלך אדום לעזור את מואב ומכאן אנו למדים שהיו מדין ומואב מריבים זה עם זה ובימי בלעם עשו שלום להתקשר על ישראל [בראשית לו, לה]. מלכותא בלא תגא. שר גדול אלא שאינו מעוטר [לעיל צט:]. שפי. אשלוייש"ם כמו דשף מדוכתיה (חולין דף מב:). שפיפון. שפייה כפולה [סוטה י.]. שתם העין. עינו נקורה ומוצאת לחוץ וחור שלה נראה פתוח ולשון משנה הוא כדי שישתום ויסתום ויגוב (ע"ז סט.) ורבותינו אמרו לפי שאמר ומספר את רובע ישראל שהקב"ה יושב ומונה רביעיותיהן של ישראל מתי תבא טפה שנולד הצדיק ממנה אמר בלבו מי שהוא קדוש ומשרתיו קדושים יסתכל בדברים הללו ועל דבר זה נסמת עינו של בלעם ויש מפרשים שתם העין פתוח העין כמו שתרגם אונקלוס ועל שאמר שתום העין ולא אמר שתום העינים למדנו שסומא באחת מעיניו היה [במדבר כד, ג].

Samson was lame **in both of his legs,** שֶׁנֶּאֱמַר ,,שְׁפִיפֹן עֲלֵי־אֹרַח הַנֹּשֵׁךְ עִקְּבֵי־סוּס" – **as it is stated:** *Dan will be a serpent on the highway,* ***slithering*** *(shefifon)* ***along the path, biting a horse's heels.***[46] בִּלְעָם סוּמָא בְּאַחַת מֵעֵינָיו הָיָה – **Bilam was blind in one of his eyes,** שֶׁנֶּאֱמַר ,,שְׁתֻם הָעָיִן" – **as it is stated:** ***[the man] with the open eye.***[47] קוֹסֵם בְּאַמָּתוֹ הָיָה – **He used to perform sorcery with his male organ,**[48] כְּתִיב הָכָא ,,נֹפֵל וּגְלוּי עֵינָיִם" – as may be deduced from the following verses: **Here,** describing Bilam, **it is written:**[49] ***fallen and with uncovered eyes.*** וּכְתִיב הָתָם ,,וְהָמָן נֹפֵל עַל־הַמִּטָּה וגו' " – **And elsewhere it is written:** ***And Haman was fallen upon the couch*** **etc.**[50]

More on Bilam's depravities:

אִיתְּמַר – **It was said:** מַר זוּטְרָא אָמַר – **Mar Zutra said:** קוֹסֵם בְּאַמָּתוֹ הָיָה – **[Bilam] used to perform sorcery with his male organ.** מַר בְּרֵיהּ דְּרָבִינָא אָמַר – **Mar the son of Ravina said:** שֶׁבָּא עַל אֲתוֹנוֹ – **[Bilam] copulated with his she-donkey.** מַאן דְּאָמַר קוֹסֵם בְּאַמָּתוֹ הָיָה כִּדְאָמָרָן – The source of **the one who said that he used to perform sorcery with his male organ is what we have said,** i.e. the two verses just cited by R' Yochanan. וּמַאן דְּאָמַר בָּא עַל אֲתוֹנוֹ הָיָה – **And** as for the source of **the one who said that [Bilam] copulated with his donkey,** כְּתִיב הָכָא ,,כָּרַע שָׁכַב" – it may be deduced from the following two verses: **Here,** in regard to Bilam, **it is written:** ***He crouched and lay down,***[51] וּכְתִיב הָתָם ,,בֵּין רַגְלֶיהָ – **and elsewhere it is written:** ***Between her legs***

NOTES

to Moab (ibid. 22:25). In spite of his pain, Bilam was so anxious to curse the Jews that he proceeded on the journey until he came to Moab. This verse describes how he limped alongside King Balak in great pain in order to find some way to curse them.

46. *Genesis* 49:17. The verse is the Patriarch Jacob's deathbed blessing of his son Dan's descendants, particularly Samson (who was a member of the tribe of Dan). R' Yochanan sees the double consonant "פ" in the word שְׁפִיפֹן (*shefifon*) as denoting *double lameness* (*Rashi*) and depicting a *slithering movement.* Samson, because of his lameness, would have to slither along the path like a viper.

Maharsha suggests that this is stated in contrast to Bilam. Despite his handicap, Bilam persevered in order to *harm* the Jews. Shimshon, on the other hand, struggled against his handicap to *save* the Jews.

47. *Numbers* 24:3,15. Bilam here describes himself as "the man with the open eye," meaning that only one of his eyes was open, i.e. could see. The other eye was "closed," i.e. blind (*Rashi*).

48. By means of certain occult phallic rites, he would conjure up the spirit of the dead and cause it to settle on his male member (*Rashi* here and to 65b ד"ה בזכורו; cf. *Tosafos* there).

According to *Yad Ramah,* Bilam could foretell the future by interpreting certain physical marks on his organ.

49. Ibid. v. 4.

50. *Esther* 7:8. Exposed as the mortal enemy of Queen Esther and the Jews, Haman trembled for his life. In desperation he fell upon the queen's couch to beg for his life. At that moment *the king returned from the palace garden to the banquet room and Haman was fallen upon the couch upon which Esther was. The king exclaimed, "Would he actually assault the queen while I am in the house!"*

From the king's reaction it is evident that Haman's position (*fallen upon the couch*) suggested that he was trying to rape the queen. Accordingly, the description of Bilam as *fallen* likewise suggests a sin committed with the male organ, in Bilam's case, sorcery. Cf. *Ben Yehoyada.*

51. *Numbers* 24:9. This reading presents difficulties, for the verse is Bilam's description of the Jewish people, not a description of Bilam. *Gra* emends the text of the Gemara, deleting our verse and substituting in its place verse 4, which was cited above: נֹפֵל [וּגְלוּי עֵינָיִם], *fallen [and with uncovered eyes].* See also *Anaf Yosef;* cf. *Rashash*.

דקאתי מיהודה מואב סיר רחצי זה גחזי שלקה על עסקי רחיצה על אדום אשליך נעלי זה דואג האדומי עלי פלשת התרועעי אמרו מלאכי השרת לפני הקב"ה רבש"ע אם יבא דוד שהרג את הפלשתי והוריש את בניך גת מה אתה עושה לו אמר להן עלי לעשותן ריעים זה לזה א) מדוע שובבה העם הזה ירושלים משובה נצחת וגו' אמר רב תשובה נצחת השיבה כנסת ישראל לנביא אמר להן נביא לישראל חזרו בתשובה אבותיכם שחטאו היכן הם אמרו להן ונביאיכם שלא חטאו היכן הם שנאמר ב) אבותיכם איה הם והנביאים הלעולם יחיו אמר להן (אבותיכם) חזרו והודו שנאמר ג) אך דברי וחוקי אשר צויתי את עבדי הנביאים וגו' שמואל אמר באו עשרה בני אדם וישבו לפניו אמר להן חזרו בתשובה אמרו לו עבד שמכרו רבו ואשה שגרשה בעלה כלום יש לזה על זה כלום אמר לו הקב"ה לנביא לך אמור להן ד) איזה ספר כריתות אמכם אשר שלחתיה או מי מנושי אשר מכרתי אתכם לו הן בעונותיכם נמכרתם ובפשעכם שלחה אמכם והיינו דאמר ריש לקיש מאי דכתיב ה) דוד עבדי ו) נבוכדנצר עבדי גלוי וידוע לפני מי שאמר והיה העולם שעתידין ישראל לומר כך לפיכך הקדים הקב"ה וקראו עבדו א) עבד שקנה נכסים עבד למי נכסים למי ז) והעולה על רוחכם היה לא תהיה אשר אתם אומרים נהיה כגוים כמשפחות הארצות לשרת עץ ואבן חי אני נאם ה' אלהים אם לא ביד חזקה ובזרוע נטויה ובחימה שפוכה אמלוך עליכם ב) אמר רב נחמן כל כי האי ריתחא לירתח רחמנא עלן ולפרוקינן ח) ויסרו למשפט אלהיו יורנו אמר רבה בר בר חנה אמר להן נביא לישראל חזרו בתשובה אמרו לו אין אנו יכולין יצר הרע שולט בנו אמר להם יסרו יצריכם אמרו לו אלהיו יורנו: ארבעה הדיוטות בלעם ודואג ואחיתופל וגחזי: בלעם ג) בלא עם דבר אחר בלעם שבלה עם בן בעור שבא על בעיר תנא הוא בעור הוא כושן רשעתים הוא לבן הארמי בעור שבא על בעיר כושן רשעתים דעבד שתי רשעיות בישראל אחת בימי יעקב ואחת בימי שפוט השופטים ומה שמו לבן הארמי שמו כתיב ט) בן בעור וכתיב י) בנו בעור אמר רבי יוחנן אביו בנו הוא לו בנביאות בלעם הוא דלא אתי לעלמא דאתי הא אחריני אתו מתניתין מני רבי יהושע היא דתניא ד) ר"א אומר יא) ישובו רשעים לשאולה כל גוים שכחי אלהים ישובו רשעים לשאולה אלו פושעי ישראל כל גוים שכחי אלהים אלו פושעי עובדי כוכבים דברי ר"א [א*] אמר לו ר' יהושע וכי נאמר ה) בכל גוים והלא לא נאמר אלא כל גוים שכחי אלהים אלא ישובו רשעים לשאולה מאן נינהו כל גוים שכחי אלהים ואף אותו רשע נתן סימן בעצמו אמר יב) תמות נפשי מות ישרים אם תמות נפשי מות ישרים תהא אחריתי כמוהו ואם לאו יג) הנני הולך לעמי יד) וילכו זקני מואב וזקני מדין תנא מדין ומואב לא היה להם שלום מעולם משל לשני כלבים שהיו בעדר והיו צהובין זה לזה בא זאב על האחד אמר האחד אם איני עוזרו היום הורג אותו ולמחר בא עלי הלכו שניהם והרגו הזאב אמר רב פפא היינו דאמרי אינשי כרכושתא ושונרא עבדו הלולא מתרבא דביש גדא טו) וישבו שרי מואב עם בלעם ושרי מדין להיכן אזול כיון דאמר להו טו) לינו פה הלילה והשבותי אתכם דבר אמרו כלום יש אב ששונא את בנו אמר רב נחמן חוצפא אפילו כלפי שמיא מהני מעיקרא כתיב טז) לא תלך עמהם ולבסוף כתיב יז) קום לך אתם אמר רב ששת חוצפא ו) מלכותא בלא תאגא היא דכתיב יח) ואנכי היום רך ומשוח מלך והאנשים האלה בני צרויה קשים ממני וגו' א"ר יוחנן בלעם ז) חיגר ברגלו אחת היה שנאמר יט) וילך שפי שמשון בשתי רגליו שנאמר כ) שפיפון עלי אורח הנושך עקבי סוס בלעם סומא באחת מעיניו היה שנאמר ח) שתום העין קוסם באמתו היה כתיב הכא כא) נופל וגלוי עינים וכתיב התם כב) והנה המן נופל על המטה וגו' איתמר מר זוטרא אמר קוסם באמתו היה מר בריה דרבינא אמר שבא על אתונו מ"ד קוסם באמתו היה כדאמרן ומ"ד בא על אתונו היה כתיב הכא ט) [א] כג) כרע שכב וכתיב התם כד) בין רגליה כרע

רש"י

דקא אתי מיהודה. דקאמר לו דוד ואתה אנוש כערכי אלופי ומיודעי שהיה קורא לאחיתופל מיודעי קרובי שהיה משבט יהודה כדוד: מואב סיר רחצי. דוד דקא אתי ממואב: סיר רחצי. גחזי שסר ונצטרע על עסקי רחיצה: על אדום אשליך נעלי. אנעיל אותם בגן עדן: אם יבא דוד שהרג את הפלשתי. וילעק לפניך על שאתה נותן חלק לדואג ואחיתופל לעוה"ב מה אתה עושה להפיס דעתו שהם היו שונאין אותו: אמר להם. עלי לפייסן ולעשותן ריעים ואהובים זה לזה והיינו התרועעי לשון ריעות: ושמואל אמר מאי תשובה נצחת כה"ג [באו] עשרה בני אדם וכו': עבד שמכרו רבו. ומאחר שמכרנו הקב"ה לנבוכדנצר וגרשנו מעליו יש לו עלינו כלום: מאי דכתיב ודוד עבדי נבוכדנצר עבדי. שקראו לאותו רשע עבד כמו שקראו לדוד דכתיב בסוף ירמיה (מג) הנני שולח ולקחתי את נבוכדנצר עבדי לא מפני שדומה זה לזה אלא גלוי וידוע לפני מי שאמר והיה העולם שעתידין ישראל לומר כבר מכרנו הקב"ה לנבוכדנצר לפיכך הקדים הקב"ה וקרא עבדי לנבוכדנצר כדי להחזיר להן תשובה: עבד למי נכסים למי. כלומר נבוכדנצר עבדי הוא וכל מה שקנה לי הוא ועדיין לא יצאתם מרשותי: והעולה על רוחכם היה לא תהיה. כל מה שאתם סבורים לא יהיה: כל כי האי ריתחא. מי יתן ויבא לנו זה הכעס בחימה שפוכה אמלוך עליכם שיגאלנו בעל כרחנו וימלוך עלינו: א"ר אבא בר כהנא. היינו תשובה נצחת דאמרו ליה אלהים יורנו שאין אנו יכולין ליסר אותו: בלא עם. שאין לו חלק עם עם: שבלה עם. שבלבל ישראל בעצתו שהשיאו לבלק כדבעינן למימר לקמן והפיל מהם כ"ד אלפים: בעור שבא על בעיר. שבא על אתונו כמו בהמה דמתרגמינן בעיר: תנא הוא בעור. אביו של בלעם הוא כושן רשעתים הוא לבן הארמי: אחת בימי יעקב. שרדף אחריו ובקש לעקור הכל: ואחת בימי שופטים. לאחר מיתת יהושע דכתיב (שופטים ג) ויחר אף ה' בישראל ויתנם ביד כושן רשעתים: בנו בעור. משמע בעור בנו של בלעם היה: בנו הוא. לבלעם בנביאות שבלעם גדול מאביו היה בנביאות: הא שאר נכרים אתו. כלומר מדקא חשיב תנא דמתניתין דבלעם שהיה נכרי בהדי הדיוטות וקאמר דאין לו חלק מכלל דשאר נכרים יש להם חלק: מתניתין מני וכו'. א"ל ר' יהושע אלו נאמר ישובו רשעים לשאולה ט) בכל הגוים משמע כדקאמרת השתא דכתיב כל גוים שכחי אלהים לא משמע אלא אותן השוכחים אלוה כגון בלעם [ושכמותו] אבל אחריני אתו כדאמרינן בריש פרקין (דף צא:) ורעו זרים צאנכם ובני נכר אכריכם לעולם הבא: מאי נינהו כל גוים שכחי אלהים. דמשום הכי בורר הקב"ה הרשעים שבהם ונותן אותם בגיהנם ואין להם חלק לעתיד אבל השאר יש להם חלק: ואף אותו רשע נתן סימן בעצמו. שאין לו חלק לעתיד: תמות נפשי מות ישרים. אם ימות מיתת עצמו תהא אחריתי כמוהו דודאי יש לו חלק עמהם: ואם לאו. דלא ימות אלא יהרג הנני הולך לעמי לגיהנם: לא היה להם שלום. דכתיב המכה את מדין בשדה מואב: צהובין. כעוסין כאדם שכועס פניו להובין: כרכושתא. חולדה: כרכושתא ושונרא. אין להם שלום מעולם: ביש גדא. מזל רע: כלום יש אב ששונא את בנו. שהוא סבור שיאמר לו הקב"ה קלל את בני דקאמר בלעם לינו פה [הלילה]: חוצפא אפילו כלפי שמיא מהני. דאהני ליה מה שהחליף פניו לומר לשלוחי בלק י) לינו פה שאמר לו הקב"ה בתחילה לא תלך והדר אמר לך: מלכותא בלא תגא. כלומר שררה גדולה ואינו חסר אלא כתר מלכות: אנכי היום רך ומשוח מלך והאנשים האלה קשים ממני. כלומר איני גדול מהם אלא משיחת מלכות: שפי. כמו (חולין דף נד:) בוקא דאטמא דשף מדוכתיה: שפיפון. משמעו שתים: שתום העין. שתום פתוח כמו שתומו ניכר כ) כלומר עינו אחת פתוחה מכלל דהאחרת סתומה והכי נמי מתרגמינן דשפיר חזי אית דמפרשי שתום כמו סתום ולאו מילתא היא: קוסם באמתו. כגון מעלה בזכורו:

מסורת הש"ס

א) [לעיל לא. מגילה טז.], ב) ר"ה לב:, ג) [גיר' הערוך בלע עם פי' שיען עלות לבלע עם ישראל ד"א בלעם בלא עם פי' שאין לו חלק עם ישראל. ערך בלע], ד) [תוספ' פי"ג], ה) [בילקוט ליתא אכן בע"י איתא בכל וגיר' זו נראה נכונה ודע דבתוספתא פרק י"ג תניא להך פלוגתא דר"א ור' יהושע בנוסחא אחריני ע"ש על נכון], ו) [לעיל לט:], ז) [סוטה י.], ח) [כל העובר על הפסוקים יראה דהך קרא כרע שכב דכתיב בפרשת בלק כ"ד פסוק ט' כרע שכב כארי וכלביא מי יקימנו בשבח לישראל נאמרה כדמפרש בתרגום ורש"י וכן בברכות יב: וע"ש דאין לענין כרע שכב שום שייכות לבלעם כלל ומצוה לתקן ולהסביר ועמ"ש בתקוני כלי שרת], ט) [צ"ל ככל], י) [בקרא דהכא לא כתיב כך ואולי כוונת רש"י על המכוון דכתיב כ"ב פסוק י"ט שבו נא בזה גם אתם הלילה], כ) [ע"ז סט: וע"ש ברש"י סט. ד"ה ותיגוב].

תורה אור השלם

א) מַדּוּעַ שׁוֹבְבָה הָעָם הַזֶּה יְרוּשָׁלַיִם מְשֻׁבָה נִצַּחַת הֶחֱזִיקוּ בַּתַּרְמִית מֵאֲנוּ לָשׁוּב: [ירמיה ח, ה]

ב) אֲבוֹתֵיכֶם אַיֵּה הֵם וְהַנְּבִאִים הַלְעוֹלָם יִחְיוּ: [זכריה א, ה]

ג) אַךְ דְּבָרַי וְחֻקַּי אֲשֶׁר צִוִּיתִי אֶת עֲבָדַי הַנְּבִיאִים הֲלוֹא הִשִּׂיגוּ אֲבֹתֵיכֶם וַיָּשׁוּבוּ וַיֹּאמְרוּ כַּאֲשֶׁר זָמַם יְיָ צְבָאוֹת לַעֲשׂוֹת לָנוּ כִּדְרָכֵינוּ וּכְמַעֲלָלֵינוּ כֵּן עָשָׂה אִתָּנוּ: [זכריה א, ו]

ד) כֹּה אָמַר יְיָ אֵי זֶה סֵפֶר כְּרִיתוּת אִמְּכֶם אֲשֶׁר שִׁלַּחְתִּיהָ אוֹ מִי מִנּוֹשַׁי אֲשֶׁר מָכַרְתִּי אֶתְכֶם לוֹ הֵן בַּעֲוֹנֹתֵיכֶם נִמְכַּרְתֶּם וּבְפִשְׁעֵיכֶם שֻׁלְּחָה אִמְּכֶם: [ישעיה נ, א]

ה) וְעַתָּה עֲשׂוּ כִּי יְיָ אָמַר אֶל דָּוִד לֵאמֹר בְּיַד דָּוִד עַבְדִּי הוֹשִׁיעַ אֶת עַמִּי יִשְׂרָאֵל מִיַּד פְּלִשְׁתִּים וּמִיַּד כָּל אֹיְבֵיהֶם: [שמואל ב' ג, יח]

ו) וְאָמַרְתָּ אֲלֵיהֶם כֹּה אָמַר יְיָ צְבָאוֹת אֱלֹהֵי יִשְׂרָאֵל הִנְנִי שֹׁלֵחַ וְלָקַחְתִּי אֶת נְבוּכַדְרֶאצַּר מֶלֶךְ בָּבֶל עַבְדִּי וְשַׂמְתִּי כִסְאוֹ מִמַּעַל לָאֲבָנִים הָאֵלֶּה אֲשֶׁר טָמָנְתִּי וְנָטָה אֶת שַׁפְרִירוֹ עֲלֵיהֶם: [ירמיה מג, י]

ז) וְהָעֹלָה עַל רוּחֲכֶם הָיוֹ לֹא תִהְיֶה אֲשֶׁר אַתֶּם אֹמְרִים נִהְיֶה כַגּוֹיִם כְּמִשְׁפְּחוֹת הָאֲרָצוֹת לְשָׁרֵת עֵץ וָאָבֶן: חַי אָנִי נְאֻם אֲדֹנָי אֱלֹהִים אִם לֹא בְּיָד חֲזָקָה וּבִזְרוֹעַ נְטוּיָה וּבְחֵמָה שְׁפוּכָה אֶמְלוֹךְ עֲלֵיכֶם: [יחזקאל כ, לב-לג]

ח) וְיִסְּרוֹ לַמִּשְׁפָּט אֱלֹהָיו יוֹרֶנּוּ: [ישעיה כח, כו]

ט) וַיִּשְׁלַח מַלְאָכִים אֶל בִּלְעָם בֶּן בְּעוֹר פְּתוֹרָה אֲשֶׁר עַל הַנָּהָר אֶרֶץ בְּנֵי עַמּוֹ לִקְרֹא לוֹ לֵאמֹר הִנֵּה עַם יָצָא מִמִּצְרַיִם הִנֵּה כִסָּה אֶת עֵין הָאָרֶץ וְהוּא יֹשֵׁב מִמֻּלִי: [במדבר כב, ה] י) וַיִּשָּׂא מְשָׁלוֹ וַיֹּאמַר נְאֻם בִּלְעָם בְּנוֹ בְעֹר וּנְאֻם הַגֶּבֶר שְׁתֻם הָעָיִן: [במדבר כד, ג] יא) יָשׁוּבוּ רְשָׁעִים לִשְׁאוֹלָה כָּל גּוֹיִם שְׁכֵחֵי אֱלֹהִים: [תהלים ט, יח] יב) מִי מָנָה עֲפַר יַעֲקֹב וּמִסְפָּר אֶת רֹבַע יִשְׂרָאֵל תָּמֹת נַפְשִׁי מוֹת יְשָׁרִים וּתְהִי אַחֲרִיתִי כָּמֹהוּ: [במדבר כג, י] יג) וְעַתָּה הִנְנִי הוֹלֵךְ לְעַמִּי לְכָה אִיעָצְךָ אֲשֶׁר יַעֲשֶׂה הָעָם הַזֶּה לְעַמְּךָ בְּאַחֲרִית הַיָּמִים: [במדבר כד, יד] יד) וַיֵּלְכוּ זִקְנֵי מוֹאָב וְזִקְנֵי מִדְיָן וּקְסָמִים בְּיָדָם וַיָּבֹאוּ אֶל בִּלְעָם וַיְדַבְּרוּ אֵלָיו דִּבְרֵי בָלָק: [במדבר כב, ז] טו) וַיֹּאמֶר אֲלֵיהֶם לִינוּ פֹה הַלַּיְלָה וַהֲשִׁבֹתִי אֶתְכֶם דָּבָר כַּאֲשֶׁר יְדַבֵּר יְיָ אֵלָי וַיֵּשְׁבוּ שָׂרֵי מוֹאָב עִם בִּלְעָם: [במדבר כב, ח] טז) וַיֹּאמֶר אֱלֹהִים אֶל בִּלְעָם לֹא תֵלֵךְ עִמָּהֶם לֹא תָאֹר אֶת הָעָם כִּי בָרוּךְ הוּא: [במדבר כב, יב] יז) וַיָּבֹא אֱלֹהִים אֶל בִּלְעָם לַיְלָה וַיֹּאמֶר לוֹ אִם לִקְרֹא לְךָ בָּאוּ הָאֲנָשִׁים קוּם לֵךְ אִתָּם וְאַךְ אֶת הַדָּבָר אֲשֶׁר אֲדַבֵּר אֵלֶיךָ אֹתוֹ תַעֲשֶׂה: [במדבר כב, כ] יח) וְאָנֹכִי הַיּוֹם רַךְ וּמָשׁוּחַ מֶלֶךְ וְהָאֲנָשִׁים הָאֵלֶּה בְּנֵי צְרוּיָה קָשִׁים מִמֶּנִּי יְשַׁלֵּם יְיָ לְעֹשֵׂה הָרָעָה כְּרָעָתוֹ: [שמואל ב' ג, לט] יט) וַיֹּאמֶר בִּלְעָם לְבָלָק הִתְיַצֵּב עַל עֹלָתֶךָ וְאֵלְכָה אוּלַי יִקָּרֵה יְיָ לִקְרָאתִי וּדְבַר מַה יַּרְאֵנִי וְהִגַּדְתִּי לָךְ וַיֵּלֶךְ שֶׁפִי: [במדבר כג, ג] כ) יְהִי דָן נָחָשׁ עֲלֵי דֶרֶךְ שְׁפִיפֹן עֲלֵי אֹרַח הַנֹּשֵׁךְ עִקְּבֵי סוּס וַיִּפֹּל רֹכְבוֹ אָחוֹר: [בראשית מט, יז] כא) נְאֻם שֹׁמֵעַ אִמְרֵי אֵל וְיֹדֵעַ דַּעַת עֶלְיוֹן מַחֲזֵה שַׁדַּי יֶחֱזֶה נֹפֵל וּגְלוּי עֵינָיִם: [במדבר כד, טז] כב) וְהַמֶּלֶךְ שָׁב מִגִּנַּת הַבִּיתָן אֶל בֵּית מִשְׁתֵּה הַיַּיִן וְהָמָן נֹפֵל עַל הַמִּטָּה אֲשֶׁר אֶסְתֵּר עָלֶיהָ וַיֹּאמֶר הַמֶּלֶךְ הֲגַם לִכְבּוֹשׁ אֶת הַמַּלְכָּה עִמִּי בַּבָּיִת הַדָּבָר יָצָא מִפִּי הַמֶּלֶךְ וּפְנֵי הָמָן חָפוּ: [אסתר ז, ח] כג) כָּרַע שָׁכַב כַּאֲרִי וּכְלָבִיא מִי יְקִימֶנּוּ מְבָרֲכֶיךָ בָרוּךְ וְאֹרְרֶיךָ אָרוּר: [במדבר כד, ט] כד) בֵּין רַגְלֶיהָ כָּרַע נָפַל שָׁכָב בֵּין רַגְלֶיהָ כָּרַע נָפָל בַּאֲשֶׁר כָּרַע שָׁם נָפַל שָׁדוּד: [שופטים ה, כז]

עין משפט נר מצוה

[א מיי' פ' י"א מהלכות עדות דין י ופ"ג מהל' תשובה דין ה]:

הגהות הגר"א

[א] גמ' כתיב הכא כרע שכב. נמחק ב' תיבות כרע שכב ונ"ב נופל:

ליקוטי רש"י

אבותיכם איה הם. ראו שלקו מכה רעה ברעב בחרב ובשבי. והנביאי' הלעולם יחיו. וא"ת אף הנביאים איה הם הרי מתו אני משיב לכם וכי הנביאים היה להם לעולם לחיות אך סופן מוכיח כי אמת היה דבריהם שכל דברי וחוקי גזירות פורענותי אשר צויתי את עבדי הנביאים עליכם הלא השיגו אבותיכם [זכריה א, ה]. באו עשרה בני אדם וישבו לפניו. ויהי בשנה השביעית בחמישי בעשור לחודש באו אנשים מזקני ישראל לדרוש את ידוד וישבו לפני. לדרוש את ה' על צרכיהם ואם אינו שומע לנו גם אנו לא נענש על עבירות שבידנו שהרי כבר מכרנו ואין לו עלינו כלום עבד שמכרו רבו ואשה שגרשה בעלה כלום יש לזה על זה כלום ומסוף הענין אתה למד מתשובה שהשיבם והעולה על רוחכם וגו' [יחזקאל כ, א]. העולה על רוחכם. שעולה על דעתכם. נהיה כגוים. נפרוק עולו מעל צוארנו מאחר ששלח מעליו. היו לא תהיה. כי כבר קבלתם עליכם מדעתכ' בימי יהושע כמו שנאמר (יהושע כד) ויאסוף יהושע את כל שבטי ישראל וכל הענין [יחזקאל כ, לב]. זו מדה טובה לישראל שלא יהיו אומרים הואיל וגלינו בין האומות נעשה כמעשיהם אני איני מניחם אלא מעמיד אני את נביאי ומחזירן לתחת כנפי שנאמר (יחזקאל כ, לב) והעולה על רוחכם היו לא תהיה וגו' חי אני וגו' אם לא ביד חזקה וגו' [ויקרא כו, מא]. בימי שפוט השופטים. לפני מלוך מלך שאול שהיו הדורות מתפרנסים על ידי שופטים ובימי אבצן היה שאמרו רבותינו אבצן זה בועז [רות א, א]. בנו בעור. כמו למעינו מים (תהלים קיד, ח). ומדרש אגדה שניהם היו גדולים מאבותיהם בלק בנו לצפור אביו בנו הוא במלכות ובלעם גדול מאביו בנביאות מנה בן פרס היה [במדבר כד, ג]. זקני מואב וזקני מדין. אל זקני מדין. והלא מעולם היו שונאים זה את זה שנאמר (בראשית לו, לה) המכה את מדין בשדה מואב שבאו מדין על מואב למלחמה אלא מיראתן של ישראל עשו שלום ביניהם [במדבר כב, ד]. המכה את מדין בשדה מואב. שבא מדין על מואב למלחמה והלך מלך אדום לעזור את מואב ומכאן אנו למדים שהיו מדין ומואב מריבים זה עם זה ובימי בלעם עשו שלום להתקשר על ישראל [בראשית לו, לה]. מלכותא בלא תגא. שר גדול אלא שאינו מעוטר [לעיל צט:]. שפי. אשלוייש"ש כמו דשף מדוכתיה (חולין דף מב:). שפיפון. שפייה כפולה [סוטה י.]. שתם העין. עינו נקורה ומוצאת לחוץ וחור שלה נראה פתוח ולשון משנה הוא כדי שישתום ויסתום ויגוב (ע"ז סט.) ורבותינו אמרו לפי שאמר ומספר את רובע ישראל שהקב"ה יושב ומונה רביעיותיהן של ישראל מתי תבא טפה שנולד הצדיק ממנה אמר בלבו מי שהוא קדוש ומשרתיו קדושים יסתכל בדברים הללו ועל דבר זה נסמת עינו של בלעם ויש מפרשים שתום העין כמו שתרגם אונקלוס ועל שאמר שתום העין ולא אמר שתום העינים למדנו שסומא באחת מעיניו היה [במדבר כד, ג].

כרע נפל שכב וגו' [א] ויודע דעת עליון השתא [א] דעת בהמתו לא הוה ידע דעת עליון הוה ידע מאי דעת בהמתו דאמרי ליה מאי טעמא לא רכבת [ב] סוסיא אמר להו שדאי להו ברטיבא אמרה ליה הלא אנכי אתונך לטעינא בעלמא אשר רכבת עלי אקראי בעלמא מעודך עד היום הזה ולא עוד אלא שאני עושה [לך] מעשה אישות בלילה כתיב הכא [ב] ההסכן הסכנתי וכתיב התם [ג] ותהי לו סוכנת אלא מאי ויודע דעת עליון שהיה יודע לכוון אותה שעה שהקב"ה כועס בה והיינו דקאמר להו נביא לישראל [ד] עמי זכר נא מה יעץ בלק מלך מואב ומה ענה אותו בלעם בן בעור מן השטים ועד הגלגל למען דעת צדקות ה' מאי למען דעת צדקות ה' אמר להן הקב"ה לישראל דעו נא כמה צדקות עשיתי עמכם שלא כעסתי כל אותן הימים בימי בלעם הרשע [ג] שאילמלא כעסתי כל אותן הימים לא נשתייר משונאיהן של ישראל שריד ופליט היינו דקאמר ליה בלעם לבלק [ה] מה אקב לא קבה אל ([ד] וגו' אותן היום [הימים] לא זעם ה') [ו] אל זועם בכל יום וכמה זעמו רגע שנאמר [ז] כי רגע באפו חיים ברצונו וגו' איבעית אימא [ח] לך עמי בא בחדריך וסגור דלתיך בעדך חבי כמעט רגע עד יעבר זעם אימת רתח בתלת שעי קמייתא כי חוורא כרבלתא דתרנגולא כל שעתא ושעתא נמי חוורא כל שעתא ושעתא אית ביה סוריקי סומקי ההיא שעתא לית ביה סוריקי סומקי ההוא מינא דהוה בשיבבותיה דרבי יהושע בן לוי דהוה קא מצער ליה יומא חד נקט [ה] תרנגולתא ואסר ליה בכרעיה ואותיב אמר כי מטא ההוא שעתא אילטייה כי מטא ההוא שעתא נמנם אמר שמע מינה לאו אורח ארעא דכתיב [ט] גם ענוש לצדיק לא טוב אפילו במיני לא איבעי ליה למימר הכי תנא משמיה דרבי מאיר בשעה שהחמה זורחת והמלכים מניחין כתריהן על ראשיהן ומשתחוים לחמה מיד כועס [י] ויקם בלעם בבקר ויחבוש את אתונו תנא משום רבי שמעון בן אלעזר אהבה מבטלת שורה של גדולה מאברהם דכתיב [כ] וישכם אברהם בבקר שנאה מבטלת שורה של גדולה מבלעם שנאמר ויקם בלעם בבקר ויחבוש את אתונו [ו] אמר רב יהודה אמר רב [א] לעולם יעסוק אדם בתורה ובמצוה אפילו שלא לשמה שמתוך שלא לשמה בא לשמה שבשכר ארבעים ושתים קרבנות שהקריב בלק זכה ויצאה ממנו רות א"ר [ז] יוסי בר הונא רות בתו של עגלון בן בנו של בלק מלך מואב היתה א"ל רבא לרבה בר מרי כתיב [ל] ייטב אלהים את שם שלמה משמך ויגדל [את] כסאו מכסאך אורח ארעא למימרא ליה למלכא הכי א"ל מעין קאמרה ליה דאי לא תימא הכי [מ] תבורך מנשים יעל אשת חבר הקיני מנשים באהל תבורך נשים באהל מאן נינהו שרה רבקה רחל ולאה אורח ארעא למימר הכי אלא מעין קאמר הכא נמי מעין קאמר ופליגא דרב יוסי בר חוני דאמר רב יוסי בר חוני בכל אדם מתקנא חוץ מבנו ותלמידו בנו משלמה ותלמידו איבעית אימא [נ] ויהי נא פי שנים ברוחך אלי ואיבעית אימא [ס] ויסמוך את ידיו עליו ויצוהו [ע] וישם דבר בפי בלעם ר"א אומר מלאך ר' יונתן אמר חכה א"ר יוחנן מברכתו של אותו רשע אתה למד מה היה בלבו ביקש לומר שלא יהו להם בתי כנסיות ובתי מדרשות [פ] מה טובו אהליך יעקב לא תשרה שכינה עליהם ומשכנותיך ישראל לא תהא מלכותן נמשכת [צ] כנחלים נטיו לא יהא להם זיתים וכרמים כגנות עלי נהר לא יהא ריחן נודף כאהלים נטע ה' לא יהיו להם מלכים בעלי קומה כארזים עלי מים לא יהיה להם מלך בן מלך [ק] יזל מים מדליו לא תהא מלכותן שולטת באומות וזרעו במים רבים לא תהא עזה מלכותן וירם מאגג מלכו לא תהא [ח] אימת מלכותן ותנשא מלכותו אמר רבי אבא בר כהנא כולם חזרו לקללה חוץ מבתי כנסיות ומבתי מדרשות שנאמר [ר] ויהפוך ה' אלהיך לך את הקללה לברכה כי אהבך ה' אלהיך קללה ולא קללות [ט] א"ר שמואל בר נחמני א"ר יונתן מאי דכתיב [ש] נאמנים פצעי אוהב ונעתרות נשיקות שונא טובה קללה שקילל אחיה השילוני את ישראל יותר מברכה שברכם בלעם הרשע אחיה השילוני קילל את ישראל בקנה שנאמר [ת] והכה ה' את ישראל כאשר ינוד הקנה במים וגו' מה קנה זה עומד במקום מים וגיזעו מחליף

כרע נפל. מה כריעה דהתם דאית ביה נפילה בעילה היא אף כריעה דהכא דכתיב נופל בעילה היא שבא על בהמתו: **דעת בהמתו לא הוה ידע.** מאי בעיא לאהדורי כדמפרש דאמרי ליה שרי בלק מאי טעמא לא רכבת אסוסיא: **ברטיבא.** באחו לרעות עשבים לחים: **אמר להו לטעינא בעלמא.** ליטא משאות ולא לרכוב: אמרה ליה אשר רכבת עלי: **אקראי בעלמא.** כשאין לי סוס מזומן: אמרה לו מעודך: **מעשה אישות.** שאתה בועלי: **סוכנת.** מחממת: **מן השטים ועד הגלגל.** משחטאו בשטים ועד שנכנסו לארץ וחטאו בגלגל עשיתי עמהם צדקות הרבה: **כל אותן הימים.** שהיה בלעם מצפה לקללם בשעה שהקב"ה כועס בה כל הקללות מתקיימות: **ה"ג לא זעם ה'.** אותן הימים לא זעם ה': **אל זועם בכל יום.** קרא הוא: **כמה זעמו רגע.** כדמפיק ליה מקרא כי רגע באפו חיים ברצונו: **בתלת שעי קמייתא.** של יום זמן קימה שכל שלש שעות זמן קימה לעמוד ממטתו וכועס הקב"ה בשעה שרואה המלכים שמשתחוים לחמה בשעה שמניחין כתריהם בראשם כדלקמן: **כרבלתא.** קירסת"א בלע"ז: **כל שעתא נמי חיורא.** רוב שעות מתלבנת ומכספת שאינה כל שעה בחוזק אדמימות: **סורייקי סומקי.** אפי' כשמכספת יש בה שורות שורות אדומות מאד כרגילותם אבל אותה שעה כולה מכספת: **גם ענוש לצדיק לא טוב.** אין נכון לצדיק שיהא מעניש ולא הוה ליה איניש נענש בשבילו: **אהבה.** שאהב [י] הקב"ה את אברהם ביטלה שורה של גדולה שחבש הוא בעצמו: **ושנאה.** ששנא בלעם הרשע את ישראל ביטלה שורה של גדולה שחבש הוא בעצמו: **מ"ב קרבנות.** בין פרים לאילים ז' פרים וז' אילים ג' פעמים הרי מ"ב בין פרים ואילים: **אורח ארעא** למימר הכי. וכי דרך ארץ כן שיאמרו [כ] וייטב אלהים שם שלמה משמך והא חלשא דעתיה דאמרי ליה שיהא גדול מאביו: **מעין שמך.** קאמר ליה ומעין כסאך ולא גדול ממש: **נשים באהל.** שרה רבקה רחל ולאה שרה ורבקה דכתיב ויביאה יצחק האהלה שרה אמו וגו' רחל ולאה דכתיב (בראשית לא) ויצא מאהל לאה ויבא באהל רחל: **אורח ארעא.** שאמרה דבורה ליעל [שתהא] ברוכה משרה ורבקה אלא מעין ברכת שרה קאמרה: **ופליגא.** האי דמשנינן שם שלמה משמך מעין פליגא דר' יוסי בר חוני: **בנו מניין.** שאינו מקנא בו: **משלמה.** דקאמרי ליה לדוד ייטב אלהים שם שלמה משמך: **ותלמידו.** איבעית אימא דקאמר ליה לאליהו ויהי נא פי שנים ברוחך אלי ונתן לו אליהו ולא נתקנא בו: **ויסמוך את ידיו עליו ויצוהו.** אע"ג דהקב"ה לא א"ל אלא וסמכת את ידך עליו חדא אזיל איהו וסמך תרתי: **מלאך.** שמסרו הקדוש ברוך הוא למלאך שלא יניחנו לקלל: **חכה.** נתן בפי בלעם שלא היה מניחו לקלל והיינו וישם: **מברכותיו אתה למד מה היה בלבו.** דכתיב ויהפוך ה' אלהיך לך את הקללה לברכה הוא היה רוצה לקללם בכך שלא יהיו בתי כנסיות ולא נתן רשות ואמר מה טובו אוהליך: **ריחו נודף.** ממלות: **וירם מאגג מלכו.** מתרגמינן ותתקף מאגג שתהא מלכותו עזה: **וכולם.** כל הברכות של בלעם חזרו לקללה כמו שהיה כוונתו מתחילה: **חוץ מבתי כנסיות ובתי מדרשות.** שלא יפסקו מישראל לעולם: **הקללה לברכה.** אחת מן הקללות הפך לברכה שלא חזרה לעולם ולא כל הקללות לברכות שחזרו: **נעתרות.** נהפכות כמו עתר שמהפך התבואה כלומר נאמנים פצעי אוהב ונהפכות מנאמנות נשיקות שונא: מחליף

עין משפט נר מצוה

ל א מיי' פ"ג מהלכות ת"ת הלכה ה ופ"י מהלכות תשובה הלכה ה סמג עשין יב טוש"ע י"ד סי' רמו סעיף כ:

תורה אור השלם

א) נְאֻם שֹׁמֵעַ אִמְרֵי אֵל וְיֹדֵעַ דַּעַת עֶלְיוֹן מַחֲזֵה שַׁדַּי יֶחֱזֶה נֹפֵל וּגְלוּי עֵינָיִם: [במדבר כד, טז]

ב) וַתֹּאמֶר הָאָתוֹן אֶל בִּלְעָם הֲלוֹא אָנֹכִי אֲתֹנְךָ אֲשֶׁר רָכַבְתָּ עָלַי מֵעוֹדְךָ עַד הַיּוֹם הַזֶּה הַהַסְכֵּן הִסְכַּנְתִּי לַעֲשׂוֹת לְךָ כֹּה וַיֹּאמֶר לֹא: [במדבר כב, ל]

ג) וַיֹּאמְרוּ לוֹ עֲבָדָיו יְבַקְשׁוּ לַאדֹנִי הַמֶּלֶךְ נַעֲרָה בְתוּלָה וְעָמְדָה לִפְנֵי הַמֶּלֶךְ וּתְהִי לוֹ סֹכֶנֶת וְשָׁכְבָה בְחֵיקֶךָ וְחַם לַאדֹנִי הַמֶּלֶךְ: [מלכים א' א, ב]

ד) עַמִּי זְכָר נָא מַה יָּעַץ בָּלָק מֶלֶךְ מוֹאָב וּמֶה עָנָה אֹתוֹ בִּלְעָם בֶּן בְּעוֹר מִן הַשִּׁטִּים עַד הַגִּלְגָּל לְמַעַן דַּעַת צִדְקוֹת יְיָ: [מיכה ו, ה]

ה) מָה אֶקֹּב לֹא קַבֹּה אֵל וּמָה אֶזְעֹם לֹא זָעַם יְיָ: [במדבר כג, ח]

ו) אֱלֹהִים שׁוֹפֵט צַדִּיק וְאֵל זֹעֵם בְּכָל יוֹם: [תהלים ז, יב]

ז) כִּי רֶגַע בְּאַפּוֹ חַיִּים בִּרְצוֹנוֹ בָּעֶרֶב יָלִין בֶּכִי וְלַבֹּקֶר רִנָּה: [תהלים ל, ו]

ח) לֵךְ עַמִּי בֹּא בַחֲדָרֶיךָ וּסְגֹר דְּלָתְךָ בַּעֲדֶךָ חֲבִי כִמְעַט רֶגַע עַד יַעֲבָר זָעַם: [ישעיה כו, כ]

ט) גַּם עֲנוֹשׁ לַצַּדִּיק לֹא טוֹב לְהַכּוֹת נְדִיבִים עַל יֹשֶׁר: [משלי יז, כו]

י) וַיָּקָם בִּלְעָם בַּבֹּקֶר וַיַּחֲבֹשׁ אֶת אֲתֹנוֹ וַיֵּלֶךְ עִם שָׂרֵי מוֹאָב: [במדבר כב, כא]

כ) וַיַּשְׁכֵּם אַבְרָהָם בַּבֹּקֶר וַיַּחֲבֹשׁ אֶת חֲמֹרוֹ וַיִּקַּח אֶת שְׁנֵי נְעָרָיו אִתּוֹ וְאֵת יִצְחָק בְּנוֹ וַיְבַקַּע עֲצֵי עֹלָה וַיָּקָם וַיֵּלֶךְ אֶל הַמָּקוֹם אֲשֶׁר אָמַר לוֹ הָאֱלֹהִים: [בראשית כב, ג]

ל) וְגַם בָּאוּ עַבְדֵי הַמֶּלֶךְ לְבָרֵךְ אֶת אֲדֹנֵינוּ הַמֶּלֶךְ דָּוִד לֵאמֹר יֵיטֵב אֱלֹהִים אֶת שֵׁם שְׁלֹמֹה מִשְּׁמֶךָ וִיגַדֵּל אֶת כִּסְאוֹ מִכִּסְאֶךָ וַיִּשְׁתַּחוּ הַמֶּלֶךְ עַל הַמִּשְׁכָּב: [מלכים א' א, מז]

מ) תְּבֹרַךְ מִנָּשִׁים יָעֵל אֵשֶׁת חֶבֶר הַקֵּינִי מִנָּשִׁים בָּאֹהֶל תְּבֹרָךְ: [שופטים ה, כד]

נ) וַיְהִי כְעָבְרָם וְאֵלִיָּהוּ אָמַר אֶל אֱלִישָׁע שְׁאַל מָה אֶעֱשֶׂה לָּךְ בְּטֶרֶם אֶלָּקַח מֵעִמָּךְ וַיֹּאמֶר אֱלִישָׁע וִיהִי נָא פִּי שְׁנַיִם בְּרוּחֲךָ אֵלָי: [מלכים ב' ב, ט]

ס) וַיִּסְמֹךְ אֶת יָדָיו עָלָיו וַיְצַוֵּהוּ כַּאֲשֶׁר דִּבֶּר יְיָ בְּיַד מֹשֶׁה: [במדבר כז, כג]

ע) וַיָּשֶׂם יְיָ דָּבָר בְּפִי בִלְעָם וַיֹּאמֶר שׁוּב אֶל בָּלָק וְכֹה תְדַבֵּר: [במדבר כג, ה] פ) מַה טֹּבוּ אֹהָלֶיךָ יַעֲקֹב מִשְׁכְּנֹתֶיךָ יִשְׂרָאֵל: [במדבר כד, ה] צ) כִּנְחָלִים נִטָּיוּ כְּגַנֹּת עֲלֵי נָהָר כַּאֲהָלִים נָטַע יְהוָה כַּאֲרָזִים עֲלֵי מָיִם: [במדבר כד, ו] ק) יִזַּל מַיִם מִדָּלְיָו וְזַרְעוֹ בְּמַיִם רַבִּים וְיָרֹם מֵאֲגַג מַלְכּוֹ וְתִנַּשֵּׂא מַלְכֻתוֹ: [במדבר כד, ז] ר) וְלֹא אָבָה יְיָ אֱלֹהֶיךָ לִשְׁמֹעַ אֶל בִּלְעָם וַיַּהֲפֹךְ יְיָ אֱלֹהֶיךָ לְּךָ אֶת הַקְּלָלָה לִבְרָכָה כִּי אֲהֵבְךָ יְיָ אֱלֹהֶיךָ: [דברים כג, ו] ש) נֶאֱמָנִים פִּצְעֵי אוֹהֵב וְנַעְתָּרוֹת נְשִׁיקוֹת שׂוֹנֵא: [משלי כז, ו] ת) וְהִכָּה יְיָ אֶת יִשְׂרָאֵל כַּאֲשֶׁר יָנוּד הַקָּנֶה בַּמַּיִם וְנָתַשׁ אֶת יִשְׂרָאֵל מֵעַל הָאֲדָמָה הַטּוֹבָה הַזֹּאת אֲשֶׁר נָתַן לַאֲבוֹתֵיהֶם וְזֵרָם מֵעֵבֶר לַנָּהָר יַעַן אֲשֶׁר עָשׂוּ אֶת אֲשֵׁרֵיהֶם מַכְעִיסִים אֶת יְיָ: [מלכים א' יד, טו]

מסורת הש"ס

א) [ברכות ז. ע"ש ע"ז ד:], ב) [צ"ל **אסוסיא**], ג) [צ"ל **שאילמלי** ועיין תוספות מגילה כח.], ד) [צ"ל ומה אזעום **לא זעם ה' מלמד שכל אותם הימים לא זעם** ה' כ"א בברכות ז. וקצת שינוי יש בע"ז ד: ע"ש], ה) [צ"ל **תרנגול'**], ו) פסחים נ: ערכין טז: סוטה כב: מז. הוריות י: נזיר כג:, ז) [צ"ל **דאמר** ר' יוסי בר הונא כך איתא בהוריות י: ע"ש וע"ע בנזיר כג: ובתוספות שם ד"ה בת בנו וכו' דלאו דוקא ע"ש וע"ע סוטה מז.], ח) ר"י יעב"ץ גרס **איומה**, ט) תענית כ., י) ס"א אברהם את הקב"ה, כ) [צ"ל ייטיב].

ליקוטי רש"י

סוכנת. לשון מחממת [ע"ז ד:]. מחממת וכן ובוקע עצים יסכן בם, (קהלת י' ט) [מ"א א, ב]. **ומה ענה אותו בלעם בן בעור.** מה אזעום לא זעם ה' (במדבר כג) שלא כעסתי כל אותן הימים. **מן השטים.** שחטאתם לי שם דעו לדקותי שלא מנעתי טובתי ועזרתי מכם עד הבאתי אתכם לגלגל וכבשתי לפניכם שם את הארץ [מיכה ו, ה]. **מן השטים ועד הגלגל.** עד באכם אל הגלגל שהפלתי לפניכם שונאיכם [ע"ז שם]. **לא זעם ה'.** אני אין כחי אלא שאני יודע לכוין השעה שהקב"ה כועס בה והוא לא כעס כל הימים הללו שבאתי אליך וזהו שנאמר (מיכה ו, ה) עמי זכר נא מה יעץ וגו' ומה ענה אותו בלעם וגו' למען דעת צדקות ה' [במדבר כג, ח]. **חבי.** התחבאי מעט עד יעבר זעם כי אמת אפקוד על שונאיך [ישעיהו כו, כ]. **כי רגע באפו.** אלמא דרגע הוי אפו. **סורייקי.** נוקיש לשון לע"ז כמו חוטין חוטין ולשון ישמעאל קורין לחוט סוריאק. **לאו אורח ארעא.** לכוין שעת זעמו [ע"ז ד:]. **בתלת שעי קמייתא.** באחד מרגעי תלת שעות ראשונות. **לצדיק לא טוב.** לענוש את הבריות [ברכות ז.]. **ויחבש את אתנו.** מכאן ששנאה מקלקלת את השורה שחבש הוא בעצמו אמר הקב"ה רשע כבר קדמך אברהם אביהם שנאמר (בראשית כב, ג) וישכם אברהם בבקר ויחבוש את חמורו [במדבר כב, כא]. **וישכם.** נזדרז למצוה. **ויחבש.** הוא בעצמו ולא צוה לאחד מעבדיו שהאהבה מקלקלת השורה [בראשית כב, ג]. **מ"ב קרבנות.** ג"פ ז' מזבחות פר ואיל במזבח. **יצאה ממנו רות.** שיצא ממנה דוד שריוה להקב"ה בשירות ותשבחות (ברכות ז: ב"ב יד:) [הוריות י:]. **מנשים באהל.** שרה שנאמר בה הנה באהל רבקה שנאמר בה ויביאה יצחק האהלה רחל ולאה שנאמר בהן ויצא מאהל לאה וגומר. **מנשים באהל תבורך.** יעל למה הן ילדו ויגדלו ואם לא יעל הרי הרשע הזה בא ומאבדן כך הוא בבראשית רבה ד"א אף יעל היתה יושבת אוהלים לפיכך הזכיר אותה בברכת אוהלים [שופטים ה, כד]. **דכתיב תבורך מנשים יעל אשת חבר הקיני.** כלומר כאותן נשים שמנינו בהן שעשו מצות שלא לשמה וכנגדן נאמר בהן אהל. **תבורך.** על שעשתה עבירה לשמה כדי להתיש כחו של אותו רשע כדי שתהא יכולה להורגו. **שרה רחל ולאה.** שאמרו לבעליהן לבא אל שפחתן ולא לשם מצוה נתכוונו אלא כדי שמתקנאות זו בזו רחל באחותה ושרה ולאה באמהות וכולן נאמר בהן אהל כדכתיבי קראי [נזיר כג:]. **ויסמך את ידיו.** בעין יפה יותר ויותר ממה שנצטווה שהקב"ה אמר לו וסמכת את ידך והוא עשה בשתי ידיו ועשאו ככלי מלא וגדוש ומלאו חכמתו בעין יפה [במדבר כז, כג]. **וישם דבר בפיו.** ומה היא השימה הזאת ומה חסר המקרא באמרו שוב אל בלק וכה תדבר אלא כשהיה שומע שאינו נרשה לקלל אמר מה אני חוזר אל בלק לצערו ונתן לו הקב"ה רסן וחכה בפיו כאדם הפוקס בהמה בחכה להוליכה אל אשר ירצה. אמר לו על כרחך תשוב אל בלק [במדבר כג, טז]. **מברכתו.** אמרו רבותינו מברכותיו של אותו רשע אנו למדים מה היה בלבו לקללם כשאמר (פסוק א) וישת אל המדבר פניו, וכשהפך המקום את פיו ברכם מעין אותן קללות שבקש לומר כו', כדאיתא בחלק [שם פסוק ה']. **ונעתרות.** ל' גודל כמו העתרת' עלי (יחזקאל לה) [משלי כז, ו]. **ונעתרות נשיקות שונא.** נעתרות לשון הפך כדאמרינן במסכת סוכה (יד.) ויעתר לו מה עתר זה מהפך את התבואה פורקא בלעז אי נמי נעתרות, לשון רבוי וייתור אינקרי"ש בלעז כמו העתרתם עלי דבריכם (יחזקאל לה) [תענית כ.].

"כָּרַע נָפַל שָׁכָב וגו׳" – *he crouched, he fell, he lay down, etc.*[1]

The Gemara discusses Bilam's powers:

"וְיֹדֵעַ דַּעַת עֶלְיוֹן" – Bilam described himself as ***one who knows the mind of the Supreme One.***[2] הַשְׁתָּא דַּעַת בְּהֶמְתּוֹ לֹא הֲוָה יָדַע – **Now [Bilam] did not** even **know** what was on **his animal's mind.** דַּעַת עֶלְיוֹן הֲוָה יָדַע – **Could he** possibly **know** what was on **the mind of the Supreme One?** Of course not! – ? –

The Gemara explains:

מַאי דַּעַת בְּהֶמְתּוֹ – **What** do we mean when we say that he did not know what was on **the mind of his animal?** דְּאָמְרֵי לֵיהּ – **For [the Moabite emissaries] said to [Bilam]:** מַאי טַעְמָא לֹא רְכַבְתְּ סוּסְיָא – **Why do you not ride a horse?**[3] אָמַר לְהוּ – **He said to them:** שְׁדַאי לְהוּ בִּרְטִיבָא – Usually I ride a horse. However, today I am riding a donkey, because **I put [my horses] in the marshland** to graze. אָמְרָה לֵיהּ, "הֲלוֹא אָנֹכִי אֲתֹנְךָ" – Thereupon, **[the she-donkey] said to [Bilam]** in front of the Moabites: ***"Am I not your she-donkey?"***[4] לְטְעִינָא בְּעָלְמָא – **"Merely for carrying burdens,"** Bilam said, trying to cut her off before she could contradict him further. "אֲשֶׁר־רָכַבְתָּ עָלַי" – ***"That you have ridden on,"*** the donkey continued, contradicting Bilam's contention that she was merely a beast of burden. אַקְרַאי בְּעָלְמָא – **"Only occasionally,"** Bilam said, implying that ordinarily he did not ride her. "מֵעוֹדְךָ עַד הַיּוֹם הַזֶּה" – ***"All your life until this day,"*** the donkey went on, contradicting Bilam's contention that he had never ridden her except on rare occasions. וְלֹא עוֹד – **"And not only that,"** she continued, אֶלָּא שֶׁאֲנִי עוֹשָׂה [לְךָ] מַעֲשֵׂה אִישׁוּת בַּלַּיְלָה – **"but at night I perform marital acts with you."** כְּתִיב הָכָא, "הַהַסְכֵּן הִסְכַּנְתִּי" – This is deduced as follows: **It is written here** that the donkey said: ***Have I been accustomed*** *(hahaskein hiskanti) to do such a thing to you,*[5] וּכְתִיב הָתָם, "וּתְהִי לוֹ־סֹכֶנֶת" – **and it is written elsewhere: *Let her be for him a warmer*** *(sochenes).*[6] To this retort of the donkey Bilam was unable to make any reply.

Thus, the donkey got the best of Bilam in their verbal sparring. How, then, could Bilam claim to "know the mind of the Supreme One," that is, to know and manipulate the mind of God to allow him to curse the Jews, when it is evident that he was unable to know and manipulate even the mind of an animal?

אֶלָּא מַאי, "וְיֹדֵעַ דַּעַת עֶלְיוֹן" – **Rather, what is the meaning of** Bilam's description of himself as ***one who knows the mind of the Supreme One?*** שֶׁהָיָה יוֹדֵעַ לְכַוֵּין אוֹתָהּ שָׁעָה שֶׁהַקָּדוֹשׁ בָּרוּךְ הוּא כּוֹעֵס בָּהּ – It means **that he knew how to ascertain the exact moment at which the Holy One, Blessed is He, becomes angry.** If Bilam cursed someone at that precise moment, the curse would be effective.[7] וְהַיְינוּ דְּקָאָמַר לְהוּ נָבִיא לְיִשְׂרָאֵל – **And that is the meaning of what the prophet** Michah **said to Israel:** "עַמִּי זְכָר נָא מַה יָּעַץ בָּלָק מֶלֶךְ מוֹאָב – ***My people, remember, please, what Balak king of Moab plotted,*** וּמֶה עָנָה אֹתוֹ בִּלְעָם בֶּן בְּעוֹר – ***and what Bilam the son of Beor answered him;*** מִן הַשִּׁטִּים עַד הַגִּלְגָּל – *[remember the period]* ***from the Shittim to the Gilgal,*** לְמַעַן דַּעַת צִדְקוֹת ה׳" – ***so that you may realize the benevolences of*** HASHEM.[8] מַאי "לְמַעַן דַּעַת צִדְקוֹת ה׳" – **What is the meaning of** ***so that you may realize the benevolences of*** *HASHEM?* אָמַר לָהֶן הַקָּדוֹשׁ בָּרוּךְ הוּא לְיִשְׂרָאֵל – **The Holy One, Blessed is He, said to Israel:** דְּעוּ נָא כַּמָּה צְדָקוֹת עָשִׂיתִי עִמָּכֶם – **Realize, please, how many benevolences I performed for you** שֶׁלֹּא כָּעַסְתִּי כָּל אוֹתָן הַיָּמִים בִּימֵי בִּלְעָם הָרָשָׁע – in **that I did not become angry all those days, in the days of the wicked Bilam** when he was seeking to curse you, שֶׁאִילְמָלֵא כָּעַסְתִּי כָּל אוֹתָן הַיָּמִים – **for had I become angry during any of those days** לֹא נִשְׁתַּיֵּיר מִשּׂוֹנְאֵיהֶן שֶׁל יִשְׂרָאֵל שָׂרִיד וּפָלִיט – **no remnant whatsoever would have remained from the enemies of Israel.**[9] הַיְינוּ דְּקָאָמַר לֵיהּ בִּלְעָם לְבָלָק, "מָה אֶקֹּב לֹא קַבֹּה אֵל וגו׳" – **This is the meaning of that which Bilam said to Balak: *How can I curse? God has not cursed,*** **etc.** *How can I anger? HASHEM has not become angry.*[10] (אוֹתָן (היום) [הַיָּמִים] לֹא זָעַם ה׳) – This teaches that throughout all **those days God did not become angry.**[11]

NOTES

1. *Judges* 5:27. Sisera, the general of the Canaanite armies oppressing Israel, was defeated in battle by the Jews, led by Deborah and Barak. Sisera fled the battlefield and came to the tent of Yael the wife of Chever the Keinite, seeking refuge. Pretending to befriend him, she welcomed him into her tent, gave him food and drink, and assured him that she would not betray his whereabouts to the pursuing Jewish army. He believed her, and fell asleep in her tent. When he was fast asleep she drove her tent pin through his temple, killing him.

In her song of victory, the prophetess Deborah describes Yael's praiseworthy action in preventing Sisera's escape and in killing him. According to *Yevamos* 103a, Yael not only fed him, she even went to the length of engaging in carnal relations with Sisera in order to keep him in the tent and put him to sleep. Yael, who was a righteous woman, did this even though it was obviously distasteful to her (see *Horayos* 10b). It was this self-sacrificing act of Yael's that Deborah praised. Since Deborah described Yael's act using the verbs "crouching" and "falling," it indicates that when Bilam describes himself as *fallen,* it was a reference to his own carnal relations, with his animal (see *Rashi*).

According to *Zohar* (cited by *Margaliyos HaYam*), Bilam's bestiality was part of an occult ritual intended to induce a state of impurity. See also *Maharal.*

2. *Numbers* 24:16.

3. When the emissaries saw how Bilam struggled with his obstinate she-donkey, which strayed from the path and finally crouched beneath him and refused to budge, they asked him, "Why did you not ride a horse, which is a more obedient animal?"

4. Ibid. 22:30. [According to its simple meaning, this verse records one continuous response made by the donkey to Bilam. The Gemara here, however, expounds it as a *series* of replies made by the donkey to several successive comments of Bilam.]

5. Ibid.

6. *I Kings* 1:2. When King David was old, he could not be made to feel warm. His courtiers persuaded him to lie beside a young woman, whose youthful body would warm him. Such a young woman, whose name was Avishag, was found. She would lie beside the king and thereby keep him warm, although they did not actually have relations.

Avishag is referred to as David's *sochenes.* Thus, the verb *sochen* (סכן) connotes lying together. Therefore, when the she-donkey said to Bilam: הַהַסְכֵּן הִסְכַּנְתִּי, she was likewise referring to a relationship with Bilam in which the two of them used to lie together, although in this case cohabitation took place. Thus, the donkey revealed that Bilam used to copulate with her.

7. The Gemara below will explain when this moment of anger occurs.

It goes without saying that this entire discussion is anthropomorphic, for God is not a human being who feels anger. The term "anger" is applied to Him to describe when His disapproval of human conduct causes Him to react forcefully, in a manner which, in a human being, we would describe as angry (*Yad Ramah*).

8. *Micah* 6:5. *From the Shittim to the Gilgal* means: I performed kindnesses for you throughout your continuous defection, from the time you sinned with the Moabite women at Shittim until now, when you sin at Gilgal by offering sacrifices to idols – see *Hosea* 4:15, 9:15, 12:12; *Amos* 4:4 (see *Rashi* here and *R' Samson Raphael Hirsch, Haftoroth* [by Dr. Mendel Hirsch, son of R' S. R. Hirsch], *Parashas Balak*; cf. *Rashi* ad loc. and to *Avodah Zarah* 4b ד״ה מן השיטים).

9. I.e. not a single Jew would have survived. The phrase "enemies of Israel" is a euphemism for the Jews themselves.

The Gemara is apparently interpreting the phrase *so that you may realize the benevolences of HASHEM* as referring back to the first phrase of the verse: *remember, please, what Balak king of Moab plotted and what Bilam the son of Beor answered him.*

10. *Numbers* 23:8.

11. The verse implies that had God permitted Himself to become angry, Bilam would have been able to curse the Jews. Thus, the verse indicates that Bilam's power lay in "seizing the moment" of God's anger to curse the Jews, and that Bilam was rendered powerless by God's refusal to become angry during that period (*Rashi*).

עין משפט
נר מצוה

ל א מיי' פ"ג מהלכות ת"ת הלכה ה ופ"ו מהלכות תשובה הלכה ה סמג עשין יב טוש"ע י"ד סי' רמו סעיף כ:

כרע נפל שכב וגו' א) ויודע דעת עליון השתא א) דעת בהמתו לא הוה ידע דעת עליון הוה ידע מאי דעת בהמתו דאמרי ליה מאי טעמא לא רכבת ב) סוסיא אמר להו שדאי להו ברטיבא אמרה ליה הלא אנכי אתונך לטעינא בעלמא אשר רכבת עלי אקראי בעלמא מעודך עד היום הזה ולא עוד אלא שאני עושה [לך] מעשה אישות בלילה כתיב הכא ב) ההסכן הסכנתי וכתיב התם ג) ותהי לו סוכנת אלא מאי ויודע דעת עליון שהיה יודע לכוון אותה שעה שהקב"ה כועס בה והיינו דקאמר להו נביא לישראל ד) עמי זכר נא מה יעץ בלק מלך מואב ומה ענה אותו בלעם בן בעור מן השטים ועד הגלגל למען דעת צדקות ה' מאי למען דעת צדקות ה' אמר להן הקב"ה לישראל דעו נא כמה צדקות עשיתי עמכם שלא כעסתי כל אותן הימים בימי בלעם הרשע ג) שאילמלא כעסתי כל אותן הימים לא נשתייר משונאיהן של ישראל שריד ופליט היינו דקאמר ליה בלעם לבלק ה) מה אקב לא קבה אל (ד) וגו' אותן היום [הימים] לא זעם ה') ו) אל זועם בכל יום וכמה זעמו רגע שנאמר ז) כי רגע באפו חיים ברצונו וגו' איבעית אימא ח) לך עמי בא בחדריך וסגור דלתיך בעדך חבי כמעט רגע עד יעבר זעם אימת רתח בתלת שעי קמייתא כי חוורא כרבלתא דתרנגולא כל שעתא ושעתא נמי חוורא כל שעתא ושעתא אית ביה סוריקי סומקי ההיא שעתא לית ביה סוריקי סומקי ההוא מינא דהוה בשיבבותיה דרבי יהושע בן לוי דהוה קא מצער ליה יומא חד נקט ה) תרנגולתא ואסר ליה בכרעיה ואותיב אמר כי מטא ההוא שעתא אילטייה כי מטא ההוא שעתא נמנם אמר שמע מינה לאו אורח ארעא דכתיב ט) גם ענוש לצדיק לא טוב אפילו במיני לא איבעי ליה למימר הכי תנא משמיה דרבי מאיר בשעה שהחמה זורחת והמלכים מניחין כתריהן על ראשיהן ומשתחוים לחמה מיד כועס י) ויקם בלעם בבקר ויחבוש את אתונו תנא משום רבי שמעון בן אלעזר אהבה מבטלת שורה של גדולה מאברהם דכתיב כ) וישכם אברהם בבקר שנאה מבטלת שורה של גדולה מבלעם שנאמר ויקם בלעם בבקר ויחבוש את אתונו ו) אמר רב יהודה אמר רב א לעולם יעסוק אדם בתורה ובמצוה אפילו שלא לשמה שמתוך שלא לשמה בא לשמה שבשכר ארבעים ושתים קרבנות שהקריב בלק זכה ויצאה ממנו רות א"ר ז) יוסי בר הונא רות בתו של עגלון בן בנו של בלק מלך מואב היתה א"ל רבא לרבה בר מרי כתיב ל) ייטב אלהים את שם שלמה משמך ויגדל [את] כסאו מכסאך אורח ארעא למימרא ליה למלכא הכי א"ל מעין קאמרה ליה דאי לא תימא הכי מ) תבורך מנשים יעל אשת חבר הקיני מנשים באהל תבורך מאן נינהו שרה רבקה רחל ולאה אורח ארעא למימר הכי אלא מעין קאמר הכא נמי מעין קאמר ופליגא דרב יוסי בר חוני דאמר רב יוסי בר חוני בכל אדם מתקנא חוץ מבנו ותלמידו בנו משלמה ותלמידו איבעית אימא נ) ויהי נא פי שנים ברוחך אלי ואיבעית אימא ס) ויסמוך את ידיו עליו ויצוהו ע) וישם דבר בפי בלעם ר"א אומר מלאך ר' יונתן אמר חכה א"ר יוחנן מברכתו של אותו רשע אתה למד מה היה בלבו ביקש לומר שלא יהו להם בתי כנסיות ובתי מדרשות פ) מה טובו אהליך יעקב לא תשרה שכינה עליהם ומשכנותיך ישראל לא תהא מלכותן נמשכת צ) כנחלים נטיו לא יהא להם זיתים וכרמים כגנות עלי נהר לא יהא ריחן נודף כאהלים נטע ה' לא יהיו להם מלכים בעלי קומה כארזים עלי מים לא יהיה להם מלך בן מלך ק) יזל מים מדליו לא תהא מלכותן שולטת באומות וזרעו במים רבים לא תהא עזה מלכותן וירם מאגג מלכו לא תהא ח) אימת מלכותן ותנשא מלכותו אמר רבי אבא בר כהנא כולם חזרו לקללה חוץ מבתי כנסיות ומבתי מדרשות שנאמר ר) ויהפוך ה' אלהיך לך את הקללה לברכה כי אהבך ה' אלהיך קללה ולא קללות ט) א"ר שמואל בר נחמני א"ר יונתן מאי דכתיב ש) נאמנים פצעי אוהב ונעתרות נשיקות שונא טובה קללה שקילל אחיה השילוני את ישראל יותר מברכה שברכם בלעם הרשע אחיה השילוני קילל את ישראל בקנה שנאמר ת) והכה ה' את ישראל כאשר ינוד הקנה במים וגו' מה קנה זה עומד במקום מים וגיזעו

מחליף

כרע נפל. מה כריעה דהתם דאית ביה נפילה בעילה היא אף כריעה דהכא דכתיב נופל בעילה היא שבא על בהמתו: דעת בהמתו לא הוה ידע. מאי בעיא לאהדורי כדמפרש דאמרי ליה שרי בלק מאי טעמא לא רכבת אסוסיא: ברטיבא. באחו לרעות עשבים לחים: אמר להו לטעינא בעלמא. לישא משאות ולא לרכוב: אמרה ליה אשר רכבת עלי: אקראי בעלמא. כשאין לי סוס מזומן: אמרה לו מעודך: מעשה אישות. שאתה בועלי: סוכנת. מחממת: מן השטים ועד הגלגל. משחטאו בשטים ועד שנכנסו לארץ וחטאו בגלגל עשיתי עמהם צדקות הרבה: כל אותן הימים. שהיה בלעם מצפה לקללכם בשעה שהקב"ה כועס בה כל הקללות מתקיימות: ה"ג לא זעם ה'. אותן הימים לא זעם ה': אל זועם בכל יום. קרא הוא: כמה זעמו רגע. כדמפיק ליה מקרא כי רגע באפו חיים ברצונו: בתלת שעי קמייתא. של יום זמן קימה שכל שלש שעות זמן קימה לעמוד ממטתו וכועס הקב"ה בשעה שרואה המלכים שמשתחוים לחמה בשעה שמניחין כתריהם בראשם כדלקמן: כרבלתא. קירשת"א בלע"ז: כל שעתא נמי חיורא. רוב שעות מתלבנת ומכספת שאינה כל שעה בחוזק אדמימות: סורייקי סומקי. אפי' כשמכספת יש בה שורות שורות אדומות מאד כרגילותם אבל אותה שעה כולה מכספת: גם ענוש לצדיק לא טוב. אין נכון לצדיק שיהא מעניש ולא הוה ליה איניש נענש בשבילו: אהבה. שאהב י) הקב"ה את אברהם ביטלה שורה של גדולה שחבש הוא בעצמו: ושנאה. ששנא בלעם הרשע את ישראל ביטלה שורה של גדולה שחבש הוא בעצמו: מ"ב קרבנות. בין פרים לאילים ז' פרים וז' אילים ג' פעמים הרי מ"ב בין פרים ואילים: אורח ארעא למימר הכי. וכי דרך ארץ כן שיאמרו כ) וייטב אלהים שם שלמה משמך והא חלשא דעתיה דאמרי ליה שיהא גדול מאביו: מעין שמך. קאמר ליה ומעין כסאך ולא גדול ממש: נשים באהל. שרה רבקה רחל ולאה שרה ורבקה דכתיב ויביאה יצחק האהלה שרה אמו וגו' רחל ולאה דכתיב (בראשית לא) ויצא מאהל לאה ויבא באהל רחל: אורח ארעא. שאמרה דבורה ליעל [שתהא] ברוכה משרה ורבקה אלא מעין ברכת שרה קאמרה: ופליגא. האי דמשנינן שם שלמה משמך מעין פליגא דר' יוסי בר חוני: בנו מניין. שאינו מקנא בו: משלמה. דקאמרי ליה לדוד ייטב אלהים שם שלמה משמך: ותלמידו. איבעית אימא דקאמר ליה לאליהו ויהי נא פי שנים ברוחך אלי ונתן לו אליהו ולא נתקנא בו: ויסמוך את ידיו עליו ויצוהו. אע"ג דהקב"ה לא א"ל אלא וסמכת את ידך עליו חדא אזיל איהו וסמך תרתי: מלאך. שמסרו הקדוש ברוך הוא למלאך שלא יניחנו לקלל: חכה. נתן בפי בלעם שלא היה מניחו לקלל והיינו וישם: מברכותיו אתה למד מה היה בלבו. דכתיב ויהפוך ה' אלהיך לך את הקללה לברכה הוא היה רוצה לקללם בכך שלא יהיו בתי כנסיות ולא נתן רשות ואמר מה טובו אוהליך: ריחו נודף. ממלות: וירם מאגג מלכו. מתרגמינן ויתקף מאגג שתהא מלכותו עזה: וכולם. כל הברכות של בלעם חזרו לקללה כמו שהיה כוונתו מתחילה: חוץ מבתי כנסיות ובתי מדרשות. שלא יפסקו מישראל לעולם: הקללה לברכה. אחת מן הקללות הפך לברכה שלא חזרה לעולם ולא כל הקללות לברכות שחזרו: נעתרות. נהפכות כמו עתר שמהפך התבואה כלומר נאמנים פצעי אוהב ונהפכות מנאמנות נשיקות שונא:

מחליף

תורה אור השלם

א) נְאֻם שֹׁמֵעַ אִמְרֵי אֵל וְיֹדֵעַ דַּעַת עֶלְיוֹן מַחֲזֵה שַׁדַּי יֶחֱזֶה נֹפֵל וּגְלוּי עֵינָיִם: [במדבר כד, טז]

ב) וַתֹּאמֶר הָאָתוֹן אֶל בִּלְעָם הֲלוֹא אָנֹכִי אֲתֹנְךָ אֲשֶׁר רָכַבְתָּ עָלַי מֵעוֹדְךָ עַד הַיּוֹם הַזֶּה הַהַסְכֵּן הִסְכַּנְתִּי לַעֲשׂוֹת לְךָ כֹּה וַיֹּאמֶר לֹא: [במדבר כב, ל]

ג) וַיֹּאמְרוּ לוֹ עֲבָדָיו יְבַקְשׁוּ לַאדֹנִי הַמֶּלֶךְ נַעֲרָה בְתוּלָה וְעָמְדָה לִפְנֵי הַמֶּלֶךְ וּתְהִי לוֹ סֹכֶנֶת וְשָׁכְבָה בְחֵיקֶךָ וְחַם לַאדֹנִי הַמֶּלֶךְ: [מלכים א' א, ב]

ד) עַמִּי זְכָר נָא מַה יָּעַץ בָּלָק מֶלֶךְ מוֹאָב וּמֶה עָנָה אֹתוֹ בִּלְעָם בֶּן בְּעוֹר מִן הַשִּׁטִּים עַד הַגִּלְגָּל לְמַעַן דַּעַת צִדְקוֹת יְיָ: [מיכה ו, ה]

ה) מָה אֶקֹּב לֹא קַבֹּה אֵל וּמָה אֶזְעֹם לֹא זָעַם יְיָ: [במדבר כג, ח]

ו) אֱלֹהִים שׁוֹפֵט צַדִּיק וְאֵל זֹעֵם בְּכָל יוֹם: [תהלים ז, יב]

ז) כִּי רֶגַע בְּאַפּוֹ חַיִּים בִּרְצוֹנוֹ בָּעֶרֶב יָלִין בֶּכִי וְלַבֹּקֶר רִנָּה: [תהלים ל, ו]

ח) לֵךְ עַמִּי בֹּא בַחֲדָרֶיךָ וּסְגֹר דְּלָתְךָ בַּעֲדֶךָ חֲבִי כִמְעַט רֶגַע עַד יַעֲבָר זָעַם: [ישעיה כו, כ]

ט) גַּם עֲנוֹשׁ לַצַּדִּיק לֹא טוֹב לְהַכּוֹת נְדִיבִים עַל יֹשֶׁר: [משלי יז, כו]

י) וַיָּקָם בִּלְעָם בַּבֹּקֶר וַיַּחֲבֹשׁ אֶת אֲתֹנוֹ וַיֵּלֶךְ עִם שָׂרֵי מוֹאָב: [במדבר כב, כא]

כ) וַיַּשְׁכֵּם אַבְרָהָם בַּבֹּקֶר וַיַּחֲבֹשׁ אֶת חֲמֹרוֹ וַיִּקַּח אֶת שְׁנֵי נְעָרָיו אִתּוֹ וְאֵת יִצְחָק בְּנוֹ וַיְבַקַּע עֲצֵי עֹלָה וַיָּקָם וַיֵּלֶךְ אֶל הַמָּקוֹם אֲשֶׁר אָמַר לוֹ הָאֱלֹהִים: [בראשית כב, ג]

ל) וְגַם בָּאוּ עַבְדֵי הַמֶּלֶךְ לְבָרֵךְ אֶת אֲדֹנֵינוּ הַמֶּלֶךְ דָּוִד לֵאמֹר יֵיטֵב אֱלֹהִים אֶת שֵׁם שְׁלֹמֹה מִשְּׁמֶךָ וִיגַדֵּל אֶת כִּסְאוֹ מִכִּסְאֶךָ וַיִּשְׁתַּחוּ הַמֶּלֶךְ עַל הַמִּשְׁכָּב: [מלכים א' א, מז]

מ) תְּבֹרַךְ מִנָּשִׁים יָעֵל אֵשֶׁת חֶבֶר הַקֵּינִי מִנָּשִׁים בָּאֹהֶל תְּבֹרָךְ: [שופטים ה, כד]

נ) וַיְהִי כְעָבְרָם וְאֵלִיָּהוּ אָמַר אֶל אֱלִישָׁע שְׁאַל מָה אֶעֱשֶׂה לָּךְ בְּטֶרֶם אֶלָּקַח מֵעִמָּךְ וַיֹּאמֶר אֱלִישָׁע וִיהִי נָא פִּי שְׁנַיִם בְּרוּחֲךָ אֵלָי: [מלכים ב' ב, ט]

ס) וַיִּסְמֹךְ אֶת יָדָיו עָלָיו וַיְצַוֵּהוּ כַּאֲשֶׁר דִּבֶּר יְיָ בְּיַד מֹשֶׁה: [במדבר כז, כג]

ע) וַיָּשֶׂם יְיָ דָּבָר בְּפִי בִלְעָם וַיֹּאמֶר שׁוּב אֶל בָּלָק וְכֹה תְדַבֵּר: [במדבר כג, ה] פ) מַה טֹּבוּ אֹהָלֶיךָ יַעֲקֹב מִשְׁכְּנֹתֶיךָ יִשְׂרָאֵל: [במדבר כד, ה] צ) כִּנְחָלִים נִטָּיוּ כְּגַנֹּת עֲלֵי נָהָר כַּאֲהָלִים נָטַע יְהוָה כַּאֲרָזִים עֲלֵי מָיִם: [במדבר כד, ו] ק) יִזַּל מַיִם מִדָּלְיָו וְזַרְעוֹ בְּמַיִם רַבִּים וְיָרֹם מֵאֲגַג מַלְכּוֹ וְתִנַּשֵּׂא מַלְכֻתוֹ: [במדבר כד, ז] ר) וְלֹא אָבָה יְיָ אֱלֹהֶיךָ לִשְׁמֹעַ אֶל בִּלְעָם וַיַּהֲפֹךְ יְיָ אֱלֹהֶיךָ לְּךָ אֶת הַקְּלָלָה לִבְרָכָה כִּי אֲהֵבְךָ יְיָ אֱלֹהֶיךָ: [דברים כג, ו] ש) נֶאֱמָנִים פִּצְעֵי אוֹהֵב וְנַעְתָּרוֹת נְשִׁיקוֹת שׂוֹנֵא: [משלי כז, ו] ת) וְהִכָּה יְיָ אֶת יִשְׂרָאֵל כַּאֲשֶׁר יָנוּד הַקָּנֶה בַּמַּיִם וְנָתַשׁ אֶת יִשְׂרָאֵל מֵעַל הָאֲדָמָה הַטּוֹבָה הַזֹּאת אֲשֶׁר נָתַן לַאֲבוֹתֵיהֶם וְזֵרָם מֵעֵבֶר לַנָּהָר יַעַן אֲשֶׁר עָשׂוּ אֶת אֲשֵׁרֵיהֶם מַכְעִיסִים אֶת יְיָ: [מלכים א' יד, טו]

מסורת הש"ס

א) [ברכות ז. ע"ש ע"ז ד:], ב) [נ"ל אסוסיא], ג) [נ"ל שאילמלי ועיין תוספות מגילה כח.], ד) [נ"ל ומה אזעום לא זעם ה' מלמד שכל אותם הימים לא זעם ה' כ"א בברכות ז. וקצת שינוי יש בע"ז ד: ע"ש], ה) [נ"ל תרנגול], ו) פסחים נ: ערכין טז: סוטה כב: מז. הוריות י: נזיר כג:, ז) [נ"ל דאמר ר' יוסי בר הונא כך איתא בהוריות י: ע"ש וע"ע בנזיר כג: ובתוספות שם ד"ה בת בנו וכו' דלאו דוקא ע"ש וע"ע סוטה מז.], ח) ר"י יעב"ץ גרס איומה, ט) תענית כ., י) ס"א אברהם את הקב"ה, כ) [נ"ל ייטיב].

ליקוטי רש"י

סוכנת. לשון מחממת [ע"ז ד:]. מחממת וכן ובוקע עצים יסכן בם, (קהלת י' ט) [מ"א א, ב]. ומה ענה אותו בלעם בן בעור. מה אזעום לא זעם ה' (במדבר כג) שלא כעסתי כל אותן הימים. מן השטים. שהטאתם לי שם דעו לדקותי שלא מנעתי טובתי ועזרתי מכם עד הבאתי אתכם לגלגל וכבשתי לפניכם שם את הארץ [מיכה ו, ה]. מן השטים ועד הגלגל. עד באכם אל הגלגל שהפלתי לפניכם שונאיכם [ע"ז שם]. לא זעם ה'. אני אין כחי אלא שאני יודע לכוין השעה שהקב"ה כועס בה והוא לא כעס כל הימים הללו שבאתי אליך וזהו שנאמר (מיכה ו, ה) עמי זכר נא מה יעץ וגו' ומה ענה אותו בלעם וגו' למען דעת צדקות ה' [במדבר כג, ח]. חבי. התחבאי מעט עד יעבר זעם כי אמת אפקוד על שונאיך [ישעיהו כו, כ]. כי רגע באפו. אלמא דרגע הוי אפו. סורייקי. נוקיים לשון לע"ז כמו חוטין חוטין ולשון ישמעאל קורין לחוט סוריאק. לאו אורח ארעא. לכוין שעת זעמו [ע"ז ד:]. בתלת שעי קמייתא. באחד מרגעי תלת שעות ראשונות. לצדיק לא טוב. לענוש את הבריות [ברכות ז.]. ויחבש את אתנו. מכאן שהשנאה מקלקלת את השורה שחבש הוא בעצמו אמר הקב"ה רשע כבר קדמך אברהם אביהם שנאמר (בראשית כב, ג) וישכם אברהם בבקר ויחבוש את חמורו [במדבר כב, כא]. וישכם. נזדרז למצוה. ויחבש. הוא בעצמו ולא צוה לאחד מעבדיו שהאהבה מקלקלת השורה [בראשית כב, ג]. מ"ב קרבנות. ג"פ ז' מזבחות פר ואיל במזבח. יצאה ממנו רות. שיצא ממנה דוד שריוה להקב"ה בשירות ותשבחות (ברכות ז: ב"ב יד:) [הוריות י:]. מנשים באהל. שרה שנאמר בה הנה באהל רבקה שנאמר בה ויביאה יצחק האהלה רחל ולאה שנאמר בהן ויצא מאהל לאה וגומר. מנשים באהל תבורך. יעל למה הן ילדו ויגדלו ואם לא יעל הרי הרשע הזה בא ומאבדן כך הוא בבראשית רבה ד"א אף יעל היתה יושבת אוהלים לפיכך הזכיר אותה בברכת אוהלים [שופטים ה, כד]. דכתיב תבורך מנשים יעל אשת חבר הקיני. כלומר כאותן נשים שמצינו בהן שעשו מצות שלא לשמה וכולן נאמר בהן אהל. תבורך. על שעשתה עבירה לשמה כדי להתיש כחו של אותו רשע כדי שתהא יכולה להורגו. שרה רחל ולאה. שאמרו לבעליהן לבא אל שפחתן ולא לשם מצוה נתכוונו אלא כדי שמתקנאות זו בזו רחל באחותה ושרה ולאה באמהות וכולן נאמר בהן אהל כדכתיבי קראי [נזיר כג:]. ויסמך את ידיו. בעין יפה יותר ויותר ממה שנצטווה שהקב"ה אמר לו וסמכת את ידך והוא עשה בשתי ידיו ועשאו ככלי מלא וגדוש ומלאו חכמתו בעין יפה [במדבר כז, כג]. וישם דבר בפיו. ומה היא השימה הזאת ומה חסר המקרא באמרו שוב אל בלק וכה תדבר אלא כשהיה שומע שאינו נרשה לקלל אמר מה אני חוזר אצל בלק לצערו ונתן לו הקב"ה רסן וחכה בפיו כאדם הפוקס בהמה בחכה להוליכה אל אשר ירצה. אמר לו על כרחך תשוב אל בלק [במדבר כג, טז]. מברכתו. אמרו רבותינו מברכותיו של אותו רשע אנו למדים מה היה בלבו לקלל כשאמר (פסוק א) וישת אל המדבר פניו, וכשהפך המקום את פיו ברכם מעין אותן קללות שבקש לומר כו', כדאיתא בחלק [שם פסוק ו']. ונעתרות. ל' גודל כמו העתרת' עלי (יחזקאל לה) [משלי כז, ו]. ונעתרות נשיקות שונא. נעתרות לשון הפך כדאמרינן במסכת סוכה (יד.) ויעתר לו מה עתר זה מהפך את התבואה פורקא בלעז אי נמי נעתרות, לשון רבוי וייתור אינקרי"ש בלעז כמו העתרתם עלי דבריכם (יחזקאל לה) [תענית כ.].

Having explained that Bilam's power lay in discerning the moment of God's anger, the Gemara discusses how long that anger lasts as well as its daily time:

,,אֵל זֹעֵם בְּכָל־יוֹם" – Scripture states:[12] *God is angered every day.* וְכַמָּה זַעְמוֹ – **And how long does His anger last?** רֶגַע – **A moment,** שֶׁנֶּאֱמַר ,,כִּי רֶגַע בְּאַפּוֹ חַיִּים בִּרְצוֹנוֹ וגו' " – **as it is stated:**[13] ***For His anger endures but a moment, life results from His favor* etc.** אִיבָּעֵית אֵימָא – Or **if you prefer, say** that the length of God's anger is derived from the following verse:[14] ,,לֵךְ עַמִּי בֹּא בַחֲדָרֶיךָ וּסְגֹר דְּלָתְךָ בַּעֲדֶךָ – ***Go, my people, enter your rooms, and close your doors behind you;*** חֲבִי כִמְעַט־רֶגַע עַד־יַעֲבָר־זָעַם" – ***hide for a moment till anger passes,*** which clearly indicates that the anger does not last longer than a moment.[15] אֵימַת רָתַח – And **when** precisely **does [God] become angry?** I.e. when does that moment of anger occur? בִּתְלַת שָׁעֵי קַמַּיְיתָא – **During the first three hours** of the day, כִּי חָוְורָא כַּרְבַּלְתָּא דְתַרְנְגוֹלָא – **when the comb of the rooster pales.**[16]

The Gemara asks:

כָּל שַׁעְתָּא וְשַׁעְתָּא נַמִּי חָוְורָא – But **at all,** i.e. most **times as well it is pale!** – ? –

The Gemara answers:

כָּל שַׁעְתָּא וְשַׁעְתָּא אִית בֵּיהּ סוּרְיָקֵי סוּמָקֵי – **At all** other **times there are red streaks in it;** i.e. some of the original red color is retained in the form of streaks, הַהִיא שַׁעְתָּא לֵית בֵּיהּ סוּרְיָקֵי סוּמָקֵי – however, **at that time,** i.e. the moment of God's anger, **there are no red streaks in it.**

A story about a sage who attempted to make use of this indicator:

הַהוּא מִינָא דַּהֲוָה בְּשִׁיבָבוּתֵיהּ דְּרַבִּי יְהוֹשֻׁעַ בֶּן לֵוִי – **There was a certain heretic who was in the neighborhood of R' Yehoshua ben Levi,** דַּהֲוָה קָא מְצַעֵר לֵיהּ – **who used to harrass [R' Yehoshua].**[17] יוֹמָא חַד נְקַט תַּרְנְגוֹלָא וְאָסַר לֵיהּ בְּכַרְעֵיהּ וְאוֹתִיב – **One day, [R' Yehoshua] took a rooster, tied it by its foot, sat it up,** and stared intently at it. אָמַר – **He said:** כִּי מָטָא הַהוּא שַׁעְתָּא – **When that moment comes** that the rooster's comb pales, אֵילַטְיֵיהּ – **I will curse [the heretic],** for then my curse will be effective. כִּי מָטָא הַהוּא שַׁעְתָּא נַמְנֵם – **When that moment came,** however, **[R' Yehoshua] dozed off.** אָמַר – **[R' Yehoshua]** thereupon **said:** שְׁמַע מִינָּהּ לָאו אוֹרַח אַרְעָא – One may **deduce from this** occurrence **that it is not proper** to have another punished on one's account, דִּכְתִיב ,,גַּם עֲנוֹשׁ לַצַּדִּיק לֹא־טוֹב" – **as it is written:**[18] ***It is also not good for a righteous person to punish,*** אֲפִילּוּ בְּמִינֵי לֹא אִיבָּעֵי לֵיהּ לְמֵימַר הָכִי – which implies that **one should not pronounce [curses] even against heretics.**[19]

More on the precise moment of God's anger:

תָּנָא מִשְּׁמֵיהּ דְּרַבִּי מֵאִיר – **A Tanna taught in the name of R' Meir:** בְּשָׁעָה שֶׁהַחַמָּה זוֹרַחַת – AT THE HOUR THE SUN SHINES in the morning, וְהַמְּלָכִים מַנִּיחִין כִּתְרֵיהֶן עַל רָאשֵׁיהֶן וּמִשְׁתַּחֲוִים לַחַמָּה – AND THE pagan KINGS PLACE THEIR CROWNS ON THEIR HEADS AND BOW TO THE SUN in worship, מִיָּד כּוֹעֵס – at that moment [GOD] IMMEDIATELY BECOMES ANGRY.

The Gemara returns to its discussion of Bilam:

,,וַיָּקָם בִּלְעָם בַּבֹּקֶר וַיַּחֲבֹשׁ אֶת־אֲתֹנוֹ" – Scripture states:[20] ***Bilam arose in the morning and saddled his she-donkey.*** תָּנָא מִשּׁוּם רַבִּי שִׁמְעוֹן בֶּן אֶלְעָזָר – **A Tanna taught in the name of R' Shimon ben Elazar:** אַהֲבָה מְבַטֶּלֶת שׁוּרָה שֶׁל גְּדוּלָּה – LOVE ANNULS THE LIMITATIONS, i.e. violates the rules of conduct IMPOSED BY HIGH POSITION, מֵאַבְרָהָם – as may be seen FROM the case of ABRAHAM, דִּכְתִיב ,,וַיַּשְׁכֵּם אַבְרָהָם בַּבֹּקֶר" – AS IT IS WRITTEN: *ABRAHAM AROSE IN THE MORNING and saddled his donkey.*[21] שִׂנְאָה מְבַטֶּלֶת שׁוּרָה שֶׁל גְּדוּלָּה – HATRED, too, ANNULS THE LIMITATIONS IMPOSED BY HIGH POSITION, מִבִּלְעָם – as may be seen FROM the case of BILAM, שֶׁנֶּאֱמַר ,,וַיָּקָם בִּלְעָם בַּבֹּקֶר וַיַּחֲבֹשׁ אֶת אֲתֹנוֹ" – AS IT IS STATED: *BILAM AROSE IN THE MORNING AND SADDLED HIS SHE-DONKEY.*[22]

The Gemara derives a lesson from Balak:

אָמַר רַב יְהוּדָה אָמַר רַב – **Rav Yehudah said in the name of Rav:** לְעוֹלָם יַעֲסוֹק אָדָם בְּתוֹרָה וּבְמִצְוָה אֲפִילּוּ שֶׁלֹּא לִשְׁמָהּ – **A person should always engage in** the study of **Torah or** the performance of **a mitzvah even if not for its own sake,** i.e. even for ulterior motives, שֶׁמִּתּוֹךְ שֶׁלֹּא לִשְׁמָהּ בָּא לִשְׁמָהּ – **because from** learning Torah and doing a mitzvah **not for its own sake he will** eventually **come** to learn Torah or do a mitzvah **for its own sake,** i.e. out of pure motives.[23] שֶׁבִּשְׂכַר אַרְבָּעִים וּשְׁתַּיִם קָרְבָּנוֹת שֶׁהִקְרִיב בָּלָק – **For as a reward for the forty-two offerings that Balak offered up** to God,[24] זָכָה וְיָצְאָה מִמֶּנּוּ רוּת – **he merited that** the proselyte **Ruth should be descended from him,** אָמַר רַבִּי יוֹסֵי בַּר הוּנָא – as **R' Yose bar Huna said:** רוּת בִּתּוֹ שֶׁל עֶגְלוֹן בֶּן בְּנוֹ שֶׁל בָּלָק מֶלֶךְ מוֹאָב הָיְתָה – **Ruth was the daughter of Eglon the grandson of Balak the king of Moab.**[25]

NOTES

12. *Psalms* 7:12.

13. Ibid. 30:6.

14. *Isaiah* 26:20.

15. The Gemara in *Avodah Zarah* 4b defines this "moment" as the amount of time it takes to pronounce the word רֶגַע (*moment*). See also *Berachos* 7a.

16. Sometime during the first three hours of the day the rooster's comb pales from its ordinary deep-red color. This is the period during which kings rise from their beds and prostrate themselves to the sun; see below (*Rashi* here and to *Berachos* 7a ד״ה בתלת; cf. *Tosafos* to *Avodah Zarah* 4b ד״ה בתלת). [Within this three-hour period, however, the moment of God's anger may vary from day to day (*HaKoseiv* in *Ein Yaakov* to *Berachos* 7a).]

17. By citing spurious Scriptural proofs to his sectarian doctrines (see *Berachos* 7a).

18. *Proverbs* 17:26.

19. See *Melo HaRoim*.

20. *Numbers* 22:21.

21. *Genesis* 22:3. Abraham was commanded by God to offer up his son Isaac as a sacrifice. Abraham's love for God transcended his fatherly mercy towards his son. In his zeal to carry out God's command, Abraham saddled his own donkey to set out to the site of the sacrifice. Ordinarily a wealthy and aristocratic person such as Abraham would not saddle his donkey himself; such lowly tasks were assigned to servants. Thus we see that Abraham's love of God led him to perform chores he would ordinarily consider beneath his dignity (*Rashi* with emendation of *Mesoras HaShas*; cf. *Maharsha* and *Yad David*).

22. I.e. Bilam, too, was a man of high station in life, yet he saddled his donkey by himself, out of his zeal to curse the Jews. Thus we see that his hatred of the Jews led him to violate the limitations his dignity ordinarily imposed upon him (*Rashi*; cf. *Maharsha*).

23. One should not become discouraged if he finds himself studying or performing mitzvos for ulterior motives, e.g. for fame or honor, for the road to Torah study and mitzvah performance for pure motives must of necessity begin with these deeds being done for ulterior motives. Only by climbing the spiritual ladder rung by rung can one hope to reach the top (*Anaf Yosef, Nefesh HaChaim* ch. 3 [following שער ג׳]; see also *Michtav MeEliyahu* III p. 115). See, however, *Tosafos* to *Taanis* 7a ד״ה וכל.

24. Balak set up seven altars in each of three places, and on each altar he offered up a bull and a ram (*Numbers* 23:12, 14, 29-30). This totals forty-two offerings (*Rashi*). Balak brought these offerings for ulterior motives, for he hoped that through them Bilam would be able to curse Israel.

25. *Tosafos* (*Nazir* 23b ד״ה בת) explain that Ruth, who lived generations after Eglon, was not actually his daughter. R' Yose bar Huna means merely that she was *descended* from Eglon.

Maharal adds that ultimately Balak's sacrifices led to the Jewish people being blessed, which in turn caused them to flourish. In reward for this he merited the descendent Ruth, the great-grandmother of David,

כרע נפל שכב וגו' א) ויודע דעת עליון השתא א) דעת בהמתו לא הוה ידע דעת עליון הוה ידע מאי דעת בהמתו דאמרי ליה מאי טעמא לא רכבת ב) סוסיא אמר להו שדאי להו ברטיבא אמרה ליה הלא אנכי אתונך לטעינא בעלמא אשר רכבת עלי אקראי בעלמא מעודך עד היום הזה ולא עוד אלא שאני עושה [לך] מעשה אישות בלילה כתיב הכא ב) ההסכן הסכנתי וכתיב התם ג) ותהי לו סוכנת אלא מאי ויודע דעת עליון שהיה יודע לכוון אותה שעה שהקב"ה כועס בה והיינו דקאמר להו נביא לישראל ד) עמי זכר נא מה יעץ בלק מלך מואב ומה ענה אותו בלעם בן בעור מן השטים ועד הגלגל למען דעת צדקות ה' מאי למען דעת צדקות ה' אמר להן הקב"ה לישראל דעו נא כמה צדקות עשיתי עמכם שלא כעסתי כל אותן הימים בימי בלעם הרשע ג) שאילמלא כעסתי כל אותן הימים לא נשתייר משונאיהן של ישראל שריד ופליט היינו דקאמר ליה בלעם לבלק ה) מה אקב לא קבה אל (ד) וגו' אותן היום [הימים] לא זעם ה') ו) אל זועם בכל יום וכמה זעמו רגע שנאמר ז) כי רגע באפו חיים ברצונו וגו' איבעית אימא ח) לך עמי בא בחדריך וסגור דלתיך בעדך חבי כמעט רגע עד יעבר זעם אימת רתח בתלת שעי קמייתא כי חוורא כרבלתא דתרנגולא כל שעתא ושעתא נמי חוורא כל שעתא ושעתא אית ביה סוריקי סומקי ההיא שעתא לית ביה סוריקי סומקי ההוא מינא דהוה בשיבבותיה דרבי יהושע בן לוי דהוה קא מצער ליה יומא חד נקט ה) תרנגולתא ואסר ליה בכרעיה ואותיב אמר כי מטא ההוא שעתא אילטייה כי מטא ההוא שעתא נמנם אמר שמע מינה לאו אורח ארעא דכתיב ט) גם ענוש לצדיק לא טוב אפילו במיני לא איבעי ליה למימר הכי תנא משמיה דרבי מאיר בשעה שהחמה זורחת והמלכים מניחין כתריהן על ראשיהן ומשתחוים לחמה מיד כועס י) ויקם בלעם בבקר ויחבוש את אתונו תנא משום רבי שמעון בן אלעזר אהבה מבטלת שורה של גדולה מאברהם דכתיב כ) וישכם אברהם בבקר שנאה מבטלת שורה של גדולה מבלעם שנאמר ויקם בלעם בבקר ויחבוש את אתונו ו) אמר רב יהודה אמר רב א) לעולם יעסוק אדם בתורה ובמצוה אפילו שלא לשמה שמתוך שלא לשמה בא לשמה שבשכר ארבעים ושתים קרבנות שהקריב בלק זכה ויצאה ממנו רות א"ר ז) יוסי בר הונא רות בתו של עגלון בן בנו של בלק מלך מואב היתה א"ל רבא לרבה בר מרי כתיב ל) ייטב אלהים את שם שלמה משמך ויגדל [את] כסאו מכסאך אורח ארעא למימרא ליה למלכא הכי א"ל מעין קאמרה ליה דאי לא תימא הכי מ) תבורך מנשים יעל אשת חבר הקיני מנשים באהל תבורך נשים באהל מאן נינהו שרה רבקה רחל ולאה אורח ארעא למימר הכי אלא מעין קאמר הכא נמי מעין קאמר ופליגא דרב יוסי בר חוני דאמר רב יוסי בר חוני בכל אדם מתקנא חוץ מבנו ותלמידו בנו משלמה ותלמידו איבעית אימא נ) ויהי נא פי שנים ברוחך אלי ואיבעית אימא ס) ויסמוך את ידיו עליו ויצוהו ע) וישם דבר בפי בלעם ר"א אומר מלאך ר' יונתן אמר חכה א"ר יוחנן מברכתו של אותו רשע אתה למד מה היה בלבו ביקש לומר שלא יהו להם בתי כנסיות ובתי מדרשות פ) מה טובו אהליך יעקב לא תשרה שכינה עליהם ומשכנותיך ישראל לא תהא מלכותן נמשכת צ) כנחלים נטיו לא יהא להם זיתים וכרמים כגנות עלי נהר לא יהא ריחן נודף כאהלים נטע ה' לא יהיו להם מלכים בעלי קומה כארזים עלי מים לא יהיה להם מלך בן מלך ק) יזל מים מדליו לא תהא מלכותן שולטת באומות וזרעו במים רבים לא תהא עזה מלכותן וירם מאגג מלכו לא תהא ח) אימת מלכותן ותנשא מלכותו אמר רבי אבא בר כהנא כולם חזרו לקללה חוץ מבתי כנסיות ומבתי מדרשות שנאמר ר) ויהפוך ה' אלהיך לך את הקללה לברכה כי אהבך ה' אלהיך קללה ולא קללות ט) א"ר שמואל בר נחמני א"ר יונתן מאי דכתיב ש) נאמנים פצעי אוהב ונעתרות נשיקות שונא טובה קללה שקילל אחיה השילוני את ישראל יותר מברכה שברכם בלעם הרשע אחיה השילוני קילל את ישראל בקנה שנאמר ת) והכה ה' את ישראל כאשר ינוד הקנה במים וגו' מה קנה זה עומד במקום מים וגיזעו
מחליף

כרע נפל. מה כריעה דהתם דאית ביה נפילה בעילה היא אף כריעה דהכא דכתיב נופל בעילה היא שבא על בהמתו: **דעת בהמתו לא הוה ידע.** מאי בעיא לאהדורי כדמפרש דאמרי ליה שרי בלק מאי טעמא לא רכבת אסוסיא: **ברטיבא.** באחו לרעות עשבים לחים: **אמר להו לטעינא בעלמא.** לישא משאות ולא לרכוב: אמרה ליה אשר רכבת עלי: **אקראי בעלמא.** כשאין לי סוס מזומן: אמרה לו מעודך: **מעשה אישות.** שאתה בועלי: **סוכנת.** מחממת: **מן השטים ועד הגלגל.** משחטאו בשטים ועד שנכנסו לארץ וחטאו בגלגל עשיתי עמהם צדקות הרבה: **כל אותן הימים.** שהיה בלעם מצפה לקללכם בשעה שהקב"ה כועס בה כל הקללות מתקיימות: **ה"ג לא זעם ה'.** אותן הימים לא זעם ה': **אל זועם בכל יום.** קרא הוא: **כמה זעמו רגע.** כדמפיק ליה מקרא כי רגע באפו חיים ברצונו: **בתלת שעי קמייתא.** של יום זמן קימה שכל שלש שעות זמן קימה לעמוד ממטתו וכועס הקב"ה בשעה שרואה המלכים שמשתחוים לחמה בשעה שמניחין כתריהם בראשם כדלקמן: **כרבלתא.** קירסת"א בלע"ז: **כל שעתא נמי חיורא.** רוב שעות מתלבנת ומכספת שאינה כל שעה בחוזק אדמימות: **סורייקי סומקי.** אפי' כשמכספת יש בה שורות שורות אדומות מאד כרגילותם אבל אותה שעה כולה מכספת: **גם ענוש לצדיק לא טוב.** אין נכון לצדיק שיהא מעניש ולא הוה ליה איניש נענש בשבילו: **אהבה.** שאהב י) הקב"ה את אברהם ביטלה שורה של גדולה שחבש הוא בעצמו: **ושנאה.** ששנא בלעם הרשע את ישראל ביטלה שורה של גדולה שחבש הוא בעצמו: **מ"ב קרבנות.** בין פרים לאילים ז' פרים וז' אילים ג' פעמים הרי מ"ב בין פרים ואילים: **אורח ארעא** למימר הכי. וכי דרך ארץ כן שיאמרו כ) וייטב אלהים שם שלמה משמך והא חלשא דעתיה דאמרי ליה שיהא גדול מאביו: **מעין שמך.** קאמר ליה ומעין כסאך ולא גדול ממש: **נשים באהל.** שרה רבקה רחל ולאה שרה ורבקה דכתיב ויביאה יצחק האהלה שרה אמו וגו' רחל ולאה דכתיב (בראשית לא) ויצא מאהל לאה ויבא באהל רחל: **אורח ארעא.** שאמרה דבורה ליעל [שתהא] ברוכה משרה ורבקה אלא מעין ברכת שרה קאמרה: **ופליגא.** האי דמשנינן שם שלמה משמך מעין פליגא דר' יוסי בר חוני: **בנו מניין.** שאינו מקנא בו: **משלמה.** דקאמרי ליה לדוד ייטב אלהים שם שלמה משמך: **ותלמידו.** איבעית אימא דקאמר ליה לאליהו ויהי נא פי שנים ברוחך אלי ונתן לו אליהו ולא נתקנא בו: **ויסמוך את ידיו עליו ויצוהו.** אע"ג דהקב"ה לא א"ל אלא וסמכת את ידך עליו חדא אזיל איהו וסמך תרתי: **מלאך.** שמסרו הקדוש ברוך הוא למלאך שלא יניחנו לקלל: **חכה.** נתן בפי בלעם שלא היה מניחו לקלל והיינו וישם: **מברכותיו אתה למד מה היה בלבו.** דכתיב ויהפוך ה' אלהיך לך את הקללה לברכה הוא היה רוצה לקללם בכך שלא יהיו בתי כנסיות ולא נתן רשות ואמר מה טובו אוהליך: **ריחן נודף.** ממלות: **וירם מאגג מלכו.** מתרגמינן ותתקף מאגג שתהא מלכותו עזה: **וכולם.** כל הברכות של בלעם חזרו לקללה כמו שהיה כוונתו מתחילה: חוץ מבתי כנסיות ובתי מדרשות. שלא יפסקו מישראל לעולם: **הקללה לברכה.** אחת מן הקללות הפך לברכה שלא חזרה לעולם ולא כל הקללות לברכות שחזרו: **נעתרות.** נהפכות כמו עתר שמהפך התבואה כלומר נאמנים פצעי אוהב ונהפכות מנאמנות נשיקות שונא:
מחליף

לז א מיי' פ"ג מהלכות ת"ת הלכה ה ופ"י מהלכות תשובה הלכה ה סמג עשין יב טוש"ע י"ד סי' רמו סעיף כ:

תורה אור השלם

א) נְאֻם שֹׁמֵעַ אִמְרֵי אֵל וְיֹדֵעַ דַּעַת עֶלְיוֹן מַחֲזֵה שַׁדַּי יֶחֱזֶה נֹפֵל וּגְלוּי עֵינָיִם: [במדבר כד, טז]

ב) וַתֹּאמֶר הָאָתוֹן אֶל בִּלְעָם הֲלוֹא אָנֹכִי אֲתֹנְךָ אֲשֶׁר רָכַבְתָּ עָלַי מֵעוֹדְךָ עַד הַיּוֹם הַזֶּה הַהַסְכֵּן הִסְכַּנְתִּי לַעֲשׂוֹת לְךָ כֹּה וַיֹּאמֶר לֹא: [במדבר כב, ל]

ג) וַיֹּאמְרוּ לוֹ עֲבָדָיו יְבַקְשׁוּ לַאדֹנִי הַמֶּלֶךְ נַעֲרָה בְתוּלָה וְעָמְדָה לִפְנֵי הַמֶּלֶךְ וּתְהִי לוֹ סֹכֶנֶת וְשָׁכְבָה בְחֵיקֶךָ וְחַם לַאדֹנִי הַמֶּלֶךְ: [מלכים א' א, ב]

ד) עַמִּי זְכָר נָא מַה יָּעַץ בָּלָק מֶלֶךְ מוֹאָב וּמֶה עָנָה אֹתוֹ בִּלְעָם בֶּן בְּעוֹר מִן הַשִּׁטִּים עַד הַגִּלְגָּל לְמַעַן דַּעַת צִדְקוֹת יְיָ: [מיכה ו, ה]

ה) מָה אֶקֹּב לֹא קַבֹּה אֵל וּמָה אֶזְעֹם לֹא זָעַם יְיָ: [במדבר כג, ח]

ו) אֱלֹהִים שׁוֹפֵט צַדִּיק וְאֵל זֹעֵם בְּכָל יוֹם: [תהלים ז, יב]

ז) כִּי רֶגַע בְּאַפּוֹ חַיִּים בִּרְצוֹנוֹ בָּעֶרֶב יָלִין בֶּכִי וְלַבֹּקֶר רִנָּה: [תהלים ל, ו]

ח) לֵךְ עַמִּי בֹּא בַחֲדָרֶיךָ וּסְגֹר דְּלָתְךָ בַּעֲדֶךָ חֲבִי כִמְעַט רֶגַע עַד יַעֲבָר זָעַם: [ישעיה כו, כ]

ט) גַּם עֲנוֹשׁ לַצַּדִּיק לֹא טוֹב לְהַכּוֹת נְדִיבִים עַל יֹשֶׁר: [משלי יז, כו]

י) וַיָּקָם בִּלְעָם בַּבֹּקֶר וַיַּחֲבֹשׁ אֶת אֲתֹנוֹ וַיֵּלֶךְ עִם שָׂרֵי מוֹאָב: [במדבר כב, כא]

כ) וַיַּשְׁכֵּם אַבְרָהָם בַּבֹּקֶר וַיַּחֲבֹשׁ אֶת חֲמֹרוֹ וַיִּקַּח אֶת שְׁנֵי נְעָרָיו אִתּוֹ וְאֵת יִצְחָק בְּנוֹ וַיְבַקַּע עֲצֵי עֹלָה וַיָּקָם וַיֵּלֶךְ אֶל הַמָּקוֹם אֲשֶׁר אָמַר לוֹ הָאֱלֹהִים: [בראשית כב, ג]

ל) וְגַם בָּאוּ עַבְדֵי הַמֶּלֶךְ לְבָרֵךְ אֶת אֲדֹנֵינוּ הַמֶּלֶךְ דָּוִד לֵאמֹר יֵיטֵב אֱלֹהִים אֶת שֵׁם שְׁלֹמֹה מִשְּׁמֶךָ וִיגַדֵּל אֶת כִּסְאוֹ מִכִּסְאֶךָ וַיִּשְׁתַּחוּ הַמֶּלֶךְ עַל הַמִּשְׁכָּב: [מלכים א' א, מז]

מ) תְּבֹרַךְ מִנָּשִׁים יָעֵל אֵשֶׁת חֶבֶר הַקֵּינִי מִנָּשִׁים בָּאֹהֶל תְּבֹרָךְ: [שופטים ה, כד]

נ) וַיְהִי כְעָבְרָם וְאֵלִיָּהוּ אָמַר אֶל אֱלִישָׁע שְׁאַל מָה אֶעֱשֶׂה לָּךְ בְּטֶרֶם אֶלָּקַח מֵעִמָּךְ וַיֹּאמֶר אֱלִישָׁע וִיהִי נָא פִּי שְׁנַיִם בְּרוּחֲךָ אֵלָי: [מלכים ב' ב, ט]

ס) וַיִּסְמֹךְ אֶת יָדָיו עָלָיו וַיְצַוֵּהוּ כַּאֲשֶׁר דִּבֶּר יְיָ בְּיַד מֹשֶׁה: [במדבר כז, כג]

ע) וַיָּשֶׂם יְיָ דָּבָר בְּפִי בִלְעָם וַיֹּאמֶר שׁוּב אֶל בָּלָק וְכֹה תְדַבֵּר: [במדבר כג, ה] פ) מַה טֹּבוּ אֹהָלֶיךָ יַעֲקֹב מִשְׁכְּנֹתֶיךָ יִשְׂרָאֵל: [במדבר כד, ה] צ) כִּנְחָלִים נִטָּיוּ כְּגַנֹּת עֲלֵי נָהָר כַּאֲהָלִים נָטַע יְהוָה כַּאֲרָזִים עֲלֵי מָיִם: [במדבר כד, ו] ק) יִזַּל מַיִם מִדָּלְיָו וְזַרְעוֹ בְּמַיִם רַבִּים וְיָרֹם מֵאֲגַג מַלְכּוֹ וְתִנַּשֵּׂא מַלְכֻתוֹ: [במדבר כד, ז] ר) וְלֹא אָבָה יְיָ אֱלֹהֶיךָ לִשְׁמֹעַ אֶל בִּלְעָם וַיַּהֲפֹךְ יְיָ אֱלֹהֶיךָ לְּךָ אֶת הַקְּלָלָה לִבְרָכָה כִּי אֲהֵבְךָ יְיָ אֱלֹהֶיךָ: [דברים כג, ו] ש) נֶאֱמָנִים פִּצְעֵי אוֹהֵב וְנַעְתָּרוֹת נְשִׁיקוֹת שׂוֹנֵא: [משלי כז, ו] ת) וְהִכָּה יְיָ אֶת יִשְׂרָאֵל כַּאֲשֶׁר יָנוּד הַקָּנֶה בַּמַּיִם וְנָתַשׁ אֶת יִשְׂרָאֵל מֵעַל הָאֲדָמָה הַטּוֹבָה הַזֹּאת אֲשֶׁר נָתַן לַאֲבוֹתֵיהֶם וְזֵרָם מֵעֵבֶר לַנָּהָר יַעַן אֲשֶׁר עָשׂוּ אֶת אֲשֵׁרֵיהֶם מַכְעִיסִים אֶת יְיָ: [מלכים א' יד, טו]

א) [ברכות ז. ע"ש ע"ז ד:], ב) [צ"ל אסוסיא], ג) [צ"ל שאילמלי ועיין תוספות מגילה כח.], ד) [צ"ל ומה אזעום לא זעם ה' מלמד שכל אותם הימים לא זעם ה' כ"א בברכות ז. וקצת שינוי יש בע"ז ד: ע"ש], ה) [צ"ל תרנגול'], ו) פסחים נ: ערכין טז: סוטה כב: מז. הוריות י: נזיר כג:, ז) [צ"ל דאמר ר' יוסי בר הונא כך איתא בהוריות י: ע"ש וע"ע בנזיר כג: ובתוספות שם ד"ה בת בנו וכו' דלאו דוקא ע"ש וע"ע סוטה מז.], ח) ר"י יעב"ץ גרס איומה, ט) תענית כ., י) ס"א אברהם את הקב"ה, כ) [צ"ל וייטיב].

ליקוטי רש"י

סוכנת. לשון מחממת [ע"ז ד:]. מחממת וכן ובוקע עצים יסכן בם, (קהלת י' ט) [מ"א א, ב]. **ומה ענה אותו בלעם בן בעור.** מה אזעום לא זעם ה' (במדבר כג) שלא כעסתי כל אותן הימים. **מן השטים.** שחטאתם לי שם דעו לדקותי שלא מנעתי טובתי ועזרתי מכם עד הבאתי אתכם לגלגל וכבשתי לפניכם שם את הארץ [מיכה ו, ה]. **מן השטים ועד הגלגל.** עד באכם אל הגלגל שהפלתי לפניכם שונאיכם [ע"ז שם]. **לא זעם ה'.** אני אין כחי אלא שאני יודע לכוין השעה שהקב"ה כועס בה והוא לא כעס כל הימים הללו שבאתי אליך וזהו שנאמר (מיכה ו, ה) עמי זכר נא מה יעץ וגו' ומה ענה אותו בלעם וגו' למען דעת צדקות ה' [במדבר כג, ח]. **חבי.** התחבאי מעט עד יעבר זעם כי אמת אפקוד על שונאיך [ישעיהו כו, כ]. **כי רגע באפו.** אלמא דרגע הוי אפו. **סורייקי.** נוקיש לשון לע"ז כמו חוטין חוטין ולשון ישמעאל קורין לחוט סוריאק. **לאו אורח ארעא.** לכוין שעת זעמו [ע"ז ד:]. **בתלת שעי קמייתא.** באחד מרגעי תלת שעות ראשונות. **לצדיק לא טוב.** לענוש את הבריות [ברכות ז.]. **ויחבש את אתנו.** מכאן שהשנאה מקלקלת את השורה שחבש הוא בעצמו אמר הקב"ה רשע כבר קדמך אברהם אביהם שנאמר (בראשית כב, ג) וישכם אברהם בבקר ויחבוש את חמורו [במדבר כב, כא]. **וישכם.** נזדרז למצוה. **ויחבש.** הוא בעצמו ולא צוה לאחד מעבדיו שהאהבה מקלקלת השורה [בראשית כב, ג]. **מ"ב קרבנות.** ג"פ ז' מזבחות פר ואיל במזבח. **יצאה ממנו רות.** שיצא ממנה דוד שריוה להקב"ה בשירות ותשבחות (ברכות ז: ב"ב יד:) [הוריות י:]. **מנשים באהל.** שרה שנאמר בה הנה באהל רבקה שנאמר בה ויביאה יצחק האהלה רחל ולאה שנאמר בהן ויצא מאהל לאה וגומר. **מנשים באהל תבורך.** יעל למה הן ילדו ויגדלו ואם לא יעל הרי הרשע הזה בא ומאבדן כך הוא בבראשית רבה ד"א אף יעל היתה יושבת אוהלים לפיכך הזכיר אותה בברכת אוהלים [שופטים ה, כד]. **דכתיב תבורך מנשים יעל אשת חבר הקיני.** כלומר כאותן נשים שמצינו בהן שעשו מצות שלא לשמה וכולן נאמר בהן אהל. **תבורך.** על שעשתה עבירה לשמה כדי להמיס כחו של אותו רשע כדי שתהא יכולה להורגו. **שרה רחל ולאה.** שאמרו לבעליהן לבא אל שפחתן ולא לשם מצוה נתכוונו אלא כדי שמתקנאות זו בזו רחל באחותה ושרה ולאה באחותה וכולן נאמר בהן אהל כדכתיבי קראי [נזיר כג:]. **ויסמך את ידיו.** בעין יפה יותר ויותר ממה שנצטווה שהקב"ה אמר לו וסמכת את ידך והוא עשה בשתי ידיו ועשאו כלי מלא וגדוש ומלאו חכמתו בעין יפה [במדבר כז, כג]. **וישם דבר בפיו.** ומה היא השימה הזאת ומה חסר המקרא באמרו שוב אל בלק וכה תדבר אלא כשהיה שומע שאינו נרשה לקלל אמר מה אני חוזר אצל בלק לצערו ונתן לו הקב"ה רסן וחכה בפיו כאדם הפוקס בהמה בחכה להוליכה אל אשר ירצה. אמר לו על כרחך תשוב אל בלק [במדבר כג, טז]. **מברכתו.** אמרו רבותינו מברכותיו של אותו רשע אנו למדים מה היה בלבו לקללם כשאמר (פסוק א) וישת אל המדבר פניו, וכשהפך המקום את פיו ברכם מעין אותן קללות שבקש לומר כו', כדאיתא בחלק [שם פסוק ו']. **ונעתרות.** ל' גודל כמו העתרת' עלי (יחזקאל לה) [משלי כז, ו]. **ונעתרות נשיקות שונא.** נעתרות לשון הפך כדאמרינן במסכת סוכה (יד.) ויעתר לו מה עתר זה מהפך את התבואה פורקא בלעז אי נמי נעתרות, לשון רבוי וייתור אינקריי"ש בלעז כמו העתרתם עלי דבריכם (יחזקאל לה) [תענית כ.].

The Gemara temporarily turns to another topic:[26]

אֲמַר לֵיהּ רָבָא לְרַבָּה בַּר מָרִי – **Rava said to Rabbah bar Mari:** כְּתִיב ,,יֵיטֵב אֱלֹהִים אֶת־שֵׁם שְׁלֹמֹה מִשְּׁמֶךָ וִיגַדֵּל [אֶת]־כִּסְאוֹ מִכִּסְאֶךָ'' – **It is written:** ***May God make the renown of Solomon greater than your renown*** (*mishimecha*)***, and may He exalt his throne higher than your throne*** (*mikisecha*).[27] אוֹרַח אַרְעָא לְמֵימְרָא לֵיהּ לְמַלְכָּא הָכִי – Now **is it proper to say such a thing to a king?**[28] אָמַר לֵיהּ – **[Rabbah bar Mari] said to [Rava]:** מֵעֵין קָאָמְרָה לֵיהּ – You misunderstand the verse; they did not say "*greater than* your renown"; ***"something of*** your renown" **is what they said to him.**[29] דְּאִי לֹא תֵּימָא הָכִי – **For if you do not say this,** ,,תְּבֹרַךְ מִנָּשִׁים יָעֵל אֵשֶׁת חֶבֶר הַקֵּינִי מִנָּשִׁים בָּאֹהֶל תְּבֹרָךְ'' – then you must translate *Judges* 5:24 in the following manner: ***May you be blessed more than the women*** (*minashim*)***, O Yael, wife of Chever the Keinite. May you be blessed more than the women in the tent*** (*minashim ba'ohel*).[30] נָשִׁים בָּאֹהֶל מַאן נִינְהוּ – Now, **who are "the women in the tent"?** שָׂרָה רִבְקָה רָחֵל וְלֵאָה – The Matriarchs: **Sarah, Rebeccah, Rachel, and Leah.**[31] אוֹרַח אַרְעָא לְמֵימַר הָכִי – **Now is it proper to say such a thing,** i.e. that Deborah said of Yael that she should be more blessed than the Matriarchs? Certainly not! אֶלָּא מֵעֵין קָאָמַר – **Rather, *"something of*** the blessing bestowed upon the Matriarchs" **is what [the verse] said.**[32] הָכָא נַמִּי מֵעֵין קָאָמַר – **Here too** in regard to the verse describing the extent of Solomon's renown, ***"something of*** your renown" **is what they said** to David.

The underlying presumption of the preceding explanation is that it would have been improper for David's courtiers to bless him that his son supersede him. The Gemara notes that this notion is not unanimously held:

וּפְלִיגָא דְּרַב יוֹסֵי בַּר חוֹנִי – **And this disagrees with Rav Yose bar Choni,** דְּאָמַר רַב יוֹסֵי בַּר חוֹנִי – **for Rav Yose bar Choni said:** בַּכֹּל אָדָם מִתְקַנֵּא חוּץ מִבְּנוֹ וְתַלְמִידוֹ – **A man is jealous of everyone except his son and his disciple.** בְּנוֹ מִשְּׁלֹמֹה – **His son,** as is evident **from** the case of **Solomon.**[33] וְתַלְמִידוֹ אִיבָּעֵית אֵימָא ,,וִיהִי־נָא פִּי־שְׁנַיִם בְּרוּחֲךָ אֵלָי'' – **And his disciple, if you prefer, say** that it is derived from the following verse: ***Let a double portion of your spirit pass on to me.***[34] וְאִיבָּעֵית אֵימָא ,,וַיִּסְמֹךְ אֶת־יָדָיו עָלָיו וַיְצַוֵּהוּ'' – **Or, if you prefer, say** that it is derived from the following verse: ***He leaned his hands upon him and commanded him.***[35]

Resuming its interrupted discussion of Bilam, the Gemara describes how he was prevented from giving vent to his desire to curse the Jews:

,,וַיָּשֶׂם . . . דָּבָר בְּפִי בִלְעָם'' – Scripture states: ***[God] put a thing*** (*davar*) ***in Bilam's mouth.***[36] What was this "thing"? רַבִּי אֶלְעָזָר אוֹמֵר מַלְאָךְ – **R' Elazar says:** It was **an angel.**[37] רַבִּי יוֹנָתָן אָמַר חַכָּה – **R' Yonasan says:** It was **a hook.**[38]

The Gemara examines *Numbers* 24:5-7, one of the speeches of praise and blessing of the Jewish people that Bilam was forced to deliver:

אָמַר רַבִּי יוֹחָנָן – **R' Yochanan said:** מִבִּרְכָתוֹ שֶׁל אוֹתוֹ רָשָׁע אַתָּה לָמֵד מֶה הָיָה בְלִבּוֹ – **From the blessing pronounced by that wicked man, – you can deduce what was in his heart:**[39] בִּיקֵּשׁ לוֹמַר שֶׁלֹּא יְהוּ לָהֶם בָּתֵּי כְנֵסִיּוֹת וּבָתֵּי מִדְרָשׁוֹת – **He sought to say that [the Jews] should not have any synagogues or study**

NOTES

who likewise caused the Jewish nation to flourish. Thus, we learn that an ill-intentioned act that leads to a positive result does not go unrewarded.

26. This seems to be a digression completely unrelated to the Gemara's discussion of Bilam. See *Maharsha,* who points out that this discussion also occurs in *Nazir* 23b and in *Horayos* 10b, and there an additional passage is cited that links it to the next passage in our Gemara; this link is omitted here. Cf. *Emes LeYaakov (R' Yaakov Kaminetsky).*

27. *I Kings* 1:47. When King David was old, his son Adoniah sought to succeed him as king, even though David desired that his other son, Solomon, should be his successor. To forestall Adoniah, David ordered that Solomon be anointed king while he, David, was still alive. This was done, and David's courtiers came to congratulate David on Solomon's coronation, saying: *May God make the renown of Solomon greater than your renown, and may He exalt his throne higher than your throne.*

28. I.e. is it not demeaning to a king to say that his renown and grandeur will be inferior to that of another king? (*Rashi*).

29. The translation follows *Rashash* who emends the word קָאָמְרָה, *she said,* to קָאָמְרֵי, *they said.*

You understand the word מִשְּׁמֶךָ to mean *more than your renown,* implying that Solomon's renown should exceed David's. Instead, it means *something of your renown* (*Rashi*), the prefix *mem* in מִשְּׁמֶךָ meaning *from* or *of;* in other words, they said to David that Solomon should have some of his renown, not that Solomon's renown should exceed his (*Yad Ramah*).

30. *Judges* 5:24. See note 1 above.

31. Scripture mentions each of the Matriarchs in connection with a tent – *Genesis* 24:67 and 31:33 (*Rashi*).

32. I.e. when the verse states מִנָּשִׁים בָּאֹהֶל תְּבֹרָךְ, it does not mean "May she be blessed *more* than the women in the tent," for it is inconceivable that Yael should be more blessed than those supreme paragons of righteousness, the Matriarchs. Rather, the prefix *mem* in מִנָּשִׁים means "something of"; in other words, Yael's blessing should be *a semblance of* the blessing of the Matriarchs (*Rashi*).

33. Rav Yose bar Choni translates the verse describing Solomon's renown as Rava originally did, namely, that Solomon's renown should exceed David's. The fact that David's courtiers would openly wish him that his son's renown should exceed his own indicates that they did not feel that in doing so they were demeaning David. This is due to their perception that David would not be jealous of Solomon's superior renown, because a father is never jealous of his son's success, even when it exceeds his own (*Rashi*).

34. *II Kings* 2:9. Before his departure from earth, the prophet Elijah offered to grant his disciple Elisha whatever the latter requested. Elisha asked for a double portion of Elijah's own prophetic powers. Elijah granted this request.

Elijah was not envious that Elisha had sought greater prophetic powers than he himself had possessed. On the contrary, Elijah sincerely desired to grant the request. This indicates that a master is not jealous when his disciple surpasses him in greatness (*Rashi*).

35. *Numbers* 27:23. Before his death Moses was told by God to appoint a successor, Joshua. God said (ibid. v. 18): *Take to yourself Joshua son of Nun, a man in whom there is spirit, and lean your hand upon him.* That is, Moses was to lean *one* hand upon Joshua [indicating that Joshua would have only half of Moses' prophetic powers]. Instead, Moses leaned *both* of his hands upon Joshua [thereby conferring a full measure of his own prophetic powers upon his successor]. The fact that Moses exceeded God's instructions in favor of his disciple Joshua proves that a master is not jealous of his disciple.

36. Ibid. 23:5.

37. I.e. the word דָּבָר here refers to an angel. God placed Bilam under the control of an angel who would not permit Bilam to speak when he sought to curse the Jews (*Rashi*). Alternatively, an angel entered his mouth and settled in his throat. When Bilam opened his mouth to speak, an angel's voice would emerge instead of Bilam's (see *Tanchuma* 12 and *Bamidbar Rabbah* 20:18). See also *Ben Yehoyada.*

38. I.e. the word דָּבָר here means a hook. God fastened a hook, so to speak, to Bilam's jaw, and whenever Bilam sought to curse the Jews, the hook was pulled and Bilam's jaw snapped shut, preventing him from speaking (*Rashi, Yad Ramah;* cf. *Rashi* to *Numbers* 23:16). See also *Maharal.*

39. Scripture states: *And HASHEM your God transformed [Bilam's] curse into a blessing for you* (*Deuteronomy* 23:6). This indicates that Bilam's blessings were the reverse of what he really had planned to say. Thus, by examining the blessings, we can deduce Bilam's true intentions (*Rashi*).

כרע נפל שכב וגו' א) ויודע דעת עליון השתא א) דעת בהמתו לא הוה ידע דעת עליון הוה ידע מאי דעת בהמתו דאמרי ליה מאי טעמא לא רכבת ב) סוסיא אמר להו שדאי להו ברטיבא אמרה ליה הלא אנכי אתונך לטעינא בעלמא אשר רכבת עלי אקראי בעלמא מעודך עד היום הזה ולא עוד אלא שאני עושה [לך] מעשה אישות בלילה כתיב הכא ב) ההסכן הסכנתי וכתיב התם ג) ותהי לו סוכנת אלא מאי ויודע דעת עליון שהיה יודע לכוון אותה שעה שהקב"ה כועס בה והיינו דקאמר להו נביא לישראל ד) עמי זכר נא מה יעץ בלק מלך מואב ומה ענה אותו בלעם בן בעור מן השטים ועד הגלגל למען דעת צדקות ה' מאי למען דעת צדקות ה' אמר להן הקב"ה לישראל דעו נא כמה צדקות עשיתי עמכם שלא כעסתי כל אותן הימים בימי בלעם הרשע ג) שאילמלא כעסתי כל אותן הימים לא נשתייר משונאיהן של ישראל שריד ופליט היינו דקאמר ליה בלעם לבלק ה) מה אקב לא קבה אל (ד) וגו' אותן היום [הימים] לא זעם ה') ו) אל זועם בכל יום וכמה זעמו רגע שנאמר ז) כי רגע באפו חיים ברצונו וגו' איבעית אימא ח) לך עמי בא בחדריך וסגור דלתיך בעדך חבי כמעט רגע עד יעבור זעם אימת רתח בתלת שעי קמייתא כי חוורא כרבלתא דתרנגולא כל שעתא ושעתא נמי חוורא כל שעתא ושעתא אית ביה סוריקי סומקי ההיא שעתא לית ביה סוריקי סומקי ההוא מינא דהוה בשיבבותיה דרבי יהושע בן לוי דהוה קא מצער ליה יומא חד נקט ה) תרנגולתא ואסר ליה בכרעיה ואותיב אמר כי מטא ההוא שעתא אילטייה כי מטא ההוא שעתא נמנם אמר שמע מינה לאו אורח ארעא דכתיב ט) גם ענוש לצדיק לא טוב אפילו במיני לא איבעי ליה למימר הכי תנא משמיה דרבי מאיר בשעה שהחמה זורחת והמלכים מניחין כתריהן על ראשיהן ומשתחוים לחמה מיד כועס י) ויקם בלעם בבקר ויחבוש את אתונו תנא משום רבי שמעון בן אלעזר אהבה מבטלת שורה של גדולה מאברהם דכתיב כ) וישכם אברהם בבקר שנאה מבטלת שורה של גדולה מבלעם שנאמר ויקם בלעם בבקר ויחבוש את אתונו ו) אמר רב יהודה אמר רב א לעולם יעסוק אדם בתורה ובמצוה אפילו שלא לשמה שמתוך שלא לשמה בא לשמה שבשכר ארבעים ושתים קרבנות שהקריב בלק זכה ויצאה ממנו רות ז) א"ר יוסי בר הונא רות בתו של עגלון בן בנו של בלק מלך מואב היתה א"ל רבא לרבה בר מרי כתיב ל) ייטב אלהים את שם שלמה משמך ויגדל [את] כסאו מכסאך אורח ארעא למימרא ליה למלכא הכי א"ל מעין קאמרה ליה דאי לא תימא הכי מ) תבורך מנשים יעל אשת חבר הקיני מנשים באהל תבורך נשים באהל מאן נינהו שרה רבקה רחל ולאה אורח ארעא למימר הכי אלא מעין קאמר הכא נמי מעין קאמר ופליגא דרב יוסי בר חוני דאמר רב יוסי בר חוני בכל אדם מתקנא חוץ מבנו ותלמידו בנו משלמה ותלמידו איבעית אימא נ) ויהי נא פי שנים ברוחך אלי ואיבעית אימא ס) ויסמוך את ידיו עליו ויצוהו ע) וישם דבר בפי בלעם ר"א אומר מלאך ר' יונתן אמר חכה א"ר יוחנן מברכתו של אותו רשע אתה למד מה היה בלבו ביקש לומר שלא יהו להם בתי כנסיות ובתי מדרשות פ) מה טובו אהליך יעקב לא תשרה שכינה עליהם ומשכנותיך ישראל לא תהא מלכותן נמשכת צ) כנחלים נטיו לא יהא להם זיתים וכרמים כגנות עלי נהר לא יהא ריחן נודף כאהלים נטע ה' לא יהיו להם מלכים בעלי קומה כארזים עלי מים לא יהיה להם מלך בן מלך ק) יזל מים מדליו לא תהא מלכותן שולטת באומות וזרעו במים רבים לא תהא עזה מלכותן וירם מאגג מלכו לא תהא ט) אימת מלכותן ותנשא מלכותו אמר רבי אבא בר כהנא כולם חזרו לקללה חוץ מבתי כנסיות ומבתי מדרשות שנאמר ר) ויהפוך ה' אלהיך לך את הקללה לברכה כי אהבך ה' אלהיך קללה ולא קללות ט) א"ר שמואל בר נחמני א"ר יונתן מאי דכתיב ש) נאמנים פצעי אוהב ונעתרות נשיקות שונא טובה קללה שקילל אחיה השילוני את ישראל יותר מברכה שברכם בלעם הרשע אחיה השילוני קילל את ישראל בקנה שנאמר ת) והכה ה' את ישראל כאשר ינוד הקנה במים וגו' מה קנה זה עומד במקום מים וגיזעו

מחליף

רש"י

ברע נפל. מה כריעה דהתם דאית ביה נפילה בעילה היא אף כריעה דהכא דכתיב נופל בעילה היא שבא על בהמתו: **דעת בהמתו לא הוה ידע.** מאי בעיא לאהדורי כדמפרש דאמרי ליה שרי בלק מאי טעמא לא רכבת אסוסיא: **ברטיבא.** באחו לרעות עשבים לחים: **אמר להו לטעינא בעלמא.** ליטא משאות ולא לרכוב: אמרה ליה אשר רכבת עלי: **אקראי בעלמא.** כשאין לי סוס מזומן: אמרה לו מעודך: **מעשה אישות.** שאתה בועלי: **סוכנת.** מחממת: **מן השטים ועד הגלגל.** משחטאו בשטים ועד שנכנסו לארץ וחטאו בגלגל עשיתי עמהם לדקות הרבה: **כל אותן הימים.** שהיה בלעם מצפה לקללכם בשעה שהקב"ה כועס בה כל הקללות מתקיימות: **ה"ג לא זעם ה'.** אותן הימים לא זעם ה': **אל זועם בכל יום.** קרא הוא: **כמה זעמו רגע.** כדמפיק ליה מקרא כי רגע באפו חיים ברצונו: **בתלת שעי קמייתא.** של יום זמן קימה שכל שלש שעות זמן קימה לעמוד ממטתו וכועס הקב"ה בשעה שרואה המלכים שמשתחוים לחמה בשעה שמניחין כתריהם בראשם כדלקמן: **ברבלתא.** קירסת"א בלע"ז: **כל שעתא נמי חיורא.** רוב שעות מתלבנת ומכספת שאינה כל שעה בחוזק אדמימות: **סורייקי סומקי.** אפי' כשמכספת יש בה שורות שורות אדומות מאד כרגילותם אבל אותה שעה כולה מכספת: **גם ענוש לצדיק לא טוב.** אין נכון לצדיק שיהא מעניש ולא הוה ליה איניש נענש בשבילו: **אהבה.** שאהב י) הקב"ה את אברהם ביטלה שורה של גדולה שחבש הוא בעצמו: **ושנאה.** ששנא בלעם הרשע את ישראל ביטלה שורה של גדולה שחבש הוא בעצמו: **מ"ב קרבנות.** בין פרים לאילים ז' פרים וז' אילים ג' פעמים הרי מ"ב בין פרים ואילים: **אורח ארעא** למימר הכי. וכי דרך ארץ כן שיאמרו כ) וייטב אלהים שם שלמה משמך והא חלשא דעתיה דאמרי ליה שיהא גדול מאביו: **מעין שמך.** קאמר ליה ומעין כסאך ולא גדול ממש: **נשים באהל.** שרה רבקה רחל ולאה שרה ורבקה דכתיב ויביאה יצחק האהלה שרה אמו וגו' רחל ולאה דכתיב (בראשית לא) ויצא מאהל לאה ויבא באהל רחל: **אורח ארעא.** שאמרה דבורה ליעל [שתהא] ברוכה משרה ורבקה אלא מעין ברכת שרה קאמרה: **ופליגא.** הא דמשנינן שם שלמה משמך מעין פליגא דר' יוסי בר חוני: **בנו מניין.** שאינו מקנא בו: **משלמה.** דקאמרי ליה לדוד ייטב אלהים שם שלמה משמך: **ותלמידו.** איבעית אימא דקאמר ליה לאליהו ויהי נא פי שנים ברוחך אלי ונתן לו אליהו ולא נתקנא בו: **ויסמוך את ידיו עליו ויצוהו.** אע"ג דהקב"ה לא א"ל אלא וסמכת את ידך עליו חדא אזיל איהו וסמך תרתי: **מלאך.** שמסרו הקדוש ברוך הוא למלאך שלא יניחנו לקלל: **חכה.** נתן בפי בלעם שלא היה מניחו לקלל והיינו וישם: **מברכותיו אתה למד מה היה בלבו.** דכתיב ויהפוך ה' אלהיך לך את הקללה לברכה הוא היה רוצה לקללם בכך שלא יהיו בתי כנסיות ולא נתן רשות ואמר מה טובו אוהליך: **ריחו נודף.** ממלות: **וירם מאגג מלכו.** מתרגמינן ותתקף מאגג שתהא מלכותו עזה: **וכולם.** כל הברכות של בלעם חזרו לקללה כמו שהיה כוונתו מתחילה: **חוץ מבתי כנסיות ובתי מדרשות.** שלא יפסקו מישראל לעולם: **הקללה לברכה.** אחת מן הקללות הפך לברכה שלא חזרה לעולם ולא כל הקללות לברכות שחזרו: **נעתרות.** נהפכות כמו עתר שמהפך התבואה כלומר נאמנים פצעי אוהב ונהפכות מנאמנות נשיקות שונא:

מחליף

עין משפט נר מצוה

ל א מיי' פ"ג מהלכות ת"ת הלכה ה ופ"י מהלכות תשובה הלכה ה סמג עשין יב טוש"ע י"ד סי' רמו סעיף כ:

תורה אור השלם

א) נְאֻם שֹׁמֵעַ אִמְרֵי אֵל וְיֹדֵעַ דַּעַת עֶלְיוֹן מַחֲזֵה שַׁדַּי יֶחֱזֶה נֹפֵל וּגְלוּי עֵינָיִם: [במדבר כד, טז]

ב) וַתֹּאמֶר הָאָתוֹן אֶל בִּלְעָם הֲלוֹא אָנֹכִי אֲתֹנְךָ אֲשֶׁר רָכַבְתָּ עָלַי מֵעוֹדְךָ עַד הַיּוֹם הַזֶּה הַהַסְכֵּן הִסְכַּנְתִּי לַעֲשׂוֹת לְךָ כֹּה וַיֹּאמֶר לֹא: [במדבר כב, ל]

ג) וַיֹּאמְרוּ לוֹ עֲבָדָיו יְבַקְשׁוּ לַאדֹנִי הַמֶּלֶךְ נַעֲרָה בְתוּלָה וְעָמְדָה לִפְנֵי הַמֶּלֶךְ וּתְהִי לוֹ סֹכֶנֶת וְשָׁכְבָה בְחֵיקֶךָ וְחַם לַאדֹנִי הַמֶּלֶךְ: [מלכים א' א, ב]

ד) עַמִּי זְכָר נָא מַה יָּעַץ בָּלָק מֶלֶךְ מוֹאָב וּמֶה עָנָה אֹתוֹ בִּלְעָם בֶּן בְּעוֹר מִן הַשִּׁטִּים עַד הַגִּלְגָּל לְמַעַן דַּעַת צִדְקוֹת יְיָ: [מיכה ו, ה]

ה) מָה אֶקֹּב לֹא קַבֹּה אֵל וּמָה אֶזְעֹם לֹא זָעַם יְיָ: [במדבר כג, ח]

ו) אֱלֹהִים שׁוֹפֵט צַדִּיק וְאֵל זֹעֵם בְּכָל יוֹם: [תהלים ז, יב]

ז) כִּי רֶגַע בְּאַפּוֹ חַיִּים בִּרְצוֹנוֹ בָּעֶרֶב יָלִין בֶּכִי וְלַבֹּקֶר רִנָּה: [תהלים ל, ו]

ח) לֵךְ עַמִּי בֹּא בַחֲדָרֶיךָ וּסְגֹר דְּלָתְךָ בַּעֲדֶךָ חֲבִי כִמְעַט רֶגַע עַד יַעֲבָר זָעַם: [ישעיה כו, כ]

ט) גַּם עֲנוֹשׁ לַצַּדִּיק לֹא טוֹב לְהַכּוֹת נְדִיבִים עַל יֹשֶׁר: [משלי יז, כו]

י) וַיָּקָם בִּלְעָם בַּבֹּקֶר וַיַּחֲבֹשׁ אֶת אֲתֹנוֹ וַיֵּלֶךְ עִם שָׂרֵי מוֹאָב: [במדבר כב, כא]

כ) וַיַּשְׁכֵּם אַבְרָהָם בַּבֹּקֶר וַיַּחֲבֹשׁ אֶת חֲמֹרוֹ וַיִּקַּח אֶת שְׁנֵי נְעָרָיו אִתּוֹ וְאֵת יִצְחָק בְּנוֹ וַיְבַקַּע עֲצֵי עֹלָה וַיָּקָם וַיֵּלֶךְ אֶל הַמָּקוֹם אֲשֶׁר אָמַר לוֹ הָאֱלֹהִים: [בראשית כב, ג]

ל) וְגַם בָּאוּ עַבְדֵי הַמֶּלֶךְ לְבָרֵךְ אֶת אֲדֹנֵינוּ הַמֶּלֶךְ דָּוִד לֵאמֹר יֵיטֵב אֱלֹהִים אֶת שֵׁם שְׁלֹמֹה מִשְּׁמֶךָ וִיגַדֵּל אֶת כִּסְאוֹ מִכִּסְאֶךָ וַיִּשְׁתַּחוּ הַמֶּלֶךְ עַל הַמִּשְׁכָּב: [מלכים א' א, מז]

מ) תְּבֹרַךְ מִנָּשִׁים יָעֵל אֵשֶׁת חֶבֶר הַקֵּינִי מִנָּשִׁים בָּאֹהֶל תְּבֹרָךְ: [שופטים ה, כד]

נ) וַיְהִי כְעָבְרָם וְאֵלִיָּהוּ אָמַר אֶל אֱלִישָׁע שְׁאַל מָה אֶעֱשֶׂה לָּךְ בְּטֶרֶם אֶלָּקַח מֵעִמָּךְ וַיֹּאמֶר אֱלִישָׁע וִיהִי נָא פִּי שְׁנַיִם בְּרוּחֲךָ אֵלָי: [מלכים ב' ב, ט]

ס) וַיִּסְמֹךְ אֶת יָדָיו עָלָיו וַיְצַוֵּהוּ כַּאֲשֶׁר דִּבֶּר יְיָ בְּיַד מֹשֶׁה: [במדבר כז, כג]

ע) וַיָּשֶׂם יְיָ דָּבָר בְּפִי בִלְעָם וַיֹּאמֶר שׁוּב אֶל בָּלָק וְכֹה תְדַבֵּר: [במדבר כג, ה] פ) מַה טֹּבוּ אֹהָלֶיךָ יַעֲקֹב מִשְׁכְּנֹתֶיךָ יִשְׂרָאֵל: [במדבר כד, ה] צ) כִּנְחָלִים נִטָּיוּ כְּגַנֹּת עֲלֵי נָהָר כַּאֲהָלִים נָטַע יְהוָה כַּאֲרָזִים עֲלֵי מָיִם: [במדבר כד, ו] ק) יִזַּל מַיִם מִדָּלְיָו וְזַרְעוֹ בְּמַיִם רַבִּים וְיָרֹם מֵאֲגַג מַלְכּוֹ וְתִנַּשֵּׂא מַלְכֻתוֹ: [במדבר כד, ז] ר) וְלֹא אָבָה יְיָ אֱלֹהֶיךָ לִשְׁמֹעַ אֶל בִּלְעָם וַיַּהֲפֹךְ יְיָ אֱלֹהֶיךָ לְּךָ אֶת הַקְּלָלָה לִבְרָכָה כִּי אֲהֵבְךָ יְיָ אֱלֹהֶיךָ: [דברים כג, ו] ש) נֶאֱמָנִים פִּצְעֵי אוֹהֵב וְנַעְתָּרוֹת נְשִׁיקוֹת שׂוֹנֵא: [משלי כז, ו] ת) וְהִכָּה יְיָ אֶת יִשְׂרָאֵל כַּאֲשֶׁר יָנוּד הַקָּנֶה בַּמַּיִם וְנָתַשׁ אֶת יִשְׂרָאֵל מֵעַל הָאֲדָמָה הַטּוֹבָה הַזֹּאת אֲשֶׁר נָתַן לַאֲבוֹתֵיהֶם וְזֵרָם מֵעֵבֶר לַנָּהָר יַעַן אֲשֶׁר עָשׂוּ אֶת אֲשֵׁרֵיהֶם מַכְעִיסִים אֶת יְיָ: [מלכים א' יד, טו]

מסורת הש"ס

א) [ברכות ז. ע"ש ע"ז ד:], ב) [צ"ל אסוסיא], ג) [צ"ל שאילמלי ועיין תוספות מגילה כח.], ד) [צ"ל ומה אזעום לא זעם ה' מלמד שכל אותם הימים לא זעם ה' כ"א בברכות ז. וקצת שינוי יש בע"ז ד: ע"ש], ה) [צ"ל תרנגול"], ו) פסחים נ: ערכין טז: סוטה כב: מז. הוריות י: נזיר כג:, ז) [צ"ל דאמר ר' יוסי בר הונא כך איתא בהוריות י: ע"ש וע"ע בנזיר כג: ובתוספות שם ד"ה בת בנו וכו' דלאו דוקא ע"ש וע"ע סוטה מז.], ח) ר"י יעב"ץ גרס איומה, ט) תענית כ., י) ס"א אברהם את הקב"ה, כ) [צ"ל ייטיב].

ליקוטי רש"י

סוכנת. לשון מחממת [ע"ז ד:]. מחממת וכן ובוקע עצים יסכן בם, (קהלת י' ט) [מ"א א, ב]. **ומה ענה אותו בלעם בן בעור.** מה אזעום לא זעם ה' (במדבר כג) שלא כעסתי כל אותן הימים. **מן השטים.** שנתאתם לי שם דעו לדקותי שלא מנעתי טובתי ועזרתי מכם עד הבאתי אתכם לגלגל וכבשתי לפניכם שם את הארץ [מיכה ו, ה]. **מן השטים ועד הגלגל.** עד באכם אל הגלגל שהפלתי לפניכם שונאיכם [ע"ז שם]. **לא זעם ה'.** אני אין כחי אלא שאני יודע לכוין השעה שהקב"ה כועס בה והוא לא כעס כל הימים הללו שבאתי אליך וזהו שנאמר (מיכה ו, ה) עמי זכר נא מה יעץ וגו' ומה ענה אותו בלעם וגו' למען דעת צדקות ה' [במדבר כג, ח]. **חבי.** התחבאי מעט עד יעבור זעם כי אמת אפקוד על שונאיך [ישעיה כו, כ]. **כי רגע באפו.** אלמא דרגע הוי אפו. **סורייקי.** נוקיים לשון לע"ז כמו חוטין חוטין ולשון ישמעאל קורין לחוט סוריאק. **לאו אורח ארעא.** לכוון שעת זעמו [ע"ז ד:]. **בתלת שעי קמייתא.** באחד מרגעי שלש שעות ראשונות. **לצדיק לא טוב.** לענוש את הבריות [ברכות ז.]. **ויחבש את אתנו.** מכאן שהשנאה מקלקלת את השורה שחבש הוא בעצמו אמר הקב"ה רשע כבר קדמך אברהם אביהם שנאמר (בראשית כב, ג) וישכם אברהם בבקר ויחבוש את חמורו [במדבר כב, כא]. **וישכם.** נזדרז למצוה. **ויחבש.** הוא בעצמו ולא צוה לאחד מעבדיו שהאהבה מקלקלת השורה [בראשית כב, ג]. **מ"ב קרבנות.** ג"פ ז' מזבחות פר ואיל במזבח. **יצאה ממנו רות.** שיצא ממנה דוד שריוה להקב"ה בשירות ותשבחות [ברכות ז: ב"ב יד:] [הוריות י:]. **מנשים באהל.** שרה שנאמר בה הנה באהל רבקה שנאמר בה ויביאה יצחק האהלה רחל ולאה שנאמר בהן ויצא מאהל לאה וגומר. **מנשים באהל תבורך.** יעל למה כן ילדו וגידלו ואם לא יעל הרי הרשע הזה בא ומאבדן כך הוא בבראשית רבה ד"א אף יעל היתה יושבת אוהלים לפיכך הזכיר אותה בברכת אוהלים [שופטים ה, כד]. **דכתיב תבורך מנשים יעל אשת חבר הקיני.** כלומר כאותן נשים שמצינו בהן שעשו מצות שלא לשמה וכולן נאמר בהן אהל. **תבורך.** על שעשתה עבירה לשמה כדי להתיש כחו של אותו רשע כדי שתהא יכולה להורגו. **שרה רחל ולאה.** שאמרו לבעליהן לבא אל שפחתן ולא לשם מצוה נתכוונו אלא כדי שמתקנאות זו בזו רחל באחותה ושרה ולאה באמהות וכולן נאמר בהן אהל כדכתיבי קראי [נזיר כג:]. **ויסמך את ידיו.** בעין יפה יותר ויותר ממה שנצטווה שהקב"ה אמר לו וסמכת את ידך והוא עשה בשתי ידיו ועשאו ככלי מלא וגדוש ומלאו חכמתו בעין יפה [במדבר כז, כג]. **וישם דבר בפיו.** ומה היא השימה הזאת ומה חסר המקרא באמרו שוב אל בלק וכה תדבר אלא כשהיה שומע שאינו נרשה לקלל אמר מה אני חוזר אצל בלק לצערו ונתן לו הקב"ה רסן וחכה בפיו כאדם הפוקס בהמה בחכה להוליכה אל אשר ירצה. אמר לו על כרחך תשוב אל בלק [במדבר כג, טז]. **מברכתו.** אמרו רבותינו מברכותיו של אותו רשע אנו למדים מה היה בלבו לקללם כשאמר (פסוק ה) וישת אל המדבר פניו, וכשהפך המקום את פיו ברכם מעין אותן קללות שבקש לומר כו', כדאיתא בחלק [שם פסוק ה]. **ונעתרות.** ל' גודל כמו העתרת' עלי (יחזקאל לה) [משלי כז, ו]. **ונעתרות נשיקות שונא.** נעתרות לשון הפך כדאמרינן במסכת סוכה (יד.) ויעתר לו מה עתר זה מהפך את התבואה פורקא בלעז אי נמי נעתרות, לשון רבוי ויתור אינקרי"ש בלעז כמו העתרתם עלי דבריכם (יחזקאל לה) [תענית כ.].

houses. Instead, he was forced to say: "מַה־טֹּבוּ אֹהָלֶיךָ יַעֲקֹב" – *How goodly are your tents, O Jacob.*[40] לֹא תִשְׁרֶה שְׁכִינָה עֲלֵיהֶם – He sought to say: **May the Divine Presence not rest upon [the Jews].** Instead, he was forced to say: "(וּ)מִשְׁכְּנֹתֶיךָ יִשְׂרָאֵל" – *your dwelling places, O Israel.*[41] לֹא תְהֵא מַלְכוּתָן נִמְשֶׁכֶת – He sought to say: **May their kingdom not endure.** Instead, he was forced to say: "כִּנְחָלִים נִטָּיוּ" – *They stretch out like streams.*[42] לֹא יִהְיוּ לָהֶם זֵיתִים וּכְרָמִים – He sought to say: **May they have no olive orchards or vineyards.** Instead he was forced to say: "כְּגַנֹּת עֲלֵי נָהָר" – *like gardens by a river.* לֹא יְהֵא רֵיחָן נוֹדֵף – He sought to say: **May their fragrance not waft.**[43] Instead he was forced to say: "כַּאֲהָלִים נָטַע ה'" – *like fragrant aloes planted by God.* לֹא יִהְיוּ לָהֶם מְלָכִים בַּעֲלֵי קוֹמָה – He sought to say: **May they have no kings of imposing stature.**[44] Instead he was forced to say: "כַּאֲרָזִים עֲלֵי־מָיִם" – *like cedars by the water,* renowned for their imposing stature. לֹא יִהְיֶה לָהֶם מֶלֶךְ בֶּן מֶלֶךְ – He sought to say: **May they not have any king who is the son of a king,** i.e. a long-lasting dynasty. Instead he was forced to say: "יִזַּל־מַיִם מִדָּלְיָו" – *May water flow from his wells,* a metaphor for children issuing from parents, indicating a stable and long-lasting dynasty. לֹא תְהֵא מַלְכוּתָן שׁוֹלֶטֶת בָּאוּמּוֹת – He sought to say: **May their kingdom not enjoy dominion over the nations.** Instead he was forced to say: "וְזַרְעוֹ בְּמַיִם רַבִּים" – *and his seed in abundant waters,* a metaphor for the conquest of many nations. לֹא תְהֵא עַזָּה מַלְכוּתָן – He sought to say: **May their kingdom not be strong.** Instead he was forced to say: "וְיָרֹם מֵאֲגַג מַלְכּוֹ" – *May his king be exalted over Agag.*[45] לֹא תְהֵא אֵימַת מַלְכוּתָן – He sought to say: **May their kingdom inspire no fear.** Instead he was forced to say: "וְתִנַּשֵּׂא מַלְכֻתוֹ" – *May his kingdom be imposingly exalted.*

Bilam's curses eventually took effect:

אָמַר רַבִּי אַבָּא בַּר כַּהֲנָא – **R' Abba bar Kahana said:** כּוּלָּם חָזְרוּ לִקְלָלָה – **All of [Bilam's blessings] were eventually transformed into the curse** he had intended, חוּץ מִבָּתֵּי כְנֵסִיּוֹת וּמִבָּתֵּי מִדְרָשׁוֹת – **except for** the curse regarding **synagogues and study houses,**[46] שֶׁנֶּאֱמַר "וַיַּהֲפֹךְ ה' אֱלֹהֶיךָ לְּךָ אֶת־הַקְּלָלָה לִבְרָכָה כִּי אֲהֵבְךָ ה' אֱלֹהֶיךָ" – **as it is stated:**[47] ***And Hashem your God transformed [Bilam's] curse into a blessing for you, because Hashem your God loved you;*** "קְלָלָה" וְלֹא "קְלָלוֹת" – the verse says ***curse,* not *curses.***[48]

Having stated that Bilam's blessings were uttered by him against his will, the Gemara unfavorably contrasts even his blessings with the curse uttered by the Jewish prophet Achiyah. The point is that Achiyah sought the Jewish people's welfare, and his feelings can be discerned even in his maledictions, whereas the reverse is true of the wicked Bilam:

אָמַר רַבִּי שְׁמוּאֵל בַּר נַחְמָנִי אָמַר רַבִּי יוֹנָתָן – **R' Shmuel bar Nachmani said in the name of R' Yonasan:** מַאי דִּכְתִיב "נֶאֱמָנִים פִּצְעֵי אוֹהֵב וְנַעְתָּרוֹת נְשִׁיקוֹת שׂוֹנֵא" – **What is the meaning of that which is written:** ***The wounds [inflicted by] a friend are trustworthy, while the kisses of an enemy are the reverse?***[49] טוֹבָה קְלָלָה שֶׁקִּילֵּל אֲחִיָּה הַשִּׁילוֹנִי אֶת יִשְׂרָאֵל – **Better was the curse with which Achiyah the Shilonite cursed Israel** יוֹתֵר מִבְּרָכָה שֶׁבֵּרְכָם בִּלְעָם הָרָשָׁע – **than the blessing with which the wicked Bilam blessed them.** אֲחִיָּה הַשִּׁילוֹנִי קִילֵּל אֶת יִשְׂרָאֵל בְּקָנֶה – **Achiyah the Shilonite cursed them with** the metaphor of **a reed,** שֶׁנֶּאֱמַר "וְהִכָּה ה' אֶת־יִשְׂרָאֵל כַּאֲשֶׁר יָנוּד הַקָּנֶה בַּמַּיִם וגו'" – **as it is stated:** ***And Hashem will smite Israel like the reed that sways in the water,* etc.**[50] מַה קָּנֶה זֶה עוֹמֵד בִּמְקוֹם מַיִם – **Just as this reed stands in a watery place,**[51] וְגִיזְעוֹ – **and its stalk**

NOTES

40. *Numbers* 24:5. According to this interpretation, the "tents" in this verse refer to the habitats of Israel's spiritual heritage, i.e. synagogues and study halls. See also *Maharsha.*

41. This refers to the Tabernacle and Temples, where God's presence dwells (*Torah Temimah* ad loc.).

42. *Numbers* 24:6. Their kingdom will stretch out, i.e. endure, like a stream.

43. I.e. may they not enjoy an enviable reputation as a result of the many mitzvos they perform (see *Rashi*; cf. *Maharsha*).

44. A man of imposing stature more readily commands respect than a slightly-built man (*Torah Temimah* ibid.).

45. A reference to Saul's victory over King Agag of Amalek – *I Samuel* ch. 15 (*Rashi* ad loc.). Alternatively, all kings of Amalek were entitled Agag (*Ramban* ibid.).

46. I.e. although Bilam was prevented from uttering the curses he had in mind, those curses eventually came to pass. Ultimately, the Jewish nation lost its Temple, its land, its reputation, its kings and its power. The only exception was Bilam's curse that there would be no synagogues or study houses; these have always survived among the Jewish people (*Rashi*).

47. *Deuteronomy* 23:6.

48. The singular form used by the verse implies that only one curse was permanently "transformed" – the other utterances (in this set) however, eventually came to pass as the intended curse. *Maharsha* explains that the statement which refers to the synagogues and study halls would be referred to as a "single" curse since it was the first one Bilam intended to utter; all the subsequent statements, being second, third and so on, were "plural" in that they were one of many.

[The Gemara here refers only to the series of blessings in *Numbers* 24:5-9; see *Torah Temimah* §9, where the reason for this is discussed.]

49. *Proverbs* 27:6. The simple meaning of the verse is that when a person suffers a "wound" at the hand of a friend, he may trust that the wound was intended for his benefit [to correct his behavior, or to save him from something worse]. By the same token, when a person receives "kisses" from his enemy, he may assume that he intends him no good [but is being nice to him only as a ploy to deceive and harm him]. Alternatively, the kisses of an enemy are considered a burden on the one being kissed, for they come without any true feelings of love (from *Rashi* and *Tosafos* to *Taanis* 20a).

50. *I Kings* 14:15. In this verse, the prophet Achiyah the Shilonite prophesied against Yarovam for leading the Jewish people astray into idolatry.

51. This provides the plant with constant moisture and nutrients.

מַחֲלִיף – **regenerates** when it is cut, וְשָׁרָשָׁיו מְרוּבִּין – **and its roots are numerous;** וַאֲפִילוּ כָּל רוּחוֹת שֶׁבָּעוֹלָם בָּאוֹת וְנוֹשְׁבוֹת בּוֹ אֵין מְזִיזוֹת אוֹתוֹ מִמְּקוֹמוֹ – **and even if all the winds of the world come and blow upon it, they cannot budge it from its place,** אֶלָּא הוּא הוֹלֵךְ וּבָא עִמָּהֶן – **rather, it** merely **sways to and fro with them;** כֵּיוָן שֶׁדּוֹמְמוּ הָרוּחוֹת – **and as soon as the winds subside,** עָמַד קָנֶה בִּמְקוֹמוֹ – **the reed** again **stands** upright **in its place.** So too the Jewish people will "sway" under the blows of its enemies, but will not be destroyed. Rather, it will revive and flourish again as soon as the storm of oppression passes. אֲבָל בִּלְעָם הָרָשָׁע בֵּרְכָן בְּאֶרֶז – **However, the wicked Bilam blessed them with** the metaphor of **a cedar.** מָה אֶרֶז זֶה אֵינוֹ עוֹמֵד בִּמְקוֹם מַיִם – **Just as this cedar tree does not stand in a watery place,**[1] וְשָׁרָשָׁיו מוּעָטִין – **and its roots are few,** וְאֵין גִּזְעוֹ מַחֲלִיף – **and its trunk does not regenerate** once it is cut off; אֲפִילוּ כָּל הָרוּחוֹת שֶׁבָּעוֹלָם בָּאוֹת וְנוֹשְׁבוֹת בּוֹ אֵין מְזִיזוֹת אוֹתוֹ מִמְּקוֹמוֹ – and **even if all the** ordinary **winds of the world come and blow upon it, they cannot budge it from its place,** כֵּיוָן שֶׁנָּשְׁבָה בּוֹ רוּחַ דְּרוֹמִית מִיָּד עוֹקַרְתּוֹ וְהוֹפַכְתּוֹ עַל פָּנָיו – but **when the** powerful **south wind blows upon it,**[2] **it immediately uproots it and overturns it.** So too the Jewish nation will, according to Bilam's blessing, not be easily brought down, but should the blow be sufficiently powerful, they will never recover.[3] וְלֹא עוֹד אֶלָּא שֶׁזָּכָה קָנֶה לִיטּוֹל מִמֶּנּוּ קוּלְמוֹס – **Moreover, the reed merited to have pens drawn from its** ranks לִכְתּוֹב מִמֶּנּוּ סִפְרֵי תוֹרָה נְבִיאִים וּכְתוּבִים – to be used **to write scrolls of the Torah, the Prophets and the Writings.**[4]

The Gemara commences a discussion of Bilam's final words of prophecy to Balak, *Numbers* 24:21-24, beginning with Bilam's remarks concerning Yisro:

"וַיַּרְא אֶת־הַקֵּינִי וַיִּשָּׂא מְשָׁלוֹ" – ***[Bilam] saw the Kenite, and he declaimed his parable.***[5] אָמַר לוֹ בִּלְעָם לְיִתְרוֹ – **Bilam said to Yisro:** קֵינִי – **Kenite!** לֹא הָיִיתָ עִמָּנוּ בְּאוֹתָהּ עֵצָה – **Were you not with us in** offering **that counsel?**[6] מִי הוֹשִׁיבְךָ אֵצֶל אֵיתָנֵי עוֹלָם – **Who placed you among the "mighty ones of the world"?**[7] וְהַיְינוּ דְּאָמַר רַבִּי חִיָּיא בַּר אַבָּא אָמַר רַבִּי סִימַאי – **And this** teaching is the same as **that which R' Chiya bar Abba said in the name of R' Simai:** שְׁלֹשָׁה הָיוּ בְּאוֹתָהּ עֵצָה – **Three** persons **were** involved **in** offering **that counsel;** אֵלּוּ הֵן בִּלְעָם אִיּוֹב וְיִתְרוֹ – **they were: Bilam, Job and Yisro.** בִּלְעָם שֶׁיָּעַץ נֶהֱרַג – **Bilam, who counseled** Pharaoh to drown the Jewish babies, **was slain;**[8] אִיּוֹב שֶׁשָּׁתַק – **Job, who was silent,** neither suggesting to Pharaoh that he drown the Jewish babies nor advising him not to do so, נִידּוֹן בְּיִסּוּרִין – **was punished by** having to undergo **suffering.**[9] וְיִתְרוֹ שֶׁבָּרַח זָכוּ בְּנֵי בָנָיו לֵישֵׁב בְּלִשְׁכַּת הַגָּזִית – **As for Yisro, who fled,**[10] **his descendants merited to sit in the Chamber of Hewn Stone** in the Temple as members of the Sanhedrin, שֶׁנֶּאֱמַר ,,וּמִשְׁפְּחוֹת סוֹפְרִים יֹשְׁבֵי יַעְבֵּץ תִּרְעָתִים שִׁמְעָתִים שׂוּכָתִים הֵמָּה הַקִּינִים הַבָּאִים מֵחַמַּת אֲבִי בֵית־רֵכָב" – **as it is stated:** ***The families of scribes, dwellers in Yabetz – the Tirathites, the Shimathites, and the Suchatites; they are the Kenites who are descended from Chammath, father of Beth Rechav.***[11] וּכְתִיב ,,וּבְנֵי קֵינִי חֹתֵן מֹשֶׁה עָלוּ מֵעִיר הַתְּמָרִים" – **And it is written:** ***The children of the Kenite, Moses' father-in-law, went up out of the city of palm-trees.***[12]

The Gemara interprets the next verse (*Numbers* 24:23):

"וַיִּשָּׂא מְשָׁלוֹ וַיֹּאמַר אוֹי מִי יִחְיֶה מִשֻּׂמוֹ אֵל" – ***He declaimed his parable and said, "Woe! Who can live*** מִשֻּׂמוֹ אֵל***!"*** (אָמַר רַבִּי שִׁמְעוֹן בֶּן לָקִישׁ אוֹי מִי שֶׁמְּחַיֶּה עַצְמוֹ בְּשֵׁם אֵל – **R' Shimon ben Lakish said:** The meaning of the passage is: **Woe to him who vivifies himself with the name "god."**)[13] אָמַר רַבִּי יוֹחָנָן – **R'**

NOTES

1. Although the verse compares the Jewish people to *cedars by the water,* the last phrase, *by the water,* issued not from the mouth of Bilam, but was added by God (*Rashi* from *Midrash Yilamdeinu,* cited in *Yalkut Shimoni* 771).

2. The south winds are the strongest winds (see *Rashi;* see *Bava Basra* 25a).

3. Thus, the "wound" (i.e. curse) inflicted by the prophet Achiyah was less injurious to Israel's long-term prospects than the "kiss" (i.e. blessing) proffered by Bilam.

Maharsha explains that the four winds represent the four kingdoms spoken of in *Daniel* 2: Babylon to the north of the Land of Israel, Persia to the east, Greece to the west and Edom to the south. Bilam's hope was that the fourth kingdom of Edom (i.e. Rome) would uproot and overturn the Jewish nation. [For explanations as to why Rome is referred to by the Sages as Edom, see ArtScroll *Daniel* pp. 105-6.]

For a lengthy analysis of the allegory of the reed and the cedar tree, see *Aruch LaNer* to 105b, who explains that the strength of the Jewish people lies in the humble and the lowly.

4. The stems of certain varieties of reeds were fashioned into quill-like pens and used in writing scrolls of Scripture (see *Rama, Yoreh Deah* 271:7; see *Aruch HaShulchan* ibid. §38 for the custom nowadays). Thus, the metaphor of a reed carries a connotation of holiness not present in the more majestic metaphor of a cedar.

5. *Numbers* 24:21. *Keni* was one of the seven names of Yisro (*Mechilta* to *Exodus* 18:1). As stated previously, the Kenites were Yisro's descendants (*Judges* 1:16; see note 12 below).

6. I.e. were you not with us in the council when Pharaoh commanded to cast the newborn Jewish babies into the Nile? [see below] (*Rashi*). Cf. *Daas Zekeinim MiBaalei HaTosafos* to *Exodus* 1:8.

7. I.e. how is it that you have merited that your descendants will sit in Jerusalem alongside the scholars of the Sanhedrin, the "mighty ones of the world"? (*Rashi*).

As the Gemara will explain below, Yisro fled rather than concur with Pharaoh's edict. Accordingly, Bilam's astonishment at Yisro's descendants' rise to eminence is perplexing. Perhaps he felt that Yisro's mere presence at the deliberations was a sin in itself (*Iyun Yaakov*). Alternatively, he was unaware of the reason for Yisro's flight (*Torah Temimah* ad loc.).

8. I.e. he was killed during the Israelite campaign against Midian (*Numbers* 31:8; see *Eitz Yosef*).

9. See *Job* chs. 1-2. One who has it within his power to protest the wrongdoing of others but remains silent is punished for it (*Eitz Yosef*). Cf. *Aruch LaNer; Ben Yehoyada; Anaf Yosef.*

[The *Brisker Rav* is reported to have commented that Job's punishment was meted out measure for measure: One who is in pain cries out, even though he knows that doing so will not alleviate his suffering. Similarly, Job should have protested Pharaoh's plan, although he knew that doing so would not change Pharaoh's mind.]

10. He protested Pharaoh's plan and then fled to Midian to escape being killed (*Eitz Yosef*; cf. *Ben Yehoyada*).

11. *I Chronicles* 2:55. See above, 104a note 4.

12. *Judges* 1:16. This verse explicitly identifies the Kenites as the descendants of Yisro.

This teaching of R' Simai – that Yisro's descendants rose to eminence on the Sanhedrin as a reward for Yisro's flight from Pharaoh – seems to be at odds with the statement by R' Yochanan on 104a that Yisro was so rewarded on account of his hospitality toward Moses. See *Maharsha* there, who reconciles the two teachings.

13. I.e. who claims to be a god, such as did Pharaoh and Hiram (*Rashi* – see *Shemos Rabbah* 9:8 and *Yalkut Shimoni* to *Ezekiel* ch. 28 respectively regarding Pharaoh's and Hiram's claims to divinity).

Alternatively, Reish Lakish's interpretation means: *Woe to him who pampers himself* [מְחַיֶּה אֶת עַצְמוֹ] i.e. who leads a hedonistic life devoid of Torah values *when [the time comes] that God emplaces* [מִשֻּׂמוֹ אֵל] the events of the redemption and rewards the righteous. [The hedonist will at that time regret his actions, because he will miss out on these rewards] (*Rashi's* second explanation, which seems to be following an alternate textual version in Reish Lakish's statement). Cf. *Rif* in *Ein Yaakov.*

A third explanation: *Woe to him who sustains himself through the Name of God,* i.e. who saves his life by reciting the Name of God. When recited in the prescribed manner, certain Divine Names can indeed effect miracles. However, people who are unworthy may not use these Names for personal gain (*Maharsha;* see *Rama* to *Yoreh Deah* 246:21 and *Gra* there §70; see also *Avos DeRabbi Nassan* 12:13).

מחליף ושרשיו מרובין ואפילו כל רוחות שבעולם באות ונושבות בו אין מזיזות אותו ממקומו אלא הוא הולך ובא עמהן כיון שדוממו הרוחות עמד קנה במקומו אבל בלעם הרשע ברכן בארז מה ארז זה אינו עומד במקום מים ושרשיו מועטין ואין גזעו מחליף אפילו כל הרוחות שבעולם באות ונושבות בו אין מזיזות אותו ממקומו כיון שנשבה בו רוח דרומית מיד עוקרתו והופכתו על פניו ולא עוד אלא שזכה קנה ליטול ממנו קולמוס לכתוב ממנו ס"ת נביאים וכתובים וירא את הקיני וישא משלו אמר לו בלעם ליתרו קיני לא היית עמנו באותה עצה מי הושיבך אצל איתני עולם והיינו דא"ר חייא בר אבא א"ר סימאי שלשה היו באותה עצה אלו הן בלעם איוב ויתרו בלעם שיעץ נהרג איוב ששתק נידון ביסורין ויתרו שברח זכו בני בניו לישב בלשכת הגזית שנאמר ומשפחות סופרים יושבי יעבץ תרעתים שמעתים סוכתים המה הקינים הבאים מחמת אבי בית רכב וכתיב ובני קיני חותן משה עלו מעיר התמרים וישא משלו ויאמר אוי מי יחיה משמו אל (אמר רשב"ל אוי מי שמחיה עצמו בשם אל) א"ר יוחנן אוי לה לאומה שתמצא בשעה שהקב"ה עושה פדיון לבניו מי מטיל כסותו בין לביא ללביאה בשעה שנזקקין זה עם זה וצים מיד כתים אמר רב ליבון אספיר ועני אשור ועני עבר עד אשור קטלי מיקטל מכאן ואילך משעבדי שיעבודי הנני הולך לעמי לכה איעצך אשר יעשה העם הזה לעמך לעם הזה לעמך מיבעי ליה א"ר אבא בר כהנא כאדם שמקלל את עצמו ותולה קללתו באחרים אמר להם אלהיהם של אלו שונא זמה הוא והם מתאוים לכלי פשתן בוא ואשיאך עצה עשה להן קלעים והושיב בהן זונות זקינה מבחוץ וילדה מבפנים וימכרו להן כלי פשתן עשה להן קלעים מהר שלג עד בית הישימות והושיב בהן זונות זקינה מבחוץ וילדה מבפנים ובשעה שישראל אוכלין ושותין ושמחין ויוצאין לטייל בשוק אומרת לו הזקינה אי אתה מבקש כלי פשתן זקינה אומרת לו בשוה וילדה אומרת לו בפחות שתים ושלש פעמים ואח"כ אומרת לו הרי את כבן בית שב ברור לעצמך וצרצורי של יין עמוני מונח אצלה ועדיין לא נאסר (יין [א] של עמוני ולא) יין של נכרים אמרה לו רצונך שתשתה כוס של יין כיון ששתה בער בו אמר לה השמיעי לי הוציאה יראתה מתוך חיקה אמרה לו עבוד לזה אמר לה הלא יהודי אני אמרה לו ומה איכפת לך כלום מבקשים ממך אלא פיעור [והוא אינו יודע שעבודתה בכך] ולא עוד אלא שאיני מנחתך עד שתכפור בתורת משה רבך שנא' המה באו בעל פעור וינזרו לבשת ויהיו שקוצים באהבם וישב ישראל בשטים ר"א אומר שטים שמה רבי יהושע אומר שנתעסקו בדברי שטות ותקראן לעם לזבחי אלהיהן רבי אליעזר אומר ערומות פגעו בהן רבי יהושע אומר שנעשו כולן בעלי קריין מאי לשון רפידים רבי אליעזר אומר רפידים שמה רבי יהושע אומר שריפו עצמן מדברי תורה שנאמר לא הפנו אבות אל בנים מרפיון ידים אמר רבי יוחנן כל מקום שנאמר וישב אינו אלא לשון צער שנא' וישב ישראל בשטים ויחל העם לזנות אל בנות מואב וישב יעקב בארץ מגורי אביו בארץ כנען ויבא יוסף את דבתם רעה אל אביהם [ב] ונאמר וישב ישראל בארץ גשן ויקרבו ימי ישראל למות וישב יהודה וישראל לבטח איש תחת גפנו ותחת תאנתו ויקם ה' שטן לשלמה את הדד האדומי מזרע המלך הוא באדום ואת מלכי מדין הרגו על חלליהם וגו' את בלעם בן בעור הרגו בחרב בלעם מאי בעי התם א"ר יוחנן שהלך ליטול שכר עשרים וארבעה אלף [שהפיל מישראל] אמר מר זוטרא בר טוביה אמר רב היינו דאמרי אינשי גמלא אזלא למיבעי קרני אודני דהוו ליה גזיזן מיניה ואת בלעם בן בעור הקוסם קוסם נביא הוא א"ר יוחנן בתחלה נביא ולבסוף קוסם אמר רב פפא היינו דאמרי אינשי מסגני ושילטי הואי איזן לגברי נגרי

הרגו

מחליף. לאחר שנקנך: אינו עומד במקום מים. והאי דכתיב כארזים עלי מים שכינה היא דאמרה איהו אמר כארזים כלומר שאין עומדין במקום מים שכינה אמרה עלי מים וכן כולהו מפרש באגדה בכה"ג כנחלים נטיו הוא אמר כנחלים פוסקין לפעמים יצאה בת קול [אמרה] נטיו הוא אמר כגנות אמרה בת קול עלי נהר הוא אמר כאהלים יצאה בת קול ואמרה נטע ה': רוח דרומית. קשה: לא עמנו היית באותה עצה. שגזר פרעה כל הבן הילוד היאורה תשליכוהו ואי היית כדלקמן: ומי הושיבך אצל איתני עולם. שעתידים בניך לישב בלשכת הגזית והיינו דכתיב איתן מושבך וכי בין איתני עולם אתה יושב מי הזקיקך לכך: שמחיה עצמו בשם אל. עושה עצמו אלוה כמו פרעה וחירם: לשון אחר מי שמחיה עצמו. כלומר אוי להם לאותן בני אדם שמחיין ומעדנין עצמן בעוה"ז ופורקין עול תורה מעל צוארם ומשמנין את עצמן: משמו אל. כשמשים הקב"ה פדיון לעצמו ומשלם גמול לצדיקים לעתיד לבא. כך שמעתי: אוי לה לאומה שתמצא. אוי לה לאומה שתהיה באותן הימים שיעלה על דעתה לעכב ישראל: מי מטיל כסות בין לביא וכו'. לעכבן שלא יזדקקו זה לזה דמסוכן הוא כלומר מי הוא שיכול לעכב את ישראל והקב"ה מכניסם: ציים. ספינות גדולות כמו (ישעיה לג) וצי אדיר (לא) בל יעברנו: וצים מיד כתים אמר רב ליבא אספיר. דכתים היינו מקום ששמו כך: עד אשור מקטל קטילי. ומאשור ואילך משעבדי להו שעבודי: וצים מיד כתים וענו אשור. דקטלי להו וענו עבר דמשעבדי להן עד אשור: כתים. רומים כלומ' אותן אומות שהביא הקב"ה בצים עתידין להרוג את כל האומות עד אשור ומאשור ואילך מניחין אותן ומשעבדין בהם (ומניחין אותן) ולעתיד קא מיירי: הן הנה היו לבני ישראל לא גרסינן אלא ה"ג הנני הולך לעמי לכה איעצך אשר יעשה העם הזה לעמך עמך לעם הזה מבעי ליה. שהשיא עצה לבלק שנכשלו בה ישראל הן הנה היו לבני ישראל בדבר בלעם: ותולה קללתו בחברו. וכך בלעם לא רצה לתלות שפלות זה בבלק שיהא הוא צריך לבקש עצה היאך יכשלו בה ישראל אלא בישראל תלה השפלות לומר שהן צריכין לעצה שיכשלו בה בני מואב שלא תתקוף ידי מואב על ישראל והיינו דכתיב אשר יעשה העם הזה לעמך. מ"ר. ל"א תולה קללתו בחברו כלומר שתלה הכתוב קללה במואב ולא רצה לכתוב כלפי ישראל כמו שאמר בלעם הרשע: קלעים. אהלים של קלעים כמו שעושין בשוקים: בערבות מואב מהר שלג. שניר: כשהיה אומר לה. ישראל כלי פשתן זה בכמה זקנה אומרת לו דמי שוויו וילדה אומרת לו בפחות מכדי שוויו וכן עושין עד ב' או עד ג' פעמים: ברור לעצמך. כל תכשיטין שאתה רוצה: צרצרי. נודות: בוער בו. שהיה משתכר ובוער בו יצר הרע: השמיעי. הוי שומעת לתשמיש: פיעור. כך היתה עבודתו של פעור שמתריזים לפניו: ה"ג כלום מבקשין ממך אלא פיעור והוא עושה ושוב אומרת לו כפור בתורת משה רבך והוא עושה: וינזרו לבשת. סרו מדרכם והלכו אחר הבשת: כאהבם. מתוך תאות אהבתם לזנות היו משוקצים שכופרין בהקב"ה: ותקראן. בגופן ותקראן [משמע] לשון מקרה: מאי רפידים. איידי דלעיל איפליגו ביה ר"א ור' יהושע במשמעות דשטים נקיט נמי רפידים דפליגי ביה בכי האי גוונא: לא הפנו אבות אל בנים. להיטיב להם: מפני רפיון ידים. של תורה ומצות והכי נמי רפידים רפיון ידים הוא כלומר מפני שרפו ידים מן התורה בא עליהם עמלק: שכר כ"ד אלפים מישראל. שהרגו בעצתו הלך ליטול מבלק ומזקני מדין: גמלא תבע קרני. כך בלעם שאל שכר ונהרג: גזו מיניה. חתכו ממנו: בלעם בן בעור הקוסם הרגו בחרב. ההוא קרא ביהושע כתיב: ולבסוף. שנתן עיניו לקלל את ישראל ניטלה ממנו נבואה ונעשה קוסם: מסגני ושילטא הואי. אשת סגנים ושרים היתה: אייזן לגברא נגר. זינתה למושכי חבל ספינה ל"א נגרי חרשים:

א) סוטה יא., ב) [שם. לעיל קד. ע"ש], ג) [פי' אותו מלכות ים נקרא ליבון אספסר ערוך ערך אספר א'], ד) [צ"ל לו], ה) [חולין ד:], ו) [בע"ז וילקוט ובתנחומא ליתא לכל זה], ז) בקרא באהבם, ח) [בכורות ה:], ט) בכורות ה:, י) [ילקוט ליתא], כ) [בע"ז וילקוט ליתא], ל) [צ"ל מצרים וכ"א בילקוט], מ) בקרא כתיב לה, נ) [צ"ל נגדו].

הגהות הגר"א

[א] גמ' של עמוני ולא יין. נמחק: [ב] שם ונאמר. נמחק:

תורה אור השלם

א) וירא את הקיני וישא משלו ויאמר איתן מושבך ושים בסלע קנך: [במדבר כד, כא]

ב) ומשפחות ספרים ישבי יעבץ תרעתים שמעתים שוכתים המה הקינים הבאים מחמת אבי בית רכב: [דברי הימים א' ב, נה]

ג) ובני קיני חתן משה עלו מעיר התמרים את בני יהודה מדבר יהודה אשר בנגב ערד וילך וישב את העם: [שופטים א, טז]

ד) וישא משלו ויאמר אוי מי יחיה משמו אל: [במדבר כד, כג]

ה) וצים מיד כתים ועני אשור וענו עבר וגם הוא עדי אבד: [במדבר כד, כד]

ו) ועתה הנני הולך לעמי לכה איעצך אשר יעשה העם הזה לעמך באחרית הימים: [במדבר כד, יד]

ז) כענבים במדבר מצאתי ישראל כבכורה בתאנה בראשיתה ראיתי אבותיכם המה באו בעל פעור וינזרו לבשת ויהיו שקוצים כאהבם: [הושע ט, י]

ח) וישב ישראל בשטים ויחל העם לזנות אל בנות מואב: [במדבר כה, א]

ט) ותקראן לעם לזבחי אלהיהן ויאכל העם וישתחוו לאלהיהן: [במדבר כה, ב]

י) מקול שעטת פרסות אביריו מרעש לרכבו המון גלגליו לא הפנו אבות אל בנים מרפיון ידים: [ירמיה מז, ג]

כ) וישב יעקב בארץ מגורי אביו בארץ כנען: [בראשית לז, א]

ל) אלה תלדות יעקב יוסף בן שבע עשרה שנה היה רעה את אחיו בצאן והוא נער את בני בלהה ואת בני זלפה נשי אביו ויבא יוסף את דבתם רעה אל אביהם: [בראשית לז, ב]

מ) וישב ישראל בארץ מצרים בארץ גשן ויאחזו בה ויפרו וירבו מאד: [בראשית מז, כז]

נ) ויקרבו ימי ישראל למות ויקרא לבנו ליוסף ויאמר לו אם נא מצאתי חן בעיניך שים נא ידך תחת ירכי ועשית עמדי חסד ואמת אל נא תקברני במצרים: [בראשית מז, כט]

ס) וישב יהודה וישראל לבטח איש תחת גפנו ותחת תאנתו מדן ועד באר שבע כל ימי שלמה: [מלכים א' ה, ה]

ע) ויקם יי שטן לשלמה את הדד האדמי מזרע המלך הוא באדום: [מלכים א' יא, יד]

פ) ואת מלכי מדין הרגו על חלליהם את אוי ואת רקם ואת צור ואת חור ואת רבע חמשת מלכי מדין ואת בלעם בן בעור הרגו בחרב: [במדבר לא, ח]

צ) ואת בלעם בן בעור הקוסם הרגו בני ישראל בחרב אל חלליהם: [יהושע יג, כב]

ליקוטי רש"י

בירכן בארז. כארזים עלי מים (במדבר כד). ארז זה אינו עומד במקום מים כו'. ואף על גב דכתיב בקרא כארזים עלי מים הוא לאו בלעם קאמר ליה דבלעם אמר כארזים והמלאך השיבו עלי מים וכן כולהו דבלעם אמר כנחלים דומינן ממייבשין וקאמר ליה המלאך נטוי דלין יבישין לעולם והיינו דכתיב ויהפוך ה' אלהיך לך את הקללה לברכה על ידי מלאך שהשיבו על ידי. אפילו כל הרוחות. שאינן קשות. רוח דרומית. שהיא קשה כדאמרינן (בבא בתרא כה:) אילמלא בן נץ שמעמידה אין כל בריה יכולה לעמוד מפניה שנאמר המבינתך יאבר נץ יפרש כנפיו לתימן [תענית כ.]. וירא את הקיני. לפי שהיה קיני תקוע אצל עמלק כענין שנאמר ויאמר שאול אל הקיני וגו' (ש"א טו, ו) הזכירו אחר עמלק נתקלל בגנזלון של בני יתרו שנאמר בהם תרעתים שמעתים סוכתים (ד"ה א, ב, נה). איתן מושבך. תמה אני מהיכן זכית לכך הלא אתה עמי היית בעצת הבה נתחכמה לו (שמות א, י) ועתה נתיישבת באיתן ומעוז של ישראל [במדבר כד, כא]. באותה עצה. דנתחכמה לו. יושבי יעבץ. תלמידי יעבץ אדם גדול בתורה היה דכתיב (דה"א ד) ויקרא יעבץ לאלהי ישראל אם ברך תברכני בתורה והרבית את גבולי בתלמידים וגו' ויבא אלהים את אשר שאל (תמורה טז.). תרעתים. מפרש במסכת סוטה תרעתים על שם שהיו יושבים בשערי ירושלים. שמעתים. ששמעו מצות אביהם דבני יונדב בן רכב משתמעו בני של יתרו כדמפרש ואזיל המה הקינים. סוכתים. על שם שהיו יושבים בסוכות כדכתיב (ירמיהו לה) ונשב באהלים ונקרי להו משפחת סופרים דהיינו סנהדרין וכן תרעתים וזקני שער [סוטה יא.]. יושבי בלשכת הגזית. ממשפחות סופרים והאי קרא מפרש ליה כולו בסיפרי בפרשת ויאמר משה לחובב. המה הקינים הבאים מחמת אבי בית רכב. וקינים הם מזרע של יתרו דכתיב ובני קיני חותן משה ובניו של יתרו בן בנו של יתרו רכב דכתיב הקינים הבאים מחמת אבי בית רכב וכתיב (ירמיהו לה) ולבית הרכבים אמר ירמיהו כי כה אמר ה' [וגו'] יען אשר שמעתם [על] מצות [יהונדב] אביכם [וגו'] לא יכרת איש ליונדב בן רכב [עומד] לפני כל הימים ואמרינן בסיפרי אפשר נכרים הם ונכנסין להיכל והרי כל ישראל לא נכנסו להיכל אלא שהיו יושבין בסנהדרין ומורין בדברי תורה מפי רבי [לעיל קד:]. מעיר התמרים. היא יריחו שניתן להם דושנה של יריחו לאוכלה עד שיבנה בית המקדש ומי שיבנה בית הבחירה בחלקו יטלנה כדי שיהא לכל ישראל חלק בבית הבחירה ונתנוה לבני יתרו ת"מ שנה והתלמידים שבהם הניחוה והלכו אצל עתניאל בן קנז הוא יעבץ במדבר יהודה אשר בנגב ערד ללמוד תורה [שופטים א, טז]. וצים. ספינות גדולות כדכתיב וצי אדיר (ישעיה לג, כא) תרגומו ובורני רבתא [במדבר כ, כג]. וצים. כדמתרגם וציים מיד כתים (במדבר כ"ד) וסיען יסתחרן מרומאי [תהלים עב, ט]. לכה איעצך. מה לך לעשות ומה היא העצה אלהיהם של אלו שונא זמה הוא כו' כדאיתא בחלק (סנהדרין קו.) תדע שבלעם השיא עצה זו להכשילם בזמה שהרי נאמר הן הנה היו לבני ישראל בדבר בלעם (לקמן לא, טז). אשר יעשה העם הזה לעמך. מקרא קצר הוא זה איעצך להכשילם ואומר לך מה שהן עתידין להרע למואב באחרית הימים [במדבר כד, יד]. וינזרו. אין נזירה בכל מקום אלא לשון פרישה. לבושת. לעכו"ס שהיא בשתם. ויהי שקוצים. לפני. כאהבם. את בנות מואב [הושע ט, י]. בדברי שטות. לזנות את בנות מואב. ערומות פגעו בהן. ותקראן משמע גופן היה פוגע בהן. שנעשו כולן בעלי קריין ולשון מקרה הוא. שריפו עצמן כו'. לפיכך בא עליהם עמלק. לא הפנו אבות אל בנים מרפיון ידים. מכאן שריפו ידיהם מן התורה [בכורות ה:]. בשטים. כך שמה. לזנות אל בנות מואב. על ידי עצת בלעם כדאיתא בחלק [במדבר כה, א]. מאי בעי התם. בלעם הלך שם ליטול שכר עשרים וארבעה אלף שהפיל מישראל בעצתו ויצא ממדין לקראת ישראל ומשיאן עצה רעה אמר להם אם כשהייתם ששים רבוא לא יכולתם להם ועכשיו בי"ב אלף אתם באים להלחם נתנו לו שכרו משלם ולא קפחוהו [במדבר לא, ח]. ולבסוף קוסם. איזהו קוסם האוחז את מקלו ואומר אם אלך אם לא אלך וכן הוא אומר עמי בעצו ישאל ומקלו יגיד לו (הושע ד, יב) [דברים יח, י].

Yochanan said: אוֹי לָהּ לָאוּמָּה שֶׁתִּמָּצֵא בְּשָׁעָה שֶׁהַקָּדוֹשׁ בָּרוּךְ הוּא עוֹשֶׂה פִּדְיוֹן לְבָנָיו – The meaning of the passage is: **Woe to the nation that will be found** hindering the Jews **at the moment that the Holy One, Blessed is He, works redemption for His children** (the Jewish people).[14] מִי מֵטִיל כְּסוּתוֹ בֵּין לָבִיא לִלְבִיאָה בְּשָׁעָה שֶׁנִּזְקָקִין זֶה עִם זֶה – **Who dares to throw his garment between a lion and a lioness at the time that they mate with one another?!**[15]

The Gemara interprets *Numbers* 24:24:

,,וְצִים מִיַּד כִּתִּים" – ***Great ships [shall go forth] from the coast of Kittim*** – אָמַר רַב – **Rav said:** לִיבּוּן אַסְפִּיר – Kittim is the land of **Libun Aspir.**[16] ,,וְעִנּוּ אַשּׁוּר וְעִנּוּ־עֵבֶר" – ***And they will afflict Assyria and they will afflict Ever*** – עַד אַשּׁוּר קַטְלֵי מִכָּאן וְאֵילָךְ מִיקְטַל – **until Assyria [the invaders] will slay;** מְשַׁעְבְּדֵי שִׁיעְבּוּדֵי – **beyond that point they will** merely **enslave.**[17]

Bilam advises Moab to seduce the Jews into immorality:

,,הִנְנִי הוֹלֵךְ לְעַמִּי לְכָה אִיעָצְךָ אֲשֶׁר יַעֲשֶׂה הָעָם הַזֶּה לְעַמְּךָ" – ***Behold, I go to my people. Come, let me advise you what this people should do to your people.***[18]

The Gemara asks:

,,עַמְּךָ לָעָם הַזֶּה" מִיבְּעֵי לֵיהּ – Why did Bilam say "what *this* people (the Jews) should do to *your* people (Moab)"? **"What *your* people should do to *this* people" is what he ought to have said!** [19] – ? –

The Gemara answers:

אָמַר רַבִּי אַבָּא בַּר כַּהֲנָא – **R' Abba bar Kahana said:** כְּאָדָם שֶׁמְּקַלֵּל אֶת עַצְמוֹ וְתוֹלֶה קִלְלָתוֹ בַּאֲחֵרִים – **Like a person who curses himself but applies his curse to others.**[20]

The Gemara details Bilam's advice:

אָמַר לָהֶם – **[Bilam] said to [the Moabites]:** אֱלֹהֵיהֶם שֶׁל אֵלּוּ שׂוֹנֵא זִמָּה הוּא – **The God of these** Jews **hates immorality.** וְהֵם מִתְאַוִּים לִכְלֵי פִּשְׁתָּן – **Furthermore,** I know that **they** [the Jews] **have a penchant for linen garments.**[21] בּוֹא וְאַשִּׂיאֲךָ עֵצָה – **Come, Let me give you** a piece of **advice:** עֲשֵׂה לָהֶן קְלָעִים – **Set up tents**[22] **for them,** i.e. the Jews, וְהוֹשֵׁיב בָּהֶן זוֹנוֹת – **and place harlots inside them,** זְקֵינָה מִבַּחוּץ וְיַלְדָּה מִבִּפְנִים – **an older one outside** each tent **and a young one inside;** וְיִמְכְּרוּ לָהֶן כְּלֵי פִשְׁתָּן – **and have them sell [the Jews] linen garments.** עָשָׂה לָהֶן קְלָעִים מֵהַר שֶׁלֶג עַד בֵּית הַיְשִׁימוֹת – Taking Bilam's advice, **[Balak] set up tents for [the Jews]** throughout the territory controlled by the Jews, all along the Jordan **from Snow Mountain** (Mt. Hermon) in the north **to Beis Hayeshimos** in the south, וְהוֹשִׁיב בָּהֶן זוֹנוֹת – **and placed harlots inside them,** זְקֵינָה מִבַּחוּץ וְיַלְדָּה מִבִּפְנִים – **an older one outside** each tent **and a young one inside.** וּבְשָׁעָה שֶׁיִּשְׂרָאֵל אוֹכְלִין וְשׁוֹתִין וּשְׂמֵחִין וְיוֹצְאִין לְטַיֵּיל בַּשּׁוּק – **When the Jews would eat, drink and be merry and go out for a walk in the marketplace** set up by the Moabites, אוֹמֶרֶת לוֹ הַזְּקֵינָה – **the older [harlot] would say to [the Jew]:** אִי אַתָּה מְבַקֵּשׁ כְּלֵי פִשְׁתָּן – **"Are you not interested in** buying **linen garments?"** זְקֵינָה אוֹמֶרֶת לוֹ בְּשָׁוֶה – **The older [harlot] would offer [the linen garment] at its full price,** וְיַלְדָּה אוֹמֶרֶת לוֹ בְּפָחוֹת – **while the young [harlot] would** call to him from inside and **offer it for less,** thereby persuading the Jew to purchase it. שְׁתַּיִם וְשָׁלֹשׁ פְּעָמִים – Pleased with his bargain purchase, the Jew would begin to frequent the store and the same episode would reoccur **two or three times.** וְאַחַר כָּךְ אוֹמֶרֶת לוֹ – **Afterwards,** i.e. after they had become friendly in this manner, **[the young harlot] would say to [the Jew]:** הֲרֵי אַתְּ כְּבֶן בַּיִת – **"Behold, you are like a member of the family,** i.e. a preferred customer! שֵׁב בְּרוֹר לְעַצְמְךָ – **Sit down** and **choose for yourself** from our merchandise at your leisure." וְצַרְצוּרֵי שֶׁל יַיִן עַמּוֹנִי מוּנָּח אֶצְלָהּ – **Pitchers of Ammonite wine were placed near her;**[23] וַעֲדַיִין לֹא נֶאֱסַר (יַיִן שֶׁל עַמּוֹנִי וְלֹא) יַיִן שֶׁל נָכְרִים – **and** at that time **(the wine of Ammonites and) the wine of gentiles had not yet been prohibited.**[24] אָמְרָה לוֹ – **She would say to him:** רְצוֹנְךָ שֶׁתִּשְׁתֶּה כּוֹס שֶׁל יַיִן – **"Would you care to drink a cup of wine?"**

NOTES

14. R' Yochanan translates מִי יְחִיֶה מִשֻּׂמוֹ אֵל as: *Woe to him who is alive when God emplaces these;* that is, woe to any nation existing at the time of the events of the final redemption that attempts to hinder the reuniting of Israel with God (*Rashi*).

15. I.e. it would be reckless to attempt to keep a lion and a lioness apart merely by throwing a garment between them. They would destroy the person who threw it. [It would certainly not prevent their mating.] Similarly, woe to the nation that attempts to keep God and the Jewish people apart when the time of their redemption arrives (*Rashi*).

16. This follows *Rashi,* who explains the enigmatic words לִיבּוּן אַסְפִּיר as the name of some foreign land (cf. *Rashash* here). *Aruch* (ע׳ אספר), however, cites a different reading: לִגְיוֹן אַסְפּוֹר, the Latin and Greek words for a legion of soldiers (see *Mussaf HaAruch* there), and understands the Gemara as explaining the word צִים – i.e. a *legion* shall go forth from the coast of Kittim (Rome).

17. I.e. in this verse Bilam foretold a Roman invasion of the Middle East, including Assyria and the territory to its east, identified here as *Ever* (see *Rashi* to *Numbers* 24:23 and *Daniel* 11:30). The war would be a bloody one, and the invaders would exterminate the populations of the lands they conquered until they got as far as Assyria. After they conquered and exterminated Assyria, they would continue their march of conquest eastward, but they would not exterminate the populations of the territories they conquered east of Assyria. Instead, they would merely enslave them (*Rashi*).

The basis for this exegesis is the repetition of the verb *afflict* (*They will afflict Assyria and they will afflict Ever*). This repetition hints at two distinct types of affliction, one involving killing and the other enslavement (*Rif* in *Ein Yaakov*).

18. *Numbers* 24:14.

19. I.e. since Bilam here is referring to his plot to have Moabite women lure the Jews into sin (see *Numbers* 31:16), the verse ought to have read: *Let me advise you what your people should do to this people,* i.e. how you should proceed in order to persuade the Jewish people to sin (*Rashi*).

20. It is considered inauspicious to mention one's name in connection with a misfortune. Accordingly, when the need arises to speak of such an occurrence, it is customary to substitute the name of another for one's own name. In a similar vein, Bilam did not wish to speak openly of the weakness of Moab by saying that they required advice on how to fend off Jewish domination. He therefore couched his proposal in euphemistic terms, as if it were the *Jews* who were seeking his advice as to the best way of bringing down *Moab* (see *Rashi*).

Alternatively, it was *Scripture* that resorted to euphemism here. In fact, Bilam said: "I shall advise you what *your* people shall do to *this* people." However, like a person who euphemistically substitutes the name of another person for his own to avoid uttering something bad regarding himself, Scripture altered Bilam's malevolent words of advice regarding the Jews and reported Bilam as having said the opposite (second explanation of *Rashi, Yad Ramah*). Cf. *Maharsha* and *Rashi* to *Numbers* 24:14.

21. *Maharsha* explains that while in Egypt, the Jews had been accustomed to wearing linen clothes, for linen grows abundantly there (see *Isaiah* 19:9 which speaks of *the flax workers* of Egypt). At the time of this episode, the Jews had not been in Egypt for forty years and were anxious to replace their old clothes with new ones.

22. Literally: hangings, i.e. stalls such as are set up at bazaars (*Rashi*).

23. Ammonite wine in particular has the quality of arousing the drinker to immorality (*Yerushalmi Sanhedrin* 52a). Indeed, the very existence of the Ammonite nation was the result of an immoral act brought about by intoxicating wine (*Genesis* 19:32-38). See also *Maharal.*

24. *Gra* deletes the parenthesized words.

[The Rishonim debate whether our Gemara refers to the general prohibition on gentile wine (סְתָם יֵינָם) or the specific prohibition on wine used as a libation for idols (יֵין נֶסֶךְ). According to the latter explanation, it was standard practice for Ammonites to pour their wine before idols prior to serving it. See *Rambam's Sefer HaMitzvos, Lo Saaseh* §194, with *Hasagos HaRamban*.]

מחליף ושרשיו מרובין ואפילו כל רוחות שבעולם באות ונושבות בו אין מזיזות אותו ממקומו אלא הוא הולך ובא עמהן כיון שדוממו הרוחות עמד קנה במקומו אבל בלעם הרשע ברכן בארז מה ארז זה אינו עומד במקום מים ושרשיו מועטין ואין גזעו מחליף אפילו כל הרוחות שבעולם באות ונושבות בו אין מזיזות אותו ממקומו כיון שנשבה בו רוח דרומית מיד עוקרתו והופכתו על פניו ולא עוד אלא שזכה קנה ליטול ממנו קולמוס לכתוב ממנו ס"ת נביאים וכתובים א) וירא את הקיני וישא משלו אמר לו בלעם ליתרו קיני לא היית עמנו באותה עצה מי הושיבך אצל איתני עולם והיינו א) דא"ר חייא בר אבא א"ר סימאי שלשה היו באותה עצה אלו הן בלעם איוב ויתרו בלעם שיעץ נהרג איוב ששתק נידון ביסורין ויתרו שברח ב) זכו בני בניו לישב בלשכת הגזית שנאמר ב) ומשפחות סופרים יושבי יעבץ תרעתים שמעתים סוכתים המה הקינים הבאים מחמת אבי בית רכב וכתיב ג) ובני קיני חותן משה עלו מעיר התמרים ד) וישא משלו ויאמר אוי מי יחיה משמו אל (אמר רשב"ל אוי מי שמחיה עצמו בשם אל) א"ר יוחנן אוי לה לאומה שתמצא בשעה שהקב"ה עושה פדיון לבניו מי מטיל כסותו בין לביא ללביאה בשעה שנזקקין זה עם זה ה) וצים מיד כתים אמר רב ג) ליבון אספיר ה) וענו אשור וענו עבר עד אשור קטלי מיקטל מכאן ואילך משעבדי שיעבודי ו) הנני הולך לעמי לכה איעצך אשר יעשה העם הזה לעמך לעם הזה לעמך מיבעי ליה א"ר אבא בר כהנא כאדם שמקלל את עצמו ותולה קללתו באחרים אמר ד) להם אלהיהם של אלו שונא זמה הוא והם מתאוים לכלי פשתן בוא ואשיאך עצה עשה להן קלעים והושיב בהן זונות זקינה מבחוץ וילדה מבפנים וימכרו להן כלי פשתן עשה להן קלעים מהר שלג עד בית הישימות והושיב בהן זונות זקינה מבחוץ וילדה מבפנים ובשעה שישראל אוכלין ושותין ושמחין ויוצאין לטייל בשוק אומרת לו הזקינה אי אתה מבקש כלי פשתן זקינה אומרת לו בשוה וילדה אומרת לו בפחות שתים ושלש פעמים ואח"כ אומרת לו הרי את כבן בית שב ברור לעצמך וצרצורי של יין עמוני מונח אצלה ה) ועדיין לא נאסר (ו) יין [א] של עמוני (ולא) יין של נכרים אמרה לו רצונך שתשתה כוס של יין כיון ששתה בער בו אמר לה השמיעי לי הוציאה יראתה מתוך חיקה אמרה לו עבוד לזה אמר לה הלא יהודי אני אמרה לו ומה איכפת לך כלום מבקשים ממך אלא פיעור [והוא אינו יודע שעבודתה בכך] ולא עוד אלא שאיני מנחתך עד שתכפור בתורת משה רבך שנא' ז) המה באו בעל פעור וינזרו לבשת ויהיו שקוצים ז) באהבם ח) וישב ישראל בשטים ח) ר"א אומר שטים שמה רבי יהושע אומר שנתעסקו בדברי שטות ט) ותקראן לעם לזבחי אלהיהן רבי אליעזר אומר ערומות פגעו בהן רבי יהושע אומר שנעשו כולן בעלי קריין מאי לשון רפידים ט) רבי אליעזר אומר רפידים שמה רבי יהושע אומר שריפו עצמן מדברי תורה שנאמר י) לא הפנו אבות אל בנים מרפיון ידים אמר רבי יוחנן כל מקום שנאמר וישב אינו אלא לשון צער י) שנא' ח) וישב ישראל בשטים ויחל העם לזנות אל בנות מואב כ) וישב יעקב בארץ מגורי אביו בארץ כנען ל) ויבא יוסף את דבתם רעה אל אביהם [ב] כ) ונאמר מ) וישב ישראל בארץ ל) גושן נ) ויקרבו ימי ישראל למות ס) וישב יהודה וישראל לבטח איש תחת גפנו ותחת תאנתו ע) ויקם ה' שטן לשלמה את הדד האדומי מזרע המלך הוא באדום פ) ואת מלכי מדין הרגו על חלליהם וגו' את בלעם בן בעור הרגו בחרב בלעם מאי בעי התם א"ר יוחנן שהלך ליטול שכר עשרים וארבעה אלף [שהפיל מישראל] אמר מר זוטרא בר טוביה אמר רב היינו דאמרי אינשי גמלא אזלא למיבעי קרני אודני דהוו ליה גזיזן מיניה צ) ואת בלעם בן בעור הקוסם קוסם נביא הוא א"ר יוחנן בתחלה נביא ולבסוף קוסם אמר רב פפא היינו דאמרי אינשי מסגני ושילטי הואי איזן לגברי נגרי

הרגו

רש"י

מחליף. לאחר שנקלן: אינו עומד במקום מים. והאי דכתיב כארזים עלי מים שכינה היא דאמרה איהו אמר כארזים כלומר שאין עומדין במקום מים שכינה אמרה עלי מים וכן כולהו מפרש באגדה בכה"ג כנחלים נטיו הוא אמר כנחלים פוסקין לפעמים יצאה בת קול [אמרה] נטיו הוא אמר כגנות אמרה בת קול עלי נהר הוא אמר כאהלים יצאה בת קול ואמרה נטע ה': רוח דרומית. קשה: לא עמנו היית באותה עצה. שגזר פרעה כל הבן הילוד היאורה בתמיה ודאי היית כדלקמן: ומי הושיבך אצל איתני עולם. שעתידים בניך לישב בלשכת הגזית והיינו דכתיב איתן מושבך וכי בין איתני עולם אתה יושב מי הזקיקך לכך: שמחיה עצמו בשם אל. עושה עצמו אלוה כמו פרעה וחירם: לשון אחר מי שמחיה עצמו. כלומר אוי להם לאותן בני אדם שמחיין ומעדנין עצמן בעוה"ז ופורקין עול תורה מעל צוארם ומשמנין את עצמן: משמו אל. כשמשים הקב"ה פדיון לעצמו ומשלם גמול לצדיקים לעתיד לבא. כך שמעתי: אוי לה לאומה שתמצא. אוי לה לאומה שתהיה באותן הימים שיעלה על דעתה לעכב ישראל: מי מטיל כסות בין לביא וכו'. לעכבן שלא יזדקקו זה לזה דמסוכן הוא כלומר מי הוא שיכול לעכב את ישראל והקב"ה מכניסם: ציים. ספינות גדולות כמו (ישעיה לג) וצי אדיר (מ) בל יעברנו: וצים מיד כתים אמר רב ליבא אספיר. דכתים היינו מקום שמו כך: עד אשור מקטל קטילי. ומאשור ואילך משעבדי להו שעבודי: וצים מיד כתים וענו אשור. דקטלי להו וענו עבר דמשעבדי להן עד אשור: כתים. רומים כלומ' אותן אומות שהביא הקב"ה בציים עתידין להרוג את כל האומות עד אשור ומאשור ואילך מניחין אותן ומשעבדין בהם (ומניחין אותן) ולעתיד קא איירי: הן הנה היו לבני ישראל לא גרסינן אלא ה"ג הנני הולך לעמי לכה איעצך אשר יעשה העם הזה לעמך לעם הזה מבעי ליה. שהשיא עצה לבלק שנכשלו בה ישראל הן הנה היו לבני ישראל בדבר בלעם: ותולה קללתו בחברו. וכך בלעם לא רצה לתלות שפלות זה בבלק שיהא הוא צריך לבקש עצה היאך יכשלו בה ישראל אלא בישראל תלה השפלות לומר שהן צריכין לעצה שיכשלו בה בני מואב שלא תתקוף ידי מואב על ישראל והיינו דכתיב אשר יעשה העם הזה לעמך. מ"ר. ל"א תולה קללתו בחברו כלומר שתלה הכתוב קללה במואב ולא רצה לכתוב כלפי ישראל כמו שאמר בלעם הרשע: קלעים. אהלים של קלעים כמו שעושין בשוקים: בערבות מואב מהר שלג. שניר: כשהיה אומר לה. ישראל כלי פשתן זה בכמה זקנה אומרת לו דמי שוויו וילדה אומרת לו בפחות מכדי שוויו וכן עושין עד ב' או עד ג' פעמים: ברור לעצמך. כל תכשיטין שאתה רוצה: צרצרי. נודות: בוער בו. שהיה משתכר ובוער בו יצר הרע: השמיעי. הוי שומעת לתשמיש: פיעור. כך היתה עבודתו של פעור שמתריזים לפניו: ה"ג כלום מבקשין ממך אלא פיעור והוא עושה ושוב אומרת לו כפור בתורת משה רבך והוא עושה: וינזרו לבשת. סרו מדרכם והלכו אחר הבשת: כאהבם. מתוך תאות אהבתם לזנות היו משוקצים שכופרין בהקב"ה: ותקראן. בגופן ותקראן [משמע] לשון מקרה: מאי רפידים. איידי דלעיל איפליגו ביה ר"א ור' יהושע במשמעות דשטים נקיט נמי רפידים דפליגי ביה בכי האי גוונא: לא הפנו אבות אל בנים. להיטיב להם: מפני רפיון ידים. של תורה ומצות והכי נמי רפידים רפיון ידים הוא כלומר מפני שרפו ידים מן התורה בא עליהם עמלק: שכר כ"ד אלפים מישראל. שהרגו בעצתו הלך ליטול מבלק ומזקני מדין: גמלא תבע קרני. כך בלעם שאל שכר ונהרג: גזו מיניה. חתכו ממנו: בלעם בן בעור הקוסם הרגו בחרב. ההוא קרא ביהושע כתיב: ולבסוף. שנתן עיניו לקלל את ישראל ניטלה ממנו נבואה ונעשה קוסם: מסגני ושילטא הואי. אשת סגנים ושרים היתה: אייזן לגברא (נ) נגר. זינתה למושכי חבל ספינה ל"א נגרי חרשים:

הרגו

מסורת הש"ס

א) סוטה יא., ב) [שם. לעיל קד. ע"ש], ג) [פי' אותו מלכות ליס נקרא ליבון אספר ערוך ערך אספר א'], ד) [צ"ל לון], ה) [חולין ד:], ו) [בע"י ובילקוט ובתנחומא ליתא לכל זה], ז) בקרא כאהבם, ח) [בכורות ה:], ט) בכורות ה:, י) [בילקוט ליתא], כ) [בע"י ובילקוט ליתא], ל) [צ"ל מצרים וכ"א בילקוט], מ) בקרא כתיב לא, נ) [צ"ל נגדי].

ליקוטי רש"י

בירכן בארז. כארזים עלי מים (במדבר כד). ארז זה אינו עומד במקום מים כו'. ואף על גב דכתיב בקרא כארזים עלי מים ההוא לאו בלעם קאמר ליה דבלעם אמר כארזים והמלאך השיבו עלי מים וכן כולהו דבלעם אמר כנחלים דזימנין מתייבשין וקאמר ליה המלאך נטיו דאין יבישין לעולם והיינו דכתיב ויהפוך ה' אלהיך לך את הקללה לברכה על ידי מלאך שהושיבו על ידי מלאך. אפילו כל הרוחות. שאין קשות. רוח דרומית. שהיא קשה כדאמרינן (בבא בתרא כה:) אילמלא בן נץ שמעמידה אין כל בריה יכולה לעמוד מפניה שנאמר המבינתך יאבר נץ יפרש כנפיו לתימן [תענית כ.]. וירא את הקיני. לפי שהיה קיני תקוע אצל עמלק כענין שנאמר ויאמר שאול אל הקיני וגו' (ש"א טו, ו) הזכירו אחר עמלק נסתכל בגדולתן של בני יתרו שנאמר בהם תרעתים שמעתים סוכתים (דה"א ב, נה). איתן מושבך. תמה אני מהיכן זכית לכך הלא אתה עמי היית בעצת הבה נתחכמה לו (שמות א, י) ועתה נתישבת באיתן ומעוז של ישראל [במדבר כד, כא]. באותה עצה. דנתחכמה לו. יושבי יעבץ. תלמידי יעבץ אדם גדול בתורה היה כדכתיב (דה"א ד) ויקרא יעבץ לאלהי ישראל אם ברך תברכני בתורה והרבית גבולי בתלמידים וגו' ויבא אלהים את אשר שאל (תמורה טז.). תרעתים. מפרש בספרי ששמעו תרועה בהר סיני ואחר כך תרעתים על שם שהיו יושבים בשערי ירושלים. שמעתים. ששמעו אלה אביהם דכתיב ויונדב בן רכב משמעתם קראו להם והם היו מבני בניו של יתרו כדמפרש ואזיל. המה הקינים. סוכתים. שם שהיו יושבים בסוכות כדכתיב (ירמיהו לה) ונשב באהלים וקרי להו משפחות סופרים דהיינו סנהדרין וכן תרעתים וכו' [סוטה יא.]. יושבי בלשכת הגזית. ממשפחות סופרים והאי קרא מפרש ליה כוליה בספרי בפרשת ויאמר משה לחובב. המה הקינים הבאים מחמת אבי בית רכב. וקינים אלו בניו של יתרו דכתיב ובני קיני חותן משה ובניו של יתרו בן בנו של רכב דכתיב הקינים הבאים מחמת אבי בית רכב וכתיב (ירמיהו לה) ולבית הרכבים אמר ירמיהו כי כה אמר ה' [וגו'] יען אשר שמעתם [על] מצות [יהונדב] אביכם [וגו'] לא יכרת איש ליונדב בן רכב [עומד] לפני כל הימים ואמרינן בסיפרי אפשר נכרים הם ונכנסין להיכל והרי כל ישראל לא נכנסו להיכל אלא שהיו יושבין בסנהדרין ומורין בדברי תורה מפי רבי [לעיל קד:]. מעיר התמרים. היא יריחו שניתן להם דושנה של יריחו לאוכלה עד שיבנה בית המקדש ומי שיבנה בית הבחירה בחלקו יטלנה כדי שיהא לכל ישראל חלק בבית הבחירה ונתנוה לבני יתרו ת"מ שנה והתלמידים שבהם הניחוה והלכו אצל עתניאל בן קנז הוא יעבץ במדבר יהודה אשר בנגב ערד ללמוד תורה [שופטים א, טז]. וצים. ספינות גדולות כדכתיב וצי אדיר (ישעיה לג, כא) תרגומו ובורני רבתא [במדבר כ, כג]. וצים. כדמתרגם וליס מיד כתים (במדבר כ"ד) וסיען יסתחרן מרומאי [תהלים עב, ט]. לכה איעצך. מה לך לעשות ומה היא העצה אלהיהם של אלו שונא זמה הוא כו' כדאיתא בחלק (סנהדרין קו.) תדע שבלעם השיא עצה זו להכשילם בזמה שהרי נאמר הן הנה היו לבני ישראל בדבר בלעם (לקמן לא, טז). אשר יעשה העם הזה לעמך. מקרא קצר הוא זה איעצך להכשילם ואומר לך מה שהן עתידין להרע למואב באחרית הימים [במדבר כד, יד]. וינזרו. אין נזירה בכל מקום אלא לשון פרישה. לבושת. לעכו"ם שהיא בשתם. ויהי שקוצים. לפני. כאהבם. את בנות מואב [הושע ט, י]. בדברי שטות. לזנות את בנות מואב. ערומות פגעו בהן. ותקראן משמע גופן היה פוגע בהן. שנעשו כולן בעלי קריין ולשון מקרה הוא. שריפו עצמן כו'. לפיכך בא עליהם עמלק. לא הפנו אבות אל בנים מרפיון ידים. מכאן שריפו ידיהם מן התורה [בכורות ה:]. בשטים. כך שמה. לזנות אל בנות מואב. על ידי עצת בלעם כדאיתא בחלק [במדבר כה, א]. מאי בעי התם. בלעם הלך שם ליטול שכר עשרים וארבעה אלף שהפיל מישראל בעצתו ויצא ממדין לקראת ישראל ומשיאן עצה רעה אמר להם אם כשהייתם ששים רבוא לא יכולתם להם ועכשיו בי"ב אלף אתם באים להלחם נתנו לו שכרו משלם ולא קפחוהו [במדבר לא, ח]. ולבסוף קוסם. איזהו קוסם האוחז את מקלו ואומר אם אלך אם לא אלך וכן הוא אומר עמי בעצו ישאל ומקלו יגיד לו (הושע ד, יב) [דברים יח, י].

הגהות הגר"א

[א] גמ' של עמוני ולא יין. נמחק: [ב] שם ונאמר. נמחק:

תורה אור השלם

א) וַיַּרְא אֶת הַקֵּינִי וַיִּשָּׂא מְשָׁלוֹ וַיֹּאמַר אֵיתָן מוֹשָׁבֶךָ וְשִׂים בַּסֶּלַע קִנֶּךָ: [במדבר כד, כא]

ב) וּמִשְׁפְּחוֹת סֹפְרִים יֹשְׁבֵי יַעְבֵּץ תִּרְעָתִים שִׁמְעָתִים שׂוּכָתִים הֵמָּה הַקִּינִים הַבָּאִים מֵחַמַּת אֲבִי בֵית רֵכָב: [דברי הימים א' ב, נה]

ג) וּבְנֵי קֵינִי חֹתֵן מֹשֶׁה עָלוּ מֵעִיר הַתְּמָרִים אֶת בְּנֵי יְהוּדָה מִדְבַּר יְהוּדָה אֲשֶׁר בְּנֶגֶב עֲרָד וַיֵּלֶךְ וַיֵּשֶׁב אֶת הָעָם: [שופטים א, טז]

ד) וַיִּשָּׂא מְשָׁלוֹ וַיֹּאמַר אוֹי מִי יִחְיֶה מִשֻּׂמוֹ אֵל: [במדבר כד, כג]

ה) וְצִים מִיַּד כִּתִּים וְעִנּוּ אַשּׁוּר וְעִנּוּ עֵבֶר וְגַם הוּא עֲדֵי אֹבֵד: [במדבר כד, כד]

ו) וְעַתָּה הִנְנִי הוֹלֵךְ לְעַמִּי לְכָה אִיעָצְךָ אֲשֶׁר יַעֲשֶׂה הָעָם הַזֶּה לְעַמְּךָ בְּאַחֲרִית הַיָּמִים: [במדבר כד, יד]

ז) כַּעֲנָבִים בַּמִּדְבָּר מָצָאתִי יִשְׂרָאֵל כְּבִכּוּרָה בִתְאֵנָה בְּרֵאשִׁיתָהּ רָאִיתִי אֲבוֹתֵיכֶם הֵמָּה בָּאוּ בַעַל פְּעוֹר וַיִּנָּזְרוּ לַבֹּשֶׁת וַיִּהְיוּ שִׁקּוּצִים כְּאָהֳבָם: [הושע ט, י]

ח) וַיֵּשֶׁב יִשְׂרָאֵל בַּשִּׁטִּים וַיָּחֶל הָעָם לִזְנוֹת אֶל בְּנוֹת מוֹאָב: [במדבר כה, א]

ט) וַתִּקְרֶאןָ לָעָם לְזִבְחֵי אֱלֹהֵיהֶן וַיֹּאכַל הָעָם וַיִּשְׁתַּחֲווּ לֵאלֹהֵיהֶן: [במדבר כה, ב]

י) מִקּוֹל שַׁעֲטַת פַּרְסוֹת אַבִּירָיו מֵרַעַשׁ לְרִכְבּוֹ הֲמוֹן גַּלְגִּלָּיו לֹא הִפְנוּ אָבוֹת אֶל בָּנִים מֵרִפְיוֹן יָדָיִם: [ירמיה מז, ג]

כ) וַיֵּשֶׁב יַעֲקֹב בְּאֶרֶץ מְגוּרֵי אָבִיו בְּאֶרֶץ כְּנָעַן: [בראשית לז, א]

ל) אֵלֶּה תֹּלְדוֹת יַעֲקֹב יוֹסֵף בֶּן שְׁבַע עֶשְׂרֵה שָׁנָה הָיָה רֹעֶה אֶת אֶחָיו בַּצֹּאן וְהוּא נַעַר אֶת בְּנֵי בִלְהָה וְאֶת בְּנֵי זִלְפָּה נְשֵׁי אָבִיו וַיָּבֵא יוֹסֵף אֶת דִּבָּתָם רָעָה אֶל אֲבִיהֶם: [בראשית לז, ב]

מ) וַיֵּשֶׁב יִשְׂרָאֵל בְּאֶרֶץ מִצְרַיִם בְּאֶרֶץ גֹּשֶׁן וַיֵּאָחֲזוּ בָהּ וַיִּפְרוּ וַיִּרְבּוּ מְאֹד: [בראשית מז, כז]

נ) וַיִּקְרְבוּ יְמֵי יִשְׂרָאֵל לָמוּת וַיִּקְרָא לִבְנוֹ לְיוֹסֵף וַיֹּאמֶר לוֹ אִם נָא מָצָאתִי חֵן בְּעֵינֶיךָ שִׂים נָא יָדְךָ תַּחַת יְרֵכִי וְעָשִׂיתָ עִמָּדִי חֶסֶד וֶאֱמֶת אַל נָא תִקְבְּרֵנִי בְּמִצְרָיִם: [בראשית מז, כט]

ס) וַיֵּשֶׁב יְהוּדָה וְיִשְׂרָאֵל לָבֶטַח אִישׁ תַּחַת גַּפְנוֹ וְתַחַת תְּאֵנָתוֹ מִדָּן וְעַד בְּאֵר שָׁבַע כֹּל יְמֵי שְׁלֹמֹה: [מלכים א' ה, ה]

ע) וַיָּקֶם יְיָ שָׂטָן לִשְׁלֹמֹה אֵת הֲדַד הָאֲדֹמִי מִזֶּרַע הַמֶּלֶךְ הוּא בֶּאֱדוֹם: [מלכים א' יא, יד]

פ) וְאֶת מַלְכֵי מִדְיָן הָרְגוּ עַל חַלְלֵיהֶם אֶת אֱוִי וְאֶת רֶקֶם וְאֶת צוּר וְאֶת חוּר וְאֶת רֶבַע חֲמֵשֶׁת מַלְכֵי מִדְיָן וְאֵת בִּלְעָם בֶּן בְּעוֹר הָרְגוּ בֶּחָרֶב: [במדבר לא, ח]

צ) וְאֶת בִּלְעָם בֶּן בְּעוֹר הַקּוֹסֵם הָרְגוּ בְנֵי יִשְׂרָאֵל בַּחֶרֶב אֶל חַלְלֵיהֶם: [יהושע יג, כב]

כֵּיוָן שֶׁשָּׁתָה בָּעַר בּוֹ – **Once he drank** and became intoxicated, **[passion] would rage within him.** אָמַר לָהּ הִשָּׁמְעִי לִי – **He would say to her: "Yield yourself to me!"** הוֹצִיאָה יִרְאָתָהּ מִתּוֹךְ חֵיקָהּ – At that point **she would bring forth her idol**[25] **from her bosom** אָמְרָה לוֹ עֲבוֹד לָזֶה – and **would say to him: "Worship this** and I will yield myself to you." אָמַר לָהּ – **He would say to her:** הֲלֹא יְהוּדִי אֲנִי – **"But I am a Jew!"** How can I worship an idol? אָמְרָה לוֹ וּמָה אִיכְפַּת לָךְ – **She would say to him: "What do you care?** כְּלוּם מְבַקְשִׁים מִמְּךָ אֶלָּא פִּיעוּר – **Are we asking you to do anything other than defecate** before the idol?" [וְהוּא אֵינוֹ יוֹדֵעַ שֶׁעֲבוֹדָתָהּ בְּכָךְ – And he would do so, for **he would not realize that it was worshiped in that manner.**] וְלֹא עוֹד – **"And not only that,"** she would continue, אֶלָּא שֶׁאֵינִי מַנַּחְתָּךְ עַד שֶׁתִּכְפּוֹר בְּתוֹרַת מֹשֶׁה רַבְּךָ – **"but I will not permit you** to cohabit with me **until you repudiate the Torah of Moses your teacher,"** and he would do so,[26] שֶׁנֶּאֱמַר ,,הֵמָּה בָּאוּ בַעַל־פְּעוֹר וַיִּנָּזְרוּ לַבֹּשֶׁת וַיִּהְיוּ שִׁקּוּצִים כְּאָהֳבָם" – **as it is stated:** ***They came to Baal-Peor, and they strayed into shame; in their lust they became detestable.***[27]

The Gemara expounds the Scriptural verses which describe how the Jews sinned with the Moabite women, *Numbers* 25:1-2: ,,וַיֵּשֶׁב יִשְׂרָאֵל בַּשִּׁטִּים" – ***Israel settled in Shittim.*** רַבִּי אֱלִיעֶזֶר אוֹמֵר – **R' Eliezer says:** שִׁטִּים שְׁמָהּ – **"Shittim" was the** actual **name of [that place].** רַבִּי יְהוֹשֻׁעַ אוֹמֵר – **R' Yehoshua says:** שֶׁנִּתְעַסְּקוּ בְּדִבְרֵי שְׁטוּת – "Shittim" means **that they engaged in matters of foolishness** (*shtus*), i.e. immorality.[28] ,,וַתִּקְרֶאןָ לָעָם לְזִבְחֵי אֱלֹהֵיהֶן" – ***And they invited the*** [Jewish] ***people to the sacrifices of their gods.*** רַבִּי אֱלִיעֶזֶר אוֹמֵר – **R' Eliezer says:** עֲרוּמּוֹת פָּגְעוּ בָּהֶן – **[The Moabite girls] met [their Jewish guests] naked.**[29] רַבִּי יְהוֹשֻׁעַ אוֹמֵר – **R' Yehoshua says:** שֶׁנַּעֲשׂוּ כּוּלָּן בַּעֲלֵי קְרָיִין – *Vatikrena* indicates that the Jews who came to the Moabite festivities were so aroused **that they all became *baalei keriin.***[30]

Having presented one dispute between R' Eliezer and R' Yehoshua concerning the meaning of the place name "Shittim," the Gemara presents a similar dispute between them concerning "Rephidim," where the Jews were attacked by Amalek (*Exodus* 17:8): מַאי לְשׁוֹן רְפִידִים – **What is** the meaning of **the word "Rephidim"?** רַבִּי אֱלִיעֶזֶר אוֹמֵר – **R' Eliezer says:** רְפִידִים שְׁמָהּ – **Rephidim was the** actual **name of [that place].** רַבִּי יְהוֹשֻׁעַ אוֹמֵר – **R' Yehoshua says:** שֶׁרִיפּוּ עַצְמָן מִדִּבְרֵי תוֹרָה – The word "Rephidim" indicates **that [the Jews] allowed themselves to weaken** (*ripu*) in their study of **the words of the Torah,** שֶׁנֶּאֱמַר ,,לֹא־הִפְנוּ אָבוֹת אֶל־בָּנִים מֵרִפְיוֹן יָדַיִם" – **as it is stated:** ***Fathers did not turn to sons because of weakness of hands.***[31]

R' Yochanan expounds a general principle:

אָמַר רַבִּי יוֹחָנָן – **R' Yochanan said:** כָּל מָקוֹם שֶׁנֶּאֱמַר ,,וַיֵּשֶׁב" – **Wherever** the word ,,וַיֵּשֶׁב", ***and he settled,*** **is mentioned** in Scripture, אֵינוֹ אֶלָּא לְשׁוֹן צַעַר – **it is nothing but an expression of pain,** i.e. it introduces a painful narrative, שֶׁנֶּאֱמַר ,,וַיֵּשֶׁב יִשְׂרָאֵל בַּשִּׁטִּים וַיָּחֶל הָעָם לִזְנוֹת אֶל־בְּנוֹת מוֹאָב" – **as,** for example, **it is stated:**[32] ***Israel settled in the Shittim, and the people began to commit harlotry with the daughters of Moab;*** ,,וַיֵּשֶׁב יַעֲקֹב בְּאֶרֶץ מְגוּרֵי אָבִיו בְּאֶרֶץ כְּנָעַן . . . וַיָּבֵא יוֹסֵף אֶת־דִּבָּתָם רָעָה אֶל־אֲבִיהֶם" – ***Jacob settled in the land of his father's sojournings, in the land of Canaan . . . and Joseph brought evil reports about [his brothers] to their father.***[33] וְנֶאֱמַר ,,וַיֵּשֶׁב יִשְׂרָאֵל . . . בְּאֶרֶץ גֹּשֶׁן . . . וַיִּקְרְבוּ יְמֵי־יִשְׂרָאֵל לָמוּת" – **And** more examples: **It is stated:** ***Israel settled*** *in the land of Egypt* ***in the region of Goshen . . . and the time approached for Israel*** [i.e. Jacob] ***to die;***[34] ,,וַיֵּשֶׁב יְהוּדָה וְיִשְׂרָאֵל לָבֶטַח אִישׁ תַּחַת גַּפְנוֹ וְתַחַת תְּאֵנָתוֹ" . . . ,,וַיָּקֶם ה' שָׂטָן לִשְׁלֹמֹה אֵת הֲדַד הָאֲדֹמִי מִזֶּרַע הַמֶּלֶךְ הוּא בֶּאֱדוֹם" – ***Judah and Israel were securely settled*** *all the days of Solomon,* ***each person under his own vine and under his own fig tree . . . And HASHEM raised up an adversary against Solomon, Hadad the Edomite, of the royal family of Edom.***[35] In each of these examples, the episode containing the word ,,וַיֵּשֶׁב" concludes in some tragedy or misfortune.[36]

NOTES

25. Literally: her fear. This was an icon of Baal Pe'or, which was worshiped by defecating before it (see Mishnah above, 60b).

26. I.e. once she had gotten the Jew to defecate to Pe'or, she proceeded to the next step of inducing him to repudiate the Torah (see *Rashi*).

27. *Hosea* 9:10. They "strayed into shame" by performing the shameful act of baring themselves and defecating before the idol (see *Rashi* and *Rashash*), and they "became detestable in their lust" for in their lust for the Moabite women they went so far as to repudiate God (*Rashi*).

Maharsha suggests that the demand of the women that the Jews deny the teachings of the Torah was aimed at the law stated in *Deuteronomy* 23:4 that Moabites may not marry Jews.

[It is noteworthy that Bilam's plan only included luring the Jews into immorality. It was the women themselves who developed the plan further to include idol worship, and they were specifically blamed for it (*Numbers* 31:16) (*Toras Chaim*).]

28. As the Gemara teaches elsewhere: "A man does not sin [with immorality] unless a spirit of foolishness enters him" (*Sotah* 3a).

29. R' Eliezer translates וַתִּקְרֶאןָ as *they encountered them,* which indicates that it was the Moabite women and nothing else, not even their clothes, that encountered the Jews (*Rashi; Maharsha*).

30. A *baal keri* is one who experienced a seminal emission. This interpretation is based on the similarity of the words *vatikrena* and *keri.*

31. *Jeremiah* 47:3. This verse is part of Jeremiah's prophecy concerning the Philistines, who were destined to be crushed by the Egyptians and the Babylonians. Jeremiah describes how the invading armies will be so numerous and terrifying that the Philistine fathers will be reduced to helplessness and will not even try to save their own children.

This is the plain meaning of the verse within its context. Here the Gemara applies it to the Jews: Whenever the Jews are weak in the study of Torah and performance of mitzvos, they are unable to save their own children, for they lack the necessary merit to do so.

Thus, the word רִפְיוֹן can refer to spiritual weakness. Accordingly, R' Yehoshua explains the name רְפִידִים in *Exodus* 17:8 as referring to the Jews' weakness in applying themselves to Torah study at the time of Amalek's attack (*Rashi*).

Maharsha points out that it is strange that the Gemara would apply the verse in *Jeremiah* to the study of Torah when in context the verse cannot bear this interpretation. Indeed *Mechilta* ad loc. and *Rashi* to *Bechoros* 5b appear to have had the reading here שֶׁרָפוּ יְדֵיהֶם (as opposed to שֶׁרִיפּוּ עַצְמָן). According to this version, it may be that the name רְפִידִים is expounded as a contraction of רִפְיוֹן יָדַיִם, and the verse from *Jeremiah* is cited merely to show that the expression רִפְיוֹן יָדַיִם is utilized in Scripture to denote weakness (see *Eitz Yosef*).]

Maharal explains that both of the foregoing disputes regarding place names hinge on the same point: R' Eliezer maintains that man by his very nature is prone to sin. R' Eliezer therefore states that these place names are no more than that – names. No deeper reason need be read into them to discover the sources of the people's sins there. R' Yehoshua, on the other hand, maintains that one's sins can always be traced to some underlying general flaw. Each place name is thus assumed to hint to that underlying flaw which resulted in the sin committed there.

32. *Numbers* 25:1.

33. *Genesis* 37:1-2. This is the beginning of the tragic tale of the sale of Joseph by his brothers.

34. Ibid. 47:27,29.

35. *I Kings* 5:5; 11:14.

36. *Toras Chaim* explains why the word וַיֵּשֶׁב, which connotes dwelling comfortably, is a prelude to trouble:

Man was put into the present world in order to prepare himself for the eternal World to Come. However, he sometimes loses sight of this goal and becomes too comfortable, regarding this world as his permanent dwelling place. He is then reminded of his true purpose here by events that disturb his complacency. See *Rashi* to *Genesis* 37:2.

מחליף ושרשיו מרובין ואפילו כל רוחות שבעולם באות ונושבות בו אין מזיזות אותו ממקומו אלא הוא הולך ובא עמהן כיון שדוממו הרוחות עמד קנה במקומו אבל בלעם הרשע ברכן בארז מה ארז זה אינו עומד במקום מים ושרשיו מועטין ואין גזעו מחליף אפילו כל הרוחות שבעולם באות ונושבות בו אין מזיזות אותו ממקומו כיון שנשבה בו רוח דרומית מיד עוקרתו והופכתו על פניו ולא עוד אלא שזכה קנה ליטול ממנו קולמוס לכתוב ממנו ס"ת נביאים וכתובים א) וירא את הקיני וישא משלו אמר לו בלעם ליתרו קיני לא היית עמנו באותה עצה מי הושיבך אצל איתני עולם והיינו א) דא"ר חייא בר אבא א"ר סימאי שלשה היו באותה עצה אלו הן בלעם איוב ויתרו בלעם שיעץ נהרג איוב ששתק נידון ביסורין ויתרו שברח ב) זכו בני בניו לישב בלשכת הגזית שנאמר ב) ומשפחות סופרים יושבי יעבץ תרעתים שמעתים סוכתים המה הקינים הבאים מחמת אבי בית רכב וכתיב ג) ובני קיני חותן משה עלו מעיר התמרים ד) וישא משלו ויאמר אוי מי יחיה משמו אל (אמר רשב"ל אוי מי שמחיה עצמו בשם אל) א"ר יוחנן אוי לה לאומה שתמצא בשעה שהקב"ה עושה פדיון לבניו מי מטיל כסותו בין לביא ללביאה בשעה שנזקקין זה עם זה ה) וצים מיד כתים אמר רב ג) ליבון אספיר ה) וענו אשור וענו עבר עד אשור קטלי מיקטל מכאן ואילך משעבדי שיעבודי ו) הנני הולך לעמי לכה איעצך אשר יעשה העם הזה לעמך עמך לעם הזה מיבעי ליה א"ר אבא בר כהנא כאדם שמקלל את עצמו ותולה קללתו באחרים אמר ד) להם אלהיהם של אלו שונא זימה הוא והם מתאוים לכלי פשתן בוא ואשיאך עצה עשה להן קלעים והושיב בהן זונות זקינה מבחוץ וילדה מבפנים וימכרו להן כלי פשתן עשה להן קלעים מהר שלג עד בית הישימות והושיב בהן זונות זקינה מבחוץ וילדה מבפנים ובשעה שישראל אוכלין ושותין ושמחין ויוצאין לטייל בשוק אומרת לו הזקינה אי אתה מבקש כלי פשתן זקינה אומרת לו בשוה וילדה אומרת לו בפחות שתים ושלש פעמים ואח"כ אומרת לו הרי את כבן בית שב ברור לעצמך וצרצורי של יין עמוני מונח אצלה ה) ועדיין לא נאסר (ו) יין [א] של עמוני ולא) יין של נכרים אמרה לו רצונך שתשתה כוס של יין כיון ששתה בער בו אמר לה השמיעי לי הוציאה יראתה מתוך חיקה אמרה לו עבוד לזה אמר לה הלא יהודי אני אמרה לו ומה איכפת לך כלום מבקשים ממך אלא פיעור [והוא אינו יודע שעבודתה בכך] ולא עוד אלא שאיני מנחתך עד שתכפור בתורת משה רבך שנא' ז) המה באו בעל פעור וינזרו לבשת ויהיו שקוצים ז) באהבם ח) וישב ישראל בשטים ח) ר"א אומר שטים שמה רבי יהושע אומר שנתעסקו בדברי שטות ט) ותקראן לעם לזבחי אלהיהן רבי אליעזר אומר ערומות פגעו בהן רבי יהושע אומר שנעשו כולן בעלי קריין מאי לשון רפידים ט) רבי אליעזר אומר רפידים שמה רבי יהושע אומר שריפו עצמן מדברי תורה שנאמר י) לא הפנו אבות אל בנים מרפיון ידים אמר רבי יוחנן כל מקום שנאמר וישב אינו אלא לשון צער י) שנא' ח) וישב ישראל בשטים ויחל העם לזנות אל בנות מואב כ) וישב יעקב בארץ מגורי אביו בארץ כנען ל) ויבא יוסף את דבתם רעה אל אביהם [ב] כ) ונאמר מ) וישב ישראל בארץ ל) גשן נ) ויקרבו ימי ישראל למות ס) וישב יהודה וישראל לבטח איש תחת גפנו ותחת תאנתו ע) ויקם ה' שטן לשלמה את הדד האדומי מזרע המלך הוא באדום פ) ואת מלכי מדין הרגו על חלליהם וגו' את בלעם בן בעור הרגו בחרב בלעם מאי בעי התם א"ר יוחנן שהלך ליטול שכר עשרים וארבעה אלף [שהפיל מישראל] אמר מר זוטרא בר טוביה אמר רב היינו דאמרי אינשי גמלא אזלא למיבעי קרני אודני דהוו ליה גזיזן מיניה צ) ואת בלעם בן בעור הקוסם קוסם נביא הוא א"ר יוחנן בתחלה נביא ולבסוף קוסם אמר רב פפא היינו דאמרי אינשי מסגני ושילטי הואי אייזן לגברי נגרי

הרגו

רש"י

מחליף. לאחר שנקלץ: אינו עומד במקום מים. והאי דכתיב כארזים עלי מים שכינה היא דאמרה איהו אמר כארזים כלומר שאין עומדין במקום מים שכינה אמרה עלי מים וכן כולהו מפרש באגדה בכה"ג כנחלים נטיו הוא אמר כנחלים פוסקין לפעמים יצאה בת קול [אמרה] נטיו הוא אמר כגנות אמרה בת קול עלי נהר הוא אמר כאהלים יצאה בת קול ואמרה נטע ה': רוח דרומית. קשה: לא עמנו היית באותה עצה. שגזר פרעה כל הבן הילוד היאורה בתמיה ודאי היית כדלקמן: ומי הושיבך אצל איתני עולם. שעתידים בניך לישב בלשכת הגזית והיינו דכתיב איתן מושבך וכי בין איתני עולם אתה יושב מי הזקיקך לכך: שמחיה עצמו בשם אל. עושה עצמו אלוה כמו פרעה וחירם: לשון אחר מי שמחיה עצמו. כלומר אוי להם לאותן בני אדם שמחיין ומעדנין עצמן בעוה"ז ופורקין עול תורה מעל צוארם ומשמנין את עצמן: משמו אל. כששם הקב"ה פדיון לעצמו ומשלם גמול לצדיקים לעתיד לבא. כך שמעתי: אוי לה לאומה שתמצא. אוי לה לאומה שתהיה באותן הימים שיעלה על דעתה לעכב ישראל: מי מטיל כסות בין לביא וכו'. לעכבן שלא יזדקקו זה לזה דמסוכן הוא כלומר מי הוא שיכול לעכב את ישראל והקב"ה מכניסם: ציים. ספינות גדולות כמו (ישעיה לג) וצי אדיר (מ) בל יעברנו: וצים מיד כתים אמר רב ליבא אספיר. דכתים היינו מקום ששמו כך: עד אשור מקטל קטילי. ומאשור ואילך משעבדי להו שעבודי: וצים מיד כתים וענו אשור. דקטלי להו וענו עבר דמשעבדי להן עד אשור: כתים. רומים כלומ' אותן אומות שהביא הקב"ה בלים עתידין להרוג את כל האומות עד אשור ומאשור ואילך מניחין אותן ומשעבדין בהם (ומניחין אותן) ולעתיד קא איירי: הן הנה היו לבני ישראל לא גרסינן אלא ה"ג הנני הולך לעמי לכה איעצך אשר יעשה העם הזה לעמך עמך לעם הזה מבעי ליה. שהשיא עצה לבלק שנכשלו בה ישראל הן הנה היו לבני ישראל בדבר בלעם: ותולה קללתו בחברו. וכן בלעם לא רצה לתלות שפלות זה בבלק שיהא הוא צריך לבקש עצה היאך

היאך יכשלו בה ישראל אלא בישראל תלה השפלות לומר שהן צריכין לעצה שיכשלו בה בני מואב שלא תתקוף ידי מואב על ישראל והיינו דכתיב אשר יעשה העם הזה לעמך. מ"ר. ל"א תולה קללתו בחברו כלומר שתלה הכתוב קללה במואב ולא רצה לכתוב כלפי ישראל כמו שאמר בלעם הרשע: קלעים. אהלים של קלעים כמו שעושין בשוקים: בערבות מואב מהר שלג. שניר: כשהיה אומר לה. ישראל כלי פשתן זה בכמה זקנה אומרת לו דמי שוויו וילדה אומרת לו בפחות מכדי שוויו וכן עושין עד ב' או עד ג' פעמים: ברור לעצמך. כל תכשיטין שאתה רוצה: צרצורי. נודות: בוער בו. שהיה משתכר ובוער בו יצר הרע: השמיעי. הוי שומעת לתשמיש: פיעור. כך היתה עבודתו של פעור שמתריזים לפניו: ה"ג כלום מבקשין ממך אלא פיעור והוא עושה ושוב אומרת לו כפור בתורת משה רבך והוא עושה: וינזרו לבשת. סרו מדרכם והלכו אחר הבשת: כאהבם. מתוך תאות אהבתם לזנות היו משוקצים שכופרין בהקב"ה: ותקראן. בגופן ותקראן [משמע] לשון מקרה: מאי רפידים. איידי דלעיל איפליגו ביה ר"א ור' יהושע במשמעות דשטים נקיט נמי רפידים דפליגי ביה בכי האי גוונא: לא הפנו אבות אל בנים. להטיב להם: מפני רפיון ידים. של תורה ומצות והכי נמי רפידים רפיון ידים הוא כלומר מפני שרפו ידים מן התורה בא עליהם עמלק: שכר כ"ד אלפים מישראל. שהרגו בעצתו הלך ליטול מבלק ומזקני מדין: גמלא תבע קרני. כך בלעם שאל שכר ונהרג: גזו מיניה. חתכו ממנו: בלעם בן בעור הקוסם הרגו בחרב. ההוא קרא ביהושע כתיב: ולבסוף. שנתן עיניו לקלל את ישראל ניטלה ממנו נבואה ונעשה קוסם: מסגני ושילטא הואי. אשת סגנים ושרים היתה: אייזן לגברא (י) נגר. זינתה למושכי חבל ספינה ל"א נגרי חרשים:

הרגו

מסורת הש"ס

א) סוטה יא., ב) [שם. לעיל קד. ע"ש], ג) [פי' אותו מלכות לים נקרא ליבון אספר ערוך ערך אספר א'], ד) [נ"ל לו], ה) [חולין ד:], ו) [בע"י וילקוט ובתנחומא ליתא לכל זה], ז) בקרא כאהבם, ח) [בכורות ה:], ט) בכורות ה:, י) [ילקוט לית'], כ) [בע"י וילקוט ליתא], ל) [נ"ל מצרים וכ"א בילקוט], מ) בקרא כתיב לא, נ) [נ"ל נגדי].

ליקוטי רש"י

בירכן בארז. כארזים עלי מים (במדבר כד). ארז זה אינו עומד במקום מים כו'. ואף על גב דכתיב בקרא כארזים עלי מים ההוא לאו בלעם קאמר ליה דבלעם אמר כארזים והמלאך השיבו עלי מים וכן כולהו דבלעם אמר כנחלים דזימנין מתייבשין וקאמר ליה המלאך נטיו דאין יבישין לעולם והיינו דכתיב ויהפוך ה' אלהיך לך את הקללה לברכה על ידי מלאך שהושיבו על ידי מלאך. אפילו כל הרוחות. שאין קשות. רוח דרומית. שהיא קשה כדאמרינן (בבא בתרא כה:) אילמלא בן נץ שמעמידה אין כל בריה יכולה לעמוד מפניה שנאמר המבינתך יאבר נץ יפרש כנפיו לתימן [תענית כ.]. וירא את הקיני. לפי שהיה קיני תקוע אצל עמלק כענין שנאמר ויאמר שאול אל הקיני וגו' (ש"א טו, ו) הזכירו אחר עמלק נסתכל בגדולתן של בני יתרו שנאמר בהם תרעתים שמעתים סוכתים (דה"א ב, נה). איתן מושבך. תמה אני מהיכן זכית לכך הלא אתה עמי היית בעצת הבה נתחכמה לו (שמות א, י) ועתה נתישבת באיתן ומעוז של ישראל [במדבר כד, כא]. באותה עצה. דנתחכמה לו. יושבי יעבץ. תלמידי יעבץ אדם גדול בתורה היה כדכתיב (דה"א ד) ויקרא יעבץ לאלהי ישראל אם ברך תברכני בתורה והרבית את גבולי בתלמידים וגו' ויבא אלהים את אשר שאל (תמורה טז). תרעתים. מפרש בספרי ששמעו תרועה בהר סיני ל"א תרעתים על שם שהיו יושבים בשערי ירושלים. שמעתים. ששמעו מצות אביהם דבני יונדב בן רכב משתעי קרא והם היו מבני בניו של יתרו כדמפרש ואזיל המה הקינים. סוכתים. על שם שהיו יושבים בסוכות כדכתיב (ירמיהו לה) ונשב באהלים וקרי להו משפחת סופרים דהיינו סנהדרין וכן תרעתים זקני שער [סוטה יא:]. ישבו בלשכת הגזית. ממשפחות סופרים והאי קרא מפרש ליה כולו בסיפרי בפרשת ויאמר משה לחובב. המה הקינים הבאים מחמת אבי בית רכב. וקינים אלו בניו של יתרו דכתיב ובני קיני חותן משה ובניו של יתרו הן הן בניו של רכב דכתיב הקינים הבאים מחמת אבי בית רכב וכתיב (ירמיהו לה) ולבית הרכבים אמר ירמיהו כי כה אמר ה' [וגו'] יען אשר שמעתם [על] מצות [יהונדב] אביכם [וגו'] לא יכרת איש ליונדב בן רכב [עומד] לפני כל הימים ואמרינן בסיפרי אפשר נכרים הם ונכנסין להיכל והרי כל ישראל לא נכנסו להיכל אלא שהיו יושבין בסנהדרין ומורין בדברי תורה מפי רבי [לעיל קד:]. מעיר התמרים. היא יריחו שניתן להם דושנה של יריחו לאוכלה עד שיבנה בית המקדש ומי שיבנה בית הבחירה בחלקו יטלנה כדי שיהא לכל ישראל חלק בבית הבחירה ונתנוה לבני יתרו ת"מ שנה והתלמידים שבהם הניחוה והלכו אצל עתניאל בן קנז הוא יעבץ במדבר יהודה אשר בנגב ערד ללמוד תורה [שופטים א, טז]. וצים. ספינות גדולות כדכתיב וצי אדיר (ישעיה לג, כא) תרגומו ובורני רבתא [במדבר כ, כג]. וצים. כדמתרגם וציס מיד כתים (במדבר כ"ד) וסיען יסתחרן מרומאי [תהלים עב, ט]. לכה איעצך. מה לך לעשות ומה היא העצה אלהיהם של אלו שונא זמה הוא כו' כדאיתא בחלק (סנהדרין קו.) תדע שבלעם השיא עצה זו להכשילם בזמה שהרי נאמר הן הנה היו לבני ישראל בדבר בלעם (לקמן לא, טז). אשר יעשה העם הזה לעמך. מקרא קצר הוא זה איעצך להכשילם ואומר לך מה שהן עתידין להרע למואב באחרית הימים [במדבר כד, יד]. וינזרו. אין נזירה בכל מקום אלא לשון פרישה. לבושת. לעכו"ם שהיא בשתם. ויהי שקוצים. לפני. כאהבם. את בנות מואב [הושע ט, י]. בדברי שטות. לזנות את בנות מואב. ערומות פגעו בהן. ותקראן משמע גופן היה פוגע בהן. שנעשו כולן בעלי קריין ולשון מקרה הוא. שריפו עצמן כו'. לפיכך בא עליהם עמלק. לא הפנו אבות אל בנים מרפיון ידים. מכאן שריפו ידיהם מן התורה [בכורות ה:]. בשטים. כך שמה. לזנות אל בנות מואב. על ידי עצת בלעם כדאיתא בחלק [במדבר כה, א]. מאי בעי התם. בלעם הלך שם ליטול שכר עשרים וארבעה אלף שהפיל מישראל בעצתו ויצא ממדין לקראת ישראל ומשיאן עצה רעה אמר להם אם כשהייתם ששים רבוא לא יכולתם להם ועכשיו בי"ב אלף אתם באים להלחם נתנו לו שכרו משלם ולא קפחוהו [במדבר לא, ח]. ולבסוף קוסם. איזהו קוסם האוחז את מקלו ואומר אם אלך אם לא אלך וכן הוא אומר עמי בעצו ישאל ומקלו יגיד לו (הושע ד, יב) [דברים יח, י].

הגהות הגר"א

[א] גמ' של עמוני ולא יין. נמחק: [ב] שם ונאמר. נמחק:

תורה אור השלם

א) וַיַּרְא אֶת הַקֵּינִי וַיִּשָּׂא מְשָׁלוֹ וַיֹּאמַר אֵיתָן מוֹשָׁבֶךָ וְשִׂים בַּסֶּלַע קִנֶּךָ: [במדבר כד, כא]

ב) וּמִשְׁפְּחוֹת סֹפְרִים יֹשְׁבֵי יַעְבֵּץ תִּרְעָתִים שִׁמְעָתִים שׂוּכָתִים הֵמָּה הַקִּינִים הַבָּאִים מֵחַמַּת אֲבִי בֵית רֵכָב: [דברי הימים א' ב, נה]

ג) וּבְנֵי קֵינִי חֹתֵן מֹשֶׁה עָלוּ מֵעִיר הַתְּמָרִים אֶת בְּנֵי יְהוּדָה מִדְבַּר יְהוּדָה אֲשֶׁר בְּנֶגֶב עֲרָד וַיֵּלֶךְ וַיֵּשֶׁב אֶת הָעָם: [שופטים א, טז]

ד) וַיִּשָּׂא מְשָׁלוֹ וַיֹּאמַר אוֹי מִי יִחְיֶה מִשֻּׂמוֹ אֵל: [במדבר כד, כג]

ה) וְצִים מִיַּד כִּתִּים וְעִנּוּ אַשּׁוּר וְעִנּוּ עֵבֶר וְגַם הוּא עֲדֵי אֹבֵד: [במדבר כד, כד]

ו) וְעַתָּה הִנְנִי הוֹלֵךְ לְעַמִּי לְכָה אִיעָצְךָ אֲשֶׁר יַעֲשֶׂה הָעָם הַזֶּה לְעַמְּךָ בְּאַחֲרִית הַיָּמִים: [במדבר כד, יד]

ז) כַּעֲנָבִים בַּמִּדְבָּר מָצָאתִי יִשְׂרָאֵל כְּבִכּוּרָה בִתְאֵנָה בְּרֵאשִׁיתָהּ רָאִיתִי אֲבוֹתֵיכֶם הֵמָּה בָּאוּ בַעַל פְּעוֹר וַיִּנָּזְרוּ לַבֹּשֶׁת וַיִּהְיוּ שִׁקּוּצִים כְּאָהֳבָם: [הושע ט, י]

ח) וַיֵּשֶׁב יִשְׂרָאֵל בַּשִּׁטִּים וַיָּחֶל הָעָם לִזְנוֹת אֶל בְּנוֹת מוֹאָב: [במדבר כה, א]

ט) וַתִּקְרֶאןָ לָעָם לְזִבְחֵי אֱלֹהֵיהֶן וַיֹּאכַל הָעָם וַיִּשְׁתַּחֲווּ לֵאלֹהֵיהֶן: [במדבר כה, ב]

י) מִקּוֹל שַׁעֲטַת פַּרְסוֹת אַבִּירָיו מֵרַעַשׁ לְרִכְבּוֹ הֲמוֹן גַּלְגִּלָּיו לֹא הִפְנוּ אָבוֹת אֶל בָּנִים מֵרִפְיוֹן יָדָיִם: [ירמיה מז, ג]

כ) וַיֵּשֶׁב יַעֲקֹב בְּאֶרֶץ מְגוּרֵי אָבִיו בְּאֶרֶץ כְּנָעַן: [בראשית לז, א]

ל) אֵלֶּה תֹּלְדוֹת יַעֲקֹב יוֹסֵף בֶּן שְׁבַע עֶשְׂרֵה שָׁנָה הָיָה רֹעֶה אֶת אֶחָיו בַּצֹּאן וְהוּא נַעַר אֶת בְּנֵי בִלְהָה וְאֶת בְּנֵי זִלְפָּה נְשֵׁי אָבִיו וַיָּבֵא יוֹסֵף אֶת דִּבָּתָם רָעָה אֶל אֲבִיהֶם: [בראשית לז, ב]

מ) וַיֵּשֶׁב יִשְׂרָאֵל בְּאֶרֶץ מִצְרַיִם בְּאֶרֶץ גֹּשֶׁן וַיֵּאָחֲזוּ בָהּ וַיִּפְרוּ וַיִּרְבּוּ מְאֹד: [בראשית מז, כז]

נ) וַיִּקְרְבוּ יְמֵי יִשְׂרָאֵל לָמוּת וַיִּקְרָא לִבְנוֹ לְיוֹסֵף וַיֹּאמֶר לוֹ אִם נָא מָצָאתִי חֵן בְּעֵינֶיךָ שִׂים נָא יָדְךָ תַּחַת יְרֵכִי וְעָשִׂיתָ עִמָּדִי חֶסֶד וֶאֱמֶת אַל נָא תִקְבְּרֵנִי בְּמִצְרָיִם: [בראשית מז, כט]

ס) וַיֵּשֶׁב יְהוּדָה וְיִשְׂרָאֵל לָבֶטַח אִישׁ תַּחַת גַּפְנוֹ וְתַחַת תְּאֵנָתוֹ מִדָּן וְעַד בְּאֵר שָׁבַע כֹּל יְמֵי שְׁלֹמֹה: [מלכים א' ה, ה]

ע) וַיָּקֶם יְיָ שָׂטָן לִשְׁלֹמֹה אֵת הֲדַד הָאֲדֹמִי מִזֶּרַע הַמֶּלֶךְ הוּא בֶּאֱדוֹם: [מלכים א' יא, יד]

פ) וְאֶת מַלְכֵי מִדְיָן הָרְגוּ עַל חַלְלֵיהֶם אֶת אֱוִי וְאֶת רֶקֶם וְאֶת צוּר וְאֶת חוּר וְאֶת רֶבַע חֲמֵשֶׁת מַלְכֵי מִדְיָן וְאֵת בִּלְעָם בֶּן בְּעוֹר הָרְגוּ בֶּחָרֶב: [במדבר לא, ח]

צ) וְאֶת בִּלְעָם בֶּן בְּעוֹר הַקּוֹסֵם הָרְגוּ בְנֵי יִשְׂרָאֵל בַּחֶרֶב אֶל חַלְלֵיהֶם: [יהושע יג, כב]

The Gemara proceeds to the Scriptural account of Bilam's death:

,,וְאֶת־מַלְכֵי מִדְיָן הָרְגוּ עַל־חַלְלֵיהֶם וגו׳ וְאֵת בִּלְעָם בֶּן־בְּעוֹר הָרְגוּ בֶּחָרֶב״ – Scripture states: *In addition to the others they slew,* ***they killed the kings of Midian:*** *Evi, Rekem, Zur, Hur and Reva, the five kings of Midian;* ***and Bilam the son of Beor they slew with the sword.***[37] בִּלְעָם מַאי בָּעֵי הָתָם – **What was Bilam doing there** [in Midian]?[38] אָמַר רַבִּי יוֹחָנָן – **R' Yochanan said:** שֶׁהָלַךְ לִיטּוֹל שְׂכַר עֶשְׂרִים וְאַרְבָּעָה אֶלֶף [שֶׁהִפִּיל מִיִּשְׂרָאֵל] – **He had gone** to Midian **to collect a reward for the twenty-four thousand [of Israel whom he had felled].**[39] אָמַר מַר זוּטְרָא בַּר טוֹבִיָּה אָמַר רַב – **Mar Zutra bar Toviyah said in the name of Rav:** הַיְינוּ דְּאָמְרֵי אִינְשֵׁי – **That is the meaning of the popular adage:**[40] גַּמְלָא אֲזַלָא לְמִיבְעֵי קַרְנֵי – **"The camel went to demand horns;** אוּדְנֵי דַּהֲווּ לֵיהּ גְּזִיזַן מִינֵּיהּ – instead, **the ears he already had were shorn from him."**[41]

The loss of Bilam's prophetic powers and his death:

,,וְאֶת־בִּלְעָם בֶּן־בְּעוֹר הַקּוֹסֵם״ – ***And Bilam the son of Beor, the sorcerer,*** *the Children of Israel slew.*[42]

The Gemara asks:

קוֹסֵם – Was Bilam, then, a mere **sorcerer?** נָבִיא הוּא – **Why, he was a prophet!** – ? –

The Gemara answers:

אָמַר רַבִּי יוֹחָנָן – **R' Yochanan said:** בַּתְּחִלָּה נָבִיא וּלְבַסּוֹף קוֹסֵם – **At the beginning** he was **a prophet, but at the end** he was merely **a sorcerer.**[43] אָמַר רַב פָּפָּא – **Rav Pappa said:** הַיְינוּ דְּאָמְרֵי אִינְשֵׁי – **That is the meaning of the popular adage:** מִסְגְּנֵי וְשִׁילְטֵי הֲוַאי – **"She who had been the wife of princes and rulers** אַיְיזַן לְגַבְרֵי נַגָּרֵי – **committed adultery with men who drag ships."**[44]

NOTES

37. *Numbers* 31:8. The verse describes the Jewish campaign against Midian.

38. After his abortive attempt to curse the Jews in Moab, Bilam told the king of Moab that he was returning home to Aram Naharaim (ibid. 24:14). How, then, did he end up in Midian at the time of the Jewish invasion?

39. I.e. whose death he had caused by persuading Moab and Midian to have their daughters seduce the Israelites into immorality. As a result of their sin, twenty-four thousand Jews died in a plague (ibid. 25:9).

The commentators puzzle over Bilam's applying to the Midianite elders for his reward when it was to Moab that he had given advice about the seduction of the Israelites. Moreover, *Rashi's* statement that Bilam went to meet Balak in Midian seems difficult, for Balak was the king of Moab, not Midian. For possible solutions to this question see *Maharsha,* as well as commentators cited in *Ein Yaakov* here and in *Otzar Meforshim* to *Numbers* 31:8. Cf. *Ramban* to *Numbers* 25:18.

40. Literally: so people say.

41. I.e. the camel's desire for horns led to the loss of his ears. Similarly, Bilam's desire for financial reward led to his death, for had he not sought a reward for helping to kill the Jews, he would not have been in Midian at the time of the Jewish invasion and would not have been killed (*Rashi*). See *The Juggler and the King* by R' Aharon Feldman, p. 49, in the name of the Vilna Gaon, for elaboration on the parable of the camel and the horns.

42. *Joshua* 13:22.

43. I.e. originally, Bilam had been a genuine prophet; however, when he undertook to curse Israel (or when he advised the Moabites to turn their daughters into harlots – *Yad Ramah*), God stripped him of his prophetic powers. Deprived of his God-given powers, Bilam practiced sorcery instead (*Rashi*). Cf. *Ramban* to *Numbers* 22:31 and 24:1.

44. This is a parable of self-degradation: not enough that a princess committed adultery, but she did so with a menial worker, one who pulls the ship by ropes through the canals and rivers (or with a carpenter, according to *Rashi*'s alternative interpretation). By doing so, she showed she had no conception of the dignity of her station. Similarly, Bilam had been a genuine prophet of God. As such he was infinitely superior to sorcerers. To switch from genuine prophecy to sorcery was the ultimate act of self-degradation (see *Rashi*).

An alternate reading: מִסְגְּנֵי וְשִׁלִּיטֵי הֲוַיָאן לְגַבְרֵי נַגָּרֵי, *she who had been the wife of princes and rulers has become the wife of carpenters.* I.e. if a woman was married to a warrior (*princes and rulers*), she is used to a husband who wields weapons. If he dies, she will remarry only if she can find another husband who wields weapons. If she cannot find another warrior, she will marry the closest thing to a warrior – a carpenter, who wields his carpentry tools, even though they are a pale imitation of a warrior's weapons. Similarly, Bilam was originally a genuine prophet and was used to the exercise of prophetic powers to foretell the future and to bestow blessings and curses. When he lost his prophetic powers, he was too accustomed to them to lead the life of a normal person. He wished to continue exercising superhuman powers and was willing to resort to sorcery to do so, even though his powers of sorcery were a very pale imitation of the powers he had enjoyed as a prophet (*Yad Ramah*).

מחליף ושרשיו מרובין ואפילו כל רוחות שבעולם באות ונושבות בו אין מזיזות אותו ממקומו אלא הוא הולך ובא עמהן כיון שדוממו הרוחות עמד קנה במקומו אבל בלעם הרשע ברכן בארז מה ארז זה אינו עומד במקום מים ושרשיו מועטין ואין גזעו מחליף אפילו כל הרוחות שבעולם באות ונושבות בו אין מזיזות אותו ממקומו כיון שנשבה בו רוח דרומית מיד עוקרתו והופכתו על פניו ולא עוד אלא שזכה קנה ליטול ממנו קולמוס לכתוב ממנו ס"ת נביאים וכתובים א) וירא את הקיני וישא משלו אמר לו בלעם ליתרו קיני לא היית עמנו באותה עצה מי הושיבך אצל איתני עולם והיינו א) דא"ר חייא בר אבא א"ר סימאי שלשה היו באותה עצה אלו הן בלעם איוב ויתרו בלעם שיעץ נהרג איוב ששתק נידון ביסורין ויתרו שברח ב) זכו בני בניו לישב בלשכת הגזית שנאמר ב) ומשפחות סופרים יושבי יעבץ תרעתים שמעתים סוכתים המה הקינים הבאים מחמת אבי בית רכב וכתיב ג) ובני קיני חותן משה עלו מעיר התמרים ד) וישא משלו ויאמר אוי מי יחיה משמו אל (אמר רשב"ל אוי מי שמחיה עצמו בשם אל) א"ר יוחנן אוי לה לאומה שתמצא בשעה שהקב"ה עושה פדיון לבניו מי מטיל כסותו בין לביא ללביאה בשעה שנזקקין זה עם זה ה) וצים מיד כתים אמר רב ג) ליבון אספיר ה) וענו אשור וענו עבר עד אשור קטלי מיקטל מכאן ואילך משעבדי שיעבודי ו) הנני הולך לעמי לכה איעצך אשר יעשה העם הזה לעמך עמך לעם הזה מיבעי ליה א"ר אבא בר כהנא כאדם שמקלל את עצמו ותולה קללתו באחרים אמר ד) להם אלהיהם של אלו שונא זימה הוא והם מתאוים לכלי פשתן בוא ואשיאך עצה עשה להן קלעים והושיב בהן זונות זקינה מבחוץ וילדה מבפנים וימכרו להן כלי פשתן עשה להן קלעים מהר שלג עד בית הישימות והושיב בהן זונות זקינה מבחוץ וילדה מבפנים ובשעה שישראל אוכלין ושותין ושמחין ויוצאין לטייל בשוק אומרת לו הזקינה אי אתה מבקש כלי פשתן זקינה אומרת לו בשוה וילדה אומרת לו בפחות שתים ושלש פעמים ואח"כ אומרת לו הרי את כבן בית שב ברור לעצמך וצרצורי של יין עמוני מונח אצלה ס) ועדיין לא נאסר (י) יין [א] של עמוני ולא) יין של נכרים אמרה לו רצונך שתשתה כוס של יין כיון ששתה בער בו אמר לה השמיעי לי הוציאה יראתה מתוך חיקה אמרה לו עבוד לזה אמר לה הלא יהודי אני אמרה לו ומה איכפת לך כלום מבקשים ממך אלא פיעור [והוא אינו יודע שעבודתה בכך] ולא עוד אלא שאיני מנחתך עד שתכפור בתורת משה רבך שנא' ו) המה באו בעל פעור וינזרו לבשת ויהיו שקוצים ז) באהבם ח) וישב ישראל בשטים פ) ר"א אומר שטים שמה רבי יהושע אומר שנתעסקו בדברי שטות ט) ותקראן לעם לזבחי אלהיהן רבי אליעזר אומר ערומות פגעו בהן רבי יהושע אומר שנעשו כולן בעלי קריין מאי לשון רפידים ט) רבי אליעזר אומר רפידים שמה רבי יהושע אומר שריפו עצמן מדברי תורה שנאמר י) לא הפנו אבות אל בנים מרפיון ידים אמר רבי יוחנן כל מקום שנאמר וישב אינו אלא לשון צער י) שנא' ח) וישב ישראל בשטים ויחל העם לזנות אל בנות מואב כ) וישב יעקב בארץ מגורי אביו בארץ כנען ל) ויבא יוסף את דבתם רעה אל אביהם [ב] י) ונאמר מ) וישב ישראל בארץ ל) גשן נ) ויקרבו ימי ישראל למות ס) וישב יהודה וישראל לבטח איש תחת גפנו ותחת תאנתו ע) ויקם ה' שטן לשלמה את הדד האדומי מזרע המלך הוא באדום פ) ואת מלכי מדין הרגו על חלליהם וגו' את בלעם בן בעור הרגו בחרב בלעם מאי בעי התם א"ר יוחנן שהלך ליטול שכר עשרים וארבעה אלף [שהפיל מישראל] אמר מר זוטרא בר טוביה אמר רב היינו דאמרי אינשי גמלא אזלא למיבעי קרני אודני דהוו ליה גזיזן מיניה צ) ואת בלעם בן בעור הקוסם קוסם נביא הוא א"ר יוחנן בתחלה נביא ולבסוף קוסם אמר רב פפא היינו דאמרי אינשי מסגני ושילטי הואי אייזן לגברי נגרי

הרגו

רש"י

מחליף. לאחר שנקלץ: **אינו עומד במקום מים.** והאי דכתיב כארזים עלי מים שכינה היא דאמרה איהו אמר כארזים כלומר שאין עומדין במקום מים שכינה אמרה עלי מים וכן כולהו מפרש באגדה בכה"ג כנחלים נטיו הוא אמר כנחלים פוסקין לפעמים יצאה בת קול [אמרה] נטיו הוא אמר כגנות אמרה בת קול עלי נהר הוא אמר כאהלים יצאה בת קול ואמרה נטע ה': **רוח דרומית.** קשה: **לא עמנו היית באותה עצה.** שגזר פרעה כל הבן הילוד היאורה בתמיה ודאי היית כדלקמן: **ומי הושיבך אצל איתני עולם.** שעתידים בניך לישב בלשכת הגזית והיינו דכתיב איתן מושבך וכי בין איתני עולם אתה יושב מי הזקיקך לכך: **שמחיה עצמו בשם אל.** עושה עצמו אלוה כמו פרעה וחירם: לשון אחר **מי שמחיה עצמו.** כלומר אוי להם לאותן בני אדם שמחיין ומעדנין עצמן בעוה"ז ופורקין עול תורה מעל צוארם ומשמנין את עצמן: **משמו אל.** כשמשים הקב"ה פדיון לעצמו ומשלם גמול לצדיקים לעתיד לבא. כך שמעתי: **אוי לה לאומה שתמצא.** אוי לה לאומה שתהיה באותן הימים שיעלה על דעתה לעכב ישראל: **מי מטיל כסות בין לביא וכו'.** לעכבן שלא יזדקקו זה לזה דמסוכן הוא כלומר מי הוא שיכול לעכב את ישראל והקב"ה מכניסם: **ציים.** ספינות גדולות כמו (ישעיה לג) וצי אדיר (מ) בל יעברנו: **וצים מיד כתים אמר רב ליבא אספיר.** דכתים היינו מקום ששמו כך: **עד אשור מקטל קטילי.** ומאשור ואילך משעבדי להו שעבודי: **וצים מיד כתים וענו אשור.** דקטלי להו וענו עבר דמשעבדי להן עד אשור: **כתים.** רומים כלומ' אותן אומות שהביא הקב"ה בלים עתידין להרוג את כל האומות עד אשור ומאשור ואילך מניחין אותן ומשעבדין בהם (ומניחין אותן) ולעתיד קא איירי: **הן הנה היו לבני ישראל** לא גרסינן אלא ה"ג **הנני הולך לעמי לכה איעצך אשר יעשה העם הזה לעמך עמך לעם הזה מבעי ליה.** שהשיא עצה לבלק שנכשלו בה ישראל הן הנה היו לבני ישראל בדבר בלעם: **ותולה קללתו בחברו.** וכך בלעם לא רצה לתלות שפלות זה בבלק שיהא הוא צריך לבקש עצה היאך יכשלו בה ישראל אלא בישראל תלה השפלות לומר שהן צריכין לעצה שיכשלו בה בני מואב שלא תתקוף ידי מואב על ישראל והיינו דכתיב אשר יעשה העם הזה לעמך. מ"ר. נ"א תולה קללתו בחברו כלומר שתלה הכתוב קללה במואב ולא רצה לכתוב כלפי ישראל כמו שאמר בלעם הרשע: **קלעים.** אהלים של קלעים כמו שעושין בשוקים: **בערבות מואב מהר שלג.** שניר: **כשהיה אומר לה.** ישראל כלי פשתן זה בכמה זקנה אומרת לו דמי שוויו וילדה אומרת לו בפחות מכדי שוויו וכן עושין עד ב' או עד ג' פעמים: **ברור לעצמך.** כל תכשיטין שאתה רוצה: **צרצרי.** נודות: **בוער בו.** שהיה משתכר ובוער בו יצר הרע: **השמיעי.** הוי שומעת לתשמיש: **פיעור.** כך היתה עבודתו של פעור שמתריזים לפניו: ה"ג כלום מבקשין ממך אלא פיעור והוא עושה ושוב אומרת לו כפור בתורת משה רבך והוא עושה: **וינזרו לבשת.** סרו מדרכם והלכו אחר הבשת: **כאהבם.** מתוך תאות אהבתם לזונות היו משוקצים שכופרין בהקב"ה: **ותקראן.** בגופן ותקראן [משמע] לשון מקרה: **מאי רפידים.** איידי דלעיל איפליגו ביה ר"א ור' יהושע במשמעות דשטים נקיט נמי רפידים דפליגי ביה בכי האי גוונא: **לא הפנו אבות אל בנים.** להיטיב להם: **מפני רפיון ידים.** של תורה ומצות והכי נמי רפידים רפיון ידים הוא כלומר מפני שרפו ידים מן התורה בא עליהם עמלק: **שכר כ"ד אלפים מישראל.** שהרגו בעצתו הלך ליטול מבלק ומזקני מדין: **גמלא תבע קרני.** כך בלעם שאל שכר ונהרג: **גזו מיניה.** חתכו ממנו: **בלעם בן בעור הקוסם הרגו בחרב.** ההוא קרא ביהושע כתיב: **ולבסוף.** שנתן עיניו לקלל את ישראל ניטלה ממנו נבואה ונעשה קוסם: **מסגני ושילטא הואי.** אשת סגנים ושרים היתה: **אייזן לגברא** (י) **נגר.** זינתה למושכי חבל ספינה נ"א נגרי חרשים:

הרגו

מסורת הש"ס

א) סוטה יא., ב) [שם. לעיל קד. ע"ש], ג) [פי' אותו מלכות ליס נקרא ליבון אספר ערוך ערך אספר א'], ד) [נ"ל לו], ה) [חולין ז:], ו) [בע"י וילקוט ובתנחומא ליתא לכל זה], ז) בקרא כאהבם, ח) [בכורות ה:], ט) בכורות ה:, י) [בילקוט לית'], כ) [בע"י וילקוט ליתא], ל) [נ"ל מצרים וכ"א בילקוט], מ) בקרא כתיב לא, נ) [נ"ל נגדי].

הגהות הגר"א

[א] גמ' של עמוני ולא יין. נמחק: [ב] שם ונאמר. נמחק:

תורה אור השלם

א) וַיַּרְא אֶת הַקֵּינִי וַיִּשָּׂא מְשָׁלוֹ וַיֹּאמַר אֵיתָן מוֹשָׁבֶךָ וְשִׂים בַּסֶּלַע קִנֶּךָ: [במדבר כד, כא]

ב) וּמִשְׁפְּחוֹת סֹפְרִים יֹשְׁבֵי יַעְבֵּץ תִּרְעָתִים שִׁמְעָתִים שׂוּכָתִים הֵמָּה הַקִּינִים הַבָּאִים מֵחַמַּת אֲבִי בֵית רֵכָב: [דברי הימים א ב, נה]

ג) וּבְנֵי קֵינִי חֹתֵן מֹשֶׁה עָלוּ מֵעִיר הַתְּמָרִים אֶת בְּנֵי יְהוּדָה מִדְבַּר יְהוּדָה אֲשֶׁר בְּנֶגֶב עֲרָד וַיֵּלֶךְ וַיֵּשֶׁב אֶת הָעָם: [שופטים א, טז]

ד) וַיִּשָּׂא מְשָׁלוֹ וַיֹּאמַר אוֹי מִי יִחְיֶה מִשֻּׂמוֹ אֵל: [במדבר כד, כג]

ה) וְצִים מִיַּד כִּתִּים וְעִנּוּ אַשּׁוּר וְעִנּוּ עֵבֶר וְגַם הוּא עֲדֵי אֹבֵד: [במדבר כד, כד]

ו) וְעַתָּה הִנְנִי הוֹלֵךְ לְעַמִּי לְכָה אִיעָצְךָ אֲשֶׁר יַעֲשֶׂה הָעָם הַזֶּה לְעַמְּךָ בְּאַחֲרִית הַיָּמִים: [במדבר כד, יד]

ז) כַּעֲנָבִים בַּמִּדְבָּר מָצָאתִי יִשְׂרָאֵל כְּבִכּוּרָה בִתְאֵנָה בְּרֵאשִׁיתָהּ רָאִיתִי אֲבוֹתֵיכֶם הֵמָּה בָּאוּ בַעַל פְּעוֹר וַיִּנָּזְרוּ לַבֹּשֶׁת וַיִּהְיוּ שִׁקּוּצִים כְּאָהֳבָם: [הושע ט, י]

ח) וַיֵּשֶׁב יִשְׂרָאֵל בַּשִּׁטִּים וַיָּחֶל הָעָם לִזְנוֹת אֶל בְּנוֹת מוֹאָב: [במדבר כה, א]

ט) וַתִּקְרֶאןָ לָעָם לְזִבְחֵי אֱלֹהֵיהֶן וַיֹּאכַל הָעָם וַיִּשְׁתַּחֲווּ לֵאלֹהֵיהֶן: [במדבר כה, ב]

י) מִקּוֹל שַׁעֲטַת פַּרְסוֹת אַבִּירָיו מֵרַעַשׁ לְרִכְבּוֹ הֲמוֹן גַּלְגִּלָּיו לֹא הִפְנוּ אָבוֹת אֶל בָּנִים מֵרִפְיוֹן יָדָיִם: [ירמיה מז, ג]

כ) וַיֵּשֶׁב יַעֲקֹב בְּאֶרֶץ מְגוּרֵי אָבִיו בְּאֶרֶץ כְּנָעַן: [בראשית לז, א]

ל) אֵלֶּה תֹּלְדוֹת יַעֲקֹב יוֹסֵף בֶּן שְׁבַע עֶשְׂרֵה שָׁנָה הָיָה רֹעֶה אֶת אֶחָיו בַּצֹּאן וְהוּא נַעַר אֶת בְּנֵי בִלְהָה וְאֶת בְּנֵי זִלְפָּה נְשֵׁי אָבִיו וַיָּבֵא יוֹסֵף אֶת דִּבָּתָם רָעָה אֶל אֲבִיהֶם: [בראשית לז, ב]

מ) וַיֵּשֶׁב יִשְׂרָאֵל בְּאֶרֶץ מִצְרַיִם בְּאֶרֶץ גֹּשֶׁן וַיֵּאָחֲזוּ בָהּ וַיִּפְרוּ וַיִּרְבּוּ מְאֹד: [בראשית מז, כז]

נ) וַיִּקְרְבוּ יְמֵי יִשְׂרָאֵל לָמוּת וַיִּקְרָא לִבְנוֹ לְיוֹסֵף וַיֹּאמֶר לוֹ אִם נָא מָצָאתִי חֵן בְּעֵינֶיךָ שִׂים נָא יָדְךָ תַּחַת יְרֵכִי וְעָשִׂיתָ עִמָּדִי חֶסֶד וֶאֱמֶת אַל נָא תִקְבְּרֵנִי בְּמִצְרָיִם: [בראשית מז, כט]

ס) וַיֵּשֶׁב יְהוּדָה וְיִשְׂרָאֵל לָבֶטַח אִישׁ תַּחַת גַּפְנוֹ וְתַחַת תְּאֵנָתוֹ מִדָּן וְעַד בְּאֵר שָׁבַע כֹּל יְמֵי שְׁלֹמֹה: [מלכים א׳ ה, ה]

ע) וַיָּקֶם יְיָ שָׂטָן לִשְׁלֹמֹה אֵת הֲדַד הָאֲדֹמִי מִזֶּרַע הַמֶּלֶךְ הוּא בֶּאֱדוֹם: [מלכים א׳ יא, יד]

פ) וְאֶת מַלְכֵי מִדְיָן הָרְגוּ עַל חַלְלֵיהֶם אֶת אֱוִי וְאֶת רֶקֶם וְאֶת צוּר וְאֶת חוּר וְאֶת רֶבַע חֲמֵשֶׁת מַלְכֵי מִדְיָן וְאֵת בִּלְעָם בֶּן בְּעוֹר הָרְגוּ בֶּחָרֶב: [במדבר לא, ח]

צ) וְאֶת בִּלְעָם בֶּן בְּעוֹר הַקּוֹסֵם הָרְגוּ בְנֵי יִשְׂרָאֵל בַּחֶרֶב אֶל חַלְלֵיהֶם: [יהושע יג, כב]

ליקוטי רש"י

בירכן בארז. כארזים עלי מים (במדבר כד). **ארז זה אינו עומד במקום מים כו'.** ואף על גב דכתיב בקרא כארזים עלי מים ההוא לאו בלעם קאמר ליה דבלעם אמר כארזים והמלאך השיבו עלי מים וכן כולהו דבלעם אמר כנחלים דזימנין מתייבשין וקאמר ליה המלאך נטיו דאין יבישין לעולם והיינו דכתיב ויהפוך ה' אלהיך לך את הקללה לברכה על ידי מלאך שהושיבו על ידי מלאך. **אפילו כל הרוחות.** שאינן קשות. **רוח דרומית.** שהיא קשה כדאמרינן (בבא בתרא כה:) אילמלא בן נץ שמעמידה אין כל בריה יכולה לעמוד מפניה שנאמר המבינתך יאבר נץ יפרש כנפיו לתימן [תענית כ.]. **וירא את הקיני.** לפי שהיה קיני תקוע אצל עמלק כענין שנאמר ויאמר שאול אל הקיני וגו' (ש"א טו, ו) הזכירו אחר עמלק נסתכל בגדולתן של בני יתרו שנאמר בהם תרעתים שמעתים סוכתים (דה"א ב, נה). **איתן מושבך.** תמה אני מהיכן זכית לכך הלא אתה עמי היית בעצת הבה נתחכמה לו (שמות א, י) ועתה נתישבת באיתן ומעוז של ישראל [במדבר כד, כא]. **באותה עצה.** דנתחכמה לו. **יושבי יעבץ.** תלמידי יעבץ אדם גדול בתורה היה כדכתיב (דה"א ד) ויקרא יעבץ לאלהי ישראל אם ברך תברכני בתורה והרבית את גבולי בתלמידים וגו' ויבא אלהים את אשר שאל (תמורה טז). **תרעתים.** מפרש בספרי ששמעו תרועה בהר סיני נ"א תרעתים על שם שהיו יושבים בשערי ירושלים. **שמעתים.** ששמעו מצות אביהם דבבני יונדב בן רכב משתעי קרא והם היו מבני בניו של יתרו כדמפרש ואזיל המה הקינים. **סוכתים.** על שם שהיו יושבים בסוכות כדכתיב (ירמיהו לה) ונשב באהלים וקרי להו משפחת סופרים דהיינו סנהדרין וכן תרעתים זקני שער [סוטה יא:]. **ישבו בלשכת הגזית.** ממשפחות סופרים והאי קרא מפרש ליה כולו בסיפרי בפרשת ויאמר משה לחובב. **המה הקינים הבאים מחמת אבי בית רכב.** וקינים אלו בניו של יתרו דכתיב ובני קיני חותן משה ובניו של יתרו הן הן בניו של רכב דכתיב הקינים הבאים מחמת אבי בית רכב וכתיב (ירמיהו לה) ולבית הרכבים אמר ירמיהו כי כה אמר ה' [וגו'] יען אשר שמעתם [על] מצות [יהונדב] אביכם [וגו'] לא יכרת איש ליונדב בן רכב [עומד] לפני כל הימים ואמרינן בסיפרי אפשר נכרים הם ונכנסין להיכל והרי כל ישראל לא נכנסו להיכל אלא שהיו יושבין בסנהדרין ומורין בדברי תורה מפי רכי [לעיל קד:]. **מעיר התמרים.** היא יריחו שניתן להם דושנה של יריחו לאוכלה עד שיבנה בית המקדש ומי שיבנה בית הבחירה בחלקו יטלנה כדי שיהא לכל ישראל חלק בבית הבחירה ונתנוה לבני יתרו ת"מ שנה והתלמידים שבהם הניחוה והלכו אצל עתניאל בן קנז הוא יעבץ במדבר יהודה אשר בנגב ערד ללמוד תורה [שופטים א, טז]. **וצים.** ספינות גדולות כדכתיב וצי אדיר (ישעיה לג, כא) תרגומו ובורני רבתא [במדבר כ, כג]. **וצים.** כדמתרגם וליס מיד כתים (במדבר כ"ד) וסיען יסתחרן מרומאי [תהלים עב, ט]. **לכה איעצך.** מה לך לעשות ומה היא העצה אלהיהם של אלו שונא זמה הוא כו' כדאיתא בחלק (סנהדרין קו.) תדע שבלעם השיא עצה זו להכשילם בזמה שהרי נאמר הן הנה היו לבני ישראל בדבר בלעם (לקמן לא, טז). **אשר יעשה העם הזה לעמך.** מקרא קצר הוא זה איעצך להכשילם ואומר לך מה שהן עתידין להרע למואב באחרית הימים [במדבר כד, יד]. **וינזרו.** אין נזירה בכל מקום אלא לשון פרישה. **לבושת.** לעכו"ם שהיא בשתם. **ויהי שקוצים.** לפני. **כאהבם.** את בנות מואב [הושע ט, י]. **בדברי שטות.** לזנות את בנות מואב. **ערומות פגעו בהן.** ותקראן משמע גופן היה פוגע בהן. **שנעשו כולן בעלי קריין** ולשון מקרה הוא. **שריפו עצמן כו'.** לפיכך בא עליהם עמלק. **לא הפנו אבות אל בנים מרפיון ידים.** מכאן שריפו ידיהם מן התורה [בכורות ה:]. **בשטים.** כך שמה. **לזנות אל בנות מואב.** על ידי עצת בלעם כדאיתא בחלק [במדבר כה, א]. **מאי בעי התם.** בלעם הלך שם ליטול שכר עשרים וארבעה אלף שהפיל מישראל בעצתו ויצא ממדין לקראת ישראל ומשיאן עצה רעה אמר להם אם כשהייתם ששים רבוא לא יכולתם להם ועכשיו בי"ב אלף אתם באים להלחם נתנו לו שכרו משלם ולא קפחוהו [במדבר לא, ח]. **ולבסוף קוסם.** איזהו קוסם האוחז את מקלו ואומר אם אלך אם לא אלך וכן הוא אומר עמי בעצו ישאל ומקלו יגיד לו (הושע ד, יב) [דברים יח, י].

א) הרגו בני ישראל [בחרב] אל חלליהם אמר רב שקיימו בו ארבע מיתות סקילה ושריפה הרג וחנק א"ל ההוא מינא לר' חנינא מי שמיע לך בלעם בר כמה הוה א"ל מיכתב לא כתיב אלא מדכתיב ב) אנשי דמים ומרמה לא יחצו ימיהם בר תלתין ותלת שנין או בר תלתין וארבע א"ל שפיר קאמרת לדידי חזי לי פנקסיה דבלעם והוה כתיב ביה בר תלתין ותלת שנין בלעם חגירא כד קטיל יתיה פנחס ליסטאה א"ל מר בריה דרבינא לבריה בכולהו לא תפיש למדרש לבר מבלעם הרשע דכמה דמשכחת ביה דרוש ביה כתיב ג) דואג וכתיב ד) דוייג אמר ר' יוחנן בתחילה יושב הקב"ה ודואג שמא יצא זה לתרבות רעה לאחר שיצא אמר ווי שיצא זה (סימן גבור ורשע וצדיק חיל וסופר) א"ר יצחק מאי דכתיב ה) מה תתהלל ברעה הגבור חסד אל כל היום אמר לו הקב"ה לדואג לא גבור בתורה אתה מה תתהלל ברעה לא חסד אל נטוי עליך כל היום וא"ר יצחק מאי דכתיב ו) ולרשע אמר אלהים מה לך לספר חוקי אמר לו הקב"ה לדואג הרשע מה לך לספר חוקי כשאתה מגיע לפרשת מרצחים ופרשת מספרי לשון הרע מה אתה דורש בהם ו) ותשא בריתי עלי פיך אמר ר' אמי אין תורתו של דואג אלא משפה ולחוץ ואמר רבי יצחק מאי דכתיב ז) ויראו צדיקים וייראו ועליו ישחקו בתחילה ייראו ולבסוף ישחקו וא"ר יצחק מאי דכתיב ח) חיל בלע ויקיאנו מבטנו יורישנו אל אמר דוד לפני הקב"ה רבש"ע ימות דואג אמר לו חיל בלע ויקיאנו אמר לפניו מבטנו יורישנו אל וא"ר יצחק מאי דכתיב ט) גם אל יתצך לנצח אמר הקב"ה לדוד ניתי דואג לעלמא דאתי אמר לפניו גם אל יתצך לנצח א) מאי דכתיב ט) יחתך ויסחך מאהל ושרשך מארץ חיים סלה אמר הקב"ה לימרו שמעתא בי מדרשא משמיה אמר לפניו יחתך ויסחך מאהל ליהוי ליה בנין רבנן ושרשך מארץ חיים סלה וא"ר יצחק ב) מאי דכתיב י) איה סופר איה שוקל איה סופר את המגדלים איה סופר כל אותיות שבתורה איה שוקל ששוקל כל קלים וחמורים שבתורה איה סופר את המגדלים שהיה סופר שלש מאות הלכות פסוקות במגדל הפורח באויר ג) א"ר ארבע מאה בעיי' בעו דואג ואחיתופל במגדל הפורח באויר [ולא איפשט להו חד] אמר רבא רבותא למבעי בעיי ד) בשני דרב יהודה כולי תנויי בנזיקין ואנן קא מתנינן טובא ה) בעוקצין וכי הוה מטי רב יהודה ו) אשה שכובשת ירק בקדירה ואמרי לה ז) זיתים שכבשן בטרפיהן טהורים אמר הויות דרב ושמואל קא חזינא הכא ואנן קא מתנינן בעוקצין תלת סרי מתיבתא ורב יהודה שליף מסאני ואתא מטרא ואנן צוחינן וליכא דמשגח בן אלא הקב"ה ליבא בעי דכתיב כ) וה' יראה ללבב אמר רב משרשיא דואג ואחיתופל לא [הוו] סברי שמעתא מתקיף לה מר זוטרא מאן דכתיב איה סופר איה שוקל איה סופר את המגדלים ואת אמרת לא הוו סברי שמעתא אלא דלא הוה סלקא להו שמעתא אליבא דהלכתא דכתיב ל) סוד ה' ליראיו א"ר אמי לא מת דואג עד ששכח תלמודו שנא' מ) הוא ימות באין מוסר וברוב אולתו ישגה רב (אשי) אמר נצטרע שנאמר נ) הצמתה כל זונה ממך כתיב התם ס) לצמיתות ומתרגמינן לחלוטין ח) ותנן אין בין מוסגר ומוחלט אלא פריעה ופרימה (סימן שלשה ראו וחצי וקראו) א"ר יוחנן שלשה מלאכי חבלה נזדמנו לו לדואג אחד ששכח תלמודו ואחד ששרף נשמתו ואחד שפיזר עפרו בבתי כנסיות ובבתי מדרשות (ט) א"ר) יוחנן דואג ואחיתופל לא ראו זה את זה דואג בימי שאול ואחיתופל בימי דוד וא"ר יוחנן דואג ואחיתופל לא חצו ימיהם תניא נמי הכי ב) אנשי דמים ומרמה לא יחצו ימיהם י) כל שנותיו של דואג לא היו אלא שלשים וארבע ושל אחיתופל אינן אלא שלשים ושלש וא"ר יוחנן בתחלה קרא דוד לאחיתופל רבו ולבסוף קראו חבירו ולבסוף קראו תלמידו בתחילה ע) קראו רבו ע) ואתה אנוש כערכי אלופי ומיודעי ולבסוף קראו חבירו פ) אשר יחדו נמתיק סוד בבית אלהים נהלך ברגש ולבסוף קראו ל) תלמידו צ) גם איש שלומי אשר בטחתי בו אוכל

הרגו אל חלליהם. מיתות הרבה משמע שתלאוהו והכיתו אש תחת הצליבה וחתכו ראשו ונפל לתוך האש תלייה היינו חנק חתיכת הראש הרג כשנפל לארץ סקילה כשנפל לאור היינו שריפה: בר תלתין ותלת. ור"ח לית ליה דר' סימאי דאמר לעיל שלשה היו באותה עצה דפרעה בלעם ואיוב ויתרו דלר' סימאי בלעם חיה יותר מן מאתים ועשר שנים דהא היה בעצת פרעה דכל הבן הילוד היאורה תשליכוהו דלרבי סימאי כל אותן מאתים ועשר שנים שהיו ישראל בגלות מצרים עד מלחמת מדין חיה בלעם: חגירא. תרגום של פיסח: כד קטל יתיה פנחס ליסטאה. שר צבא ואפילו קטליה אחר כל המלחמה נקראת על שמו: בכולהו. מלכים והדיוטות: לא תפיש ותדרוש. לגנאי: לבר מבלעם. דכל מה דמשכחת ליה לגנאי דרוש: (מ) שמא יצא זה לתרבות רעה) לאחר שיצא לתרבות רעה אמר ווי. לכך כתוב דוייג: א"ל הקב"ה לדואג והלא גבור אתה בתורה. למה תתהלל לספר לשון הרע על דוד: לא חסד תורה עליך. לא חכם בתורה אתה דכתיב (משלי לא) ותורת חסד על לשונה: מרצחים. שהרג נוב: עלי פיך. ולא בלב: בתחלה ייראו. הצדיקים היו יראים שלא ילמד אדם ממעשיו של דואג שהולך וחוטא ומצליח: ולבסוף. כשמת בחצי ימיו ושב גמולו בראשו ישחקו: חיל בלע ויקיאנו. המתן עד שתשכח תורתו: אמר לפניו ומבטנו יורישנו אל. אל תמתין לו עד שתשתכח אלא תמהר ותשכיחנו: בי מדרשא. מאהל זה בית המדרש: ושרשך מארץ חיים סלה. שורש שלו תכסח מארץ חיים דלא להוו ליה בנין רבנן: כל אותיות שבתורה. שהיה בקי בחסירות ויתירות: שוקל קלים וחמורים. יודע לדרוש בקל וחומר: במגדל הפורח באויר. מתג עליונה שלמעלה מן הלמ"ד מפני מה כפופה למטה. לשון מ"ר מפי השמועה. ל"א במגדל הפורח באויר הנכנס לארץ העמים בשידה תיבה ומגדל אם הוא טמא אם לאו. ל"א ג' מאות הלכות במגדל הפורח באויר לעשות כישוף להעמיד מגדל באויר כגון שלש מאות הלכות בנטיעות קשואין דאמרן בפירקין דלעיל (דף סח.) ולמורי נראה דה"ג שלש מאות הלכות במגדל העומד [באויר] ומשנה אחת באהלות (פ"ד משנה א) דמשתעי בהכי מגדל העומד באויר וטומאה בתוכה כלים שבתוכו טמאים וכן נראה לר': רבותא למבעא בעיי. וללמוד תורה רחמנא לבא בעי דהא בשני דרב יהודה כולהו תנויי בסדר נזיקין היה כל הגמרא שלהן לא הוה אלא בסדר נזיקין שלא היו מרבין כל כך [לדרוש]: האשה שכובשת ירק בקדירה. לא אשכחתיה במסכת עוקלין: שכובשת ירק. בחומץ או בציר טהורים דאין מקבלין טומאה ע"י עוקלין שאם נגע טומאה בשרשיו העלין טהורין שאין נעשין יד לעלין מאחר שכבשם שאין מניחין לשם אלא למראה: זיתים שכבשן בטרפיהן. איתא במסכת עוקלין (פ"ב מ"א): טרפיהן. עלין שלהן טהורין הזיתים שאין נעשין להם בית יד להכניס להם טומאה: הויות דרב ושמואל קא חזינא הכא. דלא הוה ידע מאי טעמא הן טהורין: תליסר מתיבתא. י"ג ישיבות שאנו עוסקין כולן במסכת עוקלין ויודעין אותה יפה ואפי' הכי בהם היו חסידים יותר ממנו דאלו רב יהודה כו': לא סבירי. לא היו יודעין הלכה לפרשה כתקנה בטעמא: דלא סלקא להו שמעתא כו'. שלא זכו לקבוע הלכה כמותן: ומתרגמינן לחלוטין. ואנן תנן לשון חלוטין גבי מצורע: אלופי. היינו רבי: אוכל

עין משפט נר מצוה

לא א מיי' פ"י מהל' טומאת צרעת הל' י:

תורה אור השלם

א) וְאֶת בִּלְעָם בֶּן בְּעוֹר הַקּוֹסֵם הָרְגוּ בְנֵי יִשְׂרָאֵל בַּחֶרֶב אֶל חַלְלֵיהֶם: [יהושע יג, כב]

ב) וְאַתָּה אֱלֹהִים תּוֹרִדֵם לִבְאֵר שַׁחַת אַנְשֵׁי דָמִים וּמִרְמָה לֹא יֶחֱצוּ יְמֵיהֶם וַאֲנִי אֶבְטַח בָּךְ: [תהלים נה, כד]

ג) וְשָׁם אִישׁ מֵעַבְדֵי שָׁאוּל בַּיּוֹם הַהוּא נֶעְצָר לִפְנֵי יְיָ וּשְׁמוֹ דֹּאֵג הָאֲדֹמִי אַבִּיר הָרֹעִים אֲשֶׁר לְשָׁאוּל: [שמואל א' כא, ח]

ד) וַיֹּאמֶר הַמֶּלֶךְ לְדוֹאֵג (לדויג) סֹב אַתָּה וּפְגַע בַּכֹּהֲנִים וַיִּסֹּב דּוֹאֵג הָאֲדֹמִי וַיִּפְגַּע הוּא בַּכֹּהֲנִים וַיָּמֶת בַּיּוֹם הַהוּא שְׁמֹנִים וַחֲמִשָּׁה אִישׁ נֹשֵׂא אֵפוֹד בָּד: [שמואל א' כב, יח]

ה) מַה תִּתְהַלֵּל בְּרָעָה הַגִּבּוֹר חֶסֶד אֵל כָּל הַיּוֹם: [תהלים נב, ג]

ו) וְלָרָשָׁע אָמַר אֱלֹהִים מַה לְּךָ לְסַפֵּר חֻקָּי וַתִּשָּׂא בְרִיתִי עֲלֵי פִיךָ: [תהלים נ, טז]

ז) וְיִרְאוּ צַדִּיקִים וְיִירָאוּ וְעָלָיו יִשְׂחָקוּ: [תהלים נב, ח]

ח) חַיִל בָּלַע וַיְקִאֶנּוּ מִבִּטְנוֹ יֹרִשֶׁנּוּ אֵל: [איוב כ, טו]

ט) גַּם אֵל יִתָּצְךָ לָנֶצַח יַחְתְּךָ וְיִסָּחֲךָ מֵאֹהֶל וְשֵׁרֶשְׁךָ מֵאֶרֶץ חַיִּים סֶלָה: [תהלים נב, ז]

י) לִבְּךָ יֶהְגֶּה אֵימָה אַיֵּה סֹפֵר אַיֵּה שֹׁקֵל אַיֵּה סֹפֵר אֶת הַמִּגְדָּלִים: [ישעיה לג, יח]

כ) וַיֹּאמֶר יְיָ אֶל שְׁמוּאֵל אַל תַּבֵּט אֶל מַרְאֵהוּ וְאֶל גְּבֹהַּ קוֹמָתוֹ כִּי מְאַסְתִּיהוּ כִּי לֹא אֲשֶׁר יִרְאֶה הָאָדָם כִּי הָאָדָם יִרְאֶה לַעֵינַיִם וַיְיָ יִרְאֶה לַלֵּבָב: [שמואל א' טז, ז]

ל) סוֹד יְיָ לִירֵאָיו וּבְרִיתוֹ לְהוֹדִיעָם: [תהלים כה, יד]

מ) הוּא יָמוּת בְּאֵין מוּסָר וּבְרֹב אִוַּלְתּוֹ יִשְׁגֶּה: [משלי ה, כג]

נ) כִּי הִנֵּה רְחֵקֶיךָ יֹאבֵדוּ הִצְמַתָּה כָּל זוֹנֶה מִמֶּךָּ: [תהלים עג, כז]

ס) וְהָאָרֶץ לֹא תִמָּכֵר לִצְמִתֻת כִּי לִי הָאָרֶץ כִּי גֵרִים וְתוֹשָׁבִים אַתֶּם עִמָּדִי: [ויקרא כה, כג]

ע) וְאַתָּה אֱנוֹשׁ כְּעֶרְכִּי אַלּוּפִי וּמְיֻדָּעִי: [תהלים נה, יד]

פ) אֲשֶׁר יַחְדָּו נַמְתִּיק סוֹד בְּבֵית אֱלֹהִים נְהַלֵּךְ בְּרָגֶשׁ: [תהלים נה, טו]

צ) גַּם אִישׁ שְׁלוֹמִי אֲשֶׁר בָּטַחְתִּי בוֹ אוֹכֵל לַחְמִי הִגְדִּיל עָלַי עָקֵב: [תהלים מא, י]

מסורת הש"ס

א) [עי' תוספתא בע"י], ב) [חגיגה טו:], ג) נ"א א"ר אמי, ד) תענית כד: ע"ש ברכות כ. ע"ש, ה) נ"א בשיתא סידרי, ו) [טהרות פ"ב מ"א], ז) [עוקצ' פ"ב מ"א], ח) מגילה ח: ערכין טו:, ט) [נ"ל ואמר ר'], י) לעיל סט:, כ) [אבות פ"ו מ"ג], ל) בילקוט ח"ב סוף רמז תשמא הגירסא ולבסוף קראו איש, מ) רש"ל מ"ז.

ליקוטי רש"י

מה תתהלל. ותתפאר ברעה שאתה עושה אתה הגבור בתורה. חסד אל כל היום. להציל את הנרדף על ידך [תהלים נב, ג]. ועליו ישחקו. וזה השחוק שיאמרו עליו הנה זה הגבר אשר לא שם מבטחו בהקב"ה ראו מה עלתה בו [תהלים נב, ח]. יתצך. ל' נתיצה. יחתך. לשון שבירה. ויסחך. ויעקרך. ושרשך. ישרש אחריך לעקור כל השרשים דירא"ריצינע"ר בלעז [שם ז]. קלים וחמורים. דברים הלמדין בקל וחומר שניתנו לדון מעצמן לכל אדם ולא פירשו כלום בסיני [סוכה כח.]. קלים וחמורים שאדם דן מעצמו [ב"ב קלד.]. הלכות פסוקות. הלכה כפלוני ופלוני [יבמות מב:]. במגדל הפורח באויר. יש מפרשים שדורשין גוגהו של למ"ד ודורשין בו כל זאת ויש אומרים מגדל דור הפלגה ולי נראה מגדל הפתוח לאויר גרסינן והן מהלכות אהלות מגדל של עץ שקורין משטיי"ר ועומד בפתח ופתחו פתוח לבקעה או לחצר שהוא אויר במסכת אהלות (פרק רביעי משנה א) ישנה משנה מגדל העומד באויר [חגיגה טו:]. בנזיקין הוה. למודם לא היה גדול אלא בסדר נזיקין. שכובשת ירק בקדירה. במסכת [טהרות] היא בפרק שני (משנה א') גבי ידות מיירי דקיימא לן (עוקלין פ"א מ"א) כל ידות האוכלין אם נגעה טומאה בהן נטמא גם האוכל הצריך לידות, דיד מכנים ומוציא כדאמרינן בהעור והרוטב (חולין קיח.) מכל האוכל לרבות הידות וקתני התם אשה שהיא כובשת ירק דידות שלהן טהורין דכשהיא עוצרת אותם הידות משתברות ואי אפשר ליטול הירקות בידות שלהן שנשמט ונפסק האוכל מן היד מחמת כבישה. כובשת. שול"ץ בלע"ז עוצרת שיצא המשקה שלהן ויבשו דרך אשה בכך כובשת ירק ממים שישתמרו לזמן מרובה טהורין העלין והקלחין. ואמרי לה. כי מטא לאידך בפרק שני (דעוקלין מ"א) זיתים שכבשן בטרפיהן כתרגומו עלה טרפא (בראשית ח) עלין שלהן דהיינו ידות. טהורים. הידות להביא טומאה לאוכל דתו לא חזי למהוי בית יד. הוויות דרב ושמואל. עומק גדול ולא הוה נהירא ליה.

תליסר מתיבתא. שלש עשרה ישיבות אלא בהך מתא דגמרי מסכת עוקלין. שליף חד מסאנא. משום עינוי. דחזא מידי. חס ושלום בעובדי בישי [תענית כד:]. בנזיקין הוה. לא היו גדולים בכל גמרא של ארבעה סדרים אלא בתלתא בבי. האשה שכובשת ירק או זיתים שכבשן בטרפיהן. מסכת עוקלין. טהורים. שמוקקין זיתים עם העלין כדי לאחזן בהן דהוו להו עלין יד לזיתים להביא להם טומאה כדאמרינן בהעור והרוטב (דף קי"ח.) שהיד מביאה טומאה על האוכל ואם כבשן בטרפיהן בטלה תורת יד מן העלין לפי שהכבישה מרקבתן ומרככתן ואינן ראוין שוב לאחוז בהן. הוויות דרב ושמואל קא חזינא הכא. כלומר טעם המשניות הללו קשה עלי ככל הקושיות שהיו שם רבותי מתקשין בהן בכל הגמרא. בתליסר מתיבתא. בשלש עשרה פנים יש ביינו משנה וברייתא של ששה סדרים ומסכת עוקלין גם היא בשלש עשרה פנים כגון משנת רבי ורבי חייא ומשנת בר קפרא ולוי ותנא דבי שמואל והכי אמרינן במסכת נדרים (דף מ"א.) רבי מתני הלכתא בשלש עשרה פנים [ברכות כ.]. לצמתת. לפסיקה למכירה פסוקה עולמית [ויקרא כה, כג]. פריעה ופרימה. בגדיו יהיו פרומים וראשו יהי פרוע. מוחלט. לאחר שכלו ימי ההסגר ונראה בו סימני טומאה שאמורין בו [מגילה ח:].

,,הָרְגוּ בְנֵי־יִשְׂרָאֵל [בַּחֶרֶב] אֶל־חַלְלֵיהֶם״ – *And Bilam the son of Beor, the sorcerer,* ***the Children of Israel slew by the sword with their slayings.***[1] אָמַר רַב – **Rav said:** שֶׁקִּיְּימוּ בּוֹ אַרְבַּע מִיתוֹת – The phrase *with their slayings* indicates **that [the Jews] carried out on [Bilam] the four executions** prescribed under Torah law: סְקִילָה וּשְׂרֵיפָה הֶרֶג וָחֶנֶק – **stoning, burning, beheading and strangulation.**[2]

אָמַר לֵיהּ הַהוּא מִינָא לְרַבִּי חֲנִינָא – **A certain heretic** once **said to R' Chanina:** מִי שְׁמִיעַ לָךְ בִּלְעָם בַּר כַּמָּה הֲוָה – **Have you heard how old Bilam was** when he was killed? אָמַר לֵיהּ – **[R' Chanina] said to [the heretic]:** מִיכְתַּב לֹא כְּתִיב – As far as anything being **written** in Scripture about Bilam's age, **nothing is written.** אֶלָּא מִדִּכְתִיב ,,אַנְשֵׁי דָמִים וּמִרְמָה לֹא־יֶחֱצוּ יְמֵיהֶם״ – **However from that which is written:**[3] ***Men of bloodshed and deceit shall not live out half their days,*** בַּר תְּלָתִין וּתְלַת שְׁנִין אוֹ בַּר תְּלָתִין וְאַרְבַּע – it stands to reason that he lived less than half a normal life span, that is, he was **thirty-three years old or** maybe **thirty-four.**[4] אָמַר לֵיהּ – **[The heretic] said to [R' Chanina]:** שַׁפִּיר קָאָמְרַת – **You have spoken well!** לְדִידִי חָזֵי לִי פִּנְקְסֵיהּ דְּבִלְעָם וַהֲוָה כְּתִיב בֵּיהּ – **I myself saw the chronicle of Bilam, and it was written therein:** בַּר תְּלָתִין וּתְלַת שְׁנִין בִּלְעָם חֲגִירָא כַּד קָטִיל יָתֵיהּ פִּנְחָס לִיסְטָאָה – **"Bilam the lame was thirty-three years old when he was killed by Pinchas the outlaw."**[5]

The Gemara concludes its discussion of Bilam with one final teaching:

אָמַר לֵיהּ מַר בְּרֵיהּ דְּרָבִינָא לִבְרֵיהּ – **Mar the son of Ravina said to his son:** בְּכוּלְּהוּ לֹא תַּפִּישׁ לְמִדְרַשׁ – **Concerning all** the kings and commoners listed in our Mishnah as having no share in the World to Come, **do not expatiate,** i.e. do not extend yourself to expound Scriptural hints about them in a derogatory fashion. לְבַר מִבִּלְעָם הָרָשָׁע – **The exception is the wicked Bilam:** דְּכַמָּה דְּמַשְׁכַּחַתְּ בֵּיהּ דְּרוֹשׁ בֵּיהּ – **Whatever derogatory** hints **you can discover about him** in Scripture **you should expound.**[6]

Having concluded its discussion of Bilam, the Gemara turns to the second of the four commoners listed in our Mishnah as having no share in the World to Come, Doeg.[7] The Gemara begins

NOTES

1. *Joshua* 13:22.

2. *With their slayings* suggests that Bilam suffered all the forms of slaying found among Jews, i.e. Bilam was hanged on a stake beneath which a fire was kindled, and as he was hanging he was beheaded and fell into the surrounding blaze. Thus, he suffered all four forms of execution: (a) he suffered strangulation as he hung (חֶנֶק), (b) he was beheaded (הֶרֶג), (c) he fell from the noose to the ground [just as one who is stoned is first pushed off from a height] (סְקִילָה), and (d) his body was consumed by the blaze (שְׂרֵיפָה) (*Rashi*).

Yad Ramah, however, disagrees with the foregoing explanation, for once Bilam was beheaded he was dead, and the Gemara states that he was *executed* four ways. Instead, *Yad Ramah* explains that all four punishments were carried out upon Bilam *simultaneously,* i.e. scarves were tied around his throat and pulled in opposite directions at the same moment that hot lead was poured down his throat and a stone was cast at him. Also, at that very moment he was beheaded. See also *Ben Yehoyada.* Cf. *Maharsha.*

3. *Psalms* 55:24.

4. Half of the normal life span of seventy years.

Maharal suggests that men of bloodshed and deceit do not really deserve to live at all. At the very least, it is not fitting that they should live the majority of a normal life span. Alternatively, *Maharsha* suggests that it can be assumed that one who has not repented by midlife will not do so during the second half of his life as well. There is therefore no purpose in his continuing to live.

This opinion of R' Chanina – that Bilam died in his thirties – obviously disagrees with the view of R' Simai cited on 106a that Bilam was one of Pharaoh's counselors at the time the decree was issued to throw the Jewish babies into the river, for that incident occurred at least a century before Bilam's death (see *Rashi*). [Actually, *Rashi* states that the meeting of Pharaoh's counselors occurred at the very beginning of the two-hundred-and-ten-year sojourn of the Israelites in Egypt. However, this is extremely puzzling, for it is clear from Scripture that, at the very earliest, any persecution of the Israelites did not commence until Joseph's death, seventy-one years after the Israelites came to Egypt. See *Maharshal* and *Ben Yehoyada* here, *Rashash* to *Bamidbar Rabbah* 20:14, note 24; cf. *Daas Zekeinim MiBaalei HaTosafos* to *Exodus* 1:10.]

5. The Gemara on 105a states that Bilam was lame.

Pinchas was the commander of the invading Israelite army. Thus, even if it was some other soldier who killed Bilam, since that soldier was under Pinchas' command it is considered as if Pinchas killed Bilam (*Rashi*).

6. In his *Maamar al Aggados* (printed at the beginning of the first volume of *Ein Yaakov*), *R' Moshe Chaim Luzzato* explains that when expounding verses in Scripture, the Sages followed specific guidelines known to them by tradition. (Many of these guidelines are no longer known to us, and it is for this reason that the Talmudic expositions may sometimes appear arbitrary to us. See also *Kuzari* III:73.) One known guideline states that within a section in Scripture that deals with a wicked person, all the hints and nuances concerning him are to be expounded in a derogatory fashion. Conversely, in a section about a righteous individual, the Scriptural nuances are to be expounded as complimentary. (Of course, even within these guidelines the sage must apply other exegetical rules to arrive at the correct exposition. However, one who expounds something complimentary about a wicked man or derogatory about a righteous individual is certainly missing the mark.) Thus, Mar the son of Ravina told his son that within the section concerning the wicked Bilam he should expound any and all references to Bilam in a disparaging manner. See also *Mevo HaAggados* by *Maharatz Chayes* ד״ה ואולם בפעלי הרשעים (also printed in *Ein Yaakov* ibid.).

Regarding the other kings and commoners in our Mishnah, since they were not as thoroughly wicked as Bilam, Mar instructed his son not to be as diligent in expounding hints to their faults. Alternatively, *Iyun Yaakov* suggests that Mar's instruction regarding the other kings and commoners is in line with the opinion of the "Interpreters of Verses" mentioned on 104b that these six individuals ultimately were admitted to the World to Come.

7. Doeg's sin is described in *I Samuel* chs. 21-22 and has been recounted above, on 104a note 8. In brief, it was Doeg who had informed Saul that the Kohanim of Nov had given aid to David as he fled from Saul. Indeed, the Kohanim had been unaware that David was a fugitive. Nevertheless, their protestations of innocence notwithstanding, Saul ordered all the Kohanim put to death for treason. Avner and Amasah, Saul's aides, refused to carry out the death sentence, for they knew that the Kohanim were innocent. It was Doeg himself who ultimately followed Saul's order and massacred the inhabitants of Nov, in retribution for a sin that they did not commit, but that he had fabricated. Thus, Doeg was a mass-murderer as well as a vicious slanderer, both of which are excluded from a share in the World to Come (see *Midrash Tanchuma, Metzora* §1-2 and *Midrash Shocher Tov, Psalms* 52; see also *Rambam, Hil. Teshuvah* 3:6 and *Hil. Dei'os* 7:1-3).

The Midrash (*Yalkut Shimoni, I Samuel* §131) adds some detail to the account of Doeg's sin. Doeg claimed that by inquiring of the *Urim VeTumim* David had committed treason, and by allowing him to inquire Achimelech had committed treason, for only a king is permitted to make inquiries of the *Urim VeTumim.* However, Avner and Amasa claimed that anyone who is indispensable to the Congregation of Israel, as David was, is permitted to make such inquiries. They therefore refused to carry out the sentences of death that Saul had imposed on the Kohanim. Doeg took the question to all the Rabbinical courts and they agreed unanimously with Avner and Amasa. Nevertheless, Doeg massacred the Kohanim, insisting that his view of the halachah was correct. As the Gemara states below, although Doeg was a great scholar, he did not merit to arrive at correct halachic rulings. In this case, he compounded that fault by rejecting the unanimous ruling of his fellows.

For accounts of other occasions on which Doeg slandered David, see above, 93b and *Yevamos* 76b. See also note 53.

Rambam, in his *Commentary* to our Mishnah, states that Doeg lost his share in the World to Come because he was a heretic. For an example of Doeg's heresy, see the end of note 53. See also *Arachin* 15b.

עין משפט נר מצוה

לא א מיי' פ"י מהל' טומאת צרעת הל' י:

תורה אור השלם

א) וְאֶת בִּלְעָם בֶּן בְּעוֹר הַקּוֹסֵם הָרְגוּ בְנֵי יִשְׂרָאֵל בַּחֶרֶב אֶל חַלְלֵיהֶם: [יהושע יג, כב]

ב) וְאַתָּה אֱלֹהִים תּוֹרִדֵם לִבְאֵר שַׁחַת אַנְשֵׁי דָמִים וּמִרְמָה לֹא יֶחֱצוּ יְמֵיהֶם וַאֲנִי אֶבְטַח בָּךְ: [תהלים נה, כד]

ג) וְשָׁם אִישׁ מֵעַבְדֵי שָׁאוּל בַּיּוֹם הַהוּא נֶעְצָר לִפְנֵי יְיָ וּשְׁמוֹ דֹּאֵג הָאֲדֹמִי אַבִּיר הָרֹעִים אֲשֶׁר לְשָׁאוּל: [שמואל א' כא, ח]

ד) וַיֹּאמֶר הַמֶּלֶךְ לְדוֹאֵג (לדויג) סֹב אַתָּה וּפְגַע בַּכֹּהֲנִים וַיִּסֹּב דּוֹאֵג הָאֲדֹמִי וַיִּפְגַּע הוּא בַּכֹּהֲנִים וַיָּמֶת בַּיּוֹם הַהוּא שְׁמֹנִים וַחֲמִשָּׁה אִישׁ נֹשֵׂא אֵפוֹד בָּד: [שמואל א' כב, יח]

ה) מַה תִּתְהַלֵּל בְּרָעָה הַגִּבּוֹר חֶסֶד אֵל כָּל הַיּוֹם: [תהלים נב, ג]

ו) וְלָרָשָׁע אָמַר אֱלֹהִים מַה לְּךָ לְסַפֵּר חֻקָּי וַתִּשָּׂא בְרִיתִי עֲלֵי פִיךָ: [תהלים נ, טז]

ז) וְיִרְאוּ צַדִּיקִים וְיִירָאוּ וְעָלָיו יִשְׂחָקוּ: [תהלים נב, ח]

ח) חַיִל בָּלַע וַיְקִאֶנּוּ מִבִּטְנוֹ יֹרִשֶׁנּוּ אֵל: [איוב כ, טו]

ט) גַּם אֵל יִתָּצְךָ לָנֶצַח יַחְתְּךָ וְיִסָּחֲךָ מֵאֹהֶל וְשֵׁרֶשְׁךָ מֵאֶרֶץ חַיִּים סֶלָה: [תהלים נב, ז]

י) לִבְּךָ יֶהְגֶּה אֵימָה אַיֵּה סֹפֵר אַיֵּה שֹׁקֵל אַיֵּה סֹפֵר אֶת הַמִּגְדָּלִים: [ישעיה לג, יח]

כ) וַיֹּאמֶר יְיָ אֶל שְׁמוּאֵל אַל תַּבֵּט אֶל מַרְאֵהוּ וְאֶל גְּבֹהַּ קוֹמָתוֹ כִּי מְאַסְתִּיהוּ כִּי לֹא אֲשֶׁר יִרְאֶה הָאָדָם כִּי הָאָדָם יִרְאֶה לַעֵינַיִם וַיְיָ יִרְאֶה לַלֵּבָב: [שמואל א' טז, ז]

ל) סוֹד יְיָ לִירֵאָיו וּבְרִיתוֹ לְהוֹדִיעָם: [תהלים כה, יד]

מ) הוּא יָמוּת בְּאֵין מוּסָר וּבְרֹב אִוַּלְתּוֹ יִשְׁגֶּה: [משלי ה, כג]

נ) כִּי הִנֵּה רְחֵקֶיךָ יֹאבֵדוּ הִצְמַתָּה כָּל זוֹנֶה מִמֶּךָּ: [תהלים עג, כז]

ס) וְהָאָרֶץ לֹא תִמָּכֵר לִצְמִתֻת כִּי לִי הָאָרֶץ כִּי גֵרִים וְתוֹשָׁבִים אַתֶּם עִמָּדִי: [ויקרא כה, כג]

ע) וְאַתָּה אֱנוֹשׁ כְּעֶרְכִּי אַלּוּפִי וּמְיֻדָּעִי: [תהלים נה, יד]

פ) אֲשֶׁר יַחְדָּו נַמְתִּיק סוֹד בְּבֵית אֱלֹהִים נְהַלֵּךְ בְּרָגֶשׁ: [תהלים נה, טו]

צ) גַּם אִישׁ שְׁלוֹמִי אֲשֶׁר בָּטַחְתִּי בוֹ אוֹכֵל לַחְמִי הִגְדִּיל עָלַי עָקֵב: [תהלים מא, י]

א) הרגו בני ישראל [בחרב] אל חלליהם אמר רב שקיימו בו ארבע מיתות סקילה ושריפה הרג וחנק א"ל ההוא מינא לר' חנינא מי שמיע לך בלעם בר כמה הוה א"ל מיכתב לא כתיב אלא מדכתיב ב) אנשי דמים ומרמה לא יחצו ימיהם בר תלתין ותלת שנין או בר תלתין וארבע א"ל שפיר קאמרת לדידי חזי לי פנקסיה דבלעם והוה כתיב ביה בר תלתין ותלת שנין בלעם חגירא כד קטיל יתיה פנחס ליסטאה א"ל מר בריה דרבינא לבריה בכולהו לא תפיש למדרש לבר מבלעם הרשע דכמה דמשכחת ביה דרוש ביה כתיב ג) דואג וכתיב ד) דוייג אמר ר' יוחנן בתחילה יושב הקב"ה ודואג שמא יצא זה לתרבות רעה לאחר שיצא אמר ווי שיצא זה (סימן גבור ורשע וצדיק חיל וסופר) א"ר יצחק מאי דכתיב ה) מה תתהלל ברעה הגבור חסד אל כל היום אמר לו הקב"ה לדואג לא גבור בתורה אתה מה תתהלל ברעה לא חסד אל נטוי עליך כל היום וא"ר יצחק מאי דכתיב ו) ולרשע אמר אלהים מה לך לספר חוקי אמר לו הקב"ה לדואג הרשע מה לך לספר חוקי כשאתה מגיע לפרשת מרצחים ופרשת מספרי לשון הרע מה אתה דורש בהם ו) ותשא בריתי עלי פיך אמר ר' אמי אין תורתו של דואג אלא משפה ולחוץ ואמר רבי יצחק מאי דכתיב ז) ויראו צדיקים וייראו ועליו ישחקו בתחילה ייראו ולבסוף ישחקו וא"ר יצחק מאי דכתיב ח) חיל בלע ויקיאנו מבטנו יורישנו אל אמר דוד לפני הקב"ה רבש"ע ימות דואג אמר לו חיל בלע ויקיאנו אמר לפניו מבטנו יורישנו אל וא"ר יצחק מאי דכתיב ט) גם אל יתצך לנצח אמר הקב"ה לדוד ניתי דואג לעלמא דאתי אמר לפניו גם אל יתצך לנצח א) מאי דכתיב ט) יחתך ויסחך מאהל ושרשך מארץ חיים סלה אמר הקב"ה לימרו שמעתא בי מדרשא משמיה אמר לפניו יחתך ויסחך מאהל ליהוי ליה בנין רבנן ושרשך מארץ חיים סלה וא"ר יצחק ב) מאי דכתיב י) איה סופר איה שוקל איה סופר את המגדלים איה סופר כל אותיות שבתורה איה שוקל ששוקל כל קלים וחמורים שבתורה איה סופר את המגדלים שהיה סופר שלש מאות הלכות פסוקות במגדל הפורח באויר ג) א"ר ארבע מאה בעיי' בעו דואג ואחיתופל במגדל הפורח באויר [ולא איפשט להו חד] אמר רבא רבותא למבעי בעיי ד) בשני דרב יהודה כולי תנויי בנזיקין ואנן קא מתנינן טובא ה) בעוקצין וכי הוה מטי רב יהודה ו) אשה שכובשת ירק בקדירה ואמרי לה ז) זיתים שכבשן בטרפיהן טהורים אמר הויות דרב ושמואל קא חזינא הכא ואנן קא מתנינן בעוקצין תלת סרי מתיבתא ורב יהודה שליף מסאני ואתא מטרא ואנן צוחינן וליכא דמשגח בן אלא הקב"ה ליבא בעי דכתיב כ) וה' יראה ללבב אמר רב משרשיא דואג ואחיתופל לא [הוו] סברי שמעתא מתקיף לה מר זוטרא מאן דכתיב ביה איה סופר איה שוקל איה סופר את המגדלים ואת אמרת לא הוו סברי שמעתא אלא דלא הוה סלקא להו שמעתא אליבא דהלכתא דכתיב ל) סוד ה' ליראיו א"ר אמי לא מת דואג עד ששכח תלמודו שנא' מ) הוא ימות באין מוסר וברוב אולתו ישגה רב (אשי) אמר נצטרע שנאמר נ) הצמתה כל זונה ממך כתיב התם ס) לצמיתות ומתרגמינן לחלוטין ח) ותנן ״אין בין מוסגר ומוחלט אלא פריעה ופרימה (סימן שלשה ראו וחצי וקראו) א"ר יוחנן שלשה מלאכי חבלה נזדמנו לו לדואג אחד ששכח תלמודו ואחד ששרף נשמתו ואחד שפיזר עפרו בבתי כנסיות ובבתי מדרשות (ט) א"ר) יוחנן דואג ואחיתופל לא ראו זה את זה דואג בימי שאול ואחיתופל בימי דוד וא"ר יוחנן דואג ואחיתופל לא חצו ימיהם תניא נמי הכי ב) אנשי דמים ומרמה לא יחצו ימיהם י) כל שנותיו של דואג לא היו אלא שלשים וארבע ושל אחיתופל אינן אלא שלשים ושלש וא"ר יוחנן בתחלה קרא דוד לאחיתופל רבו ולבסוף קראו חבירו ולבסוף קראו תלמידו בתחילה כ) קראו רבו ע) ואתה אנוש כערכי אלופי ומיודעי ולבסוף קראו חבירו פ) אשר יחדו נמתיק סוד בבית אלהים נהלך ברגש ולבסוף קראו ל) תלמידו צ) גם איש שלומי אשר בטחתי בו אוכל

הרגו אל חלליהם. מיתות הרבה משמע שתלאוהו והציתו אש תחתם הצליבה וחתכו ראשו ונפל לתוך האש תלייה היינו חנק חתיכת הראש הרג כשנפל לארץ סקילה כשנפל לאור היינו שריפה: בר תלתין ותלת. ור"ח לית ליה דר' סימאי דאמר לעיל שלשה היו באותה עצה דפרעה בלעם ואיוב ויתרו דלר' סימאי בלעם היה יותר מן מאתים ועשר שנים דהא היה בעצת פרעה דכל הבן הילוד היאורה תשליכוהו דלרבי סימאי כל אותן מאתים ועשר שנים שהיו ישראל בגלות מצרים עד מלחמת מדין היה בלעם: חגירא. תרגום של פיסח: כד קטל יתיה פנחס ליסטאה. שר צבא ואפילו קטליה אחר כל המלחמה נקראת על שמו: בכולהו. מלכים והדיוטות: לא תפיש ותדרוש. לגנאי: לבר מבלעם. דכל מה דמשכחת ליה לגנאי דרוש: (מ) שמא יצא זה לתרבות רעה) לאחר שיצא לתרבות רעה אמר ווי. לכך כתוב דוייג: א"ל הקב"ה לדואג והלא גבור אתה בתורה. למה תתהלל לספר לשון הרע על דוד: לא חסד תורה עליך. לא חכם בתורה אתה דכתיב (משלי לא) ותורת חסד על לשונה: מרצחים. שהרג נוב: עלי פיך. ולא בלב: בתחלה ייראו. הצדיקים היו יראים שלא ילמד אדם ממעשיו של דואג שהולך וחוטא ומצליח: ולבסוף. כשמת בחצי ימיו ושב גמולו בראשו ישחקו: חיל בלע ויקיאנו. המתן עד שתשכח תורתו: אמר לפניו ומבטנו יורישנו אל. אל תמתין לו עד שתשתכח אלא תמהר ותשכיחנו: בי מדרשא. מאהל זה בית המדרש: ושרשך מארץ חיים סלה. שורש שלו תכסח מארץ חיים דלא להוו ליה בנין רבנן: כל אותיות שבתורה. שהיה בקי בחסירות ויתירות: שוקל קלים וחמורים.

יודע לדרוש בקל וחומר: במגדל הפורח באויר. מתג עליונה שלמעלה מן הלמ"ד מפני מה כפופה למטה. לשון מ"ר מפי השמועה. ל"א במגדל הפורח באויר הנכנס לארץ העמים בשידה תיבה ומגדל אם הוא טמא אם לאו. ל"א ג' מאות הלכות במגדל הפורח באויר לעשות כישוף להעמיד מגדל באויר כגון שלש מאות הלכות בנטיעות קשואין דאמרן בפירקין דלעיל (דף סח.) ולמורי נראה דה"ג שלש מאות הלכות במגדל העומד [באויר] ומשנה אחת באהלות (פ"ד משנה א) דמשתעי בהכי מגדל העומד באויר וטומאה בתוכה כלים שבתוכו טמאים וכן נראה לר': רבותא למבעא בעיי. וללמוד תורה רחמנא לבא בעי דהא בשני דרב יהודה כולהו תנויי בסדר נזיקין היה כל הגמרא שלהן לא הוה אלא בסדר נזיקין שלא היו מרבין כל כך [לדרוש]: האשה שכובשת ירק בקדירה. לא אשכחתיה במסכת עוקצין: שכובשת ירק. בחומץ או בציר טהורים דאין מקבלין טומאה ע"י עוקצין שאם נגע טומאה בשרשיו העלין טהורין שאין נעשין יד לעלין מאחר שכבשם שאין מניחין לשם אלא למראה: זיתים שכבשן בטרפיהן. איתא במסכת עוקצין (פ"ב מ"א): טרפיהן. עלין שלהן טהורין הזיתים שאין נעשין להם בית יד להכניס להם טומאה: הויות דרב ושמואל קא חזינא הכא. דלא הוה ידע מאי טעמא הן טהורין: תליסר מתיבתא. י"ג ישיבות שאנו עוסקין כולן במסכת עוקצין ויודעין אותה יפה ואפי' הכי בהם היו חסידים יותר ממנו דאלו רב יהודה כו': לא סבירי. לא היו יודעין הלכה לפרשה כתקנה בטעמא: דלא סלקא להו שמעתא כו'. שלא זכו לקבוע הלכה כמותן: ומתרגמינן לחלוטין. ואנן תנן לשון חלוטין גבי מצורע: אלופי. היינו רבי: אוכל

מסורת הש"ס

א) [עי' תוספות בע"ז], ב) [חגיגה טו:], ג) נ"א א"ר אמי, ד) תענית כד: ע"ש ברכות כ. ע"ש, ה) נ"א בשיתא סידרי, ו) [טהרות פ"ב מ"א], ז) [עוקצי' פ"ב מ"א], ח) מגילה ח: ערכין טו:, ט) [נ"ל ואמר ר'], י) לעיל סט:, כ) [אבות פ"ו מ"ג], ל) בילקוט ח"ב סוף רמז תשמא הגירסא ולבסוף קראו איש, מ) רש"ל מ"ז.

ליקוטי רש"י

מה תתהלל. ותתפאר ברעה שאתה עושה אתה הגבור בתורה. חסד אל כל היום. להציל את הנרדף על ידך [תהלים נב, ג]. ועליו ישחקו. וזה השחוק שיאמרו עליו הנה זה הגבר אשר לא שם מבטחו בהקב"ה ראו מה עלתה בו [תהלים נב, ח]. יתצך. ל' נתיצה. יחתך. לשון שבירה. ויסחך. ויעקרך. ושרשך. ישרש אחריך לעקור כל השרשים דירא"ריליניע"ר בלעז [שם ז]. קלים וחמורים. דברים הלמדין בקל וחומר שניתנו לדון מעצמן לכל אדם ולא פירשו כלום בסיני [סוכה כח.]. קלים וחמורים שאדם דן מעצמו [ב"ב קלד.]. הלכות פסוקות. הלכה כפלוני ופלוני [יבמות מב:]. במגדל הפורח באויר. יש מפרשים שדורשין גוגהו של למ"ד ודורשין בו כל זאת ויש אומרים מגדל דור הפלגה ולי נראה מגדל הפתוח לאויר גרסינן והן מהלכות אהלות מגדל של עץ שקורין משטיי"ר ועומד בפתח ופתחו פתוח לבקעה או לחצר שהוא אויר במסכת אהלות (פרק רביעי משנה א) ישנה משנה מגדל העומד באויר [חגיגה טו:]. בנזיקין הוה. למודם לא היה גדול אלא בסדר נזיקין. שכובשת ירק בקדירה. במסכת [טהרות] היא בפרק שני (משנה א') גבי ידות מיירי דקיימא לן (עוקצין פ"א מ"א) כל ידות האוכלין אם נגעה טומאה בהן נטמא גם האוכל הצריך לידות, דיד מכניס ומוציא כדאמרינן בהעור והרוטב (חולין קיח.) מכל האוכל לרבות הידות וקתני התם אשה שהיא כובשת ירק דידות שלהן טהורין דכשהיא עוצרת אותם הידות משתברות ואי אפשר ליטול הירקות בידות שלהן שנשמט ונפסק האוכל מן היד מחמת כבישה. כובשת. שול"ץ בלע"ז עוצרת שיצא המשקה שלהן ויבשו דרך אשה בכך כובשת ירק ממים שישתמרו לזמן מרובה טהורין העלין והקלחין. ואמרי לה. כי מטא לאידך בפרק שני (דעוקצין מ"א) זיתים שכבשן בטרפיהן כתרגומו עלה טרפא (בראשית ח) עלין שלהן דהיינו ידות. טהורים. הידות להביא טומאה לאוכל דתו לא חזי למהוי בית יד. הוויות דרב ושמואל. עומק גדול ולא הוה נהירא ליה.

תליסר מתיבתא. שלש עשרה ישיבות איכא בהך מתא דגמרי מסכת עוקצין. שליף חד מסאנא. משום עינוי. דחזא מידי. חם ושלום בעובדי כישי [תענית כד:]. בנזיקין הוה. לא היו גדולים בכל גמרא של ארבעה סדרים אלא בתלתא בבי. האשה שכובשת ירק או זיתים שכבשן בטרפיהן. משנה היא במסכת עוקצין. טהורים. שמוסקין זיתים עם העלין כדי לאחוז בהן דהוו להו עלין יד לזיתים להביא להם טומאה כדאמרינן בהעור והרוטב (דף קי"ח.) שהיד מביאה טומאה על האוכל ואם כבשן בטרפיהן בחומץ בטלה תורת יד מן העלין לפי שהכבישה מרקבתן ומרככתן ואינן ראוין שוב לאחוז בהן. הוויות דרב ושמואל קא חזינא הכא. כלומר טעם המשניות הללו קשה עלי ככל הקושיות שהיו שני רבותי מתקשין בהן בכל הגמרא. בתליסר מתיבתא. בשלש עשרה פנים יש בינינו משנה וברייתא של ששה סדרים ומסכת עוקצין גם היא בשלש עשרה פנים כגון משנת רבי ורבי חייא ומשנת בר קפרא ולוי ותנא דבי שמואל והכי אמרינן במסכת נדרים (דף מ"א.) רבי מתני הלכתא בשלש עשרה פנים [ברכות כ.]. לצמיתת. לפסיקה למכירה פסוקה עולמית [ויקרא כה, כג]. פריעה ופרימה. בגדיו יהיו פרומים וראשו יהי פרוע. מוחלט. לאחר שכלו ימי הסגר ונראה בו סימני טומאה האמורין בו [מגילה ח:].

by noting an inconsistency in the Scriptural spelling of Doeg's name:

כְּתִיב ,,דֹּאֵג'' וּכְתִיב ,,דּוֹיֵג'' – **It is written:** ***Doeg;*** **yet it is** also **written:** ***Doyeg.***[8] אָמַר רַבִּי יוֹחָנָן – **R' Yochanan said:** The spellings represent God's attitudes towards Doeg during the different stages in Doeg's life: בַּתְּחִילָּה – **At first,** before Doeg sinned, יוֹשֵׁב הַקָּדוֹשׁ בָּרוּךְ הוּא וְדוֹאֵג – **the Holy One, Blessed is He, sat and worried** (*doeg*), so to speak, שֶׁמָּא יֵצֵא זֶה לְתַרְבּוּת רָעָה – **that this one,** i.e. Doeg the Edomite, **might go out to bad conduct.** לְאַחַר שֶׁיָּצָא – **After [Doeg]** actually **went out** to bad conduct, אָמַר – **[God] said:** וַוי שֶׁיָּצָא זֶה – **Alas! For this one has gone out** to bad conduct![9]

Continuing its discussion of Doeg, the Gemara presents a series of expositions of Scriptural verses by R' Yitzchak, each of which applies to Doeg. The series is preceded by a mnemonic alluding to five of those verses:

(סִימָן גִּבּוֹר וְרָשָׁע וְצַדִּיק חַיִל וְסוֹפֵר – **A mnemonic: Mighty, wicked and righteous, treasure and one who counts.**)[10]

אָמַר רַבִּי יִצְחָק – **R' Yitzchak said:** מַאי דִּכְתִיב ,,מַה־תִּתְהַלֵּל בְּרָעָה הַגִּבּוֹר חֶסֶד אֵל כָּל־הַיּוֹם'' – **What is** the meaning of **that which is written:**[11] ***Why do you pride yourself with evil, O mighty warrior? God's kindness is all day long?*** אָמַר לוֹ הַקָּדוֹשׁ בָּרוּךְ הוּא לְדוֹאֵג – **The Holy One, Blessed is He, said to Doeg:** לֹא גִּבּוֹר בַּתּוֹרָה אַתָּה – **Are you not a mighty warrior in Torah,** i.e. are you not an outstanding Torah scholar? מַה תִּתְהַלֵּל בְּרָעָה – **Why do you pride yourself with evil?**[12] לֹא חֶסֶד אֵל נָטוּי עָלֶיךָ כָּל הַיּוֹם – **Is God's lovingkindness not spread over you all day long?**[13]

R' Yitzchak's second exposition:

וְאָמַר רַבִּי יִצְחָק – **And R' Yitzchak said:** מַאי דִּכְתִיב ,,וְלָרָשָׁע אָמַר אֱלֹהִים מַה־לְּךָ לְסַפֵּר חֻקָּי'' – **What is** the meaning of **that which is written:**[14] ***But to the wicked one, God said, "To what purpose do you recount My decrees"?*** אָמַר לוֹ הַקָּדוֹשׁ בָּרוּךְ הוּא לְדוֹאֵג הָרָשָׁע – **The Holy One, Blessed is He, said to Doeg the wicked:** מַה לְּךָ לְסַפֵּר חֻקָּי – **To what purpose do you recount My decrees** and occupy yourself with the study of My Torah? כְּשֶׁאַתָּה מַגִּיעַ לְפָרָשַׁת מְרַצְּחִים וּפָרָשַׁת מְסַפְּרֵי לָשׁוֹן הָרַע – **When you arrive at the passage of murderers and the passage of those who speak** ***lashon hara,*** מַה אַתָּה דּוֹרֵשׁ בָּהֶם – **what will you expound concerning them?** How will you be able to expound those passages when you yourself massacred the Kohanim of Nov and slandered David?[15]

The Gemara expounds the latter segment of the verse just cited: ,,וַתִּשָּׂא בְרִיתִי עֲלֵי־פִיךָ'' – ***. . . and bear My covenant upon your mouth.***[16] אָמַר רַבִּי אַמִי – **R' Ami said:** אֵין תּוֹרָתוֹ שֶׁל דוֹאֵג אֶלָּא מִשָּׂפָה וְלַחוּץ – This means that **Doeg's Torah** knowledge **was merely from the lips outward,** that is, he did not internalize what he had learned.[17]

R' Yitzchak's third exposition:

וְאָמַר רַבִּי יִצְחָק – **And R' Yitzchak said:** מַאי דִּכְתִיב ,,וְיִרְאוּ צַדִּיקִים וְיִירָאוּ וְעָלָיו יִשְׂחָקוּ'' – **What is** the meaning of **that which is written,** concerning Doeg:[18] ***The righteous will see and be frightened, and they will laugh at him?*** בַּתְּחִילָּה יִירְאוּ – **At first,** when Doeg was at the height of his power, **[the righteous] were afraid,** וּלְבַסּוֹף יִשְׂחָקוּ – **but in the end,** when he died prematurely, **they laughed.**[19]

R' Yitzchak's fourth exposition:

וְאָמַר רַבִּי יִצְחָק – **And R' Yitzchak said:** מַאי דִּכְתִיב ,,חַיִל בָּלַע וַיְקִאֶנּוּ מִבִּטְנוֹ יֹרִשֶׁנּוּ אֵל'' – **What is** the meaning of **that which is**

NOTES

8. I.e. Doeg's name is spelled differently in various verses in the twenty-first and twenty-second chapters of *I Samuel*: In 21:8 and 22:9 it is spelled דֹּאֵג, whereas in ch. 22 vs. 18 and 22 it is spelled דּוֹיֵג. Why is this so?

9. Doeg was a great Talmudic scholar, as the Gemara relates below. Indeed, he was the head of the Sanhedrin in Saul's days (*Midrash Shocher Tov, Psalms* 3; *Rashi, I Samuel* 21:8) and was considered equal to all the rest of Israel in Torah scholarship (*Yalkut Shimoni, I Samuel* §121, cited by *Rashi* to 15:24). His name first appears in Scripture (ibid. and 22:9) in connection with his preparation to slander the Kohanim of Nov. At that stage, it is spelled דֹּאֵג, *Doeg,* which means worry, to reflect God's concern over his impending regression into sin. The spelling דּוֹיֵג is used in Scripture after the account of Doeg's slander (ibid. vs. 18,22). This spelling indicates God's anguish at the way this great man degenerated, for the two middle letters of דּוֹיֵג spell וָי, *alas* (*Rashi, Maharal;* cf. *Yad Ramah*).

These events are described anthropomorphically, for God does not actually worry, nor is He in doubt about how a person will turn out, nor is He affected by how a person does ultimately turn out. R' Yochanan's point is that since God knows in advance how a person will act, God is, so to speak, concerned for a person who is about to destroy himself through sin. Furthermore, since man chooses by his own free will to do either good or evil, God is, so to speak, saddened when one ultimately sins and he has to punish him (*Yad Ramah, Maharsha;* see also Mishnah above, 46a, *Rambam, Hil. Teshuvah* ch. 5 and *Otzar HaGeonim* here).

10. The series actually contains six expositions; the mnemonic lacks an allusion to the fifth of them (see *Rashash*).

11. *Psalms* 52:3. This Psalm was composed by David as an expression of condemnation of Doeg's slander.

12. Why do you take pride in slandering David? (*Rashi*).

13. The Torah is referred to in *Proverbs* (31:26) as תּוֹרַת־חֶסֶד, *the Torah of lovingkindness.* Since you are a great scholar, you are involved with God's lovingkindness all day! Why do you take pride in slandering David? (*Rashi*). [*Rashi* seems to have had the reading: לֹא חֶסֶד תּוֹרָה עָלֶיךָ – *Is the Torah's lovingkindness not upon you?*]

[Elsewhere (*Chagigah* 12b), the Gemara says: כָּל הָעוֹסֵק בַּתּוֹרָה בַּלַּיְלָה הַקָּדוֹשׁ בָּרוּךְ הוּא מוֹשֵׁךְ עָלָיו חוּט שֶׁל חֶסֶד בַּיּוֹם, *Whoever delves into Torah at night, the Holy One, Blessed is He, draws a strand of lovingkindness over him during the daytime.* Accordingly, perhaps our Gemara means that God told Doeg: Since you are an outstanding Torah scholar, is God's lovingkindness not spread over you all day as a result of your studies at night? Why, then, do you engage in slander rather than words of lovingkindness? (see *Melo HaRoim*).]

For an interesting interpretation of this passage, see *Parashas Derachim* §13. See also *Rif* in *Ein Yaakov.*

14. *Psalms* 50:16.

15. See *Rashi. Maharsha* translates the verse: *But to the wicked one, God said, "To what purpose do you count My decrees?"* This is a reference to the fact mentioned below that Doeg was able to enumerate, through Scriptural exegesis, hundreds of laws that are not stated explicitly in the Torah. God therefore told him: "To what purpose do you count the laws that are not stated explicitly, when you obviously neglect to count two explicit commandments? When you arrive at the passages of murder and *lashon hara,* what distorted expositions will you propose in order to justify your flagrant violation of their simple meaning?" (*Maharsha*; see also *Iyun Yaakov*).

16. Ibid.

17. [This is obvious from the fact that he sinned blatantly notwithstanding his erudition.] The verse implies it by saying that Doeg bore the word of God upon his mouth, rather than within his heart (*Rashi*). See *Maharsha* for another interpretation of the term *from the lips outward.*

18. Ibid. 52:8.

19. Doeg held a high position in Saul's government, acting as head of the Sanhedrin (*Shocher Tov, Psalms* 3; *Rashi, I Samuel* 21:8). The righteous feared that people might seek to emulate him, since he enjoyed honor and success. When Doeg died prematurely at the age of thirty-four (see Gemara below), the righteous laughed with relief, for it was obvious to all that Doeg had been rewarded justly for his evil deeds (*Rashi*). *Maharsha* explains that their initial fear was that Doeg might slander them, as he had slandered David and the Kohanim of Nov, and their ultimate joy was due to: וּבַאֲבֹד רְשָׁעִים רִנָּה, *Upon the destruction of evildoers there is rejoicing* (*Proverbs* 11:10). *Ben Yehoyada* explains that the worry of the righteous came from their concern that Doeg's Torah learning had not prevented his wicked deeds and that this could be taken as an indication that Torah did not prevent evilness. In fact, the reason

(א) הרגו בני ישראל [בחרב] אל חלליהם אמר רב שקיימו בו ארבע מיתות סקילה ושריפה הרג וחנק א"ל ההוא מינא לר' חנינא מי שמיע לך בלעם בר כמה הוה א"ל מיכתב לא כתיב אלא מדכתיב (ב) אנשי דמים ומרמה לא יחצו ימיהם בר תלתין ותלת שנין או בר תלתין וארבע א"ל שפיר קאמרת לדידי חזי לי פנקסיה דבלעם והוה כתיב ביה בר תלתין ותלת שנין בלעם חגירא כד קטיל יתיה פנחס ליסטאה א"ל מר בריה דרבינא לבריה בכולהו לא תפיש למדרש לבר מבלעם הרשע דכמה דמשכחת ביה דרוש ביה כתיב (ג) דואג וכתיב (ד) דוייג אמר ר' יוחנן בתחילה יושב הקב"ה ודואג שמא יצא זה לתרבות רעה לאחר שיצא אמר ווי שיצא זה (סימן גבור ורשע וצדיק חיל וסופר) א"ר יצחק מאי דכתיב (ה) מה תתהלל ברעה הגבור חסד אל כל היום אמר לו הקב"ה לדואג לא גבור בתורה אתה מה תתהלל ברעה לא חסד אל נטוי עליך כל היום וא"ר יצחק מאי דכתיב (ו) ולרשע אמר אלהים מה לך לספר חוקי אמר לו הקב"ה לדואג הרשע מה לך לספר חוקי כשאתה מגיע לפרשת מרצחים ופרשת מספרי לשון הרע מה אתה דורש בהם (ו) ותשא בריתי עלי פיך אמר ר' אמי אין תורתו של דואג אלא משפה ולחוץ ואמר רבי יצחק מאי דכתיב (ז) ויראו צדיקים וייראו ועליו ישחקו בתחילה ייראו ולבסוף ישחקו וא"ר יצחק מאי דכתיב (ח) חיל בלע ויקיאנו מבטנו יורישנו אל אמר דוד לפני הקב"ה רבש"ע ימות דואג אמר לו חיל בלע ויקיאנו אמר לפניו מבטנו יורישנו אל וא"ר יצחק מאי דכתיב (ט) גם אל יתצך לנצח אמר הקב"ה לדוד ניתי דואג לעלמא דאתי אמר לפניו גם אל יתצך לנצח (א) מאי דכתיב (ט) יחתך ויסחך מאהל ושרשך מארץ חיים סלה אמר הקב"ה לימרו שמעתא בי מדרשא משמיה אמר לפניו יחתך ויסחך מאהל ושרשך מארץ חיים סלה וא"ר יצחק (ב) מאי דכתיב (י) איה סופר איה שוקל איה סופר את המגדלים איה סופר כל אותיות שבתורה איה שוקל ששוקל כל קלים וחמורים שבתורה איה סופר את המגדלים שהיה סופר שלש מאות הלכות פסוקות במגדל הפורח באויר (ג) א"ר ארבע מאה בעיי בעו דואג ואחיתופל במגדל הפורח באויר [ולא איפשט להו חד] אמר רבא רבותא למבעי בעיי (ד) בשני דרב יהודה כולי תנויי בנזיקין ואנן קא מתנינן טובא (ה) בעוקצין וכי הוה מטי רב יהודה (ו) אשה שכובשת ירק בקדירה ואמרי לה (ז) זיתים שכבשן בטרפיהן טהורים אמר הויות דרב ושמואל קא חזינא הכא ואנן קא מתנינן בעוקצין תלת סרי מתיבתא ורב יהודה שליף מסאני ואתא מטרא ואנן צוחינן וליכא דמשגח בן אלא הקב"ה ליבא בעי דכתיב (כ) וה' יראה ללבב אמר רב משרשיא דואג ואחיתופל לא [הוו] סברי שמעתא מתקיף לה מר זוטרא מאן דכתיב ביה איה סופר איה שוקל איה סופר את המגדלים ואת אמרת לא הוו סברי שמעתא אלא דלא הוה סלקא להו שמעתא אליבא דהלכתא דכתיב (ל) סוד ה' ליראיו א"ר אמי לא מת דואג עד ששכח תלמודו שנא' (מ) הוא ימות באין מוסר וברוב אולתו ישגה רב (אשי) אמר נצטרע שנאמר (נ) הצמתה כל זונה ממך כתיב התם (ס) לצמיתות ומתרגמינן לחלוטין (ח) ותנן (א) אין בין מוסגר ומוחלט אלא פריעה ופרימה (סימן שלשה ראו וחצי וקראו) א"ר יוחנן שלשה מלאכי חבלה נזדמנו לו לדואג אחד ששכח תלמודו ואחד ששרף נשמתו ואחד שפיזר עפרו בבתי כנסיות ובבתי מדרשות ((ט) א"ר) יוחנן דואג ואחיתופל לא ראו זה את זה דואג בימי שאול ואחיתופל בימי דוד וא"ר יוחנן דואג ואחיתופל לא חצו ימיהם תניא נמי הכי (ב) אנשי דמים ומרמה לא יחצו ימיהם (י) כל שנותיו של דואג לא היו אלא שלשים וארבע ושל אחיתופל אינן אלא שלשים ושלש וא"ר יוחנן בתחלה קרא דוד לאחיתופל רבו ולבסוף קראו חבירו ולבסוף קראו תלמידו בתחילה (כ) קראו רבו (ע) ואתה אנוש כערכי אלופי ומיודעי ולבסוף קראו חבירו (פ) אשר יחדו נמתיק סוד בבית אלהים נהלך ברגש ולבסוף קראו (ל) תלמידו (צ) גם איש שלומי אשר בטחתי בו

אוכל

רש"י

הרגו אל חלליהם. מיתות הרבה משמע שתלאוהו והציתו אש תחת הצליבה ונחתכו ראשו ונפל לתוך האש תלייה היינו חנק חתיכת הראש הרג כשנפל לארץ סקילה כשנפל לאור היינו שריפה: בר תלתין ותלת. ור"ח לית ליה דר' סימאי דאמר לעיל שלשה היו באותה עצה דפרעה בלעם ואיוב ויתרו דלר' סימאי בלעם חיה יותר מן מאתים ועשר שנים דהא היה בעצת פרעה דכל הבן הילוד היאורה תשליכוהו דלרבי סימאי כל אותן מאתים ועשר שנים שהיו ישראל בגלות מצרים עד מלחמת מדין חיה בלעם: חגירא. תרגום של פיסח: כד קטל יתיה פנחס ליסטאה. שר צבא ואפילו קטליה אחר כל המלחמה נקראת על שמו: בכולהו. מלכים והדיוטות: לא תפיש ותדרוש. לגנאי: לבר מבלעם. דכל מה דמשכחת ליה לגנאי דרוש: ((מ) שמא יצא זה לתרבות רעה) לאחר שיצא לתרבות רעה אמר ווי. לכך כתוב דוייג: א"ל הקב"ה לדואג והלא גבור אתה בתורה. למה תתהלל לספר לשון הרע על דוד: לא חסד תורה עליך. לא חכם בתורה אתה דכתיב (משלי לא) ותורת חסד על לשונה: מרצחים. שהרג נוב: עלי פיך. ולא בלב: בתחלה ייראו. הצדיקים היו יראים שלא ילמד אדם ממעשיו של דואג שהולך וחוטא ומצליח: ולבסוף. כשמת בחצי ימיו ושב גמולו בראשו ישחקו: חיל בלע ויקיאנו. המתן עד שתשכח תורתו: אמר לפניו ומבטנו יורישנו אל. אל תמתין לו עד שתשתכח אלא תמהר ותשכיחנו: בי מדרשא. מאהל זה בית המדרש: ושרשך מארץ חיים סלה. שורש שלו תכסח מארץ חיים דלא להוו ליה בנין רבנן: כל אותיות שבתורה. שהיה בקי בחסירות ויתירות: שוקל קלים וחמורים. יודע לדרוש בקל וחומר: במגדל הפורח באויר. מתג עליונה שלמעלה מן הלמ"ד מפני מה כפופה למטה. לשון מ"ר מפי השמועה. ל"א במגדל הפורח באויר הנכנס לארץ העמים בשידה תיבה ומגדל אם הוא טמא אם לאו. ל"א ג' מאות הלכות במגדל הפורח באויר לעשות כישוף להעמיד מגדל באויר כגון שלש מאות הלכות בנטיעות קשואין דאמרן בפירקין דלעיל (דף סח.) ולמורי נראה דה"ג שלש מאות הלכות במגדל העומד [באויר] ומשנה אחת באהלות (פ"ד משנה א) דמשתעי בהכי מגדל העומד באויר וטומאה בתוכה כלים שבתוכו טמאים וכן נראה לר': רבותא למבעא בעיי. וללמוד תורה רחמנא לבא בעי דהא בשני דרב יהודה כולהו תנויי בסדר נזיקין היה כל הגמרא שלהן לא הוה אלא בסדר נזיקין שלא היו מרבין כל כך [לדרוש]: האשה שכובשת ירק בקדירה. לא אשכחתיה במסכת עוקלין: שכובשת ירק. בחומץ או בציר טהורים דאין מקבלין טומאה ע"י עוקלין שאם נגע טומאה בשרשיו העלין טהורין שאין נעשין יד לעלין מאחר שכבשם שאין מניחין לשם אלא למראה: זיתים שכבשן בטרפיהן. איתא במסכת עוקלין (פ"ב מ"א): טרפיהן. עלין שלהן טהורין הזיתים שאין נעשין להם בית יד להכניס להם טומאה: הויות דרב ושמואל קא חזינא הכא. דלא הוה ידע מאי טעמא הן טהורין: תליסר מתיבתא. י"ג ישיבות שאנו עוסקין כולן במסכת עוקלין ויודעין אותה יפה ואפי' הכי בהם היו חסידים יותר ממנו דאלו רב יהודה כו': לא סבירי. לא היו יודעין הלכה לפרשה כתקנה בטעמא: דלא סלקא להו שמעתא כו'. שלא זכו לקבוע הלכה כמותן: ומתרגמינן לחלוטין. ואנן תנן לשון חלוטין גבי מצורע: אלופי. היינו רבי:

אוכל

עין משפט נר מצוה

לא א מיי' פ"י מהל' טומאת צרעת הל' י:

תורה אור השלם

א) וְאֶת בִּלְעָם בֶּן בְּעוֹר הַקּוֹסֵם הָרְגוּ בְנֵי יִשְׂרָאֵל בַּחֶרֶב אֶל חַלְלֵיהֶם: [יהושע יג, כב]

ב) וְאַתָּה אֱלֹהִים תּוֹרִדֵם לִבְאֵר שַׁחַת אַנְשֵׁי דָמִים וּמִרְמָה לֹא יֶחֱצוּ יְמֵיהֶם וַאֲנִי אֶבְטַח בָּךְ: [תהלים נה, כד]

ג) וְשָׁם אִישׁ מֵעַבְדֵי שָׁאוּל בַּיּוֹם הַהוּא נֶעְצָר לִפְנֵי יְיָ וּשְׁמוֹ דֹּאֵג הָאֲדֹמִי אַבִּיר הָרֹעִים אֲשֶׁר לְשָׁאוּל: [שמואל א' כא, ח]

ד) וַיֹּאמֶר הַמֶּלֶךְ לְדוֹאֵג (לדויג) סֹב אַתָּה וּפְגַע בַּכֹּהֲנִים וַיִּסֹּב דּוֹאֵג הָאֲדֹמִי וַיִּפְגַּע הוּא בַּכֹּהֲנִים וַיָּמֶת בַּיּוֹם הַהוּא שְׁמֹנִים וַחֲמִשָּׁה אִישׁ נֹשֵׂא אֵפוֹד בָּד: [שמואל א' כב, יח]

ה) מַה תִּתְהַלֵּל בְּרָעָה הַגִּבּוֹר חֶסֶד אֵל כָּל הַיּוֹם: [תהלים נב, ג]

ו) וְלָרָשָׁע אָמַר אֱלֹהִים מַה לְּךָ לְסַפֵּר חֻקָּי וַתִּשָּׂא בְרִיתִי עֲלֵי פִיךָ: [תהלים נ, טז]

ז) וְיִרְאוּ צַדִּיקִים וְיִירָאוּ וְעָלָיו יִשְׂחָקוּ: [תהלים נב, ח]

ח) חַיִל בָּלַע וַיְקִאֶנּוּ מִבִּטְנוֹ יֹרִשֶׁנּוּ אֵל: [איוב כ, טו]

ט) גַּם אֵל יִתָּצְךָ לָנֶצַח יַחְתְּךָ וְיִסָּחֲךָ מֵאֹהֶל וְשֵׁרֶשְׁךָ מֵאֶרֶץ חַיִּים סֶלָה: [תהלים נב, ז]

י) לִבְּךָ יֶהְגֶּה אֵימָה אַיֵּה סֹפֵר אַיֵּה שֹׁקֵל אַיֵּה סֹפֵר אֶת הַמִּגְדָּלִים: [ישעיה לג, יח]

כ) וַיֹּאמֶר יְיָ אֶל שְׁמוּאֵל אַל תַּבֵּט אֶל מַרְאֵהוּ וְאֶל גְּבֹהַּ קוֹמָתוֹ כִּי מְאַסְתִּיהוּ כִּי לֹא אֲשֶׁר יִרְאֶה הָאָדָם כִּי הָאָדָם יִרְאֶה לַעֵינַיִם וַייָ יִרְאֶה לַלֵּבָב: [שמואל א' טז, ז]

ל) סוֹד יְיָ לִירֵאָיו וּבְרִיתוֹ לְהוֹדִיעָם: [תהלים כה, יד]

מ) הוּא יָמוּת בְּאֵין מוּסָר וּבְרֹב אִוַּלְתּוֹ יִשְׁגֶּה: [משלי ה, כג]

נ) כִּי הִנֵּה רְחֵקֶיךָ יֹאבֵדוּ הִצְמַתָּה כָּל זוֹנֶה מִמֶּךָּ: [תהלים עג, כז]

ס) וְהָאָרֶץ לֹא תִמָּכֵר לִצְמִתֻת כִּי לִי הָאָרֶץ כִּי גֵרִים וְתוֹשָׁבִים אַתֶּם עִמָּדִי: [ויקרא כה, כג]

ע) וְאַתָּה אֱנוֹשׁ כְּעֶרְכִּי אַלּוּפִי וּמְיֻדָּעִי: [תהלים נה, יד]

פ) אֲשֶׁר יַחְדָּו נַמְתִּיק סוֹד בְּבֵית אֱלֹהִים נְהַלֵּךְ בְּרָגֶשׁ: [תהלים נה, טו]

צ) גַּם אִישׁ שְׁלוֹמִי אֲשֶׁר בָּטַחְתִּי בוֹ אוֹכֵל לַחְמִי הִגְדִּיל עָלַי עָקֵב: [תהלים מא, י]

מסורת הש"ס

א) [עי' הנוספא בע"י], ב) [חגיגה טו:], ג) נ"א א"ר אמי, ד) תענית כד: ע"ש ברכות כ. ע"ש, ה) נ"א בשיתא סידרי, ו) [טהרות פ"ב מ"א], ז) [עוקצי' פ"ב מ"א], ח) מגילה ח: ערכין טו., ט) [נ"ל ואמר ר'], י) לעיל סט:, כ) [אבות פ"ו מ"ג], ל) בילקוט ח"ב סוף רמז תשמא הגירסא ולבסוף קראו איש, מ) רש"ל מ"ז.

ליקוטי רש"י

מה תתהלל. ותתפאר ברעה שאתה עושה אתה הגבור בתורה. חסד אל כל היום. להציל את הנרדף על ידך [תהלים נב, ג]. ועליו ישחקו. וזה השחוק שיאמרו עליו הנה זה הגבר אשר לא שם מבטחו בהקב"ה ראו מה עלתה בו [תהלים נב, ח]. יתצך. ל' נתילה. יחתך. לשון שבירה. ויסחך. ויעקרך. ושרשך. ישרש אחריך לעקור כל השרשים דירארילינע"ר בלעז [שם ז]. קלים וחמורים. דברים הלמדין בקל וחומר שניתנו לדון מעצמן לכל אדם ולא פירשו כלום בסיני [סוכה כח.]. קלים וחמורים שאדם דן מעצמו [ב"ב קלד.]. הלכות פסוקות. הלכה כפלוני ופלוני [יבמות מב:]. במגדל הפורח באויר. יש מפרשים שדורשין גוגהו של למ"ד ודורשין בו כל זאת ויש אומרים מגדל דור הפלגה ולי נראה מגדל הפתוח לאויר גרסינן והן מהלכות אהלות מגדל של עץ שקורין משטיי"ר ועומד בפתח ופתחו פתוח לבקעה או לחצר שהוא אויר במסכת אהלות (פרק רביעי משנה א) ישנה משנה מגדל העומד באויר [חגיגה טו:]. בנזיקין הוה. למודם לא היה גדול אלא בסדר נזיקין. שכובשת ירק בקדירה. במסכת [טהרות] היא בפרק שני (משנה א') גבי ידות מיירי דקיימא לן (עוקצין פ"א מ"א) כל ידות האוכלין אם נגעה טומאה בהן נטמא גם האוכל הצריך לידות, דיד מכניס ומוציא כדאמרינן בהעור והרוטב (חולין קיח.) מכל האוכל לרבות הידות וקתני התם אשה שהיא כובשת ירק דידות שלהן טהורין דכשהיא עוצרת אותם הידות משתברות ואי אפשר ליטול הירקות בידות שלהן שנשמט ונפסק האוכל מן היד מחמת כבישה. כובשת. שול"ץ בלע"ז עוצרת שילא המשקה שלהן ויבשו דרך אשה בכך כובשת ירק ממים שישתמרו לזמן מרובה טהורין העלין והקלחין. ואמרי לה. כי מטא לאידך בפרק שני (דעוקצין מ"א) זיתים שכבשן בטרפיהן כתרגומו עלה טרפא (בראשית ח) עלין שלהן דהיינו ידות. טהורים. הידות להביא טומאה לאוכל דתו לא חזי למהוי בית יד. הוויות דרב ושמואל. עומק גדול ולא הוה נהירא ליה. תליסר מתיבתא. שלש עשרה ישיבות איכא בהך מתא דגמרי מסכת עוקלין. שליף חד מסאנא. משום עינוי. חס ושלום בעובדי בישי [תענית כד:]. בנזיקין הוה. לא היו גדולים בכל גמרא של ארבעה סדרים אלא בתלתא בבי. האשה שכובשת ירק או זיתים שכבשן בטרפיהן. משנה היא במסכת עוקלין. טהורים. שמוסקין זיתים עם העלין כדי לאחוז בהן דהוו להו עלין יד לזיתים להביא להם טומאה כדאמרינן בהעור והרוטב (דף קי"ח.) שהיד מביאה טומאה על האוכל ואם כבשן בטרפיהן בחומץ בטלה תורת יד מן העלין לפי שהכבישה מרקבתן ומרככתן ואינן ראוין שוב לאחוז בהן. הויות דרב ושמואל קא חזינא הכא. כלומר טעם המשניות הללו קשה עלי ככל הקושיות שהיו שני רבותי מתקשין בהן בכל הגמרא. בתליסר מתיבתא. בשלש עשרה פנים יש בינינו משנה ובריי̇תא של ששה סדרים ומסכת עוקלין גם היא בשלש עשרה פנים כגון משנת רבי ורבי חייא ומשנת בר קפרא ולוי ותנא דבי שמואל והכי אמרינן במסכת נדרים (דף מ"א.) רבי מתני הלכתא בשלש עשרה פנים [ברכות כ.]. לצמתת. לפסיקה למכירה פסוקה עולמית [ויקרא כה, כג]. פריעה ופרימה. בגדיו יהיו פרומים וראשו יהי פרוע. מוחלט. לאחר שכלו ימי ההסגר ונראה בו סימני טומאה האמורין בו [מגילה ח:].

written:[20] ***He has swallowed treasure and will disgorge it, God shall purge it from his gut?*** אָמַר דָּוִד לִפְנֵי הַקָּדוֹשׁ בָּרוּךְ הוּא – **David said before the Holy One, Blessed is He:** רִבּוֹנוֹ שֶׁל עוֹלָם – **Master of the Universe!** יָמוּת דּוֹאֵג – **Let Doeg die** now, though he is yet young! אָמַר לוֹ – **[The Holy One, Blessed is He] said to [David]:** "חַיִל בָּלַע וַיְקִיאֶנּוּ" – ***He has swallowed treasure and will disgorge it,*** i.e. he has acquired much Torah knowledge, and has yet to forget it. Meanwhile, it protects him from premature death.[21] אָמַר לְפָנָיו – **[David] said before [the Holy One, Blessed is He]:** "מִבִּטְנוֹ יוֹרִישֶׁנּוּ אֵל" – ***God shall purge it from his gut,*** i.e. You can cause Doeg to forget prematurely the Torah he has learned, and I beseech You to do so.[22]

R' Yitzchak's fifth exposition, which provides the Scriptural source for the Mishnah's teaching that Doeg has no share in the World to Come:

וְאָמַר רַבִּי יִצְחָק – **And R' Yitzchak said:** מַאי דִּכְתִיב "גַּם־אֵל יִתָּצְךָ לָנֶצַח" – **What is** the meaning of **that which is written,** concerning Doeg:[23] ***Likewise, may God shatter you for eternity?*** אָמַר הַקָּדוֹשׁ בָּרוּךְ הוּא לְדָוִד – **The Holy One, Blessed is He, said to David:** נֵיתֵי דּוֹאֵג לְעָלְמָא דְאָתֵי – **Let Doeg** be allowed to **enter the World to Come.**[24] אָמַר לְפָנָיו "גַּם־אֵל יִתָּצְךָ לָנֶצַח" – **[David] said before [the Holy One, Blessed is He],** concerning Doeg: ***Likewise, may God shatter you for eternity,*** i.e. may He exclude you from the World to Come.[25] מַאי דִּכְתִיב "יַחְתְּךָ וְיִסָּחֲךָ מֵאֹהֶל וְשֵׁרֶשְׁךָ מֵאֶרֶץ חַיִּים סֶלָה" – And **what is** the meaning of **that which is written** at the end of that verse: ***May He cut you and tear you from the tent, and uproot you from the Land of Life, Selah?*** אָמַר הַקָּדוֹשׁ בָּרוּךְ הוּא – **The Holy One, Blessed is He, said** to David: לֵימְרוּ שְׁמַעְתָּא בֵּי מִדְרְשָׁא מִשְּׁמֵיהּ – **Let them** at least **recite a teaching in the House of Study in [Doeg's] name.** If Doeg is to be excluded from the World to Come, at least let the record of his Torah scholarship remain for posterity.[26] אָמַר לְפָנָיו – **[David] said before [the Holy One, Blessed is He],** concerning Doeg: "יַחְתְּךָ וְיִסָּחֲךָ מֵאֹהֶל" – ***May [God] cut you and tear you from the tent.***[27] לֶיהֱוֵי לֵיהּ בְּנִין רַבָּנָן – The Holy One, Blessed is He, then said to David: **Let [Doeg]** at least **have descendants who are Torah scholars.**[28] "וְשֵׁרֶשְׁךָ מֵאֶרֶץ חַיִּים סֶלָה" – David replied: ***. . . and uproot you*** (Doeg) ***from the Land of Life, Selah!***[29]

R' Yitzchak's final exposition:

וְאָמַר רַבִּי יִצְחָק – **And R' Yitzchak said:** מַאי דִּכְתִיב "אַיֵּה סֹפֵר אַיֵּה שֹׁקֵל אַיֵּה סֹפֵר אֶת־הַמִּגְדָּלִים" – **What is** the meaning of **that which is written:**[30] ***Where is the one who can count? Where is the one who can weigh? Where is the one who can count the towers?*** This verse can be interpreted in reference to Doeg:[31] "אַיֵּה סֹפֵר" כָּל אוֹתִיּוֹת שֶׁבַּתּוֹרָה – ***Where is the one who can count*** **all the letters in the Torah?**[32] "אַיֵּה שֹׁקֵל" שֶׁשּׁוֹקֵל כָּל קַלִּים וַחֲמוּרִים שֶׁבַּתּוֹרָה – ***Where is the one who can weigh*** – **for [Doeg] would weigh all the *kal vachomers* in the Torah?**[33] "אַיֵּה סֹפֵר אֶת־הַמִּגְדָּלִים" – ***Where is the one who can count the towers?*** שֶׁהָיָה סוֹפֵר שְׁלֹשׁ מֵאוֹת הֲלָכוֹת פְּסוּקוֹת בְּמִגְדָּל הַפּוֹרֵחַ בָּאֲוִיר – This too

NOTES

his Torah study did not prevent him from turning evil is that it was flawed (see Gemara below and *Sotah* 21a).

20. *Job* 20:15. The verse is part of a chapter describing the wicked and slanderers (*Maharsha*). R' Yitzchak applies it specifically to Doeg (see *Rif* in *Ein Yaakov* for the reason).

21. Torah study protects one's life, as it is written (*Proverbs* 3:18): עֵץ־חַיִּים הִיא, *It* (Torah) *is a tree of life.* However, Doeg was destined to forget what he had learned, and at that juncture he would be stripped of the Torah's protection.

R' Yitzchak's exposition is based on the unusual verb employed by the verse to describe Doeg's Torah study, *swallowing,* as opposed to *eating.* Eating denotes consuming food in a normal manner, the food being properly digested and affording nourishment to the body. Swallowing, on the other hand, denotes consuming food in a manner through which it is not digested and does not provide nourishment. When Torah is studied with pure intentions, it offers the person spiritual nourishment. However, Doeg's studies were flawed, for he studied for his own aggrandizement. Therefore, in describing his studies, Scripture uses the verb *swallowing.* Thus, God told David that whereas Doeg could not die yet since he had the merit of Torah, he was sure to disgorge (i.e. forget) his learning, since he had merely swallowed but not digested it. When that would occur, he would be vulnerable to death (see *Maharsha*).

22. Since Doeg merely "swallowed" his learning, and was therefore sure to forget it in due course, David asked God to speed the process! Indeed, as stated below, God sent an angel that made him forget his learning (*Maharsha;* see also *Yalkut Shimoni, I Samuel* §131).

23. *Psalms* 52:7.

24. I.e. I will punish Doeg in this world for his sins, so that he will merit a share in *Olam Haba* (*Maharsha*).

25. David did not consider this bitter enemy who had hounded him groundlessly worthy of entering the World to Come. [As the person most sinned against by Doeg, David's forgiveness was required before God would in any way pardon him.] Nevertheless, there is an opinion cited above (105a) that Doeg does have a share in the World to Come. As for David's complaint, God says: "It is up to Me to make friends of David and Doeg" (see 105a note 5).

26. The Gemara states in *Yevamos* (96b-97a) that any deceased Torah scholar whose teachings are repeated in his name in this world lives on in both worlds, in a certain sense [שִׂפְתוֹתָיו דּוֹבְבוֹת בַּקֶּבֶר, *his lips move in the grave*]. The Gemara derives this from the verse (*Psalms* 61:4) אָגוּרָה בְאָהָלְךָ עוֹלָמִים, *May I dwell In Your tent* (i.e. the House of Study) *in [both] worlds* (literally: forever). [See also Gemara above, 90b.] Since God granted David's request to exclude Doeg from the World to Come, He, in His infinite mercy, wanted to allow Doeg some degree of eternal life through having his teachings repeated in the Houses of Study (*Maharsha*).

27. The "tent" is an allusion to the House of Study (*Rashi*). David employed the double praise, *may He cut you and tear you from the Tent,* in requesting that Doeg be excluded from dwelling in the Tent of God in both worlds (*Maharsha*).

David argued before God that it would not be fitting for Torah lessons to be repeated in the name of a person as unworthy as Doeg (*Maharal, Nesiv HaTorah* ch. 8). Any attribution of laws to him would be tantamount to his living on (*Maharsha*).

28. This, too, would constitute some form of eternal life (see *Bava Basra* 116a).

29. *Psalms* 52:7. David prayed that Doeg's roots be torn from the Land of Life, i.e. that he not merit progeny who are Torah scholars (*Rashi*). Since the Torah is known as the Tree of Life (see note 21), those who devote their lives to its study are said to reside in the Land of Life (see *Maharsha*).

30. *Isaiah* 33:18.

31. The plain meaning of this verse within its context refers to the punishment that will befall the wicked in the Messianic era. The righteous, awed by the manifestation of God's justice, will say: Where are they today – those wise and powerful ones who counted and weighed all governmental matters and who counted the towers of each city to determine its requirements? (*Rashi* ad loc.). R' Yitzchak, however, applies this verse to Doeg.

32. [In numerous instances, the Torah varies the spelling of certain words, by including a letter (such as *vav*) when a word appears in one place, and deleting that letter when the word appears elsewhere. These intentional variations in spelling are known as חֲסֵירוֹת וִיתֵרוֹת, *deletions and additions.*] Doeg was one of those great scholars who had a reliable tradition verifying which words are meant to be written with all the letters present, and which are meant to be written with certain letters absent. Thus, he was able to count properly all the letters in the Torah (*Rashi;* see *Kiddushin* 30a).

33. A *kal vachomer,* an *a fortiori* argument, is one of the thirteen methods of Biblical hermeneutics (see Glossary). Doeg was an expert in discerning which *kal vachomers* were logically sound and which were not. Thus, he was able to "weigh" them (*Rashi;* see *Maharsha*).

א) הרגו בני ישראל [בחרב] אל חלליהם אמר רב שקיימו בו ארבע מיתות סקילה ושריפה הרג וחנק א"ל ההוא מינא לר' חנינא מי שמיע לך בלעם בר כמה הוה א"ל מיכתב לא כתיב אלא מדכתיב ב) אנשי דמים ומרמה לא יחצו ימיהם בר תלתין ותלת שנין או בר תלתין וארבע א"ל שפיר קאמרת לדידי חזי לי פנקסיה דבלעם והוה כתיב ביה בר תלתין ותלת שנין בלעם חגירא כד קטיל יתיה פנחס ליסטאה א"ל מר בריה דרבינא לבריה בכולהו לא תפיש למדרש לבר מבלעם הרשע דכמה דמשכחת ביה דרוש ביה כתיב ג) דואג וכתיב ד) דוייג אמר ר' יוחנן בתחילה יושב הקב"ה ודואג שמא יצא זה לתרבות רעה לאחר שיצא אמר ווי שיצא זה (סימן גבור ורשע וצדיק חיל וסופר) א"ר יצחק מאי דכתיב ה) מה תתהלל ברעה הגבור חסד אל כל היום אמר לו הקב"ה לדואג לא גבור בתורה אתה מה תתהלל ברעה לא חסד אל נטוי עליך כל היום וא"ר יצחק מאי דכתיב ו) ולרשע אמר אלהים מה לך לספר חוקי אמר לו הקב"ה לדואג הרשע מה לך לספר חוקי כשאתה מגיע לפרשת מרצחים ופרשת מספרי לשון הרע מה אתה דורש בהם ו) ותשא בריתי עלי פיך אמר ר' אמי אין תורתו של דואג אלא משפה ולחוץ ואמר רבי יצחק מאי דכתיב ז) ויראו צדיקים וייראו ועליו ישחקו בתחילה ייראו ולבסוף ישחקו וא"ר יצחק מאי דכתיב ח) חיל בלע ויקיאנו מבטנו יורישנו אל אמר דוד לפני הקב"ה רבש"ע ימות דואג אמר לו חיל בלע ויקיאנו אמר לפניו מבטנו יורישנו אל וא"ר יצחק מאי דכתיב ט) גם אל יתצך לנצח אמר הקב"ה לדוד ניתי דואג לעלמא דאתי אמר לפניו גם אל יתצך לנצח מאי דכתיב ט) יחתך ויסחך מאהל ושרשך מארץ חיים סלה אמר הקב"ה לימרו שמעתא בי מדרשא משמיה אמר לפניו יחתך ויסחך מאהל ליהוי ליה בנין רבנן ושרשך מארץ חיים סלה וא"ר יצחק מאי דכתיב י) איה סופר איה שוקל איה סופר את המגדלים איה סופר כל אותיות שבתורה איה שוקל ששוקל כל קלים וחמורים שבתורה איה סופר את המגדלים שהיה סופר שלש מאות הלכות פסוקות במגדל הפורח באויר א"ר ארבע מאה בעיי' בעו דואג ואחיתופל במגדל הפורח באויר [ולא איפשט להו חד] אמר רבא רבותא למבעי בעיי בשני דרב יהודה כולי תנויי בנזיקין ואנן קא מתנינן טובא בעוקצין וכי הוה מטי רב יהודה אשה שכובשת ירק בקדירה ואמרי לה זיתים שכבשן בטרפיהן טהורים אמר הויות דרב ושמואל קא חזינא הכא ואנן קא מתנינן בעוקצין תלת סרי מתיבתא ורב יהודה שליף מסאני ואתא מטרא ואנן צוחינן וליכא דמשגח בן אלא הקב"ה ליבא בעי דכתיב כ) וה' יראה ללבב אמר רב משרשיא דואג ואחיתופל לא [הוו] סברי שמעתא מתקיף לה מר זוטרא מאן דכתיב ביה איה סופר איה שוקל איה סופר את המגדלים ואת אמרת לא הוו סברי שמעתא אלא דלא הוה סלקא להו שמעתא אליבא דהלכתא דכתיב ל) סוד ה' ליראיו א"ר אמי לא מת דואג עד ששכח תלמודו שנא' מ) הוא ימות באין מוסר וברוב אולתו ישגה רב (אשי) אמר נצטרע שנאמר נ) הצמתה כל זונה ממך כתיב התם ס) לצמיתות ומתרגמינן לחלוטין ותנן אין בין מוסגר ומוחלט אלא פריעה ופרימה (סימן שלשה ראו וחצי וקראו) א"ר יוחנן שלשה מלאכי חבלה נזדמנו לו לדואג אחד ששכח תלמודו ואחד ששרף נשמתו ואחד שפיזר עפרו בבתי כנסיות ובבתי מדרשות (א"ר) יוחנן דואג ואחיתופל לא ראו זה את זה דואג בימי שאול ואחיתופל בימי דוד וא"ר יוחנן דואג ואחיתופל לא חצו ימיהם תניא נמי הכי ב) אנשי דמים ומרמה לא יחצו ימיהם כל שנותיו של דואג לא היו אלא שלשים וארבע ושל אחיתופל אינן אלא שלשים ושלש וא"ר יוחנן בתחלה קרא דוד לאחיתופל רבו ולבסוף קראו חבירו ולבסוף קראו תלמידו בתחילה קראו רבו ע) ואתה אנוש כערכי אלופי ומיודעי ולבסוף קראו חבירו פ) אשר יחדו נמתיק סוד בבית אלהים נהלך ברגש ולבסוף קראו תלמידו צ) גם איש שלומי אשר בטחתי בו אוכל

רש"י

הרגו אל חלליהם. מיתות הרבה משמע שתלאוהו והציתו אש תחת הצליבה וחתכו ראשו ונפל לתוך האש תלייה היינו חנק חתיכת הראש הרג כשנפל לארץ סקילה כשנפל לאור היינו שריפה: בר תלתין ותלת. ור"ח לית ליה דר' סימאי דאמר לעיל שלשה היו באותה עצה דפרעה בלעם ואיוב ויתרו דלר' סימאי בלעם חיה יותר מן מאתים ועשר שנים דהא היה בעצת פרעה דכל הבן הילוד היאורה תשליכוהו דלרבי סימאי כל אותן מאתים ועשר שנים שהיו ישראל בגלות מצרים עד מלחמת מדין חיה בלעם: חגירא. תרגום של פיסח: כד קטל יתיה פנחס ליסטאה. שר צבא ואפילו קטליה אחר כל המלחמה נקראת על שמו: בכולהו. מלכים והדיוטות: לא תפיש ותדרוש. לגנאי: לבר מבלעם. דכל מה דמשכחת ליה לגנאי דרוש: (מ) שמא יצא זה לתרבות רעה) לאחר שיצא לתרבות רעה אמר ווי. לכך כתוב דוייג: א"ל הקב"ה לדואג והלא גבור אתה בתורה. למה תתהלל לספר לשון הרע על דוד: לא חסד תורה עליך. לא חכם בתורה אתה דכתיב (משלי לא) ותורת חסד על לשונה: מרצחים. שהרג נוב: עלי פיך. ולא בלב: בתחלה ייראו. הצדיקים היו יראים שלא ילמד אדם ממעשיו של דואג שהולך וחוטא ומצליח: ולבסוף. כשמת בחצי ימיו ושב גמולו בראשו ישחקו: חיל בלע ויקיאנו. המתן עד שתשכח תורתו: אמר לפניו ומבטנו יורישנו אל. אל תמתין לו עד שתשתכח אלא תמהר ותשכיחנו: בי מדרשא. מאהל זה בית המדרש: ושרשך מארץ חיים סלה. שורש שלו תכסח מארץ חיים דלא להוו ליה בנין רבנן: כל אותיות שבתורה. שהיה בקי בחסירות ויתירות: שוקל קלים וחמורים. יודע לדרוש בקל וחומר: במגדל הפורח באויר. מתג עליונה שלמעלה מן הלמ"ד מפני מה כפופה למטה. לשון מ"ר מפי השמועה. ל"א במגדל הפורח באויר הנכנס לארץ העמים בשידה תיבה ומגדל אם הוא טמא אם לאו. ל"א ג' מאות הלכות במגדל הפורח באויר לעשות כישוף להעמיד מגדל באויר כגון שלש מאות הלכות בנטיעות קשואין דאמרן בפירקין דלעיל (דף סח.) ולמורי נראה דה"ג שלש מאות הלכות במגדל העומד [באויר] ומשנה אחת באהלות (פ"ד משנה א) דמשתעי בהכי מגדל העומד באויר וטומאה בתוכה כלים שבתוכו טמאים וכן נראה לר': רבותא למבעא בעיי. וללמוד תורה רחמנא לבא בעי דהא בשני דרב יהודה כולהו תנויי בסדר נזיקין היה כל הגמרא שלהן לא הוה אלא בסדר נזיקין שלא היו מרבין כל כך [לדרוש]: האשה שכובשת ירק בקדירה. לא אשכחתיה במסכת עוקצין: שכובשת ירק. בחומץ או בציר טהורים דאין מקבלין טומאה ע"י עוקצין שאם נגע טומאה בשרשיו העלין טהורין שאין נעשין יד לעלין מאחר שכבשם שאין מניחין לשם אלא למראה: זיתים שכבשן בטרפיהן. איתא במסכת עוקצין (פ"ב מ"א): טרפיהן. עלין שלהן טהורין הזיתים שאין נעשין להם בית יד להכניס להם טומאה: הויות דרב ושמואל קא חזינא הכא. דלא הוה ידע מאי טעמא הן טהורין: תליסר מתיבתא. י"ג ישיבות שאנו עוסקין כולן במסכת עוקצין ויודעין אותה יפה ואפי' הכי בהם היו חסידים יותר ממנו דאלו רב יהודה כו': לא סבירי. לא היו יודעין הלכה לפרשה כתקנה בטעמא: דלא סלקא להו שמעתא כו'. שלא זכו לקבוע הלכה כמותן: ומתרגמינן לחלוטין. ואנן תנן לשון חלוטין גבי מצורע: אלופי. היינו רבי:

לא א מיי' פי"ו מהל' טומאת צרעת הל' י:

תורה אור השלם

א) וְאֶת בִּלְעָם בֶּן בְּעוֹר הַקּוֹסֵם הָרְגוּ בְנֵי יִשְׂרָאֵל בַּחֶרֶב אֶל חַלְלֵיהֶם: [יהושע יג, כב]

ב) וְאַתָּה אֱלֹהִים תּוֹרִדֵם לִבְאֵר שַׁחַת אַנְשֵׁי דָמִים וּמִרְמָה לֹא יֶחֱצוּ יְמֵיהֶם וַאֲנִי אֶבְטַח בָּךְ: [תהלים נה, כד]

ג) וְשָׁם אִישׁ מֵעַבְדֵי שָׁאוּל בַּיּוֹם הַהוּא נֶעְצָר לִפְנֵי יְיָ וּשְׁמוֹ דֹּאֵג הָאֲדֹמִי אַבִּיר הָרֹעִים אֲשֶׁר לְשָׁאוּל: [שמואל א' כא, ח]

ד) וַיֹּאמֶר הַמֶּלֶךְ לְדוֹאֵג (לדויג) סֹב אַתָּה וּפְגַע בַּכֹּהֲנִים וַיִּסֹּב דּוֹאֵג הָאֲדֹמִי וַיִּפְגַּע הוּא בַּכֹּהֲנִים וַיָּמֶת בַּיּוֹם הַהוּא שְׁמֹנִים וַחֲמִשָּׁה אִישׁ נֹשֵׂא אֵפוֹד בָּד: [שמואל א' כב, יח]

ה) מַה תִּתְהַלֵּל בְּרָעָה הַגִּבּוֹר חֶסֶד אֵל כָּל הַיּוֹם: [תהלים נב, ג]

ו) וְלָרָשָׁע אָמַר אֱלֹהִים מַה לְּךָ לְסַפֵּר חֻקָּי וַתִּשָּׂא בְרִיתִי עֲלֵי פִיךָ: [תהלים נ, טז]

ז) וְיִרְאוּ צַדִּיקִים וְיִירָאוּ וְעָלָיו יִשְׂחָקוּ: [תהלים נב, ח]

ח) חַיִל בָּלַע וַיְקִאֶנּוּ מִבִּטְנוֹ יֹרִשֶׁנּוּ אֵל: [איוב כ, טו]

ט) גַּם אֵל יִתָּצְךָ לָנֶצַח יַחְתְּךָ וְיִסָּחֲךָ מֵאֹהֶל וְשֵׁרֶשְׁךָ מֵאֶרֶץ חַיִּים סֶלָה: [תהלים נב, ז]

י) לִבְּךָ יֶהְגֶּה אֵימָה אַיֵּה סֹפֵר אַיֵּה שֹׁקֵל אַיֵּה סֹפֵר אֶת הַמִּגְדָּלִים: [ישעיה לג, יח]

כ) וַיֹּאמֶר יְיָ אֶל שְׁמוּאֵל אַל תַּבֵּט אֶל מַרְאֵהוּ וְאֶל גְּבֹהַּ קוֹמָתוֹ כִּי מְאַסְתִּיהוּ כִּי לֹא אֲשֶׁר יִרְאֶה הָאָדָם כִּי הָאָדָם יִרְאֶה לַעֵינַיִם וַיְיָ יִרְאֶה לַלֵּבָב: [שמואל א' טז, ז]

ל) סוֹד יְיָ לִירֵאָיו וּבְרִיתוֹ לְהוֹדִיעָם: [תהלים כה, יד]

מ) הוּא יָמוּת בְּאֵין מוּסָר וּבְרֹב אִוַּלְתּוֹ יִשְׁגֶּה: [משלי ה, כג]

נ) כִּי הִנֵּה רְחֵקֶיךָ יֹאבֵדוּ הִצְמַתָּה כָּל זוֹנֶה מִמֶּךָּ: [תהלים עג, כז]

ס) וְהָאָרֶץ לֹא תִמָּכֵר לִצְמִתֻת כִּי לִי הָאָרֶץ כִּי גֵרִים וְתוֹשָׁבִים אַתֶּם עִמָּדִי: [ויקרא כה, כג]

ע) וְאַתָּה אֱנוֹשׁ כְּעֶרְכִּי אַלּוּפִי וּמְיֻדָּעִי: [תהלים נה, יד]

פ) אֲשֶׁר יַחְדָּו נַמְתִּיק סוֹד בְּבֵית אֱלֹהִים נְהַלֵּךְ בְּרָגֶשׁ: [תהלים נה, טו]

צ) גַּם אִישׁ שְׁלוֹמִי אֲשֶׁר בָּטַחְתִּי בוֹ אוֹכֵל לַחְמִי הִגְדִּיל עָלַי עָקֵב: [תהלים מא, י]

א) [עי' תוספתא בע"י], ב) [חגיגה טו:], ג) נ"א א"ר אמי, ד) תענית כד: ע"ש ברכות כ. ע"ש, ה) נ"א בשיתא סידרי, ו) [טהרות פ"ב מ"א], ז) [עוקצ' פ"ב מ"א], ח) מגילה ח: ערכין טו:, ט) [נ"ל ואמר ר'], י) לעיל סט:, כ) [אבות פ"ו מ"ג], ל) בילקוט ת"ב סוף רמז תשמא הגירסא ולבסוף קראו איש, מ) רש"ל מ"ז.

ליקוטי רש"י

מה תתהלל. ותתפאר ברעה שאתה עושה אתה הגבור בתורה. חסד אל כל היום. להציל את הנרדף על ידך [תהלים נב, ג]. ועליו ישחקו. וזה השחוק שיאמרו עליו הנה זה הגבר אשר לא שם מבטחו בהקב"ה ראו מה עלתה בו [תהלים נב, ח]. יתצך. ל' נתיצה. יחתך. לשון שבירה. ויסחך. ויעקרך. ושרשך. ישרש אחריך לעקור כל השרשים דיראצינע"ר בלעז [שם ז]. קלים וחמורים. דברים הלמדין בקל וחומר שניתנו לדון מעצמן לכל אדם ולא פירשו כלום בסיני [סוכה כח.]. קלים וחמורים שאדם דן מעצמו [ב"ב קלד.]. הלכות פסוקות. הלכה כפלוני ופלוני [יבמות מב:]. במגדל הפורח באויר. יש מפרשים שדורשין גוגהו של למ"ד ודורשין בו כל זאת ויש אומרים מגדל דור הפלגה ולי נראה מגדל הפתוח לאויר גרסינן והן מהלכות אהלות מגדל של עץ שקורין משטיי"ר ועומד בפתח ופתחו פתוח לבקעה או לאגר שהוא אויר במסכת אהלות (פרק רביעי משנה א) ישנה משנה מגדל העומד באויר [חגיגה טו:]. בנזיקין הוה. למודם לא היה גדול אלא בסדר נזיקין. שכובשת ירק בקדירה. במסכת [טהרות] היא בפרק שני (משנה א') גבי ידות מיירי דקיימא לן (עוקצין פ"א מ"א) כל ידות האוכלין אם נגעה טומאה בהן נטמא גם האוכל הצריך לידות, דיד מכנים ומוציא כדאמרינן בהעור והרוטב (חולין קיח.) מכל האוכל לרבות הידות וקתני התם אשה שהיא כובשת ירק דידות שלהן טהורין דכשהיא עוקרת אותם הידות משתברות ואי אפשר ליטול הירקות בידות שלהן שנשמט ונפסק האוכל מן היד מחמת כבישה. כובשת. שול"ץ בלע"ז עוקרת שילא המשקה שלהן ויבשו דרך אשה בכך כובשת ירק ממים שישתמרו לזמן מרובה טהורין העלין והקלחין. ואמרי לה. כי מטא לאידך בפרק שני (דעוקצין מ"א) זיתים שכבשן בטרפיהן כתרגומו עלה טרפא (בראשית ח) עלין שלהן דהיינו ידות. טהורים. הידות להביא טומאה לאוכל דתו לא חזי למסוי בית יד. הוויות דרב ושמואל. עומק גדול ולא הוה נהירא ליה.

תליסר מתיבתא. שלש עשרה ישיבות איכא בהך מתא דגמרי מסכת עוקצין. שליף חד מסאנא. משום עינוי. דחזא מידי. חס ושלום בעובדי ביש׳ [תענית כד:]. בנזיקין הוה. לא היו גדולים בכל גמרא של ארבעה סדרים אלא בתלתא בבי. האשה שכובשת ירק או זיתים שכבשן בטרפיהן. משנה היא במסכת עוקצין. טהורים. שמוסקין זיתים עם העלין כדי לאחוז בהן דהוו להו עלין יד לזיתים להביא להם טומאה כדאמרינן בהעור והרוטב (דף קי"ח.) שהיד מביאה טומאה על האוכל ואם כבשן בטרפיהן בחומץ בטלה תורת יד מן העלין לפי שהכבישה מרכבתן ומרככתן ואינן ראוין שוב לאחוז בהן. הויות דרב ושמואל קא חזינא הכא. כלומר טעם המשניות הללו קשה עלי ככל הקושיות שהיו שני רבותי מתקשין בהן בכל הגמרא. בתליסר מתיבתא. בשלש עשרה פנים יש בינינו משנה ובריתא של ששה סדרים ומסכת עוקצין גם היא בשלש עשרה פנים כגון משנת רבי ורבי חייא ומשנת בר קפרא ולוי ותנא דבי שמואל והכי אמרינן במסכת נדרים (דף מ"א.) רבי מתני הלכתא בשלש עשרה פנים [ברכות כ.]. לצמיתת. לפסיקה למכירה פסוקה עולמית [ויקרא כה, כג]. פריעה ופרימה. בגדיו יהיו פרומים וראשו יהי׳ פרוע. מוחלט. לאחר שכלו ימי ההסגר ונראה בו סימני טומאה האמורין בו [מגילה ח:].

refers to Doeg, **for he used to enumerate three hundred decided laws concerning a tower which floats in the air.**[34]

Further discussion of Doeg's scholarship:

[אָמַר רַבִּי [אַמִּי – **R' Ami said:** אַרְבַּע מֵאָה בַּעְיָא בָּעוּ דוֹאֵג וַאֲחִיתוֹפֶל בְּמִגְדָּל הַפּוֹרֵחַ בָּאֲוִיר – **Doeg and Achithophel**[35] **raised four hundred** halachic **inquiries concerning a tower which floats in the air,** [וְלֹא אִיפְּשַׁט לְהוּ חַד] – **and** the inquiries were so profound that **not** even **one was resolved by them].**[36]

A comment on R' Ami's statement:

אָמַר רָבָא – **Rava said:** רְבוּתָא לְמִבָּעֵי בְּעָיֵי – Is it a sign of **greatness to raise inquiries?**[37] בִּשְׁנֵי דְּרַב יְהוּדָה כּוּלֵּי תְּנוּיֵי בִּנְזִיקִין – **Why, in the years of Rav Yehudah, all the teaching** of the academies **was in** the Mishnaic Order of ***Nezikin.***[38] וַאֲנַן קָא מַתְנִינָן טוּבָא בְּעוּקְצִין – **We,** by contrast, **are well versed in** all six Orders of the Mishnah, down to the last Mishnaic tractate, ***Uktzin.***[39] וְכִי הֲוָה מָטֵי רַב יְהוּדָה – **Moreover, when** in the course of his lectures **Rav Yehudah would reach** the following Mishnah: ,,אִשָּׁה שֶׁכּוֹבֶשֶׁת יָרָק בַּקְּדֵירָה'' – IF A WOMAN IS PRESERVING A VEGETABLE IN A POT;[40] וְאָמְרֵי לָהּ ,,זֵיתִים שֶׁכְּבָשָׁן בִּטְרְפֵיהֶן טְהוֹרִים'' – **and others say** that it was this Mishnah:[41] OLIVES THAT ONE PRESERVED TOGETHER WITH THEIR LEAVES ARE *TAHOR;* אָמַר – **he would say:** הֲוָיוֹת דְּרַב וּשְׁמוּאֵל קָא חָזֵינָא הָכָא – **I see here** a need for **the** penetrating **inquiries of Rav and Shmuel!**[42] וַאֲנַן קָא מַתְנִינָן בְּעוּקְצִין תְּלַת סְרֵי מְתִיבָתָא – **Whereas we** nowadays **teach** Tractate ***Uktzin*** **in thirteen** different **schools** and are thoroughly proficient in it.[43] Thus, we are superior to Rav Yehudah's generation in Torah scholarship. וְרַב יְהוּדָה שָׁלִיף מְסָאנֵי וַאֲתָא מִטְרָא – **Yet** when there was a drought in his days, **Rav Yehudah would** merely **remove his shoe** as a sign of affliction **and rain would come** immediately,[44] וַאֲנַן צָוְחִינָן – **whereas we cry out**

NOTES

34. There are numerous interpretations of this phrase. *Rashi* offers four:

(a) The Hebrew letter *lamed* is composed of a *chaf* with a *vav* on top. (It is, in fact, the only letter in the Hebrew Ashuris alphabet with an upper part.) The rule is that the *vav* of the *lamed* should be slanted slightly leftward (see *Beis Yosef* to *Orach Chaim* 36 in the name of *Sefer HaManhig;* see also *Mishnas Sofrim* and *Meleches Shamayim* 26:23). Thus, the upper *vav* resembles a tower floating leftward in the air away from the *chaf* to which it is attached at its base. [Some explain that the *head* of the upper *vav* is supposed to tilt downwards, as if it is floating away from its base (see *Mishnas Sofrim* and *Meleches Shamayim* ibid.).] Doeg had such a profound understanding of even the minutest details of Torah law that he knew three hundred reasons why the *vav* of the *lamed* is supposed to slant. [For an additional discussion of this, see *Toras Chaim's* introduction to this chapter.]

(b) Doeg knew three hundred rules concerning the *tumah* and *taharah* of one who is transported outside of Eretz Yisrael in a closet (an alternative translation of מִגְדָּל) or in any other sealed container which can act as a barrier against *tumah* (see *Oholos* 8:1). Foreign lands (outside of Eretz Yisrael) were declared *tamei* by the Sages because of their concern for the presence of unmarked graves there. Thus, anyone who walks outside of Eretz Yisrael is automatically considered *tamei.* It is a matter of dispute whether this applies to one who is transported over foreign lands in a sealed container. (See the discussions between the Sages concerning this scenario in *Eruvin* 30b, *Gittin* 8b and *Nazir* 54b-55a.)

(c) Doeg knew three hundred methods of suspending a tower in the air through sorcery. A Torah scholar is required to be familiar with all methods of sorcery in order to be able to prosecute sorcerers, whose practice is prohibited by the Torah. For a similar example of such knowledge, see above, 68a, and the Gaonic Responsum quoted there by *Margaliyos HaYam* §14.

(d) The Gemara should read: שְׁלֹשׁ מֵאוֹת הֲלָכוֹת בְּמִגְדָּל הָעוֹמֵד בָּאֲוִיר, *three hundred laws concerning a tower* ***standing*** *in the [open] air.* This is a reference to a case cited in *Oholos* 4:1, which discusses the law of *tumah* that is contained in a closet standing in the open air, as opposed to inside a house.

Maharsha understands the "tower" as an allusion to the *Beis HaMikdash,* concerning which there was considerable uncertainty as to where it was supposed to be built. Since its future location was unknown, it is alluded to as "floating in the air." Doeg knew three hundred laws concerning the determination of its location (see note 36). For additional interpretations, see *Yad Ramah* and *Maharal.*

[Note that the number three hundred is often used in the Talmud as a representation of an exaggerated figure (*Rashbam, Pesachim* 119a ד״ה משוי; see *Chullin* 90b; see also *Margaliyos HaYam,* and 96b note 5).]

35. Achithophel was another one of David's enemies who lost his share in the World to Come. The Gemara discusses his downfall below. Like Doeg, he was an accomplished Torah scholar who turned sour. Note that although Doeg and Achithophel are mentioned together here, they were not contemporaries. As the Gemara states below, Doeg lived in the days of King Saul (i.e. in David's youth) whereas Achithophel lived later, in the days of David's reign. Thus, the Gemara here means that Doeg and Achithophel, each in his own days, raised four hundred inquiries concerning the tower floating in the air.

36. *Maharsha,* following his aforecited approach, understands Doeg's four hundred queries as pertaining to the site of the *Beis HaMikdash.* Although Doeg knew three hundred decided laws concerning the correct location, he was still left with four hundred unresolved queries. The Gemara in *Zevachim* (54b) relates that David, after considerable exertion, was finally able to determine with certainty the proper location, and that his accomplishment aroused Doeg's jealousy. It is to that incident that the Gemara alludes here. See *Maharal* and *Ben Yehoyada* for explanations of the significance of the number four hundred.

37. I.e. is Torah scholarship itself indicative of true greatness? (*Rashi*).

38. I.e. the yeshivos confined their most rigorous and in-depth study to the tractates found in the Mishnaic Order of *Nezikin* (*Damages*), due to the preponderance of civil disputes that they were called upon to adjudicate, and studied the other Orders more superficially (*Rashi, Yad Ramah;* cf. *Rashi* to *Berachos* 20a ד״ה בנזיקין). *Maharsha* and *Be'er Sheva* attribute the emphasis on *Nezikin* to the rule that "he who wishes to be righteous should be meticulous in the observance of matters of *Nezikin*" (*Bava Kamma* 30a). [The Mishnah is divided into six orders, the fourth of which is *Nezikin.* This order deals primarily with matters of civil law, such as damages, debts, transactions and ownership.]

39. Our elucidation follows the version of this statement cited in *Taanis* (24b).

40. These words form the opening phrase of *Tohoros* 2:1. It is explained in note 42.

41. *Uktzin* 2:1.

42. Foods are susceptible to *tumah,* whereas the inedible by-products of food, such as stems and leaves, are generally not susceptible to *tumah* (*Rambam, Hil. Tumas Ochalim* 1:1). However, stems and leaves that serve as handles to fruits or vegetables are susceptible to *tumah,* and, if they come in contact with a source of *tumah,* convey the *tumah* to the entire fruit (see *Uktzin* 1:1). Exactly when they do and do not convey *tumah* is the subject of Tractate *Uktzin.*

The first Mishnah cited (*Tohoros* 2:1) teaches that if a woman preserves a vegetable in vinegar or another preservative, the stem loses its status as a handle to the vegetable, since the pickling so softens it that it is no longer fit to carry the weight of the vegetable. It is usually left attached only to enhance the vegetable's appearance. Hence, the stem is no longer susceptible to *tumah,* nor can it serve as a conduit for conveying *tumah* to the vegetable. Similarly, the second Mishnah (*Uktzin* 2:1) teaches that if one preserved olives with their leaves, the leaves lose their status as handles to the olives, since they become very soft and flimsy through pickling. They are thenceforth *tahor* (*Rashi* here and to *Berachos* 20a ד״ה טהורים; see also *Rashi* to *Taanis* 24b).

When Rav Yehudah reached one of these Mishnahs, he would comment that to understand its reasoning properly he would need the inquiries of his teachers Rav and Shmuel. He considered their inquiries into the meaning of a Mishnah the archetype of penetrating analysis. Thus, Rav Yehudah admitted that he did not fully understand the reasoning of a Mishnah dealing with the laws of *Uktzin.*

43. *Rashi.* Alternatively: We have thirteen versions of Mishnayos and Baraisos, representing thirteen different approaches to understanding Tractate *Uktzin* (*Rashi* to *Berachos* 20a; see *Yad Ramah*). [Although the first Mishnah cited is not in Tractate *Uktzin,* the law it refers to is related to the subject of that tractate (see *Rashash* here and *Tzlach* to *Berachos* 20a).]

44. Removing one's shoes is a sign of affliction and symbolic of a major fast day (see *Yoma* 73b and 77a). As soon as Rav Yehudah would remove a single shoe, as a sign of sharing in the suffering of the community, it

עין משפט
נר מצוה

לא א מיי' פ"י מהל' טומאת צרעת הל' י:

תורה אור השלם

א) וְאֶת בִּלְעָם בֶּן בְּעוֹר הַקּוֹסֵם הָרְגוּ בְנֵי יִשְׂרָאֵל בַּחֶרֶב אֶל חַלְלֵיהֶם: [יהושע יג, כב]

ב) וְאַתָּה אֱלֹהִים תּוֹרִדֵם לִבְאֵר שַׁחַת אַנְשֵׁי דָמִים וּמִרְמָה לֹא יֶחֱצוּ יְמֵיהֶם וַאֲנִי אֶבְטַח בָּךְ: [תהלים נה, כד]

ג) וְשָׁם אִישׁ מֵעַבְדֵי שָׁאוּל בַּיּוֹם הַהוּא נֶעְצָר לִפְנֵי יְיָ וּשְׁמוֹ דֹּאֵג הָאֲדֹמִי אַבִּיר הָרֹעִים אֲשֶׁר לְשָׁאוּל: [שמואל א' כא, ח]

ד) וַיֹּאמֶר הַמֶּלֶךְ לְדוֹאֵג (לדויג) סֹב אַתָּה וּפְגַע בַּכֹּהֲנִים וַיִּסֹּב דּוֹאֵג הָאֲדֹמִי וַיִּפְגַּע הוּא בַּכֹּהֲנִים וַיָּמֶת בַּיּוֹם הַהוּא שְׁמֹנִים וַחֲמִשָּׁה אִישׁ נֹשֵׂא אֵפוֹד בָּד: [שמואל א' כב, יח]

ה) מַה תִּתְהַלֵּל בְּרָעָה הַגִּבּוֹר חֶסֶד אֵל כָּל הַיּוֹם: [תהלים נב, ג]

ו) וְלָרָשָׁע אָמַר אֱלֹהִים מַה לְּךָ לְסַפֵּר חֻקָּי וַתִּשָּׂא בְרִיתִי עֲלֵי פִיךָ: [תהלים נ, טז]

ז) וְיִרְאוּ צַדִּיקִים וְיִירָאוּ וְעָלָיו יִשְׂחָקוּ: [תהלים נב, ח]

ח) חַיִל בָּלַע וַיְקִאֶנּוּ מִבִּטְנוֹ יֹרִשֶׁנּוּ אֵל: [איוב כ, טו]

ט) גַּם אֵל יִתָּצְךָ לָנֶצַח יַחְתְּךָ וְיִסָּחֲךָ מֵאֹהֶל וְשֵׁרֶשְׁךָ מֵאֶרֶץ חַיִּים סֶלָה: [תהלים נב, ז]

י) לִבְּךָ יֶהְגֶּה אֵימָה אַיֵּה סֹפֵר אַיֵּה שֹׁקֵל אַיֵּה סֹפֵר אֶת הַמִּגְדָּלִים: [ישעיה לג, יח]

כ) וַיֹּאמֶר יְיָ אֶל שְׁמוּאֵל אַל תַּבֵּט אֶל מַרְאֵהוּ וְאֶל גְּבֹהַּ קוֹמָתוֹ כִּי מְאַסְתִּיהוּ כִּי לֹא אֲשֶׁר יִרְאֶה הָאָדָם כִּי הָאָדָם יִרְאֶה לַעֵינַיִם וַייָ יִרְאֶה לַלֵּבָב: [שמואל א' טז, ז]

ל) סוֹד יְיָ לִירֵאָיו וּבְרִיתוֹ לְהוֹדִיעָם: [תהלים כה, יד]

מ) הוּא יָמוּת בְּאֵין מוּסָר וּבְרֹב אִוַּלְתּוֹ יִשְׁגֶּה: [משלי ה, כג]

נ) כִּי הִנֵּה רְחֵקֶיךָ יֹאבֵדוּ הִצְמַתָּה כָּל זוֹנֶה מִמֶּךָּ: [תהלים עג, כז]

ס) וְהָאָרֶץ לֹא תִמָּכֵר לִצְמִתֻת כִּי לִי הָאָרֶץ כִּי גֵרִים וְתוֹשָׁבִים אַתֶּם עִמָּדִי: [ויקרא כה, כג]

ע) וְאַתָּה אֱנוֹשׁ כְּעֶרְכִּי אַלּוּפִי וּמְיֻדָּעִי: [תהלים נה, יד]

פ) אֲשֶׁר יַחְדָּו נַמְתִּיק סוֹד בְּבֵית אֱלֹהִים נְהַלֵּךְ בְּרָגֶשׁ: [תהלים נה, טו]

צ) גַּם אִישׁ שְׁלוֹמִי אֲשֶׁר בָּטַחְתִּי בוֹ אוֹכֵל לַחְמִי הִגְדִּיל עָלַי עָקֵב: [תהלים מא, י]

א) הרגו בני ישראל [בחרב] אל חלליהם אמר רב שקיימו בו ארבע מיתות סקילה ושריפה הרג וחנק א"ל ההוא מינא לר' חנינא מי שמיע לך בלעם בר כמה הוה א"ל מיכתב לא כתיב אלא מדכתיב ב) אנשי דמים ומרמה לא יחצו ימיהם בר תלתין ותלת שנין או בר תלתין וארבע א"ל שפיר קאמרת לדידי חזי לי פנקסיה דבלעם והוה כתיב ביה בר תלתין ותלת שנין בלעם חגירא כד קטיל יתיה פנחס ליסטאה א"ל מר בריה דרבינא לבריה בכולהו לא תפיש למדרש לבר מבלעם הרשע דכמה דמשכחת ביה דרוש ביה כתיב ג) דואג וכתיב ד) דויג אמר ר' יוחנן בתחילה יושב הקב"ה ודואג שמא יצא זה לתרבות רעה לאחר שיצא אמר ווי שיצא זה (סימן גבור ורשע וצדיק חיל וסופר) א"ר יצחק מאי דכתיב ה) מה תתהלל ברעה הגבור חסד אל כל היום אמר לו הקב"ה לדואג לא גבור בתורה אתה מה תתהלל ברעה לא חסד אל נטוי עליך כל היום וא"ר יצחק מאי דכתיב ו) ולרשע אמר אלהים מה לך לספר חוקי אמר לו הקב"ה לדואג הרשע מה לך לספר חוקי כשאתה מגיע לפרשת מרצחים ופרשת מספרי לשון הרע מה אתה דורש בהם ו) ותשא בריתי עלי פיך אמר ר' אמי אין תורתו של דואג אלא משפה ולחוץ ואמר רבי יצחק מאי דכתיב ז) ויראו צדיקים וייראו ועליו ישחקו בתחילה ייראו ולבסוף ישחקו וא"ר יצחק מאי דכתיב ח) חיל בלע ויקיאנו מבטנו יורישנו אל אמר דוד לפני הקב"ה רבש"ע ימות דואג אמר לו חיל בלע ויקיאנו אמר לפניו מבטנו יורישנו אל וא"ר יצחק מאי דכתיב ט) גם אל יתצך לנצח אמר הקב"ה לדוד ניתי דואג לעלמא דאתי אמר לפניו גם אל יתצך לנצח א) מאי דכתיב ט) יחתך ויסחך מאהל ושרשך מארץ חיים סלה אמר הקב"ה לימרו שמעתא בי מדרשא משמיה אמר לפניו יחתך ויסחך מאהל ליהוי ליה בנין רבנן ושרשך מארץ חיים סלה וא"ר יצחק ב) מאי דכתיב י) איה סופר איה שוקל איה סופר את המגדלים איה סופר כל אותיות שבתורה איה שוקל ששוקל כל קלים וחמורים שבתורה איה סופר את המגדלים שהיה סופר שלש מאות הלכות פסוקות במגדל הפורח באויר ג) א"ר ארבע מאה בעיי' בעו דואג ואחיתופל במגדל הפורח באויר [ולא איפשט להו חד] אמר רבא רבותא למבעי בעיי ד) בשני דרב יהודה כולי תנויי בנזיקין ואנן קא מתנינן טובא ה) בעוקצין וכי הוה מטי רב יהודה ו) אשה שכובשת ירק בקדירה ואמרי לה ז) זיתים שכבשן בטרפיהן טהורים אמר הויות דרב ושמואל קא חזינא הכא ואנן קא מתנינן בעוקצין תלת סרי מתיבתא ורב יהודה שליף מסאני ואתא מטרא ואנן צוחינן וליכא דמשגח בן אלא הקב"ה ליבא בעי דכתיב כ) וה' יראה ללבב אמר רב משרשיא דואג ואחיתופל לא [הוו] סברי שמעתא מתקיף לה מר זוטרא מאן דכתיב ביה איה סופר איה שוקל איה סופר את המגדלים ואת אמרת לא הוו סברי שמעתא אלא דלא הוה סלקא להו שמעתא אליבא דהלכתא דכתיב ל) סוד ה' ליראיו א"ר אמי לא מת דואג עד ששכח תלמודו שנא' מ) הוא ימות באין מוסר וברוב אולתו ישגה רב (אשי) אמר נצטרע שנאמר נ) הצמתה כל זונה ממך כתיב התם ס) לצמיתות ומתרגמינן לחלוטין ח) ותנן אין בין מוסגר ומוחלט אלא פריעה ופרימה (סימן שלשה ראו וחצי וקראו) א"ר יוחנן שלשה מלאכי חבלה נזדמנו לו לדואג אחד ששכח תלמודו ואחד ששרף נשמתו ואחד שפיזר עפרו בבתי כנסיות ובבתי מדרשות (ט) א"ר) יוחנן דואג ואחיתופל לא ראו זה את זה דואג בימי שאול ואחיתופל בימי דוד וא"ר יוחנן דואג ואחיתופל לא חצו ימיהם תניא נמי הכי ב) אנשי דמים ומרמה לא יחצו ימיהם י) כל שנותיו של דואג לא היו אלא שלשים וארבע ושל אחיתופל אינן אלא שלשים ושלש וא"ר יוחנן בתחלה קרא דוד לאחיתופל רבו ולבסוף קראו חבירו ולבסוף קראו תלמידו בתחילה כ) קראו רבו ע) ואתה אנוש כערכי אלופי ומיודעי ולבסוף קראו חבירו פ) אשר יחדו נמתיק סוד בבית אלהים נהלך ברגש ולבסוף קראו ל) תלמידו צ) גם איש שלומי אשר בטחתי בו

אוכל

הרגו אל חלליהם. מיתות הרבה משמע שתלאוהו והעלוהו אש תחת הצליבה וחתכו ראשו ונפל לתוך האש תלייה היינו חנק חתיכת הראש הרג כשנפל לארץ סקילה כשנפל לאור היינו שריפה: בר תלתין ותלת. ור"ח לית ליה דר' סימאי דאמר לעיל שלשה היו באותה עצה דפרעה בלעם ואיוב ויתרו דלר' סימאי בלעם היה יותר מן מאתים ועשר שנים דהא היה בעצת פרעה דכל הבן הילוד היאורה תשליכוהו דלרבי סימאי כל אותן מאתים ועשר שנים שהיו ישראל בגלות מצרים עד מלחמת מדין היה בלעם: חגירא. תרגום של פיסח: כד קטל יתיה פנחס ליסטאה. שר צבא ואפילו קטליה אחר כל המלחמה נקראת על שמו: בכולהו. מלכים והדיוטות: לא תפיש ותדרוש. לגנאי: לבר מבלעם. דכל מה דמשכחת ליה לגנאי דרוש: ((מ) שמא יצא זה לתרבות רעה) לאחר שיצא לתרבות רעה אמר ווי. לכך כתוב דויג: א"ל הקב"ה לדואג והלא גבור אתה בתורה. למה תתהלל לספר לשון הרע על דוד: לא חסד תורה עליך. לא חכם בתורה אתה דכתיב (משלי לא) ותורת חסד על לשונה: מרצחים. שהרג נוב: עלי פיך. ולא בלב: בתחלה ייראו. הצדיקים היו יראים שלא ילמד אדם ממעשיו של דואג שהולך וחוטא ומצליח: ולבסוף. כשמת בחצי ימיו ושב גמולו בראשו ישחקו: חיל בלע ויקיאנו. המתן עד שתשכח תורתו: אמר לפניו ומבטנו יורישנו אל. אל תמתין לו עד שתשתכח אלא תמהר ותשכיחנו: בי מדרשא. מאהל זה בית המדרש: ושרשך מארץ חיים סלה. שורש שלו תכסח מארץ חיים דלא להוו ליה בנין רבנן: כל אותיות שבתורה. שהיה בקי בחסירות ויתירות: שוקל קלים וחמורים. יודע לדרוש בקל וחומר: במגדל הפורח באויר. מתג עליונה שלמעלה מן הלמ"ד מפני מה כפופה למטה. לשון מ"ר מפי השמועה. ל"א במגדל הפורח באויר הנכנס לארץ העמים בשידה תיבה ומגדל אם הוא טמא אם לאו. ל"א ג' מאות הלכות במגדל הפורח באויר לעשות כישוף להעמיד מגדל באויר כגון שלש מאות הלכות בנטיעות קשואין דאמרן בפירקין דלעיל (דף סח.) ולמורי נראה דה"ג שלש מאות הלכות במגדל העומד [באויר] ומשנה אחת באהלות (פ"ד משנה א) דמשתעי בהכי מגדל העומד באויר וטומאה בתוכה כלים שבתוכו טמאים וכן נראה לר': רבותא למבעא בעיי. וללמוד תורה רחמנא לבא בעי דהא בשני דרב יהודה כולהו תנויי בסדר נזיקין היה כל הגמרא שלהן לא הוה אלא בסדר נזיקין שלא היו מרבין כל כך [לדרוש]: האשה שכובשת ירק בקדירה. לא אשכחתיה במסכת עוקלין: שכובשת ירק. בחומץ או בציר טהורים דאין מקבלין טומאה ע"י עוקלין שאם נגע טומאה בשרשיו העלין טהורין שאין נעשין יד לעלין מאחר שכבשם שאין מניחין לשם אלא למראה: זיתים שכבשן בטרפיהן. איתא במסכת עוקלין (פ"ב מ"א): טרפיהן. עלין שלהן טהורין הזיתים שאין נעשין להם בית יד להכניס להם טומאה: הויות דרב ושמואל קא חזינא הכא. דלא הוה ידע מאי טעמא הן טהורין: תליסר מתיבתא. י"ג ישיבות שאנו עוסקין כולן במסכת עוקלין ויודעין אותה יפה ואפי' הכי בהם היו חסידים יותר ממנו דאלו רב יהודה כו': לא סבירי. לא היו יודעין הלכה לפרשה כתקנה בטעמא: דלא סלקא להו שמעתתא כו'. שלא זכו לקבוע הלכה כמותן: ומתרגמינן לחלוטין. ואנן תנן לשון חלוטין גבי מצורע: אלופי. היינו רבי:

אוכל

מסורת הש"ס

א) [עי' הנוסחא בע"י], ב) [חגיגה טו:], ג) נ"א א"ר אמי, ד) תענית כד: ע"ש ברכות כ. ע"ש, ה) נ"א בשיתא סידרי, ו) [טהרות פ"ב מ"א], ז) [עוקצי' פ"ב מ"א], ח) מגילה ח: ערכין טו., ט) [נ"ל ואמר ר'], י) לעיל סט:, כ) [אבות פ"ו מ"ג], ל) בילקוט ח"ב סוף רמז תשמא הגירסא ולבסוף קראו איש, מ) רש"ל מ"ז.

ליקוטי רש"י

מה תתהלל. ותתפאר ברעה שאתה עושה אתה הגבור בתורה. חסד אל כל היום. להציל את הנרדף על ידך [תהלים נב, ג]. ועליו ישחקו. וזה השחוק שיאמרו עליו הנה זה הגבר אשר לא שם מבטחו בהקב"ה ראו מה עלתה בו [תהלים נב, ח]. יתצך. ל' נתיצה. יחתך. לשון שבירה. ויסחך. ויעקרך. ושרשך. ישרש אחריך לעקור כל השרשים דירא"רילינע"ר בלעז [שם ז]. קלים וחמורים. דברים הלמדין בקל וחומר שניתנו לדון מעצמן לכל אדם ולא פירשו כלום בסיני [סוכה כח.]. קלים וחמורים שאדם דן מעצמו [ב"ב קלד.]. הלכות פסוקות. הלכה כפלוני ופלוני [יבמות מב:]. במגדל הפורח באויר. יש מפרשים שדורשין גובהו של למ"ד ודורשין בו כל זאת ויש אומרים מגדל דור הפלגה ולי נראה מגדל הפתוח לאויר גרסינן והן מהלכות אהלות מגדל של עץ שקורין משטיי"ר ועומד בפתח ופתחו פתוח לבקעה או לחצר שהוא אויר במסכת אהלות (פרק רביעי משנה א) ישנה משנה מגדל העומד באויר [חגיגה טו:]. בנזיקין הוה. למודם לא היה גדול אלא בסדר נזיקין. שכובשת ירק בקדירה. במסכת [טהרות] היא בפרק שני (משנה א') גבי ידות מיירי דקיימא לן (עוקצין פ"א מ"א) כל ידות האוכלין אם נגעה טומאה בהן נטמא גם האוכל הצריך לידות, דיד מכניס ומוציא כדאמרינן בהעור והרוטב (חולין קיח.) מכל האוכל לרבות הידות וקתני התם אשה שהיא כובשת ירק דידות שלהן טהורין דכשהיא עורכת אותם הידות משתברות ואי אפשר ליטול הירקות בידות שלהן שנשמטו ונפסק האוכל מן היד מחמת כבישה. כובשת. שול"ץ בלע"ז עורכת שילא המשקה שלהן ויבשו דרך אשה בכך כובשת ירק ממים שישתמרו לזמן מרובה טהורין העלין והקלחין. ואמרי לה. כי מטא לאידך בפרק שני (דעוקצין מ"א) זיתים שכבשן בטרפיהן כתרגומו עלה טרפא (בראשית ח) עלין שלהן דהיינו ידות. טהורים. הידות להביא טומאה לאוכל דתו לא חזי למהוי בית יד. הוויות דרב ושמואל. עומק גדול ולא הוה נהירא ליה.

תליסר מתיבתא. שלש עשרה ישיבות איכא בהך מתא דגמרי מסכת עוקלין. שליף חד מסאנא. משום עינוי. דחזא מידי. חס ושלום בעובדי בישי [תענית כד:]. בנזיקין הוה. לא היו גדולים בכל גמרא של ארבעה סדרים אלא בתלתא בבי. האשה שכובשת ירק או זיתים שכבשן בטרפיהן. משנה היא במסכת עוקלין. טהורים. שמוסקין זיתים עם העלין כדי לאחוז בהן דהוו להו עלין יד לזיתים להביא להם טומאה כדאמרינן בהעור והרוטב (דף קי"ח.) שהיד מביאה טומאה על האוכל ואם כבשן בטרפיהן בחומץ בטלה תורת יד מן העלין לפי שהכבישה מרקבתן ומרככתן ואינן ראוין שוב לאחוז בהן. הויות דרב ושמואל קא חזינא הכא. כלומר טעם המשניות הללו קשה עלי ככל הקושיות שהיו שני רבותי מתקשין בהן בכל הגמרא. בתליסר מתיבתא. בשלש עשרה פנים יש בינינו משנה וברייתא של ששה סדרים ומסכת עוקלין גם היא בשלש עשרה פנים כגון משנת רבי ורבי חייא ומשנת בר קפרא ולוי ותנא דבי שמואל והכי אמרינן במסכת נדרים (דף מ"א.) רבי מתני הלכתא בשלש עשרה פנים [ברכות כ.]. לצמתת. לפסיקה למכירה פסוקה עולמית [ויקרא כה, כג]. פריעה ופרימה. בגדיו יהיו פרומים וראשו יהי פרוע. מוחלט. לאחר שכלו ימי ההסגר ונראה בו סימני טומאה האמורין בו [מגילה ח:].

profusely in prayer וְלֵיכָּא דְּמַשְׁגַּח בַּן – **and no one pays attention to us.** Clearly, Rav Yehudah's generation was more favored than ours by God! This demonstrates that proficiency in Torah is not necessarily indicative of true greatness. אֶלָּא הַקָּדוֹשׁ בָּרוּךְ הוּא לִיבָּא בָּעֵי – **Rather,** we must conclude that **the Holy One, Blessed is He, desires the heart,** i.e. righteousness, דִּכְתִיב ,,וַה׳ יִרְאֶה לַלֵּבָב" – **as it is written:** ***Hashem sees into the heart.***[46]

Further discussion concerning the scholarship of Doeg and Achithophel:

אָמַר רַב מְשַׁרְשִׁיָּא – **Rav Mesharshiya said:** דּוֹאֵג וַאֲחִיתוֹפֶל לֹא [הֲווּ] סָבְרֵי שְׁמַעְתָּא – **Doeg and Achithophel [did] not** really **understand** their **studies.**[47] מַתְקִיף לָהּ מָר זוּטְרָא – **Mar Zutra objected to this:** מַאן דִּכְתִיב בֵּיהּ ,,אַיֵּה סֹפֵר אַיֵּה שֹׁקֵל אַיֵּה סֹפֵר אֶת־הַמִּגְדָּלִים" – We are dealing with **one** (i.e. Doeg) **about whom it is written:**[48] ***Where is the one who can count? Where is the one who can weigh? Where is the one who can count the towers?*** וְאַתְּ אָמְרַתְּ לֹא הֲווּ סָבְרֵי שְׁמַעְתָּא – and you say that they (Doeg and Achithophel) **did not** really **understand** their **studies?!**

The Gemara concludes:

אֶלָּא דְּלֹא הֲוָה סַלְקָא לְהוּ שְׁמַעְתָּא אַלִּיבָּא דְּהִלְכְתָא – **Rather,** what Rav Mesharshiya meant was **that [Doeg's and Achithophel's] studies did not lead them to the correct halachic ruling,**[49] דִּכְתִיב ,,סוֹד ה׳ לִירֵאָיו" – **for it is written:**[50] ***Hashem's secret is to those who fear Him.***[51]

The Gemara describes Doeg's downfall:

אָמַר רַבִּי אַמִי – **R' Ami said:** לֹא מֵת דּוֹאֵג עַד שֶׁשָּׁכַח תַּלְמוּדוֹ – **Doeg did not die until he forgot his learning,** שֶׁנֶּאֱמַר ,,הוּא יָמוּת בְּאֵין מוּסָר וּבְרֹב אִוַּלְתּוֹ יִשְׁגֶּה" – **as it is stated:**[52] ***He shall die bereft of wisdom, led into error by his great folly.***[53] רַב (אַשִׁי) אָמַר – **Rav (Ashi) said:** נִצְטָרַע – **[Doeg] was afflicted with** ***tzaraas*** before he died,[54] שֶׁנֶּאֱמַר ,,הִצְמַתָּה כָּל־זוֹנֶה מִמֶּךָּ" – **as it is stated:**[55] ***You cut down (hitzmatah) all who stray from You.*** The verb *hitzmatah* alludes to *tzaraas,* as follows: כְּתִיב הָתָם ,,לִצְמִתֻת" – **It is written there,** in connection with the *Yovel* year: ***litzmisus,***[56] וּמְתַרְגְּמִינַן ,,לַחֲלוּטִין" – **which** ***Targum Onkelos*** **renders as** ***lachalutin;*** וּתְנַן אֵין בֵּין מוּסְגָּר וּמוּחְלָט אֶלָּא פְּרִיעָה וּפְרִימָה – **and we learned in a Mishnah:**[57] THERE IS NO DIFFERENCE BETWEEN A CONFINED *metzora* AND A CONFIRMED (*muchlat*) *metzora* EXCEPT the regulations concerning LETTING THE HAIR GROW AND RENDING the garments.[58] The term *muchlat,* which is used in this Mishnah in connection with *tzaraas,* has the same root as *lachalutin,* which is the *Targum* for *litzmisus.* It follows that *hitzmatah,* which has the same root as *litzmisus,* also alludes to *tzaraas.* Thus, Scripture implies that Doeg was afflicted with *tzaraas.*

The Gemara cites a series of statements by R' Yochanan concerning Doeg and Achithophel. The series is preceded by a mnemonic:

(סִימָן שְׁלֹשָׁה רָאוּ וַחֲצִי וּקְרָאוּ – **A mnemonic: Three, saw, half and called him.**)

NOTES

would begin to rain. This was due not merely to the greatness of Rav Yehudah himself, but also to the merit of his generation, for his prayers would have been ineffective if his generation had not found favor in the eyes of God (see *Taanis* 24b with *Rashi*).

46. *I Samuel* 16:7. Although Rava's generation excelled over the generation of Rav Yehudah in the breadth of its Torah knowledge, Rav Yehudah's generation was thought of more highly in Heaven (see *Berachos* 20a). This demonstrates that God does not judge people merely by the extent of their scholarship, but rather by the degree of true righteousness and total devotion to God that is in their hearts. Similarly, although Doeg may have been a brilliant scholar who could raise hundreds of insightful inquiries into the Torah subject he was studying, his intellectual brilliance did not make up for his deficiency in righteousness and devotion (*Rashi; Yad Ramah;* see also *Chagigah* 15b; and see comments of the *Gra* to *Proverbs* 16:1).

Maharsha adds that without devotion to God a person's intellect will not lead him to the truth. That is why Doeg was left with four hundred unresolved queries concerning the proper location of the Temple. In contrast, David, who was of pure heart, ascertained the truth. As the Gemara stated above (93b), God was *with* David, meaning that David's rulings were always halachically sound. The verse cited by the Gemara here — *Hashem sees into the heart* — was spoken by God to the prophet Samuel specifically in reference to David. With this statement, God explained why He chose David rather than another one of Jesse's sons to be His anointed. Thus, Rava's statement, "Is it a sign of greatness to raise inquiries?" actually means that a preponderance of unresolved queries is indicative of a lack in a person. Rava's conclusion, "Rather, the Holy One, Blessed is He, desires the heart, as it is written: *Hashem sees into the heart,*" strikes the contrast between Doeg and David.

47. I.e. they did not possess the clarity of comprehension required to understand the bases of the halachos that they studied (*Rashi*).

48. *Isaiah* 33:18. See notes 31-34.

49. I.e. they did not merit to have their opinions accepted and set down as actual halachah (*Rashi*).

50. *Psalms* 25:14.

51. God reveals the secrets of His law, that is, the correct rulings on matters of Torah law, only to one whose scholarship is accompanied by fear of God. Since Doeg did not truly fear God, he was not granted the Divine assistance required to ascertain the correct rulings in matters of Torah law and to win acceptance for those rulings (see *Sotah* 21a with *Rashi* ד״ה דסלקה; see also *Maharal, Nesiv HaTorah* ch. 14).

52. *Proverbs* 5:23.

53. The verse preceding this one states: עֲווֹנוֹתָיו יִלְכְּדֻנוֹ אֶת־הָרָשָׁע וּבְחַבְלֵי חַטָּאתוֹ יִתָּמֵךְ, *His iniquities will trap the wicked one; in the ropes of his sin will he be caught up.* In the verse cited here the phrase הוּא יָמוּת בְּאֵין מוּסָר means literally: *He shall die for lack of [accepting] rebuke.* However, R' Ami interprets it as meaning, *He shall die lacking wisdom,* thus teaching that even if a wicked person (such as Doeg) possesses wisdom during his lifetime, he will lose it before his death. The latter part of the verse, *led into error by his great folly,* refers to an incident cited in Tractate *Yevamos* (76b-77a) in which Doeg wrongly cast aspersions on the validity of David's lineage. His great folly [in desiring to disqualify David] led him to err in the laws of proper lineage (see *Maharsha*). *Ruth Rabbah* (4:8) states that during the debate over David's lineage Doeg denied heretically an oral tradition of the Sages.

54. This was a punishment for his *lashon hara,* for the Gemara states (*Arachin* 15b) that God punishes slanderers by afflicting them with *tzaraas* (*Maharsha; Toras Chaim*).

55. *Psalms* 73:27.

56. *Leviticus* 25:23. During the *Yovel* (Jubilee) year, all real estate in Eretz Yisrael reverts to its original owners, for God states: וְהָאָרֶץ לֹא תִמָּכֵר לִצְמִתֻת כִּי־לִי הָאָרֶץ, *The land shall not be sold permanently (litzmisus), for the land is mine.*

57. *Megillah* 8b. The Mishnah deals with the laws of a *metzora,* i.e. one who is afflicted with *tzaraas,* which renders him *tamei* (see *Leviticus* ch. 13). *Tzaraas* must be evaluated by a Kohen. If the Kohen finds certain symptoms of this condition present but others lacking, the *metzora* is isolated for a seven-day period, after which the development of the condition is observed and re-evaluated by the Kohen. This period of isolation is known as הֶסְגֵּר, *confinement.* If initially or upon re-evaluation the Kohen finds the condition to be a case of absolute *tzaraas,* he pronounces it to be so, a procedure known as הֶחְלֵט, *confirmation.*

58. The Torah commands (*Leviticus* 13:45): וְהַצָּרוּעַ אֲשֶׁר־בּוֹ הַנֶּגַע בְּגָדָיו יִהְיוּ פְרֻמִים וְרֹאשׁוֹ יִהְיֶה פָרוּעַ וְעַל־שָׂפָם יַעְטֶה וְטָמֵא טָמֵא יִקְרָא, *And the person in whom there is the affliction — his garments shall be torn, the hair of his head shall be unshorn, and he shall cloak himself up to his lips; and he is to call out: "Tamei, tamei."* The Mishnah teaches that these requirements apply only to a confirmed *metzora,* but not to a confined *metzora,* and that these are the only differences between their states of *tumah.* [*Tos. Yom Tov* (*Megillah* 1:7) notes that the confined *metzora* is likewise exempt from the requirement mentioned in this verse of cloaking himself up to his lips, but the Mishnah mentions only the first two requirements listed in the verse.]

עין משפט
נר מצוה

לא א מיי' פ"י מהל' טומאת צרעת הל' י':

תורה אור השלם

א) וְאֶת בִּלְעָם בֶּן בְּעוֹר הַקּוֹסֵם הָרְגוּ בְנֵי יִשְׂרָאֵל בַּחֶרֶב אֶל חַלְלֵיהֶם: [יהושע יג, כב]

ב) וְאַתָּה אֱלֹהִים תּוֹרִדֵם לִבְאֵר שַׁחַת אַנְשֵׁי דָמִים וּמִרְמָה לֹא יֶחֱצוּ יְמֵיהֶם וַאֲנִי אֶבְטַח בָּךְ: [תהלים נה, כד]

ג) וְשָׁם אִישׁ מֵעַבְדֵי שָׁאוּל בַּיּוֹם הַהוּא נֶעְצָר לִפְנֵי יְיָ וּשְׁמוֹ דֹּאֵג הָאֲדֹמִי אַבִּיר הָרֹעִים אֲשֶׁר לְשָׁאוּל: [שמואל א' כא, ח]

ד) וַיֹּאמֶר הַמֶּלֶךְ לְדוֹאֵג (לדויג) סֹב אַתָּה וּפְגַע בַּכֹּהֲנִים וַיִּסֹּב דּוֹאֵג הָאֲדֹמִי וַיִּפְגַּע הוּא בַּכֹּהֲנִים וַיָּמֶת בַּיּוֹם הַהוּא שְׁמֹנִים וַחֲמִשָּׁה אִישׁ נֹשֵׂא אֵפוֹד בָּד: [שמואל א' כב, יח]

ה) מַה תִּתְהַלֵּל בְּרָעָה הַגִּבּוֹר חֶסֶד אֵל כָּל הַיּוֹם: [תהלים נב, ג]

ו) וְלָרָשָׁע אָמַר אֱלֹהִים מַה לְּךָ לְסַפֵּר חֻקָּי וַתִּשָּׂא בְרִיתִי עֲלֵי פִיךָ: [תהלים נ, טז]

ז) וְיִרְאוּ צַדִּיקִים וְיִירָאוּ וְעָלָיו יִשְׂחָקוּ: [תהלים נב, ח]

ח) חַיִל בָּלַע וַיְקִאֶנּוּ מִבִּטְנוֹ יֹרִשֶׁנּוּ אֵל: [איוב כ, טו]

ט) גַּם אֵל יִתָּצְךָ לָנֶצַח יַחְתְּךָ וְיִסָּחֲךָ מֵאֹהֶל וְשֵׁרֶשְׁךָ מֵאֶרֶץ חַיִּים סֶלָה: [תהלים נב, ז]

י) לִבְּךָ יֶהְגֶּה אֵימָה אַיֵּה סֹפֵר אַיֵּה שֹׁקֵל אַיֵּה סֹפֵר אֶת הַמִּגְדָּלִים: [ישעיה לג, יח]

כ) וַיֹּאמֶר יְיָ אֶל שְׁמוּאֵל אַל תַּבֵּט אֶל מַרְאֵהוּ וְאֶל גְּבֹהַּ קוֹמָתוֹ כִּי מְאַסְתִּיהוּ כִּי לֹא אֲשֶׁר יִרְאֶה הָאָדָם כִּי הָאָדָם יִרְאֶה לַעֵינַיִם וַיְיָ יִרְאֶה לַלֵּבָב: [שמואל א' טז, ז]

ל) סוֹד יְיָ לִירֵאָיו וּבְרִיתוֹ לְהוֹדִיעָם: [תהלים כה, יד]

מ) הוּא יָמוּת בְּאֵין מוּסָר וּבְרֹב אִוַּלְתּוֹ יִשְׁגֶּה: [משלי ה, כג]

נ) כִּי הִנֵּה רְחֵקֶיךָ יֹאבֵדוּ הִצְמַתָּה כָּל זוֹנֶה מִמֶּךָּ: [תהלים עג, כז]

ס) וְהָאָרֶץ לֹא תִמָּכֵר לִצְמִתֻת כִּי לִי הָאָרֶץ כִּי גֵרִים וְתוֹשָׁבִים אַתֶּם עִמָּדִי: [ויקרא כה, כג]

ע) וְאַתָּה אֱנוֹשׁ כְּעֶרְכִּי אַלּוּפִי וּמְיֻדָּעִי: [תהלים נה, יד]

פ) אֲשֶׁר יַחְדָּו נַמְתִּיק סוֹד בְּבֵית אֱלֹהִים נְהַלֵּךְ בְּרָגֶשׁ: [תהלים נה, טו]

צ) גַּם אִישׁ שְׁלוֹמִי אֲשֶׁר בָּטַחְתִּי בוֹ אוֹכֵל לַחְמִי הִגְדִּיל עָלַי עָקֵב: [תהלים מא, י]

א) הרגו בני ישראל [בחרב] אל חלליהם אמר רב שקיימו בו ארבע מיתות סקילה ושריפה הרג וחנק א"ל ההוא מינא לר' חנינא מי שמיע לך בלעם בר כמה הוה א"ל מיכתב לא כתיב אלא מדכתיב ב) אנשי דמים ומרמה לא יחצו ימיהם בר תלתין ותלת שנין או בר תלתין וארבע א"ל שפיר קאמרת לדידי חזי לי פנקסיה דבלעם והוה כתיב ביה בר תלתין ותלת שנין בלעם חגירא כד קטיל יתיה פנחס ליסטאה א"ל מר בריה דרבינא לבריה בכולהו לא תפיש למדרש לבר מבלעם הרשע דכמה דמשכחת ביה דרוש ביה כתיב ג) דואג וכתיב ד) דוייג אמר ר' יוחנן בתחילה יושב הקב"ה ודואג שמא יצא זה לתרבות רעה לאחר שיצא אמר ווי שיצא זה (סימן גבור ורשע וצדיק חיל וסופר) א"ר יצחק מאי דכתיב ה) מה תתהלל ברעה הגבור חסד אל כל היום אמר לו הקב"ה לדואג לא גבור בתורה אתה מה תתהלל ברעה לא חסד אל נטוי עליך כל היום וא"ר יצחק מאי דכתיב ו) ולרשע אמר אלהים מה לך לספר חוקי אמר לו הקב"ה לדואג הרשע מה לך לספר חוקי כשאתה מגיע לפרשת מרצחים ופרשת מספרי לשון הרע מה אתה דורש בהם ו) ותשא בריתי עלי פיך אמר ר' אמי אין תורתו של דואג אלא משפה ולחוץ ואמר רבי יצחק מאי דכתיב ז) ויראו צדיקים וייראו ועליו ישחקו בתחילה ייראו ולבסוף ישחקו וא"ר יצחק מאי דכתיב ח) חיל בלע ויקיאנו מבטנו יורישנו אל אמר דוד לפני הקב"ה רבש"ע ימות דואג אמר לו חיל בלע ויקיאנו אמר לפניו מבטנו יורישנו אל וא"ר יצחק מאי דכתיב ט) גם אל יתצך לנצח אמר הקב"ה לדוד ניתי דואג לעלמא דאתי אמר לפניו גם אל יתצך לנצח א) מאי דכתיב ט) יחתך ויסחך מאהל ושרשך מארץ חיים סלה אמר הקב"ה לימרו שמעתא בי מדרשא משמיה אמר לפניו יחתך ויסחך מאהל ליהוי ליה בנין רבנן ושרשך מארץ חיים סלה וא"ר יצחק ב) מאי דכתיב י) איה סופר איה שוקל איה סופר את המגדלים איה סופר כל אותיות שבתורה איה שוקל ששוקל כל קלים וחמורים שבתורה איה סופר את המגדלים שהיה סופר שלש מאות הלכות פסוקות במגדל הפורח באויר ג) א"ר ארבע מאה בעיי' בעו דואג ואחיתופל במגדל הפורח באויר [ולא איפשט להו חד] אמר רבא רבותא למבעי בעיי ד) בשני דרב יהודה כולי תנויי בנזיקין ואנן קא מתנינן טובא ה) בעוקצין וכי הוה מטי רב יהודה ו) אשה שכובשת ירק בקדירה ואמרי לה ז) זיתים שכבשן בטרפיהן טהורים אמר הויות דרב ושמואל קא חזינא הכא ואנן קא מתנינן בעוקצין תלת סרי מתיבתא ורב יהודה שליף מסאני ואתא מטרא ואנן צוחינן וליכא דמשגח בן אלא הקב"ה ליבא בעי דכתיב כ) וה' יראה ללבב אמר רב משרשיא דואג ואחיתופל לא [הוו] סברי שמעתא מתקיף לה מר זוטרא מאן דכתיב ביה איה סופר איה שוקל איה סופר את המגדלים ואת אמרת לא הוו סברי שמעתא אלא דלא הוה סלקא להו שמעתא אליבא דהלכתא דכתיב ל) סוד ה' ליראיו א"ר אמי לא מת דואג עד ששכח תלמודו שנא' מ) הוא ימות באין מוסר וברוב אולתו ישגה רב (אשי) אמר נצטרע שנאמר נ) הצמתה כל זונה ממך כתיב התם ס) לצמיתות ומתרגמינן לחלוטין ותנן י) אין בין מוסגר ומוחלט אלא פריעה ופרימה (סימן שלשה ראו וחצי וקראו) א"ר יוחנן שלשה מלאכי חבלה נזדמנו לו לדואג אחד ששכח תלמודו ואחד ששרף נשמתו ואחד שפיזר עפרו בבתי כנסיות ובבתי מדרשות (ט) א"ר) יוחנן דואג ואחיתופל לא ראו זה את זה דואג בימי שאול ואחיתופל בימי דוד וא"ר יוחנן דואג ואחיתופל לא חצו ימיהם תניא נמי הכי ב) אנשי דמים ומרמה לא יחצו ימיהם י) כל שנותיו של דואג לא היו אלא שלשים וארבע ושל אחיתופל אינן אלא שלשים ושלש וא"ר יוחנן בתחלה קרא דוד לאחיתופל רבו ולבסוף קראו חבירו ולבסוף קראו תלמידו בתחילה י) קראו רבו ע) ואתה אנוש כערכי אלופי ומיודעי ולבסוף קראו חבירו פ) אשר יחדו נמתיק סוד בבית אלהים נהלך ברגש ולבסוף קראו ל) תלמידו צ) גם איש שלומי אשר בטחתי בו
אוכל

רש"י

הרגו אל חלליהם. מיתות הרבה משמע שתלאוהו והציתו אש תחת הצליבה וחתכו ראשו ונפל לתוך האש תלייה היינו חנק חתיכת הראש הרג כשנפל לארץ סקילה כשנפל לאור היינו שריפה: בר תלתין ותלת. ור"ח לית ליה דר' סימאי דאמר לעיל שלשה היו באותה עצה דפרעה בלעם ואיוב ויתרו דלר' סימאי בלעם חיה יותר מן מאתים ועשר שנים דהא היה בעצת פרעה דכל הבן הילוד היאורה תשליכוהו דלרבי סימאי כל אותן מאתים ועשר שנים שהיו ישראל בגלות מצרים עד מלחמת מדין חיה בלעם: חגירא. תרגום של פיסח: כד קטל יתיה פנחס ליסטאה. שר צבא ואפילו קטליה אחר כל המלחמה נקראת על שמו: בכולהו. מלכים והדיוטות: לא תפיש ותדרוש. לגנאי: לבר מבלעם. דכל מה דמשכחת ליה לגנאי דרוש: (מ) שמא יצא זה לתרבות רעה) לאחר שיצא לתרבות רעה אמר ווי. לכך כתוב דוייג: א"ל הקב"ה לדואג והלא גבור אתה בתורה. למה תתהלל לספר לשון הרע על דוד: לא חסד תורה עליך. לא חכם בתורה אתה דכתיב (משלי לא) ותורת חסד על לשונה: מרצחים. שהרג נוב: עלי פיך. ולא בלב: בתחלה ייראו. הצדיקים היו יראים שלא ילמד אדם ממעשיו של דואג שהולך וחוטא ומצליח: ולבסוף. כשמת בחצי ימיו ושב גמולו בראשו ישחקו: חיל בלע ויקיאנו. המתן עד שתשכח תורתו: אמר לפניו ומבטנו יורישנו אל. אל תמתין לו עד שתשתכח אלא תמהר ותשכיחנו: בי מדרשא. מאהל זה בית המדרש: ושרשך מארץ חיים סלה. שורש שלו תכסח מארץ חיים דלא להוו ליה בנין רבנן: כל אותיות שבתורה. שהיה בקי בחסירות ויתירות: שוקל קלים וחמורים. יודע לדרוש בקל וחומר: במגדל הפורח באויר. מתג עליונה שלמעלה מן הלמ"ד מפני מה כפופה למטה. לשון מ"ר מפי השמועה. ל"א במגדל הפורח באויר הנכנס לארץ העמים בשידה תיבה ומגדל אם הוא טמא אם לאו. ל"א ג' מאות הלכות במגדל הפורח באויר לעשות כישוף להעמיד מגדל באויר כגון שלש מאות הלכות בנטיעות קשואין דאמרן בפירקין דלעיל (דף סח.) ולמורי נראה דה"ג שלש מאות הלכות במגדל העומד [באויר] ומשנה אחת באהלות (פ"ד משנה א) דמשתעי בהכי מגדל העומד באויר וטומאה בתוכה כלים שבתוכו טמאים וכן נראה לר': רבותא למבעא בעיי. וללמוד תורה רחמנא לבא בעי דהא בשני דרב יהודה כולהו תנויי בסדר נזיקין היה כל הגמרא שלהן לא הוה אלא בסדר נזיקין שלא היו מרבין כל כך [לדרוש]: האשה שכובשת ירק בקדירה. לא אשכחתיה במסכת עוקלין: שכובשת ירק. בחומץ או בציר טהורים דאין מקבלין טומאה ע"י עוקלין שאם נגע טומאה בשרשיו העלין טהורין שאין נעשין יד לעלין מאחר שכבשם שאין מניחין לשם אלא למראה: זיתים שכבשן בטרפיהן. איתא במסכת עוקלין (פ"ב מ"א): טרפיהן. עלין שלהן טהורין הזיתים שאין נעשין להם בית יד להכניס להם טומאה: הויות דרב ושמואל קא חזינא הכא. דלא הוה ידע מאי טעמא הן טהורין: תליסר מתיבתא. י"ג ישיבות שאנו עוסקין כולן במסכת עוקלין ויודעין אותה יפה ואפי' הכי בהם היו חסידים יותר ממנו דאלו רב יהודה כו': לא סבירי. לא היו יודעין הלכה לפרשה כתקנה בטעמא: דלא סלקא להו שמעתא כו'. שלא זכו לקבוע הלכה כמותן: ומתרגמינן לחלוטין. ואנן תנן לשון חלוטין גבי מצורע: אלופי. היינו רבי:
אוכל

א) [עי' תוספתא בע"י], ב) [חגיגה טו:], ג) נ"א א"ר אמי, ד) תענית כד: ע"ש ברכות כ. ע"ש, ה) נ"א בשיתא סידרי, ו) [טהרות פ"ב מ"א], ז) [עוקצ' פ"ב מ"א], ח) מגילה ח: ערכין טו:, ט) [נ"ל ואמר ר'], י) לעיל סט:, כ) [אבות פ"ו מ"ג], ל) בילקוט מ"ב סוף רמז תשמא הגירסא ולבסוף קראו איש, מ) רש"ל מ"ז.

ליקוטי רש"י

מה תתהלל. ותתפאר ברעה שאתה עושה אתה הגבור בתורה. חסד אל כל היום. להציל את הנרדף על ידך [תהלים נב, ג]. ועליו ישחקו. זהו השחוק שיאמרו עליו הנה זה הגבר אשר לא שם מבטחו בהקב"ה ראו מה עלתה בו [תהלים נב, ח]. יתצך. ל' נתיצה. יחתך. לשון שבירה. ויסחך. ויעקרך. ושרשך. שרש אחריך לעקור כל השרשים דירא"ציניע"ר בלעז [שם ז]. קלים וחמורים. דברים הלמדין בקל וחומר שניתנו לדון מעצמן לכל אדם ולא פירשו כלום בסיני [סוכה כח.]. קלים וחמורים שאדם דן מעצמו [ב"ב קלד.]. הלכות פסוקות. הלכה פלוני ופלוני [יבמות מב:]. במגדל הפורח באויר. יש מפרשים שדורשין גוגהו של למ"ד ודורשין בו כל זאת ויש אומרים מגדל דור הפלגה ולי נראה מגדל הפתוח לאויר גרסינן והן מהלכות אהלות מגדל של עץ שקורין משטיי"ר ועומד בפתח ופתחו פתוח לבקעה או לחצר שהוא אויר במסכת אהלות (פרק רביעי משנה א) ישנה משנה מגדל העומד באויר [חגיגה טו:]. בנזיקין הוה. למודם לא היה גדול אלא בסדר נזיקין. שכובשת ירק בקדירה. במסכת [טהרות] היא בפרק שני (משנה א') גבי ידות מיירי דקיימא לן (עוקצין פ"א מ"א) כל ידות האוכלין אם נגעה טומאה בהן נטמא גם האוכל הצריך לידות, דיד מכניס ומוציא כדאמרינן בהעור והרוטב (חולין קיח.) מכל האוכל לרבות הידות וקתני התם אשה שהיא כובשת ירק ידות שלהן טהורין דכשהיא עולרת אותם הידות משתברות ואי אפשר ליטול הירקות בידות שלהן שנשמט ונפסק האוכל מן היד מחמת כבישה. כובשת. שול"ץ בלע"ז עולרת שלא המשקה שלהן ויבשו דרך אשה בכך כובשת ירק ממים שישתמרו לזמן מרובה טהורין העלין והקלחין. ואמרי לה. כי מטא לאידך בפרק שני (דעוקצין מ"א) זיתים שכבשן בטרפיהן כתרגומו עלה טרפא (בראשית ח) עלין שלהן דהיינו ידות. טהורים. הידות להביא טומאה לאוכל דמו לא לזו למהוי בית יד. הויות דרב ושמואל. עומק גדול ולא הוה נהירא ליה.

תליסר מתיבתא. שלש עשרה ישיבות היכא בהך מתא דגמרי מסכת עוקצין. שליף חד מסאנא. משום עינוי. דחזא מידי. חם ושלום בעובדי בישי [תענית כד:]. בנזיקין הוה. לא היו גדולים בכל גמרא של ארבעה סדרים אלא בתלתא בבי. האשה שכובשת ירק או זיתים שכבשן בטרפיהן. משנה היא במסכת עוקצין. טהורים. שמוסקין זיתים עם העלין כדי לאחזן בהן דהוו להו עלין יד לזיתים להביא להם טומאה כדאמרינן בהעור והרוטב (דף קי"ח.) שהיד מביאה טומאה על האוכל ואם כבשן בטרפיהן בחומץ בטלה תורת יד מן העלין לפי שהכבישה מרקבתן ומרככתן ואינן ראוין שוב לאחוז בהן. הויות דרב ושמואל קא חזינא הכא. כלומר טעם המשניות הללו קשה עלי ככל הקושיות שהיו שני רבותי מתקשין בהן בכל הגמרא. בתליסר מתיבתא. בשלש עשרה פנים יש בינינו משנה וברייתא של ששה סדרים ומסכת עוקצין גם היא בשלש עשרה פנים כגון משנת רבי ורבי חייא ומשנת בר קפרא ולוי ותנא דבי שמואל והכי אמרינן במסכת נדרים (דף מ"א). רבי מתני הלכתא בשלש עשרה פנים [ברכות כ.]. לצמיתת. לפסיקה למכירה פסוקה עולמית [ויקרא כה, כג]. פריעה ופרימה. בגדיו יהיו פרומים וראשו יהי פרוע. מוחלט. לאחר שכלו ימי ההסגר ונראה בו סימני טומאה שהמורין בו [מגילה ח:].

אָמַר רַבִּי יוֹחָנָן – **R' Yochanan said:** שְׁלֹשָׁה מַלְאֲכֵי חַבָּלָה נִזְדַּמְּנוּ לוֹ לְדוֹאֵג – **Three angels of affliction accosted Doeg** before his death: אֶחָד שֶׁשִּׁכַּח תַּלְמוּדוֹ – **one that caused** him **to forget his learning,** וְאֶחָד שֶׁשָּׂרַף נִשְׁמָתוֹ – another **one that burned his soul** וְאֶחָד שֶׁפִּיזֵּר עֲפָרוֹ בְּבָתֵּי כְנֵסִיּוֹת וּבְבָתֵּי מִדְרָשׁוֹת – **and** another **one that scattered his ashes in the synagogues and houses of study.**[59]

R' Yochanan's second statement:

[וְ]אָמַר רַבִּי יוֹחָנָן – **[And] R' Yochanan said:** דּוֹאֵג וַאֲחִיתוֹפֶל לֹא רָאוּ זֶה אֶת זֶה – **Doeg and Achithophel did not see each other,** i.e. they were not contemporaries. דּוֹאֵג בִּימֵי שָׁאוּל וַאֲחִיתוֹפֶל בִּימֵי דָוִד – **Doeg** lived **in the days of Saul, whereas Achithophel** lived **in the days of David.**[60]

R' Yochanan's third statement:

וְאָמַר רַבִּי יוֹחָנָן – **And R' Yochanan said:** דּוֹאֵג וַאֲחִיתוֹפֶל לֹא חָצוּ יְמֵיהֶם – **Doeg and Achithophel did not live out** even **half their days.**[61]

Support to this statement is adduced:

תַּנְיָא נַמִּי הָכִי – **This has also been taught in a Baraisa:** ,,אַנְשֵׁי דָמִים וּמִרְמָה לֹא־יֶחֱצוּ יְמֵיהֶם'' – Scripture states:[62] *MEN OF BLOODSHED AND DECEIT SHALL NOT LIVE OUT HALF THEIR DAYS.* This refers to Doeg and Achithophel.[63] כָּל שְׁנוֹתָיו שֶׁל דּוֹאֵג לֹא הָיוּ אֶלָּא שְׁלֹשִׁים וְאַרְבַּע – ALL THE YEARS OF DOEG'S life were no more than THIRTY-FOUR, וְשֶׁל אֲחִיתוֹפֶל אֵינָן אֶלָּא שְׁלֹשִׁים וְשָׁלֹשׁ – AND the years OF ACHITHOPHEL'S life WERE NO MORE THAN THIRTY-THREE.[64]

R' Yochanan's fourth statement:

וְאָמַר רַבִּי יוֹחָנָן – **And R' Yochanan said:** בַּתְּחִלָּה קָרָא דָוִד לַאֲחִיתוֹפֶל רַבּוֹ – **At the beginning** of their relationship, **David referred to Achithophel as his teacher;** וּלְבַסּוֹף קְרָאוֹ חֲבֵירוֹ – **subsequently, he referred to him as** merely **his colleague;** וּלְבַסּוֹף קְרָאוֹ תַּלְמִידוֹ – **and ultimately, he referred to him as his** mere **student.**[65] בַּתְּחִלָּה קְרָאוֹ רַבּוֹ – **At the beginning, [David] referred to [Achithophel] as his teacher,** as it is written:[66] ,,וְאַתָּה אֱנוֹשׁ כְּעֶרְכִּי אַלּוּפִי וּמְיֻדָּעִי'' – *But it is you – a man of my measure, my mentor and my advisor!*[67] וּלְבַסּוֹף קְרָאוֹ חֲבֵירוֹ – **Subsequently, he referred to him as his colleague,** as it is written:[68] ,,אֲשֶׁר יַחְדָּו נַמְתִּיק סוֹד בְּבֵית אֱלֹהִים נְהַלֵּךְ בְּרָגֶשׁ'' – ***Together we would take sweet counsel; in the House of God we would walk in company.***[69] וּלְבַסּוֹף קְרָאוֹ תַּלְמִידוֹ – **And ultimately, he referred to him as his student,** as it is written:[70] ,,גַּם־אִישׁ שְׁלוֹמִי אֲשֶׁר־בָּטַחְתִּי בוֹ – ***Even my ally, in whom I trusted –***

NOTES

59. *Maharsha* and *Toras Chaim* equate this description of Doeg's end with the description given in *Rosh Hashanah* (17a) of the punishment of the wicked. There, it is stated that certain sinners descend to Gehinnom and are judged there for twelve months, after which their bodies disintegrate, their souls are burned and the wind scatters their ashes under the feet of the righteous.

Some explain that spreading the ashes in the synagogues and study halls is a benefit, for the righteous who frequent these places will pray and evoke God's mercy on behalf of those sinners. Thus, R' Yochanan's statement here follows the opinion cited above (104b-105a) that Doeg, along with the other sinners listed in the Mishnah, does have a share in the World to Come. However, he has the share not by his own merit, but by the merit of the righteous who pray for him (*Ein Eliyahu* cited in *Ein Yaakov;* based on *Tanna Devei Eliyahu* ch. 3; see also *Michtav MeEliyahu* vol. I, p. 291; cf. *Maharal*).

60. Doeg reached the height of his power during Saul's reign, when he served as head of the Sanhedrin, whereas Achithophel lived at the time of Absalom's rebellion, which took place in the thirty-seventh year of David's reign (*Seder Olam Rabbah* ch. 14; see also *Radak* to *II Samuel* 15:7). Since Doeg died at a young age, as stated shortly, it is evident that Doeg died before Achithophel was born.

R' Yochanan informs us that David was fortunate in that his two most formidable enemies, Doeg and Achithophel, died young and were therefore not contemporaries. Had they been able to join forces, David might not have been able to withstand their combined onslaught (*Maharsha*).

61. I.e. just like Bilam, who was mentioned above, they died before reaching their thirty-fifth birthdays, which would have been half of the normal life span of seventy years (see *Psalms* 90:10).

62. *Psalms* 55:24. This entire psalm is understood to refer to Achithophel and his treachery.

63. Doeg was a man of bloodshed, for he slew the Kohanim of Nov. Achithophel was a man of deceit, for he betrayed David, with whom he was intimately friendly, and spearheaded Absalom's rebellion (*Maharsha*).

64. Achithophel died one year earlier than his inherent evil warranted, due to a curse David placed upon him (see *Maharal;* see also *Yerushalmi* here).

The Gemara does not cite a Scriptural source for the Mishnah's assertion that Achithophel does not have a share in the World to Come (cf. *Rashi* to 101b ד״ה ומנא לן). *Tos. Yom Tov* posits that the source is the verse cited here, which compares Achithophel to Doeg (*men of bloodshed and deceit*). This implies that just as Doeg has no share in the World to Come, so too Achithophel has no share. [Indeed, the beginning of the verse reads: וְאַתָּה אֱלֹהִים תּוֹרִדֵם לִבְאֵר שַׁחַת, *But You, God, shall lower them into the Well of Destruction,* i.e. Gehinnom.]

Achithophel's sin was his treachery against David in masterminding Absalom's rebellion (see *II Samuel* 15:12, 16:20). The reason this cost him his share in the World to Come is that it is one of the principles of our faith that the Messiah will come from the House of David, and therefore, any attempt to overthrow the House of David is in effect a denial of belief in the coming of the Messiah. Thus, Achithophel was a heretic, and his incitement against David was actually an incitement against a Principle of Faith. Although Absalom, whom he supported, was David's son, he was not David's chosen successor. Rather, Solomon was destined to become the standard bearer of the House of David (see *Rambam, Commentary to Mishnah, Principle* §12; see also below, 110a with *Maharsha* ד״ה כל החולק, *Bereishis Rabbah* 94:8 and *Shelah, Maseches Pesachim, Derush* 4). Furthermore, Achithophel's ultimate goal was not to let Absalom rule, but to manipulate Absalom to overthrow David and to then kill Absalom and seize the throne himself (see above, 101b, and *Yalkut Shimoni, II Samuel* §151).

In addition to his treachery, Achithophel emulated Doeg in slandering and attempting to use his prominence to destroy David. Like Doeg, he was a preeminent Torah scholar who went astray, blinded by jealousy of David (see *Yerushalmi* here and *Pe'ah* 1:1).

65. Since Achithophel was wicked, his scholarship declined progressively as time went on, while the scholarship of the righteous David always advanced. Hence, whereas David initially considered Achithophel his teacher, he ultimately regarded him as a mere student (*Maharsha*).

66. *Psalms* 55:14.

67. In the preceding verse, David states: כִּי לֹא־אוֹיֵב יְחָרְפֵנִי וְאֶשָּׂא, *For it is not my foe who reviles me that I could endure.* He then continues: *But it is you – a man of my measure, my mentor and my adviser.* David here addresses Achithophel, damning him for the treachery with which he replaced the intimacy, confidence and trust that David had shared with him.

When David refers to Achithophel as his *mentor,* he means his teacher of Torah (*Rashi*).

68. Ibid. v. 15.

69. Here, David continues his recollection of the friendship he once shared with Achithophel. However, in this verse, David no longer refers to Achithophel as his superior in Torah learning, but as one with whom he studies in equal company. This implies that there was a point at which their relationship shifted from one of teacher/student to one of colleagues.

70. Ibid. 41:10.

"אוֹכֵל לַחְמִי הִגְדִּיל עָלַי עָקֵב – ***who ate my bread – has raised his heel to trample me.***[1]

Having discussed Achithophel's treachery towards David in masterminding Absalom's rebellion, the Gemara turns to a discussion of the event that brought about the rebellion – the David-Bathsheba episode:[2]

אָמַר רַב יְהוּדָה אָמַר רַב – R' Yehudah said in the name of Rav: לְעוֹלָם אַל יָבִיא אָדָם עַצְמוֹ לִידֵי נִסָּיוֹן – A person should never bring himself to a test, i.e. one should not place himself in circumstances in which he will be tempted to sin, **שֶׁהֲרֵי דָּוִד מֶלֶךְ יִשְׂרָאֵל הֵבִיא עַצְמוֹ לִידֵי נִסָּיוֹן – for David, King of Israel, brought himself to a test וְנִכְשַׁל – and he stumbled,** succumbing to temptation.[3]

The Gemara explains how David brought himself to a test:

אָמַר לְפָנָיו – [David] said before [God]: רִבּוֹנוֹ שֶׁל עוֹלָם – Master of the Universe! מִפְּנֵי מָה אוֹמְרִים אֱלֹהֵי אַבְרָהָם אֱלֹהֵי יִצְחָק וֵאלֹהֵי יַעֲקֹב – "Why do [people] say in their prayers: **'the God of Abraham, the God of Isaac and the God of Jacob,' וְאֵין אוֹמְרִים אֱלֹהֵי דָוִד – and do not say, 'the God of David'?"**[4] **אָמַר – [God] said** to David: **אִינְהוּ מִינַּסּוּ לִי – "They** (Abraham, Isaac and Jacob) **were tested by Me** and withstood the tests, **וְאַתְּ לֹא מִינַּסִּית לִי – whereas you have not been tested by Me."**[5] **אָמַר לְפָנָיו – [David] said before [God]: רִבּוֹנוֹ שֶׁל עוֹלָם – "Master of the Universe! בְּחָנֵנִי וְנַסֵּנִי – Try me and test me!" שֶׁנֶּאֱמַר "בְּחָנֵנִי ה' וְנַסֵּנִי וגו' " – As it is stated:**[6] ***Try me, HASHEM, and test me, etc.*** **אָמַר – [God] said** to David: **מִינַסֵּינָא לָךְ – "I will test you, וְעָבִידְנָא מִילְּתָא בַּהֲדָךְ – and I will do something with you** that I did not do with the Patriarchs. **דִּלְדִידְהוּ לֹא הוֹדַעְתִּינְהוּ – For I did not inform them** in advance that they would be tested, **וְאִילּוּ אֲנָא קָא מוֹדַעְנָא לָךְ – whereas I am informing you דְּמְנַסֵּינָא לָךְ בִּדְבַר עֶרְוָה – that I will test you in a matter of physical temptation." מִיָּד "וַיְהִי לְעֵת הָעֶרֶב וַיָּקָם דָּוִד מֵעַל מִשְׁכָּבוֹ וגו' " – Thereupon, *It came to pass at evening time, that David arose from his bed, etc.***[7] **אָמַר רַב יְהוּדָה – Rav Yehudah said: שֶׁהָפַךְ מִשְׁכָּבוֹ שֶׁל לַיְלָה לְמִשְׁכָּבוֹ שֶׁל יוֹם** – David arose from his bed at evening, **for he had changed his night-bed into a day-bed,**[8] **וְנִתְעַלְּמָה מִמֶּנּוּ הֲלָכָה – forgetting the rule: אֵבֶר קָטָן יֵשׁ בָּאָדָם – "There is a small organ in the man; מַשְׂבִּיעוֹ רָעֵב – when he satiates it, it is starved, וּמַרְעִיבוֹ שָׂבֵעַ – and when he starves it, it is satiated."**[9] "וַיִּתְהַלֵּךְ עַל־גַּג בֵּית־הַמֶּלֶךְ וַיַּרְא אִשָּׁה רֹחֶצֶת מֵעַל הַגָּג וְהָאִשָּׁה טוֹבַת מַרְאֶה מְאֹד" – The Scriptural account continues:[10] ***And he walked upon the roof of the king's palace, and from the roof saw a woman bathing; the woman was of exceedingly beautiful appearance.*** **בַּת שֶׁבַע הֲוָה קָא חָיְיפָא רֵישָׁא תּוּתֵי חַלְּתָא – Bathsheba was shampooing her head underneath a** large **cone** that hid her from view. **אֲתָא שָׂטָן אִידַּמֵּי לֵיהּ כְּצִיפַּרְתָּא – Satan came and appeared to [David] in the form of a bird. פְּתַק בֵּיהּ גִּירָא – [David] shot an arrow at it, פַּתְקָהּ לְחַלְּתָא** – but **[the arrow]** struck and **tore open the cone. אִיגַּלְיָה** – Thus, **[Bathsheba] was exposed** to view, **וַחֲזְיָיהּ – and [David] saw her.**[11] **מִיָּד – Immediately,**[12] "וַיִּשְׁלַח דָּוִד וַיִּדְרֹשׁ לָאִשָּׁה וַיֹּאמֶר הֲלוֹא־זֹאת בַּת־שֶׁבַע בַּת־אֱלִיעָם אֵשֶׁת אוּרִיָּה הַחִתִּי – ***David sent and inquired about the woman, and was told, "Why, this is Bathsheba the daughter of Eliam, the wife of Uriah the Hittite!"***[13] וַיִּשְׁלַח דָּוִד מַלְאָכִים וַיִּקָּחֶהָ וַתָּבוֹא אֵלָיו וַיִּשְׁכַּב עִמָּהּ וְהִיא מִתְקַדֶּשֶׁת מִטֻּמְאָתָהּ – ***David sent messengers and he took her;***

NOTES

1. The phrase *who ate my bread* means "who studied my Torah" (*Rashi*), for Torah is sometimes referred to as bread, since it is the staff of life (see *Proverbs* 9:5 and *Chagigah* 14a). We learn from this verse that David eventually reached the point where he taught Achithophel Torah.

2. In chastising David for the error he committed in taking Bathsheba (see below), God told him (*II Samuel* 12:11): הִנְנִי מֵקִים עָלֶיךָ רָעָה מִבֵּיתֶךָ, *I shall give ascendancy over you to evil from within your house,* thus foretelling the rebellion of David's son Absalom. Even within the natural course of events, Achithophel's treachery resulted from the Bathsheba incident. For Bathsheba was Achithophel's granddaughter (see above, 69b) and Achithophel's animosity towards David stemmed in part from the manner in which he took Bathsheba (see *Malbim, II Samuel* 15:34).

3. When God puts a person to a test, He assists the person by providing him with the ability to withstand the test; the person must merely apply himself to the task (see *Kiddushin* 30b). However, when one brings a test upon himself, he is not necessarily awarded the Divine assistance that he might need to pass the test (*Sichos Mussar [R' Chaim Shmulevitz]* 5733:6).

4. [The phrase "The God of Abraham, the God of Isaac and the God of Jacob" is part of the first blessing of the *Shemoneh Esrei* prayer.] The Holy One, Blessed is He, is generally referred to as God of the Nation of Israel as a whole and as God of the Patriarchs – in their capacity as fathers of the nation. David felt that since he was the head of the monarchic line, and the Jewish king represents the entire nation, he too should be awarded the privilege of having God's Name affixed to his, i.e. Hashem should be called God of David (*Maharal*).

[Furthermore, on an earlier occasion, David had been promised prophetically that his name would be comparable to those of the Patriarchs (וְעָשִׂתִי לְךָ שֵׁם גָּדוֹל כְּשֵׁם הַגְּדֹלִים אֲשֶׁר בָּאָרֶץ, *I will make for you a great name, like the name of the greatest on earth – II Samuel* 7:9). This implied that God's Name would be associated with David's, as it is with the names of the Patriarchs. Yet God is never referred to as אֱלֹהֵי דָוִד, *the God of David,* but only as מָגֵן דָּוִד, *the Shield of David* (see *Pesachim* 117b). This indicates that David did not attain the spiritual level of the Patriarchs. David sought to ascertain in what aspect his devotion to God fell short of the Patriarchs' devotion, so as to be able to correct his deficiency.]

Now, God does not affix His Name to the names of the righteous during their lifetimes. However, David knew that he was not destined to have God's Name affixed to his even posthumously. He therefore asked God the reason for this (*Maharsha;* see *Toras Chaim*).

5. I.e. the Patriarchs earned the privilege of having My Name affixed to theirs because they withstood all the tests of faith to which they were subjected. Abraham was subjected to ten tests (as stated in *Avos* 5:3 and enumerated in *Avos DeRabbi Nassan* 33:2). Isaac was ready and willing to be slaughtered as an offering at My behest (*Genesis* 22). Jacob endured a life of suffering, yet he persevered in his faith (see *Rashi* to *Genesis* 43:14; see also below, 111a). You, David, on the other hand, have never been subjected to a test of faith as severe as those to which the Patriarchs were subjected.

6. *Psalms* 26:2.

7. *II Samuel* 11:2. This is the beginning of the account of the Bathsheba episode.

8. I.e. he had marital relations, which are normally reserved for nighttime, during the day. Forewarned that he would be put to a test of temptation, David engaged in relations with his own wife during the daytime, to ensure that no other woman would tempt him that day (*Rashi;* see *Orach Chaim* 240:11 with *Magen Avraham* §26; see also *Margaliyos HaYam* §3).

9. The reference here is to the male organ. The more one indulges it, the stronger its craving; the less one indulges it, the weaker its craving (*Rashi; Yad Ramah*). The same applies to all other types of physical indulgence (*Akeidas Yitzchak* §54). [Thus, David erred in thinking that increasing relations with his wife would reduce his desire. To the contrary, had he restrained himself, he might not have come to desire Bathsheba.]

10. Ibid.

11. This explains how David came to see Bathsheba bathing, for she certainly did not bathe publicly (*Maharsha*). *Yad Ramah* has the reading כִּילְּתָא, *canopy*, instead of חַלְּתָא (*cone*). Thus, Bathsheba was hidden from view by a canopy which David's arrow pushed aside. [*Maharal's* interpretation of this episode is cited below, in note 22.]

12. I.e. while gripped by temptation (*Maharsha*).

13. Ibid. v. 3. An alternative translation is: *And he said, "Why, this is Bathsheba . . ."* I.e. upon being informed who she was, David himself exclaimed, "Why, this is Bathsheba," for he knew that she was destined to be his wife (*Eitz Yosef;* see note 28).

אוכל לחמי הגדיל עלי עקב אמר רב יהודה אמר רב לעולם אל יביא אדם עצמו לידי נסיון שהרי דוד מלך ישראל הביא עצמו לידי נסיון ונכשל אמר לפניו רבש"ע מפני מה אומרים אלהי אברהם אלהי יצחק ואלהי יעקב ואין אומרים אלהי דוד אמר אינהו מינסו לי ואת לא מינסית לי אמר לפניו רבש"ע בחנני ונסני שנאמר א) בחנני ה' ונסני וגו' אמר מינסנא לך ועבידנא מילתא בהדך דלדידהו לא הודעתינהו ואילו אנא קא מודענא לך דמנסינא לך בדבר ערוה מיד ב) ויהי לעת הערב ויקם דוד מעל משכבו וגו' אמר רב יהודה שהפך משכבו של לילה למשכבו של יום ונתעלמה ממנו הלכה א) אבר קטן יש באדם משביעו רעב ומרעיבו שבע ב) ויתהלך על גג בית המלך וירא אשה רוחצת מעל הגג והאשה טובת מראה מאד בת שבע הוה קא חייפא רישא תותי חלתא אתא שטן אידמי ליה כציפרתא פתק ביה גירא פתקה לחלתא איגליה וחזייה מיד ג) וישלח דוד וידרוש לאשה ויאמר הלא זאת בת שבע בת אליעם אשת אוריה החתי וישלח דוד מלאכים ויקחה ותבא אליו וישכב עמה והיא מתקדשת מטומאתה ותשב אל ביתה והיינו דכתיב ד) בחנת לבי פקדת לילה צרפתני בל תמצא זמותי בל יעבר פי אמר איכו זממא נפל בפומיה דמאן דסני לי ולא אמר כי הא מילתא דרש רבא מאי דכתיב ה) למנצח לדוד בה' חסיתי איך תאמרו לנפשי נודי הרכם צפור אמר דוד לפני הקב"ה רבש"ע מחול לי על אותו עון שלא יאמרו הר שבכם צפור נדדתו דרש רבא מאי דכתיב ו) לך לבדך חטאתי והרע בעיניך עשיתי למען תצדק בדברך תזכה בשפטך אמר דוד לפני הקב"ה גליא וידיעא קמך דאי בעיא למכפייה ליצרי הוה כייפינא אלא אמינא דלא לימרו עבדא ג) זכי למריה דרש רבא מאי דכתיב ז) כי אני לצלע נכון ומכאובי נגדי תמיד ראויה היתה בת שבע בת אליעם לדוד מששת ימי בראשית אלא שבאה ג) אליו במכאוב וכן תנא דבי רבי ישמעאל ראויה היתה לדוד בת שבע בת אליעם אלא שאכלה פגה ד) דרש רבא מאי דכתיב ח) ובצלעי שמחו ונאספו נאספו עלי נכים [ולא ידעתי] קרעו ולא דמו אמר דוד לפני הקב"ה רבש"ע גלוי וידוע לפניך שאם היו קורעין בשרי לא היה דמי שותת ולא עוד אלא בשעה שהם עוסקין ה) בארבע מיתות ב"ד פוסקין ממשנתן ואומרים לי דוד הבא על אשת איש מיתתו במה אמרתי להם הבא על אשת איש מיתתו בחנק ויש לו חלק לעוה"ב אבל המלבין פני חבירו ברבים אין לו חלק לעולם הבא אמר רב יהודה אמר רב אפילו בשעת חליו של דוד קיים שמנה עשרה עונות שנאמר ט) יגעתי באנחתי אשחה בכל לילה מטתי בדמעתי ערשי אמסה ואמר רב יהודה אמר רב בקש דוד לעבוד ע"ז שנאמר י) ויהי דוד בא עד הראש אשר ישתחוה שם לאלהים ואין ראש אלא ע"ז שנאמר כ) והוא צלמא רישיה די דהב טב י) והנה לקראתו חושי הארכי קרוע כתנתו ואדמה על ראשו אמר לו לדוד יאמרו מלך שכמותך יעבוד ע"ז אמר לו מלך שכמותי יהרגנו בנו מוטב יעבוד ע"ז ואל יתחלל שם שמים בפרהסיא אמר מאי טעמא קנסיבת יפת תואר א"ל יפת תואר רחמנא שרייה א"ל לא דרשת סמוכין דסמיך ליה ל) כי יהיה לאיש בן סורר ומורה כל הנושא יפת תואר יש לו בן סורר ומורה דרש ר' דוסתאי דמן בירי למה דוד דומה לסוחר כותי אמר דוד לפני הקב"ה רבש"ע מ) שגיאות מי יבין [א"ל] שביקי לך ומנסתרות נקני שביקי לך גם מזדים חשוך עבדך שביקי לך אל ימשלו בי [א] אז איתם דלא לישתעו בי רבנן שביקי לך [ב] ונקיתי מפשע רב י) שלא יכתב סרחוני אמר לו א"א ומה יו"ד שנטלתי משרי עומד וצווח כמה שנים עד שבא יהושע והוספתי לו שנאמר נ) ויקרא משה להושע בן נון יהושע כל הפרשה כולה עאכ"ו ונקיתי מפשע רב אמר לפניו רבש"ע מחול לי על אותו עון כולו אמר כבר עתיד שלמה בנך לומר בחכמתו ס) היחתה איש אש בחיקו ובגדיו לא תשרפנה אם יהלך איש על הגחלים ורגליו לא תכוינה כן הבא על אשת רעהו לא ינקה כל הנוגע בה א"ל כל הכי נטרד ההוא גברא א"ל קבל עליך יסורין קבל עליו י) אמר רב יהודה אמר רב ששה חדשים נצטרע דוד ונסתלקה הימנו שכינה ופירשו ממנו סנהדרין נצטרע דכתיב ע) תחטאני באזוב ואטהר תכבסני ומשלג אלבין נסתלקה הימנו שכינה דכתיב פ) השיבה לי ששון ישעך ורוח נדיבה תסמכני ופרשו ממנו סנהדרין דכתי' צ) ישובו לי יראיך וגו' ששה חדשים מנלן דכתי' ק) והימים אשר מלך דוד על ישראל ארבעים שנה בחברון

רש"י

אוכל לחמי. לומד תורתי: שהפך משכבו של לילה לשל יום. שהיה משמש מטתו ביום כדי שיהא שבע מתשמיש ולא יהרהר אחר אשה כל היום: ונתעלמה ממנו [הלכה]. שהמשביע אברו בתשמיש רעב ומרבה תאוה: ה"ג ח) מתהלך על גג המלך ולא גרסינן והיינו: חלתא. כוורת: פתיק [ביה] גירא. בכוורת כלומר שהכה ושברה ל"א פתחה שברה ונפתחה: מתקדשת מטומאתה. אותה שעה פסק טומאתה ולא בא עליה כשהיא נדה: פקדת לילה. על מעשה לילה פקדתני אם אוכל לעמוד בנסיון של דבר עבירה: צרפתני בל תמצא. חשבת לצרפני ולא מצאתני נקי: (זמותי בל יעבר פי) איכו זממא נפל. מי יתן והיה בפי רסן ט) ואפשר לעכב את דברי שלא אומר דבר זה [של] בחנני: הר שבכם. מלך שלכם: צפור נדדתו. דעל ידי צפור נטרד כדאמר אדמי ליה כצפור: למריה. העבד נצחו לאדוניו בתוכחתו: כי אני לצלע נכון. אותו צלע היה נכון לי: שאכלה פגה. שקפץ את השעה ליזקק ע"י עבירה: נאספו עלי נכים. בעלי מומין כמו פרעה נכה (מלכים ב כג) והיו מלעיגים עלי ואני כלא יודע ל"א ולא ידעתי לא הייתי יודע כשמלעיגים כלומר פתאום בא עלי אותו עון שלא ידעתי (עד) שניתן פתחון פה לביישני: הכי גרסינן בשעה שעוסקין במיתות בית דין אומרים הבא על אשת איש מיתתו וכו': י"ח עונות. לי"ח נשיו שלא לעגנן: באנחתי אשחה. אפילו בשעת אנחתי אשחה בכל לילה: מטתי. תשמיש המטה ענין סחי ומאוס (איכה ג) קרי ליה: בדמעתי ערשי אמסה. שבשעת דמעתי אני ממאיס את מטתי בתשמיש: יאמרו מלך שכמותי. חסיד שכמותי הרגו בנו ויהו מתרעמין על מדותיו של הקב"ה ונמצא שם שמים מתחלל בפרהסיא: מוטב אעבוד ע"ז. ואחלל את השם אני לבדי ולא יחללו [אותו] כל העם: אמר ליה. חושי הארכי לדוד הקב"ה לא עביד דינא בלא דינא שמעמיד בנך להרגך דאת מאי טעמא נסבת יפת תואר דאמו של אבשלום מעכה בת תלמי מלך גשור (שמואל ב ג) ותפסה דוד במלחמה דאין לומר בעבירה באה לו דהא כתיב (מלכים א טו) רק בדבר אוריה החתי: סוחר כותי. דרכו לפנות את סחורתו מעט מעט להעמידה על דמים מועטים: שגיאות מי יבין. מי יכול להשמר משגגות: אמר לו. הקב"ה: שביקא לך. מחול לך: נסתרות. [מזיד] של צנעה: זדים. מזיד של פרהסיא: ה"ג אל ימשלו בי דלא לישתעו בי רבנן. והיינו אל ימשלו לשון משל שלא ידרשו בחטאתי חכמי הדורות ואז איתם: שלא יכתב סורחני. שתמחוק אותה פרשה מן המקרא וישתכח הדבר לעולמים: כל הפרשה. שכתובה כבר שעשית אותו חטא: על אחת כמה וכמה. שלא תעקור: תחטאני באזוב. מכלל שהיה צריך טהרת אזוב כמצורע: בחברון

תורה אור השלם

א) בְּחָנֵנִי יְיָ וְנַסֵּנִי צָרְפָה כִלְיוֹתַי וְלִבִּי: [תהלים כו, ב]

ב) וַיְהִי לְעֵת הָעֶרֶב וַיָּקָם דָּוִד מֵעַל מִשְׁכָּבוֹ וַיִּתְהַלֵּךְ עַל גַּג בֵּית הַמֶּלֶךְ וַיַּרְא אִשָּׁה רֹחֶצֶת מֵעַל הַגָּג וְהָאִשָּׁה טוֹבַת מַרְאֶה מְאֹד: [שמואל ב' יא, ב]

ג) וַיִּשְׁלַח דָּוִד וַיִּדְרֹשׁ לָאִשָּׁה וַיֹּאמֶר הֲלוֹא זֹאת בַּת שֶׁבַע בַּת אֱלִיעָם אֵשֶׁת אוּרִיָּה הַחִתִּי: וַיִּשְׁלַח דָּוִד מַלְאָכִים וַיִּקָּחֶהָ וַתָּבוֹא אֵלָיו וַיִּשְׁכַּב עִמָּהּ וְהִיא מִתְקַדֶּשֶׁת מִטֻּמְאָתָהּ וַתָּשָׁב אֶל בֵּיתָהּ: [שמואל ב' יא, ג-ד]

ד) בָּחַנְתָּ לִבִּי פָּקַדְתָּ לַּיְלָה צְרַפְתַּנִי בַל תִּמְצָא זַמֹּתִי בַּל יַעֲבָר פִּי: [תהלים יז, ג]

ה) לַמְנַצֵּחַ לְדָוִד בַּייָ חָסִיתִי אֵיךְ תֹּאמְרוּ לְנַפְשִׁי נוּדִי הַרְכֶם צִפּוֹר: [תהלים יא, א]

ו) לְךָ לְבַדְּךָ חָטָאתִי וְהָרַע בְּעֵינֶיךָ עָשִׂיתִי לְמַעַן תִּצְדַּק בְּדָבְרֶךָ תִּזְכֶּה בְשָׁפְטֶךָ: [תהלים נא, ו]

ז) כִּי אֲנִי לְצֶלַע נָכוֹן וּמַכְאוֹבִי נֶגְדִּי תָמִיד: [תהלים לח, יח]

ח) וּבְצַלְעִי שָׂמְחוּ וְנֶאֱסָפוּ נֶאֶסְפוּ עָלַי נֵכִים וְלֹא יָדַעְתִּי קָרְעוּ וְלֹא דָמּוּ: [תהלים לה, טו]

ט) יָגַעְתִּי בְּאַנְחָתִי אַשְׂחֶה בְכָל לַיְלָה מִטָּתִי בְּדִמְעָתִי עַרְשִׂי אַמְסֶה: [תהלים ו, ז]

י) וַיְהִי דָוִד בָּא עַד הָרֹאשׁ אֲשֶׁר יִשְׁתַּחֲוֶה שָׁם לֵאלֹהִים וְהִנֵּה לִקְרָאתוֹ חוּשַׁי הָאַרְכִּי קָרוּעַ כֻּתָּנְתּוֹ וַאֲדָמָה עַל רֹאשׁוֹ: [שמואל ב' טו, לב]

כ) הוּא צַלְמָא רֵאשֵׁהּ דִּי דְהַב טָב חֲדוֹהִי וּדְרָעוֹהִי דִּי כְסַף מְעוֹהִי וְיַרְכָתֵהּ דִּי נְחָשׁ: [דניאל ב, לב]

ל) כִּי יִהְיֶה לְאִישׁ בֵּן סוֹרֵר וּמוֹרֶה אֵינֶנּוּ שֹׁמֵעַ בְּקוֹל אָבִיו וּבְקוֹל אִמּוֹ וְיִסְּרוּ אֹתוֹ וְלֹא יִשְׁמַע אֲלֵיהֶם: [דברים כא, יח]

מ) שְׁגִיאוֹת מִי יָבִין מִנִּסְתָּרוֹת נַקֵּנִי: גַּם מִזֵּדִים חֲשֹׂךְ עַבְדֶּךָ אַל יִמְשְׁלוּ בִי אָז אֵיתָם וְנִקֵּיתִי מִפֶּשַׁע רָב: [תהלים יט, יג-יד]

נ) אֵלֶּה שְׁמוֹת הָאֲנָשִׁים אֲשֶׁר שָׁלַח מֹשֶׁה לָתוּר אֶת הָאָרֶץ וַיִּקְרָא מֹשֶׁה לְהוֹשֵׁעַ בִּן נוּן יְהוֹשֻׁעַ: [במדבר יג, טז] ס) הֲיַחְתֶּה אִישׁ אֵשׁ בְּחֵיקוֹ וּבְגָדָיו לֹא תִשָּׂרַפְנָה: אִם יְהַלֵּךְ אִישׁ עַל הַגֶּחָלִים וְרַגְלָיו לֹא תִכָּוֶינָה: כֵּן הַבָּא אֶל אֵשֶׁת רֵעֵהוּ לֹא יִנָּקֶה כָּל הַנֹּגֵעַ בָּהּ: [משלי ו, כז-כט] ע) תְּחַטְּאֵנִי בְאֵזוֹב וְאֶטְהָר תְּכַבְּסֵנִי וּמִשֶּׁלֶג אַלְבִּין: [תהלים נא, ט] פ) הָשִׁיבָה לִּי שְׂשׂוֹן יִשְׁעֶךָ וְרוּחַ נְדִיבָה תִסְמְכֵנִי: [תהלים נא, יד] צ) יָשׁוּבוּ לִי יְרֵאֶיךָ וְיֹדְעֵי עֵדֹתֶיךָ: [תהלים קיט, עט] ק) וְהַיָּמִים אֲשֶׁר מָלַךְ דָּוִד עַל יִשְׂרָאֵל אַרְבָּעִים שָׁנָה בְּחֶבְרוֹן מָלַךְ שֶׁבַע שָׁנִים וּבִירוּשָׁלַ͏ִם מָלַךְ שְׁלֹשִׁים וְשָׁלֹשׁ שָׁנִים: [מלכים א' ב, יא]

הגהות הגר"א

[א] גמ' אז איתם. נמחק (ועי' רש"י): [ב] שם ונקיתי מפשע רב. נמחק. ונ"ב אז איתם (וכל גירסת רבינו בגמ' כ"ה בע"י):

מסורת הש"ס

א) [סוכה נב:], ב) כד"י כפייה, ג) ע"ג עליו, ד) ב"מ נט. ע"ש, ה) ג"ה באהלות ונגעים, ו) [עי' היטב יומא פו:], ז) [יומא כב:], ח) [ל"ל ויתהלך, ט) ל"ל ואפשר.

ליקוטי רש"י

[תהלים ו, ז]. לא דרשת סמוכין. לא דברה תורה אלא כנגד יצר הרע שאם אין הקב"ה מתירה ישאנה באיסור אבל אם נשאה סופו להיות שונאה שנאמר אחריו (פסוק טו) כי תהיין לאיש וגו' וסופו להוליד ממנה בן סורר ומורה לכך נסמכו פרשיות הללו [דברים כא, יא]. שגיאות מי יבין. אני נזהרתי בהם אבל אי אפשר להזהר שלא אשגה בהם ואתה נקני מנסתרות שנסתרו ממני ולא ידעתי בחטאי בשגגה [תהלים יט, יג]. גם מזדים. מן הזדונות. אז איתם. אהיה תמים אמרו חכמים למה דוד דומה לכותי המחזר על הפתחים והם מערימים בדבר יותר מכל אדם תנו לי מים לשתות דבר שאין בו חסרון כיס משתתה אמר יש כאן בצל קטן משנתנו לו אומר יש בצל בלא מלח משנתנו לו אמר תנו לי מעט לחם שלא יזיקני הבצל כך אמר דוד בתחל' על השגגות ואחר כך על הזדונו' ואחר כך על המרדים פשעים אלו המרדים שמתכוין להכעיס וכן הוא אומר (מ"ב ג') מלך מואב פשע בי [שם יט, יד]. שנטלתי משרי. שאף יו"ד של שרי נתרעמה על השכינה עד שנתוספה ליהושע שנאמר (במדבר יג, טז) ויקרא משה להושע בן נון יהושע [בראשית יז, ה]. היחתה איש. הישא איש גחלים בשפולי בגדיו ולא ישרפו כל לשון חתיית גחלים לשון שאיבה הוא כמשמעה כשממלא הכלי בתוך המדורה [משלי ו, כז]. קבל עליך יסורין. יסור יסרני יה. על מעשה בת שבע ביסורין כגון תחת הכבשה ישלם ארבעתים (שמואל ב, י"ב) ששה חדשים נצטרע דוד [תהלים קיח, יז]. תחטאני באזוב. כמו שמטהר המצורע וטמא מת [שם נא, ט]. השיבה לי ששון ישעך. רוח הקודש שנסתלק מעלי. נדיבה. לשון נדיבות קלויות [שם יד]. ישובו לי יראיך. שפירשו הימנו סנהדרין כשנצטרע מאותו עון אף אם גרושה היא נתן עיניו בה כל הנוגע לא ינקה [שם קיט, עט].

she came to him and he lay with her – she had been purified of her tumah –[14] **"וַתָּשָׁב אֶל בֵּיתָהּ" – *and she returned to her house.***[15]

The Gemara comments:

וְהַיְינוּ דִּכְתִיב – And this incident **is** the subject of **that which is written** by David:[16] **"בָּחַנְתָּ לִבִּי פָּקַדְתָּ לַּיְלָה צְרַפְתַּנִי בַל־תִּמְצָא" – *You examined my heart, searched by night, refined me but did not find [me pure].***[17]

The Gemara expounds the end of the verse just cited:

"זַמֹּתִי בַּל־יַעֲבָר־פִּי" – *Let my scheming (zamosi) not cross my lips.* **אָמַר – [David] said: אִיכּוּ זְמָמָא נָפַל בְּפוּמֵיהּ דְּמָאן דְּסָנֵי לִי – Would that a muzzle *(zemama)* had fallen upon the mouth of my enemy,**[18] **וְלָא אָמַר כִּי הָא מִילְּתָא – and that he had not said such a thing** as a request to be tested.[19]

The Gemara presents a series of expositions by Rava concerning this incident. The first one discusses David's plea for forgiveness:

דָּרַשׁ רָבָא – Rava expounded: מַאי דִּכְתִיב "לַמְנַצֵּחַ לְדָוִד בַּה' חָסִיתִי אֵיךְ תֹּאמְרוּ לְנַפְשִׁי נוּדִי הַרְכֶם צִפּוֹר" – What is the meaning of **that which is written:**[20] ***For the Conductor, by David: In God I have taken refuge. How can you say to me, "Your mountain was moved by a bird"?***[21] **אָמַר דָּוִד לִפְנֵי הַקָּדוֹשׁ בָּרוּךְ הוּא – David said before the Holy One, Blessed is He: רִבּוֹנוֹ שֶׁל עוֹלָם – Master of the Universe! מְחוֹל לִי עַל אוֹתוֹ עָוֹן – Forgive me for that** one **sin** with Bathsheba, **שֶׁלֹּא יֹאמְרוּ – so that [others] will not say,** concerning the Jews: **הַר שֶׁבָּכֶם צִפּוֹר נִדְּדָתוּ – "Your mountain,** i.e. your king, **was caused to stray by a** mere **bird."**[22]

Rava presents the reason that David succumbed:

דָּרַשׁ רָבָא – Rava expounded: מַאי דִּכְתִיב – What is the meaning of **that which is written:**[23] **"לְךָ לְבַדְּךָ חָטָאתִי וְהָרַע בְּעֵינֶיךָ עָשִׂיתִי" – *Against You alone did I sin, and that which is evil in Your eyes did I do,* "לְמַעַן תִּצְדַּק בְּדָבְרֶךָ תִּזְכֶּה בְשָׁפְטֶךָ" – *so that You would be justified when You speak and correct when You judge?***[24] **אָמַר דָּוִד לִפְנֵי הַקָּדוֹשׁ בָּרוּךְ הוּא – David said before the Holy One, Blessed is He: גַּלְיָא וִידִיעָא קַמָּךְ דְּאִי בְּעֵיָא לְמִכְפְּיֵיהּ לְיִצְרִי הֲוָה כַּיְיפִינָא – It is revealed and known before You that had I wished to subdue my** Evil **Inclination, I could have subdued** it. **אֶלָּא אֲמִינָא – However, I said: דְּלֹא לֵימְרוּ עַבְדָּא זָכֵי לְמָרֵיהּ – Let it not be said** that **the servant bested his Master.**[25]

NOTES

14. When David saw her shampooing her hair, she was preparing to immerse in a mikveh, and she immersed herself before being called to David. Thus, David did not cohabit with her while she was a *niddah* (*Rashi, Radak* to *II Samuel* ibid.).

15. *II Samuel* 11:2.

16. *Psalms* 17:3.

17. This verse is David's expression of remorse for asking God to be tested. God "searched by night," that is, He put David to a test involving nighttime matters and sought to refine David through that test, but David was not found to be pure (*Rashi*).

18. This is a euphemism for David himself (*Maharsha*), who spoke against his own best interests when he asked for a test (see note 3). [The *mem* of זַמֹּתִי is punctuated with a *dagesh*, which makes it the equivalent of a double *mem*. The Gemara therefore associates it with זְמָמָא, *a muzzle.*]

19. The Gemara says (*Shabbos* 56a): כָּל הָאוֹמֵר דָּוִד חָטָא אֵינוֹ אֶלָּא טוֹעֶה, *Whoever says David sinned is simply in error.* The Gemara explains that it was customary in David's times for soldiers going out to battle to give their wives conditional bills of divorce, so that if any soldier failed to return from battle, his wife would be divorced retroactively from the time he left home. This was done to avoid various tragedies, including that of *agunah,* i.e. a woman unable to remarry because her husband was missing in action. At the time of this incident, the Jews were at war with the nation of Ammon, and Bathsheba's husband Uriah was away in battle. Thus, she had received a conditional divorce. Ultimately, Uriah did die in battle and the divorce took effect retroactively. Thus, Bathsheba was unwed when David took her, and as the verse stresses, she was not a *niddah*. The reason David was castigated for this act is that he should have refrained from taking Bathsheba until it became clear that she was unwed (see *Shabbos* 56a with *Rashi* and *Maharsha*).

Others explain that David's soldiers customarily gave their wives *unconditional* bills of divorce before going to battle, and remarried them upon returning. Thus, even at the time of this incident, there was no doubt that Bathsheba was unmarried. However, since the divorces were given secretly and the wives were expected to remain faithful to their former husbands and eventually remarry them, David was faulted for taking Bathsheba (*Tosafos, Shabbos* 56a ד"ה גט; see also *Kesubos* 9a,b with commentaries).

20. Ibid. 11:1.

21. We have interpreted the verse in a literal sense that accords with Rava's exposition. However, the commentators to *Psalms* offer other interpretations of the verse.

22. I.e. by Satan, who appeared in the form of a bird (*Rashi*). David prayed that he be forgiven so that the nation would be cleansed of the indignity of having a king who succumbed to this type of diversion.

Maharal explains the reference to shooting at the bird as an allusion to a diversion from the pursuit of Torah study to the indulgence in leisure. Initially, David's uninterrupted devotion to Torah served as a barrier between him and temptation. Hence, Bathsheba was "hidden from his view by a cone," i.e. her exceedingly beautiful appearance did not attract him. However, Satan's method is to ensnare a person gradually, diverting him with seemingly innocuous acts which ultimately lead to sin. Satan thus appeared as a bird, diverting David from his Torah study to a moment of leisure ("shooting at the bird"). In that moment, David's barrier to temptation was broken ("the arrow pierced the cone") and he succumbed to it.

23. *Psalms* 51:6. This verse is part of David's psalm of repentance for the Bathsheba incident.

24. I.e. I transgressed no prohibition, but merely performed a tainted act, for Bathsheba was legally divorced when I took her. Thus, I sinned against You alone, not against the Law of Israel (*Maharsha*). And I did this so that You would be justified when You speak and correct when You judge.

What did David mean by stating that he sinned in order to justify God?

25. By passing a test that his Master had apparently considered him unworthy of taking, since it was not given until he requested it (see *Rashi* and *Maharsha*). The simple meaning of this is that David therefore intentionally did not apply himself fully to the task of subduing his Inclination.

Maharal points out the difficulty in this passage. Can this rationale justify the commission of a misdeed? Furthermore, did David initially think that he could best God? And can it be that David was better able than God to assess his own character? *Maharal* explains that the Gemara does not mean to justify David's act, but to shed light on the reason for his failure. David certainly possessed the strength of character needed to resist the temptation of taking Bathsheba. Thus, had God seen fit to initiate the test, David could have withstood it. However, God did not plan to test David, and by requesting the test and seeking to reach the plateau occupied by the Patriarchs, David overstepped his bounds. He was therefore courting failure, for when a person pursues something out of consonance with God's plan he faces uncommon obstacles. Thus, David said: "If the only factor involved had been my strength of character, I could have risen to the occasion and subdued my Evil Inclination. The reason I failed is that since it was not Your will that I be as one of the Patriarchs, I encountered difficulties beyond my ability to vanquish. I was able, theoretically, to suppress my Inclination, but unable, practically, to best my Master." David initially thought that God would accede to his request to be allowed to reach the level of the Patriarchs. In that case, withstanding the test would not have involved besting his Master.

In conclusion, David cannot be compared to anyone else who sinned, for David's failure resulted not from deficiency of character – his character was as exemplary as that of the Patriarchs – but from overreaching his preordained bounds (*Maharal*).

Michtav MeEliyahu explains, somewhat differently, that David's request reflected a trace of pride in his spiritual strength, and that God therefore made him fail the test, so that he would be purged of that improper pride. See also *Avodah Zarah* 4b.

The Gemara's previous exposition, that David expressed regret

אוכל לחמי הגדיל עלי עקב אמר רב יהודה אמר רב לעולם אל יביא אדם עצמו לידי נסיון שהרי דוד מלך ישראל הביא עצמו לידי נסיון ונכשל אמר לפניו רבש"ע מפני מה אומרים אלהי אברהם אלהי יצחק ואלהי יעקב ואין אומרים אלהי דוד אמר אינהו מינסו לי ואת לא מינסית לי אמר לפניו רבש"ע בחנני ונסני שנאמר א) בחנני ה' ונסני וגו' אמר מינסנא לך ועבידנא מילתא בהדך דלדידהו לא הודעתינהו ואילו אנא קא מודענא לך דמנסינא לך בדבר ערוה מיד ב) ויהי לעת הערב ויקם דוד מעל משכבו וגו' אמר רב יהודה שהפך משכבו של לילה למשכבו של יום ונתעלמה ממנו הלכה א) אבר קטן יש באדם משביעו רעב ומרעיבו שבע ב) ויתהלך על גג בית המלך וירא אשה רוחצת מעל הגג והאשה טובת מראה מאד בת שבע הוה קא חייפא רישא תותי חלתא אתא שטן אידמי ליה כציפרתא פתק ביה גירא פתקה לחלתא איגליה וחזייה מיד ג) וישלח דוד וידרוש לאשה ויאמר הלא זאת בת שבע בת אליעם אשת אוריה החתי וישלח דוד מלאכים ויקחה ותבא אליו וישכב עמה והיא מתקדשת מטומאתה ותשב אל ביתה והיינו דכתיב ד) בחנת לבי פקדת לילה צרפתני בל תמצא זמותי בל יעבר פי אמר איכו זממא נפל בפומיה דמאן דסני לי ולא אמר כי הא מילתא דרש רבא מאי דכתיב ה) למנצח לדוד בה' חסיתי איך תאמרו לנפשי נודי הרכם צפור אמר דוד לפני הקב"ה רבש"ע מחול לי על אותו עון שלא יאמרו הר שבכם צפור נדדתו דרש רבא מאי דכתיב ו) לך לבדך חטאתי והרע בעיניך עשיתי למען תצדק בדברך תזכה בשפטך אמר דוד לפני הקב"ה גליא וידיעא קמך דאי בעיא למכפייה ליצרי הוה כייפינא אלא אמינא דלא לימרו עבדא ב) זכי למריה דרש רבא מאי דכתיב ז) כי אני לצלע נכון ומכאובי נגדי תמיד ראויה היתה בת שבע בת אליעם לדוד מששת ימי בראשית אלא שבאה ג) אליו במכאוב וכן תנא דבי רבי ישמעאל ראויה היתה לדוד בת שבע בת אליעם אלא שאכלה פגה ד) דרש רבא מאי דכתיב ח) ובצלעי שמחו ונאספו נאספו עלי נכים [ולא ידעתי] קרעו ולא דמו אמר דוד לפני הקב"ה רבש"ע גלוי וידוע לפניך שאם היו קורעין בשרי לא היה דמי שותת ולא עוד אלא בשעה שהם עוסקין ה) בארבע מיתות ב"ד פוסקין ממשנתן ואומרים לי דוד הבא על אשת איש מיתתו במה אמרתי להם הבא על אשת איש מיתתו בחנק ויש לו חלק לעוה"ב אבל המלבין פני חבירו ברבים אין לו חלק לעולם הבא אמר רב יהודה אמר רב אפילו בשעת חליו של דוד קיים שמנה עשרה עונות שנאמר ט) יגעתי באנחתי אשחה בכל לילה מטתי בדמעתי ערשי אמסה ואמר רב יהודה אמר רב בקש דוד לעבוד ע"ז שנאמר י) ויהי דוד בא עד הראש אשר ישתחוה שם לאלהים ואין ראש אלא ע"ז שנאמר כ) והוא צלמא רישיה די דהב טב ו) והנה לקראתו חושי הארכי קרוע כתנתו ואדמה על ראשו אמר לו לדוד יאמרו מלך שכמותך יעבוד ע"ז אמר לו מלך שכמותי יהרגנו בנו מוטב יעבוד ע"ז ואל יתחלל שם שמים בפרהסיא אמר מאי טעמא קנסיבת יפת תואר א"ל יפת תואר רחמנא שרייה א"ל לא דרשת סמוכין דסמיך ליה ל) כי יהיה לאיש בן סורר ומורה כל הנושא יפת תואר יש לו בן סורר ומורה דרש ר' דוסתאי דמן בירי למה דוד דומה לסוחר כותי אמר דוד לפני הקב"ה רבש"ע מ) שגיאות מי יבין [א"ל] שביקי לך ומנסתרות נקני שביקי לך גם מזדים חשוך עבדך שביקי לך אל ימשלו בי [א] אז איתם דלא לישתעו בי רבנן שביקי לך [ב] ונקיתי מפשע רב ז) שלא יכתב סרחוני אמר לו א"א ומה יו"ד שנטלתי משרי עומד וצווח כמה שנים עד שבא יהושע והוספתי לו שנאמר נ) ויקרא משה להושע בן נון יהושע כל הפרשה כולה עאכ"ו ונקיתי מפשע רב אמר לפניו רבש"ע מחול לי על אותו עון כולו אמר כבר עתיד שלמה בנך לומר בחכמתו ס) היחתה איש אש בחיקו ובגדיו לא תשרפנה אם יהלך איש על הגחלים ורגליו לא תכוינה כן הבא על אשת רעהו לא ינקה כל הנוגע בה א"ל כל הכי נטרד ההוא גברא א"ל קבל עליך יסורין קבל עליו ח) אמר רב יהודה אמר רב ששה חדשים נצטרע דוד ונסתלקה הימנו שכינה ופירשו ממנו סנהדרין נצטרע דכתיב ע) תחטאני באזוב ואטהר תכבסני ומשלג אלבין נסתלקה הימנו שכינה דכתיב פ) השיבה לי ששון ישעך ורוח נדיבה תסמכני ופרשו ממנו סנהדרין דכתי' צ) ישובו לי יראיך וגו' ששה חדשים מנלן דכתי' ק) והימים אשר מלך דוד על ישראל ארבעים שנה בחברון

אוכל לחמי. לומד תורתי: שהפך משכבו של לילה לשל יום. שהיה משמש מטתו ביום כדי שיהא שבע מתשמיש ולא יהרהר אחר אשה כל היום: ונתעלמה ממנו [הלכה]. שהמשביע אברו בתשמיש רעב ומרעבו תאוה: ה"ג ח) מתהלך על גג המלך ולא גרסינן והיינו: חלתא. כוורת: פתיק [ביה] גירא. בכוורת כלומר שהכה ושברה ל"א פתחה שברה ונפתחה: מתקדשת מטומאתה. אותה שעה פסק טומאתה ולא בא עליה כשהיא נדה: פקדת לילה. על מעשה לילה פקדתני אם אוכל לעמוד בנסיון של דבר עבירה: צרפתני בל תמצא. חשבת לצרפני ולא מצאתני נקי: (זמותי בל יעבר פי) איכו זממא נפל. מי יתן והיה בפי רסן ט) ואפשר לעכב את דברי שלא אומר דבר זה [של] בחנני: הר שבכם. מלך שלכם: צפור נדדתו. דעל ידי צפור נטרד כדאמר אדמי ליה כצפור: למריה. העבד נצחו לאדוניו בתוכחתו: כי אני לצלע נכון. אותו צלע היה נכון לי: שאכלה פגה. שקפץ את השעה ליזקק ע"י עבירה: נאספו עלי נכים. בעלי מומין כמו פרעה נכה (מלכים ב כג) והיו מלעיגים עלי ואני כלא יודע ל"א ולא ידעתי לא הייתי יודע כשמלעיגים כלומר פתאום בא עלי אותו עון שלא ידעתי (עד) שניתן פתחון פה לביישני: הכי גרסינן בשעה שעוסקין במיתות בית דין אומרים הבא על אשת איש מיתתו וכו': י"ח עונות. י"ח נשיו שלא לעגנן: באנחתי אשחה. אפילו בשעת אנחתי אשחה בכל לילה: מטתי. תשמיש המטה ענין סחי ומאוס (איכה ג) קרי ליה: בדמעתי ערשי אמסה. שבשעת דמעתי אני ממאיס את מטתי בתשמיש: יאמרו מלך שכמותי. חסיד שכמותי הרגו בנו ויהו מתרעמין על מדותיו של הקב"ה ונמצא שם שמים מתחלל בפרהסיא: מוטב אעבוד ע"ז. ואחלל את השם אני לבדי ולא יחללו [אותו] כל העם: אמר ליה. חושי הארכי לדוד הקב"ה לא עביד דינא בלא דינא שמעמיד בנך להרגך דאת מאי טעמא נסבת יפת תואר דאמו של אבשלום מעכה בת תלמי מלך גשור (שמואל ב ג) ותפסה דוד במלחמה דאין לומר בעבירה באה לו דהא כתיב (מלכים א טו) רק בדבר אוריה החתי: סוחר כותי. דרכו לפנות את סחורתו מעט מעט להעמידה על דמים מועטים: שגיאות מי יבין. מי יכול להשמר משגגות: אמר לו. הקב"ה: שביקא לך. מחול לך: נסתרות. [מזיד] של צנעה: זדים. מזיד של פרהסיא: ה"ג אל ימשלו בי דלא לישתעו בי רבנן. והיינו אל ימשלו לשון משל שלא ידרשו בחטאתי חכמי הדורות ואז איתם: שלא יכתב סורחני. שתמחוק אותה פרשה מן המקרא וישתכח הדבר לעולמים: כל הפרשה. שכתובה כבר שעשית אותו חטא: על אחת כמה וכמה. שלא תעקור: תחטאני באזוב. מכלל שהיה צריך טהרת אזוב כמצורע:

מסורת הש"ס

א) [סוכה נב:], ב) בד"ה כפייה, ג) י"ג עליו, ד) ב"מ נט. ע"ש, ה) כ"א באהלות ונגעים, ו) [עי' היטב יומא פו:], ז) [יומא כב:], ח) [נ"ל ויתהלך], ט) נ"ל ואפשר.

ליקוטי רש"י

הגדיל עלי עקב. מארב כמו (יהושע ח') ואת עקבו מים לעיר [תהלים מא, י]. בחנת לבי וגו'. ידעתי כי יש עבירה בידי ואם משפט עונשי יצא לפניך לא אצדק בדין אשר כבר בחנת לבי. פקדת לילה. לעת הערב בעון בת שבע שנאמר ויהי לעת ערב ויקם דוד וגו' (ש"ב יא). צרפתני. נסיתני. בל תמצא. לא מצאת בי חפלך. זמותי בל יעבר פי. אם תעלה עוד במחשבתי ליבחן לפניך בל יעבר פי לומר עוד בחנני ונסני כמו שאמרתי כבר כמו שנאמר (תהילים כו) בחנני ה' ונסני שאמר דוד לפני הקב"ה מפני מה אומרים אלהי אברהם ואין אומרים אלהי דוד אמר לו אני בחנתיו בי' נסיונות ונמצא שלם אמר בחנני ונסני כדאיתא במסכת שבת [תהלים יז, ג]. לך לבדך חטאתי. לפיכך בידך לסלוח ואף מה שהרעותי לאוריה לא חטאתי אלא לך שהזהרת על הדבר. למען תצדק בדברך. כח היה לי להתגבר על יצרי אלא שלא יאמרו העבד נצח את רבו שאמרתי לפניך בחנני ונסני (תהלים כ"ו) ובחנתני ולא נמצאתי שלם כדי שתצדק אתה ולא אני [תהלים נא, ו]. ובצלעי שמחו ונאספו. וכשאני צולע ששבר בא עלי שמחו ונאספו. נאספו עלי נכים. אנשי' פסחי' כמו שאנו מתרגמין נכה חגירא ומנחם חברו כמו נכאי' (ישעיה ט"ז) אימנויישי"ץ בלעז. קרעו ולא דמו. אילו היו קורעין את בשרי לא היה דמי שותת לארץ כשמלבינין פני [שם לה, טו]. דרש רבא מאי דכתיב ובצלעי. דטובה מעשה של דוד ובת שבע משלהם וספק אשת איש היא שהיוצא למלחמת בית דוד גט כריתות כותב לאשתו על מנת שאם ימות שתהא מגורשת מעכשיו ולא תיזקק ליבם וכל אותן הימים היא ספק מגורשת אם מת מגורשת מתחילה ואם לא מת לא נתגרשה. ובצלעי. בשביל אשתי זו שמתחילה חטאתי בה כמו (בראשית ב) ויבן את הצלע שמחו ונאספו. קרעו ולא דמו. אם קרעוני לא מצאו דם [ב"מ נט.]. אשחה בכל לילה מטתי. לשון סחי ומאוס (איכה ג) והיתה נבלתם כסוחה (ישעי' ה) וכו' בדמעות ומנחם חברו עם כאשר יפרש השוחה לשחות (שם ישעיהו כה) ועם מי שחו (יחזקאל מז) [תהלים ו, ז]. לא דרשת סמוכין. לא דברה תורה אלא כנגד יצר הרע שאם אין הקב"ה מתירה ישאנה באיסור אבל אם נשאה סופו להיות שונאה שנאמר אחריו (פסוק טו) כי תהיין לאיש וגו' וסופו להוליד ממנה בן סורר ומורה לכך נסמכו פרשיות הללו [דברים כא, יא]. שגיאות מי יבין. אני נזהרתי בהם אבל אי איפשר להזהר שלא אשגה בהם ואתה נקני מנסתרות שנסתרו ממני ולא ידעתי בחטאתי בשגגה [תהלים יט, יג]. גם מזדים. מן הזדונות. אז איתם. אהיה תמים אמרו חכמים למה דוד דומה לכותי המחזר על הפתחים והם מערימים בדבר יותר מכל אדם תנו לי מים לשתות דבר שאין בו חסרון כיס משתשה אמר יש כאן בצל קטן משנתנו לו אומר יש בצל בלא מלח משנתנו לו אמר תנו לי מעט לחם שלא יזיקני הבצל כך אמר דוד בתחל' על השגגות ואחר כך על הזדונו' ואחר כך על המרדים פשעים אלו המרדים שמתכוין להכעיס וכן הוא אומר (מ"ב ג') מלך מואב פשע בי [שם יט, יד]. שנטלתי משרי. שאף יו"ד של שרי נתרעמה על השכינה עד שנתוספה ליהושע שנאמר (במדבר יג, טז) ויקרא משה להושע בן נון יהושע [בראשית יז, ה]. היחתה איש. הישאב איש גחלים בשפולי בגדיו ולא ישרפו כל לשון חתיה גחלים לשון שאיבה הוא כמשמעה כשממלא הכלי בתוך המדורה [משלי ו, כז]. קבל עליך יסורין. יסור יסרני יה. על מעשה בת שבע יסורין כגון תחת הכבשה ישלם ארבעתים (שמואל ב, י"ב) ששה חדשים נצטרע דוד [תהלים קיח, יח]. תחטאני באזוב. כמו שמטהר המצורע וטמא מת [שם נא, ט]. השיבה לי ששון ישעך. רוח הקודש שנסתלק מעלי. נדיבה. לשון נדיבות קלינות [שם יד]. ישובו לי יראיך. שפירשו הימנו סנהדרין כשנצטרע מאותו עון אף אם גרושה היא נתן עיניו בה כל הנוגע לא ינקה [שם קיט, עט].

הגהות הגר"א

[א] גמ' אז איתם. נמחק (ועי' רש"י): [ב] שם ונקיתי מפשע רב. נמחק. ונ"ב אז איתם (וכל גירסת רבינו בגמ' כ"ה בע"י):

תורה אור השלם

א) בְּחָנֵנִי יְיָ וְנַסֵּנִי צָרְפָה כִלְיוֹתַי וְלִבִּי: [תהלים כו, ב]

ב) וַיְהִי לְעֵת הָעֶרֶב וַיָּקָם דָּוִד מֵעַל מִשְׁכָּבוֹ וַיִּתְהַלֵּךְ עַל גַּג בֵּית הַמֶּלֶךְ וַיַּרְא אִשָּׁה רֹחֶצֶת מֵעַל הַגָּג וְהָאִשָּׁה טוֹבַת מַרְאֶה מְאֹד: [שמואל ב' יא, ב]

ג) וַיִּשְׁלַח דָּוִד וַיִּדְרֹשׁ לָאִשָּׁה וַיֹּאמֶר הֲלוֹא זֹאת בַּת שֶׁבַע בַּת אֱלִיעָם אֵשֶׁת אוּרִיָּה הַחִתִּי: וַיִּשְׁלַח דָּוִד מַלְאָכִים וַיִּקָּחֶהָ וַתָּבוֹא אֵלָיו וַיִּשְׁכַּב עִמָּהּ וְהִיא מִתְקַדֶּשֶׁת מִטֻּמְאָתָהּ וַתָּשָׁב אֶל בֵּיתָהּ: [שמואל ב' יא, ג-ד]

ד) בָּחַנְתָּ לִבִּי פָּקַדְתָּ לַּיְלָה צְרַפְתַּנִי בַל תִּמְצָא זַמֹּתִי בַּל יַעֲבָר פִּי: [תהלים יז, ג]

ה) לַמְנַצֵּחַ לְדָוִד בַּייָ חָסִיתִי אֵיךְ תֹּאמְרוּ לְנַפְשִׁי נוּדִי הַרְכֶם צִפּוֹר: [תהלים יא, א]

ו) לְךָ לְבַדְּךָ חָטָאתִי וְהָרַע בְּעֵינֶיךָ עָשִׂיתִי לְמַעַן תִּצְדַּק בְּדָבְרֶךָ תִּזְכֶּה בְשָׁפְטֶךָ: [תהלים נא, ו]

ז) כִּי אֲנִי לְצֶלַע נָכוֹן וּמַכְאוֹבִי נֶגְדִּי תָמִיד: [תהלים לח, יח]

ח) וּבְצַלְעִי שָׂמְחוּ וְנֶאֱסָפוּ נֶאֶסְפוּ עָלַי נֵכִים וְלֹא יָדַעְתִּי קָרְעוּ וְלֹא דָמּוּ: [תהלים לה, טו]

ט) יָגַעְתִּי בְּאַנְחָתִי אַשְׂחֶה בְכָל לַיְלָה מִטָּתִי בְּדִמְעָתִי עַרְשִׂי אַמְסֶה: [תהלים ו, ז]

י) וַיְהִי דָוִד בָּא עַד הָרֹאשׁ אֲשֶׁר יִשְׁתַּחֲוֶה שָׁם לֵאלֹהִים וְהִנֵּה לִקְרָאתוֹ חוּשַׁי הָאַרְכִּי קָרוּעַ כֻּתָּנְתּוֹ וַאֲדָמָה עַל רֹאשׁוֹ: [שמואל ב' טו, לב]

כ) הוּא צַלְמָא רֵאשֵׁהּ דִּי דְהַב טָב חֲדוֹהִי וּדְרָעוֹהִי דִּי כְסַף מְעוֹהִי וְיַרְכָתֵהּ דִּי נְחָשׁ: [דניאל ב, לב]

ל) כִּי יִהְיֶה לְאִישׁ בֵּן סוֹרֵר וּמוֹרֶה אֵינֶנּוּ שֹׁמֵעַ בְּקוֹל אָבִיו וּבְקוֹל אִמּוֹ וְיִסְּרוּ אֹתוֹ וְלֹא יִשְׁמַע אֲלֵיהֶם: [דברים כא, יח]

מ) שְׁגִיאוֹת מִי יָבִין מִנִּסְתָּרוֹת נַקֵּנִי: גַּם מִזֵּדִים חֲשֹׂךְ עַבְדֶּךָ אַל יִמְשְׁלוּ בִי אָז אֵיתָם וְנִקֵּיתִי מִפֶּשַׁע רָב: [תהלים יט, יג-יד]

נ) אֵלֶּה שְׁמוֹת הָאֲנָשִׁים אֲשֶׁר שָׁלַח מֹשֶׁה לָתוּר אֶת הָאָרֶץ וַיִּקְרָא מֹשֶׁה לְהוֹשֵׁעַ בִּן נוּן יְהוֹשֻׁעַ: [במדבר יג, טז]

ס) הֲיַחְתֶּה אִישׁ אֵשׁ בְּחֵיקוֹ וּבְגָדָיו לֹא תִשָּׂרַפְנָה: אִם יְהַלֵּךְ אִישׁ עַל הַגֶּחָלִים וְרַגְלָיו לֹא תִכָּוֶינָה: כֵּן הַבָּא אֶל אֵשֶׁת רֵעֵהוּ לֹא יִנָּקֶה כָּל הַנֹּגֵעַ בָּהּ: [משלי ו, כז-כט]

ע) תְּחַטְּאֵנִי בְאֵזוֹב וְאֶטְהָר תְּכַבְּסֵנִי וּמִשֶּׁלֶג אַלְבִּין: [תהלים נא, ט]

פ) הָשִׁיבָה לִּי שְׂשׂוֹן יִשְׁעֶךָ וְרוּחַ נְדִיבָה תִסְמְכֵנִי: [תהלים נא, יד]

צ) יָשׁוּבוּ לִי יְרֵאֶיךָ וְיֹדְעֵי עֵדֹתֶיךָ: [תהלים קיט, עט]

ק) וְהַיָּמִים אֲשֶׁר מָלַךְ דָּוִד עַל יִשְׂרָאֵל אַרְבָּעִים שָׁנָה בְּחֶבְרוֹן מָלַךְ שֶׁבַע שָׁנִים וּבִירוּשָׁלִַם מָלַךְ שְׁלֹשִׁים וְשָׁלֹשׁ שָׁנִים: [מלכים א' ב, יא]

Rava illuminates the root of David's attraction to Bathsheba: דָּרֵשׁ רָבָא – **Rava expounded:** מַאי דִּכְתִיב ,,כִּי־אֲנִי לְצֶלַע נָכוֹן וּמַכְאוֹבִי נֶגְדִּי תָמִיד'' – **What is** the meaning of **that which is written:**[26] ***For I was suited for [the] rib, but my pain is always before me?***[27] רְאוּיָה הָיְתָה בַּת שֶׁבַע בַּת אֱלִיעָם לְדָוִד מִשֵּׁשֶׁת יְמֵי בְרֵאשִׁית – **Bathsheba the daughter of Eliam was suited since the Six Days of Creation to** be the wife of **David,**[28] אֶלָּא שֶׁבָּאָה אֵלָיו בְּמַכְאוֹב – **but she came to him in pain,** i.e. scandal.[29] וְכֵן תָּנָא דְּבֵי רַבִּי יִשְׁמָעֵאל – **And this was also taught in a Baraisa of the academy of R' Yishmael:** רְאוּיָה הָיְתָה לְדָוִד בַּת שֶׁבַע בַּת אֱלִיעָם – BATHSHEBA THE DAUGHTER OF ELIAM WAS SUITED TO be the wife of DAVID; אֶלָּא שֶׁאֲכָלָהּ פַּגָּה – HE MERELY TOOK HER BEFORE the time was RIPE.[30]

Rava describes the humiliation David was subjected to as a result of this episode:

דָּרֵשׁ רָבָא – **Rava expounded:** מַאי דִּכְתִיב ,,וּבְצַלְעִי שָׂמְחוּ וְנֶאֱסָפוּ נֶאֶסְפוּ עָלַי נֵכִים וְלֹא יָדַעְתִּי קָרְעוּ וְלֹא־דָמּוּ'' – **What is** the meaning of **that which is written:**[31] ***But when I limped they rejoiced and gathered,*** – ***the lame gathered against me – but I gave it no thought;*** – ***they tore [at me] and would not be silenced?***[32] אָמַר דָּוִד לִפְנֵי הַקָּדוֹשׁ בָּרוּךְ הוּא – **David said before the Holy One, Blessed is He:** רִבּוֹנוֹ שֶׁל עוֹלָם – **Master of the Universe!** גָּלוּי וְיָדוּעַ לְפָנֶיךָ שֶׁאִם הָיוּ קוֹרְעִין בְּשָׂרִי – **It is revealed and known to You that if [my enemies] were to tear my flesh,** לֹא הָיָה דָמִי שׁוֹתֵת – **my blood would not flow** out, for it has drained from the surface of my body because of their taunts about my sin.[33] וְלֹא עוֹד – **And not only** do they taunt me in their spare time, אֶלָּא בְּשָׁעָה שֶׁהֵם עוֹסְקִין בְּאַרְבַּע מִיתוֹת בֵּית דִּין – **but when they are engrossed in** the study of the laws concerning **the four** types of **execution** imposed **by the court,**[34] פּוֹסְקִין מִמִּשְׁנָתָן וְאוֹמְרִים לִי – **they interrupt their studies and say to me,** tauntingly: דָּוִד – **David!** הַבָּא עַל אֵשֶׁת אִישׁ מִיתָתוֹ בַּמֶּה – **If one cohabits with another man's wife, what is his** prescribed form of **execution?**[35] אָמַרְתִּי לָהֶם – **I said to them:** הַבָּא עַל אֵשֶׁת אִישׁ מִיתָתוֹ בְּחֶנֶק – **If one cohabits with another man's wife, his execution is by strangulation,** וְיֵשׁ לוֹ חֵלֶק לָעוֹלָם הַבָּא – **but he has a share in the World to Come.**[36] אֲבָל הַמַּלְבִּין פְּנֵי חֲבֵירוֹ בָּרַבִּים – **However, one who makes his fellow's face turn white** from shame **in public,** as you are doing to me, אֵין לוֹ חֵלֶק לָעוֹלָם הַבָּא – **has no share in the World to Come!**[37]

A comment concerning David's devotion to his marital duties even while suffering:

אָמַר רַב יְהוּדָה אָמַר רַב – **Rav Yehudah said in the name of Rav:** אֲפִילּוּ בִּשְׁעַת חָלְיוֹ שֶׁל דָּוִד – **Even during David's period of illness,** קִיֵּים שְׁמוֹנֶה עֶשְׂרֵה עוֹנוֹת – **he fulfilled** his **eighteen marital obligations,**[38] שֶׁנֶּאֱמַר ,,יָגַעְתִּי בְאַנְחָתִי אַשְׂחֶה בְכָל־לַיְלָה מִטָּתִי בְּדִמְעָתִי עַרְשִׂי אַמְסֶה'' – **as it is stated:**[39] ***I am wearied with my sigh, every night I drench my bed, with my tears I soak my couch.***[40]

Having discussed one cause of Absalom's rebellion, the Bathsheba episode, the Gemara proceeds to note another one of its causes. This is prefaced with a mention of David's reaction to the rebellion:

וְאָמַר רַב יְהוּדָה אָמַר רַב – **And Rav Yehudah said in the name of Rav:** בִּקֵּשׁ דָּוִד לַעֲבוֹד עֲבוֹדָה זָרָה – When Absalom rebelled,

NOTES

that he was not muzzled, conveys the same thought. David erred in *requesting* the test, because the request conflicted with God's will and because it reflected a trace of haughtiness. See also note 3.

26. *Psalms* 38:18.

27. Our translation of צֶלַע as *rib* accords with Rava's following exposition (see *Genesis* 2:22). See commentators to *Psalms* for other interpretations of the verse.

28. I.e. it was ordained during the six days of Creation that Bathsheba would be the wife of David. The Gemara states (*Sotah* 2a) that forty days before the formation of an embryo a Heavenly voice proclaims, "The daughter of this one is destined to marry this one." Our Gemara alludes to this predestination by calling her *Bathsheba the daughter of Eliam.* The term *rib* alludes to a wife who was predestined since Creation, since the first woman, Eve, was formed from a rib of her husband, Adam (see *Genesis* 2:22 and see *Maharsha*). For an explanation of why this particular match was ordained at the time of Creation, rather than the usual forty days before the formation of the embryo, see *Toras Chaim*.

29. Thus, David stated: I was predestined to receive this "rib," i.e. Bathsheba [but I must now suffer the painful consequences of my impulsiveness] (*Rashi*). *Maharal* notes that Bathsheba must have been David's predestined wife, for it was she who bore him Solomon, whose birth was predicted prophetically and who ultimately built the Holy Temple. It is unreasonable that Solomon would have been born to anyone other than David's predestined wife. It is because she was his predestined mate that David was attracted to her.

30. פַּגָּה is an unripe fig, and alludes to Bathsheba, for there is a species of fig known as בְּנוֹת שֶׁבַע (*Toras Chaim*). [David did not wait until the preordained time for their marriage. Had he been patient, he could have married her without any complications.]

31. *Psalms* 35:15.

32. I.e. when I stumbled and committed my misdeed, the lame – that is, people who are themselves blemished – gathered to ridicule me incessantly; but I ignored their taunts (*Rashi,* first explanation).

Note that the word וּבְצַלְעִי, *but when I limped,* can also be interpreted as, *but concerning my rib.* Thus, David alludes here to the Bathsheba episode.

33. [Rava here expounds the final words in the verse, וְלֹא־דָמּוּ, as meaning, *but they drew no blood,* interpreting דָמּוּ as related to דָּם (*blood*).] When a person is hurt by taunts, his blood drains (*Bava Metzia* 58b; see note 37).

34. I.e. stoning, burning, death by the sword and strangulation (see Mishnah above, 49b).

35. David's enemies alluded in this fashion to his initial taking of Bathsheba, which appeared outwardly like adultery. Although Bathsheba was actually divorced when David first took her (as explained in note 19), the divorce was not public knowledge and David's enemies therefore taunted him as though he had taken a married woman (*Shitah Mekubetzes*, *Kesubos* 9b).

This incident is also cited in *Bava Metzia* (59a), but there, David's enemies are described as interrupting their study of *Negaim* and *Oholos* (difficult tractates in the Order of *Tahoros*) to taunt him (see *Tosafos* ad loc. ד״ה ולא עוד and *Toras Chaim* here). *Maharsha* there sees irony in the fact that *tzaraas*, which is the subject of Tractate *Negaim,* is a punishment for *lashon hara*, yet the study of that tractate did not deter them from slandering and taunting David.

36. Before a sinner is executed, he is encouraged to confess his sin, thereby meriting a share in the World to Come (Mishnah above, 43b).

37. When one is sorely embarrassed in public, his face first turns red as the blood gathers in it, then turns white as the blood drains from it. Causing a person's blood to drain as a result of shame is in a sense like spilling his blood in murder (*Bava Metzia* 58b, with *Tosafos* ד״ה דאזיל). However, unlike a murderer, who is likely to recognize the gravity of his sin and repent, one who makes his fellow turn white from shame will most probably never appreciate the depth of his misdeed, and is thus distant from repentance. Accordingly, he will not merit a share in the World to Come. [See *Avos* 3:11 and above, 99a.]

38. David had eighteen wives (see above, 21a). Even when he was ill in the aftermath of the Bathsheba episode (see *II Samuel* ch. 12), he did not neglect his duty to his wives and paid them conjugal visits. This, despite the fact that one who falls ill is exempt from his marital obligations for up to six months (*Be'er Sheva;* see *Rambam, Hil. Ishus* 14:7; cf. *Maharal*; see also *Responsa Chasam Sofer, Even HaEzer* I:51).

39. *Psalms* 6:7.

40. According to Rav Yehudah's exposition, the word אַשְׂחֶה is interpreted as *stain* and the word אַמְסֶה as *soil.* Thus, David said: Even when I am wearied and weakened by illness, I stain my bed nightly, and even while shedding tears of anguish, I soil my couch, through the fulfillment of my marital obligations (*Rashi*; see *Hagahos R' Shlomo HaKohen*).

א) [סוכה נב:], ב) כד"י כפייה, ג) י"ג עליו, ד) ב"מ נט. ע"ש, ה) נ"א באהלות ונגעים, ו) [עי' היטב יומא פו:], ז) [יומא כב:], ח) [צ"ל ויתהלך], ט) צ"ל ואפשר.

אוכל לחמי הגדיל עלי עקב אמר רב יהודה אמר רב לעולם אל יביא אדם עצמו לידי נסיון שהרי דוד מלך ישראל הביא עצמו לידי נסיון ונכשל אמר לפניו רבש"ע מפני מה אומרים אלהי אברהם אלהי יצחק ואלהי יעקב ואין אומרים אלהי דוד אמר אינהו מינסו לי ואת לא מינסית לי אמר לפניו רבש"ע בחנני ונסני שנאמר א) בחנני ה' ונסני וגו' אמר מינסנא לך ועבידנא מילתא בהדך דלדידהו לא הודעתינהו ואילו אנא קא מודענא לך דמנסינא לך בדבר ערוה מיד ב) ויהי לעת הערב ויקם דוד מעל משכבו וגו' אמר רב יהודה שהפך משכבו של לילה למשכבו של יום ונתעלמה ממנו הלכה א) אבר קטן יש באדם משביעו רעב ומרעיבו שבע ב) ויתהלך על גג בית המלך וירא אשה רוחצת מעל הגג והאשה טובת מראה מאד בת שבע הוה קא חייפא רישא תותי חלתא אתא שטן אידמי ליה כציפרתא פתק ביה גירא פתקה לחלתא איגליה וחזייה מיד ג) וישלח דוד וידרוש לאשה ויאמר הלא זאת בת שבע בת אליעם אשת אוריה החתי וישלח דוד מלאכים ויקחה ותבא אליו וישכב עמה והיא מתקדשת מטומאתה ותשב אל ביתה והיינו דכתיב ד) בחנת לבי פקדת לילה צרפתני בל תמצא זמותי בל יעבר פי איכו זממא נפל בפומיה דמאן דסני לי ולא אמר כי הא מילתא דרש רבא מאי דכתיב ה) למנצח לדוד בה' חסיתי איך תאמרו לנפשי נודי הרכם צפור אמר דוד לפני הקב"ה רבש"ע מחול לי על אותו עון שלא יאמרו הר שבכם צפור נדדתו דרש רבא מאי דכתיב ו) לך לבדך חטאתי והרע בעיניך עשיתי למען תצדק בדברך תזכה בשפטך אמר דוד לפני הקב"ה גליא וידיעא קמך דאי בעיא למכפייה ליצרי הוה כייפינא אלא אמינא דלא לימרו עבדא ג) זכי למריה דרש רבא מאי דכתיב ז) כי אני לצלע נכון ומכאובי נגדי תמיד ראויה היתה בת שבע בת אליעם לדוד מששת ימי בראשית אלא שבאה אליו במכאוב וכן תנא דבי רבי ישמעאל ראויה היתה לדוד בת שבע בת אליעם אלא שאכלה פגה ד) דרש רבא מאי דכתיב ח) ובצלעי שמחו ונאספו נאספו עלי נכים [ולא ידעתי] קרעו ולא דמו אמר דוד לפני הקב"ה רבש"ע גלוי וידוע לפניך שאם היו קורעין בשרי לא היה דמי שותת ולא עוד אלא בשעה שהם עוסקין ה) בארבע מיתות ב"ד פוסקין ממשנתן ואומרים לי דוד הבא על אשת איש מיתתו במה אמרתי להם הבא על אשת איש מיתתו בחנק ויש לו חלק לעוה"ב אבל המלבין פני חבירו ברבים אין לו חלק לעולם הבא אמר רב יהודה אמר רב אפילו בשעת חליו של דוד קיים שמנה עשרה עונות שנאמר ט) יגעתי באנחתי אשחה בכל לילה מטתי בדמעתי ערשי אמסה ואמר רב יהודה אמר רב בקש דוד לעבוד ע"ז שנאמר י) ויהי דוד בא עד הראש אשר ישתחוה שם לאלהים ואין ראש אלא ע"ז שנאמר כ) הוא צלמא רישיה די דהב טב ו) והנה לקראתו חושי הארכי קרוע כתנתו ואדמה על ראשו אמר לו לדוד יאמרו מלך שכמותך יעבוד ע"ז אמר לו מלך שכמותי יהרגנו בנו מוטב יעבוד ע"ז ואל יתחלל שם שמים בפרהסיא אמר מאי טעמא קנסיבת יפת תואר א"ל יפת תואר רחמנא שרייה א"ל לא דרשת סמוכין דסמיך ליה ל) כי יהיה לאיש בן סורר ומורה כל הנושא יפת תואר יש לו בן סורר ומורה דרש ר' דוסתאי דמן בירי למה דוד דומה לסוחר כותי אמר דוד לפני הקב"ה רבש"ע מ) שגיאות מי יבין [א"ל] שביקי לך ומנסתרות נקני שביקי לך גם מזדים חשוך עבדך שביקי לך אל ימשלו בי [א] אז איתם דלא לישתעו בי רבנן שביקי לך [ב] ונקיתי מפשע רב ז) שלא יכתב סרחוני אמר לו א"א ומה יו"ד שנטלתי משרי עומד וצווח כמה שנים עד שבא יהושע והוספתי לו שנאמר נ) ויקרא משה להושע בן נון יהושע ח) ונקיתי מפשע רב אמר לפניו רבש"ע מחול לי על אותו עון כולו אמר כבר עתיד שלמה בנך לומר בחכמתו ס) היחתה איש אש בחיקו ובגדיו לא תשרפנה אם יהלך איש על הגחלים ורגליו לא תכוינה כן הבא על אשת רעהו לא ינקה כל הנוגע בה א"ל כל הכי נטרד ההוא גברא א"ל קבל עליך יסורין קבל עליו ט) אמר רב יהודה אמר רב ששה חדשים נצטרע דוד ונסתלקה הימנו שכינה ופירשו ממנו סנהדרין נצטרע דכתיב ע) תחטאני באזוב ואטהר תכבסני ומשלג אלבין נסתלקה הימנו שכינה דכתיב פ) השיבה לי ששון ישעך ורוח נדיבה תסמכני ופרשו ממנו סנהדרין דכתי' צ) ישובו לי יראיך וגו' ששה חדשים מנלן דכתי' ק) והימים אשר מלך דוד על ישראל ארבעים שנה
בחברון

אוכל לחמי. לומד תורתי: שהפך משכבו של לילה לשל יום. שהיה משמש מטתו ביום כדי שיהא שבע מתשמיש ולא יהרהר אחר אשה כל היום: ונתעלמה ממנו [הלכה]. שהמשביע אברו בתשמיש רעב ומרבה תאוה: ה"ג ח) מתהלך על גג המלך ולא גרסינן והיינו: חלתא. כוורת: פתיק [ביה] גירא. בכוורת כלומר שהכה ושברה ל"א פתחה שברה ונפתחה: מתקדשת מטומאתה. אותה שעה פסק טומאתה ולא בא עליה כשהיא נדה: פקדת לילה. על מעשה לילה פקדתני אם אוכל לעמוד בנסיון של דבר עבירה: צרפתני בל תמצא. חשבת לצרפני ולא מצאתני נקי: (זמותי בל יעבר פי) איכו זממא נפל. מי יתן והיה בפי רסן ט) ואפשר לעכב את דברי שלא אומר דבר זה [של] בחנני: הר שבכם. מלך שלכם: צפור נדדתו. דעל ידי צפור נטרד כדאמר אדמי ליה כצפור: למריה. העבד נלחו לאדוניו בתוכחתו: כי אני לצלע נכון. אותו לצלע היה נכון לי: שאכלה פגה. שקפץ את השעה ליזקק ע"י עבירה: נאספו עלי נכים. בעלי מומין כמו פרעה נכה (מלכים ב כג) והיו מלעיגים עלי ואני כלא יודע ל"א ולא ידעתי לא הייתי יודע כשמלעיגים כלומר פתאום בא עלי אותו עון שלא ידעתי (עד) שניתן פתחון פה לביישני: הכי גרסינן בשעה שעוסקין במיתות בית דין אומרים הבא על אשת איש מיתתו וכו': י"ח עונות. לי"ח נשיו שלא לעגנן: באנחתי אשחה. אפילו בשעת אנחתי אשחה בכל לילה: מטתי. תשמיש המטה ענין סחי ומאוס (איכה ג) קרי ליה: בדמעתי ערשי אמסה. שבשעת דמעתי אני ממאיס את מטתי בתשמיש: יאמרו מלך שכמותי. חסיד שכמותי הרגו בנו ויהו מתרעמין על מדותיו של הקב"ה ונמצא שם שמים מתחלל בפרהסיא: מוטב אעבוד ע"ז. ואחלל את השם אני לבדי ולא יחללו [אותו] כל העם: אמר ליה. חושי הארכי לדוד הקב"ה לא עביד דינא בלא דינא שמעמיד בנך להרגך דאת מאי טעמא נסבת יפת תואר דאמו של אבשלום מעכה בת תלמי מלך גשור (שמואל ב ג) ותפסה דוד במלחמה דאין לומר בעבירה באה לו דהא כתיב (מלכים א טו) רק בדבר אוריה החתי: סוחר כותי. דרכו לפנות את סחורתו מעט מעט להעמידה על דמים מועטים: שגיאות מי יבין. מי יכול להשמר משגגות: אמר לו. הקב"ה: שביקא לך. מחול לך: נסתרות. [מזיד] של צנעה: זדים. מזיד של פרהסיא: ה"ג אל ימשלו בי דלא לישתעו בי רבנן. והיינו אל ימשלו לשון משל שלא ידרשו בחטאתי חכמי הדורות ואז איתם: שלא יכתב סורחני. שתמחוק אותה פרשה מן המקרא וישתכח הדבר לעולמים: כל הפרשה. שכתובה כבר שעשית אותו חטא: על אחת כמה וכמה. שלא תעקור: תחטאני באזוב. מכלל שהיה צריך טהרת אזוב כמצורע:
בחברון

ליקוטי רש"י

הגדיל עלי עקב. מארב כמו (יהושע ח') ואת עקבו מים לעיר [תהלים מא, י]. בחנת לבי וגו'. ידעתי כי יש עבירה בידי ואם משפט עונשי יצא לפניך לא אצדק בדין אשר כבר בחנת לבי. פקדת לילה. לעת הערב בעון בת שבע שנאמר ויהי לעת ערב ויקם דוד וגו' (ש"ב יא). צרפתני. נסיתני. בל תמצא. לא מצאת בי חפצך. זמותי בל יעבר פי. אם תעלה עוד במחשבתי ליבחן לפניך בל יעבר פי לומר עוד בחנני ונסני כמו שאמרתי כבר כמו שנאמר (תהילים כו) בחנני ה' ונסני שאמר דוד לפני הקב"ה מפני מה אומרים אלהי אברהם ואין אומרים אלהי דוד אמר לו אני בחנתיו בי' נסיונות ונמצא שלם אמר בחנני ונסני כדאיתא במסכת שבת [תהלים יז, ג]. לך לבדך חטאתי. לפיכך בידך לסלוח ואף מה שהרעותי לאוריה לא חטאתי אלא לך שהזהרת על הדבר. למען תצדק בדברך. כח היה לי להתגבר על יצרי אלא שלא יאמרו העבד נצח את רבו שאמרתי לפניך בחנני ונסני (תהלים כ"ו) ובחנתני ולא נמצאתי שלם כדי שתצדק אתה ולא אני [תהלים נא, ו]. ובצלעי שמחו ונאספו. וכשאני צולע שבר בא עלי שמחו ונאספו. נאספו עלי נכים. אנשי' פסחי' כמו שאנו מתרגמינן נכה חגירא ומנחם חברו כמו נכאי' (ישעיה ט"ז) אימנויישי"ן בלעז. קרעו ולא דמו. אילו היו קורעין את בשרי לא היה דמי שותת לארץ כשמלבינין פני [שם לה, טו]. דרש רבא מאי דכתיב ובצלעי. דטובה מעשה של דוד ובת שבע משלהם וספק אשת איש היא שהיוצא למלחמת בית דוד גט כריתות כותב לאשתו על מנת שאם ימות שתהא מגורשת מעכשיו ולא תיזקק ליבם וכל אותן הימים היא ספק מגורשת אם מת מגורשת מתחילה ואם לא מת לא נתגרשה. ובצלעי. בשביל אשתי זו שמתחילה חטאתי בה כמו (בראשית ב) ויבן את הצלע שמחו ונאספו. קרעו ולא דמו. אם קרעוני לא מצאו דם [ב"מ נט.]. אשחה בכל לילה מטתי. לשון סחי ומאוס (איכה ג) והיתה נבלתם כסוחה (ישעי' ה) וכו' בדמעות ומנחם חברו עם כאשר יפרש השוחה לשחות (שם ישעיהו כה) ועם מי שחו (יחזקאל מז) [תהלים ו, ז]. לא דרשת סמוכין. לא דברה תורה אלא כנגד יצר הרע שאם אין הקב"ה מתירה ישאנה באיסור אבל אם נשאה סופו להיות שונאה שנאמר אחריו (פסוק טו) כי תהיין לאיש וגו' וסופו להוליד ממנה בן סורר ומורה לכך נסמכו פרשיות הללו [דברים כא, יא]. שגיאות מי יבין. אני נזהרתי בהם אבל אי אפשר להזהר שלא אשגה בהם ואתה נקני מנסתרות שנסתרו ממני ולא ידעתי בחטאי בשגגה [תהלים יט, יג]. גם מזדים. מן הזדונות. אז איתם. אהיה תמים אמרו חכמים למה דוד דומה לכותי המחזר על הפתחים והם מערימים בדבר יותר מכל אדם תנו לי מים לשתות דבר שאין בו חסרון כיס משנתה אמר יש כאן בצל קטן משנתנו לו אומר יש בצל בלא מלח משנתנו לו אמר תנו לי מעט לחם שלא יזיקני הבצל כך אמר דוד בתחל' על השגגות ואחר כך על הזדונו' ואחר כך על המרדים פשעים אלו המרדים שמתכוין להכעיס וכן הוא אומר (מ"ב ג') מלך מואב פשע בי [שם יט, יד]. שנטלתי משרי. שאף יו"ד של שרי נתרעמה על השכינה עד שנתוספה ליהושע שנאמר (במדבר יג, טז) ויקרא משה להושע בן נון יהושע [בראשית יז, ה]. היחתה איש. הישא איש גחלים בשפולי בגדיו ולא ישרפו כל לשון חתיית גחלים לשון [illegible] כשממלא הכלי בתוך המדורה [משלי ו, כז]. קבל עליך יסורין. יסור יסרני יה. על מעשה בת שבע יסורין כגון תחת הככשה ישלם ארבעתים (שמואל ב, י"ב) ששה חדשים נצטרע דוד [תהלים קיח, יז]. תחטאני באזוב. כמו [illegible] מת [שם נא, ט]. השיבה לי ששון ישעך. רוח הקודש שנסתלק מעלי. נדיבה. לשון נדיבות קליות [שם יד]. ישובו לי יראיך. שפירשו הימנו סנהדרין כשנצטרע מאותו עון אף אם גרושה היא נתן עיניו בה כל הנוגע לא [illegible]

תורה אור השלם

א) בחנני יי ונסני צרפה כליותי ולבי: [תהלים כו, ב]

ב) ויהי לעת הערב ויקם דוד מעל משכבו ויתהלך על גג בית המלך וירא אשה רחצת מעל הגג והאשה טובת מראה מאד: [שמואל ב' יא, ב]

ג) וישלח דוד וידרש לאשה ויאמר הלוא זאת בת שבע בת אליעם אשת אוריה החתי: וישלח דוד מלאכים ויקחה ותבוא אליו וישכב עמה והיא מתקדשת מטמאתה ותשב אל ביתה: [שמואל ב' יא, ג-ד]

ד) בחנת לבי פקדת לילה צרפתני בל תמצא זמתי בל יעבר פי: [תהלים יז, ג]

ה) למנצח לדוד ביי חסיתי איך תאמרו לנפשי נודי הרכם צפור: [תהלים יא, א]

ו) לך לבדך חטאתי והרע בעיניך עשיתי למען תצדק בדברך תזכה בשפטך: [תהלים נא, ו]

ז) כי אני לצלע נכון ומכאובי נגדי תמיד: [תהלים לח, יח]

ח) ובצלעי שמחו ונאספו נאספו עלי נכים ולא ידעתי קרעו ולא דמו: [תהלים לה, טו]

ט) יגעתי באנחתי אשחה בכל לילה מטתי בדמעתי ערשי אמסה: [תהלים ו, ז]

י) ויהי דוד בא עד הראש אשר ישתחוה שם לאלהים והנה לקראתו חושי הארכי קרוע כתנתו ואדמה על ראשו: [שמואל ב' טו, לב]

כ) הוא צלמא ראשה די דהב טב חדוהי ודרעוהי די כסף מעוהי וירכתה די נחש: [דניאל ב, לב]

ל) כי יהיה לאיש בן סורר ומורה איננו שמע בקול אביו ובקול אמו ויסרו אתו ולא ישמע אליהם: [דברים כא, יח]

מ) שגיאות מי יבין מנסתרות נקני: גם מזדים חשך עבדך אל ימשלו בי אז איתם ונקיתי מפשע רב: [תהלים יט, יג-יד]

נ) אלה שמות האנשים אשר שלח משה לתור את הארץ ויקרא משה להושע בן נון יהושע: [במדבר יג, טז]

ס) היחתה איש אש בחיקו ובגדיו לא תשרפנה: אם יהלך איש על הגחלים ורגליו לא תכוינה: כן הבא אל אשת רעהו לא ינקה כל הנגע בה: [משלי ו, כז-כט]

ע) תחטאני באזוב ואטהר תכבסני ומשלג אלבין: [תהלים נא, ט]

פ) השיבה לי ששון ישעך ורוח נדיבה תסמכני: [תהלים נא, יד]

צ) ישובו לי יראיך וידעי עדתיך: [תהלים קיט, עט]

ק) והימים אשר מלך דוד על ישראל ארבעים שנה בחברון מלך שבע שנים ובירושלים מלך שלשים ושלש שנים: [מלכים א' ב, יא]

הגהות הגר"א

[א] גמ' אז איתם. נמחק (ועי' רש"י): [ב] שם ונקיתי מפשע רב. נמחק. ונ"ב אז איתם (וכל גירסת רבינו בגמ' כ"ה בע"י):

David sought to engage in idolatry, שֶׁנֶּאֱמַר ,,וַיְהִי דָוִד בָּא עַד־הָרֹאשׁ אֲשֶׁר־יִשְׁתַּחֲוֶה שָׁם לֵאלֹהִים'' – **as it is stated:**[41] ***And David was coming to the summit*** (*rosh*), ***where he used to bow down to God;***[42] וְאֵין רֹאשׁ אֶלָּא עֲבוֹדָה זָרָה – **and** the word *rosh* **is** an allusion to **nothing other than idolatry,** שֶׁנֶּאֱמַר ,,(ו)הוּא צַלְמָא רֵאשֵׁהּ דִּי־דְהַב טָב'' – **as it is stated:**[43] ***The image – its head*** (*reisheih*) ***was of fine gold.***[44] ,,וְהִנֵּה לִקְרָאתוֹ חוּשַׁי הָאַרְכִּי קָרוּעַ כֻּתָּנְתּוֹ וַאֲדָמָה עַל־רֹאשׁוֹ'' – Now, as David considered the option of idolatry, ***behold, approaching him was Chushai the Archite, with his tunic torn and with earth upon his head.***[45] אֲמַר לוֹ לְדָוִד – **[Chushai] said to David:** יֹאמְרוּ מֶלֶךְ שֶׁכְּמוֹתְךָ יַעֲבוֹד עֲבוֹדָה זָרָה – "If you commit this act, **[people] will say: 'How can a king** as great **as you engage in idolatry?'** You will thus have also committed a great desecration of God's Name." אֲמַר לוֹ – **[David] said to [Chushai]:** מֶלֶךְ שֶׁכְּמוֹתִי יַהַרְגֵנּוּ בְּנוֹ – "If I do not do this, people will say that it is unjust that **a king** as pious **as I should be killed by his** own **son!** Thus, God's Name will be desecrated publicly.[46] מוּטָב יַעֲבוֹד עֲבוֹדָה זָרָה – **It is preferable that [a king such as I] should engage in idolatry** and desecrate the Name of Heaven as an individual, וְאַל יִתְחַלֵּל שֵׁם שָׁמַיִם בְּפַרְהֶסְיָא – **so that the Name of Heaven should not be desecrated publicly."**[47]

Chushai countered:

אָמַר – **He said** to David: מַאי טַעְמָא קָנְסִיבַת יְפַת תּוֹאַר – **Why did you marry a beautiful captive?**[48] אֲמַר לֵיהּ – **[David] replied:** יְפַת תּוֹאַר רַחֲמָנָא שַׁרְיֵיהּ – **The Torah permits** marrying **a beautiful captive.** אֲמַר לֵיהּ – **[Chushai] said to [David]:** לֹא דָרַשְׁתְּ סְמוּכִין – True, but did **you not expound** the **juxtaposition** of Scriptural passages in connection with the beautiful captive? דִּסְמִיךְ לֵיהּ ,,כִּי־יִהְיֶה לְאִישׁ בֵּן סוֹרֵר וּמוֹרֶה'' – **For** the passage **juxtaposed to [the passage permitting one to marry the beautiful captive]** states:[49] ***If a man will have a wayward and rebellious son,*** כָּל הַנּוֹשֵׂא יְפַת תּוֹאַר יֵשׁ לוֹ בֵּן סוֹרֵר וּמוֹרֶה – and this juxtaposition teaches that **anyone who marries a beautiful captive will have a wayward and rebellious son** from her.[50] Since Absalom's mother was a beautiful captive, it is not surprising that he turned out rebellious. Therefore, even if he succeeds in killing you, people will not question God's justice.

The Gemara describes David's method of praying for forgiveness:

דָּרַשׁ רַבִּי דּוֹסְתָּאי דְּמִן בִּירִי – **R' Dostai of Biri expounded:** לְמָה דָּוִד דּוֹמֶה – **To what is David comparable?** לְסוֹחֵר כּוּתִי – **To a Cuthean merchant.**[51] אָמַר דָּוִד לִפְנֵי הַקָּדוֹשׁ בָּרוּךְ הוּא – **David**

NOTES

41. *II Samuel* 15:32.

42. Understood simply, the "summit" is a reference to the summit of the Mount of Olives, which David was approaching as he fled Jerusalem to escape Absalom's cohorts. Ordinarily, when traveling towards Jerusalem David would bow down upon reaching that summit, because from there the tent containing the Holy Ark could be sighted (*Rashi* to *Samuel* loc. cit.). Here, however, David was traveling in the opposite direction. The Gemara interprets the word *rosh* as alluding to an idol. Thus, when it states that David was approaching the *rosh,* the verse means that he was contemplating idolatry.

43. *Daniel* 2:32.

44. The verse refers to a statue seen in a dream by King Nebuchadnezzar. The statue was composed of different elements, including a golden head.

Rav Yehudah here points to the fact that the head (*rosh*, or *reish* in the Aramaic language of Daniel) was that of a statue, an article generally associated with idolatry. Therefore when Scripture relates that David approached the *rosh*, it implies that he considered engaging in idolatry.

45. *II Samuel* 15:32.

46. If my son Absalom succeeds in killing me, people will say that God is unjust for allowing a wicked son to murder his righteous father. My death will thus result in a public disparagement of God's justice (*Rashi*). Let me therefore commit an act of idolatry, to create an obvious reason for my deserving to be killed (see following note).

[Although David had previously committed a transgression in taking Bathsheba prematurely, if he was to be killed his death would not be attributable to that transgression. For David had admitted his misdeed and had then been told by Nassan the Prophet (*II Samuel* 12:13): *"Hashem has also set aside your sin – you shall not die* (on its account)."]

47. If I am killed by Absalom without having committed any obvious sin, God's Name will be desecrated publicly by mass questioning of His judgment. On the other hand, if I forestall this by committing the obvious sin of idolatry, it is only I who will desecrate God's Name with my deed. The latter option is preferable to the former (see *Rashi* and see *Yevamos* 79a). [Generally, any transgression committed in public constitutes a public desecration of God's Name (see note 54 below). Nevertheless, David contended that a desecration of the Name through the act of an individual is preferable to a desecration of the Name through mass blasphemy.]

Yad Ramah and *Maharal* explain that David did not contemplate actually worshiping an idol, but merely acting as though he was worshiping one. Thus, his only misdeed would be the desecration of God's Name through the appearance of sin, and he considered this the preferable course of action (see *Aruch LaNer, Chazon Ish, Sanhedrin* 24:2 and *Rif* in *Ein Yaakov*).

According to *Maharsha*, the Gemara's reference to idolatry is to be understood not literally, but allegorically. David was not contemplating the worship of idols. However, David sought to flee Eretz Yisrael in order to escape Absalom, as he had done when he was hunted by King Saul – and leaving Eretz Yisrael is regarded as tantamount to idolatry (see *Kesubos* 110b). Chushai contended that although David had been justified in leaving Eretz Yisrael to save his life on the earlier occasion, now that he was king, his action would constitute a desecration of God's Name. David countered that remaining in Eretz Yisrael and being killed by Absalom would result in an even greater desecration of God's Name.

R' Yehonasan Eibeschutz (*Yaaros Devash* 1:11) explains the Gemara as meaning that David was contemplating retiring to private life and yielding his throne to Absalom without a fight. However, to abandon the throne and the administration of justice to a wicked person such as Absalom would have been a sin as grave as idolatry, for as stated above (7b; see note 22 there), כָּל הַמַּעֲמִיד דַּיָּין שֶׁאֵינוֹ הָגוּן כְּאִילּוּ נוֹטֵעַ אֲשֵׁרָה, *Whoever appoints an unqualified judge is considered as if he planted an asheirah* (a tree designated for idolatry).

48. Literally: one of beautiful appearance. The Torah permits a Jewish soldier to bring a gentile female prisoner of war back from the battlefield and take her as his wife. Before he could marry her, however, she had to shave her head, let her nails grow, undergo a month-long period of mourning in his home and convert to Judaism (see *Deuteronomy* 21:10-14; see also *Yevamos* 47b, and *Rambam, Hil. Melachim* 8:5). The soldier was granted the right to take the captive and live with her "only in recognition of the strength of man's Evil Inclination" (*Kiddushin* 21b).

Absalom's mother Maachah was the daughter of the gentile king Talmai of Geshur (see *II Samuel* 3:3). David captured her in battle and married her, in accordance with the aforementioned rule (*Rashi*). However, Chushai questioned David's judgment in doing so.

49. *Deuteronomy* 21:18.

50. Three passages follow in succession in *Deuteronomy* 21:10-22. The first is the passage permitting one to marry the beautiful captive; the second concerns a man who suffers domestic discord; the third concerns the incorrigibly rebellious son. The juxtaposition of these three passages alludes to a chain reaction: If one marries a beautiful captive, he will eventually come to hate her, and furthermore, the children of this misalliance will prove to be incorrigibly rebellious (*Rashi* to v. 11). For an explanation of why David did marry Absalom's mother, see *Derashos Chasam Sofer* vol. II p. 344 (*Parashas Nitzavim* 5580).

51. Cuthean merchants are effective salesmen whose modus operandi is to sell merchandise to a customer in numerous small measures, each for a nominal price [thus luring the customer into buying more than he would if he was to make one large purchase and pay for it at once] (*Rashi*). Similarly, David did not ask for forgiveness for all his sins all at once. Instead, he beseeched God to forgive a portion of his sins, and

מסורת הש"ס

א) [סוכה נב:], ב) כד"י כפייה, ג) י"ג עליו, ד) ב"מ נט. ע"ש, ה) כ"א באהלות ונגעים, ו) [עי' היטב יומא פו:], ז) [יומא כב:], ח) [צ"ל ויתהלך], ט) צ"ל ואפשר.

אוכל לחמי הגדיל עלי עקב אמר רב יהודה אמר רב לעולם אל יביא אדם עצמו לידי נסיון שהרי דוד מלך ישראל הביא עצמו לידי נסיון ונכשל אמר לפניו רבש"ע מפני מה אומרים אלהי אברהם אלהי יצחק ואלהי יעקב ואין אומרים אלהי דוד אמר אינהו מינסו לי ואת לא מינסית לי אמר לפניו רבש"ע בחנני ונסני שנאמר א) בחנני ה' ונסני וגו' אמר מינסנא לך ועבידנא מילתא בהדך דלדידהו לא הודעתינהו ואילו אנא קא מודענא לך דמנסינא לך בדבר ערוה מיד ב) ויהי לעת הערב ויקם דוד מעל משכבו וגו' אמר רב יהודה שהפך משכבו של לילה למשכבו של יום ונתעלמה ממנו הלכה א) אבר קטן יש באדם משביעו רעב ומרעיבו שבע ב) ויתהלך על גג בית המלך וירא אשה רוחצת מעל הגג והאשה טובת מראה מאד בת שבע הוה קא חייפא רישא תותי חלתא אתא שטן אידמי ליה כציפרתא פתק ביה גירא פתקה לחלתא איגליה וחזייה מיד ג) וישלח דוד וידרוש לאשה ויאמר הלא זאת בת שבע בת אליעם אשת אוריה החתי וישלח דוד מלאכים ויקחה ותבא אליו וישכב עמה והיא מתקדשת מטומאתה ותשב אל ביתה והיינו דכתיב ד) בחנת לבי פקדת לילה צרפתני בל תמצא זמותי בל יעבר פי אמר איכו זממא נפל בפומיה דמאן דסני לי ולא אמר כי הא מילתא דרש רבא מאי דכתיב ה) למנצח לדוד בה' חסיתי איך תאמרו לנפשי נודי הרכם צפור אמר דוד לפני הקב"ה רבש"ע מחול לי על אותו עון שלא יאמרו הר שבכם צפור נדדתו דרש רבא מאי דכתיב ו) לך לבדך חטאתי והרע בעיניך עשיתי למען תצדק בדברך תזכה בשפטך אמר דוד לפני הקב"ה גליא וידיעא קמך דאי בעיא למכפייה ליצרי הוה כייפינא אלא אמינא דלא לימרו עבדא ג) זכי למריה דרש רבא מאי דכתיב ז) כי אני לצלע נכון ומכאובי נגדי תמיד ראויה היתה בת שבע בת אליעם לדוד מששת ימי בראשית אלא שבאה ג) אליו במכאוב וכן תנא דבי רבי ישמעאל ראויה היתה לדוד בת שבע בת אליעם אלא שאכלה פגה ד) דרש רבא מאי דכתיב ח) ובצלעי שמחו ונאספו נאספו עלי נכים [ולא ידעתי] קרעו ולא דמו אמר דוד לפני הקב"ה רבש"ע גלוי וידוע לפניך שאם היו קורעין בשרי לא היה דמי שותת ולא עוד אלא בשעה שהם עוסקין ה) בארבע מיתות ב"ד פוסקין ממשנתן ואומרים לי דוד הבא על אשת איש מיתתו במה אמרתי להם הבא על אשת איש מיתתו בחנק ויש לו חלק לעוה"ב אבל המלבין פני חבירו ברבים אין לו חלק לעולם הבא אמר רב יהודה אמר רב אפילו בשעת חליו של דוד קיים שמנה עשרה עונות שנאמר ט) יגעתי באנחתי אשחה בכל לילה מטתי בדמעתי ערשי אמסה ואמר רב יהודה אמר רב בקש דוד לעבוד ע"ז שנאמר י) ויהי דוד בא עד הראש אשר ישתחוה שם לאלהים ואין ראש אלא ע"ז שנאמר כ) והוא צלמא רישיה די דהב טב י) והנה לקראתו חושי הארכי קרוע כתנתו ואדמה על ראשו אמר לו לדוד יאמרו מלך שכמותך יעבוד ע"ז אמר לו מלך שכמותי יהרגנו בנו מוטב יעבוד ע"ז ואל יתחלל שם שמים בפרהסיא אמר מאי טעמא קנסיבת יפת תואר א"ל יפת תואר רחמנא שרייה א"ל לא דרשת סמוכין דסמיך ליה ל) כי יהיה לאיש בן סורר ומורה כל הנושא יפת תואר יש לו בן סורר ומורה דרש ר' דוסתאי דמן בירי למה דוד דומה לסוחר כותי אמר דוד לפני הקב"ה רבש"ע מ) שגיאות מי יבין [א"ל] שביקי לך ומנסתרות נקני שביקי לך גם מזדים חשוך עבדך שביקי לך אל ימשלו בי [א] אז איתם דלא לישתעו בי רבנן שביקי לך [ב] ונקיתי מפשע רב י) שלא יכתב סרחוני אמר לו א"א ומה יו"ד שנטלתי משרי עומד וצווח כמה שנים עד שבא יהושע והוספתי לו שנאמר נ) ויקרא משה להושע בן נון יהושע כל הפרשה כולה עאכ"ו ונקיתי מפשע רב אמר לפניו רבש"ע מחול לי על אותו עון כולו אמר כבר עתיד שלמה בנך לומר בחכמתו ס) היחתה איש אש בחיקו ובגדיו לא תשרפנה אם יהלך איש על הגחלים ורגליו לא תכוינה כן הבא על אשת רעהו לא ינקה כל הנוגע בה א"ל כל הכי נטרד ההוא גברא א"ל קבל עליך יסורין קבל עליו י) אמר רב יהודה אמר רב ששה חדשים נצטרע דוד ונסתלקה הימנו שכינה ופירשו ממנו סנהדרין נצטרע דכתיב ע) תחטאני באזוב ואטהר תכבסני ומשלג אלבין נסתלקה הימנו שכינה דכתיב פ) השיבה לי ששון ישעך ורוח נדיבה תסמכני ופרשו ממנו סנהדרין דכתי' צ) ישובו לי יראיך וגו' ששה חדשים מנלן דכתי' ק) והימים אשר מלך דוד על ישראל ארבעים שנה בחברון

רש"י

אוכל לחמי. לומד תורתי: שהפך משכבו של לילה לשל יום. שהיה משמש מטתו ביום כדי שיהא שבע מתשמיש ולא יהרהר אחר אשה כל היום: ונתעלמה ממנו [הלכה]. שהמשביע אברו בתשמיש רעב ומרבה תאוה: ה"ג ח) מתהלך על גג המלך ולא גרסינן והיינו: חלתא. כוורת: פתיק [ביה] גירא. בכוורת כלומר שהכה ושברה ל"א פתחה שברה ונפתחה: מתקדשת מטומאתה. אותה שעה פסק טומאתה ולא בא עליה כשהיא נדה: פקדת לילה. על מעשה לילה פקדתני אם אוכל לעמוד בנסיון של דבר עבירה: צרפתני בל תמצא. חשבת לצרפני ולא מצאתני נקי: (זמותי בל יעבר פי) איכו זממא נפל. מי יתן והיה בפי רסן ט) ואפשר לעכב את דברי שלא אומר דבר זה [של] בחנני: הר שבכם. מלך שלכם: צפור נדדתו. דעל ידי צפור נטרד כדאמר אדמי ליה כצפור: למריה. העבד נצחו לאדוניו בתוכחתו: כי אני לצלע נכון. אותו צלע היה נכון לי: שאכלה פגה. שקפץ את השעה ליזקק ע"י עבירה: נאספו עלי נכים. בעלי מומין כמו פרעה נכה (מלכים ב כג) והיו מלעיגים עלי ואני כלא יודע ל"א ולא ידעתי לא הייתי יודע כשמלעיגים כלומר פתאום בא עלי אותו עון שלא ידעתי (עד) שניתן פתחון פה לביישני: הכי גרסינן בשעה שעוסקין במיתות בית דין אומרים הבא על אשת איש מיתתו וכו': י"ח עונות. לי"ח נשיו שלא לעגנן: באנחתי אשחה. אפילו בשעת אנחתי אשחה בכל לילה: מטתי. תשמיש המטה ענין סחי ומאוס (איכה ג) קרי ליה: בדמעתי ערשי אמסה. שבשעת דמעתי אני ממאיס את מטתי בתשמיש: יאמרו מלך שכמותי. חסיד שכמותי הרגו בנו ויהו מתרעמין על מדותיו של הקב"ה ונמצא שם שמים מתחלל בפרהסיא: מוטב אעבוד ע"ז. ואחלל את השם אני לבדי ולא יחללו [אותו] כל העם: אמר ליה. חושי הארכי לדוד הקב"ה לא עביד דינא בלא דינא שמעמיד בנך להרגך דאת מאי טעמא נסבת יפת תואר דאמו של אבשלום מעכה בת תלמי מלך גשור (שמואל ב ג) ותפסה דוד במלחמה דאין לומר בעבירה באה לו דהא כתיב (מלכים א טו) רק בדבר אוריה החתי: סוחר כותי. דרכו לפנות את סחורתו מעט מעט להעמידה על דמים מועטים: שגיאות מי יבין. מי יכול להשמר משגגות: אמר לו. הקב"ה: שביקא לך. מחול לך: נסתרות. [מזיד] של צנעה: זדים. מזיד של פרהסיא: ה"ג אל ימשלו בי דלא לישתעו בי רבנן. והיינו אל ימשלו לשון משל שלא ידרשו בחטאתי חכמי הדורות ואז איתם: שלא יכתב סורחני. שתמחוק אותה פרשה מן המקרא וישתכח הדבר לעולמים: כל הפרשה. שכתובה כבר שעשית אותו חטא: על אחת כמה וכמה. שלא תעקור: תחטאני באזוב. מכלל שהיה צריך טהרת אזוב כמצורע: בחברון

ליקוטי רש"י

הגדיל עלי עקב. ארב כמו (יהושע ח') ואת עקבו מים לעיר [תהלים מא, י]. בחנת לבי וגו'. ידעתי כי יש עבירה בידי ואם משפט עונשי יצא לפניך לא אצדק בדין אשר כבר בחנת לבי. פקדת לילה. לעת הערב בעון בת שבע שנאמר ויהי לעת ערב ויקם דוד וגו' (ש"ב יא). צרפתני. נסיתני. בל תמצא. לא מצאת בי חפצך. זמותי בל יעבר פי. אם תעלה עוד במחשבתי ליבחן לפניך בל יעבר פי לומר עוד בחנני ונסני כמו שאמרתי כבר כמו שנאמר (תהלים כו) בחנני ה' ונסני שאמר דוד לפני הקב"ה מפני מה אומרים אלהי אברהם ואין אומרים אלהי דוד אמר לו אני בחנתיו בי' נסיונות ונמצא שלם אמר בחנני ונסני כדאיתא במסכת שבת [תהלים יז, ג]. לך לבדך חטאתי. לפיכך בידך לסלוח ואף מה שהרעותי לאוריה לא חטאתי אלא לך שהזהרת על הדבר. למען תצדק בדברך. כן היה לי להתגבר על יצרי אלא שלא יאמרו העבד נצח את רבו שאמרתי לפניך בחנני ונסני (תהלים כ"ו) ובחנתני ולא נמצאתי שלם כדי שתצדק אתה ולא אני [תהלים נא, ו]. ובצלעי שמחו ונאספו. וכשאני צולע ששבר בא עלי שמחו ונאספו. נאספו עלי נכים. אנשי' פסחי' כמו שאנו מתרגמין נכה חגירא ומנחם חברו כמו נכאי' (ישעיה ט"ז) אימנוייש"ך בלעז. קרעו ולא דמו. אילו היו קורעין את בשרי לא היה דמי שותת לארץ כשמלבינין פני [שם לה, טו]. דרש רבא מאי דכתיב ובצלעי. דטובה מעשה של דוד ובת שבע משלהם וספק אשת איש היא שהיוצא למלחמת בית דוד גט כריתות כותב לאשתו על מנת שאם ימות שתהא מגורשת מעכשיו ולא תיזקק ליבם וכל אותן הימים היא ספק מגורשת אם מת מגורשת מתחילה ואם לא מת לא נתגרשה. ובצלעי. בשביל אשתי זו שמתחילה תעאתי בה כמו (בראשית ב) ויבן את הצלע שמחו ונאספו. קרעו ולא דמו. אם קרעוני לא מצאו דם [ב"מ נט.]. אשחה בכל לילה מטתי. לשון סחי ומאוס (איכה ג) והיתה נבלתם כסוחה (ישעי' ה) וכו' בדמעות ומנחם חברו עם כאשר יפרש השוחה לשחות (שם ישעיהו כה) ועם מי שחו (יחזקאל מז) [תהלים ו, ז]. לא דרשת סמוכין. לא דברה תורה אלא כנגד יצר הרע שאם אין הקב"ה מתירה ישאנה באיסור אבל אם נשאה סופו להיות שונאה שנאמר אחריו (פסוק טו) כי תהיין לאיש וגו' וסופו להוליד ממנה בן סורר ומורה לכך נסמכו פרשיות הללו [דברים כא, יא]. שגיאות מי יבין. אני נזהרתי בהם אבל אי אפשר להזהר שלא אשגה בהם ואתה נקני מנסתרות שנסתרו ממני ולא ידעתי בחטאי בשגגה [תהלים יט, יג]. גם מזדים. מן הזדונות. אז איתם. אהיה תמים אמרו חכמים למה דוד דומה לכותי הסוחר על הפתחים והם מערימים בדבר יותר מכל אדם תנו לי מים לשתות דבר שאין בו חסרון כיס משמשה אמר יש כאן בצל קטן משנתנו לו אומר יש בצל בלא מלח משנתנו לו אמר תנו לי מעט לחם שלא יזיקני הבצל כך אמר דוד בתחל' על השגגות ואחר כך על הזדונו' ואחר כך על המרדים פשעים אלו המרדים שמתכוין להכעיס וכן הוא אומר (מ"ב ג') מלך מואב פשע בי [שם יט, יד]. שנטלתי משרי. שאף יו"ד של שרי נתרעמה על השכינה עד שנתוספה ליהושע שנאמר (במדבר יג, טז) ויקרא משה להושע בן נון יהושע [בראשית יז, ה]. היחתה איש. הישא איש גחלים בשפולי בגדיו ולא ישרפו כל לשון חתיית גחלים לשון אסיפה הוא כמשמעה כשמגלה הכלי בתוך המדורה [משלי ו, כז]. קבל עליך יסורין. יסור יסרני יה. על מעשה בת שבע ביסורין כגון מחת הכבשה ישלם ארבעתים (שמואל ב, י"ב) ששה חדשים נצטרע דוד [תהלים קיח, קיז]. תחטאני באזוב. כמו שמטהר המצורע וטמא מת [שם נא, ט]. השיבה לי ששון ישעך. רוח הקודש שנסתלק מעלי. נדיבה. לשון נדיבות קלינות [שם יד]. ישובו לי יראיך. שפירשו הימנו סנהדרין כשנצטרע מאותו עון אף אם גרושה היא נתן עיניו בה כל הנוגע לא ינקה [שם קיט, עט].

הגהות הגר"א

[א] גמ' אז איתם. נמחק (ועי' רש"י): [ב] שם ונקיתי מפשע רב. נמחק. וג"ב אז איתם (וכל גירסת רבינו כגמ' כ"ה בע"י):

תורה אור השלם

א) בְּחָנֵנִי יְיָ וְנַסֵּנִי צָרְפָה כִלְיוֹתַי וְלִבִּי: [תהלים כו, ב]

ב) וַיְהִי לְעֵת הָעֶרֶב וַיָּקָם דָּוִד מֵעַל מִשְׁכָּבוֹ וַיִּתְהַלֵּךְ עַל גַּג בֵּית הַמֶּלֶךְ וַיַּרְא אִשָּׁה רֹחֶצֶת מֵעַל הַגָּג וְהָאִשָּׁה טוֹבַת מַרְאֶה מְאֹד: [שמואל ב' יא, ב]

ג) וַיִּשְׁלַח דָּוִד וַיִּדְרֹשׁ לָאִשָּׁה וַיֹּאמֶר הֲלוֹא זֹאת בַּת שֶׁבַע בַּת אֱלִיעָם אֵשֶׁת אוּרִיָּה הַחִתִּי: וַיִּשְׁלַח דָּוִד מַלְאָכִים וַיִּקָּחֶהָ וַתָּבוֹא אֵלָיו וַיִּשְׁכַּב עִמָּהּ וְהִיא מִתְקַדֶּשֶׁת מִטֻּמְאָתָהּ וַתָּשָׁב אֶל בֵּיתָהּ: [שמואל ב' יא, ג-ד]

ד) בָּחַנְתָּ לִבִּי פָּקַדְתָּ לַּיְלָה צְרַפְתַּנִי בַל תִּמְצָא זַמֹּתִי בַּל יַעֲבָר פִּי: [תהלים יז, ג]

ה) לַמְנַצֵּחַ לְדָוִד בַּייָ חָסִיתִי אֵיךְ תֹּאמְרוּ לְנַפְשִׁי נוּדִי הַרְכֶם צִפּוֹר: [תהלים יא, א]

ו) לְךָ לְבַדְּךָ חָטָאתִי וְהָרַע בְּעֵינֶיךָ עָשִׂיתִי לְמַעַן תִּצְדַּק בְּדָבְרֶךָ תִּזְכֶּה בְשָׁפְטֶךָ: [תהלים נא, ו]

ז) כִּי אֲנִי לְצֶלַע נָכוֹן וּמַכְאוֹבִי נֶגְדִּי תָמִיד: [תהלים לח, יח]

ח) וּבְצַלְעִי שָׂמְחוּ וְנֶאֱסָפוּ נֶאֶסְפוּ עָלַי נֵכִים וְלֹא יָדַעְתִּי קָרְעוּ וְלֹא דָמּוּ: [תהלים לה, טו]

ט) יָגַעְתִּי בְּאַנְחָתִי אַשְׂחֶה בְכָל לַיְלָה מִטָּתִי בְּדִמְעָתִי עַרְשִׂי אַמְסֶה: [תהלים ו, ז]

י) וַיְהִי דָוִד בָּא עַד הָרֹאשׁ אֲשֶׁר יִשְׁתַּחֲוֶה שָׁם לֵאלֹהִים וְהִנֵּה לִקְרָאתוֹ חוּשַׁי הָאַרְכִּי קָרוּעַ כֻּתָּנְתּוֹ וַאֲדָמָה עַל רֹאשׁוֹ: [שמואל ב' טו, לב]

כ) הוּא צַלְמָא רֵאשֵׁהּ דִּי דְהַב טָב חֲדוֹהִי וּדְרָעוֹהִי דִּי כְסַף מְעוֹהִי וְיַרְכָתֵהּ דִּי נְחָשׁ: [דניאל ב, לב]

ל) כִּי יִהְיֶה לְאִישׁ בֵּן סוֹרֵר וּמוֹרֶה אֵינֶנּוּ שֹׁמֵעַ בְּקוֹל אָבִיו וּבְקוֹל אִמּוֹ וְיִסְּרוּ אֹתוֹ וְלֹא יִשְׁמַע אֲלֵיהֶם: [דברים כא, יח]

מ) שְׁגִיאוֹת מִי יָבִין מִנִּסְתָּרוֹת נַקֵּנִי: גַּם מִזֵּדִים חֲשֹׂךְ עַבְדֶּךָ אַל יִמְשְׁלוּ בִי אָז אֵיתָם וְנִקֵּיתִי מִפֶּשַׁע רָב: [תהלים יט, יג-יד]

נ) אֵלֶּה שְׁמוֹת הָאֲנָשִׁים אֲשֶׁר שָׁלַח מֹשֶׁה לָתוּר אֶת הָאָרֶץ וַיִּקְרָא מֹשֶׁה לְהוֹשֵׁעַ בִּן נוּן יְהוֹשֻׁעַ: [במדבר יג, טז]

ס) הֲיַחְתֶּה אִישׁ אֵשׁ בְּחֵיקוֹ וּבְגָדָיו לֹא תִשָּׂרַפְנָה: אִם יְהַלֵּךְ אִישׁ עַל הַגֶּחָלִים וְרַגְלָיו לֹא תִכָּוֶינָה: כֵּן הַבָּא אֶל אֵשֶׁת רֵעֵהוּ לֹא יִנָּקֶה כָּל הַנֹּגֵעַ בָּהּ: [משלי ו, כז-כט]

ע) תְּחַטְּאֵנִי בְאֵזוֹב וְאֶטְהָר תְּכַבְּסֵנִי וּמִשֶּׁלֶג אַלְבִּין: [תהלים נא, ט]

פ) הָשִׁיבָה לִּי שְׂשׂוֹן יִשְׁעֶךָ וְרוּחַ נְדִיבָה תִסְמְכֵנִי: [תהלים נא, יד]

צ) יָשׁוּבוּ לִי יְרֵאֶיךָ וְיֹדְעֵי עֵדֹתֶיךָ: [תהלים קיט, עט]

ק) וְהַיָּמִים אֲשֶׁר מָלַךְ דָּוִד עַל יִשְׂרָאֵל אַרְבָּעִים שָׁנָה בְּחֶבְרוֹן מָלַךְ שֶׁבַע שָׁנִים וּבִירוּשָׁלִַם מָלַךְ שְׁלֹשִׁים וְשָׁלֹשׁ שָׁנִים: [מלכים א' ב, יא]

said before the Holy One, Blessed is He: רִבּוֹנוֹ שֶׁל עוֹלָם – **Master of the Universe!** „שְׁגִיאוֹת מִי־יָבִין" – ***Who can discern mistakes?***[52] [אָמַר לֵיהּ] – **[The Holy One, Blessed is He, said to David:]** שְׁבִיקֵי לָךְ – **"Your [unwitting sins] are forgiven."** ו„מִנִּסְתָּרוֹת נַקֵּנִי" – **And** when David continued: ***from unknown sins cleanse me,***[53] שְׁבִיקֵי לָךְ – the Holy One, Blessed is He, replied: **"Your [unknown sins] are forgiven."** „גַּם מִזֵּדִים חֲשֹׂךְ עַבְדֶּךָ" – David then proceeded: ***Also, from intentional sins spare Your servant.***[54] שְׁבִיקֵי לָךְ – The Holy One, Blessed is He, replied: **"Your [intentional sins] are forgiven** as well." „אַל־יִמְשְׁלוּ־בִי (אז איתם)" – David then said: ***Let them not rule over me*** – דְּלֹא לִישְׁתָּעוּ בִּי רַבָּנָן – that is, "Let it be Your will **that the Rabbis not talk about me."**[55] שְׁבִיקֵי לָךְ – The Holy One, Blessed is He, replied: **"You are forgiven,"** i.e. your request is granted.[56] „[אָז אֵיתָם] וְנִקֵּיתִי מִפֶּשַׁע רָב" – David concluded: ***[then I shall be perfect]***[57] ***and I shall be cleansed of great transgression*** – שֶׁלֹּא יִכָּתֵב סִרְחוֹנִי – that is, **"May my offense** in taking Bathsheba **not be written down** in Scripture."[58] אָמַר לוֹ – **[The Holy One, Blessed is He,] said to [David]:** אִי אֶפְשָׁר – "That is **impossible.** וּמַה יו״ד שֶׁנָּטַלְתִּי מִשָּׂרַי – **If even the** letter *yud* that **I removed from** the name of Abraham's wife **Sarai,** when I changed it to Sarah,[59] עוֹמֵד וְצוֹוֵחַ כַּמָּה שָׁנִים – **stood up and protested** its removal **for many years,** עַד שֶׁבָּא יְהוֹשֻׁעַ וְהוֹסַפְתִּי לוֹ – **until Joshua came along and I added [the *yud*] to his** name," שֶׁנֶּאֱמַר „וַיִּקְרָא מֹשֶׁה לְהוֹשֵׁעַ בִּן־נוּן יְהוֹשֻׁעַ" – **as it is stated:**[60] ***Moses called Hoshea the son of Nun, Joshua,***[61] כָּל הַפָּרָשָׁה כּוּלָּהּ עַל אַחַת כַּמָּה וְכַמָּה – **"how much more so** is it impossible to erase **the entire passage** of the Bathsheba episode from Scripture!"[62]

An alternate exposition of the final segment:

„וְנִקֵּיתִי מִפֶּשַׁע רָב" – ***And I shall be cleansed of great transgression*** means that אָמַר לְפָנָיו – **[David] said before [The Holy One, Blessed is He]:** רִבּוֹנוֹ שֶׁל עוֹלָם – "Master of the Universe! מְחוֹל לִי עַל אוֹתוֹ עָוֹן כּוּלּוֹ – **Forgive me for that sin in its entirety!"**[63] אָמַר – **[The Holy One, Blessed is He,] replied:** כְּבָר עָתִיד שְׁלֹמֹה בִּנְךָ לוֹמַר בְּחָכְמָתוֹ – **"Solomon your son is already destined to state, in his wisdom:**[64] „הֲיַחְתֶּה אִישׁ אֵשׁ בְּחֵיקוֹ וּבְגָדָיו לֹא תִשָּׂרַפְנָה – ***Can a man rake embers into his bosom without burning his clothes?*** אִם־יְהַלֵּךְ אִישׁ עַל־הַגֶּחָלִים וְרַגְלָיו לֹא תִכָּוֶינָה – ***Can a man walk on*** *live* ***coals without scorching his feet?*** כֵּן הַבָּא (על) [אֶל]־אֵשֶׁת רֵעֵהוּ לֹא יִנָּקֶה כָּל־הַנֹּגֵעַ בָּהּ" – ***It is the same with one who cohabits with his fellow's wife: nobody who touches her will be cleansed."*** אָמַר לֵיהּ – **[David] said to [The Holy One, Blessed is He]:** כָּל הָכִי נִטְרַד הַהוּא גַּבְרָא – **"Is that man,** i.e. myself, **so absolutely rejected** by You because of his transgression? Can I do nothing to cleanse myself entirely of it?" אָמַר לוֹ – **[The Holy One, Blessed is He,] said to [David]:** קַבֵּל עָלֶיךָ יִסּוּרִין – **"Accept suffering upon yourself,** for that will cleanse you."[65] קִבֵּל עָלָיו – **[David] accepted** suffering **upon himself.**

David's suffering:

אָמַר רַב יְהוּדָה אָמַר רַב – **Rav Yehudah said in the name of Rav:** שִׁשָּׁה חֳדָשִׁים – **For** a period of **six months,** נִצְטָרַע דָּוִד – **David was afflicted with *tzaraas*,** וְנִסְתַּלְּקָה הֵימֶנּוּ שְׁכִינָה – **the Divine Presence departed him** וּפֵירְשׁוּ מִמֶּנּוּ סַנְהֶדְרִין – **and the Sanhedrin withdrew from him.** נִצְטָרַע דִּכְתִיב „תְּחַטְּאֵנִי בְאֵזוֹב וְאֶטְהָר תְּכַבְּסֵנִי וּמִשֶּׁלֶג אַלְבִּין" – **He was afflicted with *tzaraas* – as it is written:**[66] ***Purge me with hyssop and I shall be pure, cleanse me and I shall be whiter than snow.***[67] נִסְתַּלְּקָה הֵימֶנּוּ שְׁכִינָה דִּכְתִיב „הָשִׁיבָה לִּי שְׂשׂוֹן יִשְׁעֶךָ וְרוּחַ נְדִיבָה תִסְמְכֵנִי" – **The**

NOTES

when God agreed, David proceeded with additional requests. The Gemara sees this as the meaning of the verses (*Psalms* 19:13-14): שְׁגִיאוֹת מִי־יָבִין מִנִּסְתָּרוֹת נַקֵּנִי גַּם מִזֵּדִים חֲשֹׂךְ עַבְדֶּךָ אַל־יִמְשְׁלוּ־בִי אָז אֵיתָם וְנִקֵּיתִי מִפֶּשַׁע רָב, *Who can discern mistakes? From unknown faults cleanse me! Also, from intentional sins spare Your servant; let them not rule over me. Then I shall be perfect, and cleansed of great transgression.* The Gemara goes on to interpret each segment of these verses as a plea for the absolution of a specific sort of sin. See *Midrash Shocher Tov* (ad loc.) for a slightly variant version of this exposition. See also *Toras Chaim.*

Others explain that Cuthean merchants are wise *buyers,* who are willing to pay a little extra to ensure that the seller fulfills the contract to the letter. Similarly, David was willing to "pay a little extra," that is, to endure suffering (see below) to ensure that his sin was atoned for (*Yad Ramah*).

52. *Psalms* 19:13. I.e. who can be so careful that he never sins even unintentionally? (*Rashi*).

53. Ibid. I.e. cleanse me of the sins that I committed knowingly, but are unknown to others (*Rashi*).

54. This is a reference to transgressions committed knowingly and in public (*Rashi*), which are more serious than transgressions committed privately, since a public sin causes a desecration of God's Name (*Maharsha*).

55. I.e. let the Torah scholars of future generations not expound upon the Bathsheba episode (*Rashi;* see *Rambam, Hil. Tefillah* 12:12 with *Kesef Mishneh*; see also *Tos. Yom Tov* to *Megillah* 4:10 and *Ben Yehoyada*).

The word יִמְשְׁלוּ is understood here as deriving from the word מָשָׁל, an example or parable. Hence, the verse means: Let them not present me as an example (i.e. role model) of a sinner (*Rashi*; cf. *Yad Ramah*).

56. This is not to say that God acceded immediately to every one of David's requests. Rather, when David completed his penance for his unwitting sins and was forgiven for them, he went on to do penance and beg forgiveness for the sins he committed knowingly, proceeding through one category of sin at a time (*R' Avigdor Miller*).

57. We have followed *Gra's* emendation, which correlates our text with the one cited in *Ein Yaakov*, and which appears to correspond with *Rashi's* version of the text.

58. I.e. erase the entire episode from Scripture, so that it will be forgotten forevermore. [Thus, my reputation will be cleansed of great transgression] (*Rashi*).

59. Abraham's wife originally bore the name שָׂרַי, *Sarai* (*Genesis* 11:29). Subsequently, God changed her name to שָׂרָה, *Sarah,* replacing the letter *yud* at the end of the name with the letter *hei* (ibid. 17:15).

60. *Numbers* 13:16.

61. When Moses dispatched representatives of the twelve tribes to spy out the Land of Canaan, he suspected that they were conspiring to issue an evil report about the land, as they ultimately did. He therefore changed the name of his devoted disciple, who was the representative of the tribe of Ephraim, from הוֹשֵׁעַ to יְהוֹשֻׁעַ, adding a *yud* to the name. The new name indicated: יָהּ יוֹשִׁיעֲךָ מֵעֲצַת מְרַגְּלִים, *May God save you from the conspiracy of the Spies* (*Sotah* 34b). Thus, the "missing" *yud* was replaced in Scripture.

62. The passage has already been written and therefore cannot be erased (*Rashi*).

63. The sin was partially forgiven when David admitted his misdeed (see *II Samuel* 12:13). He later asked for *complete* forgiveness, so that he would be cleansed entirely of the effects of the sin (*Maharsha*).

There are various levels of repentance and of forgiveness. It is possible for a sinner to be forgiven his misdeed and absolved of retribution, yet not find grace in the eyes of God and not have his offerings or prayers accepted. Therefore, even after achieving forgiveness for the sin, David prayed to be cleansed entirely and to be as favored by God as he was prior to the act (*Shaarei Teshuvah* 1:42).

64. *Proverbs* 6:27-29.

65. As the Gemara teaches (*Yoma* 86a), suffering cleanses a person of the effects of sin.

66. *Psalms* 51:9 (see note 23).

67. The purification process of one who is afflicted with *tzaraas* (a *metzora*) involves a ceremony in which a live bird, a cedar branch, a thread of crimson wool and a clump of hyssop are dipped into a mixture containing the blood of a slaughtered bird and spring water, which are then sprinkled seven times on the *metzora (Leviticus* 14:6). Thus, hyssop is associated with the purification of a *metzora.* Since David prays here to

אוכל לחמי הגדיל עלי עקב אמר רב יהודה אמר רב לעולם אל יביא אדם עצמו לידי נסיון שהרי דוד מלך ישראל הביא עצמו לידי נסיון ונכשל אמר לפניו רבש"ע מפני מה אומרים אלהי אברהם אלהי יצחק ואלהי יעקב ואין אומרים אלהי דוד אמר אינהו מינסו לי ואת לא מינסית לי אמר לפניו רבש"ע בחנני ונסני שנאמר [א] בחנני ה' ונסני וגו' אמר מינסנא לך ועבידנא מילתא בהדך דלדידהו לא הודעתינהו ואילו אנא קא מודענא לך דמנסינא לך בדבר ערוה מיד [ב] ויהי לעת הערב ויקם דוד מעל משכבו וגו' אמר רב יהודה שהפך משכבו של לילה למשכבו של יום ונתעלמה ממנו הלכה [א] אבר קטן יש באדם משביעו רעב ומרעיבו שבע [ב] ויתהלך על גג בית המלך וירא אשה רוחצת מעל הגג והאשה טובת מראה מאד בת שבע הוה קא חייפא רישא תותי חלתא אתא שטן אידמי ליה כציפרתא פתק ביה גירא פתקה לחלתא איגליה וחזייה מיד [ג] וישלח דוד וידרוש לאשה ויאמר הלא זאת בת שבע בת אליעם אשת אוריה החתי וישלח דוד מלאכים ויקחה ותבא אליו וישכב עמה והיא מתקדשת מטומאתה ותשב אל ביתה והיינו דכתיב [ד] בחנת לבי פקדת לילה צרפתני בל תמצא זמותי בל יעבר פי אמר איכו זממא נפל בפומיה דמאן דסני לי ולא אמר כי הא מילתא דרש רבא מאי דכתיב [ה] למנצח לדוד בה' חסיתי איך תאמרו לנפשי נודי הרכם צפור אמר דוד לפני הקב"ה רבש"ע מחול לי על אותו עון שלא יאמרו הר שבכם צפור נדדתו דרש רבא מאי דכתיב [ו] לך לבדך חטאתי והרע בעיניך עשיתי למען תצדק בדברך תזכה בשפטך אמר דוד לפני הקב"ה גליא וידיעא קמך דאי בעיא למכפייה ליצרי הוה כייפינא אלא אמינא דלא לימרו עבדא [ג] זכי למריה דרש רבא מאי דכתיב [ז] כי אני לצלע נכון ומכאובי נגדי תמיד ראויה היתה בת שבע בת אליעם לדוד מששת ימי בראשית אלא שבאה [ז] אליו במכאוב וכן תנא דבי רבי ישמעאל ראויה היתה לדוד בת שבע בת אליעם אלא שאכלה פגה [ד] דרש רבא מאי דכתיב [ח] ובצלעי שמחו ונאספו נאספו עלי נכים [ולא ידעתי] קרעו ולא דמו אמר דוד לפני הקב"ה רבש"ע גלוי וידוע לפניך שאם היו קורעין בשרי לא היה דמי שותת ולא עוד אלא בשעה שהם עוסקין [ה] בארבע מיתות ב"ד פוסקין ממשנתן ואומרים לי דוד הבא על אשת איש מיתתו במה אמרתי להם הבא על אשת איש מיתתו בחנק ויש לו חלק לעוה"ב אבל המלבין פני חבירו ברבים אין לו חלק לעולם הבא אמר רב יהודה אמר רב אפילו בשעת חליו של דוד קיים שמנה עשרה עונות שנאמר [ט] יגעתי באנחתי אשחה בכל לילה מטתי בדמעתי ערשי אמסה ואמר רב יהודה אמר רב בקש דוד לעבוד ע"ז שנאמר [י] ויהי דוד בא עד הראש אשר ישתחוה שם לאלהים ואין ראש אלא ע"ז שנאמר [כ] והוא צלמא רישיה די דהב טב [י] והנה לקראתו חושי הארכי קרוע כתנתו ואדמה על ראשו אמר לו לדוד יאמרו מלך שכמותך יעבוד ע"ז אמר לו מלך שכמותי יהרגנו בנו מוטב יעבוד ע"ז ואל יתחלל שם שמים בפרהסיא אמר מאי טעמא קנסיבת יפת תואר א"ל יפת תואר רחמנא שרייה א"ל לא דרשת סמוכין דסמיך ליה [ל] כי יהיה לאיש בן סורר ומורה כל הנושא יפת תואר יש לו בן סורר ומורה דרש ר' דוסתאי דמן בירי למה דוד דומה לסוחר כותי אמר דוד לפני הקב"ה רבש"ע [מ] שגיאות מי יבין [א"ל] שביקי לך ומנסתרות נקני שביקי לך גם מזדים חשוך עבדך שביקי לך אל ימשלו בי [א] אז איתם דלא לישתעו בי רבנן שביקי לך [ב] ונקיתי מפשע רב [ו] שלא יכתב סרחוני אמר לו א"א ומה יו"ד שנטלתי משרי עומד וצווח כמה שנים עד שבא יהושע והוספתי לו שנאמר [נ] ויקרא משה להושע בן נון יהושע כל הפרשה כולה עאכ"ו ונקיתי מפשע רב אמר לפניו רבש"ע מחול לי על אותו עון כולו אמר כבר עתיד שלמה בנך לומר בחכמתו [ס] היחתה איש אש בחיקו ובגדיו לא תשרפנה אם יהלך איש על הגחלים ורגליו לא תכוינה כן הבא על אשת רעהו לא ינקה כל הנוגע בה א"ל כל הכי נטרד ההוא גברא א"ל קבל עליך יסורין קבל עליו [ז] אמר רב יהודה אמר רב ששה חדשים נצטרע דוד ונסתלקה הימנו שכינה ופירשו ממנו סנהדרין נצטרע דכתיב [ע] תחטאני באזוב ואטהר תכבסני ומשלג אלבין נסתלקה הימנו שכינה דכתיב [פ] השיבה לי ששון ישעך ורוח נדיבה תסמכני ופרשו ממנו סנהדרין דכתי' [צ] ישובו לי יראיך וגו' ששה חדשים מנלן דכתי' [ק] והימים אשר מלך דוד על ישראל ארבעים שנה

בחברון

רש"י

אוכל לחמי. לומד תורתי: שהפך משכבו של לילה לשל יום. שהיה משמש מטתו ביום כדי שיהא שבע מתשמיש ולא יהרהר אחר אשה כל היום: ונתעלמה ממנו [הלכה]. שהמשביע אברו בתשמיש רעב ומרבה תאוה: ה"ג [ח] מתהלך על גג המלך ולא גרסינן והיינו: חלתא. כוורת: פתיק [ביה] גירא. בכוורת כלומר שהכה ושברה ל"א פתחה שברה ונפתחה: מתקדשת מטומאתה. אותה שעה פסק טומאתה ולא בא עליה כשהיא נדה: פקדת לילה. על מעשה לילה פקדתני אם אוכל לעמוד בנסיון של דבר עבירה: צרפתני בל תמצא. חשבת לצרפני ולא מצאתני נקי: (זמותי בל יעבר פי) איכו זממא נפל. מי יתן והיה בפי רסן [ט] ואפשר לעכב את דברי שלא אומר דבר זה [של] בחנני: הר שבכם. מלך שלכם: צפור נדדתו. דעל ידי צפור נטרד כדאמר אדמי ליה כצפור: למריה. העבד נלחו לאדוניו בתוכחתו: כי אני לצלע נכון. אותו צלע היה נכון לי: שאכלה פגה. שקפץ את השעה ליזקק ע"י עבירה: נאספו עלי נכים. בעלי מומין כמו פרעה נכה (מלכים ב כג) והיו מלעיגים עלי ואני כלא יודע ל"א ולא ידעתי לא הייתי יודע כשמלעיגים כלומר פתאום בא עלי אותו עון שלא ידעתי (עד) שניתן פתחון פה לביישני: הכי גרסינן בשעה שעוסקין במיתות בית דין אומרים הבא על אשת איש מיתתו וכו': י"ח עונות. לי"ח נשיו שלא לעגנן: באנחתי אשחה. אפילו בשעת אנחתי אשחה בכל לילה: מטתי. תשמיש המטה ענין סחי ומאוס (איכה ג) קרי ליה: בדמעתי ערשי אמסה. שבשעת דמעתי אני ממאיס את מטתי בתשמיש: יאמרו מלך שכמותי. חסיד שכמותי הרגו בנו ויהו מתרעמין על מדותיו של הקב"ה ונמצא שם שמים מתחלל בפרהסיא: מוטב אעבוד ע"ז. ואחלל את השם אני לבדי ולא יחללו [אותו] כל העם: אמר ליה. חושי הארכי לדוד הקב"ה לא עביד דינא בלא דינא שמעמיד בנך להרגך דאת מאי טעמא נסבת יפת תואר דאמו של אבשלום מעכה בת תלמי מלך גשור (שמואל ב ג) ותפסה דוד במלחמה דאין לומר בעבירה באה לו דהא כתיב (מלכים א טו) רק בדבר אוריה החתי: סוחר כותי. דרכו לפנות את סחורתו מעט מעט להעמידה על דמים מועטים: שגיאות מי יבין. מי יכול להשמר משגגות: אמר לו. הקב"ה: שביקא לך. מחול לך: נסתרות. [מזיד] של צנעה: זדים. מזיד של פרהסיא: ה"ג אל ימשלו בי דלא לישתעו בי רבנן. והיינו אל ימשלו לשון משל שלא ידרשו בחטאתי חכמי הדורות ואז איתם: שלא יכתב סורחני. שתמחוק אותה פרשה מן המקרא וישתכח הדבר לעולמים: כל הפרשה. שכתובה כבר שעשית אותו חטא: על אחת כמה וכמה. שלא תעקור: תחטאני באזוב. מכלל שהיה צריך טהרת אזוב כמצורע:

מסורת הש"ס

א) [סוכה נב:], ב) בד"י כפייה, ג) י"ג עליו, ד) ב"מ נט. ע"ש, ה) נ"א באהלות ונגעים, ו) [עי' היטב יומא פו:], ז) [יומא כב:], ח) [נ"ל ויתהלך], ט) נ"ל ואפשר.

ליקוטי רש"י

הגדיל עלי עקב. מארב כמו (יהושע ח') ואת עקבו מים לעיר [תהלים מא, י]. בחנת לבי וגו'. ידעתי כי יש עבירה בידי ואם משפט עונשי יצא לפניך לא אצדק בדין אשר כבר בחנת לבי. פקדת לילה. לעת הערב בעון בת שבע שנאמר ויהי לעת ערב ויקם דוד וגו' (ש"ב יא). צרפתני. נסיתני. בל תמצא. לא מצאת בי חפלך. זמותי בל יעבר פי. אם תעלה עוד במחשבתי ליבחן לפניך בל יעבר פי לומר עוד בחנני ונסני כמו שאמרתי כבר כמו שנאמר (תהילים כו) בחנני ה' ונסני שאמר דוד לפני הקב"ה מפני מה אומרים אלהי אברהם ואין אומרים אלהי דוד אמר לו אני בחנתיו בי' נסיונות ונמצא שלם אמר בחנני ונסני כדאיתא במסכת שבת [תהלים יז, ג]. לך לבדך חטאתי. לפיכך בידך לסלוח ואף מה שהרעותי לאוריה לא חטאתי אלא לך שהזהרת על הדבר. למען תצדק בדברך. כא היה לי להתגבר על יצרי אלא שלא יאמרו העבד נצח את רבו שאמרתי לפניך בחנני ונסני (תהלים כ"ו) ובחנתני ולא נמצאתי שלם כדי שתצדק אתה ולא אני [תהלים נא, ו]. ובצלעי שמחו ונאספו. וכשאני צולע שבר בא עלי שמחו ונאספו. נאספו עלי נכים. אנשי' פסחי' כמו שאנו מתרגמין נכה חגירא ומנחם חברו כמו נכאי' (ישעיה ט"ז) לימנוייש"ן בלעז. קרעו ולא דמו. אילו היו קורעין את בשרי לא היה דמי שותת לארץ כשמלבינין פני [שם לה, טו]. דרש רבא מאי דכתיב ובצלעי. דטובה מעשה של דוד ובת שבע משלהם וספק אשת איש היא שהיוצא למלחמת בית דוד גט כריתות כותב לאשתו על מנת שאם ימות שתהא מגורשת מעכשיו ולא תזקק ליבם וכל אותן הימים היא ספק מגורשת אם מת מגורשת מתחילה ואם לא מת לא נתגרשה. ובצלעי. בשביל אשתי זו שמתחילה חטאתי בה כמו (בראשית ב) ויבן את הצלע שמחו ונאספו. קרעו ולא דמו. אם קרעוני לא מצאו דם [ב"מ נט.]. אשחה בכל לילה מטתי. לשון סחי ומאוס (איכה ג) והיתה נצלתם כסוחה (ישעי' ה) וכו' בדמעות ומנחם חברו עם כאשר יפרש השוחה לשחות (שם ישעיהו כה) ועם מי שחו (יחזקאל מז) [תהלים ו, ז]. לא דרשת סמוכין. לא דברה תורה אלא כנגד יצר הרע שאם אין הקב"ה מתירה ישאנה באיסור אבל אם נשאה סופו להיות שונאה שנאמר אחריו (פסוק טו) כי תהיין לאיש וגו' וסופו להוליד ממנה בן סורר ומורה לכך נסמכו פרשיות הללו [דברים כא, יא]. שגיאות מי יבין. אני נזהרתי בהם אבל אי אפשר להזהר שלא אשגה בהם ואתה נקני מנסתרות שנסתרו ממני ולא ידעתי בחטאי בשגגה [תהלים יט, יג]. גם מזדים. מן הזדונות. אז איתם. אהיה תמים אמרו חכמים למה דוד דומה לכותי המחזר על הפתחים והם מערימים בדבר יותר מכל אדם תנו לי מים לשתות דבר שאין בו חסרון כיס משעשה אמר יש כאן בצל קטן משנתנו לו אומר יש בצל בלא מלח משנתנו לו אמר תנו לי מעט לחם שלא יזיקני הבצל כך אמר דוד בתחל' על השגגות ואחר כך על הזדונו' ואחר כך על המרדים פשעים אלו המרדים שמתכוין להכעיס וכן הוא אומר (מ"ב ג') מלך מואב פשע בי [שם יט, יד]. שנטלתי משרי. שאף יו"ד של שרי מתרעמה על השכינה עד שנתוספה ליהושע שנאמר (במדבר יג, טז) ויקרא משה להושע בן נון יהושע [בראשית יז, ה]. היחתה איש. היאכל איש גחלים בשפולי בגדיו ולא ישרפו כל לשון חתיית גחלים לשון שאיבה הוא כמשמעה כשמגלגל הכלי בתוך המדורה [משלי ו, כז]. קבל עליך יסורין. יסור יסרני יה. על מעשה בת שבע ביסורין כגון תחת הכבשה ישלם ארבעתיים (שמואל ב, י"ב) ששה חדשים נצטרע דוד [תהלים קיח, יח]. תחטאני באזוב. כמו שמטהר המצורע וטמא מת [שם נא, ט]. השיבה לי ששון ישעך. רוח הקודש שנסתלק מעלי. נדיבה. לשון נדיבות קלינות [שם יד]. ישובו לי יראיך. שפירשו הימנו סנהדרין כשנצטרע מאותו עון אף אם גרושה היא נתן עיניו בה כל הנוגע לא ינקה [שם קיט, עט].

הגהות הגר"א

[א] גמ' אז איתם. נמחק (ועי' רש"י): [ב] שם ונקיתי מפשע רב. נמחק. וג"כ אז איתם (וכל גירסת רבינו בגמ' כ"ה בע"י):

תורה אור השלם

א) בחנני יי ונסני צרפה כליותי ולבי: [תהלים כו, ב]

ב) ויהי לעת הערב ויקם דוד מעל משכבו ויתהלך על גג בית המלך וירא אשה רחצת מעל הגג והאשה טובת מראה מאד: [שמואל ב' יא, ב]

ג) וישלח דוד וידרש לאשה ויאמר הלוא זאת בת שבע בת אליעם אשת אוריה החתי: וישלח דוד מלאכים ויקחה ותבוא אליו וישכב עמה והיא מתקדשת מטמאתה ותשב אל ביתה: [שמואל ב' יא, ג-ד]

ד) בחנת לבי פקדת לילה צרפתני בל תמצא זמתי בל יעבר פי: [תהלים יז, ג]

ה) למנצח לדוד ביי חסיתי איך תאמרו לנפשי נודי הרכם צפור: [תהלים יא, א]

ו) לך לבדך חטאתי והרע בעיניך עשיתי למען תצדק בדברך תזכה בשפטך: [תהלים נא, ו]

ז) כי אני לצלע נכון ומכאובי נגדי תמיד: [תהלים לח, יח]

ח) ובצלעי שמחו ונאספו נאספו עלי נכים ולא ידעתי קרעו ולא דמו: [תהלים לה, טו]

ט) יגעתי באנחתי אשחה בכל לילה מטתי בדמעתי ערשי אמסה: [תהלים ו, ז]

י) ויהי דוד בא עד הראש אשר ישתחוה שם לאלהים והנה לקראתו חושי הארכי קרוע כתנתו ואדמה על ראשו: [שמואל ב' טו, לב]

כ) הוא צלמא ראשה די דהב טב חדוהי ודרעוהי די כסף מעוהי וירכתה די נחש: [דניאל ב, לב]

ל) כי יהיה לאיש בן סורר ומורה איננו שמע בקול אביו ובקול אמו ויסרו אתו ולא ישמע אליהם: [דברים כא, יח]

מ) שגיאות מי יבין מנסתרות נקני: גם מזדים חשך עבדך אל ימשלו בי אז איתם ונקיתי מפשע רב: [תהלים יט, יג-יד]

נ) אלה שמות האנשים אשר שלח משה לתור את הארץ ויקרא משה להושע בן נון יהושע: [במדבר יג, טז]

ס) היחתה איש אש בחיקו ובגדיו לא תשרפנה: אם יהלך איש על הגחלים ורגליו לא תכוינה: כן הבא אל אשת רעהו לא ינקה כל הנגע בה: [משלי ו, כז-כט]

ע) תחטאני באזוב ואטהר תכבסני ומשלג אלבין: [תהלים נא, ט]

פ) השיבה לי ששון ישעך ורוח נדיבה תסמכני: [תהלים נא, יד]

צ) ישובו לי יראיך וידעי עדתיך: [תהלים קיט, עט]

ק) והימים אשר מלך דוד על ישראל ארבעים שנה בחברון מלך שבע שנים ובירושלים מלך שלשים ושלש שנים: [מלכים א' ב, יא]

Divine Presence departed him – as it is written:[68] ***Return to me the joy of Your salvation, and with a generous spirit sustain me.***[69] **וּפֵרְשׁוּ מִמֶּנּוּ סַנְהֶדְרִין דִּכְתִיב ,,יָשׁוּבוּ לִי יְרֵאֶיךָ וגו׳ ״ – The Sanhedrin withdrew from him – as it is written:**[70] ***May those who fear You,*** *those who know Your testimonies,* ***return to me.***[71] **שִׁשָּׁה חֳדָשִׁים מְנָלַן – From where do we derive** that this suffering lasted **six months? דִּכְתִיב ,,וְהַיָּמִים אֲשֶׁר מָלַךְ דָּוִד עַל־יִשְׂרָאֵל אַרְבָּעִים שָׁנָה – For it is written:**[72] ***The days that David reigned over Israel were forty years;***

NOTES

be purged with hyssop, it follows that he was a *metzora* (*Rashi*; see *Rashash*).

68. *Psalms* 51:14.

69. The Divine Presence departed David as a result of his depression over his transgression, for as the Gemara states (*Shabbos* 30b): אֵין הַשְּׁכִינָה שׁוֹרָה אֶלָּא מִתּוֹךְ שִׂמְחָה, *The Divine Presence rests [upon a person] only through joy.* Hence, when David prayed, *Return to me the joy of Your salvation,* he was praying for the return of the Divine Presence (*Maharsha*; see also *Succah* 50b with *Tosafos* ד״ה חד).

70. Ibid. 119:79.

71. *Those who fear You, those who know Your testimonies,* are the members of the Sanhedrin. Since David prayed that they should return to him, it is evident that they had withdrawn from him.

Maharal points out that David was afflicted with suffering on all three levels of his existence – physically, with *tzaraas;* spiritually, with the departure of the Divine Presence; and intellectually, with the withdrawal from him of the scholars of the Sanhedrin.

72. *I Kings* 2:11.

אוכל לחמי הגדיל עלי עקב אמר רב יהודה אמר רב לעולם אל יביא אדם עצמו לידי נסיון שהרי דוד מלך ישראל הביא עצמו לידי נסיון ונכשל אמר לפניו רבש"ע מפני מה אומרים אלהי אברהם אלהי יצחק ואלהי יעקב ואין אומרים אלהי דוד אמר אינהו מינסו לי ואת לא מינסית לי אמר לפניו רבש"ע בחנני ונסני שנאמר א) בחנני ה' ונסני וגו' אמר מינסנא לך ועבידנא מילתא בהדך דלדידהו לא הודעתינהו ואילו אנא קא מודענא לך דמנסינא לך בדבר ערוה מיד ב) ויהי לעת הערב ויקם דוד מעל משכבו וגו' אמר רב יהודה שהפך משכבו של לילה למשכבו של יום ונתעלמה ממנו הלכה א) אבר קטן יש באדם משביעו רעב ומרעיבו שבע ב) ויתהלך על גג בית המלך וירא אשה רוחצת מעל הגג והאשה טובת מראה מאד בת שבע הוה קא חייפא רישא תותי חלתא אתא שטן אידמי ליה כציפרתא פתק ביה גירא פתקה לחלתא איגליה וחזייה מיד ג) וישלח דוד וידרוש לאשה ויאמר הלא זאת בת שבע בת אליעם אשת אוריה החתי וישלח דוד מלאכים ויקחה ותבא אליו וישכב עמה והיא מתקדשת מטומאתה ותשב אל ביתה והיינו דכתיב ד) בחנת לבי פקדת לילה צרפתני בל תמצא זמותי בל יעבר פי אמר איכו זממא נפל בפומיה דמאן דסני לי ולא אמר כי הא מילתא דרש רבא מאי דכתיב ה) למנצח לדוד בה' חסיתי איך תאמרו לנפשי נודי הרכם צפור אמר דוד לפני הקב"ה רבש"ע מחול לי על אותו עון שלא יאמרו הר שבכם צפור נדדתו דרש רבא מאי דכתיב ו) לך לבדך חטאתי והרע בעיניך עשיתי למען תצדק בדברך תזכה בשפטך אמר דוד לפני הקב"ה גליא וידיעא קמך דאי בעיא למכפייה ליצרי הוה כייפינא אלא אמינא דלא לימרו עבדא ג) זכי למריה דרש רבא מאי דכתיב ז) כי אני לצלע נכון ומכאובי נגדי תמיד ראויה היתה בת שבע בת אליעם לדוד מששת ימי בראשית אלא שבאה ג) אליו במכאוב וכן תנא דבי רבי ישמעאל ראויה היתה לדוד בת שבע בת אליעם אלא שאכלה פגה ד) דרש רבא מאי דכתיב ח) ובצלעי שמחו ונאספו נאספו עלי נכים [ולא ידעתי] קרעו ולא דמו אמר דוד לפני הקב"ה רבש"ע גלוי וידוע לפניך שאם היו קורעין בשרי לא היה דמי שותת ולא עוד אלא בשעה שהם עוסקין ה) בארבע מיתות ב"ד פוסקין ממשנתן ואומרים לי דוד הבא על אשת איש מיתתו במה אמרתי להם הבא על אשת איש מיתתו בחנק ויש לו חלק לעוה"ב אבל המלבין פני חבירו ברבים אין לו חלק לעולם הבא אמר רב יהודה אמר רב אפילו בשעת חליו של דוד קיים שמנה עשרה עונות שנאמר ט) יגעתי באנחתי אשחה בכל לילה מטתי בדמעתי ערשי אמסה ואמר רב יהודה אמר רב בקש דוד לעבוד ע"ז שנאמר י) ויהי דוד בא עד הראש אשר ישתחוה שם לאלהים ואין ראש אלא ע"ז שנאמר כ) והוא צלמא רישיה די דהב טב י) והנה לקראתו חושי הארכי קרוע כתנתו ואדמה על ראשו אמר לו לדוד יאמרו מלך שכמותך יעבוד ע"ז אמר לו מלך שכמותי יהרגנו בנו מוטב יעבוד ע"ז ואל יתחלל שם שמים בפרהסיא אמר מאי טעמא קנסיבת יפת תואר א"ל יפת תואר רחמנא שרייה א"ל לא דרשת סמוכין דסמיך ליה ל) כי יהיה לאיש בן סורר ומורה כל הנושא יפת תואר יש לו בן סורר ומורה דרש ר' דוסתאי דמן בירי למה דוד דומה לסוחר כותי אמר דוד לפני הקב"ה רבש"ע מ) שגיאות מי יבין [א"ל] שביקי לך ומנסתרות נקני שביקי לך גם מזדים חשוך עבדך שביקי לך אל ימשלו בי [א] אז איתם דלא לישתעו בי רבנן שביקי לך [ב] ונקיתי מפשע רב ו) שלא יכתב סרחוני אמר לו א"א ומה יו"ד שנטלתי משרי עומד וצווח כמה שנים עד שבא יהושע והוספתי לו שנאמר נ) ויקרא משה להושע בן נון יהושע כל הפרשה כולה עאכ"ו ונקיתי מפשע רב אמר לפניו רבש"ע מחול לי על אותו עון כולו אמר כבר עתיד שלמה בנך לומר בחכמתו ס) היחתה איש אש בחיקו ובגדיו לא תשרפנה אם יהלך איש על הגחלים ורגליו לא תכוינה כן הבא על אשת רעהו לא ינקה כל הנוגע בה א"ל כל הכי נטרד ההוא גברא א"ל קבל עליך יסורין קבל עליו ז) אמר רב יהודה אמר רב ששה חדשים נצטרע דוד ונסתלקה הימנו שכינה ופירשו ממנו סנהדרין נצטרע דכתיב ע) תחטאני באזוב ואטהר תכבסני ומשלג אלבין נסתלקה הימנו שכינה דכתיב פ) השיבה לי ששון ישעך ורוח נדיבה תסמכני ופרשו ממנו סנהדרין דכתי' צ) ישובו לי יראיך וגו' ששה חדשים מנלן דכתי' ק) והימים אשר מלך דוד על ישראל ארבעים שנה

בחברון

אוכל לחמי. לומד תורתי: שהפך משכבו של לילה לשל יום. שהיה משמש מטתו ביום כדי שיהא שבע מתשמיש ולא יהרהר אחר אשה כל היום: ונתעלמה ממנו [הלכה]. שהמשביע אברו בתשמיש רעב ומרבה תאוה: ה"ג ח) מתהלך על גג המלך ולא גרסינן והיינו: חלתא. כוורת: פתיק [ביה] גירא. בכוורת כלומר שהכה ושברה ל"א פתחה שברה ונפתחה: מתקדשת מטומאתה. אותה שעה פסק טומאתה ולא בא עליה כשהיא נדה: פקדת לילה. על מעשה לילה פקדתני אם אוכל לעמוד בנסיון של דבר עבירה: צרפתני בל תמצא. חשבת לצרפני ולא מצאתני נקי: (זמותי בל יעבר פי) איכו זממא נפל. מי יתן והיה בפי רסן ט) ואפשר לעכב את דברי שלא אומר דבר זה [של] בחנני: הר שבכם. מלך שלכם: צפור נדדתו. דעל ידי צפור נטרד כדאמר אדמי ליה כצפור: למריה. העבד נצחו לאדוניו בתוכחתו: כי אני לצלע נכון. אותו צלע היה נכון לי: שאכלה פגה. שקפץ את השעה ליזקק ע"י עבירה: נאספו עלי נכים. בעלי מומין כמו פרעה נכה (מלכים ב כג) והיו מלעיגים עלי ואני כלא יודע ל"א ולא ידעתי לא הייתי יודע כשמלעיגים כלומר פתאום בא עלי אותו עון שלא ידעתי (עד) שניתן פתחון פה לביישני: הכי גרסינן בשעה שעוסקין במיתות בית דין אומרים הבא על אשת איש מיתתו וכו': י"ח עונות. לי"ח נשיו שלא לעגנן: באנחתי אשחה. אפילו בשעת אנחתי אשחה בכל לילה: מטתי. תשמיש המטה ענין סחי ומאוס (איכה ג) קרי ליה: בדמעתי ערשי אמסה. שבשעת דמעתי אני ממאיס את מטתי בתשמיש: יאמרו מלך שכמותי. חסיד שכמותי הרגו בנו ויהו מתרעמין על מדותיו של הקב"ה ונמצא שם שמים מתחלל בפרהסיא: מוטב אעבוד ע"ז. ואחלל את השם אני לבדי ולא יחללו [אותו] כל העם: אמר ליה. חושי הארכי לדוד הקב"ה לא עביד דינא בלא דינא שמעמיד בנך להרגך דאת מאי טעמא נסבת יפת תואר דאמו של אבשלום מעכה בת תלמי מלך גשור (שמואל ב ג) ותפסה דוד במלחמה דאין לומר בעבירה באה לו דהא כתיב (מלכים א טו) רק בדבר אוריה החתי: סוחר כותי. דרכו לפנות את סחורתו מעט מעט להעמידה על דמים מועטים: שגיאות מי יבין. מי יכול להשמר משגגות: אמר לו. הקב"ה: שביקא לך. מחול לך: נסתרות. [מזיד] של צנעה: זדים. מזיד של פרהסיא: ה"ג אל ימשלו בי דלא לישתעו בי רבנן. והיינו אל ימשלו לשון משל שלא ידרשו בחטאתי חכמי הדורות ואז איתם: שלא יכתב סורחני. שתמחוק אותה פרשה מן המקרא וישתכח הדבר לעולמים: כל הפרשה. שכתובה כבר שעשית אותו חטא: על אחת כמה וכמה. שלא תעקור: תחטאני באזוב. מכלל שהיה צריך טהרת אזוב כמצורע:

בחברון

מסורת הש"ס

א) [סוכה נב:], ב) כד"י כפיה, ג) י"ג עליו, ד) ב"מ נט. ע"ש, ה) נ"א באהלות ונגעים, ו) [עי' היטב יומא פו:], ז) [יומא כב:], ח) [נ"ל ויתהלך], ט) נ"ל ואפשר.

ליקוטי רש"י

הגדיל עלי עקב. מארב כמו (יהושע ח') ואת עקבו מים לעיר [תהלים מא, י]. בחנת לבי וגו'. ידעתי כי יש עבירה בידי ואם משפט עונשי יצא לפניך לא אצדק בדין אשר כבר בחנת לבי. פקדת לילה. לעת הערב בעון בת שבע שנאמר ויהי לעת ערב ויקם דוד וגו' (ש"ב יא). צרפתני. נסיתני. בל תמצא. לא מצאת בי חפצך. זמותי בל יעבר פי. אם תעלה עוד במחשבתי ליבחן לפניך בל יעבר פי לומר עוד בחנני ונסני כמו שאמרתי כבר כמו שנאמר (תהילים כו) בחנני ה' ונסני שאמר דוד לפני הקב"ה מפני מה אומרים אלהי אברהם ואין אומרים אלהי דוד אמר לו אני בחנתיו בי' נסיונות ונמצא שלם אמר בחנני ונסני כדאיתא במסכת שבת [תהלים יז, ג]. לך לבדך חטאתי. לפיכך בידך לסלוח ואף מה שהרעותי לאוריה לא חטאתי אלא לך שהזהרת על הדבר. למען תצדק בדברך. כח היה לי להתגבר על יצרי אלא שלא יאמרו העבד נצח את רבו שאמרתי לפניך בחנני ונסני (תהלים כ"ו) ובחנתני ולא נמצאתי שלם כדי שתצדק אתה ולא אני [תהלים נא, ו]. ובצלעי שמחו ונאספו. וכשאני צולע ששבר בא עלי שמחו ונאספו. נאספו עלי נכים. אנשי' פסחי' כמו שאנו מתרגמין נכה חגירא ומנחם חברו כמו נכאי' (ישעיה טז) אימנויי"ץ בלעז. קרעו ולא דמו. אילו היו קורעין את בשרי לא היה דמי שותת לארץ כשמלבינין פני [שם לה, טו]. דרש רבא מאי דכתיב ובצלעי. דטובה מעשה של דוד ובת שבע משלהם וספק אשת איש היא שהיוצא למלחמת בית דוד גט כריתות כותב לאשתו על מנת שאם ימות שתהא מגורשת מעכשיו ולא תיזקק ליבם וכל אותן הימים היא ספק מגורשת אם מת מגורשת מתחילה ואם לא מת לא נתגרשה. ובצלעי. בשביל אשתי זו שמתחילה חטאתי בה כמו (בראשית ב) ויבן את הצלע שמחו ונאספו. קרעו ולא דמו. אם קרעוני לא מצאו דם [ב"מ נט.]. אשחה בכל לילה מטתי. לשון סחי ומאוס (איכה ג) והיתה נבלתם כסוחה (ישעי' ה) וכו' בדמעות ומנחם חברו עם כאשר יפרש השוחה לשחות (שם ישעיהו כה) ועם מי שחו (יחזקאל מז) [תהלים ו, ז]. לא דרשת סמוכין. לא דברה תורה אלא כנגד יצר הרע שאם אין הקב"ה מתירה ישאנה באיסור אבל אם נשאה סופו להיות שונאה שנאמר אחריו (פסוק טו) כי תהיין לאיש וגו' וסופו להוליד ממנה בן סורר ומורה לכך נסמכו פרשיות הללו [דברים כא, יא]. שגיאות מי יבין. אני נזהרתי בהם אבל אי איפשר להזהר שלא אשגה בהם ואתה נקני מנסתרות שנסתרו ממני ולא ידעתי בחטאי בשגגה [תהלים יט, יג]. גם מזדים. מן הזדונות. אז איתם. אהיה תמים אמרו חכמים למה דוד דומה לכותי המחזר על הפתחים והם מערימים בדבר יותר מכל אדם תנו לי מים לשתות דבר שאין בו חסרון כיס משששתה אמר יש כאן בצל קטן משנתנו לו אומר יש בצל בלא מלח משנתנו לו אמר תנו לי מעט לחם שלא יזיקני הבצל כך אמר דוד בתחל' על השגגות ואחר כך על הזדונו' ואחר כך על המרדים פשעים אלו המרדים שמתכוין להכעיס וכן הוא אומר (מ"ב ג') מלך מואב פשע בי [שם יט, יד]. שנטלתי משרי. שאף יו"ד של שרי נתרעמה על השכינה עד שנתוספה ליהושע שנאמר (במדבר יג, טז) ויקרא משה להושע בן נון יהושע [בראשית יז, ה]. היחתה איש. היסאב איש גחלים בשפולי בגדיו ולא ישרפו כל לשון חתיית גחלים לשון שאיבה הוא כמשמעה כשממלא הכלי בתוך המדורה [משלי ו, כז]. קבל עליך יסורין. יסור יסרני יה. על מעשה בת שבע יסורין כגון תחת הכבשה ישלם ארבעתים (שמואל ב, י"ב) ששה חדשים נצטרע דוד [תהלים קיח, קיז]. תחטאני באזוב. כמו שמטהר המצורע וטמא מת [שם נא, ט]. השיבה לי ששון ישעך. רוח הקודש שנסתלק מעלי. נדיבה. לשון נדיבות קצינות [שם יד]. ישובו לי יראיך. שפירשו הימנו סנהדרין כשנצטרע מאותו עון אף אם גרושה היא נתן עיניו בה כל הנוגע לא ינקה [שם קיט, עט].

הגהות הגר"א

[א] גמ' אז איתם. נמחק (ועי' רש"י): [ב] שם ונקיתי מפשע רב. נמחק. וצ"ל אז איתם (וכן גירסת רבינו בגמ' כ"ה בע"י):

תורה אור השלם

א) בְּחָנֵנִי יְיָ וְנַסֵּנִי צָרְפָה כִלְיוֹתַי וְלִבִּי: [תהלים כו, ב]

ב) וַיְהִי לְעֵת הָעֶרֶב וַיָּקָם דָּוִד מֵעַל מִשְׁכָּבוֹ וַיִּתְהַלֵּךְ עַל גַּג בֵּית הַמֶּלֶךְ וַיַּרְא אִשָּׁה רֹחֶצֶת מֵעַל הַגָּג וְהָאִשָּׁה טוֹבַת מַרְאֶה מְאֹד: [שמואל ב' יא, ב]

ג) וַיִּשְׁלַח דָּוִד וַיִּדְרֹשׁ לָאִשָּׁה וַיֹּאמֶר הֲלוֹא זֹאת בַּת שֶׁבַע בַּת אֱלִיעָם אֵשֶׁת אוּרִיָּה הַחִתִּי: וַיִּשְׁלַח דָּוִד מַלְאָכִים וַיִּקָּחֶהָ וַתָּבוֹא אֵלָיו וַיִּשְׁכַּב עִמָּהּ וְהִיא מִתְקַדֶּשֶׁת מִטֻּמְאָתָהּ וַתָּשָׁב אֶל בֵּיתָהּ: [שמואל ב' יא, ג-ד]

ד) בָּחַנְתָּ לִבִּי פָּקַדְתָּ לַּיְלָה צְרַפְתַּנִי בַל תִּמְצָא זַמֹּתִי בַּל יַעֲבָר פִּי: [תהלים יז, ג]

ה) לַמְנַצֵּחַ לְדָוִד בַּייָ חָסִיתִי אֵיךְ תֹּאמְרוּ לְנַפְשִׁי נוּדִי הַרְכֶם צִפּוֹר: [תהלים יא, א]

ו) לְךָ לְבַדְּךָ חָטָאתִי וְהָרַע בְּעֵינֶיךָ עָשִׂיתִי לְמַעַן תִּצְדַּק בְּדָבְרֶךָ תִּזְכֶּה בְשָׁפְטֶךָ: [תהלים נא, ו]

ז) כִּי אֲנִי לְצֶלַע נָכוֹן וּמַכְאוֹבִי נֶגְדִּי תָמִיד: [תהלים לח, יח]

ח) וּבְצַלְעִי שָׂמְחוּ וְנֶאֱסָפוּ נֶאֶסְפוּ עָלַי נֵכִים וְלֹא יָדַעְתִּי קָרְעוּ וְלֹא דָמּוּ: [תהלים לה, טו]

ט) יָגַעְתִּי בְּאַנְחָתִי אַשְׂחֶה בְכָל לַיְלָה מִטָּתִי בְּדִמְעָתִי עַרְשִׂי אַמְסֶה: [תהלים ו, ז]

י) וַיְהִי דָוִד בָּא עַד הָרֹאשׁ אֲשֶׁר יִשְׁתַּחֲוֶה שָׁם לֵאלֹהִים וְהִנֵּה לִקְרָאתוֹ חוּשַׁי הָאַרְכִּי קָרוּעַ כֻּתָּנְתּוֹ וַאֲדָמָה עַל רֹאשׁוֹ: [שמואל ב' טו, לב]

כ) הוּא צַלְמָא רֵאשֵׁהּ דִּי דְהַב טָב חֲדוֹהִי וּדְרָעוֹהִי דִּי כְסַף מְעוֹהִי וְיַרְכָתֵהּ דִּי נְחָשׁ: [דניאל ב, לב]

ל) כִּי יִהְיֶה לְאִישׁ בֵּן סוֹרֵר וּמוֹרֶה אֵינֶנּוּ שֹׁמֵעַ בְּקוֹל אָבִיו וּבְקוֹל אִמּוֹ וְיִסְּרוּ אֹתוֹ וְלֹא יִשְׁמַע אֲלֵיהֶם: [דברים כא, יח]

מ) שְׁגִיאוֹת מִי יָבִין מִנִּסְתָּרוֹת נַקֵּנִי: גַּם מִזֵּדִים חֲשֹׂךְ עַבְדֶּךָ אַל יִמְשְׁלוּ בִי אָז אֵיתָם וְנִקֵּיתִי מִפֶּשַׁע רָב: [תהלים יט, יג-יד]

נ) אֵלֶּה שְׁמוֹת הָאֲנָשִׁים אֲשֶׁר שָׁלַח מֹשֶׁה לָתוּר אֶת הָאָרֶץ וַיִּקְרָא מֹשֶׁה לְהוֹשֵׁעַ בִּן נוּן יְהוֹשֻׁעַ: [במדבר יג, טז]

ס) הֲיַחְתֶּה אִישׁ אֵשׁ בְּחֵיקוֹ וּבְגָדָיו לֹא תִשָּׂרַפְנָה: אִם יְהַלֵּךְ אִישׁ עַל הַגֶּחָלִים וְרַגְלָיו לֹא תִכָּוֶינָה: כֵּן הַבָּא אֶל אֵשֶׁת רֵעֵהוּ לֹא יִנָּקֶה כָּל הַנֹּגֵעַ בָּהּ: [משלי ו, כז-כט]

ע) תְּחַטְּאֵנִי בְאֵזוֹב וְאֶטְהָר תְּכַבְּסֵנִי וּמִשֶּׁלֶג אַלְבִּין: [תהלים נא, ט]

פ) הָשִׁיבָה לִּי שְׂשׂוֹן יִשְׁעֶךָ וְרוּחַ נְדִיבָה תִסְמְכֵנִי: [תהלים נא, יד]

צ) יָשׁוּבוּ לִי יְרֵאֶיךָ וְיֹדְעֵי עֵדֹתֶיךָ: [תהלים קיט, עט]

ק) וְהַיָּמִים אֲשֶׁר מָלַךְ דָּוִד עַל יִשְׂרָאֵל אַרְבָּעִים שָׁנָה בְּחֶבְרוֹן מָלַךְ שֶׁבַע שָׁנִים וּבִירוּשָׁלַםִ מָלַךְ שְׁלֹשִׁים וְשָׁלֹשׁ שָׁנִים: [מלכים א' ב, יא]

בחברון מלך שבע שנים ובירושלים מלך שלשים ושלש שנים וכתיב א) בחברון מלך על יהודה שבע שנים וששה חדשים וגו׳ והני ששה חדשים לא קחשיב ש״מ נצטרע א) אמר לפניו רבש״ע מחול לי על אותו עון מחול לך ב) עשה עמי אות לטובה ויראו שונאי ויבושו כי אתה ה׳ עזרתני ונחמתני א״ל בחייך איני מודיע אבל אני מודיע בחיי שלמה בנך ג) בשעה שבנה שלמה את בית המקדש ביקש להכניס ארון לבית קדשי הקדשים דבקו שערים זה בזה אמר עשרים וארבעה רננות ולא נענה אמר ג) שאו שערים ראשיכם והנשאו פתחי עולם ויבא מלך הכבוד מי זה מלך הכבוד ה׳ עזוז וגבור ה׳ גבור מלחמה ונאמר ד) שאו שערים ראשיכם ושאו פתחי עולם ויבא מלך הכבוד וגו׳ ולא נענה כיון שאמר ה) ה׳ אלהים אל תשב פני משיחך זכרה לחסדי דויד עבדך מיד נענה באותה שעה נהפכו פני שונאי דוד כשולי קדירה וידעו כל ישראל שמחל לו הקב״ה על אותו העון גחזי דכתיב ג) ו) וילך אלישע דמשק להיכא אזל ד) א״ר יוחנן שהלך להחזיר גחזי בתשובה ולא חזר אמר לו חזור בך אמר לו כך מקובלני ממך ה) א החוטא ומחטיא את הרבים אין מספיקין בידו לעשות תשובה מאי עבד איכא דאמרי אבן שואבת תלה לחטאת ירבעם והעמידה בין שמים לארץ ואיכא דאמרי שם חקק בפיה והיתה מכרזת ואומרת אנכי ולא יהיה לך וא״ד רבנן דחה מקמיה שנאמר ז) ויאמרו בני הנביאים אל אלישע הנה [נא] המקום אשר אנחנו יושבים שם לפניך צר ממנו מכלל דעד השתא לא הוו (פיישי) [צר] ו) תנו רבנן לעולם תהא שמאל דוחה וימין מקרבת לא כאלישע שדחפו לגחזי בשתי ידים גחזי דכתיב ח) ויאמר נעמן הואל ז) וקח ככרים (ויפצר) [ויפרץ] בו ויצר ככרים כסף וגו׳ ויאמר אליו אלישע מאין גחזי ויאמר לא הלך עבדך אנה ואנה ויאמר אליו לא לבי הלך כאשר הפך איש מעל מרכבתו לקראתך העת לקחת את הכסף ולקחת בגדים וזיתים וכרמים וצאן ובקר ועבדים ושפחות ומי שקל כולי האי כסף ובגדים הוא דשקל אמר רבי יצחק באותה שעה היה אלישע יושב ודורש בשמונה שרצים נעמן שר צבא מלך ארם היה מצורע אמרה ליה ההיא רביתא דאישתבאי מארעא ישראל אי אזלת לגבי אלישע מסי לך כי אתא א״ל זיל טבול בירדן א״ל אחוכי קא מחייכת בי אמרי ליה הנהו דהוו בהדיה מאי נפקא לך מינה זיל נסי אזל וטבל בירדנא ואיתסי אתא אייתי ליה כל הני דנקיט לא צבי לקבולי מיניה גחזי איפטר מקמיה אלישע אזל שקל מאי דשקל ואפקיד כי אתא חזייה אלישע לצרעת דהוה פרחא עילויה רישיה א״ל רשע הגיע עת ליטול שכר שמנה שרצים ט) וצרעת נעמן תדבק בך ובזרעך עד עולם ויצא מלפניו מצורע כשלג: י) וארבעה אנשים היו מצורעים פתח השער אמר ר׳ יוחנן גחזי ושלשה בניו תניא ח) א״ר שמעון בן אלעזר יצר תינוק ואשה תהא שמאל דוחה וימין מקרבת ט) ת״ר ג׳ חלאים חלה אלישע אחד שגירה דובים בתינוקות ואחד שדחפו לגחזי בשתי ידים ואחד שמת בו [שנא׳ כ) ואלישע חלה את חליו וגו׳] י) עד אברהם לא היה זקנה כל דחזי לאברהם אמר האי יצחק כל דחזי ליצחק אמר האי אברהם כ) בעא אברהם רחמי דליהוי ליה זקנה שנאמר ל) ואברהם זקן בא בימים עד יעקב לא הוה חולשא בעא רחמי והוה חולשא שנאמר מ) ויאמר ליוסף הנה אביך חולה עד אלישע לא הוה איניש חליש ל) דמיתפח ואתא אלישע ובעא רחמי ואיתפח שנא׳ כ) ואלישע חלה את חליו אשר ימות בו מ): **מתני׳** דור המבול אין להם חלק לעוה״ב ואין עומדין בדין שנא׳ נ) לא ידון רוחי באדם לעולם לא דין ולא רוח דור הפלגה אין להם חלק לעולם הבא שנאמר ס) ויפץ ה׳ אותם משם על פני כל הארץ נ) (וכתיב ומשם הפיצם) ויפץ ה׳ אותם בעוה״ז ע) ומשם הפיצם ה׳ לעולם הבא אנשי סדום אין להם חלק לעולם הבא שנא׳ פ) ואנשי סדום רעים וחטאים לה׳ מאד רעים בעולם הזה וחטאים לעולם הבא אבל עומדין בדין ר׳ נחמיה אומר אלו ואלו אין עומדין בדין שנאמר צ) על כן לא יקומו רשעים

רש״י

בחברון מלך שבע שנים וששה חדשים. מדהכא חשיב להו ובאידך קרא לא חשיב להו ש״מ לא היה מלכותו שלימה שנצטרע אותן ו׳ חדשים: ה״ג אבל בחיי בנך אני מודיע ולא גרסינן לך: כ״ד רננות. בין תפלה תחנה ורנה איכא כ״ד: וילך אלישע דמשק להיכא אזל: שואבת. מגבהת מתכת בלא נגיעה כעין אותה שלועזין קלאמניס״ה בלע״ז ועל ידי אותה אבן העמיד עגלים של ירבעם באויר: רבנן דחה מקמיה. התלמידים דחה מישיבתו של אלישע: צר ממנו. מכלל דעד האידנא לא הוה צר: הואל וקח. השבע שאלישע שלחך: ויפצר בו. גחזי: העת לקחת את הכסף והבגדים וגו׳. שמנה דברים קא חשיב בהאי קרא: וגחזי מי שקל כולי האי. מנעמן כסף ובגדים הוא דשקל דכתיב ויצר ככרים וגו׳: אותה שעה. היה אלישע עוסק בפרק שמונה שרצים אמר לו הגיע עת ליטול שכר פרק שמונה שרצים שעסקתי וכו׳ ולהכי כתב בהאי קרא שמנה דברים כנגד אותו פרק כלומר בכסף ובגדים שקבלת ממנו מנעמן סבור אתה לקנות דברים הללו להיותם לך שכר שמונה שרצים: יצר. תאותו אם מרחיקה ממנו לגמרי ממעט ישיבת עולם ואם מקרבה לגמרי בא לידי איסור שאינו יכול לכבוש יצרו מדבר עבירה: תינוק ואשה. דעתן קלה ואם תדחה אותם מטרדן מן העולם: חלה. חד. חליו תרי. אשר ימות בו תלת: בעא רחמי דלהוי חולשא. כדי שיהא פנאי לבניו לבא כל אחד ואחד ממקומו להיות עליו בשעת מיתה שכיון שרואין שנפל למטה יודעין שימות ומתקבצין ובאין: מתפח. מתרפא: **מתני׳** לא ידון רוחי לא דין ולא רוח. שאין עומדין בדין ואין להם רוח להיות עם הצדיקים שיש להם חלק: ויפץ [ה׳ אותם ומשם הפיצם. ויפץ] בעולם הזה ומשם הפיצם בעולם הבא: אלו ואלו. אנשי דור המבול ואנשי סדום ובהא פליג ר׳ נחמיה: רשעים

עין משפט נר מצוה

לב א מיי׳ פ״ד מהל׳ תשובה הלכה א:

ליקוטי רש״י

עשה עמי אות לטובה. שיהא ניכר לאחרים שמחלת לי. ויראו שונאי. האות ויבושו ולא שמע לו הקב״ה ליתן האות בימיו אלא בימי שלמה בנו כשדבקו השערים זה בזה ולא נפתחו עד שאמר (דה״ב ו׳) אל תשב פני משיחך זכרה לחסדי דוד עבדך [תהלים פו, יז]. על אותו עון. דבת שבע. דבקו שערים. של בית קדשי הקדשים. עשרים וארבע רננות. רנה תפילה תחינה כתובים בתפילת שלמה עד עשרים וארבע ויש אומרים עשרים וארבע ברכות דתענית ולא נהירא. אמר שאו שערים ראשיכם והנשאו פתחי עולם ויבוא מלך הכבוד. רהטו שערים בתריה למבלעיה סברי דעל עצמו אמר מלך הכבוד אמרו לו שערים מי הוא זה מלך הכבוד אמר איהו ה׳ עזוז וגבור (תהלים כד). שונאי דוד. משפחת שאול שמעי וכיוצא בו [שבת ל.]. עשרים וארבע רננות. כתיבי בפרשה, בין רנה ותחנה ותפלה ובקשה [מו״ק ט.]. אל תשב פני משיחך. מלעשות טובה עמדי ואם לא למעני עשה למענך [דה״ב ו, מב]. ויבא אלישע דמשק. להחזיר את גיחזי בתשובה [מ״ב ח, ז]. אבן שואבת. דרך אותה האבן להגביה המתכת ולתלותה באויר [ע״ז מד.]. שמגבהת את המתכת מן הארץ ומעמידתו באויר [וע״י אותו אבן העמיד העגלים של ירבעם באויר]. רבנן דחה. דוחה היה את התלמידים מפני אלישע כשהיה משמש לפניו דכתיב לאחר שפירש ממנו המקום אשר אנחנו יושבין בית המדרש של רבנן צר ממנו שנתוספו התלמידים שהיה גחזי דוחה [סוטה מז.]. ויאמרו בני הנביאים. רבותינו אמרו מכאן שהיה גיחזי דוחה התלמידים מלפניו כשנטרד באו תלמידים רבים ונדחק המקום מהם [מ״ב ו, א]. הואל. השבע שלחך [שם ה, כג]. העת לקחת את הכסף. להתעשר ולקחת ממנו בגדים וזיתים וגו׳ [מלכים ב, ה]. מי שקל כולי האי. בהאי קרא כתיב שמנה דברים כסף ובגדים וצאן ובקר ועבדים ושפחות וזיתים וכרמים. כסף ובגדים הוא דשקל. דכתיב ויצר ככרים כסף בשני חריטים ושתי חליפות בגדים. בשמנה שרצים. בפרק שמנה שרצים (שבת קז). הגיע עת ליטול שכר. תורתך בעולם הזה [שם]. וארבעה אנשים. גיחזי ובניו. פתח השער. כמו שנאמר בדד ישב מחוץ למחנה מושבו (ויקרא י״ג מ״ו) [שם ז, ג]. כדקטלינהו ינאי מלכא לרבנן. כדאמרינן בקידושין בהאומר לשלוחו (דף סו). בעלי שרוי בתוכך. נשיא היה כדאמרינן בחגיגה (דף טז:). עבדו ליה יקרא טובא. כיבדתו. כמה יפה אכסניא זו. במעשיה. טרוטות. עגולות. בכך אתה עוסק. מסתכל באשת איש. אחוי ליה בידיה. שיקבלנו. יצר. של תשמיש תקרבנו בימין שלא יקוץ בפריה ורביה וכן תינוק פן יברח ויאבד את עצמו ואשה אף היא דעתה קלה ואם ירדפוה תצא לתרבות רעה [סוטה מז.]. חליו אשר ימות בו. מכלל דחלה עוד שלא מת בו [ב״מ פז.]. אחד שגירה דובים. בעון שגירה דובים בתינוקות. חלה. חד את חליו תרי וחד אשר ימות בו [סוטה שם]. בעא אברהם רחמי. כדי שיכירו בינו ובין בנו. בעא רחמי והוה חולשא. שיחלה אדם לפני מותו ויצוה לביתו. חליש דמיתפח. ונתרפא. חליו אשר ימות בו. מכלל דחלה עוד שלא מת בו [ב״מ שם]. ויפץ ה׳ אותם משם. בעולם הזה מה שאמרו פן נפוץ נתקיים עליהם הוא שאמר שלמה (משלי י, כד) מגורת רשע היא תבואנו [בראשית יא, יח]. ומשם הפיצם. למד שאין להם חלק לעולם הבא [בראשית יא, ט].

מסורת הש״ס

א) שבת ל. ע״ש, ב) שם מו״ק ט., ג) אין זה לשון המקרא וכך הוא לשון המקרא ויבא אלישע (מ״ב ח׳) גו׳ ועיי׳ רש״א בח״א, ד) סוטה מז. [ע״ש], ה) [יומא פז.], ו) סוטה שם, ז) בקרא קח, ח) [שמחות פ״ב סוטה מז.], ט) [סוטה מז:], י) [ב״מ פז.], כ) [ב״מ פז.], ל) [לדעת הערוך בערך תפח גרס הכא ואיתפח כמו בסמוך], מ) [מכלל דחלה חלי אחריתא כך איתא בב״מ פז.], נ) [בסה״מ ל״ג].

תורה אור השלם

א) בְּחֶבְרוֹן מָלַךְ עַל יְהוּדָה שֶׁבַע שָׁנִים וְשִׁשָּׁה חֳדָשִׁים וּבִירוּשָׁלַיִם מָלַךְ שְׁלֹשִׁים וְשָׁלֹשׁ שָׁנָה עַל כָּל יִשְׂרָאֵל וִיהוּדָה: [שמואל ב׳ ה, ה]

ב) עֲשֵׂה עִמִּי אוֹת לְטוֹבָה וְיִרְאוּ שֹׂנְאַי וְיֵבֹשׁוּ כִּי אַתָּה יְיָ עֲזַרְתַּנִי וְנִחַמְתָּנִי: [תהלים פו, יז]

ג) שְׂאוּ שְׁעָרִים רָאשֵׁיכֶם וְהִנָּשְׂאוּ פִּתְחֵי עוֹלָם וְיָבוֹא מֶלֶךְ הַכָּבוֹד: מִי זֶה מֶלֶךְ הַכָּבוֹד יְיָ עִזּוּז וְגִבּוֹר יְיָ גִּבּוֹר מִלְחָמָה: [תהלים כד, ז-ח]

ד) שְׂאוּ שְׁעָרִים רָאשֵׁיכֶם וּשְׂאוּ פִּתְחֵי עוֹלָם וְיָבֹא מֶלֶךְ הַכָּבוֹד: מִי הוּא זֶה מֶלֶךְ הַכָּבוֹד יְיָ צְבָאוֹת הוּא מֶלֶךְ הַכָּבוֹד סֶלָה: [תהלים כד, ט-י]

ה) יְיָ אֱלֹהִים אַל תָּשֵׁב פְּנֵי מְשִׁיחֶךָ זָכְרָה לְחַסְדֵי דָּוִיד עַבְדֶּךָ: [דברי הימים ב׳ ו, מב]

ו) וַיָּבֹא אֱלִישָׁע דַּמֶּשֶׂק וּבֶן הֲדַד מֶלֶךְ אֲרָם חֹלֶה וַיֻּגַּד לוֹ לֵאמֹר בָּא אִישׁ הָאֱלֹהִים עַד הֵנָּה: [מלכים ב׳ ח, ז]

ז) וַיֹּאמְרוּ בְנֵי הַנְּבִיאִים אֶל אֱלִישָׁע הִנֵּה נָא הַמָּקוֹם אֲשֶׁר אֲנַחְנוּ יֹשְׁבִים שָׁם לְפָנֶיךָ צַר מִמֶּנּוּ: [מלכים ב׳ ו, א]

ח) וַיֹּאמֶר נַעֲמָן הוֹאֵל קַח כִּכָּרָיִם וַיִּפְרָץ בּוֹ וַיָּצַר כִּכְּרַיִם כֶּסֶף בִּשְׁנֵי חֲרִטִים וּשְׁתֵּי חֲלִפוֹת בְּגָדִים וַיִּתֵּן אֶל שְׁנֵי נְעָרָיו וַיִּשְׂאוּ לְפָנָיו: וְהוּא בָא וַיַּעֲמֹד אֶל אֲדֹנָיו וַיֹּאמֶר אֵלָיו אֱלִישָׁע מֵאַיִן גֵּחֲזִי וַיֹּאמֶר לֹא הָלַךְ עַבְדְּךָ אָנֶה וָאָנֶה: וַיֹּאמֶר אֵלָיו לֹא לִבִּי הָלַךְ כַּאֲשֶׁר הָפַךְ אִישׁ מֵעַל מֶרְכַּבְתּוֹ לִקְרָאתֶךָ הַעֵת לָקַחַת אֶת הַכֶּסֶף וְלָקַחַת בְּגָדִים וְזֵיתִים וּכְרָמִים וְצֹאן וּבָקָר וַעֲבָדִים וּשְׁפָחוֹת: [מלכים ב׳ ה, כג,כה-כו] ט) וְצָרַעַת נַעֲמָן תִּדְבַּק בְּךָ וּבְזַרְעֲךָ לְעוֹלָם וַיֵּצֵא מִלְּפָנָיו מְצֹרָע כַּשָּׁלֶג: [מלכים ב׳ ה, כז] י) וְאַרְבָּעָה אֲנָשִׁים הָיוּ מְצֹרָעִים פֶּתַח הַשָּׁעַר וַיֹּאמְרוּ אִישׁ אֶל רֵעֵהוּ מָה אֲנַחְנוּ יֹשְׁבִים פֹּה עַד מָתְנוּ: [מלכים ב׳ ז, ג] כ) וֶאֱלִישָׁע חָלָה אֶת חָלְיוֹ אֲשֶׁר יָמוּת בּוֹ וַיֵּרֶד אֵלָיו יוֹאָשׁ מֶלֶךְ יִשְׂרָאֵל וַיֵּבְךְּ עַל פָּנָיו וַיֹּאמַר אָבִי אָבִי רֶכֶב יִשְׂרָאֵל וּפָרָשָׁיו: [מלכים ב׳ יג, יד] ל) וְאַבְרָהָם זָקֵן בָּא בַּיָּמִים וַיְיָ בֵּרַךְ אֶת אַבְרָהָם בַּכֹּל: [בראשית כד, א] מ) וַיְהִי אַחֲרֵי הַדְּבָרִים הָאֵלֶּה וַיֹּאמֶר לְיוֹסֵף הִנֵּה אָבִיךָ חֹלֶה וַיִּקַּח אֶת שְׁנֵי בָנָיו עִמּוֹ אֶת מְנַשֶּׁה וְאֶת אֶפְרָיִם: [בראשית מח, א] נ) וַיֹּאמֶר יְיָ לֹא יָדוֹן רוּחִי בָאָדָם לְעֹלָם בְּשַׁגַּם הוּא בָשָׂר וְהָיוּ יָמָיו מֵאָה וְעֶשְׂרִים שָׁנָה: [בראשית ו, ג] ס) וַיָּפֶץ יְיָ אֹתָם מִשָּׁם עַל פְּנֵי כָל הָאָרֶץ וַיַּחְדְּלוּ לִבְנֹת הָעִיר: [בראשית יא, ח] ע) עַל כֵּן קָרָא שְׁמָהּ בָּבֶל כִּי שָׁם בָּלַל יְיָ שְׂפַת כָּל הָאָרֶץ וּמִשָּׁם הֱפִיצָם יְיָ עַל פְּנֵי כָּל הָאָרֶץ: [בראשית יא, ט] פ) וְאַנְשֵׁי סְדֹם רָעִים וְחַטָּאִים לַייָ מְאֹד: [בראשית יג, יג] צ) עַל כֵּן לֹא יָקֻמוּ רְשָׁעִים בַּמִּשְׁפָּט וְחַטָּאִים בַּעֲדַת צַדִּיקִים: [תהלים א, ה]

בְּחֶבְרוֹן מָלַךְ שֶׁבַע שָׁנִים וּבִירוּשָׁלַם מָלַךְ שְׁלֹשִׁים וְשָׁלֹשׁ שָׁנִים״ – ***in Hebron he reigned seven years and in Jerusalem he reigned thirty-three years.*** וּכְתִיב ,,בְּחֶבְרוֹן מָלַךְ עַל־יְהוּדָה שֶׁבַע שָׁנִים וְשִׁשָּׁה חֳדָשִׁים וגו׳״ – **And it is written** elsewhere:[1] ***In Hebron he reigned over Judah seven years and six months, etc.*** וְהָנֵי שִׁשָּׁה חֳדָשִׁים לֹא קָחָשִׁיב – **Now, [the first verse] does not reckon these** additional **six months** that David reigned in Hebron. Why not? שְׁמַע מִינָּהּ נִצְטָרַע – **Learn from this** omission **that he was afflicted with *tzaraas*** for six months, during which period his reign was lacking.[2]

The account of David's plea for forgiveness continues:

אָמַר לְפָנָיו – Having endured a period of suffering, **[David] said before [the Holy One, Blessed is He]:** רִבּוֹנוֹ שֶׁל עוֹלָם – **Master of the Universe!** מְחוֹל לִי עַל אוֹתוֹ עָוֹן – **Forgive me for that sin!**[3] מָחוּל לָךְ – The Holy One, Blessed is He, replied: **You are forgiven.** ,,עֲשֵׂה־עִמִּי אוֹת לְטוֹבָה וְיִרְאוּ שׂנְאַי וְיֵבֹשׁוּ כִּי־אַתָּה ה׳ עֲזַרְתַּנִי וְנִחַמְתָּנִי״ – David then requested:[4] ***Display for me a sign for good, so that my enemies may see it and be ashamed, for You, Hashem, will have helped and consoled me.***[5] אָמַר לוֹ – **[The Holy One, Blessed is He,] said to [David]:** בְּחַיֶּיךָ אֵינִי מוֹדִיעַ – **During your lifetime, I will not make it known** publicly that I have forgiven you. אֲבָל אֲנִי מוֹדִיעַ בְּחַיֵּי שְׁלֹמֹה בִּנְךָ – **However, I shall make it known** publicly **during the lifetime of your son, Solomon.**

The Gemara describes the event through which David's forgiveness was made known:

בְּשָׁעָה שֶׁבָּנָה שְׁלֹמֹה אֶת בֵּית הַמִּקְדָּשׁ – **At the time that Solomon built the Holy Temple,** בִּיקֵּשׁ לְהַכְנִיס אָרוֹן לְבֵית קָדְשֵׁי הַקֳּדָשִׁים – **he sought to bring the Ark into the Holy of Holies.** דָּבְקוּ שְׁעָרִים זֶה בָּזֶה – However, **the gates** of the Holy of Holies **clung to each other** miraculously and could not be opened.[6] אָמַר עֶשְׂרִים וְאַרְבָּעָה רְנָנוֹת – **Solomon recited twenty-four songs of prayer,**[7] וְלֹא נַעֲנָה – **but he was not answered** and the gates remained closed. אָמַר ,,שְׂאוּ שְׁעָרִים רָאשֵׁיכֶם וְהִנָּשְׂאוּ פִּתְחֵי עוֹלָם וְיָבוֹא מֶלֶךְ הַכָּבוֹד – **He said:**[8] ***Raise up your heads, O gates, and be uplifted, you everlasting entrances, so that the King of Glory may enter!*** מִי זֶה מֶלֶךְ הַכָּבוֹד ה׳ עִזּוּז וְגִבּוֹר ה׳ גִּבּוֹר מִלְחָמָה״ – ***Who is this King of Glory? HASHEM, the mighty and strong, HASHEM, the strong in battle.*** וְנֶאֱמַר ,,שְׂאוּ שְׁעָרִים רָאשֵׁיכֶם וּשְׂאוּ פִּתְחֵי עוֹלָם וְיָבֹא מֶלֶךְ הַכָּבוֹד וגו׳״ – **And it is stated** further: ***Raise up your heads, O gates, and raise up, you everlasting entrances, so that the King of Glory may enter, etc.*** וְלֹא נַעֲנָה – **Nevertheless, [Solomon] was not answered** and the gates remained closed. כֵּיוָן שֶׁאָמַר ,,ה׳ אֱלֹהִים אַל־תָּשֵׁב פְּנֵי מְשִׁיחֶךָ זָכְרָה לְחַסְדֵי דָּוִיד עַבְדֶּךָ״ – **As soon as he said:**[9] ***HASHEM, God! Turn not away the face of Your anointed one! Remember the pieties of David, Your servant*** – מִיָּד נַעֲנָה – **he was answered immediately** and the gates opened.[10] בְּאוֹתָהּ שָׁעָה נֶהֶפְכוּ פְּנֵי שׂוֹנְאֵי דָוִד כְּשׁוּלֵי קְדֵירָה – **At that moment, the faces of David's enemies**[11] **turned** dark with humiliation **like the bottom of a pot** that has been blackened by fire, וְיָדְעוּ כָּל יִשְׂרָאֵל שֶׁמָּחַל לוֹ הַקָּדוֹשׁ בָּרוּךְ הוּא עַל אוֹתוֹ הֶעָוֹן – **and all Israel knew that the Holy One, Blessed is He, had forgiven [David] for that sin.**[12]

Having concluded its discussion of Doeg and Achithophel, the Gemara now turns its attention to the last of the four commoners listed in our Mishnah as having no share in the World to Come, Geichazi:

גֵּחֲזִי דִּכְתִיב וַיֵּלֶךְ אֱלִישָׁע דַּמֶּשֶׂק – **Geichazi, as it is written: Elisha**

NOTES

1. *II Samuel* 5:5.

2. When a king is afflicted with *tzaraas,* he loses his royal status in some respects. For example, ordinarily if a king sins inadvertently he brings a special *chatas* offering [a male goat – see *Leviticus* 4:22-23] but if the king is a *metzora* he brings the same offering as a commoner [a female sheep or goat] (*Horayos* 10a; see *Haamek She'eilah* 30:2 and *Avnei Nezer, Yoreh Deah* 312:27 in footnote).

Since the verse deletes six months of the Hebron years, it would seem that David's six-month affliction occurred during his reign at Hebron. However, our Gemara has stated that the affliction was an atonement for the Bathsheba episode, which took place decades after David left Hebron for Jerusalem. We must therefore conclude that David was afflicted during his tenure in Jerusalem. The verse merely deleted six months from the record of his reign in one passage to indicate that there was a six-month gap during which his reign was not fully in force. To simplify this allusion, the year numbers were rounded off, from seven and one-half and thirty-three, to seven and thirty-three (*Tosefos Yeshanim* to *Yoma* 22b; see also *Tosafos* to *Sanhedrin* 20a ד״ה שתי, *Parashas Derachim* §10 and *Margaliyos HaYam;* cf. *Yerushalmi, Rosh Hashanah* 1:1 [2b]).

3. In the merit of my suffering, let the effects of my sin be eradicated completely (see *Maharsha*).

4. *Psalms* 86:17.

5. As related above, David's enemies used to taunt him about the Bathsheba incident. David therefore prayed to God for a public display of favor and consolation that would demonstrate to all that the sin was forgiven and would put his enemies to shame (*Maharsha*).

6. The *Midrash* (*Shemos Rabbah* 8:1) cites this incident as follows: Solomon made an Ark ten *amos* wide, and the Temple doorway was only ten *amos* wide. Thus, the Ark could not fit through the doorway, especially since people had to stand at its sides to carry it. Solomon became embarrassed and began to pray.

God caused Solomon to fall into this predicament, to set the stage for the miracle through which He would make known David's forgiveness (*Eitz Yosef* ad loc.). [See *Midrash* (ibid.) and *Shabbos* 30a for further variations in the citation of this incident.]

7. The Scriptural account of Solomon's inaugural prayer at the dedication of the Temple (*I Kings* ch. 8; *II Chronicles* ch. 6) contains twenty-four expressions of prayer, such as רִנָּה,תְּחִנָּה,תְּפִלָּה, etc. (*Rashi*).

According to *Yad Ramah,* the reference here is to the twenty-four psalms that begin with expressions of prayer, such as קְרִיאָה, צְעָקָה, שַׁוְעָה, תְּפִלָּה, תְּחִנָּה, רִנָּה.

Others explain that Solomon recited the first twenty-four chapters in the Book of *Psalms.* The twenty-fourth psalm culminates with the verses about to be cited (*Hagahos R' Elazar Moshe Horowitz* to *Shabbos* 30a).

8. *Psalms* 24:7-9.

9. *II Chronicles* 6:42.

10. The verse just cited is the final verse of Solomon's prayer at the inauguration of the Temple. The very next verse (ibid. 7:1) states: וּכְכַלּוֹת שְׁלֹמֹה לְהִתְפַּלֵּל וְהָאֵשׁ יָרְדָה מֵהַשָּׁמַיִם וַתֹּאכַל הָעֹלָה וְהַזְּבָחִים וּכְבוֹד ה׳ מָלֵא אֶת־הַבָּיִת, *Now as Solomon finished praying, the fire descended from heaven and consumed the burnt offerings and the sacrifices; and the glory of Hashem filled the House.*

11. David's enemies were the family of Saul, Shimi ben Gera and others who opposed his ascendancy to the throne (*Rashi, Shabbos* 30a).

12. The reason David's forgiveness was made known in these circumstances is the following: David had originally sought to build the Temple himself, but God decreed that David's son Solomon should be the one to build it, since David had been forced to fight many wars and Solomon was blessed with peace (see *I Chronicles* 22:7-10). David's enemies, however, claimed that God did not allow David to build the Temple due to His displeasure with David over the Bathsheba incident. God therefore chose the climax of the Temple's inauguration – the moment of bringing the Ark into the Holy of Holies – to demonstrate that the Temple was built and the Divine Presence would reside in it only in David's merit. In effect, then, the Temple was inaugurated by David. This is the meaning of the verses (*Psalms* 30:1-2): מִזְמוֹר שִׁיר־חֲנֻכַּת הַבַּיִת לְדָוִד. אֲרוֹמִמְךָ ה׳ כִּי דִלִּיתָנִי וְלֹא־שִׂמַּחְתָּ אֹיְבַי לִי, *A psalm – a song for the inauguration of the House, by David. I will exalt You, Hashem, for You have drawn me up, and not let my foes rejoice over me* (*Toras Chaim;* see *Rif* in *Ein Yaakov*).

בחברון מלך שבע שנים ובירושלים מלך שלשים ושלש שנים וכתיב א) בחברון מלך על יהודה שבע שנים וששה חדשים וגו' והני ששה חדשים לא קחשיב ש"מ נצטרע א) אמר לפניו רבש"ע מחול לי על אותו עון מחול לך ב) עשה עמי אות לטובה ויראו שונאי ויבושו כי אתה ה' עזרתני ונחמתני א"ל בחייך איני מודיע אבל אני מודיע בחיי שלמה בנך ב) בשעה שבנה שלמה את בית המקדש ביקש להכנים ארון לבית קדשי הקדשים דבקו שערים זה בזה אמר עשרים וארבעה רננות ולא נענה אמר ג) שאו שערים ראשיכם והנשאו פתחי עולם ויבא מלך הכבוד מי זה מלך הכבוד ה' עזוז וגבור ה' גבור מלחמה ונאמר ד) שאו שערים ראשיכם ושאו פתחי עולם ויבא מלך הכבוד וגו' ולא נענה כיון שאמר ה) ה' אלהים אל תשב פני משיחך זכרה לחסדי דויד עבדך מיד נענה באותה שעה נהפכו פני שונאי דוד כשולי קדירה וידעו כל ישראל שמחל לו הקב"ה על אותו העון גחזי דכתיב ג) ו) וילך אלישע דמשק להיכא אזל ד) א"ר יוחנן שהלך להחזיר גחזי בתשובה ולא חזר אמר לו חזור בך אמר לו כך מקובלני ממך ה) א החוטא ומחטיא את הרבים אין מספיקין בידו לעשות תשובה מאי עבד איכא דאמרי אבן שואבת תלה לחטאת ירבעם והעמידה בין שמים לארץ ואיכא דאמרי שם חקק בפיה והיתה מכרזת ואומרת אנכי ולא יהיה לך וא"ד רבנן דחה מקמיה שנאמר ז) ויאמרו בני הנביאים אל אלישע הנה [נא] המקום אשר אנחנו יושבים שם לפניך צר ממנו מכלל דעד השתא לא הוו (פיישי) [צר] ו) תנו רבנן לעולם תהא שמאל דוחה וימין מקרבת לא כאלישע שדחפו לגחזי בשתי ידים גחזי דכתיב ח) ויאמר נעמן הואל ז) וקח ככרים (ויפצר) [ויפרץ] בו ויצר ככרים כסף וגו' ויאמר אליו אלישע מאין גחזי ויאמר לא הלך עבדך אנה ואנה ויאמר אליו לא לבי הלך כאשר הפך איש מעל מרכבתו לקראתך העת לקחת את הכסף ולקחת בגדים וזיתים וכרמים וצאן ובקר ועבדים ושפחות ומי שקל כולי האי כסף ובגדים הוא דשקל אמר רבי יצחק באותה שעה היה אלישע יושב ודורש בשמונה שרצים נעמן שר צבא מלך ארם היה מצורע אמרה ליה ההיא רביתא דאישתבאי מארעא ישראל אי אזלת לגבי אלישע מסי לך כי אתא א"ל זיל טבול בירדן א"ל אחוכי קא מחייכת בי אמרי ליה הנהו דהוו בהדיה מאי נפקא לך מינה זיל נסי אזל וטבל בירדנא ואיתסי אתא אייתי ליה כל הני דנקיט לא צבי לקבולי מיניה גחזי איפטר מקמיה אלישע אזל שקל מאי דשקל ואפקיד כי אתא חזייה אלישע לצרעת דהוה פרחא עילויה רישיה א"ל רשע הגיע עת ליטול שכר שמנה שרצים ט) וצרעת נעמן תדבק בך ובזרעך עד עולם ויצא מלפניו מצורע כשלג: י) וארבעה אנשים היו מצורעים פתח השער אמר ר' יוחנן גחזי ושלשה בניו תניא ח) א"ר שמעון בן אלעזר יצר תינוק ואשה תהא שמאל דוחה וימין מקרבת ט) ת"ר ג' חלאים חלה אלישע אחד שגירה דובים בתינוקות ואחד שדחפו לגחזי בשתי ידים ואחד שמת בו [שנא' כ) ואלישע חלה את חליו וגו'] י) עד אברהם לא היה זקנה כל דחזי לאברהם אמר האי יצחק כל דחזי ליצחק אמר האי אברהם כ) בעא אברהם רחמי דליהוי ליה זקנה שנאמר ל) ואברהם זקן בא בימים עד יעקב לא הוה חולשא בעא רחמי והוה חולשא שנאמר מ) ויאמר ליוסף הנה אביך חולה עד אלישע לא הוה איניש חליש ל) דמיתפח ואתא אלישע ובעא רחמי ואיתפח שנא' כ) ואלישע חלה את חליו אשר ימות בו מ): **מתני'** דור המבול אין להם חלק לעוה"ב ואין עומדין בדין שנא' נ) לא ידון רוחי באדם לעולם לא דין ולא רוח דור הפלגה אין להם חלק לעולם הבא שנאמר ס) ויפץ ה' אותם משם על פני כל הארץ נ) (וכתיב ומשם הפיצם) ויפץ ה' אותם בעוה"ז ע) ומשם הפיצם ה' לעולם הבא אנשי סדום אין להם חלק לעולם הבא שנא' פ) ואנשי סדום רעים וחטאים לה' מאד רעים בעולם הזה וחטאים לעולם הבא אבל עומדין בדין ר' נחמיה אומר אלו ואלו אין עומדין בדין שנאמר צ) על כן לא יקומו רשעים

רש"י

בחברון מלך שבע שנים וששה חדשים. מדהכא חשיב להו ובאידך קרא לא חשיב להו ש"מ לא היה מלכותו שלימה שנצטרע אותן ו' חדשים: ה"ג אבל בחיי בנך אני מודיע ולא גרסינן לך: כ"ד רננות. בין תפלה תחנה ורנה איכא כ"ד: וילך אלישע דמשק להיכא אזל: שואבת. מגבהת מתכת בלא נגיעה כעין אותה שלועזין קלאמניס"ה בלע"ז ועל ידי אותה אבן העמיד עגלים של ירבעם באויר: רבנן דחה מקמיה. התלמידים דחה מישיבתו של אלישע: צר ממנו. מכלל דעד האידנא לא הוה צר: הואל וקח. השבע שאלישע שלחך: ויפצר בו. גחזי: העת לקחת את הכסף והבגדים וגו'. שמנה דברים קא חשיב בהאי קרא: וגחזי מי שקל כולי האי. מנעמן כסף ובגדים הוא דשקל דכתיב ויצר ככרים וגו': אותה שעה. היה אלישע עוסק בפרק שמונה שרצים אמר לו הגיע עת ליטול שכר פרק שמונה שרצים שעסקתי וכו' ולהכי כתב בהאי קרא שמנה דברים כנגד אותו פרק כלומר בכסף ובגדים שקבלת ממנו מנעמן סבור אתה לקנות דברים הללו להיותם לך שכר שמונה שרצים: יצר. תאותו אם מרחיקה ממנו לגמרי ממעט ישיבת עולם ואם מקרבה לגמרי בא לידי איסור שאינו יכול לכבוש יצרו מדבר עבירה: תינוק ואשה. דעתן קלה ואם תדחה אותם מטרדן מן העולם: חלה. חד. חליו תרי. אשר ימות בו תלת: בעא רחמי דלהוי חולשא. כדי שיהא פנאי לבניו לבא כל אחד ואחד ממקומו להיות עליו בשעת מיתה שכיון שרואין שנפל למטה יודעין שימות ומתקבלין ובאין: מתפח. מתרפא: מתני' לא ידון רוחי לא דין ולא רוח. שאין עומדין בדין ואין להם רוח להיות עם הצדיקים שיש להם חלק: ויפץ [ה' אותם ומשם הפיצם. ויפץ] בעולם הזה ומשם הפיצם בעולם הבא: אלו ואלו. אנשי דור המבול ואנשי סדום ובהדא פליג ר' נחמיה:

עין משפט נר מצוה

לב א מיי' פ"ד מהל' תשובה הלכה א:

ליקוטי רש"י

עשה עמי אות לטובה. שיהא ניכר לאחרים שמחלת לי. ויראו שונאי. האות ויבושו ולא שמע לו הקב"ה ליתן האות בימיו אלא בימי שלמה בנו כשדבקו השערים זה בזה ולא נפתחו עד שאמר (דה"ב ו') אל תשב פני משיחך זכרה לחסדי דוד עבדך [תהלים פו, יז]. על אותו עון. דבת שבע. דבקו שערים. של בית קדשי הקדשים. עשרים וארבע רננות. רנה תפילה תחינה כתובים בתפילת שלמה עד עשרים וארבע ויש אומרים עשרים וארבע ברכות דתענית ולא נהירא. אמר שאו שערים ראשיכם והנשאו פתחי עולם ויבוא מלך הכבוד. רהטו שערים בתריה למבלעיה סברי דעל עצמו אמר מלך הכבוד אמרו לו שערים מי הוא זה מלך הכבוד אמר איהו ה' עזוז וגבור (תהלים כד). שונאי דוד. משפחת שאול שמעי וכיוצא בו [שבת ל.]. עשרים וארבע רננות. כתיבי בפרשה, בין רנה ותחנה ותפלה ובקשה [מו"ק ט.]. אל תשב פני משיחך. מלעשות טובה עמדי ואם לא למעני עשה למען דוד [דה"ב ו, מב]. ויבא אלישע דמשק. להחזיר את גיחזי בתשובה [מ"ב ח, ז]. אבן שואבת. לקח אותו האבן והגביה המתכת ולתלותה באויר [ע"ז מג.]. שמגבהת את המתכת מן הארץ ומעמידתו באויר [ועי' אותו אבן העמיד העגלים של ירבעם באויר]. רבנן דחה. דוחה היה את התלמידים מפני אלישע כשהיה משמש לפניו דכתיב ולאמר שפירש ממנו המקום שאנחנו יושבין בית המדרש של רבנן צר ממנו שנתוספו התלמידים שהיה גחזי דוחה [סוטה מז.]. ויאמרו בני הנביאים. רבותינו אמרו מכאן שהיה גיחזי דוחה התלמידים מלפניו כשנטרד באו תלמידים רבים ונדחק המקום מהם [מ"ב ו, א]. הואל. השבע שלחך [שם ה, כג]. העת לקחת את הכסף. להתעשר ולקחת ממנו בגדים וזיתים וגו' [מלכים ב, ה]. מי שקל כולי האי. בהאי קרא כתיב שמנה דברים כסף ובגדים וצאן ובקר ועבדים ושפחות וזיתים וכרמים. כסף ובגדים הוא דשקל. דכתיב ויצר ככרים כסף בשני חריטים ושתי חליפות בגדים. בשמנה שרצים. בפרק שמנה שרצים (שבת קז). הגיע עת ליטול שכר. תורתך בעולם הזה [שם]. וארבעה אנשים. גיחזי ובניו. פתח השער. כמו שנאמר בדד ישב מחוץ למחנה מושבו (ויקרא י"ג מ"ו) [שם ז, ג]. כדקטלינהו ינאי מלכא לרבנן. כדאמרינן בקידושין בהאומר לשלוחו (דף סו). בעלי שרוי בתוכך. נשיא היה כדאמרינן בחגיגה (דף טז:). עבדו ליה יקרא טובא. כיבדתו. כמה יפה אכסניא זו. במעשיה. טרוטות. עגולות. בכך אתה עוסק. מסתכל באשת איש. אחוי ליה בידיה. שיקבלנו. יצר. של תשמיש תקרבנו בימין שלא יקוץ בפריה ורביה וכן תינוק פן יברח ויאבד את עצמו ואשה אף היא דעתה קלה ואם ירדפוה תצא לתרבות רעה [סוטה מז.]. חליו אשר ימות בו. מכלל דחלה עוד שלא מת בו [ב"מ פז.]. אחד שגירה דובים. בעון שגירה דובים בתינוקות. חלה. חד את חליו תרי וחד אשר ימות בו [סוטה שם]. בעא אברהם רחמי. כדי שיכירו בינו ובין בנו. בעא רחמי והוה חולשא. שיחלה אדם לפני מותו ויצוה לביתו. חליש דמיתפח. ונתרפא. חליו אשר ימות בו. מכלל דחלה עוד שלא מת בו [ב"מ שם]. ויפץ ה' אותם משם. בעולם הזה מה שאמרו פן נפוץ נתקיים עליהם הוא שאמר שלמה (משלי י, כד) מגורת רשע היא תבואנו [בראשית יא, יח]. ומשם הפיצם. למד שאין להם חלק לעולם הבא [בראשית יא, ט].

מסורת הש"ס

א) שבת ל. ע"ש, ב) שם מו"ק ט., ג) אין זה לשון המקרא וכך הוא לשון המקרא ויבא אלישע (מ"ב ח') גו' ועיי' רש"א במ"א, ד) סוטה מז. [ע"ש], ה) [יומא פז.], ו) סוטה שם, ז) בקרא קח, ח) [שמחות פ"ב סוטה מז.], ט) [סוטה מז:], י) [ב"מ פז.], כ) [ב"מ פז.], ל) [לדעת הערוך בערך תפח גרס הכא ואיתפח כמו בסמוך], מ) [מכלל דחלה חלי אחריתא כך איתא בב"מ פז.], נ) [בסה"מ ל"ג].

תורה אור השלם

א) בְּחֶבְרוֹן מָלַךְ עַל יְהוּדָה שֶׁבַע שָׁנִים וְשִׁשָּׁה חֳדָשִׁים וּבִירוּשָׁלַיִם מָלַךְ שְׁלשִׁים וְשָׁלשׁ שָׁנָה עַל כָּל יִשְׂרָאֵל וִיהוּדָה: [שמואל ב' ה, ה]

ב) עֲשֵׂה עִמִּי אוֹת לְטוֹבָה וְיִרְאוּ שֹׂנְאַי וְיֵבֹשׁוּ כִּי אַתָּה יְיָ עֲזַרְתַּנִי וְנִחַמְתָּנִי: [תהלים פו, יז]

ג) שְׂאוּ שְׁעָרִים רָאשֵׁיכֶם וְהִנָּשְׂאוּ פִּתְחֵי עוֹלָם וְיָבוֹא מֶלֶךְ הַכָּבוֹד: מִי זֶה מֶלֶךְ הַכָּבוֹד יְיָ עִזּוּז וְגִבּוֹר יְיָ גִּבּוֹר מִלְחָמָה: [תהלים כד, ז-ח]

ד) שְׂאוּ שְׁעָרִים רָאשֵׁיכֶם וּשְׂאוּ פִּתְחֵי עוֹלָם וְיָבֹא מֶלֶךְ הַכָּבוֹד: מִי הוּא זֶה מֶלֶךְ הַכָּבוֹד יְיָ צְבָאוֹת הוּא מֶלֶךְ הַכָּבוֹד סֶלָה: [תהלים כד, ט-י]

ה) יְיָ אֱלֹהִים אַל תָּשֵׁב פְּנֵי מְשִׁיחֶיךָ זָכְרָה לְחַסְדֵי דָּוִיד עַבְדֶּךָ: [דברי הימים ב' ו, מב]

ו) וַיָּבֹא אֱלִישָׁע דַּמֶּשֶׂק וּבֶן הֲדַד מֶלֶךְ אֲרָם חֹלֶה וַיֻּגַּד לוֹ לֵאמֹר בָּא אִישׁ הָאֱלֹהִים עַד הֵנָּה: [מלכים ב' ח, ז]

ז) וַיֹּאמְרוּ בְנֵי הַנְּבִיאִים אֶל אֱלִישָׁע הִנֵּה נָא הַמָּקוֹם אֲשֶׁר אֲנַחְנוּ יֹשְׁבִים שָׁם לְפָנֶיךָ צַר מִמֶּנּוּ: [מלכים ב' ו, א]

ח) וַיֹּאמֶר נַעֲמָן הוֹאֵל קַח כִּכָּרָיִם וַיִּפְרָץ בּוֹ וַיָּצַר כִּכְּרַיִם כֶּסֶף בִּשְׁנֵי חֲרִטִים וּשְׁתֵּי חֲלִפוֹת בְּגָדִים וַיִּתֵּן אֶל שְׁנֵי נְעָרָיו וַיִּשְׂאוּ לְפָנָיו: וְהוּא בָא וַיַּעֲמֹד אֶל אֲדֹנָיו וַיֹּאמֶר אֵלָיו אֱלִישָׁע מֵאַיִן גֵּחֲזִי וַיֹּאמֶר לֹא הָלַךְ עַבְדְּךָ אָנֶה וָאָנָה: וַיֹּאמֶר אֵלָיו לֹא לִבִּי הָלַךְ כַּאֲשֶׁר הָפַךְ אִישׁ מֵעַל מֶרְכַּבְתּוֹ לִקְרָאתֶךָ הַעֵת לָקַחַת אֶת הַכֶּסֶף וְלָקַחַת בְּגָדִים וְזֵיתִים וּכְרָמִים וְצֹאן וּבָקָר וַעֲבָדִים וּשְׁפָחוֹת: [מלכים ב' ה, כג,כה-כו]

ט) וְצָרַעַת נַעֲמָן תִּדְבַּק בְּךָ וּבְזַרְעֲךָ לְעוֹלָם וַיֵּצֵא מִלְּפָנָיו מְצֹרָע כַּשָּׁלֶג: [מלכים ב' ה, כז]

י) וְאַרְבָּעָה אֲנָשִׁים הָיוּ מְצֹרָעִים פֶּתַח הַשָּׁעַר וַיֹּאמְרוּ אִישׁ אֶל רֵעֵהוּ מָה אֲנַחְנוּ יֹשְׁבִים פֹּה עַד מָתְנוּ: [מלכים ב' ז, ג]

כ) וֶאֱלִישָׁע חָלָה אֶת חָלְיוֹ אֲשֶׁר יָמוּת בּוֹ וַיֵּרֶד אֵלָיו יוֹאָשׁ מֶלֶךְ יִשְׂרָאֵל וַיֵּבְךְּ עַל פָּנָיו וַיֹּאמַר אָבִי אָבִי רֶכֶב יִשְׂרָאֵל וּפָרָשָׁיו: [מלכים ב' יג, יד]

ל) וְאַבְרָהָם זָקֵן בָּא בַּיָּמִים וַיְיָ בֵּרַךְ אֶת אַבְרָהָם בַּכֹּל: [בראשית כד, א]

מ) וַיְהִי אַחֲרֵי הַדְּבָרִים הָאֵלֶּה וַיֹּאמֶר לְיוֹסֵף הִנֵּה אָבִיךָ חֹלֶה וַיִּקַּח אֶת שְׁנֵי בָנָיו עִמּוֹ אֶת מְנַשֶּׁה וְאֶת אֶפְרָיִם: [בראשית מח, א]

נ) וַיֹּאמֶר יְיָ לֹא יָדוֹן רוּחִי בָאָדָם לְעֹלָם בְּשַׁגַּם הוּא בָשָׂר וְהָיוּ יָמָיו מֵאָה וְעֶשְׂרִים שָׁנָה: [בראשית ו, ג]

ס) וַיָּפֶץ יְיָ אֹתָם מִשָּׁם עַל פְּנֵי כָל הָאָרֶץ וַיַּחְדְּלוּ לִבְנֹת הָעִיר: [בראשית יא, ח]

ע) עַל כֵּן קָרָא שְׁמָהּ בָּבֶל כִּי שָׁם בָּלַל יְיָ שְׂפַת כָּל הָאָרֶץ וּמִשָּׁם הֱפִיצָם יְיָ עַל פְּנֵי כָּל הָאָרֶץ: [בראשית יא, ט]

פ) וְאַנְשֵׁי סְדֹם רָעִים וְחַטָּאִים לַייָ מְאֹד: [בראשית יג, יג]

צ) עַל כֵּן לֹא יָקֻמוּ רְשָׁעִים בַּמִּשְׁפָּט וְחַטָּאִים בַּעֲדַת צַדִּיקִים: [תהלים א, ה]

went to Damascus.[13] לְהֵיכָא אָזַל – **Where was [Elisha] going?** אָמַר רַבִּי יוֹחָנָן – **R' Yochanan said:** שֶׁהָלַךְ לְהַחֲזִיר גֵּחֲזִי בִּתְשׁוּבָה – **He went** to Damascus **to bring Geichazi back in repentance.**[14] וְלֹא חָזַר – However, **[Geichazi] would not repent.** אָמַר לוֹ – **[Elisha] said to [Geichazi]:** חֲזוֹר בְּךָ – **"Repent!"** אָמַר לוֹ – **[Geichazi] replied:** כָּךְ מְקוּבְּלַנִי מִמְּךָ – "How can I repent? **Thus have I received** a tradition **from you:** הַחוֹטֵא וּמַחֲטִיא אֶת הָרַבִּים אֵין מַסְפִּיקִין בְּיָדוֹ לַעֲשׂוֹת תְּשׁוּבָה – **'He who sins and causes others to sin is not given the opportunity to repent';**[15] and I have caused others to sin."

The Gemara elaborates:

אִיבָּא מַאי עָבֵד – **What did [Geichazi] do** to cause others to sin? דְּאָמְרֵי אֶבֶן שׁוֹאֶבֶת תָּלָה לְחַטַּאת יָרָבְעָם – **Some say that he hung a magnet for the "Sin of Yarovam,"** i.e. near the Golden Calf that Yarovam had set up as an object of worship, וְהֶעֱמִידָהּ בֵּין שָׁמַיִם לָאָרֶץ – **and** thereby **suspended [the Golden Calf] between heaven and earth,** creating the impression that it had supernatural powers.[16] וְאִיכָּא דְּאָמְרֵי שֵׁם חָקַק בְּפִיהָ – **And some say that [Geichazi] engraved a** Divine **Name in the mouth of [the Calf],** וְהָיְתָה מַכְרֶזֶת וְאוֹמֶרֶת ,,אָנֹכִי'' וְ,,לֹא־יִהְיֶה לְךָ'' – **and [the Calf] would proclaim and recite:** ***I am** your God . . .* **and** ***You shall not recognize** the gods of others in My presence.*[17] וְאִיכָּא דְּאָמְרֵי רַבָּנָן דָּחָה מִקַּמֵּיהּ – **And some say** that **[Geichazi] drove the Rabbis away from the presence of [Elisha],** שֶׁנֶּאֱמַר ,,וַיֹּאמְרוּ בְנֵי־הַנְּבִיאִים אֶל־אֱלִישָׁע הִנֵּה־נָא הַמָּקוֹם אֲשֶׁר אֲנַחְנוּ יֹשְׁבִים שָׁם לְפָנֶיךָ צַר מִמֶּנּוּ'' – **as it is stated:**[18] ***The disciples of the prophets said to Elisha, "Behold, the place where we are staying before you is too cramped for us."*** מִכְּלָל דְּעַד הַשְׁתָּא לֹא הֲווּ (פיישי) [צַר] – **This implies that until now they had not been cramped.**[19]

A Baraisa discusses Elisha's treatment of Geichazi:[20]

תָּנוּ רַבָּנָן – **The Rabbis taught in a Baraisa:** לְעוֹלָם תְּהֵא שְׂמֹאל דּוֹחָה וְיָמִין מְקָרֶבֶת – ALWAYS, THE LEFT hand **SHOULD PUSH AWAY BUT THE RIGHT** hand **SHOULD DRAW CLOSE,** i.e. whenever one must rebuke another, he should not reject the other completely, but should hold out warmly the possibility of reconciliation, לֹא כֶּאֱלִישָׁע שֶׁדְּחָפוֹ לְגֵחֲזִי בִּשְׁתֵּי יָדַיִם – **UNLIKE ELISHA, WHO PUSHED GEICHAZI AWAY WITH BOTH HANDS.**[21]

The Gemara cites the verses that describe this incident:

גֵּחֲזִי – What was the incident of **Geichazi?** דִּכְתִיב ,,וַיֹּאמֶר נַעֲמָן הוֹאֵל קַח כִּכָּרָיִם (ויפצר) [וַיִּפְרָץ]־בּוֹ וַיָּצַר כִּכְּרַיִם כֶּסֶף וגו'' – **As it is written:**[22] ***Naaman said*** [to Geichazi], ***"Please, take two talents." He pressed him, and wrapped two talents of silver*** etc.[23]

NOTES

13. There is no such verse in Scripture. Rather, *II Kings* 8:7 reads: וַיָּבֹא אֱלִישָׁע דַּמֶּשֶׂק, *Elisha came to Damascus,* which is indeed the reading in the *Yerushalmi* and *Ein Yaakov* here. This verse introduces the episode in which Elisha predicted that Ben Hadad the king of Aram would die and Chazael would ascend his throne. However, it is unusual for Scripture to state that somebody *arrived* in a given place without first stating that he set out for that place. Since this verse mentions only that Elisha came to Damascus, the Gemara deduces that Elisha originally traveled to Damascus for a purpose that is unmentioned in Scripture, and only after his arrival there did the episode of Ben Hadad unfold. The Gemara therefore asks: Why did Elisha go to Damascus in the first place? (*Maharsha*).

14. Geichazi had been Elisha's disciple and attendant, but had fallen into sin, as the Gemara explains below.

15. As the Gemara states elsewhere (*Yoma* 87a), he is not given the opportunity to repent, so that he should not enter Gan Eden while his disciples are in Gehinnom. However, although the opportunity for repentance does not present itself readily, if the person does find the courage to repent he is forgiven and he receives a share in the World to Come (*Rambam, Hil. Teshuvah* 4:6; see also *Meiri*). Elisha therefore encouraged Geichazi to repent. However, Geichazi cited Elisha's teaching as an excuse to avoid repenting, for he was unwilling to invest the effort that would be required of him (*R' Avigdor Miller*).

The reason Elisha went to such lengths as traveling to Damascus for this purpose is that, as the Gemara states below, when Geichazi had sinned Elisha had rejected him too strongly, pushing him away with "both hands" (see *Yad Yosef*).

16. Geichazi attached steel plates to the sides of the Golden Calf and concealed powerful magnets at various angles above it, so that the magnets lifted it off the ground. This apparently miraculous suspension in mid-air led many onlookers to conclude that the Calf was actually a god that possessed supernatural powers. Geichazi thus led many people astray to idolatry (*Rashi, Yad Ramah*).

17. *Exodus* 20:2-3. These are the first two of the Ten Commandments. As we have seen previously in this chapter, when recited or written down in the prescribed manner, the Divine Name can cause miraculous occurrences (see, for example, 106a note 13).

[Geichazi engraved the Divine Name inside the mouth of the Calf, where it was hidden from public view, and] the Calf began to recite from the Ten Commandments. When it recited, *I am Hashem your God . . .* etc., it was actually speaking in the Name of God. However, onlookers who saw the Calf "speak" concluded that it was referring to itself, and that it possessed godly powers (*Yad Ramah;* see also *Ben Yehoyada*).

18. *II Kings* 6:1.

19. The previous passage in *II Kings* recounts how Geichazi, who had been Elisha's attendant, was banished from Elisha's presence (see Gemara below). The very next verse, which the Gemara has cited, describes how Elisha's disciples complained to him that their quarters were overly cramped. Since this is the first time that such a complaint was made, the implication is that until now there was no problem of overcrowding. Why not? Evidently, Geichazi, who had previously been the administrator of Elisha's house of study, had taken the liberty of restricting admission without Elisha's knowledge, and had prevented many qualified students from entering. Geichazi thus caused others to sin in the sense that he prevented them from studying Torah under Elisha (*Rashi, Yad Ramah;* see *Margaliyos HaYam*).

20. Scripture does not mention explicitly any of the sins just attributed to Geichazi. However, Scripture (*II Kings* ch. 5) does discuss a different sin that Geichazi committed and for which Elisha banished him permanently. Naaman, the general of the army of Aram, who had been afflicted with *tzaraas* and had been healed miraculously by Elisha, offered Elisha a handsome reward for healing him, but Elisha refused it. Naaman then took upon himself to abide by the seven Noahide commandments, becoming a גֵּר תּוֹשָׁב (see above, 96b). After Naaman departed, Geichazi chased and overtook him, and claimed that Elisha had reconsidered and would accept a talent of silver and two changes of clothing on behalf of two needy students. Naaman gave Geichazi two talents of silver and the two changes of clothing, which Geichazi kept. Elisha, who discerned Geichazi's deceit, cursed him that Naaman's *tzaraas* should cleave to him and his children forever. The Gemara will shortly elaborate on this incident. First, however, it cites a Baraisa that discusses Elisha's reaction to Geichazi's deceit.

21. Elisha's treatment of Geichazi is considered an example of excessive rejection. By cursing him with everlasting *tzaraas,* Elisha effectively banished Geichazi from the community forever, since a *metzora* is forbidden to enter any walled city in Israel [*Leviticus* 13:46; *Keilim* 1:7] (see *Anaf Yosef*).

The proper way to deal with a sinner is to rebuke him gently — with the "left," i.e. the weaker, hand — while embracing him warmly, i.e. befriending him, with the "right" hand. [If one pushes another with the left hand while pulling him with the right hand, he turns the other person around. Thus, the Gemara alludes to the most effective method of turning a person to repentance (*R' Simcha Wasserman*).]

See the parallel text in *Sotah* 47a, and *Hashmatos HaShas* here, for another example of excessive rejection and its devastating consequences. See also *Maharal* and *Ben Yehoyada.*

22. *II Kings* 5:23.

23. The simple meaning of הוֹאֵל is *please.* Thus, Naaman was eager to send the gift that Elisha had supposedly requested, and he pressed Geichazi to accept two talents of silver instead of one. However, the Gemara (*Arachin* 16a) interprets הוֹאֵל as *swear* [from the root אָלָה]. The implication is that when Geichazi asked Naaman for a talent of silver and two changes of clothing, Naaman did not believe that he had been sent by Elisha. He therefore told Geichazi: Swear that Elisha sent you,

עין משפט
נר מצוה

לב א מיי' פ"ד מהל' תשובה הלכה א:

מסורת הש"ס

א) שבת ל. ע"ש, ב) שם מו"ק ט., ג) אין זה לשון המקרא וכך הוא לשון המקרא ויבא אלישע (מ"ב ח') גו' ועיי' רש"א במ"א,ד) סוטה מז. [ע"ש], ה) [יומא פז.], ו) סוטה שם, ז) בקרא קח, ח) [שמחות פ"ב סוטה מז.], ט) [סוטה מז:], י) [ב"מ פז.], כ) [ב"מ פז.], ל) [לדעת הערוך בערך תפח גרס הכא ואיתפח כמו בסמוך], מ) [מכלל דחלה חלי אחריתא כך איתא בב"מ פז.], נ) [בסה"מ ל"ג].

בחברון מלך שבע שנים ובירושלים מלך שלשים ושלש שנים וכתיב א) בחברון מלך על יהודה שבע שנים וששה חדשים וגו' והני ששה חדשים לא קחשיב ש"מ נצטרע א) אמר לפניו רבש"ע מחול לי על אותו עון מחול לך ב) עשה עמי אות לטובה ויראו שונאי ויבושו כי אתה ה' עזרתני ונחמתני א"ל בחייך איני מודיע אבל אני מודיע בחיי שלמה בנך ב) בשעה שבנה שלמה את בית המקדש ביקש להכנים ארון לבית קדשי הקדשים דבקו שערים זה בזה אמר עשרים וארבעה רננות ולא נענה אמר ג) שאו שערים ראשיכם והנשאו פתחי עולם ויבא מלך הכבוד מי זה מלך הכבוד ה' עזוז וגבור ה' גבור מלחמה ונאמר ד) שאו שערים ראשיכם ושאו פתחי עולם ויבא מלך הכבוד וגו' ולא נענה כיון שאמר ה) ה' אלהים אל תשב פני משיחך זכרה לחסדי דויד עבדך מיד נענה באותה שעה נהפכו פני שונאי דוד כשולי קדירה וידעו כל ישראל שמחל לו הקב"ה על אותו העון גחזי דכתיב ג) ו) וילך אלישע דמשק להיכא אזל ד) א"ר יוחנן שהלך להחזיר גחזי בתשובה ולא חזר אמר לו חזור בך אמר לו כך מקובלני ממך ה) א החוטא ומחטיא את הרבים אין מספיקין בידו לעשות תשובה מאי עבד איכא דאמרי אבן שואבת תלה לחטאת ירבעם והעמידה בין שמים לארץ ואיכא דאמרי שם חקק בפיה והיתה מכרזת ואומרת אנכי ולא יהיה לך וא"ד רבנן דחה מקמיה שנאמר ז) ויאמרו בני הנביאים אל אלישע הנה [נא] המקום אשר אנחנו יושבים שם לפניך צר ממנו מכלל דעד השתא לא הוו (פיישי) [צר] ו) תנו רבנן לעולם תהא שמאל דוחה וימין מקרבת לא כאלישע שדחפו לגחזי בשתי ידים גחזי דכתיב ח) ויאמר נעמן הואל ז) וקח ככרים (ויפצר) [ויפרץ] בו ויצר ככרים כסף וגו' ויאמר אליו אלישע מאין גחזי ויאמר לא הלך עבדך אנה ואנה ויאמר אליו לא לבי הלך כאשר הפך איש מעל מרכבתו לקראתך העת לקחת את הכסף ולקחת בגדים וזיתים וכרמים וצאן ובקר ועבדים ושפחות ומי שקל כולי האי כסף ובגדים הוא דשקל אמר רבי יצחק באותה שעה היה אלישע יושב ודורש בשמונה שרצים נעמן שר צבא מלך ארם היה מצורע אמרה ליה ההיא רביתא דאישתבאי מארעא ישראל אי אזלת לגבי אלישע מסי לך כי אתא א"ל זיל טבול בירדן א"ל אחוכי קא מחייכת בי אמרי ליה הנהו דהוו בהדיה מאי נפקא לך מינה זיל נסי אזל וטבל בירדנא ואיתסי אתא אייתי ליה כל הני דנקיט לא צבי לקבולי מיניה גחזי איפטר מקמיה אלישע אזל שקל מאי דשקל ואפקיד כי אתא חזייה אלישע לצרעת דהוה פרחא עילויה רישיה א"ל רשע הגיע עת ליטול שכר שמנה שרצים ט) וצרעת נעמן תדבק בך ובזרעך עד עולם ויצא מלפניו מצורע כשלג: י) וארבעה אנשים היו מצורעים פתח השער אמר ר' יוחנן גחזי ושלשה בניו תניא ח) א"ר שמעון בן אלעזר יצר תינוק ואשה תהא שמאל דוחה וימין מקרבת ט) ת"ר ג' חלאים חלה אלישע אחד שגירה דובים בתינוקות ואחד שדחפו לגחזי בשתי ידים ואחד שמת בו [שנא' כ) ואלישע חלה את חליו וגו'] י) עד אברהם לא היה זקנה כל דחזי לאברהם אמר האי יצחק כל דחזי ליצחק אמר האי אברהם כ) בעא אברהם רחמי דליהוי ליה זקנה שנאמר ל) ואברהם זקן בא בימים עד יעקב לא הוה חולשא בעא רחמי והוה חולשא שנאמר מ) ויאמר ליוסף הנה אביך חולה עד אלישע לא הוה איניש חליש ל) דמיתפח ואתא אלישע ובעא רחמי ואיתפח שנא' כ) ואלישע חלה את חליו אשר ימות בו מ): **מתני'** דור המבול אין להם חלק לעוה"ב ואין עומדין בדין שנא' נ) לא ידון רוחי באדם לעולם לא דין ולא רוח דור הפלגה אין להם חלק לעולם הבא שנאמר ס) ויפץ ה' אותם משם על פני כל הארץ נ) (וכתיב ומשם הפיצם) ויפץ ה' אותם בעוה"ז ע) ומשם הפיצם ה' לעולם הבא אנשי סדום אין להם חלק לעולם הבא שנא' פ) ואנשי סדום רעים וחטאים לה' מאד רעים בעולם הזה וחטאים לעולם הבא אבל עומדין בדין ר' נחמיה אומר אלו ואלו אין עומדין בדין שנאמר צ) על כן לא יקומו רשעים

בחברון מלך שבע שנים וששה חדשים. מדהכא חשיב להו ובאידך קרא לא חשיב להו ש"מ לא היה מלכותו שלימה שנצטרע אותן ו' חדשים: ה"ג אבל בחיי בנך אני מודיע ולא גרסינן לך: כ"ד רננות. בין תפלה תחנה ורנה איכא כ"ד: וילך אלישע דמשק להיכא אזל: שואבת. מגבהת מתכת בלא נגיעה כעין אותה שלועזין קלאמניס"ה בלע"ז ועל ידי אותה אבן העמיד עגלים של ירבעם באויר: רבנן דחה מקמיה. התלמידים דחה מישיבתו של אלישע: צר ממנו. מכלל דעד האידנא לא הוה צר: הואל וקח. השבע שאלישע שלחך: ויפצר בו. גחזי: העת לקחת את הכסף והבגדים וגו'. שמנה דברים קא חשיב בהאי קרא: וגחזי מי שקל כולי האי. מנעמן כסף ובגדים הוא דשקל דכתיב ויצר ככרים וגו': אותה שעה. היה אלישע עוסק בפרק שמונה שרצים אמר לו הגיע עת ליטול שכר פרק שמונה שרצים שעסקתי וכו' ולהכי כתב בהאי קרא שמנה דברים כנגד אותו פרק כלומר בכסף ובגדים שקבלת ממנו מנעמן סבור אתה לקנות דברים הללו להיותם לך שכר שמונה שרצים: יצר. תאותו אם מרחיקה ממנו לגמרי ממעט ישיבת עולם ואם מקרבה לגמרי בא לידי איסור שאינו יכול לכבוש יצרו מדבר עבירה: תינוק ואשה. דעתן קלה ואם תדחה אותם מטרדן מן העולם: חלה. חד. חליו תרי. אשר ימות בו תלת: בעא רחמי דלהוי חולשא. כדי שיהא פנאי לבניו לבא כל אחד ואחד ממקומו להיות עליו בשעת מיתה שכיון שרואין שנפל למטה יודעין שימות ומתקבצין ובאין: מתפח. מתרפא: **מתני'** לא ידון רוחי לא דין ולא רוח. שאין עומדין בדין ואין להם רוח להיות עם הצדיקים שיש להם חלק: ויפץ [ה' אותם ומשם הפיצם. ויפץ] בעולם הזה ומשם הפיצם בעולם הבא: אלו ואלו. אנשי דור המבול ואנשי סדום ובהדא פליג ר' נחמיה:

ליקוטי רש"י

עשה עמי אות לטובה. שיהא ניכר לאחרים שמחלת לי. **ויראו שונאי.** האות ויבושו ולא שמע לו הקב"ה ליתן האות בימיו אלא בימי שלמה בנו כשדבקו השערים זה בזה ולא נפתחו עד שאמר (דה"ב ו') אל תשב פני משיחך זכרה לחסדי דוד עבדך [תהלים פו, יז]. **על אותו עון.** דבת שבע. **דבקו שערים.** של בית קדשי הקדשים. **עשרים וארבע רננות.** רנה תפלה תחנה כתובים בתפילת שלמה עד עשרים וארבע ויש אומרים עשרים וארבע ברכות לתענית ולא נהירא. **אמר שאו שערים ראשיכם והנשאו פתחי עולם ויבוא מלך הכבוד.** רהטו שערים בתריה למבלעיה סברי דעל עצמו אמר מלך הכבוד אמרו לו שערים מי הוא זה מלך הכבוד אמר איהו ה' עזוז וגבור (תהלים כד). **שונאי דוד.** משפחת שאול שמעי וכיוצא בו [שבת ל.]. **עשרים וארבע רננות.** כתיבי בפרשה, בין רנה ותחנה ותפלה ובקשה [מו"ק ט.]. **אל תשב פני משיחך.** מלעשות טובה עמדי ואם לא למעני עשה למענך [דה"ב ו, מב]. **ויבא אלישע דמשק.** להחזיר את גיחזי בתשובה [מ"ב ח, ז]. **אבן שואבת.** דרך אותה האבן להגביה המתכת ולתלותה באויר [ע"ז מד.]. שמגבהת את המתכת מן הארץ ומעמידתו באויר [וע"י אותו אבן העמיד העגלים של ירבעם באויר]. **רבנן דחה.** דוחה היה את התלמידים מפני אלישע כשהיה משמש לפניו דכתיב לאחר שפירש ממנו המקום אשר אנחנו יושבין בית המדרש של רבנן צר ממנו שנתוספו התלמידים שהיה גחזי דוחה [סוטה מז.]. **ויאמרו בני הנביאים.** רבותינו אמרו מכאן שהיה גיחזי דוחה התלמידים מלפניו כשנטרד באו תלמידים רבים ונדחק המקום מהם [מ"ב ו, א]. **הואל.** השבע שלחך [שם ה, כג]. **העת לקחת את הכסף.** להתעשר ולקחת ממנו בגדים וזיתים וגו' [מלכים ב, ה]. **מי שקל כולי האי.** בהאי קרא כתיב שמנה דברים כסף ובגדים וצאן ובקר ועבדים ושפחות וזיתים וכרמים. **כסף ובגדים הוא דשקל.** דכתיב ויצר ככרים כסף בשני חריטים ושתי חליפות בגדים. **בשמנה שרצים.** בפרק שמנה שרצים (שבת קז). **הגיע עת ליטול שכר.** תורתך בעולם הזה [שם]. **וארבעה אנשים.** גיחזי ובניו. **פתח השער.** כמו שנאמר בדד ישב מחוץ למחנה מושבו (ויקרא י"ג מ"ו) [שם ז, ג]. **כדקטלינהו ינאי מלכא לרבנן.** כדאמרינן בקידושין בהאומר לשלוחו (דף סו). **בעלי שרוי בתוכך.** נשיא היה כדאמרינן בחגיגה (דף טז:). **עבדו ליה יקרא טובא.** **כמה יפה אכסניא זו.** במעשיה. **טרוטות.** עגולות. **בכך אתה עוסק.** מסתכל באשת איש. **אחוי ליה בידיה.** שיקבלנו. **יצר.** של תשמיש תקרבנו בימין שלא יקוץ בפריה ורביה וכן תינוק פן יברח ויאבד את עצמו ואשה אף היא דעתה קלה ואם ירדפוה תצא לתרבות רעה [סוטה מז.]. **חליו אשר ימות בו.** מכלל דחלה עוד שלא מת בו [ב"מ פז.]. **אחד שגירה דובים.** בעון שגירה דובים בתינוקות. **חלה.** חד את חליו תרי וחד אשר ימות בו [סוטה שם]. **בעא אברהם רחמי.** כדי שיכירו בינו ובין בנו. **בעא רחמי והוה חולשא.** שיחלה אדם לפני מותו ויצוה לבניו. **חליש דמיתפח.** ונתרפא. **חליו אשר ימות בו.** מכלל דחלה עוד שלא מת בו [ב"מ שם]. **ויפץ ה' אותם משם.** בעולם הזה מה שאמרו פן נפוץ נתקיים עליהם הוא שאמר שלמה (משלי י, כד) מגורת רשע היא תבואנו [בראשית יא, יח]. **ומשם הפיצם.** למד שאין להם חלק לעולם הבא [בראשית יא, ט].

תורה אור השלם

א) בְּחֶבְרוֹן מָלַךְ עַל יְהוּדָה שֶׁבַע שָׁנִים וְשִׁשָּׁה חֳדָשִׁים וּבִירוּשָׁלַיִם מָלַךְ שְׁלֹשִׁים וְשָׁלֹשׁ שָׁנָה עַל כָּל יִשְׂרָאֵל וִיהוּדָה: [שמואל ב' ה, ה]

ב) עֲשֵׂה עִמִּי אוֹת לְטוֹבָה וְיִרְאוּ שֹׂנְאַי וְיֵבֹשׁוּ כִּי אַתָּה יְיָ עֲזַרְתַּנִי וְנִחַמְתָּנִי: [תהלים פו, יז]

ג) שְׂאוּ שְׁעָרִים רָאשֵׁיכֶם וְהִנָּשְׂאוּ פִּתְחֵי עוֹלָם וְיָבוֹא מֶלֶךְ הַכָּבוֹד: מִי זֶה מֶלֶךְ הַכָּבוֹד יְיָ עִזּוּז וְגִבּוֹר יְיָ גִּבּוֹר מִלְחָמָה: [תהלים כד, ז-ח]

ד) שְׂאוּ שְׁעָרִים רָאשֵׁיכֶם וּשְׂאוּ פִּתְחֵי עוֹלָם וְיָבֹא מֶלֶךְ הַכָּבוֹד: מִי הוּא זֶה מֶלֶךְ הַכָּבוֹד יְיָ צְבָאוֹת הוּא מֶלֶךְ הַכָּבוֹד סֶלָה: [תהלים כד, ט-י]

ה) יְיָ אֱלֹהִים אַל תָּשֵׁב פְּנֵי מְשִׁיחֶיךָ זָכְרָה לְחַסְדֵי דָּוִיד עַבְדֶּךָ: [דברי הימים ב' ו, מב]

ו) וַיָּבֹא אֱלִישָׁע דַּמֶּשֶׂק וּבֶן הֲדַד מֶלֶךְ אֲרָם חֹלֶה וַיֻּגַּד לוֹ לֵאמֹר בָּא אִישׁ הָאֱלֹהִים עַד הֵנָּה: [מלכים ב' ח, ז]

ז) וַיֹּאמְרוּ בְנֵי הַנְּבִיאִים אֶל אֱלִישָׁע הִנֵּה נָא הַמָּקוֹם אֲשֶׁר אֲנַחְנוּ יֹשְׁבִים שָׁם לְפָנֶיךָ צַר מִמֶּנּוּ: [מלכים ב' ו, א]

ח) וַיֹּאמֶר נַעֲמָן הוֹאֵל קַח כִּכָּרָיִם וַיִּפְרָץ בּוֹ וַיָּצַר כִּכְּרַיִם כֶּסֶף בִּשְׁנֵי חֲרִטִים וּשְׁתֵּי חֲלִפוֹת בְּגָדִים וַיִּתֵּן אֶל שְׁנֵי נְעָרָיו וַיִּשְׂאוּ לְפָנָיו: וְהוּא בָא וַיַּעֲמֹד אֶל אֲדֹנָיו וַיֹּאמֶר אֵלָיו אֱלִישָׁע מֵאַיִן גֵּחֲזִי וַיֹּאמֶר לֹא הָלַךְ עַבְדְּךָ אָנֶה וָאָנָה: וַיֹּאמֶר אֵלָיו לֹא לִבִּי הָלַךְ כַּאֲשֶׁר הָפַךְ אִישׁ מֵעַל מֶרְכַּבְתּוֹ לִקְרָאתֶךָ הַעֵת לָקַחַת אֶת הַכֶּסֶף וְלָקַחַת בְּגָדִים וְזֵיתִים וּכְרָמִים וְצֹאן וּבָקָר וַעֲבָדִים וּשְׁפָחוֹת: [מלכים ב' ה, כג,כה-כו]

ט) וְצָרַעַת נַעֲמָן תִּדְבַּק בְּךָ וּבְזַרְעֲךָ לְעוֹלָם וַיֵּצֵא מִלְּפָנָיו מְצֹרָע כַּשָּׁלֶג: [מלכים ב' ה, כז]

י) וְאַרְבָּעָה אֲנָשִׁים הָיוּ מְצֹרָעִים פֶּתַח הַשָּׁעַר וַיֹּאמְרוּ אִישׁ אֶל רֵעֵהוּ מָה אֲנַחְנוּ יֹשְׁבִים פֹּה עַד מָתְנוּ: [מלכים ב' ז, ג]

כ) וֶאֱלִישָׁע חָלָה אֶת חָלְיוֹ אֲשֶׁר יָמוּת בּוֹ וַיֵּרֶד אֵלָיו יוֹאָשׁ מֶלֶךְ יִשְׂרָאֵל וַיֵּבְךְּ עַל פָּנָיו וַיֹּאמַר אָבִי אָבִי רֶכֶב יִשְׂרָאֵל וּפָרָשָׁיו: [מלכים ב' יג, יד]

ל) וְאַבְרָהָם זָקֵן בָּא בַּיָּמִים וַיְיָ בֵּרַךְ אֶת אַבְרָהָם בַּכֹּל: [בראשית כד, א]

מ) וַיְהִי אַחֲרֵי הַדְּבָרִים הָאֵלֶּה וַיֹּאמֶר לְיוֹסֵף הִנֵּה אָבִיךָ חֹלֶה וַיִּקַּח אֶת שְׁנֵי בָנָיו עִמּוֹ אֶת מְנַשֶּׁה וְאֶת אֶפְרָיִם: [בראשית מח, א]

נ) וַיֹּאמֶר יְיָ לֹא יָדוֹן רוּחִי בָאָדָם לְעֹלָם בְּשַׁגַּם הוּא בָשָׂר וְהָיוּ יָמָיו מֵאָה וְעֶשְׂרִים שָׁנָה: [בראשית ו, ג]

ס) וַיָּפֶץ יְיָ אֹתָם מִשָּׁם עַל פְּנֵי כָל הָאָרֶץ וַיַּחְדְּלוּ לִבְנֹת הָעִיר: [בראשית יא, ח]

ע) עַל כֵּן קָרָא שְׁמָהּ בָּבֶל כִּי שָׁם בָּלַל יְיָ שְׂפַת כָּל הָאָרֶץ וּמִשָּׁם הֱפִיצָם יְיָ עַל פְּנֵי כָּל הָאָרֶץ: [בראשית יא, ט]

פ) וְאַנְשֵׁי סְדֹם רָעִים וְחַטָּאִים לַיְיָ מְאֹד: [בראשית יג, יג]

צ) עַל כֵּן לֹא יָקֻמוּ רְשָׁעִים בַּמִּשְׁפָּט וְחַטָּאִים בַּעֲדַת צַדִּיקִים: [תהלים א, ה]

,,וַיֹּאמֶר אֵלָיו אֱלִישָׁע מֵאַיִן גֵּחֲזִי – Scripture states further: ***Elisha said to him, "From where** [have you come], **Geichazi?"*** וַיֹּאמֶר לֹא־הָלַךְ עַבְדְּךָ אָנֶה וָאָנָה – ***And he said, "Your servant has not gone anywhere."*** וַיֹּאמֶר אֵלָיו לֹא־לִבִּי הָלַךְ כַּאֲשֶׁר הָפַךְ־אִישׁ מֵעַל מֶרְכַּבְתּוֹ לִקְרָאתֶךָ – ***And he*** [Elisha] ***said to him, "Did my spirit not accompany*** you ***when the man*** [i.e. Naaman] ***turned from upon his chariot towards you?*** הַעֵת לָקַחַת אֶת־הַכֶּסֶף וְלָקַחַת בְּגָדִים וְזֵיתִים וּכְרָמִים וְצֹאן וּבָקָר וַעֲבָדִים וּשְׁפָחוֹת" – ***Is now the time to take money and to buy clothes, olive groves and vineyards, sheep and oxen, slaves and maidservants?"***[24]

The Gemara analyzes this last verse:

וּמִי שָׁקַל כּוּלֵּי הַאי – **Did [Geichazi] take that much?** כֶּסֶף וּבְגָדִים הוּא דְשָׁקַל – **He took** only **money and clothing!** Why did Elisha list eight items?[25] אָמַר רַבִּי יִצְחָק – **R' Yitzchak said:** Elisha meant to allude to the following: בְּאוֹתָהּ שָׁעָה הָיָה אֱלִישָׁע יוֹשֵׁב וְדוֹרֵשׁ בִּשְׁמוֹנָה שְׁרָצִים – **At that time,** when Naaman came to him, **Elisha was sitting and expounding** chapter ***Shemonah Sheratzim.***[26] נַעֲמָן שַׂר צְבָא מֶלֶךְ אֲרָם הָיָה מְצוֹרָע – Now **Naaman, the general of the king of Aram, was a *metzora.*** אָמְרָה לֵיהּ הַהִיא רְבִיתָא דְּאִישְׁתַּבָּאי מֵאַרְעָא יִשְׂרָאֵל – **A certain** Jewish **girl, who had been taken captive** and carried off **from the Land of Israel, said to him:** אִי אָזְלַתְּ לְגַבֵּי אֱלִישָׁע מַסֵּי לָךְ – **"If you go to Elisha, he will heal you."** He followed her advice. כִּי אֲתָא – **When he came** to Elisha, אָמַר לֵיהּ – **[Elisha] said to him:** זִיל טְבוֹל בְּיַרְדֵּן – **"Go immerse** seven times **in the Jordan** River." אָמַר לֵיהּ – **[Naaman] said to [Elisha],** angrily: אַחוּכֵי קָא מְחַיֵּיכַתְּ בִּי – **"You are jesting with me!"**[27] אָמְרֵי לֵיהּ הַנְהוּ דַּהֲווּ בַּהֲדֵיהּ – **Those** of Naaman's aides **who were with him said to him:** מַאי נַפְקָא לָךְ מִינָּהּ – **"What does it matter to you?** זִיל נַסִּי – **Go test** his words. You have nothing to lose by the effort." אֲזַל וְטָבַל בְּיַרְדְּנָא – **He went and immersed in the Jordan,** וְאִיתַּסִּי – **and was healed.** אֲתָא – **[He]** then **came** back to Elisha אַיְיתֵי לֵיהּ כָּל הָנֵי דִּנְקִיט – and **brought him** as a gift **all those things that he had in his possession.**[28] לֹא צָבֵי לְקַבּוּלֵי מִינֵּיהּ – However, **[Elisha] did not want to accept it from him** and he sent Naaman on his way. גֵּחֲזִי אִיפְּטַר מִקַּמֵּיהּ אֱלִישָׁע – Thereupon, **Geichazi took leave of Elisha,**[29] אֲזַל – **went** to overtake Naaman, שָׁקַל מַאי דְשָׁקַל – **took what he took** from Naaman וְאַפְקִיד – **and secreted it away,** so that Elisha would not know about it. כִּי אֲתָא – **When [Geichazi] came** back to Elisha, who was expounding chapter *Shemonah Sheratzim,* חַזְיֵיהּ אֱלִישָׁע לַצָּרַעַת דַּהֲוָה פָּרְחָה עִילָוֵיהּ רֵישֵׁיהּ – **Elisha saw that *tzaraas* had sprouted upon [Geichazi's] head.**[30] אָמַר לֵיהּ – **[He] said to [Geichazi]:** רָשָׁע – **"Wicked one!** הִגִּיעַ עֵת לִיטּוֹל שְׂכַר שְׁמוֹנָה שְׁרָצִים – **Has the time come** for you **to take the reward for studying** chapter ***Shemonah Sheratzim?***[31] ,,וְצָרַעַת נַעֲמָן תִּדְבַּק־בְּךָ וּבְזַרְעֲךָ לְעוֹלָם – ***May Naaman's tzaraas cleave to you and your children forever!"*** וַיֵּצֵא מִלְּפָנָיו מְצֹרָע כַּשָּׁלֶג" – ***And he*** [Geichazi] ***departed his presence, leprous as snow.***[32]

The Gemara demonstrates that Elisha's curse was fulfilled in its entirety:

,,וְאַרְבָּעָה אֲנָשִׁים הָיוּ מְצֹרָעִים פֶּתַח הַשָּׁעַר" – Scripture states:[33] ***There were four men who were metzoraim at the opening of the gate.*** אָמַר רַבִּי יוֹחָנָן גֵּחֲזִי וּשְׁלֹשָׁה בָּנָיו – **R' Yochanan said:** These were **Geichazi and his three sons.**[34]

Having mentioned above the proper method of dealing with sinners like Geichazi, the Gemara notes other areas in which the same methodology is in order:

תַּנְיָא – **It was taught in a Baraisa:** אָמַר רַבִּי שִׁמְעוֹן בֶּן אֶלְעָזָר – R' SHIMON BEN ELAZAR SAID: יֵצֶר תִּינוֹק וְאִשָּׁה – When dealing with THE INCLINATION towards procreation, with A CHILD OR with A WOMAN, תְּהֵא שְׂמֹאל דּוֹחָה וְיָמִין מְקָרֶבֶת – THE LEFT hand SHOULD PUSH them AWAY, BUT THE RIGHT hand SHOULD DRAW them CLOSE.[35]

NOTES

and you may then take two talents of silver. The Gemara (ibid.) concludes that Geichazi was ultimately afflicted with *tzaraas* because he swore falsely, as vain oaths bring on *tzaraas. Rashi* adds that when the verse states, *He pressed him,* it means not that Naaman pressed Geichazi to accept the gift, but that Geichazi pressed Naaman to give it (see *Rashi* and *Maharsha;* see also *Rashash*).

24. *II Kings* 5:25-26.

25. Although Geichazi took enough money to buy all those items, it was unnecessary for Elisha to list them, unless he meant to allude to something (*Maharsha*).

26. Literally: eight creeping creatures. This is the fourteenth chapter of Tractate *Shabbos,* which begins with the words שְׁמֹנָה שְׁרָצִים (*Rashi*).

27. As Scripture states (*II Kings* 5:12), Naaman said: *Why, the waters of Damascus are better than all the waters of Israel; if I bathe in them, will I be healed?* [The entire story is cited at length in *II Kings* ch. 5. The Gemara will add certain details that are not mentioned explicitly in the Scriptural account.]

28. This is a reference to the huge gift that Naaman had brought along from Aram as an offering to Elisha. It consisted of ten talents of silver, six thousand golden coins and ten changes of clothing (*Maharsha;* see *II Kings* 5:5).

29. Acting as though he had personal matters to attend to (*Maharsha*).

30. Elisha knew that this was the *tzaraas* of Naaman clinging to Geichazi and he thus realized that Geichazi had accepted a gift from Naaman (*Yad Ramah;* see also note 23).

31. Elisha mentioned eight items, i.e. money, clothes and six other articles that Geichazi might purchase with them, to allude to the fact that Geichazi seemed to have seized his reward for studying *Shemonah Sheratzim* [literally: eight creeping creatures] (*Rashi*). In effect, Elisha meant that by taking this reward improperly Geichazi had prematurely seized in this world a reward for the Torah he had studied, and had thereby forfeited his reward for it in the World to Come (see *Rashi* to *Sotah* 47a ד״ה הגיע). [Elisha alluded to the eight creeping creatures simply because that was the subject they were then engaged in.]

Maharsha sees in the reference to the creeping creatures an allusion to Geichazi's affliction with *tzaraas.* Elisha meant: Just as the creeping creatures convey *tumah,* so too you, Geichazi, will convey *tumah,* for you will be a *metzora* forever.

32. Ibid. v. 27. Since the verse states that Geichazi left Elisha's presence *leprous as snow,* it implies that when he entered Elisha's presence he was somewhat leprous, albeit not as snow, for Naaman's *tzaraas* had already begun to sprout upon his head (*Maharsha*).

Maharsha explains the propriety of this particular curse for Geichazi's misdeed: Naaman considered his cure to have been effected naturally through the therapeutic power of the Jordan River, and he therefore offered Elisha compensation, just as one pays a doctor. Elisha, however, refused the gift so as to demonstrate that the cure was a miraculous one and he deserved no compensation. When Geichazi went and accepted the gift, he undermined Elisha's assertion that the cure was miraculous. Elisha therefore cursed him that the *tzaraas* should cleave to him and his children forever — and that it should never be healed through natural means (see also *Rambam, Commentary* to *Avos* 2:10).

The reason Geichazi's children were also cursed is that they were in collusion with their father (*Radak, II Kings* 5:27; see *Margaliyos HaYam*).

33. Ibid. 7:3.

34. Who were banished from the city because of their *tzaraas* (*Rashi, II Kings* ibid.; see note 21). Thus, Geichazi and his children were afflicted with *tzaraas* (see *Maharsha* and *Margaliyos HaYam*).

35. If one subdues his inclination towards procreation completely, he will not produce offspring, and that is undesirable. On the other hand, if one overindulges his inclination — even within the permissible realm — he is bound to come to sin, for having allowed his inclination free rein he will ultimately be unable to restrain himself from illicit

לב א מיי' פ"ד מהל' תשובה הלכה א:

בחברון מלך שבע שנים ובירושלים מלך שלשים ושלש שנים וכתיב א) בחברון מלך על יהודה שבע שנים וששה חדשים וגו' והני ששה חדשים לא קחשיב ש"מ נצטרע א) אמר לפניו רבש"ע מחול לי על אותו עון מחול לך ב) עשה עמי אות לטובה ויראו שונאי ויבושו כי אתה ה' עזרתני ונחמתני א"ל בחייך איני מודיע אבל אני מודיע בחיי שלמה בנך ב) בשעה שבנה שלמה את בית המקדש ביקש להכנים ארון לבית קדשי הקדשים דבקו שערים זה בזה אמר עשרים וארבעה רננות ולא נענה אמר ג) שאו שערים ראשיכם והנשאו פתחי עולם ויבא מלך הכבוד מי זה מלך הכבוד ה' עזוז וגבור ה' גבור מלחמה ונאמר ד) שאו שערים ראשיכם ושאו פתחי עולם ויבא מלך הכבוד וגו' ולא נענה כיון שאמר ה) ה' אלהים אל תשב פני משיחך זכרה לחסדי דויד עבדך מיד נענה באותה שעה נהפכו פני שונאי דוד כשולי קדירה וידעו כל ישראל שמחל לו הקב"ה על אותו העון גחזי דכתיב ג) ו) וילך אלישע דמשק להיכא אזל ד) א"ר יוחנן שהלך להחזיר גחזי בתשובה ולא חזר אמר לו חזור בך אמר לו כך מקובלני ממך ה) א החוטא ומחטיא את הרבים אין מספיקין בידו לעשות תשובה מאי עבד איכא דאמרי אבן שואבת תלה לחטאת ירבעם והעמידה בין שמים לארץ ואיכא דאמרי שם חקק בפיה והיתה מכרזת ואומרת אנכי ולא יהיה לך וא"ד רבנן דחה מקמיה שנאמר ז) ויאמרו בני הנביאים אל אלישע הנה [נא] המקום אשר אנחנו יושבים שם לפניך צר ממנו מכלל דעד השתא לא הוו (פיישי) [צר] ו) תנו רבנן לעולם תהא שמאל דוחה וימין מקרבת לא כאלישע שדחפו לגחזי בשתי ידים גחזי דכתיב ח) ויאמר נעמן הואל ז) וקח ככרים (ויפצר) [ויפרץ] בו ויצר ככרים כסף וגו' ויאמר אליו אלישע מאין גחזי ויאמר לא הלך עבדך אנה ואנה ויאמר אליו לא לבי הלך כאשר הפך איש מעל מרכבתו לקראתך העת לקחת את הכסף ולקחת בגדים וזיתים וכרמים וצאן ובקר ועבדים ושפחות ומי שקל כולי האי כסף ובגדים הוא דשקל אמר רבי יצחק באותה שעה היה אלישע יושב ודורש בשמונה שרצים נעמן שר צבא מלך ארם היה מצורע אמרה ליה ההיא רביתא דאישתבאי מארעא ישראל אי אזלת לגבי אלישע מסי לך כי אתא א"ל זיל טבול בירדן א"ל אחוכי קא מחייכת בי אמרי ליה הנהו דהוו בהדיה מאי נפקא לך מינה זיל נסי אזל וטבל בירדנא ואיתסי אתא אייתי ליה כל הני דנקיט לא צבי לקבולי מיניה גחזי איפטר מקמיה אלישע אזל שקל מאי דשקל ואפקיד כי אתא חזייה אלישע לצרעת דהוה פרחא עילויה רישיה א"ל רשע הגיע עת ליטול שכר שמנה שרצים ט) וצרעת נעמן תדבק בך ובזרעך עד עולם ויצא מלפניו מצורע כשלג: י) וארבעה אנשים היו מצורעים פתח השער אמר ר' יוחנן גחזי ושלשה בניו תניא ח) א"ר שמעון בן אלעזר יצר תינוק ואשה תהא שמאל דוחה וימין מקרבת ט) ת"ר ג' חלאים חלה אלישע אחד שגירה דובים בתינוקות ואחד שדחפו לגחזי בשתי ידים ואחד שמת בו [שנא' כ) ואלישע חלה את חליו וגו'] י) עד אברהם לא היה זקנה כל דחזי לאברהם אמר האי יצחק כל דחזי ליצחק אמר האי אברהם כ) בעא אברהם רחמי דליהוי ליה זקנה שנאמר ל) ואברהם זקן בא בימים עד יעקב לא הוה חולשא בעא רחמי והוה חולשא שנאמר מ) ויאמר ליוסף הנה אביך חולה עד אלישע לא הוה איניש חליש ל) דמיתפח ואתא אלישע ובעא רחמי ואיתפח שנא' כ) ואלישע חלה את חליו אשר ימות בו מ): **מתני'** דור המבול אין להם חלק לעוה"ב ואין עומדין בדין שנא' נ) לא ידון רוחי באדם לעולם לא דין ולא רוח דור הפלגה אין להם חלק לעולם הבא שנאמר ס) ויפץ ה' אותם משם על פני כל הארץ נ) (וכתיב ומשם הפיצם) ויפץ ה' אותם בעוה"ז ע) ומשם הפיצם ה' לעולם הבא אנשי סדום אין להם חלק לעולם הבא שנא' פ) ואנשי סדום רעים וחטאים לה' מאד רעים בעולם הזה וחטאים לעולם הבא אבל עומדין בדין ר' נחמיה אומר אלו ואלו אין עומדין בדין שנאמר צ) על כן לא יקומו רשעים

בחברון מלך שבע שנים וששה חדשים. מדהכא חשיב להו ובאידך קרא לא חשיב להו ש"מ לא היה מלכותו שלימה שנצטרע אותן ו' חדשים: ה"ג אבל בחיי בנך אני מודיע ולא גרסינן לך: כ"ד רננות. בין תפלה תחנה ורנה איכא כ"ד: וילך אלישע דמשק להיכא אזל: שואבת. מגבהת מתכת בלא נגיעה כעין אותה שלועזין קלאמניס"ה בלע"ז ועל ידי אותה אבן העמיד עגלים של ירבעם באויר: רבנן דחה מקמיה. התלמידים דחה מישיבתו של אלישע: צר ממנו. מכלל דעד האידנא לא הוה צר: הואל וקח. השבע שאלישע שלחך: ויפצר בו. גחזי: העת לקחת את הכסף והבגדים וגו'. שמנה דברים קא חשיב בהאי קרא: וגחזי מי שקל כולי האי. מנעמן כסף ובגדים הוא דשקל דכתיב ויצר ככרים וגו': אותה שעה. היה אלישע עוסק בפרק שמונה שרצים אמר לו הגיע עת ליטול שכר פרק שמונה שרצים שעסקתי וכו' ולהכי כתב בהאי קרא שמנה דברים כנגד אותו פרק כלומר בכסף ובגדים שקבלת ממנו מנעמן סבור אתה לקנות דברים הללו להיותם לך שכר שמונה שרצים: יצר. תאותו אם מרחיקה ממנו לגמרי ממעט ישיבת עולם ואם מקרבה לגמרי בא לידי איסור שאינו יכול לכבוש יצרו מדבר עבירה: תינוק ואשה. דעתן קלה ואם תדחה אותם מטרדן מן העולם: חלה. חד. חליו תרי. אשר ימות בו תלת: בעא רחמי דלהוי חולשא. כדי שיהא פנאי לבניו לבא כל אחד ואחד ממקומו להיות עליו בשעת מיתה שכיון שרואין שנפל למטה יודעין שימות ומתקבצין ובאין: מתפח. מתרפא: **מתני'** לא ידון רוחי לא דין ולא רוח. שאין עומדין בדין ואין להם רוח להיות עם הצדיקים שיש להם חלק: ויפץ [ה' אותם ומשם הפיצם. ויפץ] בעולם הזה ומשם הפיצם בעולם הבא: אלו ואלו. אנשי דור המבול ואנשי סדום ובהא פליג ר' נחמיה:

ליקוטי רש"י

עשה עמי אות לטובה. שיהא ניכר לאחרים שמחלת לי. ויראו שונאי. האות ויבושו ולא שמע לו הקב"ה ליתן האות בימיו אלא בימי שלמה בנו כשדבקו השערים זה בזה ולא נפתחו עד שאמר (דה"ב ו') אל תשב פני משיחך זכרה לחסדי דוד עבדך [תהלים פו, יז]. על אותו עון. דבת שבע. דבקו שערים. של בית קדשי הקדשים. עשרים וארבע רננות. רנה תפלה תחינה כתובים בתפלת שלמה עד עשרים וארבע ויש אומרים עשרים וארבע ברכות דתענית ולא נהירא. אמר שאו שערים ראשיכם והנשאו פתחי עולם ויבוא מלך הכבוד. רהטו שערים בתריה למבלעיה סברי דעל עצמו אמר מלך הכבוד אמרו לו שערים מי הוא זה מלך הכבוד אמר איהו ה' עזוז וגבור (תהלים כד). שונאי דוד. משפחת שאול שמעי וכיוצא בו [שבת ל.]. עשרים וארבע רננות. כתיבי בפרשה, בין רנה ותחנה ותפלה ובקשה [מו"ק ט.]. אל תשב פני משיחך. מלעשות טובה עמדי ואם לא למעני עשה למענך [דה"ב ו, מב]. ויבא אלישע דמשק. להחזיר את גיחזי בתשובה [מ"ב ח, ז]. אבן שואבת. דרך אותה האבן להגביה המתכת ולתלותה באויר [ע"ז מד.]. שמגבהת את המתכת מן הארץ ומעמידתו באויר [ועי"י אותו אבן העמיד העגלים של ירבעם באויר]. רבנן דחה. דוחה היה את התלמידים מפני אלישע כשהיה משמש לפניו דכתיב לאחר שפירש ממנו המקום אשר אנחנו יושבין בית המדרש של רבנן צר ממנו שנתוספו התלמידים שהיה גחזי דוחה [סוטה מז.]. ויאמרו בני הנביאים. רבותינו אמרו מכאן שהיה גיחזי דוחה התלמידים מלפניו כשנטרד באו תלמידים רבים ונדחק המקום מהם [מ"ב ו, א]. הואל. השבע שלחך [שם ה, כג]. העת לקחת את הכסף. להתעשר ולקחת ממנו בגדים וזיתים וגו' [מלכים ב, ה]. מי שקל כולי האי. בהאי קרא כתיב שמנה דברים כסף ובגדים וצאן ובקר ועבדים ושפחות וזיתים וכרמים. כסף ובגדים הוא דשקל. דכתיב ויצר ככרים כסף בשני חריטים ושתי חליפות בגדים. בשמנה שרצים. בפרק שמנה שרצים (שבת קז). הגיע עת ליטול שכר. תורתך בעולם הזה [שם]. וארבעה אנשים. גיחזי ובניו. פתח השער. כמו שנאמר בדד ישב מחוץ למחנה מושבו (ויקרא י"ג מ"ו) [שם ז, ג]. כדקטלינהו ינאי מלכא לרבנן. כדאמרינן בקידושין בהאומר לשלוחו (דף סו). בעלי שרוי בתוכך. נשיא היה כדאמרינן בחגיגה (דף טז:). עבדו ליה יקרא טובא. כיבדתו. כמה יפה אכסניא זו. במעשיה. טרוטות. עגולות. בכך אתה עוסק. מסתכל באשת איש. אחוי ליה בידיה. שיקבלנו. יצר. של תשמיש תקרבנו בימין שלא יקוץ בפריה ורביה וכן תינוק פן יברח ויאבד את עצמו ואשה אף היא דעתה קלה ואם ירדפוה תצא לתרבות רעה [סוטה מז.]. חליו אשר ימות בו. מכלל דחלה עוד שלא מת בו [ב"מ פז.]. אחד שגירה דובים. בעון שגירה דובים בתינוקות. חלה. חד את חליו תרי וחד אשר ימות בו [סוטה שם]. בעא אברהם רחמי. כדי שיכירו בינו ובין בנו. בעא רחמי והוה חולשא. שיחלה אדם לפני מותו ויצוה לביתו. חליש דמיתפח. ונתרפא. חליו אשר ימות בו. מכלל דחלה עוד שלא מת בו [ב"מ שם]. ויפץ ה' אותם משם. בעולם הזה מה שאמרו פן נפוץ נתקיים עליהם הוא שאמר שלמה (משלי י, כד) מגורת רשע היא תבואנו [בראשית יא, יח]. ומשם הפיצם. למד שאין להם חלק לעולם הבא [בראשית יא, ט].

מסורת הש"ס

א) שבת ל. ע"ש, ב) שם מו"ק ט., ג) אין זה לשון המקרא וכך הוא לשון המקרא ויבא אלישע (מ"ב ח') גו' ועיי' רש"א במ"א, ד) סוטה מז. [ע"ש], ה) [יומא פז.], ו) סוטה שם, ז) בקרא קח, ח) [שמחות פ"ב סוטה מז.], ט) [סוטה מז:], י) [ב"מ פז.], כ) [ב"מ פז.], ל) [לדעת הערוך בערך תפח גרס הכא ואיתפח כמו בסמוך], מ) [מכלל דחלה חלי אחריתא כך איתא בב"מ פז.], נ) [בסה"מ ל"ג].

תורה אור השלם

א) בְּחֶבְרוֹן מָלַךְ עַל יְהוּדָה שֶׁבַע שָׁנִים וְשִׁשָּׁה חֳדָשִׁים וּבִירוּשָׁלַיִם מָלַךְ שְׁלֹשִׁים וְשָׁלֹשׁ שָׁנָה עַל כָּל יִשְׂרָאֵל וִיהוּדָה: [שמואל ב' ה, ה]

ב) עֲשֵׂה עִמִּי אוֹת לְטוֹבָה וְיִרְאוּ שֹׂנְאַי וְיֵבֹשׁוּ כִּי אַתָּה יְיָ עֲזַרְתַּנִי וְנִחַמְתָּנִי: [תהלים פו, יז]

ג) שְׂאוּ שְׁעָרִים רָאשֵׁיכֶם וְהִנָּשְׂאוּ פִּתְחֵי עוֹלָם וְיָבוֹא מֶלֶךְ הַכָּבוֹד: מִי זֶה מֶלֶךְ הַכָּבוֹד יְיָ עִזּוּז וְגִבּוֹר יְיָ גִּבּוֹר מִלְחָמָה: [תהלים כד, ז-ח]

ד) שְׂאוּ שְׁעָרִים רָאשֵׁיכֶם וּשְׂאוּ פִּתְחֵי עוֹלָם וְיָבֹא מֶלֶךְ הַכָּבוֹד: מִי הוּא זֶה מֶלֶךְ הַכָּבוֹד יְיָ צְבָאוֹת הוּא מֶלֶךְ הַכָּבוֹד סֶלָה: [תהלים כד, ט-י]

ה) יְיָ אֱלֹהִים אַל תָּשֵׁב פְּנֵי מְשִׁיחֶךָ זָכְרָה לְחַסְדֵי דָּוִיד עַבְדֶּךָ: [דברי הימים ב' ו, מב]

ו) וַיָּבֹא אֱלִישָׁע דַּמֶּשֶׂק וּבֶן הֲדַד מֶלֶךְ אֲרָם חֹלֶה וַיֻּגַּד לוֹ לֵאמֹר בָּא אִישׁ הָאֱלֹהִים עַד הֵנָּה: [מלכים ב' ח, ז]

ז) וַיֹּאמְרוּ בְנֵי הַנְּבִיאִים אֶל אֱלִישָׁע הִנֵּה נָא הַמָּקוֹם אֲשֶׁר אֲנַחְנוּ יֹשְׁבִים שָׁם לְפָנֶיךָ צַר מִמֶּנּוּ: [מלכים ב' ו, א]

ח) וַיֹּאמֶר נַעֲמָן הוֹאֵל קַח כִּכָּרָיִם וַיִּפְרָץ בּוֹ וַיָּצַר כִּכְּרַיִם כֶּסֶף בִּשְׁנֵי חֲרִטִים וּשְׁתֵּי חֲלִפוֹת בְּגָדִים וַיִּתֵּן אֶל שְׁנֵי נְעָרָיו וַיִּשְׂאוּ לְפָנָיו: וְהוּא בָא וַיַּעֲמֹד אֶל אֲדֹנָיו וַיֹּאמֶר אֵלָיו אֱלִישָׁע מֵאַן גֵּחֲזִי וַיֹּאמֶר לֹא הָלַךְ עַבְדְּךָ אָנֶה וָאָנָה: וַיֹּאמֶר אֵלָיו לֹא לִבִּי הָלַךְ כַּאֲשֶׁר הָפַךְ אִישׁ מֵעַל מֶרְכַּבְתּוֹ לִקְרָאתֶךָ הַעֵת לָקַחַת אֶת הַכֶּסֶף וְלָקַחַת בְּגָדִים וְזֵיתִים וּכְרָמִים וְצֹאן וּבָקָר וַעֲבָדִים וּשְׁפָחוֹת: [מלכים ב' ה, כג,כה-כו] ט) וְצָרַעַת נַעֲמָן תִּדְבַּק בְּךָ וּבְזַרְעֲךָ לְעוֹלָם וַיֵּצֵא מִלְּפָנָיו מְצֹרָע כַּשָּׁלֶג: [מלכים ב' ה, כז] י) וְאַרְבָּעָה אֲנָשִׁים הָיוּ מְצֹרָעִים פֶּתַח הַשָּׁעַר וַיֹּאמְרוּ אִישׁ אֶל רֵעֵהוּ מָה אֲנַחְנוּ יֹשְׁבִים פֹּה עַד מָתְנוּ: [מלכים ב' ז, ג] כ) וֶאֱלִישָׁע חָלָה אֶת חָלְיוֹ אֲשֶׁר יָמוּת בּוֹ וַיֵּרֶד אֵלָיו יוֹאָשׁ מֶלֶךְ יִשְׂרָאֵל וַיֵּבְךְּ עַל פָּנָיו וַיֹּאמַר אָבִי אָבִי רֶכֶב יִשְׂרָאֵל וּפָרָשָׁיו: [מלכים ב' יג, יד] ל) וְאַבְרָהָם זָקֵן בָּא בַּיָּמִים וַיְיָ בֵּרַךְ אֶת אַבְרָהָם בַּכֹּל: [בראשית כד, א] מ) וַיְהִי אַחֲרֵי הַדְּבָרִים הָאֵלֶּה וַיֹּאמֶר לְיוֹסֵף הִנֵּה אָבִיךָ חֹלֶה וַיִּקַּח אֶת שְׁנֵי בָנָיו עִמּוֹ אֶת מְנַשֶּׁה וְאֶת אֶפְרָיִם: [בראשית מח, א] נ) וַיֹּאמֶר יְיָ לֹא יָדוֹן רוּחִי בָאָדָם לְעֹלָם בְּשַׁגַּם הוּא בָשָׂר וְהָיוּ יָמָיו מֵאָה וְעֶשְׂרִים שָׁנָה: [בראשית ו, ג] ס) וַיָּפֶץ יְיָ אֹתָם מִשָּׁם עַל פְּנֵי כָל הָאָרֶץ וַיַּחְדְּלוּ לִבְנֹת הָעִיר: [בראשית יא, ח] ע) עַל כֵּן קָרָא שְׁמָהּ בָּבֶל כִּי שָׁם בָּלַל יְיָ שְׂפַת כָּל הָאָרֶץ וּמִשָּׁם הֱפִיצָם יְיָ עַל פְּנֵי כָּל הָאָרֶץ: [בראשית יא, ט] פ) וְאַנְשֵׁי סְדֹם רָעִים וְחַטָּאִים לַייָ מְאֹד: [בראשית יג, יג] צ) עַל כֵּן לֹא יָקֻמוּ רְשָׁעִים בַּמִּשְׁפָּט וְחַטָּאִים בַּעֲדַת צַדִּיקִים: [תהלים א, ה]

The Gemara notes Elisha's punishment for rejecting Geichazi completely:

תָּנוּ רַבָּנַן – **The Rabbis taught in a Baraisa:** שְׁלֹשָׁה חֳלָאִים חָלָה אֱלִישָׁע – ELISHA TOOK ILL WITH THREE ILLNESSES at different points in his life. אֶחָד שֶׁגֵּירָה דוּבִּים בְּתִינוֹקוֹת – ONE WAS ON ACCOUNT OF INCITING BEARS AGAINST THE CHILDREN;[36] וְאֶחָד שֶׁדְּחָפוֹ לְגֵחֲזִי בִּשְׁתֵּי יָדַיִם – ONE WAS ON ACCOUNT OF PUSHING GEICHAZI AWAY WITH BOTH HANDS; וְאֶחָד שֶׁמֵּת בּוֹ – AND ONE WAS THE ILLNESS FROM WHICH HE DIED, [שֶׁנֶּאֱמַר ,,וֶאֱלִישָׁע חָלָה אֶת־חָלְיוֹ וגו׳ "] – [AS IT IS STATED:[37] *ELISHA TOOK ILL WITH HIS ILLNESS from which he would die*].[38]

The Gemara notes the historic significance of Elisha's recovery from two illnesses before succumbing to the third:

עַד אַבְרָהָם לֹא הָיָה זִקְנָה – **Until** the time of **Abraham, there were no** visible signs of **old age.** Now, Abraham's and Isaac's features appeared identical,[39] and thus, כָּל דְּחָזֵי לְאַבְרָהָם אָמַר הַאי יִצְחָק – **whoever saw Abraham would say, "That is Isaac,"** כָּל דְּחָזֵי לְיִצְחָק אָמַר הַאי אַבְרָהָם – and **whoever saw Isaac would say, "That is Abraham."** בְּעָא אַבְרָהָם רַחֲמֵי דְּלֶיהֱוֵי לֵיהּ זִקְנָה – **Abraham beseeched** God for **mercy, so that he should have** physical indications of **old age,** and from then on, visible signs of old age came into being,[40] שֶׁנֶּאֱמַר ,,וְאַבְרָהָם זָקֵן בָּא בַּיָּמִים" – **as it is stated:**[41] ***Now Abraham was old, well on in years.***[42] עַד יַעֲקֹב לֹא הֲוָה חוּלְשָׁא – **Until** the time of **Jacob, there was no feebleness** preceding death.[43] בְּעָא רַחֲמֵי וַהֲוָה חוּלְשָׁא – **[Jacob] beseeched** God for **mercy and** from then on **feebleness came into being,** שֶׁנֶּאֱמַר ,,וַיֹּאמֶר לְיוֹסֵף הִנֵּה אָבִיךָ חֹלֶה" – **as it is stated:**[44] ***And he said to Joseph, "Behold! Your father is ill."***[45] עַד אֱלִישָׁע לֹא הֲוָה אִינִישׁ חָלִישׁ דְּמִיתְּפַח – **Until** the time of **Elisha, there was never an ill person who recovered** from his illness.[46] וְאָתָא אֱלִישָׁע וּבְעָא רַחֲמֵי וְאִיתְּפַח – **Then Elisha came and beseeched** God for **mercy** when he was ill, **and he recovered,** שֶׁנֶּאֱמַר ,,וֶאֱלִישָׁע חָלָה אֶת־חָלְיוֹ אֲשֶׁר יָמוּת בּוֹ" – **as it is stated:**[47] ***Elisha took ill with his illness from which he would die,*** which implies that he had previously contracted other serious illnesses from which he had recovered.

Mishnah

The previous Mishnah concluded with a list of individuals who have no share in the World to Come. The following Mishnah lists *groups* of people who have no share in the World to Come:

דּוֹר הַמַּבּוּל אֵין לָהֶם חֵלֶק לָעוֹלָם הַבָּא – **The** people of the **Generation of the Flood have no share in the World to Come,** וְאֵין עוֹמְדִין בַּדִּין – **nor will they stand for Judgment,**[48] שֶׁנֶּאֱמַר ,,לֹא־יָדוֹן רוּחִי בָאָדָם לְעֹלָם" – **as it is stated:**[49] ***My spirit shall not contend evermore concerning man*** – לֹא דִּין וְלֹא רוּחַ – which implies, **neither judgment nor spirit.**[50]

דּוֹר הַפְּלָגָה אֵין לָהֶם חֵלֶק לָעוֹלָם הַבָּא – **The** people of the **Generation of the Dispersion have no share in the World to Come,**[51] שֶׁנֶּאֱמַר ,,וַיָּפֶץ ה׳ אֹתָם מִשָּׁם עַל־פְּנֵי כָל־הָאָרֶץ" – **as it is stated:**[52] ***HASHEM dispersed them from there***

NOTES

behavior. Therefore, the proper attitude is to strike a balance, keeping the Inclination at arm's length with the "left hand," while utilizing it with the "right hand" (*Rashi;* see *Tur Even HaEzer,* end of §25).

When dealing with a child or a woman, one must take extra care to avoid offending them, for they are highly emotional. If rebuked too harshly, they may become completely distraught, and that can lead to undesirable consequences (see *Maseches Semachos* 2:4-6). On the other hand, if they are never criticized they will acquire bad habits. Therefore, one should rebuke them with the "left hand," while offering encouragement with the "right hand." That is, the encouragement should be stronger than the rebuke (*Rashi* here and *Sotah* 47a; *Yad Ramah;* cf. *Rav Sherira Gaon,* cited in *Otzar HaGeonim* to *Sotah,* p. 270).

36. Once, upon leaving Jericho, Elisha was accosted and verbally abused by a group of worthless and contemptuous youngsters, and Elisha cursed them. As a result, two bears emerged from the forest and killed forty-two of the youngsters. For causing their deaths, Elisha was punished with an illness (*II Kings* 2:23-24). See *Sotah* 46b for a discussion of this incident.

37. Ibid. 13:14.

38. The phrase *took ill* alludes to the first illness; *with his illness* alludes to the second one; and *from which he would die* alludes to the third, mortal illness (*Rashi*).

39. The Gemara in *Bava Metzia* (87a) relates that God made Isaac's features appear similar to Abraham's to eliminate the claims of scoffers that Abraham could not have parented him at the age of one hundred years (see also *Rashi* to *Genesis* 25:19). Since there were no visible signs of old age, such as gray hair, it was difficult to distinguish Abraham from Isaac (see *Maharsha* to *Bava Metzia* 87a).

40. The primary purpose of this is to ensure that elderly people are treated respectfully by their juniors (*Midrash Tanchuma, Chayei Sarah* §1).

41. *Genesis* 24:1.

42. A previous verse (*Genesis* 18:11) already stated: וְאַבְרָהָם וְשָׂרָה זְקֵנִים בָּאִים בַּיָּמִים, *Abraham and Sarah were old, well on in years.* That verse, which describes Abraham and Sarah prior to Isaac's birth, refers to *chronological* old age. The verse cited here, which describes Abraham at a time when Isaac was already a grown man with a full beard who was seeking a wife, therefore means that Abraham was *visibly* old – for *his* beard turned white (*Maharsha* ibid.). Since Isaac was about to be married, it was especially important that father and son not be mistaken for each other (*Iyun Yaakov, Bava Metzia* 87a).

43. See *Tosafos* to *Bava Basra* 16b ד״ה שכל.

The purpose of such feebleness would be to allow the children of the dying man to travel from their respective places and be at their father's side in his last hours. Further, this would allow the father the opportunity to instruct his family [as to how they should conduct themselves after his death] (*Rashi* here and to *Bava Metzia* 87a ד״ה בעא רחמי והוה חולשא).

Pirkei DeRabbi Eliezer ch. 52 (cited by *Gilyon HaShas* to *Berachos* 53a) explains further: From the time of Creation up until Jacob's time no man would take ill before death. Rather, a man walking on the road or in the marketplace would sneeze and his soul would exit via his nostrils. This, *Pirkei DeRabbi Eliezer* says, is the origin of the custom to respond "Life!" when someone sneezes (the equivalent of our "Gesundheit" or "God bless you").

44. *Genesis* 48:1.

45. "*Behold*" indicates something new or surprising (*Margaliyos HaYam,* based on *Rashbam* to *Genesis* 25:24; cf. *Maharsha* to *Bava Metzia* 87a).

46. That is, there was never a *deathly* ill person who recovered (see *Tosafos* to *Bava Basra* 16b ד״ה שכל).

47. *II Kings* 13:14.

48. They have no share in the World to Come, but, on the other hand, they will not be resurrected to receive a punishment for their sins on the Final Day of Judgment which precedes the World to Come, because they already received their punishment through the Flood (*Yad Ramah;* see also *Tos. Yom Tov;* cf. *Meiri*).

49. *Genesis* 6:3.

50. The Mishnah interprets the word יָדוֹן, *contend,* as a derivative of דִּין, *judgment.* Furthermore, it interprets the word רוּחִי, *My spirit,* as a reference to the soul, which is the Godly spirit that lives on in the World to Come (see *Maharsha*). Thus, it infers from the phrase לֹא־יָדוֹן רוּחִי that the Generation of the Flood will neither stand for Judgment nor live on in the World to Come.

51. This refers to the generation that built the Tower of Babel and was dispersed by God (see *Genesis* 11:1-9).

[In all probability, the correct vowelization is דּוֹר הַפְּלַגָּה or דּוֹר הַפְּלָגָה (the ה is not part of the root, but is the definite article, as in the parallel case of דּוֹר הַמַּבּוּל). We have followed, however, the popular and long-accepted vowelization – דּוֹר הַפְּלָגָה.]

52. Ibid. 11:8.

בחברון מלך שבע שנים ובירושלים מלך שלשים ושלש שנים וכתיב [א] בחברון מלך על יהודה שבע שנים וששה חדשים וגו' והני ששה חדשים לא קחשיב ש"מ נצטרע [ה] אמר לפניו רבש"ע מחול לי על אותו עון מחול לך [ב] עשה עמי אות לטובה ויראו שונאי ויבושו כי אתה ה' עזרתני ונחמתני א"ל בחייך איני מודיע אבל אני מודיע בחיי שלמה בנך [ג] בשעה שבנה שלמה את בית המקדש ביקש להכנים ארון לבית קדשי הקדשים דבקו שערים זה בזה אמר עשרים וארבעה רננות ולא נענה אמר [ג] שאו שערים ראשיכם והנשאו פתחי עולם ויבא מלך הכבוד מי זה מלך הכבוד ה' עזוז וגבור ה' גבור מלחמה ונאמר [ד] שאו שערים ראשיכם ושאו פתחי עולם ויבא מלך הכבוד וגו' ולא נענה כיון שאמר [ה] ה' אלהים אל תשב פני משיחך זכרה לחסדי דויד עבדך מיד נענה באותה שעה נהפכו פני שונאי דוד כשולי קדירה וידעו כל ישראל שמחל לו הקב"ה על אותו העון גחזי דכתיב [ו] [ו] וילך אלישע דמשק להיכא אזל [ד] א"ר יוחנן שהלך להחזיר גחזי בתשובה ולא חזר אמר לו חזור בך אמר לו כך מקובלני ממך [ה] [א] החוטא ומחטיא את הרבים אין מספיקין בידו לעשות תשובה מאי עבד איכא דאמרי אבן שואבת תלה לחטאת ירבעם והעמידה בין שמים לארץ ואיכא דאמרי שם חקק בפיה והיתה מכרזת ואומרת אנכי ולא יהיה לך וא"ד רבנן דחה מקמיה שנאמר [ז] ויאמרו בני הנביאים אל אלישע הנה [נא] המקום אשר אנחנו יושבים שם לפניך צר ממנו מכלל דעד השתא לא הוו (פיישי) [צר] [ו] תנו רבנן לעולם תהא שמאל דוחה וימין מקרבת לא כאלישע שדחפו לגחזי בשתי ידים גחזי דכתיב [ח] ויאמר נעמן הואל [ז] וקח ככרים (ויפצר) [ויפרץ] בו ויצר ככרים כסף וגו' ויאמר אליו אלישע מאין גחזי ויאמר לא הלך עבדך אנה ואנה ויאמר אליו לא לבי הלך כאשר הפך איש מעל מרכבתו לקראתך העת לקחת את הכסף ולקחת בגדים וזיתים וכרמים וצאן ובקר ועבדים ושפחות ומי שקל כולי האי כסף ובגדים הוא דשקל אמר רבי יצחק באותה שעה היה אלישע יושב ודורש בשמונה שרצים נעמן שר צבא מלך ארם היה מצורע אמרה ליה ההיא רביתא דאישתבאי מארעא ישראל אי אזלת לגבי אלישע מסי לך כי אתא א"ל זיל טבול בירדן א"ל אחוכי קא מחייכת בי אמרי ליה הנהו דהוו בהדיה מאי נפקא לך מינה זיל נסי אזל וטבל בירדנא ואיתסי אתא אייתי ליה כל הני דנקיט לא צבי לקבולי מיניה גחזי איפטר מקמיה אלישע אזל שקל מאי דשקל ואפקיד כי אתא חזייה אלישע לצרעת דהוה פרחא עילויה רישיה א"ל רשע הגיע עת ליטול שכר שמנה שרצים [ט] וצרעת נעמן תדבק בך ובזרעך עד עולם ויצא מלפניו מצורע כשלג: [י] וארבעה אנשים היו מצורעים פתח השער אמר ר' יוחנן גחזי ושלשה בניו תניא [ח] א"ר שמעון בן אלעזר יצר תינוק ואשה תהא שמאל דוחה וימין מקרבת [ט] ת"ר ג' חלאים חלה אלישע אחד שגירה דובים בתינוקות ואחד שדחפו לגחזי בשתי ידים ואחד שמת בו [שנא' [כ] ואלישע חלה את חליו וגו'] [י] עד אברהם לא היה זקנה כל דחזי לאברהם אמר האי יצחק כל דחזי ליצחק אמר האי אברהם [כ] בעא אברהם רחמי דליהוי ליה זקנה שנאמר [ל] ואברהם זקן בא בימים עד יעקב לא הוה חולשא בעא רחמי והוה חולשא שנאמר [מ] ויאמר ליוסף הנה אביך חולה עד אלישע לא הוה איניש חליש [ל] דמיתפח ואתא אלישע ובעא רחמי ואיתפח שנא' [כ] ואלישע חלה את חליו אשר ימות בו [מ]: **מתני'** דור המבול אין להם חלק לעוה"ב ואין עומדין בדין שנא' [נ] לא ידון רוחי באדם לעולם לא דין ולא רוח דור הפלגה אין להם חלק לעולם הבא שנאמר [ס] ויפץ ה' אותם משם על פני כל הארץ [נ] (וכתיב ומשם הפיצם) ויפץ ה' אותם בעוה"ז [ע] ומשם הפיצם ה' לעולם הבא אנשי סדום אין להם חלק לעולם הבא שנא' [פ] ואנשי סדום רעים וחטאים לה' מאד רעים בעולם הזה וחטאים לעולם הבא אבל עומדין בדין ר' נחמיה אומר אלו ואלו אין עומדין בדין שנאמר [צ] על כן לא יקומו רשעים

רש"י

בחברון מלך שבע שנים וששה חדשים. מדהכא חשיב להו ובאידך קרא לא חשיב להו ש"מ לא היה מלכותו שלימה שנצטרע אותן ו' חדשים: ה"ג אבל בחיי בנך אני מודיע ולא גרסינן לך: כ"ד רננות. בין תפלה תחנה ורנה איכא כ"ד: וילך אלישע דמשק להיכא אזל: שואבת. מגבהת מתכת בלא נגיעה כעין אותה שלועזין קלאמניס"ה בלע"ז ועל ידי אותה אבן העמיד עגלים של ירבעם באויר: רבנן דחה מקמיה. התלמידים דחה מישיבתו של אלישע: צר ממנו. מכלל דעד האידנא לא הוה צר: הואל וקח. השבע שאלישע שלחך: ויפצר בו. גחזי: העת לקחת את הכסף והבגדים וגו'. שמנה דברים קא חשיב בהאי קרא: וגחזי מי שקל כולי האי. מנעמן כסף ובגדים הוא דשקל דכתיב ויצר ככרים וגו': אותה שעה. היה אלישע עוסק בפרק שמונה שרצים אמר לו הגיע עת ליטול שכר פרק שמונה שרצים שעסקתי וכו' ולהכי כתב בהאי קרא שמנה דברים כנגד אותו פרק כלומר בכסף ובגדים שקבלת ממנו מנעמן סבור אתה לקנות דברים הללו להיותם לך שכר שמונה שרצים: יצר. תאותו אם מרחיקה ממנו לגמרי ממעט ישיבת עולם ואם מקרבה לגמרי בא לידי איסור שאינו יכול לכבוש יצרו מדבר עבירה: תינוק ואשה. דעתן קלה ואם תדחה אותם מטרדן מן העולם: חלה. חד. חליו תרי. אשר ימות בו תלת: בעא רחמי דלהוי חולשא. כדי שיהא פנאי לבניו לבא כל אחד ואחד ממקומו להיות עליו בשעת מיתה שכיון שרואין שנפל למטה יודעין שימות ומתקבצין ובאין: מתפח. מתרפא: **מתני'** לא ידון רוחי לא דין ולא רוח. שאין עומדין בדין ואין להם רוח להיות עם הצדיקים שיש להם חלק: ויפץ [ה' אותם ומשם הפיצם. ויפץ] בעולם הזה ומשם הפיצם בעולם הבא: אלו ואלו. אנשי דור המבול ואנשי סדום ובהדא פליג ר' נחמיה:

עין משפט נר מצוה

לב א מיי' פ"ד מהל' תשובה הלכה א:

ליקוטי רש"י

עשה עמי אות לטובה. שיהא ניכר לאחרים שמחלת לי. **ויראו שונאי.** האות ויבושו ולא שמע לו הקב"ה ליתן האות בימיו אלא בימי שלמה בנו כשדבקו השערים זה בזה ולא נפתחו עד שאמר (דה"ב ו') אל תשב פני משיחך זכרה לחסדי דוד עבדך [תהלים פו, יז]. **על אותו עון.** דבת שבע. **דבקו שערים.** של בית קדשי הקדשים. **עשרים וארבע רננות.** רנה תפילה תחינה כתובים בתפילת שלמה עד עשרים וארבע ויש אומרים עשרים וארבע ברכות דתענית ולא נהירא. **אמר שאו שערים ראשיכם והנשאו פתחי עולם ויבוא מלך הכבוד.** rסבורים השערים שבתריה למבלעיה סברי דעל עצמו אמר מלך הכבוד אמרו לו שערים מי הוא זה מלך הכבוד אמר איהו ה' עזוז וגבור (תהלים כד). **שונאי דוד.** משפחת שאול שמעי וכיוצא בו [שבת ל.]. **עשרים וארבע רננות.** כמיני בפרשה, בין רנה ותחנה ותפלה ובקשה [מו"ק ט.]. **אל תשב פני משיחך.** מלעשות טובה עמדי ואם לא למעני עשה למענך [דה"ב ו, מב]. **ויבא אלישע דמשק.** להחזיר את גיחזי בתשובה [מ"ב ח, ז]. **אבן שואבת.** דרך אותה האבן להגביה המתכת ולתלותה באויר [ע"ז מד.]. שמגבהת את המתכת מן הארץ ומעמידתו באויר [וע"י אותו אבן העמיד העגלים של ירבעם באויר]. **רבנן דחה.** דוחה היה את התלמידים מפני אלישע כשהיה משמש לפניו דכתיב לאחר שפירש ממנו המקום אשר אנחנו יושבין בית המדרש של רבנן צר ממנו שנתוספו התלמידים שהיה גחזי דוחה [סוטה מז.]. **ויאמרו בני הנביאים.** רבותינו אמרו מכאן שהיה גיחזי דוחה התלמידים מלפניו כשנטרד באו תלמידים רבים ונדחק המקום מהם [מ"ב ו, א]. **הואל.** השבע שלחך [שם ה, כג]. **העת לקחת את הכסף.** להתעשר ולקחת ממנו בגדים וזיתים וגו' [מלכים ב, ה]. **מי שקל כולי האי.** בהאי קרא כתיב שמנה דברים כסף ובגדים וצאן ובקר ועבדים ושפחות וזיתים וכרמים. **כסף ובגדים הוא דשקל.** דכתיב ויצר ככרים כסף בשני חריטים ושתי חליפות בגדים. **בשמנה שרצים.** בפרק שמנה שרצים (שבת קז). **הגיע עת ליטול שכר.** תורתך בעולם הזה [שם]. **וארבעה אנשים.** גיחזי ובניו. **פתח השער.** כמו שנאמר בדד ישב מחוץ למחנה מושבו (ויקרא י"ג מ"ו) [שם ז, ג]. **כדקטלינהו ינאי מלכא לרבנן.** כדאמרינן בקידושין בהאומר לשלוחו (דף סו). **בעלי שרוי בתוכך.** נשיא היה כדאמרינן בחגיגה (דף טז:). **עבדו ליה יקרא טובא.** כידלתו. **כמה יפה אכסניא זו.** במעשיה. **טרוטות.** עגולות. **בכך אתה עוסק.** מסתכל באשת איש. **אחוי ליה בידיה.** שיקבלנו. **יצר.** של תשמיש תקרבנו בימין שלא יקוץ בפריה ורביה וכן תינוק פן יברח ויאבד את עצמו ואשה אף היא דעתה קלה ואם ירדפוה תלא לתרבות רעה [סוטה מז.]. **חליו אשר ימות בו.** מכלל דחלה עוד שלא מת בו [ב"מ פז.]. **אחד שגירה דובים.** בעון שגירה דובים בתינוקות. **חלה.** חד את חליו תרי וחד אשר ימות בו [סוטה שם]. **בעא אברהם רחמי.** כדי שיכירו בינו ובין בנו. **בעא רחמי והוה חולשא.** שיחלה אדם לפני מותו ויצוה לביתו. **חליש דמיתפח.** ונתרפא. **חליו אשר ימות בו.** מכלל דחלה עוד שלא מת בו [ב"מ שם]. **ויפץ ה' אותם משם.** בעולם הזה מה שאמרו פן נפוץ נתקיים עליהם הוא שאמר שלמה (משלי י, כד) מגורת רשע היא תבואנו [בראשית יא, יח]. **ומשם הפיצם.** למד שאין להם חלק לעולם הבא [בראשית יא, ט].

מסורת הש"ם

א) שבת ל. ע"ש, ב) שם מו"ק ט., ג) אין זה לשון המקרא וכך הוא לשון המקרא **ויבא אלישע** (מ"ב ח') גו' ועיי' רש"א בח"א, ד) סוטה מז. [ע"ש], ה) [יומא פז.], ו) סוטה שם, ז) בקרא קח, ח) [שמחות פ"ב סוטה מז.], ט) [סוטה מז:], י) [ב"מ פז.], כ) [ב"מ פז.], ל) [לדעת הערוך בערך תפח גרס הכא **ואיתפח** כמו בסמוך], מ) [מכלל דחלה חלי **אחריתא** כך איתא בב"מ פז.], נ) [בסה"מ ל"ג].

תורה אור השלם

א) בְּחֶבְרוֹן מָלַךְ עַל יְהוּדָה שֶׁבַע שָׁנִים וְשִׁשָּׁה חֳדָשִׁים וּבִירוּשָׁלַיִם מָלַךְ שְׁלֹשִׁים וְשָׁלֹשׁ שָׁנָה עַל כָּל יִשְׂרָאֵל וִיהוּדָה: [שמואל ב' ה, ה]

ב) עֲשֵׂה עִמִּי אוֹת לְטוֹבָה וְיִרְאוּ שֹׂנְאַי וְיֵבֹשׁוּ כִּי אַתָּה יְיָ עֲזַרְתַּנִי וְנִחַמְתָּנִי: [תהלים פו, יז]

ג) שְׂאוּ שְׁעָרִים רָאשֵׁיכֶם וְהִנָּשְׂאוּ פִּתְחֵי עוֹלָם וְיָבוֹא מֶלֶךְ הַכָּבוֹד: מִי זֶה מֶלֶךְ הַכָּבוֹד יְיָ עִזּוּז וְגִבּוֹר יְיָ גִּבּוֹר מִלְחָמָה: [תהלים כד, ז-ח]

ד) שְׂאוּ שְׁעָרִים רָאשֵׁיכֶם וּשְׂאוּ פִּתְחֵי עוֹלָם וְיָבֹא מֶלֶךְ הַכָּבוֹד: מִי הוּא זֶה מֶלֶךְ הַכָּבוֹד יְיָ צְבָאוֹת הוּא מֶלֶךְ הַכָּבוֹד סֶלָה: [תהלים כד, ט-י]

ה) יְיָ אֱלֹהִים אַל תָּשֵׁב פְּנֵי מְשִׁיחֶךָ זָכְרָה לְחַסְדֵי דָּוִיד עַבְדֶּךָ: [דברי הימים ב' ו, מב]

ו) וַיָּבֹא אֱלִישָׁע דַּמֶּשֶׂק וּבֶן הֲדַד מֶלֶךְ אֲרָם חֹלֶה וַיֻּגַּד לוֹ לֵאמֹר בָּא אִישׁ הָאֱלֹהִים עַד הֵנָּה: [מלכים ב' ח, ז]

ז) וַיֹּאמְרוּ בְנֵי הַנְּבִיאִים אֶל אֱלִישָׁע הִנֵּה נָא הַמָּקוֹם אֲשֶׁר אֲנַחְנוּ יֹשְׁבִים שָׁם לְפָנֶיךָ צַר מִמֶּנּוּ: [מלכים ב' ו, א]

ח) וַיֹּאמֶר נַעֲמָן הוֹאֵל קַח כִּכָּרָיִם וַיִּפְרָץ בּוֹ וַיָּצַר כִּכְּרַיִם כֶּסֶף בִּשְׁנֵי חֲרִטִים וּשְׁתֵּי חֲלִפוֹת בְּגָדִים וַיִּתֵּן אֶל שְׁנֵי נְעָרָיו וַיִּשְׂאוּ לְפָנָיו: וְהוּא בָא וַיַּעֲמֹד אֶל אֲדֹנָיו וַיֹּאמֶר אֵלָיו אֱלִישָׁע מֵאַין גֵּחֲזִי וַיֹּאמֶר לֹא הָלַךְ עַבְדְּךָ אָנֶה וָאָנָה: וַיֹּאמֶר אֵלָיו לֹא לִבִּי הָלַךְ כַּאֲשֶׁר הָפַךְ אִישׁ מֵעַל מֶרְכַּבְתּוֹ לִקְרָאתֶךָ הַעֵת לָקַחַת אֶת הַכֶּסֶף וְלָקַחַת בְּגָדִים וְזֵיתִים וּכְרָמִים וְצֹאן וּבָקָר וַעֲבָדִים וּשְׁפָחוֹת: [מלכים ב' ה, כג,כה-כו] ט) וְצָרַעַת נַעֲמָן תִּדְבַּק בְּךָ וּבְזַרְעֲךָ לְעוֹלָם וַיֵּצֵא מִלְּפָנָיו מְצֹרָע כַּשָּׁלֶג: [מלכים ב' ה, כז] י) וְאַרְבָּעָה אֲנָשִׁים הָיוּ מְצֹרָעִים פֶּתַח הַשָּׁעַר וַיֹּאמְרוּ אִישׁ אֶל רֵעֵהוּ מָה אֲנַחְנוּ יֹשְׁבִים פֹּה עַד מָתְנוּ: [מלכים ב' ז, ג] כ) וֶאֱלִישָׁע חָלָה אֶת חָלְיוֹ אֲשֶׁר יָמוּת בּוֹ וַיֵּרֶד אֵלָיו יוֹאָשׁ מֶלֶךְ יִשְׂרָאֵל וַיֵּבְךְּ עַל פָּנָיו וַיֹּאמַר אָבִי אָבִי רֶכֶב יִשְׂרָאֵל וּפָרָשָׁיו: [מלכים ב' יג, יד] ל) וְאַבְרָהָם זָקֵן בָּא בַּיָּמִים וַייָ בֵּרַךְ אֶת אַבְרָהָם בַּכֹּל: [בראשית כד, א] מ) וַיְהִי אַחֲרֵי הַדְּבָרִים הָאֵלֶּה וַיֹּאמֶר לְיוֹסֵף הִנֵּה אָבִיךָ חֹלֶה וַיִּקַּח אֶת שְׁנֵי בָנָיו עִמּוֹ אֶת מְנַשֶּׁה וְאֶת אֶפְרָיִם: [בראשית מח, א] נ) וַיֹּאמֶר יְיָ לֹא יָדוֹן רוּחִי בָאָדָם לְעֹלָם בְּשַׁגַּם הוּא בָשָׂר וְהָיוּ יָמָיו מֵאָה וְעֶשְׂרִים שָׁנָה: [בראשית ו, ג] ס) וַיָּפֶץ יְיָ אֹתָם מִשָּׁם עַל פְּנֵי כָל הָאָרֶץ וַיַּחְדְּלוּ לִבְנֹת הָעִיר: [בראשית יא, ח] ע) עַל כֵּן קָרָא שְׁמָהּ בָּבֶל כִּי שָׁם בָּלַל יְיָ שְׂפַת כָּל הָאָרֶץ וּמִשָּׁם הֱפִיצָם יְיָ עַל פְּנֵי כָּל הָאָרֶץ: [בראשית יא, ט] פ) וְאַנְשֵׁי סְדֹם רָעִים וְחַטָּאִים לַייָ מְאֹד: [בראשית יג, יג] צ) עַל כֵּן לֹא יָקֻמוּ רְשָׁעִים בַּמִּשְׁפָּט וְחַטָּאִים בַּעֲדַת צַדִּיקִים: [תהלים א, ה]

over the face of the whole earth. (וּכְתִיב ,,וּמִשָּׁם הֱפִיצָם״) – **And it is written** in the next verse: ***And from there Hashem scattered them . . .***) ,,וַיָּפֶץ ה׳ אֹתָם״ בָּעוֹלָם הַזֶּה – This redundancy implies that ***Hashem dispersed them*** – **in this world;** ,,וּמִשָּׁם הֱפִיצָם ה׳ ״ לָעוֹלָם הַבָּא – ***and from there Hashem scattered them*** – **for the World to Come.**[53]

אַנְשֵׁי סְדוֹם אֵין לָהֶם חֵלֶק לָעוֹלָם הַבָּא – **The people of Sodom have no share in the World to Come,** שֶׁנֶּאֱמַר ,,וְאַנְשֵׁי סְדֹם רָעִים וְחַטָּאִים לַה׳ מְאֹד״ – **as it is stated:**[54] ***Now the people of Sodom were wicked and sinful toward Hashem, exceedingly*** – ,,רָעִים״ בָּעוֹלָם הַזֶּה ,,וְחַטָּאִים״ לָעוֹלָם הַבָּא – ***wicked*** **in this world;** ***and sinful*** **for the World to Come.**[55] אֲבָל עוֹמְדִין בַּדִּין – **However, they will stand for judgment.**[56] רַבִּי נְחֶמְיָה אוֹמֵר – **R' Nechemiah says:** אֵלּוּ וָאֵלּוּ אֵין עוֹמְדִין בַּדִּין – **Neither these** (the people of the Generation of the Flood) **nor these** (the people of Sodom) **will stand for judgment,**[57] שֶׁנֶּאֱמַר – **as it is stated:**[58] ,,עַל־כֵּן לֹא־יָקֻמוּ –

NOTES

53. However, in contrast to the Generation of the Flood, the Generation of the Dispersal will stand for Judgment, since there is no Scriptural indication to the contrary (*Tos. Yom Tov*).

54. *Genesis* 13:13.

55. Their wickedness eradicated them from this world and their sinfulness from the World to Come (see *Yad Ramah* and *Margaliyos HaYam;* cf. *Tiferes Yisrael*).

56. Although they were punished in this world, the great magnitude of their sins requires further judgment in the next world as well (*Yad Ramah*). It is particularly fitting that they stand judgment, as they themselves perverted the administration of justice (*Maharal;* see Gemara, 109b).

57. R' Nechemiah disputes the Tanna Kamma's assertion that the people of Sodom will stand for Judgment (see *Rashi* and *Rashash*).

58. *Psalms* 1:5.

רְשָׁעִים בַּמִּשְׁפָּט וְחַטָּאִים בַּעֲדַת צַדִּיקִים" – *Therefore the wicked shall not stand up in judgment, nor the sinful in the congregation of the righteous.* "עַל־כֵּן לֹא־יָקֻמוּ רְשָׁעִים בַּמִּשְׁפָּט" זֶה דּוֹר הַמַּבּוּל – *Therefore the wicked shall not stand up in judgment* – **this is** a reference to the people of **the Generation of the Flood;**[1] "וְחַטָּאִים בַּעֲדַת צַדִּיקִים" אֵלּוּ אַנְשֵׁי סְדוֹם – *nor the sinful in the congregation of the righteous* – **these are the people of Sodom.**[2] אָמְרוּ לוֹ – **They said to [R' Nechemiah]:** אֵינָם עוֹמְדִין בַּעֲדַת צַדִּיקִים – The verse implies merely that **[the people of Sodom] shall not stand** for judgment **in the congregation of the righteous,** אֲבָל עוֹמְדִין בַּעֲדַת רְשָׁעִים – **but they shall stand** for judgment **in the congregation of the wicked.**[3]

The Mishnah continues its list of groups excluded from the World to Come:

מְרַגְּלִים אֵין לָהֶם חֵלֶק לָעוֹלָם הַבָּא) – **The Spies have no share in the World to Come.**[4] שֶׁנֶּאֱמַר "וַיָּמֻתוּ הָאֲנָשִׁים מוֹצִאֵי דִבַּת־הָאָרֶץ רָעָה בַּמַּגֵּפָה לִפְנֵי ה'" – **As it is stated:**[5] *And they died – the men who brought out an evil report about the land – in a plague before Hashem.* "וַיָּמֻתוּ" בָּעוֹלָם הַזֶּה – *And they died* – **in this world,** "בַּמַּגֵּפָה" לָעוֹלָם הַבָּא – *in a plague* – **for the World to Come.)**[6]

דּוֹר הַמִּדְבָּר אֵין לָהֶם חֵלֶק לָעוֹלָם הַבָּא – **The** people of the **Generation of the Wilderness have no share in the World to Come,** וְאֵין עוֹמְדִין בַּדִּין – **nor will they stand for judgment,** שֶׁנֶּאֱמַר "בַּמִּדְבָּר הַזֶּה יִתַּמּוּ וְשָׁם יָמֻתוּ" – **as it is stated:** *In this Wilderness they shall be consumed, and there they shall die.*[7] דִּבְרֵי רַבִּי עֲקִיבָא – These are **the words of R' Akiva.** רַבִּי אֱלִיעֶזֶר אוֹמֵר – **R' Eliezer says:** עֲלֵיהֶם הוּא אוֹמֵר "אִסְפוּ־לִי חֲסִידָי כֹּרְתֵי בְרִיתִי עֲלֵי־זָבַח" – **Concerning them it is stated:** *Gather to Me My devout ones, those who sealed a covenant with Me by sacrifice.*[8] עֲדַת קֹרַח אֵינָהּ עֲתִידָה לַעֲלוֹת – **The congregation of Korach is not destined to arise,**[9] שֶׁנֶּאֱמַר "וַתְּכַס עֲלֵיהֶם הָאָרֶץ" בָּעוֹלָם הַזֶּה – **as it is stated:**[10] *the earth covered them over* – **in this world;** "וַיֹּאבְדוּ מִתּוֹךְ הַקָּהָל" לָעוֹלָם הַבָּא – *and they were lost from among the congregation* – **for the World to Come.**[11] דִּבְרֵי רַבִּי עֲקִיבָא – These are **the words of R' Akiva.** רַבִּי אֱלִיעֶזֶר אוֹמֵר – **R' Eliezer says:** עֲלֵיהֶם הוּא אוֹמֵר "ה' מֵמִית וּמְחַיֶּה מוֹרִיד שְׁאוֹל וַיָּעַל" – **Concerning them it is stated:** *HASHEM kills and brings to life, lowers into the pit and lifts up.*[12]

Gemara A Baraisa discusses the fate of the Generation of the Flood:

תָּנוּ רַבָּנָן – **The Rabbis taught in a Baraisa:** דּוֹר הַמַּבּוּל אֵין לָהֶם חֵלֶק לָעוֹלָם הַבָּא – THE people of the GENERATION OF THE FLOOD HAVE NO SHARE IN THE WORLD TO COME, שֶׁנֶּאֱמַר "וַיִּמַח אֶת כָּל הַיְקוּם אֲשֶׁר עַל פְּנֵי הָאֲדָמָה" – AS IT IS STATED:[13] *HE BLOTTED OUT ALL EXISTENCE THAT WAS ON THE FACE OF THE GROUND ... and they were blotted out from the earth.* "וַיִּמַח אֶת־כָּל־הַיְקוּם" בָּעוֹלָם

NOTES

1. Who are referred to as wicked in the verse (*Genesis* 6:5): וַיַּרְא ה' כִּי רַבָּה רָעַת הָאָדָם, *And Hashem saw that Man's wickedness was great* (*Rashi*).

2. Who are referred to as sinful in the verse (ibid. 13:13): וְאַנְשֵׁי סְדֹם רָעִים וְחַטָּאִים, *Now the people of Sodom were wicked and sinful* (*Rashi*).

Note that the simple meaning of the verse cited by R' Nechemiah is that the wicked will not be vindicated in judgment ("they will not have a leg to stand on"), nor will the sinful be inscribed in the congregation of the righteous (see *Rashi* to *Psalms* 1:6). However, R' Nechemiah interprets the verse as alluding that certain sinners will not rise at the resurrection to stand judgment.

3. I.e. they will be resurrected and brought to judgment [among all the other sinners] (*Rashi*; see *Yad Ramah* and *Rashash*).

4. This refers to the Spies sent by Moses from the Wilderness to explore the Land of Canaan and bring back a report to the Jews. Upon their return, ten of the twelve Spies disparaged the land and convinced the people that it was unconquerable. Only Calev and Joshua defended faithfully God's promise to conquer the land for Israel. When the people were swayed by the negative report of the ten Spies and despaired of taking the land, God killed those ten in a plague and sentenced the rest of the nation to wander the Wilderness for forty years until that entire generation would die out. Only the next generation would enter the land under Joshua (see *Numbers* chs. 13-14). The Mishnah teaches that these ten spies were stricken not only from this world, but also from the World to Come.

5. *Numbers* 14:37.

6. Since the word בַּמַּגֵּפָה, *in a plague,* is not written at the beginning of the verse, together with וַיָּמֻתוּ, *And they died* (i.e. וַיָּמֻתוּ בַּמַּגֵּפָה), but rather separately at the end of the verse, it is apparently not intended merely as a description of their death, but as an allusion to another death, in the World to Come (*Maharsha*). Moreover, the reference to *a plague before Hashem* implies that the plague destroyed their potential Life in the presence of Hashem, in the World to Come (*Torah Temimah, Numbers* loc. cit.).

7. Ibid. v. 35. In this verse God informed Moses that the people of the Generation of the Wilderness, who followed the evil counsel of the spies, would perish in the Wilderness. The redundant wording of the verse indicates death in both worlds (see Gemara, 110b). [It is unclear how the verse indicates that they will not stand for judgment (see *Maharsha*).]

It seems inconceivable that Moses' entire generation, which included many righteous and pious people, was excluded from a share in the World to Come. Possibly, this refers only to those who rebelled against God in one manner or another [which may have included the bulk of the masses]. Those who were steadfast in their loyalty, although sentenced to die in the Wilderness along with the other members of their generation, could certainly not have forfeited their share in the Next World due to the sins of the others (*Margaliyos HaYam*).

8. *Psalms* 50:5. This refers to the Generation of the Wilderness, which entered the covenant with God at Sinai by offering sacrifices and sprinkling the blood, as stated in *Exodus* 24:5-8 (*Rashi* below, 110b ד"ה כורתי). [God's statement that they are to be gathered to Him implies that they will be with Him in the World to Come.]

9. From out of the ground which swallowed it up (see *Numbers* 16:33 and see *Rashash*).

The implication is that they will not emerge from the punishment to which they were condemned, to have a share in the World to Come. A Baraisa below, 109b, states this explicitly. Perhaps the phrase "is not destined to arise" means that they will not even arise to stand in judgment (*Maharsha*).

10. *Numbers* 16:33.

11. The verse reads, in its entirety: וַיֵּרְדוּ הֵם וְכָל־אֲשֶׁר לָהֶם חַיִּים שְׁאֹלָה וַתְּכַס עֲלֵיהֶם הָאָרֶץ וַיֹּאבְדוּ מִתּוֹךְ הַקָּהָל, *They and all that was theirs descended alive to the pit; the earth covered them over and they were lost from among the congregation.* The Mishnah expounds the redundancy in the latter segment of the verse as alluding to a double descent.

12. *I Samuel* 2:6. This verse is part of the thanksgiving prayer offered by Hannah when she bore her son, Samuel. In thanking God for granting her this son, she made reference to Korach, from whom Samuel was descended (see *I Chronicles* 6:18-23). [For Korach drew the courage to rebel from the prophetic knowledge that he would have a descendant as great as Samuel. He reasoned that anyone with the merit to produce such a descendant could certainly not fail (see *Rashi* to *Numbers* 16:7). Having borne this great child, who was in a sense responsible for Korach's downfall, Hannah felt obligated to pray for Korach's salvation.] She therefore said: Hashem – Who lowered Korach's congregation into the pit – please lift them up (*Maharsha*).

R' Eliezer holds that the members of Korach's congregation recognized their error as they fell into the abyss, and they repented, thus meriting a share in the World to Come (*Meiri*).

13. *Genesis* 7:23.

רשעים במשפט וחטאים בעדת צדיקים על כן לא יקומו רשעים במשפט זה דור המבול וחטאים בעדת צדיקים אלו אנשי סדום אמרו לו אינם עומדין בעדת צדיקים אבל עומדין בעדת רשעים (א) מרגלים אין להם חלק לעולם הבא שנאמר א) וימותו האנשים מוציאי דבת הארץ רעה במגפה לפני ה' וימותו בעולם הזה במגפה לעולם הבא) [א] דור המדבר אין להם חלק לעולם הבא ואין עומדין בדין שנאמר ב) במדבר הזה יתמו ושם ימותו דברי רבי עקיבא ר' אליעזר אומר עליהם הוא אומר ג) אספו לי חסידי כורתי בריתי עלי זבח [ב] עדת קרח אינה עתידה לעלות שנאמר ד) ותכס עליהם הארץ בעולם הזה ויאבדו מתוך הקהל לעולם הבא דברי ר"ע ר"א אומר עליהם הוא אומר ה) ה' ממית ומחיה מוריד שאול ויעל: **גמ'** ג) ת"ר דור המבול אין להם חלק לעולם הבא שנאמר ו) וימח את כל היקום אשר על פני האדמה וימח את כל היקום בעולם הזה וימחו מן הארץ לעולם הבא דברי ר"ע ר"י בן בתירא אומר לא חיין ולא נדונין שנאמר ז) לא ידון רוחי באדם לעולם לא דין ולא רוח דבר אחר לא ידון רוחי שלא תהא נשמתן חוזרת לנדנה ר' מנחם ג) בר יוסף אומר אפילו בשעה שהקב"ה מחזיר נשמות לפגרים מתים נשמתן קשה להם בגיהנם שנאמר ח) תהרו ד) חשש תלדו קש רוחכם אש תאכלכם ת"ר ה) דור המבול לא נתגאו אלא בשביל טובה שהשפיע להם הקב"ה ומה כתיב בהם ט) בתיהם שלום מפחד ולא שבט אלוה עליהם וכתיב י) שורו עבר ולא יגעיל תפלט פרתו ולא תשכל וכתיב יא) ישלחו כצאן עויליהם וילדיהם ירקדון וכתיב יב) ישאו בתוף וכנור וישמחו לקול עוגב וכתיב יג) יבלו [ג] ימיהם בטוב ו) ושנותם בנעימים וכתיב יג) וברגע שאול יחתו והיא גרמה שאמרו לאל יד) סור ממנו ודעת דרכיך לא חפצנו מה שדי כי נעבדנו ומה נועיל כי נפגע בו אמרו כלום צריכין אנו לו אלא לטיפה של גשמים יש לנו נהרות ומעינות שאנו מסתפקין מהן אמר הקב"ה בטובה שהשפעתי להן בה מכעיסין אותי ובה אני דן אותם שנאמר טו) ואני הנני מביא את המבול מים ר' יוסי אמר דור המבול לא נתגאו אלא בשביל גלגל העין שדומה למים [שנאמר טז) ויקחו להם נשים מכל אשר בחרו] לפיכך דן אותן במים שדומה לגלגל העין שנאמר יז) נבקעו כל מעינות תהום רבה [ד] וארבות השמים נפתחו א"ר יוחנן דור המבול ברבה קלקלו וברבה נידונו ברבה קלקלו שנאמר יח) וירא ה' כי רבה רעת האדם וברבה נידונו שנאמר יז) כל מעינות תהום רבה א"ר יוחנן שלשה נשתיירו מהם בלועה דגדר וחמי טבריא ועיניא רבתי דבירם יט) כי השחית כל בשר את דרכו על הארץ א"ר יוחנן מלמד שהרביעו בהמה על חיה וחיה על בהמה והכל על אדם ואדם על הכל א"ר אבא בר כהנא וכולם חזרו חוץ מתושלמי כ) ויאמר ז) ה' לנח קץ כל בשר בא לפני א"ר יוחנן בא וראה כמה גדול כחה של חמס שהרי דור המבול עברו על הכל ולא נחתם עליהם גזר דינם עד שפשטו ידיהם בגזל שנאמר כ) כי מלאה הארץ חמס מפניהם והנני משחיתם את הארץ וכתיב כא) החמס קם למטה רשע לא מהם ולא מהמונם ולא מהמהם ולא ח) נה בהם א"ר אלעזר מלמד שזקף עצמו כמקל ועמד לפני הקב"ה ואמר לפניו רבש"ע לא מהם ולא מהמונם ולא מהמהם ולא נה בהם (ט) ואף על נח נחתם גזר דין שנא' ולא נח בהם) תנא דבי ר' ישמעאל אף על נח נחתך גזר דין אלא שמצא חן בעיני ה' שנאמר כב) נחמתי כי עשיתם ונח מצא חן בעיני ה' כג) וינחם ה' כי עשה את האדם בארץ כי אתא רב דימי אמר אמר הקב"ה יפה עשיתי שתקנתי להם קברות בארץ מאי משמע כתיב הכא וינחם ה' וכתיב התם כד) וינחם אותם וידבר על לבם ואיכא דאמרי לא יפה עשיתי שתקנתי להם קברות בארץ כתיב הכא וינחם וכתיב התם כה) וינחם ה' על הרעה אשר דבר לעשות לעמו כו) אלה תולדות נח [נח איש צדיק תמים היה בדורותיו] א"ר יוחנן בדורותיו ולא בדורות אחרים וריש לקיש אמר בדורותיו כ"ש בדורות אחרים א"ר חנינא משל דרבי יוחנן למה הדבר דומה לחבית של יין שהיתה מונחת במרתף של חומץ במקומה ריחה נודף שלא במקומה אין ריחה נודף א"ר אושעיא משל דריש לקיש למה הדבר דומה לצלוחית של פלייטון שהיתה מונחת במקום הטנופת במקומה ריחה נודף וכ"ש במקום הבוסם ו) וימח את כל היקום אשר על פני האדמה אם אדם חטא בהמה מה חטאה תנא משום רבי יהושע בן קרחה משל לאדם שעשה חופה לבנו והתקין מכל מיני סעודה לימים מת בנו עמד (ובלבל) [ופזר] את חופתו אמר כלום עשיתי אלא בשביל בני עכשיו שמת חופה למה לי אף הקב"ה אמר כלום בראתי בהמה וחיה אלא בשביל אדם עכשיו שאדם חוטא בהמה וחיה למה לי כז) מכל אשר בחרבה מתו י) ולא דגים שבים דרש ר' יוסי דמן קסרי מאי דכתיב כח) קל הוא על פני מים תקולל חלקתם בארץ מלמד שהיה נח הצדיק מוכיח בהם ואומר להם עשו תשובה ואם לאו הקב"ה מביא עליכם את המבול ומקפה נבלתכם על המים כזיקין שנאמר קל הוא על פני מים ולא עוד אלא שלוקחין מהם קללה לכל באי עולם שנאמר כח) תקולל חלקתם בארץ לא יפנה דרך כרמים [ה] מלמד שהיו מפנים דרך כרמים כ) אמר לו ומי מעכב אמר להם פרידה אחת יש לי להוציא מכם א"כ

רש"י

רשעים דור המבול. דכתיב [בהו] כי רבה רעת האדם (בראשית ו): חטאים אנשי סדום. דכתיב בהו רעים וחטאים (שם יג): אבל עומדים הם כו'. שחיין ונדונים: **גמ'** נשמתן קשה להם בגיהנם. נשמת עצמן שורפתן דכתיב רוחכם אש תאכלכם (ישעיה לג): בשביל גלגל העין. שרואין טובתן שלימה והיו גובהין עיניהם ומנאפין אחר עיניהם: במים. שדומה לגלגל העין מעינות שנובעין ממקום קטן כמו עין: שלשה נשתיירו. מאותן מעינות של דור המבול שהיו חמין כדאמר לקמן ברותחין קלקלו ברותחין נדונו: וכולן חזרו. להזדווג עם מיניהם: חוץ מתושלמי. עוף הוא שאוחז עדיין תרבות רעה שמזדווג עם הכל. תושלמי עוף אחד ובמסכת חולין (דף סב:) גבי שמונה ספיקות איתא והרנוגא תושלמי ומרלא ודרכו של אותו עוף להרביע כל הבריות: שוקף. החמס עצמו כמקל והיינו החמס קם למטה רשע: לא מהם. אין תועלת לא בהם ולא בהמונם ולא במשאם: מהמהם. אשטרי"א בלע"ז: כי נחמתי כי עשיתם ונח. סמוכין דריש: יפה עשיתי וכו'. שאיבדתי דרך רשעים כזה: לא יפה עשיתי. דאפשר היו חוזרין: כל שכן. אילו הוה בדורות אחרים היה צדיק יותר: פלייטון. בושם שריחו נודף ואינו אפרסמון: מקיפה. מליף כמו וילף הברזל דמתרגמינן וקפא (מלכים ב ו): כזיקין. נודות: לא יפנה דרך כרמים אמרו לו ומי מעכב. [מיד] שאינו עושה אם יש בידו כח לעשות כך: [פרידה] אחת יש לי להוציא מכם. מתושלח הצדיק ימות קודם ולא יהיה נדון עמכם: א"כ

מסורת הש"ס

א) [ירושלמי ל"ג מרגלים וכו'], ב) [תוספתא פי"ג], ג) [נ"ל ברבי יוסי וכ"א בילקוט], ד) [חשש מין מוץ שנוח לידלק], ה) [תוספתא דסוטה פ"ג], ו) [אין זה בהך פסוקים אלא בסימן לו פי"א כתיב יבלו ימיהם בטוב ושניהם בנעימים], ז) [נ"ל אלהים], ח) [אין בהם נוהה אחרי מגעגע ונותן לב אלי כך פירש"י שם], ט) [בע"י ובילקוט ליתא לכל אותן עשרה תיבות], י) קידושין יג. זבחים קיג:, כ) [נ"ל אמרו וכ"א בע"י].

ליקוטי רש"י

חשש. מין מוץ דבר שנוח לידלק. רוחכם אש. מגופכם תצא רוח אש ותאכל החשש והקש [ישעיהו לג, יא]. שלום מפחד. שלא היו מזיקין שולטין בהן [איוב כא, ט]. שורו עבר. את הנקיבה. ולא יגעיל. לא יורה בה זרע פסולת שיהא חוזר ונפלט מגופה בלא הריון כל לשון הגעלה פליטה הוא וכן בל' משנה מגעילן ברותחין וכן כי שם נגעל מגן גבורים (שמואל ב, א) נפלט משיחתו והיה כאילו לא נמשח בשמן שהיו רגילין למשוח מגיני עור כדי שיהא חלק ומחליק את הרומח והחנית המכה בו והוא כמו שריס משחו מגן (ישעי' כא). תפלט פרתו. בעת תלד את ולדה. ולא תשכל. בלא עת [שם י]. ישלחו כצאן עויליהם וגו'. בעת לידתו היה הולך ומרקד מיד ואם פוגע במזיק נלחם בו והיתה אומרת לו אמו הבא לי מספריים ואחתוך שערך בהגדת בראשית, לך והדליק לי את הנר בראשית רבה [שם יא]. וברגע שאול יחתו. כשמגיע יום מותו היה מת לפי שעה בנחת בלא יסורין. יחתו. ירדו ובתרגום נחיתו [שם, יג]. ומה נועיל. מה הנאה יש לנו כי נפגע בו אין אנו צריכין לו אפי' לטיפת גשמים כי אד יעלה מן הארץ (בראשית ב) [שם פסוק טו]. מכל אשר בחרו. אף בעולת בעל אף הזכר והבהמה [בראשית ו, יב]. נבקעו. להוציא מימיהן. תהום רבה. מדה כנגד מדה הם חטאו ברבה רעת האדם (בראשית ו ה) ולקו בתהום רבה [שם ז, יא]. נשתיירו מהם. ויסכרו מעינות. כשנפתחו כתיב (ז יא) כל מעינות וכאן אין כתיב כל לפי שנשתיירו מהם אותן שיש בהם צורך לעולם כגון חמי טבריא וכיוצא בהם [שם ח, ב]. חמי טבריא. מעינות רותחין [פסחים מא.]. קץ כל בשר. כל מקום שאתה מוצא זנות ועבודה זרה אנדרלמוסיא באה לעולם והורגת טובים ורעים. כי מלאה הארץ חמס. לא נחתם גזר דינם אלא על הגזל [בראשית ו, יג]. החמס קם וגו'. החמס אשר בידכם הוא קם עליכם למטה רשע לשחתכם. לא מהם. כך אמר הקב"ה למשחית אינך זקוק להשאיר נפש [מרשעי ישראל] כי אין טובה יוצאת לא מהם ולא מבניהם ולא מהמונם. ולא נה בהם. אין בהם נוהה אחרי מגעגע ונותן לב אלי כמו וינהו כל בית ישראל אחרי ה' (שמואל א ז) ולשון ארמי הוא תמינהון לפולחנא ל' תאוה וגעגועין ומנח' חברו לשון יללה וכן וינהו כל בית ישראל פירש לשון יללה ואין בתיבה רק ה"א יסוד [יחזקאל ז, יא]. בדורותיו. יש מרבותינו דורשים אותו לשבח כל שכן שאלו היה בדור צדיקים היה צדיק יותר ויש שדורשים אותו לגנאי לפי דורו היה צדיק ואלו היה בדורו של אברהם לא היה נחשב לכלום [בראשית ו, ט]. פלייטון. בלסמ"א משחא דאפרסמא [שבת סב. ועיין רש"י כאן]. מכל אשר בחרבה. לאפוקי דגים שבים [זבחים קיג:]. קל הוא על פני מים. כשהיו הצדיקים נח ומתושלח מוכיחים אותם ואומרים להם שעתיד המבול לבא עליהם היו אומרים קלים אנו לשוט על המים ויש לנו גומא ודברים קלים לעשות מהם אניות ולשוט. תקולל חלקתם בארץ לא יפנה דרך כרמים. היו מקללים את חלקם בארץ לאמר לא יפנה דרך הטוב בדרכי הצדיקים הרמים ושוכנים ברומו של עולם ל"א כרמים הם הצדיקים ופרנסי הדור כמו ונתתי לה את כרמיה משם (הושע ב) ת"י ית פרנסהא היו מקללים את חלקם בארץ לאמר לא יפנו דרך הטוב נשבעים שלא יפנו את דרכם ל"א תקולל חלקתם מתקלקלת היתה חלקתם וכו' [איוב כח, יח].

הגהות הגר"א

[א] גמ' דור המדבר. נ"ב עליו אות ב: [ב] שם עדת קרח. נ"ב עליו אות א: [ג] שם ימיהם בטוב. נ"ל בטוב ימיהם: ושנותם בנעימים וכתיב. נמחק: [ד] שם וארבות השמים נפתחו. נמחק ונ"ב ויסכרו מעינות תהום: [ה] שם מלמד שהיו מפנים דרך כרמים. נמחק:

תורה אור השלם

א) וימתו האנשים מוצאי דבת הארץ רעה במגפה לפני יי: [במדבר יד, לז]
ב) אני יי דברתי אם לא זאת אעשה לכל העדה הרעה הזאת הנועדים עלי במדבר הזה יתמו ושם ימתו: [במדבר יד, לה]
ג) אספו לי חסידי כרתי בריתי עלי זבח: [תהלים נ, ה]
ד) וירדו הם וכל אשר להם חיים שאלה ותכס עליהם הארץ ויאבדו מתוך הקהל: [במדבר טז, לג]
ה) יי ממית ומחיה מוריד שאול ויעל: [שמואל א' ב, ו]
ו) וימח את כל היקום אשר על פני האדמה מאדם עד בהמה עד רמש ועד עוף השמים וימחו מן הארץ וישאר אך נח ואשר אתו בתבה: [בראשית ז, כג]
ז) ויאמר יי לא ידון רוחי באדם לעלם בשגם הוא בשר והיו ימיו מאה ועשרים שנה: [בראשית ו, ג]
ח) תהרו חשש תלדו קש רוחכם אש תאכלכם: [ישעיה לג, יא]
ט) בתיהם שלום מפחד ולא שבט אלוה עליהם: [איוב כא, ט]
י) שורו עבר ולא יגעל תפלט פרתו ולא תשכל: [איוב כא, י]
יא) ישלחו כצאן עויליהם וילדיהם ירקדון: [איוב כא, יא]
יב) ישאו כתף וכנור וישמחו לקול עוגב: [איוב כא, יב]
יג) יבלו בטוב ימיהם וברגע שאול יחתו: [איוב כא, יג]
[ע"פ מסוה"ש] אם ישמעו ויעבדו יכלו ימיהם בטוב ושניהם בנעימים: [איוב לו, יא]
יד) ויאמרו לאל סור ממנו ודעת דרכיך לא חפצנו: מה שדי כי נעבדנו ומה נועיל כי נפגע בו: [איוב כא, יד-טו]
טו) ואני הנני מביא את המבול מים על הארץ לשחת כל בשר אשר בו רוח חיים מתחת השמים כל אשר בארץ יגוע: [בראשית ו, יז]
טז) ויראו בני האלהים את בנות האדם כי טבת הנה ויקחו להם נשים מכל אשר בחרו: [בראשית ו, ב]
יז) בשנת שש מאות שנה לחיי נח בחדש השני בשבעה עשר יום לחדש ביום הזה נבקעו כל מעינות תהום רבה וארבת השמים נפתחו: [בראשית ז, יא]
[ע"פ הגר"א] ויסכרו מעינת תהום וארבת השמים ויכלא הגשם מן השמים: [בראשית ח, ב]
יח) וירא יי כי רבה רעת האדם בארץ וכל יצר מחשבת לבו רק רע כל היום: [בראשית ו, ה]
יט) וירא אלהים את הארץ והנה נשחתה כי השחית כל בשר את דרכו על הארץ: [בראשית ו, יב]
כ) ויאמר אלהים לנח קץ כל בשר בא לפני כי מלאה הארץ חמס מפניהם והנני משחיתם את הארץ: [בראשית ו, יג]
כא) החמס קם למטה רשע לא מהם ולא מהמונם ולא מהמהם ולא נה בהם: [יחזקאל ז, יא]
כב) ויאמר יי אמחה את האדם אשר בראתי מעל פני האדמה מאדם עד בהמה עד רמש ועד עוף השמים כי נחמתי כי עשיתם: ונח מצא חן בעיני יי: [בראשית ו, ז-ח]
כג) וינחם יי כי עשה את האדם בארץ ויתעצב אל לבו: [בראשית ו, ו]
כד) ועתה אל תיראו אנכי אכלכל אתכם ואת טפכם וינחם אותם וידבר על לבם: [בראשית נ, כא]
כה) וינחם יי על הרעה אשר דבר לעשות לעמו: [שמות לב, יד]
כו) אלה תולדת נח נח איש צדיק תמים היה בדרתיו את האלהים התהלך נח: [בראשית ו, ט]
כז) כל אשר נשמת רוח חיים באפיו מכל אשר בחרבה מתו: [בראשית ז, כב]
כח) קל הוא על פני מים תקלל חלקתם בארץ לא יפנה דרך כרמים: [איוב כד, יח]

הַזֶּה – HE BLOTTED OUT ALL EXISTENCE – IN THIS WORLD; "וַיִּמָּחוּ מִן־הָאָרֶץ" לָעוֹלָם הַבָּא – AND THEY WERE BLOTTED OUT FROM THE EARTH – FOR THE WORLD TO COME.[14] דִּבְרֵי רַבִּי עֲקִיבָא – THESE ARE THE WORDS OF R' AKIVA. רַבִּי יְהוּדָה בֶּן בְּתֵירָא אוֹמֵר – R' YEHUDAH BEN BESEIRA SAYS: לֹא חַיִּין וְלֹא נִדּוֹנִין – THEY WILL NOT COME ALIVE at the Resurrection, NOR WILL THEY BE JUDGED at the Final Judgment, שֶׁנֶּאֱמַר "לֹא־יָדוֹן רוּחִי בָאָדָם לְעֹלָם" – AS IT IS STATED:[15] *MY SPIRIT SHALL NOT CONTEND EVERMORE CONCERNING MAN* – לֹא דִּין וְלֹא רוּחַ – NEITHER JUDGMENT NOR SPIRIT.[16] דָּבָר אַחֵר – ANOTHER INTERPRETATION: "לֹא־יָדוֹן רוּחִי" – *MY SPIRIT SHALL NOT CONTEND* (*lo yadon*) means that שֶׁלֹּא תְּהֵא נִשְׁמָתָן חוֹזֶרֶת לְנִדְנָהּ – THEIR SOUL SHALL NOT RETURN TO ITS SHEATH (*nedan*), i.e. the body.[17] רַבִּי מְנַחֵם (בר יוסף) [בְּרַבִּי יוֹסֵי] אוֹמֵר – R' MENACHEM THE SON OF R' YOSE SAYS: אֲפִילוּ בְּשָׁעָה שֶׁהַקָּדוֹשׁ בָּרוּךְ הוּא מַחֲזִיר נְשָׁמוֹת לִפְגָרִים מֵתִים – EVEN AT THE TIME AT WHICH THE HOLY ONE, BLESSED IS HE, WILL RESTORE SOULS TO DEAD BODIES, i.e. the time of the Resurrection, נִשְׁמָתָן קָשָׁה לָהֶם בְּגֵיהִנָּם – THEIR SOULS WILL BE HARMFUL TO THEM IN GEHINNOM,[18] שֶׁנֶּאֱמַר "תַּהֲרוּ חֲשַׁשׁ תֵּלְדוּ קַשׁ רוּחֲכֶם אֵשׁ תֹּאכַלְכֶם" – AS IT IS STATED:[19] *YOU SHALL BE CONCEIVED OF CHAFF, BORN OF STRAW; YOUR FIERY SPIRIT SHALL CONSUME YOU.*[20]

A Baraisa discusses the root causes of the sins of the Generation of the Flood, expounding a series of verses in the Book of *Job*:[21]

תָּנוּ רַבָּנָן – **The Rabbis taught in a Baraisa:** דּוֹר הַמַּבּוּל לֹא נִתְגָּאוּ אֶלָּא בִּשְׁבִיל טוֹבָה שֶׁהִשְׁפִּיעַ לָהֶם הַקָּדוֹשׁ בָּרוּךְ הוּא – THE people of the GENERATION OF THE FLOOD BECAME ARROGANT ONLY BECAUSE OF THE BOUNTY THAT THE HOLY ONE, BLESSED IS HE, LAVISHED UPON THEM.[22] וּמַה כְּתִיב בָּהֶם – WHAT IS WRITTEN ABOUT THEM? "בָּתֵּיהֶם שָׁלוֹם מִפָּחַד וְלֹא־שֵׁבֶט אֱלוֹהַּ עֲלֵיהֶם" – *THEIR HOUSES WERE SECURE FROM TERROR, AND THE ROD OF GOD WAS NOT UPON THEM.*[23] וּכְתִיב "שׁוֹרוֹ עִבַּר וְלֹא יַגְעִל תְּפַלֵּט פָּרָתוֹ וְלֹא תְשַׁכֵּל" – AND IT IS WRITTEN in the next verse: *HIS OX IMPREGNATES, DOES NOT MISDIRECT [ITS SEED]; HIS COW CALVES, DOES NOT MISCARRY.*[24] וּכְתִיב "יְשַׁלְּחוּ כַצֹּאן עֲוִילֵיהֶם וְיַלְדֵיהֶם יְרַקֵּדוּן" – AND IT IS WRITTEN further: *THEY SEND OUT THEIR YOUNG FREELY LIKE SHEEP, AND THEIR CHILDREN FROLIC.*[25] וּכְתִיב "יִשְׂאוּ כְּתֹף וְכִנּוֹר וְיִשְׂמְחוּ לְקוֹל עוּגָב" – AND IT IS WRITTEN further: *THEY RAISE [MUSIC] WITH DRUM AND HARP, AND REJOICE TO THE SOUND OF THE FLUTE.*[26] וּכְתִיב "יְכַלּוּ יְמֵיהֶם בַּטּוֹב וּשְׁנֵיהֶם בַּנְּעִימִים" – AND IT IS WRITTEN: *THEY LIVE OUT THEIR DAYS IN COMFORT, THEIR YEARS WITH PLEASANTNESS.*[27] וּכְתִיב "וּבְרֶגַע שְׁאוֹל יֵחָתּוּ" – AND IT IS WRITTEN: *THEY GO DOWN TO THE GRAVE IN ONE SECOND.*[28] וְהִיא גָּרְמָה שֶׁאָמְרוּ לָאֵל – AND THIS prosperity CAUSED THEM TO SAY TO GOD: "סוּר מִמֶּנּוּ וְדַעַת דְּרָכֶיךָ לֹא חָפָצְנוּ – *LEAVE US! WE HAVE NO WISH TO KNOW YOUR PATHS!* מַה־שַּׁדַּי כִּי־נַעַבְדֶנּוּ וּמַה־נּוֹעִיל כִּי נִפְגַּע־בּוֹ" – *WHAT IS THE ALMIGHTY THAT WE SHOULD SERVE HIM? AND WHAT WOULD WE ACCOMPLISH BY APPROACHING HIM IN PRAYER?*[29] אָמְרוּ – THEY SAID: כְּלוּם צְרִיכִין אָנוּ לוֹ אֶלָּא לְטִיפָּה שֶׁל גְּשָׁמִים – DO WE NEED [THE ALMIGHTY] FOR ANYTHING OTHER THAN A DROP OF RAIN, i.e. our water supply? יֵשׁ לָנוּ נְהָרוֹת וּמַעְיָנוֹת שֶׁאָנוּ מִסְתַּפְּקִין מֵהֶן – Why, we do not even need Him for that! WE HAVE RIVERS AND STREAMS FROM WHICH TO SUPPLY OURSELVES.[30] אָמַר הַקָּדוֹשׁ בָּרוּךְ הוּא – Thereupon, THE HOLY ONE, BLESSED IS HE, SAID: בַּטּוֹבָה שֶׁהִשְׁפַּעְתִּי לָהֶן בָּהּ מַכְעִיסִין אוֹתִי – WITH THE VERY BOUNTY THAT I LAVISHED UPON THEM, i.e. water, THEY ARE PROVOKING ME![31] וּבָהּ אֲנִי דָן אוֹתָם – WITH THAT very bounty SHALL I PUNISH THEM! שֶׁנֶּאֱמַר "וַאֲנִי הִנְנִי מֵבִיא אֶת־הַמַּבּוּל מַיִם" – AS IT IS STATED: *AS FOR ME – I AM PREPARED TO BRING THE MABBUL OF WATER.*[32]

NOTES

14. The obvious redundancy in the verse implies a double death. Moreover, according to this exposition, the term וַיִּמָּחוּ מִן־הָאָרֶץ is interpreted as *and they were blotted out from the* ***land,*** and refers to the Land of Life, i.e. the World to Come (*Maharsha*; see also *Ramban* to *Genesis* loc. cit.).

15. *Genesis* 6:3.

16. See 107b note 50.

17. According to this interpretation, the word יָדוֹן is related to נָדָן, *sheath,* and refers to the body, which is the sheath of the soul (see *Daniel* 7:15). Thus, the verse indicates that the soul, which is the Godly spirit that is invested in the body, will nevermore be restored to any member of the Generation of the Flood, i.e. they will not come back to life at the Resurrection (see *Maharsha*).

18. At the time of the Resurrection, when the restoration of the souls will bring the bodies of the righteous back to life, the restoration of the souls of that wicked generation will not resurrect their bodies, but will merely increase the suffering of the bodies in Gehinnom (see note 20).

19. *Isaiah* 33:11. This verse is part of a passage discussing the End of the Days.

20. I.e. the relationship of your souls to your bodies will be as that of a flame to chaff and straw, for your very souls shall destroy your bodies (*Rashi, Maharsha*). R' Menachem the son of R' Yose disagrees with the opinion of R' Yehudah ben Beseira, who said that the Generation of the Flood will not be resurrected. According to R' Menachem they will be resurrected but will suffer a greater punishment than other sinners, for their souls will destroy their bodies (*Yad Ramah*).

21. *Job* 21:7 reads: מַדּוּעַ רְשָׁעִים יִחְיוּ עָתְקוּ גַּם־גָּבְרוּ חָיִל, *Why should the wicked endure, attain old age, also accomplish mightily?* That verse and the verses that follow it, which the Gemara will cite, refer to the wicked of the Generation of the Flood, who had extraordinarily happy lives until the Flood washed them away (*Maharsha*).

22. God bestowed extraordinary prosperity on that generation, but rather than taking advantage of the munificence to devote themselves to spiritual pursuits, they overindulged in materialism and thus distanced themselves from God (*Maharal*). As the Baraisa goes on to explain, their prosperity led them to grow arrogant towards God Himself.

[Perhaps this serves to explain why the Generation of the Flood will have no share in the World to Come. They were granted a foretaste of such a world, having been freed of all cares and enabled to devote themselves to spiritual pursuits. However, they spurned this heaven-sent opportunity. It stands to reason, therefore, that these persons should not be given another such opportunity for spirituality, i.e. a share in the World to Come (see *Iyun Yaakov*).]

23. Ibid. 21:9.

24. Ibid. v. 10.

25. Ibid. v. 11. I.e. they are able to allow their children to frolic outdoors without supervision, without fear of harm befalling them (see *Maharsha*).

26. Ibid. v. 12.

27. Ibid. 36:11. This verse is similar to the first segment of 21:13, which is the next verse in the sequence being cited (see *Mesoras HaShas*). *Gra* emends the text to conform with 21:13.

28. Ibid. 21:13. This too is a blessing: When the time for their death arrives, they do not endure prolonged suffering, but die quickly (*Rashi* ad loc.). [According to this explanation, the word וברגע may be read as וּבְרֹגַע, i.e. *and calmly* (see *Targum* ad loc.).]

Alternatively: This is a description of the dire consequences of their self-indulgence: They were wiped out in one second with the sudden eruption of the Flood (*Maharsha*).

29. Ibid. vs. 14-15.

30. They acknowledged God's existence, but propounded the heretical philosophy that He had abandoned the Earth to mankind and was no longer involved in governing it. Thus, the only aspect for which one might consider turning to Him in prayer would be rain, which falls from Heaven. Yet they said, "Even that is unnecessary, for we have an abundant supply of stream water!" This is the meaning of the verse, *"What is the Almighty that we should serve Him? And what would we accomplish by approaching Him in prayer?"* (*Maharsha*).

31. I.e. their prosperity is the result of the abundance of river and stream water that I have provided them, which has produced bountiful harvests and helped them attain wealth. They now have the impudence to say that since they have so much river water they are totally independent of Me!

32. *Genesis* 6:17. In a previous verse (ibid. v. 13), God said: וְהִנְנִי מַשְׁחִיתָם אֶת־הָאָרֶץ, *and I am prepared to destroy them from the earth.* In this verse,

מסורת הש"ס

א) [ירושלמי ל"ג מרגלים וכו'], ב) [תוספתא פי"ג], ג) [צ"ל ברבי יוסי וכ"א בילקוט], ד) [חשש מין מוץ שנוח לידלק], ה) [תוספתא דסוטה פ"ג], ו) [אין זה בהנך פסוקים אלא בסימן לו פי"א כתיב יכלו ימיהם בטוב ושניהם בנעימים], ז) [צ"ל אלהים], ח) [אין בהם נוהה אחרי מגעגע ונותן לב אלי כך פירש"י שם], ט) [בע"י ובילקוט ליתא לכל אותן עשרה תיבות], י) קידושין יג. זבחים קיג:, כ) [צ"ל אמרו וכ"א בע"י].

ליקוטי רש"י

חשש. מין מוץ דבר שנוח לידלק. רוחכם אש. מגופכם תלא רוח אש ותאכל החשש והקש [ישעיהו לג, יא]. שלום מפחד. שלא היו מזיקין שולטין בהן [איוב כא, ט]. שורו עבר. את הנקיבה. ולא יגעיל. לא יורה בה זרע פסולת שיהא חוזר ונפלט מגופה בלא הריון כל לשון הגעלה פליטה הוא וכן בל' משנה מגעילן ברותחין וכן כי שם נגעל מגן גבורים (שמואל ב, א) נפלט משיחתו והיה כאילו לא נמשח בשמן שהיו רגילין למשוח מגיני עור כדי שיהא חלק ומחליק את הרומח והחנית המכה בו והוא כמו שריס משחו מגן (ישעי' כא). תפלט פרתו. בעת תלד את וולדה. ולא תשכל. בלא עת [שם י]. ישלחו כצאן עויליהם וגו'. בעת לידתו היה הולך ומרקד מיד ואם פוגע במזיק נלחם בו והיתה אומרת לו אמו הבא לי מספריים ואחתוך שערך בהגדת בראשית, לך והדליק לי את הנר בראשית רבה [שם יא]. וברגע שאול יחתו. כשמגיע יום מותו היה מת לפי שעה בנחת בלא יסורין. יחתו. ירדו ובתרגום נחיתו [שם, יג]. ומה נועיל. מה הנאה יש לנו כי נפגע בו אין אנו צריכין לו אפי' לטיפת גשמים כי אד יעלה מן הארץ (בראשית ב) [שם פסוק טו]. מכל אשר בחרו. אף בעולת בעל אף הזכר והבהמה [בראשית ו, יב]. נבקעו. להוציא מימיהן. תהום רבה. מדה כנגד מדה הם חטאו ברבה רעת האדם (בראשית ו ה) ולקו בתהום רבה [שם ז, יא]. נשתיירו מהם. ויסכרו מעינות. כשנפתחו כתיב (ז יא) כל מעינות וכאן אין כתיב כל לפי שנשתיירו מהם אותן שיש בהם צורך לעולם כגון חמי טבריא וכיוצא בהם [שם ח, ב]. חמי טבריא. מעינות רותחין [פסחים מא.]. קץ כל בשר. כל מקום שאתה מוצא זנות ועבודה זרה אנדרלמוסיא באה לעולם והורגת טובים ורעים. כי מלאה הארץ חמס. לא נחתם גזר דינם אלא על הגזל [בראשית ו, יג]. החמס קם וגו'. החמס אשר בידכם הוא קם עליכם למטה רשע לשחתכם. לא מהם. כך אמר הקב"ה למשחית אינך זקוק להשאיר נפש [מרשעי ישראל] כי אין טובה יוצאת לא מהם ולא מבניהם ולא מהמונם. ולא נה בהם. אין בהם נוהה אחרי מגעגע ונותן לב אלי כמו וינהו כל בית ישראל אחרי ה' (שמואל א ז) ולשון ארמי הוא תתינהון לפולחנא ל' תאוה וגעגועין ומנח' חברו לשון יללה וכן וינהו כל בית ישראל פירש לשון יללה ואין בתיבה רק ה"א יסוד [יחזקאל ז, יא]. בדורותיו. יש מרבותינו דורשים אותו לשבח כל שכן שאלו היה בדור צדיקים היה צדיק יותר ויש שדורשים אותו לגנאי לפי דורו היה צדיק ואלו היה בדורו של אברהם לא היה נחשב לכלום [בראשית ו, ט]. פלייטון. בלשמ"א משחא דאפרסמא [שבת סב. ועיין רש"י כאן]. מכל אשר בחרבה. לאפוקי דגים שבים [זבחים קיג:]. קל הוא על פני מים. כשהיו הצדיקים נח ומתושלח מוכיחים אותם ואומרים להם שעתיד המבול לבא עליהם היו אומרים קלים אנו לשוט על המים ויש לנו גומא ודברים קלים לעשות מהם אניות ולשוט. תקולל חלקתם בארץ לא יפנה דרך כרמים. היו מקללים את חלקם בארץ לאמר לא יפנה דרך הטוב בדרכי הצדיקים הרמים ושוכנים ברומו של עולם ל"א כרמים הם הצדיקים ופרנסי הדור כמו ונתתי לה את כרמיה משם (הושע ב) ת"י ית פרנסהא היו מקללים את חלקם בארץ לאמר לא יפנו דרך הטוב נשבעים שלא יפנו את דרכם ל"א תקולל חלקתם מתקלקלת היתה חלקתם וכו' [איוב כח, יח].

רש"י

רשעים דור המבול. דכתיב [בהו] כי רבה רעת האדם (בראשית ו): חטאים אנשי סדום. דכתיב בהו רעים וחטאים (שם יג): אבל עומדים הם כו'. שחיין ונדונים: גמ' נשמתן קשה להם בגיהנם. נשמת עצמן שרפתן דכתיב רוחכם אש תאכלכם (ישעיה לג): בשביל גלגל העין. שרואין טובתן שלימה והיו גובהין עיניהם ומנאפין אחר עיניהם: במים. שדומה לגלגל העין מעינות שנובעין ממקום קטן כמו עין: שלשה נשתיירו. מאותן מעיינות של דור המבול שהיו חמין כדאמר לקמן ברותחין קלקלו ברותחין נדונו: וכולן חזרו. להזדווג עם מינייהם: חוץ מתושלמי. עוף הוא שאוחז עדיין תרבות רעה שמזדווג עם הכל. תושלמי עוף אחד ובמסכת חולין (דף סג:) גבי שמונה ספיקות איתא והרנוגא תושלמי ומרלא ודרכו של אותו עוף להרביע כל הבריות: שוקף. החמס עצמו כמקל והיינו החמס קם למטה רשע: לא מהם. אין תועלת לא בהם ולא בהמונם ולא במשאם: מהמהם. אשטרי"א בלע"ז: כי נחמתי כי עשיתים ונח. סמוכין דריש: יפה עשיתי וכו'. שאיבדתי דרך רשעים כזה: לא יפה עשיתי. דאפשר היו חוזרין: כל שכן. אילו הוה בדורות אחרים היה צדיק יותר: פלייטון. בושם שריחו נודף ואינו אפרסמון: מקיפה. מציף כמו ויצף הברזל דמתרגמינן וקפא (מלכים ב ו): כזיקין. נודות: לא יפנה דרך כרמים אמרו לו ומי מעכב. [מיד] שאינו עושה אם יש בידו כח לעשות כך: [פרידה] אחת יש לי להוציא מכם. מתושלח הצדיק ימות קודם ולא יהיה נדון עמכם: א"כ

משנה וגמרא

רשעים במשפט וחטאים בעדת צדיקים על כן לא יקומו רשעים במשפט זה דור המבול וחטאים בעדת צדיקים אלו אנשי סדום אמרו לו אינם עומדין בעדת צדיקים אבל עומדין בעדת רשעים (א) מרגלים אין להם חלק לעולם הבא שנאמר א) וימותו האנשים מוציאי דבת הארץ רעה במגפה לפני ה' (וימותו בעולם הזה במגפה לעולם הבא) [א] דור המדבר אין להם חלק לעולם הבא ואין עומדין בדין שנאמר ב) במדבר הזה יתמו ושם ימותו דברי רבי עקיבא ר' אליעזר אומר עליהם הוא אומר ג) אספו לי חסידי כורתי בריתי עלי זבח [ב] עדת קרח אינה עתידה לעלות שנאמר ד) ותכס עליהם הארץ בעולם הזה ויאבדו מתוך הקהל לעולם הבא דברי ר"ע ר"א אומר עליהם הוא אומר ה) ה' ממית ומחיה מוריד שאול ויעל: גמ' (ב) ת"ר דור המבול אין להם חלק לעולם הבא שנאמר ו) וימח את כל היקום אשר על פני האדמה וימח את כל היקום בעולם הזה וימחו מן הארץ לעולם הבא דברי ר"ע ר"י בן בתירא אומר לא חיין ולא נדונין שנאמר ז) לא ידון רוחי באדם לעולם לא דין ולא רוח דבר אחר לא ידון רוחי שלא תהא נשמתן חוזרת לנדנה ר' מנחם (ג) בר יוסף אומר אפילו בשעה שהקב"ה מחזיר נשמות לפגרים מתים נשמתן קשה להם בגיהנם שנאמר ח) תהרו (ד) חשש תלדו קש רוחכם אש תאכלכם ת"ר (ה) דור המבול לא נתגאו אלא בשביל טובה שהשפיע להם הקב"ה ומה כתיב בהם ט) בתיהם שלום מפחד ולא שבט אלוה עליהם וכתיב י) שורו עבר ולא יגעיל תפלט פרתו ולא תשכל וכתיב יא) ישלחו כצאן עויליהם וילדיהם ירקדון וכתיב יב) ישאו בתוף וכנור וישמחו לקול עוגב וכתיב יג) יבלו [ג] ימיהם בטוב (ו) ושנותם בנעימים וכתיב יג) וברגע שאול יחתו והיא גרמה שאמרו לאל יד) סור ממנו ודעת דרכיך לא חפצנו מה שדי כי נעבדנו ומה נועיל כי נפגע בו אמרו כלום צריכין אנו לו אלא לטיפה של גשמים יש לנו נהרות ומעינות שאנו מסתפקין מהן אמר הקב"ה בטובה שהשפעתי להן בה מכעיסין אותי ובה אני דן אותם שנאמר טו) ואני הנני מביא את המבול מים ר' יוסי אמר דור המבול לא נתגאו אלא בשביל גלגל העין שדומה למים [שנאמר טז) ויקחו להם נשים מכל אשר בחרו] לפיכך דן אותן במים שדומה לגלגל העין שנאמר יז) נבקעו כל מעינות תהום רבה [ד] וארבות השמים נפתחו א"ר יוחנן דור המבול ברבה קלקלו וברבה נידונו ברבה קלקלו שנאמר יח) וירא ה' כי רבה רעת האדם וברבה נידונו שנאמר יז) כל מעינות תהום רבה א"ר יוחנן שלשה נשתיירו מהם בלועה דגדר וחמי טבריא ועיניא רבתי דבירם יט) כי השחית כל בשר את דרכו על הארץ א"ר יוחנן מלמד שהרביעו בהמה על חיה וחיה על בהמה והכל על אדם ואדם על הכל א"ר אבא בר כהנא וכולם חזרו חוץ מתושלמי כ) ויאמר (ז) ה' לנח קץ כל בשר בא לפני א"ר יוחנן בא וראה כמה גדול כחה של חמס שהרי דור המבול עברו על הכל ולא נחתם עליהם גזר דינם עד שפשטו ידיהם בגזל שנאמר כ) כי מלאה הארץ חמס מפניהם והנני משחיתם את הארץ וכתיב כא) החמס קם למטה רשע לא מהם ולא מהמונם ולא מהמהם ולא (ח) נה בהם א"ר אלעזר מלמד שזקף עצמו כמקל ועמד לפני הקב"ה ואמר לפניו רבש"ע לא מהם ולא מהמונם ולא מהמהם ולא נה בהם (ט) (ואף על נח נחתם גזר דין שנא' ולא נח בהם) תנא דבי ר' ישמעאל אף על נח נחתך גזר דין אלא שמצא חן בעיני ה' שנאמר כב) נחמתי כי עשיתם ונח מצא חן בעיני ה' כג) וינחם ה' כי עשה את האדם בארץ כי אתא רב דימי אמר אמר הקב"ה יפה עשיתי שתקנתי להם קברות בארץ מאי משמע כתיב הכא וינחם ה' וכתיב התם כד) וינחם אותם וידבר על לבם ואיכא דאמרי לא יפה עשיתי שתקנתי להם קברות בארץ כתיב הכא וינחם וכתיב התם כה) וינחם ה' על הרעה אשר דבר לעשות לעמו כו) אלה תולדות נח [נח איש צדיק תמים היה בדורותיו] א"ר יוחנן בדורותיו ולא בדורות אחרים וריש לקיש אמר בדורותיו כ"ש בדורות אחרים א"ר חנינא משל דרבי יוחנן למה הדבר דומה לחבית של יין שהיתה מונחת במרתף של חומץ במקומה ריחה נודף שלא במקומה אין ריחה נודף א"ר אושעיא משל דריש לקיש למה הדבר דומה לצלוחית של פלייטון שהיתה מונחת במקום הטנופת במקומה ריחה נודף וכ"ש במקום הבושם ו) וימח את כל היקום אשר על פני האדמה אם אדם חטא בהמה מה חטאה תנא משום רבי יהושע בן קרחה משל לאדם שעשה חופה לבנו והתקין מכל מיני סעודה לימים מת בנו עמד (ובלבל) [ופזר] את חופתו אמר כלום עשיתי אלא בשביל בני עכשיו שמת חופה למה לי אף הקב"ה אמר כלום בראתי בהמה וחיה אלא בשביל אדם עכשיו שאדם חוטא בהמה וחיה למה לי כז) מכל אשר בחרבה מתו (י) ולא דגים שבים דרש ר' יוסי דמן קסרי מאי דכתיב כח) קל הוא על פני מים תקולל חלקתם בארץ מלמד שהיה נח הצדיק מוכיח בהם ואומר להם עשו תשובה ואם לאו הקב"ה מביא עליכם את המבול ומקפה נבלתכם על המים כזיקין שנאמר קל הוא על פני מים ולא עוד אלא שלוקחין מהם קללה לכל באי עולם שנאמר כח) תקולל חלקתם בארץ לא יפנה דרך כרמים מלמד שהיו מפנים דרך כרמים [ה] (כ) אמר לו ומי מעכב אמר להם פרידה אחת יש לי להוציא מכם

א"כ

הגהות הגר"א

[א] גמ' דור המדבר. נרשם עליו אות ב: [ב] שם עדת קרח. נרשם עליו אות א: [ג] שם ימיהם בטוב. צ"ל בטוב ימיהם: ושנותם בנעימים וכתיב. נמחק: [ד] שם וארבות השמים נפתחו. נמחק וצ"ב ויסכרו מעינות תהום: [ה] שם מלמד שהיו מפנים דרך כרמים. נמחק:

תורה אור השלם

א) וַיָּמֻתוּ הָאֲנָשִׁים מוֹצִאֵי דִבַּת הָאָרֶץ רָעָה בַּמַּגֵּפָה לִפְנֵי יְיָ: [במדבר יד, לז]

ב) אֲנִי יְיָ דִּבַּרְתִּי אִם לֹא זֹאת אֶעֱשֶׂה לְכָל הָעֵדָה הָרָעָה הַזֹּאת הַנּוֹעָדִים עָלָי בַּמִּדְבָּר הַזֶּה יִתַּמּוּ וְשָׁם יָמֻתוּ: [במדבר יד, לה]

ג) אִסְפוּ לִי חֲסִידָי כֹּרְתֵי בְרִיתִי עֲלֵי זָבַח: [תהלים נ, ה]

ד) וַיֵּרְדוּ הֵם וְכָל אֲשֶׁר לָהֶם חַיִּים שְׁאֹלָה וַתְּכַס עֲלֵיהֶם הָאָרֶץ וַיֹּאבְדוּ מִתּוֹךְ הַקָּהָל: [במדבר טז, לג]

ה) יְיָ מֵמִית וּמְחַיֶּה מוֹרִיד שְׁאוֹל וַיָּעַל: [שמואל א' ב, ו]

ו) וַיִּמַח אֶת כָּל הַיְקוּם אֲשֶׁר עַל פְּנֵי הָאֲדָמָה מֵאָדָם עַד בְּהֵמָה עַד רֶמֶשׂ וְעַד עוֹף הַשָּׁמַיִם וַיִּמָּחוּ מִן הָאָרֶץ וַיִּשָּׁאֶר אַךְ נֹחַ וַאֲשֶׁר אִתּוֹ בַּתֵּבָה: [בראשית ז, כג]

ז) וַיֹּאמֶר יְיָ לֹא יָדוֹן רוּחִי בָאָדָם לְעֹלָם בְּשַׁגַּם הוּא בָשָׂר וְהָיוּ יָמָיו מֵאָה וְעֶשְׂרִים שָׁנָה: [בראשית ו, ג]

ח) תַּהֲרוּ חֲשַׁשׁ תֵּלְדוּ קַשׁ רוּחֲכֶם אֵשׁ תֹּאכַלְכֶם: [ישעיה לג, יא]

ט) בָּתֵּיהֶם שָׁלוֹם מִפָּחַד וְלֹא שֵׁבֶט אֱלוֹהַּ עֲלֵיהֶם: [איוב כא, ט]

י) שׁוֹרוֹ עִבַּר וְלֹא יַגְעִל תְּפַלֵּט פָּרָתוֹ וְלֹא תְשַׁכֵּל: [איוב כא, י]

יא) יְשַׁלְּחוּ כַצֹּאן עֲוִילֵיהֶם וְיַלְדֵיהֶם יְרַקֵּדוּן: [איוב כא, יא]

יב) יִשְׂאוּ כְּתֹף וְכִנּוֹר וְיִשְׂמְחוּ לְקוֹל עוּגָב: [איוב כא, יב]

יג) יְכַלּוּ בַטּוֹב יְמֵיהֶם וּבְרֶגַע שְׁאוֹל יֵחָתּוּ: [איוב כא, יג]

[ע"פ מסוה"ש] אִם יִשְׁמְעוּ וְיַעֲבֹדוּ יְכַלּוּ יְמֵיהֶם בַּטּוֹב וּשְׁנֵיהֶם בַּנְּעִימִים: [איוב לו, יא]

יד) וַיֹּאמְרוּ לָאֵל סוּר מִמֶּנּוּ וְדַעַת דְּרָכֶיךָ לֹא חָפָצְנוּ: מַה שַּׁדַּי כִּי נַעַבְדֶנּוּ וּמַה נּוֹעִיל כִּי נִפְגַּע בּוֹ: [איוב כא, יד-טו]

טו) וַאֲנִי הִנְנִי מֵבִיא אֶת הַמַּבּוּל מַיִם עַל הָאָרֶץ לְשַׁחֵת כָּל בָּשָׂר אֲשֶׁר בּוֹ רוּחַ חַיִּים מִתַּחַת הַשָּׁמָיִם כֹּל אֲשֶׁר בָּאָרֶץ יִגְוָע: [בראשית ו, יז]

טז) וַיִּרְאוּ בְנֵי הָאֱלֹהִים אֶת בְּנוֹת הָאָדָם כִּי טֹבֹת הֵנָּה וַיִּקְחוּ לָהֶם נָשִׁים מִכֹּל אֲשֶׁר בָּחָרוּ: [בראשית ו, ב]

יז) בִּשְׁנַת שֵׁשׁ מֵאוֹת שָׁנָה לְחַיֵּי נֹחַ בַּחֹדֶשׁ הַשֵּׁנִי בְּשִׁבְעָה עָשָׂר יוֹם לַחֹדֶשׁ בַּיּוֹם הַזֶּה נִבְקְעוּ כָּל מַעְיְנוֹת תְּהוֹם רַבָּה וַאֲרֻבֹּת הַשָּׁמַיִם נִפְתָּחוּ: [בראשית ז, יא]

[ע"פ הגר"א] וַיִּסָּכְרוּ מַעְיְנֹת תְּהוֹם וַאֲרֻבֹּת הַשָּׁמָיִם וַיִּכָּלֵא הַגֶּשֶׁם מִן הַשָּׁמָיִם: [בראשית ח, ב]

יח) וַיַּרְא יְיָ כִּי רַבָּה רָעַת הָאָדָם בָּאָרֶץ וְכָל יֵצֶר מַחְשְׁבֹת לִבּוֹ רַק רַע כָּל הַיּוֹם: [בראשית ו, ה]

יט) וַיַּרְא אֱלֹהִים אֶת הָאָרֶץ וְהִנֵּה נִשְׁחָתָה כִּי הִשְׁחִית כָּל בָּשָׂר אֶת דַּרְכּוֹ עַל הָאָרֶץ: [בראשית ו, יב]

כ) וַיֹּאמֶר אֱלֹהִים לְנֹחַ קֵץ כָּל בָּשָׂר בָּא לְפָנַי כִּי מָלְאָה הָאָרֶץ חָמָס מִפְּנֵיהֶם וְהִנְנִי מַשְׁחִיתָם אֶת הָאָרֶץ: [בראשית ו, יג]

כא) הֶחָמָס קָם לְמַטֵּה רֶשַׁע לֹא מֵהֶם וְלֹא מֵהֲמוֹנָם וְלֹא מֶהֱמֵהֶם וְלֹא נֹהַּ בָּהֶם: [יחזקאל ז, יא]

כב) וַיֹּאמֶר יְיָ אֶמְחֶה אֶת הָאָדָם אֲשֶׁר בָּרָאתִי מֵעַל פְּנֵי הָאֲדָמָה מֵאָדָם עַד בְּהֵמָה עַד רֶמֶשׂ וְעַד עוֹף הַשָּׁמָיִם כִּי נִחַמְתִּי כִּי עֲשִׂיתִם: וְנֹחַ מָצָא חֵן בְּעֵינֵי יְיָ: [בראשית ו, ז-ח]

כג) וַיִּנָּחֶם יְיָ כִּי עָשָׂה אֶת הָאָדָם בָּאָרֶץ וַיִּתְעַצֵּב אֶל לִבּוֹ: [בראשית ו, ו]

כד) וְעַתָּה אַל תִּירָאוּ אָנֹכִי אֲכַלְכֵּל אֶתְכֶם וְאֶת טַפְּכֶם וַיְנַחֵם אוֹתָם וַיְדַבֵּר עַל לִבָּם: [בראשית נ, כא]

כה) וַיִּנָּחֶם יְיָ עַל הָרָעָה אֲשֶׁר דִּבֶּר לַעֲשׂוֹת לְעַמּוֹ: [שמות לב, יד]

כו) אֵלֶּה תּוֹלְדֹת נֹחַ נֹחַ אִישׁ צַדִּיק תָּמִים הָיָה בְּדֹרֹתָיו אֶת הָאֱלֹהִים הִתְהַלֶּךְ נֹחַ: [בראשית ו, ט]

כז) כֹּל אֲשֶׁר נִשְׁמַת רוּחַ חַיִּים בְּאַפָּיו מִכֹּל אֲשֶׁר בֶּחָרָבָה מֵתוּ: [בראשית ז, כב]

כח) קַל הוּא עַל פְּנֵי מַיִם תְּקֻלַּל חֶלְקָתָם בָּאָרֶץ לֹא יִפְנֶה דֶּרֶךְ כְּרָמִים: [איוב כד, יח]

Another opinion concerning the reason they were punished with water:

רַבִּי יוֹסֵי אָמַר – R' YOSE SAID: דּוֹר הַמַּבּוּל לֹא נִתְגָּאוּ אֶלָּא בִּשְׁבִיל גַּלְגַּל הָעַיִן שֶׁדּוֹמֶה לַמַּיִם – THE people of the GENERATION OF THE FLOOD BECAME ARROGANT ONLY AS A RESULT OF the freedom they exercised with THE EYEBALL,[33] WHICH RESEMBLES WATER.[34] [״וַיִּקְחוּ לָהֶם נָשִׁים מִכֹּל אֲשֶׁר בָּחָרוּ״ ,,שֶׁנֶּאֱמַר – AS IT IS STATED: *THEY TOOK FOR THEMSELVES WIVES FROM WHOMEVER THEY CHOSE.*[35]] לְפִיכָךְ דָּן אוֹתָן בְּמַיִם שֶׁדּוֹמֶה לְגַלְגַּל הָעַיִן – THEREFORE, [GOD] PUNISHED THEM WITH WATER, WHICH RESEMBLES THE EYEBALL, שֶׁנֶּאֱמַר ,,נִבְקְעוּ כָּל־מַעְיְנוֹת תְּהוֹם רַבָּה וַאֲרֻבֹּת הַשָּׁמַיִם נִפְתָּחוּ״ – AS IT IS STATED: *ALL THE FOUNTAINS OF THE GREAT DEEP BURST FORTH, AND THE WINDOWS OF THE HEAVENS WERE OPENED.*[36]

In light of these Tannaic opinions explaining how the Generation of the Flood was punished measure for measure, an Amora offers a third explanation:

אָמַר רַבִּי יוֹחָנָן – **R' Yochanan said:** דּוֹר הַמַּבּוּל בְּרַבָּה קִלְקְלוּ – **The** people of the **Generation of the Flood acted corruptly in** a manner characterized by Scripture as **"great"** *(rabbah);* וּבְרַבָּה נִידּוֹנוּ – **and they were punished in** a manner similarly characterized as **"great"** (*rabbah*). בְּרַבָּה קִלְקְלוּ שֶׁנֶּאֱמַר ,,וַיַּרְא ה׳ כִּי רַבָּה רָעַת הָאָדָם״ – **They acted corruptly in** a manner characterized by Scripture as **"great," as it is stated:**[37] ***And God saw that man's wickedness was great*** (*rabbah*). וּבְרַבָּה נִידּוֹנוּ שֶׁנֶּאֱמַר ,,כָּל־מַעְיְנוֹת תְּהוֹם רַבָּה״ – **And they were punished in** a manner characterized by Scripture as **"great," as it is stated:**[38] ***all the fountains of the great*** (*rabbah*) ***deep burst forth.*** Thus, their punishment matched their sins.[39]

A comment concerning the fountains of the deep, which opened during the Flood:

אָמַר רַבִּי יוֹחָנָן – **R' Yochanan said:** שְׁלֹשָׁה נִשְׁתַּיְּירוּ מֵהֶם – **Three of them remained** open after the Flood, and are open to this day: בְּלוּעָה דְּגָדֵר – **The whirlpool at Gader,** וְחַמֵּי טְבֶרְיָא – **the hot springs of Tiberias,** וְעֵינְיָא רַבָּתִי דְּבֵירָם – **and the great fountain of Beiram.**[40]

The Gemara discusses the perversion of the Generation of the Flood:

,,כִּי־הִשְׁחִית כָּל־בָּשָׂר אֶת־דַּרְכּוֹ עַל־הָאָרֶץ״ – Scripture states:[41] ***All flesh had perverted its way on the earth.*** אָמַר רַבִּי יוֹחָנָן – **R' Yochanan said:** מְלַמֵּד שֶׁהִרְבִּיעוּ בְּהֵמָה עַל חַיָּה – **This teaches** us **that they mounted domesticated animals upon wild animals,** וְחַיָּה עַל בְּהֵמָה – **wild animals upon domesticated animals,** וְהַכֹּל עַל אָדָם – **all** types of animals **upon humans** וְאָדָם עַל הַכֹּל – **and humans upon all** types of animals.[42] אָמַר רַבִּי אַבָּא בַּר כַּהֲנָא – **R' Abba bar Kahana said:** וְכוּלָּם חָזְרוּ – After the Flood, **all [the animals] reverted** to normal behavior, and no longer mate with different species, חוּץ מִתּוּשְׁלַמִי – **except for the** bird called ***tushlami,*** which continues to mate indiscriminately to the present day.

Further discussion of the sins that doomed the Generation of the Flood:

,,וַיֹּאמֶר (ה׳) [אֱלֹהִים] לְנֹחַ קֵץ כָּל־בָּשָׂר בָּא לְפָנַי״ – Scripture states:[43] ***And God said to Noah, "The end of all flesh has come before***

NOTES

God specified that He was prepared to bring a מַבּוּל of water. The word מַבּוּל means literally *devastation.* Thus, this verse means that God was prepared to cause the previously mentioned destruction and devastation to come through water. [The word הִנְנִי implies a special preparedness for this (see *Rashi* ad loc.).] The Gemara expounds the reason for His preparedness to make the מַבּוּל of water as being the fact that they provoked Him with water (*Torah Temimah* to *Genesis* 6:17).

33. By gazing upon their own perfect prosperity, they developed haughtiness, which in turn led them to lust after whatever they set eyes upon (*Rashi;* see *Yad Ramah*).

34. See note 36.

35. *Genesis* 6:2. The verse reads, in its entirety: וַיִּרְאוּ בְנֵי־הָאֱלֹהִים אֶת־בְּנוֹת הָאָדָם כִּי טֹבֹת הֵנָּה וַיִּקְחוּ לָהֶם נָשִׁים מִכֹּל אֲשֶׁר בָּחָרוּ, *The sons of the rulers saw that the daughters of man were good and they took for themselves wives from whomever they chose.* This indicates the immorality that characterized society at the time of the Flood: The sons of the rich and powerful took by brute force any woman who caught their fancy.

36. Ibid. 7:11. Fountains resemble the eyeball [which is moist and produces tears] inasmuch as they produce water from a small source (*Rashi*). Alternatively, the ocean, which surrounds dry land, resembles the white of the human eye surrounding the pupil. Since the members of that generation opened their eyes too widely, so to speak, exposing the whites of their eyes, God punished them in kind by causing water to cover the earth, hiding it from sight (*Maharsha;* see also *Derech Eretz Zuta* ch. 9). Note that the word עַיִן means both *eye* and *fountain* (see *Genesis* 16:7) and forms the root of the word מַעְיְנוֹת (see *Yad Ramah* and *Rashi* to *Ecclesiastes* 12:6).

37. *Genesis* 6:5.

38. Ibid. 7:11.

39. The simple meaning of this is that since they eclipsed all boundaries of decent behavior with their evil ways, they were visited with a catastrophe that transcended the normal boundaries of natural disasters. See *Aruch LaNer* for a discussion of the significance of the term רַבָּה (*great*) as regards their sins and punishment.

40. The fountains of the deep were springs of hot water, as the Gemara states below (108b). Some of these hot springs were left open after the Flood for the benefit of mankind (*Rashi* here and to *Genesis* 8:2). [After the Flood, the earth's climate deteriorated, and the health of humans was adversely affected. Therefore, the need arose at that juncture for the restorative powers of hot springs. Before the Flood, the hot springs were not needed, and therefore, God did not open them when He created the world (*Eitz Yosef* to *Bereishis Rabbah* 33:5; see also *Sforno* and *Malbim* to *Genesis* 8:22).] Scripture implies that some of the fountains remained open, for in connection with the beginning of the Flood the Torah states (*Genesis* 7:11) that ***all*** *the fountains of the great deep burst forth,* whereas in describing the end of the Flood it states merely (ibid. 8:2): *the fountains of the deep were closed* (*Bereishis Rabbah* 33:5, cited by *Rashi* to *Genesis* 8:2).

R' Yochanan does not mean that only three hot springs remained open in the entire world, but that these three remained open in Eretz Yisrael and its vicinity. There are, of course, many other hot springs in other parts of the globe (*Ben Yehoyada*).

Margaliyos HaYam points out that Flavius Josephus (*Wars of the Jews* VII:6) mentions the remarkable natural spring at Beiram, which he says had twin fountains, ice-cold water issuing forth from one and extremely hot water from the other. These waters were renowned in his time for their medicinal properties.

41. Ibid. 6:12.

42. [Thus, not only was mankind perverted, man brought perversion upon all flesh.] The Gemara implies that the animals did not seek mates of other species on their own; they were merely mounted upon other species by men. This is also the implication of the Gemara's comment below, "If man sinned, what sin did the animals commit?" However, the verse, *for all flesh has perverted its way,* implies that the animals themselves became perverted. Indeed, the *Midrash* (*Bereishis Rabbah* 28:8) explains this verse as meaning that the animals of that generation sought unusual pairings – dogs would seek out she-wolves and peacocks would mate with hens. Perhaps the intention is that after being trained by men to mate with other species the animals continued to do so on their own. Thus, the animals became perverted, but not through their own initiative (*Yefeh Einayim*). Others explain that mankind's licentious behavior permeated the world with a spirit of immorality which infected even the animals, leading them to engage in deviant behavior on their own. Thus, the animals were perverted, but man, and not they, was to blame for their perversion, for they did what nature caused them to. In contrast, man chose deviant behavior with his power of free will (*Beis HaLevi, Parashas Noach;* see also *Maharsha, Be'er Sheva* and *Hagahos Yavetz*).

43. Ibid. v. 13.

רשעים במשפט וחטאים בעדת צדיקים על כן לא יקומו רשעים במשפט זה דור המבול וחטאים בעדת צדיקים אלו אנשי סדום אמרו לו אינם עומדין בעדת צדיקים אבל עומדין בעדת רשעים ([א] מרגלים אין להם חלק לעולם הבא שנאמר א) וימותו האנשים מוציאי דבת הארץ רעה במגפה לפני ה' וימותו בעולם הזה במגפה לעולם הבא) [א] דור המדבר אין להם חלק לעולם הבא ואין עומדין בדין שנאמר ב) במדבר הזה יתמו ושם ימותו דברי רבי עקיבא ר' אליעזר אומר עליהם הוא אומר ג) אספו לי חסידי כורתי בריתי עלי זבח [ב] עדת קרח אינה עתידה לעלות שנאמר ד) ותכס עליהם הארץ בעולם הזה ויאבדו מתוך הקהל לעולם הבא דברי ר"ע ר"א אומר עליהם הוא אומר ה) ה' ממית ומחיה מוריד שאול ויעל: **גמ'** [ג] ת"ר דור המבול אין להם חלק לעולם הבא שנאמר ו) וימח את כל היקום אשר על פני האדמה וימח את כל היקום בעולם הזה וימחו מן הארץ לעולם הבא דברי ר"ע ר"י בן בתירא אומר לא חיין ולא נדונין שנאמר ז) לא ידון רוחי באדם לעולם לא דין ולא רוח דבר אחר לא ידון רוחי שלא תהא נשמתן חוזרת לנדנה ר' מנחם [ג] בר יוסף אומר אפילו בשעה שהקב"ה מחזיר נשמות לפגרים מתים נשמתן קשה להם בגיהנם שנאמר ח) תהרו [ד] חשש תלדו קש רוחכם אש תאכלכם ת"ר [ה] דור המבול לא נתגאו אלא בשביל טובה שהשפיע להם הקב"ה ומה כתיב בהם ט) בתיהם שלום מפחד ולא שבט אלוה עליהם וכתיב י) שורו עבר ולא יגעיל תפלט פרתו ולא תשכל וכתיב יא) ישלחו כצאן עויליהם וילדיהם ירקדון וכתיב יב) ישאו בתוף וכנור וישמחו לקול עוגב וכתיב יג) יבלו [ג] ימיהם בטוב [ו] ושנותם בנעימים וכתיב יג) וברגע שאול יחתו והיא גרמה שאמרו לאל יד) סור ממנו ודעת דרכיך לא חפצנו מה שדי כי נעבדנו ומה נועיל כי נפגע בו אמרו כלום צריכין אנו לו אלא לטיפה של גשמים יש לנו נהרות ומעינות שאנו מסתפקין מהן אמר הקב"ה בטובה שהשפעתי להן בה מכעיסין אותי ובה אני דן אותם שנאמר טו) ואני הנני מביא את המבול מים ר' יוסי אמר דור המבול לא נתגאו אלא בשביל גלגל העין שדומה למים [שנאמר טז) ויקחו להם נשים מכל אשר בחרו] לפיכך דן אותן במים שדומה לגלגל העין שנאמר יז) נבקעו כל מעינות תהום רבה [ד] וארבות השמים נפתחו א"ר יוחנן דור המבול ברבה קלקלו וברבה נידונו ברבה קלקלו שנאמר יח) וירא ה' כי רבה רעת האדם וברבה נידונו שנאמר יז) כל מעינות תהום רבה א"ר יוחנן שלשה נשתיירו מהם בלועה דגדר וחמי טבריא ועיניא רבתי דבירם יט) כי השחית כל בשר את דרכו על הארץ א"ר יוחנן מלמד שהרביעו בהמה על חיה וחיה על בהמה והכל על אדם ואדם על הכל א"ר אבא בר כהנא וכולם חזרו חוץ מתושלמי כ) ויאמר [ז] ה' לנח קץ כל בשר בא לפני א"ר יוחנן בא וראה כמה גדול כחה של חמס שהרי דור המבול עברו על הכל ולא נחתם עליהם גזר דינם עד שפשטו ידיהם בגזל שנאמר כ) כי מלאה הארץ חמס מפניהם והנני משחיתם את הארץ וכתיב כא) החמס קם למטה רשע לא מהם ולא מהמונם ולא מהמהם ולא [ח] נה בהם א"ר אלעזר מלמד שזוקף עצמו כמקל ועמד לפני הקב"ה ואמר לפניו רבש"ע לא מהם ולא מהמונם ולא מהמהם ולא נה בהם ([ט] ואף על נח נחתם גזר דין שנא' ולא נח בהם) תנא דבי ר' ישמעאל אף על נח נחתך גזר דין אלא שמצא חן בעיני ה' שנאמר כב) נחמתי כי עשיתם ונח מצא חן בעיני ה' כג) וינחם ה' כי עשה את האדם בארץ כי אתא רב דימי אמר אמר הקב"ה יפה עשיתי שתקנתי להם קברות בארץ מאי משמע כתיב הכא וינחם ה' וכתיב התם כד) וינחם אותם וידבר על לבם ואיכא דאמרי לא יפה עשיתי שתקנתי להם קברות בארץ כתיב הכא וינחם וכתיב התם כה) וינחם ה' על הרעה אשר דבר לעשות לעמו כו) אלה תולדות נח [נח איש צדיק תמים היה בדורותיו] א"ר יוחנן בדורותיו ולא בדורות אחרים וריש לקיש אמר בדורותיו כ"ש בדורות אחרים א"ר חנינא משל דרבי יוחנן למה הדבר דומה לחבית של יין שהיתה מונחת במרתף של חומץ במקומה ריחה נודף שלא במקומה אין ריחה נודף א"ר אושעיא משל דריש לקיש למה הדבר דומה לצלוחית של פלייטון שהיתה מונחת במקום הטנופת במקומה ריחה נודף וכ"ש במקום הבוסם ו) וימח את כל היקום אשר על פני האדמה אם אדם חטא בהמה מה חטאה תנא משום רבי יהושע בן קרחה משל לאדם שעשה חופה לבנו והתקין מכל מיני סעודה לימים מת בנו עמד (ובלבל) [ופזר] את חופתו אמר כלום עשיתי אלא בשביל בני עכשיו שמת חופה למה לי אף הקב"ה אמר כלום בראתי בהמה וחיה אלא בשביל אדם עכשיו שאדם חוטא בהמה וחיה למה לי כז) מכל אשר בחרבה מתו [י] ולא דגים שבים דרש ר' יוסי דמן קסרי מאי דכתיב כח) קל הוא על פני מים תקולל חלקתם בארץ מלמד שהיה נח הצדיק מוכיח בהם ואומר להם עשו תשובה ואם לאו הקב"ה מביא עליכם את המבול ומקפה נבלתכם על המים כזיקין שנאמר קל הוא על פני מים ולא עוד אלא שלוקחין מהם קללה לכל באי עולם שנאמר כח) תקולל חלקתם בארץ לא יפנה דרך כרמים מלמד שהיו מפנים דרך כרמים [ה] [כ] אמר לו ומי מעכב אמר להם פרידה אחת יש לי להוציא מכם א"כ

רשעים דור המבול. דכתיב [בהו] כי רבה רעת האדם (בראשית ו): **חטאים אנשי סדום.** דכתיב בהו רעים וחטאים (שם יג): **אבל עומדים הם כו'.** שחיין ונדונים: **גמ' נשמתן קשה להם בגיהנם.** נשמת עצמן שורפתן דכתיב רוחכם אש תאכלכם (ישעיה לג): **בשביל גלגל העין.** שרואין טובתן שלימה והיו גובהין עיניהם ומנאפין אחר עיניהם: **במים.** שדומה לגלגל העין מעינות שנובעין ממקום קטן כמו עין: **שלשה נשתיירו.** מאותן מעינות של דור המבול שהיו חמין כדאמר לקמן ברותחין קלקלו ברותחין נדונו: **וכולן חזרו.** להזדווג עם מיניהם: **חוץ מתושלמי.** עוף הוא שאוחז עדיין תרבות רעה שמזדווג עם הכל. תושלמי עוף אחד ובמסכת חולין (דף סג:) גבי שמונה ספיקות איתא והרנוגא תושלמי ומרדא ודרכו של אותו עוף להרביע כל הבריות: **שוקף.** החמס עצמו כמקל והיינו החמס קם למטה רשע: **לא מהם.** אין תועלת לא בהם ולא בהמונם ולא במשאם: **מהמהם.** אשטרי"א בלע"ז: **כי נחמתי כי עשיתים ונח.** סמוכין דריש: **יפה עשיתי וכו'.** שאיבדתי דרך רשעים כזה: **לא יפה עשיתי.** דאפשר היו חוזרין: **כל שכן.** אילו הוה בדורות אחרים היה צדיק יותר: **פלייטון.** בושם שריחו נודף ואינו אפרסמון: **מקיפה.** מציף כמו ויצף הברזל דמתרגמינן וקפא (מלכים ב ו): **כזיקין.** נודות: **לא יפנה דרך כרמים אמרו לו ומי מעכב.** [מיד] שאינו עושה אם יש בידו כח לעשות כך: **[פרידה] אחת יש לי להוציא מכם.** מתושלח הצדיק ימות קודם ולא יהיה נדון עמכם: א"כ

מסורת הש"ס

א) [ירושלמי ל"ג מרגלים וכו'], ב) [תוספתא פי"ג], ג) [צ"ל ברבי יוסי וכ"א בילקוט], ד) [חשש מין מוץ שנוח לידלק], ה) [תוספתא דסוטה פ"ג], ו) [אין זה בהנך פסוקים אלא בסימן לו פי"א כתיב יבלו ימיהם בטוב ושניהם בנעימים], ז) [צ"ל אלהים], ח) [אין בהם נוהה אחרי מגעגע ונותן לב אלי כך פירש"י שם], ט) [בע"י ובילקוט ליתא לכל אותן עשרה תיבות], י) קידושין יג. זבחים קיג:, כ) [צ"ל אמרו וכ"א בע"י].

ליקוטי רש"י

חשש. מין מוץ דבר שנוח לידלק. **רוחכם אש.** מגופכם תצא רוח אש ותאכל החשש והקש [ישעיהו לג, יא]. **שלום מפחד.** שלא היו מזיקין שולטין בהן [איוב כא, ט]. **שורו עבר.** את הנקיבה. **ולא יגעיל.** לא יורה בה זרע פסולת שיהא חוזר ונפלט מגופה בלא הריון כל לשון הגעלה פליטה הוא וכן בל' משנה מגעילן ברותחין וכן כי שם נגעל מגן גבורים (שמואל ב, א) נפלט משיחתו והיה כאילו לא נמשח בשמן שהיו רגילין למשוח מגיני עור כדי שיהא חלק ומחליק את הרומח והחנית המכה בו והוא כמו שרים משחו מגן (ישעי' כא). **תפלט פרתו.** בעת תלד את וולדה. **ולא תשכל.** בלא עת [שם י]. **ישלחו כצאן עויליהם וגו'.** בעת לידתו היה הולך ומרקד מיד ואם פוגע במזיק נלחם בו והיתה אומרת לו אמו הבא לי מספריים ואחתוך שערך בהגדת בראשית, לך והדליק לי את הנר בראשית רבה [שם יא]. **וברגע שאול יחתו.** כשמגיע יום מותו היה מת לפי שעה בנחת בלא יסורין. **יחתו.** ירדו ובתרגום נחיתו [שם, יג]. **ומה נועיל.** מה הנאה יש לנו כי נפגע בו אין אנו צריכין לו אפי' לטיפת גשמים כי אד יעלה מן הארץ (בראשית ב) [שם פסוק טו]. **מכל אשר בחרו.** אף בעולת בעל אף הזכר והבהמה [בראשית ו, יב]. **נבקעו.** להוציא מימיהן. **תהום רבה.** מדה כנגד מדה הם חטאו ברבה רעת האדם (בראשית ו ה) ולקו בתהום רבה [שם ז, יא]. **נשתיירו מהם.** ויסכרו מעינות. כשנפתחו כתיב (ז יא) כל מעינות וכאן אין כתיב כל לפי שנשתיירו מהם אותן שיש בהם צורך לעולם כגון חמי טבריא וכיוצא בהם [שם ח, ב]. **חמי טבריא.** מעינות רותחין [פסחים מא.]. **קץ כל בשר.** כל מקום שאתה מוצא זנות ועבודה זרה אנדרלמוסיא באה לעולם והורגת טובים ורעים. **כי מלאה הארץ חמס.** לא נחתם גזר דינם אלא על הגזל [בראשית ו, יג]. **החמס קם וגו'.** החמס אשר בידכם הוא קם עליכם למטה רשע לשחתכם. **לא מהם.** כך אמר הקב"ה למשחית אינך זקוק להשאיר נפש [מרשעי ישראל] כי אין טובה יוצאת לא מהם ולא מהמונם ולא מהמהם. **ולא נה בהם.** אין בהם נוהה אחרי מגעגע ונותן לב אלי כמו ויהיו כל בית ישראל אחרי ה' (שמואל א ז) ולשון ארמי הוא תמיהון לפולחנא ל' תאוה וגעגועין ומנח' חברו לשון יללה וכן וינהו כל בית ישראל פירש לשון יללה ואין בתיבה רק ה"א יסוד [יחזקאל ז, יא]. **בדורותיו.** יש מרבותינו דורשים אותו לשבח כל שכן שאלו היה בדור צדיקים היה צדיק יותר ויש שדורשים אותו לגנאי לפי דורו היה צדיק ואלו היה בדורו של אברהם לא היה נחשב לכלום [בראשית ו, ט]. **פלייטון.** בלסמ"א משחא דאפרסמא [שבת סב. ועיין רש"י כאן]. **מכל אשר בחרבה.** לאפוקי דגים שבים [זבחים קיג:]. **קל הוא על פני מים.** כשהיו הצדיקים נח ומתושלח מוכיחים אותם ואומרים להם שעתיד המבול לבא עליהם היו אומרים קלים אנו לשוט על המים ויש לנו גומא ודברים קלים לעשות מהם אניות ולשוט. **תקולל חלקתם בארץ לא יפנה דרך כרמים.** היו מקללים את חלקם בארץ לאמר לא יפנה דרך הטוב בדרכי הצדיקים הרמים ושוכנים ברומו של עולם ל"א כרמים הם הצדיקים ופרנסי הדור כמו ונתתי לה את כרמיה משם (הושע ב) ת"י ית פרנסהא היו מקללים את חלקם בארץ לאמר לא יפנו דרך הטוב נשבעים שלא יפנו את דרכם ל"א תקולל חלקתם מתקלקלת היתה חלקתם וכו' [איוב כח, יח].

הגהות הגר"א

[א] גמ' דור המדבר. נרשם עליו אות ב: **[ב]** שם עדת קרח. נרשם עליו אות א: **[ג]** שם ימיהם בטוב. צ"ל בטוב ימיהם: ושנותם בנעימים וכתיב. נמחק: **[ד]** שם וארבות השמים נפתחו. נמחק וצ"ל ויסכרו מעינות תהום: **[ה]** שם מלמד שהיו מפנים דרך כרמים. נמחק:

תורה אור השלם

א) וַיָּמֻתוּ הָאֲנָשִׁים מוֹצִאֵי דִבַּת הָאָרֶץ רָעָה בַּמַּגֵּפָה לִפְנֵי יְיָ: [במדבר יד, לז]

ב) אֲנִי יְיָ דִּבַּרְתִּי אִם לֹא זֹאת אֶעֱשֶׂה לְכָל הָעֵדָה הָרָעָה הַזֹּאת הַנּוֹעָדִים עָלָי בַּמִּדְבָּר הַזֶּה יִתַּמּוּ וְשָׁם יָמֻתוּ: [במדבר יד, לה]

ג) אִסְפוּ לִי חֲסִידָי כֹּרְתֵי בְרִיתִי עֲלֵי זָבַח: [תהלים נ, ה]

ד) וַיֵּרְדוּ הֵם וְכָל אֲשֶׁר לָהֶם חַיִּים שְׁאֹלָה וַתְּכַס עֲלֵיהֶם הָאָרֶץ וַיֹּאבְדוּ מִתּוֹךְ הַקָּהָל: [במדבר טז, לג]

ה) יְיָ מֵמִית וּמְחַיֶּה מוֹרִיד שְׁאוֹל וַיָּעַל: [שמואל א' ב, ו]

ו) וַיִּמַח אֶת כָּל הַיְקוּם אֲשֶׁר עַל פְּנֵי הָאֲדָמָה מֵאָדָם עַד בְּהֵמָה עַד רֶמֶשׂ וְעַד עוֹף הַשָּׁמַיִם וַיִּמָּחוּ מִן הָאָרֶץ וַיִּשָּׁאֶר אַךְ נֹחַ וַאֲשֶׁר אִתּוֹ בַּתֵּבָה: [בראשית ז, כג]

ז) וַיֹּאמֶר יְיָ לֹא יָדוֹן רוּחִי בָאָדָם לְעֹלָם בְּשַׁגַּם הוּא בָשָׂר וְהָיוּ יָמָיו מֵאָה וְעֶשְׂרִים שָׁנָה: [בראשית ו, ג]

ח) תַּהֲרוּ חֲשַׁשׁ תֵּלְדוּ קַשׁ רוּחֲכֶם אֵשׁ תֹּאכַלְכֶם: [ישעיה לג, יא]

ט) בָּתֵּיהֶם שָׁלוֹם מִפָּחַד וְלֹא שֵׁבֶט אֱלוֹהַּ עֲלֵיהֶם: [איוב כא, ט]

י) שׁוֹרוֹ עִבַּר וְלֹא יַגְעִל תְּפַלֵּט פָּרָתוֹ וְלֹא תְשַׁכֵּל: [איוב כא, י]

יא) יְשַׁלְּחוּ כַצֹּאן עֲוִילֵיהֶם וְיַלְדֵיהֶם יְרַקֵּדוּן: [איוב כא, יא]

יב) יִשְׂאוּ כְּתֹף וְכִנּוֹר וְיִשְׂמְחוּ לְקוֹל עוּגָב: [איוב כא, יב]

יג) יְכַלּוּ בַטּוֹב יְמֵיהֶם וּבְרֶגַע שְׁאוֹל יֵחָתּוּ: [איוב כא, יג]

[ע"פ מסוה"ש] אִם יִשְׁמְעוּ וְיַעֲבֹדוּ יְכַלּוּ יְמֵיהֶם בַּטּוֹב וּשְׁנֵיהֶם בַּנְּעִימִים: [איוב לו, יא]

יד) וַיֹּאמְרוּ לָאֵל סוּר מִמֶּנּוּ וְדַעַת דְּרָכֶיךָ לֹא חָפָצְנוּ: מַה שַּׁדַּי כִּי נַעַבְדֶנּוּ וּמַה נּוֹעִיל כִּי נִפְגַּע בּוֹ: [איוב כא, יד-טו]

טו) וַאֲנִי הִנְנִי מֵבִיא אֶת הַמַּבּוּל מַיִם עַל הָאָרֶץ לְשַׁחֵת כָּל בָּשָׂר אֲשֶׁר בּוֹ רוּחַ חַיִּים מִתַּחַת הַשָּׁמָיִם כֹּל אֲשֶׁר בָּאָרֶץ יִגְוָע: [בראשית ו, יז] טז) וַיִּרְאוּ בְנֵי הָאֱלֹהִים אֶת בְּנוֹת הָאָדָם כִּי טֹבֹת הֵנָּה וַיִּקְחוּ לָהֶם נָשִׁים מִכֹּל אֲשֶׁר בָּחָרוּ: [בראשית ו, ב] יז) בִּשְׁנַת שֵׁשׁ מֵאוֹת שָׁנָה לְחַיֵּי נֹחַ בַּחֹדֶשׁ הַשֵּׁנִי בְּשִׁבְעָה עָשָׂר יוֹם לַחֹדֶשׁ בַּיּוֹם הַזֶּה נִבְקְעוּ כָּל מַעְיְנוֹת תְּהוֹם רַבָּה וַאֲרֻבֹּת הַשָּׁמַיִם נִפְתָּחוּ: [בראשית ז, יא] [ע"פ הגר"א] וַיִּסָּכְרוּ מַעְיְנֹת תְּהוֹם וַאֲרֻבֹּת הַשָּׁמָיִם וַיִּכָּלֵא הַגֶּשֶׁם מִן הַשָּׁמָיִם: [בראשית ח, ב] יח) וַיַּרְא יְיָ כִּי רַבָּה רָעַת הָאָדָם בָּאָרֶץ וְכָל יֵצֶר מַחְשְׁבֹת לִבּוֹ רַק רַע כָּל הַיּוֹם: [בראשית ו, ה] יט) וַיַּרְא אֱלֹהִים אֶת הָאָרֶץ וְהִנֵּה נִשְׁחָתָה כִּי הִשְׁחִית כָּל בָּשָׂר אֶת דַּרְכּוֹ עַל הָאָרֶץ: [בראשית ו, יב] כ) וַיֹּאמֶר אֱלֹהִים לְנֹחַ קֵץ כָּל בָּשָׂר בָּא לְפָנַי כִּי מָלְאָה הָאָרֶץ חָמָס מִפְּנֵיהֶם וְהִנְנִי מַשְׁחִיתָם אֶת הָאָרֶץ: [בראשית ו, יג] כא) הֶחָמָס קָם לְמַטֵּה רֶשַׁע לֹא מֵהֶם וְלֹא מֵהֲמוֹנָם וְלֹא מֶהֱמֵהֶם וְלֹא נֹהַּ בָּהֶם: [יחזקאל ז, יא] כב) וַיֹּאמֶר יְיָ אֶמְחֶה אֶת הָאָדָם אֲשֶׁר בָּרָאתִי מֵעַל פְּנֵי הָאֲדָמָה מֵאָדָם עַד בְּהֵמָה עַד רֶמֶשׂ וְעַד עוֹף הַשָּׁמָיִם כִּי נִחַמְתִּי כִּי עֲשִׂיתִם: וְנֹחַ מָצָא חֵן בְּעֵינֵי יְיָ: [בראשית ו, ז-ח] כג) וַיִּנָּחֶם יְיָ כִּי עָשָׂה אֶת הָאָדָם בָּאָרֶץ וַיִּתְעַצֵּב אֶל לִבּוֹ: [בראשית ו, ו] כד) וְעַתָּה אַל תִּירָאוּ אָנֹכִי אֲכַלְכֵּל אֶתְכֶם וְאֶת טַפְּכֶם וַיְנַחֵם אוֹתָם וַיְדַבֵּר עַל לִבָּם: [בראשית נ, כא] כה) וַיִּנָּחֶם יְיָ עַל הָרָעָה אֲשֶׁר דִּבֶּר לַעֲשׂוֹת לְעַמּוֹ: [שמות לב, יד] כו) אֵלֶּה תּוֹלְדֹת נֹחַ נֹחַ אִישׁ צַדִּיק תָּמִים הָיָה בְּדֹרֹתָיו אֶת הָאֱלֹהִים הִתְהַלֶּךְ נֹחַ: [בראשית ו, ט] כז) כֹּל אֲשֶׁר נִשְׁמַת רוּחַ חַיִּים בְּאַפָּיו מִכֹּל אֲשֶׁר בֶּחָרָבָה מֵתוּ: [בראשית ז, כב] כח) קַל הוּא עַל פְּנֵי מַיִם תְּקֻלַּל חֶלְקָתָם בָּאָרֶץ לֹא יִפְנֶה דֶּרֶךְ כְּרָמִים: [איוב כד, יח]

Me." אָמַר רַבִּי יוֹחָנָן – **R' Yochanan said:** בֹּא וּרְאֵה כַּמָּה גָדוֹל כֹּחָהּ שֶׁל חָמָס – **Come and see how great is the power of robbery,** i.e. how far-reaching are its consequences, שֶׁהֲרֵי דּוֹר הַמַּבּוּל עָבְרוּ עַל הַכֹּל – **for the** people of the **Generation of the Flood transgressed everything** that they were commanded,[44] וְלֹא נֶחְתַּם עֲלֵיהֶם גְּזַר דִּינָם עַד שֶׁפָּשְׁטוּ יְדֵיהֶם בְּגָזֵל – **yet the decree of their punishment was not sealed upon them until they stretched forth their hands** to engage **in robbery.** שֶׁנֶּאֱמַר ,,כִּי־מָלְאָה הָאָרֶץ חָמָס מִפְּנֵיהֶם וְהִנְנִי מַשְׁחִיתָם אֶת־הָאָרֶץ" – **As it is stated:** ***for the earth is filled with robbery on account of them, and I am prepared to destroy them from the earth.***[45] וּכְתִיב ,,הֶחָמָס קָם לְמַטֵּה־רֶשַׁע לֹא־מֵהֶם וְלֹא מֵהֲמוֹנָם וְלֹא מֶהֱמֵהֶם וְלֹא־נֹהַּ בָּהֶם" – **And it is written:** ***Robbery arose as a staff of evil – neither of themselves, nor of their masses, nor of what they amassed, nor is there longing among them.***[46] אָמַר רַבִּי אֶלְעָזָר – **R' Elazar said:** מְלַמֵּד שֶׁזָּקַף עַצְמוֹ כְּמַקֵּל – **This teaches** us **that [robbery],** so to speak, **erected itself like a staff,** וְעָמַד לִפְנֵי הַקָּדוֹשׁ בָּרוּךְ הוּא – **stood before the Holy One, Blessed is He,** וְאָמַר לְפָנָיו – **and said before Him:** רִבּוֹנוֹ שֶׁל עוֹלָם – **Master of the Universe!** ,,לֹא מֵהֶם וְלֹא מֵהֲמוֹנָם וְלֹא מֶהֱמֵהֶם וְלֹא נֹהַּ בָּהֶם" – There is no value – ***neither in themselves, nor in their masses, nor in what they amassed – nor is there longing among them.***[47] (וְאַף עַל נֹחַ נֶחְתַּם גְּזַר דִּין) – **And even upon Noah was the decree of punishment sealed,** i.e. Noah was originally included in the decree of destruction, שֶׁנֶּאֱמַר ,,וְלֹא נֹחַ בָּהֶם" – **as it is stated:** ***There is no Noah*** *(longing)* ***among them.***)[48]

A Baraisa echoes this last statement:

תָּנָא דְּבֵי רַבִּי יִשְׁמָעֵאל – **A Baraisa was taught in the academy of R' Yishmael:** אַף עַל נֹחַ נֶחְתַּךְ גְּזַר דִּין אֶלָּא שֶׁמָּצָא חֵן בְּעֵינֵי ה׳ – EVEN UPON NOAH WAS THE DECREE OF PUNISHMENT PASSED, BUT HE FOUND GRACE IN THE EYES OF GOD. שֶׁנֶּאֱמַר ,,נִחַמְתִּי כִּי עֲשִׂיתִם וְנֹחַ מָצָא חֵן בְּעֵינֵי ה׳" – AS IT IS STATED: *Hashem said . . ."I HAVE RECONSIDERED MY HAVING MADE THEM." AND NOAH FOUND GRACE IN THE EYES OF HASHEM.*[49]

Two opinions concerning God's attitude towards His destruction of the Generation of the Flood:

,,וַיִּנָּחֶם ה׳ כִּי־עָשָׂה אֶת־הָאָדָם בָּאָרֶץ" – Scripture states:[50] ***Hashem reconsidered*** *(vayinachem)* ***having made man on earth.*** כִּי אֲתָא רַב דִּימִי אָמַר – **When Rav Dimi came** to Babylonia from Eretz Yisrael, **he said:** אָמַר הַקָּדוֹשׁ בָּרוּךְ הוּא – **The Holy One, Blessed is He, said:** יָפֶה עָשִׂיתִי שֶׁתִּקַּנְתִּי לָהֶם קְבָרוֹת בָּאָרֶץ – **I did well** in **that I prepared graves for them in the earth,** i.e. in that I decided to destroy them.

The Gemara comments:

מַאי מַשְׁמַע – **What indication** is there that this is the intent of the verse? כְּתִיב הָכָא ,,וַיִּנָּחֶם ה׳" – **It is written here,** in the verse just cited: ***Vayinachem Hashem,*** וּכְתִיב הָתָם ,,וַיְנַחֵם אוֹתָם וַיְדַבֵּר עַל־לִבָּם" – **and it is written there:**[51] ***He comforted*** *(vayenacheim)* ***them and spoke to their heart.*** Thus, the word *vayinachem* implies that God found comfort in His decision to destroy mankind.[52]

NOTES

44. I.e. the commandments of the Noahide Code with which all mankind was charged since Creation (see *Maharsha* and see above, 56a-57a).

45. *Genesis* 6:13. The Flood was decreed as a punishment for all the sins of that generation, particularly their immorality (see *Bereishis Rabbah* 31:2,6 and *Rashi* to *Genesis* 6:13). However, as long as a decree of punishment has not been sealed, a righteous individual can pray to be spared. In contrast, after it is sealed, the prayer of an individual is insufficient and only mass prayer can annul the decree (*Rosh Hashanah* 17b). The decree of the Flood was sealed, precluding the possibility of salvation for individuals, due to the sin of robbery. As the Gemara states shortly, even Noah was doomed by the decree, but he found grace in the eyes of God (*Maharsha*).

The reason the decree was sealed specifically because of robbery is that robbery demonstrates callousness towards man, and God restrained his harsh decree until humans began to act harshly towards each other. Another reason is that God does not finalize a decree of destruction while the possibility of repentance remains open. However, when robbery became a widespread phenomenon and was woven into the fabric of society, such an economic tangle of stolen goods was created that restitution became impossible. This precluded the possibility of full repentance, which is contingent upon restitution of that which has been stolen. It was therefore on account of robbery that the decree of destruction was irrevocably finalized (*Maharal;* cf. *Be'er Sheva*).

46. *Ezekiel* 7:11. This verse is part of a prophecy wherein God told the prophet Ezekiel about Jerusalem's forthcoming destruction at the hands of the Babylonians. God stated that the people of Jerusalem brought punishment upon themselves by their deeds. Their robbery became so widespread that it grew into a staff of Evil, i.e. a punishing rod that would smite everything in its path until nothing would remain — neither their selves, nor their mass assemblages, nor their amassed fortunes, for there was none among them who longed for a relationship with God (see *Rashi* here and to *Ezekiel* loc. cit.; see also *Mahari Kara* to *Ezekiel*). The Gemara here applies it to the people of the Generation of the Flood, who were also notorious for robbery.

47. A person's every action has repercussions in the Heavenly spheres, where an angel is created that testifies to the action, and that acts as the emissary to bestow reward or exact retribution for it. Hence, the untold acts of robbery are said to have merged into a powerful "staff" that stood before God, attesting to the depravity of that generation and arguing to be unleashed against it (*Maharsha, Toras Chaim*).

48. [The word נֹהַּ is similar to נֹחַ, for the *hei* and the *ches* are pronounced similarly and are sometimes interchangeable (see *Margaliyos HaYam*).] Since נֹהַּ is an unusual word [appearing in Scripture only this once], the Gemara reads it as נֹחַ, and understands the phrase וְלֹא־נֹהַּ בָּהֶם as meaning, "Is Noah not among them?" I.e. should Noah not share their fate? (see *Maharsha,* and note 58).

49. *Genesis* 6:7-8. This passage describes God's decision to blot out mankind through the Flood. The Tanna expounds the juxtaposition of the phrase *And Noah* to the previous verse, and reads it both as one continuous statement with the previous verse and as a separate sentence. Thus: *"I have reconsidered My having made them and Noah." And Noah found grace in the eyes of Hashem.* This teaches that Noah, too, would have been destroyed, but that he found grace in the eyes of God (see *Rashi, Yad Ramah*).

This does not mean to imply that Noah was sinful. Rather, since the world is judged according to its majority, and the sins of the masses brought a decree of destruction upon the entire world, Noah stood to be destroyed along with the sinners (*Yad Ramah, Maharsha*). Furthermore, since God had reconsidered His creation of mankind, even a righteous person's merit could not save him (*Or HaChaim* to *Genesis* loc. cit.). Only Noah was spared, due to the grace he found in the eyes of God. It is because Noah was spared by the grace of God, rather than on the basis of his own merit, that he was saved in a natural manner and not through an overt miracle (*Maharsha*; cf. *Ramban* to *Genesis* 6:19).

[The expression that God *reconsidered* does not mean that He regretted His creation of man, for God knew from the outset that man would sin. Rather, it means that He adjusted his attitude towards man's continued existence. For whereas God had previously employed His attribute of Mercy towards man, at this juncture He began to employ His attribute of Justice, through which He would punish mankind (*Rashi* to *Genesis* 6:6; see also *Yad Ramah* and *Maharal*).]

50. Ibid. v. 6.

51. Ibid. 50:21.

52. The verse just cited describes how Joseph comforted his brothers after the death of the Patriarch Jacob, and its verb *vayenacheim* clearly denotes comforting. This serves as a basis for similarly interpreting the word *vayinachem,* which describes God's attitude towards His destruction of the Generation of the Flood, as an expression of comfort.

Now, the simple meaning of the verse (ibid 6:6) is, *Hashem reconsidered having made man on earth.* However, the following verse states, apparently repetitively, ,,כִּי נִחַמְתִּי כִּי עֲשִׂיתִם", *for I have reconsidered having made them.* Rav Dimi therefore interprets וַיִּנָּחֶם as *was comforted,*

רשעים במשפט וחטאים בעדת צדיקים על כן לא יקומו רשעים במשפט זה דור המבול וחטאים בעדת צדיקים אלו אנשי סדום אמרו לו אינם עומדין בעדת צדיקים אבל עומדין בעדת רשעים (א) מרגלים אין להם חלק לעולם הבא שנאמר א) וימותו האנשים מוציאי דבת הארץ רעה במגפה לפני ה' וימותו בעולם הזה במגפה לעולם הבא) [א] דור המדבר אין להם חלק לעולם הבא ואין עומדין בדין שנאמר ב) במדבר הזה יתמו ושם ימותו דברי רבי עקיבא ר' אליעזר אומר עליהם הוא אומר ג) אספו לי חסידי כורתי בריתי עלי זבח [ב] עדת קרח אינה עתידה לעלות שנאמר ד) ותכס עליהם הארץ בעולם הזה ויאבדו מתוך הקהל לעולם הבא דברי ר"ע ר"א אומר עליהם הוא אומר ה) ה' ממית ומחיה מוריד שאול ויעל: **גמ'** ג) ת"ר דור המבול אין להם חלק לעולם הבא שנאמר ו) וימח את כל היקום אשר על פני האדמה וימח את כל היקום בעולם הזה וימחו מן הארץ לעולם הבא דברי ר"ע ר"י בן בתירא אומר לא חיין ולא נדונין שנאמר ז) לא ידון רוחי באדם לעולם לא דין ולא רוח דבר אחר לא ידון רוחי שלא תהא נשמתן חוזרת לנדנה ר' מנחם ג) בר יוסף אומר אפילו בשעה שהקב"ה מחזיר נשמות לפגרים מתים נשמתן קשה להם בגיהנם שנאמר ח) תהרו ד) חשש תלדו קש רוחכם אש תאכלכם ת"ר ה) דור המבול לא נתגאו אלא בשביל טובה שהשפיע להם הקב"ה ומה כתיב בהם ט) בתיהם שלום מפחד ולא שבט אלוה עליהם וכתיב י) שורו עבר ולא יגעיל תפלט פרתו ולא תשכל וכתיב יא) ישלחו כצאן עויליהם וילדיהם ירקדון וכתיב יב) ישאו בתוף וכנור וישמחו לקול עוגב וכתיב יג) יבלו [ג] ימיהם בטוב ו) ושנותם בנעימים וכתיב יג) וברגע שאול יחתו והיא גרמה שאמרו לאל יד) סור ממנו ודעת דרכיך לא חפצנו מה שדי כי נעבדנו ומה נועיל כי נפגע בו אמרו כלום צריכין אנו לו אלא לטיפה של גשמים יש לנו נהרות ומעינות שאנו מסתפקין מהן אמר הקב"ה בטובה שהשפעתי להן בה מכעיסין אותי ובה אני דן אותם שנאמר טו) ואני הנני מביא את המבול מים ר' יוסי אמר דור המבול לא נתגאו אלא בשביל גלגל העין שדומה למים [שנאמר טז) ויקחו להם נשים מכל אשר בחרו] לפיכך דן אותן במים שדומה לגלגל העין שנאמר יז) נבקעו כל מעינות תהום רבה [ד] וארבות השמים נפתחו א"ר יוחנן דור המבול ברבה קלקלו וברבה נידונו ברבה קלקלו שנאמר יח) וירא ה' כי רבה רעת האדם וברבה נידונו שנאמר יז) כל מעינות תהום רבה א"ר יוחנן שלשה נשתיירו מהם בלועה דגדר וחמי טבריא ועיניא רבתי דבירם יט) כי השחית כל בשר את דרכו על הארץ א"ר יוחנן מלמד שהרביעו בהמה על חיה וחיה על בהמה והכל על אדם ואדם על הכל א"ר אבא בר כהנא וכולם חזרו חוץ מתושלמי כ) ויאמר ז) ה' לנח קץ כל בשר בא לפני א"ר יוחנן בא וראה כמה גדול כחה של חמס שהרי דור המבול עברו על הכל ולא נחתם עליהם גזר דינם עד שפשטו ידיהם בגזל שנאמר כ) כי מלאה הארץ חמס מפניהם והנני משחיתם את הארץ וכתיב כא) החמס קם למטה רשע לא מהם ולא מהמונם ולא מהמהם ולא ח) נה בהם א"ר אלעזר מלמד שזקף עצמו כמקל ועמד לפני הקב"ה ואמר לפניו רבש"ע לא מהם ולא מהמונם ולא מהמהם ולא נה בהם (ט) ואף על נח נחתם גזר דין שנא' ולא נח בהם) תנא דבי ר' ישמעאל אף על נח נחתך גזר דין אלא שמצא חן בעיני ה' שנאמר כב) נחמתי כי עשיתם ונח מצא חן בעיני ה' כג) וינחם ה' כי עשה את האדם בארץ כי אתא רב דימי אמר אמר הקב"ה יפה עשיתי שתקנתי להם קברות בארץ מאי משמע כתיב הכא וינחם ה' וכתיב התם כד) וינחם אותם וידבר על לבם ואיכא דאמרי לא יפה עשיתי שתקנתי להם קברות בארץ כתיב הכא וינחם וכתיב התם כה) וינחם ה' על הרעה אשר דבר לעשות לעמו כו) אלה תולדות נח [נח איש צדיק תמים היה בדורותיו] א"ר יוחנן בדורותיו ולא בדורות אחרים וריש לקיש אמר בדורותיו כ"ש בדורות אחרים א"ר חנינא משל דרבי יוחנן למה הדבר דומה לחבית של יין שהיתה מונחת במרתף של חומץ במקומה ריחה נודף שלא במקומה אין ריחה נודף א"ר אושעיא משל דריש לקיש למה הדבר דומה לצלוחית של פלייטון שהיתה מונחת במקום הטנופת במקומה ריחה נודף וכ"ש במקום הבוסם ו) וימח את כל היקום אשר על פני האדמה אם אדם חטא בהמה מה חטאה תנא משום רבי יהושע בן קרחה משל לאדם שעשה חופה לבנו והתקין מכל מיני סעודה לימים מת בנו עמד (ובלבל) [ופזר] את חופתו אמר כלום עשיתי אלא בשביל בני עכשיו שמת חופה למה לי אף הקב"ה אמר כלום בראתי בהמה וחיה אלא בשביל אדם עכשיו שאדם חוטא בהמה וחיה למה לי כז) מכל אשר בחרבה מתו י) ולא דגים שבים דרש ר' יוסי דמן קסרי מאי דכתיב כח) קל הוא על פני מים תקולל חלקתם בארץ מלמד שהיה נח הצדיק מוכיח בהם ואומר להם עשו תשובה ואם לאו הקב"ה מביא עליכם את המבול ומקפה נבלתכם על המים כזיקין שנאמר קל הוא על פני מים ולא עוד אלא שלוקחין מהם קללה לכל באי עולם שנאמר כח) תקולל חלקתם בארץ לא יפנה דרך כרמים מלמד שהיו מפנים דרך כרמים [ה] כ) אמר לו ומי מעכב אמר להם פרידה אחת יש לי להוציא מכם

א"כ

רשעים דור המבול. דכתיב [בהו] כי רבה רעת האדם (בראשית ו): חטאים אנשי סדום. דכתיב בהו רעים וחטאים (שם יג): אבל עומדים הם כו'. שחיין ונדונים: **גמ'** נשמתן קשה להם בגיהנם. נשמת עצמן שורפתן דכתיב רוחכם אש תאכלכם (ישעיה לג): בשביל גלגל העין. שרואין טובתן שלימה והיו גובהין עיניהם ומנאפין אחר עיניהם: במים. שדומה לגלגל העין מעינות שנובעין ממקום קטן כמו עין: שלשה נשתיירו. מאותן מעינות של דור המבול שהיו חמין כדאמר לקמן ברותחין קלקלו ברותחין נדונו: וכולן חזרו. להזדווג עם מיניהם: חוץ מתושלמי. עוף הוא שאוחז עדיין תרבות רעה שמזדווג עם הכל. תושלמי עוף אחד ובמסכת חולין (דף סב:) גבי שמונה ספיקות איתא והרנוגא תושלמי ומרדא ודרכו של אותו עוף להרביע כל הבריות: שוקף. החמס עצמו כמקל והיינו החמס קם למטה רשע: לא מהם. אין תועלת לא בהם ולא בהמונם ולא במשאם: מהמהם. אשטרי"א בלע"ז: כי נחמתי כי עשיתים ונח. סמוכין דריש: יפה עשיתי וכו'. שאיבדתי דרך רשעים כזה: לא יפה עשיתי. דאפשר היו חוזרין: כל שכן. אילו הוה בדורות אחרים היה צדיק יותר: פלייטון. בושם שריחו נודף ואינו אפרסמון: מקיפה. מציף כמו ויצף הברזל דמתרגמינן וקפא (מלכים ב ו): כזיקין. נודות: לא יפנה דרך כרמים אמרו לו ומי מעכב. [מיד] שאינו עושה אם יש בידו כח לעשות כך: [פרידה] אחת יש לי להוציא מכם. מתושלח הצדיק ימות קודם ולא יהיה נדון עמהם: א"כ

א) [ירושלמי ל"ג מרגלים וכו'], ב) [תוספתא פי"ג], ג) [צ"ל ברבי יוסי וכ"א בילקוט], ד) [חשש מין מוץ שנוח לידלק], ה) [תוספתא דסוטה פ"ג], ו) [אין זה בהנך פסוקים אלא בסימן לו פי"א כתיב יבלו ימיהם בטוב ושניהם בנעימים], ז) [צ"ל אלהים], ח) [אין בהם נוהה אחרי מגעגע ונותן לב אלי כך פירש"י שם], ט) [בע"י ובילקוט ליתא לכל אותן עשרה תיבות], י) קידושין יג. זבחים קיג:, כ) [צ"ל אמרו וכ"א בע"י].

ליקוטי רש"י

חשש. מין מוץ דבר שנוח לידלק. רוחכם אש. מגופכם תצא רוח אש ותאכל החשש והקש [ישעיהו לג, יא]. שלום מפחד. שלא היו מזיקין שולטין בהן [איוב כא, ט]. שורו עבר. את הנקיבה. ולא יגעיל. לא יורה בה זרע פסולת שיהא חוזר ונפלט מגופה בלא הריון כל לשון הגעלה פליטה הוא וכן בל' משנה מגעילן ברותחין וכן כי שם נגעל מגן גבורים (שמואל ב, א) נפלט משיחתו והיה כאילו לא נמשח בשמן שהיו רגילין למשוח מגיני עור כדי שיהא חלק ומחליק את הרומח והחנית המכה בו והוא כמו שרים משחו מגן (ישעי' כא). תפלט פרתו. בעת תלד את וולדה. ולא תשכל. בלא עת [שם י]. ישלחו כצאן עויליהם וגו'. בעת לידתו היה הולך ומרקד מיד ואם פוגע במזיק נלחם בו והיתה אומרת לו אמו הבא לי מספריים ואחתוך שערך בהגדת בראשית, לך והדליק לי את הנר בראשית רבה [שם יא]. וברגע שאול יחתו. כשמגיע יום מותו היה מת לפי שעה בנחת בלא יסורין. יחתו. ירדו ובתרגום נחיתו [שם, יג]. ומה נועיל. מה הנאה יש לנו כי נפגע בו אין אנו צריכין לו אפי' לטיפת גשמים כי אד יעלה מן הארץ (בראשית ב) [שם פסוק טו]. מכל אשר בחרו. אף בעולת בעל אף הזכר והבהמה [בראשית ו, יב]. נבקעו. להוציא מימיהן. תהום רבה. מדה כנגד מדה הם חטאו ברבה רעת האדם (בראשית ו ה) ולקו בתהום רבה [שם ז, יא]. נשתיירו מהם. ויסכרו מעינות. כשנפתחו כתיב (ז יא) כל מעינות וכאן אין כתיב כל לפי שנשתיירו מהם אותן שיש בהם צורך לעולם כגון חמי טבריא וכיוצא בהם [שם ח, ב]. חמי טבריא. מעינות רותחין [פסחים מא.]. קץ כל בשר. כל מקום שאתה מוצא זנות ועבודה זרה אנדרלמוסיא באה לעולם והורגת טובים ורעים. כי מלאה הארץ חמס. לא נחתם גזר דינם אלא על הגזל [בראשית ו, יג]. החמס קם וגו'. החמס אשר בידכם הוא קם עליכם למטה רשע לשחתכם. לא מהם. כך אמר הקב"ה למשחית אינך זקוק להשאיר נפש [מרשעי ישראל] כי אין טובה יוצאת לא מהם ולא מבניהם ולא מהמונם. ולא נה בהם. אין בהם נוהה אחרי מגעגע ונותן לב אלי כמו וינהו כל בית ישראל אחרי ה' (שמואל א ז) ולשון ארמי הוא תמיהון לפולחנא ל' תאוה וגעגועין ומנח' חברו לשון יללה וכן וינהו כל בית ישראל פירש לשון יללה ואין בתיבה רק ה"א יסוד [יחזקאל ז, יא]. בדורותיו. יש מרבותינו דורשים אותו לשבח כל שכן שאלו היה בדור צדיקים היה צדיק יותר ויש שדורשים אותו לגנאי לפי דורו היה צדיק ואלו היה בדורו של אברהם לא היה נחשב לכלום [בראשית ו, ט]. פלייטון. בלסמ"א משחא דאפרסמא [שבת סב. ועיין רש"י כאן]. מכל אשר בחרבה. לאפוקי דגים שבים [זבחים קיג:]. קל הוא על פני מים. כשהיו הצדיקים נח ומתושלח מוכיחים אותם ואומרים להם שעתיד המבול לבא עליהם היו אומרים קלים אנו לשוט על המים ויש לנו גומא ודברים קלים לעשות מהם אניות ולשוט. תקולל חלקתם בארץ לא יפנה דרך כרמים. היו מקללים את חלקם בארץ לאמר לא יפנה דרך הטוב בדרכי הצדיקים הרמים ושוכנים ברומו של עולם ל"א כרמים הם הצדיקים ופרנסי הדור כמו ונתתי לה את כרמיה משם (הושע ב) ת"י ית פרנסהא היו מקללים את חלקם בארץ לאמר לא יפנו דרך הטוב נשבעים שלא יפנו את דרכם ל"א תקולל חלקתם מתקלקלת היתה חלקתם וכו' [איוב כח, יח].

הגהות הגר"א

[א] גמ' דור המדבר. נרשם עליו אות ב: [ב] שם עדת קרח. נרשם עליו אות א: [ג] שם ימיהם בטוב. צ"ל בטוב ימיהם: ושנותם בנעימים וכתיב. נמחק: [ד] שם וארבות השמים נפתחו. נמחק ונ"ב ויסכרו מעינות תהום: [ה] שם מלמד שהיו מפנים דרך כרמים. נמחק:

תורה אור השלם

א) וַיָּמֻתוּ הָאֲנָשִׁים מוֹצִאֵי דִבַּת הָאָרֶץ רָעָה בַּמַּגֵּפָה לִפְנֵי יְיָ: [במדבר יד, לז]

ב) אֲנִי יְיָ דִּבַּרְתִּי אִם לֹא זֹאת אֶעֱשֶׂה לְכָל הָעֵדָה הָרָעָה הַזֹּאת הַנּוֹעָדִים עָלָי בַּמִּדְבָּר הַזֶּה יִתַּמּוּ וְשָׁם יָמֻתוּ: [במדבר יד, לה]

ג) אִסְפוּ לִי חֲסִידָי כֹּרְתֵי בְרִיתִי עֲלֵי זָבַח: [תהלים נ, ה]

ד) וַיֵּרְדוּ הֵם וְכָל אֲשֶׁר לָהֶם חַיִּים שְׁאֹלָה וַתְּכַס עֲלֵיהֶם הָאָרֶץ וַיֹּאבְדוּ מִתּוֹךְ הַקָּהָל: [במדבר טז, לג]

ה) יְיָ מֵמִית וּמְחַיֶּה מוֹרִיד שְׁאוֹל וַיָּעַל: [שמואל א' ב, ו]

ו) וַיִּמַח אֶת כָּל הַיְקוּם אֲשֶׁר עַל פְּנֵי הָאֲדָמָה מֵאָדָם עַד בְּהֵמָה עַד רֶמֶשׂ וְעַד עוֹף הַשָּׁמַיִם וַיִּמָּחוּ מִן הָאָרֶץ וַיִּשָּׁאֶר אַךְ נֹחַ וַאֲשֶׁר אִתּוֹ בַּתֵּבָה: [בראשית ז, כג]

ז) וַיֹּאמֶר יְיָ לֹא יָדוֹן רוּחִי בָאָדָם לְעֹלָם בְּשַׁגַּם הוּא בָשָׂר וְהָיוּ יָמָיו מֵאָה וְעֶשְׂרִים שָׁנָה: [בראשית ו, ג]

ח) תַּהֲרוּ חֲשַׁשׁ תֵּלְדוּ קַשׁ רוּחֲכֶם אֵשׁ תֹּאכַלְכֶם: [ישעיה לג, יא]

ט) בָּתֵּיהֶם שָׁלוֹם מִפָּחַד וְלֹא שֵׁבֶט אֱלוֹהַּ עֲלֵיהֶם: [איוב כא, ט]

י) שׁוֹרוֹ עִבַּר וְלֹא יַגְעִל תְּפַלֵּט פָּרָתוֹ וְלֹא תְשַׁכֵּל: [איוב כא, י]

יא) יְשַׁלְּחוּ כַצֹּאן עֲוִילֵיהֶם וְיַלְדֵיהֶם יְרַקֵּדוּן: [איוב כא, יא]

יב) יִשְׂאוּ כְּתֹף וְכִנּוֹר וְיִשְׂמְחוּ לְקוֹל עוּגָב: [איוב כא, יב]

יג) יְכַלּוּ בַטּוֹב יְמֵיהֶם וּבְרֶגַע שְׁאוֹל יֵחָתּוּ: [איוב כא, יג]

[ע"פ מסוה"ש] אִם יִשְׁמְעוּ וְיַעֲבֹדוּ יְכַלּוּ יְמֵיהֶם בַּטּוֹב וּשְׁנֵיהֶם בַּנְּעִימִים: [איוב לו, יא]

יד) וַיֹּאמְרוּ לָאֵל סוּר מִמֶּנּוּ וְדַעַת דְּרָכֶיךָ לֹא חָפָצְנוּ: מַה שַּׁדַּי כִּי נַעַבְדֶנּוּ וּמַה נּוֹעִיל כִּי נִפְגַּע בּוֹ: [איוב כא, יד-טו]

טו) וַאֲנִי הִנְנִי מֵבִיא אֶת הַמַּבּוּל מַיִם עַל הָאָרֶץ לְשַׁחֵת כָּל בָּשָׂר אֲשֶׁר בּוֹ רוּחַ חַיִּים מִתַּחַת הַשָּׁמָיִם כֹּל אֲשֶׁר בָּאָרֶץ יִגְוָע: [בראשית ו, יז] טז) וַיִּרְאוּ בְנֵי הָאֱלֹהִים אֶת בְּנוֹת הָאָדָם כִּי טֹבֹת הֵנָּה וַיִּקְחוּ לָהֶם נָשִׁים מִכֹּל אֲשֶׁר בָּחָרוּ: [בראשית ו, ב] יז) בִּשְׁנַת שֵׁשׁ מֵאוֹת שָׁנָה לְחַיֵּי נֹחַ בַּחֹדֶשׁ הַשֵּׁנִי בְּשִׁבְעָה עָשָׂר יוֹם לַחֹדֶשׁ בַּיּוֹם הַזֶּה נִבְקְעוּ כָּל מַעְיְנוֹת תְּהוֹם רַבָּה וַאֲרֻבֹּת הַשָּׁמַיִם נִפְתָּחוּ: [בראשית ז, יא] [ע"פ הגר"א] וַיִּסָּכְרוּ מַעְיְנֹת תְּהוֹם וַאֲרֻבֹּת הַשָּׁמָיִם וַיִּכָּלֵא הַגֶּשֶׁם מִן הַשָּׁמָיִם: [בראשית ח, ב] יח) וַיַּרְא יְיָ כִּי רַבָּה רָעַת הָאָדָם בָּאָרֶץ וְכָל יֵצֶר מַחְשְׁבֹת לִבּוֹ רַק רַע כָּל הַיּוֹם: [בראשית ו, ה] יט) וַיַּרְא אֱלֹהִים אֶת הָאָרֶץ וְהִנֵּה נִשְׁחָתָה כִּי הִשְׁחִית כָּל בָּשָׂר אֶת דַּרְכּוֹ עַל הָאָרֶץ: [בראשית ו, יב] כ) וַיֹּאמֶר אֱלֹהִים לְנֹחַ קֵץ כָּל בָּשָׂר בָּא לְפָנַי כִּי מָלְאָה הָאָרֶץ חָמָס מִפְּנֵיהֶם וְהִנְנִי מַשְׁחִיתָם אֶת הָאָרֶץ: [בראשית ו, יג] כא) הֶחָמָס קָם לְמַטֵּה רֶשַׁע לֹא מֵהֶם וְלֹא מֵהֲמוֹנָם וְלֹא מֶהֱמֵהֶם וְלֹא נֹהַּ בָּהֶם: [יחזקאל ז, יא] כב) וַיֹּאמֶר יְיָ אֶמְחֶה אֶת הָאָדָם אֲשֶׁר בָּרָאתִי מֵעַל פְּנֵי הָאֲדָמָה מֵאָדָם עַד בְּהֵמָה עַד רֶמֶשׂ וְעַד עוֹף הַשָּׁמָיִם כִּי נִחַמְתִּי כִּי עֲשִׂיתִם: וְנֹחַ מָצָא חֵן בְּעֵינֵי יְיָ: [בראשית ו, ז-ח] כג) וַיִּנָּחֶם יְיָ כִּי עָשָׂה אֶת הָאָדָם בָּאָרֶץ וַיִּתְעַצֵּב אֶל לִבּוֹ: [בראשית ו, ו] כד) וְעַתָּה אַל תִּירָאוּ אָנֹכִי אֲכַלְכֵּל אֶתְכֶם וְאֶת טַפְּכֶם וַיְנַחֵם אוֹתָם וַיְדַבֵּר עַל לִבָּם: [בראשית נ, כא] כה) וַיִּנָּחֶם יְיָ עַל הָרָעָה אֲשֶׁר דִּבֶּר לַעֲשׂוֹת לְעַמּוֹ: [שמות לב, יד] כו) אֵלֶּה תּוֹלְדֹת נֹחַ נֹחַ אִישׁ צַדִּיק תָּמִים הָיָה בְּדֹרֹתָיו אֶת הָאֱלֹהִים הִתְהַלֶּךְ נֹחַ: [בראשית ו, ט] כז) כֹּל אֲשֶׁר נִשְׁמַת רוּחַ חַיִּים בְּאַפָּיו מִכֹּל אֲשֶׁר בֶּחָרָבָה מֵתוּ: [בראשית ז, כב] כח) קַל הוּא עַל פְּנֵי מַיִם תְּקֻלַּל חֶלְקָתָם בָּאָרֶץ לֹא יִפְנֶה דֶּרֶךְ כְּרָמִים: [איוב כד, יח]

Another interpretation of the aforecited verse: וְאִיכָּא דְּאָמְרֵי – **And some say** that God said: לֹא יָפֶה עָשִׂיתִי שֶׁתִּקַּנְתִּי לָהֶם קְבָרוֹת בָּאָרֶץ – **I did not do well** in **that I prepared graves for them in the earth.**[53] This interpretation is supported by the following: כְּתִיב הָכָא ,,וַיִּנָּחֶם" – **It is written here,** in our verse: ***Vayinachem** Hashem;* וּכְתִיב הָתָם ,,וַיִּנָּחֶם ה׳ עַל־הָרָעָה אֲשֶׁר דִּבֶּר לַעֲשׂוֹת לְעַמּוֹ" – **and it is written there:**[54] ***And Hashem relented** (vayinachem) **regarding the evil that He declared He would do to His people.*** Thus, the word *vayinachem* implies that God was regretful about having to destroy mankind.[55]

A discussion concerning Noah's righteousness:

,,אֵלֶּה תּוֹלְדֹת נֹחַ [נֹחַ אִישׁ צַדִּיק תָּמִים הָיָה בְּדֹרֹתָיו]" – Scripture states:[56] ***These are the offspring of Noah [– Noah was a righteous man, perfect in his generations].*** אָמַר רַבִּי יוֹחָנָן – **R' Yochanan said:** ,,בְּדוֹרֹתָיו" וְלֹא בְּדוֹרוֹת אֲחֵרִים – ***In his generations*** he was considered perfectly righteous, **but** he would **not** have been considered perfectly righteous **in other generations.**[57] וְרֵישׁ לָקִישׁ אָמַר – **But Reish Lakish said:** ,,בְּדוֹרֹתָיו" כָּל שֶׁכֵּן בְּדוֹרוֹת אֲחֵרִים – If ***in his generations*** he was able to be righteous, he would **certainly** have been righteous if he had lived **in other generations.**[58]

The views of R' Yochanan and Reish Lakish are elaborated upon:

אָמַר רַבִּי חֲנִינָא – **R' Chanina said:** מָשָׁל דְּרַבִּי יוֹחָנָן לְמָה הַדָּבָר דּוֹמֶה – In terms of **a parable** illustrating the opinion **of R' Yochanan, to what is the matter analogous?** לְחָבִית שֶׁל יַיִן שֶׁהָיְתָה מוּנַּחַת בְּמַרְתֵּף שֶׁל חוֹמֶץ – It is analogous **to a barrel of wine that was lying in a cellar** full **of vinegar.** בִּמְקוֹמָהּ רֵיחָהּ נוֹדֵף – While the wine is **in its place,** among the vinegar, **its aroma wafts** and is particularly noticeable, in comparison to the odor of the vinegar. שֶׁלֹּא בִּמְקוֹמָהּ אֵין רֵיחָהּ נוֹדֵף – However, when the wine is **not in its place** among the vinegar, **its aroma does not waft,** i.e. it is not so noticeable. Similarly, Noah's righteousness was noteworthy in his evil generation, but would not have attracted attention in a righteous generation. אָמַר רַבִּי אוֹשַׁעְיָא – **R' Oshaya said:** מָשָׁל דְּרֵישׁ לָקִישׁ לְמָה הַדָּבָר דּוֹמֶה – In terms of a **parable** illustrating the opinion **of Reish Lakish, to what is the matter analogous?** לִצְלוֹחִית שֶׁל פְּלַיְיטוֹן שֶׁהָיְתָה מוּנַּחַת בִּמְקוֹם הַטִּנּוֹפֶת – It is analogous **to a flask of foliatum**[59] **that was lying in a place of filth.** בִּמְקוֹמָהּ רֵיחָהּ נוֹדֵף – Even while **in its place,** among the filth, **its aroma wafts** and is noticeable; וְכָל שֶׁכֵּן בִּמְקוֹם הַבּוֹסֶם – **and** it is **certainly** even more noticeable **in a fragrant place.** Similarly, if Noah's conduct was praiseworthy in spite of the fact that he lived in an evil generation, it would certainly have been even more praiseworthy if he had lived in a more righteous generation.

A discussion of the scope of the destruction wrought by the Flood:

,,וַיִּמַח אֶת־כָּל־הַיְקוּם אֲשֶׁר עַל־פְּנֵי הָאֲדָמָה" – Scripture states:[60] ***And He blotted out all existence that was on the face of the ground.*** אִם אָדָם חָטָא בְּהֵמָה מֶה חָטְאָה – **If man** admittedly **sinned, what sin did the animals commit** to deserve destruction in the Flood?[61] תָּנָא מִשּׁוּם רַבִּי יְהוֹשֻׁעַ בֶּן קָרְחָה – **It was taught in a Baraisa in the name of R' Yehoshua ben Korchah:** מָשָׁל לְאָדָם שֶׁעָשָׂה חוּפָּה לִבְנוֹ – This is ANALOGOUS TO A MAN WHO SET UP A WEDDING CANOPY FOR HIS SON וְהִתְקִין מִכָּל מִינֵי סְעוּדָה – AND PREPARED A FEAST OF ALL KINDS of food. לְיָמִים מֵת בְּנוֹ – SOME DAYS LATER, HIS SON DIED before the wedding could take place. עָמַד (ובלבל) [וּפִזֵּר] אֶת חוּפָּתוֹ – [THE FATHER] AROSE AND SCATTERED HIS WEDDING CANOPY, as well as the feast he had prepared. אָמַר – HE SAID: כְּלוּם עָשִׂיתִי אֶלָּא בִּשְׁבִיל בְּנִי – DID I MAKE it FOR ANY PURPOSE OTHER THAN the wedding of MY SON? עַכְשָׁיו שֶׁמֵּת חוּפָּה לָמָּה לִי – NOW THAT HE HAS DIED, WHY DO I NEED A WEDDING CANOPY? אַף הַקָּדוֹשׁ בָּרוּךְ הוּא אָמַר – SO TOO, THE HOLY ONE, BLESSED IS HE, SAID: כְּלוּם בָּרָאתִי בְּהֵמָה וְחַיָּה אֶלָּא בִּשְׁבִיל אָדָם – DID I CREATE DOMESTICATED AND WILD ANIMALS FOR ANY PURPOSE OTHER THAN the benefit of MAN? עַכְשָׁיו שֶׁאָדָם חוֹטֵא – NOW THAT MAN IS SINFUL and therefore deserving of destruction, בְּהֵמָה וְחַיָּה לָמָּה לִי – WHY DO I NEED DOMESTICATED AND WILD ANIMALS?! Therefore, the animals were also destroyed

NOTES

and בָּאָרֶץ as *in the earth* (rather than *on the earth*). According to Rav Dimi's interpretation, the verse does not mean that God reconsidered having created man *upon* the earth, but that He was comforted with His decision to destroy man through the Flood and bury him *in* the earth (see *Rashi* and *Maharsha; cf. Yad Ramah*).

Others explain that the verse refers to the initial creation of man. God was comforted with the fact that He originally created man as a mortal who would return to the earth in death, for that made it feasible for Him to now destroy the sinners (*Maharal*).

53. [I.e. it is regretful that I must now destroy them and bring them back to the earth] for if they could live even longer they would retain the opportunity to repent (*Rashi*).

Alternatively: It is regretful that man is mortal; if I had created him as a spiritual being he would never have sinned (*Maharal;* see *Rashi* to *Genesis* 6:6).

54. *Exodus* 32:14.

55. The verse cited describes how God was persuaded by Moses' plea to spare the Jewish people, rather than destroy them as punishment for their sin with the Golden Calf. Its verb *vayinachem* clearly denotes relenting, or regretting a past decree. This serves as a basis for similarly interpreting the verb *vayinachem,* which describes God's attitude towards His decision to destroy the Generation of the Flood, as an expression of regret. God found it necessary to issue the decree, but He regretted that they would thereby lose the opportunity to repent (see *Maharsha*). [The expressions that God was comforted by, or that He regretted, His decision to bring the Flood, are obviously anthropomorphisms. The intent is to bring out the compassion with which God regarded His creatures, even as He decided to destroy them (see *Yad Ramah*).]

56. *Genesis* 6:9.

57. The term *in his generations* seems superfluous (see *Gur Aryeh* to *Genesis* loc. cit.; cf. *Maharsha*). Hence, R' Yochanan explains that Noah was considered righteous only in relation to the very wicked people of his times; that is, he was the outstandingly righteous person of his generations. However, later generations were not as wicked, and included many righteous persons. Had he lived in those later times, Noah would not have been regarded as perfectly righteous.

58. If Noah was able to be righteous in a generation in which everyone else was wicked, then had he lived in a generation in which his contemporaries were righteous, he would certainly have reached even greater heights (*Rashi; Yad Ramah*).

R' Yochanan and Reish Lakish agree that Noah was not as great as the righteous of later generations, such as Abraham, and was thus considered righteous only in relation to the others of his generation. They also agree that he would have been even greater if he had actually lived in a superior generation. Their dispute concerns only which of these points the verse means to emphasize with the phrase *in his generations.* For it is clear that the verse is explaining why Noah was fortunate enough to find grace in the eyes of God and be saved. According to R' Yochanan, Noah was saved simply because he was the most righteous in his generation, even though he did not rank as outstandingly righteous on an absolute scale. According to Reish Lakish, Noah was saved because he had the inherent potential to attain true perfection, and would have attained it if he had not been hampered by the sinners of his generation (*Gur Aryeh* ibid.).

59. *Rashi* to *Shabbos* 62a identifies this as the aromatic oil of balsam, but here *Rashi* states that it is some other, unidentified perfume (see *Melo HaRoim* and *Midrash Tanchuma, Parashas Noach* §5).

60. Ibid. 7:23.

61. See note 42.

רשעים במשפט וחטאים בעדת צדיקים על כן לא יקומו רשעים במשפט זה דור המבול וחטאים בעדת צדיקים אלו אנשי סדום אמרו לו אינם עומדין בעדת צדיקים אבל עומדין בעדת רשעים (א מרגלים אין להם חלק לעולם הבא שנאמר א) וימותו האנשים מוציאי דבת הארץ רעה במגפה לפני ה' וימותו בעולם הזה במגפה לעולם הבא) [א] דור המדבר אין להם חלק לעולם הבא ואין עומדין בדין שנאמר ב) במדבר הזה יתמו ושם ימותו דברי רבי עקיבא ר' אליעזר אומר עליהם הוא אומר ג) אספו לי חסידי כורתי בריתי עלי זבח [ב] עדת קרח אינה עתידה לעלות שנאמר ד) ותכס עליהם הארץ בעולם הזה ויאבדו מתוך הקהל לעולם הבא דברי ר"ע ר"א אומר עליהם הוא אומר ה) ה' ממית ומחיה מוריד שאול ויעל:

גמ' (ב ת"ר דור המבול אין להם חלק לעולם הבא שנאמר ו) וימח את כל היקום אשר על פני האדמה וימחו מן הארץ לעולם הבא דברי ר"ע ר"י בן בתירא אומר לא חיין ולא נדונין שנאמר ז) לא ידון רוחי באדם לעולם לא דין ולא רוח דבר אחר לא ידון רוחי שלא תהא נשמתן חוזרת לנדנה ר' מנחם (ג בר יוסף אומר אפילו בשעה שהקב"ה מחזיר נשמות לפגרים מתים נשמתן קשה להם בגיהנם שנאמר ח) תהרו (ד חשש תלדו קש רוחכם אש תאכלכם ת"ר (ה דור המבול לא נתגאו אלא בשביל טובה שהשפיע להם הקב"ה ומה כתיב בהם ט) בתיהם שלום מפחד ולא שבט אלוה עליהם וכתיב י) שורו עבר ולא יגעיל תפלט פרתו ולא תשכל וכתיב יא) ישלחו כצאן עויליהם וילדיהם ירקדון וכתיב יב) ישאו בתוף וכנור וישמחו לקול עוגב וכתיב יג) יבלו [ג] ימיהם בטוב (ו ושנותם בנעימים וכתיב יג) וברגע שאול יחתו והיא גרמה שאמרו לאל יד) סור ממנו ודעת דרכיך לא חפצנו מה שדי כי נעבדנו ומה נועיל כי נפגע בו אמרו כלום צריכין אנו לו אלא לטיפה של גשמים יש לנו נהרות ומעינות שאנו מסתפקין מהן אמר הקב"ה בטובה שהשפעתי להן בה מכעיסין אותי ובה אני דן אותם שנאמר טו) ואני הנני מביא את המבול מים ר' יוסי אמר דור המבול לא נתגאו אלא בשביל גלגל העין שדומה למים [שנאמר טז) ויקחו להם נשים מכל אשר בחרו] לפיכך דן אותן במים שדומה לגלגל העין שנאמר יז) נבקעו כל מעינות תהום רבה [ד] וארבות השמים נפתחו א"ר יוחנן דור המבול ברבה קלקלו וברבה נידונו ברבה קלקלו שנאמר יח) וירא ה' כי רבה רעת האדם וברבה נידונו שנאמר יז) כל מעינות תהום רבה א"ר יוחנן שלשה נשתיירו מהם בלועה דגדר וחמי טבריא ועיניא רבתי דבירם יט) כי השחית כל בשר את דרכו על הארץ א"ר יוחנן מלמד שהרביעו בהמה על חיה וחיה על בהמה והכל על אדם ואדם על הכל א"ר אבא בר כהנא וכולם חזרו חוץ מתושלמי כ) ויאמר (ז ה' לנח קץ כל בשר בא לפני א"ר יוחנן בא וראה כמה גדול כחה של חמס שהרי דור המבול עברו על הכל ולא נחתם עליהם גזר דינם עד שפשטו ידיהם בגזל שנאמר כ) כי מלאה הארץ חמס מפניהם והנני משחיתם את הארץ וכתיב כא) החמס קם למטה רשע לא מהם ולא מהמונם ולא מהמהם ולא (ח נה בהם א"ר אלעזר מלמד שזקף עצמו כמקל ועמד לפני הקב"ה ואמר לפניו רבש"ע לא מהם ולא מהמונם ולא מהמהם ולא נה בהם (ט ואף על נח נחתם גזר דין שנא' ולא נח בהם) תנא דבי ר' ישמעאל אף על נח נחתך גזר דין אלא שמצא חן בעיני ה' שנאמר כב) נחמתי כי עשיתם ונח מצא חן בעיני ה' כג) וינחם ה' כי עשה את האדם בארץ כי אתא רב דימי אמר אמר הקב"ה יפה עשיתי שתקנתי להם קברות בארץ מאי משמע כתיב הכא וינחם ה' וכתיב התם כד) וינחם אותם וידבר על לבם ואיכא דאמרי לא יפה עשיתי שתקנתי להם קברות בארץ כתיב הכא וינחם וכתיב התם כה) וינחם ה' על הרעה אשר דבר לעשות לעמו כו) אלה תולדות נח [נח איש צדיק תמים היה בדורותיו] א"ר יוחנן בדורותיו ולא בדורות אחרים וריש לקיש אמר בדורותיו כ"ש בדורות אחרים א"ר חנינא משל דרבי יוחנן למה הדבר דומה לחבית של יין שהיתה מונחת במרתף של חומץ במקומה ריחה נודף שלא במקומה אין ריחה נודף א"ר אושעיא משל דריש לקיש למה הדבר דומה לצלוחית של פלייטון שהיתה מונחת במקום הטנופת במקומה ריחה נודף וכ"ש במקום הבוסם ו) וימח את כל היקום אשר על פני האדמה אם אדם חטא בהמה מה חטאה תנא משום רבי יהושע בן קרחה משל לאדם שעשה חופה לבנו והתקין מכל מיני סעודה לימים מת בנו עמד (ובלבל) [ופזר] את חופתו אמר כלום עשיתי אלא בשביל בני עכשיו שמת חופה למה לי אף הקב"ה אמר כלום בראתי בהמה וחיה אלא בשביל אדם עכשיו שאדם חוטא בהמה וחיה למה לי כז) מכל אשר בחרבה מתו (י ולא דגים שבים דרש ר' יוסי דמן קסרי מאי דכתיב כח) קל הוא על פני מים תקולל חלקתם בארץ מלמד שהיה נח הצדיק מוכיח בהם ואומר להם עשו תשובה ואם לאו הקב"ה מביא עליכם את המבול ומקפה נבלתכם על המים כזיקין שנאמר קל הוא על פני מים ולא עוד אלא שלוקחין מהם קללה לכל באי עולם שנאמר כח) תקולל חלקתם בארץ לא יפנה דרך כרמים מלמד שהיו מפנים דרך כרמים [ה] (כ אמר לו ומי מעכב אמר להם פרידה אחת יש לי להוציא מכם

א"כ

רש"י

רשעים דור המבול. דכתיב [בהו] כי רבה רעת האדם (בראשית ו): חטאים אנשי סדום. דכתיב בהו רעים וחטאים (שם יג): אבל עומדים הם כו'. שחיין ונדונים: **גמ'** נשמתן קשה להם בגיהנם. נשמת עצמן שרפתן דכתיב רוחכם אש תאכלכם (ישעיה לג): בשביל גלגל העין. שרואין טובתן שלימה והיו גובהין עיניהם ומנאפין אחר עיניהם: במים. שדומה לגלגל העין מעיינות שנובעין ממקום קטן כמו עין: שלשה נשתיירו. מאותן מעיינות של דור המבול שהיו חמין כדאמר לקמן ברותחין קלקלו ברותחין נדונו: וכולן חזרו. להזדווג עם מיניהם: חוץ מתושלמי. עוף הוא שאוחז עדיין תרבות רעה שמזדווג עם הכל. תושלמי עוף אחד ובמסכת חולין (דף סג:) גבי שמונה ספיקות איתא והרנוגא תושלמי ומרדא ודרכו של אותו עוף להרכיע כל הבריות: שוקף. החמס עצמו כמקל והיינו החמס קם למטה רשע: לא מהם. אין תועלת לא בהם ולא בהמונם ולא במשאם: מהמהם. אשטרי"א בלע"ז: כי נחמתי כי עשיתים ונח. סמוכין דריש: יפה עשיתי וכו'. שאיבדתי דרך רשעים כזה: לא יפה עשיתי. דאפשר היו חוזרין: כל שכן. אילו הוה בדורות אחרים היה צדיק יותר: פלייטון. בושם שריחו נודף ואינו אפרסמון: מקיפה. מציף כמו ויצף הברזל דמתרגמינן וקפא (מלכים ב ו): כזיקין. נודות: לא יפנה דרך כרמים אמרו לו ומי מעכב. [מיד] שאינו עושה אם יש בידו כח לעשות כך: [פרידה] אחת יש לי להוציא מכם. מתושלח הצדיק ימות קודם ולא יהיה נדון עמכם:

א"כ

מסורת הש"ס

א) [ירושלמי ל"ג מרגלים וכו'], ב) [תוספתא פי"ג], ג) [נ"ל ברבי יוסי וכ"א בילקוט], ד) [חשש מין מוך שנוח לידלק], ה) [תוספתא דסוטה פ"ג], ו) [אין זה בהך פסוקים אלא בסימן לו פי"א כתיב יבלו ימיהם בטוב ושניהם בנעימים], ז) [נ"ל אלהים], ח) [אין בהם נוהה אחרי מגעגע ונותן לב אלי כך פירש"י שם], ט) [בע"י ובילקוט ליתא לכל אותן עשרה תיבות], י) קידושין יג. זבחים קיג:, כ) [נ"ל אמרו וכ"א בע"י].

ליקוטי רש"י

חשש. מין מוך דבר שנוח לידלק. רוחכם אש. מגופכם תצא רוח אש ותאכל החשש והקש [ישעיהו לג, יא]. שלום מפחד. שלא היו מזיקין שולטין בהן [איוב כא, ט]. שורו עבר. את הנקיבה. ולא יגעיל. לא יורה בה זרע פסולת שיהא חוזר ונפלט מגופה בלא הריון כל לשון הגעלה פליטה הוא וכן בל' משנה מגעילין ברותחין וכן כי שם נגעל מגן גבורים (שמואל ב, א) נפלט משיחתו והיה כאילו לא נמשח בשמן שהיו רגילין למשוח מגיני עור כדי שיהא חלק ומחליק את הרומח והחנית המכה בו והוא כמו שריס משחו מגן (ישעי' כא). תפלט פרתו. בעת תלד את וולדה. ולא תשכל. בלא עת [שם י]. ישלחו כצאן עוליהם וגו'. בעת לידתו היה הולך ומרקד מיד ואם פוגע במזיק נלחם בו והיתה אומרת לו אמו הבא לי מספריים ואחתוך שערך כהגדת בראשית, לך והדליק לי את הנר בראשית רבה [שם יא]. וברגע שאול יחתו. כשמגיע יום מותו היה מת לפי שעה בנחת בלא יסורין. יחתו. ירדו ובתרגום נחיתו [שם, יג]. ומה נועיל. מה הנאה יש לנו כי נפגע בו אין אנו צריכין לו אפי' לטיפת גשמים כי אד יעלה מן הארץ (בראשית ב) [שם פסוק טו]. מכל אשר בחרו. אף בעולת בעל אף הזכר והבהמה [בראשית ו, יב]. נבקעו. להוציא מימיהן. תהום רבה. מדה כנגד מדה הם חטאו ברבה רעת האדם (בראשית ו ה) ולקו בתהום רבה [שם ז, יא]. נשתיירו מהם. ויסכרו מעינות. כשנפתחו כתיב (ז יא) כל מעינות וכאן אין כתיב כל לפי שנשתיירו מהם אותן שיש בהם צורך לעולם כגון חמי טבריא וכיוצא בהם [שם ח, ב]. חמי טבריא. מעינות רותחין [פסחים מא.]. קץ כל בשר. כל מקום שאתה מוצא זנות ועבודה זרה אנדרלמוסיא באה לעולם והורגת טובים ורעים. כי מלאה הארץ חמס. לא נחתם גזר דינם אלא על הגזל [בראשית ו, יג]. החמס קם וגו'. החמס אשר בידכם הוא קם עליכם למטה רשע לשחתכם. לא מהם. כך אמר הקב"ה למשחית איך זקוק להשאיר נפש [מרשעי ישראל] כי אין טובה יוצאת לא מהם ולא מבניהם ולא מהמונם. ולא נה בהם. אין בהם נוהה אחרי מגעגע ונותן לב אלי כמו וינהו כל בית ישראל אחרי ה' (שמואל א ז) ולשון ארמי הוא תמיהון לפולחנא ל' תאוה וגעגועין ומנח' חברו לשון יללה וכן וינהו כל בית ישראל פירש לשון יללה ואין בתיבה רק ה"א יסוד [יחזקאל ז, יא]. בדורותיו. יש מרבותינו דורשים אותו לשבח כל שכן שאלו היה בדור צדיקים היה צדיק יותר ויש שדורשים אותו לגנאי לפי דורו היה צדיק ואלו היה בדורו של אברהם לא היה נחשב לכלום [בראשית ו, ט]. פלייטון. בלסמ"א משחא דאפרסמא [שבת סב. ועיין רש"י כאן]. מכל אשר בחרבה. לאפוקי דגים שבים [זבחים קיג:]. קל הוא על פני מים. כשהיו הצדיקים נח ומתושלח מוכיחים אותם ואומרים להם שעתיד המבול לבא עליהם היו אומרים קלים אנו לשיט על המים ויש לנו גומא ודברים קלים לעשות מהם אניות ולשוט. תקולל חלקתם בארץ לא יפנה דרך כרמים. היו מקללים את חלקם בארץ לאמר לא יפנה דרך הטוב בדרכי הצדיקים הרמים ושוכנים ברומו של עולם ל"א כרמים הם הצדיקים ופרנסי הדור כמו ונתתי לה את כרמיה משם (הושע ב) ת"י ית פרנסהא היו מקללים את חלקם בארץ לאמר לא יפנו דרך הטוב נשבעים שלא יפנו את דרכם ל"א תקולל חלקתם מתקלקלת היתה חלקתם וכו' [איוב כח, יח].

הגהות הגר"א

[א] גמ' דור המדבר. נרשם עליו אות ב: [ב] שם עדת קרח. נרשם עליו אות א: [ג] שם ימיהם בטוב. נ"ל בטוב ימיהם: ושנותם בנעימים וכתיב. נמחק: [ד] שם וארבות השמים נפתחו. נמחק ונ"ב ויסכרו מעינות תהום: [ה] שם מלמד שהיו מפנים דרך כרמים. נמחק:

תורה אור השלם

א) וַיָּמֻתוּ הָאֲנָשִׁים מוֹצִאֵי דִבַּת הָאָרֶץ רָעָה בַּמַּגֵּפָה לִפְנֵי יְיָ: [במדבר יד, לז]

ב) אֲנִי יְיָ דִּבַּרְתִּי אִם לֹא זֹאת אֶעֱשֶׂה לְכָל הָעֵדָה הָרָעָה הַזֹּאת הַנּוֹעָדִים עָלָי בַּמִּדְבָּר הַזֶּה יִתַּמּוּ וְשָׁם יָמֻתוּ: [במדבר יד, לה]

ג) אִסְפוּ לִי חֲסִידָי כֹּרְתֵי בְרִיתִי עֲלֵי זָבַח: [תהלים נ, ה]

ד) וַיֵּרְדוּ הֵם וְכָל אֲשֶׁר לָהֶם חַיִּים שְׁאֹלָה וַתְּכַס עֲלֵיהֶם הָאָרֶץ וַיֹּאבְדוּ מִתּוֹךְ הַקָּהָל: [במדבר טז, לג]

ה) יְיָ מֵמִית וּמְחַיֶּה מוֹרִיד שְׁאוֹל וַיָּעַל: [שמואל א' ב, ו]

ו) וַיִּמַח אֶת כָּל הַיְקוּם אֲשֶׁר עַל פְּנֵי הָאֲדָמָה מֵאָדָם עַד בְּהֵמָה עַד רֶמֶשׂ וְעַד עוֹף הַשָּׁמַיִם וַיִּמָּחוּ מִן הָאָרֶץ וַיִּשָּׁאֶר אַךְ נֹחַ וַאֲשֶׁר אִתּוֹ בַּתֵּבָה: [בראשית ז, כג]

ז) וַיֹּאמֶר יְיָ לֹא יָדוֹן רוּחִי בָאָדָם לְעֹלָם בְּשַׁגַּם הוּא בָשָׂר וְהָיוּ יָמָיו מֵאָה וְעֶשְׂרִים שָׁנָה: [בראשית ו, ג]

ח) תַּהֲרוּ חֲשַׁשׁ תֵּלְדוּ קַשׁ רוּחֲכֶם אֵשׁ תֹּאכַלְכֶם: [ישעיה לג, יא]

ט) בָּתֵּיהֶם שָׁלוֹם מִפָּחַד וְלֹא שֵׁבֶט אֱלוֹהַּ עֲלֵיהֶם: [איוב כא, ט]

י) שׁוֹרוֹ עִבַּר וְלֹא יַגְעִל תְּפַלֵּט פָּרָתוֹ וְלֹא תְשַׁכֵּל: [איוב כא, י]

יא) יְשַׁלְּחוּ כַצֹּאן עֲוִילֵיהֶם וְיַלְדֵיהֶם יְרַקֵּדוּן: [איוב כא, יא]

יב) יִשְׂאוּ כְּתֹף וְכִנּוֹר וְיִשְׂמְחוּ לְקוֹל עוּגָב: [איוב כא, יב]

יג) יְבַלּוּ בַטּוֹב יְמֵיהֶם וּבְרֶגַע שְׁאוֹל יֵחָתּוּ: [איוב כא, יג]

[ע"פ מסוה"ש] אִם יִשְׁמְעוּ וְיַעֲבֹדוּ יְכַלּוּ יְמֵיהֶם בַּטּוֹב וּשְׁנֵיהֶם בַּנְּעִימִים: [איוב לו, יא]

יד) וַיֹּאמְרוּ לָאֵל סוּר מִמֶּנּוּ וְדַעַת דְּרָכֶיךָ לֹא חָפָצְנוּ: מַה שַּׁדַּי כִּי נַעַבְדֶנּוּ וּמַה נּוֹעִיל כִּי נִפְגַּע בּוֹ: [איוב כא, יד-טו]

טו) וַאֲנִי הִנְנִי מֵבִיא אֶת הַמַּבּוּל מַיִם עַל הָאָרֶץ לְשַׁחֵת כָּל בָּשָׂר אֲשֶׁר בּוֹ רוּחַ חַיִּים מִתַּחַת הַשָּׁמָיִם כֹּל אֲשֶׁר בָּאָרֶץ יִגְוָע: [בראשית ו, יז]

טז) וַיִּרְאוּ בְנֵי הָאֱלֹהִים אֶת בְּנוֹת הָאָדָם כִּי טֹבֹת הֵנָּה וַיִּקְחוּ לָהֶם נָשִׁים מִכֹּל אֲשֶׁר בָּחָרוּ: [בראשית ו, ב]

יז) בִּשְׁנַת שֵׁשׁ מֵאוֹת שָׁנָה לְחַיֵּי נֹחַ בַּחֹדֶשׁ הַשֵּׁנִי בְּשִׁבְעָה עָשָׂר יוֹם לַחֹדֶשׁ בַּיּוֹם הַזֶּה נִבְקְעוּ כָּל מַעְיְנוֹת תְּהוֹם רַבָּה וַאֲרֻבֹּת הַשָּׁמַיִם נִפְתָּחוּ: [ע"פ הגר"א] וַיִּסָּכְרוּ מַעְיְנֹת תְּהוֹם וַאֲרֻבֹּת הַשָּׁמָיִם וַיִּכָּלֵא הַגֶּשֶׁם מִן הַשָּׁמָיִם: [בראשית ח, ב]

יח) וַיַּרְא יְיָ כִּי רַבָּה רָעַת הָאָדָם בָּאָרֶץ וְכָל יֵצֶר מַחְשְׁבֹת לִבּוֹ רַק רַע כָּל הַיּוֹם: [בראשית ו, ה]

יט) וַיַּרְא אֱלֹהִים אֶת הָאָרֶץ וְהִנֵּה נִשְׁחָתָה כִּי הִשְׁחִית כָּל בָּשָׂר אֶת דַּרְכּוֹ עַל הָאָרֶץ: [בראשית ו, יב]

כ) וַיֹּאמֶר אֱלֹהִים לְנֹחַ קֵץ כָּל בָּשָׂר בָּא לְפָנַי כִּי מָלְאָה הָאָרֶץ חָמָס מִפְּנֵיהֶם וְהִנְנִי מַשְׁחִיתָם אֶת הָאָרֶץ: [בראשית ו, יג]

כא) הֶחָמָס קָם לְמַטֵּה רֶשַׁע לֹא מֵהֶם וְלֹא מֵהֲמוֹנָם וְלֹא מֶהֱמֵהֶם וְלֹא נֹהַּ בָּהֶם: [יחזקאל ז, יא]

כב) וַיֹּאמֶר יְיָ אֶמְחֶה אֶת הָאָדָם אֲשֶׁר בָּרָאתִי מֵעַל פְּנֵי הָאֲדָמָה מֵאָדָם עַד בְּהֵמָה עַד רֶמֶשׂ וְעַד עוֹף הַשָּׁמָיִם כִּי נִחַמְתִּי כִּי עֲשִׂיתִם: וְנֹחַ מָצָא חֵן בְּעֵינֵי יְיָ: [בראשית ו, ז-ח]

כג) וַיִּנָּחֶם יְיָ כִּי עָשָׂה אֶת הָאָדָם בָּאָרֶץ וַיִּתְעַצֵּב אֶל לִבּוֹ: [בראשית ו, ו]

כד) וְעַתָּה אַל תִּירָאוּ אָנֹכִי אֲכַלְכֵּל אֶתְכֶם וְאֶת טַפְּכֶם וַיְנַחֵם אוֹתָם וַיְדַבֵּר עַל לִבָּם: [בראשית נ, כא]

כה) וַיִּנָּחֶם יְיָ עַל הָרָעָה אֲשֶׁר דִּבֶּר לַעֲשׂוֹת לְעַמּוֹ: [שמות לב, יד]

כו) אֵלֶּה תּוֹלְדֹת נֹחַ נֹחַ אִישׁ צַדִּיק תָּמִים הָיָה בְּדֹרֹתָיו אֶת הָאֱלֹהִים הִתְהַלֶּךְ נֹחַ: [בראשית ו, ט]

כז) כֹּל אֲשֶׁר נִשְׁמַת רוּחַ חַיִּים בְּאַפָּיו מִכֹּל אֲשֶׁר בֶּחָרָבָה מֵתוּ: [בראשית ז, כב]

כח) קַל הוּא עַל פְּנֵי מַיִם תְּקֻלַּל חֶלְקָתָם בָּאָרֶץ לֹא יִפְנֶה דֶּרֶךְ כְּרָמִים: [איוב כד, יח]

in the Flood.[62]

An exception to the destruction of the Flood:

״מִכֹּל אֲשֶׁר בֶּחָרָבָה מֵתוּ״ – Scripture states:[63] ***Of everything that was on dry land died.*** וְלֹא דָגִים שֶׁבַּיָּם – This implies that only creatures that live on dry land died, **but not the fish of the sea.**[64]

The Gemara focuses on Noah's exhortations to his contemporaries to repent:

דָּרַשׁ רַבִּי יוֹסֵי דְּמִן קַסָרִי – **R' Yose of Caesaria expounded:** מַאי דִּכְתִיב ״קַל־הוּא עַל־פְּנֵי־מַיִם תְּקֻלַּל חֶלְקָתָם בָּאָרֶץ״ – **What is** the meaning of **that which is written:**[65] ***He floats lightly upon the face of the waters; accursed shall be their fate on earth?*** מְלַמֵּד שֶׁהָיָה נֹחַ הַצַּדִּיק מוֹכִיחַ בָּהֶם – **This teaches that the righteous Noah used to rebuke them** (the people of his generation) וְאוֹמֵר לָהֶם – **and say to them:** עֲשׂוּ תְשׁוּבָה – **"Repent!** וְאִם לָאו – **For if** you do **not,** הַקָּדוֹשׁ בָּרוּךְ הוּא מֵבִיא עֲלֵיכֶם אֶת הַמַּבּוּל – **the Holy One, Blessed is He, will bring the Flood upon you,** וּמַקְפֶּה נִבְלַתְכֶם עַל הַמַּיִם כְּזִיקִין – **and will float your carcasses upon the waters like leather bags!"** שֶׁנֶּאֱמַר ״קַל־הוּא עַל־פְּנֵי־מַיִם״ – **As it is stated:** ***He floats lightly upon the face of the waters.***

Noah's rebuke continues:

וְלֹא עוֹד אֶלָּא שֶׁלּוֹקְחִין מֵהֶם קְלָלָה לְכָל בָּאֵי עוֹלָם – **"And not only that, but [people] will take them** (i.e. you sinners of this generation) **as** a role model for **a curse for all future generations,"**[66] שֶׁנֶּאֱמַר ״תְּקֻלַּל חֶלְקָתָם בָּאָרֶץ״ – **as it is stated:** ***Accursed shall be their fate on earth.***[67]

The Gemara expounds the final segment of the verse just cited:

״לֹא־יִפְנֶה דֶּרֶךְ כְּרָמִים״ – The verse concludes: ***He shall not clear the path of the vineyards.*** מְלַמֵּד שֶׁהָיוּ מְפַנִּים דֶּרֶךְ כְּרָמִים – **This teaches that** Noah warned his fellows about the impending Flood as **they were clearing the paths of** their **vineyards.**[68] אָמַר לוֹ – **[The people] said to [Noah]:** וּמִי מְעַכֵּב – **"Who is preventing** God from bringing the Flood upon us at this very moment?" אָמַר לָהֶם – **[Noah] said to them,** in the Name of God: פְּרֵידָה אַחַת יֵשׁ לִי לְהוֹצִיא מִכֶּם – "There is **a single dove,** i.e. one righteous person, that **I must take away from you** before I bring the Flood."[69]

NOTES

62. The two of each species that survived in the Ark were spared so that they would be preserved for the benefit of later generations of mankind (*Maharsha*).

63. Ibid. v. 22.

64. The reason is that, as Scripture states and the Gemara expounded above, all flesh perverted its way *upon the earth.* This implies that the animals on dry land became perverted, but the fish of the sea did not. This holds true not only in regard to fish, but in regard to all the sea creatures (*Be'er Sheva;* cf. *Margaliyos HaYam* and *Torah Temimah* to *Genesis* 7:22). For a further discussion of this matter, see *Torah Sheleimah* to *Genesis* 6:17.

Although the Gemara states below (108b) that the waters of the Flood were boiling hot, that refers only to the water that covered dry land. The water of the sea remained at its normal temperature, and thus, the fish were able to survive (*Maharsha;* see *Zevachim* 113b).

65. *Job* 24:18.

66. Literally: for all who come into the world.

67. That is, when people of future generations will wish to curse someone, they will say, "May the fate of the Generation of the Flood befall you."

This is indeed our practice, for the Mishnah (*Bava Metzia* 44a) teaches that we say to one who committed himself to sell or purchase an item, and retracted after the money was paid: "The One Who exacted retribution from the people of the Generation of the Flood . . . will ultimately exact retribution from someone who does not abide by his word!" (*Eitz Yosef;* cf. *Maharsha*). The Generation of the Flood is held up as an example of a group that was punished severely for dishonest dealings, for as stated above, their decree of punishment was sealed on account of robbery (*Tos. HaRosh, Bava Metzia* 48a; see also *Sma* 204:8 and *Tiferes Yisrael*, *Boaz,* to *Bava Metzia* 4:2).

68. There is no particular significance to this fact; it is merely how things occurred. The point is introduced here to shed light upon the following exchange between the people and Noah, for it explains why the people couched their rebuttal of Noah's words (cited below) in a parable involving the paths of vineyards (*Maharsha, Eitz Yosef*; cf. *Hagahos Yavetz*).

Gra deletes this phrase entirely, and it appears from *Rashi's* comments that his text did not include it.

69. This is a reference to the righteous Methuselah, who was destined to die before the Flood began, so as not to be included in the punishment visited upon the sinners (*Rashi*). Thus, Noah told the sinners that the Flood would not come during Methuselah's lifetime.

Yad Ramah has a different version of the text, according to which it was Methuselah who rebuked the sinners, generations before the Flood, and sought to move them to repentance. When they inquired what was holding back the Flood, Methuselah replied that a single dove, namely the righteous Noah, had yet to be born. Until then, God would not destroy the world, for He intended for mankind to survive through Noah. [See *Bava Kamma* 38b, for the same usage of a dove as alluding to a righteous person.]

רשעים דור המבול. דכתיב [בהו] כי רבה רעת האדם (בראשית ו): חטאים אנשי סדום. דכתיב בהו רעים וחטאים (שם יג): אבל עומדים הם כו'. שחיין ונדונים: גמ' נשמתן קשה להם בגיהנם. נשמת עצמן שורפתן דכתיב רוחכם אש תאכלכם (ישעיה לג): בשביל גלגל העין. שרואין טובתן שלימה והיו גובהין עיניהם ומנאפין אחר עיניהם: במים. שדומה לגלגל העין מעיינות שנובעין ממקום קטן כמו עין: שלשה נשתיירו. מאותן מעיינות של דור המבול שהיו חמין כדאמר לקמן ברותחין קלקלו ברותחין נדונו: וכולן חזרו. להזדווג עם מיניהם: חוץ מתושלמי. עוף הוא שאותו עדיין תרבות רעה שמזדווג עם הכל. תושלמי עוף אחד ובמסכת חולין (דף סב:) גבי שמונה ספיקות איתא והרנוגא תושלמי ומרדא ודרכו של אותו עוף להרביע כל הבריות: שוקף. החמס עצמו כמקל והיינו החמס קם למטה רשע: לא מהם. אין תועלת לא בהם ולא בהמונם ולא במשאם: מהמהם. אשטרי"א בלע"ז: כי נחמתי כי עשיתים ונח. סמוכין דריש: יפה עשיתי וכו'. שאיבדתי דרך רשעים כזה: לא יפה עשיתי. דאפשר היו חוזרין: כל שכן. אילו הוה בדורות אחרים היה צדיק יותר: פלייטון. בושם שריחו נודף ואינו אפרסמון: מקיפה. מציף כמו ויצף הברזל דמתרגמינן וקפא (מלכים ב ו): כזיקין. נודות: לא יפנה דרך כרמים אמרו לו ומי מעכב. [מיד] שאינו עושה אם יש בידו כח לעשות כך: [פרידה] אחת יש לי להוציא מכם. מתושלח הצדיק ימות קודם ולא יהיה נדון עמכם: א"כ

רשעים במשפט וחטאים בעדת צדיקים על כן לא יקומו רשעים במשפט זה דור המבול וחטאים בעדת צדיקים אלו אנשי סדום אמרו לו אינם עומדין בעדת צדיקים אבל עומדין בעדת רשעים (א) מרגלים אין להם חלק לעולם הבא שנאמר א) וימותו האנשים מוציאי דבת הארץ רעה במגפה לפני ה' (וימותו בעולם הזה במגפה לעולם הבא) [א] דור המדבר אין להם חלק לעולם הבא ואין עומדין בדין שנאמר ב) במדבר הזה יתמו ושם ימותו דברי רבי עקיבא ר' אליעזר אומר עליהם הוא אומר ג) אספו לי חסידי כורתי בריתי עלי זבח [ב] עדת קרח אינה עתידה לעלות שנאמר ד) ותכס עליהם הארץ בעולם הזה ויאבדו מתוך הקהל לעולם הבא דברי ר"ע ר"א אומר עליהם הוא אומר ה) ה' ממית ומחיה מוריד שאול ויעל:

גמ' (ב) ת"ר דור המבול אין להם חלק לעולם הבא שנאמר ו) וימח את כל היקום אשר על פני האדמה וימח את כל היקום בעולם הזה וימחו מן הארץ לעולם הבא דברי ר"ע ר"י בן בתירא אומר לא חיין ולא נדונין שנאמר ז) לא ידון רוחי באדם לעולם לא דין ולא רוח דבר אחר לא ידון רוחי שלא תהא נשמתן חוזרת לנדנה ר' מנחם (ג) בר יוסף אומר אפילו בשעה שהקב"ה מחזיר נשמות לפגרים מתים נשמתן קשה להם בגיהנם שנאמר ח) תהרו (ד) חשש תלדו קש רוחכם אש תאכלכם ת"ר (ה) דור המבול לא נתגאו אלא בשביל טובה שהשפיע להם הקב"ה ומה כתיב בהם ט) בתיהם שלום מפחד ולא שבט אלוה עליהם וכתיב י) שורו עבר ולא יגעיל תפלט פרתו ולא תשכל וכתיב יא) ישלחו כצאן עויליהם וילדיהם ירקדון וכתיב יב) ישאו בתוף וכנור וישמחו לקול עוגב וכתיב יג) יבלו [ג] ימיהם בטוב (ו) ושנותם בנעימים וכתיב יג) וברגע שאול יחתו והיא גרמה שאמרו לאל יד) סור ממנו ודעת דרכיך לא חפצנו מה שדי כי נעבדנו ומה נועיל כי נפגע בו אמרו כלום צריכין אנו לו אלא לטיפה של גשמים יש לנו נהרות ומעינות שאנו מסתפקין מהן אמר הקב"ה בטובה שהשפעתי להן בה מכעיסין אותי ובה אני דן אותם שנאמר טו) ואני הנני מביא את המבול מים ר' יוסי אמר דור המבול לא נתגאו אלא בשביל גלגל העין שדומה למים [שנאמר טז) ויקחו להם נשים מכל אשר בחרו] לפיכך דן אותן במים שדומה לגלגל העין שנאמר יז) נבקעו כל מעינות תהום רבה [ד] וארבות השמים נפתחו א"ר יוחנן דור המבול ברבה קלקלו וברבה נידונו ברבה קלקלו שנאמר יח) וירא ה' כי רבה רעת האדם וברבה נידונו שנאמר יז) כל מעינות תהום רבה א"ר יוחנן שלשה נשתיירו מהם בלועה דגדר וחמי טבריא ועיניא רבתי דבירם יט) כי השחית כל בשר את דרכו על הארץ א"ר יוחנן מלמד שהרביעו בהמה על חיה וחיה על בהמה והכל על אדם ואדם על הכל א"ר אבא בר כהנא וכולם חזרו חוץ מתושלמי כ) ויאמר (ז) ה' לנח קץ כל בשר בא לפני א"ר יוחנן בא וראה כמה גדול כחה של חמס שהרי דור המבול עברו על הכל ולא נחתם עליהם גזר דינם עד שפשטו ידיהם בגזל שנאמר כ) כי מלאה הארץ חמס מפניהם והנני משחיתם את הארץ וכתיב כא) החמס קם למטה רשע לא מהם ולא מהמונם ולא מהמהם ולא (ח) נה בהם א"ר אלעזר מלמד שזקף עצמו כמקל ועמד לפני הקב"ה ואמר לפניו רבש"ע לא מהם ולא מהמונם ולא מהמהם ולא נה בהם (ט) ואף על נח נחתם גזר דין שנא' ולא נח בהם) תנא דבי ר' ישמעאל אף על נח נחתך גזר דין אלא שמצא חן בעיני ה' שנאמר כב) נחמתי כי עשיתם ונח מצא חן בעיני ה' כג) וינחם ה' כי עשה את האדם בארץ כי אתא רב דימי אמר אמר הקב"ה יפה עשיתי שתקנתי להם קברות בארץ מאי משמע כתיב הכא וינחם ה' וכתיב התם כד) וינחם אותם וידבר על לבם ואיכא דאמרי לא יפה עשיתי שתקנתי להם קברות בארץ כתיב הכא וינחם וכתיב התם כה) וינחם ה' על הרעה אשר דבר לעשות לעמו כו) אלה תולדות נח [נח איש צדיק תמים היה בדורותיו] א"ר יוחנן בדורותיו ולא בדורות אחרים וריש לקיש אמר בדורותיו כ"ש בדורות אחרים א"ר חנינא משל דרבי יוחנן למה הדבר דומה לחבית של יין שהיתה מונחת במרתף של חומץ במקומה ריחה נודף שלא במקומה אין ריחה נודף א"ר אושעיא משל דריש לקיש למה הדבר דומה לצלוחית של פלייטון שהיתה מונחת במקום הטנופת במקומה ריחה נודף וכ"ש במקום הבוסם ו) וימח את כל היקום אשר על פני האדמה אם אדם חטא בהמה מה חטאה תנא משום רבי יהושע בן קרחה משל לאדם שעשה חופה לבנו והתקין מכל מיני סעודה לימים מת בנו עמד (ובלבל) [ופזר] את חופתו אמר כלום עשיתי אלא בשביל בני עכשיו שמת חופה למה לי אף הקב"ה אמר כלום בראתי בהמה וחיה אלא בשביל אדם עכשיו שאדם חוטא בהמה וחיה למה לי כז) מכל אשר בחרבה מתו (י) ולא דגים שבים דרש ר' יוסי דמן קסרי מאי דכתיב כח) קל הוא על פני מים תקולל חלקתם בארץ מלמד שהיה נח הצדיק מוכיח בהם ואומר להם עשו תשובה ואם לאו הקב"ה מביא עליכם את המבול ומקפה נבלתכם על המים כזיקין שנאמר קל הוא על פני מים ולא עוד אלא שלוקחין מהם קללה לכל באי עולם שנאמר כח) תקולל חלקתם בארץ לא יפנה דרך כרמים מלמד שהיו מפנים דרך כרמים [ה] (כ) אמר לו ומי מעכב אמר להם פרידה אחת יש לי להוציא מכם

א"כ

מסורת הש"ס

א) [ירושלמי ל"ג מרגלים וכו'], ב) [תוספתא פי"ג], ג) [צ"ל ברבי יוסי וכ"א בילקוט], ד) [חשש מין מוץ שנוח לידלק], ה) [תוספתא דסוטה פ"ג], ו) [אין זה בהאי פסוקים אלא בסימן לו פי"א כתיב יבלו ימיהם בטוב ושניהם בנעימים], ז) [צ"ל אלהים], ח) [אין בהם נוהה אחרי מגעגע ונותן לב אלי כך פירש"י שם], ט) [בע"י ובילקוט ליתא לכל אותן עשרה תיבות], י) קידושין יג. זבחים קיג:, כ) [צ"ל אמרו וכ"א בע"י].

ליקוטי רש"י

חשש. מין מוץ דבר שנוח לידלק. רוחכם אש. מגופכם תצא רוח אש ותאכל החשש והקש [ישעיהו לג, יא]. שלום מפחד. שלא היו מזיקין שולטין בהן [איוב כא, ט]. שורו עבר. את הנקיבה. ולא יגעיל. לא יורה בה זרע פסולת שיהא חוזר ונפלט מגופה בלא הריון כל לשון הגעלה פליטה הוא וכן בג' משנה מגעילן ברותחין וכן כי שם נגעל מגן גבורים (שמואל ב, א) נפלט משיחתו והיה כאילו לא נמשח בשמן שהיו רגילין למשוח מגיני עור כדי שיהא חלק ומחליק את הרומח והחנית המכה בו והוא כמו שרים משחו מגן (ישעי' כא). תפלט פרתו. בעת תלד את וולדה. ולא תשכל. בלא עת [שם י]. ישלחו כצאן עויליהם וגו'. בעת לידתו היה הולך ומרקד מיד ואם פוגע במזיק נלחם בו והיתה אומרת לו אמו הבא לי מספריים ואחתוך שערך כהגדת בראשית, לך והדלק לי את הנר בראשית רבה [שם יא]. וברגע שאול יחתו. כשמגיע יום מותו היה מת לפי שעה בנחת בלא יסורין. יחתו. ירדו ובתרגום נחיתו [שם, יג]. ומה נועיל. מה הנאה יש לנו כי נפגע בו אין אנו צריכין לו אפי' לטיפת גשמים כי אד יעלה מן הארץ (בראשית ב) [שם פסוק טו]. מכל אשר בחרו. אף בעולת בעל אף הזכר והבהמה [בראשית ו, יב]. נבקעו. להוציא מימיהן. תהום רבה. מדה כנגד מדה הם חטאו ברעה רבה רעת האדם (בראשית ו ה) ולקו בתהום רבה [שם ז, יא]. נשתיירו מהם. ויסכרו מעינות. כשנפתחו כתיב (ז יא) כל מעינות וכאן אין כתיב כל לפי שנשתיירו מהם אותן שיש בהם צורך לעולם כגון חמי טבריא וכיוצא בהם [שם ח, ב]. חמי טבריא. מעינות רותחין [פסחים מא.]. קץ כל בשר. כל מקום שאתה מוצא זנות ועבודה זרה אנדרלמוסיא באה לעולם והורגת טובים ורעים. כי מלאה הארץ חמס. לא נחתם גזר דינם אלא על הגזל [בראשית ו, יג]. החמס קם וגו'. החמס אשר בידכם הוא קם עליכם למטה רשע לשחתכם. לא מהם. כך אמר הקב"ה למשחית אינך זקוק להשאיר נפש [מרשעי ישראל] כי אין טובה יוצאת לא מהם ולא מבניהם ולא מהמונם. ולא נה בהם. אין בהם נוהה אחרי מגעגע ונותן לב אלי כמו וינהו כל בית ישראל אחרי ה' (שמואל א ז) ולשון ארמי הוא תתינהון לפולחנא ל' תאוה וגעגועין ומנח' חברו לשון יללה וכן וינהו כל בית ישראל פירש לשון יללה ואין בתיבה רק ה"א יסוד [יחזקאל ז, יא]. בדורותיו. יש מרבותינו דורשים אותו לשבח כל שכן שאלו היה בדור צדיקים היה צדיק יותר ויש שדורשים אותו לגנאי לפי דורו היה צדיק ואלו היה בדורו של אברהם לא היה נחשב לכלום [בראשית ו, ט]. פלייטון. בלסמ"א משחא דאפרסמא [שבת סב. ועיין רש"י כאן]. מכל אשר בחרבה. לאפוקי דגים שבים [זבחים קיג:]. קל הוא על פני מים. כשהיו הצדיקים נח ומתושלח מוכיחים אותם ואומרים להם שעתיד המבול לבא עליהם היו אומרים קלים אנו לשוט על המים ויש לנו גומא ודברים קלים לעשות מהם אניות ולשוט. תקולל חלקתם בארץ לא יפנה דרך כרמים. היו מקללים את חלקם בארץ לאמר לא יפנה דרך הטוב בדרכי הצדיקים הרמים ושוכנים ברומו של עולם ל"א כרמים הם הצדיקים ופרנסי הדור כמו ונתתי לה את כרמיה משם (הושע ב) ת"י ית פרנסהא היו מקללים את חלקם בארץ לאמר לא יפנו דרך הטוב נשבעים שלא יפנו את דרכם ל"א תקולל חלקתם מתקלקלת היתה חלקתם וכו' [איוב כד, יח].

הגהות הגר"א

[א] גמ' דור המדבר. נרשם עליו אות ב: [ב] שם עדת קרח. נרשם עליו אות א: [ג] שם ימיהם בטוב. צ"ל בטוב ימיהם: ושנותם בנעימים וכתיב. נמחק: [ד] שם וארבות השמים נפתחו. נמחק וצ"ל ויסכרו מעינות תהום: [ה] שם מלמד שהיו מפנים דרך כרמים. נמחק:

תורה אור השלם

א) וַיָּמֻתוּ הָאֲנָשִׁים מוֹצִאֵי דִבַּת הָאָרֶץ רָעָה בַּמַּגֵּפָה לִפְנֵי יְיָ: [במדבר יד, לז]

ב) אֲנִי יְיָ דִּבַּרְתִּי אִם לֹא זֹאת אֶעֱשֶׂה לְכָל הָעֵדָה הָרָעָה הַזֹּאת הַנּוֹעָדִים עָלָי בַּמִּדְבָּר הַזֶּה יִתַּמּוּ וְשָׁם יָמֻתוּ: [במדבר יד, לה]

ג) אִסְפוּ לִי חֲסִידָי כֹּרְתֵי בְרִיתִי עֲלֵי זָבַח: [תהלים נ, ה]

ד) וַיֵּרְדוּ הֵם וְכָל אֲשֶׁר לָהֶם חַיִּים שְׁאֹלָה וַתְּכַס עֲלֵיהֶם הָאָרֶץ וַיֹּאבְדוּ מִתּוֹךְ הַקָּהָל: [במדבר טז, לג]

ה) יְיָ מֵמִית וּמְחַיֶּה מוֹרִיד שְׁאוֹל וַיָּעַל: [שמואל א' ב, ו]

ו) וַיִּמַח אֶת כָּל הַיְקוּם אֲשֶׁר עַל פְּנֵי הָאֲדָמָה מֵאָדָם עַד בְּהֵמָה עַד רֶמֶשׂ וְעַד עוֹף הַשָּׁמַיִם וַיִּמָּחוּ מִן הָאָרֶץ וַיִּשָּׁאֶר אַךְ נֹחַ וַאֲשֶׁר אִתּוֹ בַּתֵּבָה: [בראשית ז, כג]

ז) וַיֹּאמֶר יְיָ לֹא יָדוֹן רוּחִי בָאָדָם לְעֹלָם בְּשַׁגַּם הוּא בָשָׂר וְהָיוּ יָמָיו מֵאָה וְעֶשְׂרִים שָׁנָה: [בראשית ו, ג]

ח) תַּהֲרוּ חֲשַׁשׁ תֵּלְדוּ קַשׁ רוּחֲכֶם אֵשׁ תֹּאכַלְכֶם: [ישעיה לג, יא]

ט) בָּתֵּיהֶם שָׁלוֹם מִפָּחַד וְלֹא שֵׁבֶט אֱלוֹהַּ עֲלֵיהֶם: [איוב כא, ט]

י) שׁוֹרוֹ עִבַּר וְלֹא יַגְעִל תְּפַלֵּט פָּרָתוֹ וְלֹא תְשַׁכֵּל: [איוב כא, י]

יא) יְשַׁלְּחוּ כַצֹּאן עֲוִילֵיהֶם וְיַלְדֵיהֶם יְרַקֵּדוּן: [איוב כא, יא]

יב) יִשְׂאוּ כְּתֹף וְכִנּוֹר וְיִשְׂמְחוּ לְקוֹל עוּגָב: [איוב כא, יב]

יג) יְכַלּוּ בַטּוֹב יְמֵיהֶם וּבְרֶגַע שְׁאוֹל יֵחָתּוּ: [איוב כא, יג]

[ע"פ מסוה"ש] אִם יִשְׁמְעוּ וְיַעֲבֹדוּ יְכַלּוּ יְמֵיהֶם בַּטּוֹב וּשְׁנֵיהֶם בַּנְּעִימִים: [איוב לו, יא]

יד) וַיֹּאמְרוּ לָאֵל סוּר מִמֶּנּוּ וְדַעַת דְּרָכֶיךָ לֹא חָפָצְנוּ: מַה שַּׁדַּי כִּי נַעַבְדֶנּוּ וּמַה נּוֹעִיל כִּי נִפְגַּע בּוֹ: [איוב כא, יד-טו]

טו) וַאֲנִי הִנְנִי מֵבִיא אֶת הַמַּבּוּל מַיִם עַל הָאָרֶץ לְשַׁחֵת כָּל בָּשָׂר אֲשֶׁר בּוֹ רוּחַ חַיִּים מִתַּחַת הַשָּׁמָיִם כֹּל אֲשֶׁר בָּאָרֶץ יִגְוָע: [בראשית ו, יז] טז) וַיִּרְאוּ בְנֵי הָאֱלֹהִים אֶת בְּנוֹת הָאָדָם כִּי טֹבֹת הֵנָּה וַיִּקְחוּ לָהֶם נָשִׁים מִכֹּל אֲשֶׁר בָּחָרוּ: [בראשית ו, ב] יז) בִּשְׁנַת שֵׁשׁ מֵאוֹת שָׁנָה לְחַיֵּי נֹחַ בַּחֹדֶשׁ הַשֵּׁנִי בְּשִׁבְעָה עָשָׂר יוֹם לַחֹדֶשׁ בַּיּוֹם הַזֶּה נִבְקְעוּ כָּל מַעְיְנוֹת תְּהוֹם רַבָּה וַאֲרֻבֹּת הַשָּׁמַיִם נִפְתָּחוּ: [בראשית ז, יא] [ע"פ הגר"א] וַיִּסָּכְרוּ מַעְיְנֹת תְּהוֹם וַאֲרֻבֹּת הַשָּׁמָיִם וַיִּכָּלֵא הַגֶּשֶׁם מִן הַשָּׁמָיִם: [בראשית ח, ב] יח) וַיַּרְא יְיָ כִּי רַבָּה רָעַת הָאָדָם בָּאָרֶץ וְכָל יֵצֶר מַחְשְׁבֹת לִבּוֹ רַק רַע כָּל הַיּוֹם: [בראשית ו, ה] יט) וַיַּרְא אֱלֹהִים אֶת הָאָרֶץ וְהִנֵּה נִשְׁחָתָה כִּי הִשְׁחִית כָּל בָּשָׂר אֶת דַּרְכּוֹ עַל הָאָרֶץ: [בראשית ו, יב] כ) וַיֹּאמֶר אֱלֹהִים לְנֹחַ קֵץ כָּל בָּשָׂר בָּא לְפָנַי כִּי מָלְאָה הָאָרֶץ חָמָס מִפְּנֵיהֶם וְהִנְנִי מַשְׁחִיתָם אֶת הָאָרֶץ: [בראשית ו, יג] כא) הֶחָמָס קָם לְמַטֵּה רֶשַׁע לֹא מֵהֶם וְלֹא מֵהֲמוֹנָם וְלֹא מֶהֱמֵהֶם וְלֹא נֹהַּ בָּהֶם: [יחזקאל ז, יא] כב) וַיֹּאמֶר יְיָ אֶמְחֶה אֶת הָאָדָם אֲשֶׁר בָּרָאתִי מֵעַל פְּנֵי הָאֲדָמָה מֵאָדָם עַד בְּהֵמָה עַד רֶמֶשׂ וְעַד עוֹף הַשָּׁמָיִם כִּי נִחַמְתִּי כִּי עֲשִׂיתִם: וְנֹחַ מָצָא חֵן בְּעֵינֵי יְיָ: [בראשית ו, ז-ח] כג) וַיִּנָּחֶם יְיָ כִּי עָשָׂה אֶת הָאָדָם בָּאָרֶץ וַיִּתְעַצֵּב אֶל לִבּוֹ: [בראשית ו, ו] כד) וְעַתָּה אַל תִּירָאוּ אָנֹכִי אֲכַלְכֵּל אֶתְכֶם וְאֶת טַפְּכֶם וַיְנַחֵם אוֹתָם וַיְדַבֵּר עַל לִבָּם: [בראשית נ, כא] כה) וַיִּנָּחֶם יְיָ עַל הָרָעָה אֲשֶׁר דִּבֶּר לַעֲשׂוֹת לְעַמּוֹ: [שמות לב, יד] כו) אֵלֶּה תּוֹלְדֹת נֹחַ נֹחַ אִישׁ צַדִּיק תָּמִים הָיָה בְּדֹרֹתָיו אֶת הָאֱלֹהִים הִתְהַלֶּךְ נֹחַ: [בראשית ו, ט] כז) כֹּל אֲשֶׁר נִשְׁמַת רוּחַ חַיִּים בְּאַפָּיו מִכֹּל אֲשֶׁר בֶּחָרָבָה מֵתוּ: [בראשית ז, כב] כח) קַל הוּא עַל פְּנֵי מַיִם תְּקֻלַּל חֶלְקָתָם בָּאָרֶץ לֹא יִפְנֶה דֶּרֶךְ כְּרָמִים: [איוב כד, יח]

א"כ לא נפנה דרך כרמים דרש רבא מאי דכתיב א) לפיד בוז לעשתות שאנן נכון למועדי רגל מלמד שהיה נח הצדיק מוכיח אותם ואומר להם דברים שהם קשים כלפידים והיו (בוזים) [מבזין] אותו אמרו לו זקן תיבה זו למה אמר להם הקב"ה מביא עליכם את המבול אמרו מבול של מה אם מבול של אש יש לנו דבר אחר ועליתה שמה ואם של מים הוא מביא אם מן הארץ הוא מביא יש לנו עששיות של ברזל שאנו מחפין בהם את הארץ ואם מן השמים הוא מביא יש לנו דבר ועקב שמו ואמרי לה עקש שמו אמר להם הוא מביא מבין עקבי רגליכם שנאמר א) נכון למועדי רגל תניא מימי המבול קשים כשכבת זרע שנאמר נכון למועדי רגל [א] אמר רב חסדא ברותחין קלקלו בעבירה וברותחין נידונו כתיב הכא ב) וישכו המים וכתיב התם ג) וחמת המלך שככה ד) ויהי לשבעת הימים ומי המבול היו על הארץ ה) מה טיבם של שבעת הימים אמר רב אלו ימי אבילות של מתושלח ללמדך שהספדן של צדיקים מעכבין את הפורענות לבא דבר אחר לשבעת ששינה עליהם הקב"ה סדר בראשית שהיתה חמה יוצאת ממערב ושוקעת במזרח דבר אחר שקבע להם הקב"ה זמן גדול ואח"כ זמן קטן ד"א לשבעת הימים שהטעימם מעין העולם הבא כדי שידעו מה טובה מנעו מהן ה) מכל הבהמה הטהורה תקח לך שבעה שבעה איש ואשתו אישות לבהמה מי אית לה ג) א"ר שמואל בר נחמני א"ר יונתן ד) מאותם שלא נעבדה בהם עבירה מנא ידע אמר רב חסדא שהעבירן לפני התיבה כל שהתיבה קולטתו בידוע שלא נעבדה בהם עבירה וכל שאין התיבה קולטתו בידוע שנעבדה בה עבירה רבי אבהו אמר מאותן הבאין מאליהן ו) עשה לך תיבת עצי גופר מאי גופר ה) אמר רב אדא ו) אמרי דבי ר' שילא זו מבליגה ואמרי לה גולמיש ז) צוהר תעשה לתיבה א"ר יוחנן אמר לו הקב"ה לנח קבע בה אבנים טובות ומרגליות כדי שיהיו מאירות לכם כצהרים ז) ואל אמה תכלנה מלמעלה דבהכי [הוא] דקיימא ז) תחתיים שנים ושלישים תעשה תנא תחתיים לזבל אמצעיים לבהמה עליונים לאדם ח) וישלח את העורב אמר ר"ל תשובה ניצחת השיבו עורב לנח אמר לו רבך שונאני ואתה שנאתני רבך שונאני מן הטהורין שבעה מן הטמאים שנים ואתה שנאתני שאתה מניח ממין שבעה ושולח ממין שנים אם פוגע בי שר חמה או שר צנה לא נמצא עולם חסר בריה אחת או שמא לאשתי אתה צריך אמר לו רשע במותר לי נאסר לי בנאסר לי לא כ"ש ומנלן דנאסרו דכתיב ט) ובאת אל התיבה אתה ובניך ואשתך ונשי בניך אתך וכתיב י) צא מן התיבה אתה ואשתך ובניך ונשי בניך אתך וא"ר יוחנן מיכן אמרו שנאסרו בתשמיש המטה ת"ר שלשה שמשו בתיבה וכולם לקו כלב ועורב וחם כלב נקשר עורב רק חם לקה בעורו כ) וישלח את היונה מאתו לראות הקלו המים א"ר ירמיה מכאן שדירתן של עופות טהורים עם הצדיקים ל) והנה עלה זית טרף בפיה ז) א"ר אלעזר אמרה יונה לפני הקב"ה רבש"ע יהיו מזונותי מרורים כזית ומסורים בידך ואל יהיו מתוקים כדבש ומסורים ביד בשר ודם מאי משמע דהאי טרף לישנא דמזוני הוא דכתיב מ) הטריפני לחם חוקי נ) למשפחותיהם יצאו מן התיבה א"ר יוחנן ח) למשפחותם ולא הם אמר רב חנא בר ביזנא אמר ליה אליעזר לשם רבא כתיב נ) למשפחותיהם יצאו מן התיבה אתון היכן הויתון א"ל צער גדול היה לנו בתיבה בריה שדרכה להאכילה ביום האכלנוה ביום שדרכה להאכילה בלילה האכלנוה בלילה האי זקיתא לא הוה ידע אבא מה אכלה יומא חד הוה יתיב וקא פאלי רמונא נפל תולעתא מינה אכלה מיכן ואילך הוה גביל לה חיזרא כי מתלע אכלה אריא אישתא זינתיה דאמר רב לא בציר משיתא ולא טפי מתריסר זינא אישתא אורשינה אשכחיניה אבא דגני בספנא דתיבותא א"ל לא בעית מזוני א"ל חזיתיך דהות טרידא אמינא לא אצערך א"ל יהא רעוא דלא תמות שנאמר ס) ואומר עם קני אגוע וכחול ארבה ימים אמר רב חנה בר לואי אמר שם רבא לאליעזר כי אתו עלייכו מלכי מזרח ומערב אתון היכי עבידיתו אמר ליה אייתי הקב"ה לאברהם ואותביה מימיניה והוה שדינן עפרא והוו חרבי גילי והוי גירי שנאמר ע) מזמור לדוד נאם ה' לאדוני שב לימיני עד אשית אויביך הדום לרגליך וכתיב פ) מי העיר ממזרח צדק יקראהו לרגלו יתן לפניו גוים ומלכים ירד יתן כעפר חרבו כקש נדף קשתו ט) נחום איש גם זו הוה רגיל דכל דהוה סלקא ליה אמר גם זו לטובה יומא חד בעו [ישראל] לשדורי דורון לקיסר אמרי בהדי מאן

א"כ לא נפנה דרך כרמים. [כלומר לא נסור ולא נפנה את דרך הכרמים] אלא כל שעה נלך בהם כלומר א"כ לא נלך דרך כבושה ולא נחזור מסורינו אלא נלך ונקלקל השורה דרכים משובשים בקוצים ודרקנים כעין שבילי כרמים: לעשתות. כמו עשתונות שיושבין שאנן וחושבין מחשבות רעות: עליתה שמה. אין אש שולט בה: מבין עקבי רגליכם. בשכבת זרע שלכם יכול למחות אתכם ל"א מבין עקבי רגליכם מן הרגל יוצא ממש מים אם היה רוצה ואי אפשר י) לכפות רגליכם בעששיות: בשכבת זרע. רותחין ועבין היו. עבין ל"ג ופי' הוא: חמת המלך שככה. נחה מרתחו ה"נ מים נחו מרותחן: סדרי בראשית. והיינו לשבעת הימים סדר שבעת ימי בראשית שינה להם: זמן קטן אחר זמן גדול. בתחילה אמר להן והיו ימיו מאה ועשרים שנה כשעבר זמן זה ולא שבו לטובה חזר וקבע להם זמן קטן: אישות לבהמה מי אית ליה. נקבה אחת נשכבת לכמה זכרים ואין זו אישות: שלא נעבדה בהן עבירה. שלא נזקקו אלא לבן זוגם: מבליגה. עץ הוא: במותר לי. אפי' באשתי אני אסור: (בני נח. שם וחם ויפת): רק. רוקק זרע מפיו לפיה של נקבה: לקה בעורו. שילא ממנו כוש: מאתו. גבי עורב לא כתיב מאתו מכאן שדירתם כו' כלומר הנאה הוא שדרים אצלם שמכירים בצדיקים כדאמרי' בדוכתי אחריתא: זית טרף בפיה. בפיה היתה שואלת מזון טרף של זית: למשפחותיהם יצאו מן התיבה. אלמא כל חד וחד בפני עצמו היה ולא היו אוכלין כולם באבוס אחד אלא משפחות [משפחות] היו שרויין: א"ל אליעזר. [עבד אברהם]: לשם רבא. גדול (א) בנו של נח: היכי הויתון. היאך הייתם יכולין להכין עניינים בכך לעשות לכל בריה ובריה תפלה: זקיתא. שם בריה: פאלי. מחתך כמו פלי פלויי במסכת נדה (דף כא:): אישתא זינתיה. חמה אחזתו וזנהו ולא היה חושש לדרוש משאר בהמות: לא בציר משיתא ולא טפי מתריסר זיינא אישתא. אין לך חמה קלה שלא תהא חמימותו יכולה לזונו ששת ימים שלא ימות בלא מאכל ואין לך חמה שיכולה לזון יותר מי"ב ימים בלי מאכל ומשתה כ"ש ואית דגרסי לא פחות משיתא ירחי ולא טפי מתריסר זנתא אשתא ואחרי קאי כלומר לא פחות מששה חדשים ולא יותר מי"ב חדשים ולא נהירא לי: אורשינא. עוף ושמו חול בלשון המקרא ואינו מת לעולם: בספנא. בחדר ספון ומתוקן לו: [נאום ה' כו']. אליעזר אמר פסוק זה. נאם ה' לאדני אמר הקב"ה לאברהם כ) שב לימיני אדני וכו': ממזרח זה אברהם. שבא מארם נהרים שהוא במזרח דכתיב (במדבר כג) מן ארם ינחני בלק מלך מואב וגו': כל דהוה סלקא ליה. כל דבר המאורע ליה: בהדי

תורה אור השלם

א) לַפִּיד בּוּז לְעַשְׁתּוּת שַׁאֲנָן נָכוֹן לְמוֹעֲדֵי רָגֶל: [איוב יב, ה]

ב) וַיִּזְכֹּר אֱלֹהִים אֶת נֹחַ וְאֵת כָּל הַחַיָּה וְאֶת כָּל הַבְּהֵמָה אֲשֶׁר אִתּוֹ בַּתֵּבָה וַיַּעֲבֵר אֱלֹהִים רוּחַ עַל הָאָרֶץ וַיָּשֹׁכּוּ הַמָּיִם: [בראשית ח, א]

ג) וַיִּתְלוּ אֶת הָמָן עַל הָעֵץ אֲשֶׁר הֵכִין לְמָרְדֳּכָי וַחֲמַת הַמֶּלֶךְ שָׁכָכָה: [אסתר ז, י]

ד) וַיְהִי לְשִׁבְעַת הַיָּמִים וּמֵי הַמַּבּוּל הָיוּ עַל הָאָרֶץ: [בראשית ז, י]

ה) מִכֹּל הַבְּהֵמָה הַטְּהוֹרָה תִּקַּח לְךָ שִׁבְעָה שִׁבְעָה אִישׁ וְאִשְׁתּוֹ וּמִן הַבְּהֵמָה אֲשֶׁר לֹא טְהֹרָה הִוא שְׁנַיִם אִישׁ וְאִשְׁתּוֹ: [בראשית ז, ב]

ו) עֲשֵׂה לְךָ תֵּבַת עֲצֵי גֹפֶר קִנִּים תַּעֲשֶׂה אֶת הַתֵּבָה וְכָפַרְתָּ אֹתָהּ מִבַּיִת וּמִחוּץ בַּכֹּפֶר: [בראשית ו, יד]

ז) צֹהַר תַּעֲשֶׂה לַתֵּבָה וְאֶל אַמָּה תְּכַלֶּנָּה מִלְמַעְלָה וּפֶתַח הַתֵּבָה בְּצִדָּהּ תָּשִׂים תַּחְתִּיִּם שְׁנִיִּם וּשְׁלִשִׁים תַּעֲשֶׂהָ: [בראשית ו, טז]

ח) וַיְשַׁלַּח אֶת הָעֹרֵב וַיֵּצֵא יָצוֹא וָשׁוֹב עַד יְבֹשֶׁת הַמַּיִם מֵעַל הָאָרֶץ: [בראשית ח, ז]

ט) וַהֲקִמֹתִי אֶת בְּרִיתִי אִתָּךְ וּבָאתָ אֶל הַתֵּבָה אַתָּה וּבָנֶיךָ וְאִשְׁתְּךָ וּנְשֵׁי בָנֶיךָ אִתָּךְ: [בראשית ו, יח]

י) צֵא מִן הַתֵּבָה אַתָּה וְאִשְׁתְּךָ וּבָנֶיךָ וּנְשֵׁי בָנֶיךָ אִתָּךְ: [בראשית ח, טז]

כ) וַיְשַׁלַּח אֶת הַיּוֹנָה מֵאִתּוֹ לִרְאוֹת הֲקַלּוּ הַמַּיִם מֵעַל פְּנֵי הָאֲדָמָה: [בראשית ח, ח]

ל) וַתָּבֹא אֵלָיו הַיּוֹנָה לְעֵת עֶרֶב וְהִנֵּה עֲלֵה זַיִת טָרָף בְּפִיהָ וַיֵּדַע נֹחַ כִּי קַלּוּ הַמַּיִם מֵעַל הָאָרֶץ: [בראשית ח, יא]

מ) שָׁוְא וּדְבַר כָּזָב הַרְחֵק מִמֶּנִּי רֵאשׁ וָעֹשֶׁר אַל תִּתֶּן לִי הַטְרִיפֵנִי לֶחֶם חֻקִּי: [משלי ל, ח]

נ) כָּל הַחַיָּה כָּל הָרֶמֶשׂ וְכָל הָעוֹף כֹּל רוֹמֵשׂ עַל הָאָרֶץ לְמִשְׁפְּחֹתֵיהֶם יָצְאוּ מִן הַתֵּבָה: [בראשית ח, יט]

ס) וָאֹמַר עִם קִנִּי אֶגְוָע וְכַחוֹל אַרְבֶּה יָמִים: [איוב כט, יח]

ע) לְדָוִד מִזְמוֹר נְאֻם יְיָ לַאדֹנִי שֵׁב לִימִינִי עַד אָשִׁית אֹיְבֶיךָ הֲדֹם לְרַגְלֶיךָ: [תהלים קי, א]

פ) מִי הֵעִיר מִמִּזְרָח צֶדֶק יִקְרָאֵהוּ לְרַגְלוֹ יִתֵּן לְפָנָיו גּוֹיִם וּמְלָכִים יַרְדְּ יִתֵּן כֶּעָפָר חַרְבּוֹ כְּקַשׁ נִדָּף קַשְׁתּוֹ: [ישעיה מא, ב]

מסורת הש"ס

א) ר"ה יב. זבחים קיג:, ב) [תוספתא דסוטה פ"י], ג) [זבחים קטז. ע"ש], ד) [פי' בשביל שלא באו על שאינן מינן עשה להן כבוד וכתב להן אישות כבאדם. ערוך ערך אשה], ה) [ר"ה כג.], ו) [גיר' הערוך רב אמר אדרא דבי ר' שילא אמרי זו כו' ע"ש ערך אדר], ז) [עירובין יח: ע"ש], ח) [כתב הבאר שבע לא ידענא פירושו ועי' מהרש"א בח"א וגם בפענח רזא קצת בדחיקות ויתכן לפרש לולא דבריהם ע"פ האמור בחולין נח. כל בריה שאין בו עצם אינו מתקיים שנים עשר חודש והכן], ט) תענית כא. ע"ש, י) נ"ל לחפות, כ) [נ"ל אדוני שב לימיני וכו'].

הגהות הב"ח

(א) רש"י ד"ה לשם רבא גדול. נ"ב ונ"ע לעיל דף סט ע"ב:

ליקוטי רש"י

לפיד בוז. אש של גיהנם עומד למי שבאן בעשתותו לומר שלום יהיה לי [איוב יב, ה]. וישכו. כמו (אסתר ב, א) כשוך חמת המלך לשון הנחת חמה [בראשית ח, א]. וחמת המלך שככה. וסתם חמה רותחת היא כדכתיב וחמתו בערה בו [ר"ה יב, א]. אלו ימי אבלות של מתושלח. כי לימים עוד שבעה. אלו שבעת ימי אבלו של מתושלח הצדיק שחס הקב"ה על כבודו ועכב את הפורענות. לא וחשוב שנותיו של מתושלח ותמצא שהם כלים בשנת שש מאות שנה לחיי נח [בראשית ז, ד]. מתושלח לדיק גמור היה כדאמרינן בחלק (סנהדרין קח:) שבעת ימים שנתלו לדור המבול הן ימי אבלו של מתושלח [סוכה נב:]. כל שהתיבה קולטתו. מהעוף למינהו. אותן שדבקו במיניהם ולא השחיתו דרכם ומאליהם באו וכל שהתיבה קולטתו הכניס בה [בראשית ו, כ]. עצי גפר. כך שמו ולמה ממין זה על שם גפרית שנגזר עליהם להמחות בו [שם ו, יד]. צהר. יש אומרים חלון ויש אומרים אבן טובה המאירה להם. ואל אמה תכלנה מלמעלה. כסויה משופע ועולה עד שהוא קצר מלמעלה ועומד על אמה כדי שיזובו המים למטה. תחתים שנים ושלשים. שלש עליות זו על גב זו עליונים לאדם אמצעים למדור בהמה תחתיים לזבל [שם ו, טז]. או שמא לאשתי אתה צריך. יצוא ושוב. הולך ומקיף סביבות התיבה ולא הלך בשליחותו שהיה חושדו על בת זוגו כמו ששנינו באגדת חלק (סנהדרין קח:) [שם ח, ז]. אתה ובניך ואשתך. האנשים לבד והנשים לבד מכאן שנאסרו בתשמיש המטה [שם ז, יח]. נח ובניו. האנשים לבד והנשים לבד לפי שנאסרו בתשמיש המטה מפני שהעולם היה שרוי בצער [שם ז,ז]. אתה ואשתך וגו'. איש ואשתו כאן התיר להם תשמיש המטה [שם ח, טז]. טרף. חטף ומדרש אגדה לשון מזון ודרשו בפיה לשון מאמר אמרה יהיו מזונותי מרורין כזית בידו של הקב"ה ולא מתוקין כדבש בידי בשר ודם [שם פסוק יא]. הטריפני. ל' מזון וכן טרף נתן ליראיו (תהלים קיא) [משלי ל, ח]. טרף בפיה. מאמר פיה ביקשה שיהא זית טרף שלה והיינו מזון. בשר ודם. נח [עירובין יח:]. פאלי. כמו פלאי פלויי שבל' גמ' (נדה כא) לשון ביקוע ביקועי חתיכותיו [איוב מא,טו]. אורשינא. וכחול ארבה ימים. עוף ושמו חול ולא נקנסה עליו מיתה שלא טעם מעץ הדעת ולבסוף אלף שנה מתחד' וחוזר לנערותו [איוב כט, יח]. נאם ה' לאדני. רבותינו דרשוהו באברהם אבינו ואני אפרשנו כדבריהם נאם ה' לאברהם שקראוהו העולם אדוני שמעני אדוני (בראשית כ"ג). שב לימיני. התעכב לתשועתי והתחולל לה' אין ישיבה אלא עכבה וכן הוא אומר ותשבו בקדש (דברים א). לימיני. לתשועת ימיני. עד אשית אויביך. אמרפל וחביריו [תהלים קי, א]. מי העיר ממזרח. אותו שצדק יקראהו לרגלו מי העיר את אברה' להביאו מארם שהוא במזרח וצדק שהיה עושה היא היתה לקראת רגליו בכל אשר הלך. יתן לפניו גוים. מי שהעירו ממקומו להסיע הוא נתן לפניו ארבעה מלכים וחיילותיהם. ירד. ירדה. יתן כעפר חרבו. רמא כעפרא קטולין קדם חרביה נתן את חרבו ועושה חללים רבים כעפר ואת קשתו נתן מרבה הרוגים ונופלים כקש נדף [ישעיהו מא, ב]. דהוי סלקי ליה. כל המאורע לו אפילו רעה [תענית כא.].

The people replied:

אִם כֵּן לֹא נְפַנֶּה דֶּרֶךְ כְּרָמִים – **"If so, we will not clear the path of the vineyards."**[1]

Further discussion of Noah's debates with the sinners of his times:

דָּרַשׁ רָבָא – **Rava expounded:** מַאי דִּכְתִיב ,,לַפִּיד בּוּז לְעַשְׁתּוּת שַׁאֲנָן נָכוֹן לְמוֹעֲדֵי רָגֶל" – **What is the** meaning of **that which is written:** ***A flame is scorned by [those with] complacent dreams, destined to stumbling feet.***[2] מְלַמֵּד שֶׁהָיָה נֹחַ הַצַּדִּיק מוֹכִיחַ אוֹתָם – **This teaches that the righteous Noah would rebuke them** וְאוֹמֵר לָהֶם דְּבָרִים שֶׁהֵם קָשִׁים כְּלַפִּידִים – **and say to them words that are harsh as flames,** וְהָיוּ (בוזים) [מְבַזִּין] אוֹתוֹ – **but they would scorn him.** אָמְרוּ לוֹ – **They said to him:** זָקֵן – **"Old man!** תֵּיבָה זוּ לָמָּה – **What is this Ark for?"** אָמַר לָהֶם – **He said to them:** הַקָּדוֹשׁ בָּרוּךְ הוּא מֵבִיא עֲלֵיכֶם אֶת הַמַּבּוּל – **"The Holy One, Blessed is He, is going to bring the** ***Mabbul*** **upon you."** אָמְרוּ – **They said:** מַבּוּל שֶׁל מָה – **"A** ***Mabbul*** **of what** will God bring?[3] אִם מַבּוּל שֶׁל אֵשׁ – **If** He brings **a** ***Mabbul*** **of fire,** יֵשׁ לָנוּ דָּבָר אַחֵר וַעֲלִיתָה שְׁמָהּ – **we have something called** ***alisah,*** which is fire resistant and will protect us.[4] וְאִם שֶׁל מַיִם הוּא מֵבִיא – **And if He brings** a *Mabbul* **of water,** the following possibilities exist: אִם מִן הָאָרֶץ הוּא מֵבִיא – **If He brings** the water up **from the ground,** יֵשׁ לָנוּ עֲשָׁשִׁיּוֹת שֶׁל בַּרְזֶל שֶׁאָנוּ מְחַפִּין בָּהֶם אֶת הָאָרֶץ – **we have iron plates with which we will cover the ground** to stanch the flow of water. וְאִם מִן הַשָּׁמַיִם הוּא מֵבִיא – **And if He brings** the water down **from the heavens,** יֵשׁ לָנוּ דָּבָר וְעָקָב שְׁמוֹ – **we have something called** ***akuv*** that will protect us."

The Gemara interjects:

וְאָמְרֵי לָהּ עָקַשׁ שְׁמוֹ – **And some say:** It was something **called** ***akush.***[5]

The narrative continues:

אָמַר לָהֶם – **[Noah] said to them:** הוּא מֵבִיא מִבֵּין עִקְבֵי רַגְלֵיכֶם – **"[God] can bring** a flood of water **from between the heels of your feet."**[6] שֶׁנֶּאֱמַר ,,נָכוֹן לְמוֹעֲדֵי רָגֶל" – **As it is stated:** ***destined to stumbling feet.***[7]

A Baraisa derives a similar teaching from this verse:

תַּנְיָא – **It taught in a Baraisa:** מֵימֵי הַמַּבּוּל קָשִׁים כְּשִׁכְבַת זֶרַע – **THE WATERS OF THE FLOOD WERE HARSH,** i.e. hot and viscous, **LIKE SEMEN,** שֶׁנֶּאֱמַר ,,נָכוֹן לְמוֹעֲדֵי רָגֶל" – **AS IT IS STATED:** ***DESTINED TO STUMBLING FEET.***[8]

A similar Amoraic teaching:

אָמַר רַב חִסְדָּא – **Rav Chisda said:** בְּרוֹתְחִין קִלְקְלוּ – It was **with a boiling** substance (semen) that **they acted corruptly** – בַּעֲבֵירָה – that is, by engaging **in immorality** –[9] וּבְרוֹתְחִין נִידּוֹנוּ – **and** it was therefore **with boiling** water that **they were punished.** כְּתִיב הָכָא ,,וַיָּשֹׁכּוּ הַמָּיִם" – This may be derived as follows: **It is written here,** concerning the end of the Flood:[10] ***The waters subsided*** (*vayashocu*); וּכְתִיב הָתָם ,,וַחֲמַת הַמֶּלֶךְ שָׁכָכָה" – **and it is written there:**[11] ***And the king's anger cooled down*** (*shachachah*). Since the word *shachachah* means *cooled down,* it follows that the word *vayashocu,* which is of the same root, means that the water cooled down. This implies that during the Flood the water was boiling hot.

The Gemara analyzes a verse concerning the onset of the Flood:

,,וַיְהִי לְשִׁבְעַת הַיָּמִים וּמֵי הַמַּבּוּל הָיוּ עַל־הָאָרֶץ" – Scripture states:[12] ***It came to pass after the seven-day period that the waters of the Flood were upon the earth.*** מָה טִיבָם שֶׁל שִׁבְעַת הַיָּמִים – **What was the nature of** this **seven-day period** that preceded the Flood? אָמַר רַב – **Rav said:** אֵלּוּ יְמֵי אֲבֵילוּת שֶׁל מְתוּשֶׁלַח – **These were the** seven **days of mourning for Methuselah,** who had just died, for the Flood was delayed until the period of mourning concluded. לְלַמֶּדְךָ שֶׁהֶסְפֵּדָן שֶׁל צַדִּיקִים מְעַכְּבִין אֶת הַפּוּרְעָנוּת לָבֹא – This comes **to teach you that eulogies for the righteous hold back an** ordained **punishment** from **coming.**[13] דָּבָר אַחֵר – **An alternative explanation:** ,,לְשִׁבְעַת" – The phrase ***after the seven-day period*** indicates שֶׁשִּׁינָּה עֲלֵיהֶם הַקָּדוֹשׁ בָּרוּךְ הוּא סֵדֶר בְּרֵאשִׁית – **that the Holy One, Blessed is He, altered upon them the natural order of** the seven days of **Creation.** שֶׁהָיְתָה חַמָּה יוֹצֵאת מִמַּעֲרָב וְשׁוֹקַעַת בַּמִּזְרָח – **For** during the Flood, **the sun would rise in the west and set in the**

NOTES

1. I.e. we will traverse this thorny path, rather than clear it of obstacles. That is to say, we will not repent, but will continue to follow our crooked path of sin (*Rashi*). Since the flood will be delayed until Methuselah dies, repentance is not of urgency (see *Yad Ramah; cf. Maharsha, Maharal*).

2. *Job* 12:5. This obscure verse is variously translated and interpreted. Our translation follows Rava's exposition, which presumes the verse to be referring to the contemptuous reaction of the Generation of the Flood to Noah's prediction of the coming deluge, and to Noah's renouncement of their complacency.

[Rava's interpretation may be based on the contextual observation that the preceding verse in Job states the following: שְׂחוֹק צַדִּיק תָּמִים, *a butt of derision – the perfectly righteous.* Since Noah is described in Scripture as צַדִּיק תָּמִים, *perfectly righteous* (see *Genesis* 6:9), the passage alludes to the fact that (like Job) Noah was a butt of derision to the members of his generation.]

3. As explained above (108a note 32), the word מַבּוּל means *devastation,* and does not necessarily refer to a flood.

4. *Rashi;* see also *Maharsha* and see *Chagigah* 27a. According to *Aruch*, (s.v. אליתא), *alisah* was a creature that could extinguish fire.

5. *Akuv/akush* is some sort of highly absorbent sponge. The people thought that these sponges would absorb the flood waters and save their lives (see *Toras Chaim*). Alternatively, *akuv/akush* is something that holds back rain (*Aruch* s.v. עקוב). [Thus, they dreamed complacently that they could not be harmed by any force God might unleash against them.]

6. I.e. He can drown you in your own semen [with which you sinned – see note 8]. Alternatively: If He so desires, He can even cause water to issue forth from your heels, which you cannot cover with iron plates (*Rashi*).

7. Ibid. 12:5. [I.e. the sinners, who dream complacently that they will not suffer, are destined to stumble over their own feet, which will be the source of their affliction.]

8. As above, the verse is interpreted as referring to something that issues from between the feet – that is, semen. However, it means that the flood waters were *similar* to semen in that they were hot and of a thick texture (see *Rashi*). This exposition is related to the Gemara's statement above (108a) that the *"fountains of the Great Deep,"* which erupted when the Flood began, consisted of many hot springs (some of which remain open to this day). Our Gemara adds that besides being hot, the water was viscous.

[It has been suggested that the *"fountains of the Great Deep"* included the many volcanoes that are scattered around the globe. Thus, in addition to the flood waters, the earth was inundated with molten lava that was expelled from the deep. Molten lava is certainly hot and viscous (*R' Avigdor Miller*).]

9. Literally: in sin. This refers to ejaculating their seed in vain (see *Niddah* 13a with *Rashi* ד״ה כאילו; see also *Maharsha* ad loc. and *Pirkei DeRabbi Eliezer* ch. 22).

10. *Genesis* 8:1.

11. *Esther* 7:10.

12. *Genesis* 7:10.

13. The eulogy of a righteous person often moves the mourners to repentance, for it brings home the realization that the merit of that righteous one no longer protects them. Thus, as long as the people mourned Methuselah, there was hope that they might repent. When the period of mourning concluded and they had not been moved, all hope was extinguished (see *Maharsha;* cf. *Rashi* to *Genesis* 7:4, *Maharal* and *Melo HaRoim*).

א"כ לא נפנה דרך כרמים דרש רבא מאי דכתיב א) לפיד בוז לעשתות שאנן נכון למועדי רגל מלמד שהיה נח הצדיק מוכיח אותם ואמר להם דברים שהם קשים כלפידים והיו (בוזים) [מבזין] אותו אמרו לו זקן תיבה זו למה אמר להם הקב"ה מביא עליכם את המבול אמרו מבול של מה אם מבול של אש יש לנו דבר אחר ועליתה שמה ואם של מים הוא מביא אם מן הארץ הוא מביא יש לנו עששיות של ברזל שאנו מחפין בהם את הארץ ואם מן השמים הוא מביא יש לנו דבר ועקב שמו ואמרי לה עקש שמו אמר להם הוא מביא מבין עקבי רגליכם שנאמר א) נכון למועדי רגל תניא מימי המבול קשים כשכבת זרע שנאמר נכון למועדי רגל [א] אמר רב חסדא ברותחין קלקלו בעבירה וברותחין נידונו כתיב הכא ב) וישכו המים וכתיב התם ג) וחמת המלך שככה ד) ויהי לשבעת הימים ומי המבול היו על הארץ [ג] מה טיבם של שבעת הימים אמר רב אלו ימי אבילות של מתושלח ללמדך שהספדן של צדיקים מעכבין את הפורענות לבא דבר אחר לשבעת ששינה עליהם הקב"ה סדר בראשית שהיתה חמה יוצאת ממערב ושוקעת במזרח דבר אחר שקבע להם הקב"ה זמן גדול ואח"כ זמן קטן ד"א לשבעת הימים שהטעימם מעין העולם הבא כדי שידעו מה טובה מנעו מהן ה) מכל הבהמה הטהורה תקח לך שבעה שבעה איש ואשתו אישות לבהמה מי אית לה [ג] א"ר שמואל בר נחמני א"ר יונתן [ד] מאותם שלא נעבדה בהם עבירה מנא ידע אמר רב חסדא שהעבירן לפני התיבה כל שהתיבה קולטתו בידוע שלא נעבדה בהם עבירה וכל שאין התיבה קולטתו בידוע שנעבדה בה עבירה רבי אבהו אמר מאותן הבאין מאיליהן ו) עשה לך תיבת עצי גופר מאי גופר [ה] אמר רב אדא [ו] אמרי דבי ר' שילא זו מבליגה ואמרי לה גולמיש [ז] צוהר תעשה לתיבה א"ר יוחנן אמר לו הקב"ה לנח קבע בה אבנים טובות ומרגליות כדי שיהיו מאירות לכם כצהרים [ז] ואל אמה תכלנה מלמעלה דבהכי [הוא] דקיימא [ז] תחתיים שנים ושלישים תעשה תנא תחתיים לזבל אמצעיים לבהמה עליונים לאדם ח) וישלח את העורב אמר ר"ל תשובה ניצחת השיבו עורב לנח אמר לו רבך שונאני ואתה שנאתני רבך שונאני מן הטהורין שבעה מן הטמאים שנים ואתה שנאתני שאתה מניח ממין שבעה ושולח ממין שנים אם פוגע בי שר חמה או שר צנה לא נמצא עולם חסר בריה אחת או שמא לאשתי אתה צריך אמר לו רשע במותר לי נאסר לי בנאסר לי לא כ"ש ומנלן דנאסרו דכתיב ט) ובאת אל התיבה אתה ובניך ואשתך ונשי בניך אתך וכתיב י) צא מן התיבה אתה ואשתך ובניך ונשי בניך אתך וא"ר יוחנן מיכן אמרו שנאסרו בתשמיש המטה ת"ר שלשה שמשו בתיבה וכולם לקו כלב ועורב וחם כלב נקשר עורב רק חם לקה בעורו כ) וישלח את היונה מאתו לראות הקלו המים א"ר ירמיה מכאן שדירתן של עופות טהורים עם הצדיקים ל) והנה עלה זית טרף בפיה [י] א"ר אלעזר אמרה יונה לפני הקב"ה רבש"ע יהיו מזונותי מרורים כזית ומסורים בידך ואל יהיו מתוקים כדבש ומסורים ביד בשר ודם מאי משמע דהאי טרף לישנא דמזוני הוא דכתיב מ) הטריפני לחם חוקי [ג] למשפחותיהם יצאו מן התיבה א"ר יוחנן [ס] למשפחותם ולא הם אמר רב חנא בר ביזנא אמר ליה אליעזר לשם רבא כתיב [ג] למשפחותיהם יצאו מן התיבה אתון היכן הויתון א"ל צער גדול היה לנו בתיבה בריה שדרכה להאכילה ביום האכלנוה ביום שדרכה להאכילה בלילה האכלנוה בלילה האי זקיתא לא הוה ידע אבא מה אכלה יומא חד הוה יתיב וקא פאלי רמונא נפל תולעתא מינה אכלה מיכן ואילך הוה גביל לה חיזרא כי מתלע אכלה אריא אישתא זינתיה דאמר רב לא בציר משיתא ולא טפי מתריסר זינא אישתא אורשינה אשכחיניה אבא דגני בספנא דתיבותא א"ל לא בעית מזוני א"ל חזיתיך דהות טרידא אמינא לא אצערך א"ל יהא רעוא דלא תמות שנאמר ס) ואומר עם קני אגוע וכחול ארבה ימים אמר רב חנה בר לואי אמר שם רבא לאליעזר כי אתו עלייכו מלכי מזרח ומערב אתון היכי עבידיתו אמר ליה אייתי הקב"ה לאברהם ואותביה מימיניה והוה שדינן עפרא והוו חרבי גילי והוי גירי שנאמר ע) מזמור לדוד נאם ה' לאדוני שב לימיני עד אשית אויביך הדום לרגליך וכתיב פ) מי העיר ממזרח צדק יקראהו לרגלו יתן לפניו גוים ומלכים ירד יתן כעפר חרבו כקש נדף קשתו [ט] נחום איש גם זו הוה רגיל דכל דהוה סלקא ליה אמר גם זו לטובה יומא חד בעו [ישראל] לשדורי דורון לקיסר אמרי בהדי מאן

א"כ לא נפנה דרך כרמים. [כלומר לא נסור ולא נפנה את דרך הכרמים] אלא כל שעה נלך בהם כלומר א"כ לא נלך דרך כבושה ולא נחזור מסורינו אלא נלך ונקלקל השורה דרכים משובשים בקוצים ובדרקנים כעין שבילי כרמים: לעשתות. כמו עשתונות שיושבין שאנן וחושבין מחשבות רעות: עליתה שמה. אין אש שולט בה: מבין עקבי רגליכם. בשכבת זרע שלכם יכול למחות אתכם ל"א מבין עקבי רגליכם מן הרגל יוציא ממש מים אם היה רוצה ואי אפשר [י] לכפות רגליכם בעששיות: בשכבת זרע. רותחין ועבין היו. עבין ל"ג ופי' הוא: חמת המלך שככה. נחה מרתחו ה"נ מים נחו מרותחן: סדרי בראשית. והיינו לשבעת הימים סדר שבעת ימי בראשית שינה להם: זמן קטן אחר זמן גדול. בתחילה אמר להן והיו ימיו מאה ועשרים שנה כשעבר זמן זה ולא שבו לטובה חזר וקבע להם זמן קטן: אישות לבהמה מי אית ליה. נקבה אחת נשכבת לכמה זכרים ואין זו אישות: שלא נעבדה בהן עבירה. שלא נזקקו אלא לבן זוגם: מבליגה. עץ הוא: במותר לי. אפי' באשתי אני אסור: (בני נח. שם וחם ויפת): רק. רוקק זרע מפיו לפיה של נקבה: לקה בעורו. שיצא ממנו כוש: מאתו. גבי עורב לא כתיב מאתו מכאן שדירתם כו' כלומר הנאה הוא שדרים אצלם שמכירים בצדיקים כדאמרי' בדוכתי אחריתא: זית טרף בפיה. בפיה היתה שואלת מזון טרף של זית: למשפחותיהם יצאו מן התיבה. אלמא כל חד וחד בפני עצמו היה ולא היו אוכלין כולם באבוס אחד אלא משפחות [משפחות] היו שרויין: א"ל אליעזר. [עבד אברהם]: לשם רבא. גדול (א) בנו של נח: היכי הויתון. היאך הייתם יכולין להכין עניינים בכך לעשות לכל בריה ובריה חפצה: זקיתא. שם בריה: פאלי. מחתך כמו פלי פלויי במסכת נדה (דף כא:): אישתא זינתיה. חמה אחזתו וזנהו ולא היה חושש לדרוש מאכל בהמות: לא בציר משיתא ולא טפי מתריסר זיינא אישתא. אין לך חמה קלה שלא תהא חמימותו יכולה לזונו ששת ימים שלא ימות בלא מאכל ואין לך חמה שיכולה לזון יותר מי"ב ימים בלי מאכל ומשתה כ"ש ואית דגרסי לא פחות משיתא ירחי ולא טפי מתריסר זנתא אשתא ואחרי קאי כלומר לא פחות מששה חדשים ולא יותר מי"ב חדשים ולא נהירא לי: אורשינא. עוף ושמו חול בלשון המקרא ואינו מת לעולם: בספנא. בחדר ספון ומתוקן לו: [נאום ה' כו']. אליעזר אמר פסוק זה. נאם ה' לאדני אמר הקב"ה לאברהם [ט] שב לימיני אדני וכו': ממזרח זה אברהם. שבא מארם נהרים שהוא במזרח דכתיב (במדבר כג) מן ארם ינחני בלק מלך מואב וגו': כל דהוה סלקא ליה. כל דבר המאורע ליה:

בהדי

א) לַפִּיד בּוּז לְעַשְׁתּוּת שַׁאֲנָן נָכוֹן לְמוֹעֲדֵי רָגֶל: [איוב יב, ה]
ב) וַיִּזְכֹּר אֱלֹהִים אֶת נֹחַ וְאֵת כָּל הַחַיָּה וְאֶת כָּל הַבְּהֵמָה אֲשֶׁר אִתּוֹ בַּתֵּבָה וַיַּעֲבֵר אֱלֹהִים רוּחַ עַל הָאָרֶץ וַיָּשֹׁכּוּ הַמָּיִם: [בראשית ח, א]
ג) וַיִּתְלוּ אֶת הָמָן עַל הָעֵץ אֲשֶׁר הֵכִין לְמָרְדֳּכָי וַחֲמַת הַמֶּלֶךְ שָׁכָכָה: [אסתר ז, י]
ד) וַיְהִי לְשִׁבְעַת הַיָּמִים וּמֵי הַמַּבּוּל הָיוּ עַל הָאָרֶץ: [בראשית ז, י]
ה) מִכֹּל הַבְּהֵמָה הַטְּהוֹרָה תִּקַּח לְךָ שִׁבְעָה שִׁבְעָה אִישׁ וְאִשְׁתּוֹ וּמִן הַבְּהֵמָה אֲשֶׁר לֹא טְהֹרָה הִוא שְׁנַיִם אִישׁ וְאִשְׁתּוֹ: [בראשית ז, ב]
ו) עֲשֵׂה לְךָ תֵּבַת עֲצֵי גֹפֶר קִנִּים תַּעֲשֶׂה אֶת הַתֵּבָה וְכָפַרְתָּ אֹתָהּ מִבַּיִת וּמִחוּץ בַּכֹּפֶר: [בראשית ו, יד]
ז) צֹהַר תַּעֲשֶׂה לַתֵּבָה וְאֶל אַמָּה תְּכַלֶנָּה מִלְמַעְלָה וּפֶתַח הַתֵּבָה בְּצִדָּהּ תָּשִׂים תַּחְתִּיִּם שְׁנִיִּם וּשְׁלִשִׁים תַּעֲשֶׂהָ: [בראשית ו, טז]
ח) וַיְשַׁלַּח אֶת הָעֹרֵב וַיֵּצֵא יָצוֹא וָשׁוֹב עַד יְבֹשֶׁת הַמַּיִם מֵעַל הָאָרֶץ: [בראשית ח, ז]
ט) וַהֲקִמֹתִי אֶת בְּרִיתִי אִתָּךְ וּבָאתָ אֶל הַתֵּבָה אַתָּה וּבָנֶיךָ וְאִשְׁתְּךָ וּנְשֵׁי בָנֶיךָ אִתָּךְ: [בראשית ו, יח]
י) צֵא מִן הַתֵּבָה אַתָּה וְאִשְׁתְּךָ וּבָנֶיךָ וּנְשֵׁי בָנֶיךָ אִתָּךְ: [בראשית ח, טז]
כ) וַיְשַׁלַּח אֶת הַיּוֹנָה מֵאִתּוֹ לִרְאוֹת הֲקַלּוּ הַמַּיִם מֵעַל פְּנֵי הָאֲדָמָה: [בראשית ח, ח]
ל) וַתָּבֹא אֵלָיו הַיּוֹנָה לְעֵת עֶרֶב וְהִנֵּה עֲלֵה זַיִת טָרָף בְּפִיהָ וַיֵּדַע נֹחַ כִּי קַלּוּ הַמַּיִם מֵעַל הָאָרֶץ: [בראשית ח, יא]
מ) שָׁוְא וּדְבַר כָּזָב הַרְחֵק מִמֶּנִּי רֵאשׁ וָעֹשֶׁר אַל תִּתֶּן לִי הַטְרִיפֵנִי לֶחֶם חֻקִּי: [משלי ל, ח]
נ) כָּל הַחַיָּה כָּל הָרֶמֶשׂ וְכָל הָעוֹף כֹּל רוֹמֵשׂ עַל הָאָרֶץ לְמִשְׁפְּחֹתֵיהֶם יָצְאוּ מִן הַתֵּבָה: [בראשית ח, יט]
ס) וָאֹמַר עִם קִנִּי אֶגְוָע וְכַחוֹל אַרְבֶּה יָמִים: [איוב כט, יח]
ע) לְדָוִד מִזְמוֹר נְאֻם יְיָ לַאדֹנִי שֵׁב לִימִינִי עַד אָשִׁית אֹיְבֶיךָ הֲדֹם לְרַגְלֶיךָ: [תהלים קי, א]
פ) מִי הֵעִיר מִמִּזְרָח צֶדֶק יִקְרָאֵהוּ לְרַגְלוֹ יִתֵּן לְפָנָיו גּוֹיִם וּמְלָכִים יַרְדְּ יִתֵּן כֶּעָפָר חַרְבּוֹ כְּקַשׁ נִדָּף קַשְׁתּוֹ: [ישעיה מא, ב]

מסורת הש"ס

א) ר"ה יב. זבחים קיג., ב) [תוספתא דסוטה פ"י], ג) [זבחים קטז. ע"ש], ד) [פי' בשביל שלא באו על שאינן מינן עשה להן כבוד וכתב להן אישות כבאדם. ערוך ערך אשה], ה) [ר"ה כג.], ו) [גיר' הערוך רב אמר אדרא דבי ר' שילא אמרי זו כו' ע"ש ערך אדר], ז) [עירובין יח: ע"ש], ח) [כתב הבאר שבע לא ידענא פירושו ועי' מהרש"א בח"א וגם בפענח רזא קצת בדחיקות ויתכן לפרש לולא דבריהם ע"פ האמור בחולין נח. כל בריה שאין בו עצם אינו מתקיים שנים עשר חודש והבן], ט) תענית כא. ע"ש, י) נ"ל לחפות, כ) [נ"ל אדוני שב לימיני וכו'].

הגהות הב"ח

(א) רש"י ד"ה לשם רבא גדול. נ"ב ול"ע לעיל דף סט ע"ב:

ליקוטי רש"י

לפיד בוז. אש של גיהנם עומד למי שאנן בעשתותו לומר שלום יהיה לי [איוב יב, ה]. וישכו. כמו (אסתר ב, א) כשוך חמת המלך לשון הנחת חמה [בראשית ח, א]. וחמת המלך שככה. וסתם חמה רותחת היא כדכתיב וחמתו בערה בו [ר"ה יב, א]. אלו ימי אבלות של מתושלח. כי לימים עוד שבעה. אלו שבעת ימי אבלו של מתושלח הצדיק שחס הקב"ה על כבודו ועכב את הפורענות. לא וחשוב שנותיו של מתושלח ותמצא שהם כלים בשנת שש מאות שנה לחיי נח [בראשית ז, ד]. מתושלח לדיק גמור היה כדאמרינן בחלק (סנהדרין קח:) שבעת ימים שנתלו לדור המבול הן ימי אבלו של מתושלח [סוכה נב:]. כל שהתיבה קולטתו. מהעוף למינהו. אותן שדבקו במיניהם ולא השחיתו דרכם ומאליהם באו וכל שהתיבה קולטתו הכניס בה [בראשית ו, כ]. עצי גפר. כך שמו ולמה ממין זה על שם גפרית שנגזר עליהם להמחות בו [שם ו, יד]. צהר. יש אומרים חלון ויש אומרים אבן טובה המאירה להם. ואל אמה תכלנה מלמעלה. כסויה משופע ועולה עד שהוא קצר מלמעלה ועומד על אמה כדי שיזובו המים למטה. תחתים שנים ושלשים. שלש עליות זו על גב זו עליונים לאדם אמצעים למדור בהמה תחתיים לזבל [שם ו, טז]. או שמא לאשתי אתה צריך. יצוא ושוב. הולך ומקיף סביבות התיבה ולא הלך בשליחותו שהיה חושדו על בת זוגו כמו ששנינו באגדת חלק (סנהדרין קח:) [שם ח, ז]. אתה ובניך ואשתך. האנשים לבד והנשים לבד מכאן שנאסרו בתשמיש המטה [שם ז, יח]. נח ובניו. האנשים לבד

east.[14] דָּבָר אַחֵר – **An alternative explanation:** There was a seven-day delay in the onset of the Flood, שֶׁקָּבַע לָהֶם הַקָּדוֹשׁ בָּרוּךְ הוּא זְמַן גָּדוֹל – **for the Holy One, Blessed is He,** first **allotted them a long period of time** to reflect and repent, וְאַחַר כָּךְ זְמַן קָטָן – **and afterwards,** when that period passed without results, **He allotted them** another **short period of time,** as a last chance for repentance.[15] דָּבָר אַחֵר – **An alternative explanation:** "לְשִׁבְעַת הַיָּמִים" – The phrase ***after the seven-day period*** teaches שֶׁהִטְעִימָם מֵעֵין הָעוֹלָם הַבָּא – **that** before the Flood **[God] gave them to taste a semblance of** the reward enjoyed by the righteous in **the World to Come,** כְּדֵי שֶׁיֵּדְעוּ מַה טּוֹבָה מָנְעוּ מֵהֶן – **so that they would realize what goodness they deprived themselves of** through their sinful ways.[16]

The Gemara analyzes one of God's instructions to Noah before the Flood:

"מִכֹּל הַבְּהֵמָה הַטְּהוֹרָה תִּקַּח־לְךָ שִׁבְעָה שִׁבְעָה אִישׁ וְאִשְׁתּוֹ" – Scripture states:[17] ***Of every clean animal take unto you seven, seven, a man and his wife.*** אִישׁוּת לִבְהֵמָה מִי אִית לָהּ – **Does an animal have matrimony,** that God should refer to a male and female as "man and wife"?[18] אָמַר רַבִּי שְׁמוּאֵל בַּר נַחְמָנִי אָמַר רַבִּי יוֹנָתָן – **R' Shmuel bar Nachmani said in the name of R' Yonasan:** מֵאוֹתָם שֶׁלֹּא נֶעֶבְדָה בָּהֶם עֲבֵירָה – God meant that Noah should take **from those** animals **with which no sin had been committed.**[19]

The Gemara analyzes this:

מְנָא יָדַע – **How did [Noah] know** which animals had never been used for sin? אָמַר רַב חִסְדָּא – **Rav Chisda said:** שֶׁהֶעֱבִירָן לִפְנֵי הַתֵּיבָה – He knew **for he led them past the Ark.** כָּל שֶׁהַתֵּיבָה קוֹלַטְתּוֹ – **Whichever one the Ark took in** בְּיָדוּעַ שֶׁלֹּא נֶעֶבְדָה בָּהֶם עֲבֵירָה – **was** thereby **known to be one with which no sin had been committed.** וְכָל שֶׁאֵין הַתֵּיבָה קוֹלַטְתּוֹ – **And whichever one the Ark did not take in** בְּיָדוּעַ שֶׁנֶּעֶבְדָה בָּהּ עֲבֵירָה – **was** thereby **known to be one with which a sin had been committed.** רַבִּי אַבָּהוּ אָמַר – **R' Abahu said:** מֵאוֹתָן הַבָּאִין מֵאֵילֵיהֶן – Noah took **from those** animals **that came** to him **of their own accord.**[20]

The Gemara discusses the construction of the Ark:

"עֲשֵׂה לְךָ תֵּבַת עֲצֵי־גֹפֶר" – Scripture states that God instructed Noah: ***Make for yourself an Ark of gopherwood.***[21] מַאי "גֹּפֶר" – **What is *gopher*?** אָמַר רַב אַדָּא אָמְרֵי דְּבֵי רַבִּי שֵׁילָא – **Rav Ada said in the name of the academy of R' Sheila:** זוּ מַבְלִיגָה – **This is** the wood known as ***mavligah.*** וְאָמְרֵי לָהּ גּוּלְמִישׁ – **And some say** it is the wood known as ***gulamish.***[22]

God further instructed Noah:

"צֹהַר תַּעֲשֶׂה לַתֵּבָה" – ***An illumination*** (*tzohar*) ***shall you make for the Ark.***[23] אָמַר רַבִּי יוֹחָנָן – **R' Yochanan said:** אָמַר לוֹ הַקָּדוֹשׁ בָּרוּךְ הוּא לְנֹחַ – **The Holy One, Blessed is He, said to Noah:** קְבַע בָּהּ אֲבָנִים טוֹבוֹת וּמַרְגָּלִיּוֹת – **Set into [the Ark] precious stones and pearls** כְּדֵי שֶׁיְּהוּ מְאִירוֹת לָכֶם כַּצָּהֳרַיִם – **so that they will illuminate** the Ark **for you as** brightly as the **noontime** (*tzaharaim*) sun.[24]

NOTES

14. According to this exposition, *after the seven-day period* does not mean that the Flood was delayed by seven days. Rather, it means that the Natural Order that had been imposed on the universe during the seven days of Creation ceased to exist with the advent of the Flood. [The Flood came after an extended period of more than one thousand years during which the seven-day order functioned] (*Rashi*). This point is also alluded to by another verse, for after the Flood ended, God told Noah (*Genesis* 8:22): עד כָּל־יְמֵי הָאָרֶץ זֶרַע וְקָצִיר וְקֹר וָחֹם וְקַיִץ וָחֹרֶף וְיוֹם וָלַיְלָה לֹא יִשְׁבֹּתוּ, *Henceforth – all the days of the earth – seedtime and harvest, cold and heat, summer and winter, day and night shall not cease.* This implies that during the Flood the normal order of day and night ceased (see *Iyun Yaakov* and *Rashi* to *Genesis* loc. cit.).

The reversal in the direction of the rising and setting of the sun represents the complete disintegration of the Natural Order of the world, which was the effect of the Flood (*Maharal*). See *Maharsha* and *Hagahos Yavetz* for explanations of the mechanics of this phenomenon.

Ben Yehoyada maintains that God visibly altered the Natural Order in order to disabuse the Generation of the Flood of their smug confidence. They assumed that they would be able to survive or prevent any catastrophe through the use of fire-resistant materials, sponges, metal plates, etc. God demonstrated to them that He has the power to unravel the laws of nature, and they could therefore not rely on any natural substance to save them from His wrath.

15. Originally, when God observed the corruption of mankind, He said (*Genesis* 6:3): *"My spirit shall not contend evermore concerning man since he is but flesh; his days shall be a hundred and twenty years."* He told Noah to build an Ark, and Noah spent the next hundred and twenty years building it and warning the world's inhabitants that unless they repented they would be destroyed. When that period passed without result, God awarded them a final seven-day period in which to repent (*Rashi;* see *Targum Onkelos* to *Genesis* loc. cit.; see also *Maharsha* ד"ה ששינה).

16. Since, in addition to having no share in the World to Come, the Generation of the Flood will not be resurrected to stand judgment, they will never witness the reward reserved for the righteous, and would not have experienced the anguish of having forfeited it. God therefore gave them a taste of it before destroying them, so that their punishment would be complete (*Maharsha;* cf. *Maharal*).

This exposition is based on the Gemara's statement above (97a) that this world will exist for six thousand years and will be desolate for the seventh thousand. Afterwards, the sublime epoch of the World to Come begins. Since a thousand years is regarded as one day by the Holy One, Blessed is He, as the Psalmist says (*Psalms* 90:4): *For a thousand years in Your eyes are but a bygone yesterday,* the seven thousand years are counted as seven days. Thus, the phrase *after the seven-day period* is an allusion to the World to Come, which is after seven thousand years, and indicates that the Flood came only after the people had been granted a taste of the World to Come (*Yad Ramah*; see 97a note 59).

17. *Genesis* 7:2.

18. [The term *wife* implies a female who mates with a single male to the exclusion of all others.] Female animals, however, generally mate with many different males (*Rashi*).

19. I.e. animals that had not mated with any animals of different species (*Rashi; Maharsha;* see also *Rashi* to *Genesis* 6:20).

Since there is no such thing as matrimony among animals, the term "man and wife" refers not to those that had a single mate, but to those that mated properly, within their own species (*Maharsha*).

20. It would seems that R' Abahu means to argue with the explanation of Rav Chisda. That is, R' Abahu says that Noah did not need to test the animals by leading them past the Ark. Rather, God caused the precise number of animals that were supposed to enter the Ark to come to Noah – seven of every clean species and two of every unclean species. Those animals that came had not been used for sin (see *Rashi* to *Zevachim* 116a ד"ה הבאין).

However, *Rashi* to *Genesis* 6:20 reconciles the statement of R' Abahu with that of Rav Chisda. *Rashi* explains that many animals came to Noah of their own accord, and he led those past the Ark, bringing in the ones that the Ark accepted. Thus, R' Abahu does not mean to argue with Rav Chisda, but to provide an additional piece of information. That is, Noah did not need to chase after animals, for God caused many animals to come to him of their own accord; only those that came to Noah were led past the Ark. The wording of our Gemara, ***from those*** *that came of their own accord,* accords with the approach of *Rashi* to *Genesis* (*Maharsha*; see also *Gur Aryeh* to *Genesis* 6:20).

In Tractate *Zevachim* (ibid.), R' Abahu cites a verse in support of his view that the animals came of their own accord. The verse states (*Genesis* 7:16): וְהַבָּאִים זָכָר וּנְקֵבָה מִכָּל־בָּשָׂר בָּאוּ, *And those that came, came male and female of all flesh.*

21. Ibid. 6:14.

22. These are species of the cedar family (see *Rosh Hashanah* 23a).

23. Ibid. v. 16.

24. Although the Ark had a window (see *Genesis* 8:6), the window did not provide light, for the earth was not lit by the celestial bodies during the Flood. The window was merely a means of egress for the birds Noah sent out after the Flood to determine if the earth was once again

גמרא

א"כ לא נפנה דרך כרמים דרש רבא מאי דכתיב א) לפיד בוז לעשתות שאנן נכון למועדי רגל מלמד שהיה נח הצדיק מוכיח אותם ואומר להם דברים שהם קשים כלפידים והיו (בוזים) [מבזין] אותו אמרו לו זקן תיבה זו למה אמר להם הקב"ה מביא עליכם את המבול אמרו מבול של מה אם מבול של אש יש לנו דבר אחר ועליתה שמה ואם של מים הוא מביא אם מן הארץ הוא מביא יש לנו עששיות של ברזל שאנו מחפין בהם את הארץ ואם מן השמים הוא מביא יש לנו דבר ועקב שמו ואמרי לה עקש שמו אמר להם הוא מביא מבין עקבי רגליכם שנאמר א) נכון למועדי רגל תניא מימי המבול קשים כשכבת זרע שנאמר נכון למועדי רגל א) אמר רב חסדא ברותחין קלקלו בעבירה וברותחין נידונו כתיב הכא ב) וישכו המים וכתיב התם ג) וחמת המלך שככה ד) ויהי לשבעת הימים ומי המבול היו על הארץ ב) מה טיבם של שבעת הימים אמר רב אלו ימי אבילות של מתושלח ללמדך שהספדן של צדיקים מעכבין את הפורענות לבא דבר אחר לשבעת ששינה עליהם הקב"ה סדר בראשית שהיתה חמה יוצאת ממערב ושוקעת במזרח דבר אחר שקבע להם הקב"ה זמן גדול ואח"כ זמן קטן ד"א לשבעת הימים שהטעימם מעין העולם הבא כדי שידעו מה טובה מנעו מהן ה) מכל הבהמה הטהורה תקח לך שבעה שבעה איש ואשתו אישות לבהמה מי אית לה ג) א"ר שמואל בר נחמני א"ר יונתן ד) מאותם שלא נעבדה בהם עבירה מנא ידע אמר רב חסדא שהעבירן לפני התיבה כל שהתיבה קולטתו בידוע שלא נעבדה בהם עבירה וכל שאין התיבה קולטתו בידוע שנעבדה בה עבירה רבי אבהו אמר מאותן הבאין מאיליהן ו) עשה לך תיבת עצי גופר מאי גופר ה) אמר רב אדא ו) אמרי דבי ר' שילא זו מבליגה ואמרי לה גולמיש ז) צוהר תעשה לתיבה א"ר יוחנן אמר לו הקב"ה לנח קבע בה אבנים טובות ומרגליות כדי שיהיו מאירות לכם כצהרים ז) ואל אמה תכלנה מלמעלה דבהכי [הוא] דקיימא ז) תחתיים שנים ושלישים תעשה תנא תחתיים לזבל אמצעיים לבהמה עליונים לאדם ח) וישלח את העורב אמר ר"ל תשובה ניצחת השיבו עורב לנח אמר לו רבך שונאני ואתה שנאתני רבך שונאני מן הטהורין שבעה מן הטמאים שנים ואתה שנאתני שאתה מניח ממין שבעה ושולח ממין שנים אם פוגע בי שר חמה או שר צנה לא נמצא עולם חסר בריה אחת או שמא לאשתי אתה צריך אמר לו רשע במותר לי נאסר לי בנאסר לי לא כ"ש ומנלן דנאסרו דכתיב ט) ובאת אל התיבה אתה ובניך ואשתך ונשי בניך אתך וכתיב י) צא מן התיבה אתה ואשתך ובניך ונשי בניך אתך וא"ר יוחנן מיכן אמרו שנאסרו בתשמיש המטה ת"ר שלשה שמשו בתיבה וכולם לקו כלב ועורב וחם כלב נקשר עורב רק חם לקה בעורו כ) וישלח את היונה מאתו לראות הקלו המים א"ר ירמיה מכאן שדירתן של עופות טהורים עם הצדיקים ל) והנה עלה זית טרף בפיה י) א"ר אלעזר אמרה יונה לפני הקב"ה רבש"ע יהיו מזונותי מרורים כזית ומסורים בידך ואל יהיו מתוקים כדבש ומסורים ביד בשר ודם מאי משמע דהאי טרף לישנא דמזוני הוא דכתיב מ) הטריפני לחם חוקי נ) למשפחותיהם יצאו מן התיבה א"ר יוחנן ח) למשפחותם ולא הם אמר רב חנא בר ביזנא אמר ליה אליעזר לשם רבא כתיב נ) למשפחותיהם יצאו מן התיבה אתון היכן הויתון א"ל צער גדול היה לנו בתיבה בריה שדרכה להאכילה ביום האכלנוה ביום שדרכה להאכילה בלילה האכלנוה בלילה האי זקיתא לא הוה ידע אבא מה אכלה יומא חד הוה יתיב וקא פאלי רמונא נפל תולעתא מינה אכלה מיכן ואילך הוה גביל לה חיזרא כי מתלע אכלה אריא אישתא זינתיה דאמר רב לא בציר משיתא ולא טפי מתריסר זינא אישתא אורשינה אשכחיניה אבא דגני בספנא דתיבותא א"ל לא בעית מזוני א"ל חזיתיך דהות טרידא אמינא לא אצערך א"ל יהא רעוא דלא תמות שנאמר ס) ואומר עם קני אגוע וכחול ארבה ימים אמר רב חנה בר לואי אמר שם רבא לאליעזר כי אתו עלייכו מלכי מזרח ומערב אתון היכי עבידיתו אמר ליה אייתי הקב"ה לאברהם ואותביה מימיניה והוה שדינן עפרא והוו חרבי גילי והוי גירי שנאמר ע) מזמור לדוד נאם ה' לאדוני שב לימיני עד אשית אויביך הדום לרגליך וכתיב פ) מי העיר ממזרח צדק יקראהו לרגלו יתן לפניו גוים ומלכים ירד יתן כעפר חרבו כקש נדף קשתו ט) נחום איש גם זו הוה רגיל דכל דהוה סלקא ליה אמר גם זו לטובה יומא חד בעו [ישראל] לשדורי דורון לקיסר אמרי בהדי מאן

רש"י

א"כ לא נפנה דרך כרמים. [כלומר לא נסור ולא נפנה את דרך הכרמים] אלא כל שעה נלך בהם כלומר א"כ לא נלך דרך כבושה ולא נחזור מסורינו אלא נלך ונקלקל השורה דרכים משובשים בקוצים ובדרקנים כעין שבילי כרמים: לעשתות. כמו עשתונות שיושבין שאנן וחושבין מחשבות רעות: עליתה שמה. אין אש שולט בה: מבין עקבי רגליכם. בשכבת זרע שלכם יכול למחות אתכם ל"א מבין עקבי רגליכם מן הרגל יוצא ממש מים אם היה רוצה ואי אפשר י) לכפות רגליכם בעששיות: בשכבת זרע. רותחין ועבין היו. עבין ל"ג ופי' הוא: חמת המלך שככה. נחה מרתחו ה"נ מים נחו מרותחן: סדרי בראשית. והיינו לשבעת הימים סדר שבעת ימי בראשית שינה להם: זמן קטן אחר זמן גדול. בתחילה אמר להן והיו ימיו מאה ועשרים שנה כשעבר זמן זה ולא שבו לטובה חזר וקבע להם זמן קטן: אישות לבהמה מי אית ליה. נקבה אחת נשכבת לכמה זכרים ואין זו אישות: שלא נעבדה בהן עבירה. שלא נזקקו אלא לבן זוגם: מבליגה. עץ הוא: במותר לי. אפי' באשתי אני אסור: (בני נח. שם וחם ויפת): רק. רוקק זרע מפיו לפיה של נקבה: לקה בעורו. שיצא ממנו כוש: מאתו. גבי עורב לא כתיב מאתו מכאן שדירתם כו' כלומר הנאה הוא שדרים אלא שמכירים בצדיקים כדאמרי' בדוכתי אחריתא: זית טרף בפיה. בפיה היתה שואלת מזון טרף של זית: למשפחותיהם יצאו מן התיבה. אלמא כל חד וחד בפני עצמו היה ולא היו אוכלין כולם באבוס אחד אלא משפחות [משפחות] היו שרויין: א"ל אליעזר. [עבד אברהם]: לשם רבא. גדול (א) בנו של נח: היכי הויתון. היאך הייתם יכולין להכין עניניהם בכך לעשות לכל בריה ובריה חפצה: זקיתא. שם בריה: פאלי. מחתך כמו פלי פלויי במסכת נדה (דף כא:): אישתא זינתיה. חמה אחזתו וזנהו ולא היה חושש לדרוש מאכל בהמות: לא בציר משיתא ולא טפי מתריסר זיינא אישתא. אין לך חמה קלה שלא תהא חמימותו יכולה לזונו ששת ימים שלא ימות בלא מאכל ואין לך חמה שיכולה לזון יותר מי"ב ימים בלי מאכל ומשתה כ"ש ואית דגרסי לא פחות משיתא ירחי ולא טפי מתריסר זנתא אשתא ואארי קאי כלומר לא פחות מששה חדשים ולא יותר מי"ב חדשים ולא נהירא לי: אורשינא. עוף ושמו חול בלשון המקרא ואינו מת לעולם: בספנא. בחדר ספון ומתוקן לו: [נאום ה' כו']. אליעזר אמר פסוק זה. נאם ה' לאדני אמר הקב"ה לאברהם כ) שב לימיני אדני וכו': ממזרח זה אברהם. שבא מארם נהרים שהוא במזרח דכתיב (במדבר כג) מן ארם ינחני בלק מלך מואב וגו': כל דהוה סלקא ליה. כל דבר המאורע ליה: בהדי

תורה אור השלם

א) לַפִּיד בּוּז לְעַשְׁתּוּת שַׁאֲנָן נָכוֹן לְמוֹעֲדֵי רָגֶל: [איוב יב, ה]

ב) וַיִּזְכֹּר אֱלֹהִים אֶת נֹחַ וְאֵת כָּל הַחַיָּה וְאֶת כָּל הַבְּהֵמָה אֲשֶׁר אִתּוֹ בַּתֵּבָה וַיַּעֲבֵר אֱלֹהִים רוּחַ עַל הָאָרֶץ וַיָּשֹׁכּוּ הַמָּיִם: [בראשית ח, א]

ג) וַיִּתְלוּ אֶת הָמָן עַל הָעֵץ אֲשֶׁר הֵכִין לְמָרְדֳּכָי וַחֲמַת הַמֶּלֶךְ שָׁכָכָה: [אסתר ז, י]

ד) וַיְהִי לְשִׁבְעַת הַיָּמִים וּמֵי הַמַּבּוּל הָיוּ עַל הָאָרֶץ: [בראשית ז, י]

ה) מִכֹּל הַבְּהֵמָה הַטְּהוֹרָה תִּקַּח לְךָ שִׁבְעָה שִׁבְעָה אִישׁ וְאִשְׁתּוֹ וּמִן הַבְּהֵמָה אֲשֶׁר לֹא טְהֹרָה הִוא שְׁנַיִם אִישׁ וְאִשְׁתּוֹ: [בראשית ז, ב]

ו) עֲשֵׂה לְךָ תֵּבַת עֲצֵי גֹפֶר קִנִּים תַּעֲשֶׂה אֶת הַתֵּבָה וְכָפַרְתָּ אֹתָהּ מִבַּיִת וּמִחוּץ בַּכֹּפֶר: [בראשית ו, יד]

ז) צֹהַר תַּעֲשֶׂה לַתֵּבָה וְאֶל אַמָּה תְּכַלֶּנָּה מִלְמַעְלָה וּפֶתַח הַתֵּבָה בְּצִדָּהּ תָּשִׂים תַּחְתִּיִּם שְׁנִיִּם וּשְׁלִשִׁים תַּעֲשֶׂהָ: [בראשית ו, טז]

ח) וַיְשַׁלַּח אֶת הָעֹרֵב וַיֵּצֵא יָצוֹא וָשׁוֹב עַד יְבֹשֶׁת הַמַּיִם מֵעַל הָאָרֶץ: [בראשית ח, ז]

ט) וַהֲקִמֹתִי אֶת בְּרִיתִי אִתָּךְ וּבָאתָ אֶל הַתֵּבָה אַתָּה וּבָנֶיךָ וְאִשְׁתְּךָ וּנְשֵׁי בָנֶיךָ אִתָּךְ: [בראשית ו, יח]

י) צֵא מִן הַתֵּבָה אַתָּה וְאִשְׁתְּךָ וּבָנֶיךָ וּנְשֵׁי בָנֶיךָ אִתָּךְ: [בראשית ח, טז]

כ) וַיְשַׁלַּח אֶת הַיּוֹנָה מֵאִתּוֹ לִרְאוֹת הֲקַלּוּ הַמַּיִם מֵעַל פְּנֵי הָאֲדָמָה: [בראשית ח, ח]

ל) וַתָּבֹא אֵלָיו הַיּוֹנָה לְעֵת עֶרֶב וְהִנֵּה עֲלֵה זַיִת טָרָף בְּפִיהָ וַיֵּדַע נֹחַ כִּי קַלּוּ הַמַּיִם מֵעַל הָאָרֶץ: [בראשית ח, יא]

מ) שָׁוְא וּדְבַר כָּזָב הַרְחֵק מִמֶּנִּי רֵאשׁ וָעֹשֶׁר אַל תִּתֶּן לִי הַטְרִיפֵנִי לֶחֶם חֻקִּי: [משלי ל, ח]

נ) כָּל הַחַיָּה כָּל הָרֶמֶשׂ וְכָל הָעוֹף כֹּל רוֹמֵשׂ עַל הָאָרֶץ לְמִשְׁפְּחֹתֵיהֶם יָצְאוּ מִן הַתֵּבָה: [בראשית ח, יט]

ס) וָאֹמַר עִם קִנִּי אֶגְוָע וְכַחוֹל אַרְבֶּה יָמִים: [איוב כט, יח]

ע) לְדָוִד מִזְמוֹר נְאֻם יְיָ לַאדֹנִי שֵׁב לִימִינִי עַד אָשִׁית אֹיְבֶיךָ הֲדֹם לְרַגְלֶיךָ: [תהלים קי, א]

פ) מִי הֵעִיר מִמִּזְרָח צֶדֶק יִקְרָאֵהוּ לְרַגְלוֹ יִתֵּן לְפָנָיו גּוֹיִם וּמְלָכִים יַרְדְּ יִתֵּן כֶּעָפָר חַרְבּוֹ כְּקַשׁ נִדָּף קַשְׁתּוֹ: [ישעיה מא, ב]

מסורת הש"ס

א) ר"ה יב. זבחים קיג:, ב) [תוספתא דסוטה פ"י], ג) [זבחים קטז. ע"ש], ד) [פי' בשביל שלא באו על שאינן מינן עשה להן כבוד וכתב להן אישות כבאדם. ערוך ערך אשה], ה) [ר"ה כג.], ו) [גיר' הערוך רב אמר אדרא דבי ר' שילא אמרי זו כו' ע"ש ערך אדר], ז) [עירובין יח: ע"ש], ח) [כתב הבאר שבע לא ידענא פירושו ועי' מהרש"א בח"א וגם בפענח רזא קצת בדחיקות ויתכן לפרש לולא דבריהם ע"פ האמור בחולין נח. כל בריה שאין בו עצם אינו מתקיים שנים עשר חודש והבן], ט) תענית כא. ע"ש, י) נ"ל לחפות, כ) [נ"ל אדוני שב לימיני וכו'].

הגהות הב"ח

(א) רש"י ד"ה לשם רבא גדול. נ"ב וצ"ע לעיל דף סט ע"ב:

ליקוטי רש"י

לפיד בוז. אש של גיהנם עומד למי ששאנן בעשתותו לומר שלום יהיה לי [איוב יב, ה]. וישכו. כמו (אסתר ב, א) כשוך חמת המלך לשון הנחת חמה [בראשית ח, א]. וחמת המלך שככה. וסתם חמה רותחת היא כדכתיב וחמתו בערה בו [ר"ה יב, א]. אלו ימי אבלות של מתושלח. כי לימים עוד שבעה. אלו שבעת ימי אבלו של מתושלח הצדיק שחס הקב"ה על כבודו ועכב את הפורענות. צא וחשוב שנותיו של מתושלח ותמצא שהם כלים בשנת שש מאות שנה לחיי נח [בראשית ז, ד]. מתושלח צדיק גמור היה כדאמרינן בחלק (סנהדרין קח:) שבעת ימים שנתלו לדור המבול הן ימי אבלו של מתושלח [סוכה נב:]. כל שהתיבה קולטתו. מהעוף למינהו. אותן שדבקו במיניהם ולא השחיתו דרכם ומאליהם באו וכל שהתיבה קולטתו הכניס בה [בראשית ו, כ]. עצי גפר. כך שמו ולמה ממין זה על שם גפרית שנגזר עליהם להמחות בו [שם ו, יד]. צהר. יש אומרים חלון ויש אומרים אבן טובה המאירה להם. ואל אמה תכלנה מלמעלה. כסויה משופע ועולה עד שהוא קצר מלמעלה ועומד על אמה כדי שיזובו המים למטה. תחתים שנים ושלשים. שלש עליות זו על גב זו עליונים לאדם אמצעים למדור בהמה תחתיים לזבל [שם ו, טז]. או שמא לאשתי אתה צריך. יצא ושוב. הולך ומקיף סביבות התיבה ולא הלך בשליחותו שהיה חושדו על בת זוגו כמו ששנינו באגדת חלק (סנהדרין קח:) [שם ח, ז]. אתה ובניך ואשתך. האנשים לבד והנשים לבד מכאן שנאסרו בתשמיש המטה [שם ז, יח]. נח ובניו. האנשים לבד והנשים לבד לפי שנאסרו בתשמיש המטה מפני שהעולם היה שרוי בצער [שם ז,ז]. אתה ואשתך וגו'. איש ואשתו כאן התיר להם תשמיש המטה [שם ח, טז]. טרף. חטף ומדרש אגדה לשון מזון ודרשו בפיה לשון מאמר אמרה יהיו מזונותי מרורין כזית בידו של הקב"ה ולא מתוקין כדבש בידי בשר ודם [שם פסוק יא]. הטריפני. ל' מזון וכן טרף נתן ליראיו (תהלים קיא) [משלי ל, ח]. טרף בפיה. מאמר פיה ביקשה שיהא זית טרף שלה והיינו מזון. בשר ודם. נח [עירובין יח:]. פאלי. כמו פלאי פלויי שבל' גמ' (נדה כא) לשון ביקוע ביקועי חתיכותיו [איוב מא,טו]. אורשינא. וכחול ארבה ימים. עוף ושמו חול ולא נקנסה עליו מיתה שלא טעם מעץ הדעת ולבסוף אלף שנה מתחד' וחוזר לנערותו [איוב כט, יח]. נאם ה' לאדני. רבותינו דרשוהו באברהם אבינו ואני אפרשנו כדבריהם נאם ה' לאברהם שקראוהו העולם אדוני שמעני אדוני (בראשית כ"ג). שב לימיני. התעכב לתשועתי והתחולל לה' אין ישיבה אלא עכבה וכן הוא אומר ותשבו בקדש (דברים א). לימיני. לתשועת ימיני. עד אשית אויביך. אמרפל וחביריו [תהלים קי, א]. מי העיר ממזרח. אותו צדק יקראהו לרגלו מי העיר את אברה' להביאו מארם שהוא במזרח וצדק שהיה עושה היא היתה לקראת רגליו בכל אשר הלך. יתן לפניו גוים. מי שהעירו ממקומו להסיע הוא נתן לפניו ארבעה מלכים וחיילותיהם. ירד. ירדה. יתן כעפר חרבו. רמא כעפרא קטולין קדם חרביה נתן את חרבו ועושה חללים רבים כעפר ואת קשתו נתן מרבה הרוגים ונופלים כקש נדף [ישעיהו מא, ב]. דהוי סלקי ליה. כל המאורע לו אפילו רעה [תענית כא.].

God further instructed Noah:

"וְאֶל־אַמָּה תְּכַלֶּנָּה מִלְמַעְלָה" – ***And to a cubit finish it from above;***[25] דִּבְהָכִי [הוא] דְקָיְימָא – **for** built **thus it would last.**[26]

"תַּחְתִּיִּם שְׁנִיִּם וּשְׁלִשִׁים תַּעֲשֶׂהָ" – God continued: ***Make it with bottom, second, and third decks.***[27] תָּנָא – **It was taught in a Baraisa:** תַּחְתִּיִּים לַזֶּבֶל – THE BOTTOM [DECK] was FOR REFUSE, אֶמְצָעִיִּים לַבְּהֵמָה – THE MIDDLE [DECK] FOR ANIMALS, עֶלְיוֹנִים לָאָדָם – and THE UPPER [DECK] FOR PEOPLE.

The Gemara proceeds to discuss what transpired when the Flood ended:

"וַיְשַׁלַּח אֶת־הָעֹרֵב" – Scripture states: *He* (Noah) ***sent out the raven,*** *and it kept going and returning until the waters dried from upon the earth.*[28] אָמַר רֵישׁ לָקִישׁ – **Reish Lakish said:** תְּשׁוּבָה נִיצַּחַת הֱשִׁיבוֹ עוֹרֵב לְנֹחַ – When he ordered the raven out on its mission, **the raven retorted to Noah** with **a winning argument.** אָמַר לוֹ – **[The raven] said to [Noah]:** רַבְּךָ שׂוֹנְאֵנִי – "Evidently, **your Master** (God) **hates me** וְאַתָּה שְׂנֵאתַנִי – **and you,** Noah, **hate me,** too. רַבְּךָ שׂוֹנְאֵנִי – **Your Master hates me,** מִן הַטְּהוֹרִין שִׁבְעָה מִן הַטְּמֵאִים שְׁנַיִם – for He instructed you to take into the Ark **seven of** each species of **the clean** animals, but only **two of** each species of **the unclean** animals. This indicates that God hates unclean animals.[29] וְאַתָּה שְׂנֵאתַנִי – **And you,** too, **hate me,** שֶׁאַתָּה מַנִּיחַ מִמִּין שִׁבְעָה – **for** when in need of a bird to send out on a dangerous mission, **you leave the species of** which there are **seven** וְשׁוֹלֵחַ מִמִּין שְׁנַיִם – **and** choose to **send** me – one **of a species of** which there are only **two!** אִם פּוֹגֵעַ בִּי שַׂר חַמָּה אוֹ שַׂר צִנָּה – **If the Master of heat or the Master of cold strikes me,** and I die of heat or cold, לֹא נִמְצָא עוֹלָם חָסֵר בְּרִיָּה אַחַת – **will the result not be** that **the world will be missing one** type of **creature** entirely? For since the only surviving ravens are myself and my mate, if I perish, there will be no male left to propagate the species.[30] אוֹ שֶׁמָּא לְאִשְׁתִּי אַתָּה צָרִיךְ – **Or, perhaps you need my wife** as your own mate and you therefore wish to send me to my death!?"[31] אָמַר לוֹ – **[Noah] said to [the raven]:** רָשָׁע – **"Wicked one!** בַּמּוּתָּר לִי נֶאֱסַר לִי – If even relations **with the** wife who is ordinarily **permitted to me are** currently **prohibited to me,** for God has prohibited cohabitation in the Ark, and I have abided by His prohibition, בַּנֶּאֱסַר לִי לֹא כָּל שֶׁכֵּן – then **with** respect to a mate that is always **forbidden to me,** i.e. your mate, **is it not certain** that I would abide by His prohibition?"[32]

The Gemara cites a source that cohabitation was prohibited for those inside the Ark:

וּמִנָּלָן דְּנֶאֶסְרוּ – **And from where do we know that [the inhabitants of the Ark] were forbidden** to cohabit? דִּכְתִיב "וּבָאתָ אֶל־הַתֵּבָה אַתָּה וּבָנֶיךָ וְאִשְׁתְּךָ וּנְשֵׁי־בָנֶיךָ אִתָּךְ" – **For it is written:**[33] ***You shall enter the Ark – you, your sons, your wife and your sons' wives with you.*** וּכְתִיב "צֵא מִן־הַתֵּבָה אַתָּה וְאִשְׁתְּךָ וּבָנֶיךָ וּנְשֵׁי־בָנֶיךָ אִתָּךְ" – **And it is written,** after the account of the Flood:[34] ***Go forth from the Ark – you and your wife, your sons and your sons' wives with you.*** The first verse lists men and women separately, whereas the latter verse lists them as couples. וְאָמַר רַבִּי יוֹחָנָן – **And R' Yochanan said:** מִיכָּן אָמְרוּ שֶׁנֶּאֶסְרוּ בְּתַשְׁמִישׁ הַמִּטָּה – **From here they learned**[35] **that [the inhabitants of the Ark] were forbidden** to engage **in cohabitation** while inside it.[36]

NOTES

habitable (*Maharsha*). Noah built into the Ark luminescent precious stones, which served as a primary source of light, just as the sun serves the earth as its primary source of light. For additional lighting, he used oil lamps (*Maharal*; see also *Gur Aryeh* to *Genesis* 6:16).

[However, the *Midrash* (*Bereishis Rabbah* 31:12) cites a dispute as to whether the צֹהַר which provided illumination was a precious stone or a window.]

25. *Genesis* 6:16.

26. With the roof of the Ark sloping upwards until it narrowed to a width of only one cubit at its peak, the waters of the Flood would run off it easily. Thus, the Ark would endure through the Flood (*Rashi* to *Genesis* loc. cit.; see also *Maharsha*). Others explain that the Ark itself was constructed in a trapezoidal shape – widest at the bottom, with its sides sloping gradually inwards until it was only one cubit wide on top. This construction helped prevent it from capsizing during the Flood (*Yad Ramah*).

27. Ibid.

28. Ibid. 8:7. Noah sent the raven out to determine whether the earth was dry, but the raven refused to leave the vicinity of the Ark and simply flew to and fro in that area (*Rashi* ad loc.).

29. And I, the raven, am counted among the unclean animals (*Leviticus* 11:15).

The reason God ordered Noah to take seven of each species of the clean (i.e. kosher) animals is that He wanted Noah to offer several of each kosher species as sacrifices after the Flood, as Noah ultimately did (see *Genesis* 8:20 with *Rashi*). Furthermore, God wanted the kosher species to propagate more plentifully, since these would be eaten by man and would always be used as offerings (*Bereishis Rabbah* 32:6 with *Yefeh Toar*).

[The Torah states (*Genesis* 7:2) that God instructed Noah: מִכֹּל הַבְּהֵמָה הַטְּהוֹרָה תִּקַּח־לְךָ שִׁבְעָה שִׁבְעָה אִישׁ וְאִשְׁתּוֹ וּמִן־הַבְּהֵמָה אֲשֶׁר לֹא טְהֹרָה הִוא שְׁנַיִם אִישׁ וְאִשְׁתּוֹ, *Of every clean animal take unto you seven, seven, a man and his wife, and of the animal that is not clean, two, a man and his wife.* *Bereishis Rabbah* (ibid.) interprets the phrase *seven, seven* as meaning seven *pairs.* However, our Gemara, which contrasts the seven of the clean with the two of the unclean, implies that the total number taken of each clean species was only seven (see *Rashash*).]

30. [This was the raven's winning argument.] The Gemara does not mean that the raven actually spoke to Noah. Rather, Noah understood that the raven's refusal to embark on its mission stemmed from a concern for the preservation of its species. For although the raven is incapable of rational thought, God endowed it with a natural instinct of self-preservation. It was through this instinct that the raven "spoke" to Noah by declining to do his bidding (*Maharal;* see also *Maharsha* and *Iyun Yaakov*; cf. *Yad Ramah*).

31. This is not a totally new argument, but a fortification of the first one. The raven said to Noah: Is the reason you are unconcerned about the future of my species that you plan to mate with my wife, and you think you will thereby propagate the species? (*Iyun Yaakov*). The raven's concern for its mate, too, was implicit in its refusal to leave the vicinity of the Ark, where it had left its mate (see *Maharal* and *Maharsha*).

32. With this retort, Noah alluded to the reason he had chosen to send out the raven. As the Gemara states shortly, all creatures in the Ark – both human and animal – were enjoined from procreating there. However, the raven violated this injunction and impregnated its mate. Noah therefore said: "Wicked one! I can be trusted to refrain from ever taking your mate. It is you who are licentious! And since you impregnated your mate, the propagation of your species is assured. [Noah knew that the raven being incubated was a male – *Ben Yehoyada*.] It is therefore most fitting that you, rather than any other creature, should be sent out on this mission." Noah thus deflected the raven's argument (*Maharsha;* see also *Or HaChaim* to *Genesis* 8:7).

Although Noah justified himself to the raven, when he needed another bird to send out, he chose the dove, for the dove and its mate are paragons of faithfulness in mating, and therefore, the dove would never suspect him of an improper motive (*Maharsha*).

The raven's suspicion of Noah was actually a projection of its own base instincts upon him. Since the raven was itself unchaste, it suspected Noah of having designs on its mate (*Maharal*).

33. *Genesis* 6:18.

34. Ibid. 8:16.

35. Literally: said (see *Rashash*).

36. Therefore, the commandment to enter the Ark stated that the men and women should enter separately, implying that they should also remain separate while inside. In contrast, the commandment to leave the Ark stated that they should leave as couples, implying that they were henceforth permitted to procreate (*Rashi* to *Genesis* loc. cit.; see *Mizrachi* to 7:7; *Yad Ramah*). *Mizrachi* (ibid.) raises the question that the Torah (ibid. 8:18), in describing their actual departure from the

א"כ לא נפנה דרך כרמים. [כלומר לא נסור ולא נפנה את דרך הכרמים] אלא כל שעה נלך בהם כלומר א"כ לא נלך דרך כבושה ולא נחזור מסורינו אלא נלך ונקלקל השורה דרכים משובשים בקוצים וברקנים כעין שבילי כרמים: **לעשתות.** כמו עשתונות שיושבין שאנן וחושבין מחשבות רעות: **עליתה שמה.** אין אש שולט בה: **מבין עקבי רגליכם.** בשכבת זרע שלכם יכול למחות אתכם ל"א מבין עקבי רגליכם מן הרגל יוציא ממש מים אם היה רוצה ואי אפשר י) לכפות רגליכם בעששיות: **בשכבת זרע.** רותחין ועבין היו. עבין ל"ג ופי' הוא: **חמת המלך שככה.** נחה מרתחו ה"נ מים נחו מרותחן: **סדרי בראשית.** והיינו לשבעת הימים סדר שבעת ימי בראשית שינה להם: **זמן קטן אחר זמן גדול.** בתחילה אמר להן והיו ימיו מאה ועשרים שנה כשעבר זמן זה ולא שבו לטובה חזר וקבע להם זמן קטן: **אישות לבהמה מי איּת ליה.** נקבה אחת נשכבת לכמה זכרים ואין זו אישות: **שלא נעבדה בהן עבירה.** שלא נזקקו אלא לבן זוגם: **מבליגה.** עץ הוא: **במותר לי.** אפי' באשתי אני אסור: (**בני נח.** שם וחם ויפת): **רק.** רוקק זרע מפיו לפיה של נקבה: **לקה בעורו.** שיצא ממנו כוש: **מאתו.** גבי עורב לא כתיב מאתו מכאן שדירתם כו' כלומר הנאה הוא שדרים אצלם שמכירים בצדיקים כדאמרי' בדוכתי אחריתא: **זית טרף בפיה.** בפיה היתה שואלת מזון טרף של זית: **למשפחותיהם יצאו מן התיבה.** אלמא כל חד וחד בפני עצמו היה ולא היו אוכלין כולם באבוס אחד אלא משפחות [משפחות] היו שרויין: **א"ל אליעזר.** [עבד אברהם]: **לשם רבא.** גדול (א) בנו של נח: **היכי הויתון.** היאך הייתם יכולין להכין עונייהם בכך לעשות לכל בריה ובריה תפלה: **זקיתא.** שם בריה: **פאלי.** מחתך כמו פלי פלויי במסכת נדה (דף כא:): **אישתא זינתיה.** חמה אחזתו וזנהו ולא היה חושש לדרוש משאר בהמות: **לא בציר משיתא ולא טפי מתריסר זיינא אישתא.** אין לך חמה קלה שלא תהא חמימותו יכולה לזונו שש ימים שלא ימות בלא מאכל ואין לך חמה שיכולה לזון יותר מי"ב ימים בלי מאכל ומשתה כ"ש ואית דגרסי לא פחות משיתא ירחי ולא טפי מתריסר זנתא אשתא ואתרי קאי כלומר לא פחות מששה חדשים ולא יותר מי"ב חדשים ולא נהירא לי: **אורשינא.** עוף ושמו חול בלשון המקרא ואינו מת לעולם: **בספנא.** בחדר ספון ומתוקן לו: **[נאום ה' כו'].** אליעזר אמר פסוק זה. נאם ה' לאדני אמר הקב"ה לאברהם כ) שב לימיני אדני וכו': **ממזרח זה אברהם.** שבא מארם נהרים שהוא במזרח דכתיב (במדבר כג) מן ארם ינחני בלק מלך מואב וגו': **כל דהוה סלקא ליה.** כל דבר המאורע ליה:

בהדי

א"כ לא נפנה דרך כרמים דרש רבא מאי דכתיב א) לפיד בוז לעשתות שאנן נכון למועדי רגל מלמד שהיה נח הצדיק מוכיח אותם ואמר להם דברים שהם קשים כלפידים והיו (בוזים) [מבזין] אותו אמרו לו זקן תיבה זו למה אמר להם הקב"ה מביא עליכם את המבול אמרו מבול של מה אם מבול של אש יש לנו דבר אחר ועליתה שמה ואם של מים הוא מביא אם מן הארץ הוא מביא יש לנו עששיות של ברזל שאנו מחפין בהם את הארץ ואם מן השמים הוא מביא יש לנו דבר ועקב שמו ואמרי לה עקש שמו אמר להם הוא מביא מבין עקבי רגליכם שנאמר א) נכון למועדי רגל תניא מימי המבול קשים כשכבת זרע שנאמר נכון למועדי רגל א) אמר רב חסדא ברותחין קלקלו בעבירה וברותחין נידונו כתיב הכא ב) וישכו המים וכתיב התם ג) וחמת המלך שככה ד) ויהי לשבעת הימים ומי המבול היו על הארץ ג) מה טיבם של שבעת הימים אמר רב אלו ימי אבילות של מתושלח ללמדך שהספדן של צדיקים מעכבין את הפורענות לבא דבר אחר לשבעת ששינה עליהם הקב"ה סדר בראשית שהיתה חמה יוצאת ממערב ושוקעת במזרח דבר אחר שקבע להם הקב"ה זמן גדול ואח"כ זמן קטן ד"א לשבעת הימים שהטעימם מעין העולם הבא כדי שידעו מה טובה מנעו מהן ה) מכל הבהמה הטהורה תקח לך שבעה שבעה איש ואשתו אישות לבהמה מי אית לה ג) א"ר שמואל בר נחמני א"ר יונתן ד) מאותם שלא נעבדה בהם עבירה מנא ידע אמר רב חסדא שהעבירן לפני התיבה כל שהתיבה קולטתו בידוע שלא נעבדה בהם עבירה וכל שאין התיבה קולטתו בידוע שנעבדה בה עבירה רבי אבהו אמר מאותן הבאין מאיליהן ו) עשה לך תיבת עצי גופר מאי גופר ה) אמר רב אדא ו) אמרי דבי ר' שילא זו מבליגה ואמרי לה גולמיש ז) צוהר תעשה לתיבה א"ר יוחנן אמר לו הקב"ה לנח קבע בה אבנים טובות ומרגליות כדי שיהיו מאירות לכם כצהרים ז) ואל אמה תכלנה מלמעלה דבהכי [הוא] דקיימא ז) תחתיים שנים ושלישים תעשה תנא תחתיים לזבל אמצעיים לבהמה עליונים לאדם ח) וישלח את העורב אמר ר"ל תשובה ניצחת השיבו עורב לנח אמר לו רבך שונאני ואתה שנאתני רבך שונאני מן הטהורין שבעה מן הטמאים שנים ואתה שנאתני שאתה מניח ממין שבעה ושולח ממין שנים אם פוגע בי שר חמה או שר צנה לא נמצא עולם חסר בריה אחת או שמא לאשתי אתה צריך אמר לו רשע במותר לי נאסר לי בנאסר לי לא כ"ש ומנלן דנאסרו דכתיב ט) ובאת אל התיבה אתה ובניך ואשתך ונשי בניך אתך וכתיב י) צא מן התיבה אתה ואשתך ובניך ונשי בניך אתך וא"ר יוחנן מיכן אמרו שנאסרו בתשמיש המטה ת"ר שלשה שמשו בתיבה וכולם לקו כלב ועורב וחם כלב נקשר עורב רק חם לקה בעורו כ) וישלח את היונה מאתו לראות הקלו המים א"ר ירמיה מכאן שדירתן של עופות טהורים עם הצדיקים ל) והנה עלה זית טרף בפיה י) א"ר אלעזר אמרה יונה לפני הקב"ה רבש"ע יהיו מזונותי מרורים כזית ומסורים בידך ואל יהיו מתוקים כדבש ומסורים ביד בשר ודם מאי משמע דהאי טרף לישנא דמזוני הוא דכתיב מ) הטריפני לחם חוקי נ) למשפחותיהם יצאו מן התיבה א"ר יוחנן ס) למשפחותם ולא הם אמר רב חנא בר ביזנא אמר ליה אליעזר לשם רבא כתיב נ) למשפחותיהם יצאו מן התיבה אתון היכן הויתון א"ל צער גדול היה לנו בתיבה בריה שדרכה להאכילה ביום האכלנוה ביום שדרכה להאכילה בלילה האכלנוה בלילה האי זקיתא לא הוה ידע אבא מה אכלה יומא חד הוה יתיב וקא פאלי רמונא נפל תולעתא מינה אכלה מיכן ואילך הוה גביל לה חיזרא כי מתלע אכלה אריא אישתא זינתיה דאמר רב לא בציר משיתא ולא טפי מתריסר זינא אישתא אורשינה אשכחיניה אבא דגני בספנא דתיבותא א"ל לא בעית מזוני א"ל חזיתיך דהות טרידא אמינא לא אצערך א"ל יהא רעוא דלא תמות שנאמר ס) ואומר עם קני אגוע וכחול ארבה ימים אמר רב חנה בר לואי אמר שם רבא לאליעזר כי אתו עלייכו מלכי מזרח ומערב אתון היכי עבידיתו אמר ליה אייתי הקב"ה לאברהם ואותביה מימיניה והוה שדינן עפרא והוו חרבי גילי והוי גירי שנאמר ע) מזמור לדוד נאם ה' לאדוני שב לימיני עד אשית אויביך הדום לרגליך וכתיב פ) מי העיר ממזרח צדק יקראהו לרגלו יתן לפניו גוים ומלכים ירד יתן כעפר חרבו כקש נדף קשתו צ) נחום איש גם זו הוה רגיל דכל דהוה סלקא ליה אמר גם זו לטובה יומא חד בעו [ישראל] לשדורי דורון לקיסר אמרי בהדי

מאן

תורה אור השלם

א) לַפִּיד בּוּז לְעַשְׁתּוּת שַׁאֲנָן נָכוֹן לְמוֹעֲדֵי רָגֶל: [איוב יב, ה]

ב) וַיִּזְכֹּר אֱלֹהִים אֶת נֹחַ וְאֵת כָּל הַחַיָּה וְאֶת כָּל הַבְּהֵמָה אֲשֶׁר אִתּוֹ בַּתֵּבָה וַיַּעֲבֵר אֱלֹהִים רוּחַ עַל הָאָרֶץ וַיָּשֹׁכּוּ הַמָּיִם: [בראשית ח, א]

ג) וַיִּתְלוּ אֶת הָמָן עַל הָעֵץ אֲשֶׁר הֵכִין לְמָרְדֳּכָי וַחֲמַת הַמֶּלֶךְ שָׁכָכָה: [אסתר ז, י]

ד) וַיְהִי לְשִׁבְעַת הַיָּמִים וּמֵי הַמַּבּוּל הָיוּ עַל הָאָרֶץ: [בראשית ז, י]

ה) מִכֹּל הַבְּהֵמָה הַטְּהוֹרָה תִּקַּח לְךָ שִׁבְעָה שִׁבְעָה אִישׁ וְאִשְׁתּוֹ וּמִן הַבְּהֵמָה אֲשֶׁר לֹא טְהֹרָה הִוא שְׁנַיִם אִישׁ וְאִשְׁתּוֹ: [בראשית ז, ב]

ו) עֲשֵׂה לְךָ תֵּבַת עֲצֵי גֹפֶר קִנִּים תַּעֲשֶׂה אֶת הַתֵּבָה וְכָפַרְתָּ אֹתָהּ מִבַּיִת וּמִחוּץ בַּכֹּפֶר: [בראשית ו, יד]

ז) צֹהַר תַּעֲשֶׂה לַתֵּבָה וְאֶל אַמָּה תְּכַלֶּנָּה מִלְמַעְלָה וּפֶתַח הַתֵּבָה בְּצִדָּהּ תָּשִׂים תַּחְתִּיִּם שְׁנִיִּם וּשְׁלִשִׁים תַּעֲשֶׂהָ: [בראשית ו, טז]

ח) וַיְשַׁלַּח אֶת הָעֹרֵב וַיֵּצֵא יָצוֹא וָשׁוֹב עַד יְבֹשֶׁת הַמַּיִם מֵעַל הָאָרֶץ: [בראשית ח, ז]

ט) וַהֲקִמֹתִי אֶת בְּרִיתִי אִתָּךְ וּבָאתָ אֶל הַתֵּבָה אַתָּה וּבָנֶיךָ וְאִשְׁתְּךָ וּנְשֵׁי בָנֶיךָ אִתָּךְ: [בראשית ו, יח]

י) צֵא מִן הַתֵּבָה אַתָּה וְאִשְׁתְּךָ וּבָנֶיךָ וּנְשֵׁי בָנֶיךָ אִתָּךְ: [בראשית ח, טז]

כ) וַיְשַׁלַּח אֶת הַיּוֹנָה מֵאִתּוֹ לִרְאוֹת הֲקַלּוּ הַמַּיִם מֵעַל פְּנֵי הָאֲדָמָה: [בראשית ח, ח]

ל) וַתָּבֹא אֵלָיו הַיּוֹנָה לְעֵת עֶרֶב וְהִנֵּה עֲלֵה זַיִת טָרָף בְּפִיהָ וַיֵּדַע נֹחַ כִּי קַלּוּ הַמַּיִם מֵעַל הָאָרֶץ: [בראשית ח, יא]

מ) שָׁוְא וּדְבַר כָּזָב הַרְחֵק מִמֶּנִּי רֵאשׁ וָעֹשֶׁר אַל תִּתֶּן לִי הַטְרִיפֵנִי לֶחֶם חֻקִּי: [משלי ל, ח]

נ) כָּל הַחַיָּה כָּל הָרֶמֶשׂ וְכָל הָעוֹף כֹּל רוֹמֵשׂ עַל הָאָרֶץ לְמִשְׁפְּחֹתֵיהֶם יָצְאוּ מִן הַתֵּבָה: [בראשית ח, יט]

ס) וָאֹמַר עִם קִנִּי אֶגְוָע וְכַחוֹל אַרְבֶּה יָמִים: [איוב כט, יח]

ע) לְדָוִד מִזְמוֹר נְאֻם יְיָ לַאדֹנִי שֵׁב לִימִינִי עַד אָשִׁית אֹיְבֶיךָ הֲדֹם לְרַגְלֶיךָ: [תהלים קי, א]

פ) מִי הֵעִיר מִמִּזְרָח צֶדֶק יִקְרָאֵהוּ לְרַגְלוֹ יִתֵּן לְפָנָיו גּוֹיִם וּמְלָכִים יַרְדְּ יִתֵּן כֶּעָפָר חַרְבּוֹ כְּקַשׁ נִדָּף קַשְׁתּוֹ: [ישעיה מא, ב]

מסורת הש"ס

א) ר"ה יב. זבחים קיג:, ב) [תוספתא דסוטה פ"י], ג) [זבחים קטז. ע"ש], ד) [פי' בשביל שלא באו על שאינן מינן עשה להן כבוד וכתב להן אישות כאדם. ערוך ערך אשה], ה) [ר"ה כג.], ו) [גיר' הערוך רב אמר אדרא דבי ר' שילא אמרי זו כו' ע"ש ערך אדר], ז) [עירובין יח: ע"ש], ח) [כתב הבאר שבע לא ידענא פירושו ועי' מהרש"א בח"א וגם בפענח רזא קצת בדחיקות ויתכן לפרש לולא דבריהם ע"פ האמור בחולין נח. כל בריה שאין בו עצם אינו מתקיים שנים עשר חודש והבן], ט) תענית כא. ע"ש, י) נ"ל לחפות, כ) [נ"ל אדוני שב לימיני וכו'].

הגהות הב"ח

(א) רש"י ד"ה לשם רבא גדול. נ"ב ול"ע לעיל דף סט ע"ב:

ליקוטי רש"י

לפיד בוז. אש של גיהנם עומד למי שאנן בעשתותו לומר שלום יהיה לי [איוב יב, ה]. **וישכו.** כמו (אסתר ב, א) כשוך חמת המלך לשון הנחת חמה [בראשית ח, א]. **וחמת המלך שככה.** וסתם חמה רותחת היא כדכתיב וחמתו בערה בו [ר"ה יב, א]. **אלו ימי אבלות של מתושלח.** כי לימים עוד שבעה. אלו שבעת ימי אבלו של מתושלח הצדיק שחס הקב"ה על כבודו ועכב את הפורענות. לא ותשוב שנותיו של מתושלח ותמצא שהם כלים בשנת שש מאות שנה לחיי נח [בראשית ז, ד]. מתושלח צדיק גמור היה כדאמרינן בחלק (סנהדרין קח:) שבעת ימים שנתלו לדור המבול הן ימי אבלו של מתושלח [סוכה נב:]. **כל שהתיבה קולטתו.** מהעוף למינהו. אותן שדבקו במיניהם ולא השחיתו דרכם ומאליהם באו וכל שהתיבה קולטתו הכניס בה [בראשית ו, כ]. **עצי גפר.** כך שמו ולמה ממין זה על שם גפרית שנגזר עליהם להמחות בו [שם ו, יד]. **צהר.** יש אומרים חלון ויש אומרים אבן טובה המאירה להם. **ואל אמה תכלנה מלמעלה.** כסויה משופע ועולה עד שהוא קצר מלמעלה ועומד על אמה כדי שיזובו המים למטה. **תחתים שנים ושלשים.** שלש עליות זו על גב זו עליונים לאדם אמצעים למדור בהמה תחתיים לזבל [שם ו, טז]. **או שמא לאשתי אתה צריך.** יצוא ושוב. הולך ומקיף סביבות התיבה ולא הלך בשליחותו שהיה חושדו על בת זוגו כמו ששנינו באגדת חלק (סנהדרין קח:) [שם ח, ז]. **אתה ובניך ואשתך.** האנשים לבד והנשים לבד מכאן שנאסרו בתשמיש המטה [שם ז, יח]. נח ובניו. האנשים לבד והנשים לבד לפי שנאסרו בתשמיש המטה מפני שהעולם היה שרוי בצער [שם ז,ז]. **אתה ואשתך וגו'.** איש ואשתו כאן התיר להם תשמיש המטה [שם ח, טז]. **טרף.** חטף ומדרש אגדה לשון מזון ודרשו בפיה לשון מאמר אמרה יהיו מזונותי מרורין כזית בידו של הקב"ה ולא מתוקין כדבש בידי בשר ודם [שם פסוק יא]. **הטריפני.** ל' מזון וכן טרף נתן ליראיו (תהלים קיא) [משלי ל, ח]. **טרף בפיה.** מאמר פיה ביקשה שיהא זית טרף שלה והיינו מזון. **בשר ודם.** נח [עירובין יח:]. **פאלי.** כמו פלאי פלויי שבל' גמ' (נדה כא) לשון ביקוע ביקועי חתיכותיו [איוב מא,טו]. **אורשינא.** וכחול ארבה ימים. עוף ושמו חול ולא נקנסה עליו מיתה שלא טעם מעץ הדעת ולבסוף אלף שנה מתחד' וחוזר לנערותו [איוב כט, יח]. **נאם ה' לאדני.** רבותינו דרשוהו באברהם אבינו ואני אפרשנו כדבריהם נאם ה' לאברהם שקראוהו העולם אדוני שמעני אדוני (בראשית כ"ג). **שב לימיני.** התעכב לתשועתי והתחולל לה' אין ישיבה אלא עכבה וכן הוא אומר ותשבו בקדש (דברים א). **לימיני.** לתשועת ימיני. **עד אשית אויביך.** אמרפל וחביריו [תהלים קי, א]. **מי העיר ממזרח.** אותו שצדק יקראהו לרגלו מי העיר את אברה' להביאו מארם שהוא במזרח וצדק שהיה עושה היא היתה לקראת רגליו בכל אשר הלך. **יתן לפניו גוים.** מי שהעירו ממקומו להסיע הוא נתן לפניו ארבעה מלכים וחיילותיהם. **ירד.** ירדה. **יתן כעפר חרבו.** רמא כעפרא קטולין קדם חרביה נתן את חרבו ועושה חללים רבים כעפר ואת קשתו נתן מרבה הרוגים ונופלים כקש נדף [ישעיהו מא, ב]. **דהוי סלקי ליה.** כל המאורע לו אפילו רעה [תענית כא.].

The fate of those who violated the ban on cohabitation:

תָּנוּ רַבָּנָן – **The Rabbis taught in a Baraisa:** שְׁלֹשָׁה שִׁמְּשׁוּ בַּתֵּיבָה – THREE COHABITED while IN THE ARK, וְכוּלָּם לָקוּ – AND ALL OF THEM WERE AFFECTED: כֶּלֶב וְעוֹרֵב וְחָם – THE DOG, THE RAVEN AND Noah's son CHAM. כֶּלֶב נִקְשַׁר – THE DOG WAS condemned to be TIED UP,[37] עוֹרֵב רָק – THE RAVEN SPITS[38] חָם לָקָה בְּעוֹרוֹ – and CHAM WAS AFFECTED IN HIS SKIN.[39]

Having discussed the raven, the Gemara contrasts it with the dove, which Noah sent out afterwards:

,,וַיְשַׁלַּח אֶת־הַיּוֹנָה מֵאִתּוֹ לִרְאוֹת הֲקַלּוּ הַמַּיִם" – Scripture states:[40] *He* (Noah) ***sent out the dove from him to see whether the waters had subsided.*** In contrast, when speaking of the raven, Scripture does not state that Noah sent it out *from him.*[41] אָמַר רַבִּי יִרְמְיָה – **R' Yirmiyah said:** מִכָּאן שֶׁדִּירָתָן שֶׁל עוֹפוֹת טְהוֹרִים עִם הַצַּדִּיקִים – **From here** we learn **that the** proper **habitat of clean birds is with the righteous.**[42]

The behavior of the dove:

,,וְהִנֵּה עֲלֵה־זַיִת טָרָף בְּפִיהָ" – Scripture states:[43] *The dove came back to him in the evening,* ***and behold, a plucked*** *(taraf)* ***olive leaf was in its bill.*** The word *taraf* alludes to food.[44] אָמַר רַבִּי אֶלְעָזָר – **R' Elazar said:** אָמְרָה יוֹנָה לִפְנֵי הַקָּדוֹשׁ בָּרוּךְ הוּא – The verse alludes that **the dove said before the Holy One, Blessed is He:** רִבּוֹנוֹ שֶׁל עוֹלָם – **"Master of the Universe!** יִהְיוּ מְזוֹנוֹתַי מְרוּרִים כַּזַּיִת וּמְסוּרִים בְּיָדְךָ – **May my food be bitter as an olive but dependent upon You,** וְאַל יִהְיוּ מְתוּקִים כִּדְבַשׁ וּמְסוּרִים בְּיַד בָּשָׂר וָדָם – **rather than sweet as honey but dependent upon flesh and blood,"** i.e. human beings.[45]

The Gemara provides the basis for this exposition:

מַאי מַשְׁמַע דְּהַאי טָרָף לִישָּׁנָא דִּמְזוֹנֵי הוּא – **What indication** is there **that the word** ***taraf*** **connotes food?** דִּכְתִיב ,,הַטְרִיפֵנִי לֶחֶם חֻקִּי" – **For it is written:**[46] ***Feed me*** *(hatrifeini)* ***my portion of bread.***[47]

The Gemara discusses the extent to which Noah cared for the animals inside the Ark:

,,לְמִשְׁפְּחֹתֵיהֶם יָצְאוּ מִן־הַתֵּבָה" – Scripture states that after the Flood, all living beings, ***by their families, came out of the Ark.***[48] אָמַר רַבִּי יוֹחָנָן – **R' Yochanan said:** לְמִשְׁפְּחוֹתָם וְלֹא הֵם – They were **by their families, not** by **themselves.**[49]

The Gemara continues:

אָמַר רַב חָנָא בַּר בִּיזְנָא – **Rav Chana bar Bizna said:** אָמַר לֵיהּ אֱלִיעֶזֶר לְשֵׁם רַבָּא – **Eliezer,** the servant of Abraham, once **said to** Noah's son, **Shem the Great:** כְּתִיב ,,לְמִשְׁפְּחֹתֵיהֶם יָצְאוּ מִן הַתֵּבָה" – **It is written:** ***by their families, came out of the Ark,***

NOTES

Ark, again lists men and women separately. However, *Iyun Yaakov* explains (on the basis of *Bereishis Rabbah* 34:5) that, although permitted to procreate, Noah did not want to do so until God swore that there would never be another Flood (see also *Eitz Yosef* and *Chizkuni*).

The reason cohabitation was forbidden for the inhabitants of the Ark is that it would have been inappropriate to procreate while the world was being destroyed. Similarly, the Sages have taught (*Taanis* 11a) that it is forbidden to engage in marital relations during a period of famine, and even one who has food must afflict himself in order to share in the suffering of his brethren (see *Maharal* and *Chasam Sofer*).

37. Dogs are subjected to the indignity of remaining attached ("tied") for some time after coitus, and are thus unable to procreate modestly (*Ben Yehoyada;* see also *Yad Ramah* and *Bereishis Rabbah* 36:11; see also *Sotah* 3b). Alternatively, dogs are commonly chained or kept on a leash by their owners in order to prevent them from attacking others (*Yad Ramah*).

38. *Rashi* explains that the raven was condemned to spit seed from its mouth into the mouth of its mate.

39. For he begot Kush (*Rashi*). Kush was Cham's firstborn and was conceived in the Ark *(Yad Ramah*). *Eitz Yosef* points out that the Gemara's statement indicates that Cham's own skin was also affected. See also *Bereishis Rabbah* 36:11 with *Matnos Kehunah,* and see *Ben Yehoyada.*

Although only humans possess the intellect to obey or disobey commandments, the animals in the Ark heeded instinctively God's will that they refrain from procreation, for they sensed innately the inappropriateness of procreating while the world was being destroyed. That the dog and the raven did not share this innate sensitivity is indicative of their dissociation with the rest of Creation. Indeed, although dogs are very faithful to their masters, they are widely shunned and feared by others. And ravens are exceedingly uncompassionate, even to their own offspring [see *Psalms* 147:9 and *Eruvin* 22a] (*Maharal*, *Chasam Sofer*).

40. *Genesis* 8:8.

41. It merely states (ibid. 8:7): וַיְשַׁלַּח אֶת־הָעֹרֵב, *And he sent out the raven.*

42. It is fitting for clean, i.e. kosher birds to take up habitat with righteous people, for these birds recognize virtuous attributes, as indicated elsewhere in the Talmud (*Rashi;* see *Sotah* 38b and *Bava Metzia* 86a). Therefore, the dove as well as the other kosher birds dwelled in the upper deck of the Ark, together with Noah and his family. That deck was reserved chiefly for humans, but also contained the creatures that associate with righteous humans. Thus, when Noah sent out the dove, he sent it *from him* (*Maharsha;* see *Bereishis Rabbah* 31:14).

43. Ibid. v. 11.

44. For טרף can be read טֶרֶף, which means *food* or *sustenance,* as the Gemara will demonstrate. Furthermore, בְּפִיהָ can be interpreted as *with its mouth.* Thus, the phrase וְהִנֵּה עֲלֵה־זַיִת טָרָף בְּפִיהָ can be understood to mean, *behold, an olive leaf was the food* [it requested] *with its mouth.* The Gemara goes on to explain this (*Rashi;* see *Ramban* and *Mizrachi* to *Genesis* loc. cit., and see *Be'er Sheva*).

45. All the dove's needs were provided for by Noah in the Ark, as the Gemara states below. Yet, it returned with an olive leaf in its mouth to demonstrate that it preferred a bitter olive leaf plucked from the wild, and thus obtained directly from the hand of God, to dependence on a human being, even one as magnanimous as Noah. This should serve as a lesson to humans, for whom it is infinitely more embarrassing to be dependent upon others: Living simply and within one's means is preferable by far to indulging in luxuries and being assisted by others (*Yad Ramah, Ramban* ibid., *Maharsha*; see *Shabbos* 118a and *Beitzah* 32b).

The dove, among other creatures, possesses innately certain good qualities (see *Eruvin* 100b). In this instance, although the dove was obviously incapable of rationalizing its action, it chose instinctively to pluck a wild olive leaf for its meal, rather than accept Noah's magnanimity (*Maharal;* see also *Gur Aryeh* to *Genesis* loc. cit.).

46. *Proverbs* 30:8.

47. The word הַטְרִיפֵנִי is a derivative of the root טרף.

48. *Genesis* 8:19.

49. The commentators offer various interpretations of this obscure statement:

Rashi explains it as meaning that while inside the Ark each species (family) of animal dwelled separately and was fed individually; different species did not eat from the same trough. This comment introduces the next segment of Gemara, which discusses the difficulty Noah and his family encountered in providing the proper food for each species.

Yad Ramah explains this comment to mean that each family of animals left the Ark complete, as no animal died in the Ark, but the individual animals did not leave the Ark complete – they were weakened considerably by the twelve-month ordeal of living in confined quarters. Thus, this comment is a continuation of the previous discussion, in which the dove's reluctance to be sustained by Noah was mentioned.

R' Yeshayah Pik, in his marginal gloss here, alludes to another explanation: The Gemara states (*Chullin* 58a) that no boneless creature lives longer than twelve months. Perforce, then, those of the boneless species that were brought into the Ark did not survive to leave it twelve months later. Rather, they entered while incubating their young and died in the Ark, and the young that were born in the Ark survived to leave it after the Flood. Thus, each *family* of animals left the Ark, but the specific creatures that entered it did not necessarily leave it.

See *Maharsha* for yet another interpretation.

א"כ לא נפנה דרך כרמים דרש רבא מאי
דכתיב (א) לפיד בוז לעשתות שאנן נכון למועדי
רגל מלמד שהיה נח הצדיק מוכיח אותם
ואמר להם דברים שהם קשים כלפידים והיו
(בוזים) [מבזין] אותו אמרו לו זקן תיבה זו
למה אמר להם הקב"ה מביא עליכם את
המבול אמרו מבול של מה אם מבול של
אש יש לנו דבר אחר ועליתה שמה ואם של
מים הוא מביא אם מן הארץ הוא מביא יש
לנו עששיות של ברזל שאנו מחפין בהם
את הארץ ואם מן השמים הוא מביא יש לנו
דבר ועקב שמו ואמרי לה עקש שמו אמר
להם הוא מביא מבין עקבי רגליכם שנאמר
(א) נכון למועדי רגל תניא מימי המבול קשים
כשכבת זרע שנאמר נכון למועדי רגל (א) אמר
רב חסדא ברותחין קלקלו בעבירה וברותחין
נידונו כתיב הכא (ב) וישכו המים וכתיב התם
(ג) וחמת המלך שככה (ד) ויהי לשבעת הימים
ומי המבול היו על הארץ (ב) מה טיבם של
שבעת הימים אמר רב אלו ימי אבילות של
מתושלח ללמדך שהספדן של צדיקים
מעכבין את הפורענות לבא דבר אחר
לשבעת ששינה עליהם הקב"ה סדר
בראשית שהיתה חמה יוצאת ממערב ושוקעת במזרח דבר אחר שקבע
להם הקב"ה זמן גדול ואח"כ זמן קטן ד"א לשבעת הימים שהטעימם מעין
העולם הבא כדי שידעו מה טובה מנעו מהן (ה) מכל הבהמה הטהורה תקח לך שבעה שבעה איש ואשתו
אישות לבהמה מי אית לה (ג) א"ר שמואל בר נחמני א"ר יונתן (ד) מאותם שלא נעבדה בהם עבירה מנא
ידע אמר רב חסדא שהעבירן לפני התיבה כל שהתיבה קולטתו בידוע שלא נעבדה בהם עבירה וכל שאין
התיבה קולטתו בידוע שנעבדה בה עבירה רבי אבהו אמר מאותן הבאין מאיליהן (ו) עשה לך תיבת עצי
גופר מאי גופר (ה) אמר רב אדא (ו) אמרי דבי ר' שילא זו מבליגה ואמרי לה גולמיש (ז) צוהר תעשה לתיבה
א"ר יוחנן אמר לו הקב"ה לנח קבע בה אבנים טובות ומרגליות כדי שיהיו מאירות לכם כצהרים (ז) ואל אמה
תכלנה מלמעלה דבהכי [הוא] דקיימא (ז) תחתיים שנים ושלישים תעשה תנא תחתיים לזבל אמצעיים
לבהמה עליונים לאדם (ח) וישלח את העורב אמר ר"ל תשובה ניצחת השיבו עורב לנח אמר לו רבך שונאני
ואתה שנאתני רבך שונאני מן הטהורין שבעה מן הטמאים שנים ואתה שנאתני שאתה מניח ממין שבעה
ושולח ממין שנים אם פוגע בי שר חמה או שר צנה לא נמצא עולם חסר בריה אחת או שמא לאשתי אתה
צריך אמר לו רשע במותר לי נאסר לי בנאסר לי לא כ"ש ומנלן דנאסרו דכתיב (ט) ובאת אל התיבה אתה
ובניך ואשתך ונשי בניך אתך וכתיב (י) צא מן התיבה אתה ואשתך ובניך ונשי בניך אתך וא"ר יוחנן
מיכן אמרו שנאסרו בתשמיש המטה ת"ר שלשה שמשו בתיבה וכולם לקו כלב ועורב וחם כלב
נקשר עורב רק חם לקה בעורו (כ) וישלח את היונה מאתו לראות הקלו המים א"ר ירמיה מכאן שדירתן
של עופות טהורים עם הצדיקים (ל) והנה עלה זית טרף בפיה (ח) א"ר אלעזר אמרה יונה לפני הקב"ה רבש"ע
יהיו מזונותי מרורים כזית ומסורים בידך ואל יהיו מתוקים כדבש ומסורים ביד בשר ודם מאי משמע
דהאי טרף לישנא דמזוני הוא דכתיב (מ) הטריפני לחם חוקי (נ) למשפחותיהם יצאו מן התיבה א"ר יוחנן
(ט) למשפחותם ולא הם אמר רב חנא בר ביזנא אמר ליה אליעזר לשם רבא כתיב (נ) למשפחותיהם יצאו מן
התיבה אתון היכן הויתון א"ל צער גדול היה לנו בתיבה בריה שדרכה להאכילה ביום האכלנוה ביום שדרכה
להאכילה בלילה האכלנוה בלילה האי זקיתא לא הוה ידע אבא מה אכלה יומא חד הוה יתיב וקא פאלי
רמונא נפל תולעתא מינה אכלה מיכן ואילך הוה גביל לה חיזרא כי מתלע אריא אישתא זינתיה
דאמר רב לא בציר משיתא ולא טפי מתריסר זינא אישתא אורשינה אשכחיניה אבא דגני בספנא דתיבותא
א"ל לא בעית מזוני א"ל חזיתיך דהות טרידא אמינא לא אצערך א"ל יהא רעוא דלא תמות שנאמר (ס) ואומר
עם קני אגוע וכחול ארבה ימים אמר רב חנה בר לואי אמר שם רבא לאליעזר כי אתו עליכו מלכי מזרח
ומערב אתון היכי עבידיתו אמר ליה אייתי הקב"ה לאברהם ואותביה מימיניה והוה זרקינן עפרא והוו חרבי
גילי והוי גירי שנאמר (ע) מזמור לדוד נאם ה' לאדוני שב לימיני עד אשית אויביך הדום לרגליך וכתיב (פ) מי
העיר ממזרח צדק יקראהו לרגלו יתן לפניו גוים ומלכים ירד יתן כעפר חרבו כקש נדף קשתו (י) נחום איש גם
זו הוה רגיל דכל דהוה סלקא ליה אמר גם זו לטובה יומא חד בעו [ישראל] לשדורי דורון לקיסר אמרי בהדי
מאן

רש"י

א"כ לא נפנה דרך כרמים. [כלומר לא נסור ולא נפנה את דרך הכרמים] אלא כל שעה נלך בהם כלומר א"כ לא נלך דרך כבושה ולא נחזור מסורינו אלא נלך ונקלקל השורה דרכים משובשים בקוצים וברקנים כעין שבילי כרמים: לעשתות. כמו עשתונות שיושבין שאנן וחושבין מחשבות רעות: עליתה שמה. אין אש שולט בה: מבין עקבי רגליכם. בשכבת זרע שלכם יכול למחות אתכם ל"א מבין עקבי רגליכם מן הרגל יוציא ממש מים אם היה רוצה ואי אפשר (י) לכפות רגליכם בעששיות: בשכבת זרע. רותחין ועבין היו. עבין ל"ג ופי' הוא: חמת המלך שככה. נחה מרתחו ה"נ מים נחו מרותחן: סדרי בראשית. והיינו לשבעת הימים סדר שבעת ימי בראשית שינה להם: זמן קטן אחר זמן גדול. בתחילה אמר להן והיו ימיו מאה ועשרים שנה כשעבר זמן זה ולא שבו לטובה חזר וקבע להם זמן קטן: אישות לבהמה מי איכא ליה. נקבה אחת נשכבת לכמה זכרים ואין זו אישות: שלא נעבדה בהן עבירה. שלא נזקקו אלא לבן זוגם: מבליגה. עץ הוא: במותר לי. אפי' באשתי אני אסור: (בני נח. שם וחם ויפת): רק. רוקק זרע מפיו לפיה של נקבה: לקה בעורו. שיצא ממנו כוש: מאתו. גבי עורב לא כתיב מאתו מכאן שדירתם כו' כלומר הנאה הוא שדרים אלא שמכירים בצדיקים כדאמרי' בדוכתי אחריתא: זית טרף בפיה. בפיה היתה שואלת מזון טרף של זית: למשפחותיהם יצאו מן התיבה. אלמא כל חד וחד בפני עצמו היה ולא היו אוכלין כולם באבוס אחד אלא משפחות [משפחות] היו שרויין: א"ל אליעזר. [עבד אברהם]: לשם רבא. גדול (א) בנו של נח: היכי הויתון. היאך הייתם יכולין להכין ענייהם בכך לעשות לכל בריה ובריה חפלה: זקיתא. שם בריה: פאלי. מחתך כמו פלי פלויי במסכת נדה (דף כא:): אישתא זינתיה. חמה אחזתו וזנהו ולא היה חושש לדרוש מאחר בהמות: לא בציר משיתא ולא טפי מתריסר זיינא אישתא. אין לך חמה קלה שלא תהא חמימותו יכולה לזונו שש ימים שלא ימות בלא מאכל ואין לך חמה שיכולה לזון יותר מי"ב ימים בלי מאכל ומשתה כ"ש ואית דגרסי לא פחות משיתא ירחי ולא טפי מתריסר זנתא אשתא ואמרי קאי כלומר לא פחות מששה חדשים ולא יותר מי"ב חדשים ולא נהירא לי: אורשינא. עוף ושמו חול בלשון המקרא ואינו מת לעולם: בספנא. בחדר ספון ומתוקן לו: [נאום ה' כו']. אליעזר אמר פסוק זה. נאם ה' לאדני אמר הקב"ה לאברהם (י) שב לימיני אדני וכו': ממזרח זה אברהם. שבא מארם נהרים שהוא במזרח דכתיב (במדבר כג) מן ארם ינחני בלק מלך מואב וגו': כל דהוה סלקא ליה. כל דבר המאורע ליה:
בהדי

א) לַפִּיד בּוּז לְעַשְׁתּוּת שַׁאֲנָן נָכוֹן לְמוֹעֲדֵי רָגֶל: [איוב יב, ה]
ב) וַיִּזְכֹּר אֱלֹהִים אֶת נֹחַ וְאֵת כָּל הַחַיָּה וְאֶת כָּל הַבְּהֵמָה אֲשֶׁר אִתּוֹ בַּתֵּבָה וַיַּעֲבֵר אֱלֹהִים רוּחַ עַל הָאָרֶץ וַיָּשֹׁכּוּ הַמָּיִם: [בראשית ח, א]
ג) וַיִּתְלוּ אֶת הָמָן עַל הָעֵץ אֲשֶׁר הֵכִין לְמָרְדֳּכָי וַחֲמַת הַמֶּלֶךְ שָׁכָכָה: [אסתר ז, י]
ד) וַיְהִי לְשִׁבְעַת הַיָּמִים וּמֵי הַמַּבּוּל הָיוּ עַל הָאָרֶץ: [בראשית ז, י]
ה) מִכֹּל הַבְּהֵמָה הַטְּהוֹרָה תִּקַּח לְךָ שִׁבְעָה שִׁבְעָה אִישׁ וְאִשְׁתּוֹ וּמִן הַבְּהֵמָה אֲשֶׁר לֹא טְהֹרָה הִוא שְׁנַיִם אִישׁ וְאִשְׁתּוֹ: [בראשית ז, ב]
ו) עֲשֵׂה לְךָ תֵּבַת עֲצֵי גֹפֶר קִנִּים תַּעֲשֶׂה אֶת הַתֵּבָה וְכָפַרְתָּ אֹתָהּ מִבַּיִת וּמִחוּץ בַּכֹּפֶר: [בראשית ו, יד]
ז) צֹהַר תַּעֲשֶׂה לַתֵּבָה וְאֶל אַמָּה תְּכַלֶּנָּה מִלְמַעְלָה וּפֶתַח הַתֵּבָה בְּצִדָּהּ תָּשִׂים תַּחְתִּיִּם שְׁנִיִּם וּשְׁלִשִׁים תַּעֲשֶׂהָ: [בראשית ו, טז]
ח) וַיְשַׁלַּח אֶת הָעֹרֵב וַיֵּצֵא יָצוֹא וָשׁוֹב עַד יְבֹשֶׁת הַמַּיִם מֵעַל הָאָרֶץ: [בראשית ח, ז]
ט) וַהֲקִמֹתִי אֶת בְּרִיתִי אִתָּךְ וּבָאתָ אֶל הַתֵּבָה אַתָּה וּבָנֶיךָ וְאִשְׁתְּךָ וּנְשֵׁי בָנֶיךָ אִתָּךְ: [בראשית ו, יח]
י) צֵא מִן הַתֵּבָה אַתָּה וְאִשְׁתְּךָ וּבָנֶיךָ וּנְשֵׁי בָנֶיךָ אִתָּךְ: [בראשית ח, טז]
כ) וַיְשַׁלַּח אֶת הַיּוֹנָה מֵאִתּוֹ לִרְאוֹת הֲקַלּוּ הַמַּיִם מֵעַל פְּנֵי הָאֲדָמָה: [בראשית ח, ח]
ל) וַתָּבֹא אֵלָיו הַיּוֹנָה לְעֵת עֶרֶב וְהִנֵּה עֲלֵה זַיִת טָרָף בְּפִיהָ וַיֵּדַע נֹחַ כִּי קַלּוּ הַמַּיִם מֵעַל הָאָרֶץ: [בראשית ח, יא]
מ) שָׁוְא וּדְבַר כָּזָב הַרְחֵק מִמֶּנִּי רֵאשׁ וָעֹשֶׁר אַל תִּתֶּן לִי הַטְרִיפֵנִי לֶחֶם חֻקִּי: [משלי ל, ח]
נ) כָּל הַחַיָּה כָּל הָרֶמֶשׂ וְכָל הָעוֹף כֹּל רוֹמֵשׂ עַל הָאָרֶץ לְמִשְׁפְּחֹתֵיהֶם יָצְאוּ מִן הַתֵּבָה: [בראשית ח, יט]
ס) וָאֹמַר עִם קִנִּי אֶגְוָע וְכַחוֹל אַרְבֶּה יָמִים: [איוב כט, יח]
ע) לְדָוִד מִזְמוֹר נְאֻם יְיָ לַאדֹנִי שֵׁב לִימִינִי עַד אָשִׁית אֹיְבֶיךָ הֲדֹם לְרַגְלֶיךָ: [תהלים קי, א]
פ) מִי הֵעִיר מִמִּזְרָח צֶדֶק יִקְרָאֵהוּ לְרַגְלוֹ יִתֵּן לְפָנָיו גּוֹיִם וּמְלָכִים יַרְדְּ יִתֵּן כֶּעָפָר חַרְבּוֹ כְּקַשׁ נִדָּף קַשְׁתּוֹ: [ישעיה מא, ב]

מסורת הש"ס

א) ר"ה יב. זבחים קיג:, ב) [תוספתא דסוטה פ"י], ג) [זבחים קטו. ע"ש], ד) [פי' בשביל שלא באו על שאינן מינן עשה להן כבוד וכתב להן אישות כבאדם. ערוך ערך אשה], ה) [ר"ה כג.], ו) [גיר' הערוך רב אמר אדרא דבי ר' שילא אמרי זו כו' ע"ש ערך אדר], ז) [עירובין יח: ע"ש], ח) [כתב הבאר שבע לא ידענא פירושו ועי' מהרש"א בח"א וגם בפענא רזא קצת בדקיקות ויתכן לפרש לולא דבריהם ע"פ האמור בחולין נח. כל בריה שאין בו עצם אינו מתקיים שנים עשר חודש והכן], ט) תענית כא. ע"ש, י) צ"ל לחפות, כ) [צ"ל אדוני שב לימיני וכו'].

הגהות הב"ח

(א) רש"י ד"ה לשם רבא גדול. נ"ב וע"ע לעיל דף סט ע"ב:

ליקוטי רש"י

לפיד בוז. אש של גיהנם עומד למי שאנן בעשתותו לומר שלום יהיה לי [איוב יב, ה]. וישכו. כמו (אסתר ב, א) כשוך חמת המלך לשון הנחת חמה [בראשית ח, א]. וחמת המלך שככה. וסתם חמה רותחת היא כדכתיב וחמתו בערה בו [ר"ה יב, א]. אלו ימי אבלות של מתושלח. כי לימים עוד שבעה. אלו שבעת ימי אבלו של מתושלח הצדיק שחס הקב"ה על כבודו ועכב את הפורענות. לא וחשוב שנותיו של מתושלח ותמצא שהם כלים בשנת שש מאות שנה לחיי נח [בראשית ז, ד]. מתושלח צדיק גמור היה כדאמרינן בחלק (סנהדרין קח:) שבעת ימים שנתלו לדור המבול הן ימי אבלו של מתושלח [סוכה נב:]. כל שהתיבה קולטתו. מהעוף למינהו. אותן שדבקו במיניהם ולא השחיתו דרכם ומאליהם באו וכל שהתיבה קולטתו הכניס בה [בראשית ו, כ]. עצי גפר. כך שמו ולמה ממין זה על שם גפרית שנגזר עליהם להמחות בו [שם ו, יד]. צהר. יש אומרים חלון ויש אומרים אבן טובה המאירה להם. ואל אמה תכלנה מלמעלה. כסויה משופע ועולה עד שהוא קצר מלמעלה ועומד על אמה כדי שיזובו המים למטה. תחתים שנים ושלשים. שלש עליות זו על גב זו עליונים לאדם אמצעים למדור בהמה תחתיים לזבל [שם ו, טז]. או שמא לאשתי אתה צריך. יצוא ושוב. הולך ומקיף סביבות התיבה ולא הלך בשליחותו שהיה חושדו על בת זוגו כמו ששנינו באגדת חלק (סנהדרין קח:) [שם ח, ז]. אתה ובניך ואשתך. האנשים לבד והנשים לבד מכאן שנאסרו בתשמיש המטה [שם ז, יח]. נח ובניו. האנשים לבד והנשים לבד לפי שנאסרו בתשמיש המטה מפני שהעולם היה שרוי בצער [שם ז,ז]. אתה ואשתך וגו'. איש ואשתו כאן התיר להם תשמיש המטה [שם ח, טז]. טרף. חטף ומדרש אגדה לשון מזון ודרשו בפיה לשון מאמר אמרה יהיו מזונותי מרורין כזית בידו של הקב"ה ולא מתוקין כדבש בידי בשר ודם [שם פסוק יא]. הטריפני. ל' מזון וכן טרף נתן ליראיו (תהלים קיא) [משלי ל, ח]. טרף בפיה. מאמר פיה ביקשה שיהא זית טרף שלה והיינו מזון. בשר ודם. נח [עירובין יח:]. פאלי. כמו פלאי פלויי שבל' גמ' (נדה כא) לשון ביקוע ביקועי חתיכותיו [איוב מא,טו]. אורשינא. וכחול ארבה ימים. עוף ושמו חול ולא נקנסה עליו מיתה שלא טעם מעץ הדעת ולבסוף אלף שנה מתחד' וחוזר לנערותו [איוב כט, יח]. נאם ה' לאדני. רבותינו דרשוהו באברהם אבינו ואני אפרשנו כדבריהם נאם ה' לאברהם שקראוהו העולם אדוני שמעני אדוני (בראשית כ"ג). שב לימיני. התעכב לתשועתי והתחולל לה' אין ישיבה אלא עכבה וכן הוא אומר ותשבו בקדש (דברים א). לימיני. לתשועת ימיני. עד אשית אויביך. אמרפל וחביריו [תהלים קי, א]. מי העיר ממזרח. אותו צדק יקראהו לרגלו מי העיר את אברה' להביאו מארם שהוא במזרח וצדק שהיה עושה היא היתה לקראת רגליו בכל אשר הלך. יתן לפניו גוים. מי שהעירו ממקומו להסיע הוא נתן לפניו ארבעה מלכים וחיילותיהם. ירד. ירדה. יתן כעפר חרבו. נתן את חרבו ועושה חללים רבים כעפר ואת קשתו נתן מרבה הרוגים ונופלים כקש נדף [ישעיהו מא, ב]. דהוי סלקי ליה. כל המאורע לו אפילו רעה [תענית כא.].

which implies that each species was tended to individually in the Ark. אַתּוּן הֵיכָן הֲוֵיתוּן – As for **yourselves, where were you,** i.e. how were you able to cope with the task of providing each species with its peculiar needs?[50] אָמַר לֵיהּ – **[Shem] said to [Eliezer]:** צַעַר גָּדוֹל הָיָה לָנוּ בַּתֵּיבָה – Indeed, **we endured great distress in the Ark.** בְּרִיָּה שֶׁדַּרְכָּהּ לְהַאֲכִילָהּ בַּיּוֹם הֶאֱכַלְנוּהָ בַּיּוֹם – Any **creature whose habit it was to be fed by day, we fed by day,** שֶׁדַּרְכָּהּ לְהַאֲכִילָהּ בַּלַּיְלָה הֶאֱכַלְנוּהָ בַּלַּיְלָה – and any creature **whose habit it was to be fed by night, we fed by night.**[51] הַאי זִקִּיתָא – With respect to **that** creature known as the *zikisa,*[52] לֹא הֲוָה יָדַע אַבָּא מָה אָכְלָה – **Father** (Noah) **did not know what it ate** and he was therefore unable to feed it. יוֹמָא חַד הֲוָה יָתִיב וְקָא פָּאלֵי רִמּוֹנָא – **One day, he was sitting and cutting up a pomegranate.** נָפַל תּוֹלַעְתָּא מִינֵּיהּ – **A worm fell out of [the pomegranate]** אָכְלָה – and **[the *zikisa*]** pounced upon it and **ate it.** מִיכָּן וְאֵילָךְ הֲוָה גָּבֵיל לָהּ חֵיזְרָא – **From then on, he would knead bran** in water[53] **for [the *zikisa*],** כִּי מִתְלַע – and **when it became wormy,** אָכְלָה – **[the *zikisa*] would eat it.**[54]

Shem's account continues:

אַרְיָא אִישְׁתָּא זַיְינְתֵיהּ – As for **the lion – a fever** seized it and **sustained it,** and it therefore refrained from devouring other animals.

The Gemara interjects:

דְּאָמַר רַב – **For Rav said:** לֹא בָּצִיר מִשִּׁיתָּא וְלֹא טְפֵי מִתְּרֵיסַר זָיְינָא אִישְׁתָּא – For **no less than six** days **and** for **no more than twelve** days **can a fever sustain** its victim.[55]

Shem's account continues:

אַוַרְשִׁינָה אַשְׁכְּחֵינֵיהּ אַבָּא דְּגָנֵי בְּסִפְנָא דְּתֵיבוּתָא – As for **the *avarshinah***[56] – **Father found it lying in** its **quarters in the Ark.**[57] אָמַר לֵיהּ – **[Father] said to it:** לֹא בָּעֵית מְזוֹנֵי – **Do you not need food?** Why are you huddled in your quarters? אָמַר לֵיהּ – **[The *avarshinah*] said to [Noah]:** חֲזִיתִיךְ דַּהֲוַת טְרִידָא – **I saw that you were preoccupied** with feeding so many animals, אֲמִינָא – so **I said:** לֹא אַצַעֲרָךְ – **I will not trouble you** with feeding me too. אָמַר לֵיהּ – Touched by its solicitude for his welfare, **[Noah] said to [the *avarshinah*]:** יְהֵא רַעֲוָא דְּלֹא תָּמוּת – **May it be the will** of God **that you never die!**

A verse demonstrates that Noah's blessing was fulfilled:

שֶׁנֶּאֱמַר ,,וָאֹמַר עִם־קִנִּי אֶגְוָע וְכַחוֹל אַרְבֶּה יָמִים'' – **As it is stated:** ***I said, "I shall die with my nest [intact], and live for many days like the chol."***[58]

Having cited this conversation between Shem and Eliezer, the Gemara cites another one:

אָמַר רַב חָנָה בַּר לִוַּאי – **Rav Chanah bar Livai said:** אָמַר שֵׁם רַבָּא לֶאֱלִיעֶזֶר – **Shem the Great said to Eliezer:** כִּי אָתוּ עֲלָיְיכוּ מַלְכֵי מִזְרָח וּמַעֲרָב – **When the kings of the East and the West converged upon you** in battle, אַתּוּן הֵיכִי עֲבֵידִיתוּ – **what did you do** to defeat them?[59] אָמַר לֵיהּ – **[Eliezer] said to [Shem]:** אַיְיתֵי הַקָּדוֹשׁ בָּרוּךְ הוּא לְאַבְרָהָם – **The Holy One, Blessed is He, brought Abraham** near Him, וְאוֹתְבֵיהּ מִימִינֵיהּ – **and,** so to speak, **seated him at His right side.**[60] וַהֲוָה שָׁדֵינַן עַפְרָא – **We would throw dust** at the enemy forces, וַהֲווּ חַרְבֵי – **and it would turn into swords;** גִּילֵי – we would throw **straw,** וַהֲוֵי גִּירֵי – **and it would turn into arrows,** which felled the enemy.[61]

The Gemara cites a verse that alludes to this incident:

שֶׁנֶּאֱמַר ,,לְדָוִד מִזְמוֹר נְאֻם ה' לַאדֹנִי שֵׁב לִימִינִי עַד־אָשִׁית אֹיְבֶיךָ הֲדֹם לְרַגְלֶיךָ'' – **As it is stated:** ***Of David, a psalm: So says HASHEM to my master: "Sit at My right, until I make your enemies a stool***

NOTES

50. *Rashi.* According to *Yad Ramah,* whose approach was mentioned in note 49, Eliezer's question was: The animals emerged from the Ark weakened by the ordeal, but what about you humans? Was your health impaired by your experience in the Ark?

Although the Gemara cites Eliezer's question as based on a Scriptural verse, it does not mean that Eliezer quoted the verse to Shem, for the Torah had not yet been given in his times. Rather, it means that Eliezer knew what had transpired with the animals in the Ark and he therefore asked Shem what the human's experience was (*Yad Ramah;* see there for another explanation; see also *Maharsha*).

51. [Thus, we were occupied around the clock.]

52. A small bird resembling the quail (*Otzar HaGeonim; Mussaf HaAruch*).

53. See *Rashi* to *Bava Metzia* 60b ד"ה מיא דחיורא.

54. This illustrates the trouble Noah took to provide each and every species with precisely what it needed (*Maharsha*).

55. The least potent fever can sustain an ill person for six days, and the most potent fever can sustain him for up to twelve days, without food or drink. [That is, the fever reduces its victim's appetite and sustains him by causing the body to consume excess fat.] The lion too was sustained by a fever for some time so that the other creatures in the Ark would be spared (*Rashi*). Noah was once late in bringing the lion his meal and the lion attacked him and rendered him lame. At that juncture, God caused the lion to develop a fever, so that it would not go on a rampage. After the fever passed, Noah was able to resume his normal feeding practice (*Maharsha* based on *Midrash Tanchuma, Noah* §9; cf. *Toras Chaim*). Others interpret Rav's statement as meaning that a fever can sustain its victim for anywhere between six and twelve *months.* [Indeed, certain animals can survive inordinate lengths of time without proper nourishment, sustained by their own fats and nutrients stored in their bodies.] Thus, the lion was ill with fever for the entire twelve months it spent in the Ark, and hardly needed to be fed (*Yad Ramah*).

56. This is a bird referred to in Scripture (*Job* 29:18) as the חול. This bird enjoys uncommon longevity, as the Gemara states shortly (*Rashi*).

57. The middle level of the Ark was composed of compartments for each species (see *Genesis* 6:14 with *Rashi*). Noah discovered the *avarshinah* huddled in its own quarters [rather than outside, where it should have come to be fed] (*Rashi*). Alternatively, it was lying in the hold of the Ark (*Yad Ramah*).

58. *Job* 29:18. The verse implies that the *chol* never dies (*Rashi*). That is, it outlives all other creatures (*Yad Ramah;* cf. *Toras Chaim* and *Bereishis Rabbah* 19:9; see also *Aruch* s.v. אורשנא).

According to the *Midrash* (*Bereishis Rabbah* ibid.), the reason the *chol* merited longevity is not Noah's blessing. Rather, when Eve gave Adam the fruit of the Tree of Knowledge, she also fed the fruit to all the animals. The only creature that refused to partake of it was the *chol,* and therefore, when God decreed that all who ate of the fruit would die, the *chol* was spared. See *Toras Chaim*, who reconciles the statement of the *Midrash* with that of our Gemara.

Maharal explains the Gemara's point as being not that Noah's blessing caused the *chol* to live long, but that the *chol* has the virtues of humility and patience, which makes it the object of many blessings and by which it merits longevity.

59. Shem referred here to the war fought by Abraham against the coalition of four kings (see *Genesis* ch. 14). The armies of four nations initially attacked those of five other nations and defeated them, taking Abraham's nephew, Lot, captive. Abraham and his servant Eliezer counterattacked and defeated the four kings. Scripture states that Abraham's army numbered three hundred and eighteen – certainly a tiny force against four powerful armies. Moreover, some Sages say (*Nedarim* 32a) that Abraham's army consisted only of himself and his servant Eliezer, whose name has the numerical value of 318. [1 (א)+ 30 (ל) + 10 (י) + 70 (ע) + 7 (ז) + 200 (ר) = 318.] Shem therefore asked Eliezer: What miracle did God do to cause you to emerge victorious? (*Maharsha*).

60. That is to say, God sent the angel Michael to help Abraham. Michael represents the Divine Attribute of חֶסֶד, *lovingkindness,* which is identified with the right side [while the attribute of justice is identified with the left] (*Ben Yehoyada;* see also *Maharsha*).

61. I.e. God would send angels of destruction upon the enemy, with their swords drawn and their bows taut (*Maharsha*). Eliezer's point was that the victory required only the minutest effort on the part of Abraham's force, since the war was actually fought by the angels (*R' Avigdor Miller*).

תורה אור השלם

א"כ לא נפנה דרך כרמים דרש רבא מאי דכתיב (א) לפיד בוז לעשתות שאנן נכון למועדי רגל מלמד שהיה נח הצדיק מוכיח אותם ואמר להם דברים שהם קשים כלפידים והיו (בוזים) [מבזין] אותו אמרו לו זקן תיבה זו למה אמר להם הקב"ה מביא עליכם את המבול אמרו מבול של מה אם מבול של אש יש לנו דבר אחר ועליתה שמה ואם של מים הוא מביא אם מן הארץ הוא מביא יש לנו עששיות של ברזל שאנו מחפין בהם את הארץ ואם מן השמים הוא מביא יש לנו דבר ועקב שמו ואמרי לה עקש שמו אמר להם הוא מביא מבין עקבי רגליכם שנאמר (א) נכון למועדי רגל תניא מימי המבול קשים כשכבת זרע שנאמר נכון למועדי רגל (א) אמר רב חסדא ברותחין קלקלו בעבירה וברותחין נידונו כתיב הכא (ב) וישכו המים וכתיב התם (ג) וחמת המלך שככה (ד) ויהי לשבעת הימים ומי המבול היו על הארץ (ב) מה טיבם של שבעת הימים אמר רב אלו ימי אבילות של מתושלח ללמדך שהספדן של צדיקים מעכבין את הפורענות לבא דבר אחר לשבעת ששינה עליהם הקב"ה סדר בראשית שהיתה חמה יוצאת ממערב ושוקעת במזרח דבר אחר שקבע להם הקב"ה זמן גדול ואח"כ זמן קטן ד"א לשבעת הימים שהטעימם מעין העולם הבא כדי שידעו מה טובה מנעו מהן (ה) מכל הבהמה הטהורה תקח לך שבעה שבעה איש ואשתו אישות לבהמה מי אית לה (ג) א"ר שמואל בר נחמני א"ר יונתן (ד) מאותם שלא נעבדה בהם עבירה מנא ידע אמר רב חסדא שהעבירן לפני התיבה כל שהתיבה קולטתו בידוע שלא נעבדה בהם עבירה וכל שאין התיבה קולטתו בידוע שנעבדה בה עבירה רבי אבהו אמר מאותן הבאין מאיליהן (ו) עשה לך תיבת עצי גופר מאי גופר (ה) אמר רב אדא (ו) אמרי דבי ר' שילא זו מבליגה ואמרי לה גולמיש (ז) צוהר תעשה לתיבה א"ר יוחנן אמר לו הקב"ה לנח קבע בה אבנים טובות ומרגליות כדי שיהיו מאירות לכם כצהרים (ז) ואל אמה תכלנה מלמעלה דבהכי [הוא] דקיימא (ז) תחתיים שנים ושלישים תעשה תנא תחתיים לזבל אמצעיים לבהמה עליונים לאדם (ח) וישלח את העורב אמר ר"ל תשובה ניצחת השיבו עורב לנח אמר לו רבך שונאני ואתה שנאתני רבך שונאני מן הטהורין שבעה מן הטמאים שנים ואתה שנאתני שאתה מניח ממין שבעה ושולח ממין שנים אם פוגע בי שר חמה או שר צנה לא נמצא עולם חסר בריה אחת או שמא לאשתי אתה צריך אמר לו רשע במותר לי נאסר לי בנאסר לי לא כ"ש ומנלן דנאסרו דכתיב (ט) ובאת אל התיבה אתה ובניך ואשתך ונשי בניך אתך וכתיב (י) צא מן התיבה אתה ואשתך ובניך ונשי בניך אתך וא"ר יוחנן מיכן אמרו שנאסרו בתשמיש המטה ת"ר שלשה שמשו בתיבה וכולם לקו כלב ועורב וחם כלב נקשר עורב רק חם לקה בעורו (כ) וישלח את היונה מאתו לראות הקלו המים א"ר ירמיה מכאן שדירתן של עופות טהורים עם הצדיקים (ל) והנה עלה זית טרף בפיה (י) א"ר אלעזר אמרה יונה לפני הקב"ה רבש"ע יהיו מזונותי מרורים כזית ומסורים בידך ואל יהיו מתוקים כדבש ומסורים ביד בשר ודם מאי משמע דהאי טרף לישנא דמזוני הוא דכתיב (מ) הטריפני לחם חוקי (נ) למשפחותיהם יצאו מן התיבה א"ר יוחנן (פ) למשפחותם ולא הם אמר רב חנא בר ביזנא אמר ליה אליעזר לשם רבא כתיב (נ) למשפחותיהם יצאו מן התיבה אתון היכן הויתון א"ל צער גדול היה לנו בתיבה בריה שדרכה להאכילה ביום האכלנוה ביום שדרכה להאכילה בלילה האכלנוה בלילה האי זקיתא לא הוה ידע אבא מה אכלה יומא חד הוה יתיב וקא פאלי רמונא נפל תולעתא מינה אכלה מיכן ואילך הוה גביל לה חיזרא כי מתלע אכלה אריא אישתא זינתיה דאמר רב לא בציר משיתא ולא טפי מתריסר זינא אישתא אורשינה אשכחיניה אבא דגני בספנא דתיבותא א"ל לא בעית מזוני א"ל חזיתיך דהות טרידא אמינא לא אצערך א"ל יהא רעוא דלא תמות שנאמר (ס) ואומר עם קני אגוע וכחול ארבה ימים אמר רב חנה בר לואי אמר שם רבא לאליעזר כי אתו עלייכו מלכי מזרח ומערב אתון היכי עבידיתו אמר ליה אייתי הקב"ה לאברהם ואותביה מימיניה והוה שדינן עפרא והוו חרבי גילי והוי גירי שנאמר (ע) מזמור לדוד נאם ה' לאדוני שב לימיני עד אשית אויביך הדום לרגליך וכתיב (פ) מי העיר ממזרח צדק יקראהו לרגלו יתן לפניו גוים ומלכים ירד יתן כעפר חרבו כקש נדף קשתו (ט) נחום איש גם זו הוה רגיל דכל דהוה סלקא ליה אמר גם זו לטובה יומא חד בעו [ישראל] לשדורי דורון לקיסר אמרי בהדי

מאן

א"כ לא נפנה דרך כרמים. [כלומר לא נסור ולא נפנה את דרך הכרמים] אלא כל שעה נלך בהם כלומר א"כ לא נלך דרך כבושה ולא נחזור מסורינו אלא נלך ונקלקל השורה דרכים משובשים בקוצים ובדרקנים כעין שבילי כרמים: לעשתות. כמו עשתונות שיושבין שאנן וחושבין מחשבות רעות: עליתה שמה. אין אש שולט בה: מבין עקבי רגליכם. בשכבת זרע שלכם יכול למחות אתכם ל"א מבין עקבי רגליכם מן הרגל יוציא ממש מים אם היה רוצה ואי אפשר (י) לכפות רגליכם בעששיות: בשכבת זרע. רותחין ועבין היו. עבין ל"ג ופי' הוא: חמת המלך שככה. נחה מרתחו ה"נ מים נחו מרותחן: סדרי בראשית. והיינו לשבעת הימים סדר שבעת ימי בראשית שינה להם: זמן קטן אחר זמן גדול. בתחילה אמר להן והיו ימיו מאה ועשרים שנה כשעבר זמן זה ולא שבו לטובה חזר וקבע להם זמן קטן: אישות לבהמה מי אית ליה. נקבה אחת נשכבת לכמה זכרים ואין זו אישות: שלא נעבדה בהן עבירה. שלא נזקקו אלא לבן זוגם: מבליגה. עץ הוא: במותר לי. אפי' באשתי אני אסור: (בני נח. שם וחם ויפת): רק. רוקק זרע מפיו לפיה של נקבה: לקה בעורו. שיצא ממנו כוש: מאתו. גבי עורב לא כתיב מאתו מכאן שדירתם כו' כלומר הנאה הוא שדרים אלא שמכירים בצדיקים כדאמרי' בדוכתי אחריתא: זית טרף בפיה. בפיה היתה שואלת מזון טרף של זית: למשפחותיהם יצאו מן התיבה. אלמא כל חד וחד בפני עצמו היה ולא היו אוכלין כולם באבוס אחד אלא משפחות [משפחות] היו שרויין: א"ל אליעזר. [עבד אברהם]: לשם רבא. גדול (א) בנו של נח: היכי הויתון. היאך הייתם יכולין להכין עונייהם בכך לעשות לכל בריה ובריה חפלה: זקיתא. שם בריה: פאלי. מחתך כמו פלי פלויי במסכת נדה (דף כא:): אישתא זינתיה. חמה אחזתו וזנהו ולא היה חושש לדרוש מאחר בהמות: לא בציר משיתא ולא טפי מתריסר זיינא אישתא. אין לך חמה קלה שלא תהא חמימותו יכולה לזונו ששת ימים שלא ימות בלא מאכל ואין לך חמה שיכולה לזון יותר מי"ב ימים בלי מאכל ומשתה כ"ש ואית דגרסי לא פחות משיתא ירחי ולא טפי מתריסר זנתא אשתא ואמרי קאי כלומר לא פחות מששה חדשים ולא יותר מי"ב חדשים ולא נהירא לי: אורשינא. עוף ושמו חול בלשון המקרא ואינו מת לעולם: בספנא. בחדר ספון ומתוקן לו: [נאום ה' כו']. אליעזר אמר פסוק זה. נאם ה' לאדני אמר הקב"ה לאברהם (כ) שב לימיני אדני וכו': ממזרח זה אברהם. שבא מארם נהרים שהוא במזרח דכתיב (במדבר כג) מן ארם ינחני בלק מלך מואב וגו': כל דהוה סלקא ליה. כל דבר המאורע ליה:

בהדי

תורה אור השלם

א) לַפִּיד בּוּז לְעַשְׁתּוּת שַׁאֲנָן נָכוֹן לְמוֹעֲדֵי רָגֶל: [איוב יב, ה]

ב) וַיִּזְכֹּר אֱלֹהִים אֶת נֹחַ וְאֵת כָּל הַחַיָּה וְאֶת כָּל הַבְּהֵמָה אֲשֶׁר אִתּוֹ בַּתֵּבָה וַיַּעֲבֵר אֱלֹהִים רוּחַ עַל הָאָרֶץ וַיָּשֹׁכּוּ הַמָּיִם: [בראשית ח, א]

ג) וַיִּתְלוּ אֶת הָמָן עַל הָעֵץ אֲשֶׁר הֵכִין לְמָרְדֳּכָי וַחֲמַת הַמֶּלֶךְ שָׁכָכָה: [אסתר ז, י]

ד) וַיְהִי לְשִׁבְעַת הַיָּמִים וּמֵי הַמַּבּוּל הָיוּ עַל הָאָרֶץ: [בראשית ז, י]

ה) מִכֹּל הַבְּהֵמָה הַטְּהוֹרָה תִּקַּח לְךָ שִׁבְעָה שִׁבְעָה אִישׁ וְאִשְׁתּוֹ וּמִן הַבְּהֵמָה אֲשֶׁר לֹא טְהֹרָה הִוא שְׁנַיִם אִישׁ וְאִשְׁתּוֹ: [בראשית ז, ב]

ו) עֲשֵׂה לְךָ תֵּבַת עֲצֵי גֹפֶר קִנִּים תַּעֲשֶׂה אֶת הַתֵּבָה וְכָפַרְתָּ אֹתָהּ מִבַּיִת וּמִחוּץ בַּכֹּפֶר: [בראשית ו, יד]

ז) צֹהַר תַּעֲשֶׂה לַתֵּבָה וְאֶל אַמָּה תְּכַלֶּנָּה מִלְמַעְלָה וּפֶתַח הַתֵּבָה בְּצִדָּהּ תָּשִׂים תַּחְתִּיִּם שְׁנִיִּם וּשְׁלִשִׁים תַּעֲשֶׂהָ: [בראשית ו, טז]

ח) וַיְשַׁלַּח אֶת הָעֹרֵב וַיֵּצֵא יָצוֹא וָשׁוֹב עַד יְבֹשֶׁת הַמַּיִם מֵעַל הָאָרֶץ: [בראשית ח, ז]

ט) וַהֲקִמֹתִי אֶת בְּרִיתִי אִתָּךְ וּבָאתָ אֶל הַתֵּבָה אַתָּה וּבָנֶיךָ וְאִשְׁתְּךָ וּנְשֵׁי בָנֶיךָ אִתָּךְ: [בראשית ו, יח]

י) צֵא מִן הַתֵּבָה אַתָּה וְאִשְׁתְּךָ וּבָנֶיךָ וּנְשֵׁי בָנֶיךָ אִתָּךְ: [בראשית ח, טז]

כ) וַיְשַׁלַּח אֶת הַיּוֹנָה מֵאִתּוֹ לִרְאוֹת הֲקַלּוּ הַמַּיִם מֵעַל פְּנֵי הָאֲדָמָה: [בראשית ח, ח]

ל) וַתָּבֹא אֵלָיו הַיּוֹנָה לְעֵת עֶרֶב וְהִנֵּה עֲלֵה זַיִת טָרָף בְּפִיהָ וַיֵּדַע נֹחַ כִּי קַלּוּ הַמַּיִם מֵעַל הָאָרֶץ: [בראשית ח, יא]

מ) שָׁוְא וּדְבַר כָּזָב הַרְחֵק מִמֶּנִּי רֵאשׁ וָעֹשֶׁר אַל תִּתֶּן לִי הַטְרִיפֵנִי לֶחֶם חֻקִּי: [משלי ל, ח]

נ) כָּל הַחַיָּה כָּל הָרֶמֶשׂ וְכָל הָעוֹף כֹּל רוֹמֵשׂ עַל הָאָרֶץ לְמִשְׁפְּחֹתֵיהֶם יָצְאוּ מִן הַתֵּבָה: [בראשית ח, יט]

ס) וָאֹמַר עִם קִנִּי אֶגְוָע וְכַחוֹל אַרְבֶּה יָמִים: [איוב כט, יח]

ע) לְדָוִד מִזְמוֹר נְאֻם יְיָ לַאדֹנִי שֵׁב לִימִינִי עַד אָשִׁית אֹיְבֶיךָ הֲדֹם לְרַגְלֶיךָ: [תהלים קי, א]

פ) מִי הֵעִיר מִמִּזְרָח צֶדֶק יִקְרָאֵהוּ לְרַגְלוֹ יִתֵּן לְפָנָיו גּוֹיִם וּמְלָכִים יַרְדְּ יִתֵּן כֶּעָפָר חַרְבּוֹ כְּקַשׁ נִדָּף קַשְׁתּוֹ: [ישעיה מא, ב]

מסורת הש"ס

א) ר"ה יב. זבחים קיג., ב) [תוספתא דסוטה פ"י], ג) [זבחים קטו. ע"ש], ד) [פי' בשביל שלא באו על שאינן מינן עשה להן כבוד וכתב להן אישות כאדם. ערוך ערך אשה], ה) [ר"ה כג.], ו) [גיר' הערוך רב אמר אדרא דבי ר' שילא אמרי זו כו' ע"ש ערך אדר], ז) [עירובין יח: ע"ש], ח) [כתב הבאר שבע לא ידענא פירושו ועי' מהרש"א בח"א וגם בפענא רזא קצת בדחיקות ויתכן לפרש לולא דבריהם ע"פ האמור בחולין נח. כל בריה שאין בו עצם אינו מתקיים שנים עשר חודש והכן], ט) תענית כא. ע"ש, י) ל"ל לחפות, כ) [ל"ל אדוני שב לימיני וכו'].

הגהות הב"ח

(א) רש"י ד"ה לשם רבא גדול. נ"ב וצ"ע לעיל דף סט ע"ב:

ליקוטי רש"י

לפיד בוז. אש של גיהנם עומד למי שאנן בעשתותו לומר שלום יהיה לי [איוב יב, ה]. וישכו. כמו (אסתר ב, א) כשוך חמת המלך לשון הנחת חמה [בראשית ח, א]. וחמת המלך שככה. וסתם חמה רותחת היא כדכתיב וחמתו בערה בו [ר"ה יב, א]. אלו ימי אבלות של מתושלח. כי לימים עוד שבעה. אלו שבעת ימי אבלו של מתושלח הצדיק שחס הקב"ה על כבודו ועכב את הפורענות. לא וחשוב שנותיו של מתושלח ותמצא שהם כלים בשנת שש מאות שנה לחיי נח [בראשית ז, ד]. מתושלח צדיק גמור היה כדאמרינן בחלק (סנהדרין קח:) שבעת ימים שנתנו לדור המבול הן ימי אבלו של מתושלח [סוכה נב:]. כל שהתיבה קולטתו. מהעוף למינהו. אותן שדבקו במיניהם ולא השחיתו דרכם ומאליהם באו וכל שהתיבה קולטתו הכנים בה [בראשית ו, כ]. עצי גפר. כך שמו ולמה ממין זה על שם גפרית שנגזר עליהם להמחות בו [שם ו, יד]. צהר. יש אומרים חלון ויש אומרים אבן טובה המאירה להם. ואל אמה תכלנה מלמעלה. כסויה משופע ועולה עד שהוא קצר מלמעלה ועומד על אמה כדי שיזובו המים למטה. תחתים שנים ושלשים. שלש עליות זו על גב זו עליונים לאדם אמצעים למדור בהמה תחתיים לזבל [שם ו, טז]. או שמא לאשתי אתה צריך. יצוא ושוב. הולך ומקיף סביבות התיבה ולא הלך בשליחותו שהיה חושדו על בת זוגו כמו ששנינו באגדת חלק (סנהדרין קח:) [שם ח, ז]. אתה ובניך ואשתך. האנשים לבד והנשים לבד מכאן שנאסרו בתשמיש המטה [שם ז, יח]. נח ובניו. האנשים לבד והנשים לבד לפי שנאסרו בתשמיש המטה מפני שהעולם היה שרוי בצער [שם ז,ז]. אתה ואשתך וגו'. איש ואשתו כאן התיר להם תשמיש המטה [שם ח, טז]. טרף. חטף ומדרש אגדה לשון מזון ודרשו בפיה לשון מאמר אמרה יהיו מזונותי מרורין כזית בידו של הקב"ה ולא מתוקין כדבש בידי בשר ודם [שם פסוק יא]. הטריפני. ל' מזון וכן טרף נתן ליראיו (תהלים קיא) [משלי ל, ח]. טרף בפיה. מאמר פיה בקשה שיהא זית טרף שלה והיינו מזון. בשר ודם. נח [עירובין יח:]. פאלי. כמו פלאי פלויי שבל' גמ' (נדה כא) לשון ביקוע ביקועי חתיכותיו [איוב מא,טו]. אורשינא. וכחול ארבה ימים. עוף ושמו חול ולא נקנסה עליו מיתה שלא טעם מעץ הדעת ולבסוף אלף שנה מתחד' וחוזר לנערותו [איוב כט, יח]. נאם ה' לאדני. רבותינו דרשוהו באברהם אבינו ואני אפרשנו כדבריהם נאם ה' לאברהם שקראוהו העולם אדוני שמעני אדוני (בראשית כ"ג). שב לימיני. התעכב לתשועתי והתחולל לה' אין ישיבה אלא עכבה וכן הוא אומר ותשבו בקדש (דברים א). לימיני. לתשועת ימיני. עד אשית אויביך. אמרפל וחביריו [תהלים קי, א]. מי העיר ממזרח. אותו שצדק יקראהו לרגלו מי העיר את אברה' להביאו מארם שהוא במזרח וצדק שהיה עושה היא היתה לקראת רגליו בכל אשר הלך. יתן לפניו גוים. מי שהעירו ממקומו להסיע הוא נתן לפניו ארבעה מלכים וחיילותיהם. ירד. ירדה. יתן כעפר חרבו. רמא כעפרא קטולין קדם חרביה נתן את חרבו ועושה חללים רבים כעפר ואת קשתו נתן מרבה הרוגים ונופלים כקש נדף [ישעיהו מא, ב]. דהוי סלקי ליה. כל המאורע לו אפילו רעה [תענית כא.].

for your feet."[62] וּכְתִיב ,,מִי הֵעִיר מִמִּזְרָח צֶדֶק יִקְרָאֵהוּ לְרַגְלוֹ – **And it is written:** ***Who aroused [Abraham] from the East, who would proclaim righteousness wherever he trod?*** יִתֵּן לְפָנָיו גּוֹיִם וּמְלָכִים יַרְדְּ – ***[The One] Who laid nations before him and made him dominate kings!*** יִתֵּן כֶּעָפָר חַרְבּוֹ כְּקַשׁ נִדָּף קַשְׁתּוֹ" – ***[The One] Who made his sword like dirt, his bow like wind-blown straw!***[63]

The Gemara relates another incident involving miraculous dirt, which occurred many generations later:

נַחוּם אִישׁ גַּם זוּ הֲוָה רָגִיל – **Nachum ish Gam Zu had the habit** דְּכָל דַּהֲוָה סַלְקָא לֵיהּ אָמַר – **that, whatever would happen to him, he would say,** גַּם זוּ לְטוֹבָה **"This, too, is for the best"** (*Gam zu letovah*).[64] יוֹמָא חַד – **One day,** בָּעוּ [יִשְׂרָאֵל] לְשַׁדּוּרֵי דּוֹרוֹן לְקֵיסָר – **[the Jews] wanted to send a gift to Caesar.** אָמְרֵי – **They said:** בַּהֲדֵי

NOTES

62. *Psalms* 110:1. The term *my master* is understood as a reference to Abraham, for this verse was composed by Eliezer [and later inserted in *Psalms* by David] (*Rashi;* cf. *Yad Ramah*). A verse later in this psalm (v. 4) alludes to Shem [Malki Tzedek – see *Genesis* 14:18] (*Yad Ramah*).

63. *Isaiah* 41:2. The verse means that God – Who aroused Abraham to leave his homeland of Aram Naharaim in the East, to travel westward to Eretz Yisrael and to proclaim monotheism wherever he would go – granted Abraham a miraculous victory over nations and kings, making the dust his sword and the wind-blown straw like arrows shot from his bow (*Rashi, Yad Ramah*).

64. Nachum was actually from a place called Gimzo, a town not far from Lod (*Rabbeinu Chananel* to *Taanis* 21a; *Aruch* s.v. גמזו, based on *II Chronicles* 28:18; *cf. Maharsha*). However, he came to be called Nachum ish Gam Zu [literally: man of Gam Zu] because he always used to say: *Gam zu letovah.* See *Toras Chaim.*

מַאן נְשַׁדַּר – With **whom should we send** the gift? נְשַׁדַּר בַּהֲדֵי נַחוּם אִישׁ גַּם זוּ – **Let us send it with Nachum ish Gam Zu,** דִּמְלוּמָּד בְּנִסִּים הוּא – **because he is accustomed to** have **miracles** performed on his behalf.[1] Nachum set out with a chest filled with precious stones and pearls.[2] כִּי מְטָא לְהַהוּא דִּיוְרָא – **When he came to a certain inn,** בְּעָא לְמֵיבַת – **he wanted to stay overnight.** אָמְרֵי לֵיהּ – **[The residents] said to [him]:** מַאי אִיכָּא בַּהֲדָךְ – **What do you have with you** in that chest? אָמַר לְהוּ – **[Nachum] said to them:** קָא מוֹבִילְנָא כְּרָגָא לְקֵיסָר – **I am transporting a tribute to Caesar.** קָמוּ בְּלֵילְיָא – **[The residents] arose during the night,** שְׁרִינְהוּ לְסִיפְטֵיהּ – **untied [Nachum's] chest,** וְשָׁקְלוּ כָּל דַּהֲוָה גַּבֵּיהּ – **took all of its contents** וּמְלַנְהוּ עַפְרָא – **and filled it with dirt.** כִּי מְטָא לְהָתָם – **When he arrived there,** at Caesar's palace, אִישְׁתַּכַּח עַפְרָא – they opened the chest and **it was found** to contain **dirt.**[3] אָמַר – **[Caesar] said,** in rage: אַחוּכֵי קָא מְחַיְּיכֵי בִּי יְהוּדָאֵי – **"The Jews are mocking me** by sending me such an insulting gift!" אַפְּקוּהוּ לְמִקְטְלֵיהּ – **They took [Nachum] out to be killed.**[4] אָמַר גַּם זוּ לְטוֹבָה – As he was being led out, **[Nachum] said, "This, too, is for the best** (*gam zu letovah*)." אֲתָא אֵלִיָּהוּ – **Elijah** the Prophet then **came** וְאִידְמֵי לְהוּ כְּחַד מִינַּיְיהוּ – **and appeared to them** (the Romans) **as one of them,** i.e. disguised as a Roman official. אָמַר לְהוּ – **[Elijah] said to [the Romans]:** דִּילְמָא הַאי עַפְרָא מֵעַפְרָא דְּאַבְרָהָם אָבִינוּ הוּא – **"Perhaps this dirt is from the dirt of our father Abraham,** which he used during his war against the four kings, דַּהֲוָה שָׁדֵי עַפְרָא הָווּ חַרְבֵי – **for [Abraham] would throw earth** at his enemies and **it would turn into swords;** גִּילֵי הָווּ גִּירֵי – he would throw **straw** and **it would turn into arrows."** בָּדוּק – **[The Romans] tested** some of the dirt, וְאַשְׁכְּחוּ הָכִי – **and they found that it was so.** הֲוָה מְחוֹזָא – **There was a** certain **district** דְּלָא הָווּ קָא יָכְלֵי לֵיהּ לְמִיכְבְּשֵׁיהּ – **that they had not been able to conquer.** שָׁדוּ מֵהַהוּא עַפְרָא עֲלֵיהּ – **They threw some of that dirt at** the defenders of **[the district]** וּכְבָשׁוּהָ – **and conquered it.** עַיְילוּהוּ לְבֵי גִּנְזָא – After their victory, **[the Romans] brought [Nachum] into** Caesar's **treasure vault** אָמְרֵי – and **said** to him: שְׁקוֹל דְּנִיחָא לָךְ – **"Take what you please!"** מַלְיֵיהּ לְסִיפְטָא דַּהֲבָא – **[Nachum] filled** his **chest with gold** and they sent him off with great honor.[5] כִּי הֲדַר אֲתָא – **When,** on his way home, **he returned** to the inn where his precious stones and pearls had been stolen, אָמְרוּ לֵיהּ הָנָךְ דִּיוְרֵי – **those residents said to him:** מַאי אַמְטֵית לְבֵי מַלְכָּא – **"What did you bring to the Emperor's palace** that he should accord you such honor?" אָמַר לְהוּ – **[Nachum] said to them:** מַאי דְּשָׁקְלִי מֵהָכָא אַמְטַאי לְהָתָם – **"Whatever I took from here, I brought there."** שָׁקְלֵי אִינְהוּ אַמְטוּ – Thereupon, **[the residents] took** some dirt from their inn קַטְלִינְהוּ לְהָנָךְ דִּיוְרֵי לְהָתָם – **and brought it there,** to Caesar. The Romans tested it in battle, but it did not possess any miraculous properties. **[The Romans] executed those residents** for attempting to defraud them.

The Gemara now discusses the second group mentioned in the Mishnah as having no share in the World to Come – the Generation of the Dispersion. The Mishnah stated: דּוֹר הַפְּלָגָה אֵין לָהֶם חֵלֶק לָעוֹלָם הַבָּא וכו׳ – **THE GENERATION OF THE DISPERSION HAS NO SHARE IN THE WORLD TO COME etc.**

The Gemara asks:

מַאי עֲבוּד – **What** exactly **did it do** wrong?[6]

The Gemara answers:

אָמְרֵי דְּבֵי רַבִּי שֵׁילָא – **[The scholars] of the academy of R' Shela say:** נִבְנֶה מִגְדָּל וְנַעֲלֶה לָרָקִיעַ וְנַכֶּה אוֹתוֹ בְּקַרְדּוּמוֹת – The Generation of the Dispersion said: **Let us build a tower, ascend to the sky, and strike it with axes,** כְּדֵי שֶׁיָּזוּבוּ מֵימָיו – **so that its water will flow!**[7]

This explanation is challenged:

מְחַכּוּ עֲלָהּ בְּמַעֲרָבָא – **They laughed at this in the West** [Eretz Yisrael]:[8] אִם כֵּן – **If** it is **so** that they built the tower in order to reach the sky, why did they build it in a valley?[9] לִיבְנוּ אַחַד בְּטוּרָא – **They should have built** it **atop one of the mountains!** –?–

The Gemara answers:

(אֶלָּא) אָמַר רַבִּי יִרְמְיָה בַּר אֶלְעָזָר – **(Rather,)**[10] **R' Yirmiyah bar Elazar said:** נֶחְלְקוּ לְשָׁלֹשׁ כִּיתּוֹת – Although everyone agreed to build a tower,[11] **they split into three groups** with regard to their

NOTES

1. Apparently, the Jews had a petition to present to Caesar and they needed to win his favor through their gift. They therefore chose a messenger who was extremely virtuous and would merit Divine assistance (*R' Avigdor Miller*).

The Gemara in *Taanis* (21a) relates some of the miracles that commonly occurred to Nachum ish Gam Zu.

2. This detail is added in *Taanis* (21a), where this incident is also recounted.

3. The parallel text in *Taanis* indicates that Nachum discovered the substitution before setting out from the inn, but with the words *gam zu letovah* on his lips, he delivered the chest full of dirt to Caesar. Some commentators emend the text in *Taanis* to conform with the version cited here, since it seems unlikely that Nachum would knowingly deliver a chest full of dirt to Caesar (see *Gevuras Ari, Eitz Yosef* and *Dikdukei Soferim* to *Taanis* 21a). However, see *Margaliyos HaYam* for an explanation of the unemended version cited in *Taanis*.

4. The parallel text in *Taanis* states that Caesar wanted to kill all the Jews.

5. *Taanis* 21a.

6. According to the Scriptural account, the Generation of the Dispersion said: *Come, let us build ourselves a city, and a tower with its top in the heavens, and let us make a name for ourselves, lest we be dispersed across the whole earth* (*Genesis* 11:4). This passage does not indicate that they committed any sin, certainly not one that would cause them to lose their share in the World to Come (*Maharsha*). The Gemara therefore asks: What exactly was their sin? [*Be'er Sheva* suggests that since their sin was directed in a most egregious way against God Himself, as the Gemara explains below, the Torah chose to conceal it for the sake of God's honor. See there for another explanation as to why their sin is not explicitly stated.]

7. The commentators ascribe a primitive mentality to the Generation of the Dispersion. According to *Yad Ramah*, they thought that they could actually create an opening in that part of the sky where the rainwater was located, thus allowing it to leak out moderately and continuously. They hoped thereby to assure themselves a constant light rainfall without having to pray to God for rain. Thus, their purpose was to make themselves independent of God.

Maharsha and *Eitz Yosef* explain that they desired to rebel against God, but were afraid that He would punish them with a second Flood [they did not rely on His oath (*Genesis* 9:11) never to inundate and destroy the world again]. Hence, they sought to create an opening in the sky to allow the rainwater to drain out, so that God could not bring another Flood. They would henceforth be able to sin with impunity.

8. This expression is a reference to R' Yose bar Chanina; see above, 17b.

9. See *Genesis* 11:2.

10. There is a question as to whether the word אֶלָּא, *rather,* belongs in the text. Since that word signals the statement of a new or revised opinion, its inclusion here would mean that because of the objection raised against the first explanation (i.e. that of the scholars of R' Sheila's academy), R' Yirmiyah is now advancing an altogether different interpretation. This is the position of *Yad Ramah*. The opposite position is taken by *Be'er Sheva*, who – like *Dikdukei Soferim* – deletes אֶלָּא from the text. He therefore maintains that R' Yirmiyah is merely adding to the first explanation. For a discussion of this opinion, see note 14 below.

11. I.e. *not* for purposes of reaching the sky, as the scholars of R' Sheila's academy held, but in order to dwell atop the tower (*Yad Ramah*). [Hence, it was unnecessary to locate the tower on a mountaintop.]

מאן נשדר בהדי נחום איש גם זו דמלומד בנסים הוא כי מטא לההוא דיורא בעא למיבת אמרי ליה מאי איכא בהדך אמר להו קא מובילנא כרגא לקיסר קמו בליליא שרינהו לסיפטיה ושקלו כל דהוה גביה ומלנהו עפרא כי מטא להתם אישתכח עפרא אמר אחוכי קא מחייכי בי יהודאי אפקוהו למקטליה אמר גם זו לטובה אתא אליהו ואידמי להו כחד מינייהו אמר להו דילמא האי עפרא מעפרא דאברהם אבינו הוא דהוה שדי עפרא הוו חרבי גילי הוו גירי בדוק ואשכחו הכי הוה מחוזא דלא הוו קא יכלי ליה למיכבשיה שדו מההוא עפרא עליה וכבשוה עיילוהו לבי גנזא אמרי שקול דניחא לך מלייה לסיפטא דהבא כי הדר אתא אמרו ליה הנך דיורי מאי אמטית לבי מלכא אמר להו מאי דשקלי מהכא אמטאי להתם שקלי אינהו אמטו להתם קטלינהו להנך דיורי: דור הפלגה אין להם חלק לעולם הבא וכו': מאי עבוד אמרי דבי רבי שילא (א) נבנה מגדל ונעלה לרקיע ונכה אותו בקרדומות כדי שיזובו מימיו א) מחכו עלה במערבא א"כ ליבנו אחד בטורא ב) (אלא) א"ר ירמיה בר אלעזר נחלקו לג' כיתות אחת אומרת נעלה ונשב שם ואחת אומרת נעלה ונעבוד עבודת כוכבים ואחת אומרת נעלה ונעשה מלחמה זו שאומרת נעלה ונשב שם הפיצם ה' וזו שאומרת נעלה ונעשה מלחמה נעשו קופים ורוחות ושידים ולילין וזו שאומרת נעלה ונעבוד עבודת כוכבים א) כי שם בלל ה' שפת כל הארץ תניא רבי נתן אומר כולם לשם עבודת כוכבים נתכוונו כתיב הכא ב) נעשה לנו שם וכתיב התם ג) ושם אלהים אחרים לא תזכירו מה להלן עבודת כוכבים אף כאן עבודת כוכבים אמר רבי יוחנן מגדל שליש נשרף שליש נבלע שליש קיים אמר רב אויר מגדל משכח אמר רב יוסף בבל ג) ובורסיף סימן רע לתורה מאי בורסיף אמר ר' אסי בור ד) שאפי: אנשי סדום אין להם חלק לעולם הבא וכו': ת"ר ה) אנשי סדום אין להן חלק לעולם הבא שנאמר ד) ואנשי סדום רעים וחטאים לה' מאד רעים בעוה"ז וחטאים לעולם הבא אמר רב יהודה רעים בגופן וחטאים בממונם רעים בגופן דכתיב ה) ואיך אעשה הרעה הגדולה הזאת וחטאתי לאלהים וחטאים בממונם דכתיב ו) והיה בך חטא לה' זו ברכת השם מאד שמתכוונים וחוטאים במתניתא תנא רעים בממונם וחטאים בגופן רעים בממונם דכתיב ו) ורעה עינך באחיך האביון וחטאים בגופן דכתיב ה) וחטאתי לאלהים לה' ז) זו ברכת השם מאד זו שפיכות דמים שנאמר ז) גם דם נקי שפך מנשה (בירושלים) הרבה מאד [וגו'] ח) ת"ר אנשי סדום לא נתגאו אלא בשביל טובה שהשפיע להם הקב"ה ומה כתיב בהם ח) ארץ ממנה יצא לחם ותחתיה נהפך כמו אש מקום ספיר אבניה ועפרות זהב לו נתיב לא ידעו עיט ולא שזפתו עין איה לא הדריכוהו בני שחץ לא עדה עליו שחל אמרו וכי מאחר שארץ ממנה יצא לחם ועפרות זהב לו למה לנו עוברי דרכים שאין באים אלינו אלא לחסרינו [מממוננו] בואו ונשכח תורת רגל מארצנו שנאמר ט) פרץ נחל מעם גר הנשכחים מני רגל דלו מאנוש נעו דרש רבא מאי דכתיב י) עד אנה תהותתו על איש תרצחו כולכם כקיר נטוי גדר הדחויה מלמד שהיו נותנין עיניהן בבעלי ממון ומושיבין אותו אצל קיר נטוי ודוחין אותו ובאים ונוטלין את ממונו דרש רבא מאי דכתיב כ) חתר בחשך בתים יומם חתמו למו לא (ראו) [ידעו] אור מלמד שהיו נותנים עיניהם בבעלי ממון ומפקידים אצלו אפרסמון ומניחים אותו בבית גנזיהם לערב באים ומריחין אותו ככלב שנא' ל) ישובו לערב יהמו ככלב ויסובבו עיר ובאים וחותרים שם ונוטלין אותו ממון [א] מ) ערום ט) הלכו מבלי לבוש ואין כסות בקרה נ) חמור יתומים ינהגו יחבלו שור אלמנה ס) גבולות ישיגו עדר גזלו וירעו ע) והוא לקברות יובל ועל גדיש ישקוד [ב] דרש ר' יוסי בציפורי אחתרין ההיא ליליא תלת מאה מחתרתא בציפורי אתו וקא מצערי ליה אמרו ליה יהבית אורחיה לגנבי אמר להו מי הוה ידענא דאתו גנבי י) כי קא נח נפשיה דרבי יוסי שפעי מרזבי דציפורי דמא [ג] אמרי כ) דאית ליה חד תורא מרעי חד יומא דלית ליה לירעי תרי יומי ההוא יתמא בר ארמלתא הבו ליה תורי למרעיה אזל שקלינהו וקטלינהו אמר להו

דאית

בהדי מאן. ביד מי נשלח: כי מטא לההוא דיירא. כשהגיע לאותו מלון: למיבת. ללון: שרינהו ל) לסיטפיה. התירו הארגזים והמרצופין ופתחום ונטלו כל מה שבתוכו: אחוכי. מלאכי: הנך דיורי. אותן בני הכפרים: א"כ ליבנו אחד בטורא. א"כ שבנו כדי לעלות לרקיע למה בנו אותו בבקעה היה להם לבנות על אחד ההרים: הפיצם ה'. פיזרם בכל העולם: שדים. יש להם צורת אדם ואוכלין ושותין כבני אדם מ): רוחין. בלי גוף וצורה: לילין. צורת אדם אלא שיש להם כנפים במסכת נדה (דף כד:): זו שאומרה נעבוד ע"ז כי שם בלל ה'. בלבל לשונם כדי שלא יהא אחד מכוון לדעת חבירו לעבוד ע"ז: שליש [נבלע]. נבלעו יסודותיה משוקעת היא בקרקע עד שליש ושליש של מעלה נשרף ושליש אמצעי קיים בקרקע ולא שיהא עומד באויר: אויר מגדל. מראש המגדל (כלומר) [כמו אוירה של עיר] מי שעומד סביב למגדל ורואה אוירה ומראה גובה שלו: משכח. שכן נגזר על אותו מקום שישכח ולכך הם עצמם שכחו את לשונם: בבל ובורסיף סימן רע לתורה. שמשכחין התלמוד מפני שעומדים באויר המגדל: למה נקרא שמה בורסיף בור שאפי. בור שנתרוקן מימיו כלומר משכח האדם כל מה שלומד: שאפי. כמו (ב"מ דף ס.) השופה את היין לשון (ירמיה מח) הורק מכלי אל כלי ומפני מה שמה בבל [שמשכחת] אמר רב יוסף כי שם בלל לפי שבלבל הקדוש ברוך הוא את לשונם לשם כך היא משכחת: סימן רע. כלומר שמס סימן שכחה היא: רעים בגופם. שטופים בזימה: השמר לך פן יהיה דבר עם לבבך בליעל וגו' והיה בך חטא. והיינו ממון: ארץ ממנה יצא לחם. ארץ שבעה וטובה היא: ותחתיה נהפך כמו אש. ואחר כן נהפכה: וכי מאחר שארץ ממנה יצא לחם. שיש לנו שיפוע לחם למה לנו עוברי דרכים: ונשכח. שלא יעברו עוברי דרכים בארצנו: פרץ. הקב"ה נחל גפרית ואש: מעם גר. ממקום הליכתו שהיה הולך למעלה והשליכו עליהם הנשכחים מני רגל ונתדלדלו (מאדם) [מארצם] ונעו לדראון: גר. קורנט"ל בלע"ז כמו (שמואל ב יד) מים הנגרים: תהותתו. תבקשו תרמיות ותואנות: תרצחו כולכם. ע"י קיר נטוי וגדר הדחויה: יומם חתמו למו. היום סותמים וסוגרין כאילו לא ידעו אור כלומר סותמין וחותמין: אפרסמון. שלהם להפקידו ביד בעלי ממון כדי שיהו מניחין פקדון שלהם בבית גנזיהם ובלילה מריחין האפרסמון וחותרין שם מנהגו של מפקיד צורר וחותם: דרש ר' יוסי. בי מדרשא חתר בחשך בתים: איחתרו תלת מאה מחתרתא. ע"י ריח אפרסמון שהיו מריחין ויודעין היכן מניחין ממונם: מי הוה ידענא דאתו גנבי ל"א מי הוה ידענא דגנבי אתון: שפעי מרזבי דציפורי דמא. דאדם גדול הוה ואיידי דאמר לעיל איחתרו מחתרתי בציפורי דאתרא דרבי יוסי התם הוה נקיט נמי הא מילתא דכי נח נפשיה כו' לאשמועינן דמצפורי הוה:

דאית

מסורת הש"ס

א) [לעיל יח: וש"נ], ב) ב"ש מ"ז, ג) [גירסת ב"ש בירשוף], ד) [גי' הערוך ערך ברסיף שפת], ה) [תוספתא פי"ג ע"ש], ו) [תוספ' פי"ג], ז) [תוספתא שם], ח) [תוספתא דסוטה פ"ג], ט) [נ"ל ילינו], י) [מ"ק כה:], כ) [נדה סט.], ל) [נ"ל לסיפטי'], מ) [חגיגה טז.].

הגהות הב"ח

(א) גמ' אמרי דבי ר' שילא אמרי נבנה:

הגהות הגר"א

[א] גמ' ערום. נרשם עליו אות ג: [ב] שם דרש רבי יוסי. נרשם על תיבת דרש אות א: [ג] שם אמרי דאית ליה חד. נרשם על תיבת אמרי אות ג':

ליקוטי רש"י

לסיפטיה. ארגז שלו. כחד מינייהו. כאחד משרי קיסר. מעפרא דאברהם הוא. כשנלחם עם המלכים. גילי. קשין [תענית כא.]. דור הפלגה אין להם חלק לעולם הבא. ומשם הפילם. למד שאין להם חלק לעולם הבא וכי אי זו קשה של דור המבול או של דור הפלגה אלו לא פשטו יד בעיקר ואלו פשטו יד בעיקר כביכול להלחם בו ואלו נשטפו ואלו לא נאבדו מן העולם אלא שדור המבול היו גזלנים והיתה מריבה ביניהם לכך נאבדו ואלו היו נוהגים אהבה וריעות ביניהם שנאמר שפה אחת ודברים אחדים למדת ששנוי המחלוקת וגדול השלום [בראשית יא, ט]. נחלקו לשלש כיתות. ודברים אחדים. באו בעצה אחת ואמרו לא כל הימנו שיבור לו את העליונים נעלה לרקיע ונעשה עמו מלחמה דבר אחר על יחידו של עולם [דבר אחר ודברים אחדים אמרו אחת לאלף ושש מאות חמשים ושש שנים הרקיע מתמוטט כשם שעשה בימי המבול בואו ונעשה לו סמוכות] [בראשית יא, א]. בבל ובורסיף. ובורסיף סמוך לבבל ואינן בני תורה כדאמרינן מאי בורסיף בור ששפו את מימיו ולא נשתייר בו כלום [סוכה לד:]. וחטאתי לאלהים. בני נח נצטוו על העריות [בראשית לט, ט]. ארץ אשר ממנה יצא לחם. נהפך מקומה כמו אש. מקום ספיר. היו אבניה. לא ידעו עיט. לא עבר עליהן חיל של ליסטין. ולא שזפתו עין איה. לפי שהיא רואה יותר משאר עופות ולכך נקרא' ראה שהיא עומדת בבבל ורואה נבילו' בארץ ישראל כך מפורש באגדת (חולין סג ע"א) כלומר לא חפרוה מרגלים. לא עדה עליו. עבר כדמתרגמינן אשר עבר בין הבתרים (בראשית טו) (נ"ל הגזרים וע' בתרגום) דעדא. פרץ נחל. על סדום ועמורה נחלי אש וגפרית. מעם גר. ממקום שהוא נובע ונוגר. הנשכחים מני רגל. אלו אנשי סדום ששיכחו תורת רגלי אורחים מארצם שהיו משכיבים האורח במטה אם היה ארוך יותר מקטעין רגליו ואם היה קצר מאריכין אותו כך מפורש באגדה. דלו. ע"י פריצת נחל זה ומאנוש נעו [איוב כח]. עיט. הוא עוף ועל שם שהוא עט ושואף הנבלות (איוב ט, כו) לטוש עלי אוכל, כמו (ש"א טו, יט) ותעט אל השלל [בראשית טו, יא]. עין איה. והראה ואת האיה וגו' היא ראה היא איה היא דיה ולמה נקרא שמה ראה שרואה ביותר [דברים יד, יג]. שחל. הארי גדול והשחל בינוני והכפיר קטן [איוב ד, י]. תהותתו. מנחם פי' מגזרת התיו לאכלה (ירמיה י"ב) ויתא ראשי עם (דברים ל"ג) עד אנה תאספו על איש ול"נ שיש לפותרו לשון הוות ויהא ה"א ותי"ו שורש כאשר יאמר מן מת מות כך נאמר מן יסוד הת הות ולשון רבים הוות והוא לשון מחשבת שבר ותרמית [תהלים סב, ד]. יומם חתמו. ורבותינו פירשו יומם חתמו למו ביום היו עושים סימנים היכן מרתפו של בית והיכן גנזיו של עשיר שהיו מפקידין אפרסמון אצל בעלי בתים עשירים ויודעים הם שיניחנו בבית גנזיו ובלילה מריחין והולכים שם וחותרים שם [איוב כד, יז]. הלכו. הם הלכוהו בלי לבוש. מבלי לבוש. שנטלו כסויו. חמור יתומים ינהגו. ועושין כל רעות האמורות בענין סוף דבר ואלוה לא ישים תפלה להודיעם עונם ולהמציאם גמולם. גבולות ישיגו. אותן שדרכן להסיג גבולות שהן קובעין שדות כנגד שדות אחרים ובלילה הם מרבים גבולותיהם שהיו עושים גדריהם בלילה בתוך תחומם. עדר גזלו וירעו. לעצמן [איוב כד, ב]. והוא לקברות יובל. סופו יובל לקבר. ועל גדיש ישקוד. כשהוא נקבר בשדות אצל הגדישים [איוב כא, לב]. לירעי תרי יומי. כל בהמות העיר. אזל יתמא. שלא היה לו שור ולקחום לרעות בהמותיהן ב' ימים [נד סט].

תורה אור השלם

א) עַל כֵּן קָרָא שְׁמָהּ בָּבֶל כִּי שָׁם בָּלַל יְיָ שְׂפַת כָּל הָאָרֶץ וּמִשָּׁם הֱפִיצָם יְיָ עַל פְּנֵי כָּל הָאָרֶץ: [בראשית יא, ט]

ב) וַיֹּאמְרוּ הָבָה נִבְנֶה לָּנוּ עִיר וּמִגְדָּל וְרֹאשׁוֹ בַשָּׁמַיִם וְנַעֲשֶׂה לָּנוּ שֵׁם פֶּן נָפוּץ עַל פְּנֵי כָל הָאָרֶץ: [בראשית יא, ד]

ג) וּבְכֹל אֲשֶׁר אָמַרְתִּי אֲלֵיכֶם תִּשָּׁמֵרוּ וְשֵׁם אֱלֹהִים אֲחֵרִים לֹא תַזְכִּירוּ לֹא יִשָּׁמַע עַל פִּיךָ: [שמות כג, יג]

ד) וְאַנְשֵׁי סְדֹם רָעִים וְחַטָּאִים לַייָ מְאֹד: [בראשית יג, יג]

ה) אֵינֶנּוּ גָדוֹל בַּבַּיִת הַזֶּה מִמֶּנִּי וְלֹא חָשַׂךְ מִמֶּנִּי מְאוּמָה כִּי אִם אוֹתָךְ בַּאֲשֶׁר אַתְּ אִשְׁתּוֹ וְאֵיךְ אֶעֱשֶׂה הָרָעָה הַגְּדֹלָה הַזֹּאת וְחָטָאתִי לֵאלֹהִים: [בראשית לט, ט]

ו) הִשָּׁמֶר לְךָ פֶּן יִהְיֶה דָבָר עִם לְבָבְךָ בְלִיַּעַל לֵאמֹר קָרְבָה שְׁנַת הַשֶּׁבַע שְׁנַת הַשְּׁמִטָּה וְרָעָה עֵינְךָ בְּאָחִיךָ הָאֶבְיוֹן וְלֹא תִתֵּן לוֹ וְקָרָא עָלֶיךָ אֶל יְיָ וְהָיָה בְךָ חֵטְא: [דברים טו, ט]

ז) וְגַם דָּם נָקִי שָׁפַךְ מְנַשֶּׁה הַרְבֵּה מְאֹד עַד אֲשֶׁר מִלֵּא אֶת יְרוּשָׁלִַם פֶּה לָפֶה לְבַד מֵחַטָּאתוֹ אֲשֶׁר הֶחֱטִיא אֶת יְהוּדָה לַעֲשׂוֹת הָרַע בְּעֵינֵי יְיָ: [מלכים ב' כא, טז]

ח) אֶרֶץ מִמֶּנָּה יֵצֵא לָחֶם וְתַחְתֶּיהָ נֶהְפַּךְ כְּמוֹ אֵשׁ: מְקוֹם סַפִּיר אֲבָנֶיהָ וְעַפְרֹת זָהָב לוֹ: נָתִיב לֹא יְדָעוֹ עָיִט וְלֹא שְׁזָפַתּוּ עֵין אַיָּה: לֹא הִדְרִיכֻהוּ בְנֵי שָׁחַץ לֹא עָדָה עָלָיו שָׁחַל: [איוב כח, ה-ח]

ט) פָּרַץ נַחַל מֵעִם גָּר הַנִּשְׁכָּחִים מִנִּי רָגֶל דַּלּוּ מֵאֱנוֹשׁ נָעוּ: [איוב כח, ד]

י) עַד אָנָה תְּהוֹתְתוּ עַל אִישׁ תְּרָצְּחוּ כֻלְּכֶם כְּקִיר נָטוּי גָּדֵר הַדְּחוּיָה: [תהלים סב, ד]

כ) חָתַר בַּחֹשֶׁךְ בָּתִּים יוֹמָם חִתְּמוּ לָמוֹ לֹא יָדְעוּ אוֹר: [איוב כד, טז]

ל) יָשׁוּבוּ לָעֶרֶב יֶהֱמוּ כַכָּלֶב וִיסוֹבְבוּ עִיר: [תהלים נט, ז]

מ) עָרוֹם יָלִינוּ מִבְּלִי לְבוּשׁ וְאֵין כְּסוּת בַּקָּרָה: [איוב כד, ז]

נ) חֲמוֹר יְתוֹמִים יִנְהָגוּ יַחְבְּלוּ שׁוֹר אַלְמָנָה: [איוב כד, ג]

ס) גְּבֻלוֹת יַשִּׂיגוּ עֵדֶר גָּזְלוּ וַיִּרְעוּ: [איוב כד, ב]

ע) וְהוּא לִקְבָרוֹת יוּבָל וְעַל גָּדִישׁ יִשְׁקוֹד: [איוב כא, לב]

objectives: אַחַת אוֹמֶרֶת נַעֲלֶה וְנֵשֵׁב שָׁם – **One** group **said, "Let us ascend** to the top of the tower **and reside there";**[12] וְאַחַת אוֹמֶרֶת נַעֲלֶה וְנַעֲבוֹד עֲבוֹדַת כּוֹכָבִים – **one** other group **said, "Let us ascend** the tower **and worship idols";**[13] וְאַחַת אוֹמֶרֶת נַעֲלֶה וְנַעֲשֶׂה מִלְחָמָה – **and one** other group **said, "Let us ascend and wage war."**[14] זו שֶׁאוֹמֶרֶת נַעֲלֶה וְנֵשֵׁב שָׁם – **That** group **which said, "Let us ascend and reside there,"** הֱפִיצָם ה׳ – **God dispersed** around the world.[15] וְזוּ שֶׁאוֹמֶרֶת נַעֲלֶה וְנַעֲשֶׂה מִלְחָמָה – **That** group **which said, "Let us ascend and wage war,"** נַעֲשׂוּ קוֹפִים וְרוּחוֹת וְשֵׁידִים וְלִילִין – **became apes,** ***ruchos, sheidim*** **and** ***lilin.***[16] וְזוּ שֶׁאוֹמֶרֶת נַעֲלֶה וְנַעֲבוֹד עֲבוֹדַת כּוֹכָבִים – **And** regarding **that** group **which said, "Let us ascend and worship idols,"** "כִּי־שָׁם בָּלַל ה׳ שְׂפַת כָּל־הָאָרֶץ" – Scripture states: ***For it was there that God confused the language of the whole earth.***[17]

Another opinion regarding the sin of the Generation of the Dispersion:

תַּנְיָא – **It was taught in a Baraisa:** רַבִּי נָתָן אוֹמֵר – R' NASSAN SAYS: כּוּלָּם לְשֵׁם עֲבוֹדַת כּוֹכָבִים נִתְכַּוְּונוּ – ALL OF [THE MEMBERS OF THE GENERATION OF THE DISPERSION] INTENDED to build the tower FOR PURPOSES OF IDOLATRY, כְּתִיב הָכָא "נַעֲשֶׂה־לָּנוּ שֵׁם" – as is evident from Scripture: IT IS WRITTEN HERE[18] that they said: *Come, let us build ourselves a city, and a tower with its top in the heavens, and* LET US MAKE A NAME (SHEM) FOR OURSELVES, וּכְתִיב הָתָם "וְשֵׁם אֱלֹהִים אֲחֵרִים לֹא תַזְכִּירוּ" – AND IT IS WRITTEN THERE:[19] *THE NAME (SHEM) OF STRANGE GODS YOU SHALL NOT MENTION.* מָה לְהַלָּן עֲבוֹדַת כּוֹכָבִים – JUST AS OVER THERE the word *shem* refers to IDOLATRY, אַף כָּאן עֲבוֹדַת כּוֹכָבִים – SO HERE in the story of the Generation of the Dispersion the word *shem* refers ALSO to IDOLATRY. Scripture thus indicates that these people built the tower for the purpose of worshiping idols.

The Gemara discusses the fate of the Tower of Babel:

אָמַר רַבִּי יוֹחָנָן – **R' Yochanan said:** מִגְדָּל שְׁלִישׁ נִשְׂרַף – As to what became of **the tower, one third** of it (i.e. the top third) **was burned,** שְׁלִישׁ נִבְלַע – **one third was swallowed up,**[20] שְׁלִישׁ קַיָּים – and **one third remains.**[21]

The Gemara describes the legacy of the tower episode:

אָמַר רַב – **Rav said:** אֲוִיר מִגְדָּל מְשַׁכֵּחַ – **The airspace of the tower causes forgetfulness** even today.[22] אָמַר רַב יוֹסֵף – **Rav**

NOTES

12. The first group desired to dwell in a high place for security purposes – their community would be difficult to conquer (*Yad Ramah*).

13. It was the practice of ancient idolaters to build their altars in high places. A great tower would well serve that practice (*Yad Ramah*).

14. The tower would be a commanding position from which to wage war against their human enemies. Their intent was not to fight against God, however (*Yad Ramah*). *Be'er Sheva* explains that this group opposed the Divine decree (*Genesis* 1:28, *Isaiah* 45:18) that man disperse to and settle all parts of the earth. By building an imposing fortress-city, they sought to rule over all the people and prevent them from leaving this central location.

Thus far, we have elucidated the Gemara according to the commentary of *Yad Ramah. Maharsha* maintains that although in R' Yirmiyah's view the tower was not built to reach the celestial source of rainwater, the Generation of the Dispersion was nonetheless very much motivated by the recent cataclysmic Flood. The first group, fearing a second deluge, sought the safety of a dwelling that would tower above the floodwater. The second group, which desired to practice idolatry, built the tower as a hedge against Divine punishment. That is, they realized that the first Flood was caused by interpersonal sins such as robbery (see *Genesis* 6:13 with *Rashi*), and concluded that had their ancestors sinned only against God He would not have destroyed the world. They therefore intended for everyone to dwell in the vicinity of the tower in one harmonious brotherhood, thereby allowing them to worship idols with impunity (see also *Bereishis Rabbah* 38:6). The third group planned to wage war against God Himself from atop the tower (see ibid.), either figuratively (*Yefei To'ar*) or, in their folly, literally (*Maharzu*). See also *Tanchuma (Genesis* 8).

Be'er Sheva, based on *Midrash Tanchuma,* disagrees with *Yad Ramah,* maintaining that the word אֶלָּא should be deleted from the text of the Gemara (see above, note 10). According to *Be'er Sheva,* then, R' Yirmiyah agrees that the tower was built to facilitate some kind of assault on the heavens, as the scholars of R' Sheila's academy maintain. R' Yirmiyah merely explains what the three groups wanted to do once they reached the heavens: One group actually sought to take up residence there; and the second group desired to bring an idol with them into heaven and worship it there, as a kind of spiritual war against the Almighty; and the third group, in its folly, wanted to attack God physically. (This interpretation follows *Osios DeR' Akiva,* cited in *Eitz Yosef.*)

See *Ramban, Rabbeinu Bachya* and *Abarbanel* for other interpretations of this episode.

15. See *Genesis* 11:9. This group, as well as the other two, was punished measure for measure (*Maharsha*).

16. *Rashi* explains that *ruchos, sheidim* and *lilin* are three types of unearthly creatures. *Ruchos* (spirits) have neither body nor form, *sheidim* (demons) have human form and eat and drink as people do, and *lilin* have human form but also have wings (see *Niddah* 24b; cf. *Chagigah* 16a, which states that *sheidim* also have wings).

Maharal explains that in daring to attack God the people showed that they were no longer worthy of the צֶלֶם אֱלֹהִים, *the image of God* in which they were created (see *Genesis* 1:27) and which demonstrates their attachment and connection to their Creator. For it is stated (*Avos* 3:18), "Beloved [to God] is man, for he is created in God's image." One who wages war with God, however, is perforce no longer His "beloved." Hence, he is stripped of the Divine image, which demonstrates attachment to the Creator, and is given one of the grotesque forms mentioned in the Gemara. (See also *Maharsha* and *Margaliyos HaYam*).

17. *Genesis* 11:9. By rendering the language of one person unintelligible to another, God prevented mankind from uniting to forge a single, universal idolatrous cult (*Rashi*). Because the people did not desire to cleave to God, Who is One, but preferred to form a separate unity for idolatrous worship, God completely alienated one from another by depriving them of a common language (*Maharal*).

18. Ibid. v. 4.

19. *Exodus* 23:13.

20. I.e. the bottom third of the tower sank into the ground, leaving the middle third to rest upon the ground (*Rashi*).

21. *Maharal* explains that the three parts of the tower correspond to the three groups of builders mentioned above. The third of the tower corresponding to the group that sought to attack God sank into oblivion, a fate that later befell another contentious cadre (Korach and his followers). The third corresponding to the group that wanted to worship idols was burned and utterly destroyed, the proper fate for idols, as it is stated with regard to the sin of idolatry: *For HASHEM, your God – He is a consuming fire, a jealous God (Deuteronomy* 4:24). Finally, the third corresponding to those who wished to reside in heaven remains, for theirs was a misguided rather than an evil design. [Other commentators explain that the middle third of the tower was left standing as a warning to future generations who would contemplate similar action (*Be'er Sheva; R' Yaakov Emden*).] Cf. *Maharsha*.

22. That is, one who stands next to the remnant of the tower, up to a distance where he sees the airspace above the tower while still looking up (*Rashi*), or, alternatively, one who stands even farther away, in the area upon which the tower would have cast a shadow had it not partially sunk and partially burned (*Maharsha*), is stricken with forgetfulness. See *Margaliyos HaYam*, who suggests that the area discussed here is the distance from the base of the tower equal to its height.

At the time they were building the tower, the Generation of the Dispersion spoke a common language (*Genesis* 11:1). God halted the building of the tower by endowing its site with the power to cause forgetfulness. He thus caused the people to forget their common language (ibid. 7), and as a result of this loss of ability to communicate they were unable to continue building (see *Rashi*).

Even today the site of the tower has the power to cause forgetfulness. *Yad Ramah* explains that God made this power permanent in order to prevent other groups from returning to the site and resuming construction of the tower.

Maharal writes that Rav's dictum, "The site of the tower causes

מאן נשדר נשדר בהדי נחום איש גם זו דמלומד בנסים הוא כי מטא לההוא דיורא בעא למיבת אמרי ליה מאי איכא בהדך אמר להו קא מובילנא כרגא לקיסר קמו בליליא שרינהו לסיפטיה ושקלו כל דהוה גביה ומלנהו עפרא כי מטא להתם אישתכח עפרא אמר אחוכי קא מחייכי בי יהודאי אפקודו למקטליה אמר גם זו לטובה אתא אליהו ואידמי להו כחד מינייהו אמר להו דילמא האי עפרא מעפרא דאברהם אבינו הוא דהוה שדי עפרא הוו חרבי גילי הוו גירי בדוק ואשכחו הכי הוה מחוזא דלא הוו קא יכלי ליה למיכבשיה שדו מההוא עפרא עליה וכבשוה עיילוהו לבי גנזא אמרי שקול דניחא לך מלייה לסיפטא דהבא כי הדר אתא אמרו ליה הנך דיורי מאי אמטית לבי מלכא אמר להו מאי דשקלי מהכא אמטאי להתם שקלי אינהו אמטו להתם קטלינהו להנך דיורי: דור הפלגה אין להם חלק לעולם הבא וכו': מאי עבוד אמרי דבי רבי שילא (א) נבנה מגדל ונעלה לרקיע ונכה אותו בקרדומות כדי שיזובו מימיו (א) מחכו עלה במערבא א"כ ליבנו אחד בטורא (ב) (אלא) א"ר ירמיה בר אלעזר נחלקו לג' כיתות אחת אומרת נעלה ונשב שם ואחת אומרת נעלה ונעבוד עבודת כוכבים ואחת אומרת נעלה ונעשה מלחמה זו שאומרת נעלה ונשב שם הפיצם ה' וזו שאומרת נעלה ונעשה מלחמה נעשו קופים ורוחות ושידים ולילין וזו שאומרת נעלה ונעבוד עבודת כוכבים (א) כי שם בלל ה' שפת כל הארץ תניא רבי נתן אומר כולם לשם עבודת כוכבים נתכוונו כתיב הכא (ב) נעשה לנו שם וכתיב התם (ג) ושם אלהים אחרים לא תזכירו מה להלן עבודת כוכבים אף כאן עבודת כוכבים אמר רבי יוחנן מגדל שליש נשרף שליש נבלע שליש קיים אמר רב אויר מגדל משכח אמר רב יוסף בבל (ג) ובורסיף סימן רע לתורה מאי בורסיף אמר ר' אסי בור (ד) שאפי: אנשי סדום אין להם חלק לעולם הבא וכו': ת"ר (ה) אנשי סדום אין להן חלק לעולם הבא שנאמר (ד) ואנשי סדום רעים וחטאים לה' מאד רעים בעוה"ז וחטאים לעולם הבא אמר רב יהודה רעים בגופן וחטאים בממונם רעים בגופן דכתיב (ה) ואיך אעשה הרעה הגדולה הזאת וחטאתי לאלהים וחטאים בממונם דכתיב (ו) והיה בך חטא לה' זו ברכת השם מאד שמתכוונים וחוטאים במתניתא תנא (ו) רעים בממונם וחטאים בגופן רעים בממונם דכתיב (ו) ורעה עינך באחיך האביון וחטאים בגופן דכתיב (ה) וחטאתי לאלהים לה' (ז) זו ברכת השם מאד זו שפיכות דמים שנאמר (ז) גם דם נקי שפך מנשה (בירושלים) הרבה מאד [וגו'] (ח) ת"ר אנשי סדום לא נתגאו אלא בשביל טובה שהשפיע להם הקב"ה ומה כתיב בהם (ח) ארץ ממנה יצא לחם ותחתיה נהפך כמו אש מקום ספיר אבניה ועפרות זהב לו נתיב לא ידעו עיט ולא שזפתו עין איה לא הדריכוהו בני שחץ לא עדה עליו שחל אמרו וכי מאחר שארץ ממנה יצא לחם ועפרות זהב לו למה לנו עוברי דרכים שאין באים אלינו אלא לחסרינו [מממוננו] בואו ונשכח תורת רגל מארצנו שנאמר (ט) פרץ נחל מעם גר הנשכחים מני רגל דלו מאנוש נעו דרש רבא מאי דכתיב (י) עד אנה תהותתו על איש תרצחו כולכם כקיר נטוי גדר הדחויה מלמד שהיו נותנין עיניהן בבעלי ממון ומושיבין אותו אצל קיר נטוי ודוחין אותו עליו ובאים ונוטלין את ממונו דרש רבא מאי דכתיב (כ) חתר בחשך בתים יומם חתמו למו לא (ראו) [ידעו] אור מלמד שהיו נותנים עיניהם בבעלי ממון ומפקידים אצלו אפרסמון ומניחים אותו בבית גנזיהם לערב באים ומריחין אותו ככלב שנא' (ל) ישובו לערב יהמו ככלב ויסובבו עיר ובאים וחותרים שם ונוטלין אותו ממון [א] (מ) ערום (ט) הלכו מבלי לבוש ואין כסות בקרה (נ) חמור יתומים ינהגו יחבלו שור אלמנה (ס) גבולות ישיגו עדר גזלו וירעו (ע) והוא לקברות יובל ועל גדיש ישקוד [ב] דרש ר' יוסי בציפורי אחתרין ההיא ליליא תלת מאה מחתרתא בציפורי אתו וקא מצערי ליה אמרו ליה יהבית אורחיה לגנבי אמר להו מי הוה ידענא דאתו גנבי (י) כי קא נח נפשיה דרבי יוסי שפעי מרזבי דציפורי דמא [ג] אמרי (כ) דאית ליה חד תורא מרעי חד יומא דלית ליה לירעי תרי יומי ההוא יתמא בר ארמלתא הבו ליה תורי למרעיה אזל שקלינהו וקטלינהו אמר להו

דאית

רש"י

בהדי מאן. ביד מי נשלח: כי מטא לההוא דיירא. כשהגיע לאותו מלון: למיבת. ללון: שרינהו (ל) לסיטפיה. התירו הארגזים והמרצופין ופתחום ונטלו כל מה שבתוכו: אחוכי. מלחקי: הנך דיורי. אותן בני הכפרים: א"כ ליבנו אחד בטורא. א"כ שבנו כדי לעלות לרקיע למה בנו אותו בבקעה היה להם לבנות על אחד ההרים: הפיצם ה'. פיזרם בכל העולם: שדים. יש להם צורת אדם ואוכלין ושותין כבני אדם (מ): רוחין. בלי גוף וצורה: לילין. צורת אדם אלא שיש להם כנפים במסכת נדה (דף כד:): זו שאומרה נעבוד ע"ז כי שם בלל ה'. בלבל לשונם כדי שלא יהא אחד מכוון לדעת חבירו לעבוד ע"ז: שליש [נבלע]. נבלעו יסודותיה משוקעת היא בקרקע עד שליש ושליש של מעלה נשרף ושליש אמצעי קיים בקרקע ולא שיהא עומד באויר: אויר מגדל. מראש המגדל (כלומר) [כמו אוירה של עיר] מי שעומד סביב למגדל ורואה אוירה ומראה גובה שלו: משכח. שכן נגזר על אותו מקום שישכח ולכך הם עצמם שכחו את לשונם: בבל ובורסיף סימן רע לתורה. שמשכחין התלמוד מפני שעומדים באויר המגדל: למה נקרא שמה בורסיף בור שאפי. בור שנתרוקן מימיו כלומר משכח האדם כל מה שלומד: שאפי. כמו (ב"מ דף ס.) השופה את היין לשון (ירמיה מח) הורק מכלי אל כלי ומפני מה שמה בבל [שמשכחת] אמר רב יוסף כי שם בלל לפי שבלבל הקדוש ברוך הוא את לשונם לשם כך היא משכחת: סימן רע. כלומר שמם סימן שכחה היא: רעים בגופם. שטופים בזימה: השמר לך פן יהיה דבר עם לבבך בליעל וגו' והיה בך חטא. והיינו ממון: ארץ ממנה יצא לחם. ארץ שבעה וטובה היא: ותחתיה נהפך כמו אש. ואחר כן נהפכה: וכי מאחר שארץ ממנה יצא לחם. שיש לנו שיפוע לחם למה לנו עוברי דרכים: ונשכח. שלא יעברו עוברי דרכים בארצנו: פרץ. הקב"ה נחל גפרית ואש: מעם גר. ממקום הליכתו שהיה הולך למעלה והשליכו עליהם הנשכחים מני רגל ונתדלדלו (מאדם) [מארצם] ונעו לדראון: גר. קורנט"ל בלע"ז כמו (שמואל ב יד) מים הנגרים: תהותתו. תבקשו תרמיות ותואנות: תרצחו כולכם. ע"י קיר נטוי וגדר הדחויה: יומם חתמו למו. היום סותמים וסוגרין כאילו לא ידעו אור כלומר סותמין וחותמין: אפרסמון. שלהם להפקידו ביד בעלי ממון כדי שיהו מניחין פקדון שלהם בבית גנזיהם ובלילה מריחין האפרסמון וחותרין שם מנהגו של מפקיד לורר וחותם: דרש ר' יוסי. בי מדרשא חתר בחשך בתים: איחתרו תלת מאה מחתרתא. ע"י ריח אפרסמון שהיו מריחין ויודעין היכן מניחין ממונם: מי הוה ידענא דאתו גנבי ל"א מי הוה ידענא דגנבי אתון: שפעי מרזבי דציפורי דמא. דאדם גדול הוה ואיידי דאמר לעיל איחתרו מחתרתי בציפורי דאתרא דרבי יוסי התם הוה נקיט נמי הא מילתא דכי נח נפשיה כו' לאשמועינן דמציפורי הוה:

דאית

תורה אור השלם

א) עַל כֵּן קָרָא שְׁמָהּ בָּבֶל כִּי שָׁם בָּלַל יְיָ שְׂפַת כָּל הָאָרֶץ וּמִשָּׁם הֱפִיצָם יְיָ עַל פְּנֵי כָּל הָאָרֶץ: [בראשית יא, ט]

ב) וַיֹּאמְרוּ הָבָה נִבְנֶה לָּנוּ עִיר וּמִגְדָּל וְרֹאשׁוֹ בַשָּׁמַיִם וְנַעֲשֶׂה לָּנוּ שֵׁם פֶּן נָפוּץ עַל פְּנֵי כָל הָאָרֶץ: [בראשית יא, ד]

ג) וּבְכֹל אֲשֶׁר אָמַרְתִּי אֲלֵיכֶם תִּשָּׁמֵרוּ וְשֵׁם אֱלֹהִים אֲחֵרִים לֹא תַזְכִּירוּ לֹא יִשָּׁמַע עַל פִּיךָ: [שמות כג, יג]

ד) וְאַנְשֵׁי סְדֹם רָעִים וְחַטָּאִים לַייָ מְאֹד: [בראשית יג, יג]

ה) אֵינֶנּוּ גָדוֹל בַּבַּיִת הַזֶּה מִמֶּנִּי וְלֹא חָשַׂךְ מִמֶּנִּי מְאוּמָה כִּי אִם אוֹתָךְ בַּאֲשֶׁר אַתְּ אִשְׁתּוֹ וְאֵיךְ אֶעֱשֶׂה הָרָעָה הַגְּדֹלָה הַזֹּאת וְחָטָאתִי לֵאלֹהִים: [בראשית לט, ט]

ו) הִשָּׁמֶר לְךָ פֶּן יִהְיֶה דָבָר עִם לְבָבְךָ בְלִיַּעַל לֵאמֹר קָרְבָה שְׁנַת הַשֶּׁבַע שְׁנַת הַשְּׁמִטָּה וְרָעָה עֵינְךָ בְּאָחִיךָ הָאֶבְיוֹן וְלֹא תִתֵּן לוֹ וְקָרָא עָלֶיךָ אֶל יְיָ וְהָיָה בְךָ חֵטְא: [דברים טו, ט]

ז) וְגַם דָּם נָקִי שָׁפַךְ מְנַשֶּׁה הַרְבֵּה מְאֹד עַד אֲשֶׁר מִלֵּא אֶת יְרוּשָׁלַיִם פֶּה לָפֶה לְבַד מֵחַטָּאתוֹ אֲשֶׁר הֶחֱטִיא אֶת יְהוּדָה לַעֲשׂוֹת הָרַע בְּעֵינֵי יְיָ: [מלכים ב' כא, טז]

ח) אֶרֶץ מִמֶּנָּה יֵצֵא לָחֶם וְתַחְתֶּיהָ נֶהְפַּךְ כְּמוֹ אֵשׁ: מְקוֹם סַפִּיר אֲבָנֶיהָ וְעַפְרֹת זָהָב לוֹ: נָתִיב לֹא יְדָעוֹ עָיִט וְלֹא שְׁזָפַתּוּ עֵין אַיָּה: לֹא הִדְרִיכֻהוּ בְנֵי שָׁחַץ לֹא עָדָה עָלָיו שָׁחַל: [איוב כח, ה-ח]

ט) פָּרַץ נַחַל מֵעִם גָּר הַנִּשְׁכָּחִים מִנִּי רָגֶל דַּלּוּ מֵאֱנוֹשׁ נָעוּ: [איוב כח, ד]

י) עַד אָנָה תְּהוֹתְתוּ עַל אִישׁ תְּרָצְּחוּ כֻלְּכֶם כְּקִיר נָטוּי גָּדֵר הַדְּחוּיָה: [תהלים סב, ד]

כ) חָתַר בַּחֹשֶׁךְ בָּתִּים יוֹמָם חִתְּמוּ לָמוֹ לֹא יָדְעוּ אוֹר: [איוב כד, טז]

ל) יָשׁוּבוּ לָעֶרֶב יֶהֱמוּ כַכָּלֶב וִיסוֹבְבוּ עִיר: [תהלים נט, ז]

מ) עָרוֹם יָלִינוּ מִבְּלִי לְבוּשׁ וְאֵין כְּסוּת בַּקָּרָה: [איוב כד, ז]

נ) חֲמוֹר יְתוֹמִים יִנְהָגוּ יַחְבְּלוּ שׁוֹר אַלְמָנָה: [איוב כד, ג]

ס) גְּבֻלוֹת יַשִּׂיגוּ עֵדֶר גָּזְלוּ וַיִּרְעוּ: [איוב כד, ב]

ע) וְהוּא לִקְבָרוֹת יוּבָל וְעַל גָּדִישׁ יִשְׁקוֹד: [איוב כא, לב]

מסורת הש"ס

א) [לעיל יז: וש"נ], ב) ב"ש מ"ז, ג) [גירסת ב"ש בירשוף], ד) [גי' הערוך ערך ברסיף שפת], ה) [תוספתא פי"ג ע"ש], ו) [תוספ' פי"ג], ז) [תוספתא שם], ח) [תוספתא דסוטה פ"ג], ט) [צ"ל ילינו], י) [מ"ק כה:], כ) [נדה סט.], ל) [צ"ל לסיפטי'], מ) [חגיגה טז.].

הגהות הב"ח

(א) גמ' אמרי דבי ר' שילא אמרי נבנה:

הגהות הגר"א

[א] גמ' ערום. נרשם עליו אות ג: [ב] שם דרש רבי יוסי. נרשם על תיבת דרש אות א: [ג] שם אמרי דאית ליה חד. נרשם על תיבת אמרי אות ג':

ליקוטי רש"י

לסיפטיה. ארגז שלו. כחד מינייהו. כאחד משרי קיסר. מעפרא דאברהם הוא. כשנלחם עם המלכים. גילי. קשין [תענית כא.]. דור הפלגה אין להם חלק לעולם הבא. ומשם הפיצם. למד שאין להם חלק לעולם הבא וכי אי זו קשה של דור המבול או של דור הפלגה אלו לא פשטו יד בעיקר ואלו פשטו יד בעיקר כביכול להלחם בו ואלו נשטפו ואלו לא נאבדו מן העולם אלא שדור המבול היו גזלנים והיתה מריבה ביניהם לכך נאבדו ואלו היו נוהגים אהבה וריעות ביניהם שנאמר שפה אחת ודברים אחדים למדת ששנוי המחלוקת וגדול השלום [בראשית יא, ט]. נחלקו לשלש כיתות. ודברים אחדים. באו בעצה אחת ואמרו לא כל הימנו שיבור לו את העליונים נעלה לרקיע ונעשה עמו מלחמה דבר אחר על יחידו של עולם [דבר אחר ודברים אחדים אמרו אחת לאלף ושש מאות חמשים ושש שנים הרקיע מתמוטט כשם שעשה בימי המבול בואו ונעשה לו סמוכות] [בראשית יא, א]. בבל ובורסיף. ובורסיף סמוך לבבל ואינן בני תורה כדאמרינן מאי בורסיף בור ששפו את מימיו ולא נשתייר בו כלום [סוכה לד:]. וחטאתי לאלהים. בני נח נצטוו על העריות [בראשית לט, ט]. ארץ אשר ממנה יצא לחם. נהפך מקומה כמו אש. מקום ספיר. היו אבניה. לא ידעו עיט. לא עבר עליהן חיל של ליסטין. ולא שזפתו עין איה. לפי שהיא רואה יותר משאר עופות ולכך נקרא' ראה שהיא עומדת בבבל ורואה נבילו' בארץ ישראל כך מפורש באגדת (חולין סג ע"א) כלומר לא חפרוה מרגלים. לא עדה עליו. עבר כדמתרגמינן אשר עבר בין הבתרים (בראשית טו) (צ"ל הגזרים וע' בתרגום) דעדא. פרץ נחל. על סדום ועמורה נחלי אש וגפרית. מעם גר. ממקום שהוא נובע ונוגר. הנשכחים מני רגל. אלו אנשי סדום ששכחו תורת רגלי אורחים מארצם שהיו משכיבים האורח במטה אם היה ארוך יותר מקטעין רגליו ואם היה קצר מאריכין אותו כך מפורש באגדה. דלו. ע"י פרצת נחל זה ומאנוש נעו [איוב כח]. עיט. הוא עוף ועל שם שהוא עט ושואף הנבלות (איוב ט, כו) לטוש עלי אוכל, כמו (ש"א טו, יט) ותעט אל השלל [בראשית טו, יא]. עין איה. והראה ואת האיה וגו' היא ראה היא איה היא דיה ולמה נקרא שמה ראה שרואה ביותר [דברים יד, יג]. שחל. הארי גדול והשחל בינוני והכפיר קטן [איוב ד, י]. תהותתו. מנחם פי' מגזרת התיו לאכלה (ירמיה י"ב) ויתא ראשי עם (דברים ל"ג) עד אנה תאספו על איש ול"נ שיש לפותרו לשון הוות ויהא ה"א ותי"ו שורש כאשר יאמר מן מת מות כך נאמר מן יסוד הת הות ולשון רבים הוות והוא לשון מחשבת שבר ותרמית [תהלים סב, ד]. יומם חתמו. ורבותינו פירשו יומם חתמו למו ביום היו עושים סימנים היכן מרתפו של בית והיכן גנזיו של עשיר שהיו מפקידין אפרסמון אצל בעלי בתים עשירים ויודעים הם שיניחנו בבית גנזיו ובלילה מריחין והולכים שם וחותרים שם [איוב כד, יז]. הלכו. הם הלכוהו בלי לבוש. מבלי לבוש. שנטלו כסותן. חמור יתומים ינהגו. ועושין כל רעות האמורות בענין סוף דבר ואלוה לא ישים תפלה להודיעם עוונם ולהמציאם גמולם. גבולות ישיגו. אותן שדרכן להשיג גבולות שהן קונין שדות כנגד שדות אחרים ובלילה הם מרגים גבולותיהם שהיו עושים גדריהם בלילה בתוך תחום. עדר גזלו וירעו. לעצמן [איוב כד עיי"ש]. והוא לקברות יובל. סופו יובל לקבר. ועל גדיש ישקוד. כשהוא נקבר בשדות אצל הגדישים [איוב כא, לב]. לירעי חד יומא. כל בהמות העיר. אזל יתמא. שלא היה לו שור וכפאוהו לרעות בהמותיהן ב' ימים [נד סט.].

Yosef said: בָּבֶל וּבוֹרְסִיף סִימָן רַע לַתּוֹרָה – **Bavel and Bursif**[23] **are a bad omen**[24] **for Torah** study.[25]

The Gemara asks:

מַאי בּוֹרְסִיף – **What is** the meaning of the word **"Bursif"?**

The Gemara answers:

אָמַר רַבִּי אַסִּי – **R' Assi said:** בּוֹר שָׁאפִי – **A pit emptied** of its contents.[26]

Having concluded its discussion of the Generation of the Dispersal, the Gemara now proceeds to the next group listed in our Mishnah as having no share in the World to Come. The Mishnah stated:

אַנְשֵׁי סְדוֹם אֵין לָהֶם חֵלֶק לָעוֹלָם הַבָּא וכו׳ – THE PEOPLE OF SODOM HAVE NO SHARE IN THE WORLD TO COME **etc.**

The Gemara offers proof of this statement:

תָּנוּ רַבָּנָן – **The Rabbis taught** in a Baraisa: אַנְשֵׁי סְדוֹם אֵין לָהֶן חֵלֶק לָעוֹלָם הַבָּא שֶׁנֶּאֱמַר – THE PEOPLE OF SODOM HAVE NO SHARE IN THE WORLD TO COME, AS IT IS STATED:[27] ,,וְאַנְשֵׁי סְדֹם רָעִים וְחַטָּאִים לַה׳ מְאֹד'' – *NOW, THE PEOPLE OF SODOM WERE EVIL AND SINFUL TOWARD HASHEM, EXCEEDINGLY.* ,,רָעִים'' בָּעוֹלָם הַזֶּה ,,וְחַטָּאִים'' לָעוֹלָם הַבָּא – Scripture implies that they were judged *EVIL* IN THIS WORLD AND *SINFUL* IN THE WORLD TO COME.

Another interpretation of that verse:

אָמַר רַב יְהוּדָה – **Rav Yehudah said:**[28] ,,רָעִים'' בְּגוּפָן ,,וְחַטָּאִים'' בְּמָמוֹנָם – Scripture means that they were ***evil*** **with their bodies** (i.e. they were excessively licentious) **and** ***sinful*** **with their money.** ,,רָעִים'' בְּגוּפָן דִּכְתִיב ,,וְאֵיךְ אֶעֱשֶׂה הָרָעָה הַגְּדֹלָה הַזֹּאת וְחָטָאתִי לֵאלֹהִים'' – They were ***evil*** **with their bodies, as it is written:** ***How can I perpetrate this great evil? I will have sinned against God!***[29] ,,וְחַטָּאִים'' בְּמָמוֹנָם דִּכְתִיב ,,וְהָיָה בְךָ חֵטְא'' – **And** they were ***sinful*** **with their money, as it is written:** ***It will be a sin upon you.***[30]

Rav Yehudah now explicates the end of *Genesis* 13:13:

,,לַה׳ '' זוּ בִּרְכַּת הַשֵּׁם – Scripture states that the people of Sodom were *evil and sinful* ***toward*** **HASHEM** – **this** refers to their **"blessing" the** Divine **Name.**[31] ,,מְאֹד'' שֶׁמִּתְכַּוְּונִים וְחוֹטְאִים – The verse concludes with the word ***exceedingly,*** which implies that the people of Sodom did not sin thoughtlessly; rather, **they meditated** first **and** then **sinned.** This indicates a far greater level of depravity, for they did not merely succumb to their lusts and desires. Rather, their sins were intentional gestures of defiance of and contempt for God.

A Baraisa discusses the wickedness of the people of Sodom:

בְּמַתְנִיתָא תָּנָא – **[A Tanna] taught in a Baraisa:** ,,רָעִים'' בְּגוּפָן ,,וְחַטָּאִים'' בְּמָמוֹנָם – The Sodomites were *EVIL* WITH THEIR MONEY AND *SINFUL* WITH THEIR BODIES.[32] ,,רָעִים'' בְּמָמוֹנָם דִּכְתִיב ,,וְרָעָה עֵינְךָ בְּאָחִיךָ הָאֶבְיוֹן'' – They were *EVIL* WITH THEIR MONEY, AS IT IS WRITTEN: *AND YOU WILL LOOK MALEVOLENTLY AT YOUR IMPOVERISHED BROTHER.*[33] ,,וְחַטָּאִים'' בְּגוּפָן דִּכְתִיב ,,וְחָטָאתִי לֵאלֹהִים'' – AND they were *SINFUL* WITH THEIR BODIES, AS IT IS WRITTEN: *I WILL HAVE SINNED AGAINST GOD.*[34]

The Baraisa now explicates the end of *Genesis* 13:13:

,,לַה׳ '' זוּ בִּרְכַּת הַשֵּׁם – Scripture states that the Sodomites were *evil and sinful* *TOWARD HASHEM* – THIS refers to their "BLESSING" THE Divine NAME.[35] ,,מְאֹד'' זוּ שְׁפִיכוּת דָּמִים שֶׁנֶּאֱמַר – The verse concludes with the word *EXCEEDINGLY*, and THIS refers to the Sodomites' SHEDDING OF BLOOD, AS IT IS STATED: ,,וְגַם דָּם נָקִי שָׁפַךְ מְנַשֶּׁה (בירושלים) הַרְבֵּה מְאֹד [וגו׳]'' – *MOREOVER, MENASHEH SHED INNOCENT BLOOD, EXCEEDINGLY MUCH* **etc.**[36]

NOTES

forgetfulness," means specifically that the place is inimical to Torah wisdom. This is because, in *Maharal's* opinion, the tower's builders were motivated by the arrogant desire for self-glorification, and so they selected the most appropriate place to achieve that end. Babylonia, the Land of Shinar, was that place, for the Gemara (*Kiddushin* 49b) teaches that "arrogance [originally] descended to Babylonia." Now, the acquisition of wisdom requires humility, for one must be willing to acknowledge his ignorance and to learn from any other person. Since the site of the tower harbors a great concentration of the spirit of arrogance, it prevents the acquisition of wisdom.

23. Bavel and Bursif were two contiguous towns whose names at some point in history were interchanged (see *Succah* 34a,b and *Rashi* to *Succah* 34b ד״ה לגיטי נשים; see also *Rashi* to *Shabbos* 36b ד״ה לגיטי נשים, and *Be'er Sheva*).

24. I.e. these two towns are emblematic of forgetfulness, which is bad (*Rashi*).

25. These places cause one to forget his Torah studies, because they are located within the site of the tower (*Rashi*).

26. "Bursif" is interpreted as a compound containing the words בּוֹר (*bor*), which means *pit*, and סִיף, which is related to שָׁאפִי (*shafi*), which means *poured out,* as in הַשּׁוֹפֶה יַיִן לַחֲבֵירוֹ, *one who pours out wine for his fellow* – i.e. he empties the bottle of its contents (*Bava Metzia* 60a). Hence, the name "Bursif" implies that those who enter the town are rendered "an emptied pit" – i.e. they are caused to forget their Torah learning (*Rashi*).

27. *Genesis* 13:13.

28. According to our text of the Gemara this statement is not part of the Baraisa, since it was made by an Amora, *Rav* Yehudah. However, according to *Ein Yaakov* and *Dikdukei Soferim,* the text should read "*Rabbi* Yehudah." He was a Tanna and would be quoted in a Baraisa. See *Rashash.*

29. *Genesis* 39:9. After Joseph was appointed chief steward of Potiphar's household, Potiphar's wife sought to seduce him, but Joseph rejected her advances, explaining that to commit adultery with his master's wife would be *a great evil.*

Just as the word *evil* in that passage connotes adultery and sexual immorality, so when Scripture describes the Sodomites as *evil*, it refers to their sexual immorality.

30. *Deuteronomy* 15:9. This verse follows a passage that teaches the laws of *shemittah,* the seventh year. In this passage, Scripture states that every seventh year all debts owed to creditors are automatically canceled. In our verse Scripture goes on to warn against refusing to lend money out of fear that the borrower will not make payment until the seventh year, at which time the entire debt will be canceled and the lender will suffer a total loss. Scripture teaches that such an attitude betrays a lack of faith in God, and is therefore accounted a *sin*, חֵטְא.

From here we see that the word *sin* connotes a transgression involving money. Hence, when Scripture describes the Sodomites as *sinful,* it implies that they transgressed in monetary matters (see *Rashi*).

31. A euphemism for cursing the Divine Name. The Sodomites blasphemed mightily.

32. Rav Yehudah mentioned (above) the Sodomites' "bodily" sins before mentioning their monetary transgressions, whereas the Baraisa here reverses the order. *Iyun Yaakov* explains that while both opinions understand that Scripture alludes to the more grievous sin last, they argue over which that might be. Rav Yehudah maintains that sins involving money are more serious, since they are offensive to both God and man. The Baraisa holds that since, on the other hand, an ill-gotten gain can be returned, monetary transgressions are less serious.

33. Ibid. 15:9; see above, note 30. The point here is that the reluctant lender is described as one who "looks malevolently" at the needy supplicant. Scripture expresses this idea with the phrase וְרָעָה עֵינְךָ, which literally means: *And your eye will be evil.* Thus, the word רָעָה, *evil,* connotes a sin involving money.

34. *Genesis* 39:9; see above, note 29. The Baraisa finds the allusion to immorality in the latter part of the verse, where Joseph proclaims that if he succumbed and committed adultery, "וְחָטָאתִי, *I will have sinned.*" From here we see that the word *sinful* connotes sexual immorality.

35. See above, note 31.

36. *II Kings* 21:16. In this verse the act of killing is modified by the adjective מְאֹד, *exceedingly.* Similarly, when Scripture uses the word *exceedingly* in describing the Sodomites' iniquities, it refers to the bloodshed they committed.

מאן נשדר בהדי נחום איש גם זו דמלומד בנסים הוא כי מטא לההוא דיורא בעא למיבת אמרי ליה מאי איכא בהדך אמר להו קא מובילנא כרגא לקיסר קמו בליליא שרינהו לסיפטיה ושקלו כל דהוה גביה ומלנהו עפרא כי מטא להתם אישתכח עפרא אמר אחוכי קא מחייכי בי יהודאי אפקוהו למקטליה אמר גם זו לטובה אתא אליהו ואידמי להו כחד מינייהו אמר להו דילמא האי עפרא מעפרא דאברהם אבינו הוא דהוה שדי עפרא הוו חרבי גילי הוו גירי בדוק ואשכחו הכי הוה מחוזא דלא הוו קא יכלי ליה למיכבשיה שדו מההוא עפרא עליה וכבשוה עיילוהו לבי גנזא אמרי שקול דניחא לך מלייה לסיפטא דהבא כי הדר אתא אמרו ליה הנך דיורי מאי אמטית לבי מלכא אמר להו מאי דשקלי מהכא אמטאי להתם שקלי אינהו אמטו להתם קטלינהו להנך דיורי: דור הפלגה אין להם חלק לעולם הבא וכו': מאי עבוד אמרי דבי רבי שילא (א) נבנה מגדל ונעלה לרקיע ונכה אותו בקרדומות כדי שיזובו מימיו [א] מחכו עלה במערבא א"כ ליבנו אחד בטורא [ב] (אלא) א"ר ירמיה בר אלעזר נחלקו לג' כיתות אחת אומרת נעלה ונשב שם ואחת אומרת נעלה ונעבוד עבודת כוכבים ואחת אומרת נעלה ונעשה מלחמה זו שאומרת נעלה ונשב שם הפיצם ה' וזו שאומרת נעלה ונעשה מלחמה נעשו קופים ורוחות ושדים ולילין וזו שאומרת נעלה ונעבוד עבודת כוכבים [א] כי שם בלל ה' שפת כל הארץ תניא רבי נתן אומר כולם לשם עבודת כוכבים נתכוונו כתיב הכא [ב] נעשה לנו שם וכתיב התם [ג] ושם אלהים אחרים לא תזכירו מה להלן עבודת כוכבים אף כאן עבודת כוכבים אמר רבי יוחנן מגדל שליש נשרף שליש נבלע שליש קיים אמר רב אויר מגדל משכח אמר רב יוסף בבל [ג] ובורסיף סימן רע לתורה מאי בורסיף אמר ר' אסי בור [ד] שאפי: אנשי סדום אין להם חלק לעולם הבא וכו': ת"ר [ה] אנשי סדום אין להן חלק לעולם הבא שנאמר [ד] ואנשי סדום רעים וחטאים לה' מאד רעים בעוה"ז וחטאים לעולם הבא אמר רב יהודה רעים בגופן וחטאים בממונם רעים בגופן דכתיב [ה] ואיך אעשה הרעה הגדולה הזאת וחטאתי לאלהים וחטאים בממונם דכתיב [ו] והיה בך חטא לה' זו ברכת השם מאד שמתכוונים וחוטאים במתניתא תנא [ו] רעים בממונם וחטאים בגופן רעים בממונם דכתיב [ו] ורעה עינך באחיך האביון וחטאים בגופן דכתיב [ה] וחטאתי לאלהים לה' [ז] זו ברכת השם מאד זו שפיכות דמים שנאמר [ז] גם דם נקי שפך מנשה (בירושלים) הרבה מאד [וגו'] [ח] ת"ר אנשי סדום לא נתגאו אלא בשביל טובה שהשפיע להם הקב"ה ומה כתיב בהם [ח] ארץ ממנה יצא לחם ותחתיה נהפך כמו אש מקום ספיר אבניה ועפרות זהב לו נתיב לא ידעו עיט ולא שזפתו עין איה לא הדריכוהו בני שחץ לא עדה עליו שחל אמרו וכי מאחר שארץ ממנה יצא לחם ועפרות זהב לו למה לנו עוברי דרכים שאין באים אלינו אלא לחסרינו [מממוננו] בואו ונשכח תורת רגל מארצנו שנאמר [ט] פרץ נחל מעם גר הנשכחים מני רגל דלו מאנוש נעו דרש רבא מאי דכתיב [י] עד אנה תהותתו על איש תרצחו כולכם כקיר נטוי גדר הדחויה מלמד שהיו נותנין עיניהן בבעלי ממון ומושיבין אותו אצל קיר נטוי ודוחין אותו עליו ובאים ונוטלין את ממונו דרש רבא מאי דכתיב [כ] חתר בחשך בתים יומם חתמו למו לא (ראו) [ידעו] אור מלמד שהיו נותנים עיניהם בבעלי ממון ומפקידים אצלו אפרסמון ומניחים אותו בבית גנזיהם לערב באים ומריחין אותו ככלב שנא' [ל] ישובו לערב יהמו ככלב ויסובבו עיר ובאים וחותרים שם ונוטלין אותו ממון [א] [מ] ערום [ט] הלכו מבלי לבוש ואין כסות בקרה [נ] חמור יתומים ינהגו יחבלו שור אלמנה [ס] גבולות ישיגו עדר גזלו וירעו [ע] והוא לקבורות יובל ועל גדיש ישקוד [ב] דרש ר' יוסי בציפורי אחתרין ההיא ליליא תלת מאה מחתרתא בציפורי אתו וקא מצערי ליה אמרו ליה יהבית אורחיה לגנבי אמר להו מי הוה ידענא דאתו גנבי [י] כי קא נח נפשיה דרבי יוסי שפעי מרזבי דציפורי דמא [ג] אמרי [כ] דאית ליה חד תורא מרעי חד יומא דלית ליה לירעי תרי יומי ההוא יתמא בר ארמלתא הבו ליה תורי למרעיה אזל שקלינהו וקטלינהו אמר להו

דאית

בהדי מאן. ביד מי נשלח: כי מטא לההוא דיירא. כשהגיע לאותו מלון: למיבת. ללון: שרינהו [ל] לסיפטיה. התירו הארגזים והמרצופין ופתחום ונטלו כל מה שבתוכו: אחוכי. מלחקי: הנך דיורי. אותן בני הכפרים: א"כ ליבנו אחד בטורא. א"כ שבנו כדי לעלות לרקיע למה בנו אותו בבקעה היה להם לבנות על אחד ההרים: הפיצם ה'. פיזרם בכל העולם: שדים. יש להם צורת אדם ואוכלין ושותין כבני אדם [מ]: רוחין. בלי גוף וצורה: לילין. צורת אדם אלא שיש להם כנפים במסכת נדה (דף כד:): זו שאומרה נעבוד ע"ז כי שם בלל ה'. בלבל לשונם כדי שלא יבא אחד מכוון לדעת חבירו לעבוד ע"ז: שליש [נבלע]. נבלעו יסודותיה משוקעת היא בקרקע עד שליש ושליש של מעלה נשרף ושליש אמצעי קיים בקרקע ולא שיהא עומד באויר: אויר מגדל. מראש המגדל (כלומר) [כמו אוירה של עיר] מי שעומד סביב למגדל ורואה אוירה ומראה גובה שלו: משכח. שכן נגזר על אותו מקום שישכח ולכך הם עצמם שכחו את לשונם: בבל ובורסיף סימן רע לתורה. שמשכחין הלמוד מפני שעומדים באויר המגדל: למה נקרא שמה בורסיף בור שאפי. בור שנתרוקן מימיו כלומר משכח האדם כל מה שלומד: שאפי. כמו (ב"מ דף ס.) השופה את היין לשון (ירמיה מח) הורק מכלי אל כלי ומפני מה שמה בבל [שמשכחת] אמר רב יוסף כי שם בלל לפי שבלבל הקדוש ברוך הוא את לשונם לשם כך היא משכחת: סימן רע. כלומר שמם סימן שכחה היא: רעים בגופם. שטופים בזימה: השמר לך פן יהיה דבר עם לבבך בליעל וגו' והיה בך חטא. והיינו ממון: ארץ ממנה יצא לחם. ארץ שבעה וטובה היא: ותחתיה נהפך כמו אש. ואחר כן נהפכה: וכי מאחר שארץ ממנה יצא לחם. שיש לנו שיפוע לחם למה לנו עוברי דרכים: ונשכח. שלא יעברו עוברי דרכים בארצנו: פרץ. הקב"ה נחל גפרית ואש: מעם גר. ממקום הליכתו שהיה הולך למעלה והשליכו עליהם הנשכחים מני רגל ונתדלדלו (מאדם) [מארצם] ונעו לדראון: גר. קוררט"ל בלע"ז כמו (שמואל ב יד) מים הנגרים: תהותתו. תבקשו תרמיות ותואנות: תרצחו כולכם. ע"י קיר נטוי וגדר הדחויה: יומם חתמו למו. היום סותמים וסוגרין כאילו לא ידעו אור כלומר סותמין וחותמין: אפרסמון. שלהם להפקידו ביד בעלי ממון כדי שיהו מניחין פקדון שלהם בבית גנזיהם ובלילה מריחין האפרסמון וחותרין שם מנהגו של מפקיד לורר וחותם: דרש ר' יוסי. בי מדרשא חתר בחשך בתים: איחתרו תלת מאה מחתרתא. ע"י ריח אפרסמון שהיו מריחין ויודעין היכן מניחין ממונם: מי הוה ידענא דאתו גנבי ל"א מי הוה ידענא דגנבי אתון: שפעי מרזבי דציפורי דמא. דאדם גדול הוה ואיידי דאמר לעיל איחתרו מחתרתי בציפורי דאתרא דרבי יוסי התם הוה נקיט נמי הא מילתא דכי נח נפשיה כו' לאשמועינן דמצפורי הוה:

דאית

מסורת הש"ס

א) [לעיל יז: וש"נ], ב) ב"ש מ"ז, ג) [גירסת ב"ש בירשוף], ד) [גי' הערוך ערך ברסיף שפת], ה) [תוספתא פי"ג ע"ש], ו) [תוספ' פי"ג], ז) [תוספתא שם], ח) [תוספתא דסוטה פ"ג], ט) [נ"ל ילינו], י) [מ"ק כה:], כ) [נדה סט.], ל) [נ"ל לסיפטי'], מ) [חגיגה טז.].

הגהות הב"ח

(א) גמ' אמרי דבי ר' שילא אמרי נבנה:

הגהות הגר"א

[א] גמ' ערום. נרשם עליו אות ב: [ב] שם דרש רבי יוסי. נרשם על תיבת דרש אות א: [ג] שם אמרי דאית ליה חד. נרשם על תיבת אמרי אות ג':

ליקוטי רש"י

לסיפטיה. ארגז שלו. כחד מינייהו. כאחד משרי קיסר. מעפרא דאברהם הוא. כשנלחם עם המלכים. גילי. קשין [תענית כא.]. דור הפלגה אין להם חלק לעולם הבא. ומשם הפיצם. למד שאין להם חלק לעולם הבא וכי אי זו קשה של דור המבול או של דור הפלגה אלו לא פשטו יד בעיקר ואלו פשטו יד בעיקר כביכול להלחם בו ואלו נשטפו ואלו לא נאבדו מן העולם אלא שדור המבול היו גזלנים והיתה מריבה ביניהם לכך נאבדו ואלו היו נוהגים אהבה וריעות ביניהם שנאמר שפה אחת ודברים אחדים למדת ששנוי המחלוקת וגדול השלום [בראשית יא, ט]. נחלקו לשלש כיתות. ודברים אחדים. באו בעצה אחת ואמרו לא כל הימנו שיבור לו את העליונים נעלה לרקיע ונעשה עמו מלחמה דבר אחר על יחידו של עולם [דבר אחר ודברים אחדים אמרו אחת לאלף ושש מאות חמשים ושש שנים הרקיע מתמוטט כשם שעשה בימי המבול בואו ונעשה לו סמוכות] [בראשית יא, א]. בבל ובורסיף. ובורסיף סמוך לבבל ואינן בני תורה כדאמרינן מאי בורסיף בור ששפו את מימיו ולא נשתייר בו כלום [סוכה לד:]. וחטאתי לאלהים. בני נח נצטוו על העריות [בראשית לט, ט]. ארץ אשר ממנה יצא לחם. נהפך מקומה כמו אש. מקום ספיר. היו אבניה. לא ידעו עיט. לא עבר עליהן חיל של ליסטין. ולא שזפתו עין איה. לפי שהיא רואה יותר משאר עופות ולכך נקרא' ראה שהיא עומדת בבבל ורואה נבילו' בארץ ישראל כך מפורש באגדת (חולין סג ע"א) כלומר לא חפרוה מרגלים. לא עדה עליו. עבר כדמתרגמינן אשר עבר בין הבתרים (בראשית טו) (נ"ל הגזרים וע' בתרגום) דעדא. פרץ נחל. על סדום ועמורה נחלי אש וגפרית. מעם גר. ממקום שהוא נובע ונוגר. הנשכחים מני רגל. אלו אנשי סדום ששיכחו תורת רגלי אורחים מארצם שהיו משכיבים האורח במטה אם היה ארוך יותר מקטעין רגליו ואם היה קצר מאריכין אותו כך מפורש באגדה. דלו. ע"י פריצת נחל זה ומאנוש נעו [איוב כח]. עיט. הוא עוף ועל שם שהוא עט ושואף הנבלות (איוב ט, כו) לטוש עלי אוכל, כמו (ש"א טו, יט) ותעט אל השלל [בראשית טו, יא]. עין איה. והראה ואת האיה וגו' היא ראה היא איה היא דיה ולמה נקרא שמה ראה שרואה ביותר [דברים יד, יג]. שחל. הארי גדול והשחל בינוני והכפיר קטן [איוב ד, י]. תהותתו. מנחם פי' מגזרת התיו לאכלה (ירמיה י"ב) ויתא ראשי עם (דברים ל"ג) עד אנה תאספו על איש ול"נ שיש לפותרו לשון הוות ויהא ה"א ותי"ו שורש כאשר יאמר מן מת מות כך נאמר מן יסוד הת הות ולשון רבים הוות והוא לשון מחשבת שבר ותרמית [תהלים סב, ד]. יומם חתמו. ורבותינו פירשו יומם חתמו למו ביום היו עושים סימנים היכן מרתפו של בית והיכן גנזיו של עשיר שהיו מפקידין אפרסמון אצל בעלי בתים עשירים ויודעים הם שיניחנו בבית גנזיו ובלילה מריחין והולכים שם וחותרים שם [איוב כד, יז]. הלכו. הם הלכוהו בלי לבוש. מבלי לבוש. שנטלו כסוין. חמור יתומים ינהגו. ועושין כל רעות האמורות בענין סוף דבר ואלוה לא ישים תפלה להודיעם עוונם ולהמציאם גמולם. גבולות ישיגו. אותן שדרכן להסיג גבולות שהן קונין שדות כנגד שדות אחרים ובלילה הם מרבים גבוליהם שהיו עושים גדריהם בלילה בתוך תחום. עדר גזלו וירעו. לעצמן [איוב כד עיי"ש]. והוא לקבורות יובל. סופו יובל לקבר. ועל גדיש ישקוד. כשהוא נקבר בשדות אצל הגדישים [איוב כא, לב]. לירעי חד יומא. כל בהמות העיר. אזל יתמא. שלא היה לו שור וכפאוהו לרעות בהמותיהן ב' ימים [נד סט.].

תורה אור השלם

א) עַל כֵּן קָרָא שְׁמָהּ בָּבֶל כִּי שָׁם בָּלַל יְיָ שְׂפַת כָּל הָאָרֶץ וּמִשָּׁם הֱפִיצָם יְיָ עַל פְּנֵי כָּל הָאָרֶץ: [בראשית יא, ט]

ב) וַיֹּאמְרוּ הָבָה נִבְנֶה לָּנוּ עִיר וּמִגְדָּל וְרֹאשׁוֹ בַשָּׁמַיִם וְנַעֲשֶׂה לָּנוּ שֵׁם פֶּן נָפוּץ עַל פְּנֵי כָל הָאָרֶץ: [בראשית יא, ד]

ג) וּבְכֹל אֲשֶׁר אָמַרְתִּי אֲלֵיכֶם תִּשָּׁמֵרוּ וְשֵׁם אֱלֹהִים אֲחֵרִים לֹא תַזְכִּירוּ לֹא יִשָּׁמַע עַל פִּיךָ: [שמות כג, יג]

ד) וְאַנְשֵׁי סְדֹם רָעִים וְחַטָּאִים לַיְיָ מְאֹד: [בראשית יג, יג]

ה) אֵינֶנּוּ גָדוֹל בַּבַּיִת הַזֶּה מִמֶּנִּי וְלֹא חָשַׂךְ מִמֶּנִּי מְאוּמָה כִּי אִם אוֹתָךְ בַּאֲשֶׁר אַתְּ אִשְׁתּוֹ וְאֵיךְ אֶעֱשֶׂה הָרָעָה הַגְּדֹלָה הַזֹּאת וְחָטָאתִי לֵאלֹהִים: [בראשית לט, ט]

ו) הִשָּׁמֶר לְךָ פֶּן יִהְיֶה דָבָר עִם לְבָבְךָ בְלִיַּעַל לֵאמֹר קָרְבָה שְׁנַת הַשֶּׁבַע שְׁנַת הַשְּׁמִטָּה וְרָעָה עֵינְךָ בְּאָחִיךָ הָאֶבְיוֹן וְלֹא תִתֵּן לוֹ וְקָרָא עָלֶיךָ אֶל יְיָ וְהָיָה בְךָ חֵטְא: [דברים טו, ט]

ז) וְגַם דָּם נָקִי שָׁפַךְ מְנַשֶּׁה הַרְבֵּה מְאֹד עַד אֲשֶׁר מִלֵּא אֶת יְרוּשָׁלִַם פֶּה לָפֶה לְבַד מֵחַטָּאתוֹ אֲשֶׁר הֶחֱטִיא אֶת יְהוּדָה לַעֲשׂוֹת הָרַע בְּעֵינֵי יְיָ: [מלכים ב' כא, טז]

ח) אֶרֶץ מִמֶּנָּה יֵצֵא לָחֶם וְתַחְתֶּיהָ נֶהְפַּךְ כְּמוֹ אֵשׁ: מְקוֹם סַפִּיר אֲבָנֶיהָ וְעַפְרֹת זָהָב לוֹ: נָתִיב לֹא יְדָעוֹ עָיִט וְלֹא שְׁזָפַתּוּ עֵין אַיָּה: לֹא הִדְרִיכֻהוּ בְנֵי שָׁחַץ לֹא עָדָה עָלָיו שָׁחַל: [איוב כח, ה-ח]

ט) פָּרַץ נַחַל מֵעִם גָּר הַנִּשְׁכָּחִים מִנִּי רָגֶל דַּלּוּ מֵאֱנוֹשׁ נָעוּ: [איוב כח, ד]

י) עַד אָנָה תְּהוֹתְתוּ עַל אִישׁ תְּרָצְּחוּ כֻלְּכֶם כְּקִיר נָטוּי גָּדֵר הַדְּחוּיָה: [תהלים סב, ד]

כ) חָתַר בַּחֹשֶׁךְ בָּתִּים יוֹמָם חִתְּמוּ לָמוֹ לֹא יָדְעוּ אוֹר: [איוב כד, טז]

ל) יָשׁוּבוּ לָעֶרֶב יֶהֱמוּ כַכָּלֶב וִיסוֹבְבוּ עִיר: [תהלים נט, ז]

מ) עָרוֹם יָלִינוּ מִבְּלִי לְבוּשׁ וְאֵין כְּסוּת בַּקָּרָה: [איוב כד, ז]

נ) חֲמוֹר יְתוֹמִים יִנְהָגוּ יַחְבְּלוּ שׁוֹר אַלְמָנָה: [איוב כד, ג]

ס) גְּבֻלוֹת יַשִּׂיגוּ עֵדֶר גָּזְלוּ וַיִּרְעוּ: [איוב כד, ג]

ע) וְהוּא לִקְבָרוֹת יוּבָל וְעַל גָּדִישׁ יִשְׁקוֹד: [איוב כא, לב]

The Gemara explains the reason for the Sodomites' moral downfall:

תָּנוּ רַבָּנָן – **The Rabbis taught** in a Baraisa: אַנְשֵׁי סְדוֹם לֹא נִתְגָּאוּ אֶלָּא בִּשְׁבִיל טוֹבָה שֶׁהִשְׁפִּיעַ לָהֶם הַקָּדוֹשׁ בָּרוּךְ הוּא – **THE PEOPLE OF SODOM BECAME ARROGANT ONLY BECAUSE OF THE BOUNTY THAT THE HOLY ONE, BLESSED IS HE, LAVISHED UPON THEM.** וּמַה כְּתִיב בָּהֶם – **WHAT IS WRITTEN** in Scripture **CONCERNING THEM?** ,,אֶרֶץ מִמֶּנָּה יֵצֵא־לָחֶם וְתַחְתֶּיהָ נֶהְפַּךְ כְּמוֹ־אֵשׁ – ***A LAND FROM WHICH BREAD COMES FORTH HAS, IN ITS STEAD, TURNED INTO SCORCHED EARTH.*** מְקוֹם־סַפִּיר אֲבָנֶיהָ וְעַפְרֹת זָהָב לוֹ – ***ITS VERY STONES YIELDED SAPPHIRES, ITS VERY DUST WAS GOLD.*** נָתִיב לֹא־יְדָעוֹ עָיִט וְלֹא שְׁזָפַתּוּ עֵין אַיָּה – ***[IT WAS] A PATH UNKNOWN TO ANY ROBBER, UNOBSERVED BY ANY SPY.*** לֹא־הִדְרִיכֻהוּ בְנֵי־שָׁחַץ לֹא־עָדָה עָלָיו שָׁחַל" – ***MIGHTY BEASTS HAD NOT TROD IT, NO LION EVER TRAVERSED IT.***[37] אָמְרוּ – **[THE PEOPLE OF SODOM] SAID:** וְכִי מֵאַחַר שֶׁ,,אֶרֶץ מִמֶּנָּה יֵצֵא־לָחֶם . . . וְעַפְרֹת זָהָב לוֹ" – **NOW, INASMUCH AS** Sodom is ***A LAND FROM WHICH BREAD COMES FORTH ... AND ITS VERY DUST IS GOLD,*** לָמָּה לָנוּ עוֹבְרֵי דְרָכִים – **WHY DO WE NEED WAYFARERS,** שֶׁאֵין בָּאִים אֵלֵינוּ אֶלָּא לְחַסְּרֵינוּ [מִמָּמוֹנֵנוּ] – **WHO COME TO US ONLY TO DEPRIVE US OF OUR MONEY?!**[38] בּוֹאוּ וּנְשַׁכַּח תּוֹרַת רֶגֶל מֵאַרְצֵנוּ – **COME, LET US CAUSE THE VERY CONCEPT OF WAYFARING TO BE FORGOTTEN IN OUR LAND** (i.e. let us undertake to mistreat all non-Sodomites so terribly that they will no longer desire to travel through our territory). שֶׁנֶּאֱמַר ,,פָּרַץ נַחַל מֵעִם־גָּר הַנִּשְׁכָּחִים מִנִּי־רָגֶל דַּלּוּ מֵאֱנוֹשׁ נָעוּ" – This sin caused their destruction, **AS IT IS STATED:** ***A STREAM BURST OUT OF ITS NORMAL COURSE [AND WAS CAST UPON THE TOWN] THAT HAD BEEN FORGOTTEN BY THE WAYFARER'S FEET. THEY WERE BANISHED, CONSIGNED TO [ETERNAL] DISGRACE.***[39]

The Gemara explains how the Sodomites murdered and robbed as part of their plan to discourage wayfarers from passing their way:

דָּרַשׁ רָבָא – **Rava expounded:** מַאי דִּכְתִיב – **What is** the meaning of that **which is written:**[40] ,,עַד־אָנָה תְּהוֹתְתוּ עַל־אִישׁ תְּרָצְחוּ כֻלְּכֶם כְּקִיר נָטוּי גָּדֵר הַדְּחוּיָה" – ***How long will you plot treacherously against man, will all of you murder with leaning wall, with toppled fence?*** מְלַמֵּד שֶׁהָיוּ נוֹתְנִין עֵינֵיהֶן בְּבַעֲלֵי מָמוֹן – **[This] teaches that [the Sodomites] would cast their eyes upon** those wayfarers and visitors who were **wealthy individuals,** וּמוֹשִׁיבִין אוֹתוֹ אֵצֶל קִיר נָטוּי – **and would seat [such a person] next to a leaning wall** וְדוֹחִין אוֹתוֹ עָלָיו – **and push [the wall] down upon [the unsuspecting wayfarer],** killing him. וּבָאִים וְנוֹטְלִין אֶת מָמוֹנוֹ – **They would** then **come and take his money.**[41]

The Gemara describes the cunning of the Sodomite thieves:

דָּרַשׁ רָבָא – **Rava expounded:** מַאי דִּכְתִיב – **What is** the meaning of that **which is written:**[42] ,,חָתַר בַּחֹשֶׁךְ בָּתִּים יוֹמָם חִתְּמוּ־לָמוֹ לֹא־יָדְעוּ אוֹר" – ***In the darkness he burrows under houses; by day they seal themselves in, never knowing the light?*** מְלַמֵּד שֶׁהָיוּ נוֹתְנִים עֵינֵיהֶם בְּבַעֲלֵי מָמוֹן – **[This] teaches that [the Sodomites] would cast their eyes upon** those wayfarers who were **wealthy individuals,** וּמַפְקִידִים אֶצְלוֹ אֲפַרְסְמוֹן – **and would deposit balsam,** which is a fragrant substance, **with [each one]** for safekeeping. וּמַנִּיחִים אוֹתוֹ בְּבֵית גִּנְזֵיהֶם – **[The unsuspecting victims] would place [these costly bailments] in their depositories,** where they safeguarded their own money and valuables. The location of these hiding places was, of course, a well-kept secret. לָעֶרֶב בָּאִים וּמְרִיחִין אוֹתוֹ כְּכֶלֶב – **In the evening [the Sodomite thieves] would come and sniff out** the location of **[the depository],** which now exuded the fragrance of balsam, acting **in the manner of a dog,** שֶׁנֶּאֱמַר ,,יָשׁוּבוּ לָעֶרֶב יֶהֱמוּ כַכָּלֶב וִיסוֹבְבוּ עִיר" – **as it is stated:**[43] ***They return toward evening, they howl like the dog and go round about the city.*** וּבָאִים וְחוֹתְרִים שָׁם – Once they located the depository **they would come and burrow there,** into the room, וְנוֹטְלִין אוֹתוֹ מָמוֹן – **and take that** valuable **property** belonging to the wayfarer.[44]

The Gemara now cites a number of verses from *Job* to describe various Sodomite atrocities:

,,עָרוֹם יָלִינוּ מִבְּלִי לְבוּשׁ וְאֵין כְּסוּת בַּקָּרָה" – ***They would allow the naked to spend the night unclothed, no garment to shield against the cold.***[45] ,,חֲמוֹר יְתוֹמִים יִנְהָגוּ יַחְבְּלוּ שׁוֹר אַלְמָנָה" – ***They drive away the orphan's donkey, take the widow's ox in pledge.***[46] ,,גְּבֻלוֹת יַשִּׂיגוּ עֵדֶר גָּזְלוּ וַיִּרְעוּ" – ***They move back boundary markers, have stolen flocks and take them out to graze.***[47] ,,וְהוּא לִקְבָרוֹת יוּבָל וְעַל גָּדִישׁ יִשְׁקוֹד" – ***He will be taken to the burial ground, be hastened to the mound.***[48]

NOTES

37. *Job* 28:5-8. In these verses Job describes Sodom at the time of her tranquility, when she was blessed with natural resources and was free of crime and dangerous animals. Our translation follows *Rashi's* commentary there; cf. *Metzudos* and *Ramban*.

38. The Sodomites perversely reasoned: Since we are more than self-sufficient with respect to all our material needs, itinerant merchants and traders are of no use to us. That they come here and sell their produce and goods to us serves no purpose other than separating us from our money (*Ben Yehoyada*).

39. Ibid. v. 4. Our translation of this verse follows *Rashi* here, who explains that God caused the destruction of Sodom by diverting a stream of fire and brimstone from its heavenly course, raining it down upon Sodom and utterly destroying the town.

The Gemara's point is that the verse explicitly describes Sodom as *[the town] that had been forgotten by the wayfarer's feet,* which implies that it was their nefarious actions against wayfarers that precipitated the Sodomites' destruction.

40. *Psalms* 62:4.

41. According to *Ben Yehoyada*, the Sodomites selected as their victims wayfarers and visitors who had no heirs. Under a specially enacted Sodomite law, the property of such people passed to the government upon their deaths. This approach lent some semblance of legality to their heinous actions. According to *Maharsha,* the Gemara does not mean that the Sodomites actually killed strangers. Rather, they would seat each victim next to a leaning wall, surreptitiously cause the wall to collapse (not upon the stranger), and then claim that the stranger was responsible for the damage. Hailed before a Sodomite court, the stranger would be found guilty and he would be ordered to pay for the wall. According to this interpretation as well, Sodomite jurisprudence was conscripted to serve in the immoral war against wayfarers.

42. *Job* 24:16.

43. *Psalms* 59:7.

44. The verse in *Job* is thus interpreted: *In the darkness [the Sodomite thief] burrows under houses* [to reach the depository, where he finds and takes the valuables of the wayfarer, who] *by day* [had bound and] *sealed* [the balsam given to him as a bailment] (*Rashi;* cf. *Eitz Yosef*).

45. *Job* 24:7. Without pity they plunder the poor, taking even their clothes away, even though this will mean that the victims have to spend the night naked, with nothing to protect them from the cold (*Metzudos* there).

46. Ibid. v. 3. They steal the donkey of the orphan, and then lead it around, brazenly, in public. They take the widow's ox as pledge for non-existing debts (*Metzudos*).

47. Ibid. v. 2. *Metzudos* interprets the second phrase: They take out the stolen flocks to graze in the very fields they obtained through moving the boundary markers, thus compounding their offense.

48. Ibid. 21:32. The verse is interpreted here as referring to the unfortunate victim of the Sodomite machinations: Robbed of everything and left to starve to death, his still-warm corpse is unceremoniously rushed to the cemetery and thrown into a pauper's grave.

The verses quoted here from *Job* (notes 42-48) to describe Sodomite practices are applied by *Yalkut* to the people of the Flood. Moreover,

בהדי מאן. ביד מי נשלח: כי מטא להההוא דיירא. כשהגיע לאותו מלון: למיבת. ללון: שרינהו לסיטפיה. התירו האלגזים והמרלופין ופתחום ונטלו כל מה שבתוכו: אחוכי. מלחקי: הנך דיורי. אותן בני הכפרים: א"כ ליבנו אחד בטורא. א"כ שבנו כדי לעלות לרקיע למה בנו אותו בבקעה היה להם לבנות על אחד ההרים: הפיצם ה'. פיזרם בכל העולם: שדים. יש להם צורת אדם ואוכלין ושותין כבני אדם [מ]: רוחין. בלי גוף וצורה: לילין. צורת אדם אלא שיש להם כנפים במסכת נדה (דף כד:): זו שאומרה נעבוד ע"ז כי שם בלל ה'. בלבל לשונם כדי שלא יהא אחד מכוון לדעת חבירו לעבוד ע"ז: שליש [נבלע]. נבלעו יסודותיה משוקעת היא בקרקע עד שליש ושליש של מעלה נשרף ושליש אמלעי קיים בקרקע ולא שיהא עומד באויר: אויר מגדל. מראש המגדל (כלומר) [כמו אוירה של עיר] מי שעומד סביב למגדל ורואה אוירה ומראה גובה שלו: משכח. שכן נגזר על אותו מקום שישכח ולכך הם עצמם שכחו את לשונם: בבל ובורסיף סימן רע לתורה. שמשכחין התלמוד מפני שעומדים באויר המגדל: למה נקרא שמה בורסיף בור שאפי. בור שנתרוקן מימיו כלומר משכח האדם כל מה שלומד: שאפי. כמו (ב"מ דף ס.) השופה את היין לשון (ירמיה מח) הורק מכלי אל כלי ומפני מה שמה בבל [שמשכחת] אמר רב יוסף כי שם בלל לפי שבלבל הקדוש ברוך הוא את לשונם לשם כך היא משכחת: סימן רע. כלומר שמש

סימן שכחה היא: רעים בגופם. שטופים בזימה: השמר לך פן יהיה דבר עם לבבך בליעל וגו' והיה בך חטא. והיינו ממון: ארץ ממנה יצא לחם. ארץ שבעה וטובה היא: ותחתיה נהפך כמו אש. ואחר כן נהפכה: וכי מאחר שארץ ממנה יצא לחם. שיש לנו שיפוע לחם למה לנו עוברי דרכים: ונשכח. שלא יעברו עוברי דרכים בארצנו: פרץ. הקב"ה נחל גפרית ואש: מעם גר. ממקום הליכתו שהיה הולך למעלה והשליכו עליהם הנשכחים מני רגל ונתדלדלו (מאדם) [מארצם] ונעו לדראון: גר. קוררט"ל בלע"ז כמו (שמואל ב יד) מים הנגרים: תהותתו. תבקשו תרמיות ותואנות: תרצחו כולכם. ע"י קיר נטוי וגדר הדחויה: יומם חתמו למו. היום סותמים וסוגרין כאילו לא ידעו אור כלומר סותמין וחותמין: אפרסמון. שלהם להפקידו ביד בעלי ממון כדי שיהו מניחין פקדון שלהם בבית גנזיהם ובלילה מריחין האפרסמון וחותרין שם מנהגו של מפקיד צורר וחותם: דרש ר' יוסי. בי מדרשא חתר בחשך בתים: איחתרו תלת מאה מחתרתא. ע"י ריח אפרסמון שהיו מריחין ויודעין היכן מניחין ממונם: מי הוה ידענא דאתו גנבי ל"א מי הוה ידענא דגנבי אתון: שפעי מרזבי דציפורי דמא. דאדם גדול הוה ואיידי דאמר לעיל איחתרו מחתרתי בציפורי דאתרא דרבי יוסי התם הוה נקיט נמי הא מילתא דכי נח נפשיה כו' לאשמועינן דמלפורי הוה:

דאית

מאן נשדר בהדי נחום איש גם זו דמלומד בנסים הוא כי מטא לההוא דיורא בעא למיבת אמרי ליה מאי איכא בהדך אמר להו קא מובילנא כרגא לקיסר קמו בליליא שרינהו לסיפטיה ושקלו כל דהוה גביה ומלנהו עפרא כי מטא להתם אישתכח עפרא אמר אחוכי קא מחייכי בי יהודאי אפקוהו למקטליה אמר גם זו לטובה אתא אליהו ואידמי להו כחד מיניהו אמר להו דילמא האי עפרא מעפרא דאברהם אבינו הוא דהוה שדי עפרא הוו חרבי גילי הוו גירי בדוק ואשכחו הכי הוה מחוזא דלא הוו קא יכלי ליה למיכבשיה שדו מההוא עפרא עליה וכבשוה עיילוהו לבי גנזא אמרי שקול דניחא לך מלייה לסיפטא דהבא כי הדר אתא אמרו ליה הנך דיורי מאי אמטית לבי מלכא אמר להו מאי דשקלי מהכא אמטאי להתם שקלי אינהו אמטו להתם קטלינהו להנך דיורי: דור הפלגה אין להם חלק לעולם הבא וכו': מאי עבוד אמרי דבי רבי שילא (א) נבנה מגדל ונעלה לרקיע ונכה אותו בקרדומות כדי שיזובו מימיו מחכו עלה במערבא א"כ ליבנו אחד בטורא (אלא) א"ר ירמיה בר אלעזר נחלקו לג' כיתות אחת אומרת נעלה ונשב שם ואחת אומרת נעלה ונעבוד עבודת כוכבים ואחת אומרת נעלה ונעשה מלחמה זו שאומרת נעלה ונשב שם הפיצם ה' וזו שאומרת נעלה ונעשה מלחמה נעשו קופים ורוחות ושידים ולילין וזו שאומרת נעלה ונעבוד עבודת כוכבים א) כי שם בלל ה' שפת כל הארץ תניא רבי נתן אומר כולם לשם עבודת כוכבים נתכוונו כתיב הכא ב) נעשה לנו שם וכתיב התם ג) ושם אלהים אחרים לא תזכירו מה להלן עבודת כוכבים אף כאן עבודת כוכבים אמר רבי יוחנן מגדל שליש נשרף שליש נבלע שליש קיים אמר רב אויר מגדל משכח אמר רב יוסף בבל ובורסיף סימן רע לתורה מאי בורסיף אמר ר' אסי בור שאפי: אנשי סדום אין להם חלק לעולם הבא וכו': ת"ר אנשי סדום אין להן חלק לעולם הבא שנאמר ד) ואנשי סדום רעים וחטאים לה' מאד רעים בעוה"ז וחטאים לעולם הבא אמר רב יהודה רעים בגופן וחטאים בממונם רעים בגופן דכתיב ה) ואיך אעשה הרעה הגדולה הזאת וחטאתי לאלהים וחטאים בממונם דכתיב ו) והיה בך חטא לה' זו ברכת השם מאד שמתכוונים וחוטאים במתניתא תנא רעים בממונם וחטאים בגופן רעים בממונם דכתיב ו) ורעה עינך באחיך האביון וחטאים בגופן דכתיב ה) וחטאתי לאלהים לה' זו ברכת השם מאד זו שפיכות דמים שנאמר ז) גם דם נקי שפך מנשה (בירושלים) הרבה מאד [וגו'] ת"ר אנשי סדום לא נתגאו אלא בשביל טובה שהשפיע להם הקב"ה ומה כתיב בהם ח) ארץ ממנה יצא לחם ותחתיה נהפך כמו אש מקום ספיר אבניה ועפרות זהב לו נתיב לא ידעו עיט ולא שזפתו עין איה לא הדריכוהו בני שחץ לא עדה עליו שחל אמרו וכי מאחר שארץ ממנה יצא לחם ועפרות זהב לו למה לנו עוברי דרכים שאין באים אלינו אלא לחסרינו [מממוננו] בואו ונשכח תורת רגל מארצנו שנאמר ט) פרץ נחל מעם גר הנשכחים מני רגל דלו מאנוש נעו דרש רבא מאי דכתיב י) עד אנה תהותתו על איש תרצחו כולכם כקיר נטוי גדר הדחויה מלמד שהיו נותנין עיניהן בבעלי ממון ומושיבין אותו אצל קיר נטוי ודוחין אותו עליו ובאים ונוטלין את ממונו דרש רבא מאי דכתיב כ) חתר בחשך בתים יומם חתמו למו לא (ראו) [ידעו] אור מלמד שהיו נותנים עיניהם בבעלי ממון ומפקידים אצלו אפרסמון ומניחים אותו בבית גנזיהם לערב באים ומריחין אותו ככלב שנאמר ל) ישובו לערב יהמו ככלב ויסובבו עיר ובאים וחותרים שם ונוטלין אותו ממון [א] מ) ערום הלכו מבלי לבוש ואין כסות בקרה נ) חמור יתומים ינהגו יחבלו שור אלמנה ס) גבולות ישיגו עדר גזלו וירעו ע) והוא לקברות יובל ועל גדיש ישקוד [ב] דרש ר' יוסי בציפורי אחתרין ההיא ליליא תלת מאה מחתרתא בציפורי אתו וקא מצערי ליה אמרו ליה יהבית אורחיה לגנבי אמר להו מי הוה ידענא דאתו גנבי כי קא נח נפשיה דרבי יוסי שפעי מרזבי דציפורי דמא [ג] אמרי דאית ליה חד תורא מרעי חד יומא דלית ליה לירעי תרי יומי ההוא יתמא בר ארמלתא הבו ליה תורי למרעיה אזל שקלינהו וקטלינהו אמר להו

דאית

מסורת הש"ס

א) [לעיל יז: וש"נ], ב) ב"ש מ"ז, ג) [גירסת ב"ש בירשוף], ד) [גי' הערוך ערך ברסיף שפת], ה) [תוספתא פי"ג ע"ש], ו) [תוספ' פי"ג], ז) [תוספתא שם], ח) [תוספתא דסוטה פ"ג], ט) [ל"ל ילינו], י) [מ"ק כה:], כ) [נדה סט.], ל) [ל"ל לסיפטי'], מ) [חגיגה טז.].

הגהות הב"ח

(א) גמ' אמרי דבי ר' שילא אמרי נבנה:

הגהות הגר"א

[א] גמ' ערום. נרשם עליו אות ב: [ב] שם דרש רבי יוסי. נרשם על תיבת דרש אות א: [ג] שם אמרי דאית ליה חד. נרשם על תיבת אמרי אות ג':

ליקוטי רש"י

לסיפטיה. ארגז שלו. כחד מינייהו. כאחד משרי קיסר. מעפרא דאברהם הוא. כשנלחם עם המלכים. גילי. קשין [תענית כא.]. דור הפלגה אין להם חלק לעולם הבא. ומשם הפיצם. למד שאין להם חלק לעולם הבא וכי אי זו קשה של דור המבול או של דור הפלגה אלו לא פשטו יד בעיקר ואלו פשטו יד בעיקר כביכול להלחם בו ואלו נשטפו ואלו לא נאבדו מן העולם אלא שדור המבול היו גזלנים והיתה מריבה ביניהם לכך נאבדו ואלו היו נוהגים אהבה וריעות ביניהם שנאמר שפה אחת ודברים אחדים למדת ששנוי המחלוקת וגדול השלום [בראשית יא, ט]. נחלקו לשלש כיתות. ודברים אחדים. באו בעצה אחת ואמרו לא כל הימנו שיבור לו את העליונים נעלה לרקיע ונעשה עמו מלחמה דבר אחר על יחידו של עולם [דבר אחר ודברים אחדים אמרו אחת לאלף ושש מאות חמשים ושש שנים הרקיע מתמוטט כשם שעשה בימי המבול בואו ונעשה לו סמוכות [בראשית יא, א]. בבל ובורסיף. ובורסיף סמוך לבבל ואינן בני תורה כדאמרינן מאי בורסיף בור ששפו את מימיו ולא נשתייר בו כלום [סוכה לד:]. וחטאתי לאלהים. בני נח נצטוו על העריות [בראשית לט, ט]. ארץ אשר ממנה יצא לחם. נהפך מקומה כמו אש. מקום ספיר. היו אבניה. לא ידעו עיט. לא עבר עליהן חיל של ליסטין. ולא שזפתו עין איה. לפי שהיא רואה יותר משאר עופות ולכך נקרא' ראה שהיא עומדת בבבל ורואה נבילו' בארץ ישראל כך מפורש באגדת (חולין סג ע"א) כלומר לא חפרוה מרגלים. לא עדה עליו. עבר כדמתרגמינן אשר עבר בין הבתרים (בראשית טו) [ל"ל הגוזרים וע' בתרגום] דעדא. פרץ נחל. על סדום ועמורה נחל אש וגפרית. מעם גר. ממקום שהוא נוטע וגוגר. הנשכחים מני רגל. אלו אנשי סדום ששכחו תורת רגלי אורחים מארצם שהיו משכיבים האורח במטה אם היה ארוך יותר מקטעין רגליו ואם היה קצר מאריכין אותו כך מפורש באגדה. דלו. ע"י פרילת נחל זה ומאנוש נעו [איוב כח]. עיט. הוא עוף ועל שם שהוא עט ושואף הנבלות (איוב ט, כו) לטוש עלי אוכל, כמו (ש"א טו, יט) ותעט אל השלל [בראשית טו, יא]. עין איה. והראה ואת האיה וגו' היא ראה היא איה היא דיה ולמה נקרא שמה ראה שרואה ביותר [דברים יד, יג]. שחל. הארי גדול והשחל בינוני והכפיר קטן [איוב ד, י]. תהותתו. מנאם פי' מגזרת התיו לאכלה (ירמיה י"ב) ויתא ראשי עם (דברים ל"ג) עד אנה תאספו על איש ול"נ שיש לפותרו לשון הוות ויהא ה"א ותי"ו שורש כאשר יאמר מן מת מות כך נאמר מן יסוד הת הות ולשון רבים הוות והוא לשון מחשבת שבר ותרמית [תהלים סב, ד]. יומם חתמו. ורבותינו פירשו יומם חתמו למו ביום היו עושים סימנים היכן מרתפו של בית והיכן גנזיו של עשיר שהיו מפקידין אפרסמון אצל בעלי בתים עשירים ויודעים הם שיניחנו בבית גנזיו ובלילה מריחין והולכים שם וחותרים שם [איוב כד, יז]. הלכו. הם הלכוהו בלי לבוש. מבלי לבוש. שנטלו כסוין. חמור יתומים ינהגו. ועושין כל רעות האמורות בענין סוף דבר ואלוה לא ישים תפלה להודיעם עוונם ולהמציאם גמולם. גבולות ישיגו. אותן שדרכן להסיג גבולות שהן קונין שדות כנגד שדות אחרים ובלילה הם מרבים גבוליהם שהיו עושים גדריהם בלילה בתוך תחום. עדר גזלו וירעו. לעצמן [איוב כד עיי"ש]. והוא לקברות יובל. סופו יובל לקבר. ועל גדיש ישקוד. כשהוא נקבר בשדות אצל הגדישים [איוב כא, לב]. לירעי חד יומא. כל בהמות העיר. אזל יתמא. שלא היה לו שור וכפאוהו לרעות בהמותיהן ב' ימים [נד סט.].

תורה אור השלם

א) עַל כֵּן קָרָא שְׁמָהּ בָּבֶל כִּי שָׁם בָּלַל יְיָ שְׂפַת כָּל הָאָרֶץ וּמִשָּׁם הֱפִיצָם יְיָ עַל פְּנֵי כָּל הָאָרֶץ: [בראשית יא, ט]

ב) וַיֹּאמְרוּ הָבָה נִבְנֶה לָּנוּ עִיר וּמִגְדָּל וְרֹאשׁוֹ בַשָּׁמַיִם וְנַעֲשֶׂה לָּנוּ שֵׁם פֶּן נָפוּץ עַל פְּנֵי כָל הָאָרֶץ: [בראשית יא, ד]

ג) וּבְכֹל אֲשֶׁר אָמַרְתִּי אֲלֵיכֶם תִּשָּׁמֵרוּ וְשֵׁם אֱלֹהִים אֲחֵרִים לֹא תַזְכִּירוּ לֹא יִשָּׁמַע עַל פִּיךָ: [שמות כג, יג]

ד) וְאַנְשֵׁי סְדֹם רָעִים וְחַטָּאִים לַיְיָ מְאֹד: [בראשית יג, יג]

ה) אֵינֶנּוּ גָדוֹל בַּבַּיִת הַזֶּה מִמֶּנִּי וְלֹא חָשַׂךְ מִמֶּנִּי מְאוּמָה כִּי אִם אוֹתָךְ בַּאֲשֶׁר אַתְּ אִשְׁתּוֹ וְאֵיךְ אֶעֱשֶׂה הָרָעָה הַגְּדֹלָה הַזֹּאת וְחָטָאתִי לֵאלֹהִים: [בראשית לט, ט]

ו) הִשָּׁמֶר לְךָ פֶּן יִהְיֶה דָבָר עִם לְבָבְךָ בְלִיַּעַל לֵאמֹר קָרְבָה שְׁנַת הַשֶּׁבַע שְׁנַת הַשְּׁמִטָּה וְרָעָה עֵינְךָ בְּאָחִיךָ הָאֶבְיוֹן וְלֹא תִתֵּן לוֹ וְקָרָא עָלֶיךָ אֶל יְיָ וְהָיָה בְךָ חֵטְא: [דברים טו, ט]

ז) וְגַם דָּם נָקִי שָׁפַךְ מְנַשֶּׁה הַרְבֵּה מְאֹד עַד אֲשֶׁר מִלֵּא אֶת יְרוּשָׁלִַם פֶּה לָפֶה לְבַד מֵחַטָּאתוֹ אֲשֶׁר הֶחֱטִיא אֶת יְהוּדָה לַעֲשׂוֹת הָרַע בְּעֵינֵי יְיָ: [מלכים ב' כא, טז]

ח) אֶרֶץ מִמֶּנָּה יֵצֵא לָחֶם וְתַחְתֶּיהָ נֶהְפַּךְ כְּמוֹ אֵשׁ: מְקוֹם סַפִּיר אֲבָנֶיהָ וְעַפְרֹת זָהָב לוֹ: נָתִיב לֹא יְדָעוֹ עָיִט וְלֹא שְׁזָפַתּוּ עֵין אַיָּה: לֹא הִדְרִיכֻהוּ בְנֵי שָׁחַץ לֹא עָדָה עָלָיו שָׁחַל: [איוב כח, ה-ח]

ט) פָּרַץ נַחַל מֵעִם גָּר הַנִּשְׁכָּחִים מִנִּי רָגֶל דַּלּוּ מֵאֱנוֹשׁ נָעוּ: [איוב כח, ד]

י) עַד אָנָה תְּהוֹתְתוּ עַל אִישׁ תְּרָצְּחוּ כֻלְּכֶם כְּקִיר נָטוּי גָּדֵר הַדְּחוּיָה: [תהלים סב, ד]

כ) חָתַר בַּחֹשֶׁךְ בָּתִּים יוֹמָם חִתְּמוּ לָמוֹ לֹא יָדְעוּ אוֹר: [איוב כד, טז]

ל) יָשׁוּבוּ לָעֶרֶב יֶהֱמוּ כַכָּלֶב וִיסוֹבְבוּ עִיר: [תהלים נט, ז]

מ) עָרוֹם יָלִינוּ מִבְּלִי לְבוּשׁ וְאֵין כְּסוּת בַּקָּרָה: [איוב כד, ז]

נ) חֲמוֹר יְתוֹמִים יִנְהָגוּ יַחְבְּלוּ שׁוֹר אַלְמָנָה: [איוב כד, ג]

ס) גְּבֻלוֹת יַשִּׂיגוּ עֵדֶר גָּזְלוּ וַיִּרְעוּ: [איוב כד, ב]

ע) וְהוּא לִקְבָרוֹת יוּבָל וְעַל גָּדִישׁ יִשְׁקוֹד: [איוב כא, לב]

A story that involves the ancient ruses of the thieves of Sodom: **דָּרַשׁ רַבִּי יוֹסֵי בְּצִיפּוֹרִי – R' Yose expounded** upon the verse, *In the darkness he burrows under houses. . .,* at a public lecture **in** the city of **Tzippori.**[49] **אִתְחַתְרִין הַהִיא לֵילְיָא תְּלַת מְאָה מַחְתָּרָתָא בְּצִיפּוֹרִי – That night, three hundred tunnels were dug in Tzippori.**[50] **וְקָא אָתוּ – [The angry victims] came** to R' Yose **מְצַעֲרֵי לֵיהּ – and accosted him. אָמְרוּ לֵיהּ – They said to him: יְהָבִית אוֹרְחֵיהּ לְגַנָּבֵי – "You gave a** wonderful **modus operandi to the thieves!" אָמַר לְהוּ – [R' Yose] said to them: מִי הֲוָה יָדַעְנָא דְּאָתוּ גַּנָּבֵי – "Did I know that thieves would come** to my lecture?![51] I thought I was speaking to an audience of honest people, who would not emulate the evil Sodomites! Had I known that there were thieves in the crowd, I would never have divulged the Sodomite tactics!"

A postscript to the above:

כִּי קָא נָח נַפְשֵׁיהּ דְּרַבִּי יוֹסֵי – When R' Yose died, שָׁפְעֵי מַרְזְבֵי דְצִיפּוֹרֵי דָּמָא – the gutters of Tzippori poured forth blood.[52]

The unjust laws of Sodom:

אָמְרֵי – [The Sodomites] said: דְּאִית לֵיהּ חַד תּוֹרָא – He who has one ox מַרְעֵי חַד יוֹמָא – must graze all the oxen of Sodom for **one day. דְּלֵית לֵיהּ –** He **who has no** oxen **לִירְעֵי תְּרֵי יוֹמֵי –** is required **to graze** the oxen of Sodom **for two days.**[53]

The Gemara relates an incident involving this law:

הַהוּא יַתְמָא בַּר אַרְמַלְתָּא – There was once **a certain orphan, the son of a widow,** who himself had no oxen. **הָבוּ לֵיהּ תּוֹרֵי לְמִרְעֵיהּ –** One day **[his Sodomite neighbors] gave him** their **oxen to graze. אָזַל שַׁקְלִינְהוּ וְקַטְלִינְהוּ –** Angry because of the burden thus placed upon him, **he went** and **took [the oxen], and killed them. אָמַר לְהוּ – He** then **said to [his neighbors]:**

NOTES

they are quoted here without comment and not in sequence. *Maharsha* suggests that these verses allude to the stories that follow in the Gemara, although the verses are not in the proper order.

49. I.e. he explained that the verse alluded to the Sodomite ruse of depositing aromatic bailments with the intended victims (see *Rashi*).

50. R' Yose's lecture on the tactics of Sodomite thievery found an unusally receptive audience. Later that night the local thieves deposited fragrant oil with the wealthy citizens of Tzippori, who, like the victims of the Sodomites, placed the bailments in their own depositories for safekeeping. Thanks to the powerful fragrance of the oil, the thieves of Tzippori were able to locate the depositories, tunnel into them and steal their wealthy townsmen's valuables (*Rashi*).

According to *Maharal,* the Gemara does not literally mean that three hundred burglaries were committed that night. Rather, that extraordinary figure alludes to the enhancement of the capacity of the community of thieves to practice their craft, which resulted from R' Yose's inadvertent instruction. [*Rashbam* (*Pesachim* 119a ד״ה משוי שלש מאות) cautions that the figure 300 should not be taken literally; rather, it is used symbolically throughout the Talmud to indicate a great quantity. See above, 95b note 19.]

51. Alternatively: Did I know that you are thieves?! (*Rashi*; according to this interpretation, the word דאתו is vowelized דְּאַתּוּ, which means *that you are*). [See *Bava Basra* 89b, where it is related that R' Yochanan ben Zakkai was once hesitant about making certain statements about thieves' methods in public, but ultimately did so.]

52. *Rashi* explains that the Gemara mentions this occurrence to teach that R' Yose not only delivered a sermon in Tzippori, but that he actually resided there. [The fact that the gutters of Tzippori ran with blood on the occasion of R' Yose's death apparently indicates that the town felt the pain of his passing more acutely than any other place, since he lived there.]

Be'er Sheva objects to *Rashi's* interpretation on the grounds that the Gemara has already mentioned elsewhere that R' Yose was a resident of Tzippori. Rather, *Be'er Sheva* maintains, this extraordinary occurrence was a sign from heaven to show the people of Tzippori that they had been wrong to reproach the saintly R' Yose for his lecture. If they suffered a wave of burglaries, it was their own fault, not R' Yose's. See also *Maharal.*

Yerushalmi Avodah Zarah 3:1 states that the blood was a miraculous reminder that R' Yose had fearlessly championed the mitzvah of circumcision even during the Roman persecutions, when circumcision had been prohibited on pain of death.

[*Ben Yehoyada* maintains that the gutters did not literally run with blood. Rather, the Gemara speaks metaphorically of the hot and bitter tears that the people of Tzippori shed upon R' Yose's passing. See there for other interpretations.]

53. The rationale for this ruling was that one who has no oxen is less burdened with work. Yet the ruling was an example of the injustice of Sodomite law, for one who owns an ox must in any event devote a certain amount of time to graze it. To require him to graze other oxen at the same time is not unreasonable, for the extra cost of time and money is negligible. On the other hand, one who possesses no oxen suffers financially when compelled to forsake his own labors and work purely on another's behalf (*Yad Ramah;* cf. *Maharsha*).

Maharal explains that this law and the ones to follow exemplify how a society's love of lucre results in perverted and corrupt legislation. The rationale behind this law was that one who owns oxen must certainly be a wealthy and fully engaged farmer. Since he has little free time, it is not fair to overburden him with communal responsibilities. On the other hand, one who owns no oxen presumably has no land to plow, and so must be idle much of the time. "Equity" dictates that such an individual should devote more time to community service than his wealthy compatriot. The Sodomites' love of money thus resulted in legislation that promoted the economic interests of the wealthy to the detriment of the poorer classes.

מאן נשדר נשדר בהדי נחום איש גם זו דמלומד בנסים הוא כי מטא לההוא דיורא בעא למיבת אמרי ליה מאי איכא בהדך אמר להו קא מובילנא כרגא לקיסר קמו בליליא שרינהו לסיפטיה ושקלו כל דהוה גביה ומלנהו עפרא כי מטא להתם אישתכח עפרא אמר אחוכי קא מחייכי בי יהודאי אפקודו למקטליה אמר גם זו לטובה אתא אליהו ואידמי להו כחד מינייהו אמר להו דילמא האי עפרא מעפרא דאברהם אבינו הוא דהוה שדי עפרא הוו חרבי גילי הוו גירי בדוק ואשכחו הכי הוה מחוזא דלא הוו קא יכלי ליה למיכבשיה שדו מההוא עפרא עליה וכבשוה עיילוהו לבי גנזא אמרי שקול דניחא לך מלייה לסיפטא דהבא כי הדר אתא אמרו ליה הנך דיורי מאי אמטית לבי מלכא אמר להו מאי דשקלי מהכא אמטאי להתם שקלי אינהו אמטו להתם קטלינהו להנך דיורי: דור הפלגה אין להם חלק לעולם הבא וכו': מאי עבוד אמרי דבי רבי שילא (א) נבנה מגדל ונעלה לרקיע ונכה אותו בקרדומות כדי שיזובו מימיו [א] מחכו עלה במערבא א"כ ליבנו אחד בטורא [ב] (אלא) א"ר ירמיה בר אלעזר נחלקו לג' כיתות אחת אומרת נעלה ונשב שם ואחת אומרת נעלה ונעבוד עבודת כוכבים ואחת אומרת נעלה ונעשה מלחמה זו שאומרת נעלה ונשב שם הפיצם ה' וזו שאומרת נעלה ונעשה מלחמה נעשו קופים ורוחות ושידים ולילין וזו שאומרת נעלה ונעבוד עבודת כוכבים [א] כי שם בלל ה' שפת כל הארץ תניא רבי נתן אומר כולם לשם עבודת כוכבים נתכוונו כתיב הכא [ב] נעשה לנו שם וכתיב התם [ג] ושם אלהים אחרים לא תזכירו מה להלן עבודת כוכבים אף כאן עבודת כוכבים אמר רבי יוחנן מגדל שליש נשרף שליש נבלע שליש קיים אמר רב אויר מגדל משכח אמר רב יוסף בבל [ג] ובורסיף סימן רע לתורה מאי בורסיף אמר ר' אסי בור [ד] שאפי: אנשי סדום אין להם חלק לעולם הבא וכו': ת"ר [ה] אנשי סדום אין להן חלק לעולם הבא שנאמר [ד] ואנשי סדום רעים וחטאים לה' מאד רעים בעוה"ז וחטאים לעולם הבא אמר רב יהודה רעים בגופן וחטאים בממונם רעים בגופן דכתיב [ה] ואיך אעשה הרעה הגדולה הזאת וחטאתי לאלהים וחטאים בממונם דכתיב [ו] והיה בך חטא לה' זו ברכת השם מאד שמתכוונים וחוטאים במתניתא תנא [ו] רעים בממונם וחטאים בגופן רעים בממונם דכתיב [ו] ורעה עינך באחיך האביון וחטאים בגופן דכתיב [ה] וחטאתי לאלהים לה' [ז] זו ברכת השם מאד זו שפיכות דמים שנאמר [ז] גם דם נקי שפך מנשה (בירושלים) הרבה מאד [וגו'] [ח] ת"ר אנשי סדום לא נתגאו אלא בשביל טובה שהשפיע להם הקב"ה ומה כתיב בהם [ח] ארץ ממנה יצא לחם ותחתיה נהפך כמו אש מקום ספיר אבניה ועפרות זהב לו נתיב לא ידעו עיט ולא שזפתו עין איה לא הדריכוהו בני שחץ לא עדה עליו שחל אמרו וכי מאחר שארץ ממנה יצא לחם ועפרות זהב לו למה לנו עוברי דרכים שאין באים אלינו אלא לחסרינו [מממוננו] בואו ונשכח תורת רגל מארצנו שנאמר [ט] פרץ נחל מעם גר הנשכחים מני רגל דלו מאנוש נעו דרש רבא מאי דכתיב [י] עד אנה תהותתו על איש תרצחו כולכם כקיר נטוי גדר הדחויה מלמד שהיו נותנין עיניהן בבעלי ממון ומושיבין אותו אצל קיר נטוי ודוחין אותו עליו ובאים ונוטלין את ממונו דרש רבא מאי דכתיב [כ] חתר בחשך בתים יומם חתמו למו לא (ראו) [ידעו] אור מלמד שהיו נותנים עיניהם בבעלי ממון ומפקידים אצלו אפרסמון ומניחים אותו בבית גנזיהם לערב באים ומריחין אותו ככלב שנא' [ל] ישובו לערב יהמו ככלב ויסובבו עיר ובאים וחותרים שם ונוטלין אותו ממון [א] [מ] ערום [ט] הלכו מבלי לבוש ואין כסות בקרה [נ] חמור יתומים ינהגו יחבלו שור אלמנה [ס] גבולות ישיגו עדר גזלו וירעו [ע] והוא לקברות יובל ועל גדיש ישקוד [ב] דרש ר' יוסי בציפורי אחתרין ההיא ליליא תלת מאה מחתרתא בציפורי אתו וקא מצערי ליה אמרו ליה יהבית אורחיה לגנבי אמר להו מי הוה ידענא דאתו גנבי [י] כי קא נח נפשיה דרבי יוסי שפעי מרזבי דציפורי דמא [ג] אמרי [כ] דאית ליה חד תורא מרעי חד יומא דלית ליה לירעי תרי יומי ההוא יתמא בר ארמלתא הבו ליה תורי למרעיה אזל שקלינהו וקטלינהו אמר להו דאית

בהדי מאן. ביד מי נשלח: כי מטא לההוא דיירא. כשהגיע לאותו מלון: למיבת. ללון: שרינהו [ל] לסיטפיה. התירו האמרגזים והמרצופין ופתחום ונטלו כל מה שבתוכו: אחוכי. מלעקי: הנך דיורי. אותן בני הכפרים: א"כ ליבנו אחד בטורא. א"כ שבנו כדי לעלות לרקיע למה בנו אותו בבקעה היה להם לבנות על אחד ההרים: הפיצם ה'. פיזרם בכל העולם: שדים. יש להם צורת אדם ואוכלין ושותין כבני אדם [מ]: רוחין. בלי גוף וצורה: לילין. צורת אדם אלא שיש להם כנפים במסכת נדה (דף כד:): זו שאומרה נעבוד ע"ז כי שם בלל ה'. בלבל לשונם כדי שלא יהא אחד מכוון לדעת חבירו לעבוד ע"ז: שליש [נבלע]. נבלעו יסודותיה משוקעת היא בקרקע עד שליש ושליש של מעלה נשרף ושליש אמצעי קיים בקרקע ולא שיהא עומד באויר: אויר מגדל. מראה המגדל (כלומר) [כמו אוירה של עיר] מי שעומד סביב למגדל ורואה אוירה ומראה גובה שלו: משכח. שכן נגזר על אותו מקום שישכח ולכך הם עצמם שכחו את לשונם: בבל ובורסיף סימן רע לתורה. שמשכחין הלמוד מפני שעומדים באויר המגדל: למה נקרא שמה בורסיף בור שאפי. בור שנתרוקן מימיו כלומר משכח האדם כל מה שלומד: שאפי. כמו (ב"מ דף ס.) השופה את היין לשון (ירמיה מח) הורק מכלי אל כלי ומפני מה שמה בבל [שמשכחת] אמר רב יוסף כי שם בלל לפי שבלבל הקדוש ברוך הוא את לשונם לשם כך היא משכחת: סימן רע. כלומר שמם סימן שכחה היא: רעים בגופם. שטופים בזימה: השמר לך פן יהיה דבר עם לבבך בליעל וגו' והיה בך חטא. והיינו ממון: ארץ ממנה יצא לחם. ארץ שבעה וטובה היא: ותחתיה נהפך כמו אש. ואחר כן נהפכה: וכי מאחר שארץ ממנה יצא לחם. שיש לנו שיפוע לחם למה לנו עוברי דרכים: ונשכח. שלא יעברו עוברי דרכים בארצנו: פרץ. הקב"ה נחל גפרית ואש: מעם גר. ממקום הליכתו שהיה הולך למעלה והשליכו עליהם הנשכחים מני רגל ונתדלדלו (מאדם) [מארצם] ונעו לדראון: גר. קוררט"ל בלע"ז כמו (שמואל ב יד) מים הנגרים: תהותתו. תבקשו תרמיות ותואנות: תרצחו כולכם. ע"י קיר נטוי וגדר הדחויה: יומם חתמו למו. היום סותמים וסוגרין כאילו לא ידעו אור כלומר סותמין וחותמין: אפרסמון. שלהם להפקידו ביד בעלי ממון כדי שיהו מניחין פקדון שלהם בבית גנזיהם ובלילה מריחין האפרסמון וחותרין שם מנהגו של מפקיד לורר וחותם: דרש ר' יוסי. בי מדרשא חתר בחשך בתים: איחתרו תלת מאה מחתרתא. ע"י ריח אפרסמון שהיו מריחין ויודעין היכן מניחין ממונם: מי הוה ידענא דאתו גנבי ל"א מי הוה ידענא דגנבי אתון: שפעי מרזבי דציפורי דמא. דאדם גדול הוה ואיידי דאמר לעיל איחתרו מחתרתי בציפורי דאתרא דרבי יוסי התם הוה נקיט נמי הא מילתא דכי נח נפשיה כו' לאשמועינן דמצפורי הוה:

תורה אור השלם

א) עַל כֵּן קָרָא שְׁמָהּ בָּבֶל כִּי שָׁם בָּלַל יְיָ שְׂפַת כָּל הָאָרֶץ וּמִשָּׁם הֱפִיצָם יְיָ עַל פְּנֵי כָּל הָאָרֶץ: [בראשית יא, ט]

ב) וַיֹּאמְרוּ הָבָה נִבְנֶה לָּנוּ עִיר וּמִגְדָּל וְרֹאשׁוֹ בַשָּׁמַיִם וְנַעֲשֶׂה לָּנוּ שֵׁם פֶּן נָפוּץ עַל פְּנֵי כָל הָאָרֶץ: [בראשית יא, ד]

ג) וּבְכֹל אֲשֶׁר אָמַרְתִּי אֲלֵיכֶם תִּשָּׁמֵרוּ וְשֵׁם אֱלֹהִים אֲחֵרִים לֹא תַזְכִּירוּ לֹא יִשָּׁמַע עַל פִּיךָ: [שמות כג, יג]

ד) וְאַנְשֵׁי סְדֹם רָעִים וְחַטָּאִים לַייָ מְאֹד: [בראשית יג, יג]

ה) אֵינֶנּוּ גָדוֹל בַּבַּיִת הַזֶּה מִמֶּנִּי וְלֹא חָשַׂךְ מִמֶּנִּי מְאוּמָה כִּי אִם אוֹתָךְ בַּאֲשֶׁר אַתְּ אִשְׁתּוֹ וְאֵיךְ אֶעֱשֶׂה הָרָעָה הַגְּדֹלָה הַזֹּאת וְחָטָאתִי לֵאלֹהִים: [בראשית לט, ט]

ו) הִשָּׁמֶר לְךָ פֶּן יִהְיֶה דָבָר עִם לְבָבְךָ בְלִיַּעַל לֵאמֹר קָרְבָה שְׁנַת הַשֶּׁבַע שְׁנַת הַשְּׁמִטָּה וְרָעָה עֵינְךָ בְּאָחִיךָ הָאֶבְיוֹן וְלֹא תִתֵּן לוֹ וְקָרָא עָלֶיךָ אֶל יְיָ וְהָיָה בְךָ חֵטְא: [דברים טו, ט]

ז) וְגַם דָּם נָקִי שָׁפַךְ מְנַשֶּׁה הַרְבֵּה מְאֹד עַד אֲשֶׁר מִלֵּא אֶת יְרוּשָׁלַיִם פֶּה לָפֶה לְבַד מֵחַטָּאתוֹ אֲשֶׁר הֶחֱטִיא אֶת יְהוּדָה לַעֲשׂוֹת הָרַע בְּעֵינֵי יְיָ: [מלכים ב' כא, טז]

ח) אֶרֶץ מִמֶּנָּה יֵצֵא לָחֶם וְתַחְתֶּיהָ נֶהְפַּךְ כְּמוֹ אֵשׁ: מְקוֹם סַפִּיר אֲבָנֶיהָ וְעַפְרֹת זָהָב לוֹ: נָתִיב לֹא יְדָעוֹ עָיִט וְלֹא שְׁזָפַתּוּ עֵין אַיָּה: לֹא הִדְרִיכֻהוּ בְנֵי שָׁחַץ לֹא עָדָה עָלָיו שָׁחַל: [איוב כח, ה-ח]

ט) פָּרַץ נַחַל מֵעִם גָּר הַנִּשְׁכָּחִים מִנִּי רָגֶל דַּלּוּ מֵאֱנוֹשׁ נָעוּ: [איוב כח, ד]

י) עַד אָנָה תְּהוֹתְתוּ עַל אִישׁ תְּרָצְּחוּ כֻלְּכֶם כְּקִיר נָטוּי גָּדֵר הַדְּחוּיָה: [תהלים סב, ד]

כ) חָתַר בַּחֹשֶׁךְ בָּתִּים יוֹמָם חִתְּמוּ לָמוֹ לֹא יָדְעוּ אוֹר: [איוב כד, טז]

ל) יָשׁוּבוּ לָעֶרֶב יֶהֱמוּ כַכָּלֶב וִיסוֹבְבוּ עִיר: [תהלים נט, ז]

מ) עָרוֹם יָלִינוּ מִבְּלִי לְבוּשׁ וְאֵין כְּסוּת בַּקָּרָה: [איוב כד, ז]

נ) חֲמוֹר יְתוֹמִים יִנְהָגוּ יַחְבְּלוּ שׁוֹר אַלְמָנָה: [איוב כד, ג]

ס) גְּבֻלוֹת יַשִּׂיגוּ עֵדֶר גָּזְלוּ וַיִּרְעוּ: [איוב כד, ב]

ע) וְהוּא לִקְבָרוֹת יוּבָל וְעַל גָּדִישׁ יִשְׁקוֹד: [איוב כא, לב]

מסורת הש"ס

א) [לעיל יז: וש"נ], ב) ב"ש מ"ז, ג) [גירסת ב"ש בירשוף], ד) [גי' הערוך ערך ברסיף שפת], ה) [תוספתא פי"ג ע"ש], ו) [תוספ' פי"ג], ז) [תוספתא שם], ח) [תוספתא דסוטה פ"ג], ט) [נ"ל ילינו], י) [מ"ק כה:], כ) [נדה סט.], ל) [נ"ל לסיפטי'], מ) [חגיגה טז.].

הגהות הב"ח

(א) גמ' אמרי דבי ר' שילא אמרי נבנה:

הגהות הגר"א

[א] גמ' ערום. נרשם עליו אות ב: [ב] שם דרש רבי יוסי. נרשם על תיבת דרש אות א: [ג] שם אמרי דאית ליה חד. נרשם על תיבת אמרי אות ג':

ליקוטי רש"י

לסיפטיה. ארגז שלו. כחד מינייהו. כאחד משרי קיסר. מעפרא דאברהם הוא. כשנלחם עם המלכים. גילי. קשין [תענית כא.]. דור הפלגה אין להם חלק לעולם הבא. ומשם הפיצם. למד שאין להם חלק לעולם הבא וכי אי זו קשה של דור המבול או של דור הפלגה אלו לא פשטו יד בעיקר ואלו פשטו יד בעיקר כביכול להלחם בו ואלו נשטפו ואלו לא נאבדו מן העולם אלא שדור המבול היו גוזלנים והיתה מריבה ביניהם לכך נאבדו ואלו היו נוהגים אהבה וריעות ביניהם שנאמר שפה אחת ודברים אחדים למדת ששנוי המחלוקת וגדול השלום [בראשית יא, ט]. נחלקו לשלש כיתות. ודברים אחדים. באו בעצה אחת ואמרו לא כל הימנו שיבור לו את העליונים נעלה לרקיע ונעשה עמו מלחמה דבר אחר על יחידו של עולם [דבר אחר ודברים אחדים אמרו אחת לאלף ושש מאות חמשים ושש שנים הרקיע מתמוטט כשם שעשה בימי המבול בואו ונעשה לו סמוכות] [בראשית יא, א]. בבל ובורסיף. ובורסיף סמוך לבבל ואינן בני תורה כדאמרינן מאי בורסיף בור ששפו את מימיו ולא נשתייר בו כלום [סוכה לד:]. וחטאתי לאלהים. בני נח נצטוו על העריות [בראשית לט, ט]. ארץ אשר ממנה יצא לחם. נהפך מקומה כמו אש. מקום ספיר. היו אבניה. לא ידעו עיט. לא עבר עליהן חיל של ליסטין. ולא שזפתו עין איה. לפי שהיא רואה יותר משאר עופות ולכך נקרא' ראה שהיא עומדת בבבל ורואה נבילו' בארץ ישראל כך מפורש באגדת (חולין סג ע"א) כלומר לא חפרוה מרגלים. לא עדה עליו. עבר כדמתרגמינן אשר עבר בין הבתרים (בראשית טו) (נ"ל הגזרים וע' בתרגום) דעדא. פרץ נחל. על סדום ועמורה נחלי אש וגפרית. מעם גר. ממקום שהוא נובע ונוגר. הנשכחים מני רגל. אלו אנשי סדום ששיכחו תורת רגלי אורחים מארצם שהיו משכיבים האורח במטה אם היה ארוך יותר מקטעין רגליו ואם היה קצר מאריכין אותו כך מפורש באגדה. דלו. ע"י פרילת נחל זה ומאנוש נעו [איוב כח]. עיט. הוא עוף ועל שם שהוא עט ושואף הנבלות (איוב ט, כו) לטוש עלי אוכל, כמו (ש"א טו, יט) ותעט אל השלל [בראשית טו, יא]. עין איה. והראה ואת האיה וגו' היא ראה היא איה היא דיה ולמה נקרא שמה ראה שרואה ביותר [דברים יד, יג]. שחל. הארי גדול והשחל בינוני והכפיר קטן [איוב ד, י]. תהותתו. מנחם פי' מגזרת התיו לאכלה (ירמיה י"ב) ויתא ראשי עם (דברים ל"ג) עד אנה תאספו על איש ול"נ שיש לפותרו לשון הוות ויהא ה"א ותי"ו שורש כאשר יאמר מן מת מות כך נאמר מן יסוד הת הות ולשון רבים הוות והוא לשון מחשבת שבר ותרמית [תהלים סב, ד]. יומם חתמו. ורבותינו פירשו יומם חתמו למו ביום היו עושים סימנים היכן מרתפו של בית והיכן גנזיו של עשיר שהיו מפקידין אפרסמון אצל בעלי בתים עשירים ויודעים הם שיניחנו בבית גנזיו ובלילה מריחין והולכים שם ומותרים שם [איוב כד, יז]. הלכו. הם הלכוהו בלי לבוש. מבלי לבוש. שנטלו כסותן. חמור יתומים ינהגו. ועושין כל רעות האמורות בענין סוף דבר ואלוה לא ישים תפלה להודיעם עונם ולהמציאם גמולם. גבולות ישיגו. אותן שדרכן להסיג גבולות שהן קונין שדות כנגד שדות אחרים ובלילה הם מרגים גבוליהם שהיו עושים גדריהם בלילה בתוך תחום. עדר גזלו וירעו. לעצמן [איוב כד עיי"ש]. והוא לקברות יובל. סופו יובל לקבר. ועל גדיש ישקוד. כשהוא נקבר בשדות אצל הגדישים [איוב כא, לב]. לירעי חד יומא. כל בהמות העיר. אזל יתמא. שלא היה לו שור וכפאוהו לרעות בהמותיהן ב' ימים [נד סט.].

א) דאית ליה תורא נשקול חד משכא דלית ליה תורא נשקול תרי משכי אמרו ליה מאי האי אמר להו סוף דינא כתחילת דינא מה תחילת דינא דאית ליה תורא מרעי חד יומא דלית ליה תורי מרעי תרי יומי אף סוף דינא דאית ליה חד תורא לשקול חד דלית ליה תורא לשקול תרי דעבר במברא ניתיב חד זוזא דלא עבר במברא ניתיב תרי דהוה ליה (תורא) [דרא] דלבני אתי כל חד וחד שקל׳ חדא א"ל אנא חדא דשקלי דהוה שדי תומי או שמכי אתו כל חד וחד שקיל חדא א"ל אנא חדא דשקלי ארבע דייני היו בסדום שקראי ושקרוראי זייפי ומצלי דינא דמחי ליה לאיתתא דחברי׳ ומפלא ליה אמרי ליה יהבה ניהליה דניעברה ניהליך דפסיק ליה לאודנא דחמרא דחבריה אמרו ליה הבה ניהליה עד דקדחא דפדע ליה לחבריה אמרי ליה הב ליה אגרא דשקל לך דמא דעבר במברא יהיב ארבעה זוזי דעבר במיא יהיב תמני זוזי זימנא חדא אתא ההוא כובס איקלע להתם אמרו ליה הב ד׳ זוזי אמר להו אנא במיא עברי אמרו ליה א"כ הב תמניא דעברת במיא לא יהיב פדיוהו אתא לקמיה דדיינא א"ל הב ליה אגרא דשקיל לך דמא ותמניא זוזי דעברת במיא אליעזר עבד אברהם איתרמי התם פדיוהי אתא לקמיה דיינא א"ל הב ליה אגרא דשקל לך דמא שקל גללא פדיוהי איהו לדיינא אמר מאי האי א"ל אגרא דנפק לי מינך הב ניהליה להאי וזוזי דידי כדקיימי קיימי הויא להו פורייתא דהוו מגני עלה אורחין כי מאריך גייזי ליה כי גוץ מתחין ליה אליעזר עבד אברהם אקלע להתם אמרו ליה קום גני אפוריא אמר להון נדרא נדרי מן יומא דמיתת אמא לא גנינא אפוריא כי הוה מתרמי להו עניא יהבו ליה כל חד וחד דינרא וכתיב שמיה עליה וריפתא לא הוו ממטי ליה כי הוה מית אתי כל חד וחד שקיל דידיה הכי אתני בינייהו כל מאן דמזמין גברא לבי הילולא לשלח גלימא הוי האי הילולא אקלע אליעזר להתם ולא יהבו ליה נהמא כי בעי למסעד אתא אליעזר ויתיב לסיפא דכולהו אמרו ליה מאן אזמנך להכא א"ל לההוא [דיתיב] אתה זמנתן [אמר דילמא שמעי בי דאנא אזמינתיה ומשלחי ליה מאניה דהאי גברא] שקל גלימיה ההוא דיתיב גביה ורהט לברא וכן עבד לכולהו עד דנפקי כולהו ואכלא איהו לסעודתא הויא ההיא רביתא דהות קא מפקא ריפתא לעניא בחצבא איגלאי מלתא שפיוה דובשא ואוקמוה על איגר שורא אתא זיבורי ואכלוה והיינו דכתיב א) ויאמר ה׳ זעקת סדום ועמורה כי רבה ואמר רב יהודה אמר רב על עיסקי ריבה: [א] מרגלים אין להם חלק לעולם הבא שנאמר ב) וימותו האנשים מוציאי דבת הארץ רעה במגפה לעולם הבא: [ב] עדת קרח אין להם חלק לעולם הבא [ג] שנאמר ג) ותכס עליהם הארץ בעולם הזה ויאבדו מתוך הקהל לעולם הבא דברי ר"ע רבי אליעזר אומר עליהם אמר הכתוב ד) ה׳ ממית ומחיה מוריד שאול ויעל: ת"ר עדת קרח אין להם חלק לעולם הבא שנאמר ותכס עליהם הארץ בעולם הזה ויאבדו מתוך הקהל לעולם הבא דברי רבי עקיבא רבי יהודה בן בתירא אומר הרי הן כאבידה המתבקשת שנאמר ה) תעיתי כשה אובד בקש עבדך כי מצותיך לא שכחתי: ו) ויקח [קרח] אמר ריש לקיש שלקח מקח רע לעצמו קרח שנעשה קרחה בישראל בן יצהר בן שהרתיח עליו את כל העולם כצהרים בן קהת בן שהקהה שיני מולידיו בן לוי בן שנעשה לויה בגיהנם וליחשוב נמי בן יעקב בן שעקב עצמו לגיהנם אמר רב שמואל בר רב יצחק יעקב ביקש רחמים על עצמו שנאמר ז) בסודם אל תבא נפשי ובקהלם אל תחד כבודי בסודם אל תבא נפשי אלו מרגלים ובקהלם אל תחד כבודי זה עדת קרח דתן שעבר על דת אל אבירם שאיבר [ד] עצמו מעשות תשובה ואון שישב באנינות פלת שנעשו לו פלאות בן ראובן בן שראה והבין אמר רב און בן פלת אשתו הצילתו אמרה ליה מאי נפקא לך מינה אי מר רבה אנת תלמידא ואי מר רבה אנת תלמידא אמר לה מאי אעביד הואי בעצה ואשתבעי לי בהדייהו אמרה [ה] ליה ידענא דכולה כנישתא קדישתא נינהו דכתיב ח) כי כל העדה כולם קדושים אמרה ליה תוב דאנא מצילנא לך אשקיתיה חמרא וארויתיה ואגניתיה גואי אותבה על בבא וסתרתה

דאית ליה תורא. כך היה מנהגם של אנשי סדום מי שהיה לו שור אחד רועה כל בהמות העיר יום א׳ ומי שאין לו בהמה מגלגלין עליו לרעות ב׳ ימים: אמר להו. יתמי למרי דתורא דאית ליה חד תורא כו׳: דעבר במברא. שהמעבורת שלהם מימיו עזין והיו דנין כך: דלא עבר במברא. אלא בא דרך אחר: דה"ל דרא דלבני. מי שהיו לו שורת לבנים ומגבל ועושה אותן היה בא כל חד וחד ונוטל אחת: שדי תומי או שמכי. מי שהיה מפזר ושוטח לפניו שומים או בצלים ליבשן כל א׳ וא׳ היה נוטל אחת: אומר לו. לנגזל מה חסרתי לך לא לקחתי ממך אלא שום אחד ונמלא קרח מכאן ומכאן: זייפא. ומצלי דין: יהבה ניהליה. וישכב עמה עד שתהיה מעוברת: עד דקדחא. עד שתצמח אזנו: דפדע. עשה לו פצע כמו פדעת במסכת ע"ז (דף כח.) כפרדור"א בלע"ז: דעבר במיא. עובר ברגליו במים: גללא. מקל ל"א אבן: א"ל. דיינא לאליעזר מאי האי: א"ל. אליעזר אגרא דמחייבת לי דשקלי לך דמא הב ליה להאי גברא דשקל לי דמא וזוזי דידי כדקיימי קיימי ל"א ה"ג ולואי כדקאי קאי כך אמר ליה דיין מי יתן שהייתי כבתחילה (א): הכי אתנו בהדייהו כל מאן דמזמן. אכסניא לבי הלולא: לשלחו לגלימיה. יפשיטו את בגדי אותו האיש שהזמינו: ואתא אליעזר. עבד אברהם: ויתיב אסיפא דכולהו. הלך וישב בסוף כולם: א"ל מאן אזמנך להכא: א"ל. אליעזר למאן דיתיב גביה את זמנתני להכא: שקל גלימיה. דיתיב לגביה ורהט לברא שהיה מתיירא שלא ישמעו אנשי המקום שאליעזר אמר שהוא זימנו ולישלחו למאניה הלך וישב לו אצל השני ואמר כמו כן וכן לכל אחד ואחד עד דאזלי כולהו ואכל אליעזר כל הסעודה: כי אריך גייצו ליה. כשהאורח ארוך יותר מן המטה מקצרין אותו בסכין גיילי לשון גוץ כן שמעתי ואית דגרסי גיידי ליה: ומתחין ליה. עד דמתפרקי אבריו: וכתיב שמיה עילויה. כדי שיכיר כל אחד וא׳ דינר שלו ויחזור ויטלנו: ורפתא לא ממטו ליה. התנו ביניהם שלא יתנו לו פת כדי שימות ברעב וכשמת אזיל כל חד וחד ושקיל לדינרא דידיה: רביתא. נערה: בחצבא. בתוך כד שלה כשיוצאת לשאוב מים: שפיוה. סכו אותה: איגר שורא. על גג החומה: כי רבה. על עסקי ריבה: רבי יהודה בן בתירא אומר ויאבדו הרי הן כאבידה המתבקשת. ובאין לעולם הבא שכך אמר דוד על בני קרח תעיתי כשה אובד בקש עבדך הם תעו כשה אובד ואתה ברחמיך הרבים בקש עבדך ותביאם לעוה"ב: מצותיך לא שכחתי. שקיימו כל מצותיך כדכתיב (במדבר טז) כי כל העדה כולם קדושים: מקח רע. התחיל בקטטה: שנעשה קרחה בישראל. שנבלעו: שהרתיח. שהכעיס: הקהה שיני מולידיו. שנתביישו אבותיו במעשיו הרעים: בקש רחמים על עצמו. שלא יהא נמנה עמהם: אלו מרגלים. דלא כתיב בהן פלוני בן יעקב: שאיבר לבבו. חזק לבבו כמו (ישעיה מו) אבירי לב: שישב באנינות. שעשה תשובה על שהיה עמהם תחילה בעצה: נעשו לו פלאות. (שפירש) [שניצל] מהם: ראה והבין. שאין מנהגן כשורה ופירש מהם: אי מר רבה. אם ינצח משה מכל מקום אתה תלמיד ואם קרח מנצח אתה תלמיד מה לך בשררה זו: הואי בעצה. אני הייתי עמהן בעצה ונשבעתי להם שאם יקראוני אלך עמהם: דכולה כנישתא קדישין. כולם צנועים וקדושים ולא יכנסו אלי אם אני פרועה:

סתרה

הגהות הב"ח

(א) רש"י ד"ה אמר ליה אליעזר וכו׳ כבתחלה הס"ד ואח"כ צ"ל ד"ה כי אריך ואח"כ ד"ה וכתיב וד"ה ורפתא ואח"כ צ"ל ד"ה הכי אתני וד"ה אזל אליעזר וד"ה א"ל מאן ואח"כ צ"ל ד"ה רביתא נערה:

הגהות הגר"א

[א] גמ׳ מרגלים אין להם כו׳ עד עדת קרח. נמחק: [ב] שם עדת קרח כו׳ לעולם הבא. נ"ב וכו׳: [ג] שם שנאמר ותכם וכו׳ עד ת"ר עדת. נמחק: [ד] שם שאבר עצמו. נמחק תיבת עצמו: [ה] אמרי ליה. נמחק תיבת ליה:

גליון הש"ס

גמ׳ הרי הן כאבידה המתבקשת. עיין מכות דף כ"ד ע"א:

תורה אור השלם

א) וַיֹּאמֶר יְיָ זַעֲקַת סְדֹם וַעֲמֹרָה כִּי רָבָּה וְחַטָּאתָם כִּי כָבְדָה מְאֹד: [בראשית יח, כ]

ב) וַיָּמֻתוּ הָאֲנָשִׁים מוֹצִאֵי דִבַּת הָאָרֶץ רָעָה בַּמַּגֵּפָה לִפְנֵי יְיָ: [במדבר יד, לז]

ג) וַיֵּרְדוּ הֵם וְכָל אֲשֶׁר לָהֶם חַיִּים שְׁאֹלָה וַתְּכַס עֲלֵיהֶם הָאָרֶץ וַיֹּאבְדוּ מִתּוֹךְ הַקָּהָל: [במדבר טז, לג]

ד) יְיָ מֵמִית וּמְחַיֶּה מוֹרִיד שְׁאוֹל וַיָּעַל: [שמואל א׳ ב, ו]

ה) תָּעִיתִי כְּשֶׂה אֹבֵד בַּקֵּשׁ עַבְדֶּךָ כִּי מִצְוֹתֶיךָ לֹא שָׁכָחְתִּי: [תהלים קיט, קעו]

ו) וַיִּקַּח קֹרַח בֶּן יִצְהָר בֶּן קְהָת בֶּן לֵוִי וְדָתָן וַאֲבִירָם בְּנֵי אֱלִיאָב וְאוֹן בֶּן פֶּלֶת בְּנֵי רְאוּבֵן: [במדבר טז, א]

ז) בְּסֹדָם אַל תָּבֹא נַפְשִׁי בִּקְהָלָם אַל תֵּחַד כְּבֹדִי כִּי בְאַפָּם הָרְגוּ אִישׁ וּבִרְצֹנָם עִקְּרוּ שׁוֹר: [בראשית מט, ו]

ח) וַיִּקָּהֲלוּ עַל מֹשֶׁה וְעַל אַהֲרֹן וַיֹּאמְרוּ אֲלֵהֶם רַב לָכֶם כִּי כָל הָעֵדָה כֻּלָּם קְדֹשִׁים וּבְתוֹכָם יְיָ וּמַדּוּעַ תִּתְנַשְּׂאוּ עַל קְהַל יְיָ: [במדבר טז, ג]

מסורת הש"ס

א) [נדה דף סט.], ב) [תוספתא פרק י"ג], ג) [סוטה יוד:].

ליקוטי רש"י

זיבורא. צירעה [ע"ז יב:]. זעקת סדום. ורבותינו דרשו הכצעקתה צעקת ריבה אחת שהרגוה מיתה משונה על שנתנה מזון לעני כמפורש בחלק (סנהדרין קט:) [בראשית יח, כא]. כאבידה המתבקשת. ונמצאת לאחר זמן [מכות כד.]. בסודם אל תבא נפשי. זה מעשה זמרי כשנתקבצו שבטו של שמעון להביא את המדינית לפני משה ואמרו לו זו אסורה או מותרת אם תאמר אסורה בת יתרו מי התירה לך אל יזכר שמי בדבר שנאמר (במדבר כה, יד) זמרי בן סלוא נשיא בית אב לשמעוני ולא כתב בן יעקב. בקהלם. כשיקהיל קרח שהוא משבטו של לוי את כל העדה על משה ועל אהרן. אל תחד כבודי. שם אל יתיחד עמהם שמי שנאמר (במדבר טז, א) קרח בן יצהר בן קהת בן לוי ולא נאמר בן יעקב אבל בדברי הימים כשנתייחסו בני קרח על הדוכן נאמר (דה"א ו, כב) בן קרח בן יצהר בן קהת בן לוי בן ישראל. אל תחד כבודי. כבוד לשון זכר הוא ועל כרחך אתה צריך לפרש כמדבר אל הכבוד ואומר אתה כבודי אל תתיחד עמם כמו (ישעיה יד, כ) לא תחד אתם בקבורה [בראשית מט, ו]. בקהלם אל תחד כבודי. בן יצהר בן קהת בן לוי. ולא הזכיר בן יעקב שבקש רחמים על עצמו שלא יזכר שמו על מחלוקתם שנאמר (בראשית מט, ו) ובקהלם אל תחד כבודי והיכן נזכר שמו על קרח בהתיחסם על הדוכן בדברי הימים שנאמר (דה"א ו, כב) בן אביאסף בן קרח בן יצהר בן קהת בן לוי בן ישראל [במדבר טז, א].

[מכאן שייך לדף קי.]

איהו הוי מלכא וכו׳. מה ראה קרח לחלוק עם משה נתקנא על נשיאותו של אליצפן בן עוזיאל שמינהו משה נשיא על בני קהת על פי הדבור אמר קרח אחי אבא ארבעה היו שנאמר (שמות ו, יח) ובני קהת וגו׳ עמרם הבכור נטלו שני בניו גדולה אחד מלך ואחד כהן גדול מי ראוי ליטול את השניה לא אני שאני בן יצהר שהוא שני לעמרם והוא מנה נשיא את בן אחיו הקטן מכולם הריני חולק עליו ומבטל את דבריו. אפיק גלימא דתכלתא. מה עשה עמד וכנס מאתים חמישים ראשי סנהדראות רובן משבט ראובן שכיניו והם אליצור בן שדיאור וחביריו וכיוצא בו שנאמר נשיאי עדה קריאי מועד ולהלן הוא אומר (במדבר א, טז) אלה קרואי העדה והלבישן טליתות שכולן תכלת באו ועמדו לפני משה אמרו לו טלית שכולה של תכלת חייבת בציצית או פטורה אמר להם חייבת התחילו לשחק עליו אפשר טלית של מין

דְּאִית לֵיהּ תּוֹרָא נִשְׁקוֹל חַד מַשְׁכָּא – "He **who had** one **ox, let him take one skin** from the dead oxen. דְּלֵית לֵיהּ תּוֹרָא נִשְׁקוֹל תְּרֵי מַשְׁכֵי – He who had no ox, let him take two skins." אָמְרוּ לֵיהּ – **[The owners of the dead oxen] said to him:** מַאי הַאי – **"What is this** ridiculous method of apportioning the skins that you are proposing?!" אָמַר לְהוּ – **He said to them:** סוֹף דִּינָא כִּתְחִילַּת דִּינָא – "It is only fair. **The rule at the end,** i.e. the rule concerning the apportionment of the skins, **ought to be like the rule at the beginning.** מַה תְּחִילַּת דִּינָא דְּאִית לֵיהּ תּוֹרָא מַרְעֵי חַד יוֹמָא – **Just as the rule at the beginning** was that he **who has** one **ox must graze** the other oxen for **one day,** דְּלֵית לֵיהּ תּוֹרֵי מַרְעֵי תְּרֵי יוֹמֵי – while he **who has no ox must graze** them for **two days,** אַף סוֹף דִּינָא דְּאִית לֵיהּ חַד תּוֹרָא לִשְׁקוֹל חַד – so **the rule at the end** should **likewise** be: He **who had one ox should take one** skin, דְּלֵית לֵיהּ תּוֹרָא לִשְׁקוֹל תְּרֵי – while he **who has no ox should take two** skins!"

Another unjust law of Sodom:

דְּעָבַר בְּמַבְרָא נֵיתִיב חַד זוּזָא – It stated: He **who crosses** the swift waters of the **ford**[1] **must pay one** *zuz,* דְּלֹא עָבַר בְּמַבְרָא נֵיתִיב תְּרֵי – while he **who does not cross the ford,** but comes a different way, **must pay two** *zuz.*

The refined form of robbery practiced by the Sodomites:

דַּהֲוָה לֵיהּ (תּוֹרָא) [דָּרָא] דִּלְבֵנֵי – If there was a person **who had a row of bricks** (he manufactured bricks), אָתֵי כָּל חַד וְחַד שָׁקִיל חֲדָא – **each and every one** of the Sodomites **would come by** and **take one** brick. אָמַר לֵיהּ – When the owner demanded restitution, **[each Sodomite] would say to him:** אֲנָא חֲדָא דִּשְׁקַלִי – **"It was** only **one** brick **that I took!** What loss did I cause you?" In this way the brick manufacturer would be dissuaded from seeking legal redress, and ultimately would lose all of his merchandise.[2] דַּהֲוָה שָׁדֵי תּוּמֵי אוֹ שׁוּמְבֵי – Similarly, if there was a person **who spread out garlic or onions** in the sun to dry, אָתוּ כָּל חַד וְחַד שָׁקִיל חֲדָא – **each and every one** of the Sodomites **would come by** and **take one** garlic or onion bulb. אָמַר לֵיהּ – Again, when the owner protested, **[each thief] would say to him:** אֲנָא חֲדָא דִּשְׁקַלִי – **"It was** only **one that I took!"**

The Gemara describes the utter depravity of the Sodomite judicial system:

אַרְבַּע דַּיָּינֵי הָיוּ בִּסְדוֹם – **There were four judges in Sodom:** שַׁקְרָאי וְשַׁקְרוּרָאי זַיְיפֵי וּמַצְלֵי דִינָא – **Shakrai, Shakrurai, Zaifai and Matzlei Dina.**[3] דְּמָחֵי לֵיהּ לְאִיתְּתָא דְּחַבְרֵיהּ וּמַפְּלָא לֵיהּ – If there was a person **who struck his fellow's wife and** as a result **she miscarried,**[4] אָמְרֵי לֵיהּ – **[the judges] would say to [the husband]:** יְהָבָהּ נִיהֲלֵיהּ – It is our verdict that **[you] shall give [your wife] to [the attacker],** דְּנִיעַבְּרָהּ נִיהֲלָךְ – **so that he may impregnate her for you** and thereby replace the unborn child whose death he caused. דְּפָסִיק לֵיהּ לְאוּדְנָא דַּחֲמָרָא דְּחַבְרֵיהּ – If there was a person **who lopped off the ear of his fellow's donkey,** אָמְרוּ לֵיהּ – **[the judges] would say to [the owner]:** הַבָה נִיהֲלֵיהּ עַד דְּקַדְחָא – **Give [the donkey] to [the damager] until** such time as **[the ear] grows back.** דְּפָדַע לֵיהּ לְחַבְרֵיהּ – If there was a person **who wounded his fellow,** אָמְרֵי לֵיהּ – **[the judges] would say to [the injured party]:** הַב לֵיהּ אַגְרָא – **Give [your assailant]** his **wage,** דִּשְׁקַל לָךְ דְּמָא – **for he let blood for you,** and this is a medical procedure for which you ordinarily pay a specialist.

Another example of the perversity of Sodomite justice:

דְּעָבַר בְּמַבְרָא יָהִיב אַרְבָּעָה זוּזֵי – Sodomite law stated that one **who crossed** the river **on a ferryboat must pay four** *zuz,* דְּעָבַר בְּמַיָּא יָהִיב תְּמָנֵי זוּזֵי – while one **who crossed in the water**[5] **must pay eight** *zuz.* זִימְנָא חֲדָא – **Once,** אָתָא הַהוּא כּוֹבֵס – **a certain launderer came** to Sodom, and was unaware of the local laws. אִיקְלַע לְהָתָם – **He happened to come there,** to the place where they collected the toll for crossing the river. אָמְרוּ לֵיהּ – **[The Sodomite officials] said to [the launderer]:** הַב אַרְבַּע זוּזֵי – **"Give** us **four** *zuz,* the cost of a ferryboat crossing." אָמַר לְהוּ – **[The launderer] said to them:** אֲנָא בְּמַיָּא עֲבָרִי – **"I** did not use the ferryboat, but **crossed in the water;** hence, I owe you nothing." אָמְרוּ לֵיהּ – **[The Sodomite officials] said to him:** אִם כֵּן הַב תְּמָנְיָא – **"If** it is **so** that you did not ride the ferry, then **give** us **eight** *zuz,* דַּעֲבַרְתְּ בְּמַיָּא – **for you crossed in the water,** and local regulations require a payment of eight *zuz* for crossing without the ferry." לֹא יָהִיב – **[The launderer] did not give** them any money, פַּדְיוּהוּ – and so **[the Sodomites]** beat, and **wounded him.** אָתָא לְקַמֵּיהּ דְּדַיָּינָא – **[The launderer]** then **came before a** Sodomite **judge** seeking damages, אָמַר לֵיהּ – but **[the judge] said to him:** הַב לֵיהּ אַגְרָא דִּשְׁקִיל לָךְ דְּמָא – **"Give [your assailant]** his **wage, since he let blood for you,** וּתְמַנְיָא זוּזֵי דַּעֲבַרְתְּ בְּמַיָּא – **and** pay an additional **eight** *zuz,* **since you crossed in the water!"**

The Gemara records Eliezer's encounter with Sodomite justice:[6]

אֱלִיעֶזֶר עֶבֶד אַבְרָהָם אִיתְרְמִי הָתָם – **Eliezer, the servant of Abraham,** once **happened** to come **there,** to Sodom. פַּדְיוּהִי – **They** assaulted and **wounded him,**[7] אָתָא לְקַמֵּיהּ דַּיָּינָא – and **he came before a** Sodomite **judge** seeking redress. אָמַר לֵיהּ – **[The judge] said to [Eliezer]:** הַב לֵיהּ אַגְרָא דִּשְׁקַל לָךְ דְּמָא – **"Give [your assailant]** his **wage, since he let blood for you."** שְׁקַל גְּלָלָא – **[Eliezer]** thereupon **took a stick,**[8] פַּדְיוּהִי אִיהוּ לְדַיָּינָא – **and he** in turn struck and **wounded the judge.** אָמַר – **[The judge] said:** מַאי הַאי – **"What is this** that you are doing?!"[9] אָמַר לֵיהּ – **[Eliezer] said to [the judge]:** אַגְרָא דְּנָפַק לִי מִינָּךְ – "You Sodomites say that every assailant deserves

NOTES

1. This is apparently *Rashi's* translation of מַבְרָא (see *Hagahos R' Yaakov Emden*), and it eliminates the question posed by *Rashash* from the Gemara below (דעבר במברא יהיב ד׳ זוזי). *Yad Ramah* renders מַבְרָא *a bridge.*

2. This is *Rashi's* interpretation. According to *Yad Ramah,* each brick was worth less than a *perutah* – that is, less than the minimum amount for which a legal action can be brought.

3. These Hebrew words are translated: Liar, Outrageous Liar, Forger and Perverter of Justice. Each judge was named after one of the four judgments presently recorded in the Gemara (*Maharsha* and *Yad Ramah;* see also *Margaliyos HaYam*).

4. The word לֵיהּ is deleted by *Dikdukei Soferim,* and our translation follows his emendation.

5. E.g. he swam across the river.

6. *Maharal* finds a connection between Eliezer's story and the preceding one, as follows: It was clearly the intention of the Sodomites to harm strangers. Nevertheless, God does not abandon the righteous, even when they are faced with the most vexing of situations. Now, whenever the Gemara mentions a "launderer," it refers to a person of low spiritual stature. Hence, the victim in the preceding episode was unworthy of being Divinely rescued from the Sodomites' evil designs. However, such was not the case with Eliezer, the loyal and righteous servant of our forefather Abraham, as the Gemara now relates.

7. *Yad Ramah* explains that Eliezer happened to have a monetary claim against one of the residents of Sodom, and when Eliezer asked for his money the debtor struck and injured him.

8. Alternatively: a stone (*Rashi*).

9. *Ben Yehoyada* explains that although the judge realized that Eliezer was acting to offset his loss, he was uncertain whether Eliezer intended to take the judge's payment himself, or whether it was to go to Eliezer's "creditor." Thus, he asked Eliezer what his intent was.

[א] דאית ליה תורא נשקול חד משכא דלית ליה תורא נשקול תרי משכי אמרו ליה מאי האי אמר להו סוף דינא כתחילת דינא מה תחילת דינא דאית ליה תורא מרעי חד יומא דלית ליה תורי מרעי תרי יומי אף סוף דינא דאית ליה חד תורא לשקול חד דלית ליה תורא לשקול תרי דעבר במברא ניתיב חד זוזא דלא עבר במברא ניתיב תרי דהוה ליה (תורא) [דרא] דלבני אתי כל חד וחד שקל' חדא א"ל אנא חדא דשקלי דהוה שדי תומי או שמכי אתו כל חד וחד שקיל חדא א"ל אנא חדא דשקלי ארבע דייני היו בסדום שקראי ושקרוראי זייפי ומצלי דינא דמחי ליה לאיתתא דחברי' ומפלא ליה אמרי ליה יהבה ניהליה דניעברה ניהליך דפסיק ליה לאודנא דחמרא דחבריה אמרו ליה הבה ניהליה עד דקדחא דפדע ליה לחבריה אמרי ליה הב ליה אגרא דשקל לך דמא דעבר במברא יהיב ארבעה זוזי דעבר במיא יהיב תמני זוזי זימנא חדא אתא ההוא כובס איקלע להתם אמרו ליה הב ד' זוזי אמר להו אנא במיא עברי אמרו ליה א"כ הב תמניא דעברת במיא לא יהיב פדיוהו אתא לקמיה דדיינא א"ל הב ליה אגרא דשקיל לך דמא ותמניא זוזי דעברת במיא אליעזר עבד אברהם איתרמי התם פדיוהי אתא לקמיה דיינא א"ל הב ליה אגרא דשקל לך דמא שקל גללא פדיוהי איהו לדיינא אמר מאי האי א"ל אגרא דנפק לי מינך הב ניהליה להאי וזוזי דידי כדקיימי קיימי הויא להו פורייתא דהוו מגני עלה אורחין כי מאריך גייזי ליה כי גוץ מתחין ליה אליעזר עבד אברהם אקלע להתם אמרו ליה קום גני אפוריא אמר להון נדרא נדרי מן יומא דמיתת אמא לא גנינא אפוריא כי הוה מתרמי להו עניא יהבו ליה כל חד וחד דינרא וכתיב שמיה עליה וריפתא לא הוו ממטי ליה כי הוה מית אתי כל חד וחד שקיל דידיה הכי אתני בינייהו כל מאן דמזמין גברא לבי הילולא לשלח גלימא הוי האי הילולא אקלע אליעזר להתם ולא יהבו ליה נהמא כי בעי למסעד אתא אליעזר ויתיב לסיפא דכולהו אמרו ליה מאן אזמנך להכא א"ל להההוא [דיתיב] אתה זמנתן [אמר דילמא שמעי בי דאנא אזמינתיה ומשלחי ליה מאניה דהאי גברא] שקל גלימיה ההוא דיתיב גביה ורהט לברא וכן עבד לכולהו עד דנפקי כולהו ואכלא איהו לסעודתא הויא ההיא רביתא דהות קא מפקא ריפתא לעניא בחצבא איגלאי מלתא שפיוה דובשא ואוקמוה על איגר שורא אתא זיבורי ואכלוה והיינו דכתיב (א) ויאמר ה' זעקת סדום ועמורה כי רבה ואמר רב יהודה אמר רב על עיסקי ריבה: [א] מרגלים אין להם חלק לעולם הבא שנאמר (ב) וימותו האנשים מוציאי דבת הארץ רעה במגפה וימותו בעולם הזה במגפה לעולם הבא: [ב] עדת קרח אין להם חלק לעולם הבא [ג] שנאמר (ג) ותכס עליהם הארץ בעולם הזה ויאבדו מתוך הקהל לעולם הבא דברי ר"ע רבי אליעזר אומר עליהם אמר הכתוב (ד) ה' ממית ומחיה מוריד שאול ויעל: ת"ר [ג] עדת קרח אין להם חלק לעולם הבא שנאמר ותכס עליהם הארץ בעולם הזה ויאבדו מתוך הקהל לעולם הבא דברי רבי עקיבא רבי יהודה בן בתירא אומר °הרי הן כאבידה המתבקשת שנאמר (ה) תעיתי כשה אובד בקש עבדך כי מצותיך לא שכחתי: (ו) ויקח [קרח] [ג] אמר ריש לקיש שלקח מקח רע לעצמו קרח שנעשה קרחה בישראל בן יצהר בן שהרתיח עליו את כל העולם כצהרים בן קהת בן שהקהה שיני מולידיו בן לוי בן שנעשה לויה בגיהנם וליחשוב נמי בן יעקב בן שעקב עצמו לגיהנם אמר רב שמואל בר רב יצחק יעקב ביקש רחמים על עצמו שנאמר (ז) בסודם אל תבא נפשי ובקהלם אל תחד כבודי בסודם אל תבא נפשי אלו מרגלים ובקהלם אל תחד כבודי זה עדת קרח דתן שעבר על דת אל אבירם שאיבר [ד] עצמו מעשות תשובה ואון שישב באנינות פלת שנעשו לו פלאות בן ראובן בן שראה והבין אמר רב און בן פלת אשתו הצילתו אמרה ליה מאי נפקא לך מינה אי מר רבה אנת תלמידא ואי מר רבה אנת תלמידא אמר לה מאי אעביד הואי בעצה ואשתבעי לי בהדייהו אמרה [ה] ליה ידענא דכולה כנישתא קדישתא נינהו דכתיב (ח) כי כל העדה כולם קדושים אמרה ליה תוב דאנא מצילנא לך אשקיתיה חמרא וארויתיה ואגניתיה גואי אותבה על בבא

וסתרתה

רש"י

דאית ליה תורא. כך היה מנהגם של אנשי סדום מי שהיה לו שור אחד רועה כל בהמות העיר יום א' ומי שאין לו בהמה מגלגלין עליו לרעות ב' ימים: אמר להו. יתמי למרי דתורא דאית ליה חד תורא כו': דעבר במברא. שהמעברות שלהם מימיו עזין והיו דנין כך: דלא עבר במברא. אלא בא דרך אחר: דה"ל דרא דלבני. מי שהיו לו שורת לבנים ומגבל ועושה אותן היה בא כל חד וחד ונוטל אחת: שדי תומי או שמכי. מי שהיה מפזר ושוטח לפניו שומים או בצלים ליבשן כל א' וא' היה נוטל אחת: אומר לו. לנגזל מה חסרתי לך לא לקחתי ממך אלא שום אחד ונמצא קרח מכאן ומכאן: זייפא. ומצלי דין: יהבה ניהליה. וישכב עמה עד שתהיה מעוברת: עד דקדחא. עד שתצמח אזנו: דפדע. עשה לו פצע כמו פדעת במסכת ע"ז (דף כח.) כפרדור"א בלע"ז: דעבר במיא. עובר ברגליו במים: גללא. מקל ל"א אבן: א"ל. דיינא לאליעזר מאי האי: א"ל. אליעזר אגרא דמחייבת לי דשקלי לך דמא הב ליה להאי גברא דשקל לי דמא וזוזי דידי כדקיימי קיימי ל"א ה"ג ולואי כדקאי קאי כך אמר ליה דיין מי יתן שהייתי כבתחילה (א): הכי אתנו בהדייהו כל מאן דמזמן. אכסניא לבי הלולא: לשלחו לגלימיה. יפשיטו את בגדי אותו האיש שהזמינו: ואתא אליעזר. עבד אברהם: ויתיב אסיפא דכולהו. הלך וישב בסוף כולם: א"ל מאן אזמנך להכא: א"ל. אליעזר למאן דיתיב גביה את זמנתני להכא: שקל גלימיה. דיתיב לגביה ורהט לברא שהיה מתיירא שלא ישמעו אנשי המקום שאליעזר אמר שהוא זימנו ולישלחו למאניה הלך וישב לו אצל השני ואמר כמו כן וכן לכל אחד ואחד עד דאזלי כולהו ואכל אליעזר כל הסעודה: כי אריך גייצו ליה. כשהאורח ארוך יותר מן המטה מקצרין אותו בסכין גיילי לשון גוץ כן שמעתי ואית דגרסי גיידי ליה: ומתחין ליה. עד דמתפרקי אבריו: וכתיב שמיה עילויה. כדי שיכיר כל אחד וא' דינר שלו ויחזור ויטלנו: ורפתא לא ממטו ליה. התנו ביניהם שלא יתנו לו פת כדי שימות ברעב וכשמת אזיל כל חד וחד ושקיל לדינרא דידיה: רביתא. נערה: בחצבא. בתוך כד שלה כשיוצאת לשאוב מים: שפיוה. סכו אותה: איגר שורא. על גג החומה: כי רבה. על עסקי ריבה: רבי יהודה בן בתירא אומר ויאבדו הרי הן כאבידה המתבקשת. ובאין לעולם הבא שכך אמר דוד על בני קרח תעיתי כשה אובד בקש עבדך הם תעו כשה אובד ואתה ברחמיך הרבים בקש עבדך ותביאם לעוה"ב: מצותיך לא שכחתי. שקיימו כל מצותיך כדכתיב (במדבר טז) כי כל העדה כולם קדושים: מקח רע. התחיל בקטטה: שעשה קרחה בישראל. שנבלעו: שהרתיח. שהכעיס: הקהה שיני מולידיו. שנתביישו אבותיו במעשיו הרעים: בקש רחמים על עצמו. שלא יהא נמנה עמהם: אלו מרגלים. דלא כתיב בהן פלוני בן יעקב: שאיבר לבבו. חזק לבבו כמו (ישעיה מו) אבירי לב: שישב באנינות. שעשה תשובה על שהיה עמהם תחילה בעצה: נעשו לו פלאות. (שפירש) [שניצל] מהם: ראה והבין. שאין מנהגן כשורה ופירש מהם: אי מר רבה. אם ינצח משה מכל מקום אתה תלמיד ואם קרח מנצח אתה תלמיד מה לך בשררה זו: הואי בעצה. אני הייתי עמהן בעצה ונשבעתי להם שאם יקראוני אלך עמהם: דכולה כנישתא קדישין. כולם צנועים וקדושים ולא יכנסו אלי אם אני פרועה:

סתרה

הגהות הב"ח

(א) רש"י ד"ה אמר ליה אליעזר וכו' כבתחלה הס"ד ואח"כ נ"ל ד"ה כי אריך ואח"כ ד"ה וכתיב וד"ה ורפתא ואח"כ נ"ל ד"ה הכי אתני וד"ה אזל אליעזר וד"ה א"ל מאן ואח"כ נ"ל ד"ה רביתא נערה:

הגהות הגר"א

[א] גמ' מרגלים אין להם כו' עד עדת קרח. נמחק: [ב] שם עדת קרח כו' לעולם הבא. נ"ב וכו': [ג] שם שנאמר ותכס וכו' עד ת"ר עדת. נמחק: [ד] שם שאבר עצמו. נמחק תיבת עצמו: [ה] אמרי ליה. נמחק תיבת ליה:

גליון הש"ס

גמ' הרי הן כאבידה המתבקשת. עיין מכות דף כ"ד ע"א:

תורה אור השלם

א) וַיֹּאמֶר יְיָ זַעֲקַת סְדֹם וַעֲמֹרָה כִּי רָבָּה וְחַטָּאתָם כִּי כָבְדָה מְאֹד: [בראשית יח, כ]

ב) וַיָּמֻתוּ הָאֲנָשִׁים מוֹצִאֵי דִבַּת הָאָרֶץ רָעָה בַּמַּגֵּפָה לִפְנֵי יְיָ: [במדבר יד, לז]

ג) וַיֵּרְדוּ הֵם וְכָל אֲשֶׁר לָהֶם חַיִּים שְׁאֹלָה וַתְּכַס עֲלֵיהֶם הָאָרֶץ וַיֹּאבְדוּ מִתּוֹךְ הַקָּהָל: [במדבר טז, לג]

ד) יְיָ מֵמִית וּמְחַיֶּה מוֹרִיד שְׁאוֹל וַיָּעַל: [שמואל א' ב, ו]

ה) תָּעִיתִי כְּשֶׂה אֹבֵד בַּקֵּשׁ עַבְדֶּךָ כִּי מִצְוֹתֶיךָ לֹא שָׁכָחְתִּי: [תהלים קיט, קעו]

ו) וַיִּקַּח קֹרַח בֶּן יִצְהָר בֶּן קְהָת בֶּן לֵוִי וְדָתָן וַאֲבִירָם בְּנֵי אֱלִיאָב וְאוֹן בֶּן פֶּלֶת בְּנֵי רְאוּבֵן: [במדבר טז, א]

ז) בְּסֹדָם אַל תָּבֹא נַפְשִׁי בִּקְהָלָם אַל תֵּחַד כְּבֹדִי כִּי בְאַפָּם הָרְגוּ אִישׁ וּבִרְצֹנָם עִקְּרוּ שׁוֹר: [בראשית מט, ו]

ח) וַיִּקָּהֲלוּ עַל מֹשֶׁה וְעַל אַהֲרֹן וַיֹּאמְרוּ אֲלֵהֶם רַב לָכֶם כִּי כָל הָעֵדָה כֻּלָּם קְדֹשִׁים וּבְתוֹכָם יְיָ וּמַדּוּעַ תִּתְנַשְּׂאוּ עַל קְהַל יְיָ: [במדבר טז, ג]

מסורת הש"ס

א) [נדה דף סט.], ב) [תוספתא פרק י"ג], ג) [סוטה יוד:].

ליקוטי רש"י

זיבורא. צירעה [ע"ז יב:]. זעקת סדום. ורבותינו דרשו הצלעקתה לעקת ריבה אחת שהרגוה מיתה משונה על שנתנה מזון לעני כמפורש בחלק (סנהדרין קט:) [בראשית יח, כא]. כאבידה המתבקשת. ונמצאת לאחר זמן [מכות כד.]. בסודם אל תבא נפשי. זה מעשה זמרי כשנתקבצו שבטו של שמעון להביא את המדינית לפני משה ואמרו לו זו אסורה או מותרת אם תאמר אסורה בת יתרו מי התירה לך אל יזכר שמי בדבר שנאמר (במדבר כה, יד) זמרי בן סלוא נשיא בית אב לשמעוני ולא כתב בן יעקב. בקהלם. כשיקהיל קרח שהוא משבטו של לוי את כל העדה על משה ועל אהרן. אל תחד כבודי. שם אל יתיחד עמהם שמי שנאמר (במדבר טז, א) קרח בן יצהר בן קהת בן לוי ולא נאמר בן יעקב אבל בדברי הימים כשנתייחסו בני קרח על הדוכן נאמר (דה"א ו, כב) בן קרח בן יצהר בן קהת בן לוי בן ישראל. אל תחד כבודי. כבוד לשון זכר הוא ועל כרחך אתה צריך לפרש כמדבר אל הכבוד ואומר אתה כבודי אל תתיחד עמם כמו (ישעיה יד, כ) לא תחד אתם בקבורה [בראשית מט, ו]. בקהלם אל תחד כבודי. בן יצהר בן קהת בן לוי. ולא הזכיר בן יעקב שבקש רחמים על עצמו שלא יזכר שמו על מחלוקתם שנאמר (בראשית מט, ו) ובקהלם אל תחד כבודי והיכן נזכר שמו על קרח בהתיחסם על הדוכן בדברי הימים שנאמר (דה"א ו, כב) בן אביאסף בן קרח בן יצהר בן קהת בן לוי בן ישראל [במדבר טז, א].

[מכאן שייך לדף קי.]

איהו הוי מלכא וכו'. מה ראה קרח לחלוק עם משה נתקנא על נשיאותו של אליצפן בן עוזיאל שמינהו משה נשיא על בני קהת על פי הדבור אמר קרח אחי אבא ארבעה היו שנאמר (שמות ו, יח) ובני קהת וגו' עמרם הבכור נטלו שני בניו גדולה אחד מלך ואחד כהן גדול מי ראוי ליטול את השניה לא אני שאני בן יצהר שהוא שני לעמרם והוא מנה נשיא את בן אחיו הקטן מכולם הריני חולק עליו ומבטל את דבריו. אפיק גלימא דתכלתא. מה עשה עמד וכנס מאתים וחמישים ראשי סנהדראות רובן משבט ראובן שכיניו והם אליצור בן שדיאור וחביריו וכיוצא בו שנאמר נשיאי עדה קריאי מועד ולהלן הוא אומר (במדבר א, טז) אלה קרואי העדה והלבישן טליתות שכולן תכלת באו ועמדו לפני משה אמרו לו טלית שכולה של תכלת חייבת בציצית או פטורה אמר להם חייבת התחילו לשחק עליו אפשר טלית של מין

to be paid. Therefore, regarding **the wage that is coming to me from you** for my letting your blood, הַב נִיהֲלֵיהּ לְהַאי – **give it to this** man who let my blood. וְזוּזֵי דִּידִי כִּדְקַיְימֵי קַיְימֵי – **And** as for **my money, it shall stay where it is!"**

Another story about Eliezer in Sodom:

דַּהֲוּו הַוְיָא לְהוּ פּוּרְיְיתָא – **[The Sodomites] had a** certain **bed** מַגְנֵי עֲלָהּ אוֹרְחִין – **upon which they would have guests sleep.** כִּי מַאֲרִיךְ – **When [a guest] was tall,** and his legs extended beyond the edge of the bed, גָּיְיזֵי לֵיהּ – **[the Sodomites] would cut him.**[10] כִּי גּוּץ – **When [a guest] was short,** and his legs did not reach the end of the bed, מַתְחִין לֵיהּ – **[the Sodomites] would stretch him.**[11] אֱלִיעֶזֶר עֶבֶד אַבְרָהָם אִקְלַע לְהָתָם – **Eliezer, the servant of Abraham, happened to come there,** to Sodom. אָמְרוּ לֵיהּ – **[The Sodomites] said to him:** קוּם גְּנֵי אַפּוּרְיָא – **"Get up** and **sleep on the bed!"** אָמַר לְהוּן – **[Eliezer] said to them:** נִדְרָא נַדְרִי – "I cannot do so, for **I have taken** the following **vow:** מִן יוֹמָא דְּמִיתַת אִמָּא לֹא גְּנֵינָא אַפּוּרְיָא – **From the day of** my **mother's death** and onward **I will not sleep on a bed,** as a sign of perpetual mourning." Thanks to this ruse, Eliezer avoided the trap they had laid for him.

The cynical and refined cruelty of the Sodomites:

כִּי הֲוָה מִתְרַמֵּי לְהוּ עַנְיָא – **Whenever a pauper happened** to come **to them,** יָהֲבוּ לֵיהּ כָּל חַד וְחַד דִּינָרָא – **each and every** Sodomite **would give him a *dinar*,** וּכְתִיב שְׁמֵיהּ עֲלֵיהּ – **and** before doing so **would write his name on [the coin].**[12] וְרִיפְתָּא לָא הֲווּ מַמְטֵי לֵיהּ – **And,** as per a prior agreement, **[the Sodomites] would not offer [the pauper] bread.**[13] כִּי הֲוָה מִית – **When [the pauper]** eventually **died** of hunger, אָתֵי כָּל חַד וְחַד – **each and every** Sodomite **came** שָׁקֵיל דִּידֵיהּ – and **took** back **his** coin.

Eliezer finds a meal in Sodom:

הָכִי אַתְנֵי בֵּינַיְיהוּ – **[The Sodomites] stipulated thus amongst themselves:** כָּל מַאן דְּמַזְמִין גַּבְרָא לְבֵי הִילוּלָא – **Anyone who invites a** non-Sodomite **man** to a wedding feast לִשְׁלַח גְּלִימָא – **shall be stripped of** his **garment.** הֲוֵי הַאי הִילוּלָא – It transpired that **there was** once **this wedding feast** in Sodom. אִקְלַע אֱלִיעֶזֶר לְהָתָם – **Eliezer happened to come there** to Sodom on that very day, וְלָא יָהֲבוּ לֵיהּ נַהֲמָא – **and,** because he was a stranger, **they did not give him bread** to eat. כִּי בָּעֵי לְמִסְעַד – However, **when he wanted to dine,** אָתָא אֱלִיעֶזֶר וְיָתֵיב לְסֵיפָא דְּכוּלְּהוּ – **Eliezer came** uninvited to the wedding feast **and sat at the end of all [the Sodomites],** who were seated at a long row of tables. אָמְרוּ לֵיהּ – **They said to him:** מַאן אַזְמְנָךְ לְהָכָא – **"Who invited you here?"** אָמַר לֵיהּ לְהַהוּא [דְּיָתֵיב] – **[Eliezer] said to the one sitting** next to him: אַתָּה זִמַּנְתָּן – **"You invited me!"**[14] אָמַר – Terrified, **[the Sodomite] said** to himself: דִּילְמָא שָׁמְעֵי בִּי דְּאֲנָא אַזְמִינְתֵּיהּ – That is a lie! Still, **perhaps [the others] will hear that I invited him,** וּמַשְׁלְחֵי לֵיהּ מָאנֵיהּ דְּהַאי גַּבְרָא – **and will strip me of my clothes.**[15] שָׁקַל גְּלִימֵיהּ הַהוּא דְּיָתֵיב גַּבֵּיהּ – Wishing to escape before his clothing was seized, **the one who was sitting next to [Eliezer] took his garment** וְרָהֵט לְבָרָא – **and ran outside.** וְכֵן עָבֵד לְכוּלְּהוּ – **And so [Eliezer] did to all of [the Sodomites],**[16] עַד דְּנָפְקֵי כּוּלְּהוּ – **until they all departed** the wedding hall, וְאָכְלָא אִיהוּ לִסְעוּדְתָּא – **and he** thereupon **ate the** entire festive **meal himself.**

A particularly heinous crime committed by the Sodomites:

דַּהֲוַת קָא מַפְּקָא הַהִיא רִבִיתָא – **There was a certain maiden** רִיפְתָּא לְעַנְיָא בְּחַצְבָּא – **who would bring out bread to the poor in** her **pitcher.**[17] אִיגְלַאי מִלְּתָא – **The matter was** eventually **discovered** by the Sodomites. שַׁפְיוּהָ דּוּבְשָׁא – Determined to punish her in a horrible manner, **they smeared her** with **honey** וְאוֹקְמוּהָ עַל אִיגַּר שׁוּרָא – **and placed her on the top of the** city **wall.** אָתָא זִיבּוּרֵי וְאַכְלוּהָ – Attracted by the honey covering her, **bees came and devoured [the maiden].** וְהַיְינוּ דִּכְתִיב ,,וַיֹּאמֶר ה' זַעֲקַת סְדֹם וַעֲמֹרָה כִּי־רָבָּה'' – **And this is** the meaning of that **which is written:**[18] ***God said, "The outcry of Sodom and Amorrah is great*** (*rabbah*)." וְאָמַר רַב יְהוּדָה אָמַר רַב – **And Rav Yehudah said in the name of Rav:** עַל עֵיסְקֵי רִיבָה – Scripture here intimates that Sodom was destroyed **because of the affair of the maiden.**[19]

The Gemara now quotes the next section of the Mishnah without comment:[20]

מְרַגְּלִים אֵין לָהֶם חֵלֶק לָעוֹלָם הַבָּא – THE SPIES HAVE NO SHARE IN THE WORLD TO COME, שֶׁנֶּאֱמַר ,,וַיָּמֻתוּ הָאֲנָשִׁים מוֹצִאֵי דִבַּת־הָאָרֶץ רָעָה בַּמַּגֵּפָה'' – AS IT IS STATED: *AND THE MEN WHO BROUGHT OUT AN EVIL REPORT ABOUT THE LAND DIED IN A PLAGUE.* ,,וַיָּמֻתוּ'' בָּעוֹלָם הַזֶּה ,,בַּמַּגֵּפָה'' לָעוֹלָם הַבָּא – *AND [THEY] DIED* – IN THIS WORLD; *IN A PLAGUE* – FOR THE WORLD TO COME.

The Gemara now discusses the next section of the Mishnah, which stated:

עֲדַת קֹרַח אֵין לָהֶם חֵלֶק לָעוֹלָם הַבָּא – THE CONGREGATION OF KORACH HAS NO SHARE IN THE WORLD TO COME,[21] שֶׁנֶּאֱמַר ,,וַתְּכַס עֲלֵיהֶם הָאָרֶץ'' בָּעוֹלָם הַזֶּה ,,וַיֹּאבְדוּ מִתּוֹךְ הַקָּהָל'' לָעוֹלָם הַבָּא דִּבְרֵי רַבִּי עֲקִיבָא – AS IT IS STATED:[22] *AND THE LAND COVERED THEM OVER* – IN THIS WORLD; *AND THEY WERE LOST FROM AMIDST THE CONGREGATION* – FOR THE WORLD TO COME. THESE ARE THE WORDS OF R' AKIVA. רַבִּי אֱלִיעֶזֶר אוֹמֵר עֲלֵיהֶם אָמַר הַכָּתוּב ,,ה' מֵמִית וּמְחַיֶּה מוֹרִיד שְׁאוֹל וַיָּעַל'' – R' ELIEZER SAYS: CONCERNING THEM SCRIPTURE

NOTES

10. [That is, they would amputate the part of his legs that dangled off the bed.] *Rashi's* text of the Gemara read: גַּיְיצֵי לֵיהּ, *they shortened him;* nevertheless, "shortening" by amputation is meant.

11. They would put the guest on a rack and stretch his body until his limbs were pulled out of place.

12. For purposes of later identifying and retrieving it (*Rashi*).

13. The Sodomites devised a sadistic strategy to eliminate the pauper: They would supply him with plenty of money, but would refuse to sell him food. To the pauper's utter horror and dismay the money would prove to be useless, and in a short while he would die of hunger (*Rashi*). One who violated this agreement and fed the poor was subject to severe retribution, as the story of the maiden (recorded below) illustrates.

14. Literally: you invited us.

15. Literally: will dispatch the clothes of that man.

16. I.e. Eliezer repeated the procedure again and again, sitting next to each guest and loudly announcing that the guest had invited him to the feast. In this manner he caused them all to flee the wedding hall (*Rashi*).

17. Whenever she had to draw water, she would hide bread in her pitcher and go out to the well. When no one was looking, she would give the bread to a pauper (*Rashi*).

18. *Genesis* 18:20.

19. The word רבה can be vowelized רַבָּה, which means *great,* or רִבָה, *maiden (Rashi*). Further, *Maharsha* explains that in Scripture זְעָקָה always refers to the *victim's* "outcry." Hence, the verse is interpreted as follows: The outcry against Sodom and Amorrah [זַעֲקַת סְדֹם וַעֲמֹרָה] emanates from the maiden [כִּי רִבָה], whom the Sodomites treated with extreme cruelty. [And with this heinous crime their doom was sealed (see *Yad Ramah*), as indicated by the following verse: *I shall descend and see: If they acted in accordance with the outcry – then destruction!*] See also *Yefeh Einayim,* who writes that the "maiden" was in fact a daughter of Lot.

20. *Hagahos HaGra* deletes this passage from the text of the Gemara.

21. *Hagahos HaGra* inserts the abbreviation וכו' (*etc.*) here, and deletes the remainder of the quotation. [Actually, the above is an inexact quote of the Mishnah; the true text reads: "The Congregation of Korach is not destined to rise."]

22. *Numbers* 16:33.

הגהות הב"ח

(א) רש"י ד"ה אמר ליה אליעזר וכו' כבתחלה הס"ד ואח"כ נ"ל ד"ה כי אריך ואח"כ ד"ה וכתיב וד"ה ורפתא ואח"כ נ"ל ד"ה הכי אתני וד"ה אזל אליעזר וד"ה א"ל מאן ואח"כ נ"ל ד"ה רביתא נערה:

הגהות הגר"א

[א] גמ' מרגלים אין להם כו' עד עדת קרח. נמחק: **[ב]** שם עדת קרח כו' לעולם הבא. נ"ב וכו': **[ג]** שם שנאמר ותכם וכו' עד ת"ר עדת. נמחק: **[ד]** שם שאבר עצמו. נמחק תיבת עצמו: **[ה]** אמרי ליה. נמחק תיבת ליה:

גליון הש"ס

גמ' הרי הן כאבידה המתבקשת. עיין מכות דף כ"ד ע"א:

תורה אור השלם

א) וַיֹּאמֶר יְיָ זַעֲקַת סְדֹם וַעֲמֹרָה כִּי רָבָּה וְחַטָּאתָם כִּי כָבְדָה מְאֹד: [בראשית יח, כ]

ב) וַיָּמֻתוּ הָאֲנָשִׁים מוֹצִאֵי דִבַּת הָאָרֶץ רָעָה בַּמַּגֵּפָה לִפְנֵי יְיָ: [במדבר יד, לז]

ג) וַיֵּרְדוּ הֵם וְכָל אֲשֶׁר לָהֶם חַיִּים שְׁאֹלָה וַתְּכַס עֲלֵיהֶם הָאָרֶץ וַיֹּאבְדוּ מִתּוֹךְ הַקָּהָל: [במדבר טז, לג]

ד) יְיָ מֵמִית וּמְחַיֶּה מוֹרִיד שְׁאוֹל וַיָּעַל: [שמואל א' ב, ו]

ה) תָּעִיתִי כְּשֶׂה אֹבֵד בַּקֵּשׁ עַבְדֶּךָ כִּי מִצְוֹתֶיךָ לֹא שָׁכָחְתִּי: [תהלים קיט, קעו]

ו) וַיִּקַּח קֹרַח בֶּן יִצְהָר בֶּן קְהָת בֶּן לֵוִי וְדָתָן וַאֲבִירָם בְּנֵי אֱלִיאָב וְאוֹן בֶּן פֶּלֶת בְּנֵי רְאוּבֵן: [במדבר טז, א]

ז) בְּסֹדָם אַל תָּבֹא נַפְשִׁי בִּקְהָלָם אַל תֵּחַד כְּבֹדִי כִּי בְאַפָּם הָרְגוּ אִישׁ וּבִרְצֹנָם עִקְּרוּ שׁוֹר: [בראשית מט, ו]

ח) וַיִּקָּהֲלוּ עַל מֹשֶׁה וְעַל אַהֲרֹן וַיֹּאמְרוּ אֲלֵהֶם רַב לָכֶם כִּי כָל הָעֵדָה כֻּלָּם קְדֹשִׁים וּבְתוֹכָם יְיָ וּמַדּוּעַ תִּתְנַשְּׂאוּ עַל קְהַל יְיָ: [במדבר טז, ג]

דאית ליה תורא. כך היה מנהגם של אנשי סדום מי שהיה לו שור אחד רועה כל בהמות העיר יום א' ומי שאין לו בהמה מגלגלין עליו לרעות ב' ימים: **אמר להו.** יתמי למרי דתורא דאית ליה חד תורא כו': **דעבר במברא.** שהמעברות שלהם מימיו עזין והיו דנין כך: **דלא עבר במברא.** אלא בא דרך אחר: **דה"ל דרא דלבני.** מי שהיו לו שורת לבנים ומגבל ועושה אותן היה בא כל חד וחד ונוטל אחת: **שדי תומי או שמכי.** מי שהיה מפזר ושוטח לפניו שומים או בצלים ליבשן כל א' וא' היה נוטל אחת: **אומר לו.** לנגזל מה חסרתי לך לא לקחתי ממך אלא שום אחד ונמלא קרח מכאן ומכאן: **זייפא.** ומטלי דין: **יהבה ניהליה.** וישכב עמה עד שתהיה מעוברת: **עד דקדחא.** עד שתצמח אזנו: **דפדע.** עשה לו פלע כמו פדעת במסכת ע"ז (דף כח.) כפרדור"א בלע"ז: **דעבר במיא.** עובר ברגליו במים: **גללא.** מקל ל"א אבן: **א"ל.** דיינא לאליעזר מאי האי: **א"ל.** אליעזר אגרא דמחייבת לי דשקלי לך דמא הב ליה לההוא גברא דשקל לי דמא וזוזי דידי כדקיימי קיימי ל"א ה"ג ולואי כדקאי קאי כך אמר ליה דיין מי יתן שהייתי כבתחילה (א): **הכי אתנו בהדייהו כל מאן דמזמן.** אכסניא לבי הלולא: **לשלחו לגלימיה.** יפשיטו את בגדי אותו האיש שהזמינו: **ואתא אליעזר.** עבד אברהם: **ויתיב אסיפא דכולהו.** הלך וישב בסוף כולם: **א"ל מאן אזמנך להכא: א"ל.** אליעזר למאן דיתיב גביה את זמנתני להכא: **שקל גלימיה.** דיתיב לגביה ורהט לברא שהיה מתיירא שלא ישמעו אנשי המקום שאליעזר אמר שהוא זימנו ולישלחו למאניה הלך וישב לו אצל השני ואמר כמו כן וכן לכל אחד ואחד עד דאזלי כולהו ואכל אליעזר כל הסעודה: **כי אריך גייזו ליה.** כשהאורח ארוך יותר מן המטה מקצרין אותו בסכין גיילי לשון גוזן כן שמעתי ואית דגרסי גיידי ליה: **ומתחין ליה.** עד דמתפרקי אבריו: **וכתיב שמיה עילויה.** כדי שיכיר כל אחד וא' דינר שלו ויחזור ויטלנו: **ורפתא לא ממטו ליה.** התנו ביניהם שלא יתנו לו פת כדי שימות ברעב וכשמת אזיל כל חד וחד ושקיל לדינרא דידיה: **רביתא.** נערה: **בחצבא.** בתוך כד שלה כשיוצאת לשאוב מים: **שפיוה.** סכו אותה: **איגר שורא.** על גג החומה: **כי רבה.** על עסקי ריבה: **רבי יהודה בן בתירא אומר ויאבדו הרי הן כאבידה המתבקשת.** ובאין לעולם הבא שכן אמר דוד על בני קרח תעיתי כשה אובד בקש עבדך הם תעו כשה אובד ואתה ברחמיך הרבים בקש עבדך ותביאם לעוה"ב: **מצותיך לא שכחתי.** שקיימו כל מצותיך כדכתיב (במדבר טז) כי כל העדה כולם קדושים: **מקח רע.** התחיל בקטטה: **שעשה קרחה בישראל.** שנבלעו: **שהרתיח.** שהכעיס: **הקהה שיני מולידיו.** שנתביישו אבותיו במעשיו הרעים: **בקש רחמים על עצמו.** שלא יהא נמנה עמהם: **אלו מרגלים.** דלא כתיב בהן פלוני בן יעקב: **שאיבר לבבו.** חזק לבבו כמו (ישעיה מו) אבירי לב: **שישב באנינות.** שעשה תשובה על שהיה עמהם תחילה בעצה: **נעשו לו פלאות.** (שפירש) [שניצל] מהם: **ראה והבין.** שאין מנהגן כשורה ופירש מהם: **אי מר רבה.** אם ינצח משה מכל מקום אתה תלמיד ואם קרח מנצח אתה תלמיד מה לך בשררה זו: **הואי בעצה.** אני הייתי עמהן בעצה ונשבעתי להם שאם יקראוני אלך עמהם: **דכולה כנישתא קדישין.** כולם צנועים וקדושים ולא יכנסו אלי אם אני פרועה: סתרה

א) דאית ליה תורא נשקול חד משכא דלית ליה תורא נשקול תרי משכי אמרו ליה מאי האי אמר להו סוף דינא כתחילת דינא מה תחילת דינא דאית ליה תורא מרעי חד יומא דלית ליה תורי מרעי תרי יומי אף סוף דינא דאית ליה חד תורא לשקול חד דלית ליה תורא לשקול תרי דעבר במברא ניתיב חד זוזא דלא עבר במברא ניתיב תרי דהוה ליה (תורא) [דרא] דלבני אתי כל חד וחד שקל' חדא א"ל אנא חדא דשקלי דהוה שדי תומי או שמכי אתו כל חד וחד שקיל חדא א"ל אנא חדא דשקלי ארבע דייני היו בסדום שקראי ושקרוראי זייפי ומצלי דינא דמחי ליה לאיתתא דחברי' ומפלא ליה אמרי ליה יהבה ניהליה דניעברה ניהליך דפסיק ליה לאודנא דחמרא דחבריה אמרו ליה הבה ניהליה עד דקדחא דפדע ליה לחבריה אמרי ליה הב ליה אגרא דשקל לך דמא דעבר במברא יהיב ארבעה זוזי דעבר במיא יהיב תמני זוזי זימנא חדא אתא ההוא כובס איקלע להתם אמרו ליה הב ד' זוזי אמר להו אנא במיא עברי אמרו ליה א"כ הב תמניא דעברת במיא לא יהיב פדיוהו אתא לקמיה דדיינא א"ל הב ליה אגרא דשקיל לך דמא ותמניא זוזי דעברת במיא אליעזר עבד אברהם איתרמי התם פדיוהי אתא לקמיה דיינא א"ל הב ליה אגרא דשקל לך דמא שקל גללא פדיוהי איהו לדיינא אמר מאי האי א"ל אגרא דנפק לי מינך הב ניהליה להאי וזוזי דידי כדקיימי קיימי הויא להו פורייתא דהוו מגני עלה אורחין כי מאריך גייזי ליה כי גוץ מתחין ליה אליעזר עבד אברהם אקלע להתם אמרו ליה קום גני אפוריא אמר להון נדרא נדרי מן יומא דמיתת אמא לא גנינא אפוריא כי הוה מתרמי להו עניא יהבו ליה כל חד וחד דינרא וכתיב שמיה עליה וריפתא לא הוו ממטי ליה כי הוה מית אתי כל חד וחד שקיל דידיה הכי אתני בינייהו כל מאן דמזמין גברא לבי הילולא לשלח גלימא הוי האי הילולא אקלע אליעזר להתם ולא יהבו ליה נהמא כי בעי למסעד אתא אליעזר ויתיב לסיפא דכולהו אמרו ליה מאן אזמנך להכא א"ל להההוא [דיתיב] אתה זמנתן [אמר דילמא שמעי בי דאנא אזמינתיה ומשלחי ליה מאניה דהאי גברא] שקל גלימיה ההוא דיתיב גביה ורהט לברא וכן עבד לכולהו עד דנפקי כולהו ואכלא איהו לסעודתא הויא ההיא רביתא דהות קא מפקא ריפתא לעניא בחצבא איגלאי מלתא שפיוה דובשא ואוקמוה על איגר שורא אתא זיבורי ואכלוה והיינו דכתיב א) ויאמר ה' זעקת סדום ועמורה כי רבה ואמר רב יהודה אמר רב על עיסקי ריבה: **[א]** מרגלים אין להם חלק לעולם הבא שנאמר ב) וימותו האנשים מוציאי דבת הארץ רעה במגפה בעולם הזה במגפה לעולם הבא: **[ב]** עדת קרח אין להם חלק לעולם הבא **[ג]** שנאמר ג) ותכס עליהם הארץ בעולם הזה ויאבדו מתוך הקהל לעולם הבא דברי ר"ע רבי אליעזר אומר עליהם אמר הכתוב ד) ה' ממית ומחיה מוריד שאול ויעל: ת"ר ג) עדת קרח אין להם חלק לעולם הבא שנאמר ותכס עליהם הארץ בעולם הזה ויאבדו מתוך הקהל לעולם הבא דברי רבי עקיבא רבי יהודה בן בתירא אומר ה) הרי הן כאבידה המתבקשת שנאמר ה) תעיתי כשה אובד בקש עבדך כי מצותיך לא שכחתי: ו) ויקח [קרח] ג) אמר ריש לקיש שלקח מקח רע לעצמו קרח שנעשה קרחה בישראל בן יצהר בן שהרתיח עליו את כל העולם כצהרים בן קהת בן שהקהה שיני מולידיו בן לוי בן שנעשה לויה בגיהנם וליחשוב נמי בן יעקב בן שעקב עצמו לגיהנם אמר רב שמואל בר רב יצחק יעקב ביקש רחמים על עצמו שנאמר ז) בסודם אל תבא נפשי ובקהלם אל תחד כבודי בסודם אל תבא נפשי אלו מרגלים ובקהלם אל תחד כבודי זה עדת קרח דתן שעבר על דת אל אבירם שאיבר **[ד]** עצמו מעשות תשובה ואון שישב באנינות פלת שנעשו לו פלאות בן שראה והבין אמר רב און בן פלת אשתו הצילתו אמרה ליה מאי נפקא לך מינה אי מר רבה אנת תלמידא ואי מר רבה אנת תלמידא אמר לה מאי אעביד הואי בעצה ואשתבעי לי בהדייהו אמרה **[ה]** ליה ידענא דכולה כנישתא קדישתא נינהו דכתיב ח) כי כל העדה כולם קדושים אמרה ליה תוב דאנא מצילנא לך אשקיתיה חמרא וארויתיה ואגניתיה גואי אותבה על בבא וסתרתה

מסורת הש"ס

א) [נדה דף סט.], ב) [תוספתא פרק י"ג], ג) [סוטה יוד:].

ליקוטי רש"י

זיבורא. צירעה [ע"ז יב:]. **זעקת סדום.** ורבותינו דרשו הכצעקתה צעקת ריבה אחת שהרגוה מיתה משונה על שנתנה מזון לעני כמפורש בחלק (סנהדרין קט:) [בראשית יח, כא]. **כאבידה המתבקשת.** ונמצאת לאחר זמן [מכות כד.]. **בסודם אל תבא נפשי.** זה מעשה זמרי כשנתקבצו שבטו של שמעון להביא את המדינית לפני משה ואמרו לו זו אסורה או מותרת אם תאמר אסורה בת יתרו מי התירה לך אל יזכר שמי בדבר שנאמר (במדבר כה, יד) זמרי בן סלוא נשיא בית אב לשמעוני ולא כתב בן יעקב. **בקהלם.** כשיקהיל קרח שהוא משבטו של לוי את כל העדה על משה ועל אהרן. **אל תחד כבודי.** שם אל יתיחד עמהם שמי שנאמר (במדבר טז, א) קרח בן יצהר בן קהת בן לוי ולא נאמר בן יעקב אבל בדברי הימים כשנתייחסו בני קרח על הדוכן נאמר (דה"א ו, כב) בן קרח בן יצהר בן קהת בן לוי בן ישראל. **אל תחד כבודי.** כבוד לשון זכר הוא ועל כרחך אתה צריך לפרש כמדבר אל הכבוד ואומר אתה כבודי אל תתיחד עמם כמו (ישעיה יד, כ) לא תחד אתם בקבורה [בראשית מט, ו]. **בקהלם אל תחד כבודי.** בן יצהר בן קהת בן לוי. ולא הזכיר בן יעקב שבקש רחמים על עצמו שלא יזכר שמו על מחלוקתם שנאמר (בראשית מט, ו) ובקהלם אל תחד כבודי והיכן נזכר שמו על קרח בהתיחסם על הדוכן בדברי הימים שנאמר (דה"א ו, כב) בן אביאסף בן קרח בן יצהר בן קהת בן לוי בן ישראל [במדבר טז, א].

[מכאן שייך לדף קי.]

איהו הוי מלכא וכו'. מה ראה קרח לחלוק עם משה נתקנא על נשיאותו של אליצפן בן עוזיאל שמינהו משה נשיא על בני קהת על פי הדבור אמר קרח אחי אבא ארבעה היו שנאמר (שמות ו, יח) ובני קהת וגו' עמרם הבכור נטלו שני בניו גדולה אחד מלך ואחד כהן גדול מי ראוי ליטול את השניה לא אני שאני בן יצהר שהוא שני לעמרם והוא מנה נשיא את בן אחיו הקטן מכולם הריני חולק עליו ומבטל את דבריו. **אפיק גלימא דתכלתא.** מה עשה עמד וכנס מאתים חמישים ראשי סנהדראות רובן משבט ראובן שכיניו והם אליצור בן שדיאור וחביריו וכיוצא בו שנאמר נשיאי עדה קריאי מועד ולהלן הוא אומר (במדבר א, טז) אלה קרואי העדה והלבישן טליתות שכולן תכלת באו ועמדו לפני משה אמרו לו טלית שכולה של תכלת חייבת בציצית או פטורה אמר להם חייבת התחילו לשחק עליו אפשר טלית של מין

STATED:[23] *HASHEM KILLS AND BRINGS TO LIFE; HE LOWERS INTO THE GRAVE AND BRINGS UP.*

The Gemara cites a Tanna who concurs with R' Eliezer's position:

תָּנוּ רַבָּנָן – The Rabbis taught in a Baraisa: עֲדַת קֹרַח אֵין לָהֶם חֵלֶק לָעוֹלָם הַבָּא שֶׁנֶּאֱמַר – THE CONGREGATION OF KORACH HAS NO SHARE IN THE WORLD TO COME, AS IT IS STATED: ,,וַתְּכַס עֲלֵיהֶם הָאָרֶץ" בָּעוֹלָם הַזֶּה ,,וַיֹּאבְדוּ מִתּוֹךְ הַקָּהָל" לָעוֹלָם הַבָּא – *AND THE LAND COVERED THEM OVER* – IN THIS WORLD; *AND THEY WERE LOST FROM AMIDST THE CONGREGATION* – FOR THE WORLD TO COME. דִּבְרֵי רַבִּי עֲקִיבָא – THESE ARE THE WORDS OF R' AKIVA. רַבִּי יְהוּדָה בֶּן בְּתֵירָא אוֹמֵר – R' YEHUDAH BEN BESEIRA SAYS: הֲרֵי הֵן כַּאֲבֵידָה הַמִּתְבַּקֶּשֶׁת – THEY ARE LIKE A LOST ARTICLE THAT IS SEARCHED FOR, שֶׁנֶּאֱמַר ,,תָּעִיתִי כְּשֶׂה אֹבֵד בַּקֵּשׁ עַבְדֶּךָ כִּי מִצְוֹתֶיךָ לֹא שָׁכָחְתִּי" – AS IT IS STATED: *I HAVE GONE ASTRAY LIKE A LOST SHEEP – SEEK OUT YOUR SERVANT, FOR I HAVE NOT FORGOTTEN YOUR COMMANDMENTS.*[24]

The Gemara expounds upon the first verse of the Korach passage (*Numbers* 16:1): *Korach son of Yitzhar son of Kehas son of Levi took, along with Dasan and Abiram, sons of Eliab, and On son of Peles, the offspring of Reuven*:

,,וַיִּקַּח [קֹרַח]" – The first two words of that passage are: ***Korach took.***[25] **אָמַר רֵישׁ לָקִישׁ – Reish Lakish** therefore **said:** שֶׁלָּקַח מִקָּח רַע לְעַצְמוֹ – The Torah implies **that [Korach] "took"** (i.e. acquired) **a bad purchase for himself.**[26]

The Gemara continues to expound upon the verse:[27]

,,קֹרַח" שֶׁנַּעֲשָׂה קָרְחָה בְּיִשְׂרָאֵל – He was called ***Korach*, for** because of him **a bald spot was made in Israel.**[28] ,,בֶּן־יִצְהָר" בֵּן שֶׁהִרְתִּיחַ עָלָיו אֶת כָּל הָעוֹלָם כַּצָּהֳרַיִם – ***Son of Yitzhar*** implies that he was **a son who excited the entire world against himself with an anger as** fierce as the heat of **noontime.**[29] ,,בֶּן־קְהָת" בֵּן שֶׁהִקְהָה שִׁינֵּי מוֹלִידָיו – ***Son of Kehas*** implies that Korach was **a son who set on edge the teeth of those who gave birth to him.**[30] ,,בֶּן־לֵוִי" בֵּן שֶׁנַּעֲשָׂה לְוָיָה בְּגֵיהִנֹּם – ***Son of Levi*** implies that Korach was **a son** on **whose** account **an escort to Gehinnom was made.**[31]

The Gemara asks:

וְלִיחְשׁוֹב נַמִּי ,,בֶּן יַעֲקֹב" – **But** why does Korach's genealogy end with Levi, the patriarch Jacob's son? **Let [Scripture] reckon also *son of Jacob,*** which could be interpreted to mean that Korach was בֵּן שֶׁעָקַב עַצְמוֹ לְגֵיהִנֹּם – **a son who caused himself to fall head over heels**[32] **into Gehinnom!**

The Gemara answers:

אָמַר רַב שְׁמוּאֵל בַּר רַב יִצְחָק – Rav Shmuel bar Rav Yitzchak said: יַעֲקֹב בִּיקֵּשׁ רַחֲמִים עַל עַצְמוֹ – **Jacob had** earlier **besought** Divine **mercy for himself,**[33] to avoid the disgrace of being eternally associated with the wicked Korach, שֶׁנֶּאֱמַר ,,בְּסֹדָם אַל־תָּבֹא נַפְשִׁי בִּקְהָלָם אַל־תֵּחַד כְּבֹדִי" – **as it is stated:**[34] ***Into their conspiracy may my soul not enter! With their congregation do not join, O my honor!*** ,,בְּסֹדָם אַל־תָּבֹא נַפְשִׁי" אֵלּוּ מְרַגְּלִים – ***Into their conspiracy may my soul not enter* – these are the Spies;**[35] ,,בִּקְהָלָם אַל־תֵּחַד כְּבֹדִי" זֶה עֲדַת קֹרַח – ***With their congregation do not join, O my honor* – this is the Congrega-**

NOTES

23. *I Samuel* 2:6.

24. *Psalms* 119:176. R' Yehudah ben Beseira maintains that the members of the Congregation of Korach do have a share in the World to Come. Although Scripture states that *they were lost from amidst the congregation,* which R' Akiva interprets as indicating that they are lost from the World to Come, R' Yehudah ben Beseira maintains that the verse does not necessarily describe a permanent loss (see *Makkos* 24a). Lost articles can be found, provided a search for them is mounted. R' Yehudah ben Beseira thus understands the verse in *Psalms* as David's plea to God to undertake a search for the Congregation of Korach, to bring them to the World to Come. David speaks on behalf of the Korachites: *I have gone astray like a lost sheep;* that is, I sinned and lost my chance to enter the World to Come. Nevertheless, *seek out Your servant* – forgive me in Your great mercy and admit me to the World to Come. And why do I deserve forgiveness? Because *I have not forgotten Your commandments,* as it is written (*Numbers* 16:3): *For the entire assembly – all of them – are holy.* [Presumably, argues R' Yehudah ben Beseira, this plea was granted and the Congregation of Korach was admitted to the World to Come] (*Rashi;* cf. *Be'er Sheva* and *Maharsha*).

25. Scripture does not specify, however, what Korach "took"; it thereby invites the Sages to expound that phrase homiletically.

26. [The Hebrew word לקח, in its Mishnaic use, can mean *purchase* or *acquire* as well as *take.*] Reish Lakish expounds וַיִּקַּח as meaning *and he acquired.* That is, Korach used his wealth in an attempt to acquire the leadership of the Jewish people, but he made a poor deal: All he got was death and dishonor – a מִקָּח רַע, *a bad purchase* (*Maharsha*). *Torah Temimah* sees here a reference to the money Korach lavished upon others in order to make them his partisans.

27. Once the first word of the verse (וַיִּקַּח, *he took*) required interpretation, the remainder of the verse is open to interpretation; indeed, the Sages often expounded upon proper names according to the narrative context (*Maharsha*; see 106b note 6).

28. Korach and his followers were miraculously swallowed up by the earth, thus leaving a bald spot among the ranks of the Jewish people [the Hebrew word קֵרֵחַ literally means *bald*] (*Rashi;* see also *Ben Yehoyada* and *Torah Temimah*).

According to *Maharsha*, the Gemara teaches that Korach became so notorious that subsequently no Jewish child was ever given his name. Thus, the name "Korach" became "bald" (i.e. absent) in Israel. Among the descendants of Esau, however, the name was perpetuated (see *Genesis* 36:16).

29. This follows *Rashi. Maharsha* explains that Korach brought anger and fury upon the Jewish people. [The name *Yitzhar* (יִצְהָר) and the word *tzaharayim* (צָהֳרַיִם, *noontime*) derive from the same root.]

30. I.e. he brought shame upon his distinguished ancestors (*Rashi*; see *Sotah* 49a). [The name *Kehas* (קְהָת) and the word *hikhah* (הִקְהָה, *set on edge*) derive from the same root.]

31. When the earth swallowed up Korach, it swallowed up his followers as well (*Numbers* 16:32-33). Thus, Korach did not descend into Gehinnom alone; he came with an escort (*Maharsha; Torah Temimah*).

32. [The name *Yaakov* (יַעֲקֹב) is related to the word *akeiv* (עָקֵב), which means *heel*. Alternatively, *Yaakov* is related to the verb *akav* (עָקַב), which can mean *outwit* (see *Genesis* 27:36 with *Targum Onkelos*). According to this understanding, the Gemara would read: "a son who outwitted himself into Gehinnom."] See also *Ohr HaChaim* to *Numbers* 16:1, end of ד"ה ויקח קרח.

33. I.e. he had prayed that Scripture not number him among Korach's forebears (*Rashi*). For a profound interpretation of this matter, see *Ohr HaChaim* ibid. (,,ובעיני יפלא למה יכנה דברים הרעים בשמות הצדיקים").

34. *Genesis* 49:6. This verse appears in the passage of prophetic "blessings" that Jacob bestowed upon his sons on his deathbed. It is addressed to Shimon and Levi (the latter was Korach's ancestor). Rav Yehudah interprets the verse as a prophetic reference to future rebellions.

35. In the Scriptural passage that gives the genealogy of the Spies (*Numbers* 13:4-16), there is no mention of their common ancestor Jacob (*Rashi*). This is because Jacob had prayed that his name not be associated with those wicked individuals.

An obvious question arises: The Gemara here states that Jacob did not want his name associated with Shimon and Levi because of the future incident of the Spies. However, the tribe of Levi did not participate in their mission, and the tribe of Shimon played no special or prominent role therein! [Indeed, *Rashi's* Biblical commentary associates this part of the verse with the episode of Zimri, the tribal prince of Shimon (see *Numbers* 25:6-8).] *Maharsha* suggests that there was a tradition that the Shimonite representative instigated the Spies' rebellion, and for that reason Jacob associated the incident with his tribe.

א) דאית ליה תורא נשקול חד משכא דלית ליה תורא נשקול תרי משכי אמרו ליה מאי האי אמר להו סוף דינא כתחילת דינא מה תחילת דינא דאית ליה תורא מרעי חד יומא דלית ליה תורי מרעי תרי יומי אף סוף דינא דאית ליה חד תורא לשקול חד דלית ליה תורא לשקול תרי דעבר במברא ניתיב חד זוזא דלא עבר במברא ניתיב תרי דהוה ליה (תורא) [דרא] דלבני אתי כל חד וחד שקל' חדא א"ל אנא חדא דשקלי דהוה שדי תומי או שמכי אתו כל חד וחד שקיל חדא א"ל אנא חדא דשקלי ארבע דייני היו בסדום שקראי ושקרוראי זייפי ומצלי דינא דמחי ליה לאיתתא דחברי' ומפלא ליה אמרי ליה יהבה ניהליה דניעברה ניהליך דפסיק ליה לאודנא דחמרא דחבריה אמרו ליה הבה ניהליה עד דקדחא דפדע ליה לחבריה אמרי ליה הב ליה אגרא דשקל לך דמא דעבר במברא יהיב ארבעה זוזי דעבר במיא יהיב תמני זוזי זימנא חדא אתא ההוא כובס איקלע להתם אמרו ליה הב ד' זוזי אמר להו אנא במיא עברי אמרו ליה א"כ הב תמניא דעברת במיא לא יהיב פדיוהו אתא לקמיה דדיינא א"ל הב ליה אגרא דשקיל לך דמא ותמניא זוזי דעברת במיא אליעזר עבד אברהם איתרמי התם פדיוהי אתא לקמיה דיינא א"ל הב ליה אגרא דשקל לך דמא שקל גללא פדיוהי איהו לדיינא אמר מאי האי א"ל אגרא דנפק לי מינך הב ניהליה להאי וזוזי דידי כדקיימי קיימי הויא להו פורייתא דהוו מגני עלה אורחין כי מאריך גייזי ליה כי גוץ מתחין ליה אליעזר עבד אברהם אקלע להתם אמרו ליה קום גני אפוריא אמר להון נדרא נדרי מן יומא דמיתת אמא לא גנינא אפוריא כי הוה מתרמי להו עניא יהבו ליה כל חד וחד דינרא וכתיב שמיה עליה וריפתא לא הוו ממטי ליה כי הוה מית אתי כל חד וחד שקיל דידיה הכי אתני בינייהו כל מאן דמזמין גברא לבי הילולא לשלח גלימא הוי האי הילולא אקלע אליעזר להתם ולא יהבו ליה נהמא כי בעי למסעד אתא אליעזר ויתיב לסיפא דכולהו אמרו ליה מאן אזמנך להכא א"ל להההוא [דיתיב] אתה זמנתן [אמר דילמא שמעי בי דאנא אזמינתיה ומשלחי ליה מאניה דהאי גברא] שקל גלימיה דההוא דיתיב גביה ורהט לברא וכן עבד לכולהו עד דנפקי כולהו ואכלא איהו לסעודתא הויא ההיא רביתא דהות קא מפקא ריפתא לעניא בחצבא איגלאי מלתא שפיוה דובשא ואוקמוה על איגר שורא אתא זיבורי ואכלוה והיינו דכתיב א) ויאמר ה' זעקת סדום ועמורה כי רבה ואמר רב יהודה אמר רב על עיסקי ריבה: [א] מרגלים אין להם חלק לעולם הבא שנאמר ב) וימותו האנשים מוציאי דבת הארץ רעה במגפה הזה במגפה לעולם הבא: [ב] עדת קרח אין להם חלק לעולם הבא [ג] שנאמר ג) ותכס עליהם הארץ בעולם הזה ויאבדו מתוך הקהל לעולם הבא דברי ר"ע רבי אליעזר אומר עליהם אמר הכתוב ד) ה' ממית ומחיה מוריד שאול ויעל: ת"ר ג) עדת קרח אין להם חלק לעולם הבא שנאמר ותכס עליהם הארץ בעולם הזה ויאבדו מתוך הקהל לעולם הבא דברי רבי עקיבא רבי יהודה בן בתירא אומר ° הרי הן כאבידה המתבקשת שנאמר ה) תעיתי כשה אובד בקש עבדך כי מצותיך לא שכחתי: ו) ויקח [קרח] ד) אמר ריש לקיש שלקח מקח רע לעצמו קרח שנעשה קרחה בישראל בן יצהר בן שהרתיח עליו את כל העולם כצהרים בן קהת בן שהקהה שיני מולידיו בן לוי בן שנעשה לויה בגיהנם וליחשוב נמי בן יעקב בן שעקב עצמו לגיהנם אמר רב שמואל בר רב יצחק יעקב ביקש רחמים על עצמו שנאמר ז) בסודם אל תבא נפשי ובקהלם אל תחד כבודי בסודם אל תבא נפשי אלו מרגלים ובקהלם אל תחד כבודי זה עדת קרח דתן שעבר על דת אל אבירם שאיבר [ד] עצמו מעשות תשובה ואון שישב באנינות פלת שנעשו לו פלאות בן ראובן בן שראה והבין אמר רב און בן פלת אשתו הצילתו אמרה ליה מאי נפקא לך מינה אי מר רבה אנת תלמידא ואי מר רבה אנת תלמידא אמר לה מאי אעביד הואי בעצה ואשתבעי לי בהדייהו אמרה [ה] ליה ידענא דכולה כנישתא קדישתא נינהו דכתיב ח) כי כל העדה כולם קדושים אמרה ליה תוב דאנא מצילנא לך אשקיתיה חמרא וארויתיה ואגניתיה גואי אותבה על בבא וסתרתה

דאית ליה תורא. כך היה מנהגם של אנשי סדום מי שהיה לו שור אחד רועה כל בהמות העיר יום א' ומי שאין לו בהמה מגלגלין עליו לרעות ב' ימים: אמר להו. יתמי למרי דתורא דאית ליה חד תורא כו': דעבר במברא. שהמעברות שלהם מימיו עזין והיו דנין כך: דלא עבר במברא. אלא בא דרך אחר: דה"ל דרא דלבני. מי שהיו לו שורת לבנים ומגבל ועושה אותן היה בא כל חד וחד ונוטל אחת: שדי תומי או שמכי. מי שהיה מפזר ושוטח לפניו שומים או בצלים ליבשן כל א' וא' היה נוטל אחת: אומר לו. לנגזל מה חסרתי לך לא לקחתי ממך אלא שום אחד ונמצא קרח מכאן ומכאן: זייפא. ומצלי דין: יהבה ניהליה. וישכב עמה עד שתהיה מעוברת: עד דקדחא. עד שתצמח אזנו: דפדע. עשה לו פצע כמו פדעת במסכת ע"ז (דף כח.) כפרדור"א בלע"ז: דעבר במיא. עובר ברגליו במים: גללא. מקל ל"א אבן: א"ל. דיינא לאליעזר מאי האי: א"ל. אליעזר אגרא דמחייבת לי דשקלי לך דמא הב ליה להההוא גברא דשקל לי דמא וזוזי דידי כדקיימי קיימי ל"א ה"ג ולואי כדקאי קאי כך אמר ליה דיין מי יתן שהייתי כבתחילה (א): הכי אתנו בהדייהו כל מאן דמזמן. אכסניא לבי הלולא: לשלחו לגלימיה. יפשיטו את בגדי אותו האיש שהזמינו: ואתא אליעזר. עבד אברהם: ויתיב אסיפא דכולהו. הלך וישב בסוף כולם: א"ל מאן אזמנך להכא: א"ל. אליעזר למאן דיתיב גביה את זמנתני להכא: שקל גלימיה. דיתיב לגביה ורהט לברא שהיה מתיירא שלא ישמעו אנשי המקום שאליעזר אמר שהוא זימנו ולישלחו למאניה הלך וישב לו אצל השני ואמר כמו כן וכן לכל אחד ואחד עד דאזלי כולהו ואכל אליעזר כל הסעודה: כי אריך גייצו ליה. כשהאורח ארוך יותר מן המטה מקצרין אותו בסכין גיילי לשון גוץ כן שמעתי ואית דגרסי גיידי ליה: ומתחין ליה. עד דמתפרקי אבריו: וכתיב שמיה עילויה. כדי שיכיר כל אחד וא' דינר שלו ויחזור ויטלנו: ורפתא לא ממטו ליה. התנו ביניהם שלא יתנו לו פת כדי שימות ברעב וכשמת אזיל כל חד וחד ושקיל לדינרא דידיה: רביתא. נערה: בחצבא. בתוך כד שלה כשיוצאת לשאוב מים: שפיוה. סכו אותה: איגר שורא. על גג החומה: כי רבה. על עסקי ריבה: רבי יהודה בן בתירא אומר ויאבדו הרי הן כאבידה המתבקשת. ובאין לעולם הבא שכך אמר דוד על בני קרח תעיתי כשה אובד בקש עבדך הם תעו כשה אובד ואתה ברחמיך הרבים בקש עבדך ותביאם לעוה"ב: מצותיך לא שכחתי. שקיימו כל מצותיך כדכתיב (במדבר טז) כי כל העדה כולם קדושים: מקח רע. התחיל בקטטה: שעשה קרחה בישראל. שנבלעו: שהרתיח. שהכעיס: הקהה שיני מולידיו. שנתביישו אבותיו במעשיו הרעים: בקש רחמים על עצמו. שלא יהא נמנה עמהם: אלו מרגלים. דלא כתיב בהן פלוני בן יעקב: שאיבר לבבו. חזק לבבו כמו (ישעיה מו) אבירי לב: שישב באנינות. שעשה תשובה על שהיה עמהם תחילה בעצה: נעשו לו פלאות. (שפירש) [שניצל] מהם: ראה והבין. שאין מנהגן כשורה ופירש מהם: אי מר רבה. אם ינצח משה מכל מקום אתה תלמיד ואם קרח מנצח אתה תלמיד מה לך בשררה זו: הואי בעצה. אני הייתי עמהן בעצה ונשבעתי להם שאם יקראוני אלך עמהם: דכולה כנישתא קדישין. כולם צנועים וקדושים ולא יכנסו אלי אם אני פרועה:

סתרה

הגהות הב"ח

(א) רש"י ד"ה אמר ליה אליעזר וכו' כבתחלה הס"ד ואח"כ צ"ל ד"ה כי אריך ואח"כ ד"ה וכתיב וד"ה ורפתא ואח"כ צ"ל ד"ה הכי אתני וד"ה אזל אליעזר וד"ה א"ל מאן ואח"כ צ"ל ד"ה רביתא נערה:

הגהות הגר"א

[א] גמ' מרגלים אין להם כו' עד עדת קרח. נמחק: [ב] שם עדת קרח כו' לעולם הבא. נ"ב וכו': [ג] שם שנאמר ותכס וכו' עד ת"ר עדת. נמחק: [ד] שם שאבר עצמו. נמחק תיבת עצמו: [ה] אמרי ליה. נמחק תיבת ליה:

גליון הש"ס

גמ' הרי הן כאבידה המתבקשת. עיין מכות דף כ"ד ע"א:

תורה אור השלם

א) וַיֹּאמֶר יְיָ זַעֲקַת סְדֹם וַעֲמֹרָה כִּי רָבָּה וְחַטָּאתָם כִּי כָבְדָה מְאֹד: [בראשית יח, כ]

ב) וַיָּמֻתוּ הָאֲנָשִׁים מוֹצִאֵי דִבַּת הָאָרֶץ רָעָה בַּמַּגֵּפָה לִפְנֵי יְיָ: [במדבר יד, לז]

ג) וַיֵּרְדוּ הֵם וְכָל אֲשֶׁר לָהֶם חַיִּים שְׁאֹלָה וַתְּכַס עֲלֵיהֶם הָאָרֶץ וַיֹּאבְדוּ מִתּוֹךְ הַקָּהָל: [במדבר טז, לג]

ד) יְיָ מֵמִית וּמְחַיֶּה מוֹרִיד שְׁאוֹל וַיָּעַל: [שמואל א' ב, ו]

ה) תָּעִיתִי כְּשֶׂה אֹבֵד בַּקֵּשׁ עַבְדֶּךָ כִּי מִצְוֹתֶיךָ לֹא שָׁכָחְתִּי: [תהלים קיט, קעו]

ו) וַיִּקַּח קֹרַח בֶּן יִצְהָר בֶּן קְהָת בֶּן לֵוִי וְדָתָן וַאֲבִירָם בְּנֵי אֱלִיאָב וְאוֹן בֶּן פֶּלֶת בְּנֵי רְאוּבֵן: [במדבר טז, א]

ז) בְּסֹדָם אַל תָּבֹא נַפְשִׁי בִּקְהָלָם אַל תֵּחַד כְּבֹדִי כִּי בְאַפָּם הָרְגוּ אִישׁ וּבִרְצֹנָם עִקְּרוּ שׁוֹר: [בראשית מט, ו]

ח) וַיִּקָּהֲלוּ עַל מֹשֶׁה וְעַל אַהֲרֹן וַיֹּאמְרוּ אֲלֵהֶם רַב לָכֶם כִּי כָל הָעֵדָה כֻּלָּם קְדֹשִׁים וּבְתוֹכָם יְיָ וּמַדּוּעַ תִּתְנַשְּׂאוּ עַל קְהַל יְיָ: [במדבר טז, ג]

מסורת הש"ס

א) [נדה דף סט.], ב) [תוספתא פרק י"ג], ג) [סוטה יוד:].

ליקוטי רש"י

זיבורא. צירעה [ע"ז יב:]. זעקת סדום. ורבותינו דרשו הצעקתה צעקת ריבה אחת שהרגוה מיתה משונה על שנתנה מזון לעני כמפורש בחלק (סנהדרין קט:) [בראשית יח, כא]. כאבידה המתבקשת. ונמצאת לאחר זמן [מכות כד.]. בסודם אל תבא נפשי. זה מעשה זמרי כשנתקבצו שבטו של שמעון להביא את המדינית לפני משה ואמרו לו זו אסורה או מותרת אם תאמר אסורה בת יתרו מי התירה לך אל יזכר שמי בדבר שנאמר (במדבר כה, יד) זמרי בן סלוא נשיא בית אב לשמעוני ולא כתב בן יעקב. בקהלם. כשיקהיל קרח שהוא משבטו של לוי את כל העדה על משה ועל אהרן. אל תחד כבודי. שם אל יתיחד עמהם שמי שנאמר (במדבר טז, א) קרח בן יצהר בן קהת בן לוי ולא נאמר בן יעקב אבל בדברי הימים כשנתייחסו בני קרח על הדוכן נאמר (דה"א ו, כג) בן קרח בן יצהר בן קהת בן לוי בן ישראל. אל תחד כבודי. כבוד לשון זכר הוא ועל כרחך אתה צריך לפרש כמדבר אל הכבוד ואומר אתה כבודי אל תתיחד עמם כמו (ישעיה יד, כ) לא תחד אתם בקבורה [בראשית מט, ו]. בקהלם אל תחד כבודי. בן יצהר בן קהת בן לוי. ולא הזכיר בן יעקב שבקש רחמים על עצמו שלא יזכר שמו על מחלוקתם שנאמר (בראשית מט, ו) ובקהלם אל תחד כבודי והיכן נזכר שמו על קרח בהתיחסם על הדוכן בדברי הימים שנאמר (דה"א ו, כב) בן אביאסף בן קרח בן יצהר בן קהת בן לוי בן ישראל [במדבר טז, א].

[מכאן שייך לדף קי.] איהו הוי מלכא וכו'. מה ראה קרח לחלוק עם משה נתקנא על נשיאותו של אליצפן בן עוזיאל שמינהו משה נשיא על בני קהת על פי הדבור אמר קרח אחי אבא ארבעה היו שנאמר (שמות ו, יח) ובני קהת וגו' עמרם הבכור נטלו שני בניו גדולה אחד מלך ואחד כהן גדול מי ראוי ליטול את השניה לא אני שאני בן יצהר שהוא שני לעמרם והוא מנה נשיא את בן אחיו הקטן מכולם הריני חולק עליו ומבטל את דבריו. אפיק גלימא דתכלתא. מה עשה עמד וכנס מאתים חמישים ראשי סנהדראות רובן משבט ראובן שכיניו והם אליצור בן שדיאור וחביריו וכיוצא בו שנאמר נשיאי עדה קריאי מועד ולהלן הוא אומר (במדבר א, טז) אלה קרואי העדה והלבישן טליתות שכולן תכלת באו ועמדו לפני משה אמרו לו טלית שכולה של תכלת חייבת בציצית או פטורה אמר להם חייבת התחילו לשחק עליו אפשר טלית של מין

tion of Korach. In this part of the verse Jacob prayed that Scripture not include him in Korach's genealogy.

The Gemara resumes its interpretation of the first verse of the Korach passage:

,,דָּתָן'' שֶׁעָבַר עַל דַּת אֵל – ***Dasan*** is one **who transgressed the law of God** by opposing Moses, God's chosen messenger.[36] ,,אֲבִירָם'' שֶׁאִיבֵּר עַצְמוֹ מֵעֲשׂוֹת תְּשׁוּבָה – ***Abiram*** is one **who fortified himself against repenting.**[37] ,,וְאוֹן'' שֶׁיָּשַׁב בַּאֲנִינוּת – ***And On*** refers to one **who sat in mourning.**[38] ,,פֶּלֶת'' שֶׁנַּעֲשׂוּ לוֹ פְּלָאוֹת – *Son of* ***Peles*** implies **that miracles were performed for him.**[39] ,,(בן) [בְּנֵי] רְאוּבֵן'' בֵּן שֶׁרָאָה וְהֵבִין – ***Sons of Reuven*** implies that On was **a son who saw and understood**[40] that the conspirators were acting improperly, and so parted company with them.

The story of how On son of Peles was saved:

אָמַר רַב – **Rav said:** אוֹן בֶּן פֶּלֶת אִשְׁתּוֹ הִצִּילַתּוּ – With regard to **On son of Peles, his wife saved him.** אָמְרָה לֵיהּ – **She said to him:** מַאי נַפְקָא לָךְ מִינָּהּ – "Why are you joining Korach's rebellion? **What will you gain from it?** אִי מַר רַבָּה אַנְתְּ תַּלְמִידָא – **If** this **master** (i.e. Moses) **is victorious, you will be a disciple,** וְאִי מַר רַבָּה אַנְתְּ תַּלְמִידָא – and if that **master** (i.e. Korach) **is victorious, you will be a disciple!** Regardless of who prevails, you will not gain power. Why, then, do you join Korach against Moses?" אָמַר לָהּ – **[On] said to [his wife]:** מַאי אֶעֱבִיד – "You are correct, but **what shall I do?** הֲוַאי בְּעֵצָה – **I took part in** their **deliberations,** וְאִשְׁתַּבַּעִי לִי בַּהֲדַיְיהוּ – **and swore to them** that I would join the rebellion when called." אָמְרָה לֵיהּ – **She said to him:**[41] יָדְעָנָא דְּכוּלָּה כְּנִישְׁתָּא קַדִּישְׁתָּא נִינְהוּ – "**I know of the entire assembly,** Korach and his followers included, that **they are holy** people,"[42] דִּכְתִיב ,,כִּי כָל־הָעֵדָה כֻּלָּם קְדֹשִׁים'' – **for it is written:** ***For the entire assembly – all of them – are holy.***[43] אָמְרָה לֵיהּ – **She said to him:** תּוּב דְּאָנָא מַצִּילְנָא לָךְ – "**Turn back**[44] from your dangerous course, **for I shall save you!"** אַשְׁקִיתֵיהּ חַמְרָא – **She gave him wine to drink** וְאַרְוִיתֵיהּ – **and caused him to be drunk,**[45] וְאַגְנִיתֵיהּ גַּוָּאֵי – **and** then **put him to bed inside** their tent. אוֹתְבָא עַל בָּבָא – **She** then **sat at the entrance** of the tent,

NOTES

36. The name *Dasan* (דָּתָן) is related to the word *das* (דָּת, *law*).

Maharsha explains that Dasan transgressed the law of God when he struck his fellow Jew (Abiram) in Egypt, as it states there (*Exodus* 2:13): *And [Moses] said to* ***the wicked one,*** *"Why do you strike your fellow?"*

37. Since it was Abiram that Dasan violently attacked, Abiram should have disassociated himself from his evil colleague and repented his own transgressions. Instead, he hardened his heart against repenting and, indeed, had a hand in every one of Dasan's misdeeds (*Maharsha*). [The name *Abiram* (אֲבִירָם) is related to the verb *ibeir* (אִיבֵּר, *strengthened* or *fortified*).]

38. [The name *On* (און) is related to the word *aninus* (אֲנִינוּת, *mourning*).] On eventually repented (i.e. mourned) his participation in the planning stage of Korach's insurrection; see below (*Rashi*). See also *Ben Yehoyada. Eitz Yosef* explains that On mourned because it was his wife who had to save him from the destruction awaiting Korach's followers; he himself lacked the strength of character to do so.

39. [The name *Peles* (פֶּלֶת) is related to the word *pela'os* (פְּלָאוֹת, *miracles*).] That On managed to be saved from Korach's fate was indeed miraculous (*Rashi*). Another connotation of *Peles: separated* (from וְהִפְלֵיתִי בַיּוֹם הַהוּא, *And on that day I shall set apart* [*Exodus* 8:18]). The name thus implies that On was separated from his fellow conspirators (*Maharsha*).

40. The name *Reuven* (רְאוּבֵן) is a compound of the words *r'eu* (רְאוּ, *see*) and *ven* (from מֵבִין, *mavin/understand*).

41. *Hagahos HaGra* deletes the word לֵיהּ, *to him,* from the text, implying that what immediately follows is the wife ruminating.

42. They are all modest and saintly, and would not approach me if I uncovered my hair (*Rashi*). See *Maharsha* and *Iyun Yaakov* for different interpretations.

43. *Numbers* 16:3.

44. *Dikdukei Soferim* cites a variant text: תִּיב דְּאָנָא מַצִּילְנָא לָךְ, *Sit* [here when they summon you], *for I shall save you.*

45. So that if he was summoned from outside the tent to join the rebellion, he would be physically unable to respond, and thus would not be in violation of his oath (*Maharsha*).

וּסְתַרְתָּה לְמַזְיָהּ – **and let down her hair.** כָּל דְּאָתָא חַזְיָהּ – **Every** member of Korach's group **who came** to summon On **saw her** sitting at the entrance of the tent with her hair uncovered, הֲדַר – and, unwilling to encounter this immodest display, **turned around** and left.[1] אַדְּהָכִי וְהָכִי אִבַּלְעוּ לְהוּ – **Meanwhile,** as On was sleeping off his intoxication, **[Korach's assembly] were swallowed up** by the earth. Thus, his wife's timely action prevented On from joining Korach's rebellion and suffering the conspirators' horrible fate.[2]

In contrast to the wife of On, Korach's spouse incited her husband against Moses:

אִיתְּתֵיהּ דְּקֹרַח אָמְרָה לֵיהּ – **Korach's wife said to him:** חֲזִי מַאי קָעָבִיד מֹשֶׁה – **"See what Moses is doing!** אִיהוּ הֲוָה מַלְכָּא – He has arrogated power and wealth for himself and his immediate family:[3] **He himself is king;** לַאֲחוּהּ שַׁוְיֵיהּ כַּהֲנָא רַבָּא – **he has appointed his brother High Priest;** לִבְנֵי אֲחוּהִי שַׁוְינְהוּ סְגָנֵי דְכַהֲנָא – **he has appointed his brother's sons deputies of the [High] Priest.** אִי אַתְיָא תְּרוּמָה – **If** ***terumah***[4] **comes** to be offered, אָמַר תֶּיהֱוֵי לַכֹּהֵן – **[Moses] said, 'It shall be for** my nephew, **the Kohen.'** אִי אָתוּ מַעֲשֵׂר – **If [the people] come** with ***maaser***,[5] דְּשָׁקֵילְתּוּ אַתּוּן – **which you** Levites **take,** אָמַר – **[Moses] said,** הָבוּ חַד מֵעַשְׂרָה לַכֹּהֵן – **'**Levites, **give one-tenth** of the *maaser rishon* you receive **to the Kohen.'**[6] וְעוֹד – **And furthermore,** דְּגַיְיז לֵיהּ לְמַזַּיְיכוּ – it is a fact **that [Moses] shaved off** all **your hair**[7] וּמִיטְלַל לְכוּ כִּי כוּפְתָּא – **and made sport of you,** treating you **as** if you were a piece of **dung,** עֵינָא יָהַב בְּמַזַּיְיכוּ – for **he had cast his eye upon your hair!"**[8]

Korach responds to this last argument:

אָמַר לָהּ – **[Korach] said to [his wife]:** הָא אִיהוּ נַמִּי קָא עָבִיד – **"But [Moses] also did** this!"[9]

Her rejoinder:

אָמְרָה לֵיהּ – **She said to him** in reply: כֵּיוָן דְּכוּלְּהוּ רְבוּתָא דִּידֵיהּ – **"Since the entire** scheme redounds to **his greatness,** אָמַר אִיהוּ נַמִּי ,,תָּמֹת נַפְשִׁי עִם־פְּלִשְׁתִּים'' – it is as if **[Moses] also said,** ***'Let me perish along with the Philistines!'***[10] וְעוֹד – **And furthermore,** דְּקָאָמַר לְכוּ עֲבִידוּ תִּכְלְתָא – it is a fact **that [Moses] said to you, 'Make** a single thread of ***techeiles*** for each corner of your garment.'[11] אִי סָלְקָא דַּעְתָּךְ תִּכְלְתָא חֲשִׁיבָא [מִצְוָה] – **Now, if it enters your mind** that ***techeiles*** **is considered a mitzvah,** אַפֵּיק גְּלִימֵי דְּתִכְלְתָא וְכַסִּינְהוּ לְכוּלְּהוּ מְתִיבְתָּךְ – then **take** whole **garments of** ***techeiles*** **and with them clothe all of your** colleagues in the **study hall."**[12]

The Gemara finds allusions to the wives of On ben Peles and Korach in Scripture:

הַיְינוּ דִּכְתִיב – **This is** the meaning of that **which is written:**[13] ,,חַכְמוֹת נָשִׁים בָּנְתָה בֵיתָהּ'' – ***She who is wise among women builds her house*** – זוֹ אִשְׁתּוֹ שֶׁל אוֹן בֶּן פֶּלֶת – **this is** a reference to **the wife of On ben Peles.** ,,וְאִוֶּלֶת בְּיָדֶ[י]הָ תֶהֶרְסֶ(ה)[וּ]'' – ***But the foolish one destroys it with her own hands*** – זוֹ אִשְׁתּוֹ שֶׁל קֹרַח – **this is** a reference to **the wife of Korach.**[14]

The Gemara now expounds upon the second verse in the Korach passage. It begins:

,,וַיָּקֻמוּ לִפְנֵי מֹשֶׁה וַאֲנָשִׁים מִבְּנֵי־יִשְׂרָאֵל חֲמִשִּׁים וּמָאתָיִם'' – ***And they stood before Moses, with two hundred and fifty men from the Children of Israel . . .***[15] מְיוּחָדִים שֶׁבָּעֵדָה – Scripture intimates

NOTES

1. The sight of a married woman's hair is an impropriety (שֵׂעָר בְּאִשָּׁה עֶרְוָה – *Berachos* 24a), and should be avoided by all other men (see *Orach Chaim* 75:2).

2. *Maharal* explains that in terms of motivation the conspirators divided into four separate groups: (a) Unlike most of the others, *Dasan and Abiram* did not seek the Kehunah, which Moshe had awarded to his brother Aaron. Rather, they were driven to rebel against Moses by a fierce brazenness, for they were, in essence, contentious individuals. (b) *The contingent of two hundred and fifty men* joined Korach solely for the purpose of acquiring the Kehunah. (c) *Korach* also sought the Kehunah, but in addition was driven by his jealousy of Moses and Aaron. (d) *On ben Peles* entered the conflict only because he did not want Moses to rule over him [Moses had assumed the position of king]; unlike Dasan and Abiram, On was not by nature a contentious person. Hence, he was susceptible to his wife's argument (above, 109b) – that removing one ruler (Moses) would result only in his subjugation to another (Korach) – and so allowed her to extricate him from the conflict.

3. Korach's wife claimed that Moses' actions were of his own volition and not in compliance with a Divine directive (*Maharsha;* see also *Bamidbar Rabbah* 18:4).

4. This is the first portion of the crop to be separated, and is given to a Kohen. See Glossary.

5. The reference is to *maaser rishon,* the "first tithe" to be separated from the crop after *terumah* is taken. It is given to a Levi (*Rashi*).

6. *Numbers* 18:26-29 require the Levite to give a tenth of the *maaser* he receives to a Kohen. This gift is called *terumas maaser.*

7. Korach's wife was referring to the consecration ceremony described in *Numbers* 8:5-22, through which the Levites assumed their status as associates of the Kohanim in serving God in the Tabernacle. God had instructed Moses to shave the entire body of each eligible Levi, after which Aaron physically lifted and waved them, one by one. Korach's wife considered the ceremony bizarre and humiliating, and she refused to believe that it had been performed at God's behest. She maintained instead that Moses had concocted the idea in order to debase the Levites by making them appear deranged (see *Rashi*).

8. She claimed: Moses had settled on eliminating your body hair as a means of insuring that you would not be as attractive as he (see *Rashi*).

9. Korach retorted: As a Levi, Moses also had his entire body shaved. If he concocted the ceremony to make us look grotesque, why did he participate therein? (*Rashi*).

10. See *Judges* 16:30. Although Korach's wife could not have quoted Samson, since she predated him, the Gemara couches her statement in terms of Samson's famous statement, as follows: Just as the blinded Samson prayed for a return of his superhuman strength in order to avenge his ill-treatment at the hands of the Philistines, and was willing to perish along with them so long as he was successful (see ibid. vs. 28-30), so Moses was willing to suffer the embarrassment of himself being completely shaven, which was necessary to mollify any recalcitrant Levi, in order to exercise supreme power over an entire tribe (*Rashi;* cf. *Maharsha*).

11. God had previously instructed Moses (*Numbers* 15:37-39) to order all Jewish males to attach *tzitzis,* fringes, to the four corners of their garments. They were to include among the fringes on each corner a thread of *techeiles,* i.e. a thread of wool dyed turquoise with the blood of an aquatic creature called the *chilazon.* It was to this order that Korach's wife was referring.

12. Korach's wife argued that if God really decreed the *techeiles* thread a mitzvah object, then why should each group of fringes contain only one such thread? On the contrary, the entire group of fringes – nay, the entire garment – should be composed of *techeiles*! Hence, the order to place a single thread of *techeiles* on each corner of their garments must be Moses' own invention! (*Rashi*).

13. *Proverbs* 14:1. According to *Dikdukei Soferim,* the entire verse should appear in the text of the Gemara before the verse is interpreted by parts.

14. The meaning is obvious: On's wife saved his life by preventing him from accompanying Korach to the fatal confrontation with Moses. Thus, she "built her house" – that is, she kept her family intact. Korach's wife, on the other hand, incited her husband to rebel against Moses, a course of action that precipitated his death. Thus, by her foolish counsel she "destroyed" her own house.

Maharsha points out that the verse was fulfilled literally in the case of Korach's wife, for Scripture states: *[The earth] swallowed them along with their houses* (*Numbers* 16:32).

15. *Numbers* 16:2.

מסורת הש"ס

א) בקרא כתיב בידיה תהרסנו, ב) [מו"ק יח:], ג) [צ"ל יוסף], ד) [ברכות כז: ע"ש], ה) פסחים קיט. ע"ש, ו) [שם], ז) ג' מאות לאו דוקא וכן כל שלש מאות בש"ס רשב"ם פסחים קיט, ח) נדרים לט: ע"ש, ט) לעיל קג., י) [לעיל קג:], כ) מגילה יד., ל) ב"ב עד ע"א.

עין משפט נר מצוה

לג א ב ג ד מיי' פ"ה מהל' ת"ת הל' א סמג עשין יג טוש"ע י"ד סי' רמב סעיף ג:

רש"י

סתרה למזיה. שערה וישבה על פתח הבית כל מי שהיה בא לקרוא רואה ראשה פרוע וחוזר: מעשר. ראשון דשקליתו אתון אמר הבו חד מי' לכהן: דגייז למזייכו. דכתיב (במדבר ח) והעבירו תער על [כל] בשרם ומשחק בכם כאילו אתם שוטים: כבופתא. רעי כמו בטולא דכופתא דאמרן לעיל (דף לח:) כגלל הזה אתם חשובים בעיניו: עינא יהב. עין נתן בשעריכם כדי שלא יהא בכם גורה כמותו: אמר לה. קרח איהו נמי משה עצמו גלח כל שערו: כיון דכולא רבותא דידיה הוא. אינו חושש אם גילח עצמו דקאמר לנפשיה תמות נפשי עם פלשתים אגוז שערי כמותם ומה לי בכך שהם מקיימין אפילו מה שאני מצוה לשחוק אגוז עכשיו כמותם כדי להפיס דעתם: ועוד דקאמר לכו. עשו פתיל תכלת בד' כנפות הבגד ואי ס"ד תכלת חשוב מפני מה לא יאמר לעשות כל הבגד כולו תכלת: אפיק גלימא דתכלתא. קח לך בגדים של תכלת וכסינהו לכולהו מתיבתך וכסה בהן בבה"מ אתה וחברותך: קנא לאשתו. אל (הסתר) [תסתרי] עם משה. קנוי היינו התראה: ונטה לו מחוץ למחנה. יצא מחוץ למחנה שלא יחשדוהו עוד: מכאן שאין מחזיקין במחלוקת. שמחל על כבודו והוא עצמו הלך לבטל מחלוקת: חולק על רבו. חולק על ישיבתו: אשר הצו על משה ועל אהרן בעדת קרח בהצותם על ה'. מעלה עליהם הכתוב כאלו היו חולקים כלפי שכינה: מריבה. תגר וקטטה לפטפט נגדו בדברים: מתרעם. אומר על רבו שנוהג לו מדה כבושה ומדת אכזרית: מהרהר. מחפה עליו דברים: אקלידי. מפתחות: וקולפי. מנעולים: דגילדי. כולם המפתחות והמנעולים של עור היו ואעפ"כ היו שלש מאות פרדות טעונות ל"א דגלדא לצורך שקים והמרצופין וכיסין של עור היו: לא מן הבלועין ולא מן השרופין. אלא במגפה מת: ולא קרח. ר"נ היו לבד קרח דכתיב חמשים ומאתים מחתות ואתה ואהרן איש מחתתו: מן הבלועים ומן השרופין היה. שנשרפה נשמתו וגוף קיים ואח"כ נתגלגל עד מקום הבלועין ונבלע דכתיב בפרשת פנחס ותבלע אותם ואת קרח עמהם ורבי יוחנן דאמר לא מן הבלועין ולא מן השרופין דריש ליה להאי ואת קרח לאחריו ואת קרח במות העדה במגפה: וקרח בהדייהו. מדכתיב ותאכל את החמשים ומאתים איש מקריבי הקטרת וקרח ממקריבי הקטרת הוה דכתיב חמשים ומאתים מחתות ואתה ואהרן איש מחתתו א"נ ואת לרבות קרח עמהם: שמש ירח עמד זבולה. לעיל מיניה כתיב ותבקע ארץ בשעת בקיעת הארץ שנבלעו בקרקע שמש וירח עלו לאותו רקיע ששמו זבול ואמרו להקב"ה אם אי אתה עושה דין לבן עמרם מקרח ועדתו: לא נצא. ונאיר לעולם: בכבודי לא מחיתם. שהרי בכל יום מלכי מזרח ומערב בשעה שמניחין כתריהן בראשם משתחוים לחמה: והאידנא לא נפקי עד דמחו להו. שכך גזר עליהם המקום כן שמעתי ל"א והאידנא לא נפקי מאחר שראו שהקפיד הקב"ה על שלא מיחה לכבודו עד דמחו להו לא נפקי שחשו לכבוד המקום על בני אדם שמשתחוים לשמש וירח: אין כל חדש תחת השמש. ואי גיהנם לא אברי עד ההוא שעתא הוה ליה חדש: לקרובי פתחה. שיקרב פתחה של גיהנם ותפתח הארץ במקום שהן: נתבצר. מלשון (ישעיה כה) עיר בצורה התקין להון הקב"ה מקום גבוה שלא העמיקו כל כך בגיהנם ולא מתו: טייעא. סוחר ישמעאל: בלועי. מקום שנתבלעו לשם עדת קרח: בזעא. ראה נקב שממנו יצא עשן: גבבא. גיזה: אמשיה. שרה אות' במים לשון (ברכות דף יד:) משי ידיה: (וכל שלשים יום. חוזר לגיהנם ועולה לשם): אמר

גמרא

וסתרתה למזיה כל דאתא חזיה הדר אדהכי והכי אבלעו להו איתתיה דקרח אמרה ליה חזי מאי קעביד משה איהו הוה מלכא לאחוה שוויה כהנא רבא לבני אחוהי שוינהו סגני דכהנא אי אתיא תרומה אמר תיהוי לכהן אי אתו מעשר דשקילתו אתון אמר הבו חד מי' לכהן ועוד דגייז ליה למזייכו ומיטלל לכו כי כופתא עינא יהב במזייכו אמר לה הא איהו נמי קא עביד אמרה ליה כיון דכולהו רבותא דידיה אמר איהו נמי א) תמות נפשי עם פלשתים ועוד דקאמר לכו עבידתו תכלתא אי ס"ד תכלתא חשיבא [מצוה] אפיק גלימי דתכלתא וכסינהו לכולהו מתיבתך היינו דכתיב ב) חכמות נשים בנתה ביתה זו אשתו של און בן פלת ואולת א) בידה תהרסנה זו אשתו של קרח ג) ויקומו לפני משה ואנשים מבני ישראל חמשים ומאתים מיוחדים שבעדה קריאי מועד שהיו יודעים לעבר שנים ולקבוע חדשים אנשי שם שהיה להם שם בכל העולם ד) וישמע משה ויפול על פניו מה שמועה שמע ב) אמר רבי שמואל בר נחמני א"ר יונתן שחשדוהו מאשת איש שנאמר ה) ויקנאו למשה במחנה א"ר שמואל בר יצחק מלמד שכל אחד ואחד קנא את אשתו ממשה שנאמר ו) ומשה יקח את האהל ונטה לו מחוץ למחנה ז) ויקם משה וילך אל דתן ואבירם אמר ר"ל מכאן שאין מחזיקין במחלוקת דאמר רב כל המחזיק במחלוקת עובר בלאו שנאמר ח) ולא יהיה כקרח וכעדתו רב אשי אמר ראוי ליצטרע כתיב הכא ח) ביד משה לו וכתיב התם ט) ויאמר ה' לו עוד הבא נא ידך בחיקך אמר ר' ג) יוסי כל החולק על מלכות בית דוד ראוי להכישו נחש כתיב הכא י) ויזבח אדוניהו צאן ובקר ומריא עם אבן הזוחלת וכתיב התם יא) עם חמת זוחלי עפר אמר רב חסדא ד) א כל החולק על רבו כחולק על השכינה שנאמר יב) בהצותם על ה' א"ר חמא ברבי חנינא ב כל העושה מריבה עם רבו כעושה עם שכינה שנאמר יג) המה מי מריבה אשר רבו בני ישראל (על) [את] ה' א"ר חנינא בר פפא ג כל המתרעם על רבו כאילו מתרעם על השכינה שנאמר יד) לא עלינו תלונותיכם כי (אם) על ה' א"ר אבהו ד כל המהרהר אחר רבו כאילו מהרהר אחר שכינה שנאמר טו) וידבר העם באלהים ובמשה טז) עושר שמור לבעליו לרעתו ה) אמר ר"ל זה עושרו של קרח יז) ואת כל היקום אשר ברגליהם ו) א"ר אלעזר זה ממונו של אדם שמעמידו על רגליו ואמר רבי לוי משוי ז) ג' מאות פרדות לבנות היו מפתחות של בית גנזיו של קרח וכולהו אקלידי וקילפי דגילדא א"ר חמא ברבי חנינא ג' מטמוניות הטמין יוסף במצרים אחת נתגלתה לקרח ואחת נתגלתה לאנטונינוס בן אסוירוס ואחת גנוזה לצדיקים לעתיד לבא וא"ר יוחנן קרח לא מן הבלועים ולא מן השרופין לא מן הבלועין דכתיב יח) ואת כל האדם אשר לקרח ולא את קרח ולא מן השרופים דכתיב יט) באכול האש את חמשים ומאתים איש ולא קרח במתניתא תנא קרח מן השרופין ומן הבלועין מן הבלועים דכתיב יט) ותבלע אותם ואת קרח מן השרופין דכתיב כ) (ותצא אש מלפני ה') [ואש יצאה מאת ה'] ותאכל את חמשים ומאתים איש וקרח בהדייהו אמר רבא ח) מאי דכתיב כא) שמש ירח עמד זבולה לאור חציך יהלכו מלמד שעלו שמש וירח לזבול אמרו לפניו רבש"ע אם אתה עושה דין לבן עמרם נצא ואם לאו לא נצא עד שזרק בהם חצים אמר להן ט) בכבודי לא מחיתם בכבוד בשר ודם מחיתם והאידנא לא נפקי עד דמחו להו י) דרש רבא מאי דכתיב כב) ואם בריאה יברא ה' ופצתה האדמה את פיה אמר משה לפני הקב"ה אם בריאה גיהנם מוטב ואם לאו יברא ה' למאי אילימא למבריה ממש והא כג) אין כל חדש תחת השמש אלא לקרובי פיתחא כד) ובני קרח לא מתו תנא כ) משום רבינו אמרו מקום נתבצר להם בגיהנם וישבו עליו ואמרו שירה ל) אמר רבה בר בר חנה זימנא חדא הוה קאזלינא באורחא אמר לי ההוא טייעא תא ואחוי לך בלועי דקרח אזיל חזא תרי בזעי דהוה קא נפק קיטרא מנייהו שקל גבבא דעמרא אמשיי' מיא ואותביה בריש רומחיה ואחלפי' התם איחרך א"ל אצית מה שמעת ושמעית דהוו קאמרי הכי משה ותורתו אמת והן בדאים אמר

תורה אור השלם

א) וַיֹּאמֶר שִׁמְשׁוֹן תָּמוֹת נַפְשִׁי עִם פְּלִשְׁתִּים וַיֵּט בְּכֹחַ וַיִּפֹּל הַבַּיִת עַל הַסְּרָנִים וְעַל כָּל הָעָם אֲשֶׁר בּוֹ וַיִּהְיוּ הַמֵּתִים אֲשֶׁר הֵמִית בְּמוֹתוֹ רַבִּים מֵאֲשֶׁר הֵמִית בְּחַיָּיו: [שופטים טז, ל]

ב) חַכְמוֹת נָשִׁים בָּנְתָה בֵיתָהּ וְאִוֶּלֶת בְּיָדֶיהָ תֶהֶרְסֶנּוּ: [משלי יד, א]

ג) וַיָּקֻמוּ לִפְנֵי מֹשֶׁה וַאֲנָשִׁים מִבְּנֵי יִשְׂרָאֵל חֲמִשִּׁים וּמָאתָיִם נְשִׂיאֵי עֵדָה קְרִאֵי מוֹעֵד אַנְשֵׁי שֵׁם: [במדבר טז, ב]

ד) וַיִּשְׁמַע מֹשֶׁה וַיִּפֹּל עַל פָּנָיו: [במדבר טז, ד]

ה) וַיְקַנְאוּ לְמֹשֶׁה בַּמַּחֲנֶה לְאַהֲרֹן קְדוֹשׁ יְיָ: [תהלים קו, טז]

ו) וּמֹשֶׁה יִקַּח אֶת הָאֹהֶל וְנָטָה לוֹ מִחוּץ לַמַּחֲנֶה הַרְחֵק מִן הַמַּחֲנֶה וְקָרָא לוֹ אֹהֶל מוֹעֵד וְהָיָה כָּל מְבַקֵּשׁ יְיָ יֵצֵא אֶל אֹהֶל מוֹעֵד אֲשֶׁר מִחוּץ לַמַּחֲנֶה: [שמות לג, ז]

ז) וַיָּקָם מֹשֶׁה וַיֵּלֶךְ אֶל דָּתָן וַאֲבִירָם וַיֵּלְכוּ אַחֲרָיו זִקְנֵי יִשְׂרָאֵל: [במדבר טז, כה]

ח) זִכָּרוֹן לִבְנֵי יִשְׂרָאֵל לְמַעַן אֲשֶׁר לֹא יִקְרַב אִישׁ זָר אֲשֶׁר לֹא מִזֶּרַע אַהֲרֹן הוּא לְהַקְטִיר קְטֹרֶת לִפְנֵי יְיָ וְלֹא יִהְיֶה כְקֹרַח וְכַעֲדָתוֹ כַּאֲשֶׁר דִּבֶּר יְיָ בְּיַד מֹשֶׁה לוֹ: [במדבר יז, ה]

ט) וַיֹּאמֶר יְיָ לוֹ עוֹד הָבֵא נָא יָדְךָ בְּחֵיקֶךָ וַיָּבֵא יָדוֹ בְּחֵיקוֹ וַיּוֹצִאָהּ וְהִנֵּה יָדוֹ מְצֹרַעַת כַּשָּׁלֶג: [שמות ד, ו]

י) וַיִּזְבַּח אֲדֹנִיָּהוּ צֹאן וּבָקָר וּמְרִיא עִם אֶבֶן הַזֹּחֶלֶת אֲשֶׁר אֵצֶל עֵין רֹגֵל וַיִּקְרָא אֶת כָּל אֶחָיו בְּנֵי הַמֶּלֶךְ וּלְכָל אַנְשֵׁי יְהוּדָה עַבְדֵי הַמֶּלֶךְ: [מלכים א' א, ט]

יא) מְזֵי רָעָב וּלְחֻמֵי רֶשֶׁף וְקֶטֶב מְרִירִי וְשֶׁן בְּהֵמֹת אֲשַׁלַּח בָּם עִם חֲמַת זֹחֲלֵי עָפָר: [דברים לב, כד]

יב) וּבְנֵי אֱלִיאָב נְמוּאֵל וְדָתָן וַאֲבִירָם הוּא דָתָן וַאֲבִירָם קְרוּאֵי הָעֵדָה אֲשֶׁר הִצּוּ עַל מֹשֶׁה וְעַל אַהֲרֹן בַּעֲדַת קֹרַח בְּהַצֹּתָם עַל יְיָ: [במדבר כו, ט]

יג) הֵמָּה מֵי מְרִיבָה אֲשֶׁר רָבוּ בְנֵי יִשְׂרָאֵל אֶת יְיָ וַיִּקָּדֵשׁ בָּם: [במדבר כ, יג]

יד) וַיֹּאמֶר מֹשֶׁה בְּתֵת יְיָ לָכֶם בָּעֶרֶב בָּשָׂר לֶאֱכֹל וְלֶחֶם בַּבֹּקֶר לִשְׂבֹּעַ בִּשְׁמֹעַ יְיָ אֶת תְּלֻנֹּתֵיכֶם אֲשֶׁר אַתֶּם מַלִּינִם עָלָיו וְנַחְנוּ מָה לֹא עָלֵינוּ תְלֻנֹּתֵיכֶם כִּי עַל יְיָ: [שמות טז, ח] טו) וַיְדַבֵּר הָעָם בֵּאלֹהִים וּבְמֹשֶׁה לָמָה הֶעֱלִיתֻנוּ מִמִּצְרַיִם לָמוּת בַּמִּדְבָּר כִּי אֵין לֶחֶם וְאֵין מַיִם וְנַפְשֵׁנוּ קָצָה בַּלֶּחֶם הַקְּלֹקֵל: [במדבר כא, ה] טז) יֵשׁ רָעָה חוֹלָה רָאִיתִי תַּחַת הַשָּׁמֶשׁ עֹשֶׁר שָׁמוּר לִבְעָלָיו לְרָעָתוֹ: [קהלת ה, יב] יז) וַאֲשֶׁר עָשָׂה לְדָתָן וְלַאֲבִירָם בְּנֵי אֱלִיאָב בֶּן רְאוּבֵן אֲשֶׁר פָּצְתָה הָאָרֶץ אֶת פִּיהָ וַתִּבְלָעֵם וְאֶת בָּתֵּיהֶם וְאֶת אָהֳלֵיהֶם וְאֵת כָּל הַיְקוּם אֲשֶׁר בְּרַגְלֵיהֶם בְּקֶרֶב כָּל יִשְׂרָאֵל: [דברים יא, ו] יח) וַתִּפְתַּח הָאָרֶץ אֶת פִּיהָ וַתִּבְלַע אֹתָם וְאֶת בָּתֵּיהֶם וְאֵת כָּל הָאָדָם אֲשֶׁר לְקֹרַח וְאֵת כָּל הָרְכוּשׁ: [במדבר טז, לב] יט) וַתִּפְתַּח הָאָרֶץ אֶת פִּיהָ וַתִּבְלַע אֹתָם וְאֶת קֹרַח בְּמוֹת הָעֵדָה בַּאֲכֹל הָאֵשׁ אֵת חֲמִשִּׁים וּמָאתַיִם אִישׁ וַיִּהְיוּ לְנֵס: [במדבר כו, י] כ) וְאֵשׁ יָצְאָה מֵאֵת יְיָ וַתֹּאכַל אֵת הַחֲמִשִּׁים וּמָאתַיִם אִישׁ מַקְרִיבֵי הַקְּטֹרֶת: [במדבר טז, לה] כא) שֶׁמֶשׁ יָרֵחַ עָמַד זְבֻלָה לְאוֹר חִצֶּיךָ יְהַלֵּכוּ לְנֹגַהּ בְּרַק חֲנִיתֶךָ: [חבקוק ג, יא] כב) וְאִם בְּרִיאָה יִבְרָא יְיָ וּפָצְתָה הָאֲדָמָה אֶת פִּיהָ וּבָלְעָה אֹתָם וְאֶת כָּל אֲשֶׁר לָהֶם וְיָרְדוּ חַיִּים שְׁאֹלָה וִידַעְתֶּם כִּי נִאֲצוּ הָאֲנָשִׁים הָאֵלֶּה אֶת יְיָ: [במדבר טז, ל] כג) מַה שֶּׁהָיָה הוּא שֶׁיִּהְיֶה וּמַה שֶּׁנַּעֲשָׂה הוּא שֶׁיֵּעָשֶׂה וְאֵין כָּל חָדָשׁ תַּחַת הַשָּׁמֶשׁ: [קהלת א, ט] כד) וּבְנֵי קֹרַח לֹא מֵתוּ: [במדבר כו, יא]

ליקוטי רש"י

אחר חוט אחד של תכלת פוטרה זו שכולה תכלת לא תפטור את עצמה [במדבר טז, א]. חכמות נשים בנתה ביתה. חכמות נקוד פתח שאינו שם דבר אלא החכמות שבנשים בונות את בתיהם שמתקיימות על ידיהן כמו אשתו של און בן פלת כמו שמפורש בפרק חלק. ואולת. ואשה שוטה. בידיה תהרסנו. תהרס ביתה זו אשתו של קרח [משלי יד, א]. קראי מועד. שהיו תלמידי חכמים כדכתיב (במדבר טז) נשיאי עדה קריאי מועד אנשי שם ועל שם שפיתם אותו רשע שנהנו מממונו הקלו בעיניו להשיאם ולהחזיק ידו במחלוקת ולמרוד בהקדוש ברוך הוא [לעיל נב.]. ויקם משה. כסבור שישאו לו פנים ולא עשו [במדבר טז, כה]. ביד משה לו. כמו עליו על אהרן דבר אל משה שיהיה הוא ובניו כהנים לפיכך לא יקרב איש זר אשר לא מזרע אהרן וגו' וכן כל לי ולו ולהם הסמוכים אצל דבור פתרונם כמו על ומדרשו על קרח ומהו ביד משה ולא כתב אל משה רמז לחולקים על הכהונה שלוקין בצרעת כמו שלקה משה בידו שנאמר (שמות ד, ו) ויוציאה והנה ידו מצורעת כשלג ועל כן לקה עוזיה בצרעת [במדבר יז, ה]. חמת זוחלי עפר. ארס נחשים המהלכים על גחונם על העפר כמים הזוחלים על הארץ זחילה לשון מרוצת המים על העפר וכן כל מרוצת דבר המשפשף על העפר והולך [דברים לב, כד]. עושר שמור לבעליו לרעתו. כעשרו של קרח שעל ידי כן נתגאה וירד לשאול [קהלת ה, יב]. שמעמידו על רגליו. שמשמח לבו. וקילפי. פותחות שקורין בלעז שרדור"א. דגלדי. של מרצופים של עור שנושאים על סוסים וחמורים וגמלים [פסחים קיט.]. מלמד שעלו שמש וירח לזבול. שחמה ולבנה ברקיע השני כדאמרינן שבעה רקיעים הם וילון רקיע שחקים זבול מכון מעון ערבות ומונה להם כסדרן וילון אינו משמש כלום רקיע יש בו חמה ולבנה כוכבים ומזלות כו' [תהלים יט, ז]. שמש ירח עמד זבולה אם אתה עושה דין לבן עמרם ממחלקותו של קרח ומשמע להו דהאי קרא במחלקותו של קרח מדריש משום דביציאת מצרים ובקריעת ים סוף משתעי בספר חבקוק וכתיב ביה מחצת ראש מבית רשע ומשמע להו דהיינו קרח וכתיב בתריה שמש ירח עמד זבולה [נדרים לט.]. אלא לקרובי פיתחא. וקריבה בעלמא ליתא בכלל אין כל חדש [נדרים לט:]. ובני קרח לא מתו. הם היו בעצה תחלה ובשעת המחלוקת הרהרו תשובה בלבם לפיכך נתבצר להם מקום גבוה בגיהנם וישבו שם [במדבר כו, יא]. נתבצר להם. לשון גבוה כמו ובצורות בשמים (דברים ט) [מגילה יד.].

that those two hundred and fifty men were **the** most **distinguished** individuals **in the Congregation** of Israel.[16] ,,קְרִאֵי מוֹעֵד'' – The verse goes on to describe the group of two hundred and fifty as people who were ***summoned for appointed times,*** **שֶׁהָיוּ יוֹדְעִים לְעַבֵּר שָׁנִים וְלִקְבּוֹעַ חֳדָשִׁים** – which implies **that they knew how to intercalate the years and establish the months** in the Jewish calendar.[17] ,,אַנְשֵׁי־שֵׁם'' – The verse concludes by calling them ***men of renown*** (literally: name), **שֶׁהָיָה לָהֶם שֵׁם בְּכָל הָעוֹלָם** – meaning **that they had a** good **name throughout the world.**[18]

The Korach passage continues:[19]

,,וַיִּשְׁמַע מֹשֶׁה וַיִּפֹּל עַל־פָּנָיו'' – *They gathered together against Moses and against Aaron and said to them, "It is too much for you! For the entire assembly – all of them – are holy, and God is among them. Why do you exalt yourselves above the Congregation of God?"* ***Moses heard and fell upon his face.***

The Gemara asks:

מַה שְּׁמוּעָה שָׁמַע – **What report did [Moses] hear** that caused him to fall upon his face?

The Gemara answers:

אָמַר רַבִּי שְׁמוּאֵל בַּר נַחְמָנִי אָמַר רַבִּי יוֹנָתָן – **R' Shmuel bar Nachmani said in the name of R' Yonasan:** **שֶׁחֲשָׁדוּהוּ מֵאֵשֶׁת אִישׁ** – He heard **that [the people] suspected him of** transgressing the prohibition against having relations with **a married woman,** ,,וַיְקַנְאוּ לְמֹשֶׁה בַּמַּחֲנֶה'' **שֶׁנֶּאֱמַר** – **as it is stated:**[20] ***They were jealous of Moses in the camp.*** **אָמַר רַבִּי שְׁמוּאֵל בַּר יִצְחָק** – And **R' Shmuel bar Yitzchak said:** **מְלַמֵּד שֶׁכָּל אֶחָד וְאֶחָד קִנֵּא אֶת אִשְׁתּוֹ מִמֹּשֶׁה** – **[This verse] teaches that each and every one** of the husbands **formally warned his wife against** secluding herself with **Moses,**[21] ,,וּמֹשֶׁה יִקַּח אֶת־הָאֹהֶל וְנָטָה־לוֹ מִחוּץ לַמַּחֲנֶה'' **שֶׁנֶּאֱמַר** – **as it is stated:** ***And Moses took the tent and pitched it outside of the camp.***[22]

Moses makes one last effort to avert strife, and the Gemara draws a lesson therefrom:

,,וַיָּקָם מֹשֶׁה וַיֵּלֶךְ אֶל־דָּתָן וַאֲבִירָם'' – The Torah states: ***Moses rose and went to Dasan and Abiram.***[23] **אָמַר רֵישׁ לָקִישׁ** – **Reish Lakish said:** **מִכָּאן שֶׁאֵין מַחֲזִיקִין בְּמַחֲלוֹקֶת** – **From here** we learn **that one should not persist in a quarrel.**[24] **דְּאָמַר רַב** – **For Rav said:** **כָּל הַמַּחֲזִיק בְּמַחֲלוֹקֶת עוֹבֵר בְּלָאו** – **Whoever persists in a quarrel violates a** Scriptural **prohibition,** ,,וְלֹא־יִהְיֶה כְקֹרַח וְכַעֲדָתוֹ'' **שֶׁנֶּאֱמַר** – **as it is stated:** ***He should not be like***

NOTES

16. The phrase, *from the Children of Israel,* is extraneous, for certainly Korach's followers came from the ranks of the Jewish people. Scripture thus implies that in terms of Torah knowledge, wisdom and other virtues, these two hundred and fifty men were the select of the congregation (*Maharsha*).

17. The Rabbis are entrusted with the task of intercalating the years (by adding leap months) and establishing the start of each new month. It is by means of these calculations that the dates of the מוֹעֲדִים (the *appointed times,* or festivals) are determined. Both tasks require a knowledge of the movements of the heavenly bodies. The two hundred and fifty men who supported Korach against Moses possessed such knowledge; therefore, they are referred to as קְרִאֵי מוֹעֵד, those men who are *summoned* when the official calculations that determine the dates of the *festivals* are to be made (*Maharsha*).

18. I.e. their importance and exalted status was known even throughout the world (*Maharsha*).

19. *Numbers* 16:3-4.

20. *Psalms* 106:16.

21. According to Torah law, if a husband suspects his wife of having committed adultery, he must formally warn her to avoid seclusion with the other man. If she disregards the warning and is observed going into seclusion with him, there is sufficient circumstantial evidence to establish the likelihood that an act of adultery has occurred, at which point she becomes prohibited to her husband until her innocence can be established (see *Numbers* 5:11-31 and *Sotah* 2a). The husband's formal warning is called קִנּוּי, *kinui,* from *Numbers* 5:14: וְעָבַר עָלָיו רוּחַ־קִנְאָה וְקִנֵּא אֶת־אִשְׁתּוֹ וְהִוא נִטְמָאָה אוֹ־עָבַר עָלָיו רוּחַ־קִנְאָה וְקִנֵּא אֶת־אִשְׁתּוֹ וְהִיא לֹא נִטְמָאָה, *A spirit of jealousy had passed over [the husband] and he had warned his wife, and she had become defiled, or a spirit of jealousy had passed over him and he had warned his wife and she had not become defiled.*

Thus, the word קנא has two connotations: jealousy and the formal warning given a suspected adulteress by her husband. The aforecited verse from *Psalms* is usually translated *They were jealous of Moses,* and is interpreted to mean that Korach and his followers were jealous of the authority Moses and Aaron had assumed (see *Ibn Ezra* there). However, R' Shmuel bar Yitzchak expounds the verse as follows: *They* (i.e. the people) *formally warned* their wives to stay away *from Moses in the camp* because they suspected their wives of committing adultery with him (see *Rashi*).

It was the humiliation of being so outrageously accused that caused Moses to fall to the ground (*Targum Yonasan ben Uziel,* cited by *Maharsha*). For explanations of how such an egregious canard could have any currency whatsoever, see following note.

22. *Exodus* 33:7, which teaches that Moses moved his tent out of the Israelite camp in order to escape further suspicion (*Rashi*). The verse thus proves R' Shmuel bar Yitzchak's point: Moshe had indeed been suspected of adultery.

We shall now present various explanations of this incredible suspicion. Some commentators take a literal approach in the matter. *Maharsha* explains that the accusation derived from the fact that Moses had separated from his wife at God's behest. The scoffers proclaimed that it was impossible for a frail mortal to abstain permanently from conjugal relations, and so Moses must have been engaging in illicit affairs. *Torah Temimah* cites *Sotah* 4b as the basis of the accusation. The Gemara there states that arrogance inevitably leads to adultery. Inasmuch as Korach and his cabal accused Moses of arrogantly seizing power and exalting himself over the people, they sought to reinforce that claim by formally accusing him of the consequent sin of adultery.

Other commentators interpret the accusation figuratively. *Shelah HaKadosh* (*parashas Korach,* p. 69b) writes that ordinarily a woman formally suspected of adultery (i.e. a *sotah*) must go to the Temple, where a Kohen administers the "bitter waters" to her. If she is innocent, she will survive and prosper; if she is guilty, the waters will kill her. Moses' enemies accused him of deliberately installing his brother and nephews in the Kehunah so that they could cover up for him were he the suspected adulterer. Moses was thereby assuring that he would be able to commit adultery with impunity.

Imrei HaTzvi (cited in *Margaliyos HaYam*) offers yet another explanation of the husbands' suspicions: When the Jewish people needed gold in order to make the Golden Calf, the husbands demanded that the wives contribute their jewelry. The women adamantly refused to comply, saying, 'We will not listen to you!" (*Pirkei DeRabbi Eliezer* 45). On the other hand, when Moses later requested that the women contribute their jewelry for the building of the Tabernacle, they responded enthusiastically (*Exodus* 35:22). It was thus evident that the wives obeyed Moses more willingly than they obeyed their own husbands, and this enraged the husbands. In their anger they determined to keep their wives away from Moses, and they did so by issuing a formal *sotah* warning to them. This warning perforce bore the legal implication that the husbands suspected their wives of committing adultery with Moses. Thus, the husbands did not actually suspect Moses of adultery; rather, such suspicions were merely the concomitance of their effort to remove their wives from Moses' sphere of influence. See also *Aderes Eliyahu* (cited in *Shaarei Aharon*) to *Numbers* 16:4.

23. *Numbers* 16:25. Before calling for the destruction of Korach and his followers, Moses betook himself to the tents of Dasan and Abiram to make a final plea that they desist (see vs. 25-27).

24. [That is, one should not perpetuate a quarrel even if he is in the right, nor should he overlook any opportunity to end the quarrel. Moses had been maliciously slandered by Dasan and Abiram (ibid. v. 3). As the aggrieved party, he could have insisted that Dasan and Abiram come and apologize to *him.* However, Moses did not adopt this attitude. On the contrary, he himself went to Dasan and Abiram to persuade them to end the controversy. Moses acted thus because he realized that one must seize any opportunity to terminate a dispute.]

וסתרתה למזיה כל דאתא חזיה הדר אדהכי והכי אבלעו להו איתתיה דקרח אמרה ליה חזי מאי קעביד משה איהו הוה מלכא לאחוה שוויה כהנא רבא לבני אחוהי שוינהו סגני דכהנא אי אתיא תרומה אמר תיהוי לכהן אי אתו מעשר דשקילתו אתון אמר הבו חד מי' לכהן ועוד דגייז ליה למזייכו ומיטלל לכו כי כופתא עינא יהב במזייכו אמר לה הא איהו נמי קא עביד אמרה ליה כיון דכולהו רבותא דידיה אמר איהו נמי (א) תמות נפשי עם פלשתים ועוד דקאמר לכו עבידיתו תכלתא אי ס"ד תכלתא חשיבא [מצוה] אפיק גלימי דתכלתא וכסינהו לכולהו מתיבתך היינו דכתיב (ב) חכמות נשים בנתה ביתה זו אשתו של און בן פלת ואולת (א) בידה תהרסנה זו אשתו של קרח (ג) ויקומו לפני משה ואנשים מבני ישראל חמשים ומאתים מיוחדים שבעדה קריאי מועד שהיו יודעים לעבר שנים ולקבוע חדשים אנשי שם שהיה להם שם בכל העולם (ד) וישמע משה ויפול על פניו מה שמועה שמע (ב) אמר רבי שמואל בר נחמני א"ר יונתן שחשדוהו מאשת איש שנאמר (ה) ויקנאו למשה במחנה א"ר שמואל בר יצחק מלמד שכל אחד ואחד קנא את אשתו ממשה שנאמר (ו) ומשה יקח את האהל ונטה לו מחוץ למחנה (ז) ויקם משה וילך אל דתן ואבירם אמר ר"ל מכאן שאין מחזיקין במחלוקת דאמר רב כל המחזיק במחלוקת עובר בלאו שנאמר (ח) ולא יהיה כקרח וכעדתו רב אשי אמר ראוי ליצטרע כתיב הכא (ח) ביד משה לו וכתיב התם (ט) ויאמר ה' לו עוד הבא נא ידך בחיקך אמר ר' (ג) יוסי כל החולק על מלכות בית דוד ראוי להכישו נחש כתיב הכא (י) ויזבח אדוניהו צאן ובקר ומריא עם אבן הזוחלת וכתיב התם (יא) עם חמת זוחלי עפר אמר רב חסדא (ד) (א) כל החולק על רבו כחולק על השכינה שנאמר (יב) בהצותם על ה' א"ר חמא ברבי חנינא (ב) כל העושה מריבה עם רבו כעושה עם שכינה שנאמר (יג) המה מי מריבה אשר רבו בני ישראל (על) [את] ה' א"ר חנינא בר פפא (ג) כל המתרעם על רבו כאילו מתרעם על השכינה שנאמר (יד) לא עלינו תלונותיכם כי (אם) על ה' א"ר אבהו (ד) כל המהרהר אחר רבו כאילו מהרהר אחר שכינה שנאמר (טו) וידבר העם באלהים ובמשה (טז) עושר שמור לבעליו לרעתו (ה) אמר ר"ל זה עושרו של קרח (יז) ואת כל היקום אשר ברגליהם (ו) א"ר אלעזר זה ממונו של אדם שמעמידו על רגליו ואמר רבי לוי משוי (ז) ג' מאות פרדות לבנות היו מפתחות של בית גנזיו של קרח וכולהו אקלידי וקילפי דגילדא א"ר חמא ברבי חנינא ג' מטמוניות הטמין יוסף במצרים אחת נתגלתה לקרח ואחת נתגלתה לאנטונינוס בן אסוירוס ואחת גנוזה לצדיקים לעתיד לבא וא"ר יוחנן קרח לא מן הבלועים ולא מן השרופין לא מן הבלועין דכתיב (יח) ואת כל האדם אשר לקרח ולא קרח ולא מן השרופים דכתיב (יט) באכול האש את חמשים ומאתים איש ולא קרח במתניתא תנא קרח מן השרופין ומן הבלועין מן הבלועים דכתיב (יט) ותבלע אותם ואת קרח מן השרופין דכתיב (כ) (ותצא אש מלפני ה') [ואש יצאה מאת ה'] ותאכל את חמשים ומאתים איש וקרח בהדייהו אמר רבא (ח) מאי דכתיב (כא) שמש ירח עמד זבולה מלמד שעלו שמש וירח לזבול אמרו לפניו רבש"ע אם אתה עושה דין לבן עמרם נצא ואם לאו לא נצא עד שזרק בהם חצים אמר להן (ט) בכבודי לא מחיתם בכבוד בשר ודם מחיתם והאידנא לא נפקי עד דמחו להו (י) דרש רבא מאי דכתיב (כב) ואם בריאה יברא ה' ופצתה האדמה את פיה אמר משה לפני הקב"ה אם בריאה גיהנם מוטב ואם לאו יברא ה' למאי אילימא למבריה ממש והא (כג) אין כל חדש תחת השמש אלא לקרובי פיתחא (כד) ובני קרח לא מתו תנא (כ) משום רבינו אמרו מקום נתבצר להם בגיהנם וישבו עליו ואמרו שירה (ל) אמר רבה בר בר חנה זימנא חדא הוה קאזילנא באורחא אמר לי ההוא טייעא תא ואחוי לך בלועי דקרח אזיל חזא תרי בזעי דהוה קא נפק קיטרא מנייהו שקל גבבא דעמרא אמשיי' מיא ואותביה בריש רומחיה ואחלפי' התם איחרך א"ל אצית מה שמעת ושמעית דהוו קאמרי הכי משה ותורתו אמת והן בדאים אמר

סתרה למזיה. שערה וישבה על פתח הבית כל מי שהיה בא לקרוא רואה ראשה פרוע וחוזר: מעשר. ראשון דשקליתו אתון אמר הבו חד מי' לכהן: דגייז למזייכו. דכתיב (במדבר ח) והעבירו תער על [כל] בשרם ומשחק בכם כאילו אתם שוטים: ככופתא. רעי כמו בטולא דכופתא דאמרן לעיל (דף נח:) כגלל הזה אתם חשובים בעיניו: עינא יהב. עין נתן בשעריכם כדי שלא יהא בכם נורה כמותו: אמר לה. קרח איהו נמי משה עצמו גלח כל שערו: כיון דכולא רבותא דידיה הוא. אינו חושש אם גילח עצמו דקאמר לנפשיה תמות נפשי עם פלשתים אגוזו שערי כמותם ומה לי בכך שהם מקיימין אפילו מה שאני מצוה לשחוק אגוזו עכשיו כמותם כדי להפיס דעתם: ועוד דקאמר לכו. עשו פתיל תכלת בד' כנפות הבגד ואי ס"ד תכלת חשוב מפני מה לא יאמר לעשות כל הבגד כולו תכלת: אפיק גלימא דתכלתא. קח לך בגדים של תכלת וכסינהו לכולהו מתיבתך וכסה בהן בהמ"ת אתה וחברותך: קנא לאשתו. אל (הסתר) [תסתרי] עם משה. קנוי היינו התראה: ונטה לו מחוץ למחנה. יצא מחוץ למחנה שלא יחשדוהו עוד: מכאן שאין מחזיקין במחלוקת. שמחל על כבודו והוא עצמו הלך לבטל מחלוקת: חולק על רבו. חולק על ישיבתו: אשר הצו על משה ועל אהרן בעדת קרח בהצותם על ה'. מעלה עליהם הכתוב כאלו היו חולקים כלפי שכינה: מריבה. תגר וקטטה לפטפט נגדו בדברים: מתרעם. אומר על רבו שנוהג לו מדה כבושה ומדת אכזרית: מהרהר. מתפה עליו דברים: אקלידי. מפתחות: וקולפי. מנעולים: דגילדי. כולם המפתחות והמנעולים של עור היו ואעפ"כ היו שלש מאות פרדות טעונות ל"א דגלדא לצורך שקים והמרצופין וכיסין של עור היו: לא מן הבלועין ולא מן השרופין. אלא במגפה מת: ולא קרח. ר"נ היו לבד קרח דכתיב חמשים ומאתים מחתות ואתה ואהרן איש מחתתו: מן הבלועים ומן השרופין היה. שנשרפה נשמתו וגוף קיים ואח"כ נתגלגל עד מקום הבלועין ונבלע דכתיב בפרשת פנחס ותבלע אותם ואת קרח עמהם ורבי יוחנן דאמר לא מן הבלועין ולא מן השרופין דריש ליה להאי ואת קרח לאחריו ואת קרח במות העדה במגפה: וקרח בהדייהו. מדכתיב ותאכל את החמשים ומאתים איש מקריבי הקטרת וקרח ממקריבי הקטרת הוה דכתיב חמשים ומאתים מחתות ואתה ואהרן איש מחתתו א"נ ואת לרבות קרח עמהם: שמש ירח עמד זבולה. לעיל מיניה כתיב ותבקע ארץ בשעת בקיעת הארץ שנבלעו בקרקע שמש וירח עלו לאותו רקיע ששמו זבול ואמרו להקב"ה אם אי אתה עושה דין לבן עמרם מקרח ועדתו: לא נצא. ונאיר לעולם: בכבודי לא מחיתם. שהרי בכל יום מלכי מזרח ומערב בשעה שמניחין כתריהן בראשם משתחוים לחמה: והאידנא לא נפקי עד דמחו להו. שכך גזר עליהם המקום כן שמעתי ל"א והאידנא לא נפקי מאחר שראו שהקפיד הקב"ה על שלא מיחה לכבודו עד דמחו להו לא נפקי שחסו לכבוד המקום על בני אדם שמשתחוים לשמש וירח: אין כל חדש תחת השמש. ואי גיהנם לא אברי עד ההוא שעתא הוה ליה חדש: לקרובי פתחה. שיקרב פתחה של גיהנם ותפתח הארץ במקום שהן: נתבצר. מלשון (ישעיה כ) עיר בצורה התקין להון הקב"ה מקום גבוה שלא העמיקו כל כך בגיהנם ולא מתו: טייעא. סוחר ישמעאל: בלועי. מקום שנתבלעו לשם עדת קרח: בזעא. ראה נקב שממנו יצא עשן: גבבא. גיזה: אמשיה. שרה אות' במים לשון (ברכות דף יד:) משי ידיה: (וכל שלשים יום. חוזר לגיהנם ועולה לשם): אמר

מסורת הש"ס

א) בקרא כתיב בידיה תהרסנו, ב) [מו"ק יח:], ג) [נ"ל יוסף], ד) [ברכות כז: ע"ש], ה) פסחים קיט. ע"ש, ו) [שם], ז) ג' מאות לאו דוקא וכן כל שלש מאות בש"ס רשב"ס פסחים קיט, ח) נדרים לט: ע"ש, ט) לעיל קג., י) [לעיל קג:], כ) מגילה יד., ל) ב"ב עד ע"א.

תורה אור השלם

א) וַיֹּאמֶר שִׁמְשׁוֹן תָּמוֹת נַפְשִׁי עִם פְּלִשְׁתִּים וַיֵּט בְּכֹחַ וַיִּפֹּל הַבַּיִת עַל הַסְּרָנִים וְעַל כָּל הָעָם אֲשֶׁר בּוֹ וַיִּהְיוּ הַמֵּתִים אֲשֶׁר הֵמִית בְּמוֹתוֹ רַבִּים מֵאֲשֶׁר הֵמִית בְּחַיָּיו: [שופטים טז, ל]

ב) חַכְמוֹת נָשִׁים בָּנְתָה בֵיתָהּ וְאִוֶּלֶת בְּיָדֶיהָ תֶהֶרְסֶנּוּ: [משלי יד, א]

ג) וַיָּקֻמוּ לִפְנֵי מֹשֶׁה וַאֲנָשִׁים מִבְּנֵי יִשְׂרָאֵל חֲמִשִּׁים וּמָאתָיִם נְשִׂיאֵי עֵדָה קְרִאֵי מוֹעֵד אַנְשֵׁי שֵׁם: [במדבר טז, ב]

ד) וַיִּשְׁמַע מֹשֶׁה וַיִּפֹּל עַל פָּנָיו: [במדבר טז, ד]

ה) וַיְקַנְאוּ לְמֹשֶׁה בַּמַּחֲנֶה לְאַהֲרֹן קְדוֹשׁ יְיָ: [תהלים קו, טז]

ו) וּמֹשֶׁה יִקַּח אֶת הָאֹהֶל וְנָטָה לוֹ מִחוּץ לַמַּחֲנֶה הַרְחֵק מִן הַמַּחֲנֶה וְקָרָא לוֹ אֹהֶל מוֹעֵד וְהָיָה כָּל מְבַקֵּשׁ יְיָ יֵצֵא אֶל אֹהֶל מוֹעֵד אֲשֶׁר מִחוּץ לַמַּחֲנֶה: [שמות לג, ז]

ז) וַיָּקָם מֹשֶׁה וַיֵּלֶךְ אֶל דָּתָן וַאֲבִירָם וַיֵּלְכוּ אַחֲרָיו זִקְנֵי יִשְׂרָאֵל: [במדבר טז, כה]

ח) זִכָּרוֹן לִבְנֵי יִשְׂרָאֵל לְמַעַן אֲשֶׁר לֹא יִקְרַב אִישׁ זָר אֲשֶׁר לֹא מִזֶּרַע אַהֲרֹן הוּא לְהַקְטִיר קְטֹרֶת לִפְנֵי יְיָ וְלֹא יִהְיֶה כְקֹרַח וְכַעֲדָתוֹ כַּאֲשֶׁר דִּבֶּר יְיָ בְּיַד מֹשֶׁה לוֹ: [במדבר יז, ה]

ט) וַיֹּאמֶר יְיָ לוֹ עוֹד הָבֵא נָא יָדְךָ בְּחֵיקֶךָ וַיָּבֵא יָדוֹ בְּחֵיקוֹ וַיּוֹצִאָהּ וְהִנֵּה יָדוֹ מְצֹרַעַת כַּשָּׁלֶג: [שמות ד, ו]

י) וַיִּזְבַּח אֲדֹנִיָּהוּ צֹאן וּבָקָר וּמְרִיא עִם אֶבֶן הַזֹּחֶלֶת אֲשֶׁר אֵצֶל עֵין רֹגֵל וַיִּקְרָא אֶת כָּל אֶחָיו בְּנֵי הַמֶּלֶךְ וּלְכָל אַנְשֵׁי יְהוּדָה עַבְדֵי הַמֶּלֶךְ: [מלכים א א, ט]

יא) מְזֵי רָעָב וּלְחֻמֵי רֶשֶׁף וְקֶטֶב מְרִירִי וְשֶׁן בְּהֵמוֹת אֲשַׁלַּח בָּם עִם חֲמַת זֹחֲלֵי עָפָר: [דברים לב, כד]

יב) וּבְנֵי אֱלִיאָב נְמוּאֵל וְדָתָן וַאֲבִירָם הוּא דָתָן וַאֲבִירָם קְרִיאֵי הָעֵדָה אֲשֶׁר הִצּוּ עַל מֹשֶׁה וְעַל אַהֲרֹן בַּעֲדַת קֹרַח בְּהַצֹּתָם עַל יְיָ: [במדבר כו, ט]

יג) הֵמָּה מֵי מְרִיבָה אֲשֶׁר רָבוּ בְנֵי יִשְׂרָאֵל אֶת יְיָ וַיִּקָּדֵשׁ בָּם: [במדבר כ, יג]

יד) וַיֹּאמֶר מֹשֶׁה בְּתֵת יְיָ לָכֶם בָּעֶרֶב בָּשָׂר לֶאֱכֹל וְלֶחֶם בַּבֹּקֶר לִשְׂבֹּעַ בִּשְׁמֹעַ יְיָ אֶת תְּלֻנֹּתֵיכֶם אֲשֶׁר אַתֶּם מַלִּינִם עָלָיו וְנַחְנוּ מָה לֹא עָלֵינוּ תְלֻנֹּתֵיכֶם כִּי עַל יְיָ: [שמות טז, ח] טו) וַיְדַבֵּר הָעָם בֵּאלֹהִים וּבְמֹשֶׁה לָמָה הֶעֱלִיתֻנוּ מִמִּצְרַיִם לָמוּת בַּמִּדְבָּר כִּי אֵין לֶחֶם וְאֵין מַיִם וְנַפְשֵׁנוּ קָצָה בַּלֶּחֶם הַקְּלֹקֵל: [במדבר כא, ה] טז) יֵשׁ רָעָה חוֹלָה רָאִיתִי תַּחַת הַשָּׁמֶשׁ עֹשֶׁר שָׁמוּר לִבְעָלָיו לְרָעָתוֹ: [קהלת ה, יב] יז) וַאֲשֶׁר עָשָׂה לְדָתָן וְלַאֲבִירָם בְּנֵי אֱלִיאָב בֶּן רְאוּבֵן אֲשֶׁר פָּצְתָה הָאָרֶץ אֶת פִּיהָ וַתִּבְלָעֵם וְאֶת בָּתֵּיהֶם וְאֶת אָהֳלֵיהֶם וְאֵת כָּל הַיְקוּם אֲשֶׁר בְּרַגְלֵיהֶם בְּקֶרֶב כָּל יִשְׂרָאֵל: [דברים יא, ו] יח) וַתִּפְתַּח הָאָרֶץ אֶת פִּיהָ וַתִּבְלַע אֹתָם וְאֶת בָּתֵּיהֶם וְאֵת כָּל הָאָדָם אֲשֶׁר לְקֹרַח וְאֵת כָּל הָרְכוּשׁ: [במדבר טז, לב] יט) וַתִּפְתַּח הָאָרֶץ אֶת פִּיהָ וַתִּבְלַע אֹתָם וְאֶת קֹרַח בְּמוֹת הָעֵדָה בַּאֲכֹל הָאֵשׁ אֵת חֲמִשִּׁים וּמָאתַיִם אִישׁ וַיִּהְיוּ לְנֵס: [במדבר כו, י] כ) וְאֵשׁ יָצְאָה מֵאֵת יְיָ וַתֹּאכַל אֵת הַחֲמִשִּׁים וּמָאתַיִם אִישׁ מַקְרִיבֵי הַקְּטֹרֶת: [במדבר טז, לה] כא) שֶׁמֶשׁ יָרֵחַ עָמַד זְבֻלָה לְאוֹר חִצֶּיךָ יְהַלֵּכוּ לְנֹגַהּ בְּרַק חֲנִיתֶךָ: [חבקוק ג, יא] כב) וְאִם בְּרִיאָה יִבְרָא יְיָ וּפָצְתָה הָאֲדָמָה אֶת פִּיהָ וּבָלְעָה אֹתָם וְאֶת כָּל אֲשֶׁר לָהֶם וְיָרְדוּ חַיִּים שְׁאֹלָה וִידַעְתֶּם כִּי נִאֲצוּ הָאֲנָשִׁים הָאֵלֶּה אֶת יְיָ: [במדבר טז, ל] כג) מַה שֶּׁהָיָה הוּא שֶׁיִּהְיֶה וּמַה שֶּׁנַּעֲשָׂה הוּא שֶׁיֵּעָשֶׂה וְאֵין כָּל חָדָשׁ תַּחַת הַשָּׁמֶשׁ: [קהלת א, ט] כד) וּבְנֵי קֹרַח לֹא מֵתוּ: [במדבר כו, יא]

עין משפט נר מצוה

לג א ב ג ד מיי' פ"ה מהל' ת"ת הל' א סמג עשין יב טוש"ע י"ד סי' רמב סעיף ג:

ליקוטי רש"י

אחר חוט אחד של תכלת פוטרה זו שכולה תכלת לא תפטור את עצמה [במדבר טז, א]. חכמות נשים בנתה ביתה. חכמות נקוד פתח שאינו שם דבר אלא החכמות שבנשים בונות את בתיהם שמתקיימות על ידיהן כמו אשתו של און בן פלת כמו שמפורש בפרק חלק. ואולת. ואשה שוטה. בידיה תהרסנו. תהרס ביתה זו אשתו של קרח [משלי יד, א]. קראי מועד. שהיו תלמידי חכמים כדכתיב (במדבר טז) נשיאי עדה קריאי מועד אנשי שם ועל שם שפיתם אותו רשע כשנהנו ממשונו הקלו בעיניו להשיאם ולהחזיק ידו במחלוקת ולמרוד בהקדוש ברוך הוא [לעיל נב.]. ויקם משה. כסבור שישאו לו פנים ולא עשו [במדבר טז, כה]. ביד משה לו. כמו עליו על אהרן דבר אל משה שיהיה הוא ובניו כהנים לפיכך לא יקרב איש זר אשר לא מזרע אהרן וגו' וכן כל לי ולו ולהם הסמוכים אצל דבור פתרונם כמו על ומדרשו על קרח ומהו ביד משה ולא כתב אל משה רמז לחולקים על הכהונה שלוקין בצרעת כמו שלקה משה בידו שנאמר (שמות ד, ו) ויוציאה והנה ידו מצורעת כשלג ועל כן לקה עוזיה בצרעת [במדבר יז, ה]. חמת זוחלי עפר. ארס נחשים המהלכים על גחונם על העפר כמים הזוחלים על הארץ וזחילה לשון מרוצת המים על העפר וכן כל מרוצת דבר המשפשף על העפר והולך [דברים לב, כד]. עושר שמור לבעליו לרעתו. כעשרו של קרח שעל ידי כן נתגאה וירד לשאול [קהלת ה, יב]. שמעמידו על רגליו. שמשמח לבו. וקילפי. פותחות שקורין בלעז שרדור"א. דגלדי. של מרצופים של עור שנושאים על סוסים וחמורים וגמלים [פסחים קיט.]. מלמד שעלו שמש וירח לזבול. שחמה ולבנה ברקיע השני כדאמרינן שבעה רקיעים הם וילון רקיע שחקים זבול מכון מעון ערבות ומונה להם כסדרן וילון אינו משמש כלום רקיע יש בו חמה ולבנה כוכבים ומזלות כו' [תהלים יט, ז]. שמש ירח עמד זבולה אם אתה עושה דין לבן עמרם ממחלוקתו של קרח ומשמע להו דהאי קרא במחלוקתו של קרח מדריש משום דביציאת מצרים ובקריעת ים סוף משתעי בספר חבקוק וכתיב ביה מחצת ראש מבית רשע ומשמע להו דהיינו קרח וכתיב בתריה שמש ירח עמד זבולה [נדרים לט.]. אלא לקרובי פיתחא. וקריבה בעלמא ליתא בכלל אין כל חדש [נדרים לט:]. ובני קרח לא מתו. הם היו בעצה תחלה ובשעת המחלוקת הרהרו תשובה בלבם לפיכך נתבצר להם מקום גבוה בגיהנם וישבו שם [במדבר כו, יא]. נתבצר להם. לשון גבוה כמו ובצורות בשמים (דברים ט) [מגילה יד.].

Korach and his assembly.[25]

The Gemara describes the potential fate of one who perpetuates a quarrel:

רַב אַשִׁי אָמַר – Rav Ashi said: רָאוּי לִיצְטָרֵעַ – Such a person deserves to be stricken with leprosy, כְּתִיב הָכָא ,,בְּיַד־מֹשֶׁה לוֹ״ – for it is written here at the conclusion of *Numbers* 17:5, *as God spoke* ***by the hand of Moses about him,***[26] **וּכְתִיב הָתָם ,,וַיֹּאמֶר ה׳ לוֹ עוֹד הָבֵא־נָא (את) יָדְךָ בְּחֵיקֶךָ״ – and it is written there,**[27] ***God said further to [Moses], "Bring your hand to your bosom,"*** *and he brought his hand to his bosom; then he withdrew it and, behold, his hand was leprous, like snow.*[28]

Korach's sin lay in challenging God's chosen messenger, Moses. It is similarly forbidden to challenge the Divinely anointed Davidic monarch:

אָמַר רַבִּי יוֹסֵי – R' Yose said: כָּל הַחוֹלֵק עַל מַלְכוּת בֵּית דָּוִד – Whoever challenges the kingship of the House of David רָאוּי לְהַכִּישׁוֹ נָחָשׁ – deserves that **a snake bite him, כְּתִיב הָכָא ,,וַיִּזְבַּח אֲדֹנִיָּהוּ צֹאן וּבָקָר וּמְרִיא עִם אֶבֶן הַזֹּחֶלֶת״ – for it is written here: *Adoniahu slaughtered sheep, cattle and fat oxen at the Stone of Zocheles,***[29] **וּכְתִיב הָתָם ,,עִם־חֲמַת זֹחֲלֵי עָפָר״ – and it is written there: ...** ***with the venom of those that creep*** (zochalei) ***in the dust.***[30]

The Gemara now discusses the moral equivalencies of those who challenge and otherwise denigrate their Torah teachers:

אָמַר רַב חִסְדָּא – Rav Chisda said: כָּל הַחוֹלֵק עַל רַבּוֹ כְּחוֹלֵק עַל הַשְּׁכִינָה – Whoever challenges his Torah teacher[31] **is like one who challenges the Divine Presence** itself, **שֶׁנֶּאֱמַר ,,בְּהַצֹּתָם עַל־ה׳ ״ – for it is stated:** ... *the same Dasan and Abiram who were summoned by the assembly, who contended against Moses and Aaron among the assembly of Korach,* ***when they contended against God.***[32] **אָמַר רַבִּי חָמָא בְּרַבִּי חֲנִינָא – R' Chama son of R' Chanina said: כָּל הָעוֹשֶׂה מְרִיבָה עִם רַבּוֹ כְּעוֹשֶׂה עִם שְׁכִינָה – Whoever picks a quarrel with his teacher**[33] **is like one who picks** a quarrel **with the Divine Presence, שֶׁנֶּאֱמַר ,,הֵמָּה מֵי מְרִיבָה אֲשֶׁר־רָבוּ בְנֵי־יִשְׂרָאֵל אֶת־ה׳ ״ – for it is stated:** ***They were the 'waters of strife,' where the Children of Israel quarreled with God.***[34] **אָמַר רַבִּי חֲנִינָא בַּר פָּפָּא – R' Chanina bar Pappa said: כָּל הַמִּתְרַעֵם עַל רַבּוֹ כְּאִילּוּ מִתְרַעֵם עַל הַשְּׁכִינָה – Whoever complains about his teacher**[35] is regarded **as if he complains**

NOTES

25. *Numbers* 17:5. In this passage God instructed Aaron's son Elazar to collect the fire-pans that had been offered by Korach's two hundred and fifty followers. Elazar was then to hammer those pans into a covering for the Altar. There, they would serve as a visible and eternal reminder of the fate that befell those who tampered with the Temple service or cast aspersions on the legitimacy of Aaron and his descendants, as it is stated: *As a reminder to the Children of Israel, so that no alien who is not of the offspring of Aaron shall draw near to bring up the smoke of incense before God, that he not be like Korach and his assembly ...*

Halachos Gedolos, Ramban and *Smag* maintain that the injunction not to be like Korach and his followers is one of the 613 mitzvos. *Rambam* disagrees; see the entire discussion in *Rambam's Sefer Hamitzvos,* General Rule 8, and the accompanying comments of *Ramban* et al. *She'iltos DeRabbi Achai* states that emulating Korach leads to hatred, a violation of *Leviticus* 19:17: *Do not hate your brother in your heart.* See also *Meshech Chochmah* on this verse, and the introduction to *Chafetz Chaim* (*Lavin* 12).

26. The plain meaning of the verse is: *As God spoke to Moses about [Aaron]* — i.e. telling Moses that Aaron and his sons were to be the Kohanim (*Rashi* there). Accordingly, the Torah should have stated simply אֶל מֹשֶׁה (*to Moses*) rather than בְּיַד מֹשֶׁה (*by the hand of Moses*). The use of the awkward latter expression is therefore understood as a deliberate connecting of this verse with another (cited below), to teach allusively that one who acts like Korach, Dasan and Abiram, who persisted in their quarrel over the Kehunah, deserves to be stricken with leprosy (see note 28 below).

27. *Exodus* 4:6.

28. At the burning bush Moses asked God to provide him with a miraculous sign with which to prove to any skeptical Jew that God had indeed chosen him to lead the people out of Egypt. God consented, and told Moses that when he brought his hand to his bosom the hand would be stricken with leprosy, and when he repeated the procedure the leprosy would completely disappear.

Rav Ashi understands that the mention of Moses' *hand* in each verse connects the two verses. Hence, the association of Moses' hand with leprosy, established in the *Exodus* verse, can be carried over to the *Numbers* verse, to produce the allusive teaching recorded in note 26 above [see *Targum Yonasan ben Uziel* and *Ramban* to *Numbers* 17:5].

29. *I Kings* 1:9. King David had sworn to his wife Bathsheba that their son Solomon would become his successor. Adoniahu, an older son of David, felt wronged and sought to seize the throne for himself. He invited all the nobles of the realm to a banquet, where he would be publicly proclaimed the new king. In the end Adoniahu's plot was foiled, and Solomon was coronated while David yet lived.

R' Yose here calls attention to the fact that the venue of Adoniahu's banquet was a place called "The Stone of Zocheles." The implication of this will be explained in the following note.

Actually, Adoniahu was himself from the House of David. How, then, can he be cited as one who challenged the Davidic kingship? *Maharsha* explains that since Solomon had already been designated to succeed King David, Adoniahu was properly considered an outside usurper.

30. *Deuteronomy* 32:24. This passage is part of Moses' Farewell Song, where he foretells how the Jews will abandon God for idols, and how God in turn will abandon the Jews to a frightful assortment of calamities. The Jews will suffer *the bloating of famine, the devouring of the fiery bolt, and bitter destruction. [God will] send against them fanged beasts, with the venom of those that creep in the dust* (*zochalei afar*).

From the above verse we see that the word *zochalei* connotes venomous snakes. Inasmuch as Scripture notes that Adoniahu planned to usurp the Davidic throne at a place bearing the name *Zocheles,* which is cognate with the word *zochalei,* we may conclude that Adoniahu was committing the kind of sin for which he deserved to be punished by *zochalei afar* — i.e. snakes.

Maharsha explains why a snakebite is fitting punishment for challenging the Davidic kingship: The primordial Serpent was initially the ruler of the animal kingdom; however, it was jealous of Adam, who was of even greater stature, and therefore engineered his downfall, and for that reason was cursed. One whose jealousy stirs him to rebel against the true Davidic king thus deserves to be bitten by a snake, for he has adopted the Serpent's ways. See *Ben Yehoyada* for other explanations.

The twelfth Article of Faith concerns the Messiah ... This Article includes the belief that there can be no king of Israel who is not descended from David and Solomon. Whoever challenges [the exclusive royal prerogative of] this dynasty denies God and His prophets (*Maimonides, Thirteen Articles of Faith*).

31. *Rashi* enigmatically explains "challenges his teacher" as "challenges [his teacher's] Torah academy." *Maharsha* explains this to mean a challenge to the Rebbe's teachings. *Be'er Sheva* maintains, however, that *Rashi* actually intends what *Rambam* states explicitly (*Hil. Talmud Torah* 5:2): *Who is considered a challenger of his teacher? Anyone who during his teacher's lifetime opens a school in which he sits, expounds and teaches [Torah] without the teacher's express permission.* To this ruling *Rama* adds: *However, it is permissible for [a student] to disagree with [his teacher] concerning any ruling or teaching if the student can cite proofs for his own opinion* (*Yoreh Deah* 242:3). See *Be'er Sheva* for a lengthy discussion of *Rama's* point.

32. *Numbers* 26:9, which explicitly equates the challenge to Moses' authority to a challenge against God Himself (*Rashi*).

33. To speak ill of him (*Rashi*).

34. Ibid. 20:13. In fact, the Children of Israel had quarreled with Moses and Aaron. Nevertheless, the verse states that they quarreled with God. This implies that contending against their teacher Moses was equivalent to contending against God (*Torah Temimah* ibid.; see also *Maharsha*).

35. He complains that his teacher is behaving too harshly toward him (*Rashi*).

וסתרתה למזיה כל דאתא חזיה הדר אדהכי והכי אבלעו להו איתתיה דקרח אמרה ליה חזי מאי קעביד משה איהו הוה מלכא לאחוה שוויה כהנא רבא לבני אחוהי שוינהו סגני דכהנא אי אתיא תרומה אמר תיהוי לכהן אי אתו מעשר דשקילתו אתון אמר הבו חד מי' לכהן ועוד דגייז ליה למזייכו ומיטלל לכו כי כופתא עינא יהב במזייכו אמר לה הא איהו נמי קא עביד אמרה ליה כיון דכולהו רבותא דידיה אמר איהו נמי א) תמות נפשי עם פלשתים ועוד דקאמר לכו עבידתו תכלתא אי ס"ד תכלתא חשיבא [מצוה] אפיק גלימי דתכלתא וכסינהו לכולהו מתיבתך היינו דכתיב ב) חכמות נשים בנתה ביתה זו אשתו של און בן פלת ואולת [א] בידה תהרסנה זו אשתו של קרח ג) ויקומו לפני משה ואנשים מבני ישראל חמשים ומאתים מיוחדים שבעדה קריאי מועד שהיו יודעים לעבר שנים ולקבוע חדשים אנשי שם שהיה להם שם בכל העולם ד) וישמע משה ויפול על פניו מה שמועה שמע [ב] אמר רבי שמואל בר נחמני א"ר יונתן שחשדוהו מאשת איש שנאמר ה) ויקנאו למשה במחנה א"ר שמואל בר יצחק מלמד שכל אחד ואחד קנא את אשתו ממשה שנאמר ו) ומשה יקח את האהל ונטה לו מחוץ למחנה ז) ויקם משה וילך אל דתן ואבירם אמר ר"ל מכאן שאין מחזיקין במחלוקת דאמר רב כל המחזיק במחלוקת עובר בלאו שנאמר ח) ולא יהיה כקרח וכעדתו רב אשי אמר ראוי ליצטרע כתיב הכא ח) ביד משה לו וכתיב התם ט) ויאמר ה' לו עוד הבא נא ידך בחיקך אמר ר' [ג] יוסי כל החולק על מלכות בית דוד ראוי להכישו נחש כתיב הכא י) ויזבח אדוניהו צאן ובקר ומריא עם אבן הזוחלת וכתיב התם יא) עם חמת זוחלי עפר אמר רב חסדא [ד] [א] כל החולק על רבו כחולק על השכינה שנאמר יב) בהצותם על ה' א"ר חמא ברבי חנינא [ב] כל העושה מריבה עם רבו כעושה עם שכינה שנאמר יג) המה מי מריבה אשר רבו בני ישראל (על) [את] ה' א"ר חנינא בר פפא [ג] כל המתרעם על רבו כאילו מתרעם על השכינה שנאמר יד) לא עלינו תלונותיכם כי (אם) על ה' א"ר אבהו [ד] כל המהרהר אחר רבו כאילו מהרהר אחר שכינה שנאמר טו) וידבר העם באלהים ובמשה טז) עושר שמור לבעליו לרעתו [ה] אמר ר"ל זה עושרו של קרח יז) ואת כל היקום אשר ברגליהם [ו] א"ר אלעזר זה ממונו של אדם שמעמידו על רגליו ואמר רבי לוי משוי [ז] ג' מאות פרדות לבנות היו מפתחות של בית גנזיו של קרח וכולהו אקלידי וקילפי דגילדא א"ר חמא ברבי חנינא ג' מטמוניות הטמין יוסף במצרים אחת נתגלתה לקרח ואחת נתגלתה לאנטונינוס בן אסוירוס ואחת גנוזה לצדיקים לעתיד לבא וא"ר יוחנן קרח לא מן הבלועים ולא מן השרופין לא מן הבלועין דכתיב יח) ואת כל האדם אשר לקרח ולא קרח ולא מן השרופים דכתיב יט) באכול האש את חמשים ומאתים איש ולא קרח במתניתא תנא קרח מן השרופין ומן הבלועין מן הבלועים דכתיב יט) ותבלע אותם ואת קרח מן השרופין דכתיב כ) (ותצא אש מלפני ה') [ואש יצאה מאת ה'] ותאכל את חמשים ומאתים איש וקרח בהדייהו אמר רבא [ח] מאי דכתיב כא) שמש ירח עמד זבולה לאור חציך יהלכו מלמד שעלו שמש וירח לזבול אמרו לפניו רבש"ע אם אתה עושה דין לבן עמרם נצא ואם לאו לא נצא עד שזרק בהם חצים אמר להן [ט] בכבודי לא מחיתם בכבוד בשר ודם מחיתם והאידנא לא נפקי עד דמחו להו [י] דרש רבא מאי דכתיב כב) ואם בריאה יברא ה' ופצתה האדמה את פיה אמר משה לפני הקב"ה אם בריאה גיהנם מוטב ואם לאו יברא ה' למאי אילימא למבריה ממש והא כג) אין כל חדש תחת השמש אלא לקרובי פיתחא כד) ובני קרח לא מתו תנא [כ] משום רבינו אמרו מקום נתבצר להם בגיהנם וישבו עליו ואמרו שירה [ל] אמר רבה בר בר חנה זימנא חדא הוה קאזלינא באורחא אמר לי ההוא טייעא תא ואחוי לך בלועי דקרח אזיל חזא תרי בזעי דהוה קא נפק קיטרא מנייהו שקל גבבא דעמרא אמשיי' מיא ואותביה בריש רומחיה ואחלפי' התם איחרך א"ל אצית מה שמעת ושמעית דהוו קאמרי הכי משה ותורתו אמת והן בדאים

אמר

סתרה למזיה. שערה וישבה על פתח הבית כל מי שהיה בא לקרוא רואה ראשה פרוע וחוזר: מעשר. ראשון דשקליתו אתון אמר הבו חד מי' לכהן: דגייז למזייכו. דכתיב (במדבר ח) והעבירו תער על [כל] בשרם ומשחק בכם כאילו אתם שוטים: ככופתא. רעי כמו בטולא דכופתא דאמרן לעיל (דף לח:) כגלל הזה אתם חשובים בעיניו: עינא יהב. עין נתן בשעריכם כדי שלא יהא בכם צורה כמותו: אמר לה. קרח איהו נמי משה עצמו גלח כל שערו: כיון דכולא רבותא דידיה הוא. אינו חושש אם גילח עצמו דקאמר לנפשיה תמות נפשי עם פלשתים אגזוז שערי כמותם ומה לי בכך שהם מקיימין אפילו מה שאני מצוה לשחוק אגזוז עכשיו כמותם כדי להפיס דעתם: ועוד דקאמר לכו. עשו פתיל תכלת בד' כנפות הבגד ואי ס"ד תכלת חשוב מפני מה לא יאמר לעשות כל הבגד כולו תכלת: אפיק גלימא דתכלתא. קח לך בגדים של תכלת וכסינהו לכולהו מתיבתך וכסה בהן בבה"מ אתה וחברותך: קנא לאשתו. אל (הסתר) [תסתרי] עם משה. קנוי היינו התראה: ונטה לו מחוץ למחנה. יצא מחוץ למחנה שלא יחשדוהו עוד: מכאן שאין מחזיקין במחלוקת. שמחל על כבודו והוא עצמו הלך לבטל מחלוקת: חולק על רבו. חולק על ישיבתו: אשר הצו על משה ועל אהרן בעדת קרח בהצותם על ה'. מעלה עליהם הכתוב כאלו היו חולקים כלפי שכינה: מריבה. תגר וקטטה לפטפט נגדו בדברים: מתרעם. אומר על רבו שנוהג לו מדה כבושה ומדת אכזרית: מהרהר. מחפה עליו דברים: אקלידי. מפתחות: וקולפי. מנעולים: דגילדי. כולם המפתחות והמנעולים של עור היו ואעפ"כ היו שלש מאות פרדות טעונות ל"א דגלדא לצורך שקים והמרצופין וכיסין של עור היו: לא מן הבלועין ולא מן השרופין. אלא במגפה מת: ולא קרח. ר"נ היו לבד קרח דכתיב חמשים ומאתים מחתות ואתה ואהרן איש מחתתו: מן הבלועים ומן השרופין היה. שנשרפה נשמתו וגוף קיים ואח"כ נתגלגל עד מקום הבלועין ונבלע דכתיב בפרשת פנחס ותבלע אותם ואת קרח עמהם ורבי יוחנן דאמר לא מן הבלועין ולא מן השרופין דריש ליה להאי ואת קרח לאחריו ואת קרח במות העדה במגפה: וקרח בהדייהו. מדכתיב ותאכל את החמשים ומאתים איש מקריבי הקטרת וקרח ממקריבי הקטרת הוה דכתיב חמשים ומאתים מחתות ואתה ואהרן איש מחתתו א"נ ואת לרבות קרח עמהם: שמש ירח עמד זבולה. לעיל מיניה כתיב ותבקע ארץ בשעת בקיעת הארץ שנבלעו בקרקע שמש וירח עלו לאותו רקיע ששמו זבול ואמרו להקב"ה אם אי אתה עושה דין לבן עמרם מקרח ועדתו: לא נצא. ונאיר לעולם: בכבודי לא מחיתם. שהרי בכל יום מלכי מזרח ומערב בשעה שמניחין כתריהן בראשם משתחוים לחמה: והאידנא לא נפקי עד דמחו להו. שכך גזר עליהם המקום כן שמעתי ל"א והאידנא לא נפקי מאחר שראו שהקפיד הקב"ה על שלא מיחה לכבודו עד דמחו להו לא נפקי שחסו לכבוד המקום על בני אדם שמשתחוים לשמש וירח: אין כל חדש תחת השמש. ואי גיהנם לא אברי עד ההוא שעתא הוה ליה חדש: לקרובי פתחה. שיקרב פתחה של גיהנם ותפתח הארץ במקום שהן: נתבצר. מלשון (ישעיה כז) עיר בצורה התקין להון הקב"ה מקום גבוה שלא העמיקו כל כך בגיהנם ולא מתו: טייעא. סוחר ישמעאל: בלועי. מקום שנתבלעו לשם עדת קרח: בזעא. ראה נקב שממנו יצא עשן: גבבא. גיזה: אמשיה. שרה אות' במים לשון (ברכות דף יד:) משי ידיה: (וכל שלשים יום. חוזר לגיהנם ועולה לשם):

אמר

מסורת הש"ס

א) בקרא כתיב בידיה תהרסנו, ב) [מו"ק יח:], ג) [צ"ל יוסף], ד) [ברכות כז: ע"ש], ה) פסחים קיט. ע"ש, ו) [שם], ז) ג' מאות לאו דוקא וכן כל שלש מאות בש"ס רשב"ם פסחים קיט, ח) נדרים לט: ע"ש, ט) [לעיל קג.], י) [לעיל קג:], כ) מגילה יד., ל) ב"ב עג ע"א.

תורה אור השלם

א) וַיֹּאמֶר שִׁמְשׁוֹן תָּמוֹת נַפְשִׁי עִם פְּלִשְׁתִּים וַיֵּט בְּכֹחַ וַיִּפֹּל הַבַּיִת עַל הַסְּרָנִים וְעַל כָּל הָעָם אֲשֶׁר בּוֹ וַיִּהְיוּ הַמֵּתִים אֲשֶׁר הֵמִית בְּמוֹתוֹ רַבִּים מֵאֲשֶׁר הֵמִית בְּחַיָּיו: [שופטים טז, ל]

ב) חַכְמוֹת נָשִׁים בָּנְתָה בֵיתָהּ וְאִוֶּלֶת בְּיָדֶיהָ תֶהֶרְסֶנּוּ: [משלי יד, א]

ג) וַיָּקֻמוּ לִפְנֵי מֹשֶׁה וַאֲנָשִׁים מִבְּנֵי יִשְׂרָאֵל חֲמִשִּׁים וּמָאתָיִם נְשִׂיאֵי עֵדָה קְרִאֵי מוֹעֵד אַנְשֵׁי שֵׁם: [במדבר טז, ב]

ד) וַיִּשְׁמַע מֹשֶׁה וַיִּפֹּל עַל פָּנָיו: [במדבר טז, ד]

ה) וַיְקַנְאוּ לְמֹשֶׁה בַּמַּחֲנֶה לְאַהֲרֹן קְדוֹשׁ יְיָ: [תהלים קו, טז]

ו) וּמֹשֶׁה יִקַּח אֶת הָאֹהֶל וְנָטָה לוֹ מִחוּץ לַמַּחֲנֶה הַרְחֵק מִן הַמַּחֲנֶה וְקָרָא לוֹ אֹהֶל מוֹעֵד וְהָיָה כָּל מְבַקֵּשׁ יְיָ יֵצֵא אֶל אֹהֶל מוֹעֵד אֲשֶׁר מִחוּץ לַמַּחֲנֶה: [שמות לג, ז]

ז) וַיָּקָם מֹשֶׁה וַיֵּלֶךְ אֶל דָּתָן וַאֲבִירָם וַיֵּלְכוּ אַחֲרָיו זִקְנֵי יִשְׂרָאֵל: [במדבר טז, כה]

ח) זִכָּרוֹן לִבְנֵי יִשְׂרָאֵל לְמַעַן אֲשֶׁר לֹא יִקְרַב אִישׁ זָר אֲשֶׁר לֹא מִזֶּרַע אַהֲרֹן הוּא לְהַקְטִיר קְטֹרֶת לִפְנֵי יְיָ וְלֹא יִהְיֶה כְקֹרַח וְכַעֲדָתוֹ כַּאֲשֶׁר דִּבֶּר יְיָ בְּיַד מֹשֶׁה לוֹ: [במדבר יז, ה]

ט) וַיֹּאמֶר יְיָ לוֹ עוֹד הָבֵא נָא יָדְךָ בְּחֵיקֶךָ וַיָּבֵא יָדוֹ בְּחֵיקוֹ וַיּוֹצִאָהּ וְהִנֵּה יָדוֹ מְצֹרַעַת כַּשָּׁלֶג: [שמות ד, ו]

י) וַיִּזְבַּח אֲדֹנִיָּהוּ צֹאן וּבָקָר וּמְרִיא עִם אֶבֶן הַזֹּחֶלֶת אֲשֶׁר אֵצֶל עֵין רֹגֵל וַיִּקְרָא אֶת כָּל אֶחָיו בְּנֵי הַמֶּלֶךְ וּלְכָל אַנְשֵׁי יְהוּדָה עַבְדֵי הַמֶּלֶךְ: [מלכים א' א, ט]

יא) מְזֵי רָעָב וּלְחֻמֵי רֶשֶׁף וְקֶטֶב מְרִירִי וְשֶׁן בְּהֵמֹת אֲשַׁלַּח בָּם עִם חֲמַת זֹחֲלֵי עָפָר: [דברים לב, כד]

יב) וּבְנֵי אֱלִיאָב נְמוּאֵל וְדָתָן וַאֲבִירָם הוּא דָתָן וַאֲבִירָם קְרִיאֵי הָעֵדָה אֲשֶׁר הִצּוּ עַל מֹשֶׁה וְעַל אַהֲרֹן בַּעֲדַת קֹרַח בְּהַצֹּתָם עַל יְיָ: [במדבר כו, ט]

יג) הֵמָּה מֵי מְרִיבָה אֲשֶׁר רָבוּ בְנֵי יִשְׂרָאֵל אֶת יְיָ וַיִּקָּדֵשׁ בָּם: [במדבר כ, יג]

יד) וַיֹּאמֶר מֹשֶׁה בְּתֵת יְיָ לָכֶם בָּעֶרֶב בָּשָׂר לֶאֱכֹל וְלֶחֶם בַּבֹּקֶר לִשְׂבֹּעַ בִּשְׁמֹעַ יְיָ אֶת תְּלֻנֹּתֵיכֶם אֲשֶׁר אַתֶּם מַלִּינִם עָלָיו וְנַחְנוּ מָה לֹא עָלֵינוּ תְלֻנֹּתֵיכֶם כִּי עַל יְיָ: [שמות טז, ח] טו) וַיְדַבֵּר הָעָם בֵּאלֹהִים וּבְמֹשֶׁה לָמָה הֶעֱלִיתֻנוּ מִמִּצְרַיִם לָמוּת בַּמִּדְבָּר כִּי אֵין לֶחֶם וְאֵין מַיִם וְנַפְשֵׁנוּ קָצָה בַּלֶּחֶם הַקְּלֹקֵל: [במדבר כא, ה] טז) יֵשׁ רָעָה חוֹלָה רָאִיתִי תַּחַת הַשָּׁמֶשׁ עֹשֶׁר שָׁמוּר לִבְעָלָיו לְרָעָתוֹ: [קהלת ה, יב] יז) וַאֲשֶׁר עָשָׂה לְדָתָן וְלַאֲבִירָם בְּנֵי אֱלִיאָב בֶּן רְאוּבֵן אֲשֶׁר פָּצְתָה הָאָרֶץ אֶת פִּיהָ וַתִּבְלָעֵם וְאֶת בָּתֵּיהֶם וְאֶת אָהֳלֵיהֶם וְאֵת כָּל הַיְקוּם אֲשֶׁר בְּרַגְלֵיהֶם בְּקֶרֶב כָּל יִשְׂרָאֵל: [דברים יא, ו] יח) וַתִּפְתַּח הָאָרֶץ אֶת פִּיהָ וַתִּבְלַע אֹתָם וְאֶת בָּתֵּיהֶם וְאֵת כָּל הָאָדָם אֲשֶׁר לְקֹרַח וְאֵת כָּל הָרְכוּשׁ: [במדבר טז, לב] יט) וַתִּפְתַּח הָאָרֶץ אֶת פִּיהָ וַתִּבְלַע אֹתָם וְאֶת קֹרַח בְּמוֹת הָעֵדָה בַּאֲכֹל הָאֵשׁ אֵת חֲמִשִּׁים וּמָאתַיִם אִישׁ וַיִּהְיוּ לְנֵס: [במדבר כו, י] כ) וְאֵשׁ יָצְאָה מֵאֵת יְיָ וַתֹּאכַל אֵת הַחֲמִשִּׁים וּמָאתַיִם אִישׁ מַקְרִיבֵי הַקְּטֹרֶת: [במדבר טז, לה] כא) שֶׁמֶשׁ יָרֵחַ עָמַד זְבֻלָה לְאוֹר חִצֶּיךָ יְהַלֵּכוּ לְנֹגַהּ בְּרַק חֲנִיתֶךָ: [חבקוק ג, יא] כב) וְאִם בְּרִיאָה יִבְרָא יְיָ וּפָצְתָה הָאֲדָמָה אֶת פִּיהָ וּבָלְעָה אֹתָם וְאֶת כָּל אֲשֶׁר לָהֶם וְיָרְדוּ חַיִּים שְׁאֹלָה וִידַעְתֶּם כִּי נִאֲצוּ הָאֲנָשִׁים הָאֵלֶּה אֶת יְיָ: [במדבר טז, ל] כג) מַה שֶּׁהָיָה הוּא שֶׁיִּהְיֶה וּמַה שֶּׁנַּעֲשָׂה הוּא שֶׁיֵּעָשֶׂה וְאֵין כָּל חָדָשׁ תַּחַת הַשָּׁמֶשׁ: [קהלת א, ט] כד) וּבְנֵי קֹרַח לֹא מֵתוּ: [במדבר כו, יא]

עין משפט נר מצוה

לג א ב ג ד מיי' פ"ה מהל' ת"ת הל' א סמג עשין יב טוש"ע י"ד סי' רמב סעיף ב:

ליקוטי רש"י

אחר חוט אחד של תכלת פוטרה זו שכולה תכלת לא תפטור את עצמה [במדבר טז, א]. חכמות נשים בנתה ביתה. חכמות נקוד פתח שאינו שם דבר אלא החכמות שבנשים בונות את בתיהם שמתקיימות על ידיהן כמו אשתו של און בן פלת כמו שמפורש בפרק חלק. ואולת. ואשה שוטה. בידיה תהרסנו. תהרס ביתה זו אשתו של קרח [משלי יד, א]. קראי מועד. שהיו תלמידי חכמים כדכתיב (במדבר טז) נשיאי עדה קריאי מועד אנשי שם ועל שם שפיתם אותו רשע כשנהנו ממונו הקלו בעיניו להשיאם ולהחזיק ידו במחלוקת ולמרוד בהקדוש ברוך הוא [לעיל נב.]. ויקם משה. כסבור שישאו לו פנים ולא עשו [במדבר טז, כה]. ביד משה לו. כמו עליו על אהרן דבר אל משה שיהיה הוא ובניו כהנים לפיכך לא יקרב איש זר אשר לא מזרע אהרן וגו' וכן כל לי ולו ולהם הסמוכים אצל דבור פתרונם כמו על ומדרשו על קרח ומהו ביד משה ולא כתב אל משה רמז לחולקים על הכהונה שלוקין בצרעת כמו שלקה משה בידו שנאמר (שמות ד, ו) ויוציאה והנה ידו מצורעת כשלג ועל כן לקה עוזיה בצרעת [במדבר יז, ה]. חמת זוחלי עפר. ארס נחשים המהלכים על גחונם על העפר כמים הזוחלים על הארץ זחילה לשון מרוצת המים על העפר וכן כל מרוצת דבר המשפשף על העפר והולך [דברים לב, כד]. עושר שמור לבעליו לרעתו. כעשרו של קרח שעל ידי כן נתגאה וירד לשאול [קהלת ה, יב]. שמעמידו על רגליו. שמשמח לבו. וקילפי. פותחות שקורין בלעז שרדור"א. דגלדי. של מרצופים של עור שנושאים על סוסים וחמורים וגמלים [פסחים קיט.]. מלמד שעלו שמש וירח לזבול. שחמה ולבנה ברקיע השני כדאמרינן שבעה רקיעים הם וילון רקיע שחקים זבול מכון מעון ערבות ומונה להם כסדרן וילון אינו משמש כלום רקיע יש בו חמה ולבנה כוכבים ומזלות כו' [תהלים יט, ז]. שמש ירח עמד זבולה אם אתה עושה דין לבן עמרם ממחלקותו של קרח ומשמע להו דהאי קרא במחלקותו של קרח מדריש משום דביציאת מצרים ובקריעת ים סוף משתעי בספר חבקוק וכתיב ביה מחצת ראש מבית רשע ומשמע להו דהיינו קרח וכתיב בתריה שמש ירח עמד זבולה [נדרים לט.]. אלא לקרובי פיתחא. וקריבה בעלמא ליתא בכלל אין כל חדש [נדרים לט:]. ובני קרח לא מתו. הם היו בעצה תחלה ובשעת המחלוקת הרהרו תשובה בלבם לפיכך נתבצר להם מקום גבוה בגיהנם וישבו שם [במדבר כו, יא]. נתבצר להם. לשון גבוה כמו ובצורות בשמים (דברים ט) [מגילה יד.].

about the Divine Presence, שֶׁנֶּאֱמַר ,,לֹא־עָלֵינוּ תְלֻנֹּתֵיכֶם כִּי (אם) עַל־ה׳״ – **for it is stated:** ***Not against us are your complaints, but against God!***[36] אָמַר רַבִּי אַבָּהוּ – **R' Abahu said:** כָּל הַמְהַרְהֵר אַחַר רַבּוֹ כְּאִילּוּ מְהַרְהֵר אַחַר שְׁכִינָה – **Whoever thinks ill of his teacher**[37] is regarded **as if he thinks ill about the Divine Presence,** שֶׁנֶּאֱמַר ,,וַיְדַבֵּר הָעָם בֵּאלֹהִים וּבְמֹשֶׁה״ – **for it is stated:** ***The people spoke against God and against Moses.***[38]

The Gemara examines the role of wealth in causing Korach's rebellion:

,,עֹשֶׁר שָׁמוּר לִבְעָלָיו לְרָעָתוֹ״ – The wise King Solomon wrote:[39] *There is a sickening evil that I have seen under the sun:* ***riches hoarded by their owner to his misfortune.*** אָמַר רֵישׁ לָקִישׁ – **Reish Lakish said:** זֶה עוֹשְׁרוֹ שֶׁל קֹרַח – **This** refers to **Korach's riches.**[40] ,,וְאֵת כָּל־הַיְקוּם אֲשֶׁר בְּרַגְלֵיהֶם״ – The Torah states:[41] *And what [God] did to Dasan and Abiram, the sons of Eliab son of Reuben, when the earth opened its mouth wide and swallowed them, their households, their tents,* ***and all the wealth*** (y'kum) ***at their feet.*** אָמַר רַבִּי אֶלְעָזָר – **R' Elazar said:** זֶה מָמוֹנוֹ שֶׁל אָדָם – **This** refers to **a person's wealth,** שֶׁמַּעֲמִידוֹ עַל רַגְלָיו – **which "stands him on his feet."**[42]

The Gemara describes the extent of Korach's wealth:

וְאָמַר רַבִּי לֵוִי – **And R' Levi said:** מַשּׂוֹי שְׁלֹשׁ מֵאוֹת פְּרָדוֹת לְבָנוֹת הָיוּ מַפְתְּחוֹת שֶׁל בֵּית גְּנָזָיו שֶׁל קֹרַח – **The keys to Korach's treasure houses were** equivalent to **the load of three hundred white mules,**[43] וְכוּלְּהוּ אַקְלִידֵי וְקִילְפֵי דְּגִילְדָא – **and all of those keys and locks were** made **of leather.**[44]

The Gemara explains how Korach became rich:

אָמַר רַבִּי חָמָא בְּרַבִּי חֲנִינָא – **R' Chama son of R' Chanina said:** שָׁלֹשׁ מַטְמוֹנִיּוֹת הִטְמִין יוֹסֵף בְּמִצְרַיִם – **Joseph concealed three treasures in Egypt:** אַחַת נִתְגַּלְּתָה לְקֹרַח – **One** treasure **was revealed to Korach,** וְאַחַת נִתְגַּלְּתָה לְאַנְטוֹנִינוּס בֶּן אַסְוִירוּס – **one was revealed to Antoninus son of Severus,**[45] וְאַחַת גְּנוּזָה לַצַּדִּיקִים לֶעָתִיד לָבוֹא – **and one is hidden away for the righteous,** to be claimed **in the future.**[46]

The Gemara discusses the fate of Korach:

וְאָמַר רַבִּי יוֹחָנָן – **And R' Yochanan said:** קֹרַח לֹא מִן הַבְּלוּעִים וְלֹא מִן הַשְּׂרוּפִין – **Korach was neither among those who were swallowed** by the earth **nor among those who were burned.**[47] לֹא מִן הַבְּלוּעִים דִּכְתִיב ,,וְאֵת כָּל־הָאָדָם אֲשֶׁר לְקֹרַח״ – It is evident that he was **not among those who were swallowed, for it is written,** *The earth opened its mouth and swallowed them and their households,* ***and all the people who were with Korach,***

NOTES

36. *Exodus* 16:8. Not long after they crossed the Red Sea, the Jews began to complain bitterly that Moses and Aaron had led them out of Egypt but had not thought to bring along sufficient provisions. God thereupon told Moses to announce that He would henceforth provide them with manna to eat. In informing them of this prospect Moses declared: *God has heard your complaints, which you complain against Him, for what are we? Not against us are your complaints, but against God!*

Thus, although the Jews complained that their teacher Moses had cruelly neglected their needs, Moses advised them that in truth they had criticized God, not himself. Scripture thus teaches that one who complains against his teacher is actually complaining against God.

37. I.e. he imputes evil to his teacher (*Rashi*).

38. *Numbers* 21:5. Heading toward Eretz Yisrael during the final year of their forty-year sojourn in the Wilderness, the Jews *spoke against God and Moses: "Why do you bring us up from Egypt to die in this Wilderness, for there is no food and no water . . .?"* Although the Jews actually addressed only Moses, their teacher, imputing to him an evil motive for bringing them into the Wilderness, the Torah regards them as having imputed ill to God as well, for it states: *The people spoke against God and against Moses* (*Yad Ramah*).

39. *Ecclesiastes* 5:12.

40. Korach's great wealth made him arrogant, and fueled his unrealistic ambition to attain the status of Moses, Aaron and Aaron's sons. This led to his infamous rebellion, which cost him his life. Thus, Korach's riches caused his misfortune (see *Maharsha*).

41. *Deuteronomy* 11:6. In this passage Moses charges the Jews to remember all the miracles they had witnessed in Egypt, at the Sea of Reeds, and in the Wilderness. He specifically mentions the supernatural demise of Korach and his followers, and refers to their wealth (see following note).

42. R' Elazar interprets the word יְקוּם (*y'kum*) as a causative form of the verb קוּם, which denotes *rising* or *standing up.* Thus, *y'kum* alludes to wealth, since a person's wealth allows him to have a standing in the world. *Maharsha* writes that the verse implies that Korach's followers relied on their wealth to launch their rebellion against Moses.

43. *Rashbam (Pesachim* 119a ד״ה משוי שלש מאות) cautions that the figure 300 should not be taken literally; rather, it is used symbolically throughout the Talmud to indicate a great quantity (see above, 96b and 106b). *Yad Ramah* also maintains that R' Levi is overstating Korach's wealth.

Ben Yehoyada argues, however, that here the figure 300 (donkeys) is not necessarily hyperbolic. He interprets "keys" to mean leather chests, in which Korach was able to transport his enormous wealth from station to station in the Wilderness. Since each donkey was able to carry two such chests, the chests totaled 600.

Maharsha points out that the kick of a white mule is particularly hard; see *Chullin* 7b. For that reason Korach chose white mules to carry his keys, for no one would be so foolhardy as to approach such dangerous creatures to steal the keys.

44. Even though the keys and locks were made of leather, which is much lighter than metal, three hundred donkeys were still required to transport them (*Rashi, Yad Ramah*).

45. This is the Roman emperor Antoninus, the close friend of Rabbi Yehudah HaNasi (see *Avodah Zarah* 10b).

46. *Ben Yehoyada* explains the matter of Joseph's three treasures: During the seven years of plenty preceding the great worldwide famine, a mighty store of grain was accumulating in Egypt under Joseph's supervision. When the famine finally struck and the other nations' grain began to spoil, the Egyptian stores were Divinely blessed in Joseph's merit. Hence, that grain, and the vast sums of money subsequently exchanged for it by a desperate and famished world population, rightfully belonged to Joseph – to do with as he pleased. Now, the purchasers of Joseph's grain divided into three groups: those who served idols, those whose hands were soiled by all manner of thievery, and those righteous gentiles who abided by the seven Noahide laws. The idolaters' money was disgusting to Joseph, and he designated a separate treasury for it. All payments from idolaters were providentially diverted to that depository, and it was this treasure that Korach took and that ultimately descended with him to the netherworld. Since the thieves' money was not as offensive as that proffered by the idolaters, it was secreted in a separate depository. This money was later revealed to the emperor Antoninus and brought to the royal treasury in Rome. The money from the good people who observed the Noahide laws deserved, however, to accrue to a holy segment. Hence, Joseph concealed their money in a third treasury, to be inherited by the righteous in the Messianic Era.

47. *Numbers* 16:32 states: *The earth opened its mouth and swallowed them and their households, and all the people who were with Korach, and the entire wealth.* Verse 35 states: *A flame came forth from God and consumed the two hundred and fifty men who were offering the incense.* Verses 17:6-15 go on to describe how on the day after these events occurred, the Jewish people complained that Moses had deliberately caused the rebels' deaths. Thereupon a plague broke out, killing an additional 14,700 persons. According to R' Yochanan, Korach perished in the plague (*Rashi*).

וסתרתה למזיה כל דאתא חזיה הדר אדהכי והכי אבלעו להו איתתיה דקרח אמרה ליה חזי מאי קעביד משה איהו הוה מלכא לאחוה שוויה כהנא רבא לבני אחוהי שוינהו סגני דכהנא אי אתיא תרומה אמר תיהוי לכהן אי אתו מעשר דשקילתו אתון אמר הבו חד מי׳ לכהן ועוד דגייז ליה למזייכו ומיטלל לכו כי כופתא עינא יהב במזייכו אמר לה הא איהו נמי קא עביד אמרה ליה כיון דכולהו רבותא דידיה אמר איהו נמי (א) תמות נפשי עם פלשתים ועוד דקאמר לכו עבדיתו תכלתא אי ס״ד תכלתא חשיבא [מצוה] אפיק גלימי דתכלתא וכסינהו לכולהו מתיבתך היינו דכתיב (ב) חכמות נשים בנתה ביתה זו אשתו של און בן פלת ואולת [א] בידה תהרסנה זו אשתו של קרח (ג) ויקומו לפני משה ואנשים מבני ישראל חמשים ומאתים מיוחדים שבעדה קריאי מועד שהיו יודעים לעבר שנים ולקבוע חדשים אנשי שם שהיה להם שם בכל העולם (ד) וישמע משה ויפול על פניו מה שמועה שמע [ב] אמר רבי שמואל בר נחמני א״ר יונתן שחשדוהו מאשת איש שנאמר (ה) ויקנאו למשה במחנה א״ר שמואל בר יצחק מלמד שכל אחד ואחד קנא את אשתו ממשה שנאמר (ו) ומשה יקח את האהל ונטה לו מחוץ למחנה (ז) ויקם משה וילך אל דתן ואבירם אמר ר״ל מכאן שאין מחזיקין במחלוקת דאמר רב כל המחזיק במחלוקת עובר בלאו שנאמר (ח) ולא יהיה כקרח וכעדתו רב אשי אמר ראוי ליצטרע כתיב הכא (ח) ביד משה לו וכתיב התם (ט) ויאמר ה׳ לו עוד הבא נא ידך בחיקך אמר ר׳ [ג] יוסי כל החולק על מלכות בית דוד ראוי להכישו נחש כתיב הכא (י) ויזבח אדוניהו צאן ובקר ומריא עם אבן הזוחלת וכתיב התם (יא) עם חמת זוחלי עפר אמר רב חסדא [ד] [א] כל החולק על רבו כחולק על השכינה שנאמר (יב) בהצותם על ה׳ א״ר חמא ברבי חנינא [ב] כל העושה מריבה עם רבו כעושה עם שכינה שנאמר (יג) המה מי מריבה אשר רבו בני ישראל (על) [את] ה׳ א״ר חנינא בר פפא [ג] כל המתרעם על רבו כאילו מתרעם על השכינה שנאמר (יד) לא עלינו תלונותיכם כי (אם) על ה׳ א״ר אבהו [ד] כל המהרהר אחר רבו כאילו מהרהר אחר שכינה שנאמר (טו) וידבר העם באלהים ובמשה (טז) עושר שמור לבעליו לרעתו [ה] אמר ר״ל זה עושרו של קרח (יז) ואת כל היקום אשר ברגליהם [ו] א״ר אלעזר זה ממונו של אדם שמעמידו על רגליו ואמר רבי לוי משוי [ז] ג׳ מאות פרדות לבנות היו מפתחות של בית גנזיו של קרח וכולהו אקלידי וקילפי דגילדא א״ר חמא ברבי חנינא ג׳ מטמוניות הטמין יוסף במצרים אחת נתגלתה לקרח ואחת נתגלתה לאנטונינוס בן אסוירוס ואחת גנוזה לצדיקים לעתיד לבא וא״ר יוחנן קרח לא מן הבלועים ולא מן השרופין לא מן הבלועין דכתיב (יח) ואת כל האדם אשר לקרח ולא קרח ולא מן השרופים דכתיב (יט) באכול האש את חמשים ומאתים איש ולא קרח במתניתא תנא קרח מן השרופין ומן הבלועין מן הבלועים דכתיב (יט) ותבלע אותם ואת קרח מן השרופין דכתיב (כ) (ותצא אש מלפני ה׳) [ואש יצאה מאת ה׳] ותאכל את חמשים ומאתים איש וקרח בהדייהו אמר רבא [ח] מאי דכתיב (כא) שמש ירח עמד זבולה לאור חציך יהלכו מלמד שעלו שמש וירח לזבול אמרו לפניו רבש״ע אם אתה עושה דין לבן עמרם נצא ואם לאו לא נצא עד שזרק בהם חצים אמר להן [ט] בכבודי לא מחיתם בכבוד בשר ודם מחיתם והאידנא לא נפקי עד דמחו להו [י] דרש רבא מאי דכתיב (כב) ואם בריאה יברא ה׳ ופצתה האדמה את פיה אמר משה לפני הקב״ה אם בריאה גיהנם מוטב ואם לאו יברא ה׳ למאי אילימא למבריה ממש והא (כג) אין כל חדש תחת השמש אלא לקרובי פיתחא (כד) ובני קרח לא מתו תנא [כ] משום רבינו אמרו מקום נתבצר להם בגיהנם וישבו עליו ואמרו שירה [ל] אמר רבה בר בר חנה זימנא חדא הוה קאזלינא באורחא אמר לי ההוא טייעא תא ואחוי לך בלועי דקרח אזיל חזא תרי בזעי דהוה קא נפק קיטרא מנייהו שקל גבבא דעמרא אמשיי׳ מיא ואותביה בריש רומחיה ואחלפי׳ התם איחרך א״ל אצית מה שמעת ושמעית דהוו קאמרי הכי משה ותורתו אמת והן בדאים אמר

רש״י

סתרה למזיה. שערה וישבה על פתח הבית כל מי שהיה בא לקרוא רואה ראשה פרוע וחוזר: מעשר. ראשון דשקליתו אתון אמר הבו חד מי׳ לכהן: דגייז למזייכו. דכתיב (במדבר ח) והעבירו תער על [כל] בשרם ומשחק בכם כאילו אתם שוטים: ככופתא. רעי כמו בטולא דכופתא דאמרן לעיל (דף נח:) כגלל הזה אתם חשובים בעיניו: עינא יהב. עין נתן בשעריכם כדי שלא יהא בכם נוה כמותו: אמר לה. קרח איהו נמי משה עצמו גלח כל שערו: כיון דכולא רבותא דידיה הוא. אינו חושש אם גילח עצמו דקאמר לנפשיה תמות נפשי עם פלשתים אגוזו שערי כמותם ומה לי בכך שהם מקיימין אפילו מה שאני מלוה לשחוק אגוזו עכשיו כמותם כדי להפיס דעתם: ועוד דקאמר לכו. עשו פתיל תכלת בד׳ כנפות הבגד ואי ס״ד תכלת חשוב מפני מה לא יאמר לעשות כל הבגד כולו תכלת: אפיק גלימא דתכלתא. קח לך בגדים של תכלת וכסינהו לכולהו מתיבתך וכסה בהן בהה״מ אתה וחברותך: קנא לאשתו. אל (הסתר) [תסתרי] עם משה. קנוי היינו התראה: ונטה לו מחוץ למחנה. יצא מחוץ למחנה שלא יחשדוהו עוד: מכאן שאין מחזיקין במחלוקת. שמחל על כבודו והוא עצמו הלך לבטל מחלוקת: חולק על רבו. חולק על ישיבתו: אשר הצו על משה ועל אהרן בעדת קרח בהצותם על ה׳. מעלה עליהם הכתוב כאלו היו חולקים כלפי שכינה: מריבה. תגר וקטטה לפטפט נגדו בדברים: מתרעם. אומר על רבו שנוהג לו מדה כבושה ומדת אכזרית: מהרהר. מחפה עליו דברים: אקלידי. מפתחות: וקולפי. מנעולים: דגילדי. כולם המפתחות והמנעולים של עור היו ואעפ״כ היו שלש מאות פרדות טעונות ל״א דגלדא לצורך שקים והמרצופין וכיסין של עור היו: לא מן הבלועין ולא מן השרופין. אלא במגפה מת: ולא קרח. ר״נ היו לבד קרח דכתיב חמשים ומאתים מחתות ואתה ואהרן איש מחתתו: מן הבלועים ומן השרופין היה. שנשרפה נשמתו וגוף קיים ואח״כ נתגלגל עד מקום הבלועין ונבלע דכתיב בפרשת פנחס ותבלע אותם ואת קרח עמהם ורבי יוחנן דאמר לא מן הבלועין ולא מן השרופין דריש ליה להאי ואת קרח לאחריו ואת קרח במות העדה במגפה: וקרח בהדייהו. מדכתיב ותאכל את החמשים ומאתים איש מקריבי הקטרת וקרח ממקריבי הקטרת הוה דכתיב חמשים ומאתים מחתות ואתה ואהרן איש מחתתו א״נ ואת לרבות קרח עמהם: שמש ירח עמד זבולה. לעיל מיניה כתיב ותבקע ארץ בשעת בקיעת הארץ שנבלעו בקרקע שמש וירח עלו לאותו רקיע ששמו זבול ואמרו להקב״ה אם אי אתה עושה דין לבן עמרם מקרח ועדתו: לא נצא. ונאיר לעולם: בכבודי לא מחיתם. שהרי בכל יום מלכי מזרח ומערב בשעה שמניחין כתריהן בראשם משתחוים לחמה: והאידנא לא נפקי עד דמחו להו. שכך גזר עליהם המקום כן שמעתי ל״א והאידנא לא נפקי מאחר שראו שהקפיד הקב״ה על שלא מיחה לכבודו עד דמחו להו לא נפקי שחסו לכבוד המקום על בני אדם שמשתחוים לשמש וירח: אין כל חדש תחת השמש. ואי גיהנם לא אברי עד ההוא שעתא הוה ליה חדש: לקרובי פתחה. שיקרב פתחה של גיהנם ותפתח הארץ במקום שהן: נתבצר. מלשון (ישעיה כה) עיר בצורה התקין להון הקב״ה מקום גבוה שלא העמיקו כל כך בגיהנם ולא מתו: טייעא. סוחר ישמעאל: בלועי. מקום שנתבלעו לשם עדת קרח: בזעא. ראה נקב שממנו יצא עשן: גבבא. גיזה: אמשיה. שרה אות׳ במים לשון (ברכות דף יד:) משי ידיה: (וכל שלשים יום. חוזר לגיהנם ועולה לשם): אמר

א) בקרא כתיב בידיה תהרסנו, ב) [מו״ק יח:], ג) [נ״ל יוסף], ד) [ברכות כז: ע״ש], ה) פסחים קיט. ע״ש, ו) [שם], ז) ג׳ מאות לאו דוקא וכן כל שלש מאות בש״ס רשב״ם פסחים קיט, ח) נדרים לט: ע״ש, ט) לעיל קג., י) [לעיל קג:], כ) מגילה יד., ל) ב״ב עד ע״א.

תורה אור השלם

א) וַיֹּאמֶר שִׁמְשׁוֹן תָּמוֹת נַפְשִׁי עִם פְּלִשְׁתִּים וַיֵּט בְּכֹחַ וַיִּפֹּל הַבַּיִת עַל הַסְּרָנִים וְעַל כָּל הָעָם אֲשֶׁר בּוֹ וַיִּהְיוּ הַמֵּתִים אֲשֶׁר הֵמִית בְּמוֹתוֹ רַבִּים מֵאֲשֶׁר הֵמִית בְּחַיָּיו: [שופטים טז, ל]

ב) חַכְמוֹת נָשִׁים בָּנְתָה בֵיתָהּ וְאִוֶּלֶת בְּיָדֶיהָ תֶהֶרְסֶנּוּ: [משלי יד, א]

ג) וַיָּקֻמוּ לִפְנֵי מֹשֶׁה וַאֲנָשִׁים מִבְּנֵי יִשְׂרָאֵל חֲמִשִּׁים וּמָאתָיִם נְשִׂיאֵי עֵדָה קְרִאֵי מוֹעֵד אַנְשֵׁי שֵׁם: [במדבר טז, ב]

ד) וַיִּשְׁמַע מֹשֶׁה וַיִּפֹּל עַל פָּנָיו: [במדבר טז, ד]

ה) וַיְקַנְאוּ לְמֹשֶׁה בַּמַּחֲנֶה לְאַהֲרֹן קְדוֹשׁ יְיָ: [תהלים קו, טז]

ו) וּמֹשֶׁה יִקַּח אֶת הָאֹהֶל וְנָטָה לוֹ מִחוּץ לַמַּחֲנֶה הַרְחֵק מִן הַמַּחֲנֶה וְקָרָא לוֹ אֹהֶל מוֹעֵד וְהָיָה כָּל מְבַקֵּשׁ יְיָ יֵצֵא אֶל אֹהֶל מוֹעֵד אֲשֶׁר מִחוּץ לַמַּחֲנֶה: [שמות לג, ז]

ז) וַיָּקָם מֹשֶׁה וַיֵּלֶךְ אֶל דָּתָן וַאֲבִירָם וַיֵּלְכוּ אַחֲרָיו זִקְנֵי יִשְׂרָאֵל: [במדבר טז, כה]

ח) זִכָּרוֹן לִבְנֵי יִשְׂרָאֵל לְמַעַן אֲשֶׁר לֹא יִקְרַב אִישׁ זָר אֲשֶׁר לֹא מִזֶּרַע אַהֲרֹן הוּא לְהַקְטִיר קְטֹרֶת לִפְנֵי יְיָ וְלֹא יִהְיֶה כְקֹרַח וְכַעֲדָתוֹ כַּאֲשֶׁר דִּבֶּר יְיָ בְּיַד מֹשֶׁה לוֹ: [במדבר יז, ה]

ט) וַיֹּאמֶר יְיָ לוֹ עוֹד הָבֵא נָא יָדְךָ בְּחֵיקֶךָ וַיָּבֵא יָדוֹ בְּחֵיקוֹ וַיּוֹצִאָהּ וְהִנֵּה יָדוֹ מְצֹרַעַת כַּשָּׁלֶג: [שמות ד, ו]

י) וַיִּזְבַּח אֲדֹנִיָּהוּ צֹאן וּבָקָר וּמְרִיא עִם אֶבֶן הַזֹּחֶלֶת אֲשֶׁר אֵצֶל עֵין רֹגֵל וַיִּקְרָא אֶת כָּל אֶחָיו בְּנֵי הַמֶּלֶךְ וּלְכָל אַנְשֵׁי יְהוּדָה עַבְדֵי הַמֶּלֶךְ: [מלכים א׳ א, ט]

יא) מְזֵי רָעָב וּלְחֻמֵי רֶשֶׁף וְקֶטֶב מְרִירִי וְשֶׁן בְּהֵמֹת אֲשַׁלַּח בָּם עִם חֲמַת זֹחֲלֵי עָפָר: [דברים לב, כד]

יב) וּבְנֵי אֱלִיאָב נְמוּאֵל וְדָתָן וַאֲבִירָם הוּא דָתָן וַאֲבִירָם קְרִיאֵי הָעֵדָה אֲשֶׁר הִצּוּ עַל מֹשֶׁה וְעַל אַהֲרֹן בַּעֲדַת קֹרַח בְּהַצֹּתָם עַל יְיָ: [במדבר כו, ט]

יג) הֵמָּה מֵי מְרִיבָה אֲשֶׁר רָבוּ בְנֵי יִשְׂרָאֵל אֶת יְיָ וַיִּקָּדֵשׁ בָּם: [במדבר כ, יג]

יד) וַיֹּאמֶר מֹשֶׁה בְּתֵת יְיָ לָכֶם בָּעֶרֶב בָּשָׂר לֶאֱכֹל וְלֶחֶם בַּבֹּקֶר לִשְׂבֹּעַ בִּשְׁמֹעַ יְיָ אֶת תְּלֻנֹּתֵיכֶם אֲשֶׁר אַתֶּם מַלִּינִם עָלָיו וְנַחְנוּ מָה לֹא עָלֵינוּ תְלֻנֹּתֵיכֶם כִּי עַל יְיָ: [שמות טז, ח] טו) וַיְדַבֵּר הָעָם בֵּאלֹהִים וּבְמֹשֶׁה לָמָה הֶעֱלִיתֻנוּ מִמִּצְרַיִם לָמוּת בַּמִּדְבָּר כִּי אֵין לֶחֶם וְאֵין מַיִם וְנַפְשֵׁנוּ קָצָה בַּלֶּחֶם הַקְּלֹקֵל: [במדבר כא, ה] טז) יֵשׁ רָעָה חוֹלָה רָאִיתִי תַּחַת הַשָּׁמֶשׁ עֹשֶׁר שָׁמוּר לִבְעָלָיו לְרָעָתוֹ: [קהלת ה, יב] יז) וַאֲשֶׁר עָשָׂה לְדָתָן וְלַאֲבִירָם בְּנֵי אֱלִיאָב בֶּן רְאוּבֵן אֲשֶׁר פָּצְתָה הָאָרֶץ אֶת פִּיהָ וַתִּבְלָעֵם וְאֶת בָּתֵּיהֶם וְאֶת אָהֳלֵיהֶם וְאֵת כָּל הַיְקוּם אֲשֶׁר בְּרַגְלֵיהֶם בְּקֶרֶב כָּל יִשְׂרָאֵל: [דברים יא, ו] יח) וַתִּפְתַּח הָאָרֶץ אֶת פִּיהָ וַתִּבְלַע אֹתָם וְאֶת בָּתֵּיהֶם וְאֵת כָּל הָאָדָם אֲשֶׁר לְקֹרַח וְאֵת כָּל הָרְכוּשׁ: [במדבר טז, לב] יט) וַתִּפְתַּח הָאָרֶץ אֶת פִּיהָ וַתִּבְלַע אֹתָם וְאֶת קֹרַח בְּמוֹת הָעֵדָה בַּאֲכֹל הָאֵשׁ אֵת חֲמִשִּׁים וּמָאתַיִם אִישׁ וַיִּהְיוּ לְנֵס: [במדבר כו, י] כ) וְאֵשׁ יָצְאָה מֵאֵת יְיָ וַתֹּאכַל אֵת הַחֲמִשִּׁים וּמָאתַיִם אִישׁ מַקְרִיבֵי הַקְּטֹרֶת: [במדבר טז, לה] כא) שֶׁמֶשׁ יָרֵחַ עָמַד זְבֻלָה לְאוֹר חִצֶּיךָ יְהַלֵּכוּ לְנֹגַהּ בְּרַק חֲנִיתֶךָ: [חבקוק ג, יא] כב) וְאִם בְּרִיאָה יִבְרָא יְיָ וּפָצְתָה הָאֲדָמָה אֶת פִּיהָ וּבָלְעָה אֹתָם וְאֶת כָּל אֲשֶׁר לָהֶם וְיָרְדוּ חַיִּים שְׁאֹלָה וִידַעְתֶּם כִּי נִאֲצוּ הָאֲנָשִׁים הָאֵלֶּה אֶת יְיָ: [במדבר טז, ל] כג) מַה שֶּׁהָיָה הוּא שֶׁיִּהְיֶה וּמַה שֶּׁנַּעֲשָׂה הוּא שֶׁיֵּעָשֶׂה וְאֵין כָּל חָדָשׁ תַּחַת הַשָּׁמֶשׁ: [קהלת א, ט] כד) וּבְנֵי קֹרַח לֹא מֵתוּ: [במדבר כו, יא]

לג א ב ג ד מיי׳ פ״ה מהל׳ ת״ת הל׳ א סמג עשין יב טוש״ע י״ד סי׳ רמב סעיף ב:

ליקוטי רש״י

אחר חוט אחד של תכלת פוטרה זו שכולה תכלת לא תפטור את עצמה [במדבר טז, א]. חכמות נשים בנתה ביתה. חכמות נקוד פתח שאינו שם דבר אלא החכמות שבנשים בונות את בתיהם שמתקיימות על ידיהן כמו אשתו של און בן פלת כמו שמפורש בפרק חלק. ואולת. ואשה שוטה. בידיה תהרסנו. תהרס ביתה זו אשתו של קרח [משלי יד, א]. קראי מועד. שהיו תלמידי חכמים כדכתיב (במדבר טז) נשיאי עדה קריאי מועד אנשי שם ועל שם שפיתם אותו רשע כשנהנו ממונו הקלו בעיניו להשיאם ולהחזיק ידו במחלוקת ולמרוד בהקדוש ברוך הוא [לעיל נב.]. ויקם משה. כסבור שישאו לו פנים ולא עשו [במדבר טז, כה]. ביד משה לו. כמו עליו על אהרן דבר אל משה שיהיה הוא ובניו כהנים לפיכך לא יקרב איש זר אשר לא מזרע אהרן וגו׳ וכן כל לי ולו ולהם הסמוכים אצל דבור פתרונם כמו על ומדרשו על קרח ומהו ביד משה ולא כתב אל משה רמז לחולקים על הכהונה שלוקין בצרעת כמו שלקה משה בידו שנאמר (שמות ד, ו) ויוציאה והנה ידו מצורעת כשלג ועל כן לקה עוזיה בצרעת [במדבר יז, ה]. חמת זוחלי עפר. ארס נחשים המהלכים על גחונם על העפר כמים הזוחלים על הארץ זחילה לשון מרוצת המים על העפר וכן כל מרוצת דבר המשפשף על העפר והולך [דברים לב, כד]. עושר שמור לבעליו לרעתו. כעשרו של קרח שעל ידי כן נתגאה וירד לשאול [קהלת ה, יב]. שמעמידו על רגליו. שמשמח לבו. וקילפי. פותחות שקורין בלעז שרדור״א. דגלדי. של מרצופים של עור שנושאים על סוסים וחמורים וגמלים [פסחים קיט.]. מלמד שעלו שמש וירח לזבול. שחמה ולבנה ברקיע השני כדאמרינן שבעה רקיעים הם וילון רקיע שחקים זבול מכון מעון ערבות ומונה להם כסדרן וילון אינו משמש כלום רקיע יש בו חמה ולבנה כוכבים ומזלות כו׳ [תהלים יט, ז]. שמש ירח עמד זבולה אם אתה עושה דין לבן עמרם ממחלקותו של קרח ומשמע להו דהאי קרא במחלקותו של קרח מדריש משום דביציאת מצרים ובקריעת ים סוף משתעי בספר חבקוק וכתיב ביה מחצת ראש מבית רשע ומשמע להו דהיינו קרח וכתיב בתריה שמש ירח עמד זבולה [נדרים לט.]. אלא לקרובי פיתחא. וקריבה בעלמא ליתא בכלל אין כל חדש [נדרים לט:]. ובני קרח לא מתו. הם היו בעצה תחלה ובשעת המחלוקת הרהרו תשובה בלבם לפיכך נתבצר להם מקום גבוה בגיהנם וישבו שם [במדבר כו, יא]. נתבצר להם. לשון גבוה כמו ובצורות בשמים (דברים ט) [מגילה יד.].

וְלֹא קֹרַח – which implies that some of Korach's followers were swallowed,[48] **but not Korach** himself. וְלֹא מִן הַשְּׂרוּפִים דִּכְתִיב ,,בַּאֲכֹל הָאֵשׁ אֵת חֲמִשִּׁים וּמָאתַיִם אִישׁ" – **And** it is also evident that Korach was **not among those who were burned,**[49] **for it is written,**[50] ***when the fire consumed the two hundred and fifty men,*** וְלֹא קֹרַח – which implies precisely two hundred and fifty men – **but not Korach** himself.[51]

A different opinion regarding Korach's fate:

בְּמַתְנִיתָא תָּנָא – **[A Tanna] taught in a Baraisa:** קֹרַח מִן הַשְּׂרוּפִין וּמִן הַבְּלוּעִין – KORACH WAS AMONG THOSE WHO WHO WERE SWALLOWED by the earth, AND AMONG THOSE WHO WERE BURNED.[52] מִן הַבְּלוּעִין דִּכְתִיב ,,וַתִּבְלַע אֹתָם וְאֶת־קֹרַח" – It is evident that he was AMONG THOSE WHO WERE SWALLOWED, FOR IT IS WRITTEN: *The earth opened its mouth* AND SWALLOWED THEM AND KORACH.[53] מִן הַשְּׂרוּפִין דִּכְתִיב – It is also evident that Korach was AMONG THOSE WHO WERE BURNED, FOR IT IS WRITTEN:[54] ,,ותצא אש מלפני ה׳ [וְאֵשׁ יָצְאָה מֵאֵת ה׳] וַתֹּאכַל אֵת הַחֲמִשִּׁים וּמָאתַיִם אִישׁ" – *A FLAME CAME FORTH FROM GOD AND CONSUMED THE TWO HUNDRED AND FIFTY MEN,* וְקֹרַח בַּהֲדַיְיהוּ – AND KORACH WAS ONE OF THEM.[55]

The sun and moon themselves protest Korach's attack on Moses:

אָמַר רָבָא – **Rava said:** מַאי דִּכְתִיב ,,שֶׁמֶשׁ יָרֵחַ עָמַד זְבֻלָה לְאוֹר חִצֶּיךָ יְהַלֵּכוּ" – **What is** the meaning of that **which is written:** ***The sun and the moon stood still in their habitation; they went for light [because of] Your arrows?***[56] מְלַמֵּד שֶׁעָלוּ שֶׁמֶשׁ וְיָרֵחַ לִזְבוּל – **[This] teaches that** when Korach and his assembly rebelled against Moses, **the sun and the moon ascended** from their heavenly abode **to** the firmament known as ***z'vul***[57] אָמְרוּ לְפָנָיו רִבּוֹנוֹ שֶׁל עוֹלָם – and **said before [God]: "Master of the Universe! אם אַתָּה עוֹשֶׂה דִּין לְבֶן עַמְרָם – If You render justice for** Moses **son of Amram** (i.e. if You publicly demonstrate that Moses is being unjustly accused and challenged by Korach and his followers), נֵצֵא – then **we will go out** and illuminate the earth. וְאִם לָאו לֹא נֵצֵא – **But if not, we will not go out** and illuminate the earth!"[58] עַד שֶׁזָּרַק בָּהֶם חִצִּים – They clung to this position **until [God] hurled arrows at them** and forced them to perform their assigned tasks, אָמַר לָהֶן – **saying to them,** בִּכְבוֹדִי לֹא מְחִיתֶם בִּכְבוֹד בָּשָׂר וָדָם מְחִיתֶם – **"For My honor you did not protest,** but **for the honor of flesh and blood you do protest!?"**[59]

NOTES

48. These were Dasan and Abiram and their households. Since their participation in the rebellion was motivated solely by a brazen desire to challenge Moses' leadership (see above, note 2), their fitting punishment was to be swallowed by the earth and descend to Gehinnom, the place specially reserved for those who sow discord (*Maharal;* cf. *Maharsha*).

49. These were the contingent of two hundred and fifty followers, who joined Korach solely for the purpose of acquiring the Kehunah (see above, note 2). Since they quested after a spiritual status of which they were unworthy, they were destroyed by a heavenly fire [in the manner of Nadav and Avihu, two of Aaron's sons who similarly overreached; see *Leviticus* 10:1-2] (*Maharal;* cf. *Maharsha*).

50. *Numbers* 26:10.

51. The proof that Korach was not included among these two hundred and fifty incense offerers is verse 16:17 above, where Moses told Korach: *Let each man take his fire-pan, and you shall place incense on them, and you shall bring before God each man with his fire-pan – two hundred and fifty fire-pans; besides you and Aaron, each man with his fire-pan.* Here Scripture explicitly excludes Korach from the group of 250 (*Rashi*).

Maharsha explains that in R' Yochanan's view Korach was spared the punishments meted out to Dasan and Abiram (being swallowed by the earth) and to the contingent of 250 (burning) because his sin was less serious than theirs. That is, it was mitigated by the fact that Korach was deluded by a vision that he would have descendants greater even than Moses and Aaron, and on that basis he challenged their authority (see *Bamidbar Rabbah* 18:8). Korach was instead killed by the plague for speaking ill of Moses and Aaron, just as the Spies were later killed by a plague for speaking ill of Eretz Yisrael. Cf. *Iyun Yaakov*, who explains that Korach was spared the two harsher punishments in the merit of his illustrious descendant Shmuel. See also *Maharal* and *Ben Yehoyada*, who take an entirely different approach in explaining R' Yochanan's opinion.

52. According to the Baraisa, Korach suffered both punishments. First, his soul was burned by a heavenly fire; then his body, which had remained intact, rolled to where the others stood and was swallowed by the earth (*Rashi*). According to *Bamidbar Rabbah* 18:14, the heavenly fire did ignite his body. Collapsing in a fiery ball, Korach rolled to the opening in the earth and fell in.

The Baraisa maintains that Korach deserved both punishments because he was the leader and instigator of the rebellion. As such, he was responsible for the sins of every contingent [see notes 2, 48 and 49 above]. Hence, had he endured only burning, his demise would not have been witnessed by those who were swallowed, and they would have gone to their deaths complaining that Korach, their leader, had escaped punishment. On the other hand, had Korach only been swallowed, those who were burned would have similarly complained. Thus, so that God's justice not have even the appearance of imperfection, Korach was burned in the presence of those who were burned, and he was swallowed up in the presence of those who were swallowed (*Maharsha,* citing *Tanchuma*).

53. *Numbers* 26:10. R' Yochanan, who maintains that Korach was not swallowed, reads this verse as follows: *The earth opened its mouth and swallowed them; and Korach* [*perished*] *when the congregation died* – i.e. when 14,700 people died in a plague on the following day (*Rashi;* cf. *Ben Yehoyada*).

54. Ibid. 16:35.

55. The verse states in full: *A flame came forth from God and consumed* (אֵת) *the two hundred and fifty men who were offering the incense.* The extraneous phrase, *who were offering the incense,* comes to include Korach, who also offered incense (see *Numbers* 16:17, cited above in note 51). Alternatively, the superfluous word אֵת in the phrase וַתֹּאכַל אֵת הַחֲמִשִּׁים וּמָאתַיִם אִישׁ comes to include Korach (*Rashi, Yad Ramah*).

56. *Habakkuk* 3:11. According to most commentators, this verse refers to Joshua's victory at Gibeon over a coalition of Canaanite kings. As the defeated Canaanites fled, God hurled huge stones at them from the sky. Afraid that the approaching nightfall would enable the enemy to escape, Joshua ordered the sun to stand still at Gibeon and the moon in the Valley of Ayalon. They did so, and the Jewish army was afforded a supernaturally long day in which to pursue the enemy (*Joshua* 10:9-14). According to this understanding, our verse would be translated: *The sun and the moon stood still in their habitation* at Joshua's bidding; the beaten Canaanites *fled by the light of Your arrows, by the shining of Your glittering spear,* a pair of metaphors for the huge stones that God hurled down at them like arrows and spears (*Targum, Radak, Abarbanel, Metzudos*).

However, because the Prophet states just above (v. 9), *You will cleave the earth,* our Gemara interprets the verse in terms of the Korach episode, as our translation indicates.

57. זְבוּל, *z'vul,* is one of the seven firmaments; see *Chagigah* 12b. The sun and the moon are ordinarily located in a different firmament, called רָקִיעַ, *rakia* (see *Nedarim* 39b: "The sun and moon ascended from *rakia* to *z'vul*").

58. *Rashba* (cited in *Anaf Yosef*) explains that the universe was created as a forum for Torah observance. Further, in challenging Moses, God's designated transmitter of the Torah, Korach was subverting the Torah itself. The sun and moon thus argued: If Korach succeeds in destroying the Torah, there will be no need for us to resume functioning, since the world will cease to exist (see *Jeremiah* 33:25 and *Shabbos* 33a).

59. God responded to the two luminaries: "Each day, when the kings of the East and West don their royal crowns, they prostrate themselves to the sun [rather than reaffirm their allegiance to Me]. Why do you not protest this affront to My honor?" (*Rashi*). See *Yad Ramah,* who writes that God includes the Jews' idolatrous worship of the Golden Calf among the affronts to His honor.

וסתרתה למזיה כל דאתא חזיה הדר אדהכי והכי אבלעו להו איתתיה דקרח אמרה ליה חזי מאי קעביד משה איהו הוה מלכא לאחוה שוויה כהנא רבא לבני אחוהי שוינהו סגני דכהנא אי אתיא תרומה אמר תיהוי לכהן אי אתו מעשר דשקילתו אתון אמר הבו חד מי' לכהן ועוד דגייז ליה למזייכו ומיטלל לכו כי כופתא עינא יהב במזייכו אמר לה הא איהו נמי קא עביד אמרה ליה כיון דכולהו רבותא דידיה אמר איהו נמי א) תמות נפשי עם פלשתים ועוד דקאמר לכו עבידתו תכלתא אי ס"ד תכלתא חשיבא [מצוה] אפיק גלימי דתכלתא וכסינהו לכולהו מתיבתך היינו דכתיב ב) חכמות נשים בנתה ביתה זו אשתו של און בן פלת ואולת א) בידה תהרסנה זו אשתו של קרח ג) ויקומו לפני משה ואנשים מבני ישראל חמשים ומאתים מיוחדים שבעדה קריאי מועד שהיו יודעים לעבר שנים ולקבוע חדשים אנשי שם שהיה להם שם בכל העולם ד) וישמע משה ויפול על פניו מה שמועה שמע ב) אמר רבי שמואל בר נחמני א"ר יונתן שחשדוהו מאשת איש שנאמר ה) ויקנאו למשה במחנה א"ר שמואל בר יצחק מלמד שכל אחד ואחד קנא את אשתו ממשה שנאמר ו) ומשה יקח את האהל ונטה לו מחוץ למחנה ז) ויקם משה וילך אל דתן ואבירם אמר ר"ל מכאן שאין מחזיקין במחלוקת דאמר רב כל המחזיק במחלוקת עובר בלאו שנאמר ח) ולא יהיה כקרח וכעדתו רב אשי אמר ראוי ליצטרע כתיב הכא ח) ביד משה לו וכתיב התם ט) ויאמר ה' לו עוד הבא נא ידך בחיקך אמר ר' ג) יוסי כל החולק על מלכות בית דוד ראוי להכישו נחש כתיב הכא י) ויזבח אדוניהו צאן ובקר ומריא עם אבן הזוחלת וכתיב התם יא) עם חמת זוחלי עפר אמר רב חסדא ד) א כל החולק על רבו כחולק על השכינה שנאמר יב) בהצותם על ה' א"ר חמא ברבי חנינא ב כל העושה מריבה עם רבו כעושה עם שכינה שנאמר יג) המה מי מריבה אשר רבו בני ישראל (על) [את] ה' א"ר חנינא בר פפא ג כל המתרעם על רבו כאילו מתרעם על השכינה שנאמר יד) לא עלינו תלונותיכם כי (אם) על ה' א"ר אבהו ד כל המהרהר אחר רבו כאילו מהרהר אחר שכינה שנאמר טו) וידבר העם באלהים ובמשה טז) עושר שמור לבעליו לרעתו ה) אמר ר"ל זה עושרו של קרח יז) ואת כל היקום אשר ברגליהם ו) א"ר אלעזר זה ממונו של אדם שמעמידו על רגליו ואמר רבי לוי משוי ז) ג' מאות פרדות לבנות היו מפתחות של בית גנזיו של קרח וכולהו אקלידי וקילפי דגילדא א"ר חמא ברבי חנינא ג' מטמוניות הטמין יוסף במצרים אחת נתגלתה לקרח ואחת נתגלתה לאנטונינוס בן אסוירוס ואחת גנוזה לצדיקים לעתיד לבא וא"ר יוחנן קרח לא מן הבלועים ולא מן השרופין לא מן הבלועין דכתיב יח) ואת כל האדם אשר לקרח ולא כל קרח ולא מן השרופים דכתיב יט) באכול האש את חמשים ומאתים איש ולא קרח במתניתא תנא קרח מן השרופין ומן הבלועין מן הבלועים דכתיב יט) ותבלע אותם ואת קרח מן השרופין דכתיב כ) (ותצא אש מלפני ה') [ואש יצאה מאת ה'] ותאכל את חמשים ומאתים איש וקרח בהדייהו אמר רבא ח) מאי דכתיב כא) שמש ירח עמד זבולה לאור חציך יהלכו מלמד שעלו שמש וירח לזבול אמרו לפניו רבש"ע אם אתה עושה דין לבן עמרם נצא ואם לאו לא נצא עד שזרק בהם חצים אמר להן ט) בכבודי לא מחיתם בכבוד בשר ודם מחיתם והאידנא לא נפקי עד דמחו להו י) דרש רבא מאי דכתיב כב) ואם בריאה יברא ה' ופצתה האדמה את פיה אמר משה לפני הקב"ה אם בריאה גיהנם מוטב ואם לאו יברא ה' למאי אילימא למבריה ממש והא כג) אין כל חדש תחת השמש אלא לקרובי פיתחא כד) ובני קרח לא מתו תנא כ) משום רבינו אמרו מקום נתבצר להם בגיהנם וישבו עליו ואמרו שירה ל) אמר רבה בר בר חנה זימנא חדא הוה קאזלינא באורחא אמר לי ההוא טייעא תא ואחוי לך בלועי דקרח אזיל חזא תרי בזעי דהוה קא נפק קיטרא מנייהו שקל גבבא דעמרא אמשיי' מיא ואותביה בריש רומחיה ואחלפי' התם איחרך א"ל אצית מה שמעת ושמעית דהוו קאמרי הכי משה ותורתו אמת והן בדאים אמר

סתרה למזיה. שערה וישבה על פתח הבית כל מי שהיה בא לקרוא רואה ראשה פרוע וחוזר: מעשר. ראשון דשקליתו אתון אמר הבו חד מי' לכהן: דגייז למזייכו. דכתיב (במדבר ח) והעבירו תער על [כל] בשרם ומשחק בכם כאילו אתם שוטים: ככופתא. רעי כמו בטולא דכופתא דאמרן לעיל (דף לא:) כגלל הזה אתם חשובים בעיניו: עינא יהב. עין נתן בשעריכם כדי שלא יהא בכם נורה כמותו: אמר לה. קרח איהו נמי משה עצמו גלח כל שערו: כיון דכולא רבותא דידיה הוא. אינו חושש אם גילח עצמו דקאמר לנפשיה תמות נפשי עם פלשתים אגזוז שערי כמותם ומה לי בכך שהם מקיימין אפילו מה שאני מצוה לשחוק אגזוז עכשיו כמותם כדי להפיס דעתם: ועוד דקאמר לכו. עשו פתיל תכלת בד' כנפות הבגד ואי ס"ד תכלת חשוב מפני מה לא יאמר לעשות כל הבגד כולו תכלת: אפיק גלימא דתכלתא. קח לך בגדים של תכלת וכסינהו לכולהו מתיבתך וכסה בהן בבה"מ אתה וחברותך: קנא לאשתו. אל (הסתר) [תסתרי] עם משה. קנוי היינו התראה: ונטה לו מחוץ למחנה. יצא מחוץ למחנה שלא יחשדוהו עוד: מכאן שאין מחזיקין במחלוקת. שמחל על כבודו והוא עצמו הלך לבטל מחלוקת: חולק על רבו. חולק על ישיבתו: אשר הצו על משה ועל אהרן בעדת קרח בהצותם על ה'. מעלה עליהם הכתוב כאלו היו חולקים כלפי שכינה: מריבה. תגר וקטטה לפטפט נגדו בדברים: מתרעם. אומר על רבו שנוהג לו מדה כבושה ומדת אכזרית: מהרהר. מחפה עליו דברים: אקלידי. מפתחות: וקולפי. מנעולים: דגילדי. כולם המפתחות והמנעולים של עור היו ואעפ"כ היו שלש מאות פרדות טעונות ל"א דגלדא לצורך שקים והמרצופין וכיסין של עור היו: לא מן הבלועין ולא מן השרופין. אלא במגפה מת: ולא קרח. ר"נ היו לבד קרח דכתיב חמשים ומאתים מחתות ואתה ואהרן איש מחתתו: מן הבלועים ומן השרופין היה. שנשרפה נשמתו וגוף קיים ואח"כ נתגלגל עד מקום הבלועין ונבלע דכתיב בפרשת פנחס ותבלע אותם ואת קרח עמהם ורבי יוחנן דאמר לא מן הבלועין ולא מן השרופין דריש ליה להאי ואת קרח לאחריו ואת קרח במות העדה במגפה: וקרח בהדייהו. מדכתיב ותאכל את החמשים ומאתים איש מקריבי הקטרת וקרח ממקריבי הקטרת הוה דכתיב חמשים ומאתים מחתות ואתה ואהרן איש מחתתו א"נ ואת לרבות קרח עמהם: שמש ירח עמד זבולה. לעיל מיניה כתיב ותבקע ארץ בשעת בקיעת הארץ שנבלעו בקרקע שמש וירח עלו לאותו רקיע ששמו זבול ואמרו להקב"ה אם אי אתה עושה דין לבן עמרם מקרח ועדתו: לא נצא. ונאיר לעולם: בכבודי לא מחיתם. שהרי בכל יום מלכי מזרח ומערב בשעה שמניחין כתריהן בראשם משתחוים לחמה: והאידנא לא נפקי עד דמחו להו. שכך גזר עליהם המקום כן שמעתי ל"א והאידנא לא נפקי מאחר שראו שהקפיד הקב"ה על שלא מיחה לכבודו עד דמחו להו לא נפקי שחסו לכבוד המקום על בני אדם שמשתחוים לשמש וירח: אין כל חדש תחת השמש. ואי גיהנם לא אברי עד ההוא שעתא הוה ליה חדש: לקרובי פתחה. שיקרב פתחה של גיהנם ותפתח הארץ במקום שהן: נתבצר. מלשון (ישעיה כז) עיר בצורה התקין להון הקב"ה מקום גבוה שלא העמיקו כל כך בגיהנם ולא מתו: טייעא. סוחר ישמעאל: בלועי. מקום שנתבלעו לשם עדת קרח: בזעא. ראה נקב שממנו יצא עשן: גבבא. גיזה: אמשיה. שרה אות' במים לשון (ברכות דף יד:) משי ידיה: (וכל שלשים יום. חוזר לגיהנם ועולה לשם): אמר

מסורת הש"ס

א) בקרא כתיב בידיה תהרסנו, ב) [מו"ק יח:], ג) [נ"ל יוסף], ד) [ברכות כז: ע"ש], ה) פסחים קיט. ע"ש, ו) [שם], ז) ג' מאות לאו דוקא וכן כל שלש מאות בש"ס רשב"ם פסחים קיט, ח) נדרים לט: ע"ש, ט) לעיל קג., י) [לעיל קג:], כ) מגילה יד., ל) ב"ב עד ע"א.

תורה אור השלם

א) וַיֹּאמֶר שִׁמְשׁוֹן תָּמוֹת נַפְשִׁי עִם פְּלִשְׁתִּים וַיֵּט בְּכֹחַ וַיִּפֹּל הַבַּיִת עַל הַסְּרָנִים וְעַל כָּל הָעָם אֲשֶׁר בּוֹ וַיִּהְיוּ הַמֵּתִים אֲשֶׁר הֵמִית בְּמוֹתוֹ רַבִּים מֵאֲשֶׁר הֵמִית בְּחַיָּיו: [שופטים טז, ל]

ב) חַכְמוֹת נָשִׁים בָּנְתָה בֵיתָהּ וְאִוֶּלֶת בְּיָדֶיהָ תֶהֶרְסֶנּוּ: [משלי יד, א]

ג) וַיָּקֻמוּ לִפְנֵי מֹשֶׁה וַאֲנָשִׁים מִבְּנֵי יִשְׂרָאֵל חֲמִשִּׁים וּמָאתָיִם נְשִׂיאֵי עֵדָה קְרִאֵי מוֹעֵד אַנְשֵׁי שֵׁם: [במדבר טז, ב]

ד) וַיִּשְׁמַע מֹשֶׁה וַיִּפֹּל עַל פָּנָיו: [במדבר טז, ד]

ה) וַיְקַנְאוּ לְמֹשֶׁה בַּמַּחֲנֶה לְאַהֲרֹן קְדוֹשׁ יְיָ: [תהלים קו, טז]

ו) וּמֹשֶׁה יִקַּח אֶת הָאֹהֶל וְנָטָה לוֹ מִחוּץ לַמַּחֲנֶה הַרְחֵק מִן הַמַּחֲנֶה וְקָרָא לוֹ אֹהֶל מוֹעֵד וְהָיָה כָּל מְבַקֵּשׁ יְיָ יֵצֵא אֶל אֹהֶל מוֹעֵד אֲשֶׁר מִחוּץ לַמַּחֲנֶה: [שמות לג, ז]

ז) וַיָּקָם מֹשֶׁה וַיֵּלֶךְ אֶל דָּתָן וַאֲבִירָם וַיֵּלְכוּ אַחֲרָיו זִקְנֵי יִשְׂרָאֵל: [במדבר טז, כה]

ח) זִכָּרוֹן לִבְנֵי יִשְׂרָאֵל לְמַעַן אֲשֶׁר לֹא יִקְרַב אִישׁ זָר אֲשֶׁר לֹא מִזֶּרַע אַהֲרֹן הוּא לְהַקְטִיר קְטֹרֶת לִפְנֵי יְיָ וְלֹא יִהְיֶה כְקֹרַח וְכַעֲדָתוֹ כַּאֲשֶׁר דִּבֶּר יְיָ בְּיַד מֹשֶׁה לוֹ: [במדבר יז, ה]

ט) וַיֹּאמֶר יְיָ לוֹ עוֹד הָבֵא נָא יָדְךָ בְּחֵיקֶךָ וַיָּבֵא יָדוֹ בְּחֵיקוֹ וַיּוֹצִאָהּ וְהִנֵּה יָדוֹ מְצֹרַעַת כַּשָּׁלֶג: [שמות ד, ו]

י) וַיִּזְבַּח אֲדֹנִיָּהוּ צֹאן וּבָקָר וּמְרִיא עִם אֶבֶן הַזֹּחֶלֶת אֲשֶׁר אֵצֶל עֵין רֹגֵל וַיִּקְרָא אֶת כָּל אֶחָיו בְּנֵי הַמֶּלֶךְ וּלְכָל אַנְשֵׁי יְהוּדָה עַבְדֵי הַמֶּלֶךְ: [מלכים א' א, ט]

יא) מְזֵי רָעָב וּלְחֻמֵי רֶשֶׁף וְקֶטֶב מְרִירִי וְשֶׁן בְּהֵמֹת אֲשַׁלַּח בָּם עִם חֲמַת זֹחֲלֵי עָפָר: [דברים לב, כד]

יב) וּבְנֵי אֱלִיאָב נְמוּאֵל וְדָתָן וַאֲבִירָם הוּא דָתָן וַאֲבִירָם קְרִיאֵי הָעֵדָה אֲשֶׁר הִצּוּ עַל מֹשֶׁה וְעַל אַהֲרֹן בַּעֲדַת קֹרַח בְּהַצֹּתָם עַל יְיָ: [במדבר כו, ט]

יג) הֵמָּה מֵי מְרִיבָה אֲשֶׁר רָבוּ בְנֵי יִשְׂרָאֵל אֶת יְיָ וַיִּקָּדֵשׁ בָּם: [במדבר כ, יג]

עין משפט נר מצוה

לג א ב ג ד מיי' פ"ה מהל' ת"ת הל' א סמג עשין יב טוש"ע י"ד סי' רמב סעיף ב:

ליקוטי רש"י

אחר חוט אחד של תכלת פוטרה זו שכולה תכלת לא תפטור את עצמה [במדבר טז, א]. חכמות נשים בנתה ביתה. חכמות נקוד פתח שאינו שם דבר אלא החכמות שבנשים בונות את בתיהם שמתקיימות על ידיהן כמו אשתו של און בן פלת כמו שמפורש בפרק חלק. ואולת. ואשה שוטה. בידיה תהרסנו. תהרס ביתה זו אשתו של קרח [משלי יד, א]. קראי מועד. שהיו תלמידי חכמים כדכתיב (במדבר טז) נשיאי עדה קריאי מועד אנשי שם ועל שם שפיתם אותו רשע כשנהנו מממונו הקלו בעיניו להשיאם ולהחזיק ידו במחלוקת ולמרוד בהקדוש ברוך הוא [לעיל נב.]. ויקם משה. כסבור שישאו לו פנים ולא עשו [במדבר טז, כה]. ביד משה לו. כמו עליו על אהרן דבר אל משה שיהיה הוא ובניו כהנים לפיכך לא יקרב איש זר אשר לא מזרע אהרן וגו' וכן כל לי ולו ולהם הסמוכים אצל דבור פתרונם כמו על ומדרשו על קרח ומהו ביד משה ולא כתב אל משה רמז לחולקים על הכהונה שלוקין בצרעת כמו שלקה משה בידו שנאמר (שמות ד, ו) ויוציאה והנה ידו מצורעת כשלג ועל כן לקה עוזיה בצרעת [במדבר יז, ה]. חמת זוחלי עפר. ארס נחשים המהלכים על גחונם על העפר כמים הזוחלים על הארץ זחילה לשון מרולת המים על העפר וכן כל מרולת דבר המשפשף על העפר והולך [דברים לב, כד]. עושר שמור לבעליו לרעתו. כעשרו של קרח שעל ידי כן נתגאה וירד לשאול [קהלת ה, יב]. שמעמידו על רגליו. שמשמח לבו. וקילפי. פותחות שקורין בלעז שרדור"א. דגלדי. של מרלופים של עור שנושאים על סוסים וחמורים וגמלים [פסחים קיט.]. מלמד שעלו שמש וירח לזבול. שחמה ולבנה ברקיע השני כדאמרינן שבעה רקיעים הם וילון רקיע שחקים זבול מכון מעון ערבות ומונה להם כסדרן וילון אינו משמש כלום רקיע יש בו חמה ולבנה כוכבים ומזלות כו' [תהלים יט, ז]. שמש ירח עמד זבולה אם אתה עושה דין לבן עמרם ממחלקותו של קרח ומשמע להו דהאי קרא במחלקותו של קרח מדריש משום דכיליאת מצרים ובקריעת ים סוף משתעי בספר חבקוק וכתיב ביה מחצת ראש מבית רשע ומשמע להו דהיינו קרח וכתיב בתריה שמש ירח עמד זבולה [נדרים לט.]. אלא לקרובי פיתחא. וקריבה בעלמא ליתא בכלל אין כל חדש [נדרים לט:]. ובני קרח לא מתו. הם היו בעלה תחלה ובשעת המחלוקת הרהרו תשובה בלבם לפיכך נתבצר להם מקום גבוה בגיהנם וישבו שם [במדבר כו, יא]. נתבצר להם. לשון גבוה כמו ובצורות בשמים (דברים ט) [מגילה יד.].

יד) וַיֹּאמֶר מֹשֶׁה בְּתֵת יְיָ לָכֶם בָּעֶרֶב בָּשָׂר לֶאֱכֹל וְלֶחֶם בַּבֹּקֶר לִשְׂבֹּעַ בִּשְׁמֹעַ יְיָ אֶת תְּלֻנֹּתֵיכֶם אֲשֶׁר אַתֶּם מַלִּינִם עָלָיו וְנַחְנוּ מָה לֹא עָלֵינוּ תְלֻנֹּתֵיכֶם כִּי עַל יְיָ: [שמות טז, ח] טו) וַיְדַבֵּר הָעָם בֵּאלֹהִים וּבְמֹשֶׁה לָמָה הֶעֱלִיתֻנוּ מִמִּצְרַיִם לָמוּת בַּמִּדְבָּר כִּי אֵין לֶחֶם וְאֵין מַיִם וְנַפְשֵׁנוּ קָצָה בַּלֶּחֶם הַקְּלֹקֵל: [במדבר כא, ה] טז) יֵשׁ רָעָה חוֹלָה רָאִיתִי תַּחַת הַשָּׁמֶשׁ עֹשֶׁר שָׁמוּר לִבְעָלָיו לְרָעָתוֹ: [קהלת ה, יב] יז) וַאֲשֶׁר עָשָׂה לְדָתָן וְלַאֲבִירָם בְּנֵי אֱלִיאָב בֶּן רְאוּבֵן אֲשֶׁר פָּצְתָה הָאָרֶץ אֶת פִּיהָ וַתִּבְלָעֵם וְאֶת בָּתֵּיהֶם וְאֶת אָהֳלֵיהֶם וְאֵת כָּל הַיְקוּם אֲשֶׁר בְּרַגְלֵיהֶם בְּקֶרֶב כָּל יִשְׂרָאֵל: [דברים יא, ו] יח) וַתִּפְתַּח הָאָרֶץ אֶת פִּיהָ וַתִּבְלַע אֹתָם וְאֶת בָּתֵּיהֶם וְאֵת כָּל הָאָדָם אֲשֶׁר לְקֹרַח וְאֵת כָּל הָרְכוּשׁ: [במדבר טז, לב] יט) וַתִּפְתַּח הָאָרֶץ אֶת פִּיהָ וַתִּבְלַע אֹתָם וְאֶת קֹרַח בְּמוֹת הָעֵדָה בַּאֲכֹל הָאֵשׁ אֵת חֲמִשִּׁים וּמָאתַיִם אִישׁ וַיִּהְיוּ לְנֵס: [במדבר כו, י] כ) וְאֵשׁ יָצְאָה מֵאֵת יְיָ וַתֹּאכַל אֵת הַחֲמִשִּׁים וּמָאתַיִם אִישׁ מַקְרִיבֵי הַקְּטֹרֶת: [במדבר טז, לה] כא) שֶׁמֶשׁ יָרֵחַ עָמַד זְבֻלָה לְאוֹר חִצֶּיךָ יְהַלֵּכוּ לְנֹגַהּ בְּרַק חֲנִיתֶךָ: [חבקוק ג, יא] כב) וְאִם בְּרִיאָה יִבְרָא יְיָ וּפָצְתָה הָאֲדָמָה אֶת פִּיהָ וּבָלְעָה אֹתָם וְאֶת כָּל אֲשֶׁר לָהֶם וְיָרְדוּ חַיִּים שְׁאֹלָה וִידַעְתֶּם כִּי נִאֲצוּ הָאֲנָשִׁים הָאֵלֶּה אֶת יְיָ: [במדבר טז, ל] כג) מַה שֶּׁהָיָה הוּא שֶׁיִּהְיֶה וּמַה שֶּׁנַּעֲשָׂה הוּא שֶׁיֵּעָשֶׂה וְאֵין כָּל חָדָשׁ תַּחַת הַשָּׁמֶשׁ: [קהלת א, ט] כד) וּבְנֵי קֹרַח לֹא מֵתוּ: [במדבר כו, יא]

The aftermath of this incident:
וְהָאִידְנָא לֹא נָפְקֵי עַד דְּמָחוּ לְהוּ – **And nowadays, [the sun and the moon] do not go out,** are not willing to illuminate at their designated times, **until they are struck** by God's arrows, thus protesting the pervasive idolatry that is a standing affront to God's honor.[60]

The Gemara discusses the phenomenon of the ground swallowing Korach and his followers:
דָּרַשׁ רָבָא – **Rava expounded:** מַאי דִּכְתִיב ,,וְאִם־בְּרִיאָה יִבְרָא ה׳ וּפָצְתָה הָאֲדָמָה אֶת־פִּיהָ'' – **What is** the meaning of that **which is written:** ***If God will create a phenomenon, and the earth will open its mouth***?[61] אָמַר מֹשֶׁה לִפְנֵי הַקָּדוֹשׁ בָּרוּךְ הוּא – **Moses said before the Holy One, Blessed is He:** אִם בְּרִיאָה גֵיהִנֹּם מוּטָב – **If Gehinnom is a creation,** i.e. if Gehinnom has already been created, so that Korach and his followers can be sent there, then **good.** וְאִם לָאו – **And if** it has **not** yet been created, ,,יִבְרָא ה׳ '' – then ***let God create it!***

The Gemara asks:
לְמַאי – **To what** purpose did Moses make such a request? אִילֵימָא לְמִבְרְיֵה מַמָּשׁ – **If you say** that he wanted God **actually to create [Gehinnom],** וְהָא ,,אֵין כָּל־חָדָשׁ תַּחַת הַשָּׁמֶשׁ'' – that cannot be, **for *there is nothing new under the sun***![62] אֶלָּא לְקָרוּבֵי פִּיתְחָא – **Rather,** Moses was praying for God **to bring close the portal** of Gehinnom.[63]

The fate of Korach's sons:
,,וּבְנֵי־קֹרַח לֹא־מֵתוּ'' – Scripture states:[64] ***But the sons of Korach did not die.*** תָּנָא – **[A Tanna] taught:** מִשּׁוּם רַבֵּינוּ אָמְרוּ – THEY SAID IN THE NAME OF OUR TEACHER, Rabbi Yehudah HaNasi: מָקוֹם נִתְבַּצֵּר לָהֶם בְּגֵיהִנֹּם – **A PLACE WAS SET UP HIGH FOR THEM IN GEHINNOM,** וְיָשְׁבוּ עָלָיו וְאָמְרוּ שִׁירָה – **AND THEY SAT ON IT AND RECITED SONGS** of praise to God for their salvation.[65]

The Gemara relates an incident involving Korach's assembly:
אָמַר רַבָּה בַּר בַּר חָנָה – **Rabbah bar bar Chanah said:** זִימְנָא חֲדָא הֲוָה קָאָזְלִינָא בְּאוֹרְחָא – **I was once walking on the road.** אָמַר לִי הַהוּא טַיְּיעָא – **A certain Arab merchant said to me:** תָּא וְאַחֲוֵי לָךְ בְּלוּעֵי דְּקֹרַח – **"Come, and I will show you** the site of **the swallowing of Korach's** assembly." אָזִיל חֲזָא תְּרֵי בִּזְעֵי – **[The Arab] went** and **spotted two cracks** in the ground דַּהֲוָה קָא נָפֵק קִיטְרָא מִנַּיְיהוּ – **from which smoke was issuing.**[66] שָׁקַל גְּבָבָא דְעַמְרָא – **He took a ball of wool shearings,** אַמְשְׁיֵיהּ מַיָּא – **soaked it in water,** וְאוֹתְבֵיהּ בְּרֵישׁ רוּמְחֵיהּ – **put** (i.e. stuck) **it on the** pointed **head of his spear** וְאַחְלְפֵיהּ הָתָם – **and passed it over [the cracks in the ground].** אִיחֲרַךְ – Even though the ball had been soaked in water, the heat was so intense that **[the wool] was singed.** אָמַר לִי – **[The Arab]** then **said to me:** אַצֵּית מַה שָּׁמְעַתְּ – **"Listen closely to what you** are about to **hear."** וּשְׁמָעִית דַּהֲווּ קָאָמְרֵי הָכִי – **I heard that they**[67] **were saying thus:** מֹשֶׁה וְתוֹרָתוֹ אֱמֶת – **"Moses and his Torah are true,** וְהֵן בַּדָּאִים – **and they**[68] **are liars!"**

NOTES

60. This is *Rashi's* second interpretation (see also *Nedarim* 39b). According to this interpretation, the thoroughly chastised sun and moon are reluctant to shine for idolaters, and they do so only under duress.

Rashi's first interpretation is that God decreed that – as a punishment – the sun and the moon should be struck daily before going out to shine.

Yad Ramah cites an alternative version that deletes לְהוּ, leaving only לֹא נָפְקֵי עַד דְּמָחוּ, *do not go out until they protest*; according to this interpretation, nowadays they protest idolatry of their own accord, but neither striking nor the method of the protest is mentioned.

61. *Numbers* 16:30. This is the usual translation of Moses' plea to God to demonstrate to the rebels in a miraculous way that he (Moses) had indeed acted truthfully.

Rava, however, is bothered by the apparent incongruity of the literal translation: *If a creation, God will create [it].*

62. *Ecclesiastes* 1:9, which teaches that nothing new will ever be created following the Six Days of Creation. How, then, could Moses beseech God to create Gehinnom *ex nihilo*? (*Rashi*).

63. Moses asked God to transport the portal of Gehinnom to the spot where Korach and his followers stood [see *Eruvin* 19a, where it is stated that one of the entrances to Gehinnom is located in that desert]. God answered Moses' prayer, and when the earth opened up under the rebels, they descended directly to Gehinnom (*Rashi*).

Of course, Gehinnom is not actually a physical place beneath the ground. For a detailed discussion of the properties of Gehinnom, see *Ramban's Shaar HaGemul.*

64. *Numbers* 26:11.

65. *Rashi* op cit. explains that Korach's sons initially joined their father's infamous mutiny against Moses. In the midst of the rebellion, however, they realized their folly and repented. When the earth opened to swallow Korach, Dasan, Abiram and their households, God miraculously provided a place of refuge for Korach's sons. As the others descended to Gehinnom, the sons of Korach landed on an elevated niche, and were spared their colleagues' fate.

Maharal explains that Gehinnom represents "non-being," whereas this world is "being." The sons of Korach were saved from Gehinnom, which means that they still had an existence. See also *Melo HaRoim.*

66. From the fire of Gehinnom.

67. Regarding who "they" are, see below, 110b note 3.

68. A euphemism for "we."

וסתרתה למזיה כל דאתא חזיה הדר אדהכי והכי אבלעו להו איתתיה דקרח אמרה ליה חזי מאי קעביד משה איהו הוה מלכא לאחוה שוויה כהנא רבא לבני אחוהי שוינהו סגני דכהנא אי אתיא תרומה אמר תיהוי לכהן אי אתו מעשר דשקילתו אתון אמר הבו חד מי' לכהן ועוד דגייז ליה למזייכו ומיטלל לכו כי כופתא עינא יהב במזייכו אמר לה הא איהו נמי קא עביד אמרה ליה כיון דכולהו רבותא דידיה אמר איהו נמי א) תמות נפשי עם פלשתים ועוד דקאמר לכו עבידתו תכלתא אי ס"ד תכלתא חשיבא [מצוה] אפיק גלימי דתכלתא וכסינהו לכולהו מתיבתך היינו דכתיב ב) חכמות נשים בנתה ביתה זו אשתו של און בן פלת ואולת א) בידה תהרסנה זו אשתו של קרח ג) ויקומו לפני משה ואנשים מבני ישראל חמשים ומאתים מיוחדים שבעדה קריאי מועד שהיו יודעים לעבר שנים ולקבוע חדשים אנשי שם שהיה להם שם בכל העולם ד) וישמע משה ויפול על פניו מה שמועה שמע ב) אמר רבי שמואל בר נחמני א"ר יונתן שחשדוהו מאשת איש שנאמר ה) ויקנאו למשה במחנה א"ר שמואל בר יצחק מלמד שכל אחד ואחד קנא את אשתו ממשה שנאמר ו) ומשה יקח את האהל ונטה לו מחוץ למחנה ז) ויקם משה וילך אל דתן ואבירם אמר ר"ל מכאן שאין מחזיקין במחלוקת דאמר רב כל המחזיק במחלוקת עובר בלאו שנאמר ח) ולא יהיה כקרח וכעדתו רב אשי אמר ראוי ליצטרע כתיב הכא ח) ביד משה לו וכתיב התם ט) ויאמר ה' לו עוד הבא נא ידך בחיקך אמר ר' ג) יוסי כל החולק על מלכות בית דוד ראוי להכישו נחש כתיב הכא י) ויזבח אדוניהו צאן ובקר ומריא עם אבן הזוחלת וכתיב התם יא) עם חמת זוחלי עפר אמר רב חסדא ד) א) כל החולק על רבו כחולק על השכינה שנאמר יב) בהצותם על ה' א"ר חמא ברבי חנינא ב) כל העושה מריבה עם רבו כעושה עם שכינה שנאמר יג) המה מי מריבה אשר רבו בני ישראל (על) [את] ה' א"ר חנינא בר פפא ג) כל המתרעם על רבו כאילו מתרעם על השכינה שנאמר יד) לא עלינו תלונותיכם כי (אם) על ה' א"ר אבהו ד) כל המהרהר אחר רבו כאילו מהרהר אחר שכינה שנאמר טו) וידבר העם באלהים ובמשה טז) עושר שמור לבעליו לרעתו ה) אמר ר"ל זה עושרו של קרח יז) ואת כל היקום אשר ברגליהם ו) א"ר אלעזר זה ממונו של אדם שמעמידו על רגליו ואמר רבי לוי משוי ז) ג' מאות פרדות לבנות היו מפתחות של בית גנזיו של קרח וכולהו אקלידי וקילפי דגילדא א"ר חמא ברבי חנינא ג' מטמוניות הטמין יוסף במצרים אחת נתגלתה לקרח ואחת נתגלתה לאנטונינוס בן אסוירוס ואחת גנוזה לצדיקים לעתיד לבא וא"ר יוחנן קרח לא מן הבלועים ולא מן השרופין לא מן הבלועין דכתיב יח) ואת כל האדם אשר לקרח ולא קרח ולא מן השרופים דכתיב יט) באכול האש את חמשים ומאתים איש ולא קרח במתניתא תנא קרח מן השרופין ומן הבלועין מן הבלועים דכתיב יט) ותבלע אותם ואת קרח מן השרופין דכתיב כ) (ותצא אש מלפני ה') [ואש יצאה מאת ה'] ותאכל את חמשים ומאתים איש וקרח בהדייהו אמר רבא ח) מאי דכתיב כא) שמש ירח עמד זבולה לאור חציך יהלכו מלמד שעלו שמש וירח לזבול אמרו לפניו רבש"ע אם אתה עושה דין לבן עמרם נצא ואם לאו לא נצא עד שזרק בהם חצים אמר להן ט) בכבודי לא מחיתם בכבוד בשר ודם מחיתם והאידנא לא נפקי עד דמחו להו י) דרש רבא מאי דכתיב כב) ואם בריאה יברא ה' ופצתה האדמה את פיה אמר משה לפני הקב"ה אם בריאה גיהנם מוטב ואם לאו יברא ה' למאי אילימא למבריה ממש והא כג) אין כל חדש תחת השמש אלא לקרובי פיתחא כד) ובני קרח לא מתו תנא כ) משום רבינו אמרו מקום נתבצר להם בגיהנם וישבו עליו ואמרו שירה ל) אמר רבה בר בר חנה זימנא חדא הוה קאזלינא באורחא אמר לי ההוא טייעא תא ואחוי לך בלועי דקרח אזיל חזא תרי בזעי דהוה קא נפק קיטרא מנייהו שקל גבבא דעמרא אמשיי' מיא ואותביה בריש רומחיה ואחלפי' התם איחרך א"ל אצית מה שמעת ושמעית דהוו קאמרי הכי משה ותורתו אמת והן בדאים אמר

סתרה למזיה. שערה וישבה על פתח הבית כל מי שהיה בא לקרות רואה ראשה פרוע וחוזר: מעשר. ראשון דשקליתו אתון אמר הבו חד מי' לכהן: דגייז למזייכו. דכתיב (במדבר ח) והעבירו תער על [כל] בשרם ומשחק בכם כאילו אתם שוטים: כבופתא. רעי כמו בטולא דכופתא דאמרן לעיל (דף לח:) כגלל הזה אתם חשובים בעיניו: עינא יהב. עין נתן בשעריכם כדי שלא יהא בכם נוה כמותו: אמר לה. קרח איהו נמי משה עצמו גלח כל שערו: כיון דכולא רבותא דידיה הוא. אינו חושש אם גילח עצמו דקאמר לנפשיה תמות נפשי עם פלשתים אגוז שערי כמותם ומה לי בכך שהם מקיימין אפילו מה שאני מצוה לשחוק אגוז עכשיו כמותם כדי להפיס דעתם: ועוד דקאמר לכו. עשו פתיל תכלת בד' כנפות הבגד ואי ס"ד תכלת חשוב מפני מה לא יאמר לעשות כל הבגד כולו תכלת: אפיק גלימא דתכלתא. קח לך בגדים של תכלת וכסינהו לכולהו מתיבתך וכסה בהן בבה"מ אתה וחברותך: קנא לאשתו. אל (הסתר) [תסתרי] עם משה. קנוי היינו התראה: ונטה לו מחוץ למחנה. יצא מתוך למחנה שלא יחשדוהו עוד: מכאן שאין מחזיקין במחלוקת. שמחל על כבודו והוא עצמו הלך לבטל מחלוקת: חולק על רבו. חולק על ישיבתו: אשר הצו על משה ועל אהרן בעדת קרח בהצותם על ה'. מעלה עליהם הכתוב כאלו היו חולקים כלפי שכינה: מריבה. תגר וקטטה לפטפט נגדו בדברים: מתרעם. אומר על רבו שנוהג לו מדה כבושה ומדת אכזרית: מהרהר. מחפה עליו דברים: אקלידי. מפתחות: וקולפי. מנעולים: דגילדי. כולם המפתחות והמנעולים של עור היו ואעפ"כ היו שלש מאות פרדות טעונות ל"א דגלדא לצורך שקים והמרצופין וכיסין של עור היו: לא מן הבלועין ולא מן השרופין. אלא במגפה מת: ולא קרח. ר"נ היו לבד קרח דכתיב חמשים ומאתים מחתות ואתה ואהרן איש מחתתו: מן הבלועים ומן השרופין היה. שנשרפה נשמתו וגוף קיים ואח"כ נתגלגל עד מקום הבלועין ונבלע דכתיב בפרשת פנחס ותבלע אותם ואת קרח עמהם ורבי יוחנן דאמר לא מן הבלועין ולא מן השרופין דריש ליה להאי ואת קרח לאחריו ואת קרח במות העדה במגפה: וקרח בהדייהו. מדכתיב ותאכל את החמשים ומאתים איש מקריבי הקטרת וקרח ממקריבי הקטרת הוה דכתיב חמשים ומאתים מחתות ואתה ואהרן איש מחתתו א"כ ואת לרבות קרח עמהם: שמש ירח עמד זבולה. לעיל מיניה כתיב ותבקע ארץ בשעת בקיעת הארץ שנבלעו בקרקע שמש וירח עלו לאותו רקיע ששמו זבול ואמרו להקב"ה אם אי אתה עושה דין לבן עמרם מקרח ועדתו: לא נצא. ונאיר לעולם: בכבודי לא מחיתם. שהרי בכל יום מלכי מזרח ומערב בשעה שמניחין כתריהן בראשם משתחוים לחמה: והאידנא לא נפקי עד דמחו להו. שכך גזר עליהם המקום כן שמעתי ל"א והאידנא לא נפקי מאחר שראו שהקפיד הקב"ה על שלא מיחה לכבודו עד דמחו להו לא נפקי שחשו לכבוד המקום על בני אדם שמשתחוים לשמש וירח: אין כל חדש תחת השמש. ואי גיהנם לא אברי עד ההוא שעתא הוה ליה חדש: לקרובי פתחה. שיקרב פתחה של גיהנם ותפתח הארץ במקום שהן: נתבצר. מלשון (ישעיה כז) עיר בצורה התקין להון הקב"ה מקום גבוה שלא העמיקו כל כך בגיהנם ולא מתו: טייעא. סוחר ישמעאל: בלועי. מקום שנתבלעו לשם עדת קרח: בזעא. ראה נקב שממנו יצא עשן: גבבא. גיזה: אמשיה. שרה אות' במים לשון (ברכות דף יד:) משי ידיה: (וכל שלשים יום. חוזר לגיהנם ועולה לשם):

א) בקרא כתיב בידיה תהרסנו, ב) [מו"ק יח:], ג) [נ"ל יוסף], ד) [ברכות כז: ע"ש], ה) פסחים קיט. ע"ש, ו) [שם], ז) ג' מאות לאו דוקא וכן כל שלש מאות בש"ס רשב"ם פסחים קיט, ח) נדרים לט: ע"ש, ט) לעיל קג., י) [לעיל קג:], כ) מגילה יד., ל) ב"ב עד ע"א.

תורה אור השלם

א) וַיֹּאמֶר שִׁמְשׁוֹן תָּמוֹת נַפְשִׁי עִם פְּלִשְׁתִּים וַיֵּט בְּכֹחַ וַיִּפֹּל הַבַּיִת עַל הַסְּרָנִים וְעַל כָּל הָעָם אֲשֶׁר בּוֹ וַיִּהְיוּ הַמֵּתִים אֲשֶׁר הֵמִית בְּמוֹתוֹ רַבִּים מֵאֲשֶׁר הֵמִית בְּחַיָּיו: [שופטים טז, ל]

ב) חַכְמוֹת נָשִׁים בָּנְתָה בֵיתָהּ וְאִוֶּלֶת בְּיָדֶיהָ תֶהֶרְסֶנּוּ: [משלי יד, א]

ג) וַיָּקֻמוּ לִפְנֵי מֹשֶׁה וַאֲנָשִׁים מִבְּנֵי יִשְׂרָאֵל חֲמִשִּׁים וּמָאתָיִם נְשִׂיאֵי עֵדָה קְרִאֵי מוֹעֵד אַנְשֵׁי שֵׁם: [במדבר טז, ב]

ד) וַיִּשְׁמַע מֹשֶׁה וַיִּפֹּל עַל פָּנָיו: [במדבר טז, ד]

ה) וַיְקַנְאוּ לְמֹשֶׁה בַּמַּחֲנֶה לְאַהֲרֹן קְדוֹשׁ יְיָ: [תהלים קו, טז]

ו) וּמֹשֶׁה יִקַּח אֶת הָאֹהֶל וְנָטָה לוֹ מִחוּץ לַמַּחֲנֶה הַרְחֵק מִן הַמַּחֲנֶה וְקָרָא לוֹ אֹהֶל מוֹעֵד וְהָיָה כָּל מְבַקֵּשׁ יְיָ יֵצֵא אֶל אֹהֶל מוֹעֵד אֲשֶׁר מִחוּץ לַמַּחֲנֶה: [שמות לג, ז]

ז) וַיָּקָם מֹשֶׁה וַיֵּלֶךְ אֶל דָּתָן וַאֲבִירָם וַיֵּלְכוּ אַחֲרָיו זִקְנֵי יִשְׂרָאֵל: [במדבר טז, כה]

ח) זִכָּרוֹן לִבְנֵי יִשְׂרָאֵל לְמַעַן אֲשֶׁר לֹא יִקְרַב אִישׁ זָר אֲשֶׁר לֹא מִזֶּרַע אַהֲרֹן הוּא לְהַקְטִיר קְטֹרֶת לִפְנֵי יְיָ וְלֹא יִהְיֶה כְקֹרַח וְכַעֲדָתוֹ כַּאֲשֶׁר דִּבֶּר יְיָ בְּיַד מֹשֶׁה לוֹ: [במדבר יז, ה]

ט) וַיֹּאמֶר יְיָ לוֹ עוֹד הָבֵא נָא יָדְךָ בְּחֵיקֶךָ וַיָּבֵא יָדוֹ בְּחֵיקוֹ וַיּוֹצִאָהּ וְהִנֵּה יָדוֹ מְצֹרַעַת כַּשָּׁלֶג: [שמות ד, ו]

י) וַיִּזְבַּח אֲדֹנִיָּהוּ צֹאן וּבָקָר וּמְרִיא עִם אֶבֶן הַזֹּחֶלֶת אֲשֶׁר אֵצֶל עֵין רֹגֵל וַיִּקְרָא אֶת כָּל אֶחָיו בְּנֵי הַמֶּלֶךְ וּלְכָל אַנְשֵׁי יְהוּדָה עַבְדֵי הַמֶּלֶךְ: [מלכים א' א, ט]

יא) מְזֵי רָעָב וּלְחֻמֵי רֶשֶׁף וְקֶטֶב מְרִירִי וְשֶׁן בְּהֵמֹת אֲשַׁלַּח בָּם עִם חֲמַת זֹחֲלֵי עָפָר: [דברים לב, כד]

יב) וּבְנֵי אֱלִיאָב נְמוּאֵל וְדָתָן וַאֲבִירָם הוּא דָתָן וַאֲבִירָם קְרִיאֵי הָעֵדָה אֲשֶׁר הִצּוּ עַל מֹשֶׁה וְעַל אַהֲרֹן בַּעֲדַת קֹרַח בְּהַצֹּתָם עַל יְיָ: [במדבר כו, ט]

יג) הֵמָּה מֵי מְרִיבָה אֲשֶׁר רָבוּ בְנֵי יִשְׂרָאֵל אֶת יְיָ וַיִּקָּדֵשׁ בָּם: [במדבר כ, יג]

יד) וַיֹּאמֶר מֹשֶׁה בְּתֵת יְיָ לָכֶם בָּעֶרֶב בָּשָׂר לֶאֱכֹל וְלֶחֶם בַּבֹּקֶר לִשְׂבֹּעַ בִּשְׁמֹעַ יְיָ אֶת תְּלֻנֹּתֵיכֶם אֲשֶׁר אַתֶּם מַלִּינִם עָלָיו וְנַחְנוּ מָה לֹא עָלֵינוּ תְלֻנֹּתֵיכֶם כִּי עַל יְיָ: [שמות טז, ח] טו) וַיְדַבֵּר הָעָם בֵּאלֹהִים וּבְמֹשֶׁה לָמָה הֶעֱלִיתֻנוּ מִמִּצְרַיִם לָמוּת בַּמִּדְבָּר כִּי אֵין לֶחֶם וְאֵין מַיִם וְנַפְשֵׁנוּ קָצָה בַּלֶּחֶם הַקְּלֹקֵל: [במדבר כא, ה] טז) יֵשׁ רָעָה חוֹלָה רָאִיתִי תַּחַת הַשָּׁמֶשׁ עֹשֶׁר שָׁמוּר לִבְעָלָיו לְרָעָתוֹ: [קהלת ה, יב] יז) וַאֲשֶׁר עָשָׂה לְדָתָן וְלַאֲבִירָם בְּנֵי אֱלִיאָב בֶּן רְאוּבֵן אֲשֶׁר פָּצְתָה הָאָרֶץ אֶת פִּיהָ וַתִּבְלָעֵם וְאֶת בָּתֵּיהֶם וְאֶת אָהֳלֵיהֶם וְאֵת כָּל הַיְקוּם אֲשֶׁר בְּרַגְלֵיהֶם בְּקֶרֶב כָּל יִשְׂרָאֵל: [דברים יא, ו] יח) וַתִּפְתַּח הָאָרֶץ אֶת פִּיהָ וַתִּבְלַע אֹתָם וְאֶת בָּתֵּיהֶם וְאֵת כָּל הָאָדָם אֲשֶׁר לְקֹרַח וְאֵת כָּל הָרְכוּשׁ: [במדבר טז, לב] יט) וַתִּפְתַּח הָאָרֶץ אֶת פִּיהָ וַתִּבְלַע אֹתָם וְאֶת קֹרַח בְּמוֹת הָעֵדָה בַּאֲכֹל הָאֵשׁ אֵת חֲמִשִּׁים וּמָאתַיִם אִישׁ וַיִּהְיוּ לְנֵס: [במדבר כו, י] כ) וְאֵשׁ יָצְאָה מֵאֵת יְיָ וַתֹּאכַל אֵת הַחֲמִשִּׁים וּמָאתַיִם אִישׁ מַקְרִיבֵי הַקְּטֹרֶת: [במדבר טז, לה] כא) שֶׁמֶשׁ יָרֵחַ עָמַד זְבֻלָה לְאוֹר חִצֶּיךָ יְהַלֵּכוּ לְנֹגַהּ בְּרַק חֲנִיתֶךָ: [חבקוק ג, יא] כב) וְאִם בְּרִיאָה יִבְרָא יְיָ וּפָצְתָה הָאֲדָמָה אֶת פִּיהָ וּבָלְעָה אֹתָם וְאֶת כָּל אֲשֶׁר לָהֶם וְיָרְדוּ חַיִּים שְׁאֹלָה וִידַעְתֶּם כִּי נִאֲצוּ הָאֲנָשִׁים הָאֵלֶּה אֶת יְיָ: [במדבר טז, ל] כג) מַה שֶּׁהָיָה הוּא שֶׁיִּהְיֶה וּמַה שֶּׁנַּעֲשָׂה הוּא שֶׁיֵּעָשֶׂה וְאֵין כָּל חָדָשׁ תַּחַת הַשָּׁמֶשׁ: [קהלת א, ט] כד) וּבְנֵי קֹרַח לֹא מֵתוּ: [במדבר כו, יא]

לג א ב ג ד מיי' פ"ה מהל' ת"ת הל' א סמג עשין יב טוש"ע י"ד סי' רמב סעיף ב:

ליקוטי רש"י

אחר חוט אחד של תכלת פוטרה זו שכולה תכלת לא תפטור את עצמה [במדבר טז, א]. חכמות נשים בנתה ביתה. חכמות נקוד פתח שאינו שם דבר אלא החכמות שבנשים בונות את בתיהם שמתקיימות על ידיהן כמו אשתו של און בן פלת כמו שמפורש בפרק חלק. ואולת. ואשה שוטה. בידיה תהרסנו. תהרס ביתה זו אשתו של קרח [משלי יד, א]. קראי מועד. שהיו תלמידי חכמים כדכתיב (במדבר טז) נשיאי עדה קריאי מועד אנשי שם ועל שם שפיתם אותו רשע כשנהנו ממונו הקלו בעיניו להשיאם ולהחזיק ידו במחלוקת ולמרוד בהקדוש ברוך הוא [לעיל נב.]. ויקם משה. כסבור שישאו לו פנים ולא עשו [במדבר טז, כה]. ביד משה לו. כמו עליו על אהרן דבר אל משה שיהיה הוא ובניו כהנים לפיכך לא יקרב איש זר אשר לא מזרע אהרן וגו' וכן כל לי ולו ולהם הסמוכים אצל דבור פתרונם כמו על ומדרשו על קרח ומהו ביד משה ולא כתב אל משה רמז לחולקים על הכהונה שלוקין בצרעת כמו שלקה משה בידו שנאמר (שמות ד, ו) ויוציאה והנה ידו מצורעת כשלג ועל כן לקה עוזיה בצרעת [במדבר יז, ה]. חמת זוחלי עפר. ארס נחשים המהלכים על גחונם על העפר כמים הזוחלים על הארץ זחילה לשון מרוצת המים על העפר וכן כל מרוצת דבר המשפשף על העפר והולך [דברים לב, כד]. עושר שמור לבעליו לרעתו. כעשרו של קרח שעל ידי כן נתגאה וירד לשאול [קהלת ה, יב]. שמעמידו על רגליו. שמשמח לבו. וקילפי. פותחות שקורין בלעז שרדור"א. דגלדי. של מרצופים של עור שנושאים על סוסים וחמורים וגמלים [פסחים קיט.]. מלמד שעלו שמש וירח לזבול. שחמה ולבנה ברקיע השני כדאמרינן שבעה רקיעים הם וילון רקיע שחקים זבול מכון מעון ערבות ומונה להם כסדרן וילון אינו משמש כלום רקיע יש בו חמה ולבנה כוכבים ומזלות כו' [תהלים יט, ז]. שמש ירח עמד זבולה אם אתה עושה דין לבן עמרם ממחלקותו של קרח ומשמע להו דהאי קרא במחלקותו של קרח מדרים משום דביליאת מארים ובקריעת ים סוף משתעי בספר חבקוק וכתיב ביה מחצת ראש מבית רשע ומשמע להו דהיינו קרח וכתיב בתריה שמש ירח עמד זבולה [נדרים לט.]. אלא לקרובי פיתחא. וקריבה בעלמא ליתא בכלל אין כל חדש [נדרים לט:]. ובני קרח לא מתו. הם היו בעצה תחלה ובשעת המחלוקת הרהרו תשובה בלבם לפיכך נתבצר להם מקום גבוה בגיהנם וישבו שם [במדבר כו, יא]. נתבצר להם. לשון גבוה כמו ובצורות בשמים (דברים ט) [מגילה יד.].

א"ל כל תלתין יומין מהדרא להו גיהנם כבשר בתוך קלחת ואמרי הכי משה ותורתו אמת והן בדאים: דור המדבר אין להם חלק לעולם הבא וכו': ת"ר (א) דור המדבר אין להם חלק לעולם הבא שנאמר (א) במדבר הזה יתמו ושם ימותו יתמו בעולם הזה ושם ימותו בעולם הבא (ב) ואמר (ב) אשר נשבעתי באפי אם יבואון אל מנוחתי דברי ר"ע ר"א אומר (ג) הן באין) לעולם הבא שנאמר (ג) אספו לי חסידי כורתי בריתי עלי זבח אלא מה אני מקיים אשר נשבעתי באפי (ד) באפי נשבעתי וחוזרני בי רבי יהושע בן קרחה אומר לא נאמר פסוק זה אלא כנגד דורות הבאים אספו לי חסידי אלו צדיקים שבכל דור ודור כורתי בריתי [א] (ה) עלי זבח) אלו חנניה מישאל ועזריה שמסרו עצמן לתוך כבשן האש עלי זבח [אלו] ר"ע וחביריו שמסרו עצמן לשחיטה על דברי תורה ר"ש בן מנסיא אומר באים הן לעולם הבא שנא' (ד) ופדויי ה' ישובון ובאו ציון ברנה אמר רבה בר בר חנה א"ר יוחנן שבקה ר"ע לחסידותיה שנאמר (ה) הלוך וקראת באזני ירושלים לאמר זכרתי לך חסד נעוריך אהבת כלולותיך לכתך אחרי במדבר בארץ לא זרועה ומה אחרים באים בזכותם הם עצמן לא כל שכן: **מתני'** עשרת השבטים אינן עתידין לחזור שנא' (ו) וישליכם אל ארץ אחרת כיום הזה מה היום הולך ואינו חוזר אף הם הולכים ואינן חוזרים דברי ר"ע ר"א אומר כיום הזה מה יום מאפיל ומאיר אף עשרת השבטים שאפילה להן כך עתידה להאיר להם: **גמ'** ת"ר (ו) עשרת השבטים (ז) אין להם חלק לעוה"ב שנאמר (ו) ויתשם ה' מעל אדמתם באף ובחמה ובקצף גדול ויתשם ה' מעל אדמתם בעוה"ז וישליכם אל ארץ אחרת לעוה"ב דברי ר"ע ר"ש בן יהודה איש כפר עכו אומר משום ר"ש אם מעשיהם כיום הזה אינן חוזרין ואם לאו חוזרין רבי אומר באים הם לעוה"ב שנאמר (ז) ביום ההוא יתקע בשופר גדול וגו' אמר רבה בר בר חנה א"ר יוחנן שבקה ר"ע לחסידותיה שנא' (ח) הלוך וקראת את הדברים האלה צפונה ואמרת שובה משובה ישראל נאם ה' ולא אפיל פני בכם כי חסיד אני נאם ה' לא אטור לעולם מאי חסידותיה דתניא (ח) קטני בני רשעי ישראל אין באין לעוה"ב שנא' (ט) כי הנה היום בא בוער כתנור והיה כל זדים וכל עושי רשעה קש ולהט אותם היום הבא אמר ה' צבאות אשר לא יעזוב להם שורש וענף שורש בעוה"ז וענף לעוה"ב דברי רבן גמליאל ר"ע אומר באים הם לעוה"ב שנא' (י) שומר פתאים ה' שכן קורין בכרכי הים לינוקא פתיא ואומר (כ) גודו אילנא וחבלוהי ברם עיקר שרשוהי בארעא שבוקו ואלא מה אני מקיים לא יעזוב להם שורש וענף שלא יניח להם לא מצוה ולא שיורי מצוה ד"א שורש זו נשמה וענף זה הגוף אבל קטני בני רשעי עובדי כוכבים [א] ד"ה אין באין לעוה"ב [ב] ור"ג נפקא ליה (ל) מותאבד כל זכר למו אתמר קטן מאימתי בא לעוה"ב ר' חייא ור"ש בר ר' חד אמר משעה שנולד וחד אמר משעה שסיפר מ"ד משעה שנולד שנא' (מ) יבואו ויגידו צדקתו לעם נולד כי עשה ומ"ד משעה שסיפר דכתיב (ט) (נ) זרע יעבדנו יסופר לה' לדור אתמר רבינא אמר משעה שנזרע דכתיב זרע יעבדנו ר"נ בר יצחק אמר משעה שנימול דכתיב (ס) עני אני וגוע מנוער נשאתי אימיך אפונה תנא משום ר"מ משעה שיאמר אמן שנא' (ע) פתחו שערים ויבא גוי צדיק שומר אמונים (י) אל תקרי שומר אמונים אלא שאומר אמן אמן

מאי

א"ל. ההוא טייעא: כל תלתין יומין מהדר להו גיהנם. הכא: ואמרי הכי משה ותורתו אמת. שנשה כמה פעמים וראה שכל ל' יום עשן יוצא משם ושומע שאומרין משה ותורתו אמת וכו': באפי לא גרסי': שנאמר. לעיל מיניה קרא מ' שנה אקוט בדור דהיינו דור המדבר: כורתי בריתי עלי זבח. והיינו דור המדבר שכרתו ברית של מקום עלי זבחים ושלמים דכתיב (שמות כד) ויזבחו זבחים שלמים וכתיב (שם) ויזרוק על העם ויאמר הנה דם הברית אשר כרת ה' עמכם: נשבעתי וחוזרני בי. והיינו אשר נשבעתי באפי מפני כעסי נשבעתי ומתחרט אני: אלו חנניה מישאל ועזריה. שמסרו עצמן למיתה בשביל בריתו של מקום: ופדויי ה'. אלו דור המדבר שנפדו ממצרים: שבקיה ר"ע לחסידותיה. שרגיל לזכות את ישראל והשתא מחייב להו דאמר לעיל (דף קח.) דור המדבר אין להם חלק לעולם הבא ולקמן מפרש מאי חסידותיה: שנאמר הלוך וקראת. כלומר שהרי היה יכול לדרוש שיש להם חלק [לעולם הבא] דכתיב הלוך וקראת וגו': **מתני'** עשרת השבטים. שהגלה סנחריב שנאמר (מלכים ב יח) וינחם בחלח ובחבור נהר גוזן וערי מדי: אין עתידים לחזור. ממקום שגלו והא דאמרינן בגמ' (ה) דירמיה החזירן לא שהחזירן כולן אלא מקצתם החזיר: שנאמר וישליכם אל ארץ אחרת כיום הזה. שכך גזר להם הקב"ה שכיון שעוזבין את תורתו הוא מגלה אותן: כיום הזה מה היום מאפיל. בבקר אפל ובצהרים מאיר א"נ בערב אפל והולך ולמחרתו מאיר אף עשרת השבטים (אין) עתידין לחזור להיות להם חלק לעולם הבא לא בניהם ובני בניהם קאמר אלא אותן שגלו עצמן אין להם חלק שרשעים גמורין הם אבל בניהם ודורות הבאים זוכין ומזכין. מ"ר: וישליכם. משמע שיהו כולם גולין במקום אחד אל ארץ אחרת והיינו עשרת השבטים שהגלם סנחריב והושיבם במקום אחד כדאמרינן (לעיל דף צד.) שהוליכם למדינת אפריקי אבל ב' השבטים לא גלו למקום אחד אלא נתפזרו בכל הארצות ועליהם הוא אומר אשרקה להם ואקבצם (זכריה י): ה"ג מתני' עשרת השבטים אין עתידין לחזור: גמ' תנו רבנן עשרת השבטים אין להם חלק לעולם הבא שנאמר ויתשם ה' מעל אדמתם וגו'. ואית דמפרשי עשרת השבטים אין להם חלק לעולם הבא היינו לימות המשיח שלא יקבלם משיח עם שאר גליות לפי שספרו בגנות ארץ ישראל

כדאמרן לעיל (שם.) כי מטו שוט וכו' ובדבר הזה נענשו מרגלים: ר"ש אומר. מאי כהיום הזה לומר לך אם מעשיהם כהיום הזה לא יהא להם חלק לעוה"ב: ואם [לאו]. שיחזרו בתשובה יחזרו גם הם מגלות ויש להם חלק לעולם הבא: האובדים בארץ אשור. אלו י' השבטים והנדחים בארץ מצרים אלו דור המדבר וכן לשון התוספתא ולא שמעתי עוד: שובה משובה. שכל ישראל עתידין לחזור: קטני בני רשעי ישראל. רשעי ישראל עצמן פשיטא דאין להם חלק לעולם הבא כדאמרי' בפ' בתרא דכתובות (דף קיא:) רפאים בל יקומו מי שמרפה עצמו מדברי תורה אבל בנים שלהם קטנים ולא חטאו פליגי בהו: שורש וענף. אלו בנים קטנים שלהם: שורש בעולם הזה. שימותו נפלים: [ב] וענף לעולם הבא. שאף על פי שאבותיהם היו רשעים הם לא חטאו: עיקר שרשוהי בארעא שבוקו. אלו הבנים קטנים שאע"פ שאבות אין להם חלק תקנה יש להם: שלא יניח. להם הקב"ה: לא מצוה ולא שיורי מצוה. לא מצוה חמורה ולא מצוה קלה הכל יהא מעביר ומשלם שכרם לאלתר כדי לטרדן מן העולם: זו נשמה. שמעמדת הגוף כשרש שמעמיד האילן: אבל קטני בני רשעי עובדי כוכבים. דוקא קאמר רשעי דאילו חסידי עובדי כוכבים פליגי בה ואיכא למ"ד הן עצמן באין ואיכא למ"ד אינן באין כדאמרן (ד' קה.) ישובו רשעים לשאולה כל גוים שכחי אלהים מכאן שאין להם חלק אמר לו רבי יהושע וכי נאמר בכל גוים והלא לא נאמר אלא כל גוים שכחי אלהים הא אין שכחי אלהים יש להן חלק [לעוה"ב]: הכי גרסינן אבל קטני רשעי עובדי כוכבים דברי הכל אינן באין: מותאבד כל זכר למו נפקא ליה. כלומר לתנא דברייתא והאי דנפקא ליה דברי הכל היא דהא שורש וענף מיבעיא ליה למר כדאית ליה ומר כדאית ליה: זרע יעבדנו יסופר לה' לדור. זרע המסופר יעבדנו לה' לדור ודור שיחזור לו ויחיה: משעה שנזרע. משעה שנקלט הזרע במעי אשה אפילו הפילה אמו ונמחה יש לו חלק לעתיד דכתיב זרע יעבדנו והכי אמר בכתובות בפ' בתרא (דף קיא.) נבלתי יקומון לרבות נפלים: עני אני וגוע מנוער. אע"פ שאני עני גויעתי חשובה גויעה וראוי לומר עלי ויגוע ויאסף כלומר שזוכה אני לעתיד לבא כצדיקים שנאמר בהן גויעה ומאימתי משעה שאני נושא אימיך ופחדך אפונה מתגלגלת ושכונה עלי והיינו מילה שבבשרו שאנו משמרים מאימתו של הקב"ה: אפונה. לשון אופן:

מאי

תורה אור השלם

א) אֲנִי יְיָ דִּבַּרְתִּי אִם לֹא זֹאת אֶעֱשֶׂה לְכָל הָעֵדָה הָרָעָה הַזֹּאת הַנּוֹעָדִים עָלָי בַּמִּדְבָּר הַזֶּה יִתַּמּוּ וְשָׁם יָמֻתוּ: [במדבר יד, לה]

ב) אֲשֶׁר נִשְׁבַּעְתִּי בְאַפִּי אִם יְבֹאוּן אֶל מְנוּחָתִי: [תהלים צה, יא]

ג) אִסְפוּ לִי חֲסִידָי כֹּרְתֵי בְרִיתִי עֲלֵי זָבַח: [תהלים נ, ה]

ד) וּפְדוּיֵי יְיָ יְשֻׁבוּן וּבָאוּ צִיּוֹן בְּרִנָּה וְשִׂמְחַת עוֹלָם עַל רֹאשָׁם שָׂשׂוֹן וְשִׂמְחָה יַשִּׂיגוּ וְנָסוּ יָגוֹן וַאֲנָחָה: [ישעיה לה, י]

ה) הָלֹךְ וְקָרָאתָ בְאָזְנֵי יְרוּשָׁלַיִם לֵאמֹר כֹּה אָמַר יְיָ זָכַרְתִּי לָךְ חֶסֶד נְעוּרַיִךְ אַהֲבַת כְּלוּלֹתָיִךְ לֶכְתֵּךְ אַחֲרַי בַּמִּדְבָּר בְּאֶרֶץ לֹא זְרוּעָה: [ירמיה ב, ב]

ו) וַיִּתְּשֵׁם יְיָ מֵעַל אַדְמָתָם בְּאַף וּבְחֵמָה וּבְקֶצֶף גָּדוֹל וַיַּשְׁלִכֵם אֶל אֶרֶץ אַחֶרֶת כַּיּוֹם הַזֶּה: [דברים כט, כז]

ז) וְהָיָה בַּיּוֹם הַהוּא יִתָּקַע בְּשׁוֹפָר גָּדוֹל וּבָאוּ הָאֹבְדִים בְּאֶרֶץ אַשּׁוּר וְהַנִּדָּחִים בְּאֶרֶץ מִצְרָיִם וְהִשְׁתַּחֲווּ לַייָ בְּהַר הַקֹּדֶשׁ בִּירוּשָׁלָיִם: [ישעיה כז, יג]

ח) הָלֹךְ וְקָרָאתָ אֶת הַדְּבָרִים הָאֵלֶּה צָפוֹנָה וְאָמַרְתָּ שׁוּבָה מְשֻׁבָה יִשְׂרָאֵל נְאֻם יְיָ לוֹא אַפִּיל פָּנַי בָּכֶם כִּי חָסִיד אֲנִי נְאֻם יְיָ לֹא אֶטּוֹר לְעוֹלָם: [ירמיה ג, יב]

ט) כִּי הִנֵּה הַיּוֹם בָּא בֹּעֵר כַּתַּנּוּר וְהָיוּ כָל זֵדִים וְכָל עֹשֵׂה רִשְׁעָה קַשׁ וְלִהַט אֹתָם הַיּוֹם הַבָּא אָמַר יְיָ צְבָאוֹת אֲשֶׁר לֹא יַעֲזֹב לָהֶם שֹׁרֶשׁ וְעָנָף: [מלאכי ג, יט]

י) שֹׁמֵר פְּתָאִים יְיָ דַּלּוֹתִי וְלִי יְהוֹשִׁיעַ: [תהלים קטז, ו]

כ) וַדִי חֲזָה מַלְכָּא עִיר וְקַדִּישׁ נָחִת מִן שְׁמַיָּא וְאָמַר גֹּדּוּ אִילָנָא וְחַבְּלוּהִי בְּרַם עִקַּר שָׁרְשׁוֹהִי בְּאַרְעָא שְׁבֻקוּ וּבֶאֱסוּר דִּי פַרְזֶל וּנְחָשׁ בְּדִתְאָא דִּי בָרָא וּבְטַל שְׁמַיָּא יִצְטַבַּע וְעִם חֵיוַת בָּרָא חֲלָקֵהּ עַד דִּי שִׁבְעָה עִדָּנִין יַחְלְפוּן עֲלוֹהִי: [דניאל ד, כ]

ל) מֵתִים בַּל יִחְיוּ רְפָאִים בַּל יָקֻמוּ לָכֵן פָּקַדְתָּ וַתַּשְׁמִידֵם וַתְּאַבֵּד כָּל זֵכֶר לָמוֹ: [ישעיה כו, יד]

מ) יָבֹאוּ וְיַגִּידוּ צִדְקָתוֹ לְעַם נוֹלָד כִּי עָשָׂה: [תהלים כב, לב]

נ) זֶרַע יַעַבְדֶנּוּ יְסֻפַּר לַאדֹנָי לַדּוֹר: [תהלים כב, לא]

ס) עָנִי אֲנִי וְגֹוֵעַ מִנֹּעַר נָשָׂאתִי אֵמֶיךָ אָפוּנָה: [תהלים פח, טז]

ע) פִּתְחוּ שְׁעָרִים וְיָבֹא גוֹי צַדִּיק שֹׁמֵר אֱמֻנִים: [ישעיה כו, ב]

מסורת הש"ס

א) [תוספ' פי"ג], ב) [צ"ל ואומר], ג) [צ"ל באין הן], ד) [חגיגה יד:], ה) [בעין יעקב ליתא], ו) תוספתא פי"ג, ז) כ"א אינם עתידין לחזור, ח) [תוספתא שם], ט) [עי' סוטה כ.], י) [שבת קיט:], כ) [מגילה יד: ערכין לג.].

הגהות הגר"א

[א] גמ' עלי זבח. נמחקו ב' תיבות הללו: [ב] שם ור"ג. נמחק (וערש"י):

גליון הש"ס

גמ' ר"א אומר הרי הן באין לעוה"ב. עיין ב"ב דף ע"ג ע"ב תוס' ד"ה ודמו:

הגהות מהר"ב רנשבורג

א] גמ' דברי הכל אין באין לעוה"ב ור"ג. מלות ור"ג נמחק וכ"ב בספרים שלפני רש"י לא היה כתוב זה דוק ותשכח: ב] רש"י ד"ה וענף לעוה"ב. מלת וענף נמחק:

ליקוטי רש"י

אספו לי חסידי. ועוד יקרא לשמי' ולארץ שיאספו לו הגליות כענין שנאמר עורי צפון ובאי תימן (שה"ש ד'). כרתי בריתי עלי זבח. שקבלו את התורה בברית וזבח כענין שנאמר הנה דם הברית אשר כרת ה' וגומר (שמות כ"ד) [שם נ, ה]. נשבעתי באפי. מדקאמר באפי משמע יכול אני לישאל עליו לפי שמחמת אפי ולא מדעת מיושבת נשבעתי יש ללמוד מכאן שהמולא פתח לנדרו לאמר לא לדעת כן נדרתי שיקרני דבר זה שאני רואה הבא לי על ידי נדרי מתירין לו [חגיגה י.]. זכרתי לך. אם הייתם שבים אלי תאוותי לרחם עליכם כי זכרת חסד נעוריך ואהבת כלילת חופתך שהכללתיך לחופה ול' הכנסה הוא כלולותיך נוצי"ש בלעז ומה הוא חסד נעוריך לכתך אחר שלוחי משה ואהרן מארץ נושבת יצאתם למדבר ואין צדה לדרך כי האמנתם בי [ירמיהו ב, ב]. וגם צדה לא עשו להם לדרך. מגיד שבחן של ישראל שלא אמרו היאך נצא למדבר בלא צדה אלא האמינו והלכו הוא שמפורש בקבלה (ירמיהו ב, ב) זכרתי לך חסד נעוריך אהבת כלולותיך לכתך אחרי במדבר בארץ לא זרועה ומה שכר מפורש אחריו (שם ג) קודש ישראל לה' וגו' [שמות יב, לט]. בשופר גדול וגו'. ובאו האובדים בארץ מלמד שלא יהו אבודים בין העובדי כוכבים [מכות כד.].

אָמַר לֵיהּ – **[The Arab] said to [Rabbah bar bar Chanah]:** כָּל תְּלָתִין יוֹמִין – **Every thirty days** מְהַדְרָא לְהוּ גֵּיהִנֹּם – **Gehinnom returns them** here,[1] כְּבָשָׂר בְּתוֹךְ קַלַּחַת – as if they were being stirred **like meat in a pot,**[2] וְאָמְרֵי הָכִי – **and they say thus:** מֹשֶׁה וְתוֹרָתוֹ אֱמֶת וְהֵן בַּדָּאִים – **"Moses and his Torah are true and they**[3] **are liars!"**

After concluding its discussion of Korach, the Gemara turns to yet another group listed in our Mishnah as having no share in the World to Come – the Generation of the Wilderness:

דּוֹר הַמִּדְבָּר אֵין לָהֶם חֵלֶק לָעוֹלָם הַבָּא וכו׳ – Our Mishnah stated: THE GENERATION OF THE WILDERNESS HAS NO SHARE IN THE WORLD TO COME, **etc.**[4]

The Gemara cites a Baraisa that elaborates on this matter:

תָּנוּ רַבָּנַן – **The Rabbis taught in a Baraisa:** דּוֹר הַמִּדְבָּר אֵין לָהֶם חֵלֶק לָעוֹלָם הַבָּא – THE GENERATION OF THE WILDERNESS HAS NO SHARE IN THE WORLD TO COME, שֶׁנֶּאֱמַר ,,בַּמִּדְבָּר הַזֶּה יִתַּמּוּ וְשָׁם יָמֻתוּ" – AS IT IS STATED: *IN THIS WILDERNESS THEY WILL CEASE TO BE, AND THERE THEY WILL DIE.*[5] ,,יִתַּמּוּ" בָּעוֹלָם הַזֶּה, ,,וְשָׁם יָמֻתוּ" בָּעוֹלָם הַבָּא – *THEY WILL CEASE TO BE* means: IN THIS WORLD; *AND THERE THEY WILL DIE* means: IN THE WORLD TO COME. (ואמר) [וְאוֹמֵר] ,,אֲשֶׁר־נִשְׁבַּעְתִּי בְאַפִּי אִם־יְבֹאוּן אֶל־מְנוּחָתִי" – MOREOVER, IT STATES: *THEREFORE I HAVE SWORN IN MY WRATH THAT THEY SHALL NOT COME TO MY RESTING PLACE.*[6] דִּבְרֵי רַבִּי עֲקִיבָא – THESE ARE THE WORDS OF R' AKIVA. רַבִּי אֱלִיעֶזֶר אוֹמֵר – R' ELIEZER SAYS: (הן באין) [בָּאִין הֵן] לָעוֹלָם הַבָּא – THEY DO COME TO THE WORLD TO COME, שֶׁנֶּאֱמַר ,,אִסְפוּ־לִי חֲסִידָי כֹּרְתֵי בְרִיתִי עֲלֵי־זָבַח" – AS IT IS STATED: *GATHER UNTO ME MY DEVOUT ONES, WHO SEAL MY COVENANT THROUGH SACRIFICE.*[7] אֶלָּא מָה אֲנִי מְקַיֵּים ,,אֲשֶׁר־נִשְׁבַּעְתִּי בְאַפִּי" – THEN HOW DO I JUSTIFY the verse: *THEREFORE I HAVE SWORN IN MY WRATH,* which implies – as R' Akiva argues – that the Generation of the Wilderness has no share in the World to Come? בְּאַפִּי נִשְׁבַּעְתִּי וְחוֹזַרְנִי בִּי – The verse means: *IN MY WRATH* HAVE I SWORN, BUT I RETRACT.[8] רַבִּי יְהוֹשֻׁעַ בֶּן קָרְחָה אוֹמֵר – R' YEHOSHUA BEN KORCHAH SAYS: לֹא נֶאֱמַר פָּסוּק זֶה אֶלָּא כְּנֶגֶד דּוֹרוֹת הַבָּאִים – THIS VERSE cited by R' Eliezer WAS NOT STATED in reference to the Generation of the Wilderness BUT rather IN REFERENCE TO COMING GENERATIONS, i.e. generations that came after the Generation of the Wilderness. R' Yehoshua ben Korchah explains: ,,אִסְפוּ־לִי חֲסִידָי" אֵלּוּ צַדִּיקִים שֶׁבְּכָל דּוֹר וָדוֹר – *GATHER UNTO ME MY DEVOUT ONES* – THESE ARE THE RIGHTEOUS ONES WHO ARE FOUND IN EVERY GENERATION. ,,כֹּרְתֵי בְרִיתִי (עלי זבח)" אֵלּוּ חֲנַנְיָה מִישָׁאֵל וַעֲזַרְיָה – *WHO SEAL MY COVENANT* – THESE ARE CHANANYAH, MISHAEL, AND AZARYAH, שֶׁמָּסְרוּ עַצְמָן לְתוֹךְ כֶּבֶשׁ הָאֵשׁ – WHO GAVE THEMSELVES UP to be cast INTO THE FIERY FURNACE.[9] ,,עֲלֵי־זָבַח" [אֵלּוּ] רַבִּי עֲקִיבָא וַחֲבֵירָיו – *THROUGH SACRIFICE* – THESE ARE R' AKIVA AND HIS COLLEAGUES, שֶׁמָּסְרוּ עַצְמָן לִשְׁחִיטָה עַל דִּבְרֵי תוֹרָה – WHO GAVE THEMSELVES UP TO BE SLAUGHTERED FOR the sake of THE WORDS OF THE TORAH.[10] רַבִּי שִׁמְעוֹן בֶּן מְנַסְיָא אוֹמֵר – R' SHIMON BEN MENASYA SAYS: בָּאִים הֵן לָעוֹלָם הַבָּא – THEY [the Generation of the Wilderness] WILL COME TO THE WORLD TO COME, שֶׁנֶּאֱמַר ,,וּפְדוּיֵי ה׳ יְשֻׁבוּן וּבָאוּ צִיּוֹן בְּרִנָּה" – AS IT IS STATED: *AND THOSE REDEEMED BY HASHEM WILL RETURN; AND THEY WILL COME TO ZION WITH GLAD SONG.*[11]

NOTES

1. Each Rosh Chodesh (*Rashbam* to *Bava Basra* 74a) they are judged in Gehinnom (*Ritva* ibid.).

The Arab knew from having studied the site that every thirty days smoke rose from those cracks and voices below could be heard saying, "Moses and his Torah are true etc." (*Rashi*).

2. As one stirs meat in a pot so that it will be well cooked (*Rashbam* loc. cit.).

3. A euphemism for "we."

According to *Mizrachi* (*Numbers* 26:11), this entire narrative would seem to deal with those of Korach's assembly who did not repent before dying. It is they who are judged every thirty days in Gehinnom. However, Korach's *sons,* who repented and did not die, but were protected on a ledge above Gehinnom when their comrades were swallowed up (as related above), later left their underground fortress and rejoined the ranks of the living. In fact, the Midrash states that they entered Eretz Yisrael and became prophets. But *Mizrachi* cites comments of *Rashi* that conflict with this interpretation. These comments do not appear in our editions (see end of note), but *Mizrachi's* version of *Rashi* to 110a ד״ה נתבצר concluded: וְלֹא מֵתוּ אֶלָּא כָּל שְׁלֹשִׁים יוֹם חוֹזְרִין לְגֵיהִנֹּם וְנִדּוֹנִין דְּהָכִי אָמְרִינַן לְקַמָּן, *and they did not die, but every thirty days they return to Gehinnom and are judged, as taught further [in the Gemara].* Accordingly, it is the sons of Korach who are judged every thirty days in Gehinnom. (See also *Maharsha* to *Bava Basra* 74a; *Maharsha* there, however, writes that the proclamation "Moses and his Torah are true . . ." is made by "the Dasan-and-Abiram group.") Our editions of *Rashi,* which do not contain those concluding comments, follow *Maharshal,* who notes that they do not appear in the *Rashi* commentary printed in the first edition of *Ein Yaakov.*

4. [The Gemara's treatment of the "Generation of the Wilderness" after "the Congregation of Korach" indicates that the Generation of the Wilderness was listed last in the Mishnah, as emended by *Hagahos HaGra* in the Mishnah (108a).]

5. *Numbers* 14:35. [This was said about the Generation of the Wilderness after they sinned in the episode of the Spies.] The verse seems to contain a redundancy: *they will cease* and *they will die.*

6. *Psalms* 95:11. This passage refers to the Generation of the Wilderness, as stated in the previous verse: *Forty years did I [God] contend with the generation* (*Rashi*). See *Maharsha* and *Rif* in *Ein Yaakov* for explanations of why *My resting place* is expounded as a reference to the World to Come.

7. Ibid. 50:5. [The word זָבַח used here generally refers to a *shelamim* offering; thus, the verse speaks of "a covenant sealed by a *shelamim* offering." Accordingly] R' Eliezer interprets this verse as a reference to the Generation of the Wilderness, who entered into a covenant with God through the offering of *shelamim* sacrifices, as related in *Exodus* 24:5-8, where it states: . . . *and they sacrificed shelamim offerings* (וַיִּזְבְּחוּ זְבָחִים שְׁלָמִים) . . . *And Moses took the blood and threw [it] upon the people, and said: "Behold the blood of the covenant which HASHEM has sealed with you . . .* (*Rashi*).

8. The verse's emphasis on *in My wrath* indicates that the oath was made in a "fit of wrath" (so to speak), but God has since "regretted" (so to speak) his wrathful oath (see *Rashi*). [The Gemara in *Chagigah* (10a) derives from this verse that making an oath with a certain mindset, and then regretting it, is grounds for its annulment.]

While R' Eliezer thus accounts for the verse in *Psalms* 95:11, he does not explain R' Akiva's other proof text – *Numbers* 14:35. See *Rif* in *Ein Yaakov* and *Anaf Yosef* for how R' Eliezer will explain this verse in *Numbers.* See also *Avos DeRabbi Nassan* 36:3, for a related Tannaic discussion.

9. Chananyah, Mishael, and Azaryah chose to be cast into a fiery kiln rather than bow to the idol erected by Nebuchadnezzar. A miracle occurred and they emerged from the kiln unharmed (see *Daniel* ch. 3; see above, 92b-93b).

They are alluded to by the words *who seal My covenant,* since they were willing to sacrifice their lives to uphold the covenant of God (*Rashi;* see also *Maharsha*). [*Ben Yehoyada* suggests that the word בְּרִיתִי, *My covenant,* is being expounded as בְּרִית י׳, *the covenant of ten,* i.e. the Ten Commandments, which open with the command forbidding idolatry.]

10. R' Akiva refused to obey the Roman decree outlawing the teaching of Torah. Knowing full well the consequences, R' Akiva continued to teach Torah until he was arrested and executed (*Berachos* 61b). A number of other sages likewise followed R' Akiva's example, such as R' Chanina ben Teradyon, who disregarded the Roman decree and convened public assemblies where he taught Torah. For this "crime" he was burned at the stake (*Avodah Zarah* 18a). Collectively, these sages who sacrificed their lives in order to teach Torah are known as the עֲשָׂרָה הֲרוּגֵי מַלְכוּת, *The ten [sages] martyred by the [Roman] government.*

These sages upheld God's covenant עֲלֵי־זָבַח, literally: *through slaughter,* i.e. even at the expense of being slaughtered by the Romans.

11. *Isaiah* 35:10. *Those redeemed by HASHEM* refers to the Generation of the Wilderness, who were redeemed by God from Egypt (*Rashi*). [And

א"ל כל תלתין יומין מהדרא להו גיהנם כבשר בתוך קלחת ואמרי הכי משה ותורתו אמת והן בדאים: דור המדבר אין להם חלק לעולם הבא וכו': ת"ר (א) דור המדבר אין להם חלק לעולם הבא שנאמר (א) במדבר הזה יתמו ושם ימותו יתמו בעולם הזה ושם ימותו בעולם הבא (ב) ואמר (ב) אשר נשבעתי באפי אם יבואון אל מנוחתי דברי ר"ע (ה) ר"א אומר (ג) הן באין) לעולם הבא שנאמר (ג) אספו לי חסידי כורתי בריתי עלי זבח אלא מה אני מקיים אשר נשבעתי באפי (ד) באפי נשבעתי וחוזרני בי רבי יהושע בן קרחה אומר לא נאמר פסוק זה אלא כנגד דורות הבאים אספו לי חסידי אלו צדיקים שבכל דור ודור כורתי בריתי [א] (ה) עלי זבח) אלו חנניה מישאל ועזריה שמסרו עצמן לתוך כבשן האש עלי זבח [אלו] ר"ע וחביריו שמסרו עצמן לשחיטה על דברי תורה ר"ש בן מנסיא אומר באים הן לעולם הבא שנא' (ד) ופדויי ה' ישובון ובאו ציון ברנה אמר רבה בר בר חנה א"ר יוחנן שבקה ר"ע לחסידותיה שנאמר (ה) הלוך וקראת באזני ירושלים לאמר זכרתי לך חסד נעוריך אהבת כלולותיך לכתך אחרי במדבר בארץ לא זרועה ומה אחרים באים בזכותם הם עצמן לא כל שכן: **מתני'** עשרת השבטים אינן עתידין לחזור שנא' (ו) וישליכם אל ארץ אחרת כיום הזה מה היום הולך ואינו חוזר אף הם הולכים ואינן חוזרים דברי ר"ע ר"א אומר כיום הזה מה יום מאפיל ומאיר אף עשרת השבטים שאפילה להן כך עתידה להאיר להם: **גמ'** ת"ר (ו) עשרת השבטים (ז) אין להם חלק לעוה"ב שנאמר (ו) ויתשם ה' מעל אדמתם באף ובחמה ובקצף גדול ויתשם ה' מעל אדמתם בעוה"ז וישליכם אל ארץ אחרת לעוה"ב דברי ר"ע ר"ש בן יהודה איש כפר עכו אומר משום ר"ש אם מעשיהם כיום הזה אינן חוזרין ואם לאו חוזרין רבי אומר באים הם לעוה"ב שנאמר (ז) ביום ההוא יתקע בשופר גדול וגו' אמר רבה בר בר חנה א"ר יוחנן שבקה ר"ע לחסידותיה שנא' (ח) הלוך וקראת את הדברים האלה צפונה ואמרת שובה משובה ישראל נאם ה' ולא אפיל פני בכם כי חסיד אני נאם ה' לא אטור לעולם מאי חסידותיה דתניא (ח) קטני בני רשעי ישראל אין באין לעוה"ב שנא' (ט) כי הנה היום בא בוער כתנור והיה כל זדים וכל עושי רשעה קש ולהט אותם היום הבא אמר ה' צבאות אשר לא יעזוב להם שורש וענף שורש בעוה"ז וענף לעוה"ב דברי רבן גמליאל ר"ע אומר באים הם לעוה"ב שנא' (י) שומר פתאים ה' שכן קורין בכרכי הים לינוקא פתיא ואומר (כ) גודו אילנא וחבלוהי ברם עיקר שרשוהי בארעא שבוקו ואלא מה אני מקיים לא יעזוב להם שורש וענף שלא יניח להם לא מצוה ולא שיורי מצוה ד"א שורש זו נשמה וענף זה הגוף אבל קטני בני רשעי עובדי כוכבים [א] ד"ה אין באין לעוה"ב [ב] ור"ג נפקא ליה (ל) מותאבד כל זכר למו אתמר קטן מאימתי בא לעוה"ב ר' חייא ור"ש בר ר' חד אמר משעה שנולד וחד אמר משעה שסיפר מ"ד משעה שנולד שנא' (מ) יבואו ויגידו צדקתו לעם נולד כי עשה ומ"ד משעה שסיפר דכתיב (ט) (נ) זרע יעבדנו יסופר לה' לדור אתמר רבינא אמר משעה שנזרע דכתיב זרע יעבדנו ר"נ בר יצחק אמר משעה שנימול דכתיב (ס) עני אני וגוע מנוער נשאתי אימיך אפונה תנא משום ר"מ משעה שיאמר אמן שנא' (ע) פתחו שערים ויבא גוי צדיק שומר אמונים (י) אל תקרי שומר אמונים אלא שאומר אמן מאי

רש"י

א"ל. ההוא טייעא: כל תלתין יומין מהדר להו גיהנם. הכא: ואמרי הכי משה ותורתו אמת. שנכה כמה פעמים ורלה שכל ל' יום עשן יולא משם ושומע שאומרין משה ותורתו אמת וכו': באפי לא גרסי': שנאמר. לעיל מיניה קרא מ' שנה אקוט בדור דהיינו דור המדבר: כורתי בריתי עלי זבח. והיינו דור המדבר שכרתו ברית של מקום עלי זבחים ושלמים דכתיב (שמות כד) ויזבחו זבחים שלמים וכתיב (שם) ויזרוק על העם ויאמר הנה דם הברית אשר כרת ה' עמכם: נשבעתי וחוזרני בי. והיינו אשר נשבעתי באפי מפני כעסי נשבעתי ומתחרט אני: אלו חנניה מישאל ועזריה. שמסרו עלמן למיתה בשביל בריתו של מקום: ופדויי ה'. אלו דור המדבר שנפדו ממצרים: שבקיה ר"ע לחסידותיה. שרגיל לזכות את ישראל והשתא מחייב להו דאמר לעיל (דף קח.) דור המדבר אין להם חלק לעולם הבא ולקמן מפרש מאי חסידותיה: שנאמר הלוך וקראת. כלומר שהרי היה יכול לדרוש שיש להם חלק [לעולם הבא] דכתיב הלוך וקראת וגו': **מתני'** עשרת השבטים. שהגלה סנחריב שנאמר (מלכים ב יח) וינחם בחלח ובחבור נהר גוזן וערי מדי: אין עתידים לחזור. ממקום שגלו והא דאמרינן בגמ' (ט) דירמיה החזירן לא שהחזירן כולן אלא מקצתם החזיר: שנאמר וישליכם אל ארץ אחרת כיום הזה. שכך גזר להם הקב"ה שכיון שעוזבין את תורתו הוא מגלה אותן: כיום הזה מה היום מאפיל. בבקר אפל ובצהרים מאיר א"נ בערב אפל והולך ולמחרתו מאיר אף עשרת השבטים (אין) עתידין לחזור להיות להם חלק לעולם הבא לא בבניהם ובני בניהם קאמר אלא אותן שגלו עצמן אין להם חלק שרשעים גמורין הם אבל בניהם ודורות הבאים זוכין ומזכין. מ"ר: וישליכם. משמע שיהו כולם גולין במקום אחד אל ארץ אחרת והיינו עשרת השבטים שהגלם סנחריב והושיבם במקום אחד כדאמרינן (לעיל דף לד.) שהוליכם למדינת אפריקי אבל ב' השבטים לא גלו למקום אחד אלא נתפזרו בכל הארצות ועליהם הוא אומר אשרקה להם ואקבצם (זכריה י): ה"ג מתני' עשרת השבטים אין עתידין לחזור: **גמ'** תנו רבנן עשרת השבטים אין להם חלק לעולם הבא שנאמר ויתשם ה' מעל אדמתם וגו'. ואית דמפרשי עשרת השבטים אין להם חלק לעולם הבא היינו לימות המשיח שלא יקבלם משיח עם שאר גליות לפי שספרו בגנות ארץ ישראל כדאמרן לעיל (שם.) כי מטו שום וכו' ובדבר הזה נענשו מרגלים: ר"ש אומר. מאי כהיום הזה לומר לך אם מעשיהם כהיום הזה לא יהא להם חלק לעוה"ב: ואם [לאו]. שיחזרו בתשובה יחזרו גם הם מגלות ויש להם חלק לעולם הבא: האובדים בארץ אשור. אלו י' השבטים והנדחים בארץ מצרים אלו דור המדבר וכן לשון התוספתא ולא שמעתי עוד: שובה משובה. שכל ישראל עתידין לחזור: קטני בני רשעי ישראל. רשעי ישראל עצמן פשיטא דאין להם חלק לעולם הבא כדאמרי' בפ' בתרא דכתובות (דף קיא:) רפאים בל יקומו מי שמרפה עצמו מדברי תורה אבל בנים שלהם קטנים ולא חטאו פליגי בהו: שורש וענף. אלו בנים קטנים שלהם: שורש בעולם הזה. שימותו נפלים: [ב] וענף לעולם הבא. שאף על פי שאבותיהם היו רשעים הם לא חטאו: עיקר שרשוהי בארעא שבוקו. אלו הבנים קטנים שאע"פ שאבות אין להם חלק תקנה יש להם: שלא יניח. להם הקב"ה: לא מצוה ולא שיורי מצוה. לא מצוה חמורה ולא מצוה קלה הכל יהא מעביר ומשלם שכרם לאלתר כדי לטרדן מן העולם: זו נשמה. שמעמדת הגוף כשרש שמעמיד האילן: אבל קטני בני רשעי עובדי כוכבים. דוקא קאמר רשעי דאילו חסידי עובדי כוכבים פליגי בה ואיכא למ"ד הן עצמן באין ואיכא למ"ד אינן באין כדאמרן (ד' קה.) ישובו רשעים לשאולה כל גוים שכחי אלהים מכאן שאין להם חלק אמר לו רבי יהושע וכי נאמר בכל גוים והלא לא נאמר אלא כל גוים שכחי אלהים הא אין שכחי אלהים יש להן חלק [לעוה"ב]: הכי גרסינן אבל קטני רשעי עובדי כוכבים דברי הכל אינן באין: מותאבד כל זכר למו נפקא ליה. כלומר לתנא דברייתא והאי דנפקא ליה דברי הכל היא דהא שורש וענף מיבעיא ליה למר כדאית ליה ומר כדאית ליה: זרע יעבדנו יסופר לה' לדור. זרע המסופר יעבדנו לה' לדור ודור שיחזור לו ויחיה: משעה שנזרע. משעה שנקלט הזרע במעי אשה אפילו הפילה אמו ונמחה יש לו חלק לעתיד דכתיב זרע יעבדנו והכי אמר בכתובות בפ' בתרא (דף קיא.) נבלתי יקומון לרבות נפלים: עני אני וגוע מנוער. אע"פ שאני עני גויעתי חשובה גויעה וראוי לומר עלי ויגוע ויאסף כלומר שזוכה אני לעתיד לבא כלדיקים שנאמר בהן גויעה ואמיתי משעה שאני נושא אמיך ופחדך אפונה מתגלגלת ושכונה עלי והיינו מילה שבבשרו שאנו משמרים מאימתו של הקב"ה: אפונה. לשון אופן: מאי

תורה אור השלם

א) אֲנִי יְיָ דִּבַּרְתִּי אִם לֹא זֹאת אֶעֱשֶׂה לְכָל הָעֵדָה הָרָעָה הַזֹּאת הַנּוֹעָדִים עָלָי בַּמִּדְבָּר הַזֶּה יִתַּמּוּ וְשָׁם יָמֻתוּ: [במדבר יד, לה]

ב) אֲשֶׁר נִשְׁבַּעְתִּי בְאַפִּי אִם יְבֹאוּן אֶל מְנוּחָתִי: [תהלים צה, יא]

ג) אִסְפוּ לִי חֲסִידָי כֹּרְתֵי בְרִיתִי עֲלֵי זָבַח: [תהלים נ, ה]

ד) וּפְדוּיֵי יְיָ יְשֻׁבוּן וּבָאוּ צִיּוֹן בְּרִנָּה וְשִׂמְחַת עוֹלָם עַל רֹאשָׁם שָׂשׂוֹן וְשִׂמְחָה יַשִּׂיגוּ וְנָסוּ יָגוֹן וַאֲנָחָה: [ישעיה לה, י]

ה) הָלֹךְ וְקָרָאתָ בְאָזְנֵי יְרוּשָׁלַיִם לֵאמֹר כֹּה אָמַר יְיָ זָכַרְתִּי לָךְ חֶסֶד נְעוּרַיִךְ אַהֲבַת כְּלוּלֹתָיִךְ לֶכְתֵּךְ אַחֲרַי בַּמִּדְבָּר בְּאֶרֶץ לֹא זְרוּעָה: [ירמיה ב, ב]

ו) וַיִּתְּשֵׁם יְיָ מֵעַל אַדְמָתָם בְּאַף וּבְחֵמָה וּבְקֶצֶף גָּדוֹל וַיַּשְׁלִכֵם אֶל אֶרֶץ אַחֶרֶת כַּיּוֹם הַזֶּה: [דברים כט, כז]

ז) וְהָיָה בַּיּוֹם הַהוּא יִתָּקַע בְּשׁוֹפָר גָּדוֹל וּבָאוּ הָאֹבְדִים בְּאֶרֶץ אַשּׁוּר וְהַנִּדָּחִים בְּאֶרֶץ מִצְרָיִם וְהִשְׁתַּחֲווּ לַייָ בְּהַר הַקֹּדֶשׁ בִּירוּשָׁלָיִם: [ישעיה כז, יג]

ח) הָלֹךְ וְקָרָאתָ אֶת הַדְּבָרִים הָאֵלֶּה צָפוֹנָה וְאָמַרְתָּ שׁוּבָה מְשֻׁבָה יִשְׂרָאֵל נְאֻם יְיָ לוֹא אַפִּיל פָּנַי בָּכֶם כִּי חָסִיד אֲנִי נְאֻם יְיָ לֹא אֶטּוֹר לְעוֹלָם: [ירמיה ג, יב]

ט) כִּי הִנֵּה הַיּוֹם בָּא בֹּעֵר כַּתַּנּוּר וְהָיוּ כָל זֵדִים וְכָל עֹשֵׂה רִשְׁעָה קַשׁ וְלִהַט אֹתָם הַיּוֹם הַבָּא אָמַר יְיָ צְבָאוֹת אֲשֶׁר לֹא יַעֲזֹב לָהֶם שֹׁרֶשׁ וְעָנָף: [מלאכי ג, יט]

י) שֹׁמֵר פְּתָאיִם יְיָ דַּלּוֹתִי וְלִי יְהוֹשִׁיעַ: [תהלים קטז, ו]

כ) וְדִי חֲזָה מַלְכָּא עִיר וְקַדִּישׁ נָחִת מִן שְׁמַיָּא וְאָמַר גֹּדּוּ אִילָנָא וְחַבְּלוּהִי בְּרַם עִקַּר שָׁרְשׁוֹהִי בְּאַרְעָא שְׁבֻקוּ וּבֶאֱסוּר דִּי פַרְזֶל וּנְחָשׁ בְּדִתְאָא דִּי בָרָא וּבְטַל שְׁמַיָּא יִצְטַבַּע וְעִם חֵיוַת בָּרָא חֲלָקֵהּ עַד דִּי שִׁבְעָה עִדָּנִין יַחְלְפוּן עֲלוֹהִי: [דניאל ד, כ]

ל) מֵתִים בַּל יִחְיוּ רְפָאִים בַּל יָקֻמוּ לָכֵן פָּקַדְתָּ וַתַּשְׁמִידֵם וַתְּאַבֵּד כָּל זֵכֶר לָמוֹ: [ישעיה כו, יד]

מ) יָבֹאוּ וְיַגִּידוּ צִדְקָתוֹ לְעַם נוֹלָד כִּי עָשָׂה: [תהלים כב, לב]

נ) זֶרַע יַעַבְדֶנּוּ יְסֻפַּר לַאדֹנָי לַדּוֹר: [תהלים כב, לא]

ס) עָנִי אֲנִי וְגֹוֵעַ מִנֹּעַר נָשָׂאתִי אֵמֶיךָ אָפוּנָה: [תהלים פח, טז]

ע) פִּתְחוּ שְׁעָרִים וְיָבֹא גוֹי צַדִּיק שֹׁמֵר אֱמֻנִים: [ישעיה כו, ב]

מסורת הש"ס

א) [תוספ' פי"ג], ב) [נ"ל ואומר], ג) [נ"ל באין הן], ד) [חגיגה יוד:], ה) [בעין יעקב ליתא], ו) תוספתא פי"ג, ז) נ"א אינם עתידין לחזור, ח) [תוספתא שם], ט) [עי' סוטה כ.], י) [שבת קיט:], כ) [מגילה יד: ערכין לג.].

הגהות הגר"א

[א] גמ' עלי זבח. נמחקו ב' תיבות הללו: [ב] שם ור"ג. נמחק (וערש"י):

גליון הש"ס

גמ' ר"א אומר הרי הן באין לעוה"ב. עיין ב"ב דף ע"ג ע"ב תוס' ד"ה ודמו:

הגהות מהר"ב רנשבורג

א] גמ' דברי הכל אין באין לעוה"ב ור"ג. מלות ור"ג נמחק וכ"ב בספרים שלפני רש"י לא היה כתוב זה דוק ותשכח: ב] רש"י ד"ה וענף לעוה"ב. מלת וענף נמחק:

ליקוטי רש"י

אספו לי חסידי. ועוד יקרא לשמי' ולארץ שיאספו לו הגליות כענין שנאמר עורי צפון ובאי תימן (שה"ש ד'). כרתי בריתי עלי זבח. שקבלו את התורה בברית וזבח כענין שנאמר הנה דם הברית אשר כרת ה' וגומר (שמות כ"ד) [שם נ, ה]. נשבעתי באפי. מדקאמר באפי משמע יכול אני לישאל עליו לפי שמחמת אפי ולא מדעת מיושבת נשבעתי יש ללמוד מכאן שהמולא פתח לנדרו לאמר לא לדעת כן נדרתי שיקרני דבר זה שאני רואה הבא לי על ידי נדרי מתירין לו [חגיגה י.]. זכרתי לך. אם הייתם שבים אלי תאותי לרחם עליכם כי זכרת חסד נעוריך ואהבת כלילת חופתך שהכללתיך לחופה ול' הכנסה הוא כלולותיך נולי"ש בלעז ומה הוא חסד נעוריך לכתך אחר שלוחי משה ואהרן מארץ נושבת ילאתם למדבר ואין לדה לדרך כי האמנתם בי [ירמיהו ב, ב]. וגם לדה לא עשו להם לדרך. מגיד שבחן של ישראל שלא אמרו היאך נלא למדבר בלא לדה אלא האמינו והלכו הוא שמפורש בקבלה (ירמיהו ב, ב) זכרתי לך חסד נעוריך אהבת כלולותיך לכתך אחרי במדבר בארץ לא זרועה ומה שכר מפורש אחריו (שם ג) קודש ישראל לה' וגו' [שמות יב, לט]. בשופר גדול וגו'. ובאו האובדים בארץ מלמד שלא יהו אבודים בין העובדי כוכבים [מכות כד.].

The Amora R' Yochanan comments on R' Akiva's statement that the Generation of the Wilderness has no share in the World to Come:

אָמַר רַבָּה בַּר בַּר חָנָה אָמַר רַבִּי יוֹחָנָן – **Rabbah bar bar Chanah said in the name of R' Yochanan:** שָׁבְקָהּ רַבִּי עֲקִיבָא לַחֲסִידוּתֵיהּ – In condemning the Generation of the Wilderness to eternal exclusion from the World to Come, **R' Akiva abandoned his** customary **generosity** of spirit.[12] שֶׁנֶּאֱמַר ,,הָלֹךְ וְקָרָאתָ בְאָזְנֵי יְרוּשָׁלַם לֵאמֹר... – **For it is stated:** ***Go and proclaim in the ears of Jerusalem, saying:*** זָכַרְתִּי לָךְ חֶסֶד נְעוּרַיִךְ אַהֲבַת כְּלוּלֹתָיִךְ – *Thus said* HASHEM: ***"I remember for your sake the kindness of your youth, the love of your bridal days,*** לֶכְתֵּךְ אַחֲרַי בַּמִּדְבָּר בְּאֶרֶץ לֹא זְרוּעָה'' – ***how you followed Me in the Wilderness, in an unsown land."***[13] וּמָה אֲחֵרִים בָּאִים בִּזְכוּתָם – Thus, R' Akiva could have expounded as follows: **Now, if others** [i.e. the people of Jerusalem] **come** to the World to Come **through their merit** [i.e. the merit of the Generation of the Wilderness], הֵם עַצְמָן לֹא כָּל שֶׁכֵּן – **is it not all the more so** that **they** [the Generation of the Wilderness] **themselves** will enter the World to Come?!

Mishnah The Mishnah proceeds to discuss the fate of the Ten Tribes of Israel, who were carried off to exile in Assyria (*II Kings* 17:6):

עֲשֶׂרֶת הַשְּׁבָטִים אֵינָן עֲתִידִין לַחֲזוֹר – **The Ten Tribes are not destined ever to return** from their place of exile, שֶׁנֶּאֱמַר ,,וַיַּשְׁלִכֵם אֶל־אֶרֶץ אַחֶרֶת כַּיּוֹם הַזֶּה'' – **as it is stated:** *And* HASHEM *uprooted them from upon their soil with anger, with rage, and with great fury,* ***and He cast them to another land, as this very day.***[14] מָה הַיּוֹם הוֹלֵךְ וְאֵינוֹ חוֹזֵר – **Just as the day goes, never to return,** אַף הֵם הוֹלְכִים וְאֵינָן חוֹזְרִים – **so they,** i.e. the Ten Tribes, **go, never to return.**[15] דִּבְרֵי רַבִּי עֲקִיבָא – These are **the words of R' Akiva.** רַבִּי אֱלִיעֶזֶר אוֹמֵר – **R' Eliezer says:** ,,כַּיּוֹם הַזֶּה'' – The phrase *as this very day* implies: מָה יוֹם מַאֲפִיל וּמֵאִיר – **Just as the day darkens and** then **becomes light,** i.e. just as the darkness of the night or early morning eventually gives way to the light of the day, אַף עֲשֶׂרֶת הַשְּׁבָטִים שֶׁאֲפֵילָה לָהֶן – **so too the Ten Tribes, for whom it is dark,** כָּךְ עֲתִידָה לְהָאִיר לָהֶם – **will likewise one day have light.**[16]

Gemara A Baraisa concerning the ultimate fate of the Ten Tribes:

תָּנוּ רַבָּנָן – **The Rabbis taught** in a Baraisa: עֲשֶׂרֶת הַשְּׁבָטִים אֵין לָהֶם חֵלֶק לָעוֹלָם הַבָּא – THE TEN TRIBES HAVE NO SHARE IN THE WORLD TO COME,[17] שֶׁנֶּאֱמַר ,,וַיִּתְּשֵׁם ה' מֵעַל אַדְמָתָם בְּאַף וּבְחֵמָה וּבְקֶצֶף גָּדוֹל'' – AS IT IS STATED:[14] *AND HASHEM UPROOTED THEM FROM UPON THEIR SOIL WITH ANGER, WITH RAGE, AND WITH GREAT FURY, and He cast them to another land, as this very day.* ,,וַיִּתְּשֵׁם ה' מֵעַל אַדְמָתָם'' בָּעוֹלָם הַזֶּה – *AND HASHEM UPROOTED THEM FROM UPON THEIR SOIL* – IN THIS WORLD; ,,וַיַּשְׁלִכֵם אֶל־אֶרֶץ אַחֶרֶת'' לָעוֹלָם הַבָּא – *AND HE CAST THEM TO ANOTHER LAND* – IN THE WORLD TO COME. דִּבְרֵי רַבִּי עֲקִיבָא – These are THE WORDS OF R' AKIVA. רַבִּי שִׁמְעוֹן בֶּן יְהוּדָה אִישׁ כְּפַר עַכּוֹ אוֹמֵר מִשּׁוּם רַבִּי שִׁמְעוֹן – R' SHIMON BEN YEHUDAH, A MAN FROM THE TOWN OF AKKO, SAYS IN

NOTES

the verse states that they *will return and they will come to Zion with glad song.* But surely they died in the Wilderness! Rather, the meaning is that they will return at the time of the Resurrection of the Dead and have a share in the World to Come.]

12. For R' Akiva was wont to exonerate the Jewish people. Yet, here he condemns the Generation of the Wilderness, though he could have expounded another verse in their favor, as the Gemara will proceed to show (see *Rashi*).

13. *Jeremiah* 2:2. God declares that the people of Jerusalem would be saved — not in their own merit — but in the merit of the Generation of the Wilderness, who in the love of their bridal days were willing to follow God out into the desert wastelands.

14. *Deuteronomy* 29:27. This verse is part of a speech by Moses wherein he warns the Jews that if they stray into idolatry God will punish them severely: The land will be laid waste, and when outsiders inquire as to the reason for the desolation, they will be told that God had punished the Jews for their idolatry, driving them from their homeland into exile, where they remain to this day.

The phrase *to another land* indicates that Moses was referring to an exile in which all the exiles were sent to a single land. This can only refer to the exile of the Ten Tribes, as the two tribes of Judah and Benjamin, who were exiled later, were dispersed across many lands (*Rashi*).

15. The phrase *as this very day* is expounded as likening the Ten Tribes to the day: Just as the day passes never to return, so also when the Messiah arrives and the Jews return to their land, the Ten Tribes will not return. This is in punishment for their having spoken disparagingly of the Land of Israel, saying that the land of their captivity surpassed the Land of Israel in beauty — see above, 94a (see *Rashi* here and to Gemara ד"ה תנו רבנן).

Although the Gemara states elsewhere (*Megillah* 14b, *Arachin* 33a) that approximately ninety years after their exile, during the reign of King Yoshiah, the Ten Tribes were brought back to the Land of Israel by Jeremiah, this refers only to *some* of the exiles. Many of them, however, remained in exile. It is to these exiles that R' Akiva refers when he says that the Ten Tribes will never return (see *Rashi*).

16. I.e. they will return from their exile at the time of the redemption.

The foregoing explanation — that the Mishnah refers to the return to the Land of Israel at the Messianic Era — follows *Rashi's* interpretation and that of *Meiri.* According to this view, the dispute between R' Akiva and R' Eliezer refers to the *descendants* of the original exiles, because the original exiles themselves will long since have died by the time the Messiah arrives.

Rashi mentions an alternate explanation in the name of his teacher, that the Mishnah refers to the World to Come. [This is also the view of *Ramban* (*Shaar HaGemul,* p. 300 in the Chavel Edition), his pupil *R' David Bonfils,* and *Ran.*] According to this interpretation, R' Akiva refers only to the original exiles, who were thoroughly wicked. Their children and descendants, however, will merit the World to Come (see *Rashi* with *Rashash;* cf. *Rif* in *Ein Yaakov;* this interpretation takes the approach, suggested in the notes to the Machon Harry Fischel Edition of *R' David Bonfils,* that the words in *Rashi* אף עשרת השבטים ... זוכין ומזכין constitute a separate, independent interpretation of the Mishnah in the name of *Rashi's* teacher, and dispute *Rashi's* own, previously cited interpretation that the Mishnah refers to the Messianic Era). Cf. *Maharal.*

It should be pointed out that the Books of *Prophets* contain numerous references to the existence of all twelve tribes in the Messianic Era. *Ramban* (*Sefer HaGeulah* ch.1) enumerates at least eight proofs that Scripture assumes a return of the Ten Tribes. Moreover, *Ezekiel* ch. 48 speaks openly of the future division of the Land among all twelve tribes. According to the latter view presented above, this poses no problem — certainly if the descendants of the Ten Tribes merit the World to Come, they can be expected to be gathered in by the Messiah.

According to the former view, however, we must assume according to R' Akiva that these prophecies refer to those members of the Ten Tribes brought back by Jeremiah — see note 15. Although at the time Jeremiah brought them back they blended in with the tribes of Judah and Benjamin, they will be identified by the Messiah and take their rightful place in Israel (*R' Moshe Eisemann,* ArtScroll *Ezekiel* pp. 572-3). See also *Margaliyos HaYam* at length.

17. Even according to the first explanation cited in the previous note that the Mishnah refers to the Messianic redemption, the present Baraisa refers to the World to Come.

Alternatively, according to the view that the Mishnah refers to the Messianic Era, the present Baraisa refers to this era as well, the term "World to Come" being used loosely (see *Rashi;* cf. *Be'er Sheva*).

א"ל כל תלתין יומין מהדרא להו גיהנם כבשר בתוך קלחת ואמרי הכי משה ותורתו אמת והן בדאים: דור המדבר אין להם חלק לעולם הבא וכו': ת"ר א) דור המדבר אין להם חלק לעולם הבא שנאמר א) במדבר הזה יתמו ושם ימותו יתמו בעולם הזה ושם ימותו בעולם הבא ב) ואמר ב) אשר נשבעתי באפי אם יבואון אל מנוחתי דברי ר"ע ר"א אומר (ג) הן באין) לעולם הבא שנאמר ג) אספו לי חסידי כורתי בריתי עלי זבח אלא מה אני מקיים אשר נשבעתי באפי ד) באפי נשבעתי וחוזרני בי רבי יהושע בן קרחה אומר לא נאמר פסוק זה אלא כנגד דורות הבאים אספו לי חסידי אלו צדיקים שבכל דור ודור כורתי בריתי [א] (ה) עלי זבח) אלו חנניה מישאל ועזריה שמסרו עצמן לתוך כבשן האש עלי זבח [אלו] ר"ע וחביריו שמסרו עצמן לשחיטה על דברי תורה ר"ש בן מנסיא אומר באים הן לעולם הבא שנא' ד) ופדויי ה' ישובון ובאו ציון ברנה אמר רבה בר בר חנה א"ר יוחנן שבקה ר"ע לחסידותיה שנאמר ה) הלוך וקראת באזני ירושלים לאמר זכרתי לך חסד נעוריך אהבת כלולותיך לכתך אחרי במדבר בארץ לא זרועה ומה אחרים באים בזכותם הם עצמן לא כל שכן: **מתני'** עשרת השבטים אינן עתידין לחזור שנא' ו) וישליכם אל ארץ אחרת כיום הזה מה היום הולך ואינו חוזר אף הם הולכים ואינן חוזרים דברי ר"ע ר"א אומר כיום הזה מה יום מאפיל ומאיר אף עשרת השבטים שאפילה להן כך עתידה להאיר להם: **גמ'** ת"ר ו) עשרת השבטים ז) אין להם חלק לעוה"ב שנאמר ו) ויתשם ה' מעל אדמתם באף ובחמה ובקצף גדול ויתשם ה' מעל אדמתם בעוה"ז וישליכם אל ארץ אחרת לעוה"ב דברי ר"ע ר"ש בן יהודה איש כפר עכו אומר משום ר"ש אם מעשיהם כיום הזה אינן חוזרין ואם לאו חוזרין רבי אומר באים הם לעוה"ב שנאמר ז) ביום ההוא יתקע בשופר גדול וגו' אמר רבה בר בר חנה א"ר יוחנן שבקה ר"ע לחסידותיה שנא' ח) הלוך וקראת את הדברים האלה צפונה ואמרת שובה משובה ישראל נאם ה' ולא אפיל פני בכם כי חסיד אני נאם ה' לא אטור לעולם מאי חסידותיה דתניא ח) קטני בני רשעי ישראל אין באין לעוה"ב שנא' ט) כי הנה היום בא בוער כתנור והיה כל זדים וכל עושי רשעה קש ולהט אותם היום הבא אמר ה' צבאות אשר לא יעזוב להם שורש וענף שורש בעוה"ז וענף לעוה"ב דברי רבן גמליאל ר"ע אומר באים הם לעוה"ב שנא' י) שומר פתאים ה' שכן קורין בכרכי הים לינוקא פתיא ואומר כ) גודו אילנא וחבלוהי ברם עיקר שרשוהי בארעא שבוקו ואלא מה אני מקיים לא יעזוב להם שורש וענף שלא יניח להם לא מצוה ולא שיורי מצוה ד"א שורש זו נשמה וענף זה הגוף אבל קטני בני רשעי עובדי כוכבים [א] ד"ה אין באין לעוה"ב [ב] ור"ג נפקא ליה ל) מותאבד כל זכר למו איתמר קטן מאימתי בא לעוה"ב ר' חייא ור"ש בר ר' חד אמר משעה שנולד וחד אמר משעה שסיפר מ"ד משעה שנולד שנא' מ) יבואו ויגידו צדקתו לעם נולד כי עשה ומ"ד משעה שסיפר דכתיב ט) נ) זרע יעבדנו יסופר לה' לדור אתמר רבינא אמר משעה שנזרע דכתיב זרע יעבדנו ר"נ בר יצחק אמר משעה שנימול דכתיב ס) עני אני וגוע מנוער נשאתי אימיך אפונה תנא משום ר"מ משעה שיאמר אמן שנא' ע) פתחו שערים ויבא גוי צדיק שומר אמונים' י) אל תקרי שומר אמונים אלא שאומר אמן מאי

רש"י

א"ל. ההוא טייעא: כל תלתין יומין מהדר להו גיהנם. הכא: ואמרי הכי משה ותורתו אמת. שנסה כמה פעמים ורואה שכל ל' יום עשן יוצא משם ושומע שאומרין משה ותורתו אמת וכו': באפי לא גרסי': שנאמר. לעיל מיניה קרא מ' שנה אקוט בדור דהיינו דור המדבר: כורתי בריתי עלי זבח. והיינו דור המדבר שכרתו ברית של מקום עלי זבחים ושלמים דכתיב (שמות כד) ויזבחו זבחים שלמים וכתיב (שם) ויזרוק על העם ויאמר הנה דם הברית אשר כרת ה' עמכם: נשבעתי וחוזרני בי. והיינו אשר נשבעתי באפי מפני כעסי נשבעתי ומתחרט אני: אלו חנניה מישאל ועזריה. שמסרו עצמן למיתה בשביל בריתו של מקום: ופדויי ה'. אלו דור המדבר שנפדו ממצרים: שבקיה ר"ע לחסידותיה. שרגיל לזכות את ישראל והשתא מחייב להו דאמר לעיל (דף קח.) דור המדבר אין להם חלק לעולם הבא ולקמן מפרש מאי חסידותיה: שנאמר הלוך וקראת. כלומר שהרי היה יכול לדרוש שיש להם חלק [לעולם הבא] דכתיב הלוך וקראת וגו': **מתני'** עשרת השבטים. שהגלה סנחריב שנאמר (מלכים ב יח) וינחם בחלח ובחבור נהר גוזן וערי מדי: אין עתידים לחזור. ממקום שגלו והא דאמרינן בגמ' כ) דירמיה החזירן לא שהחזירן כולן אלא מקצתם החזיר: שנאמר וישליכם אל ארץ אחרת כיום הזה. שכך גזר להם הקב"ה שכיון שעוזבין את תורתו הוא מגלה אותן: כיום הזה מה היום מאפיל. בבקר אפל ובצהרים מאיר א"נ בערב אפל והולך ולמחרתו מאיר אף עשרת השבטים (אין) עתידין לחזור להיות להם חלק לעולם הבא לא בניהם ובני בניהם קאמר אלא אותן שגלו עצמן אין להם חלק שרשעים גמורין הם אבל בניהם ודורות הבאים זוכין ומזכין. מ"ר: וישליכם. משמע שיהו כולם גולין במקום אחד אל ארץ אחרת והיינו עשרת השבטים שהגלם סנחריב והושיבם במקום אחד כדאמרינן (לעיל דף לד.) שהוליכם למדינת אפריקי אבל ב' השבטים לא גלו למקום אחד אלא נתפזרו בכל הארצות ועליהם הוא אומר אשרקה להם ואקבצם (זכריה י): ה"ג מתני' עשרת השבטים אין עתידין לחזור: **גמ'** תנו רבנן עשרת השבטים אין להם חלק לעולם הבא שנאמר ויתשם ה' מעל אדמתם וגו'. ואית דמפרשי עשרת השבטים אין להם חלק לעולם הבא היינו לימות המשיח שלא יקבלם משיח עם שאר גליות לפי שספרו בגנות ארץ ישראל

כדאמרן לעיל (שם.) כי מטו שוש וכו' ובדבר הזה נענשו מרגלים: ר"ש אומר. מאי כהיום הזה לומר לך אם מעשיהם כהיום הזה לא יהא להם חלק לעוה"ב: ואם [לאו]. שיחזרו בתשובה יחזרו גם הם מגלות ויש להם חלק לעולם הבא: האובדים בארץ אשור. אלו י' השבטים והנדחים בארץ מצרים אלו דור המדבר וכן לשון התוספתא ולא שמעתי עוד: שובה משובה. שכל ישראל עתידין לחזור: קטני בני רשעי ישראל. רשעי ישראל עצמן פשיטא דאין להם חלק לעולם הבא כדאמרי' בפ' בתרא דכתובות (דף קיא:) רפאים בל יקומו מי שמרפה עצמו מדברי תורה אבל בנים שלהם קטנים ולא חטאו פליגי בהו: שורש וענף. אלו בנים קטנים שלהם: שורש בעולם הזה. שימותו נפלים: [ב] וענף לעולם הבא. שאף על פי שאבותיהם היו רשעים הם לא חטאו: עיקר שרשוהי בארעא שבוקו. אלו הבנים קטנים שאע"פ שאבות אין להם חלק תקנה יש להם: שלא יניח. להם הקב"ה: לא מצוה ולא שיורי מצוה. לא מצוה חמורה ולא מצוה קלה הכל יהא מעביר ומשלם שכרם לאלתר כדי לטרדן מן העולם: זו נשמה. שמעמדת הגוף כשרש שמעמיד האילן: אבל קטני בני רשעי עובדי כוכבים. דוקא קאמר רשעי דאילו חסידי עובדי כוכבים פליגי בה ואיכא למ"ד הן עצמן באין ואיכא למ"ד אינן באין כדאמרן (ד' קה.) ישובו רשעים לשאולה כל גוים שכחי אלהים מכאן שאין להם חלק אמר לו רבי יהושע וכי נאמר בכל גוים והלא לא נאמר אלא כל גוים שכחי אלהים הא אין שכחי אלהים יש להן חלק [לעוה"ב]: הכי גרסינן אבל קטני רשעי עובדי כוכבים דברי הכל אינן באין: מותאבד כל זכר למו נפקא ליה. כלומר לתנא דברייתא והאי דנפקא ליה דברי הכל היא דהא שורש וענף מיבעיא ליה למר כדאית ליה ומר כדאית ליה: זרע יעבדנו יסופר לה' לדור. זרע המסופר יעבדנו לה' לדור ודור שיחזור לו ויחיה: משעה שנזרע. משעה שנקלט הזרע במעי אשה אפילו הפילה אמו ונמחה יש לו חלק לעתיד דכתיב זרע יעבדנו והכי אמר בכתובות בפ' בתרא (דף קיא.) נבלתי יקומון לרבות נפלים: עני אני וגוע מנוער. אע"פ שאני עני גויעתי חשובה גויעה וראוי לומר עלי ויגוע ויאסף כלומר שזוכה אני לעתיד לבא כצדיקים שנאמר בהן גויעה ומאימתי משעה שאני נושא אמיך ופחדך אפונה מתגלגלת ושכונה עלי והיינו מילה שבבשרו שאנו משמרים מאימתו של הקב"ה: אפונה. לשון אופן: מאי

תורה אור השלם

א) אֲנִי יְיָ דִּבַּרְתִּי אִם לֹא זֹאת אֶעֱשֶׂה לְכָל הָעֵדָה הָרָעָה הַזֹּאת הַנּוֹעָדִים עָלָי בַּמִּדְבָּר הַזֶּה יִתַּמּוּ וְשָׁם יָמֻתוּ: [במדבר יד, לה]

ב) אֲשֶׁר נִשְׁבַּעְתִּי בְאַפִּי אִם יְבֹאוּן אֶל מְנוּחָתִי: [תהלים צה, יא]

ג) אִסְפוּ לִי חֲסִידָי כֹּרְתֵי בְרִיתִי עֲלֵי זָבַח: [תהלים נ, ה]

ד) וּפְדוּיֵי יְיָ יְשֻׁבוּן וּבָאוּ צִיּוֹן בְּרִנָּה וְשִׂמְחַת עוֹלָם עַל רֹאשָׁם שָׂשׂוֹן וְשִׂמְחָה יַשִּׂיגוּ וְנָסוּ יָגוֹן וַאֲנָחָה: [ישעיה לה, י]

ה) הָלֹךְ וְקָרָאתָ בְאָזְנֵי יְרוּשָׁלַיִם לֵאמֹר כֹּה אָמַר יְיָ זָכַרְתִּי לָךְ חֶסֶד נְעוּרַיִךְ אַהֲבַת כְּלוּלֹתָיִךְ לֶכְתֵּךְ אַחֲרַי בַּמִּדְבָּר בְּאֶרֶץ לֹא זְרוּעָה: [ירמיה ב, ב]

ו) וַיִּתְּשֵׁם יְיָ מֵעַל אַדְמָתָם בְּאַף וּבְחֵמָה וּבְקֶצֶף גָּדוֹל וַיַּשְׁלִכֵם אֶל אֶרֶץ אַחֶרֶת כַּיּוֹם הַזֶּה: [דברים כט, כז]

ז) וְהָיָה בַּיּוֹם הַהוּא יִתָּקַע בְּשׁוֹפָר גָּדוֹל וּבָאוּ הָאֹבְדִים בְּאֶרֶץ אַשּׁוּר וְהַנִּדָּחִים בְּאֶרֶץ מִצְרָיִם וְהִשְׁתַּחֲווּ לַייָ בְּהַר הַקֹּדֶשׁ בִּירוּשָׁלָיִם: [ישעיה כז, יג]

ח) הָלֹךְ וְקָרָאתָ אֶת הַדְּבָרִים הָאֵלֶּה צָפוֹנָה וְאָמַרְתָּ שׁוּבָה מְשֻׁבָה יִשְׂרָאֵל נְאֻם יְיָ לוֹא אַפִּיל פָּנַי בָּכֶם כִּי חָסִיד אֲנִי נְאֻם יְיָ לֹא אֶטּוֹר לְעוֹלָם: [ירמיה ג, יב]

ט) כִּי הִנֵּה הַיּוֹם בָּא בֹּעֵר כַּתַּנּוּר וְהָיוּ כָל זֵדִים וְכָל עֹשֵׂה רִשְׁעָה קַשׁ וְלִהַט אֹתָם הַיּוֹם הַבָּא אָמַר יְיָ צְבָאוֹת אֲשֶׁר לֹא יַעֲזֹב לָהֶם שֹׁרֶשׁ וְעָנָף: [מלאכי ג, יט]

י) שֹׁמֵר פְּתָאיִם יְיָ דַּלּוֹתִי וְלִי יְהוֹשִׁיעַ: [תהלים קטז, ו]

כ) וְדִי חֲזָה מַלְכָּא עִיר וְקַדִּישׁ נָחִת מִן שְׁמַיָּא וְאָמַר גֹּדּוּ אִילָנָא וְחַבְּלוּהִי בְּרַם עִקַּר שָׁרְשׁוֹהִי בְּאַרְעָא שְׁבֻקוּ וּבֶאֱסוּר דִּי פַרְזֶל וּנְחָשׁ בְּדִתְאָא דִּי בָרָא וּבְטַל שְׁמַיָּא יִצְטַבַּע וְעִם חֵיוַת בָּרָא חֲלָקֵהּ עַד דִּי שִׁבְעָה עִדָּנִין יַחְלְפוּן עֲלוֹהִי: [דניאל ד, כ]

ל) מֵתִים בַּל יִחְיוּ רְפָאִים בַּל יָקֻמוּ לָכֵן פָּקַדְתָּ וַתַּשְׁמִידֵם וַתְּאַבֵּד כָּל זֵכֶר לָמוֹ: [ישעיה כו, יד]

מ) יָבֹאוּ וְיַגִּידוּ צִדְקָתוֹ לְעַם נוֹלָד כִּי עָשָׂה: [תהלים כב, לב]

נ) זֶרַע יַעַבְדֶנּוּ יְסֻפַּר לַאדֹנָי לַדּוֹר: [תהלים כב, לא]

ס) עָנִי אֲנִי וְגֹוֵעַ מִנֹּעַר נָשָׂאתִי אֵמֶיךָ אָפוּנָה: [תהלים פח, טז]

ע) פִּתְחוּ שְׁעָרִים וְיָבֹא גוֹי צַדִּיק שֹׁמֵר אֱמֻנִים: [ישעיה כו, ב]

מסורת הש"ס

א) [תוספ' פי"ג], ב) [צ"ל ואומר], ג) [צ"ל באין הן], ד) [חגיגה יוד:], ה) [בעין יעקב ליתא], ו) תוספתא פי"ג, ז) כ"א אינם עתידין לחזור, ח) [תוספתא שם], ט) [עי' סוטה כ.], י) [שבת קיט:], כ) [מגילה יד: ערכין לג.].

הגהות הגר"א

[א] גמ' עלי זבח. נמחקו ב' תיבות הללו: [ב] שם ור"ג. נמחק (וערש"י):

גליון הש"ס

גמ' ר"א אומר הרי הן באין לעוה"ב. עיין ב"ב דף ע"ג ע"ב תוס' ד"ה ודמו:

הגהות מהר"ב רנשבורג

א] גמ' דברי הכל אין באין לעוה"ב ור"ג. מלות ור"ג נמחק ונ"ב בספרים שלפני רש"י לא היה כתוב זה דוק ותשכח: ב] רש"י ד"ה וענף לעוה"ב. מלת וענף נמחק:

ליקוטי רש"י

אספו לי חסידי. ועוד יקרא לשמי' ולארץ שיאספו לו הגליות כענין שנאמר עורי צפון ובאי תימן (שה"ש ד'). כרתי בריתי עלי זבח. שקבלו את התורה בברית וזבח כענין שנאמר הנה דם הברית אשר כרת ה' וגומר (שמות כ"ד) [שם נ, ה]. נשבעתי באפי. מדקאמר באפי משמע יכול אני לישאל עליו לפי שמחמת אפי ולא מדעת מיושבת נשבעתי יש ללמוד מכאן שהמוצא פתח לנדרו לאמר לא לדעת כן נדרתי שיקרני דבר זה שאני רואה הבא לי על ידי נדרי מתירין לו [חגיגה י.]. זכרתי לך. אם הייתם שבים אלי תאוותי לרחם עליכם כי זכרת חסד נעוריך ואהבת כלולת חופתך שהכללתיך לחופה ול' הכנסה הוא כלולותיך נולי"ש בלעז ומה הוא חסד נעוריך לכתך אחר שלוחי משה ואהרן מארץ נושבת יצאתם למדבר ואין צדה לדרך כי האמנתם בי [ירמיהו ב, ב]. וגם צדה לא עשו להם לדרך. מגיד שבחן של ישראל שלא אמרו היאך נצא למדבר בלא צדה אלא האמינו והלכו הוא שמפורש בקבלה (ירמיהו ב, ב) זכרתי לך חסד נעוריך אהבת כלולותיך לכתך אחרי במדבר בארץ לא זרועה ומה שכר מפורש אחריו (שם ג) קודש ישראל לה' וגו' [שמות יב, לט]. בשופר גדול וגו'. ובאו האובדים בארץ מלמד שלא יהו אבודים בין העובדי כוכבים [מכות כד.].

THE NAME OF R' SHIMON: אִם מַעֲשֵׂיהֶם ,,כַּיּוֹם הַזֶּה'' אֵינָן חוֹזְרִין – The verse is interpreted differently: **IF THEIR DEEDS ARE** ***AS THIS DAY,*** i.e. if they do not repent, **THEY WILL NOT RETURN,**[18] וְאִם לָאו חוֹזְרִין – **BUT IF NOT,** i.e. if they do repent, then **THEY WILL RETURN.** רַבִּי אוֹמֵר – **REBBI SAYS:** בָּאִים הֵם לָעוֹלָם הַבָּא – **THEY INDEED COME TO THE WORLD TO COME,** שֶׁנֶּאֱמַר ,,בַּיּוֹם הַהוּא יִתָּקַע בְּשׁוֹפָר גָּדוֹל וגו' '' – **AS IT IS STATED:** *it will be* ***ON THAT DAY*** *that* ***A GREAT SHOFAR WILL BE BLOWN,*** **etc.** *and then will come those lost in the land of Assyria and those cast away in the land of Egypt, and they will prostrate themselves to* HASHEM *on the holy mountain in Jerusalem.*[19] אָמַר רַבָּה בַּר בַּר חָנָה אָמַר רַבִּי יוֹחָנָן – **Rabbah bar bar Chanah said in the name of R' Yochanan:** שַׁבְקָהּ רַבִּי עֲקִיבָא לַחֲסִידוּתֵיהּ – In condemning the Ten Tribes to eternal exclusion from the World to Come, **R' Akiva abandoned his** customary **generosity** of spirit.[20] שֶׁנֶּאֱמַר ,,הָלֹךְ וְקָרָאתָ אֶת־הַדְּבָרִים הָאֵלֶּה צָפוֹנָה וְאָמַרְתָּ – **For it is stated:** ***Go, proclaim these words toward the north, and say:*** שׁוּבָה מְשֻׁבָה יִשְׂרָאֵל נְאֻם־ה' – ***"Return, O wayward Israel," declares*** HASHEM, לוֹא־אַפִּיל פָּנַי בָּכֶם – ***"I will not bring My anger down upon you,*** כִּי־חָסִיד אֲנִי נְאֻם־ה' – ***because I am kind," declares*** HASHEM, לֹא אֶטּוֹר לְעוֹלָם'' – ***"I will not bear a grudge forever."***[21] This verse explicitly predicts the ultimate return of the Ten Tribes. R' Akiva could easily have cited this verse to support the thesis that the Ten Tribes would eventually come back. Since R' Akiva chose to ignore this verse and to instead maintain that the tribes will never return, it indicates that he did not view the Ten Tribes with his usual generous spirit.

The Gemara explains the statement by R' Yochanan that "R' Akiva abandoned his customary generosity of spirit":

מַאי חֲסִידוּתֵיהּ – **What was [R' Akiva's] generosity** of spirit to which R' Yochanan referred? דְּתַנְיָא – **As it was taught in a Baraisa:** קְטַנֵּי בְנֵי רִשְׁעֵי יִשְׂרָאֵל אֵין בָּאִין לָעוֹלָם הַבָּא – **THE MINOR CHILDREN OF WICKED JEWS DO NOT COME TO THE WORLD TO COME,** שֶׁנֶּאֱמַר ,,כִּי־הִנֵּה הַיּוֹם בָּא בֹּעֵר כַּתַּנּוּר – **AS IT IS STATED:** ***FOR BEHOLD, A DAY IS COMING, BURNING LIKE AN OVEN,*** וְהָיוּ כָל־זֵדִים וְכָל־עֹשֵׂה רִשְׁעָה קַשׁ – ***AND ALL THE WANTON AND ALL THE EVILDOERS WILL BE STRAW;*** וְלִהַט אֹתָם הַיּוֹם הַבָּא אָמַר ה' צְבָאוֹת – ***AND THE DAY THAT IS COMING SHALL BURN THEM UP, SAYS HASHEM OF HOSTS,*** אֲשֶׁר לֹא־יַעֲזֹב לָהֶם שֹׁרֶשׁ וְעָנָף'' – ***LEAVING THEM NEITHER ROOT NOR BRANCH.***[22] ,,שֹׁרֶשׁ'' בָּעוֹלָם הַזֶּה – ***ROOT*** – **IN THIS WORLD;** ,,וְעָנָף'' לָעוֹלָם הַבָּא – ***NOR BRANCH*** – **IN THE WORLD TO COME.**[23] דִּבְרֵי רַבָּן גַּמְלִיאֵל – These are **THE WORDS OF RABBAN GAMLIEL.** רַבִּי עֲקִיבָא אוֹמֵר – **R' AKIVA SAYS:** בָּאִים הֵם לָעוֹלָם הַבָּא – **THEY DO COME TO THE WORLD TO COME,** שֶׁנֶּאֱמַר ,,שֹׁמֵר פְּתָאִים ה' '' – **AS IT IS STATED:**[24] ***HASHEM PROTECTS THE PESA'IM,*** and *pesa'im* means "young children," שֶׁכֵּן קוֹרִין בִּכְרַכֵּי הַיָּם לִינוּקָא פַּתְיָא – **FOR IN THE COASTAL CITIES THEY CALL A YOUNG CHILD "PASYA."** The verse thus implies that God preserves young children from destruction and ensures them admittance into the World to Come.[25] וְאוֹמֵר ,,גֹּדּוּ אִילָנָא וְחַבְּלוּהִי בְּרַם עִקַּר שָׁרְשׁוֹהִי בְּאַרְעָא שְׁבֻקוּ'' – **FURTHERMORE, IT SAYS:** ***CHOP DOWN THE TREE AND DESTROY IT, BUT LEAVE ITS MAJOR ROOTS IN THE GROUND.***[26] וְאֶלָּא מָה אֲנִי מְקַיֵּים ,,לֹא־יַעֲזֹב לָהֶם שֹׁרֶשׁ וְעָנָף'' – **HOW, THEN, DO I ACCOUNT FOR** the verse ***LEAVING THEM NEITHER ROOT NOR BRANCH,*** which seems to imply the cutting off of the children of the wicked? שֶׁלֹּא יַנִּיחַ לָהֶם לֹא מִצְוָה וְלֹא שִׁיּוּרֵי מִצְוָה – It means **THAT [GOD] WILL NOT LEAVE [THE WICKED]** any reward at all, **NEITHER** for **A** major **MITZVAH NOR FOR A MINOR MITZVAH.**[27] דָּבָר אַחֵר – **AN ALTERNATIVE INTERPRETATION:** ,,שֹׁרֶשׁ'' זוּ נְשָׁמָה – ***ROOT*** – **THIS IS THE SOUL;** ,,וְעָנָף'' זֶה הַגּוּף – ***NOR BRANCH*** – **THIS IS THE BODY.**[28]

NOTES

18. As explained above, the verse is part of a passage wherein outsiders who inquire as to why Eretz Yisrael remains in a state of desolation are told that it is due to the sins of the Jews, sins which led God to exile them to foreign lands where they remain "as this very day." In other words, at the time of the response to the outsiders' inquiry, the Jews will still be in exile as a result of their sinfulness. Thus the phrase כַּיּוֹם הַזֶּה connotes a time when the Jews have not yet repented.

19. *Isaiah* 27:13. *Those lost in the land of Assyria* refers to the Ten Tribes, who were exiled by the king of Assyria (*Rashi*).

Rebbi goes further than R' Shimon and maintains that the return of the Ten Tribes is guaranteed, and does not depend on their repentance.

20. See note 12 above.

21. *Jeremiah* 3:12. In this chapter, God tells Jeremiah that though the Ten Tribes sinned grievously, their wickedness has now been surpassed by the wickedness of the remaining two tribes, who are more blameworthy in that they should have taken a lesson from the punishment that befell the northern tribes. Therefore, God instructs Jeremiah: *Go, proclaim these words toward the north,* i.e. toward Assyria in the north, where the Ten Tribes live in exile, and say, "*Return, O wayward Israel . . . I will not bear a grudge forever.*" This is a prophecy that even the Ten Tribes will eventually return (*Yad Ramah, Maharsha;* see *Rashi*).

22. *Malachi* 3:19.

23. That the wicked themselves have no share in the World to Come goes without saying. However, Rabban Gamliel states that even their small children, who are too young to have sinned themselves, will die soon after birth (see *Sifri* to *Deuteronomy* 24:16 that young children sometimes die for their fathers' sins) and will be excluded from the World to Come. This is indicated by the verse's reference to "roots" and "branches," which are metaphors for children (see *Rashi;* cf. *Maharsha*).

24. *Psalms* 116:6.

25. This verse is usually translated: *God protects fools,* פְּתִי being the Hebrew word for a fool. However, based on the word's usage in certain foreign countries, R' Akiva translates it as "young child." R' Akiva maintains that God does not punish a blameless young child for his father's sins (*Rashi* with emendation of *R' Betzalel Ronsburg;* cf. *Maharsha*).

It is to this position of R' Akiva's, which asserts that the child of a wicked man will not be punished, that the Gemara referred to previously as an example of R' Akiva's generosity of spirit.

26. *Daniel* 4:20. King Nebuchadnezzar of Babylon dreamed a dream whose meaning he, his advisers and his dream interpreters were at a loss to explain. Finally, Daniel came forward and interpreted the dream. In the dream, an angel descended from heaven and ordered that a great tree – which symbolized Nebuchadnezzar – be chopped down, but that care be taken not to uproot it. On the contrary, the roots were to be protected by a covering of iron and copper. The meaning of this dream was that Nebuchadnezzar himself was to be temporarily removed from his throne ("chopped down"), but his "roots" were to be protected, that is, his progeny would inherit his throne. The dream came true.

R' Akiva cites this verse to support his view that the young children of the wicked are not punished for the sins of their parents. [If the blameless children of a wicked gentile such as Nebuchadnezzar were spared their father's fate, then surely the blameless children of a wicked Jew are so spared!] (*Rashi*).

27. Literally: remnant of a mitzvah. I.e. God will reward the wicked while they are still alive for any good deed that they may have performed – whether major or minor – to ensure that they lose the World to Come, for since they have already received full reward for whatever good they accomplished during their lifetimes, they cannot claim any reward after death. Only punishment remains (*Rashi*; see *Deuteronomy* 7:10 and *Rashi* there).

Others are troubled by *Rashi's* translation of שִׁיּוּרֵי מִצְוָה as a "minor mitzvah." Rather, they interpret this phrase to refer to those aspects of a mitzvah which, while initially required, are not essential to the mitzvah's fulfillment, e.g. the wavings (נַעֲנוּעִים) performed while taking the *lulav.* Thus, God will reward the wicked in this world for even the minutest details of any mitzvos they may have performed, to deprive them of reward in the World to Come (*Gilyonei HaShas* to *Avodah Zarah* 3a; see also *Succah* 38a).

28. Thus, according to both of these interpretations, the passage makes no reference to the children of the wicked losing the World to Come. They indeed merit a share there.

א"ל כל תלתין יומין מהדרא להו גיהנם כבשר בתוך קלחת ואמרי הכי משה ותורתו אמת והן בדאים: דור המדבר אין להם חלק לעולם הבא וכו': ת"ר א) דור המדבר אין להם חלק לעולם הבא שנאמר א) במדבר הזה יתמו ושם ימותו יתמו בעולם הזה ושם ימותו בעולם הבא ב) ואמר ב) אשר נשבעתי באפי אם יבואון אל מנוחתי דברי ר"ע °ר"א אומר (ג) הן באין) לעולם הבא שנאמר ג) אספו לי חסידי כורתי בריתי עלי זבח אלא מה אני מקיים אשר נשבעתי באפי ד) באפי נשבעתי וחוזרני בי רבי יהושע בן קרחה אומר לא נאמר פסוק זה אלא כנגד דורות הבאים אספו לי חסידי אלו צדיקים שבכל דור ודור כורתי בריתי [א] (ה) עלי זבח) אלו חנניה מישאל ועזריה שמסרו עצמן לתוך כבשן האש עלי זבח [אלו] ר"ע וחביריו שמסרו עצמן לשחיטה על דברי תורה ר"ש בן מנסיא אומר באים הן לעולם הבא שנא' ד) ופדויי ה' ישובון ובאו ציון ברנה אמר רבה בר בר חנה א"ר יוחנן שבקה ר"ע לחסידותיה שנאמר ה) הלוך וקראת באזני ירושלים לאמר זכרתי לך חסד נעוריך אהבת כלולותיך לכתך אחרי במדבר בארץ לא זרועה ומה אחרים באים בזכותם הם עצמן לא כל שכן: **מתני'** עשרת השבטים אינן עתידין לחזור שנא' ו) וישליכם אל ארץ אחרת כיום הזה מה היום הולך ואינו חוזר אף הם הולכים ואינן חוזרים דברי ר"ע ר"א אומר כיום הזה מה יום מאפיל ומאיר אף עשרת השבטים שאפילה להן כך עתידה להאיר להם: **גמ'** ת"ר ו) עשרת השבטים ז) אין להם חלק לעוה"ב שנאמר ו) ויתשם ה' מעל אדמתם באף ובחמה ובקצף גדול ויתשם ה' מעל אדמתם בעוה"ז וישליכם אל ארץ אחרת לעוה"ב דברי ר"ע ר"ש בן יהודה איש כפר עכו אומר משום ר"ש אם מעשיהם כיום הזה אינן חוזרין ואם לאו חוזרין רבי אומר באים הם לעוה"ב שנאמר ז) ביום ההוא יתקע בשופר גדול וגו' אמר רבה בר בר חנה א"ר יוחנן שבקה ר"ע לחסידותיה שנא' ח) הלוך וקראת את הדברים האלה צפונה ואמרת שובה משובה ישראל נאם ה' ולא אפיל פני בכם כי חסיד אני נאם ה' לא אטור לעולם מאי חסידותיה דתניא ח) קטני בני רשעי ישראל אין באין לעוה"ב שנא' ט) כי הנה היום בא בוער כתנור והיה כל זדים וכל עושי רשעה קש ולהט אותם היום הבא אמר ה' צבאות אשר לא יעזוב להם שורש וענף שורש בעוה"ז וענף לעוה"ב דברי רבן גמליאל ר"ע אומר באים הם לעוה"ב שנא' י) שומר פתאים ה' שכן קורין בכרכי הים לינוקא פתיא ואומר כ) גודו אילנא וחבלוהי ברם עיקר שרשוהי בארעא שבוקו ואלא מה אני מקיים לא יעזוב להם שורש וענף שלא יניח להם לא מצוה ולא שיורי מצוה ד"א שורש זו נשמה וענף זה הגוף אבל קטני בני רשעי עובדי כוכבים [א] ד"ה אין באין לעוה"ב [ב] ור"ג נפקא ליה ל) מותאבד כל זכר למו אתמר קטן מאימתי בא לעוה"ב ר' חייא ור"ש בר ר' חד אמר משעה שנולד וחד אמר משעה שסיפר מ"ד משעה שנולד שנא' מ) יבואו ויגידו צדקתו לעם נולד כי עשה ומ"ד משעה שסיפר דכתיב ט) נ) זרע יעבדנו יסופר לה' לדור אתמר רבינא אמר משעה שנזרע דכתיב זרע יעבדנו ר"נ בר יצחק אמר משעה שנימול דכתיב ס) עני אני וגוע מנוער נשאתי אימיך אפונה תנא משום ר"מ משעה שיאמר אמן שנא' ע) פתחו שערים ויבא גוי צדיק שומר אמונים אל תקרי שומר אמונים אלא שאומר אמן

מאי

א"ל. ההוא טייעא: כל תלתין יומין מהדר להו גיהנם. הכא: ואמרי הכי משה ותורתו אמת. שנסה כמה פעמים וראה שכל ל' יום עשן יוצא משם ושומע שאומרין משה ותורתו אמת וכו': באפי לא גרסי': שנאמר. לעיל מיניה קרא מ' שנה אקוט בדור דהיינו דור המדבר: כורתי בריתי עלי זבח. והיינו דור המדבר שכרתו ברית של מקום עלי זבחים ושלמים דכתיב (שמות כד) ויזבחו זבחים שלמים וכתיב (שם) ויזרוק על העם ויאמר הנה דם הברית אשר כרת ה' עמכם: נשבעתי וחוזרני בי. והיינו אשר נשבעתי באפי מפני כעסי נשבעתי ומתחרט אני: אלו חנניה מישאל ועזריה. שמסרו עצמן למיתה בשביל בריתו של מקום: ופדויי ה'. אלו דור המדבר שנפדו ממצרים: שבקיה ר"ע לחסידותיה. שרגיל לזכות את ישראל והשתא מחייב להו דאמר לעיל (דף קח.) דור המדבר אין להם חלק לעולם הבא ולקמן מפרש מאי חסידותיה: שנאמר הלוך וקראת. כלומר שהרי היה יכול לדרוש שיש להם חלק [לעולם הבא] דכתיב הלוך וקראת וגו': **מתני'** עשרת השבטים. שהגלה סנחריב שנאמר (מלכים ב יח) וינחם בחלח ובחבור נהר גוזן וערי מדי: אין עתידים לחזור. ממקום שגלו והא דאמרינן בגמ' כ) דירמיה החזירן לא שהחזירן כולן אלא מקצתם החזיר: שנאמר וישליכם אל ארץ אחרת כיום הזה. שכך גזר להם הקב"ה שכיון שעוזבין את תורתו הוא מגלה אותן: כיום הזה מה היום מאפיל. בבקר אפל ובצהרים מאיר א"נ בערב אפל והולך ולמחרתו מאיר אף עשרת השבטים (אין) עתידין לחזור להיות להם חלק לעולם הבא לא בניהם ובני בניהם קאמר אלא אותן שגלו עצמן אין להם חלק שרשעים גמורין הם אבל בניהם ודורות הבאים זוכין ומזכין. מ"ר: וישליכם. משמע שיהו כולם גולין במקום אחד אל ארץ אחרת והיינו עשרת השבטים שהגלם סנחריב והושיבם במקום אחד כדאמרינן (לעיל דף צד.) שהוליכם למדינת אפריקי אבל ב' השבטים לא גלו למקום אחד אלא נתפזרו בכל הארצות ועליהם הוא אומר אשרקה להם ואקבצם (זכריה י): ה"ג מתני' עשרת השבטים אין עתידין לחזור: **גמ'** תנו רבנן עשרת השבטים אין להם חלק לעולם הבא שנאמר ויתשם ה' מעל אדמתם וגו'. ואית דמפרשי עשרת השבטים אין להם חלק לעולם הבא היינו לימות המשיח שלא יקבלם משיח עם שאר גליות לפי שספרו בגנות ארץ ישראל

כדאמרן לעיל (שם.) כי מטו שוש וכו' ובדבר הזה נענשו מרגלים: ר"ש אומר. מאי כהיום הזה לומר לך אם מעשיהם כהיום הזה לא יהא להם חלק לעוה"ב: ואם [לאו]. שיחזרו בתשובה יחזרו גם הם מגלות ויש להם חלק לעולם הבא: האובדים בארץ אשור. אלו י' השבטים והנדחים בארץ מצרים אלו דור המדבר וכן לשון התוספתא ולא שמעתי עוד: שובה משובה. שכל ישראל עתידין לחזור: קטני בני רשעי ישראל. רשעי ישראל עצמן פשיטא דאין להם חלק לעולם הבא כדאמרי' בפ' בתרא דכתובות (דף קיא:) רפאים בל יקומו מי שמרפה עצמו מדברי תורה אבל בנים שלהם קטנים ולא חטאו פליגי בהו: שורש וענף. אלו בנים קטנים שלהם: שורש בעולם הזה. שימותו נפלים: ב] וענף לעולם הבא. שאף על פי שאבותיהם היו רשעים הם לא חטאו: עיקר שרשוהי בארעא שבוקו. אלו הבנים קטנים שאע"פ שאבות אין להם חלק תקנה יש להם: שלא יניח. להם הקב"ה: לא מצוה ולא שיורי מצוה. לא מצוה חמורה ולא מצוה קלה הכל יהא מעביר ומשלם שכרם לאלתר כדי לטרדן מן העולם: זו נשמה. שמעמדת הגוף כשרש שמעמיד האילן: אבל קטני בני רשעי עובדי כוכבים. דוקא קאמר רשעי דאילו חסידי עובדי כוכבים פליגי בה ואיכא למ"ד הן עצמן באין ואיכא למ"ד אינן באין כדאמרן (ד' קה.) ישובו רשעים לשאולה כל גוים שכחי אלהים מכאן שאין להם חלק אמר לו רבי יהושע וכי נאמר בכל גוים והלא לא נאמר אלא כל גוים שכחי אלהים הא אין שכחי אלהים יש להן חלק [לעוה"ב]: הכי גרסינן אבל קטני רשעי עובדי כוכבים דברי הכל אינן באין: מותאבד כל זכר למו נפקא ליה. כלומר לתנא דברייתא והאי דנפקא ליה דברי הכל היא דהא שורש וענף מיבעיא ליה למר כדאית ליה ומר כדאית ליה: זרע יעבדנו יסופר לה' לדור. זרע המסופר יעבדנו לה' לדור ודור שיחזור לו ויחיה: משעה שנזרע. משעה שנקלט הזרע במעי אשה אפילו הפילה אמו ונמחה יש לו חלק לעתיד דכתיב זרע יעבדנו והכי אמר בכתובות בפ' בתרא (דף קיא.) נבלתי יקומון לרבות נפלים: עני אני וגוע מנוער. אע"פ שאני עני גויעתי חשובה גויעה וראוי לומר עלי ויגוע ויאסף כלומר שזוכה אני לעתיד לבא כלדיקים שנאמר בהן גויעה ומאימתי משעה שאני נושא אמיך ופחדך אפונה מתגלגלת ושכונה עלי והיינו מילה שבבשרו שאנו משמרים מאימתו של הקב"ה: אפונה. לשון אופן:

מאי

תורה אור השלם

א) אֲנִי יְיָ דִּבַּרְתִּי אִם לֹא זֹאת אֶעֱשֶׂה לְכָל הָעֵדָה הָרָעָה הַזֹּאת הַנּוֹעָדִים עָלָי בַּמִּדְבָּר הַזֶּה יִתַּמּוּ וְשָׁם יָמֻתוּ: [במדבר יד, לה]

ב) אֲשֶׁר נִשְׁבַּעְתִּי בְאַפִּי אִם יְבֹאוּן אֶל מְנוּחָתִי: [תהלים צה, יא]

ג) אִסְפוּ לִי חֲסִידָי כֹּרְתֵי בְרִיתִי עֲלֵי זָבַח: [תהלים נ, ה]

ד) וּפְדוּיֵי יְיָ יְשֻׁבוּן וּבָאוּ צִיּוֹן בְּרִנָּה וְשִׂמְחַת עוֹלָם עַל רֹאשָׁם שָׂשׂוֹן וְשִׂמְחָה יַשִּׂיגוּ וְנָסוּ יָגוֹן וַאֲנָחָה: [ישעיה לה, י]

ה) הָלֹךְ וְקָרָאתָ בְאָזְנֵי יְרוּשָׁלַיִם לֵאמֹר כֹּה אָמַר יְיָ זָכַרְתִּי לָךְ חֶסֶד נְעוּרַיִךְ אַהֲבַת כְּלוּלֹתָיִךְ לֶכְתֵּךְ אַחֲרַי בַּמִּדְבָּר בְּאֶרֶץ לֹא זְרוּעָה: [ירמיה ב, ב]

ו) וַיִּתְּשֵׁם יְיָ מֵעַל אַדְמָתָם בְּאַף וּבְחֵמָה וּבְקֶצֶף גָּדוֹל וַיַּשְׁלִכֵם אֶל אֶרֶץ אַחֶרֶת כַּיּוֹם הַזֶּה: [דברים כט, כז]

ז) וְהָיָה בַּיּוֹם הַהוּא יִתָּקַע בְּשׁוֹפָר גָּדוֹל וּבָאוּ הָאֹבְדִים בְּאֶרֶץ אַשּׁוּר וְהַנִּדָּחִים בְּאֶרֶץ מִצְרָיִם וְהִשְׁתַּחֲווּ לַיְיָ בְּהַר הַקֹּדֶשׁ בִּירוּשָׁלָיִם: [ישעיה כז, יג]

ח) הָלֹךְ וְקָרָאתָ אֶת הַדְּבָרִים הָאֵלֶּה צָפוֹנָה וְאָמַרְתָּ שׁוּבָה מְשֻׁבָה יִשְׂרָאֵל נְאֻם יְיָ לוֹא אַפִּיל פָּנַי בָּכֶם כִּי חָסִיד אֲנִי נְאֻם יְיָ לֹא אֶטּוֹר לְעוֹלָם: [ירמיה ג, יב]

ט) כִּי הִנֵּה הַיּוֹם בָּא בֹּעֵר כַּתַּנּוּר וְהָיוּ כָל זֵדִים וְכָל עֹשֵׂה רִשְׁעָה קַשׁ וְלִהַט אֹתָם הַיּוֹם הַבָּא אָמַר יְיָ צְבָאוֹת אֲשֶׁר לֹא יַעֲזֹב לָהֶם שֹׁרֶשׁ וְעָנָף: [מלאכי ג, יט]

י) שֹׁמֵר פְּתָאיִם יְיָ דַּלּוֹתִי וְלִי יְהוֹשִׁיעַ: [תהלים קטז, ו]

כ) וְדִי חֲזָה מַלְכָּא עִיר וְקַדִּישׁ נָחִת מִן שְׁמַיָּא וְאָמַר גֹּדּוּ אִילָנָא וְחַבְּלוּהִי בְּרַם עִקַּר שָׁרְשׁוֹהִי בְּאַרְעָא שְׁבֻקוּ וּבֶאֱסוּר דִּי פַרְזֶל וּנְחָשׁ בְּדִתְאָא דִּי בָרָא וּבְטַל שְׁמַיָּא יִצְטַבַּע וְעִם חֵיוַת בָּרָא חֲלָקֵהּ עַד דִּי שִׁבְעָה עִדָּנִין יַחְלְפוּן עֲלוֹהִי: [דניאל ד, כ]

ל) מֵתִים בַּל יִחְיוּ רְפָאִים בַּל יָקֻמוּ לָכֵן פָּקַדְתָּ וַתַּשְׁמִידֵם וַתְּאַבֵּד כָּל זֵכֶר לָמוֹ: [ישעיה כו, יד]

מ) יָבֹאוּ וְיַגִּידוּ צִדְקָתוֹ לְעַם נוֹלָד כִּי עָשָׂה: [תהלים כב, לב]

נ) זֶרַע יַעַבְדֶנּוּ יְסֻפַּר לַאדֹנָי לַדּוֹר: [תהלים כב, לא]

ס) עָנִי אֲנִי וְגֹוֵעַ מִנֹּעַר נָשָׂאתִי אֵמֶיךָ אָפוּנָה: [תהלים פח, טז]

ע) פִּתְחוּ שְׁעָרִים וְיָבֹא גוֹי צַדִּיק שֹׁמֵר אֱמֻנִים: [ישעיה כו, ב]

מסורת הש"ס

א) [תוספ' פי"ג], ב) [נ"ל ואומר], ג) [נ"ל באין הן], ד) [חגיגה יוד:], ה) [בעין יעקב ליתא], ו) תוספתא פי"ג, ז) נ"א אינם עתידין לחזור, ח) [תוספתא שם], ט) [עי' סוטה כ.], י) [שבת קיט:], כ) [מגילה יד: ערכין לג.].

הגהות הגר"א

[א] גמ' עלי זבח. נמחקו ב' תיבות הללו: [ב] שם ור"ג. נמחק (וערש"י):

גליון הש"ס

גמ' ר"א אומר הרי הן באין לעוה"ב. עיין ב"ב דף ע"ג ע"ב תוס' ד"ה ודמו:

הגהות מהר"ב רנשבורג

א] גמ' דברי הכל אין באין לעוה"ב ור"ג. מלות ור"ג נמחק וכ"ב בספרים שלפני רש"י לא היה כתוב זה דוק ותשכח: ב] רש"י ד"ה וענף לעוה"ב. מלת וענף נמחק:

ליקוטי רש"י

אספו לי חסידי. ועוד יקרא לשמי' ולארץ שיאספו לו הגליות כענין שנאמר עורי צפון ובאי תימן (שה"ש ד'). **כרתי בריתי עלי זבח.** שקבלו את התורה בברית וזבח כענין שנאמר הנה דם הברית אשר כרת ה' וגומר (שמות כ"ד) [שם נ, ה]. **נשבעתי באפי.** מדקאמר באפי משמע יכול אני לישאל עליו לפי שמחמת אפי ולא מדעת מיושבת נשבעתי יש ללמוד מכאן שהמוצא פתח לנדרו לאמר לא לדעת כן נדרתי שיקרני דבר זה שאני רואה הבא לי על ידי נדרי מתירין לו [חגיגה י.]. **זכרתי לך.** אם הייתם שבים אלי תאוותי לרחם עליכם כי זכרת חסד נעוריך ואהבת כלילת חופתך שהכללתיך לחופה ול' הכנסה הוא כלולותיך נוצ"ש בלעז ומה הוא חסד נעוריך לכתך אחר שלוחי משה ואהרן מארץ נושבת יצאתם למדבר ואין צדה לדרך כי האמנתם בי [ירמיהו ב, ב]. וגם צדה לא עשו להם לדרך. מגיד שבחן של ישראל שלא אמרו היאך נצא למדבר בלא צדה אלא האמינו והלכו הוא שמפורש בקבלה (ירמיהו ב, ב) זכרתי לך חסד נעוריך אהבת כלולותיך לכתך אחרי במדבר בארץ לא זרועה ומה שכר מפורש אחריו (שם ג) קודש ישראל לה' וגו' [שמות יב, לט]. **בשופר גדול וגו'.** ובאו האובדים בארץ מלמד שלא יהו אבודים בין העובדי כוכבים [מכות כד.].

אֲבָל קְטַנֵּי בְּנֵי רִשְׁעֵי עוֹבְדֵי כּוֹכָבִים – HOWEVER, as for THE YOUNG CHILDREN OF WICKED GENTILES i.e. idolaters דִּבְרֵי הַכֹּל אֵין בָּאִין לָעוֹלָם הַבָּא – ALL AGREE THAT THEY DO NOT COME TO THE WORLD TO COME.[29]

The Gemara explains the source for this last statement:

(ורבן גמליאל)[30] נָפְקָא לֵיהּ מ,,וַתְּאַבֵּד כָּל־זֵכֶר לָמוֹ'' – [The Tanna of the Baraisa] derives this teaching concerning the children of wicked gentiles **from** the following passage: ***You destroyed all memory of them.***[31]

The Gemara continues its discussion of the ultimate fate of Jews who die as children:

אִתְּמַר – **It was taught:** קָטָן מֵאֵימָתַי בָּא לָעוֹלָם הַבָּא – **When does** a Jewish **minor come to the World to Come,** i.e. how old must it be at death in order to be admitted into the World to Come? רַבִּי חִיָּיא וְרַבִּי שִׁמְעוֹן בַּר רַבִּי – **R' Chiya and R' Shimon bar Rebbi** dispute the matter: חַד אָמַר – **One says:** מִשָּׁעָה שֶׁנּוֹלַד – **from the moment it is born;** that is, even if it dies immediately after birth, it is admitted into the World to Come. וְחַד אָמַר – **And one says:** מִשָּׁעָה שֶׁסִּיפֵּר – **from the moment it speaks.** However, if it dies before it begins to speak, it will not be admitted into the World to Come. מַאן דְּאָמַר מִשָּׁעָה שֶׁנּוֹלַד – **The one who says from the moment it is born** שֶׁנֶּאֱמַר ,,יָבֹאוּ וְיַגִּידוּ צִדְקָתוֹ לְעַם נוֹלָד כִּי עָשָׂה'' – derives his view from Scripture, **as it is stated:** ***They shall come and relate His righteousness, that which He has done to a newborn nation.***[32] וּמַאן דְּאָמַר מִשָּׁעָה שֶׁסִּיפֵּר – **And the one who says** that a child is eligible to enter the World to Come **from the moment it speaks** דִּכְתִיב ,,זֶרַע יַעַבְדֶנּוּ יְסֻפַּר לַה' לַדּוֹר'' – also derives his view from Scripture, **for it is written:** ***The speaking seed will serve the Lord down to the latter generation.***[33]

אִתְּמַר – **It was taught:** רָבִינָא אָמַר – **Ravina said:** מִשָּׁעָה שֶׁנִּזְרַע – A child is eligible for admittance into the World to Come **from the moment it is sown,** i.e. conceived, דִּכְתִיב ,,זֶרַע יַעַבְדֶנּוּ'' – **as it is written:** ***The seed will serve Him.***[34] רַב נַחְמָן בַּר יִצְחָק אָמַר – **Rav Nachman bar Yitzchak said:** מִשָּׁעָה שֶׁנִּימּוֹל – **from the moment it is circumcised,** דִּכְתִיב ,,עָנִי אֲנִי וְגֹוֵעַ מִנֹּעַר נָשָׂאתִי אֵמֶיךָ אָפוּנָה'' – **as it is written:** ***Afflicted am I and dying since youth; I have borne Your dread, which devolved [upon me].***[35]

תָּנָא מִשּׁוּם רַבִּי מֵאִיר – **A Tanna taught in the name of R' Meir:** מִשָּׁעָה שֶׁיֹּאמַר אָמֵן – A child is eligible for admittance into the World to Come FROM THE MOMENT IT RESPONDS, "AMEN," שֶׁנֶּאֱמַר ,,פִּתְחוּ שְׁעָרִים וְיָבֹא גוֹי־צַדִּיק שֹׁמֵר אֱמֻנִים'' – AS IT IS STATED:[36] *OPEN THE GATES, AND LET ENTER THE RIGHTEOUS NATION THAT KEEPS FAITH* (*shomer emunim*). אַל תִּקְרֵי ,,שֹׁמֵר אֱמֻנִים'' – DO NOT READ *SHOMER EMUNIM, that keeps faith,* אֶלָּא שֶׁאוֹמֵר אָמֵן – BUT *SHE'OMER AMEN, that responds, "Amen."*[37]

NOTES

29. The Baraisa specifies minor children of *wicked* gentiles, for according to one Tannaic opinion cited on 105a (which is the halachically accepted view), righteous gentiles have a share in the World to Come. Certainly, then, their children have such a share (see *Rashi*).

30. *Gra* notes that *Rashi's* text omits these words.

31. *Isaiah* 26:14. The preceding verse reads: *O Hashem our God! masters other than You have dominated us, but only Your Name shall we utter!* Thus, taken in context, our verse refers to wicked gentile masters. When our verse concludes *You destroyed all memory of them,* it means that those wicked gentiles will die and leave behind no progeny to perpetuate their memory. Thus, even their young children will perish.

32. *Psalms* 22:32. According to this view, *a newborn nation* is not a reference to the Jewish people, who are not, after all, newborn, but rather to children, who are (*Yad Ramah*). The righteousness which God does to these newborns is that He admits them into the World to Come at such a tender age. Even though they have no merits of their own, their parents' merits are accounted to them (*Iyun Yaakov*).

Translated thus, the verse indicates that once a child is born, it will be admitted into the World to Come even if it dies immediately after birth. Cf. *Chidushei HaRan,* who explains this passage differently.

33. Ibid. v. 31. I.e. the speaking child will be resurrected and will live on to serve God for generations to come (*Rashi*).

Iyun Yaakov connects this to the teaching (*Succah* 42a) that as soon as a child learns to speak its father is obligated to teach it to recite the verse: *The Torah that Moses commanded us is a heritage of the Congregation of Jacob* (*Deuteronomy* 33:4).

R' David Bonfils (printed in *Sanhedrei Gedolah*) points out that the differences of opinion cited here concerning when children gain admission to the World to Come, all refer to resurrection. Everybody agrees, though, that the souls of all children who die enter the World of Souls.

34. As soon as the "seed is sown," i.e. the mother conceives, even if subsequently the fetus never develops, that soul merits the World to Come (*Rashi*).

35. Ibid. 88:16. Rav Nachman bar Yitzchak explicates the verse thus: עָנִי אֲנִי – *I am poor,* that is, an insignificant person; nevertheless, וְגֹוֵעַ, *I am a person whose death would be described as* גְוִיעָה, a term denoting the passing away of a righteous person who is destined for the World to Come (see *Rashi* to *Genesis* 25:17). Since when have I merited being described in such terms? Ever since the moment *I have borne Your dread, which devolved [upon me], that is, ever since I was circumcised as a baby, for I bear the mark of circumcision upon my flesh as a sign that I fear God (Rashi;* cf. *Yad Ramah* and *Maharsha*).

Thus, David says that ever since he was circumcised he was assured of admittance into the World to Come. This accords with the position of Rav Nachman bar Yitzchak in our Gemara.

Be'er Sheva suggests that this opinion is the source for the custom to perform circumcision on a child that died before its eighth day. See also *Yoreh Deah* 263:5 and *Gra* there.

36. *Isaiah* 26:2.

37. שֹׁמֵר אֱמֻנִים and שֶׁיֹּאמַר אָמֵן sound somewhat similar, which indicates that both meanings may be discovered in the verse. By reading the words this way, R' Meir interprets the verse to mean: *Open the gates, and let enter the righteous nation that responds, "Amen";* i.e. let the nation that responds "Amen" enter the gates of the World to Come.

Thus, once a child says, "Amen," the first time, he is assured admittance into the World to Come (see *Rama, Orach Chaim* 124:7).

מַאי אָמֵן – **What is** the meaning of the word **Amen?**[1] אָמַר רַבִּי חֲנִינָא – **R' Chanina said:** אֵל מֶלֶךְ נֶאֱמָן – It means: **God, trustworthy King.**[2] Thus, when one pronounces the word Amen, he is expressing his belief in God's sovereignty and trustworthiness. For that reason, anyone, even a small child, who says Amen thereby earns admittance into the World to Come.

The Gemara presents three verses that Reish Lakish expounds as having harsh implications for many Jews, whereas R' Yochanan expounds them in a more generous spirit:

"לָכֵן הִרְחִיבָה שְּׁאוֹל נַפְשָׁהּ וּפָעֲרָה פִיהָ לִבְלִי־חֹק" – Scripture states: ***Therefore Sheol has expanded her desire and opened wide her mouth without measure.***[3] אָמַר רֵישׁ לָקִישׁ – **Reish Lakish said** in exposition of these last two words:[4] לְמִי שֶׁמְּשַׁיֵּיר אֲפִילוּ חוֹק אֶחָד – Sheol opens her mouth **for whoever leaves even a single law** unfulfilled.[5] אָמַר רַבִּי יוֹחָנָן – **R' Yochanan said** to him: לֹא נִיחָא לְמָרַיְיהוּ דְּאָמְרַת לְהוּ הָכִי – **Their Master** [i.e. God, the Master of the Jews] **is not pleased that you say such** things **about them!**[6] אֶלָּא אֲפִילוּ לֹא לָמַד אֶלָּא חוֹק אֶחָד – **Rather,** the verse should be interpreted in the opposite sense: **Even if one learned no more than a single law,** he will be spared the punishment of Sheol.[7]

The second verse expounded harshly by Reish Lakish:

(שנאמר)[8] "וְהָיָה בְכָל־הָאָרֶץ נְאֻם־ה' פִּי־שְׁנַיִם בָּהּ יִכָּרְתוּ יִגְוָעוּ וְהַשְּׁלִשִׁית יִוָּתֶר בָּהּ" – Scripture states: ***And it shall come to pass, that in all the land, says Hashem, two-thirds in it shall be cut off and perish, and the third shall remain in it.***[9] אָמַר רֵישׁ לָקִישׁ – **Reish Lakish said** in exposition of this verse: שְׁלִישִׁי שֶׁל שֵׁם – This refers to **the third one of Shem.**[10] אָמַר לֵיהּ רַבִּי יוֹחָנָן – **R' Yochanan said to him:** לֹא נִיחָא לְמָרַיְיהוּ דְּאָמְרַתְּ לְהוּ הָכִי – **Their**

NOTES

1. [I.e. the fact that a child gains admittance into the World to Come by pronouncing the word Amen indicates that this word denotes acceptance upon oneself the sovereignty of God.] What exactly is the meaning of this word? I.e. how does it indicate such acceptance? (*Rashi*).

2. The word אָמֵן is formed by the initial letters of the three words אֵל מֶלֶךְ נֶאֱמָן (*Rashi*). [According to its plain meaning, "Amen" is simply a response confirming or accepting what has just been said (see, for example, *Numbers* 5:22).]

3. *Isaiah* 5:14. Because of the sins described in the earlier part of the passage, Sheol (which is one of the names for Gehinnom – see *Eruvin* 19a) has expanded its capacity to accommodate the vast numbers of sinners.

4. The words לִבְלִי־חֹק, *without measure,* can be rendered *without law.*

5. Reish Lakish interprets "without law" to mean that failure to fulfill even a single law condemns a person to punishment in Gehinnom.

6. God is not pleased that you interpret the verse in this manner and derive such a harsh judgment for His people. For according to your interpretation, any Jew who fails to keep even a single Torah law will be condemned to the judgment of Sheol. Very few Jews will be able to live up to such a strict standard (see *Rashi*). Alternatively, it seems more likely that R' Yochanan objected not only because of the great loss of Jews implicit in Reish Lakish's exposition, but because of the great loss of mankind in general. [God is "their Master" as well] (*Yad Ramah*).

7. R' Yochanan expounds "without law" to mean that Sheol swallows one who is "without law" altogether. But if he studies even a single law, he is spared the judgment of Sheol.

Sefer HaIkkarim (3:29) seems to interpret the descent to Sheol here to mean that the sinner is condemned to suffer there for eternity. However, the Gemara here might instead refer to judgment for a limited time in Gehinnom, after which the purified soul goes on to receive its eternal reward, as discussed extensively by *Ramban* in *Shaar HaGemul* (*Mahari,* cited by *Be'er Sheva*).

Be'er Sheva at great length cites and comments upon several approaches to understanding this dispute between R' Yochanan and Reish Lakish.

One of the approaches cited by *Be'er Sheva* is that of *R' Yosef Albo* (*Sefer HaIkkarim* 3:29). As is well known, a prime purpose of Torah and mitzvos is the refinement of character and soul, through which a person merits the World to Come. According to Reish Lakish, the entire Torah forms a single unit, all of which is essential to one's attainment of perfection. Thus, if one leaves even one aspect of Torah unfulfilled, his soul lacks the necessary perfection for admittance to the World to Come, and he must undergo the judgment of Sheol. R' Yochanan, however, considers it inconceivable that the Torah, which was given to man as a boon, should establish a standard of perfection so strict that it is almost impossible to attain, and whereby hardly anyone ever escapes Sheol. Rather, argues R' Yochanan, all aspects of Torah have the independent capacity to refine a person. Moreover, the purpose of the large number of mitzvos in the Torah is precisely to facilitate man's admittance into the World to Come. For the large variety of mitzvos makes it that much easier for a person to fulfill at least one of them in a most perfect manner, and thereby gain entry into the World to Come. [The variety of mitzvos corresponds to the variety of individual personalities and predispositions. Thus, each person can find a particular mitzvah to concentrate upon.] Indeed, this latter concept is articulated by *Rambam* in his *Commentary to the Mishnah* (end of *Makkos*) on the statement of R' Chananya ben Akashya: "The Holy One, Blessed is He, wished to confer merit upon Israel, therefore he gave them an abundance of Torah and mitzvos." *Rambam* comments there that a fundamental principle of Torah is that one who performs even one of the 613 mitzvos purely out of love for God, without any ulterior motive, merits the World to Come. Thus, the abundance of Torah and mitzvos assures every Jew that he will have perfectly performed at least one mitzvah in his lifetime and thereby merit a share in the World to Come.

Be'er Sheva himself suggests a modification of this last approach: No person actually fulfills all 613 mitzvos, as no person is bound by them all. For example, some mitzvos apply only to Kohanim, or only to a *nazir,* or are tied to some other circumstance in which a person might never find himself, such as living at a time when the Temple stands and sacrifices may be brought. Nevertheless, one can "fulfill" the entire Torah by keeping all those mitzvos that do apply to him, resolving to fulfill those that might apply to him given the appropriate circumstance, and studying those laws that cannot apply to him [see also *Menachos* 110a, which states that studying the laws of sacrifices is tantamount to bringing the offerings]. Reish Lakish maintains that in order to be spared the judgment of Sheol, one must fulfill the entirety of Torah in one of these ways. Failure to "fulfill" even one precept, however, makes it necessary for the person to be purified in Sheol before advancing to the eternal bliss of the World to Come. R' Yochanan, however, argues that if one physically performed many mitzvos and studied even one area of Torah, he might be spared the judgment of Sheol altogether. But if one failed to study any law whatsoever, then he must undergo the purification of Sheol even if he has physically performed many mitzvos. [See also *Toras Chaim,* who explains the dispute similarly.]

R' Menachem Azariah MiFano explains that Reish Lakish refers to one who treats a particular mitzvah lightly. Such an attitude is so iniquitous that the person is condemned to Sheol, regardless of whatever other mitzvos he performed. R' Yochanan, on the other hand, rejects the notion that a person who treats a single mitzvah lightly, but who otherwise faithfully and enthusiastically performed all the other mitzvos in the Torah, is condemned to Sheol for his lone transgression, grievous as this transgression is. Rather, maintains R' Yochanan, the only person who is condemned to Sheol is the one who does not perform any mitzvah with zeal and enthusiasm. If at the time of his death the person has no mitzvos to balance or cancel his sins other than mitzvos he performed as a matter of rote, without inner feeling, then those mitzvos will not be able to save him from the punishment he deserves as a result of his sins. In order to save him from Sheol, at least one of a person's mitzvos must have been performed with devotion (*Asarah Maamaros, Maamar Chikur Din* 5:3, and the commentary *Yad Yehudah* there).

See other approaches in *Be'er Sheva, Maharsha,* and *Rif* in *Ein Yaakov.*

8. *Hagahos HaGra* deletes the word שֶׁנֶּאֱמַר, *for it is stated* [since the ensuing quote is not brought in support of the preceding, but begins a new exposition].

9. *Zechariah* 13:8. [Two-thirds of the population will perish in the Messianic or pre-Messianic Era.]

10. The word וְהַשְּׁלִשִׁית, *and the third,* is expounded to mean "the third of the third one." According to Reish Lakish, our starting point is Shem. Thus, "the third of the third one" means one-third of Shem's third son. Now, Shem's third son was Arpachshad (see *Genesis* 10:22), progenitor

א) מאי אמן א"ר חנינא *אל *מלך *נאמן א) לכן הרחיבה שאול נפשה ופערה פיה לבלי חוק אמר ר"ל למי שמשייר אפי' חוק אחד ב) א"ר יוחנן ג) לא ניחא למרייהו דאמרת להו הכי אלא אפי' לא למד אלא חוק אחד [א] ד) (שנאמר) ב) והיה בכל הארץ נאם ה' פי שנים בה יכרתו ויגועו והשלישית יותר בה אמר ר"ל שלישי של שם א"ל רבי יוחנן לא ניחא למרייהו דאמרת להו הכי אלא אפי' שלישי של נח ג) כי אנכי בעלתי בכם ולקחתי אתכם אחד מעיר ושנים ממשפחה אמר ר"ל דברים ככתבן א"ל ר' יוחנן לא ניחא ליה למרייהו דאמרת להו הכי אלא אחד מעיר מזכה כל העיר כולה ושנים ממשפחה מזכין כל המשפחה כולה יתיב רב כהנא קמיה דרב ויתיב וקאמר דברים ככתבן א"ל רב לא ניחא ליה למרייהו דאמרת להו הכי אלא אחד מעיר מזכה כל העיר ושנים ממשפחה מזכין כל המשפחה חזייה דהוה קא חייף רישיה וסליק ויתיב קמיה דרב א"ל ד) ולא תמצא בארץ החיים א"ל מילט קא לייטת לי א"ל קרא קאמינא לא א תמצא תורה במי שמחיה עצמו עליה תניא רבי סימאי אומר נאמר ה) ולקחתי אתכם לי לעם ונאמר ו) והבאתי אתכם מקיש יציאתן ממצרים לביאתן לארץ מה ביאתן לארץ שנים מס' ריבוא אף יציאתן ממצרים שנים מס' ריבוא אמר רבא וכן לימות המשיח שנא' ז) וענתה שמה כימי נעוריה וכיום עלותה מארץ מצרים תניא אמר ר' אלעזר ברבי יוסי פעם אחת נכנסתי לאלכסנדריא של מצרים מצאתי זקן אחד ואמר לי בא ואראך מה עשו אבותי לאבותיך מהם טבעו בים מהם הרגו בחרב מהם מעכו בבנין ועל דבר זה נענש משה רבינו שנא' ח) ומאז באתי אל פרעה לדבר בשמך הרע לעם הזה אמר לו הקב"ה חבל על דאבדין ולא משתכחין הרי כמה פעמים נגליתי על אברהם יצחק ויעקב באל שדי ולא הרהרו על מדותי ולא אמרו לי מה שמך אמרתי לאברהם ט) קום התהלך בארץ לארכה ולרחבה כי לך אתננה ה) בקש מקום לקבור את שרה ולא מצא עד שקנה בד' מאות שקל כסף ולא הרהר על מדותי אמרתי ליצחק י) גור בארץ הזאת ואהיה עמך ואברכך בקשו עבדיו מים לשתות ולא מצאו עד שעשו מריבה שנאמר כ) ויריבו רועי גרר עם רועי יצחק לאמר לנו המים ולא הרהר אחר מדותי אמרתי ליעקב ל) הארץ אשר אתה שוכב עליה לך אתננה ביקש מקום לנטוע אהלו ולא מצא עד שקנה במאה קשיטה ולא הרהר אחר מדותי ולא אמרו לי מה שמך ואתה אמרת לי מה שמך בתחלה ועכשיו אתה אומר לי ח) והצל לא הצלת את עמך מ) עתה תראה (את) אשר אעשה לפרעה במלחמת פרעה אתה רואה ואי אתה רואה במלחמת שלשים ואחד מלכים נ) וימהר משה ויקוד ארצה וישתחו מה ראה משה ר' חנינא בן ו) גמלא אמר ארך אפים ראה ורבנן אמרי אמת ראה: תניא כמ"ד ארך אפים ראה דתניא כשעלה משה למרום מצאו להקב"ה שיושב וכותב ארך אפים אמר לפניו רבונו של עולם ז) ארך אפים לצדיקים אמר לו אף לרשעים א"ל רשעים יאבדו א"ל השתא חזית מאי דמבעי לך כשחטאו ישראל אמר לו לא כך אמרת לי ארך אפים לצדיקים

אמר

מאי אמן. כשעונין על כל ברכה וברכה אמן היאך משמע קבלת יראת שמים: **אל מלך נאמן.** בנוטריקון שמאמין עליו הקב"ה: **למי שמשייר אפילו חק אחד.** מלשמרו נידון בגיהנם: **לא ניחא ליה למרייהו.** אין הקב"ה רוצה שתהא דן את ישראל כל כך לכף חובה: **פי שנים בה יכרתו. ויגועו והשלישית יותר בה: אמר ר"ל שלישי של שם.** שב' חלקים של כל העולם יהיו נכרתים וחלק ג' יותר בה ואיזה חלק שלישי כל שלישיות שיש לשלש אנו משלשין שמנח נפרדו כל העולם וג' בנים היו לו הרי שליש בניו שם ושלישי של שם הוא ארפכשד כדכתיב בני שם עילם ואשור וארפכשד ולוד וארם ומסתמא בזרעו של ארפכשד יהיה שארית הואיל וישראל יוצאים ממנו ושלישי של ארפכשד שהוא שלישי של שם שהוא שלישי של נח יוותר וכל העולם יכרת ולדברי ר"ל נמצאו ישראל מתמעטין ביותר שמארפכשד יצאו ישראל כדכתיב בפ' נח ארפכשד הוליד את שלח ושלח הוליד את עבר ועבר הוליד את פלג עד אברהם וכשאתה מחלק לג' חלקים זרעו של ארפכשד כגון בני ישראל וישמעאל שהן בני אברהם ובני לוט ובני הרן וכן שאר האומות שיצאו ממנו לג' חלקים שמא ישראל יהיו מרובין וקרובין להיות כנגד כולם ולא יגיעו כל זרע ארפכשד להיות פי שנים אא"כ ישראל משלימין רובן או חציין ונמצאו ישראל מתמעטין בתוך פי שנים: **לא ניחא ליה למרייהו.** להקב"ה שאתה ממעט אותן כל כך אלא אפילו שלישי של נח כלומר מכל בני נח דהיינו מכל העולם כולו יותר השליש ומסתמא אותו חלק הג' שישראל בו יהיה שארית ואם אין ישראל מרובין כל כך להיות אחד מג' שבעולם יהיו הגרים וחסידי עובדי כוכבים להשלים לשליש ואם הם מרובין להיות יותר מחלק השלישית יתמעטו קצת ומ"מ לרבי יוחנן אין ישראל מתמעטין כל כך כמו לדברי ר"ש בן לקיש מ"ר ל"א שלישי של שם והשלישית משמע שני שליש לכך נאמר שלישית שלישית של שלישי לשם וכתיב ובני שם עילם ואשור וארפכשד וישראל מארפכשד הוו ושלישית מארפכשד שהוא שלישי לשם יותר היינו שלישית מישראל אלא שלישי שלישי של נח כלומר כולו ארפכשד יותר בה שהוא שלישי שלישי של נח דשם היה בן שלישי של נח דכתיב (בראשית י) ובני נח שם חם ויפת וארפכשד שלישי לשם ועיקר: **דברים ככתבן.** שלא ימלטו אלא אחד מעיר ושנים ממשפחה:

ולקחתי אחד מעיר. בשביל חסיד אחד שבעיר אקח את כל העיר כולה: **חזייה.** רב לרב כהנא: **דקא חייף רישיה.** חופף ראשו ומעדן בעצמו בשעה שהיה לו ללמוד תורה: **לא תמצא בארץ החיים.** משמע שמקללו לא תבוא לעוה"ב: **נאמר.** בפרשת וארא ולקחתי אתכם לי לעם וכתיב בתריה והבאתי אתכם אל הארץ: **מה ביאתם לארץ שנים מס' רבוא.** שלא נשתיירו מס' רבוא שיצאו ממצרים אלא ב' אנשים יהושע וכלב כדאמרינן בבבא בתרא בפ' יש נוחלין (דף קכא.) לא נגזרה גזרה לא בפחות מכ' ולא ביותר מס' שנה בהנך נמי ששים רבוא שנמנו במדבר לא אחשוב לא פחות מבן כ' שנה ויותר מס': **אף יציאתן ממצרים שנים מס' רבוא.** שמכל ס' רבוא שהיו במצרים לא נשתייר מהם אלא שנים בלבד ואותם שנים של ס' רבוא עלו [לס' רבואות שיצאו אחד מס' רבוא שהיו בהם] והשאר מתו כולם בשלשת ימי אפילה שלא יהיו מצרים רואין במפלתן של ישראל: **וכן לימות המשיח.** שלא ישארו מכל ס' רבוא אלא ב': **וענתה שמה כימי נעוריה וכיום עלותה מארץ מצרים.** עניים ושפלים יהיו כימי עלותה מארץ מצרים: **מעכו בבנין.** היו בונין אותם במקום לבנים: **ועל דבר זה נענש משה רבינו.** שכשראה שנעשה לישראל כך התחיל להתרעם ולהרהר לפני הקב"ה אמר משה לפני הקב"ה ומאז באתי: **א"ל חבל על דאבדין ולא משתכחין.** הפסד גדול יש על גדולים שאבדו ואיני יכול למצוא חסידים אחרים כמותם שאין אתה כאברהם ויצחק ויעקב שלא הרהרו אחרי מדותי: **אל שדי.** שאמרתי לו אני אל שדי פרה ורבה וגו' (בראשית לה) אני אל שדי התהלך לפני והיה תמים (שם יז) והייתי מבטיחו שכל א"י לו ולבניו ולא אמרו מה שמך כמו שעשית אתה: **בתחלה אמרת לי מה שמך.** ועכשיו הרהרת על מדותי ואמרת הצל לא הצלת את עמך: **לנטוע אהלו.** כמו [ויטע] אהלי אפדנו (דניאל יא) ולשון נטיעה שייך באהל: **עתה תראה.** הפעם תראה נפלאות שאני עושה להם: מה ראה על איזה מדה (אחת) של י"ג [מדות] ראה והשתחוה: **אמת ראה.** במדותיו שנקרא אמת ונתיירא אם נתחייבו כלייה אם הוא דן אותן בדין גמור ומיהר והתפלל עליהם שלא יהא דן אותן לפי מעשיהם: ה"ג תניא כמ"ד ארך אפים ראה דתניא כשעלה משה למרום וכו' אמר לו רשעים יאבדו ולא יהיה לך ארך אפים עליהם: **אמר לו.** הקב"ה לא כך אמרת ארך אפים לצדיקים ולא לרשעים:

אמר

מסורת הש"ס

א) [שבת קיט:], ב) [נ"ל אמר לו רבי יוחנן], ג) [כתובות דף קיא:], ד) [בע"י ליתא], ה) [ב"ב טו:], ו) י"ג גמליאל, ז) [עי' תוס' עירובין כב. ותוס' ב"ק נ: ד"ה ארך].

תורה אור השלם

א) לָכֵן הִרְחִיבָה שְּׁאוֹל נַפְשָׁהּ וּפָעֲרָה פִיהָ לִבְלִי חֹק וְיָרַד הֲדָרָהּ וַהֲמוֹנָהּ וּשְׁאוֹנָהּ וְעָלֵז בָּהּ: [ישעיה ה, יד]

ב) וְהָיָה בְכָל הָאָרֶץ נְאֻם יְיָ פִּי שְׁנַיִם בָּהּ יִכָּרְתוּ יִגְוָעוּ וְהַשְּׁלִשִׁית יִוָּתֶר בָּהּ: [זכריה יג, ח]

ג) שׁוּבוּ בָנִים שׁוֹבָבִים נְאֻם יְיָ כִּי אָנֹכִי בָּעַלְתִּי בָכֶם וְלָקַחְתִּי אֶתְכֶם אֶחָד מֵעִיר וּשְׁנַיִם מִמִּשְׁפָּחָה וְהֵבֵאתִי אֶתְכֶם צִיּוֹן: [ירמיה ג, יד]

ד) לֹא יָדַע אֱנוֹשׁ עֶרְכָּהּ וְלֹא תִמָּצֵא בְּאֶרֶץ הַחַיִּים: [איוב כח, יג]

ה) וְלָקַחְתִּי אֶתְכֶם לִי לְעָם וְהָיִיתִי לָכֶם לֵאלֹהִים וִידַעְתֶּם כִּי אֲנִי יְיָ אֱלֹהֵיכֶם הַמּוֹצִיא אֶתְכֶם מִתַּחַת סִבְלוֹת מִצְרָיִם: [שמות ו, ז]

ו) וְהֵבֵאתִי אֶתְכֶם אֶל הָאָרֶץ אֲשֶׁר נָשָׂאתִי אֶת יָדִי לָתֵת אֹתָהּ לְאַבְרָהָם לְיִצְחָק וּלְיַעֲקֹב וְנָתַתִּי אֹתָהּ לָכֶם מוֹרָשָׁה אֲנִי יְיָ: [שמות ו, ח]

ז) וְנָתַתִּי לָהּ אֶת כְּרָמֶיהָ מִשָּׁם וְאֶת עֵמֶק עָכוֹר לְפֶתַח תִּקְוָה וְעָנְתָה שָּׁמָּה כִּימֵי נְעוּרֶיהָ וּכְיוֹם עֲלֹתָהּ מֵאֶרֶץ מִצְרָיִם: [הושע ב, יז]

ח) וּמֵאָז בָּאתִי אֶל פַּרְעֹה לְדַבֵּר בִּשְׁמֶךָ הֵרַע לָעָם הַזֶּה וְהַצֵּל לֹא הִצַּלְתָּ אֶת עַמֶּךָ: [שמות ה, כג]

ט) קוּם הִתְהַלֵּךְ בָּאָרֶץ לְאָרְכָּהּ וּלְרָחְבָּהּ כִּי לְךָ אֶתְּנֶנָּה: [בראשית יג, יז]

י) גּוּר בָּאָרֶץ הַזֹּאת וְאֶהְיֶה עִמְּךָ וַאֲבָרְכֶךָּ כִּי לְךָ וּלְזַרְעֲךָ אֶתֵּן אֶת כָּל הָאֲרָצֹת הָאֵל וַהֲקִמֹתִי אֶת הַשְּׁבֻעָה אֲשֶׁר נִשְׁבַּעְתִּי לְאַבְרָהָם אָבִיךָ: [בראשית כו, ג]

כ) וַיָּרִיבוּ רֹעֵי גְרָר עִם רֹעֵי יִצְחָק לֵאמֹר לָנוּ הַמָּיִם וַיִּקְרָא שֵׁם הַבְּאֵר עֵשֶׂק כִּי הִתְעַשְּׂקוּ עִמּוֹ: [בראשית כו, כ]

ל) וְהִנֵּה יְיָ נִצָּב עָלָיו וַיֹּאמַר אֲנִי יְיָ אֱלֹהֵי אַבְרָהָם אָבִיךָ וֵאלֹהֵי יִצְחָק הָאָרֶץ אֲשֶׁר אַתָּה שֹׁכֵב עָלֶיהָ לְךָ אֶתְּנֶנָּה וּלְזַרְעֶךָ: [בראשית כח, יג]

מ) וַיֹּאמֶר יְיָ אֶל מֹשֶׁה עַתָּה תִרְאֶה אֲשֶׁר אֶעֱשֶׂה לְפַרְעֹה כִּי בְיָד חֲזָקָה יְשַׁלְּחֵם וּבְיָד חֲזָקָה יְגָרְשֵׁם מֵאַרְצוֹ: [שמות ו, א]

נ) וַיְמַהֵר מֹשֶׁה וַיִּקֹּד אַרְצָה וַיִּשְׁתָּחוּ: [שמות לד, ח]

עין משפט נר מצוה

לד א מיי' פ"ג מהל' ת"ת הלכה יג סמג עשין יב טוש"ע י"ד סי' רמו סעיף כא:

הגהות הגר"א

[א] גמ' שנאמר. נמחק:

ליקוטי רש"י

אל מלך נאמן. כך מעיד על בוראו שהוא אל מלך נאמן [שבת קיט:]. **כי אנכי בעלתי בכם.** ונקראתם בשמי שאני אדון לכם ואין כבודי להניח אתכם ביד אויבי [ירמיהו ג, יד]. **אחד מעיר.** אברור הצדיקים ואביאם לציון אף על פי שאין כולם חוזרין [סנהדרין צז:]. **ולא תמצא בארץ החיים.** במי שמחיה אלא במי שממית עצמו עליה ביגיעה וברעבון [איוב כח, כג]. **וענתה שמה.** ל' דירה כמו מעון אריות (נחום ב). **כימי נעוריה.** שישבה במצרים ימים רבים. **וכיום עלותה וגומר.** שצעקה אלי ממצרים מתוך שיעבוד וגאלתיה כן גם עתה [הושע ב, יז]. **אל שדי.** שאני כדאי לברך שהברכות שלי [בראשית לה, יא]. **ומאז באתי אל פרעה.** שאמר משה (לעיל ה, כב) למה הרעותה אמר לו הקב"ה חבל על דאבדין ולא משתכחין יש לי להתאונן על מיתת האבות הרבה פעמים נגליתי אליהם באל שדי ולא אמרו לי מה שמך ואתה אמרת מה שמו מה אומר אליהם וכשבקש אברהם לקבור את שרה לא מצא קבר עד שקנה בדמים מרובים וכן ביצחק ערערו עליו על הבארות אשר חפר וכן ביעקב (בראשית לג, יט) ויקן את חלקת השדה לנטות אהלו ולא הרהרו אחר מדותי ואתה אמרת (ה, כב) למה הרעותה [שמות ו, ט]. **עתה תראה וגו'.** הרהרת על מדותי לא כאברהם שאמרתי לו (בראשית כא, יב) כי ביצחק יקרא לך זרע, ואחר כך אמרתי לו (שם כב:) העלהו לעולה ולא הרהר אחרי לפיכך עתה תראה העשוי לפרעה תראה ולא העשוי למלכי שבעה אומות כשאביאם לארץ [שמות ו, א]. **ארך אפים.** מאריך אפו ואינו ממהר ליפרע שמא יעשה תשובה [שמות לד, ו]. **ארך אפים ראה.** כשעלה משה למרום מצאו משה להקב"ה שהיה יושב וכותב ה' ארך אפים אמר לו לצדיקים אמר לו הקב"ה אף לרשעים אמר לו רשעים יאבדו אמר לו הקב"ה חייך שתצטרך לדבר כשחטאו ישראל בעגל ובמרגלים התפלל משה לפניו בארך אפים אמר לו הקב"ה והלא אמרת לי לצדיקים אמר לו והלא אמרת לי אף לרשעים [במדבר יד, יז]. **ארך אף.** משמע מאריך רוגז וממתין מליפרע ארך אפים משמע שני רצונים אחת של טובה ואחת של רעה. **לצדיקים.** מלשלם שכר טוב לאלתר. **ולרשעים.** מלפרע מהן לאלתר [ב"ק נ:].

Master is not pleased that you say such a thing about them![11] אֶלָּא אֲפִילּוּ שְׁלִישִׁי שֶׁל נֹחַ – **Rather,** says R' Yochanan, the verse refers to **the third one of Noah.**[12]

The third verse expounded harshly by Reish Lakish: ,,כִּי אָנֹכִי בָּעַלְתִּי בָכֶם וְלָקַחְתִּי אֶתְכֶם אֶחָד מֵעִיר וּשְׁנַיִם מִמִּשְׁפָּחָה" – God declares: ***For I have become your Master, and I will take you, one from a city and two from a nation.***[13] אָמַר רֵישׁ לָקִישׁ – **Reish Lakish said** in explanation of this verse: דְּבָרִים כִּכְתָבָן – **The words** of Scripture here are meant exactly **as they are written.**[14] אָמַר לֵיהּ רַבִּי יוֹחָנָן – **R' Yochanan said to him:** לֹא נִיחָא לֵיהּ לְמָרֵייהוּ דְּאָמְרַת לְהוּ הָכִי – **Their Master is not pleased that you say such a thing about them!**[15] אֶלָּא אֶחָד מֵעִיר מְזַכֶּה כָּל הָעִיר כּוּלָּהּ – **Rather,** the meaning is that even **one** righteous person **from a city will exonerate the entire city,** וּשְׁנַיִם מִמִּשְׁפָּחָה מְזַכִּין כָּל הַמִּשְׁפָּחָה כּוּלָּהּ – **and** even **two** righteous persons **from a nation** (i.e. country) **will exonerate the entire nation** (country).[16]

An identical exchange between Rav and Rav Kahana: יָתִיב רַב כַּהֲנָא קַמֵּיהּ דְּרַב – **Rav Kahana was sitting before** his teacher **Rav,** וְיָתִיב וְקָאָמַר – **and [Rav Kahana] was sitting and saying:** דְּבָרִים כִּכְתָבָן – **The words** *one from a city and two from a region* are meant exactly **as they are written.** אָמַר לֵיהּ רַב – **Rav said to him:** לֹא נִיחָא לֵיהּ לְמָרֵייהוּ דְּאָמְרַת לְהוּ הָכִי – **Their Master is not pleased that you say such a thing about them!** אֶלָּא אֶחָד מֵעִיר מְזַכֶּה כָּל הָעִיר – **Rather,** the meaning is that even **one** righteous person **from a city will exonerate the entire city,** וּשְׁנַיִם מִמִּשְׁפָּחָה מְזַכִּין כָּל הַמִּשְׁפָּחָה – **and** even **two** righteous persons **from a region will exonerate the entire region.**

Another exchange between Rav and his student Rav Kahana: חַזְיֵיהּ דַּהֲוָה קָא חָיֵיף רֵישֵׁיהּ – **[Rav] saw that [Rav Kahana] would** first **shampoo his hair** וְסָלֵיק וְיָתִיב קַמֵּיהּ דְּרַב – **and** then **come to sit before Rav** in the study hall. אָמַר לֵיהּ – **[Rav] said to him:** ,,וְלֹא תִמָּצֵא בְּאֶרֶץ הַחַיִּים" – ***And you shall not be found in the land of the living.***[17] אָמַר לֵיהּ – **[Rav Kahana] said to him:** מֵילַט קָא לָיְיטַת לִי – **Are you indeed cursing me?!**[18] אָמַר לֵיהּ – **[Rav] replied to him:** קְרָא קָאָמֵינָא – No, **I am** merely **quoting a verse** from Scripture, which is to be understood according to the following exposition: לֹא תִמָּצֵא תּוֹרָה בְּמִי שֶׁמְּחַיֶּה עַצְמוֹ עָלֶיהָ – **The Torah is not found in one who enlivens himself over it.**[19]

The Gemara returns to the earlier discussion, and cites a Baraisa concerning the limited number of Jews who will merit the Messianic redemption:

תַּנְיָא – **It was taught in a Baraisa:** רַבִּי סִימַאי אוֹמֵר – R' SIMAI SAYS: נֶאֱמַר ,,וְלָקַחְתִּי אֶתְכֶם לִי לְעָם" – IT IS STATED: *AND I SHALL TAKE YOU UNTO ME AS A PEOPLE.*[20] וְנֶאֱמַר ,,וְהֵבֵאתִי אֶתְכֶם" – AND IT IS STATED in the very next verse: *AND I SHALL BRING YOU to the Land* [of Israel].[21] מַקִּישׁ יְצִיאָתָן מִמִּצְרַיִם לְבִיאָתָן לָאָרֶץ – By placing these two verses in juxtaposition, [THE TORAH] thereby COMPARES [THE ISRAELITES'] EXODUS from Egypt TO THEIR COMING TO THE LAND of Israel. מַה בִּיאָתָן לָאָרֶץ שְׁנַיִם מִשִּׁשִּׁים רִיבּוֹא – JUST AS THEIR COMING TO THE LAND was realized by only TWO survivors OUT OF SIX HUNDRED THOUSAND,[22] אַף יְצִיאָתָן מִמִּצְרַיִם שְׁנַיִם מִשִּׁשִּׁים רִיבּוֹא – SO TOO THEIR EXODUS FROM EGYPT was realized by only TWO survivors OUT OF every SIX HUNDRED THOUSAND.[23] אָמַר רָבָא – **Rava said:** וְכֵן לִימוֹת הַמָּשִׁיחַ – **And so it will be in the Messianic Era,**[24] שֶׁנֶּאֱמַר ,,וְעָנְתָה שָׁמָּה כִּימֵי נְעוּרֶיהָ וּכְיוֹם עֲלוֹתָהּ מֵאֶרֶץ־מִצְרָיִם" – **as it is stated:** ***And she will be humbled there as in the days of her youth, and as on the day she came up out of the land of Egypt.***[25]

The Gemara continues its discussion of Jews who perished in Egypt:

תַּנְיָא – **A Tanna taught in a Baraisa:** אָמַר רַבִּי אֶלְעָזָר בְּרַבִּי יוֹסֵי – R' ELAZAR THE SON OF R' YOSE SAID: פַּעַם אַחַת נִכְנַסְתִּי לַאֲלֶכְּסַנְדְּרִיָּא שֶׁל מִצְרַיִם – ONCE, I CAME TO ALEXANDRIA IN EGYPT. מָצָאתִי זָקֵן אֶחָד – I FOUND AN OLD Egyptian MAN, וְאָמַר לִי – AND HE SAID TO ME: בֹּא וְאַרְאֲךָ מֶה עָשׂוּ אֲבוֹתַי לַאֲבוֹתֶיךָ – "COME, LET ME SHOW YOU WHAT MY ANCESTORS DID TO YOUR ANCESTORS.

NOTES

of Abraham. If only a third of Arpachshad's descendants will remain alive, this means that only a third of Israel will survive (*Rashi,* preferred explanation).

11. I.e. to the Jewish people, for according to your explanation it emerges that two-thirds of the Jews will die!

12. Noah, not Shem, is our starting point. Thus, "the third of the third one" means the third of Noah's third son. Now, Noah's third son was Shem, whose third son was Arpachshad. Thus, the verse means that all of Arpachshad's descendants will survive, which includes all of Israel (*Rashi,* preferred explanation). [R' Yochanan interprets "the third of the third one" to be "the third *son* of the third *son.*" Reish Lakish, however, must interpret it to mean "*one-third* of the third son" (see note 9) since Reish Lakish's starting point is Shem, and Scripture records the name of only one of Arpachshad's sons (see *Genesis* 10:24; 11:12-13).]

13. *Jeremiah* 3:14, referring to the future redemption of the Jewish people. [We have translated the word מִשְׁפָּחָה here as *nation,* rather than *family,* because it refers here to a grouping larger than a city. See *Radak* ad loc. and in *Shorashim* s.v. שפח, who cites several instances in which the word מִשְׁפָּחָה is used in this sense. Cf. *Ben Yehoyada* below.]

14. That is, only one Jew from an entire city and two from an entire nation (i.e. country) will be redeemed. (Cf. *Radak* ad loc.)

15. For your exposition removes the majority of the Jews who will be alive at that time from the ranks of the redeemed!

16. And the verse means that "I will take *the entire* city in the merit of one righteous resident and *the entire nation* (i.e. country) in the merit of two righteous residents" (see *Rashi*).

17. *Job* 28:13. Rav meant to criticize Rav Kahana for shampooing his hair at a time that he should have been studying Torah (*Rashi*).

18. Rav Kahana construed the remark to mean that he would not have a share in "the land of the living" — i.e. in the World to Come (*Rashi*).

19. I.e. in one who seeks to live a life of indulgence while studying Torah. Rather, Torah is acquired by one who denies himself physical comforts and pursues Torah study single-mindedly (*Yad Ramah*; see *Rambam, Hil. Talmud Torah* 3:12).

[The word תִמָּצֵא can be rendered either *"you" will not be found,* or *"she" will not be found.* Rav explained that he meant it in the latter sense, referring to the Torah (which is a feminine noun).]

20. *Exodus* 6:7. God declares to the Israelites in Egypt that He will deliver them from their bondage and make them His special people.

21. Ibid. v. 8.

22. At the time of the Exodus there were six hundred thousand adult Jewish males from the ages of twenty to sixty (see *Exodus* 12:37). As punishment for following the counsel of the Spies and rejecting Eretz Yisrael, all these men were condemned to die in the Wilderness (*Numbers* 14:22-23) except for Joshua and Caleb (Ibid. 26:65) [*Rashi*; *Yad Ramah*; see, however, *Tosafos* to *Bava Basra* 121a ד"ה יום שכלו]. Thus, out of six hundred thousand persons who left Egypt, only two entered Eretz Yisrael (*Rashi*).

23. I.e. the number of Jews who left Egypt at the time of the Exodus was but a tiny fraction — 1/300,000 — of the original Jewish population in Egypt. The rest perished during the plague of darkness, when the Egyptians would not be able to witness the downfall of these Israelites (*Rashi*). *Maharal* explains these astronomic numbers as follows: The Jews had been in Egypt 210 years; generations of them had lived and died there before the redemption. All of these thousands and thousands of people had hoped to see the redemption in their lifetimes. Those who actually merited to see the redemption were only a tiny fraction of the very many who had expected to see it (see also *Ben Yehoyada*).

24. Only 1/300,000 of the Jews will remain at that time (*Rashi*).

25. *Hosea* 2:17, describing God's restoration of the Jewish people. I.e. Israel's numbers will be reduced in the same measure they were reduced upon her Exodus from Egypt.

[According to the simple meaning, the words וְעָנְתָה שָׁמָּה are to be

א) מאי אמן א"ר חנינא *אל *מלך *נאמן א) לכן הרחיבה שאול נפשה ופערה פיה לבלי חוק אמר ר"ל למי שמשייר אפי' חוק אחד ב) א"ר יוחנן ג) לא ניחא למרייהו דאמרת להו הכי אלא אפי' לא למד אלא חוק אחד [א] (ד) שנאמר) ב) והיה בכל הארץ נאם ה' פי שנים בה יכרתו ויגועו והשלישית יותר בה אמר ר"ל שלישי של שם א"ל רבי יוחנן לא ניחא למרייהו דאמרת להו הכי אלא אפי' שלישי של נח ג) כי אנכי בעלתי בכם ולקחתי אתכם אחד מעיר ושנים ממשפחה אמר ר"ל דברים ככתבן א"ל ר' יוחנן לא ניחא ליה למרייהו דאמרת להו הכי אלא אחד מעיר מזכה כל העיר כולה ושנים ממשפחה מזכין כל המשפחה כולה יתיב רב כהנא קמיה דרב ויתיב וקאמר דברים ככתבן א"ל רב לא ניחא ליה למרייהו דאמרת להו הכי אלא אחד מעיר מזכה כל העיר ושנים ממשפחה מזכין כל המשפחה חזייה דהוה קא חייף רישיה וסליק ויתיב קמיה דרב א"ל ד) ולא תמצא בארץ החיים א"ל מילט קא לייטת לי א"ל קרא קאמינא לא *תמצא תורה במי שמחיה עצמו עליה תניא רבי סימאי אומר נאמר ה) ולקחתי אתכם לי לעם ונאמר ו) והבאתי אתכם מקיש יציאתן ממצרים לביאתן לארץ מה ביאתן לארץ שנים מס' ריבוא אף יציאתן ממצרים שנים מס' ריבוא אמר רבא וכן לימות המשיח שנא' ז) וענתה שמה כימי נעוריה וכיום עלותה מארץ מצרים תניא אמר ר' אלעזר ברבי יוסי פעם אחת נכנסתי לאלכסנדריא של מצרים מצאתי זקן אחד ואמר לי בא ואראך מה עשו אבותי לאבותיך מהם טבעו בים מהם הרגו בחרב מהם מעכו בבנין ועל דבר זה נענש משה רבינו שנא' ח) ומאז באתי אל פרעה לדבר בשמך הרע לעם הזה אמר לו הקב"ה חבל על דאבדין ולא משתכחין הרי כמה פעמים נגליתי על אברהם יצחק ויעקב באל שדי ולא הרהרו על מדותי ולא אמרו לי מה שמך אמרתי לאברהם ט) קום התהלך בארץ לארכה ולרחבה כי לך אתננה ה) בקש מקום לקבור את שרה ולא מצא עד שקנה בד' מאות שקל כסף ולא הרהר על מדותי אמרתי ליצחק י) גור בארץ הזאת ואהיה עמך ואברכך בקשו עבדיו מים לשתות ולא מצאו עד שעשו מריבה שנאמר כ) ויריבו רועי גרר עם רועי יצחק לאמר לנו המים ולא הרהר אחר מדותי אמרתי ליעקב ל) הארץ אשר אתה שוכב עליה לך אתננה ביקש מקום לנטוע אהלו ולא מצא עד שקנה במאה קשיטה ולא הרהר אחר מדותי ולא אמרו לי מה שמך ואתה אמרת לי מה שמך בתחלה ועכשיו אתה אומר לי ח) והצל לא הצלת את עמך מ) עתה תראה (את) אשר אעשה לפרעה במלחמת פרעה אתה רואה ואי אתה רואה במלחמת שלשים ואחד מלכים נ) וימהר משה ויקוד ארצה וישתחו מה ראה משה ר' חנינא בן ו) גמלא אמר ארך אפים ראה ורבנן אמרי אמת ראה: תניא כמ"ד ארך אפים ראה דתניא כשעלה משה למרום מצאו להקב"ה שיושב וכותב ארך אפים אמר לפניו רבונו של עולם ז) ארך אפים לצדיקים אמר לו אף לרשעים א"ל רשעים יאבדו א"ל השתא חזית מאי דמבעי לך כשחטאו ישראל אמר לו לא כך אמרת לי ארך אפים לצדיקים אמר

מאי אמן. כשעונין על כל ברכה וברכה אמן היאך משמע קבלת יראת שמים: **אל מלך נאמן.** בנוטריקון שמאמין עליו הקב"ה: **למי שמשייר אפילו חק אחד.** מלשמרו נידון בגיהנם: **לא ניחא ליה למרייהו.** אין הקב"ה רוצה שתהא דן את ישראל כל כך לכף חובה: **פי שנים בה יכרתו. ויגועו והשלישית יותר בה: אמר ר"ל שלישי של שם.** שב' חלקים של כל העולם יהיו נכרתים וחלק ג' יותר בה ואיזה חלק שלישי כל שלישיות שיש לשלש אנו משלשין שמנח נפרדו כל העולם וג' בנים היו לו הרי שליש בניו שם ושלישי של שם הוא ארפכשד כדכתיב בני שם עילם ואשור וארפכשד ולוד וארם ומסתמא בזרעו של ארפכשד יהיה שארית הואיל וישראל יוצאים ממנו ושלישי של ארפכשד שהוא שלישי של שם שהוא שלישי של נח יוותר וכל העולם יכרת ולדברי ר"ל נמצאו ישראל מתמעטין ביותר שמארפכשד יצאו ישראל כדכתיב בפ' נח ארפכשד הוליד את שלח ושלח הוליד את עבר ועבר הוליד את פלג עד אברהם וכשאתה מחלק לג' חלקים זרעו של ארפכשד כגון בני ישראל וישמעאל שהן בני אברהם ובני לוט ובני הרן וכן שאר האומות שיצאו ממנו לג' חלקים שמא ישראל יהיו מרובין וקרובין להיות כנגד כולם ולא יגיעו כל זרע ארפכשד להיות פי שנים אא"כ ישראל משלימין רובן או חציין ונמצאו ישראל מתמעטין בתוך פי שנים: **לא ניחא ליה למרייהו.** להקב"ה שאתה ממעט אותן כל כך אלא אפילו שלישי של נח כלומר מכל בני נח דהיינו מכל העולם כולו יותר השליש ומסתמא אותו חלק הג' שישראל בו יהיה שארית ואם אין ישראל מרובין כל כך להיות אחד מג' שבעולם יהיו הגרים וחסידי עובדי כוכבים להשלים לשליש ואם הם מרובין להיות יותר מחלק השלישית יתמעטו קצת ומ"מ לרבי יוחנן אין ישראל מתמעטין כל כך כמו לדברי ר"ש בן לקיש מ"ר ל"א שלישי של שם והשלישית משמע שני שליש לכך נאמר שלישית שלישית של שלישי לשם וכתיב ובני שם עילם ואשור וארפכשד וישראל מארפכשד הוו ושלישית מארפכשד שהוא שלישי לשם יותר היינו שלישית מישראל אלא שלישי שלישי של נח כלומר כולו ארפכשד יותר בה שהוא שלישי שלישי של נח דשם היה בן שלישי של נח דכתיב (בראשית י) ובני נח שם חם ויפת וארפכשד שלישי לשם ועיקר: **דברים כבתבן.** שלא ימלטו אלא אחד מעיר ושנים ממשפחה:

ולקחתי אחד מעיר. בשביל חסיד אחד שבעיר אקח את כל העיר כולה: **חזייה.** רב לרב כהנא: **דקא חייף רישיה.** חופף ראשו ומעדן בעצמו בשעה שהיה לו ללמוד תורה: **לא תמצא בארץ החיים.** משמע שמקללו לא תבוא לעוה"ב: **נאמר.** בפרשת וארא ולקחתי אתכם לי לעם וכתיב בתריה והבאתי אתכם אל הארץ: **מה ביאתם לארץ שנים מס' רבוא.** שלא נשתיירו מס' רבוא שיצאו ממצרים אלא ב' אנשים יהושע וכלב כדאמרינן בבבא בתרא בפ' יש נוחלין (דף קכא.) לא נגזרה גזרה לא בפחות מכ' ולא ביותר מס' שנה בהנך נמי ששים רבוא שנמנו במדבר לא אחשוב לא פחות מבן כ' שנה ויותר מס': **אף יציאתן ממצרים שנים מס' רבוא.** שמכל ס' רבוא שהיו במצרים לא נשתייר מהם אלא שנים בלבד ואותם שנים של ס' רבוא עלו [לס' רבואות שיצאו אחד מס' רבוא שהיו בהם] והשאר מתו כולם בשלשת ימי אפילה שלא יהיו מצרים רואין במפלתן של ישראל: **וכן לימות המשיח.** שלא ישארו מכל ס' רבוא אלא ב': **וענתה שמה כימי נעוריה וכיום עלותה מארץ מצרים.** עניים ושפלים יהיו כימי עלותה מארץ מצרים: **מעכו בבנין.** היו בונין אותם במקום לבנים: **ועל דבר זה נענש משה רבינו.** שכשראה שנעשה לישראל כך התחיל להתרעם ולהרהר לפני הקב"ה אמר משה לפני הקב"ה ומאז באתי: **א"ל חבל על דאבדין ולא משתכחין.** הפסד גדול יש על גדולים שאבדו ואיני יכול למצוא חסידים אחרים כמותם שאין אתה כאברהם ויצחק ויעקב שלא הרהרו אחרי מדותי: **אל שדי.** שאמרתי לו אני אל שדי פרה ורבה וגו' (בראשית לה) אני אל שדי התהלך לפני והיה תמים (שם יז) והייתי מבטיחו שכל א"י לו ולבניו ולא אמרו מה שמך כמו שעשית אתה: **בתחלה אמרת לי מה שמך.** ועכשיו הרהרת על מדותי ואמרת הצל לא הצלת את עמך: **לנטוע אהלו.** כמו [ויטע] אהלי אפדנו (דניאל יא) ולשון נטיעה שייך באהל: **עתה תראה.** הפעם תראה נפלאות שאני עושה להם: מה ראה על איזה מדה (אחת) של י"ג [מדות] ראה והשתחוה: **אמת ראה.** במדותיו שנקרא אמת ונתיירא אם נתחייבו כלייה אם הוא דן אותן בדין גמור ומיהר והתפלל עליהם שלא יהא דן אותן לפי מעשיהם: ה"ג תניא כמ"ד ארך אפים ראה דתניא כשעלה משה למרום וכו' אמר לו רשעים יאבדו ולא יהיה לך ארך אפים עליהם: **אמר לו.** הקב"ה לא כך אמרת ארך אפים לצדיקים ולא לרשעים:

מסורת הש"ס

א) [שבת קיט:], ב) [ל"ל אמר לו רבי יוחנן], ג) [כתובות דף קיא:], ד) [בע"י ליתא], ה) [ב"ב טו:], ו) י"ג גמליאל, ז) [ע' תוס' עירובין כב. ותוס' ב"ק נ: ד"ה ארך].

תורה אור השלם

א) לָכֵן הִרְחִיבָה שְּׁאוֹל נַפְשָׁהּ וּפָעֲרָה פִיהָ לִבְלִי חֹק וְיָרַד הֲדָרָהּ וַהֲמוֹנָהּ וּשְׁאוֹנָהּ וְעָלֵז בָּהּ: [ישעיה ה, יד]

ב) וְהָיָה בְכָל הָאָרֶץ נְאֻם יְיָ פִּי שְׁנַיִם בָּהּ יִכָּרְתוּ יִגְוָעוּ וְהַשְּׁלִשִׁית יִוָּתֶר בָּהּ: [זכריה יג, ח]

ג) שׁוּבוּ בָנִים שׁוֹבָבִים נְאֻם יְיָ כִּי אָנֹכִי בָּעַלְתִּי בָכֶם וְלָקַחְתִּי אֶתְכֶם אֶחָד מֵעִיר וּשְׁנַיִם מִמִּשְׁפָּחָה וְהֵבֵאתִי אֶתְכֶם צִיּוֹן: [ירמיה ג, יד]

ד) לֹא יָדַע אֱנוֹשׁ עֶרְכָּהּ וְלֹא תִמָּצֵא בְּאֶרֶץ הַחַיִּים: [איוב כח, יג]

ה) וְלָקַחְתִּי אֶתְכֶם לִי לְעָם וְהָיִיתִי לָכֶם לֵאלֹהִים וִידַעְתֶּם כִּי אֲנִי יְיָ אֱלֹהֵיכֶם הַמּוֹצִיא אֶתְכֶם מִתַּחַת סִבְלוֹת מִצְרָיִם: [שמות ו, ז]

ו) וְהֵבֵאתִי אֶתְכֶם אֶל הָאָרֶץ אֲשֶׁר נָשָׂאתִי אֶת יָדִי לָתֵת אֹתָהּ לְאַבְרָהָם לְיִצְחָק וּלְיַעֲקֹב וְנָתַתִּי אֹתָהּ לָכֶם מוֹרָשָׁה אֲנִי יְיָ: [שמות ו, ח]

ז) וְנָתַתִּי לָהּ אֶת כְּרָמֶיהָ מִשָּׁם וְאֶת עֵמֶק עָכוֹר לְפֶתַח תִּקְוָה וְעָנְתָה שָׁמָּה כִּימֵי נְעוּרֶיהָ וּכְיוֹם עֲלֹתָהּ מֵאֶרֶץ מִצְרָיִם: [הושע ב, יז]

ח) וּמֵאָז בָּאתִי אֶל פַּרְעֹה לְדַבֵּר בִּשְׁמֶךָ הֵרַע לָעָם הַזֶּה וְהַצֵּל לֹא הִצַּלְתָּ אֶת עַמֶּךָ: [שמות ה, כג]

ט) קוּם הִתְהַלֵּךְ בָּאָרֶץ לְאָרְכָּהּ וּלְרָחְבָּהּ כִּי לְךָ אֶתְּנֶנָּה: [בראשית יג, יז]

י) גּוּר בָּאָרֶץ הַזֹּאת וְאֶהְיֶה עִמְּךָ וַאֲבָרְכֶךָּ כִּי לְךָ וּלְזַרְעֲךָ אֶתֵּן אֶת כָּל הָאֲרָצֹת הָאֵל וַהֲקִמֹתִי אֶת הַשְּׁבֻעָה אֲשֶׁר נִשְׁבַּעְתִּי לְאַבְרָהָם אָבִיךָ: [בראשית כו, ג]

כ) וַיָּרִיבוּ רֹעֵי גְרָר עִם רֹעֵי יִצְחָק לֵאמֹר לָנוּ הַמָּיִם וַיִּקְרָא שֵׁם הַבְּאֵר עֵשֶׂק כִּי הִתְעַשְּׂקוּ עִמּוֹ: [בראשית כו, כ]

ל) וְהִנֵּה יְיָ נִצָּב עָלָיו וַיֹּאמַר אֲנִי יְיָ אֱלֹהֵי אַבְרָהָם אָבִיךָ וֵאלֹהֵי יִצְחָק הָאָרֶץ אֲשֶׁר אַתָּה שֹׁכֵב עָלֶיהָ לְךָ אֶתְּנֶנָּה וּלְזַרְעֶךָ: [בראשית כח, יג]

מ) וַיֹּאמֶר יְיָ אֶל מֹשֶׁה עַתָּה תִרְאֶה אֲשֶׁר אֶעֱשֶׂה לְפַרְעֹה כִּי בְיָד חֲזָקָה יְשַׁלְּחֵם וּבְיָד חֲזָקָה יְגָרְשֵׁם מֵאַרְצוֹ: [שמות ו, א]

נ) וַיְמַהֵר מֹשֶׁה וַיִּקֹּד אַרְצָה וַיִּשְׁתָּחוּ: [שמות לד, ח]

עין משפט נר מצוה

לד א מיי' פ"ג מהל' ת"ת הלכה יג סמג עשין יב טוש"ע י"ד סי' רמו סעיף כא:

הגהות הגר"א

[א] גמ' שנאמר. נמחק:

ליקוטי רש"י

אל מלך נאמן. כך מעיד על בוראו שהוא אל מלך נאמן [שבת קיט:]. **כי אנכי בעלתי בכם.** ונקראתם בשמי שאני אדון לכם ואין כבודי להניח אתכם ביד אויבי [ירמיהו ג, יד]. **אחד מעיר.** אברור הצדיקים ואביאם לציון אף על פי שאין כולם חוזרין [סנהדרין צז:]. **ולא תמצא בארץ החיים.** במי שמחיה אלא במי שממית עצמו עליה ביגיעה וברעבון [איוב כח, כג]. **וענתה שמה.** ל' דירה כמו מעון אריות (נחום ב). **כימי נעוריה.** שישבה במצרים ימים רבים. **וכיום עלותה וגומר.** שלעקה אלי ממצרים מתוך שיעבוד וגאלתיה כן גם עתה [הושע ב, יז]. **אל שדי.** שאני כדאי לברך שהברכות שלי [בראשית לה, יא]. **ומאז באתי אל פרעה.** שאמר משה (לעיל ה, כב) למה הרעותה אמר לו הקב"ה חבל על דאבדין ולא משתכחין יש לי להתאונן על מיתת האבות הרבה פעמים נגליתי אליהם באל שדי ולא אמרו לי מה שמך ואתה אמרת מה שמו מה אומר אליהם וכשבקש אברהם לקבור את שרה לא מצא קבר עד שקנה בדמים מרובים וכן ביצחק ערערו עליו על הבארות אשר חפר וכן ביעקב (בראשית לג, יט) ויקן את חלקת השדה לנטות אהלו ולא הרהרו אחר מדותי ואתה אמרת (ה, כב) למה הרעותה [שמות ו, ט]. **עתה תראה וגו'.** הרהרת על מדותי לא כאברהם שאמרתי לו (בראשית כא, יב) כי ביצחק יקרא לך זרע, ואחר כך אמרתי לו (שם כב:) העלהו לעולה ולא הרהר אחרי לפיכך עתה תראה העשוי לפרעה תראה ולא העשוי למלכי שבעה אומות כשאביאם לארץ [שמות ו, א]. **ארך אפים.** מאריך אפו ואינו ממהר ליפרע שמא יעשה תשובה [שמות לד, ו]. **ארך אפים ראה.** כשעלה משה למרום מצאו משה להקב"ה שהיה יושב וכותב ה' ארך אפים אמר לו לצדיקים אמר לו הקב"ה אף לרשעים אמר לו רשעים יאבדו אמר לו הקב"ה חייך שתצטרך לדבר כשחטאו ישראל בעגל ובמרגלים התפלל משה לפניו בארך אפים אמר לו הקב"ה והלא אמרת לי לצדיקים אמר לו והלא אמרת לי אף לרשעים [במדבר יד, יח]. ארך אף. משמע מאריך רוגז וממתין מליפרע ארך אפים משמע שני רצונים אחת של טובה ואחת של רעה. **לצדיקים.** מלשלם שכר טוב לאלתר. **ולרשעים.** מלפרע מהן לאלתר [ב"ק נ:].

מֵהֶם טָבְעוּ בַּיָּם – SOME OF THEM THEY DROWNED IN THE SEA; מֵהֶם הָרְגוּ בַּחֶרֶב – SOME OF THEM THEY KILLED WITH THE SWORD; מֵהֶם מְעָכוּ בַּבִּנְיָן – and SOME OF THEM THEY CRUSHED by immuring them IN the walls of BUILDINGS."[26] וְעַל דָּבָר זֶה נֶעֱנַשׁ משֶׁה רַבֵּינוּ – AND IT WAS ON ACCOUNT OF THIS MATTER THAT MOSES OUR TEACHER WAS PUNISHED,[27] שֶׁנֶּאֱמַר ,,וּמֵאָז בָּאתִי אֶל־פַּרְעֹה לְדַבֵּר בִּשְׁמֶךָ הֵרַע לָעָם הַזֶּה" – AS IT IS STATED: *Moses returned to HASHEM and said, "My Lord, why have You done evil to this people, why have You sent me?* ***EVER SINCE I CAME TO PHARAOH TO SPEAK IN YOUR NAME HE HAS DONE EVIL TO THIS PEOPLE,*** *while You have not rescued Your people!"*[28] אָמַר לוֹ הַקָּדוֹשׁ בָּרוּךְ הוּא – Thereupon THE HOLY ONE, BLESSED IS HE, SAID TO [MOSES]: חֲבַל עַל דְּאָבְדִין וְלֹא מִשְׁתַּכְּחִין – ALAS FOR THOSE WHO ARE GONE AND NO MORE TO BE FOUND![29] הֲרֵי כַּמָּה פְּעָמִים נִגְלֵיתִי עַל אַבְרָהָם יִצְחָק וְיַעֲקֹב בְּאֵל שַׁדַּי – MANY TIMES DID I APPEAR TO ABRAHAM, ISAAC AND JACOB, promising the Land of Israel to them and their progeny UNDER THE NAME *EL SHADDAI*,[30] וְלֹא הִרְהֲרוּ עַל מִדּוֹתַי – YET though they did not see the fulfillment of those promises, THEY DID NOT QUESTION the justice of MY WAYS, וְלֹא אָמְרוּ לִי מַה שְּׁמֶךָ – NOR DID THEY SAY TO ME, "WHAT IS YOUR NAME?" as you did.[31] אָמַרְתִּי לְאַבְרָהָם ,,קוּם הִתְהַלֵּךְ בָּאָרֶץ לְאָרְכָּהּ וּלְרָחְבָּהּ כִּי לְךָ אֶתְּנֶנָּה" – I SAID TO ABRAHAM:[32] ***ARISE, WALK ABOUT THE LAND THROUGH ITS LENGTH AND BREADTH, FOR TO YOU WILL I GIVE IT.*** בִּקֵּשׁ מָקוֹם לִקְבּוֹר אֶת שָׂרָה וְלֹא מָצָא – Subsequently, HE LOOKED FOR A SPOT TO BURY his wife SARAH, AND COULD NOT FIND one עַד שֶׁקָּנָה בְּאַרְבַּע מֵאוֹת שֶׁקֶל כֶּסֶף – UNTIL HE PURCHASED land FOR the exorbitant price of FOUR HUNDRED SILVER *SHEKELS*.[33] וְלֹא הִרְהֵר עַל מִדּוֹתַי – STILL, although that very land had been promised to him, HE DID NOT QUESTION MY WAYS. אָמַרְתִּי לְיִצְחָק ,,גּוּר בָּאָרֶץ הַזֹּאת וְאֶהְיֶה עִמְּךָ וַאֲבָרְכֶךָּ" – I SAID TO ISAAC:[34] ***SOJOURN IN THIS LAND AND I WILL BE WITH YOU AND BLESS YOU.*** בִּקְשׁוּ עֲבָדָיו מַיִם לִשְׁתּוֹת וְלֹא מָצְאוּ – Subsequently, HIS SERVANTS SOUGHT WATER TO DRINK AND COULD NOT FIND any עַד שֶׁעָשׂוּ מְרִיבָה – UNTIL THEY QUARRELED with the local inhabitants, שֶׁנֶּאֱמַר ,,וַיָּרִיבוּ רֹעֵי גְרָר עִם־רֹעֵי יִצְחָק לֵאמֹר לָנוּ הַמָּיִם" – AS IT IS STATED:[35] ***AND THE HERDSMEN OF GERAR QUARRELED WITH ISAAC'S HERDSMEN, SAYING, "THE WATER IS OURS!"*** וְלֹא הִרְהֵר אַחַר מִדּוֹתַי – STILL, although that very land had been promised to him, HE DID NOT QUESTION MY WAYS. אָמַרְתִּי לְיַעֲקֹב ,,הָאָרֶץ אֲשֶׁר אַתָּה שֹׁכֵב עָלֶיהָ לְךָ אֶתְּנֶנָּה" – I SAID TO JACOB:[36] ***THE GROUND UPON WHICH YOU ARE LYING, TO YOU WILL I GIVE IT*** *and to your descendants.* בִּיקֵּשׁ מָקוֹם לִנְטוֹעַ אָהֳלוֹ וְלֹא מָצָא – Subsequently, HE LOOKED FOR A PLACE UPON WHICH TO PITCH HIS TENT AND COULD NOT FIND one עַד שֶׁקָּנָה בְּמֵאָה קְשִׂיטָה – UNTIL HE PURCHASED land FOR ONE HUNDRED *KESITAHS*.[37] וְלֹא הִרְהֵר אַחַר מִדּוֹתַי – STILL, though he had been promised that very land, HE DID NOT QUESTION MY WAYS. וְלֹא אָמְרוּ לִי מַה שְּׁמֶךָ – NOR DID [ANY OF THE PATRIARCHS] SAY TO ME, "WHAT IS YOUR NAME?" וְאַתָּה אָמַרְתָּ לִי מַה שְּׁמֶךָ בַּתְּחִלָּה – By contrast, RIGHT AT THE START, i.e. when I first spoke to you, YOU SAID TO ME, "WHAT IS YOUR NAME?"[38] וְעַכְשָׁיו אַתָּה אוֹמֵר לִי ,,וְהַצֵּל לֹא־הִצַּלְתָּ אֶת־עַמֶּךָ" – AND NOW YOU SAY TO ME: ***BUT YOU HAVE NOT RESCUED YOUR PEOPLE!***[39] ,,עַתָּה תִרְאֶה (את) אֲשֶׁר אֶעֱשֶׂה לְפַרְעֹה" – ***NOW YOU WILL SEE WHAT I SHALL DO TO PHARAOH.***[40] בְּמִלְחֶמֶת פַּרְעֹה אַתָּה רוֹאֶה – That is, God told Moses: THE WAR AGAINST PHARAOH, i.e. the struggle for the liberation of the slaves and their Exodus from Egypt, YOU WILL SEE, וְאִי אַתָּה רוֹאֶה בְּמִלְחֶמֶת שְׁלֹשִׁים וְאֶחָד מְלָכִים – HOWEVER YOU WILL NOT live to SEE THE WAR AGAINST THE THIRTY-ONE KINGS of Canaan, i.e. you will die before the Jewish people reach Canaan.[41]

NOTES

rendered *and she will dwell there* (*Rashi* ad loc.) or *and she will sing there* (*Radak* ad loc.). Rava, however, expounds וְעָנְתָה as deriving from the root עָנִי, meaning *humility* or *lowliness* (see *Rashi* here).]

26. It is not clear how the old Egyptian showed R' Elazar all this. *Maharsha* suggests that he showed him an ancient Egyptian chronicle that described the atrocities perpetrated by the Egyptians upon the Hebrew slaves. *Dikdukei Soferim* cites the following words from other manuscripts, left out of our text of the Gemara: הָלַךְ וְהֶרְאָה לוֹ עֲצָמוֹת וּשְׂעָרוֹת מְשׁוּקָּעוֹת בְּבִנְיָן, *He went and showed him bones and hair* [of Jewish babies] *immured in a building*.

27. I.e. it was Moses' consternation at the sight of his fellow Jews being drowned, stabbed and crushed that moved him to complain to God that God was not keeping His promise to redeem the Jewish slaves. For this complaint Moses was punished, as the Gemara will explain shortly (*Rashi*).

28. *Exodus* 5:22-23. Sent by God to admonish Pharaoh to free the Jewish slaves, Moses was chagrined to see that not only did Pharaoh not free them, he increased their persecution. This led Moses to complain to God.

Maharsha points out that Moses' complaint could not have been in reference to all three of the aforementioned persecutions, because the drowning of the babies had been ordered by Pharaoh prior to Moses' birth, and therefore could not have been a result of Moses' present mission to Pharaoh. Rather, Moses complained about the immuring of the babies into the buildings, which was a direct result of Moses' mission. As far as Moses' mission resulting in the stabbings of Jews, *Maharsha* suggests that this is alluded to by the verse which records the accusation hurled by some Jews at Moses that his petitioning of Pharaoh had "placed a sword in the hands of [the Egyptians] to murder us" (*Exodus* 5:21).

29. I.e. I sorely miss the Patriarchs, Abraham, Isaac and Jacob, whose like is no longer to be found. They were men of true faith and never questioned My ways, unlike you, who are quick to do so (*Rashi*).

30. Regarding Abraham, *Genesis* 17:1 states: *When Abram was ninety-nine years old,* HASHEM *appeared to Abram and said to him, "I am El Shaddai, walk before Me and be perfect."* In regard to Jacob it is stated, ibid. 35:11: *And God said to him, "I am El Shaddai, be fruitful and multiply."* In reference to Isaac, although we do not find a verse stating explicitly that God appeared to him with the name *El Shaddai,* we do find that God told him (Ibid. 26:3): *For to you and your offspring I will give all of these lands, and I will fulfill the oath I swore to Abraham.* This is a reference to the oath sworn to Abraham with the name *El Shaddai* (*Rashi* to *Exodus* 6:4).

In each case, God went on to promise the Patriarch that he and his seed would come to possess the Land of Israel.

31. That is, they did not ask, "By which of Your attributes ("Names") can I be assured that Your promises to me will be kept?" (see *Maharsha* here and *Be'er Mayim Chaim* to *Exodus* 6:9).

32. *Genesis* 13:17.

33. Ibid. 23:16.

34. Ibid. 26:3.

35. Ibid. v. 20.

36. Ibid. 28:13.

37. Ibid. 33:19.

38. When God first appeared to Moses in the burning bush and commanded him to go to Pharaoh and demand the release of the Jewish slaves, Moses said to God, *"When I come to the Children of Israel and say to them, 'The God of your forefathers has sent me to you,' and they say to me, 'What is His Name?' — what shall I say to them?"* (*Exodus* 3:13).

The commentators wonder why Moses was wrong in asking for God's Name, since Moses needed to know it in case the Israelites demanded that he tell it to them (*Tur* to *Exodus* 6:3, *Be'er Sheva*).

Eitz Yosef answers that the Gemara here takes the position that in stating that he was concerned that the Israelites would ask for God's Name, it was Moses himself who wished to know God's Name. God criticized him for this.

39. *Exodus* 5:23. I.e. it is this same lack of faith that prompts you now to question My ways (see *Rashi*).

40. Ibid. 6:1.

41. The Jews waged a war against thirty-one kings in their conquest of Canaan (see *Joshua* ch. 12). Moses was not permitted to live to see this war and the miracles performed then (*Rashi*).

The commentators note that Scripture gives a *different* reason for Moses' being prevented from entering the Land — his sin at the incident

א) מאי אמן א"ר חנינא *אל *מלך *נאמן א) לכן הרחיבה שאול נפשה ופערה פיה לבלי חוק אמר ר"ל למי שמשייר אפי' חוק אחד ב) א"ר יוחנן ג) לא ניחא למרייהו דאמרת להו הכי אלא אפי' לא למד אלא חוק אחד [א] (ד) שנאמר) ב) והיה בכל הארץ נאם ה' פי שנים בה יכרתו ויגועו והשלישית יותר בה אמר ר"ל שלישי של שם א"ל רבי יוחנן לא ניחא למרייהו דאמרת להו הכי אלא אפי' שלישי של נח ג) כי אנכי בעלתי בכם ולקחתי אתכם אחד מעיר ושנים ממשפחה אמר ר"ל דברים ככתבן א"ל ר' יוחנן לא ניחא ליה למרייהו דאמרת להו הכי אלא אחד מעיר מזכה כל העיר כולה ושנים ממשפחה מזכין כל המשפחה כולה יתיב רב כהנא קמיה דרב ויתיב וקאמר דברים ככתבן א"ל רב לא ניחא ליה למרייהו דאמרת להו הכי אלא אחד מעיר מזכה כל העיר ושנים ממשפחה מזכין כל המשפחה חזייה דהוה קא חייף רישיה וסליק ויתיב קמיה דרב א"ל ד) ולא תמצא בארץ החיים א"ל מילט קא לייטת לי א"ל קרא קאמינא לא *תמצא תורה במי שמחיה עצמו עליה תניא רבי סימאי אומר נאמר ה) ולקחתי אתכם לי לעם ונאמר ו) והבאתי אתכם מקיש יציאתן ממצרים לביאתן לארץ מה ביאתן לארץ שנים מס' ריבוא אף יציאתן ממצרים שנים מס' ריבוא אמר רבא וכן לימות המשיח שנא' ז) וענתה שמה כימי נעוריה וכיום עלותה מארץ מצרים תניא אמר ר' אלעזר ברבי יוסי פעם אחת נכנסתי לאלכסנדריא של מצרים מצאתי זקן אחד ואמר לי בא ואראך מה עשו אבותי לאבותיך מהם טבעו בים מהם הרגו בחרב מהם מעכו בבנין ועל דבר זה נענש משה רבינו שנא' ח) ומאז באתי אל פרעה לדבר בשמך הרע לעם הזה אמר לו הקב"ה חבל על דאבדין ולא משתכחין הרי כמה פעמים נגליתי על אברהם יצחק ויעקב באל שדי ולא הרהרו על מדותי ולא אמרו לי מה שמך אמרתי לאברהם ט) קום התהלך בארץ לארכה ולרחבה כי לך אתננה י) בקש מקום לקבור את שרה ולא מצא עד שקנה בד' מאות שקל כסף ולא הרהר על מדותי אמרתי ליצחק י) גור בארץ הזאת ואהיה עמך ואברכך בקשו עבדיו מים לשתות ולא מצאו עד שעשו מריבה שנאמר כ) ויריבו רועי גרר עם רועי יצחק לאמר לנו המים ולא הרהר אחר מדותי אמרתי ליעקב ל) הארץ אשר אתה שוכב עליה לך אתננה ביקש מקום לנטוע אהלו ולא מצא עד שקנה במאה קשיטה ולא הרהר אחר מדותי ולא אמרו לי מה שמך ואתה אמרת לי מה שמך בתחלה ועכשיו אתה אומר לי ח) והצל לא הצלת את עמך מ) עתה תראה (את) אשר אעשה לפרעה במלחמת פרעה אתה רואה ואי אתה רואה במלחמת שלשים ואחד מלכים נ) וימהר משה ויקוד ארצה וישתחו מה ראה משה ר' חנינא בן ו) גמלא אמר ארך אפים ראה ורבנן אמרי אמת ראה: תניא כמ"ד ארך אפים ראה דתניא כשעלה משה למרום מצאו להקב"ה שיושב וכותב ארך אפים אמר לפניו רבונו של עולם ז) ארך אפים לצדיקים אמר לו אף לרשעים א"ל רשעים יאבדו א"ל השתא חזית מאי דמבעי לך כשחטאו ישראל אמר לו לא כך אמרת לי ארך אפים לצדיקים
אמר

מאי אמן. כשעונין על כל ברכה וברכה אמן היאך משמע קבלת יראת שמים: אל מלך נאמן. בנוטריקון שמאמין עליו הקב"ה: למי שמשייר אפילו חק אחד. שלא למדו נידון בגיהנם: לא ניחא ליה למרייהו. אין הקב"ה רוצה שתהא דן את ישראל כל כך לכף חובה:

פי שנים בה יכרתו. ויגועו והשלישית יותר בה: אמר ר"ל שלישי של שם. שב' חלקים של כל העולם יהיו נכרתים וחלק ג' יותר בה ואיזה חלק שלישי כל שלישיות שיש לשלש אנו משלשין שמנח נפרדו כל העולם וג' בנים היו לו הרי שליש בניו שם ושלישי של שם הוא ארפכשד כדכתיב בני שם עילם ואשור וארפכשד ולוד וארם ומסתמא בזרעו של ארפכשד יהיה שארית הואיל וישראל יוצאים ממנו ושלישי של ארפכשד שהוא שלישי של שם שהוא שלישי של נח יוותר וכל העולם יכרת ולדברי ר"ל נמצאו ישראל מתמעטין ביותר שמארפכשד יצאו ישראל כדכתיב בפ' נח ארפכשד הוליד את שלח ושלח הוליד את עבר ועבר הוליד את פלג עד אברהם וכשאתה מחלק לג' חלקים זרעו של ארפכשד כגון בני ישראל וישמעאל שהן בני אברהם ובני לוט ובני הרן וכן שאר האומות שיצאו ממנו לג' חלקים שמא ישראל יהיו מרובין וקרובין להיות כנגד כולם ולא יגיעו כל זרע ארפכשד להיות פי שנים אא"כ ישראל משלימין רובן או חציין ונמצאו ישראל מתמעטין בתוך פי שנים: לא ניחא ליה למרייהו. להקב"ה שאתה ממעט אותן כל כך אלא אפילו שלישי של נח כלומר מכל בני נח דהיינו מכל העולם כולו יותר השליש ומסתמא אותו חלק הג' שישראל בו יהיה שארית ואם אין ישראל מרובין כל כך להיות אחד מג' שבעולם יהיו הגרים וחסידי עובדי כוכבים להשלים לשליש ואם הם מרובין להיות יותר מחלק השלישית יתמעטו קצת ומ"מ לרבי יוחנן אין ישראל מתמעטין כל כך כמו לדברי ר"ש בן לקיש מ"ר ל"א שלישי של שם והשלישית משמע שני שליש לכך נאמר שלישית שלישית של שלישי לשם וכתיב ובני שם עילם ואשור וארפכשד וישראל מארפכשד הוו ושלישית מארפכשד שהוא שלישי לשם יותר היינו שלישית מישראל אלא שלישי שלישי של נח כלומר כולו ארפכשד יותר בה שהוא שלישי שלישי של נח דשם היה בן שלישי של נח דכתיב (בראשית י) ובני נח שם חם ויפת וארפכשד שלישי לשם ועיקר: דברים ככתבן. שלא ימלטו אלא אחד מעיר ושנים ממשפחה:
ולקחתי

ולקחתי אחד מעיר. בשביל חסיד אחד שבעיר אקח את כל העיר כולה: חזייה. רב לרב כהנא: דקא חייף רישיה. חופף ראשו ומעדן בעצמו בשעה שהיה לו ללמוד תורה: לא תמצא בארץ החיים. משמע שמקללו לא תבוא לעוה"ב: נאמר. בפרשת וארא ולקחתי אתכם לי לעם וכתיב בתריה והבאתי אתכם אל הארץ: מה ביאתם לארץ שנים מס' רבוא. שלא נשתיירו מס' רבוא שיצאו ממצרים אלא ב' אנשים יהושע וכלב כדאמרינן בבבא בתרא בפ' יש נוחלין (דף קכא.) לא נגזרה גזרה לא בפחות מכ' ולא ביותר מס' שנה בהנך נמי ששים רבוא שנמנו במדבר לא אחשוב לא פחות מבן כ' שנה ויותר מס': אף יציאתן ממצרים שנים מס' רבוא. שמכל ס' רבוא שהיו במצרים לא נשתייר מהם אלא שנים בלבד ואותם שנים של ס' רבוא עלו [לס' רבואות שיצאו אחד מס' רבוא שהיו בהם] והשאר מתו כולם בשלשת ימי אפילה שלא יהיו מצרים רואין במפלתן של ישראל: וכן לימות המשיח. שלא ישארו מכל ס' רבוא אלא ב': וענתה שמה כימי נעוריה וכיום עלותה מארץ מצרים. עניים ושפלים יהיו כימי עלותה מארץ מצרים: מעכו בבנין. היו בונין אותם במקום לבנים: ועל דבר זה נענש משה רבינו. שכשראה שנעשה לישראל כך התחיל להתרעם ולהרהר לפני הקב"ה אמר משה לפני הקב"ה ומאז באתי: א"ל חבל על דאבדין ולא משתכחין. הפסד גדול יש על גדולים שאבדו ואיני יכול למצוא חסידים אחרים כמותם שאין אתה כאברהם ויצחק ויעקב שלא הרהרו אחרי מדותי: אל שדי. שאמרתי לו אני אל שדי פרה ורבה וגו' (בראשית לה) אני אל שדי התהלך לפני והיה תמים (שם יז) והייתי מבטיחו שכל א"י לו ולבניו ולא אמרו מה שמך כמו שעשית אתה: בתחלה אמרת לי מה שמך. ועכשיו הרהרת על מדותי ואמרת הצל לא הצלת את עמך: לנטוע אהלו. כמו [ויטע] אהלי אפדנו (דניאל יא) ולשון נטיעה שייך באהל: עתה תראה. הפעם תראה נפלאות שאני עושה להם: מה ראה על איזה מדה (אחת) של י"ג [מדות] ראה והשתחוה: אמת ראה. במדותיו שנקרא אמת ונתיירא אם נתחייבו כלייה אם הוא דן אותן בדין גמור ומיהר והתפלל עליהם שלא יהא דן אותן לפי מעשיהם: ה"ג תניא כמ"ד ארך אפים ראה דתניא כשעלה משה למרום וכו' אמר לו רשעים יאבדו ולא יהיה לך ארך אפים עליהם: אמר לו. הקב"ה לא כך אמרת ארך אפים לצדיקים ולא לרשעים:
אמר

א) [שבת קיט:], ב) [נ"ל אמר לו רבי יוחנן], ג) [כתובות דף קיא:], ד) [בע"י ליתא], ה) [ב"ב טו:], ו) י"ג גמליאל, ז) [עי' תוס' עירובין כב. ותוס' ב"ק נ: ד"ה ארך].

תורה אור השלם

א) לָכֵן הִרְחִיבָה שְּׁאוֹל נַפְשָׁהּ וּפָעֲרָה פִיהָ לִבְלִי חֹק וְיָרַד הֲדָרָהּ וַהֲמוֹנָהּ וּשְׁאוֹנָהּ וְעָלֵז בָּהּ: [ישעיה ה, יד]

ב) וְהָיָה בְכָל הָאָרֶץ נְאֻם יְיָ פִּי שְׁנַיִם בָּהּ יִכָּרְתוּ יִגְוָעוּ וְהַשְּׁלִשִׁית יִוָּתֶר בָּהּ: [זכריה יג, ח]

ג) שׁוּבוּ בָנִים שׁוֹבָבִים נְאֻם יְיָ כִּי אָנֹכִי בָּעַלְתִּי בָכֶם וְלָקַחְתִּי אֶתְכֶם אֶחָד מֵעִיר וּשְׁנַיִם מִמִּשְׁפָּחָה וְהֵבֵאתִי אֶתְכֶם צִיּוֹן: [ירמיה ג, יד]

ד) לֹא יָדַע אֱנוֹשׁ עֶרְכָּהּ וְלֹא תִמָּצֵא בְּאֶרֶץ הַחַיִּים: [איוב כח, יג]

ה) וְלָקַחְתִּי אֶתְכֶם לִי לְעָם וְהָיִיתִי לָכֶם לֵאלֹהִים וִידַעְתֶּם כִּי אֲנִי יְיָ אֱלֹהֵיכֶם הַמּוֹצִיא אֶתְכֶם מִתַּחַת סִבְלוֹת מִצְרָיִם: [שמות ו, ז]

ו) וְהֵבֵאתִי אֶתְכֶם אֶל הָאָרֶץ אֲשֶׁר נָשָׂאתִי אֶת יָדִי לָתֵת אֹתָהּ לְאַבְרָהָם לְיִצְחָק וּלְיַעֲקֹב וְנָתַתִּי אֹתָהּ לָכֶם מוֹרָשָׁה אֲנִי יְיָ: [שמות ו, ח]

ז) וְנָתַתִּי לָהּ אֶת כְּרָמֶיהָ מִשָּׁם וְאֶת עֵמֶק עָכוֹר לְפֶתַח תִּקְוָה וְעָנְתָה שָּׁמָּה כִּימֵי נְעוּרֶיהָ וּכְיוֹם עֲלֹתָהּ מֵאֶרֶץ מִצְרָיִם: [הושע ב, יז]

ח) וּמֵאָז בָּאתִי אֶל פַּרְעֹה לְדַבֵּר בִּשְׁמֶךָ הֵרַע לָעָם הַזֶּה וְהַצֵּל לֹא הִצַּלְתָּ אֶת עַמֶּךָ: [שמות ה, כג]

ט) קוּם הִתְהַלֵּךְ בָּאָרֶץ לְאָרְכָּהּ וּלְרָחְבָּהּ כִּי לְךָ אֶתְּנֶנָּה: [בראשית יג, יז]

י) גּוּר בָּאָרֶץ הַזֹּאת וְאֶהְיֶה עִמְּךָ וַאֲבָרְכֶךָּ כִּי לְךָ וּלְזַרְעֲךָ אֶתֵּן אֶת כָּל הָאֲרָצֹת הָאֵל וַהֲקִמֹתִי אֶת הַשְּׁבֻעָה אֲשֶׁר נִשְׁבַּעְתִּי לְאַבְרָהָם אָבִיךָ: [בראשית כו, ג]

כ) וַיָּרִיבוּ רֹעֵי גְרָר עִם רֹעֵי יִצְחָק לֵאמֹר לָנוּ הַמָּיִם וַיִּקְרָא שֵׁם הַבְּאֵר עֵשֶׂק כִּי הִתְעַשְּׂקוּ עִמּוֹ: [בראשית כו, כ]

ל) וְהִנֵּה יְיָ נִצָּב עָלָיו וַיֹּאמַר אֲנִי יְיָ אֱלֹהֵי אַבְרָהָם אָבִיךָ וֵאלֹהֵי יִצְחָק הָאָרֶץ אֲשֶׁר אַתָּה שֹׁכֵב עָלֶיהָ לְךָ אֶתְּנֶנָּה וּלְזַרְעֶךָ: [בראשית כח, יג]

מ) וַיֹּאמֶר יְיָ אֶל מֹשֶׁה עַתָּה תִרְאֶה אֲשֶׁר אֶעֱשֶׂה לְפַרְעֹה כִּי בְיָד חֲזָקָה יְשַׁלְּחֵם וּבְיָד חֲזָקָה יְגָרְשֵׁם מֵאַרְצוֹ: [שמות ו, א]

נ) וַיְמַהֵר מֹשֶׁה וַיִּקֹּד אַרְצָה וַיִּשְׁתָּחוּ: [שמות לד, ח]

לד א מיי' פ"ג מהל' ת"ת הלכה יג סמג עשין יב טוש"ע י"ד סי' רמו סעיף כא:

הגהות הגר"א

[א] גמ' שנאמר. נמחק:

ליקוטי רש"י

אל מלך נאמן. כך מעיד על בוראו שהוא אל מלך נאמן [שבת קיט:]. כי אנכי בעלתי בכם. ונקראתם בשמי שאני אדון לכם ואין כבודי להניח אתכם ביד אויבי [ירמיהו ג, יד]. אחד מעיר. אברור הצדיקים ואביאם לציון אף על פי שאין כולם חוזרין [סנהדרין צז:]. ולא תמצא בארץ החיים. במי שמחיה אלא במי שממית עצמו עליה ביגיעה וברעבון [איוב כח, כג]. וענתה שמה. ל' דירה כמו מעון אריות (נחום ב). כימי נעוריה. שישבה במצרים ימים רבים. וכיום עלותה וגומר. שלעקה אלי ממצרים מתוך שיעבוד וגאלתיה כן גם עתה [הושע ב, יז]. אל שדי. שאני כדאי לברך שהברכות שלי [בראשית לה, יא]. ומאז באתי אל פרעה. שאמר משה (לעיל ה, כב) למה הרעותה אמר לו הקב"ה חבל על דאבדין ולא משתכחין יש לי להתאונן על מיתת האבות הרבה פעמים נגליתי אליהם באל שדי ולא אמרו לי מה שמך ואתה אמרת מה שמו מה אומר אליהם וכשבקש אברהם לקבור את שרה לא מצא קבר עד שקנה בדמים מרובים וכן ביצחק ערערו עליו על הבארות אשר חפר וכן ביעקב (בראשית לג, יט) ויקן את חלקת השדה לנטות אהלו ולא הרהרו אחר מדותי ואתה אמרת (ה, כב) למה הרעותה [שמות ו, ט]. עתה תראה וגו'. הרהרת על מדותי לא כאברהם שאמרתי לו (בראשית כא, יב) כי ביצחק יקרא לך זרע, ואחר כך אמרתי לו (שם כב:) העלהו לעולה ולא הרהר אחרי לפיכך עתה תראה העשוי לפרעה תראה ולא העשוי למלכי שבעה אומות כשאביאם לארץ [שמות ו, א]. ארך אפים. מאריך אפו ואינו ממהר ליפרע שמא יעשה תשובה [שמות לד, ו]. ארך אפים ראה. כשעלה משה למרום מצאו משה להקב"ה שהיה יושב וכותב ה' ארך אפים אמר לו לצדיקים אמר לו הקב"ה אף לרשעים אמר לו רשעים יאבדו אמר לו הקב"ה חייך שתצטרך לדבר כשחטאו ישראל בעגל ובמרגלים התפלל משה לפניו בארך אפים אמר לו הקב"ה והלא אמרת לי לצדיקים אמר לו והלא אמרת לי אף לרשעים [במדבר יד, יח]. ארך אף. משמע מאריך רוגז וממתין מליפרע ארך אפים משמע שני רצונים אחת של טובה ואחת של רעה. לצדיקים. מלשלם שכר טוב לאלתר. ולרשעים. מלפרע מהן לאלתר [ב"ק נ:].

Another instance in which Moses was unable to fathom the ways of God:

,,וַיְמַהֵר מֹשֶׁה וַיִּקֹּד אַרְצָה וַיִּשְׁתָּחוּ'' – ***Moses hastened and bowed his head to the ground and prostrated himself.***[42] מָה רָאָה מֹשֶׁה – **What did Moses see** that caused him to bow and prostrate himself?[43] רַבִּי חֲנִינָא בֶּן גַּמְלָא אָמַר – **R' Chanina ben Gamla said:** ,,אֶרֶךְ אַפַּיִם'' רָאָה – **[Moses] saw** the Attribute of ***Slow to Anger;***[44] וְרַבָּנָן אָמְרֵי – **and the Rabbis say:** ,,אֱמֶת'' רָאָה – **He saw** the Attribute of ***Truth.***[45]

The Gemara cites support for one of these views:

תַּנְיָא כְּמַאן דְּאָמַר ,,אֶרֶךְ אַפַּיִם'' רָאָה – **A Baraisa has been taught in accordance with the one who says** that it was the Attribute of ***Slow to Anger*** **that [Moses] saw** that caused him to prostrate himself before God. דְּתַנְיָא – **For a Baraisa has taught:** כְּשֶׁעָלָה מֹשֶׁה לַמָּרוֹם – WHEN MOSES ASCENDED ON HIGH,[46] מְצָאוֹ לְהַקָּדוֹשׁ בָּרוּךְ הוּא שֶׁיּוֹשֵׁב וְכוֹתֵב ,,אֶרֶךְ אַפַּיִם'' – HE FOUND THE HOLY ONE, BLESSED IS HE, SITTING AND WRITING the words *SLOW TO ANGER* in the Torah. אָמַר לְפָנָיו רִבּוֹנוֹ שֶׁל עוֹלָם – [MOSES] SAID BEFORE HIM, "MASTER OF THE UNIVERSE! ,,אֶרֶךְ אַפַּיִם'' לַצַּדִּיקִים – Are You *SLOW TO ANGER* only AT THE RIGHTEOUS?" אָמַר לוֹ – [GOD] SAID TO HIM: אַף לָרְשָׁעִים – "I am slow to anger EVEN AT THE WICKED."[47] אָמַר לוֹ – [MOSES] SAID TO [GOD]: רְשָׁעִים יֹאבְדוּ – "LET THE WICKED PERISH!" Why should you hold back Your anger from them? אָמַר לֵיהּ – [GOD] SAID TO [MOSES]: הַשְׁתָּא חָזֵית מַאי דְּמִבָּעֵי לָךְ – "NOW YOU WILL SEE THAT WHICH YOU ARE IN NEED OF."[48] כְּשֶׁחָטְאוּ יִשְׂרָאֵל – Later, WHEN ISRAEL SINNED in the incident of the Spies and God threatened to destroy them, Moses pleaded that they be spared.[49] אָמַר לוֹ – [GOD] SAID TO [MOSES]: לֹא כָּךְ אָמַרְתָּ לִי ,,אֶרֶךְ אַפַּיִם'' לַצַּדִּיקִים – "IS THIS NOT WHAT WHAT YOU SAID TO ME: 'You should be *SLOW TO ANGER* AT THE RIGHTEOUS but not at the wicked'?" Since Israel has become wicked and followed the counsel of the Spies, why should God be merciful to them?![50]

NOTES

of the rock (*Numbers* 20:12). *Maharsha* suggests that the present decree was not accompanied by God's oath, making the decree subject to annulment through prayer. The subsequent decree at the rock, by contrast, was confirmed by a Divine oath (see *Rashi* ad loc.). This made the decree irrevocable. See also *Margaliyos HaYam*.

42. *Exodus* 34:8. Earlier Moses had asked God that He "show His face" to him (*Exodus* 33:18), i.e. that He grant Moses an unprecedented perception of the Divine reality (*Ramban* ibid.). To this God responded that He would only partially grant Moses' request; He would let Moses see His "back." In conjunction with this revelation, God proclaimed to Moses His Thirteen Attributes of Mercy (*Exodus* 34:6,7): *HASHEM, HASHEM, Almighty, Compassionate and Gracious, Slow to Anger, Abundant in Kindness and Truth; Preserver of Kindness for thousands of generations, Forgiver of Iniquity, Willful Sin, and Error, and Who Cleanses — but does not cleanse completely* . . . In the next verse it states that upon seeing this, Moses hastened to prostrate himself to God.

43. The statement of Scripture that Moses "hurriedly" fell on his face indicates that it was not in response to all Thirteen Attributes that Moses prostrated himself but rather in immediate response to one of them (*Rif* in *Ein Yaakov*). Thus, the Gemara asks which particular Attribute it was that had such a powerful impact upon Moses. [*Maharal* explains this matter differently; his interpretation of the Gemara that follows will be given on 111b; see note 1 there.]

44. Learning that God was slow to anger, Moses prostrated himself before God out of joy (*Rashi* to 111b, ד"ה אמר לפניו).

45. Learning of God's Attribute of Truth, Moses was terrified by the awful specter of God's strict justice. Truth demands that every sin be punished in full. By the dictates of Truth, the sin of the Golden Calf should result in the utter destruction of the Jewish people. Terrified for his people, Moses immediately fell on his face in supplication (*Rashi*).

Yad Ramah explains the view of the Rabbis differently. The Attribute of Truth so thrilled Moses that he fell on his face in joy, for it indicated that once God promised something, nothing would make Him change His word. Since God had promised Eretz Yisrael to the Israelites, Moses now knew that He would keep His promise, no matter how severe the sin of the Golden Calf. [See 111b note 1 for *Maharal's* explanation of this dispute.]

46. That is, to heaven, to receive the Torah from God.

47. The Hebrew word אַפַּיִם (*anger*) is plural (the singular would be אַף). The use of the plural indicates that there are two classes of people to whom God is slow to anger — the righteous and the wicked (*Maharsha* from *Eruvin* 22a, *Bava Kamma* 50b; see further in *Rif* to *Ein Yaakov* here). Moses thus asked God whether this Attribute applied towards the wicked as well, since logic dictates that God's mercy should not be directed towards them (see *Eitz Yosef*; see also *Michtav MeEliyahu* IV 138ff. which discusses the difference in perspective between Moses and God).

48. I.e. you will soon have occasion to see that you need for God to be slow to anger even at the wicked (see *Rashi* to *Numbers* 14:18).

49. Moses sent spies to Eretz Yisrael to report on the condition of the land and the best avenues for invasion. The spies reported that though the land was rich and bountiful, its inhabitants were unconquerable. This caused the people to lose faith in God's promise to bring them to Israel, as a result of which God wished to destroy the entire nation and rebuild it through the descendants of Moses. Moses pleaded with God that the nation be spared, saying: *Hashem, Slow to Anger, Abundant in Kindness, Forgiver of Iniquity, and Willful Sin; and He Who Cleanses — but does not cleanse completely, recalling the iniquity of parents upon children upon the third and fourth generations* (ibid. 14:18).

50. Although Moses had even earlier pleaded for Israel to be spared, after the sin of the Golden Calf, that plea did not consist of asking God to be slow to anger with the wicked. That incident had been the first sin of the nation, and they were therefore not yet considered a wicked people, but rather decent people who had lapsed and sinned. But by the time they sinned on the occasion of the Spies, they had sinned a number of times. Thus, on the occasion of this latest sin they were considered a wicked people (*Maharsha*).

מסורת הש"ס

א) [שבת קיט:], ב) [צ"ל אמר לו רבי יוחנן], ג) [כתובות דף קיא:], ד) [בע"י ליתא], ה) [ב"ב טו:], ו) י"ג גמליאל, ז) [עי' תוס' עירובין כב. ותוס' ב"ק נ: ד"ה ארך].

תורה אור השלם

א) לָכֵן הִרְחִיבָה שְּׁאוֹל נַפְשָׁהּ וּפָעֲרָה פִיהָ לִבְלִי חֹק וְיָרַד הֲדָרָהּ וַהֲמוֹנָהּ וּשְׁאוֹנָהּ וְעָלֵז בָּהּ: [ישעיה ה, יד]

ב) וְהָיָה בְכָל הָאָרֶץ נְאֻם יְיָ פִּי שְׁנַיִם בָּהּ יִכָּרְתוּ יִגְוָעוּ וְהַשְּׁלִשִׁית יִוָּתֶר בָּהּ: [זכריה יג, ח]

ג) שׁוּבוּ בָנִים שׁוֹבָבִים נְאֻם יְיָ כִּי אָנֹכִי בָּעַלְתִּי בָכֶם וְלָקַחְתִּי אֶתְכֶם אֶחָד מֵעִיר וּשְׁנַיִם מִמִּשְׁפָּחָה וְהֵבֵאתִי אֶתְכֶם צִיּוֹן: [ירמיה ג, יד]

ד) לֹא יָדַע אֱנוֹשׁ עֶרְכָּהּ וְלֹא תִמָּצֵא בְּאֶרֶץ הַחַיִּים: [איוב כח, יג]

ה) וְלָקַחְתִּי אֶתְכֶם לִי לְעָם וְהָיִיתִי לָכֶם לֵאלֹהִים וִידַעְתֶּם כִּי אֲנִי יְיָ אֱלֹהֵיכֶם הַמּוֹצִיא אֶתְכֶם מִתַּחַת סִבְלוֹת מִצְרָיִם: [שמות ו, ז]

ו) וְהֵבֵאתִי אֶתְכֶם אֶל הָאָרֶץ אֲשֶׁר נָשָׂאתִי אֶת יָדִי לָתֵת אֹתָהּ לְאַבְרָהָם לְיִצְחָק וּלְיַעֲקֹב וְנָתַתִּי אֹתָהּ לָכֶם מוֹרָשָׁה אֲנִי יְיָ: [שמות ו, ח]

ז) וְנָתַתִּי לָהּ אֶת כְּרָמֶיהָ מִשָּׁם וְאֶת עֵמֶק עָכוֹר לְפֶתַח תִּקְוָה וְעָנְתָה שָּׁמָּה כִּימֵי נְעוּרֶיהָ וּכְיוֹם עֲלֹתָהּ מֵאֶרֶץ מִצְרָיִם: [הושע ב, יז]

ח) וּמֵאָז בָּאתִי אֶל פַּרְעֹה לְדַבֵּר בִּשְׁמֶךָ הֵרַע לָעָם הַזֶּה וְהַצֵּל לֹא הִצַּלְתָּ אֶת עַמֶּךָ: [שמות ה, כג]

ט) קוּם הִתְהַלֵּךְ בָּאָרֶץ לְאָרְכָּהּ וּלְרָחְבָּהּ כִּי לְךָ אֶתְּנֶנָּה: [בראשית יג, יז]

י) גּוּר בָּאָרֶץ הַזֹּאת וְאֶהְיֶה עִמְּךָ וַאֲבָרְכֶךָּ כִּי לְךָ וּלְזַרְעֲךָ אֶתֵּן אֶת כָּל הָאֲרָצֹת הָאֵל וַהֲקִמֹתִי אֶת הַשְּׁבֻעָה אֲשֶׁר נִשְׁבַּעְתִּי לְאַבְרָהָם אָבִיךָ: [בראשית כו, ג]

כ) וַיָּרִיבוּ רֹעֵי גְרָר עִם רֹעֵי יִצְחָק לֵאמֹר לָנוּ הַמָּיִם וַיִּקְרָא שֵׁם הַבְּאֵר עֵשֶׂק כִּי הִתְעַשְּׂקוּ עִמּוֹ: [בראשית כו, כ]

ל) וְהִנֵּה יְיָ נִצָּב עָלָיו וַיֹּאמַר אֲנִי יְיָ אֱלֹהֵי אַבְרָהָם אָבִיךָ וֵאלֹהֵי יִצְחָק הָאָרֶץ אֲשֶׁר אַתָּה שֹׁכֵב עָלֶיהָ לְךָ אֶתְּנֶנָּה וּלְזַרְעֶךָ: [בראשית כח, יג]

מ) וַיֹּאמֶר יְיָ אֶל מֹשֶׁה עַתָּה תִרְאֶה אֲשֶׁר אֶעֱשֶׂה לְפַרְעֹה כִּי בְיָד חֲזָקָה יְשַׁלְּחֵם וּבְיָד חֲזָקָה יְגָרְשֵׁם מֵאַרְצוֹ: [שמות ו, א]

נ) וַיְמַהֵר מֹשֶׁה וַיִּקֹּד אַרְצָה וַיִּשְׁתָּחוּ: [שמות לד, ח]

גמרא

א) מאי אמן א"ר חנינא *אל *מלך *נאמן א) לכן הרחיבה שאול נפשה ופערה פיה לבלי חוק אמר ר"ל למי שמשייר אפי' חוק אחד ב) א"ר יוחנן ג) לא ניחא למרייהו דאמרת להו הכי אלא אפי' לא למד אלא חוק אחד [א] (ד) שנאמר) ב) והיה בכל הארץ נאם ה' פי שנים בה יכרתו ויגועו והשלישית יותר בה אמר ר"ל שלישי של שם א"ל רבי יוחנן לא ניחא למרייהו דאמרת להו הכי אלא אפי' שלישי של נח ג) כי אנכי בעלתי בכם ולקחתי אתכם אחד מעיר ושנים ממשפחה אמר ר"ל דברים ככתבן א"ל ר' יוחנן לא ניחא ליה למרייהו דאמרת להו הכי אלא אחד מעיר מזכה כל העיר כולה ושנים ממשפחה מזכין כל המשפחה כולה יתיב רב כהנא קמיה דרב ויתיב וקאמר דברים ככתבן א"ל רב לא ניחא ליה למרייהו דאמרת להו הכי אלא אחד מעיר מזכה כל העיר ושנים ממשפחה מזכין כל המשפחה חזייה דהוה קא חייף רישיה וסליק ויתיב קמיה דרב א"ל ד) ולא תמצא בארץ החיים א"ל מילט קא לייטת לי א"ל קרא קאמינא לא *תמצא תורה במי שמחיה עצמו עליה תניא רבי סימאי אומר נאמר ה) ולקחתי אתכם לי לעם ונאמר ו) והבאתי אתכם מקיש יציאתן ממצרים לביאתן לארץ מה ביאתן לארץ שנים מס' ריבוא אף יציאתן ממצרים שנים מס' ריבוא אמר רבא וכן לימות המשיח שנא' ז) וענתה שמה כימי נעוריה וכיום עלותה מארץ מצרים תניא אמר ר' אלעזר ברבי יוסי פעם אחת נכנסתי לאלכסנדריא של מצרים מצאתי זקן אחד ואמר לי בא ואראך מה עשו אבותי לאבותיך מהם טבעו בים מהם הרגו בחרב מהם מעכו בבנין ועל דבר זה נענש משה רבינו שנא' ח) ומאז באתי אל פרעה לדבר בשמך הרע לעם הזה אמר לו הקב"ה חבל על דאבדין ולא משתכחין הרי כמה פעמים נגליתי על אברהם יצחק ויעקב באל שדי ולא הרהרו על מדותי ולא אמרו לי מה שמך אמרתי לאברהם ט) קום התהלך בארץ לארכה ולרחבה כי לך אתננה י) בקש מקום לקבור את שרה ולא מצא עד שקנה בד' מאות שקל כסף ולא הרהר על מדותי אמרתי ליצחק י) גור בארץ הזאת ואהיה עמך ואברכך בקשו עבדיו מים לשתות ולא מצאו עד שעשו מריבה שנאמר כ) ויריבו רועי גרר עם רועי יצחק לאמר לנו המים ולא הרהר אחר מדותי אמרתי ליעקב ל) הארץ אשר אתה שוכב עליה לך אתננה ביקש מקום לנטוע אהלו ולא מצא עד שקנה במאה קשיטה ולא הרהר אחר מדותי ולא אמרו לי מה שמך ואתה אמרת לי מה שמך בתחלה ועכשיו אתה אומר לי ח) והצל לא הצלת את עמך מ) עתה תראה (את) אשר אעשה לפרעה במלחמת פרעה אתה רואה ואי אתה רואה במלחמת שלשים ואחד מלכים נ) וימהר משה ויקוד ארצה וישתחו מה ראה משה ר' חנינא בן ו) גמלא אמר ארך אפים ראה ורבנן אמרי אמת ראה: תניא כמ"ד ארך אפים ראה דתניא כשעלה משה למרום מצאו להקב"ה שיושב וכותב ארך אפים אמר לפניו רבונו של עולם ז) ארך אפים לצדיקים אמר לו אף לרשעים א"ל רשעים יאבדו א"ל השתא חזית מאי דמבעי לך כשחטאו ישראל אמר לו לא כך אמרת לי ארך אפים לצדיקים

אמר

רש"י

מאי אמן. כשעונין על כל ברכה וברכה אמן היאך משמע קבלת יראת שמים: אל מלך נאמן. בנוטריקון שמאמין עליו הקב"ה: למי שמשייר אפילו חק אחד. מלשמרו נידון בגיהנם: לא ניחא ליה למרייהו. אין הקב"ה רוצה שתהא דן את ישראל כל כך לכף חובה: פי שנים בה יכרתו. ויגועו והשלישית יותר בה: אמר ר"ל שלישי של שם. שב' חלקים של כל העולם יהיו נכרתים וחלק ג' יותר בה ואיזה חלק שלישי כל שלישיות שיש לשלש אנו משלשין שמנח נפרדו כל העולם וג' בנים היו לו הרי שליש בניו שם ושלישי של שם הוא ארפכשד כדכתיב בני שם עילם ואשור וארפכשד ולוד וארם ומסתמא בזרעו של ארפכשד יהיה שארית הואיל וישראל יוצאים ממנו ושלישי של ארפכשד שהוא שלישי של שם שהוא שלישי של נח יוותר וכל העולם יכרת ולדברי ר"ל נמצאו ישראל מתמעטין ביותר שמארפכשד יצאו ישראל כדכתיב בפ' נח ארפכשד הוליד את שלח ושלח הוליד את עבר ועבר הוליד את פלג עד אברהם וכשאתה מחלק לג' חלקים זרעו של ארפכשד כגון בני ישראל וישמעאל שהן בני אברהם ובני לוט ובני הרן וכן שאר האומות שיצאו ממנו לג' חלקים שמא ישראל יהיו מרובין וקרובין להיות כנגד כולם ולא יגיעו כל זרע ארפכשד להיות פי שנים אא"כ ישראל משלימין רובן או חציין ונמצאו ישראל מתמעטין בתוך פי שנים: לא ניחא ליה למרייהו. להקב"ה שאתה ממעט אותן כל כך אלא אפילו שלישי של נח כלומר מכל בני נח דהיינו מכל העולם כולו יותר השליש ומסתמא אותו חלק הג' שישראל בו יהיה שארית ואם אין ישראל מרובין כל כך להיות אחד מג' שבעולם יהיו הגרים וחסידי עובדי כוכבים להשלים לשליש ואם הם מרובין להיות יותר מחלק השלישית יתמעטו קצת ומ"מ לרבי יוחנן אין ישראל מתמעטין כל כך כמו לדברי ר"ש בן לקיש מ"ר ל"א שלישי של שם והשלישית משמע שני שליש לכך נאמר שלישית שלישית של שלישי לשם וכתיב ובני שם עילם ואשור וארפכשד וישראל מארפכשד הוו ושלישית מארפכשד שהוא שלישי לשם יותר היינו שלישית מישראל אלא שלישי שלישי של נח כלומר כולו ארפכשד יותר בה שהוא שלישי שלישי של נח דשם היה בן שלישי של נח דכתיב (בראשית י) ובני נח שם חם ויפת וארפכשד שלישי לשם ועיקר: דברים ככתבן. שלא ימלטו אלא אחד מעיר ושנים ממשפחה: ולקחתי אחד מעיר. בשביל חסיד אחד שבעיר אקח את כל העיר כולה: חזייה. רב לרב כהנא: דקא חייף רישיה. חופף ראשו ומעדן בעצמו בשעה שהיה לו ללמוד תורה: לא תמצא בארץ החיים. משמע שמקללו לא תבוא לעוה"ב: נאמר. בפרשת וארא ולקחתי אתכם לי לעם וכתיב בתריה והבאתי אתכם אל הארץ: מה ביאתם לארץ שנים מס' רבוא. שלא נשתיירו מס' רבוא שיצאו ממצרים אלא ב' אנשים יהושע וכלב כדאמרינן בבבא בתרא בפ' יש נוחלין (דף קכא.) לא נגזרה גזרה לא בפחות מכ' ולא ביותר מס' שנה בהנך נמי ששים רבוא שנמנו במדבר לא אחשוב לא פחות מבן כ' שנה ויותר מס': אף יציאתן ממצרים שנים מס' רבוא. שמכל ס' רבוא שהיו במצרים לא נשתייר מהם אלא שנים בלבד ואותם שנים של ס' רבוא עלו [לס' רבואות שיצאו אחד מס' רבוא שהיו בהם] והשאר מתו כולם בשלשת ימי אפילה שלא יהיו מצרים רואין במפלתן של ישראל: וכן לימות המשיח. שלא ישארו מכל ס' רבוא אלא ב': וענתה שמה כימי נעוריה וכיום עלותה מארץ מצרים. עניים ושפלים יהיו כימי עלותה מארץ מצרים: מעכו בבנין. היו בונין אותם במקום לבנים: ועל דבר זה נענש משה רבינו. שכשראה שנעשה לישראל כך התחיל להתרעם ולהרהר לפני הקב"ה אמר משה לפני הקב"ה ומאז באתי: א"ל חבל על דאבדין ולא משתכחין. הפסד גדול יש על גדולים שאבדו ואיני יכול למצוא חסידים אחרים כמותם שאין אתה כאברהם ויצחק ויעקב שלא הרהרו אחרי מדותי: אל שדי. שאמרתי לו אני אל שדי פרה ורבה וגו' (בראשית לה) אני אל שדי התהלך לפני והיה תמים (שם יז) והייתי מבטיחו שכל א"י לו ולבניו ולא אמרו מה שמך כמו שעשית אתה: בתחלה אמרת לי מה שמך. ועכשיו הרהרת על מדותי ואמרת הצל לא הצלת את עמך: לנטוע אהלו. כמו [ויטע] אהלי אפדנו (דניאל יא) ולשון נטיעה שייך באהל: עתה תראה. הפעם תראה נפלאות שאני עושה להם: מה ראה על איזה מדה (אחת) של י"ג [מדות] ראה והשתחוה: אמת ראה. במדותיו שנקרא אמת ונתיירא אם נתחייבו כלייה אם הוא דן אותן בדין גמור ומיהר והתפלל עליהם שלא יהא דן אותן לפי מעשיהם: ה"ג תניא כמ"ד ארך אפים ראה דתניא כשעלה משה למרום וכו' אמר לו רשעים יאבדו ולא יהיה לך ארך אפים עליהם: אמר לו. הקב"ה לא כך אמרת ארך אפים לצדיקים ולא לרשעים:

אמר

עין משפט נר מצוה

לד א מיי' פ"ג מהל' ת"ת הלכה יג סמג עשין יב טוש"ע י"ד סי' רמו סעיף כא:

הגהות הגר"א

[א] גמ' שנאמר. נמחק:

ליקוטי רש"י

אל מלך נאמן. כך מעיד על בוראו שהוא אל מלך נאמן [שבת קיט:]. כי אנכי בעלתי בכם. ונקראתם בשמי שאני אדון לכם ואין כבודי להניח אתכם ביד אויבי [ירמיהו ג, יד]. אחד מעיר. אברור הצדיקים ואביאם לציון אף על פי שאין כולם חוזרין [סנהדרין צז:]. ולא תמצא בארץ החיים. במי שממיה אלא במי שממית עצמו עליה ביגיעה וברעבון [איוב כח, כג]. וענתה שמה. ל' דירה כמו מעון אריות (נחום ב). כימי נעוריה. שישבה במצרים ימים רבים. וכיום עלותה וגומר. שלעקה אלי ממצרים מתוך שיעבוד וגאלתיה כן גם עתה [הושע ב, יז]. אל שדי. שאני כדאי לברך שהברכות שלי [בראשית לה, יא]. ומאז באתי אל פרעה. שאמר משה (לעיל ה, כב) למה הרעותה אמר לו הקב"ה חבל על דאבדין ולא משתכחין יש לי להתאונן על מיתת האבות הרבה פעמים נגליתי אליהם באל שדי ולא אמרו לי מה שמך ואתה אמרת מה שמו מה אומר אליהם וכשבקש אברהם לקבור את שרה לא מצא קבר עד שקנה בדמים מרובים וכן ביצחק ערערו עליו על הבארות אשר חפר וכן ביעקב (בראשית לג, יט) ויקן את חלקת השדה לנטות אהלו ולא הרהרו אחר מדותי ואתה אמרת (ה, כב) למה הרעותה [שמות ו, ט]. עתה תראה וגו'. הרהרת על מדותי לא כאברהם שאמרתי לו (בראשית כא, יב) כי ביצחק יקרא לך זרע, ואחר כך אמרתי לו (שם כב:) העלהו לעולה ולא הרהר אחרי לפיכך עתה תראה העשוי לפרעה תראה ולא העשוי למלכי שבעה אומות כשאביאם לארץ [שמות ו, א]. ארך אפים. מאריך אפו ואינו ממהר ליפרע שמא יעשה תשובה [שמות לד, ו]. ארך אפים ראה. כשעלה משה למרום מצאו להקב"ה שהיה יושב וכותב ה' ארך אפים אמר לו לצדיקים אמר לו הקב"ה אף לרשעים אמר לו רשעים יאבדו אמר לו הקב"ה חייך שתצטרך לדבר כשחטאו ישראל בעגל ובמרגלים התפלל משה לפניו בארך אפים אמר לו הקב"ה והלא אמרת לי לצדיקים אמר לו והלא אמרת לי אף לרשעים [במדבר יד, יח]. ארך אף. משמע מאריך רוגז וממתין מליפרע ארך אפים משמע שני רצונים אחת של טובה ואחת של רעה. לצדיקים. מלשלם שכר טוב לאלתר. ולרשעים. מלפרע מהן לאלתר [ב"ק נ:].

אמר לפניו רבש"ע ולא כך אמרת לי אף לרשעים והיינו דכתיב א) ועתה יגדל נא כח ה' כאשר דברת לאמר ר' חגא הוה סליק ואזיל בדרגא דבי רבה בר שילא שמעיה להההוא ינוקא דאמר ב) עדותיך נאמנו מאד לביתך נאוה קדש ה' לאורך ימים וסמיך ליה ג) תפלה למשה וגו' אמר ש"מ ארך אפים ראה א) א"ר אלעזר א"ר חנינא עתיד הקב"ה להיות עטרה בראש כל צדיק וצדיק שנאמר ד) ביום ההוא יהיה ה' צבאות לעטרת צבי ולצפירת תפארה לשאר עמו וגו' מאי לעטרת צבי ולצפירת תפארה לעושים [א] רצונו ומצפים [ב] לישועתו יכול לכל ת"ל לשאר עמו ב) למי שמשים עצמו כשירים ה) ולרוח משפט ליושב על המשפט ולגבורה משיבי מלחמה שערה ולרוח משפט זה הרודה את יצרו וליושב על המשפט זה הדן דין אמת לאמיתו ולגבורה זה המתגבר ביצרו משיבי מלחמה זה שנושא ונותן במלחמתה של תורה שערה אלו שמשכימין ומעריבין בבתי כנסיות ובתי מדרשות אמרה מדת הדין לפני הקב"ה רבש"ע מה נשתנו אלו מאלו אמר לה ו) וגם אלה ביין שגו ובשכר תעו [וגו'] פקו פליליה ואין פוקה אלא גיהנם שנאמר ז) לא תהיה זאת לך לפוקה ואין פלילה אלא דיינין שנאמר ח) ונתן בפלילים: **מתני'** ג) אנשי עיר הנדחת אין להם חלק לעוה"ב שנאמר ט) יצאו אנשים בני בליעל מקרבך וידיחו את (אנשי) [יושבי] עירם א) ואינן נהרגים עד שיהיו מדיחיה מאותה העיר ומאותו השבט ועד שיודח רובה ועד שידיחוה אנשים הדיחוה נשים וקטנים או שהודח מיעוטה או שהיה מדיחיה חוצה לה הרי אלו כיחידים ב) וצריכין ב' עדים והתראה לכל אחד ואחד זה חומר ביחידים מבמרובים ג) שהיחידים בסקילה לפיכך ממונם פלט ד) והמרובין בסייף לפיכך ממונם אבד י) הכה תכה את יושבי העיר ד) הזאת לפי חרב ה) החמרת והגמלת העוברת ממקום למקום א] הרי אלו מצילין אותה [ג] שנא' י) החרם אותה ואת כל אשר בה ואת בהמתה לפי חרב ה) מכאן אמרו נכסי צדיקים שבתוכה אובדין שבחוצה לה פליטין ו) ושל רשעים בין שבתוכה בין שבחוצה לה הרי אלו אובדין [ד] שנאמר כ) ואת כל שללה תקבוץ אל תוך רחבה וגו' אם ז) אין לה רחוב עושין לה רחוב היתה רחבה חוצה לה כונסין אותה לתוכה שנאמר כ) ושרפת באש את העיר ואת כל שללה כליל לה' אלהיך שללה ולא שלל שמים מכאן אמרו ח) ההקדשות שבה יפדו ותרומות ירקבו מעשר שני וכתבי הקדש יגנזו כליל לה' אלהיך אמר ר"ש אמר הקב"ה ט) אם אתם עושין דין בעיר הנדחת מעלה אני עליכם כאילו אתם מעלים עולה כליל לפני כ) והיתה תל עולם י) לא תעשה י) גנות ופרדסים דברי ר' יוסי הגלילי ר"ע אומר י) לא תבנה עוד לכמות שהיתה אינה נבנית אבל נעשית היא גנות ופרדסים ל) ולא ידבק בידך מאומה מן החרם שכל זמן שהרשעים בעולם חרון אף בעולם אבדו רשעים מן העולם נסתלק חרון אף מן העולם: **גמ'** ת"ר יצאו הן ולא שלוחין אנשים כ) אין אנשים פחות מב' דבר אחר אנשים ל) ולא נשים אנשים ולא קטנים בני בליעל בנים שפרקו עול שמים מצואריהם מ) מקרבך מ) ולא מן הספר יושבי עירם ולא יושבי עיר אחרת לאמר שצריכין עדים והתראה לכל אחד ואחד איתמר ר' יוחנן אמר חולקין עיר אחת לשני שבטים ור"ל אמר ט) אין חולקין עיר אחת לב' שבטים איתיביה ר' יוחנן לר"ל עד שיהו מדיחיה מאותה העיר ומאותו שבט מאי לאו אע"ג דמדיחיה מאותה העיר אי איכא מאותו שבט אין אי לא לא ש"מ חולקין עיר אחת לב' שבטים לא דנפלה ליה בירושה א"נ דיהבוה ניהליה במתנה איתיביה מ) ערים תשע מאת שני השבטים האלה מאי לאו ארבע ופלגא מהאי וארבע ופלגא מהאי וש"מ חולקין עיר אחת לב' שבטים לא ארבעה מהאי וחמש מהאי אי הכי לפרוש פרושי

קשיא

אמר לפניו וכו'. והשתא [מסתברא] כמ"ד ארך אפים ראה שכיון שראה [מדה זו] בהקב"ה שהוא ארך אפים אף לרשעים שמח: עדותיך וגו' ה' לאורך ימים. היינו מדת ארך אפים ועליה אמר משה עדותיך נאמנו מאד שראה אותו בחורב ופסוק זה מרע"ה אמרו דכתיב לעיל מיניה תפלה למשה איש האלהים וגו': יכול לכל. למי שעושין רלונו אע"פ שמתגאה: כשירים. שיריים שאין נחשבין כך אינו חשוב בעיניו ואינו מתגאה: ולרוח משפט. שופט את רוחו: שרודה ביצרו. שכועס בילרו וחוזר בתשובה מן העבירה שעבר: ומתגבר ביצרו. מרגיז יל"ט על יצה"ר אם היצה"ר אמר לו עשה עבירה זו לא דיו שנמנע מן העבירה אלא הולך ועושה מצוה ומתגבר עליו מרודהו: שערה. אלו בתי כנסיות: מה נשתנו אלו מאלו. שיש בהם מדות הללו מן השאר אמר הקב"ה ביין שגו: ואין פלילה אלא דיינין: **מתני'** יצאו אנשים בני בליעל מקרבך. שאין להם חלק לעוה"ב: וידיחו את (אנשי) [יושבי] עירם. הא אין נהרגים עד שיהיו מדיחיה מאותה העיר ואותה השבט עצמה דכתיב מקרבך מקרב אותו שבט עצמו: עד שיודח רובה. דכתיב ויושבי העיר משמע ישובה של עיר היינו רובה לישנא אחרינא עד שיודח רובה דכתיב מקרבך קרי ביה מרובך: ה"ג עד שיודח רובה עד שידיחוה אנשים: או שהיו מדיחיה חוצה לה. שלא היו מאותה העיר: הרי אלו כיחידים. שהן בסקילה וממונן פלט: וצריכים ב' עדים והתראה לכל אחד. כדיליף בגמרא [ב] יחידים בסקילה לפיכך ממונן פלט ומתוך שהחמרת עליו במיתתו הקלת עליו בממונו: הכה תכה את יושבי העיר ההיא לפי חרב החמרת והגמלת העוברת ממקום למקום מצילין. מדכתיב יושבי מכלל דשיירה של חמרים וגמלים שנשתהו בעיר ל' יום כדמפרש בגמרא דהוו להו יושבי העיר הרי אלו מצילין אם רוב אנשי העיר הודחו וחמרים וגמלים משלימין המיעוט ועושה אותם רוב מצילין עליהם שאין ממונם אבד אלא נדונים כיחידים וגורמין נמי לעשות אותה עיר הנדחת אם משלימים לעיר הנדחת לעשות רוב אלא הא פסיקא טפי דחמרת וגמלת אין דעתם מעורבת עם בני העיר להיות נדונין עמהן: ה"ג החרם אותה וכל אשר בה מכאן אמרו לדיקים וכו' ושל רשעים בין מתוכה בין מחוצה לה אבודים. בגמרא מפרש לה מדכתיב כל: ואת כל שללה תקבוץ אל תוך רחובה אין לה רחוב עושין לה רחוב. ורחובה דהשתא נמי משמע: היה רחובה חוצה לה. שמקום קבוץ בני העיר היה חוץ לעיר כונסין אותה לעיר שצריך לעשות לה רחוב בתוכה. רחוב סרטיא גדולה: את העיר ואת כל שללה ולא שלל שמים. דשלל שמים פלט: מכאן אמרו הקדשות שבתוכה יפדו. כלומר אין נשרפין אלא הרי הם כשאר הקדש שצריך פדייה כ"ש דשלל שמים הם: ותרומות ירקבו. ובגמ' מוקמי לה בתרומה ביד כהן דממון כהן הוא וחל עליה איסור דעיר הנדחת דנהי דבשריפה לא הויא עם שאר שללה דקדש אקרי ולא מזלזלינן ביה כולי האי: מעשר שני. אע"פ שהוא נאכל לישראל הואיל וקדש איקרי לא אמרי' ישרף אלא יגנזו וכן כתבי הקדש יגנזו: ה"ג כליל לה' אלהיך אר"ש אמר הקב"ה וכו' כאילו אתה מעלה עולה שהוא כליל לפני: לא תעשה גנות ופרדסין וכו'. בגמ' מפרש במאי פליגי: לכמו שהיתה. ביישוב בתים: **גמ'** יצאו הם ולא שלוחם. אם המדיחין עצמן יצאו והדיחן והרי הם מרובים ודנין בסייף אבל אם הדיחו ע"י שליח כיחידים הם בסקילה וממונם פלט: אין אנשים פחות מב'. דע"י מדיח אחד אין נעשית עיר הנדחת: בקרבך. משמע באמצע ולא מן הספר שאם היתה עיר של ספר בין מחוז עובדי כוכבים למחוז ישראל אינה נעשית עיר הנדחת דגזירת הכתוב היא שלא תעשה עיר הנדחת: יושבי העיר ולא יושבי עיר אחרת. דהיינו מדיחי' מחוצה לה: לאמר נלכה ונעבדה. משמע שצ"ל לפנינו שכך אומרים נלכה ונעבדה ואין אמירה אלא בעדים אלמא צריך עדים לכל אחד ואחד שיעידו עליהם מה שאמרו וה"נ צריך התראה לכל א' וא' מהם: חולקין עיר אחת. בתחלה כשחלקו ישראל את הארץ היו רשאין ליתן ולחלוק עיר א' לב' שבטים כגון אם אירע להם עיר בתחום ומקלת מושכת לתחום אחר שבט אחד נוטל חלק באותו קלת הארץ ע"פ הגורל נחלקה הארץ אם נפתלי עולה תחום גינוסר עולה עמו דהכי אמרינן בב"ב בפרק י"נ ומנחילין (דף קכב.): אין חולקין. אלא כולה של אותו השבט שרוב' בתחומי': מאי לאו אע"ג דמדיחיה מאותה עיר. אם יהיו מאותו שבט נעשית עיר הנדחת ואי לא שאם אינו מאותו שבט שהודחו אלא משבט אחר שבעיר אינו בסייף אלא בסקילה אלמא אפשר שיהו מן אותה העיר ולא מאותו שבט וה"ד כגון שחלקו עיר אחת לשני שבטים: לא. לעולם אימא לך דאין חולקין והיכי משכחת לה מאותה עיר ולא מאותו שבט כגון דנפלה למדיחיה בירושה מקלת העיר ע"י בת יורשת נחלה: ערים תשע מאת שני השבטים האלה. ממטה יהודה וממטה שמעון נטלו ט' ערים ונתנום ללוים: מאי לאו דשקל מהאי ד' ופלגא. שהיתה עיר א' של יהודה ושמעון ונטלו מהם אלמא חולקין עיר אחת לשני שבטים: ה"ג לא ד' מהאי וה' מהאי: א"ה לפרוש פרושי. הי ניניהו שבט דשקיל מיניה ה' והי ניניהו דשקיל מיניה ד' ומאחי כתיב ערים תשע מאת שני השבטים משמע דבשוה שקל:

קשיא

עין משפט נר מצוה

לה א מיי' פ"ד מהל' ע"ז הלכה ב סמג עשין טו:
לו ב מיי' שם הלכה ה והלכה ו:
לז ג מיי' שם הל' ב:
לח ד מיי' שם הל' ו:
לט ה מיי' שם הל' ז:
מ ו מיי' שם הל' י:
מא ז מיי' שם הל' ו:
מב ח מיי' שם הל' יג:
מג ט מיי' שם הל' ו:
מד י מיי' שם הל' ז:
מה כ ל מיי' שם הל' ב:
מו מ מיי' שם הל' ד:

הגהות מהר"ב רנשבורג

א] מתני' הרי אלו מצילין אותה שנאמר וכו' הרי אלו אובדין שנאמר וכו' כונסין אותה לתוכה שנאמר. אלו ג"פ שנאמר נמחקו: ב] רש"י ד"ה וצריכין וכו' כדיליף בגמ'. כאן הס"ד ומה"ד יחידים:

ליקוטי רש"י

יגדל נא כח ה'. לעשות דבורך. כאשר דברת לאמר. ומהו הדבור [במדבר יד, יז]. תפלה למשה. אחד עשר מזמורים מכאן עד לדוד מזמור כלם משה אמרם [תהלים צ, א]. ביום ההוא. כהתם הפושעים. יהיה ה' צבאות לעטרת צבי. לצדיקים הנשארים בה [ישעיהו כח, ה]. ולרוח משפט. יהיה הקב"ה להורות משפט ליושב על המשפט. ולגבורה. יהיה לאותן שהם משיבי מלחמ' מלחמתה של תורה [שם פסוק ו]. לרוח משפט. לשופטים את רוחן יהיה לעטרה. הרודה את יצרו. כופהו לשוב בתשובה. המתגבר על יצרו. אינו הולך אחריו לעבור עבירה. שמשכימין כו'. והיינו שערה שעושין [שנעשים שוערים] לפתוח דלתות בהשכמה ולאחר [שם עד] זמן נעילתו. גם אלה. אלו הרשעים הנידונין בגיהנם. ביין שגו. כלומר אף הם עשו כהם לפיכך דנם. מלחמתה של תורה. הוריותיה ולעמוד על בוריה ועל עיקרה [לעיל מב.]. להתוכח בתלמוד [לעיל צג:]. פקו פליליה. לגיהנם נשפטו [מגילה טו:]. וגם אלה. יושבי משפט ומשיבי מלחמה שבדור הזה כלומר טובים וחשובים שבהן ביין שגו כי עתה אין טוב בהם. פקו פליליה. הכשילו המשפט. פקו. לשון פיק ברכים (נחום ב') פוקה (שמואל א' כ"ה) [ישעיה כח, ז]. ולא תהיה וגו' לפוקה. לכשלון כמו לפיק ברכים (נחום ב' י"א) [ש"א כה, לא]. ונתן. המכה דמי ולדות. בפלילים. על פי הדיינים [שמות כא, כב]. ישבי עירם. ולא יושבי עיר אחרת מכאן אמרו אין נעשית עיר הנדחת עד שידיחוה אנשים ועד שיהיו מדיחיה מתוכה [דברים יג, יד]. החמרת והגמלת. שיירא של חמרים ושל גמלים [ב"ב ח.]. ולא ידבק בידך מאומה מן החרם. למען ישוב ה' מחרון אפו שכל זמן שעבודה זרה בעולם, חרון אף בעולם [דברים יג, יח].

מסורת הש"ס

א) עיין רש"א בח"א [מגילה טו: ע"ש כמה שינויים ועי' בפירש"י שם], ב) [ר"ה יז:], ג) [עי' תוספות לעיל מז. ד"ה ואמאי], ד) בקרא ההיא, ה) ב"ב ח., ו) [בפס"מ לא תבנה עוד], ז) [בפס"מ אפי' גנות וכו'], ח) [לעיל טז:], ט) [הא דירושלים נחלקה לשבט יהודה ובנימין ע"פ הדיבור היה. ת"י ביומא יב].

הגהות הגר"א

[א] גמ' רצונו. נמחק ונ"ב לביונו: [ב] שם לישועתו. נמחק ונ"ב לתפארתו: [ג] שם שנאמר. נמחק: [ד] שנא'. נמחק:

תורה אור השלם

א) וְעַתָּה יִגְדַּל נָא כֹּחַ אֲדֹנָי כַּאֲשֶׁר דִּבַּרְתָּ לֵאמֹר: [במדבר יד, יז]

ב) עֵדֹתֶיךָ נֶאֶמְנוּ מְאֹד לְבֵיתְךָ נַאֲוָה קֹדֶשׁ יְיָ לְאֹרֶךְ יָמִים: [תהלים צג, ה]

ג) תְּפִלָּה לְמֹשֶׁה אִישׁ הָאֱלֹהִים אֲדֹנָי מָעוֹן אַתָּה הָיִיתָ לָּנוּ בְּדֹר וָדֹר: [תהלים צ, א]

ד) בַּיּוֹם הַהוּא יִהְיֶה יְיָ צְבָאוֹת לַעֲטֶרֶת צְבִי וְלִצְפִירַת תִּפְאָרָה לִשְׁאָר עַמּוֹ: [ישעיה כח, ה]

ה) וּלְרוּחַ מִשְׁפָּט לַיּוֹשֵׁב עַל הַמִּשְׁפָּט וְלִגְבוּרָה מְשִׁיבֵי מִלְחָמָה שָׁעְרָה: [ישעיה כח, ו]

ו) וְגַם אֵלֶּה בַּיַּיִן שָׁגוּ וּבַשֵּׁכָר תָּעוּ כֹּהֵן וְנָבִיא שָׁגוּ בַשֵּׁכָר נִבְלְעוּ מִן הַיַּיִן תָּעוּ מִן הַשֵּׁכָר שָׁגוּ בָּרֹאֶה פָּקוּ פְּלִילִיָּה: [ישעיה כח, ז]

ז) וְלֹא תִהְיֶה זֹאת לְךָ לְפוּקָה וּלְמִכְשׁוֹל לֵב לַאדֹנִי וְלִשְׁפָּךְ דָּם חִנָּם וּלְהוֹשִׁיעַ אֲדֹנִי לוֹ וְהֵיטִב יְיָ לַאדֹנִי וְזָכַרְתָּ אֶת אֲמָתֶךָ: [שמואל א' כה, לא]

ח) וְכִי יִנָּצוּ אֲנָשִׁים וְנָגְפוּ אִשָּׁה הָרָה וְיָצְאוּ יְלָדֶיהָ וְלֹא יִהְיֶה אָסוֹן עָנוֹשׁ יֵעָנֵשׁ כַּאֲשֶׁר יָשִׁית עָלָיו בַּעַל הָאִשָּׁה וְנָתַן בִּפְלִלִים: [שמות כא, כב]

ט) יָצְאוּ אֲנָשִׁים בְּנֵי בְלִיַּעַל מִקִּרְבֶּךָ וַיַּדִּיחוּ אֶת יֹשְׁבֵי עִירָם לֵאמֹר נֵלְכָה וְנַעַבְדָה אֱלֹהִים אֲחֵרִים אֲשֶׁר לֹא יְדַעְתֶּם: [דברים יג, יד]

י) הַכֵּה תַכֶּה אֶת יֹשְׁבֵי הָעִיר הַהִוא לְפִי חָרֶב הַחֲרֵם אֹתָהּ וְאֶת כָּל אֲשֶׁר בָּהּ וְאֶת בְּהֶמְתָּהּ לְפִי חָרֶב: [דברים יג, טז]

כ) וְאֶת כָּל שְׁלָלָהּ תִּקְבֹּץ אֶל תּוֹךְ רְחֹבָהּ וְשָׂרַפְתָּ בָאֵשׁ אֶת הָעִיר וְאֶת כָּל שְׁלָלָהּ כָּלִיל לַייָ אֱלֹהֶיךָ וְהָיְתָה תֵּל עוֹלָם לֹא תִבָּנֶה עוֹד: [דברים יג, יז]

ל) וְלֹא יִדְבַּק בְּיָדְךָ מְאוּמָה מִן הַחֵרֶם לְמַעַן יָשׁוּב יְיָ מֵחֲרוֹן אַפּוֹ וְנָתַן לְךָ רַחֲמִים וְרִחַמְךָ וְהִרְבֶּךָ כַּאֲשֶׁר נִשְׁבַּע לַאֲבֹתֶיךָ: [דברים יג, יח]

מ) וְאֶת עַיִן וְאֶת מִגְרָשֶׁהָ וְאֶת יֻטָּה וְאֶת מִגְרָשֶׁהָ אֶת בֵּית שֶׁמֶשׁ וְאֶת מִגְרָשֶׁהָ עָרִים תֵּשַׁע מֵאֵת שְׁנֵי הַשְּׁבָטִים הָאֵלֶּה: [יהושע כא, טז]

אָמַר לְפָנָיו רִבּוֹנוֹ שֶׁל עוֹלָם – [MOSES] SAID TO [GOD], "MASTER OF THE UNIVERSE! וְלֹא כָּךְ אָמַרְתָּ לִי אַף לָרְשָׁעִים – AND DID YOU NOT SAY TO ME that You are slow to anger EVEN AT THE WICKED?!" וְהַיְינוּ דִּכְתִיב ,,וְעַתָּה יִגְדַּל־נָא כֹּחַ אֲדֹנָי כַּאֲשֶׁר דִּבַּרְתָּ לֵאמֹר'' – AND THAT IS THE MEANING OF THAT WHICH IS WRITTEN: *AND NOW, MAY THE STRENGTH OF MY LORD BE MAGNIFIED, AS YOU HAVE previously SAID, "HASHEM, Slow to Anger, Abundant in Kindness, Forgiver of Iniquity and Willful Sin, and Who Cleanses – but does not cleanse completely, recalling the iniquity of parents upon children, upon the third and fourth generations."*[1]

The Gemara cites another support for the view that Moses was moved by hearing that God was slow to anger:

רַבִּי חַגָּא הֲוָה סָלֵיק וְאָזִיל בְּדַרְגָּא דְּבֵי רַבָּה בַּר שֵׁילָא – **R' Chagga was** once **walking up the steps of the academy of Rabbah bar Shela.** שַׁמְעֵיהּ לְהַהוּא יְנוּקָא דְּאָמַר – **He heard a certain child reciting** the following verse: ,,עֵדֹתֶיךָ נֶאֶמְנוּ מְאֹד לְבֵיתְךָ נַאֲוָה־קֹדֶשׁ ה׳ לְאֹרֶךְ יָמִים'' – ***Your testimonies are very trustworthy; holiness befits Your house, O Hashem, [You] Who are [slow to anger] for many days.***[2] וְסָמִיךְ לֵיהּ ,,תְּפִלָּה לְמֹשֶׁה וגו׳ '' – **Now close by to [that verse] is** the psalm beginning with the words: ***A prayer of Moses, etc.*** indicating that the previous verse cited was also said by Moses.[3] אָמַר – **[R' Chagga] said:** שְׁמַע מִינָּהּ אֶרֶךְ אַפַּיִם רָאָה – **It is evident from this that it was the Attribute of *Slow to Anger* that Moses saw** that moved him to prostrate himself in gratitude and joy.[4]

This section concludes with a discussion of the reward destined for the righteous:

אָמַר רַבִּי אֶלְעָזָר אָמַר רַבִּי חֲנִינָא – **R' Elazar said in the name of R' Chanina:** עָתִיד הַקָּדוֹשׁ בָּרוּךְ הוּא לִהְיוֹת עֲטָרָה בְּרֹאשׁ כָּל צַדִּיק וְצַדִּיק – **In the future, the Holy One, Blessed is He, will be a crown on the head of every single righteous person,**[5] שֶׁנֶּאֱמַר ,,בַּיּוֹם הַהוּא יִהְיֶה ה׳ צְבָאוֹת לַעֲטֶרֶת צְבִי וְלִצְפִירַת תִּפְאָרָה לִשְׁאָר עַמּוֹ וגו׳ '' – **as it is stated: *On that day shall Hashem, Lord of Hosts, be for a crown of beauty and a diadem of glory to the remnant of His people etc.***[6] מַאי ,,לַעֲטֶרֶת צְבִי וְלִצְפִירַת תִּפְאָרָה'' – **What** is signified by the words ***a crown of beauty and a diadem of glory?*** לָעוֹשִׂים רְצוֹנוֹ – They teach that this reward is destined **for those who do His will,**[7] וּמְצַפִּים לִישׁוּעָתוֹ – **and** for **those who await His salvation.**[8] יָכוֹל לַכֹּל – Now, **it might have been** thought that this Divine coronation **is for anyone** who does God's will.[9] תַּלְמוּד לוֹמַר – **The verse** therefore **states** immediately afterward: ,,לִשְׁאָר עַמּוֹ'' – ***to the remnant of His people,*** לְמִי שֶׁמֵּשִׂים עַצְמוֹ כְּשִׁירַיִם – to teach that this reward is only **for one who makes himself like remnants,** i.e. he is humble.[10]

The next verse in that passage is interpreted as listing the traits of those who will receive this Divine reward:

,,וּלְרוּחַ מִשְׁפָּט לַיּוֹשֵׁב עַל־הַמִּשְׁפָּט וְלִגְבוּרָה מְשִׁיבֵי מִלְחָמָה שָׁעְרָה'' – ***And** [God will be] **for a spirit of judgment to he who sits in judgment, and for strength** [to] **those who turn back the battle to the gate** [of the foe].* ,,וּלְרוּחַ מִשְׁפָּט'' זֶה הָרוֹדֶה אֶת יִצְרוֹ – ***For a spirit of judgment:*** **This** refers **to one who controls his** Evil **Inclination.**[11] ,,לַיּוֹשֵׁב עַל־הַמִּשְׁפָּט'' זֶה הַדָּן דִּין אֱמֶת לַאֲמִיתּוֹ – ***To he who sits in judgment:*** **This** refers **to one who renders a judgment that is absolutely true.**[12] ,,וְלִגְבוּרָה'' זֶה הַמִּתְגַּבֵּר בְּיִצְרוֹ – ***And for strength:*** **This** refers **to one who overpowers**

NOTES

1. *Numbers* 14:17-18. In this verse Moses pleads with God to forgive Israel the sin of the Spies by referring to God's earlier declaration that He was *Slow to Anger.*

The dialogue recorded in this Baraisa makes it probable that it was Moses' realization that the Attribute of *Slow to Anger* applies even to the wicked that so moved him that he fell on his face in joy. [For Moses did not initially understand that God would act in this manner. When he heard from God that he would someday come to appreciate God's slowness to anger even with the wicked,] Moses realized that this meant that even if Israel were to commit some terrible sin that would classify them as wicked, God's Attribute of *Slow to Anger* would prevent Him from destroying them and afford them the chance to repent (*Rashi*). As we have seen, that is precisely what happened at the time of the sin of the Spies.

Maharal understands this entire incident in a different manner. Moses had been perplexed with the ancient question of why the righteous suffer and the wicked prosper. When he begged God to let him see God's "face," he was asking God to explain to him the answer to this question. God showed him his Attributes of Mercy, wherein the answer to Moses' query was contained. When Moses saw the answer to his question, he fell on his face in joy at the discovery of the solution to this problem. The dispute between R' Chanina and the Rabbis cited above concerns which specific Attribute contained the solution to the question. According to R' Chanina, when Moses saw Slow to Anger, he realized that in reality the prosperity of the wicked is illusory. They are temporarily granted prosperity by God because He is patient and wants to afford them the opportunity to repent. If they do not repent, they will eventually be fully punished for their sins, for while God is slow to anger, His eventual punishment of the wicked is certain. When Moses realized that the wicked do not really escape punishment, he perceived that God's ways are truly just, and he fell on his face in joy at the discovery.

The Rabbis, on the other hand, maintain that Moses was not concerned by the prosperity of the wicked, but was bothered by the fact that the righteous suffer. When he saw God's Attribute of Truth, he realized that the suffering of the righteous in this world is but a prelude to their ultimate, unimaginable reward in the World to Come, for Truth requires that the righteous receive their reward. When Moses perceived this, he prostrated himself out of joy.

2. *Psalms* 93:5. Our translation reflects R' Chagga's interpretation of the words ה׳ לְאֹרֶךְ יָמִים. [These words are usually rendered: *O Hashem, may it be for many days;* see *Radak* to verse.] R' Chagga understands the term אֹרֶךְ יָמִים here to be a reference to God's Attribute of אֶרֶךְ אַפַּיִם, *Slow to Anger* (*Rashi;* cf. *Maharsha*).

3. Ibid. 90:1. Psalm 90 begins a sequence of psalms composed by Moses, which includes Psalm 93 (*Rashi;* see *Midrash Shocher Tov* there and *Rashi* to *Bava Basra* 14b ד״ה ועל ידי משה, who states that psalms 90-100 were composed by Moses).

4. The fact that, in the verse recited by the child, Moses praised God's slowness to anger indicated to R' Chagga that it was this attribute that must have moved Moses to prostrate himself (*Rashi*). [For a different explanation, based on an emendation of the text, see *Maharsha* and *Shiyarei HaMinchah.*]

5. The reference is to the crown mentioned in Rav's famous dictum (*Berachos* 17a): "In the World to Come there is no eating or drinking . . . rather, the righteous sit with their crowns on their heads and delight in the radiance of the Divine Presence" (*Maharsha*).

6. *Isaiah* 28:5.

7. [*Gra* emends the text to read צִבְיוֹנוֹ, *His will.*] The Gemara's teaching is based on the similarity between צְבִי, *tzevi* (beauty), and צִבְיוֹנוֹ, *tzivyono* (His will).

8. [*Gra* emends the text to read וּמְצַפִּים לְתִפְאַרְתּוֹ, *and for those who await His glory* (see *Maharsha*).] צְפִירָה, *diadem,* is similar to מְצַפֶּה, *one who waits.* Thus, צְפִירַת תִּפְאָרָה (a diadem of glory) is interpreted to mean *those who await His glory.*

9. Even if he is arrogant (*Rashi, Yad Ramah*).

10. Just as people do not consider leftover scraps [of food etc.] significant, so too this righteous person does not consider himself significant (*Rashi*).

God's presence is more liable to rest on those who are humble in spirit, as stated in *Isaiah* 57:15 (*Maharsha*).

11. The words וּלְרוּחַ מִשְׁפָּט, *and for a spirit of judgment,* are interpreted as meaning: one who judges his spirit. The reference is to one who overrules his evil spirit, and repents from the sins it has led him to commit (*Rashi;* see *Rashash*).

12. Literally: one who judges a true judgment to its truth. *Tosafos* (*Megillah* 15b and *Bava Basra* 8b) explain the double expression: If witnesses are suspected of lying, a judge should not decide the case based on their evidence. First they must be thoroughly cross-examined until

אמר לפניו רבש"ע ולא כך אמרת לי אף לרשעים והיינו דכתיב א) ועתה יגדל נא כח ה' כאשר דברת לאמר ר' חגא הוה סליק ואזיל בדרגא דבי רבה בר שילא שמעיה לההוא ינוקא דאמר ב) עדותיך נאמנו מאד לביתך נאוה קדש ה' לאורך ימים וסמיך ליה ג) תפלה למשה וגו' אמר ש"מ ארך אפים ראה א) א"ר אלעזר א"ר חנינא עתיד הקב"ה להיות עטרה בראש כל צדיק וצדיק שנאמר ד) ביום ההוא יהיה ה' צבאות לעטרת צבי ולצפירת תפארה לשאר עמו וגו' מאי לעטרת צבי ולצפירת תפארה לעושים [א] רצונו ומצפים [ב] לישועתו יכול לכל ת"ל לשאר עמו ב) למי שמשים עצמו כשירים ה) ולרוח משפט ליושב על המשפט ולגבורה משיבי מלחמה שערה ולרוח משפט זה הרודה את יצרו וליושב על המשפט זה הדן דין אמת לאמיתו ולגבורה זה המתגבר ביצרו משיבי מלחמה זה שנושא ונותן במלחמתה של תורה שערה אלו שמשכימין ומעריבין בבתי כנסיות ובתי מדרשות אמרה מדת הדין לפני הקב"ה רבש"ע מה נשתנו אלו מאלו אמר לה ו) וגם אלה ביין שגו ובשכר תעו [וגו'] פקו פליליה ואין פוקה אלא גיהנם שנאמר ז) לא תהיה זאת לך לפוקה ואין פלילה אלא דיינין שנאמר ח) ונתן בפלילים: **מתני'** ג) אנשי עיר הנדחת אין להם חלק לעוה"ב שנאמר ט) יצאו אנשים בני בליעל מקרבך וידיחו את (אנשי) [יושבי] עירם א ואינן נהרגים עד שיהיו מדיחיה מאותה העיר ומאותו השבט ועד שיודח רובה ועד שידיחוה אנשים הדיחוה נשים וקטנים או שהודח מיעוטה או שהיה מדיחיה חוצה לה הרי אלו כיחידים ב וצריכין ב' עדים והתראה לכל אחד ואחד זה חומר ביחידים מבמרובים ג שהיחידים בסקילה לפיכך ממונם פלט ד והמרובין בסייף לפיכך ממונם אבד י) הכה תכה את יושבי העיר ד) הזאת לפי חרב ה) החמרת והגמלת העוברת ממקום למקום א] הרי אלו מצילין אותה [ג] שנא' י) החרם אותה ואת כל אשר בה ואת בהמתה לפי חרב ה מכאן אמרו נכסי צדיקים שבתוכה אובדין שבחוצה לה פליטין ו ושל רשעים בין שבתוכה בין שבחוצה לה הרי אלו אובדין [ד] שנאמר כ) ואת כל שללה תקבוץ אל תוך רחבה וגו' אם ז אין לה רחוב עושין לה רחוב היתה רחבה חוצה לה כונסין אותה לתוכה שנאמר כ) ושרפת באש את העיר ואת כל שללה כליל לה' אלהיך שללה ולא שלל שמים מכאן אמרו ח ההקדשות שבה יפדו ותרומות ירקבו מעשר שני וכתבי הקדש יגנזו כליל לה' אלהיך אמר ר"ש אמר הקב"ה ט אם אתם עושין דין בעיר הנדחת מעלה אני עליכם כאילו אתם מעלים עולה כליל לפני כ) והיתה תל עולם ו) לא תעשה ז) גנות ופרדסים דברי ר' יוסי הגלילי ר"ע אומר י לא תבנה עוד לכמות שהיתה אינה נבנית אבל נעשית היא גנות ופרדסים ל) ולא ידבק בידך מאומה מן החרם שכל זמן שהרשעים בעולם חרון אף בעולם אבדו רשעים מן העולם נסתלק חרון אף מן העולם: **גמ'** ת"ר יצאו הן ולא שלוחין אנשים כ אין אנשים פחות מב' דבר אחר אנשים ל ולא נשים אנשים ולא קטנים בני בליעל בנים שפרקו עול שמים מצואריהם ח) מקרבך מ ולא מן הספר יושבי עירם ולא יושבי עיר אחרת לאמר שצריכין עדים והתראה לכל אחד ואחד איתמר ר' יוחנן אמר חולקין עיר אחת לשני שבטים ור"ל אמר ט) אין חולקין עיר אחת לב' שבטים איתיביה ר' יוחנן לר"ל עד שיהו מדיחיה מאותה העיר ומאותו שבט מאי לאו אע"ג דמדיחיה מאותה העיר אי איכא מאותו שבט אין אי לא לא ש"מ חולקין עיר אחת לב' שבטים לא דנפלה ליה בירושה א"נ דיהבוה ניהליה במתנה איתיביה מ) ערים תשע מאת שני השבטים האלה מאי לאו ארבע ופלגא מהאי וארבע ופלגא מהאי וש"מ חולקין עיר אחת לב' שבטים לא ארבעה מהאי וחמש מהאי אי הכי לפרוש פרושי

קשיא

אמר לפניו וכו'. והשתא [מסתברא] כמ"ד ארך אפים ראה שכיון שראה [מדה זו] בהקב"ה שהוא ארך אפים אף לרשעים שמח: עדותיך וגו' ה' לאורך ימים. היינו מדת ארך אפים ועליה אמר משה עדותיך נאמנו מאד שראה אותו בחורב ופסוק זה מרע"ה אמרו דכתיב לעיל מיניה תפלה למשה איש האלהים וגו': יכול לכל. למי שעושין רצונו אע"פ שמתגאה: כשירים. שיריים שאין נחשבין כך אינו חשוב בעיניו ואינו מתגאה: ולרוח משפט. שופט את רוחו: שרודה ביצרו. שבועט ביצרו וחוזר בתשובה מן העבירה שעבר: ומתגבר ביצרו. מרגיז יצ"ט על יצה"ר אם היצה"ר אמר לו עשה עבירה זו לא דיו שנמנע מן העבירה אלא הולך ועושה מצוה ומתגבר עדיף מרודה: שערה. אלו בתי כנסיות: מה נשתנו אלו מאלו. שיש בהם מדות הללו מן השאר אמר הקב"ה ביין שגו: ואין פלילה אלא דיינין: **מתני'** יצאו אנשים בני בליעל מקרבך. שאין להם חלק לעוה"ב: וידיחו את (אנשי) [יושבי] עירם. הא אין נהרגים עד שיהיו מדיחיה מאותה העיר ואותה השבט עצמה דכתיב מקרבך מקרב אותו שבט עצמו: עד שיודח רובה. דכתיב ויושבי העיר משמע ישובה של עיר היינו רובה לישנא אחרינא עד שיודח רובה דכתיב מקרבך קרי ביה מרובך: ה"ג עד שיודח רובה עד שידיחוה אנשים: או שהיו מדיחיה חוצה לה. שלא היו מאותה העיר: הרי אלו כיחידים. שהן בסקילה וממונן פלט: וצריכים ב' עדים והתראה לכל אחד. כדיליף בגמרא [ב] יחידים בסקילה לפיכך ממונן פלט ומתוך שהחמרת עליו במיתתו הקלת עליו בממונו: הכה תכה את יושבי העיר ההיא לפי חרב החמרת והגמלת העוברת ממקום למקום מצילין. מדכתיב יושבי מכלל דשיירה של חמרים וגמלים שנשתהו בעיר ל' יום כדמפרש בגמרא דהוו להו יושבי העיר הרי אלו מצילין אם רוב אנשי העיר הודחו וחמרים וגמלים משלימין המיעוט ועושה אותם רוב מצילין עליהם שאין ממונם אבד אלא נדונים כיחידים וגורמין נמי לעשות אותה עיר הנדחת אם משלימים לעיר הנדחת לעשות רוב אלא הא פסיקא טפי דחמרת וגמלת אין דעתם מעורבת עם בני העיר להיות נדונין עמהן: ה"ג החרם אותה וכל אשר בה מכאן אמרו צדיקים וכו' ושל רשעים בין מתוכה בין מחוצה לה אבודים. בגמרא מפרש לה מדכתיב כל: ואת כל שללה תקבוץ אל תוך רחובה אין לה רחוב עושין לה רחוב. ורחובה דהשתא נמי משמע: היה רחובה חוצה לה. שמקום קבוץ בני העיר היה חוץ לעיר כונסין אותה לעיר שצריך לעשות לה רחוב בתוכה. רחוב סרטיא גדולה: את העיר ואת כל שללה ולא שלל שמים. דשלל שמים פלט: מכאן אמרו הקדשות שבתוכה יפדו. כלומר אין נשרפין אלא הרי הם כשאר הקדש שצריך פדייה כ"ש דשלל שמים הם: ותרומות ירקבו. ובגמ' מוקמי לה בתרומה ביד כהן דממון כהן הוא וחל עליה איסור דעיר הנדחת דנהי דבשריפה לא הויא עם שאר שללה דקדש אקרי ולא מזלזלינן ביה כולי האי: מעשר שני. אע"פ שהוא נאכל לישראל הואיל וקדש איקרי לא אמרי' ישרף אלא יגנזו וכן כתבי הקדש יגנזו: ה"ג כליל לה' אלהיך אר"ש אמר הקב"ה וכו' כאילו אתה מעלה עולה שהוא כליל לפני: לא תעשה גנות ופרדסין וכו'. בגמ' מפרש במאי פליגי: לכמו שהיתה. ביישוב בתים: **גמ'** יצאו הם ולא שלוחם. אם המדיחין עצמן יצאו והדיחו והרי הם מרובים ודנין בסייף אבל אם הדיחו ע"י שליח כיחידים הם בסקילה וממונם פלט: אין אנשים פחות מב'. דע"י מדיח אחד אין נעשית עיר הנדחת: בקרבך. משמע באמצע ולא מן הספר שאם היתה עיר של ספר בין מחוז עובדי כוכבים למחוז ישראל אינה נעשית עיר הנדחת דגזירת הכתוב היא שלא תעשה עיר הנדחת: יושבי העיר ולא יושבי עיר אחרת. דהיינו מדיחי' מחוצה לה: לאמר נלכה ונעבדה. משמע שצ"ל לפנינו שכך אומרים נלכה ונעבדה ואין אמירה אלא בעדים אלמא צריך עדים לכל אחד ואחד שיעידו עליהם מה שאמרו וה"נ צריך התראה לכל א' וא' מהם: חולקין עיר אחת. בתחלה כשחלקו ישראל את הארץ היו רשאין ליתן ולחלוק עיר א' לב' שבטים כגון אם אירע להם עיר בתחום ומקצת מושכת לתחום אחר שבט אחד נוטל חלק באותו קצת הארץ ע"פ הגורל נחלקה הארץ אם נפתלי עולה תחום גינוסר עולה עמו דהכי אמרינן בב"ב בפרק י"נ ומנחילין (דף קכב.): אין חולקין. אלא כולה של אותו השבט שרוב' בתחומי': מאי לאו אע"ג דמדיחיה מאותה עיר. אם יהיו מאותו שבט נעשית עיר הנדחת ואי לא לא שאם אינו מאותו שבט שהודחו אלא משבט אחר שבעיר אינו בסייף אלא בסקילה אלמא אפשר שיהו מן אותה העיר ולא מאותו שבט וה"ד כגון שחלקו עיר אחת לשני שבטים: לא. לעולם אימא לך דאין חולקין והיכי משכחת לה מאותה עיר ולא מאותו שבט כגון דנפלה למדיחיה בירושה מקצת העיר ע"י בת יורשת נחלה: ערים תשע מאת שני השבטים האלה. ממטה יהודה וממטה שמעון נטלו ט' ערים ונתנום ללוים: מאי לאו דשקל מהאי ד' ופלגא. שהיתה עיר א' של יהודה ושמעון ונטלו מהם אלמא חולקין עיר אחת לשני שבטים: ה"ג לא ד' מהאי וה' מהאי: א"ה לפרוש פרושי. הי ניהו שבט דשקיל מיניה ה' והי ניהו דשקיל מיניה ד' ומאחר כתיב ערים תשע מאת שני השבטים משמע דבשוה שקל:

קשיא

עין משפט
נר מצוה

לה א מיי' פ"ד מהל' ע"ז הלכה ב סמג עשין טו:
לו ב מיי' שם הלכה ה והלכה ו:
לז ג מיי' שם הל' ב:
לח ד מיי' שם הל' ו:
לט ה מיי' שם הל' ז:
מ ו מיי' שם הל' י:
מא ז מיי' שם הל' ו:
מב ח מיי' שם הל' יג:
מג ט מיי' שם הל' ו:
מד י מיי' שם הל' ז:
מה כ ל מיי' שם הל' ב:
מו מ מיי' שם הל' ד:

הגהות מהר"ב רנשבורג

א] מתני' הרי אלו מצילין אותה שנאמר וכו' הרי אלו אובדין שנאמר וכו' כונסין אותה לתוכה שנאמר. אלו ג"פ שנאמר נמחקו: ב] רש"י ד"ה וצריכין וכו' כדיליף בגמ'. כאן הס"ד ומה"ד יחידים:

ליקוטי רש"י

יגדל נא כח ה'. לעשות דבורך. כאשר דברת לאמר. ומהו הדבור [במדבר יד, יז]. תפלה למשה. אחד עשר מזמורים מכאן עד לדוד מזמור כלם משה אמרם [תהלים צ, א]. ביום ההוא. כהתם הפושעים. יהיה ה' צבאות לעטרת צבי. לצדיקים הנשארים בה [ישעיהו כח, ה]. ולרוח משפט. יהיה הקב"ה להורות משפט ליושב על המשפט. ולגבורה. יהיה לאותן שהם משיבי מלחמ' מלחמתה של תורה [שם פסוק ו]. לרוח משפט. לשופטים את רוחן יהיה לעטרה. הרודה את יצרו. כופהו לשוב בתשובה. המתגבר על יצרו. אינו הולך אחריו לעבור עבירה. שמשכימין כו'. והיינו שערה שעושין [שנעשים שוערים] לפתוח דלתות בהשכמה ולאחר [שם עד] זמן נעילתו. גם אלה. אלו הרשעים הנידונין בגיהנם. ביין שגו. כלומר אף הם עשו כהם לפיכך דנם. מלחמתה של תורה. הוריותיה ולעמוד על בוריה ועל עיקרה [לעיל מב.]. להתוכח בתלמוד [לעיל צג:]. פקו פליליה. לגיהנם נשפטו [מגילה טו:]. וגם אלה. יושבי משפט ומשיבי מלחמה שבדור הזה כלומר טובים וחשובים שבהן ביין שגו כי עתה אין טוב בהם. פקו פליליה. הכשילו המשפט. פקו. לשון פיק ברכים (נחום ב') פוקה (שמואל א' כ"ה) [ישעיה כח, ז]. ולא תהיה וגו' לפוקה. לכשלון כמו לפיק ברכים (נחום ב' י"א) [ש"א כה, לא]. ונתן. המכה דמי ולדות. בפלילים. על פי הדיינים [שמות כא, כב]. ישבי עירם. ולא יושבי עיר אחרת מכאן אמרו אין נעשית עיר הנדחת עד שידיחוה אנשים ועד שיהיו מדיחיה מתוכה [דברים יג, יד]. החמרת והגמלת. שיירא של חמרים ושל גמלים [ב"ב ח.]. ולא ידבק בידך מאומה מן החרם. למען ישוב ה' מחרון אפו שכל זמן שעבודה זרה בעולם, חרון אף בעולם [דברים יג, יח].

מסורת הש"ס

א) עיין רש"א בח"א [מגילה טו: ע"ש כמה שינויים ועי' בפירש"י שם], ב) [ר"ה יז:], ג) [עי' תוספות לעיל מז. ד"ה ואמאי], ד) בקרא ההיא, ה) ב"ק ח., ו) [בסה"מ לא תבנה עוד], ז) [בסה"מ אפי' גנות וכו'], ח) [לעיל טז:], ט) [הא דירושלים נחלקה לשבט יהודה ובנימין ע"פ הדיבור היה. ת"י ביומא יב].

הגהות הגר"א

[א] גמ' רצונו. נמחק ונ"ב לצביונו: [ב] שם לישועתו. נמחק ונ"ב לתפארתו: [ג] שם שנאמר. נמחק: [ד] שנא'. נמחק:

תורה אור השלם

א) וְעַתָּה יִגְדַּל נָא כֹּחַ אֲדֹנָי כַּאֲשֶׁר דִּבַּרְתָּ לֵאמֹר: [במדבר יד, יז]

ב) עֵדֹתֶיךָ נֶאֶמְנוּ מְאֹד לְבֵיתְךָ נַאֲוָה קֹדֶשׁ יְיָ לְאֹרֶךְ יָמִים: [תהלים צג, ה]

ג) תְּפִלָּה לְמֹשֶׁה אִישׁ הָאֱלֹהִים אֲדֹנָי מָעוֹן אַתָּה הָיִיתָ לָנוּ בְּדֹר וָדֹר: [תהלים צ, א]

ד) בַּיּוֹם הַהוּא יִהְיֶה יְיָ צְבָאוֹת לַעֲטֶרֶת צְבִי וְלִצְפִירַת תִּפְאָרָה לִשְׁאָר עַמּוֹ: [ישעיה כח, ה]

ה) וּלְרוּחַ מִשְׁפָּט לַיּוֹשֵׁב עַל הַמִּשְׁפָּט וְלִגְבוּרָה מְשִׁיבֵי מִלְחָמָה שָׁעְרָה: [ישעיה כח, ו]

ו) וְגַם אֵלֶּה בַּיַּיִן שָׁגוּ וּבַשֵּׁכָר תָּעוּ כֹּהֵן וְנָבִיא שָׁגוּ בַשֵּׁכָר נִבְלְעוּ מִן הַיַּיִן תָּעוּ מִן הַשֵּׁכָר שָׁגוּ בָּרֹאֶה פָּקוּ פְּלִילִיָּה: [ישעיה כח, ז]

ז) וְלֹא תִהְיֶה זֹאת לְךָ לְפוּקָה וּלְמִכְשׁוֹל לֵב לַאדֹנִי וְלִשְׁפָּךְ דָּם חִנָּם וּלְהוֹשִׁיעַ אֲדֹנִי לוֹ וְהֵיטִב יְיָ לַאדֹנִי וְזָכַרְתָּ אֶת אֲמָתֶךָ: [שמואל א' כה, לא]

ח) וְכִי יִנָּצוּ אֲנָשִׁים וְנָגְפוּ אִשָּׁה הָרָה וְיָצְאוּ יְלָדֶיהָ וְלֹא יִהְיֶה אָסוֹן עָנוֹשׁ יֵעָנֵשׁ כַּאֲשֶׁר יָשִׁית עָלָיו בַּעַל הָאִשָּׁה וְנָתַן בִּפְלִלִים: [שמות כא, כב]

ט) יָצְאוּ אֲנָשִׁים בְּנֵי בְלִיַּעַל מִקִּרְבֶּךָ וַיַּדִּיחוּ אֶת יֹשְׁבֵי עִירָם לֵאמֹר נֵלְכָה וְנַעַבְדָה אֱלֹהִים אֲחֵרִים אֲשֶׁר לֹא יְדַעְתֶּם: [דברים יג, יד]

י) הַכֵּה תַכֶּה אֶת יֹשְׁבֵי הָעִיר הַהִוא לְפִי חָרֶב הַחֲרֵם אֹתָהּ וְאֶת כָּל אֲשֶׁר בָּהּ וְאֶת בְּהֶמְתָּהּ לְפִי חָרֶב: [דברים יג, טו]

כ) וְאֶת כָּל שְׁלָלָהּ תִּקְבֹּץ אֶל תּוֹךְ רְחֹבָהּ וְשָׂרַפְתָּ בָאֵשׁ אֶת הָעִיר וְאֶת כָּל שְׁלָלָהּ כָּלִיל לַייָ אֱלֹהֶיךָ וְהָיְתָה תֵּל עוֹלָם לֹא תִבָּנֶה עוֹד: [דברים יג, יז]

ל) וְלֹא יִדְבַּק בְּיָדְךָ מְאוּמָה מִן הַחֵרֶם לְמַעַן יָשׁוּב יְיָ מֵחֲרוֹן אַפּוֹ וְנָתַן לְךָ רַחֲמִים וְרִחַמְךָ וְהִרְבֶּךָ כַּאֲשֶׁר נִשְׁבַּע לַאֲבֹתֶיךָ: [דברים יג, יח]

מ) וְאֶת עַיִן וְאֶת מִגְרָשֶׁהָ וְאֶת יֻטָּה וְאֶת מִגְרָשֶׁהָ אֶת בֵּית שֶׁמֶשׁ וְאֶת מִגְרָשֶׁהָ עָרִים תֵּשַׁע מֵאֵת שְׁנֵי הַשְּׁבָטִים הָאֵלֶּה: [יהושע כא, טז]

his Evil **Inclination.**[13] ,,מְשִׁיבֵי מִלְחָמָה" זֶה שֶׁנּוֹשֵׂא וְנוֹתֵן בְּמִלְחַמְתָּהּ שֶׁל תּוֹרָה – ***Those who turn back the battle:* This** refers to **one who thrusts and parries**[14] **in the battle of Torah,** i.e. a scholar who debates points of Torah law. ,,שָׁעְרָה" אֵלּוּ שֶׁמַּשְׁכִּימִין וּמַעֲרִיבִין בְּבָתֵּי כְנֵסִיּוֹת וּבָתֵּי מִדְרָשׁוֹת – ***To the gate:* These are the [Torah scholars] who come early in the morning and stay late into the evening in the synagogues and study halls.**[15]

The Gemara expounds upon the next verse:

אָמְרָה מִדַּת הַדִּין לִפְנֵי הַקָּדוֹשׁ בָּרוּךְ הוּא – **The Attribute of Justice said before the Holy One, Blessed is He:** רִבּוֹנוֹ שֶׁל עוֹלָם – **Master of the Universe!** מַה נִּשְׁתַּנּוּ אֵלּוּ מֵאֵלּוּ – **In what way are these different from those?**[16] אָמַר לָהּ – **[God] said to [the Attribute of Justice]:** ,,וְגַם־אֵלֶּה בַּיַּיִן שָׁגוּ וּבַשֵּׁכָר תָּעוּ [וגו'] פָּקוּ פְּלִילִיָּה" – ***But even these reel through wine and stagger through strong drink,* etc. *they stumble*** (*paku*) ***in judgment*** *(peliliyah)*.[17]

The end of the verse is interpreted:

וְאֵין ,,פּוּקָה" אֶלָּא גֵּיהִנֹּם – ***Pukah*** (*stumble*) **is** interpreted here as meaning **nothing but Gehinnom,** שֶׁנֶּאֱמַר ,,לֹא תִהְיֶה זֹאת לְךָ לְפוּקָה" – **as it is stated: *And this shall not be a cause of stumbling*** (*pukah*) ***to you.***[18] וְאֵין ,,פְּלִילָה" אֶלָּא דַּיָּינִין – **And *pelilah* is** interpreted here as meaning **nothing but judges,** שֶׁנֶּאֱמַר ,,וְנָתַן בִּפְלִלִים" – **as it is stated: *And he shall pay as the judges*** *(pelilim)* ***determine.***[19]

Mishnah The last Mishnah of this chapter discusses the fate of one more group which has no share in the World to Come, namely, the inhabitants of an עִיר הַנִּדַּחַת, *subverted city*.[20] This, as we have learned previously (16a, 67a), refers to a city in Eretz Yisrael in which a majority of the inhabitants worshiped idols. After stating that they have no share in the World to Come, the Mishnah goes on to delineate the laws that pertain to such a city:

אַנְשֵׁי עִיר הַנִּדַּחַת – **The inhabitants of a subverted city** אֵין לָהֶם חֵלֶק לָעוֹלָם הַבָּא – **have no share in the World to Come,** שֶׁנֶּאֱמַר – **as it is stated:** ,,יָצְאוּ אֲנָשִׁים בְּנֵי־בְלִיַּעַל מִקִּרְבֶּךָ וַיַּדִּיחוּ אֶת (אנשי) [יֹשְׁבֵי] עִירָם" – ***Lawless men have gone out from your midst and subverted the inhabitants of their city,*** *saying.*[21] וְאֵינָן נֶהֱרָגִים – **And [The inhabitants] are not beheaded**[22] עַד שֶׁיִּהְיוּ מַדִּיחֶיהָ מֵאוֹתָהּ הָעִיר – **unless those who subverted [the city] are from that**

NOTES

the truth is ascertained, and only then may the appropriate judgment be rendered. The judge should not simply rely on the formal rules of evidence — he must search out the "true" truth.

The expression "he sits in judgment" means that he does not rush into judgment but proceeds with due care (see *Maharsha*).

13. When his Evil Inclination incites him to perform a sin, he not only eschews the sin, but he performs a meritorious act instead. This is a higher level than הָרוֹדֶה אֶת יִצְרוֹ, *one who controls his inclination* (*Rashi*).

14. Literally: takes and gives.

15. Thus, they serve as the gatekeepers [of the synagogues and study halls], for they open the gates in the morning and close them at night (*Rashi* to *Megillah* 15b).

16. There are other righteous persons aside from those who possess the traits enumerated above. Why are the ones with these traits given preferential treatment? (*Rashi, Yad Ramah;* cf. *Chidushei HaGeonim* in *Ein Yaakov*).

17. *Isaiah* 28:7. Even those people who have many good deeds to their credit, if they lack the specific traits listed above, they are no better than drunkards (see *Yad Ramah*). [A virtuous person who is not immersed in Torah study (which is the antidote for the Evil Inclination [*Kiddushin* 30b]), and does not actively fight his Evil Inclination, performs his good deeds simply because he is naturally inclined to do so. Hence, in effect, he is no better than someone under the influence of drink, who acts out his base impulses.]

18. *I Samuel* 25:31. Abigail beseeches David not to execute her husband, Nabal. She argues that this act would cause David to fall into Gehinnom (*Rashi, Radak* ad loc.; see, however, *Megillah* 14a-b).

19. *Exodus* 21:22. The verse from *Isaiah* thus teaches that those who succumb to the influence of drink will not only fail to be crowned by God but will even be sent to Gehinnom. A judge who is drunk could render false decisions [and thereby deprive someone of his property or even his life] (see *Maharsha*).

[See *Megillah* 15b, where a different version of this teaching is recorded.]

20. This follows *Rashi's* reading of the Mishnah. For another view, see *Yad Ramah* and *Chidushei HaRan,* cited below in note 21.

The law regarding such a city is stated in *Deuteronomy* 13:13-19. Since many of these verses will be cited in the Mishnah and Gemara that follow, we present the passage here in its entirety:

יג. כִּי־תִשְׁמַע בְּאַחַת עָרֶיךָ אֲשֶׁר ה' אֱלֹהֶיךָ נֹתֵן לְךָ לָשֶׁבֶת שָׁם לֵאמֹר: יד. יָצְאוּ אֲנָשִׁים
בְּנֵי־בְלִיַּעַל מִקִּרְבֶּךָ וַיַּדִּיחוּ אֶת־יֹשְׁבֵי עִירָם לֵאמֹר נֵלְכָה וְנַעַבְדָה אֱלֹהִים אֲחֵרִים אֲשֶׁר
לֹא־יְדַעְתֶּם: טו. וְדָרַשְׁתָּ וְחָקַרְתָּ וְשָׁאַלְתָּ הֵיטֵב וְהִנֵּה אֱמֶת נָכוֹן הַדָּבָר נֶעֶשְׂתָה הַתּוֹעֵבָה
הַזֹּאת בְּקִרְבֶּךָ: טז. הַכֵּה תַכֶּה אֶת־יֹשְׁבֵי הָעִיר הַהִוא לְפִי־חָרֶב הַחֲרֵם אֹתָהּ וְאֶת־כָּל־
אֲשֶׁר־בָּהּ וְאֶת־בְּהֶמְתָּהּ לְפִי־חָרֶב: יז. וְאֶת־כָּל־שְׁלָלָהּ תִּקְבֹּץ אֶל־תּוֹךְ רְחֹבָהּ וְשָׂרַפְתָּ
בָאֵשׁ אֶת־הָעִיר וְאֶת־כָּל־שְׁלָלָהּ כָּלִיל לַה' אֱלֹהֶיךָ וְהָיְתָה תֵּל עוֹלָם לֹא תִבָּנֶה עוֹד:
יח. וְלֹא־יִדְבַּק בְּיָדְךָ מְאוּמָה מִן־הַחֵרֶם לְמַעַן יָשׁוּב ה' מֵחֲרוֹן אַפּוֹ וְנָתַן־לְךָ רַחֲמִים
וְרִחַמְךָ וְהִרְבֶּךָ כַּאֲשֶׁר נִשְׁבַּע לַאֲבֹתֶיךָ: יט. כִּי תִשְׁמַע בְּקוֹל ה' אֱלֹהֶיךָ לִשְׁמֹר אֶת־כָּל־
מִצְוֹתָיו אֲשֶׁר אָנֹכִי מְצַוְּךָ הַיּוֹם לַעֲשׂוֹת הַיָּשָׁר בְּעֵינֵי ה' אֱלֹהֶיךָ:

[13] *If you hear in one of your cities that* HASHEM *your God is giving you in which to live, [a report] stating:* [14] *"Lawless men have gone out from your midst and subverted the inhabitants of their city, saying: 'Let us go and worship the gods of others, [gods] that you have not known.' "* [15] *You shall inquire, question and ask thoroughly; and behold! [the report] is true and correct, this abomination was committed in your midst.* [16] *You shall smite the inhabitants of that city by the sword; destroy it and everything that is in it, as well as its animals, by the sword.* [17] *And all its booty you shall gather into its square, and you shall burn the city and all its booty in a fire, completely, to* HASHEM *your God; and it shall remain an eternal heap, it shall never again be built.* [18] *Nothing of the banned [property] shall adhere to your hand, so that* HASHEM *will turn back from His burning wrath; and He will give you mercy and be merciful to you and multiply you, as He swore to your forefathers.* [19] *For you will hearken to the voice of* HASHEM *your God, to observe all His commandments that I command you today, to do what is right in the eyes of* HASHEM *your God.*

21. *Deuteronomy* 13:14. The phrase *have gone out of your midst* connotes that they have departed [forever] from the Jewish people, and will not share in their destiny, namely, the World to Come (see *Rashi, Yad Ramah*). Although this verse refers to the subverters of the city, the subverted are treated in most respects the same as the subverters (*Rav, Commentary* to *Mishnah*).

Tosafos (47a ד"ה ואמאי) ask why people executed for idolatry as inhabitants of an *ir hanidachas* (subverted city) should be excluded from the World to Come when the Gemara above (47a) states that their very execution serves to atone for their idolatry. *Tosafos* answer that loss of a share in the World to Come is only for those inhabitants who were, for some reason, not executed; those who were executed, however, do indeed gain atonement through this punishment and thus have a share (see *Hagahos Yavetz* here for another answer; cf. *Yad Ramah* and *Chidushei HaRan*).

22. The inhabitants of a subverted city are beheaded for having worshiped idols (rather than stoned, as is ordinarily the case with idol worshipers), but only if the series of conditions listed in our Mishnah have been met. If not, they are treated as individuals who worshiped idols, and are executed by stoning, as the Mishnah will state below.

23. The verse states explicitly that *lawless men . . . subverted inhabitants of their city,* making it clear that the subverters are themselves from that city (*Rashi,* from Baraisa below). The verse also states that the lawless men *have gone out from your midst,* implying that the men who subverted the city were from the same group — i.e. tribe — as those whom they subverted (*Rashi*).

אמר לפניו רבש"ע ולא כך אמרת לי אף לרשעים והיינו דכתיב (א) ועתה יגדל נא כח ה' כאשר דברת לאמר ר' חגא הוה סליק ואזיל בדרגא דבי רבה בר שילא שמעיה להה‍וא ינוקא דאמר (ב) עדותיך נאמנו מאד לביתך נאוה קדש ה' לאורך ימים וסמיך ליה (ג) תפלה למשה וגו' אמר ש"מ ארך אפים ראה [א] א"ר אלעזר א"ר חנינא עתיד הקב"ה להיות עטרה בראש כל צדיק וצדיק שנאמר (ד) ביום ההוא יהיה ה' צבאות לעטרת צבי ולצפירת תפארה לשאר עמו וגו' מאי לעטרת צבי ולצפירת תפארה לעושים [א] רצונו ומצפים [ב] לישועתו יכול לכל ת"ל לשאר עמו [ב] למי שמשים עצמו כשירים (ה) ולרוח משפט ליושב על המשפט ולגבורה משיבי מלחמה שערה ולרוח משפט זה הרודה את יצרו וליושב על המשפט זה הדן דין אמת לאמיתו ולגבורה זה המתגבר ביצרו משיבי מלחמה זה שנושא ונותן במלחמתה של תורה שערה אלו שמשכימין ומעריבין בבתי כנסיות ובתי מדרשות אמרה מדת הדין לפני הקב"ה רבש"ע מה נשתנו אלו מאלו אמר לה (ו) וגם אלה ביין שגו ובשכר תעו [וגו'] פקו פליליה ואין פוקה אלא גיהנם שנאמר (ז) ולא תהיה זאת לך לפוקה ואין פלילה אלא דיינין שנאמר (ח) ונתן בפלילים: **מתני'** [ג] אנשי עיר הנדחת אין להם חלק לעוה"ב שנאמר (ט) יצאו אנשים בני בליעל מקרבך וידיחו את (אנשי) [יושבי] עירם [א] ואינן נהרגים עד שיהיו מדיחיה מאותה העיר ומאותו השבט ועד שיודח רובה ועד שידיחוה אנשים הדיחוה נשים וקטנים או שהודח מיעוטה או שהיה מדיחיה חוצה לה הרי אלו כיחידים [ב] וצריכין ב' עדים והתראה לכל אחד ואחד זה חומר ביחידים מבמרובים [ג] שהיחידים בסקילה לפיכך ממונם פלט [ד] והמרובין בסייף לפיכך ממונם אבד (י) הכה תכה את יושבי העיר [ד] הזאת לפי חרב [ה] החמרת והגמלת העוברת ממקום למקום [א] הרי אלו מצילין אותה [ג] שנא' (י) החרם אותה ואת כל אשר בה ואת בהמתה לפי חרב [ה] מכאן אמרו נכסי צדיקים שבתוכה אובדין שבחוצה לה פליטין [ו] ושל רשעים בין שבתוכה בין שבחוצה לה הרי אלו אובדין [ד] שנאמר (כ) ואת כל שללה תקבוץ אל תוך רחבה וגו' אם [ז] אין לה רחוב עושין לה רחוב היתה רחבה חוצה לה כונסין אותה לתוכה שנאמר (כ) ושרפת באש את העיר ואת כל שללה כליל לה' אלהיך שללה ולא שלל שמים מכאן אמרו [ח] ההקדשות שבה יפדו ותרומות ירקבו מעשר שני וכתבי הקדש יגנזו כליל לה' אלהיך אמר ר"ש אמר הקב"ה [ט] אם אתם עושין דין בעיר הנדחת מעלה אני עליכם כאילו אתם מעלים עולה כליל לפני (כ) והיתה תל עולם (י) לא תעשה [י] גנות ופרדסים דברי ר' יוסי הגלילי ר"ע אומר [י] לא תבנה עוד לכמות שהיתה אינה נבנית אבל נעשית היא גנות ופרדסים (ל) ולא ידבק בידך מאומה מן החרם שכל זמן שהרשעים בעולם חרון אף בעולם אבדו רשעים מן העולם נסתלק חרון אף מן העולם: **גמ'** ת"ר יצאו הן ולא שלוחין אנשים [כ] אין אנשים פחות מב' דבר אחר אנשים [ל] ולא נשים אנשים ולא קטנים בני בליעל בנים שפרקו עול שמים מצואריהם (מ) מקרבך [מ] ולא מן הספר יושבי עירם ולא יושבי עיר אחרת לאמר שצריכין עדים והתראה לכל אחד ואחד איתמר ר' יוחנן אמר חולקין עיר אחת לשני שבטים ור"ל אמר [ט] אין חולקין עיר אחת לב' שבטים איתיביה ר' יוחנן לר"ל עד שיהו מדיחיה מאותה העיר ומאותו שבט מאי לאו אע"ג דמדיחיה מאותה העיר אי איכא מאותו שבט אין אי לא לא ש"מ חולקין עיר אחת לב' שבטים לא דנפלה ליה בירושה א"נ דיהבוה ניהליה במתנה איתיביה (מ) ערים תשע מאת שני השבטים האלה מאי לאו ארבע ופלגא מהאי וארבע ופלגא מהאי וש"מ חולקין עיר אחת לב' שבטים לא ארבעה מהאי וחמש מהאי אי הכי לפרוש פרושי

קשיא

אמר לפניו וכו'. והשתא [מסתברא] כמ"ד ארך אפים ראה שכיון שראה [מדה זו] בהקב"ה שהוא ארך אפים אף לרשעים שמח: עדותיך וגו' ה' לאורך ימים. היינו מדת ארך אפים ועליה אמר משה עדותיך נאמנו מאד שראה אותו בחורב ופסוק זה מרע"ה אמרו דכתיב לעיל מיניה תפלה למשה איש האלהים וגו': יכול לכל. למי שעושין רצונו אע"פ שמתגאה: כשירים. שיריים שאין נחשבין כך אינו חשוב בעיניו ואינו מתגאה: ולרוח משפט. שופט את רוחו: שרודה ביצרו. שבועט בילרו וחוזר בתשובה מן העבירה שעבר: ומתגבר ביצרו. מרגיז יצ"ט על יצה"ר אם היצה"ר אמר לו עשה עבירה זו לא דיו שנמנע מן העבירה אלא הולך ועושה מצוה ומתגבר עליו מרודה: שערה. אלו בתי כנסיות: מה נשתנו אלו מאלו. שיש בהם מדות הללו מן השאר אמר הקב"ה ביין שגו: ואין פלילה אלא דיינין: **מתני'** יצאו אנשים בני בליעל מקרבך. שאין להם חלק לעוה"ב: וידיחו את (אנשי) [יושבי] עירם. הא אין נהרגים עד שיהיו מדיחיה מאותה העיר ואותה השבט עצמה דכתיב מקרבך מקרב אותו שבט עצמו: עד שיודח רובה. דכתיב ויושבי העיר משמע ישובה של עיר היינו רובה לישנא אחרינא עד שיודח רובה דכתיב מקרבך קרי ביה מרובך: ה"ג עד שיודח רובה עד שידיחוה אנשים: או שהיו מדיחיה חוצה לה. שלא היו מאותה העיר: הרי אלו כיחידים. שהן בסקילה וממונן פלט: וצריכים ב' עדים והתראה לכל אחד. כדיליף בגמרא [ב] יחידים בסקילה לפיכך ממונן פלט ומתוך שהחמרת עליו במיתתו הקלת עליו בממונו: הכה תכה את יושבי העיר ההיא לפי חרב החמרת והגמלת העוברת ממקום למקום מצילין. מדכתיב יושבי מכלל דשיירה של חמרים וגמלים שנשתהו בעיר ל' יום כדמפרש בגמרא דהוו להו יושבי העיר הרי אלו מצילין אם רוב אנשי העיר הודחו וחמרים וגמלים משלימין המיעוט ועושה אותם רוב מצילין עליהם שאין ממונם אבד אלא נדונים כיחידים וגורמין נמי לעשות אותה עיר הנדחת אם משלימים לעיר הנדחת לעשות רוב אלא הא פסיקא טפי דחמרת וגמלת אין דעתם מעורבת עם בני העיר להיות נדונין עמהן: ה"ג החרם אותה וכל אשר בה מכאן אמרו צדיקים וכו' ושל רשעים בין מתוכה בין מחוצה לה אבודים. בגמרא מפרש לה מדכתיב כל: ואת כל שללה תקבוץ אל תוך רחובה אין לה רחוב עושין לה רחוב. ורחובה דהשתא נמי משמע: היה רחובה חוצה לה. שמקום קבוץ בני העיר היה חוץ לעיר כונסין אותה לעיר שצריך לעשות לה רחוב בתוכה. רחוב סרטיא גדולה: את העיר ואת כל שללה ולא שלל שמים. דשלל שמים פלט: מכאן אמרו הקדשות שבתוכה יפדו. כלומר אין נשרפין

אלא הרי הם כשאר הקדש שצריך פדייה כ"ש דשלל שמים הס: ותרומות ירקבו. ובגמ' מוקמי לה בתרומה ביד כהן דממון כהן הוא וחל עליה איסור דעיר הנדחת דנכי דבשריפה לא הויא עם שאר שללה דקדש אקרי ולא מזלזלינן ביה כולי האי: מעשר שני. אע"פ שהוא נאכל לישראל הואיל וקדש איקרי לא אמרי' ישרף אלא יגנזו וכן כתבי הקדש יגנזו: ה"ג כליל לה' אלהיך אר"ש אמר הקב"ה וכו' כאילו אתה מעלה עולה שהוא כליל לפני: לא תעשה גנות ופרדסין וכו'. בגמ' מפרש במאי פליגי: לכמו שהיתה. ביישוב בתים: **גמ'** יצאו הם ולא שלוחם. אם המדיחין עצמן יצאו והדיחו והרי הם מרובים ודנין בסייף אבל אם הדיחו ע"י שליח כיחידים הם בסקילה וממונם פלט: אין אנשים פחות מב'. דע"י מדיח אחד אין נעשית עיר הנדחת: בקרבך. משמע באמצע ולא מן הספר שאם היתה עיר של ספר בין מחוז עובדי כוכבים למחוז ישראל אינה נעשית עיר הנדחת דגזירת הכתוב היא שלא תעשה עיר הנדחת: יושבי העיר ולא יושבי עיר אחרת. דהיינו מדיחי' מחוצה לה: לאמר נלכה ונעבדה. משמע שצ"ל לפנינו שכך אומרים נלכה ונעבדה ואין אמירה אלא בעדים אלמא צריך עדים לכל אחד ואחד שיעידו עליהם מה שאמרו וה"נ צריך התראה לכל א' וא' מהם: חולקין עיר אחת. בתחלה כשחלקו ישראל את הארץ היו רשאין ליתן ולחלוק עיר א' לב' שבטים כגון אם אירע להם עיר בתחום ומקלת מושכת לתחום אחר שבט אחד נוטל חלק באותו קלת הארץ ע"פ הגורל נחלקה הארץ אם נפלי' עולה תחום גיגוסר עולה עמו דהכי אמרינן בב"ב בפרק י"נ ומנחילין (דף קכב.): אין חולקין. אלא כולה של אותו השבט שרוב' בתחומי': מאי לאו אע"ג דמדיחיה מאותה עיר. אם יהיו מאותו שבט נעשית עיר הנדחת ואי לא לא שאם אינו מאותו שבט שהודחו אלא משבט אחר שבעיר אינו בסייף אלא בסקילה אלמא אפשר שיהו מן אותה העיר ולא מאותו שבט וה"ד כגון שחלקו עיר אחת לשני שבטים: לא. לעולם אימא לך דאין חולקין והיכי משכחת לה מאותה עיר ולא מאותו שבט כגון דנפלה למדיחיה בירושה מקלת העיר ע"י בת יורשת נחלה: ערים תשע מאת שני השבטים האלה. ממטה יהודה וממטה שמעון נטלו ט' ערים ונתנום ללוים: מאי לאו דשקל מהאי ד' ופלגא. שהיתה עיר א' של יהודה ושמעון ונטלו מהם אלמא חולקין עיר אחת לשני שבטים: ה"ג לא ד' מהאי וה' מהאי: א"ה לפרוש פרושי. הי ניניהו שבט דשקיל מיניה ה' והי ניניהו דשקיל מיניה ד' ומאחר כתיב ערים תשע מאת שני השבטים משמע דבשוה שקל:

קשיא

עין משפט
נר מצוה

לה א מיי' פ"ד מהל' ע"ז הלכה ג סמג עשין טו:
לו ב מיי' שם הלכה ה והלכה ו:
לז ג מיי' שם הל' ג:
לח ד מיי' שם הל' ו:
לט ה מיי' שם הל' ז:
מ ו מיי' שם הל' י:
מא ז מיי' שם הל' ו:
מב ח מיי' שם הל' יג:
מג ט מיי' שם הל' ו:
מד י מיי' שם הל' ז:
מה כ ל מיי' שם הל' ב:
מו מ מיי' שם הל' ד:

הגהות מהר"ב
רנשבורג

א] מתני' הרי אלו מצילין אותה שנאמר וכו' הרי אלו אובדין שנאמר וכו' כונסין אותה לתוכה שנאמר. אלו ג"פ שנאמר נמחקו: **ב]** רש"י ד"ה וצריכין וכו' כדיליף בגמ'. כאן הס"ד ומה"ד יחידים:

ליקוטי רש"י

יגדל נא כח ה'. לעשות דבורך. **כאשר דברת לאמר.** ומהו הדבור [במדבר יד, יז]. **תפלה למשה.** אחד עשר מזמורים מכאן עד לדוד מזמור כלם משה אמרם [תהלים צ, א]. **ביום ההוא.** כהתם הפושעים. **יהיה ה' צבאות לעטרת צבי.** לצדיקים הנשארים בה [ישעיהו כח, ה]. **ולרוח משפט.** יהיה הקב"ה להורות משפט ליושב על המשפט. **ולגבורה.** יהיה לאותן שהם משיבי מלחמ' מלחמתה של תורה [שם פסוק ו]. **לרוח משפט.** לשופטים את רוחן יהיה לעטרה. **הרודה את יצרו.** כופהו לשוב בתשובה. **המתגבר על יצרו.** אינו הולך אחריו לעבור עבירה. **שמשכימין כו'.** והיינו שערה שעושין [שנעשים שוערים] לפתוח דלתות בהשכמה ולאחר [שם עד] זמן נעילתו. **גם אלה.** אלו הרשעים הנידונין בגיהנם. **ביין שגו.** כלומר אף הם עשו כהם לפיכך דנם. מלחמתה של תורה. הוריותיה ולעמוד על בוריה ועל עיקרה [לעיל מב.]. להתוכח בתלמוד [לעיל צג:]. **פקו פליליה.** לגיהנם נשפטו [מגילה טו:]. **וגם אלה.** יושבי משפט ומשיבי מלחמה שבדור הזה כלומר טובים וחשובים שבהן ביין שגו כי עתה אין טוב בהם. **פקו פליליה.** הכשילו המשפט. פקו. לשון פיק ברכים (נחום ב') פוקה (שמואל א' כ"ה) [ישעיה כח, ז]. **ולא תהיה וגו' לפוקה.** לכשלון כמו לפיק ברכים (נחום ב' י"א) [ש"א כה, לא]. **ונתן.** המכה דמי ולדות. **בפלילים.** על פי הדיינים [שמות כא, כב]. **ישבי עירם.** ולא יושבי עיר אחרת מכאן אמרו אין נעשית עיר הנדחת עד שידיחוה אנשים ועד שיהיו מדיחיה מתוכה [דברים יג, יד]. **החמרת והגמלת.** שיירא של חמרים ושל גמלים [ב"ב ח.]. **ולא ידבק בידך מאומה מן החרם.** למען ישוב ה' מחרון אפו שכל זמן שעבודה זרה בעולם, חרון אף בעולם [דברים יג, יח].

מסורת הש"ס

א) עיין רש"א במ"א [מגילה טו: ע"ש כמה שינויים ועי' בפירש"י שם], ב) [ר"ה יז:], ג) [עי' תוספות לעיל מז. ד"ה ואמאי], ד) בקרא ההיא, ה) ב"ב ח., ו) [בסה"מ לא תבנה עוד], ז) [בסה"מ אפי' גנות וכו'], ח) [לעיל טז:], ט) [הא דירושלים נחלקה לשבט יהודה ובנימין ע"פ הדיבור היה. ת"י ביומא יב].

הגהות הגר"א

[א] גמ' רצונו. נמחק ונ"ב לצביונו: **[ב]** שם לישועתו. נמחק ונ"ב לתפארתו: **[ג]** שם שנאמר. נמחק: **[ד]** שנא'. נמחק:

תורה אור השלם

א) וְעַתָּה יִגְדַּל נָא כֹּחַ אֲדֹנָי כַּאֲשֶׁר דִּבַּרְתָּ לֵאמֹר: [במדבר יד, יז]

ב) עֵדֹתֶיךָ נֶאֶמְנוּ מְאֹד לְבֵיתְךָ נַאֲוָה קֹדֶשׁ יְיָ לְאֹרֶךְ יָמִים: [תהלים צג, ה]

ג) תְּפִלָּה לְמֹשֶׁה אִישׁ הָאֱלֹהִים אֲדֹנָי מָעוֹן אַתָּה הָיִיתָ לָּנוּ בְּדֹר וָדֹר: [תהלים צ, א]

ד) בַּיּוֹם הַהוּא יִהְיֶה יְיָ צְבָאוֹת לַעֲטֶרֶת צְבִי וְלִצְפִירַת תִּפְאָרָה לִשְׁאָר עַמּוֹ: [ישעיה כח, ה]

ה) וּלְרוּחַ מִשְׁפָּט לַיּוֹשֵׁב עַל הַמִּשְׁפָּט וְלִגְבוּרָה מְשִׁיבֵי מִלְחָמָה שָׁעְרָה: [ישעיה כח, ו]

ו) וְגַם אֵלֶּה בַּיַּיִן שָׁגוּ וּבַשֵּׁכָר תָּעוּ כֹּהֵן וְנָבִיא שָׁגוּ בַשֵּׁכָר נִבְלְעוּ מִן הַיַּיִן תָּעוּ מִן הַשֵּׁכָר שָׁגוּ בָּרֹאֶה פָּקוּ פְּלִילִיָּה: [ישעיה כח, ז]

ז) וְלֹא תִהְיֶה זֹאת לְךָ לְפוּקָה וּלְמִכְשׁוֹל לֵב לַאדֹנִי וְלִשְׁפָּךְ דָּם חִנָּם וּלְהוֹשִׁיעַ אֲדֹנִי לוֹ וְהֵיטִב יְיָ לַאדֹנִי וְזָכַרְתָּ אֶת אֲמָתֶךָ: [שמואל א' כה, לא]

ח) וְכִי יִנָּצוּ אֲנָשִׁים וְנָגְפוּ אִשָּׁה הָרָה וְיָצְאוּ יְלָדֶיהָ וְלֹא יִהְיֶה אָסוֹן עָנוֹשׁ יֵעָנֵשׁ כַּאֲשֶׁר יָשִׁית עָלָיו בַּעַל הָאִשָּׁה וְנָתַן בִּפְלִלִים: [שמות כא, כב]

ט) יָצְאוּ אֲנָשִׁים בְּנֵי בְלִיַּעַל מִקִּרְבֶּךָ וַיַּדִּיחוּ אֶת יֹשְׁבֵי עִירָם לֵאמֹר נֵלְכָה וְנַעַבְדָה אֱלֹהִים אֲחֵרִים אֲשֶׁר לֹא יְדַעְתֶּם: [דברים יג, יד]

י) הַכֵּה תַכֶּה אֶת יֹשְׁבֵי הָעִיר הַהִוא לְפִי חָרֶב הַחֲרֵם אֹתָהּ וְאֶת כָּל אֲשֶׁר בָּהּ וְאֶת בְּהֶמְתָּהּ לְפִי חָרֶב: [דברים יג, טו]

כ) וְאֶת כָּל שְׁלָלָהּ תִּקְבֹּץ אֶל תּוֹךְ רְחֹבָהּ וְשָׂרַפְתָּ בָאֵשׁ אֶת הָעִיר וְאֶת כָּל שְׁלָלָהּ כָּלִיל לַייָ אֱלֹהֶיךָ וְהָיְתָה תֵּל עוֹלָם לֹא תִבָּנֶה עוֹד: [דברים יג, יז]

ל) וְלֹא יִדְבַּק בְּיָדְךָ מְאוּמָה מִן הַחֵרֶם לְמַעַן יָשׁוּב יְיָ מֵחֲרוֹן אַפּוֹ וְנָתַן לְךָ רַחֲמִים וְרִחַמְךָ וְהִרְבֶּךָ כַּאֲשֶׁר נִשְׁבַּע לַאֲבֹתֶיךָ: [דברים יג, יח]

מ) וְאֶת עַיִן וְאֶת מִגְרָשֶׁהָ וְאֶת יֻטָּה וְאֶת מִגְרָשֶׁהָ אֶת בֵּית שֶׁמֶשׁ וְאֶת מִגְרָשֶׁהָ עָרִים תֵּשַׁע מֵאֵת שְׁנֵי הַשְּׁבָטִים הָאֵלֶּה: [יהושע כא, טז]

subverted,[24] וְעַד שֶׁיַּדִּיחוּהָ אֲנָשִׁים – **and unless men subverted it.**[25] הִדִּיחוּהָ נָשִׁים וּקְטַנִּים – **If women or children subverted it,** אוֹ שֶׁהוּדַּח מִיעוּטָהּ – **or if** only **a minority of [the city] was subverted,** אוֹ שֶׁהָיָה מַדִּיחֶיהָ חוּצָה לָהּ – **or if those who subverted it were** from **outside [the city],** הֲרֵי אֵלוּ כִּיחִידִים – **then [the subverted] are** treated **as individuals.**[26] וּצְרִיכִין שְׁנֵי עֵדִים וְהַתְרָאָה לְכָל אֶחָד וְאֶחָד – **And it is necessary to have two witnesses and a warning for each and every [person].**[27]

The Mishnah explains the difference in regard to punishment between individuals who committed idolatry and members of a subverted city:

זֶה חוֹמֶר בַּיְחִידִים מִבַּמְרוּבִּים – **[The following] is a stringency applying to individuals** convicted of idolatry **rather than to** the **multitudes** (i.e. inhabitants of a subverted city): שֶׁהַיְחִידִים בִּסְקִילָה לְפִיכָךְ מָמוֹנָם פָּלֵט – **For individuals** convicted of idolatry **are** put to death **by stoning; therefore, their property is spared.** וְהַמְרוּבִּין בְּסַיִיף לְפִיכָךְ מָמוֹנָם אָבֵד – **Whereas the multitude** convicted of idolatry (i.e. the inhabitants of a subverted city) **are** put to death **by the sword** (i.e. beheaded); **therefore, their property is destroyed.**[28]

The Mishnah now cites the verses regarding the destruction of the city and expounds them clause by clause:

,,הַכֵּה תַכֶּה אֶת־יֹשְׁבֵי הָעִיר (הזאת) [הַהִוא] לְפִי־חָרֶב'' – The verse states concerning the punishment of the subverted city: ***You shall smite the inhabitants of that city by the sword.*** הַחַמֶּרֶת וְהַגַּמֶּלֶת הָעוֹבֶרֶת מִמָּקוֹם לְמָקוֹם – **A donkey caravan or camel caravan that is traveling from place to place** and is temporarily residing in a city, הֲרֵי אֵלוּ מַצִּילִין אוֹתָהּ – **these can save [the city].**[29]

The verse continues:

(שנאמר)[30] ,,הַחֲרֵם אֹתָהּ וְאֶת־כָּל־אֲשֶׁר־בָּהּ וְאֶת־בְּהֶמְתָּהּ לְפִי־חָרֶב'' – ***Destroy it and everything that is in it, as well as its animals, by the sword.*** מִכַּאן אָמְרוּ – **From here they** derived the law and **said:** נִכְסֵי צַדִּיקִים שֶׁבְּתוֹכָהּ אוֹבְדִין – **The possessions of the righteous** (those who did not worship idols) **that are in [the city] are destroyed,**[31] שֶׁבְּחוּצָה לָהּ פְּלֵיטִין – **while [their possessions] that are outside [the city] are spared;** וְשֶׁל רְשָׁעִים – **whereas** the possessions **of the wicked,** בֵּין שֶׁבְּתוֹכָהּ בֵּין שֶׁבְּחוּצָה לָהּ – **both those that are in [the city] and those that are outside [the city],** הֲרֵי אֵלוּ אוֹבְדִין – **these are** all **destroyed.**[32]

The next verse states:

(שנאמר)[33] ,,וְאֶת־כָּל־שְׁלָלָהּ תִּקְבֹּץ אֶל־תּוֹךְ רְחֹבָהּ וגו' '' – ***And all its booty you shall gather into its square,* etc.**

NOTES

24. The verse states that *the inhabitants of the city* were subverted, which implies "the population of the city" – i.e. all, or at least most, of its inhabitants (*Rashi*; see there for a second exposition).

25. This is derived from Scripture's description of them as אֲנָשִׁים, *men* (Baraisa cited below). It was not strictly necessary for the verse to add this word, since the phrase בְּנֵי־בְלִיַּעַל itself means *lawless people.* Thus, the addition of the word אֲנָשִׁים, *men,* can only be to teach that the subverters must be *men,* not women or children (*Malbim* to verse).

26. I.e. they are not treated as members of an *ir hanidachas* but rather as individuals who engaged in idolatry. Thus, they are executed by stoning rather than beheading, and their property is not destroyed (*Rashi*).

27. I.e. the city cannot be condemned as an *ir hanidachas* unless there are witnesses to the idolatry of each person and unless the idolaters were warned not to engage in that idolatry (*Yad Ramah*). [Thus, the law for the inhabitants of an *ir hanidachas* is no different than the law for any other capital offense. A person cannot be executed unless his crime is attested to by two witnesses and unless he was warned not to commit the crime.] See also *Tiferes Yisrael* §32.

28. Stoning is a more severe form of execution than beheading (Gemara above, 49b). Since individuals who worship idols are stoned, the Torah spared their possessions and allowed them to pass to their heirs. However, the inhabitants of a subverted city are punished by beheading, a less severe form of execution. Because the manner of their execution is not as severe, their property is also forfeit (*Rashi*). [Accordingly, the fact that an individual's property is not forfeit is not because the individual's sin is treated more leniently than the group's. Rather, it is an outgrowth of the fact that his sin is treated more *stringently.* Since this person is punished so severely, his property is spared.]

[Some explain the reason for treating the inhabitants of an *ir hanidachas* more leniently and their property more stringently as follows: When the majority of a city's population worships idols, the individuals are not considered as being so personally sinful because they are (to some extent) being swept along by the ideas and passions of the group. However, the individual who worships idols when most around him do not is for this reason a more sinful person and he therefore deserves the more severe form of death – stoning. On the other hand, the question must be asked: Why did a person not committed to idolatry remain in a city whose inhabitants were so wicked as to commit idolatry? The Gemara below (112a) cites the statement of R' Shimon that the primary incentive for a good person residing in a morally undesirable location is economic: It is financially beneficial for him to remain there. For that reason, the person's possessions are destroyed (*Sanhedrei Ketanah,* quoted by *Margaliyos HaYam*).]

29. A city cannot be condemned unless a majority of its inhabitants engage in idolatry. When calculating the total population of the city, travelers staying in the city are included in the count; thus, if they did not participate in the idolatry, their numbers save the city from condemnation. [For example, if there were a hundred regular inhabitants of the city, fifty-one of whom engaged in idolatry, the city would ordinarily be condemned as an *ir hanidachas*. However, if a caravan of ten people was staying temporarily in the city, they would be counted as part of the city's population, raising its total to a hundred and ten and the minimum needed to condemn the city to fifty-six. If none of these ten travelers engaged in idolatry, it would mean that only fifty-one out of a hundred and ten – *less* than a majority – had engaged in idolatry. The city would therefore *not* be classified an *ir hanidachas,* and its property would not be destroyed.]

This is derived from the verse's reference to יוֹשְׁבֵי הָעִיר, *the "inhabitants" of the city* – implying, even those who merely reside in the city but are not full citizens of it. The Gemara will discuss how long the travelers must have sojourned in the city to be counted as part of its population (*Rashi*).

The same would also be true in the reverse. If only a minority of the city's regular residents engaged in idolatry, but the members of the caravan joined them in the idolatry and together they constitute a majority of the combined population, then the city is condemned as an *ir hanidachas*. The reason the Mishnah speaks of the caravans "saving the city" is only because it would be unlikely for the members of passing caravans – who have no bond with the regular residents of the city – to be swayed to idolatry by the people of the city (*Rashi*; see also *Rav;* cf. *Yad Ramah* 112a ד״ה מתני׳; *Rambam, Hil. Avodas Kochavim* 4:9 and *Kesef Mishneh* there).

30. *Rashi* deletes this word (see also *Hagahos HaGra* and *R' Betzalel Ronsburg* here). It does not appear in the standard editions of the Mishnah. See also *Maharsha.*

31. [I.e. although the people who did not worship idols are not executed, nevertheless, their property is destroyed along with the rest of the city.]

32. The Gemara (112a) will explain the source for this distinction.

33. See note 30.

אמר לפניו רבש"ע ולא כך אמרת לי אף לרשעים והיינו דכתיב ועתה יגדל נא כח ה' כאשר דברת לאמר ר' חגא הוה סליק ואזיל בדרגא דבי רבה בר שילא שמעיה לההוא ינוקא דאמר עדותיך נאמנו מאד לביתך נאוה קדש ה' לאורך ימים וסמיך ליה תפלה למשה וגו' אמר ש"מ ארך אפים ראה א"ר אלעזר א"ר חנינא עתיד הקב"ה להיות עטרה בראש כל צדיק וצדיק שנאמר ביום ההוא יהיה ה' צבאות לעטרת צבי ולצפירת תפארה לשאר עמו וגו' מאי לעטרת צבי ולצפירת תפארה לעושים [א] רצונו ומצפים [ב] לישועתו יכול לכל ת"ל לשאר עמו למי שמשים עצמו כשירים ולרוח משפט ליושב על המשפט ולגבורה משיבי מלחמה שערה ולרוח משפט זה הרודה את יצרו וליושב על המשפט זה הדן דין אמת לאמיתו ולגבורה זה המתגבר ביצרו משיבי מלחמה זה שנושא ונותן במלחמתה של תורה שערה אלו שמשכימין ומעריבין בבתי כנסיות ובתי מדרשות אמרה מדת הדין לפני הקב"ה רבש"ע מה נשתנו אלו מאלו אמר לה וגם אלה ביין שגו ובשכר תעו [וגו'] פקו פליליה ואין פוקה אלא גיהנם שנאמר לא תהיה זאת לך לפוקה ואין פלילה אלא דיינין שנאמר ונתן בפלילים:

מתני' אנשי עיר הנדחת אין להם חלק לעוה"ב שנאמר יצאו אנשים בני בליעל מקרבך וידיחו את (אנשי) [יושבי] עירם ואינן נהרגים עד שיהיו מדיחיה מאותה העיר ומאותו השבט ועד שיודח רובה ועד שידיחוה אנשים הדיחוה נשים וקטנים או שהודח מיעוטה או שהיה מדיחיה חוצה לה הרי אלו כיחידים וצריכין ב' עדים והתראה לכל אחד ואחד זה חומר ביחידים מבמרובים שהיחידים בסקילה לפיכך ממונם פלט והמרובין בסייף לפיכך ממונם אבד הכה תכה את יושבי העיר הזאת לפי חרב החמרת והגמלת העוברת ממקום למקום [א] הרי אלו מצילין אותה [ג] שנא' החרם אותה ואת כל אשר בה ואת בהמתה לפי חרב מכאן אמרו נכסי צדיקים שבתוכה אובדין שבחוצה לה פליטין ושל רשעים בין שבתוכה בין שבחוצה לה הרי אלו אובדין [ד] שנאמר ואת כל שללה תקבוץ אל תוך רחבה וגו' אם אין לה רחוב עושין לה רחוב היתה רחבה חוצה לה כונסין אותה לתוכה שנאמר ושרפת באש את העיר ואת כל שללה כליל לה' אלהיך שללה ולא שלל שמים מכאן אמרו ההקדשות שבה יפדו ותרומות ירקבו מעשר שני וכתבי הקדש יגנזו כליל לה' אלהיך אמר ר"ש אמר הקב"ה אם אתם עושין דין בעיר הנדחת מעלה אני עליכם כאילו אתם מעלים עולה כליל לפני והיתה תל עולם לא תעשה גנות ופרדסים דברי ר' יוסי הגלילי ר"ע אומר לא תבנה עוד לכמות שהיתה אינה נבנית אבל נעשית היא גנות ופרדסים ולא ידבק בידך מאומה מן החרם שכל זמן שהרשעים בעולם חרון אף בעולם אבדו רשעים מן העולם נסתלק חרון אף מן העולם:

גמ' ת"ר יצאו הן ולא שלוחין אנשים אין אנשים פחות מב' דבר אחר אנשים ולא נשים ולא קטנים בני בליעל בנים שפרקו עול שמים מצואריהם מקרבך ולא מן הספר יושבי עירם ולא יושבי עיר אחרת לאמר שצריכין עדים והתראה לכל אחד ואחד איתמר ר' יוחנן אמר חולקין עיר אחת לשני שבטים ור"ל אמר אין חולקין עיר אחת לב' שבטים איתיביה ר' יוחנן לר"ל עד שיהו מדיחיה מאותה העיר ומאותו שבט מאי לאו אע"ג דמדיחיה מאותה העיר אי איכא מאותו שבט אין אי לא לא ש"מ חולקין עיר אחת לב' שבטים לא דנפלה ליה בירושה א"נ דיהבוה ניהליה במתנה איתיביה ערים תשע מאת שני השבטים האלה מאי לאו ארבע ופלגא מהאי וארבע ופלגא מהאי וש"מ חולקין עיר אחת לב' שבטים לא ארבעה מהאי וחמש מהאי אי הכי לפרוש פרושי

קשיא

אמר לפניו וכו'. והשתא [מסתברא] כמ"ד ארך אפים ראה שכיון שראה [מדה זו] בהקב"ה שהוא ארך אפים אף לרשעים שמח: עדותיך וגו' ה' לאורך ימים. היינו מדת ארך אפים ועליה אמר משה עדותיך נאמנו מאד שראה אותו בחורב ופסוק זה מרע"ה אמרו דכתיב לעיל מיניה תפלה למשה איש האלהים וגו': יכול לכל. למי שעושין רצונו אע"פ שמתגאה: כשירים. שיריים שאין נחשבין כך אינו חשוב בעיניו ואינו מתגאה: ולרוח משפט. שופט את רוחו: שרודה ביצרו. שכובש בילרו וחוזר בתשובה מן העבירה שעבר: ומתגבר ביצרו. מרגיז יצ"ט על יצה"ר אם היצה"ר אמר לו עשה עבירה זו לא דיו שנמנע מן העבירה אלא הולך ועושה מצוה ומתגבר עליו מרודה: שערה. אלו בתי כנסיות: מה נשתנו אלו מאלו. שיש בהם מדות הללו מן השאר אמר הקב"ה ביין שגו: ואין פלילה אלא דיינין: **מתני'** יצאו אנשים בני בליעל מקרבך. שאין להם חלק לעוה"ב: וידיחו את (אנשי) [יושבי] עירם. הא אין נהרגים עד שיהיו מדיחיה מאותה העיר ואותה השבט עצמה דכתיב מקרבך מקרב אותו שבט עצמו: עד שיודח רובה. דכתיב ויושבי העיר משמע ישובה של עיר היינו רובה לישנא אחרינא עד שיודח רובה דכתיב מקרבך קרי ביה מרובך: ה"ג עד שיודח רובה עד שידיחוה אנשים: או שהיו מדיחיה חוצה לה. שלא היו מאותה העיר: הרי אלו כיחידים. שהן בסקילה וממונן פלט: וצריכים ב' עדים והתראה לכל אחד. כדיליף בגמרא [ב] יחידים בסקילה לפיכך ממונן פלט ומתוך שהחמרת עליו במיתתו הקלת עליו בממונו: הכה תכה את יושבי העיר ההיא לפי חרב החמרת והגמלת העוברת ממקום למקום מצילין. מדכתיב יושבי מכלל דשיירה של חמרים וגמלים שנשתהו בעיר ל' יום כדמפרש בגמרא דהוו להו יושבי העיר הרי אלו מצילין אם רוב אנשי העיר הודחו וחמרים וגמלים משלימין המיעוט ועושה אותם רוב מצילין עליהם שאין ממונם אבד אלא נדונים כיחידים וגורמין נמי לעשות אותה עיר הנדחת אם משלימים לעיר הנדחת לעשות רוב אלא הא פסיקא טפי דחמרת וגמלת אין דעתם מעורבת עם בני העיר להיות נדונין עמהן: ה"ג החרם אותה וכל אשר בה מכאן אמרו צדיקים וכו' ושל רשעים בין מתוכה בין מחוצה לה אבודים. בגמרא מפרש לה מדכתיב כל: ואת כל שללה תקבוץ אל תוך רחובה אין לה רחוב עושין לה רחוב. ורחובה דהשתא נמי משמע: היה רחובה חוצה לה. שמקום קבוץ בני העיר היה חוץ לעיר כונסין אותה לעיר שצריך לעשות לה רחוב בתוכה. רחוב סרטיא גדולה: את העיר ואת כל שללה ולא שלל שמים. דשלל שמים פלט: מכאן אמרו הקדשות שבתוכה יפדו. כלומר אין נשרפין אלא הרי הם כשאר הקדש שצריך פדייה כ"ש דשלל שמים הם: ותרומות ירקבו. ובגמ' מוקמי לה בתרומה ביד כהן דממון כהן הוא וחל עליה איסור דעיר הנדחת דנהי דבשריפה לא הויא עם שאר שללה דקדש אקרי ולא מזלזלינן ביה כולי האי: מעשר שני. אע"פ שהוא נאכל לישראל הואיל וקדש איקרי לא אמרי' ישרף אלא יגנזו וכן כתבי הקדש יגנזו: ה"ג כליל לה' אלהיך אר"ש אמר הקב"ה וכו' כאילו אתה מעלה עולה שהוא כליל לפני: לא תעשה גנות ופרדסין וכו'. בגמ' מפרש במאי פליגי: לכמו שהיתה. ביישוב בתים: **גמ'** יצאו הם ולא שלוחם. אם המדיחין עצמן יצאו והדיחן והרי הם מרובים ודנין בסייף אבל אם הדיחו ע"י שליח כיחידים הם בסקילה וממונם פלט: אין אנשים פחות מב'. דע"י מדיח אחד אין נעשית עיר הנדחת: בקרבך. משמע באמצע ולא מן הספר שאם היתה עיר של ספר בין מחוז עובדי כוכבים למחוז ישראל אינה נעשית עיר הנדחת דגזירת הכתוב היא שלא תעשה עיר הנדחת: יושבי העיר ולא יושבי עיר אחרת. דהיינו מדיחי' מחוצה לה: לאמר נלכה ונעבדה. משמע שצ"ל לפנינו שכך אומרים נלכה ונעבדה ואין אמירה אלא בעדים אלמא צריך עדים לכל אחד ואחד שיעידו עליהם מה שאמרו וה"נ צריך התראה לכל א' וא' מהם: חולקין עיר אחת. בתחלה כשחלקו ישראל את הארץ היו רשאין ליתן ולחלוק עיר א' לב' שבטים כגון אם אירע להם עיר בתחום ומקצת מושכת לתחום אחר שבט אחד נוטל חלק באותו קצת הארץ ע"פ הגורל נחלקה הארץ אם נפתלי עולה תחום גינוסר עולה עמו דהכי אמרינן בב"ב בפרק י"נ ומנחילין (דף קכב.): אין חולקין. אלא כולה של אותו השבט שרוב' בתחומי': מאי לאו אע"ג דמדיחיה מאותה עיר. אם יהיו מאותו שבט נעשית עיר הנדחת ואי לא לא שאם אינו מאותו שבט שהודחו אלא משבט אחר שבעיר אינו בסייף אלא בסקילה אלמא אפשר שיהו מן אותה העיר ולא מאותו שבט וה"ד כגון שחלקו עיר אחת לשני שבטים: לא. לעולם אימא לך דאין חולקין והיכי משכחת לה מאותה עיר ולא מאותו שבט כגון דנפלה למדיחיה בירושה מקצת העיר ע"י בת יורשת נחלה: ערים תשע מאת שני השבטים האלה. ממטה יהודה וממטה שמעון נטלו ט' ערים ונתנום ללוים: מאי לאו דשקל מהאי ד' ופלגא. שהיתה עיר א' של יהודה ושמעון ונטלו מהם אלמא חולקין עיר אחת לשני שבטים: ה"ג לא ד' מהאי וה' מהאי: א"ה לפרוש פרושי. הי נינהו שבט דשקיל מיניה ה' והי נינהו דשקיל מיניה ד' ואמאי כתיב ערים תשע מאת שני השבטים משמע דבשוה שקל:

קשיא

עין משפט נר מצוה

לה א מיי' פ"ד מהל' ע"ז הלכה ג סמג עשין טו:
לו ב מיי' שם הלכה ה והלכה ו:
לז ג מיי' שם הל' ב:
לח ד מיי' שם הל' ו:
לט ה מיי' שם הל' ז:
מ ו מיי' שם הל' י:
מא ז מיי' שם הל' ו:
מב ח מיי' שם הל' יג:
מג ט מיי' שם הל' ו:
מד י מיי' שם הל' ז:
מה כ ל מיי' שם הל' ב:
מו מ מיי' שם הל' ד:

הגהות מהר"ב רנשבורג

א] מתני' הרי אלו מצילין אותה שנאמר וכו' הרי אלו אובדין שנאמר וכו' כונסין אותה לתוכה שנאמר. אלו ג"פ שנאמר נמחקו: ב] רש"י ד"ה וצריכין וכו' כדיליף בגמ'. כאן הס"ד ומה"ד יחידים:

ליקוטי רש"י

יגדל נא כח ה'. לעשות דבורך. כאשר דברת לאמר. ומהו הדבור [במדבר יד, יז]. תפלה למשה. אחד עשר מזמורים מכאן עד לדוד מזמור כלם משה אמרם [תהלים צ, א]. ביום ההוא. כהתם הפושעים. יהיה ה' צבאות לעטרת צבי. לצדיקים הנשארים בה [ישעיה כח, ה]. ולרוח משפט. יהיה הקב"ה להורות משפט ליושב על המשפט. ולגבורה. יהיה לאותן שהם משיבי מלחמ' מלחמתה של תורה [שם פסוק ו]. לרוח משפט. לשופטים את רוחן יהיה לעטרה. הרודה את יצרו. כופהו לשוב בתשובה. המתגבר על יצרו. אינו הולך אחריו לעבור עבירה. שמשכימין כו'. והיינו שערה שעושין [שנעשים שוערים] לפתוח דלתות בהשכמה ולאחר [שם עד] זמן נעילתו. גם אלה. אלו הרשעים הנידונין בגיהנם. ביין שגו. כלומר אף הם עשו כהם לפיכך דנם. מלחמתה של תורה. הוריותיה ולעמוד על בוריה ועל עיקרה [לעיל מב.]. להתוכח בתלמוד [לעיל צג:]. פקו פליליה. לגיהנם נשפטו [מגילה טו:]. וגם אלה. יושבי משפט ומשיבי מלחמה שבדור הזה כלומר טובים וחשובים שבהן ביין שגו כי עתה אין טוב בהם. פקו פליליה. הכשילו המשפט. פקו. לשון פיק ברכים (נחום ב') פוקה (שמואל א' כ"ה) [ישעיה כח, ז]. ולא תהיה וגו' לפוקה. לכשלון כמו לפיק ברכים (נחום ב' י"א) [ש"א כה, לא]. ונתן. המכה דמי ולדות. בפלילים. על פי הדיינים [שמות כא, כב]. ישבי עירם. ולא יושבי עיר אחרת מכאן אמרו אין נעשית עיר הנדחת עד שידיחוה אנשים ועד שיהיו מדיחיה מתוכה [דברים יג, יד]. החמרת והגמלת. שיירא של חמרים ושל גמלים [ב"ב ח.]. ולא ידבק בידך מאומה מן החרם. למען ישוב ה' מחרון אפו שכל זמן שעבודה זרה בעולם, חרון אף בעולם [דברים יג, יח].

מסורת הש"ס

א) עיין רש"א בח"א [מגילה טו: ע"ש כמה שינויים ועי' בפירש"י שם], ב) [ר"ה יז:], ג) [עי' תוספות לעיל מז. ד"ה ואמאי], ד) בקרא ההיא, ה) ב"ב ח., ו) [בסה"מ לא תבנה עוד], ז) [בסה"מ אפי' גנות וכו'], ח) [לעיל טז:], ט) [הא דירושלים נחלקה לשבט יהודה ובנימין ע"פ הדיבור היה. ת"י ביומא יב].

הגהות הגר"א

[א] גמ' רצונו. נמחק ונ"ב לצביונו: [ב] שם לישועתו. נמחק ונ"ב לתפארתו: [ג] שם שנאמר. נמחק: [ד] שנא'. נמחק:

תורה אור השלם

א) וְעַתָּה יִגְדַּל נָא כֹּחַ אֲדֹנָי כַּאֲשֶׁר דִּבַּרְתָּ לֵאמֹר: [במדבר יד, יז]

ב) עֵדֹתֶיךָ נֶאֶמְנוּ מְאֹד לְבֵיתְךָ נַאֲוָה קֹדֶשׁ יְיָ לְאֹרֶךְ יָמִים: [תהלים צג, ה]

ג) תְּפִלָּה לְמֹשֶׁה אִישׁ הָאֱלֹהִים אֲדֹנָי מָעוֹן אַתָּה הָיִיתָ לָּנוּ בְּדֹר וָדֹר: [תהלים צ, א]

ד) בַּיּוֹם הַהוּא יִהְיֶה יְיָ צְבָאוֹת לַעֲטֶרֶת צְבִי וְלִצְפִירַת תִּפְאָרָה לִשְׁאָר עַמּוֹ: [ישעיה כח, ה]

ה) וּלְרוּחַ מִשְׁפָּט לַיּוֹשֵׁב עַל הַמִּשְׁפָּט וְלִגְבוּרָה מְשִׁיבֵי מִלְחָמָה שָׁעְרָה: [ישעיה כח, ו]

ו) וְגַם אֵלֶּה בַּיַּיִן שָׁגוּ וּבַשֵּׁכָר תָּעוּ כֹּהֵן וְנָבִיא שָׁגוּ בַשֵּׁכָר נִבְלְעוּ מִן הַיַּיִן תָּעוּ מִן הַשֵּׁכָר שָׁגוּ בָּרֹאֶה פָּקוּ פְּלִילִיָּה: [ישעיה כח, ז]

ז) וְלֹא תִהְיֶה זֹאת לְךָ לְפוּקָה וּלְמִכְשׁוֹל לֵב לַאדֹנִי וְלִשְׁפָּךְ דָּם חִנָּם וּלְהוֹשִׁיעַ אֲדֹנִי לוֹ וְהֵיטִב יְיָ לַאדֹנִי וְזָכַרְתָּ אֶת אֲמָתֶךָ: [שמואל א' כה, לא]

ח) וְכִי יִנָּצוּ אֲנָשִׁים וְנָגְפוּ אִשָּׁה הָרָה וְיָצְאוּ יְלָדֶיהָ וְלֹא יִהְיֶה אָסוֹן עָנוֹשׁ יֵעָנֵשׁ כַּאֲשֶׁר יָשִׁית עָלָיו בַּעַל הָאִשָּׁה וְנָתַן בִּפְלִלִים: [שמות כא, כב]

ט) יָצְאוּ אֲנָשִׁים בְּנֵי בְלִיַּעַל מִקִּרְבֶּךָ וַיַּדִּיחוּ אֶת יֹשְׁבֵי עִירָם לֵאמֹר נֵלְכָה וְנַעַבְדָה אֱלֹהִים אֲחֵרִים אֲשֶׁר לֹא יְדַעְתֶּם: [דברים יג, יד]

י) הַכֵּה תַכֶּה אֶת יֹשְׁבֵי הָעִיר הַהִוא לְפִי חָרֶב הַחֲרֵם אֹתָהּ וְאֶת כָּל אֲשֶׁר בָּהּ וְאֶת בְּהֶמְתָּהּ לְפִי חָרֶב: [דברים יג, טו]

כ) וְאֶת כָּל שְׁלָלָהּ תִּקְבֹּץ אֶל תּוֹךְ רְחֹבָהּ וְשָׂרַפְתָּ בָאֵשׁ אֶת הָעִיר וְאֶת כָּל שְׁלָלָהּ כָּלִיל לַייָ אֱלֹהֶיךָ וְהָיְתָה תֵּל עוֹלָם לֹא תִבָּנֶה עוֹד: [דברים יג, יז]

ל) וְלֹא יִדְבַּק בְּיָדְךָ מְאוּמָה מִן הַחֵרֶם לְמַעַן יָשׁוּב יְיָ מֵחֲרוֹן אַפּוֹ וְנָתַן לְךָ רַחֲמִים וְרִחַמְךָ וְהִרְבֶּךָ כַּאֲשֶׁר נִשְׁבַּע לַאֲבֹתֶיךָ: [דברים יג, יח]

מ) וְאֶת עַיִן וְאֶת מִגְרָשֶׁהָ וְאֶת יֻטָּה וְאֶת מִגְרָשֶׁהָ אֶת בֵּית שֶׁמֶשׁ וְאֶת מִגְרָשֶׁהָ עָרִים תֵּשַׁע מֵאֵת שְׁנֵי הַשְּׁבָטִים הָאֵלֶּה: [יהושע כא, טז]

אִם אֵין לָהּ רְחוֹב – **If [the city] has no square,** עוֹשִׂין לָהּ רְחוֹב – **they make a square for it.**[34] הָיְתָה רְחָבָהּ חוּצָה לָהּ – If **its square was outside it,** כּוֹנְסִין אוֹתָהּ לְתוֹכָהּ – **they gather it into [the city].**[35]

The verse continues:

(שנאמר)[36] ,,וְשָׂרַפְתָּ בָאֵשׁ אֶת־הָעִיר וְאֶת־כָּל־שְׁלָלָהּ כָּלִיל לַה׳ אֱלֹהֶיךָ״ – ***And you shall burn the city and all its booty in a fire, completely, to Hashem your God.*** ,,שְׁלָלָהּ״ וְלֹא שְׁלַל שָׁמַיִם – This implies, ***its booty*** (i.e. property), **but not the booty of Heaven.** מִכָּאן אָמְרוּ – **From here they** derived the law and **said:** הַהֶקְדֵּשׁוֹת שֶׁבָּהּ יִפָּדוּ – **The consecrated objects in [the city] should be redeemed,**[37] וּתְרוּמוֹת יֵרָקְבוּ – **the *terumah* portions should** be left to **rot**[38] מַעֲשֵׂר שֵׁנִי וְכִתְבֵי הַקֹּדֶשׁ יִגָּנְזוּ – and the ***maaser sheni* and holy Scriptures should be hidden away.**[39]

The verse states:

,,כָּלִיל לַה׳ אֱלֹהֶיךָ״ – *And you shall burn the city . . .* ***completely, to Hashem your God.*** אָמַר רַבִּי שִׁמְעוֹן – **R' Shimon said:** אָמַר הַקָּדוֹשׁ בָּרוּךְ הוּא – **The Holy One, Blessed is He, said:** אִם אַתֶּם עוֹשִׂין דִּין בְּעִיר הַנִּדַּחַת – **If you execute judgment against a subverted city,** מַעֲלֶה אֲנִי עֲלֵיכֶם כְּאִילּוּ אַתֶּם מַעֲלִים עוֹלָה כָּלִיל לְפָנַי – **I will regard it for you as if you are offering up before Me an *olah* that is completely burned.**[40]

The verse continues:

,,וְהָיְתָה תֵּל עוֹלָם״ – ***And it shall remain an eternal heap*** – לֹא תֵעָשֶׂה גַּנּוֹת וּפַרְדֵּסִים – **it may not** even **be made into gardens and orchards;** דִּבְרֵי רַבִּי יוֹסֵי הַגְּלִילִי – these are **the words of R' Yose HaGlili.** רַבִּי עֲקִיבָא אוֹמֵר – **R' Akiva says:** ,,לֹא תִבָּנֶה עוֹד״ – The concluding phrase of this verse states: ***it shall never again be built,***

NOTES

34. The word רְחוֹב, *square,* refers to a broad open place where the townspeople gather (*Rashi;* see *Rashi* to *Shabbos* 6a ד״ה פלטיא). Although the verse states that all the city's possessions be gathered into its square to be burned, having a city square is not a precondition for classifying a city an *ir hanidachas.* It is only necessary that the city have a square at the time it is destroyed (*Rashi* from Gemara 112a). [Thus, if a city had no square when its inhabitants engaged in idolatry, the court makes a square and then gathers all the city's property into it and burns it.]

35. If the public place of gathering was outside the city (*Rashi*), they extend the city wall to take in the square (*Rambam, Hil. Avodas Kochavim* 4:6). *Yad Ramah* states that they also tear down the section of the wall that divides the city from the square. [*Rashi*, however, seems to indicate that the phrase "they gather it into the city" is not meant literally. Rather, it is merely the Mishnah's way of saying that if the square is outside the city, they must build a new square inside the city (see *Einayim LaMishpat*).]

36. See note 30.

37. Our Mishnah speaks of objects consecrated for בֶּדֶק הַבַּיִת, *Temple maintenance,* not those designated as sacrificial offerings. (This is taught in a Baraisa on 112b.)

[An object consecrated to the Temple is the property not of its consecrator, but of the Temple.] Thus, if consecrated objects are found in an *ir hanidachas,* they are not burned because they are "the booty of Heaven," not of the city. They are instead treated like any object consecrated to the Temple for its maintenance – they are redeemed at full value, and the proceeds are spent on the Temple's maintenance (*Rashi*). Accordingly, the Mishnah could simply have said that the consecrated objects are "spared," or "not burned." The Mishnah states instead that they are "redeemed" to teach that they are treated like any other consecrated property, which may be redeemed *and used.* The forbidden *ir hanidachas* status does not take effect on them even after they are redeemed (*Yad Ramah*).

[*Ramah's* ruling is not universally accepted. *Rambam* (*Hil. Avodas Kochavim* 4:13) rules that the consecrated objects are redeemed and then burned. They are regarded as objects belonging to an *ir hanidachas* that happen to be protected from burning by their special status as sacred objects. But once their sacred status is removed through redemption, they are subject to the fate of the other objects of the city and are burned (*Kesef Mishneh;* cf. *Minchas Chinuch* 464:41). *Raavad,* however, disagrees and maintains (in agreement with *Yad Ramah*) that since sacred objects are considered the possessions of the Temple, they are not subject to the fate of the city at all. Therefore, once redeemed, they become the property of whoever redeemed them, to use as he wishes. This would seem to be the view of *Rashi* as well.]

[It should be noted that *Rashi* here uses an abbreviation whose meaning is in question. We have followed the view of *R' Yeshayah Berlin* (cited in *Margaliyos HaYam*) that the abbreviation כ״ש stands for כְּדֵי שָׁוְיָין, *for their full value.* Others understand it to mean כָּל שֶׁהוּא, *for a minimal amount*. *Rabbeinu Yehonasan* (cited in *Chamra VeChayei* and *Margaliyos HaYam* §17) cites a view that after the consecrated objects are redeemed for a token amount, the *money* is destroyed. See also *Meiri*.]

38. The foodstuffs separated as *terumah* are not burned, but are instead left to rot. The Gemara below will conclude that the Mishnah speaks of *terumah* that has already been given to a Kohen [who is an inhabitant of the *ir hanidachas*]. This *terumah* is the property of that Kohen, not of Heaven, and it therefore becomes forbidden as the property of the *ir hanidachas*. Nevertheless, since the Torah refers to *terumah* as קֹדֶשׁ, *holy* (*Leviticus* 22:10), it is not burned because this would be too great a desecration of its sanctity. Therefore, it is left to rot (*Rashi*). *Terumah* that has not yet been given to a Kohen, however, does not become forbidden because it is not the property of the person who separated it (since he must give it to a Kohen).

[According to the Gemara's conclusion, therefore, the *terumah* of which the Mishnah speaks is not really excluded from the law of *ir hanidachas*; the Mishnah merely lists its exclusion from burning along with that of הֶקְדֵּשׁוֹת, *consecrated objects,* which are excluded. *Terumah* in the possession of a Kohen is not burned merely out of consideration of its sanctity. See *Yad Ramah* (to 112b), who discusses whether this consideration is Rabbinic or Biblical.]

39. *Maaser sheni* (second tithe) is a portion separated from the crop during the first, second, fourth and fifth years of every seven-year *shemittah* cycle. This tithe is taken to Jerusalem where it is eaten, or it is redeemed for money that is taken to Jerusalem and spent on food eaten there. *Maaser sheni* foodstuffs, and any money obtained from redeeming *maaser sheni*, are not burned with the other possessions of the city but are hidden away or buried. Even though *maaser sheni* is eaten by its owner [and is therefore, according to the Tanna of our Mishnah, considered the property of the owner, not Heaven (*Yad Ramah* to 112b)], it is not burned because the Torah refers to it too as קֹדֶשׁ, *holy* [*Leviticus* 27:30] (*Rashi*). This will be elaborated more fully by the Gemara below, 112b.

As for copies of Scripture, although they are certainly the property of their owners, they may not be burned because they contain the Name of God (*Yad Ramah*).

The reason *maaser sheni* is hidden away or buried, rather than left out to rot (like *terumah*), is because people are not as careful with *maaser sheni* as they are with *terumah*. *Maaser sheni* is ordinarily theirs to eat, and we therefore fear that if *maaser sheni* is left out, it may accidentally be taken and eaten. By contrast, the *terumah* of which the Mishnah speaks is *terumah* in the hands of a Kohen (see previous note), which non-Kohanim are accustomed to avoid in any case. Although Kohanim are accustomed to eating *terumah,* they are also especially diligent [זְרִיזִים] in their observance of their priestly responsibilities, so we need not fear that *they* will eat the forbidden *terumah* (*Tos. Yom Tov;* cf. *Aruch LaNer;* and *Yad Ramah*).

40. [The verse states that the city is burned "completely to *Hashem your God.*" Thus, it partakes of the nature of a sacrificial offering, and the verse's emphasis that it is burned *completely* is indicative of its being like an *olah* – the only type of sacrifice in which the entire carcass of the animal is burned on the Altar as an offering to Hashem.] Just as an *olah* is completely consumed, with no part of it being eaten by the person who offers it, so too the *ir hanidachas* is completely destroyed, without any use or monetary benefit accruing to anyone (*Iyun Yaakov*).

אמר לפניו רבש"ע ולא כך אמרת לי אף לרשעים והיינו דכתיב א) ועתה יגדל נא כח ה' כאשר דברת לאמר ר' חגא הוה סליק ואזיל בדרגא דבי רבה בר שילא שמעיה לההוא ינוקא דאמר ב) עדותיך נאמנו מאד לביתך נאוה קדש ה' לאורך ימים וסמיך ליה ג) תפלה למשה וגו' אמר ש"מ ארך אפים ראה א"ר אלעזר א"ר חנינא עתיד הקב"ה להיות עטרה בראש כל צדיק וצדיק שנאמר ד) ביום ההוא יהיה ה' צבאות לעטרת צבי ולצפירת תפארה לשאר עמו וגו' מאי לעטרת צבי ולצפירת תפארה לעושים [א] רצונו ומצפים [ב] לישועתו יכול לכל ת"ל לשאר עמו [ג] למי שמשים עצמו כשירים ה) ולרוח משפט ליושב על המשפט ולגבורה משיבי מלחמה שערה ולרוח משפט זה הרודה את יצרו וליושב על המשפט זה הדן דין אמת לאמיתו ולגבורה זה המתגבר ביצרו משיבי מלחמה זה שנושא ונותן במלחמתה של תורה שערה אלו שמשכימין ומעריבין בבתי כנסיות ובתי מדרשות אמרה מדת הדין לפני הקב"ה רבש"ע מה נשתנו אלו מאלו אמר לה ו) וגם אלה ביין שגו ובשכר תעו [וגו'] פקו פליליה ואין פוקה אלא גיהנם שנאמר ז) לא תהיה זאת לך לפוקה ואין פלילה אלא דיינין שנאמר ח) ונתן בפלילים: **מתני'** אנשי עיר הנדחת אין להם חלק לעוה"ב שנאמר ט) יצאו אנשים בני בליעל מקרבך וידיחו את (אנשי) [יושבי] עירם ואינן נהרגים עד שיהיו מדיחיה מאותה העיר ומאותו השבט ועד שיודח רובה ועד שידיחוה אנשים הדיחוה נשים וקטנים או שהודח מיעוטה או שהיה מדיחיה חוצה לה הרי אלו כיחידים וצריכין ב' עדים והתראה לכל אחד ואחד זה חומר ביחידים מבמרובים שהיחידים בסקילה לפיכך ממונם פלט והמרובין בסייף לפיכך ממונם אבד י) הכה תכה את יושבי העיר ההיא לפי חרב החמרת והגמלת העוברת ממקום למקום הרי אלו מצילין אותה [ד] שנא' החרם אותה ואת כל אשר בה ואת בהמתה לפי חרב מכאן אמרו נכסי צדיקים שבתוכה אובדין שבחוצה לה פליטין ושל רשעים בין שבתוכה בין שבחוצה לה הרי אלו אובדין שנאמר כ) ואת כל שללה תקבוץ אל תוך רחבה וגו' אם אין לה רחוב עושין לה רחוב היתה רחבה חוצה לה כונסין אותה לתוכה שנאמר ושרפת באש את העיר ואת כל שללה כליל לה' אלהיך שללה ולא שלל שמים מכאן אמרו ההקדשות שבה יפדו ותרומות ירקבו מעשר שני וכתבי הקדש יגנזו כליל לה' אלהיך אמר ר"ש אמר הקב"ה אם אתם עושין דין בעיר הנדחת מעלה אני עליכם כאילו אתם מעלים עולה כליל לפני והיתה תל עולם לא תעשה גנות ופרדסים דברי ר' יוסי הגלילי ר"ע אומר לא תבנה עוד לכמות שהיתה אינה נבנית היא נעשית גנות ופרדסים ל) ולא ידבק בידך מאומה מן החרם שכל זמן שהרשעים בעולם חרון אף בעולם אבדו רשעים מן העולם נסתלק חרון אף מן העולם: **גמ'** ת"ר יצאו הן ולא שלוחין אנשים אין אנשים פחות מב' דבר אחר אנשים ולא נשים אנשים ולא קטנים בני בליעל בנים שפרקו עול שמים מצואריהם מקרבך ולא מן הספר יושבי עירם ולא יושבי עיר אחרת לאמר שצריכין עדים והתראה לכל אחד ואחד איתמר ר' יוחנן אמר חולקין עיר אחת לשני שבטים ור"ל אמר אין חולקין עיר אחת לב' שבטים איתיביה ר' יוחנן לר"ל עד שיהו מדיחיה מאותה העיר ומאותו שבט מאי לאו אע"ג דמדיחיה מאותה העיר אי איכא מאותו שבט אין אי לא לא ש"מ חולקין עיר אחת לב' שבטים לא דנפלה ליה בירושה א"נ דיהבוה ניהליה במתנה איתיביה מ) ערים תשע מאת שני השבטים האלה מאי לאו ארבע ופלגא מהאי וארבע ופלגא מהאי וש"מ חולקין עיר אחת לב' שבטים לא ארבעה מהאי וחמש מהאי אי הכי לפרוש פרושי

קשיא

אמר לפניו וכו'. והשתא [מסתברא] כמ"ד ארך אפים ראה שכיון שראה [מדה זו] בהקב"ה שהוא ארך אפים אף לרשעים שמח: עדותיך וגו' ה' לאורך ימים. היינו מדת ארך אפים ועליה אמר משה עדותיך נאמנו מאד שראה אותו בחורב ופסוק זה מרע"ה אמרו דכתיב לעיל מיניה תפלה למשה איש האלהים וגו': יכול לכל. למי שעושין רצונו אע"פ שמתגאה: כשירים. שיריים שאין נחשבין כך אינו חשוב בעיניו ואינו מתגאה: ולרוח משפט. שופט את רוחו: שרודה ביצרו. שבועט בילרו וחוזר בתשובה מן העבירה שעבר: ומתגבר ביצרו. מרגיז יצ"ט על יצה"ר אם היצה"ר אמר לו עשה עבירה זו לא דיו שנמנע מן העבירה אלא הולך ועושה מצוה ומתגבר עדיף מרודה: שערה. אלו בתי כנסיות: מה נשתנו אלו מאלו. שיש בהם מדות הללו מן השאר אמר הקב"ה ביין שגו: ואין פלילה אלא דיינין: **מתני'** יצאו אנשים בני בליעל מקרבך. שאין להם חלק לעוה"ב: וידיחו את (אנשי) [יושבי] עירם. הא אין נהרגים עד שיהיו מדיחיה מאותה העיר ואותה השבט עצמה דכתיב מקרבך מקרב אותו שבט עצמו: עד שיודח רובה. דכתיב ויושבי העיר משמע ישובה של עיר היינו רובה לישנא אחרינא עד שיודח רובה דכתיב מקרבך קרי ביה מרובך: ה"ג עד שיודח רובה עד שידיחוה אנשים: או שהיו מדיחיה חוצה לה. שלא היו מאותה העיר: הרי אלו כיחידים. שהן בסקילה וממונן פלט: וצריכים ב' עדים והתראה לכל אחד. כדיליף בגמרא [ב] יחידים בסקילה לפיכך ממונן פלט ומתוך שהחמרת עליו במיתתו הקלת עליו בממונו: הכה תכה את יושבי העיר ההיא לפי חרב החמרת והגמלת העוברת ממקום למקום מצילין. מדכתיב יושבי מכלל דשיירה של חמרים וגמלים שנשתהו בעיר ל' יום כדמפרש בגמרא דהוו להו יושבי העיר הרי אלו מצילין אם רוב אנשי העיר הודחו וחמרים וגמלים משלימין המיעוט ועושה אותם רוב מצילין עליהם שאין ממונם אבד אלא נדונים כיחידים וגורמין נמי לעשות אותה עיר הנדחת אם משלימים לעיר הנדחת לעשות רוב אלא הא פסיקא טפי דחמרת וגמלת אין דעתם מעורבת עם בני העיר להיות נדונין עמהן: ה"ג החרם אותה וכל אשר בה מכאן אמרו לדיקים וכו' ושל רשעים בין מתוכה בין מחוצה לה אבודים. בגמרא מפרש לה מדכתיב כל: ואת כל שללה תקבוץ אל תוך רחובה אין לה רחוב עושין לה רחוב. ורחובה דהשתא נמי משמע: היה רחובה חוצה לה. שמקום קבוץ בני העיר היה חוץ לעיר כונסין אותה לעיר שצריך לעשות לה רחוב בתוכה. רחוב פרטיא גדולה: את העיר ואת כל שללה ולא שלל שמים. דשלל שמים פלט: מכאן אמרו הקדשות שבתוכה יפדו. כלומר אין נשרפין אלא הרי הם כשאר הקדש שצריך פדייה כ"ש דשלל שמים הם: ותרומות ירקבו. ובגמ' מוקמי לה בתרומה ביד כהן דממון כהן הוא וחל עליה איסור דעיר הנדחת דנהי דבשריפה לא הויא עם שאר שללה דקדש אקרי ולא מזלזלינן ביה כולי האי: מעשר שני. אע"פ שהוא נאכל לישראל הואיל וקדש איקרי לא אמרי' ישרף אלא יגנזו וכן כתבי הקדש יגנזו: ה"ג כליל לה' אלהיך אר"ש אמר הקב"ה וכו' כאילו אתה מעלה עולה שהוא כליל לפני: לא תעשה גנות ופרדסין וכו'. בגמ' מפרש במאי פליגי: לכמו שהיתה. ביישוב בתים: **גמ'** יצאו הם ולא שלוחם. אם המדיחין עצמן ילאו והדיחן והרי הם מרודים ודנין בסייף אבל אם הדיחו ע"י שליח כיחידים הם בסקילה וממונם פלט: אין אנשים פחות מב'. דע"י מדיח אחד אין נעשית עיר הנדחת: בקרבך. משמע באמצע ולא מן הספר שאם היתה עיר של ספר בין מחוז עובדי כוכבים למחוז ישראל אינה נעשית עיר הנדחת דגזירת הכתוב היא שלא תעשה עיר הנדחת: יושבי העיר ולא יושבי עיר אחרת. דהיינו מדיחי' מחוצה לה: לאמר נלכה ונעבדה. משמע שצ"ל לפנינו שכך אומרים נלכה ונעבדה ואין אמירה אלא בעדים אלמא צריך עדים לכל אחד ואחד שיעידו עליהם מה שאמרו וה"נ צריך התראה לכל א' וא' מהם: חולקין עיר אחת. בתחלה כשחלקו ישראל את הארץ היו רשאין ליתן ולחלוק עיר א' לב' שבטים כגון אם אירע להם עיר בתחום ומקצת מושכת לתחום אחר שבט אחד נוטל חלק באותו קצת הארץ ע"פ הגורל נחלקה הארץ אם נפתלי עולה תחום גינוסר עולה עמו דהכי אמרינן בב"ב בפרק י"נ ומנחילין (דף קכב.): אין חולקין. אלא כולה של אותו השבט שרוב' בתחומי': מאי לאו אע"ג דמדיחיה מאותה עיר. אם יהיו מאותו שבט נעשית עיר הנדחת ואי לא לא שאם אינו מאותו שבט שהודחו אלא משבט אחר שבעיר אינו בסייף אלא בסקילה אלמא אפשר שיהו מן אותה העיר ולא מאותו שבט וה"ד כגון שחלקו עיר אחת לשני שבטים: לא. לעולם אימא לך דאין חולקין והיכי משכחת לה מאותה עיר ולא מאותו שבט כגון דנפלה למדיחיה בירושה מקצת העיר ע"י בת יורשת נחלה: ערים תשע מאת שני השבטים האלה. ממטה יהודה וממטה שמעון נטלו ט' ערים ונתנום ללוים: מאי לאו דשקל מהאי ד' ופלגא. שהיתה עיר א' של יהודה ושמעון ונטלו מהם אלמא חולקין עיר אחת לשני שבטים: ה"ג לא ד' מהאי וה' מהאי: א"ה לפרוש פרושי. הי ניהו שבט דשקיל מיניה ה' והי ניהו דשקיל מיניה ד' ואמאי כתיב ערים תשע מאת שני השבטים משמע דבשוה שקל: קשיא

עין משפט נר מצוה

לה א מיי' פ"ד מהל' ע"ז הלכה ב סמג עשין טו:
לו ב מיי' שם הלכה ה והלכה ו:
לז ג מיי' שם הל' ב:
לח ד מיי' שם הל' ו:
לט ה מיי' שם הל' ז:
מ ו מיי' שם הל' י:
מא ז מיי' שם הל' ו:
מב ח מיי' שם הל' יג:
מג ט מיי' שם הל' ו:
מד י מיי' שם הל' ז:
מה כ ל מיי' שם הל' ב:
מו מ מיי' שם הל' ד:

הגהות מהר"ב רנשבורג

א] מתני' הרי אלו מצילין אותה שנאמר וכו' הרי אלו אובדין שנאמר וכו' כונסין אותה לתוכה שנאמר. אלו ג"פ שנאמר נמחקו: ב] רש"י ד"ה וצריכין וכו' כדיליף בגמ'. כאן הס"ד ומה"ד יחידים:

ליקוטי רש"י

יגדל נא כח ה'. לעשות דברך. כאשר דברת לאמר. ומהו הדבור [במדבר יד, יז]. תפלה למשה. אחד עשר מזמורים מכאן עד לדוד מזמור כלם משה אמרם [תהלים צ, א]. ביום ההוא. כהתם הפושעים. יהיה ה' צבאות לעטרת צבי. לצדיקים הנשארים בה [ישעיהו כח, ה]. ולרוח משפט. יהיה הקב"ה להורות משפט ליושב על המשפט. ולגבורה. יהיה לאותן שהם משיבי מלחמ' מלחמתה של תורה [שם פסוק ו]. לרוח משפט. לשופטים את רוחן יהיה לעטרה. הרודה את יצרו. כופהו לשוב בתשובה. המתגבר על יצרו. אינו הולך אחריו לעבור עבירה. שמשכימין כו'. והיינו שערה שעושין [שנעשים שוערים] לפתוח דלתות בהשכמה ולאחר [שם עד] זמן נעילתו. גם אלה. אלו הרשעים הנידונין בגיהנם. ביין שגו. כלומר אף הם עשו כהם לפיכך דנם. מלחמתה של תורה. הוריותיה ולעמוד על בוריה ועל עיקרה [לעיל מב.]. להתוכח בתלמוד [לעיל צג:]. פקו פליליה. לגיהנם נשפטו [מגילה טו:]. וגם אלה. יושבי משפט ומשיבי מלחמה שבדור הזה כלומר טובים וחשובים שבהן ביין שגו כי עתה אין טוב בהם. פקו פליליה. הכשילו המשפט. פקו. לשון פיק ברכים (נחום ב') פוקה (שמואל א' כ"ה) [ישעיה כח, ז]. ולא תהיה וגו' לפוקה. לכשלון כמו לפיק ברכים (נחום ב' י"א) [ש"א כה, ל]. ונתן. המכה דמי ולדות. בפלילים. על פי הדיינים [שמות כא, כב]. ישבי עירם. ולא יושבי עיר אחרת מכאן אמרו אין נעשית עיר הנדחת עד שידיחוה אנשים ועד שיהיו מדיחיה מתוכה [דברים יג, יד]. החמרת והגמלת. שיירא של חמרים ושל גמלים [ב"ב ח.]. ולא ידבק בידך מאומה מן החרם. למען ישוב ה' מחרון אפו שכל זמן שעבודה זרה בעולם, חרון אף בעולם [דברים יג, יח].

מסורת הש"ס

א) עיין רש"א בח"א [מגילה טו: ע"ש כמה שינויים ועי' בפירש"י שם], ב) [ר"ה יז:], ג) [עי' תוספות לעיל מז. ד"ה ואמאי], ד) בקרא ההיא, ה) ב"ב ח., ו) [בסה"מ לא תבנה עוד], ז) [בסה"מ אפי' גנות וכו'], ח) [לעיל טז:], ט) [הא דירושלים נחלקה לשבט יהודה ובנימין ע"פ הדיבור היה. ת"י ביומא יב].

הגהות הגר"א

[א] גמ' רצונו. נמחק ונ"ב לביונו: [ב] שם לישועתו. נמחק ונ"ב לתפארתו: [ג] שם שנאמר. נמחק: [ד] שנא'. נמחק:

תורה אור השלם

א) וְעַתָּה יִגְדַּל נָא כֹּחַ אֲדֹנָי כַּאֲשֶׁר דִּבַּרְתָּ לֵאמֹר: [במדבר יד, יז]
ב) עֵדֹתֶיךָ נֶאֶמְנוּ מְאֹד לְבֵיתְךָ נַאֲוָה קֹדֶשׁ יְיָ לְאֹרֶךְ יָמִים: [תהלים צג, ה]
ג) תְּפִלָּה לְמֹשֶׁה אִישׁ הָאֱלֹהִים אֲדֹנָי מָעוֹן אַתָּה הָיִיתָ לָּנוּ בְּדֹר וָדֹר: [תהלים צ, א]
ד) בַּיּוֹם הַהוּא יִהְיֶה יְיָ צְבָאוֹת לַעֲטֶרֶת צְבִי וְלִצְפִירַת תִּפְאָרָה לִשְׁאָר עַמּוֹ: [ישעיה כח, ה]
ה) וּלְרוּחַ מִשְׁפָּט לַיּוֹשֵׁב עַל הַמִּשְׁפָּט וְלִגְבוּרָה מְשִׁיבֵי מִלְחָמָה שָׁעְרָה: [ישעיה כח, ו]
ו) וְגַם אֵלֶּה בַּיַּיִן שָׁגוּ וּבַשֵּׁכָר תָּעוּ כֹּהֵן וְנָבִיא שָׁגוּ בַשֵּׁכָר נִבְלְעוּ מִן הַיַּיִן תָּעוּ מִן הַשֵּׁכָר שָׁגוּ בָּרֹאֶה פָּקוּ פְּלִילִיָּה: [ישעיה כח, ז]
ז) וְלֹא תִהְיֶה זֹאת לְךָ לְפוּקָה וּלְמִכְשׁוֹל לֵב לַאדֹנִי וְלִשְׁפָּךְ דָּם חִנָּם וּלְהוֹשִׁיעַ אֲדֹנִי לוֹ וְהֵיטִב יְיָ לַאדֹנִי וְזָכַרְתָּ אֶת אֲמָתֶךָ: [שמואל א' כה, לא]
ח) וְכִי יִנָּצוּ אֲנָשִׁים וְנָגְפוּ אִשָּׁה הָרָה וְיָצְאוּ יְלָדֶיהָ וְלֹא יִהְיֶה אָסוֹן עָנוֹשׁ יֵעָנֵשׁ כַּאֲשֶׁר יָשִׁית עָלָיו בַּעַל הָאִשָּׁה וְנָתַן בִּפְלִלִים: [שמות כא, כב]
ט) יָצְאוּ אֲנָשִׁים בְּנֵי בְלִיַּעַל מִקִּרְבֶּךָ וַיַּדִּיחוּ אֶת יֹשְׁבֵי עִירָם לֵאמֹר נֵלְכָה וְנַעַבְדָה אֱלֹהִים אֲחֵרִים אֲשֶׁר לֹא יְדַעְתֶּם: [דברים יג, יד]
י) הַכֵּה תַכֶּה אֶת יֹשְׁבֵי הָעִיר הַהוּא לְפִי חָרֶב הַחֲרֵם אֹתָהּ וְאֶת כָּל אֲשֶׁר בָּהּ וְאֶת בְּהֶמְתָּהּ לְפִי חָרֶב: [דברים יג, טז]
כ) וְאֶת כָּל שְׁלָלָהּ תִּקְבֹּץ אֶל תּוֹךְ רְחֹבָהּ וְשָׂרַפְתָּ בָאֵשׁ אֶת הָעִיר וְאֶת כָּל שְׁלָלָהּ כָּלִיל לַייָ אֱלֹהֶיךָ וְהָיְתָה תֵּל עוֹלָם לֹא תִבָּנֶה עוֹד: [דברים יג, יז]
ל) וְלֹא יִדְבַּק בְּיָדְךָ מְאוּמָה מִן הַחֵרֶם לְמַעַן יָשׁוּב יְיָ מֵחֲרוֹן אַפּוֹ וְנָתַן לְךָ רַחֲמִים וְרִחַמְךָ וְהִרְבֶּךָ כַּאֲשֶׁר נִשְׁבַּע לַאֲבֹתֶיךָ: [דברים יג, יח]
מ) וְאֶת עַיִן וְאֶת מִגְרָשֶׁהָ וְאֶת יֻטָּה וְאֶת מִגְרָשֶׁהָ אֶת בֵּית שֶׁמֶשׁ וְאֶת מִגְרָשֶׁהָ עָרִים תֵּשַׁע מֵאֵת שְׁנֵי הַשְּׁבָטִים הָאֵלֶּה: [יהושע כא, טז]

לְכְמוֹת שֶׁהָיְתָה אֵינָהּ נִבְנֵית – which implies that **it may not be built to what it was before,** a place of structures, אֲבָל נַעֲשֵׂית הִיא גַּנּוֹת וּפַרְדֵּסִים – **but it may be made** into **gardens and orchards.**[41]

The next verse states:

,,וְלֹא־יִדְבַּק בְּיָדְךָ מְאוּמָה מִן־הַחֵרֶם" – ***Nothing of the banned [property] shall adhere to your hand.*** שֶׁכָּל זְמַן שֶׁהָרְשָׁעִים בָּעוֹלָם – **For as long as the wicked are in the world,** חֲרוֹן אַף בָּעוֹלָם – God's **anger is in the world;** אָבְדוּ רְשָׁעִים מִן הָעוֹלָם – when **the wicked perish from the world,** נִסְתַּלֵּק חֲרוֹן אַף מִן הָעוֹלָם – God's **anger disappears from the world.**[42]

Gemara The Gemara cites a Baraisa that expounds the verse: ***Lawless men have gone out from your midst and subverted the inhabitants of their city:***[43]

תָּנוּ רַבָּנָן – **The Rabbis taught in a Baraisa:** ,,יָצְאוּ" – The verse states: *Lawless men* HAVE GONE OUT *from your midst and subverted ...* הֵן וְלֹא שְׁלוּחֵין – This implies that THEY themselves went out and subverted the city, NOT THEIR AGENTS.[44] ,,אֲנָשִׁים" – The verse states: *Lawless* MEN. אֵין ,,אֲנָשִׁים" פָּחוֹת מִשְּׁנַיִם – The word *MEN* DOES NOT MEAN anything LESS THAN TWO; thus, there must have been at least two subverters for the city to be condemned as a subverted city. דָּבָר אַחֵר – ANOTHER INTERPRETATION: ,,אֲנָשִׁים" וְלֹא נָשִׁים – *MEN,* NOT WOMEN; thus, the subverters must be males. ,,אֲנָשִׁים" וְלֹא קְטַנִּים – *MEN,* NOT CHILDREN; thus, the subverters must be adults. ,,בְּנֵי־בְלִיַּעַל" – The subverters are described in the verse as *LAWLESS* men (*bnei bliyaal*). בָּנִים שֶׁפָּרְקוּ עוֹל שָׁמַיִם מִצַּוָּארֵיהֶם – This means SONS WHO CAST OFF THE YOKE OF HEAVEN FROM THEIR NECKS.[45] ,,מִקִּרְבֶּךָ" וְלֹא מִן הַסְּפָר – The verse states that they went out *FROM YOUR MIDST,* AND NOT FROM THE BORDER.[46] ,,יֹשְׁבֵי עִירָם" וְלֹא יוֹשְׁבֵי עִיר אַחֶרֶת – The verse states that they subverted *THE INHABITANTS OF THEIR CITY,* NOT THE INHABITANTS OF ANOTHER CITY. Thus, if the subverters are not themselves from the subverted city, that city is not classified a subverted city. ,,לֵאמֹר" שֶׁצְּרִיכִין עֵדִים וְהַתְרָאָה לְכָל אֶחָד וְאֶחָד – *SAYING.* This teaches THAT THERE MUST BE WITNESSES AND A WARNING issued TO EACH AND EVERY PERSON who is subverted to idolatry.[47]

The Gemara introduces an Amoraic dispute regarding the division of the Land of Israel, in which our Mishnah is cited to support one of the views:

אִיתְּמַר – **It was taught:** רַבִּי יוֹחָנָן אָמַר – **R' Yochanan said:** חוֹלְקִין עִיר אַחַת לִשְׁנֵי שְׁבָטִים – **We may divide one city between two tribes.**[48] וְרֵישׁ לָקִישׁ אָמַר – **But Reish Lakish said:**

NOTES

41. The Gemara will explain this dispute on 113a.

42. [The Mishnah apparently refers to the continuation of the verse: לְמַעַן יָשׁוּב ה׳ מֵחֲרוֹן אַפּוֹ, *so that Hashem will turn back from his burning anger* (see *Yad Ramah* to 113b). The Gemara will elaborate on this below, 113b.]

43. *Deuteronomy* 13:14.

44. If, however, they persuaded others to subvert the city, the city is not classified an *ir hanidachas,* even though the majority of its population worshiped idols as a result of their instigation. Accordingly, all those who worshiped idols are judged as individuals and executed by stoning, and their property is not destroyed (*Rashi*).

The commentators ask why the agents themselves should not be considered the subverters, since they in fact subverted the city. What difference does it make who instigated them to do it? *Yad Ramah* (see also *Meiri* and *Tos. HaRosh*) explains that the Baraisa refers to a case where the agents were not people who could cause a city to be classified an *ir hanidachas*, e.g. they were not from that city, or they were women. Since such people cannot render a city an *ir hanidachas,* as we learned in the Mishnah, the city can only be classified an *ir hanidachas* if we consider the principals (who were local men) to be the subverters. Since, however, the Torah decrees that the subverters must do the subverting themselves and not through agents, the city will in this case *not* become an *ir hanidachas.*

Others suggest that there is a Scriptural decree requiring the subverters to be acting on their own initiative, not as agents. Accordingly, subverters who preach in the name of another person cannot make a city an *ir hanidachas* (opinion cited by *Meiri; Tos. HaRosh;* see also *Shaar HaMelech, Hil. Avodas Kochavim* 4:2).

45. The word בְּלִיַּעַל, *beliyaal,* is understood to be a contraction of the words בְּלִי עוֹל, *beli ol*, which means *without a yoke* — i.e. those who have cast off the yoke of Torah (*Rashi* to *Deuteronomy* 13:14; see *Sanhedrei Ketanah* who discusses the point of this exposition; cf. *Torah Temimah* ibid. §37).

46. In order to be considered a subverted city, the city must be located within the interior of Eretz Yisrael, not along a border that divides between an area of Jewish settlement and non-Jewish settlement (*Rashi*; see *Tos. HaRosh* and *Rashash*).

[Above (16b), the Gemara also cited another reason, viz. that destruction of an entire Jewish border city would expose Eretz Yisrael to foreign invasion, for an enemy army could penetrate into Eretz Yisrael through the gap left by the destroyed city. The Gemara there explained that this latter reason follows the view of R' Shimon who "expounds the reasons for Scriptural commandments." However, both *Yad Ramah* and *Rambam (Hil. Avodas Kochavim* 4:4) cite this reason although they do not generally follow R' Shimon's view. See *Kesef Mishneh* ad loc. and *Minchas Chinuch* 464:4 for a discussion of this point.]

47. [A simple reading of the Scriptural passage of *ir hanidachas* might indicate that since the city is being judged as a whole, it is not necessary to have witnesses regarding each and every person. Rather, it is only necessary to establish that members of the city introduced idolatry into the city, and that a majority of its population worshiped the idols. Evidence of the direct subversion of any individual would not be necessary since we are not judging individuals but a city.] The Torah, however, states that the subverters "subverted the inhabitants of their city, saying: *'Let us go and worship* the gods of others . . .' " This implies that the court must be informed that the subverters said to the inhabitants, "Let us go and worship . . .," i.e. they must receive a report of a direct statement from the subverters to the subverted. Now a "report to the court" always means testimony by two witnesses. Thus, the verse states, in effect, that it is necessary to have two witnesses testify about the direct subversion of each of the inhabitants of the city [or at least the majority of them]. By the same token, we say that it is necessary for each and every person who worshiped the idol to have been warned in advance of the sinfulness and consequences of his action (*Rashi*). [I.e. since the guilt of the city is not established collectively but rather individual by individual, it is logical to assume that each individual's guilt must be established according to the rules that pertain to individuals (see *Rashi* to 112a ד״ה היכי עבדינן; see also *Yad Ramah* here). For an individual to be convicted of a capital offense, he must have received proper warning (הַתְרָאָה) prior to his commission of the crime. Thus, having established that testimony is required regarding each individual, it follows that a warning is required for each individual as well.]

[It should be noted that *Rashi's* wording here is actually somewhat obscure. *Lechem Mishneh* (*Hil. Avodas Kochavim* 4:5) understands *Rashi* to mean that the Baraisa is teaching that testimony and warning is required for each of the *subverters* (not subverted). The difficulty with this is that *Rashi* on 112a (ד״ה היכי עבדינן) states explicitly that it refers to the *subverted*, as pointed out by *Aruch LaNer*, who offers yet another interpretation of our *Rashi;* see there.]

48. R' Yochanan is referring to the original division of Eretz Yisrael among the Tribes at the time of Joshua. The tribal boundaries were decided by lot, and if a boundary line ran through an existing city, then half the city belonged to one tribe and half to the other (*Rashi*). [See *Yad Ramah,* who explains this dispute to refer to what will happen in the future when the Messiah arrives, rather than what happened in the bygone past. See further in *Meiri, Tos. HaRosh* and *Einayim LaMishpat*.]

אמר לפניו רבש"ע ולא כך אמרת לי אף לרשעים והיינו דכתיב [א] ועתה יגדל נא כח ה' כאשר דברת לאמר ר' חגא הוה סליק ואזיל בדרגא דבי רבה בר שילא שמעיה לההוא ינוקא דאמר [ב] עדותיך נאמנו מאד לביתך נאוה קדש ה' לאורך ימים וסמיך ליה [ג] תפלה למשה וגו' אמר ש"מ ארך אפים ראה [א] א"ר אלעזר א"ר חנינא עתיד הקב"ה להיות עטרה בראש כל צדיק וצדיק שנאמר [ד] ביום ההוא יהיה ה' צבאות לעטרת צבי ולצפירת תפארה לשאר עמו וגו' מאי לעטרת צבי ולצפירת תפארה לעושים [א] רצונו ומצפים [ב] לישועתו יכול לכל ת"ל לשאר עמו [ב] למי שמשים עצמו כשירים [ה] ולרוח משפט ליושב על המשפט ולגבורה משיבי מלחמה שערה ולרוח משפט זה הרודה את יצרו וליושב על המשפט זה הדן דין אמת לאמיתו ולגבורה זה המתגבר ביצרו משיבי מלחמה זה שנושא ונותן במלחמתה של תורה שערה אלו שמשכימין ומעריבין בבתי כנסיות ובתי מדרשות אמרה מדת הדין לפני הקב"ה רבש"ע מה נשתנו אלו מאלו אמר לה [ו] וגם אלה ביין שגו ובשכר תעו [וגו'] פקו פליליה ואין פוקה אלא גיהנם שנאמר [ז] לא תהיה זאת לך לפוקה ואין פלילה אלא דיינין שנאמר [ח] ונתן בפלילים: **מתני'** [ג] אנשי עיר הנדחת אין להם חלק לעוה"ב שנאמר [ט] יצאו אנשים בני בליעל מקרבך וידיחו את (אנשי) [יושבי] עירם [א] ואינן נהרגים עד שיהיו מדיחיה מאותה העיר ומאותו השבט ועד שיודח רובה ועד שידיחוה אנשים הדיחוה נשים וקטנים או שהודח מיעוטה או שהיה מדיחיה חוצה לה הרי אלו כיחידים [ב] וצריכין ב' עדים והתראה לכל אחד ואחד זה חומר ביחידים מבמרובים [ג] שהיחידים בסקילה לפיכך ממונם פלט [ד] והמרובין בסייף לפיכך ממונם אבד [י] הכה תכה את יושבי העיר [ד] הזאת לפי חרב [ס] החמרת והגמלת העוברת ממקום למקום [א] הרי אלו מצילין אותה [ג] שנא' [י] החרם אותה ואת כל אשר בה ואת בהמתה לפי חרב [ה] מכאן אמרו נכסי צדיקים שבתוכה אובדין שבחוצה לה פליטין [ו] ושל רשעים בין שבתוכה בין שבחוצה לה הרי אלו אובדין [ד] שנאמר [כ] ואת כל שללה תקבוץ אל תוך רחבה וגו' אם [ז] אין לה רחוב עושין לה רחוב היתה רחבה חוצה לה כונסין אותה לתוכה שנאמר [כ] ושרפת באש את העיר ואת כל שללה כליל לה' אלהיך שללה ולא שלל שמים מכאן אמרו [ח] ההקדשות שבה יפדו ותרומות ירקבו מעשר שני וכתבי הקדש יגנזו כליל לה' אלהיך אמר ר"ש אמר הקב"ה [ט] אם אתם עושין דין בעיר הנדחת מעלה אני עליכם כאילו אתם מעלים עולה כליל לפני [כ] והיתה תל עולם [י] לא תעשה [י] גנות ופרדסים דברי ר' יוסי הגלילי ר"ע אומר [י] לא תבנה עוד לכמות שהיתה אינה נבנית אבל נעשית היא גנות ופרדסים [ל] ולא ידבק בידך מאומה מן החרם שכל זמן שהרשעים בעולם חרון אף בעולם אבדו רשעים מן העולם נסתלק חרון אף מן העולם: **גמ'** ת"ר יצאו הן ולא שלוחין אנשים [כ] אין אנשים פחות מב' דבר אחר אנשים [ל] ולא נשים אנשים ולא קטנים בני בליעל בנים שפרקו עול שמים מצואריהם [מ] מקרבך [מ] ולא מן הספר יושבי עירם ולא יושבי עיר אחרת לאמר שצריכין עדים והתראה לכל אחד ואחד איתמר ר' יוחנן אמר חולקין עיר אחת לשני שבטים ור"ל אמר [ט] אין חולקין עיר אחת לב' שבטים איתיביה ר' יוחנן לר"ל עד שיהו מדיחיה מאותה העיר ומאותו שבט מאי לאו אע"ג דמדיחיה מאותה העיר אי איכא מאותו שבט אין אי לא לא ש"מ חולקין עיר אחת לב' שבטים לא דנפלה ליה בירושה א"נ דיהבוה ניהליה במתנה איתיביה [מ] ערים תשע מאת שני השבטים האלה מאי לאו ארבע ופלגא מהאי וארבע ופלגא מהאי וש"מ חולקין עיר אחת לב' שבטים לא ארבעה מהאי וחמש מהאי אי הכי לפרוש פרושי

קשיא

אמר לפניו וכו'. והשתא [מסתברא] כמ"ד ארך אפים ראה שכיון שראה [מדה זו] בהקב"ה שהוא ארך אפים אף לרשעים שמח: עדותיך וגו' ה' לאורך ימים. היינו מדת ארך אפים ועליה אמר משה עדותיך נאמנו מאד שראה אותו בחורב ופסוק זה מרע"ה אמרו דכתיב לעיל מיניה תפלה למשה איש האלהים וגו': יכול לכל. למי שעושין רצונו אע"פ שמתגאה: כשירים. שיריים שאין נחשבין כך אינו חשוב בעיניו ואינו מתגאה: ולרוח משפט. שופט את רוחו: שרודה ביצרו. שבועט ביצרו וחוזר בתשובה מן העבירה שעבר: ומתגבר ביצרו. מרגיז יצ"ט על יצה"ר אם יצה"ר אמר לו עשה עבירה זו לא דיו שנמנע מן העבירה אלא הולך ועושה מצוה ומתגבר עדיף מרודה: שערה. אלו בתי כנסיות: מה נשתנו אלו מאלו. שיש בהם מדות הללו מן השאר אמר הקב"ה ביין שגו: ואין פלילה אלא דיינין: **מתני'** יצאו אנשים בני בליעל מקרבך. שאין להם חלק לעוה"ב: וידיחו את (אנשי) [יושבי] עירם. הא אין נהרגים עד שיהיו מדיחיה מאותה העיר ואותה השבט עצמה דכתיב מקרבך מקרב אותו שבט עצמו: עד שיודח רובה. דכתיב ויושבי העיר משמע ישובה של עיר היינו רובה לישנא אחרינא עד שיודח רובה דכתיב מקרבך קרי ביה מרובך: ה"ג עד שיודח רובה עד שידיחוה אנשים: או שהיו מדיחיה חוצה לה. שלא היו מאותה העיר: הרי אלו כיחידים. שהן בסקילה וממונן פלט: וצריכים ב' עדים והתראה לכל אחד. כדיליף בגמרא [ב] יחידים בסקילה לפיכך ממונן פלט ומתוך שהחמרת עליו במיתתו הקלת עליו בממונו: הכה תכה את יושבי העיר ההיא לפי חרב החמרת והגמלת העוברת ממקום למקום מצילין. מדכתיב יושבי מכלל דשיירה של חמרים וגמלים שנשתהו בעיר ל' יום כדמפרש בגמרא דהוו להו יושבי העיר הרי אלו מצילין אם רוב אנשי העיר הודחו וחמרים וגמלים משלימין המיעוט ועושה אותם רוב מצילין עליהם שאין ממונם אבד אלא נדונים כיחידים וגורמין נמי לעשות אותה עיר הנדחת אם משלימים לעיר הנדחת לעשות רוב אלא הא פסיקא טפי דחמרת וגמלת אין דעתם מעורבת עם בני העיר להיות נדונין עמהן: ה"ג החרם אותה וכל אשר בה מכאן אמרו צדיקים וכו' ושל רשעים בין מתוכה בין מחוצה לה אבודים. בגמרא מפרש לה מדכתיב כל: ואת כל שללה תקבוץ אל תוך רחובה אין לה רחוב עושין לה רחוב. ורחובה דהשתא נמי משמע: היה רחובה חוצה לה. שמקום קבוץ בני העיר היה חוץ לעיר כונסין אותה לעיר שצריך לעשות לה רחוב בתוכה. רחוב סרטיא גדולה: את העיר ואת כל שללה ולא שלל שמים. דשלל שמים פלט: מכאן אמרו הקדשות שבתוכה יפדו. כלומר אין נשרפין אלא הרי הם כשאר הקדש שצריך פדייה כ"ש דשלל שמים הם: ותרומות ירקבו. ובגמ' מוקמי לה בתרומה ביד כהן דממון כהן הוא וחל עליה איסור דעיר הנדחת דנהי דבשריפה לא הויא עם שאר שללה דקדש אקרי ולא מזלזלינן ביה כולי האי: מעשר שני. אע"פ שהוא נאכל לישראל הואיל וקדש איקרי לא אמרי' ישרף אלא יגנזו וכן כתבי הקדש יגנזו: ה"ג כליל לה' אלהיך אר"ש אמר הקב"ה וכו' כאילו אתה מעלה עולה שהוא כליל לפני: לא תעשה גנות ופרדסין וכו'. בגמ' מפרש במאי פליגי: לכמו שהיתה. בישוב בתים: **גמ'** יצאו הם ולא שלוחם. אם המדיחין עצמן יצאו והדיחן והרי הם מרובים ודנין בסייף אבל אם הדיחו ע"י שליח כיחידים הם בסקילה וממונם פלט: אין אנשים פחות מב'. דע"י מדיח אחד אין נעשית עיר הנדחת: בקרבך. משמע באמצע ולא מן הספר שאם היתה עיר של ספר בין מחוז עובדי כוכבים למחוז ישראל אינה נעשית עיר הנדחת דגזירת הכתוב היא שלא תעשה עיר הנדחת: יושבי העיר ולא יושבי עיר אחרת. דהיינו מדיחי' מחוצה לה: לאמר נלכה ונעבדה. משמע שצ"ל לפנינו שכך אומרים נלכה ונעבדה ואין אמירה אלא בעדים אלמא צריך עדים לכל אחד ואחד שיעידו עליהם מה שאמרו וה"נ צריך התראה לכל א' וא' מהם: חולקין עיר אחת. בתחלה כשחלקו ישראל את הארץ היו רשאין ליתן ולחלוק עיר א' לב' שבטים כגון אם אירע להם עיר בתחום ומקצת מושכת לתחום אחר שבט אחד נוטל חלק באותו קצת הארץ ע"פ הגורל נחלקה הארץ אם נפתלי עולה תחום גינוסר עולה עמו דהכי אמרינן בב"ב בפרק י"נ ומנחילין (דף קכב.): אין חולקין. אלא כולה של אותו השבט שרוב' בתחומי': מאי לאו אע"ג דמדיחיה מאותה עיר. אם יהיו מאותו שבט נעשית עיר הנדחת ואי לא לא שאם אינו מאותו שבט שהודחו אלא משבט אחר שבעיר אינו בסייף אלא בסקילה אלמא אפשר שיהו מן אותה העיר ולא מאותו שבט וה"ד כגון שחלקו עיר אחת לשני שבטים: לא. לעולם אימא לך דאין חולקין והיכי משכחת לה מאותה עיר ולא מאותו שבט כגון דנפלה למדיחיה בירושה מקצת העיר ע"י בת יורשת נחלה: ערים תשע מאת שני השבטים האלה. ממטה יהודה וממטה שמעון נטלו ט' ערים ונתנום ללוים: מאי לאו דשקל מהאי ד' ופלגא. שהיתה עיר א' של יהודה ושמעון ונטלו מהם אלמא חולקין עיר אחת לשני שבטים: ה"ג לא ד' מהאי וה' מהאי: א"ה לפרוש פרושי. הי ניהו שבט דשקיל מיניה ה' והי ניהו דשקיל מיניה ד' ואמאי כתיב ערים תשע מאת שני השבטים משמע דבשוה שקל:

קשיא

עין משפט נר מצוה

לה א מיי' פ"ד מהל' ע"ז הלכה ב סמג עשין טו:

לו ב מיי' שם הלכה ה והלכה ו:

לז ג מיי' שם הל' ב:

לח ד מיי' שם הל' ו:

לט ה מיי' שם הל' ז:

מ ו מיי' שם הל' י:

מא ז מיי' שם הל' ו:

מב ח מיי' שם הל' יג:

מג ט מיי' שם הל' ו:

מד י מיי' שם הל' ז:

מה כ ל מיי' שם הל' ב:

מו מ מיי' שם הל' ד:

הגהות מהר"ב רנשבורג

א] מתני' הרי אלו מצילין אותה שנאמר וכו' הרי אלו אובדין שנאמר וכו' כונסין אותה לתוכה שנאמר. אלו ג"פ שנאמר נמחקו: **ב]** רש"י ד"ה וצריכין וכו' כדיליף בגמ'. כאן הס"ד ומה"ד יחידים:

ליקוטי רש"י

יגדל נא כח ה'. לעשות דבורך. **כאשר דברת לאמר.** ומהו הדבור [במדבר יד, יז]. **תפלה למשה.** אחד עשר מזמורים מכאן עד לדוד מזמור כלם משה אמרם [תהלים צ, א]. **ביום ההוא.** כהתם הפושעים. **יהיה ה' צבאות לעטרת צבי.** לצדיקים הנשארים בה [ישעיהו כח, ה]. **ולרוח משפט.** יהיה הקב"ה להורות משפט ליושב על המשפט. **ולגבורה.** יהיה לאותן שהם משיבי מלחמ' מלחמתה של תורה [שם פסוק ו]. **לרוח משפט.** לשופטים את רוחן יהיה לעטרה. **הרודה את יצרו.** כופהו לשוב בתשובה. **המתגבר על יצרו.** אינו הולך אחריו לעבור עבירה. **שמשכימין כו'.** והיינו שערה שעושין [שנעשים שוערים] לפתוח דלתות בהשכמה ולאחר [שם עד] זמן נעילתו. **גם אלה.** אלו הרשעים הנידונין בגיהנם. **ביין שגו.** כלומר אף הם עשו כהם לפיכך דנם. מלחמתה של תורה. הוריותיה ולעמוד על בוריה ועל עיקרה [לעיל מב.]. להתוכח בתלמוד [לעיל צג:]. **פקו פליליה.** לגיהנם נשפטו [מגילה טו:]. **וגם אלה.** יושבי משפט ומשיבי מלחמה שבדור הזה כלומר טובים ותשובים שבהן ביין שגו כי עתה אין טוב בהם. **פקו פליליה.** הכשילו המשפט. **פקו.** לשון פיק ברכים (נחום ב') פוקה (שמואל א' כ"ה) [ישעיה כח, ז]. **ולא תהיה וגו' לפוקה.** לכשלון כמו לפיק ברכים (נחום ב' י"א) [ש"א כה, ל]. **ונתן.** המכה דמי ולדות. **בפלילים.** על פי הדיינים [שמות כא, כב]. **ישבי עירם.** ולא יושבי עיר אחרת מכאן אמרו אין נעשית עיר הנדחת עד שידיחוה אנשים ועד שיהיו מדיחיה מתוכה [דברים יג, יד]. **החמרת והגמלת.** שיירא של חמרים ושל גמלים [ב"ב ח.]. **ולא ידבק בידך מאומה מן החרם.** למען ישוב ה' מחרון אפו שכל זמן שעבודה זרה בעולם, חרון אף בעולם [דברים יג, יח].

מסורת הש"ס

א) עיין רש"א במ"א [מגילה טו: ע"ש כמה שינויים ועי' בפירש"י שם], ב) [ר"ה יז:], ג) [עי' תוספות לעיל מז. ד"ה ואמאי], ד) בקרא ההיא, ה) ב"ב ח., ו) [בסה"מ **לא תבנה עוד**], ז) [בסה"מ **אפי' גנות וכו'**], ח) [לעיל טז:], ט) [הא דירושלים נחלקה לשבט יהודה ובנימין ע"פ הדיבור היה. ת"י ביומא יב].

הגהות הגר"א

[א] גמ' רצונו. נמחק וני"ב לצביונו: **[ב]** שם לישועתו. נמחק וני"ב לתפארתו: **[ג]** שם שנאמר. נמחק: **[ד]** שנא'. נמחק:

תורה אור השלם

א) וְעַתָּה יִגְדַּל נָא כֹּחַ אֲדֹנָי כַּאֲשֶׁר דִּבַּרְתָּ לֵאמֹר: [במדבר יד, יז]

ב) עֵדֹתֶיךָ נֶאֶמְנוּ מְאֹד לְבֵיתְךָ נַאֲוָה קֹדֶשׁ יְיָ לְאֹרֶךְ יָמִים: [תהלים צג, ה]

ג) תְּפִלָּה לְמֹשֶׁה אִישׁ הָאֱלֹהִים אֲדֹנָי מָעוֹן אַתָּה הָיִיתָ לָּנוּ בְּדֹר וָדֹר: [תהלים צ, א]

ד) בַּיּוֹם הַהוּא יִהְיֶה יְיָ צְבָאוֹת לַעֲטֶרֶת צְבִי וְלִצְפִירַת תִּפְאָרָה לִשְׁאָר עַמּוֹ: [ישעיה כח, ה]

ה) וּלְרוּחַ מִשְׁפָּט לַיּוֹשֵׁב עַל הַמִּשְׁפָּט וְלִגְבוּרָה מְשִׁיבֵי מִלְחָמָה שָׁעְרָה: [ישעיה כח, ו]

ו) וְגַם אֵלֶּה בַּיַּיִן שָׁגוּ וּבַשֵּׁכָר תָּעוּ כֹּהֵן וְנָבִיא שָׁגוּ בַשֵּׁכָר נִבְלְעוּ מִן הַיַּיִן תָּעוּ מִן הַשֵּׁכָר שָׁגוּ בָּרֹאֶה פָּקוּ פְּלִילִיָּה: [ישעיה כח, ז]

ז) וְלֹא תִהְיֶה זֹאת לְךָ לְפוּקָה וּלְמִכְשׁוֹל לֵב לַאדֹנִי וְלִשְׁפָּךְ דָּם חִנָּם וּלְהוֹשִׁיעַ אֲדֹנִי לוֹ וְהֵיטִב יְיָ לַאדֹנִי וְזָכַרְתָּ אֶת אֲמָתֶךָ: [שמואל א' כה, לא]

ח) וְכִי יִנָּצוּ אֲנָשִׁים וְנָגְפוּ אִשָּׁה הָרָה וְיָצְאוּ יְלָדֶיהָ וְלֹא יִהְיֶה אָסוֹן עָנוֹשׁ יֵעָנֵשׁ כַּאֲשֶׁר יָשִׁית עָלָיו בַּעַל הָאִשָּׁה וְנָתַן בִּפְלִלִים: [שמות כא, כב]

ט) יָצְאוּ אֲנָשִׁים בְּנֵי בְלִיַּעַל מִקִּרְבֶּךָ וַיַּדִּיחוּ אֶת יֹשְׁבֵי עִירָם לֵאמֹר נֵלְכָה וְנַעַבְדָה אֱלֹהִים אֲחֵרִים אֲשֶׁר לֹא יְדַעְתֶּם: [דברים יג, יד]

י) הַכֵּה תַכֶּה אֶת יֹשְׁבֵי הָעִיר הַהִוא לְפִי חָרֶב הַחֲרֵם אֹתָהּ וְאֶת כָּל אֲשֶׁר בָּהּ וְאֶת בְּהֶמְתָּהּ לְפִי חָרֶב: [דברים יג, טז]

כ) וְאֶת כָּל שְׁלָלָהּ תִּקְבֹּץ אֶל תּוֹךְ רְחֹבָהּ וְשָׂרַפְתָּ בָאֵשׁ אֶת הָעִיר וְאֶת כָּל שְׁלָלָהּ כָּלִיל לַייָ אֱלֹהֶיךָ וְהָיְתָה תֵּל עוֹלָם לֹא תִבָּנֶה עוֹד: [דברים יג, יז]

ל) וְלֹא יִדְבַּק בְּיָדְךָ מְאוּמָה מִן הַחֵרֶם לְמַעַן יָשׁוּב יְיָ מֵחֲרוֹן אַפּוֹ וְנָתַן לְךָ רַחֲמִים וְרִחַמְךָ וְהִרְבֶּךָ כַּאֲשֶׁר נִשְׁבַּע לַאֲבֹתֶיךָ: [דברים יג, יח]

מ) וְאֶת עַיִן וְאֶת מִגְרָשֶׁהָ וְאֶת יֻטָּה וְאֶת מִגְרָשֶׁהָ אֶת בֵּית שֶׁמֶשׁ וְאֶת מִגְרָשֶׁהָ עָרִים תֵּשַׁע מֵאֵת שְׁנֵי הַשְּׁבָטִים הָאֵלֶּה: [יהושע כא, טז]

אֵין חוֹלְקִין עִיר אַחַת לִשְׁנֵי שְׁבָטִים – We may not divide one city between two tribes.[49]

Reish Lakish's view is challenged from our Mishnah:

אֵיתִיבֵיהּ רַבִּי יוֹחָנָן לְרֵישׁ לָקִישׁ – R' Yochanan challenged Reish Lakish from the following statement of our Mishnah: **עַד שֶׁיְּהוּ מַדִּיחֶיהָ מֵאוֹתָהּ הָעִיר וּמֵאוֹתוֹ שֵׁבֶט** – The inhabitants of a subverted city are not beheaded UNLESS THOSE WHO SUBVERTED [THE CITY] ARE FROM THAT CITY AND FROM THAT TRIBE. **מַאי לָאו – Does** the Mishnah **not mean** by this **אַף עַל גַּב דְּמַדִּיחֶיהָ מֵאוֹתָהּ הָעִיר – that even though the subverters of [the city] are from that city, אִי אִיכָּא מֵאוֹתוֹ שֵׁבֶט אִין** – nevertheless, it is only **if they are from that tribe** that the city **indeed** becomes a subverted city, **אִי לָא לָא** – but **if** they are **not** from that tribe, the city does **not** become a subverted city?![50] **שְׁמַע מִינָּהּ חוֹלְקִין עִיר אַחַת לִשְׁנֵי שְׁבָטִים – Learn from this that we may divide one city between two tribes!**[51] **– ? –**

Reish Lakish answers:

לֹא – No, it is not necessary to assume this. **דְּנָפְלָה לֵיהּ בִּירוּשָּׁה – Rather, it is possible that [the property] fell to [the subverter] by inheritance** through his mother, who was not from the same tribe as his father.[52] **אִי נַמִּי – Alternatively, דִּיהֲבוּהָ נִיהֲלֵיהּ בְּמַתָּנָה – they** (i.e. one of the members of the tribe that received this city) **gave the property to [the subverter] as a gift.**[53] Thus, although the entire city was allotted to one tribe, a person from another tribe owned land in it, and he subverted the city.

Another challenge:

אֵיתִיבֵיהּ – [R' Yochanan] challenged [Reish Lakish] from the following verse in the Book of *Joshua*: **"עָרִים תֵּשַׁע מֵאֵת שְׁנֵי הַשְּׁבָטִים הָאֵלֶּה" – *Nine cities from these two tribes.***[54] **מַאי לָאו – Does** the verse **not** mean **אַרְבַּע וּפַלְגָּא מֵהַאי וְאַרְבַּע וּפַלְגָּא מֵהַאי – four-and-a-half** cities **from this** tribe, **and four-and-a-half from that** tribe?[55] **וּשְׁמַע מִינָּהּ חוֹלְקִין עִיר אַחַת לִשְׁנֵי שְׁבָטִים – Thus, learn from this that we may divide one city between two tribes! – ? –**

Reish Lakish answers:

לֹא – No. אַרְבָּעָה מֵהַאי וְחָמֵשׁ מֵהַאי – It means **four** cities **from this** tribe **and five** cities **from that** tribe.

R' Yochanan asks:

אִי הָכִי – If so, לִפְרוֹשׁ פָּרוֹשֵׁי – [Scripture] should have specified which tribe gave five and which gave four. From the fact that Scripture states that the two tribes together gave a total of nine cities, it seems that both tribes contributed an equal number, namely, four-and-a-half. **– ? –**

NOTES

49. Rather, the boundary line is adjusted so that the entire city falls within the boundary of a single tribe. Which tribe? The one to which the majority of the area would have come without the adjustment (*Rashi;* cf. *Yad Ramah*).

[The city of Jerusalem, which was divided between Judah and Benjamin, was an exception to this rule; see *Tosefos Yeshanim* to *Yoma* 12a.]

50. I.e. even if the subverters are from the same city, as stipulated in the Mishnah's first condition, it is additionally necessary that they be from the same tribe as the [majority] of the city's population. If they are not, the city does not become an *ir hanidachas,* and its people are judged as individual idolaters (*Rashi*).

51. Since the Mishnah excludes subverters who are from the same city but a different tribe, we see that it is possible for one city to belong to two different tribes. Presumably, this is as a result of one city having been divided between two tribes (*Rashi*).

52. For example, a man from the tribe of Reuven married a woman from the tribe of Judah, and she inherited land in the territory of Judah from her father. [Daughters inherit the property of their father when there are no sons (*Numbers* 27:8).] Upon her death, this property passed to her husband or son, who are members of the tribe of Reuven. [Tribal affiliation follows the father, not the mother.] Thus, we have a case of a Reuvenite who owns property in a Judean city. Should this Reuvenite subvert the members of this city, he would be a subverter from that city who was from a different tribe (*Rashi*).

53. [Seemingly, it would have been simpler for the Gemara to answer that the person *bought* property in the city, rather than received it as a gift (which is surely much rarer). It would seem from this that the Gemara is trying to find a case of acquired property that remains in the receiver's possession permanently. Bought property reverts to the seller at *Yovel* and is thus not a permanent acquisition. There are Tannaim who hold, however, that property received as a gift does not revert at *Yovel* (see Mishnah, *Bechoros* 52b) and Reish Lakish can thus explain the Baraisa to be following this view (*Aruch LaNer; Or Same'ach, Hil. Avodas Kochavim* 4:2).]

54. *Joshua* 21:16. Each of the tribes was required to give some of its cities to the Leviim (*Numbers* 35:1-8). Chapter 21 of the Book of *Joshua* describes how the tribes carried out this command. Verse 9 there states: *From the tribe of Judah and the tribe of Shimon they gave the following cities.* The next verses list the cities, and our verse (16) concludes: *nine cities from these two tribes.*

55. Since the verse does not specify how many cities each tribe contributed, but merely states that the two tribes together gave a total of nine cities, are we not to assume that the two tribes contributed an equal number of cities? Thus, it is clear that one city belonged half to Judah and half to Shimon (*Rashi*).

[Actually, there is a difficulty here noted by the commentators. When the nine cities listed in this passage are compared with the list of all the cities of Judah and Shimon given in chapter 15 of *Joshua,* it is evident that *eight* of the nine cities listed in our passage belonged to Judah. How, then, can the Gemara suggest here that each tribe contributed four-and-a-half cities?

Margaliyos HaYam suggests that the eight cities that appear to have been given to Judah in chapter 15 did not in fact all belong to Judah. In 15:32 it is stated that there were twenty-nine cities of Judah near the border of Edom. An actual tally of those cities reveals that there were thirty-eight. *Rashi* there comments that Scripture did not count the nine cities that were later given to Shimon. Thus, argues *Margaliyos HaYam,* not all the cities listed in chapter 15 did indeed belong to Judah, as some of them may have belonged to Shimon. R' Yochanan would maintain here that aside from the town of Ayin (the one obviously belonging to Shimon), three-and-a-half other towns belonged to Shimon. See *Teshuvos Meishiv Davar* II:64 for a lengthy discussion of this issue.]

The Gemara concludes:

קַשְׁיָא – That is indeed **a difficulty.**[1]

The Gemara poses a question:

אִיבַּעְיָא לְהוּ – **They inquired:** הוּדְחוּ מֵאֲלֵיהֶן – If **[the people] became subverted on their own,** i.e. without anyone convincing them to do so, מַהוּ – **what is [the law]?** Are they judged as members of a subverted city, or are they judged as individual idolaters? ,,וַיַּדִּיחוּ" אָמַר רַחֲמָנָא – Do we say that when **the Merciful One stated** in His Torah: *"Lawless men have gone out . . . **and they have subverted**. . .,"* He meant to imply that a city is classified subverted only when subverters speak to the people to worship idols, וְלֹא שֶׁהוּדְחוּ מֵאֲלֵיהֶן – **but not when they become subverted on their own?** אוֹ דִילְמָא אֲפִילוּ הוּדְחוּ מֵאֲלֵיהֶן – **Or perhaps** no such implication is intended, and the rules of a subverted city apply **even where they become subverted on their own. – ? –**

The Gemara offers a proof:

תָּא שְׁמַע – **Come, learn** the answer to this question from the following ruling of our Mishnah: הִדִּיחוּהָ נָשִׁים וּקְטַנִּים – IF WOMEN OR CHILDREN SUBVERTED [THE CITY], the inhabitants are judged as individual idolaters, not as members of a subverted city. אַמַּאי – But **why?** If self-subversion also renders a city a "subverted city," לֶיהֱוֵי כְּהוּדְחוּ מֵאֲלֵיהֶן – **let this be** the same **as if they had become subverted on their own.**[2]

The Gemara rejects this proof:

הָנָךְ בָּתַר נַפְשַׁיְיהוּ גְּרִידֵי – The two cases are not comparable, because **these** people in our case **were drawn** to idolatry **by their own inclination** and their commitment to it is therefore strong; הָנֵי בָּתַר נָשִׁים וּקְטַנִּים גְּרִידֵי – whereas **those** people in the Mishnah's case **were drawn** to idolatry **by women and children** and their commitment to it is therefore not as strong.[3]

The Gemara cites a ruling from our Mishnah and examines it. The Mishnah stated:

עַד שֶׁיּוּדַּח רוּבָּהּ – A city does not become a subverted city UNLESS A MAJORITY OF [THE CITY] HAS BEEN SUBVERTED.

The Gemara inquires:

הֵיכִי עָבְדִינַן – **How do we proceed?** What do we do with the individuals convicted of idolatry until it is ascertained whether or not a majority of the population has worshiped idols?[4]

The Gemara answers:

אָמַר רַב יְהוּדָה – **Rav Yehudah said:** דָּנִין וְחוֹבְשִׁין דָּנִין וְחוֹבְשִׁין – **We judge** the individual sinners **and imprison** them, **judge them and imprison** them, until we learn whether a majority of the populace is guilty of idolatry.[5]

This solution is challenged:

אָמַר לֵיהּ עוּלָּא – **Ulla said to [Rav Yehudah]:** נִמְצָא אַתָּה מְעַנֶּה אֶת דִּינָן שֶׁל אֵלּוּ – If you imprison them after their conviction, **it will emerge that you are delaying the judgment of these** people.[6]

Ulla therefore suggests a different procedure:

אֶלָּא אָמַר עוּלָּא – **Rather, said Ulla:** דָּנִין וְסוֹקְלִין דָּנִין וְסוֹקְלִין – **We judge** them **and stone** them, **judge** them **and stone** them, until it has been determined that a majority of the populace has been guilty of idolatry. The remainder are then judged under the rules of a subverted city.[7]

NOTES

1. The wording of the verse is indeed a difficulty according to Reish Lakish but it is not a rebuttal of his view (*Rashi, Yad Ramah*). [The word קַשְׁיָא in this context is generally used by the Gemara to denote a question for which no answer is offered, but which is not held to be a conclusive refutation. When the Gemara concludes that a challenge constitutes a rebuttal, it uses the word תְּיוּבְתָּא.]

Chidushei HaRan suggests that Reish Lakish could have answered that since the tribe of Shimon did not receive a separate territory but merely cities within the tribal borders of Judah (see *Joshua* 19:1; *Ramban* to *Genesis* 49:5; commentators to *I Chronicles* 4:27-28), Scripture did not bother to list how many cities were given by each tribe [since they were all located in the same section of the country].

2. By excluding women and children from the role of subverters, the Mishnah would seem to be ruling that subversion carried out by women and children has no legal significance; it is thus as if no one subverted the city. This case of the Mishnah is therefore equivalent to the case in question, namely, a city that no one subverted, but whose inhabitants nevertheless worshiped idols on their own. Since the Mishnah states that a city subverted by women and children is not judged a subverted city, we see that self-subversion cannot render a city an *ir hanidachas.*

3. Since their commitment to idolatry is not so firm [so that even if left to their own devices they might someday have abandoned it], the Torah did not require the destruction of the entire city. But we cannot extrapolate from this that the same holds true for a city whose populace decided on their own to serve idols. These people are certainly more committed to their decision and would not have abandoned their idolatry on their own. Thus, it is possible that the Torah does consider such a city an *ir hanidachas* (*Rashi; Yad Ramah*).

4. Individuals convicted of idolatry are executed by stoning; those convicted as part of an *ir hanidachas* are executed by beheading. However, in order to impose the punishment prescribed for a subverted city, we must first ascertain that a majority of the populace engaged in idolatry. Since we learned above that each person must be separately warned and then observed by witnesses as he engaged in idolatry, it is clear that each person must be judged separately to determine his guilt. However, if this procedure is followed, then the first person convicted of idolatry will be convicted as an individual idolater, since we do not yet know that a majority of the inhabitants have been guilty of idolatry. [Thus, he cannot be executed by beheading (*Yad Ramah*). However, if we execute him by stoning before the fate of the rest of the city is determined,] then we never have an instance in which the majority of the city's population is subject to the law of the *ir hanidachas* (*Rashi; Yad Ramah*).

5. When we find two or three people worshiping idols, we try them, convict them, and sentence them to stoning, but we refrain from carrying out the sentence until we see how many other people will be convicted of idolatry. In the interim, we imprison each person convicted of idolatry. If we find that the idolaters constitute a majority of the city, we then try them again [to determine whether they are subject] to beheading, and we [execute them and] destroy their property (*Rashi*).

[Even though a majority of the inhabitants have been convicted of idolatry, it is still necessary to try them again to determine whether they constitute an *ir hanidachas,* for there are other factors besides "majority" that have a bearing on this issue – for example, whether the subverters were men and whether they were from that city. Thus, *Rashi* states that we try them again (see also *Yad Ramah*).]

6. [Literally: you agonize his judgment (see *Machzor Vitry* to *Avos* 5:8).] Once a person is convicted of a capital crime, his sentence must be carried out that very day so as not to keep him waiting in mental agony for his execution (above, 35a). [Imposing this agony upon him violates the Scriptural injunction (*Leviticus* 19:15) against committing a perversion of justice (*Choshen Mishpat* 17:11, from *Rambam, Hil. Sanhedrin* 20:6), or the Scriptural command (*Leviticus* 19:18) to "love your neighbor as yourself" (*Yad Ramah*).] Imprisoning the convicted idolaters pending the outcome of their neighbors' trials [which may take days] violates this rule [since they know that they will be executed and it is only a question of when and how] (*Rashi; Yad Ramah*).

7. I.e. we judge each person as an individual idolater, and carry out the prescribed sentence – stoning. We continue to follow this procedure until the total number of convicted idolaters reaches half the population of the city, at which point we begin judging the remaining sinners according to the laws of an *ir hanidachas*: Anyone convicted now is executed by beheading [as would be anyone already convicted but not yet executed], and their property is destroyed (*Rashi*).

[The reason those convicted earlier are executed by stoning – even though the city may eventually be classified an *ir hanidachas,* making them subject to beheading rather than stoning – is because of the general rule of *chazakah,* which states that in dealing with matters of uncertainty, we presume the original status to remain in force until it has definitely changed. Since at the time they were convicted their

קשיא איבעיא להו הודחו מאליהן מהו וידיחו אמר רחמנא [א] ולא שהודחו מאליהן או דילמא אפילו הודחו מאליהן ת"ש הדיחוה נשים וקטנים אמאי ליהוי כהודחו מאליהן הנך בתר נפשייהו גרידי הני בתר נשים וקטנים גרידי: עד שיודח רובה: היכי עבדינן אמר רב יהודה דנין וחובשין דנין וחובשין א"ל עולא נמצא אתה מענה את דינן של אלו אלא אמר עולא דנין וסוקלין דנין וסוקלין איתמר רבי יוחנן אמר דנין וסוקלין דנין וסוקלין ור"ל אמר מרבין להן בתי דינין איני [א] והאמר ר' חמא בר יוסי א"ר אושעיא (א) והוצאת את האיש ההוא או את האשה ההיא איש ואשה אתה מוציא לשעריך ואי אתה מוציא כל העיר כולה לשעריך אלא [ב] מרבין להן בתי דינין ומעיינין בדיניהן ומסקינן להו לבית דין הגדול וגמרי להו לדינייהו וקטלי להו: הכה תכה את יושבי העיר וכו': תנו רבנן (ב) [ג] החמרת והגמלת העוברת ממקום למקום לנו בתוכה והודחו עמה אם נשתהו שם ל' יום הן בסייף וממונן אבד פחות מיכן הן בסקילה וממונן פלט ורמינהי [ג] כמה יהיה בעיר ויהיה כאנשי העיר [ד] י"ב חדש אמר רבא לא קשיא הא למיהוי מבני מתא הא למיהוי מיתבי מתא והתניא [ד] [ה] המודר הנאה מבני העיר אם יש אדם שנשתהא שם י"ב חדש אסור ליהנות ממנו פחות מיכן מותר ליהנות ממנו ביושבי העיר אם נשתהא ל' יום אסור ליהנות ממנו פחות מיכן מותר ליהנות ממנו: החרם אותה ואת כל אשר בה כו': ת"ר (ב) החרם אותה [א] ואת כל אשר בה פרט לנכסי צדיקים שבחוצה לה ואת כל אשר בה לרבות נכסי צדיקים שבתוכה שללה ולא שלל שמים ואת כל שללה לרבות נכסי רשעים שחוצה לה [ה] אמר ר"ש מפני מה אמרה תורה נכסי צדיקים שבתוכה יאבדו מי גרם להם שידורו בתוכה ממונם לפיכך ממונם אבד אמר מר (ג) ואת כל שללה תקבץ לרבות נכסי רשעים שבחוצה לה אמר רב חסדא [ו] ובנקבצים לתוכה אמר רב חסדא פקדונות של אנשי עיר הנדחת מותרין ה"ד אי לימא דעיר אחרת ואיתנהו בגוה פשיטא דמותרין לאו שללה הוא ואלא דידהו ואיתנהו בעיר אחרת אי דנקבצין לתוכה אמאי מותרין ואי אין נקבצין לתוכה הא אמרה חדא זימנא לא [ז] לעולם דעיר אחרת דמפקדי בתוכה והכא במאי עסקינן [ח] כגון דקביל עליה אחריות מהו דתימא כיון דקביל עליה אחריות כדידיה דמי קא משמע לן אמר רב חסדא [ט] בהמה חציה של עיר הנדחת וחציה של עיר אחרת אסורה [ו] עיסה [י] חציה של עיר הנדחת וחציה של עיר אחרת מותרת מאי טעמא בהמה כמאן דלא פליגא דמיא עיסה כמאן דפליגא דמיא בעי רב חסדא בהמת עיר הנדחת מהו דתיתהני בה שחיטה לטהרה מידי נבילה לפי חרב אמר רחמנא [כ] לא שנא שחטה משחט לא שנא קטלא מקטל או דלמא כיון דשחטה מהניא לה שחיטה מאי תיקו [י] בעי רב יוסף שיער נשים צדקניות מהו אמר רבא הא דרשעיות אסור [ג] תקבץ ושרפת כתיב מי שאינו מחוסר אלא קביצה ושריפה [ו] [ל] יצא זה שמחוסר תלישה וקביצה ושריפה אלא אמר רבא בפיאה נכרית היכי דמי אי דמחובר בגופה כגופה דמיא לא צריכא דתלי [י] בסיבטא כנכסי צדיקים שבתוכה דמי [מ] ואבד או דלמא כיון דעיילא ונפקא כלבושה דמי תיקו: ואת כל שללה תקבוץ אל תוך רחובה וכו': [פ] ת"ר אין לה רחוב אינה נעשית עיר הנדחת דברי רבי ישמעאל רבי עקיבא אומר אין לה רחוב עושין לה רחוב במאי קמיפלגי מר סבר רחובה מעיקרא משמע ומר סבר רחובה השתא נמי משמע:

וההקדשות

רש"י

קשיא. לשון הפסוק קשה לתרץ למ"ד חולקין אבל לא מיותבא: גרידי. בלע"ז נמשכין וכן גרים רבי בכוליה הש"ס מגריד גריד ונ"ל שהוא לשון גרידא דמפרשינן יחיד על שם שהוא יחיד משוך ומופרש הוא מן הכל ואין לאחרים סביביו ולשון ארמי הוא ואין דומה לו בפסוק (ודומה לו) אבל גורדו ומעמידו על גלדו (ר"ה ד' כז:) הוא לשון עברי ודומה לו בפסוק (איוב ב) ויקח לו חרש להתגרד בו בלע"ז ופי' לשון חטיטה שמחטט וגורד בסכין או בכל דבר וגורר ברי"ש לשון עברי הוא כמו (שבת ד' כב.) גורר אדם מטה כסא ושלחן וכן (ב"ב ד' פו.) היה מגרר ויולא מגרר ויולא: בתר נפשייהו גרידי. ומעשיהם מעשה ולדוקים ביותר הואיל ומעצמם הם נדחין ודין הוא שיעשה עיר הנדחת: אבל הנך דהודחו בתר נשים וקטנים גרידי. שאין אדוקים כ"כ: היכי עבדינן. היאך נעשין רובא נדחים הואיל דצריכין עדים והתראה לכל אחד ואחד: דנין וחובשין. כשרואין ב' או ג' מהם עובדים ע"ז לא יסקלו אותן ומניחין כל האחרים מלסקול אלא דנין אותם לסקילה וחובשין אותם בבית הסוהר וכן עושין עד שרואין אם מצטרפין לרובא וחוזרין ודנין אותם דין אחר להריגה ומאבדין את ממונם: ומענה את דינם. שלאחר שנגמר דינם אתה משהה אותם ומענה את דינם: דנין וסוקלין. עד האיך דמחזקינן להו כיחידים ודנין וסוקלין ומהאיך ואילך נתברר הדבר למפרע שהודחו רובא והוו בסייף וממונם אבד ומהאיך ואילך אי אתה רשאי למשכן למיתה חמורה: ור"ל אמר מרבין להם בתי דינין. לאו משום דאין דנין ב' ביום אחד דהא אמרת בפרק נגמר הדין (לעיל מו.) דבמיתה אחת דנין אלא משום דנפישי עדים לכל אחד ואחד ואין פנאי לחקור כל אחד ואחד ביום אחד מרבים להם בתי דינים כדי שתתקבל עדותן ביום א' ויגמור דין כולם ביום אחד: לשעריך. לב"ד שבשעריך דהיינו סנהדרי קטנה: ואי אתה מוציא. אלא בסנהדרי גדולה: אלא מרבין להם בתי דינין ומעייני בדיניהם. אם הוו מרובים ואם הודחו רוב' מעלים את כולן לב"ד הגדול: כמה יהא בעיר. משנה בהשותפין: ויהא כאנשי העיר. ליתן בצורכי העיר: למיהוי כבני מתא. שיהא נקרא כבני העיר אין נקרא בפחות מי"ב חדש אבל להקרות מיושבי העיר כיון ששהה ל' יום נקרא מאנשי העיר וקרינן בהו את יושבי העיר ההוא: והתניא. בניחותא: המודר הנאה. שאומר הרי עלי קונם אם אהנה: החרם אותה פרט לנכסי צדיקים שבחוצה לה. שאם היו צדיקים דרים בתוכה והוי להו נכסים מופקדים במקום אחר ביד אחרים אין מחרימין אותן אבל נכסים שיש להם בתוך העיר מחרימין אותן וטעמא מפורש לקמן: אמר ר"ש מפני מה וכו'. בכל דוכתי דרש ר"ש טעמא דקרא [ט]: ה"ג אמר מר ואת כל [י] (שללה) אשר בה לרבות נכסי רשעים שבחוצה לה: אמר רב חסדא ובנקבצין לתוכה. נכסי רשעים הקרובין לעיר שיכולים לקבלם לתוך העיר באותו יום עצמו שכונסין שלל העיר לרחוב לשורפן הן אבודים עמה אבל רחוקים דאין מגיעין לעיר אינן אבודים ודוקא שכבר היו לתוכה אלא שמעכשיו היו מופקדים ביד אחרים אבל לא היו מעולם בתוכה כגון דנפלה להם בירושה לא קרינא ביה שללה ואין הממון אבד: אלא דידהו. דבני עיר הנדחת ומופקדים הם בעיר אחרת: הא אמרה. רב חסדא ובנקבצין לתוכה והא אין נקבצין: דקבל עליו אחריות. בני עיר הנדחת: כמאן דלא פליגא. (א) א"א לגזית בשר בלא שחיטה ואפילו שחטה משחט אין בשחיטתו כלום דלא לשחיטה קיימא אלא למיתה ושחיטתה זו היא מיתת הבהמה ואין היתר אפילו החלי שאין של עיר הנדחת דכי שחט לסימן דעיר הנדחת אינו שוחט אלא ממית ולא מהניא ביה שחיטה: עיסה. כל אימת דבעי פליג לה ואין חלק של עיר הנדחת מעורב בו: ל"ש שחטה משחט ל"ש קטלא מקטיל. דבין בשחיטה ובין בהריגה קרינא ביה לפי חרב דאפילו שחטה מיתה בעלמא היא ולא מהני מידי או דילמא לפי חרב היינו שלא כדרך שחיטה אבל דרך שחיטה מהניא לה לטהרה מידי נבילה דנהי דלאכילה איתסרה ואיסור הנאה הוא אבל תיהני לטהרה מידי נבלה: שיער נשים צדקניות. שבעיר הנדחת מהו אי הוו בכלל ואת כל שללה תשרף או לא: רשעניות. פשיטא לן דישרף עם שלל העיר: תלישה. שצריך לגלחה: פיאה נכרית. גדיל של שערות דעלמא שעושין לנוי קא מבעי ליה לרב יוסף אם של צדקניות הוי: מחובר בגופה. שנקשר בה: כגופה דמי. וכשם שאין שורפין מלבושין שעליהן שהרי צדקניות הן כך אין שורפין אותו גדיל: דתלי בסבטא. תלה אותו גדיל ביתד ואין קשורין בה עכשיו: כיון דעיילא ונפקא. רגילה לקושרה תדיר אף על פי שלא קשרתו עכשיו כל מקום שיהא שם נדון כמלבוש שעליה דכל שעתא דעתה עליה וכשאר מלבושין דמי: רחובה מעיקרא משמע. רחובה שהיה לה מתחלה ולא שעושין לה רחוב עכשיו:

היו

מסורת הש"ס

א) לעיל טז. ע"ש, ב) [ב"ב ח. ע"ש], ג) ב"ב ז:, ד) שם ח. [תוספ' נדרים פ"ב], ה) [תוספ' פרק י"ד], ו) [ערכין ז: ושם הגירס' ר' יוסי בר' חנינא], ז) [שם הגירסא בסבתא תרגום של ויתד תהיה לך וסיכתא], ח) לעיל מה:, ט) [לעיל כא.], י) רש"א מ"ז.

הגהות הב"ח

(א) רש"י ד"ה כמאן וכו' דאי אפשר:

הגהות הגר"א

[א] גמ' ואת כל אשר בה. נמחק:

גליון הש"ס

גמ' עיסה חציה של עיר הנדחת. עי' שאגת אריה סי' פ"ט: שם יצא זה שמחוסר תלישה. עי' לעיל מו ע"ב תוס' ד"ה תלישה:

תורה אור השלם

א) וְהוֹצֵאתָ אֶת הָאִישׁ הַהוּא אוֹ אֶת הָאִשָּׁה הַהִוא אֲשֶׁר עָשׂוּ אֶת הַדָּבָר הָרָע הַזֶּה אֶל שְׁעָרֶיךָ אֶת הָאִישׁ אוֹ אֶת הָאִשָּׁה וּסְקַלְתָּם בָּאֲבָנִים וָמֵתוּ: [דברים יז, ה]

ב) הַכֵּה תַכֶּה אֶת יֹשְׁבֵי הָעִיר הַהִוא לְפִי חָרֶב הַחֲרֵם אֹתָהּ וְאֶת כָּל אֲשֶׁר בָּהּ וְאֶת בְּהֶמְתָּהּ לְפִי חָרֶב: [דברים יג, טו]

ג) וְאֶת כָּל שְׁלָלָהּ תִּקְבֹּץ אֶל תּוֹךְ רְחֹבָהּ וְשָׂרַפְתָּ בָאֵשׁ אֶת הָעִיר וְאֶת כָּל שְׁלָלָהּ כָּלִיל לַייָ אֱלֹהֶיךָ וְהָיְתָה תֵּל עוֹלָם לֹא תִבָּנֶה עוֹד: [דברים יג, יז]

עין משפט נר מצוה

מז א מיי' פ"ד מהל' עכו"ם הלכה ב סמג עשין טז:

מח ב מיי' שם הלכה ו:

מט ג מיי' שם הלכה ט:

נ ד מיי' פ"ד מהל' שכנים הלכה ה סמג עשין פב טוש"ע ח"מ סי' קסג סעיף ב:

נא ה מיי' פ"ט מהל' נדרים הלכה יז סמג לאוין רמב טוש"ע י"ד סי' ריז סעיף לב:

נב ו ז ח מיי' פ"ד מהל' עכו"ם הלכה י סמג לאוין סו:

נג ט י מיי' שם הלכה יא:

נד כ ל מ מיי' שם הלכה יב והלכה יג [ועי' כ"מ]:

ליקוטי רש"י

לשעריך. לבית דין שבשעריך דהיינו סנהדרי קטנה ואי אתה מוציא כולה אלא בסנהדרי גדולה [לעיל טז.]. לענין עבודה זרה חלק בין יחידים למרובים דעיר הנדחת בעי סנהדרי גדולה כדיליף לקמן סנהדרין (טז.) ויחיד נידון בעשרים ושלשה דכתיב (דברים יז) והוצאת את האיש ההוא וגו' אל שעריך בית דין שבשעריך [שם טו:]. החמרת והגמלת. שיירא של חמרים ושל גמלים. הרי אלו בסקילה. כדין שאר יחידים. למיהוי מיתבי מתא. בשלשים יום וגבי עיר הנדחת כתיב יושבי העיר (דברים יג) [ב"ב ח.]. ויהא כאנשי העיר. לשאת עמהם בעול [ב"ב ז:]. שער נשים צדקניות. של עיר הנדחת שלא הודחו עמה מהו ואמר רבא התם בחלק (דף קיב) פיאה נכרית שקשרה הלדקת לשערה קא מיבעיא ליה אי כגופה היא וניצול אי כממונה וקי"ל (שם) צדיקים שבתוכה יוצאין ממנה ערומים וכל ממונם נשרף דכתיב ואת כל שללה תקבוץ וגו' אלמא מספקא ליה אי כגופה אי לאו כגופה. פיאה. קליעה. בפיאה נכרית. לאו שערה ממש קאמר אלא שהיתה לה פיאה משיער אשה אחרת קשורה לשערה [דרגילות היו נשים כשערן מועט לקשור שיער נשים נכריות לשערן והוא פיאה נכרית] [ערכין ז:]. פיאה נכרית. קליעת שער תלושה ולוברתה על שערה עם קליעתה שתראה בעלת שער [שבת סד:]. עושין לה רחוב. ורחובה דהשתא נמי משמע [לעיל קיא:].

The Gemara records another set of views regarding this question:

אִיתְּמַר – **It has been stated:** רַבִּי יוֹחָנָן אָמַר דָּנִין וְסוֹקְלִין דָּנִין וְסוֹקְלִין – **R' Yochanan said: We judge** them **and stone** them, **judge** them **and stone** them, until it has been ascertained that a majority of the populace has been guilty of idolatry, as Ulla maintained. וְרֵישׁ לָקִישׁ אָמַר מַרְבִּין לָהֶן בָּתֵּי דִינִין – **However, Reish Lakish said: We set up numerous courts for them,** in order to try them all at one time.[8]

Reish Lakish's view is questioned:

אֵינִי – **Is this indeed so?** וְהָאָמַר רַבִּי חָמָא בַּר יוֹסֵי אָמַר רַבִּי אוֹשַׁעְיָא – **But R' Chama bar Yose said in the name of R' Oshaya:** "וְהוֹצֵאתָ אֶת־הָאִישׁ הַהוּא אוֹ אֶת־הָאִשָּׁה הַהִוא" – The verse states: ***And you shall take that man or that woman out*** *to your gates.*[9] אִישׁ וְאִשָּׁה אַתָּה מוֹצִיא לִשְׁעָרֶיךָ – This teaches that it is only **an** individual **man or woman that you take out to** the court **at your gates,**[10] וְאִי אַתָּה מוֹצִיא כָּל הָעִיר כּוּלָּהּ לִשְׁעָרֶיךָ – **but you cannot take** out **the entire** population of a **city to** the court at **your gates.**[11] – ? –

Reish Lakish's position is therefore reinterpreted:

אֶלָּא – **Rather,** the correct procedure is as follows: מַרְבִּין לָהֶן בָּתֵּי דִינִין – **We set up numerous courts for them,** וּמְעַיְּינִין בְּדִינֵיהֶן – by means of which **we investigate their cases** to determine whether the legal conditions for being classified a subverted city have been met,[12] וּמַסְּקִינָן לְהוּ לְבֵית דִּין הַגָּדוֹל – **and** if they have been met, **we bring them up to the Great Court** of seventy-one in Jerusalem, וְגָמְרֵי לְהוּ לְדִינַיְיהוּ – **who** try the cases, **convict them,** וְקָטְלֵי לְהוּ – **and execute them.**[13]

The Mishnah stated:

"הַכֵּה תַכֶּה אֶת־יֹשְׁבֵי הָעִיר וכו׳" – The verse states: ***YOU SHALL SMITE THE INHABITANTS OF THAT CITY* etc.** *[by the sword].* The Mishnah went on to derive from this verse that even temporary residents of the city, such as members of a passing caravan, are counted as part of the population of the city and can save it if they did not engage in the idolatry.

The Gemara now cites a Baraisa that teaches the law for travelers who did participate in the idolatry:

תָּנוּ רַבָּנָן – **The Rabbis taught in a Baraisa:** הַחַמֶּרֶת וְהַגַּמֶּלֶת הָעוֹבֶרֶת מִמָּקוֹם לְמָקוֹם – **A DONKEY CARAVAN OR CAMEL CARAVAN THAT IS TRAVELING FROM PLACE TO PLACE,** לָנוּ בְּתוֹכָהּ – **WHOSE** members **TOOK LODGING IN [A CITY]** וְהוּדְחוּ עִמָּהּ – **AND WERE SUBVERTED ALONG WITH IT,** אִם נִשְׁתַּהוּ שָׁם שְׁלֹשִׁים יוֹם – **IF THEY HAD REMAINED THERE THIRTY DAYS,** הֵן בְּסַיִיף וּמָמוֹנָן אָבֵד – **THEY ARE** put to death **BY THE SWORD** (beheaded) **AND THEIR POSSESSIONS ARE DESTROYED,** i.e. they are treated as part of the subverted city and are subject to its fate. פָּחוֹת מִיכַּן – However, if they have been there **LESS THAN THIS** time period, הֵן בִּסְקִילָה וּמָמוֹנָן פָּלֵט – **THEY ARE STONED AND THEIR POSSESSIONS ARE SPARED,** i.e. they are not treated as part of the subverted city, but rather as individuals who worshiped idols.

The Gemara cites a contradictory Mishnah:

וּרְמִינְהִי – **But contrast this with** the rule given elsewhere in **a Mishnah:**[14] כַּמָּה יְהֵא בָעִיר וִיהֵא כְּאַנְשֵׁי הָעִיר – **HOW LONG MUST ONE BE IN A CITY TO BE** treated **LIKE ONE OF THE CITIZENS OF THE CITY?**[15] שְׁנֵים עָשָׂר חֹדֶשׁ – **TWELVE MONTHS.** This contradicts the rule given in the Baraisa, that the members of a caravan are treated as part of the subverted city after a mere thirty days! – ? –

The Gemara answers:

אָמַר רָבָא – **Rava said:** לֹא קַשְׁיָא – **There is no difficulty.** הָא לְמֶיהֱוֵי מִבְּנֵי מָתָא – **This** (the Mishnah's criterion of twelve months) **is to be** considered **a citizen of the city;** הָא לְמֶיהֱוֵי מִיָּתְבֵי מָתָא – while **that** (the Baraisa's criterion of thirty days) **is to be** considered **a** mere **inhabitant of the city,** not a full citizen.[16]

The Gemara cites support for Rava's distinction:

וְהַתַנְיָא – **And this has been taught in a Baraisa:** הַמּוּדָּר הֲנָאָה מִבְּנֵי הָעִיר – **ONE WHO IS FORBIDDEN BY MEANS OF A VOW TO DERIVE BENEFIT FROM THE "CITIZENS" OF THE CITY,**[17] אִם יֵשׁ אָדָם שֶׁנִּשְׁתַּהָא שָׁם שְׁנֵים עָשָׂר חֹדֶשׁ – **IF THERE IS A PERSON** from somewhere else **WHO HAS REMAINED THERE** in the city **FOR TWELVE MONTHS,** אָסוּר לֵיהָנוֹת מִמֶּנּוּ – **HE IS FORBIDDEN TO DERIVE ANY BENEFIT FROM HIM,** for he is considered a "citizen" of the city; פָּחוֹת מִיכַּן – **LESS THAN THIS,** מוּתָּר לֵיהָנוֹת מִמֶּנּוּ – **[HE] IS PERMITTED TO DERIVE BENEFIT FROM HIM,** for he is not

NOTES

status was that of individuals, they are treated as individuals despite the possibility that they may later be reclassified as members of an *ir hanidachas* (see *Rashi*). Thus, they are executed by stoning. However, when it is later established that most of the city sinned, the *ir hanidachas* status takes effect retroactively and the remainder are then beheaded and their property is destroyed.

Seemingly, this logic should carry over to the property of those stoned before the majority was determined to have been guilty. Since the *ir hanidachas* status takes effect retroactively, their property should be destroyed. A simple reading of *Rashi's* words would indicate that this is indeed so. However, *Chazon Ish (Sanhedrin* 24:10) is uncertain about this and is inclined to say that it is not destroyed.]

According to Ulla, when the verse [and Mishnah] state that the people of an *ir hanidachas* are executed by the sword (i.e. by beheading), it refers to those executed after it has been established that the majority of the city has engaged in idolatry (*Yad Ramah*).

8. I.e. all those accused of idolatry are tried simultaneously in different courts. To do this, we set up a large number of special courts, so that their verdicts can all be reached on the same day (*Rashi*). This way, we are able to determine immediately — before any of them is executed — whether or not a majority of the city worshiped idols, and there is no agonizing delay of execution after conviction (*Yad Ramah*).

It would theoretically be possible to have one court judge many cases in one day, since a court is permitted to judge more than one capital case a day if the cases involve the same crime and the same penalty (see above, 46a). Nevertheless, it is not practical to do so because of the time involved in thoroughly examining each defendant's witnesses. Reish Lakish therefore advocates convening many courts (*Rashi*).

9. *Deuteronomy* 17:5. This verse describes the punishment of the individual idolater. He is arrested and taken for trial to the court of his city (*Rashi*), which in ancient times generally held its sessions near the city gate.

10. I.e. to a local sanhedrin, a court of twenty-three judges (*Rashi*).

11. If an entire town is involved in idolatry, then the case is beyond the jurisdiction of a local sanhedrin of twenty-three. Such a case can only be judged by the Great Sanhedrin of seventy-one. Thus, it is not possible to set up multiple courts to judge all the idolaters simultaneously and convict them under the law of *ir hanidachas* (*Rashi*).

12. E.g. whether most of the city's people have been subverted (*Rashi*).

13. The Great Sanhedrin does not just rely on the findings of the lower courts, but rather interviews all the witnesses and evaluates their testimony before reaching their own decision (*Yad Ramah*; see *Minchas Chinuch* 464:19).

14. *Bava Basra* 7b.

15. I.e. to be taxed for the town's needs (*Rashi*).

16. The verse concerning an *ir hanidachas* (*Deuteronomy* 13:16) makes reference to יוֹשְׁבֵי הָעִיר, *the inhabitants of the city.* This term includes all who reside there even if they are not taxpaying citizens who enjoy full rights and privileges. As long as one has stayed in the city for thirty days, he is considered an "inhabitant" and is subject to the punishment imposed on the people of the *ir hanidachas* (*Rashi*).

17. I.e. he declared a vow prohibiting something to himself if he should derive benefit from the citizens of this city [בְּנֵי הָעִיר] (*Rashi*; see *Yad Ramah*).

קשיא איבעיא להו הודחו מאליהן מהו וידיחו אמר רחמנא א ולא שהודחו מאליהן או דילמא אפילו הודחו מאליהן ת"ש הדיחוה נשים וקטנים אמאי ליהוי כהודחו מאליהן הנך בתר נפשייהו גרידי הני בתר נשים וקטנים גרידי: עד שיודח רובה: היכי עבדינן אמר רב יהודה דנין וחובשין דנין וחובשין א"ל עולא נמצא אתה מענה את דינן של אלו אלא אמר עולא דנין וסוקלין דנין וסוקלין איתמר רבי יוחנן אמר דנין וסוקלין דנין וסוקלין ור"ל אמר מרבין להן בתי דינין איני א) והאמר ר' חמא בר יוסי א"ר אושעיא א) והוצאת את האיש ההוא או את האשה ההיא איש ואשה אתה מוציא לשעריך ואי אתה מוציא כל העיר כולה לשעריך אלא ב מרבין להן בתי דינין ומעיינין בדיניהן ומסקינן להו לבית דין הגדול וגמרי להו לדינייהו וקטלי להו: הכה תכה את יושבי העיר וכו': תנו רבנן ב) ג החמרת והגמלת העוברת ממקום למקום לנו בתוכה והודחו עמה אם נשתהו שם ל' יום הן בסייף וממונן אבד פחות מיכן הן בסקילה וממונן פלט ורמינהי ג) כמה יהיה בעיר ויהיה כאנשי העיר ד י"ב חדש אמר רבא לא קשיא הא למיהוי מבני מתא הא למיהוי מיתבי מתא והתניא ד) ה המודר הנאה מבני העיר אם יש אדם שנשתהא שם י"ב חדש אסור ליהנות ממנו פחות מיכן מותר ליהנות ממנו ביושבי העיר אם נשתהא ל' יום אסור ליהנות ממנו פחות מיכן מותר ליהנות ממנו: החרם אותה ואת כל אשר בה כו': ת"ר ב) החרם אותה [א] ואת כל אשר בה פרט לנכסי צדיקים שבחוצה לה ואת כל אשר בה לרבות נכסי צדיקים שבתוכה שללה ולא שלל שמים ואת כל שללה לרבות נכסי רשעים שחוצה לה ה) אמר ר"ש מפני מה אמרה תורה נכסי צדיקים שבתוכה יאבדו מי גרם להם שידורו בתוכה ממונם לפיכך ממונם אבד אמר מר ג) ואת כל שללה תקבץ לרבות נכסי רשעים שבחוצה לה אמר רב חסדא ו ובנקבצים לתוכה אמר רב חסדא פקדונות של אנשי עיר הנדחת מותרין ה"ד אי לימא דעיר אחרת ואיתנהו בגוה פשיטא דמותרין לאו שללה הוא ואלא דידהו ואיתנהו בעיר אחרת אי דנקבצין לתוכה אמאי מותרין ואי אין נקבצין לתוכה הא אמרה חדא זימנא לא ז לעולם דעיר אחרת דמפקדי בתוכה והכא במאי עסקינן ח כגון דקביל עליה אחריות מהו דתימא כיון דקביל עליה אחריות כדידיה דמי קא משמע לן אמר רב חסדא ט בהמה חציה של עיר הנדחת וחציה של עיר אחרת אסורה ו) עיסה י חציה של עיר הנדחת וחציה של עיר אחרת מותרת מאי טעמא בהמה כמאן דלא פליגא דמיא עיסה כמאן דפליגא דמיא בעי רב חסדא בהמת עיר הנדחת מהו דתיתהני בה שחיטה לטהרה מידי נבילה לפי חרב אמר רחמנא כ לא שנא שחטה משחט לא שנא קטלא מקטל או דלמא כיון דשחטה מהניא לה שחיטה מאי תיקו ז) בעי רב יוסף שיער נשים צדקניות מהו אמר רבא הא דרשעיות אסור ג) תקבץ ושרפת כתיב מי שאינו מחוסר אלא קביצה ושריפה ו) ל יצא זה שמחוסר תלישה וקביצה ושריפה אלא אמר רבא בפיאה נכרית היכי דמי אי דמחובר בגופה כגופה דמיא לא צריכא דתלי ז) בסיבטא כנכסי צדיקים שבתוכה דמי מ ואבד או דלמא כיון דעיילא ונפקא כלבושה דמי תיקו: ואת כל שללה תקבוץ אל תוך רחובה וכו': ח) ת"ר אין לה רחוב אינה נעשית עיר הנדחת דברי רבי ישמעאל רבי עקיבא אומר אין לה רחוב עושין לה רחוב במאי קמיפלגי מר סבר רחובה מעיקרא משמע ומר סבר רחובה השתא נמי משמע:

והההקדשות

רש"י

קשיא. לשון הפסוק קשה לתרץ למ"ד חולקין אבל לא מיתותב: גרידי. בדל"ת נמשכין וכן גרים רבי בכוליה הש"ס מגריד גריד ונ"ל שהוא לשון גרידא דמפרשינן יחיד על שם שהוא יחיד משוך ומופרש הוא מן הכל ואין לאחרים סביביו ולשון ארמי הוא ואין דומה לו בפסוק (ודומה לו) אבל גורדו ומעמידו על גלדו (ר"ה ד' כז:) הוא לשון עברי ודומה לו בפסוק (איוב ב) ויקח לו חרש להתגרד בו בדל"ת ופי' לשון חטיטה שמחטט וגורד בסכין או בכל דבר וגורר ברי"ש לשון עברי הוא כמו (שבת ד' כב.) גורר אדם מטה כסא ושלחן וכן (ב"ב ד' פו.) היה מגרר ויוצא מגרר ויוצא: בתר נפשייהו גרידי. ומעשיהם מעשה ולדוקים ביותר הואיל ומעצמם הם נדחין ודין הוא שיעשה עיר הנדחת: אבל הנך דהודחו בתר נשים וקטנים גרידי. שאין לדוקים כ"כ: היכי עבדינן. היאך נעשין רובא נדחים הואיל דצריכין עדים והתראה לכל אחד ואחד: דנין וחובשין. כשרואין ב' או ג' מהם עובדים ע"ז לא יסקלו אותן ומניחין כל האחרים מלסקול אלא דנין אותם לסקילה וחובשין אותם בבית הסוהר וכן עושין עד שרואין אם מצטרפין לרובא וחוזרין ודנין אותם דין אחר להריגה ומאבדין את ממונם: ומענה את דינם. שלאחר שנגמר דינם אתה משהה אותם ומענה את דינם: דנין וסוקלין. עד אליין דמחזקינן להו כיחידים ודנין וסוקלין ומאליין ואילך נתברר הדבר למפרע שהודחו רובא והוו בסייף וממונם אבד ומאליין ואילך אי אתה רשאי למשכן למיתה חמורה: ור"ל אמר מרבין להם בתי דינין. לאו משום דאין דנין ב' ביום אחד דהא אמרת בפרק נגמר הדין (לעיל מו.) דבמיתה אחת דנין אלא משום דנפישי עדים לכל אחד ואחד ואין פנאי לחקור כל אחד ואחד ביום אחד מרבים להם בתי דינים כדי שתתקבל עדותן ביום א' ויגמור דין כולם ביום אחד: לשעריך. לב"ד שבשעריך דהיינו סנהדרי קטנה: ואי אתה מוציא. אלא בסנהדרי גדולה: אלא מרבין להם בתי דינין ומעייני בדיניהם. אם הוו מרובים ואם הודחו רוב' מעלים את כולן לב"ד הגדול: כמה יהא בעיר. משנה בהשותפין: ויהא כאנשי העיר. ליתן בצורכי העיר: למיהוי כבני מתא. שיהא נקרא כבני העיר אין נקרא בפחות מי"ב חדש אבל להקרות מיושבי העיר כיון ששהה ל' יום נקרא מאנשי העיר וקרינן בהו את יושבי העיר ההוא: והתניא. בניחותא: המודר הנאה. שאומר הרי עלי קונם אם אהנה: החרם אותה פרט לנכסי צדיקים שבחוצה לה. שאם היו צדיקים דרים בתוכה והוי להו נכסים מופקדים במקום אחר ביד אחרים

תוספות

אין מחרימין אותן אבל נכסים שיש להם באותה העיר מחרימין אותן וטעמא מפורש לקמן: אמר ר"ש מפני מה וכו'. בכל דוכתי דרש ר"ש טעמא דקרא ט): ה"ג אמר מר ואת כל י) (שללה) אשר בה לרבות נכסי רשעים שבחוצה לה: אמר רב חסדא ובנקבצין לתוכה. נכסי רשעים הקרובין לעיר שיכולים לקבלם לתוך העיר באותו יום עצמו שכונסין שלל העיר לרחוב לשורפן הן אבודים עמה אבל רחוקים דאין מגיעין לעיר אינן אבודים ודוקא שכבר היו לתוכה אלא שמעכשיו היו מופקדים ביד אחרים אבל לא היו מעולם בתוכה כגון דנפלה להם בירושה לא קרינא ביה שללה ואין הממון אבד: אלא דידהו. דבני עיר הנדחת ומופקדים הם בעיר אחרת: הא אמרה. רב חסדא ובנקבצין לתוכה והא אין נקבצין: דקבל עליו אחריות. בני עיר הנדחת: כמאן דלא פליגא. (א) א"א לכזית בשר בלא שחיטה ואפילו שחטה משחט אין בשחיטתו כלום דלא לשחיטה קיימא אלא למיתה ושחיטתה זו היא מיתת הבהמה ואין היתר אפילו החצי שאין של עיר הנדחת דכי שחט לסימן דעיר הנדחת אינו שוחט אלא ממית ולא מהניא ביה שחיטה: עיסה. כל אימת דבעי פליג לה ואין חלק של עיר הנדחת מעורב בו: ל"ש שחטה משחט ל"ש קטלא מקטיל. דבין בשחיטה ובין בהריגה קרינא ביה לפי חרב דאפילו שחטה מיתה בעלמא היא ולא מהני מידי או דילמא לפי חרב היינו שלא כדרך שחיטה אבל דרך שחיטה מהניא לה לטהרה מידי נבילה דנהי דלאכילה איתסרה ואיסור הנאה הוא אבל תיהני לטהרה מידי נבלה: שיער נשים צדקניות. שבעיר הנדחת מהו אי הוו בכלל ואת כל שללה תשרף או לא: רשעניות. פשיטא לן דישרף עם שלל העיר: תלישה. שצריך לגלחה: פיאה נכרית. גדיל של שערות דעלמא שעושין לנוי קא מבעי ליה לרב יוסף אם של צדקניות הוי: מחובר בגופה. שנקשר בה: כגופה דמי. וכשם שאין שורפין מלבושין שעליהן שהרי צדקניות הן כך אין שורפין אותו גדיל: דתלי בסבטא. תלה אותו גדיל ביתד ואין קשורין בה עכשיו: כיון דעיילא ונפקא. רגילה לקושרה תדיר אף על פי שלא קשרתו עכשיו כל מקום שיהא שם נדון כמלבוש שעליה דכל שעתא דעתה עליה וכשאר מלבושין דמי: רחובה מעיקרא משמע. רחובה שהיה לה מתחלה ולא שעושין לה רחוב עכשיו:

היו

עין משפט נר מצוה

מז א מיי' פ"ד מהל' עכו"ם הלכה ג סמג עשין טז:

מח ב מיי' שם הלכה ו:

מט ג מיי' שם הלכה ט:

נ ד מיי' פ"ד מהל' שכנים הלכה ה סמג עשין פב טוש"ע ח"מ סי' קסג סעיף ג:

נא ה מיי' פ"ט מהל' נדרים הלכה יז סמג לאוין רמב טוש"ע י"ד סי' ריז סעיף לג:

נב ו ז ח מיי' פ"ד מהל' עכו"ם הלכה י סמג לאוין סו:

נג ט י מיי' שם הלכה יא:

נד כ ל מ מיי' שם הלכה יב והלכה יג [ועי' כ"מ]:

ליקוטי רש"י

לשעריך. לבית דין שבשעריך דהיינו סנהדרי קטנה ואי אתה מוציא כולה אלא בסנהדרי גדולה [לעיל טז.]. לענין עבודה זרה חלק בין יחידים למרובים דעיר הנדחת בעי סנהדרי גדולה כדיליף לקמן סנהדרין (טז.) ויחיד נידון בעשרים ושלשה דכתיב (דברים יז) והוצאת את האיש ההוא וגו' אל שעריך בית דין שבשעריך [שם טז:]. החמרת והגמלת. שיירא של חמרים ושל גמלים. הרי אלו בסקילה. כדין שאר יחידים. למיהוי מיתבי מתא. בשלשים יום וגבי עיר הנדחת כתיב יושבי העיר (דברים יג) [ב"ב ח.]. ויהא כאנשי העיר. לשאת עמהם בעול [ב"ב ז:]. שער נשים צדקניות. של עיר הנדחת שלא הודחו עמה מהו ואמר רבא התם בחלק (דף קיב) פיאה נכרית שקשרה הלדקת לשערה קא מיבעיא ליה אי כגופה היא וינצל אי כממונה וקי"ל (שם) לדיקים שבתוכה יוצאין ממנה ערומים וכל ממונם נשרף דכתיב ואת כל שללה תקבוץ וגו' אלמא מספקא ליה אי כגופה אי לאו כגופה. פיאה. קליעה. בפיאה נכרית. לאו שערה ממש קאמר אלא שהיתה לה פיאה משיער אשה אחרת קשורה לשערה [דרגילות היו נשים כששערן מועט לקשור שיער נשים נכריות לשערן והוא פיאה נכרית] [ערכין ז:]. פיאה נכרית. קליעת שער תלושה ולוברתה על שערה עם קליעתה שתראה בעלת שער [שבת סד:]. עושין לה רחוב. ורחובה דהשתא נמי משמע [לעיל קיא:].

מסורת הש"ס

א) לעיל טז. ע"ש, ב) [ב"ב ח. ע"ש], ג) ב"ב ז:, ד) שם ח. [תוספ' נדרים פ"ב], ה) [תוספ' פרק י"ד], ו) [ערכין ז: ושם הגירס' ר' יוסי בר' חנינא], ז) [שם הגירסא בסבתא תרגום של ויתד תהיה לך וסיכתא], ח) לעיל מה:, ט) [לעיל כא.], י) רש"א מ"ז.

הגהות הב"ח

(א) רש"י ד"ה כמאן וכו' דאי אפשר:

הגהות הגר"א

[א] גמ' ואת כל אשר בה. נמחק:

גליון הש"ס

גמ' עיסה חציה של עיר הנדחת. עי' שאגת אריה סי' פ"ט: שם יצא זה שמחוסר תלישה. עי' לעיל מו ע"ב תוס' ד"ה תלישה:

תורה אור השלם

א) וְהוֹצֵאתָ אֶת הָאִישׁ הַהוּא אוֹ אֶת הָאִשָּׁה הַהִוא אֲשֶׁר עָשׂוּ אֶת הַדָּבָר הָרָע הַזֶּה אֶל שְׁעָרֶיךָ אֶת הָאִישׁ אוֹ אֶת הָאִשָּׁה וּסְקַלְתָּם בָּאֲבָנִים וָמֵתוּ: [דברים יז, ה]

ב) הַכֵּה תַכֶּה אֶת יֹשְׁבֵי הָעִיר הַהִוא לְפִי חָרֶב הַחֲרֵם אֹתָהּ וְאֶת כָּל אֲשֶׁר בָּהּ וְאֶת בְּהֶמְתָּהּ לְפִי חָרֶב: [דברים יג, טו]

ג) וְאֶת כָּל שְׁלָלָהּ תִּקְבֹּץ אֶל תּוֹךְ רְחֹבָהּ וְשָׂרַפְתָּ בָאֵשׁ אֶת הָעִיר וְאֶת כָּל שְׁלָלָהּ כָּלִיל לַייָ אֱלֹהֶיךָ וְהָיְתָה תֵּל עוֹלָם לֹא תִבָּנֶה עוֹד: [דברים יג, יז]

considered a "citizen" unless he resides there for at least twelve months. בְּיוֹשְׁבֵי הָעִיר – If someone vowed to prohibit himself benefit from THE "INHABITANTS" OF THE CITY, אִם נִשְׁתַּהָא שְׁלֹשִׁים יוֹם – IF [SOMEONE] HAS REMAINED in that city a mere THIRTY DAYS, אָסוּר לֵיהָנוֹת מִמֶּנּוּ – [HE] IS FORBIDDEN TO DERIVE BENEFIT FROM HIM, for such a person is considered an "inhabitant" of the city; פָּחוֹת מִיכֵּן – LESS THAN THIS, מוּתָּר לֵיהָנוֹת מִמֶּנּוּ – HE IS PERMITTED TO DERIVE BENEFIT FROM HIM, for such a person is not yet considered an "inhabitant" of the city.[18] Thus, the Baraisa explicitly states Rava's distinction, that one becomes an inhabitant of a city after a mere thirty days, but he does not become a citizen of it until he has resided there for a full twelve months.

The Mishnah continued with an elaboration of the following verse:
"הַחֲרֵם אֹתָהּ וְאֶת־כָּל־אֲשֶׁר־בָּהּ כו׳" – *DESTROY IT AND EVERYTHING THAT IS IN IT,* etc.

A Baraisa delineates the fate of property located outside the city, as well as the property of innocent people located in the city:
תָּנוּ רַבָּנַן – The Rabbis taught in a Baraisa: "הַחֲרֵם אֹתָהּ" (ואת כל אשר בה) – When the verse states: *DESTROY IT,* פְּרָט לְנִכְסֵי צַדִּיקִים שֶׁבְּחוּצָה לָהּ – IT EXCLUDES THE PROPERTY OF THE RIGHTEOUS inhabitants of the city THAT IS OUTSIDE [THE CITY].[19] That property is not destroyed. "וְאֶת־כָּל־אֲשֶׁר־בָּהּ" – On the other hand, when the verse states: *AND EVERYTHING THAT IS IN IT,* לְרַבּוֹת נִכְסֵי צַדִּיקִים שֶׁבְּתוֹכָהּ – it means TO INCLUDE THE PROPERTY OF THE RIGHTEOUS THAT IS IN [THE CITY]. This is destroyed.[20] "שְׁלָלָהּ" וְלֹא שְׁלַל שָׁמַיִם – When the next verse states: *ITS BOOTY,* it implies BUT NOT THE BOOTY OF HEAVEN.[21] "וְאֶת־כָּל־שְׁלָלָהּ" לְרַבּוֹת נִכְסֵי רְשָׁעִים שֶׁחוּצָה לָהּ – When the verse states: *AND ALL ITS BOOTY you shall gather,* it means TO INCLUDE THE PROPERTY OF THE WICKED THAT IS OUTSIDE [THE CITY].[22] All property belonging to the idolatrous residents of the city is to be destroyed, regardless of its location.

אָמַר רַבִּי שִׁמְעוֹן – R' SHIMON SAID: מִפְּנֵי מָה אָמְרָה תוֹרָה נִכְסֵי צַדִּיקִים שֶׁבְּתוֹכָהּ יֹאבְדוּ – WHY DID THE TORAH SAY THAT THE PROPERTY OF THE RIGHTEOUS THAT IS IN [THE CITY] SHOULD BE DESTROYED? After all, they did not engage in idolatry! מִי גָּרַם לָהֶם שֶׁיָּדוּרוּ בְּתוֹכָהּ – Because WHAT CAUSED THEM TO DWELL IN THAT sinful [CITY]? מָמוֹנָם – THEIR PROPERTY! לְפִיכָךְ מָמוֹנָם אָבֵד – THEREFORE, THEIR PROPERTY IS DESTROYED.[23]

The Gemara discusses the Baraisa's rulings:
אָמַר מַר – **The master said** in the Baraisa: "וְאֶת־כָּל־שְׁלָלָהּ תִּקְבֹּץ" לְרַבּוֹת נִכְסֵי רְשָׁעִים שֶׁבְּחוּצָה לָהּ – When the verse states: *AND ALL ITS BOOTY YOU SHALL GATHER,* it means TO INCLUDE THE PROPERTY OF THE WICKED THAT IS OUTSIDE [THE CITY]. אָמַר רַב חִסְדָּא – **Rav Chisda said:** וּבִנְקְבָּצִים לְתוֹכָהּ – **Only** if it is **[property] that can be gathered into the city** in time to be burned together with the city's other property.[24]

Rav Chisda discusses the fate of deposits:
אָמַר רַב חִסְדָּא – **Rav Chisda said:** פִּקְדוֹנוֹת שֶׁל אַנְשֵׁי עִיר הַנִּדַּחַת מוּתָּרִין – **The deposits of the citizens of a subverted city are permitted.**

The Gemara examines this statement:
הֵיכִי דָּמֵי – **What is the case?** אִי לֵימָא דְּעִיר אַחֶרֶת וְאִיתַנְהוּ בְּגַוָּהּ – **If you say** that Rav Chisda refers to property **of another city that is present** (i.e. deposited) **in [the subverted city],**[25] פְּשִׁיטָא דְמוּתָּרִין – then **it is obvious that [such property] is permitted,** לָאו "שְׁלָלָהּ" הוּא – because **it is not** ***its booty.***[26] There would be no need for Rav Chisda to say this. וְאֶלָּא דִידְהוּ – And if you say, **rather,** that Rav Chisda is referring to property **that is theirs,** i.e. it belongs to the residents of the subverted city,

NOTES

18. *Chidushei HaRan* demonstrates that thirty days' residence makes a caravaneer an inhabitant only in regard to being counted towards the majority and to being punished along with the city. But if members of a caravan *subverted* the inhabitants of the city, the city would not become an *ir hanidachas,* because their temporary residence does not satisfy the requirement that the subverters be of that city (see also *Minchas Chinuch* 464:9 and *Or Same'ach, Avodas Kochavim* 4:2).

19. [The word אֹתָהּ, *it,* implies an exclusion – namely, that which is actually *in* the city. However, since the Baraisa below will derive an inclusion even of property that is outside the city, the exclusion cited here is understood to refer only to the property of righteous people, i.e. people who were not guilty of idolatry.] Accordingly, the verse teaches that if there were people in the city who did not worship idols, their property outside the city is not destroyed (*Rashi*). [*Rashi* mentions here that the property was "deposited" with people living outside the city. This is because property that was never in the city, such as property inherited in another city, is in any case not subject to destruction, even if it belongs to the idolater (see below, note 24). Thus, the novelty of the ruling regarding the outside property of the righteous is only in the case of property that had once been in the city and had then been sent out and deposited in another city.]

[Our emendation of the text of the Gemara follows *Hagahos HaGra;* see also *Rashi.* These words are similarly omitted in the *Sifrei,* which expounds this verse in the identical manner.]

20. [Although they did not engage in idolatry (and are not killed), their property in the city is destroyed.]

21. This was explained by the Mishnah on 111b and will be explained further on 112b.

22. [I.e. those who were guilty of idolatry. The word כָּל, *all,* is seemingly redundant and is thus expounded to teach that even property that is not in the city should also be gathered into it and burned. See note 19.]

23. [The righteous owned property in the sinful city which they were loathe to abandon. For the sake of their economic well-being they remained in the city and exposed themselves to its pernicious influence. Since their property was the "culprit" in their remaining, it is destroyed.] See also *Genesis* 13:10-12.

In explaining the reason behind this Scriptural rule, R' Shimon follows his general policy of expounding the rationale of Scripture; see, for example, the Gemara above, 21a (*Rashi*).

[*Tos. Yom Tov* questions *Rashi's* statement on the grounds that R' Shimon's singular view in this matter is only insofar as deriving particulars of law from the exposition of the rationale. Here, however, there does not seem to be any practical consequence of this exposition, merely a moral interpretation which all might accept (see *Tosafos* to *Sotah* 14a ד״ה כדי ליגעה). Thus, it does not seem relevant to R' Shimon's unique approach to Scriptural exposition. See, however, *Minchas Chinuch* 464:26 who discusses several practical consequences of R' Shimon's exposition. See also *Aruch LaNer.*]

24. The only foreign property of the wicked that is subject to destruction is property that is located close enough to the city to be brought there in time to be burned with the rest of the city. Property that is located too far away to be brought there in time is not subject to destruction (*Rashi*).

Alternatively, the law that the foreign property of the wicked is brought to the *ir hanidachas* and burned applies only to property that had once been in the city. Such property fulfills in some sense the description of *its booty.* However, property that never physically entered the city – for example, property inherited by an idolater of the *ir hanidachas* in another city – cannot be termed *its* [the city's] *booty* and it is therefore spared and allowed to pass to the heirs of the idolaters (*Rashi,* as emended by *Maharsha* and *Rashash;* see also *Yad Ramah*). According to this explanation, the phrase וּבִנְקְבָּצִים לְתוֹכָהּ should be translated as "property that had once been gathered into it." Cf. *Rambam, Hil. Avodas Kochavim* 4:10.

25. I.e. property belonging to residents of another city that had been deposited with residents of the subverted city.

26. The Torah states (*Deuteronomy* 13:17) that שְׁלָלָהּ, *its* [the city's] *booty,* is to be gathered into the city's square and burned. Obviously, this statement only refers to the property *belonging* to the people of the *ir hanidachas.*

קשיא איבעיא להו הודחו מאליהן מהו וידיחו אמר רחמנא [א] ולא שהודחו מאליהן או דילמא אפילו הודחו מאליהן ת"ש הדיחוה נשים וקטנים אמאי ליהוי כהודחו מאליהן הנך בתר נפשייהו גרידי הני בתר נשים וקטנים גרידי: עד שיודח רובה: היכי עבדינן אמר רב יהודה דנין וחובשין דנין וחובשין א"ל עולא נמצא אתה מענה את דינן של אלו אלא אמר עולא דנין וסוקלין דנין וסוקלין איתמר רבי יוחנן אמר דנין וסוקלין דנין וסוקלין ור"ל אמר מרבין להן בתי דינין איני (א) והאמר ר' חמא בר יוסי א"ר אושעיא (א) והוצאת את האיש ההוא או את האשה ההיא איש ואשה אתה מוציא לשעריך ואי אתה מוציא כל העיר כולה לשעריך אלא [ב] מרבין להן בתי דינין ומעיינין בדיניהן ומסקינן להו לבית דין הגדול וגמרי להו לדינייהו וקטלי להו: הכה תכה את יושבי העיר וכו': תנו רבנן (ב) [ג] החמרת והגמלת העוברת ממקום למקום לנו בתוכה והודחו עמה אם נשתהו שם ל' יום הן בסייף וממונן אבד פחות מיכן הן בסקילה וממונן פלט ורמינהי (ג) כמה יהיה בעיר ויהיה כאנשי העיר [ד] י"ב חדש אמר רבא לא קשיא הא למיהוי מבני מתא הא למיהוי מיתבי מתא והתניא (ד) [ה] המודר הנאה מבני העיר אם יש אדם שנשתהא שם י"ב חדש אסור ליהנות ממנו פחות מיכן מותר ליהנות ממנו ביושבי העיר אם נשתהא ל' יום אסור ליהנות ממנו פחות מיכן מותר ליהנות ממנו: החרם אותה ואת כל אשר בה כו': ת"ר (ב) החרם אותה [א] ואת כל אשר בה פרט לנכסי צדיקים שבחוצה לה ואת כל אשר בה לרבות נכסי צדיקים שבתוכה שללה ולא שלל שמים ואת כל שללה לרבות נכסי רשעים שחוצה לה (ה) אמר ר"ש מפני מה אמרה תורה נכסי צדיקים שבתוכה יאבדו מי גרם להם שידורו בתוכה ממונם לפיכך ממונם אבד אמר מר (ג) ואת כל שללה תקבץ לרבות נכסי רשעים שבחוצה לה אמר רב חסדא [ו] ובנקבצים לתוכה אמר רב חסדא פקדונות של אנשי עיר הנדחת מותרין ה"ד אי לימא דעיר אחרת ואיתנהו בגוה פשיטא דמותרין לאו שללה הוא ואלא דידהו ואיתנהו בעיר אחרת אי דנקבצין לתוכה אמאי מותרין ואי אין נקבצין לתוכה הא אמרה חדא זימנא לא [ז] לעולם דעיר אחרת דמפקדי בתוכה והכא במאי עסקינן [ח] כגון דקביל עליה אחריות מהו דתימא כיון דקביל עליה אחריות כדידיה דמי קא משמע לן אמר רב חסדא [ט] בהמה חציה של עיר הנדחת וחציה של עיר אחרת אסורה (ו) עיסה [י] חציה של עיר הנדחת וחציה של עיר אחרת מותרת מאי טעמא בהמה כמאן דלא פליגא דמיא עיסה כמאן דפליגא דמיא בעי רב חסדא בהמת עיר הנדחת מהו דתיתהני בה שחיטה לטהרה מידי נבילה לפי חרב אמר רחמנא [כ] לא שנא שחטה משחט לא שנא קטלא מקטל או דלמא כיון דשחטה מהניא לה שחיטה מאי תיקו [ל] בעי רב יוסף שיער נשים צדקניות מהו אמר רבא הא דרשעיות אסור (ג) תקבץ ושרפת כתיב מי שאינו מחוסר אלא קביצה ושריפה (ז) [ל] יצא זה שמחוסר תלישה וקביצה ושריפה אלא אמר רבא בפיאה נכרית היכי דמי אי דמחובר בגופה כגופה דמיא לא צריכא דתלי [מ] בסיבטא כנכסי צדיקים שבתוכה דמי [מ] ואבד או דלמא כיון דעיילא ונפקא כלבושה דמי תיקו: ואת כל שללה תקבוץ אל תוך רחובה וכו': (ח) ת"ר אין לה רחוב אינה נעשית עיר הנדחת דברי רבי ישמעאל רבי עקיבא אומר אין לה רחוב עושין לה רחוב במאי קמיפלגי מר סבר רחובה מעיקרא משמע ומר סבר רחובה השתא נמי משמע:

והקדשות

רש"י

קשיא. לשון הפסוק קשה לתרץ למ"ד חולקין אבל לא מיתותב: גרידי. בדל"ת נמשכין וכן גריס רבי בכוליה הש"ס מגריד גריד ונ"ל שהוא לשון גרידא דמפרשינן יחיד על שם שהוא יחיד משוך ומופרש הוא מן הכל ואין לאחרים סביביו ולשון ארמי הוא ואין דומה לו בפסוק (ודומה לו) אבל גורדו ומעמידו על גלדו (ר"ה ד' כז:) הוא לשון עברי ודומה לו בפסוק (איוב ב) ויקח לו חרש להתגרד בו בדל"ת ופי' לשון חטיטה שמחטט וגורד בסכין או בכל דבר וגורר ברי"ש לשון עברי הוא כמו (שבת ד' כב.) גורר אדם מטה כסא ושלחן וכן (ב"ב ד' פו.) היה מגרר ויולא מגרר ויולא: בתר נפשייהו גרידי. ומעשיהם מעשה אלדוקים ביותר הואיל ומעלמם הם נדחין ודין הוא שיעשה עיר הנדחת: אבל הנך דהודחו בתר נשים וקטנים גרידי. שאין אלדוקים כ"כ: היכי עבדינן. היאך נעשין רובא נדחים הואיל דצריכין עדים והתראה לכל אחד ואחד: דנין וחובשין. כשרואין ב' או ג' מהם עובדים ע"ז לא יסקלו אותן ומניחין כל האחרים מלסקול אלא דנין אותם לסקילה וחובשין אותם בבית הסוהר וכן עושין עד שרואין אם מלטרפין לרובא וחוזרין ודנין אותם דין אחר להריגה ומאבדין את ממונם: ומענה את דינם. שלאחר שנגמר דינם אתה משהה אותם ומענה את דינם: דנין וסוקלין. עד אליין דמחזקינן להו כיחידים ודנין וסוקלין ומאליין ואילך נתברר הדבר למפרע שהודחו רובא והוו בסייף וממונם אבד ומאליין ואילך אי אתה רשאי למשכן למיתה חמורה: ור"ל אמר מרבין להם בתי דינין. לאו משום דאין דנין ב' ביום אחד דהא אמרת בפרק נגמר הדין (לעיל מו.) דבמיתה אחת דנין אלא משום דנפישי עדים לכל אחד ואחד ואין פנאי לחקור כל אחד ואחד ביום אחד מרבים להם בתי דינים כדי שתתקבל עדותן ביום א' ויגמור דין כולם ביום אחד: לשעריך. לב"ד שבשעריך דהיינו סנהדרי קטנה: ואי אתה מוציא. אלא בסנהדרי גדולה: אלא מרבין להם בתי דינין ומעייני בדיניהם. אם הוו מרודים ואם הודחו רוב' מעלים את כולן לב"ד הגדול: כמה יהא בעיר. משנה בהשותפין: ויהא כאנשי העיר. ליתן בצורכי העיר: למיהוי כבני מתא. שיהא נקרא כבני העיר אין נקרא בפחות מי"ב חדש אבל להקרות מיושבי העיר כיון ששהה ל' יום נקרא מאנשי העיר וקרינן בהו את יושבי העיר ההוא: והתניא. בניחותא: המודר הנאה. שאומר הרי עלי קונם אם אהנה: החרם אותה פרט לנכסי צדיקים שבחוצה לה. שאם היו לדיקים דרים בתוכה והוי להו נכסים מופקדים במקום אחר ביד אחרים

תוספות

אין מחרימין אותן אבל נכסים שיש להם בתוכה העיר מחרימין אותן וטעמא מפורש לקמן: אמר ר"ש מפני מה וכו'. בכל דוכתי דרש ר"ש טעמא דקרא (ט): ה"ג אמר מר ואת כל (י) (שללה) אשר בה לרבות נכסי רשעים שבחולה לה: אמר רב חסדא ובנקבצין לתוכה. נכסי רשעים הקרובין לעיר שיכולים לקבלם לתוך העיר באותו יום עלמו שכונסין שלל העיר לרחוב לשורפן הן אבודים עמה אבל רחוקים דאין מגיעין לעיר אינן אבודים ודוקא שכבר היו לתוכה אלא שמעכשיו היו מופקדים ביד אחרים אבל לא היו מעולם בתוכה כגון דנפלה להם בירושה לא קרינא ביה שללה ואין הממון אבד: אלא דידהו. דבני עיר הנדחת ומופקדים הם בעיר אחרת: הא אמרה. רב חסדא ובנקבלין לתוכה והא אין נקבלין: דקבל עליו אחריות. בני עיר הנדחת: כמאן דלא פליגא. (א) א"א לכזית בשר בלא שחיטה ואפילו שחטה משחט אין בשחיטתו כלום דלא לשחיטה קיימא אלא למיתה ושחיטתה זו היא מיתת הבהמה ואין היתר אפילו החלי שאין של עיר הנדחת דכי שחט לסימן דעיר הנדחת אינו שוחט אלא ממית ולא מהניא ביה שחיטה: עיסה. כל אימת דבעי פליג לה ואין חלק של עיר הנדחת מעורב בו: ל"ש שחטה משחט ל"ש קטלא מקטיל. דבין בשחיטה ובין בהריגה קרינא ביה לפי חרב דאפילו שחטה מיתה בעלמא היא ולא מהני מידי או דילמא לפי חרב היינו שלא כדרך שחיטה אבל דרך שחיטה מהניא לה לטהרה מידי נבילה דנהי דלאכילה איתסרה ואיסור הנאה הוא אבל תיהני לטהרה מידי נבלה: שיער נשים צדקניות. שבעיר הנדחת מהו אי הוו בכלל ואת כל שללה תשרף או לא: רשעניות. פשיטא לן דישרף עם שלל העיר: תלישה. שלריך לגלחה: פיאה נכרית. גדיל של שערות דעלמא שעושין לנוי קא מבעי ליה לרב יוסף אם של לדקניות הוי: מחובר בגופה. שנקשר בה: כגופה דמי. וכשם שאין שורפין מלבושין שעליהן שהרי לדקניות הן כך אין שורפין אותו גדיל: דתלי בסבטא. תלה אותו גדיל ביתד ואין קשורין בה עכשיו: כיון דעיילא ונפקא. רגילה לקושרה תדיר אף על פי שלא קשרתו עכשיו כל מקום שיהא שם נדון כמלבוש שעליה דכל שעתא דעתה עליה וכשאר מלבושין דמי: רחובה מעיקרא משמע. רחובה שהיה לה מתחלה ולא שעושין לה רחוב עכשיו:

היו

עין משפט נר מצוה

מז א מיי' פ"ד מהל' עכו"ם הלכה ג סמג עשין טו:

מח ב מיי' שם הלכה ו:

מט ג מיי' שם הלכה ט:

נ ד מיי' פ"ד מהל' שכנים הלכה ה סמג עשין פב טוש"ע ח"מ סי' קסג סעיף ב:

נא ה מיי' פ"ט מהל' נדרים הלכה יז סמג לאוין רמב טוש"ע י"ד סי' ריז סעיף לב:

נב ו ז ח מיי' פ"ד מהל' עכו"ם הלכה י סמג לאוין סו:

נג ט י מיי' שם הלכה יא:

נד כ ל מ מיי' שם הלכה יב והלכה יג [ועי' כ"מ]:

ליקוטי רש"י

לשעריך. לבית דין שבשעריך דהיינו סנהדרי קטנה ואי אתה מוליא כולה אלא בסנהדרי גדולה [לעיל טז.]. לענין עבודה זרה חלק בין יחידים למרובים דעיר הנדחת בעי סנהדרי גדולה כדיליף לקמן סנהדרין (טז.) ויחיד נידון בעשרים ושלשה דכתיב (דברים יז) והוצאת את האיש ההוא וגו' אל שעריך בית דין שבשעריך [שם טז:]. החמרת והגמלת. שיירא של חמרים ושל גמלים. הרי אלו בסקילה. כדין שאר יחידים. למיהוי מיתבי מתא. בשלשים יום וגבי עיר הנדחת כתיב יושבי העיר (דברים יג) [ב"ב ח.]. ויהא כאנשי העיר. לשאת עמהם בעול [ב"ב ז:]. שער נשים צדקניות. של עיר הנדחת שלא הודחו עמה מהו ואמר רבא התם בחלק (דף קיב) פיאה נכרית שקשרה הלדקת לשערה קא מיבעיא ליה אי כגופה היא וניצול אי כממונה וקי"ל (שם) לדיקים שבתוכה יולאין ממנה ערומים וכל ממונם נשרף דכתיב ואת כל שללה תקבוץ וגו' אלמא מספקא ליה אי כגופה אי לאו כגופה. פיאה. קליעה. בפיאה נכרית. לאו שערה ממש קאמר אלא שהיתה לה פיאה משיער אשה אחרת קשורה לשערה [דרגילות היו נשים כששערן מועט לקשור שיער נשים נכריות לשערן והוא פיאה נכרית] [ערכין ז:]. פיאה נכרית. קליעת שער תלושה וקושרתה על שערה עם קליעתה שתראה בעלת שער [שבת סד:]. עושין לה רחוב. ורחובה דהשתא נמי משמע [לעיל קיא:].

מסורת הש"ס

א) לעיל טז. ע"ש, ב) [ב"ב ח. ע"ש], ג) ב"ב ז:, ד) שם ח. [תוספ' נדרים פ"ב], ה) [תוספ' פרק י"ד], ו) [ערכין ז: ושם הגירס' ר' יוסי בר' חנינא], ז) [שם הגירסא בסבתא תרגום של ויתד תהיה לך וסיכתא], ח) לעיל מה:, ט) [לעיל כא.], י) רש"א מ"ז.

הגהות הב"ח

(א) רש"י ד"ה כמאן וכו' דאי אפשר:

הגהות הגר"א

[א] גמ' ואת כל אשר בה. נמחק:

גליון הש"ס

גמ' עיסה חציה של עיר הנדחת. עי' שאגת אריה סי' פ"ט: שם יצא זה שמחוסר תלישה. עי' לעיל מו ע"ב תוס' ד"ה תלישה:

תורה אור השלם

א) וְהוֹצֵאתָ אֶת הָאִישׁ הַהוּא אוֹ אֶת הָאִשָּׁה הַהִוא אֲשֶׁר עָשׂוּ אֶת הַדָּבָר הָרָע הַזֶּה אֶל שְׁעָרֶיךָ אֶת הָאִישׁ אוֹ אֶת הָאִשָּׁה וּסְקַלְתָּם בָּאֲבָנִים וָמֵתוּ: [דברים יז, ה]

ב) הַכֵּה תַכֶּה אֶת יֹשְׁבֵי הָעִיר הַהִוא לְפִי חָרֶב הַחֲרֵם אֹתָהּ וְאֶת כָּל אֲשֶׁר בָּהּ וְאֶת בְּהֶמְתָּהּ לְפִי חָרֶב: [דברים יג, טו]

ג) וְאֶת כָּל שְׁלָלָהּ תִּקְבֹּץ אֶל תּוֹךְ רְחֹבָהּ וְשָׂרַפְתָּ בָאֵשׁ אֶת הָעִיר וְאֶת כָּל שְׁלָלָהּ כָּלִיל לַיי אֱלֹהֶיךָ וְהָיְתָה תֵּל עוֹלָם לֹא תִבָּנֶה עוֹד: [דברים יג, יז]

וְאִיתַנְהוּ בְּעִיר אַחֶרֶת – **but it is** present **in another city,** this, too is problematic; אִי דְּנִקְבָּצִין לְתוֹכָהּ – for **if [the deposits] can be gathered into [the subverted city]** to be burned together with all its other property,[27] אַמַּאי מוּתָּרִין – **why,** indeed, **are they permitted?** Have we not learned that the property of the wicked that is outside the city is brought to the city and burned along with all its other property?[28] וְאִי אֵין נִקְבָּצִין לְתוֹכָהּ – **And if [the deposits] cannot be gathered into [the subverted city]** in time to be burned with it, הָא אֲמָרָהּ חֲדָא זִימְנָא – what is Rav Chisda's point in implying that such property is permitted? **He has already said this once!**[29] – ? –

The Gemara answers:

לֹא – **No!** לְעוֹלָם דְּעִיר אַחֶרֶת דְּמַפְקְדֵי בְּתוֹכָהּ – **Actually,** Rav Chisda refers to property **of another city that has been deposited in [the subverted city].** וְהָכָא בְּמַאי עַסְקִינַן – **However, with what** case **are we dealing** here? כְּגוֹן דְּקַבֵּיל עֲלֵיהּ אַחֲרָיוּת – With **a case in which [an inhabitant] of the subverted city accepted responsibility** for the property deposited with him. מַהוּ דְּתֵימָא – **You might have said** כֵּיוָן דְּקַבֵּיל עֲלֵיהּ אַחֲרָיוּת – **that since he accepted responsibility** for the deposited property, כְּדִידֵיהּ דָּמֵי – **it is considered as his own,**[30] and it should therefore be burned. קָא מַשְׁמַע לָן – **[Rav Chisda]** therefore **teaches us** that this is not so; since the deposited property does not actually belong to him but to someone from another city, it is not destroyed.[31]

Rav Chisda discusses the status of objects jointly owned by the inhabitants of a subverted city and another city:

אָמַר רַב חִסְדָּא – **Rav Chisda said:** בְּהֵמָה חֶצְיָהּ שֶׁל עִיר הַנִּדַּחַת וְחֶצְיָהּ שֶׁל עִיר אַחֶרֶת – **An animal, half of which belongs to** an inhabitant of **a subverted city and half of which belongs** to an inhabitant of **another city,** אֲסוּרָה – **is forbidden;** none of its meat may be eaten. עִיסָּה חֶצְיָהּ שֶׁל עִיר הַנִּדַּחַת וְחֶצְיָהּ שֶׁל עִיר אַחֶרֶת – **A dough, half of which belongs to** an inhabitant of **a subverted city and half of which belongs to** an inhabitant of **another city,** מוּתֶּרֶת – **is permitted;** the half belonging to the other city may be eaten. מַאי טַעְמָא – **What is the reason** that half the dough is permitted but not half the meat? בְּהֵמָה כְּמַאן דְּלָא פְּלִיגָא דָּמְיָא – **An animal is treated as though it were not divided** into parts,[32] עִיסָּה כְּמַאן דִּפְלִיגָא דָּמְיָא – whereas **a dough is treated as though it were divided** into parts, one part belonging to the inhabitant of the subverted city and the other part to the inhabitant of the other city.[33]

Having explained that the meat of an animal from a subverted city does not become permitted for consumption (even if it is properly slaughtered through *shechitah*), Rav considers how *shechitah* would affect the animal's *tumah* status:[34]

בָּעֵי רַב חִסְדָּא – **Rav Chisda inquired:** בְּהֶמַת עִיר הַנִּדַּחַת – **An animal from a subverted city,** מַהוּ דְּתִיתְהֲנֵי בָּהּ שְׁחִיטָה לְטַהֲרָהּ מִידֵי נְבֵילָה – **would its slaughter be effective in purifying it**

NOTES

27. [This follows *Rashi's* first explanation in note 24. According to *Rashi's* second explanation, this means that the property was once in the city. For the sake of simplicity, our commentary will continue to follow *Rashi's* first explanation.]

28. [By the same token, Rav Chisda is surely not speaking of property belonging to the righteous of the *ir hanidachas,* since the Baraisa has already stated that their property outside the city is not destroyed. Rav Chisda would surely not just repeat the Baraisa's ruling.]

29. Rav Chisda said in the preceding passage that property owned by the wicked outside the *ir hanidachas* is destroyed only if it can be brought to the city in time to be burned with the city's local property. This means that if it cannot be brought there, it is not destroyed (*Rashi*).

30. [Since he is responsible to pay for it if it is lost or stolen, it is tantamount to being his until he returns it. Indeed, we find such a rule in regard to *chametz* belonging to a gentile that was deposited with a Jew, where the Gemara states that it is forbidden for the Jew to hold that deposit over Pesach because his responsibility to return it makes it tantamount to being his (see *Pesachim* 5b).]

31. [The law for an *ir hanidachas* is different from the law for *chametz* on Pesach, for in regard to *chametz* the criterion is possession, not absolute ownership. The criterion in regard to *ir hanidachas,* however, is שְׁלָלָהּ, *its booty.* This connotes complete ownership, such as that of property taken by a victorious soldier from a conquered city. Mere responsibility does not qualify on this count (see *Tos. HaRosh* for an elaboration of this point; see also *Toras Chaim* and *Aruch LaNer*).

32. I.e. we do not view the animal as if it were divided into separate parts, with half belonging to the *ir hanidachas* resident and half belonging to the person from the other city. [Were we to view the animal this way, half its meat would be permitted, as will be explained in the next note.] The reason we do not view it this way is that even the theoretically permissible half cannot become fit for consumption until the animal is properly slaughtered. Now it is obviously impossible to slaughter just half an animal; thus, when slaughtering the animal one necessarily slaughters both the *ir hanidachas* part and the non-*ir hanidachas* part. The *ir hanidachas* part, however, is under sentence of death [since the Torah requires the animals of the city to be killed; see *Deuteronomy* 13:16]. Its slaughter is thus considered a form of execution, not *shechitah,* and the slaughter can therefore not permit the meat of the animal – even the half that does not belong to the *ir hanidachas* (*Rashi;* see *Chidushei HaRan*, whose difficulty with *Rashi's* explanation will be discussed in note 37 below; cf. *Yad Ramah* for a completely different explanation of this ruling; see also *Minchas Chinuch* 464:31).

[According to *Rashi,* since the reason for prohibiting the entire animal is because its *shechitah* cannot permit it, it follows that the outsider's half is forbidden only for eating (by a Jew); it should, however, be permitted for benefit (e.g. to sell to a gentile), since *shechitah* is not necessary for this purpose (*Pri Chadash,* in his notes on *Rambam*, which are printed at the end of his commentary on *Shulchan Aruch;* see *Chidushei HaRan,* who seems to say this as well). This is disputed by *Or Same'ach* to *Hil. Avodas Kochavim* 4:11.]

33. Dough is divisible. Since it is, the half belonging to the *ir hanidachas* can be separated from the other half, and that other half may then be eaten (*Rashi*).

This raises the question of how we determine which half belongs to the *ir hanidachas* and which does not. We seem, after all, to be dealing with a single dough that was jointly owned by two persons. Seemingly, such a division is possible only by recourse to the principle of בְּרֵירָה [*bereirah*], *retroactive clarification,* a legal concept that, as applied to partnerships, means that when two partners jointly own property which they subsequently divide, they are each viewed as having owned, during the time of their partnership, individual title to the very share they later receive at the division. Thus, although there was no way of knowing at the time of the original acquisition of the dough who owned which half, once they actually divide the dough, this becomes known retroactively. Consequently, the half now taken by the outsider is determined retroactively not to have been owned by a member of an *ir hanidachas.*

It should be noted, however, that the rule of *bereirah* is not universally accepted; it is the subject of a wide-ranging dispute of Tannaim and Amoraim (see *Gittin* 25a-26a; *Beitzah* 10a, 37b-38a; et al.). The view accepted as halachah is that we apply the principle of *bereirah* to matters of Rabbinic law but not to matters of Biblical law (see *Beitzah* 38a; *Rambam, Hil. Terumos* 1:21, and *Hil. Maaser* 7:1). If Rav Chisda's ruling is indeed based on the principle of *bereirah,* then it would not be accepted as halachah, since the law of *ir hanidachas* is a Biblical law. See *Shaagas Aryeh* §89 for a discussion of this problem.

Others, however, explain Rav Chisda's ruling independently of the principle of *bereirah;* see *Aruch LaNer* and *Ohr Same'ach* (*Hil. Avodas Kochavim* 4:11). See further, *Mishnas Chachamim* §20; *Mekor Chaim* 448; *Shaarei Yosher* I:7:22; and *Oneg Yom Tov*, *Orach Chaim* 34.

34. An animal that dies naturally, or that was killed in any manner other than through *shechitah* (ritual slaughter) is not only forbidden to be eaten, but its carcass is also a source of *tumah* (*Leviticus* 11:39). A dead animal of this kind is known as a נְבֵלָה, *neveilah,* and its *tumah* is thus known as *tumas neveilah. Shechitah* of a kosher animal has the effect not only of permitting its meat to be eaten, but also of preventing the carcass from becoming subject to the *tumah* of *neveilah.*

There are instances in which *shechitah* serves to prevent the carcass from becoming a source of *tumah* even though it cannot permit the meat

קשיא איבעיא להו הודחו מאליהן מהו וידיחו אמר רחמנא [א] ולא שהודחו מאליהן או דילמא אפילו הודחו מאליהן ת"ש הדיחוה נשים וקטנים אמאי ליהוי כהודחו מאליהן הנך בתר נפשייהו גרידי הני בתר נשים וקטנים גרידי: עד שיודח רובה: היכי עבדינן אמר רב יהודה דנין וחובשין דנין וחובשין א"ל עולא נמצא אתה מענה את דינן של אלו אלא אמר עולא דנין וסוקלין דנין וסוקלין איתמר רבי יוחנן אמר דנין וסוקלין דנין וסוקלין ור"ל אמר מרבין להן בתי דינין איני (א) והאמר ר' חמא בר יוסי א"ר אושעיא (א) והוצאת את האיש ההוא או את האשה ההיא איש ואשה אתה מוציא לשעריך ואי אתה מוציא כל העיר כולה לשעריך אלא [ב] מרבין להן בתי דינין ומעיינין בדיניהן ומסקינן להו לבית דין הגדול וגמרי להו לדינייהו וקטלי להו: הכה תכה את יושבי העיר וכו': תנו רבנן (ב) [ג] החמרת והגמלת העוברת ממקום למקום לנו בתוכה והודחו עמה אם נשתהו שם ל' יום הן בסייף וממונן אבד פחות מיכן הן בסקילה וממונן פלט ורמינהי (ג) כמה יהיה בעיר ויהיה כאנשי העיר [ד] י"ב חדש אמר רבא לא קשיא הא למיהוי מבני מתא הא למיהוי מיתבי מתא והתניא (ד) [ה] המודר הנאה מבני העיר אם יש אדם שנשתהא שם י"ב חדש אסור ליהנות ממנו פחות מיכן מותר ליהנות ממנו ביושבי העיר אם נשתהא ל' יום אסור ליהנות ממנו פחות מיכן מותר ליהנות ממנו: החרם אותה ואת כל אשר בה כו': ת"ר (ב) החרם אותה [א] ואת כל אשר בה פרט לנכסי צדיקים שבחוצה לה ואת כל אשר בה לרבות נכסי צדיקים שבתוכה שללה ולא שלל שמים ואת כל שללה לרבות נכסי רשעים שחוצה לה (ה) אמר ר"ש מפני מה אמרה תורה נכסי צדיקים שבתוכה יאבדו מי גרם להם שידורו בתוכה ממונם לפיכך ממונם אבד אמר מר (ג) ואת כל שללה תקבץ לרבות נכסי רשעים שבחוצה לה אמר רב חסדא [ו] ובנקבצים לתוכה אמר רב חסדא פקדונות של אנשי עיר הנדחת מותרין ה"ד אי לימא דעיר אחרת ואיתנהו בגוה פשיטא דמותרין לאו שללה הוא ואלא דידהו ואיתנהו בעיר אחרת אי דנקבצין לתוכה אמאי מותרין ואי אין נקבצין לתוכה הא אמרה חדא זימנא לא [ז] לעולם דעיר אחרת דמפקדי בתוכה והכא במאי עסקינן [ח] כגון דקביל עליה אחריות מהו דתימא כיון דקביל עליה אחריות כדידיה דמי קא משמע לן אמר רב חסדא [ט] בהמה חציה של עיר הנדחת וחציה של עיר אחרת אסורה (ו) עיסה [י] חציה של עיר הנדחת וחציה של עיר אחרת מותרת מאי טעמא בהמה כמאן דלא פליגא דמיא עיסה כמאן דפליגא דמיא בעי רב חסדא בהמת עיר הנדחת מהו דתיתהני בה שחיטה לטהרה מידי נבילה לפי חרב אמר רחמנא [כ] לא שנא שחטה משחט לא שנא קטלא מקטל או דלמא כיון דשחטה מהניא לה שחיטה מאי תיקו (י) בעי רב יוסף שיער נשים צדקניות מהו אמר רבא הא דרשעיות אסור (ג) תקבץ ושרפת כתיב מי שאינו מחוסר אלא קביצה ושריפה (ו) [ל] יצא זה שמחוסר תלישה וקביצה ושריפה אלא אמר רבא בפיאה נכרית היכי דמי אי דמחובר בגופה כגופה דמיא לא צריכא דתלי (ז) בסיבטא כנכסי צדיקים שבתוכה דמי [מ] ואבד או דלמא כיון דעיילא ונפקא כלבושה דמי תיקו: ואת כל שללה תקבוץ אל תוך רחובה וכו': (ח) ת"ר אין לה רחוב אינה נעשית עיר הנדחת דברי רבי ישמעאל רבי עקיבא אומר אין לה רחוב עושין לה רחוב במאי קמיפלגי מר סבר רחובה מעיקרא משמע ומר סבר רחובה השתא נמי משמע:

והההקדשות

רש"י

קשיא. לשון הפסוק קשה לתרץ למ"ד חולקין אבל לא מיתותב: גרידי. בדל"ת נמשכין וכן גרים רבי בכוליה הש"ס מגריד גריד וכ"ל שהוא לשון גרידא דמפרשינן יחיד על שם שהוא יחיד משוך ומופרש הוא מן הכל ואין לאחרים סביביו ולשון ארמי הוא ואין דומה לו בפסוק (ודומה לו) אבל גורדו ומעמידו על גלדו (ר"ה ד' מ:) הוא לשון עברי ודומה לו בפסוק (איוב ב) ויקח לו חרש להתגרד בו בדל"ת ופי' לשון חטיטה שמחטט וגורד בסכין או בכל דבר וגורר ברי"ש לשון עברי הוא כמו (שבת ד' כב.) גורר אדם מטה כסא ושלחן וכן (ב"ב ד' פו.) היה מגרר ויוצא מגרר ויוצא: בתר נפשייהו גרידי. ומעשיהם מעשה ואדוקים ביותר הואיל ומעצמם הם נדחין ודין הוא שיעשה עיר הנדחת: אבל הנך דהודחו בתר נשים וקטנים גרידי. שאין אדוקים כ"כ: היכי עבדינן. היאך נעשין רובא נדחים הואיל דצריכין עדים והתראה לכל אחד ואחד: דנין וחובשין. כשרואין ב' או ג' מהם עובדים ע"ז לא יסקלו אותן ומניחין כל האחרים מלסקול אלא דנין אותם לסקילה וחובשין אותם בבית הסוהר וכן עושין עד שרואין אם מצטרפין לרובא וחוזרין ודנין אותם דין אחר להריגה ומאבדין את ממונם: ומענה את דינם. שלאחר שנגמר דינם אתה משהה אותם ומענה את דינם: דנין וסוקלין. עד האיך דמחזקינן להו כיחידים ודנין וסוקלין ומהאיך ואילך נתברר הדבר למפרע שהודחו רובא והוו בסייף וממונם אבד ומהאיך ואילך אי אתה רשאי למשכן למיתה חמורה: ור"ל אמר מרבין להם בתי דינין. לאו משום דאין דנין ב' ביום אחד דהא אמרת בפרק נגמר הדין (לעיל מו.) דבמיתה אחת דנין אלא משום דנפישי עדים לכל אחד ואחד ואין פנאי לחקור כל אחד ואחד ביום אחד מרבים להם בתי דינים כדי שתתקבל עדותן ביום א' ויגמור דין כולם ביום אחד: לשעריך. לב"ד שבשעריך דהיינו סנהדרי קטנה: ואי אתה מוציא. אלא בסנהדרי גדולה: אלא מרבין להם בתי דינין ומעייני בדיניהם. אם הוו מרובים ואם הודחו רוב' מעלים את כולן לב"ד הגדול: כמה יהא בעיר. משנה בהשותפין: ויהא כאנשי העיר. ליתן בצורכי העיר: למיהוי כבני מתא. שיהא נקרא כבני העיר אין נקרא בפחות מי"ב חדש אבל להקרות מיושבי העיר כיון ששהה ל' יום נקרא מאנשי העיר וקרינן בהו את יושבי העיר הסוא: והתניא. בניחותא: המודר הנאה. שאומר הרי עלי קונם אם אהנה: החרם אותה פרט לנכסי צדיקים שבחוצה לה. שאם היו צדיקים דרים בתוכה והוי להו נכסים מופקדים במקום אחר ביד אחרים אין מחרימין אותן אבל נכסים שיש להם באותה העיר מחרימין אותן וטעמא מפורש לקמן: אמר ר"ש מפני מה וכו'. בכל דוכתי דרש ר"ש טעמא דקרא (ט): ה"ג אמר מר ואת כל (י) (שללה) אשר בה לרבות נכסי רשעים שבחוצה לה: אמר רב חסדא ובנקבצין לתוכה. נכסי רשעים הקרובין לעיר שיכולים לקבצם לתוך העיר באותו יום עצמו שכונסין שלל העיר לרחוב לשורפן הן אבודים עמה אבל רחוקים דאין מגיעין לעיר אינן אבודים ודוקא שכבר היו לתוכה אלא שמעכשיו היו מופקדים ביד אחרים אבל לא היו מעולם בתוכה כגון דנפלה להם בירושה לא קרינא ביה שללה ואין הממון אבד: אלא דידהו. דבני עיר הנדחת ומופקדים הם בעיר אחרת: הא אמרה. רב חסדא ובנקבצין לתוכה והא אין נקבצין: דקביל עליו אחריות. בני עיר הנדחת: כמאן דלא פליגא. (א) א"א לכזית בשר בלא שחיטה ואפילו שחטה משחט אין בשחיטתו כלום דלא לשחיטה קיימא אלא למיתה ושחיטתה זו היא מיתת הבהמה ואין היתר אפילו החצי שאין של עיר הנדחת דכי שחט לסימן דעיר הנדחת אינו שוחט אלא ממית ולא מהניא ביה שחיטה: עיסה. כל אימת דבעי פליג לה ואין חלק של עיר הנדחת מעורב בו: ל"ש שחטה משחט ל"ש קטלא מקטיל. דבין בשחיטה ובין בהריגה קרינא ביה לפי חרב דאפילו שחטה מיתה בעלמא היא ולא מהני מידי או דילמא לפי חרב היינו שלא כדרך שחיטה אבל דרך שחיטה מהניא לה לטהרה מידי נבילה דנהי דלאכילה איתסרה ואיסור הנאה הוא אבל תיהני לטהרה מידי נבלה: שיער נשים צדקניות. שבעיר הנדחת מהו אי הוו בכלל ואת כל שללה תשרף או לא: רשעניות. פשיטא לן דישרף עם שלל העיר: תלישה. שצריך לגלחה: פיאה נכרית. גדיל של שערות דעלמא שעושין לנוי קא מבעי ליה לרב יוסף אם של צדקניות הוי: מחובר בגופה. שנקשר בה: כגופה דמי. וכשם שאין שורפין מלבושין שעליהן שהרי לצדקניות הן כך אין שורפין אותו גדיל: דתלי בסבטא. תלה אותו גדיל ביתד ואין קשורין בה עכשיו: כיון דעיילא ונפקא. רגילה לקושרה תדיר אף על פי שלא קשרתו עכשיו כל מקום שיהא שם נדון כמלבוש שעליה דכל שעתא דעתה עליה וכשאר מלבושין דמי: רחובה מעיקרא משמע. רחובה שהיה לה מתחלה ולא שעושין לה רחוב עכשיו:

היו

מסורת הש"ס

א) לעיל טז. ע"ש, ב) [ב"ב ח. ע"ש], ג) ב"ב ז:, ד) שם ח. [תוספ' נדרים פ"ב], ה) [תוספ' פרק י"ד], ו) [ערכין ז: ושם הגירס' ר' יוסי בר' חנינא], ז) [שם הגירסא בסבתא תרגום של ויתד תהיה לך וסיכתא], ח) לעיל מה:, ט) [לעיל כא.], י) רש"א מ"ז.

הגהות הב"ח

(א) רש"י ד"ה כמאן וכו' דאי אפשר:

הגהות הגר"א

[א] גמ' ואת כל אשר בה. נמחק:

גליון הש"ס

גמ' עיסה חציה של עיר הנדחת. עי' שאגת אריה סי' פ"ט: שם יצא זה שמחוסר תלישה. עי' לעיל מו ע"ב תוס' ד"ה תלישה:

תורה אור השלם

א) וְהוֹצֵאתָ אֶת הָאִישׁ הַהוּא אוֹ אֶת הָאִשָּׁה הַהִוא אֲשֶׁר עָשׂוּ אֶת הַדָּבָר הָרָע הַזֶּה אֶל שְׁעָרֶיךָ אֶת הָאִישׁ אוֹ אֶת הָאִשָּׁה וּסְקַלְתָּם בָּאֲבָנִים וָמֵתוּ: [דברים יז, ה]

ב) הַכֵּה תַכֶּה אֶת יֹשְׁבֵי הָעִיר הַהִוא לְפִי חָרֶב הַחֲרֵם אֹתָהּ וְאֶת כָּל אֲשֶׁר בָּהּ וְאֶת בְּהֶמְתָּהּ לְפִי חָרֶב: [דברים יג, טו]

ג) וְאֶת כָּל שְׁלָלָהּ תִּקְבֹּץ אֶל תּוֹךְ רְחֹבָהּ וְשָׂרַפְתָּ בָאֵשׁ אֶת הָעִיר וְאֶת כָּל שְׁלָלָהּ כָּלִיל לַיי אֱלֹהֶיךָ וְהָיְתָה תֵּל עוֹלָם לֹא תִבָּנֶה עוֹד: [דברים יג, יז]

עין משפט נר מצוה

מז א מיי' פ"ד מהל' עכו"ם הלכה ב סמג עשין טו:
מח ב מיי' שם הלכה ו:
מט ג מיי' שם הלכה ט:
נ ד מיי' פ"ד מהל' שכנים הלכה ה סמג עשין פב טוש"ע ח"מ סי' קסג סעיף ב:
נא ה מיי' פ"ט מהל' נדרים הלכה יז סמג לאוין רמב טוש"ע י"ד סי' ריז סעיף לב:
נב ו ז ח מיי' פ"ד מהל' עכו"ם הלכה י סמג לאוין סו:
נג ט י מיי' שם הלכה יא:
נד כ ל מ מיי' שם הלכה יב והלכה יג [ועי' כ"מ]:

ליקוטי רש"י

לשעריך. לבית דין שבשעריך דהיינו סנהדרי קטנה ואי אתה מוציא כולה אלא בסנהדרי גדולה [לעיל טז.]. לענין עבודה זרה חלק בין יחידים למרובים דעיר הנדחת בעי סנהדרי גדולה כדיליף לקמן סנהדרין (טז.) ויחיד נידון בעשרים ושלשה דכתיב (דברים יז) והוצאת את האיש ההוא וגו' אל שעריך בית דין שבשעריך [שם טו:]. החמרת והגמלת. שיירא של חמרים ושל גמלים. הרי אלו בסקילה. כדין שאר יחידים. למיהוי מיתבי מתא. בשלשים יום וגבי עיר הנדחת כתיב יושבי העיר (דברים יג) [ב"ב ח.]. ויהא כאנשי העיר. לשאת עמהם בעול [ב"ב ז:]. שער נשים צדקניות. של עיר הנדחת שלא הודחו עמה מהו ואמר רבא התם בחלק (דף קיב) פיאה נכרית שקשרה הצדקת לשערה קא מיבעיא ליה אי כגופה היא וניצול אי כממונה וקי"ל (שם) צדיקים שבתוכה יוצאין ממנה ערומים וכל ממונם נשרף דכתיב ואת כל שללה תקבוץ וגו' אלמא מספקא ליה אי כגופה אי לאו כגופה. פיאה. קליעה. בפיאה נכרית. לאו שערה ממש קאמר אלא שהיתה לה פיאה משיער אשה אחרת קשורה לשערה [דרגילות היו נשים כששערן מועט לקשור שיער נשים נכריות לשערן והוא פיאה נכרית] [ערכין ז:]. פיאה נכרית. קליעת שער תלושה ומחברתה על שערה עם קליעתה שתראה בעלת שער [שבת סד:]. עושין לה רחוב. ורחובה דהשתא נמי משמע [לעיל קיא:].

from the *tumah* of ***neveilah*?**[35] ,,לְפִי־חָרֶב" אָמַר רַחֲמָנָא – *Destroy it . . . and its animals* **by the sword, said the Merciful One** in His Torah, לֹא שְׁנָא שַׁחֲטָהּ מִשְׁחַט לֹא שְׁנָא קַטְלָא מִקְטַל – and **it makes no difference whether one did this by slaughtering it** in accord with the laws of *shechitah* **or whether one did it by killing it** in any other manner.[36] אוֹ דִלְמָא כֵּיוָן דְּשַׁחֲטָהּ מְהַנְיָא לָהּ שְׁחִיטָה – **Or perhaps** we say that **since one slaughtered it** according to the rules of *shechitah,* **the *shechitah* is effective for it** in removing it from the category of *neveilah*?[37] מַאי – **What** is the law?

The Gemara concludes:

תֵּיקוּ – **[The question] remains unresolved.**

An inquiry:

בָּעֵי רַב יוֹסֵף – **Rav Yosef inquired:** שֵׂיעָר נָשִׁים צִדְקָנִיּוֹת מַהוּ – **What is [the law]** concerning **the hair of righteous women** who live in the subverted city? Is it burned along with the rest of the city's property or not?[38]

The Gemara challenges the very basis of the inquiry:

אָמַר רָבָא – **Rava said:** הָא דִּרְשָׁעִיּוֹת אָסוּר – **But is** even **[the hair] of the wicked women forbidden** and burned?[39] ,,תִּקְבֹּץ . . . וְשָׂרַפְתָּ" כְּתִיב – ***You shall gather . . . and you shall burn*** is what is **written** in Scripture,[40] מִי שֶׁאֵינוֹ מְחוּסָּר אֶלָּא קְבִיצָה וּשְׂרֵיפָה – which implies only **that which lacks nothing but gathering and burning.** יָצָא זֶה שֶׁמְּחוּסָּר תְּלִישָׁה וּקְבִיצָה וּשְׂרֵיפָה – **Excluded** from this command, therefore, **is that which lacks separation**[41] and then **gathering** and **burning.** Thus, we learn that human hair is never burned, even if it is the hair of wicked women! – ? –

Rava therefore explains the point of Rav Yosef's inquiry to be something else:

אֶלָּא אָמַר רָבָא – **Rather, said Rava:** בְּפֵיאָה נָכְרִית – Rav Yosef's inquiry is **about a wig** of a righteous woman, not her hair.

The Gemara examines this answer:

הֵיכִי דָמֵי – **What is the case?** אִי דִּמְחוּבָּר בְּגוּפָהּ – **If [the wig] is attached to her body,** i.e. she is wearing it, כְּגוּפָהּ דָּמְיָא – **it is like her body.**[42]

The Gemara answers:

לֹא צְרִיכָא דְּתָלֵי בְּסִיבְטָא – Rather, **[the inquiry] is not relevant except** to the case **where [the wig] is hanging on a peg**[43] and she is not wearing it. כְּנִכְסֵי צַדִּיקִים שֶׁבְּתוֹכָהּ דָּמֵי – We may therefore inquire: **Is [the wig] considered to be like the property of the righteous that is in [the subverted city]** וְאָבַד – **and it is** therefore **destroyed,** like all the other possessions of the righteous that are in the city? אוֹ דִלְמָא כֵּיוָן דְּעָיְילָא וְנָפְקָא – **Or** do we **perhaps** say that **since she** always **goes in and out** with it, i.e. she is always putting it on, כִּלְבוּשָׁהּ דָּמֵי – **it is considered to be like her garment** and is therefore not burned?[44]

The Gemara concludes:

תֵּיקוּ – **[The question] remains unresolved.**

A quote from the Mishnah:

,,וְאֶת־כָּל־שְׁלָלָהּ תִּקְבֹּץ אֶל־תּוֹךְ רְחֹבָהּ וכו' " – The verse states: ***And all its booty you shall gather into its square, etc.*** **The Mishnah**

NOTES

for consumption. For example, the Mishnah in *Chullin* (72b) states that the *shechitah* of a *tereifah* (an animal afflicted with a fatal flaw) removes it from the category of *neveilah,* even though its meat is forbidden to be eaten. Situations such as these are referred to by the Gemara as "its slaughter serves to purify it from [the *tumah* of] *neveilah.*"

35. Clearly, the slaughter of an animal belonging to an *ir hanidachas* cannot permit its meat for consumption, since the property of an *ir hanidachas* is forbidden for any kind of benefit. Rav Chisda now inquires whether its *shechitah* at least removes the carcass from the category of *neveilah* and thereby from the condition of *tumah* (*Yad Ramah*; see *Toras Chaim*).

36. [A *shechitah* knife is also a form of sword,] and slaughtering the animal therefore fulfills the Torah's command to *destroy . . . its animals by the sword.* Accordingly, even slaughtering the animal does not rank as *shechitah,* but only as putting it to death (*Rashi, Yad Ramah*). [Since the animal has been executed in the prescribed manner, its slaughter is considered an act of execution. This categorization supersedes the categorization of this act as *shechitah*.] Accordingly, the slaughter would not be effective even in removing the carcass from the category of *neveilah* (*Rashi*; see *Sanhedrei Ketanah*).

37. The command to destroy the animals *by the sword* may imply in a manner that would ordinarily be classified as "killing" rather than "slaughtering," and *shechitah* would therefore *not* be considered a fulfillment of this Scriptural command. If so, the *shechitah* of an *ir hanidachas* animal *would be* effective in removing the animal from the category of *neveilah.* Of course, the meat would remain forbidden for consumption and for benefit [since it is the property of an *ir hanidachas*], but it would not be *tamei* as a *neveilah* (*Rashi*).

Ran (in *Chidushim*) asks that according to the way *Rashi* explained Rav Chisda's previous ruling, Rav Chisda's question here has already been resolved in that ruling. Rav Chisda stated there that an animal that belongs half to a resident of an *ir hanidachas* and half to someone else remains completely forbidden. *Rashi* there explained the reason for this to be that since it is under sentence of death, the *shechitah* of the *ir hanidachas* part is considered "killing" rather than *shechitah* (see note 32). This assumes the view expressed by Rav Chisda in the first side of his inquiry here. But then what is Rav Chisda's question?

For this reason *Ran* explains the basis for Rav Chisda's earlier ruling somewhat differently. Since a portion of the slaughter was performed on a part of the animal that could not become permitted for consumption (because it was forbidden as property of the *ir hanidachas*), this act of *shechitah* lacks the capacity to permit any part of the animal for consumption. That, however, does not preclude it from being considered an act of *shechitah* which might at least serve to remove the carcass from the category of *neveilah.* This is the subject of Rav Chisda's present inquiry (see *Chidushei HaRan* for a fuller explanation; see also *Achiezer, Yoreh Deah* 7:8; and *Teshuvos Oneg Yom Tov, Yoreh Deah* §61 for an interesting analysis of *Ran's* view). *Pri Chadash* (cited in note 32) is of the opinion that *Rashi* means the same thing as *Ran.*

38. We learned above that although those who are innocent of idolatry are not killed, their property in the city is destroyed. Rav Yosef inquires whether the hair of the women [which can be cut off and sold for use in a wig] is considered part of the property of the city.

39. Since you inquire only about the hair of the righteous women, it is evident that you take for granted that the hair of the wicked women is burned! (*Rashi*).

40. *And all its booty you shall gather into its square, and you shall burn the city and all its booty . . .* (*Deuteronomy* 13:17).

41. Literally: plucking; i.e. removal from the head.

42. Though the righteous of an *ir hanidachas* are not killed, their property is destroyed, as we learned above. Nevertheless, the clothing they are wearing is not taken from them and burned. Rather, the clothes on their backs are spared [because they are considered subsidiary to their bodies (*Chazon Ish*, *Sanhedrin* 24:15)]. A wig, too, is an article of clothing. Thus, if they are wearing wigs [at the time a verdict is reached for the city (*Chazon Ish*)], it is obvious that the wigs are not burned, any more than the dresses they are wearing (*Rashi*).

43. Our translation follows *Rashi,* who explains the Gemara's discussion as revolving around the question of whether the woman is wearing the wig or not. *Yad Ramah*, however, explains the issue to be the degree of physical attachment to her head, i.e. whether it is pasted on to her head (with wax or the like) or merely hung from a fastening behind her ear. See also the extensive discussion of this matter in *Netziv's Haamek She'eilah* 133:5-6.]

44. [I.e. a woman considers her wig an essential part of her personal wardrobe] and is always putting it on. Thus, even when she is not actually wearing it, she has in mind to put it on, for which reason it may be considered an article of her attire (*Rashi*).

מסורת הש"ס

א) לעיל טז. ע"ש, ב) [ב"ב ח. ע"ש], ג) ב"ב ז:, ד) שם ח. [תוספ' נדרים פ"ב], ה) [תוספ' פרק י"ד], ו) [ערכין ז: ושם הגירס' ר' יוסי בר' חנינא], ז) [שם הגירסא בסכתא תרגום של ויתד תהיה לך וסיכתא], ח) לעיל מה:, ט) [לעיל כא.], י) רש"א מ"ז.

הגהות הב"ח

(א) רש"י ד"ה כמאן וכו' דאי אפשר:

הגהות הגר"א

[א] גמ' ואת כל אשר בה. נמחק:

גליון הש"ס

גמ' עיסה חציה של עיר הנדחת. עי' שאגת אריה סי' פ"ט: שם יצא זה שמחוסר תלישה. עי' לעיל מו ע"ב תוס' ד"ה תלישה:

תורה אור השלם

א) וְהוֹצֵאתָ אֶת הָאִישׁ הַהוּא אוֹ אֶת הָאִשָּׁה הַהִוא אֲשֶׁר עָשׂוּ אֶת הַדָּבָר הָרָע הַזֶּה אֶל שְׁעָרֶיךָ אֶת הָאִישׁ אוֹ אֶת הָאִשָּׁה וּסְקַלְתָּם בָּאֲבָנִים וָמֵתוּ: [דברים יז, ה]

ב) הַכֵּה תַכֶּה אֶת יֹשְׁבֵי הָעִיר הַהִוא לְפִי חָרֶב הַחֲרֵם אֹתָהּ וְאֶת כָּל אֲשֶׁר בָּהּ וְאֶת בְּהֶמְתָּהּ לְפִי חָרֶב: [דברים יג, טו]

ג) וְאֶת כָּל שְׁלָלָהּ תִּקְבֹּץ אֶל תּוֹךְ רְחֹבָהּ וְשָׂרַפְתָּ בָאֵשׁ אֶת הָעִיר וְאֶת כָּל שְׁלָלָהּ כָּלִיל לַייָ אֱלֹהֶיךָ וְהָיְתָה תֵּל עוֹלָם לֹא תִבָּנֶה עוֹד: [דברים יג, יז]

קשיא איבעיא להו הודחו מאליהן מהו וידיחו אמר רחמנא [א] ולא שהודחו מאליהן או דילמא אפילו הודחו מאליהן ת"ש הדיחוה נשים וקטנים אמאי ליהוי כהודחו מאליהן הנך בתר נפשייהו גרידי הני בתר נשים וקטנים גרידי: עד שיודח רובה: היכי עבדינן אמר רב יהודה דנין וחובשין דנין וחובשין א"ל עולא נמצא אתה מענה את דינן של אלו אלא אמר עולא דנין וסוקלין דנין וסוקלין איתמר רבי יוחנן אמר דנין וסוקלין דנין וסוקלין ור"ל אמר מרבין להן בתי דינין איני [ה] והאמר ר' חמא בר יוסי א"ר אושעיא [א] והוצאת את האיש ההוא או את האשה ההיא איש ואשה אתה מוציא לשעריך ואי אתה מוציא כל העיר כולה לשעריך אלא [ב] מרבין להן בתי דינין ומעיינין בדיניהן ומסקינן להו לבית דין הגדול וגמרי להו לדינייהו וקטלי להו: הכה תכה את יושבי העיר וכו': תנו רבנן [ו] [ג] החמרת והגמלת העוברת ממקום למקום לנו בתוכה והודחו עמה אם נשתהו שם ל' יום הן בסייף וממונן אבד פחות מיכן הן בסקילה וממונן פלט ורמינהי [ג] כמה יהיה בעיר ויהיה כאנשי העיר [ד] י"ב חדש אמר רבא לא קשיא הא למיהוי מבני מתא הא למיהוי מיתבי מתא והתניא [ז] [ה] המודר הנאה מבני העיר אם יש אדם שנשתהא שם י"ב חדש אסור ליהנות ממנו פחות מיכן מותר ליהנות ממנו ביושבי העיר אם נשתהא ל' יום אסור ליהנות ממנו פחות מיכן מותר ליהנות ממנו: החרם אותה ואת כל אשר בה כו': ת"ר [ב] החרם אותה [וא] ואת כל אשר בה פרט לנכסי צדיקים שבחוצה לה ואת כל אשר בה לרבות נכסי צדיקים שבתוכה שללה ולא שלל שמים ואת כל שללה לרבות נכסי רשעים שחוצה לה [ט] אמר ר"ש מפני מה אמרה תורה נכסי צדיקים שבתוכה יאבדו מי גרם להם שידורו בתוכה ממונם לפיכך ממונם אבד אמר מר [ג] ואת כל שללה תקבץ לרבות נכסי רשעים שבחוצה לה אמר רב חסדא [ו] ובנקבצים לתוכה אמר רב חסדא פקדונות של אנשי עיר הנדחת מותרין ה"ד אי לימא דעיר אחרת ואיתנהו בגוה פשיטא דמותרין לאו שללה הוא ואלא דידהו ואיתנהו בעיר אחרת אי דנקבצין לתוכה אמאי מותרין ואי אין נקבצין לתוכה הא אמרה חדא זימנא לא [י] לעולם דעיר אחרת דמפקדי בתוכה והכא במאי עסקינן [ח] כגון דקביל עליה אחריות מהו דתימא כיון דקביל עליה אחריות כדידיה דמי קא משמע לן אמר רב חסדא [ט] בהמה חציה של עיר הנדחת וחציה של עיר אחרת אסורה [י] עיסה חציה של עיר הנדחת וחציה של עיר אחרת מותרת מאי טעמא בהמה כמאן דלא פליגא דמיא עיסה כמאן דפליגא דמיא בעי רב חסדא בהמת עיר הנדחת מהו דתיתהני בה שחיטה לטהרה מידי נבילה לפי חרב אמר רחמנא [כ] לא שנא שחטה משחט לא שנא קטלא מקטל או דלמא כיון דשחטה מהניא לה שחיטה מאי תיקו [ל] בעי רב יוסף שיער נשים צדקניות מהו אמר רבא הא דרשעיות אסור [ג] תקבץ ושרפת כתיב מי שאינו מחוסר אלא קביצה ושריפה [מ] יצא זה שמחוסר תלישה וקביצה ושריפה אלא אמר רבא בפיאה נכרית היכי דמי אי דמחובר בגופה כגופה דמיא לא צריכא דתלי [י] בסיבטא בנכסי צדיקים שבתוכה דמי [מ] ואבד או דלמא כיון דעיילא ונפקא כלבושה דמי תיקו: ואת כל שללה תקבוץ אל תוך רחובה וכו': [ס] ת"ר אין לה רחוב אינה נעשית עיר הנדחת דברי רבי ישמעאל רבי עקיבא אומר אין לה רחוב עושין לה רחוב במאי קמיפלגי מר סבר רחובה מעיקרא משמע ומר סבר רחובה השתא נמי משמע:

והההקדשות

קשיא. לשון הפסוק קשה לתרץ למ"ד חולקין אבל לא מיתותב: גרידי. בדל"ת נמשכין וכן גרים רבי בכוליה הש"ס מגריד גריד וכ"ל שהוא לשון גרידא דמפרשינן יחיד על שם שהוא יחיד משוך ומופרש הוא מן הכל ואין לאחרים סביביו ולשון ארמי הוא ואין דומה לו בפסוק (ודומה לו) אבל גורדו ומעמידו על גלדו (ר"ה ד' כז:) הוא לשון עברי ודומה לו בפסוק (איוב ב) ויקח לו חרש להתגרד בו בדל"ת ופי' לשון חטיטה שמחטט וגורד בסכין או בכל דבר וגורר בריי"ש לשון עברי הוא כמו (שבת ד' כב.) גורר אדם מטה כסא ושלחן וכן (ב"ב ד' פו.) היה מגרר ויוצא מגרר ויוצא: בתר נפשייהו גרידי. ומעשיהם מעשה ולדוקים ביותר הואיל ומעלמם הם נדחין ודין הוא שיעשה עיר הנדחת: אבל הנך דהודחו בתר נשים וקטנים גרידי. שאין לדוקים כ"כ: היכי עבדינן. היאך נעשין רובא נדחים הואיל דצריכין עדים והתראה לכל אחד ואחד: דנין וחובשין. כשרואין ב' או ג' מהם עובדים ע"ז לא יסקלו אותן ומניחין כל האחרים מלסקול אלא דנין אותם לסקילה וחובשין אותם בבית הסוהר וכן עושין עד שרואין אם מצטרפין לרובא וחוזרין ודנין אותם דין אחר להריגה ומאבדין את ממונם: ומענה את דינם. שלאחר שנגמר דינם אתה משהה אותם ומענה את דינם: דנין וסוקלין. עד חליין דמחזקינן להו כיחידים ודנין וסוקלין ומחליין ואילך נתברר הדבר למפרע שהודחו רובא והוו בסייף וממונם אבד ומחליין ואילך אי אתה רשאי למשכן למיתה חמורה: ור"ל אמר מרבין להם בתי דינין. לאו משום דאין דנין ב' ביום אחד דהא אמרת בפרק נגמר הדין (לעיל מו.) דבמיתה אחת דנין אלא משום דנפישי עדים לכל אחד ואחד ואין פנאי לחקור כל אחד ואחד ביום אחד מרבים להם בתי דינים כדי שתתקבל עדותן ביום א' ויגמור דין כולם ביום אחד: לשעריך. לב"ד שבשעריך דהיינו סנהדרי קטנה: ואי אתה מוציא. אלא בסנהדרי גדולה: אלא מרבין להם בתי דינין ומעייני בדיניהם. אם הוו מרובים ואם הודחו רוב' מעלים את כולן לב"ד הגדול: כמה יהא בעיר. משנה בהשותפין: ויהא כאנשי העיר. ליתן בצורכי העיר: למיהוי כבני מתא. שיהא נקרא כבני העיר אין נקרא בפחות מי"ב חדש אבל להקרות מיושבי העיר כיון ששהה ל' יום נקרא מאנשי העיר וקרינן בהו את יושבי העיר ההוא: והתניא. בניחותא: המודר הנאה. שאומר הרי עלי קונם אם אהנה: החרם אותה פרט לנכסי צדיקים שבחוצה לה. שאם היו לדיקים דרים בתוכה והוי להו נכסים מופקדים במקום אחר ביד אחרים אין מחרימין אותן אבל נכסים שיש להם בתוך העיר מחרימין אותן וטעמא מפורש לקמן: אמר ר"ש מפני מה וכו'. בכל דוכתי דרש ר"ש טעמא דקרא [ט]: ה"ג אמר מר ואת כל [י] (שללה) אשר בה לרבות נכסי רשעים שבחוצה לה: אמר רב חסדא ובנקבצין לתוכה. נכסי רשעים הקרובין לעיר שיכולים לקבלם לתוך העיר באותו יום עלמו שכונסין שלל העיר לרחוב לשורפן הן אבודים עמה אבל רחוקים דאין מגיעין לעיר אינן אבודים ודוקא שכבר היו לתוכה אלא שמעכשיו היו מופקדים ביד אחרים אבל לא היו מעולם בתוכה כגון דנפלה להם בירושה לא קרינא ביה שללה ואין הממון אבד: אלא דידהו. דבני עיר הנדחת ומופקדים הם בעיר אחרת: הא אמרה. רב חסדא ובנקבלין לתוכה והא אין נקבלין: דקבל עליו אחריות. בני עיר הנדחת: כמאן דלא פליגא. (א) א"א לבזית בשר בלא שחיטה ואפילו שחטה משחט אין בשחיטתו כלום דלא לשחיטה קיימא אלא למיתה ושחיטתה זו היא מיתת הבהמה ואין היתר אפילו החלי שאין של עיר הנדחת דכי שחט לסימן דעיר הנדחת אינו שוחט אלא ממית ולא מהניא ביה שחיטה: עיסה. כל אימת דבעי פליג לה ואין חלק של עיר הנדחת מעורב בו: ל"ש שחטה משחט ל"ש קטלא מקטיל. דבין בשחיטה ובין בהריגה קרינא ביה לפי חרב דאפילו שחטה מיתה בעלמא היא ולא מהני מידי או דילמא לפי חרב היינו שלא כדרך שחיטה אבל דרך שחיטה מהניא לה לטהרה מידי נבילה דנהי דלאכילה איתסרה ואיסור הנאה הוא אבל תיהני לטהרה מידי נבלה: שיער נשים צדקניות. שבעיר הנדחת מהו אי הוו בכלל ואת כל שללה תשרף או לא: רשעניות. פשיטא לן דישרף עם שלל העיר: תלישה. שצריך לגלחה: פיאה נכרית. גדיל של שערות דעלמא שעושין לנוי קא מבעי ליה לרב יוסף אם של לדקניות הוי: מחובר בגופה. שנקשר בה: כגופה דמי. וכשם שאין שורפין מלבושין שעליהן שהרי לדקניות הן כך אין שורפין אותו גדיל: דתלי בסבטא. תלה אותו גדיל ביתד ואין קשורין בה עכשיו: כיון דעיילא ונפקא. רגילה לקושרה תדיר אף על פי שלא קשרתו עכשיו כל מקום שיהא שם נדון כמלבוש שעליה דכל שעתא דעתה עליה וכשאר מלבושין דמי: רחובה מעיקרא משמע. רחובה שהיה לה מתחלה ולא שעושין לה רחוב עכשיו:

היו

עין משפט נר מצוה

מז א מיי' פ"ד מהל' עכו"ם הלכה ב סמג עשין טו:

מח ב מיי' שם הלכה ו:

מט ג מיי' שם הלכה ט:

נ ד מיי' פ"ד מהל' שכנים הלכה ה סמג עשין פב טוש"ע ח"מ סי' קסג סעיף ב:

נא ה מיי' פ"ט מהל' נדרים הלכה יז סמג לאוין רמב טוש"ע י"ד סי' ריז סעיף לב:

נב ו ז ח מיי' פ"ד מהל' עכו"ם הלכה י סמג לאוין סו:

נג ט י מיי' שם הלכה יא:

נד כ ל מ מיי' שם הלכה יב והלכה יג [ועי' כ"מ]:

ליקוטי רש"י

לשעריך. לבית דין שבשעריך דהיינו סנהדרי קטנה ואי אתה מוליא כולה אלא בסנהדרי גדולה [לעיל טז.]. לענין עבודה זרה חלק בין יחידים למרובים דעיר הנדחת בעי סנהדרי גדולה כדיליף לקמן סנהדרין (טז.) ויחיד נידון בעשרים ושלשה דכתיב (דברים יז) והולאת את האיש ההוא וגו' אל שעריך בית דין שבשעריך [שם טז:]. החמרת והגמלת. שיירא של חמרים ושל גמלים. הרי אלו בסקילה. כדין שאר יחידים. למיהוי מיתבי מתא. בשלשים יום וגבי עיר הנדחת כתיב יושבי העיר (דברים יג) [ב"ב ח.]. ויהא כאנשי העיר. לשאת עמהם בעול [ב"ב ז:]. שער נשים צדקניות. של עיר הנדחת שלא הודחו עמה מהו ואמר רבא התם בחלק (דף קיב) פיאה נכרית שקשרה הלדקת לשערה קא מיבעיא ליה אי כגופה היא ונילול אי כממונה וקי"ל (שם) לדיקים שבתוכה יולאין ממנה ערומים וכל ממונם נשרף דכתיב ואת כל שללה תקבוץ וגו' אלמא מספקא ליה אי כגופה אי לאו כגופה. פיאה. קליעה. בפיאה נכרית. לאו שערה ממש קאמר אלא שהיתה לה פיאה משיער אשה אחרת קשורה לשערה [דרגילות היו נשים כששערן מועט לקשור שיער נשים נכריות לשערן והוא פיאה נכרית] [ערכין ז:]. פיאה נכרית. קליעת שער תלושה וקושרתה על שערה עם קליעתה שתראה בעלת שער [שבת סד:]. עושין לה רחוב. ורחובה דהשתא נמי משמע [לעיל קיא:].

stated that if the subverted city has no square, we make a square and burn the property in it.

The Gemara cites a Baraisa in which the Mishnah's ruling is disputed:

תָּנוּ רַבָּנָן – **The Rabbis taught in a Baraisa:** אֵין לָהּ רְחוֹב – IF [THE CITY] HAS NO SQUARE, אֵינָהּ נַעֲשֵׂית עִיר הַנִּדַּחַת – IT DOES NOT BECOME A SUBVERTED CITY; דִּבְרֵי רַבִּי יִשְׁמָעֵאל – these are THE WORDS OF R' YISHMAEL. רַבִּי עֲקִיבָא אוֹמֵר – R' AKIVA SAYS: אֵין לָהּ רְחוֹב עוֹשִׂין לָהּ רְחוֹב – IF IT HAS NO SQUARE, WE MAKE A SQUARE FOR IT. בְּמַאי קָמִיפַּלְגֵי – **In** regard to **what** issue **do they** [R' Yishmael and R' Akiva] **disagree?** מַר סָבַר – **One master** (R' Yishmael) **holds** ,,רְחֹבָהּ" מֵעִיקָּרָא מַשְׁמַע – that when the Torah speaks of gathering its booty into ***its square,*** **it implies** the square that was there **previously.** Thus, a city that does not have a square cannot be subjected to the destruction required by the Torah and it thus cannot be condemned as a subverted city.[45] וּמַר סָבַר – **And one master** (R' Akiva) **holds** ,,רְחֹבָהּ" הַשְׁתָּא נַמִּי מַשְׁמַע – that the phrase ***its square*** **can also imply** a square that exists **now,** at the time of the burning, even though it did not exist previously. Therefore, even though there was no square at the time of the verdict, the city can be condemned as a subverted city and a square is then cleared in which to burn the property.[46]

NOTES

45. [Clearing a place for a square afterwards would not help, since the Torah's requirement can only be fulfilled in a square that existed at the time of the city's condemnation.]

46. We have explained the Gemara according to *Rashi. Chidushei HaRan* explains the dispute to be whether the verse's reference to *its square* means a place that once functioned as the city's square (a place in which people gathered; see above, 111b note 34), or whether it merely means a place with the physical structure of a square.

קשיא איבעיא להו הודחו מאליהן מהו וידיחו אמר רחמנא א ולא שהודחו מאליהן או דילמא אפילו הודחו מאליהן ת"ש הדיחוה נשים וקטנים אמאי ליהוי כהודחו מאליהן הנך בתר נפשייהו גרידי הני בתר נשים וקטנים גרידי: עד שיודח רובה: היכי עבדינן אמר רב יהודה דנין וחובשין דנין וחובשין א"ל עולא נמצא אתה מענה את דינן של אלו אלא אמר עולא דנין וסוקלין דנין וסוקלין איתמר רבי יוחנן אמר דנין וסוקלין דנין וסוקלין ור"ל אמר מרבין להן בתי דינין איני א) והאמר ר' חמא בר יוסי א"ר אושעיא א) והוצאת את האיש ההוא או את האשה ההיא איש ואשה אתה מוציא לשעריך ואי אתה מוציא כל העיר כולה לשעריך אלא ב מרבין להן בתי דינין ומעיינין בדיניהן ומסקינן להו לבית דין הגדול וגמרי להו לדינייהו וקטלי להו: הכה תכה את יושבי העיר וכו': תנו רבנן ב) ג החמרת והגמלת העוברת ממקום למקום לנו בתוכה והודחו עמה אם נשתהו שם ל' יום הן בסייף וממונן אבד פחות מיכן הן בסקילה וממונן פלט ורמינהי ג) כמה יהיה בעיר ויהיה כאנשי העיר ד י"ב חדש אמר רבא לא קשיא הא למיהוי מבני מתא הא למיהוי מיתבי מתא והתניא ד) ה המודר הנאה מבני העיר אם יש אדם שנשתהא שם י"ב חדש אסור ליהנות ממנו פחות מיכן מותר ליהנות ממנו ביושבי העיר אם נשתהא ל' יום אסור ליהנות ממנו פחות מיכן מותר ליהנות ממנו: החרם אותה ואת כל אשר בה כו': ת"ר ב) החרם אותה [א] ואת כל אשר בה פרט לנכסי צדיקים שבחוצה לה ואת כל אשר בה לרבות נכסי צדיקים שבתוכה שללה ולא שלל שמים ואת כל שללה לרבות נכסי רשעים שחוצה לה ה) אמר ר"ש מפני מה אמרה תורה נכסי צדיקים שבתוכה יאבדו מי גרם להם שידורו בתוכה ממונם לפיכך ממונם אבד אמר מר ג) ואת כל שללה תקבץ לרבות נכסי רשעים שבחוצה לה אמר רב חסדא ו ובנקבצים לתוכה אמר רב חסדא פקדונות של אנשי עיר הנדחת מותרין ה"ד אי לימא דעיר אחרת ואיתנהו בגוה פשיטא דמותרין לאו שללה הוא ואלא דידהו ואיתנהו בעיר אחרת אי דנקבצין לתוכה אמאי מותרין ואי אין נקבצין לתוכה הא אמרה חדא זימנא לא ז לעולם דעיר אחרת דמפקדי בתוכה והכא במאי עסקינן ח כגון דקביל עליה אחריות מהו דתימא כיון דקביל עליה אחריות כדידיה דמי קא משמע לן אמר רב חסדא ט בהמה חציה של עיר הנדחת וחציה של עיר אחרת אסורה ט) עיסה י חציה של עיר הנדחת וחציה של עיר אחרת מותרת מאי טעמא בהמה כמאן דלא פליגא דמיא עיסה כמאן דפליגא דמיא בעי רב חסדא בהמת עיר הנדחת מהו דתיתהני בה שחיטה לטהרה מידי נבילה לפי חרב אמר רחמנא כ לא שנא שחטה משחט לא שנא קטלא מקטל או דלמא כיון דשחיטה מהניא לה שחיטה מאי תיקו י) בעי רב יוסף שיער נשים צדקניות מהו אמר רבא הא דרשעיות אסור ג) תקבץ ושרפת כתיב מי שאינו מחוסר אלא קביצה ושריפה ט) ל יצא זה שמחוסר תלישה וקביצה ושריפה אלא אמר רבא בפיאה נכרית היכי דמי אי דמחובר בגופה כגופה דמיא לא צריכא דתלי י) בסיבטא כנכסי צדיקים שבתוכה דמי מ ואבד או דלמא כיון דעיילא ונפקא כלבושה דמי תיקו: ואת כל שללה תקבוץ אל תוך רחובה וכו': פ) ת"ר אין לה רחוב אינה נעשית עיר הנדחת דברי רבי ישמעאל רבי עקיבא אומר אין לה רחוב עושין לה רחוב במאי קמיפלגי מר סבר רחובה מעיקרא משמע ומר סבר רחובה השתא נמי משמע:

וההקדשות

רש"י

קשיא. לשון הפסוק קשה לתרץ למ"ד חולקין אבל לא מיתותא: גרידי. בדל"ת נמשכין וכן גרים רבי בכוליה הש"ס מגריד גריד וצ"ל שהוא לשון גרידא דמפרשינן יחיד על שם שהוא יחיד משוך ומופרש הוא מן הכל ואין לאחרים סביביו ולשון ארמי הוא ואין דומה לו בפסוק (ודומה לו) אבל גורדו ומעמידו על גלדו (ר"ה ד' כז:) הוא לשון עברי ודומה לו בפסוק (איוב ב) ויקח לו חרש להתגרד בו בדל"ת ופי' לשון חטיטה שמחטט וגורד בסכין או בכל דבר וגורר ברי"ש לשון עברי הוא כמו (שבת ד' כב.) גורר אדם מטה כסא ושלחן וכן (ב"ב ד' פו.) היה מגרר ויוצא מגרר ויוצא: בתר נפשייהו גרידי. ומעשיהם מעשה ואדוקים ביותר הואיל ומעצמם הם נדחין ודין הוא שיעשה עיר הנדחת: אבל הנך דהודחו בתר נשים וקטנים גרידי. שאין אדוקים כ"כ: היכי עבדינן. היאך נעשין רובא נדחים הואיל דצריכין עדים והתראה לכל אחד ואחד: דנין וחובשין. כשרואין ב' או ג' מהם עובדים ע"ז לא יסקלו אותן ומניחין כל האחרים מלסקול אלא דנין אותם לסקילה וחובשין אותם בבית הסוהר וכן עושין עד שרואין אם מצטרפין לרובא וחוזרין ודנין אותם דין אחר להריגה ומאבדין את ממונם: ומענה את דינם. שלאחר שנגמר דינם אתה משהה אותם ומענה את דינם: דנין וסוקלין. עד האיין דמחזקינן להו כיחידים ודנין וסוקלין ומהאיין ואילך נתברר הדבר למפרע שהודחו רובא והוו בסייף וממונם אבד ומהאיין ואילך אי אתה רשאי למשכן למיתה חמורה: ור"ל אמר מרבין להם בתי דינין. לאו משום דאין דנין ב' ביום אחד דהא אמרת בפרק נגמר הדין (לעיל מו.) דבמיתה אחת דנין אלא משום דנפישי עדים לכל אחד ואחד ואין פנאי לחקור כל אחד ואחד ביום אחד מרבים להם בתי דינים כדי שתתקבל עדותן ביום א' ויגמור דין כולם ביום אחד: לשעריך. לב"ד שבשעריך דהיינו סנהדרי קטנה: ואי אתה מוציא. אלא בסנהדרי גדולה: אלא מרבין להם בתי דינין ומעייני בדיניהם. אם הוו מרובים ואם הודחו רוב' מעלים את כולן לב"ד הגדול: כמה יהא בעיר. משנה בהשותפין: ויהא כאנשי העיר. ליתן בצורכי העיר: למיהוי כבני מתא. שיהא נקרא כבני העיר אין נקרא בפחות מי"ב חדש אבל להקרות מיושבי העיר כיון ששהה ל' יום נקרא מאנשי העיר וקרינן בהו את יושבי העיר ההוא: והתניא. בניחותא: המודר הנאה. שאומר הרי עלי קונם אם אהנה: החרם אותה פרט לנכסי צדיקים שבחוצה לה. שאם היו לדיקים דרים בתוכה והוי להו נכסים מופקדים במקום אחר ביד אחרים אין מחרימין אותן אבל נכסים שיש להם באותה העיר מחרימין אותן וטעמא מפורש לקמן: אמר ר"ש מפני מה וכו'. בכל דוכתי דרש ר"ש טעמא דקרא ט): ה"ג אמר מר ואת כל י) (שללה) אשר בה לרבות נכסי רשעים שבחוצה לה: אמר רב חסדא ובנקבצין לתוכה. נכסי רשעים הקרובין לעיר שיכולים לקבלם לתוך העיר באותו יום עצמו שכונסין שלל העיר לרחוב לשורפן הן אבודים עמה אבל רחוקים דאין מגיעין לעיר אינן אבודים ודוקא שכבר היו לתוכה אלא שמעכשיו היו מופקדים ביד אחרים אבל לא היו מעולם בתוכה כגון דנפלה להם בירושה לא קרינא ביה שללה ואין הממון אבד: אלא דידהו. דבני עיר הנדחת ומופקדים הם בעיר אחרת: הא אמרה. רב חסדא ובנקבצין לתוכה והא אין נקבצין: דקבל עליו אחריות. בני עיר הנדחת: כמאן דלא פליגא. (א) א"א לגזית בשר בלא שחיטה ואפילו שחטה משחט אין בשחיטתו כלום דלא לשחיטה קיימא אלא למיתה ושחיטתה זו היא מיתת הבהמה ואין היתר אפילו החצי שאין של עיר הנדחת דכי שחט לסימן דעיר הנדחת אינו שוחט אלא ממית ולא מהניא ביה שחיטה: עיסה. כל אימת דבעי פליג לה ואין חלק של עיר הנדחת מעורב בו: ל"ש שחטה משחט ל"ש קטלא מקטיל. דבין בשחיטה ובין בהריגה קרינא ביה לפי חרב דאפילו שחטה מיתה בעלמא היא ולא מהני מידי או דילמא לפי חרב היינו שלא כדרך שחיטה אבל דרך שחיטה מהניא לה לטהרה מידי נבילה דנהי דלאכילה איתסרה ואיסור הנאה הוא אבל תיהני לטהרה מידי נבלה: שיער נשים צדקניות. שבעיר הנדחת מהו אי הוו בכלל ואת כל שללה תשרף או לא: רשעניות. פשיטא לן דישרף עם שלל העיר: תלישה. שצריך לגלחה: פיאה נכרית. גדיל של שערות דעלמא שעושין לנוי קא מבעי ליה לרב יוסף אם של צדקניות הוי: מחובר בגופה. שנקשר בה: כגופה דמי. וכשם שאין שורפין מלבושין שעליהן שהרי צדקניות הן כך אין שורפין אותו גדיל: דתלי בסבטא. תלה אותו גדיל ביתד ואין קשורין בה עכשיו: כיון דעיילא ונפקא. רגילה לקושרה תדיר אף על פי שלא קשרתו עכשיו כל מקום שיהא שם נדון כמלבוש שעליה דכל שעתא דעתה עליה וכשאר מלבושין דמי: רחובה מעיקרא משמע. רחובה שהיה לה מתחלה ולא שעושין לה רחוב עכשיו:

היו

מסורת הש"ס

א) לעיל טז. ע"ש, ב) [ב"ב ח. ע"ש], ג) ב"ב ז:, ד) שם ח. [תוספ' נדרים פ"ב], ה) [תוספ' פרק י"ד], ו) [ערכין ז: ושם הגירס' ר' יוסי בר' חנינא], ז) [שם הגירסא בסבתא תרגום של ויתד תהיה לך וסיכתא], ח) לעיל מה:, ט) [לעיל כא.], י) רש"א מ"ז.

הגהות הב"ח

(א) רש"י ד"ה כמאן וכו' דאי אפשר:

הגהות הגר"א

[א] גמ' ואת כל אשר בה. נמחק:

גליון הש"ס

גמ' עיסה חציה של עיר הנדחת. עי' שאגת אריה סי' פ"ט: שם יצא זה שמחוסר תלישה. עי' לעיל מו ע"ב תוס' ד"ה תלישה:

תורה אור השלם

א) וְהוֹצֵאתָ אֶת הָאִישׁ הַהוּא אוֹ אֶת הָאִשָּׁה הַהִוא אֲשֶׁר עָשׂוּ אֶת הַדָּבָר הָרָע הַזֶּה אֶל שְׁעָרֶיךָ אֶת הָאִישׁ אוֹ אֶת הָאִשָּׁה וּסְקַלְתָּם בָּאֲבָנִים וָמֵתוּ: [דברים יז, ה]

ב) הַכֵּה תַכֶּה אֶת יֹשְׁבֵי הָעִיר הַהִוא לְפִי חָרֶב הַחֲרֵם אֹתָהּ וְאֶת כָּל אֲשֶׁר בָּהּ וְאֶת בְּהֶמְתָּהּ לְפִי חָרֶב: [דברים יג, טו]

ג) וְאֶת כָּל שְׁלָלָהּ תִּקְבֹּץ אֶל תּוֹךְ רְחֹבָהּ וְשָׂרַפְתָּ בָאֵשׁ אֶת הָעִיר וְאֶת כָּל שְׁלָלָהּ כָּלִיל לַייָ אֱלֹהֶיךָ וְהָיְתָה תֵּל עוֹלָם לֹא תִבָּנֶה עוֹד: [דברים יג, יז]

עין משפט נר מצוה

מז א מיי' פ"ד מהל' עכו"ם הלכה ב סמג עשין טו:
מח ב מיי' שם הלכה ו:
מט ג מיי' שם הלכה ט:
נ ד מיי' פ"ד מהל' שכנים הלכה ה סמג עשין פב טוש"ע ח"מ סי' קסג סעיף ב:
נא ה מיי' פ"ט מהל' נדרים הלכה יז סמג לאוין רמב טוש"ע י"ד סי' ריז סעיף לב:
נב ו ז ח מיי' פ"ד מהל' עכו"ם הלכה י סמג לאוין סו:
נג ט י מיי' שם הלכה יא:
נד כ ל מ מיי' שם הלכה יב והלכה יג [ועי' כ"מ]:

ליקוטי רש"י

לשעריך. לבית דין שבשעריך דהיינו סנהדרי קטנה ואי אתה מוציא כולה אלא בסנהדרי גדולה [לעיל טז.]. לענין עבודה זרה חלק בין יחידים למרובים דעיר הנדחת בעי סנהדרי גדולה כדיליף לקמן סנהדרין (טז.) ויחיד נידון בעשרים ושלשה דכתיב (דברים יז) והוצאת את האיש ההוא וגו' אל שעריך בית דין שבשעריך [שם טו:]. החמרת והגמלת. שיירא של חמרים ושל גמלים. הרי אלו בסקילה. כדין שאר יחידים. למיהוי מיתבי מתא. בשלשים יום וגבי עיר הנדחת כתיב יושבי העיר (דברים יג) [ב"ב ח.]. ויהא כאנשי העיר. לשאת עמהם בעול [ב"ב ז:]. שער נשים צדקניות. של עיר הנדחת שלא הודחו עמה מהו ואמר רבא התם בחלק (דף קיב) פיאה נכרית שקשרה הלדקת לשערה קא מיבעיא ליה אי כגופה היא וניצול אי כממונה וקי"ל (שם) לדיקים שבתוכה יוצאין ממנה ערומים וכל ממונם נשרף דכתיב ואת כל שללה תקבוץ וגו' אלמא מספקא ליה אי כגופה אי לאו כגופה. פיאה. קליעה. בפיאה נכרית. לאו שערה ממש קאמר אלא שהיתה לה פיאה משיער אשה אחרת קשורה לשערה [דרגילות היו נשים כששערן מועט לקשור שיער נשים נכריות לשערן והוא פיאה נכרית] [ערכין ז:]. פיאה נכרית. קליעת שער תלושה ומחוברת על שערה עם קליעתה שתראה בעלת שער [שבת סד:]. עושין לה רחוב. ורחובה דהשתא נמי משמע [לעיל קיא:].

עין משפט
נר מצוה

נה א ב ג ד מיי׳ פ״ד מהל׳ עכו״ם הלכה יג סמג עשין טו:
נו ה ו מיי׳ פ״ו מהל׳ בכורים הלכה ד:
נז ז מיי׳ פ״ז מהל׳ בית הבחירה הלכה יד ופ״ד מהל׳ עכו״ם הלכה ד:
נח ח מיי׳ פ״ב מהל׳ מעשר שני ונטע רבעי הלכה ח סמג לאוין קלו:

והההקדשות שבה יפדו כו׳: (א) ת״ר [א]היו בה (א) (קדשי) קדשים קדשי מזבח ימותו קדשי בדק הבית יפדו ותרומות ירקבו ומעשר שני וכתבי הקדש יגנזו [ב]ר״ש אומר בהמתה ולא בהמת בכור ומעשר שללה פרט לכסף הקדש וכסף מעשר אמר מר היו בה (קדשי) קדשים קדשי מזבח ימותו ואמאי ימותו ירעו עד שיסתאבו וימכרו ויפלו דמיהן לנדבה ר׳ יוחנן אמר [א]זבח רשעים תועבה ר״ל אמר ממון בעלים הוא והכא בקדשים שחייב באחריותן [ג]ור״ש היא דאמר ממון בעלים הוא הא מדסיפא ר״ש היא רישא לאו ר״ש בקדשים קלים ואליבא דרבי יוסי הגלילי [ד]דאמר קדשים קלים ממון בעלים אבל קדשי קדשים מאי [ה]יפדו אדתני סיפא קדשי בדק הבית יפדו ליפלוג וליתני בדידה בד״א בקדשים קלים אבל קדשי קדשים [ו]יפדו כיון דאיכא חטאת שמתו בעליה דלמיתה אזלא לא פסיקא ליה בשלמא ר׳ יוחנן לא אמר כר״ל דכתיב זבח רשעים תועבה אלא ר״ל מ״ט לא אמר כר׳ יוחנן אמר לך כי אמרינן זבח רשעים תועבה הני מילי היכא דאתנהו בעינייהו אבל הכא כיון דאישתני אישתני: ר״ש אומר [ז]בהמתך ולא בהמת בכור ומעשר: במאי עסקינן [ח]אילימא בתמימין של שמים הוא אלא בבעלי מומין [ג]שללה נינהו אמר רבינא לעולם בבעלי מומין [ו]ומי שנאכל בתורת [ט]בהמתך יצאו אלו שאין נאכלין בתורת [י]בהמתך אלא בתורת בכור ומעשר [כ]דשלל שמים נינהו ופליגא דשמואל דאמר שמואל הכל קרב והכל נפדה מאי קאמר ה״ק כל שקרב כשהוא תם ונפדה כשהוא בעל מום משלל אימעיט וכל שקרב כשהוא תם ואינו נפדה כשהוא בעל מום כגון בכור ומעשר מבהמה נפקא: תרומות ירקבו: אמר רב חסדא ל״ש אלא תרומה ביד ישראל אבל תרומה ביד כהן כיון דממוניה הוא תשרף מתיב רב יוסף מעשר שני וכתבי הקדש יגנזו והא מעשר שני ביד ישראל כתרומה ביד כהן דמי וקתני יגנזו אלא אי אתמר הכי אתמר אמר רב חסדא ל״ש אלא תרומה ביד כהן אבל תרומה ביד ישראל [ד]תנתן לכהן שבעיר אחרת [ל]תנן התם [מ]עיסה של מעשר שני פטורה מן החלה דברי ר״מ וחכמים [ה]מחייבין אמר רב חסדא מחלוקת [ו]במעשר שני בירושלים דר״מ סבר [נ]מעשר שני ממון גבוה הוא ורבנן סברי ממון הדיוט הוא אבל [ס]בגבולין דברי הכל פטור מתיב רב יוסף מעשר שני וכתבי הקדש יגנזו במאי עסקינן אילימא בירושלים מי הויא עיר הנדחת והתניא [ע]עשרה דברים נאמרו בירושלים וזו אחת מהן [ז]אינה נעשית עיר הנדחת ואלא בעיר אחרת ואסקוהו לגוה הא קלטוהו מחיצות אלא לאו בגבולין וקתני יגנזו לא לעולם דעיר אחרת ואסקוהו לגוה והכא במאי עסקינן שנטמא ולפרקיה [פ]דא״ר אלעזר [ח]מניין למעשר שני שנטמא שפודין אותו אפילו בירושלים ת״ל [ב]לא תוכל שאתו ואין שאת אלא אכילה שנאמר [ג]וישא משאת מאת פניו הכא במאי עסקינן בלקוח וליפרקיה

רש״י

היו בה קדשי מזבח. כגון עולות ואשמות של רשעים בתוכה נהי דלא קרינן בהו את כל בהמתה לפי חרב דהא לא בהמתה היא אלא בהמת שמים אלא מאיסותא הוא להקריב קרבנות של רשעים הללו שהודחו הלכך ימותו כונסין אותן לכיפה ומאכילין אותן שעורין עד שכריסן נבקעת דאפילו דמיהם אסור כדלקמן: שנאמר כליל לה׳ אלהיך ל״ג: ר״ש אומר וכו׳. לקמן מפרש טעמא: זבח רשעים תועבה. ואפילו דמיהן אסורין: ור״ש הוא דאמר. בהזהב (ב״מ נו:) קדשים שחייב באחריותן ממון בעלים הוא ויש בהם אונאה הלכך לענין עיר הנדחת נמי ממון בעלים הוא ודיינינהו לפי חרב כשאר בהמות שבתוכה והלכך אסורין דמיהן בהנאה והאי דקאמר ימותו ולא אמר שיחרימו אותה עמהם משום כבוד שמים: ואליבא דרבי יוסי הגלילי דאמר. בפ״ק דב״ק (ד׳ יג:) ומעלה מעל בה׳ לרבות קדשים קלים שהם ממונו והואיל וממונו הם אסורים בהנאה דאפילו דמיהן בהמתם מיקרו אבל קדשי קדשים (ב) [ה]אמאי ירעו דהא ודאי הם עצמם אינם קרבים דזבח רשעים תועבה אלא ירעו עד שיסתאבו וימכרו ויפלו דמיהם לנדבה: אי הכי [ק]מדתני סיפא וכו׳. דקא מפליג בין קדשי מזבח לקדשי בדק הבית: ליפלוג וליתני בדידה. בקדשי מזבח עצמן בין קדשים קלים לקדשי קדשים: דלמיתה אזלא. כדאמרינן (תמורה ד׳ טו.) חמש חטאות מתות: לא פסיקא ליה. למיתני קדשי קדשים דעיר הנדחת ירעו דכיון דמתו להם אותם רשעים אי איכא חטאות שהפרישו בחייהם אזלי למיתה דכל חטאות שמתו בעליהם מתות במסכת הוריות (ד׳ ו.) מפרש טעמא אבל שאר קדשי קדשים כגון אשמות שמתו בעליהם ירעו: דאיתנהו בעינייהו. דהן עצמן ודאי אינן קרבים משום זבח רשעים תועבה: אבל הכא. דאיכא למימר ירעו ויפלו דמיהם לנדבה: כיון דאישתני. ליכא הכא זבח רשעים תועבה: ולא בהמת בכור ומעשר. שאם היו בה בכורות או מעשר בהמה שהוא של ישראל וחלבו ודמו קרב אין מחרימין אותו עמה דלא מיקרי בהמתה: שלל שמים הוא. ומשללה נפקא: אלא בבעלי מומים. שאין בהם חלק לגבוה אלא נאכלין לבעלים שללה נינהו אמאי אין מחרימין אותן עמה: לעולם בבעלי מומין. ואפ״ה אין [ר]נשרפין עמה דדרשינן לקרא הכי בהמתה למי שנאכל לבעלים בתורת בהמתם יצאו אלו שיש להם שם לווי שאין נאכלים בתורת בהמתם שאין אומרין בהמת עיר הנדחת אלא בהמת בכור ומעשר של עיר הנדחת: ופליגא. הא דרבינא אדשמואל דאמר שמואל עלה דהא מילתא דר״ש כי הוה קשיא לן במאי עסקינן הוי מתרץ הכי הכל קרב והכל נפדה: מאי קאמר ה״ק. כל שהוא קרב לגבוה כשהוא תם וכשהוא בעל מום צריך פדייה כגון שאר קדשים קלים חוץ ממעשר בהמה ובכור הנהו משללה נפקא דאין מחרימין אותם עמה דהואיל וצריכי פדייה במומן שלל שמים קרינן ביה ופליג עליה דת״ק דאמר קדשים קלים ממון בעלים הוא: וכל שקרב כשהוא תם ואינו נפדה כשהוא בעל מום. אלא נאכל לבעלים כגון בכור ומעשר ההוא לאו שלל שמים מקרו ואפילו בתמותן ולא מצי למפרך והא בתמותן שלל שמים הוא שהרי נאכל במומו והלכך אצטריך בהמתה למעוטי בכור ומעשר תמימים דמשללה ליכא למעוטינהו והיינו פליגא דאיהו מוקי לה אפילו בתמימים דקסבר בכור ומעשר בעלי מומין בהמתה קרינא ביה ובסייף: תרומה ביד ישראל. שעדיין לא נתנה לכהן דאפילו אותו ישראל רשע הוא תרומה שבידו אינה נשרפת עם שאר שללה דהא לאו דידיה הוא דשמא היה נתנה לכהן צדיק שבחוצה לה הלכך אינה נשרפת דהיינו כפקדון דעיר אחרת ואתנהו בגוה דאמר לעיל דמותרין ונהי דבאכילה לא שרינא לה דשמא היה נתנה לכהן רשע שבתוכה הלכך ירקבו אבל תרומה ביד כהן דממוניה הוא תשרף: וקתני יגנזו. אע״ג דממוניה הוא לא אמר תשרף: אלא תרומה ביד כהן. דממוניה הוא ולא מזלזלינן בה כולי האי הואיל וקדש הוא: לכהן שבעיר אחרת. כלומר לכהן שלא הודח עמהן: אבל בגבולין. שאין לה היתר אכילה אלא בפדייה ד״ה פטורה מן החלה דממון גבוה הוא ל״א אבל בגבולין דאין לה היתר אכילה בשעת חיוב חלה דהיינו בשעת גלגול העיסה לא קרינא ביה ראשית עריסותיכם (במדבר טו) ואפילו פדאה לאחר מיכן פטור מן החלה: י׳ דברים נאמרו בירושלים. בפ׳ מרובה (ב״ק פב:) חשיב להו: אלא בעיר אחרת ואסקו לגוה. שהיה אותו מעשר שני של אחד מבני עיר הנדחת והעלו אותו לירושלים קודם שהודחה ואח״כ הודחו אם כן אמאי יגנזו לשתרו נמי באכילה דהא קלטינהו מחיצות דהיינו חומה: אלא לאו בגבולין. ולא מטו ליה וקתני יגנזו ואינו יוצא לישרף בתמיה: ואם איתא. דבגבולין לד״ה ממון גבוה הוא לשתרי נמי באכילה אלא לאו ממון הדיוט הוא ונהי דבשריפה לא משום זילותא: לעולם דעיר הנדחת ואסקיה לגוה. ודקאמרת לשתרו נמי באכילה דהא קלטוהו מחיצות: הכא במאי עסקינן כשנטמא. דלאו בר אכולי בטומאה הוא דכתיב (דברים כו) לא בערתי ממנו בטמא ולקמן פריך מאי איריא עיר הנדחת אפילו בחוצה לה: ואפילו בירושלים. לאחר שנכנס ואע״ג דדרשינן (שם יד) כי ירחק ממך המקום וצרת הכסף בידך ברחוק מקום אתה פודה וצר ולא בקרוב מקום: ואין שאת אלא אכילה. וה״ק קרא כי ירחק ממך המקום או כי לא תוכל לאוכלו שנטמא וצרת הכסף בידך: בלקוח. שכבר הוציאה בהוצאה לכסף מעשר ונתנוהו ביין ושכר ובשר ונטמא אותו לקוח דההוא לית ליה פדייה וכי קאמר ר״א במע״ש גופיה שהעלה פירות מע״ש לירושלים ונטמאו: וליפרקיה

ליקוטי רש״י

היו בה קדשים. בעיר הנדחת אינן נשרפין עם שללה דכתיב (דברים יג) שללה ולא שלל שמים ומיהו מיקרב לא קרבו משום דכתיב (משלי כא) זבח רשעים תועבה ואם קדשי מזבח הן ואפילו עולות ושלמים נדבה ימותו. קדשי בדק הבית יפדו. כשאר בדק הבית והפודה אותם יאכלם שהרי לא נאסרו דלאו דידהו הוו [לעיל מז.]. קדשים שחייב באחריותן. אמר הרי עלי עולה והפרישה והוממה ומכרה. ושאינו חייב באחריותן כגון דאמר הרי זו [ב״מ נו:]. אם קיבלם בעליו עליו באחריות כגון דאמר הרי עלי עולה והפריש זו [ב״ק עא:]. ממון בעלים הן. כגון אמר הרי עלי עולה והפריש בהמה לנדרו וכו׳ דרעהו קרינן ביה דדבר הגורם לממון לרבי שמעון כממון דמי [שבועות מב:]. ושור רעהו קרינן ביה [ב״ק יב:]. בבעלי מומין שללה נינהו. היינו בהמתה דכהן אוכל את הבכור וישראל את המעשר ואין לגבוה חלק בהן [תמורה ח.]. דברי ר׳ מאיר. דאמר בפרק שני דקדושין (נד:) מעשר ממון גבוה הוא. פטורה מן החלה כדמפרש דעריסותיכם כתיב ולא של גבוה [פסחים לז:]. פטורה מן החלה. דכתיב עריסותיכם והאי דגבוה היא ואף על גב דאיכא היתר אכילה כיון דלית בה דין שאר ממון לאו דידיה הוא [סוכה לה.]. הא קלטוהו מחיצות. מעשר שני בירושלים הואיל ואינו נאכל בכל מושבות מעתה משהביאו לירושלים שוב אינו יכול לחלל לאכול בחוץ כדאמרינן במסכת מכות (כ.) מחילה לקלוט מדרבנן דמשקלטוהו מחילות שוב אינו נפדה. ר׳ אלעזר. דאם נטמא פודין אותו ואוכלין אותו בכל מקום. שאתו. כשלא תוכל לאוכלו כגון זה שניטמא ונתת בכסף [פסחים לו:]. אפילו בירושלים. שאין מעשר טהור נפדה שם דכתיב (דברים יד) כי ירחק ממך [וגו׳] ונתת בכסף ולא כשהיה בירושלים [ב״מ נג:]. אין מוכרין מעשר שני בירושלים, ואפילו לאוכלו שם בקדושה דכי ירבה ממך הדרך ונתתה בכסף כתיב (דברים יד) [פסחים עה:]. שפודין אותו אפילו בירושלים. דאי בעי פריק ואפילו בירושלים דאע״ג דמעשר שני טהור אינו נפדה בירושלים דכתיב כי ירחק ממך ונתת בכסף בריחוק מקום אתה פודה ולא בקירוב מקום (קדושין דף נו). ואין שאת אלא אכילה. והכי קאמר קרא כי ירחק ממך שיהא מעשר טהור חוץ לירושלים או אפילו הוא בירושלים אלא שאי אתה יכול לאוכלו שנטמא ונתת בכסף [מכות יט.]. בלקוח. מעשר זה ולא הוא עצמו היה מעשר אלא לצרכי סעודה שלקח בירושלים בכסף מעשר [ב״מ שם].

מסורת הש״ס

א) לעיל מז. [תוספ׳ פי״ד], ב) [תמורה ח. ע״ש], ג) [ב״מ נו.], ד) [ב״ק יג: וש״נ], ה) [גי׳ רש״י ירעו וכצ״ל], ו) [לפי גירסת רש״י דלעיל צ״ל ירעו], ז) [צ״ל בהמתה], ח) [תמורה ח. ע״ש], ט) [צ״ל בהמתה], י) [צ״ל בהמתה], כ) [בתוס׳ דבכורות דף לא. ד״ה חוץ וכו׳ משמע דגרסי הכא בסוגיא כמו דסיים הש״ס בתמורה ח. דתנן כל פסולי המוקדשין נמכרין באטליז חוץ מן הבכור והמעשר ע״ש אבל מפירש״י דהכא ד״ה לעולם בבעלי מומין וכו׳ מוכח דלא גרים להא דתנן כו׳ ומשום הכי פירש״י הכא יצאו אלו שיש להם שם לויי ורבינא הוא דמשני לה הכי כאן אבל בתמורה ח. סתמא דש״ס מייתי להא דתנן כל פסולי וכו׳ ולא ס״ל כרבינא בפי׳ הזה], ל) א״ז משנה אלא ברייתא ועיין רש״ל, מ) סוכה לה: פסחים לח. [עי׳ חולין פז: תוס׳ ד״ה תנן התם], נ) [קידושין כד. וש״נ], ס) [עי׳ תוס׳ קידושין נג: ד״ה איהו ותוס׳ בכורות ט: ד״ה ותנן ועי׳ היטב תוס׳ סוכה לה. סד״ה לפי], ע) ב״ק פב., פ) ב״מ נג. פסחי׳ לו: מכות יט:, צ) [צ״ל מאי], ק) [צ״ל אדתני], ר) נ״א נהרגין.

הגהות הב״ח

(א) גמ׳ ת״ר היו בה קדשים קדשי מזבח כצ״ל ותיבת קדשי נמחק: (ב) רש״י ד״ה ואליבא דר׳ יוסי וכו׳ קדשי קדשים ירעו כצ״ל ותיבת אמאי נמחק:

גליון הש״ס

גמ׳ ומי שנאכל בתורת בהמתך. עי׳ זבחים דף עה ע״ב תוס׳ ד״ה התפיס:

תורה אור השלם

א) זֶבַח רְשָׁעִים תּוֹעֵבָה אַף כִּי בְזִמָּה יְבִיאֶנּוּ: [משלי כא, כז]

ב) וְכִי יִרְבֶּה מִמְּךָ הַדֶּרֶךְ כִּי לֹא תוּכַל שְׂאֵתוֹ כִּי יִרְחַק מִמְּךָ הַמָּקוֹם אֲשֶׁר יִבְחַר יְיָ אֱלֹהֶיךָ לָשׂוּם שְׁמוֹ שָׁם כִּי יְבָרֶכְךָ יְיָ אֱלֹהֶיךָ: [דברים יד, כד]

ג) וַיִּשָּׂא מַשְׂאֹת מֵאֵת פָּנָיו אֲלֵהֶם וַתֵּרֶב מַשְׂאַת בִּנְיָמִן מִמַּשְׂאֹת כֻּלָּם חָמֵשׁ יָדוֹת וַיִּשְׁתּוּ וַיִּשְׁכְּרוּ עִמּוֹ: [בראשית מג, לד]

The Mishnah stated:

וְהַהֶקְדֵּשׁוֹת שֶׁבָּהּ יִפָּדוּ כו׳ – THE CONSECRATED OBJECTS IN [THE CITY] SHOULD BE REDEEMED, etc. [the *terumos* should be left to rot, and the *maaser sheni* and holy scriptures should be hidden away].

The Gemara cites a Baraisa that elaborates this ruling of the Mishnah:

תָּנוּ רַבָּנָן – **The Rabbis taught in a Baraisa:** הָיוּ בָהּ (קדשי) קֳדָשִׁים – IF THERE WERE CONSECRATED ITEMS IN [THE SUBVERTED CITY], קָדְשֵׁי מִזְבֵּחַ יָמוּתוּ – THE ITEMS CONSECRATED FOR THE ALTAR, i.e. animals designated as sacrifices, SHOULD DIE;[1] קָדְשֵׁי בֶּדֶק הַבַּיִת יִפָּדוּ – THE ITEMS CONSECRATED FOR THE MAINTENANCE OF THE TEMPLE SHOULD BE REDEEMED;[2] וּתְרוּמוֹת יִרָקְבוּ – THE *TERUMAH* PORTIONS SHOULD be left to ROT; וּמַעֲשֵׂר שֵׁנִי וְכִתְבֵי הַקֹּדֶשׁ יִגָּנְזוּ – AND THE *MAASER SHENI* AND HOLY SCRIPTURES SHOULD BE HIDDEN AWAY.[3] רַבִּי שִׁמְעוֹן אוֹמֵר – R' SHIMON SAYS: ,,בְּהֶמְתָּהּ" וְלֹא בֶּהֱמַת בְּכוֹר וּמַעֲשֵׂר – When the Torah states:[4] *Destroy it and everything that is in it, as well as* ITS ANIMALS, it implies: BUT NOT *BECHOR* OR *MAASER* ANIMALS;[5] ,,שְׁלָלָהּ" פְּרָט לְכֶסֶף הֶקְדֵּשׁ וְכֶסֶף מַעֲשֵׂר – when the Torah states:[6] *and all* ITS BOOTY, IT EXCLUDES CONSECRATED MONEY AND *MAASER* MONEY.[7]

The Gemara examines the opinion of the Tanna Kamma of the Baraisa:

אָמַר מַר – **The master said** in the Baraisa: הָיוּ בָהּ (קדשי) קֳדָשִׁים קָדְשֵׁי מִזְבֵּחַ יָמוּתוּ – IF THERE WERE CONSECRATED ITEMS IN [THE SUBVERTED CITY], THE ITEMS CONSECRATED FOR THE ALTAR SHOULD DIE.

The Gemara asks:

וְאַמַּאי יָמוּתוּ – **Now why should they die,** i.e. why should we cause their deaths? **יִרְעוּ עַד שֶׁיִּסְתָּאֲבוּ** – **Let them** be left to **graze until they develop a blemish,** **וְיִמָּכְרוּ** – **whereupon they should be sold,** **וְיִפְּלוּ דְמֵיהֶן לִנְדָבָה** – **and their proceeds should go for voluntary offerings.**[8] – ? –

The Gemara offers two explanations:

רַבִּי יוֹחָנָן אָמַר – **R' Yochanan says:** ,,זֶבַח רְשָׁעִים תּוֹעֵבָה" – The reason we do not do this is because Scripture states: ***The sacrifice of the wicked is an abomination.***[9] Thus, even if the offering were to become blemished and be redeemed, the redemption money could not be used for another offering. **רֵישׁ לָקִישׁ אָמַר** – **Reish Lakish says:** **מָמוֹן בְּעָלִים הוּא** – The reason we do not do this is because **[the offering]** of which the Baraisa speaks **is** considered **the property of** its **owner** (the person who consecrated

NOTES

1. [We do not actually kill them, but we bring about their death in the manner described below.] They are not killed outright along with the rest of the city's animals because, having been consecrated, they no longer belong to the inhabitants of the city but to "Heaven"; thus, they are not considered שְׁלָלָהּ, the city's "booty." Nevertheless, these animals cannot be offered in the Temple, because it is repugnant to offer on the Altar the sacrifices of these wicked idolaters [as the Gemara will explain below]. Therefore, the only appropriate course of action is to bring about the animals' death indirectly by resorting to the method used for certain criminals (above, 81b): Lock them in a cell and feed them barley until their stomachs burst (*Rashi;* cf. *Rashi, Kiddushin* 55b ד״ה והיא מתה, who explains that the animals are merely locked in a room until they expire; see *Rashash*). [The animals cannot be simply turned loose to roam, because in the course of time they would very likely be used in violation of the law. They must therefore be eliminated (see *Bechoros* 53a).]

[*Rashi's* explanation follows the view of R' Yochanan, which the Gemara will cite below. Reish Lakish will explain this ruling differently.

Rashi gives *olah* and *asham* as examples of the Baraisa's ruling that the sacrificial animals of an *ir hanidachas* are put to death by indirect means. In truth, the same would be true for a *chatas*. However, there is no novelty to this ruling in the case of a *chatas*, since any *chatas* whose owner has died (חַטָּאת שֶׁמֵּתוּ בְעָלֶיהָ) is subject to this fate, quite apart from the law of *ir hanidachas*, as the Gemara will state below. Thus, the novelty of the Baraisa's ruling is that if sacrificial offerings are found in an *ir hanidachas,* we bring about the deaths *even* of an *olah* and *asham,* which would otherwise be sacrificed or used to purchase sacrifices after the deaths of their owners (see note 8).]

2. I.e. these items are treated like any other items consecrated to the Temple treasury – they are sold and the proceeds are used for the repair of the Temple. The Baraisa's point is that these consecrated items are not subject to destruction (*Rashi* to Mishnah). [Thus, when our Mishnah states that consecrated objects are to be redeemed, it refers to items consecrated for Temple maintenance (see 111b note 37).]

[The term בֶּדֶק הַבַּיִת means literally: the cracks of the House [i.e. the Temple] (see *Rashi* and *Radak* to *II Kings* 12:6). Money donated to the general Temple treasury was referred to by this name because it was used for the repair and maintenance of the Temple.]

3. See 111b notes 38 and 39.

4. *Deuteronomy* 13:16.

5. If there are *bechor* or *maaser* animals belonging to the inhabitants of an *ir hanidachas*, they are not destroyed along with the city because they are not considered *its animals* (*Rashi* below ד״ה ולא בהמת בכור ומעשר). What R' Shimon means to teach by this [and the point of his dispute with the Tanna Kamma] will be explained by the Gemara below (*Rashi*).

[A *bechor* in this context is a firstborn male sheep, goat, or ox. The Torah assigns these firstborn animals a sacred status. They must be given as a gift to a Kohen, who then offers them (if unblemished) as a sacrifice in the Temple and eats their meat. (If they are blemished, the Kohen may slaughter them and their meat may be eaten anywhere.) *Maaser* here refers to the animal tithe (מַעֲשַׂר בְּהֵמָה). The calves, kids and lambs born to one's herds and flocks each year must be gathered into a pen and made to pass through an opening one at a time. Every tenth animal is designated *maaser*. A *maaser* animal is brought by its owner as an offering in the Temple, where its blood and fats are offered upon the Altar and its meat is his to eat.]

6. *Deuteronomy* 13:17.

7. I.e. neither consecrated money [money consecrated for Temple maintenance] nor *maaser sheni* money are destroyed as property of an *ir hanidachas.* R' Shimon's statement regarding consecrated money does not dispute anything said by the Tanna Kamma. R' Shimon's point of contention is in regard to *maaser* money. The Tanna Kamma rules that *maaser sheni* is hidden away and not used. Its redemption money would accordingly be treated the same way. R' Shimon disputes this and rules that *maaser* money [and so too *maaser sheni* itself] is not subject to the law of the *ir hanidachas*, for much the same reason the Gemara will give below for R' Shimon's exclusion of the *bechor* (*Chidushei HaRan;* see *Margaliyos HaYam*).

8. Once a consecrated animal becomes (permanently) blemished and no longer fit for the Altar, it may be redeemed. The sanctity of the animal is thereby transferred to the money, allowing the redeemed animal to be slaughtered for meat. The redemption money is then used to purchase another animal, and the sanctity is thereby transferred from the money to the newly purchased animal. That animal is then offered as a sacrifice.

In the case at hand, although it would be improper to offer on the Altar animals consecrated by the wicked inhabitants of the *ir hanidachas* (as explained in note 1), that does not necessitate having them die. Why not let the animals graze until they develop a permanent blemish and then redeem them and use the money to buy voluntary *olah* offerings? [If the original offerings were *olos,* the redemption money would be used to buy new *olah* offerings. If the original offerings were *ashamos*, the redemption money would be used for voluntary communal *olos*; these are offered on the Altar when it is otherwise idle (see Mishnah, *Shekalim* 6:6). This is based on a special law that any money remaining from an *asham* that is no longer needed (such as in this case, where the owners have been executed) is used to purchase voluntary communal *olah* offerings.] Thus, at least in these cases the Baraisa should not require that the animals be left to die (see *Yad Ramah*).

9. *Proverbs* 21:27. Since the offering belonged to an idolater, even the money received through its sale is abhorred by God and becomes forbidden [to use for another offering] (*Rashi;* see also *Chidushei HaRan*). Thus, the only option is to bring about the death of the animal (see above, note 1).

והההקדשות שבה יפדו כו': [א] ת"ר [א] היו בה (א) (קדשי) קדשים קדשי מזבח ימותו קדשי בדק הבית יפדו ותרומות ירקבו ומעשר שני וכתבי הקדש יגנזו [ב] ר"ש אומר בהמתה ולא בהמת בכור ומעשר שללה פרט לכסף הקדש וכסף מעשר אמר מר היו בה (קדשי) קדשים קדשי מזבח ימותו ואמאי ימותו ירעו עד שיסתאבו וימכרו ויפלו דמיהן לנדבה ר' יוחנן אמר [א] [ב] זבח רשעים תועבה ר"ל אמר ממון בעלים הוא והכא בקדשים שחייב באחריותן [ג] ור"ש היא דאמר ממון בעלים הוא הא מדסיפא ר"ש היא רישא לאו ר"ש בקדשים קלים ואליבא דרבי יוסי הגלילי [ד] דאמר קדשים קלים ממון בעלים אבל קדשי קדשים מאי [ה] יפדו אדתני סיפא קדשי בדק הבית יפדו ליפלוג וליתני בדידה בד"א בקדשים קלים אבל קדשי קדשים [ו] יפדו כיון דאיכא חטאת שמתו בעליה דלמיתה אזלא לא פסיקא ליה בשלמא ר' יוחנן לא אמר כר"ל דכתיב זבח רשעים תועבה אלא ר"ל מ"ט לא אמר כר' יוחנן אמר לך כי אמרינן זבח רשעים תועבה הני מילי היכא דאתנהו בעינייהו אבל הכא כיון דאישתני אישתני: ר"ש אומר [ז] בהמתך ולא בהמת בכור ומעשר: במאי עסקינן [ח] אילימא בתמימין שלל שמים הוא אלא בבעלי מומין [ג] שללה נינהו אמר רבינא לעולם בבעלי מומין [ד] ומי שנאכל בתורת [ט] בהמתך יצאו אלו שאין נאכלין בתורת [י] בהמתך אלא בתורת בכור ומעשר [כ] דשלל שמים נינהו ופליגא דשמואל דאמר שמואל הכל קרב והכל נפדה מאי קאמר ה"ק כל שקרב כשהוא תם ונפדה כשהוא בעל מום משלל אימעיט וכל שקרב כשהוא תם ואינו נפדה כשהוא בעל מום כגון בכור ומעשר מבהמה נפקא: תרומות ירקבו: אמר רב חסדא ל"ש אלא תרומה ביד ישראל אבל תרומה ביד כהן כיון דממוניה הוא תשרף מתיב רב יוסף מעשר שני וכתבי הקדש יגנזו והא מעשר שני ביד ישראל כתרומה ביד כהן דמי וקתני יגנזו אלא אי אתמר הכי אתמר אמר רב חסדא ל"ש אלא תרומה ביד כהן אבל תרומה ביד ישראל [ד] תנתן לכהן שבעיר אחרת [ל] תנן התם [מ] עיסה של מעשר שני פטורה מן החלה דברי ר"מ וחכמים [ה] מחייבין אמר רב חסדא מחלוקת [ו] במעשר שני בירושלים דר"מ סבר [נ] מעשר שני ממון גבוה הוא ורבנן סברי ממון הדיוט הוא אבל [ס] בגבולין דברי הכל פטור מתיב רב יוסף מעשר שני וכתבי הקדש יגנזו במאי עסקינן אילימא בירושלים מי הויא עיר הנדחת והתניא [ע] עשרה דברים נאמרו בירושלים וזו אחת מהן [ז] אינה נעשית עיר הנדחת ואלא בעיר אחרת ואסקוהו לגוה הא קלטוהו מחיצות אלא לאו בגבולין וקתני יגנזו לא לעולם דעיר אחרת ואסקוהו לגוה והכא במאי עסקינן שנטמא ולפרקיה [פ] דא"ר אלעזר [ח] מניין למעשר שני שנטמא שפודין אותו אפילו בירושלים ת"ל [ב] לא תוכל שאתו ואין שאת אלא אכילה שנאמר [ג] וישא משאת מאת פניו הכא במאי עסקינן בלקוח וליפרקיה

רש"י

היו בה קדשי מזבח. כגון עולות ואשמות של רשעים בתוכה נהי דלא קרינן בהו את כל בהמתה לפי חרב דהא לא בהמתה היא אלא בהמת שמים אלא מאיסותא הוא להקריב קרבנות של רשעים הללו שהודחו הלכך ימותו כונסין אותן לכיפה ומאכילין אותן שעורין עד שכריסן נבקעת דאפילו דמיהם אסור כדלקמן: שנאמר כליל לה' אלהיך ל"ג: ר"ש אומר וכו'. לקמן מפרש טעמא: זבח רשעים תועבה. ואפילו דמיהן אסורין: ור"ש הוא דאמר. בהזהב (ב"מ נו:) קדשים שחייב באחריותן ממון בעלים הוא ויש בהם אונאה הלכך לענין עיר הנדחת נמי ממון בעלים הוא ודיינינהו לפי חרב כשאר בהמות שבתוכה והלכך אסורין דמיהן בהנאה והאי דקאמר ימותו ולא אמר שיחרימו אותה עמהם משום כבוד שמים: ואליבא דרבי יוסי הגלילי דאמר. בפ"ק דב"ק (ד' יב:) ומעלה מעל בה' לרבות קדשים קלים שהם ממונו והואיל וממונו הם אסורים בהנאה דאפילו דמיהן בהמתם מיקרו אבל קדשי קדשים (ב) אמאי ירעו דהא ודאי הם עצמם אינם קרבים דזבח רשעים תועבה אלא ירעו עד שיסתאבו וימכרו ויפלו דמיהם לנדבה: אי הכי [ק] מדתני סיפא וכו'. דקא מפליג בין קדשי מזבח לקדשי בדק הבית: ליפלוג וליתני בדידה. בקדשי מזבח עצמן בין קדשים קלים לקדשי קדשים: דלמיתה אזלא. כדאמרינן (תמורה ד' טו.) חמש חטאות מתות: לא פסיקא ליה. למיתני קדשי קדשים דעיר הנדחת ירעו דכיון דמתו להם אותם רשעים אי איכא חטאות שהפרישו בחייהם אזלי למיתה דכל חטאות שמתו בעליהם מתות במסכת הוריות (ד' ו.) מפרש טעמא אבל שאר קדשי קדשים כגון אשמות שמתו בעליהם ירעו: דאיתנהו בעינייהו. דהן עצמן ודאי אינן קרבים משום זבח רשעים תועבה: אבל הכא. דאיכא למימר ירעו ויפלו דמיהם לנדבה: כיון דאישתני. ליכא הכא זבח רשעים תועבה: ולא בהמת בכור ומעשר. שאם היו בה בכורות או מעשר בהמה שהוא של ישראל וחלבו ודמו קרב אין מחרימין אותו עמה דלא מיקרי בהמתה: של שמים הוא. ומשללה נפקא: אלא בבעלי מומים. שאין בהם חלק לגבוה אלא נאכלין לבעלים שללה נינהו אמאי אין מחרימין אותן עמה: לעולם בבעלי מומין. ואפ"ה אין [ר] נשרפין עמה דדרשינן לקרא הכי בהמתה למי שנאכל לבעלים בתורת בהמתם יצאו אלו שיש להם שם לווי שאין נאכלים בתורת בהמתם שאין אומרין בהמת עיר הנדחת אלא בהמת בכור ומעשר של עיר הנדחת: ופליגא. הא דרבינא אדשמואל דאמר שמואל עלה דהא מילתא דר"ש כי הוה קשיא לן במאי עסקינן הוי מתרץ הכי הכל קרב והכל נפדה: מאי קאמר ה"ק. כל שהוא קרב לגבוה כשהוא תם וכשהוא בעל מום צריך פדייה כגון שאר קדשים קלים חוץ ממעשר בהמה ובכור הנהו משללה נפקא דאין מחרימין אותם עמה דהואיל וצריכי פדייה במומן שלל שמים קרינן ביה ופליג עליה דת"ק דאמר קדשים קלים ממון בעלים הוא: וכל שקרב כשהוא תם ואינו נפדה כשהוא בעל מום. אלא נאכל לבעלים כגון בכור ומעשר ההוא לאו שלל שמים מקרו ואפילו בתמותן ולא מצי למפרך והא בתמותן שלל שמים הוא שהרי נאכל במומו והלכך אצטריך בהמתה למעוטי בכור ומעשר תמימים דמשללה ליכא למעוטינהו והיינו פליגא דאיהו מוקי לה אפילו בתמימים דקסבר בכור ומעשר בעלי מומין בהמתה קרינא ביה ובסייף: תרומה ביד ישראל. שעדיין לא נתנה לכהן דאפילו אותו ישראל רשע הוא תרומה שבידו אינה נשרפת עם שאר שללה דהא לאו דידיה הוא דשמא היה נתנה לכהן צדיק שבחולה לה הלכך אינה נשרפת דהיינו כפקדון דעיר אחרת ואתנהו בגוה דאמר לעיל דמותרין ונהי דבאכילה לא שרינא לה דשמא היה נותנה לכהן רשע שבתוכה הלכך ירקבו אבל תרומה ביד כהן דממוניה הוא תשרף: וקתני יגנזו. אע"ג דממוניה הוא לא אמר תשרף: אלא תרומה ביד כהן. דממוניה הוא ולא מזלזלינן בה כולי האי הואיל וקדש הוא: לכהן שבעיר אחרת. כלומר לכהן שלא הודח עמהן: אבל בגבולין. שאין לה היתר אכילה אלא בפדייה ד"ה פטורה מן החלה דממון גבוה הוא לי"א אבל בגבולין דאין לה היתר אכילה בשעת חיוב חלה דהיינו בשעת גלגול העיסה לא קרינא ביה ראשית עריסותיכם (במדבר טו) ואפילו פדאה לאחר מיכן פטור מן החלה: י' דברים נאמרו בירושלים. בפ' מרובה (ב"ק פב:) חשיב להו: אלא בעיר אחרת ואסקו לגוה. שהיה אותו מעשר שני של אחד מבני עיר הנדחת והעלו אותו לירושלים קודם שהודחה ואח"כ הודחו אם כן אמאי יגנזו לשתרו נמי באכילה דהא קלטינהו מחילות דהיינו חומה: אלא לאו בגבולין. ולא מטו ליה וקתני יגנזו ואינו יוצא לישרף בתמיה: ואם איתא. דבגבולין לד"ה ממון גבוה הוא לשתרי נמי באכילה אלא לאו ממון הדיוט הוא ונהי דבשריפה לא משום זילותא: לעולם דעיר הנדחת ואסקיה לגוה. ודקאמרת לשתרו נמי באכילה דהא קלטוהו מחילות: הכא במאי עסקינן בשנטמא. דלאו בר אכולי בטומאה הוא דכתיב (דברים כו) לא בערתי ממנו בטמא ולקמן פריך מאי איריא עיר הנדחת אפילו בחולה לה: ואפילו בירושלים. לאחר שנכנס ואע"ג דדרשינן (שם יד) כי ירחק ממך המקום ולרת הכסף בידך ברחוק מקום אתה פודה ולר ולא בקרוב מקום: ואין שאת אלא אכילה. וה"ק קרא כי ירחק ממך המקום או כי לא תוכל לאוכלו שנטמא ולרת הכסף בידך: בלקוח. שכבר הוציאה בהוצאה לכסף מעשר ונתנוהו ביין ושכר ובשר ונטמא אותו לקוח דההוא לית ליה פדייה וכי קאמר ר"א במע"ש גופיה שהעלה פירות מע"ש לירושלים ונטמאו: וליפרקיה

עין משפט נר מצוה

נה א ב ג ד מיי' פ"ד מהל' עכו"ס הלכה יג סמג עשין טו:
נו ה ו מיי' פ"ו מהל' בכורים הלכה ד:
נז ז מיי' פ"ז מהל' בית הבחירה הלכה יד ופ"ד מהל' עכו"ס הלכה ד:
נח ח מיי' פ"ב מהל' מעשר שני ונטע רבעי הלכה ח סמג לאוין קלו:

ליקוטי רש"י

היו בה קדשים. בעיר הנדחת אינן נשרפין עם שללה דכתיב (דברים יג) שללה ולא שלל שמים ומיהו מיקרב לא קרבו משום דכתיב (משלי כא) זבח רשעים תועבה ואם קדשי מזבח הן ואפילו עולות ושלמים נדבה ימותו. קדשי בדק הבית יפדו. כשאר בדק הבית והפודה אותם יאכלם שהרי לא נאסרו דלאו דידהו הוו [לעיל מז.]. קדשים שחייב באחריותן. אמר הרי עלי עולה והפרישה והוממה ומכרה. ושאינו חייב באחריותן כגון דאמר הרי זו [ב"מ נו:]. אם קיבלם בעליו עליו באחריות כגון דאמר הרי עלי עולה והפריש זו [ב"ק עא:]. ממון בעלים הן. כגון אמר הרי עלי עולה והפריש בהמה לנדרו וכו' דרעהו קרינן ביה דדבר הגורם לממון לרבי שמעון כממון דמי [שבועות מב:]. ושור רעהו קרינן ביה [ב"ק יב:]. בבעלי מומין שללה נינהו. היינו בהמתה דכהן אוכל את הבכור וישראל את המעשר ואין לגבוה חלק בהן [תמורה ח.]. דברי ר' מאיר. דאמר בפרק שני דקדושין (נד:) מעשר ממון גבוה הוא. פטורה מן החלה. כדמפרש דעריסותיכם כתיב ולא של גבוה [פסחים לז:]. פטורה מן החלה. דכתיב עריסותיכם והאי דגבוה היא ואף על גב דאיכא היתר אכילה כיון דלית בה דין שאר ממון לאו דידיה הוא [סוכה לה.]. הא קלטוהו מחיצות. מעשר שני בירושלים הואיל ואינו נאכל בכל מושבות מעתה משהביאו לירושלים שוב אינו יכול לחלל לאכול בחוץ כדאמרינן במסכת מכות (כ.) מחילה לקלוט מדרבנן דמשקלטוהו מחילות שוב אינו נפדה. ר' אלעזר. דאם נטמא פודין אותו ואוכלין אותו בכל מקום. שאתו. כשלא תוכל לאוכלו כגון זה שניטמא ונתת בכסף [פסחים לו:]. אפילו בירושלים. שאין מעשר טהור נפדה שם דכתיב (דברים יד) כי ירחק ממך [וגו'] ונתת בכסף ולא כשהיה בירושלים [ב"מ נג:]. אין מוכרין מעשר שני בירושלים, ואפילו לאוכלו שם בקדושה דכי ירבה ממך הדרך ונתתה בכסף כתיב (דברים יד) [פסחים עה:]. שפודין אותו אפילו בירושלים. דאי בעי פריק ואפילו בירושלים דאע"ג דמעשר שני טהור אינו נפדה בירושלים דכתיב כי ירחק ממך ונתת בכסף בריחוק מקום אתה פודה ולא בקירוב מקום (קדושין דף נו). ואין שאת אלא אכילה. והכי קאמר קרא כי ירחק ממך שיהא מעשר טהור חוץ לירושלים או אפילו הוא בירושלים אלא שאי אתה יכול לאוכלו שנטמא ונתת בכסף [מכות יט.]. בלקוח. מעשר זה ולא הוא עצמו היה מעשר אלא לרכי סעודה שלקח בירושלים בכסף מעשר [ב"מ שם].

מסורת הש"ס

א) לעיל מז. [תוספ' פי"ד], ב) [תמורה ח. ע"ש], ג) [ב"מ נו.], ד) [ב"ק יב: וש"נ], ה) [גי' רש"י ירעו וכצ"ל], ו) [לפי גירסת רש"י דלעיל צ"ל ירעו], ז) [צ"ל בהמתה], ח) [תמורה ח. ע"ש], ט) [צ"ל בהמתה], י) [צ"ל בהמתה], כ) [בתוס' דבכורות דף לא. ד"ה חוץ וכו' משמע דגרסי הכא בסוגיא כמו דסיים הש"ס בתמורה ח. דתנן כל פסולי המוקדשין נמכרין באטליז חוץ מן הבכור והמעשר ע"ש אבל מפירש"י דהכא ד"ה לעולם בבעלי מומין וכו' מוכח דלא גרים להא דתנן כו' ומשום הכי פירש"י הכא יצאו אלו שיש להם שם לווי ורבינא הוא דמשני לה הכי כאן אבל בתמורה ח. סתמא דש"ס מייתי להא דתנן כל פסולי וכו' ולא ס"ל כרבינא בפי' הזה], ל) ח"ז משנה אלא ברייתא ועיין רש"ל, מ) סוכה לה: פסחים לח. [עי' חולין פז: תוס' ד"ה תנן התם], נ) [קידושין כד. וש"נ], ס) [עי' תוס' קידושין נג: ד"ה איהו ותוס' בכורות ט: ד"ה ותנן ועי' היטב תוס' סוכה לה. סד"ה לפי], ע) ב"ק פב., פ) ב"מ נג. פסחי' לו: מכות יט:, צ) [צ"ל מאי], ק) [צ"ל אדתני], ר) נ"א נהרגין.

הגהות הב"ח

(א) גמ' ת"ר היו בה קדשים קדשי מזבח כצ"ל ותיבת קדשי נמחק: (ב) רש"י ד"ה ואליבא דר' יוסי וכו' קדשי קדשים ירעו כצ"ל ותיבת אמאי נמחק:

גליון הש"ס

גמ' ומי שנאכל בתורת בהמתך. עי' זבחים דף עה ע"ב תוס' ד"ה התפיס:

תורה אור השלם

א) זֶבַח רְשָׁעִים תּוֹעֵבָה אַף כִּי בְזִמָּה יְבִיאֶנּוּ: [משלי כא, כז]

ב) וְכִי יִרְבֶּה מִמְּךָ הַדֶּרֶךְ כִּי לֹא תוּכַל שְׂאֵתוֹ כִּי יִרְחַק מִמְּךָ הַמָּקוֹם אֲשֶׁר יִבְחַר יְיָ אֱלֹהֶיךָ לָשׂוּם שְׁמוֹ שָׁם כִּי יְבָרֶכְךָ יְיָ אֱלֹהֶיךָ: [דברים יד, כד]

ג) וַיִּשָּׂא מַשְׂאֹת מֵאֵת פָּנָיו אֲלֵהֶם וַתֵּרֶב מַשְׂאַת בִּנְיָמִן מִמַּשְׂאֹת כֻּלָּם חָמֵשׁ יָדוֹת וַיִּשְׁתּוּ וַיִּשְׁכְּרוּ עִמּוֹ: [בראשית מג, לד]

it), not the property of Heaven. It is therefore subject to the law of the *ir hanidachas*. Why is the offering considered the property of the consecrator? וְהָכָא בְּקָדָשִׁים שֶׁחַיָּיב בְּאַחֲרָיוּתָן – **For here** we are dealing **with consecrated items for which [the owner] bears responsibility,** וְרַבִּי שִׁמְעוֹן הִיא – **and [this Baraisa] is** following the view of **R' Shimon** דְּאָמַר מָמוֹן בְּעָלִים הוּא – **who says that** where one is responsible for the loss of his sacrificial animal, **it is** considered **the property of the owner.**[10]

The Gemara challenges the attribution of the Tanna Kamma's ruling to R' Shimon:

הָא מִדְּסֵיפָא רַבִּי שִׁמְעוֹן הִיא – **But since the latter part** of the Baraisa **is** stated explicitly in the name of **R' Shimon,** רֵישָׁא לָאו רַבִּי שִׁמְעוֹן – it seems clear that **the first part** of the Baraisa **is not** being stated by **R' Shimon!** How then can we ascribe the Baraisa's opening ruling specifically to R' Shimon?

The Gemara concedes that the Tanna Kamma of the Baraisa cannot be R' Shimon, and therefore offers another interpretation of Reish Lakish's statement that the consecrated animals of the Baraisa are considered the property of their owners:

בְּקָדָשִׁים קַלִּים – Rather, we are dealing here **with *kodashim kalim*** offerings,[11] וְאַלִּיבָּא דְרַבִּי יוֹסֵי הַגְּלִילִי – **and** the Baraisa is **following** the view of **R' Yose HaGlili,** דְּאָמַר קָדָשִׁים קַלִּים מָמוֹן בְּעָלִים – **who said that *kodashim kalim*** offerings **are the property of** their **owners,** i.e. the persons who consecrated them.[12]

The Gemara questions this explanation based on its implication: אֲבָל קָדְשֵׁי קָדָשִׁים מַאי יִפָּדוּ – **But what** would be the law for ***kodshei kodashim*** according to this explanation? **Would they be redeemed?**[13] This would certainly follow from the previous explanation.[14] אַדְּתָנֵי סֵיפָא קָדְשֵׁי בֶּדֶק הַבַּיִת יִפָּדוּ – But if so, then **instead of the second ruling** of the Baraisa **teaching** that ITEMS CONSECRATED FOR THE MAINTENANCE OF THE TEMPLE SHOULD BE REDEEMED, לִיפְלוֹג וְלִיתְנֵי בְּדִידָהּ – **let [the Baraisa] differentiate** between the consecrated things that are put to death and those that are redeemed **and teach** this difference **in** regard to **that** case **itself** (i.e. in the case of animals consecrated for the Altar), by stating: בַּמֶּה דְבָרִים אֲמוּרִים – **"When is it said** that animals consecrated for the Altar should die, בְּקָדָשִׁים קַלִּים – only **in** the case of animals that are ***kodashim kalim.*** אֲבָל קָדְשֵׁי קָדָשִׁים יִפָּדוּ – **But** animals that are ***kodshei kodashim***[15] **should be redeemed."** Why did the Baraisa shift to the case of consecrations for Temple maintenance to teach that some consecrated items of a subverted city are redeemed?[16]

The Gemara answers:

כֵּיוָן דְּאִיכָּא חַטָּאת שֶׁמֵּתוּ בְּעָלֶיהָ – **Since** in the category of *kodshei kodashim* belonging to members of a subverted city **there is** also **the *chatas* whose owner has died,** דִּלְמִיתָה אָזְלָא – an animal **that goes to** its **death** and cannot be redeemed,[17] לֹא פְּסִיקָא לֵיהּ – **[the Tanna] could not make an absolute statement** to the

NOTES

10. If someone pledges to bring an offering with the words: הֲרֵי עָלַי, *It is hereby incumbent upon me . . .*, he becomes obligated to bring that type of offering. When he subsequently designates a specific animal to fulfill his pledge, he bears liability for that animal, because if that animal should be lost or die, he would have to provide another in its place to fulfill his pledge. Similarly, if one designates an animal to meet some sacrificial obligation (e.g. he committed a sin for which he has to bring an *asham*), he remains responsible for its loss, since he must fulfill his obligation regardless of what happens to this particular animal (*Yad Ramah*). [By contrast, if one consecrates a *specific* animal as a donated offering – without first declaring a personal obligation to give an offering – he is not obligated to make good its loss, because his pledge was only to give this *particular* animal, and this animal is no longer available for sacrifice.]

Now in *Bava Metzia* 56b, R' Shimon states that where a person is liable for the loss of his sacrificial animal, the animal is treated as his personal property even though it is consecrated (see also *Bava Kamma* 71b and *Ketzos HaChoshen* 386:7). As a result, if the animal develops a disqualifying blemish and is therefore sold, the sale is subject to the rules of אוֹנָאָה, *price fraud,* which would not be the case if the animal were considered the property of Heaven.

According to R' Shimon, therefore, since the consecrated animal is considered the property of its owner, if he is a resident of an *ir hanidachas*, the animal ought to be put to the sword along with the rest of the animals of the city. Indeed, this is what is done. The reason the Baraisa states יָמוּתוּ, *they should die* [a term that generally connotes death by indirect means], instead of יַחֲרִימוּ, *they should destroy it* [the Biblical term for killing the animals of an *ir hanidachas*], is out of respect to Heaven. Since the animal is consecrated, it would be demeaning to state explicitly that the animal is destroyed in the manner of an *ir hanidachas.* Thus, the Baraisa states merely יָמוּתוּ, *they should die*. In practice, however, the animal is killed outright (*Rashi* as explained by *Yad Ramah*; cf. *Chidushei HaRan*; see also *Minchas Chinuch* 464:35).

11. There are two classes of sacrificial offerings: *kodashim kalim* [literally: less-holy offerings] and *kodshei kodashim* [literally: most-holy offerings]. These two classes are distinguished by the stringency of their sacrificial rules. *Kodshei kodashim*, for example, can be eaten only within the Temple Courtyard, whereas *kodashim kalim* can be eaten anywhere within the walls of Jerusalem. The category of *kodashim kalim* comprises the *todah, shelamim, bechor, maaser* and *pesach* offerings.

12. Elsewhere (*Bava Kamma* 12b), R' Yose HaGlili says that one who swears falsely in regard to *kodashim kalim* is liable to the monetary penalty and *asham* offering decreed by the Torah for swearing falsely in regard to a monetary claim (see *Leviticus* 5:21). Although one who swears falsely regarding other types of consecrated property is not liable to the penalty and *asham* [because the verse in that passage speaks of *lying to one's fellow*], R' Yose HaGlili derives that *kodashim kalim,* though consecrated, are treated as the private property of their owner. Thus, if one swears falsely in denial of a claim regarding *kodashim kalim* (e.g. his fellow's claim that an animal of *kodashim kalim* held by the swearer actually belongs to the claimant), he is subject to the penalty delineated in that passage.

According to R' Yose HaGlili, if a *kodashim kalim* animal is owned by the resident of an *ir hanidachas*, it is classified as one of *its animals* and therefore becomes forbidden. Hence, even if the animal should become blemished and be sold, the proceeds would still be forbidden for benefit, like the animal itself (*Rashi*). It is to such animals that the Baraisa refers, according to Reish Lakish, when it states that sacrificial animals must die. Since they are the property of the *ir hanidachas*, they are killed by the sword (*Yad Ramah*; see note 10).

Accordingly, there is a fundamental difference between Reish Lakish's understanding of the Baraisa and R' Yochanan's. According to Reish Lakish, the animals are killed because they are the property of an *ir hanidachas* [they are therefore killed directly, not indirectly (*Rashi*)]. According to R' Yochanan, however, the animals are killed because they are disqualified sacrifices [they are therefore killed indirectly] (*Chidushei HaRan*).

13. I.e. left to graze until they develop a blemish and then be redeemed; see note 8.

14. Reish Lakish explained the Baraisa to be speaking of *kodashim kalim* when it ruled that animals consecrated for the Altar are killed. This clearly implies that *kodshei kodashim* are *not* killed. [This is because even R' Yose HaGlili agrees that *kodshei kodashim* are considered entirely the property of Heaven.] Although they themselves cannot be sacrificed – because they are the offerings of idolaters and "the sacrifices of the wicked are an abomination" (which even Reish Lakish agrees invalidates the original offering itself, as the Gemara will explain below) – nevertheless, we would allow them to graze, develop a blemish and redeem them, rather than destroy them (*Rashi*; see *Mishneh LaMelech, Hil. Shegagos* 3:7).

15. Such as the *olah* and *asham* offerings.

16. [By stating the rule of redemption only in regard to a different category of consecrated items, the Baraisa implies that everything in the category of animals consecrated for the Altar is put to death.]

17. A *Halachah LeMoshe MiSinai* teaches that there are five *chatas* offerings that are left to die [i.e. put to death indirectly]. One of these is a *chatas* whose owner has died (see *Temurah* 16a, 21a). Any *chatas* belonging to one of the guilty members of an *ir hanidachas* falls into this category, since all those who engaged in idolatry are executed.

והההקדשות שבה יפדו כו': ת"ר היו בה (קדשי) קדשים קדשי מזבח ימותו קדשי בדק הבית יפדו ותרומות ירקבו ומעשר שני וכתבי הקדש יגנזו ר"ש אומר בהמתה ולא בהמת בכור ומעשר שללה פרט לכסף הקדש וכסף מעשר אמר מר היו בה (קדשי) קדשים קדשי מזבח ימותו ואמאי ימותו ירעו עד שיסתאבו וימכרו ויפלו דמיהן לנדבה ר' יוחנן אמר זבח רשעים תועבה ר"ל אמר ממון בעלים הוא והכא בקדשים שחייב באחריותן ור"ש היא דאמר ממון בעלים הוא הא מדסיפא ר"ש היא רישא לאו ר"ש בקדשים קלים ואליבא דרבי יוסי הגלילי דאמר קדשים קלים ממון בעלים אבל קדשי קדשים מאי יפדו אדתני סיפא קדשי בדק הבית יפדו ליפלוג וליתני בדידה בד"א בקדשים קלים אבל קדשי קדשים יפדו כיון דאיכא חטאת שמתו בעליה דלמיתה אזלא לא פסיקא ליה בשלמא ר' יוחנן לא אמר כר"ל דכתיב זבח רשעים תועבה אלא ר"ל מ"ט לא אמר כר' יוחנן אמר לך כי אמרינן זבח רשעים תועבה הני מילי היכא דאתנהו בעינייהו אבל הכא כיון דאישתני אישתני: ר"ש אומר בהמתך ולא בהמת בכור ומעשר: במאי עסקינן אילימא בתמימין שלל שמים הוא אלא בבעלי מומין שללה נינהו אמר רבינא לעולם בבעלי מומין ומי שנאכל בתורת בהמתך יצאו אלו שאין נאכלין בתורת בהמתך אלא בתורת בכור ומעשר דשלל שמים נינהו ופליגא דשמואל דאמר שמואל הכל קרב והכל נפדה מאי קאמר ה"ק כל שקרב כשהוא תם ונפדה כשהוא בעל מום משלל אימעיט וכל שקרב כשהוא תם ואינו נפדה כשהוא בעל מום כגון בכור ומעשר מבהמה נפקא: תרומות ירקבו: אמר רב חסדא ל"ש אלא תרומה ביד ישראל אבל תרומה ביד כהן כיון דממוניה הוא תשרף מתיב רב יוסף מעשר שני וכתבי הקדש יגנזו והא מעשר שני ביד ישראל כתרומה ביד כהן דמי וקתני יגנזו אלא אי אתמר הכי אתמר אמר רב חסדא ל"ש אלא תרומה ביד כהן אבל תרומה ביד ישראל תנתן לכהן שבעיר אחרת תנן התם עיסה של מעשר שני פטורה מן החלה דברי ר"מ וחכמים מחייבין אמר רב חסדא מחלוקת במעשר שני בירושלים דר"מ סבר מעשר שני ממון גבוה הוא ורבנן סברי ממון הדיוט הוא אבל בגבולין דברי הכל פטור מתיב רב יוסף מעשר שני וכתבי הקדש יגנזו במאי עסקינן אילימא בירושלים מי הויא עיר הנדחת והתניא עשרה דברים נאמרו בירושלים וזו אחת מהן אינה נעשית עיר הנדחת ואלא בעיר אחרת ואסקוהו לגוה הא קלטוהו מחיצות אלא לאו בגבולין וקתני יגנזו לא לעולם דעיר אחרת ואסקוהו לגוה והכא במאי עסקינן שנטמא ולפרקיה דא"ר אלעזר מניין למעשר שני שנטמא שפודין אותו אפילו בירושלים ת"ל לא תוכל שאתו ואין שאת אלא אכילה שנאמר וישא משאת מאת פניו הכא במאי עסקינן בלקוח וליפרקיה

רש"י

היו בה קדשי מזבח. כגון עולות ואשמות של רשעים בתוכה נהי דלא קרינן בהו את כל בהמתה לפי חרב דהא לא בהמתה היא אלא בהמת שמים אלא מאיסותא הוא להקריב קרבנות של רשעים הללו שהודחו הלכך ימותו כונסין אותן לכיפה ומאכילין אותן שעורין עד שכריסן נבקעת דאפילו דמיהם אסור כדלקמן: שנאמר כליל לה' אלהיך ל"ג: ר"ש אומר וכו'. לקמן מפרש טעמא: זבח רשעים תועבה. ואפילו דמיהן אסורין: ור"ש הוא דאמר. בהזהב (ב"מ נו:) קדשים שחייב באחריותן ממון בעלים הוא ויש בהם אונאה הלכך לענין עיר הנדחת נמי ממון בעלים הוא ודיינינהו לפי חרב כשאר בהמות שבתוכה והלכך אסורין דמיהן בהנאה והאי דקאמר ימותו ולא אמר שיחרימו אותה עמהם משום כבוד שמים: ואליבא דרבי יוסי הגלילי דאמר. בפ"ק דב"ק (ד' יב:) ומעלה מעל בה' לרבות קדשים קלים שהם ממונו והואיל וממונו הם אסורים בהנאה דאפילו דמיהן בהמתם מיקרו אבל קדשי קדשים (ב) ל) אמאי ירעו דהא ודאי הם עצמם אינם קרבים דזבח רשעים תועבה אלא ירעו עד שיסתאבו וימכרו ויפלו דמיהם לנדבה: אי הכי ק) מדתני סיפא וכו'. דקא מפליג בין קדשי מזבח לקדשי בדק הבית: ליפלוג וליתני בדידה. בקדשי מזבח עצמן בין קדשים קלים לקדשי קדשים: דלמיתה אזלא. כדאמרינן (תמורה ד' טו.) חמש חטאות מתות: לא פסיקא ליה. למיתני קדשי קדשים דעיר הנדחת ירעו דכיון דמתו להם אותם רשעים אי איכא חטאות שהפרישו בחייהם אזלי למיתה דכל חטאות שמתו בעליהם מתות במסכת הוריות (ד' ו.) מפרש טעמא אבל שאר קדשי קדשים כגון אשמות שמתו בעליהם ירעו: דאיתנהו בעינייהו. דהן עצמן ודאי אינן קרבים משום זבח רשעים תועבה: אבל הכא. דאיכא למימר ירעו ויפלו דמיהם לנדבה: כיון דאישתני. ליכא הכא זבח רשעים תועבה: ולא בהמת בכור ומעשר. שאם היו בה בכורות או מעשר בהמה שהוא של ישראל וחלבו ודמו קרב אין מחרימין אותו עמה דלא מיקרי בהמתה: שלל שמים הוא. ומשללה נפקא: אלא בבעלי מומים. שאין בהם חלק לגבוה אלא נאכלין לבעלים שללה נינהו אמאי אין מחרימין אותן עמה: לעולם בבעלי מומין. ואפ"ה אין ר) נשרפין עמה דדרשינן לקרא הכי בהמתה למי שנאכל לבעלים בתורת בהמתם יצאו אלו שיש להם שם לווי שאין נאכלים בתורת בהמתם שאין אומרין בהמת עיר הנדחת אלא בהמת בכור ומעשר של עיר הנדחת: ופליגא. הא דרבינא אדשמואל דאמר שמואל עלה דהא מילתא דר"ש כי הוה קשיא לן במאי עסקינן הוי מתרץ הכי הכל קרב והכל נפדה: מאי קאמר ה"ק. כל שהוא קרב לגבוה כשהוא תם וכשהוא בעל מום צריך פדייה כגון שאר קדשים קלים חוץ ממעשר בהמה ובכור הנהו משללה נפקא דאין מחרימין אותם עמה דהואיל וצריכי פדייה במומן שלל שמים קרינן ביה ופליג עליה דת"ק דאמר קדשים קלים ממון בעלים הוא: וכל שקרב כשהוא תם ואינו נפדה כשהוא בעל מום. אלא נאכל לבעלים כגון בכור ומעשר ההוא לאו שלל שמים מקרו ואפילו בתמותן ולא מצי למפרך והא בתמותן שלל שמים הוא שהרי נאכל במומו והלכך אצטריך בהמתה למעוטי בכור ומעשר תמימים דמשללה ליכא למעוטינהו והיינו פליגא דאיהו מוקי לה אפילו בתמימים דקסבר בכור ומעשר בעלי מומין בהמתה קרינא ביה ובסייף: תרומה ביד ישראל. שעדיין לא נתנה לכהן דאפילו אותו ישראל רשע הוא תרומה שבידו אינה נשרפת עם שאר שללה דהא לאו דידיה הוא דשמא היה נתנה לכהן צדיק שבחוצה לה הלכך אינה נשרפת דהיינו כפקדון דעיר אחרת ואתנהו בגוה דאמר לעיל דמותרין ונהי דאכילה לא שרינא לה דשמא היה נתנה לכהן רשע שבתוכה הלכך ירקבו אבל תרומה ביד כהן דממוניה הוא תשרף: וקתני יגנזו. אע"ג דממוניה הוא לא אמר תשרף: אלא תרומה ביד כהן. דממוניה הוא ולא מזלזלינן בה כולי האי הואיל וקדש הוא: לכהן שבעיר אחרת. כלומר לכהן שלא הודח עמהן: אבל בגבולין. שאין לה היתר אכילה אלא בפדייה ד"ה פטורה מן החלה דממון גבוה הוא ל"א אבל בגבולין דאין לה היתר אכילה בשעת חיוב חלה דהיינו בשעת גלגול העיסה לא קרינא ביה ראשית עריסותיכם (במדבר טו) ואפילו פדאה לאחר מיכן פטור מן החלה: י' דברים נאמרו בירושלים. בפ' מרובה (ב"ק פב:) חשיב להו: אלא בעיר אחרת ואסקו לגוה. שהיה אותו מעשר שני של אחד מבני עיר הנדחת והעלו אותו לירושלים קודם שהודחה ואח"כ הודחו אם כן אמאי יגנזו לשתרו נמי באכילה דהא קלטינהו מחיצות דהיינו חומה: אלא לאו בגבולין. ולא מטו ליה וקתני יגנזו ואינו יוצא לישרף בתמיה: ואם איתא. דבגבולין לד"ה ממון גבוה הוא לשתרי נמי באכילה אלא לאו ממון הדיוט הוא ונהי דבשריפה לא משום זילותא: לעולם דעיר הנדחת ואסקיה לגוה. ודקאמרת לשתרו נמי באכילה דהא קלטוהו מחיצות: הכא במאי עסקינן כשנטמא. דלאו בר אכולי בטומאה הוא דכתיב (דברים כו) לא בערתי ממנו בטמא ולקמן פריך מאי איריא עיר הנדחת אפילו בחוצה לה: ואפילו בירושלים. לאחר שנכנס ואע"ג דדרשינן (שם יד) כי ירחק ממך המקום וצרת הכסף בידך ברחוק מקום אתה פודה וצר ולא בקרוב מקום: ואין שאת אלא אכילה. וה"ק קרא כי ירחק ממך המקום או כי לא תוכל לאוכלו שנטמא וצרת הכסף בידך: בלקוח. שכבר הוציאה בהוצאה לכסף מעשר ונתנוהו ביין ושכר ובשר ונטמא אותו לקוח דההוא לית ליה פדייה וכי קאמר ר"א במע"ש גופיה שהעלה פירות מע"ש לירושלים ונטמאו: וליפרקיה

עין משפט נר מצוה

נה א ב ג ד מיי' פ"ד מהל' עכו"ם הלכה יג סמג עשין טו:

נו ה ו מיי' פ"ו מהל' בכורים הלכה ד:

נז ז מיי' פ"ז מהל' בית הבחירה הלכה יד ופ"ד מהל' עכו"ם הלכה ד:

נח ח מיי' פ"ב מהל' מעשר שני ונטע רבעי הלכה ח סמג לאוין קלו:

ליקוטי רש"י

היו בה קדשים. בעיר הנדחת אין נשרפין עם שללה דכתיב (דברים יג) שללה ולא שלל שמים ומיהו מיקרב לא קרבו משום דכתיב (משלי כא) זבח רשעים תועבה ואם קדשי מזבח הן ואפילו עולות ושלמים נדבה ימותו. קדשי בדק הבית יפדו. כשאר בדק הבית והפודה אותם יאכלם שהרי לא נאסרו דלאו דידהו הוו [לעיל מז.]. קדשים שחייב באחריותן. אמר הרי עלי עולה והפרישה והוממה ומכרה. ושאינו חייב באחריותן כגון דאמר הרי זו [ב"מ נו:]. אם קיבלם בעליו עליו באחריות כגון דאמר הרי עלי עולה והפריש זו [ב"ק עא:]. ממון בעלים הן. כגון אמר הרי עלי עולה והפריש בהמה לנדרו וכו' דרעהו קרינן ביה דהדבר הגורם לממון לרבי שמעון כממון דמי [שבועות מב:]. ושור רעהו קרינן ביה [ב"ק יב:]. בבעלי מומין שללה נינהו. היינו בהמתה דכהן אוכל את הבכור וישראל את המעשר ואין לגבוה חלק בהן [תמורה ח.]. דברי ר' מאיר. דאמר בפרק שני דקדושין (נד:) מעשר ממון גבוה הוא. פטורה מן החלה כדמפרש דעריסותיכם כתיב ולא של גבוה [פסחים לז:]. פטורה מן החלה. דכתיב עריסותיכם והאי דגבוה היא ואף על גב דאיכא היתר אכילה כיון דלית בה דין שאר ממון לאו דידיה הוא [סוכה לה.]. הא קלטוהו מחיצות. מעשר שני בירושלים הואיל ואינו נאכל בכל מושבות מעתה משהכניסו לירושלים שוב אינו יכול לחלל לאכול בחוץ כדאמרינן במסכת מכות (כ.) מחילה לקלוט מדרבנן דמשקלטוהו מחילות שוב אינו נפדה. ר' אלעזר. דאם נטמא פודין אותו ואוכלין אותו בכל מקום. שאתו. כשלא תוכל לאוכלו כגון זה שניטמא ונתת בכסף [פסחים לו:]. אפילו בירושלים. שאין מעשר טהור נפדה שם דכתיב (דברים יד) כי ירחק ממך [וגו'] ונתת בכסף ולא כשהיה בירושלים [ב"מ נג:]. אין מוכרין מעשר שני בירושלים, ואפילו לאוכלו שם בקדושה דכי ירבה ממך הדרך ונתתה בכסף כתיב (דברים יד) [פסחים עה:]. שפודין אותו אפילו בירושלים. דאי בעי פריק ואפילו בירושלים דאע"ג דמעשר שני טהור אינו נפדה בירושלים דכתיב כי ירחק ממך ונתת בכסף בריחוק מקום אתה פודה ולא בקירוב מקום (קדושין דף נו). ואין שאת אלא אכילה. והכי קאמר קרא כי ירחק ממך שיהא מעשר טהור חוץ לירושלים או אפילו הוא בירושלים אלא שאי אתה יכול לאוכלו שנטמא ונתת בכסף [מכות יט.]. בלקוח. מעשר זה ולא הוא עצמו היה מעשר אלא לרכי סעודה שלקח בירושלים בכסף מעשר [ב"מ שם].

מסורת הש"ס

א) לעיל מז. [תוספ' פי"ד], ב) [תמורה ח. ע"ש], ג) [ב"מ נו.], ד) [ב"ק יב: וש"נ], ה) [גי' רש"י ירעו וכל"ל], ו) [לפי גירסת רש"י דלעיל צ"ל ירעו], ז) [צ"ל בהמתה], ח) [תמורה ח. ע"ש], ט) [צ"ל בהמתה], י) [צ"ל בהמתה], כ) [בתוס' דבכורות דף לא. ד"ה חוץ וכו' משמע דגרסי הכא בסוגיא כמו דקיים הש"ס בתמורה ח. דתנן כל פסולי המוקדשין נמכרין באטליז חוץ מן הבכור והמעשר ע"ש אבל מפירש"י דהכא ד"ה לעולם בבעלי מומין וכו' מוכח דלא גרים להא דתנן כו' ומשום הכי פירש"י הכא יצאו אלו שיש להם שם לווי ורבינא הוא דמשני לה הכי כאן אבל בתמורה ח. סתמא דש"ס מייתי להא דתנן כל פסולי וכו' ולא ס"ל כרבינא בפי' הזה], ל) א"ז משנה אלא ברייתא ועיין רש"ל, מ) סוכה לה: פסחים לח. [עי' חולין פז: תוס' ד"ה תנן התם], נ) [קידושין כד. וש"נ], ס) [עי' תוס' קידושין נג: ד"ה איהו ותוס' בכורות ט: ד"ה ותנן ועי' היטב תוס' סוכה לה. סד"ה לפי], ע) ב"ק פב., פ) ב"מ נג. פסחי' לו: מכות יט:, צ) [צ"ל מאי], ק) [צ"ל אדתני], ר) נ"א נהרגין.

הגהות הב"ח

(א) גמ' ת"ר היו בה קדשים קדשי מזבח כצ"ל ותיבת קדשי נמחק: (ב) רש"י ד"ה ואליבא דר' יוסי וכו' קדשי קדשים ירעו כצ"ל ותיבת אמאי נמחק:

גליון הש"ס

גמ' ומי שנאכל בתורת בהמתך. עי' זבחים דף עה ע"ב תוס' ד"ה התפיס:

תורה אור השלם

א) זֶבַח רְשָׁעִים תּוֹעֵבָה אַף כִּי בְזִמָּה יְבִיאֶנּוּ: [משלי כא, כז]

ב) וְכִי יִרְבֶּה מִמְּךָ הַדֶּרֶךְ כִּי לֹא תוּכַל שְׂאֵתוֹ כִּי יִרְחַק מִמְּךָ הַמָּקוֹם אֲשֶׁר יִבְחַר יְיָ אֱלֹהֶיךָ לָשׂוּם שְׁמוֹ שָׁם כִּי יְבָרֶכְךָ יְיָ אֱלֹהֶיךָ: [דברים יד, כד]

ג) וַיִּשָּׂא מַשְׂאֹת מֵאֵת פָּנָיו אֲלֵהֶם וַתֵּרֶב מַשְׂאַת בִּנְיָמִן מִמַּשְׂאֹת כֻּלָּם חָמֵשׁ יָדוֹת וַיִּשְׁתּוּ וַיִּשְׁכְּרוּ עִמּוֹ: [בראשית מג, לד]

effect that *kodshei kodashim* animals should be left to become blemished and then be redeemed. Rather, the Tanna would have had to add yet another distinction between *chataos* (which are left to die) and all other *kodshei kodashim* (which are left to become blemished and then redeemed). The Tanna therefore preferred to make the more clear-cut distinction between animals consecrated for the Altar and items consecrated for Temple maintenance (which are always redeemed).[18]

This concludes Reish Lakish's interpretation of the Baraisa. R' Yochanan, however, gave a different interpretation. The Gemara now examines why each rejected the interpretation of the other:

בִּשְׁלָמָא רַבִּי יוֹחָנָן לֹא אָמַר כְּרֵישׁ לָקִישׁ – Now **it is understandable why R' Yochanan did not say as Reish Lakish** did, דִּכְתִיב ,,זֶבַח רְשָׁעִים תּוֹעֵבָה" – **for it is written:** ***The sacrifice of the wicked is an abomination.***[19] אֶלָּא רֵישׁ לָקִישׁ מַאי טַעְמָא לֹא אָמַר כְּרַבִּי יוֹחָנָן – **However, why did Reish Lakish not say as R' Yochanan** that the reason the animals consecrated for the Altar are not redeemed is because the redemption money would assume the same invalidation as the animals themselves?

The Gemara answers:

אָמַר לָךְ – **[Reish Lakish] would say to you:** כִּי אַמְרִינַן ,,זֶבַח רְשָׁעִים תּוֹעֵבָה" – **When do we say** the rule that ***the sacrifice of the wicked is an abomination?*** הָנֵי מִילֵּי הֵיכָא דְּאִתְנְהוּ בְּעֵינַיְיהוּ – **Only when [the animals]** consecrated by the wicked **are present themselves.** אֲבָל הָכָא – **However, here,** where the animals of the wicked would be redeemed, כֵּיוָן דְּאִישְׁתַּנֵּי אִישְׁתַּנֵּי – **since [the offering] has been converted** into money, **it has been converted;** the money no longer bears the status of "sacrifices of the wicked."[20]

The Gemara examines the second opinion quoted in the Baraisa, that of R' Shimon:

רַבִּי שִׁמְעוֹן אוֹמֵר – **R' SHIMON SAYS:** (בהמתך) [בְּהֶמְתָּהּ] וְלֹא בֶּהֱמַת בְּכוֹר וּמַעֲשֵׂר – When the Torah states: *Destroy it and everything that is in it, as well as* ***ITS ANIMALS***, it implies: **BUT NOT *BECHOR* OR *MAASER* ANIMALS.**[21]

The Gemara analyzes this exclusion:

בְּמַאי עַסְקִינַן – **With what** sort of animals **are we dealing** here? אִילֵימָא בִּתְמִימִין – **If you say** that we are dealing **with unblemished animals,** שְׁלַל שָׁמַיִם הוּא – **[such animals] are** in any case **the "booty of Heaven,"** not of the city. It is therefore not necessary to derive a separate exclusion for them.[22] אֶלָּא בְּבַעֲלֵי מוּמִין – And if you say, **rather,** that we are dealing **with blemished animals,** ,,שְׁלָלָהּ" נִינְהוּ – **[such animals] are** certainly considered ***its booty,*** since they are no longer fit to be sacrifices and will be slaughtered and eaten by their owners.[23] How then can R' Shimon say that they are not destroyed along with the subverted city?

The Gemara answers:

אָמַר רָבִינָא – **Ravina said:** לְעוֹלָם בְּבַעֲלֵי מוּמִין – **Actually,** R' Shimon is referring **to blemished animals;** וּמִי שֶׁנֶּאֱכָל בְּתוֹרַת (בהמתך) [בְּהֶמְתָּהּ] – **but** the term *its animals* from which R' Shimon derives his exclusion implies **one that is eaten under the heading of "its animals"** – i.e. an animal that is spoken of simply as an animal of the subverted city. יָצְאוּ אֵלּוּ שֶׁאֵין נֶאֱכָלִין בְּתוֹרַת (בהמתך) [בְּהֶמְתָּהּ] – **Excluded** from this requirement, therefore, **are those** animals **that are not eaten under the heading of "its animals,"** אֶלָּא בְּתוֹרַת בְּכוֹר וּמַעֲשֵׂר – **but rather under the heading of "the *bechor* and *maaser* animals"** of that city, דִּשְׁלַל שָׁמַיִם נִינְהוּ – **for these** animals **are** treated as **"the booty of Heaven."**[24]

NOTES

18. [Accordingly, when the Baraisa speaks of Altar consecrations (according to Reish Lakish), it refers to *kodashim kalim*. These are always put to death. *Kodshei kodashim* would be subject to different rules, depending on the type of sacrifice: A *chatas* would be left to die, and an *olah* and *asham* would be left to graze until they developed a blemish and then be redeemed.]

19. *Proverbs* 21:27. Thus there is no need for R' Yochanan to seek another explanation of why the Baraisa requires the animals to die rather than be redeemed. Since Scripture states plainly that such an offering is an abomination, it is logical to assume that any money deriving from the sale of that animal is equally tainted and nothing would be gained by redeeming the animal. [Moreover, this disqualification could apply to all Altar consecrations, be they *kodshei kodashim* or *kodashim kalim.*]

20. Reish Lakish agrees that the original animals cannot be sacrificed because they are "the sacrifices of the wicked," which are an abomination (see note 14). However, Reish Lakish maintains that this invalidation adheres only to an animal designated as an offering by the wicked person, not to the money for which it is redeemed (*Chidushei HaRan*). Thus, if this were the only problem, we would allow the offerings to graze until they became blemished, redeem them, and then purchase new offerings with the redemption money. Since the taint of the wicked does not pass from the original offering to the money, the new offerings purchased with that money would also be untainted and therefore fit to sacrifice; there would be no reason for the Baraisa to require the death of the Altar animals. Accordingly, Reish Lakish must offer another reason as to why the sacrifices of the *ir hanidachas* are sent to their deaths rather than redeemed.

21. [The Gemara above quoted the opinion of R' Shimon that offerings for which one bears liability are considered the property of the owner. The Gemara inferred from this that such offerings in an *ir hanidachas* would be subject to destruction, according to R' Shimon. This rule, however, has no bearing on the *bechor* and *maaser* offerings, because the owner of these offerings does not bear any liability for them; if they are lost, disqualified or die, they are not replaced.]

22. Rather, they are excluded from the fate of the *ir hanidachas* by the word שְׁלָלָהּ, *its booty* [which excludes the property of Heaven, as taught in the Mishnah (111b) and Baraisa (112a)] (*Rashi*).

[Although the Gemara has just stated that according to some, *kodashim kalim* are considered the property of their owners and thus subject to the law of *ir hanidachas*, R' Shimon clearly does not hold this way. This is evident from the fact that he excludes from the word בְּהֶמְתָּהּ, *its animals*, only *bechor* and *maaser* offerings and not *kodashim kalim* in general, though the exclusion would logically eliminate them as well. (As the Gemara will explain below, there is more reason to assume that the *bechor* and *maaser* are the property of the *ir hanidachas* than for any other offering to be its property.) Since R' Shimon does not find it necessary to exclude *kodashim kalim* from this word, it is evident that he considers *kodashim kalim* to be the property of Heaven and hence already excluded by the word שְׁלָלָהּ, *its booty*. Therefore, the Gemara asks why unblemished *bechor* and *maaser* offerings should be treated any differently.]

23. Once a *bechor* or *maaser* animal becomes blemished and unfit for the Altar, it need not even be redeemed. The *bechor* becomes the absolute property of the Kohen to whom it was given, and the *maaser* the absolute property of its owner (see Mishnah, *Bechoros* 31a). [These become theirs to slaughter and eat, though like all blemished sacrifices, they may not be used for work (Mishnah, *Bechoros* 14a).] Thus, the blemished *bechor* or *maaser* animal certainly qualifies as the "booty of the city," not of Heaven. Why should it not be destroyed along with all the city's other animals? (*Rashi*).

24. According to R' Shimon, when the verse states: *Destroy it . . . as well as its animals,* it means animals that are commonly referred to as "its animals" and nothing else; that is, they have no status other than their status as the property of the inhabitants of the city. Animals that have some additional status, and which are thus referred to with a title other than just the name of their owner – for example, *bechor* and *maaser* animals – do not fall within this narrow definition of *its animals.* For although they belong to the inhabitants of this city, people do not refer to them simply as "So-and-so's animal," but rather as "So-and-so's *bechor* or *maaser* animal." The compound title [שֵׁם לְוַוי] accorded them removes them from the strict category of *its animals*. Thus, R' Shimon maintains, they are excluded from the law of *ir hanidachas* even though they are the property of their owners (*Rashi*).

Furthermore, although blemished *bechor* and *maaser* animals may be

והההקדשות שבה יפדו כו': [א] ת"ר [א] היו בה (א) (קדשי) קדשים קדשי מזבח ימותו קדשי בדק הבית יפדו ותרומות ירקבו ומעשר שני וכתבי הקדש יגנזו [ב] ר"ש אומר בהמתה ולא בהמת בכור ומעשר שללה פרט לכסף הקדש וכסף מעשר אמר מר היו בה (קדשי) קדשים קדשי מזבח ימותו ואמאי ימותו ירעו עד שיסתאבו וימכרו ויפלו דמיהן לנדבה ר' יוחנן אמר [א] [ב] זבח רשעים תועבה ר"ל אמר ממון בעלים הוא והכא בקדשים שחייב באחריותן [ג] ור"ש היא דאמר ממון בעלים הוא הא מדסיפא ר"ש היא רישא לאו ר"ש בקדשים קלים ואליבא דרבי יוסי הגלילי [ד] דאמר קדשים קלים ממון בעלים אבל קדשי קדשים מאי [ה] יפדו אדתני סיפא קדשי בדק הבית יפדו ליפלוג וליתני בדידה בד"א בקדשים קלים אבל קדשי קדשים [ו] יפדו כיון דאיכא חטאת שמתו בעליה דלמיתה אזלא לא פסיקא ליה בשלמא ר' יוחנן לא אמר כר"ל דכתיב זבח רשעים תועבה אלא ר"ל מ"ט לא אמר כר' יוחנן אמר לך כי אמרינן זבח רשעים תועבה הני מילי היכא דאתנהו בעינייהו אבל הכא כיון דאישתני אישתני: ר"ש אומר [ז] בהמתך ולא בהמת בכור ומעשר: במאי עסקינן [ח] אילימא בתמימין שלל שמים הוא אלא בבעלי מומין [ג] שללה נינהו אמר רבינא לעולם בבעלי מומין [ה] ומי שנאכל בתורת [ט] בהמתך יצאו אלו שאין נאכלין בתורת [י] בהמתך אלא בתורת בכור ומעשר [כ] דשלל שמים נינהו ופליגא דשמואל דאמר שמואל הכל קרב והכל נפדה מאי קאמר ה"ק כל שקרב כשהוא תם ונפדה כשהוא בעל מום משלל אימעיט וכל שקרב כשהוא תם ואינו נפדה כשהוא בעל מום כגון בכור ומעשר מבהמה נפקא: תרומות ירקבו: אמר רב חסדא ל"ש אלא תרומה ביד ישראל אבל תרומה ביד כהן כיון דממוניה הוא תשרף מתיב רב יוסף מעשר שני וכתבי הקדש יגנזו והא מעשר שני ביד ישראל כתרומה ביד כהן דמי וקתני יגנזו אלא אי אתמר הכי אתמר אמר רב חסדא ל"ש אלא תרומה ביד כהן אבל תרומה ביד ישראל [ד] תנתן לכהן שבעיר אחרת [ל] תנן התם [מ] עיסה של מעשר שני פטורה מן החלה דברי ר"מ וחכמים [ה] מחייבין אמר רב חסדא מחלוקת [ו] במעשר שני בירושלים דר"מ סבר [נ] מעשר שני ממון גבוה הוא ורבנן סברי ממון הדיוט הוא אבל [ס] בגבולין דברי הכל פטור מתיב רב יוסף מעשר שני וכתבי הקדש יגנזו במאי עסקינן אילימא בירושלים מי הויא עיר הנדחת והתניא [ע] עשרה דברים נאמרו בירושלים וזו אחת מהן [ז] אינה נעשית עיר הנדחת ואלא בעיר אחרת ואסקוהו לגוה הא קלטוהו מחיצות אלא לאו בגבולין וקתני יגנזו לא לעולם דעיר אחרת ואסקוהו לגוה והכא במאי עסקינן שנטמא ולפרקיה [פ] דא"ר אלעזר [ח] מניין למעשר שני שנטמא שפודין אותו אפילו בירושלים ת"ל [ב] לא תוכל שאתו ואין שאת אלא אכילה שנאמר [ג] וישא משאת מאת פניו הכא במאי עסקינן בלקוח וליפרקיה

רש"י

היו בה קדשי מזבח. כגון עולות ואשמות של רשעים בתוכה נהי דלא קרינן בהו את כל בהמתה לפי חרב דהא לא בהמתה היא אלא בהמת שמים אלא מאיסותא הוא להקריב קרבנות של רשעים הללו שהודחו הלכך ימותו כונסין אותן לכיפה ומאכילין אותן שעורין עד שכריסן נבקעת דאפילו דמיהם אסור כדלקמן: שנאמר כליל לה' אלהיך ל"ג: ר"ש אומר וכו'. לקמן מפרש טעמא: זבח רשעים תועבה. ואפילו דמיהן אסורין: ור"ש הוא דאמר. בהזהב (ב"מ נו:) קדשים שחייב באחריותן ממון בעלים הוא ויש בהם אונאה הלכך לענין עיר הנדחת נמי ממון בעלים הוא ודיינינהו לפי חרב כשאר בהמות שבתוכה והלכך אסורין דמיהן בהנאה והאי דקאמר ימותו ולא אמר שיחרימו אותה עמהם משום כבוד שמים: ואליבא דרבי יוסי הגלילי דאמר. בפ"ק דב"ק (ד' יב:) ומעלה מעל בה' לרבות קדשים קלים שהם ממונו והואיל וממונו הם אסורים בהנאה דאפילו דמיהן בהמתם מיקרו אבל קדשי קדשים (ג) [ל] אמאי ירעו דהא ודאי הם עצמם אינם קרבים דזבח רשעים תועבה אלא ירעו עד שיסתאבו וימכרו ויפלו דמיהם לנדבה: אי הכי [ק] מדתני סיפא וכו'. דקא מפליג בין קדשי מזבח לקדשי בדק הבית: ליפלוג וליתני בדידה. בקדשי מזבח עצמן בין קדשים קלים לקדשי קדשים: דלמיתה אזלא. כדאמרינן (תמורה ד' טו.) חמש חטאות מתות: לא פסיקא ליה. למיתני קדשי קדשים דעיר הנדחת ירעו דכיון דמתו להם אותם רשעים אי איכא חטאות שהפרישו בחייהם אזלי למיתה דכל חטאות שמתו בעליהם מתות במסכת הוריות (ד' ו.) מפרש טעמא אבל שאר קדשי קדשים כגון אשמות שמתו בעליהם ירעו: דאיתנהו בעינייהו. להן עצמן ודאי אינן קרבים משום זבח רשעים תועבה: אבל הכא. דאיכא למימר ירעו ויפלו דמיהם לנדבה: כיון דאישתני. ליכא הכא זבח רשעים תועבה: ולא בהמת בכור ומעשר. שאם היו בה בכורות או מעשר בהמה שהוא של ישראל וחלבו ודמו קרב אין מחרימין אותו עמה דלא מיקרי בהמתה: שלל שמים הוא. ומשללה נפקא: אלא בבעלי מומים. שאין בהם חלק לגבוה אלא נאכלין לבעלים שללה נינהו אמאי אין מחרימין אותן עמה: לעולם בבעלי מומין. ואפ"ה אין [ר] נשרפין עמה דדרשינן לקרא הכי בהמתה למי שנאכל לבעלים בתורת בהמתם יצאו אלו שיש להם שם לווי שאין נאכלים בתורת בהמתם שאין אומרין בהמת עיר הנדחת אלא בהמת בכור ומעשר של עיר

תוספות

הנדחת: ופליגא. הא דרבינא אדשמואל דאמר שמואל עלה דהא מילתא דר"ש כי הוה קשיא לן במאי עסקינן הוי מתרץ הכי הכל קרב והכל נפדה: מאי קאמר ה"ק. כל שהוא קרב לגבוה כשהוא תם וכשהוא בעל מום צריך פדייה כגון שאר קדשים קלים חוץ ממעשר בהמה ובכור הנהו משללה נפקא דאין מחרימין אותם עמה דהואיל וצריכי פדייה במומן שלל שמים קרינן ביה ופליג עליה דת"ק דאמר קדשים קלים ממון בעלים הוא: וכל שקרב כשהוא תם ואינו נפדה כשהוא בעל מום. אלא נאכל לבעלים כגון בכור ומעשר ההוא לאו שלל שמים מקרו ואפילו בתמותן ולא מצי למפרך והא בתמותן שלל שמים הוא שהרי נאכל במומו והלכך אצטריך בהמתה למעוטי בכור ומעשר תמימים דמשללה ליכא למעוטינהו והיינו פליגא דאיהו מוקי לה אפילו בתמימים דקסבר בכור ומעשר בעלי מומין בהמתה קרינא ביה ובסייף: תרומה ביד ישראל. שעדיין לא נתנה לכהן דאפילו אותו ישראל רשע הוא תרומה שבידו אינה נשרפת עם שאר שללה דהא לאו דידיה הוא דשמא היה נתנה לכהן צדיק שבחוצה לה הלכך אינה נשרפת דהיינו כפקדון דעיר אחרת ואתנהו בגוה דאמר לעיל דמותרין ונהי דבאכילה לא שרינא לה דשמא היה נתנה לכהן רשע שבתוכה הלכך ירקבו אבל תרומה ביד כהן דממוניה הוא תשרף: וקתני יגנזו. אע"ג דממוניה הוא לא אמר תשרף: אלא תרומה ביד כהן. דממוניה הוא ולא מזלזלינן בה כולי האי הואיל וקדש הוא: לכהן שבעיר אחרת. כלומר לכהן שלא הודח עמהן: אבל בגבולין. שאין לה היתר אכילה אלא בפדייה ד"ה פטורה מן החלה דממון גבוה הוא ל"א אבל בגבולין דאין לה היתר אכילה בשעת חיוב חלה דהיינו בשעת גלגול העיסה לא קרינא ביה ראשית עריסותיכם (במדבר טו) ואפילו פדאה לאחר מיכן פטור מן החלה: י' דברים נאמרו בירושלים. בפ' מרובה (ב"ק פב:) חשיב להו: אלא בעיר אחרת ואסקו לגוה. שהיה אותו מעשר שני של אחד מבני עיר הנדחת והעלו אותו לירושלים קודם שהודחה ואח"כ הודחו אם כן אמאי יגנזו לשתרו נמי באכילה דהא קלטינהו מחילות דהיינו חומה: אלא לאו בגבולין. ולא מטו ליה וקתני יגנזו ואינו יוצא לישרף בתמיה: ואם איתא. דבגבולין לד"ה ממון גבוה הוא לשתרי נמי באכילה אלא לאו ממון הדיוט הוא ונהי דבשריפה לא משום זילותא: לעולם דעיר הנדחת ואסקיה לגוה. ודקאמרת לשתרו נמי באכילה דהא קלטוהו מחילות: הכא במאי עסקינן כשנטמא. דלאו בר אכולי בטומאה הוא דכתיב (דברים כו) לא בערתי ממנו בטמא ולקמן פריך מאי איריא עיר הנדחת אפילו בחוצה לה: ואפילו בירושלים. לאחר שנכנס ואע"ג דדרשינן (שם יד) כי ירחק ממך המקום ונתת הכסף בידך ברחוק מקום אתה פודה ואי ולא בקרוב מקום: ואין שאת אלא אכילה. וה"ק קרא כי ירחק ממך המקום או כי לא תוכל לאוכלו שנטמא ונתת הכסף בידך: בלקוח. שכבר הוציאה בהוצאה לכסף מעשר ונתנוהו ביין ושכר ובשר ונטמא אותו לקוח דההוא לית ליה פדייה וכי קאמר ר"א במע"ש גופיה שהעלה פירות מע"ש לירושלים ונטמאו: וליפרקיה

עין משפט נר מצוה

נה א ב ג ד מיי' פ"ד מהל' עכו"ם הלכה יג סמג עשין טו:
נו ה ו מיי' פ"ו מהל' בכורים הלכה ד:
נז ז מיי' פ"ז מהל' בית הבחירה הלכה יד ופ"ד מהל' עכו"ם הלכה ד:
נח ח מיי' פ"ג מהל' מעשר שני ונטע רבעי הלכה ח סמג לאוין קלו:

ליקוטי רש"י

היו בה קדשים. בעיר הנדחת אינן נשרפין עם שללה דכתיב (דברים יג) שללה ולא שלל שמים ומיהו מיקרב לא קרבו משום דכתיב (משלי כא) זבח רשעים תועבה ואם קדשי מזבח הן ואפילו עולות ושלמים נדבה ימותו. קדשי בדק הבית יפדו. כשאר בדק הבית והפודה אותם יאכלם שהרי לא נאסרו דלאו דידהו הוו [לעיל מז.]. קדשים שחייב באחריותן. אמר הרי עלי עולה והפרישה והוממה ומכרה. ושאינו חייב באחריותן כגון דאמר הרי זו [ב"מ נו:]. אם קיבלם בעליו עליו באחריות כגון דאמר הרי עלי עולה והפריש זו [ב"ק עא:]. ממון בעלים הן. כגון אמר הרי עלי עולה והפריש בהמה לנדרו וכו' דרעהו קרינן ביה דדבר הגורם לממון לרבי שמעון כממון דמי [שבועות מב:]. ושור רעהו קרינן ביה [ב"ק יב:]. בבעלי מומין שללה נינהו. היינו בהמתה דכהן אוכל את הבכור וישראל את המעשר ואין לגבוה חלק בהן [תמורה ח.]. דברי ר' מאיר. דאמר בפרק שני דקדושין (נד:) מעשר ממון גבוה הוא. פטורה מן החלה כדמפרש דעריסותיכם כתיב ולא של גבוה [פסחים לז:]. פטורה מן החלה. דכתיב עריסותיכם והאי דגבוה היא ואף על גב דאיכא היתר אכילה כיון דלית בה דין שאר ממון לאו דידיה הוא [סוכה לה.]. הא קלטוהו מחיצות. מעשר שני בירושלים הואיל ואינו נאכל בכל מושבות מעתה משהביאו לירושלים שוב אינו יכול לחלל לאכול בחוץ כדאמרינן במסכת מכות (כ.) מחילה לקלוט מדרבנן דמשקלטוהו מחילות שוב אינו נפדה. ר' אלעזר. דאם נטמא פודין אותו ואוכלין אותו בכל מקום. שאתו. כשלא תוכל לאוכלו כגון זה שניטמא ונתת בכסף [פסחים לו:]. אפילו בירושלים. שאין מעשר טהור נפדה שם דכתיב (דברים יד) כי ירחק ממך [וגו'] ונתת בכסף ולא כשהיה בירושלים [ב"מ נג:]. אין מוכרין מעשר שני בירושלים, ואפילו לאוכלו שם בקדושה דכי ירבה ממך הדרך ונתתה בכסף כתיב (דברים יד) [פסחים עה:]. שפודין אותו אפילו בירושלים. דאי בעי פריק ואפילו בירושלים דאע"ג דמעשר שני טהור אינו נפדה בירושלים דכתיב כי ירחק ממך ונתת בכסף בריחוק מקום אתה פודה ולא בקירוב מקום (קדושין דף נו). ואין שאת אלא אכילה. והכי קאמר קרא כי ירחק ממך שיהא מעשר טהור חוץ לירושלים או אפילו הוא בירושלים אלא שאי אתה יכול לאוכלו שנטמא ונתת בכסף [מכות יט.]. בלקוח. מעשר זה ולא הוא עצמו היה מעשר אלא לוקח מעות שלקח בירושלים בכסף מעשר [ב"מ שם].

מסורת הש"ס

א) לעיל מז. [תוספ' פי"ד], ב) [תמורה ח. ע"ש], ג) [ב"מ נו.], ד) [ב"ק יב: וש"נ], ה) [גי' רש"י ירעו וכל"ל], ו) [לפי גירסת רש"י דלעיל צ"ל ירעו], ז) [צ"ל בהמתה], ח) [תמורה ח. ע"ש], ט) [צ"ל בהמתה], י) [צ"ל בהמתה], כ) [בתוס' דבכורות דף לא. ד"ה חוץ וכו' משמע דגרסי הכא בסוגיא כמו דקיים הש"ס בתמורה ח. דתנן כל פסולי המוקדשין נמכרין באטליז חוץ מן הבכור והמעשר ע"ש אבל מפירש"י דהכא ד"ה לעולם בבעלי מומין וכו' מוכח דלא גריס להא דתנן כו' ומשום הכי פירש"י הכא יצאו אלו שיש להם שם לווי ורבינא הוא דמשני לה הכי כאן אבל בתמורה ח. סתמא דש"ס מייתי להא דתנן כל פסולי וכו' ולא מ"ל כרבינא בפי' הזה], ל) א"ז משנה אלא ברייתא ועיין רש"ל, מ) סוכה לה: פסחים לח. [עי' חולין פז: תוס' ד"ה תנן התם], נ) [קידושין כד. וש"נ], ס) [עי' תוס' קידושין נג: ד"ה איהו ותוס' בכורות ט: ד"ה ותנן ועי' היטב תוס' סוכה לה. סד"ה לפי], ע) ב"ק פב., פ) ב"מ נג. פסחי' לו: מכות יט:, ק) [צ"ל מאי], ק) [צ"ל אדתני], ר) נ"א נהרגין.

הגהות הב"ח

(א) גמ' ת"ר היו בה קדשים קדשי מזבח כצ"ל ותיבת קדשי נמחק: (ב) רש"י ד"ה ואליבא דר' יוסי וכו' קדשי קדשים ירעו כצ"ל ותיבת אמאי נמחק:

גליון הש"ס

גמ' ומי שנאכל בתורת בהמתך. עי' זבחים דף עה ע"ב תוס' ד"ה התפיס:

תורה אור השלם

א) זֶבַח רְשָׁעִים תּוֹעֵבָה אַף כִּי בְזִמָּה יְבִיאֶנּוּ: [משלי כא, כז]

ב) וְכִי יִרְבֶּה מִמְּךָ הַדֶּרֶךְ כִּי לֹא תוּכַל שְׂאֵתוֹ כִּי יִרְחַק מִמְּךָ הַמָּקוֹם אֲשֶׁר יִבְחַר יְיָ אֱלֹהֶיךָ לָשׂוּם שְׁמוֹ שָׁם כִּי יְבָרֶכְךָ יְיָ אֱלֹהֶיךָ: [דברים יד, כד]

ג) וַיִּשָּׂא מַשְׂאֹת מֵאֵת פָּנָיו אֲלֵהֶם וַתֵּרֶב מַשְׂאַת בִּנְיָמִן מִמַּשְׂאֹת כֻּלָּם חָמֵשׁ יָדוֹת וַיִּשְׁתּוּ וַיִּשְׁכְּרוּ עִמּוֹ: [בראשית מג, לד]

The Gemara cites a dissenting view:

וּפְלִיגָא דִּשְׁמוּאֵל – **[This explanation]** by Ravina of R' Shimon's view **disagrees with** the explanation offered by **Shmuel.** דְּאָמַר שְׁמוּאֵל – **For** when he explained R' Shimon's view, **Shmuel said:** הַכֹּל קָרֵב וְהַכֹּל נִפְדֶּה – **"Everything may be offered and everything may be redeemed."** מַאי קָאָמַר – **What was he saying?** What did Shmuel mean by this? הָכִי קָאָמַר – **This is what he was saying:** כָּל שֶׁקָּרֵב כְּשֶׁהוּא תָּם – According to R' Shimon, **any [consecrated animal] that is offered when it is unblemished** וְנִפְדֶּה כְּשֶׁהוּא בַּעַל מוּם – **and redeemed when it is blemished,**[25] מִ,,שְׁלָלָהּ" אִימַּעִיט – **is excluded** from destruction **from** the word ***booty.***[26] וְכָל שֶׁקָּרֵב כְּשֶׁהוּא תָּם וְאֵינוֹ נִפְדֶּה כְּשֶׁהוּא בַּעַל מוּם – **And any [consecrated animal] that is offered when it is unblemished but is not redeemed when it is blemished,** כְּגוֹן בְּכוֹר וּמַעֲשֵׂר – **such as the** ***bechor*** **and** ***maaser*** animals, מִ,,בְּהֶמְתָּהּ" נָפְקָא – its exclusion **is derived from** the word ***animal.***[27]

NOTES

slaughtered and eaten, they are subject to legal limitations that do not apply to non-consecrated animals. For example, blemished *bechor* and *maaser* animals may not be sold or slaughtered in the market, nor may the meat be weighed by the *litra*-weight (see *Bechoros* 31a). Since the *bechor* and *maaser* animals are legally distinct from the ordinary animals of the city, they are not included in the category of *its animals* (*Yad Ramah*; see *Temurah* 8a where the Gemara offers this reason explicitly; *Rashi,* however, following the different reading found in the Gemara here, explains our Gemara differently).

[The reason R' Shimon excludes by this word only blemished *bechor* and *maaser* offerings is because other blemished offerings, which must be redeemed before they can be used, would be considered the property of Heaven as long as they have not been redeemed. Thus, they are excluded from destruction by the same exclusion that pertains to all consecrated items – שְׁלָלָהּ וְלֹא שְׁלַל שָׁמַיִם, *its booty, not the booty of Heaven*.]

The dispute according to Ravina: The dispute between R' Shimon and the Tanna Kamma concerns the status of blemished *bechor* and *maaser* offerings. According to the Tanna Kamma, these are put to death by the sword because they are the property of the *ir hanidachas*, whereas according to R' Shimon they are not killed because they do not conform to the strict definition of בְּהֶמְתָּהּ, *its animals.* (Although the Tanna Kamma does not explicitly speak of blemished offerings, his position on the matter is inferred from R' Shimon's response.)

Ravina's explanation of the dispute would seem to fit both the explanations of R' Yochanan and Reish Lakish. This will be explained further in the summary below (note 27).

25. For example, *kodashim kalim* other than the *bechor* and *maaser*. Should these become blemished, they must be redeemed before they can be slaughtered and eaten. *Bechor* and *maaser* offerings, however, need not be redeemed, but may be slaughtered as soon as they become blemished (*Rashi*).

26. Since they must be redeemed before the owner can slaughter them and use their meat, they are still considered the property of Heaven. They are therefore excluded from the law of destruction by the word שְׁלָלָהּ, *its booty* – which excludes the "booty of Heaven" (*Rashi*; see next note).

27. Since these types of offerings do not require redemption to permit them for consumption after becoming blemished, they are not considered the "property of Heaven" – even *before* they become blemished. The fact that they can revert to personal use without redemption demonstrates that they are considered the "city's booty" even while they are still holy (i.e. unblemished).

Accordingly, even *bechor* and *maaser* offerings that are *un*blemished [תְּמִימִין] cannot be excluded from destruction on the grounds that they are the "booty of Heaven" [שְׁלַל שָׁמַיִם]. R' Shimon therefore cites a separate exclusion for the *bechor* and *maaser* from the word בְּהֶמְתָּהּ, *its animals*. [According to Shmuel, the derivation must be somewhat different than that of Ravina, since it refers to unblemished offerings. The exclusion must therefore be that though unblemished *bechor* and *maaser* animals are considered the property of the city (שְׁלָלָהּ), they are not like its other animals in that they must be brought to the Temple, where their blood and fats are offered upon the Altar. Thus, they are not *exclusively* the city's (see *Rashi* ד״ה ולא בהמת בכור ומעשר).]

[Since Shmuel finds it necessary to apply the exclusion of בְּהֶמְתָּהּ, *its animals,* even to unblemished *bechor* and *maaser* offerings, he has no exclusion left to teach that blemished *bechor* and *maaser* animals – which are unfit for the Altar and may be slaughtered by their owners – are also excluded from the law of *ir hanidachas*.] Accordingly, Shmuel must hold that blemished *bechor* and *maaser* animals *would* be destroyed. In his view, R' Shimon excludes from destruction only *un*blemished [תְּמִימִין] *bechor* and *maaser* animals, contrary to Ravina who explained above that R' Shimon's derivation excludes from destruction even *blemished* animals (*Rashi*).

The dispute according to Shmuel: Both the Tanna Kamma and R' Shimon agree that blemished *bechor* and *maaser* offerings are destroyed along with the city's other animals. The dispute between them concerns *un*blemished animals and the status of *kodashim kalim* offerings. The Tanna Kamma holds that *kodashim kalim* offerings are considered the property of their owners and they are therefore killed by the sword as animals of the *ir hanidachas*. R' Shimon rules that *kodashim kalim* offerings are considered the "property of Heaven," and they are therefore *not* destroyed. *Bechor* and *maaser* offerings would not be excluded on this basis because the fact that they can revert to their owners' use without redemption (when they become blemished) renders them the property of the *ir hanidachas* even when they are still unblemished. Nevertheless, they are separately excluded from destruction by the word בְּהֶמְתָּהּ, *its animals* (*Rashi* ד״ה מאי קאמר as explained by *Maharshal;* cf. *Maharsha*).

An elaboration of *Rashi's* view: *Rashi* explains Shmuel to be following Reish Lakish's interpretation of the Tanna Kamma. Shmuel cannot be following R' Yochanan's interpretation because according to R' Yochanan, the Tanna Kamma considers unblemished offerings (תְּמִימִין) the property of Heaven, not of the *ir hanidachas;* they are left to die (indirectly) only because they are the "sacrifices of the wicked." Now there is nothing in R' Shimon's words to indicate that he disagrees with this rule, and we must therefore assume (according to R' Yochanan) that R' Shimon indeed agrees with the Tanna Kamma that the animals must be left to die for this reason. But if so, what does R' Shimon dispute? Both he and the Tanna Kamma agree that unblemished offerings are excluded from the law of *ir hanidachas* (but are left to die because they are "the sacrifices of the wicked"), and that blemished offerings are subject to it! Accordingly, *Rashi* explains that Shmuel does not follow R' Yochanan's interpretation of the Tanna Kamma but rather Reish Lakish's. According to Reish Lakish, the Tanna Kamma does consider *kodashim kalim* subject to the law of *ir hanidachas*. To this R' Shimon responds that the word בְּהֶמְתָּהּ, *its animals,* teaches that *kodashim kalim* (including *bechor* and *maaser*) are excluded from the law of *ir hanidachas* (*Maharshal*; cf. *Maharsha*).

It follows from this that R' Yochanan – like Ravina – must explain R' Shimon to be excluding *blemished* animals. Accordingly, both the Tanna Kamma and R' Shimon agree that *un*blemished offerings (תְּמִימִין) are considered the "booty of Heaven" (שְׁלַל שָׁמַיִם), and that they are therefore not subject to being killed by the sword. Nevertheless, they are left to die indirectly because they are invalidated offerings that cannot be redeemed. The Tanna Kamma, however, holds that blemished *bechor* and *maaser* offerings (בַּעֲלֵי מוּמִין) are certainly the "booty of the city," inasmuch as they no longer have sacrificial sanctity and do not even need to be redeemed. R' Shimon disputes this and rules (based on the word בְּהֶמְתָּהּ, *its animals*) that they are nonetheless excluded from the fate of the *ir hanidachas* because they are not completely like the other animals of the city (see *Maharshal*).

[It should be noted that although R' Yochanan must follow Ravina's explanation of R' Shimon, Ravina himself could explain the Tanna Kamma in accordance with both R' Yochanan and Reish Lakish. According to Reish Lakish's explanation, Ravina would maintain that there are *two* disputes between the Tanna Kamma and R' Shimon: In addition to the dispute regarding blemished *bechor* and *maaser* offerings, R' Shimon would also dispute the Tanna Kamma's position that *kodashim kalim* are the property of their owners. (As pointed out in note 22, the Gemara assumed even in its question that R' Shimon rejects this position.) Although *Maharshal* states that Ravina holds like R' Yochanan, he would seem to mean only that unlike Shmuel, Ravina *could* hold like R' Yochanan.]

In summary: *According to Ravina,* the dispute between R' Shimon

והההקדשות שבה יפדו כו': [א] ת"ר [א] היו בה (א) (קדשי) קדשים קדשי מזבח ימותו קדשי בדק הבית יפדו ותרומות ירקבו ומעשר שני וכתבי הקדש יגנזו [ב] ר"ש אומר בהמתה ולא בהמת בכור ומעשר שללה פרט לכסף הקדש וכסף מעשר אמר מר היו בה (קדשי) קדשים קדשי מזבח ימותו ואמאי ימותו ירעו עד שיסתאבו וימכרו ויפלו דמיהן לנדבה ר' יוחנן אמר [א] [ב] זבח רשעים תועבה ר"ל אמר ממון בעלים הוא והכא בקדשים שחייב באחריותן [ג] ור"ש היא דאמר ממון בעלים הוא הא מדסיפא ר"ש היא רישא לאו ר"ש בקדשים קלים ואליבא דרבי יוסי הגלילי [ד] דאמר קדשים קלים ממון בעלים אבל קדשי קדשים מאי [ה] יפדו אדתני סיפא קדשי בדק הבית יפדו ליפלוג וליתני בדידה בד"א בקדשים קלים אבל קדשי קדשים [ו] יפדו כיון דאיכא חטאת שמתו בעליה דלמיתה אזלא לא פסיקא ליה בשלמא ר' יוחנן לא אמר כר"ל דכתיב זבח רשעים תועבה אלא ר"ל מ"ט לא אמר כר' יוחנן אמר לך כי אמרינן זבח רשעים תועבה הני מילי היכא דאתנהו בעיניהו אבל הכא כיון דאישתני אישתני: ר"ש אומר [ז] בהמתך ולא בהמת בכור ומעשר: במאי עסקינן [ח] אילימא בתמימין שלל שמים הוא אלא בבעלי מומין [ג] שללה נינהו אמר רבינא לעולם בבעלי מומין [ו] ומי שנאכל בתורת [ט] בהמתך יצאו אלו שאין נאכלין בתורת [י] בהמתך אלא בתורת בכור ומעשר [כ] דשלל שמים נינהו ופליגא דשמואל דאמר שמואל הכל קרב והכל נפדה מאי קאמר ה"ק כל שקרב כשהוא תם ונפדה כשהוא בעל מום משלל אימעיט וכל שקרב כשהוא תם ואינו נפדה כשהוא בעל מום כגון בכור ומעשר מבהמה נפקא: תרומות ירקבו: אמר רב חסדא ל"ש אלא תרומה ביד ישראל אבל תרומה ביד כהן כיון דממוניה הוא תשרף מתיב רב יוסף מעשר שני וכתבי הקדש יגנזו והא מעשר שני ביד ישראל כתרומה ביד כהן דמי וקתני יגנזו אלא אי אתמר הכי אתמר אמר רב חסדא ל"ש אלא תרומה ביד כהן אבל תרומה ביד ישראל [ד] תנתן לכהן שבעיר אחרת [ל] תנן התם [מ] עיסה של מעשר שני פטורה מן החלה דברי ר"מ וחכמים [ה] מחייבין אמר רב חסדא מחלוקת [ו] במעשר שני בירושלים דר"מ סבר [נ] מעשר שני ממון גבוה הוא ורבנן סברי ממון הדיוט הוא אבל [ס] בגבולין דברי הכל פטור מתיב רב יוסף מעשר שני וכתבי הקדש יגנזו במאי עסקינן אילימא בירושלים מי הויא עיר הנדחת והתניא [ע] עשרה דברים נאמרו בירושלים וזו אחת מהן [ז] אינה נעשית עיר הנדחת ואלא בעיר אחרת ואסקוהו לגוה הא קלטוהו מחיצות אלא לאו בגבולין וקתני יגנזו לא לעולם דעיר אחרת ואסקוהו לגוה והכא במאי עסקינן שנטמא ולפרקיה [פ] דא"ר אלעזר [ח] מניין למעשר שני שנטמא שפודין אותו אפילו בירושלים ת"ל [ב] לא תוכל שאתו ואין שאת אלא אכילה שנאמר [ג] וישא משאת מאת פניו הכא במאי עסקינן בלקוח וליפרקיה

רש"י

היו בה קדשי מזבח. כגון עולות ואשמות של רשעים בתוכה נהי דלא קרינן בהו את כל בהמתה לפי חרב דהא לא בהמתה היא אלא בהמת שמים אלא מאיסותא הוא להקריב קרבנות של רשעים הללו שהודחו הלכך ימותו כונסין אותן לכיפה ומאכילין אותן שעורין עד שכריסן נבקעת דאפילו דמיהם אסור כדלקמן: שנאמר כליל לה' אלהיך ל"ג: ר"ש אומר וכו'. לקמן מפרש טעמא: זבח רשעים תועבה. ואפילו דמיהן אסורין: ור"ש הוא דאמר. בהזהב (ב"מ נו:) קדשים שחייב באחריותן ממון בעלים הוא ויש בהם אונאה הלכך לענין עיר הנדחת נמי ממון בעלים הוא ודיינינהו לפי חרב כשאר בהמות שבתוכה והלכך אסורין דמיהן בהנאה והאי דקאמר ימותו ולא אמר שיחרימו אותה עמהם משום כבוד שמים: ואליבא דרבי יוסי הגלילי דאמר. בפ"ק דב"ק (ד' יב:) ומעלה מעל בה' לרבות קדשים קלים שהם ממונו והואיל וממונו הם אסורים בהנאה דאפילו דמיהן בהמתם מיקרו אבל קדשי קדשים (ב) [ל] אמאי ירעו דהא ודאי הם עצמם אינם קרבים דזבח רשעים תועבה אלא ירעו עד שיסתאבו וימכרו ויפלו דמיהם לנדבה: אי הכי [ק] מדתני סיפא וכו'. דקא מפליג בין קדשי מזבח לקדשי בדק הבית: ליפלוג וליתני בדידה. בקדשי מזבח עצמן בין קדשים קלים לקדשי קדשים: דלמיתה אזלא. כדאמרינן (תמורה ד' טו.) חמש חטאות מתות: לא פסיקא ליה. למיתני קדשי קדשים דעיר הנדחת ירעו דכיון דמתו להם אותם רשעים אי איכא חטאות שהפרישו בחייהם אזלי למיתה דכל חטאות שמתו בעליהם מתות במסכת הוריות (ד' ו.) מפרש טעמא אבל שאר קדשי קדשים כגון אשמות שמתו בעליהם ירעו: דאיתנהו בעינייהו. דהן עצמן ודאי אין קרבים משום זבח רשעים תועבה: אבל הכא. דאיכא למימר ירעו ויפלו דמיהם לנדבה: כיון דאישתני. ליכא הכא זבח רשעים תועבה: ולא בהמת בכור ומעשר. שאם היו בה בכורות או מעשר בהמה שהוא של ישראל וחלבו ודמו קרב אין מחרימין אותו עמה דלא מיקרי בהמתה: שלל שמים הוא. ומשללה נפקא: אלא בבעלי מומים. שאין בהם חלק לגבוה אלא נאכלין לבעלים שללה נינהו אמאי אין מחרימין אותן עמה: לעולם בבעלי מומין. ואפ"ה אין [ר] נשרפין עמה דדרשינן לקרא הכי בהמתה למי שנאכל לבעלים בתורת בהמתם יצאו אלו שיש להם שם לווי שאין נאכלים בתורת בהמתם שאין אומרין בהמת עיר הנדחת אלא בהמת בכור ומעשר של עיר מעשר ונתנוהו ביין ושכר ובשר ונטמא אותו לקוח דההוא לית ליה פדייה וכי קאמר ר"א במע"ש גופיה שהעלה פירות מע"ש לירושלים ונטמאו: וליפרקיה

ליקוטי רש"י

היו בה קדשים. בעיר הנדחת אינן נשרפין עם שללה דכתיב (דברים יג) שללה ולא שלל שמים ומיהו מיקרב לא קרבו משום דכתיב (משלי כח) זבח רשעים תועבה ואם קדשי מזבח הן ואפילו עולות ושלמים נדבה ימותו. קדשי בדק הבית יפדו. כשאר בדק הבית והפודה אותם יאכלם שהרי לא נאסרו דלאו דידהו הוו [לעיל מז.]. קדשים שחייב באחריותן. אמר הרי עלי עולה והפרישה והוממה ומכרה. ושאינו חייב באחריותן כגון דאמר הרי זו [ב"מ נו:]. אם קיבלם בעליו עליו באחריות כגון דאמר הרי עלי עולה והפריש זו [ב"ק עא:]. ממון בעלים הן. כגון אמר הרי עלי עולה והפריש בהמה לנדרו וכו' דרעהו קרינן ביה דדבר הגורם לממון לרבי שמעון כממון דמי [שבועות מב:]. ושור רעהו קרינן ביה [ב"ק יב:]. בבעלי מומין שללה נינהו. היינו בהמתה דכהן אוכל את הבכור וישראל את המעשר ואין לגבוה חלק בהן [תמורה ח.]. דברי ר' מאיר. דאמר בפרק שני דקדושין (נד:) מעשר ממון גבוה הוא. פטורה מן החלה כדמפרש דעריסותיכם כתיב ולא של גבוה [פסחים לז:]. פטורה מן החלה. דכתיב עריסותיכם והאי דגבוה היא ואף על גב דאיכא היתר אכילה כיון דלית בה דין שאר ממון לאו דידיה הוא [סוכה לה.]. הא קלטוהו מחיצות. מעשר שני בירושלים הואיל ואינו נאכל בכל מושבות מעתה משהביאו לירושלים שוב אינו יכול לחלל לאכול בחוץ כדאמרינן במסכת מכות (כ.) מחילה לקלוט מדרבנן דמשקלטוהו מחילות שוב אינו נפדה. ר' אלעזר. דאם נטמא פודין אותו ואוכלין אותו בכל מקום. שאתו. כשלא תוכל לאוכלו כגון זה שניטמא ונתת בכסף [פסחים לו:]. אפילו בירושלים. שאין מעשר טהור נפדה שם דכתיב (דברים יד) כי ירחק ממך [וגו'] ונתת בכסף ולא כשהיה בירושלים [ב"מ נג:]. אין מוכרין מעשר שני בירושלים, ואפילו לאוכלו שם בקדושה דכי ירבה ממך הדרך ונתתה בכסף כתיב (דברים יד) [פסחים עה:]. שפודין אותו אפילו בירושלים. דאי בעי פריק ואפילו בירושלים דאע"ג דמעשר שני טהור אינו נפדה בירושלים דכתיב כי ירחק ממך ונתת בכסף בריחוק מקום אתה פודה ולא בקירוב מקום (קדושין דף נו). ואין שאת אלא אכילה. והכי קאמר קרא כי ירחק ממך שיהא מעשר טהור חוץ לירושלים או אפילו הוא בירושלים אלא שאי אתה יכול לאוכלו שנטמא ונתת בכסף [מכות יט.]. בלקוח. מעשר זה ולא הוא עצמו היה מעשר אלא לרכי סעודה שלקח בירושלים בכסף מעשר [ב"מ שם].

תוספות

הנדחת: ופליגא. הא דרבינא אדשמואל דאמר שמואל עלה דהא מילתא דר"ש כי הוה קשיא לן במאי עסקינן הוי מתרץ הכי הכל קרב והכל נפדה: מאי קאמר ה"ק. כל שהוא קרב לגבוה כשהוא תם וכשהוא בעל מום צריך פדייה כגון שאר קדשים קלים חוץ ממעשר בהמה ובכור הנהו משללה נפקא דאין מחרימין אותם עמה דהואיל וצריכי פדייה במומן של שמים קרינן ביה ופליג עליה דת"ק דאמר קדשים קלים ממון בעלים הוא: וכל שקרב כשהוא תם ואינו נפדה כשהוא בעל מום. אלא נאכל לבעלים כגון בכור ומעשר ההוא לאו שלל שמים מקרו ואפילו בתמותן ולא מצי למפרך והא בתמותן שלל שמים הוא שהרי נאכל במומו והלכך אצטריך בהמתה למעוטי בכור ומעשר תמימים דמשללה ליכא למעוטינהו והיינו פליגא דאיהו מוקי לה אפילו בתמימים דקסבר בכור ומעשר בעלי מומין בהמתה קרינא ביה ובסייף: תרומה ביד ישראל. שעדיין לא נתנה לכהן דאפילו אותו ישראל רשע הוא תרומה שבידו אינה נשרפת עם שאר שללה דהא לאו דידיה הוא דשמא היה נתנה לכהן צדיק שבתוכה לה הלכך אינה נשרפת דהיינו כפקדון דעיר אחרת ואתנהו בגוה דאמר לעיל דמותרין ונהי דבאכילה לא שרינא לה דשמא היה נתנה לכהן רשע שבתוכה הלכך ירקבו אבל תרומה ביד כהן דממוניה הוא תשרף: וקתני יגנזו. אע"ג דממוניה הוא לא אמר תשרף: אלא תרומה ביד כהן. דממוניה הוא ולא מזלזלינן בה כולי האי הואיל וקדש הוא: לכהן שבעיר אחרת. כלומר לכהן שלא הודח עמהן: אבל בגבולין. שאין לה היתר אכילה אלא בפדייה ד"ה פטורה מן החלה דממון גבוה הוא ל"א אבל בגבולין דאין לה היתר אכילה בשעת חיוב חלה דהיינו בשעת גלגול העיסה לא קרינא ביה ראשית עריסותיכם (במדבר טו) ואפילו פדאה לאחר מיכן פטור מן החלה: י' דברים נאמרו בירושלים. בפ' מרובה (ב"ק פב:) חשיב להו: אלא בעיר אחרת ואסקו לגוה. שהיה אותו מעשר שני של אחד מבני עיר הנדחת והעלו אותו לירושלים קודם שהודחה ואח"כ הודחו אם כן אמאי יגנזו לשתרו נמי באכילה דהא קלטינהו מחילות דהיינו חומה: אלא לאו בגבולין. ולא מטו ליה וקתני יגנזו ואינו יוצא לישרף בתמיה: ואם איתא. דבגבולין לד"ה ממון גבוה הוא לשתרי נמי באכילה אלא לאו ממון הדיוט הוא ונהי דבשריפה לא משום זילותא: לעולם דעיר הנדחת ואסקיה לגוה. ודקאמרת לשתרו נמי באכילה דהא קלטוהו מחילות: הכא במאי עסקינן כשנטמא. דלאו בר אכולי בטומאה הוא דכתיב (דברים כו) לא בערתי ממנו בטמא ולקמן פריך מאי איריא עיר הנדחת אפילו בחולה לה: ואפילו בירושלים. לאחר שנכנס ואע"ג דדרשינן (שם יד) כי ירחק ממך המקום וצרת הכסף בידך ברחוק מקום אתה פודה וצר ולא בקרוב מקום: ואין שאת אלא אכילה. וה"ק קרא כי ירחק ממך המקום או כי לא תוכל לאוכלו שנטמא וצרת הכסף בידך: בלקוח. שכבר הוציאה בהוצאה לכסף מעשר ונתנוהו ביין ושכר ובשר ונטמא אותו לקוח דההוא לית ליה פדייה וכי קאמר ר"א במע"ש גופיה שהעלה פירות מע"ש לירושלים ונטמאו: וליפרקיה

עין משפט נר מצוה

נה א ב ג ד מיי' פ"ד מהל' עכו"ם הלכה יג סמג עשין טו:
נו ה ו מיי' פ"ו מהל' בכורים הלכה ז:
נז ז מיי' פ"ז מהל' בית הבחירה הלכה יד ופ"ד מהל' עכו"ם הלכה ז:
נח ח מיי' פ"ב מהל' מעשר שני ונטע רבעי הלכה ח סמג לאוין קלו:

מסורת הש"ס

א) לעיל מז. [תוספ' פי"ד], ב) [תמורה ח. ע"ש], ג) [ב"מ נו.], ד) [ב"ק יב: וש"נ], ה) [גי' רש"י ירעו וכל"ן], ו) [לפי גירסת רש"י דלעיל צ"ל ירעו], ז) [צ"ל בהמתה], ח) [תמורה ח. ע"ש], ט) [צ"ל בהמתה], י) [צ"ל בהמתה], כ) [בתוס' דבכורות דף לא. ד"ה חוץ וכו' משמע דגרסי הכא בסוגיא כמו דסיים הש"ס בתמורה ח. דתנן כל פסולי המוקדשין נמכרין באטליז חוץ מן הבכור והמעשר ע"ש אבל מפירש"י דהכא ד"ה לעולם בבעלי מומין וכו' מוכח דלא גרים להא דתנן כו' ומשום הכי פירש"י הכא יצאו אלו שיש להם שם לווי ורבינא הוא דמשני לה הכי כאן אבל בתמורה ח. סתמא דש"ס מייתי להא דתנן כל פסולי וכו' ולא ס"ל כרבינא בפי' הזה], ל) א"ז משנה אלא ברייתא ועיין רש"ל, מ) סוכה לה: פסחים לח. [עי' חולין פז: תוס' ד"ה תנן התם], נ) [קידושין כד. וש"נ], ס) [עי' תוס' קידושין נג: ד"ה איהו ותוס' בכורות ט: ד"ה ותנן ועי' היטב תוס' סוכה לה. סד"ה לפי], ע) ב"ק פב., פ) ב"מ נג. פסחי' לו: מכות יט:, צ) [צ"ל מאי], ק) [צ"ל אדתני], ר) נ"א נהרגין.

הגהות הב"ח

(א) גמ' ת"ר היו בה קדשים קדשי מזבח כצ"ל ותיבת קדשי נמחק: (ב) רש"י ד"ה ואליבא דר' יוסי וכו' קדשי קדשים ירעו כצ"ל ותיבת אמאי נמחק:

גליון הש"ס

גמ' ומי שנאכל בתורת בהמתך. עי' זבחים דף עה ע"ב תוס' ד"ה התפיס:

תורה אור השלם

א) זֶבַח רְשָׁעִים תּוֹעֵבָה אַף כִּי בְזִמָּה יְבִיאֶנּוּ: [משלי כא, כז]

ב) וְכִי יִרְבֶּה מִמְּךָ הַדֶּרֶךְ כִּי לֹא תוּכַל שְׂאֵתוֹ כִּי יִרְחַק מִמְּךָ הַמָּקוֹם אֲשֶׁר יִבְחַר יְיָ אֱלֹהֶיךָ לָשׂוּם שְׁמוֹ שָׁם כִּי יְבָרֶכְךָ יְיָ אֱלֹהֶיךָ: [דברים יד, כד]

ג) וַיִּשָּׂא מַשְׂאֹת מֵאֵת פָּנָיו אֲלֵהֶם וַתֵּרֶב מַשְׂאַת בִּנְיָמִן מִמַּשְׂאֹת כֻּלָּם חָמֵשׁ יָדוֹת וַיִּשְׁתּוּ וַיִּשְׁכְּרוּ עִמּוֹ: [בראשית מג, לד]

The Gemara analyzes the next ruling of the Mishnah, which states:

תְּרוּמוֹת יֵרָקְבוּ – THE *TERUMOS* in the subverted city SHOULD be left to ROT, but they are not burned.

Terumah is separated by a person from his crop and then given to a Kohen. The non-Kohen who separates it does not own it; the Kohen who receives it does. The Gemara discusses whether the Mishnah's ruling refers to *terumah* still held by the Yisrael (i.e. non-Kohen) or *terumah* that has come into the possession of the Kohen:

אָמַר רַב חִסְדָּא – **Rav Chisda said:** לֹא שָׁנוּ אֶלָּא תְּרוּמָה בְּיַד יִשְׂרָאֵל – **They** [the Sages of the Mishnah] **did not teach** that *terumah* is left to rot rather than burned **except** where the ***terumah*** is still **in the hands of the Yisrael** who separated it;[28] אֲבָל תְּרוּמָה בְּיַד כֹּהֵן – **but** where the ***terumah*** is already **in the hands of** a **Kohen,** כֵּיוָן דְּמָמוֹנֵיהּ הוּא – **since [the *terumah*] is his property,** תִּשָּׂרֵף – **it should be burned** along with all the other property belonging to the inhabitants of the subverted city.[29]

This ruling is challenged:

מֵתִיב רַב יוֹסֵף – **Rav Yosef challenged** Rav Chisda from the Mishnah's next ruling: מַעֲשֵׂר שֵׁנִי וְכִתְבֵי הַקֹּדֶשׁ יִגָּנְזוּ – THE *MAASER SHENI* AND HOLY SCRIPTURES SHOULD BE HIDDEN AWAY. וְהָא מַעֲשֵׂר שֵׁנִי בְּיַד יִשְׂרָאֵל כִּתְרוּמָה בְּיַד כֹּהֵן דָּמֵי – **Now *maaser sheni* in the hands of a Yisrael is like *terumah* in the hands of a Kohen,** for *maaser sheni* is the property of its owner[30] just as *terumah* is the property of a Kohen. וְקָתָנֵי יִגָּנְזוּ – **Nevertheless, the Mishnah teaches that** if it belongs to an inhabitant of a subverted city, IT SHOULD BE HIDDEN AWAY, not burned. By the

NOTES

and the Tanna Kamma concerns blemished *bechor* and *maaser* offerings (בַּעֲלֵי מוּמִין). Since these do not require redemption and are the property of their owners, the Tanna Kamma rules that they are killed by the sword. R' Shimon, however, excludes them from destruction from the word בְּהֶמְתָּהּ, *its animals*, because they are not wholly like the animals of the city. All may agree, however, that *un*blemished offerings (תְּמִימִין) are not killed by the sword because they are the "booty of Heaven" (שְׁלַל שָׁמַיִם), not of the city. Nevertheless, they are left to die because they are invalidated offerings — "sacrifices of the wicked" — which cannot be redeemed because the invalidation would carry over to the money as well, as R' Yochanan explained.

[However, it is also possible for Ravina to explain the Tanna Kamma as Reish Lakish does. Thus, the Tanna Kamma would hold that *kodashim kalim* are killed by the sword because they are considered the property of their owners. He would certainly hold that blemished *bechor* and *maaser* offerings are the property of the owners and are thus also killed by the sword. R' Shimon disputes both these rulings. According to him, *kodashim kalim* are *not* killed because they are *not* the property of their owners but of Heaven. Blemished *bechor* and *maaser* offerings are not killed because they are not completely like the animals of the city and are thus excluded by the word בְּהֶמְתָּהּ.]

According to Shmuel, the dispute between R' Shimon and the Tanna Kamma concerns *un*blemished *kodashim kalim* offerings, including the *bechor* and *maaser.* The Tanna Kamma considers these the property of their owners (מָמוֹן בְּעָלִים) and therefore rules that they are killed by the sword as the animals of an *ir hanidachas*. R' Shimon considers them the property of Heaven and thus excluded from death by the word שְׁלָלָהּ, *its booty,* which excludes the "booty of Heaven" (שְׁלַל שָׁמַיִם). This, however, would not suffice to exclude *bechor* and *maaser* offerings from being killed because the fact that they can revert to the personal use of their owners without redemption (but simply by becoming blemished) qualifies them as the "booty of the city" even when they are *not* blemished. Nevertheless, R' Shimon derives from the word בְּהֶמְתָּהּ, *its animals*, that even (unblemished) *bechor* and *maaser* offerings are *not* killed. But R' Shimon and the Tanna Kamma agree that blemished *bechor* and *maaser* offerings (בַּעֲלֵי מוּמִין) are killed as animals of the *ir hanidachas.* Shmuel follows Reish Lakish's interpretation of the Tanna Kamma. See chart.

[We have explained the dispute according to *Rashi* as interpreted by *Maharshal. Maharsha* explains *Rashi* differently, but his explanation assumes that according to Reish Lakish, *kodashim kalim* are not killed by the sword but are left to die indirectly. Since this is not consistent with *Yad Ramah's* understanding of *Rashi* (which we followed above in note 10), we have followed *Maharshal's* explanation (but see *Chidushei HaRan* there).]

28. I.e. he had not yet given it to a Kohen.

29. *Terumah* in the possession of a Kohen living in the *ir hanidachas* is burned. Since the *terumah* belongs to the Kohen who received it [he may even sell it to another Kohen], it is like any other property of the *ir hanidachas* and it is therefore burned. However, if the *terumah* is still in the hands of the non-Kohen who separated it, it cannot be burned as his property since it is not his. Rather, it is like an item that is on deposit with a resident of an *ir hanidachas*. The law for deposits, as Rav Chisda taught above (112a), is that if they belong to someone outside the city, they are not burned. Accordingly, since the non-Kohen who is in possession of the *terumah* might eventually have given it to a Kohen from another city, the *terumah* cannot be burned (due to its sanctity). On the other hand, since he might eventually have given it to one of the wicked Kohanim of the *ir hanidachas,* it cannot be eaten. Consequently, it is left to rot (*Rashi*).

[See *Rashash* who questions why *Rashi* linked the prohibition to the fact that it might have been given to a *wicked* Kohen of that city. Seemingly, even if it had been given to a righteous Kohen of that city it would have been forbidden, since the property of the righteous in an *ir hanidachas* is also destroyed. See also *Sanhedrei Ketanah*.]

30. [Though he can eat it only in Jerusalem, it is his to use and to give to whomever he wishes.]

Actually, there is a dispute whether *maaser sheni* is considered the property of its owner or the property of Heaven (see Gemara below). The Gemara's question assumes the view that it is the property of its owner (*Yad Ramah*).

		קדשים תמימין UNBLEMISHED OFFERINGS	בכור ומעשר בעלי מומין BLEMISHED BECHOR AND MAASER OFFERINGS [1]
RAVINA (R' YOCHANAN)	TANNA KAMMA	PROPERTY OF HEAVEN — LEFT TO DIE INDIRECTLY [2]	PROPERTY OF *IR HANIDACHAS* — KILLED BY THE SWORD
	R' SHIMON	PROPERTY OF HEAVEN — LEFT TO DIE INDIRECTLY [2]	PROPERTY OF *IR HANIDACHAS* — BUT NOT KILLED EXCLUDED BY בְּהֶמְתָּהּ, *ITS ANIMALS* [3]
RAVINA (REISH LAKISH)	TANNA KAMMA	*KODASHIM KALIM,* PROPERTY OF *IR HANIDACHAS* — KILLED BY THE SWORD	PROPERTY OF *IR HANIDACHAS* — KILLED BY THE SWORD
	R' SHIMON	*KODASHIM KALIM,* PROPERTY OF HEAVEN — NOT KILLED [4]	PROPERTY OF *IR HANIDACHAS* — BUT NOT KILLED EXCLUDED BY בְּהֶמְתָּהּ, *ITS ANIMALS*
SHMUEL (REISH LAKISH) [5]	TANNA KAMMA	*KODASHIM KALIM* / *BECHOR* AND *MAASER* PROPERTY OF *IR HANIDACHAS* — KILLED BY THE SWORD	PROPERTY OF *IR HANIDACHAS* — KILLED BY THE SWORD
	R' SHIMON	*KODASHIM KALIM,* PROPERTY OF HEAVEN — NOT KILLED [4] *BECHOR* AND *MAASER,* PROPERTY OF *IR HANIDACHAS* — BUT NOT KILLED EXCLUDED BY בְּהֶמְתָּהּ, *ITS ANIMALS*	PROPERTY OF *IR HANIDACHAS* — KILLED BY THE SWORD

1. Other types of blemished offerings are the same as unblemished offerings because they must still be redeemed.
2. Because they are invalidated offerings.
3. Because they are not entirely like the city's animals.
4. Left to graze and become blemished, then redeemed.
5. Shmuel must follow Reish Lakish — *Rashi* as explained by *Maharshal.*

עין משפט
נר מצוה

נה א ב ג ד מיי' פ"ד מהל' עכו"ם הלכה יג סמג עשין טו:
נו ה ו מיי' פ"ו מהל' בכורים הלכה ד:
נז ז מיי' פ"ז מהל' בית הבחירה הלכה יד ופ"ד מהל' עכו"ם הלכה ד:
נח ח מיי' פ"ג מהל' מעשר שני ונטע רבעי הלכה ח סמג לאוין קלו:

ליקוטי רש"י

היו בה קדשים. בעיר הנדחת אין נשרפין עם שללה דכתיב (דברים יג) שללה ולא שלל שמים ומיהו מיקרב לא קרבו משום דכתיב (משלי כא) זבח רשעים תועבה ואם קדשי מזבח הן ואפילו עולות ושלמים נדבה ימותו. קדשי בדק הבית יפדו. כשאר בדק הבית והפודה אותם יאכלם שהרי לא נאסרו דלאו דידהו הוו [לעיל מז.]. קדשים שחייב באחריותן. אמר הרי עלי עולה והפרישה והוממה ומכרה. ושאינו חייב באחריותן כגון דאמר הרי זו [ב"מ נו:]. אם קיבלם בעליו עליו באחריות כגון דאמר הרי עלי עולה והפריש זו [ב"ק עא:]. ממון בעלים הן. כגון אמר הרי עלי עולה והפריש בהמה לנדרו וכו' דרעהו קרינן ביה דדבר הגורם לממון לרבי שמעון כממון דמי [שבועות מב:]. ושור רעהו קרינן ביה [ב"ק יב:]. בבעלי מומין שללה נינהו. היינו בהמתה דכהן אוכל את הבכור וישראל את המעשר ואין לגבוה חלק בהן [תמורה ח.]. דברי ר' מאיר. דאמר בפרק שני דקדושין (נד:) מעשר ממון גבוה הוא. פטורה מן החלה כדמפרש דעריסותיכם כתיב ולא של גבוה [פסחים לז:]. פטורה מן החלה. דכתיב עריסותיכם והאי דגבוה היא ואף על גב דאיכא היתר אכילה כיון דלית בה דין שאר ממון לאו דידיה הוא [סוכה לה.]. הא קלטוהו מחיצות. מעשר שני ירושלים הואיל ואינו נאכל בכל מושבות מעתה משהביאו לירושלים שוב אינו יכול לחלל לאכול בחוץ כדאמרינן במסכת מכות (כ.) מחיצה לקלוט מדרבנן דמשקלטוהו מחיצות שוב אינו נפדה. ר' אלעזר. דאם נטמא פודין אותו ואוכלין אותו בכל מקום. שאתו. כשלא תוכל לאוכלו כגון זה שניטמא ונתת בכסף [פסחים לו:]. אפילו בירושלים. שאין מעשר טהור נפדה שם דכתיב (דברים יד) כי ירחק ממך [וגו'] ונתת בכסף ולא כשהיה בירושלים [ב"מ נג:]. אין מוכרין מעשר שני בירושלים, ואפילו לאוכלו שם בקדושה דכי ירבה ממך הדרך ונתתה בכסף כתיב (דברים יד) [פסחים עה:]. שפודין אותו אפילו בירושלים. דאי בעי פריק ואפילו בירושלים דאע"ג דמעשר שני טהור אינו נפדה בירושלים דכתיב כי ירחק ממך ונתת בכסף בריחוק מקום אתה פודה ולא בקירוב מקום (קדושין דף נו). ואין שאת אלא אכילה. והכי קאמר קרא כי ירחק ממך שיהא מעשר טהור חוץ לירושלים או אפילו הוא בירושלים אלא שאי אתה יכול לאוכלו שנטמא ונתת בכסף [מכות יט.]. בלקוח. מעשר זה ולא הוא עצמו היה מעשר אלא לרכי סעודה שלקח בירושלים בכסף מעשר [ב"מ שם].

מסורת הש"ס

א) לעיל מז. [תוספ' פי"ד], ב) [תמורה ח. ע"ש], ג) [ב"מ נו.], ד) [ב"ק יב: וש"נ], ה) [גי' רש"י ירעו וכצ"ל], ו) [לפי גירסת רש"י דלעיל צ"ל ירעו], ז) [צ"ל בהמתה], ח) [תמורה ח. ע"ש], ט) [צ"ל בהמתה], י) [צ"ל בהמתה], כ) [בתוס' דבכורות דף לא. ד"ה חוץ וכו' משמע דגרסי הכא בסוגיא כמו דקיים הש"ס בתמורה ח. דתנן כל פסולי המוקדשין נמכרין באטליז חוץ מן הבכור והמעשר ע"ש אבל מפירש"י דהכא ד"ה לעולם בבעלי מומין וכו' מוכח דלא גרים להא דתנן כו' ומשום הכי פירש"י הכא יצאו אלו שיש להם שם לווי ורבינא הוא דמשני לה הכי כאן אבל בתמורה ח. סתמא דש"ס מייתי להא דתנן כל פסולי וכו' ולא ס"ל כרבינא בפי' הזה], ל) א"ז משנה אלא ברייתא ועיין רש"ל, מ) סוכה לה: פסחים לח. [עי' חולין פז: תוס' ד"ה תנן התם], נ) [קידושין כד. וש"נ], ס) [עי' תוס' קידושין נג: ד"ה איהו ותוס' בכורות ט: ד"ה ותנן ועי' היטב תוס' סוכה לה. סד"ה לפי], ע) ב"ק פב., פ) ב"מ נג. פסחי' לו: מכות יט:, צ) [צ"ל מאי], ק) [צ"ל אדתני], ר) נ"א נהרגין.

הגהות הב"ח

(א) גמ' ת"ר היו בה קדשים קדשי מזבח כצ"ל ותיבת קדשי נמחק: (ב) רש"י ד"ה ואליבא דר' יוסי וכו' קדשי קדשים ירעו כצ"ל ותיבת אמאי נמחק:

גליון הש"ס

גמ' ומי שנאכל בתורת בהמתך. עי' זבחים דף עה ע"ב תוס' ד"ה התפיס:

תורה אור השלם

א) זֶבַח רְשָׁעִים תּוֹעֵבָה אַף כִּי בְזִמָּה יְבִיאֶנּוּ: [משלי כא, כז]

ב) וְכִי יִרְבֶּה מִמְּךָ הַדֶּרֶךְ כִּי לֹא תוּכַל שְׂאֵתוֹ כִּי יִרְחַק מִמְּךָ הַמָּקוֹם אֲשֶׁר יִבְחַר יְיָ אֱלֹהֶיךָ לָשׂוּם שְׁמוֹ שָׁם כִּי יְבָרֶכְךָ יְיָ אֱלֹהֶיךָ: [דברים יד, כד]

ג) וַיִּשָּׂא מַשְׂאֹת מֵאֵת פָּנָיו אֲלֵהֶם וַתֵּרֶב מַשְׂאַת בִּנְיָמִן מִמַּשְׂאֹת כֻּלָּם חָמֵשׁ יָדוֹת וַיִּשְׁתּוּ וַיִּשְׁכְּרוּ עִמּוֹ: [בראשית מג, לד]

והההקדשות שבה יפדו כו': א) ת"ר א היו בה (א) (קדשי) קדשים קדשי מזבח ימותו קדשי בדק הבית יפדו ותרומות ירקבו ומעשר שני וכתבי הקדש יגנזו ב) ר"ש אומר בהמתה ולא בהמת בכור ומעשר שללה פרט לכסף הקדש וכסף מעשר אמר מר היו בה (קדשי) קדשים קדשי מזבח ימותו ואמאי ימותו ירעו עד שיסתאבו וימכרו ויפלו דמיהן לנדבה ר' יוחנן אמר א) ב זבח רשעים תועבה ר"ל אמר ממון בעלים הוא והכא בקדשים שחייב באחריותן ג) ור"ש היא דאמר ממון בעלים הוא הא מדסיפא ר"ש היא רישא לאו ר"ש בקדשים קלים ואליבא דרבי יוסי הגלילי ד) דאמר קדשים קלים ממון בעלים אבל קדשי קדשים מאי ה) יפדו אדתני סיפא קדשי בדק הבית יפדו ליפלוג וליתני בדידה בד"א בקדשים קלים אבל קדשי קדשים ו) יפדו כיון דאיכא חטאת שמתו בעליה דלמיתה אזלא לא פסיקא ליה בשלמא ר' יוחנן לא אמר כר"ל דכתיב זבח רשעים תועבה אלא ר"ל מ"ט לא אמר כר' יוחנן אמר לך כי אמרינן זבח רשעים תועבה הני מילי היכא דאתנהו בעינייהו אבל הכא כיון דאישתני אישתני: ר"ש אומר ז) בהמתך ולא בהמת בכור ומעשר: במאי עסקינן ח) אילימא בתמימין שלל שמים הוא אלא בבעלי מומין ג שללה נינהו אמר רבינא לעולם בבעלי מומין ○ ומי שנאכל בתורת ט) בהמתך יצאו אלו שאין נאכלין בתורת י) בהמתך אלא בתורת בכור ומעשר כ) דשלל שמים נינהו ופליגא דשמואל דאמר שמואל הכל קרב והכל נפדה מאי קאמר ה"ק כל שקרב כשהוא תם ונפדה כשהוא בעל מום משלל אימעיט וכל שקרב כשהוא תם ואינו נפדה כשהוא בעל מום כגון בכור ומעשר מבהמה נפקא: תרומות ירקבו: אמר רב חסדא ל"ש אלא תרומה ביד ישראל אבל תרומה ביד כהן כיון דממוניה הוא תשרף מתיב רב יוסף מעשר שני וכתבי הקדש יגנזו והא מעשר שני ביד ישראל כתרומה ביד כהן דמי וקתני יגנזו אלא אי אתמר הכי אתמר אמר רב חסדא ל"ש אלא תרומה ביד כהן אבל תרומה ביד ישראל ד תנתן לכהן שבעיר אחרת ל) תנן התם מ) עיסה של מעשר שני פטורה מן החלה דברי ר"מ וחכמים ה מחייבין אמר רב חסדא מחלוקת ו במעשר שני בירושלים דר"מ סבר נ) מעשר שני ממון גבוה הוא ורבנן סברי ממון הדיוט הוא אבל ס) בגבולין דברי הכל פטור מתיב רב יוסף מעשר שני וכתבי הקדש יגנזו במאי עסקינן אילימא בירושלים מי הויא עיר הנדחת והתניא ע) עשרה דברים נאמרו בירושלים וזו אחת מהן ז אינה נעשית עיר הנדחת ואלא בעיר אחרת ואסקוהו לגוה הא קלטוהו מחיצות אלא לאו בגבולין וקתני יגנזו לא לעולם דעיר אחרת ואסקוהו לגוה והכא במאי עסקינן שנטמא ולפרקיה פ) דא"ר אלעזר ח מניין למעשר שני שנטמא שפודין אותו אפילו בירושלים ת"ל ב) לא תוכל שאתו ואין שאת אלא אכילה שנאמר ג) וישא משאת מאת פניו הכא במאי עסקינן בלקוח וליפרקיה

היו בה קדשי מזבח. כגון עולות ואשמות של רשעים בתוכה נהי דלא קרינן בהו את כל בהמתה לפי חרב דהא לא בהמתה היא אלא בהמת שמים אלא מאיסותא הוא להקריב קרבנות של רשעים הללו שהודחו הלכך ימותו כונסין אותן לכיפה ומאכילין אותן שעורין עד שכריסן נבקעת דאפילו דמיהם אסור כדלקמן: שנאמר כליל לה' אלהיך ל"ג: ר"ש אומר וכו'. לקמן מפרש טעמא: זבח רשעים תועבה. ואפילו דמיהן אסורין: ור"ש הוא דאמר. בהזהב (ב"מ נו:) קדשים שחייב באחריותן ממון בעלים הוא ויש בהם אונאה הלכך לענין עיר הנדחת נמי ממון בעלים הוא ודיינינהו לפי חרב כשאר בהמות שבתוכה והלכך אסורין דמיהן בהנאה והאי דקאמר ימותו ולא אמר שיחרימו אותה עמהם משום כבוד שמים: ואליבא דרבי יוסי הגלילי דאמר. בפ"ק דב"ק (ד' יג:) ומעלה מעל בה' לרבות קדשים קלים שהם ממונו והואיל וממונו הם אסורים בהנאה דאפילו דמיהן בהמתם מיקרו אבל קדשי קדשים (ב) ה) אמאי ירעו דהא ודאי הם עצמם אינם קרבים דזבח רשעים תועבה אלא ירעו עד שיסתאבו וימכרו ויפלו דמיהם לנדבה: אי הכי ק) מדתני סיפא וכו'. דקא מפליג בין קדשי מזבח לקדשי בדק הבית: ליפלוג וליתני בדידה. בקדשי מזבח עצמן בין קדשים קלים לקדשי קדשים: דלמיתה אזלא. כדאמרינן (תמורה ד' טו.) חמש חטאות מתות: לא פסיקא ליה. למיתני קדשי קדשים דעיר הנדחת ירעו דכיון דמתו להם אותם רשעים אי איכא חטאות שהפרישו בחייהם אזלי למיתה דכל חטאות שמתו בעליהם מתות במסכת הוריות (ד' ו.) מפרש טעמא אבל שאר קדשי קדשים כגון אשמות שמתו בעליהם ירעו: דאיתנהו בעינייהו. דהן עצמן ודאי אינן קרבים משום זבח רשעים תועבה: אבל הכא. דאיכא למימר ירעו ויפלו דמיהם לנדבה: כיון דאישתני. ליכא הכא זבח רשעים תועבה: ולא בהמת בכור ומעשר. שאם היו בה בכורות או מעשר בהמה שהוא של ישראל וחלבו ודמו קרב אין מחרימין אותו עמה דלא מיקרי בהמתה: שלל שמים הוא. ומשללה נפקא: אלא בבעלי מומים. שאין בהם חלק לגבוה אלא נאכלין לבעלים שללה נינהו אמאי אין מחרימין אותן עמה: לעולם בבעלי מומין. ואפ"ה אין ר) נשרפין עמה דדרשינן לקרא הכי בהמתה למי שנאכל לבעלים בתורת בהמתם יצאו אלו שיש להם שם לווי שאין נאכלים בתורת בהמתם שאין אומרין בהמת עיר הנדחת אלא בהמת בכור ומעשר של עיר הנדחת: ופליגא. הא דרבינא אדשמואל דאמר שמואל עלה דהא מילתא דר"ש כי הוה קשיא לן במאי עסקינן הוי מתרץ הכי הכל קרב והכל נפדה: מאי קאמר ה"ק. כל שהוא קרב לגבוה כשהוא תם וכשהוא בעל מום צריך פדייה כגון שאר קדשים קלים חוץ ממעשר בהמה ובכור הנהו משללה נפקא דאין מחרימין אותם עמה דהואיל וצריכי פדייה במומן שלל שמים קרינן ביה ופליג עליה דת"ק דאמר קדשים קלים ממון בעלים הוא: וכל שקרב כשהוא תם ואינו נפדה כשהוא בעל מום. אלא נאכל לבעלים כגון בכור ומעשר ההוא לאו שלל שמים מקרו ואפילו בתמותן ולא מצי למפרך והא בתמותן שלל שמים הוא שהרי נאכל במומו והלכך אצטריך בהמתה למעוטי בכור ומעשר תמימים דמשללה ליכא למעוטינהו והיינו פליגא דאיהו מוקי לה אפילו בתמימים דקסבר בכור ומעשר בעלי מומין בהמתה קרינא ביה ובסייף: תרומה ביד ישראל. שעדיין לא נתנה לכהן דאפילו אותו ישראל רשע הוא תרומה שבידו אינה נשרפת עם שאר שללה דהא לאו דידיה הוא דשמא היה נתנה לכהן צדיק שבחוצה לה הלכך אינה נשרפת דהיינו כפקדון דעיר אחרת ואתנהו בגוה דאמר לעיל דמותרין והי דבאכילה לא שרינא לה דשמא היה נתנה לכהן רשע שבתוכה הלכך ירקבו אבל תרומה ביד כהן דממוניה הוא תשרף: וקתני יגנזו. אע"ג דממוניה הוא לא אמר תשרף: אלא תרומה ביד כהן. דממוניה הוא ולא מזלזלינן בה כולי האי הואיל וקדש הוא: לכהן שבעיר אחרת. כלומר לכהן שלא הודח עמהן: אבל בגבולין. שאין לה היתר אכילה אלא בפדייה ד"ה פטורה מן החלה דממון גבוה הוא ל"א אבל בגבולין דאין לה היתר אכילה בשעת חיוב חלה דהיינו בשעת גלגול העיסה לא קרינא ביה ראשית עריסותיכם (במדבר טו) ואפילו פדאה לאחר מיכן פטור מן החלה: י' דברים נאמרו בירושלים. בפ' מרובה (ב"ק פב:) חשיב להו: אלא בעיר אחרת ואסקו לגוה. שהיה אותו מעשר שני של אחד מבני עיר הנדחת והעלו אותו לירושלים קודם שהודחה ואח"כ הודחו אם כן אמאי יגנזו לשתרו נמי באכילה דהא קלטינהו מחיצות דהיינו חומה: אלא לאו בגבולין. ולא מטו ליה וקתני יגנזו ואינו יוצא לישרף בתמיה: ואם איתא. דבגבולין לד"ה ממון גבוה הוא לשתרי נמי באכילה אלא לאו ממון הדיוט הוא ונהי דבשריפה לא משום זילותא: לעולם דעיר הנדחת ואסקיה לגוה. ודקאמרת לשתרו נמי באכילה דהא קלטוהו מחיצות: הכא במאי עסקינן כשנטמא. דלאו בר אכולי בטומאה הוא דכתיב (דברים כו) לא בערתי ממנו בטמא ולקמן פריך מאי איריא עיר הנדחת אפילו בחוצה לה: ואפילו בירושלים. לאחר שנכנס ואע"ג דדרשינן (שם יד) כי ירחק ממך המקום וצרת הכסף בידך ברחוק מקום אתה פודה וצר ולא בקרוב מקום: ואין שאת אלא אכילה. וה"ק קרא כי ירחק ממך המקום או כי לא תוכל לאוכלו שנטמא וצרת הכסף בידך: בלקוח. שכבר הוציאה בהוצאה לכסף מעשר ונתנוהו ביין ושכר ובשר ונטמא אותו לקוח דההוא לית ליה פדייה וכי קאמר ר"א במע"ש גופיה שהעלה פירות מע"ש לירושלים ונטמאו: וליפרקיה

same token, we should say that *terumah* in the hands of a Kohen should also not be burned. – ? –

The Gemara therefore revises its citation of Rav Chisda:

אֶלָּא אִי אִתְּמַר – **Rather, if** something **was said** by Rav Chisda in regard to this ruling of the Mishnah, הָכִי אִתְּמַר – **this is how it was said:** אָמַר רַב חִסְדָּא – **Rav Chisda said:** לֹא שָׁנוּ אֶלָּא תְּרוּמָה בְּיַד כֹּהֵן – **They did not teach** that *terumah* is left to rot rather than burned **except** where the ***terumah*** is already **in the hands of a Kohen,**[31] אֲבָל תְּרוּמָה בְּיַד יִשְׂרָאֵל – **but** where the ***terumah*** is still **in the hands of the Yisrael** who separated it, and it had not yet been given to a Kohen, תִּנָּתֵן לְכֹהֵן שֶׁבְּעִיר אַחֶרֶת – **it should be given to a Kohen of another city.**[32]

The Gemara discusses a Baraisa regarding *maaser sheni*, which casts light on our Mishnah as well:

תְּנַן הָתָם – **We have learned there:**[33] עִיסָּה שֶׁל מַעֲשֵׂר שֵׁנִי פְּטוּרָה מִן הַחַלָּה – A DOUGH made OF *MAASER SHENI* IS EXEMPT FROM the requirement of *CHALLAH;*[34] דִּבְרֵי רַבִּי מֵאִיר – these are THE WORDS OF R' MEIR. וַחֲכָמִים מְחַיְּיבִין – THE SAGES, HOWEVER, REQUIRE that *challah* be taken from the dough.

The dispute in the Baraisa is qualified:

אָמַר רַב חִסְדָּא – **Rav Chisda said:** מַחְלוֹקֶת בְּמַעֲשֵׂר שֵׁנִי בִּירוּשָׁלַיִם – **The dispute** between R' Meir and the Sages **concerns *maaser sheni*** dough that is **in Jerusalem.** דְּרַבִּי מֵאִיר סָבַר – **For R' Meir holds** מַעֲשֵׂר שֵׁנִי מָמוֹן גָּבוֹהַּ הוּא – that ***maaser sheni*** in Jerusalem **is the property of the Most High,**[35] וְרַבָּנָן סָבְרִי מָמוֹן הֶדְיוֹט הוּא – **whereas the Rabbis hold that it is the property of the common person.**[36] אֲבָל בַּגְּבוּלִין – **However, in the provinces,** i.e. outside of Jerusalem, דִּבְרֵי הַכֹּל פָּטוּר – **everyone agrees that [*maaser sheni*] is exempt** from the requirement of *challah* because it is the property of the Most High.[37]

This explanation of the dispute is challenged:

מְתִיב רַב יוֹסֵף – **Rav Yosef challenged** this explanation **from** the statement of our **Mishnah:** מַעֲשֵׂר שֵׁנִי וְכִתְבֵי הַקֹּדֶשׁ יִגָּנְזוּ – THE *MAASER SHENI* AND HOLY SCRIPTURES in the subverted city SHOULD BE HIDDEN AWAY. בְּמַאי עַסְקִינַן – **What** location **are we dealing with** in this ruling of the Mishnah? אִילֵימָא בִּירוּשָׁלַיִם – **If you say with Jerusalem,** i.e. the *maaser sheni* and holy scriptures were from Jerusalem and Jerusalem itself became a subverted city, מִי הָוְיָא עִיר הַנִּדַּחַת – **can [Jerusalem] become a subverted city?** וְהָתַנְיָא – This cannot be, **for a Baraisa has taught:** עֲשָׂרָה דְּבָרִים נֶאֶמְרוּ בִּירוּשָׁלַיִם – TEN THINGS WERE SAID ABOUT JERUSALEM, וְזוּ אַחַת מֵהֶן – AND THIS IS ONE OF THEM:[38] אֵינָהּ נַעֲשֵׂית עִיר הַנִּדַּחַת – IT CANNOT BECOME A SUBVERTED CITY. וְאֶלָּא בְּעִיר אַחֶרֶת – **And if** you will say, **rather,** that we are dealing **with** the *maaser sheni* of **another city** וְאַסְקוּהוּ לְגַוָּהּ – **that they brought into [Jerusalem]** before that other city was subverted, הָא קְלָטוּהוּ מְחִיצוֹת – this too cannot be, **for the partitions** (i.e. walls of Jerusalem) would then already **have taken hold of it** before the subversion of the city from which it came. The *maaser sheni* would therefore remain permitted for consumption![39] We must therefore conclude that our Mishnah is not speaking of *maaser sheni* that is in Jerusalem. אֶלָּא לָאו בַּגְּבוּלִין – **Rather,** does the Mishnah **not** mean that the *maaser sheni* is **in the provinces,** i.e. in the subverted city itself? וְקָתָנֵי יִגָּנְזוּ – **And** yet **[the Mishnah] teaches that it should be hidden away,** which shows that the Tanna of our Mishnah considers

NOTES

31. Where the *terumah* is in the possession of a Kohen in the *ir hanidachas*, it really ought to be burned, for it is his property. However, since *terumah* is sacred even after it has been acquired by the Kohen [it can be eaten only by a Kohen and only when he is *tahor*], it would be demeaning to its sacred status to burn it. It is therefore left to rot (*Rashi; see Yad Ramah*).

32. I.e. to a Kohen who did not sin along with the rest of the city [not necessarily one from another city] (*Rashi*; see above, note 29).

[The Gemara now retracts its earlier assumption (note 29) that *terumah* in the hands of a Yisrael is forbidden because he might eventually have given it to a wicked Kohen. The Gemara's conclusion is that *terumah* is never forbidden unless it is actually transferred to a Kohen of the *ir hanidachas* before the city is condemned.]

33. The word תְּנַן generally denotes a Mishnah. However, there is no such Mishnah. There is, however, a Baraisa to this effect quoted in *Pesachim* 37b and *Succah* 35b (*Maharshal*).

34. There is an obligation to remove a portion from any dough made of wheat, barley, oats, spelt, or rye and give it to a Kohen. This obligation pertains to a dough that contains at least an *issaron* of flour [the volume of 43.2 eggs] (*Numbers* 15:17-21; *Rambam, Hil. Bikkurim* 6:15). The portion separated to be given to a Kohen is called *challah*. In this Baraisa, R' Meir states that if the dough is made of *maaser sheni* produce, there is no requirement of *challah*.

35. That is, of God. Elsewhere (*Kiddushin* 52b) R' Meir states that one cannot betroth a woman with *maaser sheni*. Although the owner has the right to eat it, it is not adjudged his property but the property of God, the "Most High." For this reason, dough of *maaser sheni* is not subject to the law of *challah*, for the verse (*Numbers* 15:21) states that *challah* is taken from עֲרִיסוֹתֵיכֶם, ***your** kneading trough,* not God's (*Yad Ramah*).

36. Since it is deemed the owner's property, the *maaser sheni* dough is subject to the requirement of *challah* (*Yad Ramah*).

37. *Maaser sheni* cannot be eaten outside of Jerusalem unless it is first redeemed [which results in the sanctity being transferred from the produce to the money; the money is then taken to Jerusalem and spent on food, which then acquires the sanctity from the money]. Since *maaser sheni* produce cannot be eaten outside of Jerusalem before being redeemed, it is considered the property of the Most High even according to the Sages. It is therefore not subject to the requirement of *challah* (*Rashi*).

Rashi also cites a second explanation, that a *maaser sheni* dough outside Jerusalem is exempt from the *challah* requirement simply because it is not fit to be eaten. According to this explanation, the Sages consider even *maaser sheni* outside of Jerusalem to be the property of its owner (*Rit Algazi* to *Hil. Challah* of *Ramban,* section 2, in explanation of *Rashi;* see also *Aruch LaNer*). [According to both explanations] even if the *maaser sheni* dough is later redeemed, it is exempt from the *challah* requirement, for whatever is not subject to the requirement at the time it was made into a dough remains exempt (*Rashi*; see Mishnah *Challah* 3:3,5,6).

[Our commentary to the remainder of this Gemara will follow *Rashi's* first explanation, as *Rashi* himself does (see ד״ה ואם איתא). For the explanation of the Gemara according to *Rashi's* second explanation see *Rit Algazi* and *Aruch LaNer.*]

38. The full list, and their reasons, are enumerated in *Bava Kamma* 82b (*Rashi*).

39. If the *maaser sheni* was already inside Jerusalem's walls before the city from which it came was subverted, why does our Mishnah state that it should be hidden away [to rot]? It should be permissible to eat it, since once it enters the walls of Jerusalem, the city has taken hold of it (*Rashi*); i.e. it becomes subject to the law prohibiting the removal of *maaser sheni* from Jerusalem (Mishnah, *Maaser Sheni* 3:5). Thus, even if it is considered the property of one of the idolaters of the *ir hanidachas,* it is property located outside the city that cannot be brought back to be burned – because the law of *maaser sheni* prohibits its removal from Jerusalem! As we learned above (112a), property of the wicked that cannot be brought back is not subject to destruction (*Yad Ramah, Tos. HaRosh;* see also *Chidushei HaRan*).

[*Tosafos* to *Bava Metzia* 53b (ד״ה לא פלוג רבנן) explain this last point somewhat differently. Once the walls of Jerusalem have "taken hold" of the *maaser sheni*, it is classified as the "booty of Jerusalem," not the booty of the *ir hanidachas*. Thus, it no longer becomes subject to the law of the *ir hanidachas*. (Although the property of the wicked becomes subject to destruction even if it is outside the *ir hanidachas*, this is because it is still in some measure considered the property of the *ir hanidachas*. Once *maaser sheni* enters Jerusalem, however, it can no longer be considered the property of its original city at all, since even its owner can no longer remove it from Jerusalem.)]

נה א ב ג ד מיי' פ"ד מהל' עכו"ם הלכה יג סמג עשין טו:
נו ה ו מיי' פ"ו מהל' בכורים הלכה ד:
נז ז מיי' פ"ז מהל' בית הבחירה הלכה יד ופ"ד מהל' עכו"ם הלכה ד:
נח ח מיי' פ"ב מהל' מעשר שני ונטע רבעי הלכה ח סמג לאוין קלו:

והקדשות שבה יפדו כו': [א] ת"ר [א]היו בה (א) (קדשי) קדשים קדשי מזבח ימותו קדשי בדק הבית יפדו ותרומות ירקבו ומעשר שני וכתבי הקדש יגנזו [ב] ר"ש אומר בהמתה ולא בהמת בכור ומעשר שללה פרט לכסף הקדש וכסף מעשר אמר מר היו בה (קדשי) קדשים קדשי מזבח ימותו ואמאי ימותו ירעו עד שיסתאבו וימכרו ויפלו דמיהן לנדבה ר' יוחנן אמר א) [ב]זבח רשעים תועבה ר"ל אמר ממון בעלים הוא והכא בקדשים שחייב באחריותן [ג] ור"ש היא דאמר ממון בעלים הוא הא מדסיפא ר"ש היא רישא לאו ר"ש בקדשים קלים ואליבא דרבי יוסי הגלילי [ד] דאמר קדשים קלים ממון בעלים אבל קדשי קדשים מאי [ה] יפדו אדתני סיפא קדשי בדק הבית יפדו ליפלוג וליתני בדידה בד"א בקדשים קלים אבל קדשי קדשים [ו] יפדו כיון דאיכא חטאת שמתו בעליה דלמיתה אזלא לא פסיקא ליה בשלמא ר' יוחנן לא אמר כר"ל דכתיב זבח רשעים תועבה אלא ר"ל מ"ט לא אמר כר' יוחנן אמר לך כי אמרינן זבח רשעים תועבה הני מילי היכא דאתנהו בעינייהו אבל הכא כיון דאישתני אישתני: ר"ש אומר [ז] בהמתך ולא בהמת בכור ומעשר: במאי עסקינן [ח] אילימא בתמימין שלל שמים הוא אלא בבעלי מומין [ג]שללה נינהו אמר רבינא לעולם בבעלי מומין [ה]ומי שנאכל בתורת [ט] בהמתך יצאו אלו שאין נאכלין בתורת [י] בהמתך אלא בתורת בכור ומעשר [כ] דשלל שמים נינהו ופליגא דשמואל דאמר שמואל הכל קרב והכל נפדה מאי קאמר ה"ק כל שקרב כשהוא תם ונפדה כשהוא בעל מום משלל אימעיט וכל שקרב כשהוא תם ואינו נפדה כשהוא בעל מום כגון בכור ומעשר מבהמה נפקא: תרומות ירקבו: אמר רב חסדא ל"ש אלא תרומה ביד ישראל אבל תרומה ביד כהן כיון דממוניה הוא תשרף מתיב רב יוסף מעשר שני וכתבי הקדש יגנזו והא מעשר שני ביד ישראל כתרומה ביד כהן דמי וקתני יגנזו אלא אי אתמר הכי אתמר אמר רב חסדא ל"ש אלא תרומה ביד כהן אבל תרומה ביד ישראל [ד]תנתן לכהן שבעיר אחרת [ל] תנן התם [מ] עיסה של מעשר שני פטורה מן החלה דברי ר"מ וחכמים [ה]מחייבין אמר רב חסדא מחלוקת [ו]במעשר שני בירושלים דר"מ סבר [נ] מעשר שני ממון גבוה הוא ורבנן סברי ממון הדיוט הוא אבל [ס] בגבולין דברי הכל פטור מתיב רב יוסף מעשר שני וכתבי הקדש יגנזו במאי עסקינן אילימא בירושלים מי הויא עיר הנדחת והתניא [ע] עשרה דברים נאמרו בירושלים וזו אחת מהן [ז]אינה נעשית עיר הנדחת ואלא בעיר אחרת ואסקוהו לגוה הא קלטוהו מחיצות אלא לאו בגבולין וקתני יגנזו לא לעולם דעיר אחרת ואסקוהו לגוה והכא במאי עסקינן שנטמא ולפרקיה [פ] דא"ר אלעזר [ח]מניין למעשר שני שנטמא שפודין אותו אפילו בירושלים ת"ל ב) לא תוכל שאתו ואין שאת אלא אכילה שנאמר ג) וישא משאת מאת פניו הכא במאי עסקינן בלקוח וליפרקיה

היו בה קדשי מזבח. כגון עולות ואשמות של רשעים בתוכה נהי דלא קרינן בהו את כל בהמתה לפי חרב דהא לא בהמתה היא אלא בהמת שמים אלא מאיסותא הוא להקריב קרבנות של רשעים הללו שהודחו הלכך ימותו כונסין אותן לכיפה ומאכילין אותן שעורין עד שכריסן נבקעת דאפילו דמיהם אסור כדלקמן: שנאמר כליל לה' אלהיך ל"ג: ר"ש אומר וכו'. לקמן מפרש טעמא: זבח רשעים תועבה. ואפילו דמיהן אסורין: ור"ש הוא דאמר. בהזהב (ב"מ נו:) קדשים שחייב באחריותן ממון בעלים הוא ויש בהם אונאה הלכך לענין עיר הנדחת נמי ממון בעלים הוא ודיינינהו לפי חרב כשאר בהמות שבתוכה והלכך אסורין דמיהן בהנאה והאי דקאמר ימותו ולא אמר שיחרימו אותה עמהם משום כבוד שמים: ואליבא דרבי יוסי הגלילי דאמר. בפ"ק דב"ק (ד' יב:) ומעלה מעל בה' לרבות קדשים קלים שהם ממונו והואיל וממונו הם אסורים בהנאה דאפילו דמיהן בהמתם מיקרו אבל קדשי קדשים (ב) [ו] אמאי ירעו דהא ודאי הם עצמם אינם קרבים דזבח רשעים תועבה אלא ירעו עד שיסתאבו וימכרו ויפלו דמיהם לנדבה: אי הכי [ק] מדתני סיפא וכו'. דקא מפליג בין קדשי מזבח לקדשי בדק הבית: ליפלוג וליתני בדידה. בקדשי מזבח עצמן בין קדשים קלים לקדשי קדשים: דלמיתה אזלא. כדאמרינן (תמורה ד' טו.) חמש חטאות מתות: לא פסיקא ליה. למיתני קדשי קדשים דעיר הנדחת ירעו דכיון דמתו להם אותם רשעים אי איכא חטאות שהפרישו בחייהם אזלי למיתה דכל חטאות שמתו בעליהם מתות במסכת הוריות (ד' ו.) מפרש טעמא אבל שאר קדשי קדשים כגון אשמות שמתו בעליהם ירעו: דאיתנהו בעינייהו. דהן עצמן ודאי אינן קרבים משום זבח רשעים תועבה: אבל הכא. דאיכא למימר ירעו ויפלו דמיהם לנדבה: כיון דאישתני. ליכא הכא זבח רשעים תועבה: ולא בהמת בכור ומעשר. שאם היו בה בכורות או מעשר בהמה שהוא של ישראל וחלבו ודמו קרב אין מחרימין אותו עמה דלא מיקרי בהמתה: שלל שמים הוא. ומשללה נפקא: אלא בבעלי מומים. שאין בהם חלק לגבוה אלא נאכלין לבעלים שללה נינהו אמאי אין מחרימין אותן עמה: לעולם בבעלי מומין. ואפ"ה אין [ר] נשרפין עמה דדרשינן לקרא הכי בהמתה למי שנאכל לבעלים בתורת בהמתם יצאו אלו שיש להם שם לוי שאין נאכלים בתורת בהמתם שאין אומרין בהמת עיר הנדחת אלא בהמת בכור ומעשר של עיר הנדחת: ופליגא. הא דרבינא אדשמואל דאמר שמואל עלה דהא מילתא דר"ש כי הוה קשיא לן במאי עסקינן הוי מתרץ הכי הכל קרב והכל נפדה: מאי קאמר ה"ק. כל שהוא קרב לגבוה כשהוא תם וכשהוא בעל מום צריך פדייה כגון שאר קדשים קלים חוץ ממעשר בהמה ובכור הנהו משללה נפקא דאין מחרימין אותם עמה דהואיל וצריכי פדייה בממון של שמים קרינן ביה ופליג עליה דת"ק דאמר קדשים קלים ממון בעלים הוא: וכל שקרב כשהוא תם ואינו נפדה כשהוא בעל מום. אלא נאכל לבעלים כגון בכור ומעשר ההוא לאו של שמים מקרו ואפילו בתמותן ולא מצי למפרך והא בתמותן של שמים הוא שהרי נאכל במומו והלכך אצטריך בהמתה למעוטי בכור ומעשר תמימים דמשללה ליכא למעוטינהו והיינו פליגא דאיהו מוקי לה אפילו בתמימים דקסבר בכור ומעשר בעלי מומין בהמתה קרינא ביה וכסייף: תרומה ביד ישראל. שעדיין לא נתנה לכהן דאפילו אותו ישראל רשע הוא תרומה שבידו אינה נשרפת עם שאר שללה דהא לאו דידיה הוא דשמא היה נתנה לכהן צדיק שבחוצה לה הלכך אינה נשרפת דהיינו כפקדון דעיר אחרת ואתנהו בגוה דאמר לעיל דמותרין והני דבאכילה לא שריא לה דשמא היה נתנה לכהן רשע שבתוכה הלכך ירקבו אבל תרומה ביד כהן דממוניה הוא תשרף: וקתני יגנזו. אע"ג דממוניה הוא לא אמר תשרף: אלא תרומה ביד כהן. דממוניה הוא ולא מזלזלינן בה כולי האי הואיל וקדש הוא: לכהן שבעיר אחרת. כלומר לכהן שלא הודח עמהן: אבל בגבולין. שאין לה היתר אכילה אלא בפדייה ד"ה פטורה מן החלה דממון גבוה הוא ל"א אבל בגבולין דאין לה היתר אכילה בשעת חיוב חלה דהיינו בשעת גלגול העיסה לא קרינא ביה ראשית עריסותיכם (במדבר טו) ואפילו פדאה לאחר מיכן פטור מן החלה: י' דברים נאמרו בירושלים. בפ' מרובה (ב"ק פב:) חשיב להו: אלא בעיר אחרת ואסקו לגוה. שהיה אותו מעשר שני של אחד מבני עיר הנדחת והעלו אותו לירושלים קודם שהודחה ואח"כ הודחו אם כן אמאי יגנזו לשתרו נמי באכילה דהא קלטינהו מחילות דהיינו חומה: אלא לאו בגבולין. ולא מטו ליה וקתני יגנזו ואינו יוצא לישרף בתמיה: ואם איתא. דבגבולין לד"ה ממון גבוה הוא לשתרי נמי באכילה אלא לאו ממון הדיוט הוא והני דבשריפה לא משום זילותא: לעולם דעיר הנדחת ואסקיה לגוה. ודקאמרת לשתרו נמי באכילה דהא קלטוהו מחילות: הכא במאי עסקינן כשנטמא. דלאו בר אכולי בטומאה הוא דכתיב (דברים כו) לא בערתי ממנו בטמא ולקמן פריך מאי איריא עיר הנדחת אפילו בחוצה לה: ואפילו בירושלים. לאחר שנכנס ואע"ג דדרשינן (שם יד) כי ירחק ממך המקום וצרת הכסף בידך ברחוק מקום אתה פודה וכו' ולא בקרוב מקום: ואין שאת אלא אכילה. וה"ק קרא כי ירחק ממך המקום או כי לא תוכל לאוכלו שנטמא וצרת הכסף בידך: בלקוח. שכבר הוציאה בהוצאה לכסף מעשר ונתנוהו ביין ושכר ונטמא אותו לקוח דההוא לית ליה פדייה וכי קאמר ר"א במע"ש גופיה שהעלה פירות מע"ש לירושלים ונטמאו: וליפרקיה

ליקוטי רש"י

היו בה קדשים. בעיר הנדחת אין נשרפין עם שללה דכתיב (דברים יג) שללה ולא שלל שמים ומיהו מיקרב לא קרבו משום דכתיב (משלי כא) זבח רשעים תועבה ואם קדשי מזבח הן ואפילו עולות ושלמים נדבה ימותו. קדשי בדק הבית יפדו. כשאר בדק הבית והפודה אותם יאכלם שהרי לא נאסרו דלאו דידהו הוו [לעיל מז.]. קדשים שחייב באחריותן. אמר הרי עלי עולה והפרישה והוממה ומכרה. ושאינו חייב באחריותן כגון דאמר הרי זו [ב"מ נו:]. אם קיבלם בעליו עליו באחריות כגון דאמר הרי עלי עולה והפריש זו [ב"ק עא:]. ממון בעלים הן. כגון אמר הרי עלי עולה והפריש בהמה לנדרו וכו' דרעהו קרינן ביה דדבר הגורם לממון לרבי שמעון כממון דמי [שבועות מב:]. ושור רעהו קרינן ביה [ב"ק יב:]. בבעלי מומין שללה נינהו. היינו בהמתה דכהן אוכל את הבכור וישראל את המעשר ואין לגבוה חלק בהן [תמורה ח.]. דברי ר' מאיר. דאמר בפרק שני דקדושין (נד:) מעשר ממון גבוה הוא. פטורה מן החלה כדמפרש דעריסותיכם כתיב ולא של גבוה [פסחים לז:]. פטורה מן החלה. דכתיב עריסותיכם והאי דגבוה היא ואף על גב דאיכא היתר אכילה כיון דלית בה דין שאר ממון לאו דידיה הוא [סוכה לה.]. הא קלטוהו מחיצות. מעשר שני בירושלים הואיל ואינו נאכל בכל מושבות מעתה משהביאו לירושלים שוב אינו יכול לחלל לאכול בחוץ כדאמרינן במסכת מכות (כ.) מחילה לקלוט מדרבנן דמשקלטוהו מחילות שוב אינו נפדה. ר' אלעזר. דאם נטמא פודין אותו ואוכלין אותו בכל מקום. שאתו. כשלא תוכל לאוכלו כגון זה שניטמא ונתת בכסף [פסחים לו:]. אפילו בירושלים. שאין מעשר טהור נפדה שם דכתיב (דברים יד) כי ירחק ממך [וגו'] ונתת בכסף ולא כשהיה בירושלים [ב"מ נג:]. אין מוכרין מעשר שני בירושלים, ואפילו לאוכלו שם בקדושה דכי ירבה ממך הדרך ונתתה בכסף כתיב (דברים יד) [פסחים עה:]. שפודין אותו אפילו בירושלים. דאי בעי פריק ואפילו בירושלים דאע"ג דמעשר שני טהור אינו נפדה בירושלים דכתיב כי ירחק ממך ונתת בכסף בריחוק מקום אתה פודה ולא בקירוב מקום (קדושין דף נו). ואין שאת אלא אכילה. והכי קאמר קרא כי ירחק ממך שיהא מעשר טהור חוץ לירושלים או אפילו הוא בירושלים אלא שאי אתה יכול לאוכלו שנטמא ונתת בכסף [מכות יט.]. בלקוח. מעשר זה ולא הוא עצמו היה מעשר אלא צרכי סעודה שלקח בירושלים בכסף מעשר [ב"מ שם].

א) לעיל מז. [תוספ' פי"ד], ב) [תמורה ח. ע"ש], ג) [ב"מ נו.], ד) [ב"ק יב: וש"נ], ה) [גי' רש"י ירעו וכל"ז], ו) [לפי גירסת רש"י לעיל צ"ל ירעו], ז) [צ"ל בהמתה], ח) [תמורה ח. ע"ש], ט) [צ"ל בהמתה], י) [צ"ל בהמתה], כ) [בתוס' דבכורות דף לא. ד"ה חוץ וכו' משמע דגרסי הכא בסוגיא כמו דסיים הש"ס בתמורה ח. דתנן כל פסולי המוקדשין נמכרין באטליז חוץ מן הבכור והמעשר ע"ש אבל מפירש"י דהכא ד"ה לעולם בבעלי מומין וכו' מוכח דלא גריס להא דתנן כו' ומשום הכי פירש"י הכא יצאו אלו שיש להם שם לוי ורבינא הוא דמשני לה הכי כאן אבל בתמורה ח. סתמא דש"ס מייתי להא דתנן כל פסולי וכו' ולא ס"ל כרבינא בפי' הזה], ל) א"ז משנה אלא ברייתא ועיין רש"ל, מ) סוכה לה: פסחים לח. [עי' חולין פז: תוס' ד"ה תנן התם], נ) [קידושין כד. וש"נ], ס) [עי' תוס' קידושין נג: ד"ה איהו ותוס' בכורות ט: ד"ה ותנן ועי' היטב תוס' סוכה לה. סד"ה לפי], ע) ב"ק פב., פ) ב"מ נג. פסחי' לו: מכות יט:, צ) [צ"ל מאי], ק) [צ"ל אדתני], ר) ב"ח נהרגין.

הגהות הב"ח

(א) גמ' ת"ר היו בה קדשים קדשי מזבח כצ"ל ותיבת קדשי נמחק: (ב) רש"י ד"ה ואליבא דר' יוסי וכו' קדשי קדשים ירעו כצ"ל ותיבת אמאי נמחק:

גליון הש"ס

גמ' ומי שנאכל בתורת בהמתך. ע' זבחים דף עה ע"ב תוס' ד"ה התפיס:

תורה אור השלם

א) זֶבַח רְשָׁעִים תּוֹעֵבָה אַף כִּי בְזִמָּה יְבִיאֶנּוּ: [משלי כא, כז]

ב) וְכִי יִרְבֶּה מִמְּךָ הַדֶּרֶךְ כִּי לֹא תוּכַל שְׂאֵתוֹ כִּי יִרְחַק מִמְּךָ הַמָּקוֹם אֲשֶׁר יִבְחַר יְיָ אֱלֹהֶיךָ לָשׂוּם שְׁמוֹ שָׁם כִּי יְבָרֶכְךָ יְיָ אֱלֹהֶיךָ: [דברים יד, כד]

ג) וַיִּשָּׂא מַשְׂאֹת מֵאֵת פָּנָיו אֲלֵהֶם וַתֵּרֶב מַשְׂאַת בִּנְיָמִן מִמַּשְׂאֹת כֻּלָּם חָמֵשׁ יָדוֹת וַיִּשְׁתּוּ וַיִּשְׁכְּרוּ עִמּוֹ: [בראשית מג, לד]

maaser sheni outside Jerusalem the private property of its owner.[40] This contradicts Rav Chisda, who stated that all agree that *maaser sheni* outside of Jerusalem is not considered the private property of the owner. – ? –

The Gemara answers:

לא – No. **לְעוֹלָם דְּעִיר אַחֶרֶת וְאַסְּקוּהוּ לְגַוָּהּ – Really,** the Mishnah is discussing *maaser sheni* **of another city that they brought into [Jerusalem]** before the city of origin was subverted. **וְהָכָא בְּמַאי עַסְקִינַן – But with what are we dealing here? שֶׁנִּטְמָא – With [*maaser sheni*] that became *tamei*,** which may not be eaten. It is therefore hidden away.[41]

The Gemara asks:

וְלִפְרְקֵיהּ – Why must it be hidden and go to waste? **Let it be redeemed** and eaten,[42] **דְּאָמַר רַבִּי אֶלְעָזָר – for R' Elazar has said: מִנַּיִין לְמַעֲשֵׂר שֵׁנִי שֶׁנִּטְמָא שֶׁפּוֹדִין אוֹתוֹ אֲפִילוּ בִּירוּשָׁלַיִם – From where** do we learn **that *maaser sheni* that became *tamei* may be redeemed even in Jerusalem?**[43] **תַּלְמוּד לוֹמַר ,,לֹא תוּכַל שְׂאֵתוֹ'' – For [the Torah] states** regarding the redemption of *maaser sheni: If the way be too great for you, so that* ***you will not be able "se'eiso."***[44] **וְאֵין ,,שְׂאֵת'' אֶלָּא אֲכִילָה – And** the word **"*se'eis*"** in this context **means nothing other than "eating," שֶׁנֶּאֱמַר ,,וַיִּשָּׂא מַשְׂאֹת מֵאֵת פָּנָיו'' – as is stated** in regard to the meal to which Joseph invited his brothers: ***And he took portions (mas'os) from before him.***[45] Accordingly, since *maaser sheni* that has become *tamei* can be redeemed even in Jerusalem, why would the Mishnah require it to be hidden away?

The Gemara answers:

הָכָא בְּמַאי עַסְקִינַן – With what are we dealing here? בְּלָקוּחַ – Not with *maaser sheni* itself but **with** food that was **purchased** with *maaser sheni* money; this cannot be redeemed.[46]

NOTES

40. For if he held it was the property of the Most High, the *maaser sheni* would not be subject to the law of the *ir hanidachas* and would not become forbidden to eat. Since the Tanna of our Mishnah does forbid the *maaser sheni,* he clearly considers it the property of its owner in the *ir hanidachas.*

Accordingly, it should really be burned, for burning is the proper fate for the property of an *ir hanidachas*. However, since *maaser sheni* has a certain sanctity, it would be demeaning to burn it; it is therefore hidden away (*Rashi*).

41. Although it is not burned as property of the *ir hanidachas,* it cannot be eaten because it is *tamei* (see *Yevamos* 73b, *Deuteronomy* 26:14). Thus, it is hidden away. The Gemara below will ask why our Mishnah, which teaches the laws of *ir hanidachas,* should speak of a case of *maaser sheni* that is *tamei,* which is forbidden regardless of whether it is from an *ir hanidachas* (*Rashi*).

42. Once *maaser sheni* produce is redeemed, the produce has no sanctity. As such, it may be eaten even when it is *tamei* (see Mishnah, *Maaser Sheni* 3:9).

43. *Maaser sheni* that is *tahor* cannot be redeemed inside Jerusalem. This is learned from *Deuteronomy* 14:24-25, which states in regard to the redemption of *maaser sheni*: וְכִי־יִרְבֶּה מִמְּךָ הַדֶּרֶךְ כִּי לֹא תוּכַל שְׂאֵתוֹ, כִּי־יִרְחַק מִמְּךָ הַמָּקוֹם . . . וְנָתַתָּה בַּכָּסֶף וְצַרְתָּ הַכֶּסֶף בְּיָדְךָ וְהָלַכְתָּ אֶל־הַמָּקוֹם . . . , *If the way will be too great for you, so that you will not be able to carry it, because the place* [to which the *maaser sheni* must be brought] *is far from you . . . then you shall wrap the money in your hand and go to the place* . . . From this we infer that "when the place is *far* from you, you may redeem the *maaser sheni* and take it in your hand, but not when the place is *close* to you" [i.e. when you are in Jerusalem]. R' Elazar, however, demonstrates from the following verse that *maaser sheni* that is *tamei* may be redeemed even in Jerusalem (*Rashi*).

44. The simple meaning of שְׂאֵתוֹ, *se'eiso,* is *to carry it* (see previous note). However, R' Elazar exegetically interprets as follows.

45. *Genesis* 43:34. [The verse speaks of the food served by Joseph to his brothers when they brought Benjamin to him.] We see from this verse that the Hebrew construct שְׂאֵת is used in the sense of a portion to be eaten. Taken in this sense, the *maaser sheni* verse – לֹא תוּכַל שְׂאֵתוֹ, *you will not be able "se'eiso"* – can be interpreted to mean "you will not be able to eat it." Accordingly, the verse speaks of *two* circumstances in which *maaser sheni* may be redeemed: one, where it is outside of Jerusalem (*the way will be too great for you*), and a second where it has become inedible due to *tumah* [even in Jerusalem] (*you are not able to eat it*) (*Rashi*).

46. Therefore, if this food became *tamei*, there is nothing to do with it other than to put it away and let it go to waste. When R' Elazar said that *maaser sheni* that becomes *tamei* can be redeemed even in Jerusalem, he referred to the original *maaser sheni* produce, not the food purchased with *maaser sheni* money (*Rashi*).

The Gemara questions the last assumption:

וְלִיפָּרְקֵיהּ – **But** even so, **let [the purchased food] be redeemed** and eaten, דִּתְנַן – **for we have learned in a Mishnah:**[1] הַלָּקוּחַ בְּכֶסֶף מַעֲשֵׂר שֶׁנִּטְמָא – [FOOD] that was PURCHASED WITH *MAASER* sheni MONEY, THAT BECAME *TAMEI,* יִפָּדֶה – MAY BE REDEEMED. – ? –

The Gemara answers:

כְּרַבִּי יְהוּדָה – Our Mishnah **follows** the opinion of **R' Yehudah** in that Mishnah דְּאָמַר יִקָּבֵר – **who says** that food purchased with *maaser sheni* money MUST BE BURIED if it becomes *tamei*.[2]

The Gemara asks:

אִי הָכִי – **If so,** i.e. if our Mishnah is referring to food that was purchased with *maaser sheni* money that then became *tamei,* מַאי אִירְיָא עִיר הַנִּדַּחַת – **why** does our Mishnah **teach** that it cannot be eaten but must be hidden away in regard to **a subverted city?** אֲפִילּוּ דְעָלְמָא נַמִּי – The same would be true **even** if it belonged to any city **of the world,** i.e. a city that had not been subverted![3]

The Gemara accepts this refutation and concedes that its previous explanation of the Mishnah is untenable. The Gemara therefore suggests another explanation:

אֶלָּא לְעוֹלָם בְּטָהוֹר – **Rather,** our Mishnah is **really** dealing **with** *maaser sheni* that is ***tahor.*** This *maaser sheni* belonged to an inhabitant of a subverted city, but it entered Jerusalem before the city was subverted, as we said before.[4] וּכְגוֹן דְּנָפוּל מְחִיצוֹת – The Mishnah, **however,** is speaking of **a case where the walls** of Jerusalem **fell** after the *maaser sheni* had entered the city, thereby removing the city's hold on the *maaser sheni*, וְכִדְרָבָא – **and in accord with Rava's** ruling. דְּאָמַר רָבָא – **For Rava said:** מְחִיצָה לֶאֱכוֹל דְּאוֹרַיְיתָא – The law of **the wall** of Jerusalem **in regard to eating** *maaser sheni* **is Biblical;**[5] לְקָלוֹט דְּרַבָּנָן – but the law of the wall in regard **to taking hold** of *maaser sheni* **is** only **Rabbinic.**[6] וְכִי גָּזוּר רַבָּנָן – **And when did the Rabbis decree** that the walls of Jerusalem "take hold" of *maaser sheni?*[7] כִּי אִתְנַהוּ לִמְחִיצָה – Only **when the walls** of Jerusalem **are standing.** כִּי לֵיתְנֵהוּ לִמְחִיצָה לֹא – But **when the walls** of Jerusalem **are not standing,** they did **not** so decree.[8]

The Gemara quotes the next ruling of the Mishnah:

כִּתְבֵי הַקֹּדֶשׁ יִגָּנְזוּ – HOLY SCRIPTURES SHOULD BE HIDDEN AWAY.

The Gemara discusses the authorship of this ruling:

מַתְנִיתִין דְּלָא כְּרַבִּי אֱלִיעֶזֶר – **Our Mishnah does not follow** the view of **R' Eliezer.** דְּתַנְיָא – **For a Baraisa has taught:** רַבִּי אֱלִיעֶזֶר אוֹמֵר – R' ELIEZER SAYS: כָּל עִיר שֶׁיֵּשׁ בָּהּ אֲפִילּוּ מְזוּזָה אַחַת – ANY CITY THAT HAS EVEN ONE *MEZUZAH* IN IT אֵינָהּ נַעֲשֵׂית עִיר הַנִּדַּחַת – CANNOT BECOME A SUBVERTED CITY, שֶׁנֶּאֱמַר – FOR IT IS STATED:[9] "וְשָׂרַפְתָּ בָאֵשׁ אֶת־הָעִיר וְאֶת־כָּל־שְׁלָלָהּ כָּלִיל" – *AND YOU SHALL BURN THE CITY ALONG WITH ALL ITS BOOTY IN A FIRE, COMPLETELY, TO HASHEM YOUR GOD.* וְהֵיכָא דְּאִיכָּא מְזוּזָה – **But where there is a** ***mezuzah,*** לֹא אֶפְשָׁר – **this is not possible,** דִּכְתִיב – **for it is written:** "לֹא־תַעֲשׂוּן כֵּן לַה׳ אֱלֹהֵיכֶם" – ***You shall not do so to Hashem your God.***[10]

NOTES

1. *Maaser Sheni* 3:10.

2. R' Yehudah in that Mishnah disputes the view of the Tanna Kamma and rules that food purchased with *maaser sheni* money cannot be redeemed even if it becomes *tamei*. R' Yehudah holds that the sanctity of food purchased with *maaser sheni* money is not substantial enough to be transferred to coins through redemption. We may therefore say that our Mishnah, which states that the *maaser sheni* of an *ir hanidachas* is hidden away, refers to food purchased with *maaser sheni* money that became *tamei*. [Since it can neither be eaten nor redeemed, it must be buried, which is the equivalent of hiding it away.] This ruling would reflect the view of R' Yehudah (*Rashi*).

3. R' Yehudah's rule that food purchased with *maaser sheni* money cannot be redeemed even if it became *tamei* is a general rule that has nothing to do with whether or not the food belonged to an inhabitant of an *ir hanidachas*. Why, then, does our Mishnah mention it in its delineation of the laws of *ir hanidachas*?

4. The objection put forth to this explanation above was that the *maaser sheni* should then be permitted for consumption, since having entered Jerusalem, the walls of Jerusalem have "taken hold of it," thereby prohibiting its removal from the city and exempting it from the law of the *ir hanidachas* (see 112b note 39).

5. I.e. the law that *maaser sheni* must be eaten within the walls of Jerusalem is a Biblical law (*Rashi*).

6. I.e. the law that once *maaser sheni* has entered the walls of Jerusalem it can no longer be redeemed is only Rabbinic. (This is the specific law of which Rava speaks; see *Makkos* 20a.) Similarly, the law that once *maaser sheni* has entered the walls of Jerusalem it can no longer become subject to the law of the *ir hanidachas* [since it cannot be removed from the city] is also only Rabbinic. Any law involving the principle of the walls having taken hold of *maaser sheni* is only Rabbinic (*Rashi*; see note 8).

7. Whether in regard to redemption or *ir hanidachas* (*Rashi*).

8. Thus, our Mishnah teaches that where *maaser sheni* of an *ir hanidachas* was brought to Jerusalem while the walls were still standing and the walls then collapsed, the *maaser sheni* must be hidden away. Since the *maaser sheni* entered Jerusalem while its walls yet stood, it became permissible for the owner to eat and thus his property (following the view of the Sages in the Baraisa quoted above). Since the walls are no longer standing [when the city becomes an *ir hanidachas*], they do not protect the *maaser sheni* from the fate of the *ir hanidachas*, and the *maaser sheni* is therefore forbidden. Nevertheless, we do not burn the *maaser sheni* out of deference to its holiness. We must therefore hide it [and let it rot away] (*Chidushei HaRan; Tos. HaRosh;* see also *Rashi* to Mishnah 111b and *Tosafos* to *Bava Metzia* 53b ד״ה לא פלוג רבנן; cf. *Baal HaMaor* and *Yad Ramah*).

[However, *maaser sheni* that had not yet been brought to Jerusalem would be considered the property of the Most High – as Rav Chisda stated above – and would therefore remain permissible for consumption.] Similarly, *maaser sheni* that is in Jerusalem while its walls still stand would also remain permissible, since it is property that cannot be returned to the *ir hanidachas*, which does not become subject to the fate of the city, as the Gemara stated above (112b; see note 39 there). Although the prohibition to remove *maaser sheni* from Jerusalem is only Rabbinic while the requirement to burn the property of an *ir hanidachas* is Biblical, the Rabbinic decree barring the removal of *maaser sheni* from Jerusalem is no less an impediment to returning the *maaser sheni* to its original city than a physical impediment, such as distance, would be. Just as a physical impediment displaces the Biblical requirement of burning (as the Gemara stated above in regard to deposits in another city), so too does a Rabbinic decree. Therefore, since the *maaser sheni* entered Jerusalem and became subject to this Rabbinic prohibition before the city of its origin was condemned as an *ir hanidachas*, it is excluded from the fate of the city as long as that condition exists (*Chidushei HaRan; Tos. HaRosh*).

9. *Deuteronomy* 13:17.

10. Ibid. 12:4. This verse is part of a longer passage which instructs the Israelites to destroy all the idols, altars, and sacred objects of the Canaanites. The Torah then states: *And you shall obliterate their names from that place . . . You shall not do so to Hashem your God.* We learn from this that it is forbidden to destroy anything that contains the Name of Hashem, such as a *mezuzah.* Accordingly, if there is a *mezuzah* in a subverted city, it cannot be destroyed, which in turn makes it impossible to carry out the Torah's command to destroy the *ir hanidachas* along with *everything* that is in it. R' Eliezer therefore rules that since it is impossible to carry out the letter of the law in regard to this city, the city cannot be subjected to the law of *ir hanidachas* (*Rashi*; see also *Rashi* above, 71a ד״ה ואפילו מזוזה אחת).

[This is not comparable to the situation of a city that contains animals consecrated to the Altar, which are not destroyed because they are the "booty of Heaven." In those cases even R' Eliezer would agree that the inability to destroy them does not prevent the city from being condemned as an *ir hanidachas*.] The law of *ir hanidachas* requires us to destroy only the things classified as "*its* booty" [and since con-

וליפרקיה [א] דתנן [א] הלקוח בכסף מעשר שנטמא יפדה כר"י דאמר יקבר אי הכי מאי איריא עיר הנדחת אפילו דעלמא נמי אלא לעולם בטהור וכגון דנפול מחיצות וכדרבא [ב] דאמר רבא [ב] מחיצה לאכול דאורייתא [ג] לקלוט דרבנן וכי גזור רבנן כי אתנהו למחיצה כי ליתנהו למחיצה לא: כתבי הקדש יגנזו: מתניתין דלא כר"א [ג] דתניא ר"א אומר כל עיר שיש בה אפי' מזוזה אחת אינה נעשית עיר הנדחת שנא' [א] ושרפת באש את העיר ואת כל שללה כליל והיכא דאיכא מזוזה לא אפשר דכתיב [ב] לא תעשון כן לה' אלהיכם: ר"ש אומר אמר הקב"ה וכו': לימא בדר' אבין א"ר אילעא קמיפלגי [ד] דא"ר אבין א"ר אילעא כל מקום שאתה מוצא כלל בעשה ופרט בלא תעשה אין דנין אותו בכלל ופרט דמר אית ליה דרבי אבין ומר לית ליה דרבי אבין לא דכ"ע אית להו דר' אבין והכא בהא קמיפלגי מר סבר עוד לגמרי משמע ומר סבר עוד לכמה שהיתה: אינה נבנית אבל נעשית היא גנות ופרדסים: ת"ר [ד] היו בה אילנות תלושין אסורין מחוברין מותרין של עיר אחרת בין תלושין בין מחוברין אסור מאי עיר אחרת אמר רב חסדא יריחו דכתיב [ג] והיתה העיר [ה] חרם לה' וישבע יהושע בעת ההיא לאמר ארור האיש לפני ה' אשר יקום ובנה את העיר הזאת את יריחו בבכורו ייסדנה ובצעירו יציב דלתיה תניא [ו] לא יריחו על שם עיר אחרת ולא עיר אחרת על שם יריחו דכתיב [ד] בנה חיאל בית האלי את יריחו באבירם בכורו יסדה ובשגוב צעירו הציב דלתיה תניא [ז] באבירם בכורו רשע לא היה לו ללמוד בשגוב צעירו היה לו ללמוד אבירם ושגוב מאי עבוד ([ח] מאי קאמר) ה"ק באבירם בכורו היה לו ללמוד לאותו רשע בשגוב צעירו ממשמע שנאמר באבירם בכורו איני יודע ששגוב צעירו מה ת"ל שגוב צעירו מלמד שהיה מקבר והולך מאבירם עד שגוב אחאב שושביניה הוה אתא איהו ואליהו למשאל בשלמא בי טמיא יתיב וקאמר דילמא כי מילט יהושע הכי לט לא יריחו על שם עיר אחרת ולא עיר אחרת על שם יריחו א"ל אליהו אין אמר ליה השתא לווטתא דמשה לא קא מקיימא דכתיב [ה] וסרתם ועבדתם וגו' וכתיב [ו] וחרה אף ה' בכם ועצר את השמים וגו' וההוא גברא אוקים ליה עבודת כוכבים [ט] על כל תלם ותלם ולא שביק ליה מיטרא דמיזל מיסגד ליה לווטתא דיהושע תלמידיה מקיימא מיד [ז] ויאמר אליהו התשבי מתושבי גלעד [י] חי ה' אלהי ישראל אם [כ] יהיה טל ומטר וגו' בעי רחמי והבו ליה אקלידא דמטרא וקם ואזל [ח] ויהי דבר ה' אליו לאמר לך מזה ופנית לך קדמה ונסתרת בנחל כרית [ט] והעורבים מביאים לו לחם ובשר בבקר וגו' [ל] מהיכא אמר רב יהודה אמר רב מבי טבחי דאחאב [י] ויהי מקץ ימים וייבש הנחל כי לא היה גשם בארץ כיון דחזא דאיכא צערא בעלמא כתיב [כ] ויהי דבר ה' אליו לאמר קום לך צרפתה וכתיב [ל] ויהי אחר הדברים האלה חלה בן האשה בעלת הבית בעא רחמי למיתן ליה אקלידא דתחיית המתים אמרי ליה [מ] שלש מפתחות לא נמסרו לשליח של חיה ושל גשמים ושל תחיית המתים יאמרו שתים ביד תלמיד ואחת ביד הרב אייתי הא ושקיל האי דכתיב [מ] לך הראה אל אחאב [ואתנה] מטר דרש ההוא גלילאה קמיה דרב חסדא משל דאליהו למה הדבר דומה לגברא דטרקיה לגליה ואבדיה למפתחיה דרש ר' יוסי בצפורי אבא אליהו

וליפרקיה לכוליה. ומשני כר"י דאמר לא אלים למתפס פדיונו בההיא [י] מנה גופא במס' מעשר שני (פ"ג מ"י) והיינו נמי מעשר שני דקאמר יגנז בקבורה: אלא לעולם. במעשר שני דעיר הנדחת טהור ואסקוה לגוה ודקאמר ליפתרי באכילה דהא קלטוהו מחילות אחר שנכנס לחומת ירושלים: דאמר רבא. ([ס] בשחיטת חולין פ' בהמה המקשה (דף סח): מחיצות לאכול דאורייתא. מן התורה מלוה לאכול לפנים מן החומה: אבל מחיצות לקלוט. שיהיו מחילות קולטות בין לענין פדייה בין לכל ענין מדרבנן הוא וכי גזור רבנן דתיהני קליטת מחילות למעשר דשוב אינו יכול לפדותו א] ולענין עיר הנדחת נמי שלא יהא בשריפה היכא דאיתנהו מחילות: דכתיב ואבדתם. את שמם מן המקום ההוא וגו' וסמיך ליה לא תעשון כן לה' אלהיכם ובמזוזה הואיל וכתיב בה אזכרות אי אפשר לשריפה משום קרא דלא תעשון כן ואנן בעינן שללה וליכא דהאי שלל שמים הוא: כלל בעשה ופרט בלא תעשה. כגון והיתה תל עולם כלל דאפילו גנות ופרדסים לא תעשה אלא תהיה תל עולם שהוא עשה לא תבנה עוד בנין בתים והוא לא תעשה אין דנין אותו בכלל ופרט לומר אין בכלל אלא מה שבפרט דלא תעשה פירוש הוא כלומר והיתה תל עולם לבנין קאמר אבל לגנות ופרדסים שרי אלא תרי מילי קאמר קרא דלא אמרינן פירושי קמפרש אלא מילי מילי קאמר והיתה תל עולם לגנות ופרדסים לא תבנה עוד כל בניין שבעולם ואפילו לגנות ופרדסים לא תבנה עוד ודרשינן ליה לדבר שהיה בכלל ויצא מן הכלל ללמד לא ללמד על עצמו יצא אלא ללמד על הכלל כולו יצא ולומר בנין בכלל היה ולמה יצא להקיש לך מה בנין מיוחד שהוא ישוב בני אדם אף כל בנין כגון גנות ופרדסים [ע] (לישנא אחרינא) ור' יוסי הגלילי סבר אין דנין כר' אבין ודריש הכי והיתה תל עולם מכל מילי שלא יעשה בה שום דבר ולא תבנה עוד דמשמע בנין בתים אשמועינן לאו בבנין בתים וגנות ופרדסים איסור עשה הוא דאיכא. כך שמעתי: ר"ע סבר דנין. דלא כר' אבין: דכ"ע אית להו דר' אבין. ואפילו ר"ע והא דקאמר דעיר הנדחת נעשית גנות ופרדסים לאו משום דבעלמא לית ליה דר' אבין דודאי מלתא קא מפרשי והיתה תל עולם במאי בבנין בתים דלא תבנה עוד לא משמע ליה בכל בניינין דקסבר עוד לכמו שהיתה משמע כלומר לא תחזור ולא תבנה עוד משמע כגון שהיתה מתחלה לא תבנה עוד אבל נעשה גנות ופרדסים: ומר סבר עוד לגמרי משמע. כגון דאמר לעולם ועד ועוד לשון ועד הוא [פ] שלא תבנה לעולם לשום דבר לא לבנין בתים ולא לגנות ופרדסים לא תבנה עוד: מחוברין מותרין. דתקבוץ ושרפת אמרה רחמנא מי שאינו מחוסר אלא קבילה ושריפה יצא זה שמחוסר תלישה וקבילה ושריפה: וכל אשר בה. אפילו אילנות מחוברין אשר בה נאסרין: ה"ג וישבע יהושע לאמר ארור האיש וגו'. וקרא קדריש ואזיל בבכורו ייסדנה ובצעירו יציב דלתיה וכשיעמיד דלתיה ימות בנו הקטן: לא יריחו על שם עיר אחרת. שלא יבנה יריחו ויסב שמה על שם עיר אחרת ולא עיר אחרת על שם יריחו שאפי' בנה עיר אחרת וקראה יריחו אסור לבנותה שאפי' שם יריחו ימחה לעולם וכתיב בימיו בנה חיאל בית האלי את יריחו בימיו של אחאב ועל שעבר על האלה קרי ליה בית האלי: את יריחו. ולא יריחו עצמו בנה אלא עיר אחרת על שם יריחו שקראה לה יריחו ולא אתפרש הא מנלן: באבירם בכורו יסדה. אבירם רשע כשמת אבירם הרשע לא היה לו לחיאל ללמוד שלא לבנות את יריחו: אבירם ושגוב מאי עבוד. דקרי להו רשעים: איני יודע ששגוב צעירו. מילתא באנפי נפשיה הוא ולמדרשא ממשמע שנאמר באבירם בכורו איני יודע ששגוב צעירו אלא מה ת"ל שגוב צעירו שהיה קובר והולך מאבירם ועד שגוב שהוא צעיר מכלם: אחאב שושבינו. אוהבו של חיאל היה אחאב: בי טמיא. וי"א בי טעמא בית האבל שמטעימים אותו בדברים לנחמו ובכמה דוכתין כתיב בבראשית רבה טמיא בלא עיי"ן לשון אבל: על כל תלם ותלם. שורה וערוגה ומקום גבוה הוא: ולא שביק מיטרא מיזל ומסגד. שהיה הלכלוך הולך וגדל מרוב הגשמים הבאין לעולם שאין מניחין לילך להשתחוות לעבודת כוכבים מתוך דרכים מלוכלכות בטיט: מיד ויאמר אליהו חי ה' אם יהיה השנים האלה מטר וגו'. האי קרא סמוך לקרא דחיאל בית האלי: אקלידא דמטרא. מפתח של מטר: כיון דחזא. הקב"ה דאיכא צערא בעלמא א"ל הקב"ה לאליהו לך צרפתה לגלגל הדבר שיחזיר לו מפתח של מטר כדקא מפרש ואזיל: שלש מפתחות לא נמסרו ביד שליח. על אוצרו של הקב"ה יש מפתחות ומסרם ליד שלוחים הממונים אבל ג' מפתחות יש לו בידו שלא מינה שליח עליהם מבראשית אלא בידו הם ולא רצה למסור שליח עליהם וקאמר הקב"ה לאליהו אותם ג' מפתחות עכבתי בידי מבראשית ולא מניתי שליח עליהם אלא אותך שעשיתי ממונה על אחת מהם ועתה תשאל מפתח שני יאמרו שנים ביד תלמיד ואחד ביד הרב: דטרקיה לגליה. שסתם שער שלו ואבדיה למפתחיה כך עשה אליהו נעל לשערי מטר ולבסוף אבד המפתח של גשמים שלא נפתח השער של מטר על ידו: דכתב לך הראה אל אחאב ואתנה מטר. ולא כתיב ותן מטר: אבא אליהו. חביבי וגדולי:

היה

מסורת הש"ס

א) פסחי' לו: לח. מ"ש פ"ג מ"י [ב"מ נג: זבחים מט.], ב) ב"מ שם מכות כ. [עיין תוס' ב"מ נג: ד"ה לא פלוג], ג) לעיל ע"א, ד) [מ"ק ג.], ה) [צ"ל חרם היא וכל אשר בה לה'], ו) [תוספ' פי"ד], ז) [תוספתא שם], ח) [בע"י ליתא], ט) [לעיל קג:], י) [אל אחאב], כ) [צ"ל יהיה השנים האלה טל וכו'], ל) חולין ה., מ) תענית ב., נ) [צ"ל משנה], ס) [בשחיטת חולין לא נמצא אמנם בב"מ נג: ד"ה והא אמר רבא כתב רש"י על נכון וציין במס' מכות], ע) צ"ל לא, פ) [עי' רש"י שבת לג. ד"ה לא ישמח].

ליקוטי רש"י

יקבר. דקא סבר לא אלים למיתפס פדיונו. אלא לעולם בטהור. בין מעשר בין לקוח ודקאמר נעייליה וניכליה. וכגון דנפול מחיצות. חומת ירושלים ושוב אין מעשר נאכל שם עד שיעמדו מחילות דבעינן לפני ה' תאכלנו (דברים יב) ובפדייה נמי לא דקלטוהו מחילות מלפדותו עוד משנכנס לתוכו. מחיצה לאכול דאורייתא מחיצה לקלוט דרבנן. מחילה שנאמרה בתורה לא הוזכרה אלא לאכול בתוכה ושאמרו במשנה מחילות קולטות אותם מלפדות עוד אם יצא דרבנן היא. וכי גזור רבנן כו'. דכי גזור רבנן היכא דאיתנהו וזה הוציא את המעשר לחוץ אבל כי ליתנהו לא גזור הלכך ניפרקיה [ב"מ נג:]. והיתה העיר חרם. הקדש כי היום שבת קדש וראוי להיות קדש שלל הנשלל בו [יהושע ו, יז]. בבכרו ייסדנה ובצעירו. בתחלת יסוד שיבנה בה ימות בנו הבכור ויקברנו וילך עד שימות הצעיר בגמר המלאכה היא הצבת הדלתות [שם ו, כו]. באבירם בכרו יסדה. כשיסד' מת בנו בכורו וקבר והלך וקבר כל בניו עד שמת האחרון בהצבת דלתות וכן הוא קללות של יהושע בבכורו ייסדנה ובצעירו יציב דלתיה (יהושע ו' כ"ו) [מ"א טז, לד]. חי ה'. למה סמכו כאן אלא שהלכו אליהו ואחאב לנחם את חיאל באבלו אמר אחאב לאליהו אפשר שקללת התלמיד נתקיימה וקללת משה רבינו לא נתקיימה שנאמר (דברים י"א ט"ז) וסרתם ועבדתם אלהים אחרים והשתחויתם להם וחרה אף ה' בכם ועצר את השמים והרי כל ישראל עובדין ע"ג ואין גשמים נעצרים מיד ויאמר אליהו וגו' [שם יז, א]. ונסתרת. מפני אחאב ואיזבל [שם יז, ג]. ויבש הנחל. כדי שידע צורך הגשמים ויטריח לגלות שהיה קשה בעיני הקב"ה שישראל שרוין מתים ברעב [שם יז, ז]. צרפתה. שם העיר [שם יז, ט]. חלה בן האשה. כדי שיצטרך למפתח של תחיית המתים כדאיתא בשילהי אגדתא דחלק [שם פסוק יז].

עין משפט נר מצוה

נט א מיי' פ"ז מהל' מעשר שני הלכה א ב:
ס ב מיי' שם פ"ג הל' ה סמג לאוין רסד:
סא ג מיי' שם הל' ט:
סב ד מיי' פ"ד מהל' ע"ז הלכה יג סמג עשין טו:

הגהות מהר"ב רנשבורג

א] רש"י ד"ה אבל מחיצות וכו' ולענין עיר הנדחת נמי שלא יהא בשריפה. מלת בשריפה נמחק וצ"ב בגניזה:

תורה אור השלם

א) וְאֶת כָּל שְׁלָלָהּ תִּקְבֹּץ אֶל תּוֹךְ רְחֹבָהּ וְשָׂרַפְתָּ בָאֵשׁ אֶת הָעִיר וְאֶת כָּל שְׁלָלָהּ כָּלִיל לַייָ אֱלֹהֶיךָ וְהָיְתָה תֵּל עוֹלָם לֹא תִבָּנֶה עוֹד: [דברים יג, יז]

ב) לֹא תַעֲשׂוּן כֵּן לַייָ אֱלֹהֵיכֶם: [דברים יב, ד]

ג) וְהָיְתָה הָעִיר חֵרֶם הִיא וְכָל אֲשֶׁר בָּהּ לַייָ רַק רָחָב הַזּוֹנָה תִּחְיֶה הִיא וְכָל אֲשֶׁר אִתָּהּ בַּבַּיִת כִּי הֶחְבְּאַתָה אֶת הַמַּלְאָכִים אֲשֶׁר שָׁלָחְנוּ: וַיַּשְׁבַּע יְהוֹשֻׁעַ בָּעֵת הַהִיא לֵאמֹר אָרוּר הָאִישׁ לִפְנֵי יְיָ אֲשֶׁר יָקוּם וּבָנָה אֶת הָעִיר הַזֹּאת אֶת יְרִיחוֹ בִּבְכֹרוֹ יְיַסְּדֶנָּה וּבִצְעִירוֹ יַצִּיב דְּלָתֶיהָ: [יהושע ו, יז,כו]

ד) בְּיָמָיו בָּנָה חִיאֵל בֵּית הָאֱלִי אֶת יְרִיחֹה בַּאֲבִירָם בְּכֹרוֹ יִסְּדָהּ וּבִשְׂגוּב צְעִירוֹ הִצִּיב דְּלָתֶיהָ כִּדְבַר יְיָ אֲשֶׁר דִּבֶּר בְּיַד יְהוֹשֻׁעַ בִּן נוּן: [מלכים א' טז, לד]

ה) הִשָּׁמְרוּ לָכֶם פֶּן יִפְתֶּה לְבַבְכֶם וְסַרְתֶּם וַעֲבַדְתֶּם אֱלֹהִים אֲחֵרִים וְהִשְׁתַּחֲוִיתֶם לָהֶם: [דברים יא, טז]

ו) וְחָרָה אַף יְיָ בָּכֶם וְעָצַר אֶת הַשָּׁמַיִם וְלֹא יִהְיֶה מָטָר וְהָאֲדָמָה לֹא תִתֵּן אֶת יְבוּלָהּ וַאֲבַדְתֶּם מְהֵרָה מֵעַל הָאָרֶץ הַטֹּבָה אֲשֶׁר יְיָ נֹתֵן לָכֶם: [דברים יא, יז]

ז) וַיֹּאמֶר אֵלִיָּהוּ הַתִּשְׁבִּי מִתֹּשָׁבֵי גִלְעָד אֶל אַחְאָב חַי יְיָ אֱלֹהֵי יִשְׂרָאֵל אֲשֶׁר עָמַדְתִּי לְפָנָיו אִם יִהְיֶה הַשָּׁנִים הָאֵלֶּה טַל וּמָטָר כִּי אִם לְפִי דְבָרִי: [מלכים א' יז, א]

ח) וַיְהִי דְבַר יְיָ אֵלָיו לֵאמֹר: לֵךְ מִזֶּה וּפָנִיתָ לְּךָ קֵדְמָה וְנִסְתַּרְתָּ בְּנַחַל כְּרִית אֲשֶׁר עַל פְּנֵי הַיַּרְדֵּן: [מלכים א' יז, ב-ג]

ט) וְהָעֹרְבִים מְבִיאִים לוֹ לֶחֶם וּבָשָׂר בַּבֹּקֶר וְלֶחֶם וּבָשָׂר בָּעָרֶב וּמִן הַנַּחַל יִשְׁתֶּה: [מלכים א' יז, ו]

י) וַיְהִי מִקֵּץ יָמִים וַיִּיבַשׁ הַנַּחַל כִּי לֹא הָיָה גֶשֶׁם בָּאָרֶץ: [מלכים א' יז, ז]

כ) וַיְהִי דְבַר יְיָ אֵלָיו לֵאמֹר: קוּם לֵךְ צָרְפַתָה אֲשֶׁר לְצִידוֹן וְיָשַׁבְתָּ שָׁם הִנֵּה צִוִּיתִי שָׁם אִשָּׁה אַלְמָנָה לְכַלְכְּלֶךָ: [מלכים א' יז, ח-ט] ל) וַיְהִי אַחַר הַדְּבָרִים הָאֵלֶּה חָלָה בֶּן הָאִשָּׁה בַּעֲלַת הַבָּיִת וַיְהִי חָלְיוֹ חָזָק מְאֹד עַד אֲשֶׁר לֹא נוֹתְרָה בּוֹ נְשָׁמָה: [מלכים א' יז, יז] מ) וַיְהִי יָמִים רַבִּים וּדְבַר יְיָ הָיָה אֶל אֵלִיָּהוּ בַּשָּׁנָה הַשְּׁלִישִׁית לֵאמֹר לֵךְ הֵרָאֵה אֶל אַחְאָב וְאֶתְּנָה מָטָר עַל פְּנֵי הָאֲדָמָה: [מלכים א' יח, א]

The Gemara quotes the last part of the Mishnah:
רַבִּי שִׁמְעוֹן אוֹמֵר אָמַר הַקָּדוֹשׁ בָּרוּךְ הוּא וכו׳ – **R' SHIMON SAYS: THE HOLY ONE, BLESSED IS HE, SAID, etc.**

Following R' Shimon's homiletic teaching, the Mishnah recorded the dispute between R' Yose HaGlili and R' Akiva concerning the Torah's decree that after the city is destroyed, *it shall remain an eternal heap; it shall never again be built* (*Deuteronomy* 13:17). R' Yose HaGlili maintains that the verse prohibits doing anything with the site, even planting gardens and orchards on it. R' Akiva, however, maintains that the verse only prohibits rebuilding it as a city but not making gardens and orchards. The Gemara now investigates the basis for this dispute:

לֵימָא בִּדְרַבִּי אָבִין אָמַר רַבִּי אִילְעָא קָמִיפַּלְגֵי – **Shall we say that they disagree in** regard to the rule laid down by **R' Avin in the name of R' Ila'a?** דְּאָמַר רַבִּי אָבִין אָמַר רַבִּי אִילְעָא – **For R' Avin said in the name of R' Ila'a:** כָּל מָקוֹם שֶׁאַתָּה מוֹצֵא כְּלָל בַּעֲשֵׂה וּפְרָט בְּלֹא תַעֲשֶׂה – **Wherever** in Scripture **you find a generalization as a positive commandment followed by a specification as a negative commandment,** אֵין דָּנִין אוֹתוֹ בִּכְלָל וּפְרָט – **we do not expound it as a generalization followed by a specification.**[11] דְּמַר אִית לֵיהּ דְּרַבִּי אָבִין – Shall we say that **one master** [R' Yose HaGlili] **accepts the** rule **of R' Avin,** וּמַר לֵית לֵיהּ דְּרַבִּי אָבִין – **while the** other **master** [R' Akiva] **does not accept the** rule **of R' Avin?**[12]

The Gemara rejects this explanation of the dispute and puts forth another:

לֹא – **No.** דְּכוּלֵּי עָלְמָא אִית לְהוּ דְּרַבִּי אָבִין – **Actually, everyone** [i.e. both R' Yose HaGlili and R' Akiva] **accepts the** rule **of R' Avin.** וְהָכָא בְּהָא קָמִיפַּלְגֵי – **However, here they disagree about the following:** מַר סָבַר ,,עוֹד״ לְגַמְרֵי מַשְׁמַע – **One master** [R' Yose HaGlili] **holds** that when the verse states *it shall never **again** be built,* **it implies – at all,** in *any* capacity. וּמַר סָבַר ,,עוֹד״ לִכְמָה שֶׁהָיְתָה אֵינָהּ נִבְנֵית[13] – **And the** other **master** [R' Akiva] **holds** that ***again*** **implies** that **it may not be rebuilt to what it was before,** namely, a city, אֲבָל נַעֲשֵׂית הִיא גַּנּוֹת וּפַרְדֵּסִים – **but it may be made** into **gardens and orchards.**[14]

The Gemara cites a Baraisa:

תָּנוּ רַבָּנָן – **The Rabbis taught in a Baraisa:** הָיוּ בָהּ אִילָנוֹת – **IF THERE WERE TREES IN [THE SUBVERTED CITY],** תְּלוּשִׁין אֲסוּרִין – **THE DETACHED ONES ARE PROHIBITED** מְחוּבָּרִין מוּתָּרִין – while

NOTES

secrated objects are not deemed the booty of the city, they are never subject to the law of the *ir hanidachas*]. The *mezuzos,* however, are part of the booty of the city and are therefore subject to the law of destruction. Accordingly, the prohibition to destroy them prevents the city from being classified an *ir hanidachas* according to R' Eliezer (see the end of *Rashi* ד״ה דכתיב ואבדתם, as emended by *Rashash*).

[For a discussion of why R' Eliezer does not apply to this situation the rule of עֲשֵׂה דוֹחֶה לֹא תַעֲשֶׂה, *a positive commandment supersedes a negative commandment,* see *Toras Chaim* (71a), *Minchas Chinuch* (464:46 and 142:5), *Aruch LaNer, Margaliyos HaYam* et al.]

11. The positive command at the beginning of the verse – וְהָיְתָה תֵּל עוֹלָם, *it shall remain an eternal heap* – is a general command to leave the destroyed city as it is – an eternal heap. This would seem to preclude transforming the site in any way, even by planting gardens and orchards on it. The negative command that follows – לֹא תִבָּנֶה עוֹד, *it shall not be built again* – is more specific: It prohibits *rebuilding* the city, which connotes erecting structures on the site, but not planting gardens and orchards.

Now there is a rule of Biblical hermeneutics that wherever the Torah states a general rule and then proceeds to describe a specific case where that rule applies, the specific case is not understood to be merely one example of the general rule, but is understood to be the *only* example of the rule. [In the words of the Gemara above (45b): כְּלָל וּפְרָט אֵין בִּכְלָל אֶלָּא מַה שֶּׁבִּפְרָט, *When a generalization is followed by a specification, the generalization includes only what is stated explicitly in the specification.* This is the fourth of R' Yishmael's thirteen rules of Scriptural interpretation.] R' Avin, however, states in the name of R' Ila'a that this rule does not apply where the generalization is stated as a positive commandment and the specification as a negative commandment. According to R' Avin, therefore, the general command to leave the burnt ruin of the *ir hanidachas* as an eternal heap would *not* necessarily be limited to the specific injunction not to *build* on the site (*Rashi*).

12. Rather, R' Akiva would hold that even in such a case the specification is understood to be qualifying the generalization and limiting it to the specific example given by the Torah. For this reason R' Akiva rules that it is forbidden only to *build* a structure on the site of an *ir hanidachas*, but to plant gardens and orchards on it is allowed.

R' Yose HaGlili, however, accepts R' Avin's rule and therefore does not interpret the command not to build as qualifying the more general command to leave the site an eternal heap. Rather, R' Yose HaGlili understands the command not to build to be the example that illustrates the rule. There is a different hermeneutical rule [the eighth on R' Yishmael's list] that states: כָּל דָּבָר שֶׁהָיָה בִּכְלָל וְיָצָא מִן הַכְּלָל לְלַמֵּד לֹא לְלַמֵּד עַל עַצְמוֹ יָצָא אֶלָּא לְלַמֵּד עַל הַכְּלָל כֻּלּוֹ יָצָא, *Anything that was included in the generalization but was then singled out from the generalization was not singled out to teach [only] about itself, but to teach about the entire generalization.* In our case, this means that the commandment not to build is not meant to teach anything about building per se, but rather to illustrate the *type* of activity that is prohibited by the more general positive commandment. What type of activity is building? It is an activity whose purpose is to provide for human settlement. We learn from this that the type of activity prohibited under the positive commandment is any activity whose purpose is to provide for human settlement. This includes planting gardens and orchards, since these provide for human needs.

Alternatively, R' Yose HaGlili understands the specific mention of building to be teaching that whereas all other uses of the site are forbidden only by virtue of a positive commandment, building is forbidden by a negative commandment, a more severe prohibition (*Rashi* as emended by *Maharsha;* see *R' Shlomo Algazi's* commentary on *Halichos Olam, Yavin Shemua* שער ד׳ כלל קכ״ו, for an explanation that avoids the emendation).

13. [In the standard printed editions of the Gemara, there is a colon between the words לִכְמָה שֶׁהָיְתָה and the words אֵינָהּ נִבְנֵית, dividing the rest of these words into a heading for the next passage of the Gemara. This appears to be a printer's error, since the words אֵינָהּ נִבְנֵית אֲבָל נַעֲשֵׂית הִיא גַּנּוֹת וּפַרְדֵּסִים are not an introduction to the discussion that follows and are in any case only a partial quotation of a clause that in the Mishnah begins with the earlier words לִכְמָה שֶׁהָיְתָה. By eliminating the colon, the Gemara's explanation of R' Akiva's view follows exactly the Mishnah's quotation of R' Akiva's opinion. Indeed, *Dikdukei Sofrim* notes that older editions do not have a colon at this point. We have followed this emendation in our elucidation.]

14. Thus, R' Akiva may in general agree with R' Avin that the rule of כְּלָל וּפְרָט, *generalization followed by specification,* does not apply where the generalization is a positive commandment and the specification is a negative commandment. The reason R' Akiva limits the prohibition in our case to building structures is because he understands the verse in our case to be going out of its way to make this point. The verse states that the city "shall not be built *again*." [The word עוֹד, *again*, is redundant here. This redundancy teaches, according to R' Akiva, that the prohibition is only to build it *again,* i.e. as it was before (*Chidushei HaRan*).] Now the word *"again"* connotes a repetition of what was before. This indicates that the only type of construction banned is that which would qualify as an analogue of what stood previously; gardens and orchards are not analogous to a city. Thus by adding the word עוֹד, *again,* the verse in effect qualifies its earlier statement that the site shall remain an everlasting heap, and explains that the prohibition applies only to building structures. Gardens and orchards, however, are permitted.

R' Yose HaGlili, however, interprets the word עוֹד in the sense of וָעֶד, *ever*. Accordingly, the verse is saying that the site shall not be built *ever* [paralleling the positive command of the verse, "it shall remain an *eternal* heap"]. Explained this way, the verse in no way implies that the prohibition of construction is limited to structures. Rather, it states simply that nothing may ever be built on that site – not even gardens and orchards (*Rashi*).

וליפרקיה [ס] דתנן [א] הלקוח בכסף מעשר שנטמא יפדה כר"י דאמר יקבר אי הכי מאי איריא עיר הנדחת אפילו דעלמא נמי אלא לעולם בטהור וכגון דנפול מחיצות וכדרבא [ג] דאמר רבא [ב] מחיצה לאכול דאורייתא [ג] לקלוט דרבנן וכי גזור רבנן כי אתנהו למחיצה כי ליתנהו למחיצה לא: כתבי הקדש יגנזו: מתניתין דלא כר"א [ג] דתניא ר"א אומר כל עיר שיש בה אפי' מזוזה אחת אינה נעשית עיר הנדחת שנא' [א] ושרפת באש את העיר ואת כל שללה כליל והיכא דאיכא מזוזה לא אפשר דכתיב [ב] לא תעשון כן לה' אלהיכם: ר"ש אומר אמר הקב"ה וכו': לימא בדר' אבין א"ר אילעא קמיפלגי [ד] דא"ר אבין א"ר אילעא כל מקום שאתה מוצא כלל בעשה ופרט בלא תעשה אין דנין אותו בכלל ופרט דמר אית ליה דרבי אבין ומר לית ליה דרבי אבין לא דכ"ע אית להו דר' אבין והכא בהא קמיפלגי מר סבר עוד לגמרי משמע ומר סבר עוד לכמה שהיתה: אינה נבנית אבל נעשית היא גנות ופרדסים: ת"ר [ד] היו בה אילנות תלושין אסורין מחוברין מותרין של עיר אחרת בין תלושין בין מחוברין אסור מאי עיר אחרת אמר רב חסדא יריחו דכתיב [ג] והיתה העיר [ה] חרם לה' וישבע יהושע בעת ההיא לאמר ארור האיש לפני ה' אשר יקום ובנה את העיר הזאת את יריחו בבכורו ייסדנה ובצעירו יציב דלתיה תניא [ו] לא יריחו על שם עיר אחרת ולא עיר אחרת על שם יריחו דכתיב [ד] בנה חיאל בית האלי את יריחו באבירם בכורו יסדה ובשגוב צעירו הציב דלתיה תניא [ז] באבירם בכורו רשע לא היה לו ללמוד בשגוב צעירו היה לו ללמוד אבירם ושגוב מאי עבוד ([ס] מאי קאמר) ה"ק באבירם בכורו היה לו ללמוד לאותו רשע בשגוב צעירו ממשמע שנאמר באבירם בכורו איני יודע ששגוב צעירו מה ת"ל שגוב צעירו מלמד שהיה מקבר והולך מאבירם עד שגוב אחאב שושביניה הוה אתא איהו ואליהו למשאל בשלמא בי טמיא יתיב וקאמר דילמא כי מילט יהושע הכי לט לא יריחו על שם עיר אחרת ולא עיר אחרת על שם יריחו א"ל אליהו אין אמר ליה השתא לווטתא דמשה לא קא מקיימא דכתיב [ה] וסרתם ועבדתם וגו' וכתיב [ו] וחרה אף ה' בכם ועצר את השמים וגו' וההוא גברא אוקים ליה עבודת כוכבים [ט] על כל תלם ותלם ולא שביק ליה מיטרא דמיזל מיסגד ליה לווטתא דיהושע תלמידיה מקיימא מיד [ז] ויאמר אליהו התשבי מתושבי גלעד [י] חי ה' אלהי ישראל אם [כ] יהיה טל ומטר וגו' בעי רחמי והבו ליה אקלידא דמטרא וקם ואזל [ח] ויהי דבר ה' אליו לאמר לך מזה ופנית לך קדמה ונסתרת בנחל כרית [ט] והעורבים מביאים לו לחם ובשר בבקר וגו' [ל] מהיכא אמר רב יהודה אמר רב מבי טבחי דאחאב [י] ויהי מקץ ימים וייבש הנחל כי לא היה גשם בארץ כיון דחזא דאיכא צערא בעלמא כתיב [כ] ויהי דבר ה' אליו לאמר קום לך צרפתה וכתיב [ל] ויהי אחר הדברים האלה חלה בן האשה בעלת הבית בעא רחמי למיתן ליה אקלידא דתחיית המתים אמרי ליה [מ] שלש מפתחות לא נמסרו לשליח של חיה ושל גשמים ושל תחיית המתים יאמרו שתים ביד תלמיד ואחת ביד הרב אייתי הא ושקיל האי דכתיב [מ] לך הראה אל אחאב [ואתנה] מטר דרש ההוא גלילאה קמיה דרב חסדא משל דאליהו למה הדבר דומה לגברא דטרקיה לגליה ואבדיה למפתחיה דרש ר' יוסי בצפורי אבא אליהו

היה

וליפרקיה לבוליה. ומשני כר"י דאמר לא אליס למתפס פדיונו בההיא [נ] מנה גופא במס' מעשר שני (פ"ג מ"י) והיינו נמי מעשר שני דקאמר יגנז בקבורה: אלא לעולם. במעשר שני דעיר הנדחת טהור ואסקוה לגוה ודקאמר לישתרי באכילה דהא קלטוהו מחילות אחר שנכנס לחומת ירושלים: דאמר רבא. ([ס] בשחיטת חולין פ' בהמה המקשה (דף סח)): מחיצות לאכול דאורייתא. מן התורה מלוה לאכול לפנים מן החומה: אבל מחיצות לקלוט. שיהיו מחילות קולטות בין לענין פדייה בין לכל ענין מדרבנן הוא וכי גזור רבנן דתיהני קליטת מחילות למעשר דשוב אינו יכול לפדותו אז] ולענין עיר הנדחת נמי שלא יהא בשריפה היכא דאיתנהו מחילות: דכתיב ואבדתם. את שמם מן המקום ההוא וגו' וסמיך ליה לא תעשון כן לה' אלהיכם ובמזוזה הואיל וכתיב בה אזכרות אי אפשר לשריפה משום קרא דלא תעשון כן ואנן בעינן שללה וליכא דהאי שלל שמים הוא: כלל בעשה ופרט בלא תעשה. כגון והיתה תל עולם כלל דאפילו גנות ופרדסים לא תעשה אלא תהיה תל עולם שהוא עשה לא תבנה עוד בנין בתים והוא לא תעשה אין דנין אותו בכלל ופרט לומר אין בכלל אלא מה שבפרט דלא תעשה פירוש הוא כלומר והיתה תל עולם לבנין קאמר אבל לגנות ופרדסים שרי אלא תרי מילי קאמר קרא דלא אמרינן פירושי קמפרש אלא מילי מילי קאמר והיתה תל עולם לגנות ופרדסים לא תבנה עוד כל בנינין שבעולם ואפילו לגנות ופרדסים לא תבנה עוד ודרשינן ליה לדבר שהיה בכלל ויצא מן הכלל ללמד לא ללמד על עצמו יצא אלא ללמד על הכלל כולו יצא ולומר בנין בכלל היה ולמה יצא להקיש לך מה בנין מיוחד שהוא ישוב בני אדם אף כל בנין כגון גנות ופרדסים [ע] (לישנא אחרינא) ור' יוסי הגלילי סבר אין דנין כר' אבין ודריש הכי והיתה תל עולם מכל מילי שלא יעשה בה שום דבר ולא תבנה עוד דמשמע בנין בתים אשמועינן לאו דבנין בתים וגנות ופרדסים איסור עשה הוא דאיכא. כך שמעתי: ר"ע סבר דנין. דלא כר' אבין: דכ"ע אית להו דר' אבין. ואפילו ר"ע והא דקאמר דעיר הנדחת נעשית גנות ופרדסים לאו משום דבעלמא לית ליה דר' אבין דודאי מלתא קא מפרשי והיתה תל עולם במאי בבנין בתים דלא תבנה עוד לא משמע ליה בכל בניין דקסבר עוד לכמו שהיתה משמע כלומר לא תחזור ולא תבנה עוד משמע כגון שהיתה מתחלה לא תבנה עוד אבל נעשה גנות ופרדסים: ומר סבר עוד לגמרי משמע. כגון דאמר לעולם ועד ועוד לשון ועד הוא [פ] שלא תבנה לעולם לשום דבר לא לבנין בתים ולא לגנות ופרדסים לא תבנה עוד: מחוברין מותרין. דתקבוץ ושרפת אמרה רחמנא מי שאינו מחוסר אלא קבילה ושריפה יצא זה שמחוסר תלישה וקבילה ושריפה: וכל אשר בה. אפילו אילנות מחוברין אשר בה נאסרין: ה"ג וישבע יהושע לאמר ארור האיש וגו'. וקרא קדריש ואזיל בבכורו ייסדנה ובצעירו יציב דלתיה וכשיעמיד דלתיה ימות בנו הקטן: לא יריחו על שם עיר אחרת. שלא יבנה יריחו ויסב שמה על שם עיר אחרת ולא עיר אחרת על שם יריחו שאפי' בנה עיר אחרת וקראה יריחו אסור לבנותה שאפי' שם יריחו ימחה לעולם וכתיב בימיו בנה חיאל בית האלי את יריחו בימיו של אחאב ועל שעבר על האלה קרי ליה בית האלי: את יריחו. ולא יריחו עצמו בנה אלא עיר אחרת על שם יריחו שקראה לה יריחו ולא אתפרש הא מנלן: באבירם בכורו יסדה. אבירם רשע כשמת אבירם הרשע לא היה לו לחיאל ללמוד שלא לבנות את יריחו: אבירם ושגוב מאי עבוד. דקרי להו רשעים: איני יודע ששגוב צעירו. מילתא באנפי נפשיה הוא ולמדרשא ממשמע שנאמר באבירם בכורו איני יודע ששגוב צעירו אלא מה ת"ל שגוב צעירו שהיה קובר והולך מאבירם ועד שגוב שהוא צעיר מכלם: אחאב שושבינו. אוהבו של חיאל היה אחאב: בי טמיא. וי"א בי טעמא בית האבל שמטעימים אותו בדברים לנחמו ובכמה דוכתין כתיב בבראשית רבה טמיא בלא עיי"ן לשון אבל: על כל תלם ותלם. שורה וערוגה ומקום גבוה הוא: ולא שביק מיטרא מיזל ומסגד. שהיה הגלגול הולך וגדל מרוב הגשמים הבאין לעולם שאין מניחין לילך להשתחוות לעבודת כוכבים מתוך דרכים מלוכלכות בטיט: מיד ויאמר אליהו חי ה' אם יהיה השנים האלה מטר וגו'. האי קרא סמוך לקרא דחיאל בית האלי: אקלידא דמטרא. מפתח של מטר: כיון דחזא. הקב"ה דאיכא צערא בעלמא א"ל הקב"ה לאליהו לך צרפתה לגלגל הדבר שיחזיר לו מפתח של מטר כדקא מפרש ואזיל: שלש מפתחות לא נמסרו ביד שליח. על אוצרו של הקב"ה יש מפתחות ומסרם ליד שלוחים הממונים אבל ג' מפתחות יש לו בידו שלא מינה שליח עליהם מבראשית אלא בידו הם ולא רצה למסור שליח עליהם וקאמר הקב"ה לאליהו אותם ג' מפתחות עכבתי בידי מבראשית ולא מניתי שליח עליהם אלא אותך שעשיתי ממונה על אחת מהם ועתה תשאל מפתח שני יאמרו שנים ביד תלמיד ואחד ביד הרב: דטרקיה לגליה. שסתם שער שלו ואבדיה למפתחיה כך עשה אליהו נעל לשערי מטר ולבסוף אבד המפתח של גשמים שלא נפתח השער של מטר על ידו: דכתב לך הראה אל אחאב ואתנה מטר. ולא כתיב ותן מטר: אבא אליהו. חביבי וגדולי:

מסורת הש"ס

א) פסחי' לו: לח. מ"ש פ"ג מ"י [ב"מ נג: זבחים מט.], ב) ב"מ שם מכות כ. [עיין תוס' ב"מ נג: ד"ה לא פלוג], ג) לעיל ע"א, ד) [מ"ק ג.], ה) [נ"ל חרם היא וכל אשר בה לה'], ו) [תוספ' פי"ד], ז) [תוספתא שם], ח) [בע"י ליתא], ט) [לעיל קב:], י) [אל אחאב], כ) [נ"ל יהיה השנים האלה טל וכו'], ל) חולין ה., מ) תענית ב., נ) [נ"ל משנה], ס) [בשחיטת חולין לא נמצא אמנם בב"מ נג: ד"ה והא אמר רבא כתב רש"י על נכון ועיין במס' מכות], ע) נ"ל לא, פ) [עי' רש"י שבת לג. ד"ה לא ישמח].

ליקוטי רש"י

יקבר. דקא סבר לא אלים למיתפס פדיונו. אלא לעולם בטהור. בין מעשר בין לקוח ודקאמר נעייליה וניכליה. וכגון דנפול מחיצות. חומת ירושלים ושוב אין מעשר נאכל שם עד שיעמדו מחילות דבעינן לפני ה' תאכלנו (דברים יב) ובפדייה נמי לא דקלטוהו מחילות מלפדותו עוד משנכנס לתוכו. מחיצה לאכול דאורייתא מחיצה לקלוט דרבנן. מחילה שנאמרה בתורה לא הוזכרה אלא לאכול בתוכה ושאמרו במשנה מחילות קולטות אותם מלפדות עוד אם יצא דרבנן היא. וכי גזור רבנן כו'. דכי גזור רבנן היכא דאיתנהו וזה הוציא את המעשר לחוץ אבל כי ליתנהו לא גזור הלכך ניפרקיה [ב"מ נג:]. והיתה העיר חרם. הקדש כי היום שבת קדש וראוי להיות קדש שלל הנשלל בו [יהושע ו, יז]. בבכרו ייסדנה ובצעירו. בתחלת יסוד שיבנה בה ימות בנו הבכור ויקברנו וילך עד שימות הצעיר בגמר המלאכה היא הצבת הדלתות [שם ו, כו]. באבירם בכרו יסדה. כשיסד' מת בנו בכורו וקבר והלך וקבר כל בניו עד שמת האחרון בהצבת דלתות וכן הוא קללות של יהושע בבכורו ייסדנה ובצעירו יציב דלתיה (יהושע ו' כ"ו) [מ"א טז, לד]. חי ה'. למה סמכו כאן אלא שהלכו אליהו ואחאב לנחם את חיאל באבלו אמר אחאב לאליהו אפשר שקללת התלמיד נתקיימה וקללת משה רבינו לא נתקיימה שנאמר (דברים י"א ט"ז) וסרתם ועבדתם אלהים אחרים והשתחויתם להם וחרה אף ה' בכם ועצר את השמים והרי כל ישראל עובדין ע"ג ואין גשמים נעצרים מיד ויאמר אליהו וגו' [שם יז, א]. ונסתרת. מפני אחאב ואיזבל [שם יז, ג]. ויבש הנחל. כדי שידע צורך הגשמים ויטריח לגלות שהיה קשה בעיני הקב"ה שישראל שרוין מתים ברעב [שם יז, ז]. צרפתה. שם העיר [שם יז, ט]. חלה בן האשה. כדי שיצטרך למפתח של תחיית המתים כדאיתא בשילהי אגדתא דחלק [שם פסוק יז].

עין משפט נר מצוה

נט א מיי' פ"ז מהל' מעשר שני הלכה א ב:
ס ב מיי' שם פ"ב הל' ה סמג לאוין רסד:
סא ג מיי' שם הל' ט:
סב ד מיי' פ"ד מהל' ע"ז הלכה יג סמג עשין טו:

הגהות מהר"ב רנשבורג

א] רש"י ד"ה אבל מחיצות וכו' ולענין עיר הנדחת נמי שלא יהא בשריפה. מלת בשריפה נמחק ונ"ב בגניזה:

תורה אור השלם

א) וְאֶת כָּל שְׁלָלָהּ תִּקְבֹּץ אֶל תּוֹךְ רְחֹבָהּ וְשָׂרַפְתָּ בָאֵשׁ אֶת הָעִיר וְאֶת כָּל שְׁלָלָהּ כָּלִיל לַייָ אֱלֹהֶיךָ וְהָיְתָה תֵּל עוֹלָם לֹא תִבָּנֶה עוֹד: [דברים יג, יז]

ב) לֹא תַעֲשׂוּן כֵּן לַייָ אֱלֹהֵיכֶם: [דברים יב, ד]

ג) וְהָיְתָה הָעִיר חֵרֶם הִיא וְכָל אֲשֶׁר בָּהּ לַייָ רַק רָחָב הַזּוֹנָה תִּחְיֶה הִיא וְכָל אֲשֶׁר אִתָּהּ בַּבַּיִת כִּי הֶחְבְּאַתָה אֶת הַמַּלְאָכִים אֲשֶׁר שָׁלָחְנוּ: וַיַּשְׁבַּע יְהוֹשֻׁעַ בָּעֵת הַהִיא לֵאמֹר אָרוּר הָאִישׁ לִפְנֵי יְיָ אֲשֶׁר יָקוּם וּבָנָה אֶת הָעִיר הַזֹּאת אֶת יְרִיחוֹ בִּבְכֹרוֹ יְיַסְּדֶנָּה וּבִצְעִירוֹ יַצִּיב דְּלָתֶיהָ: [יהושע ו, יז,כו]

ד) בְּיָמָיו בָּנָה חִיאֵל בֵּית הָאֱלִי אֶת יְרִיחֹה בַּאֲבִירָם בְּכֹרוֹ יִסְּדָהּ וּבִשְׂגוּב צְעִירוֹ הִצִּיב דְּלָתֶיהָ כִּדְבַר יְיָ אֲשֶׁר דִּבֶּר בְּיַד יְהוֹשֻׁעַ בִּן נוּן: [מלכים א' טז, לד]

ה) הִשָּׁמְרוּ לָכֶם פֶּן יִפְתֶּה לְבַבְכֶם וְסַרְתֶּם וַעֲבַדְתֶּם אֱלֹהִים אֲחֵרִים וְהִשְׁתַּחֲוִיתֶם לָהֶם: [דברים יא, טז]

ו) וְחָרָה אַף יְיָ בָּכֶם וְעָצַר אֶת הַשָּׁמַיִם וְלֹא יִהְיֶה מָטָר וְהָאֲדָמָה לֹא תִתֵּן אֶת יְבוּלָהּ וַאֲבַדְתֶּם מְהֵרָה מֵעַל הָאָרֶץ הַטֹּבָה אֲשֶׁר יְיָ נֹתֵן לָכֶם: [דברים יא, יז]

ז) וַיֹּאמֶר אֵלִיָּהוּ הַתִּשְׁבִּי מִתֹּשָׁבֵי גִלְעָד אֶל אַחְאָב חַי יְיָ אֱלֹהֵי יִשְׂרָאֵל אֲשֶׁר עָמַדְתִּי לְפָנָיו אִם יִהְיֶה הַשָּׁנִים הָאֵלֶּה טַל וּמָטָר כִּי אִם לְפִי דְבָרִי: [מלכים א' יז, א]

ח) וַיְהִי דְבַר יְיָ אֵלָיו לֵאמֹר: לֵךְ מִזֶּה וּפָנִיתָ לְּךָ קֵדְמָה וְנִסְתַּרְתָּ בְּנַחַל כְּרִית אֲשֶׁר עַל פְּנֵי הַיַּרְדֵּן: [מלכים א' יז, ב-ג]

ט) וְהָעֹרְבִים מְבִיאִים לוֹ לֶחֶם וּבָשָׂר בַּבֹּקֶר וְלֶחֶם וּבָשָׂר בָּעָרֶב וּמִן הַנַּחַל יִשְׁתֶּה: [מלכים א' יז, ו]

י) וַיְהִי מִקֵּץ יָמִים וַיִּיבַשׁ הַנַּחַל כִּי לֹא הָיָה גֶשֶׁם בָּאָרֶץ: [מלכים א' יז, ז]

כ) וַיְהִי דְבַר יְיָ אֵלָיו לֵאמֹר: קוּם לֵךְ צָרְפַתָה אֲשֶׁר לְצִידוֹן וְיָשַׁבְתָּ שָׁם הִנֵּה צִוִּיתִי שָׁם אִשָּׁה אַלְמָנָה לְכַלְכְּלֶךָ: [מלכים א' יז, ח-ט] ל) וַיְהִי אַחַר הַדְּבָרִים הָאֵלֶּה חָלָה בֶּן הָאִשָּׁה בַּעֲלַת הַבָּיִת וַיְהִי חָלְיוֹ חָזָק מְאֹד עַד אֲשֶׁר לֹא נוֹתְרָה בּוֹ נְשָׁמָה: [מלכים א' יז, יז] מ) וַיְהִי יָמִים רַבִּים וּדְבַר יְיָ הָיָה אֶל אֵלִיָּהוּ בַּשָּׁנָה הַשְּׁלִישִׁית לֵאמֹר לֵךְ הֵרָאֵה אֶל אַחְאָב וְאֶתְּנָה מָטָר עַל פְּנֵי הָאֲדָמָה: [מלכים א' יח, א]

THE ATTACHED ONES ARE PERMITTED.[15] שֶׁל עִיר אַחֶרֶת – But as regards THOSE OF ANOTHER CITY, בֵּין תְּלוּשִׁין בֵּין מְחוּבָּרִין אָסוּר – BOTH THE DETACHED ONES AND THE ATTACHED ONES ARE PROHIBITED.

The Gemara asks:

מַאי עִיר אַחֶרֶת – What is this **other city** to which the Baraisa refers? What city's trees are forbidden?

The Gemara answers:

אָמַר רַב חִסְדָּא – Rav Chisda said: יְרִיחוֹ – The city of **Jericho; דִּכְתִיב ,,וְהָיְתָה הָעִיר חֵרֶם [הִיא וְכָל־אֲשֶׁר־בָּהּ] לַה׳״ – for it is written:** ***The city shall be a ruin, [it and all that is in it,] unto Hashem.*** [16]

Having cited the *cherem* (decree of ruin) placed on Jericho, the Gemara expounds on that subject. The Gemara begins by citing the verse detailing the curse pronounced by Joshua on anyone who would dare violate the *cherem*:[17]

וַיַּשְׁבַּע יְהוֹשֻׁעַ בָּעֵת הַהִיא לֵאמֹר – *And Joshua adjured [the people] at that time saying,* **אָרוּר הָאִישׁ לִפְנֵי ה׳ אֲשֶׁר יָקוּם וּבָנָה אֶת־הָעִיר הַזֹּאת אֶת־יְרִיחוֹ – *"Cursed be the man before Hashem who rises up and builds this city, Jericho.*** **בִּבְכֹרוֹ יְיַסְּדֶנָּה וּבִצְעִירוֹ יַצִּיב דְּלָתֶיהָ״ – *With his oldest son he will lay its foundation and with his youngest son he will set up its gates!"*** [18]

A Baraisa elaborates on the prohibition implicit in this curse: **תַּנְיָא – A Tanna taught in a Baraisa:** לֹא יְרִיחוֹ עַל שֵׁם עִיר אַחֶרֶת – One may NEITHER build a city on the site of JERICHO WITH THE NAME OF ANOTHER CITY, וְלֹא עִיר אַחֶרֶת עַל שֵׁם יְרִיחוֹ – NOR ANOTHER CITY elsewhere WITH THE NAME OF JERICHO;[19] דִּכְתִיב ,,בְּיָמָיו בָּנָה חִיאֵל בֵּית הָאֱלִי אֶת־יְרִיחֹה – AS IT IS WRITTEN: *In his* [Ahab's] *day,* CHIEL, OF THE HOUSE OF THE CURSE,[20] BUILT JERICHO; בַּאֲבִירָם בְּכֹרוֹ יִסְּדָהּ וּבִשְׂגוּב צְעִירוֹ הִצִּיב דְּלָתֶיהָ״ – WITH AVIRAM, HIS FIRSTBORN, HE LAID ITS FOUNDATION, AND WITH SEGUV, HIS YOUNGEST, HE SET UP ITS GATES. The city Chiel built was not on the site of the ancient Jericho, as the Gemara will state below, yet Joshua's curse came to pass.[21] This corroborates the Tanna's

NOTES

15. The trees of a city are part of its property and they therefore should be burned along with all the rest of the city's property. However, the Torah states in regard to the destruction of the property of an *ir hanidachas*: וְאֶת־כָּל־שְׁלָלָהּ תִּקְבֹּץ אֶל־תּוֹךְ רְחֹבָהּ וְשָׂרַפְתָּ בָאֵשׁ אֶת־הָעִיר וְאֶת־כָּל־שְׁלָלָהּ, *And all its booty you shall gather into its square, and you shall burn the city and all its booty in a fire . . .* (*Deuteronomy* 13:17). Now the Gemara stated previously (above, 112a) that the wording of the verse, *gather . . . and . . . burn,* excludes objects that must be cut or uprooted before they can be gathered into the square to be burned. [The Gemara earlier stated this in regard to the hair of those executed. By the same token,] this verse excludes trees that are still attached to the ground, which must be cut down before they can be gathered into the city square and burned (*Rashi*).

The permission to benefit from attached trees applies only to trees that are growing from the ground. Trees that were cut and then placed in the ground (e.g. the wooden beams of a house) must be destroyed [because these are legally classified as detached (see *Chullin* 16a)] (*R' Yehonasan* cited in *Chamra VeChayei*; see *Tosafos* above, 46b ד״ה תלישה לאו כלום היא).

16. *Joshua* 6:17. [Emendation follows *Rashash;* see also *Rashi*.] Joshua, in this passage, declares that Jericho shall be a חֵרֶם לַה׳, *a ruin unto Hashem;* that is, a place left in its devastated state, forbidden for use, as a tribute to Hashem (see *Radak* to verse and in *Shorashim*).

The words וְכָל־אֲשֶׁר־בָּהּ, *and all that is in it,* imply even the trees that are in it (*Rashi*). Thus, Jericho, like an *ir hanidachas*, was a city that was to be utterly destroyed. When the Baraisa stated that the trees of another city are forbidden whether they are attached or detached, it referred to the city of Jericho.

[Seemingly, there is no point in the Baraisa teaching this lesson, since whatever happened in the days of Joshua happened and is no longer relevant. See, however, *Meiri,* who says that Jericho serves as an example of a city upon which a חֵרֶם, *ruination,* is pronounced. Should some future court or ruler declare a ban on a city and everything that is in it, all the city's trees, attached as well as detached, would be forbidden.]

17. *Rashi*.

18. Ibid. v. 26. That is, the person who dares to violate the oath by rebuilding the city will lose all his sons, the oldest as the foundation is laid and the youngest when the gates of the city are put in place (at the completion of the project).

Rambam (*Moreh Nevuchim* 3:50) explains that Joshua forbade anyone to rebuild Jericho in order that future generations would be able to view the sunken wall and recognize the magnitude of the miracle that God had wrought there. For the wall of Jericho did not crumble, but miraculously sank into the ground, leaving it an artifact of the miracle. [A Baraisa cited in *Berachos* 54a states that one who sees the sunken walls of Jericho recites the blessing: "Blessed are You, Hashem our God, King of the Universe, Who performed a miracle for our ancestors on this spot." *Tosafos* (*Berachos* 54b ד״ה אבני אלגביש) concludes that to recite this blessing it is necessary for the miracle to be discernible in the site itself and not just a memory awakened by passage through the area; i.e. some artifact that testifies to the miracle must be visible to the onlooker. See also *Magen Avraham* 218:1.]

Radak (*Joshua* 6:17) takes note of the statement of the Sages (*Yerushalmi, Berachos* 9:5) that Joshua was not commanded by God to dedicate Jericho as a *cherem* (ruin unto Hashem) but that he did so on his own. He cites two explanations of the Sages for this (*Bamidbar Rabbah* 14:1): Since Jericho was the first city of Eretz Yisrael to be conquered, Joshua considered it fitting to dedicate it to God, to teach the people the importance of dedicating the first fruits of all their efforts to God. This is in line with the Torah's command regarding the obligation of *challah*, "From the *first* of your kneading trough shall you give a portion to Hashem, for your generations" (*Numbers* 15:21). Also, since the walls of Jericho fell and the city was conquered on the Sabbath, it was only fitting that it should remain forever holy unto God (see *Aruch LaNer* and *Margaliyos HaYam* for other interpretations of this last statement of the Sages).

19. I.e. it is forbidden to build a town on the site of Jericho even if it is given another name and not called Jericho, and it is also forbidden to build a city anywhere else and call it Jericho. The very name of Jericho is to be obliterated (*Rashi*). This is derived from the seeming redundancy in Joshua's curse: *Cursed be the man before Hashem who rises up and builds this city, Jericho.* Now Joshua was located opposite Jericho when he declared the curse of Jericho. Thus, when he said *Cursed be the man . . . who . . . builds this city,* it was clear that he was referring to Jericho. Why then did he go on to identify the city by name – *this city, Jericho*? From this we learn that Joshua forbade two things: rebuilding *this city,* and building *Jericho,* i.e. this site by any name and any other site called by the name Jericho (*Maharsha, Toras Chaim;* see *Tosefta* 14:2, where this exposition of the verse is stated explicitly).

20. *I Kings* 16:34. The translation follows *Rashi* here, who relates the word אֱלִי to אָלָה, *curse.* This is also *Targum's* rendition of the phrase. *Rashi* and *Radak* to the verse also cite another interpretation that the phrase בֵּית הָאֱלִי means *the Bethelite,* i.e. from the city of Bethel.

21. *Rashi* states that he does not know the source for the Sages' understanding that the city built by Chiel was not on the site of the ancient Jericho. *Toras Chaim* explains that since the verse in *Joshua* alludes to the prohibition to rebuild the ancient site with the words הָעִיר הַזֹּאת, *this city,* and to the prohibition to build another city with the name Jericho with the word יְרִיחוֹ, *Jericho* (see note 19), then we must assume that the verse in *Kings* that states that *Chiel . . . built Jericho* refers to another city by the name of Jericho. Had the verse meant to say that he rebuilt the ancient site of Jericho, it should have said that he built אֶת הָעִיר יְרִיחוֹ, *the city Jericho* (see also *Maharsha*).

Maharal and *R' Yaakov Emden* (in his *Hagahos Yaavetz* here) suggest that the Sages' source for this is the unusual spelling of the name Jericho in the verse regarding Chiel. Elsewhere, the name is always spelled יְרִיחוֹ, with a *vav* at the end. Here, however, it is spelled יְרִיחֹה, with a *hei* at the end. This indicates that it was not the same place. (See *Margaliyos HaYam* who cites this explanation from a מדרש חסרות ויתרות, found in *Otzar HaMidrashim*.)

Maharal also suggests that the fact that the prophet Elijah paid a condolence call on Chiel when he sat in mourning for his sons (an event alluded to by Scripture, see Gemara below and note 29) indicates that Chiel had not flagrantly violated Joshua's curse but had done only

וליפרקיה [א] דתנן [א]הלקוח בכסף מעשר שנטמא יפדה כר"י דאמר יקבר אי הכי מאי איריא עיר הנדחת אפילו דעלמא נמי אלא לעולם בטהור וכגון דנפול מחיצות וכדרבא [ב] דאמר רבא [ב]מחיצה לאכול דאורייתא [ג]לקלוט דרבנן וכי גזור רבנן כי אתנהו למחיצה כי ליתנהו למחיצה לא: כתבי הקדש יגנזו: מתניתין דלא כר"א [ג] דתניא ר"א אומר כל עיר שיש בה אפי' מזוזה אחת אינה נעשית עיר הנדחת שנא' [א] ושרפת באש את העיר ואת כל שללה כליל והיכא דאיכא מזוזה לא אפשר דכתיב [ב] לא תעשון כן לה' אלהיכם: ר"ש אומר אמר הקב"ה וכו': לימא בדר' אבין א"ר אילעא קמיפלגי [ד] דא"ר אבין א"ר אילעא כל מקום שאתה מוצא כלל בעשה ופרט בלא תעשה אין דנין אותו בכלל ופרט דמר אית ליה דרבי אבין ומר לית ליה דרבי אבין לא דכ"ע אית להו דר' אבין והכא בהא קמיפלגי מר סבר עוד לגמרי משמע ומר סבר עוד לכמה שהיתה: אינה נבנית אבל נעשית היא גנות ופרדסים: ת"ר [ד]היו בה אילנות תלושין אסורין מחוברין מותרין של עיר אחרת בין תלושין בין מחוברין אסור מאי עיר אחרת אמר רב חסדא יריחו דכתיב [ג] והיתה העיר [ה] חרם לה' וישבע יהושע בעת ההיא לאמר ארור האיש לפני ה' אשר יקום ובנה את העיר הזאת את יריחו בבכורו ייסדנה ובצעירו יציב דלתיה תניא [ו] לא יריחו על שם עיר אחרת ולא עיר אחרת על שם יריחו דכתיב [ד] בנה חיאל בית האלי את יריחו באבירם בכורו יסדה ובשגוב צעירו הציב דלתיה תניא [ז] באבירם בכורו רשע לא היה לו ללמוד בשגוב צעירו היה לו ללמוד אבירם ושגוב מאי עבוד ([ס] מאי קאמר) ה"ק באבירם בכורו היה לו ללמוד לאותו רשע בשגוב צעירו ממשמע שנאמר באבירם בכורו איני יודע ששגוב צעירו מה ת"ל שגוב צעירו מלמד שהיה מקבר והולך מאבירם עד שגוב אחאב שושביניה הוה אתא איהו ואליהו למשאל בשלמא בי טמיא יתיב וקאמר דילמא כי מילט יהושע הכי לט לא יריחו על שם עיר אחרת ולא עיר אחרת על שם יריחו א"ל אליהו אין אמר ליה השתא לווטתא דמשה לא קא מקיימא דכתיב [ה] וסרתם ועבדתם וגו' וכתיב [ו] וחרה אף ה' בכם ועצר את השמים וגו' וההוא גברא אוקים ליה עבודת כוכבים [ט] על כל תלם ותלם ולא שביק ליה מיטרא דמיזל מיסגד ליה לווטתא דיהושע תלמידיה מקיימא מיד [ז] ויאמר אליהו התשבי מתושבי גלעד [י] חי ה' אלהי ישראל אם [כ] יהיה טל ומטר וגו' בעי רחמי והבו ליה אקלידא דמטרא וקם ואזל [ח] ויהי דבר ה' אליו לאמר לך מזה ופנית לך קדמה ונסתרת בנחל כרית [ט] והעורבים מביאים לו לחם ובשר בבקר וגו' [ל] מהיכא אמר רב יהודה אמר רב מבי טבחי דאחאב [י] ויהי מקץ ימים וייבש הנחל כי לא היה גשם בארץ כיון דחזא דאיכא צערא בעלמא כתיב [כ] ויהי דבר ה' אליו לאמר קום לך צרפתה וכתיב [ל] ויהי אחר הדברים האלה חלה בן האשה בעלת הבית בעא רחמי למיתן ליה אקלידא דתחיית המתים אמרי ליה [מ] שלש מפתחות לא נמסרו לשליח של חיה ושל גשמים ושל תחיית המתים יאמרו שתים ביד תלמיד ואחת ביד הרב אייתי הא ושקיל האי דכתיב [מ] לך הראה אל אחאב [ואתנה] מטר דרש ההוא גלילאה קמיה דרב חסדא משל דאליהו למה הדבר דומה לגברא דטרקיה לגליה ואבדיה למפתחיה דרש ר' יוסי בצפורי אבא אליהו

וליפרקיה לבוליה. ומשני כר"י דאמר לא אליס למתפס פדיונו בההיא [י] מנה גופא במס' מעשר שני (פ"ג מ"י) והיינו נמי מעשר שני דקאמר יגנז בקבורה: אלא לעולם. במעשר שני דעיר הנדחת טהור ואסקוה לגוה ודקאמר ליסתרי באכילה דהא קלטוהו מחילות אחר שנכנס לחומת ירושלים: דאמר רבא. ([ס] בשחיטת חולין פ' בהמה המקשה (דף סח): מחיצות לאכול דאורייתא. מן התורה מלוה לאכול לפנים מן החומה: אבל מחיצות לקלוט. שיהיו מחילות קולטות בין לענין פדייה בין לכל ענין מדרבנן הוא וכי גזור רבנן דתיהני קליטת מחילות למעשר דשוב אינו יכול לפדותו [א] ולענין עיר הנדחת נמי שלא יהא בשריפה היכא דאיתנהו מחילות: דכתיב ואבדתם. את שמם מן המקום ההוא וגו' וסמיך ליה לא תעשון כן לה' אלהיכם ובמזוזה הואיל וכתיב בה אזכרות אי אפשר לשריפה משום קרא דלא תעשון כן ואנן בעינן שללה וליכא דהאי שלל שמים הוא: כלל בעשה ופרט בלא תעשה. כגון והיתה תל עולם כלל דאפילו גנות ופרדסים לא תעשה אלא תהיה תל עולם שהוא עשה לא תבנה עוד בנין בתים והוא לא תעשה אין דנין אותו בכלל ופרט לומר אין בכלל אלא מה שבפרט דלא תעשה פירוש הוא כלומר והיתה תל עולם לבנין קאמר אבל לגנות ופרדסים שרי אלא תרי מילי קאמר קרא דלא אמרינן פירושי קמפרש אלא מילי מילי קאמר והיתה תל עולם לגנות ופרדסים לא תבנה עוד כל בניין שבעולם ואפילו לגנות ופרדסים לא תבנה עוד ודרשינן ליה לדבר שהיה בכלל ויצא מן הכלל ללמד לא ללמד על עצמו יצא אלא ללמד על הכלל כולו יצא ולומר בנין בכלל היה ולמה יצא להקיש לך מה בנין מיוחד שהוא ישוב בני אדם אף כל בנין כגון גנות ופרדסים [ע] (לישנא אחרינא) ור' יוסי הגלילי סבר אין דנין כר' אבין ודריש הכי והיתה תל עולם מכל מילי שלא יעשה בה שום דבר ולא תבנה עוד דמשמע בנין בתים אשמועינן לאו דבנין בתים וגנות ופרדסים איסור עשה הוא דאיכא. כך שמעתי: ר"ע סבר דנין. דלא כר' אבין: דכ"ע אית להו דר' אבין. ואפילו ר"ע והא דקאמר דעיר הנדחת נעשית גנות ופרדסים לאו משום דבעלמא לית ליה דר' אבין דודאי מלתא קא מפרשי והיתה תל עולם במאי בבנין בתים דלא תבנה עוד לא משמע ליה בכל בניין דקסבר עוד לכמו שהיתה משמע כלומר לא תחזור ולא תבנה עוד משמע כגון שהיתה מתחלה לא תבנה עוד אבל נעשה גנות ופרדסים: ומר סבר עוד לגמרי משמע. כגון דאמר לעולם ועד ועוד לשון ועד הוא [פ] שלא תבנה לעולם לשום דבר לא לבנין בתים ולא לגנות ופרדסים לא תבנה עוד: מחוברין מותרין. דתקבוץ ושרפת אמרה רחמנא מי שאינו מחוסר אלא קבילה ושריפה יצא זה שמחוסר תלישה וקבילה ושריפה: וכל אשר בה. אפילו אילנות מחוברין אשר בה נאסרין: ה"ג וישבע יהושע לאמר ארור האיש וגו'. וקרא קדריש ואזיל בבכורו ייסדנה ובצעירו יציב דלתיה וכשיעמיד דלתיה ימות בנו הקטן: לא יריחו על שם עיר אחרת. שלא יבנה יריחו ויסב שמה על שם עיר אחרת ולא עיר אחרת על שם יריחו שאפי' בנה עיר אחרת וקראה יריחו אסור לבנותה שאפי' שם יריחו ימחה לעולם וכתיב בימיו בנה חיאל בית האלי את יריחו בימיו של אחאב ועל שעבר על האלה קרי ליה בית האלי: את יריחו. ולא יריחו עצמו בנה אלא עיר אחרת על שם יריחו שקראה לה יריחו ולא אתפרש הא מנלן: באבירם בכורו יסדה. אבירם רשע כשמת אבירם הרשע לא היה לו לחיאל ללמוד שלא לבנות את יריחו: אבירם ושגוב מאי עבוד. דקרי להו רשעים: איני יודע ששגוב צעירו. מילתא באנפי נפשיה הוא ולמדרשא ממשמע שנאמר באבירם בכורו איני יודע ששגוב צעירו אלא מה ת"ל שגוב צעירו שהיה קובר והולך מאבירם ועד שגוב שהוא צעיר מכלם: אחאב שושבינו. אוהבו של חיאל היה אחאב: בי טמיא. וי"א בי טעמא בית האבל שמטעימים אותו בדברים לנחמו ובכמה דוכתין כתיב בבראשית רבה טמיא בלא עיי"ן לשון אבל: על כל תלם ותלם. שורה וערוגה ומקום גבוה הוא: ולא שביק מיטרא מיזל ומסגד. שהיה הלכלוך הולך וגדל מרוב הגשמים הבאין לעולם שאין מניחין לילך להשתחוות לעבודת כוכבים מתוך דרכים מלוכלכות בטיט: מיד ויאמר אליהו חי ה' אם יהיה השנים האלה מטר וגו'. האי קרא סמוך לקרא דחיאל בית האלי: אקלידא דמטרא. מפתח של מטר: כיון דחזא. הקב"ה דאיכא צערא בעלמא א"ל הקב"ה לאליהו לך צרפתה לגלגל הדבר שיחזיר לו מפתח של מטר כדקא מפרש ואזיל: שלש מפתחות לא נמסרו ביד שליח. על אוצרו של הקב"ה יש מפתחות ומסרם ליד שלוחים הממונים אבל ג' מפתחות יש לו בידו שלא מינה שליח עליהם מבראשית אלא בידו הם ולא רצה למסור שליח עליהם וקאמר הקב"ה לאליהו אותם ג' מפתחות עכבתי בידי מבראשית ולא מניתי שליח עליהם אלא אותך שעשיתי ממונה על אחת מהם ועתה תשאל מפתח שני יאמרו שנים ביד תלמיד ואחד ביד הרב: דטרקיה לגליה. שסתם שער שלו ואבדיה למפתחיה כך עשה אליהו נעל לשערי מטר ולבסוף אבד המפתח של גשמים שלא נפתח השער של מטר על ידו: דכתב לך הראה אל אחאב ואתנה מטר. ולא כתיב ותן מטר: אבא אליהו. חביבי וגדולי היה

עין משפט נר מצוה

נט א מיי' פ"ז מהל' מעשר שני הלכה א ב:
ס ב מיי' שם פ"ב הל' ה סמג לאוין רסד:
סא ג מיי' שם הל' ט:
סב ד מיי' פ"ד מהל' ע"ז הלכה יג סמג עשין טו:

הגהות מהר"ב רנשבורג

א] רש"י ד"ה אבל מחיצות וכו' ולענין עיר הנדחת נמי שלא יהא בשריפה. מלת בשריפה נמחק וצ"ב בגניזה:

תורה אור השלם

א) וְאֶת כָּל שְׁלָלָהּ תִּקְבֹּץ אֶל תּוֹךְ רְחֹבָהּ וְשָׂרַפְתָּ בָאֵשׁ אֶת הָעִיר וְאֶת כָּל שְׁלָלָהּ כָּלִיל לַייָ אֱלֹהֶיךָ וְהָיְתָה תֵּל עוֹלָם לֹא תִבָּנֶה עוֹד: [דברים יג, יז]

ב) לֹא תַעֲשׂוּן כֵּן לַייָ אֱלֹהֵיכֶם: [דברים יב, ד]

ג) וְהָיְתָה הָעִיר חֵרֶם הִיא וְכָל אֲשֶׁר בָּהּ לַייָ רַק רָחָב הַזּוֹנָה תִּחְיֶה הִיא וְכָל אֲשֶׁר אִתָּהּ בַּבַּיִת כִּי הֶחְבְּאַתָה אֶת הַמַּלְאָכִים אֲשֶׁר שָׁלָחְנוּ: וַיַּשְׁבַּע יְהוֹשֻׁעַ בָּעֵת הַהִיא לֵאמֹר אָרוּר הָאִישׁ לִפְנֵי יְיָ אֲשֶׁר יָקוּם וּבָנָה אֶת הָעִיר הַזֹּאת אֶת יְרִיחוֹ בִּבְכֹרוֹ יְיַסְּדֶנָּה וּבִצְעִירוֹ יַצִּיב דְּלָתֶיהָ: [יהושע ו, יז,כו]

ד) בְּיָמָיו בָּנָה חִיאֵל בֵּית הָאֱלִי אֶת יְרִיחֹה בַּאֲבִירָם בְּכֹרוֹ יִסְּדָהּ וּבִשְׂגוּב צְעִירוֹ הִצִּיב דְּלָתֶיהָ כִּדְבַר יְיָ אֲשֶׁר דִּבֶּר בְּיַד יְהוֹשֻׁעַ בִּן נוּן: [מלכים א' טז, לד]

ה) הִשָּׁמְרוּ לָכֶם פֶּן יִפְתֶּה לְבַבְכֶם וְסַרְתֶּם וַעֲבַדְתֶּם אֱלֹהִים אֲחֵרִים וְהִשְׁתַּחֲוִיתֶם לָהֶם: [דברים יא, טז]

ו) וְחָרָה אַף יְיָ בָּכֶם וְעָצַר אֶת הַשָּׁמַיִם וְלֹא יִהְיֶה מָטָר וְהָאֲדָמָה לֹא תִתֵּן אֶת יְבוּלָהּ וַאֲבַדְתֶּם מְהֵרָה מֵעַל הָאָרֶץ הַטֹּבָה אֲשֶׁר יְיָ נֹתֵן לָכֶם: [דברים יא, יז]

ז) וַיֹּאמֶר אֵלִיָּהוּ הַתִּשְׁבִּי מִתֹּשָׁבֵי גִלְעָד אֶל אַחְאָב חַי יְיָ אֱלֹהֵי יִשְׂרָאֵל אֲשֶׁר עָמַדְתִּי לְפָנָיו אִם יִהְיֶה הַשָּׁנִים הָאֵלֶּה טַל וּמָטָר כִּי אִם לְפִי דְבָרִי: [מלכים א' יז, א]

ח) וַיְהִי דְבַר יְיָ אֵלָיו לֵאמֹר: לֵךְ מִזֶּה וּפָנִיתָ לְּךָ קֵדְמָה וְנִסְתַּרְתָּ בְּנַחַל כְּרִית אֲשֶׁר עַל פְּנֵי הַיַּרְדֵּן: [מלכים א' יז, ב-ג]

ט) וְהָעֹרְבִים מְבִיאִים לוֹ לֶחֶם וּבָשָׂר בַּבֹּקֶר וְלֶחֶם וּבָשָׂר בָּעָרֶב וּמִן הַנַּחַל יִשְׁתֶּה: [מלכים א' יז, ו]

י) וַיְהִי מִקֵּץ יָמִים וַיִּיבַשׁ הַנַּחַל כִּי לֹא הָיָה גֶשֶׁם בָּאָרֶץ: [מלכים א' יז, ז]

כ) וַיְהִי דְבַר יְיָ אֵלָיו לֵאמֹר: קוּם לֵךְ צָרְפַתָה אֲשֶׁר לְצִידוֹן וְיָשַׁבְתָּ שָׁם הִנֵּה צִוִּיתִי שָׁם אִשָּׁה אַלְמָנָה לְכַלְכְּלֶךָ: [מלכים א' יז, ח-ט] ל) וַיְהִי אַחַר הַדְּבָרִים הָאֵלֶּה חָלָה בֶּן הָאִשָּׁה בַּעֲלַת הַבָּיִת וַיְהִי חָלְיוֹ חָזָק מְאֹד עַד אֲשֶׁר לֹא נוֹתְרָה בּוֹ נְשָׁמָה: [מלכים א' יז, יז] מ) וַיְהִי יָמִים רַבִּים וּדְבַר יְיָ הָיָה אֶל אֵלִיָּהוּ בַּשָּׁנָה הַשְּׁלִישִׁית לֵאמֹר לֵךְ הֵרָאֵה אֶל אַחְאָב וְאֶתְּנָה מָטָר עַל פְּנֵי הָאֲדָמָה: [מלכים א' יח, א]

מסורת הש"ס

א) פסחי' לו: לח. מ"ש פ"ג מ"י [ב"מ נג: זבחים מט.], ב) ב"מ שם מכות כ. [עיין תוס' ב"מ נג: ד"ה לא פלוג], ג) לעיל ע"א, ד) [מ"ק ג.], ה) [צ"ל חרם היא וכל אשר בה לה'], ו) [תוספ' פי"ד], ז) [תוספתא שם], ח) [בע"י ליתא], ט) [לעיל קב:], י) [אל אחאב], כ) [צ"ל יהיה השנים האלה טל וכו'], ל) חולין ה., מ) תענית ב., נ) [צ"ל משנה], ס) [בשחיטת חולין לא נמצא אמנם בב"מ נג: ד"ה והא אמר רבא כתב רש"י על נכון ועיין במס' מכות], ע) צ"ל לא, פ) [עי' רש"י שבת לג. ד"ה לא ישמח].

ליקוטי רש"י

יקבר. דקא סבר לא אליס למיתפס פדיונו. אלא לעולם בטהור. בין מעשר בין לקוח ודקאמר נעיילה וניכליה. וכגון דנפול מחיצות. חומת ירושלים ושוב אין מעשר נאכל שם עד שיעמדו מחילות דבעינן לפני ה' תאכלנו (דברים יב) ובפדייה נמי לא דקלטוהו מחילות מלפדותו עוד משנכנס לתוכו. מחיצה לאכול דאורייתא מחיצה לקלוט דרבנן. מחילה שנאמרה בתורה לא הוזכרה אלא לאכול בתוכה ושאמרו במשנה מחילות קולטות אותם מלפדות עוד אם יצא דרבנן היא. וכי גזור רבנן כו'. דכי גזור רבנן היכא דאיתנהו וזה הוציא את המעשר לחוץ אבל כי ליתנהו לא גזור הלכך ניפרקיה [ב"מ נג:]. והיתה העיר חרם. הקדש כי היום שבת קדש וראוי להיות קדש שלל הנשלל בו [יהושע ו, יז]. בבכרו ייסדנה ובצעירו. בתחלת יסוד שיבנה בה ימות בנו הבכור ויקברנו וילך עד שימות הצעיר בגמר המלאכה היא הצבת הדלתות [שם ו, כו]. באבירם בכרו יסדה. כשיסד' מת בנו בכורו וקבר והלך וקבר כל בניו עד שמת האחרון בהצבת דלתות וכן הוא קללות של יהושע בבכורו ייסדנה ובצעירו יציב דלתיה (יהושע ו' כ"ו) [מ"א טז, לד]. חי ה'. למה סמכו כאן אלא שהלכו אליהו ואחאב לנחם את חיאל באבלו אמר אחאב לאליהו אפשר שקללת התלמיד נתקיימה וקללת משה רבינו לא נתקיימה שנאמר (דברים י"א ט"ז) וסרתם ועבדתם אלהים אחרים והשתחויתם להם וחרה אף ה' בכם ועצר את השמים והרי כל ישראל עובדין ע"ג ואין גשמים נעצרים מיד ויאמר אליהו וגו' [שם יז, א]. ונסתרת. [שם יז, ג]. וייבש הנחל. כדי שידע צורך הגשמים ויתרנו בגלות שהיה קשה בעיני הקב"ה שישראל שרוין מתים ברעב [שם יז, ז]. צרפתה. שם העיר [שם יז, ט]. חלה בן האשה. כדי שיצטרך למפתח של תחיית המתים כדאיתא באגדת חלק [שם פסוק יז].

statement that it is forbidden to build a city anywhere and call it Jericho.

The Gemara cites a Baraisa that elaborates the verse just cited: **תַּנְיָא – A Baraisa has taught:** בַּאֲבִירָם בְּכוֹרוֹ רָשָׁע – FROM the death OF AVIRAM, HIS WICKED FIRSTBORN SON, לֹא הָיָה לוֹ לִלְמוֹד – [CHIEL] WOULD NOT HAVE been expected to have LEARNED not to build the city, בִּשְׂגוּב צְעִירוֹ הָיָה לוֹ לִלְמוֹד – but FROM the death OF SEGUV, HIS YOUNGEST SON, HE certainly SHOULD HAVE LEARNED![22]

The Gemara interrupts the Baraisa to question its assumption: **אֲבִירָם וּשְׂגוּב מַאי עֲבוּד – Aviram and Seguv – what did they do** that the Baraisa should refer to them in this manner? Where did the Tanna see anything about their wickedness?[23]

The Gemara therefore reinterprets the Baraisa:

(מאי קאמר) הָכִי קָאָמַר – This is what [the Baraisa] is saying: בַּאֲבִירָם בְּכוֹרוֹ הָיָה לוֹ לִלְמוֹד לְאוֹתוֹ רָשָׁע בִּשְׂגוּב צְעִירוֹ – **From** the death of **Aviram his firstborn, that wicked man** [Chiel] **should have learned** what would happen **to Seguv his youngest.**[24]

The Baraisa's exposition of the verse continues:[25]

מִמַּשְׁמַע שֶׁנֶּאֱמַר ,,בַּאֲבִירָם בְּכֹרוֹ" – From the implication of that which is stated: *With Aviram his firstborn,* אֵינִי יוֹדֵעַ שֶׁשְּׂגוּב צְעִירוֹ – **do I not** thereby **know that Seguv was his youngest son?**[26] מַה תַּלְמוּד לוֹמַר ,,שְׂגוּב צְעִירוֹ" – **What does [Scripture]** mean to **teach** by saying: ***Seguv his youngest son*?** מְלַמֵּד שֶׁהָיָה מְקַבֵּר וְהוֹלֵךְ מֵאֲבִירָם עַד שְׂגוּב – **This teaches that** Chiel had more than two sons, and that **he buried and kept on** burying one son after another, **from Aviram**, the eldest, **to Seguv**, the youngest.[27]

The passage in *I Kings* that follows the story of Chiel tells how the prophet Elijah pronounced a curse on Israel and thereby brought a devastating drought upon the land. The Gemara explains that the juxtaposition of the verses is not coincidental, but rather indicates that the incident of Chiel set in motion a chain of events that led to the drought:[28]

אַחְאָב שׁוּשְׁבִינֵיהּ הֲוָה – Ahab was [Chiel's] close friend. אֲתָא אִיהוּ וְאֵלִיָּהוּ לְמִשְׁאַל בִּשְׁלָמָא בֵּי טַמְיָא – **He and Elijah came to pay a condolence call** on Chiel **in the house of mourning** following the death of his sons.[29] יָתִיב וְקָאָמַר – **[Ahab] sat and said:** דִּילְמָא כִּי מֵילַט יְהוֹשֻׁעַ – **Perhaps** the reason for these terrible losses is that **when Joshua** laid a **curse** upon the person who would build Jericho, הָכִי לַט – **this is how he** laid the **curse**, i.e. this is what he prohibited: לֹא יְרִיחוֹ עַל שֵׁם עִיר אַחֶרֶת וְלֹא עִיר אַחֶרֶת עַל שֵׁם יְרִיחוֹ – **Neither Jericho by another name, nor**

NOTES

something whose prohibition he might not have been aware of. See *Margaliyos HaYam* for still other answers to this question.

22. [As we have just learned, the city that Chiel built was not on the site of the Jericho of old but a new city somewhere else that was merely called Jericho. From the Gemara below it is evident that it was not widely known that Joshua's curse applied even to such a case; Ahab had to ask the prophet Elijah if it was indeed so. Accordingly, when Chiel lost his first son, he had no reason to assume that this was for the sin of building a city by the name of Jericho on a different site. But certainly by the time he had lost all his other sons, he should have seen that Joshua's curse was being fulfilled and he should have concluded that even this was forbidden (see *Maharal* cited in note 21; *Aruch LaNer* explains this in a similar vein; cf. *Maharsha* cited in next note).]

23. I.e. how did the Tanna know that Aviram and Seguv were wicked? (*Rashi*). [*Rashi* seems to have had the reading רָשָׁע in regard to both Aviram and Seguv: בַּאֲבִירָם בְּכוֹרוֹ רָשָׁע ... בִּשְׂגוּב צְעִירוֹ רָשָׁע הָיָה לוֹ לִלְמוֹד, *From [the death of] Aviram, his wicked firstborn ... [but] from [the death of] Seguv, his wicked youngest son, he should have learned*. Indeed, such a reading is found in *Ein Yaakov*. Accordingly, *Rashi* explains the Gemara's question to be how the Tanna knew that Aviram and Seguv were *both* wicked (*Dikdukei Sofrim*).]

Maharsha, following the reading in our texts [in which it is only explicitly mentioned that Aviram was wicked], explains the Gemara as follows: The reason the Baraisa states that Chiel could not have been expected to learn from the death of Aviram, his wicked son, is because he could have attributed Aviram's death to Aviram's own wickedness. By saying that Chiel should have learned from the death of Seguv, his youngest son, the Tanna thus implies that, unlike Aviram, Seguv was righteous. The Gemara therefore asks where the Tanna saw anything in the verses to indicate that Aviram was wicked or that Seguv was righteous!

24. I.e. the word רָשָׁע, *wicked,* in the Baraisa does not refer to Aviram but to Chiel. [Although Chiel may not have known before he began that it was forbidden to build another city with the name Jericho,] he should have learned from the death of his firstborn son, Aviram, that he had done something wrong and would lose even his last son if he persisted in building the city. The fact that he did not take this to heart demonstrates that he was a רָשָׁע, *wicked person* (*Maharsha*).

Accordingly, the Baraisa should be understood as follows: "Although before Aviram's death (when Chiel began laying the foundation of the city) that wicked man (Chiel) did not have anything from which to learn (that what he was doing was forbidden), before Seguv's death he should have learned (from the death of Aviram)" that he was transgressing Joshua's curse, and he should have desisted and saved the life of his youngest son (see *Rashi* as recorded in *Ein Yaakov*). [Those who do not take their tragedies as a sign of Divine displeasure but attribute them to mere happenstance cause themselves to continue in their evil ways and thereby bring further tragedies upon themselves (*Rambam, Hil. Taaniyos* 1:3).]

[The wording found in our Gemara is somewhat awkward. From the version of *Rashi* printed in *Ein Yaakov* it is clear that he had the reading: בַּאֲבִירָם בְּכוֹרוֹ לֹא הָיָה לוֹ לְאוֹתוֹ רָשָׁע לִלְמוֹד בִּשְׂגוּב צְעִירוֹ הָיָה לוֹ לְאוֹתוֹ רָשָׁע לִלְמוֹד, which parallels the wording of the Baraisa above. See *Dikdukei Soferim* who cites this reading from old manuscripts of the Gemara.]

25. See *Rashi*. For a different interpretation of this passage, see *Yaaros Devash* II:7; see also *Aruch LaNer.*

26. [Since Scripture only mentions two sons of Chiel and identifies Aviram as the firstborn, it is clear that Seguv must have been the younger one.]

27. By stating that Seguv was the youngest, Scripture indicates that there were more than two sons, and that they died one after the other as the construction proceeded. Aviram, the eldest, died as the foundation was laid, and Seguv – the youngest and last surviving son – died as the gates were put in place. Yet Chiel never halted his construction!

28. The verse that tells of Chiel rebuilding Jericho (*I Kings* 16:34) comes at the end of a passage describing the great sins of Ahab in introducing new forms of idolatry to Israel. The very next verse (17:1) recounts Elijah's proclamation of the drought. Now the drought was clearly in punishment for the idolatry instituted by Ahab, as is evident from the context of that chapter. But if so, why does Scripture interrupt its account with the seemingly unrelated matter of the sin and punishment of Chiel? From this the Rabbis deduced that the incident of Chiel somehow led up to the drought that followed (*Maharsha*).

29. Literally: to inquire as to his welfare in the house of mourning. *Rashi* and the *Geonim* cite a variant reading: בֵּי טַעְמָא. *Rashi* says that it means *a house where they supply* [words of] *reason,* in an effort to console, i.e. a house of mourning. The *Geonim* give a different explanation. They explain that according to the laws of mourning, visitors to a house of mourning are not to say anything to the bereaved until the latter begins to speak (see *Moed Katan* 28b). However, it often happens that the bereaved find it awkward or difficult to begin the conversation. To spare them embarrassment, the custom developed in ancient times for an official of the community to be present at the house of mourning when visitors came and say to them: לִישַׁיְּילוּ רַבָּנָן טַעְמָא, *Let the Rabbis ask the reason* the bereaved are sitting in mourning. The visitors would then respond: בָּרוּךְ דַּיַּן הָאֱמֶת, *Blessed is the True Judge*, and this would open up the conversation. For this reason, a house of mourning became known as בֵּי טַעְמָא, *the house where* the word טַעְמָא (reason) *is proclaimed* (*Otzar HaGeonim* here and to *Berachos* 6b [p. 13]). See *Yad Ramah* for yet another reading and explanation.

וליפרקיה [א] דתנן [א] הלקוח בכסף מעשר שנטמא יפדה כר"י דאמר יקבר אי הכי מאי איריא עיר הנדחת אפילו דעלמא נמי אלא לעולם בטהור וכגון דנפול מחיצות וכדרבא [ב] דאמר רבא [ב] מחיצה לאכול דאורייתא [ג] לקלוט דרבנן וכי גזור רבנן כי אתנהו למחיצה כי ליתנהו למחיצה לא: כתבי הקדש יגנזו: מתניתין דלא כר"א [ג] דתניא ר"א אומר כל עיר שיש בה אפי' מזוזה אחת אינה נעשית עיר הנדחת שנא' [א] ושרפת באש את העיר ואת כל שללה כליל והיכא דאיכא מזוזה לא אפשר דכתיב [ב] לא תעשון כן לה' אלהיכם: ר"ש אומר אמר הקב"ה וכו': לימא בדר' אבין א"ר אילעא קמיפלגי [ד] דא"ר אבין א"ר אילעא כל מקום שאתה מוצא כלל בעשה ופרט בלא תעשה אין דנין אותו בכלל ופרט דמר אית ליה דרבי אבין ומר לית ליה דרבי אבין לא דכ"ע אית להו דר' אבין והכא בהא קמיפלגי מר סבר עוד לגמרי משמע ומר סבר עוד לכמה שהיתה: אינה נבנית אבל נעשית היא גנות ופרדסים: ת"ר [ד] היו בה אילנות תלושין אסורין מחוברין מותרין של עיר אחרת בין תלושין בין מחוברין אסור מאי עיר אחרת אמר רב חסדא יריחו דכתיב [ג] והיתה העיר [ה] חרם לה' וישבע יהושע בעת ההיא לאמר ארור האיש לפני ה' אשר יקום ובנה את העיר הזאת את יריחו בבכורו ייסדנה ובצעירו יציב דלתיה תניא [ו] לא יריחו על שם עיר אחרת ולא עיר אחרת על שם יריחו דכתיב [ד] בנה חיאל בית האלי את יריחו באבירם בכורו יסדה ובשגוב צעירו הציב דלתיה תניא [ז] באבירם בכורו רשע לא היה לו ללמוד בשגוב צעירו היה לו ללמוד אבירם ושגוב מאי עבוד ([ח] מאי קאמר) ה"ק באבירם בכורו היה לו ללמוד לאותו רשע בשגוב צעירו ממשמע שנאמר באבירם בכורו איני יודע ששגוב צעירו מה ת"ל שגוב צעירו מלמד שהיה מקבר והולך מאבירם עד שגוב אחאב שושביניה הוה אתא איהו ואליהו למשאל בשלמא בי טמיא יתיב וקאמר דילמא כי מילט יהושע הכי לט לא יריחו על שם עיר אחרת ולא עיר אחרת על שם יריחו א"ל אליהו אין אמר ליה השתא לווטתא דמשה לא קא מקיימא דכתיב [ה] וסרתם ועבדתם וגו' וכתיב [ו] וחרה אף ה' בכם ועצר את השמים וגו' וההוא גברא אוקים ליה עבודת כוכבים [ט] על כל תלם ותלם ולא שביק ליה מיטרא דמיזל מיסגד ליה לווטתא דיהושע תלמידיה מקיימא מיד [ז] ויאמר אליהו התשבי מתושבי גלעד [י] חי ה' אלהי ישראל אם [כ] יהיה טל ומטר וגו' בעי רחמי והבו ליה אקלידא דמטרא וקם ואזל [ח] ויהי דבר ה' אליו לאמר לך מזה ופנית לך קדמה ונסתרת בנחל כרית [ט] והעורבים מביאים לו לחם ובשר בבקר וגו' [ל] מהיכא אמר רב יהודה אמר רב מבי טבחי דאחאב [י] ויהי מקץ ימים וייבש הנחל כי לא היה גשם בארץ כיון דחזא דאיכא צערא בעלמא כתיב [כ] ויהי דבר ה' אליו לאמר קום לך צרפתה וכתיב [ל] ויהי אחר הדברים האלה חלה בן האשה בעלת הבית בעא רחמי למיתן ליה אקלידא דתחיית המתים אמרי ליה [מ] שלש מפתחות לא נמסרו לשליח של חיה ושל גשמים ושל תחיית המתים יאמרו שתים ביד תלמיד ואחת ביד הרב אייתי הא ושקיל האי דכתיב [מ] לך הראה אל אחאב [ואתנה] מטר דרש ההוא גלילאה קמיה דרב חסדא משל דאליהו למה הדבר דומה לגברא דטרקיה לגליה ואבדיה למפתחיה דרש ר' יוסי בצפורי אבא אליהו

רש"י

וליפרקיה לבוליה. ומשני כר"י דאמר לא אלים למתפס פדיונו בההיא [י] מנה גופא במס' מעשר שני (פ"ג מ"י) והיינו נמי מעשר שני דקאמר יגנז בקבורה: אלא לעולם. במעשר שני דעיר הנדחת טהור ואסקוה לגוה ודקאמר ליפרקיה באכילה דהא קלטוהו מחילות אחר שנכנס לחומת ירושלים: דאמר רבא. ([פ] בשחיטת חולין פ' בהמה המקשה (דף סח)): מחיצות לאכול דאורייתא. מן התורה מצוה לאכול לפנים מן החומה: אבל מחיצות לקלוט. שיהיו מחילות קולטות בין לענין פדייה בין לכל ענין מדרבנן הוא וכי גזור רבנן דתיהני קליטת מחילות למעשר דשוב אינו יכול לפדותו [א] ולענין עיר הנדחת נמי שלא יהא בשריפה היכא דאיתנהו מחילות: דכתיב ואבדתם. את שמם מן המקום ההוא וגו' וסמיך ליה לא תעשון כן לה' אלהיכם ובמזוזה הואיל וכתיב בה אזכרות אי אפשר לשריפה משום קרא דלא תעשון כן ואנן בעינן שללה וליכא דהאי שלל שמים הוא: כלל בעשה ופרט בלא תעשה. כגון והיתה תל עולם כלל דאפילו גנות ופרדסים לא תעשה אלא תהיה תל עולם שהוא עשה לא תבנה עוד בנין בתים והוא לא תעשה אין דנין אותו בכלל ופרט לומר אין בכלל אלא מה שבפרט דלא תעשה פירוש הוא כלומר והיתה תל עולם לבנין קאמר אבל לגנות ופרדסים שרי אלא תרי מילי קאמר קרא דלא אמרינן פירושי קמפרש אלא מילי מילי קאמר והיתה תל עולם לגנות ופרדסים לא תבנה עוד כל בניין שבעולם ואפילו לגנות ופרדסים לא תבנה עוד ודרשינן ליה לדבר שהיה בכלל ויצא מן הכלל ללמד לא ללמד על עצמו יצא אלא ללמד על הכלל כולו יצא ולומר בנין בכלל היה ולמה יצא להקיש לך מה בנין מיוחד שהוא ישוב בני אדם אף כל בנין כגון גנות ופרדסים [ע] (לישנא אחרינא) ור' יוסי הגלילי סבר אין דנין כר' אבין ודריש הכי והיתה תל עולם מכל מילי שלא יעשה בה שום דבר ולא תבנה עוד דמשמע בנין בתים אשמועינן לאו בבנין בתים וגנות ופרדסים איסור עשה הוא דאיכא. כך שמעתי: ר"ע סבר דנין. דלא כר' אבין: דכ"ע אית להו דר' אבין. ואפילו ר"ע והא דקאמר דעיר הנדחת נעשית גנות ופרדסים לאו משום דבעלמא לית ליה דר' אבין דודאי מלתא קא מפרשי והיתה תל עולם במאי בבנין בתים דלא תבנה עוד לא משמע ליה בכל בניין דקסבר עוד לכמו שהיתה משמע כלומר לא תחזור ולא תבנה עוד משמע כגון שהיתה מתחלה לא תבנה עוד אבל נעשה גנות ופרדסים: ומר סבר עוד לגמרי משמע. כגון דאמר לעולם ועד ועוד לשון ועד הוא [פ] שלא תבנה לעולם לשום דבר לא לבנין בתים ולא לגנות ופרדסים לא תבנה עוד: מחוברין מותרין. דתקבוץ ושרפת אמרה רחמנא מי שאינו מחוסר אלא קבילה ושריפה יצא זה שמחוסר תלישה וקבילה ושריפה: וכל אשר בה. אפילו אילנות מחוברין אשר בה נאסרין: ה"ג וישבע יהושע לאמר ארור האיש וגו'. וקרא קדריש ואזיל בבכורו ייסדנה ובצעירו יציב דלתיה וכשיעמיד דלתיה ימות בנו הקטן: לא יריחו על שם עיר אחרת. שלא יבנה יריחו ויסב שמה על שם עיר אחרת ולא עיר אחרת על שם יריחו שאפי' בנה עיר אחרת וקראה יריחו אסור לבנותה שאפי' שם יריחו ימחה לעולם וכתיב בימיו בנה חיאל בית האלי את יריחו בימיו של אחאב ועל שעבר על האלה קרי ליה בית האלי: את יריחו. ולא יריחו עצמו בנה אלא עיר אחרת על שם יריחו שקראה לה יריחו ולא אתפרש הא מנלן: באבירם בכורו יסדה. אבירם רשע כשמת אבירם הרשע לא היה לו לחיאל ללמוד שלא לבנות את יריחו: אבירם ושגוב מאי עבוד. דקרי להו רשעים: איני יודע ששגוב צעירו. מילתא באנפי נפשיה הוא ולמדרשא ממשמע שנאמר באבירם בכורו איני יודע ששגוב צעירו אלא מה ת"ל שגוב צעירו שהיה קובר והולך מאבירם ועד שגוב שהוא צעיר מכלם: אחאב שושבינו. אוהבו של חיאל היה אחאב: בי טמיא. וי"א בי טעמא בית האבל שמטעימים אותו בדברים לנחמו ובכמה דוכתין כתיב בבראשית רבה טמיא בלא עיי"ן לשון אבל: על כל תלם ותלם. שורה וערוגה ומקום גבוה הוא: ולא שביק מיטרא מיזל ומסגד. שהיה הלכלוך הולך וגדל מרוב הגשמים הבאין לעולם שאין מניחין לילך להשתחוות לעבודת כוכבים מתוך דרכים מלוכלכות בטיט: מיד ויאמר אליהו חי ה' אם יהיה השנים האלה מטר וגו'. האי קרא סמוך לקרא דחיאל בית האלי: אקלידא דמטרא. מפתח של מטר: כיון דחזא. הקב"ה דאיכא צערא בעלמא א"ל הקב"ה לאליהו לך צרפתה לגלגל הדבר שיחזיר לו מפתח של מטר כדקא מפרש ואזיל: שלש מפתחות לא נמסרו ביד שליח. על אוצרו של הקב"ה יש מפתחות ומסרם ליד שלוחים הממונים אבל ג' מפתחות יש לו בידו שלא מינה שליח עליהם מבראשית אלא בידו הם ולא רצה למסור שליח עליהם וקאמר הקב"ה לאליהו אותם ג' מפתחות עכבתי בידי מבראשית ולא מניתי שליח עליהם אלא אותך שעשיתי ממונה על אחת מהם ועתה תשאל מפתח שני יאמרו שנים ביד תלמיד ואחד ביד הרב: דטרקיה לגליה. שסתם שער שלו ואבדיה למפתחיה כך עשה אליהו נעל לשערי מטר ולבסוף אבד המפתח של גשמים שלא נפתח השער של מטר על ידו: דכתב לך הראה אל אחאב ואתנה מטר. ולא כתיב ותן מטר: אבא אליהו. חביבי וגדולי: היה

מסורת הש"ס

א) פסחי' לו: לח. מ"ש פ"ג מ"י [ב"מ נג: זבחים מט.], ב) ב"מ שם מכות כ. [עיין תוס' ב"מ נג: ד"ה לא פלוג], ג) לעיל ע"א, ד) [מ"ק ג.], ה) [צ"ל חרם היא וכל אשר בה לה'], ו) [תוספ' פי"ד], ז) [תוספתא שם], ח) [בע"י ליתא], ט) [לעיל קב:], י) [אל אחאב], כ) [צ"ל יהיה השנים האלה טל וכו'], ל) חולין ה., מ) תענית ב., נ) [צ"ל משנה], ס) [בשחיטת חולין לא נמצא אמנם בב"מ נג: ד"ה והא אמר רבא כתב רש"י על נכון וציין במס' מכות], ע) צ"ל לא, פ) [עי' רש"י שבת לג. ד"ה לא ישמח].

ליקוטי רש"י

יקבר. דקא סבר לא אלים למיתפס פדיונו. אלא לעולם בטהור. בין מעשר בין לקוח ודקאמר נעיילה וניכליה. וכגון דנפול מחיצות. חומת ירושלים ושוב אין מעשר נאכל שם עד שיעמדו מחילות דבעינן לפני ה' תאכלנו (דברים יב) ובפדייה נמי לא דקלטוהו מחילות מלפדותו עוד משנכנס לתוכו. מחיצה לאכול דאורייתא מחיצה לקלוט דרבנן. מחילה שנאמרה בתורה לא הוזכרה אלא לאכול בתוכה ושאמרו במשנה מחילות קולטות אותם מלפדות עוד אם יצא דרבנן היא. וכי גזור רבנן כו'. דכי גזור רבנן היכא דאיתנהו וזה הוציא את המעשר לחוץ אבל כי ליתנהו לא גזור הלכך ניפרקיה [ב"מ נג:]. והיתה העיר חרם. הקדש כי היום שבת קדש וראוי להיות קדש שלל הנשלל בו [יהושע ו, יז]. בבכרו ייסדנה ובצעירו. בתחלת יסוד שיבנה בה ימות בנו הבכור ויקברנו וילך עד שימות הצעיר בגמר המלאכה היא הצבת הדלתות [שם ו, כו]. באבירם בכרו יסדה. כשיסד' מת בנו בכורו וקבר והלך וקבר כל בניו עד שמת האחרון בהצבת דלתות וכן הוא קללות של יהושע בבכורו ייסדנה ובצעירו יציב דלתיה (יהושע ו' כ"ו) [מ"א טז, לד]. חי ה'. למה סמכו כאן אלא שהלכו אליהו ואחאב לנחם את חיאל באבלו אמר אחאב לאליהו אפשר שקללת התלמיד נתקיימה וקללת משה רבינו לא נתקיימה שנאמר (דברים י"א ט"ז) וסרתם ועבדתם אלהים אחרים והשתחויתם להם וחרה אף ה' בכם ועצר את השמים והרי כל ישראל עובדין ע"ג ואין גשמים נעצרים מיד ויאמר אליהו וגו' [שם יז, א]. ונסתרת. מפני אחאב ואיזבל [שם יז, ג]. ויבש הנחל. כדי שידע צורך הגשמים ויטריח לגלות שהיה קשה בעיני הקב"ה שישראל שרוין מתים ברעב [שם יז, ז]. צרפתה. שם העיר [שם יז, ט]. חלה בן האשה. כדי שיצטרך למפתח של תחיית המתים כדאיתא בשילהי אגדתא דחלק [שם פסוק יז].

עין משפט נר מצוה

נט א מיי' פ"ז מהל' מעשר שני הלכה א ב:
ס ב מיי' שם פ"ב הל' ה סמג לאוין רסד:
סא ג מיי' שם הל' ט:
סב ד מיי' פ"ד מהל' ע"ז הלכה יג סמג עשין טו:

הגהות מהר"ב רנשבורג

א] רש"י ד"ה אבל מחיצות וכו' ולענין עיר הנדחת נמי שלא יהא בשריפה. מלת בשריפה נמחק ונ"ב בגניזה:

תורה אור השלם

א) וְאֶת כָּל שְׁלָלָהּ תִּקְבֹּץ אֶל תּוֹךְ רְחֹבָהּ וְשָׂרַפְתָּ בָאֵשׁ אֶת הָעִיר וְאֶת כָּל שְׁלָלָהּ כָּלִיל לַייָ אֱלֹהֶיךָ וְהָיְתָה תֵּל עוֹלָם לֹא תִבָּנֶה עוֹד: [דברים יג, יז]

ב) לֹא תַעֲשׂוּן כֵּן לַייָ אֱלֹהֵיכֶם: [דברים יב, ד]

ג) וְהָיְתָה הָעִיר חֵרֶם הִיא וְכָל אֲשֶׁר בָּהּ לַייָ רַק רָחָב הַזּוֹנָה תִּחְיֶה הִיא וְכָל אֲשֶׁר אִתָּהּ בַּבַּיִת כִּי הֶחְבְּאַתָה אֶת הַמַּלְאָכִים אֲשֶׁר שָׁלָחְנוּ: וַיַּשְׁבַּע יְהוֹשֻׁעַ בָּעֵת הַהִיא לֵאמֹר אָרוּר הָאִישׁ לִפְנֵי יְיָ אֲשֶׁר יָקוּם וּבָנָה אֶת הָעִיר הַזֹּאת אֶת יְרִיחוֹ בִּבְכֹרוֹ יְיַסְּדֶנָּה וּבִצְעִירוֹ יַצִּיב דְּלָתֶיהָ: [יהושע ו, יז,כו]

ד) בְּיָמָיו בָּנָה חִיאֵל בֵּית הָאֱלִי אֶת יְרִיחֹה בַּאֲבִירָם בְּכֹרוֹ יִסְּדָהּ וּבִשְׂגוּב צְעִירוֹ הִצִּיב דְּלָתֶיהָ כִּדְבַר יְיָ אֲשֶׁר דִּבֶּר בְּיַד יְהוֹשֻׁעַ בִּן נוּן: [מלכים א' טז, לד]

ה) הִשָּׁמְרוּ לָכֶם פֶּן יִפְתֶּה לְבַבְכֶם וְסַרְתֶּם וַעֲבַדְתֶּם אֱלֹהִים אֲחֵרִים וְהִשְׁתַּחֲוִיתֶם לָהֶם: [דברים יא, טז]

ו) וְחָרָה אַף יְיָ בָּכֶם וְעָצַר אֶת הַשָּׁמַיִם וְלֹא יִהְיֶה מָטָר וְהָאֲדָמָה לֹא תִתֵּן אֶת יְבוּלָהּ וַאֲבַדְתֶּם מְהֵרָה מֵעַל הָאָרֶץ הַטֹּבָה אֲשֶׁר יְיָ נֹתֵן לָכֶם: [דברים יא, יז]

ז) וַיֹּאמֶר אֵלִיָּהוּ הַתִּשְׁבִּי מִתֹּשָׁבֵי גִלְעָד אֶל אַחְאָב חַי יְיָ אֱלֹהֵי יִשְׂרָאֵל אֲשֶׁר עָמַדְתִּי לְפָנָיו אִם יִהְיֶה הַשָּׁנִים הָאֵלֶּה טַל וּמָטָר כִּי אִם לְפִי דְבָרִי: [מלכים א' יז, א]

ח) וַיְהִי דְבַר יְיָ אֵלָיו לֵאמֹר: לֵךְ מִזֶּה וּפָנִיתָ לְּךָ קֵדְמָה וְנִסְתַּרְתָּ בְּנַחַל כְּרִית אֲשֶׁר עַל פְּנֵי הַיַּרְדֵּן: [מלכים א' יז, ב-ג]

ט) וְהָעֹרְבִים מְבִיאִים לוֹ לֶחֶם וּבָשָׂר בַּבֹּקֶר וְלֶחֶם וּבָשָׂר בָּעָרֶב וּמִן הַנַּחַל יִשְׁתֶּה: [מלכים א' יז, ו]

י) וַיְהִי מִקֵּץ יָמִים וַיִּיבַשׁ הַנַּחַל כִּי לֹא הָיָה גֶשֶׁם בָּאָרֶץ: [מלכים א' יז, ז]

כ) וַיְהִי דְבַר יְיָ אֵלָיו לֵאמֹר: קוּם לֵךְ צָרְפַתָה אֲשֶׁר לְצִידוֹן וְיָשַׁבְתָּ שָׁם הִנֵּה צִוִּיתִי שָׁם אִשָּׁה אַלְמָנָה לְכַלְכְּלֶךָ: [מלכים א' יז, ח-ט]

ל) וַיְהִי אַחַר הַדְּבָרִים הָאֵלֶּה חָלָה בֶּן הָאִשָּׁה בַּעֲלַת הַבָּיִת וַיְהִי חָלְיוֹ חָזָק מְאֹד עַד אֲשֶׁר לֹא נוֹתְרָה בּוֹ נְשָׁמָה: [מלכים א' יז, יז]

מ) וַיְהִי יָמִים רַבִּים וּדְבַר יְיָ הָיָה אֶל אֵלִיָּהוּ בַּשָּׁנָה הַשְּׁלִישִׁית לֵאמֹר לֵךְ הֵרָאֵה אֶל אַחְאָב וְאֶתְּנָה מָטָר עַל פְּנֵי הָאֲדָמָה: [מלכים א' יח, א]

another city by the name of Jericho. Therefore, Chiel, who built a city that he called Jericho, incurred Joshua's curse and lost his sons as a result.[30] אָמַר לֵיהּ אֵלִיָּהוּ – **Elijah answered [Ahab]:** אִין – **Yes,** that is how Joshua proclaimed the curse; the tragedy suffered by Chiel was Divine retribution for violating the curse. אָמַר לֵיהּ – **[Ahab] said to [Elijah]:** הַשְׁתָּא לְוָוטְתָא דְּמֹשֶׁה לֹא קָא מִקַּיְימָא – **Now** if even **the curse pronounced by Moses has not been fulfilled** – דִּכְתִיב ,,וְסַרְתֶּם וַעֲבַדְתֶּם וגו׳ " – **as it is written:**[31] *Lest your heart be seduced* ***and you turn astray and serve*** *the gods of others and prostrate yourselves to them.* וּכְתִיב ,,וְחָרָה אַף־ה׳ בָּכֶם וְעָצַר אֶת־הַשָּׁמַיִם וגו׳ " – **And** in the very next verse **it is written:** ***Then the wrath of Hashem will blaze against you, and He will restrain the heaven*** *so that there will be no rain and the ground will not yield its produce* – וְהַהוּא גַּבְרָא אוֹקִים לֵיהּ עֲבוֹדַת כּוֹכָבִים עַל כָּל תֶּלֶם וָתֶלֶם – **and** yet **that man** [Ahab][32] **has set up idols on each and every furrow** in Israel, i.e. on every elevated site around the country, וְלֹא שָׁבִיק לֵיהּ מִיטְרָא דְּמֵיזַל מִיסְגַּד לֵיהּ – **and** yet **the rains** have fallen so heavily that they **do not allow him** even **to go and** bow down to **those idols!**[33] Now if even the curse pronounced by Moses in the name of God has not been fulfilled, לְוָוטְתָא דִּיהוֹשֻׁעַ תַּלְמִידֵיהּ מִקַּיְימָא – do you expect me to believe that **the curse** pronounced **by Joshua, his student, has been fulfilled?**[34] מִיָּד ,,וַיֹּאמֶר אֵלִיָּהוּ הַתִּשְׁבִּי מִתֹּשָׁבֵי גִלְעָד . . . חַי־ה׳ אֱלֹהֵי יִשְׂרָאֵל . . . אִם־יִהְיֶה . . . טַל וּמָטָר וגו׳ " – **Thereupon,** ***Elijah the Tishbite, a resident of Gilead,*** *told Ahab:* ***"By the Living God, Lord of Israel,*** *before Whom I stand,* ***if there will be dew or rain*** *these years except through my word!"*[35] בָּעֵי רַחֲמֵי – **[Elijah]** then **beseeched** God,[36] וְהָבוּ לֵיהּ אַקְלִידָא דְּמִטְרָא – **and he was given the key for rain,**[37] וְקָם וְאָזַל – whereupon **he arose and departed.** Thus, it was the blasphemy uttered by Ahab during his condolence call on Chiel that provoked Elijah into pronouncing the curse that brought on the drought.[38] For this reason the story of Chiel is inserted by Scripture between the recounting of Ahab's sins and the story of the drought that came in punishment for them.

The Gemara now expounds the chapter about the drought. After pronouncing his oath that there would be no rain, Elijah was told by God to depart and hide in the wilderness. The Gemara quotes and expounds these verses:

,,וַיְהִי דְבַר־ה׳ אֵלָיו לֵאמֹר – ***God's word then came to him*** [Elijah] ***saying:*** לֵךְ מִזֶּה וּפָנִיתָ לְּךָ קֵדְמָה וְנִסְתַּרְתָּ בְּנַחַל כְּרִית" – ***"Go from here and turn eastward; and hide by the brook of Keris."***[39] ,,וְהָעֹרְבִים מְבִיאִים לוֹ לֶחֶם וּבָשָׂר בַּבֹּקֶר וגו׳ " – ***And the ravens would bring him bread and meat every morning,*** *and he drank from the brook.*[40] מֵהֵיכָא – **From where** did the ravens get the bread and meat? אָמַר רַב יְהוּדָה אָמַר רַב – **Rav Yehudah said in the name of Rav:** מִבֵּי טַבָּחֵי דְּאַחְאָב – **From Ahab's kitchens.**[41]

The drought worsens:

,,וַיְהִי מִקֵּץ יָמִים וַיִּיבַשׁ הַנָּחַל כִּי לֹא־הָיָה גֶשֶׁם בָּאָרֶץ" – ***And it was at the end of a year that the brook dried up, for there was no rain in the land.***[42] כֵּיוָן דַּחֲזָא דְּאִיכָּא צַעֲרָא בְּעָלְמָא – **When [God] saw that there was suffering in the world** on account of the drought, and that Elijah was not inclined to let the drought end, כְּתִיב ,,וַיְהִי דְבַר־ה׳ אֵלָיו לֵאמֹר קוּם לֵךְ צָרְפָתָה" – **it is written:** ***And the word of God came to him*** [Elijah] ***saying: "Arise, go to Tzarefas."***[43] וּכְתִיב ,,וַיְהִי אַחַר הַדְּבָרִים הָאֵלֶּה חָלָה בֶּן־הָאִשָּׁה בַּעֲלַת הַבָּיִת" – **And it is written:** ***And it was after these events that the son of the woman who was the mistress of the house took ill.***[44] בָּעָא רַחֲמֵי – When the boy died, **[Elijah] beseeched** God לְמֵיתַן לֵיהּ אַקְלִידָא דִּתְחִיַּית הַמֵּתִים – **that He give him the key of resurrection,** so that Elijah might thereby revive the dead child. אָמְרֵי לֵיהּ – **They** [God and His Court] **said to [Elijah]:** שָׁלֹשׁ מַפְתְּחוֹת לֹא נִמְסְרוּ לְשָׁלִיחַ – There are **three keys** that **were not entrusted to an agent:**[45] שֶׁל חַיָּה – The key **of childbirth,**[46] וְשֶׁל גְּשָׁמִים – the key **of rain** וְשֶׁל תְּחִיַּית הַמֵּתִים – **and** the key **of resurrection.** One key I [God] have already made an exception and given you – the key of rain. Now you request a second key,

NOTES

30. [Since Chiel had not built on the site of the ancient Jericho but had merely called his new city Jericho, Ahab was at a loss to understand why Chiel should have suffered the terrible fate decreed in Joshua's curse. He thus conjectured that Joshua must also have forbidden building a city anywhere and calling it Jericho.]

31. *Deuteronomy* 11:16-17.

32. [Ahab referred to himself as that man because when speaking of possible misfortune, one does not speak directly of himself but frames his words in terms of others (see Gemara above, 104b).]

33. The roads are so inundated with rain that they have become mires of impassable mud (*Rashi*).

34. Thus, Ahab refused to believe that the death of Chiel's sons was Divine retribution for violating Joshua's curse.

35. *I Kings* 17:1.

36. Literally: asked God for mercy.

37. This is an allegorical expression denoting God's control over rain. Since Elijah was granted the power to prevent the rains from falling, it was as if God, so to speak, locked the door of the room in which the rain was stored and gave the key to Elijah (*Yad Ramah*).

38. Although the drought was in punishment for the great sins of Ahab, had Ahab not said this, retribution would not have come at this time. God is patient and His timetable for retribution is much longer than Ahab imagined. Although God did eventually destroy the kingdom of Israel for their sins [see *II Kings* ch. 17], punishment was not destined to come in Ahab's time. Indeed, in Ahab's time there was an abundance of rain. It was only because of Elijah's oath in response to Ahab's denial that Divine retribution came upon the nation in Ahab's day (*Maharsha*).

Sanhedrei Ketanah suggests that the reason the Torah's retribution was not immediately incurred by Ahab's generation was because the lack of rain foretold by Moses was only for idolatry by the people as a whole. The idolatry of Baal instituted by Ahab was not widespread, but was confined to the king and a relatively small circle of followers. The majority of the population did not worship Baal. See also *Yaaros Devash* ibid.

39. *I Kings* 17:2.

40. Ibid. v. 6.

41. Although Elijah would ordinarily not eat meat from the house of an idolater, because the slaughter of an idolater is not valid, thus rendering the animal non-kosher, it was different in this case, for God had temporarily permitted it to him, saying: *I have commanded the ravens to feed you there* [ibid.] (see Gemara *Chullin* 5a and *Rashi* there ד״ה על פי הדבור).

42. Ibid. v. 7.

43. Ibid. vs. 8-9. When God saw that despite the suffering brought about by the drought Elijah refused to allow the rains to come (*Yad Ramah*), He set in motion a chain of events that would force Elijah to give up the right God had given him to control the rains. God dried up the brook of Keris, denying water to Elijah and forcing him to leave. He then ordered Elijah to go to a widow in the town of Tzarefas and be supported by her [thereby putting Elijah in her debt] (*Rashi*).

44. Ibid. v. 17. The verse continues: *and his illness was very great, until there was no life left in him.*

45. At the time of Creation, God entrusted the "keys" to many of His "storehouses" to agents appointed by Him. [As explained in note 37, the term "keys" refers to control. God, so to speak, entrusted control over many natural phenomena to various forces, so that they operate according to established rules.] However, God did not appoint any custodians over the keys that unlock these three matters, but chose to keep them entirely to Himself (*Rashi*; see *Rashi* and *Tosafos* to *Taanis* 2a).

46. *Tosafos* (*Niddah* 16b). However, *Tos. HaRosh* there understands this as a reference to conception.

וליפרקיה [א] דתנן [א] הלקוח בכסף מעשר שנטמא יפדה כר"י דאמר יקבר אי הכי מאי איריא עיר הנדחת אפילו דעלמא נמי אלא לעולם בטהור וכגון דנפול מחיצות וכדרבא [ב] דאמר רבא [ב] מחיצה לאכול דאורייתא [ג] לקלוט דרבנן וכי גזור רבנן כי אתנהו למחיצה כי ליתנהו למחיצה לא: כתבי הקדש יגנזו: מתניתין דלא כר"א [ג] דתניא ר"א אומר כל עיר שיש בה אפי' מזוזה אחת אינה נעשית עיר הנדחת שנא' (א) ושרפת באש את העיר ואת כל שללה כליל והיכא דאיכא מזוזה לא אפשר דכתיב (ב) לא תעשון כן לה' אלהיכם: ר"ש אומר אמר הקב"ה וכו': לימא בדר' אבין א"ר אילעא קמיפלגי [ד] דא"ר אבין א"ר אילעא כל מקום שאתה מוצא כלל בעשה ופרט בלא תעשה אין דנין אותו בכלל ופרט דמר אית ליה דרבי אבין ומר לית ליה דרבי אבין לא דכ"ע אית להו דר' אבין והכא בהא קמיפלגי מר סבר עוד לגמרי משמע ומר סבר עוד לכמה שהיתה: אינה נבנית אבל נעשית היא גנות ופרדסים: ת"ר [ד] היו בה אילנות תלושין אסורין מחוברין מותרין של עיר אחרת בין תלושין בין מחוברין אסור מאי עיר אחרת אמר רב חסדא יריחו דכתיב (ג) והיתה העיר [ה] חרם לה' וישבע יהושע בעת ההיא לאמר ארור האיש לפני ה' אשר יקום ובנה את העיר הזאת את יריחו בבכורו ייסדנה ובצעירו יציב דלתיה תניא [ו] לא יריחו על שם עיר אחרת ולא עיר אחרת על שם יריחו דכתיב (ד) בנה חיאל בית האלי את יריחו באבירם בכורו יסדה ובשגוב צעירו הציב דלתיה תניא [ז] באבירם בכורו רשע לא היה לו ללמוד בשגוב צעירו היה לו ללמוד אבירם ושגוב מאי עבוד ([ח] מאי קאמר) ה"ק באבירם בכורו היה לו ללמוד לאותו רשע בשגוב צעירו ממשמע שנאמר באבירם בכורו איני יודע ששגוב צעירו מה ת"ל שגוב צעירו מלמד שהיה מקבר והולך מאבירם עד שגוב אחאב שושביניה הוה אתא איהו ואליהו למשאל בשלמא בי טמיא יתיב וקאמר דילמא כי מילט יהושע הכי לט לא יריחו על שם עיר אחרת ולא עיר אחרת על שם יריחו א"ל אליהו אין אמר ליה השתא לווטתא דמשה לא קא מקיימא דכתיב (ה) וסרתם ועבדתם וגו' וכתיב (ו) וחרה אף ה' בכם ועצר את השמים וגו' וההוא גברא אוקים ליה עבודת כוכבים [ט] על כל תלם ותלם ולא שביק ליה מיטרא דמיזל מיסגד ליה לווטתא דיהושע תלמידיה מקיימא מיד (ז) ויאמר אליהו התשבי מתושבי גלעד [י] חי ה' אלהי ישראל אם [כ] יהיה טל ומטר וגו' בעי רחמי והבו ליה אקלידא דמטרא וקם ואזל (ח) ויהי דבר ה' אליו לאמר לך מזה ופנית לך קדמה ונסתרת בנחל כרית (ט) והעורבים מביאים לו לחם ובשר בבקר וגו' [ל] מהיכא אמר רב יהודה אמר רב מבי טבחי דאחאב (י) ויהי מקץ ימים וייבש הנחל כי לא היה גשם בארץ כיון דחזא דאיכא צערא בעלמא כתיב (כ) ויהי דבר ה' אליו לאמר קום לך צרפתה וכתיב (ל) ויהי אחר הדברים האלה חלה בן האשה בעלת הבית בעא רחמי למיתן ליה אקלידא דתחיית המתים אמרי ליה [מ] שלש מפתחות לא נמסרו לשליח של חיה ושל גשמים ושל תחיית המתים יאמרו שתים ביד תלמיד ואחת ביד הרב אייתי הא ושקיל האי דכתיב (מ) לך הראה אל אחאב [ואתנה] מטר דרש ההוא גלילאה קמיה דרב חסדא משל דאליהו למה הדבר דומה לגברא דטרקיה לגליה ואבדיה למפתחיה דרש ר' יוסי בצפורי אבא אליהו

רש"י

וליפרקיה לבוליה. ומשני כר"י דאמר לא אלים למתפס פדיונו בההיא [י] מנה גופא במס' מעשר שני (פ"ג מ"י) והיינו נמי מעשר שני דקאמר יגנז בקבורה: **אלא לעולם.** במעשר שני דעיר הנדחת טהור ואסקוה לגוה ודקאמר לישתרי באכילה דהא קלטוהו מחיצות אחר שנכנס לחומת ירושלים: **דאמר רבא.** ([ס] בשחיטת חולין פ' בהמה המקשה (דף סח): **מחיצות לאכול דאורייתא.** מן התורה מצוה לאכול לפנים מן החומה: **אבל מחיצות לקלוט.** שיהיו מחילות קולטות בין לענין פדייה בין לכל ענין מדרבנן הוא וכי גזור רבנן דתיהני קליטת מחילות למעשר דשוב אינו יכול לפדותו אן ולענין עיר הנדחת נמי שלא יהא בשריפה היכא דאיתנהו מחילות: **דכתיב ואבדתם.** את שמם מן המקום ההוא וגו' וסמיך ליה לא תעשון כן לה' אלהיכם ובמזוזה הואיל וכתיב בה אזכרות אי אפשר לשריפה משום קרא דלא תעשון כן ואנן בעינן שללה וליכא דהאי שלל שמים הוא: **כלל בעשה ופרט בלא תעשה.** כגון והיתה תל עולם כלל דאפילו גנות ופרדסים לא תעשה אלא תהיה תל עולם שהוא עשה לא תבנה עוד בנין בתים והוא לא תעשה אין דנין אותו בכלל ופרט לומר אין בכלל אלא מה שבפרט דלא תעשה פירוש הוא כלומר והיתה תל עולם לבנין קאמר אבל לגנות ופרדסים שרי אלא תרי מילי קאמר קרא דלא אמרינן פירושי קמפרש אלא מילי מילי קאמר והיתה תל עולם לגנות ופרדסים לא תבנה עוד כל בנינין שבעולם ואפילו לגנות ופרדסים לא תבנה עוד ודרשינן ליה לדבר שהיה בכלל ויצא מן הכלל ללמד לא ללמד על עצמו יצא אלא ללמד על הכלל כולו יצא ולומר בנין בכלל היה ולמה יצא להקיש לך מה בנין מיוחד שהוא ישוב בני אדם אף כל בנין כגון גנות ופרדסים [ע] (לישנא אחרינא) ור' יוסי הגלילי סבר אין דנין כר' אבין ודריש הכי והיתה תל עולם מכל מילי שלא יעשה בה שום דבר ולא תבנה עוד דמשמע בנין בתים אשמועינן לאו דבנין בתים וגנות ופרדסים איסור עשה הוא דאיכא. כך שמעתי: **ר"ע סבר דנין.** דלא כר' אבין: **דכ"ע אית להו דר' אבין.** ואפילו ר"ע והא דקאמר דעיר הנדחת נעשית גנות ופרדסים לאו משום דבעלמא לית ליה דר' אבין דודאי מלתא קא מפרשי והיתה תל עולם במאי בבנין בתים דלא תבנה עוד לא משמע ליה בכל בניין דקסבר עוד לכמו שהיתה משמע כלומר לא תחזור ולא תבנה עוד משמע כגון שהיתה מתחלה לא תבנה עוד אבל נעשה גנות ופרדסים: **ומר סבר עוד לגמרי משמע.** כגון דאמר לעולם ועד ועוד לשון ועד הוא [פ] שלא תבנה לעולם לשום דבר לא לבנין בתים ולא לגנות ופרדסים לא תבנה עוד: **מחוברין מותרין.** דתקבוץ ושרפת אמרה רחמנא מי שאינו מחוסר אלא קבילה ושריפה יצא זה שמחוסר תלישה וקבילה ושריפה: **וכל אשר בה.** אפילו אילנות מחוברין אשר בה נאסרין: ה"ג וישבע יהושע **לאמר ארור האיש וגו'.** וקרא קדריש ואזיל בבכורו ייסדנה ובצעירו יציב דלתיה וכשיעמיד דלתיה ימות בנו הקטן: **לא יריחו על שם עיר אחרת.** שלא יבנה יריחו ויסב שמה על שם עיר אחרת ולא עיר אחרת על שם יריחו שאפי' בנה עיר אחרת וקראה יריחו אסור לבנותה שאפי' שם יריחו ימחה לעולם וכתיב בימיו בנה חיאל בית האלי את יריחו בימיו של אחאב ועל שעבר על האלה קרי ליה בית האלי: **את יריחו.** ולא יריחו עצמו בנה אלא עיר אחרת על שם יריחו שקראה לה יריחו ולא אתפרש הא מנלן: **באבירם בכורו יסדה.** אבירם רשע כשמת אבירם הרשע לא היה לו לחיאל ללמוד שלא לבנות את יריחו: **אבירם ושגוב מאי עבוד.** דקרי להו רשעים: **איני יודע ששגוב צעירו.** מילתא באנפי נפשיה הוא ולמדרשא ממשמע שנאמר באבירם בכורו איני יודע ששגוב צעירו אלא מה ת"ל שגוב צעירו שהיה קובר והולך מאבירם ועד שגוב שהוא צעיר מכלם: **אחאב שושבינו.** אוהבו של חיאל היה אחאב: **בי טמיא.** וי"א בי טעמא בית האבל שמטעימים אותו בדברים לנחמו וכמה דוכתין כתיב בבראשית רבה טמיא בלא עיי"ן לשון אבל: **על כל תלם ותלם.** שורה וערוגה ומקום גבוה הוא: **ולא שביק מיטרא מיזל ומסגד.** שהיה הלכלוך הולך וגדל מרוב הגשמים הבאין לעולם שאין מניחין לילך להשתחוות לעבודת כוכבים מתוך דרכים מלוכלכות בטיט: **מיד ויאמר אליהו חי ה' אם יהיה השנים האלה מטר וגו'.** האי קרא סמוך לקרא דחיאל בית האלי: **אקלידא דמטרא.** מפתח של מטר: **כיון דחזא.** הקב"ה דאיכא צערא בעלמא א"ל הקב"ה לאליהו לך צרפתה לגלגל הדבר שיחזיר לו מפתח של מטר כדקא מפרש ואזיל: **שלש מפתחות לא נמסרו ביד שליח.** על אוצרו של הקב"ה יש מפתחות ומסרם ליד שלוחים הממונים אבל ג' מפתחות יש לו בידו שלא מינה שליח עליהם מבראשית אלא בידו הם ולא רצה למסור שליח עליהם וקאמר הקב"ה לאליהו אותם ג' מפתחות עכבתי בידי מבראשית ולא מניתי שליח עליהם אלא אותך עשיתי ממונה על אחת מהם ועתה תשאל מפתח שני יאמרו שנים ביד תלמיד ואחד ביד הרב: **דטרקיה לגליה.** שסגר שער שלו ואבדיה למפתחיה כך עשה אליהו נעל לשערי מטר ולבסוף אבד המפתח של גשמים שלא נפתח השער של מטר על ידו: **דכתב לך הראה אל אחאב ואתנה מטר.** ולא כתיב ותן מטר: **אבא אליהו.** חביבי וגדולי:

היה

מסורת הש"ס

א) פסחי' לו: לח. מ"ש פ"ג מ"י [ב"מ נג: זבחים מט.], ב) ב"מ שם מכות כ. [עיין תוס' ב"מ נג: ד"ה לא פלוג], ג) לעיל ע"א, ד) [מ"ק ג.], ה) [נ"ל חרם היא וכל אשר בה לה'], ו) [תוספ' פי"ד], ז) [תוספתא שם], ח) [בע"י ליתא], ט) [לעיל קג:], י) [אל אחאב], כ) [נ"ל יהיה השנים האלה טל וכו'], ל) חולין ה., מ) תענית ב., נ) [נ"ל משנה], ס) [בשחיטת חולין לא נמצא אמנם בב"מ נג: ד"ה והא אמר רבא כתב רש"י על נכון וציין במס' מכות], ע) נ"ל לא, פ) [עי' רש"י שבת לג. ד"ה לא ישמח].

ליקוטי רש"י

יקבר. דקא סבר לא אלים למיתפס פדיונו. **אלא לעולם בטהור.** בין מעשר בין לקוח ודקאמר נעייליה וניכליה. **וכגון דנפול מחיצות.** חומת ירושלים ושוב אין מעשר נאכל שם עד שיעמדו מחילות דבעינן לפני ה' תאכלנו (דברים יב) ובפדייה נמי לא דקלטוהו מחילות מלפדותו עוד משנכנס לתוכו. **מחיצה לאכול דאורייתא מחיצה לקלוט דרבנן.** מחילה שנאמרה בתורה לא הוזכרה אלא לאכול בתוכה ושאמרו במשנה מחילות קולטות אותם מלפדות עוד אם יצא דרבנן היא. **וכי גזור רבנן כו'.** דכי גזור רבנן היכא דאיתנהו וזה הוציא את המעשר לחוץ אבל כי ליתנהו לא גזור הלכך ניפרקיה [ב"מ נג:]. **והיתה העיר חרם.** הקדש כי היום שבת קדש וראוי להיות קדש שלל הנשלל בו [יהושע ו, יז]. **בבכרו ייסדנה ובצעירו.** בתחלת יסוד שיבנה בה ימות בנו הבכור ויקברנו וילך עד שימות הצעיר בגמר המלאכה היא הצבת הדלתות [שם ו, כו]. **באבירם בכרו יסדה.** כשיסד' מת בנו בכורו וקבר והלך וקבר כל בניו עד שמת האחרון בהצבת דלתות וכן הוא קללות של יהושע בבכורו ייסדנה ובצעירו יציב דלתיה (יהושע ו' כ"ו) [מ"א טז, לד]. **חי ה'.** למה סמכו כאן אלא שהלכו אליהו ואחאב לנחם את חיאל באבלו אמר אחאב לאליהו אפשר שקללת התלמיד נתקיימה וקללת משה רבינו לא נתקיימה שנאמר (דברים י"א ט"ז) וסרתם ועבדתם אלהים אחרים והשתחויתם להם וחרה אף ה' בכם ועצר את השמים והרי כל ישראל עובדין ע"ג ואין גשמים נעצרים מיד ויאמר אליהו וגו' [שם יז, א]. **ונסתרת.** מפני אחאב ואיזבל [שם יז, ג]. **ויבש הנחל.** כדי שידע צורך הגשמים ויטריח לגלות שהיה קשה בעיני הקב"ה שישראל שרוין מתים ברעב [שם יז, ז]. **צרפתה.** שם העיר [שם יז, ט]. **חלה בן האשה.** כדי שיצטרך למפתח של תחיית המתים כדאיתא בשילהי אגדתא דחלק [שם פסוק יז].

עין משפט נר מצוה

נט א מיי' פ"ז מהל' מעשר שני הלכה א ב:
ס ב מיי' שם פ"ב הל' ה סמג לאוין רסד:
סא ג מיי' שם הל' ט:
סב ד מיי' פ"ד מהל' ע"ז הלכה יג סמג עשין טו:

הגהות מהר"ב רנשבורג

א] רש"י ד"ה **אבל** מחיצות וכו' ולענין עיר הנדחת נמי שלא יהא בשריפה. מלת בשריפה נמחק ונ"ב בגניזה:

תורה אור השלם

א) וְאֶת כָּל שְׁלָלָהּ תִּקְבֹּץ אֶל תּוֹךְ רְחֹבָהּ וְשָׂרַפְתָּ בָאֵשׁ אֶת הָעִיר וְאֶת כָּל שְׁלָלָהּ כָּלִיל לַייָ אֱלֹהֶיךָ וְהָיְתָה תֵּל עוֹלָם לֹא תִבָּנֶה עוֹד: [דברים יג, יז]

ב) לֹא תַעֲשׂוּן כֵּן לַייָ אֱלֹהֵיכֶם: [דברים יב, ד]

ג) וְהָיְתָה הָעִיר חֵרֶם הִיא וְכָל אֲשֶׁר בָּהּ לַייָ רַק רָחָב הַזּוֹנָה תִּחְיֶה הִיא וְכָל אֲשֶׁר אִתָּהּ בַּבַּיִת כִּי הֶחְבְּאַתָה אֶת הַמַּלְאָכִים אֲשֶׁר שָׁלָחְנוּ: וַיַּשְׁבַּע יְהוֹשֻׁעַ בָּעֵת הַהִיא לֵאמֹר אָרוּר הָאִישׁ לִפְנֵי יְיָ אֲשֶׁר יָקוּם וּבָנָה אֶת הָעִיר הַזֹּאת אֶת יְרִיחוֹ בִּבְכֹרוֹ יְיַסְּדֶנָּה וּבִצְעִירוֹ יַצִּיב דְּלָתֶיהָ: [יהושע ו, יז,כו]

ד) בְּיָמָיו בָּנָה חִיאֵל בֵּית הָאֱלִי אֶת יְרִיחֹה בַּאֲבִירָם בְּכֹרוֹ יִסְּדָהּ וּבִשְׂגוּב צְעִירוֹ הִצִּיב דְּלָתֶיהָ כִּדְבַר יְיָ אֲשֶׁר דִּבֶּר בְּיַד יְהוֹשֻׁעַ בִּן נוּן: [מלכים א' טז, לד]

ה) הִשָּׁמְרוּ לָכֶם פֶּן יִפְתֶּה לְבַבְכֶם וְסַרְתֶּם וַעֲבַדְתֶּם אֱלֹהִים אֲחֵרִים וְהִשְׁתַּחֲוִיתֶם לָהֶם: [דברים יא, טז]

ו) וְחָרָה אַף יְיָ בָּכֶם וְעָצַר אֶת הַשָּׁמַיִם וְלֹא יִהְיֶה מָטָר וְהָאֲדָמָה לֹא תִתֵּן אֶת יְבוּלָהּ וַאֲבַדְתֶּם מְהֵרָה מֵעַל הָאָרֶץ הַטֹּבָה אֲשֶׁר יְיָ נֹתֵן לָכֶם: [דברים יא, יז]

ז) וַיֹּאמֶר אֵלִיָּהוּ הַתִּשְׁבִּי מִתֹּשָׁבֵי גִלְעָד אֶל אַחְאָב חַי יְיָ אֱלֹהֵי יִשְׂרָאֵל אֲשֶׁר עָמַדְתִּי לְפָנָיו אִם יִהְיֶה הַשָּׁנִים הָאֵלֶּה טַל וּמָטָר כִּי אִם לְפִי דְבָרִי: [מלכים א' יז, א]

ח) וַיְהִי דְבַר יְיָ אֵלָיו לֵאמֹר: לֵךְ מִזֶּה וּפָנִיתָ לְּךָ קֵדְמָה וְנִסְתַּרְתָּ בְּנַחַל כְּרִית אֲשֶׁר עַל פְּנֵי הַיַּרְדֵּן: [מלכים א' יז, ב-ג]

ט) וְהָעֹרְבִים מְבִיאִים לוֹ לֶחֶם וּבָשָׂר בַּבֹּקֶר וְלֶחֶם וּבָשָׂר בָּעָרֶב וּמִן הַנַּחַל יִשְׁתֶּה: [מלכים א' יז, ו]

י) וַיְהִי מִקֵּץ יָמִים וַיִּיבַשׁ הַנַּחַל כִּי לֹא הָיָה גֶשֶׁם בָּאָרֶץ: [מלכים א' יז, ז]

כ) וַיְהִי דְבַר יְיָ אֵלָיו לֵאמֹר: קוּם לֵךְ צָרְפַתָה אֲשֶׁר לְצִידוֹן וְיָשַׁבְתָּ שָׁם הִנֵּה צִוִּיתִי שָׁם אִשָּׁה אַלְמָנָה לְכַלְכְּלֶךָ: [מלכים א' יז, ח-ט] ל) וַיְהִי אַחַר הַדְּבָרִים הָאֵלֶּה חָלָה בֶּן הָאִשָּׁה בַּעֲלַת הַבָּיִת וַיְהִי חָלְיוֹ חָזָק מְאֹד עַד אֲשֶׁר לֹא נוֹתְרָה בוֹ נְשָׁמָה: [מלכים א' יז, יז] מ) וַיְהִי יָמִים רַבִּים וּדְבַר יְיָ הָיָה אֶל אֵלִיָּהוּ בַּשָּׁנָה הַשְּׁלִישִׁית לֵאמֹר לֵךְ הֵרָאֵה אֶל אַחְאָב וְאֶתְּנָה מָטָר עַל פְּנֵי הָאֲדָמָה: [מלכים א' יח, א]

the key of resurrection. יאמְרוּ שְׁתַּיִם בְּיַד תַּלְמִיד וְאַחַת בְּיַד הָרַב – Is it proper that **people should say: Two** keys **are in the hands of the student and** only **one** is **in the hands of the teacher?** אַיְיתֵי הָא וּשְׁקִיל הַאי – **Bring** back **that** key, the key of rain, **and take** in its place **this** key, the key of resurrection. Elijah was thus forced to give up his control of the rain in order to resurrect the child of his hostess. As a result, God decreed an end to the drought, דִּכְתִיב ,,לֵךְ הֵרָאֵה אֶל־אַחְאָב וְאֶתְּנָה מָטָר'' – **as is it written:** *God's Word came to Elijah:* ***Go, appear before Ahab, and I will send rain upon the earth.***[47]

The Gemara quotes a comment on Elijah's predicament:

דָּרַשׁ הַהוּא גְּלִילָאָה קַמֵּיהּ דְּרַב חִסְדָּא – **A certain Galilean expounded in the presence of Rav Chisda:** מָשָׁל דְּאֵלִיָּהוּ לְמָה הַדָּבָר דּוֹמֶה – **A parable** for the story **of Elijah: To what can this be compared?** לְגַבְרָא דְּטַרְקֵיהּ לְגַלֵּיהּ – **To a man who locked his gate** וְאַבְדֵיהּ לְמַפְתְּחֵיהּ – **and** then **lost his key.**[48]

The Gemara relates an observation made by one of the Tannaim about Elijah:

דָּרַשׁ רַבִּי יוֹסֵי בְּצִיפּוֹרִי – **R' Yose expounded in Tzippori:** אַבָּא אֵלִיָּהוּ – **"Father Elijah**[49]

NOTES

47. *I Kings* 18:1. [The verse states *and I will send rain,* rather than *and you send rain*; this indicates that God had taken control of the rains from Elijah (see *Rashi*).]

48. Elijah had been granted the power over the rains – he had been entrusted with the "key" to its "storehouse." He had used his power to cause a drought; he had, so to speak, "locked" the storehouse of rain. [He fully expected to be able to return and unlock it at his discretion.] In the end, however, Elijah himself was unable to "unlock" the door because he no longer had the key; God had forced him to give it back. Elijah was thus like the person who leaves his home and locks the gate, only to discover later that he cannot unlock it because he has lost his key (*Rashi*). Having obtained control over the rains, Elijah had felt sure that he would be able to bring back the rains. In the end, however, he was like the man who locked his door convinced that he could unlock it whenever he wished, only to have his plan frustrated by his loss of his key (*Maharal;* cf. *Maharsha* and *Ben Yehoyada*).

49. The word אַבָּא, *father,* is used here as a term of reverence and affection (*Rashi*).

וליפרקיה [א] דתנן [א] הלקוח בכסף מעשר שנטמא יפדה כר"י דאמר יקבר אי הכי מאי איריא עיר הנדחת אפילו דעלמא נמי אלא לעולם בטהור וכגון דנפול מחיצות וכדרבא [ב] דאמר רבא [ב] מחיצה לאכול דאורייתא [ג] לקלוט דרבנן וכי גזור רבנן כי אתנהו למחיצה כי ליתנהו למחיצה לא: כתבי הקדש יגנזו: מתניתין דלא כר"א [ג] דתניא ר"א אומר כל עיר שיש בה אפי' מזוזה אחת אינה נעשית עיר הנדחת שנא' [א] ושרפת באש את העיר ואת כל שללה כליל והיכא דאיכא מזוזה לא אפשר דכתיב [ב] לא תעשון כן לה' אלהיכם: ר"ש אומר אמר הקב"ה וכו': לימא בדר' אבין א"ר אילעא קמיפלגי [ד] דא"ר אבין א"ר אילעא כל מקום שאתה מוצא כלל בעשה ופרט בלא תעשה אין דנין אותו בכלל ופרט דמר אית ליה דרבי אבין ומר לית ליה דרבי אבין לא דכ"ע אית להו דר' אבין והכא בהא קמיפלגי מר סבר עוד לגמרי משמע ומר סבר עוד לכמה שהיתה: אינה נבנית אבל נעשית היא גנות ופרדסים: ת"ר [ד] היו בה אילנות תלושין אסורין מחוברין מותרין של עיר אחרת בין תלושין בין מחוברין אסור מאי עיר אחרת אמר רב חסדא יריחו דכתיב [ג] והיתה העיר [ה] חרם לה' וישבע יהושע בעת ההיא לאמר ארור האיש לפני ה' אשר יקום ובנה את העיר הזאת את יריחו בבכורו ייסדנה ובצעירו יציב דלתיה תניא [ו] לא יריחו על שם עיר אחרת ולא עיר אחרת על שם יריחו דכתיב [ד] בנה חיאל בית האלי את יריחו באבירם בכורו יסדה ובשגוב צעירו הציב דלתיה תניא [ז] באבירם בכורו רשע לא היה לו ללמוד בשגוב צעירו היה לו ללמוד אבירם ושגוב מאי עבוד ([ח] מאי קאמר) ה"ק באבירם בכורו היה לו ללמוד לאותו רשע בשגוב צעירו ממשמע שנאמר באבירם בכורו איני יודע ששגוב צעירו מה ת"ל שגוב צעירו מלמד שהיה מקבר והולך מאבירם עד שגוב אחאב שושביניה הוה אתא איהו ואליהו למשאל בשלמא בי טמיא יתיב וקאמר דילמא כי מילט יהושע הכי לט לא יריחו על שם עיר אחרת ולא עיר אחרת על שם יריחו א"ל אליהו אין אמר ליה השתא לווטתא דמשה לא קא מקיימא דכתיב [ה] וסרתם ועבדתם וגו' וכתיב [ו] וחרה אף ה' בכם ועצר את השמים וגו' וההוא גברא אוקים ליה עבודת כוכבים [ט] על כל תלם ותלם ולא שביק ליה מיטרא דמיזל מיסגד ליה לווטתא דיהושע תלמידיה מקיימא מיד [ז] ויאמר אליהו התשבי מתושבי גלעד [י] חי ה' אלהי ישראל אם [כ] יהיה טל ומטר וגו' בעי רחמי והבו ליה אקלידא דמטרא וקם ואזל [ח] ויהי דבר ה' אליו לאמר לך מזה ופנית לך קדמה ונסתרת בנחל כרית [ט] והעורבים מביאים לו לחם ובשר בבקר וגו' [ל] מהיכא אמר רב יהודה אמר רב מבי טבחי דאחאב [י] ויהי מקץ ימים וייבש הנחל כי לא היה גשם בארץ כיון דחזא דאיכא צערא בעלמא כתיב [כ] ויהי דבר ה' אליו לאמר קום לך צרפתה וכתיב [ל] ויהי אחר הדברים האלה חלה בן האשה בעלת הבית בעא רחמי למיתן ליה אקלידא דתחיית המתים אמרי ליה [מ] שלש מפתחות לא נמסרו לשליח של חיה ושל גשמים ושל תחיית המתים יאמרו שתים ביד תלמיד ואחת ביד הרב אייתי הא ושקיל האי דכתיב [מ] לך הראה אל אחאב [ואתנה] מטר דרש ההוא גלילאה קמיה דרב חסדא משל דאליהו למה הדבר דומה לגברא דטרקיה לגליה ואבדיה למפתחיה דרש ר' יוסי בצפורי אבא אליהו

וליפרקיה לבוליה. ומשני כר"י דאמר לא אלים למתפס פדיונו בההיא [י] מנה גופא במס' מעשר שני (פ"ג מ"י) והיינו נמי מעשר שני דקאמר יגנז בקבורה: **אלא לעולם.** במעשר שני דעיר הנדחת טהור ואסקוה לגוה ודקאמר ליסתרי באכילה דהא קלטוהו מחילות אחר שנכנס לחומת ירושלים: **דאמר רבא.** ([ס] בשחיטת חולין פ' בהמה המקשה (דף סח): **מחיצות לאכול דאורייתא.** מן התורה מצוה לאכול לפנים מן החומה: **אבל מחיצות לקלוט.** שיהיו מחילות קולטות בין לענין פדייה בין לכל ענין מדרבנן הוא וכי גזור רבנן דתיהני קליטת מחילות למעשר דשוב אינו יכול לפדותו **א]** ולענין עיר הנדחת נמי שלא יהא בשריפה היכא דאיתנהו מחילות: **דכתיב ואבדתם.** את שמם מן המקום ההוא וגו' וסמיך ליה לא תעשון כן לה' אלהיכם ובמזוזה הואיל וכתיב בה אזכרות אי אפשר לשריפה משום קרא דלא תעשון כן ואן בעינן שללה וליכא דהאי שלל שמים הוא: **כלל בעשה ופרט בלא תעשה.** כגון והיתה תל עולם כלל דאפילו גנות ופרדסים לא תעשה אלא תהיה תל עולם שהוא עשה לא תבנה עוד בנין בתים והוא לא תעשה אין דנין אותו בכלל ופרט לומר אין בכלל אלא מה שבפרט דלא תעשה פירוש הוא כלומר והיתה תל עולם לבנין קאמר אבל לגנות ופרדסים שרי אלא תרי מילי קאמר קרא דלא אמרינן פירושי קמפרש אלא מילי מילי קאמר והיתה תל עולם לגנות ופרדסים לא תבנה עוד כל בניין שבעולם ואפילו לגנות ופרדסים לא תבנה עוד ודרשינן ליה לדבר שהיה בכלל ויצא מן הכלל ללמד לא ללמד על עצמו יצא אלא ללמד על הכלל כולו יצא ולומר בנין בכלל היה ולמה יצא להקיש לך מה בנין מיוחד שהוא ישוב בני אדם אף כל בנין כגון גנות ופרדסים [ע] (לישנא אחרינא) ור' יוסי הגלילי סבר אין דנין כר' אבין ודריש הכי והיתה תל עולם מכל מילי שלא יעשה בה שום דבר ולא תבנה עוד דמשמע בנין בתים אשמועינן לאו דבנין בתים וגנות ופרדסים איסור עשה הוא דאיכא. כך שמעתי: **ר"ע סבר דנין.** דלא כר' אבין: **דכ"ע אית להו דר' אבין.** ואפילו ר"ע והא דקאמר דעיר הנדחת נעשית גנות ופרדסים לאו משום דבעלמא לית ליה דר' אבין דודאי מלתא קא מפרשי והיתה תל עולם במאי בבנין בתים דלא תבנה עוד לא משמע ליה בכל בניין דקסבר עוד לכמו שהיתה משמע כלומר לא תחזור ולא תבנה עוד משמע כגון שהיתה מתחלה לא תבנה עוד אבל נעשה גנות ופרדסים: **ומר סבר עוד לגמרי משמע.** כגון דאמר לעולם ועד ועוד לשון ועד הוא [פ] שלא תבנה לעולם לשום דבר לא לבנין בתים ולא לגנות ופרדסים לא תבנה עוד: **מחוברין מותרין.** דתקבוץ ושרפת אמרה רחמנא מי שאינו מחוסר אלא קבילה ושריפה יצא זה שמחוסר תלישה וקבילה ושריפה: **וכל אשר בה.** אפילו אילנות מחוברין אשר בה נאסרין: ה"ג וישבע יהושע **לאמר ארור האיש** וגו'. וקרא קדריש ואזיל בבכורו ייסדנה ובצעירו יציב דלתיה וכשיעמיד דלתיה ימות בנו הקטן: **לא יריחו על שם עיר אחרת.** שלא יבנה יריחו ויסב שמה על שם עיר אחרת ולא עיר אחרת על שם יריחו שאפי' בנה עיר אחרת וקראה יריחו אסור לבנותה שאפי' שם יריחו ימחה לעולם וכתיב בימיו בנה חיאל בית האלי את יריחו בימיו של אחאב ועל שעבר על האלה קרי ליה בית האלי: **את יריחו.** ולא יריחו עצמו בנה אלא עיר אחרת על שם יריחו שקראה לה יריחו ולא אתפרש הא מנלן: **באבירם בכורו יסדה.** אבירם רשע כשמת אבירם הרשע לא היה לו לחיאל ללמוד שלא לבנות את יריחו: **אבירם ושגוב מאי עבוד.** דקרי להו רשעים: **איני יודע ששגוב צעירו.** מילתא באנפי נפשיה הוא ולמדרשא ממשמע שנאמר באבירם בכורו איני יודע ששגוב צעירו אלא מה ת"ל שגוב צעירו שהיה קובר והולך מאבירם ועד שגוב שהוא צעיר מכלם: **אחאב שושבינו.** אוהבו של חיאל היה אחאב: **בי טמיא.** וי"א בי טעמא בית האבל שמטעימים אותו בדברים לנחמו ובכמה דוכתין כתיב בברא‍שית רבה טמיא בלא עיי"ן לשון אבל: **על כל תלם ותלם.** שורה וערוגה ומקום גבוה הוא: **ולא שביק מיטרא מיזל ומסגד.** שהיה הכלוך הולך וגדל מרוב הגשמים הבאין לעולם שאין מניחין לילך להשתחוות לעבודת כוכבים מתוך דרכים מלוכלכות בטיט: **מיד ויאמר אליהו חי ה' אם יהיה השנים האלה מטר וגו'.** האי קרא סמוך לקרא דחיאל בית האלי: **אקלידא דמטרא.** מפתח של מטר: **כיון דחזא.** הקב"ה דאיכא צערא בעלמא א"ל הקב"ה לאליהו לך צרפתה לגלגל הדבר שיחזיר לו מפתח של מטר כדקא מפרש ואזיל: **שלש מפתחות לא נמסרו ביד שליח.** על אוצרו של הקב"ה יש מפתחות ומסרם ליד שלוחים הממונים אבל ג' מפתחות יש לו בידו שלא מינה שליח עליהם מבראשית אלא בידו הם ולא רצה למסור שליח עליהם וקאמר הקב"ה לאליהו אותם ג' מפתחות עכבתי בידי מבראשית ולא מניתי שליח עליהם אלא אותך שעשיתי ממונה על אחת מהם ועתה תשאל מפתח שני יאמרו שנים ביד תלמיד ואחד ביד הרב: **דטרקיה לגליה.** שסתם שער שלו ואבדיה למפתחיה כך עשה אליהו נעל לשערי מטר ולבסוף אבד המפתח של גשמים שלא נפתח השער של מטר על ידו: **דכתב לך הראה אל אחאב ואתנה מטר.** ולא כתיב ותן מטר: **אבא אליהו.** חביבי וגדולי: היה

מסורת הש"ס

א) פסחי' לו: לח. מ"ש פ"ג מ"י [ב"מ נג: זבחים מט.], ב) ב"מ שם מכות כ. [עיין תוס' ב"מ נג: ד"ה לא פלוג], ג) לעיל ע"א, ד) [מ"ק ג.], ה) [נ"ל חרם היא וכל אשר בה לה'], ו) [תוספ' פי"ד], ז) [תוספתא שם], ח) [בע"י ליתא], ט) [לעיל קנ:], י) [אל אחאב], כ) [נ"ל יהיה השנים האלה טל וכו'], ל) חולין ה., מ) תענית ב., נ) [נ"ל משנה], ס) [בשחיטת חולין לא נמצא אמנם בב"מ נג: ד"ה והא אמר רבא כתב רש"י על נכון וליין במס' מכות], ע) נ"ל לא, פ) [עי' רש"י שבת לג. ד"ה לא ישמח].

ליקוטי רש"י

יקבר. דקא סבר לא אלים למיתפס פדיונו. **אלא לעולם בטהור.** בין מעשר בין לקוח ודקאמר נעייליה וניכליה. **וכגון דנפול מחיצות.** חומת ירושלים ושוב אין מעשר נאכל שם עד שיעמדו מחילות דבעינן לפני ה' תאכלנו (דברים יב) ובפדייה נמי לא דקלטוהו מחילות מלפדותו עוד משנכנס לתוכו. **מחיצה לאכול דאורייתא מחיצה לקלוט דרבנן.** מחילה שנאמרה בתורה לא הוזכרה אלא לאכול בתוכה ושאמרו במשנה מחילות קולטות אותם מלפדות עוד אם יצא דרבנן היא. **וכי גזור רבנן כו'.** דכי גזור רבנן היכא דאיתנהו וזה הוציא את המעשר לחוץ אבל כי ליתנהו לא גזור הלכך ניפרקיה [ב"מ נג:]. **והיתה העיר חרם.** הקדש כי היום שבת קדש וראוי להיות קדש שלל הנשלל בו [יהושע ו, יז]. **בבכרו ייסדנה ובצעירו.** בתחלת יסוד שיבנה בה ימות בנו הבכור ויקברנו וילך עד שימות הצעיר בגמר המלאכה היא הצבת הדלתות [שם ו, כו]. **באבירם בכרו יסדה.** כשיסד' מת בנו בכורו וקבר והלך וקבר כל בניו עד שמת האחרון בהצבת דלתות וכן הוא קללות של יהושע בבכורו ייסדנה ובצעירו יציב דלתיה (יהושע ו' כ"ו) [מ"א טז, לד]. **חי ה'.** למה סמכו כאן אלא שהלכו אליהו ואחאב לנחם את חיאל באבלו אמר אחאב לאליהו אפשר שקללת התלמיד נתקיימה וקללת משה רבינו לא נתקיימה שנאמר (דברים י"א ט"ז) וסרתם ועבדתם אלהים אחרים והשתחויתם להם וחרה אף ה' בכם ועצר את השמים והרי כל ישראל עובדין ע"ג ואין גשמים נעצרים מיד ויאמר אליהו וגו' [שם יז, א]. **ונסתרת.** מפני אחאב ואיזבל [שם יז, ג]. **ויבש הנחל.** כדי שידע צורך הגשמים ויטריח לגלות שהיה קשה בעיני הקב"ה שישראל שרוין מתים ברעב [שם יז, ז]. **צרפתה.** שם העיר [שם יז, ט]. **חלה בן האשה.** כדי שיצטרך למפתח של תחיית המתים כדאיתא בשילהי אגדתא דחלק [שם פסוק יז].

עין משפט נר מצוה

נט א מיי' פ"ז מהל' מעשר שני הלכה א ב:
ס ב מיי' שם פ"ב הל' ה סמג לאוין רסד:
סא ג מיי' שם הל' ט:
סב ד מיי' פ"ד מהל' ע"ז הלכה יג סמג עשין טו:

הגהות מהר"ב רנשבורג

א] רש"י ד"ה **אבל** מחיצות וכו' ולענין **עיר הנדחת נמי שלא יהא בשריפה.** מלת בשריפה נמחק וצ"ב בגניזה:

תורה אור השלם

א) וְאֶת כָּל שְׁלָלָהּ תִּקְבֹּץ אֶל תּוֹךְ רְחֹבָהּ וְשָׂרַפְתָּ בָאֵשׁ אֶת הָעִיר וְאֶת כָּל שְׁלָלָהּ כָּלִיל לַייָ אֱלֹהֶיךָ וְהָיְתָה תֵּל עוֹלָם לֹא תִבָּנֶה עוֹד: [דברים יג, יז]

ב) לֹא תַעֲשׂוּן כֵּן לַייָ אֱלֹהֵיכֶם: [דברים יב, ד]

ג) וְהָיְתָה הָעִיר חֵרֶם הִיא וְכָל אֲשֶׁר בָּהּ לַייָ רַק רָחָב הַזּוֹנָה תִּחְיֶה הִיא וְכָל אֲשֶׁר אִתָּהּ בַּבַּיִת כִּי הֶחְבְּאַתָה אֶת הַמַּלְאָכִים אֲשֶׁר שָׁלָחְנוּ: וַיַּשְׁבַּע יְהוֹשֻׁעַ בָּעֵת הַהִיא לֵאמֹר אָרוּר הָאִישׁ לִפְנֵי יְיָ אֲשֶׁר יָקוּם וּבָנָה אֶת הָעִיר הַזֹּאת אֶת יְרִיחוֹ בִּבְכֹרוֹ יְיַסְּדֶנָּה וּבִצְעִירוֹ יַצִּיב דְּלָתֶיהָ: [יהושע ו, יז,כו]

ד) בְּיָמָיו בָּנָה חִיאֵל בֵּית הָאֱלִי אֶת יְרִיחֹה בַּאֲבִירָם בְּכֹרוֹ יִסְּדָהּ וּבִשְׂגוּב צְעִירוֹ הִצִּיב דְּלָתֶיהָ כִּדְבַר יְיָ אֲשֶׁר דִּבֶּר בְּיַד יְהוֹשֻׁעַ בִּן נוּן: [מלכים א' טז, לד]

ה) הִשָּׁמְרוּ לָכֶם פֶּן יִפְתֶּה לְבַבְכֶם וְסַרְתֶּם וַעֲבַדְתֶּם אֱלֹהִים אֲחֵרִים וְהִשְׁתַּחֲוִיתֶם לָהֶם: [דברים יא, טז]

ו) וְחָרָה אַף יְיָ בָּכֶם וְעָצַר אֶת הַשָּׁמַיִם וְלֹא יִהְיֶה מָטָר וְהָאֲדָמָה לֹא תִתֵּן אֶת יְבוּלָהּ וַאֲבַדְתֶּם מְהֵרָה מֵעַל הָאָרֶץ הַטֹּבָה אֲשֶׁר יְיָ נֹתֵן לָכֶם: [דברים יא, יז]

ז) וַיֹּאמֶר אֵלִיָּהוּ הַתִּשְׁבִּי מִתֹּשָׁבֵי גִלְעָד אֶל אַחְאָב חַי יְיָ אֱלֹהֵי יִשְׂרָאֵל אֲשֶׁר עָמַדְתִּי לְפָנָיו אִם יִהְיֶה הַשָּׁנִים הָאֵלֶּה טַל וּמָטָר כִּי אִם לְפִי דְבָרִי: [מלכים א' יז, א]

ח) וַיְהִי דְבַר יְיָ אֵלָיו לֵאמֹר: לֵךְ מִזֶּה וּפָנִיתָ לְּךָ קֵדְמָה וְנִסְתַּרְתָּ בְּנַחַל כְּרִית אֲשֶׁר עַל פְּנֵי הַיַּרְדֵּן: [מלכים א' יז, ב-ג]

ט) וְהָעֹרְבִים מְבִיאִים לוֹ לֶחֶם וּבָשָׂר בַּבֹּקֶר וְלֶחֶם וּבָשָׂר בָּעָרֶב וּמִן הַנַּחַל יִשְׁתֶּה: [מלכים א' יז, ו]

י) וַיְהִי מִקֵּץ יָמִים וַיִּיבַשׁ הַנַּחַל כִּי לֹא הָיָה גֶשֶׁם בָּאָרֶץ: [מלכים א' יז, ז]

כ) וַיְהִי דְבַר יְיָ אֵלָיו לֵאמֹר: קוּם לֵךְ צָרְפַתָה אֲשֶׁר לְצִידוֹן וְיָשַׁבְתָּ שָׁם הִנֵּה צִוִּיתִי שָׁם אִשָּׁה אַלְמָנָה לְכַלְכְּלֶךָ: [מלכים א' יז, ח-ט] ל) וַיְהִי אַחַר הַדְּבָרִים הָאֵלֶּה חָלָה בֶּן הָאִשָּׁה בַּעֲלַת הַבָּיִת וַיְהִי חָלְיוֹ חָזָק מְאֹד עַד אֲשֶׁר לֹא נוֹתְרָה בּוֹ נְשָׁמָה: [מלכים א' יז, יז] מ) וַיְהִי יָמִים רַבִּים וּדְבַר יְיָ הָיָה אֶל אֵלִיָּהוּ בַּשָּׁנָה הַשְּׁלִישִׁית לֵאמֹר לֵךְ הֵרָאֵה אֶל אַחְאָב וְאֶתְּנָה מָטָר עַל פְּנֵי הָאֲדָמָה: [מלכים א' יח, א]

קפדן הוה רגיל למיתי גביה איכסי' מיניה תלתא יומי ולא אתא כי אתא א"ל אמאי לא אתא מר א"ל קפדן קרית לי א"ל הא דקמן דקא קפיד מר: (א) ולא ידבק בידך מאומה מן החרם כל זמן שרשעים בעולם חרון אף בעולם וכו': מאן רשעים אמר רב יוסף גנבי ת"ר (א) רשע בא לעולם חרון בא לעולם שנא' (ב) בבא רשע בא גם בוז ועם קלון חרפה רשע אבד מן העולם טובה באה לעולם שנא' (ג) ובאבוד רשעים רנה צדיק נפטר מן העולם רעה באה לעולם שנאמר (ד) הצדיק אבד ואין איש שם על לב ואנשי חסד נאספים באין מבין כי מפני הרעה נאסף הצדיק צדיק בא לעולם טובה באה לעולם שנאמר (ה) זה ינחמנו ממעשינו ומעצבון ידינו:

הדרן עלך כל ישראל יש להם חלק וסליקא לה מסכת סנהדרין

היה קפדן. שכעס על אחאב ואמר חי ה' אם יהיה השנים האלה טל ומטר: איכסי' מיניה. שהיה רגיל למיתי לבי מדרשו כל יומא ולא אתא בתלתא יומי: א"ל. ר' יוסי: הא דקמא דקא קפיד מר. הרי על דבר זה שאמרתי עליך (ב) קפיד שלא באת אלי ג' ימים מקפדנות שקלפת עלי: מפני הרעה. קודם שתבא הרעה הצדיק נאסף מכלל דכיון שמת הרעה באה: אבל צדיק בא לעולם פסקה הרעה שנאמר זה ינחמנו:

הדרן עלך כל ישראל וסליקא לה מסכת סנהדרין

ולא ידבק בידך מאומה מן החרם. למען ישוב ה' מחרון אפו שכל זמן שעבודה זרה בעולם חרון אף בעולם [דברים יג, יח]. הצדיק אבד. כגון יאשיהו. ואין איש שם על לב. למה נסתלק. באין מבין. אין בנותרים מבין מה ראה הקב"ה לסלקו. כי מפני הרעה. העתידה לבא אל הדור נאסף הצדיק [ישעיהו נז, א]. זה ינחמנו. ינח ממנו את עצבון ידינו עד שלא בא נח לא היה להם כלי מחרישה והוא הכין להם והיתה הארץ מוציאה קוצים ודרדרים כשזורעים חטים מקללתו של אדם הראשון ובימי נח נחה וזהו ינחמנו ינח ממנו [בראשית ה, כט].

(א) [תוס' סוטה פ"ו], (ב) ברש"י שבע"י אתה מקפיד.

תורה אור השלם

א) וְלֹא יִדְבַּק בְּיָדְךָ מְאוּמָה מִן הַחֵרֶם לְמַעַן יָשׁוּב יְיָ מֵחֲרוֹן אַפּוֹ וְנָתַן לְךָ רַחֲמִים וְרִחַמְךָ וְהִרְבֶּךָ כַּאֲשֶׁר נִשְׁבַּע לַאֲבֹתֶיךָ: [דברים יג, יח]

ב) בְּבוֹא רָשָׁע בָּא גַם בּוּז וְעִם קָלוֹן חֶרְפָּה: [משלי יח, ג]

ג) בְּטוּב צַדִּיקִים תַּעֲלֹץ קִרְיָה וּבַאֲבֹד רְשָׁעִים רִנָּה: [משלי יא, י]

ד) הַצַּדִּיק אָבָד וְאֵין אִישׁ שָׂם עַל לֵב וְאַנְשֵׁי חֶסֶד נֶאֱסָפִים בְּאֵין מֵבִין כִּי מִפְּנֵי הָרָעָה נֶאֱסַף הַצַּדִּיק: [ישעיה נז, א]

ה) וַיִּקְרָא אֶת שְׁמוֹ נֹחַ לֵאמֹר זֶה יְנַחֲמֵנוּ מִמַּעֲשֵׂנוּ וּמֵעִצְּבוֹן יָדֵינוּ מִן הָאֲדָמָה אֲשֶׁר אֵרְרָהּ יְיָ: [בראשית ה, כט]

קַפְּדָן – was a *kapdan.*[1] הֲוָה רָגִיל לְמֵיתֵי גַּבֵּיה – Now **[Elijah] used to visit [R' Yose]** every day when the latter was engaged in Torah study,[2] אִיכַּסֵּי מִינֵּיה תְּלָתָא יוֹמֵי וְלָא אֲתָא – but after R' Yose spoke of him in this manner, **[Elijah] concealed himself from him for three days and did not come.**[3] כִּי אֲתָא – **When he came** finally, אֲמַר לֵיהּ – **[R' Yose] said to him:** אַמַּאי לֹא אֲתָא מָר – **Why did the master not come** these last three days? אֲמַר לֵיהּ – **[Elijah] said to [R' Yose]:** קַפְּדָן קָרֵית לִי – **You referred to me as a *kapdan!*** Why should I come to you if you insult me?! אֲמַר לֵיהּ – **[R' Yose] replied:** הָא דְּקָמָן דְּקָא קָפֵיד מָר – **But for this very incident the master took offense!**[4]

The Gemara discusses the last part of our Mishnah, which reads:

,,וְלֹא־יִדְבַּק בְּיָדְךָ מְאוּמָה מִן־הַחֵרֶם" כָּל זְמַן שֶׁרְשָׁעִים בָּעוֹלָם חֲרוֹן אַף בָּעוֹלָם וכו' – *NOTHING OF THE BANNED [PROPERTY] SHALL ADHERE TO YOUR HAND [so that Hashem will turn back from His burning wrath . . .].* AS LONG AS THE WICKED ARE IN THE WORLD, God's ANGER IS IN THE WORLD **etc.**

The Gemara asks:

מַאן רְשָׁעִים – **Who are the wicked** to whom the Mishnah refers?[5]

The Gemara answers:

אָמַר רַב יוֹסֵף – **Rav Yosef said:** גַּנָּבֵי – **Thieves.**[6]

The Gemara cites a Baraisa:

תָּנוּ רַבָּנָן – **The Rabbis taught in a Baraisa:** רָשָׁע בָּא לָעוֹלָם – When A WICKED PERSON COMES TO THE WORLD, חָרוֹן בָּא לָעוֹלָם – Divine ANGER COMES TO THE WORLD, שֶׁנֶּאֱמַר ,,בְּבוֹא־רָשָׁע בָּא גַם־בּוּז וְעִם־קָלוֹן חֶרְפָּה" – AS IT IS STATED: *WITH THE COMING OF A WICKED PERSON COMES DERISION TOO; AND WITH SHAMEFULNESS, DISGRACE.*[7] רָשָׁע אָבַד מִן הָעוֹלָם – WHEN A WICKED PERSON IS LOST FROM THE WORLD, i.e. when he dies, טוֹבָה בָּאָה לָעוֹלָם – GOOD FORTUNE COMES TO THE WORLD, שֶׁנֶּאֱמַר ,,וּבַאֲבֹד רְשָׁעִים רִנָּה" – AS IT IS STATED: *WHEN THE WICKED PERISH THERE IS JOY.*[8] צַדִּיק נִפְטַר מִן הָעוֹלָם – On the other hand, WHEN A RIGHTEOUS PERSON DEPARTS FROM THE WORLD, רָעָה בָּאָה לָעוֹלָם – MISFORTUNE COMES TO THE WORLD, שֶׁנֶּאֱמַר ,,הַצַּדִּיק אָבָד וְאֵין אִישׁ שָׂם עַל־לֵב – AS IT IS STATED: *THE RIGHTEOUS MAN HAS PERISHED AND NO MAN TAKES TO HEART,* וְאַנְשֵׁי־חֶסֶד נֶאֱסָפִים בְּאֵין מֵבִין – *AND THE MEN OF KINDNESS ARE GATHERED IN WITHOUT ANYONE UNDERSTANDING* כִּי־מִפְּנֵי הָרָעָה נֶאֱסַף הַצַּדִּיק" – *THAT IT IS BECAUSE OF THE EVIL THAT THE RIGHTEOUS MAN IS TAKEN.*[9] צַדִּיק בָּא לָעוֹלָם – WHEN A RIGHTEOUS PERSON COMES TO THE WORLD,

NOTES

1. [A *kapdan* is a person who is easily offended and disinclined to let affronts or provocations pass. In Elijah this took the form of righteous indignation.] When Ahab contemptuously remarked that he was able to worship idols with impunity, Elijah was so outraged by his blasphemy that he immediately caused a terrible drought to descend upon the Land of Israel. This harsh reaction to Ahab's words indicates Elijah's strictness with those who give offense (*Rashi*). Had Elijah not possessed the trait of righteous indignation, he would have tried to reason with Ahab and move him to repentance rather than hurl a curse upon his head and his realm (*Maharal*). [See also *Rambam* in *Shemonah Perakim* §7, who explains that it was for this reason that God took Elijah from the world shortly afterwards. Had Elijah remained a prophet in Israel, he would have destroyed the people with his righteous indignation.]

2. Elijah would teach R' Yose Torah (*Yad Ramah*).

3. *Bereishis Rabbah* (91:9) states that when the righteous are made to suffer deprivation, it is only for three days [as seen here; see *Margaliyos HaYam.*]

4. *Rashi. Toras Chaim* [also cited in *Eitz Yosef*] explains that Elijah took umbrage at being called irascible because he felt that it was an unjustified criticism. [It is proper for a Torah sage to be zealous on behalf of God's honor.] Ahab's blasphemy called for a sharp response, not a weak and mild reaction, and Elijah was thus justified in acting as he did. R' Yose responded that Elijah's reaction to R' Yose's remark was not a defense of God's honor but of Elijah's, thus bearing out R' Yose's assessment.

Maharal understands R' Yose's reply to have been defensive rather than pointed. R' Yose was excusing himself for saying what he said by pointing out that Scripture states that Elijah did indeed react to Ahab's blasphemy with indignation. [According to *Maharal,* R' Yose did not in his response make any reference to Elijah's staying away for three days, but only to *Scripture's* account of Elijah's action. I.e. Scripture states openly that Elijah reacted to Ahab with anger.]

[What is the point of R' Yose's pointed assessment of Elijah? Perhaps it is meant to teach us not to wonder over much at our inability to perceive Divine justice in this world. When Ahab pointed to this phenomenon as evidence that Divine retribution is not to be expected, Elijah beseeched the Almighty to allow him to withhold the rains as promised. Surely, Ahab's grievous blasphemy deserved no less. Yet in the aftermath of the terrible suffering that ensued, and in the hindsight of history, Elijah's reaction appeared overly strict even to the great sage R' Yose. The swift punishment of even grievous offenses looks in retrospect like a lack of patience with human frailty. We may think we wish to see God's justice, but its consequences are often terrible, and in their aftermath we may discover that we really prefer His forbearance.]

5. It cannot refer to the idolaters of the *ir hanidachas,* for then the Mishnah, and indeed the verse itself, should have made this point in connection with the execution of the people rather than in connection with the destruction of their property. Thus, it is evident that the verse must be speaking of yet another class of wrongdoers (*Yad Ramah*).

6. This classification includes both those who steal property from others as well as those who take from the condemned property of the *ir hanidachas*. This may be seen from the fact that Achan's pilferage of the banned property of Jericho was condemned by God as "theft" (*Yad Ramah*, from *Joshua* 7:11; see also *Maharsha*, *Maharal,* and *Anaf Yosef*). [Thus, it is fitting that Scripture should allude to God's wrath over thievery in general in connection with the unauthorized usage of the condemned property of the *ir hanidachas*.]

7. *Proverbs* 18:3. [That is, the advent of the wicked brings derision and disgrace in their wake quite apart from any evil they may perpetrate.] *Rashash* explains that the word קָלוֹן, *shamefulness*, can also be understood as a cognate of the verb קלה, *burning.* The word חָרוֹן also denotes burning anger. Thus, the verse juxtaposes the coming of the wicked to burning anger, indicating that the arrival of the wicked causes God's anger to burn.

Our verse is also cited in *Bereishis Rabbah* 63:14, where the word חֶרְפָּה is understood as a reference to hunger. Hunger (famine) is a most visible sign of Divine anger. Thus, our verse indicates that the coming of the wicked leads to famine and similar displays of Divine anger.

[The expression, "When a wicked person comes into the world," would seem to refer to his birth. This is difficult to accept, however, since no person is born wicked; he becomes wicked only by his own choice. Moreover, it is inconceivable that God would punish anyone before he actually did anything wrong. Possibly, the phrase "comes into the world" is used here in the sense of emerging, i.e. when a wicked person manifests himself in the world, Divine wrath begins to flare. See *Anaf Yosef* who discusses this problem and offers another solution. See also *Ben Yehoyada*.]

8. *Proverbs* 11:10.

9. *Isaiah* 57:1. That is, it is because of the evil times that are about to come that the righteous are gathered in by God, to spare them the suffering that the world will soon endure (*Rashi* to *Taanis* 11a ד"ה הצדיק). Thus, the verse states that the death of a righteous person is a harbinger of misfortune. [See *Ahavas Tziyon* by the author of the *Noda BiYehudah* for a discussion of this phenomenon.]

קפדן הוה רגיל למיתי גביה איכסי' מיניה תלתא יומי ולא אתא כי אתא א"ל אמאי לא אתא מר א"ל קפדן קרית לי א"ל הא דקמן דקא קפיד מר: א) ולא ידבק בידך מאומה מן החרם כל זמן שרשעים בעולם חרון אף בעולם וכו': מאן רשעים אמר רב יוסף גנבי ת"ר [א] רשע בא לעולם חרון בא לעולם שנא' ב) בבא רשע בא גם בוז ועם קלון חרפה רשע אבד מן העולם טובה באה לעולם שנא' ג) ובאבוד רשעים רנה צדיק נפטר מן העולם רעה באה לעולם שנאמר ד) הצדיק אבד ואין איש שם על לב ואנשי חסד נאספים באין מבין כי מפני הרעה נאסף הצדיק צדיק בא לעולם טובה באה לעולם שנאמר ה) זה ינחמנו ממעשינו ומעצבון ידינו:

הדרן עלך כל ישראל יש להם חלק וסליקא לה מסכת סנהדרין

היה קפדן. שכעס על אחאב ואמר חי ה' אם יהיה השנים האלה טל ומטר: **איכסי' מיניה.** שהיה רגיל למיתי לבי מדרשו כל יומא ולא אתא בתלתא יומי: **א"ל.** ר' יוסי: **הא דקמא דקא קפיד מר.** הרי על דבר זה שאמרתי עליך [ב] קפיד שלא באת אלי ג' ימים מקפדנות שקלפת עלי: **מפני הרעה.** קודם שתבא הרעה הצדיק נאסף מכלל דכיון שמת הרעה באה: אבל צדיק בא לעולם פסקה הרעה שנאמר זה ינחמנו:

הדרן עלך כל ישראל וסליקא לה מסכת סנהדרין

ולא ידבק בידך מאומה מן החרם. למען ישוב ה' מחרון אפו שכל זמן שעבודה זרה בעולם חרון אף בעולם [דברים יג, יח]. **הצדיק אבד.** כגון יאשיהו. **ואין איש שם על לב.** למה נסתלק. **באין מבין.** אין בנותרים מבין מה ראה הקב"ה לסלקו. **כי מפני הרעה.** העתידה לבא אל הדור נאסף הצדיק [ישעיהו נז, א]. **זה ינחמנו.** ינח ממנו את עצבון ידינו עד שלא בא נח לא היה להם כלי מחרישה והוא הכין להם והיתה הארץ מוציאה קוצים ודרדרים כשזורעים חטים מקללתו של אדם הראשון ובימי נח נחה וזהו ינחמנו ינח ממנו [בראשית ה, כט].

[א] [תוס' סוטה פ"ו], [ב] ברש"י שבע"י אתה מקפיד.

תורה אור השלם

א) וְלֹא יִדְבַּק בְּיָדְךָ מְאוּמָה מִן הַחֵרֶם לְמַעַן יָשׁוּב יְיָ מֵחֲרוֹן אַפּוֹ וְנָתַן לְךָ רַחֲמִים וְרִחַמְךָ וְהִרְבֶּךָ כַּאֲשֶׁר נִשְׁבַּע לַאֲבֹתֶיךָ: [דברים יג, יח]

ב) בְּבוֹא רָשָׁע בָּא גַם בּוּז וְעִם קָלוֹן חֶרְפָּה: [משלי יח, ג]

ג) בְּטוּב צַדִּיקִים תַּעֲלֹץ קִרְיָה וּבַאֲבֹד רְשָׁעִים רִנָּה: [משלי יא, י]

ד) הַצַּדִּיק אָבָד וְאֵין אִישׁ שָׂם עַל לֵב וְאַנְשֵׁי חֶסֶד נֶאֱסָפִים בְּאֵין מֵבִין כִּי מִפְּנֵי הָרָעָה נֶאֱסַף הַצַּדִּיק: [ישעיה נז, א]

ה) וַיִּקְרָא אֶת שְׁמוֹ נֹחַ לֵאמֹר זֶה יְנַחֲמֵנוּ מִמַּעֲשֵׂנוּ וּמֵעִצְּבוֹן יָדֵינוּ מִן הָאֲדָמָה אֲשֶׁר אֵרְרָהּ יְיָ: [בראשית ה, כט]

טוֹבָה בָּאָה לָעוֹלָם – GOOD FORTUNE COMES TO THE WORLD, שֶׁנֶּאֱמַר ,,זֶה יְנַחֲמֵנוּ מִמַּעֲשֵׂנוּ וּמֵעִצְּבוֹן יָדֵינוּ" – AS IT IS STATED: *And he called his name Noah, saying:* ***THIS ONE WILL BRING US RELIEF FROM OUR WORK AND FROM THE TOIL OF OUR HANDS.***[10]

הדרן עלך כל ישראל יש להם חלק

**WE SHALL RETURN TO YOU,
KOL YISRAEL YESH LAHEM CHEILEK**

וסליקא לה מסכת סנהדרין

AND TRACTATE SANHEDRIN IS CONCLUDED

NOTES

10. *Genesis* 5:29. Noah grew up to be the most righteous person of his generation. His invention of the plow greatly eased the burden of farming, and in his days the curse of the earth decreed to Adam was lifted (*Rashi* to this verse). Moreover, through him the human race survived the Flood brought on by the sins of mankind (*Maharsha*). Clearly, the coming of this righteous man brought blessing to the world.

Maharsha explains that the chapter concludes with this statement because the chapter is devoted to the Messianic times and the World to Come, where the promise of Divine reward and punishment will be fulfilled. Should the length of our exile cause anyone to lose hope in the ultimate Redemption, we are directed by the prophet to look to God's oath to Noah never again to devastate the entire world, and take heart from its fulfillment that God's promise regarding the ultimate Redemption will also eventually come to pass. As the prophet says (*Isaiah* 54:9-10): *For like the waters of Noah shall this be to Me: For as I have sworn never again to pass the waters of Noah over the earth, so have I sworn not to be wrathful with you or rebuke you. For the mountains may move and the hills may falter, but My kindness shall never be removed from you and My covenant of peace shall not falter, says the One Who shows you mercy.*

Hadran – הַדְרָן

Upon the סִיּוּם, *completion*, of the study of an entire tractate, a festive meal (which has the status of a *seudas mitzvah*) should be eaten – preferably with a *minyan* in attendance. The following prayers of thanksgiving are recited by those who have completed the learning. [The words in brackets are inserted according to some customs.]

The first paragraph is recited three times.

הַדְרָן עֲלָךְ מַסֶּכֶת סַנְהֶדְרִין וְהַדְרָךְ עֲלָן. דַּעְתָּן עֲלָךְ מַסֶּכֶת סַנְהֶדְרִין וְדַעְתָּךְ עֲלָן. לָא נִתְנְשֵׁי מִנָּךְ מַסֶּכֶת סַנְהֶדְרִין וְלָא תִתְנְשֵׁי מִנָּן – לָא בְּעָלְמָא הָדֵין וְלָא בְּעָלְמָא דְּאָתֵי.

הַדְרָן *We shall return*[1] *to you, Tractate Sanhedrin, and you shall return to us. Our thoughts are on you, Tractate Sanhedrin, and your thoughts are on us. We will not forget you, Tractate Sanhedrin, and you will not forget us – neither in This World, nor in the World to Come.*

יְהִי רָצוֹן מִלְּפָנֶיךָ יי אֱלֹהֵינוּ וֵאלֹהֵי אֲבוֹתֵינוּ, שֶׁתְּהֵא תוֹרָתְךָ אֻמָּנוּתֵנוּ בָּעוֹלָם הַזֶּה וּתְהֵא עִמָּנוּ לָעוֹלָם הַבָּא. חֲנִינָא בַּר פָּפָּא, רָמִי בַּר פָּפָּא, נַחְמָן בַּר פָּפָּא, אַחָאִי בַּר פָּפָּא, אַבָּא מָרִי בַּר פָּפָּא, רַפְרָם בַּר פָּפָּא, רָכִישׁ בַּר פָּפָּא, סוּרְחָב בַּר פָּפָּא, אַדָּא בַּר פָּפָּא, דָּרוּ בַּר פָּפָּא.

יְהִי רָצוֹן *May it be Your will, HASHEM, our God, and the God of our forefathers, that Your Torah be our preoccupation in This World, and may it remain with us in the World to Come. Chanina bar Pappa,*[2] *Rami bar Pappa, Nachman bar Pappa, Achai bar Pappa, Abba Mari bar Pappa, Rafram bar Pappa, Rachish bar Pappa, Surchav bar Pappa, Adda bar Pappa, Daru bar Pappa.*

הַעֲרֶב נָא יי אֱלֹהֵינוּ אֶת דִּבְרֵי תוֹרָתְךָ בְּפִינוּ וּבְפִיפִיּוֹת עַמְּךָ בֵּית יִשְׂרָאֵל. וְנִהְיֶה [כֻּלָּנוּ,] אֲנַחְנוּ וְצֶאֱצָאֵינוּ [וְצֶאֱצָאֵי צֶאֱצָאֵינוּ] וְצֶאֱצָאֵי עַמְּךָ בֵּית יִשְׂרָאֵל, כֻּלָּנוּ יוֹדְעֵי שְׁמֶךָ וְלוֹמְדֵי תוֹרָתֶךָ [לִשְׁמָהּ]. מֵאֹיְבַי תְּחַכְּמֵנִי מִצְוֹתֶךָ, כִּי לְעוֹלָם הִיא לִי. יְהִי לִבִּי תָמִים בְּחֻקֶּיךָ, לְמַעַן לֹא אֵבוֹשׁ. לְעוֹלָם לֹא אֶשְׁכַּח פִּקּוּדֶיךָ, כִּי בָם חִיִּיתָנִי. בָּרוּךְ אַתָּה יי, לַמְּדֵנִי חֻקֶּיךָ. אָמֵן אָמֵן אָמֵן, סֶלָה וָעֶד.

הַעֲרֶב נָא *Please, HASHEM, our God, sweeten the words of Your Torah in our mouth and in the mouths of Your people, the House of Israel, and may [we all –] we, our offspring, [the offspring of our offspring,] and the offspring of Your people, the House of Israel, all of us – know Your Name and study Your Torah. Your commandment makes me wiser than my enemies, for it is forever with me.*[3] *May my heart be perfect in Your statutes, so that I not be shamed.*[4] *I will never forget Your precepts, for through them You have preserved me.*[5] *Blessed are You, HASHEM, teach me Your statutes.*[6] *Amen. Amen. Amen. Selah! Forever!*

מוֹדִים אֲנַחְנוּ לְפָנֶיךָ יי אֱלֹהֵינוּ וֵאלֹהֵי אֲבוֹתֵינוּ, שֶׁשַּׂמְתָּ חֶלְקֵנוּ מִיּוֹשְׁבֵי בֵּית הַמִּדְרָשׁ, וְלֹא שַׂמְתָּ חֶלְקֵנוּ מִיּוֹשְׁבֵי קְרָנוֹת. שֶׁאָנוּ מַשְׁכִּימִים וְהֵם מַשְׁכִּימִים, אָנוּ מַשְׁכִּימִים לְדִבְרֵי תוֹרָה, וְהֵם מַשְׁכִּימִים לִדְבָרִים בְּטֵלִים. אָנוּ עֲמֵלִים וְהֵם עֲמֵלִים, אָנוּ עֲמֵלִים וּמְקַבְּלִים שָׂכָר, וְהֵם עֲמֵלִים וְאֵינָם מְקַבְּלִים שָׂכָר. אָנוּ רָצִים וְהֵם רָצִים, אָנוּ רָצִים לְחַיֵּי הָעוֹלָם הַבָּא, וְהֵם רָצִים לִבְאֵר שַׁחַת, שֶׁנֶּאֱמַר: וְאַתָּה אֱלֹהִים, תּוֹרִדֵם לִבְאֵר שַׁחַת, אַנְשֵׁי דָמִים וּמִרְמָה לֹא יֶחֱצוּ יְמֵיהֶם, וַאֲנִי אֶבְטַח בָּךְ.

מוֹדִים *We express gratitude before You, HASHEM, our God, and the God of our forefathers, that You have established our portion with those who dwell in the study hall, and have not established our portion with idlers. For we arise early and they arise early; we arise early for the words of Torah, while they arise early for idle words. We toil and they toil; we toil and receive reward, while they toil and do not receive reward. We run and they run; we run to the life of the World to Come, while they run to the well of destruction, as it is said: But You, O God, You will lower them into the well of destruction, men of bloodshed and deceit shall not live out half their days; and I will trust in You.*[7]

---

1. **הַדְרָן עֲלָךְ** – *We shall return to you* . . . We express the hope that we will review constantly what we have learned and that, in the merit of our desire to learn, the Torah itself will long to return to us, as it were. Thus, the word is derived from הָדַר, *to return*. This is in the spirit of the Talmudic dictum that תּוֹרָה מְחַזֶּרֶת עַל אַכְסַנְיָא שֶׁלָּהּ, *the Torah returns to its inn*, i.e., the place or people where it was made welcome (*Bava Metzia* 88a).

According to *Sefer HaChaim*, the term is derived from the word הָדָר, *glory*. Thus, whatever glory we have attained is due to the Torah, and we pray that the Torah shed its glory upon us.

2. **חֲנִינָא בַּר פָּפָּא** – *Chanina bar Pappa* . . . In the simple sense, Rav Pappa was a very wealthy man who, whenever he completed a tractate, used to make great celebrations to which he invited his ten sons, as well as many others. As a result, he brought glory to the Torah, which was reflected in the scholarly attainments of his sons. The nation, therefore, honors Rav Pappa and his family by mentioning them at every *siyum*. Furthermore, esoterically, Rav Pappa symbolizes Moses and the names of his sons symbolize the Ten Commandments (*Teshuvos HaRema; Yam Shel Shelomo, Bava Kamma,* end of ch. 7).

3. *Psalms* 119:98. 4. 119:80. 5. 119:93. 6. 119:12. 7. 55:24.

יְהִי רָצוֹן לְפָנֶיךָ יי אֱלֹהַי, כְּשֵׁם שֶׁעֲזַרְתַּנִי לְסַיֵּים מַסֶּכֶת סַנְהֶדְרִין כֵּן תַּעַזְרֵנִי לְהַתְחִיל מַסֶּכְתּוֹת וּסְפָרִים אֲחֵרִים וּלְסַיְּמָם, לִלְמוֹד וּלְלַמֵּד לִשְׁמוֹר וְלַעֲשׂוֹת וּלְקַיֵּם אֶת כָּל דִּבְרֵי תַלְמוּד תּוֹרָתֶךָ בְּאַהֲבָה. וּזְכוּת כָּל הַתַּנָּאִים וַאֲמוֹרָאִים וְתַלְמִידֵי חֲכָמִים יַעֲמוֹד לִי וּלְזַרְעִי, שֶׁלֹּא תָמוּשׁ הַתּוֹרָה מִפִּי וּמִפִּי זַרְעִי וְזֶרַע זַרְעִי עַד עוֹלָם. וְתִתְקַיֵּם בִּי: בְּהִתְהַלֶּכְךָ תַּנְחֶה אֹתָךְ, בְּשָׁכְבְּךָ תִּשְׁמֹר עָלֶיךָ, וַהֲקִיצוֹתָ הִיא תְשִׂיחֶךָ. כִּי בִי יִרְבּוּ יָמֶיךָ, וְיוֹסִיפוּ לְךָ שְׁנוֹת חַיִּים. אֹרֶךְ יָמִים בִּימִינָהּ, בִּשְׂמֹאלָהּ עֹשֶׁר וְכָבוֹד. יי עֹז לְעַמּוֹ יִתֵּן, יי יְבָרֵךְ אֶת עַמּוֹ בַשָּׁלוֹם.

יְהִי רָצוֹן *May it be Your will,* H*ASHEM*, *my God, that just as You have helped me complete Tractate Sanhedrin, so may You help me to begin other tractates and books, and to complete them; to learn and to teach, to safeguard and to perform, and to fulfill all the words of Your Torah's teachings with love. May the merit of all the Tannaim, Amoraim, and Torah scholars stand by me and my children, that the Torah shall not depart from my mouth and from the mouth of my children and my children's children forever. May there be fulfilled for me the verse: When you walk, it (i.e., the Torah) will guide you; when you lie down, it will watch over you; and when you wake up, it will converse with you.*[8] *For because of me (i.e., the Torah), your days will increase, and years of life will be added to you.*[9] *Long days are in its right hand, and in its left hand are wealth and honor.*[10] H*ASHEM will give might to His people,* H*ASHEM will bless His people with peace.*[11]

If a *minyan* is present, the following version of the Rabbis' *Kaddish* is recited by one or more of those present. It may be recited even by one whose parents are still living.

יִתְגַּדַּל וְיִתְקַדַּשׁ שְׁמֵהּ רַבָּא. (Cong.– אָמֵן.) בְּעָלְמָא דִּי הוּא עָתִיד לְאִתְחַדָּתָא, וּלְאַחֲיָאָה מֵתַיָּא, וּלְאַסָּקָא יָתְהוֹן לְחַיֵּי עָלְמָא, וּלְמִבְנֵא קַרְתָּא דִירוּשְׁלֵם, וּלְשַׁכְלָלָא הֵיכְלֵהּ בְּגַוַּהּ, וּלְמֶעְקַר פָּלְחָנָא נֻכְרָאָה מִן אַרְעָא, וְלַאֲתָבָא פָּלְחָנָא דִי שְׁמַיָּא לְאַתְרֵהּ, וְיַמְלִיךְ קֻדְשָׁא בְּרִיךְ הוּא בְּמַלְכוּתֵהּ וִיקָרֵהּ, [וְיַצְמַח פֻּרְקָנֵהּ וִיקָרֵב מְשִׁיחֵהּ (Cong.– אָמֵן)] בְּחַיֵּיכוֹן וּבְיוֹמֵיכוֹן וּבְחַיֵּי דְכָל בֵּית יִשְׂרָאֵל, בַּעֲגָלָא וּבִזְמַן קָרִיב. וְאִמְרוּ: אָמֵן.

(Cong.– אָמֵן. יְהֵא שְׁמֵהּ רַבָּא מְבָרַךְ לְעָלַם וּלְעָלְמֵי עָלְמַיָּא.)

יְהֵא שְׁמֵהּ רַבָּא מְבָרַךְ לְעָלַם וּלְעָלְמֵי עָלְמַיָּא.

יִתְבָּרַךְ וְיִשְׁתַּבַּח וְיִתְפָּאַר וְיִתְרוֹמַם וְיִתְנַשֵּׂא וְיִתְהַדָּר וְיִתְעַלֶּה וְיִתְהַלָּל שְׁמֵהּ דְּקֻדְשָׁא בְּרִיךְ הוּא (Cong.– בְּרִיךְ הוּא) °לְעֵלָּא מִן כָּל (From Rosh Hashanah to Yom Kippur substitute– °לְעֵלָּא וּלְעֵלָּא מִכָּל) בִּרְכָתָא וְשִׁירָתָא תֻּשְׁבְּחָתָא וְנֶחֱמָתָא, דַּאֲמִירָן בְּעָלְמָא. וְאִמְרוּ: אָמֵן. (Cong.– אָמֵן.)

עַל יִשְׂרָאֵל וְעַל רַבָּנָן, וְעַל תַּלְמִידֵיהוֹן וְעַל כָּל תַּלְמִידֵי תַלְמִידֵיהוֹן, וְעַל כָּל מָאן דְּעָסְקִין בְּאוֹרַיְתָא, דִּי בְאַתְרָא הָדֵין וְדִי בְכָל אֲתַר וַאֲתַר. יְהֵא לְהוֹן וּלְכוֹן שְׁלָמָא רַבָּא, חִנָּא וְחִסְדָּא וְרַחֲמִין, וְחַיִּין אֲרִיכִין, וּמְזוֹנֵי רְוִיחֵי, וּפֻרְקָנָא מִן קֳדָם אֲבוּהוֹן דִּי בִשְׁמַיָּא [וְאַרְעָא]. וְאִמְרוּ: אָמֵן. (Cong.– אָמֵן.)

יְהֵא שְׁלָמָא רַבָּא מִן שְׁמַיָּא, וְחַיִּים [טוֹבִים] עָלֵינוּ וְעַל כָּל יִשְׂרָאֵל. וְאִמְרוּ: אָמֵן. (Cong.– אָמֵן.)

Take three steps back. Bow left and say ... עֹשֶׂה; bow right and say ... הוּא; bow forward and say וְעַל כָּל ... אָמֵן. Remain standing in place for a few moments, then take three steps forward.

עֹשֶׂה שָׁלוֹם בִּמְרוֹמָיו, הוּא בְּרַחֲמָיו יַעֲשֶׂה שָׁלוֹם עָלֵינוּ, וְעַל כָּל יִשְׂרָאֵל. וְאִמְרוּ: אָמֵן. (Cong.– אָמֵן.)

יִתְגַּדַּל *May His great Name grow exalted and sanctified* (Cong.– *Amen*) *in the world that will be renewed and where He will resuscitate the dead and raise them up to eternal life, and rebuild the city of Jerusalem and complete His Temple within it, and uproot alien worship from the earth, and return the service of Heaven to its place, and may the Holy One, Blessed is He, reign in His sovereignty and splendor [and cause salvation to sprout and bring near His Messiah* (Cong.– *Amen*)*] in your lifetimes and in your days, and in the lifetimes of the entire House of Israel, swiftly and soon. Now respond: Amen.*

(Cong.– *Amen. May His great Name be blessed forever and ever.*)

May His great Name be blessed forever and ever.

Blessed, praised, glorified, exalted, extolled, mighty, upraised, and lauded be the Name of the Holy One, Blessed is He (Cong.– *Blessed is He*), (From Rosh Hashanah to Yom Kippur add: *exceedingly*) *beyond any blessing and song, praise, and consolation that are uttered in the world. Now respond: Amen.* (Cong.– *Amen.*)

Upon Israel, upon the teachers, upon their disciples and upon all of their disciples' disciples and upon all those who engage in the study of Torah, who are here or anywhere else; may they and you have abundant peace, grace, kindness, and mercy, long life, ample nourishment, and salvation, from before their Father Who is in Heaven [and on earth]. Now respond: Amen. (Cong.– *Amen.*)

May there be abundant peace from Heaven, and [good] life upon us and upon all Israel. Now respond: Amen. (Cong.– *Amen.*)

Take three steps back. Bow left and say, *'He Who makes peace ...'*; bow right and say, *'may He ...'*; bow forward and say, *'and upon all Israel ... Amen.'* Remain standing in place for a few moments, then take three steps forward.

He Who makes peace in His heights, may He, in His compassion, make peace upon us, and upon all Israel. Now respond: Amen. (Cong.– *Amen.*)

---

8. *Proverbs* 6:22. 9. 9:11. 10. 3:16. 11. *Psalms* 29:11.

Appendix
Glossary
Scriptural Index

Appendix

The Messianic Era, the Resurrection of the Dead, and the World to Come

It is a general premise of Judaism that human life cannot be viewed through the narrow lens of this world, but must be seen in the far wider context of a continuum that stretches to eternity. Our present existence is but a preparatory stage for an eternal life of unimaginable sublimeness, the magnitude of which is determined by the individual's conduct in the course of his earthly sojourn.

On a global scale, human history is a progression to the supreme world order that will be reached in the Messianic Era. It is a fundamental tenet of Judaism that the Messiah – a flesh-and-blood scion of the Davidic dynasty – will come forth, gather the Jewish exiles from the lands of their dispersal and return them to Eretz Yisrael, where he will rebuild the Holy Temple and rule over the Jews as their king. The world will thenceforth forever be at peace, show obeisance to the Jewish king and seek his counsel, and be filled with the knowledge of God like the waters that cover the sea.[1] Man will still have material desires and free will, but there will be such a general outpouring of the knowledge of God that evil will disappear and people – living in peace and harmony – will strive to perfect themselves and cleave to God.[2]

Though this idyllic period is the culmination of *earthly* life, it is not the highest good achieved by the individual, who progresses to his eternal reward in "the World to Come" (see below) in a series of stages that follow earthly death. Not only does the disembodied soul live on in what is known as the עוֹלַם הַנְּשָׁמוֹת, *the World of Souls,*[3] but – as stated clearly in the Mishnah and Gemara at the beginning of Chapter *Cheilek* – it is a fundamental tenet of Judaism that God will at some point literally resurrect the dead, reuniting here on this earth the body and soul that were separated through death. This resurrection is what is meant when we speak of תְּחִיַּת הַמֵּתִים, *techiyas hameisim* [Resurrection of the Dead].[4]

◆§ עוֹלַם הַנְּשָׁמוֹת, The World of Souls

When a person dies, his disembodied soul enters the World of Souls: The souls of the righteous delight in גַּן עֵדֶן, *Gan Eden,* whereas those of the wicked are punished in גֵּיהִנֹּם, *Gehinnom.*[5] The souls remain in the World of Souls until the

NOTES

1. See at great length *Rambam* in *Hil. Melachim* chs. 11-12, based on *Deuteronomy* 30:3-10, *Isaiah* 11:9, *Zephaniah* 3:9 and many other verses; and in *Hil. Teshuvah* 9:2; and in *Commentary to the Mishnah,* Introduction to this chapter.

2. *R' Moshe Chaim Luzzato, Maamar HaIkkarim* §8. There is a dispute in the Gemara whether the Messianic Era will usher in a time of supernatural existence or whether the current natural order will prevail, albeit in an especially blessed and idyllic fashion (see Gemara 91b).

3. In the Talmud, this world of souls is referred to by the terms גַּן עֵדֶן, *Gan Eden* [Paradise], and גֵּיהִנֹּם, *Gehinnom* [Hell]. The term עוֹלַם הַנְּשָׁמוֹת, *the World of Souls,* does not appear in the Talmud, though it is used extensively by the Rishonim.

4. *Rambam's* statements in his *Yad HaChazakah* were initially misunderstood even by some of his greatest contemporaries as denying a literal resurrection and explaining "Resurrection of the Dead" to be but an allegorical reference to the immortality of the disembodied soul (see *Raavad, Hil. Teshuvah* 8:2; *Maamar Techiyas HaMeisim*). In response, *Rambam* wrote his famous treatise on the Resurrection of the Dead [*Maamar Techiyas HaMeisim*], in which he demonstrates that his words were misinterpreted. He asserts there that the cardinal Torah tenet of Resurrection of the Dead refers to the actual reunification of body and soul, and that one must not understand this in any way but its simple, literal sense (ibid. §3). *Rambam* stresses that the treatise is not meant in any way to qualify or modify what he had written previously in his *Commentary to the Mishnah* or *Yad HaChazakah,* but simply to clarify at length what he felt had already been made sufficiently clear in those earlier works. He notes that the belief in a literal resurrection is universal among traditional Jews, is mentioned repeatedly in our prayers instituted by the prophets and our greatest sages, is found extensively throughout the Talmudic and Midrashic literature, and contained in various Scriptural passages that are not to be interpreted figuratively (*Maamar Techiyas HaMeisim* §4).

5. Though Gan Eden is a real garden of delights here on this earth, as evident from verses in *Genesis* (see 2:9-10,15), its features allude to exalted spiritual concepts that can be apprehended by contemplation of those features. When the sages speak of the souls of the dead "entering Gan Eden," they mean that the soul attains those exalted levels of perception, and rises to greater spiritual heights and attachment to the Divine. Moreover, the import of some aggadic statements is that the disembodied soul initially enters the physical Gan Eden on this earth, not to partake of its physical delights, but to attain the spiritual perfection that can be achieved there (see at great length *Ramban* in *Shaar HaGemul* pp. 295-297). [*Shaar HaGemul* is part of *Ramban's* larger work *Toras HaAdam.* Our page references to *Shaar HaGemul* are to the Mosad HaRav Kook edition of *Kisvei HaRamban* vol. 2.]

Rav Saadiah Gaon explains that the terms "Gan Eden" and "Gehinnom," used to describe the reward and punishment of the soul in the Afterlife, are borrowed from the real places in this world that respectively epitomize the best and worst regions on earth (*Emunos VeDe'os,* end of 9:5).

final judgment that ushers in the Resurrection of the Dead and World to Come (see below),[6] whereupon those found deserving will live on in a resurrected bodily state in spiritual delight.[7]

◆§ יוֹם הַדִּין הַגָּדוֹל, The Great Day of Judgment

Many passages in Scripture allude to a great day of judgment at the end of days.[8] *Rashi* (to *Rosh Hashanah* 16b ד״ה ליום הדין) and, with greater elaboration, *Ramban* (in *Shaar HaGemul*) explain (based on *Rosh Hashanah* 16b) that every person comes before the heavenly tribunal at three stages of his existence: (1) every Rosh Hashanah, when man's material fortunes are decided according to his deeds during the preceding year; (2) at death, when the soul of every man is judged and his portion in Gehinnom or Gan Eden is fixed accordingly; (3) on the *Yom HaDin HaGadol,* the Great Day of Judgment, when all men are judged to determine whether they are worthy of resurrection.[9]

◆§ תְּחִיַּת הַמֵּתִים, The Resurrection of the Dead

At some point in the Messianic Era, God will resurrect the dead. *Rav Saadiah Gaon* (*Emunos VeDe'os* §7)[10] cites what he calls "the predominant belief among Jews" that the dead will be resurrected at the time of the Messianic redemption, as indicated by the plain meaning of various passages in Scripture. He notes that some people explain these passages as referring figuratively to the revival of our nation and its sovereignty. *Rav Saadiah,* however, insists that "the predominant belief among Jews" is the correct one, asserting (among other arguments) that one may not take Scriptural passages in a figurative sense without compelling reasons to do so.[11] However, according to the way many commentators understand the Gemara on 92b and 97a, it would seem that the resurrection of the dead will take place at the very end of the Messianic Era.[12]

Many assert that both views are true, explaining that the Resurrection of the Dead will occur in *two* stages. At the time of the Messianic redemption, the completely righteous (צַדִּיקִים גְּמוּרִים) will be resurrected so that they will then be able to achieve the levels they were denied in their first lives because of the adverse circumstances of this world. Later, on the

NOTES

6. This is somewhat of an oversimplification. As stated in *Rosh Hashanah* (16b-17a), there are different classes of sinners, and their punishments vary. For example, some are punished for but a short time in Gehinnom and are then advanced to a state of bliss. Others suffer for a longer period and are then released from their torment. Still others are consigned eternally to Gehinnom (see *Ramban* in *Shaar HaGemul,* p. 288).

7. *Ramban* (*Shaar HaGemul* p. 290; *Commentary* to *Leviticus* 18:29) explains that in most cases even sinners subject to *kares* have a share in the World to Come. Only those sins for which the Torah decrees *absolute kares* [הִכָּרֵת תִּכָּרֵת], such as idolatry, cause the sinner to lose his share in the World to Come.

8. See, for example, *Daniel* 7:10, 12:2 and *Malachi* 3:23.

9. *Abarbanel* (*Mayenei HaYeshuah* 8:7) argues that this third judgment seems superfluous. The judgment at death would seem to have taken everything into account. He points out that the great day of judgment mentioned so many times is in essence only a day of reckoning. The verse in *Daniel* 7:10: דִּינָא יְתִב וְסִפְרִין פְּתִיחוּ, *the judgment was set and the books were opened,* means only that the books will be opened to read the sentence before implementation. The nations that have oppressed Israel will receive their just deserts. The verse in *Daniel* 12:2 (cited below – see: *Who will be resurrected*), then, speaks of another matter. The evildoers shall be resurrected not in order to be judged, but to witness in person the glory that will be awarded the righteous.

R' Aharon Kotler (see *Mishnas R' Aharon* I, p. 252) suggests another approach to this question. At the time of death, every person is judged by the heavenly tribunal for his deeds during his life span. However, the influence of a person's actions does not terminate with his death. For example, Moses' influence is felt by us to this day; therefore, his final judgment must include his effect on subsequent generations as well as the deeds he performed while living. Conversely, the effects of a sinner's misdeeds may proliferate long after his death. Thus, the final judgment takes into account the sum total of every person's accomplishment and influence up to the last day of history.

10. *Rav Saadiah Gaon* wrote two versions of the seventh treatise (entitled "Concerning Resurrection of the Dead in This World") of his *Emunos VeDe'os.* The first version is the one found in the classic Hebrew translation of *R' Yehudah Ibn Tibbon.* The second version is the one contained in the recent Hebrew translation of R' Joseph Kafich. The citation here is from the second version, though its main points are contained in the earlier version as well. [In general, our references to the seventh treatise of *Emunos VeDe'os* will be to the later version unless otherwise noted. Also, our references will refer to the chapter divisions found in the Kafich translation (though these were not provided by *Rav Saadiah Gaon* himself, but added by a later translator).]

11. The view rejected by *Rav Saadiah* holds that the Resurrection of the Dead will not take place until the very end of the Messianic Era, whereupon the resurrected will be transported directly to the World to Come [which, in *Rav Saadiah's* view, is a new physical abode created for eternal reward, rather than a future epoch here on earth – see below, note 28]. In one place, *Rav Saadiah* applies to the proponents of the view he rejects the dictum of our Mishnah (below) that "one who denies the Resurrection of the Dead has no share in the World to Come," i.e. one who denies that the Resurrection of the Dead will occur at the time of the Messianic redemption will not merit that resurrection (*Emunos VeDe'os* 7:4). Elsewhere, however, *Rav Saadiah* seems to apply this dictum only to one who altogether denies the ultimate reward of the World to Come (op. cit. 9:4).

12. See 92b note 4 and 97a note 59.

Rambam (*Maamar Techiyas HaMeisim* §6, cited by *Yad Ramah* p. 160 column 1) apparently finds no compelling indication regarding the time of the resurrection, and writes that "[God] will resurrect the dead . . . as He wishes and whom He wishes either in the days of the Messiah or before him or after his death . . ." *Ritva* (*Niddah* 61b) writes that according to Shmuel, who holds that the natural order will continue into the Messianic Era (see Gemara 91b), the Resurrection of the Dead will not occur until after that era is complete (see also *Sefer HaIkkarim* 4:35). *Ramah* (in his letter to R' Aharon ben Meshullam of Lunel [Mechon Harry Fishel edition, p. 183]), however, argues forcefully that the continuation of the natural order into the Messianic Era in no way precludes the Resurrection of the Dead or the occurrence of any other miracles at that time. Shmuel means only that the basic workings of the world will continue according to present natural law, but occasional miracles may indeed occur, just as they have throughout history.

Great Day of Judgment, there will be a general resurrection of all people for purposes of reward and punishment (see next entry).[13]

◆ Who will be resurrected?

Daniel 12:2 states: וְרַבִּים מִיְּשֵׁנֵי אַדְמַת־עָפָר יָקִיצוּ אֵלֶּה לְחַיֵּי עוֹלָם וְאֵלֶּה לַחֲרָפוֹת לְדִרְאוֹן עוֹלָם, *And many of those who sleep in the dusty earth shall awaken; these for everlasting life, and these for shame – for everlasting abhorrence,* and the Gemara (92a) cites this verse as one of the many Scriptural sources for the Resurrection of the Dead.[14] *Yad Ramah*[15] takes this verse in *Daniel* to mean that both the righteous and the wicked will be resurrected on the Great Day of Judgment – the righteous to receive eternal reward, and the wicked to receive eternal punishment – and points out that this is indicated by the Gemara in the famous parable about the cripple and the blind man told by Rebbi to Antoninus.[16] Moreover, *Abarbanel* (*Mayenei HaYeshuah* 11a) believes that the resurrection will include all of mankind: The righteous will be resurrected so that they might enjoy the benefits they have merited. The enemies of Israel will also come alive in order to witness their own ultimate downfall.[17]

Rambam (*Commentary to the Mishnah,* Chapter *Cheilek*), however, writes that the resurrection is destined only for the righteous, and bases his opinion on a Talmudic statement.[18] This is also the view of *Ramban* and *R' Chisdai Crescas,* cited by *Abarbanel.*[19] And as regards the verse in *Daniel* cited above, these authorities might interpret it as does *Rav Saadiah Gaon,* who writes: "It does not say '*all* who sleep,' because *all* would include all of mankind, and He made this promise only to Israel. Therefore He says, *many* . . . And when it says: *these for everlasting life and these for shame . . .,* the intent is not that among those who are resurrected some will be rewarded and some punished, for those who deserve punishment will not be resurrected at the time of the Redemption. Rather, it means that those who will awaken will have everlasting life, and those who will not awaken will be *for shame – for everlasting abhorrence.* For every righteous or penitent person will live; only the unbelieving and those who died without repentance will remain. All this will happen at the time of the Redemption."[20] [See also *Ibn Ezra* to *Daniel* ad loc.]

NOTES

13. See *Ritva* to *Rosh Hashanah* end of 16b, and *Sefer HaIkkarim,* end of 4:35. See also *Zohar* and the explanation of *R' Chaim Vital,* cited in *Ben Yehoyada* to end of Gemara 92a. *Ramah's* comments to the beginning of *Cheilek* (see *Yad Ramah* pp. 160-161) clearly presume two resurrections – one in the Messianic Era and one in the World to Come. *Radbaz* (2:839) reports that the notion of two resurrections is a reliable tradition handed down from earlier authorities. He explains that the first resurrection is for the righteous who suffered and died in exile; this will take place in the early part of the Messianic era, and will afford these righteous the privilege of living the ideal life in Eretz Yisrael with the Temple and its service restored. The second resurrection will be the general one just before the seventh millennium, for purposes of general reward and punishment immediately prior to the World to Come. In a different responsum (3:1069), *Radbaz* considers this view to be generally accepted, and supports it from Scripture. [This, in fact, is essentially the view of *Rav Saadiah Gaon* himself, as we will seek to demonstrate below in note 20.]

14. *Rambam* (cited by *Abarbanel* in *Mayenei HaYeshuah* 11:9) considers this verse to be the most explicit of any in Scripture about the tenet of Resurrection of the Dead (see also *Maamar Techiyas HaMeisim* §8), and one that does not admit a figurative explanation (ibid. §4).

15. Page 159 column 2.

16. See Gemara 91a-b; cf. 91b note 4. See also *Rashi, Tosafos* and *Ritva* to *Rosh Hashanah* 16b.

17. *Abarbanel* adds that the nations of mankind that will be resurrected will realize the folly of their beliefs and will all come to acknowledge the one true belief, as seen from the words of *Zephaniah* (3:9): *For then I will turn to the nations a clear language that they will all call upon the Name of HASHEM to serve Him in unison,* and many other prophecies.

18. See *Taanis* 7a, where the Gemara states that whereas rain is for both the righteous and the wicked, "the Resurrection of the Dead is only for the righteous." Some versions read: "only for the *completely* righteous" (*Sefer HaIkkarim* 4:31). *Be'er Sheva* (to the beginning of *Cheilek,* p. 128 col. 2), however, argues that the statement in *Taanis* might refer only to attainment of the highest level of the World to Come.

19. In *Mayenei HaYeshuah* 11:9, *Shoresh* 2. [The language of *Ramban* in *Shaar HaGemul,* however, is ambiguous. As concerns *R' Chisdai Crescas's* view, see his *Or Hashem* III:4:4, p. 77.] (*Abarbanel,* loc. cit., attributes this view to *Rav Saadiah Gaon* as well. However, as we will seek to demonstrate in the next note, *Rav Saadiah* in fact agrees that the wicked will indeed be resurrected for purposes of punishment.)

Meiri (to *Avos* 4:29) describes the view that the wicked will be resurrected for judgment as "one of the traditional views held by some believers." See also *Meiri* to the Mishnah on 107b.

20. *Emunos VeDe'os* 7:2. A careful reading of various statements by *Rav Saadiah Gaon* in his *Emunos VeDe'os* strongly indicates that he propounds the view that there are two resurrections (see note 13): The first resurrection occurs at the time of the Messianic redemption, and is reserved exclusively for the righteous; whereas the second resurrection occurs with the advent of the World to Come and encompasses the wicked as well, for purposes of ultimate reward and punishment. First, this is indicated by several internal indications in the seventh treatise. Second, *Rav Saadiah* writes in the seventh treatise (as cited in our main text above) that the verse in *Daniel* (12:2) means that the righteous alone will be resurrected; yet, *Rav Saadiah* writes clearly in chapter 5 of the ninth treatise that both ultimate reward *and punishment* in the World to Come require a reunion of body and soul. The reconciliation of these two statements is that the first one refers to the resurrection *at the time of the redemption* (as stated clearly by *Rav Saadiah* there), whereas the second statement refers to the resurrection *in the World to Come,* as would appear from context. It emerges, then, that although *Rav Saadiah Gaon* interprets *Daniel* 12:2 to mean that only the righteous will be resurrected, he also interprets that verse as referring specifically to the first resurrection – the one at the time of the redemption. From a practical standpoint, however, he agrees in essence with *Yad Ramah,* though he interprets the *verse* differently. [It should be noted, though, that *Yad Ramah* – who interprets *Daniel* 12:2 as referring to a resurrection of both the righteous *and* the wicked – considers that the verse might refer to resurrection during the Messianic Era (see *Yad Ramah* p. 161 col. 1).]

◆§ The Purpose of Resurrection

Various reasons are given for the reunion of the body and soul. The parable of the cripple and the blind man[21] would suggest that the dead are resurrected so that the body and soul as a unit can stand judgment for the deeds committed in this lifetime and be punished or rewarded accordingly.

Rav Saadiah Gaon explains that the righteous of the Jewish nation are resurrected at the time of the Redemption so that they can witness that promised and long-awaited redemption.[22] Furthermore, *Rav Saadiah* writes[23] that the Jewish nation will benefit from the resurrection [at the time of the Redemption] in several ways. First, resurrection of the dead is a supreme miracle, which will greatly enhance belief in God's omnipotence.[24] Also, it will grant us a reunion of all the prophets, righteous kings of Israel, and our greatest sages, and the opportunity to actually see them. Moreover, all will be able to be reunited with departed relatives and friends. The resurrected will also be able to answer our questions regarding the nature of death, the Afterlife, and how they were resurrected, which are presently matters of confusion to many. It will also enable the Children of Israel of all generations to live together as one great nation in splendor and honor. And finally, it will be a means of strengthening belief in the World to Come, for people will realize that just as the promise of resurrection has been fulfilled, so too will all other promises pertaining to the World to Come be fulfilled.

R' Yosef Albo (*Sefer HaIkkarim* 4:31) writes that the resurrection will create another opportunity for the righteous. For it is known to God that their failure to fulfill certain aspects of the Torah did not result from their lack of will, but from the adverse conditions they were subject to in their first lives. Thus, they are resurrected and allowed to reach the heights they could not attain in their first lives.[25]

Ramchal (*Daas Tevunos* §66-76; see *Michtav MeEliyahu* IV:150-156) explains that the Resurrection of the Dead will be an overwhelming revelation of God's omnipotence, which will lead to the total purification of the body to the point of ultimately pure spiritual existence. In the process, the soul — the mover in this process — will itself reach its highest possible level.

◆§ עוֹלָם הַבָּא, *Olam Haba* [The World to Come]

This is the term by which the sages describe the principal setting for man's ultimate and eternal reward. According to *Ramah* and *Ramban*[26] and many other Rishonim, *Olam Haba* in its primary and preponderant sense refers to the eternal state of *techiyas hameisim* [the Resurrection of the Dead]. This is the era that will follow the Messianic Era, in which the souls of the deserving will be reunited with their bodies forever after to enjoy their eternal reward.[27] The famous dictum of Rav, "In the World to Come there is no eating or drinking . . . rather, the righteous sit with their crowns on their heads and delight in the radiance of the Divine Presence" (*Berachos* 17a), refers to this reunited state of body and soul. Accordingly, the eternally resurrected will not have their present physical needs and functions; rather, their bodies will be sustained through a spiritual nourishment similar to the manner in which Moses was sustained on Mount Sinai for forty days and nights without food or drink (see *Exodus* 24:18; *Deuteronomy* 9:9,18).[28]

According to *Rambam*,[29] however, the term *Olam Haba* [the World to Come] refers broadly to the entire infinite

NOTES

21. See above, note 16.

22. *Emunos VeDe'os* end of §7.

23. At the end of his first version of treatise 7.

24. See also *Or Hashem* III:4:2

25. See below, note 33.

26. The view of *Ramah* (R' Meir HaLevi Abulafia) is detailed in his commentary *Yad Ramah* to Chapter *Cheilek* and in the series of letters he wrote on this topic to the sages of Lunel (printed in *Igros HaRamah*, at the end of *Sanhedrei Gedolah* [Harry Fishel Institute] vol. 1). *Ramban's* views are detailed primarily in his *Shaar HaGemul* at the end of his treatise *Toras HaAdam* (see above, note 5).

27. See also at length *Derech Hashem* I:3, *Daas Tevunos* §66-67 and *Michtav MeEliyahu* IV:150-156. *Rabbeinu Bachya* (to *Genesis* 2:15; *Shulchan Shel Arba* [*Kisvei Rabbeinu Bachya* p. 511]) states that at *techiyas hameisim* the world will be restored to the exalted state that prevailed in the Garden of Eden before Adam's sin.

28. *Rabbeinu Bachya* (*Shulchan Shel Arba* [*Kisvei Rabbeinu Bachya* p. 512]) explains, however, that these bodies will be transformed into something other than their present flesh and blood. [See also *Rabbeinu Bachya* to *Deuteronomy*, end of 30:15.]

Sefer HaIkkarim (4:35) writes that according to *Ramban*, the resurrected *will* initially have full bodily function for as long as their resurrected bodies will have the *natural* capacity to endure. Afterwards, the bodies will be purified and elevated to an ethereal state — similar to that of Elijah, who ascended to heaven while still alive (see *II Kings* 2:11) — at which point they will no longer engage in eating and drinking and the like, but will live forever without any physical source of sustenance.

Similarly, *Rav Saadiah Gaon* takes the resurrected state to be the eternal one, and writes that the righteous who will be resurrected in the Messianic era will live normal physical lives until the end of that era. Thereupon, they will be transported to the World to Come, which (in *Rav Saadiah's* view) is a new and eternal world created for the resurrected bodies, and in which the resurrected bodies will no longer have physical needs (see *Emunos VeDe'os* 7:5-6).

29. *Rambam's* view is detailed in *Hilchos Teshuvah* ch. 8; *Commentary to the Mishnah*, introduction to this chapter; and *Maamar Techiyas HaMeisim*. Both *Rambam's* view and that of *Yad Ramah* and *Ramban* are discussed extensively by *R' Yosef Albo* in his *Sefer HaIkkarim* part 4, chs. 30-35.

period of the Afterlife.[30] For in *Rambam's* view, the principal setting for man's ultimate reward and punishment is not the world of resurrected life but the World of Souls, and it is about this world of disembodied souls that Rav spoke when he said that "the righteous sit with their crowns on their heads and delight in the radiance of the Divine Presence."[31] It is to this world of pure spirit that the soul enters upon death[32] and to which it will return after its resurrected body dies. For *Rambam* maintains that the state of resurrection is *not* permanent. Rather, those deserving of resurrection will be resurrected and live the unusually long, happy lives of the idyllic Messianic period that culminates life on this earth – eating, drinking, and procreating, just like the people born initially in that epoch.[33] Eventually, however, body and soul will again separate, with the souls of the deserving returning to the eternal World of Souls to delight in the Divine Presence forever.[34]

Fundamentally, however, all agree that man's eternal state is a sublime spiritual one – whether the spiritual life of pure soul (*Rambam*), or that of the soul reunited with an ethereal, purified body (*Ramban*).[35]

Echoing a sentiment expressed by *Rambam* in regard to the details and sequence of the Messianic era,[36] *R' Samson Raphael Hirsch* writes concerning the details of the World to Come and the Resurrection of the Dead: ". . . the true nature of these matters is concealed from man . . . In lofty matters such as the World to Come and the World of Resurrection and similar things, it is sufficient for us to hold fast with perfect faith to [the general truth of the matter, as stated in] the words of our Scriptures: *For You shall not abandon my soul to the grave* (*Psalms* 16:10), and: *also my flesh will dwell in security* (ibid. v. 9). And we should not speculate about the nature of things concealed from us, which "no eye has beheld" (*Isaiah* 64:3; see Gemara 99a) . . . The Holy One, Blessed is He, did not make a covenant with us concerning hidden matters, but only concerning what is revealed to us, to heed and fulfill His Torah [see *Deuteronomy* 29:28]. And He has assured us that we do not require for its fulfillment knowledge of matters distant from us in the heavens or in the far reaches of the sea, but only what is in our mouth and heart to fulfill them [*Deuteronomy* 30:11-14]."[37]

❦ ❦ ❦

This summary of views in no way pretends to exhaust these topics, which deserve volumes in themselves. The reader inclined to pursue these topics should study the many sources cited above, which discuss these matters at great length.

NOTES

30. *Ramban, Shaar HaGemul,* end of p. 309. *Sefer HaIkkarim* (end of 4:31) supports this broader definition from the Sabbath liturgy, which states: "There is no comparison to You, Hashem, our God, in this world; and there is none other than You in the life of the World to Come; there is nothing but You, our King, in the days of the Messiah; and there is none like You, our Redeemer, at [the time of] the Resurrection of the Dead." This progression of four stages (this world; the World to Come; the days of the Messiah; the Resurrection of the Dead), which places "the World to Come" between this world and the days of the Messiah, indicates that "the World to Come" can refer to the Afterlife in the World of Souls.

31. Thus, since many statements of the sages concerning *Olam Haba* clearly do relate to the resurrected state, in which body and soul are united, and *Rambam* interprets others as referring to the World of Souls, he is forced to define *Olam Haba* as a broad term encompassing both states.

32. The wicked – those whose sins outweigh their merits – are punished for their sins after death, and then merit the eternal reward of the soul, unless they are among those sinners about whom it is stated that they lose their share in the World to Come. The souls of this latter class of sinner are cut off entirely and eternally (*Rambam, Hil. Teshuvah* 8:1) after suffering their deserved torment in the Afterlife (*Ramban, Shaar HaGemul* pp. 291-292, in explanation of *Rambam's* view).

However, while these sinners do not have their own share in the World to Come, *Recanti* (*Leviticus* 38:19) and *Derech Hashem* (II:3:8) hold that they will be included in the collective existence of Israel through the merit of the righteous, and will be, so to speak, "onlookers" in the World to Come.

33. *Rambam* entirely rejects the notion that God would reconstitute the dead in their present form if the resurrected bodies would not perform their normal physical functions. *Rambam's* objections are addressed by *Ramban* in *Shaar HaGemul* p. 305.

In *Rambam's* view, not only will those resurrected resume their normal physical functions, but they will also rise to greater heights (which they will retain for eternity) through their further performance of mitzvos (*Shaar HaGemul* p. 310), whose fulfillment was denied them in their first lives by the adverse circumstances of this world (*Sefer HaIkkarim* 4:31). See also *Rabbeinu Bachya* in *Shulchan Shel Arba* [*Kisvei Rabbeinu Bachya* p. 511]. [Regarding the applicability of mitzvos after the Resurrection of the Dead, see *Niddah* 61b and *Ritva* there at length; see also *Rashba* (in several places, which are cited by *Maharatz Chayes* to *Niddah* loc. cit.); see also *Kovetz Shiurim* II §29.]

34. *Rambam's* view in this matter is shared by "many who are with him among the sages of Israel" (*Sefer HaIkkarim* 4:35). [*Rambam* (*Moreh Nevuchim* 2:27) indicates that the view that the resurrected state is eternal would seem to emerge from a literal interpretation of the *aggados,* but that these *aggados* should be be taken figuratively. See also *Maamar Techiyas HaMeisim,* end of §2.]

According to the author of *Chidushei HaRan* (to the beginning of this chapter), the differing approaches of *Rambam* and *Ramban* reflect conflicting views among the Talmudic and Midrashic sages in this matter. [See also *Pachad Yitzchak, Igros U'Kesavim* §51, who advances a profound analysis of *Rambam's* view.]

35. See also editor's note to *Michtav MeEliyahu* IV, pp. 154-155.

36. Concerning which he writes (*Hil. Melachim* 12:2): "All these matters and their like, no one will know how they will happen until they happen. For these matters were obscured by the prophets. Also the Sages do not have a clear tradition concerning these matters, rather [they follow] the probable meaning of the verses; and therefore they have disputes in these matters. At any rate, the order in which these things will occur and their details are not a fundamental principle of faith. A person should not occupy himself with the words of *aggados* nor study at length the *midrashim* dealing with these and similar matters, nor should he regard them as fundamentals. For they lead neither to love nor fear [of God] . . . Rather, one should await, and believe in the general fact of the matter . . ."

37. Responsum of *R' Samson Raphael Hirsch,* printed in *HaMayan, Teves* 5715; vol. 16 number 2.

Glossary

abandoned corpse – a human corpse found with no one to attend to its burial. The Torah obligates the person who finds it to bury it and allows even a **nazir** and **Kohen Gadol** to do so.

Adar – twelfth month of the Hebrew calendar.

Adar Sheni – lit. the second **Adar.** When it is deemed necessary for a leap year to be designated, an extra month is added. When this occurs there are two Adars, the second of which is *Adar Sheni.*

agav – see **kinyan agav.**

agency – the principle that an agent may act as a proxy of a principal and have his actions legally accepted on behalf of the principal.

Aggadah, aggadata – the homiletical teachings of the Sages and all non-halachic Rabbinic literature found in the Talmud.

areiv – guarantor.

akum – idolater.

Altar – the great *Altar*, which stands in the Courtyard of the **Beis HaMikdash.** Certain portions of every offering are burnt on the *Altar*. The blood of most offerings is applied to the walls of the *Altar*.

amah [pl. **amos**] – cubit; a linear measure equaling six **tefachim.** Opinions regarding its modern equivalent range between 18 and 22.9 inches.

am haaretz [pl. **amei haaretz**] – a common, ignorant person who, possibly, is not meticulous in his observance of **halachah.**

Amora [pl. **Amoraim**] – sage of the **Gemara;** cf. **Tanna.**

amud – one side of the **daf** in the **Gemara.**

Anshei Knesses HaGedolah – see **Men of the Great Assembly.**

aravos – willow branches. See **four species.**

arayos – see **ervah.**

arus – a man who is betrothed and thereby entered the **erusin** stage of marriage. See **erusin.**

arusah – a woman who has been betrothed and thereby entered the **erusin** state of marriage. See **erusin.**

asham [pl. **ashamos**] – guilt offering, an offering brought to atone for one of several specific sins; in addition, a part of certain purification offerings. It is one of the **kodshei kodashim.**

asheirah – a tree either designated for worship or under which an idol is placed.

asmachta – lit. reliance. (a) a conditional commitment made by a party who does not really expect to have to honor it; (b) a verse cited by the **Gemara** not as a Scriptural basis for the law but rather as an allusion to a Rabbinic law.

assembly – This event took place on the evening following the first day of Succos, in the year following the **shemittah** year. The entire nation would gather in one of the Temple Courtyards to hear the king read the Book of Deuteronomy.

Av – (a) fifth month of the Hebrew calendar. (b) l.c. [pl. **avos**] – see **melachah.**

av beis din – chief of the court. This position was second in importance to the **Nasi** who served as head of the **Sanhedrin.**

av [pl. **avos**] **hatumah** – primary source of **tumah,** such as an object or person possessing a degree of *tumah* sufficient to contaminate a person or utensil. Examples include **metzora, neveilah,** et al.

avi avos hatumah – a human corpse, which is the most severe source of **tumah.**

avodah [pl. **avodos**] – the sacrificial service, or any facet of it. There are four critical *avodos* to the sacrificial service. They are **shechitah, kabbalah, holachah** and **zerikah.**

avodah zarah – idol worship, idolatry.

aylonis [pl. **aylonios**] – an adult woman who never developed the physical signs of female maturity. She is therefore assumed to be incapable of bearing children.

azharah – Scriptural warning; the basic prohibition stated in the Torah, which serves to warn the potential sinner against incurring the punishment prescribed for a particular action.

baal keri [pl. **baalei keri**] – one who experienced a seminal emission. He is **tamei** (ritually impure) and must immerse himself in a **mikveh.**

bagrus – the time when a girl becomes a *bogeress* (a full adult), the final legal state of a girl's physical development. A girl automatically becomes a *bogeress* six months after she becomes a **naarah.**

bamah [pl. **bamos**] – lit. high place; altar. This refers to any altar other than the **Altar** of the Tabernacle or Temple. During certain brief periods of Jewish history, it was permitted to offer sacrifices on a *bamah*. There are two types of *bamah.* The *communal* (or: *major*) *bamah* was the altar of the public and was the only *bamah* on which communal offerings could be sacrificed. Private voluntary offerings could be brought even on a *private* (or *minor*) *bamah* which was an altar erected anywhere by an individual for private use.

Baraisa [pl. **Baraisos**] – the statements of **Tannaim** not included by **Rebbi** in the **Mishnah.** R' Chiya and R' Oshaya, the students of Rebbi, researched and reviewed the *Baraisa* and compiled an authoritative collection of them.

bechor – (a) firstborn male child; (b) a firstborn male kosher animal. Such an animal is born with sacrificial sanctity, and must be given to a **Kohen** who then offers it (if unblemished) as a *bechor* sacrifice in the **Temple** and eats its sacred meat. Unlike other sacrifices, the *bechor* is automatically sacred from birth even without designation.

bedek habayis – **Temple** Treasury.

bedi'avad – after the fact. See **lechatchilah.**

beheimah – domesticated species, livestock. In regard to various laws, the Torah distinguishes between *beheimah:* domestic species, e.g. cattle, sheep, goats; and, **chayah,** wild species, e.g. deer, antelope.

bein hashemashos – the twilight period preceding night. The legal status of *bein hashemashos* as day or night is uncertain.

beis din – court; Rabbinical court comprised minimally of three members. Such a court is empowered to rule on civil matters. See also **Sanhedrin.**

beis hamidrash – a **Torah** study hall.

Beis HaMikdash – Holy **Temple** in Jerusalem. The **Temple** edifice comprised (a) the Antechamber; (b) the **Holy** or **Heichal;** and (c) the **Holy of Holies.** See **Sanctuary.**

bereirah – retroactive clarification. This principle allows for the assignment of a legal status to a person or object whose identity is as yet undetermined, but which will be retroactively clarified by a subsequent choice.

bikkurim – the first-ripening fruits of any of the seven species (wheat, barley, grapes, figs, pomegranates, olives, dates), with which the Torah praises Eretz Yisrael. They are brought to the **Temple** and given to the **Kohanim.**

binyan av – one of the thirteen principles of Biblical hermeneutics. This principle dictates that whenever a commonality of law or essence is found in two separate areas of **Torah** law, analogies may be drawn from one area to the other, and the laws that apply to one can be applied to the other as well.

Bircas HaMazon – the blessings recited after a meal.

Bircas Kohanim – see **Priestly Blessing.**

bitul (or **bitul b'rov**) – the principle of nullification in a majority. Under certain circumstances, a mixture of items of differing legal status assumes the status of its majority component.

bogeress – a girl who has attained the age of 12½ years and is thereupon considered an adult in all aspects. See **bagrus.**

Bris Milah – ritual circumcision.

Canaanite slave – a non-Jewish slave owned by a Jew. His term of servitude is for life. While owned by the Jew, he is obligated in all the **mitzvos** incumbent upon a Jewish woman. Upon being freed, he becomes a full-fledged Jew, with a status similar to that of a convert.

chagigah offering – festival offering. Every adult Jewish male is required to bring a *chagigah* offering on the first day of the festivals of **Pesach, Shavuos** and **Succos.** It is one of the **kodashim kalim**, specifically, a type of **shelamim** offering.

chalal [f: **chalalah**] – lit. desecrated. If a **Kohen** cohabits with any woman specifically forbidden to **Kohanim,** the child of that union lacks the sanctity of a **Kohen.** The *chalal* enjoys neither the privileges of the **Kehunah** nor is subject to its restrictions.

chalifin – see **kinyan chalifin.**

chalitzah – see **yibum.**

challah – portion removed from a dough of the **five grains,** given to a **Kohen;** if *challah* is not taken, the dough is **tevel** and may not be eaten. The minimum amount of dough from which *challah* must be separated is the volume-equivalent of 43.2 eggs, which is one **issaron.** Nowadays the *challah* is removed and burned.

chametz – leavened products of the five species of grain. *Chametz* is forbidden on **Pesach.**

Chanukah – Festival of Lights. The holiday that commemorates the Maccabean victory of the Greeks. It begins on the 25th of **Kislev** and lasts for eight days.

chatas [pl. **chataos**] – sin offering; an offering generally brought in atonement for the inadvertent transgression of a **kares**-bearing sin. A *chatas* is also brought as one of various purification offerings. It is one of the **kodshei kodashim.**

chaver [pl. **chaverim**] – (a) one who observes the laws of ritual purity even regarding non-consecrated foodstuffs; (b) a Torah scholar, scrupulous in his observance of **mitzvos.** Regarding tithes, **tumah** and other matters, such as the necessity for **hasra'ah,** he is accorded a special status.

chayah – see **beheimah.**

chazakah – (a) legal presumption that conditions remain unchanged unless proven otherwise; (b) one of the methods of acquiring real estate; it consists of performing an act of improving the property, such as enclosing it with a fence or plowing it in preparation for planting; (c) "established rights"; uncontested usage of another's property establishes the right to such usage; since the owner registered no protest, acquiescence is assumed; (d) uncontested holding of real property for three years as a basis for claiming acquisition of title from the prior owner.

cheilev – The Torah forbids certain fats of cattle, sheep and goats for human consumption. These are primarily the hind fats (suet) placed on the **Altar.** See **shuman.**

cherem – a) a vow in which one uses the expression "*cherem*" to consecrate property, placing it under jurisdiction of the Temple; b) land or property upon which a ban has been declared, forbidding its use to anyone, e.g. the city of Jericho.

cheresh – lit. a deaf person; generally used for a deaf-mute who can neither hear nor speak. A *cheresh* is legally deemed mentally incompetent; his actions or commitments are not legally significant or binding.

Cheshvan – see **Marcheshvan.**

chilul Hashem – lit. profanation of God's Name. (a) Behavior which casts Jews in a negative light; (b) violation of a Torah prohibition done in the presence of ten male Jews.

Chol HaMoed – the Intermediate Days of the Festivals of **Pesach** and **Succos**; these enjoy a quasi-**Yom Tov** status.

chullin – any substance that is not sanctified. See **kodesh.**

chupah – (a) the bridal canopy; (b) a procedure for effecting **nisuin,** the final stage of marriage.

common characteristic – An exegetical derivation based on the presumption that a law found in two contexts results from characteristics common to both rather than from characteristics unique to each. Any other context possessing these common characteristics is also subject to the common law, even if the third context differs from the first two in regard to their *unique* features.

Cutheans – a non-Jewish tribe brought by the Assyrians to settle the part of **Eretz Yisrael** left vacant by the exile of the Ten Tribes. Their subsequent conversion to Judaism was considered questionable and their observance of many laws was lax.

daf – folio (two sides) in the **Gemara.**

dayyo – lit. it is sufficient. Principle which limits the application of a **kal vachomer** argument, for it states: When a law is derived from case A to case B, its application to B cannot exceed its application to A.

death penalty – this refers to a court-imposed death penalty, in contrast to one imposed by Heaven.

demai – lit. what is this; produce of **Eretz Yisrael** that is obtained from an unlearned person. By Rabbinic enactment it must be tithed since a doubt exists as to whether its original owner tithed it. However, it is assumed that **terumah** was separated from the produce.

dinar – a coin. The silver content of the coin was equivalent to ninety-six grains of barley. It was worth 1/25 the value of a gold *dinar.*

double payment – a punitive fine. A person convicted of theft is required to return both the stolen object (or its monetary equivalent) and pay the owner a fine equal to its value. If he stole a sheep or goat and slaughtered or sold it, he pays four times the value of the animal. If he stole an ox and slaughtered or sold it, he pays five times its value.

Elohim – (a) a Name of God; (b) [l.c.] sometimes used to refer to a mortal power or authority of an ordained judge.

Elul – sixth month of the Hebrew calendar.

emurin – the portions of an animal offering burnt on the **Altar.**

encumbered property – land owned by a debtor at the time he incurred a debt, but which he later sold or gave to a third party. Such land is encumbered by the debt; the creditor can retrieve it from the current owner to satisfy the debt, if the debtor defaults.

ephah [pl. **ephos**] – a measure of volume equal to three **se'ah.**

erech [pl. **arachin**] – a fixed valuation. The *erech* of a person is the amount fixed by the Torah for each of eight different groupings classified by age and gender. All individuals included in the same broad grouping have the identical *erech* valuation, regardless of their value on the slave market.

Eretz Yisrael – Land of Israel.

erusin – betrothal, the first stage of marriage. This is effected by the man giving the woman an object of value, in the presence of witnesses, to betroth her. At this point the couple is not yet permitted to have conjugal relations, but is nonetheless considered legally married in most respects and the woman requires a divorce before she can marry again; see **nisuin.**

eruv – popular contraction of **eruvei chatzeiros, eruvei tavshilin,** or **eruvei techumin.**

eruvei chatzeiros – a legal device which merges several separate ownerships **(reshus hayachid)** into a single joint ownership. This procedure allows us to view all the houses opening into the courtyard as the property of a single consortium (composed of all the residents of the courtyard). This permits all the contributing residents of the **chatzeir** to carry items during the Sabbath from the houses into the *chatzeir* and from one house to another.

eruvei tavshilin – the prepared food set aside prior to a **Yom Tov** that falls on Friday to serve as token food for the Sabbath that follows. Once this token food has been set aside, the person is allowed to complete his preparations for Sabbath on **Yom Tov.** Such preparation is generally forbidden otherwise.

eruvei techumin – a legal device that allows a person to shift his Sabbath residence from which the 2,000-**amah techum** is measured. This is accomplished by placing a specific amount of food at the desired location before the start of the Sabbath. The place where the food has been placed is then viewed as his Sabbath residence, and his *techum*-limit is measured from there.

ervah [pl. **arayos**] – (a) matters pertaining to sexual relationships forbidden under penalty of **kares** or death, as enumerated in *Leviticus* ch. 18. (b) A woman forbidden to a man under pain of one of these penalties.

esrog – see **four species**.

fines – punitive payments that do not bear a strict relation to actual damages.

five grains – wheat, barley, oats, spelt and rye.

forbidden labors of the Sabbath – see **avos melachah.**

forty lashes – see **malkus**.

Four Species – The four articles of plant-life we are commanded to take and hold in our hands on the Festival of Succos. These consist of: (a) **aravos** – willow branches; (b) **esrog** – citron; (c) **hadasim** – myrtle branches; (d) **lulav** – branch of the date palm tree.

Gaon [pl. **Geonim**] – (a) title accorded the heads of the academies in Sura and Pumbedisa, the two Babylonian seats of Jewish learning, from the late 6th to mid-11th centuries C.E. They served as the link in the chain of Torah tradition that joined the **Amoraim** to the **Rishonim;** (b) later used to describe any brilliant Torah scholar.

Gemara – portion of the Talmud which discusses the **Mishnah;** also, loosely, a synonym for the Talmud as a whole.

gematria – the numeric valuation of the Hebrew alphabet.

get [pl. **gittin**] – bill of divorce; the document that effects the dissolution of a marriage when it is placed in the wife's possession.

gezeirah shavah – one of the thirteen principles of Biblical hermeneutics. If a similar word or phrase occurs in two otherwise unrelated passages in the Torah, the principle of *gezeirah shavah* teaches that these passages are linked to one another, and the laws of one passage are applied to the other. Only those words which are designated by the **Oral Sinaitic Law** for this purpose may serve as a basis for a *gezeirah shavah.*

gifts to the poor – These include **leket, shich'chah, pe'ah, peret, oleilos** and **maaser ani.**

Golden Altar – see **Inner Altar**.

Great Court – see **Sanhedrin**.

hadasim – see **four species.**

hafarah – revocation of a woman's vow by her husband on the grounds that her vow impinges on their marital relationship or that it causes her deprivation.

hagbahah – lifting. One of the methods of acquisition used for movable objects.

halachah [pl. **halachos**] – (a) a **Torah** law; (b) [u.c.] the body of Torah law; (c) in cases of dispute, the position accepted as definitive by the later authorities and followed in practice; (d) a **Halachah LeMoshe MiSinai.**

Halachah LeMoshe MiSinai – laws taught orally to Moses at Sinai, which cannot be derived from the Written Torah.

half-shekel – While the Temple stood, every Jew was required to donate a half-*shekel* annually to fund the purchase of the various communal offerings (including among others, the daily **tamid** offerings and the holiday **mussaf** offerings).

Hashem – lit. the Name; a designation used to refer to God without pronouncing His Ineffable Name.

hasra'ah – warning. One does not incur the death penalty or lashes unless he was warned, immediately prior to commission, of the forbidden nature of the crime and the punishment to which he would be liable.

hatarah – annulment of a vow by an expert sage or a group of three competent laymen.

Havdalah – lit. distinction. The blessing recited at the conclusion of the Sabbath.

hazamah – the process by which witnesses are proven false by testimony that places them elsewhere at the time of the alleged incident. Such witnesses are punished with the consequences their testimony would have inflicted upon their intended victim.

Hebrew maidservant – a Jewish girl between the age of six and twelve sold by her father into servitude.

Hebrew servant – a Jewish man who is sold as an indentured servant, generally for a period of six years. Either he is sold by the court because he was convicted of stealing and lacks the funds to make restitution, or he sells himself for reasons of poverty.

hechsher l'tumah – rendering a food susceptible to **tumah** contamination by contact with one of seven liquids – water, dew, milk, bee honey, oil, wine or blood.

hefker beis din hefker – principle which establishes the power of Rabbinic courts to declare property ownerless.

hefker – ownerless.

Heichal – See **Beis HaMikdash.**

hekdesh – (a) items consecrated to the **Temple** treasury or as offerings; *hekdesh* can have two levels of sanctity: **monetary sanctity** and **physical sanctity.** Property owned by the Temple treasury is said to have monetary sanctity. Such property can be redeemed or can be sold by the *hekdesh* treasurers, and the proceeds of the redemption or sale become *hekdesh* in its place. Consecrated items that are fit for the Temple service (e.g. unblemished animals or sacred vessels) are deemed to have physical sanctity; (b) the state of consecration; (c) the **Temple** treasury.

hekeish – Scriptural analogy. Two subjects that are juxtaposed are compared to each other in the manner of a **gezeirah shavah.** This rule of exegesis is termed *hekeish.*

hesseis oath – lit. oath of incitement. Oath imposed by the court on one who denies the entire monetary claim made against him. This oath was required by the post-Mishnaic Rabbis on the assumption that a plaintiff would not make a totally frivolous claim.

hin – liquid measure equal to twelve **lugin.**

holachah – one of the four essential blood **avodos.** It involves carrying the blood of the offering to the **Altar.**

Holy – anterior chamber of the **Temple** edifice containing the **Shulchan, Inner Altar** and **Menorah.**

Holy Ark – the Ark holding the Tablets of the Ten Commandments and the Torah Scroll written by Moses. It stood in the **Holy of Holies.**

Holy of Holies – interior chamber of the **Temple** edifice. During most of the First Temple era, it contained the **Holy Ark;** later it was empty of any utensil. Even the **Kohen Gadol** is prohibited from entering there except on **Yom Kippur.**

Inner Altar – the gold-plated Altar which stood in the **Sanctuary.** It was used for the daily incense service and for the blood applications of inner **chataos.**

Israelites' Courtyard – an area in the Temple Courtyard, extending eleven **amos** from the eastern Courtyard wall into the Courtyard, and abutted on its west side by the **Kohanim's Courtyard.** It reached across the entire width of the Courtyard from north to south.

issaron – a dry measure equal to one-tenth of an **ephah** or approximately (depending on the conversion factor) as little as eleven or as much as twenty-one cups.

issur – prohibition.

ir hanidachas – a city in Eretz Yisrael in which the majority of the population worshiped idols. Subject to certain conditions, the city is destroyed along with all its property and its guilty inhabitants are beheaded.

Iyar – second month of the Hebrew calendar.

Jubilee – see **Yovel.**

kabbalah – (a) term used throughout the Talmud to refer to the books of the Prophets. It derives from the Aramaic root – to complain or cry out. It thus refers primarily to the admonitory passages of these books. (b) receiving the blood of a sacrificial animal that is slaughtered; one of the four blood **avodos.**

kal vachomer – lit. light and heavy, or lenient and stringent; an *a fortiori* argument. One of the thirteen principles of Biblical hermeneutics. It involves the following reasoning: If a particular stringency applies in a usually lenient case, it must certainly apply in a more serious case; the converse of this argument is also a *kal vachomer.*

kares – excision; Divinely imposed premature death decreed by the Torah for certain classes of transgression.

kav [pl. **kabim**] – a measure equal to four **lugin.**

Kehunah – priesthood; the state of being a **Kohen.**

keifel – see **double payment.**

kemitzah – the first of four essential services of a **minchah** offering, in which the **Kohen,** while closing the middle three fingers of his right hand over his palm, scoops out flour from the **minchah** to burn on the **Altar.**

kesef – (a) money; (b) Tyrian currency which is comprised solely of pure silver coins.

kesubah – (a) marriage contract; the legal commitments of a husband to his wife upon their marriage, the foremost feature of which is the payment awarded her in the event of their divorce or his death; (b) document in which this agreement is recorded.

Kesuvim – Hagiographa – Holy Writings. It consists of eleven volumes: *Psalms, Proverbs, Job, Song of Songs, Ruth, Lamentations, Ecclesiastes, Esther, Daniel, Ezra-Nehemiah, Chronicles.*

kezayis – the volume of an olive. Minimum amount of food whose consumption is considered "eating."

kiddush – (a) the benediction recited over wine before the evening and morning meals on the **Sabbath** and **Yom Tov**; (b) sanctification of **mei chatas.**

kiddushin [betrothal] – Jewish marriage conists of two stages: **erusin** and **nisuin.** *Kiddushin* is the procedure which establishes the first stage of marriage [*erusin*].

kilayim – various forbidden mixtures, including: **shaatnez** (cloth made from a blend of wool and linen); cross-breeding of animals; cross-breeding (or side-by-side planting) of certain food crops; working with different species of animals yoked together; and mixtures of the vineyard.

kilei hakerem – forbidden mixtures of the vineyard; see **kilayim.**

kinyan [pl. **kinyanim**] – formal act of acquisition; an action that causes an agreement or exchange to be legally binding.

kinyan agav – lit. acquisition by dint of; the term for the acquisition of movable property by means of the acquisition of land. The **kinyan** used for the land serves for the movable property.

kinyan chalifin – lit. acquisition by exchange. (a) Even exchange: an exchange of two items of comparable value, in which each item serves as payment for the other. The acquisition of any one of the items automatically effects the acquisition of the other. (b) Uneven exchange: An item of relatively negligible value is given in order to effect the acquisition of the other item. A kerchief or the like is traditionally used.

kinyan chatzeir – the acquisition of movable property by virtue of it being in the premises of the person acquiring it.

kinyan chazakah – see **chazakah (b).**

kinyan sudar – see **kinyan chalifin (b).**

Kislev – ninth month of the Hebrew calendar.

kodashim kalim – offerings of lesser holiness (one of the two classifications of sacrificial offerings). They may be eaten anywhere in Jerusalem by any **tahor** person. They include the **todah, shelamim, bechor, maaser** and **pesach offerings.** This category of offerings is not subject to the stringencies applied to **kodshei kodashim.**

kodesh – (a) any consecrated object; (b) the anterior chamber of the **Temple** – the **Holy;** (c) portions of sacrificial offerings.

kodshei kodashim – most-holy offerings (one of the two classifications of sacrificial offerings). They may be eaten only in the **Temple** courtyard and only by male **Kohanim.** They include the **olah** (which may not be eaten at all), **chatas, asham** and communal **shelamim.** These are subject to greater stringencies than **kodashim kalim.**

Kohanim's Courtyard – eleven-**amah**-wide area in the Courtyard of the **Beis HaMikdash** abutting the **Israelites' Courtyard** on its east side, and the **Altar** on its west side. It reached across the entire width of the Courtyard from north to south.

Kohen [pl. **Kohanim**] – member of the priestly family descended in the male line from Aaron. The Kohen is accorded the special priestly duties and privileges associated with the **Temple** service and is bound by special laws of sanctity.

Kohen Gadol – High Priest.

kometz – see **kemitzah.**

kol d'alim g'var – lit. let whoever is stronger prevail. In certain cases where neither litigant advances conclusive proof to support his claim the court withdraws and allows the stronger party to take possession of the contested property.

korban – a sacrificial offering brought in the **Beis HaMikdash.**

kor – large dry measure; a measure of volume consisting of thirty **se'ah.**

kri u'ksiv – a word in Scripture written one way but read differently by special directive to Moses at Sinai.

lashes – see **malkus** and **makkas mardus.**

leaning – see **semichah.**

lechatchilah – (a) before the fact; (b) performance of a **mitzvah** or procedure in the proper manner.

leket – gleanings; one of the various portions of the harvest which the Torah grants to the poor. *Leket* refers to one or two stalks of grain that fall from the reaper when he gathers the harvest. See **shich'chah, pe'ah, peret** and **oleilos.**

lessach – one half of a **kor.**

Levi [pl. **Leviim**] – male descendant of the tribe of *Levi* in the male line, who is sanctified for auxiliary services in the **Beis HaMikdash.** The *Leviim* were the recipients of **maaser rishon.**

libation – see **nesachim.**

litra – a liquid measure equal to the volume of six eggs.

log [pl. **lugin**] – a liquid measure equal to the volume of six eggs.

lulav – see **four species.**

ma'ah [pl. **maos**] – the smallest silver unit in Talmudic coinage. Thirty-two copper **perutos** equal one *ma'ah* and six *ma'ahs* equal a silver **dinar.**

Maariv – the evening prayer service.

maaser [pl. **maasros**] – tithe. It is a Biblical obligation to give two tithes, each known as *maaser,* from the produce of the Land of Israel. The first tithe (**maaser rishon**) is given to a **Levi.** The second tithe (**maaser sheni**) is taken to Jerusalem and eaten there or else is redeemed with coins which are then taken to Jerusalem for the purchase of food to be eaten there. In the third and sixth years of the seven year **shemittah** cycle, the *maaser sheni* obligation is replaced with **maaser ani,** the tithe for the poor.

maaser ani – see **maaser.**

maaser of animals – see **maaser beheimah.**

maaser beheimah – the animal tithe. The newborn kosher animals (specifically sheep, goats) born to one's herds and flocks are gathered into a pen and made to pass through an opening one at a time. Every tenth animal is designated as **maaser.** It is brought as an offering in the Temple and is eaten by the owner.

maaser rishon – see **maaser.**

maaser sheni – see **maaser.**

mah matzinu – lit. just as we find; a **binyan av** from one verse. Just as one particular law possesses aspect A and aspect B, so any other law that possesses aspect A should also possess aspect B.

makkas mardus – lashes for rebelliousness. This is the term used for lashes incurred by Rabbinic – rather than Biblical – law.

malkus – the thirty-nine lashes (forty minus one) imposed by the court for violations of Biblical prohibitions, where no more severe punishment is indicated.

mamzer [pl. **mamzerim**] [f. **mamzeress**] – (a) offspring of most illicit relationships punishable by **kares** or capital punishment; (b) offspring of a *mamzer* or *mamzeress.*

mamzerus – state of being a **mamzer.**

maneh – (a) equivalent to 100 **zuz;** (b) a measure of weight, equal to 17 ounces.

Marcheshvan – eighth month of the Hebrew calendar

matanos [or matnos kehunah] – lit. gifts. The Torah commands that we give the right foreleg, jaws and maw of an ox, sheep or goat that are slaughtered (for non-sacrificial purposes) to the **Kohen.** These are referred to as the "gifts."

matzah – unleavened bread; any loaf made from dough that has not been allowed to ferment or rise. One is Biblically obligated to eat *matzah* on the night of the 15th of Nissan.

mavoi – alley; specifically an alley into which courtyards open. See **shitufei mevo'os.**

mayim chayim – living water. Springwater generally has the status of *mayim chayim*. It is so designated because it issues out of the ground with a natural force which makes it "alive" and moving. It is fit to be used for three purposes for which the Torah specifies *mayim chayim*: (a) the immersion of **zavim,** (b) the sprinkling for **metzoraim,** (c) to consecrate therefrom **mei chatas.**

mayim sheuvin – drawn water; water that flows out of a vessel is designated as *sheuvin* and is unfit for use to constitute the forty **se'ah** of a **mikveh.**

mazal – fortune.

mechussar kippurim – lit. lacking atonement. The status accorded to a **tevul yom** in the interim between sunset of the day of his immersion and the time he brings his offerings. During that interval, he retains a vestige of his earlier **tumah** and is thus forbidden to enter the **Temple** Courtyard or partake of the offerings.

mei chatas – springwater consecrated by the addition of ashes of a **parah adumah.** This was used to purify individuals or objects of **tumas meis.**

me'ilah – unlawfully benefiting from **Temple** property or removing such property from the Temple ownership. As a penalty one must pay the value of the misappropriated item plus an additional one-fifth of the value. He must also bring an **asham** offering.

meis mitzvah – see **abandoned corpse.**

melachah [pl. **melachos**] – labor; specifically, one of the thirty-nine labor categories whose performance is forbidden by the Torah on the Sabbath and **Yom Tov.**

melikah – the unique manner in which bird offerings were slaughtered. *Melikah* differs from **shechitah** in two respects: (a) The cut is made with the **Kohen's** thumbnail rather than with a knife. (b) The neck is cut from the back rather than from the throat. Only birds for sacrificial purposes may be slaughtered by *melikah;* all others require *shechitah.* See **shechitah.**

melog – a married woman's property in which she retains ownership of the property itself, but her husband enjoys the right of usufruct, i.e. he owns the yield of that property.

menachos – see **minchah.**

Men of the Great Assembly – a group of 120 sages active at the end of the Babylonian exile and during the early years of the Second Temple. They were responsible for the formulation of our prayers and many other enactments.

Menorah – the seven-branched gold candelabrum which stood in the **Holy.**

meshichah – pulling, or otherwise causing an object to move; one of the methods of acquisition used for movable property.

mesirah – handing over; transferring the animal to a buyer by handing him its reins or mane; a means of acquisition used for articles too heavy to be acquired via **meshichah** or **hagbahah.**

metzora – A *metzora* is a person who has contracted **tzaraas** (erroneously described as leprosy), an affliction mentioned in *Leviticus* (Chs. 13,14). *Tzaraas* manifests itself (on people) as white or light-colored spots on the body.

mezuzah [pl. **mezuzos**] – a small scroll, containing the passages of *Deuteronomy* 6:4-9 and 11:13-21, that is affixed to the right doorpost.

midras – If someone who is **tamei** as a result of a bodily emission (e.g. a **zav, zavah, niddah,** woman who has given birth) sit or leans on a bed, couch, or chair, it acquires the same level of **tumah** as the person from whom the *tumah* emanates (i.e. **av hatumah**). This form of *tumah* transmission is called *midras.*

migo – lit. since; a rule of procedure. If one makes a claim that on its own merits the court would reject, it nonetheless will be accepted "since" had he wished to tell an untruth he would have chosen a claim that certainly is acceptable to the court.

mikveh – ritualarium; a body of standing water containing at least forty **se'ah.** It is used to purify (by immersion) people and utensils of their **tumah**-contamination. A *mikveh* consists of waters naturally collected, without direct human intervention. Water drawn in a vessel is not valid for a *mikveh.*

mil – 2,000 **amos.** A measure of distance between 3,000 and 4,000 feet.

minchah – (a) [cap.] the afternoon prayer service; (b) [pl.**menachos**] a flour offering, generally consisting of fine wheat flour, oil and frankincense, part of which is burnt on the **Altar.** See **kemitzah.**

minyan – quorum of ten adult Jewish males necessary for the communal prayer service and other matters.

Mishkan – Tabernacle, predecessor of the Temple.

mishmar [pl. **mishmaros**] – lit. watch; one of the twenty-four watches of **Kohanim** and **Leviim** who served in the Temple for a week at a time on a rotating basis. These watches were subdivided into family groups each of which served on one day of the week.

Mishnah [pl. **Mishnahs**] – (a) the organized teachings of the **Tannaim** compiled by **R' Yehudah HaNasi;** (b) a paragraph of that work.

mitzvah [pl. **mitzvos**] – A **Torah** command whether of Biblical or Rabbinic origin.

mi'un – By Rabbinic enactment, an underaged orphan girl may be given in marriage by her mother or brothers. She may annul the marriage anytime before reaching majority by declaring, before a **beis din** of three judges, her unwillingness to continue in the marriage. This declaration and process is called *mi'un.*

mixtures of the vineyard – see **kilayim.**

modeh bemiktzas – see **oath of modeh bemiktzas.**

monetary law – law dealing with financial matters rather than matters of ritual prohibition.

monetary sanctity – see **hekdesh.**

movables, movable property – property that is transportable; in contrast to real estate.

muad – lit. warned one. A bull that gores three times and whose owner was duly warned after each incident to take precautions is considered a *muad* bull. The owner must pay full damage for the fourth and all subsequent incidents. See **tam.**

muchzak – one who has physical possession of an object and who is therefore assumed to be in legal possession of it.

muktzeh – lit. set aside. (a) a class of objects which, in the normal course of events, do not stand to be used on the Sabbath or **Yom Tov.** The Rabbis prohibited moving such objects on the Sabbath or Yom Tov; (b) an animal set aside to be sacrificed for idolatry.

mum [pl. mumim] – physical defects that render a **Kohen** or sacrifice unfit.

mussaf – (a) additional sacrifices offered on the Sabbath, **Rosh Chodesh,** or **Yom Tov;** (b) [cap] the prayer service which is recited in lieu of these sacrifices.

naarah – a girl at least 12 years old who has sprouted a minimum of two pubic hairs. This marks her coming of age to be considered an adult. She is deemed a *na'arah* for six months; after that she becomes a **bogeres.**

naarus – the state of being a **naarah.**

nasi [pl. **nesiim**] – the prince. He serves as the head of the **Sanhedrin** and de facto as the spiritual leader of the people.

nazir [f. **nezirah**] – a person who takes the vow of **nezirus,** which prohibits him to drink wine, eat grapes, cut his hair or contaminate himself with the **tumah** of a corpse.

neder – a vow which renders objects, in contradistinction to actions, prohibited. There are two basic categories of vows; (a) restrictive vows; (b) vows to donate to **hekdesh.** See **hekdesh.**

negaim – spots that appear on the skin of a **metzora.**

nesachim – a libation, generally of wine, which is poured upon the **Altar.**

nesin [f. **nesinah;** pl. **nesinim**] – descendant of the Gibeonites, who deceptively concluded a peace treaty with Joshua (*Joshua* 9:3-27) and converted to Judaism.

neveilah [pl. **neveilos**] – the carcass of an animal that was not slaughtered according to procedure prescribed by the Torah. A *neveilah* may not be eaten. It is an **av hatumah.**

Neviim – Prophets; it consists of the following books: *Joshua, Judges, Samuel, Kings, Jeremiah, Ezekiel, Isaiah,* **Twelve Prophets.**

nezirus – the state of being a **nazir.**

niddah – a woman who has menstruated but has not yet completed her purification process, which concludes with immersion in a **mikveh.**

nirtza – see **retziah.**

Nissan – first month of the Hebrew calendar.

nisuin – second stage of marriage. It is effected by a procedure called **chuppah.** See **kiddushin.**

Noahide laws – the seven commandments given to Noah and his sons, which are binding upon all gentiles. These laws include the obligation to have a body of civil law, and the prohibitions against idolatry, immorality, bloodshed, blasphemy, stealing and robbing, and eating limbs from a live animal.

nossar – part of a **korban** left over after the time to eat it has passed.

olah [pl. **olos**] – burnt or elevation offering; an offering which is consumed in its entirety by the **Altar** fire. It is one of the **kodshei kodashim.**

omer – an obligatory **minchah** offering brought on the sixteenth of **Nissan.** It was forbidden to eat from the new grain crop (**chadash**) before this offering was brought.

onaah – price fraud.

onein [f. **onenes**] – a person on the day of the death of a close relative. Special laws of bereavement apply to an *onein.*

Oral Sinaitic Law – see **Halachah LeMoshe MiSinai.**

orlah – lit. sealed; fruit that grows on a tree during the first three years after it has been planted (or transplanted). The Torah prohibits any benefit from such fruit.

Outer Altar – the **Altar** that stands the Courtyard of the **Beis HaMikdash,** to which the blood of most offerings is applied, and on which the offerings are burned.

paid custodian – a **shomer** who receives remuneration for his services. He is obligated to make restitution even in the event of theft or loss.

parah adumah – lit. red cow. The ashes of the *parah adumah* are mixed with spring water. The resulting mixture is known as **mei chatas** and is used in the purification process of people or objects who have contracted **tumah** from a human corpse.

Paroches – curtain: specifically, the curtain that divided the **Holy** from the **Holy of Holies.**

parsah [pl. **parsaos**] – measure of length equal to eight thousand **amos.**

peace offering – see **shelamim.**

pe'ah – the portion of the crop, generally the corner of the field, that must be left unreaped as a gift to the poor.

peret – individual grapes which fell during harvesting. The Torah grants these to the poor. See **shich'chah, leket, pe'ah, oleilos.**

perutah [pl. **perutos**] – smallest coin used in Talmudic times. In most cases its value is the minimum that is legally significant.

Pesach – Passover. The **Yom Tov** that celebrates the Exodus of the Jewish nation from Egypt.

pesach offering – sacrifice offered on the afternoon of the fourteenth day of **Nissan** and eaten after nightfall. It is one of the **kodashim kalim.**

peter chamor – A firstborn male donkey, which must either be redeemed for a kid or lamb (which is given to a **Kohen**) or else must be decapitated.

physical sanctity – see **hekdesh.**

piggul – an offering deemed unfit by means of an improper intent to eat of it or place it on the **Altar** after the allotted time. The intention must have been present during one of the four **avodos.** Consumption of *piggul* is punishable by **kares.**

pikadon – an object deposited with a custodian for safekeeping.

pikuach nefesh – lit. saving a life; a life-threatening situation. All prohibitions (except for murder, immorality and idolatry) are waived, if necessary, in such situations.

pilgrimage festival – the title for the holidays of **Pesach, Shavuos** and **Succos,** when all Jewish males were obligated to appear at the **Beis HaMikdash** in Jerusalem.

plag haminchah – one and a quarter hours before night.

positive commandment – a Torah commandment expressed as a requirement *to do.*

poskim – authoritative decisors of Torah law.

Priestly Blessing – the blessing the **Kohanim** are obligated to confer upon the congregation. It consists of the verses designated for this purpose by the Torah (*Numbers* 6:24-26). It is recited aloud by the **Kohanim**, toward the conclusion of the **Shemoneh Esrei.**

prohibition – a negative commandment, which the Torah expresses as a command *not to do.*

prohibitory law – refers to the category of Torah law which deals with questions of permissible or forbidden status, as opposed to questions of **monetary law.**

prophets – see **Neviim.**

pundyon – a coin.

purification waters – see **mei chatas.**

rasha – (a) a wicked person; (b) a person disqualified from serving as a witness by his commission of certain transgressions.

R' – Rabbi; specifically a **Tanna,** or **Amora** of **Eretz Yisrael.**

Rebbi – R' Yehudah HaNasi; the redactor of the **Mishnah.**

red cow – see **parah adumah.**

regel – any of the three pilgrimage festivals – **Pesach, Shavuos** and **Succos.**

Reish Gelusa – Exilarch, head of the Babylonian Jewish community. Parallels the **Nasi** in **Eretz Yisrael.**

reshus harabim – lit. public domain; any unroofed, commonly used street, public area or highway at least sixteen **amos** wide and open at both ends. According to some, it must be used by at least 600,000 people.

reshus hayachid – lit. private domain; any area measuring at least four **tefachim** by four *tefachim* and enclosed by partitions at least ten *tefachim* high. According to most opinions, it needs to be enclosed only on three sides to qualify as a *reshus hayachid*. Private ownership is not a prerequisite.

resident alien – see **ger toshav.**

retziah – the process a Hebrew servant undergoes if he wishes to remain under his master after his period of servitude has ended. His right ear is placed against the doorpost and pierced with an awl. A servant who undergoes this process is known as a **nirtza** and is required to serve until his master dies or until the onset of the **Yovel** year.

revai – fruit produced by a tree in its fourth year. This is consecrated in the same manner as **maaser sheni** and must be eaten in Jerusalem or be redeemed with money which is spent in Jerusalem on food to be eaten there. See **orlah.**

revi'is – a quarter of a **log.**

ribbis – a Talmudic term for interest.

Rishon [pl. **Rishonim**] – a Torah authority of the period following the **Geonim** (approx. 1000-1500 C.E.).

rishon l'tumah – first degree of acquired **tumah.** A *rishon l'tumah* can transmit **tumah** to food and drink but not to other people or utensils.

Rosh Chodesh – (a) festival celebrating the new month; (b) the first of the month.

Rosh Hashanah – the **Yom Tov** that celebrates the new year. It falls on the first and second days of **Tishrei.**

rov – majority. A principle used in halachah to determine the origin or status of a particular object. An object of undetermined origin or status is assumed to partake of the same origin or status as that of the majority. See also **bitul b'rov.**

rova – a quarter-**kav** (one twenty-fourth of a **se'ah**).

Sadducees – heretical sect active during the Second Temple era named after Tzaddok, a disciple of Antigonas of Socho. They denied the Divine origin of the Oral Law and refused to accept the Sages' interpretation of the Torah.

Sages – (a) the collective body of Torah authorities in the Mishnaic era; (b) the anonymous majority opinion in a **Mishnah** or **Baraisa;** (c) [l.c.] Torah scholar and authority.

Sanctuary – a term applied to the **Temple** building that housed the **Holy** and the **Holy of Holies.**

Sanhedrin – (a) the High Court of Israel; the Supreme Court consisting of seventy-one judges whose decisions on questions of Torah law are definitive and binding on all courts; (b) [l.c.] a court of twenty-three judges authorized to adjudicate capital and corporal cases.

saris – (a) a male who is incapable of maturing sexually; (b) a castrated male.

se'ah – a Mishnaic measure of volume; six **kav.**

Seder [pl. **Sedarim**] – lit. order. (a) The Mishnah is divided into six *sedarim*: *Zeraim* (Plants), *Moed* (Festivals), *Nashim* (Women), *Nezikim* (Damages), *Kodashim* (Sacred Things) and *Taharos* (Ritual Purities); (b) [l.c.] ritual festive meal on **Pesach.**

sekilah – lit. stoning; one of the four forms of death penalty imposed by the court.

sela [pl. **selaim**] – a silver coin having the weight of 384 barleycorns. This is the equivalent of four **dinars.**

semichah – (a) Rabbinical ordination empowering one to serve as a judge. This ordination stretches back in an unbroken chain to Moses. (b) A rite performed with almost all personal sacrificial offerings. The owner of the offering places both his hands on the animal's head and presses down with all his might. In the case of a **chatas,** or an **asham,** he makes his confession during *semichah*. In the case of a **shelamim** or **todah** offering, he praises and thanks God.

semuchin [pl. **semuchim**] – Scriptural juxtaposition. This principle states that two consecutive verses or passages may be compared for purposes of inferring law from one to the other. It is one of the rules of exegesis employed by the Sages.

seven species – see **bikkurim.**

Seventeenth of Tammuz – a fast day. Among the tragedies that occurred on this day were: (a) Moses descended from Mount Sinai and smashed the Tablets of the Ten Commandments when he saw the people worshiping the Golden Calf. (b) Jerusalem's walls were breached by the invading Roman army three weeks before the final destruction of the Second Temple (on **Tishah B'Av**).

shaas zemaniyos – pro-rated hours. According to this reckoning the day (or night) – regardless of its length – is divided into twelve equal units (hours).

shaatnez – see **kilayim.**

Shabbos – (a) the Sabbath; (b) the Talmudic tractate that deals with the laws of the Sabbath.

Shacharis – the morning prayer service.

Shavuos – Pentecost; the festival that celebrates the giving of the Torah to the Jewish nation at Mount Sinai.

Shechinah – Divine Presence.

shechitah – (a) ritual slaughter; the method prescribed by the Torah for killing a kosher animal for consumption. It consists of cutting through most of the esophagus and windpipe from the front of the neck with a specially sharpened knife that is free of nicks. (b) One of the four essential blood **avodos.**

shekel [pl. **shekalim, shekels**] – Scriptural coin equivalent to the Aramaic **sela** or four **dinars.** In Mishnaic terminology, the Scriptural half-*shekel* is called a **shekel,** and the Scriptural **shekel** is called by its Aramaic name, **sela.**

shelamim – peace offering; generally brought by an individual on a voluntary basis; part is burnt on the **Altar,** part is eaten by a **Kohen** (and the members of his household) and part is eaten by the owner. It is one of the **kodashim kalim.**

shelichus – see **agency.**

Shemini Atzeres – the eighth and concluding day of the **Succos** celebration. In many respects, it is a **Yom Tov** in its own right.

shemittah – the Sabbatical year, occurring every seventh year, during which the land of **Eretz Yisrael** may not be cultivated.

Shemoneh Esrei – also called *Amidah*; the silent, standing prayer, which is one of the main features of the daily prayer services.

sheretz [pl. **sheratzim**] – one of eight rodents or reptiles, listed by the Torah, whose carcasses transmit **tumah.**

Shevat – eleventh month of the Hebrew calendar.

sheviis – see **shemittah.**

shevuah oaths – a formula with which one may make a self-imposed prohibition. A **shevuah oath** renders actions, in contradistinction to objects, forbidden.

shich'chah – forgotten sheaves. The Torah grants these to the poor. See **leket, pe'ah, peret** and **oleilos.**

shitufei mevo'os – incorporation of the alleys; a provision similar to **eruvei chatzeiros,** instituted to permit carrying from a courtyard into an alley on the Sabbath. It merges the different courtyards in a common ownership of a **mavoi.**

shliach tzibur – lit. messenger of the congregation; the individual leading the prayer service.

shofar – trumpet formed from the horn of a ram or certain other animals. It is a Biblical obligation to hear the blowing of a *shofar* on **Rosh Hashanah.**

shomer [pl. **shomrim**] – One who has assumed custodial responsibility for another's property.

shtar [pl. **shtaros**] – legal document.

sh'tei halechem – the offering of two wheat loaves that must be brought on **Shavuos.**

Shulchan – lit. table; the golden Table for the **lechem hapanim,** located in the **Holy.**

shuman – animal fats that are permitted for consumption. See **cheilev.**

Sifra – lit. the book; the primary collection of Tannaic exegesis, mainly halachic in nature, on the Book of *Leviticus*. It is also known as *Toras Kohanim*.

Sifri (or **Sifrei**) – lit. the books; the counterpart of the **Sifra;** it expounds on the Books of *Numbers* and *Deuteronomy*.

Sivan – third month of the Hebrew calendar.

sotah – an adulteress or a woman whose suspicious behavior has made her suspected of adultery. The Torah prescribes, under specific circumstances, that her guilt or innocence be established by having her drink specially prepared water.

sprinkling – see **haza'ah.**

stoning – see **sekilah.**

subverted city – see **ir hanidachas.**

succah – (a) the temporary dwelling in which one must live during the festival of **Succos;** (b) [cap.] the Talmudic tractate that deals with the laws that pertain to the festival of Succos.

Succos – one of the three **pilgrimage festivals,** during which one must dwell in a **succah.**

Tabernacle – a portable **Sanctuary** for the sacrificial service used during the forty years of national wandering in the Wilderness and the first fourteen years after entry into Eretz Yisrael.

taharah – a halachically defined state of ritual purity; the absence of **tumah**-contamination.

tahor – person or object in a state of **taharah.**

tam – lit. ordinary; a bull the first three times it gores another animal. See **muad.**

tamei – person or object that has been contaminated by **tumah.**

tamid – communal **olah,** offered twice daily.

Tammuz – fourth month of the Hebrew calendar.

Tanna [pl. **Tannaim**] – Sage of the Mishnaic period whose view is recorded in a **Mishnah** or **Baraisa.**

Tanna Kamma – the anonymous first opinion of a **Mishnah** or **Baraisa.**

Targum – lit. translation; the Aramaic interpretive translation of Scripture.

techum [pl. **techumim**] – Sabbath boundary; the distance of 2,000 **amos** from a person's place of residence which he is permitted to travel on the Sabbath or **Yom Tov.**

tefach [pl. **tefachim**] – handbreadth; a measure of length equal to the width of four thumbs.

tefillah – (a) prayer; (b) in Talmudic usage, **tefillah** invariably refers to **Shemoneh Esrei.**

tefillin – phylacteries; two black leather casings, each of which contains Torah passages written on parchment. It is a **mitzvah** for adult males to wear one on the head and one on the arm.

temei'ah – female for **tamei.**

Temple – See **Beis HaMikdash.**

Temple Mount – the site of the Holy **Temple.** See **Beis HaMikdash.**

temurah – The Torah forbids a person to even verbally substitute a different animal for an already consecrated sacrificial animal. This is forbidden even if the second animal is superior. If one violates this prohibition, both the animals are sacred.

tereifah [pl. tereifos] – (a) a person, animal or bird that possesses one of a well-defined group of eighteen defects which will certainly cause its death. Any of these defects renders the animal or bird prohibited for consumption even if it was ritually slaughtered. (b) A generic term for all non-kosher food.

terumah [pl. **terumos**] – the first portion of the crop separated and given to a **Kohen,** usually between 1/40 and 1/60 of the total crop. It is separated prior to **maaser,** and upon separation attains a state of sanctity which prohibits it from being eaten by a non-**Kohen,** or by a **Kohen** in a state of **tumah.**

terumah gedolah – see **terumah**

terumas maaser – the tithe portion separated by the **Levi** from the **maaser rishon** he receives and given to a **Kohen.**

tevel – produce of **Eretz Yisrael** that has become subject to the obligation of **terumah** and **tithes;** it is forbidden for consumption until *terumah* and all tithes have been designated.

Teves – tenth month of the Hebrew calendar.

tevilah – immersion in a **mikveh** for the purpose of purification from **tumah**-contamination.

tevul yom – people or utensils that had been **tamei** and underwent immersion in a **mikveh** but still retain a vestige of their **tumah** until nightfall.

Tishah B'Av – lit. the Ninth of Av; the fast day that commemorates the destruction of the First **Beis HaMikdash** and the Second one as well as other national tragedies.

Tishrei – seventh month of the Hebrew calendar.

todah [pl. **todos**] – thanksgiving offering brought when a person survives a potentially life-threatening situation.

tofes – see **toref.**

toladah [pl. **tolados**] – lit. offspring; subcategory of an **av** (pl. **avos**).

Torah – the five books of Moses; the Chumash or Pentateuch.

toref – a document's essence, specifying its date, the names of the principals and the pertinent facts particular to the document. The document's form – the **tofes** – contains the rest of the document's text.

Tosefta – a written collection of **Baraisos**.

tumah [pl. **tumos**] – legally defined state of ritual impurity affecting certain people or objects. Under specific conditions, this contamination can be transmitted to other people or objects, with the degree of *tumah* generally declining with each transmission. People or utensils in a state of *tumah* are restricted from contact and certain other forms of interaction with holy objects by a body of intricate and complex laws. People or utensils that are **tamei** can become **tahor** by being immersed in a **mikveh.**

tumas meis – the **tumah** of a human corpse.

tumas midras – see **midras**

tumas ohel – lit. roof **tumah;** the *tumah* conveyed to objects or persons when they are under the same roof as certain *tumah* conveyors, generally parts of a human corpse.

Twelve Prophets – the final book of the Prophets which consists of twelve short prophetic works: *Hosea, Joel, Amos, Obadiah, Jonah, Micah, Nahum, Habakkuk, Zephaniah, Haggai, Zechariah, Malachi.*

twofold payment – see double payment.

tzaraas – see **metzora.**

tzitzis – the fringes that by Torah law must be placed on a four-cornered garment.

tzon-barzel – lit. iron-sheep; the portion of a woman's dowry assessed prior to the marriage; its value is recorded in the **kesubah.** Should the marriage end, reimbursement is made to the woman at the property's assessed value, even if in the interim it was lost or damaged. Thus, the property's value remains preserved for the wife like *iron.*

unattended corpse – see **meis mitzvah.**

unpaid custodian – a **shomer** who receives no remuneration for his services.

variable [chatas] offering – a special type of *chatas* offering whose quality varies in accordance with the sinners financial resources. He is liable to a regular *chatas* offering of a female lamb or kid only if he is a person of means. Should he be poor, he is required to bring only two turtledoves or two young pigeons, one as a *chatas* and the other as an **olah.** If he is very poor, he brings a tenth of an **ephah** of fine flour for a **minchah.**

v'lad hatumah – derivate **tumah;** that which is contaminated by an **av hatumah.**

voluntary offering – (a) one in which a person obligates himself to bring a sacrifice but does not consecrate a specific animal for it; (b) one in which a person declares, "This animal is a sacrifice," designating a particular animal as the offering he wishes to bring. One may donate either an **olah** or a **shelamim** as a *voluntary offering.*

Women's Courtyard – the courtyard of the Temple that faced the eastern wall of the main Courtyard.

yavam – see **yibum.**

yetzer hara – Evil Inclination.

ye'ush – abandonment. This refers to an owner's despairing of recovering his lost or stolen property.

yevamah – see **yibum.**

yibum – levirate marriage. When a man dies childless, the Torah provides for one of his brothers to marry the widow. This marriage is called *yibum*. Pending this, the widow is forbidden to marry anyone else. The surviving brother, upon whom the obligation to perform the mitzvah of *yibum* falls, is called the **yavam.** The widow is called the **yevamah.** *Yibum* is effected only through cohabitation. If the brother should refuse to perform *yibum*, he must release her from her *yibum*-bond by performing the alternate rite of **chalitzah,** in which she removes his shoe before the court and spits before him and declares: *So should be done to the man who will not build his brother's house* (*Deuteronomy* 25:5-10).

Yisrael [pl. **Yisraelim**] – (a) Jew; (b) Israelite (in contradistinction to **Kohen** or **Levi**).

Yom Kippur – Day of Atonement; a day of prayer, penitence, fasting and abstention from **melachah.**

Yom Tov [pl. **Yamim Tovim**] – holiday; the festival days on which the Torah prohibits **melachah.** Specifically, it refers to the first and last days of **Pesach,** the first day of **Succos, Shemini Atzeres, Shavuos, Yom Kippur** and the two days of **Rosh Hashanah.** Outside of **Eretz Yisrael,** an additional day of **Yom Tov** is added to each of these festivals, except **Yom Kippur** and **Rosh Hashanah.**

Yovel – fiftieth year [Jubilee]; the year following the conclusion of a set of seven **shemittah** cycles. On **Yom Kippur** of that year, the **shofar** is sounded to proclaim freedom for the Jewish servants, and to signal the return to the original owner of fields sold in Eretz Yisrael during the previous forty-nine years.

zakein mamrei – a sage who refuses to accept a ruling of the Great Sanhedrin, and who continues to rule contrary to their decision.

zav [pl. **zavim**] – a man who has become **tamei** because of a specific type of seminal emission. If three emissions were experienced during a three-day period, the man must bring offerings upon his purification.

zavah [pl. **zavos**] – After a woman concludes her seven days of **niddah,** there is an eleven-day period during which any menses-like bleeding renders her a *minor zavah.* If the menstruation lasts for three consecutive days, she is a *major zavah* and must bring offerings upon her purification.

zechiyah – rule which states that one can act as a person's agent without his prior knowledge or consent if the act is clearly advantageous to the beneficiary.

zechus – unqualified benefit.

zerikah – throwing; applying the blood of an offering to the **Altar.** It is one of the four essential blood **avodos.**

zivah – the type of discharge which causes one to be a **zav** or **zavah.**

zomeim [pl. **zomemim**] – witnesses proven false through **hazamah.**

zuz [pl. **zuzim**] – (a) monetary unit equal to a **dinar;** (b) a coin of that value; (c) the weight of a *zuz* coin.

Scriptural Index

MW01152593
TALMUD BAVLI
תלמוד בבלי